T3-BXA-219

Who's Who in America®

Who's Who in America®

2008

62nd Edition

Volume 2 ✦ M-Z

Geographic Index ✦ Professional Index

890 Mountain Avenue, Suite 300
New Providence, NJ 07974 U.S.A.
www.marquiswhoswho.com

Who'sWho in America®

Marquis Who's Who®

For information, contact: Marquis Who's Who, 890 Mountain Avenue, Suite 300
New Providence, New Jersey 07974
1-908-673-1001; www.marquiswhoswho.com

WHO'S WHO IN AMERICA is a registered trademark of Marquis Who's Who LLC.

International Standard Book Number 978-0-0-8379-7011-0 (Classic Edition, Set)
978-0-0-8379-7008-0 (Classic Edition, Volume 2)
978-0-0-8379-7012-7 (Deluxe Edition, Set)
978-0-8379-7010-3 (Deluxe Edition, Volume 2)
International Standard Serial Number 0083-9396

Manufactured in the United States of America.

Table of Contents

Preface

"**WHO'S WHO IN AMERICA** *shall endeavor to list those individuals who are of current national reference interest and inquiry either because of meritorious achievement or because of the position they hold."*

Albert Nelson Marquis
Founder, 1899

Marquis Who's Who is proud to present the 62nd Edition of *Who's Who in America.* This edition features over 100,000 profiles of prominent individuals representing virtually every major field of endeavor. This edition also honors a group of "difference makers", men and women who have made profound contributions to America and the world.

In 1899, our first year of publication, Marquis biographees numbered 8,602. While the number of individuals profiled in *Who's Who in America* has grown substantially, our selection standards remain stringent. Fewer than one in 2,900 Americans are included in the 2008 edition of *Who's Who in America.*

While the vast majority of the individuals profiled on the following pages are American, *Who's Who in America* also includes the biographies of select individuals from around the world whose lives have had considerable impact and influence in America.

On the pages that follow, you will find Olympic champions, Nobel and Pulitzer Prize winners, university presidents, accomplished artists, renowned entertainers, entrepreneurs, and leaders representing hundreds of industries. Our 2008 Edition includes some long-established biographees like Bill Gates, Walter Cronkite and Meryl Streep, as well as many intriguing first-time listees. *Who's Who in America* also includes the profiles of thousands of remarkable achievers who, despite extraordinary accomplishments in everything from breakthrough medical research to cutting-edge technological innovations, have not as yet become household names.

Our profiles provide you with critical biographical information, including educational background, family history, work history, civic activity, memberships, honors, and awards. In many cases, hobbies and special interests are also listed.

One Principle Governs Selection

As in all Marquis Who's Who biographical volumes, the individuals profiled in *Who's Who in America* are selected on the basis of current reference value. Factors such as position, noteworthy accomplishments, visibility, and prominence in a field are all taken into account. An individual's desire to be listed is not sufficient reason for inclusion. Similarly, wealth and social position are not relevant criteria. Of course, Marquis Who's Who has never charged a fee for publishing a biography, nor is purchase of the book ever a factor in the selection of biographees. Final decisions concerning inclusion or exclusion are made following extensive discussion, evaluation, and deliberation.

Biographical information is gathered in a variety of manners. In most cases, we invite our biographees to submit their biographical details. In many cases, though, the information is collected independently by our research and editorial staffs, which use a wide assortment of tools to gather the most complete, accurate, and up-to-date information available. Sketches researched by Marquis Who's Who are followed by an asterisk (*).

Responding to Your Reference Needs

As a complement to the biographical profiles, the Geographic and Professional Indexes featured in Volume 2 make *Who's Who in America* an even more productive research tool. Through these indexes, users can identify and locate individuals in any of thirty-eight professional categories, as well as by country, state, or city. Each entry contains name and occupation description.

The Geographic Index lists names in the United States under state and city designations, as well as biographees in American territories. Canadian listings include provinces and cities. Names in Mexico and other countries appear by city. Biographees whose addresses are not published in their sketches are found under Address Unpublished.

The Professional Index includes categories ranging alphabetically from Agriculture to Social Science. Within each area, the names appear under geographic subheadings. Names without published addresses appear at the end of each professional area listing under Address Unpublished. If the occupation does not fall within one of the specified areas, the name is listed under Unclassified.

Some biographees have professions encompassing more than one area; each of these appears under the field best suited to the biographee's occupation. Thus, while most bankers are listed under Finance: Banking Services, investment bankers are found in Finance: Investment Services. A biographee with two or more diverse occupations is found under the area that best fits his or her professional profile.

Our Challenge

While the Marquis Who's Who editors exercise the utmost care in preparing each biographical sketch for publication, it is inevitable in a publication involving so many profiles that occasional errors will appear. Users of this publication are urged to notify the publisher of any issues so that adjustments can be made, which will not only be reflected in all subsequent editions of the book but which can now be immediately displayed via Marquis Who's Who on the Web.

We sincerely hope that this volume will be an indispensable reference tool for you. We are always looking for ways to better serve you and welcome your ideas for improvements. In addition, we continue to welcome your Marquis Who's Who nominations. Feel free to submit these via our Web site (www.marquiswhoswho.com) or by e-mail and postal mail.

Our Utmost Thanks

Without the cooperation and assistance of those profiled on the pages that follow, *Who's Who in America* would not be possible. We would like to specifically thank our biographees for reviewing and editing their profiles. As a consequence, *Who's Who in America* remains the unchallenged leader in the field of biographical reference works. For this we are truly grateful.

Key to Information

[1] GIBSON, OSCAR JULIUS, [2] physician, educator; **[3]** b. Syracuse, NY, Aug. 31, 1937; **[4]** s. Paul Oliver and Elizabeth H. (Thrun) G.; **[5]** m. Judith S. Gonzalez, Apr. 28, 1968; **[6]** children: Richard Gary, Matthew Lucas, Samuel Perry. **[7]** BA magna cum laude, U. Pa., 1960; MD, Harvard U., 1964. **[8]** Diplomate Am. Bd. Internal Medicine, Am. Bd. Preventive Medicine. **[9]** Intern Barnes Hosp., St. Louis, 1964-65, resident, 1965-66; clin. assoc. Nat. Heart Inst., NIH, Bethesda, Md., 1966-68; chief resident medicine U. Okla. Hosps., 1968-69; asst. prof. cmty. health Okla. Med. Ctr., 1969-70, assoc. prof., 1970-74, prof., chmn. dept., 1974-80; dean Coll. Medicine U. Okla., 1978-82; v.p. med. staff affairs Bapt. Med. Ctr., Oklahoma City, 1982-86, exec. v.p., 1986-88, chmn., 1988-95, chmn., CEO, 1995—; **[10]** mem. governing bd. Ambulatory Health Care Consortium, Inc., 1979-80; mem. Okla. Bd. Medicolegal Examiners, 1985—, Okla. Bd. Med. Ethics, 1994—. **[11]** Contbr. articles to profl. jours. **[12]** Bd. dirs., v.p. Okla. Arthritis Found., 1982—; trustee N. Ctrl. Mental Health Ctr., 1985—. **[13]** Served to lt. US Army, 1954-56. **[14]** Recipient R.T. Chadwick award Overlook Hosp., 1968; grantee Am. Heart Assn., 1985-86, 88, 1995-96. **[15]** Fellow Assn. Tchrs. Preventive Medicine; mem. AAAS, AMA, Am. Fedn. Clin. Rsch., Assn. Med. Colls., Masons, Shriners, Sigma Xi. **[16]** Republican. **[17]** Roman Catholic. **[18]** Achievements include research in the role of MMP inhibitors in the prevention of skin aging. **[19]** Avocations: swimming, weight lifting, traveling. **[20]** Home: 6060 N Ridge Ave Oklahoma City OK 73126 **[21]** Office: Bapt Med Ctr 1986 Cuba Hwy Oklahoma City OK 73120*

KEY

[1]	Name
[2]	Occupation
[3]	Vital statistics
[4]	Parents
[5]	Marriage
[6]	Children
[7]	Education
[8]	Professional certifications
[9]	Career
[10]	Career-related
[11]	Writings and creative works
[12]	Civic and political activities
[13]	Military
[14]	Awards and fellowships
[15]	Professional and association memberships, clubs and lodges
[16]	Political affiliation
[17]	Religion
[18]	Achievements
[19]	Avocations
[20]	Home address
[21]	Office address
[*]	Researched by Marquis Who's Who

Table of Abbreviations

The following is a list of some of the most frequently used Marquis abbreviations:

A

A Associate (used with academic degrees)
AA Associate in Arts
AAAL American Academy of Arts and Letters
AAAS American Association for the Advancement of Science
AACD American Association for Counseling and Development
AACN American Association of Critical Care Nurses
AAHA American Academy of Health Administrators
AAHP American Association of Hospital Planners
AAHPERD American Alliance for Health, Physical Education, Recreation, and Dance
AAS Associate of Applied Science
AASL American Association of School Librarians
AASPA American Association of School Personnel Administrators
AAU Amateur Athletic Union
AAUP American Association of University Professors
AAUW American Association of University Women
AB Arts, Bachelor of
AB Alberta
ABA American Bar Association
AC Air Corps
acad. academy
acct. accountant
acctg. accounting
ACDA Arms Control and Disarmament Agency
ACHA American College of Hospital Administrators
ACLS Advanced Cardiac Life Support
ACLU American Civil Liberties Union
ACOG American College of Ob-Gyn
ACP American College of Physicians
ACS American College of Surgeons
ADA American Dental Association
adj. adjunct, adjutant
adm. admiral
adminstr. administrator
adminstrn. administration
adminstrv. administrative
ADN Associate's Degree in Nursing
ADP Automatic Data Processing
adv. advocate, advisory
advt. advertising
AE Agricultural Engineer
AEC Atomic Energy Commission
aero. aeronautical, aeronautic
aerodyn. aerodynamic
AFB Air Force Base
AFTRA American Federation of Television and Radio Artists
agr. agriculture
agrl. agricultural
agt. agent
AGVA American Guild of Variety Artists
agy. agency
A&I Agricultural and Industrial
AIA American Institute of Architects
AIAA American Institute of Aeronautics and Astronautics
AIChE American Institute of Chemical Engineers
AICPA American Institute of Certified Public Accountants
AID Agency for International Development
AIDS Acquired Immune Deficiency Syndrome
AIEE American Institute of Electrical Engineers
AIME American Institute of Mining, Metallurgy, and Petroleum Engineers
AK Alaska
AL Alabama
ALA American Library Association
Ala. Alabama
alt. alternate
Alta. Alberta
A&M Agricultural and Mechanical
AM Arts, Master of
Am. American, America
AMA American Medical Association
amb. ambassador
AME African Methodist Episcopal
Amtrak National Railroad Passenger Corporation
AMVETS American Veterans
ANA American Nurses Association
anat. anatomical
ANCC American Nurses Credentialing Center
ann. annual
anthrop. anthropological
AP Associated Press
APA American Psychological Association
APHA American Public Health Association
APO Army Post Office
apptd. appointed
Apr. April
apt. apartment
AR Arkansas
ARC American Red Cross
arch. architect
archeol. archeological
archtl. architectural
Ariz. Arizona
Ark. Arkansas
ArtsD Arts, Doctor of
arty. artillery
AS Associate in Science, American Samoa
ASCAP American Society of Composers, Authors and Publishers
ASCD Association for Supervision and Curriculum Development
ASCE American Society of Civil Engineers
ASME American Society of Mechanical Engineers
ASPA American Society for Public Administration
ASPCA American Society for the Prevention of Cruelty to Animals
assn. association
assoc. associate
asst. assistant
ASTD American Society for Training and Development
ASTM American Society for Testing and Materials
astron. astronomical
astrophys. astrophysical
ATLA Association of Trial Lawyers of America
ATSC Air Technical Service Command
atty. attorney
Aug. August
aux. auxiliary
Ave. Avenue
AVMA American Veterinary Medical Association
AZ Arizona

B

B Bachelor
b. born
BA Bachelor of Arts
BAgr Bachelor of Agriculture
Balt. Baltimore
Bapt. Baptist
BArch Bachelor of Architecture
BAS Bachelor of Agricultural Science
BBA Bachelor of Business Administration
BBB Better Business Bureau
BC British Columbia
BCE Bachelor of Civil Engineering
BChir Bachelor of Surgery
BCL Bachelor of Civil Law
BCS Bachelor of Commercial Science
BD Bachelor of Divinity
bd. board
BE Bachelor of Education
BEE Bachelor of Electrical Engineering
BFA Bachelor of Fine Arts
bibl. biblical
bibliog. bibliographical
biog. biographical
biol. biological
BJ Bachelor of Journalism
Bklyn. Brooklyn
BL Bachelor of Letters
bldg. building
BLS Bachelor of Library Science
Blvd. Boulevard

BMI Broadcast Music, Inc.
bn. battalion
bot. botanical
BPE Bachelor of Physical Education
BPhil Bachelor of Philosophy
br. branch
BRE Bachelor of Religious Education
brig. gen. brigadier general
Brit. British
Bros. Brothers
BS Bachelor of Science
BSA Bachelor of Agricultural Science
BSBA Bachelor of Science in Business Administration
BSChemE Bachelor of Science in Chemical Engineering
BSD Bachelor of Didactic Science
BSEE Bachelor of Science in Electrical Engineering
BSN Bachelor of Science in Nursing
BST Bachelor of Sacred Theology
BTh Bachelor of Theology
bull. bulletin
bur. bureau
bus. business
BWI British West Indies

C

CA California
CAD-CAM Computer Aided Design–Computer Aided Model
Calif. California
Can. Canada, Canadian
CAP Civil Air Patrol
capt. captain
cardiol. cardiological
cardiovasc. cardiovascular
Cath. Catholic
cav. cavalry
CBI China, Burma, India Theatre of Operations
CC Community College
CCC Commodity Credit Corporation
CCNY City College of New York
CCRN Critical Care Registered Nurse
CCU Cardiac Care Unit
CD Civil Defense
CE Corps of Engineers, Civil Engineer
CEN Certified Emergency Nurse
CENTO Central Treaty Organization
CEO chief executive officer
CERN European Organization of Nuclear Research
cert. certificate, certification, certified
CETA Comprehensive Employment Training Act
CFA Chartered Financial Analyst
CFL Canadian Football League
CFO chief financial officer
CFP Certified Financial Planner
ch. church
ChD Doctor of Chemistry
chem. chemical
ChemE Chemical Engineer
ChFC Chartered Financial Consultant
Chgo. Chicago
chirurg., der surgeon
chmn. chairman
chpt. chapter
CIA Central Intelligence Agency
Cin. Cincinnati
cir. circle, circuit
CLE Continuing Legal Education
Cleve. Cleveland
climatol. climatological
clin. clinical
clk. clerk
CLU Chartered Life Underwriter
CM Master in Surgery
CM Northern Mariana Islands
cmty. community
CO Colorado
Co. Company
COF Catholic Order of Foresters
C. of C. Chamber of Commerce
col. colonel
coll. college
Colo. Colorado
com. committee
comd. commanded
comdg. commanding
comdr. commander
comdt. commandant
comm. communications
commd. commissioned
comml. commercial
commn. commission
commr. commissioner
compt. comptroller
condr. conductor
conf. Conference
Congl. Congregational, Congressional
Conglist. Congregationalist
Conn. Connecticut
cons. consultant, consulting
consol. consolidated
constl. constitutional
constn. constitution
constrn. construction
contbd. contributed
contbg. contributing
contbn. contribution
contbr. contributor
contr. controller
Conv. Convention
COO chief operating officer
coop. cooperative
coord. coordinator
corp. corporation, corporate
corr. correspondent, corresponding, correspondence
coun. council
CPA Certified Public Accountant
CPCU Chartered Property and Casualty Underwriter
CPH Certificate of Public Health
cpl. corporal
CPR Cardio-Pulmonary Resuscitation
CS Christian Science
CSB Bachelor of Christian Science
CT Connecticut
ct. court
ctr. center
ctrl. central

D

D Doctor
d. daughter of
DAgr Doctor of Agriculture
DAR Daughters of the American Revolution
dau. daughter
DAV Disabled American Veterans
DC District of Columbia
DCL Doctor of Civil Law
DCS Doctor of Commercial Science
DD Doctor of Divinity
DDS Doctor of Dental Surgery
DE Delaware
Dec. December
dec. deceased
def. defense
Del. Delaware
del. delegate, delegation
Dem. Democrat, Democratic
DEng Doctor of Engineering
denom. denomination, denominational
dep. deputy
dept. department
dermatol. dermatological
desc. descendant
devel. development, developmental
DFA Doctor of Fine Arts
DHL Doctor of Hebrew Literature
dir. director
dist. district
distbg. distributing
distbn. distribution
distbr. distributor
disting. distinguished
div. division, divinity, divorce
divsn. division
DLitt Doctor of Literature
DMD Doctor of Dental Medicine
DMS Doctor of Medical Science
DO Doctor of Osteopathy
docs. documents
DON Director of Nursing
DPH Diploma in Public Health
DPhil, Doctor of Philosophy
DR Daughters of the Revolution
Dr. Drive, Doctor
DRE Doctor of Religious Education
DrPH Doctor of Public Health
DSc Doctor of Science
DSChemE Doctor of Science in Chemical Engineering
DSM Distinguished Service Medal
DST Doctor of Sacred Theology
DTM Doctor of Tropical Medicine
DVM Doctor of Veterinary Medicine
DVS Doctor of Veterinary Surgery

E

E East
ea. eastern
Eccles. Ecclesiastical
ecol. ecological

econ. economic
ECOSOC UN Economic and Social Council
ED Doctor of Engineering
ed. educated
EdB Bachelor of Education
EdD Doctor of Education
edit. edition
editl. editorial
EdM Master of Education
edn. education
ednl. educational
EDP Electronic Data Processing
EdS Specialist in Education
EE Electrical Engineer
EEC European Economic Community
EEG Electroencephalogram
EEO Equal Employment Opportunity
EEOC Equal Employment Opportunity Commission
EKG electrocardiogram
elec. electrical
electrochem. electrochemical
electrophys. electrophysical
elem. elementary
EM Engineer of Mines
EMT Emergency Medical Technician
ency. encyclopedia
Eng. England
engr. engineer
engring. engineering
entomol. entomological
environ. environmental
EPA Environmental Protection Agency
epidemiol. epidemiological
Episc. Episcopalian
ERA Equal Rights Amendment
ERDA Energy Research and Development Administration
ESEA Elementary and Secondary Education Act
ESL English as Second Language
ESSA Environmental Science Services Administration
ethnol. ethnological
ETO European Theatre of Operations
EU European Union
Evang. Evangelical
exam. examination, examining
Exch. Exchange
exec. executive
exhbn. exhibition
expdn. expedition
expn. exposition
expt. experiment
exptl. experimental
Expy. Expressway
Ext. Extension

F

FAA Federal Aviation Administration
FAO UN Food and Agriculture Organization
FBA Federal Bar Association
FBI Federal Bureau of Investigation
FCA Farm Credit Administration
FCC Federal Communications Commission
FCDA Federal Civil Defense Administration
FDA Food and Drug Administration
FDIA Federal Deposit Insurance Administration
FDIC Federal Deposit Insurance Corporation
FEA Federal Energy Administration
Feb. February
fed. federal
fedn. federation
FERC Federal Energy Regulatory Commission
fgn. foreign
FHA Federal Housing Administration
fin. financial, finance
FL Florida
Fl. Floor
Fla. Florida
FMC Federal Maritime Commission
FNP Family Nurse Practitioner
FOA Foreign Operations Administration
found. foundation
FPC Federal Power Commission
FPO Fleet Post Office
frat. fraternity
FRS Federal Reserve System
FSA Federal Security Agency
Ft. Fort
FTC Federal Trade Commission
Fwy. Freeway

G

GA, Ga. Georgia
GAO General Accounting Office
gastroent. gastroenterological
GATT General Agreement on Tariffs and Trade
GE General Electric Company
gen. general
geneal. genealogical
geog. geographic, geographical
geol. geological
geophys. geophysical
geriat. geriatrics
gerontol. gerontological
GHQ General Headquarters
gov. governor
govt. government
govtl. governmental
GPO Government Printing Office
grad. graduate, graduated
GSA General Services Administration
Gt. Great
GU Guam
gynecol. gynecological

H

hdqs. headquarters
HEW Department of Health, Education and Welfare
HHD Doctor of Humanities
HHFA Housing and Home Finance Agency
HHS Department of Health and Human Services
HI Hawaii
hist. historical, historic
HM Master of Humanities
homeo. homeopathic
hon. honorary, honorable
House of Dels. House of Delegates
House of Reps. House of Representatives
hort. horticultural
hosp. hospital
HS High School
HUD Department of Housing and Urban Development
Hwy. Highway
hydrog. hydrographic

I

IA Iowa
IAEA International Atomic Energy Agency
IBRD International Bank for Reconstruction and Development
ICA International Cooperation Administration
ICC Interstate Commerce Commission
ICCE International Council for Computers in Education
ICU Intensive Care Unit
ID Idaho
IEEE Institute of Electrical and Electronics Engineers
IFC International Finance Corporation
IL, Ill. Illinois
illus. illustrated
ILO International Labor Organization
IMF International Monetary Fund
IN Indiana
Inc. Incorporated
Ind. Indiana
ind. independent
Indpls. Indianapolis
indsl. industrial
inf. infantry
info. information
ins. insurance
insp. inspector
inst. institute
instl. institutional
instn. institution
instr. instructor
instrn. instruction
instrnl. instructional
internat. international
intro. introduction
IRE Institute of Radio Engineers
IRS Internal Revenue Service

J

JAG Judge Advocate General
JAGC Judge Advocate General Corps
Jan. January
Jaycees Junior Chamber of Commerce
JB Jurum Baccalaureus
JCB Juris Canoni Baccalaureus
JCD Juris Canonici Doctor, Juris Civilis Doctor
JCL Juris Canonici Licentiatus
JD Juris Doctor

jg. junior grade
jour. journal
jr. junior
JSD Juris Scientiae Doctor
JUD Juris Utriusque Doctor
jud. judicial

K

Kans. Kansas
KC Knights of Columbus
KS Kansas
KY, Ky. Kentucky

L

LA, La. Louisiana
LA Los Angeles
lab. laboratory
L.Am. Latin America
lang. language
laryngol. laryngological
LB Labrador
LDS Latter Day Saints
lectr. lecturer
legis. legislation, legislative
LHD Doctor of Humane Letters
LI Long Island
libr. librarian, library
lic. licensed, license
lit. literature
litig. litigation
LittB Bachelor of Letters
LittD Doctor of Letters
LLB Bachelor of Laws
LLD Doctor of Laws
LLM Master of Laws
Ln. Lane
LPGA Ladies Professional Golf Association
LPN Licensed Practical Nurse
lt. lieutenant
Ltd. Limited
Luth. Lutheran
LWV League of Women Voters

M

M Master
m. married
MA Master of Arts
MA Massachusetts
MADD Mothers Against Drunk Driving
mag. magazine
MAgr Master of Agriculture
maj. major
Man. Manitoba
Mar. March
MArch Master in Architecture
Mass. Massachusetts
math. mathematics, mathematical
MB Bachelor of Medicine, Manitoba
MBA Master of Business Administration
MC Medical Corps
MCE Master of Civil Engineering
mcht. merchant
mcpl. municipal
MCS Master of Commercial Science
MD Doctor of Medicine
MD, Md. Maryland
MDiv Master of Divinity
MDip Master in Diplomacy
mdse. merchandise
MDV Doctor of Veterinary Medicine
ME Mechanical Engineer
ME Maine
M.E.Ch. Methodist Episcopal Church
mech. mechanical
MEd. Master of Education
med. medical
MEE Master of Electrical Engineering
mem. member
meml. memorial
merc. mercantile
met. metropolitan
metall. metallurgical
MetE Metallurgical Engineer
meteorol. meteorological
Meth. Methodist
Mex. Mexico
MF Master of Forestry
MFA Master of Fine Arts
mfg. manufacturing
mfr. manufacturer
mgmt. management
mgr. manager
MHA Master of Hospital Administration
MI Military Intelligence, Michigan
Mich. Michigan
micros. microscopic
mid. middle
mil. military
Milw. Milwaukee
Min. Minister
mineral. mineralogical
Minn. Minnesota
MIS Management Information Systems
Miss. Mississippi
MIT Massachusetts Institute of Technology
mktg. marketing
ML Master of Laws
MLA Modern Language Association
MLitt Master of Literature, Master of Letters
MLS Master of Library Science
MME Master of Mechanical Engineering
MN Minnesota
mng. managing
MO, Mo. Missouri
moblzn. mobilization
Mont. Montana
MP Member of Parliament
MPA Master of Public Administration
MPE Master of Physical Education
MPH Master of Public Health
MPhil Master of Philosophy
MPL Master of Patent Law
Mpls. Minneapolis
MRE Master of Religious Education
MRI Magnetic Resonance Imaging
MS Master of Science
MS, Ms. Mississippi
MSc Master of Science
MSChemE Master of Science in Chemical Engineering
MSEE Master of Science in Electrical Engineering
MSF Master of Science of Forestry
MSN Master of Science in Nursing
MST Master of Sacred Theology
MSW Master of Social Work
MT Montana
Mt. Mount
mus. museum, musical
MusB Bachelor of Music
MusD Doctor of Music
MusM Master of Music
mut. mutual
MVP Most Valuable Player
mycol. mycological

N

N North
NAACOG Nurses Association of the American College of Obstetricians and Gynecologists
NAACP National Association for the Advancement of Colored People
NACA National Advisory Committee for Aeronautics
NACDL National Association of Criminal Defense Lawyers
NACU National Association of Colleges and Universities
NAD National Academy of Design
NAE National Academy of Engineering, National Association of Educators
NAESP National Association of Elementary School Principals
NAFE National Association of Female Executives
N.Am. North America
NAM National Association of Manufacturers
NAMH National Association for Mental Health
NAPA National Association of Performing Artists
NARAS National Academy of Recording Arts and Sciences
NAREB National Association of Real Estate Boards
NARS National Archives and Record Service
NAS National Academy of Sciences
NASA National Aeronautics and Space Administration
NASP National Association of School Psychologists
NASW National Association of Social Workers
nat. national
NATAS National Academy of Television Arts and Sciences
NATO North Atlantic Treaty Organization

nav. navigation
NB, N.B. New Brunswick
NBA National Basketball Association
NC North Carolina
NCAA National College Athletic Association
NCCJ National Conference of Christians and Jews
ND North Dakota
NDEA National Defense Education Act
NE Nebraska
NE Northeast
NEA National Education Association
Nebr. Nebraska
NEH National Endowment for Humanities
neurol. neurological
Nev. Nevada
NF Newfoundland
NFL National Football League
Nfld. Newfoundland
NG National Guard
NH New Hampshire
NHL National Hockey League
NIH National Institutes of Health
NIMH National Institute of Mental Health
NJ New Jersey
NLRB National Labor Relations Board
NM, N.Mex. New Mexico
No. Northern
NOAA National Oceanographic and Atmospheric Administration
NORAD North America Air Defense
Nov. November
NOW National Organization for Women
nr. near
NRA National Rifle Association
NRC National Research Council
NS Nova Scotia
NSC National Security Council
NSF National Science Foundation
NSTA National Science Teachers Association
NSW New South Wales
nuc. nuclear
numis. numismatic
NV Nevada
NW Northwest
NWT Northwest Territories
NY New York
NYC New York City
NYU New York University
NZ New Zealand

O

ob-gyn obstetrics-gynecology
obs. observatory
obstet. obstetrical
occupl. occupational
oceanog. oceanographic
Oct. October
OD Doctor of Optometry
OECD Organization for Economic Cooperation and Development
OEEC Organization of European Economic Cooperation
OEO Office of Economic Opportunity
ofcl. official
OH Ohio
OK, Okla. Oklahoma
ON, Ont. Ontario
oper. operating
ophthal. ophthalmological
ops. operations
OR Oregon
orch. orchestra
Oreg. Oregon
orgn. organization
orgnl. organizational
ornithol. ornithological
orthop. orthopedic
OSHA Occupational Safety and Health Administration
OSRD Office of Scientific Research and Development
OSS Office of Strategic Services
osteo. osteopathic
otol. otological
otolaryn. otolaryngological

P

PA, Pa. Pennsylvania
paleontol. paleontological
path. pathological
pediat. pediatrics
PEI Prince Edward Island
PEN Poets, Playwrights, Editors, Essayists and Novelists
penol. penological
pers. personnel
PGA Professional Golfers' Association of America
PHA Public Housing Administration
pharm. pharmaceutical
PharmD Doctor of Pharmacy
PharmM Master of Pharmacy
PhB Bachelor of Philosophy
PhD Doctor of Philosophy
PhDChemE Doctor of Science in Chemical Engineering
PhM Master of Philosophy
Phila. Philadelphia
philharm. philharmonic
philol. philological
philos. philosophical
photog. photographic
phys. physical
physiol. physiological
Pitts. Pittsburgh
Pk. Park
Pky. Parkway
Pl. Place
Plz. Plaza
PO Post Office
polit. political
poly. polytechnic, polytechnical
PQ Province of Quebec
PR Puerto Rico
prep. preparatory
pres. president
Presbyn. Presbyterian
presdl. presidential
prin. principal
procs. proceedings
prod. produced
prodn. production
prodr. producer
prof. professor
profl. professional
prog. progressive
propr. proprietor
pros. prosecuting
pro tem. pro tempore
psychiat. psychiatric
psychol. psychological
PTA Parent-Teachers Association
ptnr. partner
PTO Pacific Theatre of Operations, Parent Teacher Organization
pub. publisher, publishing, published, public
publ. publication
pvt. private

Q

quar. quarterly
qm. quartermaster
Que. Quebec

R

radiol. radiological
RAF Royal Air Force
RCA Radio Corporation of America
RCAF Royal Canadian Air Force
Rd. Road
R&D Research & Development
REA Rural Electrification Administration
rec. recording
ref. reformed
regt. regiment
regtl. regimental
rehab. rehabilitation
rels. relations
Rep. Republican
rep. representative
Res. Reserve
ret. retired
Rev. Reverend
rev. review, revised
RFC Reconstruction Finance Corporation
RI Rhode Island
Rlwy. Railway
Rm. Room
RN Registered Nurse
roentgenol. roentgenological
ROTC Reserve Officers Training Corps
RR rural route, railroad
rsch. research
rschr. researcher
Rt. Route

S

S South
s. son
SAC Strategic Air Command
SAG Screen Actors Guild
S.Am. South America
san. sanitary

SAR Sons of the American Revolution
Sask. Saskatchewan
savs. savings
SB Bachelor of Science
SBA Small Business Administration
SC South Carolina
ScB Bachelor of Science
SCD Doctor of Commercial Science
ScD Doctor of Science
sch. school
sci. science, scientific
SCV Sons of Confederate Veterans
SD South Dakota
SE Southeast
SEC Securities and Exchange Commission
sec. secretary
sect. section
seismol. seismological
sem. seminary
Sept. September
s.g. senior grade
sgt. sergeant
SI Staten Island
SJ Society of Jesus
SJD Scientiae Juridicae Doctor
SK Saskatchewan
SM Master of Science
SNP Society of Nursing Professionals
So. Southern
soc. society
sociol. sociological
spkr. speaker
spl. special
splty. specialty
Sq. Square
SR Sons of the Revolution
sr. senior
S S Steamship
St. Saint, Street
sta. station
stats. statistics
statis. statistical
STB Bachelor of Sacred Theology
stblzn. stabilization
STD Doctor of Sacred Theology
std. standard
Ste. Suite
subs. subsidiary
SUNY State University of New York
supr. supervisor
supt. superintendent
surg. surgical
svc. service
SW Southwest
sys. system

T

Tb. tuberculosis
tchg. teaching
tchr. teacher
tech. technical, technology
technol. technological
tel. telephone
telecom. telecommunications
temp. temporary
Tenn. Tennessee
TESOL Teachers of English to Speakers of Other Languages
Tex. Texas
ThD Doctor of Theology
theol. theological
ThM Master of Theology
TN Tennessee
tng. training
topog. topographical
trans. transaction, transferred
transl. translation, translated
transp. transportation
treas. treasurer
TV television
twp. township
TX Texas
typog. typographical

U

U. University
UAW United Auto Workers
UCLA University of California at Los Angeles
UK United Kingdom
UN United Nations
UNESCO United Nations Educational, Scientific and Cultural Organization
UNICEF United Nations International Children's Emergency Fund
univ. university
UNRRA United Nations Relief and Rehabilitation Administration
UPI United Press International
urol. urological
US, USA United States of America
USAAF United States Army Air Force
USAF United States Air Force
USAFR United States Air Force Reserve
USAR United States Army Reserve
USCG United States Coast Guard
USCGR United States Coast Guard Reserve
USES United States Employment Service
USIA United States Information Agency
USMC United States Marine Corps
USMCR United States Marine Corps Reserve
USN United States Navy
USNG United States National Guard
USNR United States Naval Reserve
USO United Service Organizations
USPHS United States Public Health Service
USS United States Ship
USSR Union of the Soviet Socialist Republics
USTA United States Tennis Association
UT Utah

V

VA Veterans Administration
VA, Va. Virginia
vet. veteran, veterinary
VFW Veterans of Foreign Wars
VI Virgin Islands
vis. visiting
VISTA Volunteers in Service to America
vocat. vocational
vol. volunteer, volume
v.p. vice president
vs. versus
VT, Vt. Vermont

W

W West
WA, Wash. Washington (state)
WAC Women's Army Corps
WAVES Women's Reserve, US Naval Reserve
WCTU Women's Christian Temperance Union
we. western
WHO World Health Organization
WI Wisconsin, West Indies
Wis. Wisconsin
WV, W.Va. West Virginia
WY, Wyo. Wyoming

X, Y, Z

YK Yukon Territory
YMCA Young Men's Christian Association
YMHA Young Men's Hebrew Association
YM & YWHA Young Men's and Young Women's Hebrew Association
yr. year
YT Yukon Territory
YWCA Young Women's Christian Association

Alphabetical Practices

Names are arranged alphabetically according to the surnames, and under identical surnames according to the first given name. If both surname and first given name are identical, names are arranged alphabetically according to the second given name.

Surnames beginning with De, Des, Du, however capitalized or spaced, are recorded with the prefix preceding the surname and arranged alphabetically under the letter D.

Surnames beginning with Mac and Mc are arranged alphabetically under M.

Surnames beginning with Saint or St. appear after names that begin Sains, and are arranged according to the second part of the name, e.g., St. Clair before Saint Dennis.

Surnames beginning with Van, Von, or von are arranged alphabetically under the letter V.

Compound surnames are arranged according to the first member of the compound.

Many hyphenated Arabic names begin Al-, El-, or al-. These names are alphabetized according to each biographee's designation of last name. Thus Al-Bahar, Neta may be listed either under Al- or under Bahar, depending on the preference of the listee.

Also, Arabic names have a variety of possible spellings when transposed to English. Spelling of these names is always based on the practice of the biographee. Some biographees use a Western form of word order, while others prefer the Arabic word sequence.

Similarly, Asian names may have no comma between family and given names, but some biographees have chosen to add the comma. In each case, punctuation follows the preference of the biographee.

Parentheses used in connection with a name indicate which part of the full name is usually omitted in common usage. Hence, Chambers, E(lizabeth) Anne indicates that the first name, Elizabeth, is generally recorded as an initial. In such a case, the parentheses are ignored in alphabetizing and the name would be arranged as Chambers, Elizabeth Anne.

However, if the entire first name appears in parentheses, for example, Chambers, (Elizabeth) Anne, the first name is not commonly used, and the alphabetizing is therefore arranged as though the name were Chambers, Anne.

If the entire middle name is in parentheses, it is still used in alphabetical sorting. Hence, Belamy, Katherine (Lucille) would sort as Belamy, Katherine Lucille. The same occurs if the entire last name is in parentheses, e.g., (Brandenberg), Howard Keith would sort as Brandenberg, Howard Keith.

For visual clarification:

Smith, H(enry) George: Sorts as Smith, Henry George
Smith, (Henry) George: Sorts as Smith, George
Smith, Henry (George): Sorts as Smith, Henry George
(Smith), Henry George: Sorts as Smith, Henry George

Who'sWho in America®

Biographees M - Z

MA, CHUNG-PEI MICHELLE, astronomer, educator; BS, PhD, MIT, 1993. From asst. prof. to assoc. prof. physics and astronomy U. Pa., Phila., 1996—2001; assoc. prof. astronomy U. Calif., Berkeley, 2001—. Contbr. articles to profl. jours. Recipient Annie J. Cannon award, 1997, 1st prize Taiwan Nat. Violin Competition, 1983, Cottrell Scholars award Rsch. Corp., 1999, Lindback award for Disting. Tchg., U. Pa., 1999; Alfred P. Sloan fellow, 1999; Sherman Fairchild fellow, 1993. Mem. Phi Beta Kappa. Achievements include research in the formation and evolution of galaxies and large scale structure in the Universe; performed numerical simulations of the clustering of dark matter in various cosmological models of structure formation from the Early Universe until the present day; computation of the temperature variations imprinted on the cosmic microwave background radiation which provides a snapshot of the infant Universe. Office: U Calif Berkeley Dept Astronomy 601 Campbell Hall Berkeley CA 94720

MA, FAI, mechanical engineering educator; b. Canton, People's Republic of China, Aug. 6, 1954; came to U.S., 1977, naturalized, 1988; s. Rui-Qi and Shao-Fen (Luo) M. BS, U. Hong Kong, 1977; MS, PhD, Calif. Inst. Tech., 1981. Sr. rsch. engr. Weidlinger Assocs., Menlo Park, Calif., 1981-82; rsch. fellow IBM, Yorktown Heights, N.Y., 1982-83; sr. engr. Standard Oil Co., Cleve., 1983-86; prof. mech. engring. U. Calif., Berkeley, 1986—. Vis. scholar Oxford U., Eng., 1992, U. Stuttgart, Germany, 1993. Co-author: Probabilistic Analysis, 1983, Computational Mechanics, 1989; co-editor Advances in Engring., 1995--; contbr. articles to profl. jours. Young Investigator award NSF, 1987; Humboldt fellow, 1992; Fulbright awardee, 2002. Fellow: ASME. Office: U Calif Dept Mech Engring Berkeley CA 94720-1740 Business E-Mail: fma@me.berkeley.edu.

MA, L. EVE ARMENTROUT, television producer, television director, educator; b. Dec. 28, 1943; d. Edward Goodwin and Lucy McIver (Watson) Ballard; m. David Parker Armentrout, 1966 (div. 1969); 1 child, Lucy Ann; m. Jeong-Huei Ma, Jan. 1970 (div. 1986); children: William Marshall, Edward Benjamin. Student, Middlebury Coll., 1961-63; BA, San Francisco State Coll., 1968; postgrad. in Chinese, Stanford U., 1971; MA, Calif. State U., Hayward, 1972; PhD in Chinese History, U. Calif., Davis, 1977; JD, U. Calif., Hastings, 1993. Bar: Calif., 1994. Tchg. asst. history dept. U. Calif., Davis, 1973-76; rsch. assoc. anthropology dept., 1977-79; asst. prof. history dept., 1980, 1982; rsch. assoc. applied behavioral scis. dept., 1982-83; asst. prof. Mills Coll., Calif., 1988-90; pvt. practice law, 1993—99; asst. prof. Calif. State U., Hayward, 1986—88; prodr.-dir. Palomino Prodns., 2004—. Cons. Golden Gate Nat. Rec. Area, San Francisco, 1979-80, Oakland Mus., 1981, 84, ARC Assocs., Inc., Oakland, 1981-82, James R. Moore Atty. at Law, San Francisco, 1982, Pacific Ocean divsn. U.S. Army Corps. Engrs. Hawaii, 1983-86, Japan Engr., dist. U.S. Army Corps Engrs. Camp Zama, Japan, 1986-89. Author: (with others) Chinese of Oakland, 1982, sole author: Revolutionaries, Monarchists and Chinatowns, 1990, Hometown Chinatown, 2000; editor, contbr.: Farms, Firms and Runways: U.S. Military Bases, 2001; editor, contbr.: One Day, One Dollar, 1984, Chung-Hsi Liao-way T'ai (newsletter), 1986; contbr. articles to scholary volumes and jours.; prodr., host (TV series): Languages of Sound and Movement; prodr., dir. (TV series) Roots, Branches, Improvising Jerez-Style, Weaving with Spanish Threads; prodr. DVDs. Hist. and interpretive rev. com. Calif. Dept. Pks. and Recreation Multicultural Ctr., 1982-84; design rev. com. Calif. State Railroad Mus., 1982-83; vol. tchr. pub. and pvt. schs., San Francisco Bay Area, 1973-86; leader Girl Scouts USA, 1976-79, Boy Scouts Am., 1985-98; officer neighborhood assn., Richmond, Calif., 1974-87; bd. dirs. Chinese/Chinese-Am. History Assn., El Cerrito, Calif., 1979-86, Chinese Hist. Soc. Am., 1983-90, Oakland Asian Culture Ctr., 1993-97, Celebrating Culture and Cmty., 1996-04; commr. Arts and Cultural Commn. Contra Costa County, 1998-2004, Arts and Cultural Commn. City of El Cerrito, 2004. Recipient Star award, 2001, Wave award, 2006; grantee, Kellogg Found., 1977—79, Calif. Coun. Humanities grantee, 1981, 1983—84, 1998, Calif. Arts Coun., 2000—04; Nat. Def. Fgn. Lang. fellow, Stanford U., 1971, Am.-East Asian Rels. fellow, U. Calif., Davis, 1972—73. Mem. Chinese Hist. Soc. Am. (bd. dirs. 1983-90), Assn. Asian Studies, Am. Hist. Assn., Calif. Bar Assn., Contra Costa City Bar Assn., Inst. Hist. Study, Ind. Scholars Asia, U. Calif.-Berkeley Inst., East Asian Studies, Film Arts Found., others. Democrat. Address: 1355 Arlington Blvd El Cerrito CA 94530-2514 also: Palomino Prodns Calle Benavente Bajo 3 11403 Jarez Spain Office Phone: 510-236-3257, 011 34 652 388586. Business E-Mail: palopro2004@yahoo.com.

MA (XUEZHENG), MARY, retired computer company executive; married. 1 child. BA, Capital Normal U., Beijing, 1976. Bureaucrat, Chinese Academy of Sciences' Internat. Corp. bureau China State Coun., 1978—90; with Lenovo Group, 1990—, sr. v.p. Beijing & Purchase NY, 1997—2007, CFO, 2000—07, non-exec. vice-chmn., 2007—. Bd. dirs. SOHU.com; bd. dir. Lenovo Group, 1997—2007. Named Best CFO, Finance Asia; named one of most powerful women, Forbes mag., 2005, 50 Most Powerful Women in Global Bus., Fortune mag., 2005, 50 Women to Watch, Wall St. Jour., 2006. Office: Lenovo Group Haidan District No 6 Chuang Ye Road Beijing 100085 China Office Phone: 86-10-58868888.

MA, SHIJUN, engineering educator; b. Jixian, China, Sept. 29, 1932; s. Jintang and Xirong (Zhang) M.; m. Yuerui Tong, Feb. 14, 1958; children: Min Tong, Da Ma, Nian Ma. Diploma, Wuhan U., China, 1953, Huazhong U. Sci. and Tech., 1957. Asst. lectr. HUST, Wuhan, China, 1957—61; lectr. Sichuan Forestry Inst., Xichang, China, 1962—71; lectr., assoc. prof. Southwest Jiotong U., Emei, China, 1975-89; engr. Xichang Machinery Factory, China, 1972-74; prof. Southwest Jiotong U., Chengdu, China, 1990—. Vis. scholar Howard U., Washington, 1987-88. Contbr. articles to profl. jours. Recipient Sichuan Province Sci. and Tech. award Sicuhan Province, Chengdu, 1989, Thesis award The Railway Ministry, Beijing, 1985, Govt. Spl. Allowance award The State Coun., Beijing, 1993, Nat. Sci. and Tech. award, Sci. and Tech. Ministry, Beijing, 1999. Mem. (sr.) CMES. Avocations: swimming, chinese chess. Office: Sch Mech Engring SW Jiaotong U Chengdu 610031 China Home: 6101 Emmett Guards Ct Fairfax Station VA 22039 Personal E-mail: shijun_ma@yahoo.com.

MA, VU, chemist; BA, Immaculata U., Malvern, Pa., 1997. Rsch. assoc. Pharmacopiea, Princeton, NJ, 1997—99; sr. assoc. scientist Amgen, Thousand Oaks, Calif., 1999—. Achievements include patents for Vanilloid receptor ligands and their use in treatments.

MA, WENXUE, medical scientist; s. Shumin Ma and Xiuqin Liu; m. Chunyang Hou, Dec. 12, 1992; children: Duli, Yiming. MS, Zhejiang Med. U., Hangzhou, China, 1997, MD, 1989; PhD, Zhejiang U., Hangzhou, 2002. Fellow U. Nebr. Med. Ctr., Omaha; rsch. assoc. U. Wis., Madison, 2004—05; with U. Calif., San Diego, 2005—. Mem.: AAAS (assoc.), Am. Assn. for Cancer Rsch. (assoc.), Sigma Xi (assoc.). Achievements include patents pending for transmembrane superantigen staphylococcal enterotoxin A. Office: Univ Calif San Diego 3855 Health Sciences Dr #0820 La Jolla CA Office Phone: 858-822-3320. Office Fax: 858-534-7061. Personal E-mail: mawenxue@hotmail.com. E-mail: wma@ucsd.edu.

MA, XIAOMIN, communications educator; s. Deying Wang and Yongzhong Ma; m. Ziping Hu, Mar. 15, 1991; 1 child, Siqi. PhD, Beijing U. Posts & Telecom, 1999. Asst. prof. Petroleum U. China, Dongying, 1989—95, assoc. prof., 1995—99; sr. rschr. Huawei Comm. Tech. Corp., Beijing, 1999—2000; postdoctoral rsch. assoc. Duke U., Durham, NC, 2000—03; asst. prof. Oral Roberts U., Tulsa, 2003—. Cons. Motorola, Chgo., 2000—02. Contbr. articles to profl. jours. Mem. tech. program com. IEEE Wireless Comm. Conf., Maui, Hawaii, 2005. Named Scholar of the Yr., Oral Roberts U., 2004—05; recipient Excellent Tchg. award Signal & Sys. course, Petroleum U. China, 1995; grantee Analysis of MAC layer protocols for Inter-vehicle comm., Oral Roberts U., 2005—06, Application of computational intelligence to modern code, Chinese Nature Sci. Found., 1997—2000, Auditing theory for communication networks, Motorola, 2000-2002. Mem.: IEEE (corr.). Achievements include patents for methods and systems for improving utilization of traffic channel in a mobile communications network, Xiaomin Ma, Yun Liu, and K. S. Trivedi. Office: Oral Roberts University 7777 S Lewis Ave Tulsa OK 74171 Office Fax: 918-495-7648. Personal E-mail: maxiaomin@yahoo.com. Business E-Mail: xma@oru.edu.

MA, XIN-LIANG, biomedical researcher, educator; b. Taiyuan, China, Aug. 21, 1957; came to U.S., 1989; s. Ren-Chen Ma and Yu-Lang Wang; m. Yaping Guo, Jan. 28, 1986; children: Jeffrey, Joanna. MMed, Shangxi Med. U., Taiyuan, China, 1982; PhD, 4th Mil. Med. U., Xian, China, 1988. Asst. prof. Thomas Jefferson U., Phila., 1993-97, rsch. dir. emergency medicine, 1993—, assoc. prof. surgery, 1997—2002, prof. surgery, 2002—. Presenter over 100 abstracts at nat. and internat. confs. Rschr. in myocardial apoptosis after reprefusion, opposite role of nitric oxide and nitroxyl in myocardial reprefusion injury; contbr. over 100 articles to profl. jours. Fellow Soc. for Acad. Emergency Medicine (Best Basic Sci. award 1998, 2000); mem. Am. Heart Assn. Home: 12 Kyle Ct Mount Laurel NJ 08054 Office: Thomas Jefferson U 1020 Sansom St Philadelphia PA 19107 Fax: (215) 923-6225. E-mail: Xin.Ma@mail.tju.edu.

MA, YINGYU, research scientist; b. Chuma, China, Aug. 19, 1973; d. Xiaonian Ma and Shuirong Wang; m. Qing Ma. MD, Beijing Med. U., 1998; PhD, Northwestern U., Chgo., 2004. Postdoctoral fellow Roswell Pk. Cancer Inst., Buffalo, 2004—. Contbr. scientific papers to profl. jours. Recipient Achievements in Clin. Rsch. of Dermatology First prize, Bejing Med. U., 1997—98; grantee, Northwestern U. Grad. Sch., 2002—03; scholar, 1999—2004; Scholarship for Excellent Students, Bejing Med. U., 1994—95. Home: 175 North St #308 Buffalo NY 14201 Office: Roswell Park Cancer Inst Elm & Carlton Sts Buffalo NY 14263 Home Phone: 716-886-0839; Office Phone: 716-845-1257. Office Fax: 716-845-1258. Personal E-mail: yingyuma@yahoo.com. Business E-Mail: yingyu.ma@roswellpark.org.

MA, YO-YO, cellist; b. Paris, Oct. 7, 1955; m. Jill; children: Nicholas, Emily. Studied with Janos Scholz; studied with Leonard Rose, Juilliard Sch. Music, NYC, 1962; AB, Harvard U., 1976, MusD (hon.), 1991. Debut at age 9 Carnegie Hall, NYC; appeared with Pablo Casals, Isaac Stern, Leonard Bernstein, Emanuel Ax, Jaime Laredo, performs throughout world with maj. orchs.; rec. artist Sony Classical; founder & artistic dir. Silk Road Project Inc., Providence, 1998—. Peace amb. UN, 2006—. Albums include Portrait of Yo-Yo Ma, Anything Goes (with Stephanie Grapelli), Yo-Yo Ma at Tanglewood, Cello Suites Inspired By Bach, Portrait of Cello Works, Premieres, Great Cello Concertos, 1989, Japanese Melodies, 1990, Transcriptions, 1990, Hush, 1992, Made in America, 1993, The New York Album, 1994, Appalachia Waltz, 1996, The Protecting Veil/Wake Up...And Die, 1998, Plays Piazzolla, 1998, Soul of the Tango, 1998, Simply Baroque, 1999, Lulie the Iceberg, 1999, Solo, 1999, Appalachian Journey, 2000, Phantasmagoria, 2000, Yo-Yo Ma Plays the Music of John Williams, 2002, Silk Road Journeys: When Strangers Meet, 2002, Obrigado Brazil, 2003, Belle Epoque, 2003, Plays Ennio Morricone, 2004, Silke Road Journeys: Beyond the Horizon, 2004, Sounds of Yo-Yo Ma, 2004, The Dvorak Album, 2004, Vivaldi's Cello, 2004, Bach: Unaccompanied Cello Suites, 2006, Appassionato, 2006, New Impossibilities, 2007. Recipient Avery Fisher prize, 1978, Sonning Music prize, 2006; 14-time Grammy award winning artist. Office: ICM Artists 40 W 57th St Fl 16 New York NY 10019 also: Silk Road Project Inc 20 Westminster St Providence RI 02903 *

MA, ZHENQIANG, education educator; m. Shaoqin Gong, 1995; children: Alice L., David L. BS in Applied Physics, Tsinghua U., Beijing, 1991, BEE, 1991; MSEE, U. Mich., Ann Arbor, 1997, MS in Nuc. Sci., 1997, PhD, 2001. Faculty Tsinghua U., Beijing, 1991—94; rsch. asst. U. Mich., Ann Arbor, 1995—2001; R&D engr. Conexant Sys., Newport Beach, Calif., 2001—02, Jazz Semiconductor, Inc., Newport Beach, 2002; asst. prof. U. Wis., Madison, 2002—. Tech rev. rsch. panel MIT, Cambridge, 2004—; reviewer, presenter in field; mem. sci. adv. bd. Lifeboat Found., 2007—. Contbr. articles to profl. jours. Named Excellent Grad., Tsinghua U., 1991, Best Student Mentor, 1993; recipient 5.4 Youth medal, 1992, 12.9 award, 1992, Collaborative Disting. Publ. award, NASA, 2002, Best Student Paper award, ISDRS, 2005, SiRF, 2006; fellow, Ohio State U., 1994—95; scholar Grad. Student Rsch. scholar, U. Mich., Ann Arbor, 1995—2002; Rackham Travel fellow, 1996, 1998, Excellent Student scholar, Tsinghua U., 1987—91. Mem.: IEEE (session chmn. 2004, tech. program co-chmn. 2006, exec. com. 2006—, publicity chair 2007), Electrochem. Soc., IEEE Comm. Soc., IEEE Lasers and Electro-Optics Soc., IEEE Microwave Theory and Techniques Soc., IEEE Electron Devices Soc. Achievements include establishment of RF theoretical and experimental foundation of common-base heterojunction bipolar transistors; pioneer of flexible RF; development of first RF record speed flexible transistors and flexible RF components; flexible photo detectors; membrane derivation from bulk silicon; international recognition on fast flexible electronics; design of heat transfer counterbalanced power devices; development of first model for recombination enhanced impurity diffusion process, first PIN-SiGe HBT integration; discovery of recombinantion enhanced impurity diffusion process in SiGe heterojuntion bipolar transistors, unconditionally stable common-base SiGe HBTs; relation between Kirk effect and Early effect at high bias in bipolar transistors; correlation between doping profile and power gain of SiGe HBTs, analytical expression for parasitic effects on power gain degradation; power gain relation between common-source and common-gate configurations, photoconductivity on decomposed Si linked by carbon nanotube network; invention of double sided processing method on membranes derived from bulk Si; patents for novel power devices for cell phone and other portable wireless devices; patents pending for Si-based common-base power amplifier, methods of fabricating one-side and/or double-side integrated thin-film transistors on single-crystal semiconductors via layer transfer; process and device for enhanced resolution and readout speed in image sensing; solid-state high frequency high power device; first to report radiation effects on power SiGe HBTs and power MOSFETs; State-of-the-art SiGe power HBTs; analytical and graphical, full-frequency-range power gain relation between common-emitter and common-base configurations; novel bias schemes for common-base bipolar transistors to extract maximum power peformance; First SiGe/Si power MODFETs; up-scaling rule for high power semiconctor devices; research in new ballast resitor implementaion rules in power semiconductor devices; relation between maximum oscillation frequency and device structure; first thin film transistors on tranferred strained single-crystal Si; Ge profile impact on power gain of SiGe HBTs; SiGe power HBTs at L-, S-, C-, X-, Ku- and K-bands; metal film texture control method using ion beam, FET-disciplined power bipolar transistors; SiGe power HBT base region optimization method, current gain enhancement using Ge under high base doping concentrations; invention of. Avocations: swimming, travel, ping pong/table tennis, home improvement, multimedia entertainment. Office: Univ Wis 1415 Engineering Dr 3445EH Madison WI 53706 Office Phone: 608-261-1095. Office Fax: 608-261-1095. Business E-Mail: mazq@engr.wisc.edu.

MAACK, THOMAS, physiology professor; MD, U. Sao Paulo, Brazil, 1961, D in Nephrology, 1980. Prof. physiology Weill Med. Sch. of Cornell U., NYC, 1974—. Contbr. over 100 articles to profl. jours. Fellow: Am. Heart Assn.; mem.: Brazilian Acad. Scis. (life). Home: 402 E 90 St New York NY 10128 Office: Weill Med Coll of Cornell Univ 1300 York Ave New York NY 10021 Office Phone: 212-746-6343.

MAAR, ROSINA, medical products executive; BS, Ga. Inst. Tech., 1984; MD, Morehouse Sch. Medicine, 1988. Cert. internal medicine Ga., N.C. Intern and resident in internal medicine Emory U. Sch. Medicine, Atlanta, 1991; physics lab. instr. Ga. Inst. Tech., Atlanta, 1981-84; rsch. asst. Emory U., Atlanta, 1985-86; med. evaluator maternal and infant project Grady Meml. Hosp., Atlanta, 1987-88; contract physician Wesley Woods Geriatric Hosp., Atlanta, 1989-90; contract physician, program dir. Piedmont Hosp./Spinal Shepard Ctr., Atlanta, 1989-91; med. dir. Cellcor, Inc., Atlanta, 1991-92, corp. med. dir. Newton, Mass., 1992-93; med. scientist med./regulatory svcs. Quintiles, Inc., Research Triangle Park, N.C., 1993-94, dir. med. svcs., 1994-95, v.p. clin. ops., 1995—, sr. v.p. strategic mgmt., until 1999; COO Clinicor, Inc., Austin, Tex., 1999—; venture ptnr. A.M. Pappas & Associates, 2000—. Contbr. articles and abstracts to med. jours. Mem.: AMA, ACP, Am. Bd. Internal Medicine (diplomat). Office: AM Pappas and Associates PO Box 110287 7030 Kit Creek Rd Durham NC 27709

MAARBJERG, MARY PENZOLD, retired office equipment company executive; b. Oct. 2, 1943; d. Edmund Theodore and Lucy Adelaide (Singleton) Penzold; m. John Peder Maarbjerg, Oct. 20, 1966; 1 child, Martin Peder. AB, Hollins Coll., 1965; MBA, Wharton Sch., Pa., 1969. Cons. bus. and fin., Stamford, Conn., 1977-78; corp. staff analyst Pitney Bowes, Inc., Stamford, 1978-80, mgr. pension and benefit fin., 1980-81, dir. investor rels., 1981-85; v.p. planning and devel. Pitney Bowes Credit Corp., Norwalk, Conn., 1985-86, treas., v.p. planning, 1986-94; v.p. mktg. devel. and mng. dir. Asia Pacific Bowes Fin. Svcs., 1994-95, v.p. ops. and mng. dir., 1995-97; v.p. corp. svcs. Pitney Bowes, Inc., Stamford, 1997-99, v.p. real estate and adminstrn., 1999-2001, v.p. adminstrn. and process integration, 2001—05. Bd. dirs. Stanford Dental Ctr., 2003—; mem. cmty. bd. U. Conn., Stanford, 2003—; bd. dirs. Person-to-Person, 2004—, treas., 2005—. Mem. adv. com. City of Stamford Mcpl. Employees Retirement Fund, 1980-85; mem. fin. adv. com. YWCA, Stamford, 1982-86; bd. dirs. Stamford Symphony, 1985-95, Vis. Nurses Assn., 1984-86, Am. Recorder Soc., 1986-98, Am. Classical Orch., 1999-2002; bd. dirs. Stamford Partnership, chmn., 1998—2004; bd. dirs., treas. Amherst Early Music, 2000—. Fellow Royal Statis. Soc.; mem. Fin. Execs. Inst., Phi Beta Kappa. E-mail: mmaar@optonline.net.

MAAS, COREY, plastic surgeon; BS in Bio., Fla. St. Univ., Tallahassee, 1982; MD with hon., Univ. Fla. Coll. Med., Gainesville, Fla., 1986. Cert. Nat. Bd. Med. Examiners, 1987, Miss., 1987, Calif., 1991, Fla., 1996, Am. Bd. Otolaryngology, 1992, Am. Bd. Facial Plastic and Reconstructive Surgery, 1996. Gen. surg. intern St. Louis Univ. Med. Clinic, 1986—87, otolaryngology-head neck surgery resident, 1987—90, chief resident, 1990—91; fell. facial plastic and reconstructive surgery divsn. UC San Francisco Med. Clinic, 1991—92; private practice plastic surgeon San Francisco. Clin. instr., divsn. plastic surgery UC, San Francisco, 1991, assoc. clin. prof., 1992—; dir., facial plastic surgery tng. fell. Am. Acad. Facial Plastic and Reconstructive Surgery, 2000. Recipient Gold Key Scholastic Leadership honor, FSU, 1982, Sir Harold Delf Gilles Rsch. award, Am. Acad. Facial and Plastic Surgery, 1992, Nat. Cmty. Svc. award, 1994. Office: The Maas Clinic 2400 Clay St San Francisco CA 94115 Office Fax: 415-567-7011.

MAAS, DUANE HARRIS, distilling company executive; b. Tilleda, Wis., Aug. 26, 1927; s. John William and Adela (Giessel) M.; m. Sonja Johnson, Mar. 11, 1950; children: Jon Kermit, Duane Arthur, Thomas Ervin. BS, U. Wis., 1951. With Shell Chem. Corp., 1951-59; plant mgr. Fleischmann Distilling Corp., Owensboro, Ky., 1959-63, Plainfield, Ill., 1963-65; asst. to v.p. Barton Distilling Co., Chgo., 1965-68, exec. asst. to pres., 1968, v.p. adminstrn., 1968; v.p., gen. mgr. Barton Brands, Inc., Chgo., 1968— 72; pres. Leaf Confectionery div. W.R. Grace, Chgo., 1972-74; v.p., gen. mgr. Romano Bros., Chgo., 1974-79; v.p., sec.-treas. Marketing Directions Inc., Chgo., 1974-77; pres. Associated Wine Producers, Inc., 1979-80; exec. v.p., chief exec. officer Mohawk Liqueur, Detroit, 1980-86; v.p. McKesson Wine & Spirits Group of N.Y., Detroit, 1982-86; pres. Mgmt. Cons. Services Co., Chgo., 1986—, U.S. Distilled Products Co., Princeton, Minn., 1996-99, Am. Distilled Products Corp., 2001—. Chmn. Qingdao Johnson Distiller Co. Ltd., Qingdao, China, 1996-99; past pres. Bart on Distilling (Can.), Ltd.; past mng. dir. Barton Distilling (Scotland), Ltd.; past dir. Barton Distillers Europe, Barton Internat., Ltd. Sec.-treas. Plainfield Twp. Park Dist., 1967-70; chmn. Plainfield Planning and Zoning Commn., 1965-70. Served with USAAF, 1945-47. Mem.: Wis. Alumni Assn. Lutheran. Home and Office: N28W22312 Foxwood Ln Waukesha WI 53186 Home Phone: 762-522-1063; Office Phone: 262-522-6953. Personal E-mail: dhm@mcservices.com.

MAAS, JANE BROWN, advertising executive; b. Jersey City; d. Charles E and Margaret (Beck) Brown; m. Michael Maas, Aug. 30, 1957; children: Katherine, Jennifer. BA, Bucknell U., 1953; postgrad., U. Dijon, France, 1954; MA, Cornell U., Ithaca, N.Y., 1955; LittD, Ramapo Coll., 1986, St. John's U., 1988. Assoc. producer Name That Tune TV Program, NYC, 1957—64; v.p. Ogilvy and Mather Inc., NYC, 1964—76; sr. v.p. Wells, Rich, Greene, Inc., NYC, 1976—82; pres. Muller Jordan Weiss Inc., NYC, 1982—89, Earle Palmer Brown Cos., NYC, 1989—92, chmn., 1992—94, chmn. emeritus, 1994—. Co-author: (book) How to Advertise, 1975, Better Brochures, 1981, Adventures of a Advertising Woman, 1986, The New How to Advertise, 1992, Christmas in Wales: A Homecoming, 1994. Bd govs comt Scholastic Achievement, 1985—92; active Girl Scouts US, NY,

1970—76; mem adv bd William E Simon Grad Sch Bus, Univ Rochester, 1989—2005; pub dir AIA, 1993—95; trustee Bucknell Univ, Lewisburg, 1976—86, Fordham Univ, NY, 1983—91. Named Woman of the Yr, NY Advert, 1986; recipient Matrix Award, Women in Communications, 1980. Mem.: AIA (hon.), Am Assn. Advt. Agys. (bd govs), Am Archtl. Found (regent 1993—2000), Phi Beta Kappa. Avocations: creative writing, jogging. Home: 1775 York Ave New York NY 10128 Home Phone: 212-722-1221; Office Phone: 212-722-1221. Personal E-mail: janemaas@att.net.

MAAS, JOE (MELVIN JOSEPH MAAS), retired federal agency administrator; b. Washington, Feb. 29, 1940; s. Melvin Joseph and Katherine (Endress) M.; m. Constance Mary Haile, June 13, 1965; children: Christine, Michael, Kevin. BS, U. Md., 1965; postgrad., Stanford U., 1972—73. Dir. career edn. U.S. Dept. Labor, Washington, 1969-73; dep. dir. pers. SBA, Washington, 1973-76, dir. pers., 1976-82, asst. adminstr., 1982-95; founder, prin. Advancement Power, 2003—. Sr. v.p. Crave Entertainment Group, Inc., 2000 Bd. dirs., treas. Snowden Mill Assn., Silver Spring, Md., 1994-2002, pres. 2002-04; Wash. rep. Ind. Charities Am., 1995-96; bd. dirs. Amen Found., 1998—, Pres. Amen Found., 2003-05; chmn. Internat. Pers. Assn., 1982. With USMCR, 1957-64. Mem. Fed. Exec. Adminstrs. Assn., Sr. Exec. Assn., Pub. Employee Roundtable (bd. dirs. 1994—, chmn. Pub. Svc. Excellence awards 1996-98, treas. 1998-2002), Coun. Former Fed. Execs. (pres., bd. dirs. 1995-2005), Nat. Assn. Ret. Fed. Employees (chpt. pres. 1996-98, v.p. 1998-2000, state tng. officer 1997-01), Volkswagen Club (pres. Washington chpt. 1988-95). Roman Catholic. Home: 2213 Aventurine Way Silver Spring MD 20904-5253 Personal E-mail: jm73bug@aol.com.

MAAS, NORMAN LEWIS, library director; b. Jan. 22, 1948; BS in Edn., Wayne State U., 1970, MLS, 1971. Tchr. 7th grade social studies Durfee Jr. HS, Detroit, 1970; libr. I gen. info. dept. and bibliog. ctr. Main Libr. Detroit Pub. Libr., 1971, libr. I Monnier and Richard Br. Librs., 1972, libr. I older citizens ext. svcs., 1973, libr. II bookmobile svcs., 1973; libr. II cmty. info., referral svcs. Info. Pl. Svc., Detroit Pub. Libr., 1973, asst. chief dept. cmty. info., referral svcs., 1974—75, chief, coord. major libr. activity dept., 1975—90, chief gen. info., bibliog. ctr., ready reference dept., 1990; libr. dir. Pub. Librs. Saginaw, Mich., 1991—2000; exec. dir. Met. Libr. Sys., Oklahoma City, 2000—02; dir. librs. Norfolk Pub. Libr., Va., 2003—. Bd. dirs. ALA, 2005—, The Literacy Partnership. Contbr. articles to profl. publs. Bd. mem. Norfolk Literacy Partnership, 2003—, Norfolk Hist. Soc., 2004—. Named Disting. Info. and Referral Profl. of Yr., Nat. Alliances Info. and Referral Systems, 1990, Libr. Sci. Alumnus of Yr., Wayne State U., 1993; recipient Neighborhood Info. Exch., Inc. Cmty. Activist award, 1985, Libr. of Yr. award, Mich. Libr. Assn., 1998. Mem.: ALA (bd. dirs. 2005—, chair pub. com. 2005—06, mem. cmty. info. svcs. com. 2000—02), Mich. Libr. Assn., Va. Libr. Assn., Beta Phi Mu. Office: Norfolk Pub Libr Adminstrn 301 E City Hall Ave Norfolk VA 23510 Office Phone: 757-664-7328. Office Fax: 757-664-7320. E-mail: norman.maas@norfolk.gov. *

MAAS, WERNER KARL, microbiology educator; b. Kaiserslautern, Germany, Apr. 27, 1921; came to U.S., 1936, naturalized, 1945; s. Albert and Esther (Meyer) M.; m. Renata Diringer, Oct. 15, 1960; children—Peter, Andrew, Helen. AB, Harvard U., 1943; PhD, Columbia U., 1948. Postdoctoral fellow Calif. Inst. Tech., Pasadena, 1946-48; commd. officer USPHS, Tb Research Lab., Cornell U. Sch., NYC, 1948-54; asst. prof. pharmacology NYU, 1954-57, assoc. prof. microbiology, 1957-63, prof., 1963-94, prof. emeritus, 1994—, chmn. dept. basic med. scis., 1974-81. Career grantee, USPHS, 1962—94. Mem.: Am. Soc. Microbiology, Genetics Soc. Am., Am. Soc. Biol. Chemists. Home: 86 Villard Ave Hastings On Hudson NY 10706-1821 Office: 550 1st Ave New York NY 10016-6402 Home Phone: 914-478-1839; Office Phone: 212-263-5322. E-mail: maasw01@endeavor.med.nyu.edu.

MAASCH, LLOYD PALMER, physician; b. Ashippun, Wis., June 16, 1928; s. Louis and Esther Maasch; m. Patricia Ruth Maasch, Dec. 23, 1950; children: Mary Pat, Thomas, Robert, Sue Ann, Patrick. BS, Marquette U., Milw., 1950; MD, Marquette Med. Sch., Milw., 1953; MD (hon.), Med. Coll. Wic., Milw., 2003. Health officer City of Weyauwega, Wis.; county coroner Waupaca County, Waupaca, Wis., 1952—95; mem. hosp. staff Riverside Med. Ctr., Waupaca, New London Family Med. Ctr., Wis.; family physician pvt. practice, Weyauwega. Adj. prof. U. Wis. Sch. Nursing, Oshkosh; med. dir. several nursing homes, Waupaca County, 1957—. Chmn. Weyauwega (20 acre) Pk., 1968—72. Lt. USN, 1955—57. Mem.: Wolf River Area Found., Lions (election chair, Melvin Jones fellow), Am. Legion. Republican. Lutheran. Avocations: painting, collecting Indian artifacts. Home: 208 W Clark St Weyauwega WI 54983-8920

MAATHAI, WANGARI, environmentalist, consultant; b. Nyeri, Kenya, Africa, Apr. 1, 1940; children: Waweru, Wanjira, Muta. BSc, Mt. St. Scholastica, Atchison, Kans., 1964; MS in Biol. Scis., U. Pitts., 1966; PhD in Anatomy, U. Nairobi, Kenya, 1971; LLD (hon.), Williams Coll., 1990; DSc (hon.), Hobart & William Smith Coll., 1994; DAgr (hon.), U. Norway, 1997; LLD (hon.), Yale U., 2004. Lectr. U. Nairobi, 1971-82, chair, dept. veterinary anatomy, 1976, assoc. prof., dept. veterinary anatomy, 1977; ran for presidency Kenya, 1997; founder Green Belt Movement, Nairobi, 1977, coord., 1984—2002; mem. Parliament, Tetu Constituency Republic of Kenya, 2002—, asst. min. of environ., natural resources & wildlife, 2003—. Bd. dir. UN Sec. Generals Adv. Bd. on Disarmament; mem. UN Commn. on Global Governance; founding mem. GROOTS Internat., 1985; endowed chair in gender and women's studies named "Fuller-Maathai", Conn. Coll., 2000; Montgomery Fellow, Dartmouth Coll., 2001; Dorothy McCluskey vis. fellow for conservation, Yale U., 2002. Author: The Green Belt Movement, 1985, The Green Belt Movement: Sharing the Approach and the Experience, 1988, The Green Belt Movement: Sharing the Approach, 2002, Unbowed, 2006; featured in many publs. Bd. dir. Kenya Red Cross Soc., 1973-80, Jane Goodall Inst., Women and Environment Develop. Orgn., World Learning for Internat. Develop., Green Cross Internat., Worldwide Network of Women in Environ. Work; bd. dir., chmn. Environ. Liaison Ctr. Internat., Kenya, 1974-84, Nat. Coun. Women Kenya, 1976-87, chair 1981-87; active Friends of Kenyatta Nat. Hosp., Kenya, 1975; launched Kenya Jubilee 2000 coalition, 1998; mem. adv. bd. Democracy Coalition Project; mem. Earth Charter Commn.; mem. selection com., Sasakawa Environ. prize, UN Environ. Program., Kenya Recipient Women of Yr. award, 1983, Right Livelihood, 1984, Better World Soc. award, 1986, Windstar award for the Environment, 1988, Women of the World, 1989, Offeramus medal, 1990, Goldman Environ. prize, 1991, Africa prize for Leadership The Hunger Project, 1991, medal City of Edinburgh, Scotland, 1993, Jane Adams Leadership award, 1993, Golden Ark award, 1994, Juliet hollister award, 2001, Nobel Prize for Peace, 2004; co-recipient with Green Belt Movement Excellance award, Kenyen Cty. Abroad, 2001, Outstanding Vision and Commitment award, 2002, WANGO Environ. award, 2003, Sophie prize, 2004, Petra Kelly prize for Environment, 2004, J. Sterling Morton award, Conservation Scientist award, 2004, Arbor Day Found.; named to Global 500 Roll of Honor UN Environ. Program, 1990, 100 Heroines of the World, Internat. Women's Hall of Fame, 1995; elected by Earth Times as one of 100 persons in the World who have made a difference in the environ. arena, 1997; named one of 100 Most Influential People in World, Time Mag., 2005, one of most powerful women, Forbes mag., 2005. Mem. Club of Rome, Sasakawa Environ. Prize. Achievements include her work as a leader of the Green Belt Movement which has planted more than 30 million trees across Africa; awarded Nobel Peace Prize for her contribution to sustainable development, democracy, human rights, environmental conservation, peace and also for campaigning for broader women's rights; first East and Central African women to earn a PhD; first female chair and assoc. prof. of the Dept. of Veterinary Anatomy at the U. Nairobi; first female African to be awarded the Nobel Peace Prize. Office: care Green Belt Movement PO Box 67545 Nairobi Kenya

MAATMAN, GERALD LEONARD, insurance company executive; b. Chgo., Mar. 11, 1930; s. Leonard Raymond and Cora Mae (Van Der Laag) M.; children: Gerald L. Jr., Mary Ellen; m. Bernice Catherine Brummer, June 3, 1971. BS, Ill. Inst. Tech., 1951. Asst. chief engineer Ill. Inspection & Rating Bur., Chgo., 1951-58; prof., dept. chmn. Ill. Inst. Tech., Chgo., 1959-65; v.p. engring. Kemper Group, Chgo., 1966-68, pres. Nat. Loss Control Svc. Corp., 1969-74, v.p. corp. planning Long Grove, Ill., 1974-79, sr. v.p. info. svcs. group, 1979-85, exec. v.p. ins. ops., 1985-87; pres. Kemper Nat. Ins. Co., Long Grove, Ill., 1987-92, CEO, 1989-95, also bd. dirs., chmn. bd. dirs., 1991-95. Bd. dirs. Advs. for Auto and Hwy. Safety, 1992-98; chmn. bd. trustees Underwriters Labs., 1991-2002. Lt. (j.g.) USCGR, 1952-54. Mem. Knollwood Golf Club, Tau Beta Pi. Republican.

MAATSCH, DEBORAH JOAN, manufacturing executive; b. Lincoln, Nebr., Mar. 26, 1950; d. Leon F. Forst and Jarolyn J. Hoffman Forst Conrad; m. Gordon F. Maatsch, Mar. 14, 1969; children: Jason, Diana. BS, U. Nebr., Lincoln, 1976; MBA, U. Phoenix, 1997. Accredited tax advisor; IRS enrolled agt. Acct., supr. US Civil Svc., Heidelberg, Germany, 1971—73; paralegal Mattson Rickets Davies et al, Lincoln, Nebr., 1976—87; tax cons., 1981—; paralegal Wade Ash Woods & Hill, P.C., 1986—94; sr. trust adminstr. Investment Trust Co., 1994—96; compliance officer Nelson, Benson and Zellmer, Inc., 1995—96; pres. DGJD Inc., 1993—; contr. Arena Devel., Inc., 1996—2000; pres. Boyd Industries, Inc., 2001—. Mem. Park County Sr. Wellness Team, 1999—; mem. bus. adv. bd. Ponderosa HS, 1994-98. Contbr. articles to profl. jour. Event chmn., vol. Jefferson Cmty. Ctr., 1999—; bd. dirs. JCCA, 2001-03, pres., 2002-03; bd. dirs. Kids Roundup, 2002—; coord. Jefferson Hist. Preservation Fund; mem. Women's C. of C. Mem. Doane Coll. Alumni Assn. (dir. 1989-93), Nebr. Alumni Assn. Avocations: travel, outdoor activities, horses. Office: DGJD Inc PO Box 267 Jefferson CO 80456-0267 also: Boyd Industries Inc PO Box 315 Boyd TX 76023 Personal E-mail: dgjdinc@wildblue.net.

MAAZEL, LORIN, conductor, composer, violinist, music director; b. Neuilly, France, Mar. 6, 1930; s. Lincoln and Marie (Varencove) M.; m. Dietlinde Turban, 1986; 3 children; 4 children from previous marriages. Studies with, Vladimir Bakaleinikoff; student, U. Pitts., Mus. D. (hon.), 1968; H.H.D., Beaver Coll., 1973. Debut as condr., 1938; condr. Am. symphony orchs., 1939—; violin recitalist; European debut, 1953; festivals include Bayreuth, Salzburg, Edinburgh; tours include S.Am., Australia, USSR, Japan, Korea, People's Republic China; artistic dir. Deutsche Opera Berlin, 1965-71; assoc. prin. condr. New Philharm. Orch., London, 1970-72; dir. Cleve. Orch., 1972-82, condr. emeritus, 1982-86; dir. Vienna State Opera, 1982-84; music dir. Pitts. Symphony Orch., 1988-96, Orchestre Nat. de France, 1988-90, Bavarian Radio Symphony Orch., Munich, 1993-2001; music dir. NY Philharmonic, 2002-; albums include Holst: Planets, 2006. Decorated officer Legion d'Honneur 1981; Finnish Commdr. of the Lion; Portuguese Commdr.; Comdr. Cross of Merit, Germany. Achievements include 500 opera and concert performances with 150 orchestras; raised millions of dollars for benefit of UNESCO, World Wide Fund for Nature, the Red Cross, and UN High Commisioner for Refugees. Avocations: tennis, swimming, collecting American paintings and Oriental art. Office: NY Philharmonic Avery Fisher Hall 10 Lincoln Center Plaza New York NY 10023-6990 *

MABEE, CARLETON, historian, educator; b. Shanghai, Dec. 25, 1914; s. Fred Carleton and Miriam (Bentley) M.; m. Norma Dierking, Dec. 20, 1945; children: Timothy I., Susan (Mrs. Paul Newhouse). AB, Bates Coll., 1936; MA (Perkins scholar), Columbia U., 1938, PhD, 1942. With Civilian Pub. Svc., 1941-45; instr. history Swarthmore (Pa.) Coll., 1944; tutor Olivet (Mich.) Coll., 1947-49; asst. prof. liberal studies Clarkson Coll. Tech., Potsdam, NY, 1949-51, asso. prof., 1951-55; prof., 1955-61; dir. social studies divsn. Delta Coll., University Center, Mich., 1961-64; prof., chmn. dept. humanities and social scis. Rose Poly. Inst., Terre Haute, Ind., 1964-65; prof. history State U. Coll. at New Paltz, NY, 1965-80, prof. emeritus NY, 1980—. Participant in projects for Am. Friends Svc. Com., 1941-47, 53, 63; Fulbright prof. Keio U., Tokyo, 1953-54 Author: The American Leonardo, A Life of Samuel F.B. Morse, 1943, The Seaway Story, 1961, Black Freedom: The Nonviolent Abolitionists from 1830 through the Civil War, 1970, Black Education in New York State: From Colonial to Modern Times, 1979, (with Susan Mabee Newhouse) Sojourner Truth: Slave, Prophet, Legend, 1993, Listen to the Whistle: An Ancedotal History of the Wallkill Valley Railroad in Ulster and Orange Counties, N.Y., 1995; editor: (with James A. Fletcher) A Quaker Speaks from the Black Experience: The Life and Selected Writings of Barrington Dunbar, 1979, Bridging the Hudson: The Poughkeepsie Railroad Bridge and its Connecting Rail Lines, a Many-Faceted History, 2001, Gardiner and Lake Minnewaska, 2003; contbr. articles to profl. jours. Trustee Young-Morse Hist. Site, Poughkeepsie, N.Y., 1991-2002; ofcl. town historian, Gardiner, N.Y. Recipient Pulitzer prize in biography, 1944, Bergstein award for excellence in tchg. Delta Coll., 1963, Anisfield-Wolf award race rels., 1971, Gustavus Myers award for outstanding book on human rights, 1994; rsch. grantee Rsch. Found. SUNY, 1965, 67, 68, 80, Am. Philos. Soc., 1970, Nat. Inst. Edn., 1973-76, NSF, 1982-83. Mem. N.Y. State Hist. Assn., Phi Beta Kappa, Delta Sigma Rho. Methodist. Home: 2121 Route 44-55 Gardiner NY 12525-5808

MABEN, HAYWARD CLINTON, JR., cardiothoracic surgeon; b. Augusta, Ga., June 3, 1922; s. Hayward Clinton Sr. and Ethel Marie Maben; m. Carrie Mae Harris, May 3, 1959; children: Hayward Clinton III, Burton Freeman, Michael Waldo. BS, Wayne State U., Detroit, 1943; MD, Meharry Med. Coll., Nashville, 1945. Cert. Am. Bd. Surgery, 1964, Am. Bd. Thoracic Surgery, 1965. Internship Kansas City Gen. Hosp, 1945—46; pvt. practice Detroit, 1947—58; gen. surgery residency Detroit Receiving Hosp., 1958—59, Hubbard Hosp., Meharry Med. Coll., Nashville, 1959—63; thoracic and cardiovascular surgery residency Presbyn. St. Lukes Hosp., Chgo., 1963—64, Hines Veterans Adminstrn. Hosp., Ill., 1964—65; instr. surgery Meharry Med. Coll., 1961—63; pvt. practice, cardiovascular and thoracic surgery Detroit, 1965—; clin. assoc. prof. surgery Wayne State U. Med. Sch., 1969—2005; chief of surgery Kirwood Hosp., 1980—85; ret., 2005. Dept. head surgery Kirwood Gen. Hosp., Detroit, 1968—70, Southwest Detroit Hosp., 1975—78. Contbr. articles to profl. jours. 1st lt. US Army, 1944—46. Fellow: ACS, Am. Coll. Chest Physicians; mem.: NAACP (life), Wayne State Surg. Soc., Wayne County Med. Soc., Soc. Thoracic Surgeons, Nat. Med. Assn., Mich. State Med. Soc., Detroit Med. Soc., Mich. Soc. Thoracic Surgeons, Wayne State Surg. Soc., Sigma Pi Phi, Kappa Alpha Phi. Achievements include First board certified African American thoracic surgeon to practice in Michigan. Avocation: golf. Personal E-mail: hmaben@hotmail.com.

MABEY, RALPH R., lawyer; b. Salt Lake City, May 20, 1944; s. Rendell Noel and Rachel (Wilson) M.; m. Sylvia States, June 5, 1968; children: Kathryn, Rachel, Elizabeth, Emily, Sara. BA, U. Utah, 1968; JD, Columbia U., 1972. Bar: Utah 1972, U.S. Dist. Ct. Utah 1972, U.S. Ct. Appeals (10th cir.) 1976, N.Y. 1985, U.S. Supreme Ct. 1988, U.S. Ct. Appeals (4th cir.) 1988, U.S. Ct. Appeals (3d cir.) 1993. Law clk. Atty. Gen., Salt Lake City, 1970, US Dist. Ct., Salt Lake City, 1972-73; ptnr. Irvine, Smith & Mabey, Salt Lake City, 1973-79; US bankruptcy judge US Ct., Salt Lake City, 1979-83; ptnr. LeBoeuf, Lamb, Greene & MacRae LLP, Salt Lake City and NYC, 1983—2005, Mabey & Murray LC, Salt Lake City, 2005—06; sr. of counsel Stutman Treister & Glatt, LA, 2006—. Sr. lectr. Brigham Young U. Sch. Law, Provo, Utah, 1983—2005; prof. law U. Utah Coll. Law, Salt Lake City, 2007—. Mng. editor Norton Bankruptcy Law Adviser, 1983-85. With USAR, 1968-74. Mem. ABA (bus. bankruptcy com., select adv. com. on bus. reorgns.), Nat. Bankruptcy Conf., Am. Law Inst., Am. Bankruptcy Inst., Am. Coll. Bankruptcy. Republican. Mem. Lds Ch. Avocations: running, fly fishing. Home Phone: 801-295-0677. Business E-Mail: rmabey@stutman.com.

MABILANGAN, FELIPE HUGO, JR., diplomat; b. Manila, Feb. 15, 1936; s. Felipe and Felisa (Hugo) M.; m. Ada Ledesma, Dec. 8, 1943; children: Jose Antonio, Anne Marie, Lisa. BA, Balliol Coll., U. Oxford, Eng., 1959; MA, Balliol Coll., U. Oxford, 1964; diploma in internat. rels., U. Geneva, 1965. Fgn. svc. officer Philippines Ministry Fgn. Affairs, 1962-75, dir. gen., 1975-79, permanent del. to UNESCO, 1980—88, amb. to France and Portugal, 1979—88; amb. to People's Republic of China, 1990-94; permanent rep. of The Philippines to the UN, NYC, 1994—2001; sr. fgn. affairs adviser Dept. Fgn. Affairs, Republic of the Philippines, Manila, 2004—. Mem. adv. com. on adminstrv. and budgetary questions UN, 2001—03. Decorated Order of Diplomatic Merit Republic of Korea, 1978; Nat. Order of Merit France, 1988; recipient Outstanding Young Men award for govt. svc. Manila Jaycees, 1975, Gawad Mabini award Pres. of Philippines, 2001; Carnegie fellow U. Geneva, 1964-65. Mem. Manila Polo Club, Racing Club France (Paris). Office: 117 Gamboa St Legaspi Village Makati Philippines

MABRY, DONALD JOSEPH, retired academic administrator, history professor; b. Atlanta, Apr. 21, 1941; s. Jerry Leon and Eunice Leigh (Harris) M.; m. Susan Strong Johnston, July 28, 1962 (div. Oct. 1986); children: Scott, Mark; m. Paula Ann Crockett, Dec. 18, 1992. BA, Kenyon Coll., Gambier, Ohio, 1963; MEd, Bowling Green State U., 1964; PhD, Syracuse U., 1970. Instr. St. Johns River CC, Palatka, Fla., 1964—67; rsch. asst. fin. aid Syracuse U., NY, 1967—68, teaching fellow in history, 1968—69, Maxwell fellow, 1969—70, vis. lectr. dept. history, 1969—70; asst. to chancellor U. Kans., Lawrence, 1978—79; from. asst. prof. to prof. dept. history Miss. State U., Mississippi State, 1970—, asst. to pres., 1979—81, assoc. dean for budget and rsch., 1991—2001; now dir., assoc. dean Biol. Physical Sciences Rsch. Inst., Mississippi State, Miss.; ret. Sr. fellow, Ctr. for Internat. Security and Strategic Studies Miss. State U., 1981—91. Author: Mexico's Accion Nacional, 1973, The Mexican University and the State, 1982, (with others) Neighbors--Mexico and the United States, 1981; editor: The Latin American Narcotics Trade and U.S. National Security, 1989; contbr. articles to profl. jours. Mem. Am. Coun. on Edn. (exec. com. Coun. of Fellows 1980-83), South Ea. Coun. on Latin Am. Studies, Hist. Text Archive (founding editor) Avocation: computer telecommunications. Home: 206 Hiwassee Dr Starkville MS 39759-2105 Home Phone: 662-323-6852; Office Phone: 662-325-3604.

MABRY, JOSEPH M.(MIKE), JR., consumer products company executive; B math, Univ. No. Ala.; MBA, Okla. City Univ. Mgmt. positions through v.p. global services Wal-Mart, 1991—2003; sr. v.p. distbn. Lowe's Companies, Mooresville, NC, 2003—04, exec. v.p. logistics & distbn., 2004—. Office: Lowe's Companies 1000 Lowe's Blvd Mooresville NC 28117 *

MABRY, PHILIP T., political scientist, consultant; b. Spartanburg, SC, Feb. 29, 1940; s. Roy T. and Eleanor Eva (Waddell) Mabry; m. Mary E. Byars, July 3, 1961 (div. Mar. 1980); children: Tammy Kay Waldrop, Phyllis Dianne Gibbons, Sonya Kowalski; m. Amy D. Mabry, June 18; stepchildren: Philip Singh, Tina Singh. Founder Ams. for Human Rights, Greenville, SC, 1975—79; pres. Western Rsch. Cons., Euless, Tex., 1982—; dir. Western Rsch., Euless, Tex., 2000—. Cons. U.S. Dept. State, Washington, 1982—87. Contbr. news articles, interviews on Iran/Contra and Iran hostage af. Polit. activist Rep. Party, Washington, 1962—. Recipient Cert. of Appreciation, Nat. Rep. Party, 2001, Cert. of Membership, Acad. Polit. Sci., 2001, Republican Commn. Accomplishment award, Nat. Rep. Senatorial Com., D.C., 2003, U.S. Congl. Order Merit award, Nat. Rep. Congl. Com., D.C., 2005. Mem.: Acad. Polit. Sci. Republican. Avocations: golf, coin collecting/numismatics, reading, history. Home: 125 Wanda Way Apt 119 Hurst TX 76053

MABUS, RAYMOND EDWIN, JR., former ambassador, governor; b. Starkville, Miss., Oct. 11, 1948; s. Raymond Edwin and Lucille M. (Curtis) M.; m. Julia Hines, Jan. 3, 1987 (div.); children: Elisabeth, Anne BA summa cum laude, U. Miss., 1969; MA, Johns Hopkins U., 1970; JD magna cum laude, Harvard U., 1976. Bar: Tex. 1976, D.C. 1978, Miss. 1982. Law clk. US Ct. Appeals (5th Cir.), Montgomery, Ala., 1976-77; legal counsel to House Agrl. Com. US Congress, Wash., 1977-78; assoc. Fried, Frank et al., Wash., 1979-80; legis. aide to Gov. State of Miss., Jackson, 1980-83, state auditor, 1984-88, gov., 1988-92; US amb. to Saudi Arabia US Dept. State, Riyadh, 1994—96; of counsel Baker, Donelson, Bearman & Caldwell, 1996; pres. Frontline Global Resources, 1998—2002; non-exec. chmn. Foamex Internat. Inc., Linwood, Pa., 2004—07, interim pres., CEO, 2006—07. Chmn. So. Regional Edn. Bd., 1988-89 Lt. (j.g.) USN, 1970-72. Woodrow Wilson scholar Johns Hopkins U., 1969; named among Top 40 under 40 Esquire mag., 1987; recipient Martin Luther King Jr. Social Responsibility award, 1990, Miss. Assn. of Educators Friends of Edn. award, 1990. Mem. So. Govs. Assn. (chm. 1989-90). Democrat. Methodist. Avocations: spectator sports, walking, reading.

MAC, BERNIE, actor, comedian; b. Chgo., Oct. 5, 1958; m. Rhonda McCullough, Sept. 1977; 1 child, Je'Niece. Became profl. comedian, 1977. Actor: (films) Mo' Money, 1992, Who's the Man?, 1993, House Party 3, 1994, The Walking Dead, 1995, Friday, 1995, Get on the Bus, 1996, Don't Be a Menace to South Central While Drinking Your Juice in the Hood, 1996, How to Be a Player, 1997, Booty Call, 1997, The Players Club, 1998, Life, 1999, The Original Kings of Comedy, 2000, What's the Worst That Could Happen?, 2001, Ocean's Eleven, 2001, Head of State, 2003, Charlie's Angels: Full Throttle, 2003, Bad Santa, 2003, Mr. 3000, 2004, Ocean's Twelve, 2004, (voice) Lil' Pimp, 2005, Guess Who, 2005, Pride, 2007, Ocean's Thirteen, 2007; (TV films) Don King: Only in America, 1997, Honor Deferred, 2006; (TV series) Moesha, 1996; actor, prodr.: The Bernie Mac Show, 2001—06 (Image award NAACP, 2003, 2004). Recipient Outstanding Actor in a Comedy Series, NAACP Image Awards, 2006. Office: The Bernie Mac Show Attn Fox Broadcasting Publicity Dept PO Box 900 Beverly Hills CA 90213-0900 *

MACADAM, STEPHEN E., wholesale distribution executive; BS, Univ. Ky.; MS, Boston Coll.; MBA, Harvard Univ. Cons. positions through prin. McKinsey & Co., Charlotte, NC, 1988—98; sr. v.p. containerboard & packaging Georgia-Pacific Corp., 1998—2000; exec. v.p. pulp & paperboard Georgia-Pacific, 2000—01; pres., CEO Consolidated Container Co., 2001—05; dir. BlueLinx Holdings, Atlanta, 2004—, CEO, 2005—. Office: BlueLinx Holdings 4300 Wildwood Pkwy Atlanta GA 30339 *

MACAGNO, EDUARDO R., biology professor, dean; b. Argentina, 1943; arrived in US, 1956; married; 2 children. PhD, Columbia Univ., 1968. Faculty Columbia Univ., 1973—93, assoc. v.p. rsch., grad. edn., dean grad. sch. arts and sci., 1993—2000; founding dean, divsn. biology, Richard C. Atkinson prof. biology Univ. Calif. San Diego, 2001—. Rev. panel NIH, NRC. Co-editor: Jour. Neurobiology. Named one of 50 Most Important Hispanics in Govt., Edn., Hispanic Engineer and Info. Tech. mag., 2005; recipient Javits Investigator award, NIH. Office: Dean - Biological Sci-0376 UCSD 9500 Gilman Dr La Jolla CA 92093-0376 Office Phone: 858-534-4281. Office Fax: 858-534-7314. Business E-Mail: dean@biology.ucsd.edu, emacagno@ucsd.edu.

MACAHILIG, SUZANNE, pianist, educator; m. Gerard M. Lehrer, Dec. 4, 1994. BA, U. Calif., Berkeley, 1976; MusM, San Francisco Conservatory of Music, 1983; PhD, NYU, 1992; studied with, Seymout Lipkin, Jascha Zayde, Nathan Schwartz, Bernhard Abramowitsch, Adolph Baller, Berkeley, John Adams, Andrew Imbrie. Instr. East Bay Ctr. Performing Arts, Berkeley, 1976—78; lectr. NYU, 1989—95, U. Calif., Santa Cruz, 2001. Pianist: performances include Stanford U., 1979, 1980, 1981, 1982, 1986, San Francisco Conservatory, 1981, 1982, 1983, 1984, 1991, 1992, 1993, 1995, 2002, Berkeley Piano Club, 1982, Lincoln Ctr., 1984, Trinity Concert Series, 1984, NYU, 1984, 1986, 1992, 1993, Carnegie Hall, 1989, Calif. State U., 1996, Star Classics, 1996, Noon Concert, 1997, Carmel Performing Arts Festival, 1998, U. Calif. Berkeley, 1999, Nat. Steinbeck Ctr. Calif., 1999, 2000, Colton Chamber Music and Lovejoy Concerts, 2001, Colton Hall Chamber Series, 2001. Profl. artist Arts Coun. Monterey County, Calif.; instr. piano NY State Music Adjudication Guild; faculty rep. East Bay Ctr. Performing Arts, Richmond, Calif. Recipient Roger Phelps Dissertation award, NYU, 1992; Kneisel Hall Chamber Music scholar, Presser Found., 1983. Mem.: Coll. Music Soc., Am. Musicological Soc. Office: Friends of SfzPiano 340 Hazelwood Ave San Francisco CA 94127 Office Phone: 831-596-3747. Office Fax: 831-624-3029. Business E-Mail: sfzpiano@aol.com.

MACAL, ZDENEK, conductor, music director; b. Jan. 8, 1936; Student, Janacek Music Acad. Music dir. Milw. Symphony Orch., 1986-96; chief condr. Cologne Radio Orch., 1970-74; former chief condr. Prague Symphony, Hannover Radio Orch., Sydney Symphony Orch.; music dir. NJ Symphony, Newark, 1993—2002, music dir. emeritus, 2002—; music dir. Czech Philharm. Orch., 2003—. Office: NJ Symphony 2 Central Ave Newark NJ 07102-3119

MAC ALISTER, ROBERT JAMES, executive recruiter; b. NYC, Aug. 6, 1927; s. Ralph James and Ethel Burggraf Mac Alister; m. Nina Frances Koehler, Nov. 17, 1951; children: Hilary Lynn Stenger, James Kevin, Linda Ann Perez, Heather Ellen Smith. BA, Bard Coll., Annandale-on-Hudson, N.Y., 1950; MA, U. Chgo., 1958. Intern US Dept. State, Washington, 1950—51, info. specialist, 1951—52; cultural affairs assoc. US Info. Agy., Madras, India, 1952—54; steel salesperson Koehler Bros., Saginaw, Mich., 1954—55; exec. dir. Internat. Rescue Com., NYC, 1955—59; campaign aide Pell for Senator Com., Providence, 1960; legis. asst. US Senator Claiborne Pell, Washington, 1961—62; county dir. Peace Corps, Abidjan, 1962—65; chief French spkg. Africa programs US Peace Corps, Washington, 1965—67, country dir. Fort Lamy, Chad, 1967—68, dir. staff tng. Washington, 1968—69; dean student svcs. Sangamon State U., Springfield, Ill., 1969—72; exec. dir. Group Health Plan N.E. Ohio, Cleve., 1973—75; cons. USAID, Washington, 1976—77; acting dir. US Peace Corps, Kinshasa, Zaire, 1977, spl. asst. to regional dir. Africa Washington, 1978—79; program analyst USAID, Washington, 1979—82, project mgr. Dakar, Senegal, 1982—86, desk officer Washington, 1986—88, program officer, 1988—89, 1988—89; internat. devel. cons. RJM Cons., Frederick, Md., 1990—; rep. Vol. Assn. Bangldesh, Washington, 2006—. Pro bono cons. US Peace Corps, 2003; pro-bono cons. Nat. Peace Corps Assn., Washington, 2003; pro bono cons. Africare, Washington. With USN, 1944—46. Recipient John Dewey award, Bard Coll., 2000. Mem.: Nat. Peace Corps Assn. Democrat. Unitarian-Universalist. Avocation: walking. Office Phone: 301-512-8275. E-mail: bmaca@comcast.net.

MACALISTER, ROBERT STUART, retired oil industry executive; b. LA, May 22, 1924; s. Robert Stuart and Iris Grace (Doman) MacAlister; m. Catherine Vera Willby, Nov. 15, 1947 (dec. 1994); children: Rodney James, Sara Marjorie; m. Grace V. LeClerc, Dec. 2, 1995. Student, Brighton Coll., Sussex, Eng., 1945; BSME, Calif. Inst. Tech., 1947. Registered profl. engr., Tex. Petroleum engr. Shell Oil Co., 1947—56; mgmt. trainee Royal Dutch Shell, The Hague, Netherlands, 1956—57; with exec. staff, mgr. Shell Oil Co., U.S.A., 1957—68; v.p., ops. mgr. Occidental Petroleum Corp., Tripoli, Libya, 1968—71, mng. dir. various subs. London, 1971—76; mng. dir., pres. Occidental Internat. Oil, Inc., London, 1976—78; pres., chmn. bd. Can. Occidental Petroleum Ltd., Calgary, Alta., 1978—81; mng. dir. Australian Occidental Petroleum Ltd., Sydney, 1982—83, Hamilton Bros. Oil & Gas Ltd., London, 1983—86. Exe. U.K. Offshore Operators, London, 1972—78, London, 1983—86. Cubmaster Boy Scouts Am., Larchmont, NY, 1964—65, scoutmaster Houston, 1965—68. Sgt. US Army, 1944—45, ETO. Mem.: Can. Petroleum Assn. (bd. govs. 1978—81), Soc. Petroleum Engrs., Am. Assn. Petroleum Geologists, Caltech Torchbearer, Las Posas Country Club, Gold Coast Srs. Republican. Episcopalian. Avocations: carpentry, crafts, watercolor painting, golf, gardening. Home and Office: 78 Lopaco Ct Camarillo CA 93010-8846

MACALISTER, RODNEY J., President African Development Foundation; Mgr. ops., bus. devel., cmty. devel. ConocoPhillips, Central Africa; founder, pres. Bus. & Conflict Ltd., London; pres. African Devel. Found. Mem. Corp. Coun. Africa, BCIU, Nat. Fgn. Trade Coun.; founding mem. Human Rights and Bus. Roundtable Fund of Peace. Office: African Development Foundation 10th Floor 1400 Eye St NW Washington DC 20005-2248 Office Phone: 202-673-3916. Office Fax: 202-673-3810. *

MACALLASTER, ARCHIE, investment company executive; Grad., U.S. Naval Acad., 1953. Pres. Pitfield MacKay (now MacAllaster Pitfield MacKay), 1984—; CEO MacAllaster Pitfield MacKay, NYC, chmn. Trustee emeritus St. Lawrence U.; trustee Clark Fedn. Mem.: The Clark Found. Office: MacAllaster Pitfield MacKay 30 Broad St New York NY 10004 Home Phone: 203-259-4315; Office Phone: 212-422-9250.

MACALPINE, MICHELLE LEWIS, neuroscientist; b. Colorado Springs, Colo., Dec. 19, 1954; d. Arthur and Erma Lewis; m. J. David MacAlpine; children: Kira, Caylan. BA, Colo. State U., 1976; MA, U. Colo., 1983; PhD, U. Tex.-Dallas, Richardson, 1998. Owner Lariat, Ft. Collins, Colo., 1983-87, Brain Tng., Plano, Tex., 1995—; trainer Lectra, Richardson, 1987-89. Author: Word Master, 1996, Treating Developmental Delays and Autistic Spectrum Disorders, 1997, 2d edit., 1998, Brain Training: New Hope for Children with Developmental Delays, 2004, Sensory Processing Disorders, 2006. Mem.: Mensa. Democrat. Achievements include obtaining of 100% recovery rate in group of autistic children by promoting their cognitive development. Office: Brain Tng 2301 Ohio Dr #130 Plano TX 75093 Home Phone: 972-612-6140; Office Phone: 972-964-8510. Business E-Mail: braintrain@aol.com.

MACALUSO, CHRISTIE A., bishop; b. June 12, 1945; M in Sacred Theology, St. Mary's Seminary, Balt.; MA in philosophy, Trinity U., Hartford; MA in psychology, NYU; Doctoral Studies, New Sch. for Social Rsch., NYC. Ordained priest Roman Cath. Ch., 1971. Priest Archiodecese of Hartford, Conn., 1971, consecrated aux. bishop Conn., 1997, aux. bishop Conn., 1997, consecrated bishop Conn., 1997—. Office: 134 Farmington Ave Hartford CT 06105-3723

MACAN, WILLIAM ALEXANDER, IV, lawyer; b. Boston, Nov. 21, 1942; s. William A. and Carol (Whitten) M.; m. Jane Mitchell Ahern, Sept. 3, 1965; children: Sandi, Andrew. BA in Econs., Haverford Coll., 1964; LLB magna cum laude, U. Pa., Phila., 1967. Bar: Pa. 1968, US Tax Ct. 1970, NY 1999, Eng., 2000, Wales, 2000. Law clk. to judge U.S. Tax Ct., Washington, 1967-69; assoc. firm Morgan, Lewis & Bockius LLP, Phila., 1969-76, ptnr., 1976-2000, Allen & Overy LLP, NYC, 2000—04, of counsel, 2004—. Lectr. legal instns., seminars. Author publs. on tax-oriented equipment leasing, other tax subjects. Mem. ABA. Presbyterian. Office: Allen & Overy 1221 Ave of the Americas New York NY 10020 Home Phone: 618-687-3995; Office Phone: 212-610-6413. Business E-Mail: william.macan@newyork.allenovery.com.

MACARIN-MARA, LYNN, psychotherapist, consultant; b. Queens, NY, Feb. 27, 1948; d. David and Grace Macarin; m. Marvin Weingast, Sept. 2, 2000; 1 child, Leah Mara. MA, NYU, 1972; MSW, Hunter Sch. Social Work, 1980. Cert. psychoanalytic psychotherapy, hypnotherapy and hypnoanalysis. With Greenwich Inst. Psychotherapy and Psychoanalysis, 1984-87; pvt. practice, 1987—; pres. Face to Face Psychotherapy Svcs., Metuchen, N.J., 1987—; dir. family and children svcs. Ednl. Alliance, Inc., NYC, 1990-95. Adj. prof. SUNY, Staten Island, N.Y., 1972-73, New Sch. for Social Rsch., N.Y.C., 1980-81. Contbr. articles to profl. jours. Chairperson membership com. Temple Emanu-El, Edison, N.J., 1998-2001. Mem. N.J. Soc. for Clin. Social Work (newsletter editor 1997-99). Democrat. Jewish. Avocations: travel, dance, writing, painting. Office: Face to Face Psychotherapy Svcs 2 Blair Ave Metuchen NJ 08840

MACARIO, ALBERTO JUAN LORENZO, physician; b. Naschel, Argentina, Dec. 1, 1935; came to the U.S., 1974, naturalized, 1980; s. Alberto Carlos and Maria Elena (Giraudi) M.; m. Everly Conway, Mar. 16, 1963; children: Alex, Everly. MD, Nat. U. Buenos Aires, 1961. Intern Ramos Mejia Hosp., Buenos Aires, 1958—60, resident, 1960, Rivadavia Hosp., Buenos Aires, 1961—62, physician-hematologist, 1962—64; fellow NRC Argentina, Buenos Aires, 1964—69; head dept. radioactive isotopes Inst. Hematol. Investigations Nat. Acad. Medicine, Buenos Aires, 1967—69; Eleanor Roosevelt fellow Internat. Union Against Cancer Dept. Tumor Biology Karolinska Inst., Stockholm, 1969—71; mem. sci. staff Lab. Cell Biology NRC Italy, Rome, 1971—73; head lab. immunology Internat. Agy Rsch. on Cancer WHO, Lyons, France, 1973—74; rsch. scientist Brown U., Providence, 1974—76; rsch. scientist divsn. labs. and rsch. N.Y. State Dept. Health, Albany, 1976—79, chief hematology clin. lab. ctr., 1979—81; dir. clin. and exptl. immunology sect. Lab. Medicine Inst., 1981—83, rsch. physician, 1981—83; rsch. physician Wadsworth Ctr. N.Y. State Dept. Health, 1981—2006; rschr. U. Md. Biotechnology Inst., Balt., 2006—. Prof. dept. biomed. scis. Sch. Pub. Health, SUNY, Albany, 1985-2006, adj. prof. 2006-, mem. senate, 1989-94; adj. prof. pathology and lab. medicine Albany Med. Coll., 1991-2004; mem. structural and cell biology program Albany Univs. and Colls.; grant reviewer for nat. and internat. agys.; manuscript reviewer for sci. jours. Editor multivolume treatise Monoclonal Antibodies Against Bacteria and treatise Gene Probes for Bacteria; contbr. chpts. to books and encys. and articles to profl. jours. Recipient Diploma de Honor prize Nat. U. Buenos Aires, 1961, Bernardino Rivadavia prize Nat. Acad. Medicine Argentina, 1967, Ciencia e Investigation prize Argentinian Soc. Advancement Sci., 1967; Ford Found.-NAS travel fellow, 1968, Eleanor Roosevelt fellow, 1969. Mem. Internat. Soc. Microbial Ecology, Cell Stress Soc. Internat., Scandinavian Soc. Immunology, Italian Assn. Immunologists, French Soc. Immunology, Am. Assn. Immunologists, Am. Soc. Microbiology (sect. editor Manual of Clin. Lab. Immunology 4th and 5th edits. 1989-97), Am. Soc. Investigative Pathology, Assn. Internat. Union Against Cancer. Achievements include patents in field; discovered primary myeloperoxydase deficiency in leucocytes, and oscillations of antibody affinity during maturation of immune responses; developed method for immunologic identification of bacteria (archaea) that produce methane gas; discovered antigenic diversity of these microbes in natural and manufactured ecosystems; described structural topography of methanogenic archaea and population dynamics in granular microbial consortia; found novel multicellular forms of archaea; isolated for the first time ABC-transporter genes and the genes in the hsp70(dnak) locus from an archaebacterium (archaeon); devised and constructed the first integration vector for genetically engineering a methanogen useful for waste bioconversion; discovered a uni-celled organism with the main four chaperoning systems in its cytosol; found two new chaperonins in archaea; developed concept of sick chaperone or chaperonopathy as a factor contributing to the aging process and disease; discovered that archaeal hsp70 (dnaK) genes belong to various evolutionary lineages. Office: Ctr Marine Biotech Columbus Ctr 701 E Pratt St Baltimore MD 21202 Office Phone: 410-234-8849. Business E-Mail: macario@umbi.umd.edu. *I am capable of walking alone, but with my wife by me, I fly. We can both ascend toward the sky and together we reach the stars. Separately, alone, who knows, we might never have been able to rise above the mountains, perhaps not even the hills, we have conquered, flapping our wings in unison.*

MACAROL, VICTOR GEORGE, artist; s. Josephus Macarol and Gisella Zonyi. Postgrad., Johns Hopkins U., Balt., 1968—69. Prof. Kean Coll., Union, NJ, 1986, Felician Coll., Lodi, NJ, 2003. One-man shows include Galerie Zur Stockregg, Zurich, Switzerland, 1981, NJ State Mus., Trenton, 1984, Galerie Photographe, Paris, 1992, Hunterdon Mus. Art, Clinton, NJ, 1993, St. Joseph's U. Gallery, Phila., 1994, Front Rm. Gallery, Singapore, 2003, exhibited in group shows at Galerie Zur Stockeregg, 1982, Sotheby's, NYC, 1983—84, NY State Mus., 1983, Jacob K. Javits Ctr., NYC, 1989, Musée l'Elysée, Lausanne, Switzerland, 1991, Noyes Mus. Art, Oceanville, NJ, 1996, Galerie Mesmer, Basel, Switzerland, 1999, Mus. Modern Art, NYC, 2002, Represented in permanent collections NJ State Mus., Noyes Mus. Art, Bibliotheque Nat. France, Paris, Musée l'Elysée, Kunsthaus, Zurich, 1982. Recipient Disting. Artist award, NJ State Coun. Arts, 1987; fellow, 1983, 1986.

MACARTHUR, DIANA TAYLOR, advanced technology executive; b. Santa Fe, July 7, 1933; children: Elizabeth Tshursin, Alexander Tschursin. BA, Vassar Coll., Poughkeepsie, NY, 1955. Cons. economist Checchi & Co., 1957-61; v.p., dir. Thomas J. Deegan Co., 1961-62; dep. chief West Africa Peace Corps, 1963, reg. program officer for North Africa, Near East, South Asia, 1964, dir. divsn. pvt. and internat. orgns., 1965-66; pvt. cons., 1966-74; program mgr. Aerospace Divsn. Gen Elec. Co., 1974-76; pres. Consumer Dynamics, 1977-80; v.p., dir. Dynamac Internat. Inc., 1980-88, chmn., pres., CEO, 1988—; chmn., CEO Rsch. Analysis and Mgmt. Corp., 1988-92. Pres. Fgn. Traders, Inc., 1980—86. Trustee Menninger Found., Topeka, 1972-04, Santa Fe Inst., 2005-; bd. dirs. Sci. and Tech. Corp. U. N.Mex.; bd. visitors Menninger-Baylor Coll. Medicine, Meth. Hosp. Found., 2004-06; Lady Bird Johnson Wildflower Ctr., 1985-; mem. Pres.'s Com. of Adv. on Sci. and Tech., 1994-01; citizens adv. bd. to the Pres. Coun. on Youth Opportunity, 1966-70; served on CSIS Strengthening of Amer. Com., 1992, Nat. Benefits from Nat. Lab. Com., 1993, Sr. Policy on Nat. Challenges, 1996, Geopolitics of Energy Com., 2000; mem. The Chancellor's Adv. Coun. U. Sys. of Md.; bd. visitors U. Md. Biotech. Inst.; adv. com. Ctr. Strategic & Internat. Studies; bd. dirs. Atlantic Coun. USA; bus. adv. coun. Ctr. for China-US Coop., U. Denver. Mem. Coun. on Competitiveness, Business-Higher Edn. Forum (exec. com.), Tech. Coun. Md. (exec. com.), Los Alamos Nat. Lab. Found. (pres. bd. dirs.), Nat. Hispanic Cultural Ctr. Found., The Santa Fe Opera, Phi Beta Kappa. Office: Dynamac Internat Inc 2275 Research Blvd Rockville MD 20850-3268 Business E-Mail: dmacarthur@sfgrid.com.

MACARTHUR, JOHN RODERICK C. G. (RICK MACARTHUR), magazine publisher, journalist; b. N.Y.C., June 4, 1956; s. J. Roderick and Christiane (L'Etendart) MacA. BA, Columbia Coll., 1978. Reporter Wall Street Jour., Chgo., summer 1977, Washington Star, 1978, Bergen Record, Hackensack, N.J., 1978-79, Chgo. Sun Times, 1979-82; asst. fgn. editor UPI, N.Y.C., 1982; pres., pub. Harper's Mag., N.Y.C., 1983—. Author: Second Front: Censorship and Propaganda in the Gulf War, 1992, The Selling of "Free Trade": NAFTA, Washington, and the Subversion of Democracy, 1999. Bd. dirs. Com. to Protect Journalists, Overseas Press Club, Death Penalty Info. Ctr. Fellow N.Y. Inst. Humanities; mem. Econ. Club of N.Y. Office: Harper's Mag 666 Broadway Fl 11 New York NY 10012-2394

MACARTHUR, MARCIA, primary school educator; b. Birmingham, Ala., Jan. 8, 1945; d. Lee Maurance MacArthur, Jr. and Velma Bosworth Dowling; m. Francis Raborn, Aug. 8, 1970; children: Stephen Francis Raborn, Emily Louise Raborn. BA, U. Calif., Berkeley, 1968; MA, Oakland U., 1976. Flight attendant World Airways, Oakland, Calif., 1968—70; auditor No. Bancorporation, Detroit, 1973—75; dir. religious edn. Christ Ch., Los Altos Hills, Calif., 1989—90, preschool tchr., 1990—93; preschool, kindergarten tchr. Village Green Day Sch., Great Falls, Va., 1998—. Author: Parents and Children Learning Together, 1976. Parenting instr. Cabrini Coll., Wayne, Pa., 1975—76; mem. Assn. Jr. Leagues, 1976—; mem. adv. bd. United Way, Phila., 1981—84; cmty. v.p. Jr. League Phila., 1982—88; cmty. leader 4H, Los Altos, 1986—92; various bd. positions U.S. Pony Club, Great Falls, Va., 1994—2002; sustainer bd. Jr. League Washington, 2002—03; bd. mem. PTA, 1980—2002; Sunday sch. tchr. various locations, 1978—94. Mem.: Nat. Mus. Women in the Arts. Episcopalian. Avocations: hiking, travel, reading.

MACAULAY, ANN C., physician; b. Canada; Prof. family medicine McGill U., Montreal, Que., Canada, 1983—, dir. Participatory Rsch. Ctr.; physician, Herzl Family Practice Ctr. Sir Mortimer B. Davis Jewish Gen. Hosp., Montreal, Que., Canada, 1996—; inst. dir. Can. Inst. Health Rsch. Dir. Kahnawake Schools Diabetes Prevention Project, 1994—2006, Kahnawake Ctr. Rsch. & Training for Diabetes Prevention; pres. N.Am. Primary Care Rsch. Group, 2002. Fellow: Coll. Family Physicians of Can.; mem.: Inst. Medicine (assoc.). Office: Dept Family Medicine McGill U 517 Pine Ave W Montreal PQ H2W 1S4 Canada also: Herzl Family Practice Ctr Pav E Ste E0010 3755 Chemin de la Cote St Catherine Montreal PQ H3T 1E2 Canada Office Phone: 514-398-7375, 514-398-4202. E-mail: ann.macaulay@mcgill.ca.

MACAULAY, DAVID ALEXANDER, author, illustrator; b. Burton-on-Trent, Eng., Dec. 2, 1946; s. James and Joan (Lowe) M.; m. Janice Elizabeth Michel, 1970 (div.); 1 child, Elizabeth Alexandra; m. Ruth Marris, 1978 (div.); 1 child, Charlotte Valerie; m. Ruth Ellen Murray, 1997. BArch, R.I. Sch. Design, 1969. Instr. interior design R.I. Sch. Design, Providence, 1969-73, instr. two-dimensional design, 1974-76, adj. faculty dept. illustration, 1977-79; tchr. art Central Falls (R.I.) Pub. Schs., 1969-70, Newton, Mass., 1972-74; designer Morris Nathanson Design, 1969-72. Author, illustrator: Cathedral: The Story of Its Construction, 1973 (Caldecott Honor book 1973), City, 1974, Pyramid, 1975 (Christopher medal 1975), Underground, 1976, Castle, 1977 (Caldecott Honor book 1977), Great Moments in Architecture, 1978, Motel of the Mysteries, 1979, Unbuilding, 1980, Mill, 1983, Baaa, 1985, Why the Chicken Crossed the Road, 1987, The Way Things Work: From Levers to Lasers, Cars to Computers- A Visual Guide to the World of Machines, 1988, Black and White, 1990 (Caldecott medal 1991), Ship, 1993, Shortcut, 1995, Rome Antics, 1997, The New Way Things Work, 1998, Angelo, 2002; illustrator: Help! Let Me Out!, 1982, Electricity, 1983, The Amazing Brain, 1984, David Macaulay, 1997, Building Big, 2000, Angelo, 2002; cons., presenter various TV projects. Recipient Wash. Children's Book Guild award, 1977, AIA medal, 1978, Bradford Washburn meda. Boston Mus. Sci., 1993, Charles Frankel prize NEH, 1995, Chevalier of Order of Arts and Letters, France, 1995, MacArthur Fellow, John D. and Catherine T. MacArthur Found., 2006.

MACAULAY, LAWRENCE A., former Canadian government official, member of Parliament; b. St. Peters Bay, Sept. 9, 1946; s. Archibald and Bernadette MacAulay; m. Frances Elaine O'Connell, Aug. 16, 1972; children: Carolyn, Rita, Lynn. Mem. House of Commons, 1988—, apptd. assoc. critic for fisheries and oceans, 1989, apptd. critic for srs. and assoc. critic for fisheries, 1990; sec. of state for vets. Govt. of Can., 1993—96, min. labour, solicitor gen. of Can. Ottawa, 1998—2002. Mem. standing com. on forestry and fisheries, caucus com. on health and social devel.; acclaimed chair Atlantic Caucus, 1992. Roman Catholic.

MACAULAY, SUSAN JANE, lawyer, educator; b. Oceanport, NJ, Feb. 18, 1952; d. Gordon Livingston and Mary Forrest Macaulay; children: Lauren Mei, Anna Haiqiong. MusB, Oberlin Conservatory Music, 1974; JD, Loyola U., Chgo., 1984; LLM, Chgo.-Kent Coll. Law, 1990; M in Liberal Arts, U. Chgo., 1995. Bar: Ill. 1984, U.S. Dist. Ct. (no. dist.) Ill. 1984. Regional counsel Burroughs Corp., Lombard, Ill., 1984—86; atty. Borg-Warner Acceptance Corp., Chgo., 1986—86; assoc. gen. counsel Heller Fin., Inc., Chgo., 1986—94; gen. counsel ArcVentures, Inc., Chgo., 1994—95; v.p., corp. counsel Caremark Internat., Inc., Northbrook, Ill., 1995—96; sr. assoc. Skadden Arps Slate Meagher & Flom, Chgo., 1996—2001; ptnr. Gardner Carton & Douglas LLP, Chgo., 2001—06; gen. counsel Lamb Ptnrs., 2006—. Adj. prof. law Chgo.-Kent Coll. Law, 1992—. Contbr. chapters to books, articles to profl. jours. Named Ill. Leading Lawyer, The Law Bull. Ill. Superlawyers Chgo. Mag., 2004—06, Ill. Superlawyer, Chgo. Mag., 2004—06. Mem.: ABA, Chgo. Bar Assn., Families with Children from China. Avocations: classical music, local symphony orchestra member, writing. Office: Lamb Ptnrs 900 N Michigan Ste 1900 Chicago IL 60606 Home Phone: 708-771-2287; Office Phone: 312-915-2837. Office Fax: 312-915-3053. Business E-Mail: macaulay@lambllc.com.

MACAULAY, WILLIAM EDWARD, financial executive; b. NYC, Sept. 2, 1945; s. John H. and Ella M. (Cook) M.; m. Linda L. Rodger, June 17, 1967; children: Elizabeth R., Anne R. BBA cum laude, CCNY, 1966; MBA, U. Pa., 1968. Asst. v.p. Dominick & Dominick, NYC, 1968—71; v.p. Midlantic Bank, Newark, 1972—73, Oppenheimer Mgmt. Corp., NYC, 1973—75, exec. v.p., 1976—79; dir. corp. fin. Oppenheimer & Co., Inc., NYC, 1979—81, ptnr., 1976-81; gen. ptnr. Meridien Capital Co., Greenwich, Conn., 1981-92. Pres., CEO, dir. First Res. Corp., Greenwich, 1982—; chmn. Dresser Rand, Olean, NY; bd. dirs. Weatherford Inc., Dresser Inc., Dallas, So. Cross Holdings, Brisbane, Australia. Mem.: Indian Harbor Yacht Club. Presbyterian. Office: First Reserve Corp One Lafayette Pl Greenwich CT 06830-7165

MACAULEY, WILLIAM FRANCIS, lawyer; b. Boston, Sept. 12, 1943; s. Bernard Joseph and Mary Louise (Dolan) M.; m. Sheila Rose Hubbard, June 29, 1968; children: Jennifer, Douglas, Leiha, Brian. AB, U. Wash., 1966; JD, Boston U., 1969. Bar: Mass. 1969, U.S. Dist. Ct. Mass. 1970, U.S. Ct. Appeals (1st cir.) 1977, U.S. Dist. Ct. R.I. 1979, U.S. Tax Ct. 1982, U.S. Dist. Ct. Conn. 1983. Assoc. Craig & Craig, Boston, 1970-74; prin. Tyler, Reynolds & Craig, Boston, 1975-78; pres. Craig and Macauley, Boston, 1979—. Hon. trustee Boston U., bd. advisors, bd. overseers. Contbr. articles to profl. jours. Bd. dirs. YMCA Greater Boston. Mem. ABA, Mass. Bar Assn., Boston Bar Assn. Home: 55 Buttricks Hill Rd Concord MA 01742-5314 Office: Craig and Macauley Profl Corp 600 Atlantic Ave Ste 2900 Boston MA 02210-2215 Office Phone: 617-367-9500. Business E-Mail: macauley@craigmacauley.com.

MACAVERY, TRISTAN ALEXANDER (TRISTAN BLACK BEAR), small business owner, writer, actor; b. Petersburg, Va., Aug. 16, 1958; s. Carroll Alden and Mildred Harriet (Leon) Peabody. BA, Sam Houston State U., 1979. Editl. assoc Internat. Fire Svc. Tng. Assn., Stillwater, Okla., 1983—84; pub. Aegis Unicorne, Davis, Calif., 1985—92; exec. assoc. Okla. Ctr. Integrated Design and Mfg., Stillwater, 1993—95; Houston bur. chief Tex. Triangle newspaper, 1995; actor, writer, dir., prodr. ADV Films, Houston, 1996—99; owner Intangible Plastics, Columbus, Ind., 1999—. Spkr. numerous Japanese anime convs., 1996—; founding mem. Third Coast Comedy, Houston. Voice actor: Neon Genesis Evangelion, 1996—2001; author: Divine Intervention, 2001, Lion Dance, 2002, Tea for Twenty, 2003, Remnant Stew, 2004, The Improvisation Playbook, 2006; editor: Chronoscope, 2004; contbr. more than 200 articles and short stories to profl. and lit. publs. Mem.: ASTD, Soc. for Tech. Comm., Mensa. Democrat. Native Am. Shaman. Avocations: piano, voice, latch hooking. Home: 1160 Saylor Dr Apt 1C Columbus IN 47201-6131 Office: 1220 Washington St Columbus IN 47201-5746 Home Phone: 812-372-2768; Office Phone: 812-375-2370. Personal E-mail: frightfully_clever@sbcglobal.net. Business E-Mail: tristan@tamworks.net.

MACAVINTA-TENAZAS, GEMORSITA, physician; b. Numancia, Aklan, Phillippines, Dec. 18, 1938; arrived in U.S., 1967; d. Dominador Zalazar and Georgina Estrada (Tabanera) Macavinta; m. Salvador Torrefiel Tenazas Jr., Apr. 18, 1963; children: Alan, Alex, Albert, Alfred. BA, Far Ea. U., Manila, 1959, MD, 1964. Diplomate Am. Bd. Family Practice. Intern North Gen. Hosp., Manila, 1963-64; pvt. practice Manila, 1965-67; extern Chinese Gen. Hosp., Manila, 1965-67; with St. Joseph Med. Ctr., Burbank, Calif., 1967-69; chief cytotechnologist Cancer Screening Svcs., North Hollywood, Calif., 1969-73; resident in family practice medicine Health Scis. Ctr., Tex. Tech. U., Lubbock, 1974-75; staff physician VA Outpatient Clinic, LA, 1975—. Recipient physician recognition awards AMA, 1973-85, 92-94; named Mrs. Aklan, 1986, Disting. Alumna, Aklan Acad., Philippines, 1991, Most Outstanding Parent award Builders Lions Club, 1995, Citizen of Yr. Builders Lions Club, 1996, Outstanding Physician Club Filipino, 1996; inducted Asian Acad. Hall Distinction, Asian Leaders Assn. US Capital, 2007. Fellow Am. Acad. Family Physicians (bd. govs. 2003-05); mem. Philippine-Am. Assn. Family Physicians (bd. govs. 1996, 2003, 05-07, sec. 1998, sec. 1998-2002, Outstanding Leader award 2000, Mrs. Philippine Am. 2000), Am. Assn. Family Physicians, Calif. Acad. Family Physicians, Filipino Asian-Pacific VA Employees Soc. (pres. LA chpt. 1988—), Assn. Philippine Physicians in Am. (bd. govs. 2004, named Mrs. Mindanao 2002), Aklanons of Am. (pres. 1988—, bd. govs. 1998-2000, 04-06, bd. dirs. 2004—, 1st Mrs. Aklan 1986-89), Far Ea. U. Med. Alumni Assn. (life mem., asst. sec. 1988—), Far Ea. U. Dr. Nicanor Reyes Alumni Found. (life). Roman Catholic. Avocations: dance, singing, sewing, piano playing, gardening. Office: VA Outpatient Clinic 351 E Temple Los Angeles CA 90012 Office Phone: 213-253-2677. Business E-Mail: tenazas@med.va.gov.

MACAVOY, THOMAS COLEMAN, manufacturing executive, educator; b. Jamaica, NY, Apr. 24, 1928; s. Joseph V. and Edna M. Mac A.; m. Margaret M. Walsh, Dec. 27, 1952; children: Moira Mac Avoy, Ellen Mac Avoy Jennings, Christopher, Neil. BS in Chemistry, Queens Coll., 1950; MS in Chemistry, St. John's U., 1952, DSc (hon.), 1973; PhD in Chemistry, U. Cin., 1952. Chemist, Charles Pfizer & Co., Bklyn., 1957-60; mgr. electronics rsch. Corning Glass Works, NY, 1960-64, dir. phys. rsch., 1964-66, v.p. electronic products divsn., 1966-69, v.p. tech. products divsn., 1969-71, pres., 1971-83, vice-chmn., 1983-87; prof. mgmt. grad. sch. U. Va., 1988—. Patentee in field; contbr. articles to tech. jours. Trustee Corning Mus. Glass; past pres. Boy Scouts Am. With USN, 1946; with USAF, 1952-53. Recipient Silver Antelope award Boy Scouts Am., 1976, Silver Beaver award, 1975, Silver Buffalo award, 1982, Bronze Wolf award, 1988. Roman Catholic. Personal E-mail: tmacavoy@aol.com.

MACBAIN, WILLIAM HALLEY, minister, theology studies educator, academic administrator; b. Cambridge, Ont., Can., Aug. 12, 1916; s. George Alexander and Grace Ann (Wilkins) MacB.; m. Mary Ann Munday, Aug. 20, 1941; children: Grace Elizabeth MacBain Silvester, Constance Marilyn MacBain Parker. Licentiate in Theology, Toronto Baptist Sem., Ont., 1939; DD (hon.), Cen. Bapt. Sem., Toronto, 1962. Ordained to ministry Bapt. Ch., 1940. Pastor, founder Temple Bapt. Ch., Sarnia, Ont., 1937-64; pastor Forward Bapt. Ch., Toronto, 1964-73; dir., gen. sec. Fellowship Fgn. Missions, Toronto, 1973-81; chancellor Cen. Bapt. Sem., 1981-93, Heritage Bapt. Bible Coll. and Theol. Sem., Cambridge, Ont., Canada, 1993—. Pastor emeritus Forward Bapt. Ch., Toronto, 1994—; chmn. Can. Bd. Greater Europe Mission, 1963-73. Mem. Fellowship Evang. Bapt. Chs. in Can. (pres. 1953-54, 83-84) Conservative. Home: 1540 Kipling Ave Apt 903 Etobicoke ON Canada M9R 4C6 Office: Heritage Bapt Bible Coll and Theol Sem 175 Holiday Inn Dr Cambridge ON Canada N3C 3T2

MACBENN, JOSEPH VERNON, director; b. Youngstown, Ohio, Aug. 31, 1979; s. Joseph Edison and Darlene MacBenn; m. Melissa Strouble, July 8, 2006. B in Music Edn., Mt. Union Coll., Alliance, Ohio, 2001; MEd, Ohio No. U., 2005. Tchg. lic. Ohio. Orch. dir. Lima (Ohio) City Schs., 2001—. Mem.: Am. String Tchrs. Assn., Internat. Trumpet Guild, Ohio Music Edn. Assn., Kappa Kappa Psi, Mu Phi Epsilon. Avocations: music, aquariums, travel. Home: 5097 Shields Rd Canfield OH 44406 Office: Lima Sr High Orch 1 Spartan Way Lima OH 45801 Home Phone: 330-206-2300; Office Phone: 419-996-3466. Personal E-mail: orchestrajoe@hotmail.com. Business E-Mail: jmacbenn@hotmail.com.

MACBETH, ANGUS, lawyer; b. LA, May 9, 1942; BA, Yale U., 1964, LLB, 1969. Bar: NY 1970, DC 1981. Law clk. to Hon. Harold R. Tyler, Jr. US Dist. Ct. (so. dist.) NY, 1969-70, asst. US atty. criminal divsn., 1975-77; chief pollution control sect. Land and Natural Resources Divsn., US Dept. Justice, 1977-79, dep. asst. atty. gen., 1979-81; ptnr. and sr. counsel environ. law Sidley Austin LLC, Washington, 1986—. Adj. prof. law NY Law Sch., 1985—; spl. counsel Wartime Relocation and Internment Civilians Commn., 1981-83. Mem. DC Bar (steering com. energy and natural resources divsn. 1982-84), NY State Bar Assn., Phi Beta Kappa. Office: Sidley Austin LLC 1501 K St NW Washington DC 20005 Office Phone: 202-736-8271.

MACCARTHY, JOHN L., lawyer; b. St. Louis, Dec. 26, 1959; BA magna cum laude, Williams Coll., 1982; JD, Stanford U., 1985. Bar: Ill. 1985, U.S. Dist. Ct. Ill. (no. dist.) 1985. Assoc. to ptnr. Winston & Strawn LLP, Chgo., 1985—; sr. v.p., gen. counsel Nuvren Investments LLC, 2006—. Bd. dirs. Met. Family Svcs., Renaissance Soc. U. Chgo., Nature Conservancy Chgo. Mem.: Phi Beta Kappa, Order of Coif.

MACCARTHY, TALBOT LELAND, civic volunteer; b. St. Louis, Jan. 28, 1936; d. Austin Porter Leland and Dorothy (Lund) Follansbee; m. John Peters MacCarthy, June 21, 1958; children: John Leland MacCarthy, Talbot MacCarthy Payne. BA, Vassar Coll., 1958. Sec., treas. Station List Pub. Co., St. Louis, 1975-85, pres., 1985-90. Hon. trustee Robert E. Lee Meml. Assn., Arts and Edn. Coun. Greater St. Louis, pres., 1978-80, emerita; past vestry mem. St. Michael and St. George Ch., 1997-00; past trustee St. Louis Art Mus., St. Louis Merc. Libr. Assn., Family & Children's Svc. Greater St. Louis, Health and Welfare Coun., Greater St. Louis, Jr. Kindergarten St. Louis Page Park YMCA, Scholarship Found. St. Louis, Friends St. Louis Art Mus. Bd., Ch. St. Michael and St. George Sch. Bd., Mid-Am. Arts Alliance; chmn. Mo. Arts Coun., 1980-85; past chmn. Vol. Action Ctr. Greater St. Louis; past vice chmn. bd. dirs. Mary Inst.; past pres. Jr. League St. Louis; mem. Nat. Coun. Arts, 1985-91; past mem. nat. coun. for Sch. of Art Washington U.; trustee, sec. bd. Seabury-Western Theol. Sem. Recipient Woman of Achievement citation St. Louis Globe Democrat, 1979, Mo. Citizens for Arts/Arts Advocacy award, 1987, Mo. Arts Award, 1993, Honor medal, Mary Inst. and Country Day Sch., 2005. Mem. Vassar Club St. Louis (past pres.), Mary Inst. Alumnae Assn. (past pres.), Colonial Dames Am., Garden Club St. Louis, Belvedere Club (Charlevoix, Mich.; former mem. bd. dirs.). Republican. Episcopalian. Avocations: tennis, visual arts, performing arts.

MACCARTHY, TERENCE FRANCIS, lawyer; b. Chgo., Feb. 5, 1934; s. Frank E. and Catherine (McIntyre) MacC.; m. Marian Fulton, Nov. 25, 1961; children— Daniel Fulton, Sean Patrick, Terence Fulton, Megan Catherine BA in Philosophy, St. Joseph's Coll., 1955; JD, DePaul U., 1960. Bar: Ill. 1960, U.S. Dist. Ct. (no. dist.) Ill. 1961, U.S. Ct. Appeals (7th cir.) 1961, U.S. Supreme Ct. 1966. Assoc. prof. law Chase Coll. Law, Cin., 1960-61; law clk. to chief judge U.S. Dist. Ct., 1961-66; spl. asst. atty. gen. Ill., 1965-67; exec. dir. Fed. Defender Program, U.S. Dist. Ct. (no. dist.) Ill., Chgo., 1966—. Mem. nat. adv. com. on criminal rules; 7th cir. criminal jury instrn. com.; chmn. Nat. Defender Com.; chmn. bd. regents Nat. Coll. Criminal Def.; faculty Fed. Jud. Ctr., Nat. Coll. Criminal Def., Nat. Inst. Trial Advocacy, U. Va. Trial Advocacy Inst., Harvard Law Sch. Trial Advocacy Program, Western Trial Advocacy Inst., Northwestern U., U. Ill. Defender Trial Advocacy course, Nat. Criminal Def. Coll., Loyola U. Trial Advocacy Program; lectr. in field Contbr. articles on criminal law to profl. jours. Bd. dirs. U.S.O. Served as 1st lt. USMC, 1955-57 Recipient Nat. Legal Aid and Defender Assn./ABA Reginald Heber Smith award, 1986, Alumni Merit award St. Joseph Coll., 1970, Cert. of Distinction USO, 1977, Harrison Tweed Spl. Merit award Am. Law Inst./ABA, 1987, Bill of Rights award Ga. chpt. ACLU, 1986, William J. Brennan award U. Va., 1989, Alumni Svc. award DePaul U. Coll. Law, 1994, Ann. Significant Contbns. award Calif. Attys. for Criminal Justice, Defender of the Century Fed. Defenders Assn., Inns of Ct. and Ct. of Appeals (7th cir.) Professionalism award; named to Outstanding Young Men of Am., 1970. Mem. ABA (past chmn. criminal justice sect., ho. of dels., bd. govs., Charles English award criminal justice sect.), Ill. Bar Assn., Chgo. Bar Assn., 7th Cir. Bar Assn., Nat. Assn. Criminal Def. Lawyers (Disting. Svc. award 1993), Nat. Legal Aid and Defender Assn., Nat. Coll. Criminal Def. (chair), Union League of Chgo. (pres.). Democrat. Roman Catholic. Office: US Dist Ct No Dist Ill 55 E Monroe St Ste 2800 Chicago IL 60603-5802

MACCHIA, VINCENT MICHAEL, lawyer; b. Bklyn., Dec. 30, 1933; s. Vincent and Lina Rose (Cewli) M.; m. Irene Janet Audino, Feb. 27, 1965; children: Lauren, Michele, Michael. BS, Fordham U., 1955, LLB, 1958; LLM, NYU, 1967. Bar: N.Y. 1958. Assoc. Bernard Remsen Millham & Bowdish, NYC, 1959-60; atty. Equity Corp., NYC, 1961-63, Pfizer Inc., NYC, 1964, TWA, NYC, 1964-66; mem. Gifford, Woody, Palmer & Serles, NYC, 1966-85, Townley & Updike, NYC, 1985-90; of counsel Smith, Don, Alampi, Scala & D'Argenio, Ft. Lee, N.J., 1990-91; counsel Tenzer, Greenblatt, LLP, NYC, 1991-2000, Diamant, Katz Kahn & Co. LLP, NYC, 2000—02, Amper, Politziner & Mattia, P.C., NYC, 2002—06. Dir. Hudson Rev., Inc. Mem. editl. staff Fordham Law Rev., 1956-58. With USAR, 1958-64. Mem. ABA, N.Y. State Bar Assn. Republican. Roman Catholic. Home: 4 Greentree Dr Scarsdale NY 10583-7014

MACCHIAROLA, FRANK JOSEPH, academic administrator, educator; b. NYC, Apr. 7, 1941; s. Joseph John and Lucy (Bernardo) M.; m. Mary Teresa Collins, June 13, 1970; children: Joseph John, Michael Collins, Frank Joseph. BA, St. Francis Coll., 1962, L.H.D. (hon.), 1981; LL.B., Columbia U., 1965, PhD, 1970; L.H.D. (hon.), Coll. S.I., 1983; LL.D. (hon.), Dominican Coll., 1983, Manhattan Coll., 1983, St. Joseph's Coll., Molloy Coll., 1999. From fellow to prof. polit. sci. CUNY, 1964-83, v.p., 1977-78; asst. v.p. Columbia U., NYC, 1973-74; dep. dir. N.Y. State Emergency Fin. Control Bd. for N.Y.C., 1976-77; chancellor of schs. N.Y.C. Public Sch. System, 1978-83; pres., chief exec. officer N.Y.C. Partnership, Inc., 1983-87; pres. Acad. of Polit. Sci., 1987-91; prof. bus. Columbia U., NYC, 1987-91; dean Benjamin N. Cardozo Sch. of Law, Yeshiva U., NYC, 1991-96; of counsel Tannenbaum, Helpern, Syracuse and Hirschtritt, NYC, 1991—; pres. St. Francis Coll., NY, 1996—. Bd. dirs. Jeffries Group Inc.; trustee Manville Personal Injury Settlement Trust. Decorated cavalieri Order of Merit Italy; recipient cert. of merit Dirigible Soc. Am., 1976 Democrat. Roman Catholic. Office: 900 3rd Ave New York NY 10022-4728 also: 180 Remsen St Brooklyn NY 11201-4305 Office Phone: 718-489-5345. E-mail: fmacchia@stfranciscollege.edu.

MACCINI, LOUIS JOHN, economist, educator; b. Cambirdge, Mass., Aug. 3, 1942; s. Joseph and Jennie (Leccacorvi) M.; m. Carol Monterisi, June 25, 1965; children: Michael S., Sharon L. BS in Economics, Boston Coll., 1965; PhD in Economics, Northwestern U., 1970. From asst. prof. to assoc. prof. economics The Johns Hopkins U., Balt., 1969-86, prof., 1986—, chair, 1992—2007. Ad hoc com. mem. graduate fin. aid, Johns Hopkins U., editorial bd., public interest investment adv. com., law sch. com., med. sch. com., and other coms.; mem. recruting chair dept. grad. student advisor dept., and other depts. Referee Am. Econ. Review, Jour. Econ. Dynamics and Control, Oxford Econ. Papers, and others; contbr. articles to profl. jours. Grantee NSF. Mem. Am. Econ. Assn., The Econometric Soc., Internat Soc. Inventory Rsch. Office: Johns Hopkins U 3400 N Charles St Baltimore MD 21218-2680 Home Phone: 410-433-7147; Office Phone: 410-516-7607. E-mail: maccini@jhu.edu.

MACCOBY, ELEANOR EMMONS, psychology professor; b. Tacoma, May 15, 1917; d. Harry Eugene and Viva May (Johnson) Emmons; m. Nathan Maccoby, Sept. 16, 1938 (dec. Apr. 1992); children: Janice Carmichael, Sarah Maccoby Blunt, Mark. BS, U. Wash., 1939; MA, U. Mich., 1949, PhD, 1950. Study dir. div. program surveys USDA, Washington, 1942-46; study dir. Survey Rsch. Ctr. U. Mich., Ann Arbor, 1946-48; lectr., rsch. assoc. dept. social rels. Harvard U., Cambridge, Mass., 1950-58; from assoc. to full prof. Stanford (Calif.) U., 1958-87, Barbara Kimball Browning prof., 1979, chmn. dept. psychology, 1973-76, prof. emeritus, 1987—. Author: (with R. Sears and H. Levin) Patterns of Child-Rearing, 1957, (with Carol Jacklin) Psychology of Sex Differences, 1974, Social Development, 1980, (with R.H. Mnookin) Dividing the Child: Social and Legal Dilemmas of Custody, 1992, (with Buchanan and Dombusch) Adolescents after Divorce, 1996, The Two Sexes: Growing Up Apart, Coming Together, 1998; editor: (with Newcomb and Hartley) Readings in Social Psychology, 1957, The Development of Sex Differences, 1966. Recipient Gores award for Excellence in Tchg., Stanford U., 1981, Disting. Contbn. to Ednl. Research award Am. Ednl. Rsch. Assn., 1984, Lectureship award Soc. for Devel. and Behavioral Pediats., 2002. Fellow APA (pres. Divsn. 7, 1971-72, G. Stanley Hall award 1982), Soc. for Rsch. in Child Devel. (pres. 1981-83, mem. governing coun. 1963-66, Disting. Sci. Contbn. award 1987), Assn. Psychol. Ssci. (Disting. Sci. Contbns. award 1988); mem. NAS, Am. Acad. Arts and Scis., Inst. Medicine, Western Psychol. Assn. (pres. 1974-75, Lifetime Achievement award 2004), Inst. for Rsch. on Women and Gender, Social Sci. Rsch. Coun. (chmn. 1984-85), Consortium of Social Sci. Assns. (pres. 1997-98), Am. Psychol. Found. (Life Achievement award 1996). Democrat. Office: Stanford U Dept Psychology Stanford CA 94305-2130 Personal E-mail: maccoby@stanford.edu.

MACCOMBIE, BRUCE FRANKLIN, composer, college administrator; b. Providence, Dec. 5, 1943; s. Franklin S. and Florence (Corbishley) MacC.; m. Frances Holliday, Sept. 4, 1965 (div. 1970); m. Turi Gundersen, Mar. 10, 1979; 1 child, Juliana. BA, U. Mass., 1967, M of Music, 1968, DFA (hon.), 1986; PhD in Music, U. Iowa, 1971. Assoc. prof. Yale U., New Haven, 1975-80; v.p., dir. publications G. Schirmer Mus. Publs., NYC, 1980-85; assoc. dean, Amherst Coll. Humanities and Fine Arts U. Mass.; dean, provost The Juilliard Sch., NYC, 1986-92; dean Coll. Fine Arts Boston U., 1992, prof., 2002—; dir. Jazz at Lincoln Ctr., NYC, 2001. Composer numerous musical works. Recipient Goddard Lieberson award Am. Acad. Inst. Arts and Letters, N.Y.C., 1979; Sutherland Dows fellowship, Martha Baird Rockefeller Fund for Music grant. Mem. Coll. Music Soc., Charles Ives Soc. (bd. dirs.). Office: Boston U Dept Music 855 Commonwealth Ave Boston MA 02215-1303 E-mail: maccombie@hfa.umass.edu.

MAC CORMAC, EARL RONALD, retired education educator; b. NYC, Apr. 26, 1935; s. Earl Copeland and Katherine Kissel MacC.; m. Nancy Hamilton, Aug. 23, 1958; children: Ann F., Susan H. B Engring., Yale U., 1955, MA, 1959, PhD, 1961, Karlsruke U., Germany, 2003. Adminstrv. asst. Hazen Found., New Haven, 1958-61; Charles A. Dana Prof. of Philosophy Davidson (N.C.) Coll., 1961-86; Fulbright Prof. U. Madras, India, 1985-86; sci. advisor to gov. Gov.'s Office, Raleigh, NC, 1986-92; pres. N.C. Quality Leadership Found., Raleigh, 1992-94; cons. prof. of radiology Duke U. med. Ctr., Durham, NC, 1994—. Adj. prof. indsl. engring. N.C. State U., Raleigh, 1986-92; exec. dir. N.C. Bd. Sci. and Technology, Raleigh, 1986-92; mem. kuratorium Wissenschaftszentrum, North-Rhine Westphalia, 1991—; nat. Fulbright selection com. Inst. of Internat. Edn., N.Y., 1984-87. Author: (books) Metaphor and Myth in Science and Religion, 1976, A Cognitive Theory of Metaphor, 1985, Myths of Science and Technology, 1986; co-author: Decision Analysis Applied to Electrical Rate Design, 1985; co-editor: (book) Fractals in Brain, Fractals in Mind, 1995; editl. bd. John Benjamins Pubs., 1998—. Bd. dirs. Alt. Energy Corp., N.C., 1989-92; adv. bd. N.C. Solar Ctr., Raleigh. Named Outstanding Engring. Student, ASME, 1955; recipient Jefferson award for Tchg., McConnell Found., Davidson, 1971. Mem. N.C. Soc. for Electron Microscopy and Microbeam Analysis (hon.), Tau Beta Pi, Sigma Xi. Presbyterian. Avocations: tennis, golf. Home: 4413 Keswick Dr Raleigh NC 27609-6325 E-mail: ermnhm@earthlink.net.

MACCORMACK, CHARLES FREDERICK, international relief organization executive; b. Oct. 27, 1941; married; two children. AB, Middlebury Coll., 1963, EdD (hon.), 1982; MIA, Columbia U., 1965, PhD, 1974. Staff assoc. internat. div. First Nat. City Bank, Caracas, Venezuela, 1964; instr. latin-Am. politics U. N.H., Durham, 1967; asst. to dean Internat. Fellows Program Columbia U., NYC, 1967-68; rsch. fellow fgn. policy studies Brookings Instn., Washington, 1969-70; dir. internat. career tng. program Experiment Internat. Living, Brattleboro, Vt., 1970-74; v.p. programs Save the Children Fedn./Community Devel. Found., Westport, Conn., 1974-77; pres. World Learning (formerly The Experiment Internat. Living/Sch. for Internat. Tng.), Brattleboro, 1977—92; pres., CEO Save the Children Fedn., Inc., Westport, Conn., 1993—. Bd. dirs. Arthur D. Little Mgmt. Edn. Inst., Ptnrs. Internat. Edn. and Tng., Am. Forum for Global Edn., Landmark Coll., Save the Children Fedn., Inc., 1993- Mng. editor Jour. Internat. Affairs. Mem. founding com. U., 1971-72, Vt. Commn. Edn. and the Econ. Future, 1982, coun. advisors Peace Corps Future Team, 1987, Coun. Fgn. Rels., N.Y.C., global awareness adv. bd. Wheaton Coll., Norton, Mass.; mem. exec. com., chair devel. assistance com., co-chair com. refugee svcs. Am. Coun. Voluntary Internat. Action. Universidad Cen. de Venezuela Fulbright fellow, Caracas, Venezuela, 1965-66, Universidad Nacional Autonoma de Mexico NSF fellow, Mexico City, 1968-69, Edward John Noble Leadership fellow, 1963-65; Gould scholar, Middlebury scholar, Travelli scholar, 1959-63. Office: Save the Children Fedn Inc 54 Wilton Rd Westport CT 06880

MACCORMACK, JEAN F., academic administrator; d. George and Helen MacCormack. BA, Emmanuel Coll., Boston, 1969; MEd, U. Mass., Amherst, 1978, EdD, 1979. Assoc. dean Coll. of Edn. U. Mass, Boston, 1984—87, acting dean Coll. of Edn., 1984—85, assoc. chancellor, 1987—88, vice chancellor arts and fin., 1988—95, interim chancellor, 1995—96, dep. chancellor and vice chancellor arts and fin., 1996—99, chancellor Dartmouth, 1999—. Mem. South Coast Econ. Devel. Partnership, 1999, Joint CEO Group, 2000, Racial and Ethnic Access and Fairness Adv. Bd., 2001; chair South Coast Edn. Compact, 2000; mem. vis. com. U. So. Maine New Eng. Assoc. of Sch. and Coll., 2000—01; ex-officio mem. U. Mass. Dartmouth Libr. Archive Campaign, 2001; bd. mem. South Coast Health Sys., Inc., 2002; mem. marine sci. com. Fall River CEO Group, 2003, mem. med. device com., 03, mem. south coast edn. com., 03; mem. Regional Competitiveness Coun., 2003. Vice chair bd. govs. New Bedford Oceanariun, 1999, chair edn and rsch. com., 1999, trustee, chair edn. com., 2000; trustee Artworks! at Dover St., 2000, mem. edn. com, 2000, mem. pers. com., 2000; trustee Global Learning Charter Sch., 2000; bd. mem. Greater New Bedford Workforce Investment Bd., 2000, mem. legis. affairs and pub. info. com., 2000, mem. youth coun., 2000; mem. New Bedford Econ. Devel. Coun., 2000; corporator Child and Family Svcs., Inc., 2002; incorporator Home Aged People in Fall river, 2003; corporator Narragansett Fin. Corp. Citizens - Union Savs. Bank, 2003; mem. pres.'s coun. New Bedford Symphony Orch., 2003; mem. leadership coun. New Bedford Whaling Mus. Mem.: YMCA of Southeastern Mass., WHALE, Am. Assn. of State Coll. and U., U. Mass. Dartmouth Libr. Assoc. E-mail: jmaccormack@umassd.edu.

MACCORMACK, SABINE GABRIELE, history educator; b. Frankfurt, Germany, Feb. 24, 1941; came to U.S., 1978; d. Alfred and Gabriele (Buhl) Oswalt; m. Geoffrey MacCormack, June 20, 1964; 1 child, Catherine. BA in History, Oxford U., Eng., 1964, PhD, 1974; diploma in archives, U. Liverpool, Eng., 1965. Asst. prof. history U. Tex., Austin, 1979-82; asst. prof. history and classics Stanford (Calif.) U., 1982-85, assoc. prof., 1985-89; Alice Freeman Palmer prof. history U. Mich., Ann Arbor, 1989-97, Mary Ann & Charles R. Walgreen Jr. prof. study human under., 1997—; Mellon vis. prof. Inst. for Advanced Study, Princeton, N.J., 1996-98. Author: Art and Ceremony in Late Antiquity, 1981, Vision and Imagination in Early Colonial Peru, 1991, The Shadows of Poetry. Vergil in the Mind of Augustine, 1998; series editor Langs. and Cultures of the Spanish and Portuguese Worlds, 1997—; editl. cons. Viator, L.A., 1997—. Getty scholar Getty Ctr., L.A., 1991-92. Fellow Am. Acad. Arts & Scis.; mem. Am. Philos. Soc. Avocation: painting. Office: Univ Mich Dept Classical Studies Ann Arbor MI 48109 *

MACCOSS, MALCOLM, pharmaceutical executive, chemist; b. Cleator, Eng., June 2, 1947; s. John MacDonald and Ruth Victoria MacCoss; m. Sandra Eve Bramwell, Oct. 31, 1971; children: Michael John, Rachel Nicola. BSc with honors, U. Birmingham, Eng., 1968, PhD, 1971. Postdoctoral fellow U. Alta., Edmonton, Canada, 1971—76; asst. scientist Argonne Nat. Lab., Ill., 1976—80, scientist, 1980—82; asst. dir. Merck & Co, Rahway, NJ, 1986—91, dir., 1991—93, sr. dir., 1993—95, exec. dir., 1995—99, v.p. basic chemistry - Rahway, 1999—2003, v.p. drug discovery sciences - Rahway, 2003—. Adj. assoc. prof. U. Ill. Med. Ctr., Chgo., 1981—82; presenter in field. Contbr. chapters to books, articles to profl. jours. Mem. sci. adv. bd. Rider U., Lawrenceville, NJ, 2006—07. Recipient Distinguished Scientist award, U. Chgo., 1980, Thomas Alva Edison award, R & D Coun. NJ, 2004. Mem.: Am. Chem. Soc. (assoc.). Achievements include inventor or co-inventor on 91 issued US patents. Office: Merck Research Laboratories PO Box 2000 126 East Lincoln Ave Rahway NJ 07065 Home Phone: 732-780-0619; Office Phone: 732-594-7307.

MACCRACKEN, MICHAEL CALVIN, atmospheric scientist; b. Schenectady, May 20, 1942; s. Calvin Dodd MacCracken and Martha (McCracken) MacCracken Howard; m. Sandra Ann Svets, Mar. 12, 1967; children— Christopher, Ronald. B.S. in Engring., Princeton U., 1964; M.S. in Applied Sci., U. Calif.-Davis/Livermore, 1966, Ph.D. in Applied Sci., 1968. Atmospheric scientist Lawrence Livermore Nat. Lab., 1968—, prin. investigator Bay Area air quality modeling study, 1973-76, dep. div. leader atmospheric and geophys. scis. div., 1974-87, div. leader atmospheric and geophys. scis. div., 1987—; co-project leader study on global effects of nuclear exchange, 1983—; area mgr. CO2 research program Dept. Energy, 1979—, project dir. multistate atmospheric power prodn. study, 1976-79, project leader bilateral on environ. working group VIII, US/USSR, 1984—; mem. com. Internat. Climate, 1987—. Co-author: Environmental Consequences of Nuclear War, Vol. 1: Physical and Atmospheric Effects, 1986; co-author, co-editor (U.S. Dept. Energy state of the arts reports) Projecting the Climatic Effects of Increasing Carbon Dioxide, 1985; assoc. editor J. of Climate, 1987—; contbr. articles and reports to profl. publs. Bd. dirs.

Livermore Area Recreation and Park Dist., 1970-78, chmn., 1974, 78. Fannie and John Hertz Found. fellow, 1964-68. Mem. Am. Meteorol. Soc. (chmn. com. on climate variations 1983-85), Am. Geophys. Union, Am. Quaternary Assn., AAAS.

MACCRACKEN, THOMAS GREGG, musicologist; b. Norwalk, Connecticut, May 15, 1951; s. Constable and Eleanor (Dickson) MacCracken; m. Alexandra Jane (Moore-Robinson), May 28, 1988. BA, Yale Univ., 1973; PhD, Univ. of Chgo., 1985. Asst. prof. of music U. of Va., Charlottesville, 1986—90. Trustee Kinhaven Music Sch., Weston, Vt., 1974—80, 1993—98. Co-editor: (musical score) Mathurin Forestier Opera Omnia; musician: (CD recording) Pour 2 Clavecins; contbr. articles to profl. journals. Rsch. fellow, Smithsonian Instn., 1991—93. Mem.: Am. Musical Instrument Soc. (editor 1996—2006), Am. Musicological Soc., Am. Recorder Soc., Early Music Am. (bd. mem. 1990—94), Southeastern His. Keyboard Soc. (rev. editor 1991—96), Viola da Gamba Soc. of Am. (editl. bd. 1996). Presbyterian. Home: 12108 Vale Rd Oakton VA 22124

MACCRATE, ROBERT, lawyer; b. Bklyn., July 18, 1921; s. John and Flora (MacNicholl) MacC.; m. Constance Trapp, May 4, 1946; children: Christopher Robert, Barbara Constance MacCrate Gatti, Thomas John. BA, Haverford Coll., 1943, LLD (hon.), 1987; LLB, Harvard U., 1948; LLD (hon.), Union U., 1986, Dickinson Sch. Law, 1987, William Mitchell Coll. Law, 1994, Quinnipiac Coll. Law, 1995, CUNY, 2002, U. S.C., 2003. Bar: N.Y. 1949, U.S. Supreme Ct. 1955, D.C. 1965. Assoc. Sullivan & Cromwell, NYC, 1948-51, 51-55, ptnr., 1956-59, 62-91, ret., 1991—96, sr. counsel, 1997—; law sec. N.Y. Appelate Divsn. Presiding Justice David W. Peck, 1951; counsel N.Y. Gov. Nelson A. Rockefeller, 1959-62; spl. counsel U.S. Army for Investigation Mylai incident, 1969-70; counsel N.Y. State Ct. on Judiciary, 1971; mem. jud. selection com. for fed. judgeships Senator Jacob K. Javits, 1972-80; mem. jud. nominating com. N.Y. 2d Jud. Dept., 1975-82. Trustee Lawyers Com. for Civil Rights Under Law, 1976—; chmn. emeritus Fund for Modern Cts., 1978—; cons. N.Y. Profl. Edn. Project, 1994-96. Co-author: Appellate Justice in New York, 1982, Legal Education and Professional Development--an Educational Continuum, 1992, Preserving the Core Values of the American Legal Profession, 2000; contbr. articles to profl. jours. Bd. mgrs. Haverford Coll., 1971-85, emeritus 1986—. Lt. USNR, 1943-46. Recipient Justice System Improvement award Coun. for Ct. Excellence, 1988, Gold medal Nat. Inst. Social Scis., 1989. Fellow Am. Bar Found. (chmn. N.Y. state 1973-80, bd. dirs. 1989—, sec. 1992-94, v.p. 1994-96, pres. 1996-98); mem. ABA (pres. 1987-88, del. 1972-78, 89—, N.Y. State del. 1979-81, bd. govs. 1981-84, 86-89, chair task force law schs. and the profession 1989-92, chair spl. adv. com. internat. activities 1988-89, 2d cir. mem. standing com. on fed. judiciary 1984-86, mem. commn. on opportunities in profession 1993-96, mem. coun. sect. individual rights and responsibilities 1997-2000, medal 2002), N.Y. State Bar Assn. (pres. 1972-73, del. 1972—, chair com. law governing firm structure and operation 1999-2002, medal 1999), Assn. Bar City of N.Y. (v.p. 1969-71, chmn. exec. com. 1968-69, chmn. libr. com. 1977-80, chmn. 2d century com. 1989-92), Bar Assn. Nassau County, D.C. Bar Assn., N.Y. County Lawyers Assn. (Disting. Svc. award 1991), Nat. Bar Assn., Am. Coll. Trial Lawyers, Am. Soc. Internat. Law (exec. coun. 1975-80), Union Internationale des Avocats, Acad. Polit. Sci. (bd. dirs. 1975-94), Am. Judicature Soc. (pres. 1979-81, bd. dirs. and mem. exec. com. 1974-83, Justice award 1989), Practising Law Inst. (trustee and mem. exec. com. 1972-95, emeritus trustee 1995—, Seligson award 1995), Am. Law Inst. (coun. 1975—, ALI-ABA com. on continuing profl. edn. 1994-97, chair subcom. on future 1994-97), N.Y. Bar Found. (pres. 1976-91), Phi Beta Kappa. Home: 40 The Terrace Plandome NY 11030-1349 Office: Sullivan & Cromwell Rm 2421 125 Broad St New York NY 10004-2498 Home Phone: 516-627-6255.

MACDEVITT, BRIAN, lighting designer; b. Oct. 6, 1956; s. William Gerard and Julie (Powers) MacDevitt. BFA, SUNY, Purchase; studies with Bill Mintzer. Guest instr. design dept. SUNY, 1986—87. Lighting designer (Broadway plays) What's Wrong With This Picture?, 1994, Love! Valour! Compassion!, 1995, Master Class, 1995, Summer and Smoke, 1996, Sex and Longing, 1996, Present Laughter, 1996, Side Show, 1997, Proposals, 1997, The Diary of Anne Frank, 1997, Wait Until Dark, 1998, Night Must Fall, 1999, True West, 2000, The Ride Down Mt. Morgan, 2000, The Dinner Party, 2000, Judgment at Nuremberg, 2001, The Invention of Love, 2001, A Thousand Clowns, 2001, Major Barbara, 2001, Urinetown, 2001, The Women, 2001, Morning's at Seven, 2002, Into the Woods, 2002 (Tony award, best lighting design of a musical, 2002), Frankie and Johnny in the Clair de Lune, 2002, Short Talks on the Universe, 2002, Tartuffe, 2003, Nine, 2003, Long Day's Journey into Night, 2003, The Retreat From Moscow, 2003, Henry IV, 2003, Fiddler on the Roof, 2004, Match, 2004, A Raisin in the Sun, 2004, 'night Mother, 2004, Pacific Overtures, 2004, Good Vibrations, 2005, The Pillowman, 2005 (Tony award, best lighting of a play, 2005), Sweet Charity, 2005, Dog Sees God: Confessions of a Teenage Blockhead, 2005, The Wedding Singer, 2006, (plays) Oh, Coward!, 1979, A Girl's Guide to Chaos, 1986, Seven Brides for Seven Brothers, 1984, Gigi, 1984, Oliver!, 1985, Brigadoon, 1986, Can-Can, 1988, The House in Town, 2006, The Coast of Utopia, 2006 (Outer Critics Cir. award outstanding lighting design, 2007, Drama Desk award outstanding lighting design, 2007, Tony award best lighting design of a play, 2007). Mem.: United Scenic Artists. *

MACDONALD, ALAN HUGH, academic administrator; b. Ottawa, Ont., Can., Mar. 3, 1943; s. Vincent C. and Hilda C. MacDonald; children: Eric Paul Henry, Nigel Alan Christopher. BA, Dalhousie U., Halifax NS, 1963; BLS, U. Toronto, Ont., 1964. With Dalhousie U., 1964-78, law libr., 1965-67, 69-71, asst. univ. libr., 1970-72, health sci. libr., 1972-78, lectr. Sch. Libr. Svcs., 1969-78; with U. Calgary, Canada, 1979—2003, sr. advisor Info. Resources, 1999—2003, asst. to provost, 1999—2003, adj. prof. faculty comm. and culture, 2000—03, dir. Info Svcs., 1988—99, dir. librs., 1979-92, univ. orator, 1989—2003; dir. U. Calgary Press, 1984—90. Chair editl. bd. U. Calgary Press, 2001—03, libr. emeritus, 2003—; libr. N.S. Barristers Soc., 1969—74; mem. adv. bd. Nat. Libr. Can., 1972—76, Health Scis. Resource Ctr., Can. Inst. Sci. and Tech. Info., 1977—79; mem. Coun. of Prairie Univ. Librs., 1979—92, 1997—98, chair, 1984—85, 1989, 91; Bassam lectr. U. Toronto Faculty Info. Studies, 1994; Lorne MacRae lectr. Libr. Assn. Alta., 1996; mem. steering com. Alta. Libr. Knowledge Network, 1999—2002; steering com. Can. Digital Libr. Rsch. Initiative, 1999—2000. Mem. editl. bd. America: History and Life (ABC-CLIO), 1985-93. Pres. TELED Cmty. Media Access Orgn., Halifax, N.S., 1972—74; mem. Minister's Com. on Univ. Affairs, Alta., 1979—83; bd. dirs. Alta. Found. for Can. Music Ctr., 1985—92, Can. Inst. for Hist. Microreprodn., 1990—98, pres., 1996—97; bd. dirs. Calgary Learning Ctr., 1997—2004, vice-chair, 2000—04. Coun. Libr. Resources fellow, 1975; exec. fellow Univ. Microfilms Internat., 1986; recipient Disting. Acad. Librarian award Can. Assn. of Coll. and Univ. Libraries, 1988, U. Toronto Faculty of Info. Studies Alumni Jubilee award, 1999. Mem.: Order of U. Calgary, Calgary Cmty. Network Assn. (bd. dirs. 1994—99, chair 1996—99), Can. Assn. Rsch. Librs. (bd. dirs. 1981—86, v.p. 1985—86, Disting. Svc. award to rsch. librarianship 2003), Can. Assn. Info. Sci. (pres. 1979—80), Foothills Libr. Assn., Atlantic Provinces Libr. Assn. (pres. 1977—78), Can. Libr. Assn. (treas. 1977—79, pres. 1980—81, Award for Outstanding Svc. to Librarianship 1997), Australian Libr. and Info. Assn. (assoc.), Can. Health Libr. Assn. (life; treas. 1977—79), Libr. Assn. Alta. (life; v.p. 1988—89, Pres.' award 1992), AeroSpace Mus. Assn. Calgary (bd. dirs. 2002—07, exec. dir. 2003—04, sec. 2004—07, libr. 2006—). Personal E-mail: ahmacdon@ucalgary.ca.

MACDONALD, ALAN S., diversified financial services company executive; BS, Drexel U.; MS, London Sch. Econs.; PhD in Econs., Cambridge U., Eng. Economist UN Econ. Commn. for Europe, Geneva; fin. mgmt. assoc. GM, Wilmington, Del.; co-head global markets Citigroup, head corp. and investment banking U.S. and Can., head corp. banking in emerging markets, head info. bus. group, head Banco de Investimento Crefisul, head Banco Internacional de Colombia; vice chmn., head global relationship banking Citibank and Citicorp, 2000—04; COO global banking Citigroup, 2004—. Bd. dirs. Liberty Brokerage Co. Trustee NY Philharm. Orch., Hosp. for Spl. Surgery, NY. Mem.: NY Partnership (mem. high tech. com.), Am. Bankers Assn. (bd. dirs.), Am. Inst. Contemporary German Studies (trustee), Conf. Bd., Nat. Policy Assn. (trustee, mem. exec. com. new Am. realities com.), Econ. Club NY. Office: Citigroup Inc 399 Park Ave New York NY 10043

MACDONALD, BRIAN SCOTT, management consultant; b. Sudbury, Ont., Can., June 6, 1939; s. David William and Katherine Lillian (McKinnon) MacD.; m. Margaret Louise Young, Aug. 11, 1962 (dec. Apr. 1985); children— Heather Anne, David Colin, Michael Alexander BA with honors, Royal Mil. Coll., Kingston, Ont., 1961; MBA cum laude, York U., Toronto, Ont., 1980; postgrad., U. Toronto, 1980—. Tchr., cons. Bd. Edn., Ont., Can., 1966-80; exec. dir. Can. Inst. Strategic Studies, Toronto, Ont., Can., 1982-89; pres. Strategic Insight Planning and Communications, 1989—; rsch. assoc. Queens U. Centre for Def. Mgmt. Studies, 2005—. Author: Military Spending in Developing Countries: How Much is Too Much, 1997; editor: Parliament and Defence Policy, 1982, War in the 80's: Men Against High Tech, 1983, Canada's Strategies for Space, 1984, The Grand Strategy of the Soviet Union, 1984, Defence and the Canadian Economy, 1984, Canada's Strategies for the Pacific Rim, 1985, High Tech and the High Seas, 1985, Canada, the Caribbean, and Central Am., 1986, Terror, 1986, Tactics and Technology, 1987, A Grand Strategy for the United States?, 1988, Airwar 2000, 1989, Canadian Strategic Forecast 1989, 1989, Space Strategy: Three Dimensions, 1989, The New World of Robust International Peacekeeping, 2005; contbg. editor Def. Policy Rev., 1994-04. Pres. Royal Can. Arty. Assn., Toronto, 1976; vice chmn. Conf. Def. Assns., Ottawa, Ont., 1975, bd. dirs., 2005—, sr. def. analyst, 2006—; gov. Can. Corps of Commissionaires, Toronto, 1984-86; hon. aide de camp to Gov. Gen. Can., Ottawa, 1984-86; comdr. Toronto Militia Dist., 1984-86; bd. dirs. Atlantic Coun. Can., 1986—2005, sr. v.p., 1991, pres., 1999-2002; bd dirs Royal Can. Mil. Inst., 1986-87, 2004—. Served to col. Can. Army, 1957-86. Marsh-McLennan scholar, 1977, Dept. Nat. Def. scholar, 1981-82 Mem. Toronto Bd. Trade. Office: 169 Newton Dr Willowdale ON Canada M2M 2N6 Office Phone: 416-223-2192. Business E-Mail: strategicinsight@sympatico.ca.

MACDONALD, BRUCE E., military officer, lawyer; b. Cin., 1956; BA in English, Coll. Holy Cross, 1978; JD, Calif. Western Sch. Law, 1987; LLM, Harvard Law Sch., Cambridge, Mass., 1992. Bar: Calif., US Dist. Ct. (so. dist. Calif.). Advanced through grades to rear adm. USN; main propulsion asst., navigator USS Hepburn, 1979; intermediate combat sys. team tng. and advanced multi-threat team course dir. Fleet Combat Tng. Ctr., Pacific; sr. def. counsel, trial counsel, med. care recovery act claims officer Naval Legal Svc. Office, San Diego, 1987—90; command judge adv. USS Independence, 1990—92; chief operational law divsn. UN Command, Combined Forces Command, US Forces, Seoul, Republic of Korea, 1992—94; staff judge adv. US Naval Forces, Seoul, Republic of Korea, 1992—94; exec. officer Naval Legal Svc. Office N.W., 1994—96, comdr., 1999—2002; officer in charge Trial Svc. Office West Detachment Bremerton, 1996—97; fleet judge adv. Comdr. 7th Fleet, Yokosuka, Japan, 1997—99; spl. counsel to chief of naval ops., 2002—04; dep. judge adv. gen., comdr. Naval Legal Svc. Command, 2004—06; JAG USN, 2006—. Decorated Legion of Merit with two gold stars, Def. Meritorious Svc. medal, Navy Meritorious Svc. Medal with gold star, Navy Commendation Medal with gold star, Navy Achievement Medal with gold star. Office: USN 1000 Navy Pentagon Washington DC 20350-1000 *

MACDONALD, DAVID RICHARD, industrial psychologist; b. Dowagiac, Mich., May 20, 1953; s. Jerrold Brewster and Shirley Ann (Shaffer) MacD.; m. Mary Elizabeth Olson, Dec. 20, 1975 (div. Sept. 5, 1995); 1 child, Sarah Ann; m. Cathleen Jean Carlson, July 25, 1996. AS, Southwestern Mich. Coll., 1973; BBA, Western Mich. U., 1975, MA, 1976, EdS, 1979; PhD, Mich. State U., 1986. Cert. Birkman Method cons., performance technologist. Announcer, boardman WDOW AM/FM, Dowagiac, Mich., 1968—72; mgmt. devel. specialist Interstate Motor Freight Sys., Grand Rapids, Mich., 1977—79; sr. mgmt. tng. instr. GTE Gen. Telephone Co. Mich., Muskegon, 1979—82; cons. human resources devel. Steelcase, Inc., Grand Rapids, 1982—86, mgr. performance devel., 1986—96, mgr. assessment process, 1996—2004, sr. cons. mgmt. devel., 2004—; pres. Plectrum, Grand Rapids, 1997—. Cons., speaker in field; facilitator, program dir. Devel. Dimensions Internat., Pitts., 1981; facilitator Alamo Learning Systems, Southfield, Mich., 1983, 86, Wilson Learning Corp., Eden Prairie, Minn., 1983; job analysis program mgr. Barry M. Cohen & Assocs., Largo, Fla., 1985; asst. prof. grad. mgmt. Aquinas Coll., Grand Rapids, 1983—; asst. prof. Coll. Bus., Western Mich. U., Kalamazoo, 2001—; co-chair Internat. Congress on Assessment Ctr. Methods, 1998, mem. planning com., 1998, chair Internat. Task Force on Assessment Ctr. Guidelines, 1999—; asst. prof., counselor edn. and counseling psychology We. Mich. U., Kalamazoo, 2003—. Prodr. CD: The Historical Harpsichord, 1997. Co-chair United Way Steelcase campaign, Grand Rapids, 1986; bd. dirs. human resource com., Thresholds, Grand Rapids, Mich., 2001-04; mentor lang. skills, Madison Park Elem. Sch., Grand Rapids, 1997-2006, Brookside Elem. Sch., 2006—. Mem. ASTD (sec. W. Mich. chpt. 1977-79), Soc. Indsl.-Orgnl. Psychology (mem. program com. 2005, 06), Am. Psychol. Assn., Nat. Soc. for Performance and Instrn., Internat. Congress Assessment Ctr. Methods (program com., 2006), Soc. for Indsl. Orgn. Psychology (program com. ann. conf., 2006), Mensa, Phi Kappa Phi. Republican. Avocations: building harpsichords, stained glass, gardening, music. Home: 2306 Prospect Ave SE Grand Rapids MI 49507-3159 Office: PO Box 1967 Grand Rapids MI 49501-1967 Business E-Mail: dmacdona@steelcase.com.

MACDONALD, DAVID ROBERT, lawyer, pension fund administrator; b. Chgo., Nov. 1, 1930; s. James Wear and Frances Esther (Wine) M.; m. Verna Joy Odell, Feb. 17, 1962; children: Martha, Emily, David, Rachel, Rebecca. BS, Cornell U., 1952; JD, U. Mich., 1955. Bar: Ill. 1955, Mich. 1955, D.C. 1983. Practiced in Chgo., 1957-74; mem. firm Kirkland, Ellis, Hodson, Chaffetz & Masters, Chgo., 1957-62, ptnr., 1962, Baker & McKenzie, Chgo., 1962-74, 77-81; asst. sec. of Treasury for enforcement, ops. and tariff affairs Dept. Treasury, Washington, 1974-76; undersec. of Navy, 1976-77; dep. U.S. Trade Rep., 1981-83; ptnr. Baker & McKenzie, Chgo., 1983-96. Bd. dirs. Mestek, Inc (N.Y. Stock Exch.). Pres. David R. Macdonald Found., 1996—. Mem. ABA, D.C. Bar Assn., Chgo. Assn. Commerce and Industry (bd. dirs. 1977-81), Order of Coif, Econ. Club (Chgo.), Cosmos Club (Washington), Grolier Club (N.Y.C.). Home: 6605 Radnor Rd Bethesda MD 20817-6324 Office: 815 Connecticut Ave NW Washington DC 20006-4004

MACDONALD, DONALD ARTHUR, JR., physician, surgeon; b. Englewood, NJ, May 9, 1955; s. Donald Arthur and Ruth Moran M.; m. Florence Twombly Childs, June 14, 1980; children: Donald, Alexandra, Margaret, Ian. BA with highest honors, Williams Coll., 1977; MD, Dartmouth U., 1980. Diplomate Am. Bd. Ophthalmology. Intern Mary Imogene Bassett Hosp., Cooperstown, N.Y., 1980-81; resident Manhattan Eye Ear & Throat Hosp., NYC, 1981-84, attending physician, 1985—; fellow N.Y. Eye Ear & Throat Hosp., 1984-85; attending physician Riverview Med. Ctr., Red Bank, N.J., 1985—, chief dept. ophthalmology, 1995-97. Trustee Rumson (NJ) Country Day Sch., 1990-96, Monmouth County Vol. Ctr., 1996-98, Horizons Program, Rumson, 1996-98; trustee, bd. dirs. ALS Assn. Greater NY chpt.; bd. dirs. Burden Ctr. for the Aging, 2000-03. Mem. Lions, Rumson Country Club (commodore 1996-2003), Seabright Lawn Tennis and Cricket Club, St. Andrews Soc. N.Y., N.Y. Yacht Club, Monmouth Beach Club. Roman Catholic. Office: 21 Gilbert St N Tinton Falls NJ 07701-4913 Home Phone: 732-747-8217; Office Phone: 732-741-1902. E-mail: Drdonaldmadonald@mac.com.

MACDONALD, DONALD PAUL, lawyer; b. Newport, RI, Apr. 19, 1931; s. Bertram I. and Pauline E. (Toomey) MacD.; widowed; children: Theresa Carroll, Sheila Joan, D. Patrick. BA, Providence Coll., 1952; LLB, Georgetown U., 1956, LLM, 1963. Assoc. then ptnr. Smith & Pepper, Washington, 1957-61; asst. U.S. atty. Dept. Justice, Denver, 1962-67; ptnr. Carroll & MacDonald, Denver, 1967-72, Hornbein & MacDonald, Denver, 1972—. Dir. Legal Ctr., Denver, 1986—, pres., 1989—; dir. Qualife Wellness Com., Denver, 1994-2000; trustee, fellow Coll. Labor and Employment Lawyers, 1995—, pres. 1999, labor and employment law sect. mem. coun. 1985—, chair 1995-96, dir. Denver Children Advocacy Ctr., 2000-. With U.S. Army, 1952-54. Recipient Cath. Lawyers Guild St. Thomas More award, 1983. Fellow Am. Bar Found., Internat. Soc. Barristers; mem. ABA (mem. labor and employment sect., bd. govs. 1974-84), Denver Bar Assn. (pres. 1981-82), Univ. Club. Roman Catholic. E-mail: dpmacdonald@netzero.com.

MACDONALD, DONALD STOVEL, public policy advisor; b. Ottawa, Ont., Can., Mar. 1, 1932; s. Donald Angus and Marjorie (Stovel) M.; m. Ruth Hutchison, Mar. 4, 1961 (dec.); children: Leigh, Nikki, Althea, Sonja; m. Adrian Merchant Lang, Sept. 10, 1988; stepchildren: Maria (dec.), Timothy, Gregory, Andrew, Elisabeth, Amanda, Adrian. Student, Ashbury Coll., Ottawa; BA, U. Toronto, Ont., 1951; LLB, Osgoode Hall Law Sch., 1955; LLM, Harvard, 1956; diploma internat. law, Cambridge U., 1957; LLD, St. Lawrence U., U N.B. Saint John, 1990, U. Toronto, 2000, Carleton U., 2003; DEng, Colo. Sch. Mines. Bar: Called to Ont. bar 1955. Assoc. McCarthy & McCarthy, Toronto, 1957-62; M.P. for Toronto-Rosedale, 1962; reelected, 1963, 65, 68, 72, 74; parliamentary sec. to Min. of Justice, 1963-65, to Min. of Finance, 1965, to Sec. of State for External Affairs, 1966-68, to Min. of Industry, 1968; pres. Privy Coun. and Govt. House Leader, 1968-70; min. of nat. def., 1970-72; min. energy, mines and resources, 1972-75; min. of fin., 1975-77; ptnr. firm McCarthy & McCarthy, Toronto, 1977-88; high commr. for Can. to U.K., 1988-91; counsel McCarthy Tetrault, Toronto, 1991-2000. Sr. advisor UBS Bunting Warburg, Toronto, 2000-02; sr. advisor pub. policy Lang Michener Barristers and Solicitors, 2002—; spl. lectr. U. Toronto Law Sch., 1978-82, 86-88; chmn. Royal Commn. on Econ. Union and Devel. Prospects for Can., 1982-85; chmn. adv. com. competition Ont. Electricity Sys., 1995-96; chmn. Inst. for Rsch. on Pub. Policy, Montreal, 1991-97, Siemens Can. Inc., 1991-04, Atlantic Coun. of Can., 1998-02; bd. dirs. Century Mining Corp., Boise Cascade Corp., 1995-04; chmn., trustee IPC US REIT, 2001-07; trustee Clean Power Operating Trust, 2001-07; chmn. Vector Wind Energy, 2005-06; trustee Energy Savs. Income Fund, 200506; co-chmn. Trudeau Ctr. U. Toronto, 2006-; mem. adv. coun. Ctr. Am. Studies U. Western Ont., 2006-. Named Freeman of the City of London, 1990, hon. fellow Trinity Hall, Cambridge U., 1994, Companion of the Order of Can., 1994. Mem. Queen's Privy Coun. Can., Delta Kappa Epsilon. Liberal. Baptist. Office: Lang Michener Toronto Office Box 747 ste 2500 BCE place 181 Bay st Toronto ON Canada m5j 2t7 Home Phone: 905-649-2557; Office Phone: 416-307-4241. Business E-Mail: dmacdonald@langmichener.ca.

MACDONALD, DOUGLAS ANDREW, psychologist, educator; b. Barrie, Can., June 2, 1967; s. David James and Rachel Marie MacDonald; m. Clementina Iampietro, Mar. 15, 1995; children: Moriah, Sarah. BA in Psychology (hon.), U. Windsor, Ont., Can., 1990, MA in Psychology, 1992, PhD in Psychology, 1998. Practicum student Guelph Assessment and Treatment Unit, Ont., Canada, 1991; intern U. Windsor Psychol. Svc. Clinic, 1992—93, Windsor Regional Hosp., 1994—95; behavioral cons. Essex County Dist. Sch. Bd., Ont., Canada, 1995—97; psychologist Greater Essex County Dist. Sch. Bd., Windsor, 1997—2004; prof. psychology U. Detroit, 2000—; dir. clin. MA program U. Detroit Mercy, 2003—. Rsch. asst. U. Windsor, 1987—88; faculty Saybrook Grad. Sch., San Francisco, 2001—; clin. cons. Glengarda Child Family Svc., 2004—. Co-editor: (novels) Approaches to Transpersonal Measurement and Assessment, 2002; editor (rsch. assoc.): Jour. Humanistic Psychology, 2002; co-editor: Humanistic Psychologist, 2003, Internat. Jour. Transpersonal Studies, 2003—06; assoc. editor: Jour. Transpersonal Psychology, 2001, consulting editor: Australian Gestalt Jour. Cons., bd. dirs. Glengarda Child & Family Svc., Windsor, Ontario, Canada, 2000—04. Grantee, Floraglades Found., 2000—04. Mem.: APA (Carmi Harari Early Career award 2006), Can. Psychol. Assoc. Achievements include research in expression, measurement, and devel. of spirituality and assessment tools. Avocations: gardening, music, martial arts. Home: 470 Frontenac Ave N9E1M1 Windsor ON Canada Office: U Detroit Mercy Dept Psychology 4001 W McNichols Rd Detroit MI 48221 Home Phone: 519-250-4723. Business E-Mail: macdonda@udmercy.edu.

MACDONALD, FLORA ISABEL, Canadian government official; b. North Sydney, NS, Can., June 3, 1926; d. George Frederick and Mary Isabel (Royle) MacD. Attended Empire Bus. Coll.; grad., Nat. Def. Coll., 1972; DHL (hon.), Mt. St. Vincent U., 1979, various univs., Can., U.S. and UK. Exec. dir. Progressive Conservative Party Hdqs., Ottawa, Ont., Canada, 1957—66; adminstrv. officer, tutor dept. polit. studies Queen's U., 1966—72; mem. Can. Parliament for Kingston and Islands, Ont., 1972—88; Progressive Conservative spokesman for Indian affairs and no. devel. Can. Parliament, 1972; for housing and urban devel., 1974; chmn. Progressive Conservative Caucus Com. on Fed.-Provincial Rels., 1976; sec. of state for external affairs, 1979—80; min. employment and immigration, 1984—86; min. comms., 1986—89; chairperson Internat. Devel. Rsch. Ctr., 1992—97; spl. adv. Commonwealth of Learning, 1990—91. Vis. fellow Ctr. for Can. Studies, U. Edinburgh, 1989; host T.V. series North South Vision T.V., 1990-94. Bd. dirs. Carnegie Commn. Repreventing Deadly Conflict, 1994-99, Friends of the Nat. Libr., Shashtri Indo-Can. Adv. Coun., pres., 1996-2004; program advisor CARE Can., 1995-2005, Helpage Internat., London, 1996-2001; chmn. Partnership Africa-Can., 2001-04, Ottawa, Can., Future Generations, 2001-07, Franklin, W.Va.; co-chair Can Coord. Com. UN Yr. of Older Persons, 1999; hon. pres. Assn. Can. Clubs, World Federalists, Can., 2000-04; patron Commonwealth Human Rights Initiative. Decorated Companion Order of Can., Order of Ont. Mem. Nat. Mus. Scotland (hon. patron Can.), UN (Eminent Persons to study Trans-Nat. Corps. in South Africa 1989). Mem. United Ch. of Canada. Office: Ste 1103 350 Queen Elizabeth Drivewy Ottawa ON Canada K1S 3N1 E-mail: flora@intranet.ca.

MACDONALD, GORDON RHODES, retired urologist, military officer; b. Washington, Dec. 28, 1943; s. Gordon Rhodes and Sally Steele MacDonald; m. Marie Teresa Sweeney, July 2, 1966. MD, George Wash. U., DC, 1968. Medical Board Certification Am. Bd. of Urology, 1978. Surg. intern Cleve. Clinic, Ohio, 1968—69; med. dept. head USS Capricornus and USS El Paso, Norfolk, Va., 1969—70; gen. med. officer Nat. Naval Med. Ctr., Bethesda, Md., 1970—72, resident in urology, 1972—76; head urology dept. Naval Hosp., Charleston, SC, 1976—83, Naval Regional Med. Ctr., Portsmouth, Va., 1983—90, Fleet Hosp. Five, Jubail, Saudi Arabia, 1990—91, Naval Hosp. Roosevelt Roads, Ceiba, PR, 1991—99. Chmn., urology residency program Naval Regional Med. Ctr., Portsmouth, Va., 1983—90. Capt. USN, 1969—99. Mem.: Am. Urol. Assn. Home: 340 Harbour Dr #73 Humacao PR 00791-6217 Home Phone: 787-850-6728.

MACDONALD, HUGH IAN, economics professor, public policy professor, academic administrator; b. Toronto, Ont., June 27, 1929; s. Hugh and Winnifred (Mitchell) M.; m. Dorothy Marion Vernon, June 4, 1960; 5 children. B.Com., U. Toronto, 1952; MA, Oxford U., Eng., 1954, B.Phil., 1955; LLD (hon.), U. Toronto, 1974; D Univ. (hon.), Open U., UK, 1998; DLitt (hon.), Open U., Sri Lanka, 1999, Open U., Hyderabad, India, 2001, York U., Toronto, 2007. Lectr. U. Toronto, Ont., Canada, 1955—62, asst. prof., 1962—65; dean of men Univ. Coll. U. Toronto, 1956—65; chief economist Govt. Ont., Canada, 1965—67, dep. treas., 1967, dep. treas., dep. minister econ., 1968, dep. treas., dep. minister econs. and intergovtl. affairs, 1972; pres. York U., Toronto, Ont., Canada, 1974-84, prof. econ. and pub. policy, pres. emeritus, 1984—; dir. York Internat., 1984—94; dir. MPA program York U. Schulich Sch. Bus., 1994—. Past pres. World U. Svc. Can.; past chmn. Hockey Can., Commonwealth of Learning. Named Officer, Order of Can., 1977; recipient Can. Centennial medal, 1967, Queen's Silver Jubilee medal, 1977, Commemorative medal, 125th Anniversary Can. Confedn., 1992, Vanier medal for distinction in pub. svc. and excellence in pub. adminstrn., 2000, Queen's Golden Jubilee medal, 2002, Senator Boorsma medal, Southeastern Conf. Pub. Adminstrn. in U.S., 2006; Rhodes scholar, 1952. Fellow: The Commonwealth of Learning (past chmn.). Office: York U Schulich Sch Bus Rm 207 Seymour Schulich Bldg 4700 Keele St Toronto ON Canada M3J 1P3 Office Phone: 416-736-5632. Office Fax: 416-736-5643. Business E-Mail: yorkmpa@yorku.ca.

MACDONALD, J. RANDALL, information technology executive, human resources specialist; B in Polit. Sci., St. Francis Coll., M in Indsl. Rels. Human resources position Ingersoll-Rand Co., Sterling Drug Inc.; various human resources positions including exec. v.p. human resources and adminstrn. GTE (now Verizon Comm.), 1983—2000; sr. v.p. human resouces IBM, 2000—. Bd. dirs. Covance (formerly Corning Pharm. Svcs.); mem. Cornell U. Ctr. for Advanced Human Resources Study, chmn. exec. bd. bd. trustees St. Francis Coll., Pa. Fellow: Nat. Acad. Human Resources (bd. dirs. 2000—); mem.: Labor Policy Assn. (vice chmn. bd. dirs.), Pers. Roundtable, Cowdrick Group. Office: IBM 1133 Westchester Ave White Plains NY 10604 Office Phone: 800-426-4968. *

MACDONALD, JAMES ROSS, physicist, researcher; b. Savannah, Ga., Feb. 27, 1923; s. John Elwood and Antonina Jones (Hansell) Macdonald; m. Margaret Milward Taylor, Aug. 3, 1946; children: Antonina Hansell, James Ross IV, William Taylor. BA, Williams Coll., 1944; SB, MIT, 1944, SM, 1947; PhD, Oxford U., Eng., 1950, DSc, 1967. Staff Digital Computer Lab., MIT, 1946-47; physicist Armour Rsch. Found., Chgo., 1950-52; assoc. physicist Argonne Nat. Lab., 1952-53; with Tex. Instruments Inc., Dallas, 1953-74, v.p. corp. rsch. and engring., 1968-73, v.p. corp. R & D, 1973-74; cons., 1974—; dir. Simmonds Precision Products Inc., 1979-83; William Rand Kenan Jr. prof. physics U. N.C., Chapel Hill, 1974-91, prof. emeritus, 1991—. Adj. prof. biophysics U. Tex. Med. Sch., Dallas, 1954—74; mem. solid state scis. panel NRC, 1965—73; mem. adv. com. sci. edn. NSF, 1971—73; mem. vis. com. physics MIT, 1971—74; mem. external adv. com. Engring. Exptl. Sta. Ga. Inst. Tech., 1976—79. Editor, co-author: Impedance Spectroscopy-Theory, Experiment, and Applications, 2005, 2d edit., 2005; mem. editl. bd. Jour. Applied Physics, 1984—86; contbr. articles to profl. jours. Bd. dirs. League Ednl. Advancement Dallas, 1965—70; mem. Dallas Radio Commn., 1967—71; mem. sci. adv. coun. Callier Hearing and Speech Ctr., Dallas, 1974—78; mem. adv. com. Weber Rsch. Inst., 1985—90. Rhodes scholar, Oxford U., 1948—50. Fellow: AAAS, IEEE (editor Transactions Profl. Group Audio 1961—66, editor Transactions Audio and Electroacoustics 1966—73, award 1962, 1974, Edison Gold medal 1986), Am. Phys. Soc. (mem. com. edn. 1973—75, mem. com. applicaitons physics 1975—78, George E. Pake prize 1985); mem.: NAS (chmn. numerical data adv. bd. 1970—74, mem. com. motor vehicle emissions 1971—74, chmn. com. motor vehicle emissions 1973—74, mem. com. satellite power sys. 1979—81, mem. com. sci., engring., and pub. policy 1981—83, mem. commn. phys. scis., math. and applications 1985—88, mem. report rev. com. 1990—97), NAE (mem. coun. 1971—74, mem. exec. com. assembly engring. 1975—78), Audio Engring. Soc., Electrochemical Soc., Am. Inst. Physics (mem. governing bd. 1975—78), Sigma Xi, Phi Beta Kappa, Tau Beta Pi. Achievements include patents in field. Office: U NC Dept Physics and Astronomy Chapel Hill NC 27517-7549 Business E-Mail: macd@email.unc.edu.

MACDONALD, JOHN THOMAS, school system administrator; b. Utica, NY, Nov. 21, 1932; s. Gerald Clement and Mildred (Hayes) MacD.; m. Marcia Sprague Gallup; children: Terrence (dec.), Anthony, Elizabeth, Michele, Elise, Denise. BS, Northeastern U., 1958, EdM, 1960; PhD, U. Conn., 1970. Cert. elem. and secondary sch. tchr., prin., supt., Mass., Conn. Supervising prin. Noank, Ft. Hill. and Poquonnock Elem. Schs., Groton, Conn., 1962-66, Robert E. Fitch Jr. H.S., Groton, 1966-70; rsch. asst. Ednl. Resources and Devel. Ctr. U. Conn., Storrs, 1969-70; supt. schs. Wallingford (Conn.) Pub. Schs., 1970-73, Walpole (Mass.) Pub. Schs., 1973-78, Dartmouth (Mass.) Pub. Schs., 1978-86; commr. edn. State Dept. Edn., Concord, NH, 1986-90; asst. sec. for elem. and secondary edn. U.S. Dept. Edn., Washington, 1990-93; dir. state leadership ctr. Coun. of Chief State Sch. Officers, Washington, 1993-99, sr. advisor, 2000-01; prof. ednl. policy and leadership Neag Sch. Edn., U. Conn., 2001—06; dir. NE Ctr. for Ednl. Policy and Leadership. Mem. Postsecondary Edn. Commn., Concord, 1986-90, Coun. for Tchr. Edn., Concord, 1986-90, Profl. Stds. Bd., Concord, 1986-90; trustee Univ. System of N.H., Durham, 1986-90; mem. Surgeon Gen's Task Force, 1990-93; mem. White House Conf. on Indian Edn., 1990-93; mem. Interagy. Com. on Sch. Health, 1990-93, others; mem. dean's adv. coun. U. Conn., 1999—, Coll. Arts and Scis., Northeastern U., 1999—; mem. adv. coun. Va. Edn. Policy Inst., Va. Commonwealth U., 2000—; mem. adv. bd. ERIC, Washington, 1998—. Contbr. articles to profl. jours. Co-chmn. Emergency Sch.-Aide Proposals, U.S. Office Edn., 1973—75; mem. adv. com. external program rev. CDC, 1992—; mem. nat. adv. bd. ERIC Clearinghouse, 1999—; mem. Mass. Adv. Commn. for Ednl. TV, 1983—86, N.H. Task Force on Child Abuse, 1987—90; mem. Nat. Adv. Coun. Northeastern U., 1990—; mem. Galaxy Classroom Nat. Adv. Coun. Galaxy Inst. for Edn., 1992—; mem. sch. health policy initiative Ctr. for Population & Family Health Columbia U., 1992—; mem. Packard roundtable to children Ctr. for Health Policy George Washington U., 1992—; mem. adv. bd. Va. Commonwealth Policy Inst., 1999—; mem. Dean's adv. coun. Neag Sch. Edn. U. Conn., 1999—2005, Coll. Arts & Scis. Northeastern U., 1999—. Recipient Sears B. Condit award, 1958, Alumni award Northwestern U., 1973, Recognition award Coun. of Chief State Sch. Officers, 1990, Disting. Alumni award U. Conn., 2006. Fellow Phi Delta Kappa, Phi Alpha Theta; mem. N.H. Sch. Bldg. Authority, Mass. Assn. Sch. Supts. (pres. 1985-86). Office: U Conn Neag Sch Edn Dept Ednl Leadership 249 Glenbrook Rd Box U-2093 Storrs Mansfield CT 06269-2064 Personal E-mail: macmarjack@aol.com. Business E-Mail: john.macdonald@uconn.edu.

MACDONALD, KAREN CRANE, occupational therapist, geriatrics services professional; b. Denville, NJ, Feb. 24, 1955; d. Robert William and Jeanette Wilcox (Crane) M.; m. Geno Piacentini, Oct. 22, 1993. BS, Quinnipiac U., 1977; MS, U. Bridgeport, 1982; PhD, NYU, 1998. Cert. occupl. therapist. Occupational therapist, coord. of spl. care unit Jewish Home for the Elderly, Conn., 1987-92, N.Y. Inst., NYC, 1984-86; pvt. practice Fairfield County, Conn., 1977-88; occupl. therapist Rehab. Assocs., Fairfield, Conn., 1993-96. Instr. NYU, 1985—89, Quinnipiac Coll., 1986—92, Housatonic CC, Bridgeport, Conn., 2002—, Sacred Heart U., Fairfield, Conn., 2006—; lectr., cons. in field. Contbr. articles to profl. jours. Youth leader, deacon Union Meml. Ch., Stamford, Conn., 1980-88; deacon Southport Congl. Ch., 1992-94; chair consumer com. Alzheimer's Coalition of Conn., 1991-92. Teaching fellow NYU, 1983-86. Mem.: NOW, AAUW, PEO, AAAS, NY Acad. Scis., Am. Bd. Disability Analysts, Conn. Occupl. Therapy Assn. (gerontology liaison 1980—83), Am. Occupl. Therapy Assn. (coun. edn., scholar 1985), World Fedn. Occupl. Therapy, Grange, Toastmasters Internat., Pi Lambda Theta. Avocations: poetry writing, quilting. Home: 198 Glenbrook Rd Bridgeport CT 06610-1149

MACDONALD, KEN CRAIG, geophysicist; b. San Francisco, Oct. 14, 1947; m. Rachel Haymon, 1984. BS in Engring. Geoscis., U. Calif., Berkeley, 1970; PhD in Marine Geophysics, MIT/Woods Hole, 1975. Cecil H. and Ida Green postdoctoral scholar Scripps Instn. of Oceanography, 1975-76, asst. rsch. geophysicist, lectr., 1976-80; assoc. prof. U. Calif., Santa Barbara, 1980-83, prof., 1983—. Chief scientist on over 30 deep sea expeditions; prin. ALVIN diver on over 40 dives to the mid-ocean ridge. Assoc. editor Jour. of Geophys. Rsch., 1979-82, Earth and Planetary Sci. Letters, 1978-88; mem. editorial bd. Marine Sci. Revs., 1986—; editor Marine Geophys. Rschs., 1986-90; contbr. over 100 articles to profl. jours. Mem. ALVIN Rev. Com., 1979-82; mem. Ocean Sci. Bd. of NAS, 1980-83, Lithosphere Panel Advanced Ocean Drilling Project, 1983-85, Ocean Scis. Panel, NSF, 1984-86, COSOD II planning com.; mem. various RIDGE coms., RIDGE steering com., 1987-90; mem. NSF Ocean Scis. Strategic Plan for Rsch. and Edn. Com., 1993-94, U.S. Geodynamics Comm., 1997—. Regents scholar U. Calif., Berkeley, 1966-70, Mineral Tech. scholar, 1967-70, Cecil H. and Ida Green scholar Inst. Geophysics and Planetary Physics/U. Calif., San Diego, 1975-76; NSF Grad. fellow, 1970-73, World Innovation Found. fellow, 2005; recipient AAAS Newcomb-Cleveland prize, 1980, Robert L. and Bettie P. Cody prize and medal Scripps Instn. Oceanography, 1994; named U. Hawaii SOEST Disting. lectr., 1990, ISI Highly Cited Rschr., 2004. Fellow Am. Geophys. Union, Geol. Soc. Am.; mem. Phi Beta Kappa, Sigma Psi. Avocations: windsurfing, fly fishing. Office: U Calif Santa Barbara Dept Geol Sci Santa Barbara CA 93106 Business E-Mail: macdonald@geol.ucsb.edu.

MACDONALD, KENNETH R., JR., author, artist; b. NYC, Apr. 14, 1944; s. Kenneth R. and Wilma Christine (Lange) M. BA, Lehigh U., 1967; MA, W.Va. U., 1970, PhD, 1976. Instr. W.Va. U., Morgantown, 1980-81. Author: The Destiny of Man, 1978, The Gods, 1993, The Palace of Time: The Proof of God and Immortality, 1999, Henry Lange: Master Painter, 2001; exhbns. include Art's Alive (fifty Vt. artists) Festival of Fine Art, Burlington, 2003; commd. portraits KMacD Art, 2003—. Home and Studio: PO Box 1027 Middlebury VT 05753-5027

MACDONALD, KIRK STEWART, lawyer; b. Glendale, Calif., Oct. 24, 1948; s. Bruce Mace and Phyllis Jeanne MacDonald. BSCE, U. So. Calif., 1970; JD, Western State U., 1982. Bar: Calif. 1982, U.S. Dist. Ct. (cen. dist.) Calif. 1982, U.S. Ct. Appeals (9th cir.) 1982, U.S. Dist. Ct. (no. dist.) Calif. 1984, U.S. Dist. Ct. (so. dist.) Calif. 1985, U.S. Dist. Ct. (ea. dist.) Calif. 1987. Dist. engr. Pacific Clay Products, Corona, Calif., 1971-76, Nat. Clay Pipe Inst., La Mirada, Calif., 1976-82; ptnr. Gill and Baldwin, Glendale, Calif., 1982—. Mem. ABA, L.A. County Bar Assn., Water Environ. Assn., Calif. Water Environ. Assn. Avocations: travel, woodworking. Office: Gill & Baldwin Ste 405 130 N Brand Blvd Glendale CA 91203-2646 E-mail: kirk@gillandbaldwin.com.

MACDONALD, LAURIE, film company executive; m. Walter F. Parkes, 1983; 2 children. BA in English Lit., Sonoma State U., Calif. Documentary and news prodr. K-RON, NBC affiliate, San Francisco; creative exec. Columbia Pictures, 1984—85, v.p. prodn., 1985—88; head Aerial Pictures, 1988—94; exec. prodr. Amblin Entertainment, 1994; co-head motion pictures divsn. DreamWorks Pictures, 1994—. Prodr.: (films) Hayseed, 1997, Men in Black, 1997 (nominated Golden Globe best musical or comedy), Men in Black II, 2002, The Ring, 2002, The Terminal, 2004, Lemony Snicket's A Series of Unfortunate Events, 2004, The Ring Two, 2005, Just Like Heaven, 2005, The Legend of Zorro, 2005; (TV series) SFO; exec. prodr.: (films) How to Make an American Quilt, 1995, The Trigger Effect, 1996, Twister, 1996, The Mask of Zorro, 1998, Gladiator, 2000, The Time Machine, 2002, The Tuxedo, 2002, Catch Me If You Can, 2002; exec. prodr.: (films) The Island, 2005, The Lookout, 2007. Named one of 100 Most Powerful Women in Hollywood, Hollywood Reporter, 2003, 2005, 50 Most Powerful People in Hollywood, Premiere mag., 2004—05; recipient Women in Hollywood Icon award, Premiere Mag., 1999. Office: DreamWorks SKG 100 Flower St Glendale CA 91201 Office Phone: 818-733-7000. Office Fax: 818-695-7574. *

MACDONALD, LELAND LLOYD, lawyer; b. Marfa, Tex., July 19, 1931; s. John Edward and Nannye Myrtle (Barnett) M.; m. Juanice L. Koen, Nov. 22, 1958; children: David Allen, Kathryn Ann. BBA, Baylor U., 1952, LLB, 1957. Bar: Tex. 1957, U.S. Dist. Ct. (we. dist.) Tex. 1960, U.S. Ct. Appeals (5th cir.). Title analyst Shell Oil Co., Midland, Tex., 1957—60; pvt. practice Midland, 1960—64; ptnr. Kerr, Fitz-Gerald & Kerr, Midland, 1964—73, Turpin, Smith, Dyer, Saxe & MacDonald, Midland, 1973—2003; pvt. practice, 2004—. Mem. admissions com. Tex. State Bar, 1978—80, grievance com., 1976—78. Author: The Alamo Generation, 2004, Seven Sketches of Valor, 2006. Past chmn. adv. bd. Salvation Army, 1962—82. Lt. USAF, 1952—54. Fellow: Tex. Bar Found. (life); mem.: Midland County Bar Assn. (pres. 1973—74), Baylor Law Alumni Assn. (bd. dirs. 1980—86), Tex. Assn. Def. Counsel, Tex. State Bar Assn., Midland County Jr. Bar Assn. (pres. 1964—65), The Alamo Soc., Midland Jaycees (v.p. 1960), Green Tree Country Club (bd. dirs. 1983—85), Rotary (pres. 1972—73), Freemasons (writer). Baptist. Home: 1515 Community Ln Midland TX 79701-4011 Office: Ste 1310 500 W Texas Midland TX 79701-4289 Office Phone: 432-684-9990.

MACDONALD, LENNA RUTH, lawyer, business advisor; b. Providence, July 16, 1962; d. Arthur Robert and Laina Ruth (Weake) M.; m. Robert Christopher Carew, Sept. 18, 1993. BA, Brown U., Providence, 1984; postgrad., London Sch. Econs., 1984-85; JD, Emory U., Atlanta, 1988. Bar: Ohio 1988, RI, 1989, Mass. 1992, Ky. 1996. Assoc. Edwards & Angell, Providence, 1989-91, McDermott, Will & Emery, Boston, 1991-93; asst. gen. counsel, group mgr. BANC ONE N.H. Asset Mgmt. Corp., Manchester, 1993-96, BANK ONE CORP., Louisville, 1996-98; real estate counsel Vencor, Inc., Louisville, 1998-99; v.p., gen. counsel, sec. Commonwealth Industries, Inc., Louisville, 1999—2004; pres. Balnakeil Ventures LLC, Charleston, SC, 2005—. Mem. Charleston Angel Ptnrs. LLC, SC, 2005—. Mem. Mass. Bar Assn., RI Bar Assn., Ky. Bar Assn., Am. Friends London Sch. Econs., Phi Alpha Delta. Republican. Episcopalian. Personal E-mail: lmacdonald@juno.com.

MAC DONALD, MICHAEL C., printing company executive; b. Phila., July 5, 1953; BA in Polit. Sci., Rutgers U., NJ, 1975. Dist. sales mgr. Xerox Corp., Stamford, Conn., 1977, pres. North Am. solutions group, 2000—04, sr. v.p., 2000—, pres. global accounts and mktg. ops., 2004—07, pres. mktg. ops., 2007—. Bd. dirs. Xerox Capital Svcs. Bd. trustees overseers Rutgers U.; mem. US C. of C. Mem.: HealthRite (bd. dirs.), Jimmy V Found. (bd. dirs.). Office: Xerox Corp 800 Long Ridge Rd Stamford CT 06904 Office Phone: 203-968-3000. *

MACDONALD, PETER J., lawyer; b. 1957; BA, Northwestern U., 1980; JD cum laude, Boston U., 1984. Bar: Mass. 1985, NY 2001. Ptnr., vice chmn. Litigation dept, mem. exec. com. Wilmer Cutler Pickering Hale & Dorr, Boston. Former adj. prof. Northeastern Univ. Sch. Law. Editor: Boston Univ. Law Rev.; contbr. articles to profl. jours. Mem.: ABA, Boston Bar Assn. Office: Wilmer Cutler Pickering Hale & Dorr 60 State St Boston MA 02109 Office Phone: 617-526-6123. Office Fax: 617-526-5000. Business E-Mail: peter.macdonald@wilmerhale.com.

MACDONALD, PRISCILLA ANN, history professor; b. Knoxville, Tenn., Dec. 7, 1949; d. Elmer Franklin and Mae Helen Lee; m. Robert Eugene MacDonald (div.); children: Brock Glyn, Heather Mae, Megan Lee. AA in Bus. Adminstrn., Lourdes Coll., 2002, BA in Hist., 2004; MA in Hist., U. Toledo, 2006; postgrad., West Coll. Tchr. Edn. and Leadership Ariz. State U., Tempe, 2007—. Life lab Lourdes Coll., Sylvania, Ohio, 1999—2003, active Upward Bound program, 2003—04; tchg. asst. U. Toledo, 2005—06, ind. instr., 2006—. Editl. com. Lourdes Coll., 2005—; presenter in field. Vol. Rotaract Lourdes Coll., 1999—2004, Habitat for Humanity, Lourdes Coll., 2000—04, Pine Ridge Indian Reservation, SD, 2000—05. Named Student of Yr., TRIO Lourdes Coll., 2004; recipient Student Life award, Lourdes Coll., 2000. Mem.: Orgn. Am. Historians, Am. Soc. for Ethnohistory, Western Hist. Assn., Am. Hist. Assn., Phi Alpha Theta (sec. 2004—05). Democrat. Avocations: writing, crafts, sewing, movies. Home Phone: 602-687-7502. Personal E-mail: cilla112_us@yahoo.com.

MACDONALD, ROBERT RIGG, JR., retired museum director; b. Pitts., May 11, 1942; s. Robert Rigg and Ruth (Johnson) M.; m. Catherine Ronan, Nov. 27, 1965; children: Matthew, Robert, Catherine. BA, U. Notre Dame, 1964, MA, 1965, U. Pa., 1970. Asst. curator Smithsonian Instn., Washington, 1965; curator Mercer Mus., Doylestown, Pa., 1966-70; dir. New Haven Colony Hist. Soc., 1970-74, La. State Mus., New Orleans, 1974-85; dir., CEO Mus. of City of N.Y., 1985—2002; ret., 2002. Adj. prof. mus. studies NYU, 1989—; adj. prof. pub. adminstrn. Coll. Charleston, 2006—; mem. Commn. Mus. for a New Century; bd. dirs. SC Aquarium.; trustee SC Aquarium, 2004-; mem. adv. bd. Riley Inst., Coll. Charleston, 2004-; vice chair Internat. Coms. Mus. of City, Internat. Coun. Mus., 2005-. Editor: Editor: New Haven Colony Furniture, 1973, Louisiana Images 1880-1920, 1975, Louisiana Black Heritage, 1977 Louisiana Portraitures, 1979, Louisiana Legal Heritage, 1981, The Sun King: Louis XIV and the New World, On Being Homeless, A Community of Many Worlds: Arab American New Society, 2002; organizer (children's art, photographs) The Day Our World Changed: Children's Art of 9/11, The City Resilient: Photographs by Joel Meyerowitz. Decorated chevalier de l'Ordre des Arts et des Lettres (France), cruz de Caballero de la Order de Isabel La Catolica (Spain); assoc. fellow Berkeley Coll., Yale U., 1978; Hagley fellow U. Del., 1970-71; Univ. scholar U. Notre Dame, 1964-65; named to Centennial Honor Roll Am. Assn. Museums, 2006. Mem.: Mus. City N.Y. (dir. emeritus 2002—), Am. Assn. Mus. (pres. 1985—88, chmn. ethics task force 1988—91, Disting. Svc. award 2003), Am. Assn. State and Local History (coun.), Century Assn. Roman Catholic. Home: 602 Island Walk East Mount Pleasant SC 29464 Office Phone: 843-670-7440. Personal E-mail: robertrm2@gmail.com.

MACDONALD, RONALD FRANCIS, diversified financial services company executive; b. Detroit, July 23, 1946; s. Alfred and Marianne Dorothy (Paddock) MacDonald; m. Harriet Pratt Higgins, Dec. 18, 1982 (div. 1997); children: John Higgins, Peter Brewer. BS, U. Detroit, 1968; MBA, Mich. State U., 1970. V.p. No. Trust Co., Chgo., 1970—84, Bankers Trust Co., NYC, 1984—89; mng. dir. CapMAC Holdings, Inc., NYC, 1989—97, MBIA Ins. Corp., Armonk, NY, 1998—2000, Chubb Fin. Solutions Inc., NYC, 2001—02, Insurent Agy. Corp., 2005—; pres. Hartwell Cons. Co., NYC, 2002—04. Mem.: Ins. Industry Planning Forum, NY Athletic Club, Royal Oak Soc. Roman Catholic. Avocations: skiing, running, art history, reading. Personal E-mail: go2ron68@cs.com.

MACDONALD, SALLY POLK BOWERS, retired addictions therapist; b. Memphis, Tenn., Feb. 23, 1930; d. Joel Polk and Sara Louise (Nee Zearing) Bowers; m. Lemuel Coover Shattuck, Jr. (div.); children: L. C. Shattuck III, Mark Bowers Shattuck, Melissa Polk Shattuck; m. Robert Donald Macdonald, Mar. 1, 1960; 1 child, Heather Stuart Macdonald LaMarre. BA, U. Ariz., Tucson, 1950. Lic. Alcohol and Drug Abuse Counselor State of Tenn. Adminstr. Clare Found., Santa Monica, Calif., 1978—88; counselor Wilder Youth Devel. Ctr., Somerville, Tenn., 1981—90; alcohol and drug abuse therapist Profl. Care Svcs., Inc., Somerville, 1983—2006; ret., 2006. Contbr. articles various profl. jours. Founding mem. Memphis Alcohol and Drug Coun., Memphis, 1984—86, Fayette County Animal Rescue, Somerville, Tenn., 1996—98; thriftshop chmn. Women's Symphony Assn., Ojai, Calif., 1967—69; precinct com. GOP, Tucson, 1952. Mem.: AOPA, Clare Found. (bd. mem. 1977—80), Assn. Preservation Tenn. Antiquities, Fayette County Hist. Soc. Republican. Episcopalian. Avocations: birdwatching, painting, interior decorating, dog rescue. Home and Office: 612 S Somerville St Somerville TN 38068-1837

MACDONALD, SHEILA L., manufacturing executive; MBA, Harvard U., Cambridge, Mass., 1980. Prin. Tex. Transaction Mgmt. Co., Fair Winds Corp., Houston, 1990—. Chpt. 11 trustee, 1997-99; pres., CEO Bristol Resources Corp., 2000. Mailing: PO Box 27433 Houston TX 77227 Office Phone: 713-409-4933. Personal E-mail: sheilamacdonald@yahoo.com.

MACDONALD, SUSAN PRIEST, media specialist, writer; b. Lakeland, Fla., Sept. 24, 1958; d. Thomas Mitchell and Betty Jo Priest; m. Randall Malcolm MacDonald, Nov. 24, 1984; 1 child, Sarah Elizabeth. AA, South Fla. Jr. Coll., Avon Park, 1978; BA, Fla. State U., 1980, MS in Libr. Sci., 1984. Cert. profl. educator Fla. Media specialist Canal Point (Fla.) Elem. Sch., 1980—81; libr. assoc. I Del-Trail Br., Palm Beach County Libr. Sys., Delray Beach, Fla., 1981—82, libr. assoc. II West Atlantic Ave. Br., 1982—83; media specialist North Heights Elem. Sch., Rome, Ga., 1985—86, Jesse Keen Elem. Sch., Lakeland, 1986—98; sch. libr. media specialist Lawton Chiles Mid. Acad., Lakeland, 1998—. Author: Successful Keyword Searching: Initiating Research on Popular Topics Using Electronic Databases, 2001; prodr.: (TV documentary) Our Town: Lakeland, 2002. Adult vol. Campfire, Lakeland, 1986—88. Mem.: ALA, Sebring Historical Soc., Polk County Historical Assn., Polk Ednl. Media Assn. (legis. contact 1996—97, v.p. 2001—03, pres. 2003—05, 2d v.p. 2005—07), Fla. Assn. for Media in Edn., Fla. So. Coll. Women's Club, Phi Theta Kappa. Avocations: bicycling, reading, geocaching. Home: PO Box 2501 Lakeland FL 33806-2501 Office: Lawton Chiles Mid Acad 400 N Florida Ave Lakeland FL 33801-4804 Home Phone: 863-644-4177; Office Phone: 863-499-2742.

MACDONALD, TIMOTHY LEE, chemistry professor; b. Long Beach, Calif., Mar. 12, 1948; m. Deborah L. Patrick; children: Kate, Alice. BS with honors, UCLA, 1971; PhD, Columbia U., 1975. Asst. prof. chemistry Vanderbilt U., Nashville, 1977-82; assoc. prof. chemistry U. Va., Charlottesville, 1982-89, prof. chemistry, 1989—, chmn. chemistry, 1997—. Contbr. articles to profl. pubs.; patentee in field. Office: U Va Dept Chemistry Mccormick Rd Charlottesville VA 22904-0001

MACDONOUGH, ROBERT HOWARD, consulting engineer, tax specialist, consultant; b. Chgo., Jan. 24, 1941; s. John Haaf and Helen Margaret (McWilliams) MacD.; m. Joan Carol Rosecrants, Dec. 28, 1963 (div. Nov. 1975); children: John Haaf, Thomas William, Mark Peter; m. Barbara Jean Barone, Apr. 18, 2001. BS in Engring. Ops., Iowa State U., 1962; MA in Econ., Drake U., 1966. Registered profl. engr., Iowa; enrolled agent. Assoc. Mgmt. Sci. Am., Palo Alto, Calif., 1969; mng. assoc. Theo. Barry & Assoc., Los Angeles, 1970-72; mgr. indsl. engring. Advanced Memory Systems, Sunnyvale, Calif., 1972-73; mgr. planning and engring. Signetics, Sunnyvale, 1973-75; pres. Facilities Cons., Mountain View, Calif., 1976-96. Instr. H&R Block; cons. assoc. Shumaker Tax Cons., 1996-01. Fellow Nat. Tax Practice Inst.; Mem. Nat. Assn. Enrolled Agts., Calif. Soc. Enrolled Agts., Ctrl. Coast Soc. Enrolled Agts., Phi Gamma Delta.

MACDOUGAL, GARY EDWARD, corporate board member, foundation trustee; b. Chgo., July 3, 1936; s. Thomas William and Lorna Lee (McDougall) MacD.; children: Gary Edward, Michael Scott; m. Charlene Gehm, June 15, 1992. BS in Engring., UCLA, 1958; MBA with distinction, Harvard U., 1962. Cons. McKinsey & Co., LA, 1963-68, ptnr., 1968-69; chmn. bd., chief exec. officer Mark Controls Corp. (formerly Clayton Mark & Co.), Evanston, Ill., 1969-87; gen. dir. N.Y.C. Ballet, 1993-94; chmn. Gov. Task Force on Human Svcs. Reform State of Ill., 1993-97; chmn. Ill. Rep. Party, 2002. Sr. advisor and asst. campaign mgr. George Bush for Pres., Washington, 1988; chmn. Ill. Rep. Party, 2002; chmn. Bulgarian-Am. Enterprise Fund, Chgo. and Sophia, Bulgaria, 1991-93, bd. dirs., 1991—; apptd. to U.S. Commn. on Effectiveness of UN, 1992-93; bd. dirs. United Parcel Svc. Am., Inc., Atlanta; adv. dir. Saratoga Ptnrs., N.Y.; instr. UCLA, 1969. Author: Make a Difference: How One Man Helped Solve America's Poverty Problem, 2000; contbr. articles to Harvard Bus. Rev., Wall St. Jour., N.Y. Times, Chgo. Tribune, other publs., chpts. to books. Trustee Annie E. Casey Found., 1983-2006, UCLA Found., 1973-79, W.T. Grant Found., 1992-94, Russell Sage Found., 1981-91, chair, 1987-90; apptd. by Pres. Bush as pub. del., alt. rep., U.S. Del. UN 44th Gen. Assembly, 1989-90; commr. Sec. Labor's Commn. on Workforce Quality and Productivity, Washington, 1988-89; chmn. Ill. Rep. Party, 2002. Lt. USN, 1958-61. Mem. Coun. Fgn. Rels., Author's Guild, Harvard Club, Kappa Sigma. Episcopalian. Home: 505 N Lake Shore Dr Apt 3611 Chicago IL 60611-3406 Personal E-mail: gemacg@aol.com.

MACDOUGALL, GORDON PIER, lawyer; b. Bethlehem, Pa., May 31, 1930; s. Curtis Daniel and Elizabeth (Pier) MacD. AB, U. Mich., 1952; postgrad., Columbia U., 1952—55. Bar: Wis. 1955, N.Y. 1958, D.C. 1960. Atty. N.Y. Ctrl. R.R. Co., NYC, 1957—59; assoc. LaRoe, Winn & Moerman, Washington, 1959—66; pvt. practice, Washington, 1966—. Spl. asst. atty. gen. Commonwealth Pa., Washington, 1971-78; asst. counsel Pa. Pub. Utility Commn., Washington, 1975-80. Named Disting. Hoosier Gov. Edgar D. Whitcomb, Inpls., 1972. Mem. Assn. Transp. Law Profls., Transp. Lawyers Assn., Maritime Adminstrv. Bar Assn., Transp. Rsch. Forum (gen. counsel). Office: Ste 919 1025 Connecticut Ave NW Washington DC 20036-5444

MACDOUGALL, HARTLAND MOLSON, retired bank executive; b. Montreal, Que., Can., Jan. 28, 1931; s. Hartland Campbell and Dorothy (Molson) MacD.; m. Eve Gordon, Oct. 29, 1954; children: Cynthia, Wendy, Keith, Willa, Tania. Student, LeRosey, Switzerland, 1947-48, McGill U., 1949-53, Advanced Mgmt. Program, Harvard U., 1976. With Bank Montreal, various locations, 1953-84, dir., 1974, vice chmn., 1981; chmn., dir. Royal Trustco Ltd., Toronto, 1984-93. Dep. chmn. London Ins. Group, Inc., London Life Ins. Co., 1985-97; chmn., dir. Robert T. Jones Jr. Can. Scholarship Found. Founding chmn. Heritage Can., St. Michael's Hosp. Found., The Japan Soc.; past chmn. Can.-Japan Bus. Com.; gov., past pres. Coun. Can. Unity; dir. Friends of the Youth Awards Inc., U.S.; past pres. Royal Agrl. Winter Fair; mem. Internat. Coun. Music Ctr. L.A., Can. Sports Hall of Fame; bd. govs. Can. Olympic Found.; sen. Stratford Shakespearean Found.; former chmn. The Duke of Edinburgh Awards Internat. Coun.; v.p., dir. The Macdonald Stewart Found. Decorated Order of Can., comdr. Royal Victorian Order, Order of the Rising Sun, Gold and Silver Star (Japan); recipient Gabrielle Leger medal, 1978. Avocations: golf, gardening, tennis, farming. Home: 16978 Shaws Creek Rd Belfountain ON Canada L7V OE8 Office: BCE Place 181 Bay St Ste 300 PO Box 771 Toronto ON Canada M5J 2T3

MACDOUGALL, JOHN DUNCAN, thoracic surgeon; b. Indpls., Mar. 4, 1925; s. Duncan Campbell and Beulah Stewart (Ward) MacDougall; m. Inga Margaretha Tranberg, Oct. 6, 1951 (div. 1980); children: Duncan Campbell, Stewart Andrew, Eric Matthew, Victoria Suzanne MacDougall Oehmen; m. Barbara Lee Mayse, Nov. 1, 1980; children: Katherine Jane, James William. BS, Ind. U., Indpls., 1948, MD, 1951. Diplomate Am. Bd. Surgery, Am. Bd. Thoracic Surgery. Pvt. practice, Indpls., 1957-93; pres. med. staff St. Francis Hosp., Beech Grove, Ind., 1975, pres. adv. bd., 1993-95, mem. governing bd. trustees, 2003—, chmn. governing bd. trustees, 1995—2003. Chmn. bd. dirs. Med. Assurance Ind., Indpls., 1987—2000, med. cons., 1993—. Mem. Ind. Gov.'s Task Force Organ Transplantation, Indpls., 1986—89; bd. dirs. Ind. Med. History Mus., 1989—2000, 2006—; active Ind. Hist. Soc., Indpls. Mus. Art; pres. Ind. Med. Polit. Action Com., Indpls., 1992—98; mem. exec. com. dean's coun. Ind. U. Sch. Medicine, Indpls., 1988—, mem. adv. com., 1989—96, pres. dean's coun., 1992—95; pres. English Speaking Union, 1987—2001. With US Army, 1943—46, ETO. Decorated Bronze Star. Fellow: ACS; mem.: AMA (del., chmn. Ind. delegation 1994—2003), Nat. Med. Vets. Assn. (bd. dirs. 1992—2004), Orgn. State Med. Assn. Pres. (pres. 1994—95), Indpls. Med. Soc. (pres. 1978—79), Ind. State Med. Assn. (pres. 1987—88), Purdue U. Pres.'s Coun., Ind. U. Sch. Medicine J. O. Ritchery Soc., Ind. U. Arbutus Soc., Univ. Club Indpls., Meridian Hills Country Club, Contemporary Club, Indpls. Lit. Club, Masons (33d degree), Am. Legion (comdr. Paul Coble Post #26 1999—2007), Soc. Ind. Pioneers. Republican. Episcopalian. Avocations: woodworking, golf, fishing. Home: 7202 Dean Rd Indianapolis IN 46240-3628

MACDOUGALL, MALCOLM EDWARD, lawyer; b. Denver, Jan. 26, 1938; s. Malcolm W. and Helen (Harlow) MacD.; m. Phyllis R. Pomrenke, Dec. 20, 1959; children: Barry Malcolm, Christopher Scott (dec.). BS, Colo. State U., 1959; LLD, U. Colo., 1962. Bar: Colo. 1962, U.S. Dist. Ct. Colo. 1962. Law clk. to judge U.S. Ct. Appeals (10th cir.), Denver, 1962-63; atty. Denver Water Bd., 1963-65; assoc. Saunders, Snyder and Ross, Denver, 1965-68; gen. counsel Golden Cycle Corp., Colorado Springs, Colo., 1968-71; ptnr. Geddes, MacDougall and Worley, P.C., Colorado Springs, 1971-91; sole practitioner MacDougall Law Office, Colorado Springs, 1991-99; shareholder MacDougall, Woldridge & Worley, PC, Colorado Springs, 1999—. Bd. dirs. Park State Bank & Trust, Woodland Park, Colo, 1973-. Mem. Colo. Bar Assn. Republican. Office: Ste 204 530 Communication Cir Colorado Springs CO 80905 Office Phone: 719-520-9288. Business E-Mail: sandy@waterlaw.tv.

MACDOUGALL, PETER, retired lawyer; b. Boston, Sept. 22, 1937; s. Duncan Peck and Hildegard (Moebius) MacD. AB, Harvard U., 1958, LLB, 1963. Assoc. Ropes & Gray, Boston, 1964-73, ptnr., 1973-97, ret., 1997—. Sheldon fellow Harvard U., 1963-64. Mem.: Harvard (Boston). Avocations: concert and opera going, gardening, reading, travel. Home: 1720 Washington St Key West FL 33040-4916 also: 542 River Rd Westport MA 02790-5161 E-mail: pmacdougall@earthlink.net.

MACDOUGALL, PRISCILLA RUTH, lawyer; b. Evanston, Ill., Jan. 20, 1944; d. Curtis Daniel and Genevieve Maurine (Rockwood) MacDougall; m. Lester H. Brownlee, July 5, 1987. BA, Barnard Coll., 1965; grad. (hon.), U. Paris, 1967; JD, U. Mich., 1970. Bar: Wis. 1970, Ill. 1970. Asst. atty. gen. State of Wis., 1970—74; instr. Law Sch. and undergrad. campuses U. Wis., 1973—75; staff counsel Wis. Edn. Assn. Coun., Madison, 1975—; instr. Columbia Coll., Chgo., 1988—. Litigator, writer, speaker, educator women's and children's names and women's rights and employment issues. Author: Married Women's Common Law Right to Their Own Surnames, 1972; co-author: Booklet for Women Who Wish to Determine Their Own Names After Marriage, 1974, supplement, 1975, The Right of Women to Name Their Children, 1985; contbr. articles to profl. jours. Mem.: ABA, Wis. State Bar (co-founder sect. on individual rights and responsibilities, chair 1973—75, 1978—79), Legal Assn. Women Wis. (co-founder). Home: 502 Engelhart Dr Madison WI 53713-4742 Office: 33 Nob Hill Dr Madison WI 53713-2198 Office Phone: 608-276-7711 ext. 249. Business E-Mail: macdougallp@weac.org.

MACDOUGALL, VICKI LAWRENCE, law educator, writer; d. Clyde W. and Mary Ellen Lawrence; children: Katherine Erin, Emily Dyan. BA with distinction, U. Okla., Norman, 1974; JD with distinction, Okla. City U., 1976. Bar: Okla. 1977, Calif. 1977. Jud. clerkship to judge Dwain D. Box Okla. Ct. Civil Appeals, Oklahoma City, 1977—78; prof. law Okla. City U. Sch. Law, 1978—. Law rev. faculty advisor Okla. City U. Law Rev., 2004—. Author: Products Liability Law in Oklahoma, 1990, Oklahoma Product Liability Law, 2006; contbr. articles to profl. jours. Mem. PTA, Oklahoma City, 1994—2006. Mem.: Calif. Bar Assn., Okla. Bar Assn. (mem. 1977—2006), Phi Beta Kappa. Democrat. Methodist. Avocations: swimming, gardening, reading, crocheting. Office: Oklahoma City University School of Law 2501 N Blackwelder Oklahoma City OK 73106 Home Phone: 405-947-2639; Office Phone: 405-208-5187. E-mail: vmacdougall@okcu.edu.

MACDOUGALL, WILLIAM LOWELL, magazine editor; b. Des Moines, July 24, 1931; s. David Gregory and Elizabeth Jeanette (Dugan) MacD. AB, Willamette U., Salem, Oreg., 1952; M.J. in Journalism (Pulitzer scholar 1953-54), Columbia U., 1953. Reporter Washington Star, 1958-62; corr. Los Angeles Times, 1962-63; asso. editor, then London corr. U.S. News & World Report, 1964-68, asst. mng. editor Washington, 1978-86; mng. editor Artsreview mag. NEA, 1987; pres. Mid-Atlantic Media Co., Arlington, Va., 1989—. Author: American Revolutionary: A Biography of General Alexander McDougall, 1977. Served with USAF, 1954-57. Recipient George Washington medal Freedoms Found., 1978, citation U.S. Bicentennial Commn., 1976 Methodist. Office: Mid-Atlantic Media Co 5000 37th St N Arlington VA 22207-1823

MACDUFF, ILONE MARGARET, music educator; b. Berwyn, Ill., Jan. 30, 1938; d. Albert Kenneth Hinckle and Dorothy Lydia Ardina Lange; m. James Donald Macduff, Jr., Apr. 2, 1959; children: Gordon Scott, James Alexander, Charles Colin. MusB, U. Idaho, 1976. Internat. rep. Boy Scouts Am., 1983—93; mem. Thurston County (Wash.) Hist. Commrs., 1984—98; active Boy Scouts Am., Tumwater, Wash., 1968—93, dist. Cub Scout program chmn., 1973—75, mem. coun. Pow Wow staff, 1973—76; founder Cub Scout Day Camp, Tumwater Area Coun., 1973; chmn. Coun. Scout-O-Rama, 1979, 1980, 1981; mem. coun. Eagle bd. Boy Scouts Am., 1985—90; dir. monthly musicales State Captial Mus., 1970—74. Recipient Single and Double awards, Nat. Fedn. Music Clubs, 1969, 1977, Silver Beaver award, Boy Scouts Am., 1981, Disting. Commr. award, 1981, Lamb award, 1987. Mem.: Am. Coll. Musicians, Olympia Music Tchrs. Assn. (pres. 2003—04, student recitals chair 2005), Music Tchrs. Nat. Assn. (Olympia chpt. voice auditions chair 2001, 2004), Gordon Setter Club Am. (chmn. nat. dog show 2003), Puget Sound Gordon Setter Club (treas. 1998—2000, show chmn. 2003—04). Lutheran. Avocation: photography. Home: 8524 Delphi Rd SW Olympia WA 98512 Personal E-mail: delphimuse@msn.com.

MACE, MICHAEL R., academic administrator, real estate development consultant, mortgage executive; b. Billings, Mont., Oct. 4, 1951; s. Robert E. and Ruth (Fox) M.; m. Karen Marie Lawrenz, June 10, 1974; children: Ann Michelle, Joseph Michael. BBA, Mont. State U., 1975. V.p. Mace Realty & Ins., Billings, 1974-84; pres. Mut. Montago Group, Billings, 1984—; pvt. practice cons. Billings and Seattle, 1986—; pres. Mut. Trade Services, Billings and Seattle, 1988—; chief ops. exec., chmn. D&M Industries; interim pres. Rocky Mountain Coll., Billings, 2005—06, pres., 2006—. Developer in field, Billings, 1983—; mortgage banker Mut. Montago Group, 1984—; cons. in field. Mem. Nat. Assn. Realtors, Rotary. Avocations: music, fishing. Office: Rockey Moauntain Coll 1511 Poly Dr Billings MT 59102 also: 735 Grand Ave Billings MT 59101-5823 Office Phone: 406-657-1026. E-mail: president@rocky.edu. *

MACEDO DE LA CONCHA, RAFAEL, former Mexican government official; b. Mexico City, May 6, 1950; Grad., Heroic Mil. Coll.; law degree, U. Nacional Autónoma Mex., Mexico City; Dr Degree (hon.), Nat. Inst. Criminal Sci., Mex., 2003. With Mexican Army, advanced through grades to brig. gen.; legal, fiduciary and asst. dir. Nat. Bank of the Army, Air Force and Navy; judge, 1st magistrate Supreme Mil. Ct.; legal coun. fed. exec. br. Govt. of Mex., asst. chief legal counsel Presdl. staff, atty. gen. mil. justice, legal counsel Secretariat Nat. Def., atty. gen., 2000—05; prof. various subjects including Mexican positive law, polit., econ. and social problems of Mex., constl. law U. Nacional Autónoma Mex., Lat. Am. U., dir. law program. Rep. of Govt. of Mex. and Secretariat of Nat. Def. regarding arms and drug trafficking U.S. Dept. of State; rep. Secretariat of Nat. Def. before the Jt. Secretariat Com.; pres. drug abuse control commn. CICAD, 2002—03; chair, 5th mtg. mins. or justice mins. or atty. gen. Ams. REMJA, Washington, 2004. Decorated great cross Order of Isabella the Cath. Spain, Army 5th, 4th, 3d, 2d and 1st class medals, Army Spl. Class medal; recipient Mil. Tchg. award, Mexican Army, 1992, Melchor Ocampo, Nat. Acad., A.C., Blue Ribbon Gown and Eight-Cornered Academic Cap for univ. excellence, Benito Juarez knight's badge for profl. dignity, Jose Vasconcelos honor award for academic merits, Fed. Dist. Univ., award, Mex. Mil. Legion of Honor, 2000. Mem.: Mex. Nat. Legion of Honor.

MACENCZAK, LEE ANDREW, air transportation executive; m. Kimberly Carol Macenczak, Dec. 11, 1982; children: Ansley Lauren, Austin Leigh. Grad. in Mgmt., Ga. State U., Atlanta. With Delta Air Lines, Inc., Atlanta, 1985—, v.p. reservation sales & distbn. planning, 1996—98, v.p. reservation sales, 1998—99, v.p. customer svc., 1999—2000, sr. v.p. sales & distbn., 2000—04, sr. v.p., chief human resources officer, 2004, sr. v.p., chief customer svc. officer, 2004—05, exec. v.p., chief customer svc. officer, 2005—06, exec. v.p. sales & customer svc., 2006—07, exec. v.p. sales & mktg., 2007—. Office: Delta Air Lines Inc PO Box 20706 Atlanta GA 30320-6001 Office Phone: 404-715-2600. *

MACER, GEORGE ARMEN, JR., orthopedic hand surgeon; b. Pasadena, Calif., Oct. 17, 1948; s. George A. and Nevart Akullian M.; m. Celeste Angelle Lyons, Mar. 26, 1983; children: Christiana Marilu, Marina Lynn, Emily Sue. BA, U. So. Calif., 1971, MD, 1976. Diplomate Am. Bd. Med. Examiners; diplomate in orthop. surgery and hand surgery Am. Bd. Orthop. Surgery. Intern Meml. Hosp. Med. Ctr., Long Beach, Calif., 1976; resident Orthop. Hosp./U. So. Calif., 1977-81; pvt. practice Long Beach, 1983—; vol. clin. faculty orthops. U. So. Calif., LA, 1983-89, 90—; cons. hand surgery svc. Rancho Los Amigos Hosp. Downey, 1990—. Cons. Harbor UCLA Med. Ctr., Torrance, 1983—; asst. clin. prof. U. Calif. Irvine, 2004-. Joseph Boyes hand fellow, 1982. Mem. AMA, Calif. Med. Assn., Los Angeles County Med. Assn., Calif. Orthop. Assn., Western Orthop. Assn., Am. Soc. for Surgery of Hand, Am. Acad. Orthop. Surgery, So. Calif. Soc. Surgery of Hand (pres. 2004-06). Republican. Avocations: boating, skiing, scuba diving, carpentry. Office: 3918 Long Beach Blvd Ste 100 Long Beach CA 90807 Office Phone: 562-424-2600, 562-424-9000. E-mail: macer4337@aol.com.

MACERA, MICHELLE HEFFNER, marriage and family therapist; b. Balt., Oct. 2, 1975; d. George Alfred and Patricia Kratz Heffner; m. Juan Carlos Macera, July 3, 2004. PhD, W.Va. U., Morgantown, 2004. Therapist, rsch. coord. Ctr. for Hope of Sierras, Reno, 2005—07. Vis. asst. prof. W.V.a U., Morgantown, W.Va., 2004—05. Author: The Anorexia Workbook. Mem.: APA. Home Phone: 775-232-3730. Personal E-mail: mheffner@rocketmail.com.

MACER-STORY, EUGENIA ANN, writer; b. Mpls., Jan. 20, 1945; d. Dan Johnstone and Eugenia Loretta (Andrews) Macer; divorced; 1 child, Ezra Arthur Story. BS in Comms., Northwestern U., Evanston, Ill., 1965; MFA, Columbia U., NYC, 1968. Writing instr. Polyarts, Boston, 1970-72; theater instr. Joy of Movement, Boston, 1972-75; artistic dir. Magik Mirror, Salem, Mass., 1975-76, Magick Mirror Comm., 1977—. Author: Congratulations: The UFO Reality, 1978, Angels of Time, 1982, Project Midas, 1986, 2d edit., 2004, Dr. Fu Man Chu Meets the Lonesome Cowboy: Sorcery and the UFO Experience, 1991, 3d edit., 1994, Gypsy Fair, 1991, The Strawberry Man, 1991, Sea Condor/Dusty Sun, 1994, Awakening to the Light-After the Longest Night, 1995, Battles with Dragons: Certain Tales of Political Yoga, 1993, 2d edit., 1994, Legacy of Daedulus, 1995, The Dark Frontier, 1997, Troll and Other Interdimensional Invasions, 1999, Congratulations: The UFO Reality, 2000, Vanishing Questions, 2000, Carrying Thunder, 2002, Crossing Jungle River, 1998, Doing Business in the Adirondacks; True Tales of the Bizarre and Supernatural, 2003, The Merry Piper's Hollow Hills, 2003, Struck By Green Lightning aka Project Midas, 2004, reissued 2006; (poetry) Theatre Cosmos, 2005, Fast Luck Botanica & Other Such Poems, 2007; (novels) The Sin of Love, 2006, OM/NADA, 2006; (plays) Fetching the Tree, Archaeological Politics, 1986, Strange Inquiries, Divine Appliance, 1989, The Zig Zag Wall, 1990, The Only Qualified Huntress, 1990, Telephone Taps Written Up for Tabloids, 1991, Wars with Pigeons, 1992, Conquest of the Asteroids, 1993, Commander Galacticon, 1993, Meister Hemmelin, 1994, Six Way Time Play, 1994, Radish, 1996, Setting Up for the World Trade Centaur, 1996, Mister Shooting Star, 1998, Wild Dog Casino, 1999, Magic Mirror Space Installation at 515 Greenwich Street, 1999-2001, The Old Gaffer From Boise (at Gallery 113), 2000, The Redecoration According to Currier (at Gallery 113), 2001, Ars Chronicon Sylvestre, 2002, Swords of the Equinox, 2003, New Life Expo, New Yorker Hotel, NYC, 2003, Sayeed/Sayeeda, NYC, 2003, New Day, 2004, New Life Expo, 2005, Theatre For The New City, NYC, 2005, Honky Tonk Tornado Warnings, 2005, The Liberation of Little Lulu, Martin Luther King Detained in Limbo, 2006, Eternal Flowers of Ghost Mountain, Lower East Side Festival of Arts, 2006, Applied Ecological Authority, Staged Reading Theatre Cosmos, 2006, The Poison Man, 2007, Theater for the New City, 2007, others; editor Yankee Oracle Gazette, 1999; personal appearance as profl. clairvoyant (TV documentary) Haunted Houses, 1996, UFO Desk, Sta. WBAI radio shows, 1996-2001, Star People Confs., 1998—; exhbn. paintings Barcelona, Spain, 1999, 2000, 02, Magick Mirror Comm. Installation, 1999-2001, 515 Greenwich Gallery, So-Ho, NY, 1999, City Art Gallery, Stockholm, 2000, 04, Gam'Art Diffusion, Port Frejus, France, 2003, Kelikian Gallery, Beirut, 2002-03, Holland Art Fair, The Hague, 2003, BCN Art-Directe Gallery, Barcelona, Spain, 2003, Times Square Fashion Dist., Magick Mirror Space Fashion Ctr., 2003-06, Europ'art Expo, Geneva, 2006, The Other Side of Truth-Oak Island Nova Scotia, 2007; author numerous poems; contbr. articles to profl. jours. and mags. Shubert fellow, 1968. Mem. Am. Soc. Dowsers, Dramatists Guild (spkr., interviewer on radio shows and internet confs.), Theosophical Soc. Democrat. Avocations: swimming, outdoor activities, hiking. Office: Magick Mirror Comm PO Box 741 New York NY 10116-0741 Personal E-mail: e.macer-story@att.net. E-mail: magickmirr@aol.com.

MACEWAN, BONNIE, librarian, dean; b. Memphis, Sept. 10, 1950; m. Thomas Manig. BA, Whitter Coll., 1972; M, U. Denver, 1978. Humanities libr. Ctl. Mo. State Coll., Warrensburg, 1978—84; art, archaeology and music libr. U. Mo., Columbia, 1984—91; asst. dean scholarly comm. Pa. State U., University Park, 1991—98, dean collections and scholarly comm., co-dir. digital scholarly pub., 1998—2003; dean librs. Auburn U., Ala., 2006—. Mem.: ALA (vice chair, chair-elect collection mgmt. and develop. sect. 2001—02). Office: Auburn U Librs 231 Mell St Auburn University AL 36849 Office Phone: 334-844-1715. E-mail: macewbj@auburn.edu. *

MACEWAN, NIGEL SAVAGE, retired merchant banker; b. Balt., Mar. 21, 1933; s. Nigel Savage and Ellen (Wharton) MacE.; children: Alison, Nigel, Pamela, Elizabeth; m. Judith Sperry, Sept. 2, 1995. BA, Yale U., 1955; MBA, Harvard U., 1959. Assoc. Morgan Stanley & Co., NYC, 1959-62, White, Weld & Co., NYC, 1962-63; v.p. R.S. Dickson & Co., Charlotte, NC, 1963-68; chmn. Fin. Cons. Internat. Ltd., Brussels, 1965-68; successively gen. ptnr., exec. v.p., pres., dir. White, Weld & Co., NYC, 1968-78; sr. v.p., dir. Merrill Lynch, Pierce, Fenner & Smith, NYC, 1978-87; chmn. Merrill Lynch Capital Ptnrs., NYC, 1985-87; pres., CEO Kleinwort Benson, N.Am. Inc., NYC, 1987-93, also bd. dirs.; ret., 1993. Chmn. Kleinwort Benson North Am., Inc., Kleinworth Benson Holdings, Inc., Alex Brown Kleinwort Benson Realty Advs.; bd. dirs. Kleinwort Benson Group plc, Kleinwort Benson Ltd., 1987-93, Kleinworth Benson Australian Income Fund, 1992-99; adj. prof. bus. adminstrn. NYU, 1973-75. Pres. Tokeneke Tax Dist., Darien, 1978-80, later treas.; bd. dirs. Islesboro (Maine) Health Ctr., 1994-2005, Sailors Mus. and Lighthouse, Islesboro, 1993-2000; trustee coun. Island Inst., 1997-02; adv. coun. Islesboro Island Trust, 1997-, Conservation Law Found., 1998-2006. Served with USN, 1955-57. Mem. Securities Industry Assn. (chmn. NY group 1975-76), NY Yacht Club, Yale Club NY, Harvard Club of Fairfield County, Conn., Wee Burn Country Club, Tokeneke Club, Tarrantine Club (pres.) (Dark Harbor, Maine), Cruising Club Am., New Canaan Yacht Club. Republican. Episcopalian. Home: 153 Oenoke Ln New Canaan CT 06840-4518 Personal E-mail: nsmace@msn.com.

MACEY, JONATHAN R., law educator; b. 1955; BA, Harvard U., 1977; JD, Yale U., 1982; PhD (hon.), Stockholm Sch. Econs., 1996. Bar: Ga. 1986. Law clk. to Hon. Henry J. Friendly U.S. Ct. Appeals (2d cir.), NYC, 1982-83; asst. prof. Emory U., 1983-86, assoc. prof., 1986-87; vis. assoc. prof. U. Va., 1986-87; prof. Cornell U., 1987-90; vis. prof. U. Chgo., fall 1989, prof., 1990-92; J. Dupratt White prof. law Cornell U., Ithaca, NY, 1993—2004; dir. John M. Olin program in law and econs. Cornell U. Law Sch., Ithaca, 1992—2004; vis. prof. Harvard U., 1999, Yale U., 2003—04; Sam Harris prof. corp. law, fin. and securities regulation Yale U. Law Sch., 2004—. Vis. prof. Harvard U., 1999, Bocconi, Milan, 2000. Recipient Paul M. Bator prize Federalist Soc. for Law and Pub. Policy, 1995, D.P. Jacobs prize. Mem. ABA (bus. assn. and corp. gov.), Am. Law Inst., Assn. Am. Law Schs. (com. corp. law), NY Stock Exchange (legal adv. bd.), Nat. Assn. Securties Dealers (econ. adv. bd., nat. adjudicatory coun.). Office: Yale U Law Sch 127 Wall St New Haven CT 06511 Office Phone: 203-432-7913. Business E-Mail: jonathan.macey@yale.edu.

MACEY, WILLIAM BLACKMORE, oil industry executive; b. Buffalo, Aug. 1, 1920; s. Richard Charles and Doris (Bourne) M.; m. Jean Olive Mullins, Oct. 6, 1945; 1 dau., Barbara Jean. BS in Petroleum Engring, N.Mex. Sch. Mines, 1942; D.Engring. (hon.), N.Mex. Inst. Mining and Tech., 1984. Dist. engr. N.Mex. Oil Conservation Commn., 1946-48; dist. supt. Am. Republics Corp., 1948-52; chief engr. N.Mex. Oil Conservation Commn., 1952-54, state geologist, dir., 1954-56; v.p. Internat. Oil & Gas Corp. (and predecessor co., developers mineral properties), Denver, 1956-60, then pres., 1960-67; pres. Nielson Enterprises Inc., oil and gas prodn. and pipelines, livestock ranching, 1967-74; v.p., dir. Y-Tex Corp. (mfr. livestock identification tags), 1972-73; pres. GEN Oil Inc. (oil and gas prodn.), 1972-75, Col. Cody Inn (real estate and golf course devel.), 1970-73; pres., dir. Macey & Mershon Oil, Inc., 1974-93; dir. Juniper Oil and Gas Corp., Denver, 1981-83, Ruidoso (N.Mex.) State Bank Holding Co., 1987—; pres. The Macey Corp., Denver, 1985—99. Chmn. Pres.'s N.Mex. Inst. Mines and Tech., 1980-82; mem. adv. bd. U. Ariz. Heart Ctr., 1997-2002; mem. Pres.'s U. Ariz. Found. Served from 2d lt. to capt. USAAF, 1942-45. Mem.: N.Mex. Oil and Gas Assn. (exec. com. 1949—52, 1960—61), Popejoy & Pres.'s Club (U. N.Mex.), N.Mex. Jockey Club (bd. dirs. 1985—88, 1991—93, pres. 1993), Ruidoso, Tucson Country Club, Altolakes Golf and Country Club, Skyline Country Club (Tucson) (dir., treas. 1980—82, pres. 1982—83), Garden of the Gods. Episcopalian. also: 10153 Masters Dr NE Albuquerque NM 87111-5894 Office: PO Box 2210 Denver CO 80201-2210

MACFARLAND, MIRIAM KATHERINE (MIMI), computer engineer, consultant, writer, educator; b. Trenton, NJ, June 21, 1949; d. James and Merrianne (Collins) MacFarland; children: Bridget Lorraine, Chloe Merrianne Griffin. Attended, Rutgers U., Camden, NJ, 1976-78, U. Pa., Phila., 1981-83, Oxford U., Eng., 1988; B in Liberal studies with distinction, U. Okla., Norman, 2000; MFA, LI U., Southampton, NY, 2002. Cert. ITIL, 2006. Programmer analyst R&D Computer Sci. Corp., Naval Air Devel. Ctr., Warminster, Pa., 1977-81; programmer analyst NASA Ames Rsch. Ctr., Moffett Field, Calif., 1978; staff writer Aydin Controls, Inc., Ft. Washington, Pa., 1981-82; writer Banc Tec, Inc., Oklahoma City and Dallas, 1983-95; cons. engr. MCI Comm. Internat., Rye Brook, NY, 1984-86, Western Union Internat., NYC, 1984, RCA Global Comm., Ft. Lee, NJ, 1985; cons. engr., writer Siemens Med. Sys., Iselin, NJ, 1988-98; adj. asst. prof. English and writing Southampton Coll. LI U., 2000—02; instr. English Cameron U., Lawton, Okla., 2004—05; tech. writer Harris Corp., Norman, Okla., 2005—06; writer El Paso Exploration and Prodn., Houston, 2006—07. Guest spkr. U. Ctrl. Okla., Edmond, 1994, Americorp Patch project, Okla. City, 1995; mem. dean's student adv. com. U. Okla., 1999-2000. Author stories, plays, journalism, numerous lit. rev., 40 books, numerous poems; CONTACT II, Hightimes Mag., The Bloomsbury Rev.; Another Chgo. Mag.; Renovated Lighthouse; contbr. articles to books and profl. jours. Recipient Grad. Acad. Performance award, 2000—02; LI U. fellow in writing, Grad. Asst. Prof. scholar, 2001—02. Mem.: MLA, Associated Writing Programs, Soc. Technical Comm., Southampton Coll. Alumni Assn., Phi Kappa Phi. Home and Office: PO Box 722808 Norman OK 73070-9137 Office Phone: 405-364-5000. Personal E-mail: mimimacfarland@sbcglobal.net. Business E-Mail: techwriter@mimimacfarland.com.

MACFARLANE, ALASTAIR IAIN ROBERT, manufacturing executive, consultant; b. Sydney, Mar. 7, 1940; arrived in U.S., 1978; s. Alexander Dunlop and Margaret Elizabeth (Swan) M.; m. Madge McCleary, Sept. 24, 1966; children: Douglas, Dennis, Robert, Jeffrey. B in Econs. with honors, U. Sydney, Australia, 1961; MBA, U. Hawaii, Honolulu, 1964; postgrad., Columbia U., NYC, 1964; AMP, Harvard Bus. Sch., Cambridge, Mass., 1977. Comml. cadet B.H.P. Ltd., Australia, 1958-62; product mgr. H.J. Heinz Co., Pitts., 1965-66, gen. mgr. new products divsn. Melbourne, Australia, 1967-72; ptnr., dir., gen. mgr. Singleton, Palmer & Strauss McAllan Pty. Ltd., Sydney, 1972-73; dir., gen. mgr. successor co. Doyle Dane Bernbach Internat. Inc., Sydney, 1973-77, group sr. v.p. NYC, 1978-84; pres., CEO PowerBase Systems, Inc., 1984-85, Productivity Software Internat. L.P., NYC, 1985-86; divsn. pres., pub. Whittle Comm. L.P., Knoxville, Tenn., 1987-88; chmn., CEO Phyton Techs. Inc., Knoxville, 1988-94; pres., CEO Knox Internat. Corp., Knoxville, 1988-94; chmn., CEO Mich. Bulb Co., Grand Rapids, 1988-94; dir. Univ. of Sydney USA Found., 1994—; chmn., CEO Creative Pub. Internat., Inc., Minnetonka, Minn., 1997-99; sr. v.p. Pleasant Co., Middleton, Wis., 2000-2001; CEO Centric Strategies Internat., Inc., Mpls., 2001—02; sr. v.p. The Middleton Doll Co., Waukesha, Wis., 2002—04; CEO Lee Middleton Original Dolls, Inc., Columbus, Ohio, 2002—04; pres. Biz Coaching & Assocs., LLC dba Action COACH Bus. Coaching, Madison, Wis., 2004—. Ind. mgmt. cons., Melbourne, 1970—72; lectr. Faculty Econ., Politics Monash U., Melbourne, Australia, 1970—71; chmn., CEO Lansinoh, Labs., Inc., Oak Ridge, Tenn., 1994—96; dir. World Future Soc., Madison, Wis.; bd. dirs. Hilton Oceanfront Resort Hotel, Hilton Head Island, SC, U. Sydney Found.; dir. franchisee adv. bd. ActionCOACH Bus. Coaching; lectr. in field. Contbr. articles to profl. jours. V.p. Waverley Dist. Cricket Club, 1975-77. East-West Ctr. fellow, 1962-64; Australian Commonwealth scholar, Australian Steel Industry scholar, 1958-61. Fellow Australian Inst. Mgmt. (assoc.); mem. Australian Soc. Accts. (assoc.), Harvard Club N.Y.C., Blackhawk Country Club, Tenn. Nat. Golf Club. Home: 6219 S Highlands Ave Madison WI 53705 Office Phone: 608-238-7844. Business E-Mail: iainmacfarlane@actioncoach.com.

MACFARLANE, CATHY M., federal agency administrator; BS, Manhattanville Coll.; MA, Georgetown U. Counter-intelligence specialist FBI, 1980; with Nat. Inst. Justice U.S. Dept. Justice; dir. bus. devel. Jones Day, Dallas and Washington; assoc. Cassidy & Assocs.; v.p. Devillier Comm.; founder Marcom 21; exec. v.p. Direct Impact Co.; dir. pub. rels. FTC, 2001—04; asst. sec. pub. affairs U.S. Dept. Housing and Urban Devel., Washington, 2004—. Vis. scholar East China Inst. Politics and Law, Shanghai, 1987—88.

MACFARLANE, JOHN ALEXANDER, retired federal agency administrator; b. Winnipeg, Man., Can., Sept. 6, 1916; s. John MacKay and Annie Catherine (Smith) MacF.; m. Gladys Valda Church, Dec. 20, 1941; children: John Lane, Elizabeth Ann, Janet Christine. BA with honours, U. Man., Winnipeg, 1939. With stats. br. Wartime Prices and Trade Bd., Ottawa, Ont., Canada, 1940-46; supr. stats. dept. Cn. Mortgage and Housing Corp., Ottawa, 1946-65, asst. dir. econs. and stats. div., 1965-69, asst. dir. secretariat div., 1969-78; ret., 1978; treas. Caribbean and N.Am. area coun. World Alliance Ref. Chs., 1984—2002. Treas. Ottawa Valley Cricket Coun., 1946-70, 73-80, pres., 1970-73, 83-88; moderator Presbytery of Ottawa, Presbyn. Ch. Can., 1994-96, rep. elder, 1961-97. Recipient Long Svc. medal Boy Scouts Assn., 1945, Centennial medal Govt. of Can., 1967, spl. achievement award for amateur sport Govt. of Ont., 1991. Mem. Def. Cricket Club (sec.-treas. 1944-46, pres. 1951-76, 78-92). Address: New Edinburgh Square 420 Mackay St Ste 207 Ottawa ON Canada K1M 204 Personal E-mail: jamacf@sympatico.ca.

MACFARLANE, JOHN CHARLES, utilities executive; b. Hallock, Minn., Nov. 8, 1939; s. Ernest Edward and Mary Bell (Yates) MacF.; m. Eunice Darlene Axvig, Apr. 13, 1963; children: Charles, James, William. BSEE, U. N.D., 1961. Staff engr. Otter Tail Power Co., Fergus Falls, Mn., 1961-64, div. engr. Jamestown, N.D., 1964-71, div. mgr. Langdon, N.D., 1972-78, v.p. planning and control Fergus Falls, 1978-80, exec. v.p., 1981-82, pres. and chief exec. officer, 1982—, also bd. dirs., now chmn. Bd. dirs. Wells Fargo, Fergus Falls, Pioneer Mut. Ins. Co. Pres. Langdon City Commn., 1974-78; chmn. Fergus Falls Port Authority, 1985-86; bd. dirs. Minn. Assn. Commerce and Industry, Minn. Safety Coun., Edison Electric Inst., Village Family Svcs., Fargo; bd. dirs. U. N.D. Energy Rsch. Adv. Coun. Served with U.S. Army, 1962-64. Mem. Am. Mgmt. Assn., IEEE (chmn. Red River chpt.), U. N.D. Alumni Assn., Fergus Falls C. of C. Lodges: Rotary, Masons. Republican. Presbyterian.

MACFARLANE, MALCOLM HARRIS, physicist, educator; b. Brechin, Scotland, May 22, 1933; came to U.S., 1956; s. Malcolm P. and Mary (Harris) M.; m. Eleanor Carman, May 30, 1957; children: Douglas, Kenneth, Sheila, Christine. MA, U. Edinburgh, Scotland, 1955; PhD, U. Rochester, 1960. Research asso. Argonne (Ill.) Nat. Lab., 1959-60; asst. prof. physics U. Rochester, 1960-61; asso. physicist Argonne Nat. Lab., 1961-68, sr. physicist, 1968-80; prof. physics U. Chgo., 1968-80, Ind. U., Bloomington, 1980—2003, prof. emeritus, 2003—. Vis. fellow All Souls Coll., Oxford (Eng.) U., 1966-67; mem. nuclear scis. adv. com. Dept. Energy-NSF, 1983-87; cons. Ency. Brit. Contbr. articles of theoretical nuclear physics to profl. jours. Guggenheim fellow physics, 1966-67; Alexander von Humboldt Found. sr. scientist award, 1985. Fellow Am. Phys. Soc.; mem. Nuclear Physics sect. Am. Phys. Soc. (mem. exec. com. 1969-71) Home: 1008 S Meadowbrook Dr Bloomington IN 47401-4217 Office: Dept Physics Indiana U Bloomington IN 47405 Office Phone: 812-855-3709. E-mail: macfarla@indiana.edu.

MACFERRAN, ERNEST LESLIE, mechanical engineer; b. Southbend, Ind., May 19, 1945; s. Ernest Leslie Macferran Sr. and Pearl Helen (Stook) Macferran; m. Janice Carol Carr. BS in Mech. Engring., U. South Fla., Tampa, 1967. Registered profl. engr., Fla., 1975. Mech. engr. Tenn. Valley Auth., Knoxville, 1968—71, Watson and Co., Tampa, 1972—79, Carastro Aguire and Assoc., Tampa, 1980—82, Lehr Assocs., Tampa, 1983—85, Prime Design A&E, Tampa, 1986—92, Carastro and Assocs., Tampa, 1993—2001, Sch. Dist. Hillsborough County, Tampa, 2002—. Spkr. in field. Recipient Engring. Excellence award, Fla. Inst. Consulting Engrs., 2000. Mem.: ASHRAE (Engr. of Yr. 2005), Assn. Energy Engrs. Republican. Presbyterian. Achievements include invention of smoke relief hatch; discovery of LogT method for correctly field measuring air flow in rectangular ducts; research in solar heating for dehumidification instead of standard electric heating. Avocations: bicycling, fishing. Office: Sch Dist Hillsborough County 901 E Kennedy Blvd Tampa FL 33602

MACGILLIVRAY, LEONARD R., chemistry professor; BS, Saint Mary's Univ., 1994; PhD, Univ. Mo., Columbia, 1998. Rsch. assoc. Steacie Inst. Molecular Sci., Nat. Rsch. Coun. Canada, 1998—2000; adj. rsch. prof. Ottawa-Carleton Chemistry Inst., 1999—2000; assoc. prof., chemistry Univ. Iowa, Iowa City, 2000—. Recipient Margaret C. Etter Early Career award, Am. Crystallographic Assn., 2004. Mem.: Am. Chem. Soc. (Arthur C. Cope Scholar Award 2007). Office: Dept Chemistry Room 305 CB Univ Iowa Iowa City IA 52242 Office Phone: 319-335-3504. Office Fax: 319-335-1270. Business E-Mail: len-macgillivray@uiowa.edu. *

MACGINITIE, WALTER HAROLD, psychologist, educator; b. Carmel, Calif., Aug. 14, 1928; s. George Eber and Nettie Lorene (Murray) MacG.; m. Ruth Olive Kilpatrick, Sept. 2, 1950; children: Mary Catherine, Laura Anne. BA, UCLA, 1949; A.M., Stanford U., 1950; PhD, Columbia U., 1960. Tchr. Long Beach (Calif.) Unified Sch. Dist., 1950, 1955-56; mem. faculty Columbia U. Tchrs. Coll., 1959-80, prof. psychology and edn., 1970-80; Lansdowne scholar, prof. edn. U. Victoria, B.C., Canada, 1980-84. Research assoc. Lexington Sch. Deaf, N.Y.C., 1963-69; mem. sci. adv. bd. Ctr. for Study of Reading, 1977-80, chmn. 1979-80. Co-author: Gates-MacGinitie Reading Tests, 1965, 78, 89, 2000, Psychological Foundations of Education, 1968; Editor: Assessment Problems in Reading, 1972; co-editor: Verbal Behavior of the Deaf Child, 1969. Life mem. Calif. PTA. Served with USAF, 1950-54. Fellow APA, AAAS, Assn. Psychol. Sci., Nat. Conf. Rsch. on Lang. and Literacy, N.Y. Acad. Scis.; mem. Internat. Reading Assn. (pres. 1976-77, Spl. Svc. award 1981), Reading Hall of Fame (pres. 1989-90). Home and Office: PO Box 1789 Friday Harbor WA 98250-1789

MACGOWAN, BILL, information technology executive; BA in Polit. Sci., Claremont McKenna Coll., Calif. With Northrop Grumman, Allergan; v.p. human resources Corning Inc., Quest Diagnostics; head enterprise svcs. divsn. Sun Microsystems, Inc., Santa Clara, Calif., 1998, v.p. human resources Systems, Storage and Ops. bus. groups, v.p. human resources Global Ctrs. Expertise, sr. v.p. human resources, chief human resources officer, exec. v.p. people and places. Trustee Am. Found. for Blind. Office: Sun Microsystems Inc 4150 Network Cir Santa Clara CA 95054 Office Phone: 650-960-1300. *

MACGOWAN, SANDRA FIRELLI, publishing executive, consultant; b. Phila., Nov. 9, 1951; d. William Firelli and Barbara (Gimbel) Kapalcik. BS in Biology, BA in English, Pa. State U., 1973, MA in English Lit., 1978. Cert. supervisory analyst N.Y. Stock Exch. Editor McGraw-Hill Pub. Co., NYC, 1979-81; sr. acquisitions editor Harcourt Brace Jovanovich, Inc., NYC, 1981-82; sr. editor The Coll. Bd., NYC, 1982-88; v.p., head editorial CS First Boston Corp., NYC, 1988-94; v.p. supervisory analyst internat. rsch. SBC Warburg, NYC, 1994-96; v.p., supervisory analyst internat. rsch. Arnhold and S. Bleichroeder, NYC, 1996—2003; sr. v.p. Natixis Bleichroeder Inc. (formerly Arnhold and S. Bleichroeder), NYC, 2003—, mgr. Rsch. Dept., 2003—. Part time assoc. prof. pub. NYU Sch. Continuing Edn., N.Y.C., 1985—. Author: 50 College Admission Directors Speak to Parents, 1988. Democrat. Avocations: art, reading, travel. Office: Natexis Bleichroeder Fl 44 1345 Avenue Of The Americas New York NY 10105-4300 Home Phone: 212-534-5306; Office Phone: 212-698-3219. Business E-Mail: sandra.macgowan@natexisblr.us.

MACGRAW, ALI, actress; b. Pound Ridge, NY, Apr. 1, 1939; m. Robert Evans, 1970 (div.); 1 child, Joshua; m. Steve McQueen, 1973 (div.). Student, Wellesley Coll. Former editorial asst. Harper's Bazaar Mag.; former asst. to photographer Melvin Sokolsky. Actress in films including Goodbye, Columbus, 1969, Love Story, 1971, The Getaway, 1973, Convoy, 1978, Players, 1979, Just Tell Me What You Want, 1979, Natural Causes, 1994, Glam, 2001; TV mini-series The Winds of War, 1983, China Rose, 1983, Dynasty, 1985, Falcon Crest; TV movies Survive the Savage Sea, 1992, Gunsmoke, The Hollywood Fashion Machine, 1995: the Long Ride, 1993; Broadway plays Festen, 2006; author: (autobiography) Moving Pictures, 1991. Address: PO Box 284 Tesuque NM 87574-0284

MACGREGOR, DAVID BRUCE, lawyer; b. Miami Beach, Fla., Feb. 21, 1953; s. Bruce Herbert and Mary Don (Doty) MacG.; m. Carol Louise Edler, Aug. 21, 1976; children: Meredith Elder, Christine Elder, Scott Elder. BA magna cum laude, Bucknell U., 1975; JD magna cum laude, Georgetown U., 1978. Bar: Pa. 1978, US Dist. Ct. (ea. dist.) Pa., US Ct. Appeals (4th cir.). Law clk. to presiding justice US Ct. Appeals (4th cir.), Richmond, Va., 1978-79; assoc. Morgan, Lewis & Bockius LLP, Phila., 1979-85, ptnr., mem. firm energy practice group, 1985—2005; shareholder Post & Schell PC, Phila., 2005—. Mem. ABA, Pa. Bar Assn., Phila. Bar Assn. Republican. Presbyterian. Avocation: golf. Office: Post & Schell PC Four Penn Ctr 1600 JFK Blvd Philadelphia PA 19103-2808 Office Phone: 215-587-1197. Fax: 215-963-5001. Business E-Mail: dmacgregor@postschell.com.

MACGREGOR, GEORGE LESCHER, JR., freelance/self-employed writer, brokerage house executive; b. Dallas, Sept. 15, 1936; s. George Lescher and Jean (Edge) MacG.; divorced; children: George Lescher III (dec.), Michael Fordtran. BBA, U. Tex., 1958. Asst. cashier First Nat. Bank in Dallas, 1960-64, asst. v.p., 1964-68; v.p. Nat. Bank of Commerce of Dallas, 1968-70, sr. v.p., 1970-73, exec. v.p., 1973-74; pres., chief exec. officer Mountain Banks Ltd., Colorado Springs, 1974-77; chief exec. officer Highfield Fin. (U.S.A.) Ltd., 1978-83; chmn. bd., chief exec. officer, dir. Dominion Nat. Bank, Denver, 1981-84; chmn. bd., chief exec. officer Royal Dominion Ltd., Denver; chmn. bd., chief exec. officer, dir. Market Bank of Denver, 1983-84; vice chmn., dir. Bank of Aurora, Denver, 1983-84; chmn., pres., chief exec. officer Alamosa Bancorp. of Colo., Denver, 1983-84; pres., chief exec. officer Am. Interstate Bancorp., 1984-88; pres. Banco, Inc., 1984-89; sr. mng. ptnr. Scotland Co., Denver, London, 1988-91; free-lance writer, 1992—. Served with M.C. AUS, 1958-60. Mem. Am. Inst. Banking (hon.), Young Pres.'s Orgn., Coon Creek Club, Broadmoore Golf Club, Oxford Club, Phi Gamma Delta. Anglican Catholic. Home and Office: 1736 Blake St Denver CO 80202-1226 Home Fax: 303-292-9794. Personal E-mail: twotatertotts@aol.com.

MACH, JAN ELLEN WALKENHORST, literature educator, editor; b. Madison, Nebr. d. Dale Edward and Mary Moyer Walkenhorst; m. Daniel Blount (div.); 1 child, Byron K. Rupp; m. Robert Mach, 2006. BS in English Edn., U. Nebr., 1974. Cert. tchr. Tex., 1982, Nebr., 2001, coll. bd. cert. 1995. Pres. Papillion (Nebr.) Edn. Assn., 1976—79; tchr. english Papillion (Nebr.) Pub. Schs., 1974—80, Richardson (Tex.) Ind. Sch. Dist., 1982—2000, Lincoln (Nebr.) Pub. Schs., 2001—04; instr. writing, asst. acad. counselor, tchr. theory of knowledge U. Nebr., Lincoln, 2004—. Mem. core team successful strategies, English Dept. chair, site-based facilitator, tchr. cadre; mem. project to convert curriculum to software Baylor U., 1994; rater statewide writing assessment Nebr., 2003. Editor: McGraw-Hill, 2000—, DC Health. Mem.: Nat. Assn. Acad. Advisors for Athletics. Avocations: reading, politics, travel. Office: Univ Nebr Athletic Dept 1 Memorial Stadium Lincoln NE 68588 Home: 1561 Rokeby Rd Pleasant Dale NE 68423 Home Phone: 402-826-5647; Office Phone: 402-472-9985. Personal E-mail: janwalk1952@aol.com. Business E-Mail: jwalkenhorst@huskers.com.

MACHA, KEN, former professional baseball coach; m. Carolyn Virginia Macha; children: Eric, Kristin. BS in Civil Engring., Univ. Pitts. Infielder Pitts. Pirates, 1974—78, Montreal Expos, 1979—80, Toronto Blue Jays, 1981, Chunichi Dragons, Nippon Baseball League, 1983—85; minor league mgr. Boston Red Sox Organization, 1995—98; bench coach Oakland Athletics, 1999—2002, mgr., 2002—06. Named Internat. League Mgr. Yr., 1998. Achievements include mem. Am. League All-Star coaching staff, 2005. *

MACHADO, STEPHEN, science educator; s. Joseph Machado and Imelda Mahaso; m. Lidwinner Adam; children: Eugene, Stephanie, Fatima, Stephen, Leanne. BS in Agr., U. Swaziland, 1984; MS in Crop Physiology, Reading U., Eng., 1987; PhD in Agronomy, Kans. State U., 1997. Rsch. assoc. Tex. A&M U., Lubbock; rschr. Oreg. State U., Pendleton, 2001—. Chmn. Computers for Africa, Pendleton, Oreg., 2003. Achievements include research in solutions to agricultural problems. Office: Oregon State University CBARC 48037 Tubbs Ranch Rd Pendleton OR 97801 Home Phone: 541-276-6649; Office Phone: 541-278-4416. Business E-Mail: stephen.machado@oregonstate.edu.

MACHADO-ECHEZURIA, MARIANELLA PERPETUA, composer, writer, educator; b. Caracas, Venezuela, Aug. 4, 1959; arrived in U.S., 1981; d. German Machado and Isabel C. Echezuria de Ruiz. MusB, Ind. U., 1984, MusM, 1986; MusD, U. Cin., 1993, MMA, 1996, PhD in Hispanic Lit., 1998. Rsch. asst. Romulo Coll., Caracas, Venezuela, 1987—88, Biblioteca Nacional, Caracas, 1988—89; grad. tchg. asst. U. Cin., 1989—97; asst. prof. arts U. Catolica Andres Bello, Caracas, 1998—2003; asst. prof. Spanish Ea. Ky. U., Richmond, 2003—. Libr. music Cin. (Ohio) Symphony Orch., 1993—94; spkr. in field. Composer: (works) Obertura, 1987, Distonia, 1988, Las Semanas Tienen Sabados, 1988, Parafernalia, 1988, Psalm 32:10, 1990, Finneytown Suite, 1995; contbr. articles to profl. jours. Fellow, Taft Found., 1997—98; scholar, Ministry Edn., Caracas, Venezuela, 1974—80, Found. Gran Mariscal de Ayacucho, 1981—85, U. Cin., 1989—93, 1994—97; U. Rsch. Coun. fellow, 1991. Mem.: ASCAP (scholar 1993), Nat. Capital Lang. Resource Ctr., Multimedia Ednl. Resource Learning and On-line Tchg., Opera Am., Am. Composers Forum, Am. Music Ctr. Office: Eastern Ky Univ Lancaster Ave Richmond KY 40475 Home: 303 Timothy Way Apt 4 Richmond KY 40475-2724 Personal E-mail: mpme9@yahoo.com. E-mail: marianella.machado@pku.edu.

MACHASKEE, ALEX, retired newspaper publishing company executive; b. Warren, Ohio; m. Carol Machaskee. BA in Mktg., Cleve. State U., 1972, LHD (hon.), 1995, U. Akron, 1998. Sports reporter The Warren (Ohio) Tribune; asst. to pub., promo dir. to dir. labor rels. & pers. to v.p., gen. mgr. The Plain Dealer, Cleve., 1985—90, pres., pub., 1990—2006; ret., 2006. Chmn. Cleve. Coun. on World Affairs, 2006—. V.p. Mus. Arts Assn. (Cleve. Orch.); chmn. bd. United Way, 2000; mem. bd. governance, fin. and adminstrn. com. Cleve. Found.; bd. dirs. Univ. Cir. Inc., Greater Cleve. Partnership, St. Vladimir's Orthodox Theol. Sem., Crime Stoppers of Cuyahoga County, Urban League Greater Cleve.; chmn. bd. dirs. United Way Svcs., 2002—03; bd. trustees Cleve. Mus. Art; nat. bd. dirs. IOCC. Named to N.E. Ohio Bus. Hall of Fame, 2001. Mem.: Am. Soc. Newspaper Editors, Newspaper Assn. Am. Office: Plain Dealer Pub Co 1801 Superior Ave E Cleveland OH 44114-2198 Business E-Mail: publisher@plaind.com. *

MACHEN, JAMES BERNARD, academic administrator; m. Chris; children: Maggie, Michael, Lee. DDS, St. Louis U., 1968; MS, U. Iowa, 1972, PhD in Edn. Psychology, 1974. Prof., assoc. dean U. N.C., 1983-89; pres. Am. Assn. Dental Schs., 1987; dean U. Mich. Sch. Dentistry, 1989-95; provost, exec. v.p. acad. affairs U. Mich., 1995-97; pres. U. Utah, 1998—2003, U. Fla., Gainesville, 2004—. Mem. Inst. Medicine Com. in Future Dental Edn. Nat. Acad. Scis., 1993-95. Office: U Fla Office of the Pres 226 Tigert Hall PO Box 113150 Gainesville FL 32611-3150 *

MACHEN, RONALD C., lawyer; b. May 6, 1969; AB, Stanford U., 1991; JD, Harvard U., 1994. Bar: Ill. 1994, DC 1995. Clerk US Ct. of Appeals, Sixth Cir., 1995—97; asst. US Atty. US Dept. Justice, Washington, 1997—2001; lectr., Trial Adv. Howard U. Sch. Law, 1998; ptnr. Wilmer Cutler Pickering Hale and Dorr LLP, Washington, 2001—. Named one of Top 40 Lawyers Under 40, Washingtonian Mag., Litigation's Rising Stars, The Am. Lawyer, 2007; recipient Spl. Achievement award, US Dept. Justice. Mem.: Nat. Bar Assn., ABA (co-chair, Criminal Litig. Com), Edward Bennett Williams Inn of Ct., Coun. Ct. Ecvellence, Internat. Assn. Def. Counsel. Office: Wilmer Cutler Pickering Hale and Dorr LLP 1875 Pennsylvania Ave NW Washington DC 20006 Office Phone: 202-663-6881. Office Fax: 202-663-6363. Business E-Mail: ronald.machen@wilberhale.com.

MACHIDA, CURTIS A., research molecular neurobiologist, educator; b. San Francisco, Apr. 1, 1954; AB, U. Calif., Berkeley, 1976; PhD, Oreg. Health Scis. U., 1982. Postdoctoral scientist Oreg. Health Scis. U., Portland, 1982-88; asst. sci. div. neurosci. Oreg. Nat. Primate Rsch. Ctr., Beaverton, 1988-95, assoc. scie. divsn. neurosci., 1995—2002; assoc. rsch. prof. integrative biosciences Sch. Dentistry Oreg. Health Scis. U., Portland, 2002—05, rsch. prof. integrative bioscis., 2005—. Rsch. asst. prof. biochemistry and molecular biology Oreg. Health Sci. U., 1989-95, mem. faculty neurosci. and molecular and cell biology grad. programs, 1989—, adj. assoc. prof. biochemistry and molecular biology, 1995—; mem. grad. faculty biochemistry and biophysics Oreg. State U., Corvallis, 1997-01; mem. Institutional Ethics oversight com., Institutional Biosafety com., faculty bylaws com., preclin. curriculum com.; mem. Dental Sch. Rsch. Task Force; mem. biotech. program adv. com. Portland C.C. Editor Adrenergic Receptor Protocols, 1997-99, Viral Vectors for Gene Therapy: Methods and Protocols, 2000-03; mem. editl. bd. Molecular Biotechnology, Frontiers in Biosci., Internat. Jour. Biomed. Sci., World Medicine; ad-hoc reviewer Endocrinology, Molecular Pharmacology, Biochimica et Biophysica Acta, Am. Jour. Physiology, Lab. Animal Sci., NSF, BioTechs., Brain Rsch.; contbr. articles, revs., and abstracts to profl. jours. and internat. confs. Recipient Leukemia Assn. award, 1981, Tartar award Med. Rsch. Found. Oreg., 1980; NIH fellow, 1980-82, 85-87, grantee, 1989, 95, 98, 2002, 05; rsch. grantee Med. Rsch. Found. Oreg., Wills Found., Nat. Parkinson Found., Collins Med. Trust, Murdock Charitable Trust and Rsch. Corp., Nat. Am. Heart Assn. Mem. AAAS, Am. Soc. Biochemistry and Molecular Biology, Am. Soc. Microbiology, Soc. Neurosci., Am. Heart Assn. (basic scis. coun., established investigator 1994-99), Am. Soc. Gene Therapy, U.S.-Israel Binational Sci. Found. (reviewer). Achievements include patent on dopamine receptor and genes; cloning of several adrenergic receptor genes and simian retroviral infectious genomes; depositor, nucleotide sequence to EMBL and GenBank databases, and clones to American Type Culture Collection. Office: Oreg Health Sci U Sch Dentistry Dept Integrative Biosciences 611 SW Campus Dr Portland OR 97239-3097 E-mail: machidac@ohsu.edu.

MACHINA, MARK JOSEPH, economist; b. Detroit, Oct. 27, 1954; BA in Econs., Mich. State U., East Lansing, 1975, BA in Math., 1975; PhD in Econs., MIT, Boston, 1979. Asst. prof. econs. U. Calif., San Diego, 1979—84, assoc. prof. econs., 1984—88, prof. econs., 1988—. Vis. prof.

econs. Duke U., Durham, NC, 1996; jr. rsch. officer Cambridge U., 1980—81; vis. asst. prof. econs. Princeton (N.J.) U., 1981—82; instr. People's U. China, Beijing, 1987, 90, 91, 93; Kaiser vis. prof. econs. Stanford (Calif.) U., 1999. Assoc. editor: Jour. Econ. Theory, 1983—91, Econometrica, 1984—91, Quarterly Jour. Econs., 1985—91, Jour. Econ. Perspectives, 1987—90, Jour. Econ. Surveys, 1987—91; co-editor: Theory and Decision, 1986—, Jour. Math. Econs., 1999—; founding co-editor: Jour. Risk and Uncertainty, 1988—90; contbr. articles to profl. jours. Trustee U. Calif. San Diego Found., 2001—04. Fellow, Ctr. for Advanced Study in the Behavioral Scis., 1987—88; grantee, NSF, 1983—86, 1992—95, 1998—2001; Grad. fellow, 1975—78, Vis. fellow, Australian Nat. U., Canberra, 1983, Rsch. fellow, Alfred P. Sloan Found., 1984—86, Erskine fellow, U. Canterbury, Christchurch, New Zealand, 1994. Fellow: Econometric Soc., Am. Acad. Arts and Scis.; mem.: Phi Beta Kappa. Office: Univ Calif San Diego 9500 Gilman Dr La Jolla CA 92093-0508 Office Phone: 858-534-2391. Business E-Mail: mmachina@ucsd.edu.

MACHLE, EDWARD JOHNSTONE, religious studies educator, philosopher; b. Canton, China, Sept. 29, 1918; s. Edward Charles and Jean (Mawson) M.; m. Neva Hull, Aug. 29, 1942; children— Stewart, Douglas, Kathi; m. Mary Lou Reynolds, Dec. 15, 1970; 1 adopted child, Michelle; stepchildren— Rebecca, Richard, Robin. Student, Pacific Lutheran Jr. Coll., 1937; BA, Whitworth Coll., 1939; B.D., San Francisco Theol. Sem., 1942, MA, 1944; PhD, Columbia U., 1952. Ordained to ministry Presbyn. Ch., 1942; minister Concrete, Wash., 1942-43; asst. minister San Francisco, 1943-44, Mineola, N.Y., 1944-46; instr. Columbia, 1946-47; asst. prof. U. Colo., 1947-53, asso. prof., 1953-63, prof., 1963-80, emeritus, 1981—, chmn. dept., 1951-52, 56-58, 66-69. Vis. lectr. U. Alta., summer 1960, Iliff Sch. Theology, 1962, Evergreen State, 1981, Peninsula Coll., 1985-86; in-parish research dir. San Francisco Theol. Sem.; dir. music St. Andrew Presbyn. Ch., Boulder, Colo., 1961-70; guest lectr. ch. music U. Colo. Sch. Music, 1950-65; disting. faculty fellow Sheldon Jackson Coll., 1986-88 Author: Nature and Heaven in the Xunzi, 1993. Mem. Am. Phil. Assn., Soc. Asian and Comparative Philosophy, Acad. Religion. Presbyterian. Home: 11 Silver Canyon Place The Woodlands TX 77381 Personal E-mail: machle@wt.net. *Faith is largely willingness to learn of what can destroy us. Idolatry feeds on our fear of having faith. Research methods spring from the soil of our cultured idolatries. Thus, to learn, faith must at times be a traitor to "learning.".*

MACHLOWITZ, DAVID STEVEN, lawyer; b. Phila., Jan. 23, 1954; s. Roy Alan and Eleanore Machlowitz; m. Sheryl Lynn Steinberg, June 30, 1985; children: Jennifer, Kevin. BA, U. Pa., 1974; JD, Yale U., 1977. Bar: Pa. 1977, U.S. Dist. Ct. (ea. dist.) Pa. 1977, N.Y. 1981, U.S. Dist. Ct. (so. and ea. dists.) N.Y. 1981, U.S. Ct. Appeals (2d cir.) 1981. Assoc. Ballard, Spahr, Andrews & Ingersoll, Phila., 1977-80, Christy & Viener, NYC, 1981-85, Morrison, Cohen & Singer, NYC, 1985-87; asst. gen. counsel Gen. Instrument Corp., NYC, 1994—99; gen. counsel Siemens Med. Systems, Iselin, NJ, 1992—98; assoc. gen. coun. Siemens Corp., Iselin, 1993-98, dep. gen. counsel NYC, 1999—2000; sr. v.p. gen. counsel Merck-Medco Managed Care, LLC (now Medco Health Solutions), 2000—, sec., 2002—. Contbr. articles to profl. jours. including ABA Jour., 1981—. Mem. N.Y. Corp. Counsel Assn. (bd. dirs., pres.), N.J. Corp. Counsel Assn. (bd. dirs., pres.). Avocations: history, film, books, basketball. Office: Medco Health Solutions Inc 100 Parsons Pond Dr Franklin Lakes NJ 07417 *

MACHOTKA, PAVEL, psychology and art educator; b. Prague, Czechoslovakia, Aug. 21, 1936; came to U.S., 1948; s. Otakar Richard and Jarmila Marie (Mohr) M.; m. Hannelore Gothe, Apr. 6, 1963 (div. Dec. 1980); children: Danielle, Julia; m. Nina Jane Hansen, Sept. 10, 1989. AB, U. Chgo., 1956; MA, Harvard U., 1958, PhD, 1962. Instr. Harvard U., Cambridge, Mass., 1962-65; asst. prof. Med. Sch. U. Colo., Denver, 1965-70; from assoc. prof. to prof. U. Calif., Santa Cruz, 1970—, provost coll. V, 1976-79, chair acad. senate, 1992-94. Mem. editorial bd. Empirical Studies of the Arts, 1980—; author: The Nude, 1979; co-author: Messages of the Body, 1976. Precinct worker, alt. del. Dem. Party, Denver, 1968. Woodrow Wilson Nat. scholar, 1956; Fulbright fellow, 1958-60. Fellow APA, Am. Psychol. Soc.; mem. Czechoslovak Soc. for Arts and Scis. (sec.-gen. 1991-93), Internat. Assn. for Empirical Aesthetics (pres. 1980-88). Office: U Calif Santa Cruz CA 95064

MACHOVEC, FRANK J., psychologist; b. Balt., May 16, 1930; s. James Joseph and Theresa Anna MacH.; m. Evelyn Mary Stultz, May 5, 1951; 1 child, Frank. BA, U. Md., 1964; MA, Loyola U., Balt., 1965; PhD, Fielding Inst., 1979. Diplomate Am. Bd. Psychol. Hypnosis, Am. Bd. Med. Psychotherapy; lic. clin. psychologist. Asst. dir. New Sch. Psychotherapy, Washington, 1970-71; chief psychologist Victoria Hosp., Winnipeg, Man., Canada, 1973-75, Alta. Mental Health, Lethbridge, Canada, 1975-77; psychologist Alaska Psychol. Inst., Anchorage, 1977-79, State Hosp. South, Blackfoot, Idaho, 1979-81; dir. psychol. svcs. South Va. Mental Health Inst., Danville, 1981-86; dir. quality assurance Va. Dept. Mental Health, 1986-90; supr. psychology Va. Juvenile Corrections, 1991-95, ret., 1995. Prof. Piedmont Coll., Va.; instr. Jefferson Inst. Author: Hypnosis Complications, 1986, Expert Witness Survival Manual, 1987, Humor Theories, History, 1988, Interview and Interrogation, 1989, Cults and Personality, 1989, Becoming Street Smart, 1994, Spiritual Intelligence, 2003, Light from the East, 2005, Private Investigative and Security Science, 2006; contbr. numerous articles to profl. jours. and mags. With USMC, 1950—52. Avocations: writing, travel, teaching. Personal E-mail: fmacho@comcast.net.

MACHOVER, CARL, computer graphics designer, engineer, consultant; b. Bklyn., Mar. 26, 1927; s. John Herman and Rose (Alter) M.; m. Wilma Doris Simon, June 18, 1950; children: Tod, Julie, Linda. BEE, Rensselaer Poly. Inst., 1951; postgrad., NYU, 1953-56. Mgr. applied engring. Norden div. United A/C Corp., 1951-59; mgr. sales Skiatron Electronics & TV, NYC, 1959-60; v.p. mktg., dir. Info. Displays, Inc., Mount Kisco, NY, 1960-73, v.p., gen. mgr., 1973-76; pres. Machover Assocs. Corp., White Plains, NY, 1976—. Adj. prof. Rensselaer Poly. Inst.; mem. RPI H&SS adv. bd. Bradford EIMC Indsl. Adv. Bd.; pres. bd. Art & Sci. Collaborations, Inc., 1994-2004. Author: Gyro Primer, 1957, Basics of Gyroscopes, 1958; mem. editl. bd., new products editor IEEE Computer Graphics and Applications; mem. editl. bd. Computers and Graphics; editor C4 Handbook, 1989, 2d edit., 1995, The CAD/CAM Handbook, 1996; co-editor Computer Graphics Rev.; co-exec. prodr. The Story of Computer Graphics, 1999; contbr. articles to profl. jours. Mem. adv. bd. Pratt Ctr. for Computer Graphics in Design. With USNR, 1945-46. Named to Computer Graphics Hall of Fame, Fine Arts Mus. of L.I., Hempstead, N.Y., 1988; recipient Frank Oppenheimer award, Am. Soc. Engring. Edn., 1971, Orthagonal award, N.C. State U., 1988, Vanguard award, Nat. Computer Graphics Assn., 1993, Industry Lifetime Achievement award, CAD Soc., 2003. Fellow Soc. for Info. Display (pres. 1968-70), Eurographics Assn.; mem. IEEE, Assn. for Computing Machinery, Am. Inst. Design and Drafting, Soc. Mfg. Engrs., Nat. Computer Graphics Assn. (bd. dir., pres. 1989-90), Computer Graphics Pioneer, Art and Sci. Collaborators Inc. (pres. 1995—), Sigma Xi, Tau Beta Pi, Eta Kappa Nu. Home: 152 Longview Ave White Plains NY 10605-2314 Office: Machover Assocs Corp PO Box 308 152A Longview Ave White Plains NY 10605-2314 Office Phone: 914-949-3777.

MACHT, STEVEN, plastic surgeon, consultant; b. Balt., Apr. 19, 1946; m. Laurie Macht. BS in Biochemistry, U. Md., College Park, 1956; DDS, U. Md. Sch. Dentistry, Balt., 1969; MD, George Washington U. Sch. Medicine, Washington, 1972; preceptorship in Maxillofacial Surgery, Zahnart Inst., Zurich, Switzerland, 1974. Diplomate Nat. Bd. Med. Examiners, 1973, lic. dentist Md., 1969, physician DC, 1973, Md., 1976, Va., 1976, cert. Am. Bd. Surgery, 1978, Am. Bd. Plastic Surgery, 1980. Intern dept. surgery George Washington U. Hosp., Washington, 1972—73, resident surgery, 1973—76, chief surg. residency, 1976—77; asst. gen. surgery, adj. instr. dept. surgery George Washington U., 1976—77; resident then fellow plastic surgery Yale U. Sch. Medicine, New Haven, 1977—79; hand fellow Yale U., U. Conn. Hartford Hosp., 1978; instr. plastic surgery Yale U. Sch. Medicine, New Haven, 1978—79; asst. prof. plastic surgery George Washington U., Washington, 1980—84; chief dept. plastic and reconstructive surgery Bethesda Naval Hosp., Md., 1980—81; clin. asst. prof. dept. surgery Uniformed Svcs. U. Health Scis., Bethesda, 1981—88; assoc. clin. prof. dept. surgery George Washington U., 1984—89, clin. prof. dept. surgery, 1990—; pvt. practice Washington, 1990—. Cons. in plastic surgery Nat. Cancer Inst. NIH, Bethesda, Md., 1979—; chief dept. plastic and reconstructive surgery Bethesda Naval Hosp., 1980—81; cons. in plastic surgery Nat. Naval Med. Ctr, Bethesda, 1981—88; program dir., chief divsn. plastic surgery George Washington U., 1981—84; mem. exec. com. Attending Staff Physicians Assn. George Washington U. Hosp., 1986—99, pres., 1994—96; cons. FTC, Washington, 1990—91; mem. credentials com. George Washington U. Hosp., 1991—94, sec. med. staff, 1991—93; mem. pro-assurance underwriting com. Nat. Capital Reciprocal Ins. Co., Washington, 1993—. Comdr. USN, 1979—81. Grantee, Charles W Ohse Fund Yale U., 1978—79; Rex Simms Meml. scholar. Fellow: ACS; mem.: AMA (Hosp. Mgmt. Sys. Soc. rep. 1991—93, Physicians Recognition award 2001—04), ADA, Southern Med. Assn., Southeastern Surg. Congress, DC Soc. Plastic and Reconstructive Surgeons, DC Chapt. ACS, D.C. Med. Soc. (mem. fee rev. com. 1991—94, mem. grievance com. 1990—94), Assn Mil. Plastic Surgeons, Am. Soc. Plastic and Reconstructive Surgeons (mem. ednl.found. 1982—84, mem. ednl. found. 1983—86), Am. Soc. Maxillofacial Surgeons (mem. maxillofacial trauma com. 1982—84), Am. Assn. Hand Surgery (mem. govt. rels. com. 2002), Assn. Program Dirs. Office: Ste 217 2021 K St NW Washington DC 20006 Office Phone: 202-887-8120.

MACIAS, EDWARD S., chemistry professor, dean, academic administrator; b. Milw., Feb. 21, 1944; s. Arturo C. Macias and Minette (Schwenger) Wiederhold; m. Paula Wiederhold, June 17, 1967; children: Matthew Edward, Julia Katherine. AB, Colgate U., 1966; PhD, MIT, 1970. From asst. prof. to Barbara and David Thomas Disting. prof. Arts and Scis. Washington U., St. Louis, 1970—2005, Barbara and David Thomas Disting. prof. Arts and Scis., 2005—, exec. vice chancellor and dean Faculty Arts and Scis., 1995—. Cons. Meteorology Rsch., Inc., Altadina, Calif., 1978-81, Salt River Project, Phoenix, 1980-83, Santa Fe Rsch., Bloomington, Minn., 1985-88, AeroVironment, Inc., Monrovia, Calif., 1986-88. Author: Nuclear and Radiochemistry, 1981; editor: Atmospheric Aerosol, 1981; contbr. numerous articles to profl. jours. Bd. dirs. Mark Twain Summer Inst., St. Louis, 1984-87, 88-90, The Coll. Sch., St. Louis, 1984-88, Colgate U., 1997—. Grantee NSF, EPA, Electric Power Rsch. Inst., So. Calif. Edison Co., Dept. Energy, AEC. Mem. Am. Chem. Soc., Am. Assn. Aerosol Rsch. (editorial bd.), Am. Phys. Soc., AAAS. Home: 6907 Waterman Ave Saint Louis MO 63130-4333 Office: Washington U Campus Box 1094 One Brookings Dr Saint Louis MO 63130 Office Phone: 314-935-6800.

MACILVAINE, CHALMERS ACHESON, retired financial executive, former association executive; b. Bklyn., Oct. 25, 1921; s. James Andrew and Helen Marguerite (Acheson) MacI.; m. Elizabeth Jean Babcock, Mar. 26, 1943; children: Judith Anne, Joseph Chad, Martha Elizabeth. AB, Stanford U., 1943. With Kaiser Steel Corp., 1946-73, asst. controller, 1953-62, treas., 1962-70, v.p., 1967-70, v.p. finance and planning, 1970-73; also v.p., dir. subsidiaries; v.p. project financing group Bank of Am., San Francisco, 1973-74, sr. v.p., dep. head Asia div., 1974-77; sr. v.p.-fin. Peabody Coal Co., St. Louis, 1978-80; sr. v.p., dir. Stifel, Nicolaus & Co., Inc., St. Louis, 1980-83; exec. dir. Japan Am. Soc. of St. Louis, 1983-85. Pres. Bamerical Internat. Fin. Corp., 1973-74 Served to lt. (j.g.) USNR, 1943-46. Mem. Phi Beta Kappa, Sigma Chi. Clubs: Tokyo Lawn Tennis, Burns Club of St. Louis. Home: PO Box 99 Friendship ME 04547-0099

MAC INNES, DAVID HAROLD, artist, small business owner; s. Harold Boice and Julia (Storr) Mac Innes; m. Gloria Jean LePre; 1 child, Maria Alley. Grad., Cleve. Inst. Art, 1946—49. Cert. fine art/applied art Cleve. Inst. Art, 1949. Art dir. Fuller, Smith & Ross, Pitts., 1958—62, Kenyon & Eckhardt, NYC, 1964—68; creative group supr. art dir., designer L.W. Frohlich, Inc. Pharms., NYC, 1968—72; sr. art dir. Wunderman, Ricotta & Kline, NYC, 1972—75, Conahay & Lyon, NYC, 1976—80, Barnum Comm., Inc., NYC, 1983—86, Chapman Advt., Inc. (Young & Rubicam), NYC, 1986—91; creative group & studio mgr. F. Scott Kimmich, Inc., Norwalk, Conn., 1980—83; owner, artist MacInnes Comm., Rancho Palos Verdes, Calif., 1992—. Contbg. artist (exhibitions) Three Rivers Centennial Exhibit, Pitts., 1955; exhibitions include Cleve. Mus. Art, 1958, 27th New Eng. Internat., Silvermine, Conn., 1959, In Retrospect, 1996, exhibitions include paintings, graphics, Larchmont Cmty. Ctr., 1997, exhibitions include paintings, plein-air oils, acrylics A Walk in the Park, Larchmont Art Gallery, one-man shows include, Ivy Sch. Art, Pitts., 1956, large scale acrylics, Art Directors Who Paint, artists guild, NY Big Apple Show (First Artist award, Mamaroneck Artists Guild, 1993); contbg. artist, editor, cinematographer (NY experimental film exposition); pvt. collections, NYC, Pitts., Ann Arbor, Mich., Cleve., Albuquerque. Pvt. 1st class USAF, 1943—45, US, Germany. Recipient First award, Pitts. Artists in Industry, 1960, LW Frohlich Competition, 1970, First prize award, Internat. Broadcasting Assn., 1970, First prize award for painting, Mamaroneck Artists Guild, 1992, Expect the Unexpected First award, Mamaroneck Artists Gallery, 1994, 2d Prize award for monoprint, Palos Verdes Art Ctr., 2003. Mem.: DuoDecimo Soc., Advt. Artists Pitts. (bd. mem. artist, editor, designer aap comm. 1955—59), Calif. Art Edn. Assn. (assoc.; contriuting mem. 2004—06), NY Art Dirs. Club Pa. (life; various com. positions 1972—2006, students scholarship com. mem. 1985—89), Palos Verdes Art Ctr., Paletteers (assoc.), Art Dirs. Club Pitts. (bd. mem. 1958—60). Avocations: travel, museums. Office: David Mac Innes PO Box 4711 Rancho Palos Verdes CA 90275 Home Phone: 310-406-1866. Office Fax: 310-541-1039. Business E-Mail: dmacinnes2@aol.com.

MACINNES, SALLY ACKERMAN, computer education educator; b. Columbus, Ind., Nov. 12, 1946; d. Louis L. and Josephine K. Ackerman; m. James C. MacInnes, June 13, 1981; children: Todd Keenan, Jennifer Mangel, Christopher Keenan, Daniel Keenan. BA, U. Iowa, Iowa City, 1968; MS, No. Ill. U., Dekalb, 1989; postgrad., Nat. Coll. Edn., Evanston, Ill., DePaul U., Chgo., St. Xavier Coll. Cert. tchr. Computer lab. asst. York High Sch., Elmhurst, Ill.; tchr. 2nd grade Cossitt Sch., LaGrange, Ill.; library-media coord. Unit Sch. 205, Elmhurst; tchr. computer edn. Dist. 93, Hillside, Ill. Home: 915 Saylor Ave Elmhurst IL 60126-4762

MACINNIS, AL, professional sports team executive, retired professional hockey player; b. Inverness, NS, Can., July 11, 1963; Defenceman Calgary Flames, 1981-94, St. Louis Blues, 1994—2005, v.p. hockey ops., 2006—. Mem. Team Can., Olympic Games, Nagano, Japan, 1998, Salt Lake City, 2002; player NHL All-Star Game, 1985, 1987—92, 1994, 1996—2001, 2003. Named to Sporting News All-Star First Team, 1990, 1991, First All-Star Team, NHL, 1990, 1991; recipient Max Kaminsky Trophy, 1983, Conn Smythe Trophy, 1989, James Norris Meml. Trophy, 1999. Achievements include being a member of Stanely Cup Champion Calgary Flames, 1989; being a member of gold medal Canadian Hockey team, Salt Lake City Olympic Games, 2002; having his number, 2, retired by St. Louis Blues, 2006. Office: St Louis Blues Hockey Club Scottrade Ctr 1401 Clark Ave Saint Louis MO 63103 *

MACINNIS, FRANK T., construction and holding company executive, securities trader; b. Camrose, Alta., Can., Nov. 10, 1946; came to U.S., 1978; s. H. Frank and Adele M. (Irving) MacI.; m. Beverley J. McAndrews, Nov. 3, 1977; children: Christopher, Katrina, Lauren, Robbie. BA, Univ. Alta., Edmonton, 1968, LLB, 1971. Assoc. Liden, Ackroyd & Co., Edmonton, 1971-75; gen. counsel Banister-Price Internat., Tehran, Iran, 1975-77; dir. Banister-Price Overseas, London, 1977-78; exec. v.p. H.C. Price Co., Bartlesville, Okla., 1978-80; chmn., chief exec. officer H.C. Price Constrn. Co., Dallas, 1980-84; pres. Spie Group, Inc., Dallas, 1986—94; sr. v.p., CFO Comstock Group, Inc., Danbury, Conn., 1986—90, chmn., pres., CEO, 1990—94; pres. EMCOR Group Inc., Norwalk, Conn., 1994—97, chmn., CEO, 1997—. Mem. exec. com. Spie Batignolles, Paris, 1985-94; bd. dirs. The Williams Companies, ITT Industries, Inc. Served to lt. Royal Can. Navy, 1964-68; bd. dirs. Greater New York Chapter of the March of Dimes. Roman Catholic. Avocations: sports, coin collecting/numismatics, music. Office: EMCOR Group Inc 301 Merritt Seven Corporate Park 6th Fl Norwalk CT 06851-1060 Office Phone: 203-849-7800. Office Fax: 203-849-7900. *

MACINNIS, JOHN CHRISTIAN, music educator; b. Halifax, NS, Canada, July 16, 1981; s. Ritchie Fraser and Heather Elaine MacInnis; m. Victoria Lynn Cannon, June 2, 2007. MusB, Bob Jones U., Greenville, SC, 2003, MusM, 2006. Profl. tchg. cert. music edn. Am. Assn. Christian Schs., 2007. Asst. author Bob Jones U. Press, Greenville, SC, 2003—06; music tchr. Westwood Christian Sch., Miami, Fla., 2006—. Mem. civic chorale U. Miami, 2006—. Mem.: Fla. Music Educators Assn., Music Educators Nat. Conv. Home: 575 Chase Brook Dr Rock Hill SC 29732 Home Phone: 803-980-3003.

MACINTYRE, NEIL ROSS, JR., medical educator; b. San Diego, Nov. 21, 1946; s. Neil Ross and Rebecca (Torrey) MacI.; m. Suzanne Artusio, June 20, 1970; children: Catherine, Neil III, Douglas, Charles, Elizabeth, Stephen. BS cum laude, U. San Francisco, 1968; MD, Cornell U., 1972. Diplomate Am. Bd. Internal Medicine, Pulmonary Disease, Critical Care Medicine; lic. physician, NC. Intern, jr. resident, sr. resident medicine Cornell U. Med. Ctr., N.Y. Hosp., NYC, 1972-75; fellow pulmonary diseases U. Calif., San Francisco, 1978-81; med. dir. respiratory care svcs., pulmonary function lab. Duke U. Med. Ctr., Durham, N.C., 1981—, asst. prof. medicine, 1981-89, assoc. prof., 1989-95, prof., 1995—. Editor: Complications of Mechanical Ventilation, 1992, Comprehensive Respiratory Care, 1994; editorial bd. Respiratory Care, 1986—, chmn., 1990-92; co-editor in chief Problems in Respiratory Care, 1988-91; med. editor Arkos, The Jour. of Mechanical Ventilation, 1989; editorial bd. Critical Care Medicine, 1992—; contbr. articles to profl. jours., chpts. to books. Trustee Am. Respiratory Care Found., 1988—, vice chmn., 1990—. With USN, 1975-78. Fellow Am. Coll. Chest Physicians; mem. Am. Thoracic Soc. (pres. NC chpt. 1989, lab. stds. com. 1992—), Am. Assn. Respiratory Care (chmn. bd. med. advisors 1990), Am. Lung Assn. (pres. Rsch. Triangle region 1988), Am. Heart Assn. (chmn. emergency cardiac care com. 1989-90, Silver Svc. medal 1978), Soc. Critical Care Medicine, Nat. Assn. Med. Dirs. Respiratory Care (pres. 1991-93), NC Soc. Respiratory Care (hon.), Alpha Omega Alpha. Office: Duke U Med Ctr PO Box 3911 Durham NC 27710-0001

MACIOCE, FRANK MICHAEL, lawyer, financial services company executive; b. NYC, Oct. 3, 1945; s. Frank Michael and Sylvia Maria (Morea) M.; children: Michael Peter, Lauren Decker, Theodore Kenneth; m. Helen Latourette Duffin, July 9, 1988. BS, Purdue U., 1967; JD, Vanderbilt U., Nashville, 1972. Bar: NY 1973, US Dist. Ct. (so. dist.) NY 1973, US Ct. Appeals (2d cir.) 1975, US Supreme Ct. 1976. Mem. law dept. Merrill Lynch, Pierce, Fenner & Smith Inc., NYC, 1972-80, v.p., 1978-88, 1st v.p., 1988-2000, Merrill Lynch Investment Mgrs., Plainsboro, NJ, 2000—03; councilman-at-large Summit, NJ, 2004—. Mgr. corp. law dept. Merrill Lynch & Co., Inc., NYC, 1980-93, asst. gen. counsel, 1982-2000; gen. counsel investment banking group, 1993-95, ops., svcs. and tech. counsel, 1995-2000, sec. of audit, compensation and nominating coms. bd. dirs., 1978-83, sec. exec. com., 1981-83; mng. dir. Merrill Lynch Overseas Capital, N.V., Netherlands Antilles, 1980-85; sec., dir. Merrill Lynch Employees Fed. Credit Union, NYC, 1978-82; dir. Merrill Lynch Pvt. Capital Inc., NYC, 1981-87, Teleport Comm. Group Inc., NYC, 1987-92, Enhance Fin. Services Inc, NYC, 1988-92; fin. planning adv. bd. Purdue U., 1996-2000. Pres. pro tem City of Summit Common Coun., 2004, pres., 2005—06. With US Army, 1969—70. Home and Office: 22 Essex Rd Summit NJ 07901-2802 Office Phone: 908-522-0903. Personal E-mail: fmacioce@comcast.net.

MACIUSZKO, KATHLEEN LYNN, librarian, educator; b. Nogales, Ariz., Apr. 8, 1947; d. Thomas and Stephanie (Horowski) Mart; m. Jerzy Janusz Maciuszko, Dec. 11, 1976; 1 child, Christina Aleksandra. BA, Ea. Mich. U., 1969; MLS, Kent State U., 1974; PhD, Case Western Res. U., 1987. Reference libr. Baldwin-Wallace Coll. Libr., Berea, Ohio, 1974-77, dir. Conservatory of Music Libr., 1977-85; dir. bus. info. svcs. Harcourt Brace Jovanovich, Inc., Cleve., 1985-89; staff asst. to exec. dir. Cuyahoga County Pub. Libr., Cleve., 1989-90; dir. Cleve. Area Met. Library System, Beachwood, Ohio, 1990; media specialist Cleve. Pub. Schs., 1991-93, Berea (Ohio) City Sch. Dist., 1993—. Author: OCLC: A Decade of Development, 1967-77, 1984; contbr. articles to profl. jours. Named Plenum Pub. scholar, 1986. Mem. Spl. Librs. Assn. (pres. Cleve. chpt. 1989-90, v.p. 1988-89, editor newsletter 1988-89), Baldwin-Wallace Coll. Faculty Women's Club (pres. 1975), Avocation: music. Office: Midpark HS 7000 Paula Dr Middleburg Heights OH 44130

MACK, ALAN WAYNE, interior designer; b. Cleve., Oct. 30, 1947; s. Edmund B. and Florence I. (Oleksa) M. BS in Interior Design, Case Western Res. U., 1969. Designer interior design dept. Halle's, Cleve., 1969, 71-73; designer Nahan Co., New Orleans, 1973-75, Hemenway's Contract Design, New Orleans, 1975-76; ptnr. Hewlett-Mack Design Assocs., New Orleans, 1976-85; prin., dir. interior design HLM Design, Inc., 1985—2001; prin., founding ptnr. Proteus Group, Chgo., 2001—. Mem. adv. com. interior design dept. Delgado Jr. Coll., New Orleans; mktg./merchandising adv. coun. St. Mary's Dominican Coll., New Orleans; mem. friends devel. coun. U. Iowa Mus. Art, 1986-91, chair, 1990-91; chmn. adv. com. interior design program Iowa State U., 1991-96; mem. design review com. City of Iowa City, 1992-93; mem. adv. bd. Healthcare Facilities Symposiom & Expo, 2007—; mem. rev. com. Healthcare Design, 2004-07; mem. adv. bd. Healthcare Facilities Symposium, 2007—. Coauthor: audiovisual presentation Nat. Home Improvement Coun. Conf., 1981; reviewer in field. Bd. dirs. Johnson County United Way, 1991-96. Served with U.S. Army, 1969-71. Mem. ASID (profl. mem., presdl. citation 1980, treas. La. dist. chpt. 1984), Vis. Nurses Assn. (bd. dirs. 1991-96), Found. for Interior Design Edn. Rsch. (standards com. 1972-76, bd. visitors 1977-80, accreditation com. 1981-95, trustee 1996-99, chmn. bd. dirs. 1998, pres. 1999). Home: 3800 N Lake Shore Dr Ste 2G Chicago IL 60613-3313 Office Phone: 312-573-4051. Business E-Mail: amack@proteusgroup.net.

MACK, CONNIE, congressman; b. Cape Coral, Fla., Aug. 12, 1967; s. Connie Mack III and Priscilla Mack; m. Ann Mack; children: Addison, Connie Mack V. BS, U. Fla., 1993. Mem. Fla. Ho. of Reps., 2000—03, US Congress from 14th Fla. dist., 2005—; mem. budget com., internat. relations com., transp. and infrastructure com. Republican. Office: US House Reps 317 Cannon House Office Bldg Washington DC 20515-0914 Office Phone: 202-225-2536. Office Fax: 202-225-0439. *

MACK, CONNIE, III, (CORNELIUS MCGILLICUDDY III), former senator; b. Phila., Oct. 29, 1940; s. Cornelius and Susan (Sheppard)

McGillicuddy; children: Debra Lynn, Cornelius Harvey. Degree in bus., U. Fla., 1966. Mktg. Cape Coral Bank, Cape Coral, Fla., 1966-68, sr. v.p., dir., 1971-75; v.p. bus. devel. First Nat. Bank, Ft. Myers, 1968-71; pres., dir. Fla. Nat. Bank, Cape Coral, 1975-82; mem. U.S. Ho. of Reps. from 13th Dist. Fla., Washington, 1983-89; U.S. Senator from Fla Washington, 1989-2001; sr. policy advisor Shaw Pittman LLP, Washington, 2001—05, King & Spalding LLP, Washington, 2005—, co-chmn. govt. rels. group, 2005—. Chmn. joint econ. com., 1997-2001; past com. on fin., com. on banking, housing and urban affairs; bd. dirs Moody's Corp, Mutual Am. Life. Ins., Genzyme Corp., Darden Restaurants; chmn. bd., H. Lee Moffit Cancer Ctr.& Rsch. Inst., Tampa, 2001- Bd. dirs., chmn. Palmer Drug Abuse Program, Cape Coral; bd. dirs. Cape Coral Hosp. Republican. Roman Catholic. Office: King & Spalding LLP 1700 Penn Ave Washington DC 20006 Business E-Mail: cmack@kslaw.com.

MACK, DENNIS WAYNE, lawyer; b. Chgo., Sept. 11, 1943; s. Walter Andrew and Betty Jane (Klimek) M. BA, Yale U., 1965; JD, Harvard U., 1969. Bar: (NY) 1970. Assoc. firm Curtis Mallet-Prevost Colt & Mosle, NYC and Paris, 1969-78; sec., gen. counsel Dominion Textile (USA) Inc., NYC, 1978-91, v.p., 1986-91; pvt. practice NYC, 1991—; gen. counsel Knoa Corp., 2000—02. Alt. rep. Internat. Lesbian and Gay Assn. at ECOSOC of UN, 1994. Mem. dept. fin. Presbytery N.Y., 1978-83. Mem. ABA, N.Y. State Bar Assn., Bar Assn. City N.Y. (spl. com. on AIDS and the law 1996-2001). Home: 180 Riverside Dr New York NY 10024-1021

MACK, EARLE IRVING, former ambassador, real estate company executive; b. NYC, July 11, 1939; s. H. Bertram and Ruth (Kaufman) M.; m. Carol L. Dickey, July 26, 1990; children: Andrew, Beatrice. BS, Drexel U., 1959; postgrad., Fordham Law Sch., 1960-61; LHD (hon.), Yeshiva U., 1992; D in Bus. Adminstrn. (hon.), Drexel U., 2006. Sr. ptnr. The Mack Co., Fort Lee, 1964—2005; owner, breeder thoroughbred horses Fla., Ky., NJ, NY, Md., Can., Calif., 1964—; US amb. to Finland US Dept. State, Helsinki, 2004—05. Mem. adv. bd. N.Y. State Bus. Venture Partnership, 1988-98; mem. transition team for Gov. George Pataki, 1994-95; chmn., CEO, N.Y. State Coun. Arts, 1996-99, chmn. emeritus, 1999-. Prodr., co-dir. film The Children of Theater Street, 1977 (Acad. Award Feature Documentary nomination). Bd. dirs. Benjamin N. Cardozo Sch. of Law, N.Y.C., 1980-2004, chmn. exec. com., 1990, vice chmn. bd. dirs., 1991, chmn. bd. dirs., 1992-2004, chmn. emeritus, 2004; bd. dirs. N.Y.C. Ballet, 1988-2004; chmn. N.Y. State Racing Commn., 1983-89, The New 42d St., Inc., 1990-92; bd. dirs. Dance Theatre of Harlem, N.Y.C., 1987, co-chmn. bd., 1988-89; trustee N.Y. Racing Assn., Inc., 1990-2004; trustee, exec. com. Yeshiva U., 1992-2004. 1st lt. USAR, 1960—68. Recipient Can. Sovereign award Horse of Yr., 1993, Can. Sovereign award for best 3 yr. old horse, 1994, Ellis Island Medal of Honor, 1997; named One of Drexel 100, Drexel U., 1992, Commencement Spkr., 2006. Mem. Nat. Realty Com. (bd. dirs., exec. com. 1986-88), Urban Land Inst., Union League Club, Univ. Club, Reading Room Club. Avocations: skiing, swimming, jogging, nutrition. Office: 2115 Linwood Ave Ste 110 Fort Lee NJ 07024

MACK, INA LEAH, secondary school educator, pre-school administrator; b. Macon, Mo., Jan. 10, 1959; d. David Neil and Ina Bernadine Milburn; m. Gary Ray Mack, Sept. 3, 1988; children: Brittany, Cameron, Delaney. BA in Edn., Ariz. State U., 1982; MA in Edn., No. Ariz. U., 2005. Tchr. Antelope High Sch., Wellton, Ariz., 1983—86, Mt. View High Sch., Tucson, 1987—90, Snowflake High Sch., 1990—95, Northland Pioneer Coll., Holbrook, 1991—, Blue Ridge High Sch., Lakeside, 1995—. Advisor Family, Career, Cmty. Leaders Am., Lakeside, 1990—; coach various schs., 1983—93. Vol. Hope Ho., Show Low, Ariz., 2003—05. Mem.: Ariz. Family and Consumer Scis. Edn. Assn., Nat. Assn. Edn. Young Children, Ariz. Career & Tech. Edn. Assn. Republican. Baptist. Avocations: camping, motorcycling, water-skiing, scrapbooks. Office: Blue Ridge High Sch 1200 W White Mountain Rd Lakeside AZ 85929 Home: 4837 Oakwood St Lakeside AZ 85929-5537

MACK, JAMES CURTIS, II, cultural organization administrator; b. LA, Dec. 22, 1944; s. James Curtis and Ahli Christina (Youngren) M.; m. Tamara Jo Kriner, Jan. 23, 1988; children: James Curtis III, Robert Lee, Edward Albert. BA cum laude, U. So. Calif., 1967, M in Pub. Adminstrn., 1969, MA, 1976. Asst. to regional dir. VA, Los Angeles, 1973-79; exec. dir. Citizens for the Republic, Santa Monica, Calif., 1979-85; asst. sec. oceans and atmosphere U.S. Dept. Commerce, Washington, 1985-88; pres. Los Angeles World Affairs Coun., 1988—. Adj. prof. Pepperdine U. Grad. Sch. Pub. Policy, 1999—; bd. dirs. Brentwood Bank of Calif. Mem. Pres.'s Commn. on White House Fellowships, 1984-85; mem. exec. adv. bd. European Union Ctr. Calif. Col. USAFR, 1969-99. Mem. Coun. Fgn. Rels., Nat. Space Club (bd. dirs. 1987-88). Republican. Episcopalian. Avocation: philatelist. Home: 4921 Fulton Ave Sherman Oaks CA 91423 Office: LA World Affairs Coun 345 S Figueroa St Ste 313 Los Angeles CA 90071-1002 Office Phone: 213-628-2333. Business E-Mail: jcmack@lawac.org.

MACK, JEANNETTE ANA, medical technician; b. Jacksonville, Fla., July 14, 1951; d. Willie Lee and Dorothea Scott Mack; m. Luther Baker Jr. (div.); children: Luther Baker III, Calecia Baker Fowlers, Christopher Baker. AS in Bus. Sci., Fla. Tech. Coll., Jacksonville, Fla., 1987, AS in Electronics Tech. with honors, 1986. Nurse's aide St. Lukes Hosp., 1974—79; monitor tech. and patient care Meml. Hosp., 1978—86, Riverside Hosp., 1987—89; neurodiagnostic tech. Meml. Hosp., 1986—88, U. Med. Ctr., 1989—96; supr. neurodiagnostic Meml. Hosp., 1996—. Baptist. Home: 98 Lake Run Blvd Jacksonville FL 32218-0806 Office: 3625 Univ Blvd S Jacksonville FL 32216

MACK, JOHN J., diversified financial services company executive; b. Mooresville, NC, Nov. 17, 1944; s. Charles and Alice (Azouri) Mack; m. Christy King; children: John, Stephen, Jenna. BA, Duke U., 1968. Municipal bond trader and salesman Smith Barney; mem. bond dept. Morgan Stanley & Co., 1972, v.p., 1976—77, principal, 1977, mng. dir., 1979, head Worldwide Taxable Fixed Income Divsn., 1985—92; mem. bd. dirs. Morgan Stanley Group, NYC, 1987-97, chmn. operating com., 1992-97, pres., 1993-97; pres., COO Morgan Stanley Dean Witter & Co., NYC, 1997—2001; pres., CEO Credit Suisse First Boston, LLC, 2001—04; co-CEO Credit Suisse Group, NYC, 2003—04; chmn. Pequot Capital Mgmt. Inc., Westport, Conn., 2005; chmn., CEO Morgan Stanley, NYC, 2005—. Bd. dirs. Catalyst, Inc., Celiant Corp., Cousins Properties Inc.; bd. dir. NYSE, bd. exec., 2003—04; mem. internat. adv. panel Monetary Authority, Singapore; mem. chmn. adv. com. Nat. Assn. Securities Dealers (NASD); past mem. Beijing's Advisory Coun.; past dir. CICC (first investment bank in China), India Bus. Sch.; past bd. visitors Fuqua Sch. Bus., Duke U. Serves numerous positions of leadership for bus., civic and philanthropic org.; chmn. bd. trustees NY Presbyn. Hosp., U. Hosp. Columbia, Cornell; mem. bd. trustees Duke U.; trustee Doris Duke Charitable Found.; vice chmn. NYC2012; co-founder CJ Mack Found. Recipient Thomas F. Keller Disting. Leadership award, Fuqua Sch. Bus., Duke U., 1998. Office: Morgan Stanley 1585 Broadway New York NY 10036 *

MACK, JUDITH COLE SCHRIM, retired political scientist; b. Cin., Aug. 9, 1938; d. James Douglass and Cathleen (Cole) Schrim; m. Thomas H. Mack, Jan. 3, 1968; children: Robert Michael, Cathleen Cole. AB with high distinction, U. Ky., Lexington, 1960; AM, Radcliffe Grad. Sch., 1962; MPhil, Columbia U., NYC, 1988, postgrad., 1986—. Tchr. Lexington Sch., Ky., 1962-63; instr. Russian Emory U., Atlanta, 1963-64, Kent State U., Ohio, 1964-65; instr. Hunter Coll., NYC, 1988-90; adj. lectr. Barnard Coll., NYC, 1991—; instr. Douglass Coll. Rutgers U., New Brunswick, NJ, 1992—93; ret., 1993. Rsch. asst. sociology dept. U. Ky., 1961; rsch. asst. Russian and E. European Studies Ctr. UCLA, 1965—67, rsch. asst. Security Studies Ctr., 1967—68; adj. lectr. Hunter Coll., NYC, 1988; presenter in field. Chmn. state pub. affairs com. NJ Jr. Leagues, 1979—80; bd. dirs. Children's Aide Adoption Soc., Hackensack, NJ, 1979—90, v.p., 1985—90; bd. dirs. Assn. Children NJ, Newark, 1982—2003, v.p., 1983—88, chair spl. events, 1999; trustee Divsn. Youth and Family Svcs., Trenton, NJ, 1982—91, v.p., 1983—88; others; trustee Dumbarton Ho., Washington; vice chmn. vis. bd. Music Acad. of the West, Women's Aux.; active Millburn-ShortHills County Rep. Com., 1994—2003, corr. sec., 1994—96, chmn., 1996—98. Woodrow Wilson fellow, Radcliffe Coll., 1960—61, Nat. Def. fellow, 1961—62. Mem.: Am. Bd. Music Acad. West (treas.), Mortar Bd., Nat. Soc. Colonial Dames Am. (NJ treas. 1995—2001), Phi Sigma Iota, Phi Beta Kappa. Episcopalian. Avocations: bridge, cooking, ballet, theater, movies. Home: 657 Del Parque Dr Unit C Santa Barbara CA 93103 Personal E-mail: jsm22@yahoo.com.

MACK, JULIA COOPER, retired judge; b. Fayetteville, NC, July 17, 1920; d. Dallas L. and Emily (McKay) Perry; m. Jerry S. Cooper, July 30, 1943; 1 dau., Cheryl; m. Clifford S. Mack, Nov. 21, 1957. BS, Hampton Inst., 1940; LLB, Howard U., 1951; JD (hon.), U. DC, 1999. Bar: DC 1952. Legal cons. OPS, Washington, 1952-53; atty.-advisor office gen. counsel Gen. Svcs. Adminstrn., Washington, 1953-54; trial appellate atty. criminal div. Dept. Justice, Washington, 1954-68; civil rights atty. Office Gen. Counsel, Equal Employment Opportunity Commn., Washington, 1968-75; assoc. judge Ct. Appeals, Washington, 1975-89; sr. judge DC Ct. of Appeals, Washington, 1989—2001. Mem. Am., Fed., Washington, Nat. Bar Assns., Nat. Assn. Women Judges. Home: 1610 Varnum St NW Washington DC 20011-4206

MACK, MARK PHILIP, chemical company executive; b. Buffalo, Jan. 14, 1950; s. Stanley Joseph and Florence M. Mack; m. Jean Ann Merrick, June 2, 1984; 1 child, Hannah Elizabeth. BS in Chemistry, Buffalo State Coll., 1971; PhD in Chemistry, SUNY, Buffalo, 1976. Rsch. assoc. Duke U., Durham, NC, 1975-77; rsch. chemist Conoco Inc., Ponca City, Okla., 1977-80, group supr., 1980-81; group leader Conoco/DuPont, Ponca City, 1982-85; sr. supr. DuPont Polymer Products, Wilmington, Del., 1985-89; rsch. mgr. OxyChem, Houston, 1989-90; dir. tech. Occidental Chem. Corp., Houston, 1990-95, Lyondell Petrochem. Co., Houston, 1995-97, v.p. licensing, 1996-97; dir. R&D Equistar Chems., LP, 1997-99, dir. catalyst R&D, analytical chemistry and polymer sci., 1999—2002; chief scientist Lyondell/Equistar, Cin., 2002—. *Invented polymer technology that reduces the energy used in crude oil transportation in pipelines by reducing turbulence or drag. Material was named CDR or Conoco Drag Reducer and introduced in 1979 at Pump Station #1 in the Alyeska Pipeline, Prudhoe Bay, Alaska. Brought Nissan process technology to North America in the 80s and modified it to produce plastic containers and flexible packing with step-out performance for source reduction and less energy use called ALATHON polyethylene. Discovered a class of unique polymerization catalysts at EQUISTAR to produce new polymers and plastic called STAR SSC.* Patentee in field; contbr. articles to profl. jours. Recipient Linus Pauling award, SUNY-Buffalo, 1971, Outstanding Student in Chemistry award, Western N.Y. Sect. Am. Chem. Soc., 1971, Conoco Patent award, 1983, Equistar/Lyondell Inventor award, 2001, St. Labre Indian Sch. Ednl. Assn. award, 2002, Operational Excellence award, 2004; grantee Samuel B. Silbert fellowship, SUNY-Buffalo, 1974—75. Mem. AAAS, Am. Chem. Soc., Soc. Plastics Engrs., N.Y. Acad. Sci., Am. Mgmt. Assn., Product Devel. and Mgmt. Assn., World Future Soc., Sigma Xi. Home: 8483 Beckett Pointe Dr West Chester OH 45069-6440 Office Phone: 513-530-4096. Office Fax: 513-530-4267. Business E-Mail: mark.mack@equistarchem.com.

MACK, MICHAEL J., JR., manufacturing executive; B in Mech. Engring., M in Mech. Engring., Iowa State U., Ames; MBA in Fin., Ops. and Stats., U. Chgo. Registered profl. engr. Summer intern engr. John Deere Des Moines Works; various treasury positions Deere & Co., various positions in dealer systems, bus. devel., engring, purchasing, mfg. and mktg., sr. v.p. mktg. and adminstrn. Worldwide Comml. & Consumer Equipment Divsn., v.p., treas. fin. divsn., 2004, sr. v.p., CFO, 2006—. Mem. Engring. Coll. indsl. adv. bd. Iowa State U. Office: Deere & Co One John Deere Pl Moline IL 61265 Office Phone: 309-765-8000. *

MACK, RICHARD G., mathematician, consultant; s. Emil and Rose Machacek; m. Dolores Prusinski, Dec. 27, 1958; children: Richard, Nancy Holder, Robert, Sharon. BS in Edn., U. Cin., 1957; MS in Edn., U. Akron, Ohio, 1970. Cert. assessment for learning facilitator Assessment Tng. Inst., instr. ratios Lesson Lab. Tchr. Cleve. City Schs., 1957—64, Independence Local Sch., Ohio, 1964—91; curriculum dir. Parma City Schs., Ohio, 1991—2005; math. cons. Smart Consortium, Cleve., 2005—. Workshop facilitator Ednl. Rsch. Coun. Am., Cleve., 1970—73. Author: Educational Research Council, 1971, Ohio Math Academy Program, 2004. Mem.: Ohio Coun. Tchrs. Math., Nat. Coun. Tchrs. Math. Home: 6178 Castle Dr Cleveland OH 44143 Office: Smart Consortium IDRA Ctr 1375 Euclid Cleveland OH 44133

MACK, RICHARD L., lawyer, software company executive; BS in Acctg., Moorhead State U.; JD, Hamline U. Bar: 1993. Counsel administrative div. Norwest Corp.; sr. atty. Cargill, Inc., 1994—2004; sr. v.p., gen. counsel, corp. sec. Mosaic Co. (formerly IMC Global & Cargill, Inc.), 2004—. Mem.: Am. Corp. Counsel Assn., Hennepin County Bar Assn., Minnesota State Bar Assn. Office: Mosaic Co Atria Corp Ctr, Ste E490 3033 Campus Dr Plymouth MN 55441

MACK, SARA ROHRBACH, librarian, educator; b. Topton, Pa., Nov. 20, 1921; d. Jonathan H. and Alda S. (Heffner) Rohrbach; m. George Mack, June 26, 1943 (wid. Jan. 1949); 1 child, Carol Mack Foy. BS, Kutztown State Tchrs. Coll., 1943; MS in Libr. Sci., Columbia U., 1955; postgrad., Temple U. and U. Pa. Elem. tchr. Chalfont (Pa.) Pub. Sch., 1943-45; libr. Mt. Penn Jr.-Sr. High Sch., Reading, Pa., 1949-58; prof. libr. sci. Kutztown (Pa.) State Coll., 1958-82, dept. chmn., 1977-82; retired, 1982. Adj. prof. Drexel U., Phila., 1968; bd. dirs. Friends of the Reading-Berks Pub. Librs., pres., 1983-84, exec. bd., 1985—. Compiler: Inspirational Readings for Elementary Grades, 1964; contbr. articles to profl. jours, book reviewer; contbg. author: American Reference Books Annual, Along the Saucony. Trustee Kutztown U. Coun., 1983-2001, chair, 1993-95; com. chmn. Kutztown Area Hist. Soc., 1983-93, 2002-05; ch. libr. Trinity Luth. Ch., Topton, 1966-05; del. to Pa. Govs. Conf. on Librs., 1990; mem. Berks Authors Bibliography Com., 1992-98. Recipient Superior Tchg. award Kutztown State Coll., 1962, Alumni Citation, 1980, 88, Award of Merit, Pa. Libr. Assn., 1969, Outstanding Libr. Contbn. award Loisa Gonser Cmty. Libr., 2002. Mem. ALA (com. mem. 1945), Pa. Libr. Assn., Pa. Sch. Librs. Assn. (pres. 1963-65, exec. bd. 1977-80 Named Outtanding Contbr. to Sch. Libr. Programs, 1981), Ch. and Synagogue Libr. Assn. (speaker and book reviewer), Pa. Citizens for Better Librs., Emeriti Faculty Kutztown U. (coord. 1989—), Phila. Children's Reading Roundtable, Am. Assn. Univ. Women, Delta Kappa Gamma. Home: 105 Dries Rd 34 Reading PA 19605

MACK, THEODORE, lawyer; b. Ft. Worth, Mar. 5, 1936; s. Henry and Norma (Harris) M.; m. Ellen Feinknopf, June 19, 1960; children: Katherine Norma, Elizabeth Ellen, Alexandra. AB cum laude, Harvard U., 1958, JD, 1961. Bar: Tex. 1961, U.S. Supreme Ct. 1971, U.S. Ct. Appeals (5th cir.) 1967, U.S. Ct. Appeals (11th cir.) 1981, U.S. Dist. Ct. (no. dist.) Tex. 1961, U.S. Dist. Ct. (we. dist.) Tex. 1968, U.S. Dist. Ct. (so. dist.) Tex. 1968, U.S. Dist. Ct. (ea. dist.) Tex. 1999. Assoc. Mack & Mack, Ft. Worth, 1961-62, ptnr., 1963-70; dir., pres., v.p., treas., ptnr. Renfro, Mack and Hudman, P.C. and predecessors, Ft. Worth, 1970-93; spl. counsel Brackett & Ellis, P.C. and predecessors, Ft. Worth, 1993—. Trustee Ft. Worth Country Day Sch., 1976-82; bd. dirs. Beth-El Congregation, 1964-73, 75-78, pres. 1975-77; bd. dirs. Jewish Fedn. Ft. Worth, 1965-72; mem. Leadership Ft. Worth, 1973-74; bd. dirs. Sr. Citizens Ctrs., Inc., 1969-81, Family and Individual Svcs., 1981-84, Presbyn. Night Shelter Tarrant County, Inc., 1992-97; pres. Harvard Law Sch. Assn. Tex., 1976-77. Fellow Tex. Bar Found. (life); mem. Tex. Bar Assn., ABA, Am. Inn Ct. (master of the bench John C. Ford Inn), Tarrant County Bar Assn., Bar Assn. 5th Cir. Ct., Colonial County Club, Ft. Worth Club, City Club, Harvard Club (N.Y.C., Boston). Democrat. Jewish. Home: 2817 Harlanwood Dr Fort Worth TX 76109-1226 Office: Spl Counsel Brackett & Ellis PC 100 Main St Fort Worth TX 76102-3090 Office Phone: 817-339-2465. Business E-Mail: tmack@belaw.com.

MACK, WILLIAM L., real estate investment company executive; m. Phyllis Mack. BS, NYU; grad. Wharton Sch., U. Pa., 1961. Past pres., sr. mng. ptnr. The Mack Orgn.; sr. mng. ptnr. The Mack Co.; bd. dirs. Mack-Cali Realty Corp., 1997—, chmn., 2000—; founder, sr. ptnr. Apollo Real Estate Advisors LP, 1993—. Bd. dirs. Bear Stearns Companies Inc., 1997—2004, Wyndham Internat. Inc. Bd. trustees Solomon R. Guggenheim Mus., NYC; vice chmn. North Shore LI Jewish Health Sys.; trustee U. Pa., bd. overseers The Wharton Sch., endowed $10 million for the William and Phyllis Mack Ctr. for Technol. Innovation, 2001. Office: Mack-Cali Realty Corp 11 Commerce Dr Cranford NJ 07016

MACKALL, CRYSTAL L., medical researcher; BS/MD, Northeastern Ohio Universities Coll. Medicine, 1984. Medicine/pediatrics resident, Akron, Ohio; clin. assoc. Pediatric Oncology Br. Nat. Cancer Inst., 1989—92, postdoctoral sci. training Exptl. Immunology Br., 1990—96, rschr. Pediatric Oncology Br., 1996—, now also chief Pediatrics Oncoolgy Br., chief Immunology Sect. Office: Pediatric Oncology Br Ctr Cancer Rsch 10 CRC 1W 3940 Bethesda MD 20892-1104 Office Fax: 301-451-7052. Business E-Mail: cm35c@nih.gov.

MACKALL, HENRY CLINTON, lawyer; b. Ft. Lauderdale, Fla., Apr. 6, 1927; s. Douglass Sorrel and Mildred (Parker) M.; m. Mary Margaret Sullivan, June 21, 1952 (dec. Dec. 23, 2002); children: Caroline Clark, Nancy Sorrel, Lucy Parker BA, U. Va., 1950, LLB, 1952. Bar: Va. 1951. Ptnr. Mackall, Mackall & Gibb, P.C. and predecessors, Fairfax, Va., 1952—. Asst. commr. accounts Fairfax County (Va.), 1963-2006; spl. commr. in chancery for audit functions for Cir. Ct. Fairfax County, 1976-2006; substitute judge Fairfax County Ct., Juvenile and Domestic Rels. Ct. Fairfax County, 1964-69 Trustee Fairfax Hosp. Assn., 1966-75; with Va. State Bar Client Security Fund Bd., 1976-88, chmn., 1977-78; past bd. dirs. F&M Bank, No. Va. Served with AUS, 1945-46 Fellow Am. Coll. Trusts & Estate Counsel, Am. Coll. Real Estate Lawyers, Va. Law Found.; mem. ABA, Va. Bar Assn. (regional v.p. 1963-64), Fairfax County Bar Assn. (pres. 1966-67), Hist. Soc. Fairfax County (pres. 1970-72), Jamestowne Soc. (gov. 1995-97), River Bend Golf and Country Club (Gt. Falls, Va., pres. 1967-68), Georgetown Assembly Washington Democrat. Episcopalian. Home: 1032 Towlston Rd Mc Lean VA 22102-1111 Office: 4031 Chain Bridge Rd Fairfax VA 22030-4103 Home Phone: 703-759-2543; Office Phone: 703-273-0320. E-mail: mackmarhen@aol.com, mackgibb@aol.com.

MACKAY, ALEXANDER RUSSELL, neurosurgeon; s. Alexander Russell MacKay and Marjorie Mackay; m. Kathy MacKay. AB, Princeton U., NJ, 1971; MD, Harvard Med. Sch., Boston, 1975. Cert. neurosurgeon Am. Bd. Neurol. Surgery, 1984. Resident, neurol. surgery U. Calif., San Francisco, 1975—81; pvt. practice, neurol. surgery Spokane, Wash., 1981—. Med. co-dir. Gamma Knife Spokane, 2005—. Mem. St Lukes Meml. Hosp., Spokane, 1977—93. Mem.: Am. Assn. Neurol. Surgeons (licentiate), Phi Beta Kappa. Avocation: computers. Office: 711 S Cowley Ste 210 Spokane WA 99202 Home Phone: 509-747-8519; Office Phone: 509-624-5351.

MACKAY, DAVID (A.D. DAVID MACKAY), food products executive; b. Hamilton, New Zealand, Aug. 16, 1955; m. Michelle Mackay; 2 children. B of Bus., Charles Stuart U., Australia, 1977. Group product mgr. Kellogg Australia, 1985—87; category dir. ready-to-eat cereals corp. hdqrs. Kellogg Co., Battle Creek, Mich., 1987—91; mng. dir. Sara Lee Bakery, Australia, 1992—98, Kellogg Australia, Battle Creek, 1998; mng. dir. U.K. and Republic of Ireland Kellogg Co., Battle Creek, 1998—2000; sr. v.p. Kellogg USA, Battle Creek, 2000, pres., 2000—03; exec. v.p. Kellogg Co., Battle Creek, Mich., 2000—03, pres., COO, 2003—06, pres., CEO, 2007—. Bd. dir. Kellogg Co., 2005—, Fortune Brands Inc., 2006—. Office: Kellogg PO Box 3599 1 Kellogg Sq Battle Creek MI 49016-3599 *

MACKAY, GREGORY JAMES, plastic surgeon; BA, Vanderbilt U., Nashville; MD, Med. U. SC, Charleston, 1987. Cert. Am. Bd. Plastic Surgery, 1998. Intern surgery Emory U., Atlanta, 1987, resident plastic surgery, 1988—93, resident craniofacial surgery, 1993—95, asst. prof., 1999—2002; fellow U. Pa., Phila., 1995—96; asst. prof. plastic surgery Mayo Clinic Grad. Sch. Medicine, 1999—2000; staff mem. Egleston Children's Hosp., Atlanta, 2000, staff mem. plastic surgery, 2003; staff mem. Scottish Rite Children's Hosp., Atlanta, 2000, 2003, Piedmont Hosp., Ga., 2003, Northside Hosp., Ga., 2003. Contbr. articles to med. jours., chapters to books; featured: magazines Atlanta Style & Design, Jezebel. Office: 5673 Peachtree Dunwoody Rd Ste 870 Atlanta GA 30342

MACKAY, HAROLD HUGH, lawyer; b. Regina, Sask., Can., Aug. 1, 1940; s. John Royden and Grace Madeliene (Irwin) MacK.; m. Jean Elizabeth Hutchison, Dec. 27, 1963; children: Carol, Donald. BA, U. Sask., 1960; LLB, Dalhousie U., Halifax, NS, 1963; LLD (hon.), U. Regina, 2002. Bar: Sask. 1964, Queen's Counsel 1981. Assoc. MacPherson Leslie & Tyerman LLP, Regina, 1963-69, ptnr., 1969—2004, mng. ptnr., 1989-96, chmn., 1997—2003, of counsel, 2005—. Bd. dirs. Mosaic Co., Toronto-Dominion Bank; chmn. task force Future of the Can. Fin. Svcs. Sector, 1997-98; Clifford Clark vis. economist Dept. of Fin., Govt. of Can., 2002-04; non-exec. chmn. bd. Domtar Corp. Recipient Officer Order of Can., 2002. Mem. Internat. Bar Assn., Can. Bar Assn., Law Soc. Sask. Mem. United Ch. Office: 1500 1874 Scarth St Regina SK Canada S4P 4E9 Home Phone: 306-586-4089; Office Phone: 306-347-8417.

MACKAY, LEO SIDNEY, JR., healthcare company executive, former federal agency administrator; b. San Antonio, Tex., Aug. 15, 1961; s. Leo Sidney Sr. and Barbara Jean (Hodge) MacK.; m. Heather Lee Deebel, Jan. 9, 1993; children: Sarah Bley, Josiah Edward Earl. BS, U.S. Naval Acad., 1983; M Pub. Policy, J.F. Kennedy Sch. Govt., 1991; PhD, Harvard U., 1993. Commd. ensign USN, 1983, advanced through grades to lt. comdr., 1993; flight student Naval Aviation Tng. Comd., Pensacola, Fla., 1983-85; F-14 fighter pilot U.S. Navy, Virginia Beach, Va., 1985-89; grad./doctoral student Harvard U., Cambridge, Mass., 1989-92; instr. history dept. U.S. Naval Acad., Annapolis, Md., 1992-93; mil. asst. to sec. US Dept. Def., Washington, 1993-95; dir. market devel. Lockheed Martin Corp., Bethesda, Md., 1995-97; v.p. bus. devel. and strategic planning Bell Helicopter Textron, Inc., Ft. Worth, 1997—2001; dep. sec. U.S. Dept. Vets Affairs, Washington, 2001—03; COO, ACS State Healthcare Solutions Affiliated Computer Services, Inc., Atlanta, 2003—. Chair Advisory Com. on Minority Health US Dept. Health & Human Services, 2005—. Contbr. articles to profl. jours.; article reviewer Internat. Security Jour., Cambridge, Mass., 1991-94. Pres. congregation St. Martin's Luth. Ch., Annapolis, 1996-97. Kennedy fellow J.F. Kennedy Sch. Govt., Cambridge, 1989-90, guest fellow Brookings Inst., Washington, 1992-93, Internat. Affairs fellow Coun. Fgn. Rels., N.Y.C., 1995-96; MacArthur scholar MacArthur Found.,

Cambridge, 1991-92. Mem. Internat. Inst. Strategic Studies, U.S. Naval Inst., Coun. Fgn. Rels., Arlington C. of C. (bd. dirs.), U.S. Naval Acad. Alumni Assn. (nat. trustee 1995-98), Army and Navy Club. Republican. Lutheran. Avocations: reading, golf.

MACKAY, MALCOLM, executive search consultant; b. Bklyn., Nov. 6, 1940; s. John F. and Helen (Pflug) MacK.; children: Robert Livingston, Hope Winthrop. AB cum laude, Princeton U., 1963; JD, Harvard U., 1966. Bar: N.Y. 1967. Assoc. Milbank, Tweed, Hadley and McCloy, NYC, 1966-69; dep. supt. N.Y. State Ins. Dept., NYC, 1969-71, 1st dep. supt., 1971-73; vice chancellor L.I. U., Greenvale, N.Y., 1973-75; sr. v.p. Blue Cross & Blue Shield of Greater New York, 1975-77, N.Y. Life Ins. Co., NYC, 1977-89; mng. dir. Russell Reynolds Assocs., NYC, 1989—. Bd. dirs. Empire Fidelity Investments Life Ins. Co. Trustee Independence Found. Mem. Century Assn., Piping Rock Club. Home: 184 Columbia Heights Brooklyn NY 11201 Office: Russell Reynolds Assocs 200 Park Ave New York NY 10166-0005 Home Phone: 718-855-0204; Office Phone: 212-351-2140. Business E-Mail: mmackay@russellreynolds.com.

MACKAY, NEIL DUNCAN, plastics company executive, consultant; b. Chelsea, Mass., Nov. 5, 1931; s. Allan Foster and Helen May (Smith) MacKay; m. Marcia Ann McCarthy, Aug. 22, 1953 (dec. 1979); children: Duncan, Jerry, Alan, Neil, Bonnie; m. Beverly J. Burke, May 31, 1991. BSBA, Northeastern U., Boston, 1954. Gen. mgr. Plastic Molding Corp., Newtown, Conn., 1954-67; market specialist Chem. div. Uniroyal, NYC, 1967-70; project mgr. Colt Ind. Korean Project, NYC, 1970-76; pres. Automatic Injection Molding Corp., Berkeley Heights, NJ, 1976-87, Diamond Mgmt. Cons., Inc., Winchester, NH, 1988—. Bd. dir. Frazier & Son, Inc., Lor-Tech Plastics, Inc. Author: Korean Plastics, 1973. Mem. Rep. Nat. Com., Washington, 1986—92. Recipient Outstanding Performance award, Ministry Nat. Def. Republic of Korea, 1974. Mem.: Plastic Pioneers Assn., Soc. Plastics Engrs. (sec. 1963—70, treas. 1983—86), Am. Profl. Capt.'s Assn., Scottish-Am. Cultural Soc., Am. Yacht Club, Stuyvesant Yacht Club, St. Andrews Soc. N.Y. Republican. Presbyterian. Avocation: sailing. Home: 19 Lovely Ln Winchester NH 03470-2916

MACKAY, RAYMOND ARTHUR, chemist; b. NYC, Oct. 30, 1939; s. Theodore Henry and Helen Marie (Cusack) M.; m. Mary Dilberian, Aug. 13, 1966; 1 child, Chelsea Christine; children by previous marriage: Brett, Edward. BS in Chemistry, Rensselaer Poly. Inst., 1961; PhD in Chemistry, SUNY-Stony Brook, 1966. Rsch. assoc. Brookhaven Nat. Lab., Upton, NY, 1966-67; prof. Drexel U., Phila., 1969-83; chief chem. div. Chem. Research and Devel. Ctr., Aberdeen Proving Ground, Md., 1983-91; prof. chemistry, dir. ctr. advanced materials processing Clarkson U., Potsdam, NY, 1991—99, on leave as dir. Rsch. and Tech., US Army Edgewood Chem. Biol. Ctr., 199-2003; dir., mem. sr. exec. sci US Army, 2003-. Contbr. articles to profl. jours. Served to capt. US Army, 1967-69. Grantee U.S. Army, Dept. Energy, Army Rsch. Office, NSF, Acad. Applied Scis., 1972-83, 95—, NATO, 1982-86, NYSSTF, 1991—. Mem. Am. Chem. Soc., Internat. Assn. Colloid and Interface Scientists (past. pres.), Sigma Xi. Office: US Army Chemical Biological Ctr Aberdeen Providing Ground Aberdeen Proving Ground MD 21010 Home Phone: 410-876-0767; Office Phone: 410-436-3250. Business E-Mail: raymond.mackay@us.army.mil.

MACKAY, WILLIAM ANDREW, judge; b. Halifax, NS, Can., Mar. 20, 1929; s. Robert Alexander and Mary Kathleen (Junkin) MacK.; m. Alexa Eaton Wright, July 7, 1954; 1 dau., Margaret Kathleen. BA, Dalhousie U., 1950, LLB, 1953, LLM, 1954, Harvard U., 1970; LLD (hon.), Meml. U. Nfld.; LLD, St Francis Xavier U., NS, Dalhousie U. Bar: N.S.; Named queen's counsel. Fgn. service officer Dept. External Affairs, Ottawa, Ont., Canada, 1954-57; asst. sec. Royal Com., Ottawa, 1955-57; sucessively asst. prof., assoc. prof., prof. law, dean Faculty of law Dalhousie U. (Halifax), N.S., Canada, 1957-69, v.p. N.S., 1969-80, pres., vice-chancellor N.S., 1980-86; ombudsman N.S., Canada, 1986-88; judge trial divsn. Fed. Ct. Can., Ottawa, 1988—2004, dep. judge trial divsn., 2004—. Chmn. Assn. Atlantic Univs., Halifax, 1981-83; v.p. Assn. Univs. and Colls. Can., 1982-83, pres., 1983-85; pres. Conf. Gov. Bodies Legal Profession Can., 1968-69, Assn. Can. Law Tchrs., 1964-65 Chmn. N.S. Human Rights Com., Halifax, 1967-86; chmn. N.S. Commns. on Salary and Allowances of Elected Provincial Ofcls., 1974, 78, 81, 83, 84, 85; chmn. N.S. Task Force on AIDS, 1987-88. Mem. Can. Bar Assn. Home: 601 6369 Coburg Rd Halifax NS Canada B3H 4J7 Office: Fed Ct Ottawa ON Canada K1A 0H9 E-mail: andrewmackay@earthlink.ca.

MACKEN, DANIEL LOOS, cardiologist, educator; b. Rochester, NY, May 7, 1933; s. Daniel Edward and Mary Frances (Loos) Macken; m. Maria Luisa Medina de Palma, Nov. 16, 1979; children: Daniel Edward, Mary Frances Loos. BA, Holy Cross Coll., Worcester, Mass., 1955; post grad., Yale U., 1956-57; MD, U. Mass, Boston, 1960. Diplomate Am. Bd. Cardiovascular Disease. Resident Roosevelt and Columbia-Presbyn. Hosp., NYC, 1960—63; fellow Am. Heart Assn., 1964—65; dir. coronary care unit Walter Reed Gen. Hosp., Washington, 1968; staff rsch. physician Walter Reed Army Inst. Rsch., Washington, 1970; instr. Columbia U., NYC, 1966—78. Vis. lectr. U. Saigon, Vietnam, 1969; pres. Medica Found., Inc., NYC, 1971—; bd. dirs. Medica Endowment Fund. Contbr. chapters to books, articles to profl. jours.; student editor: Jour. History Medicine and Allied Scis., 1956—57. Lt. col. M.C. US Army, 1967—70, Vietnam. Decorated Bronze Star, Vietnam Cross. Fellow: N.Y. Acade. Medicine, Royal Soc. Medicine, Am. Coll. Cardiology, Harvey Soc.; mem.: AMA, Am. Heart Assn., Assn. Mil. Surgeons U.S., Met. Gov. Island Officers Club. Roman Catholic. Office: Columbia-Presbyn Med Ctr 161 Ft Washington Ave New York NY 10032-3713 Office Phone: 212-751-4343.

MACKENZIE, CHARLES SHERRARD, academic administrator; b. Quincy, Mass., Aug. 21, 1924; s. Charles Sherrard and Dorothy MacKenzie; m. Florence Evelyn Phelps Meyer, Aug. 28, 1964 (dec. 1981); 1 child, Robert Walter Meyer; m. Lavonne Rudolph Gaiser, Mar. 30, 1985. Student, Boston U., 1942-43; BA, Gordon Coll., 1946; M.Div., Princeton Theol. Sem., 1949, ThD, 1955, PhD, 1957; LHD, Grove City Coll., 1997; postgrad., U. Paris, 1953. Ordained to ministry Congl. Christian Ch., 1949. Pastor Carversville (Pa.) Christian Ch., 1948-51; fellow faculty Princeton Theol. Sem., 1949-51, 53-54, Princeton U., 1954-64; pastor First Presbyn. Ch., Avenel, NJ, 1954-64, Broadway Presbyn. Ch., Columbia U., NYC, 1964-67, First Presbyn. Ch., Stanford U., San Mateo, Calif., 1967-71; pres. Grove City (Pa.) Coll., 1971-91, chancellor, 1991-92; advisor to pres., prof. philosphy Reformed Seminary, Orlando, Fla., 1992—; sr. min. Eastminster Presbyn. Ch., Wichita, Kans., 1993. Bd. dirs. Covenant Life Ins. Co., C.S. Lewis Inst.; cons. Oxford Project, 1992—, Provident Mutual Ins. Co.; lectr. Oxford U., 1965, U. Hamburg, 1968, Columbia U., 1964-67, Stanford U., 1967-71, U. Pitts., 1990-93; adv. Provident Mutual Ins. Co. Author: The Anguish and Joy of Pascal, 1973, Freedom, Equality, Justice, 1980, The Trinity and Culture, 1985. Bd. dirs. Knox Fellowship, Frontline, Orlando; mem. Human Relations Commn., San Mateo, 1968-70; mem. Indsl. Devel. Council, Grove City, 1972-75. Served with USAF, 1951-53. Mem. Presbyn. Coll. Union, Am. Assn. Pres.'s Ind. Colls. and Univs. (dir., pres.), Nat. Assn. Ind. Colls. and Univs. (mem. secretariat 1985-91), Freedoms Found. (nat. jury), Soc. Christian Philosphers, Duquesne Club (Pitts.), Univ. Club Boston, Citrus Club (Orlando), Evangelical initiative Notre Dame U., Rockford Inst. Main St. com. (De Toqueville award 1998). Republican. Address: 1231 Reformation Dr Oviedo FL 32765-7197

MACKENZIE, DONALD MURRAY, health facility administrator; b. Toronto, Ont., Can., June 5, 1947; s. Donald Alexander and June Cameron MacKenzie; m. Marilyn Adele McNaughton, Jan. 3, 1970; children: Jennifer, Katherine, Kenneth. BA in Econs., U. Toronto, 1968, MA in Polit. Sci., 1970, D Health Adminstr., 1974. Exec. asst. Mt. Sinai Hosp., Toronto, 1974-76, successively asst. exec. dir., assoc. exec. dir., v.p., 1974-89; pres. North York Gen. Hosp., Toronto, 1989—2002; asst. prof. U. Toronto, 1989—; internat. healthcare cons., 2002—. Chair Cardiac Care Network Ont., 2001-2002; founding dir. OH Africa, bd. dirs. Neuchâtel Jr. Coll., The Seeing Eye; trustee R. Alan Hay Awards. Editor: History of Canadian Hospitals, 1972; contbr. articles to profl. jours. Bd. dirs. Cancer Care Ont., 1989-99. Mem. Can. Coll. Health Svc. Execs. (cert., various coms.), Can. Cancer Soc. (hon. life, pres. Ont. div. 1989-91, award of merit 1988), Ont. Hosp. Assn. (chmn. 1999-2000), York Club. Anglican. Avocations: golf, tennis, canoe tripping. Personal E-mail: mmackenzie55@hotmail.com.

MACKENZIE, GEORGE ALLAN, medical products executive; s. George Adam and Annette Louise MacKenzie; m. Valerie Ann Marchand, June 30, 1971; children from previous marriage: Richard Michael, Barbara Wynne. Student, Jamaica Coll., Kingston, 1944-48. Commd. flying officer Canadian Air Force, 1951, advanced through grades to lt. gen., 1978; comdr. Canadian Forces Air Command, Winnipeg, Man., 1978-80, resigned, 1980; exec. v.p., COO Gendis Inc., 1980-89, pres., COO, 1989-99, pres., CEO, 1999—2002; bd. dirs. Sony of Can. Ltd., Willowdale, Ont., Canada; pres., CEO CANUSA MedExpress Ltd., 2003—. Mem. regional adv. bd. Carleton U. Decorated comdr. Order of Mil. Merit, Order St. Johns, Can. Decoration, Knight of St. Lazarus of Jerusalem. Mem. United Services Inst. Can. (hon. v.p.), Can. Corps Commissionaires (gov.), Police Chiefs Rsch. Found. (co-chmn.), Manitoba Club, Royal Mil. Inst. Manitoba. Home: 383 Christie Rd Winnipeg MB Canada R2N 4A5 Personal E-mail: gallanmac@hotmail.com.

MACKENZIE, JOHN, retired oil industry executive; b. 1919; BS, N.Y. U., 1948. Accountant S.Am. Devel. Co., NYC, 1938-41; financial comptroller French Oil Ind. Agy.-Groupment D'Achat des Carburants, N.Y., 1946-53; v.p., treas. George Hall Corp., 1954-56; asst. treas. Am. Petrofina, Inc., 1956-61, sec., 1961-64, v.p., sec., 1964-68, sr. v.p., sec., 1968-84; ret., 1984. Decorated comdr. Order of Crown (Belgium) Address: 3861 Frio Way Frisco TX 75034-8469

MACKENZIE, LEWIS WHARTON, military officer; b. Truro, NS, Can., Apr. 30, 1940; s. Eugene Murdock and Shirley Helena (Wharton) MacK.; m. Dora Rosalie McKinnon; 1 child, Kimm Katheryn. Student, NATO Def. Coll., Rome, 1977; BA in Polit. Sci., U. Man., Winnipeg, Can., 1988; PhD (hon.), St. Francis Xavier U., 1993; LLB (hon.), St. Mary's U., 1993, Acadia U., 1993, U. Calgary, 2000. Commd. 2d lt. Can. Armed Forces, 1960, advanced through grades to major gen., 1992; teamsite comdr. Internat. Commn. Control and Supervision, Vietnam, 1972; co. comdr. UN Emergency Peace Keeping Force, Cairo, 1973; exec. asst. to comdr. Can. Forces Europe, Lahr, Fed. Republic Germany, 1974-77; comdr. Nicosia dist. UN Peacekeeping Force, Cyprus, 1978; commdg. officer 1st bn. Princess Patricia's Can. Light Infantry, Calgary, 1977-79; faculty mem. Can. Forces Staff Coll., Toronto, 1979-82; dep. chief staff for tng. Can. Army, Montreal, 1983-85; dir. pers. careers officers Can. Armed Forces, Ottawa, 1985-87; dir. Combat Related Employment of Women, Ottawa, 1987-88; comdr. combat tng. ctr. Can. Armed Forces, Gagetown Can. Forces Base, N.B., 1988-1990; pres. MGen MacKenzie Enterprises Inc., MGen MacKenzie Comms. Inc., 1993—. Comdr. UN Peacekeeping Force, Ctrl. Am., 1990-91, chief of staff Unprotection force, Yugoslavia, 1992, comdr. UN forces to open Sarajevo airport for humanitarian relief, 1992; host TV documentary A Soldier's Peace; bd. dirs. Magnifoam Internat., MEDEMERG Inc., Crowflight Minerals Inc., Eurocontrol Technics, Inc.; chmn. bd. adv. Athlone Globel Security Inc. Author: Peacekeeper, Road to Sarajevo, 1993. Bd. advisors Can. Fedn. for AIDS Rsch.; patron Saving Our Mil. Heritage, The Normandy Project, Internat. Comty. for Relief of Starvation and Suffering, Can., St. Anne's Vet.'s Hosp. Found., Tony Stacey Ctr.; bd. dirs. Last Post Fund, Vet.'s Rideln, Juno Beach Centre Assn. Decorated Meritorious Svc. Cross (2) (Can.); invested Order of Ont., 2002, Order of Can., 2007, Serving Brother Order of St. John, 1993; recipient Birks gold medal Xavier Jr. Coll., Sydney, N.S., Can., 1960, Vimy award, 1993, medal of honour UN Assn., 1994, World Peace award, 1993; named Canadian of Yr., Tourism Industry Assn. of Can., 1992; Internat. fellow U.S. Army War Coll., 1982-83; Nat. Sports Car champion, 1981; Nat. Formula Ford B Class champion, 1995-96; named to McLean's Honor Roll., 1993. Avocation: motor racing. Home and Office: RR2 Carp 2379 Upper Dwyer Hill Rd Ontario Canada K0A 1L0 Office Phone: 613-256-1151. Business E-Mail: lewmac@ntl.sympatico.ca.

MACKENZIE, NANCI, gas company executive; m. Len Mackenzie, 1988. Co-founder (with Sue Palmer) Lucky Lady Oil Co., 1976—82; founder, pres. USGT/Aquila (formerly U.S. Gas Transp. before sale to Aquila), Dallas, 1986—2001; pres. Aquila Dallas Marketing LP. Recipient Entrepreneur of the Yr, 1998. Mem.: Nat. Assn. Women's Bus. Owners, Am. Gas Assn. Office: Aquila Inc 20 W Ninth St Kansas City MO 64105

MACKENZIE, RONALD ALEXANDER, anesthesiologist; b. Detroit, Mar. 31, 1938; s. James and Elizabeth Mackenzie; m. Nancy Lee Vogan, Aug. 25, 1962; children: Margaret, James. BS, Alma Coll., 1961; DO, Kansas City Coll., 1967. Diplomate Am. Bd. Anesthesiology. Resident in anesthesiology Detroit Osteo. Hosp., 1970-72, Cleve. Clinic, 1972-73, Mayo Clinic, Rochester, Minn., 1973-74, cons. in anesthesia, 1974—87, vice-chmn. anesthesiology, 1988—99, chmn. GYN/ENT anesthesia, 1998—99; pres. ceo Am. Soc. Anesthesiologists. Vice-chmn. dept. anesthesiology Mayo Clinic, 1988-98. Pres. Minn. Orch., Rochester, 1987-89. Fellow Am. Coll. Anesthesiologists; mem. Am. Soc. Anesthesiologists (bd. dirs. 1983-87, sec. 1991-97, 1st v.p. 1998, pres.-elect 1999), Sigma Xi. Avocations: sailing, photography. Office: Mayo Clinic 200 1st St SW Rochester MN 55905-0002

MACKERODT, FRED, public relations specialist; b. Bklyn., Sept. 17, 1938; s. Leroy and Margaret (Murphy) M.; m. Christy Woods, June 7, 1987. Student, NYU, 1958-59. Freelance writer, photographer, NYC and Barcelona, Spain, 1968-73; editor Cars Mag., Popular Publs. Inc., NYC, 1973-76; pres. Fred Mackerodt. Inc. (pub. relations and publicity), NYC, 1976—, Stone House Farm, Inc., 2001—. Contbg. editor Popular Mechanics, 1987—; contbr. articles to popular mags. Spl. dep. sheriff Indian River County, Fla., 1994—2001. Mem. Aviation and Space Writers Am., Internat. Motor Press Assn., Publicity Club N.Y., Wings Club, N.Y. Zool. Soc. (aquarium field assoc. 1971—) Home: 940 Craigville Rd Chester NY 10918 Address: Apt 612 205 W 86th St New York NY 10024-3362 E-mail: fmackerodt@fredmackerodt.com.

MACKERRAS, SIR CHARLES (ALAN MACLAURIN), conductor; b. Schenectady, NY, Nov. 17, 1925; s. Alan Patrick and Catherine Mackerras; m. Helena Judith Wilkins, 1947; 2 children. Student, Sydney Conservatorium Music, Australia, 1938-42; student with Vaclav Talich, Prague Acad. Music, 1947-48; DMus (hon.), U. Hull, 1990, U. Nottingham, 1991, U. Brno, Czech Republic, 1994, York U., Eng., 1994, Griffith U., Brisbane, Australia, 1994, Oxford U., Eng., 1997, Prague Acad. Music, 1999, Napier U., Scotland, 2000, U. Sydney, 2003, U. Melbourne, 2003, Janácek Acad. Music, Brno, 2004, U. London, 2005. Prin. oboist Sydney (Australia) Symphony Orch., 1943-46; staff condr. English Nat. Opera (formerly Sadler's Wells Opera), London, 1948-54, musical dir., 1970-77; prin. condr. BBC Concert Orch., 1954-56; first condr. Hamburg Opera, 1966-69; chief guest condr. BBC Symphony Orch., 1976-79; chief condr. Sydney Symphony Orch., Australian Broadcasting Commn., 1982-85; prin. guest condr. Royal Liverpool Philharm. Orch., 1986-88, Scottish Chamber Orch., 1992-95, condr. laureate, 1995—; music dir. Orch. of St. Luke's, 1998-2001, music dir. emeritus, 2001—; pres. Trinity Coll. Music, London, 2000. Freelance condr. with most Brit. and many continental orchs.,c oncert tours, Russia, South Africa, N. Am., Australia, 1957—66, U.S. coast-to-coast, 1983; prin. guest condr. San Francisco Opera, 1993—96, prin. guest condr. emeritus, 1996—; prin. guest condr. Royal Philharm. Orch., 1993—96, Czech Philharm. Orch., 1997—2003, Philharmonia Orch., 2002—; mus. dir. Welsh Nat. Opera, 1987—92, condr. emeritus, 1993—; appearances at internat. festivals and opera houses, frequent radio and TV broadcasts; condr. comml. recordings, notably Handel, Mozart operas and symphonies, Janáček, Brahms, Beethoven, Dvořák, Mahler and Schubert. Published ballet arrangements Pineapple Poll (Sullivan), Lady and the Fool (Verdi), reconstrn. Sullivan's Lost Cello Concerto, contbr. appendices to book Charles Mackerras: A Musicians' Musician, by Nancy Phelan, articles to Opera Mag., other jours. Decorated comdr. Order of Brit. Empire, Knight Bachelor, medal of merit Czech Republic, Companion Order of Australia, Companion of Honor; named Australian of Yr. in the UK, 2007; recipient Evening Std. award for opera, 1977, Janacek medal, 1978, Gramophone Record of Yr. award, 1977, 1980, 1999, Grammy award for best opera recording, 1981, Gramophone Best Opera Recording award, 1983, 1984, 1994, 1999, prix, Fondation Jacques Ibert, 1983, Record of Yr. award, Stereo Rev., 1983, Chocs de l'Annèe award, 1998, Edison award, Preis der Deutschen Schallplattenkritik, Prix Caecilia, 1999, Conducting award, Royal Philharm. Soc., 1999, Chopin prize and lifetime achievement award, Cannes Classical awards at Midem, 2000, award, Assn. Brit. Orchs., 2001, Disting. Musician award, Inc. Soc. Musicians, 2002, Gold medal, Royal Philharmonic Soc., 2005, Listeners' award, BBC Radio 3, 2005, 1st recipient Queen's medal for music, 2005, Classic FM Gramophone Lifetime Achievement award, 2006; hon. fellow, Royal Acad. Music, 1969, Royal Coll. Music, 1997, Royal No. Coll. Music, 1999, St. Peter's Coll., Oxford, 1999, Cardiff U., 2003, Royal Welsh Coll. Music and Drama, 2005. Office: Askonas Holt Ltd Lonsdale Chambers 27 Chancery Ln London WC2A 1PF England Office Phone: 44 0207 400 1710.

MACKESEY, DANIEL R., lawyer; b. Ithaca, NY, July 14, 1954; m. Jennifer Mackesey; 2 children. BA in Anthropology cum laude, Cornell U., 1977; JD, U. Va. Sch. Law, 1980. Bar: DC 1980, Va. 1980, admitted to practice: All Va. State Cts. Assoc. David & Hagner, 1982—85; v.p., sr. counsel Artery Organization, Inc., 1985—88, sr. v.p., gen. counsel, 1988—92; counsel Piper & Marbury, Washington, 1992—96; founding ptnr. Jefferson Law Firm, PLC, McLean, Va., 1996—2001; mng. mem. Womble Carlyle Sandridge & Rice PLLC, Tyson Corner, Va., 2001—, mem. firm mgmt. com. (ex-officio), chair firm. leadership com., mem. recruiting com., mem. professionalism com. Recipient NCAA Top Five award. Mem.: Va. State Bar (mem. real property sect., mem. corp. counsel sect.), ABA (mem. law practice mgmt. sect.). Office: Womble Carlyle Sandridge & Rice PLLC 8065 Leesburg Pike 4th Fl Vienna VA 22182-2738 Office Phone: 703-790-4682. Office Fax: 703-918-2242. Business E-Mail: dmackesey@wcsr.com.

MACKEY, JEFFREY ALLEN, priest; b. Kingston, NY, July 12, 1952; s. Allen William and Vivian Mathilda (Hornbeck) M.; m. Martha LaVonne Webster, Dec. 18, 1971; children: Guy Linwood, Kenyon Paul, Geoffrey Joel. BS, Nyack Coll., 1974; D of Sacred Lit., Ridgedale Theol. Sem., 1975; MDiv, Macon Baptist Sem., Ga., 1976; D Ministry, Mansfield Div., 1985, Grad. Theol. Found., 1990; cert. of theol. studies, Gen. Theol. Sem., 1993; postgrad., Grad. Theol. Found., 1991—, U. of the South; DHL, St. Paul Theol. Sem., 2000; DLitt, Evangel U., 2003; DD, Grad. Theol. Found., 2005. Ordained to ministry Congl. Christian Ch., 1974; ordained priest Episcopal Ch., 1993. Min. music Neversink Valley Bapt. Ch., Huguenot, NY, 1969-70; pastor Ponckhockie Congl. Ch., Kingston, 1971-74, The Alliance Ch., Andover, 1974-76; acad. dean Macon (Ga.) Bible Inst., 1976-78; min. Oak Grove Gospel Tabernacle, Williamsport, Pa., 1977-80, 69th St. Alliance Ch., Phila., 1980-83; sr. min. Vestavia Alliance Ch., Birmingham, Ala., 1983-87, Hope Alliance Ch., New Hartford, NY, 1987-91; assoc. rector Grace Ch., Utica, NY, 1991-96, vicar Waterville, NY, 1995-96; rector Trinity Episcopal Ch., DeRidder, La., 1996-97; vicar Polk Meml. Episcopal Ch., Leesville, La., 1996-97; rector St. Mark the Evangelist Ch., North Bellmore, NY, 1997-99; registrar/Bible faculty Nyack Coll., Manhattan Campus, NYC, 1999-2000, assoc. dean for acad. affairs, 2000-2001, acad. dean, 2001—03, asst. v.p., dean Coll. Arts and Scis., 2003—05; v.p., acad. dean Trinity Sch. Ministry, 2005—07; interim rector St. Mark's Episcopal Ch., Orchard Park, NY, 2007—. Adj. prof. Cranmer Theol. Ho., Shreveport, La., 1997, Nyack Coll., 1998—99; asst. priest St. John's Episcopal Ch., Kingston, NY, 2000—02; interim rector St. John's Ch., Kingston, 2002—03, St. Gregory's, Woodstock, NY, 2003—04. Author: A Worship Manifesto, 1986, Indicatives and Imperatives, 1987, Christ's Centripetal Cross, 1990; co-author: Where Love and People Are, 1990, Prophet of Justice, Prophet of Life: Essays on William Stringfellow, 1997, A Diary of Three Decades: Grace Church, Utica, N.Y., 1963-96, 1999, And Jesus Everything: Conversations with A.B. Simpson, 2000, A Heart for the Future, 2004, Hidden Mirth, 2005; contbr. numerous articles to profl. jours. Mem. Alcohol and Drug Abuse Prevention Treatment Program, Birmingham, 1987—88; chaplain N. Bellmore Vol. Fire Dept., 1998—99; trustee Cathedral of St. John the Divine, NYC, 2002—. Mem. Fellowship Christian Sch. Adminstrs., Evang. Theol. Soc., Am. Assn. Sch. Adminstrs., Am. Guild Organists, Anglican Assn. of Biblical Scholars, Order of Preachers (Anglican), Inst. for Advanced Theology, Soc. Biblical Lit. Avocations: piano, collecting art and statues, hymn writing, walking, auto restoration. Personal E-mail: parsonsmanor@msn.com.

MACKEY, JOHN P., food products executive; s. Bill and Margaret Mackey; m. Deborah Morin. Student, Trinity Coll., San Antonio, Tex., U. of Texas, Austin. Owner Safer Way Natural Foods, Austin, 1978—80; co-founder, chmn., CEO Whole Foods Market Inc., Austin, 1980—, pres., 2001—04. Named Overall Nat. Entrepreneur of Yr., Ernst & Young, 2003. Achievements include hiking entire Applachian Trail (2168 miles), 2002. Avocations: yoga, meditation, scuba diving. Office: Whole Foods Market Inc 550 Bowie St Austin TX 78703-4677 *

MACKEY, NATHANIEL, poet and poetry professor; Author: (books of poetry) Four for Trane, 1978, Septet for the End of Time, 1983, Eroding Witness: Urbana and Chicago, 1985, School of Udhra, 1993, Song of the Andoumboulou: 18-20, 1994, Whatsaid Serif, 1998, Splay Anthem, 2006. *

MACKEY, PAMELA ROBILLARD, lawyer; b. Harlingen, Tex., July 16, 1956; d. Gregory Leo and Rosanne Elizabeth (Niland) Robillard; m. Craig W. Mackey, Dec. 30, 1983. BS in Journalism with honors, U. Colo., Boulder, 1981; JD with highest honors, George Washington U., 1985. Bar: Colo. 1985, US Dist. Ct. (dist. Colo.) 1985. Assoc. Davis, Graham & Stubbs, Denver, 1985-87, Haddon, Morgan & Foreman, P.C., Denver, 1987—89; dep. state pub. defender Office of State Pub. Defender, Colo., 1989—94; shareholder Haddon, Morgan, Mueller, Jordan, Mackey & Foreman, P.C., Denver, 1994—. Exec. editor George Wash. Law Rev., 1984-85. Fellow ABA; mem. Colo. Bar Assn., Denver Bar Assn. (mem. conciliation panel), Colo. Women's Bar Assn. (bd. dirs. 1986-90, 94-95; pres. 1995-96), Colo. Criminal Def. Bar (newsletter editor 1988), NACDL. Democrat. Roman Catholic. Avocations: skiing, golf. Office: Haddon Morgan Mueller Jordan Mackey & Foreman PC 150 E Tenth Ave Denver CO 80203 Office Phone: 303-831-7364. E-mail: pmackey@hmflaw.com.

MACKEY, PATRICIA ELAINE, university librarian; b. Balt., July 29, 1941; d. Timothy and Hazel Mozelle (Davis) M. BA in Anthropology, CUNY, 1978; MLS, Columbia U., 1981. Asst. libr. I, European Exch. Sys., Mainz-Kastel, Germany, 1966-68; interlibr. loan asst. Poly. U., Bklyn., 1968-72, Rockefeller U., NYC, 1972-73, sr. libr. asst., 1974-80, libr., 1981-91, univ. libr., 1991—. Mem. various libr. coms., N.Y.C., 1991—. Chair pub. svc. scholars program Hunter Coll. CUNY, 1992—; trustee Met. N.Y. Libr. Coun., 2000—, also 1st v.p. Named to, Hunter Coll. Hall of

Fame, 2002. Mem.: ALA, Assn. Coll. and Rsch. Librs., N.Y. State Libr. Assn., Hunter Coll. Alumni Assn. (bd. dirs. 1998—, 2d v.p. 1998—2002). Democrat. Roman Catholic. Avocations: reading, chess, gardening. Office: Rockefeller U Libr RU Box 263 1230 York Ave New York NY 10021-6307 Home Phone: 212-988-8359; Office Phone: 212-327-8909. Business E-Mail: rmackey@mail.rockefeller.edu.

MACKEY, THOMAS CLYDE, historian; b. Radford, Va., Aug. 17, 1956; s. Howard and Blanche M. BA, Beloit Coll., 1978; PhD, Rice U., 1984. Golieb postdoctoral fellow NYU Sch. Law, NYC, 1984-85; vis. asst. prof. Mich. State U., East Lansing, 1985-86; asst. prof. U. Nebr., Lincoln, 1986-88, Ea. Mont. Coll., Billings, 1988-89; vis. asst. prof. Kans. State U., Manhattan, 1989-90, asst. prof., 1990-91; asst. prof. history, adj. asst. prof. law U. Louisville, 1991-95, assoc. prof. history, adj. prof. law, 1995—. Author: Red Lights Out: A Legal History of Prostitution, Disorderly Houses and Vice Districts, 1870-1917, 1987, Pornography on Trial, 2002, Pursuing Johns: Criminal Law Reform, Defending Character and New York City Committee of Fourteen, 1920-1930, 2005. NEH travel grantee, 1992. Mem. Am. Soc. Legal History, Soc. Historians of the Gilded Age and Progressive Era (com. mem.), Orgn. Am. Historians, Am. Hist. Assn. Republican. Office: U Louisville Dept History Louisville KY 40292-0001 Home Phone: 502-891-1557; Office Phone: 502-852-3892. Business E-Mail: thomasmackey@louisville.edu.

MACKEY, WILLIAM ARTHUR GODFREY, analytical testing company executive; b. Glasgow, Scotland, Mar. 23, 1946; came to U.S., 1970; s. William Arthur and Joan Margaret (Sykes) M.; m. Bianca Ann Dell'Isola, June 9, 1973 (dec. Nov. 1993). BSc in Engring., U. London, 1968, MSc in Engring., 1970; MBA, Harvard U., 1972. Prodn. engr. Rolls-Royce PLC, Glasgow, 1969-70; securities analyst Tucker, Anthony & R.L. Day, Inc., Boston, 1972-74; sr. project engr. Fafnir Bearing divsn. Textron Inc., New Britain, Conn., 1974-76; mfg. contr. Loctite Corp., Newington, Conn., 1976-78, mgr. ops. and mktg. divisional, 1978-80, mgr. corp. productivity improvement, 1980-83; pres., CEO Signum Microsystems, Inc., Bloomfield, Conn., 1983-84, 91-97; worldwide product mgr. Otis Elevator Co., Farmington, Conn., 1985-87; pres., CEO Axiom Labs., Inc., Bloomfield, CT, 1998—. Sr. cons. Coopers & Lybrand, L.L.P., Hartford, Conn., 1988-91; bd. dirs. Axiom Labs., Inc., Bloomfield, Conn.; chmn., Assn. Promoting Edn. and Conservation in Amazonia, Inc., West Hartford, Conn., 1997—. Vice chmn. Conn. Com. Newcomen Soc. in U.S., Exton, Pa., 1980—; mem. Wadsworth Atheneum, Hartford, 1975—, coun., 1994—; mem. World Affairs Coun., Hartford, Conn., 1984—, bd. dirs., 1992-98; chief staff City of New Haven Blue Ribbon Commn., 1990; bd. dirs. West Hartford (Conn.) Taxpayers Assn., 1995—; vol. mem. classical music staff WWUH Radio. Rolls-Royce scholar, 1964-69, 70-72. Fellow Pres.'s Coll. U. Hartford; mem. ACLU, Alliance Francaise, Soc. Mfg. Engrs. (vice chmn. Hartford chpt. 1991-95, 98—, chmn. 1996, 97, Pres.'s award 1992, SME Conn. Day award, 1998), Conn. Bus. and Industry Assn., Greater Hartford C. of C., MIT Enterprise Forum Conn., Concord Coalition, Harvard Bus. Sch. Club No. Conn. (bd. dirs. 1991—), Imperial Coll. City Guilds Coll. Assn., St. Andrews Soc. Conn., U.S. Amateur Ballroom Dancers Assn., Royal Scottish Automobile Club (Glasgow), Masons, Mensa. Republican. Congregationalist. Avocations: economics and current affairs, modern chamber music, ballroom dancing, special-interest automobiles and motorcycles. Home: 61 Tunxis Rd West Hartford CT 06107-2948 E-mail: mackeyw@gmail.com.

MACKEY CATOE, MARGARET EMMIE, library media specialist; b. Lancaster, SC, Aug. 2, 1947; d. Furman Robert and Margaret Edna (Stogner) M; m. Samuel B. Catoe, Jan. 20, 2007. BA, Winthrop Coll., 1968, MEd, 1980; MAT, U. S.C., 1975. Tchr. English, social studies Alexander Graham Jr. H.S., Charlotte, NC, 1968—69; grad. tchg. asst. U. S.C., Columbia, 1969—71; tchr. English, chemistry Andrew Jackson H.S., Kershaw, SC, 1971—82; libr. media specialist Heath Springs Elem. Sch., SC, 1968—86, Andrew Jackson H.S., 1986—2006; ret., 2006. Mem. ALA, S.C. Assn. Sch. Librs. (treas. 1989-91), Lancaster County Librs. Assn. (pres. 1991-93), Libr. Media Specialist Network (pres. 1987-88), Assn. Sch. Librs., Young Adult Libr. Svcs. Assn. Presbyterian. Avocations: reading, computers, travel. Personal E-mail: mmackey@infoave.net.

MACK-HARVIN, DIONNE L., library director; b. SC, June 18, 1972; BA in History and African-Am., SUNY, Brockport; MA in Africana Studies, SUNY, Albany, 1995, MLS in Info. Sci., 1996. Libr. Queens Coll., NY, 1996; libr. Crown Heights Libr. Bklyn. Pub. Libr., NY, 1996, asst. branch libr. NY, branch mgr. NY, regional libr. NY, dir. Ctrl. Libr. NY, chief of staff NY, 2005—06, interim dir. NY, 2006—07, exec. dir., 2007—. Office: Bklyn Pub Libr Ctrl Libr Grand Army Plaza Brooklyn NY 11238 E-mail: d.mack@brooklynpubliclibrary.org. *

MACKICHAN, MARGARET ANNA, artist, art educator; b. Charleston, W.Va., Feb. 27, 1948; d. Kenneth Allen and Lois Alma (Deyton) MacK.; 1 child, Jemma Moccasin. BFA, U. Nebr., 1970; MA, U. N.Mex., 1974, MFA, 1977. Assoc. VISTA, Ky., 1966-67; photographer Ky., 1968—87, Rosebud (S.D.) Reservation, 1987-92; founding dir. Great Plains Art Inst., Sinte Gleska U., Rosebud Reservation, SD, 1987. Curatorial intern Internat. Mus. of Photography, George Eastman House, Rochester, N.Y., 1971-72; artist-in-community Western Nebr. Art Ctr., Scottsbluff, 1978-79; instr. Nebr. Western Coll., Scottsbluff, 1978-79; vis. prof. Nebr. Wesleyan U., Lincoln, 1980-87; participant Annual Plains Indian Seminar, 1987-98. Co-author: In the Kingdom of Grass, 1992. Recipient 1st prize photography Mademoiselle Mag., 1970, Vreeland award U. Nebr., 1970, Artist grant Nebr. Arts Coun./Nebr. Com. on Humanities, 1978, Artist fellowship Mid-Am. Arts Alliance, 1983, Outstanding Svc. in Art Edn. award S.D. Gov., 2003. Fellow Ctr. for Great Plains Study; mem. Soc. for Photographic Edn., Nat. Am. Art Studies Assn., Scottish Soc. Artists. Presbyterian. Avocations: walker horses, Lakota arts, Scottish dancing, banjo, bagpipes. Home: PO Box 6 Mission SD 57555-0006 Office: Sinte Gleska University PO Box 105 Mission SD 57555-0105

MACKIE, LANDON KELLER, lawyer; BBA in Fin., Tex. Tech U., 1991; JD, Mass. Sch. Law, 1995. Bar: Mass. 1995, Tex. 1999. Assoc. Barrett, Burke, Wilson, Castle, Daffin & Frappier, L.L.P., Addison, Tex. Named a Rising Star, Tex. Super Lawyers mag., 2006. Office: Barrett Burke Wilson Castle Daffin & Frappier LLP 15000 Surveyor Blvd Ste 100 Addison TX 75001 Office Phone: 972-386-5040. E-mail: kellerm@bbwcdf.com. *

MACKIN, CHARLES PHILIP, JR., lawyer; b. Boston, Dec. 13, 1947; s. Charles Philip and Mary Patricia (Sparkes) M.; m. Deborah Ann Huey, Oct. 18, 1980; children: Emily K., Claire E.S. BA, St. Anselm Coll., 1969; JD, Loyola U., New Orleans, 1972; MGA, U. Pa., 1987; grad., U.S. Army War Coll., 1990. Bar: Pa. 1972, U.S. Ct. Mil. Appeals 1973, U.S. Ct. Appeals (D.C. cir.) 1977, U.S. Supreme Ct. 1977, U.S. Ct. Appeals (3rd cir.) 1985. Asst. dist. atty., Coudersport, Pa., 1978-81; sr. dep. atty. gen. Office of Atty. Gen. of Pa., Harrisburg, 1982-86, chief dep. atty. gen., 1986-89; dep. chief counsel for investigations Dept. Auditor Gen. of Pa., Harrisburg, 1989-91, dep. auditor gen., 1991-96. Capt. USMC, 1972-77. Mem. Pa. Bar Assn., Army Navy Club (Washington). Office: 3400 Trindle Rd Camp Hill PA 17011 Office Phone: 717-214-3700.

MACKINNEY, ARCHIE ALLEN, physician; b. St. Paul, Aug. 16, 1929; s. Archie Allen and Doris (Hoops) MacK.; m. Shirley Schaefer, Apr. 9, 1955; children— Julianne, Theodore, John. BA, Wheaton Coll., Ill., 1951; MD, U. Rochester, 1955. Intern, resident in medicine U. Wis. Hosp., 1955-59; clin. assoc. NIH, 1959-61; clin. investigator VA, 1961-64; asst. prof. medicine U. Wis., Madison, 1964-68, assoc. prof., 1968-74, prof., 1974-98, med. alumni prof., 1987. Mentor class of '03 U. Wis. Med. Sch.; chief hematology VA Hosp., Madison, 1964-98, chief nuclear medicine, 1964-73, 78-79 Author (editor): Pathophysiology of Blood, 1984, Hematology for Students, 2002; contbr. articles to profl. jours. Trustee Intervarsity Christian Fellowship, 1985-88. Served with USPHS, 1959-61. Danforth assoc., 1962 Mem. Am. Soc. Hematology, Am. Fedn. Clin. Research, Central Soc. Clin. Research. Republican. Baptist. Home: 190 N Prospect Ave Madison WI 53705-4071 Office: 2500 Overlook Ter Madison WI 53705-2254

MACKINNON, CATHARINE ALICE, lawyer, educator, writer; d. George E. and Elizabeth V. (Davis) MacKinnon. BA in Govt. magna cum laude with distinction, Smith Coll., 1969; JD, Yale U., 1977, PhD in Polit. Sci., 1987. Prof. law U. Mich., Ann Arbor, 1990—, Elizabeth A. Long Prof. Law. Long term vis. prof. U. Chgo., 1997-2005; co-dir. LAW Project Equality Now, 2001-05; fellow Ctr. for Advanced Study, 2005-06; vis. prof. various univs. Author: Sexual Harassment of Working Women, 1979, Feminism Unmodified, 1987, Toward a Feminist Theory of the State, 1989, Only Words, 1993, Sex Equality, 2001, Women's Lives, Men's Laws, 2005, Are Women Human? and other international dialogues, 2006; co-author: In Harm's Way, 1997, Directions in Sexual Harassment Law, 2003. Mem.: AAAS (assoc.), Am. Bar Found. (Disting. Rsch. award 2007). Office: U Mich Law Sch 625 S State St Ann Arbor MI 48109-1215 Office Phone: 734-647-3595. Office Fax: 734-764-8309. E-mail: camtwo@umich.edu.

MACKINNON, DOUGLAS JEROME, retired radio and magazine publishing executive; b. Battle Creek, Mich., Dec. 19, 1930; s. Alexander Duncan and Ella Francis MacKinnon; m. Mary Lou Nolan-MacKinnon, Sept. 14, 1953; children: Kathy, Don, Margaret, Brian, Craig, Chris. Grad., A.B. Davis HS, Mt. Vernon, NY. With KIOA, Des Moines, 1953—64; with radio sta. Indpls., 1964—65; pub. Iowa Scene Mag., Des Moines, 1965—70, 1982—94; sales dir. Thrifty Rental Car/Oil Co., Des Moines, 1970—72; with WYOO Radio, Mpls.-St. Paul, 1972—75, KHOW-KITE, KRGO-KTEX Radio, Denver, San Antonio and Salt Lake City, 1975—82. Nat. program dir. Double Day Broadcasting, Denver, Mpls. and San Antonio. Judge advocate Mil. Order Purple Heart, Des Moines, 2004—07, sgt.-at-arms, 2003—. Served with USMC, 1951—53, Korea. Named to Iowa Rock 'n' Roll Hall of Fame, Okoboji, 2003. Avocations: amateur radio, oil painting. Home: 2409 50th St Des Moines IA 50310 Personal E-mail: kioagudguy1@aol.com.

MACKINNON, JAMES GORDON, economist, educator; b. Charlottetown, PEI, Can., Jan. 4, 1951; s. James William and Marion Elizabeth MacKinnon; m. Susan Gentleman, Nov. 23, 1985. BA with honors, York U., 1971; MA, Princeton U., 1974, PhD, 1975. Asst. prof. Queen's U., Kingston, Ont., Canada, 1975—78, assoc. prof., 1978—82, prof., 1982—, Sir Edward Peacock prof. econometrics, 1991—. Mem. editl. bd. Can. Jour. Econs., 1984—87, assoc. editor Jour. Applied Econometrics, 1989—91, Jour. Econometrics, 1991—2007, software rev. editor Jour. Applied Econometrics, 1991—. Fellow: Royal Soc. Can., Econometric Soc.; mem.: Can. Econs. Assn. (pres.-elect 2000—01, pres. 2001—02, past pres. 2002—03). Office: Queen's U Dept Econs Kingston ON Canada K7L 3N6 Home Phone: 613-531-9854; Office Phone: 613-533-2293. Business E-Mail: jgm@econ.queensu.ca.

MACKINNON, JOHN ALEXANDER, lawyer; b. Glen Ridge, NJ, Feb. 5, 1949; s. John and Carol McNeir (Cox) M.; m. Anne Rider Patterson, Aug. 19, 1972; children: Lindsay Rider, John William. BA, Williams Coll., 1971; JD, U. Va., Charlottesville, 1974. Assoc. Brown & Wood, NYC, 1974-82, ptnr., 1983-2001; ptnr. securities law Sidley Austin Brown & Wood LLP, NYC, 2001—06, Sidley Austin LLP, NYC, 2006—. Adv. bd. Mutual Fund Dir. Forum. Trustee, Tuxedo Park Libr., NY, 1982-89; mem. chmn., bd. zoning appeals, Tuxedo Park, 1987-89. Mem. ABA, Assn. of the Bar of NYC, The Tuxedo Club. Office Phone: 212-839-5300, 212-839-5534. Business E-Mail: jmackinnon@sidley.com.

MACKINNON, KEVIN SCOTT, lawyer; b. San Jose, Calif., June 29, 1958; s. Hector Neil and Margie Lou (Riggs) MacK.; m. Hanna T. Piech, Sept. 1, 1984. BA, U. Calif., Santa Barbara, 1980; JD, U. Santa Clara, 1983. Assoc. Fisher & Hurst, Chgo., 1983-84, Isham, Lincoln & Beale, Chgo., 1984-86, Schiff, Hardin & Waite, Chgo., 1986; sr. corp. counsel, staff dir. McDonald's Corp.; ptnr. Katten Muchin Zavis Rosenman, Chgo. Mem.: ABA, Lawyers for Creative Arts (v.p.), Internat. Franchise Assn., Chgo. Bar Assn., Internat. Trademark Assn.

MACKINNON, MALCOLM D(AVID), retired insurance company executive; b. Guelph, Ont., Can., Mar. 9, 1931; came to U.S., 1955; s. A.L. and Jean (Butchart) MacK.; m. Betty Campbell, June 18, 1955; children: Sandra, Katherine, Donald. BA, U. Toronto, 1953. Cert. CLU, chartered fin. analyst. With Prudential Ins. Co., 1954-94, v.p. Newark, 1979-81, sr. v.p., 1981—94; ret., 1994. Commentator pub. radio. Trustee Kean Coll., Union, N.J., 1990-93, Millburn Free Pub. Libr., 1996-2005, pres., 1997-2000; chmn. Milburn Short Hills chpt. ARC, 1992-94. Fellow Soc. Actuaries; mem. Canoe Brook Country Club (Summit, N.J.). Home: 23 Grosvenor Rd Short Hills NJ 07078-1639

MACKINNON, REBECCA, media consultant, researcher; Grad. magna cum laude, Harvard U. Taiwan stringer Newsweek mag., 1991—92; bur. asst. CNN, Beijing, 1992—93, assoc. prodr., 1993—96, prodr., correspondent, 1997—98, bur. chief, 1998—2001, Tokyo, 2001—03; media cons., 2004—; fellow Shorenstein Ctr. on the Press Harvard U., 2004; rsch. fellow Berkman Ctr. for Internet and Society Harvard Law Sch., 2004—; co-founder Global Voices Online. Office: Harvard Law Sch Baker House 1587 Massachusetts Ave Cambridge MA 02138 Office Phone: 617-495-7547. Office Fax: 617-812-7950. E-mail: rmackinnon@cyber.law.harvard.edu.

MACKINNON, RODERICK, neuroscientist, educator; b. Burlington, Mass., 1956; married. BA, Brandeis U., 1978; MD, Tufts U., 1982, PhD (hon.), 2002. Postdoctoral fellow Beth Israel Hosp., Harvard U., 1985—86, Brandeis U., 1986—89; from asst. to prof. dept. neurobiology Harvard Med. Sch., 1989—96; John D. Rockefeller Jr. prof. lab. molecular neurobiology and biophysics Rockefeller U., 1996—. Recipient W. Alden Spencer award, Young Investigator award, Biophysical Soc., 1995, Newcomb Cleveland prize, AAAS, 1998, Albert Lasker Basic Med. Rsch. award, 1999, Lewis S. Rosentiel award, 2000, Gairdner Found. Internat. award, 2001, Nobel prize for chemistry, 2003; grantee, Howard Hughes Med. Inst. Chevy Chase, Md., 1997—. Mem.: NAS, Alpha Omega Med. Honor Soc. Avocation: trout fishing. Office: Rockefeller Univ 1230 York Ave New York NY 10021 also: Howard Hughes Med Inst 4000 Jones Bridge Rd Chevy Chase MD 20815-6789 Office Phone: 212-327-7288.

MACKINNON, STEPHEN R., Asian studies administrator, educator; b. Columbus, Nebr., Dec. 2, 1940; s. Cyrus Leland and Helen (Wigglesworth) MacKinnon; children: Rebecca, Cyrus R.; m. Anne Feldhaus, Dec. 21, 2005. BA, Yale U., New Haven, Conn., 1963, MA, 1964; PhD, U. Calif., Davis, 1971. Acting instr. Chinese U., Hong Kong, 1968-69; dir. Asian Studies, prof. history Ariz. State U., Tempe, 1971—; vis. assoc. Chinese Acad. Social Sci., Beijing, 1979-81, 85. Mem. US State Dept. Selection Bd., Washington, 1991, Nat. Com. on US-China Rels., NYC, 1991—; cons. PBS film documentary "Dragon and Eagle." Author: Power/Politics China, 1980; co-author: Agnes Smedley, 1988, China Reporting, 1987; co-editor: Chinese Women Revolution, 1976 (ALA notable book 1976), Scars of War, 2001, China At War, 2007; lectr. on China to local orgns. and TV, 1981—. Commr. Phoenix Sister Cities, 1986-91; bd. dirs. Com. on Fgn. Rels., Phoenix, 1988—; bd. dirs. Marshall Fund Ariz., 1995—. Rsch. fellow Am. Coun. Learned Socs., Hong Kong, 1978, Fulbright Found., India, 1977-78; rsch. sr. Com. on Scholarly Com. People's Republic China, Washington-Beijing, 1992, Pacific Cultural Found., 1999, Am. Inst. Indian Studies, 2003, Fulbright-Hays ACLS, China, 2005-. Mem. Assn. Asian Studies (bd. dirs. 1990-91), Am. Hist. Assn. (program com. 1990-91). Avocations: tennis, hiking, jazz. Office: Ariz State U Dept History Tempe AZ 85287-4302 Office Phone: 480-965-6692. Business E-Mail: stephen.mackinnon@asu.edu.

MACKINNON, SUSAN, plastic surgeon; b. Can., Jan. 31, 1950; married; 4 children. MD, Queen's U., Kingston, Can., 1975. Cert. in plastic surgery. Surgery residency Queen's U., 1978; surgery residency divsn. plastic surgery U. Toronto, 1980, neurosurgery fellowship dept. surgery, 1981; hand surgery fellowship Union Meml. Hosp., Balt., 1982; Shoenberg prof., surgery chief divsn. plastic and reconstructive surgery Wash. U. Sch. Medicine. Surgeon Barnes-Jewish Hosp., St. Louis Children's Hosp.; with Barnes-Jewish West County Hosp. Contbr. chapters to books, articles to profl. jours. Named a Top Dr., Wash. U.; named to, Best Dr.'s in Am., 2002, 2005, 2006; recipient Medal award in surgery, Royal Coll. Physicians and Surgeons Can., 1988, Outstanding Clinician award, Wash. U. Sch. Medicine III Humanity Program. Mem.: Am. Assn. Plastic Surgeons (treas. 2003—05, v.p. 2005, pres. 2007—, awards com. chair), Am. Assn. Hand Surgery (v.p. 2003, pres.-elect 2004, pres. 2005). Achievements include completing the first donor nerve allotransplant, a procedure that can restore function to severely injured limbs that previously were considered irreparable; research in peripheral nerve surgery in hand/upper extremity and lower extremity; carpal tunnel syndrome; tarsal tunnel syndrome; thoracic outlet syndrome; nerve transplant; facial palsy. Office: Wash U Sch Medicine 600 S Euclid Ave Campus Box 8238 Saint Louis MO 63110 also: Plastic and Reconstructive Surgery Ctr Ctr for Advance Medicine 4921 Parkview Pl Ste G Fl 6 Saint Louis MO 63110 Office Phone: 314-362-4586. Office Fax: 314-362-4536. *

MACKINTOSH, FREDERICK ROY, oncologist; b. Miami, Fla., Oct. 4, 1943; s. John Harris and Mary Carlotta (King) MacK.; m. Judith Jane Parnell, Oct. 12, 1961 (div. Aug. 1977); children: Lisa Lynn, Wendy Sue; m. Claudia Lizanne Flournoy, Jan. 7, 1984; 1 child, Gregory Warren. BS, MIT, 1964, PhD, 1968; MD, U. Miami, 1976. Intern then resident in gen. medicine Stanford (Calif.) U., 1976-78, fellow in oncology, 1978-81; asst. prof. med. U. Nev., Reno, 1981-85, assoc. prof., 1985-92, prof. medicine, 1992—. Contbr. articles to profl. jours. Fellow ACP; mem. Am. Soc. Clin. Oncology, Am. Cancer Soc. (pres. Nev. chpt. 1987-89, Washoe chpt. 1988-90), No. Nev. Cancer Coun. (bd. dirs. 1981-92), No. Calif. Cancer Program (bd. dirs. alt. 1983-87, bd. dirs. 1987-91). Avocations: bicycling, sporting clays. Office: Med Sch Assocs North Ste 302 1500 E 2nd St Reno NV 89502 Home Phone: 775-853-2347; Office Phone: 775-784-7500. E-mail: roy.mackintosh@va.gov.

MACKLEM, MICHAEL KIRKPATRICK, publisher; b. Toronto, Ont., Can., July 12, 1928; s. Hedley Clark and Mary Eileen (Kirkpatrick) M.; m. Anne Woodburne Hardy, Dec. 30, 1950; children— Timothy Street, Nicholas Hardy. BA, U. Toronto, 1950; AM (Charles Scribner fellow), Princeton U., 1952, PhD (Porter Ogden Jacobus fellow, Royal Soc. Can. fellow), 1954. Instr., English Yale U., New Haven, 1954-55; staff editor Ency. Canadiana, 1955-58; asst. to dir. Humanities Research Council of Can., 1958-60; gen. mgr. Oberon Press, Ottawa, Ont., 1966-85. Pres. Michael, Hardy, Ltd., Ottawa, 1972— Author: The Anatomy of the World: Relations Between Natural and Moral Law from Donne to Pope, 1958, God Have Mercy: The Life of John Fisher of Rochester, 1967, Cinderella, 1969, Voyages to New France 1615-1618, 1970, Voyages to New France 1599-1603, 1971, The Sleeping Beauty, 1973, Jacques the Woodcutter, 1977, Liberty and the Holy City, 1978, The Oberon Reader, 1991, The Oberon Poetry Collection, 1992. Can. Council fellow, 1964-65 Mem.: Order Can. (apptd. mem.). Home: 555 Maple Ln Ottawa ON Canada K1M 0N7 Office: Oberon Press 205-145 Spruce St Ottawa ON Canada K1R 6PI E-mail: oberon@sympatico.ca.

MACKLIN, CROFFORD JOHNSON, JR., lawyer; b. Columbus, Ohio, Sept. 10, 1947; s. Crofford Johnson, Sr. and Dorothy Ann (Stevens) M.; m. Mary Carole Ward, July 5, 1969; children: Carrie E., David J. BA, Ohio State U., 1969; BA summa cum laude, U. West Fla., 1974; JD cum laude, Ohio State U., 1976. Bar: Ohio 1977, U.S. Tax Ct. 1978. Acct. Touche Ross, Columbus, 1976-77; assoc. Smith & Schnacke, Dayton, 1977-81, shareholder, 1988-89; sole practice Dayton, 1981-82; ptnr. Porter, Wright, Morris & Arthur, Dayton, 1983-88, Thompson, Hine LLP, 1989—, practice group leader pers. and succession planning, 2001—06. Adj. faculty Franklin U., 1977; adj. prof. U. Dayton Law Sch., 1981. Contbr. articles to profl. jours. Bd. dirs. Great Lakes Nat. Bank Ohio, 1997, Easter Seals, 1984-86. Served to capt. USMCR, 1969-74. Fellow Am. Coll. Trust and Estate Counsel; mem. ABA, Dayton Bar Assn. (chmn. probate com. 1981-83), Dayton Trust & Estate Planning (pres. 1983-84), Ohio Bar Assn. Presbyterian. Home: 7276 Wetherington Dr West Chester OH 45069 Office: Thompson Hine LLP 2000 Courthouse Pla NE PO Box 8801 Dayton OH 45401-8801 Home Phone: 513-759-0504; Office Phone: 937-443-6730.

MACKLIN, PHILIP ALAN, retired physics professor; b. Richmond Hill, NY, Apr. 13, 1925; s. Egbert Chalmer and Margaret Griswold (Collins) M.; m. Cora Baldwin Galindo, Sept. 5, 1953 (dec. Feb. 2005); children: Susan, Steven, Peter. BS cum laude, Yale U., 1944; MA, Columbia U., 1949, PhD, 1956. Physicist Carbide & Carbon Chems. Corp., Oak Ridge, 1946-47; research scientist AEC, Columbia U., 1949-51; instr. physics Middlebury Coll., Vt., 1951-54, acting chmn. dept., 1953-54; mem. faculty Miami U., Oxford, Ohio, 1954—, prof. physics, 1961-93, chmn. dept., 1972-85, prof. emeritus, 1993—; ret., 1993. Research scientist Armco Steel Co., summers 1955-56; vis. prof. U. N.Mex., summers 1957-68, Boston U., fall 1985-86; physicist Los Alamos Sci. Labs., summers 1960-62; participant NSF summer insts., 1970-71; vis. scientist MIT, 1985-86 Author publs. in field; patentee in field. Vestryman Holy Trinity Episcopal Ch., Oxford, 1959-61, 67, 71-73, 75-77, mem. fin. com., chmn. blood assurance program, 1980—, lector, 1989—. With USN, 1944-46. Mem. AAAS, LWV of Oxford (treas. 1986-88, dir. governance 1997—), Am. Phys. soc., Forum Physics and Soc., Kiwanis (bd. dirs. 1994-97), Torch Club of Butler County (pres. 1982-83, 96-97, mem. editl. adv. com. The Torch), 1809 Club (pres. 1964-65), Campus Ministry Ctr. (trustee 1994-2002), Union of Concerned Scientists, Ctr. for Voting and Democracy (charter), Membership Assn. Miami U. Art Mus. (exec. com. 1999-2002), Phi Beta Kappa (pres. Iota of Ohio chpt. 1987-88), Sigma Xi, Sigma Pi Sigma, Omicron Delta Kappa. Democrat. Home: 211 Oakhill Dr Oxford OH 45056-2710 Office: Culler Hall Miami Univ Oxford OH 45056 Office Phone: 513-529-5625. E-mail: macklipa@muohio.edu.

MACKLIN, RUTH, bioethics educator; b. Newark, Mar. 27, 1938; d. Hyman and Frieda (Yaruss) Chimacoff; m. Martin Macklin, Sept. 1, 1957 (div. June 1969); children: Meryl, Shelley Macklin Taylor. BA with distinction, Cornell U., 1958; MA in Philosophy, Case Western Res. U., 1966, PhD in Philosophy, 1968. Instr. in philosophy Case Western Res. U., Cleve., 1967—68, asst. prof., 1968—71, assoc. prof., 1971—76; assoc. for behavioral studies The Hastings Ctr., Hastings-on-Hudson, NY, 1976—80; vis. assoc. prof. Albert Einstein Coll. Medicine, Bronx, NY, 1977—78, assoc. prof., 1978—84, prof. dept. epidemiology and social medicine, 1984—. Cons. NIH, 1986—; advisor WHO, Geneva, 1989—; mem. White House Adv. Com. on Human Radiation Experiments, Washington1994;

chair ethical rev. com. UNAIDS, Geneva, 1996—2001. Author: Man, Mind and Morality, 1982, Mortal Choices, 1987, Enemies of Patients, 1993, Surrogates and Other Mothers, 1994, Against Relativism, 1999, Double Standards in Medical Research, 2004; contbr. articles to ethics, law and med. jours. Fellow: APHA, Am. Soc. Law, Medicine and Ethics, Inst. Medicine NAS, The Hastings Ctr., Am. Philosophys. Assn. (life); mem.: Am. Soc. Bioethics and Humanities (bd. dirs. 1997—99), Internat. Assn. Bioethics (bd. dirs., pres. 1999—2001). Democrat. Office: A Einstein Coll Medicine Dept Epidemiology Population Health 1300 Morris Park Ave Bronx NY 10461-1926 E-mail: macklin@aecom.yu.edu.

MACKLIS, ROGER MILTON, physician, educator, researcher; b. Stratford, Conn., Mar. 12, 1956; m. Carol Clark, July 25, 1987; children: Andrew Clark, Paul Clark. BS, MS, Yale U., 1978; MD, Harvard U., 1983. Diplomate Am Bd Radiation Oncology. Instr. Harvard Med. Sch., Boston, 1988-89, asst. prof. radiation oncology, 1989-93; dep. div. chief Children's Hosp., Boston, 1990-93; chmn. dept. radiation oncology Cleve. Clinic Found., 1993—. Biomedical consult, Boston, 1989—; assoc prof hist med Case Western Res Univ, 1995—; prof. medicine Cleve. Clin. Lerner Coll. of Medicine, 2004—. Author: (book) Manual of Introductory Clinical Medicine, 1984; contbr. articles to profl jours. Recipient Resident Research Award, ASTRO, 1988, Jr Faculty Research Award, Am Cancer Soc, 1990. Mem.: Soc Chairs of Acad Radiation Oncology Programs (treas, vpres, pres), Am Soc Therapeutic Radiology and Oncology, Am Soc Clin Oncology (Young Investigator Award 1987), Radiation Research Soc. Achievements include research in research on new approaches to cancer treatment involving radioactively labeled molecules and novel technologies for minimizing medical errors in oncology. Office: Cleve Clinic Found Dept Radiation Oncology 9500 Euclid Ave Cleveland OH 44195-0001 Home Phone: 440-442-4252; Office Phone: 216-444-5576. Business E-Mail: macklir@ccf.org.

MACKNIGHT, CAROL BERNIER, educational association administrator; b. Quincy, Mass., Apr. 12, 1938; d. Harold Nelson and Marguerite (Norris) Bernier; m. William J. MacKnight, Aug. 19, 1967. BS, Ithaca Coll., NYC, 1960; MM, Manhattan Sch. Mus., NYC, 1961; Dipl., Fontainebleau Sch. Music/Art, France, 1968; EdD, U. Mass., 1973. Asst. to supt. Falmouth (Mass.) pub. schs., 1975-76; dir. bus., mgmt., engring. prog. Sch. Bus. Adminstrn. U. Mass., Amherst, 1976-79, assoc. dir. continuing edn., 1979-82, dir. Office Instructional Tech., 1982—93. Trustee New Eng. Regional Computer Program, Inc., 1986—92; bd. dirs. Info. Sys. and Bus. Exch., 1992—93; keynote spkr. Australian Soc. for Computers in Learning In Tertiary Edn. Conf., Adelaide, 1996; conf. chair various confs., 2002—. Editor: Jour. Computing in Higher Edn., 1988—, Jour. Info. Sys. for Mgrs., 1992—93; mem. editl. rev. bd.: Jour. of Computer-Based Instrn., 1988—2002, author/editor: computer progs.; contbr. articles to profl. jours. Grantee, CDC, 1986, Regents of Boston, 1988; Lilly Fellow Mentor, 1991—92. Mem. ACM, Assn. for Computing Machinery, Educom, Soc. Applied Learning Techs. (bd. dirs. 2003-05, conf. chair e-learning 2004, conf. chair gaming and simulation 2006), New England Regional Computer Program. Avocations: music, photography, tennis, hiking, skiing. Office: Norris Consulting and Pub PO Box 2593 Amherst MA 01004 Business E-Mail: cmacknight@oit.umass.edu.

MACKNIGHT, WILLIAM JOHN, chemist, educator; b. NYC, May 5, 1936; s. William John and Margaret Ann (Stuart) M.; m. Carol Marie Bernier, Aug. 19, 1967 BS, Rochester U., 1958; MA, Princeton U., 1963, PhD, 1964. Rsch. assoc. Princeton U., 1964-65; asst. prof. chemistry U. Mass., Amherst, 1965-69, assoc. prof. chemistry, 1969-74, prof. chemistry, 1974-76, dept. head polymer sci., 1976-85, prof. polymer sci. and engring., 1985-88, 95-96, head dept. polymer sci. and engring., 1988-95, disting. univ. prof., 1996-98, Wilmer D. Barret disting. prof., 1998-99, Wilmer D. Barret Disting. prof. emeritus, 1999—. Mem. sci. and tech. adv. bd. Alcoa, Pitts., 1984-86, Diversitech Gen., Akron, Ohio, 1985-89; mem. panel for materials sci. Nat. Bur. Standards, Washington, 1983-89. Author: Polymeric Sulfur and Related Polymers, 1965; Introduction to Polymer Viscoelasticity, 3d edit., 2005. Served to lt. USN, 1958-61 Recipient Ford prize in high polymer physics Am. Phys. Soc., 1984, award for disting. svc. in the advancement of polymer sci. Japan Soc. for Polymer Sci., 1998; Guggenheim fellow, 1985, Internat. Rsch. award Soc. Plastics Engrs., 2007. Fellow: AAAS, Am. Phys. Soc. (exec. com. 1975—76); mem.: Am. Chem. Soc. (award in polymer chemistry 1997, Herman F. Mark award, polymers chemistry divsn. 2002, Flory award, polymer chemistry divsn. 2006), Nat. Acad. Engring., Cosmos Club. Avocations: music, sports. Home: 127 Sunset Ave Amherst MA 01002-2019 Office: U Mass Polymer Sci & Engring Dept Conte Bldg Amherst MA 01003 Home Phone: 413-549-5150; Office Phone: 413-577-1412. Business E-Mail: wmacknight@polysci.umass.edu.

MACKOWSKI, JOHN JOSEPH, retired insurance company executive; b. Westport, Mass., Feb. 1, 1926; s. John J. and Victoria K. (Skript) Mieczkowski; m. Ruth Williams, Feb. 3, 1951; children: Martha, John Matthew, Daniel, Joan. AB, Duke U., 1948; student, Harvard Advanced Mgmt. Program, 1970-71. With Ins. Co. of N.Am., Boston, Phila., Chgo., 1948-51; with Atlantic Mut. Ins. Co., NYC, 1951-88, chmn., CEO, to 1988. Bd. dirs. Transatlantic Holdings, Inc. 1st lt. USMCR, 1943-46. Mem. Sawgrass Club (Ponte Vedra Beach, Fla.), Acoaxet Country Club (Westport Harbor, Mass.), Spindle Rock Yacht Club, Sigma Chi, Beta Lambda. Episcopalian. Home: 19 Village Walk Cir Ponte Vedra Beach FL 32082-3500 also: 19 Village Walk Cir Ponte Vedra FL 32082-3543 E-mail: jmackowski@aol.com.

MACKS, RYAN JEFFREY, psychologist; b. Silver Spring, Md., June 14, 1977; s. Marshall Jay and Nancy Howe Macks. PhD, U. of Va., 2004; BA in Psychology (magna cum laude), Dickinson Coll., 1999. Staff psychologist Cin. Children's Hosp. Med. Ctr., Cin., 2004—. Vol. staff mem. Save The Animals Found. (S.T.A.F.), Cin., 2004—06. Libertarian. Home: 4572 Lakes Edge Apt 1 West Chester OH 45069-8665 Home Phone: 513-531-2704. Personal E-mail: littlekingryan@hotmail.com.

MACKWELL, STEPHEN JOSEPH, geophysicist, educator; b. Christchurch, New Zealand, June 5, 1956; arrived in U.S., 1984; s. Alan Gordon Mackwell and Mary Veronica (Carter) Francis; m. Kathleen Garland, March 27, 2004. BSc in Physics and Math., U. Canterbury, Christchurch, New Zealand, 1978, MSc in Physics, 1979; diploma of edn., Christchurch Tchrs. Coll., New Zealand, 1979; PhD in Geophysics, Australian Nat. U., Canberra, 1985. Postdoctoral assoc. Cornell U., Ithaca, NY, 1984—86, rsch. fellow, 1984—87; asst. prof. Pa. State U., University Park, 1987—92, assoc. prof., 1992—98; prof. exptl. geophysics Bayerisches Geoinst., Germany, 1998—2000, dir., 2000—02, Lunar and Planetary Inst., Houston, 2002—. Program dir. for geophysics, divsn. of earth sci., NSF, Washington, 1993-94, expert cons., 1995; panelist proposal rev. NASA, Houston, 1994-95; expert rev. Geoscis. Rsch. program, Dept. Energy, 1993; mem. rev. panel Planetary Geology and Geophysics program, NASA, 1994-96, 2002-, group chief, 1996-98, 2004, panel chief, 2005—. Assoc. editor Jour. Geophys. Rsch. - Solid Earth, 1992—97, mem. editl. bd. Physics of the Earth and Planetary Interiors, 1992—98, Tectonophysics, 2002; editor: (Solid Earth) Geophys. Rsch. Letters, 2000—01; editor-in-chief Geophys. Rsch. Letters, 2002—05; contbr. articles to profl. jours. Recipient Stipendiat der Alexander von Humboldt-Stiftung, Bayreuth, Germany, 1996; grantee, NSF, 1988—98, NASA, 1993—98. Fellow: Mineral. Soc. Am.; mem.: AAAS, Am. Geophys. Union (mem. meetings program com. 1988—91, mem. mineral acquisition and distbn. subcom. 1989—90, mem. phys. properties of Earth materials com., tectonophysics section 1989—91, mem. mineral physics com. 1990—92, mem. 75th anniversary com. 1992—94, mem. meetings com. 1992—96, mem. mineral and rock physics com. 2000—03, mineral physics editor for EOS trans. 1990—92, editor-in-chief, frontiers in mineral physics 1988). Office: Lunar & Planetary Inst USRA Ctr Advanced Space Studies 3600 Bay Area Blvd Houston TX 77058

MACLACHLAN, DOUGLAS LEE, marketing educator; b. Hollywood, Calif., Aug. 27, 1940; s. Alexander D. and Patricia E. (Culver) MacL.; m. Natalie Bowditch Knauth, July 23, 1966; children: Heather Bowditch, Trevor Douglas. AB in Physics, U. Calif., Berkeley, 1962, MBA, 1965, MA in Stats., 1970, PhD in Bus. Adminstrn., 1971; student, Hastings Sch. Law, 1965—66. Instr. bus. adminstrn. U. Calif., Berkeley, 1969-70; v.p. Hartec Corp., Newport Beach, Calif., 1965-70; from acting asst. prof. to Marion B. Ingersoll endowed prof. mktg. U. Wash., Seattle, 1970—2007, Marion B. Ingersoll endowed prof. mktg., 2007—, chair dept. mktg. and internat. bus., 2006—. Vis. prof. bus. adminstrn. U. Calif., Berkeley, 1974; vis. prof. Institut Europeen des Affaires, Fontainebleau, France, 1982—83, Cath. U. Leuven, Belgium, 1991—92, Koc U., Istanbul, 2001; dir. Univ. Book Store, 1985—2002, 2004—. Contbr. articles to profl. jours.; mem. editl. bd.: Jour. Mktg. Rsch., 1975-81. Mem. Am. Mktg. Assn. (dir. Puget Sound chpt. 1975-77, 90-91, pres. 1978-79), Informs, Am. Statis. Assn., Assn. Consumer Rsch., Clan MacLachlan Soc. (pres. n.w. br. 1995—), Alpha Kappa Psi, Kappa Delta Rho, Beta Gamma Sigma. Home: 16305 Inglewood Rd NE Kenmore WA 98028-3908 Office: U Washington Box 353200 Seattle WA 98195-3200 Office Phone: 206-543-4369.

MACLACHLAN, KYLE, actor; b. Yakima, WA, Feb. 22, 1960; m. Desiree Gruber, Apr. 20, 2002. BFA, U. Wash., 1982. Actor: (films) Dune, 1984, Blue Velvet, 1986, The Hidden, 1987, Don't Tell Her It's Me, 1990, The Doors, 1991, Twin Peaks: Fire Walk with Me, 1992, Where the Day Takes You, 1992, Rich in Love, 1993, The Trial, 1993, The Flintstones, 1994, Showgirls, 1995, The Trigger Effect, 1996, Mad Dog Time, 1996, One Night Stand, 1997, Hamlet, 1999, Perfume, 2001, Me Without You, 2001, Miranda, 2002, Northfork, 2003, Touch of Pink, 2004, (voice) Free Jimmy, 2006; TV series Twin Peaks, 1990-91 (Golden Globe award, 1991), Sex and the City, 2000-02, In Justice, 2006, Desperate Housewives, 2006; TV movies: Against the Wall, 1994, Roswell, 1994, Moonshine Highway, 1996, Thunder Point, 1996, Route 9, 1998, The Spring, 2000, Jo, 2002, Mysterious Island, 2005; dir. (TV series) Tales from the Crypt, 1989; TV guest appearance Miami Vice, 1988. Address: Industry Entertainment Ste 300 955 S Carrillo Dr Los Angeles CA 90048 also: ICM 8942 Wilshire Blvd Beverly Hills CA 90211

MACLACHLAN, PATRICIA, author; b. Cheyenne, Wyo., Mar. 3, 1938; d. Philo and Madonna (Moss) Pritzkau; m. Robert MacLachlan, Apr. 14, 1962; children: John, Jamie, Emily. BA, U. Conn., 1962. Tchr. English Bennett Jr. High Sch., Manchester, Conn., 1963-79. Vis. lectr. Smith Coll., Northampton, Mass., 1986. Author: The Sick Day, 1979, Arthur, for the Very First Time, 1980 (Golden Kite award Soc. Children's Book Writers 1980), Moon, Stars, Frogs, and Friends, 1980, Through Grandpa's Eyes, 1980, Cassie Binegar, 1982, Mama One, Mama Two, 1982, Tomorrow's Wizard, 1982, Seven Kisses in a Row, 1983, Unclaimed Treasures, 1984 (Boston Globe/Horn Book award 1984), Sarah, Plain and Tall, 1985 (Golden Kite award 1985, Scott O'Dell Historical Fiction award 1985, John Newbery medal 1986, Jefferson Cup award Va. Libr. Assn. 1986, Christopher award 1986, Garden State Children's Book award N.J. Libr. Assn. 1988), The Facts and Fictions of Minna Pratt, 1988 (Parent's Choice award Parent's Choice Found. 1988), Three Names, 1991, Journey, 1991, All the Places to Love, 1993, Baby, 1993, Skylark, 1994, What You Know First, 1995, Caleb's Story, 2001, More Perfect Than The Moon, 2004, Who Loves Me?, 2005; author (screenplays): Sarah Plain and Tall, 1988, Skylark, 1992, Journey, 1992. Bd. dirs. Children's Aid Family Svc. Agency, 1970-80. Recipient numerous awards for children's fiction. Office: Curts Brown Ltd c/o Marilyn Marlow 10 Astor Pl Fl 3D New York NY 10003-6935

MACLAINE, SHIRLEY, actress; b. Richmond, Va., Apr. 24, 1934; d. Ira O. and Kathlyn (MacLean) Beatty; m. Steve Parker, Sept. 17, 1954 (div. 1982); 1 child, Stephanie Sachiko. Broadway appearances include Me and Juliet, 1953, Pajama Game, 1954, films appearances The Trouble With Harry, 1954, Artists and Models, 1954, Around the World in 80 Days, 1955-56, Hot Spell, 1957, The Matchmaker, 1957, The Sheepman, 1957, Some Came Running, 1958 (Fgn. Press award 1959), Ask Any Girl, 1959 (Silver Bear award as best actress Internat. Berlin Film Festival), Career, 1959, Can-Can, 1959, The Apartment, 1959 (Best Actress prize Venice Film Festival), Children's Hour, 1960, The Apartment, 1960, Two for the Seesaw, 1962, Irma La Douce, 1963, What A Way to Go, The Yellow Rolls Royce, 1964, John Goldfarb Please Come Home, 1965, Gambit and Woman Times Seven, 1967, The Bliss of Mrs. Blossom, Sweet Charity, 1969, Two Mules for Sister Sara, 1969, Desperate Characters, 1971, The Possession of Joel Delaney, 1972, The Other Half of the Sky: A China Memoir, 1975, The Turning Point, 1977, Being There, 1979, A Change of Seasons, 1980, Loving Couples, 1980, Terms of Endearment, 1983 (Acad. award 1984, Golden Globe-Best Actress), Cannonball Run II, 1984, Madame Sousatzka, 1988 (Best Actress Venice Film Festival, Golden Globe-Best Actress), Steel Magnolias, 1989, Waiting For the Light, 1990, Postcards From the Edge, 1990, Defending Your Life, 1991, Used People, 1992, Wrestling Ernest Hemingway, 1993, Guarding Tess, 1994, Evening Star, 1995, Mrs. Winterbourne, 1996, Carolina, 2003, Bewitched, 2005, In Her Shoes, 2005, Rumor Has It..., 2005; TV appearances Shirley's World, 1971-72, Shirley MacLaine: If They Could See Me Now, 1974-75, Gypsy in My Soul, 1975-76, Where Do We Go From Here?, 1976-77, Shirley MacLaine at the Lido, 1979, Shirley MacLaine...Every Little Movement, 1980 (Emmy award 1980), TV movie appearances Out On A Limb, 1987, The West Side Waltz, 1995, Joan of Arc, 1999, These Old Broads, 2001, Hell on Heels: The Battle of Mary Kay, 2002, TV mini-series Salem Witch Trials, 2002; (directorial debut) Bruno, 2000; co-dir. documentary: China The Other Half of the Sky; star U.S. tour stage musical Out There Tonight, 1990; author: Don't Fall Off the Mountain, 1970, The New Celebrity Cookbook, 1973, You Can Get There From Here, 1975, Out on a Limb, 1983, Dancing in the Light, 1985, It's All in the Playing, 1987, Going Within: A Guide for Inner Transformation, 1989, Dance While You Can, 1991; editor: McGovern: The Man and His Beliefs, 1972, My Lucky Stars, 1995, The Camino, 2000, Out On A Leash: Exploring The Nature of Reality and Love, 2003. Address: C/O ICM 8942 Wilshire Blvd Beverly Hills CA 90211-1934

MACLAREN, ROY, retired Canadian government official; b. Vancouver, BC, Can., Oct. 26, 1934; s. Wilbur and Anne (Graham) MacLaren; m. Alethea Mitchell, June 25, 1959; children: Ian, Vanessa, Malcolm. BA, U. B.C., 1955; MA, U. Cambridge, Eng., 1957; postgrad., Harvard U., 1974; MDiv, U. Toronto, 1991, DCL (hon.), 1996; DHL (hon.), U. N. Ala.; LLD (hon.), U. N.B., U. P.E.I. Fgn. svc. officer Can. Diplomatic Svc., 1957-69; dir. corporate pub. affairs Massey-Ferguson Ltd., Toronto, Ont., 1969-74; chmn., CEO Ogilvy & Mather, Toronto, 1974-76; chmn. C.B. Media Ltd., 1976-93; mem. Parliament of Can., 1979-84, 88-96, parliamentary sec. to min. of energy, mines and resources, 1980-82, min. of state (fin.), 1983-84, min. of nat. revenue, 1984, min. of internat. trade, 1993-96; high commr. for Can. to U.K. of Gt. Britain and No. Ireland, 1996-2000; ret., 2000. Bd. dirs. Brascan, Algoma Ctrl., Pacific Safety Products. Author: (book) Canadians in Russia: 1918-19, 1976, Canadians on the Nile, 1882-1898, 1978, Canadians Behind Enemy Lines, 1939-1945, 1981, Honourable Mentions, 1986, African Exploits: The Diaries of William Stairs, 1998, Commissions High, 2006; contbr. articles to profl. jours. Commr. Trilateral Commn.; chmn. Can. Inst. Internat. Affairs, Can.-India Bus. Coun.; coun. mem. Internat. Inst. Strategic Studies, Ditchley Found. Hon. col. 7th Toronto Rgt. Royal Can. Arty. Mem.: Pratt's (London), White's (London), Rideau Club (Ottawa), Toronto Club, Royal Can. Yacht Club. Address: 425 Russell Hill Rd Toronto ON Canada M5P 2S4

MACLAREN, WILLIAM GEORGE, JR., engineering executive; b. Chgo., May 6, 1928; s. William George, Sr. and Dorothy Pauline (Costello) MacLaren; m. Marie Lorraine Logan, Sept. 15, 1951 (div. Dec. 1977); children: Vanessa Ann MacLaren-Wray, Jon Mark, Scott William; m. Mary Patricia Loftus, Dec. 22, 1977 (div. Oct. 1995); m. Brigitte Hildegard Krakau, Apr. 19, 1997. BS in Indsl. Engring., U. Pitts., 1951; MS in Indsl. Engring., Syracuse U., NYC, 1958; PhD in Indsl. Mgmt., Columbia Pacific U., 1989. Commd. 2nd lt. USAF, 1951, advanced through grades to major gen., 1974; comdr. 5BW Minot AFB, ND, 1972-74; chief of staff 15 AF, 1975; comdr. Pacific Comm. Area, 1975-78; vice comdr. Air Force Comm. Command, 1978-79; dir. Command Control and Comm. Hdqs. USAF, 1979-81; dir. Comm. and Info. Sys. NATO, 1981-84; ret. USAF, 1984; v.p. Gia, Inc., Arlington, Va., 1984-90, 93-95; dir. gen. NATO/NATO Air Command and Control Mgmt. Agy., Brussels, 1990-93; v.p. BEI, Inc., Alexandria, Va., 1995—. Contbr. articles to profl. jours. Regional bd. dirs. Boy Scouts Am., Minot, ND, 1972—74. Named Disting. Engring. Alumnus, U. Pitts., 1986. Mem.: AIAA, Inst. Indsl. Engrs., Am. Def. Preparedness Assn., Armed Forces Comm. and Electronics Assn. (regional v.p. 1975—78, Gold medal 1983), Air Force Assn., Rotary, Order of Daedalians (chpt. pres. 1976—78, merit award 1979). Republican. Avocations: golf, bicycling, flying. Office: SAIC 1800 Diagonal Rd Ste 430 Alexandria VA 22314-2840 Home: 91 Clark Ct Dover DE 19901 Personal E-mail: wilmack@aol.com.

MACLAUGHLIN, FRANCIS JOSEPH, lawyer; b. Davenport, Iowa, Oct. 5, 1933; s. Francis Joseph and Sylvia (Boone) MacL.; m. Joan Elizabeth Pfeiffer, Oct. 17, 1959; children: Lisa Ann, Christine Ann, Francis Joseph BA, Yale U., 1955; JD, U. Mich., 1958. Bar: Ill. 1958, Calif. 1963. Assoc. Graham, Califf, Harper & Benson, Moline, Ill., 1958-59, Lillick, McHose & Charles, Los Angeles, 1963-70, ptnr. LA, 1970-90, White and Case, 1990—. Lt. USN, 1959-63 Mem. ABA, Calif. Bar Assn., Los Angeles County Bar Assn., Maritime Law Assn. U.S. Republican. Office: White & Case 633 W 5th St Ste 1900 Los Angeles CA 90071-2087 Home Phone: 310-459-2165; Office Phone: 213-553-7900. Personal E-mail: rusty1933@charter.net.

MACLAY, DONALD MERLE, retired lawyer; b. Belleville, Pa., Feb. 16, 1934; s. Robert Barr and Grace Virginia (Royer) M.; m. Nancy Margaret Hixenbaugh, Sept. 13, 1958; children: Susan Jo (dec.), Timothy Dean. AB magna cum laude, Grove City Coll., 1956; LLB, U. Pa., 1961. Bar: D.C. 1968, Pa. 1970. Commd. fgn. svc. officer U.S. Dept. State, 1961; assigned Am. embassy, Cotonou, Dahomey (Benin), 1962-64, Am. Consulate Gen., Frankfurt, Fed. Republic Germany, 1964-66, U.S. Dept. State, Washington, 1966-69; dir. courses of study Am. Law Inst.-ABA Com. on Continuing Profl. Edn., Phila., 1969-87, dep. exec. dir., 1987-99, ret., 1999. Served with U.S. Army, 1956-58. Mem.: Am. Law Inst. Democrat. Presbyterian. Home: 936 Church Rd Springfield PA 19064-3935

MACLEAN, BABCOCK, lawyer; b. NYC, Jan. 26, 1946; s. Charles Chalmers and Lee Selden (Howe) MacL.; m. Cynthia Gannon, Feb. 15, 1983. BA, Yale U., 1967; MA, Columbia U., 1970; JD, Case Western Res. U., 1975; LLM in Taxation, NYU, 1987. Bar: Ohio 1975, N.Y. 1983. Assoc. Hadley, Matia, Mills & MacLean, Cleve., 1976-77, mem., 1977-83; tax editor Rsch. Inst. Am., NYC, 1983-85; assoc. Robinson Brog, NYC, 1985-86, mem., 1987—. Adj. asst. prof. taxation Pace U., N.Y.C., 1983-84; adv. bd. Rsch. Inst. Am., 1992-97. Pres. Soc. Preservation of Long Is. Antiquities, 2005—. Mem. ABA (sect. taxation), N.Y. State Bar Assn. (sect. taxation), Assn. Bar City N.Y. (personal income taxation com. chair, 2006—), Yale Club, St. Anthony Club, N.Y. Yacht Club, Seawanhaka Corinthian Yacht Club, St. Andrew's Soc. N.Y., Pilgrims of the U.S. Home: 40 Lloyd Lane Lloyd Harbor NY 11743 Office: Robinson Brog 1345 Avenue Of The Americas New York NY 10105-0143 Home Phone: 212-956-4090; Office Phone: 212-603-6315.

MACLEAN, BARBARA HUTMACHER, retired journalist, writer; b. Toledo, Dec. 16, 1926; d. Norman Eugene and Betty Lucille Price; div. 1971; m. E. Fraser MacLean, Aug. 30, 1977; children: Beth, Jessica, Cary, David, Clay. Student, Rockford Coll., 1945, Western Mich. Coll., 1946. Reporter News-Leader, Richmond, Va., 1962; editor-writer News-Chronicle, Thousand Oaks, Calif., 1963-70, Star-Free Press, Ventura, Calif., 1971-75, Daily Dispatch, East London, South Africa, 1974-78, Wenatchee (Wash.) World, 1980-92, ret., 1992. Exchange journalist The Examiner, Huddersfield, Eng., 1983, China Daily, Beijing, 1988, The Times, Windhoek, Namibia, 1991. Author: In Black and White: Voices of Apartheid, 1980 (Eng.), 1983, I Can't Do What? Voices of Pathfinding Women, 1997, Strike A Woman, Strike A Rock: Fighting for Freedom in South Africa, 2004. Named Woman of Achievement AAUW, 1997; recipient Nat. Headliners award, 1968, 1st Social Issues Reporting award Soc. of Profl. Journalists, 1989. Home: 50 Harborview Dr #3 Port Townsend WA 98368 Personal E-mail: barbhm@olympus.net.

MACLEAN, BRIAN W., insurance company executive; Dir. planning Corp. Fin. dept. Travelers Cos. Inc. (formerly Travelers Ins. Group Holdings, Inc.), St. Paul, 1988, CFO claim svcs., 1993—96, CFO comml., 1996—99, pres. select accounts, 1999—2002, exec. v.p. claim svcs., 2002—05, co-COO, 2005, exec. v.p., COO, 2005—. Office: Travelers Cos Inc 385 Washington St Saint Paul MN 55102 Office Phone: 651-310-7911. *

MACLEAN, DOUG, former professional hockey coach, former sports team executive; b. Summerside, PEI, Can., Apr. 12, 1954; m. Jill MacLean; children: Clark, Mackenzie. Student, P.E.I.; M in Ednl. Psychology, We. Ont. Asst. coach London Knights of OHL, 1984-85, St. Louis Blues, 1986-87, 87-88, Washington Capitals, 1988-89, 89-90, Detroit Red Wings, 1990-91, asst. gen. mgr., 1992-93, 93-94; gen. mgr. Adirondack, Red Wing orgn., 1992-93, 93-94; dir. player devel., scout Fla. Panthers, 1994-95, head coach, 1995—98; gen. mgr Columbus Blue Jackets, 1998—2007, pres., 1998—2007, head coach, 2003—04.

MACLEAN, JOHN, professional hockey coach, former professional hockey player; b. Oshawa, Ont., Can., Nov. 20, 1964; m. Adrienne MacLean; children: John Carter, Kyle Christopher. Right wing NJ Devils, 1983-97, San Jose Sharks, 1997-98, NY Rangers, 1998—2000, Dallas Stars, 2000—02; asst. coach NJ Devils, 2002—. Named to Meml. Cup All-Star team, 1982-83; played in NHL All-Star game, 1989, 91. Achievements include mem. Stanley Cup Champion, NJ Devils, 1995. Office: NJ Devils 33 Fl 744 Broad St Newark NJ 07102 *

MACLEAN, JOHN RONALD, lawyer; b. Pueblo, Colo., Jan. 19, 1938; s. John Ronald and Mary Victoria (Curlin) MacL.; m. Carol Jean Turner, Aug. 18, 1962; children— Leslie Carol, John Ronald. Student. U. Okla., 1956; BS, U.S. Mil. Acad., 1961; JD, Vanderbilt U., 1967. Bar: Tex. 1967; cert. in personal injury trial law Tex. Bd. Legal Splzn. Practicing atty. Turner & MacLean, Cleburne, Tex., 1967-68; county atty. Johnson County, Tex., 1968-76; dist. atty. 18th Jud. Dist. Tex., 1976-84; dist. judge 249th Jud. Dist. Tex., 1984-91; pvt. practice MacLean & Boulware, 1992—. Pres. Johnson County United Fund, 1976 With US Army, 1961—64. Fellow Tex. Bar Found.; mem. Tex. Bar Assn., Johnson County Bar Assn. (pres. 1969), Am. Bd. Trial Advocates (past nat. dir.), Tex. Trial Lawyers Assn.,

Vanderbilt U. Law Sch. Bar Assn. (past pres.), Elks. Democrat. Methodist. Home: 1216 W Westhill Dr Cleburne TX 76033-6021 Office: 11 N Main St Cleburne TX 76033-5543 Office Phone: 817-645-3700.

MAC LEAN, LLOYD DOUGLAS, surgeon; b. Calgary, Alta., Can., June 15, 1924; s. Fred Hugh and Azilda MacL.; m. Eleanor Colle, June 30, 1954; children: Hugh, Charles, Ian, James, Martha. B.Sc. (Viscount Bennett scholar), U. Alta., 1947, MD (Viscount Bennett scholar), 1949; PhD, U. Minn., 1957. Resident U. Minn. Hosps., Mpls., 1950-56; instr. dept. surgery U. Minn., Mpls., 1956-58, asst. prof. surgery, 1958-59, asso. prof., 1959-62; prof. McGill U., Montreal, Que., Canada, 1962—, chmn. dept. surgery, 1968-73, 77-82, 87-88. Surgeon-in-chief Ancker Hosp., St. Paul, 1957-62, Royal Victoria Hosp., Montreal, 1962-88; Edward Archibald prof. surgery McGill U., 1988-93, prof. surgery 1993—. Contbr. numerous articles on surgery, shock, host resistance and transplantation to profl. jours. Decorated officer Order Can. Fellow Royal Soc. Can.; mem. ACS (pres. 1993-94), Am. Surg. Assn. (pres. 1993), Ctrl. Surg. Assn. (pres. 1982-83), Am. Physiol. Soc., Am. Assn. Thoracic and Cardiovasc. Surgery, Soc. Surgery of Alimentary Tract. Home: # 1402-80 Berlioz Montreal PQ Canada H3E 1N9 Personal E-mail: lloydm@citenet.net.

MACLEAN, STEVE(N) G., astronaut; b. Ottawa, Ont., Can., Dec. 14, 1954; m. Nadine Wielgopolski; 3 children. BS in Physics with honors, York U., Toronto, Ont., 1977, PhD, 1983; DSc (hon.), Royal Military Coll., Saint-Jean, Quebec, York U., Toronto, Acadia U. Worked in sports adminstrn. & pub. rels. York U., Toronto, 1974—76; mem. Can. Nat. Gymnastics Team, 1976—77; astronaut Can. Space Agy., 1983—88, program mgr., Advanced Space Vision Sys., 1987—93, astronaut advisor to strategic technolgies in automation and robotics program, 1988—91, program mgr. orbiter space vision sys., chief sci. advisor for Internat. Space, 1993—94; acting dir.-gen. Can. Astronaut Program, 1994—96; astronaut NASA, Johnson Space Ctr., Houston, 1996—. Adj. instr. York U., Toronto, 1980—83; adj. prof. Inst. Aerospace Studies U. Toronto, 1993; payload specialist, Space Shuttle Columbia Mission STS-52, 1992; crew mem. Space Shuttle Atlantis (STS-115), 2006. Achievements include research in electro-optics, laser-induced fluorescence of particles and crystals and multi-photon laser spectroscopy; second Canadian to walk in space; first Canadian to operate Canadarm2. Avocations: hiking, canoeing, flying, parachuting, gymnastics. Office: Astronaut Office/CB NASA Johnson Space Ctr Houston TX 77058

MACLEAY, THOMAS H., insurance company executive; Various investment mgmt., corp. planning and fin. positions Nat. Life Group, 1976—91, CFO, 1991, bd. dirs., 1996—, pres., COO, 1996—2001, chmn., pres., CEO, 2001—. Chmn. Sentinel Group Funds, Inc.; bd. dirs. Chittenden Trust Co., Life Office Mgmt. Assn. Trustee, chmn. fin. com. Air Force Aid Soc.; bd. dirs. Ctrl. Vt. Econ. Devel. Corp. Office: Nat Life Group One National Life Dr Montpelier VT 05604 Office Phone: 800-732-8939. *

MACLEISH, PETER R., neuroscientist; PhD. Prof. medicine Morehouse Sch. Medicine Neuroscience Inst., Atlanta, dir., 1996—, George H.W. Bush & Barbara P. Bush chair, 1996—. Mem.: Inst. Medicine. Office: Morehouse Sch Medicine Neuroscience Inst 720 Westview Dr SW Atlanta GA 30310 Office Phone: 404-756-5785. Office Fax: 404-752-0141. E-mail: pmacleish@msm.edu.

MACLEISH, RODERICK, JR., lawyer; b. Boston, Oct. 31, 1952; AB with honors, Vassar Coll., 1975; JD cum laude, Boston U., 1978. Bar: Mass. 1979, US Court Appeals, 1st Cir., US Court Appeals, 11th Cir., US Dist. Ct. for the Dist. Mass. Law clerk to Hon. Joseph L. Tauro US Dist. Ct. Mass., 1978-79; shareholder, atty. Greenberg Traurig, LLP, Boston. Lectr. and guest spkr. in the field. Editor Boston U. Law Rev., 1977-78; contbr.articles to profl. publs. Mem. civil justice adv. bd. US Dist. Ct., 1995; bd. dir. Cotting Sch., Lexington, Mass., 1990—, Internat. Assn. for the Right to Effective Treatment, 1988—92, Greater Boston Legal Svcs., 1988—90; founder, chmn. bd. dirs. The Mass. 9/11 Fund, Inc., 2002; mem. adv. com. Alliance for the Mental Ill of Mass. Inc., 1988—90. Named one of Top 10 Litigators, Nat. Law Jour., 2003; recipient Award for Outstanding Advocacy in a successful 10-yr. pro bono litigation effort on behalf of Bridgewater State Hospital Clients, Alliance for the Mentally Ill of Mass., 1988, Civil Rights award, Mass. Coalition of Families and Advocates for the Retarded, 1997. Fellow: Mass. Bar Found. Office: Greenberg Traurig LLP One International Pl Boston MA 02110 Office Phone: 617-310-6000. Office Fax: 617-310-6001. Business E-Mail: macleishr@gtlaw.com.

MACLELLAN, STEVE, bank executive; Chief exec. pvt. client svcs. J.P. Morgan Chase & Co. Office: JP Morgan Chase & Co 270 Park Ave New York NY 10017-2070

MACLENNAN, BERYCE WINIFRED, psychologist; b. Aberdeen, Scotland, Mar. 14, 1920; came to U.S., 1949, naturalized, 1965; d. William and Beatrice (MaCrae) Mellis; m. John Duncan MacLennan, Nov. 29, 1944. BSc with honors, London Sch. Econs., 1947; PhD, London U., 1960. Diplomate Am. Bd. Clin. Psychology, cert. group therapist, trauma specialist. Group psychotherapist, youth specialist cons., NYC and Washington, 1949-63; dir. Ctr. for Prevention Juvenile Delinquency and New Careers, Washington, 1963-66; sect. chief NIMH, Mental Health Study Ctr., Adelphi, Md., 1967-70, chief, 1971-74; regional adminstr. Mass. Dept. Mental Health, Springfield, 1974-75; sr. mental health adv. GAO, Washington, 1976-90; pvt. practice, specialist psychotherapy Bethesda, Md., 1990—. Clin. prof. George Washington U., 1970-2002; group therapy cons. DC Mental Health Svcs., 1993-2002, Washington Assessement and Therapy Svcs., 1992-2006; lectr. Montgomery CC, 1988-91, Washington Sch. Psychiatry Geropsychiatric Program, 1997—; tech. adv. com. Prince George's County Mental Health Assn., 1968-84; cons. Washington Bus. Group on Health, 1990-91, KOBA, 1991; leader Trauma Psychotherapy Groups, 2002-03, Hebrew Home Rsch. Inst. Elder Housing Socialization and Memory Improvement Groups, 2000-02. Mem. NIMH Prevention Intervention Rsch. Task Force, 1990-91, Montgomery County Victims Assistance Programs, 1990-95; v.p. Compliance, Federally Employed Women, 1979-81; pres. Glenecho chpt. Older Women's League, 1993-94; mem. Montgomery County Disaster Outreach Team, 2004—. Fellow APA, Am. Orthopsychiat. Assn.; disting. fellow Am. Group Psychotherapy Assn.; mem. Washington Mushroom Club. Democrat.

MACLENNAN, DAVID HERMAN, research scientist, educator; b. Swan River, Man., Can., July 3, 1937; s. Douglas Henry and Sigridur (Sigurdson) MacL.; m. Linda Carol Vass, Aug. 18, 1965; children: Jessica Lynn (dec.), Jeremy Douglas, Jonathan David. BSA, U. Man., 1959; MS, Purdue U., 1961, PhD, 1963; DSc (hon.), U. Man., 2001. Postdoctoral fellow Inst. Enzyme Research, U. Wis., Madison, 1963-64; asst. prof. U. Wis., Madison, 1964-68; assoc. prof. U. Toronto, 1969-74, prof., 1974-93, J.W. Billes prof. med. rsch., 1987—, Univ. prof., 1993—, acting chmn., 1978-80, chmn., 1980-90; prin. investigator Can. Genetic Diseases Network of Ctrs. of Excellence, 1991—. Med. adv. bd. Muscular Dystrophy Assn. Can., 1976-87; scientists' rev. panel Med. Rsch. Coun. Can., 1988-90; chmn. molecular biology and pathology grants com. Heart and Stroke Found. Can., 1995-99; rsch. rev. panel U. Ottawa Heart Inst., 1991-95; med. rev. panel Gairdner Found., 1999-2001, med. adv. bd., 2001-2005; cons. Merck, Sharp and Dohme, West Point, Pa., 1992-98. Assoc. editor Can. Jour. Biochemistry, 1972-76; mem. editl. bd. Jour. Biol. Chemistry, 1975-80, 82-87; contbr. articles on muscle membrane biochemistry to profl. jours. Decorated Officer Order of Can.; recipient Gairdner Found. Internat. award, 1991; Can. Med. Rsch. Coun. scholar, 1969-71, I.W. Killam Meml. scholar, 1977-78; recipient I.W. Killam Meml. prize Health Scis., 1997, Jonas Salk award Ont. March of Dimes, 1998, Salute to the City award, City of Toronto, 2002, Rick Gallop award Heart and Stroke Found. Ont., 2002. Fellow Royal Soc. Can., Royal Soc. London (Glaxo-Wellcome prize 2000), NAS (fgn. assoc.); mem. Can. Biochem. Soc. (Ayerst award 1974), Am. Soc. Biol. Chemists, Biophys. Soc. (Nat. Lectr. award 1990), Japanese Biochem. Soc. (hon.). Office: U Toronto-Banting & Best Med Rsch 112 College St Toronto ON Canada M5G 1L6 Home: 292 Airdrie Rd Toronto ON Canada M4G 1N3 E-mail: david.maclennan@utoronto.ca.

MACLEOD, ANGUS, retired internist; b. Romford, Essex, Eng., Apr. 24, 1943; came to U.S., 1967; s. Malcolm Macleod and Jean (Littlefair) McKean; m. Gwynne Louise Grellner, May 23, 1969 (div. Aug. 1987); children: Kenneth, Anne, Stephen. MB, ChB, Glasgow U., 1967. Diplomate Am. Bd. Internal Medicine. Intern Luth. Hosp., St. Louis, 1967—68; resident in internal medicine St. Louis U., 1969, 1971—73, fellow in cardiology, 1973—74; physician Grandel Med. Group, St. Louis, 1974—2000, ret., 2000. Instr., then asst. prof. medicine St. Louis U.; chmn. dept. medicine Lutheran Hosp., St. Louis; pres. Grandel Med. Group, St. Louis. Capt. U.S. Army, 1969-71. Decorated Bronze Star. Fellow: ACP; mem.: St. Louis Met. Med. Soc., Mo. State Med. Soc. E-mail: corvus1745@yahoo.com.

MACLEOD, HUGH ANGUS MCINTOSH, optical science educator, physicist, consultant; b. Glasgow, Scotland, June 20, 1933; came to U.S., 1979; s. John and Agnes (Maclure) M.; m. Ann Turner, May 25, 1957; children: Hugh, Ivor, Charles, Eleanor, Alexander. BSc with honors, U. Glasgow, 1954; D of Tech., Coun. for Nat. Acad. Awards, 1979; D honoris causa, U. Aix-Marseille, 1997. Chartered physicist. Grad. apprentice Sperry Gyroscope Co. Ltd., Brentford, Eng., 1954-56, engr., 1956-60; chief engr. Williamson Mfg. Co. Ltd., London, 1961-62; sr. physicist Mervyn Instruments Ltd., Woking, Eng., 1963; tech. mgr. Sir Howard Grubb Parsons & Co. Ltd., Newcastle upon Tyne, Eng., 1964-70; reader in thin-film physics Newcastle upon Tyne Poly., 1971-79; assoc. prof. U. Aix-Marseille III, France, 1979; prof. optical scis. U. Ariz., Tucson, 1979-95, prof. emeritus, 1995—; pres. Thin Film Ctr., Inc., Tucson, 1992—; dir. Precision Optics Corp., Inc., 1997—2002. Author: Thin-Film Optical Filters, 2001; editor Jour. Modern Optics, London, 1988-93; contbr. over 200 articles to profl. jours., chpts. to books. Recipient John Matteucci award, Assn. Indsl. Metallizers, Coaters and Laminators, 2000, Life for Thin Film award, European Vacuum Coaters Workshop, 2004. Fellow Inst. Physics (London), Optical Soc. Am. (dir.-at-large 1987-89, Esther Hoffman Beller award 1997), SPIE-Internat. Soc. Optical Engring. (Gold medal 1987), Am. Vacuum Soc., Soc. Vacuum Coaters (Nathaniel H. Sugerman Meml. award 2002). Anglican. Avocation: piano. Home: 2745 E Via Rotunda Tucson AZ 85716-5227 Office: Thin Film Ctr Inc 2745 E Via Rotonda Tucson AZ 85716-5227 Business E-Mail: angus@thinfilmcenter.com.

MACLEOD, JAMES L., minister, finance company executive, art gallery owner; b. Oakdale, La., Apr. 27, 1937; s. William Lasater and Sara Louise (Macaulay) MacLeod. BA, Washington and Lee U., 1959; MA, BD, Emory U., 1968; D, Miss. State U., 1972. Ordained to ministry Presbyn. Ch., 1963. Minister U.S.-So. Presbyn. Ch., 1963—85, minister assoc. reform synod, 1985—; educator Ga. State Schs., 1972—91; pres. Brunswick Fin., Ga., 1991—, Brunswick Gallery, 1993—; min. First Assoc. Reformed Presbyn. Ch., Augusta, Ga., 1988—99. Author: (book) Great Dr. Waddel, 1985, A Season of Grace, 1974, Presbyterian Tradition in the South, 1978. Councilman City of Brunswick, 1994—, mayor pro tem, 1996—; mem. Soc. Cin., Washington, 1970. Scholar, NEH, 1986. Fellow: Soc. Antiquaries Scotland; mem.: NEA, Ga. Assn. Edn., Fulbright Alumni Assn., Pinnacle Club, Phi Delta Kappa. Democrat. Home: 508 Walker Road Augusta GA 30901

MACLEOD, JOHN AMEND, lawyer; b. Manila, June 5, 1942; s. Anthony Macaulay and Dorothy Lillian (Amend); m. Ann Klee; children: Kerry, Jack. BBA, U. Notre Dame, 1963, JD, 1969. Bar: D.C. 1969, U.S. Supreme Ct. 1980. Assoc. Jones, Day, Reavis & Pogue, Washington, 1969-73, ptnr., 1974-79, Crowell & Moring LLP, Washington, 1979—. Mem. mgmt. com., 1979-82, 83-86, 91-94, 99-2000, 00-06, chmn.firm, 1984-85, 93-94., 2000-06, chmn. emeritus, 2006—. Editor-in-chief Notre Dame Law Rev., 1968-69; contbr. articles to profl. jours. Trustee Energy Mineral and Law Found., 1979—2002; bd. dirs. St. Francis Ctr., 1982—91, Notre Dame Law Assn., 1981—86. Served to lt. US Army, 1963—65. Recipient disting. mining lawyer award Nat. Mining Assn., 1995, forest industry victory of yr. award Am. Forest and Paper Assn., 1994. Mem. ABA, D.C. Bar Assn., Ptnrs. Leadership Forum, Metro. Club (Washington). Home: 4040 Swartz Rd Maurertown VA 22644-2320 Office: Crowell & Moring LLP 1001 Pennsylvania Ave NW Washington DC 20004-2595

MACLEOD, LINDA ANN, secondary school educator; b. Kansas City, Dec. 30, 1946; d. William Glennon Price and Victoria Murdza; children: Angela Renee, Sara Kristen. BA in Art Edn., U. Mo., 1969, MA in Secondary Edn., 1983, degree in Edn., 1988. Tchr. art Consolidated Sch. Dist. 2, Raytown, Mo., 1980—. Torchbearer Olympics, 2002. Recipient Nat. Merit award, Knights Pythias, 2003. Mem.: Raytown (Mo.) Cmty. Tchrs. Assn. (sec. 1986—87), Mo. State Tchrs. Assn., Kans. City (Mo.) Ski Club (trip capt. 1986—). Roman Catholic. Avocations: tennis, art, skiing, volleyball. Office: Raytown South Sr High Sch 8211 Sterling Ave Raytown MO 64138-2690

MACLEOD, ROBERT ANGUS, microbiology educator, researcher; b. Athabasca, Alta., Can., July 13, 1921; s. Norman John and Eleonora Pauline Bertha (Westerhoff) MacL.; m. Patricia Rosemarie Robertson, Sept. 1, 1948; children— Douglas John, Alexander Robert, Kathleen Mary, David Gordon, Michael Norman, Susan Joan BA with honors in Chemistry, U. B.C., Vancouver, Can., 1943, MA in Chemistry and Biology, 1945; PhD in Biochemistry, U. Wis., Madison, 1949. Asst. prof. Queen's U., Kingston, Ont., Canada, 1949-52; sr. biochemist Fisheries Research Bd. Can., Vancouver, B.C., 1952-60; assoc. prof. to prof., chmn. dept. microbiology Macdonald Coll., McGill U., Ste. Anne de Bellevue, Que., Canada, 1960-86, prof. emeritus, 1986—. Cons. Def. Research Bd., Ottawa, Ont., 1965—75; assoc. editor Can. Jour. Microbiology, Ottawa, 1965—70. Author tech. papers. Recipient Harrison prize, Royal Soc. Can., 1960. Fellow: Royal Soc. Can.; mem.: Am. Soc. Microbiology (hon.), Can. Soc. Microbiologists (hon.; pres. 1976—77, award 1973). Avocations: swimming, fishing. Home: 10 Slate St Stittsville ON Canada K2S 1Y5 E-mail: ramacl@sympatico.ca.

MACLEOD, WILLIAM BENTLEY, economics, law professor; b. Iserlohn, Germany, 1954; came to U.S., 1995; m. Raisa Nones (div.); children: Raisa, Gabriela; m. Janet Marion Currie, May 18, 1997; children: Joana, Daniel. BA magna cum laude, Queen's U., Kingston, Ont., Can., 1975, MSc in Math., 1979; PhD in Econs., U. B.C., Vancouver, Can., 1984. From asst. prof. to assoc. prof. Queen's U., 1982-90; assoc. prof. U. Montreal, 1990-92, prof. econs., 1992-96, Boston Coll., 1996-97; prof. econs. and law U. So. Calif., LA, 1997—2006, dir. Ctr. for Law, Econs. and Orgn., 1997—2006, chair jr. recruiting, 2000—03; program dir., personnel and behavioral econs. IZA, Bonn, Germany, 2003—07; prof. dept. econs. Columbia U., NY, 2005—, co-dir., chair jr. recruiting, 2005—06. Cons. Ind. Power Prodrs. Ont., Toronto, 1990-92, Human Resources Can., Ottawa, Ont., 1993-95; Harold Innis Meml. lectr., 1996; vis. prof. econs. and law Calif. Inst. Tech., 2002, Princeton U., 2003-04; bd. dirs. We. Econs. Assn. Assoc. editor: Jour. Econ. Behavior and Orgn., 2002—; editor: Jour. Labor Econs., 2003—; contbr. articles to profl. jours. NSF grantee, 1997-03, 06. Fellow Econometric Soc.; mem. AAAS, Am. Econs. Assn., Soc. Labor Economists (H. Gregg Lewis prize 2002), Assn. Comparative Sys., Econ. Sci. Assn., Am. Law and Econs. Assn., Western Econs. Assn. (bd. dirs. 2003-06). Office: Columbia U Dept Econs MC3308 420 W 118th St New York NY 10027-7296

MACLIN, AMY, editor; Staff editor NY Times Syndication Sales Corp. Contbr. US Weekly, 2000; author: (article) State of Grace, 2004; contbr. (chapters to books) Diverse Issues -- Diverse Answers: Reading, Writing, & Thinking About Social Issues, 2006.

MACLIN, SAMUEL TODD, diversified financial services company executive; With Chem. NY Corp., Chem. Banking Corp., Chase Manhattan Corp.; exec. v.p. J.P. Morgan Chase & Co., chmn., CEO Tex. Region and head mid. market banking, head comml. banking, 2004—. Office: JP Morgan Chase & Co 270 Park Ave New York NY 10017-2070

MAC LOW, MORDECAI-MARK, astrophysicist; b. NYC, Mar. 9, 1963; s. Jackson Mac Low and Iris Lezak. BA, Princeton U., 1983; PhD, U. Colo., 1989. Rsch. asst. U. Colo., Boulder, 1983—88; NRC fellow NASA Ames Rsch. Ctr., Moffett Field, Calif., 1989-90; rsch. assoc. U. Calif., Berkeley, 1991-92, U. Chgo., 1992-95; sci. Max-Planck-Inst. für Astronomie, Heidelberg, Germany, 1995-99; asst. curator of astrophysics Am. Mus. Natural History, NYC, 1999—2002, assoc. curator astrophysics, 2002—07, curator astrophysics, curator-in-charge dept. astrophysics, 2005—, chair divsn. phys. sics., 2007—. Adj. asst. prof. Columbia U., 1999—2002, adj. assoc. prof., 2003—07, adj. prof., 2007—; mem. grant rev. panels NSF and NASA, chair panels; mem. adv. com. tchr. renewal for urban sci. tchg. program Am. Mus. Natural History and CUNY; mem. several conf. sci. organizing coms.; spkr. in field; reviewer in field. Contbr. articles to popular mags. and profl. jours. Grantee, NSF, 1999—, NASA, 1999—. Mem.: Internat. Astron. Union, Am. Phys. Soc., Am. Astron. Soc. (mem. com. employmenht 2001—04). Office: Am Mus Natural History Dept Astrophysics CPW & 79th St New York NY 10024-5192 Home Phone: 212-932-2639. Business E-Mail: mordecai@amnh.org.

MACMAHON, THOMAS P., healthcare company executive; B in mktg., St. Peter's Coll., NJ; MBA, Fairleigh Dickinson U., 1975. Joined Roche Bio-Med. Labs. as mktg. rsch. analyst, 1969; v.p. pub. affairs and planning Hoffman-La Roche Inc., Nutley, NJ, 1982—83, v.p. and gen. mgr. diagnostics systems unit, 1983—86, pres. Roche Diagnostics Group, 1988—96, mem. exec. com., 1988—96, sr. v.p., 1993—96; vice chmn. Lab. Corp. Am. Holdings, Burlington, NC, 1995—96, chmn., 1996—, CEO, pres., 1997—2007. Named to The Pinnacle (highest award), Fairleigh Dickinson U., 2001. Office: Lab Corp Am Holdings 358 S Main St Burlington NC 27215 *

MACMANUS, SUSAN ANN, political science professor, researcher; b. Tampa, Fla., Aug. 22, 1947; d. Harold Cameron and Elizabeth (Riegler) MacM. BA cum laude, Fla. State U., 1968, PhD, 1975; MA, U. Mich., 1969. Instr. Valencia C.C., Orlando, Fla., 1969-73; rsch. asst. Fla. State U., 1973-75; asst. prof. U. Houston, 1975-79, assoc. prof., 1979-85, dir. MPA program, 1983-85; rsch. assoc. Ctr. Pub. Policy, 1982-85; prof., dir. PhD progam Cleve. State U., 1985-87; prof. pub. adminstrn. and polit. sci. U. South Fla., Tampa, 1987—, chair dept. govt. and internat. affairs, 1987-93, disting. univ. prof., 1999. Vis. prof. U. Okla., Norman, 1981—; field rsch. assoc. Brookings Inst., Washington, 1977—82, Princeton (N.J.) U., 1979—, Cleve. State U., 1982—83, Westat, Inc., Washington, 1983—; summer field rsch. assoc. Columbia U., NYC, 1979, Nat. Acad. Pub. Adminstrn., Washington, 1980. Author: Revenue Patterns in U.S. Cities and Suburbs: A Comparative Analysis, 1978, Reapportionment and Representation in Florida: A Historical Collection, 1991, Doing Business with Government: Federal, State, Local and Foreign Government Purchasing Practices for Every Business and Public Institution, 1992, Federal Aid to Houston, 1993, Young v. Old: Generational Combat in the 21st Century, 1996, Targeting Senior Voters, 2000; co-author (with others): Governing A Changing America, 1984; co-author: (with Francis T. Borkowski) Visions for the Future: Creating New Institutional Relationships Among Academia, Business, Government, and Community, 1989; co-author: (with Elizabeth R. MacManus) Citrus, Sawmills, Critters & Crackers: Life in Early Lutz and Central Pasco County, 1998, The Lutz Depot, 2000; editor: Mapping Florida's Political Landscape: The Changing Art and Politics of Reapportionment and Redistricting, 2002; co-editor (with Thomas R. Dye): Politics in States and Communities, 11th edit., 2003; co-editor: (with Dano Moreno and Kevin Hill) Florida's Politics: Ten Media Markets, One Powerful State, 2004; writer: manuals in field, mem. editl. bd.: various jours; contbr. articles to profl. jours., chapters to books. Bd. dirs. Houston Area Women's Ctr., 1977, past pres., v.p. fin., treas.; mem. LWV, Gov.'s Coun. Econ. Advisers, 1988-90, Harris County (Tex.) Women's Polit. Caucus, Houston; bd. dirs. USF Rsch. Found., Inc.; chair Fla. Elections Commn., 1999-2003; mem. Fla. Gov.'s Coun. Econ. Advisers, 2000—. Recipient U. Houston Coll. Social Scis. Tchg. Excellence award, 1977, Herbert J. Simon award for best article in 3d vol., Internat. Jour. Pub. Adminstrn., 1981, Theodore & Venette Askounes-Ashford Disting Scholar award U. South Fla., 1991, Disting. Rsch. Scholar award, 1991, Tchg. Excellence award, 1999; Ford Found. fellow, 1967-68; grantee Valencia C. C. Faculty, 1972, U. Houston, 1976-77, 79, 83; Fulbright Rsch. scholar, Korea, 1989; Choice mag. award, 1996; named Disting. Univ. Prof., 1999; rsch. fellow Fla. Inst. of Govt., 2000—. Mem. Am. Polit. Sci. Assn. (program com. 1983-84, chair sect. intergovtl. rels., award 1989, mem. exec. coun. 1994—, pres.-elect sec. urban politics 1994-95, pres. sect. urban politics 1995-96), So. Polit. Sci. Assn. (v.p. 1990-91, pres.-elect 1992-93, pres. 1993-94, V.O. key award com. 1983-84, best paper on women and politics 1988, Diane Blair award 2001), Midwest Polit. Sci. Assn., Western Polit. Sci. Assn., Southwestern Polit. Sci. Assn. (local arrangements com. 1982-83, profession com. 1977-80), ASPA (nominating com. Houston chpt. 1983, bd. mem. Suncoast chpt., pres.-elect 1991, Lilly award 1992), Policy Studies Orgn. (mem. editl. bd. jour. 1981—, exec. coun. 1983-85), Women's Caucus Polit. Sci. (portfolio pre-decision rev. com. 1982-83, projects and programs com. 1981, fin.-budget com. 1980-81), Fla. Polit. Sci. Assn. (pres. 1997-98, Manning Dauer Disting. Fla. Polit. Sci. award 2001), Acad. Polit. Sci., Mcpl. Fin. Officers Assn., Phi Kappa Phi (Artist/Scholar award U. South Fla. 1997), Phi Beta Kappa, Pi Sigma Alpha (mem. exec. coun. 1994-96, pres. 2000-02), Pi Alpha Alpha. Methodist. Home: 2506 Collier Pky Land O Lakes FL 34639-5228 Office: U South Fla Dept Polit Sci Tampa FL 33620 E-mail: samacmanus@aol.com.

MACMASTER, ROBERT ELLSWORTH, historian, educator; b. Winthrop, Mass., Oct. 10, 1919; s. Joseph Oscar and Ruby (Slocomb) MacM.; m. Ann Elizabeth Lynch, Apr. 28, 1942; children— Angus Michael, Martha Ann, David Joseph. AB, Harvard, 1941, A.M., 1948, PhD, 1952. Mem. faculty MIT, 1952-90, prof. history and lit., 1967-90, prof. emeritus, 1990—, chmn. history faculty, 1970-72. Author: Danilevsky: A Russian Totalitarian Philosopher, 1967; contbr. articles on L.N. Tolstoi to publs. Served with AUS, 1941-46. Mem. Am. Assn. Advancement Slavic Studies. Home: 461 Main St Hingham MA 02043-4701 Office: MIT Dept History Cambridge MA 02139

MACMEEKEN, JOHN PEEBLES, foundation executive, educator; b. Aug. 15, 1924; s. John West and Esther (Strong) M.; m. Mary Swanberg, Nov. 26, 1949; children: Carol B. Macmeeken Luther, John W., Susan G. Student, U. Calif., Berkeley, 1941-43, Ind. U., 1943-44; JD, Harvard U., 1948. Bar: Calif. 1948. Assoc. Chickering & Gregory, San Francisco, 1948-60, ptnr., 1960-82, Pettit & Martin, San Francisco, 1982-93; v.p. Zynk Indsl. Corp., 1995-98; pres. Found. for Books to China, 1993—, SOAR Bus. Inst., 1998—. Bd. dirs. Lanark West Corp.; pres. Clinton U., San Francisco, 1995-97; lectr. law Fudan U., Shanghai, China, East China

Normal U., Shanghai, Nanking U., China, Zhongshan U., Guangzhou; sec. Twan Co. LLC, Sian Tien Dao Yuan. Sgt. U.S. Army, 1943-45. Mem. Nat. Com. on US-China Rels., Calif. Bar Assn., Outlook Club Calif. Republican. Congregationalist. Home: 5708 Glenbrook Dr Oakland CA 94618-1724 Office Phone: 510-428-2145. Personal E-mail: jmacmeeken@aol.com.

MACMILLAN, DAVID W.C., chemistry professor; b. Bellshill, Scotland, 1968; BS in Chemistry, Univ. Glasgow, 1991; PhD, Univ. Calif., Irvine, 1996; postdoctoral studies, Harvard Univ., 1996—98. Asst. to assoc. prof. Calif. Inst. Tech., Pasadena, 2000—03, prof., 2003—04, Earle C. Anthony prof. chemistry, 2004—06; A. Barton Hepburn prof., inorganic chemistry Princeton Univ., 2006—. Cons. Abbott Rsch. Labs., Ill., 2000—, Johnson & Johnson, Calif., NJ, 2000—, Bayer Pharm., Conn., 2001—, Merck Rsch. Labs., 2001, Amgen Pharm. Worldwide, 2002—, Gilead Pharm., Calif., 2003—. Recipient Boehringer-Ingelheim New Investigator award, 2000, Astra-Zeneca Excellence in Chemistry award, 2001, Eli-Lilly New Investigator award, 2001, Glaxo Smithkline Chemistry Scholar award, 2001, Pfizer Award for Excellence in Synthesis, 2002, Bristol-Meyers Squibb Award for Organic Synthesis, 2002, Corday-Morgan Medal, Royal Soc. Chemistry, 2004, Elias J. Corey Award for Outstanding Contribution in Organic Synthesis by a Young Investigator, 2005, Tetrahedron Young Investigator award, 2005, Mukaiyama award, 2006, Thieme-IUPAC Prize in Synthetic Organic Chemistry, 2006. Mem.: Am. Chem. Soc. (Arthur C. Cope Scholar award 2007). Office: Dept Chemistry Princeton Univ Princeton NJ 08544 *

MACMILLAN, ROBERT SMITH, electronics engineer; b. LA, Aug. 28, 1924; s. Andrew James and Moneta (Smith) M.; m. Barbara Macmillan, Aug. 18, 1962; 1 child, Robert G. BS in Physics, Calif. Inst. Tech., 1948, MS in Elec. Engring., 1949, PhD in Elec. Engring./Physics cum laude, 1954. Rsch. engr. Jet Propulsion Lab., Calif. Inst. Tech., Pasadena, 1951-55, asst. prof. elec. engring., 1955-58; assoc. prof. elec. engring. U. So. Calif., LA, 1958-70; mem. sr. tech. staff Litton Sys., Inc., Van Nuys, Calif., 1969-79; dir. sys. engring. Litton Data Command Sys., Agoura Hills, Calif., 1979-89; pres. The Macmillan Group, La Canada Flintridge, Calif., 1989—. Treas., v.p. Video Color Corp., Inglewood, 1965-66; cons. fgn. tech. div. USAF, Wright-Patterson AFB, Ohio, 1957-74, Space Tech. Labs., Glendale, Calif., 1956-60, Space Gen. Corp., El Monte, Calif., 1960-63. With Air Corps US Army, 1943—46. Recipient Nat. Patriot's medal, Nat. Rifle Assn., 2002, Rep. Senatorial medal of freedom, 2004. Mem.: IEEE, Am. Phys. Soc., Am. Inst. Physics, Eta Kappa Nu, Tau Beta Pi, Sigma Xi. Republican. Presbyterian. Achievements include research in ionospheric, radio-wave, propagation; very low frequency radio-transmitting antennas; optical coherence and statistical optics. Home: 350 Starlight Crest Dr La Canada Flintridge CA 91011-2839 Office: The Macmillan Group 350 Starlight Crest Dr La Canada Flintridge CA 91011-2839 Home Phone: 818-790-4809; Office Phone: 818-790-4809. Office Fax: 818-952-1735. Personal E-mail: rsmacmillan08@aol.com.

MACMILLAN, STEPHEN P., health products executive; b. July 19, 1963; married; 2 children. BA in econ., Davidson Coll.; grad. advanced mgmt. program, Harvard Bus. Sch. Various mktg. positions Procter & Gamble; with over the counter div. McNeil Consumer and Specialty Pharm. Johnson & Johnson Corp., mktg. dir. J&J/Merck over-the-counter franchise worldwide England; mgr. dir. Johnson & Johnson MSD (Merck), England, 1995; v.p., mktg. and profl. sales McNeil Consumer and Splty. Pharm. Johnson & Johnson Corp., 1997; pres. Johnson & Johnson-Merck Consumer Pharmaceuticals; sector v.p. global splty. ops. Pharmacia & Upjohn, 1999—2003; COO Stryker Corp., 2004—05, pres., CEO, 2005—. Office: Stryker Corp 2725 Fairfield Rd Kalamazoo MI 49002 *

MACMILLAN, WHITNEY, retired food products and import/export company executive; married; 2 children. BA, Yale Univ., 1951; D (hon.), Mont.State Univ., Bozeman, 2002. With Cargill, Wayzata, Minn., 1951—95, chmn., CEO, 1977—95, chmn. emeritus, 1995. Bd. dirs. Deluxe Corp., Minn.; exec. fellow, tchr. Univ. St. Thomas Grad. Sch. Bus., Minn. Named one of 400 Richest Americans, Forbes Mag., 2005; recipient Outstanding Alumni award, Blake Sch., 1997, 400 Richest Americans, Forbes Mag., 2006. Mem.: Care Internat., Trilateral Commn., Coun. Fgn. Affairs.

MACMILLEN, RICHARD EDWARD, biological sciences educator, researcher; b. Upland, Calif., Apr. 19, 1932; s. Hesper Nichols and Ruth Henrietta (Golder) MacM.; m. Ann Gray, June 12, 1953 (div. 1975); children: Jennifer Kathleen, Douglas Michael; m. Barbara Jean Morgan, Oct. 23, 1980; 1 child, Ian Richard. BA, Pomona Coll., Claremont, Calif., 1954; MS, U. Mich., 1956; PhD, UCLA, 1961. From instr. to assoc. prof. Pomona Coll., Claremont, Calif., 1960-68, Wig Disting. prof., 1965; assoc. prof., then prof. U. Calif., Irvine, 1968—, chair dept. population and environ. biology, 1972-74, chair dept. ecology and evolutionary biology, 1984-90, prof. emeritus, 1993—. Award panel NSF, Washington, 1976-80; coord. U. Calif. Multi-Campus Supercourse in Environ. Biology, White Mountain Rsch. Sta., 1996-97, tchg. participant, 1998—; rev. panel, EPA Star grad. fellowship program, 2002, 04; budget com., Jackson County Fire Dist. 5, 2001—; Alumni Admissions vol., Pomona Coll., 2001—; SMART vol. Talent Elem. Sch., 2007-; vol. morphologist US Fish and Wildlife Svc. Forensics Lab., 2004—. Contbr. numerous articles to profl. jours. Chair sci. adv. bd. Endangered Habitats League, 1991-93. Recipient Rsch. award NSF, 1961-83; Fulbright-Hays Advanced Rsch. fellow Monash U., Australia, 1966-67. Fellow AAAS; mem. Am. Soc. Mammalogists (life), Ecol. Soc. Am. (cert. sr. ecologist), Am. Ornithologists Union (life), Cooper Ornithol. Soc. (life, bd. dirs. 1982-84). Democrat. Avocations: fly fishing, camping, hiking, nature photography. Home: 705 Foss Rd Talent OR 97540-9758 Home Phone: 541-512-9884. Business E-mail: bidmac@jeffnet.org. *As world human populations continue to increase, our natural world continues to degrade. It is incumbent upon all of us to accept the responsibility of stewarding our land and its biota as precious and renewable resources.*

MACMURREN, HAROLD HENRY, JR., psychologist, lawyer; b. Jersey City, Sept. 18, 1942; s. Harold Sr. and Evelyn (Almone) MacM.; m. Margaret Bartro, Nov. 21, 1970. BA, William Paterson Coll., Wayne, NJ, 1965; MA, Jersey City Coll., 1973; EdD, St. Johns U., NYC, 1985; JD, Rutgers U., 1989. Cert. secondary tchr., N.J.; Bar: N.J. 1989. Instr. Wanaque (N.J.) Bd. Edn., 1965-66, cons. psychologist, 1983-84; instr. Elmwood Park (N.J.) Bd. Edn., 1967-70; coll. faculty mem., psychologist Assoc. Clinic, Jersey City, 1971-72; cons. psychologist Rockaway (N.J.) Bd. Edn., 1972-83; intern lawyer Environ. Law Clinic, Newark, 1988-89; cons. psychologist Pequannock (N.J.) Bd. Edn., 1984—; pvt. practice law, 2000—. Coord. child study team Sandyston Walpack Sch. Sys.; adj. prof. William Paterson U.; spkr., writer in field. Mem. ABA, NEA, N.J. Edn. Assn., N.J. Psychologists Assn., N.J. Bar Assn., Sierra Club, Phi Delta Kappa. Avocations: reading, travel, skiing, hiking. Home: 4 Systema Pl Sussex NJ 07461-2833 Office: PO Box 2510 22 Wantage Ave Branchville NJ 07890 Office Phone: 973-948-3500. Personal E-mail: macmurrenesq@earthlink.net.

MACMURREN, MARGARET PATRICIA, secondary school educator, consultant; b. Newark, Nov. 4, 1947; d. Kenneth F. and Doris E. (Lounsberry) Bartro; m. Harold MacMurren, Nov. 21, 1970. BA, Paterson State U., 1969; MA, William Paterson Coll., 1976; postgrad., Jersey City State Coll., 1976—. Tchr. Byram (N.J.) Twp. Schs., 1969-77; learning cons., child study team coord. Andover Regional Schs., Newton, N.J., 1977—. Mem.: NEA, Andover Regional Edn. Assn. (pres. 1986—87), Sussex County Assn. Learning Cons. (pres. 1982—83, 1993—94, sec.-treas. 1991—92, v.p. 1992—93), N.J. Learning Assn., N.J. Edn. Assn. Avocations: skiing, dance, weightlifting, travel, reading. Home: 4 Systema Pl Sussex NJ 07461-2833 Office: Andover Regional Schs 707 Limecrest Rd Newton NJ 07860-8801 Office Phone: 973-940-1234 246. Business E-Mail: haroldm@nac.net.

MACNAIR, DAVID CAMERON, marketing executive; s. Hugh Alexander Wilson and Winifred Neville MacNair; m. Lisa Marie McKain, June 30, 1984; children: Margaret Lauren, Elizabeth Cameron. BA, Claremont McKenna Coll., Calif., 1981; MBA, U. Wash., Seattle, 1984. Sales rep. Polaroid, Seattle, 1986—89, mktg. mgr. film Cambridge, Mass., 1989—90, mktg. mgr. worldwide new products, 1990—92; sr. product mgr. health care Sunbeam, Schaumburg, Ill., 1992—94, dir. mktg. internat., 1994—95, dir. mktg. health care products Delray Beach, Fla., 1995—97; v.p. mktg. InSinkErator divsn. Emerson, Racine, Wis., 1997—. Brand officer Emerson Electric, St. Louis, 2004—. Patentee food waste disposer trim shell, others. Bd. dirs. Racine Art Mus., 2003—, co-chair mktg. com., 2004—, mem. edn. com., 2005—. Recipient Bottom Line Design award, Bus. 2.0 mag., 2007. Avocations: hiking, boating, travel. Home: 1137 Dawes St Libertyville IL 60048 Office: InSinkErator divsn Emerson 4700 21st St Racine WI 53406 Office Phone: 262-554-3532. Office Fax: 262-554-3639. Personal E-mail: dcm4@aol.com.

MACNAUGHTON, ANGUS ATHOLE, finance company executive; b. Montreal, July 15, 1931; s. Athole Austin and Emily Kidder (MacLean) MacN.; children: Gillian Heather, Angus Andrew. Student, Lakefield Coll. Sch., 1941-47, McGill U., 1949-54. Auditor Coopers & Lybrand, Montreal, 1949-55; acct. Genstar Ltd., Montreal, 1955, asst. treas., 1956-61, treas., 1961-64, v.p., 1964-70, exec. v.p., 1970-73, pres., 1973-76, vice chmn., chief exec. officer, 1976-81, chmn. or pres., chief exec. officer, 1981-86; pres. Genstar Investment Corp., 1987—. Bd. dirs. Barrick Gold Corp., Genstar Investment Corp., Varian Semicondr. Assocs., Inc., San Ramon Med. Ctr.; past pres. Montreal chpt. Tax Execs. Inst. Bd. govs. Lakefield Coll. Sch.; past chmn. San Francisco Bay Area coun. Boy Scouts Am.; bd. dirs. San Francisco Opera; trustee World Affairs Coun. of No. Calif. Mem. Pacific Union Club, Villa Taverna (San Francisco), Mt. Royal Club (Montreal), Toronto Club. Office: 4 Embarcadero Ctr Ste 1900 San Francisco CA 94111-4191

MACNEE, WALTER M., finance company executive; BA, B.Ed, Queens Univ.; MBA, York Univ. Mgmt. positions through sr. v.p. Toronto Dominion Bank, 1983—2001; pres. MasterCard Canada, 2001—04; exec. v.p. Canadian Imperial Bank of Commerce, 2004—06; pres., Americas MasterCard Worldwide, Purchase, NY, 2006—. Office: MasterCard Worldwide 2000 Purchase St Purchase NY 10577 *

MACNEIL, IAN RODERICK, lawyer, educator; b. NYC, June 20, 1929; s. Robert Lister and Kathleen Gertrude (Metcalf) Macneil; m. Nancy Carol Wilson, Mar. 29, 1952; children: Roderick, Jennifer, Duncan (dec.), Andrew. BA magna cum laude, U. Vt., 1950; LLB magna cum laude, Harvard U., 1955. Bar: N.H. 1956-02. Law clk. Hon. Peter Woodbury, 1955-56; asso. Sulloway Hollis Godfrey & Soden, Concord, NH, 1956-59; mem. faculty Cornell U. Law Sch., Ithaca, NY, 1959-72, 74-80, Ingersoll prof. law, 1976-80; Wigmore prof. law Northwestern U. Sch. Law, Chgo., 1980-99, prof. emeritus, 1999—. Vis. prof. U. East Africa, 1965-67, Duke U., 1971-72; prof. law, mem. Inst. Advanced Studies, U. Va., 1972-74; vis. fellow Centre for Socio-legal Studies and Wolfson Coll., Oxford U., 1979; hon. vis. fellow faculty law U. Edinburgh, 1979, 87; Rosenthal lectr. Northwestern U. Sch. Law, 1979; Braucher vis. prof. Harvard U., 1988-89. Author: Bankruptcy Law in East Africa, 1966, Contracts: Exchange Transactions and Relations, 3d edit., with Paul J. Gudel, 2001. The New Social Contract, 1980, American Arbitration Law: Reformation Nationalization Internationalization, 1992; co-author: Federal Arbitration Law, 1994. Served with U.S. Army, 1951-53. Guggenheim fellow, 1978-79. Fellow Soc. Antiquaries (Scotland), Am. Acad. Arts and Scis.; mem. Scottish Soc. No. Studies, The Scottish Medievalists, Standing Coun. Scottish Chiefs. Home: 95/6 Grange Loan Edinburgh EH9 2ED Scotland

MACNEIL, ROBERT BRECKENRIDGE WARE, retired journalist, writer; b. Montreal, Que., Can., Jan. 19, 1931; came to U.S., 1963; s. Robert A.S. and Margaret Virginia (Oxner) MacN.; m. Rosemarie Anne Copland, 1956 (div. 1964); children: Catherine Anne, Ian B.; m. Jane J. Doherty, May 29, 1965 (div. 1983); children: Alison N., William H.; m. Donna P. Richards, Oct. 20, 1984. Student, Dalhousie U., 1949-51; BA, Carleton U., 1955; LHD (hon.), William Patterson Coll., 1977, Beaver Coll., Bates Coll., 1979, Lawrence U., 1980, Bucknell U., 1982, George Washington U., Kings Coll., Trinity Coll., U. Maine, 1983, Brown U., 1984, Colby Coll., Carleton Coll., U. S.C., 1985, Franklin and Marshall Coll., 1987, Nazareth Coll., Washington Coll., 1988, Kenyon Coll., 1990, U. Western Ont., 1992, U. Miami, Clark U., 1994, U. L.I., 1995, Columbia U., 1995, Princeton U., 1995, The Cooper Union, 1996, U. Toronto, 1997, Mt. Allison U., 1998; LHD (hon.), Dalhousie U., 2000. Radio actor CBC, Halifax, N.S., Canada, 1950-52, radio/TV announcer, 1954-55; announcer Sta.-CJCH, Halifax, 1951-52; announcer, news writer Sta. CFRA, Ottawa, Ont., Canada, 1952-54; sub-editor to filing editor Reuters News Agy., London, 1955-60; news corr. NBC, London, 1960-63, Washington, 1963-65, NYC, 1965-67; corr. Panorama program BBC, London, 1967-71, 73-75; sr. corr. Nat. Public Affairs Center for TV, Washington, 1971-73; exec. editor, co-anchor MacNeil/Lehrer Report, Sta. -WNET-TV, NYC, 1975—, MacNeil/Lehrer News Hour, PBS, 1983-95, ret., 1995; host America at a Crossroads, PBS, 2006—. Author: The People Machine, The Influence of Television on American Politics, 1968, The Right Place at the Right Time, 1982, Wordstruck, 1989, Burden of Desire, 1992, The Voyage, 1995, Breaking News, 1998, Looking For my Country, 2003; co-author: The Story of English, 1986, Do You Speak American?, 2005; editor The Way We Were 1963, 1988. Trustee Freedom Forum Newseum. Decorated Officer Order of Can., 1998; inductee TV Acad. Hall of Fame, 1999; recipient Lifetime Achievement award Overseas Press Club, 1995, Broadcaster of Yr. Internat. Radio and TV Soc., 1991, Paul White award Radio TV News Dirs. Assn., 1990, Medal of Honor U. Mo. Sch. Journalism, 1980; Catto fellow The Aspen Inst. Fellow AAAS, The MacDowell Colony (chmn. 1993); mem. AFTRA, Assn. Radio and TV News Analysts, Writers Guild Am., Century Club (NYC). Office: c/o MacNeil-Lehrer Prodns 2700 S Quincy St Ste 240 Arlington VA 22206-2226 E-mail: wordstruck2@cs.com.

MACNEILL, FREDERICK DOUGLAS, artist; b. Boston, Sept. 28, 1929; s. Frederick Douglas and Agnes (Thompson) MacN.; m. Anita Concetta Venti, Sept. 1, 1961; children: John, Paul. Student, Vesper George Sch. of Art, 1952-54, Arthur Safford, Alphonse Shelton. One man shows include Guild Boston Artists, 1980, 82; exhibited in group shows at Springfield (Mass.) Mus. Fine Art, 1965, Hobe Sound Gallery, Miller Gallery, Cin., Guild Boston Artists, 1982, Hobe Sound N. Gallery (formerly Payson Waldron Gallery), Portland, Maine, 1982, Nat. Wildlife Art Mus, Jackson, Wyo., 1994, Mus. of SW, Midland, Tex., 1992, Gibbs Mus. Art, Charleston, SC, Mystic Maritime Gallery and Mus., Mystic, Conn., 1995; represented in permanent and pvt. collections; painting included in Crucifixion in American Art; also book cover. Recipient Marion Quimby award Ogunquit Art Assn., 1975, Elliot Liskin award Rockport Art Assn., 1984, John Chetcutti, 1985, Silver medal of honor, 1985, Guild of Boston Artists award, 1988, Arts for the Pk. Top 100 award, 1991-92, 94, 2004, Bernard Cory Meml. award Rockport Art Assn., 2007, others. Mem. Am. Artists Profl. League, Allied Artists Am., Acad. Artists of Am., Guild Boston Artists, Concord Art Assn., North Shore Art Assn. (Gloucester Coop. Bank award 2005, Gift Cert. award 2006, Alden Bryan Meml. award 2006), Rockport Art Assn. (Helen Van Wyk Gold medal, 2000, Marguerite Pearson Gold medal, 2002, Virginia Karl Meml. award 2004, Maurice E. Goldberg Meml. award 2005, Popular Vote award 2006), Salmagundi Club (NYC, Martin Hannon Meml. award). Home: 23 Dana Rd Concord MA 01742-3408 Personal E-mail: macneillartist1@aol.com.

MACNEILL, JAMES WILLIAM, environmental energy and management consultant; b. Sask., Can., Apr. 22, 1928; s. Leslie William and Helga Ingeborg (Nohlgren) MacN.; m. Phyllis Beryl Ferguson, Nov. 30, 1953; children: Catherine Anne, Robin Lynne. BA, U. Sask., 1949, BE Mech., 1958, LLD (hon.), 1988; Diplome, U. Stockholm, 1951; DSc (hon.), McGill U., 1992; D of Environ. Studies (hon.), U. Waterloo, 1993; LHD (hon.), Lakehead U., 1994. Spl. adv. on constl. rev. Privy Council Office, Govt. Can., Ottawa, Ont., 1969-70; asst. sec. Can. Ministry of State for Urban Affairs, Ottawa, 1970-73, permanent sec., 1973-76; Can. AEP, Can. commr.-gen. UN Human Settlements Conf., Vancouver, B.C., 1975-78; dir. environ. directorate OECD, Paris, 1978-84; sec. gen. World Commn. Environment and Devel., Geneva, 1984-87; sr. fellow Inst. Research Pub. Policy, Ottawa, 1987-93; pres. J.W. MacNeill and Assocs., 1987-98; chmn. Internat. Inst. for Sustainable Devel., 1994-99. Spl. advisor to adminstrn. UN Devel. Program, 1994-97; chmn. ind. insp. panel World Bank, 1997-2002; mem. adv. panel BP Caspian Devel., 2003--. Author: Environmental Management, 1971, Beyond Interdependence, 1991. Apptd. officer Order of Can., 1995. Recipient Saskatchewan Achievement award, 1984, Silver medal City of Paris, 1983, Climate Inst. award, 1991, Swedish WASA award, 1991, Lifetime Achievement award Govt. of Can., 1994, Candlelight award UN, 2002, Elizabeth Haub award for internat. environ. diplomacy, 2005. Mem. Assn. Profl. Engrs. Ont., Assn. Profl. Engrs. Sask. Personal E-mail: jwmacneill@hotmail.com.

MACOPIYO, LABAN ADERO, geographer, researcher, ecologist; b. Kisumu, Nyanza, Kenya, June 23, 1969; arrived in U.S., 2002; s. Stephen Opiyo Omolo and Rachel Adero Opiyo; m. Beldinah Rachel Ochola, May 16, 2001; 1 child, Serabi Akinyi Opiyo. BSc in Geography, U. Nairobi, 1993, MSc in Geography, 2000; student in Rangeland Ecology, Tex. A&M U., 2002—. Geog. info. sys. analyst Internat. Livestock Rsch. Inst., Nairobi, Kenya, 1998—2000; geog. info. sys. analyst and scientist Internat. Ctr. Insect Physiology and Ecology, Nairobi, 2000—02; rsch. asst. Tex. A&M U., College Station, Tex., 2002—. Mem. Geog. Info. Tech. Cmty. USAID, Washington, 2002—. Scholar, Swiss Agy. Devel. and Cooperation, 1994, U.S. AID, 2002—05; Jim Ellis fellowship, Global Livestock Collaborative Rsch. Support Program, 2003. Mem.: AAAS, African Students Assn. (v.p. 2003—04), Geo-info. Soc. Kenya (treas. 2000—01), Environ. Info. Sys. Program in Sub-Saharan Africa, Assn. Am. Geographers, Phi Kappa Phi. Office: Texas A&M University 2126 TAMU Animal Industries Building College Station TX 77843 Home Phone: 979-862-9298; Office Phone: 979-458-3215. Business E-Mail: lmacopiyo@cnrit.tamu.edu.

MACOVSKI, ALBERT, electrical engineer, educator; b. NYC, May 2, 1929; s. Philip and Rose (Winogr) Macovski; m. Adelaide Paris, Aug. 5, 1950; children: Michael, Nancy. BEE, City Coll. N.Y., 1950; MEE, Poly. Inst. Bklyn., 1953; PhD, Stanford U., 1968. Mem. tech. staff RCA Labs., Princeton, NJ, 1950—57; asst. prof., then assoc. prof. Poly. Inst. Bklyn., 1957—60; staff scientist Stanford Rsch. Inst., Menlo Park, Calif., 1960—71; fellow U. Calif. Med. Center San Francisco, 1971—72; prof. elec. engring. and radiology Stanford U., 1972—, endowed chair, Canon USA prof. engring., 1991—. Dir. Magnetic Resonance Sys. Rsch. Lab.; cons. to industry. Author. Recipient award for color TV cirs., Inst. Radio Engrs., 1958; spl. fellow, NIH, 1971. Fellow: IEEE (Zworykin award 1973), Internat. Soc. Magnetic Resonance in Medicine (trustee 1991—94, gold medal 1997), Optical Soc. Am., Am. Inst. Med. Biol. Engring.; mem.: NAE, Am. Assn. Physicists in Medicine, Inst. Medicine, Eta Kappa Nu, Sigma Xi. Jewish. Achievements include patents in field. Office: Stanford Univ Dept Elec Engring Stanford CA 94305 Home: 620 Sand Hill Rd Apt 407B Palo Alto CA 94304 Office Phone: 650-723-2708. Business E-Mail: macovski@stanford.edu.

MACPHAIL, ANDREW B., professional sports team executive; b. Bronxville, NY, Apr. 5, 1953; m. Lark MacPhail; children: William Reed, Andrew Hamilton. Grad., Dickinson Coll., 1976. Bus. mgr. Gulf Coast League Bradenton Rookie affiliate Chgo. Cubs, 1976-77, asst. parks ops., 1977, with dept. player devel., 1978, asst. dir. dept. player devel., asst. dir. scouting, pres., CEO, 1994—2006; asst. gen. mgr. Houston Astros, 1982-85; v.p. player pers. Minn. Twins, 1985-86, exec. v.p., gen. mgr., 1986-94; pres. baseball ops. Balt. Orioles, 2007—. Named Maj. League Exec. of Yr., The Sporting News, 1991, Am. League Exec. of Yr., UPI, 1991; winner World Series Championship as general manager of the Twins, 1987, 91. Office: Balt Orioles Oriole Park at Camden Yards 333 W Camden St Baltimore MD 21201 *

MACPHEE, CRAIG ROBERT, economist, educator; b. Annapolis Royal, NS, Can., July 10, 1944; came to U.S., 1950; s. Craig and Dorothy (Seney) MacP.; m. Kathleen Gray McCown, Feb. 6, 1966 (div. 1981); children: Paul, Heather, Rob; m. Andrea Joy Sime, June 26, 1983. BS, U. Idaho, 1966; MA, Mich. State U., 1968, PhD, 1970. Asst. prof., then assoc. prof. econs. U. Nebr., Lincoln, 1969-89, prof., 1989—, chmn. econs. dept., 1980—83, 1989—98. Econ. affairs officer UN, Geneva, 1975-77; internat. economist US Dept. Labor, Washington, 1983-84; econ. adv. Republic of Ga., 1998-2001, Republic of Montenegro, 2001, Mongolia, 2006; cons. in field. Author: Economics of Medical Equipment and Supply, 1973, Restrictions on International Trade in Steel, 1974, Roll Over Joe Stalin, 2005. Mem. Am. Econ. Assn., Nebr. Econ. and Bus. Assn., Phi Eta Sigma, Omicron Delta Epsilon. Avocations: running, skiing, sailing, reading. Home: 631 Hazelwood Dr Lincoln NE 68510-4325 Office: U Nebr Coll Bus Dept Econs Lincoln NE 68588-0489 Office Phone: 402-472-2449. Business E-Mail: cmacphee@unl.edu.

MACPHERSON, GRANT, chef; Chef The Regent, The Ritz Carlton, Four Seasons; exec. chef Datai Hotel, Raffles Hotel, Bellagio, Las Vegas, Wynn Macau, Wynn Las Vagas. Team capt. Singapore Nat. Team; participant St. Mortiz Gourmet Festival, Cape Gourmet, South Africa, Lanesborough, London, Crystal Cruises Alaskan Food and Wine Sailing, James Beard House, NYC, Labortario Del Galileo, Washington, The Masters, Sydney, Consentino Winery Anniversary Celebration, Napa, Calif.; chef's coun. Chef's for Humanity, 2005—. Featured in Cuisine Scene, Bon Appétit mag., Ansett Chefs, Foie Gras, Art Culinaire. Nominee Premier's award, Canada; recipient Gold medal, Culinary Olympics, 1992. Office: Country Club Wynn Las Vagas 3131 Las Vegas Blvd S Las Vegas NV 89109 Office Phone: 702-770-7000. *

MACPHERSON, ROBERT DUNCAN, mathematician, educator; b. Lakewood, Ohio, May 25, 1944; s. Herbert G. and Jeanette (Wolfenden) MacP. BA, Swarthmore Coll., 1966; MA, PhD, Harvard U., 1970; DSc (hon.), Brown U., 1994, U. Lille, France, 1993. Instr. Brown U., Providence, 1970-72, asst. prof., 1972-74, assoc. prof., 1974-77, prof., 1977-85, Florence Pirce Grant prof., 1985-87; prof. MIT, Cambridge, Mass., 1987-94, Inst. Advanced Study, 1994—. Mem. Inst. des Hautes Etudes Sci., Paris, France, 1974-75, 76-77, 80-81, Steklov Math Inst., Moscow, USSR, 1980; vis. prof. U. Rome, 1985, 2000, U. Chgo., 1991, Max-Planck Inst. for Math, 1992; chmn. NRC Bd. Math. Scis., 1997-2000; mem. sci. adv. com. Math Sci. Rsch. Inst., 2004-. Co-author: Stratified Morse Theory, 1988, Nilpotent Orbits, 1989; contbr. numerous articles to profl. jours. Chmn. Former Soviet Union Aid Fund, 1991-96. Mem.: NAS (Math award 1992), Nat. Orgn. of Gay and Lesbian Sci. and Tech. Profs., Soc. for Applied and Indsl. Math., Am. Math. Soc. (Steele prize 2002), Am. Philos. Soc., Am. Acad. Arts and Scis., Moscow Math. Soc. (hon.), Phi Beta

Kappa. Home: 19 Haslet Ave Princeton NJ 08540-4913 Office: Inst for Advanced Study Princeton NJ 08540 Business E-Mail: rdm@ias.edu.

MACQUEEN, ROBERT MOFFAT, solar physicist; b. Memphis, Mar. 28, 1938; s. Marion Leigh and Grace (Gilfillan) MacQ.; m. Caroline Gibbs, June 25, 1960 (div. Dec. 1997); children: Andrew, Marjorie; m. Marsha Anne Sime, Mar. 9, 1998. BS, Rhodes Coll., 1960; PhD, Johns Hopkins U., 1968. Asst. prof. physics Rhodes Coll., 1961-63; instr. physics and astronomy Goucher Coll., Towson, Md., 1964-66; sr. research scientist Nat. Ctr. for Atmospheric Research, Boulder, Colo., 1967-90, dir. High Altitude Obs., 1979-86, asst. dir., 1986-87, assoc. dir., 1987-89; prof. physics Rhodes Coll., Memphis, 1990—; prin. investigator NASA Apollo program, 1971-75, NASA Skylab program, 1970-76, NASA Solar Maximum Mission, 1976-79, NASA/ESA Internat. Solar Polar Mission, 1978-83; affiliate scientist NCAR, 1994—. Lectr. U. Colo., 1968-79, adj. prof., 1979-90; mem. com. on space astronomy Nat. Acad. Scis., 1973-76, mem. com. on space physics, 1977-79; mem. Space Sci. Bd., 1983-86 Recipient Exceptional Sci. Achievement medal NASA, 1974 Fellow Optical Soc. Am.; mem. Am. Astron. Soc. (chmn. solar physics div. 1976-78), Assn. Univ. Research Astronomy (dir.-at-large 1984-93, chmn. bd. 1989-92), Am. Assn. Physics Tchrs., Sigma Xi. E-mail: rmac@rhodes.edu.

MAC RAE, ALFRED URQUHART, physicist, electrical engineer; b. NYC, Apr. 14, 1932; s. Farquhar and Eliza J. (Urquhart) Mac R.; m. Peggy M. Hazard, May 13, 1967; children: Susan, Pamela. BS in Physics, Syracuse U., 1954, PhD in Physics, 1960. Dir. integrated circuit devel. Bell Labs., Murray Hill, NJ, 1979-83, dir. satellite communications systems Homdel, NJ, 1983-95; pres. Mac Tech., Berkeley Heights, NJ, 1995—. Sr. rsch. fellow Potomac Inst. New Zealand; chair NASA Internat. Technology Studies, 1997-98; mem. adv. com. to bd. trustees N.J. Inst. Tech., 1981-85. Bd. editor: Vacuum Sci. and Tech, 1965-67, Rev. Sci. Instruments, 1969-71; contbr. articles to jours.; patentee in field. Bd. dirs. Summit Area ARC, 1996-2004, chmn., 2001-02. Fellow IEEE (mem., chmn. numerous coms. 1969—, Third Millenium medal 2000), Am. Phys. Soc., Nat. Acad. Engring.; mem. Bohmische Phys. Soc., IEEE Electron Devices Soc. (pres. 1986-87, chmn. field awards coun. 1989-93, Ebers award 1994, Disting. Svcs. award 1996). Office: 72 Sherbrook Dr Berkeley Heights NJ 07922-2346 Personal E-mail: a.macrae@ieee.org.

MACRAE, CAMERON FARQUHAR, III, lawyer; b. NYC, Mar. 21, 1942; s. Cameron F. and Jane B. (Miller) MacR.; m. Ann Wooster Bedell, Nov. 30, 1974; children: Catherine Fairfax, Ann Cameron. AB, Princeton U., 1963; LLB, Yale U., 1966. Bar: N.Y. 1966, D.C. 1967, U.S. Dist. Ct. (so. dist.) N.Y. 1975. Atty.-advisor Office of Gen. Counsel to Sec. Air Force, Washington, 1966-69; assoc. Davis, Polk & Wardell, NYC, 1970-72; dep. supt. and counsel N.Y. State Banking Dept., NYC, 1972-74; sr. ptnr. LeBeouf, Lamb, Greene & MacRae, LLP, NYC, 1975—2004, vice-chmn., 1995—2000, sr. of counsel, 2005—. Dir. Nat. Integrity Life Ins. Co., 2000—. Note and comment editor Yale Law Jour., 1965-66. Trustee, sec. St. Andrew's Dune Ch., 1982—; hon. chmn. Clear Pool Inc., 1990-94. Capt. USAF res., 1966-69. Mem.: DC Bar Assn., Jupiter Island Club, Cottage Club (Princeton, NJ), Shinnecock Hills Golf Club (Southampton), Bathing Corp. Southampton, Meadow Club (v.p., bd. govs.), Union Club (NYC). Democrat. Episcopalian. Office: LeBoeuf Lamb Greene & MacRae LLP 125 W 55th St New York NY 10019-5369 Office Phone: 212-424-8080. E-mail: cfmacrae@llgm.com.

MACRAE, ELIZABETH (ELIZABETH MACRAE HALSEY), counselor, actor; b. Columbia, SC, Feb. 22, 1936; d. James and Dorothy (Hendon) MacRae; m. Charles Day Halsey, Jr., 1969; m. Nedrick Young, 1965 (dec. 1968); children: Benjamin Young(dec.), Beryl MacRae Young-(dec.). Student, Herbert Berghof Studio, NYC, 1956—58, Arts Students League, 1958, U. So. Calif., LA, 1965, Marymount Manhattan Coll., NYC, 1989—91, Breakthrough at Gracie Sq. Hosp., 1990—91. Cert. Alcoholism and Alcohol Abuse, Credentialed Alcoholism Counselor 1992. Intern Arms Acres, Carmel, NY, 1990; counselor chem. dependency Breakthrough at Gracie Sq. Hosp., 1990; adult counselor Manhattan Bowery Corp., 1991—93; program dir., counselor alcoholism outpatient clinic Freedom Inst., 1993—98. Actor: (plays) off Broadway, 1956, New. Eng. Stock, 1957, 1963, (as Elizabeth MacRae): (films) Everything's Ducky, 1961, Love in a Goldfish Bowl, 1961, The Incredible Mr. Limpet, 1964, The Wild Westerners, 1962, For Love or Money, 1963; (TV series) Route 66, 1969, 1972, 1974; (films) The Conversation, 1974; (TV series) Naked City, 1960, 77 Sunset Strip, 1961, Harrigan and Son, 1961, Surfside 6, 1961, Maverick, 1961, Asphalt Jungle, 1961, Dr. Kildare, 1962, Hawaiian Eye, 1962, Stoney Burke, 1962, Death Valley Days, 1962, Sam Benedict, 1962, Gunsmoke, 1961—64, The Untouchables, 1962, Burke's Law, 1963, Rawhide, 1963, The Virginian, 1964, The Fugitive, 1964, I Dream of Jeannie, 1965, Gomer Pyle, USMC, 1966—68, Andy Griffith, 1967, Bonanza, 1968, Judd for the Defense, 1969, Rheingold Theatre - England, 1969, Kojak, 1974, Petrocelli, 1974, Mannix, 1974, Rhoda, 1976, Barnaby Jones, 1976, General Hospital, 1969, 1971; (TV films), 1974; (TV series) Days of Our Lives, 1976—77, All My Children, 1978, Guiding Light, 1980, Another World, 1980, 1989, Search for Tomorrow,: (live TV) The Verdict is Yours, 1958—59, Ellery Queen, 1960, Ninotshka, 1960. Vol. Help Line, NYC, 1982. Recipient Disting. Counselor award, Freedom Inst., 2003. Mem.: AFTRA, SAG, Nat. Assn. Alcoholism and Drug Abuse Counselors, Actors Equity, Acad. Motion Picture Arts and Scis., Nat. Soc. Colonial Dames Am. (N.C. chpt.). Home: 1405 Raeford Rd Fayetteville NC 28305 Office Phone: 910-485-5061. E-mail: chalsey@nc.rr.com.

MACRAE HALSEY, ELIZABETH See **MACRAE, ELIZABETH**

MACRI, THEODORE WILLIAM, book publisher; b. NYC; s. Francis Carl and Emma Julia (Fantini) M.; m. Joan Michele Damato; children: Alicia, Theodore William AB, Villanova U.; MA, NYU. With Doubleday & Co. Inc., NYC, dir. domestic rights, 1978-82, editorial group dir., 1982-83, asst. to pres., 1983; v.p., pub. R.R. Bowker Co., 1983-85; v.p., dir. subs. rights Contemporary Books, Inc., 1985-90; v.p. Carol Pub. Group, Inc., NYC, 1990-94; pres. Ted Macri Assocs., 1994—. Bd. dirs. CUNY Ctr. for Pub., Nat. Book Awards Mem. N.Y. County Republican Com.; mem. men's com. Mus. Natural History, N.Y.C. Served to lt. (j.g.) USNR. Named Disting. Alumnus Villanova U. Mem. Assn. Am. Pubs. (edn. com.), Am. Bookseller's Assn. Clubs: N.Y. Athletic (N.Y.C.). Republican. Roman Catholic. Office: 180 Central Park S Ste 441 New York NY 10019-1562 Home Phone: 203-834-8722. Personal E-mail: papatwm@aol.com.

MACRIS, MICHAEL, lawyer; b. Jackson Heights, NY, July 12, 1949; Student, Cornell U.; BA with distinction, Stanford U., 1971; JD, Columbia U., 1974. Bar: N.Y. 1975, Conn. 1976. Mem. Cahill Gordon & Reindel LLP, NYC. Bd. editors Columbia Law Rev., 1973-74; co-editor ERISA & Benefits Law Jour., 1992-99. Harlan Fiske Stone scholar. Fellow: Am. Coll. Employee Benefits Counsel (charter); mem.: ABA (group vice chmn. employee benefit plans and compensation arrangements, real property, probate and trust law sect.), Phi Beta Kappa. Office: Cahill Gordon & Reindel LLP 80 Pine St Fl 19 New York NY 10005-1790 Home Phone: 203-453-1704; Office Phone: 212-701-3409. E-mail: mmacris@cahill.com.

MACSAI, JOHN, retired architect; b. Budapest, Hungary, May 20, 1926; came to U.S., 1947, naturalized, 1954; s. Ferenc and Margit (Rosenfeld) Lusztig; m. Geraldine Marcus, May 7, 1950; children: Pamela, Aaron, Marian, Gwen. Baccalaureate summa cum laude, Kolcsey Gimnasium, Budapest, 1944; student, Atelier Art Sch., Budapest, 1941-43, Poly. U., 1945-47; BArch magna cum laude, Miami U., Oxford, Ohio, 1949. Archtl. designer Skidmore, Owings & Merrill, Chgo., Pace Assos., Chgo., Raymond Loewy Assos., Chgo., 1949-55; ptnr. Hausner & Macsai, Chgo., 1955-71, Campbell & Macsai, Chgo., 1971-74; prin. John Macsai & Assocs. Architects, Inc., Chgo., 1975-90, O'Donnell Wicklund Pigozzi & Peterson, Chgo., 1991-2000, ret., 2000. Prof. architecture U. Ill., Chgo., 1970-76, prof. emeritus, 1997—. Author: High Rise Apartment Buildings: A Design Primer, 1972, Housing, 1976, Housing, 2d edit., 1982, Housing, Russian edit., 1980, Housing, Mexican edit., 1984; co-author: Designing Environments for the Aged, 1977, Housing for a Maturing Population, 1983, (ency.) Highrise Apartment Buildings, 1988, East European Modernism, 1996; contbr. articles to profl. jours.; prin. works include Nat. Opinion Rsch. Ctr., U.Chgo., 1967, High Energy Physics Bldg., 1968, Social Svcs. Ctr., 1970, Harbor House, 1965, Malibu East, 1972, Waterford apt. bldg., 1976, U. Chgo. faculty townhouses, 1986, Fairfield Ct. housing for the elderly, 1988, Evanston Pl. apt. bldg and city garage, 1991, 2960 N. Lake Shore Dr. Housing for the Elderly, 1991; staff arch. Tel Tanninim Archaeol. Project, Israel, 1996—2000, Elike Archaeol. Project, Greece, 2001; exhibitions include Gallery 1756, Chgo., 1991—2005, Chgo. Cultural Ctr., 2000, Cliffdwellers Club, 2002; author: (monthly article) Evanston Round Table. Fellow AIA (13 design award citations Chgo. chpt.). Jewish. Home: 1501 Hinman Ave Apt 3B Evanston IL 60201-4675 Personal E-mail: gerry.macsai@gmail.com.

MACTAGGART, TERRENCE JOSEPH, education educator, researcher, former academic administrator; b. Buffalo, Sept. 20, 1946; s. Joseph Carol and Genieve Mary (Quinn) MacT. BA in English and Philosophy, Canisius Coll., Buffalo, 1967; MA in Lit., St. Louis U., 1971, PhD in Lit., 1976; MBA, St. Cloud State U., Minn., 1986. Prof. Blackburn Coll., Carlinville, Ill., 1973-74; dir. Webster U., St. Louis, 1974-77; acting dean U. Alaska, Fairbanks, 1977-79; dean St. Cloud State U., Minn., 1979-83; v.p. Met. State U., St. Paul, 1983-86; vice chancellor Minn. State U. System, St. Paul, 1986-87, chancellor, 1991-95, U. Wis., Superior, 1987-91; prof. English Minn. State U., St. Paul, 1991-95; chancellor U. Maine Sys., Bangor, 1996—2001, interim chancellor, 2006—07; prof. U. Maine, 2002—. Fulbright Scholar in Thailand, 1996. Editor: Cost Effective Assessment of Prior Learning, 1983; contbr. articles on higher edn. to profl. jours. Sgt. U.S. Army, 1969-71, Viet Nam. NDEA fellow, 1968-72. Mem. Phi Beta Kappa. Avocations: cross country skiing, sailing. Office: U Maine Sys 16 Central St Bangor ME 04401-5106 *

MACTAS, MARK V., diversified financial services company executive; BA in Math and Econ., Lehigh Univ., Bethlehem, Penn. Former internat. consul, later mng. dir. global health and welfare bus. Towers Perrin, NYC, 1997, former v.p., former pres., chmn., CEO, 2001—. Office: Towers Perrin One Stamford Plaza Stamford CT 06901

MACTAVISH, CRAIG, professional hockey coach, former professional hockey player; b. London, Ont., Can., Aug. 15, 1958; m. Debbie MacTavish; children: Nathan, Sean, Brianna. Center Boston Bruins, 1980-85, Edmonton Oilers, 1985-94, NY Rangers, 1994, Phila. Flyers, 1994-96, St. Louis Blues, 1996-97; asst. coach NY Rangers, 1997—99, Edmonton Oilers, 1999—2000, head coach, 2000—. Achievements include being a member of Stanely Cup Champion Edmonton Oilers, 1987, 1988, 1990, NY Rangers, 1994. Office: Edmonton Oilers Rexall Place 11230-110 St Edmonton AB Canada T5G 3H7

MACTAVISH, SUSANNE HANNA, retired library and information scientist; b. Atlanta, Jan. 6, 1947; d. Albert Kenneth and Mary Ann Hanna; m. Nelson Thomas Henderson, May 4, 1974 (div. Sept. 3, 1993); children: Russell Evan Henderson, Andrea Renee Henderson; m. Douglas Stewart MacTavish, Aug. 1, 1998; 1 child, Ian Stewart. BA, DePauw U., Greencastle, Ind., 1969; MS in Lib. Sci., Case Western Res. U., Cleve., 1970. Libr. Denver Pub. Libr., 1970—72; info. officer, libr. US CIA, 1972—81; mgr. libr. svcs. Gen. Electric Co., Gaithersburg, Md., 1981—93; project lead Lockheed Martin, Falls Church, Va., 1993—2001, ethics officer Gaithersburg, 2001—07; ret., 2007. Mem.: ALA (life), Internat. Orgn. Standardization/Internat. Electrotech. Commn. (joint tech. com., one sub com. twenty-four), Libr. Adminstrn. and Mgmt. Assn. (pres. 1990—91, councilor 2005—), Ethics Officer Assn., Beta Phi Mu, Delta Zeta (v.p. 1968—69). Methodist. Home: 568 Rifes Ford Rd Verona VA 24482 Personal E-mail: sue.mactavish@northriver.coop.

MACTIER, ANN DICKINSON, state agency administrator; b. Ravenna, Nebr., June 29, 1922; d. Robert Smith and Carrie (Clark) Dickinson; m. James Allan Mactier, Feb. 26, 1944; children: James Allan II, Judith Ann, Robert Dickinson. BS, Northwestern U., 1944; BA, U. Nebr., Omaha, 1963, MA, 1969; EdD (hon.), U. Nebr., 2005. Owner, mgr. Ponca Hills Riding Acad., Omaha, 1966-73; cmty. coord. Coll. Fine Arts, U. Nebr., Omaha, 1974-75; mem. Nebr. State Bd. Edn., 1996—, v.p., 2001—. Mem. Omaha Jr. League, 1944—57; mem. exec. com. Riverfront Devel. Corp., Omaha, 1973—79; founder, pres. Florence Arts Coun., Omaha, 1975—79; mem. Omaha Pub. Schs. Bd. Edn., 1983—98; mem. steering com. Coun. Urban Bds. Edn., 1996—98; bd. dirs. Coun. Great City Schs., 1984—89. Home: 3811 N Post Rd Omaha NE 68112-1209 Office Phone: 402-453-4580. E-mail: ann@mactier.omhcoxmail.com.

MACURDY, JOHN EDWARD, bass; b. Detroit, Mar. 18, 1929; s. Blanchard Archibald and Dorathea Rosalie (Radtke) Macurdy; m. Justine May Votypka, Apr. 12, 1958; children: Allison Anne, John Blanchard. Student, Wayne State U., 1947; student of Avery Crew, Detroit, 1946. Mem. N.Y.C. Opera, 1959-62, Met. Opera, 1962—. Appeared in U.S., Europe, including San Francisco Opera, La Scala; performances include world premieres Mourning Becomes Electra, Met. Opera, 1967, opening night Anthony and Cleopatra, Met. Opera, 1966, Wuthering Heights, Santa Fe Opera, 1958, Six Characters in Search of an Author, N.Y.C. Opera, 1959, Griffalkin, Tanglewood Festival, 1957; Am. premieres Capriccio, Santa Fe Opera, 1958, Murder in the Cathedral, Empire State Music Festival, Bear Mountain Park, N.Y., 1959, Inspector General, N.Y.C. Opera, 1960; appeared with numerous orchs.; film Don Giovanni, 1979; participant 40th Anniversary Sud-Deutsche Rundfunk, 100th Anniversary Gala Met. Opera, 1983. Served with USAF, 1950-54. Recipient medal for artistic merit during Mich. Week City of Detroit, 1969, Arts Achievement award Wayne State U., 2003; inducted into Acad. Vocal Hall of Fame, 1985. Mem.: Bohemian Club of San Francisco. Presbyterian. Office: 73 Tall Oaks Ct Stamford CT 06903-1515

MAC WATTERS, VIRGINIA ELIZABETH, singer, music educator, actress; b. Phila. d. Frederick-Kennedy and Idoleein (Hallowell) Mac W.; m. Paul Abée, June 10, 1960. Grad., Phila. Normal Sch. for Tchrs., 1933; student, Curtis Inst. Music, Phila., 1936. With New Opera Co., NYC, 1941-42; artist-in-residence Ind. U. Sch. Music, 1957-58; assoc. prof. U. Ind. Sch. Music, 1958-68, prof. voice, 1968-82, prof. emeritus, 1982—. Singer: leading roles Broadway mus. Rosalinda, 1942-44, Mr. Strauss Goes to Boston, 1945, leading opera roles New Opera Co., N.Y.C., 1941-42, San Francisco, 1944, N.Y.C. Ctr., 1946-51; leading soprano for reopening of Royal Opera House, Covent Garden, London, 1947-48, Guatemala, El Salvador, Cen. Am., 1948-49; debut at Met. Opera, N.Y.C., 1952; TV spls. on NBC include Menotti's Old Maid and the Thief, 1949, Would-be Gentleman (R. Strauss), 1955; leading singer with Met. Opera Co. on coast to coast tour of Die Fledermaus, 1951-52, Met. Opera debut, N.Y.C., 1952, leading soprano Cen. City Opera Festival, Colo., 1952-56; performed with symphony orchs. in U.S., Can., S.Am.; concert recitalist U.S., Can., 1950-62; opened N.Y. Empire State Music Festival in Ariadne auf Naxos (Strauss), 1959; soloist Mozart Festival, Ann Arbor, Mich. Recipient Mile award Album Familiar Music, 1949, Ind. U. Disting. Tchg. award, 1979; named One of 10 Outstanding Women of the Yr.; Zeckwer Hahn Phila. Mus. Acad. scholar, 1941-42; MacWatters chair donated by New Auer Grand Concert Hall, U. Ind. Sch. Music. Mem. Nat. Fedn. of Music Clubs, Nat. Soc. Arts and Letters, Nat. Soc. Lit. and Arts, Soc. Am. Musicians, Nat. Assn. Tchrs. of Singing, Internat. Platform Assn., Sigma Alpha Iota. Clubs: Matinee Musical (hon. mem. Phila., Indpls. chpts.). Achievements include having only original recorded version of Zerbinetta aria from Ariadne auf Naxos (Strauss). Home: 3800 Arlington Rd Bloomington IN 47404-1347 Office: Ind U Sch Music Bloomington IN 47405

MACWILLIAMS, KENNETH EDWARD, investment banker; b. Newburyport, Mass., Aug. 21, 1936; s. Harold Freeman and Helen (Melia) MacW.; children: Robert Hovey, James Stuart; m. Natalya V. Fedorova, Aug. 29, 2004. BA, Harvard U., 1958, MBA, 1962. V.p. Morgan Guaranty Trust Co., NYC, 1962-71; sr. assoc. Goldman Sachs & Co., NYC, 1971-74; mng. dir., domestic merchant banking group Manfacturers Hanover Trust Co., NYC, 1975-82; chmn., chief exec. officer Prudential Capital Corp. subs. Prudential Ins. Co. Am., Newark, 1982-90; pres. Prudential Equity Mgmt. Assn. subs. Prudential Ins. Co. Am., Newark, 1990-92; founder, pres. Woodrow Wilson Assocs., NYC, 1993—. Personal E-mail: macwilliams@earthlink.net.

MACWILLIAMS, MICHAEL BROUGHTON, lawyer; b. Balt., Oct. 17, 1966; s. Roger W. and Bette Burk (Broughton) MacW. BSME, Va. Tech. U., 1989; JD, U. Balt., 1994. Tech. rep. ARCO Chem. Co., Chgo., 1989-91; assoc. Goodell, DeVries, Leecy & Gray, Balt., 1994—2001, Venable LLP, Balt., 2001—03, ptnr., comml., intellectual property litig., 2003—. Editor-in-chief Balt. Law Rev. Mem. Md. State Bar Assn. (tech. task force 1997—). Avocation: sailboat racing. Office: Venable LLP 1800 Mercantile Bank & Trust Bldg 2 Hopkins Plz Baltimore MD 21201 Office Phone: 410-244-7514. Office Fax: 410-244-7742. Business E-Mail: mbmacwilliams@venable.com.

MACWILLIAMS, MICHAEL L., JR., environmentalist, educator; s. Michael L. MacWilliams, Sr. and Susan MacWilliams. BA in English, U. Notre Dame, 1997; BS in Engring. & Environ. Sci., U. Notre Dame, Ind., 1997; MS in Civil & Environ. Engring., Stanford U., Calif., 1998; PhD in Civil & Environ. Engring., Stanford U., 2004. Environ. cons. in field, San Francisco, 2001—; consulting asst. prof., dept. civil & environ. engring. Stanford U., 2004—. Mem. strategic planning com. No. Calif. Coun. Fedn. Fly Fishers, 2000—07. Mem.: Am. Geophys. Union, Golden Gate Angling & Casting Club (conservation dir. 2000—04).

MACY, BILL (WILLIAM MACY GARBER), actor; b. Revere, Mass., May 18, 1922; s. Michael and Mollie (Friedopfer) Garber; m. Samantha Harper. BS in Edn., NYU, 1954; studied with Lee Strasberg, NYC. Appeared in (stage prodns.) The Roast, 1980, I Ought To Be in Pictures, 1980-81, An American Comedy, 1983, The Man Who Came to Dinner, Oh! Calcutta!, The Balcony, The Cannibals, The Tempest, America Hurrah, (films) The Producers, 1968, The Late Show, 1977, The Jerk, 1979, Serial, 1980, My Favorite Year, 1982, Bad Medicine, 1985, Sibling Rivalry, 1990, The Doctor, 1991, Me, Myself and I, 1992, Analyze This, 1999, Surviving Christmas, 2004, The Holiday, 2006, (TV series) Maude, 1972-78, Hanging In, 1979, Nothing in Common, 1987. Served with U.S. Army, 1943-46. Mem. Actors' Equity Assn., Screen Actors Guild, AFTRA. Avocations: photography, tennis, reading. *

MACY, WILLIAM H., actor; b. Miami, Mar. 13, 1950; m. Felicity Huffman, Sept. 6, 1997; children: Sofia Grace, Georgia Grace. Attended, Bethany Coll. Founding mem. St. Nicholas Theater, Chgo., Atlantic Theatre Co., NYC. Actor: (TV series) The Awakening Land, 1978, Kate & Allie, 1984, Spenser: For Hire, 1985, The Equalizer, 1985, L.A. Law, 1986, Law & Order, 1990, Civil Wars, 1991, Bakersfield P.D., 1993, Frasier, 1993, ER, 1994, Superman, 1996, King of the Hill, 1997, The Lionhearts, 1998, Hercules, 1998, Sports Night, 1998, Batman Beyond, 1999, Out of Order, 2003; writer: thirtysomething, 1987; writer, actor Above Suspicion, 1995; dir., actor: Lip Service, 1988; actor: (TV films) The Cradle Will Fall, 1983, The Boy Who Loved Trolls, 1984, The Dining Room, 1984, The Murder of Mary Phagan, 1988, In the Line of Duty: Siege at Marion, 1992, A Private Matter, 1992, The Water Engine, 1992, The Heart of Justice, 1993, Texan, 1994, The Writing on the Wall, 1994, In the Shadow of Evil, 1995, Andersonville, 1996, The Night of the Headless Horseman, 1999, It's a Very Merry Muppet Christmas Movie, 2002, Reversible Errors, 2004; writer, actor: The Con, 1998; A Slight Case of Murder, 1999; Door to Door, 2002 (Screen Actors Guild award best actor, 2003, Emmy award best actor in a TV movie, 2003, Emmy award best writing TV movie, 2003); actor, writer, actor: (TV films) The Wool Cap, 2004; writer Every Woman's Dream, 1996; Just a Walk in the Park, 2002; actor: (films) Foolin' Around, 1980, Somewhere in Time, 1980, Without a Trace, 1983, The Last Dragon, 1985, Radio Days, 1987, House of Games, 1987, Things Change, 1988, Homicide, 1991, Shadows and Fog, 1992, Benny & Joon, 1993, Searching for Bobby Fischer, 1993, Twenty Bucks, 1993, Being Human, 1993, The Client, 1994, Oleanna, 1994, Murder in the First, 1995, Roommates, 1995, Tall Tale, 1995, Evolver, 1995, Mr. Holland's Opus, 1995, Down Periscope, 1996, Fargo, 1996, Hit Me, 1996, Ghosts of Mississippi, 1996, Colin Fitz, 1996, Air Force One, 1997, Boogie Nights, 1997, Wag the Dog, 1997, Jerry and Tom, 1998, Pleasantville, 1998, Psycho, 1998, The Secret of NIMH 2: Timmy to the Rescue, 1998, A Civil Action, 1998, Happy, Texas, 1999, Mystery Men, 1999, Magnolia, 1999, Panic, 2000, State and Main, 2000, Jurassic Park III, 2001, Focus, 2001, Welcome to Collinwood, 2002, The Cooler, 2003, Seabiscuit, 2003, Cellular, 2004, Sahara, 2005, Edmond, 2005, Thank You for Smoking, 2006, (voice) Doogal, 2006, Bobby, 2006, Inland Empire, 2006, (voice) Everyone's Hero, 2006, He Was a Quiet Man, 2007, Wild Hogs, 2007; exec. prodr.: Transamerica, 2005. Spokesperson United Cerebral Palsy. Office: Creative Artist Agency 9830 Wilshire Blvd Beverly Hills CA 90212 *

MACYS, SONJA, science association director; b. 1971; Exec. dir. Tucson Audubon Soc. Mem., Found. Bd. Rsch. Ranch Found.; mem., environ. adv. com. Raœl Grijalva; mem., exec. com. Sonoran Joint Venture, US Fish & Wildlife Svc. Named an 40 Under 40, Tucson Bus. Edge, 2006. Office: Tucson Audubon Society 300 E University Blvd 120 Tucson AZ 85705 Office Phone: 520-622-5622. Office Fax: 520-623-3476.

MACZULSKI, MARGARET LOUISE, event marketing professional, meeting manager; b. Detroit, Apr. 01; d. Bohdan Alexander and Olga Louise (Martinuick) Maczulski. BS, Mich. State U.; cert. E-Commerce Mgmt., DePaul U., 2000. Cert. meeting mgr. Mgr. meetings Nat. Assn. Realtors, Mktg. Inst., Chgo., 1977-82, mgr. mktg., 1982-83; regional sales mgr. Fairmont Hotels, Chgo., 1982; dir., mgr. trade shows and confs. Capital Cities Am. Broadcasting Co./Pub. Div., Wheaton, Ill., 1983-85; mgr. meeting and conf. planning Soc. Human Resource Mgmt., Alexandria, Va., 1985-90; mgr. meeting and conv. planning Kraft Foods, Glenview, Ill., 1990-95; cons. meetings and spl. events Chgo., 1996-98; sr. mgr. meeting and travel svcs. Coll. Am. Pathologists, Northfield, Ill., 1998-2000; conv. mgr. Common, A User Group, 2001—02, cons. spl. events, 2002—. Mem. Meeting Planners Internat., Greater Washington Soc. Assn. Execs. (past chmn. site inspection com.), Soc. Corporate Meeting Planners, Am. Soc. Assn. Execs., Mich. State U. Alumni Assn. (treas. D.C. chpt. 1987-90), Soc. for Corp. Mtg. Planners, Assn. Forum, Profl. Conf. Mgmt. Assn. Republican. Roman Catholic. Avocations: piano, swimming, skiing. Home: 16830 W Serranda Dr Libertyville IL 60048 Personal E-mail: gwenraz@hotmail.com.

MADAN, DEEPAK S., engineering executive; s. S. M. and K. S. Madan; m. A. P. Madan; 1 child, N. S. B Technology/Metall. Engr., Indian Inst. Technology, Kanpur, India, 1982; MS Materials Engr., Rensselaer Poly.

Inst., 1986, PhD Materials Engr., 1988. Rsch. fellow Rensselaer Poly. Inst., Troy, NY, 1982-87; sr. materials engr. Elkem Metals Co., Pitts., 1987-95; v.p. new bus. devel. F.W. Winter, Inc. & Co., Camden, NJ, 1995—2007; v.p. tech. and new bus. devel. Magnesium Elektron Powders, Manchester, NJ, 2007—. Spkr. at tech. meetings and seminars. Patentee in field; editor tech. books; contbr. articles to profl. jours. Mem.: Am. Welding Soc., Am. Powder Metallurgy Inst. (past chmn. local chpt.), Am. Soc. Metals. Avocations: photography, travel, computers. Office: Magnesium Elektron Powders 100 Ridgeway Blvd Manchester NJ 08759 Office Phone: 908-330-8176.

MADARA, JAMES LEE, dean, pathologist, educator, epitheliologist; b. Altoona, Pa., Sept. 16, 1950; s. Daniel Rodman and Margaret Jane (Hauser) M.; m. Victoria Mollenkopf, May 14, 1975; children: J. Maxwell, Alexis Lindsy. BA, Juniata Coll., 1971; MD, Hahnemann Med., 1975. Cert. anatomic and clin. pathology. Intern Deaconess Hosp., Boston, 1975—76, resident in pathology, 1976—78; fellow in internal medicine Harvard Med. Ctr., Boston, 1978—80; instr. pathology Harvard Med. Sch., Boston, 1980-81, asst. prof. pathology, 1981-85, assoc. prof. pathology, 1985-91, prof. pathology, 1993-97; assoc. prof. of health scis. and tech. Harvard-M.I.T., Boston, 1986-91; Timmie prof., chmn. dept. pathology & lab. medicine Emory U. Sch. Medicine, Atlanta, 1997—2002; dean, v.p. for medical affairs Pritzker Sch. of Med. and Div. of Biological Sciences, U. of Chicago, Chicago, Ill., 2002—, Sara and Harold Lincoln Thompson disting. svc. prof. Assoc. editor Gastroenterology, 1986-91; mem. editl. bd. Jour. Clin. Investigation, 1987—; editor-in-chief Am. Jour. Pathology, 2000; contbr. over 160 articles to profl. jours. Grantee NIH, 1980—. Mem. Am. Soc. for Clin. Investigation (elected), Am. Soc. for Cell Biology, Am. Gastroenterological Assn. (rsch. coun. 1988-90, Ross Rsch. scholar award 1982), Am. Physiol. Soc., Am. Assn. Pathology (Parke/Davis award 1990), Assn. Am. Physicians. Achievements include description of functional sequellae of neutrophil-epithelial cell interactions; recognition that tight junctions between epithelial cells are regulated under physiological conditions. Office: Biological Sci U Chicago 5812 S Ellis St Chicago IL 60637 Office Fax: 773-702-1897. E-mail: jmadara@bsd.uchicago.edu.

MADARIAGA, MIGUEL G., epidemiologist; b. Moquegua, Peru, Feb. 19, 1970; s. Luis Madariaga and Gloria Rios; m. Ana Cynthia Monge, May 18, 1998; children: Andrea, Isabella. B in Medicine, Nat. U., Lima, 1994; MD, Nat. U. Mayor de San Marcos, Lima, Peru, 1994. Cert. internist Am. Bd. Internal Medicine, 2001, infectious diseases Am. Bd. Internal Medicine, 2003, lic. Ill. Health Dept., 2001, Iowa Bd. Med. Examiners, 2003, Nebr. Health and Human Svcs. Sys., 2003, physician asst. supr. lic. Nebr. Health and Human Svcs. Sys., cert. HIV specialist Am. Acad. HIV Medicine, 2004. Intern Chgo. Med. Sch., North Chicago, 1998—99, resident internal medicine North Chgo., 1999—2001; fellow infectious diseases Rush U., Chgo., 2001—03; asst. prof. medicine U. Nebr. Med. Ctr., Omaha, 2003—. Relevance reviewer Am. Bd. Internal Medicine, Phila., 2004—; resource contact q fever HHS, Raleigh, NC, 2005; tech. reviewer W.Va. U., Morgantown, 2002—04; dep. dir. Nebr. Biocontainment Unit, Omaha, 2007—. Contbr. numerous articles to profl. jours., chapters to books; reviewer (med. jours. including Jour. Pediats., Lancet Infectious Diseases Jour. and Clin. Infectious Diseases Jour.). Voluntary physician One World Health Clinic, Omaha, 2006—. Recipient Outstanding Med. Intern, Chgo. Med. Sch., 1999, Oustanding Med. Resident, 2001, Chancellor Diversity award, U. Nebr. Med. Ctr., 2006—; fellow, Royal Soc. Tropical Medicine and Hygiene, 2004—06. Mem.: Am. Soc. Microbiology (corr.), Infectious Diseases Soc. Am. (corr.), Internat. Union Agaist TB and Lung Disease (corr.), Peruvian Coll. Physicians (assoc.). Achievements include research in role of Q fever as a biological weapon. Home: 16018 Capitol Ave Omaha NE 68118 Office: Univ Nebr Med Ctr 985400 Nebraska Medical Center Omaha NE 68198-5400 Home Phone: 402-697-5134; Office Phone: 402-559-8650.

MADDALONI, MARTIN J., retired labor union administrator; BA, George Meany Ctr. Nat. Labor Coll., 2004. Bus. mgr. Steamfitters Local 420; v.p., Phila. internat. rep. United Assn. Journeyman and Apprentices Plumbing and Pipe Fitting Industry U.S. and Can., Wash., DC, 1988—97, gen. pres., 1997—2004. V.p. AFL-CIO, 1995. Office: United Assn 901 Massachusetts Ave NW Washington DC 20001-4307 also: 1717 K St NW Ste 207 Washington DC 20036 Office Phone: 202-628-5823.

MADDEN, DAVID, author; b. Knoxville, Tenn., July 25, 1933; s. James Helvy and Emile (Merritt) M.; m. Roberta Margaret Young, Sept. 6, 1956; 1 son, Blake Dana. BS, U. Tenn., 1957; MA, San Francisco State Coll., 1958; postgrad., Yale Drama Sch., 1959-60. Faculty Appalachian State Tchrs. Coll., Boone, NC, 1957-58, Centre Coll., Danville, Ky., 1960-62, U. Louisville, 1962-64, Kenyon Coll., Gambier, O., 1964-66, Ohio U., Athens, 1966-68; writer-in-residence La. State U., Baton Rouge, 1968-92, dir. creative writing program, 1992-94, dir. U.S. Civil War Ctr., 1992-99, Donald and Velvia Crumbley prof. creative writing, 1999—. Alumni prof. La. State U., 1994. Author: (novels) Cassandra Singing, 1969, Bijou, 1974, The Suicide's Wife, 1978, Pleasure Dome, 1979, On the Big Wind, 1980, Sharpshooter: A Novel of the Civil War, 1996, (stories) The Shadow Knows (Nat. Coun. on Arts selection), 1970, The New Orleans of Possibilities (lit. criticism) Wright Morris, 1964, Poetic Image in Six Genres, 1969, James M. Cain, 1970, A Primer of the Novel, 1980, Writers' Revisions, 1981, Cain's Craft, 1985, Revising Fiction, 1988, Rediscoveries II, 1988; asst. editor: The Kenyon Rev., 1964-66; editor: Remembering James Agee, 1974; co-editor: (with P. Bach) Classics of Civil War Fiction, 1991, Beyond the Battlefield, 2000, The Legacy of Robert Penn Warren, 2000, Thomas Wolfe's Civil War, 2004, Losses of the Sultana, 2004, Touching the Web of Southern Novelists, 2006, Primer of the Novel, 2006. Served with AUS, 1953-55. Recipient Rockefeller grant in fiction, 1969; John Golden fellow in playwriting, 1959; recipient Robert Penn Warren award for excellence in fiction. Mem. Authors League, Associated Writing Programs (bd. dirs.). Democrat. Office: La State U Dept English Baton Rouge LA 70803-0001 Home Phone: 225-344-3630; Office Phone: 225-344-3630. Business E-Mail: dmadden@lsu.edu.

MADDEN, JAMES D., forensic engineer; b. Jersey City; s. Louis A. and Ann Madden. BSChemE, U. S.C., 1963, ME, 1966. Lic. profl. engr., Ohio; cert. diplomate forensic engr. Process engr. Monsanto Co., Alvin, Tex., 1966-67; process and project engr. Union Carbide Corp., Houston, 1967-70; systems engr. M.W. Kellogg Co., Houston, 1970-73, prin. systems engr., 1974-77; sr. process engr. Litwin Co., Houston, 1973-74; sr. project engr. Davy Powergas, Houston, 1977-78, supervising project engr., 1978-79; mgr. equipment engring. DM Internat., Houston, 1979-80, project engring. mgr., 1980-83; owner, forensic engr. Madden Accident Analysis and Forensic Engring., Parma, Parma Heights and Brecksville, Ohio, 1983—. NSF rsch. grantee, 1963; NASA fellow, 1963-65; named to Outstanding Young Men Am., 1973. Mem. ASME, NSPE, AIChE, Soc. Automotive Engrs., Nat. Fire Protection Assn., Inst. Transp. Engrs., Am. Soc. Agrl. Engrs., Bldg. Ofcls. and Code Adminstrs. Internat., Nat. Acad. Forensic Engrs., Sigma Xi, Sigma Pi Sigma, Tau Beta Pi, Omicron Delta Kappa. Office: 10175 Brecksville Rd Cleveland OH 44141-3205

MADDEN, JANICE FANNING, economics professor; b. Fall River, Mass., Jan. 30, 1947; d. Richard and Concorde Roseanne (Thibault) Fanning; m. Paul Charles Madden, June 6, 1969; children: Patrick, Erin. BA, U. Denver, 1969; MA, Duke U., 1971, PhD, 1972. Prof. regional sci., sociology and real estate U. Pa., Phila., 1972—; economist Nat. Commn. on Employment and Unemployment Stats., Washington, 1978; cons. Abt Assn., Cambridge, Mass., 1979-81, U.S. Dept. Justice, Washington, 1984-88, EEOC, Washington, 1979-91; dir. women's studies U. Pa., 1988—91, 2002—04, Robert C. Daniels Found. chair in urban studies Phila., 1990—2000, vice provost grad. edn., 1991—99. Bd. dirs. Econsult Corp., Phila., 1980—2003; co-dir. Temple-Penn Phila. Econ. Monitoring Project, Phila., 1987—91; dir. MGA Program, 2000—02. Author: The Economics of Sex Discrimination, 1973, Post-Industrial Philadelphia: Structural Changes in the Metropolitan Economy, 1990, Work, Wages and Poverty: Income Distribution in Post-Industrial Philadelphia, 1991, Changes in Income Inequality within U.S. Metropolitan Areas, 2000, Mommies and Daddies in the Fast Track, 2004; contbr. articles to profl. jours. Adv. coun. mem. Office Employment and Tng., Phila., 1981—84; commr. Fellowship Commn., Phila., 1981—82; bd. dirs. Career Alternatives for Women, Jenkintown, Pa., 1979—82, Friends Select Sch., 1991—2000, 2002—, Am. Acad. Polit. and Social Scis., 2001—. Vis. scholar, U. Indonesia, 1991, Fed. Res. Bank Phila., 1999—2000, 2005; Rsch. grantee, Manpower Devel., 1971—72, Spencer Fedn., 1974, Nat. Inst. Edn., 1974—76, US Dept. of Commerce, 1978—80, NIMH, 1978—80, William Penn Found., 1988—91, W.E. Upjohn Found., 1993—95, NSF, 1993—95, Brookings Inst., 1998—2000, HUD, 2004—05, James B. Duke fellow, Duke U., 1966—71, Boettcher scholar, U. Denver, 1965—69. Mem.: Assn. Pub. Policy and Mgmt., Regional Sci. Assn., Am. Econs. Assn. Home: 2031 Spruce St Philadelphia PA 19103-5623 Office: U Pa 3718 Locust Walk Philadelphia PA 19104-6209 Home Phone: 215-546-5144; Office Phone: 215-898-6739. Business E-Mail: madden@ssc.upenn.edu.

MADDEN, JEROME ANTHONY, lawyer; b. Memphis, Aug. 24, 1948; s. Bernard Clark and Virginia Ann (Golas) M.; m. Cynthia S. Madden, June 27, 1992; 1 child, Clark John. BA, The Franciscan U. Steubenville, Ohio, 1971; JD summa cum laude, U. Dayton, Ohio, 1978; LLM, Georgetown U. Law Ctr., DC, 2005. Bar: Ohio 1978, D.C. 1979, U.S. Dist. Ct. D.C. 1979, U.S. Ct. Appeals (D.C. cir.) 1980, U.S. Ct. Claims 1984, U.S. Ct. Appeals (Fed. cir.) 1984, U.S. Supreme Ct. 1984, U.S. Ct. Appeals (7th and 11th cirs.) 1987, U.S. Ct. Appeals (4th and 5th cirs.) 1988, U.S. Ct. Appeals (9th cir.) 1991, U.S. Ct. Appeals (2d & 10th cirs.) 1992, U.S. Ct. Appeals (1st cir.) 1993. Law clk. to chief justices O'Neill and Leach Ohio Supreme Ct., Columbus, 1978-79; assoc. Cadwalader, Wickersham & Taft, Washington, 1979-85; sr. trial counsel US Dept. Justice, Washington, 1985-91, trial atty. comml. litig. br., 1998—2006; counsel, then acting sr. counsel, then supervisory counsel FDIC Appellate Litigation Sect., Comml. Litigation Unit, Washington, 1991-98; counsel litig. divsn. Office of Comptroller of Currency, Washington, 2006—. Adj. prof. George Washington U. Sch. Law, Washington, 2000-2003. Editor-in-chief U. Dayton Law Rev., 1977-78. Served with USMCR, 1970-76. Mem. D.C. Bar Assn. Roman Catholic. Avocation: golf. Home: 1502 Powells Tavern Pl Herndon VA 20170-2831 Office: Office of Comptroller of Currency 250 E St SW Rm 8068 Washington DC 20219 Office Phone: 202-874-4619. Business E-Mail: jerome.madden@occ.treas.gov.

MADDEN, JOHN, sportscaster, retired professional football coach; b. Austin, Minn., Apr. 10, 1936; s. Earl and Mary O'Flaherty M.; m. Virginia Madden; children: Mike, Joe. BS, Calif. Poly. U., 1959, MA, 1961. Player Phila. Eagles, 1959; asst. coach Hancock Jr. Coll., Santa Maria, Calif., 1960-62, head coach, 1962-64; defensive coord. Calif. State U., San Diego, 1964-66; linebacker coach Oakland Raiders, Am. Football League (now Am. Football Conf., Nat. Football League), 1967-69, head coach, 1969-79; head coach NFL Pro Bowl team Am. Football Conf., 1971, 73, 74, 75; head coach 6 Western divsn. Am. Football Conf. championship teams, Super Bowl champions, 1976; sports commentator, football analyst CBS Sports, 1979-93; appears in TV and radio commls.; sports commentator, football analyst Fox Sports, 1994—2002, Monday Night Football (ABC), 2002—06, NBC Sunday Night Football, 2006—. Author: Hey, Wait a Minute, I Wrote a Book!, 1984; One Knee Equals Two Feet (and Everything Else You Wanted To Know About Football), 1987, One Size Doesn't Fit All, 1993; co-author (with Dave Anderson) All Madden: Hey, I'm Talking Pro Football, 1996, (with Peter Kaminsky) John Madden's Ultimate Tailgating, 1998, (with Bill Gutman) John Madden's Heroes of Football, 2006; developer (software) John Madden Football, 1988, John Madden Football II, 1993. Named Coach of Yr. Am. Football League, 1969, Sports Personality of Yr., Am. Sportscasters Assn., 1985; recipient Emmy awards for sports broadcasting, 1982, 83, 85, 86, 87, 88, Pete Rozelle Radio-TV award, 2002; elected to Pro Football Hall of Fame, 2006 Office: c/o NBC Sports 30 Rockefeller Plaza New York NY 10014 *

MADDEN, JOHN J., lawyer; b. NYC, May 27, 1946; s. John L. and Bertha M.; m. Mary A. O'Neill, June 19, 1976; children: Elisabeth, Samuel. BA, U. Pa., 1968; JD cum laude, Fordham U., 1975. Bar: NY 1976, US Dist. Ct. (So. Dist.) NY 1976; avocat a la cour de Paris 1994. From assoc. to ptnr. Shearman & Sterling LLP, NYC, 1975—83, ptnr., 1983—, co-head mergers and acquisitions group, 1987—91, head mergers and acquisitions group, 1995—2001, mng. ptnr. European Offices Paris, 1991-95, co-mng. ptnr., 2004—. Articles editor Law Review, Fordham Law Sch. Trustee St. David's Sch., N.Y.C., 1981-91 Served to 1st lt., Infantry platoon leader, 101st Airbourne Divsn. US Army, 1969—71, Vietnam. Mem. ABA, N.Y. Bar Assn., Assn. Bar City of N.Y., Internat. Bar Assn., Cercle de l'Union Interalliee (Paris), World Policy Inst. (bd. advisors 2004—) Office: Shearman & Sterling LLP 599 Lexington Ave New York NY 10022-6069 Office Fax: 646-848-7055. Business E-Mail: jmadden@shearman.com.

MADDEN, JOHN PATRICK, lawyer; b. NYC, Sept. 9, 1945; s. Eugene Patrick and Eileen Mary (Gaughan) M.; m. Sally Williams, Apr. 21, 1984; children: Samuel, Christopher. Student in Mechanical Engineering, U. Maine, 1966; student in Structural Engineering, U. Wash., 1967, Purdue Univ., 1968; student in Environmental Engineering, George Washington Univ., 1975; BCE, Manhattan Coll., 1967; MSCE, NYU, 1969; JD, St. John's U. Sch. Law, NYC, 1978; EC Trade Law, Trinity Coll., Cambridge Univ., England, 1976; Comecon Trade Law, Univ. Warsaw, Poland, 1976. Bar: US Patent and Trademark Office 1978, NY State Ct. 1979, NJ State Ct. 1982, US Dist. Ct. (so. and ea. dists.) NY 1982, US Dist. Ct. NJ 1982, US Supreme Ct. 1985; solicitor Law Soc. England and Wales, 2003; cert. Accredited Mediator Chartered Inst. Arbitrators, London, 2002; accredited mediator, CEDR, London, 2002; Large Complex Case Panel, Am. Arbitration Assn., 1996; constrn. arbitrator, 1983, Am. Arbitration Assn., comml. mediator, 1990, internat. arbitrator, 1993; US D.O.D. qualified instr., Nuclear Def. Design, 1967. Engr., 1966—75; law clk., assoc. Buckley, Treacy, Shaffel Mackey & Abbate, NYC, 1977-80; cons. Contractors Consulting Svcs. Inc., Greatneck, N.Y., 1980-81; ptnr. Madden, Sciarra & Muirhead, N.Y., N.J., 1981-82, Canfield, Venusti, Madden & Rossi, NYC, 1979—. Lectr. in field; arbitrator and mediator conciliator in field. Contbr. articles to profl. jours. V.p. N.Y.C. Jaycees, 1975-95. ROTC USAF, 1963-65. Mem. ABA (pub. contract law sect., forum com. on constrn. industry), Internat. Bar Assn. (mem. alternative dispute resolution com., internat. constrn. projects com.), London Ct. Internat. Arbitration, Swiss Arbitration Assn., Am. Trial Lawyers Assn., NY State Bar Assn., NY State Trial Lawyers Assn., Assn. of Bar of City of NY, Chartered Inst. Arbitrators, Union Internationale Des Avocats, Am. Arbitration Assn., NJ State Bar Assn., Nat. Arts Club, Fidelity & Surety Law com. Office: Canfield Venusti Madden & Rossi 230 Park Ave Rm 2525 New York NY 10169-2599 E-mail: johnpmadden@cs.com.

MADDEN, JOSEPH DANIEL, trade association executive; b. NYC, Dec. 25, 1921; s. Thomas A. and Margaret (McFadden) M.; m. Eileen M. MacDonnell, Sept. 8, 1951; children: Joseph Daniel, Jr., Maureen A. BS, Fordham U., 1951; MBA, N.Y. U., 1956. Credit investigator Dun & Bradstreet, NYC, 1947-48; credit mgr. Devoe & Raynolds Co., NYC, 1948-50, Admiral Corp., NYC, 1950-51; nat. credit mgr. Standard Toch Chems., Inc., SI, N.Y., 1951-52; with chems. and plastics div. Union Carbide Corp., Midland, Mich., 1952-62; mgr. Detroit sales office, 1958-60; sr. staff adminstr. Soc. Plastics Industry, Washington, 1962-69; exec. v.p. Drug, Chem. and Assoc. Techs. Assn., Robbinsville, NJ, 1969-88, cons. assn. mgmt., 1988—. With U.S. Army, 1942-43. Mem. AARP (past pres. local chpt., v.p.), Am. Soc. Assn. Execs. (cert.), N.Y. Soc. Assn. Execs. (past bd. dirs., Exec. of Yr. award 1988), Soc. Friendly Sons of St. Patrick, Kiwanis (past pres. Bayside, sec.), Am. Legion, Toastmasters Internat. (past pres. local club). Home: 211-37 18th Ave Bayside NY 11360-1529 Personal E-mail: jdmadden21@verizon.net.

MADDEN, M. STUART, lawyer, educator; b. Washington, Dec. 1, 1948; s. Murdaugh S. and Louise M. BA, U. Pa., Kenney, 1971; MA, London Sch. Econs., 1972; JD, Georgetown U., 1976. Bar: DC 1976. Assoc. Reed, Smith, Shaw & McClay, Washington, 1976-78, Weil, Gotshal & Manges, Washington, 1978-80, Santarelli & Gimer, Washington, 1980-83; ptnr. Santarelli & Bond, Washington, 1983-85; prof. law Pace U. Sch. Law, White Plains, NY, 1986—, Disting. prof. law, 1986-2007. Co-editor Jour. Products and Toxics Liability, 1984—95; co-author: Madden and Owen on Products Liability, 3d edit., 2000, (with Boston) Law of Environmental and Toxic Torts, 2005; editor: Exploring Tort Law, 2005; contbr. articles to profl. jours. Mem. ABA, Am. Law Inst. Office: 359 Rich Ave Mount Vernon NY 10552 Office Phone: 914-837-4451. Personal E-mail: maddenmstuart@aol.com.

MADDEN, MARTIN GERARD, former state legislator; b. Washington, May 24, 1949; s. Anthony M. and Catherine W. Madden; m. Julia Gatewood Spangler, July 29, 1988; children: Donald Gerard, Thomas Martin, Christina Lynne, Marguerite Allen Spangler. BA in Econs., Iona Coll., 1971. Mem. Md. Ho. of Dels., Annapolis, 1991-94, Md. Senate, Annapolis, 1995—2002; senate minority leader State of Md. Gen. Assembly, Annapolis, 1999—2001, mem. Senate Budget and Taxation com. Mem. Budget and Tax com.; co-chmn. joint com. on welfare reform. Chmn. Critical Area Commn. for Atlantic and Chesapeake Bays, 2003—. Republican. Roman Catholic. Avocation: folk art collector. Office: 1804 West St Annapolis MD 21401 Personal E-mail: themaddens@hotmail.com.

MADDEN, MICHAEL DANIEL, finance company executive; b. Buffalo, Feb. 16, 1949; s. Daniel Francis and Miriam (Catron) M.; m. Mary Madden, May 1, 1976; children: Daniel, Kristina, Megan, Michael. BA in Econs. magna cum laude, Le Moyne Coll., 1971; MBA with distinction, U. Pa., 1973. Assoc. Kidder, Peabody & Co., NYC, 1973-77, v.p., 1977-80, mng. dir., 1980-85, global head investment banking, 1985-88; head investment banking Lehman Bros., NYC, 1989—93; exec. mng. dir. Global Capital Markets Kidder, Peabody Co., NYC, 1993-94; vice chmn., chief origination officer Paine Webber Inc., NYC, 1995-96; chmn., CEO Hanover Capital LLC, NYC, 1996—; ptnr. Beacon Group, NYC; sr. ptnr. Questor Mgmt., NYC, 1999—2005; mng. ptnr. Black Eagle Ptnrs., NYC, 2005—. Bd. dirs. Geologistics Corp., Transonic Sys. Inc., Chef Solutions Inc., Pinn Oak Mining, Freeport Properties, Inc. Bd. dirs. Cath. TV Ctr., NYC, 1981-85, Canisius Prep. Sch., Buffalo, 1992—; chmn. bd. trustees LeMoyne Coll., Syracuse, NY, 1987—. Mem. Am. Petroleum Inst., MBA Assn., Univ. Club, The Creek, Longboat Key Club. Republican. Roman Catholic. Avocations: boxing, hunting, tennis, coin collecting/numismatics, fishing. Office: Black Eagle Ptnrs 1285 6th Ave New York NY 10019 Office Phone: 212-554-4600. Business E-Mail: mmadden@blackeaglepartners.com.

MADDEN, MICKEY, musician; b. Austin, Tex., May 13, 1979; Bassist Kara's Flowers (name changed to Maroon 5, 2001), 1994—; signed to Reprise Records, 1997—99, Octone Records, 2001—. Musician (as Kara's Flowers): (albums) Fourth World, 1997; musician: (as Maroon 5) Songs About Jane, 2002, 1.22.03.Acoustic, 2004, Live Friday the 13th, 2005, It Won't Be Soon Before Long, 2007, (songs) Harder to Breathe, 2003, This Love, 2004 (MTV Video Music award for Best New Artist, 2004, Grammy award, Best Group Pop Performance, 2006), She Will Be Loved, 2004, Shiver, 2005, contbr. to Spider-Man 2 soundtrack, 2004. Recipient World Music award for Best New Group, 2004, MTV Europe award for Best New Act, 2004, Grammy award for Best New Artist (with Maroon 5), 2005. Address: Maroon 5 PO Box 884564 San Francisco CA 94188 Office: Octone Records Rm 500 560 Broadway New York NY 10012 Office Phone: 646-613-0200. E-mail: maroon5@maroon5.com.

MADDEN, MURDAUGH STUART, lawyer; b. Morgantown, W.Va., Feb. 26, 1922; s. Joseph Warren and Margaret (Liddell) M.; m. Constance Viens McKenna, May 12, 1999; children by previous marriage: Liddell Louise, Murdaugh Stuart Jr., Michael Mann. Student, Oberlin Coll., 1939-40; BA, George Washington U., 1942; JD, Harvard U., 1948. Bar: D.C. 1948, Va. 1948, U.S. Supreme Ct. 1953. Asst. counsel Bur. Aero., Washington, 1948-50; sole practice Washington, 1950-61, 71—; sr. ptnr. Shaw, Pittman, Potts, Trowbridge & Madden, Washington, 1961-71. Sr. counsel Humane Soc. U.S., Atlantic Devel. Co. and related corps. Author: (with Sherman L. Cohn) The Legal Status and Problems of the American Abroad, 1966. Trustee Inst. for Study Nat. Behavior, Princeton, N.J., Friends of India Com., Washington; pres. World Fedn. for Protection Animals, The Netherlands; v.p. World Soc. forProtection Animals, London. With USAAF, 1942-45, ETO. Mem. ABA (past chmn. internat. and comparative law com. internat. transp., chmn. subcom. on charitable orgns. internat. law sect. 1985—), D.C. Bar Assn., (past dir., past chmn. com. bar ethics), Va. Bar Assn., The Barristers, Am. Soc. Internat. Law, Harvard Law Sch. Assn., Oberlin Alumni Assn., Metropolitan Club, Harvard Club N.Y., Internat. Lawn Tennis Club U.S., Chevy Chase Club, Phi Sigma Kappa. Episcopalian. Home: 2530 Queen Annes Ln NW Washington DC 20037-2148 Office: 2100 L St NW Washington DC 20037-1525

MADDEN, PALMER BROWN, lawyer; b. Milw., Sept. 19, 1945; m. Susan L. Paulus, Mar. 31, 1984. BA, Stanford U., 1968; JD, U. Calif., Berkeley, 1973. Bar: Calif. 1973, U.S. Dist. Ct. (no. dist.) Calif. 1973, U.S. Supreme Ct. 1982. Ptnr. McCutchen, Doyle Brown & Enersen, Walnut Creek, 1985-98; prin. ADR Svcs., Alamo, Calif., 1999—. Pres. State Bar Bd. Govs., 2000-01. Chair bd. govs. Continuing Edn. of the Bar, 1997; judge pro tem Contra Costa Superior Ct., 1991-98; pres. Contra Costa Coun., 1995, Kennedy-King Found., 1994; bd. dirs. Episcopal Homes Found., 2001-05, Bay Area Legal Aid, 2005—, Bar Fund, 2006—. Mem. Contra Costa County Bar Assn. (pres. 1996-97). Democrat. Episcopalian. Office: ADR Svcs 3000 Danville Blvd # 543 Alamo CA 94507 Office Phone: 925-838-8593. Business E-Mail: pbm@netvista.net.

MADDEN, PAUL ROBERT, lawyer, director; b. St. Paul, Nov. 13, 1926; s. Ray Joseph and Margaret (Meyer) Madden; m. Rosemary R. Sorel, Aug. 7, 1974; children: Margaret Jane, James Patrick, William M., Derek R Sorel, Lisa T. Schoutsen. Student, St. Thomas Coll., 1944; AB, U. Minn., 1948; JD, Georgetown U., 1951. Bar: Ariz. 1957, Minn. 1951, D.C. 1951. Assoc. Hamilton & Hamilton, Washington, 1951-55; legal asst. to commr. SEC, Washington, 1955-56; assoc. Lewis and Roca, Phoenix, 1957-59, ptnr., 1959-90, Beus, Gilbert & Morrill, Phoenix, 1991-94, Chapman and Cutler, Phoenix, 1994-97; of counsel Gallagher & Kennedy, Phoenix, 1997—. Nat. co-chmn. Youth for Eisenhower, 1951—52; sec. Minn. Fedn. Coll. Rep. Clubs, 1947—48; chmn. 4th dist. Minn. Young Rep. Club, 1948; mem. Ariz. Rep. Com., 1960—62; bd. dir. Ind. Devel. Authority of City of Prescott, 2002—; past bd. dir. Yavapai Coll. Dist. Governing Bd., Prescott, sec., 2003—06; hon. life mem., mem. adv. bd. Cath. Cmty. Found., Cath. Social Svcs. No. Ariz., 2002—; bd. dir., pres. Ariz. Club, Phoenix, 1990—93; bd. dir. People Who Care, Prescott, 2001—, Yavapai Symphony Assoc., Prescott, 2004—, Found. Jr. Achievement Ctr. Ariz., Phoenix; mem. nat. bd. visitors Embry Riddle Aero. U., Prescott, 2002—, U. Ariz. Law Sch.; past bd. dir., past chmn. Mesa Air Group, Inc., Camelback Charitable Trust, Found. Sr. Living; past bd. dir., vice chmn. Ctrl. Ariz.

chpt. ARC; past bd. dir., past pres. Jr. Achievement Ctrl. Ariz., Inc.; past bd. dir. The Samaritan Found., Phoenix, St. Joseph the Worker, Phoenix, Hidden Valley Homeowners Assn., Prescott, 2002—04. With USNR, 1946—48. Mem.: ABA, Ariz. Bar Assn., Maricopa County Bar Assn., Yavapai County Bar Assn., The Barristers Club (Washington), Phi Delta Phi. Home: 1565 Range Rd Prescott AZ 86303 Office: Gallagher & Kennedy PA 101 E Gurley Ste 214 Prescott AZ 86301 Office Phone: 928-445-5800. Business E-Mail: prm@gknet.com.

MADDEN, PETER J., advertising executive; Founder, pres. AgileCat: Comms. Catalysts, Phila. Named one of 40 Under 40, Phila. Bus. Jour., 2006. Office: AgileCat 2nd Fl 4390 Main St Philadelphia PA 19127 Office Phone: 215-508-2082. Office Fax: 215-508-3558. E-mail: peter@agilecat.com.

MADDEN, RICHARD BLAINE, forest products executive; b. Short Hills, NJ, Apr. 27, 1929; s. James L. and Irma (Twining) M.; m. Joan Fairbairn, May 24, 1958; children: John Richard, Lynne Marie, Kathryn Ann, Andrew Twining. BS, Princeton U., 1951; JD, U. Mich., 1956; MBA, NYU, 1959; PhD (hon.), St. Scholastica Coll., 1994. Bar: Mich. 1956, N.Y. 1958. Gen. asst. treas.'s dept. Socony Mobil Oil Corp., NYC, 1956-57, spl. asst., 1958-59, fin. rep., 1960; asst. to pres. Mobil Chem. Co.; also dir. Mobil Chems. Ltd. of Eng., 1960-63; exec. v.p., gen. mgr. Kordite Corp.; also v.p. Mobil Plastics, 1963-66; v.p. Mobil Chem. Co., NYC, 1966-68, group v.p., 1968-70; asst. treas. Mobil Oil Corp., 1970-71; chmn. Mobil Oil Estates Ltd., 1970-71; pres., chief exec. Potlatch Corp., San Francisco, 1971-77, chmn. chief exec. officer, 1977-94; ret., 1994. From lectr. to adj. assoc. prof. fin. N.Y.U., 1960-63; bd. dir., pres., Knight Grand Cross Magistral Grace in Obedience Order of Malta, Western Assn.; bd. govs., chmn. audit com., mem. adminstrv. compensation and labor rels. com. San Francisco Symphony. Former bd. dir. Smith-Kettlewell Eye Rsch. Inst., trustee emeritus, former chmn. Am. Enterprise Inst.; former mem. bd. Nat. Park Found.; hon. trustee Com. Econ. Devel. Lt. (j.g.) USNR, 1951-54. Mem. N.Y. Bar Assn., Mich. Bar Assn. Clubs: Bohemian (San Francisco); Lagunitas (Ross, Calif.); Metropolitan (Washington). Roman Catholic. Office Phone: 415-461-0683.

MADDEN, ROBERT EDWARD, surgeon, educator; b. Oak Park, Ill., Sept. 16, 1925; s. Joseph Edward and Gertrude Celelia (McGowan) M.; m. Susan Ann Hale, May 24, 1958; children: Robert Joseph, Lisa Marie, Karen Louise, Kevin Francis. BS in Medicine, U. Ill., Chgo., 1950, MS in Biochemistry, 1952, MD, 1952. Diplomate Am. Bd. Surgery, Bd. Thoracic Surgery. Assoc. in surgery U. Ill. Coll. Medicine, Chgo., 1957-58; sr. surgeon Nat. Cancer Inst., Bethesda, Md., 1959-60; asst. prof. surgery N.Y. Med. Coll., NYC, 1961-66, assoc. prof., 1966-71, prof. Valahlla, 1971—. Mem. N.Y. State Health Rsch. Coun., Albany, 1976—; med. coord. N.Y. State Dept. Health, 1998—2007. Author: (with Lippincott) Problems In General Surgery, 1988; editor: Gastrointestinal Bleeding, 1987; editor-in-chief N.Y. Med. Quarterly, 1979-90; contbr. articles to profl. jours. With U.S. Army, 1943-46. Recipient Borden Undergrad. Rsch. award Borden Corp., 1952; postdoctoral fellow Am. Cancer Soc., 1958-59. Fellow ACS (com. on cancer 1993-97); mem. Am. Soc. for Vascular Surgery, Soc. Internat. Chirurgie, Am. Assn. Cancer Edn. (pres. 1979), N.Y. Cancer Soc. (pres. 1975-76), N.Y. State Cancer Programs Assn. (pres. 1975-76), Knights of Holy Sepulchre, Knights of the Order of Malta, Pi Gamma Mu. Republican. Roman Catholic. Home: 6 Crows Nest Rd Bronxville NY 10708-4802 Office: NY Med Coll Munger Pavilion Valhalla NY 10595 Office Phone: 914-493-7615. E-mail: remadden@bellatlantic.net.

MADDEN, STEVEN, footwear designer; b. NY, 1958; m. Wendy Madden. Attended, U. Miami. Founder Steven Madden Ltd., 1990, CEO, 1990—2002, creative & design chief, 2002—. Owner, Friedman accessories divsn. Steven Madden Ltd., 2006—, creative dir., Rule shoe line, creative dir., Natural Comfort sneaker collection. Office: Steven Madden Ltd 52-16 Barnett Ave Long Island City NY 11104 Office Phone: 718-446-1800. Office Fax: 718-446-5655.

MADDEN, TERESA DARLEEN, insurance agency owner; b. Dallas, Aug. 4, 1960; d. Tommy Joe Frederick Dodd and Mary Helen (Sterner) Smith; m. Kim Ashley Madden, June 2, 1989. Student, Tex. Tech U., 1978-81. Cert. ins. counselor, 1985, risk mgr., 2006. With personal lines svc. Charles R. Ervin Ins., Midland, Tex., 1981, Bryant Scalf Ins., Richardson, Tex., 1981-82; with comml. ins. svc. Street & Assocs. Inc., Dallas, 1982-84; with comml. ins. sales/svc. Hotchkiss Ins., Dallas, 1984-85; mgr. sales Abbott-Rose Ins. Agy., Dallas, 1985-89; owner Glenn-Madden & Assocs. Ins., Dallas, 1990—. Bd. dirs. Ind. Ins. Agents of Dallas, 2004—06, exec. bd., 2006—. Methodist. Office: Glenn Madden & Assocs Inc 13601 Preston Rd Ste 106E Dallas TX 75240-4906 Business E-Mail: dmadden@glenn-maddeninsurance.com.

MADDEN, THOMAS A., finance educator; BBA, Ind. U. of Pa.; MBA, U. Pitts. CPA, Mich. Audit mgr. Coopers & Lybrand, 1975; various positions including v.p. corp. devel., v.p. fin., asst. corp. contr. Rockwell Internat., 1981—97; sr. v.p. Meritor Automotive, Inc., 1997—2000; sr. v.p., CFO ArvinMeritor, Inc., Troy, Mich., 2000—01; exec. v.p., CFO Ingram Micro Inc., Santa Ana, Calif., 2001—05; lectr. acctg. U. Calif. Irvine Paul Merage Sch. Bus., 2005—. Bd. dirs. Mindspeed Technologies, Inc. Office: U Calif Irvine Paul Merage Sch Bus Irvine CA 92697-3125

MADDEN, THOMAS JAMES, lawyer, educator; b. Trenton, NJ, Sept. 13, 1941; m. Irene Lyons. BEE, Villanova U., 1964; JD with honors, Cath. U., 1968. Bar: NJ 1968, DC 1968, US Patent Office 1968. Atty. adv. Naval Air Sys. Command, 1968—69; dep. gen. counsel Dept. Justice Law Enforcement Assistance Adminstrn., 1970—71, gen. counsel, 1972—79; dir. Nat. Adv. Commn. on Criminal Justice Stds. and Goals, 1971—73; adv. US Office Mgmt. and Budget on Fed. Assistance Programs, Washington, 1979—80; gen. counsel Dept. Justice Office Justice Assistance Rsch. and Stats., 1980; from assoc. to ptnr. Kay Scholer, Fierman, Hays and Handler, Washington, 1980—84; ptnr., gov. contract, intellectual property litig. Venable, LLP (formerly Venable, Baetjer, Howard & Civiletti), Washington, 1984—. Adj. prof. contract law Am. U., 1980-85; gen. counsel Nat. Coun. Juvenile and Family Ct. Judges; adv. panel on streamlining and codifying fed. acquisition laws Dept. Def., 1991-93; mem. Procurement Round Table, 1998—, vice chmn., 2002— Contbr. articles to profl. jours. Pres. US Ct. Fed. Claims Bar Assn., 1999-2000. Recipient Louis Brownlow award Am. Soc. for Pub. Adminstrn., 1982, Disting. Svc. award Dept. Justice Law Enforcement Assistance Adminstr., 1973, Wilson Cowen award US Ct. Fed. Claims, 1998. Fellow Am. Bar Found.; mem. ABA (chmn. pub. contract law sect. 1988-89, pres. fellows of pub. contract law sect. 1992-93), DC Bar Assn., Fed. Bar Assn. (pres. DC chpt. 1982-83). Office: Venable LLP 575 7th St N W Washington DC 20004 Home Phone: 703-821-8566; Office Phone: 202-344-4803. Business E-Mail: tmadden@venable.com.

MADDEN, WALES HENDRIX, JR., lawyer; b. Amarillo, Tex., Sept. 1, 1927; s. Wales Hendrix and Kathryn (Nash) Madden; m. Alma Faye Cowden, Nov. 8, 1952; children: Wales Hendrix III, Straughn. BA, U. Tex., 1950, LLB, 1952. Bar: Tex. 1952. Pvt. practice, Amarillo. Mem. Tex. Constl. Revision Commn., 1973. Mem. Tex. Coll. and Univ. Sys. Coord. Bd., 1964—69, Amarillo Area Found., Cal Farley's Boys Ranch, Pres.'s Export Coun., 1981, Select Com. Higher Edn., 1985, 1987; chmn. SWST regional panel Pres.'s Commn. White Ho. Fellowships, 1989—90; chmn. Tex. Water Devel. Bd., 2002; mem. Gov.'s Com. Ad Valorem Taxes, 1996; bd. regents Amarillo Coll., 1958—59, U. Tex., 1959—65; trustee Trinity U., San Antonio; chmn. bd. Internat. Food and Agrl. Devel., 1990—94. With USNR. Named Outstanding Man of Amarillo, 1972, Disting. Alumnus, U. Tex., 1979, U. Tex. Law Sch., 1986. Mem.: ABA, State Jr. Bar Tex. (pres. 1956), State Bar Tex. (Outstanding 50 Year Lawyer award 2003), Amarillo Bar Assn. (pres. 1956), Friar Soc., Amarillo C. of C. (pres. 1968), Tex. Philos. Soc., Sigma Alpha, Phi Eta Sigma, Phi Delta Theta, Phi Alpha Delta. Presbyterian. Avocation: mountain climbing. Home and Office: PO Box 15288 Amarillo TX 79105-5288 Office Phone: 806-374-2422.

MADDIN, ROBERT, metallurgist, educator; b. Hartford, Conn., Oct. 20, 1918; s. Isadore I. and Mae (Jacobs) Levine; married, July 8, 1945; children: Leslie, Jill. BS in Metall. Engring., Purdue U., 1942; DEng., Yale U., 1948. Registered profl. engr., Pa. Asst., assoc. prof. Johns Hopkins U., Balt., 1949-55; prof. U. Pa., phila., 1955-73, univ. prof., 1973-83; vis. prof. Harvard U., Cambridge, Mass., 1983-87, curator, 1987—; vis. prof. Oxford (Eng.) U., 1970, vis. fellow Wolfson Coll., 1987. Vis. prof. U. Birmingham, Eng., 1953-54; vis. scholar Hebrew U., Jerusalem, 1976; hon. prof. Beijing Sci. and Engring. U., 1986; hon. mem. Japan Metals, hon. prof. Dali U., 2006. Editor-in-chief Math., Sci., and Engring, 1965-82; contbr. more than 250 publs. to profl. jours. 1st Lt. USAF, 1942-45. Disting. Sr. Sci. fellow A. von Humboldt Found., Germany, 1989-90, Disting. Alumnus Purdue U., 1974; recipient Pomerance award Archaeol. Inst. Am., 1994, medal of merit U. Pa. Fellow Am. Soc. Metallurgists, TMS. Avocation: history early metallurgy. Personal E-mail: robertmaddin@comcast.net.

MADDOCK, JEROME TORRENCE, library and information scientist; b. Darby, Pa., Feb. 7, 1940; s. Richard Cotton and Isobel Louise (Mezger) M.; m. Karen Rhueama Weygand, Oct. 2, 1965. BS in Biology, Muhlenberg Coll., 1961; MS in Info. Sci., Drexel U., 1968. Editl. assoc. Biol. Abstracts, Phila., 1962—63; mgr. rsch. info. Merck & Co., West Point, Pa., 1963—72; sr. cons. Auerbach Assocs., Inc., Phila., 1972—79; mgr. libr. and info. svcs. Solar Energy Rsch. Inst., Golden, Colo., 1979—88; mgr. info. svcs. Transp. Rsch. Bd., Washington, 1988—99; project mgr. IHS Enterprise Solutions, Boulder, Colo., 1999—2001; ind. cons., 2002—; faculty online U. Phoenix, 1999—. Del. Gov.'s Conf. on Libr. and Info. Svc., Pa., 1978; mem. blue ribbon panel to select archivist of U.S., Washington, 1979; U.S. del. to ops. com. on transp. rsch. info. Orgn. for Econ. Cooperation and Devel., 1988-99. Bd. dirs. Paoli (Pa.) Pub. Libr., 1976-77, Boulder Friends of Jazz, 2003—; bd. trustees Louisville County Pub. Libr., 2002-07, pres. 2004. With USAFR, 1962-68. Mem. AAAS, Am. Soc. Info. Sci. (chmn. 1974-75), Elks, Beta Phi Mu, Pi Delta Epsilon. Republican. Episcopalian. Achievements include projection of information science operations 10 years into the future. Home: 545 W Laurel Ct Louisville CO 80027-1116

MADDOCK, LAWRENCE HILL, retired language educator, writer; b. Ogden, Utah, July 14, 1923; s. Lawrence J. and Nellie (Hill) Maddock. Student, U. Fla., 1941-42; BA, George Peabody Coll., 1946, PhD, 1965; MA, U. So. Calif., 1949. Tchr. pub. schs., Jacksonville, Fla., 1949-52; instr. U. Fla., Gainesville, 1952-53; asst. prof. California (Pa.) State Coll., 1955-56, assoc. prof., 1956-64, N.E. La. State Coll., Monroe, 1964-67, U. West Fla., Pensacola, 1967-90. Author: The Door of Memory, 1974, revised, 2003, John Maddock: Mormon Pioneer, 1996; contbr. chpts. to books and articles to profl. jours. Mem. MLA (bibliographer 1978-93), Thomas Wolfe Soc., Mormon History Assn. Republican. Mem. Lds Ch. Home: 1012 Gerhardt Dr Pensacola FL 32503-3222

MADDOCK, PATRICK JEROME, lawyer; b. Devils Lake, ND, Sept. 19, 1938; s. John and Sophie (Duchscherer) M.; m. Susan Gail Robbins, Sept. 30, 1970; children: Stacey Kost, Melissa, Daniel. BSBA, U. N.D., 1962, LLB, 1964. Bar: N.D. 1964. Atty. Camrud Law Firm, Grand Forks, N.D., 1964—. Lectr. in field. Author articles on profl. liability. Cpl. USMC, 1956-58. Mem. N.D. Bar Assn. (Recognition of Svc. award 1993), Rotary (past pres.). Avocations: farming, antiques, hunting, old cars. Home: 3128 Olson Dr Grand Forks ND 58201-7567 Office: Camrud Law Firm 500 1st Bank Bldg 600 Demers Ave Grand Forks ND 58201-4599

MADDON, JOE, professional baseball coach; b. Sept. 19, 1954; BS in Econ., Lafayette Coll., Easton, Pa., 1976. Mgr. Idaho Falls Minor League Baseball, 1981, Salem Minor League Baseball, Peoria Minor League Baseball, Midland Minor League Baseball, 1985—86; coord. Calif. Angels Arizona Instrnl. League, 1984—93; roving hitting instructor Calif. Angels, 1987—93, dir. player develop., 1994, bullpen coach, 1994, first base coach, 1995, bench coach, 1996, interim mgr., 1996, 1999, bench coach, 2000—05; mgr. Tampa Bay Devil Rays, 2005—. Office: Tampa Bay Devil Rays One Tropicana Dr Saint Petersburg FL 33705

MADDOW, RACHEL, radio personality, political activist; BA, Stanford U., 1994; PhD in Politics, Oxford U. Host The Big Breakfast, WRSI, Northhampton, Mass., 2002—04; co-host (with Chuck D. & Liz Winstead) Unfiltered, Air Am. Radio, NYC, host The Rachel Maddow Show, 2005—. Fellow AIDS Legal Referral Panel, San Francisco; grantee John Gardner Pub. Svc. Fellowship, Ludlam Health Policy Fellowship; Rhodes Scholar, 1995. Office: Air America Radio 641 Avenue Of The Americas Fl 4 New York NY 10011-2038

MADDOX, ALVA HUGH, retired state supreme court justice; b. Andalusia, Ala., Apr. 17, 1930; s. Christopher Columbus and Audie Lodella Maddox; m. Virginia Roberts, June 14, 1958; children: Robert Hugh, Jane Maddox. AB in Journalism, U. Ala., Tuscaloosa, 1952, JD, 1957. Bar: Ala. 1957. Law clk. to Judge Aubrey Cates, Ala. Ct. Appeals, Montgomery, 1957-58; field examiner Chief Atty.'s Office, VA, Montgomery, 1958-59; law clk. to Judge Frank M. Johnson, U.S. Dist. Ct., Montgomery, 1959-61; pvt. practice Montgomery, 1961-65; cir. judge, spl. cir. judge Montgomery Cir. Ct., 1963, asst. dist. atty., 1964; legal advisor to govs. including George C. Wallace, Lurleen B. Wallace, Albert P. Brewer, State of Ala., Montgomery, 1965-69; assoc. justice Supreme Ct. Ala., Montgomery, 1969-2001; ret., 2001. Author: Billy Boll Weevil: A Pest Becomes A Hero, 1976, Alabama Rules of Criminal Procedure, 1991, supplements, 1992—. Founder youth jud. program YMCA, Montgomery, 1978, also mem. metro. bd. dir. 2d lt. USAF, 1952-54, col. USAF Res. ret. Recipient Man of Yr. award YMCA, 1988, Disting. Program Svc. award, 1989, Srs. of Achievement award Montgomery Coun. on Aging, 1999. Mem.: ABA, Am. Inns of Ct. (former trustee), Hugh Maddox Inn of Ct. Montgomery (charter, founding mem.), Christian Legal Soc., Inst. Jud. Adminstrn., Ala. Bar Assn. (Jud. award of merit 1997), Order of Samaritan/U. Ala. Law Sch., Kiwanis. Baptist. Office: 3137 Hathaway Pl Montgomery AL 36111-1707

MADDOX, DAVID M., management consultant, career military officer; Advanced through grades to gen. US Army; comdr. 14th Armored Cavalry Regiment, Germany, 1st Squadron, 11th Armored Cavalry Regiment, Fulda, 2nd Armored Cavalry Regiment, Nuremberg, 18th Infantry Div., Bad Kreuznach, V Corps, Frankfurt, NATO's Ctrl. Army Group; comdr.-in-chief U.S. Army, Europe, 1992—94; ret., 1995. Cons. Gateway Mgmt. Group Inc., Blue Bell, Pa. Recipient Vance R. Wanner Meml. Award, 2004. Mem.: NAE. Office: Gateway Mgmt Group Inc 1200 DeKalb Pike Blue Bell PA 19422 Office Phone: 215-561-4000.

MADDOX, FREDERICK LYNN, mathematics educator; b. Fayette, Ala., Nov. 9, 1975; s. Freddie Odean and Jo Ann (Corbett) Maddox. BEd in math. and history, U. North Ala., Florence, 1998, ME in math. Math. tchr., dept. chair Lyman Ward Mil. Acad., Camp Hill, Ala., 2000—05; math. tchr. Lamar County HS, Vernon, Ala., 2005—. Mem.: NEA, Ala. Edn. Assn., Nat. Coun. Tchrs. Math. Baptist. Home: 186 Monroe St Millport AL 35576 Office: Lamar County HS 8990 Hwy 18 Vernon AL 35592

MADDOX, JERRY AVEN, retired catalog executive, writer; b. Atlanta, Sept. 27, 1935; s. George Ernest and Emilie Marion (Peeples) Maddox; m. Roberta Ann Eddy; children: Lamont Edward, Ryan Allen, Jolie Aven. BBA in Fin. and Acctg., Emory U., Atlanta, 1957, JD, 1964. Catalog mgmt. exec. Sears, Roebuck & Co., Atlanta, 1957—89; substitute tchr. DeKalb County Sch. Sys., Atlanta, 1992—2000. Author: (geneology books) Descendants of John Allen, 1997, The Peeples Family, Descendants of William Peeples, 1999, (historical fiction) Song of the Ogeechee, 2002, From Salacoa to Tahlequah, 2004, (nonfiction) The Legacy of Ludovic Grant, 2007. Page Congressman James C. Davis, Washington, 1951; adminstrv. bd. Dunwoody United Meth. Ch., 1972—81; coach nat. age group U.S. Swimming, 1978—88; v.p., sec. DeKalb County Jaycees, Ga., 1964—70; life mem. Dunwoody Preservation Trust, Inc., 2004. With U.S. Marine Corps. active duty and reserves, 1957—63. Named one of Outstanding Atlantans, Heritage Pub. Co., 1977—78. Mem.: Corpus Cordis Aureum, Clan Grant, Mil. Order Stars and Bars (Lt. Comdr. Gen. William J. Hardee chpt. 2002—03, The Jackson medal 2000), Ft. Delaware Soc. (life), Nat. Eagle Scout Assn. (life), Eddy Family Assn. (life; rec. sec. 1995—2000), St. Andrews Soc., Belle Meade Hunt Club (equestrian), SCV (comdr. maj. Charles A. Dunwoody camp 2002—06), St. David's Welsh Soc. Ga., Phi Alpha Delta, Pi Kappa Alpha, Alpha Kappa Psi. Republican. Avocation: distance running. Home: 4917 Cambridge Dr Dunwoody GA 30338-5007

MADDOX, LAUREN M., federal agency administrator; B, Creighton U.; M, Northwestern U. Sr. v.p. Comm. Fedn. Am. Hospitals; sr. Comm. adv. US Rep. Newt Gingrich, US Rep. J.C. Watts, Jr.; sr. comm. adv. to US Rep. Joel Hefley US Congress; comm. dir. Ho. Rep. Conf.; prin. PodestaMattoon; asst. sec. for comm. & outreach US Dept. Edn., Washington, 2006—. Office: 400 Maryland Ave SW Rm 7C115 Washington DC 20202-1510 Office Phone: 202-401-0404. Office Fax: 202-401-8607. *

MADDOX, NADANA, secondary school educator; m. John Maddox, Sept. 1, 1969; children: Brian D., Gregory D. BA, Southwestern Okla. State U., Weatherford, Okla., 1972; MS in Sch. Counseling, East Ctrl. U., Ada, Okla., 2002. Tchr., counselor Walters (Okla.) Pub. Schs., 1984—2004; project dir. Osage County Interlocal Coop., Hominy, Okla., 2004—. Avocations: travel, baseball, reading. Office Phone: 918-885-2667.

MADDOX, ODINGA LAWRENCE, II, head of religious order; b. Akron, Ohio, Aug. 23, 1964; s. Odinga Lawrence and Shirley Jean (Shavers) Maddox; m. Nancy Malone, Apr. 21, 1983; children: Terrell, Lawrence III, Shelly, Carissa, Joshua. AST in theology, Berean Bible Coll., 1995; BA in pastorial min., Bethany Divinity Coll., 2000; MA in pastoral min., Bethany Seminary, 2005. Ordained deacon 1996; cert. peace officer State of Ohio. Peace officer Comml. Protective Svcs., Akron, Ohio, 1984—96; pastor St. Paul AMEZ Ch., Coraopolis, Pa., 1996—98, Price Meml. AMEZ Ch., Atlantic City, 1998—. Auditor NJ Conf. AMEZ Ch., Atlantic City, 2002—; dean Camden Dist. Sch. of Min., Camden, NJ, 2002—. Mem. Salvation Army, Coraopolis, Pa., 1996—98. Recipient Black Hist. Acad. award, Asbury United Meth. Ch., 1999, Faithful Svc. award, Minister's Home Detention Program, 2003, Cmty. Involvement award, NAACP, 2005. Mem.: NAACP, Pan-Meth. Alliance (pres. 2001). Avocations: reading, fishing, power walking. Office: Price Meml AME Zion Ch 525 Atlantic Ave Atlantic City NJ 08401 E-mail: amezionite@aol.com.

MADDOX, ROBERT NOTT, chemical engineer, educator; b. Winslow, Ark., Sept. 29, 1925; s. R.L. and Mabel (Nott) M.; m. Paula Robinson, Oct. 6, 1951 (dec. Apr. 1984); children: Deirdre O'Neil, Robert Dozier; m. Pauline Razook, Nov. 30, 1987. Student, Iowa State Coll., 1944-45; BS, U. Ark., 1948; MS, U. Okla., 1950; PhD, Okla. State U., 1955; Sc.D. (hon.), U. Ark., 1991. Registered profl. engr., Okla. Mem. faculty Sch. Chem. Engring., Okla. State U., 1950-51, 52-58, prof., head dept., 1958-77, Leonard F. Sheerar prof., 1976-86, dir. phys. properties lab., 1976-86. Design engr. process div. Black, Sivalls & Bryson, Inc., Oklahoma City, 1951-52; adminstrv. v.p., tech. dir. Fluid Properties Research, Inc., 1972-85; chem. engring. cons. Author: Gas and Liquid Sweetening, 1971, rev. ed. 1978, 83, (with J. Erbar) Gas Conditioning and Processing Vol. 3 - Computer Techniques and Applications, 1981, rev. ed. (with L. Lilly), 1988, (with A. Hines) Mass Transfer - Fundamentals and Applications, 1985; also numerous tech. papers. Served with USNR, 1944-45. Recipient award for personal achievement Chem. Engring. mag., 1988; Phillips lectr. in chem. engring. edn., Oklahoma State U., 1989; inducted into Engring. Hall of Fame, U. Ark., 1989, Okla. Higher Edn. Hall of Fame, 1996; Dr. Robert N. Maddox Professorship in Chem. Engring. established in his honor by Gas Processors Suppliers Assn. at Okla. State U., 1989, Founders award Am. Inst. of Chemical Engineers, 1994 Fellow AIChE (chpt. pres. 1956-57, André Wilkins Meml. award 1981, Founder's award 1994); mem. NSPE, Okla. Soc. Profl. Engrs. (chpt. pres. 1961-62, dir. 1966-68, Engr. of Yr. 1972), Am. Inst. Mining Engrs., Soc. Petroleum Engrs., Acad. Chem. Engrs., Am. Chem. Soc. (treas. indsl. and engring. chemistry div. 1966-68, chmn. div. 1970, Stewart award 1971), Gas Processors Assn. (Hanlon award 1985, Svc. citation 1987, Meritorious Svc. award 1998), Gas Processors Suppliers Assn. (editorial adv. bd. Engring. Data Book 1972—), Sigma Xi, Omega Chi Epsilon (nat. pres. 1968-70), Tau Beta Pi, Alpha Chi Sigma, Omicron Delta Kappa, Sigma Nu (high coun. 1966-70, regent 1972-74, Hall of Honor 1988). Episcopalian (lay reader, vestryman). Clubs: Elks, Masons. Home: 1710 Davinbrook Ln Stillwater OK 74074-2339

MADDREY, WILLIS CROCKER, medical educator, internist, academic administrator, consultant, researcher; b. Roanoke Rapids, NC, Mar. 29, 1939; s. Milner Crocker and Sara Jean (Willis) M.; m. Ann Marie Matt; children: Jeffrey, Gregory, Thomas. BS, Wake Forest U., 1960; MD, Johns Hopkins U., 1964. Diplomate: Am. Bd. Internal Medicine. Intern Osler Med. Service Johns Hopkins Hosp., Balt., 1964-65, asst. resident, 1965-66, 68-69, chief resident, 1969-70; fellow in liver disease Yale U., 1970-71; asst. prof. medicine Johns Hopkins U., Balt., 1971-75, assoc. prof., 1975-79, prof., 1980—82, asst. dean Sch. Medicine, 1975-79, assoc. dir. dept. medicine, 1979-82; prof., chmn. dept. medicine Jefferson Med. Coll., Phila., 1982-90; v.p. clin. affairs U. Tex. Southwestern Med. Ctr., Dallas, 1990-93, exec. v.p. clin. affairs, 1993—. Assoc. editor: Medicine, 1972-82, Hepatology, 1988-95, mem. editl. bd., 1981-84, 86-87, Gastroenterology, 1982-87, Am. Jour. Medicine, 1978-88; contbr. articles to profl. jours. Bd. dirs. Am. Liver Found., 1978-81, Dallas County Med. Soc., 1996-98; trustee Magee Rehab. Hosp., Phila., 1982-87. With USPHS, 1966-68. Mem. ACP (bd. regents 1986-92, pres. 92-93), Am. Soc. Clin. Investigation, Am. Gastroenterol. Assn., Am. Assn. Study Liver Disease (pres. 1981). Republican. Office: U Tex Southwestern Med Ctr 5323 Harry Hines Blvd Dallas TX 75390-8570 Office Phone: 214-648-2024.

MADDUX, GREGORY ALAN, professional baseball player; b. San Angelo, Tex., Apr. 14, 1966; Grad., H.S., Las Vegas. Baseball player Chgo. Cubs, 1986—92, 2004—06, Atlanta Braves, 1992—2003, LA Dodgers, 2006, San Diego Padres, 2006—. Named Nat. League Pitcher of Yr., Sporting News, 1993, Nat. League Innings Pitched Leader, 1991—95, Nat. League Earned Run Avg. Leader, 1993—95, 1998; named to All-Star team, 1988, 1992, 1994—98, 2000, All-Time Rawlings Gold Glove Team, 2007; recipient Cy Young award, Baseball Writers Assn. Am., 1992, 1993, 1994, 1995, Gold Glove award, 1990—2002, Gold Glove Award, 2004—06. Achievements include being a mem. of World Series Championship team, 1995; becoming 13th pitcher in MLB history to throw 3,000 strikeouts, 2005. *

MADDUX, VERNON RAY, retired history professor; s. Raymond Dockery Maddux and Ada Ruth Holloway; 1 child, Tiffany Jane Henry. BA, Southwestern State Coll., Weatherford, Okla., 1966; MA in Am. History, U. Okla., Norman, 1994. History prof. Oklahoma City CC, 2000—. Author: (history book) Cattle King of Colorado, John Hittson, 1994, In Dull Knife's Wake, 2003. Bd. mem. Cleve. County Hist. Soc., Norman, 2007. Lt. col. USMC, 1966—87. Mem.: ARC (assoc.). Office: Oklahoma City CC S May Ave Oklahoma City OK Home Phone: 405-364-0506.

MADEIRA, FRANCIS KING CAREY, conductor, educator; b. Jenkintown, Pa., Feb. 21, 1917; s. Percy Childs and Margaret (Carey) M.; m. Jean E. Browning, June 17, 1947. Grad., Avon Old Farms, 1934; student, Julliard Grad. Sch., 1937-43; DFA (hon.), Providence Coll., 1966; DHL, R.I. Coll., 1969; MusD (hon.), Brown U., 1976. Instr. music Brown U., 1943-46, asst. prof. music, 1946-56, assoc. prof. music, 1956-66. Founder, condr. R.I. Philharm. Orch., 1945-78; concert pianist recitals and condr. concerts, U.S. and Europe; also guest condr. U.S. and fgn. orchs. World premiere Trilogy (JFK-MLK-RFK) (by Ron Nelson), R.I. Philharmonic Orch., 1969. Mem. music panel Maine State Arts Commn., 1987-90; bd. trustees Saco River Festival Assn., 1988-94; mem. adv. bd., trustee Portland (Maine) Symphony Orch., 1996—. Recipient Gov.'s award for excellence in arts, 1972; John F. Kennedy award for svc. to cmty., 1978, Maestro award R.I. Philharm. Orch., 1998, Millennium Reflections award R.I. Philharm. Orch., 1999, John Hazen White Sr. Leadership award R.I. Philharm. Orch., 2003, Citizen Citation award Mayor or Providence, R.I., 2003.

MADER, CHARLES LAVERN, chemist; b. Dewey, Okla., Aug. 8, 1930; s. George Edgar and Naomia Jane (Harer) M.; m. Emma Jean Sinclair, June 12, 1960; 1 child, Charles L. II. BS, Okla. State U., 1952, MS, 1954; PhD, Pacific Western U., 1980. Fellow Los Alamos (N.Mex.) Nat. Lab., 1955—; JIMAR sr. fellow U. Hawaii, Honolulu, 1985-94; pres. Mader Cons. Co., Honolulu, 1985—. Author: Numerical Modeling of Detonation, 1979, Numerical Modeling of Water Waves, 1988, Numerical Modeling of Explosives and Propellants, 1997, 3rd edit. 2007, Numerical Modeling of Water, 2d edit., 2004; editor: Los Alamos Explosives Performance Data, 1982, LASL Phermex Data, vol. 1, 1980, vol. 2, 1980, vol. 3, 1981; contbr. numerous articles to profl. jours.; author 70 reports. Scoutmaster Boys Scouts Am., Los Alamos, 1971-85. Fellow Am. Inst. Chemists; mem. Am. Chem. Soc., Combustion Inst., Tsunami Soc. (editor 1985—2006), Marine Tech. Soc., Sigma Xi, Pi Mu Epsilon, Phi Lambda Upsilon. Methodist. Achievements include development and definition of field of numerical modeling of explosives and water waves. Office: Mader Consulting Co 1049 Kamehame Dr Honolulu HI 96825-2860 also: 214 Barranca Rd Los Alamos NM 87544-2410 also: PO Box 5930 Avon CO 81620-5930 Office Phone: 808-396-9855. Personal E-mail: mccohi@aol.com.

MADEWELL, JOHN EDWARD, radiologist; Student, Ctrl. State Coll., Oklahoma City, 1960-69; MD, U. Okla., 1969. Intern Madigen Gen. Hosp., Tacoma, 1969-70; resident in diagnostic radiology Walter Reed Med. Ctr., Washington, 1970-73; fellow in radiol. pathology Armed Forces Inst. Pathology, Washington, 1973-74; radiologist Pa. State Geisinger Health Sys.; prof., chmn. dept. radiology Milton S. Hershey Med. Ctr./Pa. State U., 1987—; exec. dir. Univ. Physicians/Pa. State U., Hershey, 1996-97. Mem. Am. Coll. Radiology, Am. Roentgen Ray Soc., Assn. Univ. Radiologists, Internat. Skeletal Soc., Radiologic Soc. N.Am. Office: Pa State U Coll Medicine Hershey MC Dept Radiol H066 PO Box 850 Hershey PA 17033-0850

MADGETT, NAOMI LONG, poet, editor, publisher, educator; b. Norfolk, Va., July 5, 1923; d. Clarence Marcellus and Maude Selena (Hilton) Long; m. Julian F. Witherspoon, Mar. 31, 1946 (div. Apr. 1949); 1 child, Jill Witherspoon Boyer; m. William H. Madgett, July 29, 1954 (div. Dec. 1960); m. Leonard P. Andrews, Mar. 31, 1972 (dec. May 1996). BA, Va. State Coll., 1945; MEd, Wayne State U., 1955; PhD, Internat. Inst. for Advanced Studies, 1980; LHD (hon.), Siena Heights Coll., 1991, Loyola U., 1993; DFA (hon.), Mich. State U., 1994. Reporter, copyreader Mich. Chronicle, Detroit, 1946; svc. rep. Mich. Bell Telephone Co., Detroit, 1948-54; tchr. English pub. high schs. Detroit, 1955-65, 66-68; rsch. assoc. Oakland U., Rochester, Mich., 1965-66; mem. staff Detroit Women Writers Conf. Ann. Writers Conf., 1968—; lectr. English U. Mich., 1970-71; assoc. prof. English Eastern Mich. U., Ypsilanti, 1968-73, prof., 1973-84, prof. emeritus, 1984—; editor-pub. Lotus Press, 1974—. Editor Lotus Poetry Series, Mich. State U. Press, 1993-98. Author: (poetry) Songs to a Phantom Nightingale (under name Naomi Cornelia Long), 1941, One and the Many, 1956, Star by Star, 1965, 2d edit., 70, (with Ethel Tincher and Henry B. Maloney) Success in Language and Literature B, 1967, Pink Ladies in the Afternoon, 1972, 2d edit., 90, Exits and Entrances, 1978, A Student's Guide to Creative Writing, 1980, Phantom Nightingale: Juvenilia, 1981, Octavia and other Poems (Creative Achievement award Coll. Lang. Assn.), 1988, Remembrances of Spring: Collected Early Poems, 1993, Octavia: Guthrie and Beyond, 2002, Connected Islands, 2004, (autobiography) Pilgrim Journey, 2006; editor: (anthology) A Milestone Sampler: 15th Anniversary Anthology, 1988, Adam of Ife: Black Women in Praise of Black Men, 1992; In Her Lifetime tribute Afrikan Poets Theatre, 1989 Participant Creative Writers in Schs. program. Recipient Esther R. Beer Poetry award Nat. Writers Club, 1957, Disting. English Tchr. of Yr. award, 1967; Josephine Nevins Keal award, 1979; Mott fellow in English, 1965, Robert Hayden Runagate award, 1985, Creative Artist award Mich. Coun. for the Arts, 1987, award Nat. Coalition 100 Black Women, 1984, award Nat. Coun. Tchrs. English Black Caucus, 1984, award Chesapeake/Virginia Beach chpt. Links, Inc., 1981, Arts Found. Mich. award, 1990, Creative Achievement award Coll. Lang. Assn., 1988; Arts Achievement award Wayne State U., 1985, The Black Scholar Award of Excellence, 1992; Am. Book award, 1993, Mich. Artist award, 1993; Creative Contbrs. award Gwendolyn Brooks Ctr. Black Lit. and Creative Writing Chgo. State U., 1993, Lifetime Achievement award Furious Flower, 1994, George Kent award, 1995, Lifetime Achievement award Gwendolyn Brooks Ctr., 2003; Naomi Long Madgett Poetry award named for her, 1993—, Alain Locke award Detroit Inst. Arts, Friends of African and African Am. Art, 2003, Creative Scholarship award, Coll. Lang. Assn.; inducted Sumner H.S. Hall of Fame, St. Louis, 1997, Nat. Lit. Hall Fame for Writers of African Descent, Chgo. State U., 1999, Mich. Women's Hall of Fame, 2002; named Poet Laureate, City of Detroit, 2001—, Mayor's award Literary Excellence, 2005; named one of 23 Enterprising Women, Detroit Hist. Soc., 2004; Bronze Bust created by Artis Lane unveiled at Charles H. Wright Mus. African Am. History, 2005. Mem. NAACP, Coll. Lang. Assn., So. Poetry Law Ctr., Langston Hughes Soc., Charles H. Wright Mus. of African Am. History, Detroit Working Writers, Detroit Inst. Arts, Fred Hart Williams Geneal. Soc., Coll. Lang. Assn. (Creative scholar, 2007), Alpha Kappa Alpha. Congregationalist. Home: 18080 Santa Barbara Dr Detroit MI 48221-2531 Office: PO Box 21607 Detroit MI 48221-0607 Office Phone: 313-861-1280. Personal E-mail: nlmadgett@aol.com. *I have tried to set an example of excellence in the use of language, especially the language of poetry. If I can leave behind some enduring work—my own words and the words of others I have published—I will consider myself amply rewarded for my labors. The truly great people I have known have given a great deal of themselves in the service of others, have not been puffed up by their own importance, and have maintained integrity in their personal and professional lives. They have been my models.*

MADIA, WILLIAM JUUL, chemist; b. Pitts., May 20, 1947; s. William Anthony and Joanna (VanKerchkoven) M.; m. Audrey Marie Madia, May 23, 1970; children: Joseph Anthony, Benjamin Paul, William Byron. BS in Chemistry, Ind. U. of Pa., 1969, MS in Nuclear Chemistry, 1970; PhD in Radiochemistry, Va. Polytech. Inst., 1975. With Battelle, 1975—; chemist, researcher Battelle Columbus (Ohio) div., 1975-77, assoc. sect. mgr., 1977-80, sect. mgr., 1980-83, mgr. office of nuclear waste isolation, 1983-85; pres. Battelle Project Mgmt. div., 1985-86; sr. v.p. Battelle Meml. Inst., 1988-89, 89—; pres. Battelle Tech. Internat., 1988-89, corp. sr. v.p., 1990-91, gen. mgr. environ. systems and tech. divsn., corp. sr. v.p., 1992-94; dir. Pacific Northwest Nat. Lab., 1994—99, Oak Ridge Nat. Lab., Tenn., 2000—03; pres., CEO UT- Battelle, Oak Ridge, Tenn., exec. v.p., 2003—. Mem. adv. bd. Ohio State U. Coll. Engring.; bd. dirs. Mason & Hanger. Mem. editl. bd. R&D Mag.; contbr. articles to profl. jours. Bd. dirs. Franklin U., 1987-94, Franklin County Children Svcs., 1988-94; editorial adv. bd. High Tech. Bus., 1988—; bd. dirs. Tri-City Indsl. Devel. Coun., Washington Roundtable; hon. bd. dirs. Mid-Columbia Edn. Alliance; adv. bd. Jr. Achievement Greater Tri-Cities; bd. dirs. Reading Found.; co-chair Tri-Cities Corp. Coun. Arts; mem. exec. com. Children's Ctr. Capital Campaign. With U.S. Army, 1970-72. Mem. AAAS, Indsl. Rsch. Inst. (fed. sci. and tech. com.), Midwest Rsch. Inst. (trustee), Nat. Renewable Energy Lab. (bd. govs.), Brookhaven Sci. Assocs. (bd. dirs.), U.S. Dept. Energy Lab. Ops. Bd., Washington Tech. Alliance. Roman Catholic. Office: Battelle 505 King Ave Columbus OH 43201

MADIGAN, JOHN WILLIAM, publishing executive; b. Chgo., June 7, 1937; s. Edward P. and Olive D. Madigan; m. Holly Williams, Nov. 24, 1962; children: Mark W., Griffith E., Melanie L. BBA, U. Mich., 1958, MBA, 1959. Fin. analyst Duff & Phelps, Chgo., 1960—62; audit mgr. Arthur Andersen & Co., Chgo., 1962—67; v.p. investment banking Paine, Webber, Jackson & Curtis, Chgo., 1967—69; v.p. corp. fin. Salomon Bros., Chgo., 1969—74; v.p., CFO, dir. Tribune Co., Chgo., 1975—81, exec. v.p., 1981—91; pub. Chgo. Tribune, 1990—94; pres., CEO Tribune Pub. Co., Chgo., 1991—94; pres., COO Tribune Co., Chgo., 1994—95, pres., 1994—2001, CEO, 1995—2002, chmn., 1996—2004; spl. ptnr. Madison Dearborn Ptnrs. LLC, 2005—. Bd. dir. AP, AT&T Wireless Svcs.; former dir. Morgan Stanley. Trustee Rush-Presbyn.-St. Luke's Med. Ctr., Mus. TV and Radio in N.Y., Northwestern U., Ill. Inst. Tech.; mem. bd. overseers Hoover Instn. Mem.: Chgo. Coun. on Fgn. Rels. (chmn.), Robert R. McCormick Tribune Found. Office: Madison Dearborn Ste 3800 Three First National Plz Chicago IL 60602

MADIGAN, JOSEPH EDWARD, financial executive, director, consultant; b. Bklyn., June 26, 1932; s. James Peter and Mary (Goldman) M.; m. Catherine Cashman, July 26, 1980; children: Kerri Ann, Kimberly Ann Burquest, Elizabeth Ann Laginess. BBA cum laude, Baruch Coll., CUNY, 1958; MBA, NYU, 1963. Adminstrv. asst. Assoc. Metals & Minerals Corp., 1961-63; fin. analyst, fgn. exch. trader, corp. portfolio trader AMAX, Inc., 1963-65; mgr. corp. portfolio, dir. cash mgmt., asst. treas. TWA, Inc., 1965-68; treas. Borden, Inc., 1968-76, v.p., treas., 1976-80; exec. v.p., chief fin. officer, dir. Wendy's Internat., Inc., Dublin, Ohio, 1980-87. Bd. dirs Columbus Show Case World Wide, Scioto Properties LLC. Chmn. bd. Lexford Residential Properties, 1997-99. With USN, 1951-55. Mem. Fin. Execs. Internat., Nat. Investor Rels. Inst., Baruch Coll.-CUNY Alumni Assn., NYU Alumni Assn., Imperial Golf Club, Allendale Country Club, Beta Gamma Sigma. Republican. Roman Catholic. Home and Office: 5555 Heron Point Dr Unit 2102 Naples FL 34108

MADIGAN, KATHRYN GRANT, lawyer; b. Paterson, NJ, May 4, 1953; d. William Joseph and Patricia (McCaffrey) Grant; m. Robert James Madigan Jr., Oct. 28, 1978; children: R. James III, Grant Daniel. BA, U. Colo., 1975; JD, Union U., Albany, NY, 1978. Bar: N.Y. 1979, U.S. Dist. Ct. (no. dist.) N.Y. 1979. Asst. gen. counsel Security Mut. Life Ins. Co. N.Y., Binghamton, 1978-85; law asst. trial part Broome County Surrogate's Ct., Binghamton, 1985-86; ptnr. Madigan & Madigan, Binghamton, 1986, Levene Gouldin and Thompson, Binghamton, cofounder Elder Law Group. Mem. N.Y. State Conf. of Bar Leaders, 1987—. V.p. Southern Tier Zool. Soc., Binghamton, 1980-82; co. chmn. Broome County United Way, Binghamton, 1980, 82, acct. exec., Network for Children, Binghamton, 1986; mem. Harpur Forum, 1987—, Broome County Status of Women Coun., 1988. Recipient Bus. woman of the Yr. award Am. Bus. Women, 1988; named Woman Achievement Broome County Status of Women, Coun., 1988. Mem. N.Y. State Bar Assn. (chmn. subcom. on law student membership 1979-82, del. 1983-86, 89, exec. com. corp. counsel sect. 1982, pres.-elect 2006-07; award of merit 1985, 86, named outstanding young lawyer award young lawyers sect. 1987), Broome County Bar Assn. (pres. 1988-89, bd. dirs. 1981-89, chmn. continuing edn. com. 1984—, gender bias in cts. com. 1987), Ms. Demeanors Rugby Club (founder, pres. 1976-78), Binghamton Women's Rugby Club (founder, pres. 1978-82), Phi Beta Kappa. Democrat. Roman Catholic. Avocations: hiking, music, literature. Mailing: Levene Gouldin and Thompson PO Box F 1706 Binghamton NY 13902 Office Phone: 607-763-9200. Office Fax: 607-763-9212. E-mail: kmadigan@binghamtonlaw.com.

MADIGAN, LISA, state attorney general; m. Pat Byrnes; 1 child, Rebecca. BA, Georgetown U., 1988; student, Loyola U. Asst. dean adult, continuing edn., dir. Sr. Acad. Lifelong Learning Wrights Family Coll. Wilbur Wright Coll., with positive alts. project; litigator Sachnoff & Weaver, Ltd., Chgo.; mem. Ill. Senate, Springfield, 1998—2002, mem. senate appropriations com., edn. com., joint com. adminstrv. rules; atty. gen. State of Ill., 2002—. Former vol. tchr., South Africa. Bd. dirs. AIDS Living Rememberance Com. Named one of Top 40 Lawyers Under 40, Nat. Law Jour., 2005. Mem. Ill. Bar Assn., Women's Bar Assn. Ill., Chgo. Bar Assn. Republican. Office: Office of Atty General James R Thompson Ctr 100 W Randolph St Chicago IL 60601 Office Phone: 312-814-3000.

MADIGAN, MICHAEL JOSEPH, state legislator; b. Chgo., Apr. 19, 1942; m. Shirley Roumagoux; children: Lisa, Tiffany, Nicole, Andrew. Ed., U. Notre Dame, Loyola U., Chgo. Mem. Ill. Ho. of Reps., 1971—, majority leader, 1977-80, minority leader, 1981-82, house spkr., 1983-94, Dem. leader, 1995-96, ho. spkr., 1997—; private atty. Sec. to Alderman David W. Healey; hearing officer Ill. Commerce Commn.; del. 6th Ill. Constnl. Conv.; trustee Holy Cross Hosp.; ex officio mem. adv. com. to pres. Richard J. Daley Coll.; adv. com. Fernley Harris Sch. for Handicapped; committeeman 13th Ward Democratic Orgn.; chmn. Ill. Dem. Party, 1998-. Mem. Council Fgn. Relations, City Club Chgo. Democrat. Office: House Reps 300 State Capital Bldg Springfield IL 62706-0001 *

MADIS, ERIC STEPHEN, musician; b. Derby, Conn., Dec. 5, 1953; s. Frederick Madis and Isabelle Bellis-Saran; m. Eileen Mercedes Damian, Sept. 2, 1989; 1 child, Alika Damian. BA in Physiol.-Psychology, U. Ill., Urbana, 1975. Luthier Rosewood Guitar Shop, Champagne, Ill., 1976—78; musician Dallas, 1978—81; founder, musician Denver, 1981—84; pub., founder, musician Seattle, 1984—; founder, pres. Luna Records, Seattle, 1991—. Instr. Denver Free U., 1983—84, U. Wash., 1984—97, Nat. Guitar Workshop, 1998—; founder, sr. instr. Tang Soo Do MDK Seattle, Shoreline, Wash., 1992—. Contbr. articles to profl. jours.; composer, musician: albums Nine Shades of Blue, 1991, Traveling Light, 1997, Third Step, 2002, Wood, Wires & Bone, 2003. Steward Victory Creek Seattle Pub. Utilities, 2006—. Recipient New Folk award, Kerrville Nat. Folk Festival, Tex., 1981; scholar, Ill. Wesleyan U., 1971; Ill. Dept. Edn. scholar, 1971. Mem.: Victory Music (writer 1989—2007), Wash. Blues Soc., US Korean Martial Arts Fedn. (fourth degree black belt 2007). Avocations: martial arts, Hawaiian culture, running, languages, music. Home and Studio: 11756 12th Ave NE Seattle WA 98125

MADISON, ANNE CONWAY, marketing, public relations professional; b. Balt., Mar. 13, 1963; d. Earl Cranston Jr. and Nancy C.; 1 child, Ryan Douglas. BS in Comm., Wittenberg U., 1985. Pub. rels. specialist Springfield (Ohio) Met. Housing Authority, 1984-85; account rep. CT Corp. Sys., Washington, 1985-86; pub. rels. asst. Ryland, Columbia, Md., 1986-88, comm. coord., 1988-90, mgr. mktg. comm., 1990-92, dir. mktg. comm., 1992-94, v.p. comm., 1994—2003; v.p. mktg. and comm. ESIC, Inc., Columbia, 2003—05; v.p. corp. comm. Choice Hotels Internat., Silver Spring, Md. Bd. dirs., officer Domestic Violence Cr. of Howard County, Columbia, 1987-96; bd. dirs. Norbel Sch., Nat. Family Resiliency Ctr. Named Vol. of Yr. Domestic Violence Ctr., 1988, recipient Spirit award, 1992; named one of Top 100 Women in Md., The Daily Record, 1996. Mem. Pub. Rels. Soc. Am., Nat. Investor Rels. Inst. Republican. Roman Catholic. Office Phone: 301-592-6723. Personal E-mail: acmadison@comcast.net. Business E-Mail: anne_madison@choicehotels.com.

MADISON, DEBORAH LEAFY, writer, chef; b. West Hartford, Conn., June 21, 1945; d. John Herbert and Winifred (Law) Madison; m. Dan Welch, Mar. 17, 1979 (div. Nov. 1986); m. J. Patrick McFarlin, May 29, 1991. BA, U. Calif., Santa Cruz, 1968. Founding chef The Greens Restaurant, San Francisco, 1978-83, Cafe Escalera, Santa Fe, N.Mex., 1990-93; menu cons. Rancho San Miguel, Baja Sur, Mex., 1996. Cons. to various restaurants, 1986—. Author: The Greens Cookbook, 1986 (Andre Simon award 1987), The Savory Way, 1990 (Best Cookbook of Yr. Julia Childs award 1991), The Vegetarian Table: America, 1996, Vegetarian Cooking for Everyone, 1997 (James Beard Award), This Can't be Tofu, 2000, Local Flavors: Cooking and Eating from America's Farmers' Markets, 2002, Vegetarian Suppers from Deborah Madison's Kitchen, 2005; adv. editor Saveor, 1994—; contbg. author books; contbr. articles to profl. jours. Bd. dirs. Santa Fe Area Farmers Mkt., 1990—; mem. Student Nutrition Action Com., Santa Fe, 1995—. Named to Honor Roll of Am. Chefs, Food and Wine Mag., 1983; recipient Contessa Premium Foods Whos Who of Food and Beverage in Am. award, James Beard Found., 2005. Mem. Internat. Assn. Culinary Professions, The Chef's Collaborative (founder), Les Dames D'Escoffier (MFK Fisher Mid-Career award 1994). Avocations: gardening, reading.

MADISON, EDDIE LAWRENCE, JR., public relations consultant, editor, writer; b. Tulsa, Sept. 8, 1930; s. Eddie Lawrence Sr. and Laverta (Pyle) M.; m. Davetta Jayn Cooksey, Nov. 17, 1956; children: Eddie Lawrence III, Karyn Devette, David Cooksey. B in Journalism, Lincoln U., Jefferson City, Mo., 1952; MA, U. Tulsa, 1959. Editor-in-chief, gen. mgr. Okla. Eagle, Tulsa, 1954-59; assoc. editor Chgo. Daily Defender, 1959-61; dep. editor Assoc. Negro Press, Chgo., 1961-63; sect. editor Chgo. Tribune, 1963-65; dir. domestic pub. affairs Paris Air Show Newsletter, U.S. Dept. Commerce; dep. dir. publs. divsn. Domestic and Internat. Bus., U.S. Dept. Commerce, Washington, 1965-69; mgr. cmty. svcs. Evening Star Broadcasting Co., Washington, 1969-78; asst. editor Bus. Am. Mag., Washington, 1978-81; press asst. Ho. of Reps., Washington, 1981-82; pub. affairs specialist U.S. Dept. HHS, Washington, 1982-92, mgr. HHS radio, 1991-92; asst. prof., chmn. dept. comm. Lincoln U., 1992-99; exec. editor, CEO, Okla. Eagle, Tulsa, 2001—; pres., CEO Three Elms & Assoc., Inc., Tulsa, 2001—. Founder Nat. Broadcast Assn. for Cmty. Affairs, Washington, 1974, 1st pres., 1974-77. Correspondent, Native Am. Times. Pres. Brightwood Civic Assn., Washington, 1969-72; mem. media adv. com. Mo. Arts Coun., 1996-99; mem. tobacco coalition and assist coms. Am. Cancer Soc., 1993-99; Hist. Preservation Commn., 1997-99; bd. dirs. Opportunities Industrialization Ctr., Washington, 1971-77, D.C. United Way, 1972-77, Boy Scouts Am., Washington, 1972-77. With U.S. Army, 1952-54; corr., Army Times, columnist, Recon Observer, Ellsworth AFB, S.D. Recipient Lifetime Achievement award, Tulsa Assn. Black Journalists, 2005. Mem. Alpha Phi Alpha (pres. Washington chpt. 1969-72, nat. dir. pub. rels. 1985-91, co-chair nat. pub. policy com. 1973, v.p. Montgomery County chpt. 1987-89, pres. Jefferson City Beta Zeta Lambda chpt. 1993, assoc. editor Sphinx mag., award of merit Ea. region 1992). Methodist. Avocations: photography, aerobics, jazz. Home: 4355 S Braden Ave Tulsa OK 74135-6337 Office: The Okla Eagle 624 E Archer St Tulsa OK 74120-1000 Address: Three Elms & Assocs PO Box 161 Tulsa OK 74101-0161 Office Phone: 918-582-7124 224. Fax: 918-852-8905. E-mail: emadsept@cox.net.

MADISON, GEORGE W., lawyer, corporate financial executive; b. Jersey City, Oct. 17, 1953; BS, NYU, 1975; MBA, Columbia U., 1977, JD, 1980. Law clk. to Hon. Nathaniel R. Jones U.S. Ct. Appeals (6th cir.) Ohio, Cin., 1980-81; assoc. Shearman & Sterling, NYC, 1981-87; with Mayer, Brown & Platt, NYC, 1987-89, ptnr., 1989-96; exec. v.p., corp. sec., gen. counsel Comerica Inc., Detroit, 1997—2003; exec. v.p., gen. counsel TIAA-CREF, NYC, 2003—. Bd. visitors Law Sch. Columbia U. Recipient Invaluable Pro Bono Legal Svcs. award, NAACP, 1997, Diversity 2000 award, MCCA, 1998, Learned Hand award, Am. Jewish Com., 2003, Disting. Svc. award, Detroit Met. Bar Assn., 2003, Pres. Choice award, State Bar Mich., 2003. Mem. ABA (chmn. com. corp. gen. counsel), Am. Judicature Soc., Am. Law Inst., Am. Corp. Counsel Assn., Assn. of Bar of City of N.Y. (mem. exec. com.). Office: TIAA-CREF 730 Third Ave New York NY 10017 Office Phone: 212-916-4750. Business E-Mail: gmadison@tiaa-cref.org. *

MADISON, GRACE LENORE, retired medical/surgical nurse, psychologist, educator; b. Albert Lea, Minn., July 29, 1924; d. Ernest and Gertrude Abbie (Gordy) Clubb; m. Eldon Harold Madison, June 15, 1946; children: Paul Ernest, Curtis John, Roger Dale, Carol Ann. BA in Psychology, So. Ill. U., Edwardsville, 1969, MA in Psychology, 1971. RN Minn., 1945; cert. clin. psychologist Ill., 1973. Pedist. staff nurse Sacramento City Hosp., 1945; spl. duty surg. nurse U. Minn. Hosp., 1945—46, nurse technician x-ray therapy, 1946—48, spl. duty heart surgery nurse, 1951—53; guest lectr. Coll. Home and Scis., Lahore, Pakistan, 1958; tchr. English Dacca, Bangladesh, 1959—60; staff nurse Mpls. Gen. Hosp., 1961—63, Alton Meml. Hosp., Ill., 1964; grad. rsch. asst. So. Ill. U., 1969—70, grad. tchr. asst., asst. project dir. Sch. Nursing, 1971—72; ret., 1972. Psychology instr. Florissant Valley CC, Mo., 1973—77, Belleville Area Coll., Ill., 1974—75. Unitarian. Achievements include patents for Empathy Game. Avocations: travel, writing. Home: 1828 Stanford Pl Edwardsville IL 62025-2633

MADISON, JAMES RAYMOND, lawyer; b. White Plains, NY, Apr. 27, 1931; s. Raymond S. and Katherine (Sherwin) M.; m. Mary Massey, Sept. 19, 1953; children: Michael, Matthew, Molly. BS, Stanford U., 1953, LLB, 1959. Bar: Calif. 1960, U.S. Dist. Ct. (no. dist.) Calif. 1960, U.S. Ct. Appeals (9th cir.) 1960, U.S. Dist. Ct. (ctrl. dist.) Calif. 1970, U.S. Supreme Ct. 1973, U.S. Dist. Ct. (ea. dist.) Calif. 1981, U.S. Dist. Ct. (so. dist.) Calif. 1988. Assoc. Orrick, Herrington & Sutcliffe, San Francisco, 1959-67, ptnr., 1968-95; pvt. practice Menlo Park, Calif., 1996—. Trustee Antioch U., Yellow Springs, Ohio, 1980-87; bd. dirs. Planned Parenthood Alameda/San Francisco, 1984-89; pres. Calif. Dispute Resolution Coun., 2001. Lt. (j.g.) USN, 1953-56. Mem. ABA, ASCE, State Bar Calif., Bar Assn. San Francisco, San Mateo County Bar Assn., Am. Arbitration Assn. (large complex case panel arbitrators and mediators, No. Calif. regional adv. coun.), Mediation Soc., Calif. Dispute Resolution Coun., Dispute Rev. Bd. Found., Coll. Comml. Arbitrators. Democrat. Episcopalian. Avocation: soccer. Office: 750 Menlo Ave Ste 250 Menlo Park CA 94025-4758 Home Phone: 650-324-3491; Office Phone: 650-614-0160. E-mail: jrmcoach@aol.com.

MADISON, JOHN MARK, pulmonologist, educator; b. Springfield, Ill., Nov. 1, 1953; s. Thomas Alvin and Georgie Lou (Huss) Madison; m. Paula Jean Drach, Nov. 30, 1985; children: Lindsey R., Elliot C.T. BA, Carleton Coll., 1975; MD, Harvard U., 1979. Cert. internal medicine and pulmonary diseases Md. Resident in internal medicine Washington U., St. Louis, 1982; fellow in pulmonary medicine U. Calif., San Francisco, 1985, instr., 1985—87, asst. prof., 1987—90; asst. prof. medicine U. Mass. Med. Sch.,

Worcester, 1990—95, assoc. prof. medicine, 1995—2005, prof. medicine, 2005—, chief divsn. pulmonary allergy and critical care medicine, 2005—. Mem. editl. bd.: Am. Jour. Respiratory, Cell and Molecular Biology, 1998—2003, Chest, 2006—; contbr. articles to profl. jours. Mem.: Am. Coll. of Chest Physicians, AM. Thoracic Soc. Avocations: skiing, travel. Home: 75 Wyndhurst Dr Holden MA 01520 Office: U Mass Med Sch 55 Lake Ave N Worcester MA 01655 Business E-Mail: mark.madison@umassmed.edu.

MADISON, OLIVIA, librarian, dean; BS, Iowa State U., 1972; MLS, U. Mo., Columbia, 1975. Faculty mem. Iowa State U., Ames, 1975—, chair monographs and cataloging depts., assoc. dir. pub. svcs. collections, interim libr. dean, 1997, dean libr. svcs., 1998—. Mem.: Internat. Fedn. Libr. Assns. Office: Univ Libr Corner of Osborn Dr & Morrill Rd Iowa State U Ames IA 50011-2140 Office Phone: 515-294-3642. Office Fax: 515-294-5525. E-mail: omadison@iastate.edu. *

MADISON, ROBERT PRINCE, architect; b. Cleve., July 28, 1923; s. Robert J. and Nettie (Brown) M.; m. Leatrice L. Branch, Apr. 16, 1949; children: Jeanne Marie, Juliette Branch. Student, Howard U., 1940—43, HHD, 1987; BArch, Western Res. U., 1948; MArch, Harvard U., 1952; DFA (hon.), Cleve. State U., 2000; HHD (hon.), Kent State U., 2001; DSc (hon.), Case We. Res. U., 2004. Mem. various archtl. firms, 1948; instr. Howard U., Washington, 1952—54; chmn., CEO Robert P. Madison Internat., architects, engrs. and planners, Cleve., 1954—. Trustee Am. Automobile Assn.; vis. prof. Howard U., 1961-62; lectr. Western Res. U., 1964-65; mem. U.S. architects del. Peoples Repub. China, 1974 Prin. works include U.S. Embassy Dakar, Senegal, West Africa, 1966, State of Ohio Computer Ctr., 1988, Cuyahoga County Jail, 1990, Continental Airlines Hub Concourse, Cleve. Internat. Airport, 1991. Mem. tech. adv. com. Cleve. Bd. Edn., 1960—; mem. adv. com. Cleve. Urban Renewal, 1963—; mem. fine arts adv. com. to mayor, Cleve.; mem. archtl. adv. coun. Cornell U.; trustee Case Western Res. U., Cleve. Opera, 1990, NCCJ, 1990, Commn. on Higher Edn., 1990, Cleve. (Ohio) Orch., 1998, Cleve. (Ohio) Arts Prize, 2001; bd. dirs. Jr. Achievement Greater Cleve.; trustee Cuyahoga County Hosp. Found., 1983—, Univ. Circle Inc., Midtown Corridor Inc.; mem. Ohio Bd. Bldg. Standards, 1986, Cleveland Heights City Planning Commn., 1987. 1st lt., inf. AUS, 1943-46. Decorated Purple Heart; Fulbright fellow, 1952-53; recipient Disting. Svc. award Case Western Res. U., 1989, Disting. Archtl. Firm award Howard U., 1989, Entrepreneur of Yt. award Ernst Young, Inc., Merrill Lynch, 1991, Arch. of Yr. Nat. Tech. Assn., 1996, Martin Luther King Jr. Corp. award African-Am. Archives Aux. Western Res. Hist. Soc., 1997, Disting. Alumni award Case We. Res. U., 1997; named to Corp. Hall of Fame, Ohio Assembly of Couns., 1991, Pres. award Kent State U., 1999; named to Cleve. Bus. Hall of Fame, 2002. Fellow AIA (chpt. pres.; nat. task force for creative econs. 1976, mem. jury of fellows 1983-85, mem. nat. judicial coun. 1993, Gold Medal Firm award Ohio 1994, Gold Medal award Ohio 1997, Whitney M. Young Jr. award 2002); mem. Architects Soc. Ohio, Epsilon Delta Rho, Alpha Phi Alpha, Sigma Pi Phi. Office: Robert P Madison Internat Inc 2930 Euclid Ave Cleveland OH 44115-2416 Home: 18975 Van Aken Blvd Apt 410 Shaker Heights OH 44122-3539 Office Phone: 216-861-8195. Business E-Mail: rmadison@rpmadison.com.

MADISON, T. JEROME, business executive; b. NYC, June 2, 1940; s. Theodore H. and Eleanor E. (Eveland) M.; m. Marsha A. Heeb, Sept. 26, 1964 (dec.); children: Jillian, Kimberly, Ryan. BS, U. Pa., 1962; MBA, Monmouth U., 1975. CPA NJ. Mgr. KPMG, Newark and Princeton, NJ, 1970-75, Abbott Labs., North Chicago, Ill., 1976; asst. corp. contr. Rhone-Poulenc Rorer (now Sanofi-Aventis), Ft. Washington, Pa., 1977-78; corp. contr. Aventis, Ft. Washington, Pa., 1979-82; v.p. fin. Cytogen Corp., Princeton, 1982-86; pres., CEO, dir. Outwater & Wells Ventures, Inc., 1981-85, Atlantic Capital Resources Group, Inc., 1985-87, Founders Ct. Inc., 1986—, Montgomery Ptnrs., 1991—2005. Chmn, CEO Pilling Co., 1986—91, AxCell Bioscis. Corp., 1996—97, Trinity Tech. Ptnrs., 1997—2006, Trinity Ptnrs., S.A.; chmn. Somerset Ctrl. Corp.; bd. dirs. ProMed Sys. Flight Officer USN, 1962-66. Office: Founders Court 1 Washington Crossing Rd Ste 11 Pennington NJ 08534

MADIX, ROBERT JAMES, chemical engineer, educator; b. Beach Grove, Ind., June 22, 1938; s. James L. and Marjorie A. (Strohl) M.; children: Bradley Alan, David Eric, Micella Lynn, Evan Scott. BS, U. Ill., 1961; PhD, U. Calif., 1964. NSF postdoctoral fellow Max Planck Inst., Göttingen, Fed. Republic of Germany, 1964-65; asst. prof, chem. engr. Stanford (Calif.) U., 1965-72, assoc. prof., chem. engr., 1972-77; prof. chem. engring. Stanford U., 1977—, chmn., chem. engr., 1983-87, prof. chemistry, 1981—, Charles Lee Powell prof., 1990—2006, Charles Lee Powell prof. emeritus, 2006; sr. rsch. fellow divsn. engring. and applied sci. Harvard U., Cambridge, Mass., 2006. Cons. Monsanto Chem., St. Louis, 1975-84, Shell Oil Co., Houston, 1985-86; Peter Debye lectureship Cornell U., 1985; Eyring lectr. chemistry Ariz. State U., 1990; Barnett Dodge lectr. Yale U., 1996; disting. prof. lectr. U. Tex., Austin, 1980; Walter Robb Disting. lectr. Pa. State U., 1996; chmn. Gordon Rsch. Conf. on Reactions on Surfaces, 1995; sr. rsch. fellow divsn. engring. and applied scis. Harvard U., 2006. Assoc. editor Catalysis Rev., 1986—, Catalysis Letters, 1992—, Rsch. on Chem. Intermediates, 1994—; contbr. articles to profl. jours. Recipient Alpha Chi Sigma award AIChemE, 1990, Paul Emmett award Catalysis Soc. N.Am., 1984, Humboldt U.S. Sr. Scientist prize, 1978; Ford Found. fellow, 1969-72. Mem. AIChE, Internat. Precious Metal Inst. (Henry J. Alber award 1997), Am. Chem. Soc. (Irving Langmuir Disting. Lectr. award 1981, Arthur Adamson award 1997, Am. Phys. Soc., Am. Vacuum Soc., Calif. Catalysis Soc.

MADJID, A. HAMID, retired science educator; b. Tashkent, Russia, Aug. 16, 1922; arrived in US, 1966; s. A. Madjid and Emilia (Madjid) Zabuli; m. Anni Neukomm-Madjid, Dec. 31, 1958; children: Torai, A. Hamid Jr. BA, Cornell U.; DSc, Swiss Fed. Inst. Tech. Sec., sci. adv. to pres., coord. Afghan scholarships, head indsl. planning Afghan Nat. Bank, Munich, 1948—55; sr. rsch. assoc. Swiss Fed. Inst. Tech., Zurich, 1955—66; asst. assoc. prof., dir. thermionic emission lab, co-head of sci. program Pa. State U., University Park, 1966—90; ret., 1990. Chair various com. Pa. State U., 1977—86. Contbr. articles various profl. jours. Mem. Am. European Swiss Phys. Soc., 1966—90; chair Harris Twp. Planning Commn., Pa., 1982—86; mem. State Coll. Area Sch. Dist. Curriculum Coun., 1987; dir. A.M. Zabuli Charitable Found., 1998, Renaissance Charitable Found., 1999. Mem.: AAAS, Am. Assn. of Naval Engrs., US Holocaust Meml. Mus., Heritage Found., Nat. Rifle Assn. Achievements include research in electron emission from metal, semi conductor and insulator surfaces and the transport and optical properties of such substances; patents for layer structured switching and negative resistance devices; development of methods of involving undergraduate students in basic scientific rsch. Avocation: growing bonsai trees. Home and Office: 326 Harris Dr State College PA 16801 Office Phone: 814-466-7127.

MADLE, ROBERT ALBERT, writer; b. Phila., June 2, 1920; s. Vincent Robert and Mary Virginia (Kidwell) M.; m. Billie Franklin Lindsay, Nov. 7, 1943 (dec. Dec. 1997); children: Robert, Richard, Jane, Mary Anne; m. Ana Lisseth Martinez, Feb. 28, 2002; 1 stepchild, Sarah Nicole Martinez. BS, Drexel U., 1951, MBA, 1953. Asst. to sales mgr. Masland Duraleather, Phila., 1951—53; asst. to dir. indsl. rels. Chadbourne Hosiery, Charlotte, NC, 1953—54; mgr. pers. and credit Shaw Mfg. Co., Charlotte, 1954—56; pers. rsch. specialist U.S. Army, Washington, 1956—59; rsch. psychologist, program mgr. USN, Washington, 1959—80. Sci. fiction rsch. cons. Paramount Prodns., other film cos.; rsch. cons. projects Yesterday's Tomorrows and Study on Hugo Gernsback, Smithsonian Inst.; spkr. in field Co-author: Science Fiction Fandom, 1994; contbr. articles to sci. fiction and sports mags.; condr. search svcs. rare books in field of sci. fiction and fantasy lit.; cons. editor profl. fantasy mags., including Mag. of Horror, Bizarre Mystery, Startling Mystery, Famous Sci. Fiction. With U.S. Army, 1942-46. Named Guest of honor World Sci. Fiction Conv., Miami, 1977, U. Md. Sci. Fiction Conv., 1982, Boston Sci. Fiction Conv., 1996; rep. Am. sci. fiction Brit. Worldcon, 1957; recipient E.E. Evans Sci. Fiction Achievement award, 1974, Sam Moskowitz Achievement award, 2002 Mem.: Phila. Sci. Fiction Soc. (founder), First Fandom (pres. 1959—82, Hall of Fame 1990), Washington Sci. Fiction Assn., Sci. Fiction Writers Am. Achievements include development of survey on science fiction's predictions of atomic energy. Home: 4406 Bestor Dr Rockville MD 20853-2137 Office Phone: 301-460-4712.

MADLOCK, YVONNE, city health department administrator; m. Lawrence Madlock; 3 children. BS, Wellesley Coll.; MAT, Wesleyan U., Middletown, Conn.; studied, U. Tex. Sch. Pub. Health. Adminstr., bur. personal health svcs. Shelby Co. Divsn. Health Svcs., Memphis, dir., 1995—. Bd. pres. Cmty. Inst. for Early Childhood; bd. dirs. W. Tenn. Area Health Edn. Ctr., Memphis Leadership Inst., Cmty. Found. of Greater Memphis, Shelby Co. Ground Water Quality Control Bd. Mem.: Nat. Assn. City and County Health Officials (bd. dirs.). Office: Shelby Co Divsn Health Svcs 814 Jefferson Ave Memphis TN 38103 Business E-Mail: HealthDirector@co.shelby.tn.us.

MADNI, ASAD MOHAMED, engineering executive; b. Bombay, Sept. 8, 1947; came to US, 1966; s. Mohamed Taher and Sara Taher (Wadiwalla) M.; Gowhartaj Shahnawaz, Nov. 11, 1976; 1 child, Jamal Asad. Gen. cert. edn., U. Cambridge, Eng., 1964; AAS in Electronics, RCA Insts., Inc., 1968; BS in Engring., UCLA, 1969, MS in Engring., 1972; postgrad. exec. inst., Stanford U., 1984; cert. in engring. mgmt., Calif. Inst. Tech., 1987; PhD in Engring., Calif. Coast U., 1987; sr. exec. program, MIT, 1990. chartered engr. Engring. Coun., UK. Sr. instr. Pacific States U., LA, 1969—71; sr. electronics auditor Pertec Corp., Chatsworth, Calif., 1973—75; project engr., sr. engr., program mgr., dir. advanced programs Microwave divsn. Systron Donner, Van Nuys, Calif., 1975—82, dir. engring., 1982—92; gen. mgr. Microwave and Instrument divsn. Systron Donner, Van Nuys, Calif., 1985—90; chmn., pres., CEO Systron Donner Corp., 1990—92; pres., CEO Sensors and Controls Group BEI Electronics, Inc., 1992—93, BEI Sensors & Sys. Co., 1993—2006; pres. BEI Techs. Inc., 2000—06, COO, 2000—06; exec. mng. dir., chief tech. officer Crocker Capital, 2006—. Vice-chmn. IEEE-MTTS, San Fernando Valley chpt., 1991-92, chmn., 1992-94; tech. advisor Test and Measurement World, Boston, 1982-90; adv. Calif. State U. Northridge, Coll. Elec. Engring. and Computer Sci.; bd. adv. dept. mech. and aerospace engring. UCLA, UCLA WINMEC, chmn. dept. elec. engring. UCLA; adv. bd. UCLA RFID Group, UCLA Ctr. for Embedded Network Sensing; chmn. adv. bd. elec. engring. dept. U. So. Calif., mem. indsl. adv. bd. TCI Coll. of Tech., Northwestern U., McCormick Sch. Engring. and Applied Sci.; adj. prof. U. N.Mex. Sch. Engring., Albuquerque, 2004—, Ryerson U. Sch. Engring. and Computer Sci., Toronto, Can., 2007-; disting. coll. prof. TCI Coll. Tech., NY, 2007-. Mem. editl. rev. bd. Microwave Sys. News and Comms. Tech., 1982—90, chmn. West coast, 1982—90, mem. editl. review bd. SENSORS Jour., 2001—06, mem. tech. review com. World Automation Congress, 1996—, mem. editl. rev. bd. IEEE Sys. Jour., 2006—. Named George Washington Engr. of Yr., LA Coun. of Engrs. and Scientists, 2003; recipient Joseph F. Engelberger Best Paper award, World Automation Congress, 2000, Disting. Alumni award, Calif. Coast U., 2001, Profl. Achievement award, UCLA, 2002, Alumnus of Yr. award, UCLA Sch. Engring. and Applied Sci., 2004, Dist. Engring. Achievement award, San Fernando Valley Engrs. Coun., 2004, Achievement medal, Inst. Elec. Engrs., 2005, Lifetime Achievement award, World Automation Compress and AutoSoft Jour., 2006, Marconi medal, TCI Coll. Tech., 2007. Fellow: AAAS, IEEE (adv. bd. MTT-S San Fernando Valley chpt. 1993—2001, tech. review com. aerospace conf. 1994—, 3d Millennium medal), AIAA (life; vice chair honors and awards L.A. sect. 2000—01, sr.), Inst. Engring. and Tech., Soc. Automotive Engrs., NY Acad. Scis., Inst. Advancement Engring., Instn. Elec. Engrs. U.K. (chartered elec. engr., Achievement medal 2005); mem.: NRA (life), MIT Soc. Sr. Execs. (life), UCLA Engring. Alumni Assn. (life; pres. 2006—, bd. govs. 2003—), TCI Coll. Tech. Alumni Assn. (life), MIT Alumni Assn. (life), UCLA Alumni Assn. (life), Calif. Rifle and Pistol Assn. (life), Assn. Old Crows (life gold cert. of merit 1992). Home and Office: 3281 Woodbine St Los Angeles CA 90064-4836 Personal E-mail: ammadni@yahoo.com. *Personal philosophy: There is no substitute for talent and vision complemented by perseverance, dedication and integrity.*

MADONNA, (MADONNA LOUISE VERONICA CICCONE), singer, actress, producer; b. Bay City, Mich., Aug. 16, 1958; d. Sylvio and Madonna Ciccone; m. Sean Penn, Aug. 16, 1985 (div. Sept. 14, 1989); m. Guy Ritchie, Dec. 22, 2000; 2 children: Lourdes, Rocco, 1 adopted child, David Student, U. Mich., 1976-78. Dancer Alvin Ailey Dance Co., NYC, 1979; CEO Maverick Records, LA, 1992—. Singer: (albums) Madonna, 1983, Like a Virgin, 1985, True Blue, 1986, You Can Dance, 1987, Like a Prayer, 1989, I'm Breathless: Music From and Inspired by the Film Dick Tracy, 1990, The Immaculate Collection, 1990, Erotica, 1992, Bedtime Stories, 1994, Something to Remember, 1995, Ray of Light, 1998 (Grammy award for Best Pop Album 1999), Music, 2000, GHV2: Greatest Hits Volume II, 2002, American Life, 2003, Confessions on a Dancefloor, 2005 (Best Electronic/Dance Album, Grammy Awards, 2007), I'm Going to Tell You a Secret, 2006, The Confessions Tour- Live From London, 2007; (soundtracks) Who's That Girl, 1987, Evita, 1996; actor (films) A Certain Sacrifice, 1980, Vision Quest, 1985, Desperately Seeking Susan, 1985, Shanghai Surprise, 1986, Who's That Girl, 1987, Bloodhounds of Broadway, 1989, Dick Tracy, 1990, Shadows and Fog, 1992, Body of Evidence, 1992, A League of Their Own, 1992, Dangerous Game, 1993, Blue in the Face, 1995, Four Rooms, 1996, Girl 6, 1996, Evita, 1996 (Golden Globe, 1997), The Next Best Thing, 2000, Swept Away, 2002; (documentaries) Truth or Dare, 1991, I'm Going to Tell You a Secret, 2005; (voice) Arthur and the Invisibles, 2006; Broadway theater debut in Speed-the-Plow, 1987, stage appearance in Up for Grabs, 2002; (TV appearances) Happy Birthday Elizabeth: A Celebration of a Life, 1997, Will & Grace, 2003; author: Sex, 1992, (children's books) The English Roses, 2003, Mr. Peabody's Apples, 2003, Yakov and the Seven Thieves, 2004, Adventures of Abdi, 2004, Lotsa de Casha, 2005. Recipient World's Best Pop Artist award, World Music Awards, 2007, Best-Selling US Artist, 2007, Ivor Novello award for Internat. Hit of Yr., Brit. Acad. Composers & Songwriters, 2007. *

MADORY, RICHARD EUGENE, lawyer; b. Kenton, Ohio, May 14, 1931; s. Harold Richard and Hilda (Strictland) Madory; m. Barbara Jean Madory, Sept. 25, 1955; children: Richard Eugene, Terry Dean, Michael Wesly. BS in Edn., Ohio State, Columbus, 1952; JD, Southwestern U., 1961. Bar: Calif. 1961, U.S. Ct. Mil. Appeals, U.S. Supreme Ct., U.S. Dist. Ct. (ctrl. dist.) Calif. With Madory, Booth, Zell & Pleiss, Santa Ana, Calif., 1962—, now pres., v.p., sec.-treas. Lectr. continuing edn. Bar of State of Calif. Col. USMC. Fellow: Am. Coll. Trial Lawyers; mem.: ABA, Nat. Bd. Trial Advocacy, Am. Bd. Trial Advs., So. Calif. Def. Counsel Assn., LA County Bar Assn., Orange County Bar Assn. Office: Ste 205 17822 17th St Tustin CA 92780-2152 Office Phone: 714-832-3772. Business E-Mail: madory@pacbell.net.

MADOW, LEO, psychiatrist, educator; b. Cleve., Oct. 18, 1915; s. Solomon Martin and Anna (Meyers) Madow; m. Jean Antoinette Weisman, Apr. 16, 1942 (dec.); children: Michael, Robert; m. Barbara N. Young, Dec. 26, 2000. AB, Western Res. U., 1937, MD, 1942; MA, Ohio State U., 1938. Diplomate Am. Bd. Psychiatry and Neurology. Intern Phila. Gen. Hosp., 1942-43; resident Phila. Gen. Hosp., Jefferson Hosp., Inst. Pa. Hosp., 1943-46; practice medicine specializing in psychiatry Phila., 1948—; prof., chmn. dept. neurology Med. Coll. Pa., Phila., 1958-65, prof., chmn. dept. psychiatry and neurology, 1965-70, prof., chmn. dept. psychiatry, 1970-81, clin. prof. psychiatry Hershey Med. Ctr., 1982—; sr. cons. psychiatry Inst. Pa. Hosp., Phila., 1975—. Tng. analyst, past pres. Phila. Psychoanalytic Inst.; past pres., mem. med. staff Inst. Pa. Hosp. Author: Anger, 1972, Love, 1983, Guilt, 1989; editor: Dreams, 1970, Sensory Deprivation, 1970, Psychomimetic Drugs, 1971, Integration of Child Psychiatry with Basic Resident Program, 1975. Served to capt. US Army, 1944—46. Named Outstanding Educator, Am. Med. Coll. Pa., 1972. Fellow: ACP, Am. Coll. Psychoanalysts (pres. 1989—90, Laughlin award 1990), Am. Coll. Psychiatrists, Am. Psychiat. Assn. (life), Phila. Psychiat. Soc. (past pres., Lifetime Achievement award 1991); mem.: Phila. Psychoanalytic Soc. (past pres.), Am. Neurol. Assn., Am. Psychoanalytic Assn., Phi Soc., Alpha Omega Alpha. Home and Office: 2401 Pennsylvania Ave Philadelphia PA 19130 Office Phone: 215-235-5253. Personal E-mail: leomadow@aol.com.

MADRA, SATBIR SINGH, materials researcher, mechanical engineer; arrived in U.S., 1995; s. Bhupinder Singh and Satwant Kaur Madra. BSME, Punjab U., 1993; MSME, San Jose State U., Calif., 1997. Lectr. San Jose State U., Calif., 1996—97; process devel. engr. R&D Watkins Johnson Co., Scotts Valley, Calif., 1997—99; sr. staff engr. Wj Comm., Inc., San Jose, 1999—2002, sr. rsch. scientist, 2002—05; sr. mgr. Semiconductor Package, 2005—06, RFID Engring., 2005—06; v.p. tech. Silitronics, Inc., San Jose, Calif., 2006—, sr. v.p., 2006—. Presenter in field. Contbr. articles to profl. jours. Mem.: ASME, IEEE, Materials Rsch. Soc., Internat. Microelectronics And Packaging Soc., Pi Tau Sigma. Avocations: tennis, travel, hockey. Office: Silitronics Inc 85 Great Oaks Blvd San Jose CA 95119 Office Phone: 408-360-9100. Business E-Mail: satbir.madra@silitronics.com.

MADRAS, BERTHA KALIFON, federal official, neuroscientist, researcher; b. Montreal, Que., Can., Dec. 9, 1942; m. Peter Madras, June 21, 1964; children: Cynthia Gumbert, Claudine D. BSc in Chemistry with honors, McGill U., 1963, PhD, 1967. Chair divsn. neurochemistry New Eng. Primate Rsch. Ctr.; postdoctoral fellow Tufts U., Boston, 1966-67; postdoctoral fellow rsch. assoc. MIT, Cambridge, 1967-69, 72-74; asst. prof. U. Toronto, 1979—80, Harvard Med. Sch., Boston, 1986-90, assoc. prof., 1990-99, prof. psychobiology dept. psychiatry, 1999—2006, assoc. dir. pub. edn. divsn. addictions, 1998—2006; dep. dir. demand reduction Office Nat. Drug Control Policy, Washington, 2006—. Sci. adv. com. Brookhaven Nat. Lab., Upton, N.Y., 1998—; rev. com., cons. Nat. Inst. Drug Abuse, chair B study sect., 1998-99; MDCN-5 MNPS rev. com.; cons. Ont. Mental Health Found., 1984-90, chmn. fellowships and awards com., 1988-90; chmn. radiation safety Harvard U., 1995-99, acting dir. Primate Ctr., 1998-99; chmn. faculty affairs Harvard Med. Sch.; mem. Dana Alliance Brain Initiatives; mem. NIH coms.; mem. sci. adv. bd. Nat. Inst. Drug Abuse Medications Devel., Addiction Studies Inst. Journalists; mem. sci. and tech. adv. com. Brookhaven Nat. Lab. and others; spkr. HS students and judges numerous drug and addiction topics. Author: (book chpt.) Dopamine, 1984, over 130 sci. manuscripts and book chpts.; editor: Neurosci.; mem. editl. bd. Synapse, 1991-04; featured in Better World Report one of 25 tech. transfer innovations; contbr. articles to profl. jours.; dir. exhibit (CD and play) Mus. Sci., Boston. Sci. fair judge. Recipient Rsch. grants Nat. Inst. Drug Abuse, 1992—, 94—, Sci. Edn. Partnership award grant, 1992-94, Parkinson's Disease Found., 1990-91, Nat. Inst. Neurol. Disease and Stroke, 1994, 99—, NIMH, Dana Alliance Brain Initiatives, Merit award NIH Nat. Inst. Drug Abuse, Sr. Scientist award, Pub. Svc. award Nat. Inst. Drug Abuse. Mem. Soc. Neurosci., Coll. Probs. Drug Dependence. Achievements include development of a marker for Parkinson's disease and attention deficit hyperactivity disorder, a probe for cocaine binding sites in brain; developed a PET imaging SPECT for living brain; developed a PET and SPECT imaging drug to monitor Parkinsonism in brain; research on how the brain responds and adapts to drugs; developed novel diagnostic and therapeutic agents for substance abuse and other brain disorders; co-developer of CD-ROM on how drugs affect brain; 16 patents in field. Office: Office Nat Drug Control Policy 750 17th St NW Rm 609 Washington DC 20503

MADRID, CIRILO L., health facility administrator; b. Clint, Tex., Mar. 18, 1945; s. Leandro L. and Felicitaz L. Madrid; m. Grace Avila Madrid, Jan. 23, 1971; children: Michelle, Melinda, Jesus. AA, Glendale CC, 1967; BA, Ariz. State U., 1969; MEd, U. Tex., El Paso, 1981; PhD, Hamilton U., 2002. Psychiat. tech. St. Mary's Hosp., Tucson, 1970—71; CEO Aliviane No-Ad, Inc., El Paso, 1971—, Family Reintegration Tex., El Paso, 1995—2000, New Beginnings of Tex., El Paso, 2000—. Mem. Lt. Gov. Drug Bd. State of Tex., Austin, 1978—81, Nat. Drug Coun. Ctr. Substance Abuse Tex., Wash., 2003—. Author: Mi India, 1981, Changing Heart of America, 2002; contbr. articles various profl. jours. Mem. Eastside Polit. Action Com., El Paso, 1995—; leg. chair. ASAP of Tex., Austin, 2002—; elected off. Ysleta Sch. Bd., El Paso, 1976—81. Combat medic US Army, 1969—70, South Vietnam. Recipient Carlos Finlay award, Pub. Health Svc., 1996, TCADA award, State of Tex., 1997, Tex. Chem. Found. award, 2000. Mem.: VFW, Tex. Assn. Drug Abuse Counselors, Assn. of Substance Svcs. Roman Catholic. Achievements include development of promising chem. dependence prevention approaches; evident based treatment approaches for hispanic addicts; chem. dependence training approaches for ethnic minorities. Avocations: running, weight training, poetry, comedy. E-mail: cmadrid@aliviane.org.

MADRID, PATRICIA A., former state attorney general; BA in English and Philosophy, U. N.Mex., 1969, JD, 1973; cert., Nat. Jud. Coll., U. Nev., 1978. Bar: N.Mex. Dist. judge State of N.Mex., 1978—84, atty. gen., 1999—2006. Chmn. Western Conf. of Attys. Gen.; exec. cons. Dickstein Shapiro, LLP, Washington. Named Latina Atty. of Yr., Nat. Hispanic Bar Assn., 2001, N.Mex. Power Broker, N.Mex. Bus. Weekly; recipient Mary V. Orozco Abriendo Caminos award, Latina Lawyers Bar Assn., 2003, Trailblazer award, N.Mex. Commn. on the Status of Women, Las Primeras award, MANA, 2004, Woman of the Yr. in Govt. award, Capital Bus. and Professional Women of Santa Fe, 2004, Exec. Dir. award, Animal Protection of N.Mex., 2004. Democrat. Mailing: 2219 Vista Larga Dr Albuquerque NM 87106 Office Phone: 505-243-0503. E-mail: patriciamadrid100@yahoo.com.

MADRY-TAYLOR, JACQUELYN YVONNE, educational association administrator; d. Arthur Chester and Janie (Cowart) Madry; 1 child, Jana LeMadry. BA, Fisk U., 1966; MA, Ohio State U., 1969; EdD, U. Fla., 1975. Cert. Inst. for Ednl. Mgmt., Harvard U., 1981. Tchr. Spanish Terry Parker Sr. High Sch., Jacksonville, 1967-72; instr. U. Fla., Gainesville, 1972-75; asst. to v.p. for acad. affairs. Morris Brown Coll., Atlanta, 1975-76; dean for instructional svcs. No. Va. Community Coll., Annandale, Va., 1976-83; dean undergrad. studies Bridgewater (Mass.) State Coll., 1983-92, exec. asst. to acting pres., 1988, acting v.p. acad. affairs, 1988-90; dir. Acad. Leadership Acad. Am. Assn. State Coll. and Univs., Washington, 1992-94; dir. ednl. programs and svcs. United Negro Coll. Fund Hdqs., 1994-97; pres. JYM Assocs., 1999—; sr. advisor Nat. Assn. for Equal Opportunity in Higher Edn., 1997—2003. Cons. to colls., univs. and orgns., 1997-99; cons. W.K. Kellog Found., 1993-97; bd. dirs. Bridgewater State Coll. Early Learning Ctr., 1984-88; evaluator U.S. Dept. State/Fgn. Svc., Washington, 1982—, U.S. Dept. Edn., 1989—; pres. JYM Assocs., 1999—. Vice chmn. No. Va. Manpower Planning Coun., Fairfax County, Va., 1981. Recipient Cert. Achievement Bridgewater State Coll. Black Alumni, 1988, Women Helping Women award Soroptimist Internat., 1983, Outstanding Young Women Am. award, 1976, 78; named Personalities of South, 1977; recipient Outstanding Tchr./Student Rels. Humanitarian award B'nai B'rith, 1972. Mem. Pub. Mem. Assn. U.S. Fgn. Svc., Soroptimist Internat., Boston Club (v.p. 1986-88), Jack and Jill of Am., Inc., Am. Assn. of Univ. Women, Phi Delta Kappa, Alpha Kappa Alpha, Links Inc. (Reston, Va. chpt.). Methodist. Avocations: playing piano, bike riding. Home and Office: 12274 Angel Wing Ct Reston VA 20191-1119 Fax: 703-716-4364. E-mail: jkemt@aol.com.

MADSEN, ANDREW H., food service executive; Grad., DePauw Univ., 1978. V.p., mktg. Gen. Mills Inc.; v.p., gen. mgr. James River Corp., 1993—97; pres. Internat. Master Publishers, 1997—98; exec. v.p. mktg., Olive Garden div. Darden Restaurants Inc., Orlando, Fla., 1998—2002, sr. v.p., pres. Olive Garden div., 2002—04, pres., COO, 2004—. Mailing: Darden Restaurants Inc PO Box 593330 Orlando FL 32859-3330 Office: Darden Restaurants Inc 5900 Lake Ellenor Dr Orlando FL 32809 *

MADSEN, BARBARA A., state supreme court justice; b. Renton; BA, U. Wash., 1974; JD, Gonzaga U., 1977. Pub. defender King and Snohomish Counties, 1977—82; staff atty. Seattle City Atty.'s Office, 1982—84, spl. prosecutor, 1984—88; judge Seattle Mcpl. Ct., 1988—92; justice Wash. Supreme Ct., Olympia, 1993—. Chair Wash. State Gender and Justice Commn., Supreme Ct. Circulation Com., Ct. Personnel Com.; co-chair Internal Rules Com., Death Penalty Rules Com.; mem. Ct. Budget Com., Administrative Com., Reporter of Decisions Com. Active in Judges in the Classroom prog., Tacoma Public Sch. Recipient Wash. Women Lawyers Vanguard award, 1998, Wash. Women Lawyers Found. award, 2001, Presidents award, Nat. Assn. of Women Judges, 2002, Equal Justice Coalition Judicial award, 2004, Access to Justice award of distinction for public svc., 2006. Mem.: Judicature Soc., Nat. Assn. of Women Judges, Am. Judges Assn. Office: Wash Supreme Ct PO Box 40929 Olympia WA 98504-0929 *

MADSEN, BRIGHAM DWAINE, history professor; b. Magna, Utah, Oct. 21, 1914; s. Brigham and Lydia (Cushing) M.; m. Betty McAllister, Aug. 11, 1939; children— Karen Madsen Loos, David B., Linda Madsen Dunning, Steven M.; m. Lola Kastler, Dec. 1, 2001; m. Mary Harriman, June 7, 2003. BA, U. Utah, 1938; MA, U. Calif., Berkeley, 1940, PhD, 1948. Prin. Grade Sch. and Jr. High Sch., Pingree, Idaho, 1938-39; assoc. prof. history Brigham Young U., Provo, Utah, 1948-54; pres., mgr. Madsen Bros. Constrn. Co., Salt Lake City, 1954-61; prof. history Utah State U., Logan, 1961-64; asst. dir. tng. Peace Corps, Washington, 1964-65; first dir. tng. Vols. in Service to Am., Washington, 1965; dean div. continuing edn. U. Utah, Salt Lake City, 1965-66, dep. acad. v.p., 1966-67, adminstrv. v.p., 1967-71, dir. libraries, 1971-73, prof. history, 1973-84, chmn. dept. history, 1974-75. Author: Bannock of Idaho, 1958, The Lemhi: Sacajawea's People, 1980, Corinne: Gentile Capital of Utah, 1980, The Northern Shoshoni, 1980, (with Betty M. Madsen) North to Montana: Jehus, Bullwhackers and Muleskinners on the Montana Trail, 1980; Gold Rush Sojourners in Great Salt Lake City, 1849 and 1850, 1983, The Shoshoni Frontier and the Bear River Massacre, 1985, Chief Pocatello: The "White Plume", 1986, Glory Hunter: A Biography of Patrick Edward Connor, 1990, Against the Grain: Memoirs of a Western Historian, 1998; editor: The Now Generation, 1971, Letters of Long Ago, 1973, A Forty-niner in Utah: Letters and Journal of John Hudson, 1982, B.H. Roberts: Studies of the Book of Mormon, 1985, Exploring the Great Salt Lake: The Stansbury Expedition of 1849-50, 1989, The Essential B.H. Roberts, 1999. 1st lt., inf. AUS, 1943-46. Mem. Phi Beta Kappa, Phi Kappa Phi., Phi Alpha Theta. Home: 451 Bishop Federal Ln Apt 4117 Salt Lake City UT 84115-2222 E-mail: mimih02@aros.net, mimih@01exmission.com.

MADSEN, DOROTHY LOUISE (MEG), writer; b. Rochester, NY; d. Charles Robert and Louise Anna Agnes Meyer; m. Frederick George Madsen, Feb. 17, 1945 (dec.) BA, Mundelein Coll., Chgo., 1978; grad., U.S. Army Command and Gen. Staff Coll., 1960. Feature writer Gannett Newspapers, Rochester Democrat & Chronicle, NY, 1937—41; pub. rels. rep. Rochester Tel. Corp., 1941—42; exec. dir. LaPorte chpt. ARC, Ind., 1964; dir. adminstrv. svcs. Bank Mktg. Assn., Chgo., 1971—74; exec. dir. Eleanor Women's Found., Chgo., 1974—84; founder Meg Madsen Assocs., Chgo., 1984—88, women's career counselor; founder Eleanor Women's Forum, Clearinghouse Internat., Eleanor Intern Program Coll. Students and Returning Women. Chief global radiotelephone and radioteletype top secret encrypted conf. ctr. war dept. gen. staff Pentagon, Washington, 1944—46; conf. aide to Pres. Harry S Truman, Washington, 1945. Lt. col. WAC, 1942-47, 67-70 Decorated Legion of Merit, Meritorious Svc. award Mem.: Res. Officers Assn. (life), Mundelein Alumnae Assn., Ret. Officers Assn. (life), Phi Sigma Tau (charter mem. Ill. Kappa chpt.). Achievements include Aide to Pres. Truman during Sigsaly encoded phone conf. with Prime Min. Winston Churchill and U.S. Joint Chiefs Staff concerning terms of German surrender, WWII, Apr. 25, 1945. Home and Office: 1030 N State St Apt 25H Chicago IL 60610-2831 E-mail: megmadsenchgo@aol.com.

MADSEN, GEORGE FRANK, lawyer; b. Sioux City, Iowa, Mar. 24, 1933; s. Frank O. and Agnes (Cuhel) M.; m. Magnhild Norstog; 1 child, Michelle Marie. BA, St. Olaf Coll., 1954; LLB, Harvard U., 1959. Bar: Ohio 1960, Iowa 1961, U.S. Dist. Ct. (no. and so. dists.) Iowa, U.S. Ct. Appeals (8th cir.), U.S. Supreme Ct. 1991. Trainee Cargill, Inc., Mpls., 1954; assoc. Durfey, Martin, Browne & Hull, Springfield, Ohio, 1959-61; assoc., then ptnr. Shull, Marshall & Marks, Sioux City, 1961-85; ptnr. Marks & Madsen, Sioux City, 1985-97, Marks, Madsen & Hirschbach, Sioux City, 1998-99, Mayne, Marks, Madsen & Hirschbach, LLP, Sioux City, 1999-2001. Author, editor: Iowa Title Opinions and Standards, 1978; contbg. author: The American Law of Real Property, 1991. Sec., bd.dirs. Sioux City Boys Club, 1969-76; mem. Sioux City Zoning Bd. Adjustment, 1963-65; active Iowa Mo. River Preservation and Land Use Authority, 1992-2001, pres., 1997-2001. Lt. USAF, 1954-56. Fellow Iowa State Bar Found.; mem. ABA, Iowa Bar Assn., Woodbury County Bar Assn., Nat. Wildlife Assn., Mont. Wildlife Assn., Pheasants Forever, Phi Beta Kappa (past pres. Siouxland chpt.), Rotary Internat. Avocations: hunting, swimming, reading. Office: PO Box 3661 Sioux City IA 51102-3661

MADSEN, MATTHEW J., lawyer; b. Feb. 26, 1969; BBA in Fin., U. Iowa, 1991; JD, Stanford U., Calif., 1998. Bar: Mo. 1998. Atty. Lewis, Rice & Fingersh, LC, St. Louis, 2004—. Contbr. articles to profl. jours. Outside gen. counsel St. Louis Cmty. Found.; mem. planned giving adv. coun. ARC St. Louis Area; mem. gift planning coun. Cardinal Glennon Children's Hosp. Named one of Top 100 Attys., Worth mag., 2006. Mem.: Estate Planning Coun. St. Louis, Bar Assn. Met. St. Louis, ABA (real property, probate and trust law sect.). Office: Lewis Rice & Fingersh LC 500 N Broadway Ste 2000 Saint Louis MO 63102 Office Phone: 314-444-7878. Office Fax: 314-612-7878. E-mail: mmadsen@lewisrice.com.

MADSEN, MICHAEL, actor; b. Chicago, Sept. 25, 1958; m. Georganne LaPierre (div.); m. Jeannine Bisignano (div.); 1 child, Christian; m. De Anna Morgan Apr. 15, 1996; 4 children. Films include: Wargames, 1983, The Natural, 1984, Racing with the Moon, 1984, The Killing Time, 1987, Shadows in the Storm, 1988, Iguana, 1988, Blood Red, 1989, Kill Me Again, 1990, The Doors, 1991, The End of Innocence, 1991, Thelma and Louise, 1991, Fatal Instinct, 1992, Inside Edge, 1992, Reservoir Dogs, 1992, Straight Talk, 1992, Almost Blue, 1992, Free Willy, 1993, A House in the Hills, 1993, Money for Nothing, 1993, Trouble Bound, 1993, Wyatt Earp, 1994, The Getaway, 1994, Dead Connection, 1994, Species, 1995, Free Willy II: The Adventure Home, 1995, The Winner, 1996, Red Line, 1996, Mullholland Falls, 1996, Man With a Gun, 1996, The Last Days of Frankie the Fly, 1996, Rough Draft, 1997, The Maker, 1997, Donnie Brasco, 1997, Catherine's Grove, 1997, Papertrail, 1997, The Girl Gets Moe, 1997, Executive Target, 1997, The Thief and the Stripper, 1998, Supreme Sanction, 1998, The Florentine, 1998, Species II, 1998, Fait Accompli, 1998, The Thief & the Stripper, 1998, Flat Out, 1998, Ballad of the Nightingale, 1998, The Florentine, 1999, Detour, 1999, The Stray, 1999, Luck of the Draw, 2002, The Alternate, 2000, The Price of Air, 2000, Love.com, 2000, Ides of March, 2000, The Ghost, 2000, Fall, 2000, Choke, 2000, Bad Guys, 2000, Extreme Honor, 2001, Pressure Point, 2001, Outlaw, 2001, L.A.P.D.: To Protect and to Serve, 2001, Die Another Day, 2002, Welcome to America, 2002, The Real Deal, 2002, Where's Angelo, 2003, My Boss's Daughter, 2003, Kill Bill: Vol. 1, 2003, Vampires Anonymous, 2003, Hunt for the Devil, 2003, Blueberry, 2004, Kill Bill: Vol. 2, 2004, Sin City, 2005, Chasing Ghosts, 2005, (voice) The Chronicles of Narnia: The Lion, the Witch and the Wardrobe, 2005, BloodRayne, 2005; TV movies include: Special Bulletin, 1983, War and Remembrance, 1988, Montana, 1990, Baby Snatcher, 1992, Beyond the Law, 1994, Supreme Sanction, 1999, The Inspectors 2: A Shred of Evidence, 2000, Sacrifice, 2000, High Noon, 2000, 44 Minutes: The North Hollywood Shoot-Out, 2003, Frankenstein, 2004; TV series include: Our Family Honor, 1985-86, Vengeance Unlimited, 1998, Big Apple, 2001, Tilt, 2005; author: The Complete Poetic Works of Michael Madsen, Vol 1: 1995-2005. also: Creative Artists Agy Michael Manchal 9830 Wilshire Blvd Beverly Hills CA 90212-1804

MADSEN, STEPHANIE D., psychology professor; b. Mpls., May 21, 1974; d. Michael Christian and Karen Storey; m. Joseph P. Madsen, Oct. 1, 2000; 1 child, A. BA in Psychology, Carleton Coll., Northfield, Minn., 1996; MA in Child Psychology, U. Minn., Mpls., 1999, PhD in Child Psychology, 2001. Cert. in Interview Coding U. Calif. Berkley, 1999. Asst. prof. psychology McDaniel Coll., Westminster, Md., 2001—07, assoc. prof. psychology, 2007—. Cons. in field. Recipient Scholarly Publications award, McDaniel Coll., 2003. Mem.: Soc. Tchg. Psychology, Soc. Rsch. Adolescence, Soc. Rsch. Child Devel. Office: McDaniel Coll Psychology Dept 2 College Hill Westminster MD 21157 Office Phone: 410-386-4674. Business E-Mail: smadsen@mcdaniel.edu.

MADSEN, VIRGINIA, actress; b. Chgo., Sept. 11, 1963; d. Cal Madsen; m. Danny Huston, Sept. 2, 1989 (div. 1992); 1 child, Jack. Represented by Creative Artists Agy., Beverly Hills, Calif. Actor: (films) Class, 1983, Dune, 1984, Electric Dreams, 1984, Creator, 1985, Fire with Fire, 1986, Modern Girls, 1986, Slam Dance, 1987, Zombie High, 1987, Mr. North, 1988, Hot to Trot, 1988, Heart of Dixie, 1989, The Hot Spot, 1990, Highlander II—The Quickening, 1991, Becoming Colette, 1992, Candyman, 1992, Blue Tiger, 1994, Caroline at Midnight, 1994, The Prophecy, 1995, Ghosts of Mississippi, 1996, The Rainmaker, 1997, Ambushed, 1998, Ballad of the Nightingale, 1998, The Florentine, 1998, The Haunting, 1999, After Sex, 2000, Lying in Wait, 2000, Almost Salinas, 2001, American Gun, 2002, Artworks, 2003, Tempted, 2003, Nobody Knows Anything!, 2003, Sideways, 2004 (Screen Actors Guild Award, outstanding performance by cast in motion picture, 2005), Firewall, 2006, A Prairie Home Companion, 2006, The Number 23, 2007, The Astronaut Farmer, 2007; (TV films) A Matter of Principle, 1984, The Hearst and Davies Affair, 1985, Long Gone, 1987, Gotham, 1988, Third Degree Burn, 1989, Ironclads, 1991, Victim of Love, 1991, Love Kills, 1991, A Murderous Affair: The Carolyn Warmus Story, 1992, Linda, 1993, Bitter Vengeance, 1994, The Apocalypse Watch, 1997, Children of Fortune, 2000, The Inspector General, 2000, Crossfire Trail, 2001, Just Ask My Children, 2001, Tempted, 2003, Brave New Girl, 2004; (TV miniseries) Mussolini: The Untold Story, 1985; (TV series) American Dreams, 2002-03, Smith, 2006-; TV appearances include The Hitchhiker, 1987, Moonlighting, 1989, Earth 2, 1994, Star Trek: Voyager, 1998, Frasier, 1999, The Practice, 2001, (voice) Justice League, 2002, Dawson's Creek, 2003, CSI: Miami, 2003, Boomtown, 2003. Democrat. *

MADURA, JAMES ANTHONY, surgeon, educator; b. Campbell, Ohio, June 10, 1938; s. Anthony Peter and Margaret Ethel (Sebest) M.; m. Loretta Jayne Sovak, Aug. 8, 1959; children: Debra Jean, James Anthony II, Vikki Sue. BA, Cogate U., 1959; MD, Western Res. U., 1963. Diplomate Am. Bd. Surgery. Intern in surgery Ohio State U., Columbus, 1963—64, resident in surgery, 1966—71; asst. prof. surgery Ind. U., Indpls., 1971—76, assoc. prof. Surgery, 1976—80, prof. Surgery, 1980—, J.S. Battersby prof. surgery, 2001—. Dir. gen. surgery Ind. U. Sch. Medicine, Indpls., 1985—, vice-chmn., 1985—. Contbr. articles to profl. jours. Bd. dir. Indpls. Opera. Capt. med. corps US Army, 1965—66, Vietnam, 85th Evacuation Hosp. Fellow Am. Coll. Surgeons; mem. Cen. Surg. Assn., Western Surg. Assn., Soc. Surgery Alimentary Tract, Midwest Surg. Assn., Internat. Biliary Assn., Assn. Acad. Surgeons, The Columbia Club. Republican. Roman Catholic. Home: 9525 Copley Dr Indianapolis IN 46260-1422 Personal E-mail: jmadura1@comcast.net. Business E-Mail: jmadura@iupui.edu.

MADVA, STEPHEN ALAN, lawyer; b. Pitts., July 27, 1948; s. Joseph Edward and Mary (Zulick) M.; m. Denise C. Creedon; children: Alexander, Elizabeth. BA cum laude, Yale U., 1970; JD, U. Pa., 1973. Bar: Pa. 1973, US Dist. Ct. (ea. dist.) Pa. 1975, US Ct. Appeals (3d cir.) 1976, US Supreme Ct. 1985, N.Y. 1990. Asst. defender Defender Assn. Phila., 1973—75, fed. defender, 1975—77, also bd. dirs.; assoc. Montgomery, McCracken, Walker & Rhoads, Phila., 1977—81, ptnr., 1981—, mem. mgmt. com., 1993—, chmn. litig. sect., 1993—2002, vice chmn., 2002—03, chmn., 2003—. Bd. dirs. Ferag-Ams., LLC, chmn., 2004-; bd. dirs. WRH Mktg. Ams., LLC., chmn. 2004-. Bd. dirs. Ctrl. Phila. Devel. Corp., St. Christopher's Hosp. for Children, chmn., 2004—; bd. dirs. St. Christopher's Found. for Children, Opera Co. of Phila., v.p., 2002—04, chmn., 2004—; bd. dirs. Police Athletic League, Phila. C. of C., Cmty. Legal Svcs., Kimmel Ctr. Performing Arts, 2007. Fellow Internat. Soc. Barristers, Am. Coll. Trial Lawyers; mem. ABA, Internat. Assn. Def. Counsel, Pa. Bar Assn. (ho. of dels.), Phila. Bar Assn. (bd. govs. 2002-, fed. cts. com., chmn. commn. on jud. selection and retention,), Def. Rsch. Inst., Hist. Soc. Pa., Phila. C. of C. (bd. dirs.), Yale Alumni Assn. (schs. com.), Yale Rowing Assn., Union League of Phila., Sunday Breakfast Club. Democrat. Avocations: tennis, distance running, opera, classical music. Office: Montgomery McCracken Walker & Rhoads LLP 123 S Broad St Fl 24 Philadelphia PA 19109-1099 Home: 608 Spruce St Philadelphia PA 19106 Office Phone: 215-772-7600. Business E-Mail: smadva@mmwr.com.

MADZIK, ELIZABETH MAY, hospital administrator; b. St. Louis, Mo., Sept. 21, 1965; d. William J. and Nadine Madzik; children: Derek Embry, Nathaniel Embry. Student, St. Leo U., 2003—. Client liaison Receivables Mgmt., Arlington, Tex., 1996—99; denials mgmt. mgr. Presbyn. Hosp. Dallas, 1999—2005, privacy and compliance officer, 2005—. Dir. bd. dirs. HM Caps, Inc., 2004—. Author: Dark Passion Deef Reflections, Book of Poetry, 2006. Exec. bd. mem. Parkway Elem. Sch. PTA, Ft. Worth, 2000—03; mem. Am. Ex-Prisoners of War, Ft. Worth, 2001. Mem.: Health Care Compliance Assn., Healthcare Fin. Mgmt. Assn., Phi Theta Kappa. Mem. Lds Ch. Avocations: reading, exercise, poetry, dance, music. Home: 1728 Wild Willow Trail Fort Worth TX 76134 Office: THR - Presbyn Hosp Dallas 8200 Walnut Hill Ln Dallas TX 75231 Home Phone: 817-568-9304. Personal E-mail: madzik@sbcglobal.net. Business E-Mail: elizabethmadzik@texashealth.org.

MAEDA, J. A., data processing executive, consultant; b. Mansfield, Ohio, Aug. 24, 1940; d. James Shunso and Doris Lucille Maeda; m. Robert Lee Hayes; 1 child, Brian Sentaro Hayes. BS in Math., Purdue U., 1962, postgrad., 1962—63, Calif. State U., Northridge, 1968—75; cert. profl. designation in tech. of computer operating systems and tech. of info. processing, UCLA, 1971. Cons., rsch. asst. computer ctr. Purdue U., West Lafayette, Ind., 1962-63; computer operator, sr. tab operator, mem. faculty Calif. State U., Northridge, 1969, programmer cons., tech. asst. II, 1969-70, supr. acad. applicatons, EDP supr. II, 1970-72, project tech. support coord. programmer II, office of the chancellor, 1972-73, tech. support coord. statewide timesharing tech. support, programmer II, 1973-74, acad. coord., tech. support coord. instrn., computer cons. III, 1974-83; coord. user svcs. info. ctr., mem. tech. staff IV CADAM INC subs. Lockheed Corp., Burbank, Calif., 1983-86, coord. user svcs., tech. specialist computing dept., 1986-87; v.p., bd. dirs. Rainbow Computing, Inc., Northridge, 1976-85; dir. Aki Tech/Design, Northridge, 1976—. Mgr. mktg. thaumaturge Taro Quipu Cons., Northridge, 1987—; tech. cons. Digital Computer Cons., Chatsworth, Calif., 1988; computer tech., fin. and bus. mgmt., sys. integration, 1988—90; tech. customer software support Collection Data Sys., Westlake, Calif., 1991; sr. tech. writer info mgmt. divsn. Sterling Software, 1992—2000; sr. tech. writer, quality analyst Computer Assocs. Internat., Inc., 2000—. Author, editor more than 460 user publs., tutorials, reference manuals, user guides, CD graphics/packaging; contbr. articles and photos to profl. jours. Mem.: DECUS (ednl. spl. interest group 1977—83, ednl. steering com. RSTS/E 1979—82), SHARE, IEEE, Soc. for Tech. Comm. Avocations: photography, photojournalism, vintage automobiles.

MAEDER, MICHAEL C., endocrinologist; b. Brownsville, Tex., Aug. 11, 1945; s. Charles E. and Betty L. Maeder; m. Jan Zipf; children: Michael Robert, Melissa. BA, Depauw U., Greencastle, Ind., 1967; MD, Ohio State U., Columbus, Ohio, 1971. Diplomate in internal medicine and in endocrinology and metabolism Am. Bd. Internal Medicine. Internal medicine resident U. Fla., Gainesville, 1971—74; fellow in endocrinology Ohio State U., Columbus, 1976—78; endocrinologist Mt. Auburn Internists Inc., 1978—95, Hyde Park Internists Inc., Cin., 1996—2006. Major US Army, 1974—76. Avocations: bicycling, hiking, golf. Home: 7019 Sprucewood Ct Cincinnati OH 45241 Office: Hyde Park Internists Inc 2727 Madison Rd #208 Cincinnati OH 45209 Office Phone: 513-321-0833. Office Fax: 513-321-6063. E-mail: mcmaeder@pol.net.

MAEHARA, PAULETTE V., fundraising executive; b. Happy, Tex. married; 2 children. BA, U. Hawaii. Cert. Fund Raising Exec. (CFRE), Assn. Exec. (CAE). Exec. U. Hawaii Found., March of Dimes Birth Defects Found., Hawaii Chap.; v.p. devel. Project HOPE; exec. Am. Red Cross; CEO Epilepsy Found.; pres., CEO Assn. of Fundraising Profls. (AFP). Exec. com. Internat. Bur. for Epilepsy, Internat. Svc. Agencies, chair membership com.; bd. dirs. Nat. Health Coun.; mem. Assn. Com. of 100, US C. of C. Recipient Best Direct Mail Program award, Direct Mktg. Assn. of Am., 1994. Mem.: Am. Soc. of Assn. Execs. (bd. dirs. 2000—02, vice chair exec. bd. dirs. 2001, sec., treas. 2003, past chair Exec. Mgmt. Coun., bd. chair 2005—). Office: Assn of Fundraising Profls 1101 King St, Ste 700 Alexandria VA 22314 Office Phone: 703-684-0410. Office Fax: 703-684-0540.

MAEHL, WILLIAM HARVEY, retired historian; b. Bklyn., May 28, 1915; s. William Henry and Antoinette Rose (Salamone) M.; m. Josephine Scholl McAllister, Dec. 29, 1941; children: Madeleine, Kathleen. BSc, Northwestern U., 1937, MA, 1939; PhD, U. Chgo., 1946. Asst. prof. history St. Louis U., 1941-42, Tex. A&M U., College Sta., 1943, De Paul U., Chgo., 1944-49; historian Dept. of Def., Karlsruhe, Stuttgart, Fed. Rep. Germany, 1950-52; chief briefing office U.S. hdqrs. U.S. Hdqs. European Command, Frankfurt, Germany, 1952-53; chief historian Arty. Sch., Okla., 1954; with War Plans Office, Hdqs. No. Air Materiel Area for Europe, Burtonwood, England, 1954-55; assoc. prof. European history Nebr. Wesleyan U., Lincoln, 1955-57, prof., 1958-62, 65-68; prof. German history Auburn (Ala.) U., 1968-81, prof. emeritus, 1981—. Vis. prof. U. Nebr., 1962, U. Auckland, New Zealand, 1963-64, Midwestern U., Wichita Falls, Tex., 1965. Author: German Militarism and Socialism, 1968, History of Germany in Western Civilization, 1979, A World History Syllabus, 3 vols., 1980, August Bebel, Shadow Emperor of the German Workers, 1980, The German Socialist Party: Champion of the First Republic, 1918-33, 1986;; contbr. poetry to Question of Balance, Tears of Fire, Disting. Poets Am., Best Poems of 1995, Journey of Mind; contbr. articles to profl. jours.; chpts. to books. Grantee Nebr. Wesleyan U., 1959, Auburn U., 1969-73, 79-80, Am. Philosophical Soc., 1973-74, Deutscher Akademischer Austauschdienst, 1978. Mem.: Am. Hist. Assn., Phi Alpha Theta, Phi Kappa Phi.

MAEHL, WILLIAM HENRY, historian, academic administrator, consultant; b. Chicago Heights, Ill., June 13, 1930; s. William Henry and Marvel Lillian (Carlson) M.; m. Audrey Mae Ellsworth, Aug. 25, 1962; 1 child, Christine Amanda. BA, U. Minn., 1950, MA, 1951; postgrad., King's Coll., U. Durham, Eng., 1955—56; PhD, U. Chgo., 1957; LHD (hon.), Fielding Inst., 1993. Asst. prof. Montclair (N.J.) State Coll., 1957-58, Washington Coll., Chestertown, Md., 1958-59, U. Okla., Norman, 1959-64, assoc. prof., 1964-70, prof. English history, 1970-86; dean Coll. Liberal Studies, 1976-86, vice provost for continuing edn. and public service, 1979-86; pres. The Fielding Inst., Santa Barbara, Calif., 1987-93, pres. emeritus, 1993—. Prin. investigator Project for a Nation of Lifelong Learners, Regents Coll., Albany, N.Y., 1994-97; vis. prof. U. Nebr., summer 1965; vis. fellow Wolfson Coll. Oxford (Eng.) U., spring 1975; fellow Salzburg Seminar in Am. Studies, 1976. Author: The Reform Bill of 1832, 1967, Lifelong Learning at Its Best: Innovative Practices in Adult Credit Programs, 2000; contbg. author: Encyclopedia of Education, 2d edit., 2003, Encyclopedia of Distributed Learning, 2004; editor: R.G. Gammage, Chartist Reminiscences, 1981, Continuum: Jour. of the Nat. Continuing Edn. Assn., 1980-83, also articles. Mem. coun. Nat. Ctr. for Adult Learning, 1990—2001; bd. dirs. Alliance for Alternative Degree Programs, 1988—90; trustee Coun. for Adult and Exptl. Learning, 1990—94, Southwestern Coll., 2000—02. Fulbright fellow, 1955-56; Leverhulme Rsch. fellow, 1961-62; grantee Am. Philos. Soc., 1961-62, 67-68, 71, 76. Fellow: Assn. Grad. Liberal Studies Programs, Royal Hist. Soc.; mem.: Adult Higher Edn. Alliance. Office: PO Box 31757 Santa Fe NM 87594-1757

MAEHR, KATE, social services organization executive; m. Sam Maehr; 2 children. B, Macalester Coll.; M in Pub. Policy and Adminstrn., U. Wis. Mng. editor nonprofit lit. pub. house, Mpls.; dir., individual giving Greater Chgo. Food Depository, dir. devel., 1999—2006, exec. dir., 2006—. Named one of Chgo.'s 40 under 40 to watch, Crain's Chgo. Bus. Fellow: Leadership Greater Chgo. Office: Greater Chicago Food Depository 4100 W Ann Lurie Pl Chicago IL 60632 Office Phone: 773-247-3663. *

MAEHR, MARTIN LOUIS, psychology professor; b. Guthrie, Okla., June 25, 1932; s. Martin J. and Regina (Meier) M.; m. Jane M. Pfeil, Aug. 9, 1959; children— Martin, Michael, Katherine BA, Concordia Coll., 1953, MA, 1959; PhD, U. Nebr., 1960. Counselor U. Nebr., Lincoln, 1959-60; asst. prof. to assoc. prof. Concordia Sr. Coll., Fort Wayne, Ind., 1960-67; assoc. prof. ednl. psychology U. Ill., Urbana, 1967-70, prof., 1970—, chmn. dept. ednl. psychology, 1970-75, assoc. dean grad. and internat. programs prof., 1975-77, research prof., dir. Inst. Research on Human Devel., prof. ednl. psychology, 1977-88, assoc. dir. Office Gerontology and Aging Studies, 1980-82; prof. edn. and psychology U. Mich., Ann Arbor, 1988—, chair combined program edn. and psychology, 1988-92. Vis. prof. U. Queensland, Australia, 1981; vis. prof., cons. to dean Faculty Edn. U. Tehran, Iran, 1973-74 Author: Sociocultural Origins of Achievement, 1974, (with Jane Maehr) Being a Parent in Today's World, 1980, (with L.A. Braskamp) The Motivation Factor, 1986, (with Carol Midgley) Transforming School Cultures, 1996; editor: Advancement in Motivation and Achievement series; contbr. articles to profl. jours. Lutheran. Office Phone: 734-647-0627. Business E-Mail: mlmaehr@umich.edu.

MAEKAWA, KOJI OGURA, technology company administrator; b. Fukui, Japan, Sept. 11, 1954; s. Eiji and Toshiko M.; m. Yukiko Ogura, Nov. 30, 1995. BSChemE, Tokyo U. of Agr. & Tech., 1979; MBA, U. St. Thomas, St. Paul, 1992. Analytical engr., Analytical Lab. Sumitomo 3M, Sagamihara, Japan, 1979-81, chem. engr., Corporate Lab., 1982-87; process engr., Optical Storage Divsn. 3M, St. Paul, 1988—92, sr. process devel. engr., 1993—96; technical team leader Imation Corp. Adv. Imaging Technology, St. Paul, 1997-98, bus. devel. mgr., 1998-99, program mgr., 1998—2000; program mgr., bus. devel. mgr. PDF Solutions, San Jose, Calif., 2000—05, account gen. mgr., 2006—. Intellectual property translator (English/Japanese), language soc. Minn. Mining Mfg., 1993—; cons. Expert Magnetics Corp., Chiba, Japan, 1993—. Patentee in field. Mem. Am. Japanese Soc. Avocations: golf, gardening. Office: Ste 700 333 W San Carlos St San Jose CA 95110 Office Phone: 408-938-4409. Business E-Mail: kojim@pdf.com.

MAELAND, ARNULF JULIUS, research scientist; b. Aakrehamn, Norway, Apr. 21, 1933; came to U.S., 1952; s. Erling Magnus and Dagny Marie M.; m. Gunhild Olaug, June 18, 1955; children: Lynn Solveig, David Erling, Kerry Brynhild. BS, Augsburg Coll., 1955; MS, Tufts U., 1959; PhD, U. Vt., 1965. NATO postdoctoral fellow Inst. Atomic Energy, Kjeller, Norway, 1965-66; NAS-NRC postdoctoral rsch. assoc. Army Materials Rsch. Ctr., Watertown, Mass., 1966-68; prof. Worcester (Mass.) Polytechnic Inst., 1968-75; adj. prof. N.J. Inst. Tech., Newark, 1981—84; sr. rsch. assoc. Allied Corp., Morristown, N.J., 1975-90; vis. sr. rsch. fellow Inst. Energy Tech., Kjeller, Norway, 1992—. Chmn. Gordon Rsch. Confs., Kingston, R.I., 1999; advisor Internat. Sci. and Tech. Ctr., Moscow, 1998—; program evaluator Norwegian Rsch. Coun., Oslo, Norway; cons. Norsk Hydro, Oslo, 2000—; hydrogen program reviewer DOE; mem. adv. bd. Tubitak Energy Inst., Turkey. Editor: Hydrides for Energy Storage, 1977; contbr. articles to profl. jours. Rsch. grantee Aluminum Assn., 1969-75. Mem.: Am. Physics Soc. Mem. Missionary Alliance Ch. Achievements include patents in field. Avocations: stamp collecting/philately, travel, classical music. Home: 305 Cactus Hill Ct Royal Palm Beach FL 33411 Office: Inst Energy Tech Kjeller N-2027 Norway Office Phone: 476-380-6000. Personal E-mail: arnulf@ife.no. E-mail: arnulf@juno.com.

MAES, PAUL JOEL, dentist; b. Bozeman, Mont., Mar. 29, 1952; s. Joseph Paul Maes and Alice Mae Ehlman; m. Nancy Susan Gallagher (div.); children: Jacob Paul, Joshua William, Jeffrey Gallagher, Justin Timothy. BA, U. Mont., Missoula, 1974; BS in Dentistry, U. Minn., Mpls., 1976, DDS, 1978. Dentist USN, San Diego, 1978—81; pvt. practice Helena, Mont., 1981—2006; group practice South Hills Dental, Helena, 2006—. Trustee Shodair Hosp., Helena, 1990—2001; co-founder Helena Coop. Dental Clinic, 1991, chmn. dental adv. bd., 1992—; pres. Mont. chpt. Donated Dental Svcs., 1996—; founder Shodair Classic All Star Soccer Game, Mont., 2000; bd. dirs. Holter Mus. Art, Helena, 2006—. Lt. comdr. USNR, 1978—81. Master: Acad. Gen. Dentistry (Nat. Humanitarian award 1999); fellow: Am. Coll. Dentists; mem.: ADA, Mont. Dental Assn., Mont. Study Club. Avocations: backpacking, photography, bicycling. Office: South Hills Dental 2480 Tracy Dr Helena MT 59601 Office Phone: 406-443-2780. Office Fax: 406-443-5902.

MAES, PETRA JIMENEZ, state supreme court justice; widowed; 4 children. BA, U. N.Mex., 1970, JD, 1973. Bar: N.Mex. 1973. Pvt. pratice law, Albuquerque, 1973-75; rep., then office mgr. No. N.Mex. Legal Svcs., 1975-81; dist. judge 1st Jud. Dist. Ct., Santa Fe, Los Alamos, 1981-98; chief judge, 1984-87, 92-95; assoc. justice N.Mex. Supreme Ct., 1998—, chief justice, 2003—04. Mem. N.Mex. Commn. on Access to Justice; mem. nat. rev. bd. U.S. Conf. Cath. Bishops. Mem.: Nat. Hispanic Bar Assn., N. Mex. Hispanic Bar Assn., N. Mex. Women's Bar Assn., N. Mex. Bar Assn. Office: Supreme Court NMex PO Box 848 Santa Fe NM 87504-0848 Office Phone: 505-827-4883. *

MAESTRONE, FRANK EUSEBIO, diplomat; b. Springfield, Mass., Dec. 20, 1922; s. John Battista and Margaret Carlotta (Villanova) M.; m. Jo Colwell, Jan. 20, 1951; childen: Mark, Anne. BA, Yale U., 1943; grad., Naval War Coll., 1963. With Fgn. Svc., Dept. State, 1948-84; assigned to Vienna and Salzburg, Austria, 1948, 1954, Hamburg, Germany, 1949, Khorramshahr, Iran, 1960; with NATO, Paris, 1963, dep. asst. sec. gen. Brussels, 1968—71; counselor of embassy for polit. affairs Am. Embassy, Manila, 1971-73; Dept. State adviser to pres. Naval War Coll., 1973; min.-counselor Am. Embassy, Cairo, 1974, amb. to Kuwait, 1976-79; diplomat-in-residence U. Calif., San Diego, 1979; spl. rep. of Pres., dir. U.S. Sinai Support Mission, 1980; exec. dir. World Affairs Coun., San Diego, 1984-86; adj. prof. internat. rels., amb.-in-residence U.S. Internat. U., San Diego, 1986-90. Mem. bd. San Diego World Affairs Coun., 2005. With AUS, 1943-46. Decorated chevalier du Merite Agricole (France). Mem. Internat. Inst. Strategic Studies. Home Phone: 858-457-1656; Office Phone: 858-457-1656. Personal E-mail: fmaestrone@prodigy.net.

MAFFEI, FRANK ANTHONY, pediatrician, educator; b. Bronx, NY, June 23, 1965; s. Vito and Maria Maffei; m. Lynn Catherine Voisinet, Sept. 19, 1992; children: Luke, Katelyn, Marisa, Matthew, Annaleigh. MD, Albert Einstein Coll. Medicine, NYC, 1992. Diplomate Am. Bd. Pediats., 1995, pediat. emergency medicine Am. Bd. Pediats., 1998, pediat. critical care Am. Bd. Pediats., 2002. Pediat. and pediatric emergency medicine physician Children's Hosp. Pitts., 1992—98; pediatric critical care physician U. Rochester Golisano Children's Hosp., NY, 1998—2004, Janet Weis Children's Hosp. at Geisinger, Danville, Pa., 2004—. Named Fellow of Yr., Children's Hosp. Pitts., 1996; recipient Excellence Clin. Tchg. award, U. Rochester Sch. Medicine, 1998—2001, Golden Apple Tchg. award, Janet Weis Children's Hosp. Residency, 2005; Lowell A. Glasgow Dean's Tchg. fellow, U. Rochester Sch. Medicine, 2003—04. Fellow: Am. Assn. Pediats.; mem.: Am. Coll. Pediatricians, Alpha Omega Alpha. Achievements include research in pediatric menigitis, pediatric sepsis, pediatric life-threatening asthma.

MAFFEI, GREGORY B., media company executive, former computer software company executive; b. NYC, May 24, 1960; s. Ralph J. and Sheila (Quinn) M. AB, Dartmouth Coll., 1982; MBA, Harvard U., 1986. Analyst Dillon, Read & Co., Inc., NYC, 1982-84, assoc.; pres. Beacon Hill Cons. Co., Boston, 1984; dir. bus. devel & investments Microsoft Corp., Redmond, Wash., 1993—94, treas., 1994—96, v.p. corp. devel., 1996—97, sr. v.p., fin. & adminstrn., CFO, 1997—2000; non-exec. chmn. Expedia, Inc., Bellevue, Wash., 1999—2002; pres., CEO 360 networks, Inc., Vancouver, BC, Canada, 2000—05, chmn., 2000—05; pres., CFO Oracle Corp., Redwood City, Calif., 2005; pres., CEO Liberty Media Corp., Englewood, Colo., 2006—. Bd. dir. Starbucks Corp., Seattle, 1999—, Electronic Arts Inc., Redwood City, Calif., 2003—, Liberty Media Corp., Englewood, Colo., 2005—. Bd. trustee Seattle Pub. Libr. George F. Baker scholar Harvard U., 1986. Roman Catholic. Office: Liberty Media Corp 12300 Liberty Blvd Englewood CO 80112 *

MAFFEO, ALPHONSE A., anesthesiologist; b. 1947; MD, SUNY Syracuse, 1972. Diplomate Am. Bd. Anesthesiology. Intern Harrisburg Hosp., 1972-73; res. anesthesiology Mass Gen. Hosp., Boston, 1973-75; physician Lehigh Valley Hosp., Allentown, Pa., 1977—, chmn. anesthesiology, 1990-2001. Clin. assoc. prof., assoc. chmn. anesthesiology Pa. St. U. Hershey Med. Ctr., 1994—2001. Fellow ABA, Am. Coll. Anesthesiologists, mem. Am. Soc. Anesthesiologists. Office: Allentown Anesthes Assn Inc 1245 S Cedar Crest Blvd Ste 301 Allentown PA 18103-6258

MAFFEO, PINO, chef; b. 1970; Grad., Newbury Culinary Coll., 1991. Task force chef Marriott Corp., 1991—92; chef Cafe Katie, San Francisco, 1992; chef de partie Molhern and Shackern, San Francisco; chef de cuisine Inn at the Opera, San Francisco; co-exec. chef Sage, Boston, 1996—99; chef de cuisine AZ, NYC, 1999—2002; co-exec. chef Pazo, NYC, 2002—03; exec. chef Restaurant L, Boston, 2004—. Guest appearances (TV series) The Early Show, Food Network, Simply Ming. Named Best New Chef: Up and Coming, Boston Mag., 2005; named one of Boston's Rising Stars, StarChefs.com, 2006, Boston's Best New Faces, Boston Globe Mag., 2004, Boston's Top Tastemakers, Boston Mag., 2004; recipient Best New Chef award, Food and Wine Mag., 2006. Office: Restaurant L 234 Berkeley St Boston MA 02116 Office Phone: 617-266-4680. *

MAFFEO, VINCENT ANTHONY, lawyer, director; b. NJ, Jan. 22, 1951; s. Michael Anthony and Marie Maffeo; m. Debra Maffeo, Dec. 16, 1972. BA summa cum laude, Bklyn. Coll., 1971; JD, Harvard U., 1974. Bar: NY 1975, Calif. 1982, Va. 1988, DC 1988, Mich. 1994. Assoc. Simpson Thacher & Bartlett, NYC, 1974—77; legal counsel Comms. Sys. divsn. ITT, Hartford, Conn., 1977—79; v.p., gen. counsel Bus. Comms. divsn. ITT, Des Plaines, Ill., 1979—80; asst. counsel western region ITT, 1980—83; group counsel ITT Europe, Inc., 1983—86; v.p. gen. coun. ITT Defense Inc., 1987—91; v.p., gen. coun. ITT Automotive, Inc., 1992—95; sr. v.p., gen. counsel ITT Corp., 1995—. Bd. dir. Fund for Modern Courts, 1997—. Trustee Sacred Heart Univ.; bd. dir. Pro Bono Partnership, Fundacion Chile. Lt. Judge Adv. Gen. Corps. USNR, 1975. Mem.: ABA, N.Y.State Bar Assn., Calif. State Bar, Phi Beta Kappa. Office: ITT Industries Inc 4 W Red Oak Ln White Plains NY 10604-3617 Business E-Mail: vince.maffeo@itt.com.

MAFFITT, JAMES STRAWBRIDGE, lawyer; b. Raleigh, NC, Oct. 29, 1942; s. James Strawbridge III and Lois (Handy) M.; children: Amy Maffitt Barkley, Margaret Maffitt Kramer; m. Frances Holton, Aug. 15, 1981. BA, Washington and Lee U., 1964, LLB, 1966. Bar: Va. 1966, Md. 1969. Assoc. Apostolou, Place & Thomas, Roanoke, Va., 1966-67; trust officer Mercantile-Safe Deposit & Trust Co., Balt., 1967-71; from assoc. to ptnr. Cable, McDaniel, Bowie & Bond, Balt., 1971-82; ptnr. Maffit & Rothschild, Balt., 1982-85, Anderson, Coe & King, Balt., 1986-90, Miles & Stockbridge, Easton, Balt., 1990—. Chmn. Acad. Art Mus., 1994—97, bd. dirs., 1993—99; trustee Grayce B. Kerr Fund, Inc., 1998—; bd. dirs. Chesapeake Coll., 2002—, Leadership Md., 2002—04, United Fund of Talbot County, 1994—98, pres., 1997—98. Fellow Md. Bar Found.; mem. ABA (ho. dels. 1986-88), Md. Bar Assn. (bd. govs. 1989-91), Va. Bar. Assn., Balt. City Bar Assn. (pres. 1985-86), Wednesday Law Club, Talbot Country Club. Republican. Episcopal. Avocation: golf. Home: 6272 Country Club Dr Easton MD 21601 Office: Miles & Stockbridge 101 Bay St Easton MD 21601-2748 also: Miles & Stockbridge 10 Light St Baltimore MD 21202-1407 Office Phone: 410-820-0222. E-mail: jmaffitt@milesstockbridge.com.

MAGADAN, DAVID JOSEPH, retired professional baseball player; b. Tampa, Fla., Sept. 30, 1962; m. Monique Magadan; children: Jordan, Christian. Student, U. Ala. 1st baseman-3d baseman N.Y. Mets, NYC, 1986—92, Fla. Marlins, Miami, 1993; 1st-baseman-3d-baseman-designated hitter Seattle Mariners, 1993; 1st baseman-3d baseman Fla. Marlins, 1994, Houston Astros, 1995; 1st baseman-3d baseman-designated hitter Oakland Athletics, Calif., 1997—99, San Diego Padres, 1999—2001; asst. coach Boston Red Sox, 2006—. Drafted Boston Red Sox, declined, 1980. Chmn. No Small Affair-South. Named Coll. Player of Yr., Baseball Am., 1983, All-Southeast Conf., 1983; recipient Payson award for humanitarian svc., N.Y. chpt. Baseball Writers' Assn. Am., Golden Spikes award, USA Baseball, 1983. Achievements include leading U. Ala. to championship game 1983 Coll. World Series, 1983; leading NCAA divsn. 1 with .525 batting average, 1983. Office: Boston Red Sox 4 Yawkey Way Boston MA 02215-3496

MAGANA, MELANIE G, psychologist, consultant; b. New York, NY, Feb. 21, 1954; d. Anthony Dominic Thomas Guggenheimer; m. John R Magana, Oct. 4, 2003; children: Justin Anthony Moss, Timothy Andrew Moss. MS in Sch. Psychology, Nat. U., San Diego, Calif., 1995. Lic. Psychologist Calif., 2000. Sch. psychologist Oceanside Unified Sch. Dist., Oceanside, Calif., 1996, Chino Valley Unified Sch. Dist., Chino, Calif., 1996—2006; pvt. practice Resilience Through Edn., 2006—. Parenting instr. Chino Human Services, Chino, Calif., 2000—; cons. in trauma and loss in children. Mem.: APA (assoc.), Calif. Assn. Sch. Psychologists, Nat. Assn. Sch. Psychologists. Roman Catholic. Home Phone: 909-854-0311. Personal E-mail: ottermgm@sbcglobal.net.

MAGANZINI, BROTHER JOHN BERNARD, academic administrator; b. Somerville, Mass., Nov. 11, 1947; s. Bernard Louis and Eva (Alo) M. BS, St. Francis Coll., 1982; MS, Fordham U., 1987, postgrad., 1987—. Tchr. spl. religious edn. Kennedy Meml. Hosp. Day Program, Brighton, Mass., 1980-81; parish asst. Our Lady Queen of Peace, Hewitt, N.J., 1981; tchr. Holy Cross Sch., Bronx, N.Y., 1982, St. Anthony's Grade Sch., Washington, 1982-83; dir. religious edn. Holy Cross Parish & Sch., Bronx, 1983-84, tchr., 1984-88, dept. chmn., tchr., 1990-93, asst. prin., 1993—; tchr. East Boston (Mass.) Ctrl. Cath. Sch., 1988-90; asst. dir. Franciscan Sch. Arch St., 2003—. With U.S. Army, 1967-69. Recipient John J. Duffy award Archdiocese of N.Y., 1987, Call to the Brotherhood award, Religious Bors. Conf. Mem. Cath. Edn. Assn., Am. Assn. Pastoral Counselors, Spiritual Dirs. Internat., Order of Friars Minor, Holy Name Province, 11th Armored Cavalry's Vets. Vietnam and Cambodia. Avocations: music, theater, youth work. Address: Saint Anthony Shrine 100 Arch St Boston MA 02110-1111 Home Phone: 617-542-6440; Office Phone: 617-542-6440. Personal E-mail: magsofm@aol.com.

MAGAOAY, MICHAEL Y., state representative; b. Waialua, Hawaii, Aug. 13, 1953; m. Felimar C. Visaya; children: Chanel, Michael. BEE, U. of Hawaii, 1976. Chief elec. engr., estimator, project mgr. George S. Okano Elec. Contracting Corp., 1976—86; mgr., chief engr. of facilities and bldg. svcs. Queen's Med. Ctr., 1986—89; dir. engring. and sales Am. Techs., Inc., 1989—94; project mgr., estimator Am. Electric Co., 1994—96; sr. project engr. A-1 A-lectrician, Inc., 1997—. Chairperson St. Michael's Sch. Bd., Waialua, Hawaii, 1995—98; elected mem. C. of C. of Hononlulu Neighborhood Bd. #27, 1998, 2000, chmn., 1999—2000; pres., bd. dirs. Aloha Ke Akua HS, 1996—; mem. pastoral coun. St. Michael's Ch., 1995—98; corp. bd. mem. Cath. Charities, 1998—2003. Mem.: Engring. Alumni Assn. (treas. 1992, sec. 1993, v.p. 1994, pres. 1995, bd. dirs. 2003—), Hawaii Soc. of Hosp. Engrs. (pres. 1989), IEEE, Mililani Lions Club (1st v.p. 1994, pres. 1995, 2d v.p. 1993, 3d v.p. 1992). Democrat. Office: State Capitol Rm 418 415 S Beretania St Honolulu HI 96813 E-mail: repmagaoay@Capitol.hawaii.gov.

MAGARGEE, W(ILLIAM) SCOTT, III, lawyer; b. Abington, Pa., Sept. 3, 1940; m. Annette Bruno, (dec.); children: Scott, Todd, Ashley. AB, Princeton U., 1962; LLB, Yale U., 1966. Bar: Pa. 1966, U.S. Dist. Ct. (ea. dist.) Pa. 1966, U.S. Tax Ct. 1973. Assoc. Dechert LLP, Phila., 1966-75, ptnr., 1975—2005, of counsel, 2006—. Bd. dirs. United Way Southeastern Pa., 2006—, CC Phila. Found., pres., 2000—04. Fellow Am. Coll. Employee Benefits Counsel; mem. ABA (sect. taxation, real estate, probate, trust law), Phila. Bar Assn., Princeton Club Phila., Princeton Univ. Alumni Coun. (chmn. 1985-87), Phila. Club, Glassan Club. Office: Dechert LLP Cira Ctr 2929 Arch St Philadelphia PA 19104

MAGARIEL, DALE L., law librarian; b. St. Louis, Dec. 4, 1951; d. David Lee and Carol Hart; m. Larry K. Magariel, Jan. 8, 1972. BS in Libr. Mgmt., Park U., 1977. Law libr. Morrison, Hecker, Curtis, Kuder & Parrish, Kansas City, Mo., 1977—81; dir. libr. svcs. Stinson Morrison Hecker LLP, Kansas City, Mo., 1983—. Office: Stinson Morrison Hecker LLP 1201 Walnut Ste 2900 Kansas City MO 64106 E-mail: dmagariel@stinsonmoheck.com.

MAGAW, JOHN W., former federal agency administrator; b. Columbus, Ohio, 1935; m. Helen Mahley; 5 children. BA in Edn., Otterbein Coll., 1957. Patrolman State of Ohio, Columbus, 1958-66; joined US Secret Svc., US Dept. Treasury, Columbus, 1967, spl. agt., 1967, head protection for U.S. President and First Lady Washington, 1986—92, dir., 1992-93, Bur. Alcohol, Tobacco & Firearms, US Dept. Justice, Washington, 1993—99; spl. advisor to dir. Fed. Emergency Mgmt. Agy, Washington, 1999—2001, acting dep. dir., 2001, acting dir., 2001, acting exec. dir., Office Nat. Preparedness, 2001—02; under sec. for security U.S. Dept. Transp., Washington, 2002. Mem. Homeland Security Advisory Coun., 2006—. Bd. trustees Otterbein Coll., Westerville, Ohio. Recipient Presdl. Rank Meritorious award, 1991, 1999, Presdl. Rank Disting. award, 1995. Mem. Fed. Investigators Assn., Internat. Assn. Chiefs of Police (exec. com. adv. com. for internat. policy).

MAGAZINE, ALAN HARRISON, association executive, consultant; b. Cambridge, Mass., May 16, 1944; s. Arnold Lloyd and Ruth Magazine; m. June Ann O'Donohue, June 20, 1971 (div. Feb. 1984); children: Sarah Elizabeth, David Michael; m. Cynthia Louise Cordiner, Aug. 30, 1984. BA, Monmouth Coll., 1966; MPA, Kent State U., 1968; PhD, U. Md., 1976. Sr. cons. Real Estate Rsch. Corp., Washington, 1969-72; exec. dir. Nat. Ctr. for Pub. Svc. Internships, Washington, 1972-75; nat. policy coord. Internat. City Mgmt. Assn., Washington, 1973-76; dep. asst. dir. U.S. Commn. on Fed. Paperwork, Washington, 1976-78; dir. office of intergovernmental rels. EPA, Washington, 1978-81; dir. Bus.-Higher Edn. Forum, Washington, 1981-86; pres. Coun. on Competitiveness adv. com. Congl. Tech. Policy Task Force, 1986-89; adv. bd. George Mason U. Ctr. Conflict Resolution, 1986-89; pres. Health Industry Mfgs. Assn., 1990-99; cons. in field, 1999—2001; sr. advisor Coun. on Competitiveness, 1999—2003; prin., sr. advisor New Economy Strategies, 2003—04. Bd. dir. Dickinson Coll., Clark Ctr. Pub. Policy, Congrl. Econ. Leadership Inst., Healthcare Tech. Inst. Bd. Advisors, Sunrise Techs. Internat., Inc., Eyetel Corp., PLC Med. Inc., Innotech, USA; mem. adv. bd. Brookings Inst. Ctr. Econ. Progress and Employment, 1986-89; mem. U.S. China Joint Commn. on Commerce and Trade, 1996-97 Author: Environmental Management in Local Government, 1977. Bd. dir. Met. Washington Coun. of Govts., 1972-79; mem. Fairfax County Bd. Suprs., Va., 1972-79; chmn. No. Va. Transp. Commn., 1974-75; mem. No. Va. Planning Dist. Commn., Fairfax, 1976-79; mem. Dickinson Coll. Parents Coun., 1994-98, bd. dir. Clark Ctr. for the Study of Contemporary Issues. With USAFR, 1968-71. Ford Found. fellow, 1970-71. Democrat. Jewish. Avocation: photography.

MAGAZINER, ELLIOT ALBERT, musician, conductor, educator; b. Springfield, Mass., Dec. 25, 1921; m. Sari Fromkin; 2 children. Student, Nat. Orch. Assn., 1937-40, Princeton U., 1943, Juilliard School of Music, 1946-50. Music dir., prof. music Manhattanville Coll., Purchase, NY, 1970—. Faculty Westchester Conservatory Music, Summit Music Festival, 2001. Debut: Town Hall, NYC, 1952; staff artist, concertmaster CBS-TV and Radio; Networks: condrs. Reiner, Ansermet, Beecham, Stokowski; condr., sr. violin instr. Westchester Conservatory of Music; vis. condr. Dubuque Symphony; soloist N.Y. Philharm. Symphony, Symphony of the Air, Kol Visrael, symphonies in Chgo., Ft. Myers, Dubuque, York, St. Petersburg, Lincoln Ctr., NYC, 2002; recitals in N.Y.C., Washington, Detroit, Amsterdam, Paris, Jerusalem; star of CBS-TV, The Violin. Recs.: Charles Ives Sonata #2, Charles Ives Trio (with Frank Glazer and David Weber); Vivaldi Concerto in C and Concerto in B (with orchestre Symphonique de Paris); conductor Westchester All County Festival Orch. Mem. AAUP, N.Y. TV Musicians (pres.), CBS Musicians Fund (sec.) Avocation: collecting unique and ancient instruments. Home: 250 Garth Rd Apt 2b3 Scarsdale NY 10583-3954 Office: Manhattanville Coll 2900 Purchase St Purchase NY 10577-2131 Office Phone: 914-694-2200 ext 6267.

MAGAZINER, FRED THOMAS, lawyer; b. Phila., July 4, 1947; s. Henry Jonas and Reba (Henken) M.; m. Phyllis Heller, June 28, 1970; children: Daniel, Andrew. BA, Columbia U., 1969, JD, 1976. Bar: Pa., U.S. Dist. Ct. (ea. dist.) Pa., U.S. Ct. Appeals (3rd cir.), U.S. Claims Ct. Law clk. to judge Max Rosenn U.S. Ct. Appeals (3rd cir.), Phila., 1976-77; assoc. Dechert, Price & Rhoads, Phila., 1977-84, ptnr., 1984—. Mem. ABA, Pa. Bar Assn., Phila. Bar Assn., Am. Law Inst. Democrat. Jewish. Home: 1021 W Cliveden St Philadelphia PA 19119-3702 Home Phone: 215-849-7009; Office Phone: 215-994-2587. Business E-Mail: fred.magaziner@dechert.com.

MAGAZINER, HENRY JONAS, architect, writer; b. Phila., Sept. 13, 1911; s. Louis and Selma (Jonas) M.; m. Reba Henken, June 19, 1938; children: Ellen Louise (Mrs. Alan I. Widiss), Fred Thomas. BArch, U. Pa., 1936. Cert. Nat. Coun. Arch. and Registration Bds. Draftsman Phila. City Planning Project, 1936-37; draftsman Louis Magaziner (Architect), Phila., 1937-39, architect, 1946-48; chief Architects' Squad, Day & Zimmermann, Inc., Burlington, Iowa, 1940-41; architect Albert Kahn (Architect), Detroit, 1942; designer Wright Aero. Corp., Wood Ridge, N.J., 1943-45; ptnr. Louis & Henry Magaziner, Phila., 1948-56; architect, planner pvt. practice, 1956-72; regional hist. architect, archtl. historian Mid-Atlantic region Nat. Pk. Svc., Phila., 1972-87; pvt. practice architecture, 1987—. Archtl. adviser Phila. Hist. Commn., 1970-75, mem. archtl. com., 1979-85, chmn. archtl. com., 1972-75. Author: The Golden Age of Ironwork, 2000, Our Liberty Bell, 2007. Mem. Carpenters' Co. of City and County of Phila., mem. mng. com. historic Carpenters' Hall, 2000-02; v.p. Phila. Health and Welfare Coun., 1957-61, Phila. chpt. Victorian Soc. Am., 1975; v.p. city planning Germantown Comty. Coun., 1957-62; bd. dirs. Downtown Children's (day care) Ctr., 1956-73, v.p., 1960-61; bd. dirs. Allens Ln. Art Ctr., 1945-67, Neighborhood Ctr. Phila., 1956-74, Hist. Soc. Pa., 1970-74, Chestnut Hill Hist. Soc., 1970-80, Phila. chpt. Assn. for Preservation Tech., 1991-98, Clean Air Coun., 1980-92, Center City Residents Assn., 1995-96; bd. dirs. Maxwell Mansion Mus., pres., 1964-67; trustee Stewardsom Meml. Fellowship in Arch., 1958-90. Recipient Presdl. award for Excellence in Design for the Govt., 1988, James Biddle award Preservation Alliance for Greater Phila., 1999; named to Germantown Hall of Fame, 1994. Fellow AIA (mem. com. on hist. resources, John Harbeson award 2000); mem. ASTM (mem. com. on hist. preservation stds. 1981-90), Am. Inst. Conservation, Assn. for Preservation Tech., Ea. Nat. Pk. and Monument Assn., Fellows in Am. Studies (pres. 1983-84), Nat. Trust for Hist. Preservation, Soc. Archtl. Historians (bd. dirs. 1977-80, mem. editl. bd. 58 vol. Buildings of the United States 1992-98), Bldg. Conservation Internat., Victorian Soc. Am., T-Square Atelier (pres. 1963-65), Pa. Soc. Architects, Pa. Acad. Fine Arts, Libr. Co. Phila., Sierra Club, Athenaeum of Phila., Preservation Action. Home: 2 Franklin Town Blvd Apt 2404 Philadelphia PA 19103-1237 Office Fax: 215-545-8397. *I do hope that we can pass on to future generations a prejudice-free America having a natural environment without pollution and a man-made environment with its best elements both preserved and appreciated. Achieving these objectives is an unending struggle but one certainly worth winning. God willing, I expect to continue to fight for these ends.*

MAGBOUL, MAGBOUL M., anesthesiologist, educator; MBBS, U. Khartoum, Sudan, 1974. Cons. anesthetist, asst. prof. King Saud U., Riyadh, Saudi Arabia, 1998—2001; asst. prof. U. Iowa, Iowa City, 2001—.

Mem.: Royal Coll. Surgeons and Physcians Ireland. Achievements include invention of magboul laryngoscope. Office: Univ Iowa 200 Hawkins Dr Iowa City IA 62242 Business E-Mail: m-magboul@uiowa.edu. E-mail: mmagboul@gmail.com.

MAGDEN, RONALD EARNEST, education educator; b. Aug. 30, 1926; BA, U. Idaho, Moscow, 1949, MA, 1955; PhD, U. Wash., Seattle, 1964. Tchr. Am. history Orofino HS, Idaho, 1949—51, Renton HS, Wash., 1954—63; tchr. trainer Seattle U., 1962—64; chmn. social sci. divsn. Tacoma CC, 1964—83; tchr. trainer U. Zagreb, Croatia, 1972, SUNY, Buffalo, 1972. Co-author: The Working Waterfront, 1983, Harts Lake School: Symbol of Pioneer Education, 1984, To Live in Dignity: Histories of Unions, 1985, More Voices, New Stories: Buddhism Comes to Seattle, 2002; author: A History of Seattle Waterfront Workers, 1991, The Working Longshoreman, 1991, Furusato: A History of the Tacoma and Pierce County Japanese, 1989; contbr. articles to profl. publs. Vol. tchr. McNeil Island Fed. Penitentiary, 1967—77, Women's Treatment Ctr., 1978—83. Scholar, Am. Coun. Learned Socs., 1960, Asian Soc., 1961, NEH, 1966—67, Civil Liberties Pub. Edn., 2001; fellow in history, Nat. Def. Act, 1962. Mem.: Tacoma Hist. Soc. (pres. 2000—05). Mailing: Tacoma Hist Soc 3703 N 22d St Tacoma WA 98406-5306

MAGDON-ISMAIL, MALIK, computer science professor; US, 1989; s. Hamim and Fathima Magdon-Ismail; m. Fathima Zainab Muhsin, July 17, 1999; children: Zain, Deen. BS summa cum laude, Yale U., New Haven, Conn., 1992; PhD, Calif. Inst. of Tech., Pasadena, 1998. Postdoctoral rsch. scholar Calif. Inst. of Tech., Pasadena, 1998—2000; prof. computer sci. Rensselaer Poly. Inst., Troy, NY, 2000—. CEO, chief tech. officer Swooge LLC, Albany, NY, 2006—; chief tech. officer Gold Finger Mgmt. LLC, Hong Kong, 2003—. Contbr. articles to profl. jours. Recipient Wilts prize for best PhD thesis in elec. engring., Calif. Inst. of Tech., 1998, Grant Funding awards to study social comm. networks, NSF, ONR, KDD, 2003, 2004, 2005, 2006. Mem.: IEEE, Assn. for Computing Machinary, Phi Beta Kappa. Achievements include patents pending for Remote Caller ID Projection Device. Avocations: bridge, squash, badminton, tennis, travel. Office: Rensselaer Poly Inst 110 8th St Troy NY 12180 Office Phone: 518-276-4857. Office Fax: 518-276-4033. E-mail: magdon@cs.rpi.edu.

MAGE, ROSE GOLDMAN, immunologist, educator; d. Abraham and Augusta (Wagner) Goldman; m. Michael Gordon Mage, June 12, 1955; children: Dan, Gene, Anita. BS, Cornell U., Ithaca, NY, 1956; PhD, Columbia U., NYC, 1963. Postdoctoral fellow NIAID, NIH, Bethesda, Md., 1963—65, career investigator, 1965—, sect. chief, 1988—. Adj. prof. George Washinton U., Washington, 1976—. Contbr. chapters to books, more than 195 articles to scholarly and profl. jours. Fellow AAAS; mem. Am. Assn. Immunologists, Am. Soc. Microbiology. Office Phone: 301-496-6113. Personal E-mail: rmage@comcast.net.

MAGEE, ALAN, artist; b. Newtown, Pa., May 26, 1947; s. Richard Forrest and Rena (Cook) M.; m. Monika Gabriele Ruth Siekmann, Jan. 4, 1969. Student, Tyler Sch. of Art, 1965-66, Phila. Coll. Art, 1967-69. One-person shows include Allport Assocs. Gallery, Larkspur, Calif., 1978, 81, Clark Gallery, Lincoln, Mass., 1979, Staempfli Gallery, N.Y.C., 1980, 82, 90, FIAC Grand Palais, Paris, 1983, Norton Gallery and Sch. of Art, West Palm Beach, Fla., 1983, San Jose Mus. Art, 1983, Newport Art Mus., 1984, Farnsworth Art Mus., Rockland, Maine, 1984, Ark. Art Ctr., Columbus Mus. of Art, Ohio Chgo. Art Inst., U. Maine, 1985, Fresno Art Ctr., 1985, L.A., 1986, Schmidt-Bingham Gallery, N.Y.C., 1986, 88, 89, Allport Assocs. Gallery, San Francisco, 1986, Joan Whitney Payson Gallery at Westbrook Coll., Portland, Maine, 1990, Staempfli Gallery, NY, 1990, Farnsworth Art Mus., 1991, James A. Michener Art Mus., Bucks County, Pa., 1991, Ringling Sch. Art & Design, Sarasota, Fla., 1992, Fine Arts Ctr. at Cheekwood, Nashville, 1992, Edith Caldwell Gallery, San Francisco, 1992, 93, 95, 96, 97, Edith Lambert Gallery, Santa Fe, 1995, Hollis Taggart Gallery, N.Y.C., 2000, Berlin Philharm. Hall, 2000, Forum Gallery, L.A., 2001, 02, Forum Gallery, N.Y., 2003, James A. Michener Art Mus., 2003; 30-Yr. Retrospective traveling exhbn. James A. Michener Art Mus., 2003, Farnsworth Art Mus., 2004, Mus. of Tex. Tech U., 2004, Frye Art Mus., 2005, Luxemburg Embassy, Berlin, 2005, Forum Gallery, NY, 2006, Goethe Inst., NY, 2006, Sardoni Art Mus., Pa., 2006, Galerie Raab, Berlin, 2007, Ctr. for Maine Contemporary Art, Rockport, 2007, Forum Gallery, LA, 2007; group shows include Farnsworth Art Mus., Rockland, Maine, 1985, Akron (Ohio) Mus. of Art, 1985, Maine Coast Artists, Rockport, 1985, Ark. Art Ctr, Little Rock, 1985, Smithsonian Instn., Nat. Air and Space Mus., Washington, 1985, Wunderlich & Co., N.Y.C., 1986, Light Gallery, N.Y.C., 1986, Schmidt-Bingham Gallery, N.Y.C., 1986, 88, Mus. Fine Arts, Springfield, 1986, Butler Inst. Am. Art, Youngstown, Ohio, 1987, Am. Acad. and Inst. Arts and Letters, N.Y.C., 1987, Nat. Invitational Drawing Exhbn., 1989, Staempfli Gallery, N.Y.C., 1990, Albrecht Art Mus., St. Joseph, 1990, NAD, N.Y.C., 1990, Edith Caldwell Gallery, San Francisco, 1993, 94, 95, 96, Nora Eccles Harrison Mus. Art, Logan Utah, 1992, Portland Mus. of Art, 1993, Creiger Dane Gallery, Boston, 1995, Phila. Art Mus., 1995, Forum Gallery, N.Y.C, 1996, Nat. Mus. Am. Art, Washington, 1997, Hollis Taggart Gallery, N.Y., 1998, Hackett, Feedman Gallery, San Francisco, 1998, Portland Mus. Art, 1998, Farnsworth Art Mus., 1998, Art Inst. Chgo., 1999, Katonah Mus. Art, 1999, U. Rochester, 1999, O.P. FotoGalery, Hong Kong, 1999, others; prin. commd. works include portrait of Senate Majority Leader George Mitchell 2003 and Alan Magee, Maine, 2002, Tapestry for Riverview Psychiat. Ctr., Maine, and others; commns. include mural U. Maine, 1997, Maine State House, 1999; pub. collections include Farnsworth Art Mus., Rockland, Arco Collection, Lucasfilm, Bank of Japan, Mobil Oil, Janss Collection, L.A., Achenbach Collection, Palace of the Legion of Honour, San Francisco, Art Inst. Chgo., Portland (Maine) Mus. of Art, Rutgers U. Art Mus.; author: Stones and Other Works, 1987, Alan Magee 1981-91, Archive, Monotypes, Alan Magee, 2000, 03, Alan Magee - paintings, sculpture, graphics, 2003, Alan Magee: Maine Master, 2003, Time Pieces, 2006, Beyond Recognition: The Art of Alan Magee, 2006, Alan Magee: From the Underground River, 2007, (with Barry Lopez) Resistance, 2005; contbr. articles to profl. jours.; TV: Visions of Darkness and Light, 1988. Recipient Richard and Hinda Rosenthal Found. award N.Y.C., Am. Book award, Nevelson award, 1982; The Leo Meissner prize NAD, 1990. Personal E-mail: info@alanmagee.com.

MAGEE, CHARLES THOMAS, international consultant, retired diplomat; b. Clifton Forge, Va., Mar. 6, 1932; s. Charles Thomas and Dorothy Elizabeth (McPherson) M.; m. Maideh Mazda, May 30, l959; 1 child, Maya. BA, Harvard U., 1953. Vice consul Am. Consulate, Windsor, Can., 1961-63; polit.-mil. affairs officer Am. Emb., Paris, 1964-66; polit. officer Soviet desk Dept. State, 1966-68; adv. Russian language and area studies Garmisch, Germany, 1968—69; polit. officer Am. Embassy, Moscow, 1969—71; dep. dir. for ops. Exec. Secretariat Dept. State, Washington, 1971-72, officer-in-charge French desk, 1972-74; chief internal polit. affairs, exec. asst. to amb. Am. Embassy, Paris, 1974—77, dep. chief mission Sofia, Bulgaria, 1977-80; chief jr. officer div. Bur. Pers. Dept. State, 1980-82, fgn. svc. insp., 1982-83; cons. gen. U.S. Consulate Gen., Leningrad, USSR, 1984-86; spl. asst. internat. affairs to mayor City of San Francisco, 1986-87; dir. Russian lang. ops. U.S. Del. to Negotiations on Nuclear and Space Arms with USSR, Geneva, 1988-91; sr. program officer for Russia Citizens Democracy Corps, Washington, 1992—93; amb. mission to Latvia Orgn. Security and Coop. Europe, 1994-97, amb. mission to Ukraine, 1998-99. Ofcl. election observer, Ukraine, 1998, 2002, 04, 06, Russia, 2000, 03, 04, Latvia, 2002, Azerbaijan, 2005; polling supr., Bosnia and Herzegovina, 2000; head Orgn. for Security and Coop. in Europe election observation mission to Macedonia, 2000, Azerbaijan, Moldova, Bulgaria, 2001; field rep Census Bur., 2005; cons. Acad. Arrangements Abroad, N.Y.C., 1987—, Dept. of State, 1989—, Seabourn Cruise Line, San Francisco, 1989-92, Acad. Travel Abroad, Washington, 1995; asst. prof. Dept Navy, 1959-61. Active duty USN, 1953—59, lt. comdr. USNR. Mem. Am. Fgn. Svc. Assn., Harvard Club. Home and Office: 4518 Albemarle St NW Washington DC 20016-2016 Home Phone: 202-966-7038. Personal E-mail: ctmagee32@aol.com.

MAGEE, CHRISTOPHER L., systems engineer; PhD in Metallurgy and Materials Sci., Carnegie Inst. Tech. Exec. dir. Ford/MIT Strategic Tech. Partnership MIT, Cambridge, prof., Engring. Systems Divsn. Lectr. in field; prof. MIT. Ford Tech. fellow, 1996. Mem. NAE. Achievements include vehicle design, concepts and processes, systems engineering, application of computer-aided engineering and vehicle crashworthiness. Office: Engring Sys Div MIT Bldg E40-293 77 Massachusetts Ave Cambridge MA 02139-4307 Fax: 617-452-3760. E-mail: cmagee@MIT.edu.

MAGEE, DONALD EDWARD, retired national park service administrator; b. Trenton, NJ, Sept. 24, 1937; s. Donald A. and Anna C. (Bocskowics) M.; m. Linda Kimball, June 27, 1964; children: Kevin, Bonnie Magee Burch, Gale. BS in Forestry Mgmt., U. Mass., 1964. Pk. ranger Bryce Canyon (Utah) Nat. Pk., 1966-68; area mgr. Sunset Crater Nat. Monument, Flagstaff, Ariz., 1968-73; mgmt. analyst Nat. Capital Region, Washington, 1973-80; supt. Stones River Nat. Battlefield, Murfreesboro, Tenn., 1980-89, USS Ariz. Meml., Pearl Harbor, Hawaii, 1989-95; ret., 1995. With USN, 1956-58. Recipient Excellence of Svc. award Dept. of Interior, 1991. Home: 95-457 Kaukoe St Mililani HI 96789-1865

MAGEE, JOHN FRANCIS, research and development company executive; b. Bangor, Maine, Dec. 3, 1926; s. John Henry and Marie (Frawley) M.; m. Dorothy Elma Hundley, Nov. 19, 1949; children: Catherine Anne, John Hundley, Andrew Stephen. AB, Bowdoin Coll., 1947; MS, U. Maine, 1952; MBA, Harvard U., 1948; LLD, Bowdoin Coll., 1996. With Arthur D. Little, Inc., Cambridge, Mass., 1950-98, v.p., 1961-72, pres., 1972-86, chief exec. officer, 1974-88, chmn., 1986-98, also dir., 1968-98. Author: Physical Distribution Systems, 1967, Industrial Logistics: Analysis and Management of Physical Supply and Distribution Systems, 1968, (with D. M. Boodman) Production Planning and Inventory Control, 1968; (with W. Capacino and W. Rosenfield) Modern Logistics Management, 1985. Trustee Emerson Hosp., Thompson Island Outward Bound Edn. Ctr., chair, 1995—2000; emeritus trustee Bowdoin Coll.; hon. trustee Woods Hole Oceanographic Instn.; chmn. trustees Bowdoin Coll., 1990—94; overseer emeritus Mus. Sci., Boston. Officer USN, 1944—46. Recipient Disting. Leadership award, MIT, 1977. Fellow: Inst. for Ops. Rsch. and Mgmt. Sci., Phi Beta Kappa (life); mem.: Am. Soc. Metals (disting. life mem.), Inst. Mgmt. Scis. (pres. 1971—72), Ops. Rsch. Soc. Am. (pres. 1966—67, Kimball medal 1978), Comml. Club (pres. 1992—94), Somerset Club (Boston), The Country Club (Brookline, Mass.), Concord (Mass.) Country Club (gov. 1971—74), Phi Kappa Psi. Avocation: painting. Personal E-mail: magjfmagee@verizon.net.

MAGEE, KATHLEEN S., foundation executive; b. NJ; m. William Preston Magee, Jr.; 5 children. BSN, Coll. Misericordia, Pa.; MEd, U. Md.; MSW, Norfolk State U. Nurse, social worker; co-founder (with William P. Magee, Jr.) Operation Smile, 1982, pres., bd. dir. Featured guest Montel Williams, guest appearances Dateline NBC, CBS Sunday Morning, 48 Hours, NBC Nightly News. Bd. gov. World of Children; adv. bd. World Healing Inst.; founder, organizer World Journey of Hope, 1999. Co-recipient Common Wealth award disting. svc., 2001; named to Mad. Mission Hall of Fame, 2004; recipient Conrad N. Hilton Humanitarian prize, 1996, Servants of Peace award, 1997, Golden Plate award, Am. Acad. Achievement, 1999, Kellogg's Hannah Neil World of Children award, 1999, Lifetime Volunteer Achievement award, Operation Smile, 2005. Office: Operation Smile 6453 Tidewater Dr Norfolk VA 23509

MAGEE, STEPHEN PAT, economics professor, finance professor; b. Wichita, Kans., Mar. 17, 1943; s. Lawrence Patrick and Edna Willard (Brock) M.; m. Naneska Nall, Aug. 20, 1965 (div. Dec. 1987); children: Christopher Sean Patrick, Theodore Parker; m. Frances Jean Toepperwein, July 28, 1988. BA in Econs., Tex. Tech. U., 1965, MA in Econs., 1966; PhD in Econs., MIT, 1969. Asst. prof. U. Calif., Berkeley, 1969-71; assoc. prof. U. Chgo., 1971-76; economist The White House, Washington, 1972-73; rsch. fellow Brookings Insts., Washington, 1973-74; prof. fin. and econs. U. Tex., Austin, 1976—, chmn. fin., 1980-84, McDermott prof., 1980-84, Fred H. Moore prof., 1984-92, Charles and Sarah Seay prof., 1992-94; Bayless/Enstar Corp. chairholder, 1994—. Econ. adv. bd. U.S. Sec. Commerce, Washington, 1978-79, NSF, 1979; expert witness Mesa Petroleum, Avis Rent-a-Car, El Paso Natural Gas, Kodak, Proctor & Gamble, AB Dick, Exxon; vis. prof. bus. U. Chgo., 1990-91, 1997; expert effects of lawyers on U.S. economy and corp. litigation damages, securities, energy, microeconomics, intellectual property and internat. econs.; lectr. in field. Author: International Trade (transl. to Japanese, Chinese, Korean), 1980, Black Hole Tariffs and Endogenous Policy Theory, 1989; mem. editl. bd. Rev. Econs. and Stats., 1972-79, Jour. Internat. Econs., 1977-79, Econs. and Politics, 1988-94, Rev. Internat. Econs., 1992-94; contbr. articles to profl. jours. including Fortune Mag., Wall St. Jour. Capt. US Nat. Soccer Champions, 1999—2006. Grantee NSF, 1972-77; recipient Joe Beasley Tchg. award U. Tex. Grad. Sch. Bus., 1980, 2000, Outstanding Career Rsch. Contbn. award, 1990, named TopCore MBA prof., 1986. Avocations: soccer, drag racing, photography. Home: 1801 Lanaca St Austin TX 78701 Office Phone: 512-656-6666. Business E-Mail: magee@mail.utexas.edu.

MAGEE, THOMAS HENRY, radiologist, educator; b. Newport, RI, Nov. 26, 1958; s. Francis Robert and Anne Louise (Moriarty) M.; m. Christina Marie (Lapolla), June 7, 1987. BA, Wesleyan Univ., 1977-81; MD, NY. Med. Coll., 1982-86. Diplomate Am. Bd. Radiology. Staff radiologist Bethesda Naval Hosp., Md., 1991-94; asst. prof. medicine Uniformed Svc. Sch. of Med., Bethesda, Md., 1991-94, Kans. U. Sch. of Med., Kans. City, Kans., 1994—; staff radiologist Menorah Med. Pk., Overland Pk., Kans., 1994—; asst. prof. radiology U. Mo., Kans. City, Mo., 1997—2006; clin. prof. radiology U. Miami, 2006—. Pres. Rockhill Radiology, 1999; bd. examiner Am. Bd. Radiology; reviewer prof. jours., Am. Coll. Radiology. Contbr. articles to profl. jours. including Radiology, Jour. of Computer Assisted Tomography, Am. Jour. Roentgenology. Lt. comdr. USNR, 1991-94. Recipient: Jonas N. Muller Award, NY Med. Coll., 1986. Fellow Am. Coll. Radiology; mem. Am. Roentegen Ray Soc., Radiol. Soc. N.Am. (moderator, cert. of merit 1990); Kansas City Roentegen Ray Soc. (pres.), Internat. Skeletal Soc., Am. Bd. Radiology (bd. examiner, 2005). Avocations: stamp collecting/philately, tennis. Home: 185 Lanternback Island Dr Satellite Beach FL 32937-4704 Office: Neuroskeletal Imaging Melbourne FL Personal E-mail: tmageerad@cfl.rr.com.

MAGEE, THOMAS HUGH, lawyer; b. Rochester, NY, Aug. 15, 1943; s. Edward Charles and Jane Kathleen (Cranmer) M.; m. Judith Joy Stone, Oct. 2, 1982; 1 child, Michael Julian. BSME, U. Rochester, NYC, 1965; JD, Syracuse U., 1973. Bar: NJ 1974, US Dist. Ct. NJ 1974, US Ct. Appeals (DC cir.) 1975, NY 1981, US Supreme Ct. 1978, US Patent and Trademark Office. Sr. patent counsel RCA Corp., Princeton, NJ, 1973-86, GE/RCA Licensing Operation, Princeton, 1986-88; corp. counsel E.I. duPont de Nemours & Co., Wilmington, Del., 1988—. Lt. USN, 1965-70, Capt. USNR (ret.), 1991. Decorated Navy commendation medal with combat V Vietnam. Mem. Am. Intellectual Property Law Assn. (com. chair 1974—), Phila. Intellectual Property Law Assn. (com. chmn. 1974—), NJ Patent Law Assn., Justinian hon. law soc., Phi Alpha Delta. Republican. Presbyterian. Avocations: tennis, handball, coin collecting/numismatics. Home: 721 Severn Rd Wilmington DE 19803-1724 Office: E I duPont de Nemours & Co Barley Mill Plz BMP 25-1372 Wilmington DE 19880 Office Phone: 302-892-0795. Business E-Mail: thomas.h.magee@usa.dupont.com.

MAGEE, WILLIAM PRESTON, JR., plastic surgeon; b. NJ; m. Kathleen S. Magee; 5 children. BS, Mt. St. Mary's Coll., Maryland; DDS, U. Md.; MD, George Washington U. Resident gen. surgery U. Va. Med. Sch.; resident plastic surgery Ea. Va. Grad. Sch. Medicine; pvt. practice Norfolk, Va.; co-founder (with Kathleen S. Magee) Operation Smile, 1982, CEO; co-dir. Inst. Craniofacial and Plastic Surgery Children's Hosp. of King's Daughters, chmn. Plastic Surgery Dept.; assoc. prof. plastic surgery Ea. Va. Med. Sch. Contbr. chapters to books, articles to med. jours.; guest appearances NBC Nightly News, Dateline NBC, Fox News, Leeza, The Rosie O'Donnell Show, Hour of Power, 48 Hours, CBS Sunday Morning, Touched by an Angel. Bd. dirs. Operation Smile; founder, organizer World Journey of Hope, 1999; bd. dirs. talksurgery.com. Co-recipient Common Wealth award disting. svc., 2001; named to Med. Mission Hall of Fame, 2003; recipient Conrad N. Hilton Humanitarian prize, 1996, Servants of Peace award, 1997, Golden Plate award, Am. Acad. Achievement, 1999, Frank Annunzio award, Christopher Columbus Fellowship Found., 2002. Mem.: Am. Soc. Plastic Surgeons (Disting. Svc. award 1998), Va. Soc. Plastic and Reconstructive Surgeons (pres. 1991—93), AMA (Pride in the Profession award 2000). Office: Operation Smile 6435 Tidewater Dr Norfolk VA 23509

MAGENHEIM, MARK JOSEPH, physician, epidemiologist, educator; b. Deland, Fla., Nov. 1, 1947; s. Milton David and Dolores Ella (Raithel) M. BA cum laude, Wash. U., 1969; MPH, Yale U., 1971; MD with honors, McMaster U., 1974. Diplomate Am. Bd. Preventive Medicine, Am. Bd. Pub. Health, Am. Bd. Family Medicine. Health officer, prof. Oreg. State U., Corvallis, 1976-78; prof. cmty. health U. Sierra Leone, Freetown, West Africa, 1978-81; asst. prof. McMaster U., Hamilton, Ont., Canada, 1978-83; asst. state health officer State of Fla., Tallahassee, 1989-91; health officer, dir. County Health Dept., Sarasota, Fla., 1984—2003; med. dir. Hospice of S.W. Fla., Sarasota, 1994-99; CEO, med. dir. Suncoast Cmtys. Blood Bank, 2003—. Chair adv. com. HIV and STD prevention CDC, 1997—2000. Author, editor Clinics in Geriatric Medicine, 1986, (with others) Practice of Geriatrics, 1986; contbr. articles to profl. jours. Med. dir., instnl. rev. bd. Sarasota Meml. Hosp., 1992—. Recipient Surgeon Gen.'s medallion of excellence, USPHS, 1989, award of commendation, CDC, 1989, Leadership award, 1991—92, numerous grants. Fellow: Royal Soc. Tropical Medicine and Hygiene; mem.: Fla. Assn. Blood Banks (treas.), Fla. Soc. Preventive Medicine, Fla. Med. Assn. (Roy Baker Leadership award 2000), Fla. Pub. Health Assn., Fla. Pub. Health Leadership Inst., Pub. Health Leadership Soc. (chair 1993—95). Avocations: tennis, music, bicycling, international travel. Home: 4571 Robin Hood Trail W Sarasota FL 34232-2640 Office: Suncoast Communities Blood Bank 1760 Mound St Sarasota FL 34236 Office Phone: 941-954-1600 ext 1029. Personal E-mail: markomag@comcast.net. Business E-mail: mmagenheim@scbb.org.

MAGER, ARTUR, retired aerospace executive; b. Nieglowice, Poland, Sept. 21, 1919; arrived in U.S., 1939, naturalized, 1944; s. Herman and Ella (Kornbluh) M.; m. Phyllis R. Weisman, Aug. 19, 1942; 1 child, Ilana Gail. BS, U. Mich., 1943; MS, Case Inst. Tech., 1951; PhD in Aeros., Calif. Inst. Tech., 1953. Aero. rsch. scientist NASA Lewis Labs., Cleve., 1946-51; rsch. scientist Marquardt Corp., Van Nuys, Calif., 1954-60; dir. Nat. Engring. Sci. Co., Pasadena, Calif., 1960-61; dir. spacecraft scis. Aerospace Corp., El Segundo, Calif., 1961-64, gen. mgr. applied mechanics divsn., 1964-68, v.p., gen. mgr. engring. sci. ops., 1968-78, v.p. engring. group, 1978-82, cons., 1982—. Mem. BSD Re-entry Panel, 1961—63; mem. NASA com. missile and space vehicle aerodynamics, 1963—65; mem. adv. com. AFML, 1971—72; mem. NASA Adv. Coun., 1982—86; chmn. NASA Space Applications Adv. Com., 1982—86; mem. Aeros. and Space Engring. Bd. NRC, 1982—87; mem. Space Sta. Task Force NRC, 1983—87, mem. Shuttle Critically and Hazard Analysts Rev. Bd., 1986—88; mem. DSB NASP Task Force, 1987—88, AFSB Hypersonic Task Force, 1987—88. Contbr. articles to profl. jours. Mem. alumni fund coun. Calif. Inst. Tech., 1972—74; trustee West Coast U., 1980—92; mem. devel. disabilities bd. Area X, 1976—80, chmn., 1976—78; 1st v.p. Calif. Assn. Retarded, 1983—85; pres. Exceptional Children's Found., 1970—72; bd. councilors U. So. Calif. Sch. Engring., 1976—86. Recipient Disting. Alumni award, U. Mich., 1969, Golden Rule award, Calif. Assn. Retarded, 1977, 1989. Fellow: AAAS, AIAA (chmn. L.A. sect. 1967—68, bd. dirs. 1975—77, pres. 1980—81), Inst. Advanced Engring.; mem.: Nat. Acad. Engring., Technion Soc., Sigma Xi. Home and Office: 1353 Woodruff Ave Los Angeles CA 90024-5129 Personal E-mail: ap.mager1@verizon.net.

MAGER, EZRA PASCAL, investment company executive; b. NYC, Nov. 1, 1941; s. Harold and Naomi (Levinson) M.; m. Sarah Johnson, Mar. 25, 1964 9div.); 1 child, Emma Rachel; m. Reeva Starkman, May 14, 1972; children: Camilla Elizabeth, Michael Johanon. BA, Cornell U., 1963; MBA, Harvard, 1966. Successively v.p., sr. v.p., exec. v.p. and dir. Seiden & DeCuevas, Inc., NYC, 1966-73; exec. v.p., dir. Furman Selz Mager Dietz & Birney, Inc., NYC, 1973-90; vice chmn. United Auto Group, Inc., NYC, 1990-96, Cross Continent Auto Retailers, Inc., NYC, 1996-97, First Team Auto Corp., NYC, 1997-98; CEO EPM Advisory LLC, NYC, 1998—; pres. The Torrey Funds, 1998—2004. Trustee Baron de Hirsch Fund, The Textile Mus., Washington. Mem. N.Y. Soc. Security Analysts, Alpha Delta Phi. Clubs: Harvard (N.Y.C.). Democrat. Home: 141 E 72d St New York NY 10021-4315 Office: EPM Advisory LLC 509 Madison Ave Penthouse New York NY 10022 Office Phone: 212-223-2333. Business E-Mail: epmager@epmadvisory.com.

MAGERKO, MARGARET HARDY (MAGGIE), lumber company executive; b. Pitts., Dec. 7, 1965; d. Joseph Hardy; m. Peter Magerko. Student, W.Va. U. Pres. Nemacolin Woodlands Resort & Spa, 1987—, 84 Lumber Co., Eighty Four, Pa., 1994—. Named one of 400 Richest Ams., Forbes mag., 2006. Office: 84 Lumber Co 1019 Route 519 Eighty Four PA 15330 Business E-Mail: magerkom@84lumber.com.

MAGGIOLO, ALLISON JOSEPH, lawyer; b. New River, NC, Aug. 29, 1943; s. Allison and Florence Celeste (Vago) M. Cert., U. Paris-Sorbonne, 1965; AB, Brown U., 1966; JD, U. Louisville, 1975. Bar: Ky. 1976, U.S. Dist. Ct. (we. dist.) Ky. 1981. Ops. mgr., stockbroker Bache & Co., Louisville, 1970-73; ptnr. Reisz, Blackburn, Manly & Treitz, Louisville, 1976-78, Greenebaum Boone Treitz Maggiolo & Brown, Louisville, 1978-91, Wyatt, Tarrant & Combs, LLP, Louisville, 1991—. Workshop panelist Fin. Adv. Coun., 1994; panelist Seminar on Defaulted Bond Issues, 1987-89, Bond Counsel and the Corp. Trustee, 1990-92, Defaults and Workouts, 1993. Author: Indenture Trustee Liability and Defaulted Bond Issues, 1987, Minimizing Indenture Trustee Liability and Defaulted Bond Issues, 1991, Bond Default Resolution, 1993; co-author: The legal Aspects of Doing International Business in Kentucky, 1990. Mem. exec. com. St. Louis Com. Fgn. Rels., 1979—, chmn., 1991—96; bd. dirs. Ky. Show, Louisville, 1978—91, Ky. Opera, Louisville, 1978—91, mem. hon. coun., 1991—; bd. dirs. Glassworks Found., 2002—03. Decorated Bronze Star. Mem. Internat. Bar Assn., Nat. Assn. Bond Lawyers, Bond Attys. Workshop (planning com. 1991-93), Pendennis Club, Wynn Stay Club, Jefferson Club. Office: Wyatt Tarrant & Combs LLP PNC Plz Louisville KY 40202-2823

MAGGIPINTO, V. ANTHONY, lawyer; b. Tucson, Apr. 15, 1943; s. William Vito and Elizabeth Maria Maggipinto; m. Maria Teresa, Aug. 31,

1976; children: Marshall Albert Nicholas, Spencer William Jonathan. AB cum laude, Southampton Coll., 1970; JD, Fordham U., 1976. Bar: Fla. 1977, N.Y. 1978, U.S. Dist. Ct. (ea. and so. dists.) N.Y. 1979, U.S. Ct. Appeals (2d cir.) 1980; ordained deacon Cath. Ch., 2007. Asst. to pres. Interpub. Group of Cos., NYC, 1965-66; asst. dean of admission Southampton (N.Y.) Coll., 1971-73; investigative aide N.Y. State Com. on Jud. Conduct, NYC, 1974-76; asst. state atty. Dade County State Atty., Miami, Fla., 1977-78; asst. dist. atty. Suffolk Dist. Atty., Hauppage, N.Y., 1978-80; asst. county atty. Suffolk County Atty., Hauppauge, 1980-84; sole practice Riverhead and St. James, N.Y., 1982—. Mem. spl. coms. on discovery, civil litigation U.S. Dist. Ct. (ea. dist.) N.Y., Bklyn., 1983-90, 95—, arbitrator, 1986—, Civil Justice Reform Act adv. group, 1990-95, chair jury task force, 1993—, commendation U.S. Dist. Ct., 1997. Mem. appeals bd. SSS, 1982—2001, vice chmn., 1986—97, chmn., 1997—2001. With submarine svc. USN, 1961—65. Recipient Disting. Alumni award L.I. U., 1990. Mem.: Southampton Coll. Alumni Assn. (exec. com. 1997—2004, pres. 2001—02), Navy League (judge adv. L.I. coun. 1992—), U.S. Naval Inst., Fla. Bar Assn., Suffolk County Bar Assn., N.Y. State Bar Assn. (exec. com. real property sect. 1997—2002), Nissequogue Golf Club (counsel 1980—2004, bd. govs.). Republican. Roman Catholic. Avocations: hiking, horseback riding. Office: 1212 Roanoke Ave Riverhead NY 11901-2740

MAGGS, PETER BLOUNT, lawyer, educator; b. Durham, NC, July 24, 1936; s. Douglas Blount and Dorothy (Mackay) M.; m. Barbara Ann Widenor, Feb. 27, 1960; children: Bruce MacDowell, Gregory Eaton, Stephanie Ann, Katherine Ellen. AB, Harvard U., 1957, JD, 1961; postgrad. (exchange student), Leningrad State U., USSR, 1961-62. Bar: D.C. 1962. Research assoc. Law Sch. Harvard U., 1963-64; asst. prof. law U. Ill., 1964-67, assoc. prof., 1967-69, prof., 1969-88, William and Marie Corman prof., 1988-98, Peer & Sarah Pedersen prof., 1998—2002, acting dean, 1990, Clifford M. and Bette A. Carney chair in law, 2002—; dir. Rule of Law Program Washington, 1994. Fulbright lectr. Moscow State U., 1977; reporter Uniform Simplification of Land Transfers Act; vis. prof. George Washington U., 1998. Author: (with others) The Mandelstam File, 1996; co-translator Civil Code of the Russian Federation, translation, 2003, Civil Code of the Republic of Armenia, translation, 1999, Intellectual Property (in Russian), 2000, Internet and Computer Law, 2001, Trademark and Unfair Competition, 2002; designer talking computers for the blind. Fulbright rsch. scholar, Yugoslavia, 1967; Fulbright disting. chair, Trento, 2002; East-West Ctr. fellow, 1972, Guggenheim fellow, 1979. Mem. ABA, D.C. Bar, Am. Assn. Advancement Slavic Studies, Assn. Am. Law Schs., Am. Law Inst. (consultative group, UCC Article 2), Internat. Acad. Comparative Law. Office: U Ill Coll Law 504 E Pennsylvania Ave Champaign IL 61820-6909 Office Phone: 217-333-6711. E-mail: p-maggs@uiuc.edu.

MAGID, CREIGHTON (CHIP) REID, lawyer; b. Cedar Rapids, Iowa, Dec. 11, 1961; s. Frank N. and Marilyn (Young) M. AB, Princeton U., 1984; JD, U. Mich., 1987. Bar: Iowa 1987, Minn. 1987, Mont. 1988, U.S. Dist. Ct. Minn., U.S. Dist. Ct. (no. dist.) Iowa. Ptnr., trial, regulatory, tech. group Dorsey & Whitney PLLP, Mpls., 1987—, and co-chmn., products and tech. liability litig. group. Mem. Mpls. Rowing Club (pres. 1991-95). Avocation: rowing. Office: Dorsey & Whitney Ste 1500 50 S 6th St Minneapolis MN 55402-1498 Office Phone: 612-340-5661. Office Fax: 612-340-2868. Business E-Mail: magid.chip@dorsey.com.

MAGIDSON, JAY, statistician; b. Chgo., Mar. 18, 1947; s. Samuel and Shirley Arlene (Weininger) M.; m. Elizabeth Katherine Morgan, Oct. 26, 1976; children: Jeremy, Jenna. BA, U. Ill., 1969; MS in Bus., U. Wis., 1971; PhD in Mgmt., Northwestern U., 1976. Sr. analyst Ill. Bell Tel. Co., Chgo., 1971-72; sr. statistician Abt Assocs., Inc., Cambridge, Mass., 1976-81; founder, pres. Statis. Innovations, Inc., Belmont, Mass., 1981—. Presenter seminars; cons. A.C. Nielsen Co., Chgo., Nat. Geog. Soc., Washington, 1984—, Beneficial Mgmt. Corp., Peapack, NJ, 1989—; instr. Boston U., Tufts U.; mem. govt. adv. panel USDA, 1984; expert reviewer govt. panel NIH, Washington, 1989, 91, NSF, Washington, 1982, 87. Author: Reforming Schools, 1980, SPSS PC+ SI-CHAID version 5.0 for DOS and 6.0 for Windows Computer Manual; editor: Analyzing Qualitative/Categorical Data, 1978, Advances in Factor Analysis and Structural Equation Models, 1979; designer CHAID market segmentation computer package, GOLDMINER (graphical ordinal logit displays based on monotonic regression) computer package, latent gold program for latent class modeling, TYPE-O-GRAPHIC profiler statis. modeling program; contbr. articles to profl jours.; mem. editl. rev. bd. Jour. Direct Mktg., Evanston, Ill., 1988—, Jour. Targeting, Measurement and Analysis for Mktg.; computer sect. editor Jour. Mktg. Rsch., 1983-85. Coach youth basketball, baseball and soccer teams. Mem. Am. Statis. Assn., Assn. for Psychol. Type. Achievements include patent for Apparatus and Method for Graphical Display of Statistical Effects in Categorical and Continuous Outcome Data. Office: Statistical Innovations Inc 375 Concord Ave Belmont MA 02478-3048

MAGIELNICKI, ROBERT L., lawyer; b. Perth Amboy, NJ, Mar. 28, 1947; s. Leon C. and Dorothy M. (Hudanish) M.; m. Kathleen J. Urban, June 14, 1969; children: Robert Jr., Kimberly, Peter, Matthew. AB with honors, Rutgers U., 1967; JD with distinction, Cornell U., 1970. Bar: N.Y. 1971, U.S. Supreme Ct. 1974, D.C. 1990. Commd. lt. USN, 1968; assoc. Donovan Leisure Newton & Irvine, NYC, 1970-71, 74-80; asst. staff judge advocate U.S. Naval Base Subic Bay, Republic of Philippines, 1971-73; asst. prof. law U.S. Naval Acad., Annapolis, Md., 1973-74; assoc. litigation and antitrust counsel Gen. Electric Co. Hdqrs., Fairfield, Conn., 1980-83, counsel, 1989-90; divsn. gen. counsel Gen. Electric Factory Automation Products, Charlottesville, Va., 1983-88; ptnr. Kutak Rock, Washington, 1990-2000, Schnader Harrison Segal & Lewis LLP, Washington, 2000—03, Sheppard Mullin Richter & Hampton LLP, Washington, 2003—. Avocations: tennis, golf, swimming, reading. Office: Sheppard Mullin Richter & Hampton LLP 11th Fl East 1300 I St NW Washington DC 20005-3314 Home Phone: 703-709-0621; Office Phone: 202-218-0002. E-mail: rmagielnicki@sheppardmullin.com.

MAGILL, FRANK JOHN, federal judge; b. Verona, ND, June 3, 1927; s. Thomas Charles and Viola Magill; m. Mary Louise Timlin, Nov. 22, 1955; children: Frank Jr., Marguerite Connolly, R. Daniel, Mary Elizabeth, Robert, John. BS in Fgn. Svc., Georgetown U., 1951, LLB, 1955; MA, Columbia U., 1952. Ptnr. Nilles, Hansen, Magill & Davies, Ltd., Fargo, ND, 1955—86; judge US Ct. Appeals (8th cir.), Fargo, 1986—2000, sr. judge, 2000—. Chmn. fin. disclosure com. US Jud. Conf., 1993—98. Fellow: Am. Coll. Trial Lawyers; mem.: Cass County Bar Assn. (Pres. 1970). Republican. Avocations: tennis, sailing, skiing. Home: 501 7th St S Apt 301 Fargo ND 58103-2761 Office: Quentin N Burdick US Courthouse 655 1st Ave N Ste 320 Fargo ND 58102-4932 Home Phone: 701-232-3930; Office Phone: 701-297-7250. Fax: 701 297-7255. E-mail: frank_magill@ca8.uscourts.gov. *

MAGILL, KENT B., lawyer; b. Kansas City, Mo., Dec. 2, 1952; m. Teresa A. Magill. BS, Kent State U., 1975; JD, U. Iowa, 1977. Bar: Mo. 1977, Kans. 1987, US Dist. Ct. Dist. Kans. Assoc. Shughart, Thomson & Kilroy, Kansas City, Mo., 1977—80, atty., 1980—89; assoc. gen. counsel, v.p. The Marley Co., Mission Woods, Kans., 1989—92; v.p., gen. counsel, sec. Layne Christensen Co., Mission Woods, Kans., 1992—2000; assoc. gen. counsel Interstate Brands Corp., 2000—02, v.p., gen. counsel, sec., 2002—, Interstate Bakeries Corp., Kansas City, Mo., 2002—. Office: Interstate Bakeries Corp 12 E Armour Blvd Kansas City MO 64111

MAGILL, SAMUEL HAYS, academic administrator, consultant; b. Decatur, Ga., July 19, 1928; s. Orrin Rankin and Ellen Howe (Bell) M.; children: Samuel Hays Jr., Katherine Magill Walters, Suzanne Magill Weintraub. AB, U. N.C., 1950; BD, Yale U., 1953; PhD, Duke U., 1962; LHD (hon.), Stockton State Coll., 1990; EdD (hon.), Monmouth U., 2005. Ordained to ministry Congl. Christian Ch., 1953; gen. sec. Davidson Coll. YMCA, 1953-55; dir. student activities U. N.C., Chapel Hill, 1955-58, asst. dean student affairs, 1958-59; chaplain Dickinson Coll., 1962-63, asst. prof. religion, 1962-66, asso. prof. religion, 1966-68, dean coll., 1963-68; pres. Council Protestant Colls. and Univs., Washington, 1968-70; exec. asso., chief office acad. affairs Assn. Am. Colls., 1971-76; pres. Simon's Rock Early Coll., Great Barrington, Mass., 1976-79, Monmouth U., West Long Branch, NJ, 1980-93, pres. emeritus, 1993—; higher edn. cons., 1993-98; assoc. dir. gift planning U. N.C., 1999—2004, major gifts officer, 2004—06. Adj. prof. Duke U., 1996. Trustee Jersey Shore Med. Ctr., 1985-93; bd. overseers N.J. Gov.'s Schs., 1986-93; bd. dirs., pres. Falconbridge Homeowners Assn., 2003-06. Guerney Harris Kearns fellow in religion, 1960-61; Danforth Found. spl. grad. fellow, 1959-61. Fellow Soc. Values in Higher Edn. (dir. 1969-81); mem. Am. Assembly Collegiate Sch. Bus. (accreditation task force 1989-90), NCAA (pres.'s commn. 1990-93), Am. Coun. Edn. (commn. leadership devel. 1982-85, commn. on minority affairs 1986-89), Harvard Inst. Ednl. Mgmt., Assn. Ind. Colls. and Univs. N.J. (dir. 1980-93, exec. com. 1983-93, chair 1987-89), Order of Golden Fleece U. N.C., Fearrington Dem. Club (co-chair 1997-98), Delta Psi. Home: 319 Burlage Creek Chapel Hill NC 27514 Personal E-mail: smagill@nc.rr.com.

MAGINN, JOHN LEO, retired insurance company executive; b. Omaha, Feb. 17, 1940; s. Walter J. and Ruth C. (Sawtelle) M.; m. Carol Varnes, Aug. 3, 1963; children: Mary Kay, Karen, Colleen, Matthew. BSBA, Creighton U., 1961; MS, U. Minn., 1962. Chartered fin. analyst. Investment analyst Continental Casualty, Chgo., 1962-64, Mut. Omaha Ins. Co., 1964-68, asst. v.p., 1968-69, 2d v.p., 1969-76, v.p., asst. treas., 1976-82, exec. v.p., 1982-87, treas., 1982-2000, exec. v.p., chief ins. officer, 1987-2000; sr. advisor Summit Strategies, Inc., 2000—03; pres. Maginn Assocs. Pres. Mut. Asset Mgmt. Co.; bd. dirs. Companion Life Ins. Co., Rye, N.Y., Kirkpatrick, Pettis, Smith, Polian, Omaha. Editor, author: Managing Investment Portfolios, 1983, 2d edit., 1990. Sgt. U.S. Army, 1957-65. Mem. CFA Inst. (bd. dirs. 1991, chmn. bd. govs.), Inst. Chartered Fin. Analysts (C. Steward Sheppard award 1990). Republican. Roman Catholic. Office Phone: 402-384-8200.

MAGINNIS, ROBERT P., bishop; b. Phila., Dec. 22, 1933; Student, St. Charles Borromeo Sem., Overbrook, Pa. Ordained priest Roman Cath. Ch. 1961. Titular bishop Diocese of Siminina, 1996—; auxiliary bishop Diocese of Phila., 1996—. Office: 222 N 17th St Philadelphia PA 19103

MAGLACAS, A. MANGAY, nursing researcher, educator; BSN, Vanderbilt U.; MPH, U. Minn.; DPH, Johns Hopkins U.; DSc (hon.), U. Ill. Former chief sci. for nursing devel. health manpower divsn. WHO, Geneva, Switzerland, 1976-89, regional nurse adviser Southeast Asia Office Delhi, India, 1972-75. Internat. health/nursing cons., 1989—; adj. prof. Coll. Nursing, U. Ill., Chgo., 1990-2000; various vis. prof. positions in several countries, 1990—. Former mem., bd. dirs. Internat. Coun. Nurses, 1989-93; fgn. assoc. NAS Inst. Medicine, 1988—. Rockefeller fellow, 1964-67; Fulbright-Smith-Mundt scholar, 1952-54; recipient Outstanding alumni award Vanderbilt U., 1986, Internat. Pub. Health Leadership award Johns Hopkins U., 1992, Outstanding Profl. award for Nursing, Profl. Regulation Commn. of Philippines, 2000, Profl. Recognition award U. Philippines, 1989, Disting. Achievement award Philippine Nurses Assn., 1989, Outstanding Alumni award U. Philippines Sch. Nursing, 1987, Disting. Leadership award USA Commn. on Grads. of Fgn. Nursing Schs., 2002; named Woman of Yr. Am. Rsch. Inst. Bd. Internat. Rsch., 1988, named Most Outstanding Paulinian St. Paul's U., Philippines, 2002. Fellow Royal Coll. Nursing U.K. (hon.). Office: 70 Rue De La Prulay CH-1217 Meyrin Geneva Switzerland E-mail: amelia_maglacas@yahoo.com.ph.

MAGLIOCCA, LARRY ANTHONY, education educator; b. New Castle, Pa., Sept. 3, 1943; s. Anthony Norman Magliocca and Madeline Rose Ross; m. Judie Alene Kerr, Sept. 1, 1964 (div.); children: Jeannine Marie, Seth Bryan; m. Phyllis Marion Gentry, May 9, 1981 (div.); 1 child, Nicholas Rossi; m. Karen Elizabeth Sanders, Jan. 23, 1996. BSEd, Slippery Rock State Coll., 1967; MEd, U. Pitts., 1970; PhD, Ohio State U., 1978. Dir. Youth Devel. Ctr. of Pa., New Castle, 1967-70; state cons. S.D. Dept. Pub. Inst., Pierre, SD, 1970-73; coord. Balt. City Pub. Schs., 1973-76; exec. dir. Ctr. for Spl. Needs Population, Columbus, Ohio, 1979—; assoc. prof. Ohio State U., Columbus, 1988—, charter faculty Primary Care Inst., 2000—; adj. faculty Saybrook Grad. Sch., San Francisco, 2000—. Charter faculty Ohio Primary Care Inst., 2000—; vis. lectr. Melbourne (Australia) State Coll., 1978-79; adj. faculty Johns Hopkins U., Balt., 1974-76, Saybrook Grad. Sch., San Francisco, 2000—; blue ribbon task force, Chgo. City Pub. Schs., 1985; sr. ptnr. The Compact. Author: Teaching Mainstreamed Students, 1982, 2d edit., 1988, Strategic Teaching, 1991; contbr. articles to profl. jours.; editor The Directive Teacher jour., 1976-84; author/designer instructional materials in math. problem solving, 1992. Founder Young Scientists Club, Westerville, Ohio, 1990-92; rsch. fellow Internat. Sys. Inst., 1994-96. Mem.: Internat. Soc. Systems Sci. (v.p. 2002—), Coun. for Exceptional Children, Am. Assn. for Artificial Intelligence, Soc. for Gen. Systems Rsch. Democrat. Unitarian-Universalist. Avocations: poetry, travel, fly fishing. Office: Ctr Spl Needs Populations 700 Ackerman Rd Ste 440 Columbus OH 43202-1559 E-mail: magliocca.1@osu.edu.

MAGNAN, SARAH E., court reporter; d. Henry Joseph and Loretta Agnes Magnan; m. Tommy Bentley. AS, Champion Coll., Burlington, Vt., 1986. Court reporter State of N.H., Manchester, 1987—93, Lyon Reporting, Inc., Atlanta, 1993—. Mem.: Nat. Ct. Reporters Assn. Home: 4515 Otha Way Lilburn GA 30047 Office Phone: 770-458-5500. E-mail: slmagnan@aol.com.

MAGNANO, SALVATORE PAUL, retired finance company executive, treasurer; b. Portland, Conn., Jan. 10, 1934; s. Salvatore and Lucy (Dimodica) M.; m. Lois Jewel Johnson, July 16, 1955; children: Paul C., Mark J., Peter E B.Metall. Engring., Rensselaer Poly. Inst., Troy, NY, 1955; MBA, Northwestern U., Chgo., 1959. Div. controller Sanders Assocs., Inc., Nashua, NH, 1962-73; v.p., controller Teledyne Mec, Palo Alto, Calif., 1973-75; div. controller Sanders Assocs., Inc., Nashua, 1975-79, grp. controller, 1979-81, grp. v.p., controller, 1981-86, v.p. fin. and treas., 1986-96; ind. fin. and adminstrv. cons., 1996—; ret. Pres. Boys and Girls Club of Greater Nashua, 1988-89, bd. dirs., 1981—, sec. bd. dirs., 2004; bd. dirs. Boys and Girls Club of Greater Nashua Charitable Found., 1991—; trustee Daniel Webster Coll., Nashua, 1993—, sec. bd. trustees, 2005-06; trustee Congl. Ch. of Hollis, 2002—; bd. dirs., treas. N.H. Prostate Cancer Coalition, 2006—. Lt. USN, 1955-57 Mem. Fin. Execs. Inst. (life mem.), Beta Gamma Sigma (award for excellence 1959). E-mail: spm-ljm@charter.net.

MAGNANTI, THOMAS L., management and engineering educator; b. Omaha, Oct. 7, 1945; s. Leo A. and Florence L. Magnanti; m. Beverly A. McVinney, June 10, 1967; 1 child, R. Randall. BS in chem. engring., Syracuse U., 1967; MS in stats., Stanford U., 1969, MS in math., 1971, PhD in ops. rsch., 1972; Doktor honoris causa, Linköping U., 1995; PhD (hon.), U. Montreal, Universite Catholique de Louvain. Asst. prof. Alfred P. Sloan Sch. Mgmt. MIT, Cambridge, Mass., 1971-75, assoc. prof., 1975-79, prof., 1979-85, George Eastman prof. of mgmt. sci., 1985—, head mgmt. sci. area, 1982-88, co-dir. Ops. Rsch. Ctr., 1986—, founding co-dir. Leaders for Mfg. Program, 1988-94, prof. dept. elec. engring. and computer sci., 1995—, founding co-dir. Sys. Design and Mgmt. Program, 1995—, founding dir., Leaders for Mfg. Program, dean Sch. Engring., 1999—; rsch. fellow, vis. prof. Ctr. for Ops. Rsch. and Econometrics Univ. Catholique de Louvain, 1976-77, 89. Vis. scientist Bell Labs., 1977, GTE Labs., 1989; vis. scholar Grad. Sch. Bus. Adminstrn., Harvard U., 1980-81; mem. corp. mfg. staff Digital Equipment Corp., 1990; mem. editl. bd. Jour. Computational Optimization and Applications; mem. adv. bd. North Holland Handbooks in Ops. Rsch. and Mgmt. Sci.; bd. dirs. Ford Design Inst., Emptoris Inc; mem. internat. advisory bd., Linköping Univ. Author: Applied Mathematical Programming, 1977, Network Flows, 1993; editor: Jour. Ops. Rsch., 1983-87; co-editor: Math. Programming, 1981-83; assoc. editor SIAM Jour. Algebraic and Discrete Methods, 1981-83, Mgmt. Sci., 1978-81, Ops. Rsch., 1978-81, SIAM Jour. Applied Math., 1976-81, Math. Programming, 1988—; adv. editor Transp. Sci., 1985—, Mktg. Sci., Math. of Artificial Intelligence, 1987-91; contbr. numerous articles to profl. jours. Mem. NSF Sci. and Tech. Exchange Delegation to Soviet Union, 1977, NSF Rsch. Initiation Grant panels, 1985, 90; advisor NSF program on decision, risk and mgmt. sci., 1988, 89; mem. mfg. studies bd. Nat. Rsch. Coun., 1993—; mem. internat. adv. bd. Linkopeg U., Sweden; mem. pres. coun. Olin Coll.; mem. adv. bd. Harvard Bus. Sch., Stanford Sch. Engring. Recipient Gordon Billard award MIT, 1992, Irwin Sizer Award; Mgmt. Program Exch. grantee IREX, Curriculum Devel. grantee Sloan Found., 1990-94. Mem. IEEE (com. on large scale systems 1979-83), TIMS (mem. and chmn. various coms.), NAE, Am. Acad. Arts and Sciences, Ops. Rsch. Soc. Am. (pres. 1988-89, mem. and chmn. various coms., coun. mem. computer sci. tech. sect. 1983-87, co-organizer 1st doctoral consortium 1983, plenary speaker conf. on telecom. 1983, Lanchester prize 1993, Kimball medal 1994), Tau Beta Pi, Pi Mu Epsilon, Phi Kappa Phi. Achievements include research in network analysis and optimization, network design and combinatorial optimization, and applications in manufacturing, telecommunications, and transportation; development of new engineering/management programs. Home: 33 School St Hopkinton MA 01748-2003 Office: MIT Ops Rsch Ctr 77 Massachusetts Ave Cambridge MA 02139-4307

MAGNER, JEROME ALLEN, performing company executive; b. Bklyn., Mar. 14, 1929; s. Herman and Evelyn I. (Wolfe) M.; m. Frances Ogens, Mar. 22, 1953; children: Merrill, Steven. BBA cum laude, CCNY, 1951. Asst. to treas., chief acct. Grayson-Robinson Stores, Inc., S. Klein Dept. Stores, Inc., NYC, 1951-59; contr. Food Fair Properties, NYC, 1959-61; v.p., contr. Am. Leisure Products Corp., NYC and Providence, 1961-69; sr. v.p. fin., treas., CFO, Nat. Amusements Inc., NE Theatre Corp., Dedham, Mass., 1969—. Mem. Nat. Assn. Theatre Owners (bd. dirs.), CCNY Alumni Assn. Office: Nat Amusements Inc 200 Elm St Dedham MA 02026-4536 Business E-Mail: jmagner@nationalamusements.com.

MAGNER, MARJORIE J. (MARGE MAGNER), investment company executive; b. Bklyn., Apr. 29, 1949; BS in Psychology, Brooklyn Coll., NY, 1968; MS, Purdue U., 1974; D of Mgmt. (hon.), Purdue University, 2004. Mng. dir. Chem. Tech. Divsn. Chemical Bank; from mem. staff Commercial Credit to chmn., CEO Citigroup, NYC, 1987—2003; COO Global Consumer Group, Citigroup Inc., NYC, 2002—03, chmn., CEO, 2003—05; co-founder Brysam Global Partners, 2007—. Bd. dirs. Gannett Co., 2006—, The Charles Schwab Corp., 2006—, Accenture, 2006—; chmn. bd. trustees Bklyn. Coll. Found.; mem. dean's adv. coun. Krannert Sch. Mgmt. Purdue U. Bd. dirs. Welfare to Work Partnership, Dress for Success Worldwide, Port Discovery Children's Mus., Balt., Md. Bus. Roundtable Edn. Named one of 50 Most Powerful Women in Am. Bus., Fortune mag., 2001, 2002, 2003, 2004, 25 Most Power Women in Banking, US Banker mag., 2003, 2004, 2005, World's 100 Most Powerful Women, Forbes mag., 2005; recipient Am. Found. for the Blind Helen Keller Achievement award, 2001. *

MAGNER, TIMOTHY J., federal agency administrator, educator; married; 2 children. BA, Coll. William and Mary, 1988; MEd, Harvard U. Tchr. Walsingham Acad., Williamsburg, Va., Leysin, Switzerland, Paris, 1992—93; tech. training specialists Fairfax County Pub. Schs., Va.; Internet specialist, program mgr. K-12 ArtsEdge, Kennedy Ctr., 1995—97; dir. tech. Framingham Pub. Schs., Mass., 1997; with Nat. Retail Fedn., Washington, 1999; mgr. online learning PBS, Alexandria, Va.; dir. Schs. Interoperability Framework Assn., Washington, 2001—03; exec. dir. K-12 edn. Microsoft Corp., 2003—04; dep. dir. ednl. tech. US Dept. Edn., Washington, 2004—05, dir. Office of Ednl. Tech., 2006—; dep. exec. dir. Coun. of Chief State Sch. Officers, 2005—06. Prof. ednl. tech. Framingham State Coll.; adj. prof. George Mason U. Office: US Dept Edn 400 Maryland Ave, SW Washington DC 20202 Office Phone: 202-205-4280. *

MAGNES, HARRY ALAN, physician; b. Orange, NJ, Dec. 3, 1948; s. Sam and Shirley (Daniels) Magnes; m. Patricia Bruce, Mar. 25, 1989; 1 child, Carlos Fontiveros. AB in Biology magna cum laude, Brown U., Providence, 1970; MD, Yale U., New Haven, Conn., 1974; M in Med. Mgmt., Tulane U., New Orleans, 1998; cert. in med. mgmt., Am. Coll. Physician Execs., 1997. Diplomate Am. Bd. Internal Medicine, Am. Bd. Med. Mgmt. Intern, resident internal medicine U. Iowa Hosps. and Clinics, 1974—77; ptnr., med. dir., pres., CEO Gallatin Med. Clinic, Downey, Calif., 1997—2001; pres., CEO Gallatin Med. Corp., Downey, Calif., 1992—94; med. dir., bd. dirs. Gallatin Med. Found., Downey, Calif., 1993—2001; chief med. officer Gallatin Med. Group, 2000—01, Physician Assocs. of Greater San Gabriel Valley, Pasadena, Calif., 2001—05; CEO Lovelace Med. Group, Albuquerque, 2005—. Staff physician Downey Cmty. Hosp., 1977—96, Presbyn. Intercmty. Hosp., 1992—2001; clin. instr. Rancho Los Amigos Hosp., Downey, 1981—83; chairperson bd. dirs. Primehealth of So. Calif., 1997—99; sec.-treas. Calif. Health Network, 1998—99; project adv. bd. VA/UCLA/RAND Calif. Med. Group, IPA Governance Project, 1997—98; prin. investigator Reach Asthma Rsch. Project, 2002; bd. dirs. Calif. Health Network; bd. govs. Lovelace Clinic Found., 2006—, Lovelace Med. Ctr., 2006—. Author: Rheumatic Fever in Connecticut, 1974. Bd. dirs. N.Mex. Symphony Orch., 2007—. James Manning scholar Brown U., 1968. Mem.: Greater Albuquerque Med. Assn., N.Mex. Med. Soc., Med. Group Mgmt. Assn., Am. Med. Group Assn. (policy com. 1994—98, legis. com. 1997—2000), Sigma Xi, Phi Beta Kappa, Delta Omega. Avocation: racquetball. Office Phone: 505-262-3085. Business E-Mail: harry.magnes@lovelace.com.

MAGNESS, RHONDA ANN, retired microbiologist; b. Stockton, Calif., Jan. 30, 1946; d. John Pershing and Dorothy Waneta (Kelley) Wetter; m. Barney LeRoy Bender, Aug. 26, 1965 (div. Jan. 1977); m. Gary D. Magness, Mar. 5, 1977; children: Jay D.(dec.), Troy D. BS, Calif. State U., Sacramento, 1977. Med. asst. C. Fred Wilcox, MD, Stockton, 1965-66; clk. typist Dept. of U.S. Army, Ft. Eustis, Va., 1967, Def. Supply Agy., New Orleans, 1967-68; med. asst. James G. Cross, MD, Lodi, Calif., 1969, Arthur A. Kemalyan, MD, Lodi, 1969-71, 72-77; med. sec. Lodi Meml. Hosp., 1972; lab. aide Calif. State U., Sacramento, 1977; phlebotomist St. Joseph's Hosp., Stockton, 1978-79; microbiologist Dameron Hosp. Assn., Stockton, 1980—2004. Active Concerned Women Am., Washington, 1987—. Mem.: San Joaquin County Med. Assts. Assn., Calif. Assn. Clin. Lab. Technologists, Nat. Audubon Soc., Nat. Geog. Soc., Jobs Daus. (chaplain 1962—63). Baptist. Avocations: birdwatching, sewing, reading. Home: 9627 Knight Ln Stockton CA 95209-1961

MAGNUS, BURKE, broadcast executive; b. 1967; m. Colleen Magnus; children: Burke, Quinn. BA in History, Holy Cross Univ., Springfield, Mass., 1988; MS in Sports Mgmt., Univ. Mass., 1993. Former legal asst., 1988—93; intern CBS Sports, 1993—94; program assoc. ESPN, program planner, program mgr., dir. brand mgmt. men's college basketball, motorsports and other sports, v.p., gen. mgr. ESPNU Network, 2004—. Office: ESPNU ESPN Plz 935 Middle St Bristol CT 06010

MAGNUSON, NANCY, librarian; b. Seattle, Aug. 15, 1944; d. James Leslie and Jeanette (Thomas) M.; 2 sons, Daniel Johnson, Erik Johnson. BA in History, 1977; MLS, U. Wash., 1978. With. King County Libr. System, Seattle, 1973-80; rsch. asst. Free Libr. Phila., 1980-81; asst. libr. Haverford (Pa.) Coll., 1981-87; libr. dir. Goucher Coll., Balt., Md., 1987—. Contbr. to profl. publs. Mem. ALA (com. on status of women in librarianship, various others), Online Computer Libr. Ctr. Users Coun., Md. Libr. Assn., Congress Acad. Libr. Dirs., NOW, Women's Internat. League for Peace and Freedom, Balt. Bibliophiles, Jane Austen Soc. N.Am. Democrat. Office: Goucher Coll Julia Rogers Libr 1021 Dulaney Valley Rd Baltimore MD 21204-2753

MAGNUSON, ROGER JAMES, lawyer; b. St. Paul, Jan. 25, 1945; s. Roy Gustaf and Ruth Lily (Edlund) M.; m. Elizabeth Cunningham Shaw, Sept. 11, 1982; children: James Roger, Peter Cunningham, Mary Kerstin, Sarah Ruth, Elizabeth Camilla, Anna Clara, John Edlund, Britta Kristina. BA, Stanford U., 1967; JD, Harvard U., 1971; BCL, Oxford U., 1972. Bar: Minn. 1973, U.S. Dist. Ct. Minn. 1973, U.S Ct. Appeals (8th, 9th, 10th, 11th cirs.) 1974, U.S. Supreme Ct. 1978. Chief pub. defender Hennepin County Pub. Defender's Office, Mpls., 1973; ptnr., trial group Dorsey & Whitney, Mpls., 1972—, and head, strategic litig. group. Dean Oak Brook Coll. of Law and Govt. Policy, 1995—; chancellor Magdalen Coll., 1999—. Author: Shareholder Litigation, 1981, Are Gay Rights Right, The White-Collar Crime Explosion, 1992, Informed Answers to Gay Rights Questions, 1994; Internat. Judicial Asst. in Civil Matters (1999), contbr. articles to profl. jours. Elder, Straitgate Ch., Mpls., 1980—. Fellow, Ctr. of Internat. Legal Studies, Mem. Christian Legal Soc., The Am. Soc. Writers of Legal Subjects, Mpls. Club, White Bear Yacht Club. Republican. Office: Dorsey & Whitney LLP 50 S 6th St Ste 1500 Minneapolis MN 55402-1498 Home Phone: 651-429-0579; Office Phone: 612-340-2738. Office Fax: 612-340-2807. Business E-Mail: magnuson.roger@dorsey.com.

MAGNUSON, TERRY R., geneticist, educator; Grad. in biology, U. Redlands. Postdoctoral work U. Calif., San Francisco; prof. genetics to dir. develop. biology ctr. Case Western Reserve U., 1984—2000; Sarah Graham Kenan prof., founding chair dept. genetics, Sch. Medicine U. NC, Chapel Hill, 2000—; dir. Carolina Ctr. for Genome Sciences, Chapel Hill; dir., cancer genetics Lineberger Comprehensive Cancer Ctr., Chapel Hill. Mem. adv. panels NIH Genetic Basis Disease Review Com., 1990—95, chair, 1993—95; program project site visits/RFA panels/Ad Hoc panel mem. (36), Ad Hoc counsel mem. NICHD, Mouse Chromosome 7 com., 1991—94, co-chair, 1992—93; mem. NRC panel on establishing guidelines for use of human embryonic stem cells; mem. adv. com., Human Embryonic Stem Cell Rsch. NRC and Inst. Medicine, 2006—; co-instructor, Molecular Embryology of the Mouse Cold Spring Harbor Lab., 1995—96, co-dir., Molecular Embryology of the Mouse, 1997—98; mem. organizing com. Cold Spring Harbor/Heidelberg Mouse Molecular Genetics Mtg., 2003—; bd. dir. Pharm. Products Developments Svc. Co., 2001—; bd. overseers Jackson Lab., 2004—. Contbr. articles to profl. jours.; co-editor-in-chief Genesis: The Journal of Genetics and Development, 1999—, mem. editl. adv. bd. Development, 1986—93, 1999—, Mammalian Genome, 1995—. Recipient Nat. Rsch. Svc. award, NICHD, 1979—82, New Investigator award, 1982—85, March Dimes Basil O'Conner award, 1984—86, NIH Merit award, 1999; Postdoctoral Fellow, NSF, 1978—79, Pew Scholar in Biomedical Sciences, 1985—89. Fellow: Am. Acad. Arts & Scis.; mem.: Genetics Soc. Am. (bd. dir. 2004), Soc. for Developmental Biology (bd. dir. 2000—06), Internat. Mammalian Genome Soc. (secretariat 1999—2001, founding mem.). Office: Dept Genetics U NC at Chapel Hill CB#7264 Lineberger Cancer Ctr 102 Mason Farm Rd Chapel Hill NC 27599-7264 Office Phone: 919-843-6475. Office Fax: 919-843-6365. Business E-Mail: trm4@med.unc.edu. *

MAGOR, LOUIS ROLAND, conductor; b. Auburn, Nebr., May 16, 1945; s. John William and Eleanor Lucille (Niemann) M. B.Mus. Edn., Northwestern U., 1967, Mus.M., 1974. Choral dir. Avoca Jr. High Sch., Wilmette, Ill., 1968-70; choral dir. Niles North High Sch., Skokie, Ill., 1970-73; dir. San Francisco Symphony Chorus, 1974-82, Schola Cantorum, 1982-85, San Francisco Boys Chorus, 1985-88; artistic dir. Seattle Bach Choir, 1990—2001. Founder The Louis Magor Singers; mem. faculty San Francisco Conservatory of Music, 1976-78, San Francisco State U., 1979-80 Founder West Seattle Children's Chorus, 1990—; condr. Sing-It-Yourself Messiah, 1979-91, Calif. Symphony Chorus, 1990-92; exec. prodr. Sandy Bradley's Potluck, 1995-96; co-founder, mng. dir. Kenyon Hall, 1993—. Mem. Pi Kappa Lambda. Personal E-mail: louis@magor.com.

MAGORIAN, JAMES, poet, writer; b. Palisade, Nebr., Apr. 24, 1942; s. Jack and Dorothy (Gorthey) M. BS, U. Nebr., 1965; MS, Ill. State U., 1969; postgrad., Oxford U., 1972, Harvard U., 1973. Author children's books: School Daze, 1978, 17%, 1978, The Magic Pretzel, 1979, Ketchup Bottles, 1979, Imaginary Radishes, 1980, Plucked Chickens, 1980, Fimperings and Torples, 1981, The Witches' Olympics, 1983, At the City Limits, 1987, The Beautiful Music, 1988, Magic Spell #207, 1988; author numerous books of poetry, including: Ideas for a Bridal Shower, 1980, The Edge of the Forest, 1980, Spiritual Rodeo, 1980, Tap Dancing on a Tight Rope, 1981, Training at Home to Be A Locksmith, 1981, The Emily Dickinson Jogging Book, 1984, Keeper of Fire, 1984, Weighing the Sun's Light, 1985, Summer Snow, 1985, The Magician's Handbook, 1986, Squall Line, 1986, The Hideout of the Sigmund Freud Gang, 1987, Haymarket Square, 1998, Dragon Bones, 1999, Millennial Journal, 2000, Voices, 2006, (novels) America First, 1992, Hearts of Gold, 1996, (poetry) The Bookbinder's Daughter, 2007; contbr. poems and stories to numerous publs. Home and Office: 2626 North 49th St 402 Lincoln NE 68504

MAGOVERN, JAMES ANTHONY, thoracic surgeon; b. San Antonio, June 8, 1954; MD, U. Pitts., 1980. Diplomate Am. Bd. Thoracic Surgery, Am. Bd. Surgery. Intern Johns Hopkins, Balt., 1980-81, resident in surgery, 1981-82, Pa. State U. Coll. Medicine, Hershey, 1982-89; fellow in rsch. cardiothoracic surgery Milton S. Hershey Med. Ctr., 1985-87; with Allegheny Gen. Hosp., Pitts. Prof. surgery Drexel U. Sch. Med. Mem. Assn. Acad. Surgery, Am. Coll. Cardiology, Am. Coll. Surgeons, Am. Heart Assn., Soc. Thoracic Surgery, Am. Assn. Thoracic Surgery. Office: 490 E North Ave Ste 302 Pittsburgh PA 15212-4740 Business E-Mail: jmagover@wpahs.org.

MAGOWAN, PETER ALDEN, professional sports team and retail executive; b. NYC, Apr. 5, 1942; s. Robert Anderson and Doris (Merrill) Magowan; m. Jill Tarlau (dec. July 1982); children: Kimberley, Margot, Hilary; m. Deborah Johnston, Aug. 14, 1982. BA, Stanford U., 1964; MA, Oxford U., Eng., 1966; postgrad., Johns Hopkins U., 1967—68. Store mgr. Safeway Stores Inc., Washington, 1968—70, dist. mgr. Houston, 1970—71, retail ops. mgr. Phoenix, 1971—72, divsn. mgr. Tulsa, 1973—76, mgr. internat. divsn. Toronto, Ont., Canada, 1976—78, mgr. western region San Francisco, 1978—79, CEO Oakland, Calif., 1980—93, chmn. bd. dirs., 1980—98; pres., mng. gen. ptnr. San Francisco Giants, 1993—; ret. Safeway Stores Inc., 2005. Bd. dirs. Daimler Chrysler Corp, Caterpillar. Office: San Francisco Giants 24 Willie Mays Plz San Francisco CA 94107-2199 Office Phone: 415-972-1950. Business E-Mail: scasabat@sfgiants.com.

MAGRATH, C. PETER, educational association executive; b. NYC, Apr. 23, 1933; s. Laurence Wilfrid and Giulia Maria (Dentice) M.; m. Deborah C. Howell, 1988; children: Valerie Ruth, Monette Fay. BA summa cum laude, U. N.H., 1955; PhD, Cornell U., 1962. Faculty Brown U., Providence, 1961-68, prof. polit. sci., 1967-68, assoc. dean grad. sch., 1965-66; dean Coll. Arts and Scis. U. Nebr., Lincoln, 1968-69, dean faculties Coll. Arts and Scis., 1969-72, interim chancellor, 1971-72, prof. polit. sci., 1968-72, vice-chancellor for acad. affairs, 1972; pres. SUNY, Binghamton, 1972-74, prof. polit. sci., 1972-74; pres. U. Minn., Mpls., 1974-84, U. Mo. System, 1985-91, Nat. Assn. State Univs. and Land Grant Colls., Washington, 1991—2005, sr. presdl. adv. to the Coll. Bd., 2006—. Author: The Triumph of Character, 1963, Yazoo: Law and Politics in the New Republic, The Case of Fletcher v. Peck, 1966, Constitutionalism and Politics: Conflict and Consensus, 1968, Issues and Perspectives in American Government, 1971; (with others) The American Democracy, 2d edit., 1973; (with Robert L. Egbert) Strengthening Teacher Education, 1987; contbr. articles to profl. jours. With AUS, 1955—57. Mem. Assn. Am. Univs. (chmn. 1985-86, bd. dirs. Salzburg Sem. 2000-05), Am. Assn. C.C.s (trustee), Phi Beta Kappa, Phi Kappa Phi, Pi Gamma Mu, Pi Sigma Alpha, Kappa Tau Alpha. Office: Coll Bd 1233 20th St NW Washington DC 20036-2375 Office Phone: 202-741-4701. Office Fax: 202-741-4743. Business E-Mail: pmagrath@collegeboard.org. *True personal success cannot be measured by public acclaim, recognition, or status. It grows out of an ability to recognize right from wrong, and to maintain principles of fairness and understanding in all human relationships - regardless of one's role in life. In my case I have tried to fulfill this ideal; I have been willing to exercise leadership by asserting my judgments and views openly and directly on the educational and human issues that came my way.*

MAGRATH, KATHLEEN BARRY, retired municipal official; b. Raymond, Neb., Aug. 10, 1930; d. Leo D. Barry and Eileen K. Larkin; m. Frank J. Magrath, June 6, 1953 (dec. Dec. 13, 1992); children: Maureen, Teresa, Patricia, Timothy, Cecilia, Mary Kathleen. BS in Chemistry, Mt. Marty Coll., Yankton, SD, 1952; MPA, Nova Southeastern U., Ft. Lauderdale, Fla., 1978, D in Pub. Adminstrn., 1979. Cert. med. technologist S.D., 1952. Med. technologist St. Catherine Hosp., McCook, Nebr., 1952—53, St. Joseph's Hosp., South Bend, Ind., 1953—54; adminstrv. asst. Dade County Sch. Bd., Miami, Fla., 1974—84; dir. child care ctr. Riviera Presbyn. Ch., Miami, 1980—82; mem. and vice chair Dade County Sch. Bd., Miami, 1984—86; coord. portfolio program Barry U., Miami, 1987—92, adj. prof. orgnl. comms., 1987—89. Founding mem. Greater Miami Urban League Fair Housing Group, 1966—70; mem. Dade County Cmty. Rels. Bd., Miami, 1983—90; dir. Fla. Sch. Bds. Assn., Talahassee, 1985—86; mem. Dade County Property Adjustment Bd., Miami, 1986. Contbr. book reviews to Miami Herald, 1966—68; poet:. Mem. Archdiocese of Miami Synod, 1986—89; mem. local and state bds. PTA, 1970—74; vol. Fairchild Tropical Bot. Gardens, 1998—. Recipient Svc. award, Music Edn. Dade County Schs., 1985, Outstanding Svc. to Edn., Kappa Delta Pi, 1985, Recognition cert., Fla. Women's Hall of Fame, 1986, Women Helping Women cert. of Appreciation, Soroptimist Internat. of the Ams., 1991, Vol. of Yr., Homestead Mid. Sch., 2002—03. Democrat. Roman Catholic. Avocations: watercolor, drawing, volunteering, reading. Home: 7730 SW 134th St Miami FL 33156 E-mail: KBM810@aol.com.

MAGRAW, DANIEL BARSTOW, JR., lawyer, educator; b. Mpls., Sept. 14, 1946; s. Daniel Barstow Sr. and Jean Best (Grismer) M.; m. Pia Agnes Lodberg (div. 1977); 1 child, Kim; m. Lucinda Ann Low, Jan. 3, 1981; children: Kendra, Caitlin, Sean. AB in econs., Harvard U., 1968; JD, U. Calif., Berkeley, 1976. Bar: Calif. 1976, D.C. 1978, Colo. 1986. Economist, bus. cons. Am. Peace Corps, Madras, India, 1968-72; law clk. to Hon. James R. Browning San Francisco, 1976-77; atty. Covington & Burling, Washington, 1978-83; prof. law U. Colo., Boulder, 1983-92; dir. internat. environ. law office EPA, Washington, 1992—2001; pres. & CEO Ctr. Internat. Environ. Law, Washington, 2001—. Lectr. U. Calif. Law Sch., 1977. Mem. study group internat. bus. transactions U.S. Dept. State; mem. expert roster U.N. ctr. transnational corp. Mem.: Internat. Law Assn. (rapporteur, Long Range Transboundary Air Pollution), Am. Soc. Internat. Law (rapporteur, panel on State responsibility), Am. Law Inst., ABA (past chmn. Internat. Law & Practice sect., mem. standing com. environ. law). Office: Ctr for Internat Environ Law Suite 300 1367 Connecticut Ave Washington DC 20036 Office Phone: 202-785-8700. Business E-Mail: dmagraw@ciel.org.

MAGRILL, JOE RICHARD, JR., religious organization administrator, minister; b. Marshall, Tex., Aug. 7, 1946; s. Joe Richard and Mary Belle (Chadwick) M. BA summa cum laude, East Tex. State U., 1967; MDiv, Princeton Theol. Sem., 1970, MTh, 1972; MLS, Rutgers U., 1971. Ordained to ministry Cumberland Presbyn. Ch., 1970. Stated supply min. Newsome (Tex.) Cumberland Presbyn. Ch., 1966-67; Christian edn. asst. United Presbyn. Ch., Carlstadt, NJ, 1967-70; order libr. Princeton (N.J.) Theol. Sem., 1969-72; head libr., prof. Memphis Theol. Sem., 1972-79; pastor Brookhaven Cumberland Presbyn. Ch., Nashville, 1987-89; asst. to stated clk. Gen. Assembly Office, Cumberland Presbyn. Ch., Memphis, 1979-83, supr. ctrl. acctg. div., 1980-87, editor The Cumberland Presbyn., 1984-87, chief exec. bd. stewardship, 1989—2007, mem. Gen. Assembly Coun., 1993—2007, chief exec. Cumberland Presbyn. Investment Loan Program, Inc., 1999—2007. Mem. Trinity Presbytery of Cumberland Presbyn. Ch., 1970—; sec.-treas. Hist. Found. Cumberland Presbyn. Ch., Memphis, 1974—; bd. dirs. Hist. Found. Presbyn. Ch. U.S., Montreat, N.C., 1980-83. Editor: In the Valley of the Cauca, 1981, One Family Under God, 1982, Family of Faith, 1998. Recipient achievement award Hist. Found. Cumberland Presbyn. Ch., 1980; scholar Phi Alpha Theta, 1967, Am. Theol. Libr. Assn., 1970. Democrat. Avocations: computers, historical research. Personal E-mail: jrm@cumberland.org.

MAGRILL, ROSE MARY, library director; b. Marshall, Tex., June 8, 1939; d. Joe Richard and Mary Belle (Chadwick) M. BS, East Tex. State U., 1960, MA, 1961; MS, U. Ill., 1964, PhD, 1969. Asst. to dean women E. Tex. State U., Commerce, 1960-61, librarian II, 1961-63; teaching asst. U. Ill., Urbana, 1963-64; instr. to asst. prof. E. Tex. State U., Commerce, 1964-67; asst. prof. Ball State U., Muncie, 1969-70; asst. prof. to prof. U. Mich., Ann Arbor, 1970-81; prof. U. N. Tex., Denton, 1981-99; dir. libr. E. Tex. Bapt. U., Marshall, 1987-2001. Accreditation site visitor ALA, Chgo., 1975—; cons. in field. Co-author: Building Library Collections, 4th edit. 1974, Library Technical Services, 1977, Building Library Collections, 5th edit. 1979, Acquisition Management and Collection Development in Libraries, 2d edit. 1989; author: Family of Faith, 1998. Treas. Mission Synod of Cumberland Presbyn. Ch., 1989—; mem. bd. fin. Trinity Presbytery, 1989—98; sec. Nat. Conv. Cumberland Presbyn. Women, 2000—02; co-moderator of gen. assembly Cumberland Presbyn. Ch., 2007; trustee Memphis Theol. Sem., 1988—98; sec.-treas. Harrison County Hist. Commn., 1995—; trustee Hist. Found., 1999—. Recipient award, Cumberland Presbyn. History, 1995, Spaulding History award, 2006. Mem.: ALA (RTSD Resources Sect. Pub. award 1978), Tex. Libr. Assn., Marshall (Tex.) Regional Med. Ctr. Aux. (treas. 2004—), Presbyn. Hist. Soc. of S.W. (bd. dirs. 2000—, chmn. bd. 2003—05, sec. 2005—). Home: 203 Pitts ave Marshall TX 75672-4719

MAGRO, CYNTHIA MARIA, pathologist; BS, U. Man., MD, 1985. Medical diplomate, diplomate Am. Bd. Cytopathology, Am. Bd. Dermatopathology, Am. Bd. Anatomic Pathology. Intern Harvard Med. Sch., Boston, 1985—87, resident, 1987—89, fellow, 1989—91; asst. prof. U. Winnipeg, 1991—93; asst. clin. prof. pathology Harvard Med. Sch., Boston, 1995—98; assoc. clin. prof. dermatology U. Hosps., Case Western Res. U., Cleve., 1998—99; assoc. prof. pathology Thomas Jefferson U., Phila., 1999—2000; prof. Ohio State U., Columbus, 2000—, dir. dermatopathology, 2000—. Author: (textbook) The Melanocytic Proliferations: A Comprehensive Textbook of Pigmented Lesions (Am. Assn. Pubs. award for Excellence, 2001); contbr. 133 publs. in field. Mem.: Am. Soc. Dermatopathology (chair edn. com. 2000—02). Achievements include research in neelanocytic, lymphoproliferative and inflammatory disorders of the skin and malignant disorders of skin; inflammatory lung disease; interstitrol lung disease and lung transplantation. Office Phone: 212-746-6434.

MAGRUDER, JACK, retired academic administrator; m. Sue Brimer; children: Julie Magruder Lochbaum, Kerry, Laura Magruder Mann. BS in Chemistry and Math., Truman State U., 1957; postgrad., La. State U., 1959; MA in Chemistry and Sci. Edn., U. No. Iowa, 1960; EdD in Chemistry and Sci. Edn., U. No. Colo., 1966; grad., Harvard U. Inst. Ednl. Mgmt., 1992. Asst. prof. chemistry Truman State U., Kirksville, Mo., 1964—86, prof., head divsn. sci., 1986—89, acting dean instrn., 1989—91, v.p. acad. affairs, 1991—94, pres., 1994—2003; ret., 2003. Cons.-evaluator Higher Learning Commn. North Ctrl. Assn. Colls. and Schs.; chmn. com. on transfer and articulation Mo. Coord. Bd. for Higher Edn.; past pres. Coun. of Pub. Liberal Arts Colls., Coun. Pub. Higher Edn. for Mo. Mem.: Sci. Tchrs. Mo., Am. Chem. Soc., Sigma Beta Delta, Phi Kappa Phi, Phi Delta Kappa, Beta Gamma Sigma, Phi Beta Kappa. E-mail: wjm@truman.edu.

MAGUAD, BEN ABRICO, management educator; arrived in US, 2000; s. Camilo Jalipa and Ascencion Abrico Maguad; m. Narinee Petchploysri, Dec. 8, 1985; children: Melanie, Maverick. Diploma cum laude, U. Santo Tomas, Manila, 1980; PhD in Bus. and Mgmt., U. South Australia, Adelaide, 1998. Clk. Bank of Philippine Islands, Makati, 1980—81; secondary tchr. Adventist English Sch., Bangkok, 1983—88; prof. Hong Kong Adventist Coll., Kowloon, 1988—98, Caribbean Union Coll., Maracas, Trinidad and Tobago, 1998—2000, Andrews U., Berrien Springs, Mich., 2000—. Contbr. articles to profl. jours. Deacon to head deacon Bangkok Adventist Hosp. Ch., 1981—83; deacon Adventist English Ch., Bangkok, 1983—88, Pioneer Meml. Ch., Berrien Springs, Mich., 2001—; elder to head elder Bayview Ch. of Seventh-day Adventists, Hong Kong, 1988—98. Scholar, Rockefeller Found., 1981—83; Rector's grant, U. Santo Tomas, 1976—80. Mem.: Am. Soc. Quality, South East Asia Club (co-sponsor 2001—). Seventh-Day Adventist. Office: Andrews Univ 100 Old US Hwy 31 Berrien Springs MI 49104-0022 Home Phone: 269-473-2863; Office Phone: 269-471-3103.

MAGUIRE, CHARLOTTE EDWARDS, retired pediatrician; b. Richmond, Ind., Sept. 1, 1918; d. Joel Blaine and Lydia (Betscher) Edwards; m. Raymer Francis Maguire, Sept. 1, 1948 (dec.); children: Barbara, Thomas Clair II (dec.). Student, Stetson U., 1936—38, U. Wichita, 1938—39; BS, Memphis Tchrs. Coll., 1940; MD, U. Ark., 1944; LHD (hon.), Fla. State U., 2002. Intern, resident Orange Meml. Hosp., Orlando, Fla., 1944—46, med. staff., 1944—69, instr. nurses, 1947—57; resident Bellevue Hosp. and Med. Ctr., NYU, NYC, 1954—55; staff mem. Fla. Santarium and Hosp., Orlando, 1946—56, Holiday House and Hosp., Orlando, 1950—62; mem. courtesy and cons. staff West Orange Meml. Hosp., Winter Garden, Fla., 1952—67; active staff, chief dept. pediat. Mercy Hosp., Orlando, 1965—68; med. dir. childrens med. svcs., asst. sec. Fla. Dept. Health and Rehab. Svcs., 1969—71, med. dir. med. svcs. and basic care, 1975—84; med. exec. dir., med. svcs. divsn. worker's compensation Fla. Dept. Labor, Tallahassee, 1984—87; chief of staff physicians and dentists Ctrl. Fla. divsn. Children's Home Soc. Fla., 1947—56; dir. Orlando Child Health Clinic, 1949—58; pvt. practice Orlando, 1946—68; asst. regional dir. HEW, 1970—72; ret., 1987. Asst. dir. health and sci. affairs Dept. Health Edn. & Welfare, Atlanta, 1971-72, Washington, 1972-75; pediat. cons. Fla. Crippled Children's Commn., 1952-70, dir., 1968-70; med. dir. Office Med. Svcs. and Basic Care, sr. physician Office of Asst. Sec. Ops., Fla. Dept. Health and Rehab. Svcs.; clin. prof. dept. pediat. U. Fla. Coll. Medicine, Gainesville, 1980-87; mem. Fla. Drug Utilization Rev., 1983-87; real estate salesperson Investors Realty, 1982-2003; bd. dirs. Stavros Econ. Ctr. Fla. State U., Tallahassee; pres.'s coun. Fla. State U., U. Fla., Gainesville; Charlotte Edwards Maguire eminent scholar chair and scholarships for qualified students, 1999. Mem. profl. adv. com. Fla. Ctr. for Clin. Svcs. at U. Fla., 1952-60; del. to Mid-century White House Conf. on Children and Youth, 1950; U.S. del from Nat. Soc. for Crippled Children to World Congress for Welfare of Cripples, Inc., London, 1957; pres. of corp. Eccleston-Callahan Hosp. for Colored Crippled Children, 1956-58; sec. Fla. chpt. Nat. Doctor's Com. for Improved Med. Svcs., 1951-52; med. adv. com. Gateway Sch. for Mentally Retarded, 1959-62; bd. dirs. Forest Park Sch. for Spl. Edn. Crippled Children, 1949-54, mem. med. adv. com., 1955-68, chmn., 1957-68; mem. Fla. Adv. Coun. for Mentally Retarded, 1965-70; dir. ctrl. Fla. poison control Orange Meml. Hosp.; mem. orgn. com., chmn. com. for admissions and selection policies Camp Challenge; participant 12th session Fed. Exec. Inst., 1971; del. White House Conf. on Aging, 1980; dir. Stavros Econ. Ctr. Fla. State U.; trustee Fla. State U. Found., 1998—, mem. campaign com. Charlotte Edwards Maguire Eminent Scholarship named in her honor Fla. State U., Charlotte Edwards Maguire MLS Med. Libr., Fla. State U. Coll. Medicine named in her honor, 2005; named Outstanding Woman in Our Cmty. AAUW, Tallahassee, 2002; recipient David M. Solomon Disting. Pub. Svc. award Am. Geriatric Soc., 2005, Torch award Fla. State U., 2005. Mem. AMA (life), Nat. Rehab. Assn., Am. Congress Phys. Medicine and Rehab., Fla. Soc. Crippled Children and Adults, Ctrl. Fla. Soc. Crippled Children and Adults (dir. 1949-58, pres. 1956-57), Am. Assn. Cleft Palate, Fla. Soc. Crippled Children (trustee 1951-57, v.p. 1956-57, profl. adv. com. 1957-68), Mental Health Assn. Orange County (charter mem.; pres. 1949-50, dir. 1947-52, chmn. exec. com. 1950-52, dir. 1963-65), Fla. Orange County Heart Assn., Am. Med. Women's Assn., Am. Acad. Med. Dirs., Fla. Med. Assn. (life, chmn. com. on mental retardation), Orange County Med. Assn., Orange Med. Soc. (life), Fla. Pediat. Soc. (pres. 1952-53), Fla. Cleft Palate Assn. (counselor-at-large, sec.), Nat. Inst. Geneal. Rsch., Nat. Geneal. Soc., Assn. Profl. Genealogists, Tallahassee Geneal. Soc., Fla. State U. Found. Inc. (bd. dirs. Stavoris Ctr. for Econ. Edn.), Capital City Tiger Bay Club, Fla. Econs. Club, Francis Eppes Soc. Fla. State U., Econ. Club Fla., Governors Club. Home: 4158 Covenant Ln Tallahassee FL 32308-5765

MAGUIRE, GREGORY, writer; m. Andy Newman; children: Luke, Alex, Helen. PhD in English and Am. Lit., Tufts U., 1990. Fellow Bread Loaf Writers Conf., Middlebury, Vt., 1978; prof., assoc. dir. Ctr. for the Study of Children's Lit., Simmons Coll., 1979—86; co-dir., founding bd. mem. Children's Lit. New England, Inc., 1986—; artist-in-residence Isabella Stewart Gardner Mus., Boston, 1994; fellow Blue Mountain Ctr., NY, The Hambidge Ctr., Ga., 1998, The Va. Ctr. for the Creative Arts, 1999. Author: (novels) Wicked: The Life and Times of the Wicked Witch of the West, 1995, Confessions of an Ugly Stepsister, 1999, Lost, 2001, Mirror Mirror, 2003, Son of a Witch, 2005, (children's novels) The Dream Stealer, 1983 (named one of the Children's Books of the Yr., Child Study Children's Books Com., 1983, named a Nat. Coun. Tchrs. of English Tchr.'s Choice, 1984), Missing Sisters, 1994 (named a Parents Choice Hon. book, 1994), The Good Liar, 1996, The Hamlet Chronicles, Seven Spiders Spinning (named an ALA Notable book, 1994, Judy Lopez Meml. Award Hon. book, 1995), Six Haunted Hairdos, Five Alien Elves, Four Stupid Cupids, Three Rotten Eggs, A Couple of April Fools, Leaping Beauty: And Other Animal Fairy Tales, 2004; contbr. articles to profl. mags. including the Boston Rev., Christian Sci. Monitor, The Horn Book Mag., others. Office: William Reiss - Literary Agt John Hawkins and Assocs 71 W 23rd St Ste 1600 New York NY 10010 Address: Jennifer Suitor - Publicist HarperCollins 10 E 53rd St New York NY 10022

MAGUIRE, JAMES HARVEY, physician; b. Easton, Pa., Nov. 25, 1948; s. James I. and Elizabeth C. (Updegrove) Maguire. AB, Princeton U., 1970; MD, Harvard U., 1974, MPH, 1978. Cert. internal med, infectious disease. Rsch. assoc. Harvard Sch. Pub. Health, Boston, 1978-81; instr. in medicine Harvard Med. Sch. Pub. Health, 1982-85; asst. prof. Medicine Tropical Pub. Health, Boston, 1985-92, assoc. prof. medicine, 1992-2001; physician, clin. dir. infectious disease Brigham Womens Hosp., Boston, 1992-2001; chief parasitic disease br. Ctrs. for Disease Control and Prevention, Atlanta, 2001—05; prof., dir. internat. health divsn. U. Md. Sch. Medicine, Balt., 2005—. Editor: Parasitic Diseases, 1993; sect. editor: Am. Jour. Tropical Medicine and Hygiene, 2002—. Mem.: Am. Epidemiol. Soc., Infectious Disease Soc. Am., Am. Soc. Tropical Medicine and Hygiene (councillor 2000—04, Ben Kean medal 2001). Avocation: tennis. Home Phone: 410-667-0411. Business E-Mail: jmaguire@epi.umaryland.edu.

MAGUIRE, JOANNE M., aerospace transportation executive; BS, Mich. State Univ.; MS, UCLA. Positions with TRW Space & Electronics, 1975—2003, prog. mgr. Defense Support, dep. gen. mgr. Defense Systems div., v.p., gen. mgr. Space & Tech. div., v.p., gen. mgr. Space & Laser Programs div., v.p., dep. bus. develop.; v.p., deputy Space Systems Co. Lockheed Martin Corp., Bethesda, Md., 2003—06, exec. v.p. Space Systems Co., 2006—. Bd. dir. Space Found., INROADS Inc. Named one of Most Powerful Women in Bus., Fortune mag., 2006; recipient Outstanding Leadership award, Women in Aerospace, 1999. Mem.: AIAA, Soc. Women Engineers. Office: Lockheed Martin Corp 6801 Rockledge Dr Bethesda MD 20817 *

MAGUIRE, JOHN DAVID, academic administrator, educator, writer; b. Montgomery, Ala., Aug. 7, 1932; s. John Henry and Clyde (Merrill) M.; m. Lillian Louise Parrish, Aug. 29, 1953; children: Catherine Merrill, Mary Elizabeth, Anne King. AB magna cum laude, Washington and Lee U., 1953, Litt.D. (hon.), 1979; Fulbright scholar, Edinburgh U., Scotland, 1953-54; B.D. summa cum laude, Yale U., 1956, PhD, 1960; postdoctoral research, U. Tübingen, Germany, 1964-65, U. Calif., Berkeley, 1968-69, Silliman U., Philippines, 1976-77; HLD (hon.), Transylvania U., 1990. Dir. Internat. Student Ctr., New Haven, 1956-58; mem. faculty Wesleyan U., Middletown, Conn., 1960-70, assoc. provost, 1967-68; vis. lectr. Pacific Sch. Religion and Grad. Theol. Union, Berkeley, 1968-69; pres. SUNY Coll. at Old Westbury, 1970-81, Claremont (Calif.) Grad. U., 1981-98. Sr. fellow Claremont Grad. U. Sch. Politics and Econs.; trustee (charter) Keck Grad. Inst. Applied Life Scis., 1997-98, (hon) Claremont Grad. U., 1998-, Union Theological Seminary, 2003-; dir. nat. project Renewing Democracy through Interracial/Multicultural Comty. Bldg., 1998—; mem. adv. coun. Pacific Oaks Coll., Ga. State U., 1999-, The Advancement Project; sr. adv. Claremont Mus. Art; nat. co-dir. Inst Democratic Renewal/Project Change's joint antiracism venture, 2002-. Author: The Dance of the Pilgrim: A Christian Style of Life for Today, 1967; also numerous articles. Mem. Conn. adv. comt. US Comn. Civil Rights, 1961—70; participant White House Conf. on Civil Rights, 1966; advisor Martin Luther King Cent. Social Change, Atlanta, 1968—, permanent trustee, 1968—, 1st chmn. bd. dirs., 1968—; bd. dirs. Nassau County Health and Welfare Coun., 1971—81, pres., 1974—76; trustee United Bd. Christian Higher Ed in Asia, 1975—81, Inst. Int. Ed., 1980—86; charter trustee Tomas Rivera Policy Inst., Claremont, Calif., 1984—, vice chmn., 1987—94, treas., 1995—; with Asn. Ind. Calif. Cols. and Univs., 1985—98, chmn., 1990—92, mem. exec. comt., 1992—98; with Calif. Achievement Coun., 1985—94, chmn., 1990—94; with Transylvania Univ. Bingham Trust, 1987—, Lincoln Found. and Lincoln Inst. Land Policy, Inc., 1987—94; The JL Found., 1988—; with Educ. Found. African Ams., 1991—99; bd. dirs. Asn. Am. Cols. and Univs., 1981—86, chmn., 1984—85; bd. dirs. Legal Def. and Edn. Fund NAACP, 1991—, west coast div., 1981—91, Thacher Sch., Ojai, Calif., 1982—94, vice chmn., 1986—90; with Salzburg Seminar, 1992—96; charter mem. Pacific Coun. Int. Policy, 1995—; mem. Am. Comt. US-Soviet Rels., 1981—92, Blue Ribbon Calif. Comn. Teaching Profession, 1984—86; mem. gov. coun. Aspen Inst. Wye Faculty Seminar, 1984—94; mem. Coun. Fgn. Rels., 1983—; mem. adv. bd. RAND Cent. Research Immigration Policy, 1994—97, Peter F. Drucker Found. Non-Profit Mgt, 1990—, Andrew Young Sch. Policy Ga. State Univ., 1999—, The Eureka Communities, 1998—; mem. Pres.'s Adv. Coun. Comn. on Calif. Master Plan Higher Educ., 1986—87, Los Angeles Educ. Alliance Restructuring Now, 1992—98, Calif. Bus. Higher Educ. Forum, 1992—98; leader Idyllwild Sch. Summer Poetry Festival, 1998—. Recipient Julia A. Archibald High Scholarship award Yale Div. Sch., 1956; Day fellow Yale Grad. Sch., 1956-57; Kent fellow, 1957-60; Howard Found. postdoctoral fellow Brown U. Grad. Sch., 1964-65; Fenn lectr., 7 Asian countries, 1976-77; recipient Conn. Prince Hall Masons' award outstanding contbns. human rights in Conn., 1965; E. Harris Harbison Gt. Tchr. prize Danforth Found., 1968 Fellow Soc. Values Higher Edn. (pres. 1974-81, bd. dirs. 1972-88); mem. Phi Beta Kappa, Omicron Delta Kappa Democrat. Office: Claremont Grad U Inst for Dem Renewal 170 E 10th St Claremont CA 91711-5909 Office Phone: 909-607-9220. Business E-Mail: john.maguire@cgu.edu.

MAGUIRE, MARGARET LOUISE, lawyer; b. Bklyn., Oct. 31, 1944; d. William L. and Elizabeth L. (Steinbugler) M.; 1 child, William Egginton. BA, Marymount Coll., 1965; MA, Colgate U., 1969; JD, U. Louisville, 1977. Bar: Ky. 1977, D.C. 1987. Counsel 1st Ky. Nat. Corp., Louisville, 1977-79; atty. Fed. Res. Bd., Washington, 1979-80; dep. to chmn. FDIC, Washington, 1980-86; atty., cons. The Secura Group, Washington, 1986—. Co-author: Bank Holding Companies: A Practical Guide to Bank Acquisitions and Mergers, 1978-79. Office: The Secura Group Ste 950 1921 Gallows Rd Vienna VA 22182

MAGUIRE, MARTIE (MARTHA ELENOR ERWIN MAGUIRE), musician; b. York, Pa., Oct. 12, 1969; d. Paul and Barbara Erwin; m. Ted Seidel, 1995 (div.); m. Gareth MaGuire, Aug. 10, 2001. Student, So. Meth. U. Performer Blue Night Express, 1984—89; fiddle player, violinist, vocalist Dixie Chicks, 1989—. Musician: (albums) Thank Heavens for Dale Evans, 1990, LIttle Ol' Cowgirl, 1992, Shouldn't a Told You That, 1993, Wide Open Spaces, 1998 (Album of Yr., Acad. Country Music, 1998, Best Country Album, Grammy Awards, 1998, Best Country Artist Clip of Yr., Billboard Awards, 1998, Maximum Vision Clif of Yr., Billboard Awards, 1998, Best Selling Album, Can. Country Music Award, 1999, Song of Yr. (Country), WB Radio Music Awards, 1999, Album of Yr., Acad. Country Music, 1999), Fly, 1999 (Best Country Album, Grammy Awards, 1999, Best Selling Album, Can. Country Music Awards, 2000, Internat. Album, British Country Music Awards, 2000, Country Album of Yr., Billboard Awards, 2000, Album of Yr., Acad. Country Music Awards, 2000, Album of Yr., CMA, 2000), Home, 2002 (Favorite Country Album, Am. Music Awards, 2002, Best Recording Package, Grammy Awards, 2002, Best Country Album, Grammy Awards, 2002), Top of the World Tour: Live, 2003 (Best Country Group Vocal Performance, Grammy Awards, 2005), Taking the Long Way, 2006 (Album of Yr. and Best Country Album, Grammy Awards, 2007), (songs) Not Ready to Make Nice, 2006 (Record of Yr., Song of Yr., Best Performance by a Duo or Group with Vocal, Grammy Awards, 2007); performer: (documentary) Dixie Chicks: Shut Up and Sing, 2006. Named Top New Country Artist, Billboard, 1998, Most Significant New Country Act, Country Monitor, 1998, Group of Yr., CMA, 1998, Top Vocal Group, Acad. Country Music, 1998, Internat. Rising Star, British Country Music Awards, 1999, Country Artist of Yr., Rolling Stone, 1999, Artist of Yr. (Country), WB Radio Music Awards, 1999, Favorite New Artist (Country), AMA, 1999, Vocal Group of Yr., CMA, 1999, Country Artist of Yr., Billboard, 1999, 2000, Vocal Group of Yr., CMA, 2000, Entertainer of Yr., 2000, ACM, 2000, 2001, Vocal Group of Yr., 2001, Favorite Musical Group or Band, People's Choice Awards, 2001, Favorite Country Band, Am. Music Award, 2002, Vocal Group of Yr., Country Music Assn. Award, 2002, Country Duo/Group of Yr., Billboard, 2002; named one of 100 Most Influential People, Time Mag., 2006; recipient Horizon award, CMA, 1998, others. *

MAGUIRE, MILDRED MAY, retired chemistry professor; b. Leetsdale, Pa., May 7, 1933; d. John and Mildred (Sklarsky) Magura. BS in Chemistry, Carnegie-Mellon U., 1955; MS in Phys. Chemistry, U. Wis., 1960; PhD in Phys. Chemistry, Pa. State U., 1967. Devel. chemist Koppers Co., Monaca, Pa., 1955-58; rsch. chemist Am. Cyanamid Co., Stamford, Conn., 1960-63; asst. prof. chemistry Waynesburg Coll., Pa., 1967-70, assoc. prof., 1970-74, prof., 1974—2006, prof. emeritus, 2006. Cons. Pitts. Energy Tech. Ctr., summers 1978-86; faculty rsch. participant Oak Ridge Assoc. Univs., 1978-80, 82-85; Leverhulme vis. prof. U. Leicester, Eng., 1980-81, 1989; US del. Internat. Conf. Phys. Chemists, China, 1996, Sci. and Tech. Conf., India, 1997; vis. prof. chemistry U. Wis., Madison, 2004, 06. Contbr. articles to sci. jours., chpt. to book. Sec. Waynesburg Women's Club, 1981-82; citizen amb. People to People Program, 1996, 97. Recipient Woman of the Yr. award AAUW, Waynesburg, 1983; Cottrell grantee Rsch. Corp. N.Y., 1970-71; Leverhulme vis. fellow U.K., 1980-81; Curie Internat. fellow AAUW, U.K., 1980-81; Robert West Superconductor Rsch. Grantee, Univ. Wis., 2001-05. Mem. AAUP, AAAS, Am. Chem. Soc.; Spectroscopy Soc. of Pitts.; Pitts. Soc. of Analytical Chemists. Avocations: gardening, painting, swimming, classical music, reading. Home: 1550 Crescent Hills 6th St Ext Waynesburg PA 15370-1654 Office: Waynesburg Coll College St Waynesburg PA 15370 Office Phone: 724-852-3278 ext. 254. Personal E-mail: mmaguire@alltel.net, mmaguire@windstream.net.

MAGUIRE, ROBERT FRANCIS, III, real estate investor; b. Portland, Oreg., Apr. 18, 1935; s. Robert Francis Jr. and Jean (Shepard) M. BA, UCLA, 1960. Vice pres. Security Pacific Nat. Bank, LA, 1960-64; chmn. Maguire Ptnrs., LA, 1964—. Exec. bd. med. scis. UCLA. Bd. dirs. Los Angeles County Mus. Art; trustee UCLA Found., Bard Coll.; bd. dirs. St. John's Hosp., Music Ctr. Bd. Govs., Calif. Presidential Citation of Excellence, Am. Inst. Achitects; Real Estate Exec. Yr., NACORE. Mem.: California (Los Angeles); Valley (Montecito, Calif.), L.A. Country. E-mail: robert.maguire@maguirepartners.com.

MAGUIRE, TOBEY (TOBIAS VINCENT MAGUIRE), actor; b. Santa Monica, Calif., June 27, 1975; s. Vincent and Wendy Maguire; 1 child, Ruby. Actor: (films) The Wizard, 1989, This Boy's Life, 1993, Healer, 1994, SFW, 1994, Revenge of the Red Baron, 1994, Joyride, 1996, The Ice Storm, 1997, Deconstructing Harry, 1997, Pleasantville, 1998 (Saturn Award for best performance by a younger actor, 1999), Fear and Loathing in Las Vegas, 1998, Ride with the Devil, 1999, The Cider House Rules, 1999, Wonder Boys, 2000 (Toronto Film Critics Assn. Award for best male supporting performance, 2000), Don's Plum, 2001, Spider-Man, 2002, Spider-Man 2, 2004, The Good German, 2006, Spider-Man 3, 2007; voice (films) Cats & Dogs, 2001; actor: (TV films) Tales from the Whoop: Hot Rod Brown Class Clown, 1990, Spoils of War, 1994, A Child's Cry for Help, 1994, Seduced by Madness: The Diane Borchardt Story, 1996, (short film) Duke of Groove, 1996 (Oscar nomination for best short film, 1996); (TV series) Great Scott!, 1992; actor, exec. prodr.: (films) Seabiscuit, 2003; (TV films) Rock of Ages, 2003; prodr.: (films) 25th Hour, 2002, Whatever We Do, 2003; guest appearences on: Blossom, 1991, Roseanne, 1991, Eerie, Indiana, 1991, Wild & Crazy Kids, 1992, Walker, Texas Ranger, 1994, Tracey Takes On, 1996. Office: c/o SFM 1122 S Robertson Blvd Los Angeles CA 90036 also: c/o Creative Artists Agency 9830 Wilshire Blvd Beverly Hills CA 90212-1825 *

MAGURNO, RICHARD PETER, lawyer; b. Suffern, NY, June 29, 1943; s. Eugene and Rose (Foresta) M. BS, Georgetown U., 1964; MS, U. Wis., 1965; JD, Fordham U., 1968. Bar: N.Y. 1970, Fla. 1982, U.S. Supreme Ct. 1974, U.S. Ct. Appeals (2d, 5th, 11th cirs.) 1976, U.S. Dist. Ct. (so. and ea. dists.) N.Y. 1979. Atty. Eastern Air Lines, NYC, 1970-73, sr. atty., 1973-76, gen. atty., 1976-79, dir. legal Miami, Fla., 1980, v.p. legal, asst. sec., 1980-84, gen. counsel, sr. v.p. legal, sec., 1984-88; ptnr. Lord Day & Lord, Barrett Smith, 1989-94; gen. counsel, sr. v.p. legal Trans World Airlines, St. Louis, 1994-98; aviation cons., 1998-2000; gen. counsel, sr. v.p., sec. AirTran Airways, 2000—. Author: Romantic Suffern, 1773-1973, 1973. Served in Peace Corps, 1968-69. Mem. ABA, Fla. Bar Assn. Democrat. Roman Catholic.

MAH, SILVIA ARMITANO, director, educator; b. Caracas, Venezuela, Nov. 21, 1973; arrived in US, 1991; d. Ernesto Amadei and Shirley McDaniel Armitano; m. Edward Anthony Mah, June 27, 1998; children: Alexio Nicolas, Matteo Andreas, Sofia Alegria. BS in Biology with honors, Pepperdine U., Malibu, Calif., 1995; PhD, U. Calif. San Diego, La Jolla, 2004. Rsch. technician Abilene Christian U., Tex., field tchg. asst. marine biology, 1996; tchg. asst. invertebrate zoology and cell biology Pepperdine U., Malibu, Calif., 1993—95, lab coord., 1996; field technicain Smithsonian Instn., Washington, 1995; expdn. organizer Royal Ont. Mus., Ontario, Canada, 1997; grad. rsch. asst. U. Calif. San Diego, La Jolla, 1997—2004, head tchg. asst. structural biochemistry, 2003, teams in engring. svc. program dir., 2005—; terraclima outreach program coord. Scripps Instn. Oceanography, La Jolla, 2004—05; sci. cons. Encinitas Sch. Dist. - Mission Estancia Elem. Sch., Calif., 2004—05. Founding mem. Scripps Women in Sci. and Scripps Cmty. Outreach Program for Edn.ope) Scripps Instn. Oceanography, U. Calif. San Diego, La Jolla, 2000—02, career mentor, 2001—02; rsch. mentor U. Calif. San Diego, La Jolla, 2001—04, coord./instr. for sci. outreach, 2002—03; sci. fair judge Greater San Diego Sci. and Engring. Fair, 2004. Membersip chair Am. Women in Sci., San Diego, 2005. Recipient Tchg. Asst. Excellence in Tchg. award, Divsn. Biol. Scis., U. Calif. San Diego, 2003, Outstanding Sr. Rschr. award, Pepperdine U., 2005; fellow Travel award, Am. Soc. for Cell Biology Minorities Affairs Com., 2001—02; scholar, U. ND Alumni Found., 1996; Summer Undergraduate Rsch. in Biology Summer fellow, Pepperdine U., 1994, Advanced Tng. in Molecular Marine Biology fellow, Office Naval Rsch., 1995, Minority Grad. Rsch. fellow, NSF, 1997—2001, Shirley Boyd Meml. Fund fellow, Scripps Instn. Oceanography, U. Calif. San Diego, 2001. Mem.: Golden Key. Office: University of California San Diego 9500 Gilman Dr La Jolla CA 92093-0403 Home Phone: 858-720-9895; Office Phone: 858-822-4164. Personal E-mail: samah@ucsd.edu. Business E-Mail: samah@uccsd.edu.

MAHADEVA, MANORANJAN, financial executive, accountant; b. Colombo, Sri Lanka, Feb. 12, 1955; arrived in US, 1977; s. Kandiah and Rupavathy (Ponniah) M.; m. Donna Sue Martin, May 12, 1986; 1 child, Danielle. BBA, U. Tex., 1981; MBA, Tex. A&M U., 1985. Accrdited in bus. valuation, AICPA; cert. mgmt. acct. and cert. fin. mgmt. Inst. Mgmt. accts., fraud examiner, cash mgr., internal auditor 2002, lic. real estate broker Tex., cert. CPA. Asst. contr. Presbyn. Village North, Dallas, 1981-84; CFO Dallas Meml. Hosp., 1984-86; exec. dir. Associated Orthopedics & Sports Medicine, Plano, Tex., 1986-95; CFO Access Med. Supply Inc., Plano, 1988-95; mng. dir. YNM Corp., Plano, 1987-95; practice adminstr. Tex. Orthopaedic Assocs., Dallas, 1995-96; dir. project mgmt. Physician Reliance Network, Dallas, 1996-99; dir. valuations, bus. devel. US Oncology, Houston, 1999—2001, dirp. fin. planning, 2001—03, dir. regional fin., 2003—. CFO Access Med. Supply, Inc., 1988—96. Mem. editl. rev. bd. Jour. Accountancy and Strategic Fin., mem. editl. rev. bd., column editor Today's CPA; mem. editl. rev. bd.: Fin. Analyst Jour. Mem. Leadership Plano Class 8, 1990-91, bd. dirs., mem. exec. bd., 1991-97, chmn. exec. bd., 1992-93; mem. Mental Health Assn. Collin County, Tex. State Bd. of Physical Therapy Examiners; bd. dirs. Nat. Assn. Cmty. Leadership, vice chair, 1995-97, chair-elect, 1997-98, chair, 1998-99; bd. dirs. Am. Heart Assn., Inst. Mgmt. Accts., 2002—, Then, 2004; bd. dirs., treas. Crisis Ctr. of Collin County; chmn. emergency svcs. Coalition of Collin County; steering com. Leadership USA, 1996-97. Recipient Nat. Disting. Leadership award, 1994; Presdl. scholar Wayne (Nebr.) State U., 1977-78; Mano Mahadeva Day proclaimed in his honor Mayor of Plano, 1999. Mem. CFA Inst., Nat. Assn. Accts. (bd. dirs. North Dallas chpt. 1985-86), Am. Hosp. Assn., Internat. Students Assn., Am. Arbitration Assn. (mem. panel of neutrals), Houston Soc. Fin. Analysts, Plano C. of C. (chmn. cmty. edn. com.), Leadership Plano Alumni Assn. (bd. dirs.), Toastmasters, Lions (past pres. Plano, Lion of Yr. award 1993), Rotary (sec., program chmn., pres. Plano 1996-97, Rotarian of Yr. award 1995, Paul Harris fellow 1998), Delta Sigma Pi, Beta Gamma Sigma. Avocations: reading, tennis, playing drums, jogging, cooking. Office: US Oncology 16825 Northchase Dr Ste 1400 Houston TX 77060-6005 Home: 4113 Aldenham Dr Plano TX 75024 Office Phone: 469-467-4372.

MAHADEVAN, KUMAR, marine life administrator, researcher; b. Madras, Tamilnadu, India, Sept. 29, 1948; came to U.S., 1971; s. Sockalingam Ponnusamy and Pankajam (Nadar) M.; m. Linda Claire Goggin, Sept. 27, 1980; children: Andrew, Alexander, Chad, Vijayan. BS, Madras U., 1967; MS, Annamalai U., Chidambaram, India, 1971; PhD, Fla. State U., 1977. Instr. Chingleput (India) Med. Coll., 1967-68, Lakshman's Coll., Madras, 1968-69; rsch. asst. Fla. State U., Tallahassee, 1971-75; staff scientist Conservation Cons., Inc., Palmetto, Fla., 1975-78; sr. scientist Mote Marine Lab., Sarasota, Fla., 1978-79, dir. divsn., 1979—86, interim co-dir., 1984; pres. Mote Marine Found., Sarasota, Fla., 1986—; trustee Mote Sci. Found., Sarasota, Fla., 1999—. Mem. Coun. on Ocean Affairs, Washington, 1989-91, steering com. Gulf of Mex. Program, Atlanta, 1988-96; mem. South Atlantic and Gulf States Coastal Protection Commn., 1990-93; vice chmn. NOAA Marine Rsch. Bd., Gulf of Mex., 1992-96. Contbr. articles to profl. jours. Mem. sch. adv. bd., Sarasota, 1988-89; mem. tech. adv. bd. Myakka River, Sarasota, 1987-90; legis. liason Parents Assn. of Sarasota Schs., 1988-89; bd. dirs. Jason Found. for Edn., 1991-2004, Health Care Sarasota, 1997-98; vice chmn. Fla. Ocean Alliance, 2000—; mem. Fla. Gov.'s Ocean Com., 1997-98; mem. adv. bd. Harte Inst. for Gulf of Mex. Studies, 2001—; active Sarasota Cmty. Video Archives Hall of Fame, 2005. Nat. Merit scholar Univ. Grants Commn., India, 1969-71. Fellow Explorers Club (nat.); mem. N.Am. Benthological Soc., Oceanographic Soc., World Aquaculture Soc., Deep Sea Biol. Soc. (hon.), Fla. Acad. Scis. (councillor 1975), So. Assn. Marine Labs (pres. 1990, exec. bd. 1986-91, treas. 1995—), Assn. Marine Labs Caribbean (pres. 1987-88, exec. bd. 1984—), Nat. Assn. Marine Labs. (pres. 1994-95), Sci. and Environ. Coun. Sarasota (chmn. 2003-06, Fla. Coastal Ocean Observing Systems Rsch. Consortium (chmn. 2006-07), Greater Sarasota C. of C. (dir. 2005—), Sarasota Rotary Club, Nat. Marine Sanctuary Found. (dir., 2007—).Sigma Xi. Republican. Avocations: racquetball, fishing, gardening. Office: Mote Marine Lab 1600 Ken Thompson Pky Sarasota FL 34236-1096 Home Phone: 941-346-9338. Business E-Mail: kumar@mote.org.

MAHADY, JOSEPH M., former pharmacy products company executive; Pres. Am. Home Products Corp., Madison, NJ; pres., North Am. & Global bus. Wyeth Pharmaceuticals, 1997—, sr. v.p. Office: Wyeth Pharm Five Giralda Farms Madison NJ 07940-0874 also: Wyeth Phar North Am & Global Bus 500 Arcola Rd Collegeville PA 19426 Office Phone: 484-865-5476, 973-660-5771.

MAHAFFEY, JOHN CHRISTOPHER, medical association executive; b. Jefferson City, Mo., July 20, 1953; s. Fred Turner and Betty Cord (Woodfill) Mahaffey; children: Michael, Katherine. BA, Western Ill. U., Macomb, 1975; MS, DePaul U., 1999. Legis. aide Congressman Harold R. Collier, Washington, 1972-73; legis. asst. Nat. Assn. Retail Druggists, Washington, 1975-76; dir. Commn. and Meetings Nat. Assn. Bds. of Pharmacy, Chgo., 1976-80; pres., CEO Assn. Forum, Chgo., 1980—2002; exec. dir. Am. Coll. Foot and Ankle Surgeons, Park Ridge, Ill., 2002—. Bd. dirs. Healthcare Assocs. Credit Union, 2003—. Commr. City of Park Ridge (Ill.) Econ. Devel. Commn., 1990—94, 1996—2000; mem. exec. com. Chgo. Convention and Tourism Bur., Chgo., 1993—2002. Recipient Disting. Alumni award, Western Ill. U., Macomb, 1993. Fellow: Am. Soc. Assn. Execs. (Key award 1994); mem.: U.S. C. of C., Assn. Com. 100. Presbyn. Office: Am Coll Foot and Ankle Surgeons 8725 W Higgins Rd Chicago IL 60631 Office Phone: 773-693-9300.

MAHAFFEY, MARCIA HIXSON, retired educational administrator; b. Scobey, Mont. d. Edward Goodell and Olga Marie (Frederickson) Hixson; m. Donald Harry Mahaffey (div. Aug. 1976); 1 child, Marcia Anne (dec.); m. George Justin Fair, Mar. 26, 1997 (div. June 9, 2004). BA in English, U. Wash.; MA in Secondary Edn., U. Hawaii, 1967. Cert. secondary and elem. tchr., adminstr. Tchr. San Lorenzo (Calif.) Sch. Dist., 1958-59, Castro Valley (Calif.) Sch. Dist., 1959-63, vice prin., 1963-67, Sequoia Union HS Dist., Redwood City, 1967-77, asst. prin., prin., 1977-91, ret., 1991. Tchr. trainer Project Impact Sequoia Union HS Sch. Dist., Redwood City, 1986-91; supr.'s task force for dropout prevention, 1987-91, Sequoia Dist. Goals Commn. (chair subcom. staff devel. 1988) chair, Sequoia Union HS Dist. Grading Com., 1976-1984; mentor tchr. selection com., 1987-91; mem. Stanford Program Devel. Ctr. Com., 1987-91; chair gifted and talented Castro Valley Sch. Dist.; family svcs. bd., San Leandro, Calif. Vol. Am. Cancer Soc., San Mateo, Calif., 1967, Castro Valley, 1965; chair Carlmont H.S. Site Coun., Belmont, Calif., 1977—91; active Nat. Trust for Hist. Preservation; Neighborhood Beautification project dir. Bridle Trails Cmty. Club, 1999—2001; mem. Golden Grads. scholarship com. Roosevelt HS, Seattle, 2000—, co-chair, 2004—; founder Colonial Williamsburg, 2006; Sunday sch. tchr. Hope Luth. Ch., San Mateo, 1970—76. Recipient Life Mem. award Parent, Tchr., Student Assn., Belmont, 1984, Svc. award, 1989, Exemplary Svc award Carlmont High Sch., 1989, 92; named Woman of the Week, Castro Valley, 1967, Outstanding Task Force Chair Adopt A Sch. Program San Mateo (Calif.) County, 1990. Mem.: DAR, AAUW, ASCD, Acad. Am. Poets, Sequoia Dist. Mgmt. Assn. (pres. 1975, treas. 1984—85), Assn. Calif. Sch. Adminstrs. (Project Leadership plaque 1985), Mohave County Landowners' Assn., Animal Welfare Advocacy, Libr. of Congress Assocs. (charter), Met. Mus. Art, Smithsonian Instn., Am. Heritage-The Soc. of Am. Historians, Woodrow Wilson Internat. Ctr. Scholars, The Heritage Found., White Ho. Hist. Assn. (charter), Am. Mus. Natural History (charter), Alpha Xi Delta (Order of Rose award 1997), Delta Kappa Gamma. Avocations: painting, travel, tap dancing, redecorating, poetry. *Personal philosophy: Life is short, so make haste to be kind to one another.*

MAHAFFEY, REDGE ALLAN, movie producer, director, writer, actor, scientist, business executive; b. Bethesda, Md., Dec. 15, 1949; s. George Newton and Lila Katherine (Drum) M.; m. Ellen Cecilia Cranston, May 30, 1973 (div. Dec. 1980); m. Patricia Jane Guy, Apr. 29, 1984 (div. Sept. 1994); children: Travis Guy, Morgan Nicole; m. Veronica Bird, Sept. 24, 1994; children: Ryan Alexander, Ramsey Blake. BS, U. Md., 1971, MS, 1973, PhD, 1976. NRC postdoctoral fellow Nat. Acad. of Scis., Washington, 1976-77; research physicist Naval Research Lab., Washington, 1977-78; sr. research physicist Sachs/Freeman Assocs., Bladensburg, Md., 1978-79, dir. research Bowie, Md., 1979-81, exec. v.p., chief scientist Largo, Md., 1981-91, 1999—, also bd. dirs. Landover, Md., 1985—; mng. ptnr. Ramsway Pictures, 1991—; pres. WHOH, Davidsonville, Md., 1993—. Instr. George Washington U., Washington, 1979-80, Prince George's Coll., 1987; pres. Capitol Contracts, Bowie, 1981-83. Author: A Higher Education, 1989, Me, Myself and I, 1992, Deadly Rivals, 1992; exec. prodr., writer Deadly Rivals, 1992, Quest of the Delta Knights, 1993; prodr., actor, writer, dir. Life 101, 1995 (hon. mention Atlantic City Film Festival 1997), First Encounter, 1997; prodr., actor, dir., writer She's Too Tall, 1998 (Best Comedy award Atlantic City Film Festival 1998); contbr. articles on lasers and particle beams to sci. jours., also short stories, essays and poems to mags.; patentee laser, x-rays and particle beams. Recipient

Research Publ. award Naval Research Lab., 1978, 1st Place Novel Internat. Lit. Awards, 1988, award of merit Internat. Soc. for Advancement of Poetry, 1990. Mem. IEEE, Am. Phys. Soc., Mensa, Intertel, Nat. Writer's Club, Internat. Platform Assn., Internat. Soc. Phil. Enquiry, Writer's Assn. Anne Arundel County, Bethesda Writer's Ctr., Inst. Noetic Scis. Clubs: Sea Dragons Martial Arts(Washington) (treas. 1984-85, instr. 1987-91). Republican. Avocations: martial arts, softball, basketball. Office: SFA Inc 2200 Defense Hwy Crofton MD 21114 Office Phone: 301-858-1244. E-mail: redge@sfa.com.

MAHAJAN, ARVIND, finance educator; b. Delhi, India, Nov. 24, 1951; arrived in U.S., 1974; s. Vedavrata and Shakuntala Mahajan; m. Vanita Mahajan, Jan. 16, 1983; children: Aseem K., Sia S. B of Commerce in Acctg. and Fin., U. Delhi, 1972; MBA in Fin., U. Scranton, 1975; PhD in Fin., Ga. State U., 1980. Fin. officer Raisina Press, Delhi, 1972—74; instr., rsch. asst. Ga. State U., Atlanta, 1976—79; sr. cons. Mfrs. Hanover Trust Co., NYC, 1987—88; asst. prof. fin. Tex. A&M U., College Station, 1980—86, assoc. prof., 1986—92, prof., 1992—94, Lamar Savings prof. fin., 1994—, assoc. dir. acad. programs Ctr. Internat. Bus. Studies and CIBER, 1990—99. Vis. prof. Group Ecole Superieure de Commerce, Rennes, France, 2000, Johannes Kepler U., Linz, Austria, 1992—99, Group Ecole Superieure de Commerce, Dijon, France, 1991; faculty mem. Acad. Future Internat. Leaders, 1998—2000. Contbr. articles to rsch. jours. and confs. Pres. Coalition Support Pub. Schs., College Station, 2003. Avocations: travel, reading, music. Office: Tex A&M U Mays Bus Sch College Station TX 77843

MAHAJAN, ASHUTOSH, library and information scientist; B in Tech., Indian Inst. Tech., New Delhi, India, 2003. Grad. asst. Lehigh U., Bethlehem, Pa., 2003—04, tchg. asst., 2004—05, grad. asst. libr. and tech. svcs., 2006—. Sys. adminstr. Coral lab. Lehigh U., 2004—, rsch. asst. SAS inst., 2005—06; cons. in field. Recipient Nat. Top 1% in Physics Olympiad award, Indian Assn. Physics Teachers, 1999; scholar, Nat. Coun. Ednl. Rsch. and Tng., India, 1999—2003. Mem.: Asha for Edn. (web mgr. Lehigh chpt. 2005—06), Iforms Computing Soc., Inst. Ops. Rsch. and Mgmt. Scis., Clean Energy and Water for All (web mgr. 2006—07), India Club Lehigh U. (sec. 2004—05), Phi Beta Delta. Avocations: hiking, running, puzzles. Home Phone: 610-758-2995.

MAHAJAN, SUBHASH, electronic materials educator; b. Gurdaspur, India; m. Sushma Sondhi, Sept. 3, 1965; children: Sanjoy, Sunit, Ashish. BS with highest honors, Panjab U., India, 1959; BE in Metallyrgy with highest honors, Indian Inst. Sci., 1961; PhD in Materials Sci. and Engring., U. Calif., 1965. Rsch. asst. U. Calif., Berkeley, 1961-65; rsch. metallurgist U. Denver, 1965-68; Harwell fellow Atomic Energy Rsch. Establishment, Harwell, England, 1968-71; mem. tech. staff AT&T Bell Labs., Murray Hill, NJ, 1971-83, rsch. mgr., 1981-83; prof. electronic materials dept. material sci. and engring. Carnegie Mellon U., Pitts., 1983-97; prof. electronic materials Ariz. State U., Tempe, 1997—, assoc. chair, 1999, interim chair and chair dept. chem. and materials engring., 2000—06, dir. Sch. Materials, 2006—, Regents' prof., 2007. Mem. site panel Materials Rsch. Lab., 1993; vis. prof. U. Antwerp, Belgium, 1991, Ecole Ctrl. Lyon, Ecully, France, 1993; lectr., spkr., patentee, cons. in field. Editor: Handbook on Semiconductors, vol. 3, 1994, Acta Materialia, 2001; editor: (with V.G. Keramidas) Electrochemical Society Symposium Volume, 1983; editor: (with L.C. Kimerling) The Concise Encyclopedia of Semiconducting Materials and Related Technologies, 1992; editor: (with D. Bloor, R.J. Brook and M.C. Flemings) The Encyclopedia of Advanced Materials, 1994; editor: (with K.H. Jurgen Buschow, Robert W. Cahn et al) Encyclopedia of Materials: Science and Technology, 2001; coordinating editor: The Acta Materiala Jours., 2004—; contbr. more than 200 articles to profl. jours. Mem. materials rsch. adv. com. divsn. materials rsch. NSF, 1989-92. Fellow TMS, Am. Soc. Metals Internat. (trustee bd., Albert Sauveur Achievement award); mem. NAE, Materials Rsch. Soc. (editor symposium volume 1983, organizer symposium Am. Assn. Crystal Growers), Electrochem. Soc. (mem. electronics divsn. 1973-86, divisional editor 1976-86), Minerals, Metals and Materials Soc. (mem. phys. metallurgy com. 1976-83, vice chmn. mech. metallurgy com. 1978-79, mem. 1975-80, mem. electronic materials com. 1990-94, chmn. electronic, magnetic and photonic materials com. 1984-86, tech. dir. bd., John Bardeen award, The Educator award), Sigma Xi. Home: 8824 S Poplar St Tempe AZ 85284-4521 Office: Ariz State U Sch Materials Tempe AZ 85287 Home Phone: 480-345-9192; Office Phone: 480-727-9322. Business E-Mail: smahajan@asu.edu.

MAHALAWICH, ANNE MARY, retired mathematics educator; b. Norwich, Conn., Mar. 10, 1922; d. Dimitry and Emilia Pisarko; m. Nicholas Mahalawich, Nov. 24, 1945. BS, Willimantis State Tehrs. Coll., 1943, MS, 1967. Mem. RSVP, 1980—2006; mem. bd. Otis Libr.; pres. Taxpayer's Assn. Mem.: New London Retired Tchrs. (pres.), Norwich Tchrs. League (pres. 1972—73), AARP (pres.), Beta Sigma Phi (Profl. Woman of Yr. 1989), Phi Beta Kappa, Delta Kappa Gamma (pres.). Ea. Orthodox. Home: 7838 Naples Heritage Dr Naples FL 34112 Personal E-mail: amahalawich@aol.com.

MAHALEY-JOHNSON, HOSANNA, school system administrator; b. 1968; BA, Marquette U., Milw., 1991; MEd, U. Ill., Chgo. Chief of staff Chgo. Pub. Schools, 2001—, dir. New Schools Devel., dir. Renaissance 2010 initiative, 2006—. Bd. dirs. City Yr. Chgo.; bd. advisors Chgo. Comty. Trust. Named one of 40 Under 40, Crain's Chgo. Bus., 2006. Office: Chgo Pub Schools 5th Fl 125 S Clark St Chicago IL 60603 Office Phone: 773-553-1530. Office Fax: 773-553-2199.

MAHAN, CLARENCE, federal agency administrator, writer; b. Dayton, Ohio, Jan. 1, 1939; s. Clarence Mahan and Elsie (Crouch) Dlitz; m. Suky Mahan, May 27, 1962; children: Sean M., Christiane Elizabeth. BA, U. Md., 1963; MA, Am. U., 1968; MBA, Syracuse U., 1969. Dep. comptroller U.S. Army, Japan, 1974-76; dep. chief program and budget Defense Commn. Agy., Arlington, Va., 1976; aide Asst. Sec. Army, Washington, 1976-77; chief operating appropriations Dept. AF, Washington, 1979-80; dir. fin. and acctg. Dept. Energy, Washington, 1980-81, dep. comptroller, 1981-82; dir. fiscal and contracts mgmt. EPA, Washington, 1982-83, dep. comptroller, 1983-85, dir. Rsch. Program Mgmt. Office, 1985-95. Instr., lectr. in field. Author: Classic Irises and the Men and Women Who Created Them, 2007; contbr. articles to profl. jours. and hort. mags. With U.S. Army, 1959-62, Korea. Mem. Am. Iris Soc. (bd. dirs., 2d v.p. 1991-95, 1st. v.p. 1995-98, pres. 1998-2001), Hist. Iris Preservation Soc. (pres. 1991-93), Soc. Japanese Irises (pres. 1989-92), Reblooming Iris Soc. (bd. dirs. 1986-94, pres. 2002-05). Democrat. Home and Office: 7311 Churchill Rd Mc Lean VA 22101-2001 Business E-Mail: cemahan@aol.com.

MAHAN, DAVID JAMES, retired academic administrator; b. St. Louis, May 29, 1934; s. John William and Eleanor (Johnson) M.; m. Jane E. Pyle, Nov. 28, 1957; children: Elizabeth Mahan-Shaw, Kathryn Goodman. BA, Okla. Baptist Coll., 1956; MA, Washington U., St. Louis, 1962, EdD, 1968. Cert. elem., secondary English tchr., Mo., cert. elem. prin., Mo., cert. supt., Mo. Adminstr., tchr. St. Louis Pub. Schs., 1958-90, supt., 1990-96; supt. in residence U. Mo., St. Louis, 1996-99. Co-author: The Faculty Team: School Organization for Results, 1971. Bd. dirs. Commerce and Growth Assn., St. Louis, 1990—, Asthma and Allergy Found. Am., St. Louis, 1990—, St. Louis Symphony Soc., 1992—, Boy Scouts Am., 1992—. Home: 5 Portland Ct Saint Louis MO 63108-1293

MAHAN, GERALD DENNIS, physicist, researcher; s. Thomas Finley and Julia Kay (Swails) M.; m. Sally Ann Spaugh, Feb. 20, 1965; children—Christopher Parker, Susan Thayer, Roy Finley AB, Harvard U., 1959; PhD in Physics, U. Calif.-Berkeley, 1964. Rsch. physicist GE, Schenectady, 1963-67, part-time, 1967-84; assoc. prof. physics U. Oreg., Eugene, 1967-73; prof. physics Ind. U., Bloomington, 1973-82, disting. prof., 1982-84; disting. prof. physics U. Tenn., Knoxville, 1984—2001, Penn State U., University Park. Guest prof. Niels Bohr Inst., Copenhagen, 1977-78 Author: Many-Particle Physics, 1981; contbr. articles to profl. jours. Alfred Sloan fellow, 1968-70. Fellow Am. Phys. Soc.; mem. NAS, AAAS. Office: Penn State U 104 Davey Lab University Park PA 16802 Business E-Mail: gmahan@psu.edu.

MAHAN, JAMES CAMERON, judge; b. El Paso, Tex., Dec. 16, 1943; m. Eileen Agnes Casale, Jan. 13, 1968; 1 child, James Cameron Jr. BA, U. Charleston, 1965; JD, Vanderbilt U., 1973. Bar: Nev. 1974, U.S. Dist. Ct. Nev. 1974, U.S. Ct. Appeals (9th cir.) 1975, U.S. Tax Ct. 1980, U.S. Supreme Ct. 1980. Assoc. Lee & Beasey, Las Vegas, Nev., 1974-75; mem. firm John Peter Lee Ltd., Las Vegas, 1975-82; sr. ptnr. Mahan & Ellis, Chartered, Las Vegas, 1982-99; dist. ct. judge 8th Jud. Dist. Nev., Las Vegas, 1999—2002; U.S. dist. judge, 2002—. Adj. prof. law Boyd Sch. Law, U. Nev., Las Vegas, 2005—. With USN, 1966-69. Office: 333 Las Vegas Blvd S Las Vegas NV 89101 Home Phone: 702-645-3627; Office Phone: 702-464-5520. E-mail: james_mahan@nvd.uscourts.gov.

MAHAN, MARY HOYLE, retired physical educator; b. Boston, July 19, 1939; d. Frederick John and Mary Dwyer Hoyle; m. J. Roger Mahan Jr., Mar. 21, 1970 (dec. June 1999). BS in Phys. Edn., Bridgewater State Coll., 1960; MS in Phys. Edn., U. N.C., 1963; EdD, Nova U., 1975. Tchr. phys. edn. Stoughton Jr. High Sch., Mass., 1960—62; tchr. phys. edn., coach Locust Valley Jr./Sr. High Sch., NY, 1963—65; prof. phys. edn., coach Ctrl. Conn. State U., New Britain, 1965—71, Miami-Dade C.C. North, 1971—2001, assoc. athletic dir., dept. chair, prof., 1980—2001, ret., 2001. CEO, pres. The Teaching Well, Ftr. Lauderdale, Fla., 2000—. Bd. trustees Bridgewater State Coll. Found., 2002—, Lake Isle Woods Assn., Centerville, 2004—; edn. found. Villanova U., Pa., 2003—. Named Weymouth High Sch. Hall Fame, Bridgewter State Coll. Hall Fame, Fla. C.C. Activities Assn. Hall Fame; recipient 3 Outstanding Faculty awards, Miami-Dade C.C., 1985, Case Prof. of Yr., U. Tex., 1996, Endowed Tchg. Chair, Bowden award, Cheshle Acad., Natycaa Billmiller award. Mem.: Nat. Assn. Coll. Directors of Athletics, Am. Alliance Health, Phys. Edn., Recreation and Dance, Am. Coll. Sports Medicine, Delta Psi Kappa. Independent. Roman Catholic. Avocations: golf, interior decorating, travel. Home (Winter): 3750 Galt Ocean Dr #2007 Fort Lauderdale FL 33308 Home (Summer): 30 Crestview Cir Centerville MA 02632

MAHANEY, MICHAEL C., library director; m. Lee Mahaney; 1 child, Kate. BA with honors, SUNY, Buffalo, MLS with honors, 1976. With Buffalo & Erie County Pub. Libr., NY, 1973—, with Ctrl. Libr. NY, asst. dep. dir. cmty. rels. NY, 1990—2000, dep. dir., COO NY, 2000—02, dir. NY, 2003—. V.p. Explore and More, East Aurora, NY, pres.; bd. trustees NY Ctr. for Books and Reading. Mem. pres.'s adv. coun. Erie CC. Mem.: ALA, NY Libr. Assn. Office: Buffalo & Erie County Pub Libr 1 Lafayette Sq Buffalo NY 14203-1887 Office Phone: 716-858-7179. Office Fax: 716-858-6544. E-mail: mahaneym@buffalolib.org. *

MAHANI, MOHAMMAD SHADBAKHT, engineering educator; b. Teheran, Iran; s. Mahmood Shadbakht and Shamsi Torkzad Sanian; children: Mehdy, Bita, Dariush. Degree in mgmt., Air Force Acad., Teheran, 1973; BS, U. Ill., Chgo., 1990; MS, U. Ill., 1991. Rsch. asst. U. Ill., Chgo., 1990—91; educator Wilbur Wright Coll., Chgo., 1991—93; dir., educator Acad. Lang. and Computer Sci., Chgo., 1993—; prof. DeVry U., Chgo., 1998—. Mem.: Alpha Chi Iota (advisor, award 2003), Eta Kappa Nu. Achievements include design of unique method of teaching and learning English as a second language. Home: 6534 W Montrose Ave # 1-E Harwood Heights IL 60706 Office: DeVry Univ 3300 N Campbell Ave Chicago IL 60618 Office Phone: 773-777-7797. E-mail: mmahani@chi.devry.edu.

MAHAR, ELLEN PATRICIA, law librarian; b. Washington, Jan. 15, 1938; d. Richard A. and Lina Mahar. BA, St. Joseph Coll., Emmitsburg, Md., 1959; MLS, U. Md., 1968. Asst. librarian Covington & Burling, Washington, 1971-73, libr. dir., 1978-92; librarian Shea & Gardner, Washington, 1974-78; mgr. info. ctr. Assn. Comml. Real Estate, Herndon, Va., 1992-94; head libr. Caplin & Drysdale Chtd., Washington, 1994—. Co-editor: Legislative History of the Securities Act of 1933 and the Securities Act of 1934, 11 vols., 1973. Mem. Am. Assn. Law Libraries, Spl. Libraries Assn., Law Librarians' Soc. Washington. Office: Caplin & Drysdale Chtd 1 Thomas Cir NW Fl 11 Washington DC 20005-5802

MAHARIDGE, DALE DIMITRO, journalist, educator, writer; b. Cleve., Oct. 24, 1956; s. Steve and Joan (Kopfstein) Maharidge. Student, Cleve. State U., 1974—75. Freelance reporter various publs., Cleve., 1976, Cleve. Plain Dealer, 1978—80; reporter The Gazette, Medina, Ohio, 1977—78, Sacramento Bee, 1980—91; vis. prof. Stanford U., Palo Alto, Calif., 1992—2002; asst. prof. Columbia U. Grad. Sch. Journalism, NYC, 2002—. Art colony resident Yaddo Residency, 2004. Author: Journey to Nowhere: The Saga of the New Underclass, 1985, Journey to Nowhere: The Saga of the New Underclass repub. with introduction by Bruce Springsteen, 1996, And Their Children After Them, 1989 (Pulitzer Prize for gen. nonfiction, 1990), The Last Great American Hobo, 1993, The Coming White Minority: California, Multiculturism and the Nation's Future, 1996, The Coming White Minority: California's Eruptions and the Nation's Future, Vintage Books edit., 1999, Homeland, 2004, Denison, Iowa: Searching for the Soul of America Through the Secrets of a Midwest Town, 2005; contbr. articles to profl. jours. Grantee, Open Soc. Inst., 2006; Freedom Forum grantee, 1995, Nieman fellow, Harvard U., 1988, Pope Found. grantee, 1994. Democrat. Office Phone: 212-854-3854. Personal E-mail: dmaharidge@yahoo.com.

MAHER, BILL, television personality and producer, comedian; b. NYC, Jan. 20, 1956; s. Bill and Julie (Berman) M. BA in English, Cornell U., 1978. Creator, host Politically Incorrect, Comedy Central, NYC, 1993-96, Politically Incorrect, ABC, 1996—2002; host Real Time With Bill Maher, HBO, 2003—. Performances include (theatre) Seymour Glick is Alive But Sick (Steve Allen); (stand-up) The Bob Monkhouse Show, Late Night with David Letterman, The Tonight Show Anniversary Show, The Tonight Show, HBO Spl., 1989, 92, 95, 97, 2000, 03; (TV shows) Steve Allen's Music Room, Alice, Sara, Max Headroom, Hard Knocks, Newhart, Murder, She Wrote, The Midnight Hour, Say What?; (TV movies) Out of Time, Rags to Riches, Club Med; (films) D.C. Cab, Rat Boy, House II, Cannibal Women in the Avocado Jungle of Death, Pizza Man; author: (books) True Story, 1994, Does Anybody Have a Problem With That? Politically Incorrect's Greatest Hits, When You Ride Alone You Ride with bin Laden, 2002, New Rules: Polite Musings from a Timid Observer, 2005. Recipient CableACE award Nat. Acad. Cable Programming, 1990, CableACE award for best talk show series, 1995, CableACE award for best talk show host, 1995, President's award for championing free speech, LA Times Press Club, 2002, Johnny Carson Prodr. of Yr. award, Prodrs. Guild Am., 2007. Office: Brillstein Grey Entertainment Ste 350 9150 Wilshire Blvd Beverly Hills CA 90212 *

MAHER, BRENDAN ARNOLD, retired psychology educator, editor; b. Widnes, Eng., Oct. 31, 1924; came to US, 1955; s. Thomas F. and Agnes (Power) M.; m. Winifred Barbara Brown, Aug. 27, 1952; children: Rebecca, Thomas, Nicholas, Liam, Niall. BA with honours, U. Manchester, Eng., 1950; MA, Ohio State U., 1951, PhD, 1954; student, U. Ill. Med. Sch., 1952-53; AM (hon.), Harvard, 1972; DPhil (hon.), U. Copenhagen, 1998. Diplomate Am. Bd. Examiners in Profl. Psychology. Psychologist Her Majesty's Prison, Wakefield, England, 1954-55; instr. Ohio State U., Ohio, 1955-56; asst. prof. Northwestern U., 1956-58; asso. prof. La. State U., La., 1958-60; lectr. Harvard, 1960-64; chmn. Ctr. Rsch. Personality, 1962-64; prof. U. Wis., 1964-67, 71-72; vis. fellow U. Copenhagen, 1966-67, vis. fellow and rsch. scientist, 1979, 96-98; prof. psychology Brandeis U., 1967-72; dean Brandeis U. (Grad. Sch.), 1969-71, dean faculty, 1971-72; E. C. Henderson prof. psychology Harvard U., 1983-99, E.C. Henderson rsch. prof., 1999—2004, E.C. Henderson prof. emeritus, 2004—, prof., 1972—, chmn. dept. psychology and social relations, 1973-78, chmn. dept. psychology, 1987-89, dean Grad. Sch. Arts and Scis., 1989-92; assoc. psychologist McLean Hosp., Belmont, Mass., 1968-77, psychologist, 1977-84; prof. emeritus, 2004—. Cons. in medicine Peter Bent Brigham Hosp., Boston, 1977-85; cons. in psychology Mass. Gen. Hosp., 1977-2002. Author: Principles of Psychopathology, 1966, Introduction to Research in Psychopathology, 1970, A Passage to Sword Beach, 1996; co-editor: National Research Council: Rsch. Doctorate Programs in the United States, 1995; editor Progress in Exptl. Personality Rsch., 1964-87, Jour. Cons. and Clin. Psychology, 1972-78; cons. editor Rev. Personality and Social Psychology, Clin. Psychology Rev. Served with Brit. Royal Navy, 1943-47. Recipient Zubin award for rsch. in psychopathology, 1998. Fellow AAAS, Am. Psychol. Soc.; mem. Brit. Psychol. Assn. (chartered psychologist UK), Soc. Rsch. in Psychopathology (pres. 1985-87), Phi Beta Kappa. Office: Harvard U William James Hall Cambridge MA 02138 also: Giffords Island Mahone Bay NS Canada Business E-Mail: bam@wjh.harvard.edu.

MAHER, DAVID WILLARD, Internet company executive; b. Chgo., Aug. 14, 1934; s. Chauncey Carter and Martha (Peppers) M.; m. Jill Waid Armagnac, Dec. 20, 1954; children: Philip Armagnac, Julia Armagnac. BA, Harvard, 1955, LLB, 1959. Bar: NY 1960, Ill. 1961, Wis. 1996, US Patent Office 1961. Pvt. practice, Boston, NYC, 1958-60; assoc. Kirkland & Ellis, and predecessor firm, 1960-65, ptnr., 1966-78, Reuben & Proctor, 1978-86, Isham, Lincoln and Beale, 1986-88, Sonnenschein, Nath & Rosenthal, Chgo., 1988—2003; ret., 2003; chmn. bd. dirs. Publ. Interest Registry, 2003—04, sr. v.p law and policy, 2004—. Dir. BBB Chgo. and No. Ill., 2004—; lectr. DePaul U. Sch. Law, 1973—79, Loyola U. Law Sch., Chgo., 1980—84. Contbr. articles to profl. jours. Vis. com. U. Chgo. Div. Sch., 1986—. 2nd lt. USAF, 1955—56. Recipient Torch of Integrity award, Better Bus. Bureau, Chgo. and N. Ill., Inc. Fellow Am. Bar Found. (life); mem. ABA, Am. Law Inst., Wis. State Bar, Chgo. Bar Assn., Chgo. Lit. Club. Roman Catholic. Home: 501 N Clinton St Apt 1503 Chicago IL 60610-8886 Office: Pub Interest Registry 1775 Wiehle Ave Ste 102A Reston VA 20190 Office Phone: 312-876-8055. Business E-Mail: dmaher@pir.org.

MAHER, JAMES VINCENT, JR., physics professor, academic administrator; b. NYC, Aug. 25, 1942; s. James Vincent and Anne (Cunneen) M.; m. Angela Beth Braunstein, Aug. 13, 1966; children: Robin, James. BS in Physics, U. Notre Dame, 1964; MS in Physics, Yale U., 1965, PhD in Physics, 1969. Postdoctoral fellow Argonne (Ill.) Nat. Lab., 1968-70; asst. prof. U. Pitts., 1970-74, assoc. prof., 1974-80, prof., 1980—, fellow Ctr. for Philosophy of Sci., dept. chair physics and astronomy, 1991-94, provost and sr. vice-chancellor, 1994—. Dir. Scaife nuclear physics lab., 1979-80. Contbr. over 100 articles to profl. jours. Intellectual property task force Assn. Am. Univs., 1998—99; task force on accreditation Nat. Assn. State Univs. and Land Grant Colls., 1997—2000; commr. Med. States Commn. Higher Edn., 2004—. Grantee Dept. Energy, NSF. Fellow AAAS, Am. Phys. Soc.; mem. Am. Crystal Growth Assn. (pres. Pitts. chpt. 1989-92, exec. com. 1988-93), Sigma Xi. Democrat. Roman Catholic. Home: 1313 Denniston Ave Pittsburgh PA 15217-1330 Office: U Pitts Office of the Provost Pittsburgh PA 15260 Office Phone: 412-624-4223. Business E-Mail: jvmaher@pitt.edu.

MAHER, JOHN, literature educator, writer; b. Cedar Rapids, Iowa, Apr. 25, 1945; s. Rose F. (Hopkins) Maher. BS, So. Ill. U., 1972; MA, Ariz. State U., 1976; PhD, Pacific W. U., 1992. Tchg. asst. So. Ill. U., 1972; tchr. Phoenix Union H.S. Dist., Ariz., 1976—82, Mesa Sch. Dist., 1982—97; adj. prof. Ctrl. Ariz. Coll., 1990—2002; ret., 2002. Author: Twentieth Century Campfire Culture, 1999. Chmn. Pinal County Transp. Com., 1990—; mem. Gov. Task Force on Transp., 2001. With US Army, 1963—65. Mem.: C.A.A.R.S. Corvette Club (founder). Democrat. Roman Catholic. Avocation: Grand Canyon hiking. Home: 131 W Canyon St Apache Junction AZ 85220

MAHER, JONATHAN BANNON, finance executive; b. Manhattan, NY, June 21, 1981; s. Richard Donald and Marianne Bannon Maher. BA in Bus. Adminstrn., U. San Diego, 2005. Cert. Oracle Developer, Oracle Corp., Calif., 2000; EMT NJ. Founder, CEO Host1, NYC, 1993—. Cons. Bear Stearns, NYC, 2005. Named a Master Scuba Diver, Nat. Assn. Underwater Instrs. Achievements include patents pending for structure & interface for building an information management application. Office: One Columbus Pl S 46A New York NY 10019 Home Phone: 646-496-5104; Office Phone: 646-496-5104. Business E-Mail: jonathan.maher@host1.com.

MAHER, L. JAMES, III, molecular biologist; b. Mpls., Nov. 28, 1960; s. Louis James and Elizabeth Jane (Crawford) M.; m. Laura Lee Moseng, July 2, 1983; children: Elizabeth Lillian, Christina Ailene. BS in Molecular Biology, U. Wis., 1983, PhD in Molecular Biology, 1988. Fellow U. Wis., Madison, 1983-84, rsch. asst., 1984-88; postdoctoral fellow Calif. Inst. Tech., Pasadena, 1988-91; asst. prof. molecular biology Eppley Inst., U. Nebr. Med. Ctr., Omaha, 1991-95; assoc. prof. biochem. molecular biology Mayo Clinic Coll. Medicine, Rochester, Minn., 1995-2000, prof., 2000—02, vice chmn., 2002—, assoc. dean for academic affairs, 2003—. Editorial bd. Antisense and Nuclear Acid Drug Design, 1991—, Nucleic Acids Rsch. Jour., 1988—; contbr. articles to profl. jours. Musician, Madison Symphony Orch., 1983-88, Calif. Inst. Tech. Symphony Orch., L.A., 1988-91. Gosney fellow, 1988; Am. Cancer Soc. postdoctoral fellow, 1988. Mem. AAAS, Phi Beta Kappa. Evangelical Christian Ch. Achievements include research in chemical and biochemical agents designed to artificially regulate the flow of genetic information in biological systems. Office: Mayo Clinic Coll Medicine Dept Biochem and Molec Biol 200 1st St SW Rochester MN 55905-0001 Home Phone: 507-287-0275; Office Phone: 507-284-9041. Business E-Mail: maher@mayo.edu.

MAHER, LOUIS JAMES, JR., geologist, educator; b. Iowa City, Iowa, Dec. 18, 1933; s. Louis James and Edith Marie (Ham) M.; m. Elizabeth Jane Crawford, June 7, 1956; children: Louis James, Robert Crawford, Barbara Ruth. BA, U. Iowa, 1955, MS, 1959; PhD, U. Minn., 1961. Mem. faculty dept. geology and geophysics U. Wis.-Madison, 1962—, prof., 1970—2003, chmn. dept., 1980-84, prof. emeritus, 2003—. Contbr. articles to profl. jours. With US Army, 1956—58, with counter intelligence corps US Army, 1957—58, Duty Sta., La Rochelle, France. Danforth fellow, 1955-61; NSF fellow, 1959-61; NATO fellow, 1961-62 Fellow AAAS, Geol. Soc. Am.; mem. Am. Quaternary Assn., Ecol. Soc. Am., Wis. Acad. Sci., Arts and Letters, Sigma Xi. Episcopalian. Office: U Wis Dept Geology and Geoph 1215 W Dayton St Madison WI 53706-1600 Office Phone: 608-262-9595. E-mail: maher@geology.wisc.edu.

MAHER, THOMAS GEORGE, academic administrator, producer, media educator; b. St. Louis, Feb. 18, 1947; s. Dale Russell and Dorothy Leone M.; m. (div.). AB, St. Louis U., 1969, MA, 1971; PhD, U. So. Calif., 1985. Cert. C.C. tchr. and supr., Calif. Tchg. fellow St. Louis U., 1969-71; assoc.

prof. Chaffey Coll., Rancho Cucamonga, Calif., 1974-79, media dir., 1980-84; assoc. producer Corp. for C.C. TV, Orange, Calif., 1979-80; assoc. dir. instrnl. tech. Calif. State Poly. U., Pomona, 1984-89; dir. office media svcs. U. Ill., Chgo., 1989-94; dir. office instrnl. svcs. Colo. State U., Ft. Collins, 1994—2006, interim v.p. divsn. ednl. outreach, 2000—02, dir. ebs and digital media, 2006—. Cons. Rsch. Comm., Ltd., Boston, 1984-94; book reviewer Focal Press, Inc., Boston, 1985-94. Writer: (TV series) Project: Universe, 1978 (Emmy award nomination 1979), The Business of Management, 1981; assoc. producer, dir., writer (TV series) Oceanus: The Marine Environment, 1979 (Emmy award 1980); exec. producer (TV program) For the People: Local Gov. Budget Making, 1992 (Cert. Merit, Chgo. Internat. Film/Video Festival 1992); producer, dir. (live nat. video teleconference, moderated by Sen. Bill Bradley) Campus Line-up with Carol Moseley Braun, 1992; instrnl. designer (interactive videodisc) Smog Check Multimedia Simulation Test, 1993 (INVISION Merit award, New-Media Multimedia awards, 1993); prodr., dir. numerous additional refereed ednl. TV shows, 1974—. 1st lt. USAF, 1971-74. Grantee Air Force, 1967-69; Mary Clemmens scholarship St. Louis U., 1965-67, Educare scholar U. So. Calif., 1983-84; grantee numerous competitive contracts. Mem. Acad. TV Arts and Scis. (judge coll. Emmy awards, 1989), Am. Ednl. Research Assn., Assn. for Ednl. Comm. and Tech, Alpha Sigma Nu, Psi Chi. Democrat. Roman Catholic. Avocations: reading, computers, running, theater, piano. Office: Colorado State U Mail Stop 1018 Fort Collins CO 80523-1018 Home Phone: 970-568-3777; Office Phone: 970-491-3315. Business E-Mail: thomas.maher@colostate.edu.

MAHER, VIRGINIA JONES, art historian, educator; b. Milw., Oct. 11, 1941; d. Frederick Thomas Murphy and Virginia June Harmon; m. William H. Jones, Aug. 22, 1964 (dec. Nov. 23, 1982); children: William H. Jones Jr., Michael J. Jones, Megan Jones Townsend; m. J. Thomas Maher, III, May 14, 1994. BS, U. Wis., Milw., 1964, MA in Art History, 1994, cert. art mus. studies, 1994. Tchr. French and English Custer HS, Milw., 1964; curatorial asst. Kohler Art Ctr., Sheboygan, Wis., 1993; curator fine arts commn. Cathedral of St. John, Milw., 1995—2003; instr. art history Cardinal Stritch U., Milw., 1997—99, Peninsula Art Sch., Fish Creek, Wis., 2001—; lectr. art history Milw. Art Mus., 2004—. Guest art curator Miller Art Mus., Sturgeon Bay, Wis., 2000—; bd. dirs. Peninsula Art Sch., chmn. acquisitions com., 2002—; lectr. in field. Organizer Friends of Art History, Milw., 2000—03; hist. preservation Jr. League Evanston, Ill., 1980—81, lectr. art in the sch., 1978—80; mem. dean's adv. com. Inst. Visual Arts U. Wis. Milw., 2004; bd. dirs. Wis. Heritages Inc., Milw., 1996—99, Am. Heritage Soc. Milw. Art Mus., 1994—98. Named Writer of Yr. award, Metalsmith Mag., 1998; recipient Grad. of Last Decade (G.O.L.D.) award, U. Wis., Milw., 2000. Mem.: Nat. Mus. Women in Arts, Collectors' Corner Milw. Art Mus., Contemporary Art Soc. Milw. Art Mus., Womans Club Wis., Alpha Phi. Roman Catholic. Avocations: art collecting, painting, gardening. Home: 5611 Schauer Rd Sturgeon Bay WI 54235 Personal E-mail: vmaher@itol.com.

MAHERAS, THOMAS G., diversified financial services company executive; b. Chgo., Nov. 25, 1962; BBA in Fin., U. Notre Dame, 1984. Various positions including head mortgage-backed securities, head high yield trading desk Salomon Smith Barney (Citigroup), 1984—96, vice chmn., head global fixed income, 1996—2004; CEO global capital markets, global corp. & investment banking group Citigroup Inc., NYC, 2004—06, co-pres. global corp. & investment banking group, 2007, co-chmn., co-CEO Citi Markets & Banking, 2007—. Mem. borrowing adv. com. U.S. Treasury Dept. Mem.: Bond Market Assn. (bd. dirs., mem. exec. com.). Office: Citigroup Inc Global Corp and Investment Banking Group 399 Park Ave New York NY 10043 *

MAHESH, VIRENDRA BHUSHAN, endocrinologist; b. India, Apr. 25, 1932; came to U.S., 1958, naturalized, 1968; s. Narinjan Prasad and Sobhagyawati; m. Sushila Kumari Aggarwal, June 29, 1955; children: Anita Rani, Vinit Kumar. BSc with honors, Patna U., India, 1951; MSc in Chemistry, Delhi U., India, 1953, PhD, 1955; DPhil in Biol. Sci, Oxford U., 1958. James Hudson Brown Meml. fellow Yale U., 1958-59; asst. rsch. prof. endocrinology Med. Coll. Ga., Augusta, 1959-63, assoc. rsch. prof., 1963-66, prof., 1966-70, Regents prof., 1970-86, Robert B. Greenblatt prof., 1979-99, chmn. endocrinology, 1972-86, chmn., Regents prof. physiology and endocrinology, 1986-99, chmn. physiology and endocrinology, 1986-99, regents prof., chmn. emeritus physiology and endocrinology, 1999—, Robert B. Greenblatt prof. emeritus endocrinology, 1999—. Dir. Ctr. for Population Studies, 1971-99; mem. reproductive biology study sect. NIH, 1977-81, mem. human embryology and devel. study sect. NIH, 1982-86, 90-93, chmn., 1991-93. Contbr. articles to profl. jours., chpts. to books; editor: The Pituitary, a Current Review, Functional Correlates of Hormone Receptors in Reproduction, Recent Advances in Fertility Research, Hirsuitism and Virilism, Regulation of Ovarian and Testicular Function, Excitatory Amino Acids: Their Role in Neuroendocrine Function; mem. editl. bd. Steroids, 1963—, Jour. of Clin. Endocrinology and Metabolism, 1976-81, Jour. Steroid Biochemistry and Molecular Biology, 1991—, Assisted Reproductive Tech./Andrology, 1993-98, Endocrinology, 1999-2003; mem. adv. bd. Maturitas, 1977-81; editor-in-chief Biology of Reprodn., 1999-2004, cons. editor, 2004—. Recipient Rubin award Am. Soc. Study Sterility, 1962, Billings Silver medal, 1965, Best Tchr. award freshman class Sch. Medicine, Med. Coll. Ga., 1969, Outstanding Faculty award Sch. Medicine, 1992, Outstanding Faculty award Sch. Grad. Studies, 1981, 94, Disting. Tchg. award, 1988, Excellence in Rsch. award Grad. Faculty Assembly, 1987-91, 93-95, Disting. Scientist award Assn. Scientist Indian Origin in Am., 1989, Lifetime Achievement award Sch. Medicine, 1997, Lifetime Achievement award Med.Coll. Ga. Rsch. Inst., 2006; rsch. grantee NIH, 1960-2000. Fellow Am. Soc. Exptl. Biology (bd. dirs. 2004-07); mem. AAUP, Chem. Soc. (Eng.), Soc. Biochem. and Molecular Biol., Soc. Neurosci., Endocrine Soc., Soc. for Gynecologic Investigation, Internat. Soc. Neuroendocrinology, Soc. for Study Reproduction (Carl G. Hartman award 1996, Disting. Svc. award 2005), Am. Physiol. Soc. (chmn. endocrinology and metabolism sect. 2004-06), Internat. Soc. Reproductive Medicine (pres. 1980-82), Soc. Exptl. Biology and Medicine, Am. Fertility Soc., Am. Assn. Lab. Animal Sci., NY Acad. Scis., Sigma Xi. Home Phone: 256-882-7130. Business E-Mail: vmahesh@mail.mcg.edu.

MAHESWARANATHAN, PONN, physicist, educator; b. Colombo, Sri Lanka, Dec. 15, 1954; arrived in U.S., 1980, naturalized, U.S., 1998; s. Sithamparanathar and Kamalambikai Ponnampalam; m. Shyamala Navaratnam, July 2, 1987; children: Mithunan, Niruban. BS, Peradeniya U., Sri Lanka, 1978; MS, Purdue U., 1982, PhD, 1985. Asst. lectr. U. Peradeniya, 1978-79, U. Jaffna, Sri Lanka, 1979-80; asst. prof. physics Winthrop U., Rock Hill, SC, 1985-92, assoc. prof., 1992—2003, prof., 2003—. Contbr. articles to profl. jours. Grantee, Winthrop Rsch. Coun., 1992, 1998, 2000, 2001, 2007, SC Dept. Edn., 2006, 2007. Mem.: Am. Phys. Soc. Hindu. Achievements include discovery of of enhancement of electromechanical coupling; piezoelectric constant in Cd1-x MnxTe. Home: 1750 Colony Rd Rock Hill SC 29730-3810 Office: Winthrop U 101 Sims Rock Hill SC 29733-0001 Home Phone: 803-327-1262; Office Phone: 803-323-4940. Business E-Mail: mahesp@winthrop.edu.

MAHEY, JOHN ANDREW, retired museum director; b. DuBois, Pa., Mar. 30, 1932; s. Manasseh A. and Bernyce (Holdar) M. Student, Columbia U., 1950-52; BA, Pa. State U., 1959, MA, 1962. Asst. dir. Peale Mus., Balt., 1964-69; dir. E.B. Crocker Art Gallery, 1969-72, Cummer Gallery of Art, 1972-75, Meml. Art Gallery of U. Rochester, 1975-79; chief curator Philbrook Art Center, Tulsa, 1979-84; dir. San Antonio Mus. Art, 1984-89, Flint (Mich.) Inst. of Arts, 1989-96; ret., 1996. Contbr. articles on artists to art his. jours.; author exhbn. catalogs. Fulbright scholar, 1962 Mem. Phi Beta Kappa, Phi Alpha Theta. Home: 4645 N Progress Ave Harrisburg PA 17119 E-mail: mahey@aol.com.

MAHINKA, STEPHEN PAUL, lawyer; b. Hazleton, Pa., June 25, 1949; s. Stephen and Mary (Stanziola) M.; m. Nancy Marie Casper, Aug. 30, 1975; 1 child, Alexandra Kathryn. AB, Johns Hopkins U., 1971; JD, Harvard U., 1974. Bar: Pa. 1974, D.c. 1975, U.S. Dist. Ct. D.C. 1975, U.S. Ct. Appeals (D.C. cir.) 1976. Law clk. to chief justice Mass. Appeals Ct., Boston, 1974-75; assoc. Morgan, Lewis & Bockius, 1975-81, ptnr., 1981—. Chmn. Life Sci. Interdisciplinary Group; mem. Antitrust and FDA Healthcare Groups, Fin. Com. Contbr. articles to Food and Drug Law Jour., Antitrust Law Jour.; contbr. treatise chpt.: Nat. Labor Rels. Act: Law & Practice, 1995, Winning Antitrust Strategies, 2004; mem. editl. bd. Food and Drug Law Jour., 1992-95. Trustee Johns Hopkins U., Balt., 1974-79. Mem. ABA (chair com. labor exemptions, sect. antitrust law, Chgo., 1983-87), Regulatory Affairs Profls. Soc., Phi Beta Kappa. Republican. Roman Catholic. Office: Morgan Lewis & Bockius LLP 1111 Pennsylvania Ave Washington DC 20004 Home Phone: 703-759-4461; Office Phone: 202-739-5205. Office Fax: 202-739-3001. Business E-Mail: smahinka@morganlewis.com.

MAHLE, CHRISTOPH ERHARD, electrical engineer; b. Stuttgart, Germany, Mar. 7, 1938; came to U.S., 1968; s. Ernst Johannes and Else (Wurth) M.; m. Mary Heavenrich, Mar. 23, 1975; children: Lisa, Charles. Diploma engring., Swiss Fed. Inst. Polytech., Zurich, 1961, D of Sci. Tech., 1966. Rsch. asst. Swiss Fed. Inst. Tech., Zurich, Switzerland, 1961-67; with tech. staff Comsat Labs., Clarksburg, Md., 1968-71, sect. head, 1971-73, dept. mgr., 1973-81, dir., 1981-83, exec. dir., 1983-94, v.p., 1995-96; ret., 1996. Patentee in field; contbr. articles to profl. jours. Fellow IEEE. Avocations: music, mountain climbing. E-mail: chrismahle@usa.net.

MAHLEN, TATUM L., voice educator; d. William C. Young and Rhonda R. Moen, Jon L. Moen (Stepfather); m. DuWayne L. Mahlen, Jr.; children: Jasa E., Sasha A., Gabriel J. MusB, U. S.D., 1998. Vocal dir. Mitchell Sch. Dist., 2000—06, Hastings H.S., Minn., 2006—. Choir dir. Mitchell Wesleyan Ch., 2004—. Mem.: Am. Choral Dirs. Assn. (state R&S show choir chair 2004—06). Home: 5020 142d Path W Apple Valley MN 55124 Office: Hastings HS Zoo Gen Sieben Hastings MN 55033 E-mail: tmahlen@hastings.k12.mn.us.

MAHLENDORF, URSULA RENATE, literature educator; b. Strehlen, Silesia, Germany, Oct. 24, 1929; arrived in US, 1953; Student, Oberschule an der Hamburgerstraße, Bremen, Fed. Republic Germany, 1950, U. Tübingen, Fed. Republic Germany, 1950-52, Brown U., Providence, 1953-57, MA in English Lit., 1956, PhD in German Lit., 1958; student, Bonn U., Fed. Republic Germany, 1953, London U.; grad., New Directions in Psychoanalysis, Washington, 2002. Teaching asst. Brown U., Providence, 1953-57; from acting instr. to prof. German U. Calif., Santa Barbara, 1957—93, prof. women's studies, 1988—93, assoc. dir., campus coord. edn. abroad program, 1967—69, chmn. dept. Germanic and Slavic langs. and lits., 1980-83, assoc. dean Coll. Letters and Sci., 1986-89, emeritus, 1993—. Chmn. symposium in honor of Harry Slochower, 1977; campus coord. edn. abroad program U. Calif., 1967-69, assoc. dir., 1969-72; co-chair Nietzsche symposium Dept. Germanic and Slavic Langs. and Lits., U. Calif., Santa Barbara, 1981. Author: The Wellsprings of Literary Creation, 1985; editor: (with John L. Carleton) Man for Man: A Multi-Disciplinary Workshop on Affecting Man's Social and Psychological Nature through Community Action (Charles C. Thomas), 1973, Dimensions of Social Psychiatry, 1979, (with Arthur Lerner) Life Guidance through Literature, 1992, (in German) Surviving Childhood; assoc. editor Am. Imago, Am. Jour. Social Psychiatry, Jour. Evolutionary Psychology; contbr. more than 90 articles to profl. jours. Recipient Alumni Tchg. award, 1981; rsch. grantee, U. Calif., 1974—, Fulbright fellow, 1951—52, Festschrift named in her honor, 2004. Mem. MLA, Am. Assn. for Aesthetics and Art Criticism (past pres. Calif. div.), Assn. for applied Psychoanalysis (profl. mem.), Am. Assn. Social Psychiatry (councillor 1977-81), Internat. Assn. Social Psychiatry (treas. 1978-83). Avocations: sculpting, woodcarving. Home: 1505 Portesuello Ave Santa Barbara CA 93105-4626 Office: U Calif Dept Germanic Semitic Slavic Studies Santa Barbara CA 93106 Office Phone: 805-893-2131. Business E-Mail: mahlendo@gss.ucsb.edu.

MAHLER, HALFDAN THEODOR, physician, health organization executive; b. Vivild, Denmark, Apr. 21, 1923; s. Magnus and Benedicte (Suadicani) M.; m. Ebba Fischer-Simonsen, Aug. 31, 1957; children: Per Bo, Finn. MD, U. Copenhagen, 1948, degree in pub. health; LLD (hon.), U. Nottingham, Eng., 1975; MD (hon.), Karolinska Inst., Stockholm, 1977; Docteur, U. Scis. Sociales de Toulouse, France, 1977; DPH (hon.), Seoul Nat. U., 1979; ScD (hon.), U. Lagos, Nigeria, 1979, Emory U., 1989; MD (hon.), Warsaw Med. Acad., 1980; LHD (hon.), U. Nat. Federico Villareal, Lima, Peru, 1980, U. Gand, Belgium, 1983, CUNY, 1989; MD (hon.), Charles U., Prague, 1982, Mahidol U., Bangkok, Thailand, 1982, Aarhus U., Denmark, 1988, U. Copenhagen, 1988, Aga Khan U., Pakistan, 1989; LHD (hon.), U. Nat. Autonoma de Nicaragua, 1983; PhD (hon.), Semmelweis U., Budapest, Hungary, 1987; LLD (hon.), McMaster U., Can., 1989; DSc (hon.), SUNY, 1990; MD (hon.), U. Newcastle Upon Tyne, 1990; LLD (hon.), U. Exeter, 1990, U. Toronto, 1990; DPH (hon.), U. Goteborg, 2005. Specialized tng. in TB; active field of internat. pub. health work; planning officer mass Tb campaign Ecuador, 1950-51; sr. officer nat. Tb program WHO, India, 1951-61, chief Tb unit, Hdqrs., Geneva, 1962-69, sec. to expert adv. panel on Tb, 1962-69, dir. project systems analysis, 1969-70, asst. dir.-gen. div. health services and div. family health, 1970-73, dir.-gen., 1973-88, dir. gen. emeritus, 1988; sec. gen. Internat. Planned Parenthood Fedn., 1989-95. Contbr. articles to profl. jours. Decorated Grand Officier de l'Ordre Nat. du Benin, 1975, Grand Officier de l'Ordre Nat. du. Voltaique, Upper Volta, 1978, comdr. de l'Ordre Nat. du Mali, 1982, Grand Officer de l'Ordre du Merite de la Rep. du Senegal, 1982, comdr. 1st class Order White Rose (Finland), Grand Officier de l'Ordre nat. malgache, Madagascar, 1987, Grand Cross Icelandic Order of the Falcon, 1988, Grand Cordon of Order Sacred Treasure, Japan, 1988, Bourgeoisie d'Honneur, Geneva, Switzererland, Grand Croix De L'Ordre De Merite, Luxenbourg, 1990, Grand Cross Ordem do Merito Medico, Brazil, 2003; recipient Jana Evangelisty Purkyne medal (Presdl. award) Prague, 1974, Comenius U. Gold medal Bratislava, 1974, Carlo Forlanini gold medal Federazione Italiana contro la Tubercolosi et le Malattie Polmonari Sociali Rome, 1975, Ernest Carlsens Found. Prize Copenhagen, 1980, Georg Barfred-Pedersen prize Copenhagen, 1982, Hagedorn medal and prize Denmark, 1986, Freedom From Want medal Roosevelt Inst., 1988, Storkors Af Dannebrogsordenen, Denmark, 1988; hon. prof. U. Nat. Mayor de San Marcos, Lima, Peru, U. Chile Faculty of Medicine, Beijing Med. Coll., Rep. of China, Shanghai Med. U.; Bartel World Affairs fellow Cornell U., 1988; U.N. Population award, 1995, Andrija Stampar award, 1995. Fellow Royal Coll. Physicians (London), Faculty Community Medicine of Royal Colls. Physicians U.K. (hon.), Indian Soc. for Malaria and other Communicable Diseases (hon.), Royal Soc. Medicine (London) (hon., U.K.-U.S. Hewitt award 1992), London Sch. Hygiene and Tropical Medicine (hon.); mem. Med. Assn. Argentina (hon.), Latin Am. Med. Assn. (hon.), Italian Soc. Tropical Medicine (hon.), Belgium Soc. Tropical Medicine (assoc.), Societe medicale de Geneve (hon.), Union Internat. contre la Tuberculose (hon.), Soc. Francaise d'Hygiene, de Medecine sociale et de Genie sanitaire (hon.), Uganda Med. Assn. (hon. life), Coll. Physicians and Surgeons, Bangladesh Royal Coll. Gen. Practitioners (ad eundem), List of Honour of the Internat. Dental Fedn., Am. Pub. Health Assn. (hon.), Nat. Acad. Medicine Mex. (hon.), Nat. Acad. Buenos Aires (hon.), Swedish Soc. Medicine (hon.), Brit. Medal Assn. (hon. fgn. corr. 1990), Inst. Medicine (NAS U.S.A.). Achievements include research in epidemiology and control of Tb, polit., social, econ, and technol. priorities in health sector, application of systems analysis to health care problems. Home and Office: Chemin de Pont-Céard 12 CH-1290 Versoix Switzerland Office Fax: 022 755 26 10. Business E-Mail: halfdan.mahler@bluewin.ch.

MAHLEY, ROBERT W., health facility administrator; b. July 23, 1941; m. Linda Mahley; children: Stephen, Leslyn. BS, Maryville Coll., Tenn., 1963; PhD, Vanderbilt U., 1968, MD, 1970; MD (hon.), U. Gsoteborg, Sweden. Instructor biology Maryville Coll., Tenn., 1963—64; MD and PhD program Vanderbilt U., 1964—70, pathology intern, 1970—71; staff Nat. Heart, Lung, and Blood Inst., NIH, Bethesda, Md., 1971—75, head, comparative atherosclerosis and arterial metabolism sect., lab. exptl. atherosclerosis, 1975—79; dir., sr. investigator Gladstone Inst. of Cardiovascular Disease, San Francisco, 1979—; prof. pathology and medicine U. Calif., San Francisco, 1979—; pres. J. David Gladstone Inst., U. Calif., San Francisco, 1992—; sr. investigator Gladstone Inst. of Neurological Disease, San Francisco, 1998—. Contbr. articles to profl. jours. Recipient Heinrich Wieland prize, George Lyman Duff Meml. Lectureship, Am. Heart Assn. award, CIBA-GEIGY award in Biomedical Rsch., Metropolitan Life award for Medical Rsch. in Alzheimer's Disease, Nat. Cholesterol Education Program DeWitt S. Goodman award for Basic Science Achievement, Distinguished Alumnus Award, Vanderbilt U. Sch. Medicine. Fellow: Am. Acad. Arts & Sciences; mem.: NAS, Am. Soc. for Clinical Investigation, Assn. Am. Physicians, IOM. Office: J David Gladstone Inst 1650 Owens St San Francisco CA 94158 Office Phone: 415-794-2000. Office Fax: 415-355-0826. Business E-Mail: rmahley@gladstone.ucsf.edu.

MAHLMAN, JERRY DAVID, retired meteorologist; b. Crawford, Nebr., Feb. 21, 1940; s. Earl Lewis and Ruth Margaret (Callendar) M.; m. Janet Kay Hilgenberg, June 10, 1962; children: Gary Martin, Julie Kay. AB, Chadron State Coll., Nebr., 1962, LHD (hon.), 2000; MS, Colo. State U., 1964, PhD, 1967. Instr. Colo. State U., Ft. Collins, 1964-67; from asst. prof. to assoc. prof. Naval Postgrad. Sch., Monterey, Calif., 1967-70; rsch. meteorologist NOAA Geophys. Fluid Dynamics Lab., Princeton, NJ, 1970-84, lab. dir., 1984-2000; lectr. with rank of prof. Princeton U., NJ, 1980—2002; sr. rsch. fellow Nat. Ctr. for Atmospheric Rsch., Boulder, Colo., 2001—. Chmn. panel on mid-atmosphere program NAS-NRC, 1982-84, mem. climate rsch. com., 1986-89, mem. panel on dynamic extended range forecasting, 1987-90; mem. U.S.-USSR Commn. on Global Ecology, 1989-92; mem. Bd. on Global Change, 1991-95, Bd. on Sustainable Devel., 1995-2000, Commn. to Review U.S. Climate Change Program Strategic Plan, 2002-03; U.S. rep. world climate rsch. program Joint Sci. Commn., 1991-96. Contbr. over 100 articles to profl. jours. Bd. dirs. Lawrence Non-Profit Housing Inc., 1978-88. Recipient Disting. Authorship award Dept. Commerce, 1980, 81, Gold medal, 1986, Disting. Svc. award Chadron State Coll., 1984, Presdl. Rank award disting. exec. 1994, Honor Alumnus award Colo. State U. 1995, Climate Protection award EPA, 2000. Fellow Am. Geophys. Union (Jule Charney lectr. 1993), Am. Meterol. Soc. (awards com. 1984, 95, chmn. 2000, chmn. upper atmosphere com. 1979, assoc. editor Jour. Atmospheric Sci. 1979-86, councilor 1991-94, Editor's award 1978, Carl-Gustaf Rossby Rsch. medal 1994, disting. lectr. 1999), Blue Key Nat. Honor Soc., Lambda Delta Lambda (life), Phi Kappa Phi (life), Sigma Delta Nu (life), Sigma Xi. Home: 460 Golden Ln Longmont CO 80501 Office: Nat Ctr for Atmospheric Rsch PO Box 300 Boulder CO 80307-3000 Business E-Mail: jmahlman@ucar.edu. *

MAHLUM, DALE DUANE, state legislator, small business owner; b. Bowman, ND, June 12, 1930; s. Lloyd S. and Ragna (Paulson) M.; m. Sandra Sue Little, Dec. 21, 1956; children: Douglas, Connie, Thomas, Dee Ann, Michele. BS, U. Mont, 1956. Mgr. Super Foods, Kalispell, Mont., 1958—93; store owner Ace Hardware, Missoula, Mont., 1959-93; thoroughbred farm owner, breeder Missoula, Mont.; mem. Mont. Senate, Dist. 35, Helena, 1996—2003. Chmn. Mont. Bank Bd., Missoula, 1974—; bd. dirs. Mont. Hardware Implement, Helena, St. Patricks Hosp., Missoula; chmn. adv. bd. sch. bus U. Mont., Missoula, 1985-88. Mem. Western Mont. Fair Commn., Missoula, 1974-94. With USN, 1950-54. Mem. Mont. Thoroughbreds Breeders Assn. (pres.), Thoroughbred Owners/Breeders Assn. Republican. Lutheran. Home: 10955 Us Highway 93 N Missoula MT 59808-9227 Office: Mont Legislature PO Box 201706 Helena MT 59620-1706 Office Phone: 406-549-3115. Personal E-mail: mal51732@aol.com.

MAHMOOD, AKHTAR HASAN, physicist, educator, researcher; b. Dhaka, Bangladesh, Mar. 26, 1969; s. Mohammad Ahsan Ali and Selima Akhtar. BSc with honors, Edinboro U. Pa., 1992; MSc, SUNY, Albany, 1994, PhD, 1998. Rsch. asst. SUNY, Albany, 1994-98, lab. instr., 1994-97, rsch. scientist high energy physics lab., 1998-99; lectr. U. Tex. Pan Am., Edinburg, 1998-99, asst. prof., dir. Ctr. High Energy Physics, 1999—2004; asst. prof. Edinboro U., Pa., 2004—. Grant reviewer NASA, 1999, NSF, 2000, 02, State of La. Bd. Regents, 2003; book reviewer Prentice Hall, McGraw Hill, 2001. Contbr. over 250 articles to profl. jours. Recipient Provost Scholar award Rsch. Coll. Sci. and Engring 2000, Outstanding Faculty award, 2000, Cos&E Rsch. Excellence award, 2000; rsch. grantee Tex. Higher Edn. Coord. Bd., 1999, Rsch. grantee U. Tex. Pan Am., 1999, Faculty Rsch. grantee, 1999-2002; NSF grantee, 2002, rsch. grantee Edinboro U. Pa. Faculty Senate, 2005, Pa. State Sys. Higher Edn. Faculty Devel. Coun., 2005. Mem. AAAS, CLEO, Am. Phys. Soc., Assn. Computing Machinery, Coun. Undergrad. Rsch., NY Acad. Scis., GriphyN, Virtual Data Grid Lab., Sigma Xi, Pi Mu Epsilon, Phi Kappa Phi. Muslim. Achievements include discovery of several new subatomic particles. Office: Edinboro U Pa Dept Physics Edinboro PA 16444 Home Phone: 814-734-4030; Office Phone: 814-732-1237. Business E-Mail: mahmood@edinboro.edu.

MAHMOOD, NAFEESA F., physician, consultant; MD, Punjab U., Lahore, Pakistan. Lic. Nat. Bd. Med. Examiners; cert. personal trainer Am. Coun. Exercise. Faculty, staff physician U. Minn., Mpls.; cons. internal medicine Mayo Clinic Outreach, Rochester, Minn.; med. dir., CEO, pres. New You Med. Aesthetics, LLC, St. Paul. Academic faculty, staff physician U. Ill., Urbana-Champaign, adviser, preceptor, clin. instructor, Chgo.; genomics liason Mayo Clinic, spkr. women's seminars in hypertention. Contbr. articles to profl. jours. Recipient Shield Healing Skills From God award, U. Ill. dept. medicine, Outstanding Clinician for Oustanding Diagnostic Skills & Clin. Achievement award, Certificate Commendation For Outstanding Clin. Performance award, U. Ill. dept. internal medicine. Mem.: Am. Soc. Laser Medicine and Surgery, Day Spa Assn., Am. Coll. Sports Medicine, ACP, Aerobics and Fitness Assn. of Am. (assoc.), Am. Acad. Aesthetic Medicine (assoc. Mem.), Am. Acad. Anti Aging Medicine (assoc. Membership), Am. Acad. Cosmetic Surgery (assoc.). Achievements include research in angiotensin II and amiodarone induced apoptosis of type 2 alveolar epithelail cells, duet to blockade of AT1 receptors by losartan and L compound. Avocations: jogging, exercise, reading, music, baking.

MAHMOOD, TALLAT, oncologist, hematologist; b. Lahore, Pakistan, Apr. 9, 1968; arrived in U.S.A., 1994; d. Mahmood Ali and Furrukh Begum Khan; m. Shahid H. Khan, Jan. 29, 1993; children: Aquila, Nadir, Mohsin. MD, Aga Khan U., 1991. Diplomate Am. Bd. Internal Medicine, Oncology, and Hematology. Clin. fellow Tulane U. Med. Ctr., New Orleans, 1997—99, rsch. fellow, 1999—2000; staff physician Marquette (Mich.) Gen. Hosp., 2000—. Contbr. articles to profl. jours. Mem.: AMA, Am. Soc. Hematology, Am. Soc. Oncology. Avocations: skiing, golf. Office: Marquette General Hospital 1414 W Fair Ave Ste 332 Marquette MI 49855

MAHMOODI, HAMID, engineer; s. Teimoor Mahmoodi and Fatemeh Dehghan. BSEE, Iran U. Sci. and Tech., 1998; MS in Elec. and Computer Engring., U. Tehran, 2000. Design engr. IUST Electronic Rsch. Ctr., Tehran, Iran, 1998—99; grad. rsch. asst. Purdue U., West Lafayette, Ind., 2001—. Author: (tech. jour. paper) Estimation of Delay Variations Due to Random-Dopant Fluctuations in Nanoscale CMOS Circuits. Recipient Best Paper award, Internat. Conf. on Computer Design, 2004. Mem.: Toastmasters Internat., Gigascale Systems Rsch. Corp., Semiconductor Rsch. Corp., IEEE. Achievements include patents pending for Dynamic Logic Styles Using Independent Gate Control in Double-Gate SOI Technologies; First Level Supply Gating for Low Power Scan-Based Testing; research in low power, robust and high performance circuit design in nano-scaled technologies, low power and robust memory design, circuit design with nano-scaled devices. Avocations: swimming, cooking. Home Phone: 765-496-4824; Office Phone: 765-494-0750. Business E-Mail: mahmoodi@ecn.purdue.edu.

MAHMOODZADEGAN, NAVID A., investment banker; b. 1969; JD, Harvard U. Assoc., corp. securities dept. Irell & Manella Law; assoc. to ptnr., tech. group Donaldson, Lufkin & Jenrette, 1995; exec. dir., media and tech. Credit Suisse First Boston; head, media investment banking UBS Warburg, LA, 2000—06, global head, media investment banking, 2006—. Recipient Rainmaker Prize in media investment banking, Dealmaker mag., 2006. Office: UBS Media Investment Banking 1999 Ave of Stars Los Angeles CA 90067 Office Phone: 310-556-6700. *

MAHMOUD, ADEL A., physician, molecular biologist, educator; b. Cairo, Aug. 24, 1941; arrived in US, 1972; s. Abdel Fattah and Fathia (Osman) Mahmoud; m. Sally L. Hodder, Jan. 31, 1993. Grad., Cairo U., 1958, MD, 1963; PhD, U. London, 1971. Asst. lectr. Ain Shams U., Cairo, 1965—68; WHO fellow U. London, 1969—72; rsch. assoc., prof. Case Western Res. U., Cleve., 1973—87, prof., chmn. dept. medicine, 1987—98; physician-in-chief Univ. Hosps., Cleve., 1987—98; pres. vaccines Merck & Co. Inc., Whitehouse Sta., NJ, 1998—2006; prof. dept. molecular biology and Woodrow Wilson Sch. Princeton U., 2007—. Editor: The Eosinophil in Health and Disease, 1979, Tropical and Geographical Medicine, 1990, Schistosomaisis, Tropical Medicine Sci. and Practice, Vol. 1, 2001, Biological Threats and Terrorism: Assessing the Science and Response Capabilities, 2002. Fellow: Infectious Diseases Soc. Am.; mem.: Inst. Medicine, Assn. Am. Physicians, Am. Soc. Clin. Investigations. Office: Princeton Univ 228 Lewis Thomas Lab Princeton NJ 08544 Office Phone: 609-258-8557. Business E-Mail: amahmoud@princeton.edu.

MAHMUD, SHIREEN DIANNE, photographer; b. Chittagong, Pakistan, Oct. 4, 1949; came to U.S., 1974; d. Mohammed Mazhurul Qudus and Mumtaz Mahal Begum; m. Abdul Wazed Mahmud, Apr. 10, 1966 (div. 1996); children: Sharmin, Anita. BA in Mass Comm., U. Hartford, 1982. Part-time med. sec., Middletown, Conn., 1979—82; freelance photographer, 1985—; typist Aetna Ins. Co., Middletown, 1991. Prodr. feature program Storer Cable Comm., Clinton, Conn., 1991-95; mem. Bridgeport Regional Bus. Coun., 1997; realtor Buyer's Capital. Literacy vol. Russell Libr., Middletown, Conn. Mem. AAUW, Nat. League Am. Pen Women, Internat. Soc. Poets (Hall of Fame award 1997), Conn. Soc. Poets, Conn. Songwriter's Assn., Internat. Platform Assn. Office Phone: 860-306-9090. E-mail: sdshireen@optonline.net.

MAHOLIC, NANCY L., nurse; b. Bradford, Pa., Jan. 25, 1937; d. George Edward and Leona Dolores Cuthbertson; m. James Andrew Maholic, Nov. 12, 1955; children: James Jr., Jeffrey, Julie. AA, Bucks County C.C., Newtown, Pa., 1980; degree, Upper Bucks Nursing Sch., Upper Black Eddy, Pa., 1981. Teller Bradford Nat. Bank, 1957—62, Springfield (Ohio) Bank, 1964—66; office mgr. Woodrow Mfg. Co., Springfield, 1968—70; coord. adjustment svcs. for the blind, dept. head Bucks county Assn. for the Blind, 1970—78; staff nurse Doylestown (Pa.) Hosp., 1981—2003; patient coord. Doylestown Women's Health, 1990—2003; pvt. duty nurse Bayada Nurses, Langhorne, Pa., 2003—. Preceptor Doylestown Hosp., 1983—2003. Youth choir dir. United Meth. Ch., Ivyland, Pa., 1970—74; parish nurse St. John's United Meth. Ch., 1999—, lay leader, 2005—. Named Bayada Employee of Month, 2005; recipient Nurse Excellence award, Doylestown Hosp., 1993. Republican. Avocations: music, reading. Home: 19 Meadow Ln Richboro PA 18954 Personal E-mail: nursecubby@aol.com.

MAHON, ARTHUR JOSEPH, lawyer; b. NYC, Jan. 13, 1934; s. Arthur Logan and Mary Agnes (Craine) M.; m. Myra E. Murphy, Aug. 10, 1957; children: Maura, Madonna, Arthur, Nancy. BA, Manhattan Coll., 1955; JD, NYU, 1958. Bar: NY, Fla., DC. Adj. prof. law NYU Sch. of Law, NYC, 1964-78; ptnr. Mudge, Rose, Guthrie, Alexander & Ferdon, NYC, 1970-94; counsel Donovan Leisure Newton & Irvine, NYC, 1994-98, McDermott, Will & Emery, 1998—2007. Trustee Manhattan Coll., NYC, 1988-03, Adrian and Jesse Archbold Charitable Trust, NYC, 1976-, NY Presbyn. Hosp., NYC, 1994—, Alvin Ailey Am. Dance Theatre, 1998—; mem. joint bd. NY Hosp.-Cornell Med. Ctr., NYC, 1990-98; com. on trust and estate gift plans Rockefeller U., NYC, 1984—; bd. dirs. United Way Internat., 1988-94, Alexandria, Va., chmn. planned giving and endowments com. Archdiocese, NYC, 1982-97; bd. overseers Cornell Med. Coll., NYC, 1986—, chmn., 1992-95, vice chmn., 1990-91, 96-; dir. Am. Skin Assn., NYC, 1989-00; v.p., dir. Cath. Communal Fund, Archdiocese of NY, 1997—, trustee Inner City Scholarship Fund, 1998—. Served to capt. USAF, 1958-60. Root-Tilden scholar NYU. Mem. N.Y. State Bar Assn., Bar Assn. City of N.Y., D.C. Bar Assn. Home: 41 Middle Beach Rd W Madison CT 06443-3016 Office: McDermott Will & Emery 340 Madison AVe 14th Fl New York NY 10017-4613 E-mail: famg@rcn.com.

MAHON, KATHERINE A. (KIT MAHON), public relations executive, writer; d. Thomas Patrick Mahon and Winifred Marie Collins. BA, Hunter Coll., NYC; postgrad., Columbia U., NYU. Dir. fundraising and pub. rels. Girl Scout Coun. Greater NY, NYC, 1956—69; dir. comm. Girls Club Am., NYC, 1968—77; supr. Campbell Soup Co., Camden, NJ, 1977—91. Dir. pubs. rels. Fedn. Protestant Welfare Agys., NYC, 1959—66. Mem.: Women Execs. Pub. Rels., Pub. Rels. Soc. Am. (NY chpt. publicity com.). Home: 447 Watergate Maple Shade NJ 08052

MAHON, MALACHY THOMAS, SR., lawyer, educator; b. NYC, Jan. 4, 1934; s. James and Alice (Rooney) M.; m. Margaret Phyllis Kirwan, Jan. 25, 1958 (dec. 1993); children: Veronica Mahon Grover, Laura Mahon Chandonnet, Malachy. BA, Manhattan Coll., 1954; JD, Fordham U., 1960. Bar: N.Y. 1960. Law clk. to chief magistrate John M. Murtagh, NYC, 1959-60; law clk. to justice Tom C. Clark U.S. Supreme Ct., 1960-61; assoc. Hale Russell & Stentzel, NYC, 1961-62, Mudge Rose Guthrie & Alexander, NYC, 1979-80; of counsel Farrell, Fritz, Caemmerer, Cleary, Barnosky & Armentano, Mineola, NY, 1982-83, Havens & Lombard, Flushing, NY, 1994-95; prof. Fordham U. Law Sch., 1962-68; prof. law Hofstra U. Law Sch., 1968—, founding dean, 1968-73, S.B. Wilzig disting. prof. banking, 1985—. Vis. prof. U. Tex. Law Sch., 1973-74; exec. dir., spl. N.Y. State asst. atty. gen. Meyer Investigation of State Police Murder Coverup Charges Against the Spl. Attica Prison Riot Prosecutor's Office, 1975; chief counsel N.Y. Gov.'s Spl. Com. on Criminal Offenders, 1966; mem. Nassau County Bd. Ethics, 1983-96, chmn., 1989-96; chmn. merit selection com. EDNY Bankruptcy Judges, 1985-88. Staff author: Mental Illness, Due Process and the Criminal Defendant, 1968; monthly comml. law columnist: N.Y. Law Jour. 1976-78. Served with U.S. Army, 1954-56. Mem. ABA, N.Y. State Bar Assn., Assn. Bar City N.Y., Am. Law Inst. Home: 14 Duke Of Gloucester Manhasset NY 11030-3210 Office: Hofstra U Law Sch Hempstead NY 11550 Office Phone: 516-463-5864. Business E-Mail: lawmtm@hofstra.edu.

MAHON, ROBERT, photographer; b. Wilmington, Del., Dec. 28, 1949; s. Clifton and Mary Veronica (Figash) M.; m. Carol Joyce, Apr. 24, 1983. BA in Am. Studies, U. Del., 1971. One-man shows include Twining Gallery, N.Y.C., 1985, Mercer Coll., Trenton, N.J., 1993, Anne Reid Gallery, Princeton, 1996, N.J. State Mus., 1997, Dana Libr. Rutgers U., Newark, 1998, RVC Coll., N.J., 2001, PhilosophyBox, N.Y.C., 2004, Witherspoon Gallery, Princeton, N.J., 2005, Rittenhouse, Phila., 2006, 3000BC, 2007, Schotland Gallery, Flemington, NJ, 2007, exhibited in group shows at Whitney Mus. Am. Art, 1982, Phila. Mus. Art, 1982, 1995, Am. Ctr., Paris, 1982, Mus. Modern Art, NYC, 1983—85, 1993, Kolnischer Kunstverein, 1983, Art Inst., Chgo., 1985, Twining Gallery, 1985—86, 1988—89, N.J. State Mus., 1990, 1997, 2002, 1999, Guggenheim Soho, 1994, Sandra Gering Gallery, N.Y.C., 1996, Newark Mus., 1997, 2002, Korn Gallery Drew U., Madison, N.J., 1999, N.Y. Pub. Libr., 1999, Guild Hall, East Hampton, N.Y., 1999, others, Represented in permanent collections Phila. Mus. Art, Mus. Modern Art, Met. Mus. Art, N.Y. Pub. Libr., Humanities Rsch. Ctr., U. Tex., Austin, Princeton U. Libr., Princeton U. Art Mus., Harvard U. Art Mus., N.J. State Mus., Newark Mus., Montclair Art Mus., Rutgers U., Dana Libr., Zimmerli Mus., Noyes Mus., also pvt. collections, exhibitions include 100 NJ Artists Nat. Tour, 2002—03. Guggenheim grantee, 1985; RCIP Printmaking fellow, 1996. Home: PO Box Q Stockton NJ 08559-0390 E-mail: mailbox@robertmahon.net.

MAHON, STEPHEN C., lawyer; b. New Rochelle, NY, 1964; BA, Vanderbuilt U., 1986, JD, 1989. Bar: NY 1989, DC 1992, Ohio 1993, US Ct. Appeals, DC Cir. 1993. Ptnr., corp. transactions & securities regulation Squire, Sanders & Dempsey, LLP, Cin., NY, mem., mgmt. com. Bd. dir. Entrepreneurship Inst. Bd. dir. Cin. Zoo & Botanical Garden. Mem.: Cin. Bar Assn. Office: Squire Sanders & Dempsey LLP 312 Walnut St Ste 3500 Cincinnati OH 45202-4036 Address: Squire Sanders & Dempsey LLP 350 Park Ave New York NY 10022-6022 Office Phone: 513-361-1230. Fax: 216-479-8780; Office Fax: 513-361-1201. Business E-Mail: smahon@ssd.com.

MAHONE, BARBARA JEAN, automotive executive; BS, Ohio State U., 1968; MBA, U. Mich., 1972; program for mgmt. devel., Harvard U., 1981. Sys. analyst GM, Detroit, 1968-71, sr. staff asst., 1972-74, mgr. career planning, 1975-78, dir. pers. adminstrn. Rochester, NY, 1979-81, mgr. indsl. rels. Warren, Ohio, 1982-83, dir. human resources mgmt. Chevrolet-Pontiac-Can. group, 1984-86, dir. gen. pers. and pub. affairs Inland divsn. Dayton, Ohio, 1986-88, gen. dir. pers. Indland Fisher Guide divsn. Detroit, 1989-91, gen. dir. employee benefits, 1991-93, dir. human resources truck group Pontiac, Mich., 1994—2000, exec. dir. human resources, 2001—. Chmn. Fed. Labor Rels. Authority, Washington, 1983-84, Spl. Panel on Appeals; dir. Metro Youth; mem. bd. govs. U. Mich. Alumni. Bd. dirs. ARC, Rochester, 1979-82, Urban League Rochester, 1979-82, Rochester Aea Multiple Sclerosis; mem. human resources com. YMCA, Rochester, 1980-82; mem. exec. bd. Nat. Coun. Negro Women; mem. allocations com. United Way Greater Rochester. Recipient Pub. Rels. award Nat. Assn. Bus. and Profl. Women, 1976, Mary McLeod Bethune award Nat. Coun. Negro Women, 1977, Senate resolution Mich. State Legislature, 1980; named Outstanding Woman, Mich. Chronicle, 1975, Woman of Yr., Nat. Assn. Bus. and Profl. Women, 1978, Disting. Bus. Person, U. Mich., 1978, one of 11 Mich. Women, Redbook mag., 1978. Mem. Nat. Black MBA Assn. (bd. dirs., nat. pres. Disting. Svc. award, bd. dirs., nat. pres. Outstanding MBA), Women Econ. Club (bd. dirs.), Indsl. Rels. Rsch. Assn., Internat. Assn. for Pers. Women, Engring. Soc. Detroit. Republican. Home: 2697 Melcombe Cir Unit 402 Troy MI 48084

MAHONE, GLENN R., lawyer; b. Apr. 22, 1945; m. Andrea Mahone; 2 children. BS, Pa. State U., 1968; JD, Duquesne U., 1973; LLM, Yale U., 1975. Bar: Pa. 1973. With Reed Smith LLP, 1973—80, 1991—; now ptnr., mem. exec. com.; broadcast industry exec., 1980—91. Dir. Matthews Internat. Corp.; chmn. Allegheny County Airport Authority. Trustee Duquesne U., Westminster Coll.; chmn. Manchester Bidwell Corp. Mem.: Homer S. Brown Law Assn., Allegheny County Bar Assn., Nat. Bar Assn., ABA. Office: Reed Smith LLP 435 Sixth Ave Pittsburgh PA 15219 Office Phone: 412-288-4240. Office Fax: 412-288-3063. Business E-Mail: gmahone@reedsmith.com.

MAHONEY, ANDREA NOEL, lawyer; BS in Mktg., Okla. State U., Stillwater, 1991; JD, Okla. City U., 1995. Atty. Olsen & Traeger, LLP, Denver, 2001—. Office: Olsen & Traeger LLP 650 S Cherry St Ste 850 Denver CO 80246

MAHONEY, ANN DICKINSON, fundraiser; b. Topeka, Sept. 12, 1961; d. Jacob Alan II and Ruth (Curd) Dickinson; m. Michael James Mahoney, May 29, 1993; children: James Junius Castle, Catherine Lane, Grace Dickinson, Christopher Michael Hayes. AB in History, Grinnell Coll., 1983; postgrad., McGill U., Montreal, Que., Can., 1985. Analyst, corp. fin. dept. E.F. Hutton & Co., Inc., NYC, 1983-85; pres., owner The Dark Side, NYC, 1985-87; asst. dir. individual giving Meml. Sloan-Kettering Cancer Ctr., NYC, 1987-88, dir. spl. gifts, 1988-91; assoc. dir. devel. Sch. Humanities and Scis. Stanford (Calif.) U., 1991-96; ind. fundraising cons., 1996—. Devel. asst. regional office Brandeis U., NYC, 1987. Vol. interviewer Grinnell Coll., NYC, San Francisco, 1983—; chair No. Calif. adv. bd. Nat. Found. for Tchg. Entrepreneurship, 2000-02. Mem.: Peninsula Assn. Retarded Children and Adults Aux. (bd. dirs. 1998—2002, pres. 2000), Pacific Rsch. Inst. Pub. Policy, Nat. Soc. Fund Raising Execs., San Francisco Ballet Aux., Friends of Filoli (Woodside, Calif.), Hist. Topeka Assn., Jr. League San Francisco (com. chmn. 1996—98), Menlo Circus Club, Hayden Lake (Idaho) Country Club, Spokane Club, Villa Taverna (San Francisco). Republican. Episcopalian. Personal E-mail: admahone@pacbell.net.

MAHONEY, CAROLYN RAY, academic administrator; b. Memphis, Dec. 22, 1946; d. Stephen and Myrtle (Gray) Boone; m. Charles Augustus Mahoney, May 20, 1972; children: Cindy Rae, Megan Ruth, Carolyn Bernadette. BS, Sienna Coll., 1970; MS in Math., Ohio State U., 1972, PhD in Math., 1983. Asst. prof. math. Denison U., Granville, Ohio, 1984-87; founding faculty prof. math. Calif. State U., San Marcos, 1989—2000; dean sch. math. sci. and tech. Eiizabeth City State, Elizabeth City, NC, provost, vice chancellor academic affairs; pres. Lincoln U., Jefferson City, Mo., 2005—. Mem. Coll. Bd. Tst Devel. Com., Princeton, N.J., 1986-89; advisory com. Coll. Bd. Math. Scis., 1992—; vis. asst. prof. math. Ohio State U., Columbus, 1987-89; instr. South African Program Denison U., Granville, 1987; math. campus coord. Young Scholars Program, Columbus, 1987—; cons., researcher regarding increasing the numbers and achievement of minorities and women in math. at all levels; dir. Middle Sch. Math. and Sci. San Marcos, 1992—. Contbr. articles to Jour. Combinatorial Theory, Soc. Indsl. and Applied Math. Newsletter. Active Edn. Commn. of States Task Force on Improving Achievement of Minorities in Higher Edn., 1990. Grantee NSF, 1987, 90, 92, Math. Assn. Am., 1992, Charles A. Dana Found, 1989, Ohio Bd. Regents, 1989, Math. Scis. Edn. Bd., 1989; named to State of Ohio Women's Hall of Fame, 1989. Mem. Am. Math. Soc., Assn. for Women in Math., Math. Assn. Am., Nat. Assn. Mathematicians, Phi Kappa Phi. Office: Lincoln Univ 820 Chestnut St Jefferson City MO 65102-0029 E-mail: president@lincolnu.edu.

MAHONEY, CATHERINE ANN, artist, educator; b. Macon, Mo., Nov. 18, 1948; d. Joe H. and Berniece Joyce (Garnett) Dickson; m. Michael W. Mahoney, July 19, 1969; children: Karin Lynn Mahoney Broeker, Ryan Michael. BS in Edn. with honors, Truman U., Kirksville, 1969. Mo. state life cert. for tchg. art. Elem./secondary art instr. Bucklin (Mo.) R-I Schs., 1970-74; pvt. art instr. Groom (Tex.) Artist's Assn., 1974-75; substitute tchr. Gasconade R-I Schs., Hermann, Mo., 1977-89; pvt. art instr. Colorful Brushes Studio, Hermann, Mo., 1987—; elem./secondary art instr. Crosspoint Christian Schs., Union, Mo., 1994-98. Pres. City of Hermann Arts Coun., 1983-87, membership chmn., 1980-82; dir. Summertime Children's Watercolor Workshops, Colorful Brushes, Hermann, 1987—; artist-in-residence Mo. State Fair, 2005. One-woman shows at Truman U., Kirksville, 1969, Capitol City Art Guild, Jefferson City, Mo., 1983, Kolbe Gallery of Art, Hermann, 1984, Colorful Brushes Studio, Hermann, 1987-94; designer Sister Cities Emblem City of Hermann/Arolsen, Germany, 1989, 20 foot hist. mural, Gasconade County, 2000; works published in: Best of Watercolor: Texture, 1998, The Artful Home II, 2004, Art Resource Book IV, Mo. Life Mag, 2005, Guild's Source Book of Residenital Art 4, 2006. Pres. Hermann Parent-Tchr. Orgn., 1985—87; leader 4-H, Girl and Boy Scouts, Hermann, 1982—95; organist, pianist, tchr. Hermann Cath. and Bapt. Chs., 1977—97, E. Free Ch., 1997—2007. Named Outstanding Young Woman of Yr., Hermann Jaycees, 1984, 1st place award Mo. Artists Collection, Mo. Pub. Svc., Sedalia, Mo., 1992, 3d place award and purchase prize Watercolor USA, Springfield (Mo.) Art Mus., 1995, 1st place award Arts Rolla Art Show, 1999, 2004, 1st pl. watercolor Top 50 Exhbn., Sedalia Excellence award, Tex. Watercolor Soc. and Traveling Exhbn., 2005. Mem.: Mo. Watercolor Soc. (signature mem. 1998—2007, bd. dir. 1998—2007, M. Graham Mdse. award 2003, Daniel Smith award 2006), Oil Painters Am., St. Louis Artist Guild (mem. art sect., Hon. Mention 1993, 1998, 2002), Watercolor USA Honor Soc. (hon. Art Show award 1995), Okla. Watercolor Assn. (assoc. included Art Show 1989), Nat. Watercolor Soc. (assoc. included Nat. Art Show 1995). Avocations: piano, reading, embroidery, sewing, knitting. Home and Office: Colorful Brushes Studio 1058 Stonehill Hermann MO 65041 Office Phone: 573-486-2444. Personal E-mail: camahoney@ktis.net.

MAHONEY, DAVID L., former pharmaceutical wholesale and healthcare management company executive; b. Brighton, Mass., June 24, 1954; s. Thomas H.D. and K. Phyllis (Norton); m. Winn Canning Ellis, Sept. 26, 1992. AB in English, Princeton U., 1975; MBA, Harvard U., 1981. Asst. gen. mgr. Ogden Food Svc. Corp., LA, 1975-76, concessions mgr. East Boston, Mass., 1976-77, gen. mgr., 1977-78, ops. analyst, 1978-79; assoc. McKinsey & Co., San Francisco, 1981-86, prin., 1986-90; v.p. strategic planning McKesson Corp., San Francisco, 1990-94, pres. HDS, Inc., 1994-95, pres. pharm. svcs., 1995-97, group pres. pharm svcs. & internat. group, 1997-99; exec. v.p., CEO pharm. svcs. bus. McKesson HBOC, 1999, co-CEO, 1999-2001; CEO iMcKesson, 2000-01. Bd. dirs. Symantec Corp., Corcept Therapeutics, Tercica, Inc., KQED, Live Oak Sch., SF-MOMA, Mercy Corps. Mem.: Young Pres. Orgn., City Club of San Francisco. Avocations: outdoor activities, photography. Office: Pier 5 The Embracaders Ste 102 San Francisco CA 94111

MAHONEY, GEORGE LEFEVRE, lawyer; b. Washington, Mar. 28, 1952; s. George Francis Xavier and Elaine (LeFevre) M.; m. Lucinda Stuart, July 11, 1986. BA, U. Va., 1974, JD, 1978. Bar: N.Y. 1979, U.S. Dist. Ct. (so. and ea. dists), N.Y. 1979, U.S. Ct. Appeals (5th cir.), 1980, U.S. Ct. Appeals (2d cir.) 1981, U.S. Ct. Appeals (D.C. cir.) 1991. Assoc. Satterlee & Stephens, NYC, 1978-82; asst. gen. counsel Dow Jones & Co., Inc., NYC and Princeton, N.J., 1982—93; corp. sec., gen. counsel Media General, Inc., Richmond, Va., 1993—, v.p., 2006—.

MAHONEY, GEORGE R., JR., lawyer; b. Oct. 18, 1942; m. Linda L. Mahoney. AB, Ohio Wesleyan U.; LLB, Duke U. Gen. counsel Family Dollar Stores Inc., 1976—77, v.p., gen. counsel, sec., 1977—84, sr. v.p., gen. counsel, sec., 1984—91, dir., 1987—, exec. v.p., gen. counsel, sec., 1991—2005.

MAHONEY, JAMES E., information technology executive; BS in Info. Sys., Boise State Univ., 1981. Joined Micron Technology, Boise, Idaho, 1981, various mgmt. positions in info. sys., v.p. info. sys., 1997—. Achievements include being involved in devel. of software applications for Fab, Probe, Assembly, Test, Sales, Shipping, Fin. and Plant ops. depts. Office: VP Info Sys Micron Tech 8000 S Federal Way Boise ID 83716-9632

MAHONEY, JAMES R., federal agency administrator; b. Syracuse, NY; m. Taya Mahoney; 2 children; 6 children from previous marriage. BS in Physics, LeMoyne Coll., Syracuse; PhD in Meteorology, MIT. Faculty pub. health Harvard U.; co-founder Environ. Rsch. and Tech., Inc., 1968—84; dir. environ. industries ctr. Bechtel Group Inc., San Francisco, 1984—88; dir. Nat. Acid Precipitation Assesement Program, 1988; sr. exec. Internat. Tech. Group, LA, 1991—99; pres. Consulting and Ventures Group, 2000—01; asst. sec. for oceans and atmosphere US Dept. Commerce, Washington, 2002—; and dep. adminstr. NOAA, Washington, 2002—. Mem.: NAS (com. mem., co-chmn. bd. on atmospheric sci. and climate), Am. Meteorol. Soc. (pres. 1990—91). Office: US Dept Commerce Oceanic and Atmospheric Rsch 1315 East-West Hwy Silver Spring MD 20910-3279

MAHONEY, JOËLLE KATHERINE, astrological consultant, communications educator; b. Amiens, France, Jan. 6, 1948; came to U.S., 1953; d. Louis James and Regine (LeClercq) Dennis; m. John William Christopher Mahoney, Aug. 14, 1971. AA, Boro Manhattan C.C., 1971; BA, Adelphi U., 1982; postgrad., Hofstra U., 1989—. Profl. cert. in astrology; cert. master practitioner neurolinguistic programming; cert. neurolinguistics programming. Tri-lingual translator N.A. Bogdan Co., NYC, 1967-71; practicing astrologer Long Island, NY, 1971-74; founding pres. Astrological Rsch. Centre and Tng. Inst. Ltd., Mineola, NY, 1974-84; internat. astrological cons. Brewster, NY, 1984—. Pres. French Regional Alliance for Nat. Costume Edn., 1999—. Author: Concept I, II and III, 1974, In Search of Time, 1989. Vol. fund raiser Americares, New Canaan, Conn., 1991-94, Silver Hill Hosp., New Canaan, 1992-94, City Harvest, N.Y.C., 1995-97; amb. All Nations Universal Pageant Orgn., 1998-99. Named Mrs. France, 1996, Mrs. All Nations Universal, 1997; named amb.-at-large All Nations Universal Orgn., 1998. Mem. Astrologers Guild Am. (pres. 1980-83), Congress of Astrological Orgns. (v.p. 1981-84). Avocations: equitation, painting, writing, exercise, animal welfare. Home: 5 Fair Meadow Dr Brewster NY 10509-4617

MAHONEY, JOHN, actor; b. Blackpool, Eng., June 20, 1940; MA in English, Western Ill. U.; student, Quincy Coll.; trained for the theater, St. Nicholas Theatre, Chgo. Stage performances include The Water Engine, 1977, The Hothouse, Taking Steps, Death of a Salesman, Orphans, 1985 (Theater World award), The House of Blue Leaves, 1986 (Tony award, Clarence Derwent award), The Subject Was Roses, 1991, The Drawer Boy, 2005, Prelude to a Kiss, 2007; films include Mission Hill, 1982, Voyeur, 1984, Code of Silence, 1985, The Manhattan Project, 1986, Streets of Gold, 1987, Tin Men, 1987, Suspect, 1987, Moonstruck, 1987, Frantic, 1988, Betrayed, 1988, Eight Men Out, 1988, Say Anything, 1989, Love Hurts, 1990, The Russia House, 1990, Barton Fink, 1991, Article 99, 1992, In the Line of Fire, 1993, Striking Distance, 1993, Reality Bites, 1994, The Hudsucker Proxy, 1994, The American President, 1995, Mariette in Ecstasy, 1996, Primal Fear, 1996, She's the One, 1996, Antz (voice), 1998, The Iron Giant (voice), 1999, The Broken Hearts Club, 2000, Almost Salinas, 2001, Atlantis: The Lost Empire (voice), 2001, Atlantis: Milo's Return (voice), 2003, Zodiac, 2007; TV series: Lady Blue, 1985-86, H.E.L.P., The Human Factor, 1991, Frasier, 1993-2004; TV movies

Chicago Story, 1981, Listen to your Heart, 1983, Dance of the Phoenix, 1984, The Killing Floor, 1984, First Steps, 1985, Trapped in Silence, 1986, Favorite Son, 1988, (TNT) Dinner at Eight, 1989, (HBO) The Image, 1990, The 10 Million Dollar Getaway, 1991, The Secret Passion of Robert Clayton, 1992; TV special The House of Blue Leaves, 1987. Served AUS Recipient award SAG, 2000. *

MAHONEY, JOHN J., office supply company executive; BA, Coll. Holy Cross, Worcester, Mass.; MBA, Northeastern U., Boston. Ptnr. Ernst & Young; exec. v.p., CFO Staples Inc., Framingham, Mass., 1996—97, exec v.p., CFO, chief adminstrv. officer, 1997—2006, vice chmn., CFO, 2006—. Bd. dirs. ADVO, 2001—, non-exec. chmn. bd., 2004—; bd. dirs. Tweeter. Office: Staples Inc 500 Staples Dr Framingham MA 01701 *

MAHONEY, JOHN L., English literature educator; b. Somerville, Mass., Feb. 4, 1928; AB, Boston Coll., 1950, AM, 1952, DHL (hon.), 2003; PhD, Harvard U., 1957. From instr. English to prof. Boston Coll., 1955—94, Rattigan prof. English, 1994—2002, prof. emeritus, 2002—. Chmn. dept. English, Boston Coll., 1962-67, 69-70, dir. PhD program in English, 1970-75, 82-85, mem. ednl. policy com. Grad. Sch. Arts and Scis., 1985-87; vis. prof. English Harvard U. summer sch., 1963, 65, 67, 71, 80, 83, 86; cons. for self-study Weston Coll. Schs. of Philosophy and Theology, Boston Coll., 1965; sem. leader programs for women, Boston Coll., Newton Coll., 1976, 78, 79; mem. numerous acad. coms. and couns.; cons., mem. English adv. com. Commonwealth of Mass., 1968-70; mem. acad. coun. Coll. of Advancing Studies, Boston Coll., 1969—, univ. core curriculum devel. com., 1991-97; trustee St. John's Sem., Brighton, Mass., com. on acad. affairs, 1980-86; sec. bd. trustees Katharine Gibbs Sch., Boston, 1982-90; mem. adv. bd. Jesuit Inst., Boston Coll., 1987—2005; mem. Boston Coll. Coun. the Arts, 1997-2007, mem. edn. com. Religion and the Arts. Author: The Whole Internal Universe: Imitation and the New Defense of Literature in British Criticism, 1660-1830, 1985, The Persistence of Tragedy: Episodes in the History of Drama, 1985, The Logic of Passion: The Literary Criticism of William Hazlitt, rev. edit., 1981, Wordsworth: A Poetic Life, 1997, Wordsworth and the Critics, 2001, Wordsworth of Rydal: Religious Experience and Religious Practice, 2003; editor, author intro. and notes: The Enlightenment and English Literature, 1980, The English Romantics: Major Poetry and Critical Theory, 1978, An Essay of Dramatic Poetry and Other Critical Writings by John Dryden, 1965, William Duff's Essay on Original Genius, 1964; contbr. Imagination and the Ways of Genius (in Approaches to Hazlitt), 1986, Teaching the Immortality Ode with Coleridge's Dejection: An Ode (in Approaches to Teaching Wordsworth's Poetry), 1986, Teaching Shelley's Skylark and the Defence of Poetry (in Approaches to Teaching Shelley's Poetry), 1990, and others; editor: (with J. Robert Barth, S.J.) Coleridge, Keats, and the Imagination: Romanticism and Adam's Dream, 1990, Seeing Into the Life of Things: Essays on Literature and Religion, 1998; CD recs. Boston College Poetry Reading Series: Poetry of Faith, 2003, Freedom: America's Literary Voices, 2005, Poetry of Ireland, 2007; mem. editl. bd. Boston Coll. Mag., 1981-90; author articles, papers delivered at profl. confs.; reviewer for Studies in Romanticism, The Wordsworth Circle, European Romantic Rev., Nineteenth Century Contexts, So. Humanities Rev., Coll. Lit., Religion and the Arts 1650-1850; series editor Fordham U. Press Series on Religion and Lit., 1997-2005. Active Sacred Heart Parish, Lexington, Mass., del. to Lexington Coun. Chs., 1968, chmn. parish coun., 1969-72, mem. parish coun., 1995-98, 2005—, vice chmn., 1996-98, mem. religious edn. commn., 1974-79, 90-93, sem. leader Christian Youth Edn., 1969-73, lector, 1972—; mem. Archdiocese of Boston Commn. for Promotion of Parish Couns., 1969-74, Benjamin Mays Mentor Ahana program, 1993-2003. Boston Coll. Grad. Sch. fellow, 1950-52; Boston Coll. Faculty rsch. grantee, 1964, 68, 86, 92, 96, 97, 98, Mellon Found. grantee for rsch. and faculty devel., 1981-82; grantee rsch. Am. Philos. Soc., 1987; recipient Boston Coll. Campus Coun. Tchr. of Yr. award, 1966, Boston Coll. alumni award for excellence in edn., 1978, Andrè Favat award Mass. Coun. Tchrs. English, 1988, Prof. of Yr. award Coun. for Advancement and Support of Edn. Mass., 1989, Ann. Wordsworth Meml. Lectr., Rydal Ch., 2003. Mem. AAUP (pres. Boston Coll. chpt. 1962), MLA, N.E. Soc. Eighteenth Century Studies, Wordsworth-Coleridge Assn. Am., Keats-Shelley Assn. Am., The Johnsonians, Alpha Sigma Nu, Phi Beta Kappa (Tchg. award Boston Coll. 1994). Office Phone: 617-552-3720. Business E-Mail: mahoneyj@bc.edu.

MAHONEY, KATHLEEN MARIE, social studies educator; b. West Palm Beach, Fla., Nov. 6, 1951; d. Nelson Levinus and Jane Elizabeth Van Son; m. Neil David Mahoney; children: Neil, Erin, Matthew. EdB, Loyola U., New Orleans, 1973; MEd in Curriculum and Instrn., Fla. Atlantic U., Boca Raton, 1974. Cert. guidance counselor 1977. Social studies tchr. Suncoast HS, Riviera Beach, Fla., 1974—75, Lakeshore Cath. Acad., Waukegan, Ill., 1986—90, Oak Grove Sch. # 68, Green Oaks, Ill., 1990—; career edn. counselor Pontotoc Cmty. Schs., Miss., 1975—77; guidance counselor Oxford Pub. Schs., Miss., 1977—79. Mem.: Nat. Coun. Social Studies. Home: 1604 Churchill Ct Libertyville IL 60048 Office: Oak Grove Sch 1700 Oplaine Rd Libertyville IL 60048-1599

MAHONEY, KATHLEEN MARY, lawyer; b. Methuen, Mass., Oct. 24, 1954; d. Joseph Patrick and Beatrice Evelyn (Blackington) M.; m. Mark Dennis Schmitt, May 26, 1979; children: Alexis Anne Schmitt, Brynne Elizabeth Schmitt. BA, Keene State Coll., NH, 1976; JD, Syracuse U., NY, 1979. Bar: Minn. 1979, U.S. Dist. Ct. Minn. 1980, U.S. Ct. Appeals (8th cir.) 1985, U.S. Supreme Ct. 1988. Instr. Sch. of Law Hamline U., St. Paul, 1979-80; law clk. to hon. justice Douglas K. Amdahl Minn. Supreme Ct., St. Paul, 1980-81; law clk. to hon. judge Neal P. McCurn U.S. Dist. Ct. (no. dist.) N.Y., Syracuse, 1981-83; spl. asst. atty. gen. Atty. Gen.'s Office State of Minn., St. Paul, 1983-89; assoc. Oppenheimer, Wolff & Donnelly, St. Paul, 1989-91, sr. assoc., 1991-93, ptnr., 1994—2002, chair labor and employment practice group, 1995-97, mng. ptnr., 1997-2000, Larson-King, LLP, St. Paul, 2002—04; v.p., dep. gen. counsel Nash-Finch Co., Mpls., 2004—06, interim gen. counsel, sec., 2006, sr. v.p., gen. counsel, sec., 2006—. Cons. George Banzhaf Co., Milw., 1979-80; adj. prof. Hamline U. Sch. of Law, 1987-89. Mem. Dist. 621 Study Adv. Com., Shoreview, Minn., 1989-91, chair, 1991-93; mem. Turtle Lake Sch. Adv. Com., Shoreview, 1988-96; mem. exec. com., bd. dirs. Voyageurs Regional Nat. Park Assn., 1993-95; mem. Class of '93; bd. dirs. St. Paul Vol. Ctr., 1994-99; leader Girl Scouts Am., 1993-99; mem. Leadership St. Paul.; bd. dirs. Girl Scout Council St. Croix Valley, 2001—. Mem. ABA, Minn. Bar Assn., Ramsey County Bar Assn. Office: Nash-Finch Co 7600 France Ave S Minneapolis MN 55435

MAHONEY, KEVIN J., lawyer; b. Boston, Oct. 7, 1962; BA, U. Mass., 1986; JD, New Eng. Sch. Law, 1989. Bar: Mass. 1989, U.S. Dist. Ct. Mass. 1992; Black Belt 1981. Jud. law clk. Conn. Superior Ct., 1989—90; asst. dist. atty. Middlesex County, Mass., 1991—93; assoc. Lecomte, Emanuelson, Tick & Doyle, Boston, 1993; pvt. practice. Staff mem.: New Eng. Law Rev., 1987—88, symposium editor:, 1988—89; contbr. articles to profl. jours. Recipient Am. Jurisprudence Book award for Clin. Evidence, 1988. Mem.: Mass. Assn. Criminal Def. Lawyers, Nat. Assn. Criminal Def. Lawyers (mem. champion adv. com., mem. forensic evidence fraud task force, mem. law enforcement misconduct com.). Avocations: weightlifting, hunting, mountain climbing, literature, politics. Office: Law Offices of Kevin J Mahoney PC 545 Concord Ave Ste 22 Cambridge MA 02138 Office Phone: 617-492-0055. Fax: 617-492-6886. *

MAHONEY, KEVIN J., social worker, educator; BA, St. Louis U.; MSW, U. Conn.; PhD, U. Wis., Madison. Chief rsch. and program devel. Conn. Dept. on Aging, 1978—87; assoc. prof. Boston Coll. Grad. Sch. Social Work, Chestnut Hill, Mass., 1999—, dir. Ctr. for Study of Home and Cmty. Life; nat. program dir. Cash & Counseling. Faculty mem. Yale U., U. Conn., U. Calif., San Francisco, U. Md.; spkr. in field. Contbr. articles to profl. jours. Recipient Flynn Prize for Social Work Rsch., 2007. Mem.: Gerontological Soc. Am. (sec., Maxwell Pollack award 2004). Office: Ctr for Study of Home and Cmty Life Boston Coll Grad Sch Social Work 314 Hammond St Chestnut Hill MA 02467-3807 also: Boston Coll McGuinn Hall, Rm 306 140 Commonwealth Ave Chestnut Hill MA 02467 Office Phone: 617-552-4039. Office Fax: 617-552-1975. E-mail: kevin.mahoney@bc.edu.

MAHONEY, KIMBERLY LYNNE, event and facility executive; b. Johnson City, NY, Nov. 1969; d. Dewitt Duncan and Selina Faye Smith; m. Michael Mahoney, June 24, 2000. BA, U. Ky., 1992; MEd, U. Ga., 1994; PhD, Ohio State U., 2006. Facility mgmt. intern Charlotte Coliseum, NC, 1994; event coord. Charlotte Conv. Ctr., NC, 1994—95; account mgr. Show Pros Entertainment Svcs., Inc., Charlotte, NC, 1995—97, regional mgr. Greensboro, NC, 1997—98; guest services mgr. Schottenstein Ctr., Ohio State U., Columbus, 1998—2000, asst. dir. event svcs. and adminstrn., 2000—03; asst. commr. Ohio H.S. Athletic Assn., 2003—05; instr. Univ. S.C., 2005—06, asst. prof., 2006—07; vis. asst. prof. Ohio State U., 2007—. Cons., trainer NFL Jacksonville Jaguars, 2002—03; lectr. Ohio State U., 2003; cons. OHSAA, 2006—, Schottenstein Ctr., 2006—. Office: Ohio State Univ PAES Bldg A238 305 W 17th Ave Columbus OH 43210-1224 Office Phone: 614-247-6535. Business E-Mail: mahoney.82@osu.edu.

MAHONEY, MARGARET ELLERBE, foundation executive; d. Charles Hallam and Leslie Nelson (Savage) M. BS magna cum laude, Vanderbilt U., 1946; LHD (hon.), Meharry Med. Coll., 1977, U. Fla., 1980, Med. Coll. Pa., 1982, Williams Coll., 1983, Smith Coll., 1985, Beaver Coll., 1985, Brandeis U., 1989, Marymount Coll., 1990, Mt. Sinai Sch. Medicine, 1992, Rush U., 1993, SUNY, Bklyn., 1994, N.Y. Med. Coll., 1995. Fgn. affairs officer State Dept., Washington, 1946-53; exec. assoc., assoc. sec. Carnegie Corp., NYC, 1953-72; v.p. Robert Wood Johnson Found., Princeton, NJ, 1972-80; pres. Commonwealth Fund, NYC, 1980-94, MEM Assocs., Inc., NYC, 1995—. Spkr. in field. Contbr. articles to profl. jours. Trustee Carnegie Found. Advancement of Tchg., 1963—2001, John D. and Catherine T. MacArthur Found., 1985—2002, Smith Coll., 1988—93, Columbia U., 1991—96, Arthur Ashe Found., 1997—2005; vis. fellow Sch. Archtl. and Urban Planning, Princeton U., 1973—80; bd. dirs. Coun. on Found., 1982—88, Skillbuilders Fund, 1993—99, adv. dir., 1999—; bd. dirs. Alliance for Aging Rsch., 1986—99, Overseas Devel. Coun., 1988—2001, Nat. Found. Ctrs. for Disease Control and Prevention, Inc., 1994—2004; mem. MIT Corp., 1984—89, N.Y.C. Commn. on the Yr. 2000, 1985—87; chmn. Nat. Found. Ctrs. for Disease Control and Prevention, Inc., 1996—98; bd. govs. Am. Stock Exch., 1987—92, Am. Skin Assn., 1994—, Classroom Inc., 1996—2005, Buckminster Fuller Inst., 2005, 2007—; mem. adv. bd. Office of Med. Examiner, NYC, 1987—; vice chmn. N.Y.C. Mayor's Com. for Pub./Pvt. Partnerships, 1990—93; mem. vestry Parish of Trinity Ch., 1982—89, 1991—95. Recipient Frank H. Lahey Meml. award, 1984, Women's Forum award, 1989, Walsh McDermott award, 1992, Disting. Grantmaker award Coun. Founds., 1993, Edward R. Loveland award ACP, 1994, Spl. Recognition award AAMC, 1994, Merit medal Lotos Club, 1994, Terrance Keenan Leadership award in health philanthropy Grantmakers in health, 1995, Distinction award Am. Skin Assn., 1998, Rsch. Am. award, 1999, Hon. Classmate Class of 1976 award Princeton U., 2001, Picker Inst. award, 2003. Mem. AAAS, Inst. Medicine of NAS, Am. Acad. Arts and Scis., Am. Philos. Soc., Coun. Fgn. Rels., Fin. Women's Assn. NY, NY Acad. Medicine, NY Acad. Scis., Alpha Omega Alpha. Office: MEM Assocs Inc 521 5th Ave 29th Fl New York NY 10175-0088 Home: 659 76th St Apt 5B New York NY 10021 Office Phone: 212-297-0500.

MAHONEY, MARGARET ELLIS, advertising executive; b. Detroit, Mar. 17, 1929; d. Seth Wiley and Mildred Elizabeth (Hill) Ellis; m. Stephen Bedell Smith, Mar. 15, 1956 (div. Oct. 1962); 1 child, Laura Elizabeth; m. Patrick John Mahoney, Sept. 1, 1972 (dec.). BA, Butler U., 1953. Copywriter Hook Drugs Inc., Indpls., 1953; continuity dir. Sta. WXLW, Indpls., 1954-57; ptnr. Steve Smith and Assocs. Advt., Indpls., 1956-62; account mgr. Sive Advt., Cin., 1963-64, Associated Advt., Cin., 1964-65; copywriter SupeRX Drugs Inc., Cin., 1965-72; promotion writer U.S. News and World Report, Washington, 1974; asst. mgr. advt. Drug Fair, Alexandria, Va., 1975-82; dir. advt. Cosmetic and Fragrance Concepts Inc./DBA Cosmetic Ctrs., Beltsville, Md., 1982-89; advt., prodn. cons. Nat. Red Cross, Galladet U., Washington, 1989-94; asst. to real estate agt. Carmel, Ind., 1994-96; editl. cons., mem. svc. rep., acct. clk. Angie's List, Carmel, Ind., 1996—. Vestrywoman St. Matthews Episcopal Ch., Cin., 1969-71; vol. jr. achievement hosp. chmn. Sleepy Hollow Citizens Assn., Falls Church, Va., 1973; vol. resident assoc. program Smithsonian Instn., Washington, 1989-94; chmn. membership and pub. rels. Friends Chinn Park Regional Libr., Woodbridge, Va., 1991-94; vol. Indpls. Art Ctr. Gift Shop, 1997—, Prince William Symphony Orch., Prince William County Voter Registration Bd. Mem. Potomac Valley Aquarium Soc. (past treas., past sec., editor jour.), Am. Cichlid Assn. (nat. pub. rels. chair 1985-90), Delta Delta Delta. Avocations: swimming, reading, needlecrafts, travel, computers. Home: 9850 Greentree Dr Carmel IN 46032-9099 Office Phone: 317-803-3961.

MAHONEY, MAUREEN A., academic administrator; PhD in Human Devel. and Family Studies, Cornell U., 1977. Prof. psychology Hampshire Coll., Amherst, Mass.; dean Smith Coll., Northampton, Mass., 1996—. Office: Smith Coll Dean of the College College Hall 21 Northampton MA 01063 *

MAHONEY, MAUREEN E., lawyer; b. Ind., Aug. 28, 1954; d. James Edward and Marian Ruth (Hanselman) M. m. William H. Crispin; children: Brad, Abigail. BA, Ind. U., 1974; JD, U. Chgo., 1978. Bar: Ill. 1978, Va. 1983, U.S. Dist. Ct. (no. dist.) Calif. 1980, U.S. Dist. Ct. D.C. 1981, U.S. Dist. Ct. (ea. dist.) Va., U.S. Ct. Appeals D.C. 1981, U.S. Ct. Appeals (8th cir.) 1982, U.S. Ct. Appeals (4th cir.) 1983, U.S. Ct. Appeals (5th cir.) 1986, U.S. Ct. Appeals (9th cir.) 1987, U.S. Supreme Ct. 1987. Law clk. to presiding judge US Ct. Appeals (7th cir.), Chgo., 1978-79; law clk. to Justice William Rehnquist US Supreme Ct., Washington, 1979-80; ptnr. Latham & Watkins LLP, Washington, 1980-91, 93—; dep. solicitor gen. US Dept. Justice, Washington, 1991—93. Named one of America's top 50 women litigators, Nat. Law Jour., 100 Most Influential Lawyers, 2006, The 50 Most Influential Women Lawyers in Am., 2007; recipient Rex Lee Advocacy Award, J. Rueben Clark Law Soc. Mem. ABA, Washington Bar Assn., Ill. Bar Assn., Va. Bar Assn., Am. Acad. of Appellate Lawyers, Am. Coll. of Trial Lawyers. exec. comm. Supreme Court Historical Soc. Office: Latham & Watkins LLP 555 Eleventh St NW Suite 1000 Washington DC 20004-1305 *

MAHONEY, MAURICE JEREMIAH, medical educator; b. Washington, Aug. 4, 1935; s. Maurice Mahoney and Julia Johnson; m. Blanche Katz, May 23, 2004; children: Tatyana Renner, Karen, Cydney, Matthew, Allison, Linnea. AB, Cornell U., 1957; MD, U. Pitts., 1962; JD, U. Conn., 1994. Bar: Conn. 1994; diplomate Med.Genetics Am. Bd. of Med. Genetics, 1982, Pediats. Am. Bd. of Pediat., 1967. Prof. of genetics Yale U., New Haven, 1970—; dir. human investigation com. Yale U. Sch. of Medicine, 2000—. Editl. bd. Am. Jour. of Med. Genetics, NYC, 1977—94, Fetal Diagnosis and Therapy, Basel, Switzerland, 1984—, Jour. of BioLaw & Bus., Denville, NJ, 1997—; bd. dirs. Am. Soc. of Human Genetics, Bethesda, Md., 1981—84, Soc. for Inherited Metabolic Disorders, Washington, 1984—87; fellow Am. Pediat. Soc., The Woodlands, Tex., 1983—, Am. Coll. of Med. Genetics, Bethesda, Md., 1993—. Editor: (medical text book) Medicine of the Fetus & Mother. Capt. US Army, 1966—68, Ft. McClellan, AL USA. Fellow, AAAS, 1998—2005. Avocations: kayaking, triathlon, opera, bioethics. Home: 526 Riverdale Dr Stratford CT 06615 Home Phone: 203-375-4535; Office Phone: 203-785-2661. Office Fax: 203-785-7673. Personal E-mail: maurice.mahoney@yale.edu.

MAHONEY, MICHAEL JAMES, investment company executive; b. Spokane, Wash., July 18, 1960; s. James Lyle and Frances Edith (Castle) Mahoney; m. Ann Dickinson, May 29, 1993; children: James Junius Castle, Catherine Lane, Grace Dickinson, Christopher Michael Hayes. BA in History cum laude, Whitman Coll., 1982; MBA, Stanford U., 1991. Analyst corp. fin. dept. E.F. Hutton & Co., Inc., NYC, 1982—85; assoc. cons. Bain & Co., Inc., Boston, 1985—87, cons., 1987—89; summer assoc. Goldman, Sachs & Co., NYC, 1990; investment analyst G.T. Global (acquired by AIM Funds), San Francisco, 1991—93; portfolio mgr., lead mgr. G.T. Global Telecom. Fund, 1993—99; sr. portfolio mgr. AIM Funds, San Francisco, 1998—99; founding ptnr. J&M Investments, Menlo Park, Calif., 1996—; sr. analyst, portfolio mgr., dir. Dresdner RCM Global Investors, San Francisco, 1999—2000; chief strategy officer Neon Yoyo, Inc. (acquired by Interwoven, Inc.), San Francisco, 2000; dir. Interwoven, Inc., Sunnyvale, Calif., 2000—01; mng. dir., sr. portfolio mgr., bd. dirs. Falcon Point Capital LLC (formerly EGM), San Francisco, 2001—, sr. mng. dir., 2004—. Guest lectr. in investments Stanford Grad. Sch. of Bus., 1994—; frequent print and TV commentator on the telecomms. industry and investing, 1993—; profiled in Investment Visionaries by Peter Tanous, 2003. Pres. Spokane County Young Reps., 1976-78; campaign mgr. Malone for U.S. Senate, Boston, 1988; bd. overseers Whitman Coll., investment com. 1999—. Recipient Pete Reid award, Whitman Coll., 1997. Mem. O'Mahony Records Soc., Ea. Wash. Geneal. Soc., Pacific Rsch. Inst. for Pub. Policy (mem. tech. adv. bd.), Stanford Alumni Assn. (life), Guardsmen, Menlo Circus Club (Atherton, Calif.), Villa Taverna (San Francisco), Spokane Club (Washington), Lincoln Club of No. Calif., Hayden Lake Country Club (Idaho), Phi Beta Kappa, Sigma Chi (com. chmn. 1979-80). Office: Falcon Poiunt Capital LLC Two Embarcadero Ctr Ste 1300 San Francisco CA 94111 Business E-Mail: mmahoney@fptcap.com.

MAHONEY, MICHAEL ROBERT TAYLOR, art historian, educator; b. Worcester, Mass., Jan. 24, 1935; s. Michael J. and Mary (Taylor) M. BA, Yale U., 1957; PhD, U. London, 1965. Finley fellow Nat. Gallery Art, 1962-64; fellow Harvard Center Italian Studies, Villa I Tatti, 1963; museum curator Nat. Gallery Art, 1964-69; prof. fine arts, chmn. dept. Trinity Coll., Hartford, Conn., 1969-86, Genevieve Harlow Goodwin prof. fine arts, 1974-99. Incorporator Hartford Pub. Library, 1970-99; elector Wadsworth Atheneum, Hartford, 1974-85 Author: The Drawings of Salvator Rosa, 1977, (with Jean Cadogan) Wadsworth Atheneum Paintings II: Italy and Spain; editor: National Gallery of Art Report and Studies in the History of Art, 1968-69. Trustee Cesare Barbieri Found., Trinity Coll., 1977-99, Watkinson Libr., Trinity Coll., 1985-99, Somerset House Art History Found., NYC, 1985-2004; bd. govs. Hill-Stead Mus., Farmington, Conn., 1992-95; mem. adv. coun. Am. Friends of Georgian Group, 1996—.

MAHONEY, ROBERT WILLIAM, electronic and security systems manufacturing executive; b. N.Y.C., Sept. 10, 1936; s. Francis Joseph and Margaret (Colleton) M.; m. Joan Marie Sheraton, Oct. 3, 1959; children: Linda Marie, Stephen Francis, Brian Michael. BS, Villanova U., 1958, MBA, Roosevelt U., Chgo., 1961. With sales dept. NCR, Inc., Phila., 1961-70, sales mgr., Allentown, Pa. and Atlanta, 1971-76, v.p., Dayton, Ohio, 1977-80; pres. NCR Can. Ltd., Toronto, 1981-82; sr. v.p. Diebold, Inc., Canton, Ohio, 1983-84, pres., COO, 1984-85, pres., CEO, 1985-88, CEO, 1988-99, chmn. bd., 1988-2000, also bd. dirs.; Chmn. Fed. Reserve Bank Cleveland; bd. dirs. Timken Co., Sherwin-Williams Co., Cin. Bell. Bd. dirs. Timken Mercy Med. Ctr., Canton, 1983—, Northeast Ohio Council, Cleve., 1986—, Profl. Football Hall of Fame, Canton, 1987—, Stark County Devel. Bd., Canton, 1986—, Canton Symphony Orch., 1985, Jr. Achievement, Canton, 1984, Akron (Ohio) U. Econ. Devel. Bd., 1982; trustee Canton City Schs., 1986, Mount Union Coll., 1988—, Ohio Found. Ind. Colls., 1988—; mem. adv. bd. C. of C. Leadership Canton, 1987. Served with USN, 1958-61. Republican. Roman Catholic. Clubs: Firestone Country (Akron); Brookside Country (Canton).

MAHONEY, SUZANNE MARIE **See SOMERS, SUZANNE**

MAHONEY, TIM (TIMOTHY EDWARD MAHONEY), congressman; b. Aurora, Ill., Aug. 15, 1956; m. Terry.Mahoney; 1 child. BA in Computer Sci & Bus., W. Va. U., 1978; MBA, George Washington U., 1983. V.p., Mktg. and Sales Rodime Inc.; pres. Rodime Systems, Rodime Inc., 1986—89; co-founder Union Atlantic, 1995—98, Ctr. for Creative Entrepreneurship; co-founder, COO, chmn. vFinance, Inc., Boca Raton, Fla., 1998—; mem. US Congress from 16th Fla. dist., 2007—, mem. fin. svcs. com., agrl. com. Mem.: Fla. Cattleman's Assn., New Democrat Coalition, Blue Dog Coalition. Democrat. Meth. Office: 1541 Longworth House Office Bldg Washington DC 20515 also: 18500 Murdock Cir Ste 536 Port Charlotte FL 33948 *

MAHONEY, WILLIAM FRANCIS, editor, writer; b. Joliet, Ill., Jan. 24, 1935; s. Cletus George and Mildred Marie (Ochs) Mahoney; m. Carroll Frances Johnson, June 28, 1958; children: Erin Michele Alderfer, Kevin William, Megan Ann, Sheila Marie Startup, Nora Aileen Petchkofski. BS in Journalism, Marquette U., 1957. Reporter Ft. Wayne (Ind.) News Sentinel, 1958-59; pub. rels. mgr. Motorola, Inc., Franklin Park, Ill., 1959-66; sr. acct. exec. Young & Rubicam, Inc., Chgo., 1966-68; pub. info. dir. ABA, Chgo., 1969-71; investor rels. mgr. Chemetron Corp., Chgo., 1971-76; corp. comm. dir. Scott Paper Co., Phila., 1976-80; pub. rels. dir. Esmark Inc., Chgo., 1980-81; prin. Mahoney & Mitchell Incorp., Phila., 1981-89, Investor Rels. Ptnrs., Livingston, NJ, 1993—, prin., editl. dir. VI LLC, 2004—. Author: Investor Relations: The Professional's Guide to Financial and Marketing Communications, 1991, The Active Shareholder, 1993, The Strategy and Practice of Investor Relations, 1997; author, editor: The Investor Relations Guide, 1999, The IR Book, Capital Markets and Valuation, 2003; exec. editor Shareholder Value Mag., 2000-2003; Investor Rels. Update, 1981-99, Valuation Issues. Mem. Nat. Investor Rels. Inst., Vesper Club. Republican. Roman Catholic. Home: 716 S Brandywine St West Chester PA 19382 Home Phone: 610-430-7057. Personal E-mail: wfmahoney35@verizon.net. Business E-Mail: wfmahoney@vi-llc.com.

MAHONY, ROGER MICHAEL, archbishop; b. Hollywood, Calif., Feb. 27, 1936; s. Victor James and Loretta Marie (Baron) Mahony. AA, Our Lady Queen of Angels Sem., 1956; BA, St. John's Sem. Coll., 1958, BST, 1962; MSW, Cath. U. Am., 1964. Priest Roman Cath. Ch., 1962, ordained bishop, 1975, created cardinal priest, 1991. Asst. pastor St. John's Cathedral, Fresno, Calif., 1962, 1968—73, rector, 1973—80; adminstr. St. Genevieve's Parish, Fresno, Calif., 1964—67, pastor, 1967—68; titular bishop of Tamascani, aux. bishop of Fresno Fresno, Calif., 1975—80; chancellor Diocese of Fresno, 1970—77, vicar gen., 1975—80; bishop Diocese of Stockton, Calif., 1980—85; archbishop Archdiocese of L.A., 1985—, cardinal priest, 1991—; diocesan dir. Cath. Charities and Social Svc., Fresno, 1964—70; exec. dir. Infant of Prague Adoption Svc., Cath. Welfare Bur., Fresno, 1964—70. Faculty extension divsn. Fresno State U., 1965—67; sec. U.S. Cath. bishops ad hoc com. on farm labor Nat. Conf. Bishops, 1970—75; chmn. com. on pub. welfare and income maintenance Nat. Conf. Cath. Charities, 1969—70; adminstrv. com. Nat. Conf. Cath. Bishops, 1976—79, 1982—85, 1987—90, 1992—95, 1998—2001, com. migration and refugees, 1976—95, chmn. com. farm labor, 1981—92, com. moral evaluation of deterrence, 1986—88, cons. com., chmn. for prolife activities, 1990—95; com. social devel. and world peace U.S. Cath.

Conf., 1985—93, chmn. internat. policy sect., 1987—93; com. justice and peace Pontifical Couns., 1984—98, chmn. com. domestic policy, 1998—2001, pastoral care of migrants and itinerant people, 1986—91, social comms., 1989—. Active Mexican-Am. Coun. for Better Housing, 1968—72, Fed. Commn. Agrl. Workers, 1987—93, Urban Coalition of Fresno, Calif., 1968—72, Fresno County Econ. Opportunities Commn., Calif., 1964—65, Fresno County Alcoholic Rehab. Com., Calif., 1966—67, Fresno City Charter Rev. Com., 1968—70, Fresno Redevel. Agy., 1970—75, L.A. 2000 Com., 1985—88, Blue Ribbon Com. Affordable Housing City of L.A., LA, 1988; mem. commn. to draft an ethics code L.A. City Govt., 1989—90; trustee St. Agnes Hosp., Fresno, 1969—73, Cath. U. Am., 1984—88, 1998—; named chaplain to Pope Paul VI, 1967; chaplain St. Vincent de Paul Soc., 1964—70; bd. dirs. West Coast Regional Office Bishops Com. for Spanish-Speaking, 1967—70; chmn. Calif. Assn. Cath. Charities Dirs., 1965—69; trustee St. Patrick's Sem., Archdiocese of San Francisco, 1974—75; bd. dirs. Fresno Cmty. Workshop, 1965—67, Rebuild L.A., 1992—95. Named Young Man of Yr., Fresno Jr. C. of C., 1967. Mem.: Canon Law Soc. Roman Catholic. Office: Archdiocese LA 3424 Wilshire Blvd Los Angeles CA 90010-2241

MAHONY, SHEILA ANNE, retired communications executive; b. Yonkers, NY, Jan. 30, 1942; d. Paul Ambrose and Grace (Sullivan) M.; m. Charles A. Riggs, July 7, 1983; stepchildren: Charles Riggs, Julia Riggs Shultis. BA, Newton Coll. Sacred Heart, Mass., 1963; JD, Fordham U., 1967. Asst. corp. counsel Law Dept. City of N.Y., NYC, 1967—72; regional dir. Cable TV Info. Ctr., The Urban Inst., Washington, 1972—74, gen. counsel, 1974-75, exec. dir., 1976-77, Carnegie Commn. on Future of Pub. Broadcasting, NYC, 1977-79, Cablevision Systems Corp., Woodbury, NY, 1980—95, sr. v.p. comm. and pub. affairs, 1995—99, exec. v.p. comm., govt. and pub. affairs, 1999—2004, dir., 1988—2005. Mem. exec. com. CSPAN, 2000—04. Author: Keeping PACE With the New Television, 1979. Dir. C-SPAN, Washington, 1990-2004, Found. for Minority Interests in Media, N.Y.C., 1992-2003; bd. dirs. Lustgarten Found., 2000—, Legal Aid Soc. of N.Y., 2000-2004. Office: Cablevision Systems Corp 1111 Stewart Ave Bethpage NY 11714-3581

MAHOOD, KEN, music educator; s. Kenneth Mahood Sr. and Helen Mahood; children: Jonathan Scott, Jason Kenneth. BS Music, The King's Coll., 1969; MusM, Manhattan Sch. Music, 1971; PhD of Music Theory, Met. Coll., 1981; PhD of Music, Concordia Coll., 1999; EdD, Am. U., 2001. Assoc. dir. music Christian Fellowship Ch., Ashburn, Va., 1981—2005; exec. dir. edn. KME Internat., Inc., Leesburg, Va., 1983—; dir. music ministries The Ch. of the Valley, Strasburg, Va., 2005—. Adj. faculty prof. No. Va. C.C. Recipient 20 yr. Achievement Award, Assn. Of Music Students, 2001. Mem.: Music Educators Nat. Conf., Am. Coll. Musicians, Music Tchrs. Nat. Assn. Office: KME Internat Inc PO Box 1616 Leesburg VA 20177 Personal E-mail: drken@musikdok.com.

MAHOOD, MARIE I., counselor, educator; b. Hackensack, NJ, Aug. 25, 1961; d. James George and Marie Josephine (Karlovsky) Mahood. BA in English, Montclair State U., 1983, MA in Counseling and Sch. Social Work, 1991. Lic. profl. counselor NJ; cert. secondary tchr. NJ. English tchr. Marylawn of the Oranges HS, South Orange, NJ, 1983—87; grad. asst., counselor Montclair State Coll., Upper Montclair, NJ, 1989—90, asst. to dir. Women's Ctr., 1990—91; counselor, tchr. Hudson County CC, Jersey City, 1992—. Mem.: ACA, NEA, NJ Counseling Assn., NJ Edn. Assn., Nat. Acad. Adv. Assn., Psi Chi, Kappa Delta Pi, Phi Kappa Phi. Democrat. Roman Catholic. Avocations: reading, writing, pets. Office: Hudson County CC 70 Sip Ave Jersey City NJ 07306

MAHORNER, JAMES G., lawyer; b. DeLand, Fla., Jan. 28, 1932; s. James Glennon and Sue Mahorner; m. Brenda Johnson (div. May 1992); children: John G., James G., Mary Christine Gore, Amy Caprice, Ted G. JD, Stetson U., DeLand, FL; BSEE, US Naval Acad., Annapolis, MD. Bar: Fla. Atty. Pvt. Practice, Fla., 1975—; gen. counsel Dept. of HRS, Fla., 1970—74; trial counsel Dept. of Agr., Fla., 1965; ptnr. Dickens, Linn, and Mahorner, Tallahassee, Fla., 1967—70, White, Phipps, Linn, Furnell and Mahorner, Tallahassee, Fla., 1965—67; atty. State Attorney's Gen. Office, Fla., 1960—65. Mem.: Mensa. Democrat-Npl. Avocations: chess, bridge, tennis. Office: 234 9th Avenue South Jacksonville Beach FL 32250 Home: PO Box 50774 Jacksonville Beach FL 32240-0774 E-mail: jgmahorner@netzero.net.

MAHRAUN, DANIEL ALLEN, musician, director; b. Muscatine, Iowa, Feb. 2, 1971; s. Donald Gene and Janet Gail Mahraun. MusB in Edns., Wartburg Coll., 1993; MusM in Conducting, U. No. Iowa, 1995, MusM in Performance, 1996; PhD in Musical Arts, U. Colo., Boulder, 2003. Vocal music dir. Clear Lake Jr. HS, Iowa, 1995—97; dir. choral activities Bethany Coll., Lindsborg, Kans., 2000—. Chancel choir dir. Bethany Luth. Ch., Lindsborg, 2004—. Study grant, Evang. Luth. Ch. Am., 2002, Burmeister grant, Bethany Coll., 2003. Mem.: Herbert Howells Soc., Assn. Luth. Ch. Musicians, Coll. Music Soc., Music Educators Nat. Conf., Am. Choral Dirs. Assn., Luth. Concerned N.Am. D-Liberal. Lutheran. Avocations: hiking, art, films, theater. Office: Bethany Coll 421 N First St Lindsborg KS 67456 Home Phone: 785-227-3329; Office Phone: 785-227-3380 x 8334. Business E-Mail: mahraund@bethanylb.edu.

MAHSMAN, DAVID LAWRENCE, writer, church administrator; b. Quincy, Ill., Aug. 16, 1950; s. Alvin Henry and Dorothy Marie (Schnack) M.; m. Lois Jean Mohn, July 27, 1975. BS in Journalism, So. Ill. U., 1972; MDiv, Concordia Theol. Seminary, Fort Wayne, Ind., 1983; STM, Concordia Sem., St. Louis, 1995. Staff writer Paddock Publs., Arlington Heights, Ill., 1972-73, Decatur (Ill.) Herald & Rev., 1973-76; press asst. Hon. Tom Railsback U.S. Ho. Reps., Washington, 1976-79, campaign press sec. Hon. Dan Coats Ft. Wayne, Ind., 1979-80, 82; pastor Trinity Luth. Ch., Glen Cove, NY, 1983-85; dir. news and info. Luth. Ch.-Mo. Synod, St. Louis, 1985—2005; exec. editor, contbr. Luth. Witness, St. Louis, 1985—2005; exec. editor Reporter, St. Louis, 1985—2005; asst. to exec. dir. Bd. Mission Svcs. Mo. Synod, 2005—. Mem. Inter-Luth. task force on pornography Luth. Coun. U.S.A., 1986; mem. Washington adv. coun. Mo. Synod, Office of Govt. Info., Washington, 1987-2000. Editor: Augsburg Today: This We Believe, Teach and Confess, 1997. Recipient Jacob Scher Investigative Reporting award Women in Comm., 1974, Commendation award Concordia Hist. Inst., 1988, 98, 1st Place Reporting award Evang. Press Assn., 2003. Mem. Concordia Hist. Inst. (life). Republican. Lutheran. Avocations: travel, photography. Office: Luth Ch-Mo Synod 1333 S Kirkwood Rd Saint Louis MO 63122-7226 E-mail: david.mahsman@lcms.org.

MAI, WILLIAM FREDERICK, plant nematologist, educator; b. Greenwood, Del., July 23, 1916; s. William Frederick and Laurana (Owens) M.; m. Barbara Lee Morrell, June 2, 1941; children: Virginia Mai Abrams, William Howard Mai, Eliabeth Hardy Mai. BS, U. Del., 1939; PhD, Cornell U., 1945. Asst. prof. Cornell U., Ithaca, N.Y., 1946-49, assoc. prof., 1949-52, prof., 1952-81, Liberty Hyde prof. plant pathology, 1981-83, prof. emeritus, 1983—. Cons. Nat. Acad. Scis., Internat. Potato Ctr., Brands Co., AID. Author (with H.H. Lyon), Pictoral Key to Genera of Plant Parasitic Nemtodes, 1960, 5th edit. 1993, Plant Parasitic Nematodes, 1971; editor: Control of Plant Parasitic Nematodes, 1968. Coach Little League Baseball and Football, Ithaca, 1955—60; chmn. Community Orgn., 1960—65. Recipient award of distinction Internat. Plant Protection Conf., 1979; Paul Harris fellow Rotary Found., 1997. Fellow Am. Phytopath. Soc. (pres. Northeastern div. 1968-69 award of merit Northeastern div); mem. AAAS, Soc. Nematologists (pres. 1969 hon. life), Helminthological Soc. Washington, Soc. European Nematologists, Potato Assn. Am. Lodges: Rotary. Home: Apt 203 103 Bundy Rd Ithaca NY 14850 Office: Cornell U Dept Plant Pathology Ithaca NY 14853

MAIBACH, BEN C., JR., consumer products company executive; b. Bay City, Mich., 1920; With Barton-Malow Co., Detroit, 1938—, v.p., dir.-in-charge field ops., 1949-53, exec. v.p., 1953-60, pres., 1960-76, chmn. bd., 1976; chmn. and dir. Barton-Malow Ent.; chmn. bd. Cloverdale Equipment Co. Trustee Barton-Malow Found, Maibach Found., 1967—; chmn. Apostolic Christian Woodhaven, Detroit; bishop Apostolic Christian Ch., Mich., Ont., Fla.; bd. dirs. S.E. Mich. chpt. ARC, Rural Gospel and Med. Missions of India. Home: 29711 Wentworth St Apt 207 Livonia MI 48154-3887 also: 5525 Azure Way Sarasota FL 34242-1857

MAIBACH, BEN C., III, construction company executive; b. May 5, 1946; BS, Mich. State U., 1969. With Barton-Malow Corp., Oak Park, Mich., 1964—, v.p. field ops., 1964-68, systems analyst, programmer, 1968-70, project adminstr., 1970-72; officer mgr., purchasing agt. Barton-Malow Co., Oak Park, Mich., 1972-73, v.p., 1973-76, exec. v.p., 1976-81, pres., 1981—. Office: Barton Malow Co 26500 American Dr Southfield MI 48034

MAIDA, ADAM JOSEPH CARDINAL, cardinal; b. East Vandergrift, Pa., Mar. 18, 1930; Student, St. Vincent Coll., Latrobe, Pa., St. Mary's U., Balt., Lateran U., Rome, Duquesne U. Ordained priest Roman Cath. Ch., 1956, consecrated bishop Roman Cath. Ch., 1984. Bishop, Green Bay, Wis., 1984—89; archbishop Detroit, 1990—; created cardinal, 1994—; appt. superior Cayman Islands, 2000. Home and Office: Archdiocese of Detroit 1234 Washington Blvd Detroit MI 48226-1825

MAIDIQUE, MODESTO ALEX, academic administrator; b. Havana, Cuba, Mar. 20, 1940; s. Modesto Maidique and Hilda Rodriguez; children: Ana Teresa, Mark Alex. BS, MIT, 1962, MS, 1964, PhD, 1970. Instr. MIT, Boston, 1976-79; v.p., gen. mgr. Analog Devices Semiconductor, Boston, 1970-76; asst. prof. Harvard U., Boston, 1976-81; assoc. prof. Stanford U., Palo Alto, Calif., 1981-84; sr. ptnr. Hambrecht and Quist Venture Ptnrs., Palo Alto, Calif., 1981-86; co-founder, dir. U. Miami (Fla.) Innovation and Entepreneurship Inst., 1984-86; pres. Fla. Internat. U., Miami, 1986—. Mem. Pres.'s Edn. Policy Adv. Com.; chmn. Beacon Coun., 1992-93. Recipient Citizenship award HEW, 1973, Teaching award Stanford U., 1983 Mem. IEEE, Assn. Cuban Engrs. Republican. Roman Catholic. Office: Florida International Univ Office of President University Park PC 528 Miami FL 33199-0001 Fax: 305-348-3660. E-mail: maidique@fiu.edu.

MAIDMAN, RICHARD HARVEY MORTIMER, lawyer; b. NYC, Nov. 17, 1933; s. William and Ada (Seegle) M.; m. Lynne Rochelle Lateiner, Apr. 3, 1960 (div. Sept. 1987); m. Gail Lowe Haymes, Sept. 27, 1998; children: Patrick, Mitchel, Dagny. BA, Williams Coll., 1955; JD, Yale U., 1959; postgrad., NYU Grad. Sch. Bus., 1957, NYU Grad. Sch. Law, 1960-77. Bar: NY 1961, Fla. 1961, US Dist. Ct. 1962, 79, US Ct. Appeals 1966, US Supreme Ct. 1978. Assoc. Saxe, Bacon & O'Shea, NYC, 1962-64; ptnr. Weiner, Maidman & Goldman, NYC, 1964-67; pvt. practice NYC and Fla., 1968—96; mng. gen. ptnr. Richard and David Maidman, NYC, 1972—; of counsel Maidman and Mittelman LLP, 1996—; chmn. Townhouse Mgmt. Co., 2002—, Fashion Wear Realty Co., Inc., 2004—. Of counsel Shwal, Thompson & Bloch, NYC and Geneva, 1976-87; pres. MBS Equities, Inc., 1970-88, Fashion Wear Realty Co., Inc., NYC, 1975-2004, chmn., 2004—; Barcelona Hotel Ltd., Miami Beach, Fla., 1975-84, New Haven Projects Co., 1987—; dir., gen counsel The Farr Companies, Washington, 1990-92; legis. counsel Theodore R. Kupferman, 17th Congl. Dist. NY, 1966-68; receiver Halloran House Hotel, NYC, 1981; prin. Manhattan Parking Sys. Group, NYC, 1990-2007. Contbr. articles to profl. jours. Mem. ABA, NY State Bar Assn., Fla. Bar Assn., Assn. of the Bar of the City of NY, NYC Real Estate Bd. NY. Home: Steamboat Landing 27 Astor Ln Sands Point NY 11050-2602 also: 9 E 79th St New York NY 10021-0123 Office: 70 E 55th St New York NY 10022-3222 Office Phone: 212-755-0500. Personal E-mail: rhmm59@aya.yale.edu. Business E-Mail: richard@maidman.org.

MAIDMENT, KAREN E., bank executive; b. 1958; married; 2 children. Grad., Galt Collegiate Inst., 1977; B in Commerce, McMaster U. Chartered acct., 1983. With Clarkson Gordon, 1981; CFO Clarica Life Insurance Co., 1988; exec. v.p., CFO BMO Fin. Grp., 2000—03, sr. exec. v.p., 2003—. Mem., Mgmt. Bd. Exec. Com. BMO Fin. Grp. Pres. Canadian Fedn. U. Women; bd. mem. Cambridge Chamber of Commerce; hon. chair Easter Seals' Ball. Named Canada's CFO of Yr., Fin. Executives Internat. Can. and PricewaterhouseCoopers LLP, 2006; named one of 25 Women to Watch, US Banker, 2006; named to Power 50 list, Fin. Post, 2004, 2005, 2006; recipient Women of Distinction award, YWCA, 2001, Mgmt. Achievement award, McGill U., 2004, Wayne C. Fox Disting. Alumni award, McMaster U. Michael G. Degroote Sch. of Bus., 2004. Fellow: Inst. Chartered Accountants; mem.: Waterloo-Wellington Chartered Accountants Assn. (pres.). Office: BMO Financial Group Corporate Communications Media and Publi 302 Bay St 11th Fl Toronto ON Canada M5X 1A1 Office Phone: 416-867-3996. *

MAIDON, CAROLYN HOWSER, director; b. Chgo., May 13, 1946; d. Lloyd Earl and Esther Lillian (Beck) Howser; m. Charles Randall Maidon, Nov. 21, 1970; children: Randall Scott, April Janel. BS in Edn., Okla. State U., 1968; MS in Edn., N.C. State U., 1984, postgrad., 1987—. Tchr. biology and English Cary (N.C.) High Sch., 1968-71; grad. instr. N.C. State U., Raleigh, 1984-85, asst. affirmative action officer, 1985-89, asst. dir. univ. undesignated program, 1989-95; dir. tchr. edn., 1995-99; coord. MentorNet N.C. State U., Raleigh, 2000—; chief, tchr. edn. sect. N.C. Dept. Pub. Instrn., 1999-2000. Home: 4204 Belnap Dr Apex NC 27502-5378 Office: NC State U PO Box 7632 Raleigh NC 27695-7632

MAIENSCHEIN, FRED, retired physicist; b. Belleville, Ill., Oct. 28, 1925; s. Fred and Ethel (Forsythe) M.; m. Joyce Kylander, Aug. 14, 1948; children: Jane, Jon. BS in Chem. Engring, Rose Hulman Inst. Tech., 1945; MS in Physics, Ind. U., 1948, PhD in Physics, 1949. Physicist Oak Ridge Nat. Lab., 1951-60, assoc. dir. engring. physics div., 1960-66; co-dir. Oak Ridge Electron Linear Accelerator, 1965-74, dir. engring. physics div., 1966-90, ret., 1990. Mem. com. reactor physics Nuclear Energy Agy., 1962-89; mem. adv. com. radiation aspects of SST, FAA, 1969-74; mem. subcoms. Nat. Com. Radiation Protection, 1959-71. Contbr. articles profl. jours., chpts. in books. Fellow Am. Nuclear Soc.; mem. Am. Phys. Soc., AAAS, Soc. Neurosci., Tau Beta Pi. Home: 838 W Outer Dr Oak Ridge TN 37830-8402

MAIER, CHARLES STEVEN, history professor; b. NYC, Feb. 23, 1939; s. Louis and Muriel (Krailsheimer) M.; m. Pauline Alice Rubbelke, June 17, 1961; children: Andrea Nicole, Nicholas Winterer, Jessica Elizabeth Heine. AB, Harvard U., 1960, PhD, 1967; postgrad., St. Anthony's Coll., Oxford, Eng., 1960—61. Instr. history Harvard U., Cambridge, Mass., 1967-69, asst. prof., 1969-73, lectr., 1973-75, prof. history, 1981-91, Krupp Found. prof. European studies, 1991—2002, Leverett Saltonstall prof. history, 2002, dir. Ctr. for European Studies, 1994-2001, 2006; vis. prof. U. Bielefeld, Germany, 1976; assoc. prof. history Duke U., Durham, NC, 1976-79, prof., 1979-81. Rsch. fellow Lehrman Inst., NYC, 1975-76; mem. assoc. staff Brookings Instn., Washington, 1978-84; mem. coun. Fondation Jean Monnet pour l'Europe, Lausanne, Switzerland; mem. joint comm. on We. Europe Social Sci. Rsch. Coun. and Am. Coun. Learned Socs., 1978-84, chmn., 1979-81; mem. German Am. Acad. Coun., Bonn, Germany and Washington, 1998-2001; chair selection com., Am. Acad. Berlin, 2001-05; vis. prof. Sch. Advanced Studies in Social Scis., Paris, 2007. Author: Recasting Bourgeois Europe, 1975 (Am. Hist. Assn. George Louis Beer award 1976, Herbert Baxter Adams award 1977), In Search of Stability, 1987, The Unmasterable Past, 1988, Dissolution: The Crisis of Communism and the End of East Germany, 1997, Among Empires: American Ascendancy and its Predecesssons, 2006; editor: The Origins of the Cold War and Contemporary Europe, 1978, rev. edit., 1990, (with Dan S. White) The Thirteenth of May and the Advent of de Gaulle's Republic, 1967, (with Leon Lindberg) The Politics of Inflation and Economic Stagnation, 1985, Changing Boundaries of the Political, 1987, The Marshall Plan and Germany, 1991. contbr. numerous essays, chpts. to books, book reviews, 1970-2007. Decorated comdr.'s cross Order of Merit, Germany; fellow NEH, 1977-78, German Marshall Fund, 1980-81, Guggenheim Found., 1984-85; rsch. grantee MacArthur Found., 1988-89; recipient Alexander von Humboldt Found. Rsch. prize, 2003; fellow Woodrow Wilson Ctr. for Scholars, Washington, D.C., 1989. Mem. Coun. on Fgn. Rels., Am. Hist. Assn., Soc. Italian Hist. Studies, Soc. Historians of Am. Fgn. Rels., Am. Acad. Arts and Scis., Phi Beta Kappa. Office: Harvard U Ctr for European Studies Cambridge MA 02138 Office Phone: 617-495-4303. Business E-Mail: csmaier@fas.harvard.edu.

MAIER, GERALD JAMES, gas industry executive; b. Regina, Sask., Can., Sept. 22, 1928; s. John Joseph and Mary M. Student, Notre Dame Coll., Wilcox, U. Man., U. Alta., U. Western Ont.; LLD (hon.), U. Alta., 1999; LLD, U. Calgary, 2005. With petroleum and mining industries Can., U.S., Australia, U.K.; responsible for petroleum ops. Africa, United Arab Emirates, S.E. Asia; past chmn., pres., CEO TransCan. PipeLines, Calgary, Canada, 1985-99; vice-chmn. NOVA Chems. Corp., Calgary, 1998-2000. Bd. dirs. Stream-Flo Industries, Ltd., Master Flo Valve Inc., Bow Valley Energy Ltd., Willbros Group, Inc.; chmn. Can. Nat. Com. for World Petroleum Congresses, 1991—94, Van Horne Inst. for Internat. Transp., 1992—2000. Chmn. bd. dirs. Notre Dame Coll. Named Hon. Col. (ret.) King's Own Calgary Rgt., Resource Man of Yr. Alta. Chamber of Resources, 1990, Officer Order of Can., 2004; named to Can. Petroleum Hall of Fame, 1999; recipient Can. Engr.'s Gold medal Can. Coun. Profl. Engrs., 1990, Disting. Alumni award U. Alta., 1992, Mgmt. award McGill U., 1993, Centennial award Alta. Assn. Engrs., Geologists and Geophysicists, 1994, Hal Godwin award U. Calgary, 1999, Can. Bus. Leader award U. Alta., 1999, Can. Engring. Leader award U. Calgary, 2003, Alta. Centennial medal, 2005. Fellow Can. Acad. Engring.; mem. Assn. Profl. Engrs., Geologists and Geophysicists Alta. (past pres.), Can. Inst. Mining and Metallurgy (Past Pres.'s Meml. medal 1971). Avocations: golf, downhill skiing, shooting, fishing. Office: Granmar Investments Ltd 88 Massey Pl SW Calgary Canada T2V 2G8

MAIER, KAREN MARIE, school librarian; b. Philip, SD, Dec. 8, 1956; d. Clell and Cheryl Joan Baker; m. Gary Lee Maier, Dec. 23, 1978; children: Pamela Ann, Robert James, Crystal Lea, Jonathan Walter. A in English, Presentation Coll., Aberdeen, SD, 1995, B in Bus. Mgmt., 1998. Libr. student asst. Presentation Coll., 1994—97, tech. svcs./circulation libr., 1998—. Libr. tech./dept. liaison Presentation Coll., 2001—, sys. libr., 1999—, S.D. Libr. Network, Spearfish, 1999—. Avocations: reading, knitting. Office: Presentation Coll 1500 N Main St Aberdeen SD 57401 Office Phone: 605-229-8498. E-mail: Karen.Maier@presentation.edu.

MAIER, PAULINE, historian, educator; b. Apr. 27, 1938; d. Irvin Louis and Charlotte (Winterer) Rubbelke; m. Charles Steven Maier, June 17, 1961; children: Andrea Nicole, Nicholas Winterer, Jessica Elizabeth Heine. AB, Radcliffe Coll., 1960; postgrad., London Sch. Econs., 1960-61; PhD in History, Harvard U., 1968; LLD (hon.), Regis Coll., 1987; DHL (hon.), Williams Coll., 1993. Asst. prof. then assoc. prof. history U. Mass., Boston, 1968-77; Robinson-Edwards prof. history U. Wis., Madison, 1977-78; prof. history MIT, Cambridge, Mass., 1978—, William R. Kenan Jr. prof. history, 1990—. Dept. head, MIT, 1979-88, mem. coun. Inst. Early Am. History, 1982-84; trustee Regis Coll., 1988-93; trustee Commonwealth Sch., 1991-96; bd. mgrs. Old South Meeting House, 1987-97, bd. advisors Internat. Ctr. Jefferson Studies, 2000-. Author: From Resistance to Revolution: Colonial Radicals and the Development of American Opposition to Britain, 1765-1766, 1972, The Old Revolutionaries: Political Lives in the Age of Samuel Adams, 1980, The American People: A History, 1986, American Scripture: Making the Declaration of Independence, 1997; co-author: Inventing America, 2002, 2d edit. 2006. Recipient Douglass Adair award Claremont Grad. Sch.-Inst. Early Am. History, 1976, Kidger award New Eng. History Tchrs. Assn., 1981; fellow Nat. Endowment Humanities, 1974-75, 88-89, Charles Warren fellow, 1974-75, Guggenheim fellow, 1990. Mem. Orgn. Am. Historians (mem. exec. bd. 1978-82), Am. Hist. Assn. (mem. nominations com. 1983-85, chmn. 1985), Soc. Am. Historians, Am. Antiquarian Soc. (mem. exec. coun. 1984-89), Colonial Soc. Mass. (mem. exec. coun. 1990-93), Mass. Hist. Soc., Am. Acad. Arts and Scis., The Hist. Soc. (bd. govs. 1998—). Home: 60 Larchwood Dr Cambridge MA 02138-4639 Office: MIT E51-279 77 Massachusetts Ave Cambridge MA 02139-4307 Home Phone: 617-868-2281; Office Phone: 617-253-2646. Business E-Mail: pmaier@mit.edu.

MAIER, RONALD VITT, surgeon, educator; b. Wheeling, W.Va., Oct. 23, 1947; BS, U. Notre Dame, 1969; MD, Duke U., 1973. Intern Parkland Meml. Hosp., Dallas, 1973-74; resident U. Wash. Hosps., Seattle, 1974-78; rsch. assoc. Scripps Rsch. Found., La Jolla, Calif., 1978-81; surgeon-in-chief HMC, Seattle, 1993—; vice chair U. Wash., Seattle, 1994—. Jane and Donald D. Trunkey prof., 2005—. Office: Dept Surgery 359796 Harborview Med Ctr 325 9th Ave Seattle WA 98104-2499 Office Phone: 206-744-3299. Business E-Mail: ronmaier@u.washington.edu.

MAIESE, KENNETH, neurologist, neuroscientist; b. Audubon, NJ, Dec. 5, 1958; s. Charles and Margaret (Fioretti) M. BA summa cum laude, U. Pa., 1981; MD, Cornell U., 1985. Intern N.Y. Hosp., 1985—86, resident neurology, 1986—89, asst. attending physician, 1989—94; asst. prof. Cornell U. Med. Coll., NYC, 1989—94; assoc. prof. dept. neurology, anatomy and cell biology Ctr. Molecular Toxicology and Medicine Wayne State U., Detroit, 1994—99, dir. lab. molecular and cellular cerebral ischemia Ctr. Molecular Toxicology, 1994—, prof. dept. neurology, anatomy, cell biology Ctr. Molecular Toxicology, 1999—. Dir. neurol. diagnosis NY Hosp., 1991—94; chmn. nat. brain/stroke consortium Am. Heart Assn., 2000—01, exec. coun., 2001—, nat peer rev. steering com., 2002—, mem. rsch. com., 2003—; mem. study sect. cell death and injury NIH/CDIN, 2003—; mem. neurobiology study sect. Vet.'s Adminstrn., 2004—; spkr. in field. Author: Neurology and General Medicine, 1989, Neurological and Neurosurgical ICU Medicine, 1988; editor-in-chief Current Neurovascular Rsch., 2002—; editor: Neuronal and Vascular Plasticity, 2003; mem. editl. bd. Letters in Drug Design and Discovery, 2002—, Histology and Histopathology, 2002—, Jour. Histological Histopathology, 2002—, Drug Design Revs., 2003—, Medicinal Chemistry, 2004—, Current Drug Targets-Heme Agts., Jour. Heart Digest, 2005—, Internat. Jour. Molecular Medicine, 2005—, Ctrl. Nervous Sys. Agts., Medicinal Chemistry, 2006—, Open Neurosci. Jour., 2007—, Open Biochem. Jour., 2007—; editl. bd. contbr. The Merck Manual Profl. Home Edit., 2007; contbr. articles to profl. jours. Joseph Collins scholar, 1981-85, Grupe Found. scholar, 1985; grantee NIH, 1990—, Nat. Stroke Assn., 1992-94, Alzheimer's Assn., 1994—, Am. Heart Assn., 1995—, United Cerebral Palsy Found., 1995—, Janssen Found., 1995—; recipient Young Scientist award Jours. Cerebral Blood Flow, 1991, Hoechst Investigator award, 1993, Robert G. Siekert award in stroke, 1994, Johnson and Johnson Disting. Investigator award, 1996-98, Maiese Lab. Neurosci. Tng. award J & J/Janssen, 1998, Boehringer Investigator award, 1999, NIH/NIEHS award, Learn Found. award, 2002-03, MI Challenge award, Bugher Found. award, 2005, Am. Diabetes Assn. award, 2006, NIH/NIA award, 2007; named one of Am.'s Top Physicians, 2005-06, Best of US Physicians, 2006. Mem. NIH (minority edn. tng. 2002—, spl. emphasis cellular pathophysiologyspl., emphasis panel cellular degeneration 2004—), Am. Acad. Neurology, NY Acad. Scis., Assn. for Rsch. in Nervous and Mental Diseases, Am. Neurol. Assn. (elected), Soc. Neurosci., Internat. Acad. Cardiology (sci. com. 2003-, Bugher Found. award 2005-), Am. Diabetes Assn. (Sr. Investigator award 2006), Alzheimer's Soc. UK, Diabetes Found. UK, Rsch. Coun. Hong Kong, Rsch. Coun. Spain, NIH Applied Metabolom Techs., Austrian Sci. Fund. Roman Catholic. Achievements include rsch. in imidazole receptors, cerebral ischemia, nitric oxide toxicity, growth factor neuroprotection, signal cellular transduction mechanisms, metabotropic glutamate receptors, gene regulation, and gene therapy, patents in field. Office: Wayne State U Sch Medicine 8C-1 U Health Ctr Dept Neur 4201 Saint Antoine St Detroit MI 48201-2153 Business E-Mail: kmaiese@med.wayne.edu.

MAIKISH, CHARLES JOHN, engineer, lawyer; b. NYC, May 8, 1946; s. Charles Francis and Anna Marie (Ross) M.; m. Linda Teresa LeVoci, Apr. 5, 1970; children: Nicole, Charles N., Christopher. BS in Engring., Manhattan Coll., 1966; BA, St. Joseph's Coll., Yonkers, NY, 1968; JD, NYU, 1974; AMP, Harvard U., 1989. Bar: N.Y. 1975, U.S. Dist. Ct. (so. and ea. dists.) N.Y. 1975, U.S. Ct. Appeals (2nd cir.) 1981. Engr. Port Authority of N.Y. and N.J., NYC, 1968-74, atty., 1974-78, prin. atty. litigation, 1978-85, dir. office of ferry transp., 1985-89, asst. dir. world trade and econ. devel., 1989, sr. exec. in charge of the recovery, reconstruction, and repositioning of the World Trade Center after the February 1993 bombing, 1993—96; v.p. facilities mgmt. Columbia U., NYC, 1997; exec. v.p. Global Real Estate Business Services JP Morgan Chase, NYC, 1999—2005; exec. dir. Lower Manhattan Construction Command Ctr., NYC, 2005—07. Adj. lectr. Real Estate Inst. NYU, 1975-78, adj. asst. prof., 1978-83, adj. assoc. prof., 1978—. Recipient De La Salle Medal, Manhattan Coll., 2006. Mem. ABA, Internat. Marine Transit Assn., N.Y. State Trial Lawyers Assn., Rockland Country Club (Sparkhill, N.Y.). Avocations: golf, sailing. *

MAIKON, MARC STEVEN, podiatrist; BA, Grinnell Coll., 1980; BS, U. Iowa, 1982; DPM, U. Osteo. Medicine, Des Moines, 1989. Cert. Am. Coun. Cert. Podiatric Physicians and Surgeons. Podiatrist, owner Family Foot Care Ctr. PLC, Cedar Rapids, Iowa, 1991—. Mem. Am. Coll. Foot Surgeons, Am. Podiatric Med. Assn., Iowa Podiatric Med. Soc., C. of C. Cedar Rapids, Rotary Internat. Office: Family Foot Ctr 3359 Center Point Rd NE Cedar Rapids IA 52402-5568 Home: 1750 Emerald Ct Robins IA 52328-9651

MAILER, NORMAN KINGSLEY, writer, playwright, film director; b. Long Branch, NJ, Jan. 31, 1923; s. Issac Barnett and Fanny (Schneider) M.; m. Beatrice Silverman, 1944 (div. 1952); 1 dau., Susan; m. Adele Morales, 1954 (div. 1962); children: Danielle, Elizabeth; m. Jeanne Campbell, 1962 (div. 1963); 1 dau., Kate; m. Beverly Bentley, 1963 (div. 1980); children: Michael, Steven; m. Carol Stevens, 1980 (div. 1980); 1 dau., Maggie; m. Norris Church, 1980; 1 son, John Buffalo. SB cum laude, Harvard U., 1943; postgrad., Sorbonne, Paris, France, 1947-48. Columnist Village Voice, 1946, Commentary, 1962-63, Esquire, 1962-63; contbg. editor Dissent, 1953-69; co-founding editor Village Voice, 1955. Author: No Percentage, 1941, The Naked and the Dead, 1948, Barbary Shore, 1951, The Deer Park, 1955, The White Negro: Superficial Reflections on the Hipster, 1957, Advertisements for Myself, 1959, Deaths for the Ladies and Other Disasters, 1962, The Presidential Papers, 1963, An American Dream, 1965, Cannibals and Christians, 1966, Why Are We in Vietnam?, 1967 (Nat. Book award nomination 1967), The Short Fiction of Norman Mailer, 1967, The Bullfight, 1967, The Armies of the Night, 1968 (Pulitzer prize for non-fiction 1969, George Polk award 1969), Miami and the Siege of Chicago, 1968 (Nat. Book award for non-fiction 1968), The Idol and the Octopus, 1968, Of a Fire On The Moon, 1970, King of the Hill, 1971, The Prisoner of Sex, 1971, The Long Patrol, 1971, Existential Errands, 1972, St. George and the Godfather, 1972, Marilyn, 1973, The Faith of Graffiti, 1974, The Fight, 1975, Some Honorable Men, 1975, Genius and Lust, 1976, A Transit to Narcissus, 1978, The Executioner's Song, 1979 (Pulitzer Prize for fiction 1980, Nat. Book Critics Circle award nomination 1979, Am. Book award nomination 1980), Of a Small and Modest Malignancy, Wicked and Bristling with Dots, 1980, Of Women and Their Elegance, 1980, Pieces and Pontifications, 1982, Ancient Evenings, 1983, Tough Guys Don't Dance, 1984, The Last Night, 1984, Harlot's Ghost, 1991, How the Wimp Won the War, 1991, Oswald's Tale, 1995, Portrait of Picasso as a Young Man, 1995, The Gospel According to the Son, 1997, The Spooky Art: Thoughts on Writing, 2003, The Castle in the Forest, 2007; co-author: (with John Buffalo Mailer) The Big Empty, 2005; author: (plays) The Deer Park: A Play, 1967, Strawhead, 1985; editor: Genius and Lust: A Journey Through the Major Writings of Henry Miller, 1976; screenwriter: (films) The Executioner's Song, 1982 (Emmy award nomination outstanding adapted screenplay 1983); screenwriter, prodr., dir., actor: (films) Wild 90, 1967, Maidstone: A Mystery, 1971; screenwriter, prodr.: (films) Beyond the Law, 1968; screenwriter, dir.: (films) Tough Guys Don't Dance, 1987; actor: (films) Ragtime, 1981. Served with AUS, 1944-46. Recipient Edward MacDowell medal MacDowell Colony, 1973, Nat. Arts Club Gold medal, 1976, Emerson-Thoreau Medal for lifetime of literary achievement, 1989, Golden Plate award, Acad. Achievement, 2004, Nat. Book Found. medal for disting. contbn. to Am. letters, 2005; Legion of Honor France, 2006; Nat. Inst. and Am. Acad. grantee, 1960; Pappas fellow U. Pa., 1983. Mem. PEN Am. Ctr. (pres. 1984-86), Nat. Inst. Arts and Letters. *

MAILLOUX, ROBERT JOSEPH, physicist; b. Lynn, Mass., June 20, 1938; s. Joseph H. and Nora S. M.; m. Marlene Schirf, Jan. 14, 1967; children: Patrice, Julie, Denise. BS, Northeastern U., 1961; SM, Harvard U., 1962, PhD, 1965. Physicist NASA Electronics Rsch. Ctr., Cambridge, Mass., 1965—70, Air Force Cambridge Rsch. Labs., Bedford, Mass., 1970—77, Rome Air Devel. Ctr., Bedford, 1977—80, chief antennas and components divsn., electromagnetic directorate, 1990—91; sr. scientist Air Force Rsch. Lab., 1992—2004; rsch. prof. U. Mass., 2006—. Lectr. Tufts U., Boston, 1985-, rsch. prof. U. Mass. Amherst, 2006-. Author: Phased Array Antenna Handbook; editor History of Wireless; guest editor IEEE/AP-S Transactions Spl. Issue on Phased Array Antennas, 1999; contbr. chpts. to 8 textbooks, articles to sci. jours. Served with C.E. U.S. Army, 1966-68. Recipient Air Force Marcus O'Day paper award, 1971, Engineer of Yr. award Rome Air Devel. Ctr., 1988, fellow 1988 Fellow IEEE (chmn. tech. com. 1997 phased array symposium, spl. achievement award 1969, 76, nat. lectr., assoc. editor Trans. on Antennas and Propagation 1984-92, Harry Diamond award 1991, Fred Diamond award 1997, Third Millenium medal, 2000, Disting. Achievement award 2005); mem. Antenna and Propagation Soc. (chmn. Boston chpt. 1968, nat. meetings chmn. 1977-80, adcom mem. 1977-80, v.p. 1982, pres. 1983), Internat. Sci. Radio Union (Commn. B tech. activities chmn. 1980—), Sigma Xi (pres. Hanscom chpt. 1980-81), Eta Kappa Nu, Tau Beta Pi. Achievements include 12 patents in field. Office: AFRL/SNH 31 Grenier St Hanscom Afb MA 01731-3008

MAIMAN, MITCHELL, oncologist, gynecologist; b. Bklyn., 1957; s. Irwin and Gloria (Pepper) Maiman; m. Judith E. Levy, 1985. MD, SUNY-Health Sci. Ctr., 1981. Diplomate Am. Bd. Obstetrics and Gynecology with subspecialty in gynecologic oncology. Resident Einstein Coll. Medicine, Bronx, 1981—85; fellow Univ. Hosp., Bklyn., 1985—87; pvt. practice oncology, gynecology SI, NY, 1987—. V.p. women's health S.I. Univ. Hosp., chmn. dept. ob-gyn., 1999—; prof. SUNY, Bklyn. Office: 256 Mason Ave Staten Island NY 10305-3408 Office Phone: 718-226-9269. Business E-Mail: mmaiman@siuh.edu.

MAIMON, ELAINE PLASKOW, academic administrator; b. Phila., July 28, 1944; d. Louis J. and Gertrude (Canter) Plaskow; m. Morton A. Maimon, Sept. 30, 1967; children: Gillian Blanche, Alan Marcus. AB, U. Pa., 1966, MA, 1967, PhD, 1970. Asst. prof. Haverford Coll., 1971-73; lectr. Arcadia U., Glenside, Pa., 1973-75, asst. prof., dir. writing, 1975-77, assoc. prof., 1977-83, assoc. dean, 1980-84, assoc. v.p., prof. English, 1984-86; adj. assoc. prof. U. Pa., Phila., 1982-83; assoc. dean of coll. Brown U., Providence, 1986-88; dean, prof. English Queens Coll. CUNY, Flushing, NY, 1988-96; campus CEO, provost Ariz. State U. West, Phoenix, 1996—2004; v.p. Ariz. State U., 1996—2004; chancellor U. Alaska, Anchorage, 2004—07; pres. Govs. State U., University Park, Ill., 2007—. Nat. bd. cons. NEH, 1977-81; mem. adv. bd. Cox Comm., 1997-2001; bd. dirs. Arrowhed Cmty. Bank. Co-author: Writing in the Arts and Sciences, 1981, A Writer's Resource, 2003; co-editor: Readings in the Arts and Sciences, 1984, Thinking, Reasoning and Writing, 1989, A Writer's Resource, 2003, 2d edit., 2007, The New McGraw Hill Handbook, 2007, Writing Intensive, 2007. Trustee Heard Mus., Phoenix, 1999—2005. Recipient Golden Heart award, Today's Ariz. Woman, 2000, Women of Distinction award, YMCA, Maricopa County, 2001, YWCA award in Edn., 2002, World award, Girl Scouts Am., Ariz. Cactus-Pine Coun., 2002, Woman of Vision award, Phoenix Bus. Jour.; Elaine Maimon award for Excellence in Writing named in her honor, Arcadia U., 1994. Mem.: MLA (exec. com., tchg. of writing divsn.), Am. Assn. Colls. and Univs. (exec. bd. 2002—06), Conf. on Coll. Composition Comm. (exec. com. 1985—87), ACE Nat. Commn. Women, Nat. Coun. Tchrs. English (nominating com. 1986—87, teaching of writing divsn. 1991), Phi Beta Kappa. Office: Govs State U Office of Pres 1 University Parkway University Park IL 60466-0975 Home Phone: 907-562-2084; Office Phone: 907-786-1437. Business E-Mail: elaine.maimon@uaa.alaska.edu.

MAIN, DAVID C., lawyer; b. Des Moines, Feb. 29, 1948; BA, DePauw Univ., 1970; MTS, Harvard Divinity Sch., 1973; JD, Georgetown Univ., 1976. Bar: DC 1977, Va., US Dist. Ct. (DC), US Ct. Appeals (DC cir.), US Supreme Ct. Staff mem. U.S. Senate Rep. Policy Com., 1974—76; health counsel to U.S. Senator Richard S. Schweiker, 1976—79; counsel U.S. Senate Subcom. on Health & Scientific Rsch., 1977—79; atty., chmn. managed care practice Gardner Carton & Douglas; atty., chmn. health care practice Crowell & Moring; ptnr., co-chmn. Healthcare practice Pillsbury Winthrop Shaw Pittman, McLean, Va. Founder & coord. Healthcare Tech. Network of Greater Washington; counsel Health Mgmt. Academy. Contbr. articles to profl. jours. Mem.: Am. Health Lawyers Assn., Md. BioScience Alliance, DC Hosp. Assn., Phi Beta Kappa. Office: Pillsbury Winthrop Shaw Pittman 1650 Tysons Blvd Mc Lean VA 22102-4859 Office Phone: 703-770-7518. Office Fax: 702-770-7901. Business E-Mail: david.main@pillsburylaw.com.

MAIN, EDNA DEWEY (JUNE MAIN), education educator; b. Hyannis, Mass., Sept. 1, 1940; d. Seth Bradford and Edna Wilhelmina (Wright) Dewey; m. Donald John Main, Sept. 9, 1961 (dv. Dec. 1989); children: Alison Teresa Main Ronzon, Susan Christine Main Leddy, Steven Donald. Degree in merchandising, Tobe-Coburn Sch., NYC, 1960; BA in Edn., U. North Fla., Jacksonville, 1974, MA in Edn., 1979, M in Adminstrn. and Supervision, 1983; PhD in Curriculum and Instrn., U. Fla., Gainsville, 1990. Asst. buyer Abraham & Straus, Bklyn., 1960-61; asst. mdse. mgr. Interstate Dept. Stores, NYC, 1962-63; tchr. Holiday Hill Elem. Sch., Jacksonville, Fla., 1974-86; instr. summer sci. inst., 1984—92; prof. edn. Jacksonville U., 1992—, dir. masters program in integrated learning and ednl. tech. Instr. U. Fla., 1987—90, U. North Fla., 1990—92; cons. Assn. Internat. Schs. Africa, 1994—97. Co-author: (book) Developing Critical Thinking Through Science, Book I, 2001, Developing Critical Thinking Through Science, Book II, 2002. Rep. United Way, 1981—86; tchr. rep., chpt. leader White Ho. Young Astronaut Program, 1984—85; team leader NSF Shells Elem. Sci. Project. Named Fla. Prof. of the Yr., Carnegie Found., 2002, Prof. of Yr., Jacksonville U., 2003; recipient Innovative Excellence in Tchg., Learning and Tech. award, Internat. Coll. Conf., 1999, Outstanding Alumni award, U. North Fla., 1999, Eve award for Edn., 2001, Apple Disting. Educator award, 2003—05. Mem.: Internat. Soc. Tech. Edn., Soc. Info. Tech. and Tchr. Edn., ASCD, NSTA (Sci. Tchrs. Achievement Recognition award 1983), Kappa Delta Pi, Phi Delta Kappa, Phi Kappa Phi. Episcopalian. Office: Jacksonville U 2800 University Blvd N Jacksonville FL 32211-3394 Personal E-mail: main750@bellsouth.net.

MAIN, JACK, military officer; b. Caldwell, Idaho, Dec. 3, 1957; s. Lyal Mainard Main and Marlyn Gay Wisdom; m. Marie Annette Aubert, June 27, 2004; children: Anthony Michael Smith, Theresa Denise Yapp, Tawnya Marie McGregor, Melissa Ann, Nicole Kathleen Aubert, TaLeigha Dawn Gervais children: John Dundas Gervais Jr. AAC, Lewis and Clark State Coll., Lewiston, Idaho, 1990. Enlisted US Army, 1975, drill sgt., 1989—99, 1st sgt., 1999—; carpenter Leone and Keemble, Spokane, Wash., 1991—. Decorated 4 Army Achievement medal, 3 Army Commendation medal, Good Conduct medal, 7 Army Res. Component Achievement medals, Nat. Def. medal w ith Bronze stars, Humanitarian Svc. medal, Global War on Terrorism svc. campaign medal, 3 - Army Acommodation medals, Purple Heart US Army, Ranger Tab, Airborne Wings, Air Assault medal, Expert Inf. badge, Drill Sgt. badge, Iraq Campaign medal; recipient Arm Forces Res. medal, 1988, Combat Action badge, 2004. Home: 12808 E Mission Spokane WA 99216 Home Phone: 509-891-2905. Personal E-mail: angelfaceandme@aol.com.

MAIN, JAMES L., lawyer; b. Chgo., Sept. 24, 1947; BS in Engring. Sci., Fla. State U.; JD with honors, U. Fla., 1974; LLM in Taxation, NYU, 1978. Ptnr. Holland & Knight LLP, Jacksonville, Fla., leader private equity funds practice group, pres. Mem. U. Fla. Law Review, 1973—74. Bd. dir., pres. Rotary Club, Deerwood, 2006—07. Mem.: Jacksonville Bar Assn., ABA, Fla. Bar, Omicron Delta Kappa, Order of the Coif, Phi Kappa Phi. Office: Holland & Knight LLP 50 N Laura St Ste 3900 Jacksonville FL 32202 Office Phone: 904-798-7319. Business E-Mail: jamesmain@hklaw.com.

MAIN, MICHAEL DEE, information developer; b. Anderson, Ind., Oct. 12, 1956; s. John Dyson and Marilyn Anne (Miller) M.; m. Deborah Lee Holland, Oct. 19, 1996. BA in English, Ind. U., 1979, MLS, 1981. System svcs. libr. Ind. U. Librs., Bloomington, 1981-85, acquisitions libr., 1985-96, info. technologist, 1996-98; br. libr. mgr. Ind. U. Journalism Libr., Bloomington, 1985; info. developer CDI Info. Svcs./IBM, Beaverton, Oreg., 1998—2002, Summit Info. Sys., Corvallis, Oreg., 2002—. Entrepreneurial cons. Star Thrower Pub., 1996—. Author: (electronic novel) Apollo: An American Life, 1997. Writer's fellow Nat. Endowment for Arts and Ind. Arts Commn., 1992-93. Mem. Soc. Tech. Comm., Ind. Arts Commn. (contbg. artist, advisor 1993—), Sierra Club, Audubon Soc., Nature Conservancy, Amnesty Internat. Buddhist (ordained Karma Kagyu Lineage Holder 2000). Avocations: collecting music, music criticism, web consulting and design. Home: 726 NW Lee St Newport OR 97365 Office: Summit Info Sys 4500 SW Research Way Corvallis OR 97339 Office Phone: 541-758-5899 x6406. Business E-Mail: michael.main@star-thrower.com.

MAIN, ROBERT GAIL, communications educator, training services executive, television and film producer, retired military officer; b. Bucklin, Mo., Sept. 30, 1932; s. Raymond M. and Inez L. (Olinger) M.; m. Anita Sue Thoroughman, Jan. 31, 1955; children: Robert Bruce, David Keith, Leslie Lorraine. BS magna cum laude, U. Mo., 1954; grad. with honors, Army Commd. Gen. Staff Coll., 1967; MA magna cum laude in Comm., Stanford U., Calif., 1968; PhD, U. Md., 1978. Commd. 2d lt. US Army, 1954, advanced through grades to lt. col., 1968; mem. faculty Army Commd. Gen. Staff Coll., 1968-70; chief speechwriting and info. materials divsn. US Army Info. Office, 1971, chief broadcast and film divsn., 1972-73; dir. def. audiovisual activities Office of Info. for Armed Forces, 1973-76; ret., 1976; prof. instrnl. tech. Calif. State U., Chico, 1976—, dept. chair, 1993-98, prof. emeritus. Cons. in field. Author: Rogues, Saints and Ordinary People, 1988; prodr. (TV documentary) Walking Wounded, 1983, Army Info. Films, Army Radio Series, 1972-73; contbr. articles on computer based tng. and telecoms. to scientific and profl. jours. Decorated Legion of Merit, Meritorious Svc. medal, Commendation medal with oak leaf cluster, combat Inf. Badge; Vietnamese Cross of Gallantry; recipient Freedom Found. awards, 1972, 73, 74; Bronze medal Atlanta Film Festival, 1972; Best of Show award Balt. Film Festival, 1973; Creativity award Chgo. Indsl. Film Festival, 1973; Cine gold award Internat. Film Prodrs. Assn., 1974; named an Outstanding Prof. Calif. State U., 1987-88. Mem. Phi Eta Sigma, Alpha Zeta, Phi Delta Gamma, Omicron Delta Kappa, Alpha Gamma Rho. Personal E-mail: rmain75@aol.com.

MAIN, TIMOTHY L., electronics company executive; b. 1957; BS, Mich. State U.; M in Internat. Mgmt., Am. Grad. Sch. Internat. Mgmt. Comml. lending officer internat. divsn. Nat. Bank Detroit; mgr. prodn. control Jabil Circuit Inc., St. Petersburg, Fla., 1987, ops. mgr., 1987-89, project mgr., 1989-91, v.p. bus. devel., 1991, sr. v.p. bus. devel., pres., 1999—, CEO, 2000—. Bd. dirs. Jabil Circuit Inc., 1999—. Office: Jabil Cir 10560 9th St N Saint Petersburg FL 33716

MAINELLA, FRAN (FRANCES P. MAINELLA), educator, former federal agency administrator; b. Groton, Conn., 1947; BS cum laude, U. Conn.; MS cum laude in Counseling, Ctrl. Conn. State Coll.; PhD in Pub. Svc. (hon.), Ctrl. Conn. State U., 2002. H.S. phys. edn. tchr. Vernon Pub. Sch., Rockville, Conn., 1969—77; asst. ctr. dir. Tallahassee Parks and Recreation Dept., 1977—78; dir. recreation Town of Lake Park, Fla., 1978—83; exec. dir. Fla. Recreation and Park Assn., Tallahassee, 1983—89; dir. divsn. Recreation and Parks Fla. Dept. Environ. Protection, Tallahassee, 1989—2001; dir. Nat. Park Svc. US Dept. Interior, Washington, 2001—06; vis. scholar Clemson U., SC, 2006—. Spkr. in field. Contbr. numerous articles to profl. publs. Co-chair Com. for Preservation of the White House, mem. adv. coun. on hist. preservation; bd. trustees John F. Kennedy Ctr. for Performing Arts; liaison White House Hist. Soc.; sec., treas. Nat. Park Found.; mem. Am. Folklife Bd.; past pres. Nat. Assn. State Park Dirs.; past bd. mem. Am. Acad. Park and Recreation Adminstr.; past mem. Fla. Commn. Ttourism; past officio bd. mem. Fla. Recreation and Park Assn.; past mem. Gov.'s Mansion adv. com.; past bd. mem. Fla. Gov.'s Coun. on Phys. Fitness and Sports; past sec., bd. dirs. Spl. Olympics; past pres. Tallahassee Soc. Assn. Execs.; past chair United Way Drive for Tallahassee Soc. Assn. Execs.; past bd. dirs. Tallahassee Leon County Convention and Visitors Bur.; bd. dirs. Ford's Theatre Soc., Wolf Trap Found. for Performing Arts. Recipient Disting. Svc. award, Nat. Assn. Recreation Resource Planners, 1996, Woman of Distinction award, Girl Scout Coun. of Apalachee Bend, 1998, Pugsley medal, Am. Acad. Park and Recreation Adminstrn., 1998, Disting. Svc. award, Nat. Assn. State Park Dirs., 1999, Senator Bob Williams award, State of Fla., 2001, Sheldon Coleman Outdoors award, 2002, Walter T. Cox Pub. Svc. Achievement award, Clemson U., 2002. Mem.: Nat. Recreation and Park Assn. (congress planning com. 1984, 1987, past chair coun. exec. dirs., pres. 1997—, Harold D. Meyer Profl. award 2000). E-mail: fmainella@clemson.edu.

MAINES, CHARLES JOHN, electronics manager; b. Fairfax, July 25, 1980; s. George Markham and Linda Olson Maines. AA in Arts, Grand Rapids CC, 2003; BBA in Fin. high hons., Davenport U., Grand Rapids, 2004—06; Cert. of Completion - Mandarin Chinese, Worldlink Edn., Beijing, 2005. Asst. assembly mgr. TACK Electronics, Inc., Grand Rapids, 1996—. Mem.: West Mich. Mensa. Conservative. Christian Reformed Ch. Avocation: travel. Home: 7440 Kettle Lake Dr SE Alto MI 49302 Office: TACK Electronics Inc 4910 Kraft Ave SE Grand Rapids MI 49512 Home Phone: 616-868-7112; Office Phone: 616-698-0960. Office Fax: 616-698-0970; Home Fax: 616-698-0970.

MAINES, NATALIE LOUISE, musician; b. Lubbock, Tex., Oct. 14, 1974; d. Lloyd and Tina M.; m. Michael Tarabay, May 9, 1997 (div. Jan. 1999); m. Adrian Pasdar, June 24, 2000; children: Jack Slade, Beckett Finn. Student, Tex. Tech.; grad., Berklee Coll. Music, Boston, 1995. Performer Dixie Chicks, 1995—. Singer: (albums) Wide Open Spaces, 1998 (Maximum Vision Clip of Yr., Billboard, 1998, Best New Country Artist Clip of Yr., Billboard, 1998, Best Country Album, Grammy Awards, 1998, Album of Yr., Acad. Country Music, 1998, Best Selling Album, Can. Country Music Awards, 1999, Song of Yr. (Country), WB Radio Music Awards, 1999, Album of Yr., ACM, 1999), Fly, 1999 (Best Country Album, Grammy Awards, 1999, Best Selling Album, Can. Country Music Awards, 2000, Internat. Album, British Country Music Awards, 2000, Country Album of Yr., Billboard, 2000, Album of Yr., ACM, 2000, Album of Yr., CMA, 2000), Home, 2002 (Favorite Country Album, Am. Music Awards, 2002, Best Recording Package, Grammy Awards, 2002, Best Country Album, Grammy Awards, 2002), Top of the World Tour: Live, 2003 (Best Country Group Vocal Performance, Grammy awards, 2005), Taking the Long Way, 2006 (Album of Yr. and Best Country Album, Grammy Awards, 2007), (songs) Not Ready to Make Nice, 2006 (Record of Yr., Song of Yr., Best Performance by a Duo or Group with Vocal, Grammy Awards, 2007); performer: (documentary) Dixie Chicks: Shut Up and Sing, 2006. Named Most Significant New Country Act, Country Monitor, 1998, Top New Country Artist, Billboard, 1998, Group of Yr., CMA, 1998, Top Vocal Group, Acad. Country Music, 1998, Country Artist of Yr., Rolling Stone, 1999, Top Country Artist, Billboard, 1999, Internat. Rising Star, British Country Music Awards, 1999, Artist of Yr., WB Radio Music Awards, 1999, Favorite New Artist (Country), AMA, 1999, Vocal Group of Yr., CMA, 1999, Country Artist of Yr., Billboard, 1999, Entertainer of Yr., CMA, 2000, ACM, 2000, 2001, Vocal Group of Yr., 2001, Favorite Musical Group or Band, People's Choice Award, 2002, Vocal Group of Yr., Country Music Assn. Awards, 2002; named one of 100 Most Influential People, Time Mag., 2006; recipient Horizon award, CMA, 1998. *

MAINWARING, THOMAS LLOYD, transportation executive, director; b. Cleve., Aug. 25, 1928; s. Hugh Trevor and Mary Beatrice (Ottman) M.; m. Gladys Fraser Mehr, June 10, 1983; children by previous marriage—Kevin, James, Eileen, Scott, Bruce BA, Albion Coll., 1950; MBA, Western Res. U., 1958. C.P.A., Ohio. Controller Cleve. Cartage Co., 1959-61, v.p., treas., 1961-64; controller Associated Truck Lines, Inc., Vandenberg Ctr., Grand Rapids, Mich., 1964-69; v.p. fin. Associated Transport, Inc., NYC, 1969-70, exec. v.p. fin. and adminstrn., 1970-72; pres. Ryder Truck Lines Inc., Jacksonville, Fla., 1972-78, exec. v.p., chief operating officer, 1978-81, chief exec. officer, 1981-84; pres. Freight System div. Ryder System Inc., Miami, Fla., 1984-86; cons. trucking industry affairs Arlington, Va., 1986-88; pres., chief oper. officer H & M Internat. Transp., Inc., 1989-91, vice chmn., 1991-92; transp. cons., 1992-93; pres., gen. mgr. E.I. Kane Intermodal Transport, Inc., Balt., 1993-95, vice chmn., 1995, transp. cons., 1996—99; COO, Am. C. of C. Execs., 0200—2001; mgmt. cons., 2002—03; treas. & CFO AICHI-USA 2005 World Expn., Inc., 2003—06; exec. v.p. Shanghai-USA 2010 Work Expo., Inc., 2000—. Bd. dirs. Trucking Mgmt., Inc. Mem. exec. com. United Way Jacksonville, 1981-84; trustee Albion Coll., 1977; bd. dirs. Goodwill Industries North Fla. Served with AUS, 1950-53. Mem. Am. Trucking Assn. (nat. acctg. and fin. council 1964, pres. 1971, chmn. ATA Found. 1986-88, exec. com. 1985-88), Fla. Trucking Assn. (bd. dirs. 1973, pres. 1979), Am. Mgmt. Assn. (lectr. seminars), Jacksonville Area C. of C. (bd. govs., com. of 100, v.p. internat. 1984), Cen. and So. Motor Freight Tariff Assn. (bd. dirs. 1981-84, pres. 1983, exec. com. transp. rsch. bd. 1987-89), Sigma Nu. Home: Apt 711 South 1600 S Eads St Arlington VA 22202

MAINWARING, WILLIAM LEWIS, publishing company executive, author; b. Portland, Oreg., Jan. 17, 1935; s. Bernard and Jennie (Lewis) M.; m. Mary E. Bell, Aug. 18, 1962; children: Anne Marie, Julia Kathleen, Douglas Bernard. BS, U. Oreg., 1957; postgrad., Stanford U., 1957-58. With Salem (Oreg.) Capital Jour., 1958-76, editor, pub., 1962-76; pub. Oreg. Statesman, 1974-76; pres. Statesman-Jour. Co., Inc., Salem, 1974-76, Westridge Press, Ltd., 1977—, MediAmerica, Inc., Portland, 1981-96, CEO, 1988—91. Bd. dirs. MediAmerica, Inc. Author: Exploring the Oregon Coast, 1977, Exploring Oregon's Central and Southern Cascades, 1979, Exploring the Mount Hood Loop, 1992, Government, Oregon-Style, 1996, rev. edit., 1997, 99. Pres. Salem Beautification Coun., 1968, Marion-Polk County United Good Neighbors, 1970, Salem Social Svcs. Commn., 1978-79, Salem Hosp. Found., 1978-81, Marion Hist. Found., 2002-03. 2d lt. AUS, 1958; capt. Res. Ret. Mem. Salem Area C. of C. (pres. 1972-73), Oreg. Symphony Soc. Salem (pres. 1973-75), Salem City Club (pres. 1977-78), Sigma Chi. Republican. Presbyterian. Home and Office: 1090 Southridge Pl S Salem OR 97302-5947

MAIOCCHI, CHRISTINE, lawyer; b. NYC, Dec. 24, 1949; d. George and Andreina (Toneatto) M.; m. John Charles Kerecz, Aug. 16, 1980; children: Charles George, Joan Christine. BA in Polit. Sci., MA in Polit. Sci., Fordham U., 1971, JD, 1974; postgrad., NYU, 1977—. Bar: N.Y. 1975, U.S. Dist. Ct. (so. and ea. dists.), N.Y. 1975, U.S. Ct. Appeals (2nd cir) 1975. Law clk. to magistrate U.S. Dist. Ct. (so. dist.) N.Y., NYC, 1973-74; atty. corp. legal dept. The Home Ins. Co., NYC, 1974-76; asst. house counsel corp. legal dept. Allied Maintenance Corp., NYC, 1976; atty. corp. legal dept. Getty Oil Co., NYC, 1976-77; v.p., mgr. real estate Paine, Webber, Jackson & Curtis, Inc., NYC, 1977-81; real estate mgr. GK Techs., Inc., Greenwich, Conn., 1981-85; real estate mgr., sr. atty. MCI Telecom. Corp., Rye Brook, N.Y., 1985-93; real estate and legal cons. Wallace Law Registry, 1994-96; sr. assoc. counsel Met. Transp. Authority, 1996-99, dep. gen. counsel, 1999—2005, gen. counsel, 2005—. Lectr. Practicing Law Inst., NYC, 1999—. Mem.: ABA, CoreNet Global, Indsl. Devel. Rsch. Coun. (program v.p. 1985, Profl. award 1987), Nat. Assn. Corp. Real Estate Execs. (pres. 1983—84, treas. 1984—86, bd. dirs. 1995—, exec. v.p. N.Y. chpt. 2000—01), The Corp. Bar (sec. real estate divsn. 1987—89, chmn. 1990—92), Women's Bar Assn. Manhattan, NY. Bar Assn., Dobbs Ferry Women's Club (program dir. 1981—92, 1994—96, publicity dir. 1992—94), Jr. League Club. Avocations: sports, theater, gardening. Home: 84 Clinton Ave Dobbs Ferry NY 10522-3004 E-mail: cmaiocch@mtahq.org.

MAIOCCO, KENNETH JOSEPH, dermatologist; b. Bridgeport, Conn., Oct. 3, 1941; s. John Paul Maiocco and Jane Marie Pilgoste; m. Maxine Marie Gormley, Dec. 7, 1967; children: David, Mark, Dana, Adam. BS, Fairfield U., Conn., 1963; MD, U. Rochester, NY, 1967. Diplomate Am. Bd. Dermatology, 1976. Dir. pub. health Trumbull Health Dept., 1976—2006. Vol. skin cancer screening clinic Health Dept. Trumbull, Trumbull and Westport, Colo. Maj. US Army, 1971—73. Decorated Commendation medal; named Top Dr. for Women, Conn. Mag., 2002. Mem.: Conn. Dermatology and Dermatol. Surgery Soc., Fairfield County Med. Assn., Conn. State Med. Soc., Am. Acad. Dermatology, Dermatology Found. Scholar's Cir., Gaelic Am. Club, Brooklawn Country Club. Avocations: golf, boating, skiing, model trains. Office: 4639 Main St Bridgeport CT 06606-1838

MAIOLINI, GLORIA J., nursing case manager, poet, writer; d. Harriet Yvonne and Matthew Boyd; 1 child, Galen R. Young Jr. AS Nursing, C.C. Allegheny County, 1994; BS in Health Arts, U. St. Frances, 2000. Health ins. assoc.; cert. case mgr., gerontol. nurse. RN FMC Carswell, Bur. Prisons, Fort Worth, Tex., 1995—95; nurse Heritage Shadyside Nursing Rehab Ctr., Pitts., 1996—99; unit mgr. St. Joseph's Nursing Rehab Ctr., Pitts., 1997—98; RN case mgr. Highmark Blue Shield, Pitts., 1998—2005, Peidmont Geriatric Hosp., Richmond, Va., 2006—. Author numerous poems. Coord. United Way, Pittsburgh, 2000—03. Recipient Editor's Choice award/Outstanding Achievement Poetry, Poetry.com, 2001, Editor's Choice award, Internat. Libr. Poetry, 2002—04, 2005, 2006, merit award, outstanding achievement award. Mem.: Acad. Cert. Case Mgr., Ams. Health Ins. Plans (Wash. DC) (health ins. assoc. designation), Internat. Soc. Poets, Broadcast Music (BMI), Internat. Songwriters Assn. Avocation: exercise. Personal E-mail: iwrktolive1@cs.com.

MAIONE, DONNA, fashion designer; Degree with honors, FIT. With various cos. Liz Claiborne, Macy's; prin., owner Donna Maione Studio, 1988—; ptnr. DMI, 1992—. Office: 525 7th Ave Fl 19 New York NY 10018-4901

MAIORIELLO, RICHARD PATRICK, retired otolaryngologist; b. Mar. 17, 1936; s. Gesumino Theodore and Angelina (Del Rossi) M.; m. Susan Hemenway, Mar. 6, 1979; children: Gabriel, Angela, Richard. AB, U. Pa., 1960; MD, Jefferson Med. Coll., 1964; MS, Thomas Jefferson U., 1972. Diplomate Nat. Bd. Med. Examiners, Am. Bd. Otolaryngology. Commd. 2d lt. USAF, 1963, advanced through grades to col., 1977, ret., 1979; intern Keesler Hosp., 1965-67; chief flight medicine USAF Base, Bitburg, Fed. Republic Germany, 1965-68; resident in otolaryngology Thomas Jefferson Hosp., Phila., 1968-71, 72-73; dir. med. edn. Andrews AFB, 1974-78; assoc. prof. uniformed svcs. Univ. Health Scis., 1978-79; assoc. prof. Northeastern Ohio U. of Medicine, 1983—; mem. staff Aultman Hosp., 1979—; assoc. staff Timken Mercy Med. Ctr., 1981—, Union Hosp., 1988—; retired, 2001. Cons. otolaryngology to Surgeon Gen., 1977—; pres. Mid-Ohio Dressage Assn. With USNR, 1954-58. Decorated Air Force Commendation medal. Fellow ACS, Am. Soc. Head and Neck Surgery; mem. Am. Acad. Otolaryngology, Am. Acad. Facial Plastic and Reconstructive Surgery, Am. Assn. Cosmetic Surgery, Vail Cosmetic Surg. Soc., Hanoverian Soc. (exec. v.p.), U.S. Dressage Fedn. (chmn. all-breeds coun.), Centurion Club. Republican. Roman Catholic.

MAIR, BRUCE LOGAN, interior designer, architectural firm executive; b. Chgo., June 5, 1951; s. William Logan and Josephine (Lee) M. BFA, Drake U., 1973; postgrad., Ind. Wesleyan U., 1990—. Mgr., head designer Reifers of Indpls., 1973-79; pres. Interiors Internat., Indpls., 1979-87; sr. designer Kasler Group, Indpls., 1987-89; dir. devel. Tillery Interiors and Imports, Greenwood, Ind., 1990, v.p. Indpls., 1990-92; owner Mair Interior Design Group, Indpls., 1992—. Pres. Tokens Inc., Indpls., 1982-88, Meg-A-Wat Enterprises Inc., Indpls., 1985-87, Luxury Ice Creams Inc., Indpls., 1986-87. Cover designer Indpls. Home and Garden mag., 1978, feature designer 1980; feature designer Builder mag., 1979; co-designer feature Indpls. At Home mag., 1979. Campaigner Anderson for Pres., 1980. Mem. Am. Soc. Interior Designers (profl., treas. Ind. chpt. 1982-83, Pres. awards 1981-82), U.S. Rowing Assn. (master 1987—), St. Joseph Hist. Neighborhood Assn., Columbia Club (rowing crew coxswain 1986—), Highland Model A Club, Tower Harbor Yacht Club (Douglas, Mich.), Royal Palm Yacht Club Ft. Myers, Alpha Epsilon Pi. Avocations: sculling, historic preservation, model a ford restoration, fishing, farming. Office Phone: 239-476-9404. E-mail: BruceMairID@aol.com.

MAISEL, DAVID, entertainment company executive; b. 1961; Mgr. entertainment and media practice The Boston Cons. Group; with Creative Artists Agy.; dir. corp. devel. and strategic planning The Walt Disney Co.; pres. Livent, Inc.; mng. dir. Chello Broadband, 1999—2001; head corp. strategy and bus. devel. Endeavor Talent Agy., 2001—03; pres., COO Marvel Studios, 2004—05, vice chmn., 2005—07, chmn., 2007—; exec. v.p. corp. devel., Office Chief Exec. Marvel Entertainment Inc., 2005—. Office: Marvel Studios 9242 Beverly Blvd Ste 350 Beverly Hills CA 90210 *

MAISEL, WILLIAM HOWARD, cardiologist, internist; b. Mar. 26, 1966; BS in Biology, MIT, Cambridge, Mass.; MPH, Harvard Sch Pub. Health, Boston, Mass.; MD, Cornell U., 1992. Intern, internal medicine Brigham & Women Hosp., Boston, 1992—93, resident, internal medicine, 1993—95, fellow, cardiovascular, 1996—99, fellow, cardiac electrophysiology; clin. fellow, medicine Harvard Med. Sch., Boston, asst. prof. medicine; attending staff physician, cardiovascular divsn. Beth Israel Deaconess Med. Ctr., Boston. Ad hoc reviewer Am. Jour. Cardiology, Annals Internal Medicine, Circulation, Jour. Am. Coll. Cardiology, Jour. Cardiovascular Electrophysiology, Jour. Interventional Cardiac Electrophysiology, New England Jour. Medicine, Pacing and Clin. Electrophysiology; contbr. articles tp profl. jours., chapters to books. Mem.: Heart Rhythm Soc., Am. Heart Assn., AMA, Am. Coll. Cardiology, Mass. Med. Soc. Office: Beth Israel Deaconess Med Ctr 185 Pilgrim Rd Baker 4 Boston MA 02215 Office Phone: 617-632-7457. Office Fax: 617-632-7620. *

MAISSEL, LEON ISRAEL, physicist, engineer; b. Cape Town, South Africa, May 31, 1930; came to U.S., 1956; s. Charles and Emily (Cohen) M.; m. Raina Eve Corren, Jan. 26, 1956; children: Simon, Gerda, Joseph. B.Sc., U. Cape Town, 1949, M.Sc., 1951; PhD, U. London, 1955. Staff scientist Philco Corp., Phila., 1956-60; adv. physicist IBM Corp., Poughkeepsie, NY, 1960-63, sr. engr., 1963-81, sr. tech. staff mem., 1981-93; patent writer, 1994—. Author, editor: Handbook of Thin Film Technology, 1969, An Introduction to Thin Films, 1970; contbr. articles profl. jours.; patentee in field. Recipient Outstanding Invention award IBM Corp., 1968; recipient Outstanding Contbn. award IBM Corp., 1969 Fellow IEEE; mem. Am. Vacuum Soc. (Dir. 1966-68) Lodges: B'nai B'rith. Democrat. Jewish. Home: 16 Smoke Rise Ln Wappingers Falls NY 12590-1240 Personal E-mail: maissel@att.net. *Most people, properly trained, can solve well-defined problems. The ability to deal with poorly-defined problems is much rarer and is the key to success in science.*

MAISTER, DAVID HILTON, consultant; b. London, July 21, 1947; came to U.S., 1973; s. Alfred and Bertha (Spanglett) M. BS in Soc. Sci., U. Birmingham, Eng., 1968; MSc, London Sch. Econs., 1971; DBA, Harvard U., 1976. Asst. prof. U. B. C., Can., 1976-78; assoc. prof. Harvard Bus. Sch., Mass., 1979-85; pres. Maister Assocs., Boston, 1985—; cons. to profl. svc. firms. Author: The Owner Operator, 1975, The Motor Carrier Industry, 1977, The Domestic Airline Industry, 1977, Management of Owner Operator Fleets, 1979, Cases in Operations Management, 2 vols., 1982, Professional Service Firm Management, 1987, Success Strategies for the Design Professions, 1987, Merging the Professional Service Firm, 1993, The Professionalism, 1997, The Trusted Advisor, 2000, Practice What You Preach, 2001, First Among Equals, 2002. Home and Office: 90 Commonwealth Ave Boston MA 02116-3040 Home Phone: 617-536-0474; Office Phone: 617-262-5968. Personal E-mail: david@davidmaister.com.

MAISTO, JOHN F., former ambassador; b. Braddock, Pa., Aug. 28, 1938; married; 3 children. BSFS, Georgetown U., 1961; MA, San Carlos Coll., Guatemala, 1962. With BiNational Ctr., Cordoba, Argentina, 1963-66; asst. cultural affairs officer USIA, Cochabamba, Bolivia, 1966-68; with Fgn. Svc., 1968—; adminstrv. asst. Fgn. Svc. Inst. Dept. State, 1968-69; econ. and comml. officer U.S. Embassy, La Paz, Bolivia, 1969-71; internat. rels. officer Ops. Ctr., 1971-72; spl. asst. Office of Counselor, 1972-73; internat. rels. officer office Andean affairs, bur. inter-Am. affairs Dept. State, 1973-75; polit. officer U.S. Embassy, San Jose, Costa Rica, 1975-78, Manila, 1978-82; dep. dir. office Philippine affairs, bur. East Asian and Pacific affairs Dept. State, 1982-84, dir., 1984-86; dep. chief of mission and charge d'affaires Am. Embassy, Panama, 1986-89; dep. permanent U.S. rep. to OAS, 1989-92; dep. asst. sec. state for Ctrl. Am. and Panama U.S. Dept. State, 1992-93; U.S. amb. to Nicaragua, 1993-96; U.S. amb. to Venezuela, 1997—2000; fgn. policy advisor U.S. so. commd., 2000—01; spl. asst. to Pres., sr. dir. for western hemisphere affairs Nat. Security Coun., 2001—03; U.S. permanent rep. to OAS US Dept. State, Washington, 2003—07. Office Phone: 202-647-9430.

MAITI, AMITESH, physicist; b. Bahrampur, India, Dec. 8, 1964; came to U.S., 1986; s. Achalesh and Sanchita (Roy) M.; m. Baishali Guha; 1 child, Esha. BS in Physics with honors, Presidency Coll., 1986; MS in Physics, U. N.C., 1988; PhD in Physics, U. Calif., Berkeley, 1992. Rsch. assoc. physics N.C. State U., Raleigh, 1992-95; applications scientist Molecular Simulations, Inc., Burlington, Mass., 1997—. Adj. asst. prof. Vanderbilt U., Nashville, 1995-97; spkr. in field. Contbr. articles to profl. jours. U. Calif. Regents fellow, 1988, fellow U. N.C. Bd. Govs., Chapel Hill, 1987, sr. rsch. fellow Oak Ridge (Tenn.) Nat. Lab., 1995-97; Victor F. Lenzen Meml. scholar U. Calif., 1990, Iishan scholar U. Calcutta, India, 1986; recipient Scindia Gold medal U. Calcutta, 1985. Mem. Am. Phys. Soc., Materials Rsch. Soc. Office: Molecular Simulations Inc 200 Wheeler Rd Burlington MA 01803-5501 Fax: 781-229-9899.

MAITLAND, GUY EDISON CLAY, lawyer; b. London, Dec. 28, 1942; (mother Am. citizen); s. Paul and Virginia Francesca (Carver) M. BA, Columbia U., 1964; JD, NY Law Sch., 1968; LLD (hon.), SUNY Maritime Coll., Ft. Schuyler, 2007. Bar: NY 1969, US Dist. Ct. (so. and ea. dists.) NY 1969, US Ct. Appeals (2d and DC cirs.) 1969. Assoc. Burlingham, Underwood & Lord, NYC, 1969-74; admiralty counsel Union Carbide Corp., NYC, 1974-76; exec. v.p., gen. counsel, officer Liberian Svcs., Inc., NYC and Reston, Va., 1976-99; pres. Trust Co. of the Marshall Islands, Inc., 1990—; mng. ptnr. Internat. Registries, Inc., 2000—. Del. UN Conf. on Trade and Devel., Manila, 1979, Belgrade, 1983; participant London Conf. on Limitation of Maritime Liability, 1976; mem. legal com. Internat. Maritime Orgn. (UN) London, 1980—; del. UN Conf. on Law of the Sea, 1976-82, London UN Maritime Law Conf., 1984; co-founder The Admiralty-Fin. Forum, NYC, 1986. Contbr. articles on maritime law, US shipping policy. Mem. NY Rep. State Exec. Com., 1974-76; del. Rep. Nat. Conv., Kansas City, 1976; sec. NY Rep. County Com., 1976-87, vice chmn., 1988—, mem. exec. com., 1974-76; co-chmn. Citizens for Reagan, NY State, 1979-80; trustee Am. Mcht. Marine Mus. Found. at US Mcht. Marine Acad., King's Point, Nat. Maritime Hist. Soc., chmn., 2000-01; trustee NY Maritime Coll. at Ft. Schuyler Found., Inc.; bd. dirs. Coast Guard Found.; del. UN Geneva Conf. on Arrest of Vessels, 1999; bd. dirs. Seamen's Ch. Inst., NYC, Ctr. for Seafarers Rights, McLean Container Ctr. at King's Point, Inc.; mem. adv. com. Am. Maritime History Project. Mem. ABA, Assn. of Bar of City of NY (chmn. admiralty com. 1982-85), Maritime Law Assn. US (chmn. com. on intergovtl. orgns. 1987-95). Office: Internat Registries Inc 437 Madison Ave 32d Fl New York NY 10022-7001

MAITLAND, WENDY, real estate company executive, psychotherapist; MA in Social Work. Psychotherapist, priv. practice, Greenwich Village; former broker, v.p. The Corcoran Group; sr. v.p. Brown Harris Stevens, 2007—; mng. dir. I.D. Marketing Group, 2007—; mng. ptnr. Restaurant 5 Ninth, NYC; founding mem. Fatty Crab. Office: Brown Harris Stevens 2 Fifth Ave New York NY 10011 *

MAIWALD, DIANE CECILE, dermatologist; b. Huntington, L.I., N.Y., Apr. 4, 1947; d. Ernest John and Cecelia Ann (Kuskowski) M. B.A., Fordham U., 1969; M.D., Emory U., 1975. Diplomate Am. Bd. Dermatology. Intern, Stonybrook U. Affiliated Hosps., N.Y., 1975-76; resident Louisville Med. Sch. Assoc. Hosps., 1976-78, Wayne State U., 1978-79; practice medicine specializing in dermatology, Toledo, Ohio, 1979—. Bd. dirs. Goodwill Industries, Toledo, 1983. Mem. Am. Acad. Dermatology. Mem. Soc. Friends. Office: 3450 W Central Ave Ste 118 Toledo OH 43606-1403

MAIWURM, JAMES JOHN, lawyer; b. Wooster, Ohio, Dec. 5, 1948; s. James Frederick and Virginia Anne (Jones) M.; m. Wendy S. Leeper, July 31, 1971; children: James G., Michelle K. BA, Coll. Wooster, 1971; JD, U. Mich., 1974. Bar: Ohio 1974, D.C. 1986, Md. 1987, N.Y., 1987. Ptnr. Squire, Sanders & Dempsey, Cleve. and Washington, 1974-90; ptnr., group head Crowell & Moring, Washington, 1990-98; ptnr. Squire, Sanders & Dempsey, Washington, 1998-99; chmn., CEO Kaiser Group Internat., Inc., Fairfax, Va., 1999-2000; mng. ptnr. Squire, Sanders & Dempsey LLP, Washington, 2001—03, firmwide mng. ptnr., 2003—. Bd. dirs. George Mason U. Coll. Visual and Performing Arts. Contbr. articles to profl. jours. Mem. ABA, DC Bar Assn., Leadership Washington, The Tower Club (bd. govs. 2003-). Home: 9419 Brian Jac Ln Great Falls VA 22066-2002 Office: Squire Sanders & Dempsey LLP 14th fl 8000 Towers Crescent Vienna VA 22182 Business E-Mail: jmaiwurm@ssd.com.

MAIZE, JOHN CHRISTOPHER, dermatologist, educator; b. Elizabeth, NJ, July 23, 1943; s. Donald Adam and Caroline Marie (Costanzo) Maize; m. Janice Lee Bentley, May 21, 1966; children: Sandra Kristine Tolly, John C. Jr., Jennifer Lee. MD, U. Mich., 1968. Cert. Am. Bd. Dermatology. Intern U. Mich., Ann Arbor, 1968—69, residency in dermatology, 1968—72; asst. prof. dermatology SUNY, Buffalo, 1972—77, assoc. prof., 1977—80, Med. U. SC, Charleston, 1980—83, prof., 1983—89, prof., chmn. dept. dermatology, 1989—2003, clin. prof., 2003—. Author: Pigmented Lesions of the Skin, 1987, Cutaneous Pathology, 1998; editor-in-chief Am. Jour. Dermatology, 1986—90. Fellow: Am. Soc. Dermapathology (pres. 1995), Am. Acad. Dermatology; mem.: Am. Bd. Dermatology (dir. 1990—99, pres. 1999), S.C. Dermatol. Assn. (pres. 2001), S.C. Med. Assn., Internat. Soc. Dermatopathology (sec. 1987—89, pres. 1989—91), Am. Dermatol. Assn. Roman Catholic. Avocations: fishing, golf, travel. Office: 266 W Coleman Blvd Unit 101 Mount Pleasant SC 29464 Home Phone: 843-881-1007; Office Phone: 843-388-6911. E-mail: jmaizesr@ameripath.com.

MAJEED, D. HADAYAI S., publishing executive, writer; b. Milwaukee, Wis., Jan. 14, 1955; d. Fred J. and Evelyn L. Spencer; m. Abdul H. Abdullah, Jan. 28, 1998. BA in Biology, U. Ark., 1976. Prin., owner Spencer-Majeed, Ltd., Conley, Ga., 1995—; adminstr. Baitul Salaam Network, Inc., Atlanta, 1997—. Author: Emerging Victorious: A Dialogue on Polygamy/Polygyny in America (nominated Writer of Yr., Ga. Writers, 2000). Mem. coun. Masjid Al Mu minun, Atlanta, 2002—04. Nominee Noble Peace prize, 2005; recipient Real Life is Drug Free award, State of Ga., 1997. Mem.: 1000 Peace Women 2005 (assoc.). Independent. Islam. Home Phone: 404-366-6610; Office Phone: 404-366-6610.

MAJER, JOHN M., psychologist, educator; PhD, DePaul U., Chgo., 2004. Rsch. assoc., cons. Ctr. Cmty. Rsch., DePaul U., Chgo., 2004—. Mem.: APA. Achievements include research in clinical-community psychology investigations. Office: Richard J Daley Coll 7500 S Pulaski Rd Chicago IL 60652 Office Phone: 773-838-7677. E-mail: jmajer@ccc.edu.

MAJERONI, RONALD L., pastoral counselor, consultant; b. Erie, Pa., Aug. 1, 1945; s. Lamar Edward Majeroni and Marian Juanita (Herman) Venesky; m. Barbara Ann Berkley, June 24, 1967; children: Timothy, Heather, Raymond, Keith. BS in Forestry, Pa. State. U., State Coll., 1967; MDiv in Pastoral Care, Luth. Sch. Theology, Gettysburg, Pa., 1972; DMin Pastoral Counseling, Luth. Sch. Theology, Chgo., 1999. Ordained word and sacrament Luth. Ch. Am., Pitts., 1972, diplomate Am. Assn. Pastoral Counselors, 2005; cert. mental health counseor State NY, 2006. Parish pastor Forks Zion, Lechburg, Pa., 1972—75, St. Andrews, Carnegie, 1975—79, Atonement, Phila., 1979—83, Good Shepherd, Erie, Pa., 1983—86, Harrison Valley Parish, Pa., 1987—88; resident counselor Samaritan Pastoral Counseling Ctr., Buffalo, 1989—92, pastoral counselor, 1992—2005, supr., cons., clin. dir., 2005—. Fin. vol. Samaritan Pastoral Counseling Ctr., North Tonawanda, NY, 1989—; song, workship leader Amherst Luth. Ch., NY, 2002—. Mem.: Double T Archery Club. Republican. Lutheran. Avocations: hunting, fishing, carpentry, archery. Office: Samaritan Pastoral Counseing Ctr 322 Old Falls Rd North Tonawanda NY 14120

MAJERUS, PHILIP WARREN, physician; b. Chgo., July 10, 1936; s. Clarence Nicholas and Helen Louise (Mathis) Majerus; m. Janet Sue Brakensiek, Dec. 28, 1957; children: Suzanne, David, Juliet, Karen; m. Elaine Michelle Flansburg, 1996. BS, Notre Dame U., 1958; MD, Washington U., 1961. Resident in Medicine Mass. Gen. Hosp., Boston, 1961—63; research assoc. NIH, Bethesda, Md., 1963—66; asst. prof. biochemistry Washington U., St. Louis, 1966—75, asst. prof. medicine, 1966—69, assoc. prof. medicine, 1969—71, prof. medicine, 1971—, dir. div. hematology, 1973—, prof. biochemistry, 1976—. Mem. editl. bd. numerous jours. and profl. mags.; contbr. articles to profl. jours. Recipient Faculty Rsch. Assoc. award, Am. Cancer Soc., 1966—75, Disting. Career award for contbns. to hemostasis, Internat. Soc. for Thrombosis and Hemostasis, 1985, Alumni Faculty award, Washington U. Sch. Medicine, 1986, The Robert J. and Claire Pasarow Found. award, 1994, Bristol-Myers Squibb prize for cardiovascular rsch., 1998, numerous others. Fellow: ACP; mem.: Inst. of Medicine of NAS, Am. Soc. Clin. Investigation (pres. 1981—82), Am. Soc. Biol. Chemists, Am. Fedn. Clin. Rsch., Am. Soc. Hematology (pres. 1991), Assn. Am. Physicians, Am. Acad. Arts and Scis., Alpha Omega Alpha, Sigma Xi. Home: 7220 Pershing Ave Saint Louis MO 63130-4248 Office: Wash Univ Sch of Med Dept Int Med Saint Louis MO 63110

MAJERUS, RICK, men's college basketball coach; b. Sheboygan, Wis., Feb. 17, 1948; s. Raymond and Alyce Majerus BS, Marquette U., 1970, MS, 1979. Asst. coach Marquette U., 1971—83, head coach, 1983—86; asst. coach Milw. Bucks, 1986—87; head coach Ball State U., 1987—89, U. Utah, Salt Lake City, 1989—2003, St. Louis U., 2007—; analyst ESPN College Basketball, 2004—07. Asst. coach USA Dream Team 2, summer 1994. Named Coach of Yr. Hoop Scoop, 1989, UPI Coach of Yr., 1991, Coach of Yr. Basketball Times, 1991, Kodak Dist. Coach of Yr., 1991, 93, 95, Utah Sports Person of Yr. 1992, Playboy Coach of Yr., 1992, Western Athletic Conf. Coach of Yr., 1994, 95. Office: St Louis U Mens Basketball Athletics Dept 3672 W Pine Mall Saint Louis MO 63108 Office Fax: 314-977-3272. *

MAJESTY, MELVIN SIDNEY, psychologist, consultant; b. New Orleans, June 6, 1928; s. Sidney Joseph and Marcella Cecilia (Kieffer) M.; m. Bettye Newanda Gordon, Dec. 18, 1955; 1 child, Diana Sue. BA, La. State U., 1949; MS, Western Res. U., 1951; PhD (USAF Inst. Tech. fellow), Case-Western Res. U., 1967. Commd. 2d lt. USAF, 1951, advanced through grades to lt. col., 1968; program mgr., asst. dir. tng. rsch. Air Force Human Resources Lab., 1967-69; dir. faculty and profl. ednl. rsch. USAF Acad., 1969-72; dir. plot tng. candidate selection program Officer Tng. Sch., Air Tng.Command, 1972-76; ret. USAF, 1976; personnel selection cons. to Calif. State Pers. Bd., Sacramento, 1976-92. Patentee listening center; founded pers. testing for ballistic missile and space systems; directed largest study of fighter pilot selection since World War II; pioneered use of phys. testing as replacement for the maximum age requirement in law enforcement jobs; developed phys. fitness tests and established psychol. screening standards for state highway patrol officer and police officers; contbr. numerous articles to profl. publs. With U.S. Army, WWII, 1944-46, Korea, Vietnam, USAF, 1951-76. Decorated Commendation medal (2), Meritorious Svc. medal (2), Am. Campaign medal, WWII Victory medal, WWII Overseas Occupation medal, Ballistic Missile badge, numerous others. Mem.: DAV, VFW, APA, Veterans for

Peace, Reserve Officers Assn., Mil. Officers Assn. Am., Am. Family Assn., Am. Legion, Mil. Order Fgn. Wars, Vietnam Vets. Am., Amvets, Bible Soc., Nat. Assn. Uniformed Svc. Office: 801 Capitol Mall Sacramento CA 95814-4806

MAJETTE, DENISE, former congresswoman; b. Bklyn., May 18, 1955; d. Voyd and Olivia Majette; m. Rogers Mitchell Majette; 2 children. BA, Yale U., 1976; JD, Duke U., 1979. Atty. Legal Aid Soc. Winston-Salem, NC, 1981—83; law asst. Ga. Ct. Appeals, 1984—89; ptnr. Jenkins Nelson & Welch, 1989—92; spl. asst. atty. gen. State of Ga., 1991—92; adminstrv. law juste Ga. State Bd. Workers' Compensation, 1992; judge State Ct. of DeKalb County, 1993—2002; congresswoman 4th Dist. Ga. U.S. Ho. Reps., 2003—05; mem. budget, edn. and workforce, and small bus. ho. coms. Grad. Leadership DeKalb, 1992; mem. Kidney Caucus; former com. mem. Miller Grove PTA; past mem. vestry Episcopal Ch. of Holy Cross; former pres. DeKalb Lawyers Assn.; mem. Childcare Com. YMCA, Decatur; mem. adv. bd. Jr. League DeKalb County; mem. Congl. Black Caucus, Congl. Caucus on India and Indian Ams.; mem. steward bd. Antioch AME Ch. Recipient Judge's Cmty. Recognition award, Black Law Students' Assn., Ga. State U. Coll. Law, 2001, You Go Girl award, Ga. Assn. Black Women Attys., 2003. Democrat. Home: PO Box 33678 Decatur GA 30033-0678

MAJOR, CLARENCE LEE, writer, painter, poet, educator; b. Atlanta, Dec. 31, 1936; s. Clarence and Inez (Huff) M.; m. Pamela Ritter, May 8, 1980. BS, SUNY, Albany; PhD, Union Inst. Prof. U. Colo., Boulder, 1977-89, U. Calif., Davis, 1989—. Author: All-Night Visitors, 1969, 2d version, 1998, Dictionary of Afro-American Slang, 1970, No, 1973, Reflex and Bone Structure, 1975, rev. edit., 1996, Emergency Exit, 1979, My Amputations, 1986, Such Was the Season, 1987, Painted Turtle: Woman with Guitar, 1988, Fun and Games, 1990, Calling the Wind, 1993, Juba to Jive: A Dictionary of African American Slang, 1994, Dirty Bird Blues, 1996; poetry: Swallow the Lake, 1970 (Nat. Coun. on the Arts award 1970), Symptoms & Madness, 1971, Private Line, 1971, The Cotton Club, 1972, Inside Diameter: The France Poems, 1985, Surfaces and Masks, 1988, Some Observations of a Stranger at Zuni in the Latter Part of the Century, 1989, Parking Lots, 1992, The Garden Thrives, 1996, Configurations: New and Selected Poems, 1958-1998, 1998 (Nat. Book Award Bronze medal 1999), Clarence Major and His Art: Portraits of an African American Postmodernist, 2001, Necessary Distance, 2001, Come By Here: My Mother's Life, 2002, Waiting for Sweet Betty, 2002, Conversations with Clarence Major, 2002, One Flesh, 2003; one man shows include Kresge Mus., Mich., 2001, Hamilton Club Gallery, Paterson, NJ, 2006-07; group shows include Schacknow Mus. Fine Art, Plantation, Fla., 2003, Exploding Head Gallery, Calif., 2003-06; contbr. articles to Washington Post Book World, L.A. Times Book Rev., N.Y. Times Book Rev. Recipient Nat. Council on Arts award, Washington, 1970; Western States Book award, Western States Found., Santa Fe, 1986; Fulbright grantee, 1981-83. Office: U Calif Dept English 281 Voorhies Hall Davis CA 95616

MAJOR, JOHN CHARLES, judge; s. William and Elsie M.; m. Hélène Provencher, 1959; children: Suzan, Peter, Paul, Steven. BComm, Loyola Coll., Montreal, 1953; LLB, U. Toronto, 1957, LLD (hon.), 2005, Concordia U., 2003, U. Calgary, 2005. Bar: Alta. 1958, Queen's Counsel, 1972. With Bennett, Jones & Verchere, Calgary, 1957-91, sr. ptnr., 1967; sr. counsel City of Calgary Police Svc., 1975-85; counsel McDonald Commn., 1978-82; sr. counsel Province of Alta., 1987, Alta. Ct. Appeal, 1991; justice Supreme Ct. of Can., Ottawa, Ont., Canada, 1992—95. Fellow: Am. Coll. Trial Lawyers. Avocation: golf. Office: Bennett Jones LLP 4500 855-2 Str SW Calgary AB Canada T2P 4K7 Office Phone: 403-298-3166. Business E-Mail: jmajor@bennettjones.ca.

MAJOR, PATRICK WEBB, III, principal; b. Wai, Maharastra, India, Mar. 12, 1947; s. Patrick W. Jr. and Alice (Seeland) M.; m. Daphnelynn Jantz, June 26, 1971; children: Mindy Joy, Matthew Patrick Webb. BA in BE, Columbia Internat. U., 1969; BA, Biola U., 1972; MA, Point Loma Nazarene U., 1979; postgrad., U. Calif., Irvine. Cert. secondary tchr., adminstr., Calif. Prin. Omega High Sch., Bakersfield, Calif., 1980-84; headmaster Bakersfield Christian Life Schs., 1984-86; prin. North Kern Christian Sch., Wasco, Calif., 1986-88; prin., adminstr. Yucaipa (Calif.) Christian Schs., 1988-2000; prin. Christian H.S., El Cajon, Calif., 2000—03; adminstr. First Bapt. Ch. of Lakewood (Calif.) Schs., 2003—. Chmn. ACSI So. Calif. Accreditation Commn., 1998-2003. Mem. ASCD, Assn. Christian Schs. Internat. (former dist. rep., exec. bd. 1992-2001), Ctrl. Redwood League (pres. 1985-86), CIF Ctrl Sect., Internat. Fellowship Christian Sch. Adminstrs. Business E-Mail: administrator@fbcoles.org.

MAJORAS, DEBORAH PLATT, commissioner; m. John Majoras. BA summa cum laude, Westminster Coll.; JD, U. Va., 1989. Law clk. to Hon. Stanley S. Harris US Dist. Ct., DC; dep. asst. atty. gen. US Dept. Justice, Antitrust Divsn., 2000—01, prin. dep. asst. atty. gen., 2002—03; ptnr. antitrust sec., mem. tech. issues practice Jones Day, Washington, DC, 2004; chmn. FTC, Washington, DC, 2004—. Chair Internat. Competition Network's (ICN) Merger Working Group. Mem.: ABA (mem. Antitrust Law Sec.). Avocations: golf, shopping. Office: FTC 600 Pennsylvania Ave NW Washington DC 20580 Office Phone: 202-326-2100. E-mail: chairman@ftc.gov. *

MAJORS, NELDA FAYE, physical therapist; b. Houston, Aug. 3, 1938; d. Columbus Edward and Mary (Mills) M. Cert. in Phys. Therapy, Hermann Sch. Phys. Therapy, Houston, 1960; BS, U. Houston, 1963. Lic. phys. therapist, Tex. Staff therapist Tex. Med. Ctr. Hermann Hosp., Houston, 1960-61; phys. therapist Chelsea Orthopedic Clinic, Houston, 1961-63; dir. phys. therapy Meml. Hosp. Southwest, Houston, 1963-75; owner, pres. Nelda Majors, Inc., Houston, 1975—. Profl. adv. bd. Logos Home Health Agy., Houston, 1985-86; adv. dir. Prime Bank, Houston; sec.-treas., bd. dirs. Dominion Media Corp.; realtor, State of Ariz., 2005-. Ptnr. Houston Proud Ptnr., 1986—; founder, pres. Instnl. Safety Advs. Inc., 1994—; bd. dirs. Texans for the Improvement of Long Term Care Facilities, 1995—; mem. founders cir. Crosswalk Am. Christian Orgn., 2006. Named All Am. Softball Pitcher, Amateur Softball Assn., 1964, All-Regional and All-State Pitcher, Tex. Amateur Softball Assn., 1954-70; named to Houston Amateur Softball Assn. Softball Hall of Fame, 1994, Houston Softball Legends Hall of Fame, 2002. Mem. Am. Phys. Therapy Assn. (pvt. practice sect.), Ams. for Separation of Ch. and State, Tex. Phys. Therapy Assn., U. Houston Alumni Assn., Nat. Assn. Realtors, E. Cullen Soc. (U. Houston), Crosswalk Am. (founders circle), Rotary Club (Houston, Meml. Spring br.), Phi Kappa Phi. Clubs: U. Houston Cougar. Avocations: softball, bicycling, travel, golf, reading. Personal E-mail: nmajors370@aol.com.

MAJTENYI, STEVEN ISTVAN, retired civil engineer, consultant; b. Elek, Hungary, Jan. 20, 1936; came to U.S., 1962; s. Vilmos Gyorgy and Edit (Laczo) M.; m. Joan E. Zimmerman, Jan. 21, 1972; children: Vivian Claire, Juliet Eve. Student, U. Poitiers, France, 1962; MSc, Cornell U., 1965, PhD, 1969. Registered profl. engr., Ohio. Tchg. and rsch. asst. Cornell U., Ithaca, N.Y., 1964-68; soils engr. TAMS, NYC, 1968-71; hwy. rsch. engr. U.S. Dept. Transp./FHWA, Washington, 1971-76; hwy. engr. The World Bank, Washington, 1976-81; sr. cons. The World Bank, U.S. Dept. Transp./FHWA, Washington, 1981-95; procurement expert UN, NYC, 1995-98; civil engring. cons. Gahanna, Ohio, 1998—; ret., 2001. Speaker in field. Contbr. articles to profl. jours. Josephine de Karman scholar, 1962-64. Fellow: ASCE (life). Roman Catholic. Achievements include participation in the development of numerous technical ideas in the U.S. Government and private industry; improvement of procurement documents in numerous countries worldwide. Home: 167 Highmeadow Dr Gahanna OH 43230-1791

MAJUMDAR, ARUNAVA, mechanical engineer, educator; BTech, Indian Inst. Tech., Bombay, 1985; MS in Mech. Engring., U. Calif., Berkeley, 1987, PhD in Mech. Engring., 1989. Rsch. asst. U. Calif., Berkeley, 1985-89; asst. prof. Ariz. State U., 1989-92, U. Calif., Santa Barbara, 1992—96, prof. Berkeley, 1996—, vice chair Dept. Engring., 1999—2002, Almy and Agnes Maynard Chair Prof. mech. engring. Co-chmn. U.S.-Japan seminar on Molecular and Microscale Transport Phenomena, NSF, 1993; co-chmn. 22nd Internat. Thermal Conductivity Conf., Ariz. State U., Tempe, 1993. Reviewer Internat. Jour. Heat and Mass Transfer, Internat. Jour. Wear, NSF, Am. Chem. Soc. Petroleum Rsch. Fund, Solid State Electronics, Am. Inst. Physics, Soc. Photo-Instrumentation Engrs., Biotechnology Progress; contbr. over 20 articles to sci. jours. Scroeder-Scovill-Duncan scholar Indian Inst. Tech., 1982-84, D. K. Merchant scholar, 1984-85; Regents fellow U. Calif., Berkeley, 1985-86; recipient Young Investigator award NSF, 1992—; grantee NSF, 1990—, 91— (two grants), 92— (two grants). Mem. NAE, ASME (sec. K-8 com. fundamentals heat transfer heat transfer divsn., reviewer Jour. Heat Transfer, Jour. Tribology, Jour. Applied Mechanics, Melville medal 1992), AAAS, Am. Vacuum Soc., Materials Rsch. Soc. Achievements include research in heat generation and transport in nanometer scale devices and structures, nanomechanics of ductile grinding of brittle materials, contact mechanics of surfaces and application to microtribology, thermal and mechanical property measurement of very thin films. Office: U Callif Mailstop 1740 5131 Etcheverry Hall Berkeley CA 94720 Office Phone: 510-643-8199. E-mail: majumdar@me.berkeley.edu.

MAJUMDAR, MUKUL KUMAR, economist, educator; b. Krishnagar, India, Dec. 6, 1944; came to U.S., 1965, naturalized, 1971; s. Nirmal Kanti and Sita (Mitra) M.; m. Malabika Dutta, Aug. 8, 1969. BA in Econs. with honors 1st class, Calcutta U., India, 1966; PhD in Econs, U. Calif., Berkeley, 1970. Asst. prof. econs. Stanford U., 1969-72; lectr. London Sch. Econs., 1972-73; asso. prof. Cornell U., 1973-77, prof., chmn. dept. econs., 1977—, Warshow prof. econs., 1983—. Ford rotating research prof. U. Calif., Berkeley, 1976-77 Coordinating editor: The Rev. Econ. Studies, 1976—; asso. editor: Jour. Math. Econs, 1974—, Jour. Econ. Theory, 1977—. Recipient Coll. de France medal, 1989; Guggenheim fellow, 1976-77. Fellow Econometric Soc. Office: Cornell U Dept Econs Uris Hall Ithaca NY 14850 Office Phone: 607-255-3640. Business E-Mail: mkm5@cornell.edu.

MAK, LINDA L., dermatologist; BSc with honors, U. Wis.; PhD, Johns Hopkins U. Contbr. articles to profl. jours. Mem.: Am. Acad. Pediats., Johns Hopkins Med. and Surg. Assn., Am. Acad. Cosmetic Surgery, Royal Coll. Surgeons Eng. Achievements include research in HIV vaccine development and gene therapy.

MAKADOK, STANLEY, management consultant; b. NYC, Mar. 30, 1941; s. Jack and Pauline (Speciner) Makadok; m. Neilia A. David, Nov. 12, 1989; 1 child from previous marriage, Richard. BME, CCNY, 1962; MS in Mgmt. Sci., Rutgers U., 1964. Bus. sys. analyst Westinghouse Electric Corp., Balt., 1964—65; project engr., corp. cons. Am. Cyanamid Corp., Pearl River, NY, Wayne, NJ, 1965—68; v.p., bus. devel. and planning Pepsico Inc. and affiliates, Purchase, NY, Miami, Fla., 1968—75; mgr. fin. and planning cons. Coopers & Lybrand, NYC, 1975—77; pres. Century Mgmt. Cons., Inc., Yardley, Pa., 1977—. Contbr. articles to profl. jours. Office: Century Mgmt Cons Inc 1449 Wheatsheaf Rd Yardley PA 19067-3939 Office Phone: 215-321-5699.

MAKADON, ARTHUR, lawyer; b. Phila., Mar. 11, 1943; BA, Pa. State U., 1964, LLB cum laude, 1967. Bar: Pa. 1968. Law clk. to Hon. Joseph S. Lord III US Dist. Ct., 1967-68; chief asst. dist. atty. litig. Office Phila. Dist. Atty., 1970-73; ptnr. Ballard, Spahr, Andrews & Ingersoll, Phila., chmn., 2002—. Adj. prof. law U. Pa., 1973-83. Editor U. Pa. Law Rev., 1966-67. Trustee U. Pa., 1996—; chair Mayor's Task Force on Police Corruption, Phila., 1998, 1999; bd. mem. Pa. Conv. Ctr. Mem. ABA, Pa. Bar Assn., Phila. Bar Assn., Order of Coif. Avocations: golf, running. Office: Ballard Spahr Andrews & Ingersoll 1735 Market St Fl 51 Philadelphia PA 19103-7599 Office Phone: 215-864-8200. Office Fax: 215-864-9760. E-mail: makadon@ballardspahr.com. *

MAKAROV, DANIL VICTOR, urologist; b. Kiev, Ukraine, July 11, 1976; s. Victor Illych and Galina Anna Makarov. BA, Yale U., New Haven, Conn., 1994—98; MD, Johns Hopkins U., Balt., 1998—2002. Internship dept. surgery Johns Hopkins U. Sch. Medicine, Balt., 2002—03, urology housestaff Brady Urol. Inst., 2003—. Interviewer Yale U. Alumni Schs. Com., Balt., 2001—. Recipient Lawton Calhoun Cup, Pierson Coll., Yale U., 1998, Found. Merit award, Am. Soc. Clin. Oncology, 2006; Mini-grant, Nat. Kidney Found. Md., Inc, 2005—. Mem.: Am. Urol. Assn. (assoc.; candidate mem., 1st Prize award for clin. investigation 2006), Alpha Omega Alpha, Phi Beta Kappa. Achievements include research in use of nuclear morphometry to detect unfavorable biopsy pathology in men with small volume, low-grade prostate cancer undergoing expectant management. Office: Brady Urol Inst 600 N Wolfe St Marburg 144 Baltimore MD 21287 Home Phone: 410-752-6526. Business E-Mail: dmakarov@jhmi.edu.

MAKAROV, IOURI, advertising executive; b. Ukraine, Dec. 2, 1946; arrived in U.S., 1993; m. Sofia Gaisinskaia, Dec. 19, 1970; 1 child, Ganna Makarova. Journalist and mem. editl. bd. Izvestia, Moscow, 1985—93; creative supr. YAR Comm., Inc, NYC, 1993—98; creative dir. and v.p. Kang & Lee Advt., 1998—. Author: He wasn't, he didn't attend, he didn't participate. (All-Russian Theatrical Union award, 1985); Mousetrap (Best of NY, 1995); creative dir.: TV commercial; contbr. U.S. Census 2000 advertising campaign (Golden Effie, 2001); author: (plays) He Was Not, He Didn't Attend, He Didn't Participate, 1985, Front Page Picture, 1987, (films) Criminal Talent, 1988, Hostage, 1990, Deadly Game of Love, 1991. Recipient Telly award, ATRT TV Comml. Home Phone: 718-891-9180; Office Phone: 212-375-8150.

MAKE, ISABEL ROSE, multicultural studies educator, adult education educator, small business owner; b. Phila., Oct. 6, 1947; d. Aaron M. and Lillian (Simon) Rose; children: Jonathan David, Jeremy Simon. BA, Geog Wash. U., 1969; EdM, Temple U., 1970; EdD, W.Va. U., 1975. Cert. tchr., Pa., Mich., W.Va., Mass. Dir. learning ctr. Kirkbride Elem. Sch., Phila., 1970-71, Huron High Sch., Ann Arbor, 1971-73; learning disabilities tutor Brookline (Mass.) Pub. Schs., 1976-82; ednl. cons. Newton, Mass., 1982-84; child care cons. Isabel Make Assocs., Newton, 1984-88; adj. prof. reading C.C. Denver, 1989—92; adj. prof. multicultural studies, critical thinking and creativity Metro State Coll., Denver, 1992—2002; pres. Top Hat Gourmet, 1992—2000; bus. lectr. on The Art of Corp. Giving, 1993; lectr. adult edn. South Fla. Lib. Sys., 2001—. Ednl. counselor Phila. Home for Emotionally Disturbed Girls, 1970; cons. Ann Arbor Pub. Schs., 1971; child care cons. Newton Cmty. Schs., 1985; founding mem. Denver Parenting Ctr., 1989—92; chair legis. and regulations subcom. Commonwealth of Mass., Boston, 1984-88; adj. prof. Met. State Coll., 1992-2002, C.C. Denver, 1992-96. Founder Temple Shalom Nursery Sch., Newton, 1975; chmn. childcare task force The U. Hosp., Boston U. Med. Ctr., 1985-88; bd. dirs. Greenwood Village Arts and Humanites Coun., 1991—2001; mem. at large Colo. Consortium Community Arts Couns., 1992, Greenwood Village Arts and Humanities Coun. (chair A Space of my Own, Parent-Child Art Day), 1991—; mem. steering com. Colo. Alliance for Arts in Edn., 1993; co-chair Teen Arts Adv. Bd., 1999-, Greenwood Village, Colo., 1999-; founding mem. Delray Cultural Roundtable, 2005—, Delray Film Festival, 2005. Democrat. Jewish. Avocations: gourmet cooking, swimming. Home and Office: 1584 Estuary Trail Delray Beach FL 33483 Home Phone: 561-243-2108; Office Phone: 561-243-2108.

MAKEEV, MAXIM A., physicist; b. Moscow, Mar. 11, 1970; s. Alexander N. and Vera M. Makeev. MS, Moscow Engring. Physics Inst., 1993; PhD, U. Notre Dame, 1999. Rsch., tchg. asst. U. Notre Dame, Ind., 1994—99; rsch. assoc. U. So. Calif., LA, 1999—2001, 2003—05; rsch. asssoc. La. State U., Baton Rouge, 2001—03; rsch. assoc. NASA Ames Rsch. Ctr., Moffett Field, Calif., 2005—. Mem.: Materials Rsch. Soc., Am. Phys. Soc. Achievements include contributions to development of methodologies for large-scale parallel simulations; research in statistical mechanics, surface science, nano-science. Office: NASA Ames Rsch Ctr MS 229-1 Moffett Field CA 94035-1000 Business E-Mail: makeev@usc.edu, mmakeev@mail.arc.nasa.gov.

MAKEL, LARRY A., lawyer; b. Vestaburg, Pa., Dec. 7, 1953; BA cum laude, Washington & Jefferson Coll., 1975; JD, W.Va. Univ., 1978; LLM, NYU, 1980. Bar: W.Va. 1978, Pa. 1978, Tex. 1981, DC. Asst. atty. gen. Commonwealth of Pa., 1978—79; ptnr., Banking, Bus. Law & Internat. Bus. Transactions practices, mem. exec. com. Patton Boggs LLP, Dallas. Former counsel & legis. liaison S.W. Chpt. Nat. Comml. Fin. Assn. Mem.: ABA (past chmn. Acquisition Fin. Subcommittee), State Bar Assn. Pa., State Bar Tex. (past vice chmn. Comml. Fin. Svc. Subcommittee), Dallas Bar Assn., Am. Coll. Comml. Fin. Attys. Office: Patton Boggs LLP Suite 3000 2001 Ross Ave Dallas TX 75201-8001 Office Phone: 214-758-1560. Office Fax: 214-758-1550. Business E-Mail: lmakel@pattonboggs.com.

MAKELA, JONATHAN JAMES, engineering educator; BS in Elec. Engring with honors, Cornell U., Sch. Elec. Engring., Ithaca, NY, 1999, PhD in Elec. & Computer Engring., 2003. Student researcher The Cleve. Clinic Found., 1995, 1996; co-op engr. 3M Co., 1997; undergraduate researcher Cornell U., Sch. Elec. & Computer Engring., Ithaca, NY, 1998—99, grad. rsch. asst., 1999—2002; Nat. Rsch. Coun. Rsch. Assoc., Thermospheric and Ionospheric Rsch. and Applications group Naval Rsch. Lab., Washington, 2002—04; with U. Ill, Urbana-Champaign, 2004—, asst. prof., dept. elec. & computer engring., 2004—, asst. rsch. prof., Coordinated Sci. Lab., 2004—. Mem. academic excellence workshop Cornell U., 1998, tchg. asst. fellow, 2000—01, head cooperative learning trainer, Learning Initiatives for Future Engineers, 2000—02; Discovery Station vol. Nat. Air and Space Mus., 2002—04; co-convener in the field, 2002—; sci. definition team member, Communication/Navigation Outage Forecasting System (C/NOFS) satellite, 2002—; team mem. calibration/validation effort for the Special Sensor Ultraviolet Spectrographic Imager (SSUSI), 2002—, Special Sensor Ultraviolet Limb Imager (SSULI) on the next generation Defense Meteorological Support Program (DMSP) satellites, 2002—; presenter in field; invited lectr. in field. Contbr. articles to profl. publications; referee for papers in several profl. publications, panel reviewer for proposals at NSF and NASA, reviewer for proposals Journal of Geophysical Research, Geophysical Research Letters, Radio Science, Annales Geophysicae, Planetary and Space Science, Journal of Atmospheric and Solar-Terrestrial Physics, and Advances in Space Research. Recipient Einwecther award for outstanding service to the Coll. Engring, 1999, Editors' Citation for Excellence in Refereeing for Geophysical Rsch. Letters, 2005; Cornell U. Grad. Rsch. Fellowship, 1999—2002, NSF Grad. Rsch. Fellowship, 1999—2002, NRC Post-Doctoral Rsch. Associateship, 2002—04. Mem.: Am. Geophysical Union, IEEE. Achievements include development of new instrumentation to forcast the weather in the ionosphere. Office: Dept Elec & Computer Engrng U Ill 316 Coordinated Science Laboratory 1308 W Main St Urbana IL 61801-2307 Office Phone: 217-265-9470. Office Fax: 217-333-4303. Business E-Mail: jmakela@uiuc.edu. *

MAKEN, SONNY, real estate company executive, real estate developer; b. India, Sept. 27, 1975; arrived in U.S., 1989; s. Mani and Pam Maken; m. Debbie Maken, Mar. 2, 2002; children: Hannah, Abigail. BS in Internat. Econs., Georgetown U., 1997. Cert. commercial investment mgr. Chief legal assoc. No. Trust Inc., Chgo., 1997—99; lead subrogation specialist Grotefeld & Denenberg, LLC, Chgo., 1999—2001; pres., CEO The Maken Group, Inc., Palm Beach, Fla., 2001—; CEO Maken Hotel Group, Inc., Palm Beach, 2006—. Recipient Diamond Cir. award, Coldwell Banker Real Estate Inc., 2002, Pres. Cir. award, 2003, Coldwell Baker Real Estate Inc., 2004; scholar, Gen. Mills Corp., 1995—97, United Meth. Ch., 1995—97. Mem.: CCIM (corr.), Fla. Assn. Realtors (assoc.; mem. 2001), C. of C. Palm Beaches, Georgetown Club Palm Beach (corr.), Georgetown Alumni Interviewer Program (corr.), Georgetown Club Miami (corr.). Avocations: golf, sailing, antique cars. Office: The Maken Group Inc Ste 215 6299 West Sunrise Blvd Sunrise FL 33313 also: Ste 203 2247 Palm Beach Lakes Blvd West Palm Beach FL 33409 Home Phone: 561-767-0220; Office Phone: 561-721-9855. Office Fax: 561-721-9854. Business E-Mail: sonnymaken@themakengroup.com.

MAKEPEACE, MARY LOU, foundation administrator, former mayor; 2 children. BA in Journalism, U. ND, 1962; MPA, U. Colo., Colorado Springs, 1980. Tchr. Am. Sch., Tananarive, Madagascar; asst. to Def. Attaché Am. Embassy, Prague, Czechoslavakia; adult edn. officer Ramstein AFB, Germany; case worker, adminstr. El Paso County Dept. Social Svcs., 1974-82; exec. dir. Cmty. Coun. Pikes Peak Region, 1982-84; dist. 1 rep. City Colorado Springs, 1985-97, vice mayor, 1997, mayor, 1997—2003; exec. dir. Leadership Pike's Peak, Colo. Springs, 2003—04, Gill Found. Gay and Lesbian Fund, Colo., 2004—. Exofficio mem. Econ. Devel. Coun. Bd. Dirs.; chair Econ. Devel. Com., Task Force City Svcs. to Srs., urban affairs com. Pikes Peak Area Coun. Govts.; apptd. Colo. Space Adv. Coun.; adj. prof. U. Colo.; ex-dir. leadership Pikes Peak Mem. steering com. Imagination Celebration; sr. advisor Palmer Found., Pikes Peak Partnership; mem. Nat. League Cities Leadership Tng. Coun.; past mem. Colo. Mcpl. League Exec. Bd., 1st United Meth. Ch. Gates Found. fellow, 1992; recipient Svc. Mankind award Centennial Sertoma Club, 1985, Mary Jean Larson Cmty. Svc. award Girl Scouts Wagon Wheel Coun., 2002, Spence Vanderlin Pub. Ofcl. award Am. Pub. Power Assn., 2002, Outstanding Cmty. award Econ. Devel. Corp., 2003; named Super Woman Women's Health Ctr., 1988, Best City Councilmem. Springs Mag., 1991; honored Women in Your Life dinner Women's Found. Colo., 2002. Mem. Am. Soc. Pub. Adminstrn., Pi Alpha Alpha. Personal E-mail: maryloum@gillfoundation.org.

MAKER, CAROL JUNE, gifted and talented education educator; b. Caneyville, Ky., Aug. 7, 1948; d. Arnold David and Bernice (Smith) Shartzer. BS, Western Ky. U., 1970; MS, So. Ill. U., 1971; PhD, U. Va., 1978. Cert. elem. edn. tchr. Tchr. Caneyville (Ky.) Pub. Schs., 1970; tchr. of gifted Edwardsville (Ill.) Pub. Sch., 1971; regional supr. Ill. Office Edn., Springfield, 1971-74; adminstrv. intern U.S. Office Edn., Washington, 1974-75; grad. instr. U. Va., Charlottesville, 1976-77, off-campus instr., 1977-78; asst. prof. U. N.Mex., Albuquerque, 1978-81, U. Ariz., Tucson, 1981-83, assoc. prof., 1983-96, prof., 1996—. Vis. scholar Hong Kong Inst. Edn., 2004; spkr. and keynote spkr. Author: Teaching Models in Education of Gifted, 1982, 3d edit., 2005, Curriculum Development for the Gifted, 1982, Curriculum Development and Teaching Strategies for Gifted Learners, 2d edit., 1996; co-author: Intellectual Giftedness in Disabled Persons, 1985, Nurturing Giftedness in Young Children, 1996, Thinking Skills and Problem Solving: An Inclusive Approach, 2004, The Discover Project: Improving Assessment and Currilulum for Diverse Gifted Learners, 2005;

editor: (book series) Critical Issues in Education of Gifted, Vol. I, 1986, Vol. II, 1989, Vol. III, 1994; mem. editl. bd. Jour. for Edn. of Gifted, 1977—, Gifted Edn. Internat., 1985—, Eurasian Jour. Ednl. Rsch., 2003—, Internat. Jour. Evaluation and Rsch. in Edn., 2004—, Jour. Inst. Ednl. Rsch. in Belgrade, 2005—. Mem. H.S. task force Tucson (Ariz.) Unified Sch. Dist., 1983, 85; mem. task force gifted concerns Ariz. State Bd. Edn., Phoenix, 1985-87; steering com. China-U.S. Conf. Edn., 1996-97; bd. dirs. Arts Genesis, Inc., Tucson, 1994-97, Am. Logos Found., 1997-2003; coord. U.S.-China Interactive Learning Ctr., 1996. Fulbright scholar U. de las Ams., Mexico City, 1987; Rsch. grantee U.S. Dept. Edn., Office of Bilingual Edn., 1987-89, 93-96, U.S. Dept. Edn., Javits Gifted Edn. Program, 1993-01, Shonto Prep. Acad., 1996-2000, Met. Sch.Dist. of Seoul, Korea, 2004, 05. Mem. Nat. Assn. for Gifted (bd. dirs., sec. 1972-89), Ariz. Assn. for Gifted and Talented (bd. dirs., sec. 1981-87), World Coun. for Gifted and Talented (com. chair 1986-93), Coun. for Exceptional Children (com. chair 1975-94). Democrat. Avocations: photography, yoga, hiking, gardening. Home: 503 E 2nd St Tucson AZ 85705-7870 Office: Univ Ariz Dept Special Edn & Rehab Tucson AZ 85721-0001 Office Phone: 520-621-7822. Personal E-mail: junemaker@hotmail.com.

MAKHIJA, MOHAN, nuclear medicine physician; b. Bombay, Oct. 1, 1941; came to US, 1969; m. Arlene Zambito, Nov. 11, 1978. MD, Bombay U., 1965. Diplomate Am. Bd. Nuc. Medicine, Am. Bd. Radiology; cert. spl. competence in nuc. radiology. Resident in radiology Morristown Meml. Hosp., NJ, 1972—75; resident in nuc. medicine Yale-New Haven Hosp., 1975; fellow Yale U. Sch. Medicine, New Haven, 1976—77; jr. attending physician Helene Fuld Med. Ctr., Trenton, NJ, 1977—78; acting dir. dept. nuc. medicine Monmouth Med. Ctr., Long Branch, NJ, 1978, dir. nuc. medicine sect., 1979—2000, asst. attending radiology, 1978—80, assoc. attending radiology, 1980—83, attending radiologist, 1983—2000, St. Peter's U. Hosp., New Brunswick, NJ, 2001—, Robert Wood Johnson U. Hosp., New Brunswick, 2001—. Sr. instr. Hahneman U., Phila., 1978-80, clin. asst. prof., 1980-83, clin. assoc. prof., 1983-91, clin. prof., 1991-94, clin. prof. radiologic scis. Med. Coll. Pa. and Hahnemann U., 1994-2000; clin. prof. radiology U. Medicine and Dentistry NJ-Robert Wood Johnson Med. Sch., 2002—; radiol. cons. to NJ State Bd. Med. Examiners., 1994; mem. Commn. Radiation Protection NJ, 2004—. Contbr. articles to profl. jours. Mem. NJ Commn. on Radiation Protection, 2004—. Fellow: ACP (spkr. ho. of dels. 1992—93), Am. Coll. Radiology, Am. Coll. Nuc. Physicians; mem.: Med. Soc. NJ (trustee 2003—), Assn. Med. Specialties NJ (sec. 2001—02, pres. 2003—04), Soc. Nuc. Medicine (bd. govs. Gt. NY chpt. 1992—98), Indo-Am. Soc. Nuc. Medicine (pres. 1992—92), Radiol. Soc. NJ (chmn. nuc. medicine 1988—94, treas. 1994—95, sec. 1995—96, v.p. 1996—97, pres.-elect 1997—98, pres. 1998—99, chmn. nominting com. 2001—02, chmn. fellowship com. 2002—), Monmouth County Med. Soc. (pres. 1991—92). Home: 5 High Ridge Rd Ocean NJ 07712-3460 Office: St Peter's U Hosp 254 Easton Ave New Brunswick NJ 08901 Home Phone: 732-493-4467. Personal E-mail: mmakhija@aol.com.

MAKI, ATSUSHI, economics professor; b. Kanagawa, Japan, Jan. 14, 1948; s. Sadao and Eiko (Yamaguchi) M.; m. Michie Yabu, Feb. 28, 1975; children: Chiori, Hisashi. BA, Keio U., Japan, 1971; MA, Keio U., 1973, PhD, 1993. Asst. prof. Keio U., Tokyo, 1973-79, assoc. prof., 1979-87, prof., 1987—. Guest rsch. officer Ministry Posts and Telecom., 1988-90; vis. scholar Harvard U., Cambridge, Mass., 1982-84, 2001, George Washington U., 2001, U. Sydney, Australia, 2002; vis. prof. Osaka U., Japan, 1989, Ecole Superieure des Scis. Econs. et Commls., France, 1994, 2005, Tokyo Internat. U., 2005-07; vis. fellow Australian Nat. U., Canberra, 1990, Massey U., New Zealand, 1991, U. Western Australia, Perth, 1993, Victoria U., Wellington, New Zealand, 1997, Bur. Labor Stats., Washington, 2001. Author: Consumer Preferences and Measurement of Demand, 1983, Japanese Consumer Behavior, 1998, Applied Econometrics, 2001. Recipient award Japan Found., 1996; Abe fellow SSRC, 2001; Ministry of Edn. grant-in-aid, 1997-99, 2003-07. Mem. Am. Econ. Assn., Econometric Soc., Japanese Econ. Assn., Japan Assn. Stats., Japan Soc. Household Econs., Royal Econ. Soc. Home: 107-8 Terao Kawagoe-shi Saitama 350-1141 Japan Office: Keio U 2-15-45 Mita Minato-ku Tokyo 108-8345 Japan Business E-Mail: maki@fbc.keio.ac.jp.

MAKI, DENNIS G., epidemiology educator; b. River Falls, Wis., May 8, 1940; m. Gail Dawson, 1962; children: Kimberly, Sarah, Daniel. BS in Physics with honors, U. Wis., 1962, MS in Physics, 1964, MD, 1967. Diplomate Am. Bd. Internal Medicine, Am. Bd. Infectious Diseases, Am. Bd. Critical Care Medicine. Physicist, computer programmer Lawrence Radiation Lab., AEC, Livermore, Calif., 1962; intern, asst. resident Harvard Med. unit Boston City Hosp., 1967-69, chief resident, 1972-73; with Hosp. Infections sect. Ctrs. for Disease Control, USPHS, Atlanta, 1969-71; acting chief nat. nosocomial infections study Ctr. for Disease Control, USPHS, Atlanta, 1970-71; sr. resident dept. medicine Mass. Gen. Hosp., 1971-72, clin. and research fellow infectious disease unit, 1973-74; asst. prof. medicine U. Wis., Madison, 1974-78, assoc. prof., 1978-82, prof., 1982—; hosp. epidemiologist, U. Wis. Hosp. and Clinic, Madison, 1974—; Ovid O. Meyer prof. medicine U. Wis., Madison, 1975—, head sec. infectious diseases, 1979—2007, attending physician Ctr. for Trauma and Life Support, 1976—. Clinician, rschr., educator in field; mem. program com. Intersci. Conf. on Antimicrobial Agts. and Chemotherapy, 1987-94; mem. Am. Bd. Critical Care Medicine, 1989-95. Sr. assoc. editor Infection Control and Hosp. Epidemiology, 1979-93; mem. editl. bd. Jour. Lab. and Clin. Investigation, 1980-86, Jour. Critical Care, 1985-96, Jour. Infectious Diseases, 1988-90, Critical Care Medicine, 1989-94, 97—, Mayo Clinic Procs., 2002—; contbr. articles to med. jours. Recipient 1st award for disting. rsch. in Antibiotic Rev., 1980, Internat. CIPI award, 1994, SHEA lectr., 1999, numerous tchg. awards and hon. lectrs. Master ACP; fellow Infectious Diseases Soc. Am. (coun. 1993-96, citation 2000), Am. Acad. Microbiology, Soc. for Critical Care Medicine, Surg. Infection Soc., Wis. Acad. Scis., Arts and Letters; mem. Soc. Hosp. Epidemiologists Am. (pres. 1990), Ctrl. Soc. for Clin. Rsch., Am. Soc. Microbiology, Am. Fedn. Clin. Rsch., Alpha Omega Alpha (nat. bd. dirs. 1983-89). Office: U Wis Hosp and Clinics H4/574 Madison WI 53792 Fax: 608-833-0327. Personal E-mail: dgmaki@yahoo.com. Business E-Mail: dgmaki@medicine.wisc.edu.

MAKI, HOPE MARIE (COUNTESS HOPE MARIE MAKI), artist, educator; b. St. Joseph, Mo., Jan. 14, 1938; 3 children. Host TV art show Channel 6, Fort Walton Beach, Fla.; owner art sch., gallery; tchr. art, 1957—. Exhibited in shows at Arts-Inter-Salon Int des Sekneurs de L'Art, Chateauneuf du Pape, France, 1994, Salon Int des Seigneurs de L'Art, Palais des Congres Marseille, 1994, Mountserrat Gallery, N.Y.; represented in permanent pvt. and pub. collections; created art for the blind, 1963—; author, illustrator: Trader Jon His Life, 2001 Named One of Best New Poets Am. Poetry Assn., 1987, 88, 89; recipient Award of Poetic Achievement, Amherst Soc., recognition of outstanding achievements in art edn. Cox Comm., 2000; poem placed in spl. collection Statue of Liberty Nat. Monument, 1992 Mem. Nat. Mus. Women in Arts Avocation: poetry. Home and Office: 3985 Langley Ave Pensacola FL 32504-8371

MAKI, KAZUMI, physicist, researcher; b. Takamatsu, Japan, Jan. 27, 1936; s. Toshio and Hideko M.; m. Masako Tanaka, Sept. 21, 1969. BS, Kyoto U., 1959, PhD, 1964. Research asso. Inst. for Math. Scis., Kyoto U., 1964; research asso. Fermi Inst., U. Chgo., 1964-65; asst. prof. physics U. Calif., San Diego, 1965-67; prof. Tohoku U., Sendai, Japan, 1967-74; vis. prof. Universite Paris-Sud, Orsay, France, 1969-70; prof. physics U. So. Calif., Los Angeles, 1974—. Vis. prof. Inst. Laue-Langevin, U. Paris-Sud, France, 1979-80, Max Planck Inst. fur Festkorper Forschung, Stuttgart, Germany, 1986-87, U. Paris-7, 1990, Hokkaido U., Sapporo, Japan, 1993, Centre de Recherche sur Tres Basses Temperatures, Grenoble, France, 1993-94, Instituto de Ciencia de Materiales, Madrid, Spain, 1994, Max Planck Inst. Phys. Complex Sys., Dresden, Germany, 2001-02. Assoc. editor Jour. Low Temperature Physics, 1969-91; contbr. articles to profl. jours. Guggenheim fellow, 1979-80, Japan Soc. Promotion of Sci. fellow, 1993; Fulbright scholar, 1964-65; recipient Nishina prize, 1972, Alexander von Humboldt award, 1986-87, John Bardeen prize, 2006. Fellow Japan Soc. Promotion of Sci., Am. Phys. Soc.; mem. AAAS, Phys. Soc. Japan. Office: U So Calif Dept Physics and Astronomy Los Angeles CA 90089-0484 Office Phone: 213-740-8405. Business E-Mail: kmaki@usc.edu.

MAKIMURA, YASUHIRO, history professor; b. Nov. 20, 1971; BA, Harvard U., Cambridge, Mass., 1993; MCH, Cambridge U., Eng., 1995; PhD, Columbia U., NYC, 2005. Asst. prof. Iona Coll., New Rochelle, NY, 2003—. Japan Found. fellow, 1998—2000, Hegmea Ctr. fellow, Columbia U., 2001—03. Mem.: Assn. Asian Studies, Am. Hist. Assn.

MAKINEN, MARVIN WILLIAM, biophysicist, educator; b. Chassell, Mich., Aug. 19, 1939; s. William John and Milga Katarina (Myllyla) M.; m. Michele de Groot, July 30, 1966; children: Eric William, Stephen Matthew. AB, U. Pa., 1961; postgrad., Free U. Berlin, 1960-61; MD, U. Pa., 1968; DPhil, U. Oxford, Eng., 1976. Diplomate Am. Bd. Med. Examiners. Intern Columbia-Presbyn. Med. Ctr., NYC, 1968-69; rsch. assoc. NIH, Bethesda, Md., 1969-71; vis. fellow U. Oxford, Eng., 1971-74; asst. prof. biophysics U. Chgo., 1974-80, assoc. prof., 1980-86, prof. biochemistry and molecular biology, 1986—, chmn. dept., 1988-93. Established investigator Am. Heart Assn., 1975-80; lectr. in field. Contbr. numerous articles to profl. jours. Sr. surgeon USPHS, 1969-71. John Simon Guggenheim fellow 1997-98, John E. Fogarty Sr. Internat. fellow, 1984-85, European Molecular Biology Orgn. sr. fellow, 1984-85, NIH spl. fellow, 1971-74, Berquist fellow Am. Scandinavian Found., 1970. Fellow Am. Inst. Chemists; mem. Am. Chem. Soc., Biophys. Soc., Am. Soc. Biochemistry and Molecular Biology, The Protein Soc., AAAS. Office: U Chgo Dept Biochemistry/Mol Biol 920 E 58th St Chicago IL 60637-5415 Home Phone: 773-684-6507; Office Phone: 773-702-1080. Business E-Mail: makinen@uchicago.edu.

MAKINO, SHINJI, virologist, educator; DVM, Iwate U., Morioka, Japan, 1979; PhD in Virology, U. Tokyo Inst. Med. Sci., 1984. Scientist Sealy Ctr. Vaccine Devel. U. Tex. Med. Br., Galveston, mem. Ctr. Biodefense and Emerging Infectious Disease, prof. dept. microbiol. and immunology. Contbr. articles to profl. jours., chapters to books. Achievements include discovery of the method the SARS virus uses to prevent production of a protein the immune system would normally use to defend against viruses. Office: Dept Microbiol and Immunology U Tex Med Br 301 Univ Blvd Galveston TX 77555-1019 E-mail: shmakino@utmb.edu.

MAKKER, SUDESH PAUL, physician; b. Sargodha, Punjab, India, June 8, 1941; came to U.S., 1966; s. Manohar Lal and Daya Wati (Kharbanda) M.; m. Donna Mae Stohs, Feb. 15, 1969; children: Vishal, Kirin. Fellow of Sci., Panjab U., 1959; MD, All India Inst. med. Scis., New Dehli, 1964. Bd. cert. Am. Bd. Pediatrics, Am. Bd. Pediatric Nephrology. Intern in internal medicine All India Inst. of Med. Scis., New Dehli, 1965, resident in internal medicine, 1966; rotating intern Queens Gen. Hosp., NYC, 1966-67; resident in pediatrics U. Chgo. (Ill.) Hosps., 1967-69; rsch. fellowship in pediatric nephrology Case Western Res. U., 1969-71; fellowship in pediatric nephrology U. Calif., San Francisco, 1971; instr. to asst. prof. pediatrics Case Western Res. U., Sch. Medicine, Cleve., 1971-76, assoc. prof., div. head pediatric nephrology, 1976-83; prof., div. head pediatric nephrology U. Tex. Health Sci. Ctr., San Antonio, 1983-91; prof., sect. chief pediatric nephrology U. Calif., Davis Sch. Medicine, Davis, 1991—. Mem. ad hoc com. on nat. standards for dialysis and transplantation in children Am. Soc. Pediatric Nephrology; ad hoc com. on hypertension in the young Am. Heart Assn., N.E. Ohio Chpt.; mem. end stage renal disease program Crippled Children Svcs. State of Ohio; mem. rsch. grants com. and pub. edn. com. Kidney Found. of Ohio; vis. prof. U. Pa. Children's Hosp., Phila., 1981, U. So. Calif., L.A., 1981, U. Calif. Sch. Medicine, San Francisco, 1982, U. Mich., Ann Arbor, 1990, and many others. Editor: (textbook) Pediatric Nephrology, 1992; editorial bd.: Internat. Jour. Pediatric Nephrology, Indian Jour. Pediatrics; contbr. over 80 articles to profl. jours. Mem. AAAS, Am. Soc. Investigative Pathology, Am. Acad. Pediatrics, Am. Soc. Nephrology, The Soc. for Exptl. Biology and Medicine, Am. Assn. Immunologists, Soc. for Pediatric Rsch., Am. Pediatric Soc., Sigma Chi, Sigma Xi. Avocations: tennis, hiking, reading, photography. Office: Univ Calif Davis Med Ctr Pediatric Nephrology 2516 Stockton Blvd Sacramento CA 95817-2208

MAKKI, S. KAMI, education educator; MS in Eng, U. NSW, 1991; PhD, U. Queensland, Austrasia, 1997. Lectr. Royal Melbourne Inst. of Tech., Melbourne, Australia, 1997—2000, Queensland U. of Tech., Brisbane, Australia, 2000—03; asst. prof. U. Toledo, 2003—. Home Phone: 419-530-8154; Office Phone: 419-530-8154. Office Fax: 419-530-8146. Business E-Mail: kmakki@eng.utoledo.edu.

MAKKI, SHAMILA, project manager engineer, researcher; arrived in US, 2003; d. Seyed Rouholloh Mohammad Makki and Esmat Ghaem Maghami. M in Civil Engring., U. Queensland, Brisbane, 1999, grad. diploma in info. tech., 2002, M in Info. Tech. and Civil Engring., 2003; PhD in Elec. Engring., Fla. Internat. U., Miami. Civil engr., estimator Telecommunication Co., Tehran, 1990—95; civil engr. rsch. asst. Civil Engring. Dept., Brisbane, Australia, 1998—99; info. tech. rsch. scholar Sch. Info. Tech., Brisbane, 1999—2001, project mgmt. rsch., 2002—03; project mgmt. engr. Horizon Electronics, Inc., Miami Lakes, 2003—. Recipient several Tech. Contbn. and Leadership awards, NSF, 2003—07. Mem.: ACM, IEEE, Eta Kappa Nu, Phi Kappa Phi, Delta Epsilon Iota (life). Avocations: reading, sports, cooking. Office: Inst Electrical and Computer Engring Fla Internat U 10555 W Floyer St Miami FL 33174 Personal E-mail: shamilamakki@gmail.com.

MAKOUS, BRUCE B., fundraiser, writer; b. Phila., June 24, 1953; s. Norman and Dorothy Makous; m. Barbara H. Makous, Oct. 17, 1981; children: Dyani, Kacie. BA in Lit., Oberlin Coll., 1976; MA in Cultural Adminstrn., NYU, 1986. CLU, ChFC. Gen. mgr. 78th Street Theatre Lab., NYC, 1979-81; comm. cons. Price Waterhouse Nat. Offices, NYC, 1981-84; dir. info. svcs. Theatre Comm. Group, NYC, 1984-86; mng. dir. Attic Theatre, Detroit, 1986-89, Players Theatre Columbus, Ohio, 1989-90; founder, pres. Makous Mktg. & Fundraising, Phila., 1990-93; dir. devel. Am. Coll., Bryn Mawr, Pa., 1993-98, dir. planned giving, 1998-99; dir. major and planned gifts Drexel U., Phila., 1999-2000, asst. v.p. for major and planned gifts, 2000—01; maj. gifts and planned giving officer Am. Assn. for Cancer Rsch., 2001—; v.p. devel. Multiple Sclerosis Assn. Am., Cherry Hill, NJ, 2007—. Lectr. Wayne State U., Detroit, 1988-89, Assn. Fundraising Profls. Villanova U., Pa., 1998-2001, Am. Coll., Bryn Mawr, Pa., 2002-2004; Planned Giving Coun. Greater Phila., 2007-. Author: Riding the Brand, 2004, Virtually Dead, 2006; co-prodr. Back in the World, 1987 (award for best play outside N.Y. Nat. Theatre Critics Assn. 1987); assoc. editor Boulevard lit. mag., 1991—. Grad. Leadership, Inc. Class of 1992, 1991-92. Mgmt. for Arts Rev. scholar NYU, 1983-86. Mem. Nat. Com. on Planned Giving, Mystery Writers of Am., Assn. Fundraising Profls. (pres. 2000-01, treas. 2004). Democrat. Roman Catholic. Home: 7905 Cadillac Ln Philadelphia PA 19128 Office: Multiple Sclerosis Assn Am 706 Haddonfield Rd Cherry Hill NJ 08002 Office Phone: 267-251-9060, 800-532-7667 X 148. Personal E-mail: bruce@brucemakous.com. Business E-Mail: bmakous@msassociation.org.

MAKOUS, NORMAN, retired internist, cardiologist, educator; b. Chgo., July 22, 1924; s. Lawrence Alonzo and Ruth (Luehring) M.; m. Dorothy Murl Bowlin, Sept. 25, 1948 (dec. July 25, 2003); children: David, Bruce, Catherine, Monte, Joseph, Martin, John, Virginia, Dorothy, Margaret; m. Eleanor B. Sullivan Feb. 21, 2004. BS, U. Wis., 1945, MD, 1947. Diplomate in internal medicine and cardiovascular diseases Am. Bd. Internal Medicine. Mixed intern Rsch. Hosp., Kansas City, Mo., 1947—48, resident in internal medicine, 1948—50; fellow in cardiovasc. disease U. Vt., Burlington, 1950—51; resident in internal medicine U.S. Naval Hosp., Camp Lejeune, NC, 1951—52; dir. cardiac catheterization lab. Kansas City, Mo., 1955—56; fellow in cardiovasc. disease Pa. Hosp., Phila., 1953—54, assoc. cardiologist, assoc. physician to hosp., 1960—72, cardiologist, physician to hosp., 1972—2000, cons., 2000—01; pvt. practice Kansas City and Independence, Mo., 1956—59, Phila., 1959—2001; assoc. in medicine U. Pa., Phila., 1959—71, asst. prof. clin. medicine, 1971—74, clin. asst. prof. medicine, 1974—2000; clin. asst. prof. medicine Thomas Jefferson U., Phila., 1994—; ret., 2006. Physician advisor Keystone Profl. Rev. Orgn., 1986-93; mem. cons. Pa. Bur. Disability Determination, 1981-2001; cardiology cons. Phila. City Solicitor's Office, 1986-2005; mem. peer rev. panel Jour. Cardiopulmonary Rehab., 1990; mem. adv. group Greater Delaware Valley Regional Med. Program, 1971-75. Contbr. articles to med. jours., chpts. to books. Founder, acting chmn. Southeastern Pa. Regional High Blood Pressure Control Program, 1978-80; mem. interim bd. Health Sys. Agy. Southeastern Pa., 1975-77, chmn. adv. coun., 1979-80; trustee Edna B. Kynett Meml. Found., Phila., 1963—, v.p., 1994-96, pres., 1997—2004; pres. Home and Sch. Assn., Our Lady of Lourdes Parish, Phila., 1972-73, mem. parish pastoral coun., 1991-95, co-chmn., 1993-95; trustee Vis. Nurse Assn. Greater Phila., 1997-2000. Lt. USNR, 1943-45, 50-52, Res., 1952-62. Recipient Legion of Honor, Chapel of Four Chaplains, 1980, Spl. Achievement award Southeastern Pa. Regional High Blood Pressure Control Program. Fellow ACP, Am. Coll. Cardiology, Am. Soc. Internal Medicine; mem. AMA, Pa. Med. Soc. (chmn. profl. liability ins. appeals com. 1986-91), Phila. County Med. Soc. (standing com. Med. Econs., 1979-86, pres. Center City br. 1980-81, sec. 1990-91, chmn. membership and orgn. com. 1991-2000, Cristol award 1994), Am. Heart Assn. (fellow coun. clin. cardiology, pres. Southeastern Pa. affiliate 1988-89, bd. govs., program chmn. 1988-92, pres. Pa. affiliate 1981-82, Disting. Svc. award Pa. affiliate 1982, Disting. Achievement award Pa. affiliate, 1986, Disting. Achievement award Southeastern Pa. affiliate 1988, Vol. of Yr. award Southeastern Pa. affiliate 1988), Pa. Soc. Internal Medicine (pres. 1983-84). Avocations: tennis, cinematography. Office: 243 Freedom Blvd Coatesville PA 19320 Office Phone: 610-466-9441. Personal E-mail: drnmakous@aol.com.

MAKOUS, WALTER LEON, visual scientist, educator; s. Lawrence and Ruth Lorraine (Luehring) Makous; m. Marilyn Ann Carlson, Feb. 2, 1958 (div. 1973); children: Ann, James, Matthew; m. Joyce Brown Menconi, 1974 (div. 1981); m. Barbara Anne Duggins, Apr. 29, 1982. BS, U. Wis., 1958; MSc, Brown U., Providence, 1961, PhD, 1964. Mem. staff IBM, Yorktown Heights, NY, 1963-66; asst. prof. psychology U. Wash., 1966-69, lectr. in physiology and biophysics, 1966-69, assoc. prof. psychology, 1969-74, prof. psychology, 1974-79; prof. psychology, ophthalmology and visual sci. U. Rochester, 1979-95; prof. brain and cognitive sci., ophthalmology & visual sci., 1995—; dir. Ctr. for Visual Sci. U. Rochester, 1979-90. Northwest rep, charter mem steering comt West Coast Regional Consortium Univs in Neurosciences, 1976—79; mem coun on energy saving through more efficient lighting NAS-NRC, 1978—79, night vision coun, 1985—86; chmn ctr symp Univ Rochester, 1981—82; sensory processes panelist NSF, Washington, 1977—82, mem adv comt applied sci and research applicaitons policy, 1978—81; rev comt Presidential Young Investigator Award Program, 1984; vis scientist IBM Research, 1970—71. Editor (consult ed): Sensory Processes, 1977—79, Jour of the Optical Soc Am, 1982—86; contbr. articles to profl jours. With USNR, 1953—55. Grantee, Nat Eye Inst, 1969—2006, NSF, 1959—62, 1981—82. Fellow: AAAS, Optical Soc. Am. (ed vision and color 1982—86, mem coord vision and physiological optics comt 1983—89, coord vision and med optics comt 1983—89, publs comt 1985—89, chmn fellows and hon mems comt 1986, feature ed applied vision 1989—90); mem.: Am Nat Standards Inst/Human Factor & Ergonomics Soc-100 (rev comt 1992—2006, chmn. visual displays 2002—06), Assn. Rsch. in Vision and Ophthalmology (chmn sect psycho-physics 1977). Office: U Rochester Ctr for Visual Sci Rochester NY 14627 Office Phone: 585-275-2460. Business E-Mail: walt@cvs.rochester.edu.

MAKOVSKY, KENNETH DALE, public relations executive; s. Jack and Minnie (Freedman) Makovsky; m. Phyllis Ann Peck, Oct. 15, 1972; children: Evan, Matthew. BA, Washington U., St. Louis, 1962, JD, 1965. Asst. account exec. Curtis Hoxter Inc., NYC, 1965—66; account exec. Ruder & Finn Inc., NYC, 1966—69, Harshe-Rotman & Druck, NYC, 1970—72, v.p., 1973—75, sr. v.p., 1975—79, sr. v.p., dep. gen. mgr. N.Y. office, 1979; founder, pres. Makovsky and Co., Inc., NYC, 1979—; founder, past pres. Internat. Pub. Rels. Exch.; chmn. Makovsky & Co., Inc., NYC. Contbr. articles to profl. pubs. Nat. bd. govs. Am. Jewish Com. N.Y., 1999—, nat. pub. rels. com. chmn., 1981—; speechwriter 17th Dist. Congl. Campaign, NYC, 1972; v.p. Am. Jewish Com. N.Y., NYC, 1985—, N.Y. bd. dirs., 1978—; adv. com. S.I. Newhouse Sch. Pub. Commn., 1996—, Washington U. Nat. Arts and Sci. Coun., 1998—; bd. trustees Inst. PR, 2000—. Recipient Gold Quill IABC, 1990, Cipra award Inside Pub. Rels., 1994, PRSA's Silver Anvil, PRSA-NY's Big Apple award; named Pub. Rels. All Star, Inside Pub. Rels., 1992; co. named one of ten fastest growing pub. rels. firms in U.S., O'Dwyer Rankings, 1985, 86, 87, 89, 90, 91, one of four top pub. rels. firms in N.Y.C., Small Agy. Yr. Inside Pub. Rels., 1990, among 12 Best Managed Firms in U.S., 1993, 94, among the 12 top strategic counseling firms in U.S., 1995, one of the 8 hot bus.-to-bus. agys., 1996, one of the 8 best managed agys., 1997, one of the 12 top investor relations agys., 1997, among the 15 top tech. agys., 1997, best managed PR agy. in U.S., 1998, among 16 top investor relations agys., 1998, among 9 top bus.-to-bus., 1998, 16 nat. capabilities agys., 1998, among 12 best managed agys., 1999, one of 12 top bus.-to-bus. mktg., 1999, among 12 top investor relations agys., 1999, one of 15 top agys. in N.Y.C., 1999, among top 8 bus.-to-bus. mktg., 1999. Mem.: Inst. Pub. Rels. (bd. trustees), Arthur Page Soc., Nat. Investors Rels. Inst., Pub. Rels. Soc. Am. (Silver Anvil award for Chem. Spltys. Mfrs. Assn. 1978, award for Am. Superconductor 1994), Nat. Arts Sci. Coun., Washington U. Alumni Club N.Y.C. (pres. 1970). Avocations: theater, movies, travel. Office: Makovsky and Co Inc 575 Lexington Ave Fl 15 New York NY 10022-6104 Personal E-mail: kmakovsky@makovsky.com.

MAKRIS, MARGARET LUBBE, retired elementary school educator; b. Everett, Wash., July 17, 1930; d. Fred Roy and Edna (McFarland) Lubbe; m. Andreas Makris, June 12, 1959 (dec. Feb. 2005); children: Christos, Myron. BA, San Francisco State U., 1956; MEd, U. Md., College Park, 1970. Tchr. San Francisco Pub. Schs., 1954—56; recreation dir. U.S. Army Spl. Svcs. Staff, Germany, 1956—58; tchr. St. Louis Pub. Schs., 1959—61, Montgomery County Pub. Schs., Rockville, Md., 1961—86; ret., 1986. Co-sponsor Makris Violin Competition, Salonika, Greece, 1996; founder Andreas Makris Music Endowment-Nat. Philharm., Strathmore Hall Music Ctr., 2005, Andreas and Margaret Makris Music Scholarship Fund, Md. Classic Youth Orchestras, Bethesda, 2006; co-sponsor Makris Clarinet Competition, Colo. State U., Ft. Collins, 2003, Makris Wood Wind Competition, Colo. State U., 2004; bd. dirs. Nat. Philharm., 2005. Mem.: Heritage Found. (Washington), Pres. Club. Republican. Achievements include the donation of Andreas Makris violin crafted by Nicolaus Gagliano in Italy 1732 to the Heritage Foundation Washington, 2006. Home: 11204 Oak Leaf Dr Silver Spring MD 20901

MAKROGIANNIS, SOKRATIS, physicist, researcher; s. Konstantinos Makrogiannis and Stamatina Lagadianou. PhD, U. Patras, Greece, 2002. Rsch. scholar Wright State U., Dayton, 2003—05; postdoctoral rsch. fellow U. Pa., 2005—. Engring. cons. AIIS Inc., Centerville, Ohio, 2003—04. Contbr. articles to profl. jours. Visiting scholar, U. Brussels, 2000—01. Mem.: IEEE. Home Phone: 215-307-0115. Personal E-mail: smakrogiannis@yahoo.com.

MAKUPSON, AMYRE PORTER, broadcast executive; b. River Rouge, Mich., Sept. 30, 1947; d. Rudolph Hannibal and Amyre Ann (Porche) Porter; m. Walter H. Makupson, Nov. 1, 1975; children: Rudolph Porter, Amyre Nisi. BA, Fisk U., 1970; MA, Am. U., Washington, 1972. Asst. dir. news Sta. WGPR-TV, Detroit, 1975-76; dir. pub. rels. Mich. Health Maintenance Orgn., Detroit, 1976-77; mgr. pub. affairs, news anchor Sta. WKBD-TV, Southfield, Mich., 1977—2004, Children's Miracle Network Telethon, 1989—. Mem. Co-Ette Club, Inc., Met. Detroit Teen Conf. Coalition; mem. adv. com., bd. dirs. Alzheimers Assn.; bd. dirs. com. March of Dimes; bd. dirs. Providence Hosp. Found., Sickle Cell Assn., Covenant House Mich., AAA, Home Fed. Savs. Bank, Skillman Found. Recipient 6 Emmy awards 4 Best Commentary/Best Anchor, Best Interview/Discussion Show, 26 Emmy nominations NATAS, Editl. Best Feature award AP, Media award UPI, Oakland County Bar Assn., TV Documentary award, Detroit Press Club, Bishop Gallagher award Mental Illness Rsch. Assn., Svc. award Arthritis Found. Mich., Mich. Mchts. Assn., DAV, Jr. Achievement, City of Detroit, Salvation Army, Spirit award City of Detroit, Spirit award City of Pontiac, Golden Heritage award Little Rock Bapt. Ch., 1993, Neal Shine award outstanding contbn. Nat. Soc. Fund-raising Execs., Virginia Merrick award outstanding contbn. Christ Child Soc., Outstanding Achievement award Tuskegee Airmen, Best Feature Story award Mich. Assn. Broadcasters; named Media Person of the Yr., So. Christian Leadership Conf., 1994, Humanitarian of the Yr., March of Dimes, 1995, Michiganian of the Yr., Detroit News, Outstanding Woman of the Yr., GM Women's Club. Mem. Pub. Rels. Soc. Am., Am. Women in Radio and TV (Outstanding Achievement award 1981, Outstanding Woman in TV Top Mgmt. 1993, Mentor award 1993), Women in Comm., Nat. Acad. TV Arts and Scis., Detroit Press Club, Ad-Craft, Howard U. Nat. Gold Key Honor Soc. (hon.). Roman Catholic. Office: 26955 W 11 Mile Rd Southfield MI 48034-2292

MALA, THEODORE ANTHONY, physician, consultant; b. Santa Monica, Calif., Feb. 3, 1946; s. Ray and Galina (Liss) M.; children: Theodore S., Galina T.; 1 adopted child, Christine A. Lindholm. BA in Philosophy, DePaul U., 1972; MD, Autonomous U., Guadalajara, Mex., 1976; MPH, Harvard U., 1980. Spl. asst. for health affairs Alaska Fedn. Natives, Anchorage, 1977-78; chief health svcs. Alaska State Divsn. Corrections, Anchorage, 1978-79; assoc. prof., founder, dir. Inst. for Circumpolar Health Studies, U. Alaska, Anchorage, 1982-90; founder Siberian med. rsch. program U. Alaska, Anchorage, 1982, founder Magadan (USSR) med. rsch. program, 1988; commr. Health and Social Svcs. State of Alaska, Juneau, 1990-93; pres., CEO Ted Mala, Inc., Anchorage, 1993-97; pres., ptnr. Mexican-Siberian Trading Co., Monterrey, Mex., 1994-96; CEO, Confederated Tribes of Grand Ronde, Oreg., 1998-99; dir. tribal rels. Southcentral Found., Anchorage, 1999—, 2000—. Traditional healing dir. Southcentral Found., Anchorage, 2000—; Alaska rsch. and publs. com. Indian Health Svc., USPHS, 1987-90; advisor Nordic Coun. Meeting, WHO, Greenland, 1985; mem. Internat. Organizing Com., Circumpolar Health Congress, Iceland, 1992-93; chmn. bd. govs. Alaska Psychiat. Inst., Anchorage, 1990-93; cabinet mem. Gov. Walter J. Hickel, Juneau, 1990-93; advisor humanitarian aid to Russian Far East U.S. Dept. State, 1992-96; cons. USAID on U.S.-Russian Health Programs, 1994; apptd. adv. com. Sec. of Health and Human Svc. on Minority Health for the U.S., 2000—; mem. coun. pub. reps. NIH, 2002-05. Past columnist Tundra Times; contbr. articles to profl. jours. Trustee United Way Anchorage, 1978-79; chmn. bd. trustees Alaska Native Coll., 1993-96. Recipient Gov.'s award, 1988, Outstanding Svc. award Alaska Commr. Health, 1979, Ministry of Health citation USSR Govt., 1989, Citation award Alaska State Legislature, 1989-90, 94, Commendation award State of Alaska, 1990, Alaska State Legislature, 1994, Honor Kempton Svc. to Humanity award, 1989, citation Med. Comty. of Magadan region, USSR, 1989; Nat. Indian fellow U.S. Dept. Edn., 1979. Mem. Assn. Am. Indian Physicians (pres.), N.Y. Acad. Scis., Internat. Union for Circumpolar Health (permanent sec.-gen. 1987-90, organizing com. 8th Internat. Congress on Circumpolar Health 1987-90), Russian Acad. Polar Medicine (elected). Avocations: cross country skiing, hiking, photography, travel. Office Phone: 907-729-4955. E-mail: tmala@post.harvard.edu. *Personal philosophy: Progress in the North will come only when circumpolar countries put aside their geopolitical thinking and work together as one northern family.*

MALACH, MONTE, physician; b. Jersey City, Aug. 15, 1926; s. Charles and Yetta (Pascher) M.; m. Ann Elaine Glazer, June 15, 1952 (dec. June 1989); children: Barbara Sandra, Cathie Tara, Matthew David. BA, MD, U. Mich., 1949. Diplomate Am. Bd. Internal Medicine, Nat. Bd. Med. Examiners. Intern Beth Israel Hosp., Boston, 1949-50, resident, 1950-51, chief resident, 1951-52; chief med. resident Kings County Hosp., Bklyn., 1954-55; practice medicine specializing in internal medicine and cardiology Bklyn., 1955—2001; dir. CCU Bklyn. Hosp., 1965-91, dir. emeritus CCU, 1991—; med. dir., clin. coord. Medicare IPRO Downstate N.Y., 1990—2005; cardiology cons., 2005—. Pres. profl. staff Bklyn. Hosp., 1966-69, chmn. med. bd., 1971-72; attending staff Caledonian Hosp., pres. profl. staff, 1984-85; pres. profl. staff Bklyn. Hosp.-Caledonian Hosp., 1987-89, chmn. med. bd., 1988-89; cons. Kings County Hosp.; tchg. fellow Tufts U. Med. Sch., 1951-52; instr. medicine Downstate Med. Ctr., Bklyn., 1955-59, clin. asst. prof. medicine, 1959-68, clin. assoc. prof., 1969-76, clin. prof., 1976—; clin. prof. medicine NYU Med. Ctr., 1994—; bd. dirs. Bay St. Landing One Owners Corp., 1985-87; v.p. Ocean View Condos, 1989-90, pres., 1990-95; med. dir. IPRO Medicare Rev., N.Y. State, 1990—, IPRO N.Y. State Peer Rev., 1990-2006. Kings County committeeman Dem. Party, 1964, 65. Served with USNR, 1944-46, to 1st lt. M.C. U.S. Army, 1952-54. Recipient 1st Prize for Crisis Mgmt. Habitat Mag., 1987. Fellow Am. Coll. Chest Physicians, ACP (master, Laureate award 2000), Am. Coll. Cardiology (task force Health Care Quality Improvement Initiative 1996—); mem. AMA (chmn. sect. coun. internal medicine 1980), N.Y. Heart Assn., Am. Soc. Internal Medicine (master, trustee 1975-79, sec.-treas. 1979—, pres. elect 1981, pres. 1982-83, chmn. investment com. 1985-93), N.Y. State Soc. Internal Medicine (pres. 1973-74, dir. 1966-84, chmn. Bklyn. chpt., v.p. 1971, award of merit 1978), Bklyn. Soc. Internal Medicine (mem. council 1965, pres. 1969-72), Med. Soc. State of N.Y. (chmn. sect. internal medicine 1976, chmn. med. care ins. com. 1988-93), Federated Council for Internal Medicine (chmn. 1979-80), Med. Soc. County Kings (censor 1985-91). Office Phone: 917-522-1201. Office Fax: 917-522-1201. Personal E-mail: montemalach@hotmail.com. *There is a place for hard work, scrupulous ethics and a pride of accomplishment. A great marriage and a fine close family are buffers against adversity.*

MALACHOWSKI, NICOLE, pilot; b. 1974; Grad., Air Force Acad., 1996. F-15E (Strike Eagle fighter jet) pilot Royal Air Force, Lakenheath, Eng., 494th Fighter Squadron; No. 3 right wing pilot Thunderbirds, US Air Force Air Demonstration Squadron, 2005—. Served in Operation Iraqi Freedom, 2005. Achievements include being the first female demonstration pilot in the 52 year history of the Thunderbirds, US military high performance jet team. Office: USAFADS 4445 Tyndall Ave Nellis Afb NV 89191

MALACHOWSKI, ROBERT MICHAEL, retired pediatrician; b. Abilene, Tex., July 27, 1944; s. Edward Michael Malachowski and Ruth Eileen Chesterman; m. Louise Mary Noel, July 2, 1966; children: Robert Michael Jr., Carol Louise Mercer, William Edward, Patrick Noel. MD, Loyola U., Chgo., 1969. Diplomate Am. Bd. of Pediats. Pvt. practice pediatrician, Indpls., 1974—2002; ret. Lt. comdr. USN. Mem.: Alpha Omega Alpha. Home: 5722 Brendon Forest Dr Indianapolis IN 46226 Home Phone: 317-545-9467. Personal E-mail: babydocmd@comcast.net.

MALAFRONTE, DONALD, health facility administrator, consultant; b. Bklyn., Dec. 16, 1931; s. Pasquale and Amalia (Castaldo) M.; m. Diane Freedenberg, Jan. 7, 1960 (dec. Nov. 14, 1970); children: Philip, Victor.; m. Hillary Demby, Oct. 30, 1982. BS, NYU, 1954. Reporter L.I. Daily Press, 1956-58; reporter, editor Newark Star-Ledger, 1958-65, art columnist, 1963-70; adminstrv. asst. to mayor of Newark, 1965-70; dir. Newark Model Cities Program, 1967-70, Newark Community Devel. Adminstrn., 1968-70; chief urban field operations N.J. Regional Med. Program, 1970-73; pres. Urban Health Inst., Roseland, NJ, 1973—. Cons. to hosps., local govts., 1970— Author articles in field. Served with AUS, 1954-56. Recipient Joyce Kilmer fiction prize NYU, 1953 Office: Urban Health Inst 101 Eisenhower Pky Roseland NJ 07068-1028 Home: 1056 5th Ave New York NY 10028-0112 Office Phone: 973-228-9000.

MALAMUD, DEBORAH C., law educator; b. 1955; BA in Religion magna cum laude, Wesleyan U., 1976; grad. work in Anthropology, U. Chgo., 1978—81, JD cum laude, 1986. Bar: Pa. 1987, DC 1988. Law clk. to Hon. Louis H. Pollack US Dist. Ct. Ea. Dist. Pa., Phila., 1986—87; law clk. to Hon. Harry A. Blackman US Supreme Ct., Washington, 1988—89; assoc. Bredhoff & Kaiser, DC, 1987—88, 1989—92; asst. prof. law U. Mich. Law Sch., 1992—97, prof., 1997—2003, James E. and Sarah A. Degan prof. law; prof. NYU Sch. Law, 2003—, An-Bryce prof. law. Vis. prof. NYU, 2002, Yale U., 2002—03. Mem.: Am. Soc. Legal History, Law and Soc. Assn. Office: NYU Sch Law Vanderbilt Hall Rm 310 40 Washington Sq S New York NY 10012-1099 Office Phone: 212-992-8902. E-mail: deborah.malamud@nyu.edu.

MALAMUTH, NEIL MOSHE, psychology and communication educator; BA in Psychology summa cum laude, UCLA, 1972, MA in Psychology, 1972, PhD in Social Psychology and Personality, 1975. Lectr. dept. psychology, UCLA and postdoctoral fellow Ctr. for Behavioral Therapy, Beverly Hills, Calif., 1975-77; asst. prof. psychology U. Man., Winnipeg, Can., 1977-80, assoc. prof., 1980-82; prof. comm. and psychology, chairperson dept. comm. U. Mich., Ann Arbor, 1991-94; tchg. asst. dept. psychology UCLA, 1971-73, rsch. assoc. Ctr. for Computer-Based Behavioral Studies, 1973-75, assoc. prof., 1982-86, assoc. dir. Ctr. for Study of Women, 1986-87, prof. comm. and psychology, 1982-91, 94—, chairperson comm. studies program and speech dept., 1984-91, 94—. Vis. scholar Stanford (Calif.) U., fall 1988; mem. rev. com. on violence and stress NIMH, 1989-93; Lady Davis sr. fellow Hebrew U. Jerusalem, spring 1995; participant leadership inst. Freedom Forum, Columbia U., summer 1992; participant workshop for deans and chairpersons Annenberg Programs, Washington, winter 1993; presenter various profl. and ednl. confs., most recently Oakland (Mich.) U., 1994, Nat. Assn. for Devel. of Work with Sex Offenders, Durham (Eng.) U., 1994, Soc. for Sci. Study of Sex., Miami, Fla., 1994, Ctr. for Study of Evolution and Origins of Life, UCLA, 1994, Ctr. for Evolutionary Psychology, Santa Barbara, Calif., 1995, Tel Aviv U., 1995, Bar-Ilan U., Israel, 1995, Hebrew U. Jerusalem, 1995, NRC, Washington, 1995, Soc. Exptl. Social Psychology, Washington, 1995, Nat. Assn. for Treatment of Sexual Aggression, New Orleans, 1995, Polish Nat. Acad. Sci., Warsaw U., 1995. Co-author: An Instructor's Manual and Guide for Teaching a Course in Social Psychology, 1976, Pornography, 1993; co-editor Sites and Insights in Psychology, 1976; co-editor, contbr. chpt. to: Pornography and Sexual Aggression, 1984, Sex, Power, Conflict: Evolutionary Feminist Perspectives, 1996; contbr. chpt. to: Aggression in Children and Youth, 1984, Handbook of Research on Rape and Sexual Assault, 1984, Media Violence and Pornography: An International Perspective, 1984, The psychology of Women: Ongoing Debates, 1987, Public Communication and Behavior, Vol. 2, 1989; contbr. or co-contbr. various chpts., also numerous articles; mem. editl. bd. Motivation and Emotion, 1983-89, Comm. Rsch., 1986-92, Jour. Sex Rsch., 1982-99, Sexual Abuse: A Jour. and Treatment, 1995-99; assoc. editor Comm. Concepts Series, 1989-98, Jour. Rsch. in Personality, 1990-93; co-editor issue Jour. Social Issues, 1986. Recipient John Kendall award for Outstanding Contbns. to Psychology, Gustavus Coll., Minn., 1987; rsch. grantee Social Sci. and Humanities Rsch. Coun. Can., 1979-81, NIMH, 1986-89, 89-91, 91-92; named one of 7 scholars among top 100 rschrs. in 4 categories of eminence Personality and Social Psychology Bull., 1992. Fellow APA, Am. Psychol. Soc.; mem. Internat. Comm. Assn. (presenter 1994, Top 5 Conf. Paper award mass comm. divsn. 1987), Internat. Soc. for Rsch. on Aggression, Soc. for Psychol. Study of Social Issues, Soc. for Sci. Study of Sex, Phi Beta Kappa. Office: UCLA Comm Studies Program 334 Kinsey Hall Los Angeles CA 90095-0001

MALAN, CHRIS J., lawyer; b. 1955; m. Laurie Jensen; 4 children. BA cum laude, Weber State Coll., 1980; JD, Univ. Idaho, 1982. Bar: 1983. Assoc. Campbell & Neeley, 1983—86, Fowler & Purser, 1986—87; corp. counsel Flying J Inc., 1987—90; gen. counsel, sec. JB's Restaurants, 1990—92; v.p., gen. counsel, sec., mgr. of lands Flying J Oil & Gas Inc., 1992—. Editor (rsch.): Idaho Law Rev., 1982. Trustee Weber State Univ., 2003—; bd. dir. Weber State Univ. Alumni Assn., 2001—, v.p., 2002—03, pres., 2003—04. Mem.: Utah State Bar (chmn. corp. counsel sect. 1993—94), Montana Petroleum Assn. (bd. dir. 1997—2003, v.p. 2000—01), Utah Assn. Profl. Landmen, Utah Petroleum Assn., Rocky Mountain Mineral Law Found., Am. Inn of Ct. II (charter mem. & barrister 1985). Office: Flying J Oil & Gas 333 W Center St North Salt Lake UT 84054 Office Phone: 801-624-1000.

MALANDRINO, CATHERINE, apparel designer; b. Grenable, France; m. Bernard Aiden. Grad., Esmond. With Dorothee Biss, Louis Feraud, Emanuel Ungaro, Et Vous; head designer Diane Von Furstenberg, NYC, 1998; founder, chief designer Catherine Malandrino brand, 1998—. Named to 500 People Who Most Impact the Hamptons list, Hamptons Mag., 2007. Achievements include designing famous Am. flag dress exhibited at Zandra Rhodes' Fashion and Textile Mus., London, 2003; opening boutiques all over the country and worldwide, including Paris and Tokyo. Office: Aidan Industries Inc 275 W 39th St Fl 3 New York NY 10018-3195 *

MALANEY, STEPHANIE J., reading specialist; b. Lafayette, Ind., Feb. 7, 1949; d. George Walter Joseph and Audrey (Fisher) Schneider; m. Michael J. Malaney; children: Amanda Lynn, Kyle Patrick, Ryan Elliot. BS Elem. Edn., U. Wis., Oshkosh, 1990, MS Elem. Edn., 1992; MSE Reading, U.Wis., Oshkosh, 1997; MS Ednl. Adminstrn., U.Wis., Madison, 2004. Tchr. grades 1-3 Appleton Area Sch. Dist., Wis., 1990—92, instrnl. lead tchr. and dist. leader social studies program, 1992—95, tchr. 6th grade, 1995—98, reading specialist, 1998—. Docent Ontagami Hist. Soc. Grignon Mansion, Appleton, 2002—, Hearthstone (Hist. Site), Appleton, 2005—. Mem.: NEA, AAUW (pres. Appleton chpt. 2004—06, state nominating com.), Wis. Edn. Assn. (bd. dirs., mem. budget/fin. com.), Mid East Reading Coun. (pres. 2004—06). Avocations: reading, gardening, walking, travel, history research. Home: 307 E McArthur St Appleton WI 54911 Office: Appleton Area Sch Dist 2505 W Capitol Dr Appleton WI 54914 Office Phone: 920-832-4608. Office Fax: 920-993-7078. Business E-Mail: malaneystephan@aasd.k12.wi.us.

MALANGA, GERARD ANTHONY, sports medicine physician, director; b. Montclair, NJ, Feb. 24, 1961; s. Lorenzo and Antoinette Malanga; m. Carrie Helen Rowe, May 6, 1989; children: Tara, Grace, Luke, John. BA in Biology cum laude, Villanova U., Pa., 1983; MD, U. Medicine and Dentistry NJ, Newark, 1987. Resident U. Medicine and Dentistry NJ, 1989—92; fellow in sports medicine Mayo Clinic, Rochester, Minn., 1992—93, sr. assoc. cons., 1993—96; dir. sports, spine and orthop. rsch. Kessler Inst. Rehab., West Orange, NJ, 1996—2004; dir. pain mgmt. Overlook Hosp., Summit, NJ, 2005—; dir. sports medicine Mountaineer Hosp., Montclair, NJ, 2005—; dir. NJ Sports Medicine Inst., Verona, 2005—. Assoc. prof. phys. medicine and rehab. U. Medicine and Dentistry NJ/NJ Med. Sch., 2003—; Rhala A. Helm MD disting. lectr. U. Tex., SW Med. Ctr., 2005. Editor: Whiplash, 2002, Musculoskeletal Physical Exam, 2005. Named Tchr. of Yr., Mayo Clinic, 1995; named one of Top Drs. in NY Metro Area, 2003—05, Best Drs. in Am., 2003—06; recipient Dean Charles Brown award, NJ Med. Sch., 1987. Fellow: Am. Coll. Sports Medicine, Am. Acad. Physicians Rehab.; mem.: N.Am. Spine Soc. (chmn. patient edn. com. 1996—), Physicians Assn. Sport, Spine and Occupl. Rehab. (disting.), Alpha Omega Alpha. Avocations: basketball, reading. Office: NJ Sports Medicine Inst 799 Bloomfield Ave Ste 304 Verona NJ 07044 Office Phone: 973-571-0001. E-mail: gmalanga@armnji.net.

MALANGONI, MARK ALAN, surgeon, educator; b. East Chicago, Ind., Nov. 3, 1949; s. Roland G. and Cornelia (Marza) M.; m. Nancy Knapp, Aug. 12, 1972; children: Joseph, Michael, Jonathan. AB in Zoology cum laude, Ind. U., 1971, MD, 1975. MD; diplomate Am. Bd. Surgery. Asst. prof. surgery Med. Coll. Wis., Milw., 1980-84, assoc. program dir., gen. surgery, 1981-84; assoc. prof. Surgery U. Louisville, 1984-90, chief surgery Humana Hosp., 1985-90; prof. surgery Case Western Res. U., Cleve., 1990—. Chmn. dept. surgery MetroHealth Med. Ctr., Cleve., 1990—. Merit Rev. grantee VA, Louisville, 1985-88. Fellow Am. Coll. Surgeons; mem. Cen. Surg. Assn., So. Surg. Assn., Am. Surg. Assn., Phi Beta Kappa, Alpha Omega Alpha. Office: MetroHealth Med Ctr 2500 Metrohealth Dr # 914 Cleveland OH 44109-1998 Office Phone: 216-778-4558.

MALANI, ASHOK K., physician; b. Jadcharla, India, Dec. 17, 1969; s. Jugal K. and Kamala Malani; m. Hemalata Malani, Feb. 1, 1972; children: Khushi, Gyan. MBBS, Osmania Med. Coll., 1992; MS in Gen. Surgery, Postgraduate Inst. Med. Edn. and Rsch., 1996; MD in Internal Medicine, 2003. Jr. resident in gen. surgery Postgraduate Inst. Med. Edn. and Rsch., Chandigarh, India, 1993—96, sr. resident in surgery, 1996; sr. resident in surg. oncology Nizams Inst. Med. Scis., Hyderabad, India, 1996—97; resident in surgery and oncology Leighton Hosp., Crewe, England, 1998; resident in breast and surg. oncology Royal Free Hosp., London, 1998—2000; resident in internal medicine Coney Island Hosp., Bklyn., 2000—03, alt. del., com. interns and residents, 2001—03, mem. grad. med. edn. com., 2003, mem. quality control exec. com., 2003; attending physician, internal medicine St. Mary Hosp., Kankakee, Ill., 2003—05, mem. continuing med. edn., libr. and cancer com., 2004; attending physician, internal medicine Riverside Med. Ctr., Kankakee, 2003—05; pvt. practice Momence, Ill., 2003—05; hospitalist in hematology, oncology Heartlands Regional Med. Ctr., St. Joseph, Mo., 2005—. Hematology com. mem. US Oncology, Dallas, 2005—, US Oncology Rsch., Houston, 2005—. Contbr. scientific papers, abstracts, publs. in field. Com. mem. Coney Island Hosp., Bklyn., 2000—03, edn. com., quality control com., alt. del. com. of interns and residents New York, NY, 2001—03. Master: Post Grad. Inst. (life); fellow: Royal Coll. Surgeons, Royal Coll. Physicians and Surgeons of Glasgow (life); mem.: AMA (assoc.), ACP (assoc.). Office: St Joseph Oncology Inc 902 N Riverside Rd Saint Joseph MO 64507 Home Phone: 816-364-2906. Personal E-mail: drmalani@yahoo.com.

MALARO, MARIE C., retired museum administrator, lawyer; b. Jan. 1933; BA, Regis Coll., 1954; LLB, Boston Coll., 1957. Legal counsel Smithsonian Inst., Washington; prof. mus. studies George Washington U., Washington, dir. Grad. Prog. in Mus. Studies, prof. emeritus, 1997—. Bd. mem. Hospice of Queen Anne's, patient volunteer; bd. mem. Mus. Eastern Shore Life, Hist. Soc. Queen Anne's County. Named to Centennial Honor Roll, Am. Assn. Museums, 2006. E-mail: mmalaro@gwu.edu. *

MALATESTA, MARY ANNE, lawyer; b. Wapakoneta, Ohio, Aug. 7, 1954; d. Leo J. Jr. and Ellen E. Malatesta. BA in English, Ohio State U., 1976; JD, U. Colo., 1979. Bar: Colo. 1979, U.S. Dist. Ct. Colo. 1979, U.S. Ct. Appeals (9th cir.) 1989, U.S. Appeals (10th cir.) 1990, U.S. Dist. Ct. Ariz. 1992. Dep. dist. atty. 1st Jud. Dist., Golden, Colo., 1979-84; assoc. Tilly & Graves, P.C., Denver, 1985-88, shareholder, 1988-93; asst. atty. gen. Office Atty. Gen. State of Colo., Denver, 1994—. Mem. faculty Nat. Inst. Trial Advocacy, South Bend, Ind., 1989-90, asst. team leader, 1990-93, team leader, 1994—; lectr. U. Denver, 1990, 91, 97—; guest faculty U. Colo., 1992—; organizer Victims of Violence seminar; mem. faculty Am. Bd. Trial Advocates seminar, 1992, Domestic Violence Prosecution Tng. Course, 1994, Child Advocates Tng. Course, 1996; master Am. Inns of Ct. Judge William E. Doyle Inn, 1994—, Women's Leadership Forum, 1996-2000. Founder, mem. Facio ut Des, Denver, 1987-94. Mem. Colo. Bar Assn., Denver Bar Assn. (professionalism com. 1990—, co-chair professionalism com. 1994-99, professionalism conciliation panel mem. 1999—), Colo. Women's Bar Assn. Avocations: hiking, horseback riding, spectator sports.

MALAYERY, NASRIN, educational consultant; b. Tehran, Iran, Jan. 27, 1943; U.S. citizen, 1990; d. Mahmoud Malayery and Ghamar Narjis Kia. BA with spl. honors in history, George Washington U., 1964; EdM in Edn. and Social Studies, Boston U., 1967, EdM in Media and Tech., 1977, EdD in Media Tech., 1986. Editor in-house mgmt. jour. Oil Consortium, Employee Comm., Tehran, 1970-74; mgr. documents and publs. Iran-UNESCO Adult Literacy Program, Tehran, 1974-76; instr., instrnl. designer Shiraz (Iran) U. Med. Sch., 1977-81; ednl. cons. WHO Eastern Mediterranean Regional Orgn., Alexandria, Egypt, 1981-87; sr. ednl. cons. Compaq Computer Corp., Littleton, Mass., 1987—. Mem. Internat. Soc. for Performance Improvement, Nat. Mus. of Women in the Arts (assoc.), Libr. of Congress Assocs., Phi Beta Kappa. Avocations: writing, reading, gardening, ballet, yoga. Home: 2228 Dominion Dr Fort Mitchell KY 41017-2017

MALBON, CRAIG CURTIS, pharmacology educator, dean; b. Providence, June 1, 1950; s. Elroy Willis and Edith Roberta (Curtis) M.; children: Lindsey Gei Sook, Hailey Sook Yee; m. Hsien-yu Wang, June 26, 1993. BA, Mass. State Coll., Worcester, 1972; PhD, Case Western Reserve U., 1976. NIH postdoctoral fellow sect. physiological chemistry Brown U., Providence, 1976-77, research assoc. sect. physiological chemistry, 1977, asst. prof. research sect. physiological chemistry, 1978; asst. prof. dept. pharmacology SUNY Sch. Medicine, Stony Brook, 1978-83, assoc. prof., 1983-90, prof., 1990—; leading univ. prof. Sch. Medicine SUNY, Stony Brook, 1993—, vice chmn. dept. pharmacology, 1988-89, prof. dept. pharmacology Stony Brook, 1990—, assoc. dean biomed. scis. Sch. Medicine, 1989-93, v.p. rsch., 1993-97; vice dean Univ. Hosp. and Med. Ctr. SUNY, Stony Brook, 1993—2005. Bd. dir. diabetes & metabolic diseases rsch. program NIH, Stony Brook, NY, mem. cell biology & physiology study sect., Bethesda, Md., 1981—86; bd. dir. LI High Tech. Incubator; mem. sci. adv. bd. Brookhaven Nat. Lab. DOE, 1998—2005. Mem. editl. bd. Am. Jour. Physiology, 1985—, assoc. editor, 1993-99; mem. editl. bd. Jour. Biol. Chemistry, 1988-93; contbr. articles to profl. jours. Mem. Marine Biol. Lab., Inc., Woods Hole, Mass., 1986; bd. dirs. Faculty/Student Assn., Inc., Stony Brook, 1979-82. Recipient nat. rsch. Svc. award NIH, 1976-80, career devel. award, 1981-86; rsch. award Am. Cancer Soc., 1998. Mem. Biophys. Soc., N.Y. Acad. Scis., Am. Physiol. Soc. (editl. bd. 1986, assoc. editor 1990), Am. Soc. for Biochemistry and Molecular Biology (editl. bd. 1988), Biochem. Soc. (U.K.) (hon.), Sigma Xi. Home: PO Box 2726 East Setauket NY 11733-0852 E-mail: craig@pharm.sunysb.edu.

MALCOLM, EDITH, elementary school educator; b. Dec. 14, 1952; BA, Nova Southea. U., Ft. Lauderdale, Fla.; tchg. cert., Sam Sharpe Tchrs. Coll., Jamaica, WI. Elem. tchr. St. Lucie Sch. Bd., Port St. Lucie, Fla.; adj. tchr. IRCC, Ft. Pierce, Fla. Named Tchr. of Week, Palm Beach Post, 1999, Ida Baker Outstanding Minority Tchr., Palm Beach, 2000. Mem.: Fla. Edn. Assn., Internat. Reading Assn., Nat. Coun. Tchrs. English. Home: 673 SW Sail Ter Port Saint Lucie FL 34953

MALCOLM, GLORIA J., small business owner; b. Atlanta, Apr. 16, 1956; d. George and Norella Camp; m. Ericka Monique Malcolm. B in Bus. Mgmt., DeKalb Coll., Atlanta; PhD in Edn. Leadership, Nova Southeastern U. Cert. notary pub. Team leader MS Soc., Atlanta; cons., advisor Home Testing Inst., NYCq; rep., organizer Nielsen TV, Dunedin, Fla.; mem. Alliance Orgn., Memphis; assoc., advisor Joyner Hutcheson Rsch., Atlanta; owner, pres. GJM Profl. Cleaning Svc., Inc., Union City, Ga., College Park, Ga., 1988—2004; floor supr., U-scan coord. Kroger Co., Atlanta, 2005—. Bd. dirs. Atlanta FCU. Active United Food Comml. Unions, Home Inst., MS Walk Soc., Am. Stroke Assn.; mem. ARC, Nat. Geog. Soc.; mem. svcs. Mt. Carmel Bapt. Ch., Atlanta; bd. dirs. St. Matthew's Ch. Mem.: NAFE, Bldg. Trader Assn., United Negro Coll. Assns., Rep. Senate Leadership, Am. Stroke Assn., Piedmont Conservancy Com., Nat. Home Garden Club. Avocations: travel, reading, volleyball, tennis, bicycling. Office: GJM Profl Cleaning Svcs Inc 2171 Red Oak Cir Union City GA 30291

MALCOLM, MARK, automotive executive; m. Patty Malcolm; 2 children. Grad., Dartmouth Coll.; MBA, U. of Chgo., 1977. Mgmt. positions through dir. worldwide acctg., Visteon CFO, & head vehicle ops. fin. Ford Motor Co., dir. fin. & strategy global purchasing, 2002—04; exec. v.p., contr. Ford Motor Credit, 2004—06; lead automotive analyst Cerberus Capital mgmt., 2006—07; pres., CEO Tower Automotive, Novi, Mich., 2007—. Office: Tower Automotive 27175 Hagerty Rd Novi MI 48377 *

MALCOLM, STEVEN J., petroleum pipeline company executive; b. St. Louis, Sept. 1948; m. Gwen Malcolm; 1 child. BCE, U. Mo.-Rolla, 1970; attended, Northwestern U. With Cities Gas Co.; dir., bus. develop. Williams Nat. Gas Co., 1984—86, dir. gas mgmt., 1986—89; v.p., gas mgmt. & supply Williams Field Svcs. Co., 1989—93, sr. v.p., gen. mgr., 1994—98; pres., CEO Williams Energy Svcs. LLC, 1998—2001; pres., COO Williams Companies, Tulsa, Okla., 2001—02, chmn., pres., CEO, 2002—. Bd. mem. Tulsa Area United Way, Tulsa Community Found., Tulsa Metro Chamber, St. John Medical Ctr.; bd. of trustees U. Tulsa. Mem.: Nat. Energy Svc. Assn., Gas Processors Assn. Office: Williams 1 Williams Ctr Tulsa OK 74172 *

MALDACENA, JUAN MARTIN, physicist, researcher; b. Buenos Aires, Sept. 10, 1968; married; 2 children. Student, U. Buenos Aires, 1985—88, Inst. Balseiro, U. Cuyo, Bariloche, Argentina, 1988—91; PhD program, Princeton U., 1992—96. Rsch. assoc. Rutgers U., 1996—97; vis. assoc. prof. Harvard U., 1997, Tomas D. Cabot assoc. prof., 1998—99, prof. physics, 1999—2001; prof. natural sci. Inst. for Advanced Study, Princeton, NJ, 2001—. Contbr. artilces to profl. jours. Named a Disting. Lectr., Stanford U., 2004; recipient UNESCO Husein prize for Young Scientists, 1999, Sackler prize in Physics, 2000, Xanthopoulas prize in general relativity, 2001, Pius XI medal, 2002, Edward A. Bouchet award, Am. Phys. Soc., 2004, Dannie Heineman Prize for Math. Physics, 2007; Sloan Fellowship, 1998, Packard Fellowship in Sci. and Engring., 1998, MacArthur Fellowship, 1999. Fellow: Am. Acad. Arts & Scis. Office: Inst for Advanced Study Sch Natural Sciences 1 Einstein Dr Princeton NJ 08540 Office Phone: 609-734-8307. Office Fax: 609-951-4489. E-mail: malda@ias.edu. *

MALDE, HAROLD EDWIN, retired federal government geologist; b. Reedsport, Oreg., July 9, 1923; s. Emil and Bessie May (Alspaugh) M.; m. Caroline Elizabeth Rose, Dec. 21, 1954; children: Margaret Jean, Melissa Ruth. AB, Willamette U., 1947; postgrad., Harvard U., 1947-48, U. Colo., 1948-51. Geologist U.S. Geol. Survey, Denver, 1951-87; affiliate prof. U. Idaho, 1968—76, 1987—91. Mem. Colo. com. for Nat. Register Hist. Places, 1972-80; vol. photographer Nature Conservancy, 1987—2007; mem. paleoanthropology del. to Peoples Republic China, Nat. Acad. Scis., 1975, mem. various coms. for study surface mining, 1973-79; mem. oil shale environ. adv. panel US Dept. Interior, 1976-80; seasonal geologic studies Valsequillo Archeol. Nat. Sci. Found. Harvard U., Puebla, Mex., 1964-73, 2004. Contbr. numerous sci. papers to profl. lit. Served to ensign USNR, 1942-44. Recipient Meritorious Service award U.S. Dept. Interior, 1979, Oak Leaf award Nature Conservancy, 1993. Fellow Geol. Soc. Am. (Kirk Bryan award 1970, assoc. editor 1982-88), AAAS, Ariz.-Nev. Acad. Sci., Explorers Club; mem. Am. Quaternary Assn., Assn. Earth Sci. Editors. Democrat. Unitarian Universalist. Home: 842 Grant Pl Boulder CO 80302-7415 E-mail: halmalde@msn.com.

MALDEN, KARL (MLADEN SEKULOVICH), actor; b. Chgo., Mar. 22, 1912; s. Peter and Minnie (Sebera) Sekulovich; m. Mona Graham, Dec. 18, 1938; children— Mila, Carla. Student, Goodman Theatre, Chgo., 1935-38. Pres. Acad. of Motion Arts and Scis., 1989-92; mem. Citizens Stamp Com., U.S. Govt., Washington. Actor, 1935—; stage plays include Golden Boy, 1938, Gentle People, 1939, Key Largo, 1940, Flight to the West, 1942, Uncle Harry, 1940, All My Sons, 1949, A Streetcar Named Desire, 1950, Desire Under the Elms, 1952, Desperate Hours, 1954; in motion pictures, 1940—, films include: Boomerang, Gunfighter, 1945, Halls of Montezuma, 1950, A Streetcar Named Desire (Acad. award for best supporting actor, Oscar award, 1951), 1951, Ruby Gentry, 1952, I Confess, 1953, On the Waterfront, 1954, Baby Doll, 1956, Desperate Hours, 1957, Fear Strikes Out, 1957, The Hanging Tree, 1959, Pollyanna, 1960, One Eyed Jacks, 1961, Parrish, The Adventures of Bullwhip Griffin, 1967, Patton, 1970, Beyond the Poseidon Affair, 1978, Meteor, 1979, Sting II, 1982, Twilight Time, 1982, Billy Galvin, 1987, Nuts, 1987; TV films include: Word of Honor, 1981, Miracle on Ice, 1981, Intent to Kill, 1983, Fatal Vision, 1984 (Emmy award), My Father My Son, 1988, The Hijacking of the Achille Lauro, 1989, Call Me Anna, 1990, Absolute Strangers, 1991, Back to the Streets of San Francisco, 1992; dir.: Time Limit, 1957, Billion Dollar Brain, 1967, Hot Millions, 1968, Hotel, Cat O'Nine Tails, 1971, Wild Rovers, 1971, Summertime Killer, 1973, Nuts, 1987; star TV series Streets of San Francisco, 1972-77, Skag, 1980. Recipient Donaldson award, 1950, Critic's award, 1950, Lifetime Achievement Award, Screen Actors Guild, 2003; Barrington Station post office in L.A. renamed in his honor, 2005. Address: 1845 Mandeville Canyon Rd Los Angeles CA 90049-2222

MALDONADO, FRANCISCO JAVIER, electrical research engineer; s. Sostenes Maldonado and Maria Díaz; m. Norma Angelica Portillo, Dec. 17, 1990; children: Mayra Lizeth, Frida Katherine, Samantha Melissa. B in Indsl. Engring. in Electronics, Inst. Tecnológico de Veracruz, Mexico, 1981—85; MSEE, Chihuahua Inst. Tech., Mexico, 1988; DEng, U. Tex. at Arlington, 2002. Rschr. Xomox S.A. de C.V., Chihuahua, 1987—88; tech. support engr. Zenith Data Systems, Chihuahua, 1988—90; rsch. prof. Chihuahua Inst. Tech., 1988—2001, 2003—05; rsch. asst. Automation and Robotics Rsch. Inst. at the UTA, Fort Worth, Tex., 1998—99, Image Processing and Neural Networks Lab., Arlington, 2000—01; elec. engr. Williams-Pyro, Inc., Fort Worth, 2001—02, elec. rsch. engr., 1995—. Reviewer neurocomputing jour. Elsevier, 2005; part-time prof. U. Autonoma de Chihuahua, 2005. Several grants for devel. of monitoring systems and control (Mex.), COSNET. Mem.: IEEE. Achievements include research in the development of pruning algorithm for designing MLP based upon a modified version of the Schmidt procedure. This pruning method was used for proposing two pseudogenetic algorithms; development of the principal investigator and collaborator in several SBIR projects (program of Small Business Research Innovations) developing hardware design in wireless applications and embedding neural networks; harware development and software simulation of industrial and mobile robots. Office: Williams-Pyro Inc 200 Greenleaf St Fort Worth TX 76107 Home Phone: 817-303-3147; Office Phone: 817-872-1500 ext. 129. Personal E-mail: frankmald@hotmail.com.

MALDONADO, KIRK FRANCIS, lawyer; b. Omaha, Mar. 7, 1950; s. Manuel and Orpha Mae (Kovar) Maldonado. BA, U. Nebr.-Omaha, 1975; JD, Creighton U., 1978; MLT, Georgetown U., 1981. Bar: Nebr. 1978, Calif. 1982. Atty. Employee Plans and Exempt Orgns. Divsn. Office of Chief Counsel IRS, Washington, 1978—81; assoc. Gibson, Dunn & Crutcher, Newport Beach, Calif., 1982—85; prin. Stradling, Yocca, Carlson & Rauth, Newport Beach, 1985—89, Riordan & McKinzie, Costa Mesa, Calif., 1989—2001; ptnr. Bobeck Phleger & Harrison LLP, 2001—03; mem. Sherman & Howard, LLC, Denver, 2003—. Contbr. articles to profl. jours. Mem.: ABA (employee benfits com.), State Bar Calif. Office: Sherman & Howard LLC 633 17th St Ste 3000 Denver CO 80202 E-mail: kmaldonado@sah.com.

MALDONADO-BEAR, RITA MARINITA, economist, educator; b. Vega Alta, PR, June 14, 1938; d. Victor and Marina (Davila) Maldonado; m. Larry Alan Bear, Mar. 29, 1975. BA, Auburn U., 1960; PhD, NYU, 1969. With Min. Wage Bd. & Econ. Devel. Adminstr., Govt. of P.R., 1969-70; asst. prof. econs. Manhattan Coll., 1970-72; assoc. prof. econs. Bklyn. Coll., 1972-75; assoc. prof. fin. & econs., undergrad./grad. divsn. Stern Sch. Bus. NYU, 1975-81, prof., 1981—2004, prof. emerita, 2004—. Vis. assoc. prof. fin. Stanford (Calif.) Grad. Bus. Sch., 1973-74; acting dir. markets, ethics & law, NYU, 1993-94; cons. Morgan Guaranty Trust Co., N.Y.C., 1972-77, Bank of Am., N.Y.C., 1982-84, Res. City Bankers, N.Y.C., 1978-87, Swedish Inst. Mgmt., Stockholm, 1982-91, Empresas Master of P.R., 1985-90. Author: Role of the Financial Sector in the Economic Development of Puerto Rico, 1970; co-author: Free Markets, Finance, Ethics and Law, 1994, Financing Economic Development in the Economy of Puerto Rico: Restoring Growth, 2006; contbr. chpts. to books including The Economy of Puerto Rico: Restoring Growth, 2006; contbr. articles to profl. jours. Bd. dirs. Medallion Funding Corp., 1985-87; mem. NYU Senate and Faculty Coun., 1995-2003, chair fin. com., 1996-2000; apptd. adv. bd. dirs. equity & diversity in ednl. environs. Mid. States Commn. Higher Edn., 1991—; trustee Securities Industry Assn., N.Y. Dist. Econ. Edn. Found., 1994—; chair NSF, Nat. Vis. Com. Curriculum Devel. Project Networked Fin. Simulation, 1995—; econ. cons. Inst. Women of Color, Nat. Coun. Black Women Cmty. Svcs. Fund, 2000—; trustee Bd. Edn., Twp. Mahwah, N.J., 1991-92. P.R. Econ. Devel. Adminstrn. fellow, 1960-65, Marcus Nadler fellow, NYU, 1966-67, Phillips Lods Dissertation fellow, 1967-68. Mem. Am. Econs. Assn., Am. Fin. Assn., Metro. Econ. Assn. N.Y., Assn. Social Econs. (trustee exec. coun. 1994-96). Home: 95 Tam O Shanter Dr Mahwah NJ 07430-1526 Office: Mgmt Edn Ctr 44 W 4th St Ste 9-190 New York NY 10012-1106 Business E-Mail: rmaldona@stern.nyu.edu, rmaldona@stern-nyu.edu.

MALDONADO-CLASS, JOAQUIN, language educator; b. Manati, PR, Nov. 15, 1959; s. Juan Maldonado-Rodriguez and Albina Class-Santiago; m. Katherine Velez-Andujar, June 30, 1990; 1 child, Sebastian Gioachino Maldonado-Velez. BA, Universidad Central de Bayamon, PR, 1982, MA, 1993; PhD summa cum laude, U. PR, Rio Piedras, 2004. Cert. Spanish tchr. PR. Spanish tchr. Escuela Superior Catolica, Bayamon, 1986—89, Escuela Angel Sandin Martinez, Vega Baja, PR, 1989—93, Escuela Emilio R. Delgado, Corozal, PR, 1993—2000; assoc. prof. Spanish Truman State U., Kirksville, Mo., 2000—. Spanish instr. Universidad Interamericana, Bayamon, 1998—2000; texts author Editorial Norma, Catano, PR, 1998—2001. Author: (textbook) Sueños y Palabras 7, 2000, Sueños y Palabras 12, 2002. Tutor Casa Hogar Sagrados Corazones, Bayamon, 1985—86; missionary Fathers of Holy Spirit, French Guyana, 1984—85; co-dir. Servidores de Jesus, Vega Baja, PR, 1987—2000. Rsch. grantee, U. PR, 1999—2000. Mem.: L.Am. Studies Assn. Roman Catholic. Office: Truman State U 100 E Normal Kirksville MO 63501 Office Phone: 660-785-4500. Business E-Mail: jmaldona@truman.edu.

MALDONADO-MENDOZA, IGNACIO EDUARDO, molecular biologist, researcher; b. Merida, Yucatan, Mexico, July 31, 1966; s. Higinio Maldonado-Alcocer and Edith Esther Mendoza-Oliveros; m. Melina Lopez-Meyer, Aug. 14, 1992; children: Daniel Maldonado-Lopez, Rebeca Maldonado-Lopez. BSc in Chemistry, Autonomous U. of Yucatan, Merida, 1988; MSc, CICY, Merida, 1992; PhD, Tex. A&M U., 1996. Postdoctoral fellow Samuel Roberts Noble Found., Ardmore, Okla., 1997—99; prof. CIIDIR-IPN Sinaloa Unit, Guasave, Sinaloa, Mexico, 2000—03, assoc. head, 2000—03; postdoctoral assoc. Boyce Thompson Inst. for Plant Rsch., Ithaca, NY, 2003—. Supernumerary prof. Universidad de Occidente, Guasave, 2001—03; assoc. prof. CICY, Merida, 1992; plant biotechnology cons. Nat. Coun. for Sci. and Tech. CONACyT-Mexico, Guasave, 2001—03. Contbr. articles to profl. publs., chpts. to books. Recipient Candidate to Rschr. award, Nat. Sys. of Researchers, Mexico, 1992—96, award, 2001—; fellow, Nat. Coun. of Sci. and Tech. (CONACyT-Mexico), 1989—92, Biotechnology Short-Term Fellowship, UNESCO, 1991, Nat. Coun. for Sci. and Tech., CONACyT, Mexico, 1992—96; grantee, Nat. Poly. Inst., 2000—03, Unesco, Mexico, 2001—02, State Coun. for Sci. and Tech. CECyT-Sinaloa, Mexico, 2001—03; Repatriation fellow, Nat. Coun. for Sci. and Tech., CONACyT, Mexico, 2000. Mem.: AAAS (corr.), ASPB (corr.), Phi Kappa Phi. Roman Catholic. Achievements include first to molecular detail a fungal gene (phosphate transporter from arbuscular mycorrhiza) in an in vitro system. Avocations: reading, travel, movies, world music, volleyball. Office: Boyce Thompson InstPlant Research Tower Rd Ithaca NY 14853-1801 Home Phone: 011 52 687 8720612. Personal E-mail: ignacioemaldonado@yahoo.com.mx. E-mail: iem3@cornell.edu.

MALE, ALAN THOMAS, engineering educator, foundation administrator; b. Birmingham, Eng., Sept. 3, 1937; came to U.S., 1968; s. Albert Leslie and Olive (Caddel) M.; m. Beryl Glover, Sept. 20, 1958; children: Andrew James, Christopher John. BSc, U. Birmingham, 1958, PhD, 1962. Registered profl. engr. Pa., Ky.; chartered engr. U.K. Lectr. U. Birmingham, 1960-67; supr. Westinghouse Astronuclear Lab., Pitts., 1968-70; from mgr. metals processing to mgr. processing rsch. Westinghouse Rsch. Labs., Pitts., 1970-83; mgr. advanced processing Westinghouse Sci. & Tech. Ctr., Pitts., 1990-91; prin., tech. mgr. Concurrent Techs. Corp., Johnstown, Pa., 1992-96; dir. Ctr. for Robotics and Mfg. Systems U. Ky., assoc. dean rsch. and grad. studies College of Engring., 1996—2002, prof. mech. engring., 1996—. Pres. Anvil Techs. LLC, Lexington, Ky., 2003—. Holder 16 patents in field. Fellow Inst. Materials (award 1977), Soc. Mfg. Engrs. (life, internat. dir. 1991-99, pres. N.Am. mfg. rsch. inst. 1988-89, Frederick W. Taylor Rsch. medal 1989, internat. pres. 1997-98), ASM Internat. (life); mem. ASME, Am. Welding Soc. Republican. Methodist. Avocations: freemasonry, carpentry, fishing. Home: 3390 Mantilla Dr Lexington KY 40513-1039 Office Phone: 859-257-6262. Business E-Mail: atmale@engr.uky.edu.

MALE, AYN ROCHELLE, psychologist, researcher; b. NYC, June 7, 1947; d. Robert Senft and May Marcia Silver-Senft; m. Kenneth Ira Male, Sept. 1, 1947; children: Addie, Jessie. BA in Psychology, SUNY, Stone Brook, 1969; MS in Spl. Edn., Fordham U., NYC, 1973; PhD in Sch. Psychology, CUNY, Flushing, NY, 1991. Cert. mental health counselor NY. Tchr. NYC Bd. Edn., Bronx, 1969—78, spl. edn. tchr. Queens, 1979—90, sch. psychologist Flushing, 1991—2003; ret., 2003. Adj. instr. CCNY, NYC, part-time supr., SUNY, Geneseo. Mem.: Nat. Assn. Sch. Psychologists. Avocation: painting. Home: 67-38 199 St Fresh Meadows NY 11365

MALECHA, MARVIN JOHN, architect, academic administrator; b. Lonsdale, Minn., June 26, 1949; s. George and Barbara Malecha; m. Cynthia Marie Miller, Aug. 8, 1970; children: Peter, Michelle. Student, St. Thomas Coll.; BArch, U. Minn.; MArch, Harvard U. Registered architect, Calif. Designer Wallace and Mundt Architects, Edina, Minn., 1969-73, Hugh Stubbins and Assocs., Cambridge, Mass., 1973-76; instr. Cambridge Urban Awareness Program, 1973-76, Boston Archtl. Ctr., 1974-76; asst. chmn., asst. prof. dept. arch. Coll. Environ. Design Calif. State Poly. U., Pomona, 1976-77, chmn., assoc. prof., 1979-82, prof., dean Coll. Environ. Design, 1982-94; dean Coll. Design N.C. State U., 1994—. Chmn. Univ. Fall Conf. com. Calif. State Poly. U., 1984; mem. steering com. Architects for Social Responsibility; mem. bd. advisors Tchrs. cert. program City Bldg. Edn. Program, planning com. So. Calif. Assn. Govts.; vis. critic UCLA, 1985, U., Minn., 1981-83, 87, U. So. Calif., 1980-87, Calif. Poly. State U., San Luis Obispo, 1979-87, Clemson U., 1988, Columbia U., 1993, U. Tenn., 1994, U. Md., 1995, Miss. State U., 1995, U. Wis., Milw., 1996, Roger Williams U., 1997; lectr. to schs. and archtl. assns.; cons. in architecture and research, Claremont, Calif., 1976—; master juror Nat. Council Archtl. Registration Bds.; mem. edn. equity com. Calif. State U. System, 1985-86; pres. Calif. Coun. Archtl. Edn., 1986-88; mem. accreditation vis. team for collegiate programs in landscape architecture, 1988—; bd. dirs. Nat. Archtl. Accreditation Bd.; campus architect cons. U. Calif., Riverside, 1990-94. Author: Reconfiguration in the Study and Practice of Architecture, Form of Performance, The Fabric of Architecture, The Pomona Method; co-sgner, author internat. protocol for internat. exch. in arch. edn.; contbr. articles to profl. jours. Mem. Art and Liturgy com. Our Lady Assumption Ch., Claremont, Calif., 1982-94; mem. bldg. and real estate com. Archdiocese of Raleigh; bd. dirs. United Arts Raleigh, City Gallery Raleigh, 1995—; nat bd. dirs. Am. Inst. Architects; master juror workgroup, bd. dirs. Downtown Raleigh Alliance. Recipient Ellerbe Archtl. award, 1972, Hon. Mention Mass. Housing Dept., 1976, Topaz medallion for excellence in archtl. edn., 2003, Prize for Creative Integration of Practice and Edn. in the Acad., Nat. Coun. Archtl. Registration, 2002; Rotch scholar, 1980. Fellow AIA (bd. dirs. L.A. chpt. 1982-83, chmn. state and nat. awards coms. 1983-85, chmn. Monterey design conf. com., Henry Adams award 1973, mem. steering com. archs. in edn. com. 1991, chair archs. in edn. com. 1994-95, adv. bd. ArchVoices, presdl. citation L.A. chpt. 1987, mem. Calif. coun. 1994, nat. bd. dirs. 2005, Excellence in Arch. Edn. award), European Assn. for Arch. Educators (hon.), Soc. Am. Registered Archs., Assn. Collegiate Schs. Arch. (v.p. 1988-89, chair ann. meeting, pres. 1988-89, adminstrs. conf. Wash. 1985, Disting. Prof. 2002), Calif. Coun. Archtl. Edn. (pres. 1988-89), Golden Key (hon. mem. N.C. chpt.). Office: NC State U Coll Design PO Box 7701 Raleigh NC 27695-0001 Office Phone: 919-515-8300. E-mail: marvin_malecha@ncsu.edu.

MALEE, THOMAS, lawyer; BA, Carroll Coll., Helena, Mont., 1970; JD, U. Mont., 1975. Bar: Mont. 1975, US Dist. Ct. Mont. 1975, US Ct. Appeals (9th cir.) 1986, US Supreme Ct. 1988. Staff atty. State of Mont. Legis. Counsel, Helena, Mont., 1975-76; asst. atty. gen. State of Mont., Helena, 1976; pvt. practice Seattle, Tacoma area, Wash., 1977-78, Helena, 1979-82, Billings, Mont., 1982—. Internat. biathlon referee. Mem. State Bar of Mont. (ins. com. 1988—). Roman Catholic. Avocations: skiing, exercise. Office: 1109 N 22nd St Ste 103A Billings MT 59101-0253 Office Phone: 406-245-8304. E-mail: tmalee@usa.com.

MALEK, FREDERIC VINCENT, finance company executive; b. Oak Park, Ill., Dec. 22, 1936; s. Fred W. and Martha (Smickilas) M.; m. Marlene A. McArthur, Aug. 5, 1961; children: Fred W., Michelle A. BS, U.S. Mil. Acad., 1959; MBA, Harvard U., 1964; D of Humanities (hon.), St. Leo Coll., St. Petersburg, Fla., 1970. Assoc. McKinsey & Co., Inc., LA, 1964-67; chmn. exec. com. Triangle Corp., Columbia, SC, 1967-69; dep. under sec. HEW, Washington, 1969-70; spl. asst. to Pres. U.S., Washington, 1970-73; dep. dir. U.S. Office of Mgmt. and Budget, Washington, 1973-75; with Marriott Corp., Washington, 1975-88, sr. v.p., 1975-77, exec. v.p., 1978-88; pres. Marriott Hotels and Resorts, 1981-88, Northwest Airlines, Mpls., 1989-90, vice chmn., 1990-91, also bd. dirs.; campaign mgr. Bush-Quayle '92, 1991-92; co-chmn. CB Richard Ellis, 1989-96; chmn. Lodging Opportunities Fund, 1991—, Thayer Capital Ptnrs., 1992—, Thayer Hotel Investors, 1994—. Chmn. 1996 Rep. Presdl. Trust, 1995-96; bd. dirs. Automated Data Processing Corp., CB Richard Ellis; dir. with rank of amb., 1990 Econ. Summit, 1989—; adj. prof. U. S.C., 1986-89; lectr. Kennedy Sch. Govt., Harvard U., 1976 Mem. Pres.'s Commn. on White House Fellows, 1971-75, White House Domestic Coun., 1974-75, Pres.'s Commn. on Pers. Interchange, 1974-76; dep. dir. com. for Re-election of Pres., 1972; Pres.'s Commn. on Pvt. Sector Initiatives, 1982-85, dir. conv. Bush for Pres., 1988; mem. Nat. Coun. on Surface Transp. Rsch., 1993-95; nat. adv. bd. Nat. Ctr. Econ. Edn. of Children, 1980-82; mem. Pres.'s Coun. on Phys. Fitness and Sports, 1986-91. Named Bus. Statesman of Yr. Harvard Bus. Sch. Club Washington, 2000, Citizen of Yr. Boy Scouts Am. Nat. Capitol Coun., 2000, Am. Friends of Czech Republic Civil Soc. Vision award, Woodrow Wilson award for corp. citizenship, 2004; named to Washington Bus. Hall of Fame, 2005. Mem. Am.-Israel Friendship League (bd. trustees 1991—), Aspen Inst. (bd. trustees 1996—). Episcopalian. Avocations: bicycling, skiing. Office: 1455 Pennsylvania Ave NW Washington DC 20004-1008 Home Phone: 703-522-6848; Office Phone: 202-371-0150. Business E-Mail: fmalek@thayercapital.com.

MALEK, MANU, information scientist, educator; BSEE, U. Tehran, Iran; MSc in Elec. Engring. and Computer Sci., PhD in Elec. Engring. and Computer Sci., U. Calif., Berkeley. Disting. mem. tech. staff Lucent Technologies Bell Labs.; mem. faculty to industry prof. computer sci. and telecom. mgmt. Stevens Inst. Tech., Hoboken, NJ, 2001—. Adj. prof. elec. engring., computer sci. and telecom. mgmt. Stevens Inst. Tech., dir. cert. in cybersecurity prog.; hon. dir. Computer Networks Forensics Lab. Shandong Acad. Scis., Jinan, China, 2005—. Contbr. articles to profl. jours.; editor network mgmt.: IEEE Transactions on Comm., 1989—92, founder, editor-in-chief: Jour. Network and Systems Mgmt., 1992—, editor. Fellow; IEEE (Third Millennium medal 2000); mem.: NY Acad. Scis., Sigma Xi, Internat. Fedn. Info. Processing, IEEE Comm. Soc. (disting. lectr.), Eta Kappa Nu. Achievements include patents in field. Office: Dept Computer Sci Stevens Inst Tech Castle Point on Hudson Hoboken NJ 07030 E-mail: mmalek@stevens.edu.

MALEK, MARLENE ANNE, foundation administrator; b. Oakland, Calif., June 22, 1939; d. William and Yolanda (Stella) McArthur; m. Frederic Malek; children: Frederic William, Michelle A. Olson. Degree in Nursing, Marymount U. Pres. Friends Cancer Rsch., Washington, 2000—. Vice chmn. bd. dirs. Marymount U., Arlington, Va.; presdl. appointee bd. dirs. Kennedy Ctr., 2002—; bd. dirs. Nat. Mus. Women in Arts, Vital Voices Global Partnership, Best Friends Found., MD Anderson Cancer Ctr., Houston; bd. overseers Duke U. Cancer Ctr.; mem. Nat. Dialogue on Cancer. Episcopalian. Avocations: cross country skiing, bicycling.

MALENKA, BERTRAM JULIAN, physicist, researcher; b. NYC, June 8, 1923; s. Morris and Mollie (Wichtel) M.; m. Ruth D. Stolper, Mar. 28, 1948; children: David Jonathan, Robert Charles. AB, Columbia, 1947; MA, Harvard, 1949, PhD, 1951. Research fellow Harvard, 1951-54; asst. prof. physics Washington U., St. Louis, 1954-56; assoc. prof. Tufts U., Medford, Mass., 1956-60; faculty Northeastern U., Boston, 1960—, prof. physics, 1962-93, prof. emeritus, 1993—. Mem. sci. adv. group Harvard-Mass. Inst. Tech. Cambridge Electron Accelerator, 1956— Mem. vis. com. dept.

conservation Mus. Fine Arts, Boston, 1997—; mem. collections mgmt., 2004—; mem. vis. com. Art of the Ams. Dept. Mem. Am., Italian phys. socs., N.Y. Acad. Scis., Phi Beta Kappa, Sigma Xi. Achievements include research and publications on theory of nuclear forces and structure of nucleus, explanation polarization phenomena in high-energy scattering, gamma radiation, electric polarization deuteron, accelerator design. Home: 16 Rutledge Rd Belmont MA 02478-3323 Office: Northeastern Univ Dept Of Physics Boston MA 02115 E-mail: bjm11@verizon.net.

MALENKA, ROBERT C., psychiatrist, educator; b. Boston, June 21, 1955; PhD in Neuroscis., MD, Stanford U., 1983. Resident in psychiatry Stanford Sch. Medicine; postdoctoral work U. Calif., San Francisco, asst. prof. psychiatry and physiology, prof. psychiatry and physiology; dir. Ctr. for Neurobiology of Addiction; assoc. dir. Ctr. for Neurobiology and Psychiatry; Pritzker prof. psychiatry and behavioral scis., dir. Pritzker Lab. Stanford U. Sch. Medicine, 1999—; lectr. in field. Scientific adv. bd. Renovis, Inc., 2000—, Merck, Inc., 2000—; Wendy and Stanley Marsh lectr., 2002. Mem. editl. bd. jours.:; co-author: (textbook) Molecular Neuropharmacology: A Foundation for Clinical Neuroscience, 2001; contbr. articles to profl. jours. Mem. Nat. Adv. Coun. on Drug Abuse. Recipient Alfred P. Sloan rsch. fellowship, 1990, Young Investigator award, Nat. Alliance for Rsch. in Schizophrenia and Depression, 1990, 1992, Scholars award in neurosci., McKnight Endowment Fund for Neurosci., 1990, Investigator award in neurosci., 1997, Soc. for Neurosci. Young Investigator award, 1993, Daniel H. Efron award, Am. Coll. Neuropsychopharmacology, 1998, Dargut and Milena Kemali Found. Internat. prize in neurosci., 2000, MERIT award, NIMH, 2001—11, Basic Neuroscience Rsch. award, Collegium Internationale Neuropsychopharmacologicum, 2002. Mem.: Am. Acad. Arts & Sciences, Inst. Medicine, Soc. for Neurosci. (program com.). Office: Stanford U Sch Medicine Psychiatry and Behavioral Scis MSLS P104 Mail Code 5485 Stanford CA 94305-5485 E-mail: malenka@stanford.edu.

MALERNEE, JAMES KENT, JR., financial consultant; b. Durango, Colo., June 15, 1947; s. James Kent and Norma Virginia (Calhoon) M.; m. Charlean Ann Born, Aug. 21, 1971 (div. May 1, 1992). BS in Engring., U. Tex., Austin, 1970; PhD in Bus. Adminstrn., U. Tex., 1977; MBA, So. Meth. U., 1972. Petroleum engr. Tex. R.R. Commn., 1970-71; instr. fin. U. Tex., 1973-75; lectr. fin. U. Tulsa, 1975-76; assoc. Mgmt. Analysis Ctr., Northbrook, Ill., 1977-80, v.p., 1980—; sr. v.p. The MAC Group, 1987-89; also dir. MAC Rsch.; co-founder Cornerstone Rsch., NYC, mng. dir., 1989-2000, pres., CEO, 2000—07, chmn., 2007—. Lectr. mgmt. Stanford GSB, 1983; leader seminars on mergers and acquisitions and corp. strategy; guest speaker in field of strategy; speaker on damages in securities litigation P.L.I. and ABA; expert witness in securities and fin.; bd. dirs. RealPage; adv. bd. U. Tex. Bus. Sch. Contbr. articles to profl. jours. Named one of Outstanding Young Men Am. U.S. Jaycees, 1977. Mem. Fin. Mgmt. Assn. (v.p. 1981-82, bd. dirs. 1983-85), Assn. Corp. Growth. Home: 208 E 51st St # 123 New York NY 10022-6557 Office: Cornerstone Rsch 599 Lexington Ave New York NY 10022-6030 *

MALESKI, CYNTHIA MARIA, lawyer; b. July 4, 1951; d. Richard Anthony and Helen Elizabeth (Palovcak) Maleski; m. Andrzej G. Groch, Aug. 7, 1982; 1 child, Elizabeth Maria. Student, U. Rouen, France, 1970; BA summa cum laude, U. Pitts., 1973; JD, Duquesne U., 1976. Bar: Pa. 1976, U.S. Dist. Ct. (we. dist.) Pa. 1976, U.S. Supreme Ct. 1980, U.S. Ct. Appeals (3d cir.) 1984. Indsl. rels. adminstr. Allegheny Ludlum Industries, Inc., Brackenridge, Pa., 1972—74; law clk. Conte, Courtney, Tarasi & Price, Pitts., 1974, Paul Hammer, Pitts., 1974—76; solo practice Natrona Heights, Pa., 1978—92, 1995—. Adj. prof. law Sch. Law Duquesne U., Pitts., 1998—; ins. commnr. Penna, 1992—; mem. Gov.'s cabinet, 1992—95; v.p., regulatory coun. Highmark Blue Cross/Blue Shield, 1995—99; assoc. dir. pers. Mercy Hosp., Pitts., 1976—77, dir. legal affairs, 1977—81, gen. counsel, 1981—92; spl. master Allegheny County Ct. Common Pleas, 1989; bd. dirs. legal adv. bd. Cath. Health Assn., 1980—82; gen. counsel, vice chmn. nat. assembly of reps. Nat. Confedn. Am. Ethnic Groups, 1980—; health law cons. and lectr. Co-author: The Legal Dimensions of Nursing Practice, 1982 (Nurses' Book of Month Club award, 1982); contbr. articles to publs. Mem. Allegheny-Kiski Hist. Soc., 1995—; mem. exec. bd. Pa. Fedn. Women, 2003—; elected mem. Allegheny County Dem. Com., 1986—89; corp. sec., pres. Duquesne U. Tamburitzans, Pitts., 1985—92; vice chmn. Czechoslovak room com. Nationality Rooms Program, U. Pitts., Pitts., 1983; v.p. Slovak League Am., 1990—; mem. adv. bd. Children's and Youth Svcs., Allegheny County, 1984—92; soloist, spkr. various groups Pitts. Slovakians. Named Disting. Alumnus, 1993; recipient Acad. Excellence award, Duquesne U., 1976; scholar, U. Rouen, 1970; Allegheny Ludlum Industries scholar, 1969—73, Andrew Mellon scholar, 1969—73, tuition scholar, U. Pitts., 1969—73, tuition remission grantee, Duquesne U., 1975, 1976. Mem.: ABA, St. Thomas More Soc. (bd. govs. 1980—), Slavic Edn. Assn. (nat. treas. 1981—86), Allegheny County Bar Assn., Pa. Bar Assn. (commn. on women 1996—, exec. women's coun.), Soc. Hosp. Attys. We. Pa., Soc. Hosp. Attys. of Hosp. Assn. Pa. (v.p.), Women Execs. in State Govt. (mem. nat. bd. 1994), Nat. Health Lawyers Assn., Am. Soc. Hosp. Attys., Nat. Slovak Soc., 1st Cath. Slovak Ladies' Assn. (nat. trustee), First Cath. Slovak Union, Slovak Cath. Sokols, Polish Falcons, Phi Beta Kappa. Roman Catholic. Home: 137 Oak Manor Dr Natrona Heights PA 15065-1949 Office: 2413B Freeport Rd Box 263 Natrona Heights PA 15065-0046 Office Phone: 724-224-6800.

MALEY, ABIGAIL JOY, zoologist, researcher; d. Charles Edward Maley and Joyce Marie Steck. BA in Zoology magna cum laude, Ohio Wesleyan U., Delaware, 2006. William Stull asst. mus. curator Ohio Wesleyan U., 2004—06; rsch. asst. U. Ill., Champaign, 2006—. Mem.: Phi Sigma, Sigma Xi, Phi Beta Kappa, Theta Alpha Kappa. Avocation: acting.

MALFA, FRANCES, lawyer; b. Bklyn., Dec. 16, 1969; BBA, Baruch Coll., 1991; JD, Touro Coll., 1994. Bar: NJ 1994, NY 1995, US Dist. Ct. Ea. Dist. NY, NY Dist. Ct. So. Dist. NY. Ptnr. Wilson, Elser, Moskowitz, Edelman & Dicker LLP, NYC. Office: Wilson Elser Moskowitz Edelman & Dicker LLP 23rd Fl 150 E 42nd St New York NY 10017-5639 Office Phone: 212-490-3000 ext. 2296. Office Fax: 212-490-3038. Business E-Mail: malfaf@wemed.com.

MALGIERI, LEWIS JOSHUA, psychologist, consultant; b. Syracuse, NY, Nov. 10, 1943; s. Severino Vincenzino and Maria Francesca Malgieri; life ptnr. Kathleen Anne Stevens; children: Donald Wayne Stevens, Brian Michael Stevens, Scott Matthew Stevens. BA in Psychology, SUNY, Buffalo, 1968; MA in Psychology, Roosevelt U., 1974; PhD in Clin. Psychology (hon.), New Sch. For Social Rsch., 1991; postgrad. in Neuropsychology, Greystone Park Psychiat. Hosp., 1995. Neuropsychology cert. in biofeedback NJ Biofeedback Assn., 1981, cert. psychologist NJ State Bd. Psychol. Examiners, 1993, NY State Bd. Psychol. Examiners, 2001, hypnotherapist Wellness Inst. Seattle, 1995, lic. FCC amateur radio operator. Psychologist NY State Assn. for Retarded Citizens, Geneva, 1974—77, Rahway State Prison, NJ, 1985—93; prin. clin. psychologist Greystone Park Psychiat. Hosp., NJ, 1993—2001; chief psychologist Oswego Hosp., NY, 2001—. With US Army, 1969—71, Viet Nam. Named Grad. Asst., Roosevelt U., 1969—74; scholar, Syracuse U., 1962. Mem.: APA (Med. Corps. Psychologist Honor award 2002), Ctrl. NY Psychol. Assn. Roman Catholic. Home: 103 Pineledge Rd Camillus NY 13031 Office: Oswego Hospital 74 Bunner St Oswego NY 13126 Office Phone: 315-343-8162 ext. 108, 315-529-3758. Personal E-mail: fermi1001@aol.com.

MALGIERI, NICK, food service executive, educator, chef, writer; b. Newark, Sept. 30, 1947; s. Nufre and Antoinette (LoConte) M. BA in French, Seton Hall U., 1970; AOS in Culinary Arts, Culinary Inst., Hyde Park, NY, 1973. Pastrycook Seehotel Meierhof, Zurich, 1973-74, Hotel de Paris, Monte Carlo, 1974, Sporting Club, Monte Carlo, 1974-76, Hotel la Reserve, Beaulieu, France, 1974; pastry chef Windows on the World, NYC, 1976-79; asst. pastry chef Hotel Waldorf Astoria, NYC, 1979; chmn. baking dept. NY Restaurant Sch., NYC, 1979-83; dir. baking program Inst. Culinary Edn., NYC, 1984—; founder, owner Total Heaven Baking Co. Exec. chef Paine Webber; pastry chef Board Room; cons. Inhilco, Inc.; guest lectr. Smithsonian Instn.; Am. spokesperson for Switzerland tourism. Author: Nick Malgieri's Perfect Pastry, 1989, Great Italian Desserts, 1990, How to Bake, 1995 (James Beard Found. Cookbook award/Best Book on Baking/Desserts of 1995), Chocolate, 1998 (IACP/Julia Child cookbook award 1998, Salon Internat. du Livre award), Cookies Unlimited, 2000, Perfect Cakes, 2002 (100 Best Books of 2002 Pub. Weekly), A Baker's Tour: Nick Malgieri's Favorite Baking Recipes from Around the World, 2005, Perfect Light Desserts, 2006; contbr. articles and recipes to newspapers and profl. jours. Recipient Toque award City of Phila., 2006. Mem. Internat. Assn. Culinary Profls. Found. (former trustee), Internat. Assn. Culinary Profls. (cert. culinary profl., chmn. certification 1989-91), Amicale Culinaire de Monaco, Societe Culinaire Philanthropique N.Y., Federazione Italiana dei Cuochi, James Beard Found. (coord. competitions 1991-95), N.Y. Assn. Cooking Tchrs. (former bd. dirs., Ann. honor 2000), Bakers Dozen East (founding mem.). Home: 277 W 10th St New York NY 10014-2562 Office: Inst of Culinary Education 50 W 23d St New York NY 10010

MALHERBE, ABRAHAM JOHANNES, retired religious studies educator, writer; b. Pretoria, South Africa, May 15, 1930; arrived in US, 1951; s. Abraham Johannes and Cornelia Aletta (Meyer) Malherbe; m. Phyllis Melton, May 28, 1953; children: Selina, Cornelia, Abraham Johannes VII. BA, Abilene Christian U., 1954; STB, Harvard U., 1957; student, U. Utrecht, The Netherlands, 1960-61; ThD, Harvard U., 1963; LLD (hon.), Pepperdine U., 1981; LHD (hon.), Centre Coll., 1990; STD (hon.), Providence Coll., 1994; DD (hon.), U. Pretoria, 2000. Minister Ch. of Christ, Lexington, Mass., 1956-63; asst. and assoc. prof. Abilene (Tex.) Christian U., 1963-67; vis. scholar Harvard Divinity Sch., Cambridge, Mass., 1967-68; assoc. prof. Abilene Christian U., 1968-69, Dartmouth Coll., Hanover, NH, 1969-70, Yale Divinity Sch., New Haven, 1970-77, prof., 1977-81, Buckingham prof., 1981-94, assoc. dean acad. affairs, 1987-89, prof. emeritus, 1994—. Guest prof. U. Pretoria, South Africa, 1989, 98, 2005. Author: (book) Social Aspects of Early Christianity, 1983, Moral Exhortation, 1986, Paul and the Thessalonians, 1987, Ancient Epistolary Theorists, 1988, Paul and the Popular Philosophers, 1989, The Letters to the Thessalonians, 2000; cons.: Anchor Bible Dictionary, 1992; inspiration for books Greeks, Romans and Christians: Essays in Honor of Abraham J Malherbe, 1990, Early Christianity and Classical Culture: Comparative Studies in Honor of Abraham J. Malherbe, 2003; mem. editl. bd.: Bible Rev., 1986—, Novum Testamentum, 1991—, Religious Studies Rev., 1980—2002, co-founder: Restoration Quar., 1957; contbr. articles to profl. jours. Recipient Teaching Award, Abilene Christian U., 1965, 1967, Outstanding Alumni Citation, 1996, NEH award, 1973; Abraham J. Malherbe scholarship developed in his honor, Yale U. Sch. Divinity, 1997—, Abraham J. Malherbe rsch. fellowship developed in his honor, U. Tex. Dept. Classics, Austin, 2002—, Abraham J. Malherbe doctoral fellowship, Yale U. Sch. Divinity, 2004—. Mem.: Studiorum Novi Testamenti Societas, Soc. Bibl. Lit., South African New Testament Soc. (hon.). Ch. Of Christ. Home: 71 Spring Garden St Hamden CT 06517-1913 Business E-Mail: abraham.malherbe@yale.edu.

MALHI, GURBAX SINGH, Canadian government official; b. India; m. Devinder Brar, Mar. 16, 1976; children: Gurinder, Harinder. BA in Polit. Sci., English, History, Punjab U., India; BA in Polit. Sci., English and History. Prior com. appts. Ho. of Commons Standing Com. for Govt. Ops., Standing Com. on Procedure and Ho. Affairs, Spl. Com. on Code of Conduct for MPs and Senators, Subcom. on Bus. of Supply, Pearson Airport Subcom., Limoousine Subcom.; assoc. mem. Com. for Fgn. Affairs; with Justice, Legal Affairs, Human Rights, Industry Coms.; mem. Scrutiny of Regulations Com.; chmn. Ho. of Commons Standing Com. for Libr. of Parliament; former pres. Bramalea-Gore-Malton Fed. Liberal Assn.; elected Ho. of Commons, 1993, re-elected, 1997, 2000, 2004, apptd. parliamentary sec. to min. of nat. revenue, 2005—; mem. Standing Com. on Human Resources Devel. Founder, chair Canada-South Asia Parliamentary Friendship Group. Active Toronto Real Estate Bd., Canadian Real Estate Assn.; former dir. Malton Neighborhood Svcs., 2004; appointed parliamentary sec. to min. of human resources. Recipient Queen's Golden Jubilee medal, Can., Amb. of Peace award. Office: 8500 Torbram Rd # 44 Brampton ON L6T 5C6 Canada Office Phone: 905-790-9211. E-mail: malhig@parl.gc.ca.

MALHOTRA, ASHOK KUMAR, philosophy educator; b. Ferozepur, India, 1940; came to the U.S., 1963, naturalized, 1977. s. Nihal Chand and Vidya (Wanti) M.; m. Nina Judith Finestone, Oct. 24, 1966 (dec.); children: Raj Kumar, Ravi Kumar. BA, U. Rajasthan, 1961, MA, 1963; PhD, U. Hawaii, 1969. Asst. prof. SUNY, Oneonta, 1967-70, assoc. prof., 1970-80, prof., 1980—, chmn. philosophy dept., 1975-80. Vis. prof. SUNY-Buffalo, summer 1970, Kurukshetra U. and Birla Inst., Pilani, India, spring 1980; grants reviewer NEH, 1978—; bd. dirs. SUNY Press editorial, 1989-93, dir. SUNY study abroad, program to India, 1980—; cons. TV series Kung Fu: The Legend Continues., 1992. Author: Sartre's Existentialism in Nausea and Being and Nothingness, 1978, Sartre's Existentialsim as Literature and Philosophy, 1995, Pathways to Philosophy: A Multidisciplinary Approach, 1996, Culture and Self, 1997, Transcreation of the Bhagavad Gita, 1998, Instant Nirvana, 1999, An Introduction to Yoga Philosophy, 2001, Wisdom of the Tao Te Ching, 2006; TV appearances include ABC World News Now, NBC News, JAIN TV, Doordarshan TV, ZEE TV (India), Natraj TV (Holland), All India Radio, NPR. Founder Ninash Found. Oneonta; established Indo-Internat. Sch., Dundlod, Rajasthan, Mahapura, Rajasthan and Kuran, Gujarat, India; founder, chmn. Yoga and Meditation Soc., SUNY, Oneonta. Recipient Excellence in Tchg. award and Disting. Tchg. Prof. award United Univ. Profession; Friend of Ednl. award City of Oneonta, 1998, Disting. Alumni award East-West Ctr., 2000, Jewel of India award 2002, Bharat Excellence award Friendship Forum of India, 2002, Spiritual Leadership award, 2006; East-West Ctr. fellow, 1963-65, 66-67; N.Y. State Dept. Edn. grantee, 1967-69, NEH grantee, 1979. Mem. Am. Philos. Assn., Soc. Asian and Comparative Philosophy, Assn. Asian Studies, N.Y. State Asian Studies Soc., Internat. Phenomenol. Soc., Yoga and Meditation Soc. (founder, chair). Home: 17 Center St Oneonta NY 13820-1445 Office Phone: 607-436-3220. E-mail: malhotak@oneonta.edu.

MALHOTRA, MADHU BALA, psychiatrist; b. New Delhi, June 10, 1951; arrived in U.S., 1974; d. Faqir Chand and Krishna Khandpur; m. Amjed Hussain; 1 child, Saira H. Amjed. MBBS, India. Unit chief inpatient psychiatry Jamaica Hosp., Richmond Hill, NY. Mem.: Am. Assn. Psychiatrists from India, Am. Psychiat. Assn. Office: Jamaica Hosp 8900 Van Wyck Expressway Richmond Hill NY 11418

MALHOTRA, NARESH KUMAR, marketing educator; arrived in U.S., 1975; s. Har Narian and Satya (Kakkar) M.; m. Veena Bahl, Aug. 13, 1980; children: Ruth Veena, Paul Naresh. *Dr. Malhotra converted from Hinduism to Christianity on March 19, 1978. He is a Bible preacher, teacher, and evangelist. He has preached the Gospel in 27 countries and has been blessed to see more than 132,000 people pray to accept the Lord Jesus Christ as their personal Savior. He frequently travels overseas to share his faith in the Lord Jesus Christ. He is a Deacon and member of the First Baptist Church, Atlanta. He has been married to Veena for over 27 years and they have two children, Ruth and Paul.* BTech with honors, Indian Inst. Tech., Bombay, 1971; MBA, I.I.M., Ahmedabad, India, 1973; MS, PhD, SUNY, Buffalo, 1979. Mgmt. cons. ASCI, Hyderabad, India, 1971-73; asst. prof. Ga. Tech. Inst., Atlanta, 1979—, assoc. prof. mgmt., coord. mktg., 1982-87, 89—, prof., 1988, Regents' prof., 1992—. Organizer several nat. and internat. mktg. mgmt. confs. Author: Marketing Research: An Applied Orientation (N.Am., European, Internat., Australia and New Zealand, Indian, Spanish, Portuguese, Chinese, Russian, French, Japanese, Bahasa Indonesia and Hungarian edits.), Basic Marketing Research: A Decision-Making Approach; contbr. articles to profl. jours. Lay preacher of the Gospel. Recipient Outstanding Mktg. Educator, Acad. of Mktg. Sci., 2005. Fellow Acad. Mktg. Sci. (disting., program chmn. 1984-85, 85-86, v.p. programs 1988-90, chmn. bd. 1990-92, pres. 1994-96, chmn. found. 1996-98, Top Rsch. Jour., Jour. Mktg. Rsch., Jour. Acad. Mktg. Sci., Jour. Healthcare Mktg., Internat. Mktg. Rev.), Decision Scis. Inst. (track chmn. 1984-86); mem. Am. Mktg. Assn. (track chmn. 1983-84), Am. Statis. Assn. Republican. Baptist. Achievements include globally top ranked researcher based on four independent publication rankings. Avocations: reading, writing, outdoor activities. Home: 1956 Lenox Rd NE Atlanta GA 30306-3035 Office: Ga Tech Inst Coll Mgmt Atlanta GA 30332-0520 Office Phone: 404-894-4358. Business E-Mail: naresh.malhotra@mgt.gatech.edu.

MALHOTRA, YOGESH, information scientist, consultant, information technology executive, computer engineer; b. India, Jan. 11, 1964; arrived in US, 1988, naturalized; B Engring. with distinction, Delhi Coll. Engring., India, 1984; MBA in Econ. and Info. Sys. summa cum laude, U. Nev., Las Vegas, 1993; PhD Bus. Adminstrn., Info. Sys. and Control Sys. magna cum laude, U. Pitts., 1998. Cert. computing profl., info. sys. security profl.; chartered engr. Exec. engr. Suzuki Maruti Udyog Ltd., Gurgaon, India, 1984—87; sys. analyst Tata Unisys Ltd., New Delhi, 1987—89; sr. sys. analyst JK Technosoft, Neepz, India, 1989; sr. cons. info. sys. Bank Am., Nev., 1990—91; prin. founder, pres., chief knowledge architect @BRINT-.COM, The Biztech Network, Pitts., 1994—98; founder, chmn., chief knowledge officer Brint.com L.L.C., 1998—2001; founding chmn., chief knowledge architect BRINT Inst. LLC, 2001—; asst. prof. mgmt. info. and decision Syracuse U., 2001—05, asst. prof. acctg. and info. sys., 2005—. Coun. ptnr., Inter-Agency Benchmarking & Best Practices Coun. US Fed. Govt., 1995—99; advisor, cons. Intel, Br. Telecom, Ziff Davis, Hewlett Packard, Arthur Andersen, South Korean, Vision Korea Nat. Campaign, Govt. of Netherlands, U.S. Fed. Govt, and, Govt. of Mex., 1995—2001, NSF, 2003—05, UN, Philips, Netherlands, 1996—; founder, editor-in-chief The Knowledge Mgmt. Think Tank, 1997—2001; advisor Govt. of Netherlands, 1998; mem. internat. advisory bd. Knowledge Mgmt. Jour., London, 1998—; disting. faculty BrainTrust, San Francisco, 1998, advisory bd. mem., 98; invited rsch. faculty INSEAD, France, 1998; faculty exec. edn. program Carnegie Mellon U., 1998, Northwestern U., Kellogg Grad. Sch. Mgmt., 2000; founding mem. Ziff Davis Internet Commerce Standard, 1999—2000; assoc. editor Info. Resources Mgmt. Jour., Hershey, Pa., 2001—03; cons., advisor Intel Corp., 2002, NSF, 2002, Syracuse U., 2002—, UN, 2003; founder The Knowledge Mgmt. Network, 2002—; editl. adv. bd. The Learning Orgn., 2004—05; bd. dir. Commonwealth Ctr. e-Governance, India; invited rsch. faculty Queen's U. Sch. Bus., Canada, 2006; spkr. in field. Author (and editor): Knowledge Management and Virtual Organizations, 2000; author: Knowledge Management and Business Model Innovation, 2001; contbr. articles to profl. jours. Grantee, Intel Corp., 2001, UN, 2003, Kaufman Found., 2003, Snyder Innovation Mgmt. Ctr., 2003, 2004, 2005, Ctr. for Creation and Mgmt. of Digital Ventures, 2003, 2004, Brethen Ops. Mgmt. Inst., 2005. Mem.: Info. Sys. Security Cert. Consortium, Info. Sys. Audit and Control Assn., Info. Sys. Security Assn., Assn. Info. Sys., Inst. Cert. Computing Profls., Inst. Engrs. (life), Phi Kappa Phi, Beta Gamma Sigma. Achievements include development of global research and practices for two new technology management disciplines, business technology and knowledge management. Avocations: information systems, e-business, knowledge management. Office: Syracuse U Sch Mgmt Syracuse NY 13244 Home Phone: 315-798-4636; Office Phone: 315-443-3571, 315-382-7275. Business E-Mail: yogesh@syr.edu.

MALI, PAUL, publisher, retired management educator; b. Hartford, Conn., July 6, 1926; m. Mary S. Mali; children: Faith, Dawn. BS in Engring., U. Conn., 1953, MS, 1962, PhD in Mgmt. and Engring., 1967; postgrad., Cornell U., 1964. Cert. mgmt. cons. Inst. Mgmt. Cons. Elec. engr. Gen. Dynamics, Groton, Conn., 1953—67, dir., 1961—67; prof. mgmt. Entrepreneurial, New London, Conn., 1961—67, U. Hartford, Conn., 1967—94; minister/co-pastor Bible Student ch., New London, Conn., 1994—; prof. Swiss Inst. Tech., Hebrew U.; pub. Horizon Publs.; mgmt. cons. to IBM, Westinghouse, U.S. Steel, United Tech., Aetna, Hanes, Alcan Aluminum, Combustion Engring. Founding fellow Acad. Disting. Engrs. and Hall of Fame of U. Conn. Author: various profl. books, including Writing and Word Processing for Scientists and Engineers, 1981, MBO Updated, 1986, (ministerial books) Magnetic Amplifiers, 1960, The Bible as a Rising Civilization, 1998, Ten Bad Mistakes About God, 2000, Terrorism and the Permission of Evil, 2002, Biblical View on Human Cloning, others, 2002, Spirituality: The Roadmap to Heaven, Spiritual Leadership for Every Christian, 2007. Pres. Good Samaritan Fund, New London, Conn., 1994—; bd. dirs. 12 state cmty. colls., Conn., 1981—88. Named to, U. Conn. Acad. Disting. Engrs. and Hall of Fame, 2004. Mem.: Am. Mgmt. Assn., Tau Beta Pi, Beta Gamma Sigma, Phi Delta Kappa, Eta Kappa Nu. Achievements include having September 14th named Dr. Paul Mali day in Connecticut by Governer Rell and the state General Assembly. E-mail: malipnm@aol.com.

MALICAY, MANUEL ALABAN, physician; b. Zamboonga City, The Philippines, Aug. 13, 1947; arrived in US, 1973; s. Bernardino Malicay Agan and Juliana (Alaban) Malicay; m. Lourdes V. Manzano, Jan. 12, 1974; children: Mark, Marlo, Brian, Michael, Margaret. BS, Far Eastern U., Manila, 1967, MD, 1972. Rsch. and tchg. fellow Far Eastern U., Manila, 1972-73; intern St. Francis Hosp., Evanston, Ill., 1973-74; resident in internal medicine Vets. Hosp., Hines, Ill., 1974-76; pvt. practice Bolingbrook, Ill., 1976—; physician Hinsdale (Ill.) Hosp., 1976-97, 1976—, Good Samaritan Hosp., Downers Grove, Ill., 1977—, vice chmn. dept. medicine, 1998—2001, chmn. Clin. Quality Coun., 1999-2001; asst. prof. in medicine Rush Med. Coll., Chgo., 2004—. Chmn continuing med educ comt IPMS, 1998—; prin. clin. investigator Dynacirc Assessment Trial Analysis, 1990, The Safety and Efficacy of Cardizem SR as anti-anginal medication, 1991, Comparative Outcome Study of Metformin vs. conventional approach, 1996, Lantus GOAL AIC Clin. Trials, 2003, REACH Registry, 2004—; spkr., bureau mem. Novartis Pharm. Corp., 2003, Abbott Pharm. Editor: IPMS Today, 1989—91. Trustee Far Ea. U. Sch. Med. Alumni Found., 1993—2001, v.p., 2002—04; pres. Class of 1972 Far Ea. U. Dr. N. Reyes Med. Alumni Found.; chmn. continuing med. edn. Far Ea. U. DNR Sch. Med. Alumni Found., 2005—; co-chmn. physician adv. bd. Nat. Rep. Congl. Com., 2002—. Named Most Outstanding Silver Jubilarian, Far Eastern U. Dr N Reyes Med. Alumni Found., 1997, Physician of Yr., Nat. Rep. Congl. Com., 2003. Fellow: ACP; mem.: AMA, Far Eastern U. Med. Alumni Assn. Ill. (pres. 1991—93, co-chair conv. ann. reunion and sci. seminar 1993, Outstanding Alumnus 1995), Assn. Philippine Physicians Am. (co-chair 25th ann. conv. and sci. seminar 1996, gov. 1996—2001), Ill. Med. Soc. (del. 1990—, coun. on econs. com. 2002—), DuPage County Med. Soc. (bd. dirs. 1986—), Ill. Philippine Med. Soc. (seminar program dir. 1994, pres. 1994—96, chmn CME comt 1998—, program dir. Primary Care Update 1999, 2001, Disting Leadership Award 1996, Disting Physician Award Organized Med 1999, Disting Serv Award 2001). Avocations: tennis, dance. Home: 2 S 676th Ave Vendome

Oak Brook IL 60521 Office: 402 W Boughton Rd Bolingbrook IL 60440-1872 Address: 47 6th Ave La Grange IL 60525-2499 Office Phone: 630-759-3782. Personal E-mail: mmalicaymd@hotmail.com.

MALICK, TERRENCE (DAVID WHITNEY II), film director; b. Waco, Tex., Nov. 30, 1943; m. Jill Jakes (div. 1978); m. Michele Malick, 1985 (div. 1998); m. Alexandra Wallace, 1998. Student, Harvard U., Oxford U.; MFA, Am. Film Inst. Dir., prodr., writer (films) Badlands, 1973 (Golden Seashell award 1974); dir., writer, Lanton Mills, 1969, Days of Heaven, 1978 (Best Dir. award Cannes Film Festival 1979, nominee Golden Globe award 1979, N.Y. Film Critics Circle award 1978), The Thin Red Line, 1998 (Acad. award nomination for Best Dir., Golden Berlin Bear award 1999, Chgo. Film Critics Assn. award 1999, Golden Satellite award, 1999), The New World, 2005; prodr. (films) Endurance, 1999, The Endurance, Shackleton's Legendary Antartic Expedition, 2000, Happy Times, 2001, The Beautiful Country, 2004, Undertow, 2004, Amazing Grace, 2006, The Unforseen, 2007; writer (films) Drive, He Said, 1971, Deadhead Miles, 1972, Pocket Money, 1972, The Gravy Train, 1974, Bear's Kiss, 2002 Office: Creative Artists Agy 9830 Wilshire Blvd Beverly Hills CA 90212 *

MALIFRANDO, FRANK, healthcare executive, theater producer, consultant, film producer, international real estate investor, publisher; b. NYC, Feb. 16, 1954; s. Frank Malifrando and Michele Michelin Kuhn. BS, Southwest U., LA, 1986, MS in Health Scis., 2004. Cert. media comm. Boston U., 1991. CEO Spring Fed Corp., NYC, 1982—88, Kalanakila Prodns., Hawaii, 1985—91, Thunder Key Inc., 1982—89; mktg. dir. Mus. Edits. West, LA, 1988—91; dir. of devel. No. Calif. Svc. League, 1997—99; exec. dir. Keith Haring AIDS Interfaith Chapel, 1994—2000, Grace Cathedral, San Francisco; dir. devel. Life Lines Ministries, San Francisco, 1997—98; dir. of career svcs. Computer Learning Ctr., 1999—2001; project dir., designer Career Acceleration Mentor Program, 2000—01; exec. dir. fundraising arm Seton Med. Ctr., Seton Med. Ctr. Coastside, Dau. Charity Healthcare Sys., Seton Health Svcs. Found., Daly City, Calif., 2001—04, Marin Gen. Hosp., Novato Cmty. Hosp., Marin Cmty. Health Found., San Rafael, Calif., 2004—; owner Restaurant Spring Fed., NYC; personal mgr. of photographer Kenn Duncan. Dir. of programs Alma DelFina Group, San Francisco, 1995—2000; CEO Artist Alliance Against AIDS, 1996; bd. dirs. Bethany Ctr. Prodr.: Red Shoes, Kenn Duncan, 1984, (fine art reproductions) Hula Kahiko Series, 1986 (Pele Award of Excellence, 1986), Dance Cos., 1984 (Nat. Ann. Print award and Comm. Arts award, 1984); prodr., dir.: (documentaries) Poets and Painters, A Night at the Palace, 1994; Willie by Madaglia Cruz, starring Sean San Jose, 1996; In Conversation with David Henry Hwong, 1996; Awakening New Futures (behind bars), 1997; The making of an event: Charity Ball-150 Years for Daughters of Charity Seton Medical Center, 2001. Exec. dir., bd. mem. Marin Cmty. Health Found.; bd. dirs. Seton Health Svcs. Found., Bethany Ctr.; mem. adv. bd. Philanthropy Leadership Coun., Washington. Recipient Radiant Baby Gold Pin, Keith Haring Found., 1995, Canon Pastor award, Grace Cathedral, San Francisco, 1995, Pele award for excellence, Advertising Assn. of Hawaii, 1984, Cert. of Design Excellence, Print's Regional Design Annual, 1986, Black and White award, Assn. Honolulu Artist, 1987, Resolution recognition, State of Calif., 2003. Mem.: Dir.'s Coun. Devel.-Sutter Health, San Francisco C. of C., Seniors RSVP/San Francisco (adv. bd.), Brisbane C. of C., Half Moon Bay C. of C., Daly City C. of C. Achievements include creator and founder of the AIDS Interfaith Chapel in Grace Cathedral, San Francisco. Office: Marin Cmty Health Found Box 8010 San Rafael CA 94012-8080 Address: 4000 Civic Ctr Dr Ste 150 San Rafael CA 94903 Office Phone: 415-492-4735. E-mail: malifrf@sutterhealth.org.

MALIK, JOHN STEPHEN, lawyer; b. Bryn Mawr, Pa., Sept. 15, 1958; s. John and Mary M. (Pisko) M. BA, St. Joseph's U., 1980; JD, Del. Law Sch., 1983. Bar: Del. 1984, Pa. 1984, U.S. Dist. Ct. Del. 1984, N.J. 1985, U.S. Ct. Appeals (3d cir.) 1990, U.S. Supreme Ct. 1989. Adj. faculty Widener U., Wilmington, 1984-86; sole practice Wilmington, 1985—. Mem. ATLA, Nat. Assn. Criminal Def. Lawyers, Del. Assn. Criminal Def. Lawyers, Del. Bar Assn. Democrat. Roman Catholic. Office: 100 E 14th St Wilmington DE 19801-3210 Office Phone: 302-427-2247. Business E-Mail: jmalik@malik-law.com.

MALIK, OM, former venture capitalist, blog website company executive, journalist; Honors Degree in Chemistry, St. Stephens' Coll., New Delhi, 1986. Position with Quick Nikkei News; sr. editor, founding mem. Forbes.com, 1999; with Hambrecht & Quist Asia Pacific, 1999—2000; sr. writer Red Herring, 2000; co-founder Masala.com; sr. writer Business 2.0, San Francisco, 2003—06; founder Giga Omni Media, Inc., San Francisco, 2006—; exec. editor GigaOm.com, 2006—. Guest appearances Business Week TV, BBC TV and Radio, CNNfn, CNBC and TechTV; contbr. articles to publications, including Economic Times, The Week, Wall Street Journal, Brandweek, Crains, NY Business; author: Broadbandits: Inside the $750 Billion Telecom Heist, 2003. Co-recipient Single News Category award for 'Enron's Burnout', Am. Soc. Bus. Publication Editors, 2001; named one of Top 25 Web Celebs, Forges mag., 2007; recipient Excellence in Journalism award, Soc. Profl. Journalists, N. Calif., 2001, Gold award for individual profile category, Am. Soc. Bus. Publication Editors, 2001. *

MALIK, OM PARKASH, electrical engineering educator, researcher; b. Sargodha, Punjab, India, Apr. 20, 1932; arrived in Can., 1966; s. Arjan Dass and Kesar Bai (Ahuja) M.; m. Margareta Fagerstrom, Dec. 22, 1968; children: Ola Parkash, Mira, Maya. Nat. Diploma in Elec. Engring., Delhi Poly., India, 1952; M in Engring., Roorkee U., India, 1962; PhD, London U., 1965; D.I.C., Imperial Coll., London, 1966. Registered profl. engr., Ont., Alta. Asst. engr. Punjab State Elec. Bd., 1953-61, asst. to chief engr., 1957-59; rsch. engr. English Elec. Co., England, 1965-66; asst. prof. U. Windsor, Ont., Canada, 1966-68; assoc. prof. U. Calgary, Alta., Canada, 1968-74, prof. Alta., 1974-97, faculty prof. Alta., 1997—2000, assoc. dean student affairs, faculty engring. Alta., 1995-98, assoc. acad. dean faculty engring. Alta., 1979-90, acting dean Alta., 1981, prof. emeritus Alta., 1997—. Cons. prof. Huazhong U. Sci. and Tech., Wuhan, People's Republic China, 1986—; chief judge Can. Wide Sci. Fair, 2003. Assoc. editor Can. Elec. and Computer Engring. Jour., 1988-97, mng. editor, 1998-2003; contbr. 400 articles to profl. jours. Indsl. tng. scholar Govt. India, 1952-53, sr. indsl. tng. scholar Confedn. Brit. Industries, 1959-60; recipient vol. svc. award APEGGA, 1990, Rsch. Excellence award Elec. and Computer Engring. Dept. U. Calgary, 1996, Can. Pacific Rwy. engring. medal Engring. Inst. Can., 1997, Disting. Lifetime Leadership award Faculty Engring. U. Calgary, 2001, Alberta Ingenuity Fund Rsch. Excellence award, 2002; admitted Order of U. Calgary, 2006. Fellow IEEE (life, chmn. life mems. com. 2004-05, chmn. Western Can. coun. 1983-84, chmn. student activities Can. region 1979-82, chmn. life mems. com., mem. Found., Centennial medal 1984, Western Can. Coun. Merit award 1986, Third Millennium medal 2000, A.G.L. McNaughton award 2001), Inst. Elec. Engrs., Can. Acad. Engring., World Innovation Found.; mem. IEEE Power Engring. Soc. (electric machinery com. 2002-, vice chmn. 2006-2007, chair 2007-, machine theory subcom. 1979-2004, excitation sys. subcom. 1988—, chmn. 2004-2007, sys. dynamic performance com. 1988—, energy devel. and power generation com. 1990—), Assn. Profl. Engrs., Geologists and Geophysicists Alta. (Vol. Svc. award 1990, Alta. Ingenuity Rsch. Excellence award), Assn. Profl. Engrs. Ont., Am. Soc. Engring. Edn., Can. Elec. Assn. (assoc., controls com. 1977-92, chmn. digital control com. 1977-85, chmn. edn. com. 1983-85, mem. expert sys. com. 1989-94), Confederacion Panamericana de Ingenieria Mecanica, Electica y Ramas Afines (v.p. 1987-00, bd. dirs. region I, 1991-93), U. Calgary Emeritus Assn. (v.p. 2002-03, pres. 2003-04), Internat. Fed. Automatic Control (chmn. power plants and power sys. control commn. 2002-). Hindu. Home: 4 6841 Coach Hill Rd SW Calgary AB Canada T3H 3T9 Office: U Calgary Dept Elec & Computer Engring 2500 University Dr NW Calgary AB Canada T2N 1N4 Home Phone: 403-217-6412; Office Phone: 403-220-6178. Personal E-mail: maliko@ucalgary.ca.

MALIK, WAHEED AHMAD, cardiologist; s. Gohar Sultana Malik; m. Samina Ahmed Malik, Oct. 24, 1996; children: Danial Ahmed, Harris Ahmed, Waleed Ahmed. MB & BChir, Army Med. Coll., Rawalpindi, Pakistan, 1986; MD, Ednl. Commn. Fgn. Med. Grads., 1993. Diplomate Am. Bd. Internal Medicine, 2001, Am. Bd. Nuc. Cardiology, 2002. Nuc. cardiologist and dir. Advanced Cardiology Ctr., Rockville, Md., 2002—. Mem.: Am. Soc. Nuc. Cardiology. Office: Advanced Cardiology Center 11119 Rockville Pike Ste 100 Rockville MD 20852 Home Phone: 240-686-4521; Office Phone: 301-816-9000. Office Fax: 301-816-8616; Home Fax: 301-816-8616. Personal E-mail: waheed5@verizon.net.

MALIN, HOWARD GERALD, podiatrist; b. Providence, Dec. 2, 1941; s. Leon Nathan and Rena Rose (Shapiro) M. AB, U. R.I., 1964; MA, Brigham Young U., 1969; BSc, Calif. Coll. Podiatric Medicine, 1969, DPM, 1972; MSC, Pepperdine U., 1978; MD (hon.), Internat. U. Sch. Medicine, Winnipeg, Man., Can., 2001. Diplomate Am. Bd. Podiatric Pub. Health, Am. Bd. Podiatric Orthopedics, Am. Acad. of Wound Care Mgmt. Extern in podiatry VA Med. Ctr., Wadsworth, Kans., 1971-72, Marine Corps Res. Dept., San Diego, 1972; resident in podiatric medicine and surgery N.Y. Coll. Podiatric-Medicine, NYC, 1972-73; resident in podiatric surgery, instr. in podiatric surgery N.Y. Coll. Podiatric Medicine, NYC, 1973-74; pvt. practitioner in podiatric medicine and surgery Bklyn., 1974-77; mem. staff Prospect Hosp., Bronx, NY, 1974-77; chief podiatry service, mem. staff, cons. sports medicine David Grant U.S. Air Force Med. Ctr., Travis AFB, Calif., 1977-80; chief podiatric sect., mem. staff VA Med. Ctr., Martinsburg, W.Va., 1980—. Instr. ednl. devel. program VA Med. Ctr., Martinsburg, W.Va., 1980—; clin. prof. med. sci. Alderson-Broaddus Coll., U. Osteopathic Medicine and Health Scis.; adj. faculty Barry U. Sch. Podiatric Medicine; adj. clin. prof. Ohio Coll. Podiatric Medicine, dir. extern program; clin. asst. prof. surgery W.Va. U. Sch. Medicine. Mem. editl. rev. bd. Jour. Contemporary Podiatric Physician, 1991—. Lt. Col. USAFR, ret. Fellow Am. Soc. Podiatric Dermatology (past archivist), Am. Coll. Foot Orthopedics (emeritus), Am. Coll. Podiatric Physicians, Am. Coll. Podiatric Radiology (archivist, past pres.), Am. Soc. Podiatric Medicine (asst. exec. dir. emeritus, past pres., archivist), Am. Podiatric Med. Writers Assn. (pres., archivist), Am. Coll. Foot and Ankle Pediat. (past pres., archivist, historian), Am. Profl. Wound Care Assn., Royal Soc. for Promotion Health, Royal Soc. Medicine (life), Coll. Cert. Wound Specialists; mem. Am. Acad. Podiatric Sports Medicine (assoc.), Assn. Mil. Surgeons US (life), Am. Coll. Podiatric Surgery (assoc.), Phi Kappa Theta, Phi Kappa Psi. Home and Office: 2250 Bear Den Rd Ste 210 Frederick MD 21701-9408 Office Phone: 304-263-0811 Ext. 3770.

MALIN, IRVING, language educator, critic; b. NYC, Mar. 18, 1934; s. Morris and Bertha (Silverman) M.; m. Ruth Lief, Dec. 18, 1955; 1 child, Mark. BA, Queens Coll., 1955; PhD, Stanford U., 1958. Acting instr. English Stanford U., 1955-58; instr. Ind. U., 1958-60; from instr. to prof. CCNY, 1960-72, prof., 1972—. Cons. Jewish Publ. Soc., 1964, Am. Quar., 1964, NEH, 1972, 79, 80, 81, 82, B'nai B'rith, 1974-75, Yaddo, 1975-77, Jewish Book Coun., 1976, 79, PEN, 1978-82, Princeton U. Press, 1979, Fairleigh Dickinson Press, 1980, Wayne State U. Press, 1980, Internat. Coun. Exch. of Scholars, 1980-81, Duke U. Press, 1981, Jewish Daily Forward, 1981, U. Pitts. Press, 1981, Papers on Lang. and Lit., 1981, U. Ga. Press, 1983, UMI Rsch., 1989, Gordian Press, 1990, Ctr. for Study of Higher Edn., 1990, Mosiac, 1991, MacArthur Found., 1996, U. of S.C. Press, 1998, Purdue U. Press, Lafayette, Ind., 1999; adv. bd. James Purdy Soc.; cons. U. Tex.2005 Author: William Faulkner: An Interpretation, 1957, New American Gothic, 1962, Jews and Americans, 1965, Saul Bellow's Fiction, 1969, Nathanael West's Novels, 1972, Isaac Bashevis Singer, 1972; co-editor: Breakthrough: A Treasury of Contemporary American Jewish Literature, 1964, William Styron's The Confessions of Nat Turner: A Critical Handbook, 1970, The Achievement of William Styron, 1975, William Goyen, 1997, Into the Tunnel, 1998, Garrett's Elizabethan Trilogy, 1998; editor: Psychoanalysis and American Fiction, 1965, Saul Bellow and the Critics, 1967, Truman Capote's In Cold Blood: A Critical Handbook, 1968, Critical Views of Isaac Bashevis Singer, 1969, Contemporary American-Jewish Literature: Critical Essays, 1973, Conrad Alken's Prose, 1982; co-editor: Underwords: Perspectives on Don DeLillo's Underworld, 2002; adv. editor: Studies in American Jewish Literature, Jour. Modern Literature, Review of Contemporary Fiction, Saul Bellow Jour., 20th Century Literature; reviewer: Hollins Critic, So. Quar.; co-editor Paul Bowles, 1986, Spl. Issue of 20th Century Lit., James Dickey Spl. Issue of S.C. Rev., 1994, Pynchon and Mason and Dixon, 2000, So. Novelists on Stage and Screen So. Quar., 1995, James Dickey's Fiction Spl. Tex. Rev., 1996, Leslie Fiedler and American Culture, 1999, Torpid Smoke: The Stories of Vladimir Nabokov, 2000. Fellow Yaddo, 1963, Nat. Found. for Jewish Culture, 1963-64, Huntington Libr., 1978. Mem. MLA, AAUP, Am. Studies Assn., Am. Jewish Hist. Soc., Melville Soc., Authors League Am., Soc. Study of So. Lit., Poe Studies Assn., English Inst., Nathaniel Hawthorne Soc., N.Y. Acad. Scis., Poetry Soc. Am., Popular Culture Assn., Nat. Book Critics Circle, Sherwood Anderson Soc., Internat. Assn. Univ. Prof. English, Kafka Soc., English-Speaking Union, Multi-Ethnic Lit. U.S. Soc., Hastings Ctr., Am. Jewish Congress, Assoc. Writing Programs, Nat. Coun. Tchrs. of English, Vladimir Nabokov Soc., Phi Beta Kappa. Jewish. Home: 96-13 68th Ave Forest Hills NY 11375-5039 Office: CCNY Dept English New York NY 10031

MALIN, ROBERT ABERNETHY, retired investment company executive; b. Mt. Vernon, NY, Dec. 13, 1931; s. Patrick Murphy and Caroline Cooper (Biddle) M.; m. Gail Lassiter, Nov. 5, 1960; children: Alison Campbell, Robert Lassiter. AB, Dartmouth Coll., 1953, MBA, 1954. Asst. to comptr. Biddle Purchasing Co., NYC, 1958-59; with Blyth & Co., Inc., NYC, 1960-71, v.p., 1965-71, dir., 1968-71, sr. v.p., mem. exec. com., 1971-72; sr. v.p. corp. fin. Reynolds Securities Inc., NYC, 1972-74, dir., 1973-74; mng. dir. First Boston Corp., NYC, 1974-90; gen. ptnr. Tiedemann Investment Group, NYC, 1991-96; mng. dir. SeaBridge Investment Advisors, Summit, NJ, 1997—2006; ret., 2006. Mem. adv. coun. Fin. Acctg. Stds. Bd., 1973-78. Served as lt. (j.g.) USNR, 1954-57. Mem.: Securities Industry Assn. (acctg. com.), Investment Bankers Assn. Am., The Moorings Club, Morris County Club, Beacon Hill Club. Republican. E-mail: malinrobta@aol.com.

MALINA, MICHAEL, lawyer; b. Bklyn., Mar. 20, 1936; s. William and Jean (Kutlowitz) M.; m. Anita May Oppenheim, June 22, 1958; children: Rachel Lynn, Stuart Charles, Joel Martin. AB, Harvard U., 1957, LLB, 1960. Bar: N.Y. 1961, U.S. Dist. Ct. (so. and ea. dists.) N.Y. 1962, U.S. Ct. Appeals (2d, 3d, 4th, 9th, and D.C. cirs.) 1965, U.S. Supreme Ct. 1965, U.S. Tax Ct. 1991. Assoc. Kaye, Scholer, Fierman, Hays & Handler, NYC, 1960-69, ptnr., 1969—. Contbr. articles to profl. jours. Mem. ABA (antitrust sect.), N.Y. State Bar Assn. (chmn. antitrust sect. 1998-99), Assn. Bar City N.Y. (profl. ethics com. 1985-88), Phi Beta Kappa. Democrat. Jewish. Home: 12 Innes Rd Scarsdale NY 10583-7110 Office: Kaye Scholer Fierman Hays & Handler 425 Park Ave New York NY 10022-3506

MALING, GEORGE CROSWELL, JR., physicist; b. Boston, Feb. 24, 1931; s. George Croswell and Marjory Maling; m. Norah J. Horsfield, Dec. 29, 1960; children: Ellen P., Barbara J., Jeffrey C. AB, Bowdoin Coll., 1954; SB, MIT, 1954, SM, 1954, PhD in Physics, 1963. Rsch. asst., postdoctoral fellow MIT, 1957—65; adv. physicist IBM Corp., Poughkeepsie, NY, 1965—71, sr. physicist, 1971—92; pres. Empire State Software Sys., Ltd., 1992—93; dir. Noise Control Found., Inc., Poughkeepsie, 1975—2006; chmn. com. SI-acoustics Am. Nat. Std. Com., 1976—79; dir. Internat. Noise Control Engring. Found., Inc., 1993—2006; mng. dir. Inst. of Noise Control Engring., 1994—2001; ret. Pres. Internat. Noise Control Engring. Found., 1999—. Editor: Noise/News, 1972—92; mng. editor: Noise/News Internat., 1993—, assoc. editor: Jour. Acoustical Soc. Am., 1976—83, editor tech. proc.; contbr. articles to profl. jours. Recipient Raleigh medal, Inst. Acoustics U.K., 1999, Dist. Noise Ctrl. Eng., INCE, 2001. Fellow: AAAS, IEEE, Audio Engring. Soc., Acoustical Soc. Am. (exec. coun. 1980—83, Silver medal in noise 1992); mem.: Nat. Acad. Engring., Internat. Inst. Noise Control Engring. (editor-in-chief 2002—, bd. dirs. 1980—86, v.p. comms. 1997—, bd. dirs.), Inst. Noise Control Engring. (bd. dirs. 1972—77, pres. 1975, award 2001). Personal E-mail: maling@alum.mit.edu.

MALINOWSKA-SEMPRUCH, KASIA, director; b. Bialystok, Poland, Mar. 5, 1966; d. Ryszard Malinowski and Irena Malinowska; m. Stas Sempruch, Apr. 28, 1996; children: Alan Sempruch, Kaya Sempruch. BA, Rutgers U., New Brunswick, NJ, 1990; MSW, U. Pa., Phila., 1992. Assoc. prof. Sch. Social Work, Crakow, 1992—93; program officer HIV Devel. Program, UN Devel. Program, NYC, 1993—95, program coord. Warsaw, 1995—98; program dir. Internat. Harm Reduction Devel. Program, Open Soc. Inst., NYC, 1999—. Vis. assoc. Albert Einstein Coll. Medicine, NYC, 2005—; task force mem. Millennium Project Task Force on HIV/AIDS, TB, Malaria and Access to Essential Medicines, 2002—05; reference group mem. UN Reference Group HIV/AIDS Prevention and Care Among Injecting Drug Users, 2002—; mem. subcom. Latin Am. grants program Tides Found., Fund Drug Policy Reform, NYC, 2002; mem. tech. rev. panel Global Fund to Fight AIDS, Tb and Malaria, 2002—05; vice chair bd. Internat. Coun. AIDS Svc. Orgns., Toronto, 2001—; mem. exec. bd. Social AIDS Com., Warsaw, 1996—; mem. steering com. AIDS and Mobility Project, Netherlands, 1987—88; regional organiser European Ctr. Social Welfare Policy, Vienna, 1993; internat. adv. com. mem. Awards Action on Human Rights and HIV/AIDS, 2004—; faculty mem. Salzburg Cornell Seminar, 2003—06; spkr. and present in field to numerous confs. on HIV/AIDS and related diseases. Editl. bd. mem. Internat. Jour. of Drug Policy; contbr. numerous articles to profl. jours. Recipient Gold Order medal, Polish Ministry Justice, 2000, Silve Badge award, Assn. Nurses for Malopolska Region, 2001. Mem.: Internat. AIDS Soc., Can. HIV/AIDS Legal Network. Office: Open Soc Inst 400 W 59th St New York NY 10019 Office Phone: 212-548-0344. Office Fax: 212-548-4617. Business E-Mail: kmalinowska@sorosny.org.

MALINOWSKI, ARTHUR ANTHONY, lawyer, arbitrator; b. Chgo., Apr. 4, 1929; s. Ignatius and Sophie (Data) M. BS in Econs., DePaul U., 1956, JD, 1960; MS in Indsl. Rels., Loyola U., 1958; PhD, Ill. Inst. Tech., 1972; LLM in Labor Law, Chgo. Kent Coll. Law, 1981. Bar: Ill. 1960. Instr. indsl. rels. Loyola U., Chgo., 1963-69, prof., 1969-94; prof. emeritus, 1994—; mem. Ill. Office Collective Bargaining, Chgo., 1973-83. Lectr. dept. econs. Ill. Inst. Tech., Chgo., 1965-68. Mem. Ill. Bar Assn., Indsl. Rels. Rsch. Assn., Nat. Acad. Arbitrators, Knights Malta, Phi Alpha Delta, Alpha Sigma Nu, Pi Gamma Mu, Iota Sigma Epsilon, Beta Gamma Epsilon. Home: 9240 Major Ave Morton Grove IL 60053-1552 Office: Loyola U of Chgo One E Pearson Ste 460 Chicago IL 60611-2147 Office Phone: 312-913-6613.

MALINOWSKI, DARIUSZ PIOTR, horticulturist, educator; s. Ryszard Wojciech Malinowski and Gabriela Maria Malinowska. Degree in Horticulture, Warsaw Agrl. U., Poland, 1989; PhD in Natural Scis., Swiss Fed. Inst. Tech., Zurich, Switzerland, 1995. Asst. prof. Tex. A&M U., College Station, 2001—. Mem.: Am. Forage and Grasslands Coun. (assoc. Emerging Scientist award 1998, Merit award 2006), Am. Soc. Agronomy (assoc.). Achievements include research in discovery of chemical modifications in the rhizosphere of grasses infected with shoot-located Neotyphodium spp. fungal endophytes. Office: Texas Agricultural Experiment Station 11708 Hwy 70W Vernon TX 76385 Home Phone: 940-553-4462; Office Phone: 940-552-9941. Business E-Mail: d-malinowski@tamu.edu.

MALINOWSKI, MARYELLEN, photographer, artist; b. Oak Park, Ill., Oct. 10, 1961; d. Richard A. and Mary Jo (Curran) Lamz; m. Preston Malinowski; children: Nicole, Brielle, Demi. Student, Internat. Acad. Merch./Design, Chgo., 1985, Maine Photog. Workshops, Rockport, 1996, Elgin CC, Ill., 1993—2004. Owner, dir. The Infrared Light Gallery, St. Charles, Ill., 1994—; prin., owner Enlighten Pub., St. Charles, 2004—. Spkr. in field. Author: The Sacred Light, 1999; exhibited infrared photography in shows. Founder, bd. dirs. The Sacred Light Found. Recipient awards for photography; People's Choice award Women's Work Exhbn., Woodstock, 1995, 1st place Georgetown Internat. Fine Art Exhbn., Washington, 1997; recipient Ill. Women's Works Scholarship, 1996. Mem. Kodak Profl. Network, Luminos Printmakers Guild, Theosophical Soc., Nat. Mus. Women in Arts. Home: 6N779 IL RT 31 Saint Charles IL 60175 Office: Infrared Light Gallery PO Box 1281 Saint Charles IL 60175 Home Phone: 630-584-8668; Office Phone: 800-571-2730, 630-584-8068. Business E-Mail: maryellen@infraredlight.com.

MALINOWSKI, MATTHEW J., lawyer; b. Lansing, Mich., Sept. 22, 1976; BA with honors, Michigan State U., 1998; JD, Emory U., 2003. Bar: Va. 2003, US Dist. Ct. (Ea. Dist.), Va. Assoc., pharm. products and toxic torts group & product liability group Spriggs & Hollingsworth, Washington, 2003—. Mem.: Va. State Bar Assn. Office: Spriggs & Hollingsworth 1350 I St NW Ste 900 Washington DC 20005 Office Phone: 202-898-5800. Office Fax: 202-682-1639. Business E-Mail: mmalinowski@spriggs.com.

MALINS, DONALD CLIVE, biochemist, researcher; b. Lima, Peru, May 19, 1931; came to U.S., 1947; s. Richard Henry and Mabel (Madeline) M.; m. Mary Louise Leiren, 1962; children: Christopher W., Gregory S., Timothy J. BA, U. Wash., 1953; BS in Chemistry, Seattle U., 1954; PhD in Biochemistry, U. Aberdeen, 1967, DSc, 1976. Dir. environ. conservation div. Nat. Marine Fisheries Svc., Seattle, 1974-87; sr. scientific cons. U.S. Dept. Justice, Washington, 1989-91; sci. cons. NOAA, 1990-92; prin. scientist, dir. molecular epidemiology program Pacific N.W. Rsch. Inst., Seattle, 1992—2001, dir. biochem. oncology program, 2001—06, prin. scientist emeritus, 2006—; rsch. prof. dept. chemistry Seattle U., 1972-95. Affiliate prof. dept. environ. and occupl. health sci. U. Washington, 1984—, Coll. Ocean & Fishery Scis. U. Washington, 1974-91; editor-in-chief Aquatic Toxicology, 1980-95; lectr., speaker in field. Mem. editl. bd. Tech. in Cancer Rsch. and Treatment, 2001—; mem. editl. bd. Tech. in Cancer Rsch. and Treatment, 2001—; contbr. articles to profl. jours.; inventor in field. Bd. dirs. Am. Oceans Campaign, 1989-91; adv. bd. Internat. Jt. Commn., 1990-91. Recipient U.S. Dept. Commerce Gold medal, 1982. Mem. NAS, Am. Soc. Biochemistry and Molecular Biology, Am. Assn. for Cancer Rsch.

MALINSKY, MARCI ANN, education educator; b. New Orleans, July 10, 1950; d. Walter Henry Tekippe and Mary Margaret Martin; m. Robert A. Malinsky, July 13, 1991; stepchildren: Matthew, Craig, Jennifer. BA in Edn., U. New Orleans, 1972; MA in Adminstrn., Coll. St. Thomas, St. Paul, 1983; PhD in Curriculum and Instrn., U. New Orleans, 2001. Tchr. Orleans Parish Sch., New Orleans, 1972—2001; asst. prof. Ark. State U., Jonesboro, Ark., 2001—05. Mem.: Nat. Sci. Tchrs. Assn., Internat. Reading Assn., Kappa Delta Pi. Roman Catholic. Avocations: reading, bridge. Home: 1607 Roleson Ln Jonesboro AR 72404 Office Phone: 870-972-3059. Personal E-mail: mmalinsky@cox-internet.com.

MALIPIERO, VICTORIA SCHNEIDER, opera singer; d. Donald Francis and Alice Eva (Billig) Snyder; m. Riccardo Malipiero, Dec. 21, 1988 (dec. Nov. 2003). MusB magna cum laude, Eastman Sch. Music, Rochester, NY, 1974, MusM, 1980; postgrad., U. Pisa, Italy, 1982; diploma in opera, Stuttgart Conservatory, Germany, 1984. Performer's cert. Eastman Sch. Music, 1978. Singer: (Operas) Stuttgart State Opera, 1980—85, La Scala, 1985, 1990, 1993, Genova Opera, 1986, 1988, Holland Festival Opera, 1987, 1990, Bologna Opera, 1987, 1988, 1995, Vienna Musikverein, 1992, Paris Chatelet Theater, 1993, Frankfurt Opera, 1999—2000, Rome Opera, 2001, others; singer: (soloist) Italian RAI Radio Broadcasts, 1984—2006, Schoenberg Festival, 2003, Musica in Alto Lario Festival, 2005, Master Classes on Lake Como, 2007; singer: (radio recs.) Schoenberg Lied der Waldtaube, Mahler Lieder eines fahrenden Gesellen, Dallapiccola An Mathilde, R. Malipiero Due Arie da L'Ultima Eva, Liederétudes. Flagstad Grant, Kirsten Flagstad Found., 1979—80. Mem.: Nat. Assn. Tchrs. Singing, Coll. Music Soc., Amici della Scala Milan (hon.), Pi Kappa Lambda, Sigma Alpha Iota. Home: 2848 Dove Pond Dr Grapevine TX 76051 Office: Via Pusgnano SNC 22010 Cremia Italy Office Phone: (011) 39-0344-82790.

MALIS, ANDREW GARY, telecommunications industry executive; ScB in Computer Sci., Brown U., Providence, 1975; ScM in Applied Math. and Computer Sci., Harvard U., Cambridge, Mass., 1979. Mem. tech. staff Mitre Corp., Bedford, Mass., 1975-78; divsn. engr. Bolt Beranek and Newman, Cambridge, Mass., 1979-93; cons. engr. Ascom Nexion, Acton, Mass., 1993-96; sr. cons. engr. Cascade Comm./Ascend Comm./Lucent Techs., Westford, Mass., 1996-2000; chief technologist Vivace Networks, Inc., San Jose, Calif., 2000—03, Tellabs, San Jose, 2003—06; dir. Verizon Commn., Waltham, Mass., 2006—. Chmn. working group Internet Engring. Task Force, Reston, Va., 1993—, ATM Forum, St. Louis, 1998-2000; mem. tech. adv. bd. Megisto Sys., Inc., Germantown, Md., 2000—; cons. Coun. Tech. Advisors, Gerson Lehrman Group, NYC, 2000—; pres., chmn. Multi-Protocol Label Switching Forum, Fremont, Calif., 2002-03; chmn., pres. MFA Forum, Fremont, Calif. 2003—; spkr., chmn. numerous telecom.-related confs. Contbr. articles to sci. jours., including Procs. IEEE, IEEE Comm.; author telecom. stds. documents, 1981—. Bd. dirs., past pres. Temple Emanuel, Andover, Mass., 1986—. Recipient spl. tech. achievement award Frame Relay Forum, 1994, Disting. Svc. award, 1999; Spotlight award ATM Forum, 2000. Mem. IEEE, Internet Soc., Sigma Xi. Democrat. Jewish. Achievements include patent for method and apparatus for enabling flow control over multiple networks having disparate flow control capability. Office: Verizon Commn 40 Sylvan Rd Waltham MA 02451 Office Phone: 781-466-2362. Personal E-mail: amalis@gmail.com. Business E-Mail: andrew.g.malis@verizon.com.

MALISHENKO, TIMOTHY PETER, aerospace company executive; s. John and Myra Phillys (Morris) M.; m. Jane Baxter, Mar. 17, 1968; 1 child, Andrew. BSBA, Ohio State U., 1968; MBA in Supply Chain Mgmt., Mich. State U., 1969; MS in Sys. Mgmt., U. So. Calif., 1972; postgrad., Nat. War Coll., Washington, 1986. Commd. 2d lt. USAF, 1968, advanced through grades to maj. gen., 1998, chief contracts and acquisition NATO E-3A Early Warning Sy. Brunssum, Netherlands, 1979-82, dep. dir. R&D contracting Aero. Sys. Divsn. Wright-Patterson AFB, Ohio, 1982-84, dir. contracting, dep. aero. equipment, 1984-86, chief contract support divsn. Office Asst. Sec. Washington, 1987-88, chief, sys. and logistics contracting divsn., 1988-89, asst. dep. asst. sec. for contracting, 1989-90, dir. contracting Electronic Sys. Ctr. Hanscom AFB, Mass., 1990-93, dep. dir. contracting Hdqrs. Air Force Materiel Command Wright-Patterson AFB, Ohio, 1993-94, dir. contracting Hdqrs. Air Force Materiel Command, 1994-95; dep. asst. sec. for contracting USAF, Pentagon, Washington, 1995-97, dir. def. contract mgmt. agy., 1997—2001; v.p., contracts and pricing, integrated def. sys. Boeing Co., Seal Beach, Calif., 2001—03, corp. v.p., contracts and pricing Chgo., 2003—. Contbr. articles to profl. jours. Served to maj. gen. USAF. Decorated Def. Disting. Legion of Merit with oak leaf cluster, Def. Meritorious Svc. medal. Personal E-mail: tim@malishenko.com. Business E-Mail: timothy.p.malishenko@boeing.com.

MALITZ, SIDNEY, psychiatrist, educator; b. NYC, Apr. 20, 1923; s. Benjamin and Etta (Cohen) Malitz. Student, NYU, 1940-42, Tulane U., 1942-43; BM, Chgo. Med. Coll., 1946, MD, 1947. Diplomate Am. Bd. Psychiatry and Neurology. Intern St. Mary's Hosp., Huntington, W.Va., 1946-47; sr. intern Bethesda Hosp., Cin., 1947-48; resident N.Y. State Psychiat. Inst., NYC, 1948-51, sr. rsch. psychiatrist, 1954-56, acting prin. rsch. psychiatrist, 1956-58, acting chief psychiat. rsch., chief dept. exptl. psychiatry, 1958-64, chief psychiat. rsch. dept. exptl. psychiatry, 1964-72, dep. dir., 1972-75, acting dir., 1975-76, 81-84, dep. dir., 1976-78, dir. dept. biol. psychiatry, 1984-91. In charge psychiat. drug clinic Vanderbilt Clinic Presbyn. Hosp., NYC, 1956—75; asst. attending psychiatrist, 1960—66, assoc. attending psychiatrist, 1966—71, attending psychiatrist, 1971—93, acting dir. psychiatry svc., 1975—76, NYC, 1981—84, NYC, 1993—, consulting psychiatrist; asst. dept. psychiatry Coll. Physicians and Surgeons Columbia U., NYC, 1955—57, assoc., 1957—59, asst. clin. prof., 1959—65, assoc. prof., 1965—69, prof., 1969—93, prof. emeritus, 1993, vice chmn. dept. psychiatry, 1972—75, acting chmn., 1975—76, vice chmn., 1976—78, spl. instr., 1993—; panel impartial psychiat. experts N.Y. State Supreme Ct., 1960—; cons. U.S. Pharmacopeia, Rush Found., LA, 1968—75; cons. divsn. med. scis. NRC, Washington, 1967—70; mem. ad hoc rev. com. to select Nat. Drug Abuse Rsch. Ctrs. Ctr. Studies Narcotic and Drug Abuse, NIMH, 1972—73. Contbr. articles to profl. jours. Recipient Leonard Caemmer award, N.Y. State Psychiat. Inst., 1984. Fellow: Am. Psychiat. Assn. (chmn. com. biol. psychiatry 1961—62, program com. 1961—62, sec.-treas. chpt. 1962—63, com. rsch. 1966—68, pres. chpt. 1969—70, chmn. Coun. R&D 1971—73, mem. history and libr. com. 1989—91), Am. Coll. Neuropsychopharmacology (life), Royal Soc. Medicine (life); mem.: AMA (cons. coun. drugs 1960—70), AAAS (coun. 1969—72), Vidonian Soc. (pres. 1989—93), N.Y. Psychiat. Soc. (v.p. 1989—91, pres. 1991—92), N.Y. Acad. Scis., Benjamin Rush Soc. (life; pres.-elect 1989, pres. 1990—91), Am. Psychopath. Assn. (life), Assn. Rsch. Nervous and Mental Disease (life), Am. Coll. Psychoanalysts (life), N.Y. Acad. Medicine (life), Collegium Internationale Neuropsychopharmacologicum (life), N.Y. Soc. Clin. Psychiatry (life), N.Y. County Med. Socs. (life), Soc. Biol. Psychiatry (life), Group Advancement Psychiatry (rsch. com. 1986—91), Royal Coll. Psychiatrists, Am. Coll. Psychiatrists (archivist-historian 1978—2002, liaison to Royal Coll. Psychiatrists 1985—2004, Bowis award 1989), Alpha Omega Alpha. Office: Columbia U Dept Psychiatry 161 Fort Washington Ave New York NY 10032-3713 E-mail: lithopha@optonline.net.

MALIWACKI, JOHN M., secondary school educator; BS in Environ. Edn., Cornell U., Ithaca, NY, 1979; MAT in Biology, Binghamton U., NY, 1984. Cert. tchr. sci. NY. Sci. tchr. Jennie F. Snapp Mid. Sch., Endicott, NY, 1980; tchr. sci. Vestal H.S., NY, 1981—85; lead tchr. sci. Maine-Endwell Mid. Sch., NY, 1986—. Mem.: Sci. Tchrs. Assn. NY State. Office: Maine-Endwell Middle School 1119 Farm to Market Rd Endwell NY 13760

MALKASIAN, GEORGE DURAND, JR., obstetrician, educator; b. Springfield, Mass., Oct. 26, 1927; s. George Dur and Gladys Mildred (Trombley) M.; m. Mary Ellen Koch, Oct. 16, 1954; children: Linda Jeanne, Karen Diane, Martha Ellen. AB, Yale U., 1950; MD, Boston U., 1954; MS, U. Minn., 1963. Diplomate Am. Bd. Ob-Gyn. Intern Worcester (Mass.) City Hosp., 1954-55; resident in ob-gyn Mayo Grad. Sch. Hosp., Rochester, Minn., 1955-58, 60-61; mem. faculty Mayo Med. Sch., 1962—, prof. ob-gyn, 1976—, chmn. dept. ob-gyn, 1976-86. Author articles in field. Served to lt. comdr. M.C., USNR, 1958-60. Named Tchr. of Yr., Mayo Grad. Sch. Medicine, 1973, 77, Alumnus of Yr., Boston U. Sch. Med., 1990. Fellow Royal Coll. Obstetricians and Gynecologists (ad eundum); mem. ACS, Am. Coll. Ob-Gyn (pres. 1989-90), Am. Ob-Gyn Soc., Am. Radium Soc., Soc. Ob-Gyn, Assn. Profs. Ob-Gyn., N.Am. Ob-Gyn. Soc., Ctrl. Assn. Ob-Gyn, Minn. Soc. Ob-Gyn, Internat. Fedn. Ob-Gyn (v.p. 1997-2000), Zumbro Valley Med. Soc. (exec. dir. 1996-2002). Home: 211 NW 2nd St #503 Rochester MN 55901 Office: Mayo Clinic 200 1st St SW Rochester MN 55905-0001

MALKI, HEIDAR A., dean; arrived in US, 1979; s. Karim A. and Rokhsareh A. Malki; m. Layla F. Niaki, June 12, 1962; 1 child, Armeen. PhD, U. Wis., Milw., 1990. Prof. U. of Houston, 1991—2005, assoc. dean, 2004—. Adviser Mind and Vision Computing, Houston, 1992—2000. Author: (textbook) Control Systems Technology (Best Paper award, 1998). Named Alumnus of Yr., 2005; recipient Invited Paper award, Sci. Am., 1997, Rsch. in Outstanding Faculty award. Mem.: IEEE, Am. Soc. Engring. Edn. (zone chair 1997—98, Best Paper award). Office: U Houston 4800 Calhoun Rd Houston TX 77204-4020 Office Phone: 713-743-4075. Office Fax: 713-743-4032. Business E-Mail: malki@uh.edu.

MALKIEL, BURTON GORDON, economist, educator; b. Boston, Aug. 28, 1932; s. Sol and Celia (Gordon) Malkiel; m. Judith Ann Atherton, July 16, 1954 (dec. 1987); 1 child, Jonathan; m. Nancy Weiss, July 31, 1988. BA, Harvard, 1953, MBA, 1955; PhD, Princeton, 1964. Assoc. Smith Barney & Co., NYC, 1958—60; asst. prof. dept. econs. Princeton U., 1964—66, assoc. prof., 1966—68, prof., 1968—81, Rentschler prof. econs., 1969—81, chmn. dept. econs., 1974—75, 1977—81, Chem. Bank chmn.'s prof. econs., 1988—; dean Sch. Orgn. and Mgmt., Yale U., 1981—87. Mem. Pres.'s Coun. Econ. Advisors, 1975—77; bd. dirs. Vanguard Group Internat. Author: The Term Structure of Interest Rates, 1966, The Inflation-Beater's Investment Guide, 1980, Global Bargain Hunting, 1998, A Random Walk Down Wall Street, 9th edit., 2007, The Random Walk Guide to Investing, 2003; author: (with others) Strategies and Rational Decisions in the Securities Options Market, 1969, The Index Fund Solution, 1999. 1st lt. US Army, 1955—58. Mem.: Am. Fin. Assn. (dir., pres. 1978). Home: 76 North Rd Princeton NJ 08540-2430 Office: Princeton U Dept Econs Princeton NJ 08544-0001 Office Phone: 609-258-6445. Business E-Mail: bmalkiel@princeton.edu.

MALKIEL, NANCY WEISS, dean, historian, educator; b. Newark, Feb. 14, 1944; d. William and Ruth Sylvia (Puder) Weiss; m. Burton G. Malkiel, July 31, 1988. BA summa cum laude, Smith Coll., 1965; MA, Harvard U., 1966, PhD, 1970. From asst. to assoc. prof. history Princeton (N.J.) U., 1969-82, prof., 1982—, master Dean Mathey Coll., 1982-86, dean coll., 1987—. Author (as Nancy J. Weiss): (book) Charles Francis Murphy, 1858-1924: Respectability and Responsibility in Tammany Politics, 1968; author: (with others) Blacks in America: Bibliographical Essays, 1971, The National Urban League, 1910-1940, 1974, Farewell to the Party of Lincoln: Black Politics in the Age of FDR, 1983 (Berkshire Conf. of Women Historians prize, 1984), Whitney M. Young Jr., and the Struggle for Civil Rights, 1989. Trustee Woodrow Wilson Nat. Fellowship Found., 1975—, chmn. bd. trustees, 1999—; trustee Smith Coll., Northampton, Mass., 1984—94. Fellow, Woodrow Wilson Found., 1965, Charles Warren Ctr. Studies in Am. History, 1976—77, Radcliffe Inst., 1976—77, Ctr. Advanced Study Behavioral Scis., 1986—87. Mem.: So. Hist. Assn., Orgn. Am. Historians (chmn. status women hist. profession 1972—75), Am. Hist. Assn., Phi Beta Kappa. Democrat. Jewish. Office: Princeton U Office Dean Of College Princeton NJ 08544-0001

MALKIN, BARRY, film editor, consultant; b. NYC, Oct. 26, 1938; s. Richard and Helen (Kandix) M.; m. Stephanie Byer; 1 child, Sacha Janine. BA, Adelphi U., 1960. Freelance film editor Sacha Prodns., Inc., NYC, 1964—. Editor: (films) The Rain People, 1969, Cotton Comes to Harlem, 1970, They Might Be Giants, 1971, Who is Harry Kellerman?, 1971, Cops and Robbers, 1973, The Godfather Part 2, 1974, One Summer Love, 1976, Somebody Killed Her Husband, 1978, Last Embrace, 1979, One Trick Pony, 1980, Windows, 1980, Four Friends, 1981, Hammett, 1982, Rumble Fish, 1983, The Cotton Club, 1984 (Acad. award nominee for best film editing 1984), Peggy Sue Got Married, 1986, Gardens of Stone, 1987, Big, 1988, New York Stories ("Life Without Zoe"), 1989, The Freshman, 1990, The Godfather Part III, 1990 (Acad. award nominee for best film editing 1990), Honeymoon in Vegas, 1992, It Could Happen to You, 1994, Jack, 1996, The Rainmaker, 1997, Isn't She Great, 1999, Lucky Numbers, 2000, The Big Bounce, 2003, The Treatment, 2005, The Skeptic, 2006. Mem. Acad. Motion Picture Arts and Scis., Motion Picture Editors Guild, Am. Cinema Editors. Home and Office: 275 Central Park W New York NY 10024-3015 E-mail: cpwblackie@aol.com.

MALKIN, CARY JAY, lawyer; b. Chgo., Oct. 6, 1949; s. Arthur D. and Perle (Slavin) Malkin; m. Lisa Kimley, Oct. 27, 1976; children: Dorothy R., Victoria S., Lydia R. BA, George Washington U., 1971; JD, Northwestern U., 1974. Bar: Ill. 1974, U.S. Dist. Ct. (no. dist.) Ill. 1974, N.Y. 2001. Assoc. Mayer, Brown & Platt, Chgo., 1974—80, ptnr., 1991—2002, Mayer, Brown, Rowe & Maw LLP, Chgo., 2002—07, Mayer Brown LLP, Chgo., 2007—. Chmn. spl. events com. Mental Health Assn., 1984—85; mem. steering com. Endowment Campaign Latin Sch. Chgo., 1990—91, trustee, 1991—2000, nat. trustee, 2000—02, sr. trustee, 2002—; chmn. Campaign Latin Sch. Chgo., 1995—98; mem. exec. com. Friends Prentice Women's Hosp., 1991—92; bd. dirs. SOS Children's Village Ill., 1992—96; mem. M. S. Weiss fund bd. Children's Meml. Hosp., 1993—96, mem. Graziano fund bd., 1993—96; trustee Field Mus., 1999—, mem. fin. com., 2002—05, mem. investment com., 2003—05, mem. budget com., 2005—, mem. founder's coun., 1995—, chmn. founder's coun., 1999—2003. Mem.: Saddle and Cycle Club (bd. govs. 1998—2001, 2006—), Chgo. Club, Phi Beta Kappa, Order of Coif. Home: 233 E Walton St Chicago IL 60611-1526 Office: Mayer Brown LLP 71 S Wacker Dr Chicago IL 60606

MALKIN, EVGENI, professional hockey player; b. Magnitogorsk, Russia, July 31, 1986; s. Vladimir and Tatiana Malkin. Center Metallurg Magnitogorsk (Russian Super League), 2003—06, Pitts. Penguins, 2006—. Mem. Team Russia, Olympic Games, Torino, Italy, 2006; player NHL YoungStars Game, 2007. Named NHL Rookie of Yr., Sporting News, 2007; named to All-Rookie Team, NHL, 2007; recipient Calder Trophy, 2007. Achievements include being drafted in the first round (2nd overall) in the NHL Entry Draft, 2004; being a member of silver medal Team Russia, World Junior Championships, 2006. Office: c/o Pitts Penguins 66 Mario Lemieux Pl Pittsburgh PA 15219 *

MALKIN, JOSEPH M., lawyer; b. NYC, Jan. 26, 1947; BA, Claremont Men's Coll., 1968; JD, Yale U., 1972. Bar: Calif. 1972, U.S. Dist. Ct. (ctrl. dist.) Calif. 1972, U.S. Dist. Ct. (no. dist.) Calif. 1972, U.S. Fed. Cts. 1972, U.S. Ct. Appeals (9th cir.) 1973, U.S. Supreme Ct. 1976. Mem. O'Melveny & Myers, San Francisco; ptnr. in charge-San Francisco Office Orrick, Herrington & Sutcliffe LLP, San Francisco, co-chmn. energy & project fin. group. Editor Yale Law Jour., 1970-72. Recipient Carter, Ledyard and Milburn prize Yale Law Sch., 1970. Mem. ABA, Bar Assn. San Francisco. Office: Orrick, Herrington & Sutcliffe LLP The Orrick Building 405 Howard St San Francisco CA 94105 Office Phone: 415-773-5505. Office Fax: 415-773-5759. Business E-Mail: jmalkin@orrick.com.

MALKIN, MARJORIE J., recreational therapist, educator; b. New Haven, May 28, 1946; d. Jacob K. and Charlotte S. Malkin; m. Timothy J. Brossart, May 26, 1996; 1 child, Jace Andrew Brossart; 1 child from previous marriage, Daniel Jacob Klotz. BA cum laude, Mt. Holyoke Coll., South Hadley, Mass., 1967; MEd, U. Ga., Athens, 1983, EdD, 1986. Cert. therapeutic recreation specialist Nat. Coun. Therapeutic Recreation Cert., 1983. Recreation therapist Athens Gen. Hosp., 1983—87; dir. activity therapy CPC Palm Bay Hosp., Fla., 1987—88; dir. adjunctive therapy Charter Hosp., Paducah, NY, 1988—89; prof., grad. coord. So. Ill. U., Carbondale, 1989—. Vis. asst. prof. Murray State U., Ky., 1988—89; cons. Ill. Dept. Human Svcs., Springfield, 1995—2002; cons., trainer U. Costa Rica, San Jose, 1996—97, Togliatti Social & Econ. Coll., Russia, 1998—2001, Samara Tech. Coll., Russia, 1998—2001; invited spkr., Barretstown, Ireland, 2007—. Contbr. chapters to books, articles to profl. jours. Named Outstanding Vol., Spl. olympics, 2002; recipient Profl. Knowledge award, Ill. Recreational Therapy Assn., 1997, 2001; scholar, Leisure Careers Found., 1985—86; Tom and Ruth Rivers grantee, World Leisure and Recreation Assn., 1985. Mem.: Am. Therapeutic Recreation Assn. (internat. rels. team co-leader, past chair rsch. com. 2005—07, bd. dirs. 1992—94, Presdl. award for Outstanding Profl. Contbns. 1991—92, Best Rsch. presentation 1995), US Equestrian Fedn. (nat. lic. horse show judge and steward 1979—2007), Kappa Delta Pi. Achievements include research in suicidal and depressed women; adolescent and family substance abuse; equine assisted therapy. Avocations: swimming, horseback riding, gardening, cooking, reading. Home: 335 Old US Hwy 51 Makanda IL 62958 Office: So Ill U 307 Pulliam Hall Carbondale IL 62901-4632 Office Phone: 618-453-4331. Office Fax: 618-453-1829. Business E-Mail: mmalkin@siu.edu.

MALKIN, MICHAEL M., lawyer; b. New Haven, Nov. 1, 1944; s. Eli B. and Gladys (Pollak) M.; children: Andrea, Lisa, Daniel. BA, U. N.Mex., 1966; JD, NYU, 1969. Bar: N.Y. 1970, U.S. Dist. Ct. (so. dist.) N.Y. 1971, U.S. Dist. Ct. (ea. dist.) N.Y. 1971, U.S. Ct. Appeals (2d cir.) 1972, U.S. Supreme Ct. 1984. Assoc. Weil, Lee & Bergin, NYC, 1970-76, Weil, Guttman & Davis, NYC, 1976-77, ptnr., 1977-82, Weil, Guttman, Davis & Malkin, NYC, 1982-86, Weil, Guttman & Malkin, NYC, 1986-95, Weil, Guttman & Malkin, LLP, NYC, 1995—2001. Judge Giles Sutherland Rich Moot Ct. Competition, N.Y.C., 1982; arbitrator Civil Ct. of City N.Y., 1984-88. Mem. editl. bd. Trademark Reporter, 1973-75, 88-90, contbg. editor, 1974-75. Mem. N.Y. State Bar Assn., U.S. Trademark Assn., Phi Delta Phi, Alpha Epsilon Pi. Office Phone: 480-513-2859. Business E-Mail: mikemalkin@cox.net.

MALKIN, MICHELLE, columnist; b. Phila., Oct. 20, 1970; d. Apolo and Rafaela Maglalang; married; 2 children. B, Oberlin Coll., Ohio, 1992. Editorial writer, columnist LA Daily News, 1992—94; editorial bd. Seattle Times, 1996—99. Author: Invasion: How America Still Welcomes Terrorists, Criminals and Other Foreign Menaces to Our Shores, 2002 (NY Times bestseller), In Defense of Internment: The Case for Racial Profiling in World War II and the War on Terror, 2004 (NY Times bestseller), Unhinged: Exposing Liberals Gone Wild, 2005; syndicated columnist, commentator Fox News Channel, polit. blogger michellemalkin.com, 2004— (rated as one of the best polit. blogs in 2005, Forbes Mag. and The Week Mag.). Warren Brookes Fellow, Competitive Enterprise Inst., 1995. Avocations: fishing, piano, crocheting. Mailing: Creators Syndicate Ste 700 5777 W Century Blvd Los Angeles CA 90045 E-mail: writemalkin@gmail.com. *

MALKIN, MOSES MONTEFIORE, retired employee benefits administration company, diversified financial services company executive; b. Revere, Mass., Sept. 18, 1919; s. Irving and Annie (Helfant) M.; m. Hannah Lacob, Oct. 11, 1941. AB, U. N.C., 1941; BSME, Columbia U., 1948. Enrolled actuary; CLU. Engr. GE, Schenectady, NY, 1948-50; engr. Gen. Bronze, Inc., Jersey City, 1950-51; v.p. Malkin Warehouse, Inc., New Haven, 1951-57; pvt. practice actuary and adminstr. New Haven, 1957—72; chmn., actuary Profl. Pensions, Inc., Middletown, Conn., 1973—93; ret., 1993. Presenter pension issues at numerous confs., 1970-80. Pres., founder Milford, Conn., 1962, Milford Child Guidance Clinic, 1966; pres. Clifford Beers Child Guidance, New Haven, 1971, Jewish Family Svc., New Haven, 1973. With U.S. Army, 1941-45, ETO. Mem. Am. Acad. Actuaries (ret. mem.), Am. Soc. Pension Actuaries (ret. mem., instr. 1984), Am. Soc. CLUs (ret. mem.), Phi Beta Kappa, Tau Beta Pi. Jewish. Address: 1514 Heron Dr Sun City Center FL 33573-4707

MALKIN, PETER LAURENCE, lawyer, investor; b. NYC, Jan. 14, 1934; s. Samuel and Gertrude (Greenberger) Malkin; m. Isabel L. Wien, July 10, 1955. Grad. cum laude, Poly. Prep. Country Day Sch., 1951; AB summa cum laude, Harvard Coll., Cambridge, Mass., 1955; LLB magna cum laude, Harvard U. Law Sch., Cambridge, 1958. Bar: NY 1958, Conn. 1976, Fla. 1977. Sr. ptnr., chmn. Wien & Malkin LLC, NYC, 1958—; mng. Empire State Bldg. Assocs. LLC, 1961—; chmn. W & M Properties, Inc., NYC, 1965—. Ptnr. NYC Partnership, NYC, 2001—; founding chmn. Grand Ctrl. Partnership Inc. & 34th Street Partnership, Inc.; founding dir., sec. Fashion Ctr. Bus. Improvement Dist.; dir. Realty Found. NY, 1981—, v.p., 1995—; mem. adv. com. Greenwich Japanese Sch., Conn., 1992—2005; mem. NYC Mayor's Bus. Adv. Coun., 1997—2002; gov. Real Estate Bd., NYC, 1993—2005; co-founder, hon. co-chmn. Com. Encouraging Corp. Philanthropy, 1998—; emeritus dir. US Trust Corp. Chmn. Met. Aircraft Noise Mitigation Commn., 1990—; vice-chmn. Harvard Law Sch. Fund, 1967-71, chmn. nat. scholarship com., 1975-76, chmn. NYC com., 1981-83; founder, bd. dir. Urban League Southwestern Fairfield County, 1969-73, treas., 1969-71; bd. dir., exec. com. Lincoln Ctr. Performing Arts, 1979—; bd. dir. Inst. Internat. Edn., 1983-89, hon. 1994—; bd. dir. Greenwich Ctr. Arts, 2004—; mem. adv. bd. Conn. Trust Hist. Preservation, 2007—; trustee Nat. Trust Hist. Preservation, 1988-91, adv. coun., 1997—, trustee emeritus, 2005—; founding chmn. Greenwich Green & Clean, Inc., 1986—, Greenwich Adopt-A-Road, 1996-; founding pres. Greenwich Tree Conservancy, 2006—; chmn., co-founder Merritt Pkwy. Conservancy, 2002—; v.p., exec. com. Greenwich chpt. NAACP, 1967-69; trustee Citizens Budget Commn., NYC, 1971-91, Jewish Communal Fund, NY, 1976-81; dean's coun., Harvard U., 1987-95; chmn. capital campaign and chmn. dean's coun. Kennedy Sch. Govt., 1995—, overseers com. to visit Kennedy Sch. Govt., 1976-82, 83-89, 90—, to visit Harvard Law Sch. 1977-83; exec. com. Program Ctr. Jewish Studies, 1974-80; bd. overseers Harvard Coll., 1989-95, overseers com. univ resources, 1972—, exec. com., 1985—; dean's adv. com. Harvard Law Sch., 1988-90; elected dir. Harvard Alumni Assn., 1981-83; chmn. schs. and scholarship com. Harvard Coll., Greenwich, 1973-79; exec. com. Assn. Better NY, 1972—; founder NY leadership com. Harvard Coll. Fund. Brandeis U. fellow, 1970—; recipient Outstanding Young Man award, NYC Jaycees, 1969; named Man of Yr., Hist. Soc. Greenwich, Conn., 1993, Man of Yr., Greenwich Rotary, 2005; recipient Nat. Preservation Honor award Nat. Trust Hist. Preservation, 1987, Pres. award Grad. Sch. and Univ. Ctr. CUNY, 1989, Crain's All-Star award, 1994, Nacore Disting. Man of Yr. award, 1995; Murray Hill Archl. award, 1996, PENCIL award for outstanding commitment to NYC Pub. Schs., 2003, Lincoln Ctr. Outstanding Vol. Leader award, 2004. Mem. Harvard Law Sch. Assn. NYC (trustee 1968-70, v.p. 1973-74), Assn. Bar City NY, Century Assn., Links NY, The Hasty Pudding Inst. 1770, AD Hon., Harvard Varsity Club (Cambridge), Harvard Club NYC (bd. mgrs. 1979-81), Harvard Club (Fairfield County, Conn., v.p. 1974-75, bd. dirs. 1976-80), Bailwick Club (hon. life, founding pres.), Blind Brook Club, Conn. Golf Club, Indian Harbor Yacht Club, Phi Beta Kappa. Office: 60 E 42d St New York NY 10165-0015 Business E-Mail: plmalkin@wienmalkin.com.

MALKIN, STANLEY LEE, neurologist; b. Pitts., Nov. 11, 1942; s. Maurice and Bessie Beatrice (Serbin) M.; m. Candace N. Conard; children: Justin Ross, Keith Richard. BA with honors, U. Pa., 1964; MD, U. Pitts., 1968. Diplomate Am. Bd. Psychiatry and Neurology, Nat. Bd. Med. Examiners. Intern Montefiore Hosp., Pitts., 1968-69; resident in neurology Columbia-Presbyn. Med. Ctr., NYC, 1969-72; chief neurology svc., Wright-Patterson AFB, Dayton, 1972-74; practice medicine specializing in neurology NYC; attending staff Mt. Sinai Hosp.; former dir. Neuro-

Diagnostic Lab., Englewood; asst. clin. prof. neurology Mt. Sinai Sch. Medicine; founder Bergen-Passaic Tomography Ctr., Fairlawn, N.J. Neurology cons. Regent Hosp.; med. dir. Pain Suppression Labs., Inc.; med. dir. Efficient Health Systems, Inc.-N.Y.C, Healthline; founder, med. dir., exec. v.p. Hosp. Diagnostic Equipment Corp., 1987—; pres. Cancer Treatment Holdings, Inc, 1993-95, dir. 1993-94, sr. med. dir. 1995-97; founder Montvale Med. Imaging Assocs. (N.J.), N.Y. Med. Imaging, N.Y.C., Hosp. Diagnostic Equipment Corp. Co-mcpl. coord. Ft. Lee Citizens for McGovern, 1972; ptnr. Sall/Myers Med. Assocs., prin. 1995—; mem. Edgewater Rent Control Bd., 1978. Maj. M.C. USAF, 1972-74. Recipient Comdr.'s Recognition award for care of repatriated prisoners of war, 1973; award Am.'s Top Physicians Consumers' Rsch. Coun. Am., 2004-05. Fellow Royal Soc. Medicine; mem. Am. Acad. Neurology, Am. Assn. Electrodiagnostic Medicine, Am. Soc. Neuro-Imaging (charter), EEG and Clin. Neurosci. Soc., Am. Headache Soc. (rev. bd.), Nat. Headache Found., Internat. Headache Soc., Nat. Neurotrauma Soc., N.Y. Acad. Scis., NYU Bellevue Psychiat. Soc., European Fedn. Neurol. Socs. Office: 60 E 42d St Ste 2214 New York NY 10165

MALKINSON, FREDERICK DAVID, dermatologist, educator; b. Hartford, Conn., Feb. 26, 1924; s. John Walter and Rose Malkinson; m. Una Zwick, June 15, 1979; children by previous marriage: Philip, Carol, John. Student, Loomis Inst., 1937-41; 3 yr. cert. cum laude, Harvard U., 1943, DMD, 1947, MD, 1949. Intern Harvard-Beth Israel Hosp., Boston, 1949-50; resident in dermatology U. Chgo., 1950-54, from instr. to assoc. prof. dept. dermatology, 1954-68; prof. medicine and dermatology U. Ill., Chgo., 1968-71; chmn. dept. dermatology Rush Med. Coll. and Rush-Presbyn.-St. Luke's Med. Ctr. (now Rush U. Med. Ctr.), Chgo., 1968-92, Clark W. Finnerud, M.D. prof. dept. dermatology, 1981-95, 95—; trustee Sulzberger Inst. Dermatol. Comm. and Edn., 1976-96; pres. Sulzberger Inst. Dermatol. Communication and Edn., 1983-88, 93-96; prof. emeritus Rush U. Med. Ctr., Chgo., 2000—. Editor: Year Book of Dermatology, 1971-78; chief editor: AMA Archives of Dermatology, 1979-83; bd. editors, 1976-84, Jour. AMA, 1979-83; editorial cons. World Book Medical Encyclopedia, 1991-2000; contbr. articles to profl. jours., chpts. to books. Active Evanston (Ill.) Libr. Bd., 1988-94, pres., 1993-94. With M.C. USNR, 1950-52. Grantee, U.S. Army, 1955—61, USPHS, 1962—70. Fellow AAAS; mem. Am. Acad. Dermatology (v.p. 1987-89, dir. 1964-67), Am. Dermatol. Assn., Soc. Investigative Dermatology (v.p. 1978-79, dir. 1963-68), Am. Fedn. Med. Rsch., Cen. Soc. Clin. Rsch., Radiation Rsch. Soc., Assn. Profs. of Dermatology (dir. 1982-85), Dermatology Found. (exec. com., trustee 1980-93, pres. 1983-85, Lifetime Career Educator award 2006), Nat. Coun. on Radiation Protection and Measurements (mem. com. on cutaneous radiobiology 1986-92), Chgo. Dermatol. Soc. (pres. 1964-65, Gold Medal award 1992, established ann. lectureship, 2004), Chgo. Lit. Club (v.p. 1997-99, 2000-03, pres. 1999-2000). Office: Rush Univ Med Ctr Dept Dermatology 707 S Wood St 220 Annex Bldg Chicago IL 60612 Office Fax: 312-942-7778.

MALKOVICH, JOHN, actor; b. Christopher, Ill., Dec. 9, 1953; m. Glenne Headley, 1982 (div. 1988); m. Glenne Headly, Aug. 2, 1982 (div. 1988); m. Nicoletta Peyran, 1989; children: Amandine and Lorwy. Student, Eastern Ill. U., Ill. State U. Co-founder Steppenwolf Theatre, Chgo., 1976 Made N.Y.C. theatrical debut in True West, 1982 (Obie award, Clarence Derwent award); other theatrical appearances include: Death of a Salesman, 1984, Burn This, 1987, States of Shock; dir. Balm in Gilead, 1984-85, Arms and the Man, 1985, The Caretaker, 1986, Coyote Ugly, (Chgo., Kennedy Ctr. for Performing Arts, Washington) 1985, Libra, 1994, Steppenwolf, 1994; appeared in films Places in the Heart, 1984, The Killing Fields, 1984, Eleni, 1985, Making Mr. Right, 1987, Glass Menagerie, 1987, Empire of the Sun, 1987, Miles From Home, 1988, Dangerous Liaisons, 1988, The Sheltering Sky, 1990, Queen's Logic, 1991, The Object of Beauty, 1991, Shadows and Fog, 1992, Jennifer 8, 1992, Of Mice and Men, 1992, In The Line Of Fire, 1993 (Academy award nomination best supporting actor 1993), Alive, 1993, Touchstone, 1994, Para De La Nuages, 1994, Mary Reilly, 1994, Mulholland Falls, 1996, Der Unhold, 1996, The Portrait of a Lady, 1996, Primary Colors, 1997, Con Air, 1997, The Man in the Iron Mask, 1998, Rounders, 1998, Le Temps retrouvé, 1999, The Libertine, 1999, Ladies Room, 1999, Joan of Arc, 1999, Being John Malkovich, 1999 (American Comedy Award, 2000), Shadow of the Vampire, 2000, Les Ames Forte, 2001, Knockaround Guys, 2001, Je rentre a la Maison, 2001, Ripley's Game, 2002, Hotel, 2001, The Dancer Upstairs, 2002, Johnny English, 2003, The Hitchhiker's Guide to the Galaxy, 2005, Colour Me Kubrick, 2005, Klimt, 2006, The Call, 2006, Eragon, 2006; exec. prodr. The Accidental Tourist, 1988, Somewhere Else, 2000; prodr. Ghost World, 2000, The Loner, 2001, Found in the Street, 2001, The Dancer Upstairs, 2002, Ripley's Game, 2002, Johnny English, 2003, A Talking Picture, 2003, The Libertine, 2004, Kill the Poor, 2006, Art School Confidential, 2006; co-exec. prodr. The Accidental Tourist, 1988; The Dancer Upstairs, 2002; appeared in TV films Word of Honor, 1981, American Dream, 1981, Death of a Salesman, 1985 (Emmy award 1986), Heart of Darkness, 1994, RKO 281, 1999, Les Miserables, 2000, Napoleon, 2002. *

MALKOVICH, MARK PAUL, III, musician, performing company executive; b. Eveleth, Minn., July 10, 1930; s. Mark II and Mary Frances (Greben) M.; m. Joan Shewring, Feb. 7, 1959; children: Mark IV, Erik, Kent, Kara. BS in Chemistry, Columbia U., 1952, MS, 1953; studied piano with Dorothy Crost Bourgin, Chgo. Mus. Coll., 1947-50; William Beller ch. Piano Dept., Columbia U., 1951-54; Adele Marcus, Juilliard Sch., 1959-62; MusD (hon.), Salve Regina, 1993; DFA, U. RI, 1994; MusD, Cath. U. Am., 1999. Pres. Chem. Gum Industries, Ltd., NYC, 1964—69. Artistic and gen. dir. Newport Music Festival, 1975—; exec. dir. Palm Beach Festival, Fla., 1984-86; guest lectr. TV and radio appearances and adjudicator at music competitions; pres. Chopin Found. of U.S., Miami, Fla., 1985; presented N.Am. debuts of Bella Davidovich, Jean-Philippe Collard, Dmitry Sitkovevsky, Andrei Gavrilov, Mikhail Pletnev, others; founder Sports US*A*SR; negotiator/agt. for USSR leading hockey players Fetisov, Krutov, Larionov, Makarov, 1989. Recipient Individual Achievement award Bus. Vols. for the Arts, RI, 1998; named to RI Heritage Hall of Fame, 2000; named hon. citizen, Tbilisi, Republic of Ga., hon. prof. Tbilisi Conservatoire. Mem. Harvard Mus. Assn., Newport Reading Rm., Newport Hist. Soc., Spouting Rock Beach Assn., Royal Arts Found. (pres.), Clambake Club. Office: care Newport Music Festival PO Box 3300 Newport RI 02840-0992 Office Phone: 401-846-1133. Business E-Mail: staff@newportmusic.org.

MALKOWICZ, STANLEY BRUCE, urologist; b. Passaic, NJ; s. Stanley Jacob and Jeanne (iracki) M.; m. Denise Elaine Ewald, Sept. 22, 1985. BA, U. Vt., 1977; MD, U. Pa., Phila., 1981. Intern in surgery Hosp. U. Pa., Phila., 1981-82, resident in surgery, 1982-83, resident in urology, 1983-86, chief resident in urology, 1986-87; fellow in urologic oncology U. So. Calif., LA, 1987-88, Hosp. U. Pa., Phila., 1988-90, asst. prof. surgery, 1990-95, assoc. prof., 1995—2003, prof. urology, 2003—; chief urology Phila. VA Med. Ctr. Assoc. scientist Wistar Inst. Anatomy and Biology, Phila., 1988—; Nat. Kidney Found. rsch. fellow, 1983-84; Am. Found. Urologic Disease rsch. scholar, 1988-90. Contbr. articles to profl. jours. Mem. AAAS, Am. Urologic Assn., Am. Assn. GU Surgeons, Am. Soc. Clin. Oncology, Soc. Univ. Urologists, Urodynamics Soc., Assn. Academic Surgeons, Soc. Pelvic Surgeons (treas.-sec.), Soc. Urologic Oncology, Urol. Rsch. Soc., Phila. Urol. Soc. (pres.), S.E. Pa. Am. Cancer Soc. (pres.), Sigma Xi. Presbyterian. Avocations: camping, reading, cooking. Office: Hosp U Pa Philadelphia PA 19104-4206 Home Phone: 610-525-0117; Office Phone: 215-662-7330.

MALKS, BETTY F., social worker; d. Benjamin Fishman and Bertha Finkelstein; m. Joshua B. Malks, Aug. 28, 1988; children: Nicole Shana Rosen, Brannon Benjamin. BA, U. Md., College Park, 1967; MSW, Adelphi U., LI, NY, 1982. LCSW N.Y., 1982; cert. exec. mgmt. devel. U. Calif., Berkeley, 1994. Dir. enriched housing programs Associated Y's of Greater N.Y., NYC, 1983—88; social svcs. program mgr. County of Santa Clara, San Jose, Calif., 1993—97, dir. dept. aging and adult svcs., 1997—. Chair Elder and Dependent Adult Law Enforcement Protocol Task Force, San Jose, 1999—2002, Fin. Institutions Team to Combat Elder Fin. Abuse, San Jose, 2003—; founder Fin. Abuse Specialist Team, San Jose, 1999, Vets. Resource Faire, San Jose, 1999; panelist Second World Conf. on Family Violence, Prague, Czech Republic, 2003, Internat. Assn. Geriatrics and Gerontology Conf., Rio de Janeiro, 2005; N.Am. regional rep. Internat. Network for Prevention of Elder Abuse, 2003—; chair First Aging Summit Calif. Social Work Edn. Ctr., Long Beach, Calif., 2004; project dir. Faith-based Initiative for Elder Abuse Awareness in Diverse Communities, San Jose, 2006—; presenter in field. Contbr. articles to profl. jours. Congl. del. White House Conf. on Aging, 2005; bd. dirs. Jewish Cmty. Rels. Coun., San Jose, 1990—93, Coun. on Aging, San Jose, 1992—93, Women's Fund of Silicon Valley, San Jose, 2002—04; chair Sr. Citizen's Commn., San Jose, 1992—94; charter mem. Nat. Holocaust, Washington, 1998—. Named Woman of Achievement, Women's Fund of Silicon Valley, 2001; recipient commendation, Santa Clara County Bd. Dirs., 2000, award for outstanding svc. to the disabled cmty., Internat. Assn. Workforce Profls., Am.'s Crown Communities award for creation of the FAST team, Am. City and County mag., 2001, President's award, Nat. Assn. Adult Protective Svcs., 2004. Mem.: Internat/Network for Prevention of Elder Abuse, Am. Soc. on Aging, Nat. Com. for Prevention of Elder Abuse. Avocations: exercise, travel. Home Phone: 831-477-1818; Office Phone: 408-975-4848. Business E-Mail: betty.malks@ssa.sccgov.org.

MALKUS, DAVID STARR, mathematician; b. Chgo., June 30, 1945; s. Willem V.R. Malkus and Joanne (Gerould) Simpson; m. Evelyn R. (div.); children: Christopher, Annelise, Byron, Renata. AB, Yale U., 1968; PhD, Boston U., 1976. Mathematician U.S. Nat. Bur. Standards, Gaithersburg, Md., 1975-77; asst. prof. math. Ill. Inst. Tech., Chgo., 1977-83, assoc. prof., 1983-84; assoc. prof. mechanics U. Wis., Madison, 1984-87, prof., 1987—2002, chmn. Rheology Rsch. Ctr., 1991-94, prof. emeritus, 2002—. Chair prof. Nanjing (People's Republic China) Aero. Inst., 1986. Co-author: Concepts and Applications of Finite Element Analysis, 1989; contbr. articles to Computer Methods Applied Mech. Engring., Jour. Computational Physics. Achievements include research on finite element methods--reduced and selective integration techniques, a unification of concepts. Home: 2710 Mason St Madison WI 53705-3716 Home Phone: 608-232-1455. Business E-Mail: malkus@engr.wisc.edu.

MALL, SANFORD J., lawyer; Cert.: Nat. Elder Law Found. (elder law atty.), Soc. Sr. Advs. (sr. adv.). Founder, sr. ptnr. Mall Malisow & Cooney PC, Farmington Hills, Mich. Instr. estate planning Cert. Fin. Planning prog. Coll. Fin. Planning, Denver. Named one of Top 100 Attys., Worth mag., 2006. Mem.: State Bar Mich. (chair elder law & disability rights sect.). Office: Mall Malisow & Cooney PC 30445 Northwestern Hwy Ste 250 Farmington Hills MI 48334 Office Phone: 248-538-1800. Office Fax: 248-538-1801. E-mail: sjmjd@teclf.com.

MALL, SHANKAR, engineering mechanics educator, researcher; came to U.S., 1974; s. Hari Das and Methul Mall; m. Raj Kumari, Dec. 2, 1965; 1 child, Sharal. BSME, Banaras Hindu U., Varanasi, 1964, MS, 1966; PhD, U. Wash., 1977. Engr. in tng. Kisha Seizo Kaisha, Osaka, Japan, 1966-67; lectr. mech. engring. Banaras Hindu U., 1967-74; rsch. asst. U. Wash., Seattle, 1974-77; asst. prof. U. Maine, Orono, 1978-81, assoc. prof., 1981-83, U. Mo., Rolla, 1983-86; prof., head Air Force Inst. Tech., Wright-Patterson AFB, Ohio, 1986-98; prof., prin. materials rsch. engr. Air Force Rsch. Lab., Wright-Patterson AFB, 1998—. Rsch. engr. NASA Langley Research Ctr., Hampton, Va., 1981-82. Author several chapters in technical books; author: (more than 250 technical papers), editor technical book, metal matrix composites. Tech. program chair of tech. conf. Am. Inst. of Aeronautics and Astronautics, Reston, Va., 2001; organizer of several tech. symposia ASME; pres., sch. of engring. faculty coun. Air Force Inst. of Tech., Wright-Patterson AFB, Ohio; dir. of honors and awards ASME, Dayton Chapter, Ohio, 1987—89. Recipient Elected Membership of Honor Soc., Tau Beta Pi, Simga Xi, Sigma Gamma Tau, Outstanding Paper, Jour. of Composites and Tech., 1995, Outstanding Paper Award, Fatigue and Fracture of Engring. Materials and Structures, Internat. Jour., 2002, Outstanding Engr. and Scientist, Affiliated Societies Coun., Dayton, OH, 1997, Stone Award for Leadership, Air Force Inst. of Tech., 1990, Tenure, U. of Maine, 1981, U. of Missouri-Rolla, 1986, Air Force Inst. of Tech., 1989, Listed in, Who Who's in Engring., Who Who's in Tech., Who Who's in Am. Edn., Am. Men and Women of Sci.; fellow Fellow, ASME, 1993, Assoc. Fellow, Am. Inst. of Aeronautics and Astronautics, 1991; grantee More than 2 million dollars of rsch. grants, Nat. Funding agencies and Laboratories, 1994-2004. Fellow ASME, AIAA (assoc.); mem. Sigma Xi, Tau Beta Pi. Achievements include Supervised, guided and advised more than 100 PhD and MS Dissertations and Theses. Home: 2374 N Knoll Dr Dayton OH 45431-2454 Office: Dept Aeronautics & Astronautics Air Force Inst Technol Wright Patterson Afb OH 45433

MALL, WILLIAM JOHN, JR., aerospace transportation executive, retired military officer; b. Pitts., Jan. 13, 1933; s. William John and Margaret (Henry) M.; m. Vivian Lea Fenton; children— Michele, William, Catherine BBA, U. Pitts., 1954; MBA, George Washington U., 1966; sr. mgrs. in govt. program, Harvard U., 1980. Commd. officer USAF, 1954, advanced through grades to maj. gen., 1981; insp. gen. Mil. Airlift Command., Scott AFB, Ill., 1978, comdr. 436 wing Dover AFB, Del., 1979; DCS personnel Mil. Airlift Command, Scott AFB, Ill., 1979-81; comdr. Air Rescue Service, Scott AFB, Ill., 1981-83, 23d AF/MAC, Scott AFB, Ill., 1983-85; assigned to Hdqrs USAF, Bolling AFB, DC, 1985-86; ret.; dir. integrated logistics support div. Douglas Aircraft Co., Long Beach, Calif., 1987-89, gen. mgr. human resources, 1989-91; exec. dir. LAX Two Corp., LA, 1991-99. Decorated Legion of Merit, Bronze Star, Air medal Mem. Airlift Assn., Daedalians, Jolly Green Pilots Assn. Avocations: tennis, sailing. Office: LAX Two Corp 200 World Way Los Angeles CA 90045-5859

MALLAPRAGADA, SURYA K., science educator; d. Nageswara Rao and Padma Mallapragada; m. Balaji Narasimhan, Dec. 14, 2000. BTech in Chem. Engring., Indian Inst. Tech., Bombay, 1993; PhD, Purdue U., West Lafayette, Ind., 1996. Asst. prof. Iowa State U., Ames, 1996—2001, assoc. prof., 2001—06, prof., 2006—. Program dir. Ames Lab., 2004—. Contbr. articles to profl. jours. Recipient Non-tenured faculty award, 3M, 2001, Career award, NSF, 2001, TR100 award, MIT's Tech. Rev., 2002, Global Indus Technovator award, MIT Indsl. Bus. Club, 2003, Rising Star award, Big 12 U. Consortium, 2007. Fellow: Am. Inst. Med. and Biol. Engring. (life); mem.: AIChE (chair food pharm. and bioengring. divsn. 2007—), Sigma Xi (life; nominating com. mem. 2001—02), Tau Beta Pi (life; advisor 1996—2000). Achievements include patents for nerve regeneration; methacrylic acid copolymers. Office: Iowa State Univ 3035 Sweeney Hall Ames IA 50011-2230 Office Phone: 515-294-7407. Business E-Mail: suryakm@iastate.edu.

MALLARD, CARRIE CHARLENE, science educator; b. Canton, Ill., Apr. 12, 1976; d. Robert Darwin and Barbara Charlene Mallard. BS, U. Ill., 1998, MS, 2001. Grad. tchg. asst. dept. agrl. and consumer econ. U. Ill., Champaign/Urbana, 1998—99, grad. rsch. asst. dept. animal scis., 1998—2001, vis. vet. rsch. asst. dept. clin. medicine, 2001—03; life sciences instr. Lincoln Trail Coll., Robinson, Ill., 2003—. Contbr. articles to profl. jours. Mem.: Nat. Mastitis Coun., Am. Dairy Assn. Avocations: travel, scrapbooking, reading. Office: Lincoln Trail Coll 11220 State Hwy 1 Robinson IL 62454 Home Phone: 618-544-4659; Office Phone: 618-544-8657.

MALLARD, STEPHEN ANTHONY, retired utilities executive; b. Jersey City, Sept. 15, 1924; s. Stephen F. and Gertrude V. (Donahue) M.; m. Winifred Anne Carey, June 7, 1947; children: Stephen Kevin, Catherine Anne, Eileen Rosemary Mallard McClenahan. M.E., Stevens Inst. Tech, Hoboken, NJ, 1948, MSE.E., 1951. Registered profl. engr. With elec. distbn., system planning and devel. Pub. Service Electric and Gas Co., Newark, 1951-77, v.p. system planning, 1977-80, sr. v.p. planning and research, 1980-88, sr. v.p. transmission systems, 1989; pvt. practice engring. Nutley, N.J., 1990—. Advisor Brookhave Nat. Lab.; cons. Manhattan Coll. Bd. dirs. Met. chpt. ARC, Fairfield, N.J., 1985—, bd. dirs. No. N.J. chpt., 1988—; bd. dirs. Essex County Grand Jury Assn., 1978-87. With USN, 1944-46, PTO. Fellow IEEE; mem. Nat. Soc. Profl. Engrs., Conf. Internationale des Grands Reseaux Electriques a Haute Tension, Eta Kappa Nu, Tau Beta Pi Roman Catholic. Home and Office: 68 High St Nutley NJ 07110-1134 Office Phone: 973-667-2350. E-mail: samallardnj@aol.com.

MALLERY, DAVID, education association executive, consultant; b. Sugar Hill, NH, Aug. 3, 1923; s. Otto Tod and Louise Marshall Mallery; m. Judith Chappell Mallery, June 15, 1956; children: Roger, Diane Mallery Cusick. BA, Haverford Coll., Pa., 1945, PhD (hon.), 1995; MA, Middlebury Coll., Vt., 1950. Tchr. English Germantown Friends Sch., Phila., 1946-58; seminar leader Friends Coun. on Edn., Phila., 1959-94; dir. profl. devel. Nat. Assn. Ind. Schs., Washington, 1959—. Edn. cons., 1959—; tchr. Bell Tel./U. Pa. Inst. for Humanistic Studies for Execs., 1960's. Author: High School Students Speak Out, 1960's, Ferment on the Campus, 1960's. Edn. advisor Tracy S. Voorhees, Pres. Eisenhower's rep. on Cuban refugee crisis, 1959-60; founding trustee Am. Film Inst., 1967-79. Lt. (j.g.) USNR, 1943-46, WW II. Recipient Klingenstein award Columbia U. Tchrs. Coll., 1996. Avocations: films, theater, music, international networking. Home and Office: 9006 Crefeld St Philadelphia PA 19118-3607 Office Phone: 215-242-0731. Business E-Mail: mallery@davidseminars.com.

MALLETT, EDWARD A., lawyer; Grad., Dartmouth Coll.; JD, U. Tex. Bar: Tex. Ptnr. Mallett Guiberson Saper, LLP, Houston. Lectr. U. Houston Sch. Law, Nat. Criminal Defense Coll. Contbr. articles to profl. jours. Office: Mallett Guiberson Saper, LLP 600 Travis St, Ste 1900 Houston TX 77002 Office Phone: 713-236-1900. E-mail: edward@mgscounsel.com. *

MALLEY, RAYMOND CHARLES, retired foreign service official, industrial executive; b. Cambridge, Mass., Dec. 22, 1930; s. William and Evangeline (Vautour) M.; m. Rita Ann Masse, May 26, 1951 (dec. June 1989); children: Keith, Bruce, Gregory; m. Josette Lucile Vidril Murphy, Aug. 11, 1995. AA, Boston U., 1950, BS, 1952; MA Equivalent, U. Geneva, 1955; MA, PhD ABD, Fletcher Sch. Law & Diplomacy, Tufts U. and Harvard U., Mass., 1956. Economist, fin. analyst Texaco, Inc., NYC, 1957—61; fgn. svc. officer U.S. Dept. State, AID, Washington & fgn. posts, 1961—82; dir. U.S. Trade and Devel. Program, Washington, 1980; v.p. Silopress, Inc., Sioux City, Iowa, 1982—87; pres. Silopress Can., 1985—87; cons., advisor Labat-Anderson Internat., Arlington, Va., 1988—93; sr. group advisor, N.Am. and S.Am. rep. Halla Bus. Group, Seoul, Republic of Korea, NYC, Washington, 1991—. Fed. exec. fellow Brookings Instn., 1973—74; chmn. Halla Am. Inc., 1996—2001. Mem. exec. bd. Coll. of Mgmt., L.I. U., Brookville, NY, 1994—. 2nd lt., 1st lt., capt. then maj. USAFR. Recipient Nat. Def. Svc. medal, USAFR, Korean War. Mem. Acadian Cultural Soc., Am. Fgn. Svc. Assn., Diplomatic and Consular Officers Ret., Harvard Club. Roman Catholic. Avocation: tennis.

MALLIA, MARIANNE, medical writer; b. Davenport, Iowa, Feb. 14, 1948; d. Norman Bramblett and Mary Jane (Hilkemeyer) Hagar; 1 child from previous marriage, Lindsay Sharyn. BA in English, U. Iowa, 1970. Cert. tchr., editor in life sci. Tchr. tech. writing Houston Ind. Sch. Dist., 1970—76; med. writer Tex. Heart Inst., Houston, 1976—; editl. cons. Tex. Heart Inst. Jour., Houston, 1977—87, head sci. publ., 1986—, sr. med. writer, 1994—. Instr. Sch. Allied Health Sci. and Sch. Pub. Health U. Tex., 1990—94. Editor: Techniques in Cardiac Surgery, 1984; editor: (with Denton A. Cooley) Surg. Treatment of Aortic Aneurysms, 1985; editor: (essays) Reflections and Observation, Denton A. Cooley, MD, 1985; author: (handbook) Heart Owner's Handbook, 1995; bd. editors: Life Sci., 2002. Fellow: Am. Med. Writers Assn. (core curriculum cert. 1984, instr. 1985—, advanced curriculum cert. 1989, honor roll workshop leader 1992—, bd. dir., exec. com. 1996—2005, pres. 2002—03, writer advanced core curriculum, Award Tchg. Excellence 1998); mem.: Women in Comm. (Matrix award 1996—2000), Coun. Biology Editors, Pi Beta Phi. Avocations: classic cars. Office: Tex Heart Inst PO Box 20345 Houston TX 77225-0345 Office Phone: 832-355-6776. Business E-Mail: mmallia@heart.thi.tmc.edu.

MALLIN, JOEL, lawyer; m. Sherry Vogel. BS, Cornell U.; LLB, Columbia U. Bar: NY 1961. Atty. Joel Mallin LLP, NYC. Chmn. Aldrich Mus., Conn. Named one of Top 200 Collectors, ARTnews Mag., 2004—. Mem.: Manhattan Theatre Club. Avocation: collector of modern & contemporary art, particularly sculpture. Office: 110 East 59th St New York NY 10022-1304 Home: 60 Pound Ridge Rd Pound Ridge NY 10576 Office Phone: 212-715-0569, 212-486-0511. E-mail: jmallin@aol.com.

MALLING, HEINRICH VALDEMAR, retired geneticist; b. Copenhagen, Apr. 21, 1931; came to US, 1963; s. Henry August Valdemar and Jenny Bolette (Hansen) M.; m. Bodil Jensen, June 15, 1955 (div. June 1968); children: Tove, Soren, Jakob, Mikael; m. Martha Hale Shackford, July 18, 1969; children: Richard, Kevin, Kirsten. PhD, U. Copenhagen, 1957, Lic. Sci., 1962. Rsch. staff Leo Pharm., Copenhagen, 1957—58; postdoctoral fellow Inst. Genetics U. Copenhagen, 1958—61, assoc. prof. Inst. Genetics, 1961—63; rsch. staff mem. Oak Ridge Nat. Lab., Tenn., 1963—72; sect. head Nat. Inst. Environ. Health Sci., Research Triangle Park, NC, 1972—76, 1982—, lab. chief, 1976—82; dir. HuMutagen LLC, 2004—; ret., 2004. Adj. prof. NC State U., Raleigh, 1972-78, U. NC, Chapel Hill, 1976—; dir. Environ. Mutagen Info. Ctr., Oak Ridge, 1968-72; pres. Humutagen LLC, 2005; vis. prof. Flinders U., 2004-05; CEO HUMutagen, 2005— Editorial bd. Environ. and Molecular Mutagenesis, 1989—, Mutation Rsch., 1971—; contbr. articles to profl. jours. Nation chief YMCA Indian Guides, Knoxville, Tenn, 1970, Raleigh, 1974. Recipient Sci. award Environ. Mut. Soc., Washington, 1980; Grad. fellow U. Copenhagen, 1953-57, postdoctoral fellow NSF, 1958-61. Mem. Environ. Mutagen Soc. (com. 1989—), Med. Rsch. Coun. (Can., grant revs. 1987—). Democrat. Lutheran. Achievements include patent in transgenic mice for study of mammalian mutagenesis; first to demonstrate mammalian liver microsomes can active non-mutagenic carcinogens to mutagens, first to develop transgenic mutation systems based on recoverable vectors; first to develop transgenic mutation stys. based on recoverable vectors. Home: 3200 Winged Elm Ln Chapel Hill NC 27514-9530 Office: Nat Inst Environ Health Sci PO Box 12233 Durham NC 27709-2233 Office Phone: 919-541-3378. Business E-Mail: malling@niehs.nih.gov.

MALLISON, HOWARD DANFORD, retired corporate communications specialist; b. Scotland Neck, NC, Sept. 13, 1932; s. Howard Winford and Myrtle Dean (Jernigan) Mallison; m. Norma Mae Gibbs, Apr. 30, 1955; children: Howard Danford II, N. Daniele Daniel. Lic. ins. agt. Va., 1958. Comm. specialist Dept. Army Civil Svc., 1953—58, 1962—79; life and casualty agt. Allstate Ins. Co., Portsmouth, Va., 1958—62; coord. support ctr. S.W.I.F.T., Belgian Internat. Co., Culpeper, Va., 1979—85; ret., 1985. Author of poems. Staff sgt. USAF, 1950—53. Decorated Korean Svc. medal USAF, Korean Svc. medal with 2 Bronze campaign stars; recipient Good Conduct medal. Mem.: NRA, Rivanna Rifle & Pistol Club. Avocations: walking, gun enthusiast, travel.

MALLON, KELLIE JANE, special education educator; b. Silver Spring, Md., Apr. 18, 1969; d. James A. and Barbara E. Mallon. B, St. Leo Coll., Fla., 1994; Master's degree, Nova Southeastern U., 1997. Cert. profl. tchr. Fla. Specific learning disabilities and spl. edn. tchr. Pasco County Sch. Bd., New Port Richey, Fla., 1996—. Sec. Schwettman Alternative Sch. Adv. Bd., New Port Richey, 1997—2004. Recipient After Sch. Activities grant, Pasco County Sch. Bd., 1997—98, Svc. Learning grant, Fla. Dept. of Edn. Mem.: CEC (assoc.; specific learning disability divsn. 2001—02). Roman Catholic. Avocations: reading, rescue animal advocate. Home: 6618 Crossbow Ln New Port Richey FL 34653 Office: Pasco County Sch Bd 7227 Land O' Lakes Blvd Land O Lakes FL 34638 Home Phone: 727-848-0373; Office Phone: 727-774-2000. Personal E-mail: kmallon@ij.net. E-mail: kmallon@pasco.k12.fl.us.

MALLON, THOMAS, writer; b. Glen Cove, NY, Nov. 2, 1951; s. Arthur Vincent and Caroline (Moruzzi) M. AB, Brown U., 1973; AM, Harvard U., 1974, PhD, 1978. Asst. prof. English Vassar Coll., Poughkeepsie, NY, 1979-85, assoc. prof., 1985-89, lectr. in English, 1989-91; lit. editor Gentlemen's Quar., NYC, 1991-95, writer-at-large, 1995-99; mem. Nat. Coun. on Humanities, 2002—05; dep. chmn. NEH, Washington, 2005—06; prof. English George Washington U., Washington, 2007—. Author: Edmund Blunden, 1983, A Book of One's Own, 1984, Arts and Sciences, 1988, Stolen Words, 1989, Aurora 7, 1991, Rockets and Rodeos, 1993, Henry and Clara, 1994, Dewey Defeats Truman, 1997, Two Moons, 2000, In Fact, 2001, Mrs. Paine's Garage, 2002, Bandbox, 2004, Fellow Travelers, 2007. Recipient Ingram Merrill award, 1994, Nat. Book Critics Cir. citation for excellence in reviewing, 1998, Great Lakes Book award for fiction, 1998; Rockefeller Found. fellow, 1986-87, Guggenheim fellow, 2000-2001. Mem. PEN Am., Phi Beta Kappa. Home: 801 25th St NW Washington DC 20037 Personal E-mail: TVMallon@aol.com.

MALLONEE, SUE, epidemiologist, researcher; m. Joseph P. Mallonee, 1989; children: Joseph P., Scott D. Makintubee, Lauren. BSN, Okla. Bapt. U., Shawnee, 1977; MPH in Epidemiology, U. Okla., Oklahoma City, 1985. RN Okla. Staff nurse Stillwater Med. Ctr., Okla., 1977—78; pub. health nurse Lincoln County Health Dept., Chandler, Okla., 1978—81; staff epidemiologist Okla. State Dept. Health, Oklahoma City, 1981—87, chief injury prevention svc., 1987—2004, dir. sci. affairs, 2004—. Adj. asst. prof. dept. biostatistics and epidemiology U. Okla. Coll. Pub. Health, Oklahoma City, 1990—; co-chair Addressing Violence in Okla. Coalition, Oklahoma City, 1993—95; nat. adv. com. for injury prevention and control Nat. Ctr. for Injury Prevention and Control, Ctr. for Disease Control, Atlanta, 1994—97, steering com. rsch. agenda, 2000—01; mem. Okla. Child Death Rev. Com., Oklahoma City, 1995—2000; external adv. bd. mem. Iowa Injury Prevention Rsch. Ctr., Iowa City, 1996—; com. on injury prevention and control NAS, Inst. Medicine, Washington, 1997—98; injury rsch. grant rev. com. Centers for Disease Control and Prevention, Atlanta, 2000—04; mem. Okla. Domestic Violence Fatality Rev. Bd., Oklahoma City, 2000—04; internat. sci. com. 8th World Congress on Injury Prevention and Safety Promotion, Durban, South Africa, 2005—06; scholar Nat. Pub. Health Leadership Inst., Raleigh-Durham, NC, 2005—06; editl. bd. Centers for Disease Control Morbidity and Mortality Weekly Reports, Atlanta, 2005—. Lay chaplain United Meth. Ch. of the Servant, Oklahoma City, 1989—94. Recipient Profile in Excellence award, Okla. Bapt. U., 2003, Spl. Contributions award, Okla. U. Coll. Pub. Health, 2004. Mem.: APHA (assoc. Pub. Health Svc. award Injury Control and Emergency Health Sect. 2002), U. Okla. Coll. Pub. Health Alumni Assn. (assoc.), Okla. Pub. Health Assn. (assoc.; pres.-elect 2007—, Epidemiology award 1993, Exceptional Merit award 1985), Coun. of State and Territorial Epidemiologists (assoc.), State and Territorial Injury Prevention Dirs. Assn. (assoc.; treas., v.p., pres. 1993—2003, Outstanding Svc. award 2004), Pub. Health Leadership Soc. (assoc.), Delta Omega (assoc.; Xi chpt.). Office: Oklahoma State Department of Health 1000 NE 10th St Oklahoma City OK 73117 Office Phone: 405-271-4200. Business E-Mail: suem@health.ok.gov.

MALLORY, ARTHUR LEE, dean, retired state official; b. Springfield, Mo., Dec. 26, 1932; s. Dillard A. and Ferrell (Claxton) M.; m. Joann Peters, June 6, 1954; children: Dennis Arthur (dec.), Christopher Lee, Stephanie Ann, Jennifer Lyn. BS, S.W. Mo. State Coll., 1954; MEd, U. Mo., 1957, EdD, 1959; HHD, S.W. Bapt. Coll., Mo., 1972. History supr. U. Mo. Lab. Sch., Columbia, 1956-57; asst. to supt. schs. Columbia, 1957-59; asst. supt. schs. Parkway Sch. Dist., St. Louis County, Mo., 1959-64; dean evening div. U. Mo., St. Louis, 1964; pres. S.W. Mo. State U., Springfield, 1964-70, dean Coll. Edn., 1991-94; commr. edn. Mo. Dept. Edn., Jefferson City, 1971-87. Dir. Internat. House, U. Mo., Columbia, 1956-59; chmn. bd. Mo. Coun. on Econ. Edn., 2000—. V.p. Ozarks coun. Boy Scouts Am., 1967, pres. Gt. Rivers coun., 1972-73, Greene County Assn. for Retarded Citizens, 1989—, pres., 1991-96, mem. north ctrl. region exec. bd., 1984—; bd. dirs. Meml. Cmty. Hosp., Mid-Continent Regional Ednl. Lab., Ozark Pub. Telecoms. Inc., 1989—; chmn. bd. Mo. Coun. on Econ. Edn.; bd. regents Mo. State Univs.; trustee Pub. Sch. Retirement, William Jewell Coll., 1972-74; chmn. com. bds. So. Bapt. Conv., 1972-73, mem. com. or bds., 1981—; mem. exec. bd. Mo. Bapt. Conv., 1972-75, 77-80, 2d v.p., 1995-96, pres., 1996-97; trustee Southwestern Bapt. Theol. Sem., Fort Worth, 1995—; mem. adv. com. Young Audiences, Inc., 1986, ARC Bd., Greene County, 1986, Children's Svcs. Commn., chmn., 1986—, Edn. Commn. U.S.; bd. dirs. Ozark Pub. TV; chmn. bd. advisors Windemere Bapt. Assembly, 1992—, chmn. bd. trustees, 2000—; chmn. Mo. Coun. for Econ. Edn., 2000—. With U.S. Army, 1954-56. Recipient Disting. Service award Mo. Jr. C. of C., 1966; Disting. Service award U. Mo., 1976; Faculty/Alumni award U. Mo., 1976; Silver Beaver award Boy Scouts Am., 1983, Good Shepherd and Cross, 1986, Disting. Citizen award, 1986; hon. life mem. Mo. Congress Parents and Tchrs.; named Springfield's Outstanding Young Man of Yr., 1965; Champion of Excellence PUSH, 1978 Mem. Am. Assn. State Colls. and Univs., N. Central Assn. Colls. and Secondary Schs., Council Chief State Sch. Officers, Mo. Assn. Sch. Adminstrs., NEA, Mo. Tchrs. Assn. So. Baptist (deacon). Clubs: Masons (33 deg.), Rotary. Business E-Mail: arthurmallory@missouristate.edu.

MALLORY, CHARLES KING, III, lawyer; b. Norfolk, Va., Nov. 16, 1936; s. Charles King Mallory Jr. and Dorothy Pratt (Williams) Swanke; m. Florence Beale Marshall; children: King, Raburn, Anne, Richard. BA, Yale U., 1958; JD, Tulane U., 1961. Bar: La. 1961, Calif. 1965, D.C. 1972. Ptnr. Monroe & Lemann, New Orleans, 1965-72; acting exec. dir. SEC, Washington, 1972; dep. asst. sec. U.S. Dept. Interior, Washington, 1973, acting asst. sec., 1974; v.p., gen. counsel Middle South Svcs., Inc., New Orleans, 1975-79; ptnr. Hunton & Williams, Washington, 1979—. Gen. counsel Com. on the Present Danger, 1987-91. Mem. Reagan-Bush Transition Team, Washington, 1980-81, Grace Commn. on Pvt. Sector Survey Cost in the Fed. Govt., Washington, 1983-84. Served to lt. USNR, 1961-65. Mem. ABA, La. Bar Assn., Calif. Bar Assn., D.C. Bar Assn., Energy Bar Assn., Nat. Assn. Bond Lawyers. Republican. Episcopalian. Office: Hunton & Williams 1900 K St NW 12th Floor Washington DC 20006-1110 E-mail: kmallory@hunton.com.

MALLORY, FRANK LINUS, lawyer; b. Calgary, Alta., Can., May 5, 1920; s. Frank Louis and Anna Amy (Allstrum) M.; m. Jean Ellen (Lindsey), Jan. 29, 1944; children: Susan Mallory Remund, Ann M. Kenney, Bruce R. AB, Stanford U., 1941, LLB, 1947. Bar: Calif., 1948. Assoc. Gibson, Dunn, and Crutcher, LA, 1947-54; ptnr. L.A. and Orange County, 1955-88. Cert. specialist taxation law Calif. Bd. Legal Splty., 1973-89. Pres. town hall of L.A., 1970; Boys Republic, Chino, Calif., 1962-64; pres. Braille Inst. Am., L.A., 1988-92; Lt.(j.g.), USNR, 1942-46. Mem. ABA, Los Angeles County Bar Assn., Orange County Bar Assn., Newport Harbor Yacht Club, Big Canyon Country Club, Transpacific Yacht Club (staff commodore), Order of Coif, Phi Beta Kappa. Republican. Home: 25382 Sea Bluffs Dr 205 Dana Point CA 92629

MALLORY, MARK L., mayor, former state legislator; b. Cin., Apr. 2, 1962; s. William L. Mallory. Student, Xavier U.; BS in Adminstrv. Mgmt., U. Cin. Dept. mgr. Hamilton County Pub. Libr. Graphic Prodn., Cin., 1981—95; rep. dist. 31 Ohio Ho. Reps., Columbus, 1995—98; mem. Dist. 9 Ohio State Senate, Columbus, 1998—2005, asst. minority whip, 2000—03, asst. minority leader, 2003—05; mayor City of Cin., 2005—. Bd. trustees Friar's Club; advisory coun. 4C for Children; advisory bd. Ronald McDonald House of Cin. Recipient Devel. Leadership award, Bowhay Inst. for Legis. Leadership, 1996, Myrl Shoemaker Legis. of the Year award, 1998, Excellence in Correctional Edn. award, Correctional Edn. Assn., 1999, Pub. Svc. award, Gothic Lodge 122, 2000, Legis. of the Year award, Nat. Assn. Social Workers, 2001, Wolfe award of Excellence, OH Assn. Elected Officials, 2002, Pub. Svc. award, Nat. Assn. Grad. & Profl. Students, 2003, Passport to Excellence award, Phi Delta Kappa, 2003, Andrew Carnegie award, OH Library Coun., 2003, Legis. of the Year award, OH Community Corrections Assn., 2004. Mem. NAACP, Libr. Staff Assn., Black Male Coalition, Friends of Pub. Libr., Urban League of Cin., Pub. Libr. Staff Assn., Internat. TV Assn. Achievements include being the first African American directly elected by the people of Cincinnati, 2005. Office: Office of Mayor 801 Plum St Cincinnati OH 45202

MALLORY, ROBERT MARK, controller, finance company executive; b. Mattoon, Ill., Apr. 15, 1950; s. Robert Monroe and Betty Ann (Mudd) M.; m. Diana Marie Burde, Aug. 19, 1972; 1 child, Laura Elizabeth. BS in Accountancy, U. Ill., 1972; MBA, Northwestern U., 1985. CPA Ill. Staff acct. Price Waterhouse, Chgo., 1972-74, sr. acct., 1974-77, mgr., 1977-79; dir. internal audit Mark Controls Corp., Skokie, Ill., 1979-81, corp. contr., 1981-86, v.p., contr., 1986-88; contr., dir. planning Tribune Co., Chgo., 1988-91, v.p., contr., 1991—. Bd. dirs. Met. Family Svcs. Mem. AICPA (Elijah Watts Sells award 1972), Ill. CPA Soc., Fin. Execs. Internat. (bd. dirs.), Internat. Newspaper Fin. Execs. (bd. dirs.), Beta Gamma Sigma. Methodist. Home: 3312 Lakewood Ct Glenview IL 60026-2505 Office: Tribune Co 435 N Michigan Ave Chicago IL 60611-4066 Home Phone: 847-998-1467. Personal E-mail: mallory435@aol.com.

MALLORY, TROY L., accountant; b. Sesser, Ill., July 30, 1923; s. Theodore E. and Alice (Mitchell) M.; m. Magdalene Richter, Jan. 26, 1963. Student, So. Ill. U., 1941-43, Washington and Jefferson Coll., 1943-44; BS, U. Ill., 1947, MS, 1948. Staff sr. supr. Scovell, Wellington & Co., CPAs, Chgo., 1948-58; mgr. Gray Hunter Stenn CPAs, Quincy, Ill., 1959-62, ptnr., 1962-99. Mem. fin. com. United Fund, Adams County, 1961-64; bd. dirs. Woodland Home for Orphans and Friendless, 1970—2005, pres., 1981-84, 87-90. Served with 84th Inf. Divsn. AUS, 1942-45. Decorated Purple Heart, Bronze Star. Mem. AICPA, Ill. CPA Soc., Quincy C. of C. (bd. dirs. 1970-76), Rotary (bd. dirs. Quincy 1967-70, pres. 1978-79), Shriners (bd. dirs. Quincy 1982-85, pres. 1988), Royal Order Jesters (Ct. 20 dir. 1997), Railsplitters Soc. (pres. 1993). Home: 2229 Jersey St Quincy IL 62301-4341

MALLOW, MATTHEW J., lawyer; b. Bklyn., 1943; AB, Brown U., 1964; JD, NYU, 1967, LLM, 1968. Bar: NY 1967. Ptnr. corp. fin. Skadden, Arps, Slate, Meagher & Flom LLP, NYC. Guest lectr. Harvard Bus. Sch. Bd. trustee Brown U., 1990—96, 1997—, treas., 1999—; represented Bard Coll. in the creation of the Bard HS Early Coll., 2001; rep. of the city council pres. to the bd. trustees Metropolitan Mus. Art, 1978—85. Mem.: Assn. Bar City NY (exec. com. 1971—75, vice-chmn., grievance com. 1976—77, chmn. securities regulation com. 2003—06). Office: Skadden Arps Slate Meagher & Flom LLP 4 Times Sq New York NY 10036 Office Phone: 212-735-3930. Office Fax: 917-777-3930. Business E-Mail: mmallow@skadden.com.

MALLOW CORBETT, STEPHANIE, pharmacist, educator; b. Jacksonville, Fla., June 13, 1977; d. William Michael and Denise Marie Mallow; m. Sean Thomas Mallow, June 20, 2004; 1 child, Soren Michael Corbett. PharmD, Albany Coll. Pharmacy, NY, 2001. Lic. pharmacist Vt. State Bd. Pharmacy, 2001, Tex. State Bd. Pharmacy, 2007. Pharmacy intern Kaiser Permanente, Latham, NY, 1993—99, Rite Aid Pharmacy, Saratoga Springs, NY, 2000—01; clin. pharmacist (part-time) Fletcher Allen Health Care, Burlington, Vt., 2001—03, pharmacy practice resident, 2001—02, critical care pharmacy resident, 2002—03; adj. asst. prof. clin. pharmacy Mass. Coll. Pharmacy, Boston, 2004—06; critical care pharmacotherapy fellow U. Vt. Coll. Medicine, Burlington, 2003—05, critical care rsch. cons., 2005—06; asst. prof. U. Houston Coll. Pharmacy, 2006—; clin. pharmacist, surg. icu Meth. Hosp., Houston, 2006—. Contbr. articles to profl. jours. Recipient Dr. Vojech E. Andic award, Albany Coll. of Pharmacy, 2000, Lilly Achievement award, Albany Coll. Pharmacy, 2001, Pharmacy Intervention award, Fletcher Allen Health Care, 2002, Presdl. Citation award, Soc. Critical Care Medicine, 2006, Presidential Citation award, 2007; fellow, Soc. Critical Care Medicine, Ortho Biotech, 2004—05. Mem.: Am. Soc. Health Sys. Pharmacists, Vt. Soc. Health Sys.Pharmacists, Am. Pharm. Assn., Soc. Critical Care Medicine (chair clin. pharmacy/pharmacology sect. membership com. 2005—), Am. Coll. Clin. Pharmacy (chair critical care prn, comm. com. 2004—06), Am. Assn. Colleges Pharmacy, Internat. Soc. Pharmcoeconomic and Outcomes Rsch. Achievements include research in survival of propofol infusion syndrome in a head injured patient; patient knowledge and pursuit of medical care following traumatic splenectomy is influenced by co-morbidities and time lapse since injury; dexmedetomidine does not improve patient satisfaction when compared to propofol during mechanical ventilation; do proton pump inhibitors increase the incidence of nosocomial pneumonia and related infectious complications when compared with histamine-2 receptor antagonists in critically ill trauma patients?. Office: UH Coll Pharmacy TMC 1441 Moursund St Ste 308 Houston TX 77030 Home Phone: 713-838-2288; Office Phone: 713-795-8369. Office Fax: 713-795-8383. Business E-Mail: smallowcorbett@uh.edu.

MALLOY, COURTNEY L., research scientist, educator; b. Burbank, Calif. PhD, U. So. Calif., LA. Sr. project mgr. Vital Rsch., LLC, LA, 2004—. Asst. adj. prof. U. So. Calif., LA, 2003—. Achievements include research in educational reform, partnerships, charter schools. Office: Vital Research LLC 6380 Wilshire Blvd Ste 1609 Los Angeles CA 90048

MALLOY, DANNEL PATRICK, mayor; m. Cathy Malloy; children: Dan, Ben, Sam. LLB, Boston Coll. Bar: Conn., Mass., N.Y., U.S. Dist. Ct. Conn., U.S. Dist. Ct. (ea. and so. dists.) N.Y. Asst. dist. atty. Bklyn., N.Y. Dist. Atty.'s Office, 1980-84; ptnr. Abate & Fox, Stamford, Conn., 1984-95; mayor City of Stamford, 1995—. Mem. bd. fin. City of Stamford, 1983-94, Stamford Bd. Edn., 1994-95; spl. master Conn. Superior Ct.; lectr. Family Law Tng. Seminar. Past bd. dirs. Teen Life Ctr., Liberation Programs, Inc., CTE; treas. Conn. Conf. Municipalities, 1997-98, v.p.; vice chair mayors and pub. schs. task force U.S. Conf. Mayors; mem. fair policy steering com. Nat. League of Cities, 1997-98, mem. task force on youth and edn; chmn. Dem. Mcpl. Ofcls. Orgn.; mem. Dem. Nat. Com., mem. exec. com.; mem. adv. bd. U.S. Conf. Mayors. Mem. ABA, ATLA, Nat. Trial Lawyers Assn., Conn. Bar Assn., Conn. Trial Lawyers Assn. Democrat. Office: 10th Fl Govt Center 888 Washington Blvd Stamford CT 06902

MALLOY, EDWARD ALOYSIUS, academic administrator; b. Washington, May 3, 1941; s. Edward Aloysius and Elizabeth (Clark) Malloy. BA, U. Notre Dame, 1963, MA, 1967, ThM, 1969; PhD, Vanderbilt U., 1975. Ordained to ministry Cath. Ch., 1970. Instr. U. Notre Dame, South Bend, Ind., 1974—75, asst. prof., 1975—81, assoc. prof., 1981—88, prof. theology, 1988—, assoc. provost, 1982—86, pres. elect, 1986, pres., 1987—2005, pres. emeritus, 2005—. Established chair Cath. Studes in name of Edward A. Malloy Vanderbilt U., 1997; editl. adv. bd. The Presidency mag.; bd. dir. Nat. Com. on Higher Edn. and Health of Youth; co-chmn. Nat. Inst. on Alcohol Abuse and Alcoholism; chmn. Nat. Commn. on Substance Abuse and Sports; regent U. Portland, 1985—; bd. govs., trustee Notre Dame, Australia, 1990—. Author: Culture & Commitment: The Challenge of Today's University, 1992, Notre Dame: The Unfolding Vision, 1994, Monk's Reflection: A View from the Dome, 1999, Monk's Travels People, Places & Events, 2004, Monk's Notre Dame, 2005; co-author: Colleges and Universities as Citizens, 1999. Chmn. Am. Coun. Edn.; mem. Pres. Adv. Coun. on Drugs, 1989—; adv. bd. AmeriCorps and Nat. Civilian Cmty. Corps, 1994—97; interim chmn. Ind. Commn. Cmty. Svc., 1994—97; active Boys and Girls Clubs Am., 1997—; trustee U. St. Thomas, 1997—, Vanderbilt U., 1999; bd. advisors Bernadin Ctr., 1997—2005; founding dir., bd. dir. Points of Light Found.; past chmn. Campus Impact; bd. regents U. Portland, 1985; bd. govs. Notre Dame Australia, 1990; mem. Bishopps and pres. com. Assn. Cath. Colls. and Univs., 1988—2005; bd. dirs. Internat. Fedn. Cath. Univs., 1988—2005, NCAA Found., 1989—. Mem.: Nat. Assn. Ind. Colls. and Univs. (bd. dirs. 1997), The Conf. Bd., Assn. Governing Bds. of Univs. and Colls. (vice chair 1996—2004), Bus.-Higher Edn. Forum, Am. Soc. Christian Ethics, Cath. Theol. Soc. Roman Catholic. Office: Univ Notre Dame Pres Emeritus Notre Dame IN 46556 Office Phone: 574-631-6755.

MALLOY, EDWARD MICHAEL, diplomat, educator; b. NYC, Oct. 4, 1936; s. Michael Malloy and Mollie McHale; m. Iris Ortolja, Jan. 24, 1970; children: Tara Nicole, Matthew S. BS, Manhattan Coll., 1958; MS, Adelphi U., 1962, MIT, 1970; PhD, George Washington U., 1978. Aerospace engr. Sperry Gyroscope, Garden City, NY, 1958—62; educator U.S. Peace Corps., Nigeria, 1963—65; fgn. svc. officer U.S. State Dept., Washington, 1966—98; lectr. George Washington U., Washington, 1998—99; info. tech. policy adviser U.S. Agy. Internat. Devel., Washington, 1999—. Diplomatic svc. in U.S. Embassies in Indonesia, France, Yugoslavia, Brazil, Germany, Japan. Home: 6212 Crathie Ln Bethesda MD 20816-1004

MALLOY, ELLEN ANN, athletic trainer; d. William Francis Thomas and Janet Day Malloy. BS in Health and Phys. Edn., Bridgewater State Coll., Mass., 1977; MEd in Sports Medicine and Athletic Tng., U. Va., Charlottesville, 1979. Cert. EMT Mass., 1981; health and phys. edn. tchr. Mass., 1977, lic. athletic trainer Mass., 1984, cert. instr. ARC, 2003. Am. Heart Assn., 2000. Head women's athletic trainer, head baseball athletic trainer Duke U., Durham, NC, 1979—81; head athletic trainer Regis Coll., Weston, Mass., 1981—83, Sports Innovation and Diagostic Ctr., Charlottesville, 1984—86, Noble and Greenough Sch., Dedham, Mass., 1988—2003, Thayer Acad., Braintree, Mass., 2003—. Dir. sports medicine Europa Cup Hockey, Wellesley, Mass., 2001—. Vol. Spl. Olympics, Charlottesville, 1978—79; vol. athletic trainer Bay State Games, Boston, 1981—2000, Boston Marathon, Boston, 1981—2004, Jimmy Fund Walk, Boston, 2000—06; participant Doug Flutie Walk for Autism, Natick, Mass., 2004; vol. Meals on Wheels, Cohasset, Mass., 2000—06. Recipient Robert J. Agostini award, Noble & Greenough Sch., 1990, 1997. Mem.: Ind. Sch. Athletic Trainer's Assn. (pres. 1990—97), Ea. Athletic Trainer's Assn., Nat. Athletic Trainer's Assn. (cert.), State of Mass. - Allied Health (licentiate), Cohasset Golf Club (Mother-Daughter Champion 1975—79), Cohasset Golf Club (Father-Daughter Champion 1975—79), Cohasset Golf Club (Lincoln Bowl Champion 1975), Cohasset Golf Club (Women's Club Champion 1990—92), Cohasset Golf Club (Mixed Scotch Club Champion 1984), Cohasset Sailing Club (Lincoln Bowl Champion 1985, Father-Daughter Champion 1988—92, Mother-Daughter Champaion 1988—92, Mixed Scotch Club Champion 1989), Hatherly Country Club (Women's Tennis Club Champion 1969), South Shore Women's Golf League (Mother-Daughter Champion 1988), U. of Va. Alumni Assn. (life). Independent. Roman Catholic. Avocations: golf, tennis, hockey, sailing, sewing. Office: Thayer Acad 745 Washington St Braintree MA 02184 Home Phone: 781-383-0686; Office Phone: 781-843-3580. Office Fax: 781-848-1027. Business E-Mail: emalloy@thayer.org.

MALLOY, INA ARLENE, secondary school educator, photographer; m. K. O. Malloy; children: Bryanne, Zachary, Elyse. MS, Quinnipiac U., 2003; BFA, Temple U., 1982. Lic. tchr. K-12 art Conn., 1982, N.J., 1982, Pa., 1982. Tchr. photography Amity H.H., Woodbridge, Conn., 1998—. Mem. Beth Ahm Congregation, Windsor, Conn., 2003—06. Mem.: N.J. Art Edn. Assn. (life scholar 2003). Office: Amity Regional HS 25 Newton Rd Woodbridge CT 06082 Office Phone: 203-397-4830. Business E-Mail: inamalloy_x@yahoo.com.

MALLOY, JOHN RICHARD, lawyer, chemicals executive; b. Boston, Nov. 26, 1932; s. Thomas Francis and Mary (Field) M.; m. Maraleta Ellerson, May 24, 1960; children: Maureen, John, Megan, Elizabeth. BA, St. John's Sem., Brighton, Mass., 1954; LLB, Boston Coll., 1957. Bar: Mass. 1957. With chief counsel's office IRS, 1961—64; atty. advisor Tax Ct. of U.S., 1964—65; legal dept. Du Pont, 1965—73, asst. comptroller taxes, 1973—75; v.p., dir. fin. Remington Arms Co., Inc., Bridgeport, Conn., 1975-78; chief counsel, energy and raw materials E. I. du Pont de Nemours and Co., Wilmington, Del., 1978-79, asst. gen. counsel legal, 1979-83, dir. pub. affairs, 1983-85, v.p. pub. affairs, 1983-85, sr. v.p. external affairs, 1985-92, sr. v.p., spl. counsel to chmn. bd., 1992-93; ret., 1993. Chmn. Jobs for Del. Grads, Wilmington, 1985-97, Del. Compensation Commn., 1988-96; trustee Med. Ctr. of Del., Christiana, 1985—, dir., 2004—, Del. Pension Fund, 1993-99; bd. dirs. Del. Cmty. Found., 1996-2000, Children's Beach House, 1993-2000; mem. Minner Commn., Del., 1993-96; chmn. Ursuline Acad., 1978-84, Del. Coun. on Transp., 1994-2001, Riverfront Devel. Corp., 2002—05; trustee Archmere Acad., 2001-05. With JAGC US Army, 1958—60. Mem. ABA, Fed. Bar Assn. Democrat. Roman Catholic. Avocations: tennis, golf, skiing.

MALLOY, MICHAEL P., lawyer; b. Providence, July 18, 1959; s. Judge Edward Francis and Patricia Marie Malloy; m. Jamie Marie Azzara, Aug. 20, 1983; children: Christofer, Nicholas, Michael, Cara. BA summa cum laude, Boston Coll., 1981, JD cum laude, 1984. Bar: Pa. 1984. Assoc. Drinker Biddle & Reath LLP, Phila., 1984-93, ptnr., 1993—, ptnr., head investment mgmt. group. Coach numerous childrens athletics teams. Mem. ABA, Phila. Bar Assn. (co-chair investment com.). Avocations: tennis, paddle tennis, racketball. Office: Drinker Biddle & Reath LLP One Logan Square 18th & Cherry Sts Philadelphia PA 19103-6996 Office Phone: 215-988-2978. Office Fax: 215-988-2757. Business E-Mail: michael.malloy@dbr.com.

MALLOY, MICHAEL PATRICK, law educator, consultant; b. Haddon Heights, NJ, Sept. 23, 1951; s. Francis Edward and Marie Grace (Nardi) Malloy; divorced; 1 child, Elizabeth; m. Susie Pieratos, Jan. 1992; children: Michael Emil, Nicholas Charles, Edward Francis, Theodora Marie, Sophia Grace. BA magna cum laude (scholar), Georgetown U., Washington, DC, 1973, PhD, 1983; JD (scholar), U. Pa., Phila., 1976. Bar: NJ 1976, US Supreme Ct. 1991. Rsch. assoc. Inst. Internat. Law and Econ. Devel., Washington, 1976—77; atty. advisor Office Fgn. Assets Control US Dept. Treasury, Washington, 1977—80, spl. asst. Office Gen. Counsel, 1985; atty. advisor Office Comptr. Currency, Washington, 1981; spl. counsel SEC, Washington, 1981—82; asst. prof. NY Law Sch., NYC, 1982—83; assoc. prof. Seton Hall U. Sch. Law, Newark, 1983—86, prof., assoc. dean, 1986—87; prof. Fordham U. Sch. Law, NYC, 1987—96, dir. grad. studies, 1990—94; prof. U. Pacific McGeorge Law Sch., Sacramento, 1996—2002, disting. prof. and scholar, 2003—, dir. Ctr. Global Bus. and Devel., 2004—. Law lectr. Morin Ctr. Banking and Fin. Law Studies Boston U. Law Sch., 1986—90, 1995—96, 2001; vis. prof. U. Salzburg, Austria, 2000, 2005—, Macao U. Sci. and Tech., 2006—; vis. prof. Sch. Law Suffolk U., 2001—02; cons. bank regulation and pvt. internat. law matters. Author: Corporate Law of Banks, 2 vols., 1988, Economic Sanctions and U.S. Trade, 1990, The Regulation of Banking, 1992, Banking Law and Regulation, 3 vols., 1994, Fundamentals of Banking Regulation, 1998, International Banking, 1998, Banking and Financial Services Law, 1999;: 2d edit., 2005, Hornbook on Bank Regulation, 1999, U.S. Economic Sanctions: Theory and Practice, 2001, Principles of Bank Regulation, 2003, Global Issues in Contract Law, 2007; contbr. articles, revs. and comments to profl. jours. Mem.: L'Association des Auditeurs et Anciens Auditeurs de l'Academie de Droit International de la Haye, Hegel Soc. Am., Assn. Am. Law Schs. (chair-elect and program chair 2001—02, chair sect. fin. insts. and consumer fin. svcs. 2002—03), Internat. Law Assn. (com. chair Am. br. 1995—97), Am. Soc. Internat. Law (exec. coun. 1986—89), Phi Beta Kappa. Office: U of Pacific McGeorge Sch Law 3200 5th Ave Sacramento CA 95817-2705 Home Phone: 916-481-3250; Office Phone: 916-716-7645. Personal E-mail: malloympm@aol.com.

MALLOY, MICHAEL TERRENCE, journalist, reporter; b. Chgo., Feb. 26, 1936; s. Medard Valentine and Lucille (Zehrol)M.; m. Ruth Gwendolyn Lor, June 5, 1965; children: Linda Jo, Terrence. Student, Reed Coll., 1953-54, Columbia U., 1966-67; BA, U. Toronto, 2001. Police reporter City News Bur. Chgo., 1956-58; reporter, then bur. chief and chief corr. S.E. Asia UPI, Japan, Laos, India, Vietnam and Thailand, 1960-66; reporter Nat. Observer, Washington, 1968-76, mng. editor, 1976-77; reporter Asian Wall St. Jour., Manila, 1977-80, mng. editor, Hong Kong, 1980-84; mng. editor Dow Jones Can., Toronto, Ont., 1984-94; chief corr. Dow Jones India Report, 1995-97. Author: Racing Today, 1967, The Art of Retirement, 1967. With U.S. Army, 1958-60. E-mail: mikemalloy@idirect.ca.

MALLOY, WILLIAM XAVIER, pharmacist; b. Terre Haute, Ind., May 18, 1953; s. William Mosel and Rita Jean Malloy; m. Leanne Foli, Aug. 16, 1975; 1 child, Katherine Marie. BS, Purdue U., W.Lafayette, Ind., 1973—76; MS, Butler U., Indpls., 1979—80; PharmD, Shenandoah U., Winchester, Va., 2000—03. Lic. pharmacotherapy specialist Bd. Pharm. Specialties, 1992. Asst. dir. pharmacy clinical svcs. Union Hosp. Health Grp., Terre Haute, Ind., 1990—2001; clin. pharmacy mgr. Wishard Health Svc., Indpls., 2001—02; coord. clin. pharmacy svcs. Cmty. Health Network, Indpls., 2002—. Pres. Ind. Bd. Pharmacy, Indpls., 1998—99, Ind. Pharmacists Alliance, Indpls., 2004—06. Vol. People Helping People-Guatemala Med. Mission, Indpls., 2005—06; bd. dirs. Am. Cancer Soc., Terre Haute, 1985—86; founding mem., vol. Light Ho. Mission Med. Clinic, Terre Haute, 1998—2002. Recipient Outstanding Tchr. award, Ind. U. Sch. Medicine, 1997, 2001—02, Ind. Hosp. Pharmacist of Yr. award, Ind. Pharmacists Alliance, 1998, 2006, Glen J. Sperandio award for advancement of pharmacy, Purdue U. Sch. Pharmacy, 2002, Disting. Alumnus award, Butler U. Coll. Pharmacy, 2005. Mem.: Ind. Pharmacists Alliance (assoc.; pres. 2003—06), Am. Coll. Clin. Pharmacists (assoc.), Nat. Assn. Bds. Pharmacy (assoc.; nat. del. Ind. 1993—97), Am. Soc. Health Sys. Pharmacists (assoc.; del. 1990—91). Avocations: scuba diving, running, travel. Home: 6792 Black Oak Ct W Avon IN 46123 Office: Cmty Health Network 1500 N Ritter Ave Indianapolis IN 46219 Home Phone: 317-272-1032. Personal E-mail: wmalloy@indy.rr.com.

MALLUCHE, HARTMUT HORST, nephrologist, medical educator; b. Jan. 1, 1943; arrived in U.S., 1975, naturalized, 1985; s. Harald E. and Renate (Muenzberg) M.; children: Nadine, Danielle, Tiffany. Abitur, Albertus Magnus Coll., Koenigstein, Germany, 1963; postgrad., Phillips U., Marburg/Lahn, Fed. Republic Germany, 1963—65, U. Innsbruck, Austria, 1965—66, U. Vienna, 1966; MD, J.W. Goethe U., Frankfurt, Fed. Republic Germany, 1969. Diplomate German Bd. Internal Medicine. Intern County Hosp., Aichach, Germany, 1969—70; resident in internal medicine, fellow in nephrology Cen. Internal Medicine, Univ. Hosp., Frankfurt Am Main, Germany, 1970—75; asst. prof. medicine U. So. Calif., Calif., 1975—78, assoc. prof., 1978—81; prof., dir. divsn. nephrology, bone and mineral metabolism U. Ky. Med. Ctr., Lexington, 1981—. Cons. NIH, FDA; mem. Va. Merit Rev. Bd. Nephrology; program dir. Gen. Clin. Rsch. Ctr. Author: (monograph) Atlas of Mineralized Bone Histology, 1986; editor: Clinical Nephrology; contbr. articles to profl. jours. and books. Grantee, NIH, 1982—, Shriner's Hosp. for Crippled Children, 0192—. Fellow: ACP; mem.: AAAS, Internat. Soc. Bone Morphometry (founder), Internat. Soc. Nephrology, Am. Fedn. Clin. Rsch., European Dialysis and Transplantation Assns., Am. Soc. Physiol. endocrinology, Am. Soc. Bone and Mineral Rsch., Am. Soc. Clin. Investigation, Am. Soc. Nephrology. Office Phone: 859-323-5049 221.

MALM, ROGER CHARLES, lawyer; b. Hot Springs, SD, July 8, 1949; s. Harry Milton and Angeline Mae (Johnson) M.; m. Sandra M. Metz, July 15, 1972; children: Andrew, Elliott, Nicholas. BA, St. Olaf Coll., 1971; JD, U. ND, 1974. Bar: N.D. 1974, Ariz. 1975, Minn. 1980, U.S. Dist. Ct. N.D. 1974, U.S. Dist. Ct. Ariz. 1976, U.S. Ct. Appeals (9th cir.) 1981, U.S. Supreme Ct. 1981, U.S. Ct. Appeals (8th cir) 1982, U.S. Dist. Ct. Minn. 1985, U.S. Claims Ct. 1985, U.S. Tax Ct. 1988. Ptnr. Brink, Sobolik, Severson, Malm & Albrecht, P.A., Hallock, Minn., 1980—; county atty. Kittson County, Minn., 1995—. Pres. N.W. Minn. County Atty.'s Coun; mem. Minn. Commn. Jud. Selection, 2007—. Hospice dir. Kittson County Hospice, Inc., 1984—; bd. dirs. Cmty. Theatre, Hallock, 1987—, Greater Grand Forks Cmty. Theater, 1991-95, N.W. Minn. Found., 2004—. Mem. ABA, Ariz. Bar Assn., N.D. Bar Assn., Minn. Bar Assn. (mem. bd. govs. 1993-2000). Lutheran. Avocations: skiing, sailing. Office: Brink Sobolik Severson Malm & Albrecht PO Box 790 Hallock MN 56728-0790 Office Phone: 218-843-3686. Personal E-mail: brinklaw@brinklawyers.com.

MALMANGER, CURTIS A., mathematician, educator; b. Fairmont, Minn., July 15, 1947; s. Alvin L. and Evelyn M. Malmanger; m. Susan A. Resman, Mar. 22, 1969; children: Heidi S. Braughler, Mark C., Kipp A., Benn J., April M. Meachum. BS in Math. Edn., Bemidji State U., Minn., 1969, MS in Math. Edn., 1973; PhD, U. No. Colo., Greeley, Colo., 1988. Tchr. math. Pillsbury Bapt. Bible Coll., Owatonna, Minn., 1973—84; prof. Maranatha Bapt. Bible Coll., Watertown, Wis., 1988—. Home: 206 Herman St Watertown WI 53098 Office: Maranatha Bapt Bible Coll 745 West Main St Watertown WI 53094 Home Phone: 920-262-1586; Office Phone: 920-206-2363. Business E-Mail: cmalmanger@mbbc.edu.

MALMGREN, HARALD BERNARD, economist; b. Boston, July 13, 1935; s. Berndt Birger and Magda Helena (Nilsson) M.; m. Patricia A. Malmgren, 1959 (div. 1975); children: Karen Philippa, Britt Patricia, Erika Nina; m. Linda V. Einberg, Oct. 3, 1987; children: Markus Harald, Liivia Linda, Viivianne Vaike. BA summa cum laude, Yale U., 1957; postgrad., Harvard U., 1959; PhD, Oxford U., 1961. Asst. prof. dept. engring. and econs. Cornell U., Ithaca, NY, 1961—62; head econ. group Inst. for Def. Analyses, Washington, 1962—64; asst. U.S. trade rep. Exec. Office Pres. The White House, Washington, 1964—69; sr. fellow Overseas Devel. Coun., 1969—71; amb., dep. U.S. trade rep., 1972—75; sr. fellow Woodrow Wilson Internat. Ctr. for Scholars, Washington, 1975—76; prof. George Washington U., Washington, 1976—77; pres. Malmgren, Inc., Washington, 1977—; mng. dir. Malmgren, Golt, Kingston, Ltd., London, 1979—99; chmn. Malmgren O'Donnell, London, 1998—2001, Cordell Hull Inst., Washington, 2001—. Adv. coun. Ctr. Strategic and Internat. Studies, Washington, 1987-97; adv. Senate Fin. Com., Washington, 1970-71, 75-76, Interaction Coun., 1985—. Author: International Economic Peace Keeping, 1972; co-author: Assisting Developing Countries, 1972; editor: Pacific Basin Development, 1972; bd. editors: The International Economy, 1987—, The Washington Quarterly, 1987-95, The World Economy, 1980-90; contbr. articles to profl. jours. Mem. Am. Econ. Assn., Met. Club, Reform Club. Home: Summerfield Farm 7620 Cannonball Gate Rd Warrenton VA 20186-7304 Office Phone: 202-466-8740. Business E-Mail: hm@malmgrenglobal.com.

MALMQUIST, CARL PHILLIP, psychiatrist; b. St. Paul, Mar. 10, 1934; s. Phillip C. and Lillian Viola (Kahler) M.; m. Arlyn Virginia Bodal (dec. 1984); children: Derek, Jay. BA summa cum laude, U. Minn., 1954, MD, 1958, MS in Philosophy of Sci., 1961. Diplomate Am. Bd. Psychiatry and Neurology, Am. Bd. Child Psychiatry, Am. Bd. Adult Psychiatry; cert. forensic psychiatry, added qualification in forensic psychiatry. Intern Columbia Med. Ctr., NYC, 1963—64, U. Minn., Mpls., 1962—63; assoc. prof. dept. psychiatry U. Mich., 1965—67; assoc. prof. Inst. Child Devel. U. Minn., 1967—70, prof., dir. child and adolescent psychiatry, 1971—72, prof. criminal justice, 1972—80, prof. social psychiatry, dept. sociology, 1980—. Cons. Hennepin County Dist. Ct., Mpls., 1967—; mem. commn. of mentally disabled ABA, 1985. Author: Handbook of Adolescence, 1980 (Guttmacher award 2007), Homicide: Psychiatric Perspectives, 1996, 2d edit., 2006; mem. editl. bd. Psychiat. Anns., 1981; contbr. articles to profl. jours. Fellow Am. Psychiat. Assn. (disting. sr.; commn. on jud. action 1994—), Am. Coll. Psychiatrists, Am. Orthopsychiat. Assn., Am. Acad. Child Psychiatry, Am. Acad. Psychiatry and Law (Segmour Pollock Disting. Achievement award 2004), Am. Coll. Forensic Psychiatry; mem. Group for Advancement Psychiatry, Am. Psychopathol. Assn. Episcopalian. Home: 5010 Bruce Ave Minneapolis MN 55424-1318 Office: Univ Minn 6600 France Ave S Ste 545 Minneapolis MN 55435-1804 Office Phone: 952-926-6654. Business E-Mail: malmqu01@atlas.socsci.umn.edu.

MALMSTAD, JOHN EARL, literature and language professor; b. Bismarck, ND, June 25, 1941; s. Manley Ellsworth and Joyce Evelyn (David) M. BA summa cum laude with distinction and departmental honors in Russian Lang. and Lit., Northwestern U., 1963; MA in Slavic Langs. and Lits., Princeton U., 1965, PhD in Slavic Langs. and Lits., 1969; AM (hon.), Harvard U., 1985. Instr. Columbia U., NYC, 1968-69, asst. prof. Russian Lit., 1969-73, assoc. prof., 1973-79, prof. dept. slavic langs. and lits., 1979-85; Samuel Hazzard Cross prof. Slavic langs. and lits. Harvard U., Cambridge, Mass., 1985—, assoc. dean, 1993-94. Vis. assoc. prof. Stanford U., 1971-72, U. Calif. Berkeley, 1977-78; vis. prof. Harvard U., fall 1982; cons., referee NEH translation awards; lectr. in field; attendee internat. symposia. Editor: (with others) The Poetry of Mikhail Kuzmin (3 vols.), 1977, The Poetry of Andrei Bely (3 vols.), 1982-85, Gibel Senatora, 1986, Vladislav Khodasevich Sobranie sochinenii, 1983, Andrei Bely, Spirit of Symbolism, 1987, Readings in Russian Modernism to Honor Vladimir Markov, 1993, Mikhail Kuzmin: Zhizn' Tvorchestvo, Epokha, 1996, Andrey Bely-Ivanov-Razumnik Perepiska, 1998, Mikhail Kuzmin: A Life in Art, 1999, K.N. Bugaeva Vospominaniia o Belom, 2001, Andrey Bely Stikhotvoveniia i poemy, 2 vol., 2006, Andrey Bely Perepiska s M.N. Movozovoi, 2006; Russian book rev. editor Slavic Rev., 1975-86; assoc. editor Russian Rev., 1986-88; mem. editl. bd. Feniks, Opyty, Novoe Literaturnoe obozrenie, Experiment, Philologica, Diaspora; manuscript rev. profl. jours., univ. presses; contbr. articles to profl. jours. Woodrow Wilson fellow, 1963, NDFL fellow Columbia U., 1963-66, Princeton U., 1967-68, Fulbright-Hays fellow, 1966-67, spring 1981, spring 1987, Woodrow Wilson Dissertation fellow, 1966, ACLS rsch. fellow, 1972, Rsch. fellow Russian Inst. Columbia U., summer 1977, 79, 83, 84, IREX fellow, 1975, John Simon Guggenheim fellow, 1980-81; ACLS grant-in-aid, summer, 1980, IREX/ACLS grantee exch. Acad. Scis. USSR, fall 1981, spring 1987, 91, IREX travel grantee Moscow, 1992, Am. Coun. Internat. Edn. grantee, Moscow, 2003. Mem. MLA, Am. Assn. Advancement of Slavic Studies, Assn. Tchrs. of Slavic and East European Langs., Inst. d'Etudes Slaves (Paris), Phi Beta Kappa. Avocations: fine arts, ballet, reading. Home: 8A Cogswell Ave Cambridge MA 02140-2001 Office: Harvard U Dept Slavic Langs/Lit Barker Ctr, 12 Quincy St Cambridge MA 02138 E-mail: malmstad@fas.harvard.edu.

MALOF, KEVIN K., lawyer; b. Cin., Nov. 27, 1967; BS, Miami U., 1990; JD, Salmon P. Chase Coll. Law, 2000. Bar: Ohio 2000. Sr. assoc. Frost Brown Todd LLC, Cin. Mem. Nat. Moot Ct. Bd., 1998—2000. Mem. Miami Twp. Zoning Bd.; bd. mem. NWCCSAY Soccer; coach Miami Twp. Soccer, Miami Twp. Baseball. Named one of Ohio's Rising Stars, Super Lawyers, 2006. Mem.: Ohio State Bar Assn., Cin. Bar Assn., ABA. Office: Frost Brown Todd LLC 2200 PNC Ctr 201 E Fifth St Cincinnati OH 45202-4182 Office Phone: 513-651-6431. Office Fax: 513-651-6981.

MALONE, ADAM, lawyer; b. Albany, Ga., Nov. 22, 1972; BA, No. Ga. Mil. Coll., Dahlonega, Ga., 1996; JD, John Marshall Law Sch., Atlanta, Ga., 2000. Bar: St. of Ga. 2000. Asst. dist. atty. intern Clayton Co. Dist. Atty., 1999—2000; judicial clerk intern Ga. St. Ct. Appeals, Atlanta; atty., personal injury and liability Malone Law Office, Atlanta, 2001—, now ptnr. Mem.: ABA, So. Trial Lawyers Assn. (bd. gov. 2001—03, co-chmn. mem. com. 2001—), Gen. Trial Lawyers Assn., Lawyers Found. Ga., Assn. Trial Lawyers Am., Atlanta Bar Assn., Ga. Bar Assn., Melvin B. Belli Soc., Red Clay Democrats. Office: Malone Law Office Ste 300 Two Ravinia Dr Atlanta GA 30346 Fax: 770-390-7560.

MALONE, ALICIA JANE, minister, theologian; b. Akron, Ohio, July 7, 1953; d. Clifford David Malone, Sr. and Veralene Malone; 1 child, Aaron D. MA, Ashland Theol. Sem., Ohio, 1996, MDiv, 2001, D in Ministry, 2005; postgrad., Moody Bible Inst., Stow, Ohio, 1982—90, McCleary Theol. Ctr., Cleve., 1991—94. Cert. clin. pastoral edn. Stenographer Babcock & Wilcox Co., Barberton, Ohio, 1971—75, Navy nuc. corr., 1976—80; chaplain intern Akron Gen. Hosp., Ohio, 1995—, chaplain assoc. Acad. tchr. Mt. Olive Bapt. Ch., Akron, 1982—2006; execd. dir. Bondage Breakers, Inc., Akron, 1991—2006; mentor, counselor Cmty. Health Ctr., Akron, 2005—. Author: What God Can't Do Just Can't Be Done, 1996, Bondage Breakers, Inc A Model, 2005. Recipient Harold K. Stubbs Justice award for social adv., Leona Ferris Caring award for social adv., Womens History award, Akron City Coun. Mem.: Am. Bapt. Akron Assn. (exec. com. 1991—2006). Avocations: chess, gardening, martial arts. Home: 1365 Peckham St Akron OH 44320 Office: Bondage Breakers Inc 680 E Market St Ste 305 Akron OH 44304

MALONE, BEVERLY LOUISE, nursing administrator, former dean; b. Aug. 25, 1948; d. Dorothy Black; children: Tosha Manuel, Jelani Manuel. BSN, U. Cin., 1970; MS, Rutgers U., 1972; PhD, U. Cin., 1981. Lic. clin. psychologist. Asst. adminstr. for nursing, U. Hosp. U. Cin., 1983—86, adj. asst. prof., 1983-86; dimension faculty Union of Experimenting Colls. & Univs., Cin., 1985-88; dean, prof. nursing N.C. A&T State U., Greensboro, 1996—99, interim vice chancellor for acad. affairs, 1996—99; dep. asst. sec. for health US Dept. Health & Human Services, Washington, 2000—01; gen. sec. Royal Coll. Nursing, 2001—07; CEO Nat. League for Nursing, NYC, 2007—. Mem. N.C. Commn. on Health Svcs., 1991—; bd. trustees Moses Cone Hosp., 1988—; chair Statewide Nursing Edn. Task Force, 1988-91. Mem. ANA (bd. dirs. 1990-94, pres. 1996-2000). Office: Nat League for Nursing 61 Broadway 33rd Fl New York NY 10006

MALONE, CAROLYN LUCIA MARINO, education educator; b. Manhattan, Kans., July 14, 1944; d. John and Viola (Rolander) Marino; 1 child, Jesse David Marino Kramer. PhD in History of Art and Medieval Studies, U. Calif., Berkeley, 1973. Vis. lectr. U. Mich., Ann Arbor, 1972, Harvard U., Cambridge, Mass., 1973; asst. prof. U. Mass., Amherst, Mass., 1974, Vassar Coll., Poughkipsie, NY, 1974—75, Princeton U., NJ, 1975—81; assoc. prof. U. So. Calif., LA, 1981—. Author: (excavations and archtl. interpretation) Les Fouilles de Saint Bénigne de Dijon (1976-1978) et le problème de l'église de l'an mil, Bulletin Monumental 138, 1980 (Courtland-Elliott prize, Medieval Acad. Am., 1982), (liturgical and political interpretation) Facade as Spectacle: Ritual and Ideology at Wells Cathedral, Brill Series: Studies in Medieval and Reformation Traditions, 2004. Fellow excavations, Saint-Bénigne in Dijon, Samuel H. Kress Found., 1976, Nat. Endowment for Humanities, 1977—78, Am. Coun. Learned Socs., 2002, Am. Assn. of U. Women, 2002; St.-Bénigne fellow, Graham Found., 1998. Mem.: So. Calif. Art Historians Assn. (assoc.; v.p., pres. 1996—99), Medieval Assn. of the Pacific (assoc.; bd. dirs. 1986—89), Medieval Acad. of Am. (assoc.), Phi Beta Kappa (hon.). Home: 476 36th St Manhattan Beach CA 90266 Office: Univ Southern Calif Dept History of Art Los Angeles CA 90089 Home Phone: 310-545-1694; Office Phone: 213-740-4569. Personal E-mail: cmalone@usc.edu.

MALONE, CLAUDINE BERKELEY, financial and management consultant; b. Louisville, May 9, 1936; d. Claude McDowell and Mary Katharine (Smith) M.; BA, Wellesley Coll., 1963; MBA, Harvard U., 1972. CPA, Md. Systems engr. IBM Corp., Washington, 1964; sr. systems analyst Crane Co., Chgo., 1966; contr., mgr. data processing Raleigh Stores, Washington, 1967-70; asst. prof. Harvard U., 1972-76, assoc. prof., 1977-81; pres., CEO, Fin. & Mgmt. Consulting Inc., McLean, Va., 1981-; vis. prof., Georgetown U., 1982-84, U. Va., 1984-87; dir. Scott Paper Co., Houghton Mifflin Co., Campbell Soup Co., Boston Co., Dart Group Inc., Hasbro Inc., 1994-, Novell Inc., 2003-, Apollo Investment Corp., 2007-; trustee Penn Mut. Life Ins. Co. Chmn. Bus. for Reagan-Bush Com. Mass., 1980; trustee Wellesley Coll., 1982-. Recipient Candace award, 1982. Mem. Assn. Women CPA's, UN Assn., Wellesley Coll. Alumnae Assn., Washington Wellesley Club. Episcopalian. *

MALONE, DAVID MICHAEL, diplomat, educator; b. Ottawa, Canada, Feb. 7, 1954; s. Paul Thomas Malone and Deirdre Lavalette Ingram. BA, U. Montreal, 1972; MPA, Harvard U., Cambridge, Mass., 1980; DPhil, Oxford U., Eng., 1997. Various positions in Can. fgn. ministry and at Can. diplomatic missions in Cairo, Amman and Kuwait Govt. of Can., 1975—90; Can. rep. UN/ECOSOC, NY and Geneva, 1990—92; amb., dep. permanent rep. Can. Permanent Mission to the UN, NYC, 1992—94; dir. gen., policy, internat. orgn. and global issues bureaus Can. Ministry of Fgn. Affairs and Internat. Trade, Ottawa, Canada, 1994—98; pres. Internat. Peace Acad., NYC, 1998—2004; asst. dep. min. global issues Fgn. Affairs Can., 2004—06; high commr. for Can. to India and amb. of Can. to Bhutan and Nepal, 2006—. Adj. prof. law NYU Sch. Law, 1999—2004; adj. prof. internat. rels. Institut des Etudes Politiques (Sciences Po), Paris, 2001—04. Author: The UN Security Council from the Cold War to the Twenty First Century; contbr. articles to profl. jour. Address: Can High Commn 7/8 Shantypath Chanakyapuri New Delhi 110 021 India Office Phone: 91-11-4178-2000. Business E-Mail: david.malone@international.gc.ca.

MALONE, DAVID ROY, retired educational association administrator, director; b. Beebe, Ark., Nov. 4, 1943; s. James Roy and Ila Mae (Griffin) M.; m. Judith Kaye Huff, June 20, 1965 (div. Feb. 1990); m. Deborah W. Thomas, Jan. 23, 2004; 1 child, Michael David. BSBA, U. Ark., 1965, JD, 1969, MBA, 1982. Bar: Ark. 1969, US Dist. Ct. (we. dist.) Ark. 1969, US Tax Ct. 1972, US Ct. Appeals (8th cir.) 1972, US Supreme Ct. 1972. Pvt. practice, Fayetteville, Ark., 1969-72; atty. City of Fayetteville, 1969-72; asst. prof. bus. U. Ark., Fayetteville, 1972-76, asst. dean law, 1976-91; mem. Ark. Ho. of Reps., 1980-84, Ark. Senate, 1984—2002; exec. dir. U. Ark. Found., 1991—2002, Ark. Tchr. Ret. Sys., 2003—06; ret., 2006. Chair Senate edn. com., 1997-2002, co-chair legis. coun., 1999-2000; bd. dirs. Bank of Elkins, 1976-98, S.W. Edn. Devel. Lab., Austin, Tex., 1988-94; legal adv. coun. So. Regional Edn. Bd., Atlanta, 1991-2002. Contbr. articles to profl. jours.; bd. dirs. Ark. Law Rev., 1978-92; contbg. author U. Ark. Press, 1989. Mayor City of Fayetteville, 1979-80; mem. Jud. Article Task Force, Little Rock, 1989-91; chair Motor Voter task force, 1994-95; bd. dirs. Music Festival Ark., 1989-91, Washington County Hist. Soc., 1993-96; bd. dirs. Walton Arts Ctr. Found., 1994-2000, chmn., 1994-98; chmn. bd. dirs. Washington County Law Libr., 1970-84; chmn. Ark. Tuition Trust Authority, 1997-99. Recipient Svc. award, Ark. Mcpl. League, 1980, Disting. Svc. award, U. Ark., 1988, Lucas Svc. award, Ark. Alumni Assn., 1998, award, Walton Coll. Bus., U. Ark., 2004. Mem. Ark. Bar Assn. (ho. of dels. 1977-81, award of merit 1980, exec. 1981-82, Outstanding Lawyer-Citizen award 1990), Washington County Bar Assn., Ark. Inst. Continuing Legal Edn. (bd. dirs. 1979-88), Fayetteville C. of C. (bd. dirs. 1984-89), Ark. Genealogy Soc. (bd. dirs. 1990-92). Democrat. Methodist. Avocations: genealogy, stamp collecting/philately. Home: 3411 Sassafras Hill Rd Fayetteville AR 72703 Mailing: PO Box 1366 Fayetteville AR 72702-1366 Personal E-mail: davidr_malone@yahoo.com.

MALONE, JAMES HIRAM, graphics designer, journalist, writer; b. Winterville, Ga., Mar. 24, 1930; s. Ralph and Sarah Lena (Echols) M.; m. Mary Louise Liebaert, 1972 (div. 1982); children: Andrew Ralph, Matthew Martin. Student, Morehouse Coll., 1949-50, Coll. Art and Design, 1959-62. Art dir., prodn. mgr. Better Brochures, Inc., Detroit, 1963-65; graphics mgr. Fed. Dept. Stores, Detroit, 1965-69; sr. art cons. Northgate Ad Agy., Detroit, 1969-75; sr. graphics designer Montgomery Ward Regional Hdqs., Southfield, Mich., 1975-80; layout/prodn. designer K-Mart Internat. Hdqs., Troy, Mich., 1980-83; ad/promotions creative dir. Atlanta Jour./Constitution, 1983-90; fine art prodr., painter Bianco Art Collections of Atlanta, Marietta, Ga., 1990-92; cartoonist, newspaper columnist/reporter Atlanta News Leader, Union City, Ga., 1992—. Author, artist: Ralph cartoon strip, 1998, Here and There Poetry, Blues Poetry, 1954, Grandma Sarah's Closet, 1960, Brother, 1970, Malone's Atlanta, 1986, No-Job Dad, 1992, The Cart, 1994, April Mae Jones Coloring Book, 1999; contbr. The Total Cartoonist, 1983, Lure of the Local, 1997, Landscape Narratives, 1998, (novel) If I Live, 2003, (juvenile) Joey Grows and Knows, 2005; co-author songs Talk to Your Child, Willie Lives in the Streets, 1986, Homeless Hope, 1987, The TAP Song, 1995, artist: (literacy drawings) Say (Simply Apply Yourself), 1988, contr. Word-Up Anthology, 1990, (paintings) BIG (Black Inventors Gifts), 1991; one-man shows include AAA Art Gallery, Detroit, 1963-67, Richard Russell Hall Gallery, Atlanta, 1985, C.W. Hill Gallery, Atlanta, 1990, Walker St. Gallery, Atlanta, 1992, Alma Simmons Gallery, 1986-94, The Atlanta Project Collaboration Ctr., 1994, Atlanta's Auburn Ave. Rsch. Libr., African Am. Culture and History Gallery, 1999, Tchg. Mus. South, 1999-2001, Decatur Bapt. Ch., 2000; exhibited in group shows at Red Cross European Exchange Touring Art Exhbn., 1949, Atlanta U., 1949, 53-55, Contemporary Art Studio Gallery, Detroit, 1962, 64-67, 75, Detroit Mus. Art, 1968, Wayne State Coll. Cmty. Gallery, Detroit, 1969, Kumarsi Mart Art Gallery, Detroit, 1970, Scarab Club Mus., Detroit, 1974, United Auto Workers, Detroit, 1977, Salon Internat. De La Caricature, Montreal, Can., 1980-83, 85-86, 88, Artistic Directions Gallery, Atlanta, 1983, Nexus Gallery, Atlanta, 1984, 89, Ctr. Creative Studies Coll. Art and Design Alumni Exhibits, Detroit, 1986-92, Spelman Coll., Atlanta, 1987, Mattress Factory, 1987, 89, Nat. Black Arts Festival, Atlanta, 1988-92, Ga. State U., 1989, Ruth Hall Hodges Gallery, Atlanta, 1990-93, TULA Galleries, Atlanta, 1990, Seven Stages, 1990, 96, EarthFactory, Atlanta, 1991, Art Station, Atlanta, 1991, Atlanta Life, 1992, Trinity Art Gallery, 1992, Samari Art Gallery, 1993, Mobile (Ala.) Coll., 1993-94, Albany Mus. Art, 1994, Alma Simmons Gallery, Atlanta, 1994, Atlanta Project Hdqs., 1994, Avery Gallery, 1995; Buttermilk Bottom Art Proj., 1995-96, Atlanta's Civic Ctr., 1995-96, Alma Simmons Gallery, 1995-96, Atlanta's Auburn Ave Rsch. Libr., African Am. Culture and History Gallery, 1996, City Hall East Gallery, 1996-97, Atlanta Olympic Park, 1997, Eddies' Alley, 1997, Miles Gallery, 1997, House of Colors, 1998, Annie McPheeters Art Gallery, 1999, Tchg. Mus. South, 1999-2007, Atlanta Hartsfield Airport, 2000, New Orleans Art Galleries, 2000, Kennesaw State U. Gallery, 2000, Southwest

Cafe Gallery, 2005, Homecoming: 20th Century African Am. Masters, 2005, Walt Disney's movie scenery, 2001-, Motion Through Art, 2002, Pilgrimage to Paradise, Gallery on Greene, 2002, Youth Gallery, 2003, Atlanta Biennial, 2003, Mills Srs. Ctr. Collection, 2003, Habersham Gardens, 2004, South Fulton Art Show, 2004; represented in permanent collections including Atlanta U., Hatch-Billups, N.Y., Ga. Artists Register, Atlanta, Bianco Collections, Ga. Rsch. libr. African-Am. culture and history, 1995, RepoHistory Assn., 1996, neighborhood schs. mentor Fed. Dept. Stores, Detroit, 1964-69; motivator, sch. lectr. Atlanta Jour./Constitution, 1983-90, minority job fairs guide, 1985; bd. dirs. Neighborhood Planning Unit J, Atlanta, 1984—, Bankhead Hwy. Revitalization Project, Atlanta, 1990—; arts cons. Fulton County Arts Task Force, Atlanta, 1990—; com. chmn. Jimmie Carter's West Fulton and Douglass Atlanta Cluster Project, 1992—; active Feed The Homeless, Inc., Atlanta Olympics Com., Atlanta Mayor's Bicycle Paths Commn., 1995; com. chmn. Atlanta-Fulton County Action Authority Assn., 1994, North Ave Civic League Assn., 2002, The Atlanta Contemporary Studios, 2003. Recipient George H. Clapp Meml. Found. award Art Inst. Pitts., 1949, Nat. Art award, Scholastic Art Awards Contest, Atlanta U. Nat. Art award, 1949, Nat. Cartoonist Soc. scholar, 1958, Editorial Cartoon award Nat. Newspapers Pubs. Assn., 1973, Bronze Jubilee Cmty. award WPBA TV, Atlanta, 1986, Alumni Art award Ctr. Creative Studies, Coll. Art and Design, Detroit, 1986, Atlanta Symphony Art award, 1986, Youth Motivation award Merit Employment Assn., 1987-89, So. Drawl Art Exhbn. award, 1993, Atlanta'a Centennial Olympic Park Art award, 1997, Annie L. McPheeters Cmty. Medallion award, 1998, Million Man March Srs. award, 1998, Cmty. award Together Atlanta, 1999; grantee Atlanta Jour./Constitution, 1986, Nexus Family History Artbook Project, 1994, Avant Gardening Tour 2000, Daimler/Chrysler Art award, 2002. Mem. Assn. Am. Cultures, 1980, High Mus. Art, 1st World Writers (v.p. 1993-94), Internat. Black Writers (cons., pres. 1996), Atlanta Writing Resource Ctr., Nat. Conf. Artists, Friends of Atlanta/Fulton County Libr., Buttermilk Bottom Cmty. Assn. (cons., v.p. 1996, pres. 1998), Individual Visual Artists' Coalition, Laughing Trees Assn. (CEO 2000), Keep Atlanta Beautiful (bd. mem. 2004). Democrat. Baptist. Avocations: poetry, photography, tennis, rummage sales, reading. Home: 1796 North Ave NW Atlanta GA 30318-6441 Home Phone: 404-794-0948. Personal E-mail: j.l.t.malone@att.net. E-mail: laughingtrees@worldnet.att.net.

MALONE, JEAN HAMBIDGE, educational consultant; b. South Bend, Ind., Nov. 23, 1954; d. Craig Ellis and Dorothy Jane (Piechorowski) Hambidge; m. James Kevill Malone, July 8, 1978; children: Julia Mae, James Kevill III, John Thomas. BS in Edn., Butler U., 1976, MS in Edn., 1977. Tchr. Indpls. Pub. Schs., 1977-78; dir. student center and activities Butler U., Indpls., 1978-87. Trustee Eisenhower Meml. scholarship, 1977-80; bd. dirs. Heritage Place of Indpls., 1983-88, Ind. Office Campus Ministries, 1985-87, 89—91, Campfire of Cen. Ind., 1980-84, 86-87, Intercollegiate YMCA, Indpls., 1985-87, 89-90, Indpls. Jr. League, 1989—, Indpls. Urban Parish Coop, 1987-90, v.p., pres., 1991, 92; bd. dirs. Gennesaret Free Clinic of Indy, 1992-94; mem. overseers coun. Camp Delafield Children with Dyslexia, 1993-95, bd. pres., 1997-2000; bd. dirs. Dyslexia Inst. Ind., 1996—, bd. pres., 1997-2000; mem. Commn. Youth Archdiocec, 2000-01; community adv. for the homeless of Indpls. Recipient Outstanding Faculty award, Butler U., 1980. Mem. Ind. Assn. Women Deans (v.p. bd. dirs. 1987-88), Adminstrs. and Counselors (bd. dirs. 1982-83), Internat. Dyslexia Assn. (mem. Ind. br. 1992—), Kappa Delta Pi, Phi Kappa Phi, Alpha Lambda Delta, Kappa Kappa Gamma. Roman Catholic. Office: 5256 N Illinois St Indianapolis IN 46208-2636 Personal E-mail: jhmalone2@aol.com.

MALONE, JIMMY, radio personality; m. April Malone; 1 child, Angela. Radio host WMJI, Cleve., 1961—. Stand-up comedian. Co-host (radio shows) Knuckleheads in the News, 1961—, The Lanigan & Malone Show, 1991—. Active Cleve. Scholar Program, Providence House, Greater Cleve. Hunger Task Force. Co-recipient (with John Lanigan) Large Market Personality of Yr., NAB Marconi Radio Awards, 2003; named Radio and TV Coun. Students' Boradcaster of Yr.; named to, Shaker Heights Alumni Hall of Fame. Office: WMJI 105.7 4th Fl 6200 Oak Tree Blvd Independence OH 44131 also: WMJI 105.7 FM 6th Fl 310 W Lakeside Ave Cleveland OH 44113 E-mail: malone@wmji.com.

MALONE, JOHN C., media company executive; b. Milford, Conn., Mar. 7, 1941; m. Leslie. BS in Elec. Engring. and Econ., Yale U., 1963; MS in Indsl. Mgmt., John Hopkins U., 1964, PhD in Ops. Rsch., 1967; LHD (hon.), Denver U., 1992. With econ. planning rsch. and devel. Bell Telephone Labs/AT&T, 1963—68; joined McKinsey & Co., 1968; group v.p. Gen. Instrument Corp., 1970—73; formerly pres. Jerrold Electronics Corp. (subs. Gen. Instrument Corp.); pres., CEO Tele-Comms., Inc., Denver, 1973—96; chmn., CEO Tele-Comms., Inc (merged with AT&T Corp.), Denver, 1996-99; chmn. Liberty Satellite, 1996—2000, Liberty Media Corp., Denver, 1990—, CEO, 2005—06. Bd. dirs. IAC/InterActiveCorp., 2001—04, Bank of New York, 1986—, UnitedGlobalCom, Inc., Discovery Communications, CATO Inst., Cablevision Systems Corp.; bd. dirs. Liberty Media Corp.; bd. dirs. The Nature Conservancy; bd. dirs., chmn. emeritus Cable Television Laboratories, Inc. Bd. dirs. Nature Conservancy, CATO Inst. Named Man of Yr. award, TVC Mag., 1981; named one of Forbes' Richest Americans, 2006; recipient Wall Street Transcript's Gold award for cable industry's best CEO, 1982, 1985, 1986, 1987, Wall Street Transcript Silver award, 1984, 1989, NCTA Vanguard award, 1983, Women In Cable Betsy Magness Fellowship Honoree, U. Pa. Wharton Sch. Sol C. Snider Entrepreneurial Ctr. Award of Merit for Disting. Entrepreneurship, Am. Jewish Com. Sherrill C. Corwin Human Rels. award, Comm. Tech. Mag. Svc. and Tech. award, Bronze award, Fin. World CEO of Yr. Competition, 1993, Hopkins Disting. Alumnus award, 1994. Mem.: Nat. Cable. TV Assn. (dir. 1974—77, treas. 1977—78, dir. 1980—93, Vanguard award 1983). Office: Liberty Media Corp 12300 Liberty Blvd Englewood CO 80112 *

MALONE, JOHN I., pediatrics educator, biomedical researcher; b. Altoona, Pa., Oct. 10, 1941; s. W. Paul and Olive (Romine) M.; m. Gloria Joyce Cromer, Sept. 5, 1964; children: John Irvin Jr., Michael A., Jennifer A., W. Andrew. BS, Pa. State U., 1963; MD, U. Pa., 1967. Diplomate Am. Bd. Pediatrics, Am. Bd. Pediatric Endocrinology; cert. diabetes educator. Straight pediatric intern Children's Hosp. Phila., 1967-68, resident, 1968-69, research fellow div. biochem. devel. and molecular diseases, 1969-71; instr. pediatrics U. Pa. Sch. Medicine, Phila., 1971-72; chief resident Hosp. of U. Pa., 1971-72; asst. prof. U. South Fla. Coll. Medicine, Tampa, 1972-76, assoc. prof., 1976-80, chief divsn. pediatric diabetes & metalbolic diseases, 1976—, prof., 1980—, co-dir. Diabetes Ctr., 1979—. Co-dir. Fla. Camp for Children and Youth with Diabetes, Tampa, 1973—2005; mem. clin. and sci. adv. bd. Children's Diabetes Found., Denver, 1976-86; dir. Suncoast Regional PKU Program, 1976—, Suncoast Regional Diabetes Program, 1976—, chief pediat. endocrinology, diabetes and metabolism, 1995-2005; mem. Fla. Gov.'s Diabetes Adv. Coun., 1979-2003; mem. Internat. Study Group Diabetes in Children and Adolescents, Paris, 1982—; vis. prof., cons. in pediat. endocrinology Uniformed Svcs. U. Health Scis., Bethesda, Md., 1990-98. Contbr. over 110 articles Sci., New Eng. Jour. Medicine, Jour. Pediatrics, Am. Jour. Human Genetics, Am. Jour. Diseases of Children, Diabetes, Jour. Fla. Med. Assn., Diabetes Care, Jour. Clin. Investigation, Jour. Clin. Psychiatry, European Jour. Pediatrics, Proc. NAS, Pediatrics Rsch., Pediatrician, Diabetes Care, Pediatrics, Am. Jour. Med. Scis., Am. Jour. Med. Genetics, Clin. Pediatrics, also chpts. to books. Bd. dir. Diabetes Trust Fund, Birmingham, Ala., 2002—. Mem. AAAS, Am. Acad. Pediatrics, Am. Diabetes Assn. (program chmn. youth coun. 1987-88), Lawson Wilkins Pediatric Endocrine Soc., So. Soc. for Pediatric Rsch. (pres. 1986-87), Am. Fedn. for Clin. Rsch., Soc. for Pediatric Rsch., N.Y. Acad. Sci., Am. Inst. Nutrition, Am. Pediatric Soc., Am. Soc. for Clin. Nutrition, Soc. for Inherited Metabolic Disorders. Achievements include research in metabolic causes of diabetes associated complications; development and prevention of diabetes in relatives of patients with insulin-dependent diabetes. Office: U South Fla Coll Medicine 12901 Bruce B Downs Blvd Tampa FL 33612-4742 Office Phone: 813-974-5777. E-mail: jmalone@hsc.usf.edu.

MALONE, JOSEPH JAMES, mathematics professor, researcher; b. St. Louis, Sept. 9, 1932; s. Joseph James and Aurelia Theresa (Schomaker) M.; m. Dorothy Sue Cleary, Nov. 24, 1960; children: Michael, Barbara, Philip, Patrick. BS, St. Louis U., 1954, MS, 1958, PhD, 1962. Instr. math. Rockhurst Coll., Kansas City, Mo., 1960-62; asst. prof. U. Houston, 1962-67; assoc. prof. Tex. A&M U., College Station, 1967-70, prof., 1970-71, Worcester (Mass.) Poly. Inst., 1971-2000, prof. emeritus, 2000—, chmn. dept. math., 1971-78. Contbr. articles to profl. jours. Mem. pub. schs. bd. Town of Westborough (Mass.), 1974-83, 84-87, fin. com., 1992-98, selectman, 1998-2001, fin. com., 2001—. With U.S. Army, 1954-56. Mem. Am. Math. Soc., Math. Assn. Am. Democrat. Roman Catholic. Achievements include research in near-ring theory and group theory. Home: 45 Adams St Westborough MA 01581-3610 Office: Worcester Poly Inst 100 Institute Rd Worcester MA 01609-2280 E-mail: jjmalone@wpi.edu.

MALONE, NANCY, actress; b. Queens Village, NY; d. James and Bridget (Sheilds) M. Freelance actress, dir., producer, writer. Performer (TV series) The First Hundred Years, Naked City, The Long, Hot Summer (Best Performance by an Actress award); Broadway debut in Time Out For Ginger, other stage performances include Major Barbara, The Makropoulis Secret, A Touch of the Poet, The Trial of the Catonsville Nine; touring performances include The Chalk Garden, The Seven Yr. Itch, A Place For Dolly; actress (films) The Violators, I Cast No Shadow, An Affair of the Skin, Intimacy, The Trial of the Cantonsville Nine, The Man Who Loved Cat Dancing, Capricorn One; producer (TV series) including Bionic Woman, 1978, Husbands, Wives and Lovers, 1978, The Great Pretender, 1984, (special) Bob Hope: The First 90 Years, 1993 (Emmy award, Outstanding Variety, Musical or Comedy Special, 1993), Womanspeak, 1983; dir. (TV series) Dynasty, 1984-87, Hotel, 1984-87, Colbys, 1985, Cagney and Lacey, 1987, Star Trek Voyager, 1997, Burning Zone, 1997, Fame l.A. 1997-98, Rosie O'Niel (Emmy nomination), Sisters (Emmy nomination), Melrose Place, 1992-99, Beverly Hills, 1990-2000, Picket Fences, Judging Amy, 1999-, Resurrection Blvd., 2000-02; producer, dir. (film) There Were Times Dear, 1986 (John Muir Trustees award, Cine Golden Eagle, Blue Ribbon); founder Nancy Malone Prodns., 1975, Lilac Prodns., 1979. Fellow Leaky Found.; mem. Am. Film Inst. (mem. founder), Women in Film (trustee, Chrystal award, Founders award 1996). Office: Guild Mgmt PHA 9911 W Pico Blvd Los Angeles CA 90035-2703 Home: 4604 Ledge Ave Toluca Lake CA 91602-1536

MALONE, NICHOLAS SHERLON, systems analyst, consultant; b. Huntington, W.Va., Aug. 6, 1958; s. Clarence Edward Malone and Ernestine (Queen) Vaughn; m. Julie Stratton, Mar. 4, 1985 (div. Dec. 3, 1990); m. Tracy Lynne Prunty, Dec. 21, 1991; children: Nicolle Morgynne, Shannon Darby. BA in Polit. Sci., Marshall U., Huntington, 1981; JD, Rocheville U., Richmond, Va., 2005. Owner Mgmt. Resources, 1977—. Dir. W.Va. Sci. Fiction Assn., Charleston, 1980-86. Author: (book) Social Alternatives in Rsch., 1982, Comp. Security Program, 1990; contbr. articles to profl. jours. Rsch. analyst W.Va. Code Reform Orgn., Charleston, 1979, W.Va. GOP, Huntington, 1980; Nat. Orgn. Reform Marijuana Laws, Huntington, 1985-86; project mgr. UN Edn. Orgn./Non Govt. Orgns. Soc., N.Y., 1981-82; bd. dirs. UN Ednl. Orgn., N.Y., 1979-82, MARCON, 1983-90. Served With USMC, 1979-92. Recipient Gold Star award Michelien du France, 1981, award Rikido-USA, 1981, Nat. Top 10 award Role Playing Games Assn., 1978, 79, 80, 81, Nat. Top 100 Rating United Fedn. Fighting Arts 1975, 76, 77, 78; inducted into Naidh Nasc, 1999. Mem. NRA, Am. Soc. Transp. and Devel., Assn. Computing Machines, Am. Soc. Industry Security, Millennium Soc., Boy Scouts Am., Soc. Noble Celts. Republican. Mem. Daoist Ch. Avocations: martial arts, gourmet cooking, sca, chess, hunting. Office: Mgmt Resources Int 9450 Tuxford Rd Richmond VA 23236 Office Phone: 804-320-0370. Business E-Mail: nix@iolinc.net.

MALONE, ROBERT K., lawyer; b. Bklyn., 1959; BA, Cath. Univ. Am., 1981; JD, Seton Hall Univ., 1984. Bar: NJ 1985. Staff to Hon. Bill Bradley US Senate, Wash., 1979—81; law clk. to Hon. William H. Gindin US Bankruptcy Ct. Dist. NJ, 1985—86; ptnr., vice chmn. corp. restructuring practice group Drinker Biddle & Reath LLP, Florham Pk., NJ. Office: Drinker Biddle & Reath LLP 500 Campus Dr Florham Park NJ 07932-1047 Office Phone: 973-549-7080. Office Fax: 973-360-9831. Business E-Mail: robert.malone@dbr.com.

MALONE, ROBERT ROY, artist, art educator; b. McColl, SC, Aug. 8, 1933; s. Robert Roy and Anne (Matthews) M.; m. Cynthia Enid Taylor, Feb. 26, 1956; 1 child, Brendan Trevor. BA, U. N.C., 1955; MFA, U. Chgo., 1958; postgrad., U. Iowa, 1959. Instr. art Union U., Jackson, Tenn., 1959-60, Lambuth Coll., 1959-61; asst. prof. art Wesleyan Coll., Macon, Ga., 1961-67, assoc. prof., 1967-68, W.Va. U., 1968-70, So. Ill. U., Edwardsville, 1970-75, prof., 1975—2000, prof. emeritus, 2000—. Oneman shows at Gallery Illien, Atlanta, 1969, De Cinque Gallery, Miami, 1968, 71, Ill. State Mus., Springfield, 1974, U. Del., Newark, 1978, Elliot Smith Gallery, St. Louis, 1985, Merida Galleries, Louisville, 1985, Yvonne Rapp Gallery, Louisville, 1990, 92-93, 96, 98, 2000, 04, St. John's Coll., Santa Fe, 1991, Uzelac Gallery, Pontiac, Mich., 1997, others; group shows include Bklyn. Mus., 1966, Assoc. Am. Artists Gallery, NYC, 1968, Mus. d'Art Modern, Paris, 1970, DeCordova Mus., 1973-74, St. Louis Art Mus., 1985, Wake Forest U., 1985, New Orleans Mus. Art, 1990, Dakota Internat., Vermillion, 1994, Springfield Art Mus., Mo., 2004; represented in permanent collections including Smithsonian Instn., Washington, USIA, Washington, Libr. of Congress, Calif. Palace of Legion of Honor, San Francisco, NY Pub. Libr., NYC, Victoria and Albert Mus., London, Chgo. Art Inst., Indpls. Mus. Art, Humana Inc., Louisville, State of Ill. Ctr., Chgo., Speed Mus., Louisville, N. Ill. U., Capital Devel. Bd., Ill.; co-editor: Contemporary American Printmakers, 1999 (English and Chinese edits.). Recipient numerous regional, nat. awards in competitive exhbns.; Ford fellow, 1977, So. Ill. U. at Edwardsville sr. research scholar, 1976, 1984. Home: 600 Chapman St Edwardsville IL 62025-1260

MALONE, ROBERT WALLACE, surgeon; s. Edgar Wallace and Nancy Adams Malone; m. Jill Glasspool, Feb. 17, 1979; children: William Zachary, Spencer James. AA, Santa Barbara C.C., Calif., 1982; BS in Biochemistry, U. of Calif., Davis, 1984; MS in Biology, U. of Calif., La Jolla, 1989; MD, Northwestern U., Chgo., 1991. Rsch. scientist Vical, Inc, San Diego, 1989; pathology resident U. of Calif., Davis, 1991—92, rsch. fellow, 1992—93, asst. prof. pathology, 1993—97; asst. prof, pathology U. of Md., Sch. of Medicine, Balt., 1997—2000; chief of lab. sci., dir. of tissue banking USUHS Clin. Breast Care Program, Bethesda, Md., 2000—01; pres. and founder Gene Delivery Alliance, Inc, Rockville, Md., 2001; assoc. dir, clin. rsch. Dynport Vaccine Co., LLC, Frederick, Md., 2002—; assoc. prof. of surgery Uniformed Services U. of the Health Sci., Bethesda, Md., 2001. Cons. Inovio, Oslo, 2001—02; sr. cons. Mgmt. Systems Designers, Inc, Vienna, 2001—02; med. dir. Molecular Histology, Montgomery Village, Md., 2002. Contbr. chpts. to books. Recipient Trainee Investigator award, Am. Fedn. for Clin. Rsch., 1993, Svc. to the Coll. award, Santa Barbara C.C., 1981—82, Giannini Found. fellow, Bank of Am., Giannini Found., 1992—93, Henry Christian Award for Excellence in Rsch., Am. Fedn. for Clin. Rsch., 1992, 1st Pl., Northwestern AOA Rsch. Symposium competition for Med. Students, Northwestern U. AOA, 1989; fellow Edmonson Summer fellow, UC Davis Dept. of Med. Pathology, 1984, Pre-Doctoral fellow, USPHS, 1986—88; grantee Pres.'s Undergraduate Fellowship grantee, U. Calif.-Davis, 1983—84, Med. Scholars Program grantee, Univ of Calif. Davis Med. Ctr., 1992—93, Grant for RNA structure modeling, San Diego Supercomputer Ctr., 1988; scholar MD./Ph.D. scholar, Northwestern U., 1984—86. Mem.: AAAS, European Gene Therapy Soc., Bioelectrochem. Soc., NY Acad. of Sci., Gene Therapy/Molecular Biology Internat. Soc. Achievements include invention of electroporative gene delivery into lung; patents for direct DNA delivery; genetic (DNA) vaccination; mucosal polyncleotide vaccination; invention of nuclease inhibitors for non-viral gene therapy; patents pending for nuclease inhibitors fo non-viral gene therapy; invention of skin electroporation for genetic vaccination. Avocations: carpentry, kayacking, animal husbandry, mountain climbing. Personal E-mail: gtinventor@hotmail.com. E-mail: maloner@dynport.com.

MALONE, THOMAS FRANCIS, academic administrator, meteorologist; b. Sioux City, Iowa, May 3, 1917; s. John and Mary (Hourigan) M.; m. Rosalie Doran, Dec. 30, 1942; children: John H., Thomas Francis, Mary E., James K., Richard K., Dennis P. BS, S.D. Sch. Mines, 1940, D.Eng., 1962; Sc.D., MIT, 1946; L.H.D., St. Joseph Coll., West Hartford, Conn., 1965; Sc.D. (hon.), Bates Coll., 1988; Sc.D. (hon.), Wesleyan U., 2007. Instr. MIT, 1942-43, asst. prof., 1943-51, assoc. prof., 1951-56; dir. Travelers Rsch. Ctr., Travelers Ins. Co., Hartford, Conn., 1955-56, dir. rsch., 1956-69, sr. v.p., 1968-70, chmn. bd., 1961-70; dean Grad. Sch., U. Conn., Storrs, 1970-73; chmn. bd. Ctr. for Environment and Men, 1970-71; dir. emeritus Holcomb Rsch. Inst., Butler U., Indpls., 1983—; scholar in residence St. Joseph Coll., 1983-91; Nat. Scis. fellow Resources for Future, 1983-84; Univ. Disting. scholar N.C. State U., 1991—98. Chmn. bd. Univ. Corp. for Atmospheric Rsch., 1973—76; mem. Conn. Weather Control Bd., 1959—73; mem. panel on sci. and tech. com. on sci. and astronautics U.S. Ho. of Reps., 1960—70; nat. adv. com. cmty. air pollution HEW, 1962—66; mem. sci. info. coun. NSF, 1962—66; rep. Am. Geophys. Union to U.S. Nat. Commn. for UNESCO, 1963—73, chmn. U.S. Nat. Commn., 1965—67; mem. nat. adv. com. on oceans and atmosphere, 1972—75; mem. Conn. Rsch. Commn., 1965—71; mem. com. application sci. and tech. New Eng. Coun.; chmn. Nat. Motor Vehicle Safety Adv. Coun., 1967—70; mem. sci. adv. com. climate impact assessment and response program UN Environ. Program, 1992—; mem. adv. com. on accreditation Conn. Dept. Higher Edn., 2000—02; mem. acad. adv. bd. S.D. Sch. Mines and Tech., 1991—2002; bd. dirs. Conn. Acad. for Edn., 2001—02. Editor: Compendium of Meteorology, 1951; contbg. editor: Environment, 1992-99; bd. editors: Jour. of the Marine Tech. Soc., 1995-99. Bd. dirs. Engrs. Joint Coun., 1968-70; bd. govs. Ins. Inst. Hwy. Safety, 1968-70; mem. oversight rev. bd. Nat. Acid Precipitation Assessment Program, 1990-96; corporator Hartford Sem., 2003—. Recipient Spl. Citation for Patriotic Svc. US War Dept., 1946, Robert M. Losey award Inst. Aero. Sci., 1960, Charter Oak Leadership medal Greater Hartford C. of C., 1962, Charles Franklin Brooks award, 1964, Cleveland Abbe award Am. Meteorol. Soc., 1968, Conn. Conservationist of Yr. award, 1966, Guy E. March Silver medal S.D. Sch. Mines, 1976, Internat. Meteorol. Orgn. prize, 1984, Internat. St. Francis Assissi prize for environment, 1991, AAAS Internat. prize, 1994, Irving award Distance Edn. Consortium, 1997, Disting. Alumni award S.D. Sch. Mines, 1998, Living Legend award St. Joseph Coll., 2006; named to S.D. Hall of Fame, 2003; named KEN Practitioner of Yr., Entuovation Internat., 2003; N.C. State U. disting. scholar, 1990-99, emeritus, 1999- Fellow AAAS (internat. sci. coop., 1994), N.Y. Acad. Scis., Am. Meteorol. Soc. (pres. 1960-62), Am. Geophys. Union (past pres., sec. internat. participation 1964, Waldo E. Smith award 1986); mem. NAS (chmn. geophysics rsch. bd. 1969-76, chmn. bd. on internat. orgns. and programs, dep. fgn. sec. 1969-73, fgn. sec. 1978-82), NRC (space application bd. 1973-77), Am. Acad. Arts and Scis., Internat. Coun. Sci. Unions (v.p., sec.-gen. sci. com. problems environ. 1970-76, treas. 1978-82) Am. Geog. Soc. (coun. 1971-77), Royal Irish Acad. (hon.), Conn. Acad. Sci. and Engring. (exec. scientist 1987-91, 97-2000, Lifetime Disting. Svc. award, 2004, Man of Century award 2007), Acad. Polit. Scis., Sigma Xi (bd. dirs. 1983-96, pres. 1988-89, dir. Sigma Xi Ctr. 1992-95, chief scientist 1996-98). Home: 275 Steele Rd Apt 504B West Hartford CT 06117 Office Phone: 860-920-6357. Personal E-mail: tfmalone@aol.com.

MALONE, THOMAS W., business educator, researcher; b. Roswell, N.Mex., June 2, 1952; s. Ernest P. Jr. and Virginia Malone; m. Joan L. Goldberg, Aug. 28, 1988; children: Robert, Laura. BA in Math. Scis. magna cum laude, Rice U., 1974; MA in Psychology, Stanford U., 1977, MS in Engring.-Econ. Sys., 1979, PhD in Psychology, 1980. Cons. for computer-based instrn. Region IV Edn. Svc. Ctr., Houston, 1974-75; rsch. intern Xerox Corp., Palo Alto Rsch. Ctr., Calif., 1979-80, mem. rsch. staff, 1980-83; from asst. prof. to assoc. prof. MIT, Sloan Sch. Mgmt., Cambridge, Mass., 1983-89, Patrick J. McGovern prof. info. sys., 1989—, Patrick J. McGovern prof. mgmt., 2004—, dir. Ctr. Coord. Sci., 1989—2006, head info. tech. group, 2000—, dir. Ctr. Collective Intelligence, 2006—. Vis. prof. Harvard Bus. Sch., Boston, 1992, IESE Bus. Sch., Barcelona, 2001-02; co-dir. Initiative on Inventing the Orgns. of 21st Century, MIT, Sloan Sch. Mgmt., 1994-99, Douglas Drane Career Devel. assoc. prof. info. tech. and mgmt., 1985; co-founder, cons. Palladian Software, Cambridge, 1984-88, Agility Sys., Waltham, Mass., 1989-91; mem. adv. bd. Perot Sys. Corp., Dallas, 1992-98; co-founder, chmn. Phios Corp., Cambridge, 1996—, CEO, 1998-99; mem. adv. bd. ELance, Inc., Sunnyvale, Calif., 2000—, Oco Corp., Wayland, Mass., 2000—; bd. dir. Seriosity, Inc.; spkr. and presenter in field. Author: The Future of Work, 2004, others; contbr. articles to profl. jours.; patentee in field. Scholar U.S. Presdl. Scholars Commn., 1970; grad. fellow NSF, 1976. Mem. Assn. for Computing Machinery (program chair conf. on computer supported coop. work 1993-94), Phi Beta Kappa. Office: MIT Sloan Sch Mgmt E53-333 Cambridge MA 02142 Office Phone: 617-253-6843. Business E-Mail: malone@mit.edu.

MALONE, THOMAS WILLIAM, lawyer; b. Seattle, Sept. 16, 1946; s. James Edward and Marie Cecilia (Anderson) M.; m. Drexel Cox, June 19, 1978; children: Jason, Cary, Jane Marie. BA, U. Wash., 1968, JD, 1972; MBA, Golden Gate U., 1982. Bar: Wash. 1972, U.S. Ct. Appeals (9th cir.) 1972, U.S. Tax Ct. 1980, U.S. Ct. Claims 1981, U.S. Supreme Ct. 1980. Prin. Treece Richale Malone PS, Seattle, 1973—2000, Malone, Galvin & Spicer PS, Seattle, 2001—05. Pres. Seattle Marine Bus. Coalition, 1983-86; bd. dirs. Ballard Cmty. Hosp., 1982-91, North Seattle C.C. Found., 1989-97, chmn. 1992-93; bd. dirs. Swedish Med. Ctr.-Ballard Found., 1991-95; chmn. bd. dirs. Ballard Cmty. Hosp., 1986-88; bd. dirs. Swedish Med. Ctr., 1992-2006; gov. Swedish Found., 2001-; vice-chmn. Swedish Health Systems, 1995, chair 1996-99; chmn. City of Seattle Fair Campaign Practices Commn., 1986-92; bd. ethics City of Seattle, 1986-92; chmn. City of Seattle Ethics and Elections Com., 1992; trustee Seattle C.C. Dist., 1997—, chmn. 1998-2000. Mem. ABA, Wash. Bar Assn., Seattle-King County Bar Assn., Ballard C. of C. (pres. 1981-84). Office: Malone and Assocs PS 10202 5th NE #201 Seattle WA 98125

MALONE, WILLIAM GRADY, retired lawyer; b. Minden, La., Feb. 19, 1915; s. William Gordon and Minnie Lucie (Hortman) M.; m. Marion Rowe Whitfield, Sept. 26, 1943; children: William Grady, Gordon Whitfield, Marion Elizabeth, Helen Ann, Margaret Catherine. BS, La. State U., 1941; JD, George Washington U., 1952. Bar: Va. 1952, U.S. Supreme Ct. 1971. Statis. analyst Dept. Agr., Baton Rouge, 1941; investigator VA, Washington, 1946-59, legal officer, dep., gen. counsel, asst. gen. counsel, 1959-79; pvt. practice law Arlington, Va., 1979-97. Editor: Fed. Bar News, 1972-73. Pres. Aurora Hills Civic Assn., 1948-49; spl. asst. to treas. Com. of 100, 1979-81, chmn., 1982-83; pres. Children's Theater, 1968-69;

trustee St. George's Episc. Ch., 1979—; chmn. Arlington County Fair Assn., 1979-83. Lt. col. AUS, 1941-46, ETO. Decorated Legion of Merit; recipient Disting. Svc. award, 1979, 3 Superior Performance awards, 1952-72, Outstanding Alumni award George Washington Law Sch., 1978 Mem. Fed. Bar Assn. (pres. D.C. chpt. 1970-71, nat. pres. 1978-79), Va. Bar Assn., Arlington County Bar Assn., Nat. Lawyers Club (dir.), Arlington Host Lions, Ft. Myer Officers Club. Home: Apt 1523 900 N Taylor St Arlington VA 22203 Personal E-mail: wgmalone@juno.com. *Success is not measured by dollars accumulated but by service to others.*

MALONEY, CAROLYN BOSHER, congresswoman; b. Greensboro, NC, Feb. 19, 1948; d. R.G. and Christine (Clegg) Bosher; m. Clifton H.W. Maloney, 1976; children: Christina, Virginia. BA, Greensboro Coll., 1968. Cmty. affairs coord. welfare edn. prog. Bd. Edn., NYC, 1972—75, spl. asst. ctr. career and occupl. edn., 1975—76; legis. aide housing com. NY State Assembly, 1977, sr. prog. analyst cities com., 1977—79; exec. dir. adv. coun. Office of NY State Senate Minority Leader Manfred Ohrenstein, 1979—82, dir. spl. projects, 1980—82; mem. City Coun. from Dist. 8, NYC, 1983-93, US Congress from 14th NY dist., 1993—, chair Ho. Dem. Caucus Task Force on Homeland Security, 2003—, ranking Ho. Dem. mem. joint econ. com., 2005—, mem. fin. svcs. com., chair subcommittee on fin. instns. and consumer credit, mem. oversight and govt. reform com., ranking minority mem. census subcommittee, 1999—. Mem. US del. Fourth World Conf. on Women, Beijing, Internat. Conf. on Population and Devel., The Hague, Netherlands. Active Assn. for a Better NY, Manhattan Women's Polit. Caucus. Decorated Mil. Order of the Purple Heart; recipient Spl. Impact award, Healthy Mothers, Healthy Babies, 2000, Women's Leadership award, UN Family Planning, 2002, Disting. Pub. Svc. award, Nat. Family Planning and Reproductive Health Assn., Ellis Island Medal of Honor, Global Peace award, Peace Action, Queens Women of Distinction award, Queen's Women's Polit. Caucus. Mem.: Hadassah (Myrtle Wreath award), NOW, NAACP. Democrat. Presbyterian. Office: US House Reps 2331 Rayburn House Office Bldg Washington DC 20515-3214 Office Phone: 202-225-7944, 212-860-0606. Office Fax: 202-225-4709, 212-860-0704. *

MALONEY, DON, professional sports team executive, retired professional hockey player; b. Lindsay, Ont., Can., Sept. 5, 1958; m. Toni Maloney; 1 child, Don. Left wing NY Rangers, 1979—89, Hartford Whalers, 1989, NY Islanders, 1989—91, asst. gen. mgr., 1991—92, gen. mgr., v.p. hockey ops., 1992—95; eastern profl. scout San Jose Sharks, 1996—97; asst. gen. mgr. NY Rangers, 1997—2007, v.p. player personnel, 2000—07; gen. mgr. Phoenix Coyotes, 2007—. Asst. gen. mgr. Team Can., World Hockey Championships, Helsinki, Finland, 2003, Czech Republic, 04. Office: Phoenix Coyotes Hockey Club 6751 N White Out Way, #200 Glendale AZ 85305 *

MALONEY, ELLEN CLAIRE, elementary school educator; b. Buffalo, Jan. 12, 1946; d. Eugene Michael and Norma Ann Gooley; m. John Charles Maloney, Aug. 9, 1986; children: Matthew Donovan Lennert, Elizabeth Anne Lennert, Patrick O'Neal Johnson. MEd, U. San Diego, Calif., 1978. Elem. tchr. San Diego Unified Sch. Dist., 1978—. Reader, sodality mem. St. Rita's Cath. Ch., San Diego, 1986—2006; mem. Whispering Winds Aux., San Diego, 2001—06. Named Tchr. of Yr., Encanto Elem., 1995, 1997, Zamorano Elem., 2002, 2004, 2005. Office: San Diego Unified Sch Dist 4100 Normal Ave San Diego CA 92105 Home Phone: 619-262-3904; Office Phone: 619-725-8000.

MALONEY, JAMES HENRY, community development executive, former congressman; b. Quincy, Mass., Sept. 17, 1948; s. James Henry Jr. and Katherine Smith (Murphy) M.; m. Mary Angela Draper, Aug. 16, 1980; children: Adele, Anna, Ellen. BA cum laude, Harvard U., 1972; JD, Boston U., 1980. Vol. VISTA, Gary, Ind., 1969—70; exec. dir. Cmty. Action Com. Danbury, Conn., 1974—78; atty. Pinney, Payne, VanLenten, Burrell, Wolfe & Dillman, P.C., Danbury, 1980—86; ptnr. Dice, Maloney & Lenz, P.C., Danbury, 1986—93, Maloney, Leaphart & Assocs., PC, Danbury, 1995—97; mem. Conn. Senate, Hartford, 1987—95, 105-107th Congresses from 5th Conn. dist., 1997—2003, mem. armed svcs. com., mem. fin. svcs. com.; pres., gen. counsel Conn. Inst. Cmtys., Inc., 2003—; CEO Main St. Devel. Corp., 2003—. Democrat. Roman Catholic. Avocation: sailing. Office Phone: 203-743-9760. E-mail: JamesHMaloney@aol.com.

MALONEY, JOHN JOSEPH, writer; b. NYC, Jan. 15, 1929; s. John J. and Breda T. (O'Leary) M.; m. Helen Martin; children: Peter, Elizabeth, Mary Ellen. BA, Fordham Coll., 1951. City editor Patent Trader, Mt. Kisco, N.Y., 1953-59; news bureau mgr. N.Y. Stock Exchange, NYC, 1959-63; dir. pub. rels. Lehman Bros., NYC, 1963-71, Warnaco, Inc., Bridgeport, Conn., 1971-77; v.p. charge of media rels. Citigroup (formerly Citicorp/Citibank), NYC, 1977-91; writer Easton, Conn., 1991—. Cons. capital formation markets Kenyan govt., 1991, Bulgarian govt., 1999. With U.S. Army, 1951-53. Avocation: sailing. Home: 65 Sport Hill Pkwy Easton CT 06612-2239

MALONEY, KRISTEN, gymnast; b. Hacketstown, NJ, Mar. 10, 1981; d. Richard and Linda. Mem. U.S. Gymnastics Team, 1994—2001, UCLA Gymnastics Team, 2000—. Mem. U.S. World Championships Team, 1997, 99, U.S. Gymnastics Team Sydney Olympics, 2000. Recipient numerous awards, 1st pl. Am. Classic, 1997, 98, 1st pl. (3) Foxsport Challenge, Sydney, 1997, 1st team, 1st balance beam, 1st floor exercise 1st AA, Internat. Team Championships, 1998, 1st team, 1st AA, Pacific Alliance Champaionships, Winnipeg, Can., 1998, 1st balance beam Goodwill Games, 1998, others. Mem. Parketts Club. Avocations: reading, music, movies, shopping. Office: UCLA Women's Gymnastics PO Box 24044 Los Angeles CA 90024

MALONEY, MARYNELL, lawyer; b. Hutchinson, Kans., Jan. 14, 1955; d. Robert Edgar and Marian Ellen (Benson) Baker; m. Michael D. Maloney, Nov. 30, 1977; children: Michelle M., Erica O., Dennis Jr. BA, Oberlin Coll., 1975; MA, Trinity U., San Antonio, 1978; JD, St. Mary's U., San Antonio, 1980. Cert. by Tex. bd. of legal specialization. Assoc. Law Offices Pat Maloney, P.C., San Antonio, 1981-82; ptnr., owner Maloney & Maloney, San Antonio, 1982—. Bd. dirs. San Antonio Internat. Keyboard Competition, 1988-90; bd. govs. St. Peters/St. Joseph's Children's Home, San Antonio, 1989-92. Mem. ACLU of Tex. (bd. dirs. 1990—, v.p. 1995-96, SACLU 1990—), Am. Trial Lawyers Assn., State Bar Tex., Tex. Trial Lawyers Assn. (assoc. bd. dirs. 1989-90, bd. dirs. 1991-2002, dir. emeritus 2002—, cert. personal injury trial law), San Antonio Bar Assn., San Antonio Trial Lawyers Assn. (pres. 1991-92). Democrat. Avocations: reading, writing, films. Office: Maloney & Maloney PC 2000 Milam 115 E Travis San Antonio TX 78205 Office Phone: 210-227-7000. Business E-Mail: marynell@maloneyandmaloney.com.

MALONEY, MAUREEN MURPHY, social sciences educator; b. NYC, Nov. 16, 1941; d. Cyril Bernard Murphy and Monique Louissiane Jacques; m. Paul K. Maloney, Dec. 5, 1964; children: Jennifer, Paula, Edward. Diploma, Holy Name Sch. Nursing, 1962; BS in Psychology, Sacred Heart U., 1982; M in Applied Psychology, Fairfield U., 1986; D Ednl. Leadership summa cum laude, U. Bridgeport, 2003. RN N.J. Head nurse neurosurgery Columbia Presbyn. Med. Ctr., NYC, 1962—65; prof. Housatonic C.C., Bridgeport, Conn., 1993—, chmn. dept. behavioral and social scis., 2006—. Adj. prof. Norwalk C.C., 1987—93. Recipient award for Tchg. Excellence and Disting. Svc., Housatonic Coll., 2004. Mem.: APS, ASCD, APA, AAUP, Am. Psychological Soc. Roman Catholic. Avocations: reading, skiing, tennis, classical music, opera. Office: Housatonic CC 900 Lafayette Ave Bridgeport CT 06608

MALONEY, MICHAEL PATRICK, lawyer, mediator, arbitrator; b. Syracuse, NY, June 1, 1944; s. Randolph Bartholomew and Alice Mary (Loban) M.; m. Jane McBurney, May 21, 1977; children: Christopher, Kara. AB, Georgetown U., 1966; MBA, Cornell U., 1968, JD, 1971. Bar: N.Y. 1972. Assoc. Donovan Leisure Newton and Irvine, NYC, 1971-78; asst. dir. div. market regulation SEC, Washington, 1978-79; sr. v.p., gen. counsel, sec. Orion Capital Corp., NYC, 1979-98; pres. OSOWA Enterprises, LLC, 1998—. Sec., bd. dirs. Carden Sch. Maui; bd. dirs. Interquest Detection Canines of Hawaii. Mem.: Am. Corp. Counsel Counsel Assn., Am. Soc. Corp. Secs. Home: 891 Holopuni Rd Kula HI 96790 E-mail: osowa@aol.com.

MALONEY, MILFORD CHARLES, retired internal medicine educator; b. Buffalo, Mar. 15, 1927; s. John Angelus Maloney and Winifred Hill; m. Dione Ethyl Sheppard. BS, Canisius Coll., 1947, postgrad., 1947-49; MD, U. Buffalo, 1953. Diplomate Am. Bd. Internal Medicine. Rsch. chemist Buffalo Electrochem. Co., 1947-49; intership Mercy Hosp./Georgetown U., 1953-54; med. residency Buffalo VA Hosp., 1954-56; cardiology fellow Buffalo Gen. Hosp., 1956-57; chmn. dept. medicine Mercy Hosp., 1969-94, program dir., internal medicine residency Buffalo, 1972-89; with steering com. Assn. Program Dirs. in Internal Medicine, 1976, coun. mem., 1977-80; clin. prof. medicine SUNY, Buffalo, 1981-94; trustee Am. Soc. Internal Medicine, 1984-90, edn. leader, European seminar, 1987, edn. leader, So. Am. seminar, 1988; faculty instr. Christopher Wren Assn. Coll. William and Mary, Williamsburg, Va., 1997—. Bd. dirs. Internal Medicine Ctr. for Advancement and Rsch. Edn., Ctr. Excellence in Aging and Geriatric Health, Williamsburg, Va., Heart Assn. Western NY, Buffalo, 1969; sr. cancer rsch. physician Roswell Park Meml. Cancer Inst., 1959-62; mem. internal medicine liaison com. NY State, 1980-90; faculty instr., mem. curriculum com. Christopher Wren Assn. Coll. William & Mary, Williamsburg, Va., 1997-99. Editor newsletter N.Y. State Soc. Internal Medicine, 1972-78. Bd. dirs. Health Sys. Agy. Western N.Y., Buffalo, 1981; mem. exec. com., bd. dirs. Blue Cross Western N.Y., Buffalo, 1987; mem. bd. regents Canisius Coll., Buffalo, 1987—; mem. pres. assocs. SUNY, Buffalo; founding mem. Greater Williamsburg Va. Symphony Soc., 1998; bd. dirs. Va. Symphony, Norfolk, 2001; bd. dirs., dir. devel. Williamsburg Ctr. for Excellence in Aging and Geriatric Health, 2004. Capt. M.C., U.S. Army, 1957-59. Recipient award of merit N.Y. State Soc. Internal Medicine, 1980, Man of Yr. award Heart Assn. Western N.Y., 1982, ann. honoree award Trocaire Coll., 1986, Disting. Alumni award Canisius Coll., 1991, Berkson Excellence award in tchg. and art of medicine, SUNY at Buffalo, 1992, Outstanding Med. Tchg. Attending award Mercy Hosp./SUNY Med. Residents, 1994, Lifetime Career Achievement award Med. Alumni Assn. SUNY, Buffalo, 2005, Heritage award Mercy Hosp. Found., Buffalo, N.Y., 2005; named to Sports Hall of Fame, Canisius Coll., 1978. Master ACP (pres. emeritus, Upstate Physician Recognition award 1989); fellow Am. Coll. Cardiology; mem. AMA (SUNY rep. 1986-94, rep. to sect. med. schs. at ann. meetings 1984-94, chmn. sect. on internal medicine 1990-91), Am. Soc. Internal Medicine (bd. dirs. Internal Medicine Ctr. for Advancement of Rsch. Edn. 1988-91, trustee 1984-90, pres. 1990-91, chmn. long range planning com., rep. to Federated Coun. on Internal Medicine 1990-91, rep. nat. practice parameters and guidelines com. 1989-91, Scroll of Honor benefactor for Internal Medicine Ctr. for Advancement of Rsch. and Edn. 1991), Va. State Soc. Internal Medicine (ex officio mem. exec. com., bd. dirs.), N.Y. State Soc. Internal Medicine (pres. 1974-75), Alumni Assn. SUNY (pres. 1975), Med. Soc. County Erie (pres. 1991-82), Va. Soc. Internal Medicine (hon.), Greater Williamsburg Va. Symphony Soc. (founding mem. 1998, editor newsletter 1998-2003). Home: 116 Cove Point Ln Williamsburg VA 23185-8613 E-mail: mcmaloney@widomaker.com.

MALONEY, PATSY LORETTA, nursing educator; b. Murfreesboro, Tenn., Feb. 19, 1952; d. Buford Leon Browning and Ina (Bush) DuBose; m. Richard J. Maloney, July 26, 1975; children: Katherine Nalani, Nathaniel Allen, Elizabeth Maureen. BS in Nursing, U. Md., 1974; MA, Cath. U., DC, 1984, MS in Nursing, 1984; EdD, U. So. Calif., 1994. Commd. 1st lt. U.S. Army, 1974, advanced through grades to lt. col., 1989; asst. chief nurse evenings and nights DeWitt Army Hosp., Ft. Belvoir, Va.; chief nurse, tng. officer 85th EVAC Hosp., Ft. Lee, Va.; clin. head nurse emergency rm./PCU Tripler Army Med. Ctr., Honolulu, chief nursing edn.; chief surg. nursing sect. and acute care nursing sect. Madigan Army Med. Ctr., Tacoma, 1991-94; dir. Ctr. for Continued Nursing Learning Pacific Luth. U., Tacoma, 1994—. Asst. prof., dir. continuing nursing edn. Pacific Luth. U., Tacoma, 1994—2000, assoc. prof., 2000—. Mem. Emergency Nurses Assn., Nat. Nursing Staff Devel. Orgn., Acad. Med. Surg. Nurses, Sigma Theta Tau, Phi Kappa Phi. Home: 7002 53rd St W Tacoma WA 98467-2214 Office: Pacific Luth U Continuing Nursing Edn Tacoma WA 98467 Office Phone: 253-535-7685. Business E-Mail: malonepl@plu.edu.

MALONEY, ROBERT E., JR., lawyer; b. San Francisco, Sept. 17, 1942; s. Robert E. and Mara A. (Murphy) M.; children: Michael, Sarah, Paul. BA magna cum laude, U. Portland, 1964; JD summa cum laude, Willamette U., Salem, Oreg., 1967. Bar: Oreg., Wash., U.S. Dist. Ct. Oreg., U.S. Dist. Ct. (we. dist.) Wash., U.S. Dist. Ct. (ea. dist.) Wash., U.S. Ct. Appeals (9th cir.). Ptnr. Lane Powell PC, Portland, 1967—; chmn., profl. svcs. counsel Bounce Back Oreg., 2003. Mem. bd. visitors Willamette U. Law Sch., 1985-98, chair, 1993-95, mem. exec. com., 1992-97; past chair, mem. exec. com. Portland Trial Dept.; lawyers del. 9th Cir. Jud. Conf., 1995-98; chmn., pres. adv. coun. U. Portland, 2001—; mem. adv. com. Oreg. Ct. Appeals, 2004-. Bd. dirs. Oreg. chpt. Multiple Sclerosis Soc., 1995-02, Children's Cancer Assn., 2002—, Oreg. Ind. Coll. Found., 2004—, chmn., Oreg. Lawyers Against Hunger, 1997-99; judge pro tem Multnomah County Cir. Ct., 1994-98. Mem. ABA (co-chair products liability com., trial practice com. 1988-93), Nat. Assn. R.R. Trial Counsel, Fedn. Ins. Corp. Counsel, Oreg. Assn. Def. Counsel (bd. dirs. 1988-95 sec. 1991-92, v.p. 1993-94, pres. 1994), Fed. Bar Assn. (exec. com. Oreg. divsn. 1988-96, pres. 1994-95), Multnomah Athletic Club. Republican. Roman Catholic. Office: Lane Powell PC 601 SW Second Ave Ste 2100 Portland OR 97204-3158 Office Phone: 503-778-2105. Office Fax: 503-778-2200. Business E-Mail: maloneyr@lanepowell.com.

MALONEY, ROBERT KELLER, ophthalmologist, medical educator; b. May 1, 1958; AB in Mathematics summa cum laude, Harvard U., 1979; MA in Philosophy, Politics and Econs., Oxford U., Eng., 1981; MD, U. Calif., San Francisco, 1985. Diplomate Am. Bd. Ophthalmology. Rsch fellow dept. physiology Cambridge (Eng.) U., 1985; intern U. Calif., LA, 1985-86; resident Wilmer Ophthal. Inst. Johns Hopkins Hosp., Balt., 1986-89; Heed fellow cornea and refractive surgery Emory U., Dept. Ophthalmology, Atlanta, 1989-91; clin. prof. ophthalmology Jules Stein Eye Inst. Sch. Medicine U. Calif., 2005—, assoc. prof. ophthalmology Jules Stein Eye Inst. Sch. Medicine, 1991—2004; dir. Maloney Vision Inst., LA, Calif., 1998—. Bd. dirs. Lasik Inst., Calhoun Vision; cons. in field. Contbr. numerous articles to profl. jours.; presenter and spkr. in field; assoc. editor (N.Am.) Jour. Refractive and Corneal Surgery, 1991-95; internat. editl. bd. European Jour. Implant and Refractive Surgery, 1995; reviewer Am. Jour. Ophthalmology, Ophthalmology, Archives of Ophthalmology, Jour. Cataract and Refractive Surgery, Ophthalmic Surgery and Lasers; editl. bd. Ophthalmology Times. Rhodes scholar, 1979, Heed Found. fellow, 1989-90, Heed/Knapp fellow, 1990-91, John Harvard scholar, 1978; recipient Detur and Edward Whitaker prizes, Harvard U., Rsch. to Prevent Blindness Career Devel. award, 1992, Mericos Whittier award, 1997, VISX Star Surgeon award, 1999, 2000. Mem. Am. Acad. Ophthalmology (long-range planning com. 1989-92, quality of care com. 1987-91, retina preferred practice pattern subcom., refractive errors preferred practice pattern subcom.; chmn. ann. meeting program com. for young ophthalmologists, 1990-92; adv. group to ad hoc com. on orgnl. design 1991, young ophthalmologists' com. 1992-94; Honor award 1993, 97, Sr. Achievement award 2002, Secretariat award 2003), Assn. Rsch. in Vision and Ophthalmology, Internat. Soc. Refractive Surgery (Disting. Lans Refractive Surgery award 2001), Calif. Assn. Ophthalmology, Max Fine Corneal Soc., Phi Beta Kappa. Office: Maloney Vision Inst Ste 900 10921 Wilshire Blvd Los Angeles CA 90024 Office Phone: 310-208-3937. Business E-Mail: info@maloneyvision.com.

MALONEY, SEAN M., computer company executive; Mgr. applications engrng. Intel U.K. Intel Corp., country mgr. Intel U.K., dir. mktg. Intel Europe, gen. mgr. Asia Pacific ops., tech. asst. to chmn. and chief exec., 1992—95, mgr. sales and mktg. activities Asia Pacific, 1995—98, sr. v.p., mgr. sales org., 1999—2001, exec. v.p., dir. sales org., 2001, exec. v.p., gen. mgr. Intel Comm. Group, 2001—04, exec. v.p., co-mgr. mobility group, 2004—06, exec. v.p., chief sales & mktg. officer, 2006—. Bd. dirs. Cadence Design Sys., U.S./China Bus. Coun. Office: 2200 Mission College Blvd Santa Clara CA 95052 *

MALONEY, SEAN PATRICK, state official, lawyer; b. Sherbrooke, Que., Can., July 30, 1966; s. James Francis and Joan Caroline (Daley) Maloney; life ptnr. Randy Florke; 3 adopted children. Student, Georgetown Sch. Fgn. Svc., Washington, 1984-86; BA, U. Va., 1988, JD, 1992. Bar: NY 1993, DC 1994. Assoc. Willkie Farr & Gallagher LLP, NYC, 1992-97, 2003—07; asst. to Pres., staff sec. The White House, Washington, 1997—2000; v.p., gen. counsel Kiodex, Inc., NYC, 2000, COO, 2000—03; 1st dep. sec. to Gov. State of NY, Albany, 2007—. Grantee Next Generation Leadership fellowship, Rockefeller Found., 2002—03. Avocations: soccer, running. Office: Office of Gov State Capitol Albany NY 12224 *

MALONEY, THERESE ADELE, retired insurance company executive; b. Sept. 15, 1929; d. James Henry and F. Adele (Powers) M. BA in Econs., Coll. St. Elizabeth, Convent Station, NJ, 1951; AMP, Harvard U., 1981. CPCU. With Liberty Mut. Ins. Co., Boston, 1951-94, asst. v.p., asst. mgr. nat risks, 1974-77, v.p., asst. mgr. nat. risks, 1977-79, v.p., mgr. nat. risks, 1979-86, sr. v.p. underwriting mktg. and adminstrn., 1986-87, exec. v.p. underwriting, policy decision, 1987-94, also bd. dirs.; pres. and bd. dirs. subs. Liberty Mus. (Bermuda) Ltd., 1981-94, LEXCO Ltd.; cons. Exec. Svc. Corp., 1994—2002. Bd. dirs., dep. chmn. Liberty Mut. (U.K.) Ltd., London; bd. dirs. Liberty Mut. Ins. Co., Liberty Mut. Fire Ins. Co., Liberty Mut. Life Assurance Co., Liberty Fin. Cos.; mem. faculty Inst. Northeastern U., Boston, 1969—74; mem. adv. bd., risk mgmt. studies Ins. Inst. Am., 1977—83; mem. adv. coun. Suffolk U. Sch. Mgmt., 1984—96; mem. adv. coun. to program in internat. bus. rels. Fletcher Sch. Law and Diplomacy, 1985—94; cons. Exec. Svc. Corp., Boston, 1994—2002. Trustee Coll. St. Elizabeth, N.J., 1993-02. Mem. Soc. CPCUs (past pres. Boston chpt.), Univ. Club, Boston Club, Neighborhood Club of Quincy. Personal E-mail: therese.maloney@verizon.net.

MALONEY, WILLIAM JAMES, dentist, educator; b. White Plains, NY, Feb. 16, 1967; BS, Siena Coll., Loudonville, NY, 1989; DDS, NYU, 1992. Faculty NYU Coll. Dentistry, NY, 2000—. Contbr. articles to profl. jours. Mem.: ADA. Office: 12 Ellis Pl Ossining NY 10562 Business E-Mail: maloneydentistry@aol.com.

MALOOF, FARAHE PAUL, lawyer; b. Boston, Feb. 10, 1950; s. Farahe and Emily Suzanna (Puchy) M.; divorced; children: Alexandre F., Melissa F. BS, Georgetown U., 1975, JD, 1978. Bar: D.C. 1978, Va. 1981, Md. 1990. Assoc. Corcoran & Rowe, Washington, 1978-82; ptnr. Berliner & Maloney, Washington, 1982-84; internat. legal counsel Advocacia Oliveira Ribeiro, Sao Paulo, Brazil, 1984-85; sole practice Washington, 1985-86; prin. Maloof & Assocs., Washington, 1986-97; of counsel Haas & Anderson, P.C., McLean, Va., 1997-99; mem. Brincefield Hartnett Maloof & Paleos, P.C., Alexandria, Va., 2000—02; prin. Maloof & Assocs., Alexandria, 2003—04; ptnr. Redmon, Peyton & Braswell, LLP, Alexandria, 2004—. Lectr. Am. U., Washington, 1984-85, Internat. Law Inst., Washington, 1986-87. Active Reagan-Bush campaign, Washington, 1984, Frank Wolf re-election campaign, Arlington, Va., 1986, Bush-Quayle campaign, Washington, 1988. Served to cpl. USMC, 1968-70, Vietnam. Mem. ABA, Va. Bar Assn., D.C. Bar Assn. (litigation and corps. sects.), Fed. Bar Assn. (immigration law sect.), Georgetown U. Alumni Assn. (co-chmn. 1983-84). Republican. Roman Catholic. Avocations: tennis, water-skiing. Home: 1506 Dewberry Ct Mc Lean VA 22101-5629 Office: Redmon Peyton & Braswell LLP Ste 301 510 King St Alexandria VA 22314 Office Phone: 703-684-2000. Business E-Mail: fpmaloof@rpb-law.com.

MALOOF, GAVIN PATRICK, professional sports team executive; b. Oct. 9, 1956; s. George and Colleen Maloof. Student, N.Mex. Mil. Inst., Roswell, N.Mex.; BA in Speech and Comm., Trinity U., San Antonio, 1979. Co-owner NBA Houston Rockets, 1979-82, Women's NBA Sacramento Monarchs, Sacramento Knights, ARCO Arena, NBA Sacramento Kings, 1999—; pres. World League of Am. Football Birmingham Fire, 1990—92; vice chmn. Maloof Cos. Co-recipient Most Involved Execs. award, World Sports Humanitarian Hall of Fame, 2001. Avocation: golf. Office: Sacramento Kings Arco Arena One Sports Pky Sacramento CA 95834 *

MALOOF, GILES WILSON, academic administrator, educator, author; b. San Bernardino, Calif., Jan. 4, 1932; s. Joseph Peters and Georgia (Wilson) M.; m. Mary Anne Ziniker, Sept. 5, 1958 (dec. Oct. 1976); children: Mary Jane, Margery Jo. BA, U. Calif., Berkeley, 1953; MA, U. Oreg., 1958; PhD, Oreg. State U., 1962. Petroleum reservoir engr. Creole Petroleum Corp., Venezuela, 1953—54; mathematician electronics divsn. rsch. dept. U.S. Naval Ordnance Rsch. Lab., Corona, Calif., 1958—59; asst. prof. math. Oreg. State U., Corvallis, 1962—68, rsch. assoc. dept. oceanography, 1963—68, vis. prof. math., 1977—78; prof. math. Boise State U., Idaho, 1968—, head dept., 1968—75, dean grad. sch., 1970—75. Author, reviewer of coll. textbooks; contbr. to profl. jours. Served with Ordnance Corps, AUS, 1950, 54-56. Recipient Carter award, 1963, Mosser prize, 1966, Oreg. State U., Alumni Found. scholar Tchg. award Boise State U., 2000. Mem. Math. Assn. Am., Am. Math. Soc., Soc. Indsl. and Applied Math., N.W. Coll. and Univ. Assn. for Sci. (dir., pres. 1990-92), N.W. Sci. Assn. (trustee 1977-80), Assn. We. Univs. (edn. and rsch. com. 1993-2001), Sigma Xi, Pi Mu Epsilon, Phi Kappa Phi. Home: 1400 Longmont Ave Boise ID 83706-3730 E-mail: giles@diamond.boisestate.edu.

MALOOF, JOSEPH, professional sports team owner; s. George and Colleen Maloof. Co-owner NBA Houston Rockets, 1979-82, NBA Sacramento Kings, 1999—, Women's NBA Sacramento Monarchs, Sacramento Knights, ARCO Arena; ptnr., pres. Maloof Cos. Bd. govs. NBA, 1999—; bd. mem. Coors Distbr. Coun. Co-recipient Most Involved Execs. award, World Sports Humanitarian Hall of Fame, 2001. Avocation: tennis. Office: Sacramento Kings Arco Arena One Sports Pky Sacramento CA 95834 *

MALOOF, SAM, woodworker; b. Chino, Calif., Jan. 24, 1916; m. Alfreda Ward, 1948 (dec. 1998); m. Beverly Wingate, 2001. With VORTOX, 1934—39, Harold Graham Industrial Designer, 1940—41; graphic artist Millard Sheets, 1946—48; design project in Iran and Lebanon US State Dept., 1959, design project in El Salvador, 1963. Former pres. So. Calif. Designer; former trustee Southeast Region Am. Craft Coun., former chmn. Acad. Fellows; former bd. dir. US sect. World Craft Congress. Exhibitions include Calif. Design I-XI, 1954—71, Smithsonian Inst., Washington, 1970, Renwick Gallery, Smithsonian Am. Art Mus., 1971, 1992, 2004, Mus. Contemporary Art, Chgo., 1976, Vatican Mus., Rome, 1978, Vice

President's House, Washington, DC, 1980, J.M. Kohler Arts Ctr., Sheboygan, Wis., 1983, Barnsdell Art Ctr., LA, 1984, Anderson Ranch Arts Ctr., Aspen, Colo., 1984—85, Euphat Gallery, Cupertino, Calif., 1986, Joanne Lyon Gallery, Apsen, 1987, Laguna Beach Mus. Art, 1988, Dallas Mus. Art, 1989, University Art Gallery, Riverside, Calif., 1993, LA County Fair, 1993, Chgo. Internat. New Art Forms Exposition, Navy Pier Joanne Rapp Gallery, 1993, Wustum Mus. Fine Arts, 1993, Connell Gallery, Atlanta, Ga., 1996, Craft and Folk Art Mus., LA, 2003, Ruth Chandler Williamson Gallery at Scripps Coll., 2004, public collections, Minn. Art Mus., 1959, Oakland Art Mus., Calif., 1969, 1984, Fine Art Mus., Boston, 1976, The White House, 1981, St. Louis Art Mus., 1983, Carter Presdl. Library, 1985, Dallas Art Mus., 1986, Met. Mus. Art, NYC, 1988, Phila. Mus. Art, 1981, 1991, Renwick Gallery, 1992, Toledo Mus. Art, Ohio, 1992. Served with US Army, 1941—45. Mailing: c/o Sam and Alfreda Maloof Found for Arts and Crafts 5131 Carnelian St Alta Loma CA 91701

MALOOLEY, DAVID JOSEPH, electronics and computer technology educator; b. Terre Haute, Ind., Aug. 20, 1951; s. Edward Joseph and Vula (Starn) Malooley. BS, Ind. State U., 1975; MS, Ind. U., 1981. Supr. Zenith Radio Corp., Paris, Ill., 1978—79; assoc. prof., electronics and computer tech. Ind. State U., Terre Haute, 1979—; cons. in field. Served to 1st lt. US Army, 1975—78. Mem.: Nat. Fire Protection Assn., Nat. Assn. Indsl. Tech., Soc. Mfg. Engrs., Instrument Soc. Am. (sr.), Epsilon Pi Tau, Pi Lambda Theta, Phi Delta Kappa. Democrat. Home: 11420 Spring Creek Rd Terre Haute IN 47805-9679 Office: Ind State U Dept Electronics and Computer Tech Terre Haute IN 47809-0001 Office Phone: 812-237-3395. Business E-Mail: dmalooley@indstate.edu.

MALOON, JERRY L., lawyer, physician; b. Union City, Ind., June 23, 1938; s. Charles Elias and Bertha Lucille (Creviston) M.; children: Jeffrey Lee, Jerry Lee II. BS, Ohio State U., 1960, MD, 1964; JD, Capital U. Law Sch., 1974. Intern Santa Monica (Calif.) Hosp., 1964-65; tng. psychiatry Ctrl. Ohio Psychiat. Hosp., 1969, Menninger Clinic, Topeka, 1970; clin. dir. Orient (Ohio) Devel. Ctr., 1967-69, med. dir., 1971-83; assoc. med. dir. Western Electric, Inc., Columbus, 1969-71; cons. State Med. Bd. Ohio, 1974-80; pvt. practice law Columbus, 1978—; pres. Jerry L. Maloon Co., L.P.A., 1981—. Medicolegal cons., 1972—; pres. Maloon, Maloon & Barclay Co., L.P.A., 1990-95; guest lectr. law and medicine Orient Devel. Ctr. and Columbus Devel. Ctr., 1969-71; dep. coroner Franklin County (Ohio), 1978-84 Dean's coun. Capital U. Law Sch. Capt. M.C., AUS, 1965-67. Fellow: Columbus Bar Found., Am. Coll. Legal Medicine; mem.: ATLA, AMA, ABA, Am. Profl. Practice Assn., Columbus Trial Lawyers Assn., Ohio Trial Lawyers Assn., Columbus Bar Assn., Ohio Bar Assn., Ohio State U. Alumni Assn., U.S. Trotting Assn., The Country Club at Muirfield Village, Ohio State U. Pres.'s Buckeye Club. Office: 9155 Moors Pl North Dublin OH 43017 Home: 9155 Moors Pl N Dublin OH 43017-8220 Office Phone: 614-798-1616. Personal E-mail: maloonmdjd@columbus.rr.com.

MALORATSKY, LEO G., electrical engineer; b. Zaporoghe, USSR, Apr. 28, 1939; arrived in US, 1989; s. German M. Maloratsky and Slava I. Grinberg; m. Helena A. Vinitsky, Oct. 3, 1968; children: Artem, Anna. MSEE, Moscow Aviation Inst., 1962; PhD, Moscow Int. Telecomm., 1967. Rsch. scientist Electrotech. Inst., Moscow, 1962—79; asst. prof. Moscow Inst. Radio, Electronics and Automation, 1969—88; sr. rsch. scientist Automation Lab., Moscow, 1979—89; vis. scholar Northeastern U., Boston, 1989; sr. engr. M/A-COM, Boston, 1990; v.p. REC, Boston, 1991—92; staff engr. Allied Signal, Ft. Lauderdale, Fla., 1992—97; prin. engr. Rockwell Collins, Melbourne, Fla., 1997—. Author: Microminiaturization of Microwave Components and Devices, 1976, Passive RF and Microwave Integrated Circuits, 2003; co-author: Design and Calculation of Microwave Stripline Elements, 1972, Design of Microwave Devices, 1983, Microwave Devices and Screens, 1990. Mem.: IEEE. Home: 2160 N Hwy A1A Apt 205 Indialantic FL 32903 Office: Rockwell Collins PO Box 1080 Melbourne FL 32902 Personal E-mail: lhmal@earthlink.net.

MALORZO, THOMAS VINCENT, lawyer; b. Rome, NY, Jan. 10, 1947; s. Vincent T. and Helene Adeline Malorzo; m. Catherine Marie Malorzo, Dec. 28, 1968; children: Amy, Craig, Mary, Thomas Jr. BA, Walsh U., Canton, Ohio, 1969; JD, Cleve. State U., 1979. Bar: Ohio 1979, U.S. Dist. Ct. (no. dist.) Ohio 1980, U.S. Patent Office 1980, Tex. 1981, U.S. Dist. Ct. (no. dist.) Tex. 1981, U.S. Ct. Appeals (7th cir.) 1994, U.S. Dist. Ct. (ea. dist.) Tex., 1998, U.S. Dist. Ct. (so. dist.) Tex., 2000. Analytical chemist Glidden-Durkee divsn. SCM Corp., 1969—79; environ. regulations analyst Diamond Shamrock Corp., Dallas, 1979-81; ind. counsel, agt. Southwestern Life Ins. Co., Dallas, 1981-83; staff atty. NCH Corp., Irving, Tex., 1983-89; gen. counsel Wormald US, Inc., Dallas, 1989-90; patent atty. Otis Engring. Corp., Carrollton, Tex., 1990-93; pvt. practice Addison, Tex., 1993-95; ptnr. Falk, Vestal & Fish LLP, 1995; pvt. practice Dallas, 1996-97; of counsel Bennett & Weston P.C., 1997—2002; prin. atty. Malorzo & Tapscott, 2002; sole practitioner Dallas, 2002—04; fee title atty. Blue Star Title, Arlington, Tex., 2004—05, Title Tex., 2005—, Stewart Title, 2005—. Asst. prof. law Dallas/Ft. Worth Sch. Law, Irving, Tex., 1990-92. Dist. com. Circle 10 Boy Scouts Am., Dallas, 1985-2003; first aid team ARC, Cleve., 1972-80. Recipient Dist. Award of Merit, Boy Scouts Am., 1990, Silver Beaver award Boy Scouts Am., 1997. Mem. State Bar Tex. (chmn. trademark com. intellectual property sect. 1989). Office: 1521 N Cooper St Ste 130 Arlington TX 76011 Home Phone: 214-358-1493; Office Phone: 214-597-3247. Personal E-mail: patents@prodigy.net.

MALOTT, JOHN RAYMOND, writer, consultant, not-for-profit executive; b. Kankakee, Ill., Nov. 5, 1946; s. Raymond Roderick and Ruth Pearl (Jacobs) M.; m. Hiroko Iwami, Nov. 23, 1971; children: David Iwami, Rumi Justine. BA, Northwestern U., 1967; grad., Nat. War Coll., 1983. Civilian advisor US Dept. State, Vietnam, 1969-70, China desk officer Washington, 1970-71, Am. consul Kobe, Japan, 1971-73, 1st sec. Am. Embassy Tokyo, 1974-77, Sri Lanka desk officer Washington, 1977-78, India desk officer, 1978-80; Am. consul Bombay, 1980-82; with Nat. War Coll. Washington, 1982-83; dep. dir. Japan Affairs, 1983-85; spl. asst. to Under Sec. State Econ. Affairs, 1985-86; Am. consul gen. Osaka, Japan, 1986-89; dir. Japan Affairs Washington, 1989-91; sr. seminar, 1991-92; dep. asst. sec. state South Asian Affairs, 1992-93; sr. advisor to Undersec. State for Econ. Affairs, Washington, 1993-95; U.S. amb. to Malaysia Dept. State, 1995-98; exec. chmn. Malott & Assocs., 1999—; pres. World Affairs/Coun. of Orange County, 2000—02; mng. dir. Manatt Jones Global Strategies, 2003—06; sr. advisor Manatt, Phelps & Phillips, LLP, 2003—06; pres., CEO Japan-Am. Soc. Wash., DC, 2006—. Author: Partners, 1992. Recipient Vietnam Svc. award, 1970, Meritorious Honor award Dept. State, 1982, Superior honor award, 1991. Presbyterian. Home: 5911 Reservoir Heights Ave Alexandria VA 22311-1017 Office Phone: 202-833-2210. Business E-Mail: jmalott@us-japan.org.

MALOUF, MARK E., structural engineer, consultant; s. John R. and Renée Malouf; m. Kimberley K. Skinner, May 10, 1984; children: Isabelle, John-Mark. BSCE, U. Okla., 1982, MSCE, 1984. Registered profl. engr. Project engr., mgr. Alpha Tower Design, Richardson, Tex., 1984—91, v.p. engring., 1991—92; pres. Malouf Engring. Internat., Dallas, 1992—. Exec. com. Electronics Industry Assn., Washington, 1988—, Telecom. Industry Assn., Washington, 1988; spkr. in field. Telecom com. City of Plano, Tex., 1997; treas. Tau Beta, Okla., 1982. Mem.: ASCE, Internat. Assn. Spatial Structures, Am. Coun. Cons. Engrs. Avocations: tennis, horseback riding, hiking. Office: Malouf Engring Internat Inc 17950 Preston Rd Ste 720 Dallas TX 75252

MALOUF, STEPHEN FERRIS, lawyer; b. Dallas, Nov. 14, 1953; s. Edward Junior and Marie (Moossy) M. BA, U. Dallas, 1977; JD, St. Mary's U., San Antonio, 1982. Bar: Tex., US Dist. Ct. (no., so. & we. dists. Tex.), US Ct. Appeals (5th cir.). Atty. Tex. Ct. Appeals, Dallas, 1982; assoc. Windle, Turley Law Office, Dallas, 1983-84, 1985-87, Boyd Waggoner Law Office, Dallas, 1984-85; with Milgrim, Thomajan & Lee, Dallas, 1988—90; pvt. practice Dallas, 1990—. Mem. ABA, Assn. Trial Lawyers Am., Dallas Trial Lawyers Assn., Tex. Bar Assn. Roman Catholic. Avocations: painting, music. Office: Law Offices of Stephen F Malouf Ste 1600 3811 Turtle Creek Blvd Dallas TX 75219 Office Phone: 214-969-7373. Office Fax: 214-969-7648. E-mail: smalouf@smalouf.com.

MALOUFF, FRANK JOSEPH, health care association executive; s. Phillip Francis and Lillian Aileen Malouff; m. Virginia Lynn Frye, Aug. 24, 1968; children: Lynnea, Joseph, J. Daniel, David. BS in Journalism, U. Colo., Boulder, 1969; MS in Health Adminstrn., U. Colo., Denver, 1974; LLD (hon.), Ohio Coll. Podiatric Medicine, 1988. Program adminstr. U. Colo. Health Scis. Ctr., Denver, 1974-83; exec. dir. Ohio Podiatric Med. Assn., Columbus, 1983-89, Am. Podiatric Med. Assn., Bethesda, Md., 1989-98, Am. Soc. Therapeutic Radiology and Oncology, Fairfax, Va., 1998—2002; prin. and CEO JVF Mgmt., Chantilly, Va., 2002—; exec. dir. Neurology Ctr. of Fairfax, 2004—. Bd. dirs. Neurologic Disease Found., Fairfax, Va.; lectr. in field Leader Boy Scouts Am., various locations; mem. Fairfax County Med. Res. Corps. 1st lt. US Army, 1969—72, Korea. Mem. Am. Soc. Healthcare Edn. and Tng. (officer 1977-81, Disting. Svc. award 1982, past dir.), Am. Soc. Assn. Execs., Area 26 Coun., Spl. Olympics Va. Roman Catholic. Avocation: lay church ministry. Office: JVF Mgmt PO Box 2234 Centreville VA 20122

MALOUIN, JEAN-LOUIS, adult education educator; b. Three-Rivers, Que., Can., Oct. 5, 1943; m. Hélène Pépin; children: Pascale, Philippe. B in Commerce, Université Laval, Que., 1965, MSc, 1966; PhD, UCLA, 1970. Prof. Bus. Sch., U. Laval, 1966-89, dir. OSD dept., 1971-75, 78-79, assoc. dean acad. affairs, 1979-84, dean, 1984-89; dean faculty of bus. U. Alta., Edmonton, Alta., Canada, 1989-92; dean faculty of adminstrn. U. Ottawa, Ottawa, Ont., Canada, 1992-2000. Coord. Can. Consortium for the Support of the Sea PhD program; bd. dirs. Corel Corp., 1997—2003, Acerra Corp. Editor: The Generation of Scientific Administrative Knowledge, 1986; co-author: L'Innovation Technologique dans les PME Manufacturières: études de cas enquête, 1992. Bd. dirs. Centre québécois de Productivité, du Vêtement, Montréal, 1983-86, Nat. Rsch. Ctr., London, 1986-87, Banff Sch. Advancement Mgmt., 1989-92. Mem. Can. Fedn. Deans (v.p. 1987), Edmonton C. of C. (bd. dirs. 1989-92). Home: 1410 Clay Ct Gloucester ON Canada K1C 4T2 Business E-Mail: malouin@uottawa.ca.

MALOVANY, HOWARD, lawyer; b. Dayton, Ohio, July 6, 1950; m. Cynthia Jane Shilt, Sept. 18, 1976. BA, Ohio State U., 1972; JD, U. Toledo, 1977; MBA, U. Dayton, 1985. Bar: Ohio 1977, Ill. 1997. Staff atty., asst. sec. Nat. Cash Register Corp., Dayton, 1977-85; counsel Outboard Marine Corp., Waukegan, Ill., 1985-89, asst. sec., counsel, 1989—93, sec., sr. counsel, 1993—96; asst. sec., sr. counsel William Wrigley Jr. Co., Waukegan, 1996-98, sec., gen. counsel Chgo., 1998-2001, v.p., sec., gen. counsel, 2001—. Mem.: ABA, Am. Soc. Corp. Secretaries (mem. corp. practice & technology com. 1995—97), Toledo Internat. Law Soc. (founder), Ohio State Bar Assn., Ill. State Bar Assn. Office: William Wrigley Jr Co 410 N Michigan Ave Chicago IL 60611-4213 Office Phone: 312-645-4223. Business E-Mail: hmalovany@wrigley.com. *

MALOZZI, JASON ANTHONY, mathematics professor; b. Bethlehem, Pa., Jan. 16, 1977; s. Carol Malozzi. MSc in Math., Lehigh U., Bethlehem, 2001. Instr. to asst. prof. math. Lehigh Carbon C.C., Schnecksville, Pa., 2002—. Mem.: Pa. State Assn. Two-Yr. Coll. (assoc.; sec. 2005—07). Office: Lehigh Carbon Cmty Coll 4525 Education Park Dr Schnecksville PA 18078 Home Phone: 610-769-4670; Office Phone: 610-799-1597. Office Fax: 610-799-1527. Business E-Mail: jmalozzi@lccc.edu.

MALPHURS, ROGER EDWARD, biomedical marketing executive; b. Lake Worth, Fla., Dec. 15, 1933; s. Cecil Edward and Muriel Thelma (Ward) M.; m. Carolyn Sue Calapp, Feb. 2, 1963(div. 1993); children: Steven, Brian, Darren, Regina, Victoria. BS, U. Utah, 1961; D of Chiropractic, Palmer Coll. Chiropractic West, 1990. Cert. med. technologist; lic. chiropractor, Calif., Ariz. Supr. spl. chemistry Cen. Pathology Lab., Santa Rosa, Calif., 1968-73; mgr. lab. Cmty. Hosp., Santa Rosa, 1973-76; supr. chem., staff asst. Meml. Hosp., Santa Rosa, 1976-85; pres., CEO R.E. Malphurs Co., Sunnyvale, Calif., 1972—95; tech. writer Maximus, Inc., Rancho Cordova, Calif., 2004—07. Owner, developer REMCO Mktg. Assocs., Santa Rosa, 1970—71; pvt. commodity trader, 1974—; owner Better Bus. Forms and Typeset, Santa Rosa, Calif., 1977—81; commodity pool operator, 1979—81; dept. mgr. immunochemistry Spectra Labs, Fremont, Calif., 1990—95; clin. trials cons. hematology, tech. writer Abbott Diagnostics, Santa Clara, Calif., 1995—2000; tech. writer Healtheon/WebMD, Santa Clara, Calif., 2000—01; tech. writer, project mgr. Hewlett-Packard, Roseville, Calif., 2000—04. Author: A New, Simple Way to Win at Blackjack, 1972. Served as squadron commdr. CAP USAF Aux., 1982-84. Mem. APHA, Am. Chiropractic Assn., Calif. Chiropractic Assn., Optimists Internat. (youth awards chmn. 1969-74), Toastmasters (sec./treas. 1988-89), Rep. Senatorial Inner Circle. Republican. Avocations: flying, computers, pistol shooting, painting, writing.

MALT, RONALD BRADFORD, lawyer; b. Boston, Aug. 1, 1954; s. Ronald A. and Geraldine (Sutton) M.; m. Sharon Lynn Harford, Feb. 14, 1981; 2 children. AB, Harvard U., 1976, JD, 1979. Bar: Mass. 1979. Assoc. Ropes & Gray, Boston, 1979-86, ptnr., 1987—, policy com., 1993—, chmn., 2004—; dir. Fenway Ptnrs., Inc., NYC, 1999—. Asst. treas. Butler Capital Corp., N.Y.C., 1983—; sec. to adv. bd. Mezzanine Lending Assocs., N.Y.C., 1983—. Mem. corp. Mass. Gen. Hosp., Boston, 1989—; trustee Butler Found., 1989—, Butler Fund for the Environment, 2004-, Black River Environ. Improvement Assn., Inc., 1991—. Republican. Episcopalian. Office: Ropes & Gray One International Pl Boston MA 02110 Office Phone: 617-951-7318. Office Fax: 617-951-7050. Business E-Mail: bmalt@ropesgray.com.

MALTAS, CARLA JO, music educator, education educator; d. Carl I. and Corinne L. Maltas. B Music Edn., U. Nebr., Lincoln, 1984, MusM, 1991; PhD in Music Edn., U. Okla., Norman, 2004. Nat. Kodaly cert., Master Orff Schulwerk. K-12 vocal music tchr. Humboldt Pub. Sch., Nebr., 1984—87; K-5 gen. music tchr. Columbus Pub. Sch., Nebr., 1987—2000; grad. asst. music U. Okla., 2000—03; asst. prof. music edn. Ball State U., Muncie, Ind., 2003—06, U. Ctrl. Mo., Warrensburg, 2006—. Lectr. in field; judge music competitions. Author: (children's opera) 3 Little Pigs From School, 2005 (Bennie award, 05), The Lonely Empress, 2006. Mus. dir. various cmty. theaters, 1988—2006; keyboard player Columbus Jazz Orch., 1988—2000; pres. Friends of Music, Columbus, 1991—96, Columbus Edn. Assn., 1993—96, Columbus Area Arts Coun., 1995—2000. Named New Leader of Future, Nebr. State Edn. Assn., 1992, Outstanding Elem. Educator, Columbus Edn. Assn., 1999. Mem.: Am. Orff Schulwerk, Coll. Music Soc., Nat. Assn. Music Educators. Avocations: music, theater, writing, travel.

MALTBY, FLORENCE HELEN, library science educator; b. Sumner, Iowa, Mar. 2, 1933; d. Harold George and Blanche Theresa (Gritzner) Garland; m. George Robert Maltby, June 3, 1964 (dec. Oct. 1985); 1 child, Patricia Garland Maltby Clark. BA, U. No. Iowa, Cedar Falls, 1954; MS in Libr. Sci., U. Ill., 1960, cert. advanced study librarianship, 1967. Cert. literary braille transcriber. Elem. sch. libr. Barrington (Ill.) Pub. Sch., 1954-57, USAF Dependent Sch. Europe, Sculthorpe, Eng., 1957-58, Ramstein, Fed. Republic of Germany, 1958-59, Wiesbaden, Fed. Republic of Germany, 1960-61; grad. asst. U. Ill., Champaign, 1959-60; reference asst., instr. Libr. Cen. Mich. U., Mt. Pleasant, 1961-63; asst. prof. libr. sci. Southwest Mo. State U., Springfield, 1963-66, 67-80, assoc. prof. libr. sci., 1980-97; instr. libr. sci. U. Ill., Champaign, 1966-67; archivist Diocese of Springfield-Cape Girardeau, 2001—04, 2006—. Evaluator North Cen. Assn., Springfield, 1989, Dept. Elem. and Secondary Edn., Mo. Sch. Improvement, 1989; com. mem. Children's Lit. Festival, Springfield, 1990, treas., 1991. Contbr. to Masterplots II: Juvenile and Young Adult Fiction, 1991, 97. Mem. AAUP, ALA, Assn. Libr. and Info. Sci. Edn., Mo. Assn. Sch. Librs. (mem. standards rev. com. for state sch. libr. media standards 1994), Assn. Cath. Diocesan Archivists, Beta Phi Mu, Alpha Beta Alpha, Kappa Delta Pi. Roman Catholic. Avocations: reading, piano, organ.

MALTER, JAMES SAMUEL, pathologist, educator; b. Tooele, Utah, May 18, 1956; s. Robert Henry Malter and Evvajean (Harris) Mintz; m. Elaine Gadzicki, May 26, 1988. AB, Dartmouth Coll., 1979; MD, Washington U., 1983. Diplomate Am. Bd. Clin. Pathology. Resident in pathology U. Pa., Phila., 1983-88, chief resident, 1987-88; asst. prof. pathology Tulane U., New Orleans, 1988-91; dir. exptl. pathology Tulane Med. Ctr., New Orleans, 1988-91, dir. Blood Ctr., 1989-91; asst. prof. pathology Sch. Medicine U. Wis., Madison, 1991-97; med. dir. Blood Bank U. Wis. Hosp. & Clinic, Madison, 1991—; prof. pathology Sch. Medicine U. Wis., Madison, 1997—. Mem. editl. bd. Hepatology jour., 1991—. Recipient Nat. Rsch. Svc. award NIH, 1986-88, Clin. Investigator award NCI-NIH, 1988-91, Ind. Investigator award NIH, 1991—. Mem. Am. Assn. Blood Banks, Am. Assn. Pathologists, Am. Coll. Pathologists (diplomate). Office: U Wis Hosp & Clinic Dept of Pathology 600 Highland Ave # B4 263 Madison WI 53792-0001

MALTER-HOFFMAN, KELLY A., finance company executive, consultant; b. Fair Lawn, NJ, June 4, 1978; d. Frank and Ruth Malter; m. Richard E. Hoffman, June 14, 2003; 1 child, Isabella Caroline Hoffman. BS in Fin., U. NC, Wilmington, 2000. Cert. Series 7, 66 NASD. Regional cons. Banc of Am. Capital Mgmt., Charlotte, NC, 2001—05; internat. bus. devel. HFL, Newmarket, England, 2005—. Internat. bus. cons. Hoffman & Assocs., Lake Wylie, SC, 2006—. Family readiness group USAR, Rock Hill, SC, 2000; founder Informed-Choice, NYC, 2006. Avocations: travel, tennis. Home Phone: 704-905-1413. Business E-Mail: kelly@hoffmanltd.com.

MALTIN, LEONARD, commentator, writer; b. NYC, Dec. 18, 1950; s. Aaron Isaac and Jacqueline (Gould) M.; m. Alice Tlusty, Mar. 15, 1975; 1 child, Jessica Bennett. BA, NYU, 1972. Mem. faculty New Sch. for Social Rsch., NYC, 1973-81; curator Am. Acad. Humor, NYC, 1975-76; guest curator dept. film Mus. Modern Art, NYC, 1976; film critic and corr. Entertainment Tonight, Hollywood, Calif., 1982—; columnist Modern Maturity, 1996-99; film critic Playboy Mag., 1998—2004. Adj. prof. Sch. Cinema & TV, U. So. Calif., 1998—. Author: Movie Comedy Teams, 1970, rev. edit., 1985, Behind the Camera (reprinted as The Art of the Cinematographer), 1971, The Great Movie Shorts (reprinted as Selected Short Subjects), 1971, The Disney Films, 1973, rev. edit., 2000, The Great Movie Comedians, 1978, Of Mice and Magic: A History of American Animated Cartoons, 1980, rev. edit., 1987, The Great American Broadcast, 1997; co-author: Our Gang: The Life and Times of the Little Rascals, 1977, reprinted as The Little Rascals: The Life and Times of Our Gang, 1992; editor: Leonard Maltin's Movie & Video Guide, 1969, rev. annually, Leonard Maltin's Movie Encyclopedia, 1994, Leonard Maltin's Family Film Guide, 1999; producer, writer, host (video) Cartoons for Big Kids, 1989; writer (TV spl.) Fantasia: The Making of a Disney Classic, 1990; writer, host (video) The Making of The Quiet Man, 1992, The Making of High Noon, 1992, Cartoon Madness: The Fantastic Max Fleischer Cartoons, 1993, Cliffhanger!, 1993; co-host Hot Ticket, 2001-04; co-prodr., host (film series) Walt Disney Treasures, 2001—. Recipient Distinction award, Am. Soc. Cinematographers, 2005. Mem. Authors Guild, Soc. for Cinephiles (pres. 1990-91, Man of Yr. 1973), L.A. Film Critics Assn. (pres. 1995-96). Office: c/o Entertainment Tonight Paramount TV 5555 Melrose Ave Los Angeles CA 90038-3112

MALTZ, ROBERT, surgeon; b. Cin., July 21, 1935; s. William and Sarah (Goldberg) M.; m. Sylvia Moskowitz, Aug. 24, 1958; children: Mark Edward, Deborah Lynn, Steven Alan, David Stuart. BS in Zoology, U. Cin., 1958, MD, 1962. Diplomate Am. Bd. Otolaryngology. Intern Cin. Gen. Hosp., 1962-63; resident Barnes Hosp., St. Louis, 1965-69; asst. prof. surgery Stanford U. Med. Ctr., Palo Alto, Calif., 1969-71; asst. prof. otolaryngology U. Cin. Med. Ctr., 1971-75, assoc. prof. otolaryngology, 1975—; dir. dept. otolaryngology Jewish Hosp., Cin., 1992—. Chief divsn. head and neck surgery, dept. otolaryngology and maxillofacial surgery U. Cin. Med. Ctr., 1972-76; bd. dirs. Cancer Control Coun., U. Cin. Med. Cntr.; cons. Bur. Crippled Children's Svcs., State of Ohio; on staff Univ. Hosp., Cin., Jewish Hosp., Cin., Children's Hosp. Med. Ctr., Bethesda Hosp., Cin.; del. to numerous profl. confs.; mem. health affairs adv. com. Cmty. Mut. Ins. Co.; mem. mng. bd. PIE Mut. Ins. Co.; bd. dirs. UCATS, 1995-98; trustee Health Found. Greater Cin., 1997-2006, vice-chmn., 2000-01, chmn. 2001-03, chmn. program com., 2000-01; instr. short term courses in field; pres.-elect alumni exec. coun. U. Cin. Coll. Medicine, 1998-2000, pres., 2000-02. Contbr. articles to profl. jours. Bd. dirs. Jewish Cmty. Rels. Coun.; bd. trustees Cin. Art Acad., 1998—; faculty adv. com. U. Cin.; trustee Health Found. Fund, 2002-, vice-chmn., 2002-03, chmn., 2003—05. Capt. USAF, 1963-65, PTO. USPHS fellow, 1968-69; Eli Lilly Co. grantee, 1971-76, Burroughs Wellcome Co., 1972. Fellow ACS, Am. Acad. Facial and Reconstructive Surgery (edn. com. 1972, future plans com. 1973-75, sci. program com., budget and fin. com. 1975, chmn. credentials com., no. sect. 1980-85), Royal Soc. Health, Internat. Cosmetic Surgeons, Am. Acad. Cosmetic Surgeons, Am. Assn. Cosmetic Surgeons (sec.-treas. 1976-81); mem. Am. Acad. Otolaryngology and Head and Neck Surgery, Am. Coun. Otolaryngology, Soc. Univ. Otolaryngologists, Pan-Am. Assn. Oto-Rhino-Laryngology and Broncho-Esophagology, Ohio State Med. Assn., Cin. Acad. Medicine (trustee 1992-95, treas. 1993-95, pres. 1996-97, chmn. pub. rels. com. 1980, chmn. comm. com. 1994-96, chmn. sply. soc. com. 1995, legis. com. 1985, editl. bd. 1994-96, jud. com. 1995—2004, chmn. managed care med. dirs. com. 1997-2002), U. Cin. Alumni Assn. (bd. govs., sec. 1994, fin. v.p. 1995, 1st v.p. 1996, pres. 1997-98), Acad. Medicine Found. (bd. dirs., v.p., pres. 2002—2004), Cin. Ear, Nose and Throat Soc., Losantiville Country Club (bd. govs. 1996-2002, pres. 1999-2001), Omicron Delta Kappa, Sigma Sigma, Sigma Alpha Mu. Avocations: tennis, golf, travel. Home: 2601 Willowbrook Dr Cincinnati OH 45237-3725 Office: 11135 Montgomery Rd Cincinnati OH 45249 Personal E-mail: maltz@cinci.rr.com.

MALTZAN, MICHAEL THOMAS, architect; b. Roslyn Heights, NY, Oct. 10, 1959; s. William George and Jacqueline (Cain) M.; m. Amy Louise Murphy, Sept. 25, 1988. Student, Wentworth Inst. Tech., 1977-79; BFA, RISD, 1984, BArch, 1985; MArch with letter of distinction, Harvard U., 1988. Lic. arch., Calif. Architect The Architects, Glastonbury, Conn., 1978-80, Williamd D. Warner Assocs., Exeter, RI, 1980-83, Steven Lerner Assocs., Providence, 1983-84, Schwartz/Silver Assocs., Boston, 1984-86, Machado-Silvetti Assocs., Boston, 1986-88, Frank O. Gehry Assocs., LA, 1988-95; pvt. practice architecture LA, 1995—. Prof. RISD, Providence, 1987, Harvard U., Cambridge, Mass., 1988; co-instr. UCLA, 1989, U. Waterloo, 1993, RISD, 1995, Harvard U., 1999, USC, 2002; vis. prof. GSD, 2003; invited jury critic Harvard U., RISD, Ariz. State U., Tempe, Calif. Coll. Arts and Crafts, San Francisco, U. So. Calif., L.A., UCLA, Iowa State U., Ames, Miami (Ohio) U. Prin. works include Inner-City Arts, LA, 1994 (PA award), Getty Digital Lab., 1997, Feldman-Horn Ctr. Arts, 1997 (AIA award), Hergott-Shepard Residence, 1998 (AIA awards), Kidspace Mus., Pasadena, Calif., 1998 (PA award), UCLA Hammer Mus.,

1999, MOMA ONS, 2002 (AIA awards), World Trade Ctr. Team, 2002, Fresno (Calif.) Met. Mus., 2002 (AIA award), Giardini Di Porta Nuova, Milan, Italy, 2004, Vancouver (Can.) Art Gallery, 2004. Recipient Collegiate Gold medal AIA, Young Archs. award. Fellow: AIA. Office: Michael Maltzan Architecture 2801 Hyperion Ave Studio 107 Los Angeles CA 90027-2571 Office Phone: 323-913-3098. Office Fax: 323-913-5932.

MALTZMAN, IRVING MYRON, psychology professor; b. Bklyn., May 9, 1924; s. Israel and Lillian (Mass) M.; m. Diane Seiden, Aug. 21, 1949; children— Sara, Kenneth, Ilaine. BA, NYU, 1946; PhD, State U. Iowa, 1949. Mem. faculty UCLA, 1949—, assoc. prof., 1957—60, prof. psychology, 1961—94, chmn. dept., 1970—77, prof. emeritus, 1994—. Co-author: Handbook of Contemporary Soviet Psychology, 1969, Alcoholism: A Review of it Characteristics, Etiology, Treatments, and Controversies, 2000. Fellow: APA, AAAS; mem.: Psychonomic Soc., APS, Phi Beta Kappa, Sigma Xi. Home: 11260-22B Overland Ave Culver City CA 90230-5559 Office Phone: 310-825-2909.

MALUCHNIK, ROSEMARY PELLICORE, elementary school educator; b. Chgo., Ill., Oct. 25, 1947; d. Henry Joseph Pellicore and Genevieve Gorski; m. Jerome Anthony Maluchnik, June 22, 1980; 1 child, Joshua Anthony. BS in Edn., Northern Ill., 1969; MS in Edn., 1971. Tchr. Elgin Pub. Schools, 1969—84, 1995—. Mentor to new tchrs., 2001, 02, 03, 04, 05, 06; contbr. to kindergarten curriculum, 1995—96. Mem.: NEA, Elgin Tchr. Assn., Internat. Reading Assn., Ill. Edn. Assn. Home: 221 W Beech Dr Schaumburg IL 60193

MALUGEN, J.T. (JOE THOMAS), retail executive; BS, Univ. Mo., Columbia; JD, Samford Univ.; LLM in taxation, NYU. Atty., Ala., 1978—92, Mo., 1978—92; co-founder, chmn., CEO Movie Gallery Inc., Dothan, Ala., 1985—, pres., 2002—. Bd. dir. Helen Keller Found.; mem. dean's adv. bd. Cumberland Sch. Law Samford Univ.; mem. dean's strategy council NYU Sch. Law. Office: Movie Gallery Inc 900 W Main St Dothan AL 36301 *

MALVEAUX, FLOYD JOSEPH, dean; BS, Creighton U., 1961; MS, Loyola U.; PhD in Microbiology and Pub. Health, Mich. State U., 1968; MD, Howard U., 1974; postgrad., Washington Hosp. Ctr., 1974—76, Johns Hopkins U., 1976—78. Asst. prof. microbiology Howard U. Med. Sch., Washington, 1968—70, chmn. microbiology, assoc. prof. microbiology and medicine, 1989—94, dean, v.p. health affairs, prof. microbiology and medicine, 1995—; mem. faculty Johns Hopkins U., Balt., 1984—89. Founder, pres. Urban Asthma and Allergy Ctr., Balt., 1986—89; mem. numerous med. panels; lectr. in field. Contbr. articles to profl. jours. Recipient Nat. Rsch. Svc. award, NIH, Clemens von Pirquet Rsch. award, Georgetown U. Sch. Medicine, 1991; grantee, Nat. Inst. Allergy and Infectious Diseases, Nat. Heart, Lung and Blood Inst. of NIH, Hasbro Children's Found., Robert Wood Johnson Found.; Vivian B. Allen Found. fellow. Mem.: NAACP (life), Inst. Medicine, Kappa Alpha Psi, Sigma Pi Phi, Sigma Xi, Alpha Omega Alpha. Office: Howard U Med Sch 520 W St NW Washington DC 20059-0001

MALVEAUX, JULIANNE MARIE, academic administrator, economist, writer; b. San Francisco, Sept. 22, 1953; d. Paul and Proteone Marie (Alexandria) M. BA, Boston Coll., 1974, MA, 1975; PhD, MIT, 1980. Jr. staff economist Coun. Econ. Advisors, The White House, Washington, 1977-78; rsch. fellow Rockefeller Found., NYC, 1978-80; asst. prof. New Sch. Social Rsch., NYC, 1980-81, San Francisco State U., 1981-85; assoc. prof. U. Calif., Berkeley, 1989-91; syndicated columnist King Features Syndicate, 1990—2002; CEO Last Word Productions, Inc., 1996—2007; pres. Bennett Coll., Greensboro, NC, 2007—. Vis. scholar U. Calif., Berkeley, 1985-89, Stanford U., 1987-89; spkr. in field. Co-editor: Slipping Through the Cracks: The Status of Black Women, 1986, The Paradox of Loyalty: An African American Response to the War on Terrorism, 2002; author: Sex, Lies, and Stereotypes: Perspectives of a Mad Economist, 1994, Wall Street, Main Street, and the Side Street: A Mad Economist Takes a Stroll, 1999; editor: Voices of Vision: African American Women on the Issues, 1996; co-author: Unfinished Business: A Democrat and A Republican Take On the 10 Most Important Issues Women Face, 2002; contbr. articles to profl. jours. Founder, chmn. San Francisco Anti-Apartheid Com., 1985-86; bd. dirs. Coleman Advs. for Children and Youth, San Francisco, 1985-88, Dem. Women's Forum, San Francisco, 1986-88, San Francisco chpt. NAACP, 1984, Washington chpt. Nat. Rainbow Coalition, 1986-88; pres. San Francisco Bus. and Profl. Women's Club, 1987-89, San Francisco Leadership Forum, 1989-90; nat. v.p. Nat. Assn. Negro Bus. and Profl. Women's Clubs, Washington. Named one of Am.'s Top 100 Black Bus. and Profl. Women, Dollar and Sense Mag., 1985, one of 5 Black Women Who Make it Happen, Nat. Council Negro Women and Frito-Lay, 1987; postdoctoral fellow NRC, 1985-86. Roman Catholic. Office: Bennett Coll Office of Pres 900 E Washington St Greensboro NC 27401 also: Last Word Productions Inc 1318 Corcoran St NW Washington DC 20009 Office Phone: 202-462-1932, 336-517-2225.

MALY, KURT JOHN, computer science educator; b. Modling, Austria, Aug. 20, 1944; came to U.S., 1969; s. Anton and Editha (Gneist) M.; m. Christiana Peterlik, Mar. 18, 1972; 1 child, Angela Claudia. Diplom Ingenieur summa cum laude, U. Tech., Austria, 1968; MS, Courant Inst. NYU, 1970, PhD, 1973. Asst. prof. U. Minn., Mpls., 1972-78, assoc. prof., 1978-85, acting head, 1980-82, head, 1982-85; eminent prof., chmn. computer sci. Old Dominion U., Norfolk, Va., 1985—, Kaufman prof., 1991—. Hon. prof. Chengdu U. of Sci. and Tech., People's Republic of China, 1986—, Hefei U., People's Republic of China, 1991—, Guangxi Computer Inst., People's Republic of China, 1993—; bd. dirs. Inst. of Info. Tech., Ctr. for Innovative Tech., Blacksburg, Va., 1988-92; bd. dirs., exec. co-dir. Microelectronic and Info. Scis. Ctr., Mpls., 1980-85. Author: Fundamentals of the Computing Sciences, 1978; assoc. editor: Jour. for Microcomputer Application Tech., PRC; contbr. articles to profl. jours. Served with Austrian Air Force, 1963-64. Fellow Sorbonne U., Paris, 1966, Courant Inst., N.Y.C., 1968-72. Mem. Assn. Computing Machinery, IEEE, Sigma Xi. Roman Catholic. Office: Old Dominion U Norfolk VA 23529 Home Phone: 757-481-4986; Office Phone: 757-683-4817. E-mail: maly@cs.odu.edu.

MALY, MICHAEL KIP, lawyer; b. San Antonio, Tex., July 18, 1945; BA with honors, U. Tex., 1967; JD, U. Calif., 1975. Bar: Calif. 1975, U.S. Dist. Ct. Calif. (no., so., ea., ctrl. dist.). Mng. ptnr. Winston & Strawn LLP, San Francisco, 2003—. Spkr. in field; mem. arbitration panel San Francisco Superior Ct. Contbr. articles to profl. jours. Lt USN, 1967—72. Mem.: ABA. Office: Winston & Strawn LLP 101 California St San Francisco CA 94111-5802 Office Phone: 415-591-1424. Office Fax: 415-591-1400. Business E-Mail: mmaly@winston.com.

MALY, WOJCIECH P., engineering educator, researcher; b. Inowroclaw, Poland, Jan. 5, 1946; came to U.S., 1979; s. Feliks and Maria (Gordzialkowska) M.; m. Halina Zarembowska, Apr. 11, 1970; 1 child, Katarzyna. MSc, Tech. U. Warsaw, 1970; PhD, Polish Acad. Sci., Warsaw, 1975. Asst. prof. Tech. U. Warsaw, 1975-86; assoc. prof. dept. elec. and computer engrng. Carnegie Mellon U., Pitts., 1986-90, prof., 1990-96, Whitaker prof., 1996—. Author: Atlas of IC Technologies, 1986; contbr. chpts. to books, numerous articles to profl. jours. Recipient Teare Tchg. award Carnegie Mellon U., 1989; SRC Tech. Excellence award Semicondr. Rsch. Corp., 1993. Fellow IEEE. Roman Catholic. Achievements include development of methodologies of design for manufacturability of integrated circuits; patents in field. Office: Carnegie Mellon U ECE Dept 5000 Forbes Ave Pittsburgh PA 15213-3890

MAMAT, FRANK TRUSTICK, lawyer; b. Syracuse, NY, Sept. 4, 1949; s. Harvey Sanford and Annette (Trustick) M.; m. Kathy Lou Winters, June 23, 1975; children: Jonathan Adam, Steven Kenneth. BA, U. Rochester, 1971; JD, Syracuse U., 1974. Bar: D.C. 1976, U.S. Ct. Appeals (D.C. cir.) 1976, Fla. 1977, U.S. Supreme Ct. 1979, US. Dist. Ct. (ea. dist.) 1983, U.S. Ct. Appeals (6th cir.) 1983, Mich. 1984, U.S. Dist. Ct. (no. dist.) Ind. 1984. Atty. NLRB, Washington, 1975—79; assoc. Proskauer, Rose, Goetz & Mendelsohn, Washington, NYC and L.A., 1979—83, Fishman Group, Bloomfield Hills, Mich., 1983—85, ptnr., 1985—87; sr. ptnr. Honigman, Miller, Schwartz and Cohn, 1987—94; pres., CEO Morgan Daniels Co., Inc., West Bloomfield, Mich., 1994—; ptnr. Clark Klein & Beaumont, P.L.C., Detroit, 1995—96, Clark Hill, P.L.C., Detroit, 1996—2003, mem. exec. com., 1999—2001; ptnr. Dickinson Wright, PLLC, 2003—. Bd. dirs. Mich. Food and Beverage Assn., Air Conditioning Contractors of Am., Air Conditioning Contractors of Mich., Am. Subcontractors Assn., Mich. Mfrs. Assn. Labor Counsel, Jewish Vocat. Svcs., Constrn. Fin. Mgmt. Assn., Mich. Assn. Home Builders. Gen. counsel Rep. Com. of Oakland County, 1986—; chmn. Constrn. Code Commn. Mich., 1993—; bd. dirs. 300 Club, Mich., 1984-90; pres. 400 Club, 1990-93, chmn., 1993—; mem. Associated Gen. Contractors Labor Lawyers Coun.; mem. Rep. Nat. Com. Nat. Rep. Senatorial Com., Presdl. Task Force, Rep. Labor Coun., Washington; city dir. West Bloomfield, 1985-87; pres. West Bloomfield Rep. Club, 1985-87; chmn. bd. trustees Am. Soc. Edn. Found., 2005—; fin. com. Rep. Com. of Oakland County, 1984-93; pres. Oakland County Lincoln Rep. Club, 1989-90; bd. dirs. camping svcs. and human resources com. YMCA, 1989-93, Anti-Defamation League, 1989—; vice chmn. Lawyers for Reagan-Bush, 1984; v.p. Fruehauf Farms, West Bloomfield, Mich., 1985-88; mem. staff Exec. Office of Pres. of US Inquiries/Comments, Washington, 1981-83. Fellow Coll. Labor and Employment Attys.; mem. ABA, FBA, Mich. Bar Assn., Fla. Bar Assn. (labor com. 1977—), Rep. Nat. Lawyers Assn., Mich. Bus. and Profl. Assn., Am. Acad. Constrn. and Labor Attys. (exec. dir. 1998—), Am. Subcontractors Assn. (Southeastern Mich., bd. dirs.), Founders Soc. Detroit Bar Assn., Assn. Corp. Growth (Detroit chpt.), Oakland County Bar Assn., Mich. Infrastructure and Transp. Assn., Constrn. Mgmt. Fin. Assn., B'nai B'rith (v.p. 1982-83, trustee 1987-88, bd. dirs. Detroit Barristers unit 1983-91, pres. 1985-87), Am. Soc. Employers (chmn. 2003-05, chmn. ednl. found. 2005—), Oakpointe Country Club, Detroit Soc. Clubs, Skyline Club, Fairlane Club, Detroit Athletic Club, Renaissance Club, Econ. Club Detroit. Office: Dickinson Wright PLLC 500 Woodward Ave Ste 4000 Detroit MI 48226 also: Morgan Daniels Co Inc 5484 Crispin Way Rd West Bloomfield MI 48323-3402 Home Phone: 248-626-4107; Office Phone: 313-223-3169. Personal E-mail: fmamat@aol.com. Business E-Mail: fmamat@dickinsonwright.com.

MAMER, JAMES MICHAEL, secondary school educator; b. LA, Oct. 8, 1948; s. James Robert and Annette (Babue) M.; m. Jessica Puma, Aug. 31, 1963. BA in Polit. Sci., Calif. Poly. U., Pomona, 1970; MA in Internat. Studies, Immaculate Heart Coll., 1990. Tchr. Irvine (Calif.) Unified Sch. Dist., 1978—. Mentor tchr. Irvine Sch. Dist., 1988-95. Mem. editl. bd. Global Pages, L.A., 1991-96. Recipient Global Teaching award Western Internat. Studies Consortium, L.A., 1991, Am. Coun. Internat. Edn. award, 1998, Human Rights Edn. award Internat. Studies Edn. Project, 2004; Fulbright-Hays grantee, India, 1977; Coe fellow, 1984. Mem. Nat. Coun. Social Studies (Nat. Social Studies Tchr. of Yr. 1992), Irvine Tchrs. Assn. Democrat. Avocation: reading. Home: 29102 Kommers Ln Silverado CA 92676-9726 Personal E-mail: jmamer@earthlink.net.

MAMER, JOHN WILLIAM, business educator; b. July 4, 1954; BA, BS, U. Calif., Davis, 1975; MS, U. Calif., Berkeley, 1978, PhD, 1982. Analyst Manalytics Inc., 1977-78; rsch. intern Xerox Corp., 1979-80; from asst. prof. to prof. U. Calif., LA, 1981-96, prof., 1996—. Lectr. in field. Referee Mgmt. Sci., 1982—, Ops. Rsch., 1984—, Jour. Econ. Dynamics and Control, 1984, 88; contbr. over 15 articles to profl. jours. Mem. Inst. Mgmt. Sci. (organizing chmn. 1994, arangements chmn. 1995), Ops. Rsch. Soc. Am. Office: The Anderson School UCLA PO Box 951481 Los Angeles CA 90095-1481

MAMER, STUART MIES, lawyer; b. East Hardin, Ill., Feb. 23, 1921; s. Louis H. and Anna (Mies) M.; m. Donna E. Jordan, Sept. 10, 1944; children: Richard A., John S., Bruce J. AB, U. Ill., 1942, JD, 1947. Bar: Ill. bar 1947. Assoc. Thomas & Mulliken, Champaign, 1947-55; partner firm Thomas, Mamer & Haughey, Champaign, 1955—. Lectr. U. Ill. Coll. Law, Urbana, 1965-85; Mem. Atty. Registration and Disciplinary Commn. Ill., 1976-82 Chmn. fund drive Champaign County Community Chest, 1955; 1st pres. Champaign County United Fund, 1957; Pres., dir. U. Ill. McKinley Found., Champaign, 1957-69; trustee Children's Home and Aid Soc. of Ill., v.p., 1977-96. Served as pilot USAAC, 1943-45. Mem. Am. Coll. Trust and Estate Counsel (bd. regents 1984-90), Pillar of Champaign County Bar Assn., Phi Beta Kappa, Phi Gamma Delta. Republican. Presbyterian. Home: 101 W Windsor Rd # 3105 Urbana IL 61802-6663 Office: Thomas Mamer & Haughey LLP 30 E Main St Fl 5 Champaign IL 61820-3629 Office Phone: 217-351-1500. Business E-Mail: smamer@tmh-law.com.

MAMET, DAVID ALAN, playwright, scriptwriter; b. Chgo., Nov. 30, 1947; s. Bernard Morris and Lenore June (Silver) Mamet; m. Lindsay Crouse, Dec. 1977 (div.); m. Rebecca Pidgeon, Sept. 22, 1991. BA, Goddard Coll., Plainfield, Vt., 1969; DLitt (hon.), Dartmouth Coll., 1996. Artist-in-residence Goddard Coll., 1971-73; artistic dir. St. Nicholas Theatre Co., Chgo., 1973-75; guest lectr. U. Chgo., 1975, 79, NYU, 1981; assoc. artistic dir. Goodman Theater, Chgo., 1978; assoc. prof. film Columbia U., 1988. Chmn. bd. Atlantic Theater Co. Author: (plays) The Duck Variations, 1971, Sexual Perversity in Chicago, 1973 (Village Voice Obie award, N.Y. Drama Critics Cir. award), Reunion, 1973, Squirrels, 1974, American Buffalo, 1976, A Life in the Theatre, 1976, The Water Engine, 1976, The Woods, 1977, Lone Canoe, 1978, Prairie du Chien, 1978, Lakeboat, 1980, Donny March, 1981, Edmond, 1982 (Village Voice Obie award, 1983), The Disappearance of the Jews, 1983, The Shawl, 1985, Glengarry Glen Ross, 1984 (Pulitzer prize for drama, N.Y. Drama Critics Cir. award), Speed-the-Plow, 1987, Bobby Gould in Hell, 1989, The Old Neighborhood, 1991, Oleanna, 1992, The Cryptogram, 1994, Ricky Jay and His 52 Assistants, 1994, Death Defying Acts, 1995, Boston Marriage, 1999, Romance, 2005, November, 2007; dir.: (plays) Dangerous Corner, 1995; author: (screenplays) The Postman Always Rings Twice, 1979, The Verdict, 1980, The Untouchables, 1986, House of Games, 1986, We're No Angels, 1987, Homicide, 1991, Hoffa, 1991, Oleanna, 1994, The Edge, 1996, The Spanish Prisoner, 1996, Wag the Dog, 1997, Ronin, 1998, The Winslow Boy, 1999, State & Main, 2000, Lakeboat, 2001, Hannibal, 2001; co-author (with Shel Silverstein) Things Change, 1987; author: (novels) The Village, 1994, The Old Religion, 1996, Wilson: A Consideration of the Sources, 2001, (non-fiction) True and False: Heresy and Common Sense for the Actor, 1996, 3 Uses of the Knife: On the Nature and Purpose of Drama, 1996, The Wicked Son: Anti-Semitism, Self-Hatred and the Jews, 2006, Bambi vs. Godzilla: On the Nature, Purpose and Practice of the Movie Business, 2007, (children's books) Warm and Cold with drawings by Donald Sultan, 1985, Passover, The Duck and the Goat, 1996, The Duck and the Goat, Jafsie & John Henry, 1999, Bar Mitzvah, 1999, Henrietta, 1999, (essays) Writing In Restaurants, 1986, SomeFreaks, 1989, On Directing Film, 1990, The Cabin, 1992, Make-Believe-Town, 1996, (poetry) The China Man, 1999, The Hero Pony, 1990; dir.: (films) House of Games, 1986, The Winslow Boy, 1988, Things Change, 1988, Homicide, 1991, Oleanna, 1994, The Spanish Prisoner, 1996, State and Main, 2000, Catastrophe, 2000; writer, dir. (films) Heist, 2001, assoc. prodr. Hoffa, 1992; exec. prodr.: (TV films) Lansky, 1999, A Life in the Theater, 1993; prodr.: Lip Service, 1988; creator, writer (TV series) The Unit, 2006. Recipient Outer Critics Circle award for contbn. to Am. theater, 1978, Acad. award nominee for best screenplay adaptation, 1983, 1998, Common Wealth Award Distinguished Svc., 2004, Screen Laurel Award, Writers Guild Am., 2005; Rockefeller grantee, 1977, CBS Creative Writing fellow, Yale U. Drama Sch, 1976—77. Office: David Mamet 2 Northfield Plz Northfield IL 60093-1294 *

MAMLOK, WALTER JOSEPH, music educator, musician; b. Bronx, NY, Jan. 4, 1949; s. Julius Alvin and Ruth Mamlok; m. Carol Diane Rubin, Aug. 26, 1972; children: Charna Beth Westervelt, Elena Susanne. B in Music Edn., U. Hartford, 1971; MS, Ctrl. Conn. State U., 2000. Cert. profl. educator Conn. State Bd. Edn., 1994. Music tchr. Wethersfield (Conn.) Bd. Edn., 1971—75, 1976—80, Wolcott (Conn.) Bd. Edn., 1975—76; mgmt. Kemp Enterprises, South Windsor, Conn., 1980—88; music tchr. Newtown (Conn.) Bd. Edn., 1988—99, Meridan (Conn.) Bd. Edn., 1999—2001; music tchr. gr 6-12 Capitol Region Ednl. Coun., Hartford, Conn., 2001—04; mid. sch. music tchr. Bloomfield (Conn.) Bd. Edn., 2004—. Dir., condr. Strictly Swing Jazz Band, Bloomfield, 1977—; bass clarinetist Local 400 Pops Band, Rocky Hill, Conn., 1988—; musician Capital Winds Ensemble, Hartford, 1990—; clarinetist Klezical Tradition Klezmer Band, Fairfield, Conn., 1994—. Contbr. articles to profl. jours. Mem. Dem. Town Com., Bloomfield, 2004; v.p. bd. dirs. Temple Beth Sholom, Manchester, 1985—95, tchr., 1991—99; pres. Temple Beth Sholom Nursery Sch., Manchester, Conn., 1982—86. Mem.: Music Educators Technologists Assn. (treas., sec., charter), Conn Music Educators Assn., Conn. Edn. Assn. (assoc.), Music Educators Nat. Conf. (assoc.). Democrat. Jewish. Avocations: music, sports. Home: 1 South Ridge Dr Bloomfield CT 06002-5009 Office: Bloomfield Board of Education 390 Park Ave Bloomfield CT 06002 Office Phone: 860-286-2433 2313. Personal E-mail: wmamlok@comcast.net. Business E-Mail: wmamlok@blmfld.org.

MAMPRE, VIRGINIA ELIZABETH, communications executive; b. Chgo., Sept. 12, 1949; d. Albert Leon and Virginia S. (Joboul) M. BA with honors, U. Iowa, 1971; Masters degree, Ind. U., 1972; spl. cert., Harvard U., 1981, Purdue U., 1999. Cert. tchr. Harris Intern WTTW-TV Sta., Chgo., 1972, asst. dir., 1972-73; prod. and dir. WSIU/WUSI-TV Sta., Carbondale, Ill., 1973-74; instr. So. Ill. U., Carbondale, 1972-77; prog. and prod. mgr. WSIU/WUSI-TV, Carbondale, 1974-77; prog. dir. KUHT-TV Sta., Houston, 1977-83; pres. Victory Media, Inc., Houston, 1984-89, Mampre Media Internat., Houston, 1984—. Cons. Corp. Pub. Broadcasting, Washington, 1981—83; bd. dirs. TVPC; program bd. Ea. Ednl. Network; spkr., presenter in field Europe, Asia, Australia, S. Am. Contbg. author/editor to mags. including Focus, 1989, News & Views, 1987-88, In the Black, 1984-93, Festivals; creator: (report card campaign) Multi-media, U.S., 1985—; exec. prodr. TV spls., pub. affairs and info., 1977-83 (awards 1978-91). Pres. Child Abuse Prevention Coun., Houston, 1984—97; chmn. exhbns. Mayor's 1st Hearing, Children and Youth, Houston, 1985—88; rep. Houston 2nd World Conf. on Mayors, Japan, 1989; bd. govs. Houston Read Commn., pres., 1995—2001, chair adv. bd., 1993—2001; mem. nat. faculty Ctr. Children's Issues, 1995—97; pres. Episcopal Ch. Women, 2002—, 2006; pres. bd. dirs. Houston Fin. Coun., 1983—; bd. dirs. Child Abuse Prevention Network, 1990—97; chmn. bd. dirs., gala chair Crime Stoppers Houston, 1984—99; founder, bd. dirs. Friends of WSIU-TV, 1974—77; chmn. St. Kevork/ACYO Nat. Sports Fair, St. John the Divine, 1990; mem. exec. bd. Nat. Com. To Prevent Child Abuse, 1990—97; pres., bd. dirs. Fedn. Houston Profl. Women Found., 1996; bd. dirs. Humanities Tex., 1998—, Tex. Coun. Humanities, Operation Rainbow, 1997—, pres. bd. gala chair; bd. dirs. Kellogg Fellows Leadership Alliance; adv. bd. Southwest Area Media Project. Fellow W.K. Kellogg Leadership Found., Battle Creek, Mich., 1987-90; recipient award for Excellence Pres. Pvt. Sector, White House, Washington, 1987, Ohio State U., Columbus, 1983, Feddersen award for excellence in Pub. TV Ind. U., Bloomington, 1981, Heritage award Child Abuse Prevention Coun., 1990, Dona J. Stone Founders award Nat. Assn. for Prevention of Child Abuse, 1990; named among Outstanding Women Vols. for community, civic and profl. contbns., Fedn. Houston Profl. Women, 1989; honoree Woman on Move, 1997. Mem.: Houston Culinary Guild (pres. 2006—), Internat. Festivals Events. Assn. (officer 1994—2003, sec. 1994—, bd. dirs. 1995—2002, creator Mampre Media Internat. Leadership Devel.), Profls. in Culinary Arts (pres. 2002—04, bd. dirs.), TV Program Conf. (sec. bd. 1990—), Ctr. Bus. Women's Devel., Nat. Assn. Programming TV Execs., Nat. Assn. Ednl. Broadcasters (presenter nat. conv. 1975—76), Houston Fed. Profl. Women (del. 1986—93, chmn. 1994—, pres.), Am. Women in Radio and TV (bd. dirs. 1985—, nat. v.p. 1986—90, award 1987, pres. Houston chpt. 1990), Kellogg Fellows Leadership Alliance (bd. trustees), Dau. of the King, Christ in the Arts (chair), Dephians, Tex. Lyceum (v.p., bd. dirs. 1990—96). Republican. Episcopalian. Avocations: photography, swimming, sailing, languages, travel. Office: Mampre Media Internat 5123 Del Monte Dr Houston TX 77056-4391 Office Phone: 713-960-9849. Personal E-mail: mampremedi@aol.com.

MAMTANI, MANJU RAMESHLAL, geneticist, researcher; b. Nagpur, India, Oct. 12, 1974; arrived in U.S., 2004; d. Rameshlal Tekchand and Savitri Rameshlal Mamtani; m. Hemant Kulkarni, Feb. 23, 2004. MBBS, Indira Gandhi Govt. Med. Coll., Nagpur U., India, 1997; MD, Govt. Med. Coll. Nagpur U., India, 2003. Cert. Maharashtra Med. Coun., 1997. Rsch. fellow U. Tex. Health Sci. Ctr., San Antonio, 2004—. Patron mem. Lata Med. Rsch. Found., Nagpur, 2001—; joint sec. Thalassemia Soc. India, Nagpur, 2001—. Kathak dance. Achievements include several international research publications related to thalassemia, sickle cell anemia, neonatal lead toxicity and type 2 diabetes. Avocations: travel, dancing, painting. Home: 7458 Louis Pasteur Dr Apt #1205 San Antonio TX 78229 Office: UTHSCSA 7703 Floyd Curl Dr San Antonio TX 78229 Home Phone: 210-614-1268; Office Phone: 210-567-0103. Business E-Mail: mamtani@uthscsa.edu.

MAMUT, MARY CATHERINE, retired entrepreneur; b. Calabria, Italy, Oct. 17, 1923; came to U.S., 1928; d. Carmelo Charles and Caterina (Tripodi) Cogliandro; m. Michael Matthew Mamut, May 15, 1954; children: Anthony Carl, Charles Terrance. Student, Stenotype Comml. Coll., 1946-50. Sec. to pres. Thomas Goodfellow, Inc., Detroit, 1942-50; asst. to v.p. R.G. Moeller Co., Detroit, 1951-52; sec. to pres. United Steel Supply Co., Detroit, 1952-54; sec. to libr. Farmington (Mich.) Schs., 1962-68; real estate agt., 1969; owner, mgr. Crystal Fair, Birmingham, Mich., 1969-88, ret. Mich. Tchr. Stenotype Comml. Coll., Detroit, 1952-54. Vol. Henry Ford Mus., Dearborn, Mich., 1989-90, Greenfield Village, 1989-90, West Bloomfield Libr., 1993-95. Recipient World Lifetime Achievement award Am. Biog. Inst. U.S.A., 1993. Mem. Am. Bus. Women's Assn., Birmingham-Bloomfield C. of C., Profl. Secs. Internat, NAFE. Roman Catholic. Avocations: reading, music, art, theater. Home: 7423 Coach Ln West Bloomfield MI 48322-4022

MAN, DANIEL, plastic surgeon; married; 3 children. MD, Tel Aviv U., 1973. Lic. Maine, 1976, Del., 1976, Ky., 1978, Fla., 1981, cert. in Plastic and Reconstructive Surgery Am. Bd. Plastic Surgery, 1981. Intern in gen. surgery Tel Hashomer Hosp., Ramat Gan, Israel, 1972—73; resident in gen. surgery Montefiore Hosp., Bronx, NY, 1974—76; resident in surgery Wilmington Gen. Hosp., Del., 1976—78; resident in plastic and reconstructive surgery U. Louisville, 1978—80; pvt. practice Boca Raton, Fla., 1981—. Presenter in field; profl. interviewee in field various mags., newspapers, and TV programs. Author: The Art of Man: Faces of Plastic Surgery, 1998, The New Art of Man: Faces of Plastic Surgery, 2002, Man at Work: A Photographic of Plastic Surgery and Art, 2006; contbr. books, anthologies, and profl. jours. in field. Named Dr. Man Day in his honor, Boca Raton, Fla., 2001; recipient Humanitarian of Yr. award, Palm Beach County Victim Svcs., 2001, Letter of Recognition for Humanitarian Contbns., Fla. State Senator M. Mandy Dawson, 2001, Fla. State Senator

Tom Rossin, 2001, US Congressman Robert Wexler, 2001, US Senator Bill Nelson, 2001, US Senator Bob Graham, 2001, Gov. Jeb Bush, Fla., 2001; Hand fellowship, U. Louisville, 1978—80, Microvascular fellowship, 1980. Fellow: Am. Soc. Laser Surgery and Medicine; mem.: AMA, Y-ME Fla. (founding bd. mem. 1982—87, med. advisor 1982—87), Lipolysis Soc. N.Am., Broward County Soc. Plastic Surgeons, Palm Beach County Soc. Plastic Surgeons, Palm Beach County Med. Soc., Am. Soc. Aesthetic Plastic Surgery, Am. Soc. Plastic Surgeons. Office: 851 Meadows Rd Ste 222 Boca Raton FL 33486 Office Phone: 561-395-5508.

MAN, LAWRENCE KONG, architect, art dealer; b. Kowloon, Hong Kong, July 4, 1953; s. Hon-Kwong Man and Sau-Ching Luk. Student, U. Redlands, 1971-72; BArch, U. Oreg., 1977; MArch, Harvard U., 1978. Registered architect, Mass., Calif. Designer, project architect Shepley Bulfinch Richardson & Abbott, Boston, 1978-86; project designer, project architect E. Verner Johnson & Assoc., Boston, 1987-91; owner Lawrence Man Architect, Cambridge, Mass., 1992-95, LA, 1994—. Prin. works include Kromka House, L.A., Calif., LMAN Studio, L.A., Chu House, Downey, Calif., Fong House, San Marino, Calif., Tighe Summer House, Sagamore Beach, Mass, Frozen Fusion Juice Bar, L.A. schs., Fed. Credit Union, L.A., Pub. Mus. Grand Rapids, Mich. (AIA Grand Valley Disting. Bldg. award 1997), LCP Studio, Somerville, Mass., New Asia Restaurants, Danvers and Arlington, Mass., Tai Pan Restaurant, Cambridge, Mass. (Honor award AIA 1993, New Eng. award Excellence in Architecture 1993, Design Excellence award Nat. Orgn. Minority Architects 1993), Ti-Sales Office, Sudbury, Mass. (Design Excellence award Nat. Orgn. Minority Architects 1993), Dental Clinic, Reading, Mass. (AIA Interior Architecture award 1992, Interior Design Project award Am. Soc. Interior Designers 1991, Boston Exports citation AIA 1990, Boston Soc. of Architects/New Eng. Healthcare Assembly honor award, 1994), Mus. Ctr. Union Terminal, Cin. (Reconstrn. award 1991), Ramesses Pavilion Boston Mus. Sci. (Double Vision award/Double Silver Soc. Environ. Graphics 1990), Smithsonian South Quadrangle Mus., Washington (Boston Exports award/citation AIA 1990, Honor award AIA 1989), U. Vt. Student Ctr., Burlington, Campus Ctr. Study and Libr. addition Franklin & Marshall Coll., Andover (Mass.) Co. Corp. Hdqs., Emerson Hosp., Concord, Mass., pvt. residences, others. Avocations: dance, travel, music. Office: 949 Chung King Rd Los Angeles CA 90012 Office Phone: 213-628-3883. Business E-Mail: info@lawrencemanarchitects.com. *There are ups and downs in life. It is more rewarding to experience them all, no matter how hard it may get sometimes. It allows you to become a more complete person. That is, in my view, a true achievement.*

MAN, PANG LING, retired psychiatrist; b. Hong Kong, China; arrived in U.S., 1963; s. Kwong Cheung and Loy-Ho Man; m. Hope Man, Mar. 8, 1958; children: Ching, Dick, Linda. Degree, Queen Coll., Hong Kong, 1953; MD, Sun Yat-Sen U., 1958. Intern, resident U. Hosp., Goungzhou, China, 1958—60; intern Grace Hosp., Winnipeg, Canada, 1963—64; resident Worcester State Hosp., Mass., 1964—67; instr. psychiatry U. Louisville, 1967—71; asst. prof. psychiatry Wayne State U., Detroit, 1971—78, assoc. prof. psychiatry, 1978—98, ret., 1998. Dir. rsch. Northville Regional Psychiatric Hosp., Mich., 1971—98, asst. dir. edn., 1971—90. Author: Handbook of Acupuncture Anesthesia, 1973; contbr. articles to profl. jours. Vol. physician Chinatown Free Clinic, Detroit, 1971—90. Fellow: Am. Psychiatric Assn., Am. Bd. Neurology and Psychiatry. Avocations: golf, travel, swimming, ping pong/table tennis, dance. Home: 6504 Horsemans Canyon Dr Walnut Creek CA 94595

MANABE, SHARI A, physical education educator; BS, Ind. State U., 1991, MS, 1993, U. Hawaii, Manoa, 2001. Lic. tchr. Hawaii, cert. adapted phys. edn. educator Nat. Consortium for Phys. Edn. and Recreation for People with Disabilities, 2001. Secondary tchr. King Kekaulike H.S., Pukalani, Hawaii, 1995—96, Lahaina Intermediate Sch., Hawaii, 1996—97, Lokelani Intermediate Sch., Kihei, Hawaii, 1997—2001, Ctrl. Mid. Sch., Honolulu, 2001—03, Aiea Intermediate Sch., Hawaii, 2003—. Mem.: AAHPERDe (assoc.), Hawaii Assn. for Health, Phys. Edn., Recreation and Dance (life). Office: Aiea Intermediate Sch 99-600 Kulawea St Aiea HI 96701

MANABE, SYUKURO, meteorologist; b. Shikoku-chuo-shi, Ehime-ken, Japan, Sept. 21, 1931; arrived in U.S., 1958; s. Seiichi and Sueko (Akashi) M.; m. Nobuko Nakamura, Jan. 21, 1962; children: Nagisa M., Yukari C. BS, Tokyo U., 1953, MS, 1955, PhD, 1958; DSc (hon.), McGill U., 2004. Rsch. meteorologist, gen. circulation rsch. sect. U.S. Weather Bur., Washington, 1958-63; sr. rsch. meteorologist Geophys. Fluid Dynamics Lab. Environ. Sci. Services Adminstrn., Washington, 1963-68; sr. rsch. meterologist geophys. fluid dynamics lab. NOAA, Princeton, NJ, 1968-95, mem. sr. exec. svc. of U.S.A., geophys. fluid dynamics lab., 1979-95, sr. scientist, geophys. fluid dynamics lab., 1995-97; dir. global warming rsch. program Frontier Rsch. Sys. for Global Change, Yokohama, Japan, 1997—2001; sr. meteorologist Program in Atmospheric and Oceanic Sciences Princeton U., 2002—. Lectr. with rank of prof. Princeton U., 1968-98; vis. prof., faculty of sciences, Geophysical Inst., U. Tokyo, 1983, vis. prof. Sch. Environ. Sci., Nagoya (Japan) U., 2006. Contbr. articles to peer-reviewed publications. Recipient Gold medal U.S. Dept. Commerce, 1970, Presdl. Rank Meritorious Exec. award Pres. of U.S., 1989, Blue Planet prize Asahi Glass Found., 1992, Asahi prize Asahi Shimbun Cultural Found., 1995, Volvo Environ. prize Volvo Found., 1997, Milutin Milankovitch medal, European Geophys. Soc., 1998. Fellow AAAS, Am. Geophys. Union (Revelle medal 1993); mem. NAS, Acad. Europaea (fgn.), Royal Soc. Can. (fgn.), Am. Meteorol. Soc. (hon., Meisinger award 1967, 2nd half century award 1977, C.G. Rossby Rsch. medal 1992), Royal Meteorol. Soc. (hon.), Japan Meteorol. Soc. (hon., Fujiwara award 1966). Achievements include first numerical modeling study of global warming. Home: 6 Governors Ln Princeton NJ 08540-3666 Office: Princeton U Sayre Hall Forrestal Campus PO Box CN710 Princeton NJ 08544-0710 Business E-Mail: manabe@splash.princeton.edu.

MANAS, GERALD BENNETT (JERRY MANAS), information technology manager; b. Phila., Mar. 15, 1960; s. Sidney Ralph and Barbara M. Manas; m. Sharon Erica Olson, Sept. 10, 1989; 1 child, Elizabeth Rose. Student, Temple U., 1978-79. Cert. project mgmt. Am. Mgmt. Assn., project mgmt. profl. Project Mgmt. Inst., Microsoft Project Users Group. Programmer Alfred Angelo, Inc., Willow Grove, Pa., 1978-81, Pepper, Hamilton & Scheetz, Phila., 1981-82; programmer, analyst Hurst Performance, Warminster, Pa., 1982-85; sys. analyst C&D Power Sys., Plymouth Meeting, Pa., 1985-87; mgr. product devel. Centennial Sys., Wayne, Pa., 1987-89; mgr. edn. Responsive Software Solutions, Wayne, 1989-90; client mgr. Alliance Cons., Phila., 1990—2003, Rohm and Haas, Phila., 2003—; pres. Marengo Group, LLC, 2007—. Pres. Manas Comm., Inc., Phila., 1994—96; chmn. round table Del. Valley Computer Users Group, Phila., 1987—88; co-founder Project Mgmt. Thought Leadership. Author: Napoleon on Project Management: Timeless Lessons in Planning, Execution, and Leadership, 2006, (songs) Sept. Forever, 1996; contbr. articles to profl. jours. Vol. contbr. Project Mgmt. Inst. Mem.: Nat. Acad. Songwriters, Alliance Francaise Phila., Delaware Valley Entrepreneur's Club (pres., founder 1994—96). Democrat. Jewish. Avocations: music, art, photography, writing, french studies.

MANASSAH, JAMAL TEWFEK, electrical engineer, educator, management consultant; b. Haifa, Palestine, Feb. 23, 1945; s. Tewfek George and Alia Nasrallah (Kardoush) M.; m. Azza Tarek H.I. Mikdadi, Mar. 16, 1979; children: Tala, Nigh. BSc, Am. U., Beirut, Lebanon, 1966; MA, Columbia U., NYC, 1968, PhD, 1970. Mem. Inst. Advanced Study, Princeton, N.J., 1970-72, 74-79; asst. prof. Am. U. Beirut, 1972-75; chief sci. adviser Kuwait Inst. Sci. Rsch., 1976-81; COO Kuwait Found., 1979-81; prof. dept. elec. engring. CUNY, NYC, 1981—. Cons. Columbia Radiation Labs., N.Y.C., 1970-73, Ford Found., N.Y.C., 1973-79, NSF, Washington, 1978-83; chmn. Internat. Symposium Series, Kuwait, 1979-81; mng. dir. Khayatt and Co., Inc., N.Y.C., 1982; organizing com. Chem. Rsch. Applied to World Needs II, 1980-83; mem. Welfare Assn., Geneva, 1984-92; steering com. Internat. Workshop on Laser Physics, 1993-2000. Editor: Alternate Energy Sources (2 vols.) 1981; (with others) Advances in Food Producing Systems for Arid and Semiarid Lands (2 vols.), 1981, Innovations in Telecommunication (2 vols.), 1982, (with others) Transient Coherent Phenomena, 1995, Elementary Mathematical and Computational Tools for Electrical and Computer Engineering Using MATLAB®, 2001, 06, (with others) Coherent and Nonlinear Optics and Spectroscopy, 2002; mem. editl. bd. Internat. Jour. Laser Physics, 1994—, Laser Physics Letters, 2004—; contbr. articles to profl. jours. Commr. Lebanese Boy Scouts Assn., Beirut, 1972-75; adviser internat. program NSF, 1979-83; bd. dirs. CUNY Rsch. Found., 2001-03. Columbia U. faculty fellow, 1966-68, Pfister fellow, 1968-70; grantee NSF, 1982-87; recipient ABI Key award, 1987, Commemorative medal of honor, 1988; named Man of Yr., 1990. Mem. Assn. Mems. of Inst. for Advanced Study, Princeton Club. Christian Orthodox. Achievements include discovery of resonant absorption coefficient frequency shift; collective Lamb shift, pion minus condensation in nuclear matter, blackbody frequency shift; dynamical Lorenz shift, reflectivity frequency shift, induced coherent pulse compression, induced spectral broadening; induced frequency shift, three-photons frequency shift, twin peaks in second harmonics generation; induced waveguiding and focusing, time-space superspike, non-linear compression of noise correlation time, soliton phases; coherently inhibited amplification, induced channeling, delayed reflectivity, two-color photon echos; superradiance without inversion, pressure induced optical cavities, periodicity enhanced precocious superradiant transition, acousto-induced reflectivity shift; research in statistical field theory, nonlinear and quantum optics, photonics, ultrafast phenomena and new technologies assessment. Home: 55 E 87th St Apt 15G New York NY 10128-1051 Office: CUNY Dept Elec Engring Convent Ave New York NY 10031 Office Phone: 212-650-8133. Business E-Mail: manassah@ccny.cuny.edu.

MANASSE, HENRI RICHARD, JR., pharmaceutical executive; b. Amsterdam, The Netherlands, Nov. 27, 1945; came to U.S., 1954, naturalized, 1963; s. Henri David and Janny Lynn (Borst) M.; m. Arlynn Hem, Aug. 9, 1969; children: Bryan, Sheralynn. BS in Pharmacy, U. Ill., Chgo., 1968; MA, Loyola U., Chgo., 1972; PhD, U. Minn., 1974; DSc (hon.), Campbell U., 1997, Union U., 1997, Mercer U., 1998, LI U., NY, 2004. Lic. pharmacist, Ill. Rsch. pharmacist Xttrium Labs., Chgo., 1968-69; asst. to dean Coll. Pharmacy U. Ill., Chgo., 1969-72, asst. prof. pharmacy adminstrn., 1974-77, assoc. dean, 1977-80, acting dean, 1980-81, dean, prof., 1981-93, interim vice chancellor for health svcs., 1992-93; prof. coll. pharmacy and medicine U. Iowa, v.p. for health scis., 1993-96; exec. v.p.-designate Am. Soc. Health-Sys. Pharmacists, 1996—, CEO, exec. v.p., 1997—. Sr. policy fellow Ctr. on Drugs and Pub. Policy, U. Md., 1988—; mem. Ill. Bd. Pharmacy, Springfield, 1982-94; pub. mem. Am. Soc. Hosp. Pharmacists Commn. on Credentialling, Bethesda, Md., 1984-86; chair bd. dirs. Nat. Patient Safety Found., 1999-2001, chair bd. govs., 2006; mem. adv. bd. PEW Found. Health Professions Edn. Reform Commn.; bd. dirs. Am. Soc. Cons. Pharmacists Rsch. and Edn. Found.; pres. Coun. on Credentialing in Pharmacy, 1998—02; mem. quality quest prize selection com. Am. Hosp. Assn.; co-chair safe practices steering com. Nat. Quality Forum, 2001-04, adv. com. on exec. leadership; mem. sentinel events adv. com. JCAHO Sentinel, 2002—; cons. FDA Adv. Com. on Risk Mgmt. and Drug Safety, 2003-07; expert on patient safety Bd. Pharmacy Practice, profl. sec., 2005—, Internat. Pharm. Fedn.; JCAHO mem. Internat. Adv. Com. on Patient Safety. Mem. editl. bd. Am. Jour. Hosp. Pharmacy, 1990-92; contbr. chpts. to books and articles to profl. jours. Pres. Downers Grove Sch. Bd. Caucus, Ill., 1984-85; bd. dirs. med. svc. Westside Holistic Ctr., Chgo., 1979-89. Recipient Lederle Faculty award Lederle Pharm. Co., 1975, Outstanding Achievement award U. Minn., 1998; named Alumnus of Yr., U. Ill. Alumni Assn., 1983. Jesse E Stewart Svc. award, U. of Illinois, 2004, Harvey A.K. Whitney Lecture award, 2007. Fellow: Inst. Medicine Chgo.; mem.: NAS, Am. Soc. Assn. Execs., Am. Pharm. Assn., Inst. Medicine, Am. Soc. Health Sys. Pharmacists (H.A.K. Whitney award 2007), Am. Assn. Colls. Pharmacy (pres., adminstrv. bd. 1982—86, bd. dirs. 1984—86, pres. 1988—89). Baptist. Avocations: computers, international travel. Home: 10118 Vanderbilt Cir Rockville MD 20850-4674 Office: ASHP 7272 Wisconsin Ave Bethesda MD 20814 Home Phone: 301-947-3296; Office Phone: 301-657-3000. Business E-Mail: hrmjr@ashp.org.

MANASSON, VLADIMIR ALEXANDROVICH, physicist; b. Chernovtsy, Ukraine, Mar. 4, 1952; arrived in US, 1991; s. Alexander and Chaya (Finkelsteyn) Manasson; m. Katrine Kokhanovskaya, Aug. 2, 1975; children: Alexander, Julia. BSEE, Moscow Inst. Electronic Mfg., 1973, MSEE, 1974; PhD in Physics, Chernovtsy U., 1984. Entr. Acad. Scis. Ukraine Material Sci. Inst., 1975-78, sr. engr., 1978-80, jr. rsch. assoc., 1980-85, sr. rsch. assoc., 1985-90; rsch. scientist Phys. Optics Corp., Torrance, Calif., 1991-94, sr. scientist, 1994-95; leader antenna devel. WaveBand Corp., Irvine, Calif., 1996—98, dir. rsch., 1999—2000, 2nd v.p. R&D, 2000—05; chief scientist, leader antenna devel. Sierra Nevada Corp., 2005. Grantee, NSF, 1993—94, 1997, 1998, 2003, 2004, Dept. Def., 1994, 1995, 1996, 1997, 1998, 1999, 2001, 2002, 2003, 2004, U.S. Dept. Commerce, 1997, Nat. Rsch. Coun./Nat. Acad. of Sci., 1995, 1998, L.A. Regional Tech. Alliance, 1999, NASA, 2001, 2002, DOE, 2002, 2003. Mem.: IEEE. Achievements include patents for several photosensitive devices and antennae. Avocations: piano improvising, reading. Office: 15245 Alton Pkwy Ste 100 Irvine CA 92618 Business E-Mail: vladimir.manasson@sncorp.com.

MANATT, CHARLES TAYLOR, lawyer; b. Chgo., June 9, 1936; BS, Iowa State U., 1958; JD, George Washington U., 1962. Bar: Calif. 1962, U.S. Supreme Ct. 1967, D.C. 1985. Ptnr. Manatt, Phelps & Phillips, Washington, now chmn.; U.S. ambassador Dominican Republic, 1999—2001. Bd. editors George Washington Law Rev., 1960-62. Pres. Calif. Bankers Assn.; chmn. Nat. Democratic Inst., Calif. Dem. Com., Nat. Dem. Com., Internat. Found. for Election Sys.; chmn. bd. trustees George Washington U.; bd. dirs. Mayo Clinic; trustee Mus. Am. History. Mem. ABA, Calif. State Bar, L.A. County Bar Assn., San Fernando Valley Bar Assn. (pres. 1971-72), Century City Bar Assn., Phi Delta Phi, Delta Sigma Rho. also: Manatt Phelps & Phillips Trident Ctr E Tower 11355 W Olympic Blvd Los Angeles CA 90064-1614 Office: Manatt Phelps Phillips 700 12th St NW Ste 1100 Washington DC 20005-4075

MANATT, RICHARD, retired education educator; b. Odebolt, Iowa, Dec. 13, 1931; s. William Price and Lucille (Taylor) M.; m. Sally Jo Johnson, Aug. 20, 1952; children— Tamra Jo, Ann Lea, Joel Price; m. Jacquelyn M. Nesset, Feb. 25, 1970; 1 child, Megan Sue. BSc, Iowa State U., 1953, MS, 1956; PhD, U. Iowa, 1964. Prin. Oskloosa (Iowa) Schs., 1959-62; rsch. assoc. U. Iowa, Iowa City, 1962-64; mem. faculty Iowa State U., Ames, 1964—, prof., 1972—, chmn. dept. edn. adminstrn., 1970-80, 93-98, dir. Sch. Improvement Model Projects, 1980—, prof., 1998—2002, prof. emeritus, 2002—. Cons. performance evaluation for public and independent schs.; disting. vis. prof. Calif. State U., L.A. Author: Educator's Guide to the New Design, When Right is Wrong, Fundamentalists and the Public Schools, Clinical Manual for Teacher Performance Evaluation Compendias of Professional Growth Plans, (computer software program) Computer Assisted Teach Evaluation/Supervision. Served with AUS, 1953-55. Named Disting. Prof., Nat. Acad. Sch. Execs., 1979, Regents' Prof. Edn., 1994; recipient faculty citation Iowa State U. Alumni Assn., 1998, Margaret White Grad. Faculty award, 2001, Pres.'s award NAACP, 2002. Mem. NEA, NASSP, ASCD (Outstanding Cons. 1981), Am. Assn. Sch. Adminstrs., Phi Kappa Phi, Phi Delta Kappa, Delta Chi. Democrat. Methodist. Home: 2926 Monroe Dr Ames IA 50010-4362 Office Phone: 515-232-0202. Business E-Mail: rmanatt@iastate.edu.

MANBECK, HARVEY B., agricultural and biological engineer, educator; b. Reading, Pa., Jan. 11, 1942; m. Glenda Manbeck; children: Eric, Christina. BS, Pa. State U., 1963, MS in Agrl. Engring., 1965; PhD in Engring., Okla. State U., 1970. Rsch. assoc. agrl. engring. dept. Pa. State U., 1965, instr. agrl. engring. dept., 1966, prof. agrl. engring., 1980-96; asst. prof. agrl engring. dept. U. Ga., 1970-75, assoc. prof. agrl. engring. dept., 1977-80; assoc. prof., extension agrl. engr. Ohio State U., 1975-77; adminstrv. intern rsch. office Pa. Agrl. Experiment Sta., 1991-92; Disting. prof. agrl. engring. Pa. State U., 1996—2004, Disting. prof. emeritus Pa., 2004—, interim head agrl. and biol. engring. dept. Pa., 1996—98. Vis. prof. agrl. engring. U. Manitoba, 1986-87, Shenyang Agrl. U., 1988; interim dir. Housing Rsch. Ctr., Pa. State U., 1995. Contbr. chpts. to books and articles to profl. jours. Coach Little League Baseball, 1981-84, leader YMCA Indian Princess Longhouse, 1983-85, Webelo's Cub Scouts 1984, com. mem. Troop 31 Boy Scouts of Am. 1985—. Recipient Outstanding and Premier Tchg. award, Outstanding Rsch. award Coll. of Engring., Pa. State U., Atherton Excellence in Tchg. award Pa. State U., Black award for rsch. excellence Coll. Agrl. Scis., Pa. State U. Mem. ASCE, Am. Soc. Agrl. Engrs. (mem. structures group, vice chair 1978-79, chair, 1979-81, Pa. State sect. sec.-treas. 1983-84, chair 1985-86, trustee 1992-94, tech. dir. S.E. divsn. 1993-95, Henry Giese S & E award 1990), Nat. Frame Builders Assn. (mem. editl. rev. com. for the post-frame profl., chair 1988—), Ga. Soc. Profl. Engrs (state dir. at large 1974-75, named Outstanding Young Engr. of the Year, 1972, recipient Outstanding Chpt. Pres. award, 1974, various other coms.), Ohio Soc. Profl. Engrs., Forest Products Rsch. Soc., Gamma Sigma Delta (internat. sec. 1998—), Alpha Epsilon, Sigma Xi, numerous others. Achievements include development of standard designs and specs for hardwood glulam highway bridges, authorship of national engineering practice for post-frame structural diaphragm design, development of FEM for predicting thermal pressures in grain bins, development of FEM for predicting structural performance of wood-framed, metal-clad diaphragm evaluation of creep response of wood I-joist floor systems, lateral stability of composite wood I-joists and development of standards for ventilation of confined space storage systems in agriculture. Home: 912 Anna St Boalsburg PA 16827-1214 Office: Penn State U 210 Agr Engring Bldg University Park PA 16802 Business E-Mail: Hmanbeck@psu.edu.

MANCALL, ELLIOTT LEE, retired neurologist, educator; b. Hartford, Conn., July 31, 1927; s. Nicholas and Bess Tuch M.; m. Jacqueline Sue Cooper, Dec. 27, 1953; children: Andrew Cooper, Peter Cooper. BS, Trinity Coll., Hartford, 1948; MD, U. Pa., 1952. Diplomate Am. Bd. Psychiatry and Neurology. Intern Hartford Hosp., 1952-54; clk. in neurology Nat. Hosp. Nervous Disease, London, 1954-55; asst. resident neurology Neurol. Inst. NY, 1955-56; resident in neuropathology Mass. Gen. Hosp., 1956-57, clin. and rsch. fellow, 1957-58; tchg. fellow neuropathology Harvard Med. Sch., 1956-57; from asst. prof. neurology to assoc. prof. Jefferson Med. Coll., 1958-65; prof. medicine Hahnemann Med. Coll. and Hosp., 1965-76; prof. neurology Med. Coll. Pa.-Hahnemann U., 1993-95; prof. neurology, chmn. dept. Hahnemann Med. Coll. and Hosp., 1976-93; prof. neurology Jefferson Med. Coll., Phila., 1995—, interim chmn. dept. neurology, 1997—2003; prof. emeritus, 2006—. Dir. Hahnemann U. ALS Clinic, 1985-95; chmn. bd. dirs. Phila. Profl. Stds. Rev. Orgn., 1981-84. Author: (with others) The Human Cerebellum: A Topographical Atlas, 1961; (with B.J. Alpers) Clinical Neurology, 1971, Essentials of the Neurological Examination, 1971, 81; contbr. articles to profl. jours. With USN, 1945—47. Recipient Christian R. and Mary F. Lindback award, 1969, Oliver Meml. prize ophthalmology U. Pa., 1952. Fellow Am. Acad. Neurology (alt. del. to AMA 1982-86, gen. editor CONTINUUM 1991-2003, A.B. Baker award for excellence in neurol. edn. 1997, Presdl. award 2003); mem. Am. Neurol. Assn., Am. Assn. Neuropathology, Assn. Rsch. in Nervous and Mental Diseases, Soc. Neurosci., AAUP, Pa. Med. Peer Rev. Orgn. (dir. 1979-84), Phila. Neurol. Soc., Alpers Soc. Clin. Neurology, Coll. Physicians Phila., Sydenham Coterie, Phila. County Med. Soc., Pa. State Med. Soc., AMA (sec.-treas. sect. coun. neurology 1983-86), Am. Med. Soc. on Alcoholism, Neurology Intersoc. Liaison Group, Intersoc. Com. Neurol. Resources, Assn. Univ. Prof. Neurology (pres. 1988-90), Soc. for Exptl. Neuropathology, Am. Bd. Med. Specialities (exec. bd., chmn. com. study of evaluation procedures, 1992-99, rep. accreditation com. continuing med. edn. 1998-2004, chair accredidation coun., 2003-05), Am. Bd. Psychiatry and Neurology (v.p. 1990, del. to Am. Bd. Med. Spltys., dir. 1983-91, emeritus dir. 1991—, cons. 2004-), Pa. Blue Shield (profl. adv. coun. 1991-98). Democrat. Jewish. Home: PO Box 498 Lafayette Hill PA 19444-0498 Office: Ste 200 900 Walnut St Philadelphia PA 19107 Office Phone: 215-955-0707. Business E-Mail: elliott.mancall@jefferson.edu.

MANCALL, JACQUELINE COOPER, library and information scientist, educator; b. Phila., Mar. 31, 1932; d. Morris and Bertha Cooper; m. Elliott Lee Mancall, Dec. 27, 1953; children: Andrew Cooper, Peter Cooper. BA, U. Pa., 1954; MS, Drexel U. Sch. Libr. and Info. Sci., 1970, PhD, 1979. Adminstr. Miquon Sch., Pa., 1966—67, libr., 1967—76; tchg. asst. Drexel U., Phila., 1976—78, rsch. assoc., 1978, asst. prof., assoc. prof., 1979—89, prof., 1989—. Chair Phila. Children's Reading Round Table, 1982—84, mem. steering com., 1979—89; mem. faculty coun. Drexel U., 1984—89, chair faculty coun., 1987—89, mem. senate, 2000—05, chair senate, 2001—02; mem. sch. libr. survey com. State Libr. Pa., 1993; cons. Author (with M.C. Drott): Measuring Student Information Use: A Guide for School Library Media Specialists, 1963; author: (with E.S. Aversa) Management of Online Search Services in Schools, 1989; author: (with Sandra Hughes-Hassell) Collection for Management Youth, 2005; rsch. editor: Sch. Libr. Media quar., 1982—88, mem. editl. bd.: Jour. Libr. and Info. Sci. Edn., 1981—86, mem. editl. adv. bd.: Multimedia Schs.; contbg. editor: Cath. Libr. World, 1981—85; contbr. chapters to books, articles to profl. jours. Bd. dirs. Friends of William Jeannes Meml. Libr., Plymouth Meeting, Pa., 1976—79; pres. bd. dirs. Miquon Sch., 1964—66. Recipient Harold M. Myers award for Outstanding Svc., Drexel U., 1990, Ann. award, Phila. Sch. Libr., 1994. Mem.: ALA (adv. com. office info. tech. 1995—97, continuing edn. task force 1995—98, co-chair ICONect evaluation com. 1996—2000, libr. congress nat. digital libr. adv. com. 1997, pub. awareness com. 1997—99, dir. KidsConnect 2000—02), Am. Assn. Sch. Libr. (chmn. continuing edn. com. 1985—87, rsch. stats. com. 1988—92, v.p./pres.-elect 1993, pres. 1994, Disting. Svc. award 1999), Pa. Sch. Librs. Assn. (chmn. profl. std. com. 1980—82, bd. dirs. 1984—87, chmn. profl. std. com. 1991—, Outstanding Contbr. award 1997), Phi Delta Kappa, Beta Phi Mu, Pi Gamma Mu. Democrat. Jewish. Office: Drexel U Coll Info Sci & Tech Philadelphia PA 19104 Office Phone: 215-895-2473. Business E-Mail: jackie.mancall@drexel.edu.

MANCHESTER, KENNETH EDWARD, electronics executive, consultant; b. Winona, Minn., Mar. 22, 1925; s. Laurence Edwin and Daisy Idel (Finley) M.; m. Bonnie Lee Hardgrave, June 24, 1946; children: Cynthia Lee, David Scott. AB, San Jose State Coll., 1949; MS, Stanford U., 1950, PhD, 1955. Sr. chemist Shell Devel. Co., Emeryville, Calif., 1955-62; head chemistry sect. Sprague Electric Co., North Adams, Mass., 1962-63, head chemistry dept., 1963-69, dir. semiconductor rsch., devel. and engring., 1969-79, dir. quality assurance and reliability Worcester, Mass., 1979-85, v.p. corp. R & D North Adams, 1985-89, Sprague fellow, 1985; cons. semiconductor industry, 1989—. Lectr. Rensselaer Poly. Inst., Troy, N.Y., 1967. Contbr. articles to profl. jours.; patentee in field. Chmn. com. Troop

70 Boy Scouts Am. Sgt. U.S. Army Ground Forces, 1943-46, ETO. Mem. Am. Chem. Soc., AIME, Optimist Club, Sigma Xi. Democrat. Avocations: woodworking, golf. Personal E-mail: ken@machester.bz.

MANCHESTER, PAUL BRUNSON, economist; b. Winsted, Conn., Oct. 7, 1942; s. Elbert Grant and Eleanor Elizabeth (Jones) M.; m. Ruth Elaine Garbisch, Oct. 25, 1969; children: Sarah H., Daniel P. BA, Yale U., 1964; PhD, U. Minn., 1973. Vol. Peace Corps, Colombia, 1964-66; teaching assoc. U. Minn., Mpls., 1966-69; asst. prof. Mary Washington Coll., Fredericksburg, Va., 1971-74; cons. U.S. Dept. Treasury, Washington, 1974-75; asst. prof. Cath. U. Am., Washington, 1974-78; cons. Robert R. Nathan Assocs., Washington, 1975-78; economist joint econ. com. U.S. Congress, Washington, 1978-89; econ. adviser to Tenn. senator U.S. Senate, Washington, 1988; sr. economist U.S. League Savs. Insts., Washington, 1989-90; economist Office Thrift Supervision, Washington, 1990-91; fin. economist U.S. Dept. HUD, Washington, 1991—2007, mem. fin. instns. regulatory divsn., 2007—. Contbr. articles to profl. jours. Pres. Woodmoor-Pinecrest Citizens' Assn., Silver Spring, Md.; del. Allied Civic Group, Silver Spring. Mem. Am. Econ. Assn., Soc. Govt. Economists, Nat. Economists Club (v.p. 1985, 87, bd. dirs. 1989-92), Yale Club Washington (bd. dirs., v.p. 2004-2007). Lutheran. Avocations: tennis, skiing, bowling. Home: 105 Lexington Dr Silver Spring MD 20901-2546 Office: US Dept HUD 451 7th St SW Rm 8212 Washington DC 20410-0001

MANCHIN, JOE, III, (JOSEPH MANCHIN III), governor, former state official; b. Farmington, W. Va., Aug. 24, 1947; s. John and Mary Manchin; m. Gayle Conelly; children: Heather, Joseph IV, Brooke. BS in Bus. and Econs., W.Va. U., 1970. Operator Manchin's Carpet Center, Marion County, W.Va., 1970; mem. W.Va. Ho. of Dels., 1982—86, W.Va. State Senate, 1986—92; sec. of state State of W.Va., Charleston, 2001—05, gov., 2005—. Past chmn. banking and ins. com. W.Va. State Senate, past vice chair fin. com., past chair rule making rev. Democrat. Office: Office of Governor 1900 Kanawha Blvd East Charleston WV 25305 Office Phone: 304-558-8860. *

MANCILLA, FAUSTINA RAMIREZ, retired psychologist; b. Tijuana, Mexico, Feb. 15, 1943; d. Domingo Gomez and Carmen Castillo Ramirez; m. Armando Hernandez Mancilla, Nov. 30, 1957; children: Irene M. Torres, Alice M. Kincaid, Edward, Sergio Armando, Jaime. BA in Liberal Studies, Loyola Marymount U., LA, 1980, MA in Counseling and Guidance, 1986, MA in Counseling Psychology, Marriage and Family, 1986, MA in Ednl. Psychology, 1987, MA in Sch. Adminstrn., 1993; MA in Profl. Adminstrv. Svcs., Azusa Pacific U., Azusa, Calif., 1999; PhD in Behavioral Studies, Azusa Pacific U., 2000. Guidance tech. Culver City Unified Sch. Dist., Calif., 1980—84; tchr. k-5, bilingual Lennox Sch. Dist., 1984—85, tchr. spl. edn., 1985—86; bilingual sch. psychologist Santa Monica/Malibu Unified Sch. Dist., 1986—90; asst. prin. Lennox Sch. Dist., 1990—91, sr. psychologist, 1991—93, dir. pupil pers. svcs., 1993—97; dist. psychologist Murrieta Valley Unified Sch. Dist., 1997—99; coord., prin., infant cir., presch. grasp Riverside County Office Edn., 1999—2003; interim dir. pupil svcs. Murrieta Valley Unified Sch. Dist., 1999—99; coord., site adminstr., interagency assessment and tng. ctr. Riverside County Office Edn., 2003—05. Early childhood devel. cons. Riverside County Office Edn., 2003—06. Cert. parent trainer instr. Ctr. Improvement Children, LA, 1986—90; trainer trainer Los Padres Richstone Family Ctr., Lawndale, 1987—90; cert. interpreter/translator trainer Loyola Marymount U., LA, 1990—2006; cert. trainer spl. projects bilingual edn. San Diego County Dept. Edn., 1995—96; trainer trainers tchg. strategies young children Dept. Edn. -Nat. Project, 1993—96. Recipient Outstanding Bilingual Psychologist award, Santa Monica/Malibu Unified Sch. Dist., 1989, Outstanding Svc. award, Supr. and Trainer, Loyola Marymount U., 1994, 1996, Outstanding Svc. award, Dist. Adv. Coun., Lennox Sch. Dist., 1997. Mem.: Calif. Assn. Sch. Psychologists, Assn. Calif. Sch. Adminstrs. (assoc.), Nat. Assn. Sch. Psychologists (assoc.), Kappa Delta Phi (hon.). Avocations: travel, dance, painting. Home: 31597 Vignes Court Winchester CA 92596 Office: Riverside County Office of Education 3939 Thirteenth Street Riverside CA 92502-0868 Home Phone: 951-325-5032; Office Phone: 951-826-4600.

MANCINI, ERNEST ANTHONY, geologist, educator, researcher; b. Reading, Pa., Feb. 27, 1947; s. Ernest and Marian K. (Filbert) M.; m. Marilyn E. Lee, Dec. 27, 1969; children: Lisa L., Lauren N. BS, Albright Coll., 1969; MS, So. Ill. U., 1972; PhD, Tex. A&M U., 1974. Petroleum exploration geologist Cities Svc. Oil Co., Denver, 1974-76; asst. prof. geology U. Ala., Tuscaloosa, 1976-79, assoc. prof., 1979-84, prof., 1984—, Disting. Rsch. prof., 2005—. State geologist, oil and gas supr. State Ala., Tuscaloosa, 1982-96; regional dir. Ea. Gulf Region of the Petroleum Tech. Transfer Coun., 1995—; founding dir. Ctr. Sedimentary Basin Studies, U. Ala., 1998—. Contbr. articles to profl. jours. Geol. Soc. Am. fellow; recipient Nat. Coun. Citation Albright Coll., 1983, Pratt-Haas Disting. Lectr. Am. Assn. Petroleum Geologists, 1987-88. Mem. Geol. Soc. Am. (past chmn. S.E. sect.), Am. Assn. Petroleum Geologists (A.I. Levorsen petroleum geology Meml. award Gulf Coast Assn., geol. socs. sect. 1980, chair rsch. com. 2001-04, assoc. editor, 2003-04, editor, 2004-07, Disting. Educator award 2000), Assn. Am. State Geologists (hon., past pres.), Am. Geol. Inst. (past pres., Ian Campbell medal 2004), Nat. Assn. State Univs. and Land-Grant Colls. (past chair, mineral and energy resources sect. mem. bd. natural resources), Soc. Econ. Paleontologists and Mineralogists Gulf Coast sect. (hon., past pres.), Paleontol. Soc. (past pres. southeast sect.), Ala. Geol. Soc. (past pres.), Gulf Coast Assn. Geol. Scis. (hon., Outstanding Educator award 1998), Sigma Xi (past chpt. pres.), Phi Kappa Phi (past chpt. pres.), Phi Sigma. Presbyterian. Home: 15271 Four Winds Loop Northport AL 35475-3325 Office: U Ala Dept Geol Scis PO Box 870338 Tuscaloosa AL 35487-0338 Business E-Mail: emancini@geo.ua.edu.

MANCINI, JOHN, editor, publishing executive; b. NYC; m. Laura Litterello; 2 children. BA in Comm. Arts, LI Univ-C.W. Post. Reporter Greenwich Time, 1982—83; copy editor Stamford Advocate, Conn., 1983—85; presentation editor NY Times, 1995; dep. met. editor NY Post, 1995—96, met. editor, 1999—2001; founding editor-in-chief LI Voice, 1996—99; editorial asst. Newsday, 1980—82, copy editor, graphics editor, Sunday news editor, night city editor, day city editor, NY edition, 1985—95, met. editor, 2001—03, asst. mng. editor/NY, 2003—04, exec. v.p., editor, 2004—. Office: Newsday 235 Pinelawn Rd Melville NY 11747-4250 Office Phone: 631-843-4177. Office Fax: 631-843-4719. Business E-Mail: john.mancini@newsday.com. *

MANCINO, DOUGLAS MICHAEL, lawyer; b. May 8, 1949; s. Paul and Adele (Brazaitis) M.; m. Carol Keith, June 16, 1973. BA, Kent State U., 1971; JD, Ohio State U., 1974. Bar: Ohio 1974, U.S. Tax Ct. 1977, Calif. 1981, D.C. 1981. Assoc. Baker & Hostetler, Cleve., 1974-80; ptnr. Memel & Ellsworth, LA, 1980-87, McDermott, Will & Emery, LA, 1987—. Bd. dirs. Health Net of Calif. Inc. Author: Taxation of Hospitals and Health Care Organizations, 2000, (with others) Hospital Survival Guide, 1984, Navigating the Federal Physician Self-Referral Law, 1998; (with F. Hill) Taxation of Exempt Organizations, 2002; co-author quar. tax column Am. Hosp. Assn. publ. Health Law Vigil, (with L. Burns) Joint Ventures Between Hosps. and Physicians, 1987; contbr. articles to profl. jours. Chmn. bd. dirs. The Children's Burn Found.; bd. dirs. Kent State U. Found., Inc. Mem. ABA (tax, bus., real property, probate and trust sects., chair exempt orgns. com. 1995-97, coun. dir. 1999—), Calif. State Bar Assn. (tax, bus. law sects.), Ohio Bar Assn., Calif. State Bar, D.C. Bar Assn., Am. Health Lawyers Assn. (bd. dirs. 1986-95, pres. 1993-94), Calif. Soc. for Healthcare Attys., Bel Air Country Club, The Regency Club, Calif. Yacht Club. Office: McDermott Will & Emery 2049 Century Park E Fl 34 Los Angeles CA 90067-3101 E-mail: dmancino@mwe.com.

MANCINO, JOHN GREGORY, software company executive; b. NYC, Nov. 14, 1946; s. John D. and Carmela A. Mancino. BA, Colgate U., 1968. Chief appraiser Rusciano Appraisers & Cons., NYC, 1968-70; v.p. Pisces Prodns., Boulder, Colo., 1971-73; v.p. ops. Celestial Seasonings, Inc., Boulder, Colo., 1973-84, also dir.; dir. Strategic Info. Group, 1994—; founder, owner DeviceWorks Co., 2002—. Bd. dirs. Computer Connection, Inc., Mr. Software, Inc., Spruce St. Mktg., Inc., Fortune 44 Co., Inc.; pres., bd. dirs. Decision Makers Software, 1984—; chmn. Generation 5 Tech., 1985-89, Preferred Bus. Investments, Ltd., 1986-90; founder, dir. Device-Works Co., 2002—. Author: (software) Tattletale, 1991. Office: 214 Mountain Meadows Rd Boulder CO 80302-9256 E-mail: mancino@decismkr.com.

MANCOFF, NEAL ALAN, lawyer; b. Chgo., May 7, 1939; s. Isadore and Sarah (Leviton) M.; m. Alys Belofsky, June 26, 1966; children: Wesley, Frederick, Daniel. BBA, U. Wis., 1961; JD, Northwestern U., 1965. Bar: Ill. 1965, U.S. Dist. Ct. (no. dist.) Ill. 1965. Assoc. Aaron Aaron Schimberg & Hess, Chgo., 1965-72, ptnr., 1972-80, Schiff Hardin & Waite, Chgo., 1980—. Author: Qualified Deferred Compensation Plans, l983, Nonqualified Deferred Compensation Agreements, l987. Lst lt. U.S. Army, l961-62. Mem. Chgo. Bar Assn. (chmn. employee benefits com. l984). Office: Schiff Hardin LLC 7500 Sears Tower Chicago IL 60606

MANCUSO, J(OHN) JAMES, librarian; b. Olean, NY, Apr. 19, 1958; s. Frank A. and Josephine (Romano) M. m. Kathleen M. Petrie, June 29, 1985; children: Nicholas, Victoria, Benjamin. BA, Syracuse U., 1979, MLS, 1983. Bibliographic asst. Ctrl. Libr. Coun., Syracuse, N.Y., 1980-83; quality control specialist BRS, Latham, N.Y., 1983-86; asst. dir. libr. Capital Dist. Libr. Coun., Albany, N.Y., 1986-2000; libr. Mid-Am. Bapt. Theol. Sem., Schenectady, N.Y., 2000—. Reference libr. Schenectady County Pub. Libr., Schenectady, N.Y., part-time 1993-2001; book reviewer Pub. Rsch. Quar., 1995-97. Editor, compiler: Directory of Repositories, 2000; contbr. articles to profl. jours.; inventor Orderly Arrangement of Knowledge (OAK)libr. classification sys.; designer Internet web-sites. Ch. libr. 1st Presbyn. Ch., Schenectady, 1993— Mem. N.Y. Libr. Assn. (legis. com. 1992-97, sect. on mgmt. of resources and tech. smart Dewey fellow 1992), Hudson-Mohawk Libr. Assn. (pres. 1993-97), Capital Area Archivists N.Y. (v.p. 1992-94). Republican. Avocations: victorian architecture, genealogy, seashells, calligraphy. Office: Mid-Am Bapt Theol Sem 2810 Curry Rd Schenectady NY 12303 Office Phone: 518-355-4000. E-mail: jimancuso@mabtsne.edu.

MANCUSO, JOSEPH EDWARD, medical psychotherapist; b. Rockford, Ill., Dec. 1, 1955; s. Robert and Anne Mancuso. Student, Bradley U., Peoria, Ill., 1974-76; BA in Psychology, Marquette U., 1984, MEd in Ednl. Psychology, 1987. Diplomate Am. Bd. Med. Psychotherapists; LCSW, Wis.; lic. profl. counselor, alcohol and drug abuse counselor, Wis. Child care worker Community Care Svcs. Inc., Milw., 1978—79; day care dir. Mich. Street Day Care, Milw., 1979—80; adminstrv. unit clk. Milw. Jewish Nursing Home, 1980—81; day care tchr. St. Mary's Children's Sch., Milw., 1983—84; psychotherapist Wis. Correctional Svcs., Milw., 1984—90; coord. alcohol and other drug abuse St. Mary's Psychiat. Hosp., Milw., 1990-92; pvt. practice Lighthouse Clinic, Milw., 1993—2004; emergency rm. social worker Sinai Samaritan Med. Ctr., Milw., 1994-99; intake psychotherapist psychiat. svcs. Behav. Health Intake Ctr.-Sinai Samaritan Med. Ctr., Milw., 1999-2000; childrens psychotherapist Sinai Samaritan Med. Ctr., Milw., 2000—02, adult psychotherapist, 2002—03, geriatric psychotherapist, 2003; program psychotherapist Aurora Psychiat. Hosp., Wauwatosa, Wis., 2003—. Cons., presenter in field. Cartoonist, published and shown in galleries throughout Milw. Mem. APA, Wis. Psychol. Assn. (assoc.), Am. Ednl. Rsch. Assn. Avocations: hiking, drawing, birdwatching, writing. Home: 1612 E Hartford Ave Milwaukee WI 53211-3036 Office: Aurora Psychiat Hosp 1220 Dewey Ave Wauwatosa WI 53213 Office Phone: 414-454-6695.

MANCUSO, JULIA, skier, Olympic athlete; b. Reno, Nev., Mar. 9, 1984; d. Ciro and Andrea Mancuso. Mem. U.S. Winter Olympics Team, 2006; designer Super Jules Underwear. Mem.: U.S. Ski Team. Achievements include Am. record for medals and gold medals, Jr. World Championships Downhill Skiing; bronze medal in Super-G and Giant Slalom, World Championships, 2005; gold medal in Giant Slalom, Olympic Winter Games, Torino, 2006. Avocations: surfing, water-skiing, mountain biking, kite-boarding. Office: US Ski and Snowboard Assn 1500 Kearns Blvd Park City UT 84060

MANCUSO, MARIO, federal agency administrator; b. 1969; BA, Harvard U., 1991; JD, NYU Sch. Law, 1995. Law clk. to Hon. Thomas C. Platt US Dist. Ct. (ea. dist.) NY; atty. Ropes & Gray Internat. Law Firm, 1995—2005; spl. counsel US Dept. Def., 2005, dep. asst. sec. for spl. ops. & combating terrorism, 2005—07; under sec. for ind. & security US Dept. Commerce, 2007—. Served in US Army, Operation Iraqi Freedom. Office: US Dept Commerce Bur Industry & Security 14th St and Constitution Ave NW Washington DC 20230 Office Phone: 202-482-4811. *

MANCUSO, MICHAEL JOHN, retired corporate financial executive; Grad., Villanova U.; MBA, Ea. Coll. Exec. in fin. mgmt. space systems divsn. GE; CFO land systems divsn. Gen. Dynamics, Falls Church, Va., 1993-94, v.p., contr., 1994-97, sr. v.p., CFO, 1997—2006. Bd. dir. SPX Corp., 2005—, Agere Systems Inc., 2006—, Shaw Group Inc., 2006—. Mailing: SPX Corp Bd Directors 13515 Ballantyne Corp Pl Charlotte NC 28277

MANCUSO, PETER, medical educator; b. Somerville, NJ, July 15, 1962; s. Joseph and Anita Mancuso; m. Alison Maud Hightower, Sept. 17, 1987; children: Jonathan Hightower, Christopher Hightower, Amanda Catherine. BS, Purdue U., West Lafayette, Ind., 1985; MS, U. Tenn., Knoxville, 1987, PhD, 1996. Food scientist Ragu Foods, Shelton, Conn., 1987—90, rsch. food scientist, 1990; grad. student rsch. and tchg. asst. U. Tenn., Knoxville, 1990—96; postdoctoral rsch. fellow U. Mich. Med. Ctr., Ann Arbor, 1997—99; asst. prof. U. Mich., Ann Arbor, 2000—. Rsch. asst., U. Tenn. Grad. Sch. Medicine, 1994—96, grantee, NIH, 1997—98, rsch. fellow, Am. Lung Assn. of Mich., 1999—2000, rsch. grantee, Am. Lung Assn., 2001—03, NIH-Heart, Lung, and Blood Inst., 2006—. Mem.: Am. Assn. of Immunologists (assoc.), Am. Thoracic Soc. (assoc.). Lutheran. Achievements include research in role of leptin in pulmonary innate host defense. Avocation: cycling. Office: U Mich 109 S Observatory Dr Ann Arbor MI 48109 Office Phone: 734-615-5158. Office Fax: 734-936-7283.

MAND, MARTIN GARY, financial executive; b. Norfolk, Va., Sept. 26, 1936; s. Meyer J. and Lena (Sutton) M.; m. Shelly Cohen, Aug. 29, 1965; children: Gregory S., Michael E., Brian C. BS in Commerce, U. Va., 1958; MBA, U. Del., 1964. Various fin. staff and mgmt. positions E.I. du Pont de Nemours & Co., Wilmington, Del., 1961-81, v.p. taxes and fin. svcs., 1981-84, v.p., comptr., 1984-88, v.p., treas., 1989-90; sr. v.p., CFO, Nortel Networks, Mississauga, Ont., Canada, 1990—93, exec. v.p., CFO, 1993—94; chmn. pres., CEO Mand Assocs., Ltd., Wilmington, 1995—. Bd. dirs. Mizuho Corp Bank U.S.A., NYC, Townsends, Inc., Wilmington, Del., Factory Card and Party Outlet, Naperville, Ill.; pres. Fin. Execs. Rsch. Found., 1988—90. Co-author: (book) Partnering for Performance: Unleashing the Power of Finance in the 21st Century Organization, 2000. Lt. USN, 1958-61. Mem. Fin. Execs. Inst., Am. Mgmt. Assn. (chmn. fin. coun.). Office: 618 Berwick Rd Ste 100 Wilmington DE 19803-2204 Office Phone: 302-478-5644. Personal E-mail: mandassociates@comcast.net.

MANDABACH, CARYN, television producer; m. Paul Mandabach; children: Marisa, Jon. Pres. Carsey-Werner Co., Studio City, Calif., 1987—; co-founder Oxygen Media, NYC, 1998—. Exec. prodr., prodr.: (TV series) The Cosby Show, Roseanne, A Different World, Grace Under Fire, Cybill, Third Rock from the Sun, That '70s Show, God, the Devil and Bob, Normal, Ohio, Grounded for Life, You Don't Know Jack, The Downer Channel, That '80s Show, 2002, Are We There Yet?, 2003, Whoopi, 2003, The Tracy Morgan Show, 2003, Game Over, 2004, Good Girls Don't..., 2004, (TV films) Are We There Yet, 2003, These Guys, 2003, Blue Aloha, 2004, (films) Let's Go to Prison, 2006. Bd. dirs. The Center Theatre Group, The Curtis Sch., AFI Third Decade C. Recipient Emmy for The Cosby Show, Humanitas award, People's Choice award, Peabody award. Office: Oxygen Media 75 9th Ave New York NY 10011-7006 *

MANDARICH, DAVID D., real estate corporation executive; b. 1948; With Majestic Savs. and Loan, 1966-67, MDC Holdings Inc., Denver, 1977—, bd. dir., 1980—89, 1994—, chmn. Richmond Am. Homes, 1990—93, exec. v.p. real estate, 1993—94, co-COO, 1994—96, COO, 1996—, pres., 1999—. Office: MDC Holdings 4350 S Monaco St Denver CO 80237 *

MANDEL, ADRIENNE ABRAMSON, state legislator; b. Irvington, NJ, Sept. 30, 1936; d. Nathaniel and Florence (Lebovitz) Abramson; m. Emanuel Mandel, 1958; children: Lisa Mandel-Trupp, David. BA, Rutgers U., 1958; MA, George Washington U., 1984. Exec. program cert.: Harvard U., JF Kennedy Sch. Govt. 2003. Chairwoman, vice chairwoman Precinct 13-56, 1979-94; parole officer, social svc. case worker N.J. Dept. Inst. & Agencies, 1958-60; survey interviewer U.S. Census Bur., 1973-77; monitoring and evaluation specialist Divsn. Labor Svc., Montgomery County Govt., 1979-81; asst. dir. Sr. Ctr. Divsn. Elder Affairs, Dept. Family Resources, 1981-84; staff asst. Office Chief Adminstr., 1984-85; legis. rep. Office Intergovt. Rels., 1985-94; mem. Md. State Legislature, 1995—, mem. commerce govt. matters com., 1995—2002, mem. health and govt. ops. com., 2003—, dep. majority whip, 2003—. Pres. Women's Caucus, 2002-03; bi-county chair Montgomery County Del., 1999—; health issues chair Nat. Order Women Legislators, 1999—; mem. exec. bd. Nat. Found. Women Legislators, 2004—. Named one of Md. Top 100 Women, The Daily Record, 2002, 2004; recipient Woman of Valor award, B'nai B'rith Women, 1972, MD Profl. Driver Educators Legis. of Year, 1998, MD League Conservation Voters Environ. Leadership award, Nat. Capitol Homecare Assn. Pres. award, 2001, MD Nurses Assn. Legislator of Yr., 2002, Montgomery County NOW Legislator of Yr., 2003, Significant Contribution to Med. Cmty. award, Montgomery County Med. Soc., 2005. Mem. Women's Polit. Caucus, Mothers Against Drunk Driving, Md. Govt. Rels. Assn., Montgomery County Ethnic Heritage Festival, LWV, Alpha Psi Omega, Delta Phi Delta.

MANDEL, BABALOO, scriptwriter; b. NYC; 6 children. Screenwriter: (with Lowell Ganz) Night Shift, 1982, (with Bruce Jay Friedman) Splash, 1984 (Academy award nomination best original screenplay 1984), (with Dan Aykroyd) Spies Like Us, 1985, Vibes, 1988, Parenthood, 1989, City Slickers, 1991, A League of Their Own, 1992, (with Billy Crystal) Mr. Saturday Night, 1992, Greedy, 1994, City Slickers II: The Legend of Curley's Gold, 1994, (with Billy Crystal) Forget Paris, 1995, Multiplicity, 1996, Father's Day, 1997, Edtv, 1999, Where the Heart Is, 2000, Robots, 2005, Fever Pitch, 2005; writer: (TV series) Happy Days, 1974-84, Laverne and Shirley, 1976-83,Herndon, 1983; writer, assoc. prodr.: Gung Ho, 1986; creator (TV series) Knight and Daye, 1989; appearances include (film) Splash, 1984, (TV) Naked Hollywood, 1991. Office: Creative Artists Agy 9830 Wilshire Blvd Beverly Hills CA 90212-1804

MANDEL, BRETT H., community organization executive, writer; m. Laura Weinbaum; children: Rose, Ariel, Sidney. BA, Hamilton Coll.; MGA, U. Pa. Assoc. Pa. Economy League; asst. to policy dir. Phila. Independent Charter Commn.; former dir. fin. and policy analysis City of Phila. Office of Controller; exec. dir. Phila. Forward. Author: Minor Players, Major Dreams, 1997, This Heaven? The Magic of the Field of Dreams, 2002; co-author: Philadelphia: A New Urban Direction, 1999 (Nat. Assn. of Local Govt. Auditors Special Project Award, 1999). Commr. Greater Phila. Men's Adult Baseball League. Named one of 40 Under 40, Phila. Bus. Jour., 2006. Office: Phila Forward 1700 Market St, Ste 3130 Philadelphia PA 19103 Office Phone: 215-563-3881. Office Fax: 215-563-1566.

MANDEL, CAROL, university librarian; b. Bklyn., Dec. 18, 1946; d. Irwin Daniel and Charlotte Mandel; m. Vincent T. Covello. BA magna cum laude, U. Mass., 1968; MSLS with honors, Columbia U., 1970, MA in Art History, 1975. Reference libr. Northeastern U. Libr., Boston, 1970; architecture and fine arts cataloger Columbia U. Librs., NYC, 1971-75, asst. to head original monographs cataloging dept., 1975-77, head original monographs cataloging dept., 1977-79, dir. tech. svcs., 1986-91, dir. tech. and networked info. svcs., 1991-93, dep. univ. libr., 1993—99; assoc. exec. dir. Assn. Rsch. Librs., Washington, 1979-83; asst., assoc. univ. libr. assess svcs. U. Calif., San Diego Librs., 1983-86; dean libr. NYU, 1999—. Mem. coop. cataloging coun. Libr. Congress, 1993-95, mem. seminar on copy cataloging, 1992, cons., 1985; reviewer, panelist, site visitor NEH, 1978-94; panelist NEA Title II-C grant program Dept. Edn., 1982, 84, 86, 89; mem. pres.'s commn. on tech. processing Rsch. Librs. Group, 1991, mem. bibtech steering com., 1988-90; presenter in field. Contbr. articles to profl. publs. Grantee NEH, 1980-83, 83-86, 89-93, 93—, Dept. Edn., 1989-95. Mem. ALA (vice chair tech. svcs. dirs. of large rsch. librs. discussion group 1992, editorial bd. 1993—, chair various coms., Margaret Mann citation for outstanding profl. achievement in cataloging or classification 1994), Assn. Rsch. Librs. (cons. 1983-86, project dir. microform project, CONSER A&I coverage project), Coun. on Libr. Resources (chair bibliographic svcs. study com. 1987-93, cons.), Ctr. for Rsch. Librs. (mem. access adv. panel 1992—). Office: Columbia U Librs 535 W 114th St New York NY 10027-7035 also: NYU The Elmer Holmes Bobst Library Rm 1134 70 Washington Sq S New York NY 10012 Office Phone: 212-998-2444. Office Fax: 212-995-4070. E-mail: carol.mandel@nyu.edu. *

MANDEL, GAIL, immunologist; BS in Immunology, UCLA, PhD. Faculty Harvard Med. Sch., Tufts-New England Med. Ctr.; disting. prof. SUNY, StonyBrook, 1997—2006; investigator Howard Hughes Med. Inst., 2006—; sr. scientist Oreg. Health & Sci. Univ., Portland, 2006—. Recipient Jacob Javits award, NIH, McKnight Investigator award in Neurosciences. Fellow: AAAS, Am. Acad. Arts & Scis. Office: Oreg Health Sci Univ Vollum Inst L-474 3181 SW Sam Jackson Park Rd Portland OR 97239 *

MANDEL, HAROLD GEORGE, pharmacologist, educator; b. Berlin, June 6, 1924; came to U.S., 1937, naturalized, 1944; s. Ernest A. and Else (Crail) M.; m. Marianne Klein, July 25, 1953; children: Marcia Mandel Halgren, Audrey Lynn Todd. BS, Yale U., 1944, PhD, 1949. Lab. instr. in chemistry Yale U., 1942-44, 47-49; rsch. assoc. dept. pharmacology George Washington U. Sch. Medicine and Health Scis., 1949-50, asst. rsch. prof., 1950-52, assoc. prof. pharmacology, 1952-58, prof., 1958—, chmn. dept. pharmacology, 1960-96. Advanced Commonwealth Fund fellow Molteno Inst. Cambridge (Eng.) U., 1956; Commonwealth Fund fellow U. Auckland (N.Z.) and U. Med. Scis., Bangkok, Thailand, 1964; Am. Cancer Soc. Eleanor Roosevelt Internat. fellow Chester Beatty Research Inst. London, 1970-71; Am. Cancer Soc. scholar U. Calif., San Francisco, 1978-79; fellow Med. Research Council toxicology unit, Carshalton, Eng., 1986; Burroughs Wellcome Rsch. travel grant, Carshalton, 1988; hon. rsch. fellow dept. biochemistry and molecular biology U. Coll., London, 1993,

96, 97; mem. com. problems drug safety NRC-NAS, 1965-76, mem. com. on toxicology, 1978-82, mem. various panels, 1981-86; mem. cancer chemotherapy com. Internat. Union Against Cancer, 1966-73, fellow, Lyon, France, 1989; mem. external rev. com. Howard U. Cancer Research Center, 1972-74; cons. Bur. Drugs, FDA, 1975-79, EPA, 1978-82; mem. toxicology adv. com. FDA, 1975-78; mem. med. research service merit rev. bd. in alcoholism and drug dependence VA, 1975-78; mem. cancer spl. program adv. com. Nat. Cancer Inst., 1974-78, chmn., 1976-78; mem. Nat. Large Bowel Cancer Project Working Cadre, 1980-84; mem. Kettering award selection com. GM Cancer Rsch. Found., 1979-81; bd. advisors Roswell Park Cancer Inst., Buffalo, 1972-74. Editorial bd.: Jour. Pharmacology and Exptl. Therapeutics, 1960-65, field editor, 1978-94; editorial bd.: Molecular Pharmacology, 1965-69, Rsch. Comm. in Chem. Pathology, Pharmacology, 1972-98, Cancer Drug Delivery, Selective Cancer Therapeutics, 1983-92, Cancer Research, 1974-76, assoc. editor, 1977-81. Served with AUS, 1944-46. Recipient John J. Abel award in pharmacology Eli Lilly and Co., 1958, Disting. Achievement award Washington Acad. Scis., 1958, Golden Apple Teaching award AMA, 1969, 85, 97, Sci. Emeritus award Soc. Biology & Medicine, 1999. Fellow AAAS; mem. Am. Chem. Soc., Am. Soc. Biochemistry and Molecular Biology, Am. Soc. Pharmacology and Exptl. Therapeutics (pres. 1973-74), Am. Assn. Cancer Rsch., Assn. Med. Sch. Pharmacology Chairs (pres. 1976-78), Nat. Caucus of Basic Biomed. Sci. Chairs (chmn. 1991—), Citizens Pub. Rsch. and Edn. Funding (sec. 1996-99), Cosmos Club (Washington), Sigma Xi, Alpha Omega Alpha. Democrat. Achievements include research, numerous publs. on cancer chemotherapy, mechanism of growth inhibition, antimetabolites, drug disposition, chemical carcinogenesis. Home: Apt 302 4956 Sentinel Dr Bethesda MD 20816-3594 Office: George Washington U Sch Medicine and Health Scis Dept Pharmacology and Physiology 2300 I St NW Washington DC 20037-2336 Home Phone: 301-320-4450; Office Phone: 202-994-3542. Business E-Mail: phmhgm@gwumc.edu. E-mail: hgmandel@verizon.net.

MANDEL, HERBERT MAURICE, civil engineer; b. Port Chester, NY, May 11, 1924; s. Arthur William and Rose (Schmeiser) M.; m. Charlotte Feldman, Aug. 22, 1954; children: Rosanne Mandel Levine, Elliott D., Arthur M. BSCE, Va. Poly. Inst., 1948; M Engring., Yale U., 1949. Registered profl. engr., N.Y., Conn., Fla., Md., Mich., Minn., Ohio, Pa., Va., W.Va. Structural engr. Madigan Hyland Co., LI, NY, 1949—50; mem. Parsons, Brinckerhoff, Quade & Douglas, Inc., 1950—86; v.p. GAI Cons., Inc., Monroeville, Pa., 1986—2004, prin. staff cons., 1993—2004, sr. staff cons., 2004—. Resident engr., Chgo., 1961, Atlanta, 1962, project. mgr., N.Y.C., 1963-70, Honolulu, 1970-74, v.p., 1974, sr. v.p., Pitts., 1977-86; mem. faculty Yale U., 1948-49; adj. faculty Bklyn. Poly. Inst., 1956-64, U. Pitts., 1986; gen. chmn. 6th Internat. Bridge Conf., Pitts., 1989. Prin. works include (prin.-in-charge) Williamstown-Marietta Bridge, W.Va.-Ohio, Dunbar Bridge, W.Va., I-64 Bridge over Big Sandy River, W.Va.-Ky., Davis Creek Bridge, Charleston, W.Va., Tygart R. Bridge, W.Va., Easley Bridge, Bluefield, W.Va., Fayette Sta. Bridge, Fayetteville, W.Va., Mon Valley Expwy., W.Va., King Coal Hwy, W.Va., Romney Bridge, W.Va., (project mgr.) Newport Bridge, Narragansett Bay, R.I., (designer/project engr.) Hackensack River Bridge, N.J., Housatanic River Bridge, Conn., Arthur Kill Vertical Lift R.R. Bridge, S.I., N.Y., 62d St. Bridge, Pitts., Savannah River Cantilever Bridge, Ga., I-84 Bridges, Danbury, Conn., (structural rehab. designer) Avondale Bridge, N.J, Lincoln Bridge, N.J., B&O R.R. Bridge, Vincennes, Ind., Hawk St. Viaduct, Albany, N.Y., Congress Ave. Bridge, Austin, Tex., Ohio St. Bridge, Buffalo, Panhandle Bridge, Pitts.; project dir. design and constrn. Pitts. Light Rail Transit Sys., 1977-84; designer Elizabeth R. Tunnel, Norfolk, Va., 1950. Served to 1st lt. U.S. Army, 1943-46, 50-52, ETO. Fellow ASCE, Soc. Am. Mil. Engrs.; mem. NSPE, Engrs. Soc. We. Pa. (exec. com. Internat. Bridge Conf. 1986—, gen. chmn. 1988-89), Am. Rlwy. Engring. and Maintenance of Way Assn. (steel structures specifications com. 1974—), Profl. Engrs. in Pvt. Practice (bd. govs. 1994-96, profl. devel. coun. 1995-97), Pa. Profl. Engrs. in Pvt. Practice (state vice-chmn. 1992-94, chmn. 1994-96), Pa. Soc. Profl. Engrs. (dir. Pitts. chpt. 1995-98), Internat. Assn. Bridge and Structural Engring., Assn. for Bridge Constrn. and Design, Engrs. Club Pitts., Tau Beta Pi, Chi Epsilon, Omicron Delta Kappa, Phi Kappa Phi, Pi Delta Epsilon, Scabbard and Blade. Jewish. Home: 920 Parkview Dr Pittsburgh PA 15243-1116 Office: GAI Cons Inc 385 Waterfront Dr E Homestead PA 15120-5005 Home Phone: 412-561-4881. Business E-Mail: h.mandel@gaiconsultants.com.

MANDEL, HOWIE, actor, comedian; b. Toronto, Ont., Can., Nov. 29, 1955; m. Terry Mandel, Mar. 1980; children: Jacklyn Perry, Riley, Alex. Actor: (films) Gas, 1981, The Funny Farm, 1983, (voice) Gremlins, 1984, A Fine Mess, 1986, Walk Like a Man, 1987, Little Monsters, 1989, (voice) Gremlins 2: The New Batch, 1990, Magic Kid II, 1994, Spin Cycle, 2000, Tribulation, 2000, (voice) The Tangerine Bear, 2000, Hansel & Gretel, 2002, (voice) Pinocchio 3000, 2004, (TV series) Laugh Trax, 1982, (voice) Muppet Babies, 1984-91, St. Elsewhere, 1983, 85, 88, Good Grief, 1990-91, The Amazing Live Sea-Monkeys, 1992; exec. prodr.: Howie Mandel on Ice, 1997, The Legend of Willie Brown, 1998, The Howie Mandel Show, 1998, Hidden Howie, 2005-; host: Howie Mandel's Sunny Skies, 1995, Deal or No Deal, 2005-; comedian various nighclubs and venues; opening act for Diana Ross, Las Vegas. Office: c/o 3 Arts Entertainment 9460 Wilshire Blvd 7th Fl Beverly Hills CA 90212

MANDEL, IRWIN DANIEL, dentist; b. Bklyn., Apr. 9, 1922; s. Samuel A. and Shirley (Blankstein) M.; m. Charlotte Lifschutz, Apr. 1, 1944; children: Carol, Nora, Richard. BS, CCNY, 1942; DDS, Columbia U., 1945; DSc (hon.), U. Medicine and Dentistry N.J., 1981, U. Göteborg, 1984, Columbia U., 1996. Rsch. asst. Dental Sch. Columbia U., 1946-48, mem. faculty Dental Sch., 1946—, prof. dentistry, dir. div. preventive dentistry Dental Sch., 1969-84, dir. Ctr. Clin. Rsch. in Dentistry Dental Sch., 1984-91, assoc. dean rsch., 1991-92; prof. emeritus Dental Sch., 1992—; pvt. practice dentistry, 1946-68; vis. prof. various dental schs.; chmn. oral biology and medicine study sect. Nat. Inst. Dental Rsch., 1974-76. Co-author: The Plaque Diseases, 1972; contbr. over 250 articles to profl. jours., chpts. to books. Active local chpt. Peace Action, Physicians for Social Responsibility. Lt. Dental Corps USNR, 1945-46, 52-54. Recipient Career Scientist award, N.Y.C. Health Rsch. Coun., 1969—72, Leadership award in periodontology, Tufts U. Dental Sch., 1971, Internat. award, U. Conn. Sch. Dental Medicine, 1979, Seymour J. Kreshover NIDR Lectr. award, 1986, Townsend Harris medal, CCNY, 2000. Fellow AAAS, Am. Coll. Dentists; mem. ADA (chmn. coun. dental rsch. 1978-80, Gold medal for excellence in rsch. 1985), Dental Soc. (Henry Spenadel award 1973, Jarvie-Burkhart Internat. award 1990), Am. Assn. Dental Rsch. (pres. 1980), Am. Assn. Pub. Health Dentists (Disting. Svc. award 1991), Fed. Dentair Internat. (W. D. Miller prize 1992), Internat. Assn. Dental Rsch. (Salivary Rsch. award 1994, Disting. Svc. award 2001), N.Y. Acad. Scis., Sigma Xi, Omicron Kappa Upsilon. Home and Office: 1305 Holly Ln Cedar Grove NJ 07009 Personal E-mail: irwindmandel@optonline.net.

MANDEL, JACK N., manufacturing executive; b. Austria, July 16, 1911; s. Sam and Rose M.; m. Lilyan, Aug. 14, 1938 (dec.) Student, Fenn Coll., 1930-33. Founder, former pres., chmn. Premier Indsl. Corp., Cleve.; chmn., pres. Manbro Corp.; exec. dir. Parkwood Corp.; gen. ptnr. Courtland Assocs. Former mem. exec. com. NCCJ; former life trustee Wood Hosp.; trustee Fla. Soc. for Blind; life trustee South Broward Jewish Fedn., Cleve. Jewish Welfare Fedn.; former pres., life trustee Montefiore Home for Aged; pres. adv. bd. Barry U.; hon. trustee Hebrew U.; trustee Tel Aviv U. Mus. of the Diaspora; life trustee The Temple, Woodruff Found.; trustee Cleve. Play House. Mem. Beachmont Country Club, Commede Club, Union Club. Office: Parkwood Corp 2829 Euclid Ave Cleveland OH 44115-2413 Office Phone: 216-875-6502.

MANDEL, JOEL EMANUEL, orthopedist; b. BKlyn., Mar. 1, 1930; s. Morris and Minnie Mandel. BA, N.Y. U., 1951; MS, Ga. Inst. Tech., 1952; MD, Chgo. Med. Sch., 1956. Diplomate Am. Bd. Med. Examiners, Am. Bd. Orthop. Surgery, Am. Bd. Profl. Disabled Cons. Intern D.C. Gen. Hosp., 1956—57; resident in gen. surgery VA Hosp., 1957—58; resident in orthopedic surgery D.C. Gen. Hosp., 1958—60, N.Y. U., Bellevue, 1960—61; pres., founding ptnr. The New City (N.Y.) Orthopedic Group, P.C., 1961—85; med. dir. Post-Trauma Med. Svcs., New Windsor, NY, 1985—. Host weekly radio program Medicine Today, 1973—76. Mem. editl. bd. Jour. Disability, 1990—93, Disability, 1995—96. Bd. govs. Rockland County (N.Y.) Health Complex, 1977—88; mem. coord. coun. Rockland County Emergency Med. Svc., 1977—81. Recipient Rockland County Dist. Svc. award, 1973. Fellow: ACS, NY State Soc. Surgeons, Am. Acad. Orthop. Surgeons, Internat. Coll. Surgeons, Am. Acad. Disability Evaluating Physicians (bd. dirs. 1988—93, sec. 1990—93); mem.: Rockland County Med. Soc. (dir. pub. rels. 1967—73, exec. com. 1967—76, peer rev. com. 1973—85, pres. 1974—75, chmn. bd. censors 1975—76), Orange County Med. Soc. (peer rev. com. 1987—, exec. com. 1994—), Ea. Orthop. Assn., NY State Soc. Orthop. Surgeons (bd. dirs. 1976—82). Avocations: sailing, windsurfing, computer science, astronomy. Office: Post-Trauma Med Svc PC 833 Blooming Grove Tpk New Windsor NY 12553 Office Phone: 845-561-2000. E-mail: bonedoc@frontiernet.net.

MANDEL, JOSEPH DAVID, academic administrator, lawyer; b. NYC, Mar. 26, 1940; s. Max and Charlotte Lee (Goodman) M.; m. Jean Carol Westerman, Aug. 18, 1963; children: Jonathan Scott, Eric David. AB, Dartmouth Coll., 1960, MBA with distinction, 1961; JD, Yale U., 1964. Bar: Calif. 1965. Law clk. U.S. Ct. Appeals, 9th cir., LA, 1964-65; lectr. law U. So. Calif. Law Ctr., LA, 1965-68; assoc. atty. Tuttle & Taylor, LA, 1965-69, mem., 1970-82, 90-91, of counsel, 1984-90; vice chancellor UCLA, 1991—2007, lectr. in law, 1993, 2001—02, spl. asst. chancellor legal affairs, 2007—; v.p., gen. counsel, sec. Natomas Co., San Francisco, 1983. Bd. dirs. LRN, The Legal Knowledge Co., 1993-2005. Mem. bd. editors Yale Law Jour., 1962-64. Pres. Legal Aid Found., L.A., 1978-79; trustee Southwestern U. Sch. Law, 1982, UCLA Pub. Interest Law Found., 1981-82, L.A. County Bar Found., 1974-79, 82, Coro Found., 1989-92, UCLA Armand Hammer Mus. Art and Cultural Ctr., 1995—, Geffen Playhouse, Inc., 1995-98, Coro So. Calif. Ctr., 1985-92; bd. dirs. pub. coun., 1989-94, cmty. v.p., 1992-94; mem. L.A. Bd. Zoning Appeals, 1984-90, vice-chmn., 1985-86, 89-90, chmn., 1986-87; mem. L.A. City Charter Reform Commn., 1996-99; bd. dirs. Western Justice Ctr. Found., 1989—, v.p., 1992-95, 1st v.p., 1995-97, sr. v.p., 1997-99, pres., 1999-03; bd. dirs. Harvard Water Polo Found., 1990-96; bd. govs. Inner City Law Ctr., 1991-05; chair Blue Ribbon Screening Com. to Select Insp. Gen., L.A. Police Commn., 1999; mem. bd. overseers Inst. for Civil Justice, RAND, 1999—, bd. dirs. Children's Law Ctr. L.A., 2003-. Recipient Maynard Toll award Legal Aid Found. of L.A., 1991, Shattuck-Price award L.A. County Bar Assn., 1993, West Coast Liberty award Lambda Legal Def. and Edn. Fund, 1994, Cmty. Achievement award Pub. Coun., 1996, Stanley Mosk Liberty Through Justice award ADL, 2003; named One of Calif.'s 100 Most Influential Attys. by Calif. Bus. Jour., 2000. Mem. State Bar Calif. (legal svcs. trust fund commn. 1985-87, chmn. 1985-86), Yale U. Law Sch. Assn. (exec. com. 1983-88, 90-96, v.p. 1986-88, chmn. planning com. 1990-92, pres. 1992-94, chmn. exec. com. 1994-96), mem. alumni Coun. Dartmouth Coll., 1992-95, Dartmouth Coll. Assn. Alumni (exec. com. 1997-2002, v.p. 2001-02), L.A. Co. Bar Assn. (trustee 1974, 1975-81, v.p. 1977-78, sr. v.p. 1978-79, pres.-elect 1979-80, pres. 1980-81, chair pro bono coun. 1986-87), Order of Coif. Democrat. Home: 15478 Longbow Dr Sherman Oaks CA 91403-4910 Office: UCLA Office of the Chancellor 2135 Murphy Hl Los Angeles CA 90095-1405 Office Phone: 310-206-1355. Business E-Mail: jmandel@conet.ucla.edu.

MANDEL, JUDITH LYNN, primary school educator; b. Mpls., June 20, 1936; d. Lloyd L. and Gussie Miller Elzas; m. Seymour L. Mandel (div.); children: Lloyd J., Paula J. Cert. of X-Ray Tech., U. Minn., Mpls., 1958; BEd, Nat. Lewis U., Evanston, Ill., 1979. Substitute tchr. pub. schs., Wilmette and Winnetka, Ill., 1979—83; tchr. 2d grade Solomon Schechter Sch., Skokie, Ill., 1984—85; tchr. Haugan Sch., Chgo., 1986—90, Patrick Henry Sch., Chgo., 1991—. Vol. in pediatrics dept. Evanston Hosp., Ill.; den mother cub scouts Boy Scouts Am., Wilmette; leader brownie troop Girl Scouts U.S., Wilmette. Mem.: Chgo. Tchrs. Union, North Shore Sr. Ctr., Chgo. Bot. Gardens, Kappa Delta Pi, Alpha Epsilon Phi. Jewish. Avocations: rug hooking, exercise, reading, antiques, gardening. Home: 245 Essex Pl Wilmette IL 60091 Personal E-mail: judylyn2@aol.com.

MANDEL, KARYL LYNN, accountant; b. Chgo., Dec. 14, 1935; d. Isador J. and Eve (Gellar) Karzen; m. Fredric H. Mandel, Sept. 29, 1956; children: David Scott, Douglas Jay, Jennifer Ann. Student, U. Mich., 1954-56, Roosevelt U., 1956-57; AA summa cum laude, Oakton Community Coll., 1979. CPA, Ill; registered investment advisor; lic. life ins. provider. Pres. Excel Transp. Service Co., Elk Grove, Ill., 1958-78; tax mgr. CTB, Ltd., CPAs, Northbrook, Ill., 1981-83; tax ptnr. Chunowitz, Teitelbaum & Mandel, CPAs, Riverwoods, Ill., 1984—. Sec-treas. Lednam, Inc., Coffee Break, Inc.; mem. acctg. curriculum adv. bd. Oakton C.C., Des Plaines, Ill., 1987—; pres. Lednam Enterprises, LLC, 2001—. Contbg. author: Ill. CPA's News Jour., Acctg. Today. Recipient State of Israel Solidarity award, 1976. Mem. AICPA, Am. Soc. Women CPA, Women's Am. ORT (pres. Chgo. region 1972-74, v.p. midwest dist. 1975-76, nat. endowment com., nat investment adv. com.), Ill. CPA Soc. (chmn. estate and gift tax com. 1987-89, legis. contact com. 1981-82, pres. North Shore chpt., bd. dirs. 1989-91, award for Excellence in Acctg. Edn.), Chgo. Soc. Women CPA, Chgo. Estate Planning Coun., Nat. Assn. Women Bus. Owners, Lake County Estate Planning Coun., Greater North Shore Estate Planning Coun. Office: 302 Saunders Rd Ste 300 Riverwoods IL 60015 Office Phone: 847-444-1040. Business E-Mail: klm@ctbltd.com.

MANDEL, LESLIE ANN, investment advisor, writer; b. Washington, July 29, 1945; d. Seymour and Marjorie (Syble) Mandel; m. Arthur Herzog III, Oct. 27, 1999. BA in Art History, U. Minn., 1967; cert., N.Y. Sch. Interior Design, 1969. Cert. Brailled Libr. Congress. Pres. Leslie Mandel Enterprises, Inc., NYC, 1968—; sr. v.p. Maximum Entertainment Network, L.A. and NYC, 1988-90; pres. Rich List Co., 1968—; pres., CEO Mandel Airplane Funding and Leasing Corp., NYC, Hong Kong, China and Mongolia, 1990—; CEO Mandel-Khan Inc., Ulaanbaatar, Mongolia, 1994—, Travel Safe: keep hers, keep his, 2002—. Fin. advisor Osmed, Inc., Mpls., 1986—, Devine Comm./Allen & Co., NY, Del., Utah, N.Mex., NY, N.Y. WUWV, Utah KBER, WKTC-AM-FM, 1984—89, Am. Kefir Corp., NYC, 1983—89, Shore Group (Internat., Guyana), Flight Internat., 1991—; owner The Rich List Co., 150 internat. catalogs, mags. and fundraising lists; joint venture Mongolian Ind. Broadcasting Channel, Ulaanbaatar, 1995; pres., owner Mandel Airplane Funding and Leasing Corp.; rep. Israeli Govt. IAI Satellite, China, Romania, Costa Rica, Mongolia, Amos Satellite Network, China, 1992—; advisor rep. Gt. Wall Corp., Long March Corp., China, 1992—, Chinese Silk, 1993—, Am. Oil Refinery, 1993—; bd. dirs. Coastal Equipment Co., Bristol Airlines; cons. Exclusive Miat Airlines, Mongolia; purchasing agt. People's Republic of China-Aircraft; advisor Aeropostalis, Mexico, 1994—95; photographer; lectr. UN Internat. Direct Mail; advisor Aruba Airlines, Mexicana Airlines; aircraft agt., bd. dirs. Lazorlines Landing Equipment, 1997—; lease Estafada Airlines 757-200-C, 2000—, Chile Airlines 757-200C, 2002; advisor Guyana 2000 Airlines; ptnr. Laserline/Vulcan Power Plant, China, 2005, Greece, 2005—, Nicaragua, 2005—, Trinidad and Tobago, 2005—, Pakistan, 2005—, Turkmenistan, 2005—, Hungary, 2005—. Photographer: Vogue, 1978, New Earth Times, 1995, Fortune mag.; Braille transcriber: The Prophet (Kalil Gibran), 1967, Getting Ready for Battle (R. Prawe Jhabuala), 1967; exec. prodr. film: Hospital Audiences, 1975 (Cannes award 1976); author: Hungry at the Watering Hole, Gardiners Island, 1636-1990, 1989, Expedition: In the Steps of Ghengis Kahn, 1994; advisor Port Libertè Ptnrs., 1988-94; contbr. articles to profl. jours. Fin. advisor Correctional Assn., Osborn Soc., 1977—; founder, treas. Prisoners Family Transportation and Assistance Fund, N.Y., 1972-77; judge Emmy awards of Acad. TV Arts and Scis., N.Y.C., 1970; bd. dirs. Prisoners Assn., 1990; chmn. U.S.A. com. Violeta B. de Chamarro for Pres. of Nicaragua Campaign. Recipient Inst. for the Creative and Performing Arts fellowship, N.Y.C., 1966, Appreciation cert. Presdl. Inaugural Com., Washington, 1981. Fellow N.Y. Women in Real Estate, Explorers Club (lectr. on Mongolia, fin. com., housing, student, hospitality and Lowell Thomas coms., reciprocity com., legacy com.); mem. Com. on Am. and Internat. Fgn. Affairs, Lawyers Com. on Internat. Human Rels., Bus. Exec. Nat. Security, Venture Capital Breakfast Club, The Coffee Club House, Sigma Delta Tau, Sigma Epsilon Sigma. Democrat. Avocations: painting, writing, fishing, canoeing, horseback riding, breeding cockatiels. Home: 4 E 81st St New York NY 10028-0235 Office: Mandel-Khan Inc PO Box 97 care Boldbaatar Mandel Kahn Ulaanbaatar 210648 Mongolia also: Leslie Mandel Enterprises PO Box 294 Wainscott NY 11975-0294 also: PO Box 294 Wainscott NY 11975-0029 Office Phone: 212-737-8917. Personal E-mail: mandelair@aol.com. E-mail: richlistco@aol.com, leslie_mandel@yahoo.com.

MANDEL, MARTIN LOUIS, lawyer; b. LA, May 17, 1944; s. Maurice S. and Florence (Byer) Mandel; m. Duree Dunn, Oct. 16, 1982; 1 child, Max Andrew. BA, U. So. Calif., 1965, JD, 1968; LLM, George Washington U., 1971. Bar: Calif. 1969, U.S. Claims Ct. 1971, U.S. Tax Ct. 1971, U.S. Dist. Ct. (ctrl. dist.) Calif. 1972, U.S. Supreme Ct. 1972. With office of gen. counsel IRS, Washington, 1968-72; ptnr. Stephens, Jones, LaFever & Smith, LA, 1972-77, Stephens, Martin & Mandel, 1977-79, Fields, Fehn, Feinstein & Mandel, 1979-83; sr. v.p., gen. counsel Investment Mortgage Internat., Inc., 1983-84; ptnr. Feinstein, Gourley & Mandel, 1984-85, Mandel & Handin, San Francisco, 1985—2000; gen. counsel LA Express Football Club, 1983-85; prin., owner Law Offices Martin L. Mande, 2000—. Instr. corps. U. West LA, 1973—83. Mem.: ABA, Los Angeles County Bar Assn., LA Athletic Club, Phi Delta Phi. Office: 2905 N Sepulveda Blvd A #319 Manhattan Beach CA 90266 Business E-Mail: martin@tmgtalent.com.

MANDEL, MORTON, molecular biologist; b. Bklyn., July 6, 1924; s. Barnet and Rose (Kliner) M.; m. Florence H. Goodman, Apr. 1, 1952; children: Robert, Leslie. BCE, CUNY, 1944; MS, Columbia U., 1949, PhD in Physics, 1957. Scientist Bell Telephone Labs., Murray Hill, NJ, 1956-57; asst. prof. physics dept. Stanford (Calif.) U., 1957-61; scientist Gen. Telephone & Telegraph, Mountain View, Calif., 1961-63; rsch. assoc. dept. genetics Stanford U., 1963-64; rsch. fellow Karolinska Inst., Stockholm, 1964-66; assoc. prof. sch. of medicine U. Hawaii, Honolulu, 1966-68, prof., 1968—; founder, dir. Hawaii Biotechnology Group, Inc., 1982-95. Cons. Fairchild Semiconductor, Hewlett Packard, Lockheed, Rheem, Palo Alto, Calif., 1957-61. Contbr. articles to profl. jours. Lt. (j.g.) USN, 1944-46. Recipient Am. Cancer Soc. Scholar award Am. Cancer Soc., 1979-80, Eleanor Roosevelt Internat. Cancer fellowship, 1979; named NIH Spl. fellow Karolinska Inst., 1964-66. Fellow Am. Phys. Soc.; mem. Sigma Xi. Achievements include citation classics; optimal conditions for mutagenesis by N-methyl-N-nitro-N-nitrosoguanidine in E. coli K12; calcium dependent bacteriophage DNA infection. Office: Dept Biochemistry 1960 E West Rd Honolulu HI 96822-2319 Home: 250 Hammond Pond Pkwy Apt 303N Chestnut Hill MA 02467-1519 E-mail: mandel321@jacaro.com.

MANDEL, SHELDON LLOYD, dermatologist, educator; b. Mpls., Dec. 6, 1922; s. Maurice and Stelle R. M.; m. Patricia E., Oct. 15, 1978; 1 child, Melissa A. MA in Spl. Edn., St. Thomas U., St. Paul; BA, U. Minn., Mpls., 1943, BS, 1944, BM, MD, U. Minn., Mpls., 1946. Diplomate Am. Bd. Dermatology, 1953. Intern U. Okla., 1946-47; resident Valley Forge (Pa.) Gen. Hosp., 1947—49, VA Hosp., Mpls., 1949—51, VA Hosp. and U. Minn., Mpls., 1949—51; pvt. practice dermatology Mpls., 1951—; prof. clin. dermatology U. Minn., Mpls., 1970—. Contbr. articles to profl. jours. Capt. MC, U.S. Army, 1947-49. Fellow Royal Soc. Medicine (Britain), Am. Acad. Dermatology (life); mem. AMA, Minn. Med. Soc., Noah Worcester Dermatol. Soc. (bd. dirs. 1988-91), Internat. Dermatol. Soc. Address: Downtown Dermatology PA 825 Nicollet Mall Ste 1629 Minneapolis MN 55402-2705

MANDEL, STEPHEN, JR., investment company executive; m. Susan Mandel; children: Katie, Tom. BA, Philips Exeter Acad., 1974; MA, Dartmouth Coll., 1978; MBA, Harvard U., 1982. Sr. cons. Mars and Co., 1982—84; retail analyst Goldman, Sachs & Co., 1985—87, v.p., retail analyst NY, 1987—90; sr. mng. dir. Tiger Mgmt. Corp., 1990—97; CEO Lone Pine Capital, 1998—. Trustee The Children's Sch., Stamford, Conn., Philips Exeter Acad. Office: Lone Pine Capital LLC 2 Greenwich Plz Greenwich CT 06830-6353 *

MANDELBAUM, HAROLD NEIL, accountant; b. Englewood, NJ, Sept. 13, 1967; s. Diane M. (Kaufman) Kubik; m. Shari Patt, Sept. 9, 1995. BA in Econs., Syracuse U., 1990; BS in Acctg., William Paterson Coll., 1993. CPA; CFP; cert. personal fin. specialist; lic. ins. N.Y.; lic. securities. Broker Lehman Brothers, NYC, 1990—91; acct. NSCSA Am. Inc., SI, NY, 1992; acct., fin. cons. Joseph A. Salamo, CPA, NYC, 1992—96, Harold N. Mandelbaum CPA, PFS, CFP, NYC, 1996—. Mem. AICPA, N.Y. State Soc. CPA. Office: 555 5th Ave Fl 9 New York NY 10017-2416 Business E-Mail: hnmandelbaum@nyc.rr.com.

MANDELBAUM, JAY, diversified financial services company executive; B, Princeton U., NJ; MBA, Harvard Bus. Sch. Cons. McKinsey & Co.; v.p. corp. devel. Primerica Corp., 1992; sr. exec. v.p. Pvt. Client Sales and Mktg. Salomon Smith Barney, vice chmn., CEO Pvt. Client Grp., 2000—02; head strategy and bus. devel. Bank One Corp., 2002; officer J.P. Morgan Chase & Co., exec. v.p. strategy. Office: JP Morgan Chase & Co 270 Park Ave New York NY 10017-2070

MANDELBROT, BENOIT B., mathematician, research scientist, educator; b. Warsaw, Nov. 20, 1924; arrived in US, 1958, naturalized, 2000; s. Charles and Belle (Lurie) M.; m. Aliette Kagan, Nov. 5, 1955; children: Laurent, Didier. Diploma, Ecole Polytechnique, Paris, 1947; MS in Aeronautics, Calif. Inst. Tech., 1948; PhD in Math., U. Paris, 1952; DSc (hon.), Syracuse U., 1985, Laurentian U., Ont., Can., 1986, Boston U., 1987, SUNY, 1988, U. Bremen, Germany, 1988, U. Guelph, Ont., Can., 1989, Pace U., 1989, U. Dallas, 1992, Union Coll., 1993, U. Buenos Aires, 1993, U. Tel Aviv, 1995, Open U., UK, 1998, Athens U. Bus. and Fin., 1998, U. St. Andrews, Scotland, 1999, Emory U., Atlanta, 2002, Politecnico di Torino, Italy, 2005, U. Bari, 2007; AM (hon.), Yale U., 2000. Postdoctoral mem. and Rockefeller scholar Inst. for Advanced Study, Princeton, NJ, 1953—54; jr. prof. math. U. Geneva, 1955-57, U. Lille and Ecole Polytechnique, Paris, 1957-58; rsch. staff mem. IBM Watson Rsch. Ctr., Yorktown Heights, NY, 1958-74, IBM fellow, 1974-93, IBM fellow emeritus, 1993—; vis. prof. engring. Yale U., New Haven, 1970, prof. math. scis., 1987—99, Sterling prof., 1999—2004, Sterling prof. emeritus, 2005—; Battelle fellow Pacific Northwest Nat. Lab, 2005—07. Vis. prof. econs. Harvard U., 1962-63, applied math., 1963-64, 84-87, U. Paris, 1966, physiology Einstein Coll. Medicine, 1970, Coll. France, 1973, math., 1979-80, Inst. Hautes Etudes Sci. Bures, 1980, Mittag-Leffler Inst., Sweden, 1984, 2001, 02, 04, Max Planck Inst. Math, Bonn, Germany, 1988, Cambridge, 1990, 2005, Oxford U., 1990, Imperial Coll., London, 1991; Hitchcock prof. U. Calif., Berkeley, 1992; visitor MIT, 1953, Inst. lectr., 1964-; spkr. and organizer profl. confs. Author: Logique, langage et théorie de l'information, 1957, Les objets fractals: forme, hasard et dimension, 1975, 4th edit., 1995, Fractals: Form, Chance and Dimension, 1977, The Fractal Geometry of Nature, 1982, La Geometria della Natura, 1987, Fractals and Scaling in Finance: Discontinuity, Concentration, Risk, 1997, Fractales, hasard et finance, 1997, Multifractals and 1/f Noise: Wild Self-Affinity in Physics, 1999, Nel mondo dei frattali, 2001, Gaussian Self-Affinity and Fractals: Globality, The Earth, 1/f Noise and R/S, 2002, (with M.L. Frame) Fractals, Graphics and Mathematics Education, 2002, (with R.L. Hudson) The (Mis)Behavior of Markets: A Fractal View of Risk, Ruin, and Reward, 2004, Fractals and Chaos: The Mandelbrot Set and Beyond, 2004,; contbr. articles to profl. jours. Recipient Franklin medal Franklin Inst., 1986, Alexander von Humboldt Preis, 1987, Caltech disting. svc. award, 1988, Moet-Hennessy Sci. and Art prize, 1988, Harvey prize, 1989, Nev. prize U. Nev. Sys., 1991, Wolf prize for physics, 1993, Honda prize, 1994, Medal of City of Paris, 1996, John Scott award City of Phila., 1999, L.F. Richardson medal European Geophys. Soc., 2000, Sven Berggren prize, Lund, Sweden, 2002, Japan prize for Sci. and Tech., 2003, Fin. Times (Germany) award, 2004, Waclaw Sierpinski prize, 2005 Wladislaw Orlicz medal, 2005, Casimir Funk award Piasa, 2005; Guggenheim fellow, 1968. Fellow AAAS, IEEE (Charles Proteus Steinmetz medal 1988), Am. Acad. Arts and Scis., European Acad. Arts, Scis. and Humanities, Am. Phys. Soc., French Physics Soc. (hon.), Inst. Math. Stats., Econometric Soc., Am. Geophys. Union, Am. Statistic Assn.; mem. NAS U.S.A. (Barnard medal 1985), Am. Philos. Soc., Internat. Statis. Inst. (elected,), Am. Math. Soc., Norwegian Acad. Sci. and Letters (fgn. mem.), Sigma Xi (nat. lectr. 1980-82, Procter prize 2002). Achievements include origination of theory of fractals, a nascent interdisciplinary theory of roughness; this theory provides mathematical conjectures including very difficult ones, and also provides practical tools to handle financial data, mountains, clouds, fractures of metals, dynamic attractors, and all other shapes and phenomena in nature or man's works that are equally irregular or broken-up at all scales; the best known fractal is called Mandelbrot set. Personal E-mail: benoit.mandelbrot@yale.edu.

MANDELKER, LAWRENCE ARTHUR, lawyer; b. NYC, Dec. 2, 1943; s. Murray and Sally (Levine) M.; m. Carolyn Anne Bareish, Oct. 4, 1970; children: Daniel H., Benjamin E BA, Queens Coll., CUNY, 1964; JD, NYU, 1968. Bar: N.Y. 1968, Pa. 1981, U.S. Dist. Ct. (so. and ea. dists.) N.Y. 1973, (ea. dist.) Wis. 1980, (no. dist.) N.Y., 1995, U.S. Ct. Appeals (2d cir.) 1979, (9th cir.) 1989. Law sec. NYC Civil Ct., 1970—71, NY State Supreme Ct., 1972; mem. Kantor, Davidoff, Wolfe, Mandelker & Kass, P.C.; chmn. character and fitness com. 9th Jud. Dist.; counsel NY State Athletic Commn., 1995—2001. Mem. Lewisboro Bd. Assessment Rev., NY, 1979—, chmn., 1984—; chmn. Lewisboro Bd. Ethics. Former mem. bd. editors: NY Law Jour.; contbr. articles to profl. jours. Served as staff sgt. USAR, 1968-74. Mem. Assn. Bar City NY (past chmn., pastspl. com. election law, task force jud. selection 2006, coun. jud. adminstrn., past com. state cts. superior jurisdiction, civil ct. com., task force jud. selection 2003, 06, task force constl. conv.), NYU Law Alumni Assn. (pres.). Home: 206 Todd Rd Katonah NY 10536-2410 Office: Kantor Davidoff Wolfe Mandelker & Kass PC 51 E 42nd St New York NY 10017-5404 Office Phone: 212-682-8383. Business E-Mail: mandelker@kantorlawonline.com.

MANDELKORN, ROBERT MARC, ophthalmologist; b. Detroit, Aug. 23, 1948; s. Ben and Rose Mandelkorn; m. Mary Beth Danneffel, Sept. 28, 2001; 1 child, Rachel Sophia. MD, U. Louisville, 1974. Ophthalmologist pvt. practice, Pitts., 1980—2000; dir. eye clinic VA Outpatient Clinic, Fort Myers, Fla., 2001—. Fellow: ACS, Royal Coll. Ophthalmologists, Am. Glaucoma Soc., Am. Acad. Ophthalmology (Achievement award 2006). Achievements include patents for Mandelkorn Punctal Gauge/Dilator System; invention of Mandelkorn Suture Lysis Lens; Mandelkorn Iridotomy/Capsulotomy Lens. Office: Veterans Affairs Outpatient Clinic 3033 Winkler Ave Ext Fort Myers FL 33916 Home Phone: 239-482-0489; Office Phone: 239-939-3939 6360.

MANDELL, FLOYD A., lawyer; b. Chgo., June 17, 1948; s. Marvin M. and Estelle (Witt) M.; m. Pamela Sue Cohen, Aug. 31, 1975; children: Chad, Craig. BA magna cum laude, No. Ill. U., 1970; JD, U. Ill., Champaign, 1973. Bar: Ill. 1973, Fla. 1973. Assoc. Dettishell, McAuliffe & Hifestiter, Chgo., 1973-76; sr. ptnr. Katten Muchin Zavis Rosenman, Chgo., 1976—. Dir. Chgo. Bar Assn., 1978-80; planning chmn. Ill. Continuing Legal Edn., Intellectual Property Litigation, Chgo., 1985—. Cpl. USAR, 1969-73. Office: Katten Muchin Zavis Rosenman 525 W Monroe St Ste 1600 Chicago IL 60661-3693 Office Fax: 312-577-8982. E-mail: floyd.mandell@kmzr.com.

MANDELL, GERALD LEE, internist, educator; b. NYC, Aug. 20, 1936; s. Herman and Sylvia (Keller) M.; m. Judith Rensin Mandell, Dec. 22, 1960; children: James, Pamela, Scott. BA, Cornell U., 1958; MD, Cornell U., NYC, 1962. Diplomate Am. Bd. Internal Medicine. Intern, resident NY Hosp. Cornell Med. Ctr., NYC, 1965-67; instr. Med. Coll., Cornell U., NYC, 1968-69; asst. prof. U. Va., Charlottesville, 1969-71, assoc. prof., 1972-75, prof., 1976—, Owen R. Cheatham prof. sci., 1981—, chief infectious diseases, 1970—2002. Editor: Principles and Practice of Infectious Diseases, 1979, 6th edit., 2005. Lt. comdr. USPHS, 1963-65. Recipient MERIT award NIH, 1986; named Outstanding Alumnus, Cornell Med. Coll, 2002. Master ACP; fellow AAAS, Infectious Diseases Soc. Am. (pres. 1994, Maxwell Finland award 2000), Nat. Inst. Allergy and Infectious Diseases (adv. coun.), Inst. Medicine; mem. Assn. Am. Physicians, Am. Soc. Clin. Investigation (emeritus prof. 2006—), Phi Beta Kappa, Alpha Omega Alpha. Avocations: photography, tropical fish, sculling.

MANDELL, GORDON KEITH, aerospace engineer; b. NYC, Mar. 6, 1947; s. Bertram Herman and Maria Catherine (O'Hagan) M. BS, MIT, 1969, MS, 1970. Rsch. aerospace engr. MIT, Cambridge, 1970—72; aero. cons. Eagle River, Alaska, 1972—76; designated engring. rep., 1976—82; aerospace engr. FAA, Anchorage, 1982—2007; ind. rschr., 2007—. Author/editor: Topics in Advanced Model Rocketry, 1973; mng. editor Model Rocketry mag., Cambridge, 1968-72; contbr. articles to profl. jours. Fellow, NSF, 1969; scholar, Grumman Aerospace Corp., 1965. Mem.: Search for Extraterrestrial Intelligence Inst., Nat. Space Soc., Nat. Assn. Rocketry, Planetary Soc., Tau Beta Pi, Sigma Gamma Tau, Sigma Xi. Avocations: rural living, model building, home computing. Home: PO Box 671388 Chugiak AK 99567-1388 Office: PO Box 671388 Chugiak AK 99567-1388

MANDELL, JAMES, health facility executive, urologist, educator; b. SI, NY, Feb. 20, 1945; s. Gustave and Rose (Zimmerman) M.; m. Valerie Steele, Jan. 20, 1967; children: Joshua Lindstrom, Jeremy Hill, Bethany Shalom. AA, U. Fla., 1965; MD, U. Fla. Coll. Medicine, 1970; MS, Union U., 1999. Am. Bd. Diplomate Urology 1979. Intern U. Fla. Sch. Medicine, Gainesville, 1970-71, resident in surgery, 1971-72; resident in urology U. NC Sch. Medicine, Chapel Hill, 1974-77, fellow in pediatric urology, 1977-78, asst. prof. surgery and pediatrics, 1979-84, assoc. prof., 1984-85; dir. pediatric urology NC Meml. Hosp., Chapel Hill, 1979-85; instr. surgery Harvard U. Med. Sch., Boston, 1978-79, asst. prof. surgery (urology), 1985-90, assoc. prof. surgery, urology, 1990-94, prof. surgery (urology); prof. surgery and pediat., chief divsn. urology, exec. med. dir. Albany Med. Coll., NY, 1994-97, dean NY, 1996-2000; fellow in surgery (urology) Children's Hosp., Boston, 1978-79, asst. in surgery (urology), 1985-90, sr. assoc. surgery, 1990-94, CEO, pres., 2000—. Contbr. numerous articles to med. jours., chpts. to books. Lt. comdr. M.C., USNR, 1972-74. Fellow ACS, Am. Acad. Pediatrics; mem. Am. Urol. Assn. (New England sec.), Soc. Pediatric Urology (exec. com. 1988-92), Soc. Univ. Urologists (pres. 2001-02). Avocations: fishing, skiing, tennis. Office: Children's Hosp Boston Dept Urology Hunnewell 3 300 Longwood Ave Boston MA 02115-5724 Office Phone: 518-355-2080, 617-355-6000. Office Fax: 617-730-0474. Business E-Mail: james.mandell@childrens.harvard.edu.

MANDELL, JOEL, lawyer; b. Hartford, Conn., July 1, 1939; s. Max Edward and Harriet (Shafer) Mandell; m. Ellen Solomon, Aug. 23, 1964; children: Peter, Ross, Jason. BA, U. Conn., 1961, JD, 1966. Bar: Conn. 1966, U.S. Dist. Ct. Conn. 1967, U.S. Supreme Ct. 1971. Ptnr. Rosenthal, Clayman & Mandell, Hartford, 1966-72; prin. Levy & Droney, Farmington & West Hartford, Conn., 1972—2005; spl. counsel comml. svcs. CATIC, 2005—. Mem. Town of Simsbury Charter Revision Commn., 1990—92, Simsbury Housing Authority, 1992—93; selectman Town of Simsbury, 1993—, dep. 1st selectman, 1999—; bd. dirs. Farmington Valley Jewish Congregation, Simsbury, Conn., 1980—83. Mem.: Real Estate Exch., Conn. Assn. Real Estate Profls. (panel mem. 1991, real estate exch. panel moderator 1996, 2000, real estate exchange panel moderator 2002), New Eng. Land Title Assn. (panel mem. 1991, 2000—01, 2000, 2007, bd. dirs. 1996—, treas. 2007), Conn. Bar Assn. (real estate exec. com. 1978—2001, chmn. 1995—97, emeritus 2001—), Am. Legion Simsbury, KP (chancellor comdr. 1981—82). Office: CATIC 101 Corporate Pl Rocky Hill CT 06067-1895 Office Phone: 860-257-0606. Personal E-mail: joelmandell@mac.com. Business E-Mail: joelmandell@catie-e.com.

MANDELSTAM, CHARLES LAWRENCE, lawyer; b. Brookline, Mass., July 6, 1927; s. Felix and Sarah (Odence) M.; m. Gloria Messinger, June 2, 1957; children: Emily F., Peter D. BA, Harvard Coll., 1949; LLB, Yale U., 1952. Bar: Conn. 1952, NY 1953, DC 1953. Mem. staff office gen. counsel Internat. Ladies' Garment Workers Union, NYC, 1952—56; assoc. Kaye, Scholer, Fierman, Hays & Handler, NYC, 1956—60; ptnr. Dornbush Mensch Mandelstam & Schaeffer, LLP, NYC, 1968—2004, McLaughlin & Stern, LLP, NYC, 2004—. Comment editor Yale Law Jour., 1951-52; contbr. articles Yale Law Jour., 1951, 52 Bd. dirs. Samuel Rubin Found., 1975-2005 Mem. Assn. Bar City N.Y., Phi Beta Kappa. Home: 27 W 86th St New York NY 10024-3615 Office: 260 Madison Ave New York NY 10016 Office Phone: 212-873-7732.

MANDELSTAM, STANLEY, physicist; b. Johannesburg, Dec. 12, 1928; came to U.S., 1963; s. Boris and Beatrice (Liknaitzky) M. BSc, U. Witwatersrand, Johannesburg, 1952; BA, Cambridge U., Eng., 1954; PhD, Birmingham U., Eng., 1956. Boese postdoctoral fellow Columbia U., NYC, 1957-58; prof. math. physics U. Birmingham, 1960-63; asst. rsch. physicist U. Calif., Berkeley, 1958-60, prof. physics, 1963-94, prof. emeritus, 1994—. Vis. prof. physics Harvard U., Cambridge, Mass., 1965-66, Univ. de Paris, Paris Sud, 1979-80, 84-85. Editorial bd. The Phys. Rev. jour., 1978-81, 85-88; contbr. articles to profl. jours. Recipient Dirac medal and prize Internat. Ctr. for Theoretical Physics, 1991. Fellow AAAS, Royal Soc. London, Am. Phys. Soc. (Dannie N. Heineman Math. Physics prize 1992). Jewish. Office: U Calif Dept Physics Berkeley CA 94720-7300

MANDELSTAMM, JEROME ROBERT, lawyer; b. St. Louis, Apr. 3, 1932; s. Henry and Estelle (London) M.; m. Carolyn A. White; stepchildren: John M. Gagliardi, Maria A. Amundson, Amy E. Gagliardi. AB, U. Pa., Phila., 1954; LLB, Harvard U., Cambridge, Mass., 1957. Bar: Mo. 1957. Since practiced in, St. Louis; ptnr. Greenfield, Davidson, Mandelstamm & Voorhees, 1969—81, Schmitz, Mandelstamm, Hawker & Fischer, 1981—82; pvt. practice St. Louis, 1982—. Bd. dirs. Legal Aid Soc. City and County St. Louis, 1967-75; pres. Legal Svcs. Eastern Miss. Inc., 1969-70; bd. dirs. Lawyers Reference Service Met. St. Louis, 1976-83, chmn., 1978-83; bd. dirs. Mo. Legal Aid Soc., 1977-82; mem. 22d Jud. Cir. Bar Com., 1983-85, gen. chmn., 1984-85. Mem. St. Louis County Bd. Election Commrs., 1973-77. Served with AUS, 1957. Mem. ABA, Mo. Bar Assn., Am. Arbitration Assn. (panel of arbitrators 1984-2003), Bar Assn. Met. St. Louis (v.p. 1974-75, treas. 1975-76, Legal Svcs. Ea. Mo. Inc. F. Wm. McCalpin Wall of Justice award, 2002, William L. Weiss award for Svcs. to the Bar and the Cmty. 2004). Home: 7217 Princeton Saint Louis MO 63130-3000 Office: 1010 Market St Ste 1600 Saint Louis MO 63101-2082

MANDERS, KARL LEE, neurosurgeon; b. Rochester, NY, Jan. 21, 1927; s. David Bert and Frances Edna (Cohan) Mendelson; m. Ann Laprell, July 28, 1969; children: Karlanna Butler, Maidena Fulford;children from previous marriage: Karl, Kristine Myers, Kerry. Student, Cornell U., 1946; MD, U. Buffalo, 1950. Diplomate Am. Bd. Neurol. Surgery, Am. Bd. Clin. Biofeedback, Am. Bd. Hyperbaric Medicine, Am. Bd. Pain Medicine, Nat. Bd. Med. Examiners. Intern U. Va. Hosp., Charlottesville, 1950-51, resident in neurol. surgery, 1951-52, Henry Ford Hosp., Detroit, 1954-56; pvt. practice Indpls., 1956—. Med. dir. Cmty. Hosp. Rehab. Ctr. Pain, 1973—92; chief hosp. med. and surg. neurology Cmty. Hosp., 1983, 93; coroner Marion County, Ind., 1977—85, 1992—96. With USN, 1952—54, Korea. Recipient cert. Achievement, Dept. Army, 1969, Disting. Physician award, Cmty. Hosp., 1997, Cert. of Distinction, Ind. State Med. Assn., Am.'s Top Surgeon award, Cosumers Rsch. Coun. Am., 2002. Fellow: ACS, Harvey Cushing Soc., Am. Acad. Neurology, Internat. Coll. Surgeons; mem.: AMA, Marion County Med. Soc., Ind. Med. Soc., James McClure Surg. Soc., Am. Bd. Med. Psychotherapists (mem. profl. adv. coun.), James A. Gibson Anat. Soc., Internat. Soc. Aquatic Medicine, Interurban Neurosurg. Soc., Ctrl. Neurol. Soc., Am. Acad. Pain Medicine, Midwest Pain Soc. (pres. 1988), Am. Pain Soc., Nat. Assn. Med. Examiners, Royal Soc. Medicine, Ind. Coroners Assn. (pres. 1979), Soc. Computerized Tomography and Neuroimaging, Am. Soc. Stereotaxic and Functional Neurosurgery, N.Am. Spine Soc., Internat. Back Pain Soc., Pan Am. Med. Assn., Acad. Psychosomatic Medicine, Biofeedback Soc. Am., Pan Pacific Surg. Assn., Soc. Cryosurgery, Am. Assn. Biofeedback Clinicians, Am. Acad. Forensic Sci., Undersea Med. Soc., Am. Holistic Med. Assn. (co-founder), Am. Soc. Contemporary Medicine and Surgery, Am. Coll. Angiology, NY Acad. Scis., Am. Assn. Study Headache, Internat. Assn. Study Pain, Congress Neurol. Surgery, Highland Country Club, Brendonwood Country Club. Home and Office: 5845 High Fall Rd Indianapolis IN 46226-1018 Home Phone: 317-547-2369; Office Phone: 317-546-6691. Personal E-mail: annlmanders@comcast.net.

MANDERSCHEID, LESTER VINCENT, agricultural economics educator; b. Andrew, Iowa, Oct. 9, 1930; s. Vincent John and Alma (Sprank) M.; m. Dorothy Helen Varnum, Aug. 29, 1953; children: David, Paul, Laura, Jane. BS, Iowa State U., 1951, MS, 1952; PhD, Stanford U., 1961. Grad. asst. Iowa State U., Ames, 1951-52, Stanford (Calif.) U., 1952-56; asst. prof. Mich. State U., East Lansing, 1956-65, assoc. prof., 1965-70, prof., 1970-73, prof., assoc. chmn., 1973-87, prof., chmn., 1987-92, prof., 1992-95, prof. emeritus, 1996—, coord. Grad. Sch., 1993—. Reviewer Tex. A&M Agrl. Econ. Program, College Station, 1989; cons. Consortium Internat. Earth Sci. Info. Network, Ann Arbor, 1990. Co-author: Improving Undergraduate Education, 1967; contbr. articles to jours. in field. Pres. parish coun. St. Thomas, East Lansing, 1984-87; coll. coord. United Way, East Lansing, 1983-84; pres. bd. dirs. Cristo Rey Cmty. Ctr., 1998-2001. Recipient Disting. Faculty award Mich. State U., 1977. Mem. Am. Agrl. Econ. Assn. (pres. 1988-89, bd. dirs. 1982-85, excellence in teaching award 1974), Am. Statis. Assn., Am. Evaluation Assn., Am. Econ. Assn., University Club, Sigma Xi (pres. 1986-87), Phi Kappa Phi (pres. 1979-80). Roman Catholic. Home: 2372 Burcham Dr East Lansing MI 48823-3885 Office: Mich State U Dept of Agrl Econs Circle Dr East Lansing MI 48824-1039 Office Phone: 517-355-0301. Business E-Mail: mandersc@msu.edu.

MANDERSCHEID, RONALD WILLIAM, program administrator; b. LaCrosse, Wis., Sept. 28, 1943; s. William Joseph and Norene Elsine (Batteen) M.; m. Frances Elizabeth Fedkiw, Sept. 1, 1973; children: William Derrick, Kristen Elizabeth, Erika Marie. BA maxima cum laude, Loras Coll., 1965; MA, Marquette U., 1967; PhD, U. Md., 1975; Cert., Fed. Exec. Inst., 1986. Rsch. asst. U. Md., College Park, 1970—72; rsch. assoc. NIMH, Adelphi, Md., 1972—75, sr. rsch. sociologist, 1975—80, chief evaluation rsch. sect. Rockville, Md., 1980—81, chief stats. rsch. br., 1981—92; acting dir. divsn. state and cmty. sys. devel. Ctr. Mental Health Svcs., Rockville, 1992—93, chief survey & analysis, 1992—2006; dir. mental health and substance use program Constella Group, Rockville, 2006—. Cons. George Washington U., Washington, 1978-83, WHO, 1993—, Pan Am. Health Orgn., 1995—, Columbia U., 1998-2001; mem. Internat. Consortium Mental Health Policy & Rsch., 2000—; adj. prof. dept. mental health Bloomberg Sch. Pub. Health, Johns Hopkins U., Balt., 2006—. Author, editor: Mental Health in the United States, 1987, 90, 92, 94, 96, 98, 2000, 02, 04; editor: System Science and the Future of Health, 1976; prodr.: Making the Numbers Work for You, 1987; spl. editor Jour. of Washington Acad. Scis., 2000, Internat. Jour. Mental Health, 1998, 2005, 07; contbr. articles to profl. jours. Active West Montgomery Citizens Assn., Potomac, Md., 1983—. With U.S. Army, 1967-69. Decorated Army Commendation medal; recipient Disting. Alumni award, Loras Coll., 1998, Sec. Disting. Svc. award, Dept. Health and Human Sevcs., 1999, 2004, 2005, 2006, Mental Health Stats. Improvement Program Leadership award, 2001, 2006, Irving Blumberg Humanitarian award, Am. Assn. for Psychosocial Rehab., 2002. Fellow Washington Acad. Scis. (life, pres. 1987-88), World Acad. Art and Sci.; mem. APHA (chair mental health 1997-98, Mental Health Sect. award 2000, Mental Health Chairperson's Disting. Svc. award 2001, Consumer Leadership award 2003), N.Y. Acad. Scis., Am. Sociol. Assn. (chmn. various coms. 1983-91, chmn. com. fed. stds. sociologists 1983-88), Soc. for Gen. Sys. Rsch. (chmn. Washington chpt. 1976—), Ea. Sociol. Soc. (exec. com. 1979-84, chmn. various coms., Peter Gellman award 1984), D.C. Sociol. Soc. (pres. 1992-93), Fed. Exec. Inst. Alumni Assn. (exec. bd. 1997-2005, chair policy issues com. 1995-2000, pres. 2003, pres. found. 2003—, Meritorious Svc. award 1999), Soc. Applied Sociology (Nat. Sociol. Practice award 1995), Nat. Assn. State Mental Health Program Dirs. (Disting. Svc. tribute 2006), Am. Coll. Mental Health Adminstrs. (Saul Feldman Lifetime Achievement award 2003, Disting. Svc. award 2006, exec. bd. 2007-), Nat. Coun. Cmty. Behavioral Helathcare (Pub. Svc. award 2006), Cosmos Club, Farmington Country Club, Alpha Kappa Delta (pres. 1972-73), Delta Epsilon Sigma, Phi Kappa Phi. Avocations: coin collecting/numismatics, reading. Office: Constella Group 6003 Exec Blvd Ste 400 Rockville MD 20852 Office Phone: 240-514-2607. Office Fax: 240-514-2601. Business E-Mail: rmanderscheid@constellagroup.com.

MANDERSON, EASTON L., orthopedist, surgeon; arrived in U.S., 1963; s. Caleb Sterling and Beatrice Anita Manderson; m. Lois Constance Manderson; children: Tanya Michelle, Mario Sean, Keisha Anita Rochelle. BS cum laude, Howard U., 1967, MD, 1971. Diplomate Am. Bd. Orthopedic Surgery, Am. Bd. Ind. Med. Examiners. Rotating intern Freedmen's Hosp., Howard U., 1971—72; orthop. resident Howard U., 1972—75; pediat. orthop. fellow/resident Johns Hopkins U. Med. Sch.; med. officer DC Gen. Hosp., Washington, 1975—2001, chief orthopedic surgery, 1995—2001; pvt. practice Riggs Orthopedic Clinic, Washington, 1978—. Clin. instr. Howard U. Med. Sch., Washington, 1975—90, asst. prof., 1990—. Contbr. articles to profl. jours. Fellow: ACS, Am. Acad. Orthopedic Surgeons. Achievements include patents for extra medullary rod fixateur for long bone fracture; sub muscular and incision technique; jigless intra medullary nail with easy locking; intra medullary screw for fusion of ankles with complex deformities. Avocations: jogging, weight-lifting, reading. Office: Riggs Orthopaedic Clinic 1140 Varnum St NE Washington DC 20017 Office Phone: 202-526-5300.

MANDIBERG, DAVID MICHAEL, sculptor; b. Detroit, June 30, 1942; s. Jack Norman and Helen (Jaffe) M. Student, Art Students League, NYC, 1965-68, San Francisco Art Inst., 1970-71, Ctr. for Creative Studies, Detroit, 1991-93; BA, Wayne State U., 1981. Tchr. sculpture Cunniff Studio Gallery, Lake Orion, 1995-96. One-man shows include Cunniff Studio Gallery, Lake Orion, Mich., 1989, 91, 93-95, 97, Swann Gallery, Detroit, 1997, 99; exhibited in group shows at Detroit Artists Market, 1970, Helen Cunniff Studio Gallery, Lake Orion, 1987, 88, 90, Detroit Focus Gallery, 1988, Ariel Gallery, N.Y.C., 1988, 89, Sculptors Guild Mich., Detroit, 1993, 2006, 2007, Gallery One Twenty Eight, N.Y.C., 1994, 96, Scarab Club, Detroit, 1998, Mus. Contemporary Art, Pontiac, Mich., 1999, State of the Art Gallery, Ithaca, N.Y., 2002, See Spot Gallery, Ithaca, 2003; represented in permanent collections Rosemary McNaughton, Toronto, Can., Helen Cunniff, Lake Orion, Mich., Swords into Plowshares Peace Ctr., Detroit, Dr. Jack Levine, N.Y.C., Sol Lewitt, N.Y.C., Takao Nagai, Chgo., Irving Berg, Detroit, Joan Brace, Lake Orion, Mich., Mus. New Art, Detroit; sculptures include life-size David, Life, Psalm, Reality, Peace at Swords into Ploughshares Peace Ctr., Detroit, busts of William Clinton, Andy Warhol, Dr. Elliot Luby, Dr. Jack and Helen Mandiberg; Progress-3 part woodcarving, Stardom; TV appearances include Metro Art and Book Talk, Channel 11, Media One, 1999. Recipient 12 award ribbons Metro Carvers Mich., 1994-97, 2d place award for sculpture Sister Kenny Inst., Mpls., 1991; scholar Art Students League, 1966-67. Mem. Sculptors Guild Mich. (treas. 1992-97), Metro Carvers Mich., Detroit Blues Soc. (bd. dirs. 1994-96), Met. Detroit Recorder Soc., Nat. Sculpture Soc. Avocations: playing piano, guitar and recorder, italian, tennis. Home: Apt 101 2688 Patrick Henry St Auburn Hills MI 48326-2241 Studio: Ste 318 40 W Howard St Pontiac MI 48342-1293 E-mail: dmandiberg@aol.com.

MANDILE, MICHAEL ANGELO, investment advisor; b. Mpls., Dec. 2, 1948; s. Dominic Anthony and Irene Mary Mandile; m. Nikki-Lynn Anderson Mandile. BS, Huron Coll., SD, 1970. Fin. advisor Merrill-Lynch, Mpls., 1970—72; fin. advisor, v.p. Smith Barney, Mpls., 1972—. Avocation: gardening. Office Phone: 612-349-4832.

MANDL, HERBERT JAY, rabbi; b. Balt., Jan. 9, 1945; s. Sigmund and Ruth (Lefkowitz) M.; m. Barbara Sue Toltzis, Aug. 18, 1968; children: Aron M., Seth S., Debra A., Miriam D. AB, Johns Hopkins U., Balt., 1965; MHL, Jewish Theol. Sem., 1967, DDiv, 1994; PhD, U. Montreal, 1981. Ordained rabbi, 1969. Lectr. U. Alta., Edmonton, 1969-71; sr. rabbi Beth Shalom Synagoge, Edmonton, Alta., Can., 1969-71; asst. rabbi Congregation Shaar Hashomayim, Montreal, Que., Can., 1971-77; sr. rabbi Kehilath Israel Synagogue, Kansas City, Mo., 1977—; chaplain Overland Park Police Dept., Kans., 2000—. Adj. prof. U. Mo., Kansas City, 1978-80, Rockhurst Coll., adj. prof., 1989—; chaplain Kansas City Police Dept., 1988—. Bd. dirs. Shalom Geriatric Group, Kansas City, 1985-1990, Jewish Fedn., Kansas City, 1977—; chmn. State Mo. Health Facilities Rev. Commn., Jefferson City, 1980-86; chmn. Kansas State Holocaust Commn., Topeka, 1987—; mem. Kansas City Sister City Commn., 1980—, Kans. Pub. Disclosure Commn., 1991-97. Mem. Rabbinical Assembly (com. Jewish law and standards 1989-94), Internat. Order Police Chaplains, Rabbinical Assn. Kansas City (pres. 1980-81, 94-96), Union for Traditional Judaism (panelist on Jewish law 1985—), B'nai Brith, Rabbinic Cabinet United Jewish Cmtys., Fedn. of North Am. Office: Kehilath Israel Synagogue 10501 Conser St Shawnee Mission KS 66212-2600 Personal E-mail: hjm18@aol.com.

MANDL, ROBERT, application developer; b. Romania; s. Paul and Eva Mandl. BSc in Math., Physics, and Linguistics, Hebrew U., 1963, MSc in Math., 1965; student, MIT, Cambridge, Mass., MSEE, 1969, PhD in Engring., 1970. Sr. software engr. Softech, Waltham, Mass., 1980—83; mgr. software engring. Analogic Corp., Peabody, Mass., 1983—89; sr. software engr. Info. Engring., Bedford, Mass., 1990; cons. AT&T Bell Labs., North Andover, Mass., 1991—95; prin. engr. Digital Equipment Corp., Littleton, Mass., 1996—2001; ind. rschr. Cambridge, 2001—.

Presenter in field. Author software; compiler, editor: MIT Folk Dance Club Song Book, 1975; contbr. articles to profl. jours. Mem.: IEEE, NY Acad. Sci., IEEE Computer Soc., Linguistic Soc. Am., Math. Assn. Am., Sigma Xi. Avocations: languages, running, hambo, dance. Home: Box 397199 Cambridge MA 02139

MANDL, WILLIAM JOHN, electronics engineer, researcher; b. Los Angeles, Calif., Apr. 8, 1939; s. Bernard William Mandl and Teresa Rodia; m. Mary Louise Mullins, Nov. 25, 1950; children: Kathryn Ingrid McCarron, Stephen William, Joseph William. AA, East LA Coll., 1957—59; BS, Calif. State U. at LA, 1959—62; MS, U. of So. Calif., 1963—65. Rsch. engr. Rockwell Internat., Downey, Calif., 1960—64; sr. rsch. engr. RCA, Van Nuys, Calif., 1964—67, Litton Systems, Woodland Hills, Calif., 1967—69; v.p. mktg. Macrodata, Los Angeles, 1969—76; new products mktg. mgr. EM&M, Woodland Hills, Calif., 1976—78; pres. Hometech Corp., Los Angeles, 1978—81; dir. of engring. Aerojet, Azusa, Calif., 1981—94; pres. Amain Electronics Co., Reno, 1994—. Asst. prof. of engring. Calif. State U. at LA, 1964—67. Contbr. articles to profl. jours. Recipient 1998 SBIR Phase II Quality award, US Army, 1998. Achievements include patents for method and apparatus for multiplexed oversampled analog to digital modulation; system for digitally driving addressable pixel matrix; residential monitoring and control system; low power EPROM logic cell and log arrays there of; garbage collection system for a symbolic digital processor. Home: 5429 Greenview Ct Reno NV 89502 Office: Amain Electronics Co 3983 South McCarran Blvd Unit 466 Reno NV 89502 Home Phone: 775-857-1016; Office Phone: 775-825-6001. Office Fax: 775-825-6002; Home Fax: 775-825-6002. Personal E-mail: wmandl@aol.com.

MANDLER, GEORGE, psychologist, educator; b. Vienna, June 11, 1924; came to U.S., 1940, naturalized, 1943; s. Richard and Hede (Goldschmied) M.; m. Jean Matter, Jan. 19, 1957; children: Peter Clark, Michael Allen. BA, NYU, 1949; MS, Yale U., 1950, PhD, 1953; post grad., U. Basel, Switzerland, 1947-48. Asst. prof. Harvard U., 1953-57, lectr., 1957-60; prof. U Toronto, 1960—65; prof. psychology U. Calif., San Diego, 1965-94, chmn. dept. psychology, 1965-70, disting. prof. emeritus, 1994—; dir. Ctr. Human Info. Processing, U. Calif., San Diego, 1965-90. Hon. rsch. fellow Univ. Coll. London., 1977-78, 82-90, vis. prof., 1990—. Author: Mind and Emotion, 1975, (German edit.), 1980, Mind and Body, 1984, (Japanese edit.), 1987, Cognitive Psychology, 1985, Japanese edit., 1991, Human Nature Explored, 1997, Interesting Times, 2001, Consciousness Recovered, 2002, A History of Modern Experiemental Psychology, 2007; co-author: (with W. Kessen) The Language of Psychology, (Italian edit.), 1959, (with J.M. Mandler) Thinking: From Association to Gestalt, 1964; contbr. articles and revs. to profl. jours.; editor: Psychol. Rev., 1970-76. Served with U.S. Army, 1943-46. Fellow Ctr. for Advanced Study in Behavioral Scis., 1959-60; vis. fellow Oxford U., Eng., 1971-72, 78; Guggenheim fellow, 1971-72. Fellow AAAS, Am. Acad. Arts and Scis.; mem. AAUP, Am. Assn. Advancement Psychology (1974-82); Psychonomic Soc. (governing bd., chmn. 1983), Am. Psychol. Soc., Am. Psychol. Assn. (pres. div. exptl. psychology 1978-79, pres. div. gen psychology 1982-83, mem. coun. reps. 1978-82, William James prize 1986), Internat. Union Psychol. Scis. (U.S. com. 1985-90), Soc. Exptl. Psychologists, Fedn. Behavioral Psychol. and Cognitive Scis. (pres. 1981). Home: 1406 La Jolla Knoll La Jolla CA 92037-5236 Office: U Calif San Diego Dept Psychology La Jolla CA 92093-0109 also: 3 Perrins Lane London NW3 1QY England Business E-Mail: gmandler@ucsd.edu.

MANDLER, JEAN MATTER, psychologist, educator; b. Oak Park, Ill., Nov. 6, 1929; d. Joseph Allen and May Roberts (Finch) Matter; m. George Mandler, Jan. 19, 1957; children: Peter Clark, Michael Allen. Student, Carleton Coll., 1947-49; BA with highest honors, Swarthmore Coll., 1951; PhD, Harvard U., 1956. Rsch. assoc. lab. social rels. Harvard U., 1957-60; rsch. assoc. dept. psychology U. Toronto, Ont., Canada, 1961-65; assoc. rsch. psychologist, lectr. U. Calif. at San Diego, La Jolla, 1965-73, assoc. prof., 1973-77, prof. psychology, 1977-88, prof. cognitive sci., 1988—96, disting. prof., 1996—2000, disting. rsch. prof., 2000—; mem. adv. com. memory and cognitive processes NSF, 1978-81. Hon. rsch. fellow U. Coll., London, 1978-89, vis. prof., 1990—; hon. mem. Med. Rsch. Coun. Cognitive Devel. Unit, 1982-98. Author: (G. Mandler) Thinking: From Association to Gestalt, 1964, Stories, Scripts and Scenes, 1984, The Foundations of Mind: Origins of Conceptual Thought, 2004 (APA Divsn. 7 Eleanor Maccoby Book award 2005, Cognitive Devel. Soc. Best Authored Book award 2006); assoc. editor Psychol. rev., 1970-76; mem. editl. bd. Child Devel., 1976-89, Discourse Processes, 1977-94, Jour. Exptl. Psychology, 1977-85, Text, 1979-97, Jour. Verbal Learning and Verbal Behavior, 1980-88, Lang. and Cognitive Processes, 1985—, Cognitive Devel., 1990-99, Jour. Cognition and Devel., 1999—; contbr. articles to profl. jours Pres. San Diego Assn. Gifted Children, 1968-71; v.p. Calif. Parents for Gifted, 1970-71; mem. alumni council Swarthmore Coll., 1975-78. Recipient Disting. Scientific Contrbn. award, Am. Psychol. Assn., 2007; NIMH research grantee, 1968—81, NSF research grantee, 1981—99. Fellow: APA (mem. exec. com. divsn. 3 1983—85), Am. Acad. Arts and Scis.; mem.: Soc. Exptl. Psychologists, Cognitive Devel. Soc., Cognitive Sci. Soc., Psychonomic Soc. (mem. governing bd. 1982—87, chmn. 1985—86), Phi Beta Kappa. Office: U Calif San Diego Dept Cognitive Sci 9500 Gilman Dr La Jolla CA 92093-0515 Business E-Mail: jmandler@ucsd.edu.

MANDLES, MARTINN HEROE, facility services company executive; b. Tacoma, Nov. 1, 1940; m. Connie Mandles; children: Melanie, Valarie Barsky. BS in Engring., Stanford U., 1964. Pilot U.S. Navy, 1964—68; dir., western corp. opers. Microdot Inc., 1969—72; v.p., mem. mgmt. com. ABM Industries Inc., LA, 1973—91, exec. v.p., mem. bd. dirs., exec. com., 1992—96, chmn. bd., 1997—. Dir. Nat. Multi-Housing Coun., Washington, 1988—90, Bldg. Owners & Mgrs. Assn. of Greater L.A., 1995—. Founding dir. Century City C. of C., 1971—, chmn. bd., 1994; trustee Jewish Big Brothers & Sisters Assn., 1977—; charter mem. Fraternity of Friends of the L.A. Music Ctr., 1978—; trustee The Hebrew U. of Jerusalem, 1996—, vice chmn., dir. western region Am. Friends, 1996—. Lt. comdr. USN. Named Century City Citizen of Yr., Century City C. of C., 1986. Mem.: The Regency Club (L.A.), Hillcrest Country Club (L.A.). Home: 2465 Century Hill at 10100 Galaxy Way Los Angeles CA 90067

MANDRELL, BARBARA ANN, singer, entertainer, actress, producer, writer; b. Houston, Dec. 25, 1948; d. Irby Matthew and Mary Ellen (McGill) M.; m. Kenneth Lee Dudney, May 28, 1967; children: Kenneth Matthew, Jaime Nicole, Nathaniel. Grad. high sch. Country music singer and entertainer, 1959—, performed throughout U.S. and in various fgn. countries; mem., Grand Ole Opry, Nashville, 1972—; star TV series Barbara Mandrell and the Mandrell Sisters, 1980-82, Barbara Mandrell: Get to the Heart, 1987; albums include Midnight Oil, Treat Him Right, He Set My Life To Music (Grammy award, Dove award 1983), This Time I Almost Made It, This is Barbara Mandrell, Midnight Angel, Barbara Mandrell's Greatest Hits, Christmas at Our House, 1987, Morning Sun, 1990, Greatest Country Hits, 1990, Standing Room Only, 1993; star TV series Barbara Mandrell and the Mandrell Sisters, 1980-82, TV movie Burning Rage, 1984, TV specials Barbara Mandrell, Something Special, 1985, The Lady is A Champ, (TV) The Wrong Girl, 1999, Stolen from the Heart, 2000; guest star TV series The Commish, Touched By an Angel, Dr. Quinn, Medicine Woman, Baywatch, Diagnosis Murder, (TV series) Sunset Beach, 1997-98, Touched By an Angel, 1994, Love Boat: The Next Wave, 1998, others; author (with George Vecsey): Get To the Heart: My Story, 1990; co-exec. (TV) Get to the Heart: The Barbara Mandrell Story, 1997; discs include No Nonsense, 1990, Key's in the Mailbox, 1991, The Best of Barbara Mandrell, 1992, The Ultimate Barbara Mandrell, 1994, The Barbara Mandrell Collection, 1995, Fooled By a Feeling, 1995. Named Miss Oceanside, Calif., 1965; Named Most Promising Female Singer, Acad. Country and Western Music, 1971; Female Vocalist of Yr., 1978; Female Vocalist of Yr., Music City News Cover Awards, 1979; Female Vocalist of Yr., Country Music Assn., 1979, 81, Entertainer of Yr., 1980, 81, 95; People's Choice awards (9), 1983-87. Mem. Musicians Union, Screen Actors Guild, AFTRA, Country Music Assn. (v.p.) Mem. Order Eastern Star. Home: PO Box 620 Hendersonville TN 37077-0620 Office: Creative Artists Agy 3310 W End Ave Fl 5 Nashville TN 37203-1028

MANDY, STEPHEN HOWARD, dermatologist, educator; b. Balt., Jan. 6, 1943; s. Arthur Jerome and Sylvia Bliss Mandy; 1 child, Ashley Jacqueline. BA, George Washington U., 1962, MD, 1966. Cert. dermatology Am. Bd. Dermatology, 1972. Intern U. Fla., Gainesville, 1966—67; resident ob-gyn. Sinai Hosp., Balt., 1967—68; resident dermatology Johns Hopkins, Balt., 1968—69, U. Miami, Fla., 1969—71, clin. prof. dermatology, 1982—. Chmn. bd. Dermatologics For Vet. Medicine, Miami, 1976—92; pres. Am. Soc. for Dermatologic Surgery, Rolling Meadows, Ill., 2000—01. Contbr. articles to profl. jours. Maj. USAF, 1971—73. Jewish. Avocations: wine collector, skiing, equestrian, travel, photography. Office: South Beach Dermatology 555 Washington Ave Ste 210 Miami Beach FL 33139 Home Phone: 305-532-8811; Office Phone: 305-672-1233. Office Fax: 305-673-6422.

MANDYAM, GIRIDHAR DHATI, electronics engineer; b. Dallas, Tex., Oct. 15, 1967; s. Mandyam Dhati and Revathi Srinath; m. Chitra Mandyam, Feb. 1, 1973; 1 child, Atulya Dhati. BSEE, So. Meth. U., Dallas, 1985—89; MSEE, U. So. Calif., LA, 1991—93; PhD, U. N.Mex, Albuquerque, 1994—96. Engr. Rockwell Internat., Richardson, Tex., 1989—91, Qualcomm Inc., San Diego, Calif., 1993—94; mem. of group tech. staff Tex. Instruments, Dallas, Tex., 1996—98; sr. rsch. engr. Nokia Rsch. Ctr., Irving, Tex., 1998—2000, prin. scientist, 2000—02, dir., 2002—04, San Diego, 2004—06; chief technologist, N.Am. Nokia Mobile Phones, Irving, Tex., 2006; v.p. tech. Qualcomm Inc., San Diego, 2006; v.p. Qaulcomm Inc., San Diego, 2006—. Adj. prof. U. Tex. at Dallas, Richardson, 2001—. Mem.: IEEE. Achievements include patents for 14 issued US patents. Home Phone: 858-780-0672.

MANEA, NORMAN, writer, educator; b. Suceava, Bukovina, Romania, July 19, 1936; came to U.S., 1988; s. Marcu and Janeta (Braunstein) M.; m. Josette-Cella Boiangiu, June 28, 1969. MS in Engring., Inst. Constrn., Bucharest, Romania, 1954. Engr., Romania, 1959-74; writer, 1969-86; fellow Deutscher Akademischer Austauschdienst, West Berlin, Germany, 1987; fellow Internat. Acad. Scholarship and the Arts Bard Coll., Annandale On Hudson, NY, 1989-92, writer in residence, 1992-96, Francis Flournoy prof. in European studies and culture, 1997—. Author: October, eight o'clock, 1992, On Clowns: The Dictator & the Artist, 1992, Compulsory Happiness, 1993, The Black Envelope, 1995, The Hooligan's Return, 2003; contbr. articles, stories to profl. jours. Recipient MacArthur Found. award, 1992, Nat. Jewish Book award Jewish Book Coun., 1993, Literary Lion award Nat. Pub. Libr., 1993, Nonino Internat. Lit. prize, Italy, 2002, Napoli prize for internat. fiction, 2004, Holtzbrinck prize Am. Acad. in Berlin, 2005, Anfora Italian prize, 2006, Medicis Fgn. Lit. prize France, 2006; Guggenheim grantee, 1992; Fulbright fellow, 1988; named Commdr. Order Cultural Merit, Pres. Romania, 2007. Mem. Am. PEN, Berlin Acad. Art. Office: Bard Coll Dept Lang and Lit Annandale On Hudson NY 12504

MANEKER, MORTON M., lawyer; b. NYC, Nov. 14, 1932; s. Arthur and Estelle (Hochberg) M.; m. Roberta S. Wexler, 1985; children: Meryl Colle, Amy Jill, Marion Kenneth. AB, Harvard U., 1954, LLB, 1957. Bar: NY 1957. Assoc. Shearman & Sterling, NYC, 1957—62; trial atty. antitrust divsn. Dept. Justice, 1962—63; ptnr. Proskauer Rose LLP, NYC, 1963—94; ret., 1994. Trustee Beth Israel Hosp., NYC, 1977—2001. Mem. Am. Law Inst., N.Y. State Bar Assn., Harmonie Club. Jewish. Home: 30 E 65th St New York NY 10021-7013 Office Phone: 212-439-9737. Personal E-mail: maneker@aol.com.

MANEKER, ROBERTA S(UE), public relations executive; b. NYC, July 9, 1937; d. Maxwell Roy and Esther (Gerson) Scheff; m. Hannan Wexler, June 4, 1961 (div. 1983); children: Daniel, Joanna Bayer; m. Morton M. Maneker, June 1, 1985. BA, Oberlin Coll., 1957. Mng. editor True Love mag., NYC., 1960-62; publicity dir. Capt. Kangaroo, CBS, NYC., 1962-66; syndicated columnist Oleg Cassini, NYC., 1967-69; freelance writer, NYC., 1967-70; dir. pub. rels. Direct Mktg. Assn., NYC, 1983-85, v.p. pub. rels., 1985-87; v.p. pub. rels. Christie's, NYC, 1987-91, sr. v.p. corp. comm./mktg., 1991-94; freelance cons. mktg. and pub. rels., 1995—; mktg. dir. Phillips Auctioneers, 2000-01; mktg. cons. Lechters, Inc., 2000, dir. 1991-2001; corr. NY Art & Antiques Mag., 1997—. Contbr. articles to publs. Ford Found. scholar, 1953-57. Trustee Jewish Home and Hosp., 1996-04, chmn. Manhattan Divsn., 2000-03; pres. Oberlin Coll., 1997-2006, mem. exec. com., 2004-2006, hon. trustee, 2006—; chmn. vis. com. Allen Meml. Art Mus., 2002—. Mem. Oberlin Coll. Alumni Assn. (pres. 1989-91), Phi Beta Kappa

MANELLA, NORA MARGARET, judge; BA in Italian with high honors, Wellesley Coll., Mass., 1972; JD, U. So. Calif., 1975. Bar: Calif. 1976, U.S. Ct. Appeals (5th cir.) 1976, D.C. Ct. Appeals 1978, U.S. Dist. Ct. (ctrl., so., no. and ea. dists.) 1980-81, U.S. Ct. Appeals (9th cir.) 1982. Law clk. to Hon. John Minor Wisdom U.S. Ct. Appeals (5th cir.), New Orleans, 1975-76; legal counsel Subcom. on Constn., Senate Com. on Judiciary, Washington, 1976-78; assoc. O'Melveny & Myers, Washington and L.A., 1978-82; asst. U.S. atty. U.S. Dept. Justice, LA, 1982—90, trial asst. major crimes, 1982-85, dep. chief, criminal complaints, 1986-87, chief criminal appeals, 1988-90; judge L.A. Mcpl. Ct., 1990—92, L.A. Superior Ct., 1992-93, U.S. Dist. Ct. (ctrl. dist.) Calif., LA, 1998—2006; justice pro tem Calif. Ct. of Appeal 2d appellate dist. LA, 1992, assoc. justice, 2006—; U.S. Atty. (ctrl. dist.) Calif. U.S. Dept. Justice, LA, 1994—98. Instr. U.S. Atty. Gen. Advocacy Inst., 1984-86, Calif. Jud. Coll., 1992-93; mem. Atty. Gen.'s Adv. Com., 1994-95. Mem. editl. bd. State Bar Criminal Law Newsletter, 1991-92. Mem. adv. bd. Monroe H.S. and Govt. Magnet, 1991-94; acad. specialist USAID Delegation, 1993; judge L.A. Times Cmty. Partnership Awards, 1993; bd. councilors Law Sch. U. So. Calif., 1996—. Mem. Am. Law Inst., Calif. Judges Assn., Nat. Assn. Women Judges, Calif. Women Lawyers, Women Lawyers L.A., Order of Coif, Phi Beta Kappa. Office: Calif Ct of Appeal 2d Appellate Dist LA 300 South Spring St Los Angeles CA 90013 Office Phone: 213-830-7443. Business E-Mail: arlene.chavez@jud.ca.gov.

MANELLI, DONALD DEAN, scriptwriter, film and television producer; s. Daniel Anthony and Mignon Marie (Dean) M.; m. Susan Linda Allen, June 16, 1964 (div. Aug. 1973); children: Daniel, Lisa. BA, U. Notre Dame, 1959. Communications specialist Jewel Cos., Melrose Park, Ill., 1959; script writer Coronet Films, Chgo., 1960-62; freelance writer Chgo., 1962-63; creative dir. Fred A. Niles Communications Ctrs., Chgo., 1963-67; sr. writer Wild Kingdom NBC-TV, Chgo., 1967-70; freelance film writer, producer Chgo., 1970-76; pres. Donald Manelli & Assocs., Inc., Chgo. and Paris, 1976—. Screenwriter, prodr. more than 225 documentary films, 1970—, numerous episodes Wild Kingdom, 1967-82 (Emmy award 1969, 70). Recipient numerous awards various orgns. including N.Y. Internat. Film Festival, Houston Internat. Film Festival, Berlin, Paris, Venice Internat. Film Festivals, CINE, 1976—. Mem. Writers Guild Am. Roman Catholic. Avocations: photography, travel, tennis. also: 1 Rue Goethe 75116 Paris France Office: Donald Manelli And Associates 175 N Harbor Dr Ste 4901 Chicago IL 60601-7892 Business E-Mail: dmanelli@earthlink.net. *A simple truth is played out in most lives: what we believe ourselves to be, we are. We may be tested with our own failed efforts and plain bad luck, but our personal vision gives us strength. Success brings satisfaction and the responsibility to help others form and follow their own visions.*

MANES, STEPHEN GABRIEL, concert pianist, educator; b. Bennington, Vt., Apr. 11, 1940; s. Julius H. and Edna E. (Silberstein) M.; m. Frieda Green, July 7, 1963; children: Sonya Ruth, Daniel Ira. BS, Juilliard Sch. Music, 1961, MS, 1963; postgrad. (Fulbright fellow), Acad. Music, Vienna, 1963-64. Vis. instr. music Oberlin Coll. Conservatory, Ohio, 1966-67; asst. prof. Ball State U., Muncie, Ind., 1967-68; prof. music U. Buffalo-SUNY, 1968—, chair, 1989-93, 99—; co-music dir. Sebago-Long Lake Region Chamber Music Festival, North Bridgton, Maine, 1982-85. Concert piano soloist maj. orchs. U.S. and abroad; debuts in Washington, 1962, N.Y.C., 1963, Vienna, Austria, 1964, Berlin, 1975, Amsterdam, 1975, London, 1975, chamber music concerts, radio, TV appearances, four-hand piano recitals with Frieda Manes in U.S., Australia, Can. and P.R.; rec. artist Orion Master Records, 1974—, Spectrum Records, 1986—; mem. Baird Piano Trio, 1986-90, 2000—. Recipient Kosciuszko Chopin prize, 1960, Town Hall award Concert Artists Guild, 1962; finalist Leventritt Internat. Competition, 1962; Harriet Cohen Internat. Beethoven prize, 1964 Mem. Music Tchrs. Nat. Assn., Coll. Music Soc., Am. Fedn. Musicians. Home: 89 High Park Blvd Amherst NY 14226-4210 Office: U Buffalo-SUNY Dept of Music 222 Baird Hall Buffalo NY 14260-4700

MANESS, ELEANOR PALMER, researcher; b. Raleigh, NC, June 24, 1935; d. Oren Alston and Lillian Way Palmer; m. Charles B. Maness, Feb. 1, 1955 (dec. July 1989); children: Reid, Brian, Teresa. BA, Meredith Coll., 1958. Tchr. St. Timoth Sch., Raleigh, 1958—64; rsch. analyst N.C. State U., Raleigh, 1966—99; cons., 1999—. Contbr. articles to sci. jours. Recipient L.M. Ware Rsch. award, Am. Soc. for Hort. Sci., 1974, Excellence in Environment Rsch. award, Fed. Hwy. Adminstrn., 1997. Presbyterian. Avocations: hiking, swimming, gardening, rock hunting, fishing. Home: 2104 Gray Walsh Dr Wilmington NC 28405

MANESS, GEORGE ANDREW, music educator; s. George Edward and Sidney Helen (Greer) Maness; m. Donna Lee Andrews, Feb. 7, 1986; children: Emily Kim, John Alexander. BA in Music, Marietta Coll., Ohio, 1975; diploma in profl. music magna cum laude, Berklee Coll. Music, Boston, 1980. Owner Absolutely Music/Four Guys in Tuxes, Boston, 1983—; asst. prof. Berklee Coll. Music, 1986—. Cons. Cape Cod Conservatory, Falmouth, Mass., 2005. Mem.: Am. Fed. Tchrs., Meeting Profls. Internat., Am. Fedn. Musicians, Mensa. Avocations: money management, history, philosophy, classic film. Home and Office: 67 Swing Ln Ste 1 Falmouth MA 02540 Office Fax: 617-482-3234.

MANETTA, AMEDA AVRILL, social sciences educator; d. Malcolm James and Mabel Manetta; children: Lola P Sutherland, Morgan J. J. Sutherland. BA in Sociology, The U. of Western Ont., London, Ont., Can., 1988; BSW, The U. of Western Ont., 1989; MSW, U. of Windsor, Ont., 1990; PhD, Va. Commonwealth U., 1997. Faculty Stephen F. Austin State U., Nacogdoches, Tex., 1997—98; assoc. prof. Winthrop U., Rock Hill, SC, 1998—. Bd. dirs. Safe Passage, Inc, Rock Hill, SC, 2003—. Contbr. articles to profl. jours., chapters to books. Mem. profl. adv. bd. Home Care Connections, Richmond. Grantee, Winthrop Faculty grantee, 1999, Stephen F. Austin Faculty grantee, 1998. Mem.: NASW (bd. dirs. 2001), Coun. on Social Work Edn., Am. Assn. of Suicidology. Office: Winthrop University 128 Bancroft Bldg Rock Hill SC 29733 Business E-Mail: manettaa@winthrop.edu.

MANETTA, RICHARD L., chemicals executive, lawyer; b. 1945; BA, U. Mich.; JD, Wayne State U. Legal advisor Detroit City Coun., 1973—74; chief supervising asst./corp. counsel City of Detroit Law Dept., 1974—78; asst. gen. counsel for automotive safety and product litigation Ford Motor Co., 1989—94, asst. gen. counsel for discovery, 1994—99, assoc. gen. counsel for litigation, 1999—2000, dep. gen. counsel, dir. regulatory compliance, 2000—01; corp. v.p., gen. counsel The Dow Chem. Co., Midland, Mich., 2001—04, corp. v.p., spl. counsel to pres., 2004—05. Spkr. in field. Recipient Pres. award, Nat. Bar Assn., 2001, award, Wolverine Bar Assn., 2001, Access to Justice award, State of Mich., 2003. Fellow: Mich. State Bar Found. (life); mem.: ABA, Mich. Gen. Counsel Assn., Mich. State Bar. Home: 59 Lake Shore Rd Grosse Pointe MI 48236

MANEY, JACK LOGAN, mathematician, educator; b. Crookston, Minn., Nov. 26, 1976; s. Daniel and Ardis Maney, George High (Stepfather); m. Geraldean Lynn Baxter, Aug. 7, 2005. BS in Math., ND State U., 1999; PhD in Math., N.D. State U., 2004. Grad. tchg. fellow ND State U., Fargo, 2003—04; asst. prof. math. U. SD, Vermillion, 2004—. Mem.: Math. Assn. Am., Am. Math. Soc., Sigma Xi. Democrat. Avocations: computers, mathematics. Office: U SD Dept Math Scis 414 E Clark St Vermillion SD 57069 Home Phone: 605-202-0688; Office Phone: 605-677-5997. Business E-Mail: jmaney@usd.edu.

MANEY, MICHAEL MASON, lawyer; b. Taihoku, Japan, Aug. 13, 1936; s. Edward Strait and Helen M. M.; m. Suzanne Cochran, Oct. 22, 1960; 1 child, Michele. BA, Yale U., 1956; MA, Fletcher Sch. Law and Diplomacy, Tufts U., 1957; LL.B., U. Pa., 1964. Bar: N.Y. 1966, D.C. 1977. Case officer CIA, 1957-61; law clk. Justice John Harlan, Supreme Ct. U.S., Washington, 1964-65; asso. Sullivan & Cromwell, NYC, 1965-70, ptnr., 1971—77, 1981—2003, mng. ptnr. Washington, 1977-81, sr. counsel, 2004—. Law fellow Salzburg Seminar in Am. Studies, 1967; mem. bd. overseers Fletcher Sch. Law and Diplomacy. 1st lt. USAF, 1957-61. Mem. ABA, Am. Law Inst., Am. Coll. Trial Lawyers, N.Y. State Bar Assn., Union Club, Madison Beach Club, Madison Country Club, Met. Opera Club, New Haven Country Club. Address: 48 Neptune Ave Madison CT 06443-3210 Office: Sullivan & Cromwell LLP 125 Broad St New York NY 10004-2498

MANFREDA, JOHN J., federal agency administrator; b. DC; m. Rosemary Manfreda; 3 children. Grad., U. Md.; JD, Am. U., 1970; M in Tax Law, Georgetown U., 1974. Bar: DC, U.S. Ct. Appeals DC. With Bur. Alcohol and Tobacco Tax and Trade, US Dept. Treasury, 1970—2003, staff atty., 1970—78, assoc. chief counsel for alcohol and tobacco, 1978—96, chief counsel for alcohol and tobacco, 1996—2003, dep. adminstr., 2003—05, adminstr., 2005—. Office: Alcohol and Tobacco Tax and Trade Bur Pub Info Officer 1310 G St NW Ste 300 Washington DC 20220 *

MANFREDI, ZACHARY-JOHN A., political scientist; s. K.S. Manfredi. BS in Internat. Studies, Phil., Emory Univ., Atlanta, 2007; MPhil. student, Oxford Univ., 2007—. Pres., Emory chpt. Amnesty Internat.; pres. Paperclips for Peace in Sudan. Rhodes Scholar. Avocations: tai chi, yoga. *

MANGA, MICHAEL, earth science educator, geophysicist; b. Hamilton, Ont., Can., July 22, 1968; s. Pran and Louise Manga; m. Susan Storch. BSc in Geophysics, McGill U., Montreal, Que., Can., 1990; SM in Engring. Scis., Harvard U., 1992, PhD in Earth and Planetary Scis., 1994. Miller rsch. fellow Miller Inst. Basic Rsch. in Scis., Berkeley, Calif., 1994—96; asst. prof. dept. geol. scis. U. Oreg., Eugene, 1996—2001; assoc. prof. dept. earth & planetary scis. U. Calif., Berkeley, 2001—. Contbr. articles to sci. jours.; assoc. editor: Jour. Geophys. Rsch., 2001—05, mem. editl. bd.: Geology, 2004—; editor: Revs. Geophysics, 2005—. Named a MacArthur fellow, John D. and Catherine T. MacArthur Found., 2005; named one of Brilliant 10, Popular Sci. mag., 2003; recipient CAREER award, NSF, 1997—2001; fellow, Sloan Found., 2001. Fellow: Geol. Soc. Am. (Donath medal 2003), Am. Geophys. Union (James B. Macelwane medal 2002).

Office: Dept Earth and Planetary Sci Univ Calif Berkeley 173 McCone Hall Berkeley CA 94720-4767 Office Phone: 510-643-8532. Office Fax: 510-643-9980. E-mail: manga@seismo.berkeley.edu. *

MANGAN, JOHN LEO, retired electric power industry executive, international trade specialist; b. Lakewood, Ohio, May 24, 1920; s. Mark A. and Celia M. Mangan; m. Mildred J. Livingston, June 21, 1946; children: John, Scott. BSME, Carnegie Inst. Tech., 1942. Registered profl. engr., Mass., N.Y. Turbine design engr. Gen. Electric Co., Lynn, Mass., 1946-48, turbine application and sales engr. Fitchburg and Lynn, Mass., Schenectady, St. Louis, 1948-55, mgr. gas turbine indsl. sales Schenectady, 1955-60, mgr. gas turbine product planning, 1960-64, mgr. turbine bus. strategy devel., 1966-86; mgr. turbine indsl. customer requirements Boeing Co., Seattle, 1964-66. Contbr. articles profl. jours., chpts. in books; inventor in field. Mem. com. Boy Scouts Am., 1955-59, 64-66; bd. dirs. United Way Schenectady County, Inc., 1991-96, chmn., 1992-93. 1st lt. U.S. Army, 1942-46. Recipient Profl. and Social Activities award GE, 1977, cert. of merit N.Y. State Assembly, 1995. Fellow ASME (v.p. 1975-79, bd. govs. 1983-87, Gas Turbine citation, Centennial medal 1980, Dedicated Svc. award 1988); mem. Internat. Combustion Engine Coun. (permanent com. 1974-81, v.p. 1977-81), Mohawk Golf Club (Schenectady). Home: 1345 Ruffner Rd Niskayuna NY 12309-2505

MANGAN, MICHAEL D., corporate financial executive; BME, Gen. Motors Inst.; MBA, Amos Tuck Sch., Dartmouth Coll. Fin. mgmt. positions through group CFO GMAC Gen. Motors Corp., 1981—94; exec. v.p., CFO The Ryland Group Inc., 1994—99; v.p. investor rels. The Black & Decker Corp., Towson, Md., 1999—2000, sr. v.p., CFO, 2002—. Past. bd. dir. Gen. Motors Acceptance Corp. Office: The Black & Decker Corp 701 E Joppa Rd Towson MD 21286 *

MANGAN, TERENCE JOSEPH, retired federal agency administrator; b. Utica, NY, Feb. 17, 1938; BA, St. Mary's Coll., 1961; MA, St. Albert's Coll., 1965; postgrad. in pub. adminstrn., U. So. Calif., 1972-76; Grad., FBI Nat. Acad., N.W. Law Enforcement Exec., 1986. Cert. Wash. State Criminal Justice Tng. Commn., Calif.; cert. Gov.'s Rev. Team Child Abuse Svscs., 1986. With Seaside Police Dept., Calif., 1967—72, Lakewood Police Dept., Calif., 1972-76, chief, dir. cmty. safety Calif., 1976; chief Bellingham Police Dept., Wash., 1976—87, Spokane Police Dept., Wash., 1987—98; ret., 1998; mem. FBI Leadership Devel. Inst. FBI Acad., Quantico, Va., 1998—2006; program mgmt. FBI Nat. Exec. Inst. and Major City Chiefs Program. Past chair Wash. Stae Criminal Justice Tng. Commn., working group counter-terrorism, futures; mem. Mgmt. Adv. Group Organized Crime and Narcotics Enforcement; apptd. to death investigations coun. Spl. Task Force on Child Abuse, Gov.'s Criminal Justice Adv. Bd.; master mentor Waspc's Exec. Leadership Inst., coord. N.W. Law Enforcement Command Coll. Program; mem. Wash. Law Enforcement Exec. Forum, past chair; mem. Wash. State Inst. Cmty. Oriented Policing. Mem. archdiocesan steering com. Ann. Catholic Appeal, 1982; chair fund-raising drives Am. Cancer Soc., Am. Heart Assn., Salvation Army, Easter Seal Soc., Assn. Retarded Citizens; bd. advs. Holy Names Ctr.; exec. bd. Inland Empire coun. Boy Scouts Am.; bd. dirs. Spokane Goodwill Industries, United Way, Whatcom County, Calif. Paul Harris fellow Rotary Internat., 1986; recipient citation U.S. Secret Svc., 1969, Congl. Com. Internal Security, 1971, Svc. award City of Seaside, 1972, Disting. Svc. award City of Lakewood, Wash. Assn. Sheriffs and Police Chiefs, 1978-81, Cmty. Svc. award Wash. Toastmasters Internat., 1980, Pres. award Pacific Luth. U., 1981; named Police Officer of Yr. Nat. Exch. Club, 1979, Lawman of Yr. VFW, 1980, Law Enforcement Officer of Yr. VFW, 1980. Secret Svc. Honor award, 1998, Defender of Freedom award, 1998. Mem. Internat. Assn. Chiefs of Police (life)(com. terrorism), Nat. Coun. Crime and Delinquency, Wash. Assn. Sheriffs and Police Chiefs (life mem.; past pres.), Internat. Peace Artch Law Enforcement Coun., VFW (life). Roman Catholic. Office: FBI Acad L Msu Rm 112 Quantico VA 22135-0001 Home Phone: 703-878-0724; Office Phone: 703-632-3164. Business E-Mail: tmangan@fbiacademy.edu.

MANGANELLO, TIMOTHY M., auto parts company executive; B of Mech. Engring., U. Mich.; postgrad., Harvard U.; grad., Chrusler Inst. Program. Product engring. mgr. Chrysler Corp., 1973—81; sales mgr. PT Components, 1981—88; v.p. ops. BorgWarner TorqTransfer Systems, Inc., Muncie, Ind., 1995—99, pres., gen. mgr. Chgo., 1999—2001; v.p. Borg-Warner, Inc., 1999—2001, exec. v.p., 2001—02, pres., COO, 2002—03, pres., CEO, 2003, chmn., CEO, 2003—. Mem. bd. dir. Bemis Co., Inc. Office: Borgwarner 3850 Hamlin Rd Auburn Hills MI 48326-2872 *

MANGANO, LOUIS, lawyer; b. Passaic, NJ, Sept. 19, 1939; s. Salvatore and Mary Mangano; m. Arlene M. Triolo, Sept. 20, 1964; children: Kenneth L., Eileen M., Louis M., Michael S. BS in Bus. Adminstrn., Seton Hall U., 1970; MA in Criminal Justice, John Jay Coll., 1973; JD, Seton Hall U., 1979. Bar: N.J. 1981, U.S. Dist. Ct. N.J. 1981, U.S. Supreme Ct. 1985. With Elmwood Park (N.J.) Police Dept., 1966-83; pvt. practice atty. Elmwood Park, 1981—. Adj. prof. Fairleigh Dickinson U., Rutherford, N.J., 1973-75, Jersey City (N.J.) State Coll., 1973-75; asst. prof. William Paterson Coll., Wayne, N.J., 1983-84. Trustee, pres. Elmwood Park (N.J.) Bd. Edn., 1980-83, 89-93; borough atty. for Elmwood Park, N.J., 2005—. With U.S. Army, 1959-61. Mem. Bergen County Bar Assn. Office: PO Box 305 395 River Dr Elmwood Park NJ 07407-1622 Office Phone: 201-796-2727.

MANGANO, PHILIP F., federal agency administrator; b. 1947; Dir. homeless services City of Cambridge, Mass.; with Soc. Action Ministries of Greater Boston; founding exec. dir. Mass. Housing and Shelter Alliance, 1990—2002; exec. dir. US Interagy. Coun. on Homelessness, 2002—. Breadline vol. St. Anthony's Shrine, Boston. Named a Pub. Official of Yr., Governing mag., 2006. Office: US Interagy Coun on Homelessness Fed Ctr SW 409 3rd St SW Ste 310 Washington DC 20024 Office Phone: 202-708-4663. Office Fax: 202-708-1216.

MANGASARIAN, OLVI LEON, research scientist, educator; b. Baghdad, Iraq, Jan. 12, 1934; s. Leon Ohannes and Josephine Mangasarian; m. Claire Natalie Garabedian, June 14, 1959; children: Leon Charles, Jeffrey Thomas, Aram Andrew. BSE, Princeton U., 1954, MSE, 1955; PhD, Harvard U., Cambridge, Mass., 1959. Mathematician Shell Devel. Co., Emeryville, Calif., 1959—67; prof. U. Wis., Madison, 1967—2003, John von Neumann prof. emeritus, 2003—; rsch. scientist U. Calif. at San Diego, La Jolla, 2002—. Author: (scientific book) Nonlinear Programming, 1969 (INFORMS Lanchester prize for Math. Programming in Machine Learning and Data Mining, 2000). Home Phone: 608-233-1352; Office Phone: 608-262-6593. Business E-Mail: olvi@cs.wisc.edu.

MANGELSDORF, THOMAS KELLY, psychiatrist, consultant; b. St. Louis; s. Albert Henry and Hazel (Kelly) M.; m. Helen Louise Kareth, Apr. 12, 1958 (div. Jan. 1986); children: Ellen S., Steven T., Thomas K. Jr., Laura E. BS, U. Notre Dame, 1952; MD, St. Louis U., 1956. Diplomate Am. Bd. Psychiatry and Neurology (examiner 1968, 95); forensic expert in psychiat. trauma. Cons. in mental health various municipalities and pvt. practice, 1972—. Author and editor computerized system to interpret Minn. Multiphasic Personality Inventory profiles. Served to capt. U.S. Army, 1960-62. Fellow: Am. Psychiat. Assn. Avocation: sailing. Home Phone: 314-997-5440; Office Phone: 314-997-5440. Personal E-mail: tkm18@sbcglobal.net.

MANGER, WILLIAM MUIR, internist, educator, writer, research scientist; b. Greenwich, Conn., Aug. 13, 1920; s. Julius and Lilian (Weissinger) M.; m. Lynn Seymour Sheppard, May 30, 1964; children: William Muir, Jr., Lilian Wade (Mrs. Porter Fleming), Stewart Sheppard, Charles Seymour. BS, Yale U., 1944; MD, Columbia U., 1946; PhD, Mayo Found., U. Minn., 1958. Diplomate Nat. Bd. Med. Examiners, Am. Bd. Internal Medicine. Intern Presbyn. Hosp., NYC, 1946-47, resident, 1949-50, asst. physician, 1957—2001; fellow internal medicine Mayo Found., 1950-55; dir. Manger Rsch. Found., 1961-77; clin. asst. attending physician Columbia divsn. Bellevue Hosp., 1964-68; asst. attending physician NYU Bellevue Hosp., 1969-77, assoc. attending physician, 1977-83, attending physician, 1983—; instr. medicine Columbia U. Coll. Physicians and Surgeons, 1957-66, assoc. medicine, 1966-70, lectr. emeritus, 1991—. Asst. attending physician Presbyn. Hosp., 1966—68; asst. clin. prof. medicine NYU Med. Ctr., 1968—75, assoc. clin. prof. medicine, 1975—83, clin. prof. medicine, 1983—; mem. devel. com. Mayo Clinic, 1981; vice chmn. bd. Manger Hotels, Inc., 1957—73, 1990—2004; former mem. nat. high blood pressure edn. program NIH. Co-author: Chemical Quantitation of Epinephrine and Norepinephrine in Plasma, 1959, Pheochromocytoma, 1977, Clinical and Experimental Pheochromocytoma, 1996, 100 Questions and Answers About Hypertension, 2001, Our Greatest Threats, 2006; author: Catecholamines in Normal and Abnormal Cardiac Function, 1982; editor, co-author: Hormones and Hypertension, 1966; editor: Am. Lecture Series in Endocrinology, 1962-75; guest editor First Irvine H. Page Internat. Hypertension Rsch. Symposium, 1990; contbr. articles to profl. and lay jours. Mem. bd. govs. St. Albans Sch., Washington, 1958-64, 83-89, chmn., 1962-64, 67-69; trustee Found. Rsch. in Medicine and Biology, 1971-77, Buckley Sch., 1975-85, Lycee Francais, NY, 1996-98, Found. for Advancement Internat. Rsch. in Microbiology, 1977-82, Thyroid Found., 1980-85; mem. bd. visitors Boston U. Med. Sch., 1992—; trustee Found. for Depression and Manic Depression, 1978-89, pres., 1980-89; elder Presbyn. Ch., 1968-70, 92-93, trustee, 1962-67, 80-84, deacon, 1959-61; founder Values Initiative Tchg. About Lifestyle program to combat obesity, 2002. Lt. (j.g.) MC, USNR, 1947-49. Recipient Mayo Found. Alumni award for Meritorious Rsch., 1955, Disting. Alumnus award, 1992, Alumni Svc. award St. Albans Sch., 2007. Fellow ACP, Acad. Psychosomatic Medicine, Am. Geriatric Soc., Coun. on Geriatric Cardiology, NY Acad. Medicine (admission com. 1976-78, edn. com. 1979-92) Am. Coll. Cardiology, Am. Coll. Clin. Pharmacology, Royal Soc. Health, Am. Inst. Chemists; Nat. Hypertension Assn. (founder, trustee, chmn. 1977—), AMA, Am. Soc. Internal Medicine, NY State Med. Soc., NY County Med. Soc., Am. Heart Assn. (fellow coun. on circulation and coun. for high blood pressure rsch.), Inter-Am. Soc. Hypertension, Internat. Soc. Hypertension, Am. Soc. Hypertension (designated hypertension specialist), Am. Thoracic Soc., NY Acad. Sci., AAAS, Am. Physiol. Soc., Am. Chem. Soc., Am. Soc. Pharmacology and Exptl. Therapeutics, Am. Soc. for Clin. Pharmacology and Therapeutics, Clin. Autonomic Rsch. Soc., Am. Autonomic Soc., Med. Strollers, NYC, Endocrine Soc., Pan Am. Med. Assn., Harvey Soc., Soc. Exptl. Biology and Medicine, Rsch. Discussion Group (founding mem., sec.-treas. 1958-80), Am. Fedn. Clin. Rsch. Am. Soc. Nephrology, Royal Soc. Medicine (affiliate), Fellows Assn. Mayo Found. (v.p., pres. 1953), Mayo Alumni Assn. (v.p. 1981-82, exec. com. 1981-89, pres. elect 1982-85, pres. 1985-87), Chatecholamine Club (founder, sec.-treas. 1967-80, pres. 1981-82), Pheochromocytom Rsch. Support Orgn. (pres. and treas. 2005—), Drs. Mayo Soc., Plummer Soc., Albert Gallatin Assocs., The 1941 Soc., New Eng. Soc., SAR (chmn. admissions com. 1959-67, bd. mgrs. 1959-67, 69-70), Soc. Colonial Wars, Soc. of the Cin., Sigma Xi, Nu Sigma Nu, Phi Delta Theta, Explorers, Meadow (L.I., NY), Univ. Club, NY Athletic Club (NYC), Southampton Bathing Corp. Achievements include research on the mechanism of salt-induced hypertension, the mechanism whereby potassium lowers blood pressure and prevents stroke, and on pheochromocytoma. Home: 8 E 81st St New York NY 10028-0201 Home Phone: 212-772-3068; Office Phone: 212-689-0873. Fax: 212-447-7032. Personal E-mail: nathypertension@aol.com.

MANGES, JAMES HORACE, investment banker; b. NYC, Oct. 8, 1927; s. Horace S. and Natalie (Bloch) M.; m. Joan Brownell, Oct., 1969 (div.); m. Mary Seymour, 1974 (div. Oct. 2000); children: Alison, James H. Jr. Grad., Phillips Exeter Acad., 1945; BA, Yale U., 1950; MBA, Harvard U., 1953. With Kuhn, Loeb & Co., NYC, 1954-77, ptnr., 1967-77; mng. dir. Lehman Bros., Kuhn Loeb Inc., NYC, 1977-84, Shearson Lehman, Inc., NYC, 1984-90; adv. dir. Lehman Bros., NYC, 1990-96. Dir. Baker Industries, 1967—77, Proudfoot PLC (U.K.), 1996—98; dir., exec. com. Metromedia, Inc., 1970—86. Trustee The Episcopal Sch., 1978-92, St. Bernard's Sch., 1985-2000, Phillips Exeter Acad., 1985-89, mem. trustee coun., 1989-95; mem. Ctr. Strategic and Internat. Studies, Washington. Mem. Bond Club, Yale Club (N.Y.C.), Century Country Club (Purchase, N.Y.), Harvard Club (N.Y.C.). Home: 888 Park Ave New York NY 10021-0235 Office: #2016 45 Rockefeller Plz New York NY 10111-0100

MANGIA, ANGELO JAMES, lawyer; b. Bklyn. AB in Govt. cum laude, Georgetown U., Washington, DC, 1975; JD, St. John's U., Jamaica, NY, 1978. Bar: NY 1979, US Dist. Ct. (so. and ea. dists.) NY 1979, US Ct. Appeals (2d cir.) 1985. Atty. Town of North Hempstead, NY, 1982; counsel senate com. on crime State of NY, 1983-85, counsel senate com. on banks, 1985-88; chief counsel to majority NY State Senate, 1989-94; mng. dir. Sandler, O'Neill & Ptnrs., L.P., NYC, 1995-2001; pres., CEO Std. Funding Corp., Woodbury, NY, 2001—. Trustee LI U., NY, 2006—. Mem. bd. editors NY Law Jour., 1994-96. Recipient Outstanding Work in Field of Criminal Justice Legis. award NY State Bar Assn., 1985, Disting. Svc. award Civil Trial Inst./St. John's Law Sch., 1987, Luther Gulick award for Outstanding Achievement in Pub. Svc. Long Island U., 1992; Toll fellow, 1991. Mem.: Nassau County Bar Assn. Office: 335 Crossways Park Dr Woodbury NY 11797 Office Phone: 516-364-0200 x222. Business E-Mail: amangia@standardfunding.com.

MANGIAPANE, JOSEPH ARTHUR, retired consulting company executive, physicist; b. NYC, Aug. 1, 1926; s. Michael and Rose D'Amico M.; m. Marcia Balut, Oct. 30, 1954 (div. Apr. 1974); children: Rosemarie, Michael, Diana, Joseph J., Susan. BS, Fordham U., 1950. Stress analyst Republic Aviation, Farmingdale, NY, 1951-55; pvt. practice tech. cons., 1955-58; sect. mgr. Aerojet-Gen., Sacramento, 1958-61; project engr. Pratt & Whitney Aircraft, East Hartford, Conn., 1961-71; pvt. practice tech. cons., 1971-79; pres. Joseph A. Mangiapane & Assocs., Inc., Tampa, Fla., 1979-92; ret., 1992. Contbr. articles to profl. jours. Served as cpl. USAAF, 1945-47, ETO. Fellow: AIAA (assoc.); mem.: Pine Acres Club (Wethersfield, Conn. chpt.) (pres. 1968—69), Equestrian Order of the Holy Sepulchre of Jerusalem (Southeastern Lieutenancy) (knight 2004). Republican. Roman Catholic. Avocations: reading, photography, genealogy. Home: 5410 Aragon Ct Tampa FL 33624-4884 Personal E-mail: jam26ram50@aol.com.

MANGIERI, MARK LOUIS, computer engineer; b. Commack, NY, Aug. 16, 1960; s. Daniel Dominic and Jolene Theresa Mangieri; m. Jonica Ellen Stuart, May 22, 1982; children: Michael, Joseph. BA in Computer and Info. Sci., U. Houston Clear Lake, 1982. Programmer, analyst engring., scientific Ford Aerospace, Houston, 1983—88; electronic engr., aviation survival tech. NASA Johnson Space Ctr., Houston, 1988—94, computer engr., 1994—. Author: Government Furnished Equipment software, Advanced Resistive Exercise Device Softeware, 2006; contbr. articles to profl. jours. Recipient Group Achievement award, NASA, 1996, 1997, 2000, Space Flight Awareness award, 2001, Space Act award, 2003, 2004, 2006. Mem.: AIAA (space conf. track co-chair 2005). Republican. Avocations: boating, travel. Office: NASA Johnson Space Ctr 2101 NASA Pkwy Houston TX 77058 Home: 11903 Mighty Redwood Dr Houston TX 77059 Office Phone: 281-483-6126.

MANGIN, CHARLES-HENRI, electronics company executive; b. Riom, France, Apr. 16, 1942; s. Louis Eugene and Monique (Mathivon) M.; m. Marguerite Stern, Nov. 27, 1974; children: Charlotte, Louis-David, Maxence. MBA, Ecole Superieure de Commerce, Reims, France, 1965. Computer salesman IBM, Paris, 1967-68; asst. to pres. EDC, Rome, 1969-71; gen. mgr. CEGI, Paris, 1971-77; pres. CEERIS, Paris, 1977-81, CEERIS Internat., Inc., Old Lyme, Conn., 1982—. Cons. The Mitre Corp., Washington, 1973-78, Coyne & Bellier, Paris, 1973-76, IITRI, Chgo., 1979-81, PRC, London, 1980-81. Author: Lebanon, 1965, The Atlantic Facade, 1973, Flights Over Europe, 1974, Surface Mount Technology, 1986, Managing the SMT Challenge, 1990; contbg. editor Electronic Packaging and Prodn., 1988-91; contbr. articles to profl. jours. Mem. Surface Mount Tech. Assn., N.Y. Yacht Club, Ocean Cruising Club, Cruising Club Am., Ski Club (Les Arcs, France). Roman Catholic. Avocations: sailing, skiing, opera. Office: Ceeris Internat Inc PO Box 939 Old Lyme CT 06371-0939 Personal E-mail: strellaencore@aol.com.

MANGINI, ERIC, professional football coach; b. Hartford, Conn., Jan. 19, 1971; s. Carmine and Nancy Mangini; m. Julie Mangini; children: Jake, Luke. BA in Polit. Sci., Wesleyan Coll., 1994. Asst. coach Cleve. Browns, 1995—96, Balt. Ravens (formerly Cleve. Browns), 1996—97; defensive asst., quality control coach NY Jets, 1997—99; defensive backs coach New England Patriots, 1999—2005, defensive coord., 2005—06; head coach NY Jets, 2006—. Founder The Carmine & Frank Mangini Found., 2006—. Achievements include asst. coach, Super Bowl Champion New England Patriots, 2001, 2003, 2004. Office: c/o NY Jets 1000 Fulton Ave Hempstead NY 11550

MANGINO, CHRISTINE, academic administrator; BA, Hofstra U., Hempstead, NY, 1990, MA, 1996; EdD, St. John's U., Jamaica, NY, 2004. Prof. Hostos C.C., Bronx, NY, 2004—, coord. unit, 2004—. Co-pres. North Merrick SEPTA, North Merrick, NY, 2006—. Fellow, St. John's U., 2002—03. Home Phone: 516-546-1996; Office Phone: 718-518-4161. Personal E-mail: csmangino@yahoo.com. Business E-Mail: cmangino@hostos.cuny.edu.

MANGION, RICHARD MICHAEL, health facility administrator; b. Haverhill, Mass., Apr. 26, 1941; s. Michael Anthony and Evelyn (Cote) M.; m. Gail Elizabeth Donne, Apr. 27, 1968; children: Catherine Jean, James Richard, Ian Kyle. BBA, Suffolk U., 1963; MBA, Syracuse U., 1965; MPH, U. Calif., Berkeley, 1972. Asst. adminstr. Nashua (N.H.) Meml. Hosp., 1972-75, assoc. adminstr., 1975-77; pres. and chief exec. officer Harrington Meml. Hosp., Southbridge, Mass., 1977—. Lectr. U. N.H., Durham, 1972-74. Pres. Tri-Community Devel. Corp., Southbridge, 1983-88. Capt. USAF, 1966-70. Fellow Am. Coll. Health Care Execs. (regent Mass. area B 1995-99); mem. Am. Hosp. Assn., Mass. Hosp. Assn., Ctrl. Mass. Hosp. Coun. (pres. 1982-84), Ctrl. Mass. Health Care Found., Tri-Cmty. C. of C. (pres. 1983-84). Clubs: Hosp. Supts. Lodges: Rotary. Democrat. Roman Catholic. Avocations: tennis, swimming, hiking. Home: 50 Old Village Rd Sturbridge MA 01566-1069 Office: Harrington Meml Hosp 100 South St Ste 1 Southbridge MA 01550-4047 Home Phone: 508-347-3155; Office Phone: 508-765-9771 x 3451. E-mail: rmangion@harringtonhospital.org.

MANGLA, SUNDEEP, radiologist, research scientist; s. Kishan Chand and Sushila Mangla; m. Minh-Nhut Yvonne Dang, Oct. 4, 2003; children: Ronin Tai Satyam, Leila Mai Saraswati. BS, U. Akron, Ohio, 1988; MD, N.E. Ohio U., Rootstown, 1992. Resident in diagnostic radiology Coll. Medicine, N.E. OH U., Canton, 1992—97; fellow in diagnostic neuroradiology U. So. Calif., LA, 1997—98; fellow in interventional neuroradiology and neuroendovascular surgery Yale U., New Haven, 1998—99, U. Iowa, Iowa City, 1999—2000; asst. prof. interventional neuroradiology Columbia and Cornell Univs., NYC, 2000—03; dir. interventional neuroradiology, radiology rsch. SUNY Downstate Health Sci. Ctr., Bklyn., 2003—. Dir. radiology rsch. SUNY Downstate Health Sci. Ctr., 2006—. Contbr. articles to profl. jours. Local educator stroke awareness SUNY Health Sci. Ctr., Bklyn., 2003—06. Grantee, Columbia U., NY, 2002—03. Mem.: Neurocritical Care Soc., Am. Soc. Neuroradiology, Am. Soc. Interventional and Therapeutic Neuroradiology. Achievements include patents pending for endovascular and endoluminal robotics, nano-robotics. Avocations: tennis, basketball, travel, cooking, international and independent cinema. Home Phone: 718-270-4141; Office Phone: 718-270-4141. Office Fax: 718-270-7241. Business E-Mail: smangla@downstate.edu.

MANGLONA, JOHN A., commonwealth supreme court justice; b. Rota, Northern Marianas, June 12, 1959; m. Mona V. Monglona; 2 children. BA in Polit. Econ., U. Calif., Berkeley, 1981; JD, Creighton U., 1984; LLM in Taxation, U. Pacific, 1988. Pvt. practice; assoc. judge Commonwealth Superior Ct., 1998—2000; justice Commonwealth Supreme Ct., 2000—. Designated justice Guam Supreme Ct., 1999—2003. Office: House Justice Guma Hustisia, Imwaal Aweewe PO Box 502179 Saipan MP 96950-2179 Business E-Mail: supreme.court@saipan.com. *

MANGLONA, RAMONA V., judge, former attorney general; b. 1967; BA, U. Calif., 1990; JD, U. N.Mex., 1996. Bar: New Mex. Bar Assn. 1997, No. Mariana Islands Bar Assn. 1997. Asst. atty. gen., 1997—2002; atty. gen. No. Mariana Islands, Saipan, 2002—03; assoc. judge Commonwealth Superior Ct., 2003—. Home Phone: 670-235-5443; Office Phone: 670-236-9751. *

MANGO, WILFRED GILBERT, JR., construction, real estate company executive; b. Weehawken, NJ, July 11, 1940; s. Wilfred Gilbert and Mildred B.M.; children from previous marriage; Christian P., Peter H.; m. Charlene Holt, Feb. 14, 1985; children: Alison L., David H. BS, Lehigh U., 1963; MBA, NYU, 1969. With Hurdman & Cranstown, NYC, 1963-69; dir. fin. Thomas Crimmins Contracting Co., NYC, 1969-77; v.p. fin., mgr. fin. controls ITT Teleplant, Inc., NYC, 1977-78; v.p. fin. George A. Fuller Co. div. Northrop Corp., NYC, 1978-81, now pres., CEO, dir., 1981—; chmn., CEO Fuller Internat. Devel., Ltd. Past chmn. bd. trustees Marymount Manhattan Coll., The Stanwich Sch., Greenwich, Conn.; adv. bd. N.Y. Real Estate Inst.; bus. adv. coun. emeritus Lehigh U.; bus. coun. Lighthouse for the Blind; mem. Urban Land Inst. Mem.: Bell Haven Club, Univ. Club, Lehigh U. N.Y. Club. Home: 40 Carrington Dr Greenwich CT 06831-3119 Business E-Mail: wmango@fullerdev.com.

MANGOLD, JOHN FREDERIC, manufacturing executive, retired military officer; b. La Grange, Ill., Jan. 24, 1927; s. John Frederic and Helvig Victoria (Anderson) M.; m. Margaret Ellen Gore, Oct. 25, 1947; children: John, Andrew, Jennifer. BS, U.S. Naval Acad., 1947; MSEE, U.S. Naval Postgrad. Sch., Monterey, Calif., 1958. Registered profl. engr., Conn. Commd. ensign USN, 1947, advanced through grades to comdr., 1962, comdg. officer nuclear submarine U.S.S. Halibut, 1962—63, comdg. officer nuclear tng. unit, 1963—67, ret., 1967; v.p. mfg. Combustion Engring., Inc., Windsor, Conn., 1972—78, group pres., 1982—86, v.p. utility boilers, 1990—91; pres. Vetco, Inc., Ventura, Calif., 1978—82; cons., 1992; pres. Detrex Corp., Southfield, Mich., 1992—93, ret., 1993. Bd. dirs. Detrex Corp. Mem. IEEE, U.S. C. of C. (energy com. 1984-87). Republican.

MANGOLD, SYLVIA PLIMACK, artist; b. NYC, Sept. 18, 1938; d. Maurice and Ethel (Rein) Plimack; m. Robert Mangold. Student, Cooper Union, 1956-59; BFA, Yale U., 1961. Exhibited one-person shows Daniel Weinberg Gallery, San Francisco, 1974, 75, Fischbach Gallery, N.Y.C., 1974, 76, Fischbach, 1974, 76, Annemarie Verna Gallery, Zurich, 1978, 91, 97, Droll-Kolbert Gallery, N.Y.C., 1978, 80, Young Hoffman Gallery, Chgo., 1980, Ohio State U., Columbus, 1980, Pa. Acad., 1981, Contemporary Arts Mus., Houston, 1981, Madison Art Ctr., (Wis.), 1982, Brooke Alexander, Inc., 1982, 83, 84, 85, 86, 89, 92, 95, Duke Art Mus., N.C., 1982, Rhona Hoffman Gallery, Chgo., 1982, 85, Tex. Gallery, 1986, Fuller Goldeen Gallery, San Francisco, 1987, U. Mich, Ann Arbor, 1992, Minn. Inst. Arts, 1992, Grunwald Ctr. for Graphic Arts, UCLA, 1992, Neuberger Mus. Art, SUNY Purchase, 1993, Davison Art Ctr., Wesleyan U., Middletown, Conn., 1993, Albright-Knox Art Gallery, Buffalo, 1994, Wadsworth Atheneum, Hartford, Conn., 1994, Blaffer Gallery U. Houston, 1994, Mus. Fine Arts, Boston, 1994, Herbert F. Johnson Museum, 1998, Cornell U., Ithaca, N.Y., 1998, Alexander and Bonin, N.Y., 2000, 2003; group shows at Young Hoffman Gallery, Chgo., 1979, Walker Art Ctr., Mpls., 1979, Droll-Kolbert Gallery, 1979, Denver Art Mus., 1979, U. So. Calif., 1979, Honolulu Acad. Art, 1979, Oakland Mus., (Calif.), 1979, Univ. Art Mus. of U. Tex.-Austin, 1979, Cornell U., Ithaca, N.Y., 1979, The New Museum of Contemporary Art, N.Y.C., 1979, Nat. Museum, Belgrade, Yugoslavia, 1979, Internat. Biennial Ljibljana, Yugoslavia, Phoenix Art Mus., 1979, Art Latitute Gallery, N.Y.C., 1980, Thorpe Intermedia Gallery, Sparkhill, N.Y., 1980, U. Colo. Art Galleries, Boulder, 1980, Nina Freudenheim Gallery, Buffalo, 1980, U.S. Pavillion of Venice Biennial, 1980-81, Indianapolis Museum of Art, 1980, Civici Musei e Gallerie di Storia e Arte, Sala Ajace, Udine, Italy, 1980, Young Hoffman, Chicago, 1980-81, Delahurty, Dallas, 1980, Museum of Modern Art, 1981, Wesleyan U. Art Gallery, 1981, Davison Art Ctr., Middleton, Conn., 1981, Virginia Museum of Fine Arts, Richmond, 1981, Oakland Museum, Calif., 1981, Inst. Contemporary Art of U. Pa., Phila, 1980-81, Yale U. Art Gallery, 1981, San Antonio Mus. Art, 1981, Indpls. Mus. Art, 1981, Tucson Mus. Art, 1981, Pa. Acad., 1981, Mus. Art of Carnegie Inst., Pitts., 1981, Brooke Alexander, Inc., N.Y.C., 1982, Ben Shahn Ctr. Visual Arts, 1982, Castle Gallery, Coll. of New Rochelle, N.Y., 1983, Thomas Segal Gallery, Boston, 1982-83, Siegel Contemporary Art, N.Y., 1983, Freedman Gallery, Albright Coll., Reading, Pa., 1983, Fuller Goldeen, San Francisco, 1983, Yale U. Art Gallery, New Haven, 1983-84, 86, Wilcox Gallery, Swarthmore, Pa., 1984, The Hudson River Mus., Yonkers, N.Y., 1984, Sardonia Art Gallery, Wilkes Coll., Wilkes-Barre, Pa., 1985, Kent State U. Gallery, Ohio, 1985, Brooke Alexander, N.Y., 1985, John C. Stoller Co., Minn., 1985, Knight Gallery, Spirit Sq. Arts Ctr., Charlotte, N.C., 1986, Mus. Art, R.I. Sch. Design, Providence, 1986, Yale U. Gallery, 1986, CUNY, 1986-87, Lorence Monk Gallery, N.Y.C., Vanguard Gallery, Phila., 1986-87, Aldrich Mus., Ridgefield, 1986-87. Flander's Contemporary Art, Mpls., 1987, Annemarie Verna Galerie, Zurich, 1988, U. N.C., 1988, R.I. Sch. Design, 1988, Grace Borgenicht Gallery, N.Y.C., 1988, Fay Gold Gallery, Atlanta, 1988, U. N.C., Greensboro, Three Rivers Arts Festival, Pitts., 1989, Cin. Art Mus., New Orleans Mus. Art, Denver Art Mus., Pa. Acad. Fine Arts, 1989, U. Mich., 1992, Mpls. Inst. Arts, 1992, Grunwald Ctr. Graphic Arts, UCLA, L.A., Neuberger Mus. Art, SUNY Purchase, 1993, Davison Art Ctr., 1993, Montgomery Glasoe Fine Art, Mpls., 1993, Yale U. Art Gallery, New Haven, 1993, Daniel Weinberg Gallery, Santa Monica, Calif., 1993, Museum of Fine Arts, Boston, 1993, Barbara Mathes Gallery, N.Y.C., 1993, Nina Freudenheim Gallery, Buffalo, 1993, Kansas City Gallery of Art, U. Mo., 1994, Midtown Payson, N.Y.C., 1994, Katonah Museum of Art, N.Y., 1994, Rhona Hoffman Gallery, Chgo., 1994, Feigen Inc., Chgo., 1994, Brooke Alexander, N.Y.C., 1994, Elga Wimmer Gallery, N.Y.C., 1995, Aargauer Kunsthaus Aarau, Austria, 1995, The Am. Acad. of Arts and Letters, N.Y.C., 1995, Andre Zarre Gallery, N.Y.C., 1996, Aspen Art Museum, Colo., 1996, The Am. Acad. of Arts and Letters, N.Y.C., 1996, Anne Marie Verna Gallery, Zurich, Switzerland, 1997, Queens Museum of Art, 1997, Aspen Art Museum, 1997, U. Gallery, Fine Arts Ctr., U. Mass., Amherst James Graham & Sons, N.Y.C., 1997, The Museum of Modern Art, 1997, Seattle Art Museum, 1997, State U. N.Y., 1998, N.Y.C. Dowd Fine Arts Gallery, 1998, The Am. Acad. of Fine Arts and Letters, 1998, Karen McCready Fine Art, 1999, Alexander and Bonin, N.Y.C., 1999, Henry Art Gallery, Seattle, 2000, Small Work, Nina Freudenheim Inc., Buffalo, Whitney Mus., 2006, and numberous others; exhibited in permanent collections, Albright-Knox Art Gallery, Buffalo, Allen Meml. Art Mus., Oberlin, Ohio, Bklyn. Mus., Dallas Mus. Fine Arts, Detroit Inst. Art, Mus. Fine Arts, Houston, Indpls. Mus. Art, Madison (Wis.) Art Ctr., Milw. Art Mus., Yale U. Art Gallery, Mus. Modern Art, N.Y.C., Mus. Fine Arts, U. Utah, Tampa (Fla.) Mus., Walker Art Mus., Mpls., Whitney Mus. Am. Art, N.Y., Weatherspoon Art Gallery, Greensboro, N.C., Wadsworth Athenaeum, Hartford, U. Mich., Utah Mus. Fine Art, Museum of Fine Arts, Boston, N.Y.C. Public Library, Smith Coll. Museum, Northampton, Mass., Achenbach Found. for Graphic Arts, San Francisco, St. Louis Art Museum, The Tampa Museum, Art Inst. Chgo., Modern Art Mus. Fort Worth Tex., Indpls. Mus. Art, Telfair Mus. Art, Savannah Ga. Achievements include work reviewed in newspapers and mags. Office Phone: 212-367-7474. Business E-Mail: gallery@alexanderandbonin.com.

MANGONE, GERARD J., international maritime law educator; b. NYC, Oct. 10, 1918; s. Gerard Francis and Viola (Schumm) M.; m. Emma Haddad, Apr. 13, 1958; children— Cleopatra, Regina, Flaminia. AB, CCNY, 1938; MA, Harvard U., Cambridge, Mass., 1947, PhD (Charles Summer prize), 1949. Asst. prof. polit. sci. Wesleyan U., Middletown, Conn., 1948-51; assoc. prof. Swarthmore Coll., 1951-56; prof. polit. sci. and internat. relations Syracuse U., 1956-67; dir. grad. overseas tng. program, exec. officer Maxwell Center Study Overseas Operations, 1958-60; exec. asst. to dean Maxwell Grad. Sch., 1961-64, asso. dean dir. internat. relations program, 1961-67; dean Coll. Liberal Arts, v.p., provost Temple U., Phila., 1967-69; sr. fellow Woodrow Wilson Internat. Ctr., 1970-72; prof. internat. law U. Del., Newark, 1972-74, dir. Ctr. for Study of Marine Policy, 1973-89, H. Rodney Sharp prof. internat. law and orgn., 1975-89, univ. rsch. prof. internat. and maritime law, 1989—, prof. legal studies, 2001—, coord. grad. studies, 1976-79; adj. prof. Maine Maritime Acad., 1992—94. Vis. prof. Trinity Coll., Mt. Holyoke Coll., Yale, Princeton, Johns Hopkins; Tagore law prof. U. Calcutta, 1979; disting. lectr. U. Ind., 1980; vis. scholar U. Western Australia, 1983, 87, Peking U., 1984, Capetown U., 1986, 89, U. Natal, 1989, Hanyang U., 1994, Hong Kong U., 1997; mem. Presdl. Commn. Trust Territory Pacific, 1963; cons. AID, 1965-67, Nat. Commn. Marine Resources and Engring. and State Dept., 1967-73, UN, 1965, US Corps Engrs., 1975; vice chmn. exec. com. Commn. Study Orgn. Peace; exec. dir. Pres.' Commn. on UN, 1970-71; dir. diploma program, shipping and pt. mgmt. Pt. of Singapore, 1990-97; founder Gerard J. Mangone Marine Policy Ctr., 2003. Author: The Idea and Practice of World Government, 1951, A Short History of International Organization, 1954, The Elements of International Law, 2d edit, 1967, Marine Policy for America, 1977, 2d edit., 1989, Law for the World Ocean, 1981, Mangone's Concise Marine Almanac, 2d edit., 1991, United States Admiralty Law, 1997; co-author, editor: The Art of Overseasmanship, 1958, The Overseas Americans, 1960, European Political Systems, 1960, UN Administration of Economic and Social Programs, 1966, Energy Policies of the World, 3 vols, 1976-79, Internat. Straits of the World, 14 vols., 1978-2004; editor: Future of Gas and Oil from Sea, American Strategic Minerals, 1984; editor in chief: Marine Policy Reports, 1981-91, Internat. Jour. Marine and Coastal Law, 1991—. Capt. AUS, 1942-46, maj. res., 1946-54. Mem. Am. Soc. Internat. Law, Internat. Law Assn., Maritime Law Assn., Port of Wilmington Maritime Soc. (bd. dirs. 1980-, chmn. 1989, Francis Alison award 1983), Alison Soc. (sec. 1990—), Del. Acad. Sci. (pres. 1993), Cosmos Club (Washington), Harvard Club (NYC). Home: 201 Unami Trl Newark DE 19711-7508 Office: Univ Del Grad Coll Marine Studi Newark DE 19716 Office Phone: 302-831-8087. Business E-Mail: gmangone@udel.edu.

MANGOUNI, NORMAN, publishing executive; b. Detroit, Oct. 19, 1932; s. Nazareth Lazarus and Isabelle (Garabedian) M.; m. Anahid Apelian, May 10, 1964; 1 child, Marie-Isabelle. AB, U. Mich., 1954; MS, Columbia U., 1955; postgrad., U. Mich., 1957-58. Reporter Ann Arbor (Mich.) News, 1957-59; editor Mich. Alumnus, U. Mich., Ann Arbor, 1959-62; sr. editor Coll. Entrance Exam. Bd., NYC, 1962-64; dir. fin. aid U. Miami, Coral Gables, Fla., 1965-66; dir. State U. N.Y. Press, Albany, 1966-78; pres., gen. editor Scholars' Facsimiles & Reprints, Ann Arbor, Mich., 1972—; pres. Caravan Books, Ann Arbor, Mich., 1972—, Acad. Resources Corp., Las Vegas, Nev., 1988—; corr. DuPont-Columbia Survey and Awards, 1976-78; rep. to com. on standards in field of library work, documentation and related pub. practices Am. Nat. Standards Inst., 1974-78. Exec. asst. to majority caucus Mich. State Senate, 1964; dir. summer session Am. Coll. Switzerland, 1979, 81, 82. Co-translator: The Gaucho Martin Fierro, 1974; contbr. articles to profl. jours.; mem. editorial bd. Ararat mag, 1962-66, 77-78. Served to lt. USAF, 1955-57. Mem. Mensa, Phi Sigma Kappa, Sigma Delta Chi, Phi Alpha Delta. Home: PO Box 5934 Carefree AZ 85377 Office Phone: 480-575-9945. E-mail: maxinmin@umich.edu.

MANGRAVITE, RONALD, education educator, writer; MFA, UCLA, LA; BA (highest hons.), U. Calif., Berkeley; prep., Lawrenceville Sch., NJ. Instr. Juilliard Sch., NYC, 1974—76; assoc. artistic dir. Attic Theatre, Detroit, 1985—90; instr. Am. Film Inst., LA, 1991—2000, U. of Miami, Coral Gables, 2001—02; theatre, film critic Miami New Times, New Times Broward/Palm Beach, Miami, 2001—05; asst. prof. U. Miami, Coral Gables. Author: (plays) Back in the Saddle premiered NY, 1981, Behind the Chutes premiered NY, 1981, The Lewis & Clark Expedition, premiered Ashland, OR, 1983, The Rewrite premiered San Francisco, 1983, Jean Baptiste Pointe du Sable: Black Man in the Wilderness premiered Detroit, 1988, Madame Cadillac premiered Detroit, 1989, The Great Divide, 2005; dir.(writer): (short film) The Queen of the Sea, 2002, My Father's Hopes (Silver Palmetto Piccolo Spoleto Short Film Festival, 2004); screenwriter (films) Kennedy Boulevard, 2006; screenwriter, prodr.: (films) For Liberty, 2007; co-author: The Screenwriter's Manual, 2005, The Complete Screenwriter's Manual, 2006. Recipient First prize, Fla. Press Assn., 2003, Silver Palmetto, Piccolo Spoleto Festival, 2004 for My Father's Hopes, Best Film, Miami Film Festival Collaboration Film Contest, 2002 for The Queen of the Sea, Best Screenplay, 2002 for The Queen of the Sea, Best of the Fest citation, Silver Images Film Festival, 2002 for My Father's Hopes. Mem.: U. Film and Video Assn., Dramatists Guild (assoc.). Office: Univ of Miami 5100 Brunson Dr Coral Gables FL 33146 Home Phone: 305-529-1977; Office Phone: 305-284-5219. Business E-Mail: mangravite@miami.edu.

MANGUM, GARTH LEROY, retired economist; b. Delta, Utah, July 23, 1926; s. James L. and Golda (Elder) M.; m. Marion Poll, Nov. 20, 1953; children: Stephen, David, Mary, Elizabeth. BS, Brigham Young U., 1956; MPA, Harvard U., 1958, PhD, 1960; JD, U. Utah, 1989. Instr. econs. Harvard U., 1960; asso. prof. econs. Brigham Young U., 1960-63; sr. staff analyst Presdl. R.R. Commn., 1961; research dir., subcom. employment and manpower U.S. Senate, 1963-64; exec. dir. President's Com. Manpower, 1964-65; exec. sec. Nat. Com. Tech., Automation and Econ. Progress, 1965-66; research prof. econs. George Washington U., 1967-71; co-dir. George Washington U. (Center Manpower Policy Studies), 1967-69; Max McGraw prof. econs. and mgmt. U. Utah, Salt Lake City, 1969-97, prof. emeritus, 1997—, dir. Inst. Human Resource Mgmt., 1969-90. Adj. prof. edn. leadership Brigham Young U., 2003—; lectr. U. Tel Aviv, Israel, 1969, 84, Am. Seminar at Salzburg, 1975, U. South Africa, 1977, Monash U., Australia, 1984; spl. mediator Fed. Mediation and Conciliation Svc., 1962-63; mem. Adv. Coun. Vocat. Edn., 1966-67; vice chmn. Nat. Manpower Policy Task Force, 1966-69, chmn., 1969-71; mem. Nat. Coun. on Employment Policy, 1976—, chmn., 1979-81, sec.- treas., 1990-2002; chmn. Nat. Inst. Career Edn., 1976-81; cons. internat. agencies, fed., state and local govts., bus. firms, govts. of, Saudi Arabia, Kuwait, Jordan, Omen, Yemen, Bahrain, United Arab Emirates, Indonesia, Yugoslavia, Romania, Uganda, Nigeria, Israel, South Africa, Russia, Brazil, Argentina, Chile, Uruguay, Mexico, Philippines, Taiwan, Republic of Korea, China, others; cons. AID, ILO, World Bank; also arbitrator; v.p. Retired Faculty Assn., U. SC, 2006-. Author: The Operating Engineers: Economic History of a Trade Union, 1964, MDTA, Foundation of Federal Manpower Policy, 1968, The Emergence of Manpower Policy, 1969, Federal Work and Training Program in the 1960's, 1969, Economic Opportunity in the Ghetto, 1970, Human Resources and Labor Markets, 1971, Career Education: What It Is and How To Do It, 1972, A Decade of Manpower Development and Training, 1973, Career Education and the Elementary School Teacher, 1973, Career Education in the Middle/Junior High School, 1973, Manpower Planning for Local Labor Markets, 1974, Career Education for the Academic Classroom, 1975, Employability, Employment and Income, 1976, Career Education in the High School, 1976, Your Child's Career, 1977, The Lingering Crisis of Youth Unemployment, 1978, Coming of Age in the Ghetto, 1978, Job Market Futurity, 1979, The Coal Industry and its Industrial Relations, 1985, Capital and Labor in American Copper, 1992, Labor Struggle in The Post Office, 1992, The Mormons War on Poverty, 1993, Union Resilience in Troubled Times, 1994, Portable Pension Plans for Casual Labor Markets, 1995, Transnational Industrial Marriages, 1996, The Rise, Fall and Replacement of Industry-Wide Bargaining in the Basic Steel Industry, 1996, Programs in Aid of the Poor, 8th edit., 2003, On Being Poor in Utah, 1997, The Public Employment Svc. In a One Stop World, 1998, Poverty Ain't What It Used To Be, 1999, Confronting The Youth Demographic Challenge, 2000, The Persistance of Poverty in the United States, 2003, Struggling at the Golden Door: International Refugees in Utah, 2007; also articles, monographs.; editor: The Manpower Revolution: Its Policy Consequences, 1965, Automation and Economic Progress, 1966, Metropolitan Impact of Manpower Programs, 1973, The T in CETA, 1981, Of Heart and Mind: Social Policy Essays in Honor of Sar A. Levitan, 1996, Utah's Poor: Solutions for Today's Economyy, 2005 With USAAF, 1944-45. Mem. Ch. of Jesus Christ of Latter-day Saints (missionary 1950-53, bishop 1971-78, other positions). Home: 2130 Ridgewood Way Bountiful UT 84010-1632 Personal E-mail: garthmangum@msn.com.

MANGUM, MYLLE BELL, information technology executive; b. Thomas, Ga. BA, Emory U., 1970. Tchr. N. Syracuse Sch. Sys., NY; computer programmer and systems analyst Gen. Electric Corp., 1972, gen. mgr. systems ops.; pres. BellSouth Internat., 1990; bd. dirs., exec. v.p. strategic mgmt. Holiday Inn Worldwide, 1992, exec. v.p. mktg.; pres. global systems and sr. v.p. strategic planning and expense mgmt. Carlson Wagonlit Travel; CEO MMS Incentives, 1999, True Mktg. Services, Internat. Banking Technologies, 2003—. Bd. dirs. Scientific Atlanta, Payless ShoeSource, Inc., Haverty Furniture Companies, The Barnes Group, Inc., Respironics, Inc., Emageon, Inc. Bd. trustees Piedmont Coll., Boys & Girls Club; adv. bd. Emory Bus. Sch.; mem. bd. Ga. Ctr. Advanced Telecommunications Tech. Named Decision Maker of Yr., Bus. to Bus. mag., Marketer of Yr., Am. Mktg. Assn.-Atlanta chpt.; named one of Divas 2000, Bus. to Bus. mag., 100 Most Influential Atlantans, Atlanta Bus. Chronicle; recipient Woman of Yr. Tech., (WIT) Women in Tech., 2004. Mem.: Soc. Internat. Bus. Fellows, Committee of 200 (former pres.). Office: Internat Banking Tech Ste 300 1770 Indian Trail Norcross GA 30093 Office Phone: 770-381-2023. Office Fax: 770-381-2123.

MANHART, MARCIA Y(OCKEY), art museum director; b. Wichita, Kans., Jan. 14, 1943; d. Everett W. and Ruth C. (Correll) Yockey; children: Caroline Manhart Sanderson, Emily Alexandrea Morrison. BA in Art, U. Tulsa, 1965, MA in Ceramics, 1971. Dir. edn. Philbrook Art Ctr., Tulsa, 1972-77, exec. v.p., asst. dir., 1977-83, acting dir., 1983-84; exec. dir. Philbrook Mus. Art (formerly Philbrook Art Ctr.), Tulsa, 1984—2003; exec. dir., trustee The Judith and Jean Pape Charitable Foun., 2004—. Instr. Philbrook Art Ctr. Mus. Sch., Tulsa, 1963-72; gallery dir. Alexandre Hogue Gallery, Tulsa U., 1967-69; NEH Challenge Grant panelist, 1991, presenter to AAM Conv., 1991; MAAA Craft Fellowship panelist, 1988, 93, NEA Craft Fellowship panelist, 1990; NEA spl. exhbn. panelist, 1996; curator nat. touring exhibit Nature's Forms/Nature's Forces: The Art of Alexandre Hogue, 1984-85; co-curator internat. exhbn.: The Eloquent Object, 1987-90; curator Sanford and Diane Besser Collection exhbn., 1992. Author essays in field. Vis. com. Smithsonian Instn./Renwick Gallery, Washington, 1986; cultural negotiator Gov. George Nigh's World Trade Mission (Okla.), China., 1985; com. mem. State Art Coll. of Okla., 1985—; mem. Assocs. of Hillcrest Med. Ctr., 1983-88, exec. com., 1985-88; com. mem. Neighborhood Housing Services, 1985-87; mem. City of Tulsa Arts Commn., 1996-2003; steering com. Harwelden Isnt. for Aesthetic Edn., 1983; com. mem. River Parks Authority, 1976; mem. Jr. League of Tulsa Inc., 1974-78; adv. panel mem. Nat. Craft Planning Project, NEA, Washington, 1978-81; craft adv. panel mem. Okla. Arts and Humanities Council, 1974-76; juror numerous art festivals, competitions, programs; reviewer Inst. Mus. Services, Washington, 1985, 88, 92, 95, 98; auditor Symposium on Language & Scholarship of Modern Crafts, NEA and NEH, Washington, 1981; nominator MacArthur Fellows Program, 1988; panelist Lila Wallace Reader's Digest Internat. Artists Fellowship, 1992, panelist Pew Charitable Trust, 1996. Recipient Harwelden award for Individual Contbrn. in the Arts, 1989, Gov.'s award State of Okla., 1992. Mem. Gillespie County Hist. Soc. (bd. dirs. 2005—), Phi Beta Kappa. Home: 105 S Cherry St Fredericksburg TX 78624 Office Phone: 830-997-7347. E-mail: mmanhart@austin.rr.com.

MANHEIM, CAMRYN, television and film actress; b. Caldwell, NJ, Mar. 8, 1961; d. Jerry and Sylvia Manheim; 1 child, Milo Jacob. BFA, UC Santa Cruz, 1984; MFA, NYU, 1987. Actor: (TV series) The Practice, 1997—2004 (Emmy award for Outstanding Supporting Actress in a Drama Series, 1998, Golden Globe award for Best Performance by an Actress in a Supporting Role, 1999); (TV films) Jackie's Back!, 1999, The Loretta Claiborne Story, 2000, Jenifer, 2001; (TV miniseries) The 10th Kingdom, 2000, A Girl Thing, 2001, Elvis, 2005; actor, prodr. (TV films) Kiss My Act, 2000; actor: (films) Bonfire of the Vanities, 1990, The Road to Wellville, 1994, Jeffrey, 1995, Eraser, 1996, Romy and Michele's High School Reunion, 1997, David Searching, 1998, Wide Awake, 1998, Mercury Rising, 1998, Happiness, 1998 (Nat. Bd. Rev. award, 1998), Fool's Gold, 1998, Joe the King, 1999, What Planet are You From?, 2000, East of A, 2000, The Laramie Project, 2002, Just Like Mona, 2003, Scary Movie 3, 2003, Twisted, 2004, Marilyn Hotchkiss' Ballroom Dancing and Charm School, 2005, Dark Water, 2005, An Unfinished Life, 2005; guest appearances Law and Order, Touched By an Angel, New York Undercover, Ally McBeal, Oh Baby, Chicago Hope, Will and Grace; writer: (off-Broadway play) Wake Up, I'm Fat, 1995; theater appearances include N.Y. Shakespeare Festival, Lincoln Ctr., Yale Repertory, N.Y. Theatre Workshop, Classic Stage Co., Home for Contemporary Theater. Office: Creative Artists Agy 9830 Wilshire Blvd Beverly Hills CA 90212

MANHEIMER, HEIDI, cosmetics company executive; Diploma in Bus. Mgmt., Ithaca Coll., 1985. Various buying and mgmt. positions Bloomingdales; v.p. cosmetics Barneys NY; with Bluemercury.com, 1999; gen. mgr. Beauty.com; exec. v.p. Shiseido Cosmetics (Am.) Ltd., pres., 2002—06, CEO, 2006—. Bd. dirs. Fragrance Found. Recipient Skin Sense award, Skin Cancer Found., 2005. Office: Shiseido Cosmetics Am Ltd 178 Bauer Dr Oakland NJ 07436-3131

MANHOLD, JOHN HENRY, dental educator, consultant; b. Rochester, NY, Aug. 20, 1919; s. John Henry and Helen Martha (Shulz) Manhold; m. Beverly Schecter, 1953 (div. 1969); 1 child; m. Enriqueta Andino, Mar. 20, 1971. BA, U. Rochester, 1940; MD, Harvard U., 1944; MA, Washington U., 1956. Instr. Coll. Medicine Tufts U., Boston, 1948—50; asst. prof., chmn. gen. and oral pathology Coll. Dentistry U. Washington, St. Louis, 1954—56; from asst. prof. to prof., chmn. dept. gen. and oral pathology Seton Hall Coll. Medicine and Dentistry (now U. Medicine and Dentistry NJ, Newark, 1956—87; med. dir. Woog Internat., 1987—89; ret., 1989. Cons. Johnson & Johnson, New Brunswick, NJ, 1960—70, Richardson-Vicks, Shelton, Conn., 1981—87, Los Produits Associes, Geneva, 1965—87, Health Care Devel. Group NJ, 1990—2005, Health Care Devel. Group Pa., 1990—2005, Consumer Comm. Network NY, 1990—2005, Consumer Comm. Network Conn., 1990—; lectr. in field. Author: Introductory Psychosomatic Dentistry, 1956, Outline of Pathology, 1960; editor: Clinical Oral Diagnosis, 1965; author: Tissue Respiration and Oxigenating Agents, 1977, Practical Dental Management: Patients and Practice, 1984, El Tigre, 2007; author: (in 4 langs.) Illustrated Dental Terminology: A Lexicon for the Dental Profession, 1985; author: (with others) Handbook of Pathology, 1987; editor: Clinical Preventive Dentistry Jour., 1979—92; contbr. articles to profl. jours. Named Disting. Alumni, Harvard U., 1989; named to Sr. Soc. Harvard Sch. Dental Medicine, 1984; recipient Pres. award, Alumni Assn. U. Medicine and Dentistry NJ, 1980, Letter Appreciation, Asara Mihara former min. Japan, 1980, Cert. Achievement, U. Md., 1965. Fellow: Acad. Psychosomatic Medicine (sec. 1975—76, treas. 1976—77, pres. 1977—78), Internat. Coll. Dentists, Am. Coll. Dentists; mem.: APA, Western Writers of Am., Soc. SW Authors, Internat. Assn. Dental Rsch., Am. Soc. Clin. Pathologists, St. Petersburg Yacht Club, Sigma Xi. Home and Office: 26027 N 44th Ave Phoenix AZ 85083 Office Phone: 623-434-6647. E-mail: kupferce@cox.net.

MANI, MARC, plastic surgeon; BA, Harvard U., 1990; MD, Baylor Coll. Med. Sch. Diplomate Am. Bd. Plastic Surgery, 2002. Co-owner & med. dir. M Aesthetics Spa, LA; ptnr. Aesthetic Surg. Ptnrs., Santa Barbara, Calif. Featured doctor, contbr. Make Me Heal web portal (MakeMeHeal.com). Featured in (documentaries) Plastic Surgery Beverly Hills, The Learning Channel, 2005, (TV series) Dr. Phil, NBC, Plastic Surgery: Before & After, Discovery Health Channel, Extra: Hollywood Makeovers, NBC, Brand New You, Showtime. Named one of Top Plastic Surgeons in Southern Calif., Fashionlines. Mem.: AMA, Am. Soc. Aesthetic Plastic Surgeons, Am. Soc. Plastic Surgeons. Office: M Aesthetics/Spa Ground Fl 9201 Sunset Blvd Los Angeles CA 90069 also: Aesthetic Surg Ptnrs 427 Pueblo St Santa Barbara CA 93105 Office Phone: 310-203-0511, 805-682-7222. Office Fax: 310-859-9820. E-mail: mmanimd@post.harvard.edu. *

MANI, NANDITA S., medical librarian; b. Edmonton, Alberta, Canada, Jan. 31, 1978; d. Rajam Subra and Anu Subra Mani; m. Scotia Meeshan Roopnarine; 1 child, Maya Mani Roopnarine. BA, U. Concordia, Edmonton, Alberta, Can., 1999; M in Libr. and Info. Sci., Wayne State U., Detroit, 2003, postdoc. in Instrnl. Tech., 2006—. Cert. computer sys. tech. Northern Alberta Inst. Tech., 2000. Sys. analyst Cross Cancer Inst., Edmonton, Alberta, Canada, 1999—2001; info. sys. libr. Shiffman Med. Libr. Wayne State U., Detroit, 2003—05; med. libr. Sladen Libr. Henry Ford Hosp., 2005—. Presenter at profl. confs. Contbr. articles to profl. jours. Mem.: Met. Med. Libr. Group (chair pub. rels. 2007—), Med. Libr. Assn. (mem. minority student scholarship jury 2006—), Beta Tau, Beta Phi Mu. Office: Henry Ford Hosp Sladen Libr K-17 2799 W Grand Blvd Detroit MI 48202 Office Phone: 313-916-5335. Business E-Mail: nmani@wayne.edu.

MANIAS, WILLIAM G., oil industry executive; b. Concord, NH, Feb. 24, 1962; m. Gretchen Manias; 2 children. BSCE, Princeton Univ.; MS, La. State Univ.; MBA, Rice Univ. Fin. mgmt. positions J.P. Morgan, 1992—2001; v.p. bus. develop. & strategic planning El Paso Field Services, 2001—04; CFO GulfTerra Energy Partners LP, 2004; v.p. corp. develop. Enterprise Product Partners LP, 2004—06; v.p., CFO TEPPCO Partners LP, Houston, 2006—. Office: TEPPCO Partners LLP 1100 Louisiana St Houston TX 77002 *

MANIBUSAN, JOAQUIN V.E., JR., magistrate judge; b. Sinajana, Guam, Dec. 10, 1949; s. Joaquin and Alejandrina M.; m. Eileen Bordallo; children: Joaquin III, Erwin, Michael, Maria. BA in Polit. Sci., U. Calif., Berkeley, 1971, JD, 1974. Asst. atty. gen. Govt. of Guam, 1975-77; pvt.

practice Guam, 1977-95; judge Superior Ct. of Guam, Agana, Guam, 1995—2004; magistrate judge Dist. of Guam, 2004—. Vice-chmn., mem. Chalan Pago (Guam)-Ordot Mcpl. Planning Coun.; mem. Ret. Srs. Vol. Program; chmn., mem. Guam chpt. ARC; mem. Chalan Pago Parish Coun. Mem. Jr. Holy Name Soc. (pres.), Knights of Alter (v.p.). Office: Dist Ct of Guam 3d Floor US Courthouse Hagatna GU 96910

MANILOW, BARRY (BARRY ALAN PINCUS), singer, composer; b. NYC, June 17, 1946; s. Harold Pincus and Edna M. Student, N.Y. Coll. Music. Former positions include mailroom CBS; film editor WCBS-TV. Dir. music Callback series, Ed. Sullivan's Pilots; dir. music, condr., arranger, producer for Bette Midler, singer and composer; recorded hit songs: Can't Smile Without You, I Write the Songs, At the Copa (Grammy award, best male pop performance, 1979), Mandy, Looks Like We Made It, Let Me Be Your Wings; albums include Barry Manilow I, 1973, Barry Manilow II, 1974, Tryin' to Get the Feeling, 1975, This One's For You, 1976, Live, 1977, Even Now, 1977, One Voice, 1979, Barry, 1980, A Nice Boy Like Me, 1980, If I Should Love Again, 1981, Here Comes the Night, 1982, Oh, Julie!, 1982, 2 A.M. Paradise Cafe, 1984, Manilow, 1985, Swing Street, 1987, Live on Broadway, 1987, Barry Manilow, 1989, Because It's Christmas, 1990, Showstoppers, 1991, Live in Britain, 1993, Singin' with The Big Bands, 1994, Summer of '78, 1996, Manilow Sings Sinatra, 1998, Here at the Mayflower, 2001, A Christmas Gift of Love, 2002, 2 Nights Live, 2004, The Essential Barry Manilow, 2005, Love Songs of the 50's, 2006; (video) The Best of Me: The Greatest Hits Tour, 1993; star TV movie Copacabana, 1985, Because It's Christmas: Barry Manilow, 1991; appeared TV specials The Barry Manilow Special (Emmy award, 1977), The Second Barry Manilow Special, also Big Fun on Swing Street, 1988, Barry Manilow: SRO on Broadway, 1989; TV appearances include Murphy Brown, 1993, Ally McBeal, 2001, Will & Grace, 2003, American Idol, 2004, Dancing With the Stars, 2006; Broadway prodn.: Barry Manilow at the Gershwin, 1989; author Sweet Life: Adventures on the Way to Paradise; recipient Spl. Tony award, 1977, Ruby award After Dark mag. 1976, Photoplay Gold medal award 1976. Recipient Emmy award for Individual Performance in a variety or music program (Music and Passion), 2006. Office: William Morris Agy 1325 Ave of the Americas New York NY 10019

MANIN, YURI IVANOVICH, mathematician; b. Simferopol, Crimea, Russia, Feb. 16, 1937; s. Ivan Gavrilovich and Rebecca Zinovievna (Miller) M.; m. Marianna Z. Rosenfeld (div.); 1 child, Dimitri Yurievic; m. Xenia Glebovna Semenova, May 30, 1975. MS, Moscow U., 1958; PhD in Math., Math. Inst., Acad. Scis., Moscow, 1960. Leading rsch. scientist Steklov U., 1960—; prof. & chair mathematics Moscow U., 1965—91; dir. Max Planck Inst. for Mathematics, Bonn, 1995—2005; trustee prof. mathematics Northwestern U., 2002—. Vis. prof. Harvard U., MIT, Coll. de France, Montreal (Que., Can.) U., Utrecht (The Netherlands) U., others. Author: Cubic Forms, 1972, Mathematics and Physics, 1981, Gauge Fields and Complex Geometry, 1988, Frobenius Manifolds, Quantum Cohomology and Moduli Spaces, 1999. Recipient award Moscow Math. Soc., 1963, Lenin award for work in algebraic geometry USSR Govt., 1967, Brouwer medal Netherlands Math. Soc., 1987, Erwin Plein Nemmers prize in mathematics, Northwestern U., 1994, King Faisal Internat. prize in sci., 2002. Fellow Am. Acad. Arts and Scis.; mem. Acad. Scis. Russia (corr.), Royal Acad. Scis. of the Netherlands (fgn. mem.), Academia Europaea, Acad. de Scis. Inst. France (fgn.), Order Pour le Mérite Germany. Avocations: literary criticism, studies in psycholinguistics. Office: Northwestern U 2033 Sheridan Rd Evanston IL 60208 Business E-Mail: manin@mpim-bonn.mpg.de.

MANION, BONNIE J., volunteer, poet, composer; b. South Bend, Ind., Apr. 13, 1942; d. Serge A. and Inez (Reed) Rivard; m. Paul T. Manion, Aug. 12, 1961; children: Christine, Sheila, Stephanie, Michael, Daniel, John Brian. BS in Elem. Edn., DePaul U., 1965; grad. lay ministry leadership program, Cath. Diocese, Peoria, Ill., 1988. Cert. elem. tchr. Ill. Author: Soul Search, 2002; contbr. of poetry to jours. Host family Rotary Internat., Hoopeston, Ill., 1985, 1995, 1996, 2002; vol. Hosp. Auxillary, Little League, United Way, Lions Club, local libr.; Hoopeston Music Boosters; vol. Dem. Party, Danville, Ill., 1972—2004; tchr. CCD programs St. Anthony's, Hoopeston, 1969—89, lay pastoral care min., 1985—2006; presenter diocesan programs Cath. Diocese, Peoria, Ill., 1980—2005. Recipient Pere Marquette Medal, Cath. Diocese, Peoria, 2001. Mem.: Ill. State Poetry Soc., St. Davids' Christian Writers' Assn., Mary Hartwell Catherwood Book Club. Avocations: painting, hiking.

MANION, DANIEL ANTHONY, federal judge; b. South Bend, Ind., Feb. 1, 1942; s. Clarence E. and Virginia (O'Brien) Manion; m. Ann Murphy Manion, June 29, 1984. AB, U. Notre Dame, 1964; JD, Ind. U., 1973. Bar: Ind., US Dist. Ct. (no. dist.) Ind., US Dist. Ct. (so. dist.) Ind. Dir., indsl. devel. Ind. Dept. Commerce, 1968—73; dep. atty. gen. State of Ind., 1973—74; from assoc. to ptnr. Doran, Manion, Boynton, Kamm & Esmont, South Bend, 1974—86; judge US Ct. Appeals (7th cir.), South Bend, 1986—. Mem. Ind. State Senate, Indpls., 1978—82; dir. St. Joseph Bank & Trust Co., 1979—86. With US Army, 1965—66. Office: US Ct Appeals US Courthouse & Federal Bldg 204 S Main St Rm 301 South Bend IN 46601-2122 *

MANION, KAY DAUREEN, financial and office manager; b. St. Francis, Kans., Feb. 7, 1943; d. Edward William and Martha Dankenbring; children: Todd, Jon, Bandel. AS in Mktg. and Art, Western Nebr. C.C., 1990; postgrad., Colby CC, Kans., 1992-95, Fort Hayes State U., 1997—. Various banking positions, Kans. and Nebr., 1960-73; mgr. Alliance (Nebr.) Area C. of C., 1974-79; bridal cons., dept. mgr. Hatch Drug, Alliance, 1980-85; bridal cons. Herbergers, Scotts Bluff, 1986-88; salesperson, script writer Sta. KIMB, Kimball, 1989-90; med. records analyst Dunn Med. Equipment and Svcs., Inc., Colby, 1990-93; graphic designer Quad County Star, Oakley, Kans., 1993-95; news asst., advt. sales rep. Sherman County Star, Goodland, Kans., 1995-97; fin. and office mgr. Steinke Farm Svcs., Holdredge, Nebr., 2000—. Freelance creative designer, 1988—; dir. tng. H.S. Distributive Edn. Clubs Am., Alliance, 1980-85, CETA, Alliance, 1976-79; advt. mgr. Russell Daily News, Russell Record, 1997-99. Bd. dirs., sec. Alliance Cmty. Improvement Com., Alliance, 1974-79; mem. Oakley Tourism Com., 1994-96. Named Businesswoman of Yr. Alliance Area C. of C., 1978, One of the Oustanding Young Women in Am., 1976, 78; recipient Disting. Svc. award Jaycees, Alliance, 1979. Mem. Am. Legion Aux., Eagles Ladies' Aux., Phi Theta Kappa. Republican. Methodist. Avocations: art, drawing, photography, nature, music. Home: P O Box 193 Logan KS 67646-0193

MANIRE, JAMES MCDONNELL, lawyer; b. Memphis, Feb. 22, 1918; s. Clarence Herbert and Elizabeth (McDonnell) M.; m. Nathalie Davant Latham, Nov. 21, 1951 (dv. 1979); children: James McDonnell, Michael Latham, Nathalie Manire Willard; m. Nancy Whitman Colbert, Dec. 30, 1995. LL.B., U. Va., 1948. Bar: Tenn. 1948, U.S. Supreme Ct. 1957. Pvt. practice, Memphis, 1948—; city atty., 1968-71; of counsel Williams, McDaniel, Wolfe & Womack, Memphis, 2001—. Editor in chief Va. Law Rev., 1947-48. Served to lt. comdr. USNR, 1941-46. Fellow Am. Coll. Trial Lawyers, Am. Bar Found. (life); mem. Tenn. Bar Assn. (pres. 1966-67), Memphis and Shelby County Bar Assn. (pres. 1963-64, Lawyer's Lawyer award 1995), Tenn. Bar Found. (charter), 6th Circuit Jud. Conf. (life), Raven Soc., Memphis Hunt and Polo Club. Home: 2927 Frances Pl Memphis TN 38111-2401 Office: 5521 Murray Rd Memphis TN 38119-3717

MANIS, MELVIN, psychologist, educator; b. NYC, Feb. 18, 1931; s. Alex and Hanna (Oyle) M.; m. Jean Denby, May 28, 1954; children: Peter Eugene, David Denby. AB in Psychology, Franklin and Marshall Coll., 1951; PhD, U. Ill., 1954. Instr. psychology U. Pitts., 1956-58; rsch. psychologist Ann Arbor VA Med. Ctr., Mich., 1958-89; prof. psychology U. Mich., Ann Arbor, 1966-98, assoc. chmn. dept., 1990-91; ret., 1998. Author: Cognitive Processes, 1966, An Introduction to Cognitive Psychology, 1971; editor Jour. Personality and Social Psychology, 1980-84. With USPHS, 1954—56. Mem.: APA, Soc. Exptl. Social Psychology, Racquet, Phi Beta Kappa. Democrat. Jewish. Home: 20 Harvard Pl Ann Arbor MI 48104-1726 Business E-Mail: Melmanis@umich.edu.

MANISCALCO-FEICHTL, MARIA, pharmacist, educator; d. Rosario Maniscalco and Dorothy D'Amico; m. Daniel James Feichtl. PharmD, St. John's U., Jamaica Queens, NY, 1997. Cert. specialty residency ambulatory care Nova S.E. U., 2003, immunization Am. Pharmacists Assn., 2006, asthma Am. Pharmacists Assn., 2000. Pharmacist Stop and Shop Supermarket, Holbrook, NY, 1997—2002; ambulatory care resident Nova S.E. U. Coll. Pharmacy, Fort Lauderdale, 2002—03, asst. prof., pharmacy practice, 2003—. Bd. mem. South Fla. Am. Lung Assn., Fort Lauderdale, 2005—; dir. cmty. pharmacy residency program Nova S.E. U. Clinic Pharmacy, Fort Lauderdale, 2005—. Contbr. articles to profl. jours. Bd. mem. South Fla. Am. Lung Assn., Fort Lauderdale, 2005—; co-chair recruitment Am. Lung Assn. AsthmaWalk, Fort Lauderdale, 2002—. Recipient Comm. award, Roche Pharmaceuticals, 1997, Resident Yr., SFSHP, 2003; grantee, Am. Pharmacists Assn., 2005; Rsch. grant, Nova S.E. U., 2004. Mem.: APHA, BCPA (bd. mem. 2003—05), AACP, AACP, FPA (orgnl. affairs coun. mem. 2003—04), ASHP. Achievements include research in medication therapy managment. Office: Nova SE Univ Coll Pharmacy 3200 South University Drive Fort Lauderdale FL 33324 Office Phone: 954-262-1360. Office Fax: 954-262-2278. Business E-Mail: maniscal@nsu.nova.edu.

MANISCALCO-THEBERGE, MARY ELIZABETH, surgeon, medical educator; b. Portsmouth, Va., Sept. 1, 1956; d. Joseph Jack and Elizabeth Mary Maniscalco; m. Daniel Martin Theberge, June 23, 1984; children: Matthew John Theberge, Danielle Elizabeth Theberge. BS, Old Dominion U., 1978; MD, Ea. Va. Med. Sch., 1981. Diplomate Am. Bd. Surgery, Am. Bd. Critical Care. Intern gen. surgery Eisenhower Army Med. Ctr., 1981—82, resident gen. surgery, 1982—86; commd. 2d lt. US Army, 1981, advanced through grades to col., 1999; attending surgeon Frankfurt Army Regional Med. Ctr., 1986—89; trauma critical care fellow Washington Hosp. Ctr., 1989—90; surg. critical care fellow Walter Reed Army Med. Ctr., 1990—91, attending surg. intensivist, 1991—2003, attending surgeon, 1990—2006, spl. intensivist, 1991—2006, dir. surg. intensive care unit, 1993—95, chief gen. surgery svcs., 1994—2001, chair dept. surgery Washington, 2001—06; sr. surg. investigator Office of Med. Insp., VA Health Adminstrn. Dept., Washington, 2007—. Cons. to surgeon gen. US Army, 1994—2002. Mem. forward in hope com. St. Thomas a Becket Cath. Ch., Reston, Va., 2003. Recipient William Clements award for excellence in edn., Uniformed Svcs. U., Bethesda, Md., 1994, Disting. Alumni award, Old Dominion U., 2003, Legion of Merit, 2006. Fellow: ACS (pres. Med. Washington chpt. 2003—04, mem. com.); mem.: AMA, Assn. Women Surgeons, Soc. Critical Care Medicine (chmn. coun. local chpt.), Am. Soc. Breast Surgeons. Office: Office of Med Insp VA Health Adminstrn VA Affairs 810 Vermont Ave NW Washington DC 20420 Business E-Mail: mary.maniscalco@va.gov.

MANJILI, MASOUD H., immunologist, educator; b. Manjil, Iran, Sept. 23, 1962; arrived in U.S., 1999; s. Mahmoud Hajizadeh Manjili and Farandokht Kamran; m. Fariba Azimi, Sept. 26, 1962; children: Saeed H. children: Razieh H., Fahimeh H. DVM, U. Tehran Vet. Sch., Iran, 1990; PhD, Vet. Sch., Sydney, Australia, 1996. Rsch. asst. U. Sydney, 1996—96; asst. prof. Razi Vaccine & Serum Rsch. Inst., Hessarak, Tehran, Iran, 1997—99; rsch. affiliate Roswell Pk. Cancer Inst., Buffalo, 1999—2002, instr., 2003—04; asst. prof. Massey Cancer Ctr., Va. Commonwealth U., Richmond, 2004—, mem. scientist, 2006—; mng. editor Frontiers in Biosci., 2005—. Cons. Pasteur Inst., Tehran, 1997—99. Editor: Frontiers in Biosci., 2005—; contbr. articles to profl. jours. Recipient The AACR Inglenook Scholars-in-Training award, 2003; grantee, The N.Y. State Breast Cancer Rsch. and Edn. Fund, 2001, Roswell Pk. Alliance Found., 2003, NIH, 2005—, Susan G. Komen Breast Cancer Found., 2005—. Mem.: Internat. Soc. Biol. Therapy of Cancer, North Am. Hyperthermia Soc., Am. Assn. Immunologists, Am. Assn. for Cancer Rsch. Achievements include research in HSP110-HER-2/neu chaperone complex vaccine induces protective immunity against spontaneous mammary tumors in HER-2/neu transgenic mice. Office: Va Commonwealth U Sch Medicine/Massey Cancer Ctr Dept Microbiology and Immunology Box 980037 Richmond VA 23298 Home Phone: 804-364-6056; Office Phone: 804-828-8779. Business E-Mail: mmanjili@vcu.edu.

MANKEL, FRANCIS XAVIER, retired principal, priest; b. Knoxville, Tenn., Nov. 8, 1935; s. George Whitehead Sr. and Willia Frances (Duncan) M. BA, St. Ambrose U., Davenport, Iowa, 1957; STB, St. Mary's Sem. and U., Balt., 1959, STL, 1961; MEd, Loyola Coll., Balt., 1965. Ordained priest, Roman Cath. Ch., 1961. Assoc. pastor Our Lady of Fatima Ch., Alcoa, Tenn., 1961—62, Holy Ghost Ch., Knoxville, 1962-67; tchr. Knoxville Cath. H.S., 1961—67, prin., 1967-79; pastor Sacred Heart Ch., Lawrenceburg, Tenn., 1979-84, St. John Neumann Ch., Knoxville, 1984-87, Sacred Heart Cathedral, Knoxville, 1987-97, Holy Ghost Ch., Knoxville, 1997—. Chancellor Cath. Diocese Knoxville, 1988-96, vicar gen., 1988-98, 1999-2007; reverend monsignor, 2006; supt. Cath. Schs., Diocese of Knoxville, 1989-92. Bd. dirs. Knoxville area chpt. ARC, 1986—2005; sch. bd. Knoxville Cath. HS, 1967—79, 1984—85, 1987—; com. mem. Sacred Heart Cathedral Sch., Knoxville, 1987—97, St. Joseph Sch., Knoxville, 1997—. Mem. Knoxville Ministerial Assn. Home and Office: 111 Hinton Ave Knoxville TN 37917-6418 Office Phone: 865-522-2205. Personal E-mail: hgchurch@bellsouth.net.

MANKIEWICZ, THOMAS FRANK, screenwriter, director, producer; b. LA, June 1, 1942; s. Joseph Leo and Rosa M. Student, Phillips Exeter Acad., NH, 1955—59, Yale U., New Haven, 1959—63. Filmmaker-in-residence Dodge Coll. Film and Media Arts, Chapman U., Orange, Calif., 2006. Author: (book, Broadway musical) Georgy!, 1970; screenwriter: (teleplay, musical spl.) Movin' with Nancy, 1967, The Sweet Ride, 1968, (teleplay, musical spl.) The Beat of the Brass, 1968, Diamonds Are Forever, 1971, Live and Let Die, 1973, The Man With the Golden Gun, 1974, The Eagle Has Landed, 1976, The Cassandra Crossing, 1977, Ladyhawke, 1985; screenwriter, co-prodr.: Mother, Juggs and Speed, 1976; creative cons.: Superman, 1978, Superman II, 1980; dir. (teleplay, tv pilot) Hart to Hart, 1979-80, (screenplay) Dragnet, 1987, Delirious, 1991, (cable tv series) Tales from the Crypt, 1992, (cable tv movie) Taking the Heat, 1993; exec. prodr. Hot Pursuit, 1985. Bd. dirs. William Holden Wildlife Found., L.A., 1995—. Mem. Greater L.A. Zoo Assn. (bd. trustees 1997—, chmn. 2002--), Motion Picture Acad. Arts and Scis. (bd. govs. 1979-81), Thoroughbred Owners Calif. (bd. dirs. 2005). Avocations: wildlife conservation, thoroughbred horse racing and breeding. E-mail: mankone@earthlink.net.

MANKIN, HENRY JAY, orthopedist, educator, health facility administrator; b. Pitts., Oct. 9, 1928; s. Hyman Isaac and Mary (Simons) M.; m. Carole Jane Pinkney, Aug. 20, 1952; children: Allison Joan, David Philip, Keith Pinkney. BS magna cum laude, U. Pitts., 1952, MD, 1953; MA (hon.), Harvard U., 1973. Diplomate Am. Bd. Orthopaedic Surgery (mem. bd. 1976-82, pres. bd. 1980-81). Intern U. Chgo. Clinics, 1953-54; resident orthopaedics Hosp. for Joint Diseases, NYC, 1957-60; instr. orthopaedics U. Pitts. Sch. Medicine, 1960-62, asst. prof., 1962-64, assoc. prof., 1964-66; dir., prof. orthopaedics Hosp. for Joint Diseases and Mt. Sinai Sch. Medicine, 1966-72; chief orthopaedics Mass. Gen. Hosp., Boston, 1972-96, chief orthopaedic oncology, 1972—. Edith M. Ashley prof. orthopaedics Harvard Med. Sch., 1972—; mem. surgery B study sect. NIH, 1969-73; mem. adv. com. on surg. treatment FDA, 1973-75; corporator Boston Five Cent Savs. Bank, 1982-83; mem. exec. com. Am. Bd. Med. Spltys., 1982-85; adv. council on grad. med. edn., 1986-96; mem. Nat. Arthritis Avd. Bd., 1986-89; mem. human resources and research rev. group A Nat. Inst. Arthritis, Metabolism and Digestive Diseases, 1981-85, chmn., 1983-85. Assoc. editor Arthritis and Rheumatism, 1967-77, Jour. Bone and Joint Surgery, 1967-82; mem. editorial bd. Jour. Orthopaedic Research, 1982-85; trustee Jour. Bone and Joint Surgery, 1985-91, chmn. bd., 1988-91; contbr. more than 600 articles to profl., med. jours. Served to lt. comdr. USNR, 1955-57. Fellow ACS, Royal Coll. Surgeons (hon.); mem. Am. Acad. Orthopaedic Surgeons, Acad. Orthopaedic Soc. (pres. 1991-92), Am. Orthopaedic Assn. (pres. 1982-83), Orthopaedic Research Soc. (pres. 1969-70), Musculoskeletal Tumor Soc. (pres. 1991-92), Brit. Orthopaedic Research Soc., Argentine Orthopaedic Assn. (hon.), N.Y. Acad. Medicine (chmn. orthopaedic sect. 1971-72), Am. Rheumatism Assn., Soc. Internat. Chirurgerie Orthopaedice et Traumatologia, Hip Soc., Interurban, Forum Orthopaedic clubs, Brit. Orthopaedic Assn. (hon.), Can. Orthopaedic Assn. (hon.), Australian Orthopaedic Assn. (hon.), N.Z. Orthopaedic Assn. (hon.), Japanese Orthopaedic Assn. (hon.), Israel Orthopaedic Assn. (hon.), Thai Orthopaedic Assn (hon.).

MANKIN, ROBERT STEPHEN, diversified financial services company executive; b. NYC, Mar. 26, 1939; s. Samuel Harry Mankin and Dorothy (Rosenblum) Goldstein; m. Joyce Marie Cabel, June 13, 1971 (div.); children: Seth Howard, Laura Nicole, Gina Danielle; m. Ruth Irwin, July 20, 2002. BA cum laude, Bklyn. Coll., 1961; MBA, Bernard Baruch Coll., 1970; Dr. Profl. Studies with distinction, Pace U., 1982. Mgr. ABC, NYC, 1969-71, Babcock and Wilcox, NYC, 1971-74; v.p. Chase Manhattan Bank, NYC, 1974-84; sr. v.p. 1st Interstate Bank, NYC, 1984-87; mng. dir., co-head fixed income, mem. mgmt. com. Nomura Securities Internat., NYC, 1987-94; mng. dir. Paine Webber, NYC, 1994-95; pres., CEO Lakeside Fin. Svcs., Hoboken, NJ, 1995—; COO Thomson Fin. Electronic Settlements Group, Boston, 1997-98; acting pres. Ocwen Tech. Exch., West Palm Beach, Fla., 1999; CEO Sutton Strategic, LLC, 2001—02. Bd. dirs., sec. Nomura Mortgage Capital Corp., N.Y.C.; bd. dirs., pres., CEO Nomura Asset Capital Corp., N.Y.C., 1988-94; trustee Hudson Inst., 2004— Contbr. articles to profl. jours. Mem. Planning Forum, Assn. for Computing Machinery, Assn. Computer Programmers and Analysts (chmn. bd. 1971).

MANKIW, (NICHOLAS) GREGORY, economics professor, former federal official; b. Trenton, NJ, Feb. 3, 1958; s. Nicholas and Dorothy (Sawchak) Mankiw; m. Deborah Jean Roloff, June 16, 1984. AB, Princeton U., 1980; PhD, MIT, 1984. Staff economist Coun. Econ. Advisers, Washington, 1982-83; instr. MIT, Cambridge, 1984-85; asst. prof. econs. Harvard U., Cambridge, 1985-87, prof. econs., 1987—; mem., chmn. Coun. Econ. Advisers Exec. Office of the Pres., Washington, 2003—05. Research assoc. Nat. Bureau of Economic Research; adviser Fed. Reserve Bank of Boston, Congressional Budget Off.; mem. test devel. comm. ETS. Author: Macroeconomics, 1992, Principles of Economics, 1998; contbr. articles Am. Economic Review, Jour. of Polit. Economy, Quarterly Jour. of Economics, The NY Times, The Financial Times, The Wall Street Journal, Fortune. Recipient Presidential Young Investigator award NSF, 1986. Fellow Am. Acad. Arts & Scis. Office: Harvard U Dept Econs Littauer 223 Cambridge MA 02138 *

MANKOFF, DAVID ABRAHAM, nuclear medicine physician; b. July 10, 1959; BS in Physics summa cum laude, Yale U., 1981; MD, PhD in Bioengring., U. Pa., 1988. Diplomate Am. Bd. Internal Medicine, Am. Bd. Nuclear Medicine. Rsch. scientist UGM Med. Sys., Phila., 1988-89, dir. engring., 1989-90; rsch. assoc. nuclear medicine sect. U. Pa., Phila., 1988-90; resident in internal medicine U. Wash., Seattle, 1990-92, resident in nuclear medicine, 1992-96, asst. prof. radiology, 1996—2001, assoc. prof. radiology, 2001, assoc. prof. medicine, 2002—06, assoc. prof. bioengring., 2005—06; prof. radiology, medicine, and bioengring. Seattle Cancer Care Alliance, 2006—.

MANKOFF, RONALD MORTON, retired lawyer; b. Gettysburg, SD, Oct. 13, 1931; s. Harry B. and Sarah (Frank) M.; m. Joy Faith Shechtman, Nov. 3, 1959; children: Jeffrey Walker, Douglas Frank. BSL, U. Minn., JD, 1954; LLM in Taxation, NYU, 1959. Bar: Minn. 1954, Tex. 1959. With Leonard, Street & Deinard, Mpls., 1957-58; research analyst Inst. Jud. Adminstrn., NYC, 1958-59; assoc. Lyne, Blanchette, Smith & Shelton, Dallas, 1959-60; ptnr. Durant and Mankoff, Dallas, 1960-85; pres. Brice & Mankoff P.C., Dallas, 1985-89, Mankoff, Hill, Held & Metzger, L.L.P., Dallas, 1989-95; chmn./gen. counsel RAC Fin. Group, Inc. (now 1st Plus Fin Group, Inc.), 1994-96. Lectr. law So. Meth. U., 1974-77; speaker in field. Contbr. articles to profl. jours. Mem. Dallas Mcpl. Libr., 1973—75, Mayor's Task Force on Child Care, 1984; chmn. bd. Dallas chpt. Am. Cancer Soc., 1976—77, bd. dirs. Tex. divsn., 1981—94; chmn. Dallas Crusade, 1974—75, bd. dirs., mem. exec. com., 1963—88; mem. exec. com. Nat. Pooled Income Fund, Coun. Jewish Welfare Fedns. and Funds, 1975—77; adv. dir. Dallas Cmty. Chest Trust Fund, 1976—78; chmn. Found. Dallas Jewish Fedn., 1976—77; pres. Temple Emanu-el Dallas, 1977—79; bd. dirs. Jewish Fedn. Greater Dallas, 1977—79, 1999—2002, Dallas Civic Opera, 1981—83, World Union Progressive Judaism, 1981—90; mem. S.W. regional liaison com. IRS, 1980—83; mem. exec. com. Union Am. Hebrew Congregations, 1979—89, trustee, 1979—97, chmn. nat. coll. com., 1983—87, vice chmn. bd. dirs., 1984—88, vice chmn. devel. commn., 1997—99; sec. Dallas Assembly, 1979—84; mem. exec. com. Jewish Cmty Rels. Coun., 1982—83, Com. for Qualified Judiciary, 1982—; sec. Child Care Partnership, 1984—86, bd. dirs., 1986—88, Dallas Women's Found., 1985—89, mem. adv. coun., 1989—, chair adv. coun., 1997—99; bd. dirs. Am. Jewish Com., 1982—88, pres. Dallas chpt., 1986—90; bd. dirs. Tex. coun. Girl Scouts U.S., 1982—85; bd. dirs. Goodwill Industries of Greater Dallas, 1979—83, Title One Home Improvement Lender's Assn., 1994—96; bd. govs. Dallas Symphony Assn., 1988—92, 1998—; chmn. Temple Emanu El Found., 1988—95; bd. dirs. Dallas Inst. Humanities and Culture, 1998—2005, mem. adv. com., 2005—; bd. dirs. Ctr. for Interreligious Understanding, 2001—05, Cardio-Pulmonary Rsch. Inst., 2002—, Jane's Due Process, Inc., 2002—07, Cmty. Home for Adults Found., 2001—, Am. Film Inst., Dallas, 2007—; adv. bd. Rockridge Inst., 2006—. Lt. (j.g.) USN, 1954—57. Mem. ABA, State Bar Tex., Dallas Bar Assn., Columbian Country Club (bd. dirs. 1967-73), LaJolla Country Club, Crescent Club, Park Cities Club, Zeta Beta Tau, Delta Sigma Rho. Democrat. Jewish. Home: 22 Lakeside Pk Dallas TX 75225 also: 8510 El Paseo Grande La Jolla CA 92037 Home Phone: 214-368-6860. Personal E-mail: ron@mankoff.com.

MANLEY, AUDREY FORBES, retired academic administrator, pediatrician, retired military officer; b. Jackson, Miss., Mar. 25, 1934; d. Jesse Lee and Ora Lee (Buckhalter) Forbes; m. Albert Edward Manley, Apr. 3, 1970. AB with honors (tuition scholar), Spelman Coll., Atlanta, 1955; MD (Jesse Smith Noyes Found. scholar), Meharry Med. Coll., 1959; MPH, Johns Hopkins U.-USPHS traineeship, 1987; LHD (hon.), Tougaloo Coll., Miss., 1990, Meharry Med. Coll., Nashville, 1991; LLD (hon.), Spelman Coll., 1991, Tskegee U., 1998; DSc (hon.), Coll. New Rochelle, 1998, Morehouse Coll., 2002, U. Del., 2002. Diplomate: Am. Bd. Pediatrics. Intern St. Mary Mercy Hosp., Gary, Ind., 1960; from jr. to chief resident in pediatrics Cook County Children's Hosp., Chgo., 1960—62; NIH fellow neonatology U. Ill. Rsch. and Ednl. Hosp., Chgo., 1963—65; staff pediatrician Chgo. Bd. Health, 1963—66; practice medicine specializing in pediatrics Chgo., 1963—66; assoc. Lawndale Neighborhood Health Ctr. North, 1966—67; asst. med. dir., 1967—69; asst. prof. Chgo. Med. Coll., 1966—67; instr. Pritzker Sch. Medicine, U. Chgo., 1967—69; asst. dir.

ambulatory pediatrics, asst. dir. pediatrics Mt. Zion Hosp. and Med. Center, San Francisco, 1969—70; med. cons. Spelman Coll., 1970—71, med. dir. family planning program, chmn. health careers adv. com., 1972—76; med. dir. Grady Meml. Hosp. Family Planning Clinic, 1972—76; commd. officer, advanced though grades to rear adm. USPHS, 1976—97; chief genetic diseases services br. Office Maternal and Child Health, Bur. Community Health Services, Rockville, Md., 1976—81; acting assoc. adminstr. clin. affairs Office of Adminstr. Health Resources and Services Adminstrn., 1981—83, chief med. officer, dep. assoc. adminstr. planning, evaluation and legis., 1983—85; sabbatical leave USPHS Johns Hopkins Sch. Hygiene and Pub. Health, 1986—87; dir. Nat. Health Service Corps.; asst. surgeon gen. US Dept. Health & Human Services, 1988, dep. asst. sec. for health, 1989—93, acting asst. sec. health, 1993, dep. asst. sec. health & intergovtl. affairs, 1993—94, dep. surgeon gen., acting dep. asst. sec. for minority health, 1994—95, acting surgeon gen., 1995—97; pres. Spelman Coll., 1997—2002, pres. emerita, 2003—04; pres. History Makers, 2003. Mem. U.S. del. UNICEF, 1990-94, Am. Acad. Family Physicians (pub. adv. bd.), Am. Coun. Learned Socs., Am. Med. Assn. Minority Affairs Consortium (sr. advisor), Ctrs. for Disease Control Found. (bd. visitors), Morehouse Sch. Medicine (clin. Prof. Pediats., Pub. Health Lectr.), Rollins Sch. Pub. Health Emory U (Commrs., Adv. Coun., Ga. Leadership Commn. Organ, Tissue, Blood Marrow donation amont African Ams. Author numerous articles, reports in field; artist permanent collections Nat. Acads. Sci., Spelman Coll. Alumnae Hall of Fame, 2005. Trustee Spelman Coll., 1966-70; The Coll. Fund (UNCF com. Archives, Hist. Govtl. Affairs Com.), Coun. Fgn. Rels., bd. dirs. coun. Ind. Colls.; bd. dirs. March of Dimes, 1998, Nat. Merit Scholarship Corp., Nat. Minority Mil. Mus. Found. Edl. Adv. Coun., Am. Cancer Soc. Found., CDC Found., Compas Compact, Downtown Atlanta Chpt. Rotary, Atlanta 2000 Adv. Com., Quality Edn. for Minorities; adv. bd. Atlanta Regional Health Summit, Commerce Club, Ga. Found. Ind., Food and Drug Adv. Com., publ. advisory bd. Am. Acad. Family Physicians, sr. advisor AMA Minority Affairs Consortium, bd. visitors CDC Found., hon. advisor coun., charter mem. The Children's Inn at NIH, mem. Coun. on Fgn. Rels., Adv. Com., vaccine and biologics com. Food and Drug Adminstrn., mem. Health Careers Exploring Advisory Com., Tribal Colls.; chair, advisory group Univ. S.Carolina Rural Health Initiative. Rear adm. USPHS, ret. USPHS. Recipient Meritorious Svc. award USPHS, 1981, Mary McLeod Bethune award Nat Coun. Negro Women, 1979, Dr. John P. McGovern Ann. Lectureship award Am. Sch. Health Assn., Disting. Alumni award Meharry Med. Coll., 1989, Spelman Coll. 108 Founder's Day Convocation, 1989, Disting. Svc. medal USPHS, 1992, Hildrus A. Poindexter award OSG/PHS, 1993, numerous other svc. and achievement awards; named to African Americans in Sci., Engring., and Medicine Portrait Collection, Nat. Acads., 2005. Fellow Am. Acad. Pediatrics; mem. Nat. Inst. Medicine of Nat. Acad. Sci., Nat. Med. Assn., APHA, AAUW, AAAS, Coun. Fgn. Rels., Spelman Coll. Alumnae Assn. (Hall of Fame 2005), Meharry Alumni Assn., African Am. Collection Portraits of NAS, Operation Crossroads Africa Alumni Assn., Atlanta C. of C., Rotary, Delta Sigma Theta (hon.), Phi Beta Kappa. Address: 5820 Hannah Brook St Andiente North Las Vegas NV 89081 Personal E-mail: amanley009@aol.com. E-mail: amanley007@netaccess.com.

MANLEY, DAVID BOTT, III, lawyer; b. Jacksonville, Fla., June 19, 1953; s. David Bott and Bernadette Claire Manley; m. Gayle Aileen Whitney, Nov. 1, 1978; children: David Jeremiah, Alexandra Ina Claire. BA with honors magna cum laude, U. Ga., 1975, JD, 1982. Bar: Ga. 1983, U.S. Dist. Ct. (no. dist.) Ga. 1983, U.S. Ct. Appeals (11th cir.) 1986. Auditor So. Hostess Sys., Inc., Augusta, Ga., 1975-76; prosecutorial asst. fraud investigator State Ga., Atlanta, 1976-79; assoc. Gadrix & Green, P.C., Atlanta, 1982-83, Lowe, Barham, Eubanks & Lowe, Atlanta, 1983-85; mem. Barham & Manley, Atlanta, 1985-89; dir., ptnr. Campbell Martin & Manley, LLP, Atlanta, 1989—. Corp. counsel Highland Homes, Inc., Dallas and Atlanta, 1990—, Mast Advt. and Pub. Inc., Houston and Nashville, 1991—; corp. sec., counsel Agrisel USA, Inc., Atlanta and Hong Kong, 1998—; mem. Ga. Law Related Edn. Constorium of Carl Vinson Inst. Govt., U. Ga., 2000—. Pres. U.S. Jaycees, Mt. Park/Lilburn, 1985; cert. coach Lucky Shoals Youth Athletic Assn., Norcross, Ga., 1992-98; bd. dirs Fulton County, Ga. Dept. Family and Children's Svcs. (commendation, bd. resolution for bravery, 1978); svc. provider Parent to Parent of Ga.; mem. Dekalb Vol. Lawyers Found., Lawyers Found. Ga. Named Jaycee of Yr., U.S. Jaycees-Mt. Park/Lilburn, Ga., 1984. Mem. ABA, State Bar Ga. (legis. com. corp. and banking law sect. 1987-88, mem. corp. and banking law sect. 1987—, adv. mem. law revision com. 1989-90, mem. trial sect. 1984—, mem. real property sect. 1996—, advocate for spl. needs children 1996—), Nat. Youth Sports Coaches Assn. (continuing mem. 1996—), Sandy Springs Bar Assn. (treas. 1987-88, pres. 1988-89, dir. 1989-90), Omicron Delta Kappa. Avocations: coaching youth sports, model railroading, photography, collecting, travel. Home: 4390 Flippen Trl Norcross GA 30092-3902 Office: Campbell Martin & Manley LLP 990 Hammond Dr NE Ste 800 Atlanta GA 30328-5510 E-mail: dbmanley@chb-cmm.com.

MANLEY, EDWARD HARRY, JR., professional association administrator, food products executive, retired military officer; b. SI, NY, Sept. 12, 1941; s. Edward H. and Dorothy I.; m. Judith Manley; children: Deborah Szymchack, Michael E. BS, Cornell U., 1975; MS, Rollins Coll., 1978. Cert. HACCP mgr., 2003. Joined USN, 1959, commd. ensign, 1970, advanced through grades to lt. comdr., 1979; food svc. dir. Naval Hosp., Annapolis, Md., 1972-73; asst. food svc. dir. Nat. Naval Med. Ctr., Bethesda, Md., 1971-72; food svc. dir. Naval Regional Med. Ctr., Orlando, Fla., 1975-80, ret., 1980; food svc. dir. North Broward Hosp., Pompano Beach, Fla., 1981-89; pres. Creative Food Concepts, Inc.; founder Workaholics Internat. Network, 1999—; pres. VIP Food Safety; HACCP and food safety tng. worldwide. Mem. adv. bd. Mid-Fla. Tech. Food Svc. Program, 1978-80, Atlantic Vo-Tech Dietetic Program, 1981-89; chmn. Skills Std. Bd., Hospitality and Tourism; presenter in field. Author: Restaurant University in a Binder, 2006, HACCP Implementation Manual, 2007, Restaurant Manager's Handbook, 2007. Mem. evaluation team Hennessey award US Air Force, 1982; mem. adv. bd. Broward C.C., 1985—. Ed Manley Scholarship Fund established, 1984; named Disting. Health Care Food Svc. Adminstr., 1985, Master Cert. Food Exec., 2002; recipient Peter Gust Economou award, 1987. Mem. Internat. Food Svc. Execs. Assn. (pres. Orlando br. 1979-80, pres. South Fla. br. 1983-84, internat. sec.-treas. 1986-87, chmn. bd. 1988-1989, pres. 1989—, Mem. of Yr. Orlando br. 1978, South Fla. br. 1984, Disting. Svc. award 1984, Dignified Order of Dinner Gong 2001), Cornell Soc. Hotelmen (pres. Ctrl. Fla. chpt. 1976-80), Cornell Hotel Soc. (treas. Las Vegas 2001—03), Fla. Restaurant Assn. (bd. dir. 1980), Am. Soc. Hosp. Food Svc. Adminstrn. (sec. South Fla. chpt.), Cornell of Ctrl. Fla. Club, Naval Tng. Ctr. Officers Club (pres. 1978-80), Pompano Sq. Mall Walkers Club (founder). Home and Office: 2609 Surfwood Dr Las Vegas NV 89128-1282 Office Phone: 702-430-9217. Personal E-mail: hq@workaholic.org.

MANLEY, FRANK, language educator, writer; b. Scranton, Pa., Nov. 13, 1930; s. Aloysius F. and Kathryn L. (Needham) M.; m. Carolyn Mary Holliday, Mar. 14, 1952; children: Evelyn, Mary. BA, Emory U., 1952, MA, 1953; PhD, Johns Hopkins U., 1959. Instr., then asst. prof. Yale U., New Haven, 1959-64; assoc. prof., then prof. dept. English Emory U., Atlanta, 1964-2000, chmn. dept., 1968-70, Candler prof. English, 1982-2000, dir. creative writing program, 1990-2000, retired, 2000. Editor: The Anniversaries (John Donne), 1963, (with R. Sylvester) De Fructu qui ex Doctrina Percipitur, 1967, All Fools (George Chapman), 1968, A Dialogue of Comfort (St. Thomas More), vol. 12, 1977 and Epistola ad Pomeranum, vol. 7, 1990, Yale edit. More's complete works; author: Resultances, 1980 (Devins award for poetry 1980), Two Masters (co-winner Gt. Am. New Play Contest 9th Ann. Humana Festival New Am. Plays 1985), (with F. Watkins) Some Poems and Some Talk About Poetry, 1985, Within the Ribbons: 9 Stories, 1989, (play) The Trap, 1993, The Cockfighter: a Novel, 1998, Among Prisoners: Stories, 2000, (poems) The Emperors, 2001, True Hope: A Novel, 2002. With US Army, 1953—55. Guggenheim Found. fellow, 1966-67, 78-79; recipient NEH transl. program fellowship, 1981-83, Nat. Endowment Arts Creative Writing Fellowship in Fiction, 1995-97, Disting. Teaching award, 1984, Univ. scholar/tchr. of yr. award, 1989, Disting. Alumnus award The Marist Sch., 1993, Miller Playmaker award Theater Emory, 2007. Roman Catholic. Home: 401 Adams St Decatur GA 30030-5207 also: Doublehead Gap Rd Ellijay GA 30540 Business E-Mail: fmanley@emory.edu.

MANLEY, JAMES L., molecular biologist, educator; PhD. Julian Clarence Levy prof. life scis. Columbia U., NYC. Contbr. articles to sci. jours.; editor: Molecular and Cellular Biology; assoc. editor: Gene Expression. Fellow: Am. Acad. Arts & Scis. Office: Dept Biol Scis Columbia U 1117 Fairchild Ctr MC 2410 New York NY 10027 E-mail: jlm2@columbia.edu.

MANLEY, JOAN A(DELE) DANIELS, retired publishing executive; b. San Luis Obispo, Calif., Sept. 23, 1932; d. Carl and Della (Weinmann) Daniels; m. Jeremy C. Lanning, Mar. 17, 1956 (div. Sept. 1963); m. Donald H. Manley, Sept. 12, 1964 (div. 1985); m. William G. Houlton, May 31, 1991. BA, U. Calif., Berkeley, 1954; DBA (hon.), U. New Haven, 1974; LLD (hon.), Babson Coll., 1978. Sec. Doubleday & Co., Inc., NYC, 1954-60; sales exec. Time Inc., 1960-66, v.p., 1971-75, group v.p., 1975-84, also bd. dir.; circulation dir. Time-Life Books, 1966-68, dir. sales, 1968-70, pub., 1970-76; chmn. bd. Time-Life Books Inc., 1976-80. Vice chmn. bd. Book-of-the-Month Club, Inc., N.Y.C., until 1984; supervising dir. Time-Life Internat. (Nederland) B.V., Amsterdam, until 1984; mem. exec. bd. Coll. Letters and Sci. U. Calif., Berkeley, Calif., 2005— Past trustee Mayo Found., Rochester, Minn., Nat. Repertory Orch., William Benton Found.; former mem. adv. coun. Stanford U. Bus. Sch., Haas Sch. Bus. U. Calif. Named to Direct Mktg. Hall of Fame, 1993; U. Calif.-Berkeley fellow, 1989. Mem. Assn. Am. Pubs. (past chmn.).

MANLEY, JOHN FREDERICK, political scientist, educator; b. Utica, NY, Feb. 20, 1939; s. John A. and Gertrude Manley; children from previous marriage: John, Laura; m. Kathy Lynn Sharp, 1991; 1 child, Cole Sharp Manley. BS, Le Moyne Coll., 1961; PhD, Syracuse U., 1966. Asst. prof. polit. sci. U. Wis., 1966, assoc. prof., 1969-71; prof., chmn. dept. polit. sci. Stanford U., 1977-80. Fellow Center for Advanced Study in Behavioral Scis., 1976-77; vis. prof. Stanford in Oxford, 1996. Author: The Politics of Finance, 1970, American Government and Public Policy, 1976; author, co-editor: The Case Against the Constitution, 1987. Congressional fellow, 1963-64; Brookings Instn. fellow, 1965-66; Guggenheim fellow, 1974-75; Fulbright fellow U. Bologna, 1992. Office: 152 Greens Farms Rd Westport CT 06880-6215 Office Phone: 203-341-9410. E-mail: manley48@msn.com.

MANLEY, JOHN HUGO, computer company executive, educator; b. Highland Park, Mich., July 9, 1932; s. Hugo Edward and Linda Amelia (Kuure) M.; m. Josephine Theresa Catanzaro, Sept. 3, 1958; children: Lisa Linn, Michele Ann, John David, Marc Darrin. B. Metall. Engring., Cornell U., 1955; MS Indsl. Engring., U. Pitts., 1965, PhD, 1971. Metall. engr. GE, Schenectady, NY, 1955—56; commd. 2d lt. USAF, 1956, advanced through grades to lt. col., 1973, ret., 1976; asst. to dir. Johns Hopkins Applied Physics Lab., Laurel, Md., 1976—80; exec. ITT Corp., Stratford, Conn., 1980—83; v.p. Nastec Corp., Southfield, Mich., 1983—85; dir. emeritus Software Engring. Inst. Carnegie Mellon U., Pitts., 1985—87; pres., chmn. Computing Tech. Transition, Inc., Wilmington, Del., 1983—2004; prof. emeritus mfg. and info. tech. sys. engring., dir. mfg. sys. engring. program U. Pitts., 1987—2002. Tech. adv. bd. Tartan Inc., Pitts.; com. on nat. weather svc. modernization NRC, 1991-94. Editor-in-chief Jour. Systems and Software, 1978-82; contbr. articles to profl. jours. Pres. Point Field Community Assn., Millersville, Md., 1979-80; v.p. Greater Severna Park Coun., Severna Park, Md., 1980. Lt. col. USAF, 1955-76, Vietnam. Decorated Legion of Merit, Bronze Star. Mem. IEEE Computer Soc. (TC exec. bd.), Soc. Mfg. Engrs., Gulf Harbour Golf & Country Club. Republican. Episcopalian.

MANLEY, JUDITH L., director; b. Columbus, Ohio; B in Bus., Ohio State U., 1970; MEd, Xavier U., 1986. Copy writer advt. agy., Columbus, 1970—74; program asst. Ohio State U., Columbus, 1974—. Advisor, counselor, tchr. dept. Spanish and Portuguese Ohio State U., Columbus, 1991—. Author poems. Commr. Greater Hilltop Area Commn., Columbus, 1989—; bd. dirs. Greater Hilltop Cmty. Devel. Corp., Columbus, 1989—2006; alumnae Leadership Columbus, Columbus, 1993; citizens' adv. coun. Columbus Devel. Ctr.; alumna Citizen's Police Acad., Columbus. Named Vol. of the Month, Children's Hosp., Columbus, 2002; recipient Pres.'s Vol. Svc. award, 2003, 2004, 2005, 2006, Va. Denman Vol. award, 2004. Mem.: ACA, Am. Assn. Tchrs. Spanish and Portuguese. Avocations: writing, photography, music, theater.

MANLEY, KELLI JO, writer, photographer; b. Wichita, Kans., May 13, 1959; d. Harvey Joe Starlin and Betty Lou Mesplay; m. David Byron Manley, Jan. 11, 2003; 1 child, Tyler; m. Duane Harold Belcher (div.); children: Kail Starlin, Kasha Belcher. Mental health worker Heartland Behavioral, Nev., 1993—96, Mo., 1993—96, Raphael Hosp., Nev., 1984—87, Mo., 1984—87, Truman Med. Ctr. East, Lee's Summit, Mo., 1980—86; devel. asst. State Hosp., Nev., 1978—79, Mo., 1978—79; apt. mgr. Erwin Estates, Everett, Wash., 1998—2002. Gen. svc. rep. Narcotics Anonymous, Nev., 1996—98, Mo., 1996—98. Author of poems; jewelry designer, author (book) How To Make Your Own Earings, 2007, freelance photographer, 1972—. Hospice vol. Judith Hayes Ranch, Maricopa, Ariz., 2004. Recipient Employee of Month, Heartland Behavioral, 1994. Mem.: Gallping Gooses Motorcycle Club. Avocations: rock collecting, camping, fishing, motorcycling.

MANLEY, LAWRENCE G., literature educator; BA, Dartmouth Coll.; MA, PhD, Harvard Univ. Faculty Yale Univ., 1976—, dir. grad. studies, Renaissance studies, 1985—86, dir. grad. studies, English dept., 1987—90, chair, Renaissance Studies program, 1991—98, dir., undergrad. studies in English, 2004—, William R. Kenan Jr. prof., English, 2005—. Grantee Andrew W. Mellon Found. Fellowship, Guggenheim Found. Fellowship. Fellow: Am. Acad. Arts & Scis. Avocation: instrument-rated pilot. Office: English Dept Yale Univ PO Box 208302 New Haven CT 06520-8302 Office Phone: 203-432-2249. Business E-Mail: lawrence.manley@yale.edu. *

MANLEY, RICHARD WALTER, insurance company executive; b. Malone, NY, Dec. 26, 1934; s. Walter E. and Ruth (St. Mary) Manley; m. Linda Kimberlin, Dec. 18, 1965; children: Stephanie, Christopher. BS in Bus., U. So. Miss., 1960. Cert. real estate broker. Account exec. Colonial Life and Accident, Hattiesburg, Miss., 1960-63, dist. mgr. Oklahoma City, 1963-66, regional dir. Denver, 1966-76, zone dir., 1976-82; pres. Commonwealth Gen. Group, Denver, 1982-98, Manley Properties Inc., Denver, 1982-90, Richard W. Manley Commonwealth Gen. Grps., Inc., Denver, 1982—. Bd. dirs. Mercy Hosp., Denver, 1982—87; cons. Capitol Am. Life Ins. Co., Cleve., 1987—96. With USAF, 1956—59. Mem.: Cherry Hills C. of C., Rotary, Alpha Tau Omega. Roman Catholic. Avocations: golf, racquetball, running. Home: 6510 E Lake Pl Englewood CO 80111-4411 Office Phone: 303-220-1114. Personal E-mail: dickmanley@speakeasy.net.

MANLY, MARC EDWARD, lawyer, energy executive; b. Knoxville, Tenn., Mar. 11, 1952; s. William Donald and Jane (Wilden) M.; m. Colby A. Chapman, July 20, 1974; children: Justin C., Allison C. BA summa cum laude, Amherst Coll., 1974; MA in Econs., U. Mich., 1977, JD magna cum laude, 1977. Bar: Ill. 1978, DC 1988, US Dist. Ct. (no. dist. Ill.) 1978. Assoc. Sidley & Austin, Chgo., 1978—85, ptnr., 1986—94; v.p., solicitor gen. to v.p., chief counsel consumer svcs. group AT&T, 1995—2000; mng. dir. law & govtl. holdings, gen. counsel, sec. Newpower Holdings, Inc., 2000—02; exec. v.p., chief legal officer Cinergy Corp., 2002—06; group exec., chief legal officer Duke Energy, Charlotte, NC, 2006—. Mem. ABA, Order of Coif, Phi Beta Kappa. Office: Duke Energy 526 S Church St Charlotte NC 28202-1904 Office Phone: 704-594-6200. *

MANLY, ROBERT W., IV, food products executive; Grad., Stanford U., Calif.; MBA, Harvard Bus. Sch. Asst. to pres. IBP, Inc., 1981—86; exec. v.p. Smithfield Foods, Inc., 1986—96, 2006—, interim CFO, 2007; pres., COO Smithfield Packing, 1994—95; pres. Premium Std. Farms, 1996—2006. Office: Smithfield Foods Inc 200 Commerce St Smithfield VA 23430 Office Phone: 757-365-3000. *

MANLY, SAMUEL, lawyer; b. Louisville, Aug. 8, 1945; s. Samuel III and Nell Thornton (Montgomery) M.; m. Tacie Jarrett Bond, Aug. 8, 1970 (div. 1978); children: Julie Elder, Elizabeth Meriwether. BA cum laude, Yale U., 1967; JD, U. Va., 1970. Bar: Ky. 197l, U.S. Dist. Ct. (we. and ea. dists.) Ky. l972, U.S. Dist. Ct. (so. dist.) Ind. 1972, U.S. Dist. Ct. (we. dist.) Mich. 1995, U.S. Ct. Appeals (6th cir.) 1972, U.S. Ct. Appeals (10th cir.) 1997, U.S. Supreme Ct. 1997. Pres. Madison House, U. Va., Charlottesville, 1968-70; assoc. Greenebaum Doll & McDonald, Louisville, 1970-76; ptnr. Reisz Blackburn Manly & Treitz, Louisville, 1976-78; sr. ptnr. Manly & Sears, Louisville, 1978-81, Manly & Heleringer, Louisville, 1981-84; pvt. practice Law Offices of Samuel Manly, Louisville, 1984—. Sec., gen. counsel Gibbs-Inman Co., Louisville, 1972-78; contract atty. FDIC, Washington, 1976-84; counsel Winston Products Co., 1988—; dir. defender svcs. U.S. Dist. Ct. (we. dist.) Ky., 1992-94; mem. Ky. Criminal Justice Coun., 2002—; mem. clin. rules com. Supreme Ct. Ky., 2007—. Contract atty. Jefferson County, 1977—78, City of Louisville, 1978—83. Capt. USAR, 1967—86. Fellow: Ky. Bar Found. (life); mem.: ATLA, ABA (com. on products liability, subcom uninsured mfrs. sect. ligitation, com. on self-insurers and risk mgrs. sect. tort and ins. law practice), Am. Bankruptcy Inst., Assn. Fed. Def. Attys., Am. Judicature Soc., Comml. Law League of Am., Fed. Bar Assn., Ky. Acad. Trial Lawyers, Nat. Assn. Criminal Def. Lawyers, Ky. Assn. Criminal Def. Lawyers (bd. dirs., exec. com. 1986—, pres. 2001—03), Louisville Bar Assn., Ky. Bar Assn. (com. on legal ethics 1978—84, 1996—98), Louisville Boat Club. Republican. Avocations: classical music, fishing, golf. Home: 407 S Sherrin Ave Louisville KY 40207-3817 Office: Law Offices of Samuel Manly 239 S 5th St Ste 1606 Louisville KY 40202-3208 Office Phone: 502-585-4619. Personal E-mail: lawmanlouisville@aol.com.

MANLY, SARAH LETITIA, retired state legislator, ophthalmic photographer, angiographer; b. Greenville, SC, Feb. 1, 1927; d. Victor Harris and Elsie Clippard (Burnett) Gillespie; m. Basil Manly IV, Sept. 11, 1947; children: Sarah Manly Cornish, Basil V, Jean Manly McDowell, Mary Manly Mounce. BS cum laude, Furman U., 1947; postgrad., MIT, 1972; MEd, Clemson U., 1974; postgrad., Cambridge U., Eng., 1981. Cert. physics tchr., Pa., S.C.; cert. retinal angiographer. Ward sec. Roper Hosp., Charleston, S.C., 1947; analytical chemist Parker Labs., Charleston, 1948; tchr. sci. Upper Darby (Pa.) Sch. Dist., 1961-63; tchr. physics Sch. Dist. Greenville (S.C.) County, 1963-64, 70-76; ophthalmic photographer Basil Manly IV, MD, Greenville, 1976-96; lectr. physics Clemson (S.C.) U., 1979-81. Cons. MIT, Cambridge, 1972-75, Georgetown U., Washington, 1974-76, NASA, Houston, 1974-76. Editor, cons. physics study guides MIT, 1972-75; editor lab. materials NASA, 1974-76; contbr. articles to profl. jours. Trustee Sch. Dist. Greenville County, 1976-88. Named S.C. Legislator of Yr., S.C. Sch. Bds. Assn., 1991, Hon. Alumnus of Phi Beta Kappa, 1994. Mem. Greenville County Med. Aux. (sec. 1953-54), Delta Kappa Gamma. Democrat. Baptist. Avocations: travel, reading, volunteering. Home: 201 Robin Ln Greenville SC 29605

MANN, ALFRED, pharmaceutical executive; b. Portland, Oreg., 1925; MS in Physics, UCLA; DHL (hon.), U. So. Calif., 2001, Johns Hopkins U., 2001. Chmn., CEO MannKind Corp., Sylmar, Calif.; chmn., co-CEO Advanced Bionics Corp.; chmn. emeritus MiniMed Inc.; founder, chmn. Med. Rsch. Group, Inc.; chmn., CEO Siemens-Pacesetter, Inc. and predecessor Pacesetter Sys., Inc.; pres. Spectrolab, Heliotek. Chmn. bd. trustees Alfred Mann Found., 1985—, Alfred Mann Inst., U. So. Calif.; U. So. Calif. trustee mem. bd. overseers Keck U. So. Calif. Sch. Medicine; chmn. So. Calif. Biomed. Coun., Second Sight, LLC, Allecure Corp., Quallion, LLC, CTL Immunotherapy, Inc., Pharm. Discovery Co., Inc. Named Man of Yr., WISE Sr. Svcs., 1999, Humanitarian of Yr., House Ear Inst., 1999; named one of 10 Most Influential People on Tch Coast, L.a. Times, 1999, Forbes' Richest Americans, 2006; recipient Spirit of Edison award for cmty. svc., Thomas Edison State Coll., 1999, Vision of the Future award, RP Internat., 1999, Reynolds Soc. Achievement award, Harvard Med. Sch., 1999. Fellow: Am. Inst. Med. and Biol. Engring.; mem.: NAE. Office: MannKind Corp 28903 N Ave Paine Valencia CA 91355 also: Alfred Mann Found PO Box 905 Valencia CA 91380

MANN, BRUCE ALAN, lawyer, investment banking executive; b. Chgo., Nov. 28, 1934; s. David I. and Lillian (Segal) M.; m. Naomi Cooks, Aug. 31, 1980; children: Sally Mann Stull, Jonathan Hugh, Andrew Ross. BBA, U. Wis., 1955, SJD, 1957. Bar: Wis. 1957, N.Y. 1958, Calif. 1961. Assoc. Davis, Polk & Wardwell, NYC, 1957-60, Pillsbury, Madison & Sutro, San Francisco, 1960-66, ptnr., 1967-83; adminstrv. mng. dir. L.F. Rothschild Unterberg Towbin, San Francisco, 1983-87; ptnr. Morrison & Foerster, San Francisco, 1987—; sr. mng. dir. W.R. Hambrecht & Co., San Francisco, 1999—2003. Cons. SEC, 1978; vis. prof. law Georgetown U., 1978; lectr. in field. Author: (with Mattson) California Corporate Practice and Forms, 1999; contbr. articles to profl. jours. Served with USAR, 1957. Mem.: NASD (gov.-at-large 1981—83), ABA (chmn. fed. regulation of securities com. 1981—83, mem. bus. law sect. coun. 1996—99, standing com. on ethics and profl. responsibility 1997—2003, chmn. com. on venture capital 2000—03), Bar Assn. San Francisco (bd. dirs. 1974—75), State Bar Calif., Am. Law Inst., The Family Club. Office: Morrison & Foerster 425 Market St Ste 3100 San Francisco CA 94105-2482 E-mail: bmann@mofo.com.

MANN, CEDRIC ROBERT, retired science administrator, oceanographer; b. Auckland, New Zealand, Feb. 14, 1926; came to Can., 1949; s. Duncan and Winifred Mary (Hood) M.; m. Muriel Frances May, Dec. 19, 1950; 1 child, Robin Carl B.Sc., U. N.Z., Auckland, 1948, M.Sc., 1950; PhD, U. B.C., Vancouver, Can., 1953; D.Eng., N.S. Tech. Coll., Halifax, Can., 1972. Physicist Naval Research Establishment, Halifax, N.S., Can., 1953-61; oceanographer Atlantic Oceanographic Lab., Halifax, N.S., Can., 1961-75, dir., 1975-78; dir. gen. Bedford Inst. Oceanography, Halifax, N.S., Can., 1978-79, Inst. Ocean Scis., Sidney, B.C., Can., 1979-87. Assoc. prof. Dalhousie U., Halifax, 1961-75; chmn. sci. adv. bd. Intergovtl. Oceanographic Commn., Paris, 1978-81; mem. Can. Climate Planning Bd., Ottawa, 1983-86; chmn. Sea Use Council, Seattle, 1981-86. Contbr. articles to profl. jours. Fellow Royal Soc. Can.; mem. Can. Meteorol. and Oceanographic Soc. (life, recipient J.P. Tully medal in Oceanography, 1994). Anglican. Avocations: golf, gardening. Home: 301-2373 Henry Ave Sidney BC Canada V8L 2B4

MANN, CLARENCE CHARLES, retired realtor; b. Oradell, NJ, Oct. 15, 1929; s. Clarence Theodore and Martha Barbara (Koster) M.; m. Joan Elizabeth Schnoor, Nov. 25, 1951 (div. Jan. 1985); 1 child, Gary John; life ptnr., Stephen Garrett. BA, NYU, 1951; MA, U. Pa., 1958, Am. U., Beirut, Lebanon, 1963. Commd. 2d. lt. U.S. Army, 1951, advanced through grades to col., ret., 1977; def. attache to Jordan, 1973-77; mktg. mgr. Litton Industries, Middle East, 1977-81; mktg. mgr. Mid-East Hughes Aircraft Co., Fullerton, Calif., 1981-91; dir. relocation ERA Gem Realty, Tucson, 1992-97; realtor Realty Execs., Tucson, 1997—2005; ret., 2005. Author: Abu Dhabi: Birth of an Oil Shaikhdom, 1964. Decorated Legion of Merit. Avocations: music, gardening, travel. Personal E-mail: reloweb@aol.com.

MANN, CLIFTON, secondary school educator; s. Jimmy and Linda Mann. Masters, U. Memphis, 1998. Tchr. Memphis City Schs., 1997—2004; HS tchr. geography, history Shelby County Schs., Collierville, Tenn., 2005—. Tchr. adv. com. Facing History and Ourselves, Memphis, 1998—2004. Office: Collierville HS 1101 N Byhalia Collierville TN 38017 Home Phone: 901-682-7792; Office Phone: 901-853-3310.

MANN, DAVID SCOTT, lawyer; b. Cin., Sept. 25, 1939; s. Henry M. and Helen Faye M.; m. Elizabeth Taliaferro, Oct. 5, 1963; children: Michael, Deborah, Marshall. AB cum laude, Harvard Coll., 1961, LLB magna cum laude, 1968. Bar: Ohio 1968. Assoc. Dinsmore & Shohl, Cin., 1968-74, ptnr., 1974-83, Taliaferro and Mann, Cin., 1983-92; councilman City of Cin., 1974-92, mayor, 1980-82, 91; mem. 103d Congress 1st Ohio dist., Washington, 1993-94; mem. armed svcs. com., mem. jud. com. Washington; of counsel Thompson, Hine and Flory, Cin., 1995-96; pvt. practice Mann & Mann, LLC, Cin., 1997—. Adj. prof. Coll. Law U. Cin., 1995—2002. Editor Harvard Law Rev., 1966-68, notes editor, 1967-68; contbr. articles to profl. jours. Mem., chmn. Cin. Bd. Health, 1972-74. With USN, 1961-65. Mem. Cin. Bar Assn. Democrat. Methodist. Home: 568 Evanswood Pl Cincinnati OH 45220-1527 Office Phone: 513-621-2888. Business E-Mail: david@mannandmannlaw.com.

MANN, DAVID WILLIAM, minister; b. Elkhart, Ind., Apr. 17, 1947; s. Herbert Richard and Kathryn (Bontrager) M.; m. Brenda Marie Frantz, June 7, 1969; children: Troy, Todd, Erika. BA, Bethel Coll., 1969; MS, Nat. Louis U., 1986. Ordained to ministry Missionary Ch., 1978. Campus life dir. Youth for Christ, Elkhart, 1969-77; denominational youth dir. Missionary Ch., Ft. Wayne, Ind., 1977-81, Christian edn. dir., 1981-88, U.S. dir. missions, 1990—; assoc. dir. World Ptnrs., Ft. Wayne, 1988-90. Dir. Missionary Ch. Vol. Svc., Ft. Wayne, 1983—, World Ptnrs. USA, 1998—. Author: (with others) Youth Leaders Source Book, 1985; contbr. articles to profl. jour. Mgr. Little League, Ft. Wayne, 1981-89, bd. dirs. 1986. Recipient Alumnus of the Year award, Bethel Coll., 2003. Mem. Nat. Assn. Evangelicals, Evangelical Fellowship of Mission Agys. (nat. bd. dirs. 1999—), Denominational Execs. in Christian Edn. (chmn. 1988), Aldersgate Pub. Assn. (bd. dirs. 1985, 87), Nat. Christian Edn. Assn. (exec. com. 1987-89). Avocations: baseball, skiing, fishing, woodworking. Office: Missionary Ch PO Box 9127 Fort Wayne IN 46899-9127 Home Phone: 260-396-2509; Office Phone: 260-747-2027. E-mail: manndw@aol.com.

MANN, ERIC LOUIS, retired military officer, mathematics professor, researcher; b. July 22, 1952; BA in Math., Albion Coll., 1974; MSc in Sys. Mgmt. and Logistics Sys., U. So. Calif., 1980; MAT in Elem. Tchg. and Ednl. Tech., Colo. Coll., 1997; post grad. diploma in Ednl. Psychology, U. Conn., 2002, student, 2003—. Cert. Elem. Tchr. (kindergarten through eighth grade) NH, Elem. Tchr. (kindergarten through sixth grade) Conn., Mid. Sch. Math. Tchr. Conn., Mid. Sch. Earth Sci. Tchr. Conn. Advanced through grades to lt. col. USAF, 1975—96, ret. lt. col., 1996; intern tchr. Rockrimmon Elem., 1996—97; tchr. Atkinson Acad., NH, 1997—98, editor, pub. In Their Own Words; sci., math, Am. history tchr. Bow Meml. Mid. Sch., NH, 1998—2002, gifted and talented coord., 2001—02, mathcounts, math. team coach, Jason project coord., conv. coord., math. olympiads, continental math. league, Mandelbrot competition, space explorers mission to moon coord., bridge builders club supr., physics course coord., FIRST LEGO team organizer, gifted and talented resource website developer, editor lit. jour., chess club establisher; math. tchr. Hall Meml. Sch., Willington, Conn., 2002—03; vis. prof. Purdue U., 2005. Adj. prof. U. Conn., 2003—, webmaster project M3, 2003, editor project M3 newsletters, moderator on-line profl. discussion bd. project M3, rsch. assoc. project M3, 03, on-line course developer, mentor, 04; presenter in field, 2004—05. Contbr. articles to profl. jours. in field, manuals in field. Decorated Group Achievement award NASA, Commendation medals USAF, Achievement medals, Meritorious Svc. medals, Orgnl. Excellence awards, Outstanding Unit awards, Air Force Assn. award, Dept. Def. Joint Svc. Commendation medal, Master Space Ops. badge, Named one of Twelve Airmen of Air Force award, Named 1st Space Wing Jr. Officer of Quarter, Named Hdqs. North Am. Def. Command Jr. Officer of Quarter, Named Hdqs. Air Force Space Command Jr. Officer of Quarter, Named Strategic Air Command Communication Area Airman of Quarter; Quality of Life Improvement grant, USAF, New Boston Air Sta., 1990, Space Explorers On-line Simulation Project, Jefferson Pilot Fin. grant, Bow Meml. Mid. Sch., 1990, FIRST LEGO League grant, Bow PTO, 2001, Blue Chip Sch. Tech. grant, State of Conn., Hall Meml. Sch., 2003. Mem.: NSTA, Sch. Sci. and Math. Assn., Ind. Coun. Tchrs. Math., Nat. Coun. Tchrs. Math., Nat. Coun. Suprs. Math., Ind. Assn. for Gifted, Nat. Assn. Gifted Children, Assn. Supervision and Curriculum Devel., Kappa Delta Pi, Pi Lambda Theta.

MANN, FRANK BERT, artist, educator; b. Washington, Apr. 22, 1950; s. Frank Bert and Wilda Vendetta Kaufman. BS, High Point Univ., 1972; BA, George Washington Univ., 1978; MFA, Pratt Inst., 1981. Guest lectr. Corcoran Sch. of Art, Washington, 1979, Pa. State U., Reading, 1986-87, Pratt Inst., Bklyn., 1987-88, Parsons Sch. Art & Design, NYC, 1996-97, Iona Coll., New Rochelle, NY, 2005. Exec. dir. Colaborative Projects, Inc., NY, 1987-88, Basicarts Network, NY, 1989-90; vis. artist Coalition for the Homeless Camp, 1997, Children's Friends for Life, NY, 1997, Project for St. Cyrils Ch., NY, 1992. Author: Eye of the Painter, 1997; illustrator (film) Nerves, 1993; exhibitions include Biennale Internat., Florence, Italy, 2001 (Lorenzo Il Magnifico medal in painting, 2001), Represented in permanent collections Guggenheim Mus., NYC, Mus. Contemp. Art, Nice, France, live interview series and DVD, A Special Program in Three Parts: The Art of Frank Mann, 2005. U.S. rep. Biennale Internazionale, Florence, 1999, 2001. Recipient Mable Sanger Webb award, Ford Found., 1980, Lorenzo le Magnifico medal, Internat. Dell'Arte Contemporanea, 2001; grantee, NY State Coun. Arts, 1988, NY City Dept. Cultural Affairs, 1989. Mem.: Assn. D'Art Internat., Contemporary Artists' Guild, Am. Soc. Contemporary Artists (v.p. 2003—), Drawing Soc., Artists Equity (bd. dirs. 2000—03, v.p. 2003—), Am. for the Arts. Lutheran. Home and Office: 212 E 34th St Apt 3E New York NY 10016-4846 Office Phone: 212-689-9003. Personal E-mail: fmann100@hotmail.com.

MANN, GEORGE STANLEY, diversified financial services company executive, real estate company officer; b. Toronto, Ont., Can., Dec. 23, 1932; s. David Philip and Elizabeth (Green) M.; children: Michael, Tracy. Attended, North Toronto Collegiate Sch.; LLD (hon.), U. Windsor. Ptnr. Mann & Martel Co. Ltd., 1959-68, CEO, 1968-70, United Trust Co., 1970-76; pres. Unicorp Canada Corp., Toronto, 1972-76, chmn. bd., 1976-90; dir. Nat. Bank Canada, 1978-91; chmn. bd. Union Gas Ltd., 1986-93; owner Townsview Properties Ltd., Toronto, 1984—. Bd. govs. Mt. Sinai Hosp., Toronto. Mem. Oakdale Golf & Country Club (Toronto), High Ridge Country Club (Palm Beach, Fla.), Mar-a-Lago Club (Palm Beach, Fla.), Trump Internat. Golf Club (Palm Beach, Fla.). Avocation: golf. Home: #10 Bellair St Ste 302 Toronto ON Canada M5R 3T8 also: 505 South County Rd Palm Beach FL 33480 Office: 2 St Clair Ave W Ste 1004 Toronto ON Canada Office Phone: 416-922-1500.

MANN, JACK MATTHEWSON, bottling company executive; b. Marshall, Tex., Apr. 14, 1932; s. Jack Slater and Mary (Matthewson) M.; m. True Sandlin, Sept. 4, 1954 (div. 1989); children: Jack, Robert, Daniel, Nathaniel; m. Glenda Copeland Grimes, Sept. 17, 2005. Student, N.Mex. Mil. Inst., 1952; BBA, U. Tex., 1954; MBA, Harvard U., 1960. Credit analyst Republic Nat. Bank, Dallas, 1959; chem. coord. Humble Oil and Refining Co., Baytown, Tex., 1960-61; asst. sales mgr. The Made-Rite Co., Marshall, Tex., 1957-58; asst. gen. mgr. The Made Rite Co., Marshall, Tex., 1961-63, gen. mgr. Longview, Tex., 1963-92, pres., 1972—, owner, chmn., 1982—; v.p. Longview Econ. Devel. Corp., 1994-2000, treas., 1995-96, pres., 1996-97. Mem. pres.'s adv. coun. Le Tourneau U., 1994—97; mem. devel. coun. U. Tex.-Tyler Longview U. Ctr., 2000—, pres., 2004—06. Exec. com. Rep. Party Tex., 1962-65; mem. Trinity Episcopal Ch., Longview, 1963-, sr. warden, jr. warden, treas.; mem. exec. bd. Episcopal Diocese Tex., Houston, 1974-76; mem. small bus. adv. com. Tex. Dept. Commerce, 1988-91. Mem.: Nat. Dr. Pepper Bottlers Assn. (pres. 1983—85), Tex. Soft Drink Assn. (pres. 1972), Longview C. of C. (dir. 1965—68, 1984—86), Pinecrest Country Club, Longview Summit Club (gov. 1982—94). Avocation: University of Texas athletics. Office: The Made Rite Co PO Box 3283 Longview TX 75606-3283 Home: 21 Tallwood Ln Longview TX 75605 Home Phone: 903-663-4238.

MANN, JAMES BROOKS, lawyer; b. Houston, July 31, 1957; s. George Solomon and Brooksine (Thompson) M. BA, Cornell U., 1979; JD, Harvard U., 1982. Bar: D.C. 1982, U.S. Supreme Ct. 1987, U.S. Ct. Appeals (D.C. cir.) 1982, U.S. Ct. Appeals (fed. cir.) 1983, U.S. Ct. Appeals (5th cir., 6th cir., 10th cir.) 1987, U.S. Ct. Appeals (3rd, 4th cir., 9th cir., 11th cir.) 1988. Assoc. Ivins, Phillips & Barker, Washington, 1982-84, Lane & Edson, Washington, 1984-85; gen. counsel and acting dep. staff dir. U.S. Commn. Civil Rights, Washington, 1985-87; dep. asst. atty. gen. tax div. Dept. of Justice, Wash., 1987; assoc. Societe Generale, NYC. Mem. Telluride Assn. (trustee 1977—). Republican. Office: Societe Generale 1221 Ave of Americas New York NY 10020 Office Phone: 212-278-7001. Office Fax: 212-278-7731. Business E-Mail: james.mann@sgcib.com.

MANN, JAMES ROBERT, former congressman; b. Greenville, SC, Apr. 27, 1920; s. Alfred Cleo and Nina (Griffin) M.; m. Virginia Thomason Brunson, Jan. 15, 1945; children— James Robert, David Brunson, William Walker, Virginia Brunson. BA, The Citadel, 1941, LL.D. (hon.), 1978; JD, U. S.C., 1947. Bar: S.C. 1947, U.S. Ct. Appeals (4th cir.) 1948, U.S. Supreme Ct. 1970. Practice in, Greenville, 1947—; del. S.C. Ho. of Reps. from, Greenville County, 1949-52; solicitor 13th Jud. Circuit, 1953-63; mem. 91st-95th Congresses 4th Dist. SC. Sec. Greenville County Planning Commn., 1963-67; Trustee Greenville Hosp. System, 1965-68; bd. govs. Greenville Shriners Hosp., 1983-90. Served to lt. col. AUS, 1941-46; col. USAR ret. Mem. Am., S.C., Greenville County bar assns., Am. Judicature Soc., Greater Greenville C. of C. (pres. 1965), V.F.W. (dep. comdr. 1951-52), Am. Legion. Lodges: Mason; Shriners; Kiwanis; Elks; Woodmen of World. Democrat. Baptist. Office: 414 Univ Park Greenville SC 29601

MANN, JOHN MARTIN, minister; b. McKeesport, Pa., Nov. 18, 1946; s. Glenn Grant and Mary Dorothy (Flaherty) M. BA, Clarion State Coll., 1967; MDiv, Duke U., 1970, ThM, 1972; D Ministry, Wittenberg U., 1976. Ordained to ministry Luth. Ch. in Am., 1972. Pastor 1st Luth. Ch., Edinboro, Pa., 1971-82; sr. pastor St. John's Luth. Ch., Erie, Pa., 1982-91; sem. pastor Luth. Theol. Sem., 2006—. Instr. Edinboro State Coll., 1971-82; adj. prof. religion Thiel Coll. Greenville, Pa., 1980-82, baccalaureate preacher, 1980-84, trustee, 1974-80, 82—; chmn. synod vocations examining com. NW Pa.-W.Va. Synod, 1984-88; chmn. intersynodical candidacy com. NW Pa.-Allegheny Synods, 1988-90; chmn. ch. vocations examining com. NW Pa. Synod, 1990—; chmn. Luth. Coalition of Erie, 1990-91; dean Cond. I, Northwestern Pa. Synod, 1991—, adj. faculty postgrad/ Family Systems Seminars, 2004; mem. faculty Clergy Seminars with Larry Foster. Contbr. articles to profl. jours. Bd. dirs. Luth. Home, Erie, 1976-79, 82—, Inter-Ch. Ministries NW Pa., 1979-84, South Erie Hillside Cmty. Orgn., 1982—, Holy Trinity Cmty. Ctr., Erie, 1984-88, Nesting Inn, 1988—, Hospice Met. Erie, 1988—, Westminster Counseling Ctr., Mpls.; chmn. Erie City Strategy for Luths., 1989—; pastor Trinity Luth. Ch., Canton, Ohio, 1992—2006; pres. UrbanArk Urban Ministry Coalition; active ELCA NE Ohio Synod, ecumenical com., chmn. synod outreach com., 1998—, dean conf., Canton, mission planner, Urban Strategy com.; founding chmn. Interfaith Roundtable of Canton and NW Neighborhood Assn.; covenant commr. Youngstown Roman Cath. Diocese, NE Ohio Synod; bd. dirs. Westminster Counseling Ctr. Recipient Outstanding Young Man of Am. award Jaycees, 1982. Mem. Luth. Assn. Larger Chs., Am. Assn. Pastoral Counselors, Luth. Campus Ministry Assn., Interdenominational Ministerial Assn. (sec.), Canton Downtown Pastors Assn., Synod Evangelism Com. Office: Trinity Luth Ch 415 Tuscarawas St W Canton OH 44702-2017 Office Phone: 651-641-3216. E-mail: jmann001@luthersem.edu. *In a global environment where fundamentalist religions create division and terrorism, we need a constructive, reappropriation of faith in God.*

MANN, KATINKA, artist; b. NYC, June 28, 1925; Vis. artist Morris & Rose Markowitz Polaroid Corp. at Boston Mus. Fine Arts, 1983. One-woman shows include Ctrl. Hall Gallery, Port Washington, N.Y., 1974, 76, 77, 79, N.Y.C., 1982, 84, Hansen Gallery, N.Y.C., 1976, 77, 79, Heckscher Mus., Huntington, N.Y., 1977, Fairleigh Dickinson U., Hackensack, N.J., 1985, Real Art Ways, Hartford, Conn., 1985, Marymount Manhattan Coll., N.Y.C., 1986, Islip Art Mus., East Islip, N.Y., 1986, Phlia. Art Alliance, 1987, Silvermine Galleries, New Canaan, Conn., 1987, Dowling Coll. Gallery, Oakdale, N.Y., 1987, Art Gallery Port Washington Libr., Port Washington, N.Y., 1996, Space 504 Gallery, N.Y.C., 1998, Heckscher Mus. Art, Roslyn, N.Y., 2001; exhibited in numerous group shows including most recently A.I.R. Gallery, N.Y.C., 2000, Martin Art Gallery, Muhlenberg Coll., Allentown, Pa., 2002, Hofstra Art Mus., Hempstead, N.Y., 2002, Hillwood Art Mus., Brookville, N.Y., 2003, El Instituto Nacional de Bellas Artes, San Miguel de Allende, Mex., 2003, Nasau County Mus. Art, Roslyn, N.Y., 2004, Heckscher Mus. Art, Huntington, N.Y., 2003; represented in permanent collections Bklyn. Mus., Islip Art Mus., Polaroid Internat. Corp., Boston, Russ Togs Corp., N.Y., Nassau C.C., Guggenheim Mus., N.Y.C., Mus. Modern Art, N.Y.C., Princeton Univ., Nat. Mus. Am. Art, Smithsonian Instn., Washington, Brit. Mus., London, Phila. Mus. Art, N.Y. Pub. Libr., N.Y.C., San Francisco Mus. Modern Art, Houston Mus. Fine Arts, numerous pvt. collections. Mem. Am. Abstract Artists (treas. 1989-96, 2002—). Home: 290 9th Ave Apt 13H New York NY 10001 Office Phone: 212-989-2230. Personal E-mail: katinkamann5@aol.com.

MANN, KENNETH HENRY, marine ecologist; b. Dovercourt, Essex, Eng., Aug. 15, 1923; arrived in Can., 1967, naturalized, 1973; s. Harry and Mabel (Ashby) M.; m. Isabella Gilmour Ness, Apr. 18, 1946; children: Ian Malcolm, Sheila Helen, Colin Gilmour. BSc, U. London, 1949, DSc, 1965; PhD, U. Reading, 1953. Lectr. zoology, then reader U. Reading, Eng., 1949-64; 64-67; sr. biologist marine ecology lab. Bedford Inst. Oceanography, Dartmouth, Can., 1967-72, dir. marine ecology lab., 1980-87, sr. rsch. scientist, 1987-93, emeritus rsch. scientist, 1993—. Prof., chmn. biology Dalhousie U., Halifax, N.S., Canada, 1972—80, adj. prof. biology, 1980—2002. Author: Leeches: Their Structure, Physiology, Ecology and Embryology, 1961, Ecology of Coastal Waters: A Systems Approach, 1982, Ecology of Coastal Waters: Implications for Management, 2000; co-author (with J. Lazier): Dynamics of Marine Ecosystems: Biological-Physical Interactions in the Sea, 1991, 3d edit., 2005; co-author: (with R.S. Barnes) Fundamentals of Aquatic Ecology, 1991, Korean edit., 2002; editor, contbr.: (with T. Platt and R. Ulanowicz) Mathematical Models in Biological Oceanography, 1981, (with F. Wulff and J.G. Field) Network Analysis in Marine Ecology, 1989, (with A. Payne, K. Brink and R. Hilborn) Benguela Trophic Functioning, 1992; editor Jour. Animal Ecology, 1966—67. Served with Royal Air Force, 1942-46. Fellow Royal Soc. Can.; mem. Am. Soc. Limnology and Oceanography. Home: 23 Woodward Cres Halifax NS Canada B3M 1J6 Office: Bedford Inst Oceanography Box 1006 Dartmouth NS Canada B2Y 4A2 Office Phone: 902-426-3696. Personal E-mail: ken.mann@ns.sympatico.ca.

MANN, KENNETH WALKER, retired minister, psychologist; b. Nyack, NY, Aug. 22, 1914; s. Arthur Hungerford and Ethel Livingston (Walker) M. AB, Princeton U., 1937; STB, Gen. Theol. Sem., NYC, 1942; MS, U. Mich., 1950, PhD, 1956. Ordained priest Episcopal Ch., 1942; diplomate Am. Assn. Pastoral Counselors; lic. clin. psychologist, Calif., Conn.; lic. marriage, family and child counselor, Calif. Vicar in Valley Cottage, Pearl River, NY, 1941-43; priest in charge Yonkers, NY, 1943-45; ret. minister, 1945—. Dir. youth work and Christian edn. Diocese L.A., 1945-47; curate in Beverly Hills, Calif., 1947-49; counselor Bur. Psychol. Svcs., U. Mich., 1951-52; chaplain, clin. psychologist dept. psychiatry St. Luke's Hosp., N.Y.C., also priest-psychotherapist Cathedral St. John Divine, N.Y.C., psychol. examiner ministerial candidates Diocese N.Y., 1952-58; assoc. chaplain Hosp. Good Samaritan, L.A., 1958-65; exec. pastoral svcs., exec. coun. Episc. Ch. N.Y.C., 1965-70; program officer Acad. Religion and Mental Health, N.Y.C., 1970-72; sr. adviser profl. affairs Inst. Religion and Health, 1972-74; sr. psychol. staff Silver Hill Found., New Canaan, Conn., 1974-84; pres. Rockland County (N.Y.) Mins. Assn., 1942-43; exec. sec. social svc. commn. Diocese N.Y., 1943-45; chmn. div. pastoral svcs. Diocese L.A., 1958-65; field dir. Western region Acad. Religion and Mental Health, 1958-61; assoc. nat. chaplain U.S. Power Squadrons, 1956-57. Author: On Pills and Needles, 1969, Deadline for Survival—A Survey of Moral Issues in Science and Medicine, 1970; contbr. articles to profl. jours. Pres. Adoption Inst. LA, 1964; edn. com. Calif. Heart Assn., 1962-64; trustee, treas. Acad. Religion and Mental Health, 1954-59, profl. bd., 1960-70; trustee Vis. Nurse Assn. LA, 1963-65, Children's Home Soc. Calif. in LA, 1964-65, North Conway Inst., 1966-80. USPHS grantee, 1950-51. Fellow AAAS; mem. APA (chmn. com. rels. between psychology and religion 1956-58), Western Psychol. Assn., Calif. Psychol. Assn., L.A. County Psychol. Assn., N.Y. Acad. Scis., Planetary Soc., Assembly Episc. Hosps. and Chaplains, Upper Nyack Tennis Club, Princeton Club N.Y., Exch. Club Beverly Hills (pres.). Republican. Home: 32 Tallman Ave Nyack NY 10960-1606 *I have strongly held to the principle that the total "health" of mankind cannot be considered apart from the values and aspirations by which people live, and by which they may even be prepared to die. Amidst the confusions that exist today over loyalties, traditions, and ideals, many are asking: What is the right way to behave? How should I think? What kind of person am I supposed to be? To help such people in quandary to live responsibly, and still be true to their individuality, is a large task, but it is one that is central to a religious ministry. It has always been my chief concern.*

MANN, LAURA ANN, soprano; MusB, Eastman Sch. Music, 1965, MusM, 1972; Dr.Mus.Arts, U. Md., 1995; studied with Herbert Brauer Kammersanger, Berlin, Germany; studied with Edwin McArthur, NYC; studied with Edith Lang Kammersangerin, Lubeck, Germany; studied with David Garvey, studied with Stefan Scaggiari and Rayburn Wright, studied with Julius Huehn, studied with Anna Kaskas, studied with John Maloy, studied with Kammersanger Hans Hotter, studied with Louise Urban, studied with Leon Major, studied with Rhoda Levine, studied with Ted van Griethaesen, studied with Franchelle Dorn, studied with Kammersanger Heinz Rehfuss, studied, studied with Gerd Albrecht, studied with Christof Perick, studied with Richard Woitach. Prin., owner vocal studio Vocal Advancement, Fairfax, Va., 1979—. Prof. voice Tex. A&I U., Kingsville, Tex., 1984—85; asst. prof. voice Tex. Tech. U., Lubbock, Tex., 1984—86; vis. prof. voice We. Carolina U., Cullowhee, NC, 1986—88; prof. voice Anne Arundel C.C., Annapolis, Md., 1989—94; adj. prof. voice and opera George Mason U., Fairfax, Va., 1995—2001, dir. opera, 1995—, mem. women's studies faculty, 1998—, tchr. stage movement, French, German diction; presenter in field; lectr. in field; clinician and adjudicator. Singer: (CD) The Joy of Christmas, 1996, Operas, (albums) Christ Is Born, Laura Mann In Recital, Songs of Light and Joy, 2002, (CD) Laura Mann in Concert, 1999, (one-act, one-person opera/monodrama) The White Cliffs; soloist: Berlin Philharm., Swiss Chamber Orch., Prague Chamber Ensemble, Rochester Philharm., Buffalo Philharm., Richmond Symphony, Oklahoma City Symphony, Asheville Symphony, Dallas Baroque Ensemble, Kennedy Ctr. Concert Hall, German Embassy, French Embassy, Mexican Embassy. Broadcaster, Christian Sci. Media Svcs. Sta. WTNT-TV. Named a Internat. Opera Singers Competition Semi-Finalist, Ctr. Contemporary Opera, NYC; recipient Performer's Cert. in Voice and Opera, Eastman Sch. Music, Senatorial award, U. Md. Coll. Pl., 1995; grantee, Prince George's Arts Coun., 1993—96, Va. Commn. Arts, 2000—, Fulbright grant, Martha Rockefeller grant. Mem.: Music Tchrs. Nat. Assn., Internat. Alliance for Women in Music, Opera Am., Nat. Acad. Recording Arts and Scis., South Tex. Assn. Tchrs. Singing, Nat. Assn. Tchrs. Singing, Pi Kappa Lambda. Office: Music Dept George Mason Univ 4400 University Dr Fairfax VA 22030-4422 Office Phone: 703-217-8615, 703-995-1586. Personal E-mail: opera_tunity@peoplepc.com.

MANN, LOUIS EUGENE, financial planner; b. Balt., Jan. 24, 1947; s. Manfred and Ruth Eleanor (Kates) M.; m. Marjorie Ruth Friedman, Mar. 23, 1971; children: Lisa Renee, Brian Michael. Student, Balt. Poly. Inst., 1964, Towson State Coll., 1964-67; postgrad., U. Pa., 1969-70; CFP, Coll. for Fin. Planning, 1993. CFP; securities lics.; lic. ins. broker, NJ, Pa.; registered investment adv. Clk. Food Fair Stores, Inc., Balt., 1964-68; v.p. Friendly Grocer, Inc., Cherry Hill, N.J., 1968-79; sales mgr. Frito-Lay Inc., Cinnaminson, N.J., 1979-82; salesman N.Y. Life Ins. Co., Cherry Hill, 1982-89; ptnr. Custom Fin. Svcs., Marlton, N.J., 1988-93; registered investment advisor, pres. Louis E. Mann Fin. Svcs., Inc., Mt. Laurel, NY, 1993—; comptroller Shusterman & Davis, LLC, Phila., 1996-2000; exec. v.p. Orion Fin. Svcs. LLC, Phila., 2001. Developer: (math. formula) Law of Squares of Consecutive Numbers, 1963. Mgr., coach Greentree Athletic Assn., Mount Laurel, N.J., 1985-94; pres. Congregation Beth Tikvah Men's Club, Marlton, 1988-89, 90-91, 94-95, bd. dirs., exec. bd. mem., 1994-95. Recipient Coll. scholarships State of Md.-Senatorial and Ednl., 1964. Mem. Delaware Valley Inst. CFPs, Fin. Planning Assn., Million Dollar Round Table (membership com. 1984), Rotary Club of Moorestown (com. chmn., bd. dirs. 1984-94, 1st v.p. 1996-97, pres. 1997-98), Rotary Internat. (dist. planned giving chmn. Dist. 7500, 1994-95, asst. dist. ann. giving chair dist. 7500 2001-03), Fedn. Jewish Men's Clubs (trustee Mid-Atlantic region 1995-96) Democrat. Jewish. Avocations: sports, music, gardening, reading. Home: 121 Colony Pl Mount Laurel NJ 08054-2404 Home Phone: 856-778-0418; Office Phone: 856-988-5453. Personal E-mail: manncfp@aol.com. Business E-Mail: louis@mannfinacial.net.

MANN, MARION, pathologist, educator; b. Atlanta, Mar. 29, 1920; s. Levi James and Cora (Casey) Mann; m. Ruth Maurine Reagin, Jan. 16, 1943; children: Marion Jr., Judith Walk. BS in Edn., Tuskegee Inst., Ala., 1940; MD, Howard U., 1954; PhD, Georgetown U., 1961; grad., 1965, U.S. Army War Coll., 1970; DSc (hon.), Georgetown U., 1979, U. Mass., 1984, Tuskegee U., 1998; grad., U.S. Army War Coll., 1970. Diplomate Nat. Bd. Med. Examiners, Am. Bd. Pathology. Intern USPHS Hosp., Staten Island, NY, 1954—55; resident Georgetown U. Hosp., 1956—60; practice medicine, specializing in pathology Washington, 1961—; instr. pathology Georgetown U., 1960—61; professorial lectr. Georgetown U. Sch. Medicine, 1970—73; asst. prof. pathology Howard U. Coll. Medicine, 1961—67, assoc. prof., 1967—70, prof., 1970, dean, 1970—79; v.p. rsch. Howard U., 1988—91. Capt. US Army, 1942—50, brig. gen. Res. US

Army. Mem.: Nat. Acad. Scis., Inst. Medicine, Sigma Pi Phi, Alpha Omega Alpha. Mem. United Ch. Of Christ. Home: 1453 Whittier Pl NW Washington DC 20012-2845 Office: 520 W St NW Washington DC 20059-0001

MANN, MERLIN DEAN, III, blogger; b. Cin., Nov. 26, 1966; m. Cudworth Madeline Stiness, Dec. 21, 2005. BA, New Coll. Fla., 1990. Web developer; telemarketer; musician Bacon Ray, Tallahassee, 1994—99; blog host, creator 43Folders.com. Contbr. articles to WIRED, Make, Popular Sci., MacWorld.; featured in (media) NY Times Mag., Washington Post, Time, Wall St. Jour. Named one of Top 10 Blogs on Web, Technorati, 100 Blogs We Love (43Folders), PC World mag., Top 25 Web Celebs, Forbes mag., 2007. *

MANN, MICHAEL E., physicist, educator, climatologist; b. Amherst, Mass., Dec. 28, 1965; s. Larry N. and Paula (Finesod) M. AB in Applied Math and Physics (honors), U. Calif., Berkeley, 1989; MS in Physics, MPhil in Physics, Yale U., 1991, MPhil in Geology and Geophysics, 1993, PhD in Geology and Geophysics, 1998. Rsch. asst., dept. chemistry Univ. Calif., Berkeley, 1985-88, rsch. asst., dept. materials sci., 1988-89; teaching asst., dept. physics Yale Univ., New Haven, Con., 1989-90, rsch. asst., 1990, teaching asst., 1990—96; Alexander Hollaender Disting. postdoctoral rsch. fellow Dept. Energy, 1996—98; adj. asst. prof., dept. geosciences U. Mass., 1997—98, rsch. asst. prof., dept. geosciences, 1998—99; asst. prof., dept. environ. sciences U. Va., 1999—2005; assoc. prof., dept meterology (joint appt. dept. geosciences and earth and environ. systems inst.) Pa. State U., 2005—, dir., Earth System Sci. Ctr., 2005—. Invited lectr. in field; scientific advisor to US Govt. (White House OSTP) on climate change, 1999—2000; invited advisor NOAA Global Change and Climate Panel, Boulder, Colo., 1999; mem. of Working Group, Internat. PAGES/CLIVAR, 2000—; panel mem. NOAA Climate Change Data and Detection Program, 2000—; IAMAS delegate for US/Internat. Comm. on Climate, 2002—; mem. steering com. NSF Marine Earth Systems History Panel, 2003—; chair organizing com. NAS, Frontiers of Sci. symposium, 2003; co-chair Workshop on Past Millennia Climate Variability, Wengen, Switzerland, 2006; provided testimony to US House of Representatives, Energy and Commerce Com. hearing, 06. Contbr. articles to profl. jours., chpts. to books;refereed Nature, Science, Climatic Change, Geophysical Research Letters, Jour. Climate, JGR-Oceans, JGR-Atmospheres, Paleoceanography, Climate Dynamics, Eos, Internat. Jour. Climatol., Water Resources Research, Holocene, Atmospheric & Solar-Terrestrial Physics, GSA Today, Earth and Planetary Science Letters, Global & Planetary Change, Water Resources Research, Climate Research, NRC/NAS, NSF, NOAA, DOE grant programs; public outreach to CBS, NBC, ABC, CNN, CNN headline news, The Weather Channel, BBC, NPR, PBS, WCBS, Time, Newsweek, Life, US News & World Report, Economist, Scientific American, New Scientist, National Geographic, Discover, Science News, Science, Rolling Stone, Mother Jones, Cosmos, Popular Science, USA Today, New York Times, New York Times "Science Times", Washington Post, Wall Street Journal, Boston Globe, London Times, Irish Times, Le Monde, AP, UPI, Reuters, Scripps Howard, and numerous other television/print media.; mem. editl. adv. bd, Scientific American, Scientific American 50, 2003-, The Holocene, 2005-; editor, Jour. of Climate, 2000-02; co-founder, contbr. (website) RealClimate.org, 2004-(named one of the top 25 Sci. and Tech. website, Scientific American, 2005). Named one of 50 Leading Visionaries in Sci. and Tech., Scientific American, 2002, Website: RealClimate.org (co-founded, 2004) chosen as one of top 25 Science and Technology websites, 2005; recipient Josiah Willard Gibbs prize for outstanding rsch. and scholarship in Physics, Yale U., 1989, Phillip M. Orville prize for outstanding dissertation in the earth sciences, Yale U., 1997, Article (Mann, et. al Global-scale temperature patterns and climate forcing over the past six centuries, Nature, 1998) selected for fast moving fronts, Inst. Scientific Information, 2002, Outstanding Scientific Paper award for article: Observed and Simulated Multidecadal Variability in the Northern Hemisphere, Climate Dynamics, 2000), NOAA Office of Oceanic and Atmospheric Research (OAR), 2002, John Russell Mather Paper award article: Mann, et. al. A Distinctly Interdecadal Signal of Pacific Ocean-Atmosphere Interaction, Journal of Climate), Assn. Am. Geographers, 2005. Mem. Am. Meteorol. Soc.(com. on probability & statistics, 2003-05), Am. Geophysical Union (mem. adv. bd., Earth Interactions, 2001-02), European Geophysical Soc., Geol. Soc. Am., Am. Physical Soc., AAAS, Sigma Xi Research conducted with colleagues concluded that the Northern Hemisphere was the warmest it has been in 2,000 years. The research was known as the "hockey-stick" graph because it compared the sharp curve of the hockey blade to the recent sharp rise in temperatures and the stick's long shaft to centuries of previous climate stability. Office: Pa State U Dept Meterology University Park PA 16802 Office Phone: 814-863-4075. Office Fax: 814-865-3663. Business E-Mail: mann@psu.edu.

MANN, MICHAEL KENNETH, film director, producer; b. Chgo., Feb. 5, 1943; m. Summer Mann, 1974; 4 children. Student, U. Wis., London Film Sch. Dir.: (documentaries) 17 Days Down the Line, 1972; screenwriter, dir. (films) The Keep, 1983, Manhunter, 1986, screenwriter, exec. prodr., dir. Thief, 1981, screenwriter, prodr., dir. The Last of the Mohicans, 1992, Heat, 1995 (Dir., Screenwriter, Prodr. Acad. award nominee), The Insider, 1999, Ali, 2001, Miami Vice, 2006, dir., prodr. Collateral, 2004, prodr. The Aviator, 2004, screenwriter (TV films) River of Promises, 1977, screenwriter, dir. The Jericho Mile, 1979 (Best Dir. award Dir. Guild Am., Emmy award, 1979), screenwriter Swan Song, 1980, screenwriter, exec. prodr., dir. L.A. Takedown, 1989, screenwriter, exec. prodr. (TV miniseries) Drug Wars: The Camarena Story, 1990 (Emmy award, 1990), screenwriter (TV series) Police Story, 1973, Starsky and Hutch, 1975, Bronk, 1975, screenwriter, dir. Vega$, 1978, screenwriter, exec. prodr. Miami Vice, 1984; exec. prodr.: (TV series) Robbery Homicide Division, 2002—03. Mem.: Dirs. Guild, Writers Guild. Office: c/o Creative Artists Agy 9830 Wilshire Blvd Beverly Hills CA 90212-1804

MANN, MICHAEL MARTIN, engineering executive; b. NYC, Nov. 28, 1939; s. Herbert and Rosalind (Kaplan) M.; m. Mariel Joy Steinberg, Apr. 25, 1965. BSEE, Calif. Inst. Tech., 1960, MSEE, 1961; PhD in Elec. Engrng. and Physics, U. So. Calif., 1969; MBA, UCLA, 1984. Cert. bus. appraiser, profl. cons., mgmt. cons., lic. real estate broker, Calif. Mgr. high power laser programs office Northrop Corp., Hawthorne, Calif., 1969-76; mgr. high energy laser systems lab. Hughes Aircraft Co., El Segundo, Calif., 1976-78, mgr. E-0 control systems labs., 1978-83, asst. to v.p., space & strategic, 1983-84; exec. v.p. Helionetics Inc., Irvine, Calif., 1984-85, pres., chief exec. officer, 1985-86, also bd. dirs.; ptnr. Mann Kavanaugh Chernove, 1986-87; sr. cons. Arthur D. Little, Inc., 1987-88; chmn. bd., pres., CEO, Blue Marble Devel. Group, Inc., 1988—; exec. assoc. Ctr. Internat. Cooperation and Trade, 1989—91; sr. assoc. Corp. Fin. Assocs., 1990—91; exec. assoc. Reece and Assocs., 1991—92; mng. dir. Blue Marble Ptnrs. Ltd, 1991—; chmn. bd. dirs., CEO Blue Marble Ptnrs., 1992—; chmn., CEO, En Compass Techs., Inc., Torrance, Calif., 1994-98; chmn. En Compass Knowledge Systems, Inc., 2000—. Mem. Army Sci. Bd., Dept. Army, Washington, 1986-91; chmn. Ballistic Missile Def. Panel, Directed Energy Weapon Panel, Rsch. and New Initiatives Panel; cons. Office of Sec. of Army, Washington, 1986—, Inst. of Def. Analysis, Washington, 1978—, Dept. Energy, 1988—, Nat. Riverside Rsch. Inst., 1990—; bd. dirs. Datum, Inc.,1988—, Fail-Safe Tech., Corp., 1989-90, Safeguard Health Enterprises, Inc., 1988—, Am. Video Communications, Inc., Meck Industries, Inc., 1987-88, Decade Optical Systems, Inc., 1990—, Forum Mil. Application Directed Energy, 1992—, Am. Bus. Consultants, Inc., 1993—; chmn. bd. Mgmt. Tech., Inc. 1991—, Encompass Tech., Inc., 1994-98; bd. dirs., mem. adv. bd. Micro-Frame, Inc., 1988-91; chmn. bd. HLX Laser, Inc., 1984-86; bd. dirs. Cons's. Roundtable, 1992—, Am. Bus. Cons., Inc., 1993—, Country Home Bakers, Inc., 1999—, C.L.E.A.R., Inc., 1999—; chmn. TEC, 1999—; rsch. assoc., mem. extension teaching staff U. So. Calif., L.A., 1964-70; chmn. Ballistic Missile Def. Subgroup, 1989-90, Tactical Directed Energy Weapons Subgroup, 1988-90; chmn., chief exec. officer Mgmt. Tech., Inc., 1991—; dir. Am. Bus. Cons., Inc., 1993—; faculty mem. Asia Pacific Inst., 1998—; faculty Nat. Technol. U., 1997—. Mem. editl. bd. Calif. High-Tech Funding Jour., 1989-90; contbr. articles to profl. jours.; patentee in field. Adv. com. to Engrng. Sch., Calif. State U., Long Beach, 1985—; chmn. polit. affairs Am. Electronics Assn., Orange County Coun., 1986-87, exec. com., 1986-88; adv. com. Calif. congressmen, 1985—; dean's coun. UCLA Grad. Sch. Mgmt., 1984-85; bd. dirs. Archimedes Circle U. Soc. Calif., 1983-85, Ctr. for Innovation and Entrepreneurship, 1986-90, Caltech/MIT Venture Forum, 1987-91; chmn. adv. coun., adj. prof., indsl. and sys. engrng. U. So. Calif., 1996—; bd. examiners Nat. Quality Award, 1998—2000. Hicks fellow in Indsl. Rels. Calif. Inst. Tech., 1961, Hewlett Packard fellow. Mem. IEEE (sr.), So. Calif. Tech. Execs. Network, Orange County CEO's Network, Orange County CEO's Roundtable, Pres. Roundtable, Nat. Assn. Corp. Dirs., Aerospace-Def. CEO's Roundtable, Am. Def. Preparedness Assn., Security Affairs Support Assn., Acad. Profl. Cons. and Advisors, Internat. Platform Assn., Inst. Mgmt. Cons. (bd. dirs. So. Calif. chpt.), Pres. Assn., Cons. Roundtable Forum for Corp. Dirs., King Harbor Yacht Club, Fourth of July Yacht Club. Republican. Avocations: sailing, photography, writing. Home: 4248 Via Alondra Palos Verdes Peninsula CA 90274-1545 Office: Encompass Knowledge Sys Inc 100 Corporate Pointe Ste 210 Culver City CA 90230 Home Phone: 310-375-6391; Office Phone: 310-981-9200. E-mail: mmmann@encompassknowledge.com.

MANN, OSCAR, retired physician, internist, educator; b. Paris, Oct. 13, 1934; arrived in U.S., 1953; s. Aron and Helen (Biegun) Mann; m. Amy S. Mann, July 19, 1964; children: Adriana, Karen. AA with distinction, George Washington U., 1958; MD cum laude, Georgetown U., 1962. Diplomate Am. Bd. Med. Examiners, Am. Bd. Internal Medicine, Am. Bd. Cardiovasc. Disease, cert. advanced achievement in internal medicine. Intern Georgetown U. Med. Ctr., Washington, 1962-63, jr. asst. med. resident, 1963-64, clin. fellow in cardiology with Proctor Harvey program, 1965-66; sr. asst. resident in medicine Georgetown svc. D.C. Gen. Hosp., Washington, 1964-65; clin. prof. medicine Georgetown U. Sch. Medicine, 1985—; nat. chmn. med. alumi fund Georgetown U. Med. Sch., Washington, 1993-95; pvt. practice internal medicine and cardiology, Washington, 1966-99. Mem. med. nursing com. Georgetown U. Med. Ctr., mem. adv. com. CME, mem. tchg. adv. com., opthalmology dept. rev. com., surgery dept. rev. com., faculty com., search com. for a new dean for acad. affairs; appointed coun. to the dean Georgetown U. Sch. Medicine, 1977—; mem. Instnl. Self Study Task Force. Author: A Journey of Hope, 2005; contbr. articles to profl. jours. Nat. chmn. med. alumni fund Georgetown U., 1997—99. With US Army, 1953—55, with US Army, 1953—55. Recipient Mead Johnson Postgrad. Scholar ACP, 1964—65, Physicians Recognition award, AMA, 1987—96, Advanced Achievement in Internal Medicine, 1987, John Carroll award, Georgetown U., 1999. Fellow: ACP, Am. Coll. Chest Physicians, Am. Coll. Cardiology; mem.: AMA, Med. Soc. D.C., Am. Heart Assn. (coun. clin. cardiology), Am. Soc. Internal Medicine, Georgetown U. Alumni Assn. (bd. govs. 1993—, chair med. alumni bd. 1995—, nat. chmn. med. alumni fund 1997—99), Cosmos Club, Phi Delta Epsilon, Alpha Omega Alpha. Home: 5137 Yuma St NW Washington DC 20016 E-mail: oscarmann@comcast.net.

MANN, RICHARD ALAN, physician, educator; b. Bklyn., Dec. 18, 1952; s. Daniel Isaac and Claire Ethel (Spiller) M.; m. Judith Fleischer, Aug. 6, 1977; 1 child, David Michael Mann. BS in Math., Union Coll., Schenectady, NY, 1973; MS in Biophysics, SUNY, Buffalo, 1975; MD, Albert Einstein Coll. Medicine, The Bronx, NY, 1979. Diplomate Am. Bd. Internal Medicine. Intern Grad. Hosp. U. Pa., Phila., 1979-80; resident Temple U. Hosp., Phila., 1980—82; clin. nephrology fellow Hosp. U. Pa., Phila., 1982—83, rsch. fellow, 1983—86; asst. prof. medicine Rutgers U. Med. Sch., New Brunswick, NJ, 1986—93; assoc. prof. medicine, microbiology and molecular genetics; physician Robert Wood Johnson Med. Sch., New Brunswick, 1993—, med. dir. Kidney/Pancreas Transplant Program, 1999—; mem. grad. program in microbiology and molecular genetics Rutgers U., Piscataway, NJ, 1989—. Antiviral drug adv. com. FDA, Rockville, Md., 1993—; spl. study sect. NIH, Bethesda, Md., 1994; NIH Reviewers Res.; State Dept. Task Force, Operation Desert Storm, 1991. Contbr. over 50 articles, chpts. and abstracts to profl. jours. Recipient Young Investigator award Nat. Kidney Found., 1987, Nat. Med. award Kidney and Urology Found. Am., 2004, named one of Best Drs. in Am., 1996-2007, others; grantee NIH, 1988-93, William Lightfoot Schultz Found., 1987-88, UMDNJ Found., 1987-88. Mem. Am. Soc. Nephrology (co-chair basic immunology free comm. session 1989, 90), Am. Fedn. for Clin. Rsch., Am. Heart Assn. (Coun. on the Kidney in Cardiovascular Disease), Nat. Kidney Found., Nephrology Soc. N.J., Am. Assn. for Lab. Animal Sci., Am. Soc. Transplantation, Alpha Omega Alpha (Acad. Excellence and Outstanding Tchg. award 1995). Office: UMDNJ Robert Wood Johnson Med Sch Acad Health Sci Ctr CN-19 New Brunswick NJ 08903 Business E-Mail: mannri@umdnj.edu.

MANN, RICHARD O., public relations consulting company executive; b. NYC, July 1, 1933; s. Otto and Ruth (Buchwald) M.; m. Anne Marie Seidenschwang, Apr. 28, 1956; children: Melinda, Susan, Carolyn. BA in History and Polit. Sci., Hofstra U., Hempstead, NY, 1955. Reporter Newsday, Garden City, NY, 1951-56; pub. rels. v.p., cons. Carl Byoir & Assoc., NYC, 1957—76; v.p. corp. affairs Mack Trucks, Inc., Allentown, Pa., 1976-79; v.p. pub. rels. Transway Internat., NYC, 1979—85; pres. Mann Assoc., Danbury, Conn., 1985—. Track and field ofcl., U.S. Internat. meets, including 1984 Olympics, 1970—. 1st lt. US Army, 1956—57. Mem. Met. Golf Writers Assn. Republican. Presbyterian. Avocations: golf, sports. Home and Office: 63 Woodcrest Ln Danbury CT 06810 E-mail: romsport@sbcglobal.net.

MANN, ROANNE L., federal judge; b. 1951; BA, Yale U., 1972; JD, Stanford U., 1975. Bar: N.Y. 1975. Asst. dist. atty. Manhattan Dist. Atty.'s Office, NYC, 1975-76; law clk. U.S. Ct. Appeals for D.C. Circuit, Washington, 1976-77; spl. asst. to asst. atty. gen. civil divsn. U.S. Dept. Justice, Washington, 1977-78; asst. U.S. atty., chief appeals, sr. litigation counsel U.S. Atty.'s Office for So. Dist. N.Y., NYC, then dept. chief criminal divsn., 1978-86; ptnr. Stein, Zauderer, Ellenhorn, Frischer & Sharp, NYC, 1986-94; magistrate judge for ea. dist. N.Y., U.S. Magistrate Ct., Bklyn., 1994—. Mem.: Fed. Bar Coun. Office: US Magistrate Ct 225 Cadman Plz E Brooklyn NY 11201-1818 Office Phone: 718-613-2350.

MANN, SALLY, photographer; b. Lexington, Va., 1951; married; children: Emmett, Jessie, Virginia. Student, Putney Sch., 1966-69, Bennington Coll., 1969-71, Praestegaard Film Sch., Denmark, 1971-72, Aegean Sch. Fine Arts, Greece, 1971-72; BA summa cum laude, Hollins Coll., 1974, MA, 1975; DFA (hon.), Corcoran Coll., 2006. Guest lectr. Honolulu Acad. Arts, 1989, Women Photog. Conf., 1989, Md. Inst. Art, 1989, Bard Coll., 1989, San Francisco Cameraworks, 1990, Photog.-Retrospect/Prospect Conf., 1990, others; instr. Maine Photog. Workshops, 1985-89, Palm Beach Photog. Workshops, 1987-89, Ctr. Photog. Woodstock, 1988, 90, Internat. Ctr. Photog., N.Y., 1989, Image Found., Honolulu, 1989, Okla. Arts Found., 1989, Friends Photog. Workshops, 1990. One-woman shows include Cleve. Ctr. Contemporary Art, 1990, Edwynn Houk Gallery, Chgo., 1990, 92, Tartt Gallery, Washington, 1990, Md. Art Pl., Balt., 1991, Houk Friedman, N.Y., 1992-94, Mus. Contemporary Photog., Chgo., 1993-94, Mus. Modern Art, N.Y., 1991, Milw. Mus. Art, 1991, Whitney Mus. Am. Art, N.Y., 1991, Met. Mus. Art, N.Y., 1991, Frumpkin Adams Gallery, N.Y., 1994, Elizabeth Leach Gallery, Portland, Oreg., 1994, Bard Coll., Mass., 1994, Wellesley Coll., Mass., 1995, Edwynn Houk Gallery, N.Y., 1997, Gagosian Gallery, Calif., 1997; exhibited in group shows Corcoran Gallery Art, Washington, 1977, Va. Mus. Fine Arts, Richmond, 1988, New Orleans Mus. Art, 1990; represented in permanent collections Addison Gallery Am. Art, Andover, Mass., Balt. Mus. Art, Birmingham (Ala.) Mus. Art, Boston Mus. Fine Art, In Response to Place: Photographs from The Nature Conservancy's Last Great Places, Corcoran Gallery Art, 2001, Hirshhorn Mus. and Sculpture Garden, Nat. Mus. Am. Art, Smithsonian Inst., Washington, Met. Mus. Art, N.Y., Mus. Modern Art, N.Y., Whitney Mus. Am. Art, N.Y., San Francisco Mus. Art, Va. Mus. Fine Arts, Richmond, Gagosian Gallery, NYC, 2006, others; author/photographer: (with Ann Beattie) Second Sight: The Photographs of Sally Mann, 1984, (with Reynolds Price) At Twelve: Portraits of Young Women, 1988, Imediate Family, 1992, Still Time, 1994, What Remains, 2003. Fellow Nat. Endowment Arts, 1982, 88, 92, Guggenheim Found., 1987, Southeastern Ctr. Contemporary Arts, 1989, Artists Visual Arts, 1989; named Best Photographer in Am., Time Mag., 2001.

MANN, SAM HENRY, JR., retired lawyer; b. St. Petersburg, Fla., Aug. 2, 1925; s. Sam Henry and Vivian (Moore) M.; m. Mary Joan Bishop, Sept. 7, 1948; children: Vivian Louise, Sam Henry III, Wallace Bishop. BA, Yale U., New Haven, Conn., 1948; LLB, Fla. U., Gainesville, 1951, JD, 1967. Bar: Fla. 1951, U.S. Dist. Ct. (mid. and so. dists.) Fla. 1951, U.S. Ct. Appeals (5th cir.) 1955, U.S. Ct. Appeals (11th cir.) 1996, U.S. Supreme Ct. 1971. Ptnr. Greene, Mann, Rowe, Stanton, Mastry & Burton, St. Petersburg, 1951-84, Harris, Barrett, Mann & Dew, St. Petersburg, 1984—, ret., 2001. Trustee, v.p. Mus. Fine Arts, St. Petersburg, 1980-94, Eckerd Coll., St. Petersburg, 1976-79, Webb Sch., Bell Buckle, Tenn., 1966-75; bd. dirs. Regional Cmty. Blood Ctr., St. Petersburg, 1966-93, Fla. Blood Svcs., 1993-94, mem. emeritus 1996—; mem. Disting. Alumni Soc. Webb Sch.; mem., chmn. H. Milton Rogers Heart Found.; bd. dirs., pres. Family and Children's Svc., Inc., 1956-61. Lt. (j.g.) USNR, 1943-48. Fellow Am. Coll. Trial Lawyers, Am. Bar Found., Fla. Bar Found.; mem. ABA, Fla. Bar Assn., Fla. Supreme Ct. Hist. Soc., Am. Counsel Assn., Def. Rsch. Inst., Internat. Assn. Def. Counsel, Pinellas County Trial Lawyers Assn., Nat. Assn. Railroad Trial Counsel, Fla. Def. Lawyers Assn., Assn. Hostp. Attys., Bay Area Vanderbilt, St. Petersburg Bar Assn., Yale and U. Fla. Alumni Assns., Phi Alpha Delta, Delta Kappa Epsilon. Republican. Presbyterian. Avocations: travel, boating, gardening. Home: 531 Brightwaters Blvd NE Saint Petersburg FL 33704 Office: Harris Barrett Mann Dew Pa 8083 38th Ave N Saint Petersburg FL 33710-1029 Office Phone: 727-892-3100. Personal E-mail: mjbmann@aol.com.

MANN, THEODORE R., lawyer; b. Czechoslovakia, Jan. 31, 1928; came to U.S., 1929, naturalized, 1930; s. Aaron and Bertha (Schreiber) M.; m. Rowena Joan Weiss, 1954; children: Julie Ellen, Rachel Beth, Marcus Eliyahu. Pvt. practice, Phila., 1953—2005; counsel Pa. Securities Commn., 2005—07. Chmn., pres. Nat. Jewish Cmty. Rels. Adv. Coun., 1976-80; Conf. Pres. Major Am. Jewish Orgns., 1978-80; Nat. Conf. Soviet Jewry, 1981-83; Am. Jewish Congress, 1984-88; founding chmn. Mazon-A Jewish Response to Hunger, 1985-90, Project Nishma, 1988-97; exec. com. chair Israel Policy Forum, 1997-2001; trustee internat. coun. New Israel Fund, 2002-. Alumni fellow, Temple U. Home and Office: 2401 Pennsylvania Ave 17A4 Philadelphia PA 19130 E-mail: tedm@netreach.net.

MANN, THOMAS, reference librarian; b. Chgo., Feb. 21, 1948; BA, St. Louis U., 1966; MLS, La. State U., 1979; PhD, Loyola U., Chgo., 1975. Pvt. investigator B & L Assocs., Baton Rouge, 1976—77; reference libr. La. State U. Libr., Baton Rouge, 1979—80, Mullen Libr., Cath. U. Am., Washington, 1980—81, Libr. Congress, Washington, 1981—. Author: A Guide to Library Research Methods, 1987, Library Research Models, 1993, The Oxford Guide to Library Research, 2005. Mem.: Cosmos Club. Office: Library of Congress 101 Independence Ave SE Washington DC 20540-4660 Home Phone: 202-833-1749; Office Phone: 202-707-5173.

MANN, THOMAS EDWARD, political scientist; b. Milw., Sept. 10, 1944; s. Edward Emil and Eleanor (Hoffman) M.; m. Sheilah Rosenhack, June 4, 1976; children: Edward Matthew, Stephanie Rachael. BA, U. Fla., 1966; MA, U. Mich., 1968, PhD, 1977. Staff assoc. Am. Polit. Sci. Assn., Washington, 1970-76, asst. dir., 1977-81, exec. dir., 1981-87; co-dir. congress project Am. Enterprise Inst., Washington, 1979-81; dir. govtl. studies Brookings Instn., 1987-99, W. Averell Harrimann sr. fellow in Am. governance, 1991—. Mem. bd. overseers Nat. Election Study, 1987-94, chmn., 1990-94. Author: Unsafe At Any Margin, 1978; co-author: Vital Statistics on Congress, 1980-2006; Renewing Congress, 1992, 93, The New Campaign Finance Sourcebook, 2005, The Broken Branch, 2006; co-editor: The New Congress, 1981, The American Elections of 1982, 1983, Media Polls in American Politics, 1992, Values and Public Policy, 1994, Elections at Home and Abroad, 1994, Congress, the Press, and the Public, 1994, Intensive Care: How Congress Shapes Health Policy, 1995,Campaign Finance Reform, A Source Book, 1997, The Permanent Campaign and Its Future, 2000, Governance for a New Century: Japanese Challenges, American Experience, 2002, Inside the Campaign Finance Battle, 2003, Party Lines: Competition, Partisanship, and Congressional Redistricting, 2005; editor: A Question of Balance: The President, The Congress and Foreign Policy, 1990. Mem. Democratic Nat. Com.'s Commn. on Presdl. Nomination and Party Structure, 1975-78; mem. tech. com. Dem. Nat. Com. Commn. on Presdl. Nominations, 1981-82, The Fairness Commn., 1985. U. Mich. NDEA grad. fellow, 1966-69; Am. Polit. Sci. Assn. Congl. fellow, 1969-70 Fellow Am. Acad. Arts and Scis., Nat. Acad. Pub. Adminstrn.; mem. Coun. on Fgn. Rels., Phi Beta Kappa (Frank J. Goodnow award, Charles E. Merriam award). Home: 6508 Goldleaf Dr Bethesda MD 20817-5837 Office: Brookings Instn 1775 Massachusetts Ave NW Washington DC 20036-2103 Home Phone: 301-229-8928. Business E-Mail: tmann@brookings.edu.

MANN, TRUE SANDLIN, psychologist, consultant; b. Longview, Tex., Aug. 4, 1934; d. Bob Murphy and Stella True (Williams) Sandlin; m. Jack Matthewson Mann, Sept. 4, 1954 (div. Dec. 1989); children: Jack Matthewson Jr., Bob Sandlin, Daniel Williams, Nathaniel Currier. BS, Stephen F. Austin State U., Nacogdoches, Tex., 1973, MA, 1977; PhD, East Tex. State U., 1982. Lic. psychologist, Tex., Ark. Instr. Stephen F. Austin State U., 1975-76, vis. asst. prof. psychology, 1986-87; instr. East Tex. State U., Commerce, 1980-81; postdoctoral fellow Southwestern Med. Sch., Dallas, 1982-83; pvt. practice, Longview, Tex., 1983-92; psychologist dept. family practice U. Tex. Health Sci. Ctr., Tyler, 1990-92; dir. psychol. svcs. St. Michael's Hosp., Texarkana, Tex., 1992-93; cons. psychologist, Longview, 1993—. Weekly newspaper columnist HARBUS, Cambridge Mass., 1959-60; cons. Made-Rite Co., Longview, 1989—. Mem. candidate com. Assoc. Reps. Tex., Austin, 1990—; bd. dirs. Mental Health Assn. Tex., 1977-82, 84-92, Longview Symphony, 1995-99, Dallas Opera Guild, 1999—, Longview Mus. of Art, 1995; mem. Leadership Tex., 1988—. Mem. APA, Tex. Psychol. Assn., N.E. Tex. Field Ornithologists. Episcopalian. Avocations: photography, travel, history. Home: 1906 N 4th St Longview TX 75601-3202 Office: 1203 Montclair St Longview TX 75601-3565

MANN, WILLIAM CRAIG, lawyer; b. Norwalk, Ohio, Nov. 17, 1953; s. Abraham and Shirley (Smith) M. BA, Case Western Res. U., Ohio, 1976; JD, U. Dayton, Ohio, 1979. Bar: Ohio 1979, U.S. Dist. Ct. (no. dist.) Ohio 1979, U.S. Supreme Ct. 1986, U.S. Dist. Ct. (so. dist.) Ohio 1988. Law clk. Ohio Supreme Ct., Ohio, 1985-86; pvt. practice Cleve., 1986-87; assoc. Wolske and Blue, Columbus, Ohio, 1987-97; ptnr. Sunbury, Mann & Young, Columbus, Ohio, 1997-99; of counsel Mitchell, Allen, Catalano & Boda, Columbus, 1997—. Spkr. various orgns. in field, including Ohio Legal Ctr. Inst., Ohio Acad. of Trial Lawyers; mem. Ohio Supreme Ct. commn. on professionalism, 1997-2002 Contbr. articles to profl. jours. Bd.

dirs. United Way, Huron County, Ohio, 1983; mem. exec. and cen. coms. Huron County Dem. Com., 1976-79. Mem. Ohio State Bar Assn. (ethics com. 1987—), Columbus Bar Assn., Ohio Acad. Trial Lawyers (pres. 2001—), Franklin County Trial Lawyers Assn. (pres. 2001-2002. Avocations: football, history, economics. Home: 2041 Ramblewood Ave Columbus OH 43235-7340 Office: Mitchell Allen Catalano & Boda 580 S High St Ste 200 Columbus OH 43215 Home Phone: 614-442-6634; Office Phone: 614-224-4114. Personal E-mail: mannlaw99@aol.com.

MANNA, MARTIN, public relations executive, marketing executive; b. 1972; Pres. Chaldean Am. Chamber of Commerce, Farmington Hills, Mich., 2003—; co-founder Bank of Mich.; mng. ptnr. Interlink Media, Farmington Hills, Mich. Co-publisher The Chaldean News. Named one of 40 Under 40, Crain's Detroit Bus., 2006. Office: Chaldean American Chamber of Commerce 30095 Northwestern Hwy Ste 102 Farmington Hills MI 48334 Office Phone: 248-538-3700. Office Fax: 248-932-9161.

MANNE, HENRY GIRARD, lawyer, consultant, economist, educator, retired dean; b. New Orleans, May 10, 1928; s. Geoffrey and Eva (Shainberg) M.; m. Bobbette Lee Taxer, Aug. 19, 1968; children: Emily Kay, Geoffrey Adam. BA, Vanderbilt U., 1950; JD, U. Chgo., 1952; LL.M., Yale U., 1953, J.S.D., 1966; LLD, U. Seattle, 1987, U. Francisco Marroquin, Guatemala, 1987, George Mason U., 2000. Bar: Ill. 1952, N.Y. 1969. Practice in, Chgo., 1953-54; assoc. prof. St. Louis U. Law Sch., 1956-57, 59-62; vis. prof. law U. Wis., Madison, 1957-59; prof. George Washington U. Law Sch., 1962-68; Kenan prof. law and polit. sci. U. Rochester, 1968-74; disting. prof. law, dir. Law and Econs. Center, U. Miami Law Sch., 1974-80; prof. law Emory U. Law and Econs. Ctr., Atlanta, 1980-86; dean Law Sch., chmn. Law and Econs. Ctr. George Mason U., 1986-96, univ. prof., 1986-99, dean emeritus, 2000—. Vis. prof. law U. Wis., Madison, 1957-59, Stanford (Calif.) Law Sch., 1971-72, U. Chgo. Law Sch., 2000-02; dir. Econs. Insts. Fed. Judges, 1976-89. Author: Insider Trading and the Stock Market, 1966, (with H. Wallich) The Modern Corporation and Social Responsibility, 1973, (with E. Solomon) Wall Street in Transition, 1974, Med. Malpractice Guidebook: Law and Economics, 1985; editor: (with Roger LeRoy Miller) Gold, Money and the Law, 1975; editor: Economic Policy and the Regulation of Corporate Securities, 1968, The Economics of Legal Relationships, 1975; editor: (with James Dorn) Econ. Liberties and the Judiciary, 1987; contbr. to Wall St. Jour. Served to 1st lt. USAF, 1954—56. Recipient Salvatori award Excellence in Acad. Leadership, 1994, award for excellence in pvt. enterprise edn. Freedom Found., 1992; named Cultural Laureate of Va., 1992; Adj. scholar Cato Inst. Fellow Am. Law and Econs. Assn. (hon. life; named one of four Founders of Law and Econs.), Mont Pelerin Soc., Order of Coif, Phi Beta Kappa. Achievements include pioneered work in economics of corporation law, including first economic analysis of a "market for corporate control" and of insider trading. Avocation: golf. Office Phone: 239-596-7972. E-mail: Henry@themannes.com.

MANNELLA, CARMEN A., research scientist; b. Buffalo, June 15, 1947; s. Patrick and Nicolina Mannella; m. Linda J. Thomann, Apr. 8, 1950; children: Marc P., Susan N. BS in Physics, Canisius Coll., Buffalo, 1969; PhD in Biophysics, U. Pa., Phila., 1974. Rsch. scientist Wadsworth Ctr., Albany, NY, 1979—, assoc. dir. rsch. and tech., 2007—. Prof. U. Albany, Albany, 1986—; adj. prof. Rensselaer Poly. Inst., Troy, NY; mem., sr. health rsch. svc. Health Rsch., Inc., Rensselaer, NY, 2001—. Mem. editl. bd.: Jour. Bioenergetics and Biomembranes, 1992—. Recipient Disting. Alumnus award, Canisius Coll., 2000; fellow, Roswell Pk. Cancer Inst., Buffalo, 1974—76, St. Louis U. Med. Sch., 1976—78; grantee, NSF, 1981—99, 1991—99; Peter Coleman fellow, Ben Gurion U., Beer Sheeva, Israel, 2006. Mem.: Albany Conf. Found. (bd. dirs. 1989), Mitochondrial Rsch. Soc. (mem. sci. adv. bd. 2001), Biophysical Soc. (chair bioenergetics subgroup 2001—04), DiGamma, Alpha Sigma Nu, Sigma Xi. Achievements include research in development of electron tomography & application to mitochondria other biological structures characterization of mitochondrial channel, VDAC by electron crystallography & other biophysical techniques. Office: Wadsworth Center Empire State Plaza Albany NY 12201-0509 Home Phone: 518-439-1098; Office Phone: 518-474-2462. Office Fax: 518-402-5381. Personal E-mail: carmmann@aol.com. E-mail: carmen@wadsworth.org.

MANNELLI, PAOLO, psychiatrist, educator; b. Grosseto, Italy, Mar. 1, 1959; arrived in US, 2000; s. Mauro Mannelli and Preziosa Giovannetti; m. Jill Baron; 1 child, Etan. MD, U. Cattolica Sacro Cuore, Rome, Italy, 1990. Diplomate Italian Bd. Psychiatry and Psychotherapy, 1990. Rsch. fellow Langley Porter psychiat. inst. U. Calif., San Francisco, 1989—90; resident U. Cattolica Sacro Cuore, 1990, asst. prof. psychiatry, 1990—2002; rsch. assoc. prof. psychiatry Thomas Jefferson U., Phila., 2000—04; assoc. prof. psychiatry Duke U., Durham, NC, 2004—. Contbr. chapters to books, articles to profl. jours. Grantee, NIH, 2003—06; scholar, Rotary, 1989—90. Mem.: Am. Acad. Addiction Psychiatry, Am. Soc. Addiction Medicine. Achievements include research in drug addiction and comorbid psychiatric disorders.

MANNELLY, PATRICK J., former beverage company executive; With Johnston Coca-Cola Bottling Group, The Coca-Cola Co.; group v.p. Ea. N.Am. group; divsn. gen. mgr. So. Calif. divsn.; CFO Western N.Am. group; corp. v.p., fin. & adminstrn. Coca-Cola Enterprises, Inc., Atlanta, 1998, CFO, 1999—2004.

MANNERS, PAMELA ANN, psychology professor; b. Oklahoma City, Aug. 7, 1949; d. Don Manners and Patricia Ann Sheridan; m. David James Smart, May 16, 1985; children: Kerry Anne Smart, Dawn Michelle Koren, Ian Andrew Robert Clarke, Nathan Richard Manners Clarke. BS, U. Okla., Norman, 1971, MEd, 1979, PhD, 1985. Elem. sch. tchr. Dept. of Def., RAF Sculthorpe, Norfolk, England, 1971—72; reading specialist Moore Pub. Schs., Okla., 1977—81; assoc. prof. Troy U., Ala., 1985—. Supplement writer, reviewer Worth Pub., NYC, 2002—. Bd. mem. Ho. of Ruth Women's Shelter, Dothan, Ala., 1995—2000. Mem.: Am. Ednl. Rsch. Assn. New Party. Episcopalian. Avocations: reading, knitting. Office: Troy University 219 Gab Troy AL 36082 Home Phone: 334-566-9392; Office Phone: 334-670-3272. Business E-Mail: pmanners@troy.edu.

MANNERS, PAMELA JEANNE, secondary school educator; b. Holyoke, Mass., Mar. 20, 1951; d. Francis Edward and Helen Mary (Kurtyka) Herbert; div. 1985; children: Tracy, Kristen. BA, U. So. Miss., 1986, MEd, 1993. Cert. elem. edn. K-3, 4-8, secondary Eng., Social Studies; cert. elem. prin., secondary prin., elem. and secondary adminstrn. Registrar Michel Mid. Sch., Biloxi, Miss., 1987-88, tchr. Eng. and Social Studies, 1988-90, tchr. reading/law related edn., 1990-95; curriculum coord. Biloxi Pub. Schs., 1995-98; administrator Fernwood Jr. High Sch., Biloxi Pub. Schs., 1998-2000; dir. ABA Reading Curriculum Program, 1989-95; prin. Michel Jr. H.S., Biloxi Pub. Schs., 2000—04, Biloxi H.S., 2004—. Law-related edn. trainer Miss. Law-Related Edn. Ctr., Jackson, 1990-2002; law-related trainer Ctr. Civic Edn., Calabasas, Calif., 1993; law-related trainer Constitutional Right Found., 1994-2002. Participant program Lawyer in Every Class Miss. Bar Assn., Jackson, 1990-93 On-site target grantee Miss. Bar/Dept. Justice, 1992; A+ Site recognition U.S. Dept. Edn. Mem. Leadership Gulf Coast C. of C. (edn. com. 1996—). Roman Catholic. Office: Biloxi Pub Schs 1845 Richard Dr Biloxi MS 39532 Home Phone: 228-388-5068. Business E-Mail: pamela.manners@biloxischools.net.

MANNES, ELENA SABIN, film and television producer, television director; b. NYC, Dec. 3, 1943; d. Leopold Damrosch and Evelyn (Sabin) M. BA, Smith Coll., 1965; MA, Johns Hopkins U., 1967. Rschr. Pub. Broadcast Lab. Nat. Ednl. TV, NYC, 1968-70; writer Sta. WPIX-TV, NYC, 1970-73; assignment editor Sta. ABC-TV, NYC, 1973-76; prodr., writer Sta. WCBS-TV, NYC, 1976-80; prodr. CBS News, NYC, 1980-87, Pub. Affairs TV/Bill Moyers PBS Documentaries, NYC, 1987-90. Ind. documentary dir. and prodr., 1987—. Recipient Emmy award NATAS, 1984, 85, 87, 90, 94, 96, 2002, Peabody award, 1985, Cine Golden Eagle award, 1988, 90, 93, 94, 95, 99, Robert F. Kennedy Journalism award, 1989, DGA awards, 1987, 90. Mem. Writers Guild Am., Dirs. Guild Am., Am. Film Inst. (dir. Workshop for Women). Avocations: tennis, still photography.

MANNICK, JOHN ANTHONY, surgeon; b. Deadwood, SD, Mar. 24, 1928; s. Alfred and Catherine Elizabeth (Schuster) M.; m. Alice Virginia Gossard, June 9, 1952; children— Catherine Virginia, Elizabeth Eleanor, Joan Barbara. BA, Harvard U., 1949, MD, 1953. Diplomate: Am. Bd. Surgery (dir. 1971-77). Intern Mass. Gen. Hosp., 1953-54, resident in surgery, 1956-60; instr. in surgery to asst. prof. Med. Coll. Va., 1960-64; asso. prof. to prof. surgery Boston U., 1964-76, chmn. div. surgery, 1973-76; Moseley prof. surgery Harvard U., 1976-94, Moseley Disting. prof. surgery, 1994—; dir. ednl. programs Harvard Med. Internat., 1994-96; chmn. dept. surgery Peter Bent Brigham Hosp. and Brigham and Women's Hosp., Boston, 1976-94. Mem. surgery, anesthesiology and trauma study sect. NIH, 1978-82, mem. medicine study sect., 1967-70; rsch. com. Med. Found., Inc., 1970-76. Author: (with others) Modern Surgery, 1970, Core Textbook of Surgery, 1972, Surgery of Ischemic Limbs, 1972, The Cause and Management of Aneurysms, 1990; mem. editorial bd. AMA Archives of Surgery, 1973-84, Clin. Immunology and Immunopathology, 1972-84, Surgery, 1982-97, Brit. Jour. Surgery, 1982-92, European Jour. Vascular Surgery, 1988-96, Shock, 1997—; mem. editl. bd. Advances in Surgery, 1979—, editor, 1984-86; mem. editl. bd. Jour. Vascular Surgery, 1984-97, assoc. editor, 1990-97; also articles. Served to capt. M.C. USAF, 1954-56. Markle scholar in acad. medicine, 1961-66 Fellow ACS (gov.), Royal Coll. Surgeons (hon., Eng.), Royal Coll. Surgeons (hon., Edinburgh), Royal Coll. Surgeons (hon. Ireland), Vascular Soc. Gt. Britain and Ireland (hon.); mem. Am. Fedn. Clin. Rsch., Am. Assn. Immunologists, Am. Soc. Exptl. Pathology, Soc. Clin. Investigation, Soc. Clin. Surgery, Soc. Univ. Surgeons (Lifetime Achievement award 2005), Soc. Surg. Chmn. (sec. 1985-87, pres. 1987-88), Am. Surg. Assn. (pres. 1989-90), Internat. Cardiovascular Soc. (recorder N.Am. chpt., 1973-76, pres. N.Am. chpt. 1991-92, internat. v.p. 1993, Disting. Svc. award 2002), Soc. Vascular Surgery (pres. 1981), N.E. Surg. Soc., New Eng. Soc. Vascular Surgery (pres. 1994-95), Royal Coll. Surgeons (hon., Australasia) So. Surg. Assn., So. Soc. Vascular Surgery (hon.), Surg. Infection Soc., Halstead Soc., Lifeline Found. (pres. 1997-2002), Shock Soc. (Sci. Achievement award 2000), Phi Beta Kappa. Home: 81 Bogle St Weston MA 02493-1056 Office: 75 Francis St Boston MA 02115-6110 Office Fax: 617-582-6169.

MANNINEN, PETER R., chemist; BS in Chemistry, Mich. State Univ., 1985; grad. studies, Ctrl. Mich. Univ., Western Mich. Univ. Rsch. scientist Mich. Molecular Inst., Pharmacia (now Pfizer); sr. assoc. organic chemist Eli Lilly & Co., Indianapolis. Co-recipient Fred Kagan Lead Finding award, 1995. Mem.: Am. Chem. Soc. (31st Northeast Regional Indsl. Innovation award 2003, Award for Team Innovation 2007). Achievements include recipient 1 US patent, inc. being co-inventor linezolid, which became the basis of Zyvox. *

MANNING, BRENT V., lawyer; b. Preston, Idaho, Jan. 18, 1950; s. Leon W. and Gwen Manning; m. J. Christine Coffin, Oct. 25, 1969; children: Justin, Britten, John. BA, Idaho State U., 1972; JD, Harvard U., 1975. Bar: Colo. 1975, Utah 1981, Idaho 2004, US Ct. Appeals (10th cir.) 1978. Assoc. Holme Roberts & Owen, Denver, 1975-80, ptnr., 1980-97, Salt Lake City, 1981-97; founding ptnr. Manning Curtis Bradshaw & Bednar, LLC, Salt Lake City, 1997—. Mem. panel mediators and arbitrators US Dist. Ct. Utah, 1993—; mediation and settlement judge pro tempore 3d Jud. Dist. State of Utah, 1996—; mem. jud. nominating commn. 2d Jud. Dist. Ct. Utah., judge pro tem, 2000-2003. Trustee Bountiful Davis Art Found., Utah, 1985-91, Utah Tibetan Resettlement Project; chmn. "...and Justice for All" campaign. Mem. Utah Bar Assn. (chmn. continuing legal edn. com. 1988, mem. disciplinary com. 1991-93, chmn. cts. and judges com. 1996-97, Am. Inns of Ct. (pres. 1997-98, master of bench 1988—), Am. Alpine Club (NYC) Democrat. Avocations: mountain climbing, bicycling, skiing, running. Home: 2079 Maple Grove Way Bountiful UT 84010-1005 Office: Manning Curtis 3d Fl Newhouse Bldg 10 Exchange Pl Salt Lake City UT 84111-2714 Business E-Mail: BManning@mc2b.com.

MANNING, CHARLES W., university chancellor; b. Mar. 18, 1943; s. Charles Manning; m. Sharon Fischer; children: Shannon, Charles, Kelly. BS in Chemistry, McDaniel Coll., 1965; PhD in Analytical Chemistry, U. Md., 1969; postgrad., Johannes Gutenberg U., Mainz, Germany, 1969—70. Sr. staff assoc. Nat. Ctr. Higher Edn. Mgmt. Systems, Boulder, Colo., 1971-74; asst. provost, asst. prof. chemistry U. Mo., Kansas City, 1974-79; assoc. exec. dir. acad. affairs Colo. Commn. Higher Edn., Denver, 1979-81, dep. exec. dir., 1982-88; v.p. acad. affairs U. No. Colo., Greeley, 1981-82; exec. vice chancellor Okla. State Regents for Higher Edn., Oklahoma City, 1988-90; chancellor U. System W.Va., Charleston, 1991-2000, Tenn. Bd. Regents, Nashville, 2000—. Cons. as v.p. for planning and fin. Fed. U., Ceara, Brazil, 1976-77; presenter in field. Contbr. articles to profl. jours. Capt. U.S. Army, 1970-71. Office: Tenn Bd Regents 1415 Murfreesboro Pike Ste 350 Nashville TN 37217-2829

MANNING, CHRISTOPHER ASHLEY, finance educator, consultant; b. LA, June 26, 1945; s. Ashley and Vivian LaVerne (Wagner) M.; m. Cathy Ann Nichols, July 30, 1977 (div. Sept. 1993). BS, San Diego State U., 1967; MBA, Northwestern U., 1971; PhD, UCLA, 1983. Corp. loan officer Security Pacific Nat. Bank, LA, 1971-75; v.p. fin. Solitude Ski Resort, Bravo Ski Corp., Salt Lake City, 1975-78; pres. Sequoia Spa Co., LA, 1976-79, Manning and Co., LA, 1971-86, Manning's Little Red Piano Shop, LA, 1971-86; instr. corp. fin. Pepperdine U., LA, 1979-83; instr. corp. fin. and real estate Long Beach State U., Calif., 1983-86; assoc. prof. fin. Loyola Marymount U., LA, 1986-92, prof. fin., 1992—. Mng. prin. Denver office Houlihan Valuation Advisors, 1993-94; founder, mng. prin. Manning Advisors. Mem. editl. bd. Jour. of Real Estate Rsch., 1988-90, 91-93, 94-96, 97-99, 2003—; contbr. articles to profl. jours. 1st lt. US Army, 1967—70. Decorated Bronze Star. Mem.: Am. Real Estate Soc. (bd. dirs. 1994—96, 1997—99, v.p./program chair 2000—01, bd. dirs. 2000—, pres.-elect 2001—02, pres. 2002—03), Phi Eta Sigma, Beta Gamma Sigma. Republican. Episcopalian. Home and Office: Manning Advisors 29438 Quailwood Dr Palos Verdes Peninsula CA 90275-4929 Office Phone: 310-541-0353. Personal E-mail: chrismanning1@verizon.net. Business E-mail: cmanning@lmu.edu.

MANNING, DAVID GEOFFREY, ambassador; b. Dec. 5, 1949; m. Catherine Manning. With Mex. and C.Am. Dept. British Fgn. and Commonwealth Office, 1972—74, third sec. to second sec. Warsaw, 1974—77, second sec. to first sec. New Delhi, 1977—80, with Soviet Dept., 1980—82, dep. head Policy Planning Dept., 1982—84, first sec. Paris, 1984—88, counselor-on-loan to Cabinet Office, 1988—90, counselor, head of chancery Moscow, 1990—93, head Ea. Dept., 1993—94, head Policy and Planning staff, 1994—95, dep. undersecretary, 1998—2000; fgn. policy adv. to Prime Min., London, 2001—03; amb., mem. UK Del. to NATO, Brussels, 2001; British amb. to Israel, Tel Aviv, 1995—98, to the US, Washington, 2003—. UK mem. Internat. Conf. on Former Yugoslavia, 1994. Recipient Knight Comdr., Order of St. Michael and St. George. Office: Embassy of Britain 3100 Mass Ave NW Washington DC 20008

MANNING, DENNIS J., insurance company executive; m. Kathy Manning; 3 children. BBA, Notre Dame U. Ins. agent Guardian Life Ins. Co. Am., Houston, 1983—91, v.p. life mktg., agy. distbn., 1991—2000, COO, 2000—02, pres., 2002—, CEO, 2003—. Bd. trustees Forman Sch., Litchfield, Conn. With US Army, in Vietnam. Office: 7 Hanover Sq New York NY 10004-2616 *

MANNING, ELI (ELISHA NELSON MANNING), professional football player; b. Jan. 3, 1981; s. Archie and Olivia Manning. BA in Mktg., U. Miss., 2003. Quarterback N.Y. Giants, East Rutherford, NJ, 2004—. Recipient Maxwell award, 2003, Johnny Unitas Golden Arm award, 2003. Achievements include selected #1 overall NFL Entry Draft, 2004; comes from a prestigious family with brother Peyton and father Archie both great NFL quarterbacks. Office: c/o New York Football Giants Giants Stadium East Rutherford NJ 07073

MANNING, ERIC, computer scientist, educator, dean, researcher; b. Windsor, Ont., Can., Aug. 4, 1940; g. George Gorman and Eleanor Katherine (Koehler) M.; m. Betty Golding, Sept. 16, 1961; children: David, Paula; m. Eileen Walker, Sept. 10, 2005. BSc, U. Waterloo, Ont., 1961, MSc, 1962; PhD, U. Ill., 1965. Registered profl. engr., B.C. With MIT and Bell Tel. Labs., 1965-68; prof. computer sci. U. Waterloo, 1968-86, founding dir. computer comms. networks group, 1973-82; founding dir. Inst. for Computer Rsch., 1982-86; prof., dean engring. U. Victoria, B.C., Canada, 1986-92, prof. computer sci., elec. engring., 1993-2000, New Media Ctr./Nortel Networks Prof. Network Performance, 2000—03; prin. scientist, strategic advisor Syscor R&D Inc., 2003—05. NewMIC Chief Scientist, Networks Cluster, 2000-03; dir. Natural Sci. and Engring. Rsch. Coun. Can., exec. com., chair strategic grants com., 1982-87; dir. Comm. Rsch. Ctr., Govt. of Can., 1995-97, Consortium for Software Engring. Rsch., Ottawa, 1997-99; trustee B.C. Advanced Sys. Found., 1986-93; dir. Sci. Coun. B.C., 1988-91; bd. dirs. Can. Microelectric Corp.; adv. com. on artificial intelligence NRC, 1987-91; internat. rsch. adv. com. Alta. Informatics Cir. Rsch. Excellence, 2002-, chair, 2007—; IBM chair computer sci. Keio U., Yokohama, 1992-93; hon. prof. South East U., Nanjing, China; guest prof. Tokyo U. Tech., 2005— Author: Fault Diagnosis of Digital Systems, 1970; contbr. articles to profl. jours V.p. Greater Victoria Concert Band, 1995-96; trumpet sect., Sooke Philharm. & 5th Field Arty. Band, Royal Can. Arty. Fellow IEEE, Engring. Inst. Can.; mem. Assn. Computing Machinery (mem. snowbird com. 1999—), Assn. Profl. Engrs. B.C., Soc. for Computer Simulation, Can. Inst. for Advanced Rsch. (adv. com. on artificial intelligence and robotics 1986-90), Can. Assn. for Computer Sci. (pres. 1994-2000), Can. Soc. for Fifth Generation Rsch. (trustee 1987-88), B.C. Microelectronics Soc. (bd. dirs. 1986-87). Avocations: amateur radio, scuba diving, sailing, flying, musical performance. Home: 440 Simcoe St #1431 Victoria BC Canada V8V 1L3 Office: U Victoria Faculty Engring PO Box 3055 Victoria BC Canada V8W 3P6 Home Phone: 250-386-8039. Business E-Mail: eric.manning@engr.uvic.ca.

MANNING, FREDERICK JAMES, insurance company executive; b. Chgo., Oct. 20, 1947; s. Herbert and June Betty (Cohen) M.; m. Gail Hilary Phillips, Feb. 9, 1980; children: Elizabeth Sarah, David Charles. BS, U. Pa., 1969; JD, Harvard U., 1972. CPA. Treas. The Marmon Group, Inc., Chgo., 1973-77; chmn. bd. dirs., chief exec. officer Celtic Life Ins. Co., Chgo., 1978—; also chmn. bd. dirs., pres., chief exec. officer Celtic Group, Inc., Chgo., chmn., pres., ceo. Bd. dirs. Engineered ControlsInternat.Inc., mem. of Adv. Com. Kellogg Grd. Sch. of Mgmt. (dispute resolution research ctr.). Trustee Michael Reese Health Trust; trustee, v.p., asst. sec. Pritzker Family Philanthropic Fund; mem., pres. coun. U. Pa.; mem. adv. com. Dispute Resolution Rsch. Ctr., Kellogg Grad. Sch. Mgmt., Northwestern U., Evanston, Ill.; bd. trustee, mem. fin. and audit com., mem. investment com. Children's Meml. Med. Ctr., Michael Reese Health Trust, Newberry Library. Mem. Young Pres. Orgn., World Pres.'s Orgn., Chief Exec. Orgn., Std. Club, East Bank Club, Met. Club, Northmoor Country Club (Highland Park, Ill.), member of bd. dir. Exec. Com., Governance Com., Policy Com., Membership Com. & Fin. Com.(co-chmn.) AHIP. Office: Celtic Life Ins Co 233 S Wacker Dr Ste 700 Chicago IL 60606-6393 Office Phone: 312-332-5401.

MANNING, GEORGE TAYLOR, lawyer; b. June 27, 1948; s. Howard M.; children: Nell, Taylor; m. Catherine Zick, Apr. 9, 1999. BA, U. NC, 1970; JD, Columbia U., 1973. Bar: NY 1974, DC 1982, GA 2001. Assoc. Chadbourne, Parke & Whiteside, NYC, 1973-78, ptnr. NYC and Washington, 1982-85; asst. US Atty. So. Dist., NYC, 1978-82; ptnr. Jones, Day, Reavis & Pogue, Washington, 1985—99; ptnr.-in-charge Atlanta office Jones Day, 2000—. Office: Jones Day Ste 800 1420 Peachtree St NE Atlanta GA 30309-3053 Office Phone: 404-581-8400. Business E-Mail: gtmanning@jonesday.com.

MANNING, J. RICHARD, lawyer; b. Seattle, Nov. 2, 1932; BA, Seattle U., 1954; LLB, Gonzaga U., 1960. Bar: Wash. 1960. Pvt. practice, Seattle. Chmn. Seattle adv. coun. Am. Arbitration Assn., 1985—96, Bd. Govs., 1997—2000; Mem. Law Adv. Bd. Gonzaga U., 1988—; pres. Wash. State Bar Assn., 2002—03. Chair US Supreme Ct. Hist. Soc., Wash., 2005—. Recipient Nat. Outstanding Svc. award, Am. Arbitration Assn., 1988, Wash. Law and Politics Super Lawyer award, Top 100 Lawyers award, 2002—04. Mem.: ABA, Wash. State Bar Assn. (pres. 2003), Assn. Trial Lawyers Am., King County Bar Found. (pres. 1991—93), Am. Judicature Soc., King County Bar Assn. (pres. 1995—96). Office: 925 Logan Bldg 500 Union St Seattle WA 98101 Office Phone: 206-623-6302. Business E-Mail: jmb@seanet.com.

MANNING, JEROME ALAN, retired lawyer; b. Bklyn., Dec. 31, 1929; s. Emanuel J. and Dorothy (Levine) M.; m. Naomi Jacobs, Oct. 31, 1954; children: Joy, Stephen, Susan. BA, NYU, 1950, LLB, 1952; LLM, Yale U., 1953. Bar: N.Y. 1953, Fla. 1977. Assoc. Joseph Trachtman, NYC, 1956-61; ptnr. Stroock & Stroock & Lavan, NYC, 1961-96; prof. NYU Sch. Law, 1956-96. Editor: NYU Law Rev.; author: Estate Planning, 1980, rev. edit., 2005, Estate Planning for Laymen, 1992. Trustee N.Y.U. Sch. Law. Capt. USAF, 1953-56. Home: 1661 Pine St #911 San Francisco CA 94109-3457 Office Phone: 212-806-6030. Personal E-mail: jmanning@stroock.com.

MANNING, JOHN F., law educator; b. LA, Apr. 11, 1961; AB in History summa cum laude, Harvard U., 1982, JD magna cum laude, 1985. Bar: Pa. 1986, Calif. 1990. Law clk. to Judge Robert H. Bork US Ct. Appeals DC Cir., 1985; atty.-advisor Office Legal Counsel US Dept. Justice, 1986—88; law clk. to Justice Antonin Scalia US Supreme Ct., 1988; assoc. Gibson, Dunn & Crutcher, Washington, 1989—91; asst to US Solicitor Gen., 1991—94; prof. Columbia Law Sch., NYC, 1994—2004, Harvard Law Sch., Cambridge, Mass., 2004—. Office: Harvard Law Sch 1563 Massachusetts Ave Cambridge MA 02138 Office Phone: 617-495-5547. Business E-Mail: jmanning@law.harvard.edu.

MANNING, JOHN WARREN, III, retired surgeon, medical educator; b. Phila., Nov. 24, 1919; s. John Warren Jr. and Edith Margaret (Reagan) M.; m. Muriel Elizabeth Johnson, Oct. 11, 1944; children: John, Melissa, Susan. BS in Chemistry with honors, Ursinus Coll., 1940; MD, U. Pa., 1943; postgrad., 1978. Diplomate Am. Bd. Surgery. Naval intern Pa. Naval Hosp., 1946; resident Saginaw (Mich.) Gen. Hosp., 1947-50; preceptor Dr. H.M. Bishop, 1950-52; pvt. practice Saginaw, 1950—. Sr. staff mem. Saginaw Gen. Hosp., St. Luke's Hosp., Saginaw; past chief of surgery, chmn. tissue com. St. Mary's Hosp., Saginaw; cons. VA Hosp., Saginaw; assoc. clin. prof. surgery Mich. State U., assoc. prof. surgery, 1976-92, prof. emeritus, 1992—; mem. search com. Saginaw Coop. Hosp. Contbr.

articles to profl. publs. Lt. USN, 1942-46, PTO. Fellow ACS; mem. AMA, Mich. State Med. Soc., Saginaw Surg. Soc., Soc. Abdominal Surgeons, Am. Coll. Angiology, Soc. Am. Gastrointestinal Endoscopic Surgeons. Office Phone: 989-793-0712.

MANNING, JOHN WILLARD, lawyer; b. Miles City, Mont., Mar. 8, 1950; s. Frank Willard Manning and Mary Kathryn (Williams) Murphy; m. Margaret Jean Connors, Dec. 11, 1987; children: Dan Marsh, Sean Marsh, Megan Marsh, Molly Manning. AB, Dartmouth Coll., 1972; JD, Stanford U., 1975. Bar: N.Y. 1977, Mont. 1983. Assoc. Davis Polk & Wardwell, NYC, 1975-80, Dorsey & Whitney, Great Falls, Mont., 1980-83, ptnr., corp. practice group, 1984—, ptnr.-in-charge, Great Falls and Missoula offices. Bd. dirs. Neighborhood Housing Services, Great Falls, 1986-, Native Am. Ctr., Great Falls, 1987-90, Mont. Overthrust Energy Found., Great Falls, 1983-. Mem. Mont. Securities Task Force, Mont. Venture Capital Network. Avocations: skiing, golf, sports. Office: Dorsey & Whitney 507 Davidson Bldg 8 Third St N Great Falls MT 59403-1566 also: Dorsey & Whitney Ste 600 Millenium Bldg 125 Bank St Missoula MT 59802-4407 Office Phone: 406-727-3632, 406-721-6025. Office Fax: 406-727-3638, 406-543-0863. Business E-Mail: manning.jack@dorsey.com.

MANNING, KENNETH ALAN, lawyer; b. Buffalo, July 22, 1951; s. Jack Edwin and Dorothea Ann (Ruhland) Manning; children: Michael John, Kathyrn Ann. BS in Engring. Sci., SUNY, Buffalo, 1974, JD, 1977. Bar: N.Y. 1978, U.S. Dist. Ct. (we. dist.) N.Y. 1978, U.S. Dist. Ct. (no. dist.) N.Y. 1980, U.S. Ct. Appeals (2d cir.) 1983, U.S. Ct. Appeals (3d cir.) 1988. Confidential law asst. to assoc. justice Appellate Divsn. 4th Dept., Buffalo, 1977—79; assoc. Phillips, Lytle, Hitchcock, Blaine & Huber, Buffalo, 1979—84; ptnr. Phillips Lytle LLP, Buffalo, 1985—. Vol. Lawyers Project, Erie County, 1985-2002, Criminal Appeals Program, Erie County, 1988-89; mem. Western N.Y. region NCCJ. Woodburn fellow SUNY, Buffalo, 1973-76. Mem. ABA (TIP sect.), N.Y. State Bar Assn. (ins. negligence sect.), Erie County Bar Assn., Gyro Club (pres. 1988), Park Club. Avocations: sports, hunting. Home: 167 Leicester Rd Buffalo NY 14217-2113 Office: Phillips Lytle LLP 3400 HSBC Ctr Buffalo NY 14203-2887 Office Phone: 716-847-7041.

MANNING, KENNETH PAUL, specialty chemical company executive; b. NYC, Jan. 18, 1942; s. John Joseph and Edith Helen (Hoffmann) M.; m. Maureen Lambert, Sept. 12, 1964; children: Kenneth J., John J., Elise, Paul, Carolyn, Jacqueline. BME, Rensselaer Poly. Inst., 1963; postgrad., George Washington U., 1965-66; MBA in Ops. Rsch., Am. U., 1968. With W.R. Grace & Co., NYC, 1973-87, v.p. European consumer divsn., 1975-76, pres. ednl. products divsn., 1976-79, pres. real estate divsn., 1979-81, v.p. corp. tech. group, 1981-83, pres., CEO, Ambrosia Chocolate Co. divsn. Milw., 1983-87; group v.p. Sensient Technologies Corp., Milw., 1987-89, exec. v.p., dir., 1989-92, pres., COO, dir., 1992-96, pres., CEO, dir., 1996—, chmn., CEO, 1997—. Bd. dirs. Badger Meter, Inc., Milw., Sealed Air Corp., Saddle Brook, N.J. Served as lt. USN, 1963-67; rear adm. USNR, ret. Decorated Legion of Merit, Nat. Def. medal, others. Mem. ASME, Am. Chem. Soc., Navy League, U.S. Naval Inst., Naval Res. Assn., Milw. Metro Assn. Commerce, Knights of Malta. Republican. Roman Catholic. Office: Sensient Techs Corp 777 E Wisconsin Ave Milwaukee WI 53202-5304

MANNING, MARTHA MARY, writer, psychologist; b. Chgo., Aug. 18, 1952; d. John Eugene and Mary Louise M.; m. Brian J. Depenbrock, Oct. 20, 1973; 1 child, Keara. BA with high honors, U. Md., College Park, 1974; MA, Cath. Univ. Am., 1978, PhD, 1981. Postdoctoral fellow McLean Hosp./Harvard Med. Sch., Boston, 1981-83; asst. prof. George Mason U., Fairfax, Va., 1983-88; pvt. practice Alexandria, Va., 1994-96. Psychology instr., 1989-93. Author: A Season of Mercy, 1985, Undercurrents: A Life Beneath the Surface, 1995, Chasing Grace, 1996; co-author: Restoring Intimacy: A Patients Guide to Maintaining Relationships During Depression, 1999, All Seasons Pass: Grieving & Miscarriage, 2000; columnist, Salt of the Earth, 1993-96; contbr. to popular mags. including Health, Mirabella, New Woman, Ladies' Home Jour., Glamour, U.S. Cath., N.Y. Times Book Review, Family Therapy Networker, Washington Post. Recipient Merit award Associated Ch. Press, 1994, 96, Best Mag. Column Cath. Press Assn., 1995, Presdl. award for Patient Advocacy, Am. Psychiat. Assn., 1996, Stephen Logan award Nat. Alliance for Mentally Ill. Office: Arielle Eckstut James Levine Comm Inc care FWI 307 7th Ave 1904 New York NY 10001

MANNING, MICHAEL J., lawyer; b. Wichita, Kans., July 18, 1944; BA, U. Kans., 1966; JD, Washburn U., 1969. Bar: Kans. 1969, DC 1970. Mem. Fulbright & Jaworski LLP, Washington. Mem.: ABA, Fed. Energy Assn., D.C. Bar, Phi Alpha Delta. Office: Fulbright & Jaworski Market Sq 801 Pennsylvania Ave NW Fl 3-5 Washington DC 20004-2623

MANNING, MICHAEL NICHOLAS, actor, singer, guitarist, broadcaster, journalist; b. Cin., Apr. 5, 1958; s. Nicholas George and Catherine. BA in psychology, U. Cin., 1999. Regional mktg. and develop. mgr. SCA Wolff Sys., Redmond, Wash., 1986—90; mktg. and pub. rels. cons. Manning & Assoc., Dallas, 1989—90, KERA-TV 13 (PBS), Dallas, 1990—2003; news anchor, reporter CBS Radio Network, NYC, 1999—2000; prodr. CBS Westwood One affiliates, 1990—95; comml. copywriter, scriptwriter, host Saturday Main Event Weekend Music mag., 1990—95, dir. mktg. and promotions, 1995—98; news anchor WBAP News Network / Talk 820 AM (ABC Network), NYC, 2001—03; helicopter reporter WLWT-TV5 (NBC), Cin., 2003—04. Strategic cons. alt. plan of reorgn. US Airways, Crystal City, Va., 2004. Author: (poems) No Artificial Flowers During the Mowing Season, 1990, (short stories) Bread Crumbs for Sale, 2006; contbg. editor: Airways mag., 1995—; actor(voice over): (pilot for cable TV series) When Dreams Come True, 2004, (radio and TV) in 6,000 and more commls.; contbr. numerous mag. articles; actor, narrator: Turning Back Time: A Tribute to the 35th Anniversary of "Bullitt" with Steve McQueen; actor: Out of Our Heads Improv Comedy Group, 2003—04; interviewed for: Billboard mag., 1996. Founding mem. Legacy Found. Hole in the Wall Gang Camp, New Haven, 2007, Hole in the Wall Gang Capt, New Haven, 2007; chmn. pub. rels. No. Tex. chpt. Lupus Found. Am., 1987—93, bd. dirs.; mem. adv. bd. Families for the Rainforest, Carrollton, Tex., 1998—2005. Nominee Best Program Major Market, Nat. Assn. Broadcasters Conv., 1996; recipient Vol. Svc. award, Lupus Found. Am., 1993. Mem.: AFTRA (actor 2003—), Pan Am World Airways Hist. Found. (mus. com. 2006—). E-mail: michaelmanninginfo@gmail.com.

MANNING, PETER KIRBY, criminal justice educator; b. Salem, Oreg., Sept. 27, 1940; s. Kenneth Gilbert and Esther Amelia (Gibbard) M.; m. Victoria Francis Shaughnessy, Sept. 1, 1961 (div. 1981); children— Kerry Patricia, Sean Peter, Merry Kathleen; m. Betsy Cullum-Swan, Aug. 4, 1991 (div. 1997). BA, Willamette U., 1961; MA, Duke U., 1963, PhD, 1966; MA (hon.), Oxford U., Eng., 1983. Instr. sociology Duke U., 1964-65; asst. prof. sociology U. Mo., 1965-66, Mich. State U., East Lansing, 1966-70, assoc. prof. sociology and psychiatry, 1970-74, prof., 1974—; prof. criminal justice, 1993—. Beto chair lectr. Sam Houston State U., 1990; Ameritech lectr. E. Ky. U., 1993; vis. lectr. U. Las Andes, Meridá Venezuela, 2001—03, 2005; vis. prof. U. Victoria, 1968, MIT, 1982, SUNY, Albany, 1982, U. Mich., 1990—91, York U., Toronto, 1999; vis. sr. scholar Northeastern U. Coll. Criminal Justice, 2001, E.V. and E.M. Brooks chair; cons. Nat. Inst. Law Enforcement and Criminal Justice, U.S. Dept. Justice, Rsch. Triangle Inst., NSF, Nat. Health and Med. Rsch. Coun., Australia, 1980—, Social Sci. Rsch. Coun. Eng., AID, Jamaica, 1991, Sheehy com. Police Pay and Performance, England, 1993. Author: Sociology of Mental Health and Illness, 1975, Police Work, 1977, 2d edit., 1997, The Narcs' Game, 1980, 2d edit., 2003, Semiotics and Fieldwork, 1987, Symbolic Communication, 1988, Organizational Communication, 1992, Private Policing, 1999, Policing Contingencies, 2003, others; also book chpts., articles in profl. jours.; cons. editor series: Principal Themes in Sociology; co-editor Sage Series in Qualitative Methods, Crime, Law and Social Change, 2004—; mem. editl. bd. numerous jours. in social scis. Recipient Bruce Smith Sr. award Acad. Criminal Justice Scis., 1993, O.W. Wilson award, 1997, Charles H. Cooley award Mich. Sociol. Assn., 1994; NDEA fellow, 1962-64, NSF fellow, 1965, fellow Balliol Coll., Oxford U., 1982-83, vis. fellow Wolfson Coll., Oxford U., 1981, 82-83, fellow, 1984-86; Am. Bar Found. rsch. fellow, 1998; Rockefeller resident, Bellagio, Italy, 2000. Mem. Am. Soc. Criminology, Am. Sociol. Assn., Acad. Criminal Justice Scis., Brit. Soc. Criminology, Internat. Sociol. Assn., Midwest Sociol. Soc., Soc. Study Social Problems, Soc. Study Symbolic Interaction (spl. recognition award 1990, v.p. 1992-93, program chair 1993), Internat. Soc. Semiotics and Law. Office: Northeastern U Coll Criminal Justice Boston MA 02115 Office Phone: 617-373-7748. Personal E-mail: manningpk@hotmail.com.

MANNING, PEYTON WILLIAMS, professional football player; b. New Orleans, Mar. 24, 1976; s. Archie and Olivia Manning; m. Ashley Thompson, Mar. 17, 2001. BA in Speech Comm., U. Tenn., 1998. Quarterback Indpls. Colts, 1998—. Founder PeyBack Found., 1999—. Co-recipient NFL MVP award, AP, 2003; named NFL Offensive Player of Yr., 2004, NFL Pro Bowl MVP, 2004, Walter Payton NFL Man of Yr., 2005, Super Bowl XLI MVP, 2007; named to Am. Football Conf. Pro-Bowl Team, 1999—2006, NFL All-Pro Team, AP, 2003—06; recipient Espy Award for Best Coll. Football Player, 1998, Am. Dream award, Hudson Inst., 2001, Henry P. Iba Citizen Athlete award, 2002, Bert Bell award, Maxwell Club, 2003, 2004, John Wooden trophy, Athletes for a Better World, 2004, NFL MVP award, AP, 2004, Espy Award for Best NFL player, 2004, Byron "Whizzer" White Humanitarian award, 2005, Espy award, Best Championship Performance, 2007. Achievements include led NFL in completions and passing yards 2000, 2003; holds the NFL single season record for most touchdown passes (49), 2004; holds the NFL single season record for best passing rating (121.1), 2004. Office: Indianapolis Colts PO Box 535000 Indianapolis IN 46253-5000 also: Indianapolis Colts 7001 West 56th Strreet Indianapolis IN 46254 *

MANNING, ROBERT HENDRICK, retired audio-visual services executive; b. Soerabaja, Java, Indonesia, Aug. 23, 1941; s. William and Gertrude (Unk) Manning. BS, No. Mich. U., 1974. Lic. capt. USCG. Instr. sailing USCG Acad., New London, Conn., 1959-63; dir. audio visual/media svcs. No. Mich. U., Marquette, 1965-93, capt. univ. rsch. vessel, 1977-79, dir. audio visual svcs. emeritus; dir. devel. Bresnan Comm. Co., Marquette, 1993-97. Host (TV series) Ask the Doctors, Sta. WNMU-TV, 1977—98. Pub. rels. dir. Charter Comm., 2000—02. Mem.: Marquette-Alger County Med. Soc. (hon.; exec. dir. 1975—2000). Avocations: astronomy, sailing, amateur radio. Home and Office: PO Box 309 Marquette MI 49855-0309

MANNING, ROBERT THOMAS, internist, educator; b. Wichita, Kans., Oct. 16, 1927; s. Thomas Earl and Mary Francis (Schlegel) M.; m. Jane Bell, July 29, 1949; children: Mary Kay Fausch, Phillip Trenton, Susan Ann Shiba. AB, Wichita U., 1950; MD, Kans. U., 1954; DHL, Med. Coll. Hampton Rds., 1991. Diplomate Am. Bd. Internal Medicine. Intern Kansas City (Mo.) Gen. Hosp., 1954-55; resident Kans. U., Kansas City, 1955-58; from asst. prof. to prof. Kans. U. Med. Ctr. Sch. of Medicine, Kansas City, 1958-71, assoc. dean students, 1969-71; dean Eastern Va. Med. Sch., Norfolk, Va., 1971-74, chmn., prof. internal medicine, 1974-77; prof. internal medicine U. Kans. Sch. of Medicine, Wichita, 1977-93; prof. emeritus U. Kans. Sch. Medicine, Wichita, 1993—; assoc. dean, clin. affairs U. Kans. Sch. of Medicine, Wichita, 1985-89; chmn. internal medicine U. Kans. Sch. Medicine, Wichita, 1987—89; pres. Wesley Med. Rsch. Inst., 1986-88. Nat. cons. surgeon gen. USAF, 1973-78. Author: Major's Physical Diagnosis, 9th edit., 1982; contbr. articles to profl. jours. Pres. Kans. Health Ethics, Inc., 1994-96. With US Army Air Corps, 1945—47. Recipient Advanced Achievement award Am. Bd. Internal Medicine, 1987. Fellow ACP (laureate Kans. chpt., bd. govs. Kans. 1984-88); mem. Am. Fedn. Clin. Rsch., Cen. Soc. Clin. Rsch., Am. Assn. Study Liver Disease, Sigma Xi, Alpha Omega Alpha. Presbyterian. Avocations: woodworking, golf. Home: 126 Trail Of The Flowers Georgetown TX 78628-4814 Personal E-mail: rmannsun@suddenlink.net.

MANNING, SYLVIA, language educator; b. Montreal, Que., Can., Dec. 2, 1943; came to U.S., 1967; d. Bruno and Lea Bank; m. Peter J. Manning, Aug. 20, 1967; children— Bruce David, Jason Maurice BA, McGill U., 1963; MA, Yale U., 1964, PhD in English, 1967. Asst. prof. English Calif. State U.-Hayward, 1967-71, assoc. prof., 1971-75, assoc. dean, 1972-75; assoc. prof. U. So. Calif., 1975-94, prof., assoc. dir. Ctr. for Humanities, 1975-77, assoc. dir. Ctr. for Humanities, 1975-77, chmn. freshman writing, 1977-80, chmn. dept. English, 1980-83, vice provost, exec. v.p., 1984-94; prof. English U. Ill., Champaign, 1994—, v.p. for acad. affairs, prof. English, 1994—, interim chancellor Chgo., 1999-2000, chancellor, 2000—. Author: Dickens as Satirist, 1971; Hard Times: An Annotated Bibliography, 1984. Contbr. essays to mags. Woodrow Wilson fellow, 1963-64, 66-67 Mem. MLA, Dickens Soc. Office: U of Ill Office of Chancellor 2833 University Hall 601 S Morgan St Chicago IL 60607-7100 Office Phone: 312-413-3350.

MANNING, W. ROBERT, JR., bank executive; B in Acctg. and Fin., U. Akron, Ohio, MBA, JD, U. Akron, Ohio; grad. with honors, Stonier Grad. Sch. Banking. With Nat. City Corp., 1977—, various mgmt. positions in fin. acctg., retail banking and trust and investments, mgr. retail delivery systems' planning and automation divsn., group mgr. customer focus initiative, sr. v.p., mgr. consumer loan svcs. and consumer lending divsns., exec. v.p., mgr. retail svcs. and direct banking, head Best in Class initiative, sr. v.p. lending svcs. Office: Nat City Corp Nat City Ctr 1900 E Ninth St Cleveland OH 44114-3484 Office Phone: 216-222-2000. *

MANNING, WILLIAM DUDLEY, JR., retired specialty chemical company executive; b. Tampa, Fla., Mar. 7, 1934; s. William Dudley and Rebecca (Reid) M.; m. Carol Randolph Gillis, June 30, 1962; children: Carol Randolph, Rebecca Barrett, Anne Gillis. BA in Chemistry, Fla. State U., 1957. Sales rep. Amoco Chem. Co., St. Louis and Cleve., 1959-63; sales engr. The Lubrizol Corp., Tulsa, 1963-64, southwestern regional sales mgr., 1964-66, mgr. chem. product sales Wickliffe, Ohio, 1966-72, sales mgr., western U.S., 1972, gen. sales mgr., asst. div. head-sales, 1972-79, mktg. mgr., asst. div. head-sales, 1979-80, v.p. mktg., 1980-81, v.p., bus. devel. div., 1981-85, sr. v.p. sales and mktg., 1985-87; pres. Lubrizol Petroleum Chems. Co., Wickliffe, 1987-94; sr. v.p., asst. to pres. The Lubrizol Corp., 1994; cons., investor, 1994—. Bd. dirs. NYCO Am. LLC, Spartanburg, SC, Robbins and Myers, Dayton, Ohio, UNIFRAX Corp., Niagara Falls, N.Y. Trustee Vocat. Guidance Svcs., Cleve., 1991-2000, Borromeo Sem., 2000—. With USAR, 1957-63. Mem. Soc. Automotive Engrs. (assoc.), Kirtland Country Club (v.p. 1986-88, pres. 1988-89), Tavern Club (trustee 1986-91), Chagrin Valley Hunt Club, Sand Ridge Golf Club. Republican. Roman Catholic. E-mail: wdmann@compuserve.com.

MANNING, WILLIAM FREDERICK, retired photographer; b. Gardner, Mass., Aug. 18, 1920; s. Seth Newton and Jennie May (Bennett) M.; m. Yvonne J.C. Wilshire, Feb. 29, 1964; children: Pamela Ann, Jeffrey Newton. AA, Boston U., 1950, BS in Comm., 1952. With AP, Boston, 1951-53; photographer UPI, Boston, 1953-88; ret., 1988. Contbr. photos to books, mags., newspapers throughout the world. Served with USN, 1940-46, PTO. Recipient Look 1st Prize All Sports award, 1958; Pictures of the Yr. award U. Mo., 1964, 74; Nat. Headliners Club award for outstanding syndicate photography, 1974. Mem. Boston Press Photographers Assn., Nat. Headliners Club, Delta Kappa Alpha. Congregationalist. Home: 23 Sunset Dr Beverly MA 01915-2319

MANNINO, EDWARD FRANCIS, lawyer, educator; b. Abington, Pa., Dec. 5, 1941; s. Sante Francis and Martha Anne (Hines) M.; m. Mary Ann Vigilante, July 17, 1965 (div. 1990); m. Antoinette K. O'Connell, June 25, 1993; children: Robert John, Jennifer Elaine. BA with distinction, U. Pa., 1963, LLB magna cum laude, 1966. Bar: Pa. 1967. Law clk. 3d cir. U.S. Ct. Appeals, 1966-67; assoc. Dilworth, Paxson, Kalish & Kauffman, Phila., 1967-71, ptnr., 1972-86, co-chmn. litigation dept., 1980-86, sr. ptnr., 1982-86; sr. prin. Elliott, Mannino & Flaherty, PC, Phila., 1986-90; chmn. Mannino Griffith PC, Phila., 1990-95; sr. ptnr. Wolf, Block, Schorr & Solis-Cohen, Phila., 1995-98; ptnr., chair litig. practice Akin, Gump, Strauss, Hauer & Feld LLP, Phila., 1998—. Hearing examiner disciplinary bd. Supreme Ct. Pa., 1986—89, mem. adv. com. on appellate ct. rules, 1989—95; lectr. Temple U. Law Sch., 1968—69, 1971—72; mem. Phila. Mayor's Sci. and Tech. Adv. Com., 1976—79; project mgr. Pa. Environ. Master Plan, 1973; chmn. Pa. Land Use Policy Study Adv. Com., 1973—75; chmn. adv. com., hon. faculty history dept. U. Pa., 1980—85, lectr. Am. history, 2001—. Author: Lender Liability and Banking Litigation, 1989, Business and Commercial Litigation: A Trial Lawyer's Handbook, 1995, The Civil RICO Primer, 1996; mem. editl. bd. Litig. mag., 1985-87, Comm. Lending Litig. News, 1988-2001, Bank Bailout Litig. News, 1989-93, Bus. Torts Reporter, 1988-2005, Practical Litigator, 1989-2003, Civil RICO Report, 1991-2001; contbr. articles to profl. jours. Pres. parish coun. Our Mother of Consolation Ch., 1977-79; bd. overseers U. Pa. Sch. Arts and Scis., 1985-89, chmn. recruitment and retention of faculty com.; commonwealth trustee Temple U., 1987-90, audit, bus. and fin. coms. Named one of Nation's Top Litigators Nat. Law Jour., 1990, Pa.'s Top Ten Trial Lawyers, 1999, Best Lawyers in Am., Am.'s Leading Bus. Lawyers. Fellow Am. Bar Found., ABA (chmn. various coms.), Am. Law Inst., Hist. Soc. U.S. Dist. Ct. Ea. Dist. Pa. (bd. dirs.), Pa. Bar Assn., Phila. Bar Assn. (gov. 1975), Pa. Soc., Order of Coif, Phi Beta Kappa, Phi Beta Kappa Assocs. Democrat. Roman Catholic. Office: Akin Gump Strauss Hauer Et Al One Commerce Sq Ste 2200 2005 Market St Philadelphia PA 19103-7014 Office Phone: 215-965-1340. Office Fax: 215-965-1210. Business E-Mail: emannino@akingump.com.

MANNINO, J. DAVIS, psychologist, educator, author; b. Patchoque, NY, Sept. 27, 1949; s. Joseph I. and Adrienne Adele (Davis) M. BA magna cum laude, SUNY, Stony Brook, 1971; MSW summa cum laude, San Francisco State U., 1974; EdD in Counseling and Ednl. Psychology, U. San Francisco, 1989. Lic. psychotherapist, Calif.; lic. clin. social worker, Calif., marriage, family and child counselor. Instr. U. Malaysia, 1974-76; dir. refugee programs City San Francisco, 1979-82; instr. U. San Francisco, 1979-85; pvt. practice specializing in psychology San Francisco, Sonoma Counties, 1979—. Cons. foster care Calif. State Legis., 1980, cmty. rels., San Francisco Police Dept., 1982-87, Hospice Sonoma County, 1990, Sonoma County Mental Health, 1990; forensic task force on AIDS, San Francisco Pub. Health Dept., 1984-85; child abuse investigation supr. City of San Francisco, 1985-88; supr. Reasonable Efforts to Families Unit; project coord. Edna McConnell Clark Found. Family Mediation Demonstration Grant, 1987-88; prof. human sexuality, death and dying, Intro. to Psychology Santa Rosa Jr. Coll., 1990—, chair dept. behavioral scis.; commr. Calif. Bd. Behavioral Sci. Examiners, 1990. Author: Grieving Days, Healing Days, 1997, Sexually Speaking, 1998, Sexual Themes and Variations, The New Millennium, 2000; contbr. articles to profl. jours.; local psychology columnist Art of Caregiving, 1986—. Mem. APA, NASW (diplomate clin. social work), Orthopsychiat. Assn., Am. Assn. Counseling and Devel., Am. Soc. Sex Educators, Counselors and Therapists, Soc. for Sci. Study Sexuality, Calif. Assn. Marriage Family and Child Therapists, Golden Gate Bus. Assn. (ethics com. 1986, Disting. Svc. award, 1985), Am. Assn. Marriage and Family Therapists, Nat. Register Clin. Social Workers, Lions (bd. dirs. San Francisco chpt. 1986). Avocations: running, gym and fitness, writing, gardening. Office: PO Box 2880 Guerneville CA 95446-2880 Office Phone: 707-524-1742. E-mail: psychdavis@aol.com. *Personal philosophy: A life is to be enjoyed not endured. How people get through life is a piece of art not a piece of cake. Everyday is a canvas and our actions brushstrokes, let our brushstrokes be bold each day.*

MANNIX, CHARLES RAYMOND, law educator; b. Elizabeth, NJ, Aug. 2, 1950; s. Charles Raymond and Helen Joan (French) M. BA, Duquesne U., 1972, MA, JD, Duquesne U., 1976; MPA, Harvard U., 1998. Bar: Iowa 1976, NY 1996, Va. 1980, DC 1980, NH 2006, Vt. 2007, US Ct. Claims 1976, US Tax Ct. 1976, US Ct. Mil. Appeals 1976, US Ct. Internat. Trade 1976, US Ct. Appeals (4th and 5th cirs.) 1977, US Ct. Appeals (DC cir.) 1977, US Dist. Ct. Va. 1980, US Dist. Ct. NH 2006, US Supreme Ct. 1980, US Ct. Appeals (DC cir.) 1980, US Ct. Appeals (fed. cir.) 1982, NY 1996, Supreme Ct. Vt., 2007. Commd. 2d lt. USAF, 1973, advanced through grade to col., 2004; intern UN Office of Legal Affairs, NYC, 1975; res. legal advisor Air Force Surgeon Gen., 2001—06; assoc. dean, COO, Dartmouth Med. Sch., Hanover, NH, 2004—, asst. prof. medicine, 2004—. Adj. faculty Georgetown U., Washington, 1984-99; assoc. prof. and chmn. dept. med. jurisprudence, 1987-2004, asst. prof. mil. medicine, v.p. and gen. counsel Uniformed Svcs. U. Health Scis, 1987-2004. Decorated Commendation medal with 2 oak leaf clusters, USAF, 1978, Nat. Def. medal with 2 stars, Reserve medal with "m", 2002, Meritorious Svc. medal with 2 oak leaf clusters, 2003, Global War on Terror medal, 2004, Legion Merit, 2006, Army Commondation, 2004. medal of Outstanding Unit award, AF Organizational Excellence award, Uniformed Svcs. U. Helath Scis. Disting. Svc. medal. Mem. ABA, ATLA, DC Bar Assn., Va. State Bar Assn., Vt. Bar Assn., NH Bar Assn., Am. Soc. Internat. Law, Am. Soc. Law and Medicine, Am. Arbitration Assn. (arbitrator), Am. Acad. Hosp. Attys., Nat. Assn. Coll. and Univ. Attys., NY State Bar Assn., Bar Assn. City of NY, Assn. Mil. Surgeons US, Harvard Club NY and Boston. Office: Office of the Dean Dartmouth Med Sch 1 Rope Ferry Rd Hanover NH 03755 Office Phone: 802-649-8920. Personal E-mail: charlesmannix@msn.com.

MANNIX, KEVIN LEESE, lawyer, school system administrator; b. Queens, NY, Nov. 26, 1949; s. John Warren Sr. and Editta Gorrell M.; m. Susanna Bernadette Chiocca, June 1, 1974; children: Nicholas Chiocca, Gabriel Leese, Emily Kemper. BA, U. Va., 1971, JD, 1974. Bar: Oreg. 1974, U.S. Ct. Appeals (9th cir.) 1976, U.S. Supreme Ct. 1978, Guam 1979. Law clk. to judge Oreg. Ct. Appeals, Salem, 1974—75; asst. atty. gen. Oreg. Dept. Justice, Salem, 1975—77, Govt. of Guam, Agana, 1977—79; judge adminstrv. law Oreg. Workers' Compensation Bd., Salem, 1980—83; assoc. Lindsay, Hart, Neil & Weigler, Portland, Oreg., 1983—86; pres. Kevin L. Mannix Profl. Corp., Salem, 1986—. Chmn. St. Joseph Sch. Bd., Salem, 1981-86; pres. Salem Cath. Schs. Corp., 1985; v.p. Salem Cath. Schs. Found., 1985-88, pres., 1988-90, 91-94, 2000—; pres. bd. dirs. Blanchet Sch., 1995-; vice chair Oreg. Rep. Party, 1998-2000, chmn., 2003-05; state rep., 1989-97, 99-2001; state sen., 1998-99. Mem. Oreg. State Bar Assn., Rotary (bd. dirs. East Salem 1985-89, pres. 1987-88), KC. Republican. Avocations: photography, scuba diving, travel. Home: 375 18th St NE Salem OR 97301-4307 Office: 2009 State St Salem OR 97301-4349 Office Phone: 503-364-1913.

MANNO, ROBERT, composer, conductor; b. Bryn Mawr, Pa., July 27, 1944; s. John B. and Isabel S. Manno; m. Magdalena Golczewski, Feb. 27, 1983; children: Nina Endler, Thom. MusB, Manhattan Sch. Music, NYC, 1968; MusM, NYU, NYC, 1973. Mem. chorus NYC Opera, 1967—77, Met. Opera, NYC, 1977—2001; co-dir. Windham Chamber Music Festival, 1997—; asst. condr. Met. Opera, 2002. Music dir., condr. Catskill Mountain Chamber Orch., Hunter, NY, 2004—. Composer musical scores. Music cons. Catskill Mountain Found., Hunter, NY, 2004. Democrat. Home: 740 County Route 32C Windham NY 12496 Office: Windham Chamber Music Festival PO Box 771 Windham NY 12496 Home Phone: 518-734-3868; Office Phone: 518-734-3868.

MANNWEILER, MARY-ELIZABETH, painter; b. Norwood, Ohio, June 23, 1916; d. Wilbur Lawrence Young Davis and Augusta Minnis (Newman) Davis; m. Robert Mays Lang, Sr., May 25, 1940 (dec. July 1981); children: Robert Mays Lang, Jr., Gary Davis Lang, Julianna Elizabeth Lang Crawford; m. Gordon Bannatyne Mannweiler, Apr. 17, 1982 (dec. Aug. 2001). Student, Miami U., Oxford, Ohio, 1935-37. Portrait painter; permanent collections; donated (with husband) stained glass window to Congl. Ch., Naugatuck, Conn. Past pres. Athena Club, Freeport, N.Y., Woodbury (Conn.) Woman's Club, 1977-78, Watertown (Conn.) Art League; past dir. Waterbury (Conn.) Symphony Orch.; pres. Mary Elizabeth and Gordon Mannweiler Found., Naugatuck, Conn.; trustee YMCA, Naugatuck; mem. scholarship com. Naugatuck H.S., 2003. Recipient blue ribbons for artwork; Paul Harris fellow Rotary, 2001; music room named in honor of Mr. and Mrs. Mannweiler Conn. Jr. Republic, Litchfield, 1997m Meml. Vol. award Naugatuck YMCA, 2005. Mem. DAR (regent Ruth Floyd Woodhull chpt. 1966-67, pres.). Home: 435 Hillside Ave Naugatuck CT 06770-2727

MANNY, CARTER HUGH, JR., architect, foundation administrator; b. Michigan City, Ind., Nov. 16, 1918; s. Carter Hugh and Ada Gage (Barnes) M.; m. Mary Alice Kellett, Dec. 6, 1942 (dec. Jan. 1994); children: Elizabeth, Carter Hugh III; m. Maya Moran, Dec. 27, 1995. AB magna cum laude, Harvard U., 1941, Indsl. Adminstr., 1942; Taliesin fellow, Scottsdale, Ariz., 1946; BS in Architecture, Ill. Inst. Tech., 1948. With Murphy/Jahn (name formerly Naess & Murphy and C.F. Murphy Assocs.), Chgo., 1948-83, partner, 1957-61; dir. 1st Citizens Bank, Michigan City, Ind., 1970-86; sr. v.p. Murphy/Jahn (name formerly Naess & Murphy and C.F. Murphy Assocs.), 1978-83. Mem. adv. com. on architecture Art Inst. of Chgo., 1982—, oversight com. Ill. Inst. Tech. Sch. of Architecture, Chgo., 1989-94; trustee Graham Found. Advanced Studies in Fine Arts 1956-74, exec. dir., 1972-93, hon. trustee, 1994—. Projects include O'Hare Internat. Airport, Chgo., FBI Hdqrs, Washington, First Nat. Bank Chgo, Chgo. Civic Center, Chgo. Bd. Trade. Fellow AIA (pres. Chgo. chpt. 1973, dir. Ill. coun. 1972-73), Soc. Archtl. Historians (dir. 1982-85), Chgo. Bldg. Congress (dir. 1978-83); mem. Phi Beta Kappa, Mich. City Yacht Club, Arts Club, Cliff Dwellers Club (Chgo., hon.). Home: 50 Parftridge Dr San Rafael CA 94901

MANOFF, RICHARD KALMAN, advertising executive, writer, public health service officer, consultant; b. Bklyn., June 24, 1916; s. Kalman and Sarah (Glatman) M.; m. Lucy B. Deutscher, Nov. 27, 1942; children: Robert K., Gregory P. BS, CCNY, 1937, postgrad., 1940. Asst. regional dir. War Manpower Commn., 1942-45; marketing dir. Welch Grape Juice Co., 1949-53; v.p. Kenyon & Eckhardt Advt., NYC, 1953-56; pres., chmn. bd. Richard K. Manoff Inc. Advt., NYC, from 1956; now pres. Manoff Internat. Inc.; spl. adv. mktg. and communications to exec. dir. UNICEF, 1980—. Dir. Thomas J. Lipton, Inc.; adj. prof. dept. health Scis. Sargent Coll. Allied Health Professions, Boston U., 1978—; lectr. pub. health Columbia U. Sch. Medicine, 1982-83; Mem. U.S. del. FAO World Conf., Rome, Italy, 1966; spl. advisor UNICEF and WHO, 1968-78; cons. spl. mission to Food and Agr. Ministry, Govt. India, AID, 1969; Ford Found. offices Pub. Edn. Pub. Broadcasting for children's TV; participant 1st World Conf. on Social Communication for Devel. Mass Communications, Mexico, 1970, 7th Asian Advt. Congress, Delhi, 1970, 3d Western Hemisphere Nutrition Congress, Fla., 1971, Internat. Conf. Nutrition, Nat. Devel. and Planning, Mass. Inst. Tech., 1971, Symposium Eating Patterns and Their Influence on Purchasing Behavior and Nutrition, Nev., 1971, Nutrition Workshop, AID, 1971, 9th Annual Summer Workshop Family Planning, 1971, 4th & 5th Seminar Workshop on Mgmt. and Planning of Population Family Planning Programs, 1971, New Products Symposium, 1971, Communication Seminar series Cornell U., 1971, Exploration The Frontiers of Nutritional Edn. Seminar, 1972, 9th Internat. Congress of Nutrition, Mexico, 1972, East-West Center Comml. Resources Conf. on Family Planning, Hawaii, 1972; Protein adv. group UN Systems Annual Mtg., 1973; mem. panel White House Conf. Food, Nutrition and Health, 1969; mem. Sec.'s Adv. Com. on Population Affairs, Dept. HEW, 1971-76; mem. adv. com. Population Reference Bur., Washington, 1977—, Population Inst., 1980—; mem. Nelson A. Rockefeller's Commn. on Critical Choices for Ams.; cons. HRSA Healthy Start Campaign to reduce infant mortality, 1991; bd. dirs. Population Comm. Internat.; Martin J. Forman Meml. lectr., Washington, 1993. Author: Social Marketing: New Imperative for Public Health, 1985. Bd. dirs. Planned Parenthood World Population, Pathfinder Fund, Boston, 1977-80, United Nutrition Edn. Found., Alexandria, Va., 1978—; mem. com. on internat. nutrition programs NAS-NRC, 1973; founder, mem. Com. for Shakespeare Festival, NYC; bd. visitors Grad. Sch. and Univ. Ctr., CUNY; mem. adv. bd., cons. to the pres. Henry J. Kaiser Family Found., 1987-91; dir. City Coll. Fund, 1990—. Recipient 5th Ann. Global award for media excellence Population Inst., China, 1985, Townsend Harris medal Alumni Assn. CCNY, 1986. Mem. Am. Assn. Advt. Agys. (gov. 1967—, sec.-treas. 1975—), Population Comms. Internat. (dir. 1992—), Friars Club, Harmonie Club (NYC), Century Assn. Home: 322 E 57th St New York NY 10022-2949

MANOOGIAN, RICHARD ALEXANDER, consumer products company executive; b. Long Branch, NJ, July 30, 1936; s. Alex and Marie (Tatian) Manoogian; m. Jane Manoogian; children: James, Richard, Bridget. BA in Econs, Yale U., 1958. Asst. to pres. Masco Corp., Taylor, Mich., 1958-62, exec. v.p., 1962-68, pres., 1968-85, chmn. bd., CEO, 1985—. Chmn., dir. Mascotech, Inc., Trimas Corp.; dir. First Chgo. NBD Corp., Bank One Corp., Ford Motor Co., Metaldyne Corp., Detroit Renaissance, Am. Bus. Conf. Chmn. Alex & Marie Manoogian Found.; pres. & treas. Richard & Jane Manoogian Found.; co-founder Mackinac Island Cmty. Found., 2003; trustee U. Liggett Sch., State Dept. Fine Arts Comsn., Founder's Soc., Detroit Inst. Arts, Center for Creative Studies; trustee coun. Nat. Gallery Art. Mem. Yale Alumni Assn. Clubs: Grosse Pointe Yacht, Grosse Pointe Hunt, Country Club Detroit, Detroit Athletic. Office: Masco Corp 21001 Van Born Rd Taylor MI 48180-1300 *

MANOS, CHRISTOPHER LAWRENCE, lawyer, mediator; b. Ft. Bragg, NC, July 1, 1952; m. B.J. Osmon, June 14, 1974; children: Monica, Kelly. BS, U.S. Mil. Acad., 1974; JD, U. N.D., 1982. Bar: Mont. 1983, U.S. Dist. Ct. (Mont.) 1983, U.S. Ct. Appeals (9th cir.) 1983. Assoc. to ptnr. Moore, O'Connell, Refling & Manos, Bozeman, Mont., 1982-92; ptnr. Biglen & Manos, Big Timber, Mont., 1992—97, Manos law firm, 1997; part-time dep. county atty. Sweet Grass county, 1992—98; county atty, 1998—2001. Trainer for mediators Ctr. for Collaborative Solutions and Alternative Dispute Resolution Assocs., Bozeman and Palo Alto, Calif., 1990—. Contbr. articles to profl. jours. Bd. dirs. Mont. Pub. TV, Bozeman, 1985-92, Mont. Coun. for Internat. Visitors, Bozeman, 1992; mem. Mont. Stat Bar Dispute Resolution Com., Helena, Mont., 1989—. Capt. U.S. Army, 1974-79. Col. USAR (ret.), 1979-2004. Mem. Assn. Conflict Resolution, Am. Arbitration Assn., State Bar Mont. (pres. 2001-02), Soc. Profls. in Dispute Resolution. Office Phone: 406-442-7660.

MANOS, THOMAS G., investment company executive; b. Toronto, Ohio, Feb. 10, 1923; s. George A. and Louise G. (Clappas) Manos. BSBA, Kent State U., Ohio, 1950; MA, Hiram Coll., Ohio, 1950. Registered pub. acct., Ohio. Theater mgr. Manos Theatres Inc., Newton Falls, Ohio, 1940—41, 1946—49; open-hearth laborer Treadwell Constrn., Midland, Pa., 1941—42; with US mil. 11th Airborne Divsn., 1942—46; pub. acct. Data Processors Inc., Warren, Ohio, 1949—90; pres. Thedic Corp., Brookfield, Ohio, 2006—. 1st lt. US Army, 1942—46, PTO. Decorated Bronze star; recipient Nat. Leadership award, Bus. Adv. Coun., 2006. Home: 1076 S Park Dr Brookfield OH 44403

MANOSEVITZ, MARTIN, psychologist; b. Mpls., June 22, 1938; s. Julius and Ethel (Cohen) M.; m. Carolyn Heather Margulius, Sept. 17, 1959; children— Bradley, Jason. BA, U. Minn., Mpls., 1960, PhD, 1964. Diplomate in clin. psychology, psychoanalysis Am. Bd. Profl. Psychology. Asst. prof. psychology Rutgers U., 1964-67; asst. prof. psychology U. Tex., Austin, 1967-69, assoc. prof., 1969-75, prof., 1975-87; pvt. practice clin. psychology Austin, 1975-99, Aspen, Colo., 1999—. Adj. prof. psychology U. Tex., 1987-93; dir. psychol. svcs. CPC Capital Hosp., Austin, 1987-93, Shoal Creek Hosp., Austin, 1994-99; allied profl. staff Aspen Valley Hosp., 2000—; bd. dirs. Given Inst., Aspen. Trustee Austin-Travis County Mental Health-Mental Retardation Center, 1978-80. Fellow APA (bd. dirs. divsn. psychoanalysis, 1999-2000, membership chmn. 1997-2000, bd. mem. at large 1999-2000, treas. 2003-05), Acad. Psychoanalytic Psychology; mem. Colo. Psychol. Assn. (bd. dirs. 2005-06, pres.-elect 2006-07, pres 2007), Austin Soc. for Psychoanalytic Psychology (pres. 1994-95), Denver Psychoanalytic Soc. Office: 225 N Nill St Ste 206 Aspen CO 81611 Mailing: PO Box 7976 Aspen CO 81612 E-mail: mmanosev@earthlink.net.

MANOWITZ, PAUL, biochemist, researcher, educator; b. Monticello, NY, Dec. 13, 1940; s. Jacob M. and Rose (Levine) M.; m. Joyce L. Swartz, June 16, 1968; children: Neal J., Lauren H. BA in Chemistry with honors, Cornell U., 1962; PhD in Biochemistry, Brandeis U., 1967. Fellow NYU Sch. Medicine, 1967-70, instr., 1970-72; asst. prof. psychiatry U. Medicine and Dentistry N.J. Robert Wood Johnson Med. Sch., Piscataway, 1972-78, assoc. prof. psychiatry, 1978-96, prof. psychiaty, 1996—. Rsch. cons. VA Med. Ctr., Lyons, N.J., 1987—. Mem. editl. bd. Jour. of Studies on Alcohol, 1993—2003; contbr. articles to profl. jours. Mem. AAAS, Internat. Soc. for Biomed. Rsch. on Alcoholism, Am. Soc. Human Genetics, Am. Soc. Neurochemistry, Soc. Biol. Psychiatry, Rsch. Soc. on Alcoholism. Home: 7 Guernsey Ln East Brunswick NJ 08816-3506 Office: U Medicine and Dentistry NJ Robert Wood Johnson Med Sch 671 Hoes Ln Piscataway NJ 08854-5627 Office Phone: 732-235-4347.

MANSBERGER, ARLIE ROLAND, JR., surgeon; b. Pitts., Oct. 13, 1922; s. Arlie Rol and Mayme (Smith) M.; m. Anna Ellen Piel, July 27, 1946; children— Ellen Lynn, John Arlie, Leigh Ann. BA, Western Md. Coll., 1943, D.Sc. (hon.), 1974; MD, U. Md., 1947, D.Sc. (hon.), 1978. Diplomate: Am. Bd. Surgery (dir., vice chmn.). Intern U. Md. Hosp., 1947-49, resident in surgery, 1947-54; chief wound shock br. biophysics div. Army Chem. Center, 1954-56; instr. surgery U. Md., 1956-59, asst. prof., 1959-61, asso. prof., 1961-69, prof. surgery, 1969-73; clin. dir. shock-trauma unit, 1962-73; prof. surgery, chmn. dept. Med. Coll. Ga., Augusta, 1973-91; prof. surgery emeritus, chmn., 1991—. Cons. surgeon Dwight David Eisenhower Army Med. Center, VA Hosp. Editor: Essence of General Surgery, 1975; chmn. editorial bd.: Bull. U. Md, 1971-73; editor-in-chief: The Am. Surgeon, 1973-89; surg. editor: Resident and Staff Physician, 1979-91; contbr. articles to profl. jours., chpts. to books. Trustee Western Md. Coll., 1971—, Med. Research Found. Ga., 1973-91; bd. dirs. Nicholas J. Pisican Found., 1993—. Served to col. U.S. Army, 1943-46, 54-56. Recipient Man of Yr. award U. Md., 1970, 72, Golden Apple teaching award U. Md., 1968, 72, Disting. Faculty award Med. Coll. Ga., 1979, Gold Medal Alumni award U. Md., 1989, Disting. Svc. award (medal) Southeastern Surg. Congress, 1990. Fellow A.C.S. (gov.); mem. Am. Surg. Assn., Soc. Univ. Surgeons, So. Surg. Assn., Soc. Internationale de Chirurgie, Am. Assn. Surgery of Trauma, Southeastern Surg. Congress, Soc. Surgery of Alimentary Tract, AMA, Soc. Consultants to Armed Forces, Med. Assn. Ga. (editorial bd. 1987-92), Am. Bd. Family Practice (bd. dirs. 1987-92), 29th Div. Assn., Alpha Omega Alpha (Tchg. award 2001). Episcopalian. Home: One 7th St Unit 1502 Augusta GA 30901-1343 Office: Dept Surgery Med Coll Ga Augusta GA 30912 Personal E-mail: ellenmansberger@aol.com.

MANSBRIDGE, JANE JEBB, political scientist, educator; b. NYC, Nov. 19, 1939; d. Ronald and Georgia St. Claire (Mullen) Mansbridge; m. Christopher Jencks; 1 child, Nathaniel Mansbridge Jencks. BA, Wellesley Coll., 1961; MA, Harvard U., 1966, PhD, 1971. Asst. prof. polit. sci. U. Chgo., 1973-80; assoc. prof. Northwestern U., Evanston, Ill., 1980-86, prof. polit. sci., 1986-91, Jane W. Long prof. arts and scis., 1991-96; prof. J.F. Kennedy Sch. Govt. Harvard U., 1996-98, Adams prof. polit. leadership and democratic values, 1998—. Author: Beyond Adversary Democracy, 1980, Why We Lost the ERA, 1986; editor: Beyond Self-Interest, 1990; editor: (with Susan M. Okin) Feminism 2 vols., 1994; editor: (with Aidon Morris) Oppositional Consciousness, 2001; mem. editl. bd. Signs, Jour. Polit. Philosophy, Jour. Social Philosophy, Gender and Politics, Social Justice Rsch. Russell Sage Found. scholar, 1991-92; fellow Inst. for Advanced Study, 1985-86, Rockefeller Humanities, 1982-83, NSF, 1971-72, Ctr. Advanced Study in the Behavioral Scis., 1997-98, 2001-02, Radcliffe medal Radcliffe Grad. Soc., 2004; fellowship Radcliffe Inst. Advanced Study, 2004-05. Mem. Am. Acad. Arts and Scis., Am. Polit. Sci. Assn. (v.p. 1992-93, program chair 1990, exec. com. 1987-89, coun. 1987-89, pres. Women's Caucus 1996, Schuck award 1988, Kammerer award 1987), Soc. Advancement of Socio-Econs. (pres. 1992-93), Internat. Polit. Psychology Assn. (governing coun. 1993-94). Office: JF Kennedy Sch Govt 79 JFK St Cambridge MA 02138-5801 Office Phone: 617-495-9343.

MANSELL, DARREL LEE, JR., language educator; b. Canton, Ohio, Apr. 9, 1934; s. Darrel Lee and Virginia (Shepherd) M.; m. Elizabeth Meihack, Jan. 1957 (div. July 1970); 1 child, Benjamin Lloyd; m. Adriana Saviane, July 16, 1983. BA, Oberlin Coll., 1956; student, Oxford U., 1961—62; PhD, Yale U., 1963; MA (hon.), Dartmouth Coll., 1975. Instr. Dartmouth Coll., Hanover, NH, 1962-64, asst. prof., 1964-68, assoc. prof., 1968-74, prof., 1974-99, prof. emeritus, 1999—. Author: The Novels of Jane Austen, 1973; contbr. articles to scholarly jours. Mem.: Jane Austen Soc. N.Am. (founding patron), Phi Beta Kappa. Home: 2 Dana Rd Hanover NH 03755-2227 Office: Dartmouth Coll Dept English Hanover NH 03755

MANSELL, HENRY J., archbishop; b. NYC, Oct. 10, 1937; Student, Cathedral Coll., St. Joseph's Sem. and Coll., N.Am. Coll., Gregorian U.; BA, St. Joseph Sem., Yonkers, 1959; Lic. Sacred Theology, Gregorian U., Rome, 1963; postgrad., Catholic U. Am., 1965. Ordained priest, NY, 1962; parish priest in various parishes NYC & Westchester County; auxiliary bishop Archdiocese of NY, 1992—95; titular bishop Marazanae, NYC, 1993-95; bishop Diocese of Buffalo, NY, 1995—2003; archbishop Archdiocese of Hartford, Conn., 2003—. Dir. Office of Parish Councils, 1972. Office: Archdiocese of Hartford 134 Farmington Ave Hartford CT 06105-3784

MANSELL, JOYCE MARILYN, retired special education educator; b. Minot, ND, Dec. 17, 1934; d. Einar Axel and Gladys Ellen (Wall) Alm; m. Dudley J. Mansell, Oct. 31, 1954; children: Michael, Debra Mansell Richards. BS, U. Houston, 1968; MEd, Sam Houston State U., 1980. Cert. provisional elem. tchr. 1-8, provisional mentally retarded tchr., provisional lang. and/or learning disabilities tchr., profl. elem. tchr. gen. 1-9, reading specalist. From 1st grade tchr. to 3rd grade tchr. Johnson Elem. Sch., 1968-77; spl. edn. tchr. mentally retarded/learning disabled Meml. Parkway Jr. HS, 1982-86, Waller Mid. Sch., 1986-90; spl. edn. tchr. mentally retarded Royal Mid. Sch., Tex., 1990-95, Royal HS, 1995-96; ret., 1996. Tchr. Am. sign lang. for retarded students in pub. schs. Lutheran. Avocations: painting, bridge, reading, fishing, travel. Home: 2155 Paso Rello Dr Houston TX 77077-5622 Personal E-mail: dmansell@houston.rr.com.

MANSELL, JUSTIN DENNIS, optical engineer, consultant; b. LA, Oct. 21, 1973; s. Dennis Mansell and Mary Lou Dowling; m. Tahmina Rahman Mansell, Mar. 21, 2004; 1 child, Rhianna Jada. BSEE, MSEE, Western Res. U., Ohio, 1996; PhD in Elec. Engring., Stanford U., Calif., 2002. Intern Sandia Nat. Labs., Albuquerque, 1993—96, NASA Glenn Rsch. Ctr., Ohio Aerospace Inst., Cleve., 1993—94; rsch. asst. Stanford U., Robert L. Byer's Rsch. Group, 1996—2002; engring. cons. Wavefront Sciences Corp., Albuquerque, 1996—99; founder, v.p., chief tech. officer AgilOptics, Inc. (formerly Intellite, Inc.), 2000—02; pres., founder Mansell & Assocs., LLC, 2002—06; chief engr. Qynergy Corp., 2002—03; v.p., chief tech. officer MZA Assocs. Corp., 2004—; pres., founder Active Optical Sys., LLC, 2005—. Contbr. articles to profl. jours. Pres. N.Mex Gymnastics Judges Assn., Albuquerque, 2003—05. Mem.: SPIE (assoc.), IEEE (assoc.), USA Gymnastics (assoc.), Optical Soc. Am. (assoc.). Achievements include patents for automated pupil remapping with binary optics; silicon micromachined deformable mirror; apparatus and method for evaluating a target larger than a measuring aperture of a sensor; sub-lens spatial resolution Shack-Hartmann wavefront sensing; patents pending for new concepts in advanced optics. Avocation: gymnastics coach. Office: Active Optical Systems LLC 2021 Girard Ste 150 Albuquerque NM 87106 Home Phone: 505-883-0970; Office Phone: 505-245-9970 184. Personal E-mail: jmansell@mansellassociates.com. Business E-Mail: jmansell@aos-llc.com.

MANSELL, KEVIN B., retail executive; b. St. Louis; Student, U. Mo. With Venture Store divsn. May Dept. Stores, 1975, positions in merchandising and buying; divisional mdse. mgr. Kohl's Corp., Menomonee Falls, Wis., 1982—87, gen. mdse. mgr., 1987, sr. exec. v.p. merchandising and mktg., 1998—99, pres., 1999—, bd. dirs., 1999—. Office: Kohls Corp N56 W17000 Ridgewood Dr Menomonee Falls WI 53051-5660 Office Phone: 262-703-7000. *

MANSFIELD, CHRISTOPHER CHARLES, lawyer; b. 1950; m. Laura Mansfield; children: Carolyn, Brendan. BA in Econs., Boston Coll., 1972, JD, 1975. Bar: Mass. 1975. With Liberty Mut. Ins. Co., Boston, 1975—, assoc. gen. counsel, 1981—83, v.p., gen. counsel, 1985—88, sr. v.p., gen. counsel, 1988—, bd. dirs. Bd. dirs. Employers Ins. Co., Wausau, New Eng. Legal Found.; bd. overseers RAND Corp. Inst. Civil Justice. Trustee Trust Fund Commn., Dedham, Mass.; bd. dirs. Pine St. Inn, Boston. Office: Liberty Mut Ins Co PO Box 140 175 Berkeley St Boston MA 02117-5066 *

MANSFIELD, EDWARD PATRICK, JR., advertising executive; b. Warren, Pa., Oct. 29, 1947; s. Edward Patrick and Frieda (Dahler) M.; m. Norma L. Johnson, Apr. 17, 1971. AS in Acctg., Jamestown Bus. Coll., 1967; BS in Mktg. Advt., Myers U., 1970. Promotion mgr., ad dir. The News-Herald, Lake County, Ohio, 1973-77; dir. advt. The Eagle, Butler, Pa., 1977-78; dir. mktg. Baltimore Mag., 1978-79; dir. advt. The Washingtonian, Washington, 1979—. Founder, chmn. Warm-A-Heart Fund, 1988—; bd. dirs. Columbia Lighthouse for the Blind, 1988—, chmn., 1988-93; bd. dirs. The Lighthouse. Avocations: amateur radio, boating. Home: 347 Cottswold Pl Riva MD 21140-1528 Office: Washingtonian Mag 1828 L St NW Ste 200 Washington DC 20036-5169 Home Phone: 410-956-5328; Office Phone: 202-296-3600. Business E-Mail: emansfield@washingtonian.com.

MANSFIELD, GORDON HALL, federal agency administrator; BA, Villanova U., 1964; JD, U. Miami, 1973. Commd. U.S. Army, 1964, co. comdr. 101st Airborne Divsn. Vietnam; lawyer Ocala, Fla.; various positions including assoc. exec. dir. govt. rels. Paralyzed Vets. Am., 1981—89, exec. dir. Washington, 1993—2001; asst. sec. for fair housing and equal opportunity US Dept. Housing & Urban Devel., Washington, 1989—93; asst. sec. for cong. & legis. affairs US Dept. Veterans Affairs, Washington, 2001—04, dep. sec., 2004—. Decorated Bronze Star, Purple Heart (2), Combat Infantryman's badge, Presdl. Unit Citation. Office: US Dept Veterans Affairs 810 Vermont Ave NW Rm 1004 Washington DC 20420

MANSFIELD, JAMES NORMAN, III, lawyer; b. Chattanooga, Feb. 15, 1951; s. James Norman and Doris June (Hilliard) M.; m. Terry Ann Thomas, Dec. 28, 1975; children: Seth Thomas, James Norman, Scott Michael. BA, U. Tenn., Chattanooga, 1973; MA, La. State U., 1976, JD, 1979. Bar: La. 1979, U.S. Dist. Ct. (we. dist.), La. 1979. Shareholder Liskow and Lewis, Lafayette and New Orleans, La., 1979—. Pres. Raven Soc., Chattanooga, 1973; pres. sch. bd. St. Thomas More H.S. Mem. ABA, La. Bar Assn., La. Min. Law Inst. (adv. coun. mem.), Am. Assn. Profl. Landmen, Lafayette Assn. Petroleum Landmen, Order of Coif. Roman Catholic. Avocations: photography, golf, fishing. Home: 103 Asbury Cir Lafayette LA 70503-3632 Office: Liskow & Lewis PO Box 52008 Lafayette LA 70505-2008 Office Phone: 337-232-7424.

MANSFIELD, KAREN LEE, lawyer; b. Chgo., Mar. 17, 1942; d. Ralph and Hilda (Blum) Mansfield; children: Nicole Rafaela, Lori Michele. BA in Polit. Sci., Roosevelt U., 1963; JD, DePaul U., 1971; student U. Chgo., 1959-60. Bar: Ill. 1972, U.S. Dist. Ct. (no. dist.) Ill. 1972. Legis. intern Ill. State Senate, Springfield, 1966-67; tchr. Chgo. Pub. Schs., 1967-70; atty. CNA Ins., Chgo., 1971-73; law clk. Ill. Apellate Ct., Chgo., 1973-75; sr. trial atty. U.S. Dept. Labor, Chgo., 1975—, mentor Adopt-a-Sch. Program, 1992-95. bd. dirs. Chgo. lawyer chpt. Am. Constn. Soc., 2006-. Contbr. articles to profl. jours. Vol. Big Sister, 1975-81; bd. dirs. Altgeld Nursery Sch., 1963-66, Ill. div. UN Assn., 1966-72, Hull House Jane Addams Ctr., 1977-82, Broadway Children's Ctr., 1986-90, Acorn Family Entertainment, 1993-95; active Oak Park Farmers' Market Commn., 1996-02; rsch. asst. Citizens for Gov. Otto Kerner, Chgo., 1964; com. mem. Ill. Commn. on Status of Women, Chgo., 1964-70; del. Nat. Conf. on Status of Women, 1968; candidate for del. Ill. Constl. Conv., 1969. Mem. Chgo. Coun. Lawyers, Women's Bar Assn. Ill., Lawyer Pilots Bar Assn., Fed. Bar Assn., Am. Constn. Soc. (bd. dirs. Chgo. Lawyer chpt.), Friends of Gamelan (performer), 99's Internat. Orgn. Women Pilots (legis. chmn. Chgo. area chpt. 1983-86, legis. chmn. North Ctrl. sect. 1986-88, Legis. award 1983, 85). Unitarian. Home: 204 S Taylor Ave Oak Park IL 60302-3307 Office: US Dept Labor Office Solicitor 230 S Dearborn St Fl 8 Chicago IL 60604-1505

MANSFIELD, LORRAINE J., lawyer; JD, U. Wyo., Laramie, 1979. Bar: Wyo. 1979, Nev. 1981, US Ct. Appeals (10th cir.) 1980, US Ct. Appeals (9th cir.) 1983, US Ct. of Claims, 1990, US Supreme Ct. 1985. Law clk. Wyo. Supreme Ct., Laramie, 1980; sole practitioner law Las Vegas, 1981—. Arbitrator 8th Jud. Cir., Las Vegas, 1992—. Contbr. articles to profl. jours. Avocation: sailing. Office: Mansfield Law Office 6655 W Sahara Ave # B 200 Las Vegas NV 89146 Office Phone: 702-222-4009. Personal E-mail: lorrainemansfield1@yahoo.com.

MANSFIELD, WILLIAM L., manufacturing executive; BS, Drexel Univ.; MBA, Lehigh Univ. Mgmt. positions through v.p. Valspar Corp., Mpls., 1977—91, v.p. packaging & coatings, 1991—98, sr. v.p. packaging & indsl. coatings, 1998—2000, sr. v.p. arch., automotive, specialty & packaging coatings, 2000—02, exec. v.p., 2002—04, exec. v.p., COO, 2004—05, pres., CEO, 2005—. Office: Valspar Corp 1101 3d St S Minneapolis MN 55415 *

MANSI, JOSEPH ANNEILLO, public relations company executive; b. Oct. 8, 1935; s. Joseph C. and Vinnie (Chirico) M.; m. Mary P. Fusco, Aug. 1, 1959; children: Karen M. D'Attore, Jeanine V. Dimenna. BS, NYU, 1957. Newsman Internat. News Service, UPI, 1953-58; mem. pub. relations staff Lawrence Orgn., NYC, 1960-63; acct. supr. Philip Lesly Co., NYC, 1963-67; dir. corp. communications Ward Foods, Inc., NYC, 1967-72; dir. pub. relations Metromedia Inc., NYC, 1973-75; pres. Corp. Relations Network, Inc., NYC, 1975-80; mng. ptnr. KCSA Pub. Rels. Worldwide, NYC, 1980—. Trustee North Shore Hist. Mus., Five Towns Coll. With AUS, 1958—60. Mem. Pub. Rels. Soc. Am. (accredited). Home: 10 Beatrice Ln Glen Cove NY 11542-1202 Office: KCSA Pub Rels Worldwide 800 2nd Ave New York NY 10017-4709 Home Phone: 516-759-9007; Office Phone: 212-896-1205. Personal E-mail: jmansi@kcsa.com.

MANSKE, PAUL ROBERT, orthopedic hand surgeon, educator; b. Ft. Wayne, Ind., Apr. 29, 1938; s. Alfred R. and Elsa E. (Streufert) M.; m. Sandra H. Henricks, Nov. 29, 1975; children: Ethan Paul, Claire Bruch, Louisa Hendricks. BA, Valparaiso U., 1960, DSc (hon.), 1985; MD, Washington U., St. Louis, 1964. Diplomate Am. Bd. Surgery. Intern U. Wash., Seattle, 1964-65, resident in surgery, 1965-66; resident in orthopedic surg. Washington U., St. Louis, 1969-72; hand surgery fellow U. Louisville, 1971; instr. orthopedic surgery Washington U. Med. Sch., St. Louis, 1972-76, asst. prof. orthopedic surgery, 1976-83, prof., 1983—, chmn. dept., 1983-95. Editor-in-chief Jour. Hand Surgery, 1996—; contbr. over 215 articles to profl. jours. Lt. comdr. USN, 1966-69, Vietnam. Fellow AMA, Am. Acad. Orthopaedic Surgery (Elizabeth Winston Lanier award, 1985Am. Orthopaedic Assn.; mem. Am. Soc. Surgery of the Hand, Alpha Omega Alpha. Office: Washington Univ Sch Medicine Dept Orthop Surgery Box 8233 660 S Euclid Ave Saint Louis MO 63110-1036 *

MANSKE, SUSAN E., investment advisor; Grad., U. of Wis.; MBA, Marquette U. Chartered Fin. Analyst. Portfolio mgr. Ford Motor Co.; mgr., fixed income Ameritech Corp., 1987, dir., capital markets, dir., risk mgmt., chief investment officer, 1998—2000; v.p., chief investment officer Boeing Co., 2001—03, The John D. and Catherine T. MacArthur Found., 2003—. Mem. bd. dirs. Ednl. Dist. 181 Found. Named a Woman to Watch, Crain's Chgo. Bus., 2007. Mem.: Investment Bd. of United Way/Crusade of Mercy. Office: The John D and Catherine T MacArthur Found Office of Grants Mgmt 140 S Dearborn St Chicago IL 60603-5285 Office Phone: 312-726-8000. Office Fax: 312-920-6258. *

MANSNERUS, LAURA, news correspondent; Staff writer NY Times, editor Week in Review, corr. Trenton Bur. Office: NY Times Trenton Bur PO Box 021 Trenton NJ 08625-0021 also: NJ State House 125 W State St Trenton NJ 08625-0021

MANSON, HAROLD CRAIG, former federal agency administrator, former judge; b. Mo., 1954; m. Penny Manson. Grad., USAF Acad., 1976; JD, U. Pacific McGeorge Sch. Law, 1981. Atty. Downey, Brand, Seymour & Rohwer, 1989—93; gen. counsel, Dept. Fish & Game State of Calif., Sacramento, 1993—98; judge Sacramento County Superior Ct., Calif., 1998—2002; asst. sec. for fish, wildlife & parks US Dept. Interior, Washington, 2002—05; Disting. visitor & lectr. in law U. Pacific McGeorge Sch. Law, 2006—. Adj. prof. McGeorge Sch. Law, 1992—2001. Mem Calif. Rep. Party State Ctrl. Com., 1991—95. Served in USAF, 1976—89. Recipient Pacific McGeorge Alumnus of Yr. award, 2004.

MANSON, JOANN ELISABETH, endocrinologist; b. Cleve., Apr. 14, 1953; d. S. Stanford and Therese (Palay) M.; m. Christopher N. Ames, June 12, 1979; children: Jennifer, Jeffrey, Joshua Simon. AB magna cum laude, Harvard U., 1975; MD, Case Western Res. U., 1979; MPH, Harvard Sch. Pub. Health, 1984, DPH, 1987. Bd. cert. internal medicine; bd. cert. in subspecialty of endocrinology and metabolism. Intern and resident internal medicine NEDH, Harvard Med. Sch., Boston, 1979-82; fellowship in endocrinology U. Hosp. Boston, Mass., 1982-84; rsch fellow in medicine Brigham and Women's Hosp., Boston, 1984-87, co-dir. women's health, divsn. preventive medicine, 1993—, chief divsn. preventive medicine, 1999—; staff physician, consulting endocrinologist Harvard Vanguard Med. Assocs., Peabody, Mass., 1986—2003; prof. medicine Harvard Med. Sch., Boston, 1999—, Elizabeth Brigham prof. women's health, 2003—. Mem. editl. bd.: Jour. Women's Health, 1996—, Menopause, 2004—; contbr. chapters to books, more than 600 articles to profl. jours.; author, editor: several books and textbooks. Vol. physician Lynn (Mass.) Shelter for the Homeless, 1989-93; med. adv. bd. Harvard Health Letter, Boston, 1992—, Greater Boston (Mass.) Diabetes Soc., 1993—, Harvard Women's Health Watch, Boston, 1993—; vol. Am. Heart Assn., 1992—. Named Hero in Women's Health, Am. Health for Women Mag., 1997; named one of Top 10 Champions of Women's Health, Ladies Home Jour., 2000, Top Docs for Women, Boston mag., 2001; recipient Connors award for oustanding leadership in women's health, 1999—, Woman in Sci. award, Am. Med. Women's Assn., 2003, Henry I. Bowditch award for excellence in pub. health, Mass. Med. Soc., 2002, Women's Profl. Achievement award, Harvard Coll., 2006. Fellow ACP, ACE; mem. AMA, Am. Med. Women's Assn., Am. Heart Assn., Am. Diabetes Assn., Women's Health Initiative (mem. steering com.), Assn. Am. Physicians, Alpha Omega Alpha. Avocations: reading, hiking, music, travel. Home: 14 Washington St Beverly MA 01915-5820 Office: Brigham and Women's Hosp 900 Commonwealth Ave E Fl 3 Boston MA 02215-1204 Home Phone: 978-927-6764; Office Phone: 617-278-0871. Business E-Mail: jmanson@rics.bwh.harvard.edu.

MANSON, JOSEPH LLOYD, III, lawyer; b. Richmond, Va., May 5, 1949; s. Joseph Lloyd Jr. and Nan Smith (Copley) M.; divorced; children: Martha Stuart, Joseph Scott, Rachel Smith. BS, U. Va., 1970; JD, Emory U., 1974. Assoc. Verner, Liipfert, Bernhard & McPherson, Washington, 1974—80; ptnr. Verner, Liipfert, Bernhard, McPherson & Hand, 1981—2002, co-chmn. exec. com., 1998—2001; ptnr. Piper, Rudnick, 2002—05, Baker & Hostetler, 2005—. Pres., CEO, bd. dirs. Barrow Grocery Co., DBM Group; mem. internat. bd. advisors Thailand Creative and Design Ctr. Founder Alexandria Youth Sports Found., 1993, Emory U. Law Sch. Coun.; bd. dirs. Mesa Air Group; trustee St. Stephens and St. Agnes Sch. Found. 2d lt. U.S. Army, 1973. Mem. ABA (ry. and airline labor law com., co-chmn. mgmt. 1993-94), D.C. Bar Assn. Republican. Episcopalian. Avocations: music, tennis, theater, movies. Office: Baker & Hostetler 1050 Connecticut Ave NW Washington DC 20036 Office Phone: 202-861-1543. Business E-Mail: jmanson@bakerlaw.com.

MANSON, MARILYN (BRIAN HUGH WARNER), singer, musician; b. Canton, OH, Jan. 5, 1969; s. Hugh and Barbara Warner; m. Dita Von Teese, Dec. 3, 2005 (separated Dec. 2006). Music journalist, 1987—89; co-founded band Marilyn Manson & the Spooky Kids, 1989; band signed to Nothing Records as Marilyn Manson, 1992. Founder art movement Celebritarian Corp., 1996. Singer: (albums) Portrait of an American Family, 1994, Smells Like Children, 1995, Antichrist Superstar, 1996, Remix & Repent, 1997, Mechanical Animals, 1998, The Last Tour on Earth, 1999, Holy Wood (In the Shadow of the Valley of Death), 2000, The Golden Age of Grotesque, 2003, Lest We Forget, 2004, Eat Me, Drink Me, 2007, (songs) The Beautiful People, 1996 (one of 100 Greatest Videos Ever Made, MTV, 1999), The Dope Show, 1998 (Rolling Stone Best Video of Yr., Billboard Maximum Vision award, 1998); composer: WWF Smackdown! theme song, 2001—; co-author: (autobiography) The Long Hard Road Out of Hell, 1998; contbr.: film soundtracks From Hell, 2001, The Matrix, 1999, Book of Shadows: Blair Witch 2, 2000, Resident Evil, 2002, Queen of the Damned, 2002, Bowling for Columbine, 2002; actor: (films) Lost Highway, 1997, Jawbreaker, 1998, Party Monster, 2003, The Heart is Deceitful Above All Things, 2004, Rise, 2005, Living Neon Dreams, 2005, (video games) Area 51 (voice only), 2005; actor, dir., exec. prodr. (films) Doppelherz, 2003. Rev. Church of Satan, 1994. Nominee 3 Grammy Awards, 5 MTV Video Music awards; named one of 100 Greatest Artists of Hard Rock, VH1, 2000; recipient 4 S. Fla. Slammies. Avocations: painting, writing. Office: Interscope Geffen A&M Records 2220 Colorado Ave Santa Monica CA 90404 *

MANSON, ZYNORA DAVIS, music educator, minister; b. Richmond, Va., Sept. 9, 1954; d. Henry and Ada Ellis Davis; m. Isaiah Jacob Manson, Aug. 8, 1993; children: Elizabeth Nicole, Chenaniah Jacob, Lateisha Rene', Isaiah Jacob Jr. BS in Music Edn., Norfolk State U., 1979. Profl. collegiate cert. Va., 1979. Sec. Henrico County Govt., Richmond, Va., 1972—73; tchr. music Fairfax County Pub. Schs., 1979—86, Henrico County Pub. Schs., Richmond, 1986—. Composer: (music book and music cd's) Catch Zynora's SOL Songs. Pastor Bethany Bapt. Ch., Sandston, Va., 1996—2005. Finalist Tchr. award of Excellence, REB, 2005; named Jacob L. Adams Tchr. of Yr., 1991, 1992, Henrico Music Educator of Yr., 2002; recipient Telly award, Henrico County Pub. Schs., Channel 36, 2001, Disting. Communicator award, Channel 36, Henrico County, 2001. Mem.: Va. Music Educators Assn. (assoc.). Democrat. Baptist. Avocations: walking, travel, skating. Home: 1070 Nash Rd Sandston VA 23150 Office: Prophetic Full Tone Praise Ministries In 1070 Nash Rd Sandston VA 23150 Home Phone: 804-737-7042; Office Phone: 804-737-7042. Office Fax: 804-737-7042. Personal E-mail: pftpm@aol.com.

MANSOUR, KAMAL A., cardiothoracic surgeon; b. Nov. 25, 1929; m. Sylvia Cleopatra Sideros, June 19, 1956; 1 child, Sylvia Frederica. M.B., B.Ch., Ein Shams U., Cairo, Egypt, 1954. Diplomate Am. Bd. Surgery, Am. Bd. Thoracic Surgery; lic. physician, Ga. Intern Tanta (Egypt) Gen. Hosp., 1954-55; surgeon Bapt. Hosp., Ajlun, Jordan, 1956-60, Gaza, Egypt, 1961-62; asst. resident in surgery Ch. Home & Hosp., Balt., 1962-63; asst. and chief resident in surgery Ga. Bapt. Hosp., Atlanta, 1963-66; asst. and chief resident cardio thoracic surgery Emory U. Hosp., Atlanta, 1966-68; pvt. practice specializing in cardiothoracic surgery Atlanta, 1968—. Active staff Emory U. Hosp., Grady Meml. Hosp., Crawford W. Long Hosp., Henrietta Egleston Children's Hosp., VA Hosp., Piedmont Hosp.; chief cardiothoracic surgery VA Med. Ctr., Atlanta; instr. surgery Emory U. Sch. Medicine, 1968-71, asst. prof. surgery, 1971-76, assoc. prof. surgery, 1976-87, prof. cardiothoracic surgery, 1987—. Contbr. numerous articles to profl. jours. Fellow ACS, Am. Coll. Cardiology, Am. Coll. Chest Physicians, Am. Coll. Angiology, Southeastern Surg. Congress; mem. Council on Critical Care, Am. Assn. Thoracic Surgery, Am. Heart Assn., Soc. Thoracic Surgeons, So. Thoracic Surg. Assn. Internat. Coll. Surgeons (vice regent Ga.), Am. Thoracic Soc., Ga. Surg. Soc., AMA, Med. Assn. Ga., Med. Assn. Atlanta, N. Am. Soc. Pacing and Electrophysiology (founding mem.), Internat. Soc. for Diseases of the Esophagus, Gen. Thoracic Surg. Club. Home: 823 Lullwater Rd NE Atlanta GA 30307-1239 Office: The Emory Clinic 1365 Clifton Rd NE Atlanta GA 30322-1013 Office Phone: 404-778-3755. E-mail: kamal_mansour@emoryhealthcare.org.

MANSOUR, TAG ELDIN, pharmacologist, educator; b. Belkas, Egypt, Nov. 6, 1924; came to U.S., 1951, naturalized, 1956; s. Elsayed and Rokaya (Elzayat) M.; m. Joan Adela MacKinnon, Aug. 6, 1955; children—Suzanne, Jeanne, Dean. DVM, Cairo U., 1946; PhD, U. Birmingham, Eng., 1949, DSc, 1974. Lectr. U. Cairo, 1950-51; Fulbright instr. physiology Howard U., Washington, 1951-52; sr. instr. pharmacology Case Western Res. U., 1952-54; asst. prof., assoc. prof. pharmacology La. State U. Med. Sch., New Orleans, 1954-61; assoc. prof., prof. molecular pharmacology Stanford U. Sch. Medicine, 1961—, chmn. dept. pharmacology, 1977-91; Donald E. Baxter prof., 1977-98, prof. emeritus, 1999—. Cons. USPHS, WHO, Nat. Acad. Scis.; Mem. adv. bd. Med. Sch., Kuwait U.; Heath Clarke lectr. London Sch. Hygiene and Tropical Medicine, 1981 Author: Chemotherapeutic Targets in Parasites, 2002; contrbr. sci. articles to profl. jours. Commonwealth Fund fellow, 1965; Macy Found. scholar NIMR, London, 1982. Fellow AAAS; mem. Am. Soc. Pharmacology and Exptl. Therapeutics, Am. Soc. Biochemistry and Molecular Biology, Am. Heart Assn., Sierra Club, Stanford Faculty Club. Office: Stanford Sch Medicine Dept Molecular Pharm CCSR 269 Campus Dr Stanford CA 94305-5174

MANSOURI, LOTFOLLAH (LOTFI MANSOURI), retired performing company executive; b. Tehran, June 15, 1929; s. Hassan and Mehri (Jalili) M.; m. Marjorie Anne Thompson, Sept. 18, 1954; 1 child, Shireen Melinda. AB, UCLA, 1953. Asst. prof. UCLA, 1957-60; resident stage dir. Zurich Opera, 1960-65; chief stage dir. Geneva Opera, 1965-75; gen. dir. Can. Opera Co., Toronto, Ont., 1976-88, San Francisco (Calif.) Opera, 1988—2001, gen. dir. emeritus, 2001—; dramatic coach Music Acad. West, Santa Barbara, Calif., 1959; dir. dramatics Zurich Internat. Opera Studio, 1961-65, Centre Lyrique, Geneva, 1967-72; artistic adviser Tehran Opera, 1973-75; opera adviser Nat. Arts Centre, Ottawa, Ont., 1977; v.p. Opera America, 1979—. Operatic cons. dir. Yes, Giorgio, MGM, 1981; dir. opera sequence for film Moonstruck (Norman Jewison), 1987; stage dir. Fla. Grand Opera Mus. Acad. of West. Guest dir. opera cos. including Met. Opera, San Francisco Opera (70 prodns.), N.Y.C. Opera, Lyric Opera of Chgo., L.A. Opera, guest dir. opera cos. San Diego Opera, guest dir. opera cos. including Teatro Colon, Buenos Aires, Utah Opera, Canadian Opera Co. (30 new prodns.), Houston Grand Opera, La Scala, Covent Garden, Verona Opera, Kirov Opera, Australian Opera, Vienna Staatsoper, Vienna Volksoper, Salzburg Festival, Amsterdam Opera, Holland Festival, Nice (France) Opera, Festival D'Orange, France, Verona Arena Festival; co-author: An Operatic Life, 1982. Decorated chevalier Order Arts and Letters (France), 1992. Mem. Am. Guild Mus. Artists, Can. Actors Equity Assn. Achievements include initiating above-stage projection of subtitles as a simultaneous translation of opera, 1983. Office: Columbia Artists Management Llc 1790 Broadway # 6 New York NY 10019-1412 Home Phone: 415-386-3442; Office Phone: 415-387-9967. E-mail: lotfimansouri@hotmail.com.

MANSUETO, JOSEPH DANIEL, publisher; b. East Chicago, Ind., Sept. 3, 1956; s. Mario Daniel and Sara Wilda (Smart) M. BBA, U. Chgo., 1978, MBA, 1980. Securities analyst Harris Assocs., Chgo., 1983-84; founder, chmn., prin. Morningstar, Chgo., 1984—, CEO, 1984—96, 2000—. Named one of Forbes' Richest Americans, 2006; recipient Rosenthal Award for Excellence in Investment Research, Univ. Chgo., 1992, KPMG Peat Marwick High Tech Entrepreneur of Yr. award, 1993, Disting. Entrepreneurial Alumnus award, Univ. Chgo., 2000. Office: 225 W Wacker Dr Chicago IL 60606 Office Phone: 312-696-6000.

MANTEI, LORRAINE E., school system administrator; b. Albuquerque, Feb. 27, 1961; d. Chester T. and Ella Strange Mantei; m. Richard E. Tuck, July 6, 2001; m. Donald G. Keene (div.); children: Cassandra D. Keene, Pamela Preston, Kendall Keene, Daniel Keene. BS, U. So. Ind., Evansville, 1986; MEd, Tex. A&M U., Commerce, 1999. Tchr. Duncanville Ind. Sch. Dist., Tex., 1994—2000, Arlington Ind. Sch. Dist., Grand Prairie, 2000—02; asst. prin. Dallas Ind. Sch. Dist., 2002—05; supr., prin. La Academia de Estrellas Charter Sch., 2006—. Mem. arts commn. bd. City of DeSoto, 2004—; precinct chair Dallas Dem. Party, 2004—; v.p. DeSoto Dining & Dialogue, Tex., 2005—. Mem.: ASCD, Hispanic Woman's Network, Tex. Elem. Prins. and Suprs. Assn. Democrat. Avocations: reading, walking, travel.

MANTEL, ALLAN DAVID, lawyer; b. NYC, June 27, 1951; s. Bernard and Ruth (Weichman) M.; m. Janet Mantel, June 17, 1985; children: Bernard, Elizabeth. BA, NYU, 1973; JD, SUNY, Buffalo, 1976. Bar: N.Y. 1977, U.S. Dist. Ct. (so. and ea. dists.) N.Y. 1977. Assoc. Rosenthal & Herman P.C., NYC, 1977-82; ptnr. Rosenthal, Herman & Mantel, NYC, 1983-94, Hofheimer, Gartlir & Gross, LLP, NYC, 1995-98, Stein Riso Mantel LLP, NYC, 1999—. Fellow Am. Acad. Matrimonial Lawyers (NY chpt. pres. 2007-); mem. ABA (family law sect.), NY State Bar Assn. (equitable distbn. com.), Assn. Bar City NY (matrimonial law com.), NY County Lawyers Assn. (matrimonial law and comml. law sects.), Buffalo Law Sch. SUNY (dean's adv. counsel 2007-). Jewish. Office: Stein Riso Mantel LLP 405 Lexington Ave New York NY 10174-0002 Office Phone: 212-599-1515. Business E-Mail: allan.mantel@steinrisomantel.com.

MANTEL, SAMUEL JOSEPH, JR., management educator, consultant; b. Indpls., Nov. 17, 1921; s. Samuel Joseph and Beatrice Smith (Talmas) M.; m. Dorothy Jean Friedland, June 28, 1950 (dec. July 27, 2005); children— Michael Lee, Samuel Joseph, III, Margaret Irene, Elizabeth Baer. AB, Harvard U., 1948, MPA, 1950, PhD, 1952. Asst. prof. social sci. Ga. Inst. Tech., 1953-56; asst. prof., then assoc. prof. econs., dir. Econs.-in-Action program, Case Western Res. U., 1956-69; prof. mgmt. and quantitative analysis U. Cin., 1969-89, prof. emeritus quantitative analysis and ops. mgmt., 1989—, Joseph S. Stern prof. mgmt., 1973—89, prof. emeritus, 1989, exec. dir. Grad. Ctr. for Mgmt. of Advanced Tech. and Innovation, 1987—89, emeritus, 1989. Mgmt. cons., condr. mgmt. seminars. Author: Cases in Managerial Decisions, 1964, Project Management: A Managerial Approach, 1985, 6th edit., 2006, Operations Management for Pharmacists: Strategy and Tactics, 1992, Project Management in Practice 2d edit., 2005; contbr. chapters to books, articles to profl. jours. Vice pres. Jewish Fedn. Cin., 1978-80; past pres., life mem. Cin. Hillel Found., Cleve. Hillel Found.; historian Rockdale Temple, 1969-77; mem. mgmt. and adminstrn. com. Anti-Defamation League, B'nai B'rith, 1976; trustee Jewish Hosp., Cin., 1975-84, Sarah Marvin Found. for Performing Arts, 1990—; mem. mgmt. adv. com. Cin. Police Dept., 1991-92. Maj. USMCR, 1942-46, 51-53. Decorated D.F.C. with 2 oak leaf clusters, Air medal with 11 oak leaf clusters; Econs.-in-Action fellow, 1955; fellow Inst. Policy Rsch., 1980; named Prof. of Year, Delta Sigma Pi, 1974. Mem. IEEE, Project Mgmt. Inst., Iota Epsilon, Beta Gamma Sigma. Home: 608 Flagstaff Dr Cincinnati OH 45215-2525 Personal E-mail: mantelsj@email.uc.edu. E-mail: mantelsj@earthlink.net.

MANTELLO, JOSEPH, theater director; b. Rockford, Ill., Dec. 27, 1962; Studied acting, N.C. Sch. Arts, 1984; studied directing, Cir. Repertory Co. Co-founder Edge Theater, NYC, 1984. Dir.: (plays) Imagining Brad, 1989, Nebraska, 1991, Coq au Vin, 1991, Babylon Gardens, 1991, Three Hotels, 1993, Fat Men in Skirts, 1994, Blue Window, 1996, The Santaland Diaries, 1996, God's Heart, 1997, Schmucks, 1998, Lillian, 1998, Corpus Christi, 1998, Bash, 1999, The Mineola Twins, 1999—2000, The Vagina Monologues, 1999—2003, Another American: Asking & Telling, 1999, Assassins, 2001, A Man of No Importance, 2002; (Broadway plays) What's Wrong with the Picture?, 1994, Love! Valour! Compassion!, 1994—97 (Obie award), Proposals, 1997, Design for Living, 2001, Take Me Out, 2002 (Lucille Lortel award for outstanding dir., 2003, Drama Desk award nom. for outstanding dir. of a play, 2003, Tony award best dir. of a play, 2003), Frankie and Johnny in the Clair de Lune, 2002, Wicked, 2003—04 (Tony nom. best dir. of a musical, 2004, Drama Desk award best book of a musical, 2004), Assassins, 2004— (Tony award best dir. of a musical, 2004), Glengarry Glen Ross, 2005; actor: Angels in America, 1994 (Drama Desk award for best featured actor in a play, 1994). Recipient Outer Critics Cir. award, Helen Hayes award, Clarence Derwent award, Joe A. Callaway award. Office: Creative Artists Agy 9830 Wilshire Blvd Beverly Hills CA 90212

MANTEUFFEL, ROBERT LEE, lawyer; b. St. Francis, Kans., July 15, 1955; s. Walter Junior and Winnie Belle Manteuffel; m. Martha Ann Hatten, Mar. 8, 1980; children: Jessica Ann, Laura Alean. BA in Math. with distinction, Va. Mil. Inst., Lexington, 1977; MS in Ops. Rsch., USAF Inst. Tech., Wright-Patterson AFB, Ohio, 1985; JD, So. Meth. U., Dallas, 1991. Bar: Tex. 1991, US Dist. Ct. (no. dist.) Tex. 1992, US Dist. Ct. (so. dist.) Tex. 1994, US Dist. Ct. (ea. dist.) Tex. 1994, US Dist. Ct. (we. dist.) Tex. 1994. Commd. lt. US Army, 1977, advanced throug grades to capt., various positions Ft. Bliss, Tex., 1978—88; clk., atty. Bailey & Williams, Dallas, 1990—92; atty. Fowler, Wiles & Keith, LLP, Dallas, 1992—98, Kane Russell Coleman & Logan P.C., Dallas, 1998—. Mng. staff editor Southwestern Law Jour., 1990—91. Mem. adv. bd. West Dallas Youth and Family Ctr., 1995—2001. Named one of Outstanding Young Men of Am., 1985; recipient Mil. Parachute Badge, 1975, Silver medal for Army scholarship, Am. Legion, 1976, medal, Am. Vets. of WWII, 1977, John H. French medal, Va. Mil. Inst., 1977, Jackson-Hope medal (first honor), 1977, Army Svc. ribbon, 1977, Overseas Svc. ribbon, 1982, Army Commendation medal, 1982, Meritorious Svc. medal, 1988; Hatton W. Sumners scholar, So. Meth. U. and Hatton W. Sumners Found., 1988—91. Mem.: Dallas Bar Assn. (chair libr. com. 2002), State Bar Tex., Coll. State Bar Tex., Berkner Area Exch. Club (pres. club 2004—05), Rotary (bd. dirs. Dallas Market Ctr. club 2002—05), Kappa Alpha Order, Omega Rho, Va. Mil. Inst. Alumni Assn., Phi Delta Phi. Republican. Methodist. Avocations: music, reading, jogging, swimming, bicycling. Home: 4817 Copper Mountain Ln Richardson TX 75082 Office: Kane Russell Coleman & Logan PC 1601 Elm St Ste 3700 Dallas TX 75201 Office Fax: 214-777-4299. Business E-Mail: rmanteuffel@krcl.com.

MANTEY, ELMER MARTIN, food company executive; b. Malone, Tex., July 20, 1926; s. Edward G. and Margaret H. Mantey; m. Donna May Scritsmier, Dec. 27, 1948; children: Patricia Mantey Rooks, Carol Mantey Callis, Cynthia Mantey Stockdale. BS in Chemistry with honors, Bradley U., 1949. Chemist, plant mgr. Am. Petrochem. Co., Mpls., 1949—63, v.p. ops., 1963—66; v.p. Polychem. Group Whittaker Corp., LA, 1966—69, pres. textile divsn., 1969—71; CEO, pres., chmn. bd. dirs. Favorite Labs. Inc., Memphis, 1971—89; chmn. emeritus; bd. dirs. Craig Halum Corp., 1971—92. Bd. dirs. A.M. Todd Co., dir. emeritus; bd. dirs. The Dupps Co.; chmn. emeritus Chrichton Coll. Trustee John Brown U., 1991-2000. Served with USN, 1944-46. Mem.: Crescent Club, Rotary. Home: 3535 Kirby Rd Apt D 109 Memphis TN 38115-3713 Personal E-mail: emantey@aol.com.

MANTHE, CORA DE MUNCK, real estate company executive; b. Alton, Iowa, Oct. 10, 1928; d. Cornelius John and Bessie Bell (Miller) De Munck; m. Carl Robert Manthe, Apr. 5, 1952 (dec. Dec. 1987); children: Barry Paul, David Glenn. BA in Econs., U. Iowa, Iowa City, 1950; postgrad., U. Wis., Madison and Oshkosh, 1972-75; grad., Realtors Inst., 1983. Cert. residential appraiser. Rsch. analyst Dept. Def., Washington, 1951-52; social work investigator Dane County, Madison, 1960-62; civic hostess Welcome Wagon, Beaver Dam, Wis., 1963-70; real estate broker "C" Manthe Realty, Ltd., Beaver Dam, 1979—, property mgr., investment mgr., pres., treas., 1982—. Invited amb. World Forum Fedn., 2007. Deacon Grace Presbyn. Ch., 1974-77, elder, 1979-82, ruling elder, 1989-92; staff worker Kohl Senate Campaign, 1994; with Crystal Cathedral, 2005. Mem. AAUW (life), Beaver Dam C. of C., U. Iowa Alumni Assn. (life), Optimist Internat. (life). Avocations: bridge, golf, travel, reading. Home and Office: 404 Declark St Beaver Dam WI 53916-1714 *Attendance at meetings, classes, family reunions throughout the world has consumed time. The Crystal Cathedral California Hour of Power Television Ministry has been a participating meeting place for me since the early 70s. The International Platform Association in wAshington, D.C., featuring classes in Speech, Journalism, Art, Acting, etc. has been attended. Charitable work includes Optimist International and the American Association of University Women with their emphasis on Women's issues has taken time and endeavors.*

MANTHEI, RICHARD DALE, retired lawyer, health products executive; b. Olivia, Minn., Dec. 23, 1935; s. Alvin R. and Sidonia (Klatt) M.; m. Karen J. Peterson, Sept. 6, 1959 (dec. Mar. 1985); children: Steven, Jana, Kari, John, Rebecca; m. Lynn E. Graham, Aug. 9, 1986. BS in

Pharmacy (Rexall award 1960), S.D. State U., 1960; JD, U. Minn., 1967. Bar: DC 1987, US Supreme Ct. 1987. Sales rep. Eli Lilly & Co., Indpls., 1962-64, atty., 1967-70; atty., then asst. corp. sec., dir. regulatory affairs Am. Hosp. Supply Corp., Evanston, Ill., 1970-79, corp. sec., dep. gen. counsel, 1979-85; assoc. gen. counsel Baxter Travenol Labs., Deerfield, Ill., 1986-87; ptnr. Burditt, Bowles & Radzius, Washington, 1987-90, McKenna & Cuneo, Washington, 1990-96; sr. v.p. regulatory scis. C.R. Bard, Inc., Murray Hill, NJ, 1996-2000. Author articles in field.; Editorial adv. staff: Med. Devices and Diagnostic Industry, 1979. Mem. bd. edn. Libertyville H.S., 1984-87; mem. governing bd. Spl. Edn. Dist. of Lake County, Ill., 1985-87; trustee N.J. Ctr. for Visual Arts. With AUS, 1954-56. Mem. Health Industry Mfrs. Assn. (chmn. law sect. 1976), Health Industry Assn. (chmn. legal com. 1973), Am. Soc. Corp. Secs. (corp. practices com. 1983-88, group pres. 1985-86, Chgo. regional group 1986-87), D.C. Bar Assn., Univ. Club (Evanston, Ill., bd. dirs. 1984-86). Home: 11608 Stonewall Jackson Dr Spotsylvania VA 22553

MANTHEY, FRANK ANTHONY, physician, director; b. NYC, Dec. 2, 1933; s. Frank A.J. and Josephine (Roth) M.; m. Douglas Susan Falvey, Sept. 14 1958 (div. 1979, dec. 1989); children: Michael P., Susan M., Peter J.; m. Doris Jean Pulley, Oct. 11, 1979. BS, Fordham U., 1955; MD, SUNY, Syracuse, 1958. Diplomate Am. Bd. Anesthesiology, Am. Bd. Med. Examiners. Intern Upstate Med. Ctr., Syracuse, 1958-59; resident in anesthesiology Yale-New Haven Med. Ctr., 1962-64; physician Yale-New Haven Hosp., 1964-75; pvt. practice medicine Illmo, Mo., 1975-79; dir. Manthey Med. Clinic, Elkton, Ky., 1979—. Clin. instr. anesthesiology Yale U. Med. Sch., New Haven, 1964-69, asst. clin. prof. anesthesiology, 1969-75; cons. Conn. Dept. Aeros., Hartford, 1969-70; sr. med. examiner Fed. Aviation Adminstrn., Illmo, 1975-79. Contbr. articles to profl. jours. Chmn. gen. works Little Folks Fair, Guilford, Conn., 1967-71; mem. Rep. Town Com., Guilford, 1969-75; chmn. Guilford Sch. Bldg. Com., 1973-75; mem. Todd County (Ky.) Bd. of Health, 1999—. Capt. USAF (M.C.), 1956-62. Mem.: Flying Physicians Assn. (v.p. NE chpt. 1973—75, v.p. nat. 1974—75, 1979—80, bd. dirs. 1970—73, 1975—78, bd. dirs. nat. 1975—78), Aerospace Med. Assn. (assoc. fellow 1973—75), Ky. Med. Assn., Aircraft Owners and Pilots Assn., Mercedes Benz ClubAm., Alpha Kappa Kappa. Avocations: stamp collecting/philately, coin collecting/numismatics, aviation, auto restoration, skiing. Home: 105 Sunset Dr Elkton KY 42220-9257 Office: Manthey Family Practice Clinic 203 Allensville St PO Box 368 Elkton KY 42220-0368 Office Phone: 270-265-2531. Personal E-mail: giantsinky@earthlink.net.

MANTHEY, THOMAS RICHARD, lawyer; b. St. Cloud, Minn., May 5, 1942; s. Richard Jesse and Dolores Theresa (Terhaar) M.; m. Janet S. Barth, Dec. 18, 1965; children: Molly, Andrew, Luke. BA cum laude, St. John's U., Collegeville, Minn., 1964; JD cum laude, Harvard U., 1967. Bar: Minn. 1967. Assoc. Dorsey & Whitney, Mpls., 1967-73, ptnr. real estate dept., 1974—, also mem. Indian and gaming law practice group, chmn. real estate workout practice group. Contbr. articles to profl. jours. Capt. U.S. Army, 1968-70. Mem. Minn. State Bar Assn. (real estate sect.), Hennepin County Bar Assn. (real estate sect.). Roman Catholic. Avocations: volleyball, golf, fishing. Home: 9958 Wellington Ln Woodbury MN 55125-8459 Office: Dorsey & Whitney 50 S 6th St Ste 1500 Minneapolis MN 55402-1553

MANTIONE, KIRK JOHN, research scientist, consultant; b. Amityville, NY, Aug. 19, 1970; s. John and Kathleen Mantione; m. Michelle Ann McLoone, May 22, 1999; 1 child, Sydney Ann. MS, SUNY, Stony Brook, 2000. Sr. rsch. specialist SUNY Neuroscience Rsch. Inst., Old Westbury, 2000—. Cons. Kiernan Wellness Ctr., Rockaway Park, NY, 2003—. Recipient Promising Inventor award, NY State Rsch. Found., 2003. Achievements include patents for nitric oxide from plant products; endogenous morphine. Avocation: surfing. Home Phone: 631-475-5004.

MANTLE, RAYMOND ALLAN, lawyer; m. Judith Ann LaGrange, Nov. 26, 1967; children: Amanda Lee, Rachel Ann, Leah Amy. BSBA summa cum laude, BA summa cum laude, Kent State U., 1961; LLB cum laude, NYU, 1964. Bar: N.Y. 1964, N.J. 1976, Fla. 2005, U.S. Supreme Ct. Asst. counsel Gov. Nelson A. Rockefeller, NYC, 1964-65; assoc. Paul Weiss Rifkind Wharton & Garrison, 1967-69; mem. Varet & Fink P.C. (formerly Milgrim Thomajan & Lee, P.C.), NYC, 1969-95; ptnr. Piper & Marbury L.L.P., NYC, 1995-98; mem. Reitler Brown & Rosenblatt LLC (formerly Brock Silverstein, LLC), 1998—2003, counsel, 2004—06. Lectr. in computer law field. Contbr. author: Doing Business in China and Intellectual Property China, 1990—. Capt. US Army, 1965—67. Mem.: Fla. Bar, N.Y. State Bar Assn. (co-chmn. ann. meeting seminar on intellectual property 2000—05, co-chair intellectual property sect. internat. com. 2004—05, exec. com. intellectual property sect.). Republican. Methodist. Office: 4745 Sutton Park Ct Ste 602 Jacksonville FL 32224 Office Phone: 904-821-4885. Business E-Mail: rmantle@rmantlelaw.com.

MANTONYA, JOHN BUTCHER, lawyer; b. Columbus, Ohio, May 26, 1922; s. Elroy Letts and Blanche (Butcher) M.; m. Mary E. Reynolds, June 14, 1947 (dec. 1987); children: Elizabeth Claire, Mary Kay, Lee Ann; m. Carole L. Lugar, Sept. 28, 1989. AB cum laude, Washington and Jefferson Coll., 1943; postgrad., U. Mich. Law Sch., 1946—47; JD, Ohio State U., 1949. Bar: Ohio 1949. Assoc. A.S. Mitchell, Atty., Newark, Ohio, 1949—50, C.D. Lindrooth, Newark, 1950—57; ptnr. firm Lindrooth & Mantonya, Newark, 1957—74; firm John B. Mantonya, 1974—81, John B. Mantonya, L.P.A., 1981—. Mem. North Fork Local Bd. Edn., 1962-69; adv. com. Salvation Army, Licking County, 1965—, Mayor of Utica, Ohio, 1953-59. Served with AUS, 1943-45. Mem. ABA, Ohio Bar Assn., Licking County Bar Assn. (pres. 1967), Phi Delta Phi, Beta Theta Pi. Home: 11055 Reynolds Rd Utica OH 43080-9549 Office: 3 N 3rd St Newark OH 43055-5506 Business E-Mail: jb.mantonya@alltel.com.

MANTOVANI, JOHN F., pediatric neurologist; b. St. Louis, Jan. 17, 1949; s. John F. and Marinelle Mantovani; children: John R. and Ann Marie. BA cum laude, U. Evansville, 1971; MD, U. Mo., 1974. Diplomate Am. Bd. Pediat., Am. Bd. Psychiatry and Neurology in child neurology and in neurodevel. disabilities. Resident pediat., neurology, fellow child neurology Washington U.-St. Louis Children's Hosp., 1974-79; practitioner adult and child neurology Dean Clinic, Madison, Wis., 1979-84; dir. child neurology, vice chmn. dept. pediatrics St. John's Mercy Med. Ctr., St. Louis, 1984—; med. dir. St. John's Mercy Children's Hosp., St. Louis, 2006—. Clin. asst. prof. neurology U. Wis., Madison, 1980-84; instr. clin. pediatrics and neurology Washington U., 1985-95, asst. prof., 1995-99, assoc. prof., 1999—; vice chmn. neurodevel. disabilities com. Am. Bd. Psychiatry and Neurology. Mem. editl. bd., vice chmn. Dev. Med. and Child Neurology; Contbr. articles to profl. jours. Fellow Am. Acad. Pediatrics, Am. Acad. Cerebral Palsy and Devel. Medicine (bd. dirs. 1994-2003, v.p. 1997-98, pres.-elect 1999, pres. 2000); mem. AMA, Am. Acad. Neurology (vice chmn. Neurodevel. Disabilities Exam. com.), Child Neurology Soc., Alpha Omega Alpha. Office: St John's Mercy Med Ctr 621 S New Ballas Rd Ste 5009 Saint Louis MO 63141-8232

MANTSCH, HENRY HORST, chemistry professor; b. Mediasch, Transylvania, Romania, July 30, 1935; emigrated to Can., 1968; s. Heinrich Johann and Olga Augusta (Gondosch) M.; m. Amy Emilia Kory, Nov. 2, 1959; children: Monica, Marietta. BSc, U. Cluj, Transylvania, 1958, PhD, 1964. Rsch. scientist Romanian Acad. Sci., Cluj, 1958-65, Tech. U. Munich, Germany, 1966-68; with NRC, Ottawa, Can., 1968-72; prof. biochemistry U. Cluj, 1973-74, Liebig U., Giessen, Germany, 1975-76; head molecular spectroscopy NRC, Ottawa, 1977—; mem. Can. Rsch. Coun., Ottawa, 1977-91, Winnipeg, 1992—2002; sci. counsellor Can. Embassy, Berlin, 2002—. Adj. prof. Carleton U., Ottawa, 1978-90, U. Ottawa, 1990-92, U. Manitoba, Winnipeg, 1992—. Contbr. articles to profl. jours.; patentee in field. Recipient medal Ministry of Edn., Bucharest, 1972, Humboldt Found. medal Bonn, 1980, Herzberg award, 1984, Marcus Marci medal, 1998; Chem. Inst. Can. fellow, 1979, Royal Soc. Can. fellow, 1982. Mem. Am. Biophys. Soc., Soc. Applied Spectroscopy, Chem. Inst. Can. (chmn. biol. chem. divsn. 1980-81), Can. Spectroscopy Soc. (nat. exec. com. 1981-90), Can. Biophys. Soc. (sec. 1999—). Office: Can Embassy Leipziger Platz 17 10117 Berlin Germany E-mail: henry.mantsch@international.gc.ca.

MANTUANO, TONY, chef; Chef Dal Pescatore, Canetto Sul'Oglio, Italy, Albergo del Sole, Maleo, Italy, Al Bersagliere, Goito, Italy, Da Romano, Viareggio, Italy; owner, exec. chef Spiaggia, Chicago, 1984—, Tuttaposto; mgr. Mangia, Kenosha, Wis. Guest chef Celebrity Chef Tour, 2006. Co-author: The Spiaggia Cookbook: Eleganza Italiana in Cucina, 2004 (named one of 25 best cookbooks of 2004, Food & Wine Mag.); appearances include CNN, PBS, The Frank DeCaro Show, Food Talk with Rocco DiSirito. Nominee Best Chef: Midwest, James Beard Found., 2002, 2003, 2004; named, 2005; recipient Good Eating award, Chgo. Tribune. Office: Spiaggia 1 Magnificent Mile 980 N Mich Ave Level 2 Chicago IL 60611 *

MANTYLA, KAREN, distance learning consultant; b. Bronx, NY, Dec. 31, 1944; d. Milton and Sylvia (Diamond) Fischer; 1 child, Michael Alan. Student, Rockland C.C., Suffern, NY, 1962, NYU, 1967, Mercer U., 1981. Coord. mktg. Credit Bur., Inc., Miami, Fla., 1973—79; dist. mgr. Rsch. Inst. Am., NYC, 1979—80, regional dir., 1980—85, mgr. field sales, 1985—86, mgr. nat. sales, 1986—87, mgr. nat. accounts, 1989; v.p. sales Bur. Bus. Practice/Paramount Comm., Inc., Waterford, Conn., 1989—93; pres. Quiet Power, Inc., Washington, 1993—. Author: Consultative Sales Power, 1995, Interactive Distance Learning Exercises That Really Work, 1999, The 2000/2001 ASTD Distance Learning Yearbook, 2000, Blending e-Learning: The Power is in the Mix, 2001; co-editor The 2001/2002 ASTD Distance Learning Yearbook; co-author: Distance Learning: A Step-By-Step Guide for Trainers, 1997, Blending E-Learning: The Power is in the Mix, 2001. Bd. dirs. Federal Govt. Distance Learning Assn. Named to Distance Learning Hall of Fame, Fed. Govt. Distance Learning Assn., 2003. Mem. ASTD, Sales and Mktg. Execs. (past bd. dirs. N.Y. chpt., v.p. Ft. Lauderdale chpt. 1979), U.S. Distance Learning Assn. (editor Distance Learning News, mem. tech. and comm. com. Fla. chpt.), Nat. Assn. Women Bus. Owners, U.S. C. of C., Women Entrepreneurs. Avocations: antiques, tennis, writing, swimming. Office: Quiet Power Inc South Bldg Ste 900 601 Pennsylvania Ave NW Washington DC 20004-2401 Office Phone: 202-661-4646. Personal E-mail: quietpower@aol.com.

MANTZ, ARLAN W., physics professor; b. Slatington, Pa., July 25, 1940; s. Harold H. and Irene A. (Herber) M.; m. Barbara Dae Mantz, Dec. 28, 1963; 1 child, Yves Andre. BA, Catawba Coll., 1962; MSc, Ohio State U., 1966, PhD, 1969. Sr. scientist Air Force Avionics Lab., Ohio, 1966-73; postdoctoral fellow Labo Aime Cotton, Orsay, France, 1973-74; sr. scientist Digilab, Inc., Cambridge, Mass., 1974-76; engring. mgr. Laser Analytics Inc., Bedford, Mass., 1976-79, pres., gen. mgr., 1979-89; assoc. prof. Franklin and Marshall Coll., Lancaster, Pa., 1990-95; Oakes Ames prof. physics Conn. Coll., New London, 1995—. Editl. adv. bd. Spectrochemica Acta, 1990, revs. editor, 1995. Mem.: Am. Phys. Soc. Avocation: sailing. Office Phone: 860-439-5030. Business E-Mail: awman@conncoll.edu.

MANUEL, CHARLES B., JR., lawyer; b. Sept. 24, 1949; BA, Harvard U., 1971, JD, 1975. Bar: NY 1977, US Supreme Ct. 1982, US Dist. Ct. (so. & ea. dists.) NY 1978, US Ct. of Appeals 2nd cir. 1981, US Ct. Internat. Trade 1991, US Ct. of Appeals 1st 1998, US Ct. of Appeals 6th cir. 2004, US Dist. Ct. (no. dist.) NY. Mem. Morgan, Lewis & Bockius, NYC; ptnr. Manuel & Rosenfeld LLP. Office: Manuel & Rosenfeld LLP 350 5th Ave Empire State Bldg 59th Fl New York NY 10118 Office Phone: 212-601-2606. Office Fax: 212-601-2605.

MANUEL, CHARLIE (CHARLES FUQUA MANUEL JR.), professional baseball manager; b. Northfork, W.Va., Jan. 4, 1944; children: Charles Jr., Julie. Outfielder Minn. Twins, 1963-74; with LA Dodgers, 1974-75, Yakult Swallows and Kintetsu Buffaloes, Japan, 1976-81; scout Minn. Twins, 1982; mgr. class A Wisconsin Rapids, 1983; various coaching and mgr. positions, 1983-99; mgr. Cleve. Indians, 1999—2002; special asst. to gen. mgr. Phila. Phillies, 2003—04, mgr., 2004—. Inducted Salem-Roanoke Baseball Hall of Fame, 1995. Office: c/o Philadelphia Phillies 1 Citizens Bank Way Philadelphia PA 19148

MANUEL, PETER JAY, poet, singer/songwriter, dramatist, language professor, librettist; b. Framingham, Mass. s. John Lewis and Jane Dorothy (Bohlin) Manuel. BA English, U. So. Maine, 1982, MFA in Creative Writing, 2005. Adj. prof. English So. Maine CC, South Portland, 2003—. Organizer Geno's Live Poets' Soc., Portland, 2000—05, Word Cirkus, 2006—07. Mem. Trinity touring performance poetry act, 2002—05. Green Independent. Jewish. Avocation: art. Home: 312 Congress St # 4 Portland ME 04101 Office: So Maine C C 2 Fort Rd South Portland ME 04106 Office Phone: 207-741-5500. E-mail: pjm@gwi.net.

MANUEL, RALPH NIXON, retired private school executive; b. Frederick, Md., Apr. 21, 1936; s. Ralph Walter and Frances Rebecca (Nixon) M.; m. Sarah Jane Warner, July 22, 1960; children: Mark, David, Stephen, Bradley. AB, Dartmouth Coll., 1958; M.Ed., Boston U., 1967; PhD, U. Ill., 1971. Assoc. dean Dartmouth Coll., Hanover, NH, 1971-72, dean of freshmen, 1972-75, dean, 1975-82; pres. Culver (Ind.) Acad. and Culver Edn. Found., 1982-99. Bd. dirs. Ind. Sch. Cen. States, 1986-99, chair, 1993-95. Mem. Assn. Mil. Colls. and Schs. of U.S. (pres., bd. dirs.), Nat. Assn. Ind. Schs. (bd. dirs. 1995-99).

MANUEL, VIVIAN, public relations executive; b. Queens County, NY, May 6, 1941; d. George Thomas and Vivian (Anderson) M. BA, Wells Coll., 1963; MA, U. Wyo., Laramie, 1965. Mgmt. analyst Dept. Navy, 1966-68; account supr. GE Co., NYC, 1968-72, corp. rep. bus. and fin., 1972-76; dir. corp. comm. Standard Brands Co., NYC, 1976-78; pvt. cons. NYC, 1978-80; pres. V M Comm. Inc., NYC, 1980-97; pub. info. officer Mont. Dept. Commerce, Helena, 1997—2002; adminstr. Gough, Shanahan, Johnson & Waterman, Helena, 2003—04. Mem. com. Girls Club N.Y., 1983—84; mem. adv. bd. Glenholme Sch., 1991—92; mem. allocation com. United Way Mont., 1998—; bd. dirs. Am. Lung Assn. of No. Rockies, 1999—2002; trustee Wells Coll., 1983—90. Mem. AAUW, N.Y. Women in Comms. (bd. v.p. 1983-85, chair Matrix awards 1985), Women Execs. in Pub. Rels. (bd. dirs. 1985-88), Women's Econ. Roundtable. Address: 109 Oakwood Ln Helena MT 59601-6024

MANUELLA, FRANK, art and design educator; b. NYC; BFA, Cooper Union U., 1963; M in Comm. Design, Pratt Inst., 1982. Pres. Manuella & Assocs., NYC, 1963-82; prof. art & design U. Tex., Edinburg, 1982—. Asst. prof. design Pratt Inst., N.Y.C., 1975-82; adv. bd. U. Tex. Press, 1982—, coun. mem., 1989-92, officer Phi Kappa Phi, 1990-92, faculty senator, 1986-93. Solo exhbns. include U. Tex. Gallery, 1991, 92, Reynosa, Mex., 1993, McAllen Internat. Mus., 1994. Recipient gov.'s award for acad. excellence, State of Tex., 1989; Fulbright grantee, 1993. Office: U Tex Dept Art 1201 W University Dr Edinburg TX 78539-2909

MANVILLE, GRETA CRAIG, writer; b. Clarinda, Iowa, June 12, 1932; d. William Donald Craig and Eunice Catherine Nolan; m. Wallace Carruthers Manville, Jr., Feb. 1, 1953. BA, San Jose State U., 1975, MA, 1978. Asst. treas. Argonaut Ins. Co., Menlo Park, Calif., 1962-75; exec. mgr. quality control Consol. Freightways, Menlo Park, 1977-91; freelance writer Sun City West, Ariz., 1991—. Bd. dirs., lit. contest coord. Ariz. Authors Assn., 2006—. Author: The Man on the Train, 1994 (3rd prize S.W. Writers Workshop 1994), Murder On-Line, 1998, Death Key, 2000; co-author: The Purgatory Trail, 1993 (1st prize S.W. Writers Workshop 1993), Death Key, 2000 (1st place mystery/suspense category Authorlink website New Authors Awards Competition, 2000); author (poetry) Passage, 1999 (Grand prize Sparrowgrass Poetry Forum, 1999). SteinbeckFellowship, San Jose State U., 2002—03. Mem. AAUW (newsletter editor Sun City West br. 1999-2000, 06-07). Republican. Methodist. Avocations: duplicate bridge, golf. Personal E-mail: gmanville@aol.com.

MANVILLE, STEWART ROEBLING, archivist; b. White Plains, NY, Jan. 15, 1927; s. Leo and Margaret (Roebling) Manville; m. Ella V. Grainger, Jan. 19, 1972 (dec.). Student, U. Wyo., 1944-46; BS, Columbia U., 1962. Various office positions, NYC, 1947-51, 56-58; asst. stage dir. several European opera houses, 1951-55; editor Jas. T. White & Co., 1959-63; archivist, curator Percy Grainger Library, White Plains, 1963—. Author: The Manville/Manvel Families in America; contbr. articles to mags. and newspapers. Mem.: SAR, Archivists Round Table Met. NY, St. Nicholas Soc. NY, Westchester Trails Assn. (pres. 2001—05), Brit. Music Soc., Société des Antiquaires de Picardie, Victorian Soc. Am. (past. dir. N.Y. chpt.), Nat. Trust Hist. Preservation. Mem. Soc. Of Friends. Office: 7 Cromwell Pl White Plains NY 10601-5005 Office Phone: 914-948-7436.

MANYAK, MICHAEL JOHN, urologist, educator, researcher; b. Flint, Mich., Mar. 25, 1951; m. Rebecca Bruning; children: Rachel, Susannah, Timothy. BA, U. Notre Dame, 1973; MD, U. of East, Manila, 1979. Intern, then resident in gen. surgery Booth Meml. Med. Ctr., Flushing, N.Y., 1980-82; resident in urology George Washington Univ. Med. Ctr., Washington, 1982-84, chief resident, 1984—85, instr. urology, 1988—89, asst. prof., 1989—91, assoc. prof., 1991—95, prof. urology engring. microbiology and tropical medicine, 1996—; v.p. med. affairs Cxtogen Corp., 2005—. Mem. adv. bd. Nat. Kidney and Urological Disease, 1992—. Contbr. articles to profl. jours. Adv. bd. aerospace medicine NASA. Fellow Nat. Cancer Inst., 1985-88; scholar Am. Urol. Assn., 1986-88. Fellow Explorers Club (nat. bd. dirs. 1996-06, chmn. sci. adv. bd., Sweeney medal); mem. Internat. Soc. Cryptozoology (field med. advisor), Am. Urol. Assn. (chmn. tech. coun. 1995). Office: Cytogen Corp 650 Coll Rd U St Princeton NJ 08540 Office Phone: 609-750-8281. Business E-Mail: mmanyak@cytogen.com.

MANYAM, BALA VENKATESHA, medical researcher, neurology educator; arrived in US, 1972, naturalized, 1980; s. Kolar Venktesha and Swarnam (Venktesha) Iyer; m. Rani Manyam; 1 child, Shaila. MB, BS, Bangalore Med. Coll., 1967. Diplomate Am. Bd. of Psychiatry and Neurology. With Thomas Jefferson U., Phila., 1975-83, 83-84, asst. prof. pharmacology, 1981-83, assoc. prof. pharmacology, 1983-84; staff neurologist VA Med. Ctr., Wilmington, Del., 1975-80, asst. chief neurology, 1982-84; assoc. prof. neurology Sch. of Medicine So. Ill. U., Springfield, 1984-92, prof., 1992—99, dir. neurology residency program, 1993—99; prof., dir. Plummar Movement Disorder Ctr., Scott & White Clinic, Tex. A&M U. HSC Coll. Medicine, 1999—2005; disting. rsch. prof. Hindu U. of Am., 2006—. Founding dir. Parkinson's Disease & Movement Disorders Clinic, Springfield, 1984—99; mem. NIH/NCCAM Coun., 2004—; adj. prof. neurology SI U. Sch. Medicine. Contbr. numerous articles to profl. jours.; mem. editl. bd. Phytotherapy Rsch., patentee in field. Grantee NIH, VA, various founds. Fellow Am. Acad. Neurology; mem. Am. Neurologic Assn. Hindu. Achievements include research in drug development from herbs for neurological diseases; patents in field. Avocations: creative writing, history of medicine, collecting old coins and stamps, photography, Indian art.

MANZ, CHARLES CRAIG, management educator; BA, Mich. State U., 1974, MBA, 1975; PhD, Penn State U., 1981. Nirenberg prof. bus. leadership U. Mass., Amherst, 1997—. Author: The Art of Self-Leadership: Strategies for Personal Effectiveness in Your Life and Work, 1983, Mastering Self-Leadership: Empowering Yourself for Personal Excellence, 1992, 4th edit., 2007, The Power of Failure: 27 Ways to Turn Life's Setbacks Into Success, 2002, Emotional Discipline: The Power to Choose How You Feel, 2003; co-author: Superleadership, 1990, Business Without Bosses: How Self-Managing Teams are Building High-Performance Companies, 1993, Company of Heroes: Unleashing the Power of Self-Leadership, 1996, For Team Members Only, 1997, The Leadership Wisdom of Jesus: Practical Lessons for Today, 1998, 2005, Teamwork and Group Dynamics, 1999, The Wisdom of Solomon at Work: Ancient Virtues for Living and Leading Today, 2001, The New Super Leadership: Leading Others to Lead Themselves, 2001, Fit to Lead: The Proven 8-Week Solution for Shaping Up Your Body, Your Mind and Your Career, 2004, Temporary Sanity: Instant Self-Leadership Strategies for Turbulent Times, 2005, The Greatest Leader Who Wasn't: A Leadership Fable, 2005. Office: U Mass Sch of Mgmt Amherst MA 01003

MANZANARES, J. ROBERT, ambassador; b. Colo. BA, Adams State Coll., Alamosa, Colo.; MPA in City Adminstrn., U. Colo., Boulder. Regional mgmt. officer US Dept. State, Abidjan, Cote d'Ivoire, mgmt. officer Mexico City, Reykjavik, Iceland, acting dep. chief of mission, mgmt. counselor Tel Aviv, advance officer for presdl. internat. visits Adminstrns. of Pres. Ronald Reagan and Pres. George H.W. Bush, sr. watch officer Ops. Ctr., dir. adminstrn. NSC, 1993—94, exec. dir. Bur. African Affairs, 1998—2000, exec. dir. to exec. secretariat Office of Sec. of State Colin Powell, dep. chief of mission, charge d'Affaires US Embassy Spain, 2003—06, acting nat. coord. for the Summits of the Ams., acting permanent US rep. to OAS, 2007—. Office: Bur Western Hemisphere Affairs US Dept State Rm 5914 2201 C St NW Washington DC 20520 Office Phone: 202-647-9422. *

MANZANARES, LAWRENCE, city attorney; b. Colo. BA, U. Denver, 1979; JD, Harvard Law Sch., 1982. Private practice atty., corp. law comml. litig., 1982—92; judge Denver Co. Ct., 1992—98; appointed Denver District Ct. Bench, 1998—2007; city atty. City of Denver, 2007—. Mem. bd. dir. Colo. Hispanic Bar Assn., Colo. I Have A Dream Found.; former bd. mem., pres. Latin Am. Rsch. Svc. Agy. Mem. Citizens Budget Task Force Denver Publ. Schs. Recipient Judicial Excellence award, Denver Bar Assn. Office: City Attys Office Rm 353 1437 Bannock St Denver CO 80202

MANZARI, LAURA LYNN, law educator; b. NYC, Jan. 4, 1959; d. Charles John and Rose Marie (Lepik) Slepetis; m. Peter Michael Manzari, Aug., 19, 1988. BA, Queen's Coll., 1979, MLS, 1986; JD, St. John's U., 1982. Bar: N.Y. 1983. Claim atty. Allstate Ins. Co., Lake Success, N.Y., 1984-85; law libr. Parker Chapin Flattau & Klimpl, NYC, 1985; libr. Pace U., NYC, 1987-89; assoc. prof. L.I. U., Greenvale, 1989—, dept. head Libr. and Info. Sci. Libr., 2000—. Contbr. articles to profl. jours. Mem. ALA, AAUW, Greater N.Y. Assn. Coll. and Rsch. Librs., Nassau County Libr. Office: LI U B Davis Schwartz Meml Libr Greenvale NY 11548 Business E-Mail: manzari@liu.edu.

MANZO, EDWARD DAVID, lawyer; b. NYC, 1950; BS in Physics, Poly. Inst. Bklyn., 1972; JD cum laude, SUNY, Buffalo, 1975. Bar: N.Y. 1976, Ill. 1979, U.S. Patent and Trademark Office 1976, U.S. Ct. Appeals (fed. cir.) 1982, U.S. Supreme Ct. 1982. Assoc. Darby & Darby, P.C., NYC, 1975-77; group patent counsel Schlumberger Ltd., NYC, 1977-79; ptnr. Cook, Wetzel & Egan, Chgo., 1979-85, 88-90, Jenner & Block, 1985-88; sr. ptnr. Cook McFarron & Manzo, Ltd., Chgo., 1990-99; sr. ptnr., exec.

v.p., treas., CFO Cook, Alex, McFarron, Manzo, Cummings & Mehler, Ltd., Chgo., 1999—. Instr. DePaul U., Chgo., 1989-91, 2002-03; mem. adv. bd. DePaul Law Sch., 2002—. Author (with others); Intellectual Property Law in Illinois, 1988-90; editor-in-chief Claim Constrn. in Fed. Cir., 2006, 07; contbr. articles to profl. jours. Bd. dirs. Concertante di Chgo., 1997-2004; Lake Forest Symphony, 2004-; grantor Edward Manzo Patent Law scholarship DePaul Law Sch., 2001-03, Law Lectures, 2004-06. Jaeckle Fleishman grantee, 1973. Mem. Am. Intellectual Property Law Assn., Intellectual Property Law Assn. Chgo. (chmn. litigation com. 2002-05, bd. mgrs. 2005-07, chmn. membership com. 2007—), Stradivari Soc., Sicilian Am. Cultural Assn. (treas. 1996-98, v.p. 1998-99, pres. 2000-02) Office: Cook Alex McFarron Manzo Cummings & Mehler Ltd 200 W Adams St Ste 2850 Chicago IL 60606-5206 Office Phone: 312-236-8500. Business E-Mail: emanzo@cookalex.com.

MANZULLO, DONALD A., congressman, lawyer; b. Rockford, Ill., Mar. 27, 1944; s. Frank A. Sr. and Catherine M.; m. Freda Teslik; children: Neil, Noel, Katie. BA in Polit. Sci./Internat. Rels., American U., 1967; JD, Marquette U. Law Sch., 1971. Atty., 1970—; mem. U.S. Congress from 16th Ill. Dist., 1993—. Mem. House Com. on Internat. Rels., subcom. internat. econ. policy and trade, subcom. on Asia and the Pacific, House Com. on small bus., chmn. on subcom. on tax, fin. and exports, Banking Com. and its capital markets, securities and govt.-sponsored enterprises subcom. Mem. No. Ill. Alliance for Arts, Friends of Severson Dells, Citizens Against Govt. Waste, Rep. Nat. Com. Recipient George Washington honor medal for excellence in pub. comm. Freedoms Found., Valley Forge, Pa., 1991. Mem. ABA, Ill. Bar Assn., Ogle County Bar Assn. (pres. 1971, 73), Nat. Legal Found., Acad. Polit. Sci., Ill. Press Assn., Ill. C. of C., Oregon City C. of C., Nat. Land Inst., Nat. Fedn. Ind. Bus., Ogle County Hist. Soc., Aircraft Owners and Pilots Assn., Ogle County Pilots Assn., Ill. Farm Bur., Ogle County Farm Bur. Republican. Office: US House Reps 2228 Rayburn House Office Bldg Washington DC 20515-1316 *

MAO, AIWU, physician, radiologist; b. Shanghai, June 1956; s. Zhen Long Mao and Peifang Shi; m. Feng Ping Zhou; 1 child, Yiming. MD, Shanghai Secondary Mil. Med. U. Internship Shanghai Tian Shan Hosp., 1976—77; resident St. Luke's Hosp., 1982—87; asst. dir., attending physician Xian Xia Hosp.; dep. dir. St. Luke's Hosp., dep. dir. The Interventional Dept. Prof. Shanghai Secondary Med. Sch., Shanghai Worker's Med. Sch.; cons. YueYang Hosp., Rui Jing Hosp. Editor: Interventional Radiology-Non Vascular, Chinese Med. Jour. of the Lenient Treatment of Cancer, Jour. of Interventional Radiology, International Therapy of Cancer; contbr. articles to profl. jours. Named Top Ten Physicians of Shanghai, 2004; recipient Progress of Sci. and Tech. of Shanghai award, The Shanghai People's Gov., 1999, 2000, 2001, 2002, Outstanding Person of Health, Dept. China, 2003, Outstanding Specialist, Shanghai, 2003. Mem.: The Chinese Anti-Cancer Assn. Achievements include patents in field. Avocations: music, travel.

MAO, HO-KWANG (DAVE MAO), geophysicist, educator; b. Shanghai, June 18, 1941; arrived in US, 1964, naturalized, 1976; s. Sen and Tak-chun (Hu) M.; m. Agnes Liu, Feb. 10, 1968; children: Cynthia, Linda, Wendy. BS, Nat. Taiwan U., Taipei, 1963; MS, U. Rochester, NY, 1966, PhD, 1968. Rsch. asst., tchg. asst. U. Rochester, 1964-67, rsch. assoc., 1967-68; postdoctoral fellow Carnegie Instn. Geophys. Lab., Washington, 1968-70, rsch. assoc., 1970-72, geophysicist, 1972—. Mem. physics adv. com. Lawrence Livermore Nat. Lab., Calif., 1999—; dir. Nat. Rsch. Ctr. High Pressure Jilin U., China, 2001—; vis. prof. dept. geophys. scis. and James Franck Inst. U. Chgo., 2001—; Guangbiao Chair prof. Zhejiang U., China, 2005—; Einstein prof. Chinese Acad. Scis., 2005—. Recipient P.W. Bridgman Gold Medal award Internat. Assn. for Advancement of High Pressure Sci. and Tech., 1989, Gregori Aminoff prize Royal Swedish Acad. Sci., 2005, Balzan prize, Italy and Switzerland, 2005. Fellow Am. Geophys. Union (Inge Lehmann medal 2007), Am. Phys. Soc., Geochemical Soc., European Assn. Geochemistry, Mineral. Soc. Am. (award 1979, Roebling medal 2005); mem. AAAS, NAS (Arthur L. Day prize and lectureship 1990), Academia Sinica, Chinese Acad. Scis. (fgn.), Sigma Xi. Office: Carnegie Instn Geophys Lab 5251 Broad Branch Rd NW Washington DC 20015-1305 Office Phone: 202-478-8960. Office Fax: 202-478-8901. E-mail: mao@gl.ciw.edu. *

MAO, LI, molecular biologist, educator; b. Nanjing, China, July 16, 1957; s. Xiqiu Mao and Yihe Huang; m. Jialing Xu, Dec. 25, 1982; children: Melissa Shanshan, Roger Tiger. MD, Nanjing Med. U., China, 1977—82. Diplomate China, 1982. Attending surgeon Nanjing Med. U. Hosp., China, 1989—95; rsch. fellow Johns Hopkins Med. Sch., Balt., 1992—95; asst. prof., medicine U. Tex., M.D. Anderson Cancer Ctr., Houston, 1995—99, assoc. prof., medicine, 1999—2004, prof., medicine, 2004—; exec. v.p., chief tech. officer Cangen Internat., Irvine, Calif., 2001—02. Advisor Panacea Pharmaceuticals, Washington, 2003—. Mem.: AACR (corr.). Office: Univ Texas MD Anderson Cancer Ctr Unit 432 PO Box 301402 Houston TX 77230-1402 Home Phone: 713-668-3815; Office Phone: 713-792-6363. Office Fax: 713-796-8655. E-mail: lmao@mdanderson.org.

MAO, RUIXUAN (RICK MAO), dean; arrived in US, 1986; s. Junye Mao and Wenhua Wu; m. Mi Hu, Oct. 6, 1980; m. Kangquan Zhou, Nov. 15, 1967 (div. May 9, 1980); children: Shufan, Guxia, Guyang Alex. BS, S.W. China Teachers U., Chongqing, 1964; MS, U. Tenn., Knoxville, 1986, PhD, 1993. Asst. prof. to assoc. prof. English S.W. China Teachers U., Chongqing, Sichuan, China, 1964—86; grad. asst. U. Tenn., Knoxville, 1986—89, instr. Chinese, 1989—90, grad. tchg. asst., 1990—92; asst. prof. English and coord. English edn. Philander Smith Coll., Little Rock, 1992—95, chair of divsn. of edn., assoc. prof. of edn., 1995—98; assoc. dir. instl. rsch. and planning The Ross Sch., East Hampton, NY, 1998—2002; dean liberal arts and social sci. Elgin C.C., Ill., 2002—05, dean comms. and behavioral sci., 2005—. Dir. instn. and rsch. srs. S.W. China Teachers U., Chongqing, 1982—86, dir. internship program, 1982—86; English editor natural sci. series S.W. China Teachers U. Jour., 1979—86; translator Chinese edit. Sci. Am. Jour., 1980—85; editor Internat. Edn. Jour., Knoxville, Tenn., 1986—. Editor: (textbooks) English (Volumes I-VIII), 1973—75, Tunnel English (Volumes 1-3), 1974, Teacher's Manual for English (Volumes 1-6), 1976. Recipient Multicultural Presentation award, Little Rock Dist. U.S. Army Corps of Engrs., 1993, Extraordinary Contbn. award, The Ross Sch., 2002; grantee, Ark. State Dept. Higher Edn., 1995—98, Ill. C.C. Bd., 2003—, Historically Black Colls.and Univs., 1997; Hilton A. Smith fellow, U. Tenn., Knoxville, 1988—89. Mem.: Rotary (Elgin Breakfast chpt.). Avocations: bridge, ping pong/table tennis. Office: Elgin CC 1700 Spartan Dr Elgin IL 60123 Home Phone: 847-742-1443; Office Phone: 847-214-7455. Office Fax: 847-622-3048. Business E-Mail: rmao@elgin.edu.

MAO, WEIDONG, communications engineer, technology executive; arrived in U.S., 1986; BS, Beijing U., 1986; PhD in Elec. Engring., Princeton U., NJ, 1991. Sr. mem. rsch. staff Philips Electronics, Briarcliff Manor, NY, 1990—94; dir. telecom. unit Gen. Instrument, Horsham, Pa., 1994—97; co-founder, chief tech. officer MoreCom, Horsham, 1997—2000; v.p. tech. Liberate Tech., San Carlos, Calif., 2000—03; fellow Comcast, Phila., 2003—. Key contbr. Moving Picture Expert Group, 1990—96; invited spkr. Nat. Cable TV Assn., 2004; panelist Cable TV Labs., 2004. Wallace Meml. fellowship, Princeton U., 1989—90. Mem.: Soc. Motion Picture and TV Engrs., Soc. Cable Telecomm. Engrs., IEEE. Achievements include invention of digital TV system with synchronized www content; channel changer in a switched video system; apparatus and method for web-casting over digital TV; pioneer of digital cable, video on demand, and interactive television. Office: Comcast Cable 1500 Market St Philadelphia PA 19102 Business E-Mail: weidong_mao@cable.comast.com.

MAPEL, DOUGLAS WAYNE, epidemiologist, educator, pulmonologist, critical care specialist; b. Torrejon U.S. AFB, Madrid, Spain, Apr. 14, 1961; m. Cynthia Caruso-Mapel; children: Xena, Sierra. BS in Chemistry, U. Tex., Arlington, 1984; MD, U. Tex., Galveston, 1988; MPH, U. N.Mex., 1996. Diplomate Am. Bd. Internal Medicine, Am. Bd. Pulmonary Diseases, Am. Bd. Critical Care Medicine. Resident Tex. Tech. U., Lubbock, 1988—92; fellow U. N.Mex., Albuquerque, 1992—96, asst. prof., 1996—2000, clin. prof., 2001—; med. dir. Lovelace Respiratory Rsch. Inst., Albuquerque, 2001—03, Lovelace Clinic Found., Albuquerque, 2003—; sr. ptnr. Progressive Med. Intensivists, 2003—06; founding ptnr. Critical Care Cons. of Ariz., 2006—. Co-author: (book) Rom's Occupational Medicine, 1998, Occupational Disorders of the Lung, 2001; contbr. articles to profl. jours., scientific papers. Fellow: Am. Coll. Chest Physicians (Clin. Rsch. award 2004); mem.: ACP, Am. Thoracic Soc. Home: PO Box 67050 Albuquerque NM 87193 Office: Lovelace Clin Found 2309 Renard Pl SE Ste 103 Albuquerque NM 87106 Office Phone: 505-262-7857. Business E-Mail: doug@lcfresearch.org.

MAPEL, PATRICIA JOLENE, farmer, consultant; b. Lake City, Iowa, June 24, 1933; d. John Gilbert and Blanche Evelyn (Taylor) Sharkey; m. J.R. Mapel, Sept. 1, 1952 (dec. 1992); children: Pati Jo, Mark L., Grant L., Penelope R., Kay Collene. Student, Wesley Meml. Hosp. Sch. of Nursing, 1951-52. Ptnr. farming, Lake City, Iowa, 1953-92; ptnr., pres. Mapel Farms Ethanol, Inc., Lake City, Iowa, 1984-92; house dir. Delta Delta Delta Simpson Coll., Indianola, Iowa, 1993-2001, 2002—. Cons. Dept. of Energy, Kansas City, 1981; demonstrator, educator Iowa Cen. Community Coll., Ft. Dodge, Iowa. Contbr. articles to profl. jours. Bd. dirs. Cen. Sch. Preservation, Inc., Lake City, 1984-90. Mem. Entre Nous Music Club, Eastern Star. Democrat. Mem. Ch. of Christ. Avocations: sewing, leathercraft. Home: 705 N C St Indianola IA 50125-1274 also: 3046 21st Ave N Fort Dodge IA 50501-7370

MAPEL, WILLIAM MARLEN RAINES, retired bank executive; b. Maryville, Mo., Sept. 17, 1931; s. William and Evelyn (Raines) M.; m. Gail Manchee, June 21, 1958; children: Daniel B., Susan L., Stephen W. BA, Yale U., 1953. Indsl. relations asst. Union Carbide Corp., NYC, 1953-57; with Citibank (N.A.), NYC, 1957-88, asst. cashier, 1959-62, asst. v.p., 1962-64, v.p., 1964-69, sr. v.p., 1969-88. Bd. dirs. Atlantic Salmon Fedn., Que.-Labrador Found. Bd. Miramichi Salmon Assn. Mem. U.S. Srs. Golf Assn., Wentworth-By-The-Sea Country Club, Pine Valley Golf Club, Anglers Club, Wolf's Head, Delta Kappa Epsilon. Home: PO Box 2063 New Castle NH 03854

MAPES, GLYNN DEMPSEY, newspaper editor; b. NYC, July 15, 1939; s. John George and Dorothy (Glynn) M.; m. Elizabeth Adlum, Apr. 13, 1963; children— Timothy Glynn, Susannah Glynn. BA, Williams Coll., 1961. Reporter Wall St. Jour., San Francisco, 1965-67, bur. chief Phila., 1967-70, fgn. editor NYC, 1970-71, bur. chief, 1971-75, Page One editor, 1975-88, Reports editor, 1988-89, bur. chief London, 1989-93, money and investing editor NYC, 1993-99, asst. mgn. editor, 1999—. Bd. dirs., singer Bronx Opera Co. Lt. (j.g.) USN, 1961—65. Mem.: London Concert Choir, Collegiate Chorale. Democrat. Home: 37 W 12th St Apt 2H New York NY 10011-8503 Office: Wall St Jour 200 Liberty St New York NY 10281-1003 E-mail: gmapes@pipeline.com.

MAPES, WILLIAM RODGERS, JR., lawyer; b. Cleve., Nov. 29, 1952; s. William R. and Marian (Atkins) M. BS in Bus. Adminstrn., Miami U., Oxford, Ohio, 1974; JD, Am. U., 1977. Bar: D.C. 1978, U.S. Ct. Appeals (D.C. cir.) 1979, U.S. Ct. Appeals (fed. cir.) 1980, U.S. Ct. Appeals (5th cir.) 1981, U.S. Supreme Ct. 1982, U.S. Ct. Appeals (3d cir.) 1985, U.S. Ct. Appeals (4th cir.) 1987, U.S. Ct. Appeals (6th cir.) 1988. Ptnr. Ross, Marsh & Foster, Washington, 1984—2000, Duane Morris, Washington, 2000—05, Duncan, Weinberg, Genzer & Pembroke, Washington, 2005—. Bd. dirs. Holy Land Christian Ecumenical Found., 1999-2004. Mem. ABA (editor nat. resources sect. newsletter 1984-89), Energy Bar Assn. Avocations: boating, tennis, bicycling. Home: 5714 Greenlawn Dr Bethesda MD 20814-1828 Office: Duncan Weinberg Genzer Pembroke 1615 M St NW #800 Washington DC 20036 Home Phone: 301-530-0275; Office Phone: 202-467-6370. Business E-Mail: wrm@dwgp.com.

MAPES, WILLIAM W., auditor; b. July 19, 1958; AAS, Genesee CC, Batavia, NY, 1987; degree in bus. mgmt., SUNY; BSc, Empire State Coll., Saratoga Springs, NY, 1997. Cert. govt. auditing profl., Inst. Internal Auditors. Intelligence ops. US Army and Army Res., various cities, 1979—82; sr. acct. NY State Edn. Dept., Albany, NY, 1994—2000; sr. auditor Office State Comptroller, Albany, 2000—07. Co-author: Anatomy of a Scandal, 2005 (award, 2005), Medicaid Reimbursements to School Districts, 2006 (award, 2006). Recipient Various awards Op. Desert Storm, US Army, S.W. Asia, 1991. Mem.: Assn. Govt. Accts., Am. Mensa.

MAPLE, M. BRIAN, physics professor; b. Nov. 20, 1939; BS in Physics with distinction, San Diego State U., 1963, AB in Math with distinction, 1963; MS in Physics, U. Calif., San Diego, 1965, PhD in Physics, 1969. Asst. rsch. physicist U. Calif., San Diego, 1969—75, asst. prof. physics, 1973—75, assoc. prof. physics, 1975—81, prof. physics, 1981—90, assoc. rsch. physicist Inst. for Theoretical Physics Santa Barbara, 1980, Bernd T. Matthias endowed chair in physics San Diego, 1990—, dir. Ctr. Interface and Materials Sci., 1990—; Bernd T. Matthias scholar Ctr. for Materials Sci. Los Alamos Nat. Lab., N.Mex., 1993; dir. Inst. for Pure and Applied Phys. Scis. U. Calif., 1995—, chair dept. physics, 2004—, disting. prof. physics, 2005—. Vis. scientist U. Chile, Santiago, 1971, 1973; vis. prof. Inst. de Fisica Jose Balseiro, San Carlos de Bariloche, Argentina, 1974; lectr. in field; mem. rev. com. materials sci. and tech. divsn. Argonne Nat. Lab., 1983-90, chmn., 1987; mem. rev. com. Office of Basic Energy Scis. Rev. of the Materials Sci. Program at Lawrence Livermore Nat. Lab., 1985; mem. exec. com. High Flux Isotope Reactor User's Group, Oak Ridge Nat. Lab., 1984-91; mem. user's com. Francis Bitter Nat. Magnet Lab., 1984-87; mem. rev. com. materials scis. program rev. Ames Lab., 1990-93; mem. scientific adv. bd. CONNECT, 1990—; mem. adv. coun. Glenn T. Seaborg Inst. for Transactinium Sci. Lawrence Livermore Nat. Lab., 1991—. Co-editor: Applied Physics A, 1983-93, Superconductivity in d- and f-Band Metals, 1980, Valence Fluctuations in Solids, 1982, Superconductivity in Ternary Compounds, Vols. 32, 34, 1982, Proceedings of the Internat. Conf. on Strongly Correlated Electron Sys., 1994; guest editor Spl. Issue of Materials Rsch. Soc. Bulletin on High Tc Superconductors, 1989, 2d Spl. Issue of Materials Rsch. Soc. Bulletin on High Tc Superconductors, 1990, Handbook on the Physics and Chemistry of Rare Earths, Vols. 30, 31, High Temperature Superconductors, 2001; mem. editl. bd. Superconductivity Review. Recipient Lockheed Leadership scholarship, 1958-60, Rotary Club scholarship, 1958-60, Calif. State scholarship, 1961-62, John Simon Guggenheim Meml. Found. fellowship, 1984, Disting. Alumnus of Yr. award U. Calif., San Diego, 1987, Disting. Alumnus of Yr. award San Diego State U. Coll. Scis., 1988; inducted into Chula Vista HS Hall of Fame, 1990; Bernd T. Matthias Endowed Chair in Physics 1990; Bernd T. Matthias prize, Internat. Conf. on Materials and Mechanisms of Superconductivity and High Temperature Superconductors, 2000; hon. prof. Trzebiatowski Inst. for Low Temperature and Structure Rsch., Polish Acad. of Sci., 2006. Fellow AAAS (Alexander v. Humboldt Rsch. award, Germany 1998, Frank H. Spedding award 1999), Am. Physical Soc. (various positions selection com. for internat. prize on new materials, 1982-91, mem. exec. com. divsn. condensed matter physics 1985-89, vice-chmn. to chmn. divsn. 1986-88, mem. com. on mtgs. 1992-96, David Adler Lectureship award 1996, James C. McGroddy prize for New Materials 2000); mem. National Academy of Sciences, Am. Vacuum Soc., Materials Rsch. Soc., Calif. Catalysis Soc., Nat. Acad. Sci. (elected mem.), Sigma Xi. Achievements include research in experimental condensed matter physics including superconductivity, magnetism, valence fluctuation and heavy fermion phenomena, strongly correlated election phenomena low temperature and high pressure physics, surface science and catalysis. Office: U Calif San Diego Dept Physics IPAPS 0319 9500 Gilman Dr La Jolla CA 92093-0319

MAPLE, MARILYN JEAN, educational media coordinator; b. Turtle Creek, Pa., Jan. 16, 1931; d. Harry Chester and Agnes (Dobbie) Kelley; 1 child, Sandra Maple. BA, U. Fla., 1972, MA, 1975, PhD, 1985. Journalist various newspaper including Mountain Eagle, Jasper, Ala., Boise (Idaho) Statesman, Daytona Beach (Fla.) Jour., Lorain (Ohio) Jour.; account exec. Frederides & Co., NYC; prodr. hist. films Fla. State Mus., Gainesville, 1967-69; writer, dir., prodr. med. and sci. films and TV prodns. for 6 medically related colls. U. Fla., Gainesville, 1969—. Pres. Media Modes, Inc., Gainesville. Author: On the Wings of a Butterfly; columnist Health Care Edn. mag.; contbr. Fla. Hist. Quar. Recipient Blakslee award, 1969, spl. award, 1979; Monsour lectr., 1979. Mem. Health Edn. Media Assn. (bd. dirs., awards 1977, 79), Phi Delta Kappa, Kappa Tau Alpha. Office: U Fla PO Box 16J Gainesville FL 32602-0016 Home: 125 Deep Lake Tr Melrose FL 32666 Personal E-mail: mmaple@atlantic.net.

MAPLES, MARY LOU, elementary school educator; Tchr. kindergarten Lessie Moore Elem. Sch., Pineville, La., 1974-97; early childhood Title I supr. Media Ctr., Pineville, 1997—. Recipient La. Tchr. of Yr. award La. Dept. Edn., 1992. Office: Media Ctr PO Box 1230 Alexandria LA 71309-1230 E-mail: maplesml@cox-internet.com.

MAPLES, MICHAEL D., federal agency administrator, military officer; b. Bonham, Tex., 1949; m. Lynn; children: Meredith, Katherine, Elizabeth. Graduate, US Mil. Acad., 1971; MA in Organizational Behavior, Pacific Lutheran U. Commd. 2d. lt. US Army, 1971, advanced through grades to lt. gen., 2005; stationed at Ft. Lewis, Wash., Republic of Korea; tng. mgmt. officer Ft. Sam Houston, Tex.; various assignments Desert Shield/Desert Storm; sr. military aide to sec. US Army; comdr. Babenhausen, Hungary; dep. chief staff ops. US Army Europe, Tazar, Hungary, asst. chief of staff G3, V Corps Heidelberg, Germany; asst. divsn. comdr. (support) 1st Armored Divsn. US Army Europe & Seventh Army, Germany; dir. mil. support, Office Dep. Chief of Staff for Ops. & Plans US Army, dir. ops., readiness & mobilization, Office Dep. Chief of Staff for Ops. & Plans Washington, 2000—01; commdg. gen. US Army Field Artillery Ctr., Ft. Sill, Okla., 2001—03; vice dir., dir. mgmt. The Joint Staff, The Pentagon, 2003—05; dir. Def. Intelligence Agy., Washington, 2005—. Decorated Legion of Merit with oak leaf cluster, Bronze Star medal, Def. Superior Svc. award with oak leaf cluster, Meritorious Svc. medal with three oak leaf clusters, Army Commendation medal with oak leaf cluster, Army Achievement medal, French Croix du Guerre with silver star. Office: Def Intelligence Agy 7400 Def Pentagon Washington DC 20301

MAPLES, PHILIP G., museum director; s. Philip B Maples and Jessie Hazel Galligan; m. Karen E Ritz, Mar. 26, 1977; children: Philip C, Susan E. MA, SUNY, Brockport, NY, 1976. Curator of decorative arts Mattatuck Mus., Waterbury, Conn., 1971—72; asst. curator for registration Old Mus. Village of Smith's Clove, Monroe, NY, 1972; hist. rschr. and preparator Cayuga County Historian's Office, Auburn, NY, 1972—73; curator/dir. Arcade Hist. Soc., Arcade, NY, 1989—92, Baker-Cederberg Mus. and Archives, Rochester, NY, 1989—. Author: (institutional history) To Serve the Community: a Sesquicentennial History of Rochester General Hospital, 1847 to 1997, (monograph) Outline for an Emergency Medical Services History Program, Organizing a Healthcare History Program; contbr. articles in field to profl. jours. Fellow: Co. of Mil. Historians. Office: Baker-Cederberg Museum and Archives 333 Humboldt St Rochester NY 14610 Home Phone: 385-266-9034; Office Phone: 385-922-1847. Office Fax: 585-922-0018. Personal E-mail: p_maples@msn.com. Business E-Mail: phil.maples@viahealth.org.

MAPLESDEN, CAROL HARPER, marriage and family therapist, music educator; b. Phila., Aug. 27, 1947; d. Emmitt Dewain and Helen Esther (Davison) Harper; m. James Paul Maplesden, May 27, 1967; children: Andrew James, Elizabeth Elvira. *Carol is a descendant of the Pusey family who came to Pennsylvania with William Penn in 1682. Several served in the Revolutionary War. They were business proprietors in Pennsylvania, Delaware, and Maryland, notably Henry E. Pusey, of Wilmington, Delaware (1838-1921) and Ralph Shelton and John Chandler, VA founders, and Capt. James Shelton of Va. in Revolutionary War. Husband James, formerly of Philadelphia Police Department, is a descendant of Richard Maplesden (Jamestown 1607), William Bradford, William Brewster and Richard Warren, who arrived on the Mayflower in 1620. Son, Andrew, received Bachelor of Business Adminstration at Temple University in 1994. Daughter Elizabeth, graduate Temple University Tyler School of Art 2004, is an award winning graphic designer.* BA, Holy Family Coll., Phila., 1979; MA, La Salle U., Phila., 1984. Cert. counselor Nat. Bd. Cert. Counselors, lic. profl. counselor of mental health Del., Pa. Child, youth and family therapist People Acting To Help, Phila., 1983—86, Benjamin Rush Cmty. Mental Health, Phila., 1987-88; clin. dir. N.E. Treatment, Phila., 1988-89; outpatient supr. Interact Com. Mental Health, Phila., 1989; program supr. Cath. Charities Christopher House, Trenton, N.J., 1989-90; dir. Carden Family Inst., Phila., 1984—, CEO, 1984—, instr. keyboard, organist, vocal performer, vocal choir and handbell choir dir. Carden music dlv., 1993—. Seminar lectr. in Phila. area. Author: (piano course and audio tape) Young Beginnings Piano Course, Part I, 1993. Mem.: DAR, APA, ACA, NRC (hon. bus. chmn. 2004), Internat. Assn. Marriage and Family Counselors, Daus. Am. Colonists (chpt. regent 2006—), Daughters Union Vets. Civil War (Pa. state pres. 2001—02). Republican. Methodist. Avocations: history studies, genealogy, crafts. Office Phone: 215-741-4234.

MAPOTHER, THOMAS CRUISE See CRUISE, TOM

MAPP, ALF JOHNSON, JR., writer, historian, educator; b. Portsmouth, Va., Feb. 17; s. Alf Johnson and Lorraine (Carney) M.; m. Hartley Lockhart, Mar. 28, 1953; 1 son, Alf Johnson III; m. Ramona Hartley Hamby, Aug. 1, 1971. AA, Coll. William and Mary, 1945, AB summa cum laude, 1961; LLD (hon.), Old Dominion U., 2005. Editorial writer Portsmouth Star, 1945-46, assoc. editor, 1946-48, editorial chief, 1948-54; news editor, editorial writer Virginian-Pilot, Norfolk, 1954-58; free-lance writer, 1958—; lectr. Old Dominion U., 1961-62, instr., 1962-67, asst. prof. English and history, 1967-73, assoc. prof. English, journalism, creative writing, history, 1973-79, prof., 1979-82, eminent prof., 1982-89, eminent scholar, 1989-92, eminent scholar emeritus, 1992—, Louis I. Jaffe prof. English, 1990-92; Louis I. Jaffe prof. emeritus, 1992—. Radio commentator WSAP, Portsmouth, Va., 1947-48; profl. lectr., 1984—; frequent analyst or guest on radio and TV including individual stas. and Universal Studio and BBC radio networks, CBS-TV, 1985—, C-SPAN, 1998—, PBS, 2001, NPR, 2001, CNN, 2001—, World-Wide Ave Maria Network, 2005.; mem. Nat. Jefferson-Hemings Scholars commn., 2001-2002. Host (TV series) Jamestown to Yorktown, 1975—77; author: The Virginia Experiment, 1975, 4th edit., 2007, Frock Coats and Epaulets, 1963, 5th edit., 1996, America Creates Its Own Literature, 1965, Just One Man, 1968, The Golden Dragon: Alfred the Great and His Times, 1974, 4th edit., 1990, Thomas Jefferson: A Strange Case of Mistaken Identity, 1987, 3d edit., 1989 (Book-of-Month Club feature selection, 1987), Thomas Jefferson: Passionate Pilgrim, 1991, 3d edit., 1993 (Book-of-Month Club feature selection, 1991), (novel) Bed of Honor, 1995, 2d edit., 2000, Three Golden Ages: Discovering the Creative Secrets of Renaissance Florence, Elizabethan England, and America's Founding, 1998, Faiths of Our Fathers: What America's Founders Really Believed, 2003; co-author: Chesapeake Bay in the Revolution, 1981, Portsmouth: A Pictorial History, 1989, Constitutionalism: Founding and Future, 1989, Constitutionalism and Human Rights, 1991, Great American Presidents, 1995; mem. editl. bd. Jamestown Found., 1967—, author lyrics for symphonic composition, world debut with Va. Symphony, 1998; contbr. to NY Times, Wall St. Jour., other newspapers and mags. Mem. Portsmouth-Norfolk County Savs. Bond Com, 1948-51, Va. Com. on Libr. Devel., 1949-50; mem. publs. com. 350th Anniversary of Rep. Govt. in the Western World, 1966-69, War of Independence Commn., 1967-83; chmn. Portsmouth Revolutionary Bicentennial Com., 1968-81; chmn. awards jury Baruch award United Daus. Confederacy-Columbia U., 1976, mem., 1980; chmn. Portsmouth Mus. and Fine Arts Commn., 1983-85, Southeastern Va. Anglo-Am. Friendship Day, 1976, Bicentennial Commemoration of Cornwallis' Embarkation for Yorktown, 1981, World Premiere of Mary Rose Marine Archeol. Exhibit, 1985; mem. grant rev. com. Va. Commn. for the Arts, 1986-87; bd. dirs. Portsmouth Pub. Libr., 1948-58, v.p., 1954-56; bd. dirs. Va. Symphony, 1986-87, trustee, 1987—; mem. taxes and mandates com. City of Portsmouth, 1982-86; mem. adv. com. City Mgr. of Norfolk, 1988-94; bd. dirs. Portsmouth Area Cmty. Chest, 1948-52, Va. YMCA Youth and Govt. Found., 1950-52; mem. All-Am. cities com. for award-winning city Nat. League Municipalities, 1976; bd. advisors Ctr. Study Interactive Learning, Pasadena, Calif., 1993—; mem. steering com. Old Dominion U. Friends of the Libr., 1994-2002, dir., 1995-2002; trustee Coun. for Am.'s First Freedom, 1994-98; chair ad hoc com. Joint Portmouth-Suffolk Libr., 1999-2004; dir. Va. R.R. Mus., 2000-. Named Portsmouth Young Man of Year, 1951; recipient honor medal Freedoms Found., 1951, Disting. Rsch. award Old Dominion U., 1987, Great Citizen award Hampton Roads 8 Cities, 1987, Notable Citizen award Portsmouth, Va., 1987; English award Old Dominion Coll., 1961; Troubadour, Great Tchrs. award, 1969; Outstanding Am. Educator award, 1972, 74; Nat. Bicentennial medal Am. Revolution Bicentennial Adminstrsn., 1976; medal Comité Francais du Bicentenaire de l'Independence des Etats-Unis, France, 1976; (with Ramona Mapp) Nat. Family Svc. award Family Found. Am., 1980; Laureate award Commonwealth of Va., 1981; Disting. Alumnus award Old Dominion U., 1982; Liberty Bell award Portsmouth Bar Assn., 1985; Old Dominion U. Triennial Phi Kappa Phi Scholar award, 1986, 91; History medal Great Bridge Chpt. DAR, Nat. Notary medal, 2007; Portsmouth Downtown Merchants award, 1984, 85, Nat. Founders and Patriots award, 1995; Old Dominion U. Outstanding Achievement award, 1995; Gladstone Hill Friend of the Arts award (with Ramona H. Mapp), 1995, Richard Hakluyt award for Am. history, 1996, First Freedom Tchg. Excellence awrd named in his honor Coun. for Am.'s 1st Freedom, 2005; named to Order of the Crown of Charlemagne, 1993. Mem. Am. Hist. Assn., Va. Hist. Soc., Portsmouth Hist. Soc. (historiographer 1975-82, v.p. 1982-84, pres. 1985), Norfolk Hist. Soc. (dir. 1965-72), No. Neck Hist. Soc., Hist. Socs. Eastern Va. (dir. 1971—), SAR, Am. Assn. U. Profs., Authors Guild, Va. Library Assn. (legislative com. 1950-51), Poetry Soc. Va. (pres. 1974-75, adv. com. 1976—), Va. Writers Club, Assn. Preservation of Va. Antiquities, Order of Cape Henry (dir. 1970—, nat. pres. 1975-76), Jamestowne Soc. (chief historian 1975-77, internat. sec. state 1978-79), English Speaking Union (dir. 1976-77), Modern Lang. Assn., Order of First Families Va. 1607-1624 (councillor 1996-99), Nat. Historians Circle, Phi Theta Kappa, Delta Phi Omega (chpt. pres. 1961), Phi Kappa Phi. Baptist. Home: Willow Oaks 2901 Tanbark Ln Portsmouth VA 23703-4828 Office Phone: 757-484-6273. Personal E-mail: amapp@cox.net.

MAPP, EDWARD CHARLES, speech educator; b. NYC, Aug. 17, 1929; s. Edward Cameron and Estelle Viola (Sampson) Mapp; children: Andrew, Elmer, Everett. BA, CCNY, 1953; MS, Columbia U., 1956; PhD, NYU, 1970. Tchr. Bd. Edn., NYC, 1957-64; dir. librs. N.Y.C. Tech. Coll. CUNY, 1964-77, dean of faculty Borough of Manhattan CC NYC, 1977-81, prof. speech and communication, 1983-92, prof. emeritus, 1994—; vice chancellor City Colls. Chgo., 1982-83. Commr. N.Y.C. Commn. Human Rights, 1987—94, vice chair, 1992—94; treas. univ. faculty senate CUNY, 1974—77; model, 1994—2002. Compiler Books for Occupational Education Programs, 1971, Directory of Blacks in Performing Arts, 1978, Directory of Blacks in Performing Arts, 2d edit., 1990; editor: (book) Puerto Rican Perspectives, 1974; author: African-Americans and the Oscar, 2003, Blacks in American Films: Today and Yesterday, 1972, Wednesday at Weeksville, 2005; co-author: (book) A Separate Cinema, 1992; columnist: Movie/TV Mktg., 1979—91. Mem. Bklyn. Borough Pres. Adv. Panel, 1981—84; mem. exec. com. Com. Pub. Higher Edn., NYC, 1978—81; bd. dirs. UN Assn. N.Y., 1975—78; trustee N.Y. Met. Ref. and Rsch. Agy., 1980—82. Named Comms. Educator of Yr., City Coll. N.Y., 2005; named to Black Collectors Hall of Fame, 1992; recipient Founders Day award, NYU, 1970, award, Acad. Motion Picture Arts and Scis., 1996. Mem.: Theatre Libr. Assn., Audelco, Friends Thirteen (bd. dirs. 2000—, 1st vice chmn. 2003—05, chmn. 2005—), Archons Colophon (convenor 1985—86). Democrat.

MAPSTONE, MARK, neuropsychologist, educator; s. Jeffrey and Linda Mapstone; m. Heather Mapstone; children: Kendall, Sheridan. BS, Hobart Coll., Geneva, NY, 1989; MA, Boston U., 1990; PhD, Northwestern U., Chgo., 2000. Lic. clin. psychologist NY. Tech. assoc. MIT, Cambridge, Mass., 1990—96; resident psychology Rush-Presbyn. St. Lukes Hosp., Chgo., 1999—2000; fellow clin. neuropsychology U. Rochester Med. Ctr., NY, 2000—01, fellow exptl. therapeutics, 2001—02, asst. prof. neurology, 2002—. Grantee Career Devel. award, NIH, 2004; John Henry Hobart fellow in Ethics and Social Justice, Hobart Coll., 2004. Mem.: Soc. for Neuroscience, Internat. Neuropsychol. Soc., Delta Chi. Office: Univ Rochester Medical Center 601 Elmwood Ave Box 673 Rochester NY 14642

MAQSOOD, AHSAN, cardiologist, researcher; s. Maqsood Ul Hassan and Parveen Maqsood; m. Madiha Ahsan, Dec. 11, 1995; children: Mahnoor Ghumman, Aleena Ghumman. MD, Army Med Coll., Pakistan, 1994. Diplomate internal medicine Am. Bd. Internal Medicine, 2002, cardiology Am. Bd. Internal Medicine, 2005. Ho. staff CMH, Rawalpindi, Punjab, Pakistan, 1995, MH, 2005—06; med. officer KRL, 1996—97; medicine resident NBIMC, 1999—2002, cardiology fellow, 2002—05, interventional fellow, 2005—. Chief cardiology fellow NBIMC, Newark, 2004—05. Fellow: ACC (licentiate). Achievements include research in Qrs association with LV functin in paced rhythm; clinical significance of borderline elevated troponin. Office: Newark Beth Israel Med Ctr 201 Lyons Ave Newark NJ 07112 Home Phone: 908-868-9828; Office Phone: 973-926-7000. Office Fax: 973-926-7852. Personal E-mail: ahsanmaqsood@hotmail.com.

MAQUAT, LYNNE E., biomedical researcher; Grad., U. Conn.; PhD in Biochemistry, U. Wis., Madison. Postdoctoral rschr. McArdle Lab. Cancer Rsch. U. Wis., Madison; rsch. scientist Roswell Pk. Cancer Inst.; mem. faculty to prof. biochemistry and biophysics James P. Wilmot Cancer Ctr. U. Rochester Med. Ctr., NY, 2000—. Contbr. articles to profl. jours.; mem. editl. bd.: RNA, Molecular and Cellular Biology, RNA Biology. Recipient Davey Meml. award, Outstanding Cancer Rsch., 2002. Fellow: Am. Acad. Arts & Scis.; mem.: Am. Soc. Cell Biology (mem. pub. info. com. 1992—), RNA Soc. (dir. 2000—02, pres. 2006—). Office: Dept Biochemistry and Biophysics U Rochester Sch Medicine and Dentistry 601 Elmwood Ave Box 712 Rochester NY 14642 E-mail: Lynne_Maquat@urmc.rochester.edu.

MARA, JOHN KEVIN, professional sports team executive; b. NYC, Dec. 1, 1954; s. Wellington Timothy and Ann (Mumm) Mara; m. Denise Walter; children: Lauren, Courtney, John Jr., Christine, Erin. BS in Mktg., Boston Coll., 1976; JD, Fordham U., 1979. Atty. Vedder, Price, Kaufman, Kammholz & Day, Shea & Gould; exec. v.p., gen. counsel NY Giants, East Rutherford, NJ, 1991—2005, pres., CEO, 2005—. Bd. dirs. St. Vincent's Hosp., The Sch. Holy Child, Catholic Community Services. Office: NY Giants Giants Stadium East Rutherford NJ 07073 *

MARABLE, MANNING, social science educator, writer; b. Dayton, Ohio, May 13, 1950; s. James Palmer and June (Morehead) M.; m. Leith Patricia Mullings, June 1, 1996; children from previous marriage: Malaika, Joshua, Sojourner. AB in History, Earlham Coll., Richmond, Ind., 1971; MA in History, U. Wis., Madison, 1972; PhD in History, U. Md., College Park, 1976; D (hon.), SUNY, New Paltz, 2000; PhD (hon.), John Jay Coll. CUNY, NYC, 2006. Lectr. Black studies Smith Coll., Northampton, Mass., 1974-76; assoc. prof., chair polit. sci. dept. Tuskegee (Ala.) Inst., 1976-78; assoc. prof. Africana Studies Ctr. Cornell U., Ithaca, NY, 1979-82; prof. econs. and history Fisk U., Nashville, 1982-83; prof. sociology, chair dept. Africana and Hispanic studies Colgate U., Hamilton, NY, 1983-86; prof. sociology Purdue U., West Lafayette, Ind., 1986-87; prof., chair dept. Black studies Ohio State U., Columbus, 1987-89; prof. polit. sci., rsch. assoc. Ctr. Studies of Ethnicity and Race U. Colo., Boulder, 1989—93; prof. history, pub. affairs, polit. sci. Columbia Univ., NYC, 1993—, dir. Inst. Rsch. in African-Am. Studies, 1993—2003, dir. Ctr. Contemporary Black History, 2002—. Luce disting. prof. Williams Coll., Williamstown, 1982, Williamstown, Mass., 84. Author: How Capitalism Underdeveloped Black America, 1983, Race, Reform and Rebellion, 1984, Black American Politics, 1985 (book of yr. Socialist Rev. jour. 1986), W.E.B. Du Bois: Black Radical Democrat, 1986 (book of yr. Gustavus Myers Ctr., U. Ark. 1987), African and Caribbean Politics, 1987, Beyond Black and White: Transforming African-American Politics, 1995, (Book of Yr.Gustavus Myers Ctr. Study Human Rights, Univ. Ark., 1996), Speaking Truth to Power: Essays on Race, Resistance & Radicalism, 1996, Black Liberation in Conservative America, 1997, Black Leadership, 1998, Let Nobody Turn Us Around, 2000, The Great Wells of Democracy: The Meaning of Race in American Life, 2002, Living Black History: How Re-Imagining the African-American Past Can Remake America's Racial Future, 2006; editor: Souls: A Critical Journal of Black Politics, Culture and Society, 1990- present; co-editor (with Myrlie Evers Williams) The Autobiography Of Medgar Evers: A Hero's Life and Legacy Revealed Through His Writings, Letters, and Speeches, 2005; mem. editl. bd. Rev. Black Economy, 1983-87, Jour. Sport and Social Issues, 1983-87, The Witness, 1984—94. Recipient Arthur J. Felberbaum award, Brecht Forum, 1989; grantee, Columbus Found., 1989, Open Soc. Inst., 2002, Ford Found., 2007. Office: 758 Schermerhorn Extension Columbia Univ 1200 Amsterdam Ave New York NY 10027 Office Phone: 212-854-7002. Business E-Mail: mm247@columbia.edu.

MARABLE, SIMEON-DAVID, artist; b. Phila., May 10, 1948; s. Daniel Berry and Marsima (Maddela) M.; m. Pamela Joyce Sorenson, June 1, 1969; children: Simeon-David dePaul, Daniel-Dale Christopher (dec.), Jason-Andrew Bartley, Jo Anna Lee, Benjamin Arthur Kurtis. BA in Art and English, Lea Coll., Minn., 1970; postgrad., Tyler Sch. Art, Phila. Art tchr. 7-8th grade Pennsbury Sch. Sys., Pa., 1970—88; Art tchr. 9-10th grade Charles H. Boehm H.S., Pennsbury, 1988—, Medill Bair H.S., Pennsbury, 1990—; Art tchr. 9-12th grade Pennsbury H.S. W, 2002—. Tchr. Neshaminy Adult Edn., 1972-82; resident artist Middletown Hist. Assn., 1976, Three Arches Corp., 1975, treas.; founder, creator Rivulet Art 2000. Permanent collections include Albert Lea (Minn.) Libr., chapel Ft. Dix, N.J., pencil/charcoal Am. Eagle superimposed over outline Levittown, Pa., James A. Michener Mus., 2003; portraits of Mr. Mike Schmidt, Mr. Lee Elia; creator Phila. City of Champs logo, 50th anniversary logo Fairless Hills, Pa. 1951-2001 Celebration; creator children's ednl. programs Falls Twp. 300th Pa. statehood; artwork represented in Middletown Twp. calendar, 1992, Falls Twp. calendar, 1992; creator Olde Phila. Ednl. Program and Pa. Statehood Program, Nat. Rep. Conv., Phila., 2000; creator scale model homes exhibit Pa. Hist. Mus., 2002; author: Levittown Pennsylvania 1952-2002 A Garden Community, 2002; sketch presented to Gov. of Pa. 2002, papers written of John S. Levitt, 2005, Raymond Fletcher Proffitt, profl. pilot and close friend of William J. Levitt, 2005. Vol. Rep. Nat. Conv., Phila., 2000; mgr. Boys Soccer League, Boys Little League, Middletown Twp.; sr. Babe Ruth coach, mgr. Langhome Athletic Assn., 1988-89; sr. coach Babe Ruth League, 1989; J.V. baseball coach, 1989; mem. Presdl. Task Force; elected to Nat. Trust for Hist. Preservation, 1995; involved with ednl. program Honoring the 200th Anniversary U.S. Constn. Commemorative Olde Phila. Constn. Atty.; curator Levittown Exhibit, Pa.; pres. Levittown Internationally Known Communities Inc., 2003—; program dir. Dream of America 1952 Photographs and Memorabilia of Levittown and Bucks County, Pa., Snowball Gate Dr. Levittown Exhibit Ctr., 2003. Served with USAR, 1970. Named Artist of Yr., Albert Lea Lions Club, 1970, Dir. Archtl. Planning and Cmty. Design, The Bucks Hub Conf.; recipient Rep. Senatorial Am. Spirit medal, Rep. Party, US Senate, 2007. Mem. Buck County Art Educators (pres. 1973-74), Levittown Artists Assn., Nat. Soc. Arts and Lit., Internat. Platform Assn. Roman Catholic. Achievements include development of Levitt Mobile that houses memorabilia and photog. of the 1950's in Buck's Co., Pa. Home: 18 Spindletree Rd Levittown PA 19056-2215 Office: Levittown Exhibit Ctr North 283 Snowball Dr Levittown PA 19056 Office Phone: 215-945-4558. Personal E-mail: amx_12345@hotmail.com.

MARADUDIN, ALEXEI A., physics professor; b. San Francisco, Dec. 14, 1931; BS, Stanford U., 1953, MS, 1954; PhD in Physics, Bristol U., 1957; D (hon.), U. Pierre et Marie Curie, Paris, 1986. Rsch. assoc. physics U. Md., College Park, 1956—57, rsch. asst. prof., 1957—58; asst. rsch. prof. Inst. Fluid Dynamics & Applied Math., 1958—60; physicist Westinghouse Rsch. Labs., Churchill Borough, Pa., 1960—65; cons. semiconductor br. U.S. Naval Rsch. Lab., Washington, 1958—60, Los Alamos Sci. Lab., N.Mex., 1965—67, 1983—89, Gen. Atomic Divsn. Gen. Dynamics Corp., 1965—71; prof. physics U. Calif., Irvine, 1965—, chmn. dept., 1968—71. Recipient Alexander von Humboldt U.S. Sr. Scientist award, 1980—81. Fellow: AAAS, Am. Phys. Soc., Optical Soc. Am., Inst. Physics (U.K.); mem.: Phi Beta Kappa, Sigma Xi, Tau Beta Pi. Office: U Calif Irvine Dept Physics & Astronomy Frederick Reines Hl # 2180 Irvine CA 92697-4575 Office Phone: 949-824-5943. Business E-Mail: aamaradu@uci.edu.

MARAMAN, KATHERINE ANN, judge; b. Los Alamos, N.Mex., Aug. 13, 1951; d. William Joseph and Katherine Ann (Thorpe) Maraman. BA, Colo. Coll., Colo. Springs, 1973; JD, U. N.Mex., Albuquerque, 1976. Bar: N.Mex. 1976, Guam 1978, Trust Territory Pacific Islands, Commonwealth of No. Mariana Islands, US Ct. Appeals (9th cir.), US Supreme Ct. Draftsperson N.Mex. Legis. Coun. Svc., Santa Fe, 1976—77; atty. Brooks & Klitzkie, P.C., Agana, Guam, 1977—84; pvt. practice Agana, 1985—88; counsel Office of Gov., Agana, 1988—94; judge Superior Ct., Agana, 1994—2007; assoc. justice Guam Supreme Ct., 2007—. Mem. asst. legis. counsel Guam Legis., Agana, 1977—80, mem. minority counsel, 1981—87; bd. dirs. Pub. Defender Svc. Corp., Agana, 1988—94. Trustee Guam Ter. Law Libr., 1994—; counsel Rep. Party, Agana, 1981—94; deacon First Presbyn. Reformed Ch., Agana; bd. dirs. Guam Rehab. and Workshop, Inc., Tumon, Guam, 1983—95. Mem.: Mem. Guam Bar Assn. Office: Guam Supreme Ct Guam Judicial Ctr 120 W O'Brien Dr Ste 300 Hagatna GU 96910-5174

MARAMOROSCH, KARL, virologist, educator; b. Vienna, Jan. 16, 1915; came to U.S., 1947, naturalized, 1952; s. Jacob and Stefanie Olga (Schlesinger) M.; m. Irene Ludwinowska, Nov. 15, 1938; 1 dau., Lydia Ann. MS magna cum laude in Entomology, Agrl. U., Warsaw, Poland, 1938; student, Poly. U. Bucharest, Rumania, 1944-46; fellow, Bklyn. Bot. Garden, 1947-48; PhD (predoctoral fellow Am. Cancer Soc. 1948-49), Columbia, 1949. Civilian internee in Rumania, 1939-46; asst., then assoc. Rockefeller U., NYC, 1949-61; sr. entomologist Boyce Thompson Inst., Yonkers, NY, 1961-74, program dir. virology and insect physiology, 1962-74; prof. microbiology Waksman Inst., Rutgers U., New Brunswick, NJ, 1974-85; prof. entomology Cook Coll., Rutgers U., New Brunswick, 1985—, Robert L. Starkey prof., 1983—; vis. prof. agr. U. Wageningen, Netherlands, 1953, Cornell U., 1957, Rutgers U., 1967-68, Fordham U., 1973, Hokkaido U., Sapporo, Japan, 1980, Justus Liebig U., Giessen, Ger., 1983. Mendel lectr. St. Peters Coll., Jersey City, 1963; virologist FAO to Philippines, 1960; Disting. Vis. prof. Fudan U., Shanghai, 1982; cons. FAO-UN, World-wide survey, 1963; chmn. U.S.-Japan Coop. Seminar, 1965, 74, 85; mem. panel food and fiber Nat. Acad. Scis., 1966; cons. rice virus diseases AID-IRRI, Hyderabad, India, 1971; cons. UNDP, Bangalore, India, 1978-79; virologist FAO/UNDP, Sri Lanka, 1981, 82, 83, Mauritius, 1985; AIBS lectr., 1970-72, Found. Microbiology Nat. lectr., 1972-73, Fulbright Disting. prof., Yugoslavia, 1972, 78; mem. tropical medicine and parasitology study sect. NIH, 1972-76; chmn. 1st-3d Internat. Confs. Comparative Virology, 1969, 73, 76. Author: Comparative Symptomatology of Coconut Diseases of Unknown Etiology, 1964; editor: Biological Transmission of Disease Agents, 1962, Insect Viruses, 1968, Viruses, Vectors and Vegetation, 1969, Comparative Virology, 1971, Mycoplasma Diseases, 1973, Viruses, Evolution and Cancer, 1974, Invertebrate Immunity, 1975, Legume Diseases in the Tropics, 1975, Invertebrate Tissue Culture: Research Applications, 1976, Invertebrate Tissue Culture: Applications in Medicine, Biology and Agriculture, 1976, Aphids as Virus Vectors, 1977, Insect and Plant Viruses: An Atlas, 1977, Viruses and Environment, 1978, Practical Tissue Culture Applications, 1979, Leafhopper Vectors and Plant Disease Agents, 1979, Vectors of Plant Pathogens, 1980, Invertebrate Systems in Vitro, 1980, Vectors of Disease Agents, 1981, Mycoplasma Diseases of Trees and Shrubs, 1981, Mycoplasma and Allied Pathogens of Plants, Animals and Human Beings, 1981, Plant Diseases and Vectors: Ecology and Epidemiology, 1981, Invertebrate Cell Culture Applications, 1982, Pathogens, Vectors and Plant Diseases: Approaches to Control, 1982, Subviral Pathogens of Plants and Animals, 1985, Viral Insecticides for Biological Control, 1985, Biotechnology Advances in Insect Pathology and Cell Culture, 1987, Mycoplasma Diseases of Crops, 1988, Invertebrate and Fish Tissue Culture, 1988, Biotechnology for Biological Control of Pests and Vectors, 1991, Viroids and Satellites: Molecular Parasites at the Frontier of Life, 1991, Plant Diseases of Uncertain Etiology, 1992, Insect Cell Biotechnology, 1994, Arthropod Cell Culture Systems, 1994, Forest Trees and Palms: Diseases and Control, 1996, Invertebrate Cell Culture: Novel Directions and Biotechnology Applications, 1997, Invertebrate Cell Culture: Looking Toward the XXI Century, 1997, Biotechnology and Plant Protection in Forestry Sci., 1998, Maintenance of Human, Animal, and Plant Pathogen Vectors, 1999; Methods in Virology, 1964-84, Advances in Virus Research, 1972—, Archives of Virology, 1973-78, Intervirology, 1973-77, Advances in Cell Culture, 1979-89, Jour. Virological Methods, 1980-; editor in chief Jour. NY Entomol. Soc, 1972-84; assoc. editor: Virology, 1964-68, 75-79. Recipient Sr. Rsch., Lalor Found., 1957, Nat. Ciba-Geigy award in agr., 1976, Wolf prize in agr., Wolf Found., Israel, 1980, Jurzykowski prize in biology, 1980, Disting. Svc. award, Am. Inst. Biol. Scis., 1983, Khailshanker Durlabhji award, Jaipur, 1993, Lifetime Achievement award, Soc. In Vitro Biology, 2001, Gold Shield award, Egyptian Soc. Biol. Control, 2007. Fellow AAAS (hon., Campbell award 1958), Entomol. Soc. Am. (L.O. Howard Disting. Achievement award 2006), Am. Phytopath. Soc., NY Acad. Scis. (A. Cressy Morrison prize natural sci. 1951, chmn. divsn. microbiology 1956-60, rec. sec. 1960-61, v.p. 1962-63), Nat. Acad. Scis. India (hon.); mem. Harvey Soc., Growth Soc., Phytopath. Soc., Indian, Japan, Can. phytopath. socs., Leopoldina Acad., Internat. Com. Virus Nomenclature, Electron Microscopy Soc., Am. Soc. Microbiology (Waksman award 1978), Soc. In Vitro Biology (Tissue Culture Assn., pres. N.E. br. 1978-81, pres. history br. 1988-90, Disting. Lifetime Achievement award 2001), Soc. Invertebrate Pathology (founder's lectr., Adelaide 1990, Founder's honoree Sapporo 1998), Internat. Assn. Medicinal Forest Plants (pres. 1989—), Sigma Xi (pres. Rugers chpt. 1978). Home: 17 Black Birch Ln Scarsdale NY 10583-7456 Office: Rutgers U Dept Entomology New Brunswick NJ 08901 Office Phone: 732-932-9329. Business E-Mail: maramors@rci.rutgers.edu.

MARAN, STEPHEN PAUL, astronomer; b. Bklyn., Dec. 25, 1938; s. Alexander P. and Clara F. (Schoenfeld) Maran; m. Sally Ann Scott, Feb. 14, 1971; children: Michael Scott, Enid Rebecca, Elissa Jean. BS, Bklyn. Coll., 1959; MA, U. Mich., 1961, PhD, 1964. Astronomer Kitt Peak Nat. Obs., Tucson, 1964-69; project scientist for orbiting solar observatories NASA-Goddard Space Flight Center, Greenbelt, Md., 1969-75; head advanced systems and ground observations br. NASA-Goddard Space Flight Ctr., 1970-77, mgr. Operation Kohoutek, 1973-74, sr. staff scientist Lab. for Astronomy and Solar Physics, 1977-95; asst. dir. Space Scis. for Info. and Outreach, 1995—2004. Cons. Westinghouse Rsch. Labs., 1966; vis. lectr. U. Md., College Park, 1969—70; sr. lectr. UCLA, 1976; A. Dixon Johnson lectr. sci. comm. Pa. State U., 1990; lectr. astronomy cruises and eclipse tours. Author (with John C. Brandt): New Horizons in Astronomy, 1972, 2d edit., 1979, Arabic edit., 1979; author: (with Jacqueline Mitton) Gems of Hubble-Superb Images from the Hubble Telescope, 1996; author: Astronomy for Dummies, 1999, 2d edit., 2005, German edit., 2000, 2d German edit., 2004, French edit., 2001, Chinese edit., 2001, Russian edit., 2004, Dutch edit., 2005; editor: Physics of Nonthermal Radio Sources, 1964, The Gum Nebula and Related Problems, 1971, Possible Relations Between Solar Activity and Meteorological Phenomena, 1975, New Astronomy and Space Science Reader, 1977, A Meeting with the Universe, 1981, Astrophysics of Brown Dwarfs, 1986, The Astronomy and Astrophysics Encyclopedia, 1991, Astrophys. Letters, 1974—77; assoc. editor:, 1977—85, Earth, Extraterrestrial Scis., 1969—79, contbg. editor: Air & Space/Smithsonian, 1990—; mem. editl. adv. bd. Astronomy Mag., 1997—, Astronomy and Geophysics, 1997—; contbr. articles to pop. mags. Named Disting. Visitor, Boston U., 1970; recipient Group Achievement award, NASA, 1969, 1974, Exceptional Achievement medal, 1991, Klumpke-Roberts award, Astron. Soc. Pacific, 1999; vis. scholar, Univ. Ctr. Ga., 1997. Fellow: AAAS; mem.: Am. Geophys. Union, Am. Phys. Soc., Royal Astron. Soc., Internat. Astron. Union (editor daily newspaper 1988, Minor Planet 9768 named Stephenmaran in his honor 2000), Am. Astron. Soc. (press officer 1985—, Harlow Shapley vis. lectr. 1981—, George Van Biesbroeck prize 2007). Office: Am Astronomical Soc Ste 400 2000 Florida Ave NW Washington DC 20009 Office Phone: 202-328-2010 116. Business E-Mail: maran@aas.org.

MARANGOZ, SALIH, orthopedist; b. Gaziantep, Turkey, Sept. 25, 1976; s. M. Ihsan and F. Sema Marangoz. MD, Hacettepe U., Ankara, Turkey, 2000. Resident in orthopaedic surgery Hacettepe U., Ankara, Turkey, 2001—05; clin. fellow in pediatric orthopaedic surgery N.Y. U., Hosp. Joint Diseases, N.Y.C., 2006—. Fellow, EFORT, 2005. Office: NY Univ Hosp Joint Diseases 301 East 17th St New York NY 10003 Business E-Mail: salih.marangoz@yahoo.com.

MARANO, ANTHONY JOSEPH, cardiologist; b. White Plains, NY, Apr. 14, 1934; s. Anthony Joseph and Mary Antoinette (Perrotta) M.; m. Mary Regina Marbach, Aug. 23, 1958; children— Thomas, Kathryn, Michele. BA, Williams Coll., 1956; MD, Cornell Med. Coll., 1960. Diplomate Am. Bd. Internal Medicine, Am. Bd. Cardiovasc. Disease. Intern Bellevue

Hosp., NYC, 1960-61; resident St. Luke's Hosp., NYC, 1961-63; NIH fellow in cardiology Mt. Sinai Hosp., NYC, 1963-64, rsch. assoc., 1964-75; clin. assoc. in medicine Coll. Physicians and Surgeons, NYC, 1970-86; pres. med. staff White Plains Hosp., 1984-86, chief cardiology, 1985-91, chief cardiology emeritus, 1991—, bd. dirs., 1983-88; cons. in cardiology Burke Rehab. Ctr.; med. dir., founder Paramedic Ambulance, White Plains, 1976-82. Contbr. articles to profl. jours. Trustee Pace U., NYC, 1975—, Home Savs. Bank, White Plains, 1973-90; bd. dirs. YMCA, White Plains, 1978-82; team physician White Plains HS, 1967—; cons. physician Dept. Pub. Safety, White Plains, 1968—; cons. physician City of White Plains Sch. System, 1994-98; bd. dirs. Westchester County Sports Hall of Fame, 1993—; alumni trustee Tyng Found., Williams Coll., 1994—. Tyng scholar Williams Coll., 1952-59; recipient Outstanding Achievement award Emergency Med. Svcs. Coun., 1982, YMCA Ctrl. Westchester Cmty. Svc. award, 2006; named to White Plains HS Hall of Fame, 1998; Anthony J. Marano MD Cardiac Care Unit at White Plains Hosp. Ctr. named in his honor, 2005. Fellow ACP, Am. Coll. Cardiology; mem. AMA, Am. Coll. Sports Medicine, Am. Heart Assn., NY State Heart Assn. (bd. dirs. 1982-85), Westchester Heart Assn. (v.p. 1983-86, pres. 1987-90), Univ. Club (White Plains, pres. 1970-71) Westchester Country Club (Harrison, NY), Phi Beta Kappa. Avocations: gardening, swimming. Home: 46 Eagle Ct White Plains NY 10605-5116 Office: 15 North Broadway White Plains NY 10605 Office Phone: 914-948-8838.

MARANO, RICHARD MICHAEL, judge; b. Waterbury, Conn., June 22, 1960; s. Albert Nicholas and Angeline Domenica (Viotti) M.; m. Eileen N. Barry. BA, Fairfield U., 1982; JD, Seton Hall U., 1985. Bar: Conn. 1985, US Dist. Ct. Conn. 1985, US Tax Ct. 1986, US Supreme Ct. 1990, US Ct. Appeals (2d cir.) 1991; cert. criminal trial advocate. Assoc. Moynahan, Ruskin, Mascolo & Mariani, Waterbury, 1985-87; ptnr. Marano & Diamond, Waterbury, 1987—2001, Marano Law Offices, 2001—04; superior ct. judge, 2004—. Bd. of examiners Nat. Bd. Trial Advocacy, 1999-04. Author: History of the Order Sons of Italy of Waterbury, Connecticut, 1995, Connecticut Criminal Legal Forms, 1999, Vote Your Conscience: The Last Campaign of George McGovern, 2003; co-author: Growing Up Italian and American in Waterbury, 1997; co-editor: Counsel for the Defense, 1991-93, editor, 1993-98; contbr. law articles to Conn. Bar Jour. Bd. dirs. Italian-Am. Dem. Club, Waterbury, 1988-04, Ctrl. Naugatuck Valley HELP, 1992-05, Anderson Boys Club, 1989-02, pres. 1996-98; bd. dirs. Waterbury Housing Police Fund, 1992-94, Waterbury Crime Stoppers Inc., 1994-97; pres. Conn. Young Dems., 1981-82; state coord. McGovern for US Presdl. campaign, 1983-84; campaign mgr. Orman for Congress, 1984; active Oxford Dem. Town Com., 2002-04; commr. Waterbury Pub. Assistance, 1986-88, Waterbury Fire Bd., 1996-98; justice of peace, Waterbury, 1989-99; gen. counsel Waterbury Dem. Town Com., 1990-96; trustee Our Lady of Lourdes Ch., 1993—; alderman City of Waterbury, 1988-90; mem. adv. bd. Housatonic coun. Boy Scouts Am., 2004-06, v.p., 2006—07, pres. 2007-; mem. bldg. com. Oxford HS, 2004. Mem. Conn. Criminal Def. Lawyers Assn. (pres. 1998-99), Conn. Italian-Am. Bar Assn. (pres. 1993-95), Waterbury Bar Assn. (bd. dirs. 1993-2002, pres. 1996-98), New Haven County Bar Assn., Nat. Italian-Am. Bar Assn. (Conn. del. 1993-2004), Sons of Italy (pres. lodge #66 1994-96), Unico Club (pres. Waterbury chpt. 1997-99), Cath. Lawyers Guild, Conn. Acad. Cert. Trial Lawyers, Nat. Eagle Scout Assn. (life), Alpha Mu Gamma, Pi Sigma Alpha. Roman Catholic. Home: 24 Lake Dr Oxford CT 06478-1172 Personal E-mail: richardmarano@aol.com.

MARANO, THOMAS, diversified financial services company executive; b. 1962; Grad., Columbia U., 1983. Joined Bear Stearns, 1983; temp. aide to CEO Bear Stearns Asset Mgmt.; global head of mortgages and asset-backed securities Bear Stearns Companies Inc., head high-grade structured credit strategies fund, 2007—. Office: Bear Stearns Cos Inc 383 Madison Ave New York NY 10179 Office Phone: 212-272-2000. *

MARANO, THOMAS J., marketing professional; b. 1952; married; 3 children. BE, U. Va.; M Systems Mgmt., U. SC. Variety of mktg. & operational mgmt. roles, including v.p. Apple Computer Corp., and Pepsi-Cola Co.; v.p. sales & mktg. fountain divsn. Coca-Cola, USA; pres., COO AHL Services, Inc., Atlanta, 1995—2001, Innotrac Corp., 2002—03; pres., CEO Coffeecol Inc., 2004—06; CEO Air Serve Corp., 2006—. Bd. dirs. Innotrac Corp., 2005—. *

MARAVIGLIA, BRUNO, physicist, researcher; b. Pescia/Pistoia, Tuscany, Italy, Apr. 29, 1938; s. Narciso and Nada (Guidi) M.; m. Maria Antonietta Macri, Jan. 31, 1992; 1 child, Beatrice. Master's degree, U. Florence, Italy, 1962; postgrad., La Sapienza U., Rome, 1964. Researcher Nat. Inst. Nuclear Physics, Rome, 1962-68; asst. prof. dept. physics Duke U., Durham, NC, 1969-70; assoc. prof. Inst. Physics La Sapienza U., Rome, 1970-79, prof. physics, 1980—, dir. Postgrad. Sch. Med. Physics, 1986—, dir. dept. physics, 1992-95. Vis. prof. dept. physics U. B.C., Vancouver, Can., 1977-78; dir. magnetic resonance and brain function E. Fermi Sch. Physics., 1998 Editor: Physics of NMR Spectroscopy, 1988, Nuclear Magnetic Double Resonance, 1992, (book procs.) XXIII Congress Ampere, 1986; contbr. over 170 articles to profl. jours.; mem. editorial bd. Jour. Magnetic Resonance, 1992-99, Magnetic Resonance in Medicine, 1986—, Applied Magnetic Resonance, 1990—, Solid State Nuclear Magnetic Resonance, 1995—. Mem. coun. Mus. of Physics and Sci. Ctr. E. Fermi, Rome, 2000—. Mem. Internat. Soc. Magnetic Resonance (com. mem. 1985—), Soc. Magnetic Resonance in Medicine, Italian Phys. Soc., Groupement Ampere (v.p. 1986-94, pres. 1994-2000). Avocations: skiing, hiking, archaeology. Home: Via Jacopo Sannazzaro 82 00141 Rome Italy Office: La Sapienza U Dept Physics P le Aldo Moro 2 00185 Rome Italy Office Phone: +39-06-4454859. E-mail: bruno.maraviglia@romal.infn.it.

MARAVOLO, NICHOLAS C., biology professor; b. Chgo., Dec. 4, 1940; s. Nicholas and Mary Ann Maravolo. SB, U. Chgo., 1962, MS, 1964, PhD, 1966. Prof. biology Lawrence U., Appleton, Wis., 1966—. Author: numerous articles in refereed jours. Mem.: Am. Biological Lichenological Soc., Am. Assn. Plant Biology. Office: Lawrence Univ PO Box 599 Appleton WI 54912 Business E-Mail: nicholas.c.maravolo@lawrence.edu.

MARAYNES, ALLAN LAWRENCE, filmmaker, television producer; b. NYC, Apr. 26, 1950; s. Harry and Dorothy (Kaufman) Maraynes; m. Bitsy Healy, Oct. 14, 1978; children: Sean, Megan, Matthew. BA, Queens Coll., 1972; MA, Loyola U., LA, 1974. Assoc. prodr. CBS News, NYC, 1976-77, prodr. 60 Minutes, 1974-88, writer, dir. 60 Minutes, 1976-88; pres. No. Films, NYC, 1988-90; exec. prodr. "SST" program ABC, NYC, 1989; prodr. 20/20 ABC News, NYC, 1990-93, sr. investigative prodr. 20/20, 1994-96; sr. investigative prodr. Dateline NBC, NYC, 1996—. Lectr. New Sch., NYC, 1979, Columbia U., NYC. Author: (plays) A Straight Line to the Market Place, 1975, (screenplays) Smithereens, 1999, Track Rats, 2005. Recipient Emmy award, NATAS, 1981, 1985, 1988, 1989, 1991, 1993, 1995, 1997, 1998, 2002, 2004, 2005, George Foster Peabody award, 1989, 2000, Edward R. Murrow award, 1997, 1998, 2000, Investigative Reporters and Editors award, 1997, 2000—01, DuPont Columbia Journalism award, 2000, 2006, George Polk award, 2000, Overseas Press Club award, 2002. Mem.: NATAS, Writers Guild Am. Office: NBC 30 Rockefeller Plz Fl 2 New York NY 10112-0036 E-mail: ALLAN.MARAYNES@NBC.COM.

MARAZITA, MARY LOUISE, genetics researcher; b. Cheboygan, Mich., June 13, 1954; m. Richard T. McCoy, 1984; 5 children. BS, Mich. State U., East Lansing, 1976; PhD in Genetics, U. NC, Chapel Hill, 1980. Fellow U. So. Calif., 1980-82; statistician, instr. UCLA, 1982-86; asst. prof. human genetics Med. Coll. Va., 1986-93; dir. Cleft Palate-craniofacial Ctr. U. Pitts., 1993-00, dept. chair oral biology, 1999—, asst. dean for rsch. Sch. Dental Medicine, 2000-2001, assoc. dean rsch., 2001—. Instr. biomath. U. Calif., 1984-86; asst. prof. dentistry Med. Coll. Va., 1992-93; assoc. prof. human genetics and oral biology U. Pitts., 1993-97, prof. human genetics and oral and maxillofacial surgery, 1997—, prof. psychiatry, 2003—. Fellow Am. Coll. Med. Genetics, Am. Cleft Palate Assn., Am. Soc. Human Genetics, Internat. Genetic Epidemiol. Soc., Internat. Assn. Dental Rsch. Achievements include research in genetics of cleft lip, cleft palate and other craniofacial anomalies, including statistical genetic analysis and gene mapping studies. Office: U Pitts Dept Oral Biology/Genetics Ste 500 Cellomics Bldg/100 Technology Dr Pittsburgh PA 15219 Business E-Mail: marazita@pitt.edu.

MARBAIS, PETER CHRISTIAN, language educator; b. East Liverpool, Ohio, July 1, 1973; s. James and Margaret Marbais. BA, Ohio Wesleyan U., Delaware, 1995; MA, Kent State U., Ohio, 1998, PhD, 2005. Instr. English Hutchinson (Kans.) CC, 2000—06; asst. prof. Mt. Olive (NC) Coll., 2006—. Mem.: Internat. John Bunyan Soc., Am. Soc. Eighteenth-Century Studies. Home: 5134 Berry Rose Way Cary NC 27511 Office: Mount Olive Coll 634 Henderson St Mount Olive NC 28365 Office Phone: 919-658-7850. Business E-Mail: pmarbais@moc.edu.

MARBLE, DUANE FRANCIS, geography educator, researcher; b. Seattle, Dec. 10, 1931; s. Francis Augustus and Beulah Belle (Simmons) M.; m. Jacquelynne Hardester, Aug. 18, 1957; children: Kimberley Eileen Wood, Douglas Craig. BA, U. Wash., 1953, MA, 1956, PhD, 1959. Asst. prof. real estate U. Oreg., Eugene, 1959; asst. prof. regional sci. U. Pa., Phila., 1960-63; from assoc. prof. geography to prof. geography Northwestern U., Evanston, Ill., 1963-73, assoc. dir. Transp. Ctr., 1966-73; prof. geography and computer sci. SUNY at Buffalo, Amherst, NY, 1973-87; prof. geography and natural resources Ohio State U., Columbus, 1987-98, prof. emeritus, 1998—; Courtesy prof. U. Oreg., 2003—07. Chmn. com. on geog. data sensing and processing Internat. Geog. Union, 1980-88; bd. dirs. Castlereagh Enterprises, Phoenix; founder Internat. Symposium Spatial Data Handling; founder Assn. Am. Geographers-Marble Fund Geographic Sci.; cons. on geog. info. systems to U.S. Bur. Census, UN, also pvt. orgns. Editor: Intro Readings in GIS, 1990, Taylor & Francis, 1990-95; author computer program (best software award Assn. Am. Geogs. 1990); mem. editl. bd. Annals of Assn. Am. Geography, 2000-05, Internat. Jour. of Geographic Info. Sys., 1987-97. Vice-chair Florence Urban Renewal Adv. Com.; mem. Florence Transit Adv. Com., 2007—. Named GIS Educator of Yr., UCGIS, 2007; recipient Legend in Leadership award, Environ. Sys. Rsch. Inst., 1997, Making a Difference award, 2004. Mem.: Univ. Consortium for Geographic Info. Sci., Assn. Am. Geographers (sr. assoc. 2005, honors 1993, Geog. and Info. Sci. and Sys. Disting. Career award 2007). Home: 2226 Primrose Ln Florence OR 97439-7627 Personal E-mail: dmarble@oregonfast.net.

MARBURGER, JOHN HARMEN, III, federal official; b. SI, NY, Feb. 8, 1941; s. John H., Jr. and Virginia A. (Smith) M.; m. Carol Preston Godfrey, June 12, 1965; children: John Harmen, Alexander Godfrey. BA in Physics magna cum laude, Princeton U., 1962; PhD in Applied Physics (NASA trainee), Stanford U., 1967; LHD (hon.), Hofstra U., 2000; DS (hon.), Stony Brook U., 2002, Moscow State U., 2002. Physicist Goddard Space Flight Center, NASA, 1962—63; asst. prof. physics & elec. engring. U. So. Calif., Los Angeles, 1966—69, assoc. prof., 1969—75, prof., 1975—80, chmn. physics dept., 1972—75; interim dean Coll. Letters, Arts and Sciences, U. So. Calif., LA, 1976—77, dean, 1977—80; pres. SUNY, Stony Brook, 1980—94, prof. physics & elec. engring., 1994—98; pres. Brookhaven Sci. Assoc., 1998—2001; dir. Brookhaven Nat. Labs, 1998—2001; asst. to the Pres., dir. Office Sci. & Tech. Policy, Exec. Office of the Pres., Washington, 2001—. Cons. laser fusion program Lawrence Livermore Labs., 1972-76; chmn. N.Y. State fact finding panel on Shoreham Nuclear Power Facility, 1983; chmn. bd. trustees Universities Rsch. Assn., 1988-94; co-chair NASULGC Bd. on Oceans and Atmosphere, 1992-93; bd. dirs. N.Y. State Edn. and Rsch. Network, Inc., 1986-98; bd. dirs., chair L.I. Rsch. Inst., 1989-95; bd. dirs. L.I. High Tech. Incubator Corp., 1992-98, chair 1994-98. Contbr. articles to tech. publs. Bd. dirs. Mus. at Stony Brook, 1980-92, 94-98, L.I. Assn., Inc., 1983-93, 98—, Action Com. for L.I., 1980-83, L.I. Forum for Tech., Inc., 1980—, Rsch. Found. SUNY, 1990—; bd. trustees Princeton U., 1985-89; chmn. N.Y. State Energy Office Rev. Commn., 1980-81, Suffolk County (N.Y.) Task Force on Priorities in Fin., 1980-81; campaign chmn. United Way of L.I., 1991-92. Recipient Shuichi Kusaka Meml. Prize Princeton U., 1962 Fellow AAAS, APS; mem. Assn. of Colls. and Univs. State of N.Y. (pres. 1988-90), Coleman Chamber Music Assn. (bd. dirs. 1969-80). Office: Office Sci & Tech Policy EEOB 17th & Pennsylvania Ave NW Washington DC 20502

MARBURG-GOODMAN, JEFFREY EMIL, lawyer; b. Taipei, Taiwan, Feb. 20, 1957; s. Samuel and Lisl (Marburg) Goodman. BA, Amherst Coll., 1979; JD, Harvard U., 1983; postgrad., U. Aix-Marseille, France, 1983-84. Bar: N.Y. 1986, U.S. Dist. Ct. (so. and ea. dists.) N.Y. 1988. Assoc. Shearman & Sterling, Paris, 1984, NYC, 1985-89; legal counsel US AID, US Dept. State, Washington, 1991-2000, asst. gen. counsel, 2000—06; gen. counsel Creative Assocs. Internat., Inc., Washington, 2006—. Spkr. in field. Co-author: International Procurement Year In Review; contbr. articles pub. to profl. jour. Mem. nat. steering com. Clinton-Gore '96, Gore 2000, Kerry, 2004. Rotary fellow, 1984. Mem.: ABA (conv. panel spkr. 2003, 2004, 2006, internat. law and pub. contract sects., co-chair internat. procurement com. 2007—), Harvard Club, Phi Beta Kappa. Avocations: running, weightlifting, music, theater, travel. Home: 1401 17th St NW PH Apt1008 Washington DC 20036-6400 Office: Creative Assocs Internat Inc 5301 Wisconsin Ave NW Ste 700 Washington DC 20015 Office Phone: 202-572-1334. Business E-Mail: jeffreym@caii.com.

MARBURY, RITCHEY MCGUIRE, III, engineering executive, surveyor; b. Albany, Ga., May 18, 1938; s. Ritchey McGuire and Shirley Kathryn (VanHouten) M.; m. Fonda Gayle Starnes, June 16, 1962; children: Mary Kathryn, Ritchey McGuire IV. BCE, Ga. Tech. Inst., 1960, M in City Planning, 1966. Registered profl. engr., Ga., Fla., Idaho, Ala.; land surveyor, Ga. V.p. Marbury Engring. Co., Albany, Ga., 1965-78, pres., chmn. bd., 1981—; pres. Marbury, Ritter, Scott & Turner, Inc., Albany, 1970-78, 81-92, Marbury Assocs., Inc., 1991—, Idaho Boise Mission of Latter-day Saints Ch., 1978-81; sr. prin. EMC Engring. Svcs., 2004—. Presenter seminars on total quality mgmt. to nat. convs. of Am. Cons. Engrs. Coun., Design Constrn. Quality Inst., Sml. Firm Coalition of Cons. Engrs., Assn. for Project Mgrs. Exec. bd. Boy Scouts Am., Southwest Ga., 1982—. Served to 1st lt. U.S. Army, 1963-65. Mem. NSPE (South Ga. chpt. pres. 1993-95), Am. Cons. Engrs. Coun., Surveying and Mapping Soc. of Ga. (bd. dirs. 1966-78), Ga. Planning Assn., Home Builders Assn. (bd. dirs. 1985-86), Rotary. Mem. Lds Ch. Avocations: fishing, writing, music, computer, golf. Home: 1824 Green Valley Dr Albany GA 31707-3116 Office: 2334 Lake Park Dr Albany GA 31707-3132 Office Phone: 229-435-6133. Business E-Mail: ritchey_marbury@emc-eng.com. *Always be a role model of Christlike behavior and do those things that make a significant differenc for good. Do what's right simply because it's the right thing to do. The greatest results come through kindness.*

MARBURY, STEPHON, professional basketball player; b. Feb. 20, 1977; children: Stephanie, Xaviera. Student, Ga. Inst. Tech., 1996. Guard Minn. Timberwolves, 1996—98; guard, forward N.J. Nets, 1998—2001; guard Phoenix Suns, 2002—04, N.Y. Knicks, 2004—. Mem. U.S. Olympic Basketball Team, Athens, 2004. Hosts The Stephon Marbury Basketball Classic. Named National High School Player of the Year (Abraham Lincoln H.S.) by Parade Magazine, 1995; named one of New York's Influentials, New York Mag., 2006; named to 1996-97 NBA All-Rookie First Team, NBA All-Star game, 2001, 2003. Office: c/o NY Knickerbockers 2 Pennsylvania Plz New York NY 10121 *

MARBUT, ROBERT GORDON, communications, electronic security and broadcast executive, investor; b. Athens, Ga., Apr. 11, 1935; s. Robert Smith and Laura Gordon (Powers) M.; m. Margo Susan Spitz, Sept. 24, 1989; children: Robert Gordon, Laura Dodd, Michael Powers, Marcy Lizbeth. B Indsl. Engring., Ga. Inst. Tech., 1957; MBA with distinction, Harvard U., 1963. Registered profl. engr., Calif. Engr. Esso Standard Oil Co., Baton Rouge, 1957; corp. dir. engring. and plans Copley Press, La Jolla, Calif., 1963-70; v.p. Harte-Hanks Newspapers, Inc., San Antonio, 1970-71; pres., CEO Harte-Hanks Comm., Inc., San Antonio, 1971-91, also dir., 1971-91, vice chmn. bd. dirs., 1991; founder, chmn., CEO Argyle Comm., Inc, San Antonio, 1992—; founder, CEO, dir. Argyle TV Holding, Inc., San Antonio, 1993-95; co-founder, chmn., CEO Argyle TV, Inc., San Antonio, 1994-97; chmn., co-CEO Hearst-Argyle TV, Inc., NYC, 1997-2000, chmn., 2001—02; co-mng. ptnr. Argyle Global, LP, 2001—; founder, chmn., CEO SectecGLOBAL, Inc., 2002—. Dir. AP, 1979—88, vice chmn., 1987—88; chmn. Newspaper Advt. Bur., 1988—90, exec. com. dir., 1974—89, 1982—90; bd. dirs. Valero Energy Corp., Tupperware, Inc., Hearst-Argyle TV, Inc., Bus. Execs. Nat. Security; mem. adv. bd. U. Ga. Henry W. Grady Sch. Journalism, 1975—83, Ga. Tech., 1978—81, 1998—; founding mem. Am. Bus. Conf., 1981—89; mem. U. Tex. Centennial commn., 1981—83; pres. adv. coun. U. Tex. Coll. Comm., 1982—83; bd. dirs. Up With People, 1983—2001, exec. com., 1984—2001; instr. Armstrong Coll., 1951, Calif. State U., LA, 1964, Woodbury Coll., 1964. Author: (with Healy, Henderson and others) Creative Collective Bargaining, 1965. Coordinating chmn. San Antonio Target 90 commn., 1983-84; campaign chmn. United Way, San Antonio, 1985, chmn. bd. trustees 1988-89; vice chmn. Tex. select com. on Tax Equity, 1987-89; mem select com. Tex. Revenues, 1991-92; mem. Tex. World Trade Coun., 1986-87. Capt. USAF, 1958-61. Salzburg Inst. Am. Studies sr. fellow, 1997—; recipient Isaiah Thomas award Rochester Inst. Tech., 1980, EXCEL award in comm., 1987, People of Vision award, 1991; selected to Acad. Disting. Engring. Alumni Ga. Tech., 1995. Mem. Am. Newspaper Publs. Assn. (chmn. task group on future, chmn. telecomm. com. 1974-81, bd. dirs. 1976-84, chmn. future task group), So. Newspaper Pubs. Assn. (pres. 1979-80, dir. 1975-81, treas. 1977), Am. Newspaper Pubs. Assn. Found. (trustee 1976-79), Tex. Daily Newspaper Assn. (pres. 1979, Tex. Newspaper Leader of Yr., 1981), N.Y. Met. Club, Doubles, San Antonio Country Club, Argyle Club, Greater San Antonio C. of C., Delta Tau Delta (Alumni Achievement award 2000), Omicron Delta Kappa, Phi Eta Sigma. Office: Hearst-Argyle Television Inc 200 Concord Plaza Dr Ste 700 San Antonio TX 78216-6941

MARCALI, JEAN GREGORY, retired chemist; b. Jermyn, Pa., May 29, 1926; d. John Robert and Anna Marie Gregory; m. Kalman Marcali, Oct. 6, 1956; children: Coleman, Frederick. Student, U. Pa., 1948—52, U. Del., 1971—72. Microanalyst E.I. du Pont de Nemours & Co., Deepwater, NJ, 1943-60, tech. info. analyst, organic chems. dept., 1960-64, tech. info. analyst info. systems dept. Wilmington, Del., 1964-67, sr. adviser tech. info., 1967-70, supr. tech. info., 1970-82, 85-89, supr. adminstrv. svcs. Ctrl. Rsch. Dept., 1982-85, cons., 1989-92, ret., 1992. Sec. Alfred I. Dupont Elem. PTA, 1971, pres. 1972; pres. PTA Brandywine Sch. Dist., 1973; mem. Wilmington Dist. Rep. Com., 1976—, Winterthur Mus., 1996—. Mem. Am. Chem. Soc. (treas. divsn. chem. info. 1976-81, chmn.-elect 1981, chmn. 1982, 83, divsn. councilor 1983-90), Am. Chem. Soc. (com. on chem. abstracts svc. 1983-85, 87-93, mem. joint bd. coun. com. on chem. abstracts svc. 1994-96, 98, 99, 2000, Del. sec. chem. lit. topical group, chmn. 1979-80, chem. vets. chmn.-elect 1999), Order Ea. Star, Du Pont Country Club, Winterthur Mus. Guild. Lutheran. Home: 312 Waycross Rd Wilmington DE 19803-2950

MARCANO, MARIANO, mathematics professor; b. Cidra, PR; s. Luz M. Velazquez and Mariano Marcano; m. Judith Rivera, June 6, 1998. BS, U. PR, Cayey, 1986; MS, U. PR, Rio Piedras, 1990; PhD, SUNY, Stony Brook, 1998. Asst. prof. U. PR, Rio Piedras, 1998—2003, assoc. prof., 2003—; vis. asst. prof. Duke U., Durham, 2000—01. Fellowship, U. PR, 1990, W. Burghardt Turner Fellowship, SUNY, 1993—98, Rsch. Grant, NIH, 1995—97, 2004—. Mem.: Am. Physiol. Soc., Soc. for Indsl. and Applied Math., Soc. for Math. Biology. Office: U PR PO Box 23355 San Juan PR 00931-3355 Office Phone: 787-764-0000 4698. Business E-Mail: mmarcano@uprrp.edu.

MARCANTEL, BERNARD NORMAN, lawyer, judge; b. Oberlin, La., July 14, 1923; s. Emile Peter and Florence Ida (Reed) M.; m. Martha Tabb de Gravelles, June 23, 1946 (dec.); children: David Emile, Nancy Tabb, Gregory Norman, Peter Camille; m. Nancy Magoon, May 2, 1998 (dec.). BS, U. Southwestern La., 1946; JD, U. Chgo., 1949, Tulane U., 1950. Bar: La. 1950, U.S. Dist. Ct. (ea. and we. dists.) La. 1951, U.S. Ct. Appeals (5th cir.) 1978. Dist. atty. 31st Jud. Dist., Jennings, La., 1953-78; ptnr. Marcantel, Marcantel & Wall, Jennings, 1978—. Judge City of Jennings, 1985-93; judge pro tem 15th Jud. Dist., Crowley, Lafayette and Abbeville, La., 1990-91, 3d Cir. Ct. Appeals, Lake Charles, La., 1992, judge pro tem 1994—). Assoc. editor U. Chgo. Law Rev., 1947-48. With AUS, 1942-46, ETO. Mem. ABA, La. Bar Assn. Democrat. Roman Catholic. Avocations: fishing, hunting. Home: 1331 N Cutting Ave Jennings LA 70546-4201 Office: 302 E Nezpique St Jennings LA 70546-5354 Office Phone: 318-824-7380.

MARCDANTE, KAREN JEAN, medical educator; b. Milw., Sept. 15, 1955; d. Willard Karl and Beth Elaine (Maule) Kohn; m. Mark Wendelberger, Aug. 5, 1978 (div. Sept. 1985); m. Anthony Marcdante, Oct. 17, 1998. Student, Marquette U., Milw., 1973-76; MD, Med. Coll. Wis., Milw., 1980. Diplomate Am. Bd. Pediat. & Pediat. Crit. Care. Resident in pediat. Med. Coll. Wis. affiliated hosps., Milw., 1980-83; instr. pediat. Med. Coll. Wis., Milw., 1983-85, asst. prof. pediat., 1987-94, assoc. prof. pediat., 1994-2000, prof. pediat., 2000—, assoc. dean curriculum, 1997—2003, vice-chair edn. dept. pediat., 1994—; fellow in pediatric critical care U. Calif., San Francisco, 1985-87; vice chief staff Children's Hosp. Wis., Milw., 1995-97. Dir. Respiratory Care Svcs., 1992-98, Transport Program, 1998—; chief dept. pediat. Children's Hosp. Wis., 1991-95, dept. critical care 1993-95, mem. numerous coms., including care mgmt. steering com., 1994-, critical care com., 1991—, pres.-elect, 2003-05; pres. med. dental staff, 2005-07. Contbr. numerous articles to profl. jours. Recipient New Investigator award Assn. Am. Med. Colls., 1992, Cert. Leadership award YWCA and Marquette Electronics Found., 1992, Laureate award Ctrl. Group Ednl. Affairs, 2004; grantee Dept. HHS, 1996—. Mem. Am. Acad. Pediat. (pub. rels. chair Wis. chpt. 1988-91, sec.-treas. 1990-95, v.p. 1995-96, chair careers and opportunities 1996-2001), Soc. Critical Care Medicine (chair task force on quality improvement pediat. 1994-96, quality indicator devel. work group 1997-98, Presdl. citation 1996, 97), Coun. on Med. Student Edn. in Pediat. (co-chair task force on tchg. methods 1991-96, nominating com. 1993-95, exec. com. 1996-99, sec.-treas. 1997-99). Business E-Mail: kwendel@mcw.edu.

MARCEAU, JUDITH MARIE, retired elementary school educator, small business owner; b. Gardner, Mass., Aug. 10, 1946; d. George Joseph and Bernice Victoria (Johnson) Babineau; m. James Victor Krymowski, Aug. 20, 1976 (div. Mar. 1985); children: Kathryn Victoria, Kenneth James; m. Glenn Francis Marceau, Aug. 30, 1989. Grad., Sch. Worcester Art Mus., 1967; BFA, Clark U., 1971. Tchr. elem. art Quabbin Regional Pub. Schs., Barre, Mass., 1967-70, Gardner (Mass.) Pub. Schs., 1970—2003, ret., 2003; propr. Babineau's Corner Antiques Shop, Hubbardston, 2003—. Author, editor: Fascinating Facts of Gardner, 1977, 2d edit., 1999,

Hubbardston as Seen Through the Eyes of its Children, 1987; author numerous poems. Active Hubbarston Hist. Commn.; vol. Hubbarston Recycling Initiative; bd. dirs. Gardner Edn. Assn., 1975-86; bd. dirs. Youth Advocacy and Counseling Ctr., Gardner, 1979-82. Recipient Outstanding Edn. citation City of Gardner, 1994, 2000, Commendation cert. Mayor of City of Gardner, Achievement cert. Gardner Pub. Sch. Com., 2004; named Woman of Year AARP Worcester County, Mass., 2006. Mem. Mass. Tchrs. Assn., Nat. Tchrs. Assn. Achievements include my third grade class 2000-01 petitioned for a bill to declare offical state colors to be cranberry, green and blue for Mass. This became a law signed by Gov. Mitt Romney in Dec. 2004 (students in 7th). Avocations: writing history, poetry, antiques, watercolor painting, sketching. Office Phone: 978-632-2840.

MARCEAU, YVONNE, ballroom dancer, educator; b. Chgo., July 13, 1950; BFA, U. Utah, 1972; AA, Imperial Soc. Ballroom Dance. Ballet dancer Ballet West; ptnr. with Pierre Dulaine, 1976; founder, artistic dir. Am. Ballroom Theatre, NYC, 1984-93; educator dance divsn. Julliard Sch., NYC, 1993—. Guest tchr. Sch. Am. Ballet, NYC; tchr. ballroom dancing Juilliard Sch. Appearances include The Smithsonian Inst., JFK Ctr. for Performing Arts, N.Y. State Theater, N.Y.C., Sadlers Wells, London, (Broadway and London show) Grand Hotel, 1989-92, toured with Pierre Dulaine and Am. Ballroom Theatre worldwide, choreographer (films) Mona Lisa Smile, 2003. Recipient Recipient Brit. Theatrical Arts Championships 4 times, Spl. Astaire award, Dance Educator awards, Outstanding Achievement in Dance award Nat. Coun. Dance Am., 1992, Dance Mag. award, 1993, Edn. award, Americans for the Arts, 2005. Office: Am Ballroom Theater Co 4th Fl 25 W 31st St New York NY 10001 Office Phone: 212-244-9442. Office Fax: 212-244-9299. E-mail: info@dancingclassrooms.com. *

MARCEAUX, LINDA D'AUGEREAU, elementary school educator; b. Abbeville, La., Sept. 27, 1947; d. Charles d'Augereau, Jr. and Hazel Marie Bellot d'Augereau; m. Alex John Marceaux, Aug. 31, 1968; 1 child, Jana Nichole. BA, U. Southwestern La., 1988. Cert. elem. edn. grades 1-8, spl. edn. mild/moderate grades 1-12 generic Dept. Edn. State La. Spl. edn. grades 4th-6th behavior disorder/resource Lafayette Parish Sch. Bd., La., 1988—91, educator 4th grade, 1991—2000, educator 6th grade math, 2000—01, educator 8th grade math, 2001—03, educator 7th -8th grade math. honors, 2003—. Mem. Student La. Assn. Educators U. Southwestern La., Lafayette, 1983—88; membership chair Coun. for Exceptional Children, 2001—02; mem. Lafayette Parish Assn. Educators, 1988—; pres. Student Coun. for Exceptional Children, U. SW La., 1986—88. Sponsor Jr. Nat. Young Leaders Conf., 2004—; v.p. KC Aux., Abbeville, La., 1983—85; pres. Parents for Progress, Meaux, La., 1983—85; coach/advisor Vermilion Boys Football League Cheerleaders, Abbeville, 1983—86; coach/asst. Vermilion Girls Basketball, Abbeville, 1985—87; cheerleader coach Milton Mid. Sch., 1992—2000; co-organizer, co-chair Wives of Workers, Tex. City, Tex., 1972—74; mem. Sch. Crisis Team, 2004. Nominee Outstanding Inclusion Tchr., Coun. for Exceptional Children, 1998—99, Tchr. award, Lafayette Edn. Found., 1999; recipient Coach's award, Universal Cheerleading Assn., 1999. Mem.: La. Tchrs. Math. (math tournament com., Prin.'s award com., sch. crisis team 2001), La. Fedn. Coun. Exceptional Children (state membership chair 2002—05, state exec. bd. 2001—04), Lafayette Paris Assn. Classroom Tchrs., La. Assn. Educators. Roman Catholic. Avocations: woodworking, motorcycling, travel. Home: 410 Quail Dr Lafayette LA 70508 Office: Paul Breaux Mid Sch Lafayette LA 70508

MARCEL-CALDERON, LINDA, music educator; m. Gene Calderon. MusB, Brigham Young U.; MusM, SUNY, Potsdam; EdD, Columbia U. Assoc. prof. music Bergen C.C., Paramus, NJ, 1987—. Author: Discover the Power of Music Listening, 2001. Recipient award, NISOD, 2005; Princeton U. fellow, 2005—. Mem.: Coll. Music Soc. Office: Bergen CC 400 Paramus Rd Paramus NJ 07652-1508 Office Phone: 201-447-7143. Business E-Mail: lmarcel@bergen.edu.

MARCELLA, JOSEPH, information scientist; BA in Biochemistry, Temple U., 1970. Computer operator/sys. programmer, asst. mgr. King Kullen Grocery Co./Gen. Fire & Casualty, LI, 1971-72; asst. v.p., electronic banking Bank of Am., Las Vegas, 1972-83; sr. v.p., dir. info. svcs. Norwest/Wells of Nev., Las Vegas, 1983-96; chief info. officer, dir. info. technologies City of Las Vegas, 1997—. Bd. dirs., past pres. Bank Adminstrn. Inst.; past pres., v.p. Nev. Clearing House Assn.; bd. dirs. Western Payments Alliance; mem. Rules Com. Nat. Automated Clearning House, Task Force to Build Acad. Advanced Tech., Focus Sch. Partnership program. Mem. South Nev. Entities Tech. Alliance (bd. dirs.). Office: City Las Vegas Dept Info Techs City Hall 5th Fl 400 Stewart Ave Las Vegas NV 89101-2927

MARCELLO, MATTHEW T., III, lawyer; b. Cranston, RI, July 12, 1946; BS, Cornell U., 1968; JD, Harvard U., 1972. Bar: RI 1972. Assoc. Hinckley, Allen & Snyder, Providence, 1972—77, ptnr., 1978—. Contbr. articles to profl. jours. Bd. mem. Billy Andrade/Brad Faxon Charities for Children, RI Sponsoring Edn.; bd. mem. & vice chmn. Landmark Med. Ctr. Named Best Lawyers Am. Mem. ABA, Am. Coll. Real Estate Lawyers, R.I. Bar Assn., Phi Kappa Phi. Office: Hinckley Allen & Snyder LLP 50 Kennedy Plz Ste 1500 Providence RI 02903 Office Phone: 401-274-2000. Office Fax: 401-277-9600. E-mail: mmarcello@haslaw.com.

MARCH, BOYD LEE, political science professor, researcher; b. Macon, Mo., Apr. 11, 1958; s. Virgil Boyd and Ruby Marceine March; m. Debra Lynn Branson, Apr. 21, 1984; children: William, Benjamin. BA, Truman State U., Kirksville, Mo., 1980, MA, 1983; PhD, U. Mo., Columbia, 1993. Asst. city mgr. City of Kirksville, 1983—84; city mgr. City of Marceline, Mo., 1984—85; asst. exec. dir. Mo. Local Govt. Retirement, Jefferson City, 1985—86; city adminstr. City of Willow Springs, Mo., 1986—87; adj. instr. Buena Vista Coll., Creston, Iowa, 1987—88; John H. Harland prof. polit. sci. Young Harris Coll., Ga., 1993—. Dir. Vietnam Vets. Oral History Project, Young Harris, 2001—. Author: If You Ain't Cav, 2005. Moderator candidate forum LWV, Hiawassee, Ga., 1993—; spkr. vets. support, 1995—. Named Faculty Mem. of Yr., Young Harris Coll., 1994, 1995, 1997, 2000, 2005, 2006, 2007; recipient Vulcan Tchg. award, Vulcan Techs., 2005. Methodist. Office: Young Harris Coll PO Box 456 Young Harris GA 30582 Office Phone: 706-379-5143. Office Fax: 706-379-4314. Business E-Mail: leem@yhc.edu.

MARCH, JAMES GARDNER, social sciences educator; b. Cleve., Jan. 15, 1928; s. James Herbert and Mildred (MacCorkle) M.; m. Jayne Mary Dohr, Sept. 23, 1947; children: Kathryn Sue, Gary Clifton, James Christopher, Roderic Gunn. BA, U. Wis., Madison, 1949; MA, Yale U., New Haven, Conn., 1950, PhD, 1953; PhD (hon.), Copenhagen Sch. Econs., Denmark, 1978, Swedish Sch. Econs., Helsinki, Finland, 1979, U. Wis., Milw., 1980, U. Bergen, Norway, 1980, Uppsala U., Sweden, 1987, Helsinki Sch. Econs., Finland, 1991, Dublin City U., Ireland, 1994, Göteborg U., Sweden, 1998, U. Poitiers, France, 2001, Budapest U. Econs., Hungary, 2003, York U., Toronto, 2007. From asst. prof. to prof. Carnegie Inst. Tech., 1953-64; prof. psychology, sociology, dean Sch. Social Scis. U. Calif., Irvine, 1964-70; prof. mgmt., higher edn., polit. sci. and sociology Stanford (Calif.) U., 1970-95, prof. emeritus, 1995—. Cons. in field; mem. Nat. Council Ednl. Research, 1975-78, Nat. Sci. Bd., 1968-74; mem. sociol.-social psychology panel NSF, 1964-66; social sci. tng. com. NIMH, 1967-68; mem. math. social sci. com. Social Sci. Research Council, 1958-60; mem. Assembly Behavioral and Social Sci., NRC, 1973-79, chmn. com. on aging, 1977-82, chmn. com. on math., sci., tech. edn., 1984-86 Author: (with H.A. Simon) Organizations, 1958, 2nd edit., 1993, (with R.M. Cyert) A Behavioral Theory of the Firm, 1963, 2nd edit., 1992, Handbook of Organizations, 1965; (with B.R. Gelbaum) Mathematics for the Social and Behavioral Sciences, 1969; (with M.D. Cohen) Leadership and Ambiguity, 1974, 2nd edit., 1986, Academic Notes, 1974; (with C.E. Lave) An Introduction to Models in the Social Sciences, 1975; (with J.P. Olsen) Ambiguity and Choice in Organizations, 1976, Aged Wisconsin, 1977, Autonomy as a Factor in Group Organization, 1980, Pleasures of the Process, 1980, Slow Learner, 1985; (with R. Weissinger-Baylon) Ambiguity and Command, 1986, Decisions and Organizations, 1988; (with J.P. Olsen) Rediscovering Institutions, 1989, Minor Memos, 1990, A Primer on Decision Making, 1994, Fornuft og Forandring, 1995; (with J.P. Olsen) Democratic Governance, 1995; The Pursuit of Organizational Intelligence, 1999, (with M. Schulz and X. Zhou) The Dynamics of Rules, 2000, Late Harvest, 2000; (with M. Augier) The Economics of Choice, Change and Organization, 2002, (with M. Augier), Models of a Man, 2004, Footprints, 2005, Valg, Vane ag Vision, 2005, (with T. Weil) On Leadership, 2005; contbr. articles to profl. jours. Fellow Ctr. Advanced Study in Behavioral Scis., 1955-56, 73-74; recipient Wilbur Lucius Cross medal Yale U., 1968, Viipuri prize, Finland, 2004, Herbert Simon award, Hungary, 2005; decorated knight 1st class Royal Norwegian Order of Merit, comdr. Order of Lion of Finland. Mem. NAS, APA, Nat. Acad. Edn., Accademia Italiana di Economia Aziendale, Royal Swedish Acad. Scis., Norwegian Acad. of Sci. and Letters, Am. Acad. Arts and Scis., Am. Econ. Assn., Am. Polit. Sci. Assn. (v.p. 1983-84, John Gaus award 1997, Wildavsky award 2004), Am. Sociol. Assn., Acad. Mgmt. (Disting. Scholar award 1999), Russell Sage Found. (trustee 1985-94, chmn. 1990-93), Finnish Soc. Scis. and Letters, Citigroup Behavioral Scis. Rsch. Coun. (chmn. 1994-2000), Am. Philos. Soc., Phi Beta Kappa, Sigma Xi. Home: 501 Portola Rd Box 8136 Portola Valley CA 94028 Office Phone: 650-424-4344. Business E-Mail: march@stanford.edu.

MARCH, KATHLEEN PATRICIA, judge, lawyer; b. May 18, 1949; married; 2 children. BA, Colo. Coll., 1971; JD, Yale U., 1974. Bar: N.Y. 1975, Calif. 1978. Law clk. to hon. judge Thomas J. Griesa U.S. Dist. Ct. (so. dist.) N.Y., 1974-75; assoc. Cahill, Gordon & Reindel, NYC, 1975-77; asst. U.S. atty. criminal div. Office of U.S. Atty. Cen. Dist. Calif., LA, 1978-82; assoc. Adams, Duque & Hazeltine, LA, 1982-85; ptnr. Demetriou, Del Guercio & Lovejoy, LA, 1985-88; judge US Bankruptcy Ct. Cen. Dist. Calif., LA, 1988—2002; founder Bankruptcy Law Firm, LA, 2002—. Contbr. articles to profl. jours. Mem.: ABA, Fin. Lawyers Assn., L.A. Bankruptcy Forum (bd. dirs.), Nat. Assn. Women Judges, Women Lawyers Assn., L.A. County Bar Assn., Fed. Bar Assn., Phi Beta Kappa. Bd. editors: Yale U. Law Jour. Office: Bankruptcy Law Firm 10524 W Pico Blvd Ste 212 Los Angeles CA 90064 Office Phone: 310-559-9224. Office Fax: 310-559-9133. Business E-Mail: kmarch@bkylawfirm.com.

MARCH, KEVIN P., electronics executive; BS in Econs., U. Pitts., 1983, MBA, 1984. Various positions including dir. fin., contr. semiconductor units Tex. Instruments, Inc., Dallas, 1984—97, v.p. fin. planning, mgr. global ops., 1997—2002, contr., 2002—03, sr. v.p., CFO, 2003—. Mem. Fin. Exec. Internat., Conf. Bd.'s Coun. Fin. Exec. Office: Tex Instruments Inc PO Box 660199 Dallas TX 75266-0199 Office Phone: 972-995-2011. Office Fax: 972-995-4360. *

MARCH, MICHAEL F., propulsion systems analyst, consultant; b. Detroit, Mar. 3, 1962; s. Stanley and Dorothy M. AAS in Archtl. Design, Macomb C.C., Warren, Mich., 1983; BS in Mech. Engring., Lawrence Technol. U., 1986; ME, U. Fla., 1994. Sr. analytical engr. United Techs. Corp.-Pratt & Whitney, West Palm Beach, Fla., 1986-93; pvt. practice propulsion analysis cons. Tullahoma, Tenn., 1994—. Mem. ASME.

MARCHAK, MAUREEN PATRICIA, anthropology and sociology educator, academic administrator; b. Lethbridge, Alta., Can., June 22, 1936; d. Adrian Ebenezer and Wilhelmina Rankin (Hamilton) Russell; m. William Marchak, Dec. 31, 1956; children: Geordon Eric, Lauren Craig. BA, U. B.C., Vancouver, Can., 1958, PhD, 1970. Asst. prof. U. B.C., Vancouver, 1972-75, assoc. prof., 1975-80, prof., 1980—, head dept. anthropology and sociology, 1987-90, dean faculty arts, 1990-96, disting. scholar in residence Peter Wall Inst., 2000—, prof., dean emerita of arts, 2001—; sr. rsch. fellow Ctr. Internat. Rels. Liu Inst. for Study of Global Issues, 2002—; interim dir., 2005—06. Author: Ideological Perspectives on Canada, 1975, 2d edit., 1981, 3d edit., 1988, In Whose Interests, 1979, Green Gold, 1983 (John Porter award 1985), The Integrated Circus, The New Right and The Restructuring of Global Markets, 1991, Logging the Globe, 1995, Falldown, Forest Policy in British Columbia, 1999, Racism, Sexism and the University, the Political Science Affair at UBC, 1996, God's Assassins. State Terrorism in Argentina in the 1970's, 1999 (Wallace J. Ferguson prize, Hon. Mention), Reigns of Terror, 2003, Global Pieces, 2006; author, co-editor: Uncommon Property, 1987; mem. editl. bd. Can. Rev. Sociology and Anthropology, Montreal, 1971-74, Studies in Polit. Economy, Ottawa, Ont., Can., 1980-87, Current Sociology, 1980-86, Can. Jour. Sociology, 1986-90, B.C. Studies, 1988-90, 2000-04. Bd. dir., chair ethics com. Univ. Hosp., 1992-93; trustee Cedar Lodge Trust Soc., 1989-92; mem. adv. coun. Ecotrust, 1991-93, bd. dir., 1993-97, Eco-trust Can., 1995-99; chmn. bd. dir. B.C. Bldgs. Corp., 1992-95; mem. B.C. Forest Appeals Commn., 1992-2002; bd. govs. U. B.C., 1999-2001; bd. dir. Pub. Svc. Employees for Environ. Ethics, 2002-04; mem. sector study steering com. Can. Coun. Profl. Fish Harvesters, 2002—05. Named Woman of Distinction, YWCA, 1999. Fellow Royal Soc. Can. (v.p. Acad. II 1994-98, pres. Acad. II 1998-2000); mem. Can. Sociology and Anthropology Assn. (pres. 1979-80, other offices), Internat. Sociol. Assn., Can. Polit. Sci. Assn., Assn. for Can. Studies, Forest History Soc. (mem. exec. com. 1991-92). Avocations: hiking, swimming, travel, listening to music. Home: 4455 W 1st Ave Vancouver BC Canada V6R 4H9 Home Phone: 604-228-1375. E-mail: patricia.marchak@gmail.com.

MARCHAND, MICHAEL J., judge, career military officer; b. Rice, Minn. BA, St. John's U., Collegeville, Minn., 1970; JD, U. Minn.; grad., Armed Forces Staff Coll., Indsl. Coll. Armed Forces. Commd. JAGC, U.S. Army, 1974, asst. staff judge advocate Ft. Sam Houston, Tex., 1974—77, US Army Forces Command, Ft. McPherson, Ga., 1977—79; instr., sr. instr. contract law JAG Sch., Charlottesville, Va., 1980—83; dep. staff judge advocate U.S. Army Transp. Ctr. and Ft. Eustis, Ft. Eustis, Va., 1983—85; plans officer Office of the JAG, Washington, 1986—88; staff judge advocate 6th Inf. Divsn. (Light) Alaska, 1988—91, U.S. Army Garrison, Ft. Polk, La., 1991—93; chief adminstrv. law divsn. Office of JAG, Washington, 1994—95, exec. to JAG, 1995—97, asst. JAG for civil law and litigation, 1997—98; comdr. U.S. Army Svcs. Agy., 1998—2001; chief judge U.S. Army Ct. Criminal Appeals, 1998—2001; asst. JAG, JAGC U.S. Army, 2001—. Decorated Legion of Merit, Meritorious Svc. medal with 3 oak leaf clusters, Army Commendation medal with one oak leaf cluster, Army Achievement medal with one oak leaf cluster, Nat. Def. Svc. medal with one svc. star, Army Staff Identification Badge. Office: Office of JAG US Army Pentagon Washington DC 20310-1500

MARCHANT, GARY ELVIN, lawyer; b. Squamish, BC, Can., July 5, 1958; came to U.S., 1986; s. Leonard Roy and Elsie Christine (Anderson) M. BSc, U. B.C., 1980, PhD, 1986; MPP, Harvard U., 1990, JD magna cum laude, 1990. Bar: Mass. 1991, D.C. 1993. Assoc. Kirkland & Ellis, Washington, 1990-95, ptnr., 1995—99; assoc. prof. Ariz. State U. Coll. Law, Tempe, Ariz., 1999—2003, dir. Ctr. Study Law, Sci. & Tech., 2001—, prof., 2003—. Editor-in-chief, Harvard Jour. Law & Tech.; editor, Harvard Environ. Law rev.; assoc. ed., Nonlinearity in Biology, Toxicology and Medicine; contr. articles to profl. jours. Mem. ABA, Def. Rsch. Inst., Air and Waste Mgmt. Assn., Environ. Law Inst., AAAS, Soc. Risk Analysis, N.Y. Acad. Sci., Soc. Social Studies of Sci. Office: Ariz State U Sch Law PO Box 877906 Tempe AZ 85287-7906 Office Phone: 480-965-3246. Business E-Mail: gary.marchant@asu.edu. *

MARCHANT, KENNY, congressman; b. Bonham, Tex, Feb. 23, 1951; m. Donna Marchant; children: Luke, Matthew, Kenny, Dallas. BA, So. Nazarene U., Bethany, Okla., 1974; attended, Nazarene Theol. Sem., Kansas City, Mo., 1975—76; DHL (hon.), So. Nazarene U., Bethany, Okla., 1999. Mem. City Coun., Carrollton, Tex., 1980—84; mayor Carrollton, Tex., 1984—87; mem. Tex. State Ho. Reps., Austin, 1987—2004, US Congress from 24th Tex. dist., 2005—, mem. transp. and infrastructure com., mem. edn. and the workforce com., mem. govt. reform com. Mem. adv. bd. Children's Med. Ctr. Named Top Ten Legislator, Tex. Monthly mag., Citizen of Yr., Metrocrest C. of C., Legislator of Yr., Tex. Mcpl. League. Republican. Nazarene. Office: US Ho Reps 501 Cannon Ho Office Bldg Washington DC 20515-4324 Office Phone: 202-225-6605. *

MARCHASE, RICHARD BANFIELD, cell biologist, educator, research administrator; b. Sayre, Pa., Mar. 12, 1948; s. Nicholas and Vivian H. (Banfield) M.; m. Gail C. Andrews, Sept. 2, 2006; children: Nicholas Darrow, Allison Elizabeth. BS in Engring., Cornell U., 1970; PhD in Biophysics, Johns Hopkins U., 1976; postgrad., Duke U., 1978. Muscular Dystrophy Assn. postdoctoral fellow divsn. neurology Duke U. Med. Ctr., 1976-77, USPHS postdoctoral fellow dept. anatomy, 1977-78, asst. prof. anatomy, 1978-86; assoc. prof. cell biology U. Ala.-Birmingham, 1986—90, prof., 1990—, chmn., 1992—2000, sr. assoc. dean biomed. rsch., 2000—06, v.p. rsch. and econ. devel., 2004—. Contbr. chpts. to books, articles to profl. jours. Recipient Hamilton Watch award Cornell U., 1970, award Juvenile Diabetes Found., 1995-2002; Grad. fellow NSF, 1970-73, Danforth Found. grad. fellow, 1973-76; Nanaline H. Duke scholar, 1982-85; grantee USPHS 1979-, NSF, Presdl. Young Investigator grant, 1982-87. Mem. AAAS, Am. Soc. Cell Biology, Am. Soc. Zoology, Assn. of Anatomy, Cell Biology, and Neurobiology Chairpersons (pres. 1995-96), Am. Assn. Anatomists, Fed. Am. Soc. Exptl. Biology (bd. dirs. 2000— v.p. sci. policy, 2005, pres.-elect 2007), Sigma Xi. Office: U Ala Birmingham 720 AB Birmingham AL 35294-0001 Home: 4012 Lenox Rd Birmingham AL 35213 Office Phone: 205-934-1294. Business E-Mail: marchase@uab.edu.

MARCHENKO, TAMARA G., music educator; b. NEvelsk, Russia, Aug. 4, 1951; arrived in US, 1996; d. Georgy Davidovich and Galina Grigoryevna Khachikyan; m. Yury Marchenko (div.); 1 child, Leon;. BA in Piano, N.A. Rimskiy-Korsakov Coll. Music, Krasnodar, Russia, 1981; MusM, Kuban State U., Krasnodar, Russia, 1973. Care giver to elderly pvt. practice, LA, 1996—98; salesperson Jons Market, LA, 1998—99; tchr. music Sunflower Montessori Sch., LA, 2000—; pianist El Redentor Luth. Ch., LA, 2000—04; dir. choir, organist Ctrl. Luth. Ch., Van Nuys, Calif., 2002—05; tchr. aide LA Unified Sch. Dist., North Hollywood, Calif., 2005—; dir. music All Saints Luth. Ch., Sun Valley, Calif., 2005—; tchr. music Winds of Hope, Sun Valley, 2006—. Organist St. Barnabas the Apostle Anglican Ch., Sun Valley, 2006—. Mem.: Am. Guild Organists. Avocations: reading, exercise, music. Personal E-mail: marchenkomusic@netzero.com.

MARCHESE, LISA MARIE, lawyer, educator; b. Seattle, Sept. 13, 1962; d. John Sebastian and Joanne Spino Marchese. BA, Cath. U. Am., Washington, DC, 1984; JD, Georgetown U. Law Ctr., Washington, DC, 1987. Bar: Wash. 1988, Oreg. 2003, US Supreme Ct. 1998, US Dist. Ct. (ea. and we. dists.) Wash. 1998, US Ct. Appeals (9th cir.) 2003. Legis. counsel Hon. Daniel J. Evans, Washington, 1983—88; sr. dep. pros. atty. King County Prosecutor's Office, Seattle, 1989—98; ptnr. Stafford Frey Cooper, 1998—2006, Dorsey & Whitney LLP, Seattle, 2006—. Adj. law prof. U. Wash. Law Sch., 1999—, Seattle U. Sch. Law, 2000—; faculty mem. Nat. Inst. Trial Advocacy, 1999—; bd. mem. Wash. Women Lawyers, 2000—02; spkr. in field. Contbr. articles to various law jours. Mem.: Washington Women Lawyers, Phi Beta Kappa. Roman Cath. Avocations: sports, opera, reading, golf. Office: Dorsey & Whitney LLP US Bank Ctr 1420 Fifth Ave 3400 Seattle WA 98101 Office Phone: 206-903-8800, 206-903-2379. Business E-Mail: marchese.lisa@dorsey.com.

MARCHESE, MICHAEL JAMES, JR., radiation oncologist; b. NYC, Mar. 9, 1955; s. Michael James Sr. and Mabel Gladys (Rosero) M.; m. Kathryn Allen, Aug. 7, 1982 (div. May 1993); 1 child, Michael James III; m. Kathleen Spahr, Oct. 18, 1997; 1 child, Melissa June, Jessica Maria. BA magna cum laude, NYU, 1976; MD, Baylor Coll. Medicine, 1979. Diplomate Am. Bd. Radiology. Intern Monmouth Med. Ctr., Hahnemann Med. Coll., Long Branch, NJ, 1979—80; resident and chief resident radiation therapy Presbyn. Hosp., Columbia U. Coll. Physicians and Surgeons, NYC, 1980—83, asst. attending physician radiation oncology, 1983—87; resident brachytherapy svc. Meml. Sloan Kettering Cancer Ctr., Cornell U. Med. Coll., NYC, 1982; asst. clin. prof. radiation oncology Columbia U. Coll. Physicians & Surgeons, NYC, 1983—84, asst. prof. radiation oncology, 1984—87; attending staff radiology/radiation oncology Cmty. Med. Ctr., Toms River, NJ, 1987—96, Kimball Med. Ctr., Lakewood, NJ, 1994—, Med. Ctr. Ocean County, Brick, NJ, 1996—; dir. Ocean Radiation Therapy Ctr., Toms River, NJ, 1997—2005, Ctr. for Advanced Radiation Oncology, Toms River, NJ, 2005—. Investigator Nat. Cancer Inst., 1983-87, investigator radiation therapy oncology group, 1983-87, 95—, physician surveyor, 1983-85, investigator cancer and leukemia group B, 1986-87, investigator Ea. Coop. Oncology Group, 1995—; physician surveyor practice accreditation program Am. Coll. Radiology, 1986-87; Cancer liason Am. Coll. Surgeons, Kimball Med. Ctr., 2001-04. Author: (with others) Radiation Therapy of Gynecological Cancers, 1987, Frontiers of Radiation Therapy and Oncology, vol. 22, 1988; contbr. articles to profl. jours. Bd. dirs. Am. Cancer Soc., Ocean County, N.J., 1993—2004, v.p., 1993-94, pres., 1994-98, chief med. officer, 2000-01. Recipient Resident/Fellow award Am. Radium Soc., Travel award European Soc. Therapeutic Radiology and Oncology, Clin. Oncology Career Devel. award Am. Cancer Soc., Physician of Yr., Am. Cancer Soc., 1998. Fellow Am. Coll. Radiation Oncology; mem. Am. Soc. Therapeutic Radiology and Oncology, Am. Soc. Clin. Oncology, Acad. Medicine N.J., Radiation Rsch. Soc., N.Y. Acad. Sci., Ocean County Med. Soc. (trustee 1997—, treas. 2005—), Med. Soc. N.J. (del. 2000—). Roman Catholic. Home: 44 Lake Shore Dr Red Bank NJ 07701-5840 Office: Center for Advanced Radiation Oncology 512 Lakehurst Rd Toms River NJ 08755-5029 Office Phone: 732-240-0053. Personal E-mail: mjmmd44@yahoo.com.

MARCHESI, VINCENT THOMAS, biochemist, educator; b. NYC, Sept. 4, 1935; married, 1959; six children. BA, Yale U., 1957, MD, 1963; PhD in Pathology, Oxford U., Eng., 1961. Intern, resident in pathology Wash. U., St. Louis, 1963-65; rsch. assoc. cell biology Rockefeller U., NYC, 1965-66; staff assoc. Nat. Cancer Inst., Bethesda, Md., 1966-68; chief sect. chem. pathology Nat. Inst. Arthritis, Metabolism & Digestive Disorders, 1968—72; assoc. prof. pathology Sch. Medicine Yale U., New Haven, 1972-73, prof. pathology and cell biology Sch. Medicine, chmn. dept. biology, 1973—89; chief pathology Yale-New Haven Hosp., New Haven, 1973—79; dir. Boyer Ctr. Molecular Medicine, Yale U. Sch. Medicine, New Haven, 1989—. Cons. Miles Pharm., West Haven, Conn., 1982—. Editor-in-chief FASEB Jour., 1996—; editor: Laboratory Investigation, —, Molecular Mag., —, BCMD, —. Bd. dirs. Am. Cyanamid, N.J., 1992-94. Lt. comdr. USPHS, 1966-68. Recipient Borden Undergrad. Med. Rsch. award, Yale U., 1963, Parke Davis Meritorious award in exptl. pathology, 1973, Karl Landsteiner award, 1983, Rous-Whipple Rsch. award, Am. Assn. Pathology, 1989. Mem. Inst. Medicine-NAS, Am. Soc. Cell Biology, Am. Assn. Pathologists (former pres.), Am. Assn. Immunologists, Am. Soc. Investigative Pathology, Am. Soc. Biological Chem., Biophysical Soc. Avocations: tennis, history. also: Boyer Ctr Molecular Medicine 295 Congress Ave Rm 109 New Haven CT 06519-1418

MARCHI, JON, retired brokerage house executive, rancher, venture capitalist; b. Aug. 6, 1946; s. John Robert and Joan Trimble (Toole) M.; m. Mary Stewart Sale, Aug. 12, 1972 (div. 1999); children: Aphia Jessica, Jon Jacob. Student, Claremont Men's Coll., 1964-65; BS, U. Mont., 1968, MS, 1972. Sec., treas. Marchi, Marchi & Marchi, Inc., Morris, Ill., 1968-69; account exec. D. A. Davidson & Co., Billings, Mont., 1972-75, asst. v.p., office mgr., 1976-77, v.p. mktg. and adminstrn. Great Falls, Mont., 1977—. Sec., dir., v.p. fin. svcs. and exec. devel. D. A. Davidson Realty Corp., Great Falls, 1978-85, chmn. rsch. com., 1980; bd. dirs. Ligocyte Corp., Bozeman, Mont., Big Sky Airlines, Billings, chmn. bd. dirs., 1995; bd. dirs. Implemax Equipment Co., Inc., Bozeman, Energy Overthrust Found., Mansfield Found., Mont. Beverages, Mont. Venture Capital Network, Direct Advantage, Inc., Hamilton, Mont., Mont. Naturals Internat., Inc., Eclipse Techs., Inc., Mont. Small Bus. Investment Corp., Phillips Environ. Corp., Bozeman, Mont.; chmn., dir. Devel. Corp. Mont., Helena, 1995; cattle rancher, Polson, Mont., 1986—; dir. Mont. Econ. Devel. Action Group, 2001-; guest lectr. London Sch. Econs., London, 2004. Chmn. Mont. Gov.'s Subcom. for Venture Capital Devel., Mont. Cmty. Fin. Corp., Helena, Mont. Facility Fin. Corp.; chmn. investment com. State of Mont. Sci. and Tech. Alliance, 1985—; chmn. seed capital com. State of Mont., bd. dirs. job svc. com.; mem. Mont. Peoples Action; sec.-treas. Valley View Assn., 1987—; trustee sch. dist. # 35, Polson, Mont., 1990—, chmn., 1991—; bd. dirs. Mont. Entrepreneurship Ctr., Missoula, Mont., 1990—; pres., dir. sec.-treas. Mont. Pvt. Capital Network, Bozeman, Mont., 1990—, pres., 1992—; chmn., dir. Mont. Naturals Internat., Inc., 1991; dir. Mont. State Rural Devel. Coun., 1992, Mont. SBA Adv. Coun., 1992; dir. Ctr. Econ. Renewal and Tech. Transfer Mont. State U., Bozeman, 1994—; del. to White House Conf. on Small Bus., Washington, 1994-95; chmn. Glacier Venture Fund, Helena, Mont., 1996—; mem. investment adv. com. DCC Growth Fund, Washington, 1998—. With U.S. Army, 1969-71; dir. Mont. State U., Billings, Coll. of Bus. Bd., 1995-, Mont. Econ. Devel. Action Group, 2001-; mem. Gov.'s Com. Tax Restructuring, 2002-, Gov.'s Task Force on Access to Capital, 2002-; mem. Frontier Fund, Kalispell, Mont., 2006; regional dir. Mus. of Rockies, Bozeman, Mont.; appointed chmn. Mont. Facility Fin. Auth.; dir. Greater Northern Drilling Corp., Billings, Mont., 2007, treas. Named Amb. of Yr., State of Mont., 2003, Alumni of Yr., U. Mont. Sch. Bus., 2004; named to Mont. Acad. Disting. Entrepreneurs, U. Mont., 2003. Mem. Nat. Cattlemen's Assn. (fgn. trade com.), Am. Wagyu Assn. (bd. dirs. 2000—, 1st v.p.), Can. Wagyu Assn., Polson C. of C. (bd. dirs.), Valley View Assn. (bd. dirs.), Mont. Cattle Feeders Assn., Mont. Angus Assn., Western Mont. Angus Assn., Am. Angus Assn., Western Mont. Stockgrowers Assn., Securities Industry Assn., Mont. Stock Growers Assn., Mont. Ambassadors (dir. 1995, pres. 2001—), Polson C. of C. (dir.), Acme Angels, Leadership Great Falls Club, Ski Club, Mont. Club, Helena Wilderness Riders Club, Rotary. Episcopalian. Office: Marchi Angus Ranches 7783 Valley View Rd Polson MT 59860-9302 Business E-Mail: jonmarchi@marchiangos.com.

MARCHI, SERGIO SISTO, Canadian government official; b. Buenos Aires, May 12, 1956; s. Ottavio and Luisa (D'Agostinis) M.; m. Laureen Storozuk, Oct. 1, 1983. BA with honors, York U., Toronto, 1979. Alderman City of North York, 1982-84; M.P. for York West dist. Ho. of Commons, Ottawa, 1984-99, min. citizenship and immigration, 1993-96; min. of environment, 1996-97; min. internat. trade Govt. Canada, 1997-99; Canadian amb. of UN and WTO Permanent Missions of Can. to Office of UN, Geneva, 2000—05; chmn. WTO Coun. for Trade in Svcs., 2000—01; chair working party on accession of Ukraine WTO, 2000—; mem. policy adv. commn. WIPO, 2000—; chair gen. coun. WTO, 2002—03; pres. Legacy House of Investments, Geneva. Mem. cabinet coms. on treasury bd., social policy and program review. Mem. Cabinet Com. on Treas. bd., Social Policy and Program Review; vice chmn. North York Planning Bd., Toronto, 1982-84, Standing Com. on Transport, Ottawa, 1990-93; chmn. Nat. Liberal Caucus, Ottawa, 1990-93. Liberal Party Can.

MARCHIONINI, GARY JOSEPH, information science educator; b. Altoona, Pa., Sept. 12, 1949; s. Arthur and Claudia (Serventi) M.; m. Suzanne Bernhardt, July 10, 1970; children: Brian, Deanna. BA, Western Mich. U., 1971; MEd, Wayne State U., 1974, PhD, 1981. Tchr. math. East Detroit (Mich.) Pub. Schs., 1971-78; inservice specialist, rschr. Wayne State U., Detroit, 1978-82, asst. prof. inst. tech., 1982-83; asst. prof. info. sci. U. Md., College Park, 1983-90, assoc. prof. info. sci., 1990-95, prof. info. sci., 1995-98; Boshamer prof. info. sci. U. N.C., Chapel Hill, 1998—. Expert NSF, Washington, 1989-90; adj. prof. George Washington U., Washington, 1992. Author: Information Seeking in Electronic Environments, 1995; contbr. articles to profl. jours. Grantee: NSF, 1987-90, Harvard U., Annenberg Corp. Pub. Broadcasting, 1988-93, Coun. on Libr. Resources, 1990-91, Nat. Libr. Medicine, 1992, NASA, 1993-94. Mem. Assn. for Computing Machinery, Am. Soc. for Info. Sci. (Rsch. award 1997), Am. Ednl. Rsch. Assn., Assn. for Advancement Computers in Edn. Office: U NC 203 Maning Hill Chapel Hill NC 27599-0001

MARCHUK, NEIL, automotive executive; First degree in Bus. Commerce, U. Windsor, Can.; MBA, U. Paisley, UK. Pers. and indsl. rels. mgr. ITT Can.; with DuPont, 1980—92, human resources dir. Greater China, 1995—99, dir. corp. human resources; v.p. human resources Can. bus. to dir. human resources and adminstrn. China ops. SC Johnson, 1992—95; exec. v.p. human resources TRW Automotive Holdings Corp. Mem. Overseas Schs. Adv. Bd. Office: TRW Automotive Holdings Corp 12001 Tech Center Dr Livonia MI 48150 Office Phone: 734-855-2600. *

MARCIALIS, ANGELO VINCENT, musician, educator; b. Bronx, NY, Nov. 19, 1958; s. Vincent John and Mary Concetta Marcialis. BA in Music, Berklee Coll. Music, 1980; MA in Edn. and Music, Manhattanville Coll., 1991. Cert. state cert. adjudicator NY State Sch. Music Assn., tchr. mentor NY State Union Tchrs. Regional dir. Music on the Move, Staten Island, NY, 1982—84; dir. of bands Chester (N.Y.) Union Free Sch. Dist., 1985—87, Enlarged City Sch. Dist. Middletown, NY, 1987—2003; dir. ensembles Washingtonville (NY) Sch., 2003—. Historian, archivist, trumpeter, jazz clnician Orange County (N.Y.) Music Educators Assn., 1987—. Author: Supplementary Method for Beginning Trumpet Players, 1992. Recruiter Green Party, Orange County, 2000. Named Tchr. of Yr., Middletown, 1991. Mem.: N.Y. State Band Dirs. Assn., Internat. Trumpet Guild, N.Y. State Music Assn. Avocations: gardening, baseball, hiking, bicycling, herptology. Home: 3712 Whispering Hills Chester NY 10918-1530 Office: Washingtonville Sch 38 W Main St Washingtonville NY 10992 Office Phone: 845-497-2200 ext 21197. Personal E-mail: trumpethead@hotmail.com.

MARCIALIS, ROBERT LOUIS, planetary astronomer; b. NYC, Sept. 14, 1956; s. Louis Angelo and Joan Regina (Dippolito) M. SB in Aero. and Astronautical Engring., MIT, 1978, SB in Earth and Planetary Scis., 1980; MS in Physics and Astronomy, Vanderbilt U., 1983; PhD in Planetary Scis., U. Ariz., 1990. Tchg. asst. dept. earth and planetary scis. MIT, Cambridge, 1976—80; lab. instr. dept. physics and astronomy Vanderbilt U., Nashville, 1981, 1982—83, rsch. asst. Arthur J. Dyer Obs., 1981—82; rsch. asst. Lunar and Planetary Lab. U. Ariz., Tucson, 1983—86, rsch. assoc., 1986—90; postdoctoral fellow Jet Propulsion Lab., Pasadena, Calif., 1990—92; adj. faculty Pima C.C., Tucson, 1992—; sr. rsch. specialist U. Ariz., 1996—. Founding mem. Pluto/Charon Mut. Eclipse Season Campaign. Contbr. articles to Nature, Bull. Am. Astron. Soc., Astron. Jour., Minor Planet Circular, Lunar and Planetary Sci., Sci., Jour. Brit. Astron. Assn., Astrophys. Jour., Icarus, also others. Instr. water safety ARC, 1981-82; ednl. counselor MIT, 1983—; fastpitch softball umpire, 1975—. Rsch. fellow NASA, 1986-89. Mem. AAAS, Am. Astron. Soc., Am. Geophys. Union, Astron. Soc. Pacific, Internat. Occultation Timing Assn., Sigma Pi Sigma. Roman Catholic. Achievements include discovery of water ice on surface of Pluto's moon Charon; construction of an albedo map for surface of Pluto; research on Pluto, Charon and Triton, icy satellites, outer solar system formation and evolution, solar system photometry, occultation astronomy, construction and calibration of Imager for Mars Pathfinder, cameras for the Mars Polar Lander and Mars Phoenix missions and Mars Odyssey gamma ray spectrometer. Office: U Ariz Lunar Planetary Lab Tucson AZ 85721-0001 E-mail: umpire@lpl.arizona.edu.

MARCIL, WILLIAM CHRIST, SR., publisher, broadcast executive; b. Rolette, ND, Mar. 9, 1936; s. Max L. and Ida (Fuerst) M.; m. Jane Black, Oct. 15, 1960; children: Debora Jane, William Christ Jr. BSBA, U. N.D., 1958. Br. mgr. Community Credit Co., Mpls., 1959-61; with Forum Comms. Co., Fargo, N.D., 1961—, pres., pub., CEO, 1969—. Pres. Forum Comm. Found.; past bd. dirs. North Ctrl. region Boy Scouts Am. With U.S. Army, 1958-59. Mem. Inland Newspaper Press Assn., N.D. Press Assn., Am. Newspaper Pubs. Assn. (past dir., chmn.), Fargo Morehead C. of C., N.D. State C. of C. (past pres.), U.S. C. of C. (past chmn.), Sigma Delta Chi, Lambda Chi Alpha. Lodges: Masons, Shriners, Elks. Republican. Office: Forum Comm Co 101 5th St N Fargo ND 58102-4826 Home: 1618 S 8th St Fargo ND 58103

MARCIN, ROBERT H., automotive executive; BBA, SUNY, 1971; MBA, Calif. State U., 1973. With Ford Aerospace, San Jose, Calif., 1973—89; exec. v.p., dir., external & employee affairs First Nationwide Fin. Corp., 1989—93; dir., compensation planning office Ford Motor Co., 1993—95, dir., internat. labor affairs, 1995—98, exec. dir., labor affairs, 1998—2000; sr. v.p., human resources Visteon Corp., Dearborn, Mich., 2000—03, sr. v.p., corp. relations, 2003—. Bd. dirs. Med-i-bank, Inc., Am. Soc. Employers, Mich. Office: Visteon Corp 1700 Rotunda Dr Dearborn MI 48120

MARCINIAK, MACARY WECK, pharmacist, educator; PharmD, U. NC, Chapel Hill, 2000. Bd. cert. pharmacotherapy specialist Bd. Pharm. Specialties, Washington, 2003, cert. internat. smoking cessation specialist U. Pitts. Sch. Pharmacy, 2001, clinician assisted tobacco cessation specialist U. Calif. San Francisco Sch. Pharmacy, 2003, Smallpox vaccinator and adverse event, take site monitor NY State Dept. Health, 2003. Assoc. prof. pharmacy practice Albany Coll. Pharmacy, NY, 2001—. Named Club/Orgn. Advisor of Yr., Albany Coll. Pharmacy Student Govt. Assn., 2006; recipient Outstanding Commitment award, Am. Lung Assn. Northeastern NY, 2003, Walter Singer Svc. award, Capital Area Pharmacists Soc., 2004. Mem.: Am. Assn. Colls. Pharmacy, Pharmacists Soc. State NY (chair acad. pharmacy coll. academicians 2006—, Disting. Young Pharmacist award 2003), Am. Coll. Clin. Pharmacy, Am. Pharmacists Assn. (new practitioner officer, cmty. and ambulatory practice sect. 2002—04, cert. pharmaceutical care for patients with Diabetes 2000, cert. pharmacy-based immunization delivery 2000, cert. over the counter advisor pharmacy-based self-care svcs. 2005, Mortar and Pestle Professionalism Essay award Acad. Student Pharmacists 2001), Phi Lambda Sigma (chpt. v.p. 1998—99), Phi Delta Chi (grand v.p. for collegiate affairs 2003—05). Conservative. Pentecostal. Office: Albany College Pharmacy 106 New Scotland Ave Albany NY 12208 Office Phone: 518-694-7337. Office Fax: 518-694-7302. Business E-Mail: marcinim@acp.edu.

MARCO, CURA A., medical educator; s. Jorge and Martha Cura; m. Natalia Martinez, Aug. 17, 1970; children: Victoria Cura, Emilia Cura. MD, Cath. U. Cordoba, Argentina, 1995. Cert. Am. Bd. Radiology, 2003. Asst. prof. U. Tex. Health Sci. Ctr., San Antonio, 2005—. Contbr. articles to profl. jours. Fellow Interventional Radiology, Columbia U., 2003. Mem.: Am. Roentgen Ray Soc. (Cert. Merit 2005), Soc. Interventional Radiology (assoc.), Am. Coll. Radiology (assoc.), Radiol. Soc. N.Am. (assoc. Cert. Merit 2002, Cum Laude award 2002), Am. Heart Assn. (assoc.). Home Phone: 210-842-8938; Office Phone: 210-567-5564.

MARCOCCIA, LOUIS GARY, accountant, academic administrator; b. Syracuse, NY, Nov. 6, 1946; s. George A. and Rose J. (Misita) M.; m. Susan Evelyn Miller, June 21, 1974; 1 child: Rachel Kathryn. BS, Syracuse U., 1968, MS, 1969; EdD, U. Pa., 2003. CPA NY. Acct. Price Waterhouse & Co., Syracuse, NY, 1969-75; dir. internal audit Syracuse U., 1975-76, comptroller, 1976-82, v.p., comptroller, 1982-95, sr. v.p. bus., and fin., 1985—95, sr. v.p. bus., fin. and adminstrv. svcs., 1995—2006, exec. v.p., CFO, 2006—. Bd. dirs. Syracuse Bd. Chase Manhattan Bank, Syracuse Divsn., 1985-2001, Lincoln Life and Annuity Co. N.Y., Univ. Hill Corp., Upstate Med. Univ. Found.; pres. Syracuse U. Hotel and Conf. Ctr., LLC; spkr. Harvard U. Inst. Ednl. Mgmt., 1984-88, 90-91. Pres. parish coun. St. Michael's Ch., Syracuse, 1985-88; pres. Syracuse U. Theatre Corp., 1987—; bd. dirs. Friends of Burnet Park Zoo, 1987-93, Syracuse U. Press., 1982—, Syracuse Sports Corp., 1990-91. Mem. AICPA, N.Y. Soc. CPA, Nat. Assn. Accts., Fin. Execs. Inst., Inst. Internal Auditors. Clubs: Drumlins (pres. 1976—); Century. Republican. Roman Catholic. Avocations: swimming, tennis. Home: Hedge Ln Cazenovia NY 13035 Office: Syracuse U Off ExecVP and CFO 900 S Crouse AveSte 620 Syracuse NY 13244-2130 Business E-Mail: lmarcocc@syr.edu.

MARCOGLIESE, RICHARD J., energy executive; BSChemE, NYU. Various operational and tech. supervisory positions Benicia refinery, Baton Rouge refinery, refining and supply hdqs. and Bayway refinery Exxon; v.p., gen. mgr. Benicia refinery Valero Energy Corp., sr. v.p. strategic planning San Antonio, 2001—02, sr. v.p. refining ops., 2002, exec. v.p. refining ops. Office: Valero Energy Corpn PO Box 696000 San Antonio TX 78269-6000 *

MARCOPOULOS, GEORGE JOHN, history professor; b. Salem, Mass., June 30, 1931; s. John George and Urania Christou (Moustakis) M. BA, Bowdoin Coll., 1953; MA, Harvard U., 1955, PhD, 1966. Instr. Tufts U., Medford, Mass., 1961-66, asst. prof., 1966-71, assoc. prof., 1971-92, prof., 1992—2006, prof. emeritus, 2006. Contbr. articles to profl. jours. and Am. Ann. yearbooks. Bd. dirs. Gerondelis Found., Inc., Lynn, Mass., 1987—, treas., 1994—. Recipient Seymour Simcher award for disting. tchg. and advising Tufts U., 1997, 2006, Outstanding Contbn. to Grad. Studies award Tufts U., 2006; Mellon Faculty Devel. grantee Tufts U., 1983. Mem. Phi Beta Kappa. Greek Orthodox. Avocations: music, films, reading, performing arts, excursions. Home Phone: 781-862-4463; Office Phone: 617-627-3758. Business E-Mail: gjm1953@comcast.net.

MARCOSSON, THOMAS I., management consultant, advertising executive; b. NYC, Jan. 31, 1936; s. Mark and Mollie (Schreiber) M.; m. Carla F. Hunt, May 15, 1988; children: Mark, Susan, Samuel, Jill. Student, Union Coll., Schenectady, 1953-55; BS, NYU, 1959. CPA NY. Mgr. Touche Ross & Co., NYC, 1959-63; v.p. fin., dir. Superior Surg. Mfg. Co., Inc., Huntington, NY, 1964-66; div. pres., gen. mgr. OEI div., Vernitron Corp., Great Neck, NY, 1967-71; controller Allied Maintenance Corp., NYC, 1972-75, v.p. fin., 1975-82; chief fin. officer Remco Maintenance Corp., NYC, 1982-84, exec. v.p., chief operating officer, 1984-88; pres. MBW Advt. Network Inc., NYC, 1988-89; founder, pres. Dunmarc Assocs., Inc., NYC, 1989—; pres., dir. Square Arch Realty Corp., NYC, 1986—2004. Exec. v.p. Greater Talent Network, Inc., 1991—; co-founder, dir. Village Alliance Bus. Improvement Dist., 1993-2004. Office: 437 5th Ave 7th Fl New York NY 10016 Office Phone: 212-645-4200. Personal E-mail: tmarcosson@gmail.com.

MARCOTTE, MICHAEL STEVEN, municipal official; b. New Orleans, Jan. 17, 1951; s. Steven Stephen and Gloria Catherine (DeValcourt) Marcotte; m. Mary Jane Kilgore, May 28, 1972; children: Matthew David, Margaret Katherine. BA, M of Environ. Engring., Rice U., 1973. Cert. profl engr. Tex, Colo. Engr., sr. engr., mgr. Turner, Collie & Braden, Inc., Houston, 1973—82; chief maintenance engr. water divsn. City of Houston, 1982—83, mng. engr. water divsn., 1984—85, asst. to dir. Pub. Works dept., 1985—87, exec. asst. to dir. Pub. Works dept., 1987—88, acting dir. dept. planning and devel., 1988—89; dir. Dallas Water Utilities, 1989—95; dir. econ. devel. City of Dallas, 1995—97; chief engr. D.C. Water & Sewer Authority, 1997—2004; dir. pub. works City Houston, 2004—. Fellow: ASCE; mem.: Houston Galveston Area Coun., Am. Acad. Water Resource Engrs., Am Acad Environ Engrs (trustee), Tex Water Conservation Asn (bd dirs), Water Environ Fedn (life), Am Water Works Assn. (life; trustee Rsch. Found.). Presbyterian. Avocation: high school and college sports official. Home: 204 Travis St Apt 2D Houston TX 77002-1775 Office: City Houston 611 Walker 25th Fl Houston TX 77002 Home Phone: 713-226-8029; Office Phone: 713-837-0037. Personal E-mail: marcottem@prodigy.net.

MARCOTTE, PAUL JOHN, neurosurgeon, educator; b. Ottawa, Ont., Can., Oct. 15, 1958; (parents Can. and Am. citizens); s. Paul John and Elinor Ann (Simeone) M. BSc, U. Ottawa, 1980, MD, 1984. Intern Ottawa Civic Hosp., 1984-85; resident U. Ottawa, 1985-90, asst. prof., 1990-92; fellow in spinal surgery Barrow Neurol. Inst., Phoenix, 1991-92; assoc. prof. U. Pa., Phila., 1993—. Contbr. articles to profl. jours., chpts. to books. Fellow: ACS, Royal Coll. Physicians and Surgeons (Can.); mem.: Can. Congress Neurol. Surgeons, Am. Assn. Neurol. Surgeons, Congress Neurol. Surgeons. Roman Catholic. Avocations: hockey, model railroading, automobiles. Office: Hosp U Pa 3400 Spruce St Philadelphia PA 19104-4206

MARCOULLIS, ERATO KOZAKOU, ambassador; b. Limassol, Cyprus, Aug. 3, 1949; m. George Marcoullis; 1 child, Panos. Degree in law, U. Athens, Greece, 1972; degree in pub. law and polit. scis., Dept. Pub. Law and Polit. Scis., 1975; PhD Social Scis., U. Helsinki, Finland, 1979. Practice law, 1973—74; advisor Permanent Mission of Cyprus UN, 1980—83, attaché Permanent Mission of Cyprus, 1983—88; consulate gen. Cyprus, 1982—83; amb. extraordinary and plenipotentiary with concurrent accreditation to Finland, Lithuania, Latvia, Sweden, Iceland, Norway, Denmark, and Estonia, 1996—98; mem. 1st polit. divsn. Cyprus question Ministry Fgn. Affairs, 1989—93, dir. office of permanent sec., 1993—96, amb. extraordinary and plenipotentiary to U.S. with concurrent accreditation to Can., Brazil, Guyana, Jamaica Washington, 1998—2003. Office: Embassy of Cyprus 2211 R St NW Washington DC 20008

MARCOUX, CARL HENRY, insurance company executive, writer, historian; b. San Francisco, Jan. 6, 1927; s. Henry Roderick and Margaret (Carlin) M.; m. Ana Virginia Penate-Melara, Nov. 11, 1967; children: Eric Henry, Grant Reynold. BA, Stanford U., 1950; MBA, Golden Gate U., San Francisco, 1958; MA in Latin Am. History, U. Calif., Irvine, 1988; PhD in Latin Am. History, U. Calif., Riverside, 1994. Gen. mgr. Nat. Union Ins. Co., Pitts., 1953-68; exec. v.p. Transam. Ins. Co., 1968-85. Author: (novels) Sailing West, 2001. Served with U.S. Mcht. Marine, 1944-46; USAF, 1951-53. Mem. Stanford Alumni Assn. Republican. Home: 1967 Port Cardigan Pl Newport Beach CA 92660-5347

MARCOUX, JULIA A., midwife; b. St. Helens, Eng., Aug. 7, 1928; d. Robert Patrick and Margaret Mary Theresa (White) Ashall; m. Albert Marcoux, Apr. 23, 1955; children: Stephen, Ann Marie, Richard, Michael, Maureen, Patrick, Margaret, Julie. Diploma, Withington Hosp., Manchester, England, 1950; grad., Cowley Hill Hosp., St. Helens, England, 1952; BS in Pub. Adminstrn., St. Joseph's Coll. RN, Conn.; lic. midwife, Conn. Nurse, labor, delivery rm. and nursery Day Kimbal Hosp., Putnam, Conn.; sch. nurse Marianapolis Prep. Sch., Thompson, Conn.; occupational nurse U.S. Post Office, Hartford, Conn.; pvt. duty and gerontology nurse Conn. Cons. in field. Contbr. articles to profl. jours. Named Internat. Cath. Family of Yr., 1982.

MARCOUX, WILLIAM JOSEPH, lawyer; b. Detroit, Jan. 20, 1927; s. Lona J. and Anna (Ransom) C.; m. Kae Marie Sanborn, Aug. 23, 1952; children: Ann K., William C. BA, U. Mich., 1949, JD, 1952. Bar: Mich. 1953. Pvt. practice, Pontiac, Mich., 1953; assoc. McKone, Badgley, Domke and Kline, Jackson, Mich., 1953-65, ptnr., 1965-75; dir. Marcoux, Allen, Schomer, Bower, Nichols, Kendall and Lindsey, PC, Jackson, Mich., 1975—. Mem. exec. bd. Great Sauk Trail council Boy Scouts Am., pres., 1965-66; bd. dirs. Jackson County United Way, pres., 1983-84. Served with USNR, 1945-46. Recipient Silver Beaver award Boy Scouts Am., 1969, Disting. Citizen award Land O'Lakes coun. Boy Scouts Am., 1991. Fellow Am. Coll. Trial Lawyers, Mich. State Bar Found.; mem. Mich. State Bar Assn., Jackson County Bar Assn. (pres. 1979-80), Jackson Rotary Club (pres. 1963-64), Country Club of Jackson, Clark Lake Yacht Club (commodore 1959). Methodist. Home: 1745 Malvern Dr Jackson MI 49203-5378 Office: Marcoux Allen et al PO Box 787 Jackson MI 49204-0787 Office Phone: 517-787-4100. Business E-Mail: wmarcoux@marcouxallen.com.

MARCOVICI, MICHAEL, investment company executive; b. 1969; V.p., private banking and investment group Merrill Lynch & Co., Chgo. Named one of 40 Under Forty, Crain's Bus. Chgo., 2005. Office: Merril Lynch & Co Ste 2500 33 W Monroe St Chicago IL 60603-5409 *

MARCOVITZ, LEONARD EDWARD, retail executive; b. Bismarck, ND, Sept. 6, 1934; s. Jacob and Frieda Marcovitz. Asst. mgr. Greengard's Clothing, Mandan, ND, 1955-58; mgr. K-G Men's Stores, Inc., Bismarck, 1958-61, Billings, Mont., 1961-69, v.p. store ops., 1969-73; pres. Leonard's Men's Stores, Yakima, Wash. and Billings, Mont., 1973-77; chief exec. officer K-G Retail div. Chromalloy Am. Corp., Englewood, Colo., 1977-81; pres. DeMarcos Men's Clothing, Casper, Wyo., 1982—, Idaho Falls, Idaho, 1984—, Billings, Mont., 1986-96, Twin Falls, Idaho, 1996—, Ft. Collins, Colo., 1999—, Boise, Idaho, 2000, DeMarcos, Men's Clothing, Boise Town Square, 2002. With N.D. Nat. Guard, 1954—61, with Mont. Nat. Guard, 1961—63. Mem. Menswear Retailers Am. (past dir.), Order of Demolay (Degree of Chevalier 1952, Internat. Master Councilor 1953, Demolay Dad 1959), Elks. Home: PO Box 777035 Henderson NV 89077

MARCUCCIO, PHYLLIS ROSE, retired educational association administrator, editor; b. Hackensack, NJ, Aug. 25, 1933; d. Filippo and Rose (Henry) Marcuccio. AB, Bucknell U., 1955; MA, George Washington U., 1976. Trainee Time, Inc., 1956—57; art prodn. for mags. of Med. Econs., Inc., 1958—60; mem. staff Nat. Sci. Tchrs. Assn., Washington, 1961—99; assoc. editor Sci. and Children, 1963, editor, 1964—93, dir. divsn. elem. edn., 1974—78, dir. divsn. program devel. and continuing edn., 1978—83, pub., 1993—99; dir. publs. Nat. Sci. Tchrs. Assn., 1983—99, assoc. exec. dir., 1990—99; pub. Dragonfly, 1996—99. Lectr., cons. in field. Author (photographer, illustrator numerous articles); co-author: Investigation in Ecology, 1972; editor: Science Fun, 1977, Science Fun, 2d edit., 1994; Selected Readings for Students of English as a Second Language, 1966; compiler: Opportunities for Summer Studies in Elementary Science, 1968, Opportunities for Summer Studies in Elementary Science, 2d edit., 1969, pub.: Sci. and Children, 1993—99, Dragonfly Mag., 1997—99. Apptd. commr. Rockville (Md.) Housing Authority, 1981—91, chairperson, 1984—86; bd. dirs. Nat. Sci. Resource Ctr., NAS, 1986—96, Hands on Sci. Outreach, Inc., 1991—2001; pres. East Rockville Civic Assn., 2000—; elected mem. City Coun. of Rockville, 2005—. Recipient Citizenship medal, DAR, 1951, Golden Lamp award, Edpress, 1998. Mem.: AAAS,

NSTA (life), Pocono Environ. Edn. Ctr. (bd. dirs. 1989—98), Sci. Tchg. Assn. N.Y. (Outstanding Svc. to Sci. Edn. award 1987), Ednl. Press Assn. Am. (regional dir. 1969—71, sec. 1979—, Disting. Achievement award 1969, 1971—74, 1976, 1977, Eleanor Fishburn award 1978, Disting. Achievement award 1980, 1988, 1993, 1995), The Washington Forum, Washington edn. Press Assn. (treas. 1966—67, pres. 1975—76), Ohio Coun. Elem. Sch. Sci. (life), Nat. Assn. Industry Edn. Coop. (bd. dirs. 1980—86), Nat. Press Club (Silver Owl), Am. Nature Study Soc., Coun. Elem. Sci. Internat. (Internat. award for outstanding contbns. sci. edn. 1971, 1972, 1986, 1994), Kiwanis Internat., Sigma Delta Chi, Phi Delta Kappa, Phi Delta gamma, Theta Alpha Phi. Home: 406 S Horners Ln Rockville MD 20850-1556 E-mail: marcu@erols.com.

MARCUM, DEANNA BOWLING, library administrator; b. Salem, Ind., Aug. 5, 1946; d. Anderson and Ruby (Mobley) Bowling; m. Thomas P. Marcum, June 13, 1974; 1 child, Ursula. BA, U. Ill., 1967; MA, So. Ill. U., 1969; MLS, U. Ky., 1971; PhD, U. Md., 1991. Tchr. Deland-Weldon HS, Ill., 1967-68; instr. English U. Ky., Lexington, 1969-70, cataloging librarian, 1970-73, asst. to dir., 1973-74; asst. dir. pub. svcs. Joint U. Librs., Nashville, 1974-77; mgmt. tng. specialist Assn. Rsch. Librs., Washington, 1977-80; sr. cons. Info. Systems Cons., Inc., Washington, 1980-81; v.p. Coun. Libr. Resources, Washington, 1981-89; dean Libr. and Info. Sch., Cath. U., Washington, 1989-92; dir. pub. svcs. and collections mgmt. Libr. of Congress, Washington, 1993-95, assoc. libr., 2003—; pres. Coun. Libr. Resources and Info., Washington, 1995—2003; chair Fed. Library and Info. Ctr. Com., Washington. Adv. bd. So. Edn. Found., Atlanta, 1986-91; chmn. grants com. Coun. on Libr. resources, Washington, 1990-94. Author: Good Books in a Country Home, 1993, Development of Digital Libaries, An American Perspective, 2001, Digital Library Development: View from Kanazawa, 2005; co-author: (with Richard Boss) The Library Catalog, 1980, On-Line Acquisitions Systems, 1981; contbr. articles to profl. jours. Pres., Commn. on Preservation and Access, 1995—. Mem. ALA, Am. Studies Assn., Orgn. Am. Historians, Am. Antiquarian Soc. (adv. bd. 1989—), Beta Phi Mu, Phi Kappa Phi. Office: Coun on Libr and Info Resources Ste 500 1755 Massachusetts Ave NW Washington DC 20036-2124 Home Phone: 301-933-9503; Office Phone: 202-707-6240. E-mail: dmarcum@loc.gov.

MARCUS, ABIR A., psychiatrist; arrived in US, 1995; d. Assaad Aziz Abdel-Sayed and Nadra Nassry Sourial; divorced; 1 child, Gina Marie. MD with honors, Ain Shams U., Cairo, 1991. Diplomate Am. Bd. Psychiatry and Neurology, Am. Bd. Med. Specialties, lic. psychiatrist NJ, NY. Intern Ain Shams Med. Sch., Cairo, 1992—93, instr. forensic medicine and toxicology, 1994—95; resident in psychiatry NJ Med. Sch., Newark, 1996—2000; fellow, asst. prof. Robert Wood Johnson, Piscataway, NJ, 2000—01; pvt. practice Little Silver and NYC, 1999—. Adj. asst. prof. Robert Wood Johnson Med. Sch., Piscataway, 2001—; task force com. for curriculum devel. in psychotherapy tng. for residents U. Medicine and Dentistry NJ Med. Sch., Newark, 1999—2000; cons. CPC Behavioral Health Care, Red Bank, NJ, 2001—; cons. in field. Contbr. articles to profl. jours. Recipient Physician's Recognition award, AMA, 1999, 2005; scholar, Nat. Inst. Drug Abuse. Mem.: Am. Psychoanalytic Assn. (assoc. mem.), Neurosci. Edn. Inst., Am. Soc. Clin. Psychopharmacology, NJ Psychiat. Assn. (pres. resident chpt. 1999, pres. 2000, early career psychiatry com., pub. edn. com., disaster preparedness com., resident and med. student com.), Am. Psychiat. Assn., Am. Acad. Addiction Psychiatry, Am. Soc. Addiction Medicine. Avocations: reading, travel, ballroom dancing, salsa dancing. Office: 34 Sycamore Ave # 2C Little Silver NJ 07739 Office Phone: 732-530-3122. Personal E-mail: abirmarcus@aol.com. Business E-Mail: drmarcus@birovenusmedicalspa.com.

MARCUS, ALAN C., public relations consultant; b. NYC, Feb. 26, 1947; s. Percy and Rose (Fox) M.; m. Judith Lamel. June 21, 1979; 1 child, Allison. Student, Hun Sch. of Princeton, 1965. Dir. pub. rels. Bergen County Rep. Com., Hackensack, N.J., 1968; clk. N.J. Gen. Assembly, Trenton, 1969, sec. to majority party of assembly, 1970; pres. The Marcus Group, Inc., Secaucus, 1971—. Adj. prof. Rutger U. Grad. Sch., 1986-88. Trustee Nat. Leukemia Assn., 1978-82, Hun Sch. of Princeton, 1977-88, Passaic River Coalition, 1980-82. Recipient Youth Enterprise award Jim Waiter Corp., 1972. Mem. Pub. Rels. Soc. Am. (pres., bd. dirs. N.J. chpt. 1976-77, N.J. chpt. Pres. award 1975), N.J. C. of C., N.J. Bus. and Industry Assn., N.J. Press Assn., Alpine Country Club. Office: 300 Lighting Way Secaucus NJ 07094-3672 also: 50 W State St Trenton NJ 08608-1220

MARCUS, ANDREA CANDACE SILLS, lawyer; b. Brookline, Mass., Nov. 23, 1947; d. Benjamin and Mary Natalie (Rogers) Sills; m. Lawrence I. Marcus, Aug. 9, 1974; children: David, Anthony, Rebecca. Grad. with honors, Norwalk Hosp. Sch. Nursing, 1973; BSN, U. Miami, Coral Gables, Fla., 1985, MSN, 1987; JD, Sch. of Law, U. Miami, 1991. Bar: Fla., US Dist. Ct. (so. dist.) Fla., US Supreme Ct. 2004; cert. arbitrator, 2004, clin. nurse specialist oncology nurse/adult health; ARNP, Fla.; RN, Conn. Head nurse, mem. psychotherapeutic team Hall-Brooke Hosp., Westport, Conn., 1973-75; founder, bd. dir. Hospice of Boca Raton, Boca Raton, Fla., 1978—81; staff RN oncology Boca Raton Cmty. Hosp., 1983—84, psychiat. nurse liaison, 1984—89; patient care coord. Hospice by the Sea, Boca Raton, 1973-75; law clk. Legal Aid Soc. of Palm Beach County, 1989—91, atty., 1991—93; asst. counsel Interim Svcs. Inc., Ft. Lauderdale, Fla., 1993-95; assoc. atty. Krathen & Roselli, 1995-96; atty. Gary, Williams, Parenti, Lewis & McManus, Fort Pierce, Fla., 1996-97; assoc. Mitchell H. Katler & Assocs., P.A., Coconut Creek, Fla., 1997—98; trial atty. Figueroa, Gonzalez & Hoecker, West Palm Beach, 1998—2000; ptnr. McIntosh, Sawran, Peltz & Cartaya, Ft. Lauderdale, 2000—. Co-editor OnCare, 1987-88. Mem. Ambs. Program U. Miami; bd. dir. Estancia Homeowners Assn.; treas. Palm Beach County Med.Soc. Aux., Diabetes Assn. Palm Beach County; mem. svc. & rehab. com., steering com. Am. Cancer Soc.; mem. psychosocial support team Boca Raton Cmty. Hosp. Fellow Fla. Bar Found.; mem. ABA, ATLA, ANA, Fla. Nurses Assn., Am. Assn. Corp. Counsel, Nat. Health Lawyers Assn., Am. Bd. Forensic Examiners, Am. Assn. Nurse Attys., Am. Soc. Law, Medicine and Ethics, Internat. Nurses Cancer Care, Am. Inn Ct. (Spellman chpt.), Oncol. Nurses Soc., Nurses Alliance Prevention Nuc. War, Health & Law Soc., Stephen Booher Inn of Ct., Def. Rsch. Inst., Fla. Def. Lawyers Assn., Broward County Bar Assn., Fla. Med. Malpractice Claims Coun., Am. Soc. Healthcare Risk Mgmt., U. Miami Alumni Club, Sigma Theta Tau, Phi Alpha Delta. Home: 6913 Corto Cir Boca Raton FL 33433-2730 Office Phone: 954-765-1001. Business E-Mail: cmarcus@mspcesq.com.

MARCUS, BERNARD, lawyer, arbitrator, mediator; b. Wilkes-Barre, Pa., Mar. 10, 1924; m. Frances Frank; children: Kate, Aaron, Charles, Mary. Student, U. Pa., 1941-43, Carnegie-Mellon U., 1943-44; LL.B., Harvard U., 1948; postgrad., Loyola U. of South, New Orleans, 1958. Bar: D.C. 1949, La. 1958. Atty. legis. reference service Library of Congress, 1949-50; acting counsel small bus. com. Ho. of Reps., 1950; atty. NLRB, Washington, Cin., Buffalo and New Orleans, 1950-57; assoc. Deutsch, Kerrigan & Stiles, New Orleans, 1957-58, ptnr., 1958-95, mng. ptnr., 1985-89, emeritus ptnr., 1995—2004; of counsel Lehmann, Norman & Marcus, New Orleans, 2004—. Cons. Dept. State, 1965-69; labor arbitrator Am. Arbitration Assn.; arbitrator Fed. Med. and Concil. Svc. Author: Congress and the Monopoly Problem, 1950; contbr. to casebooks. Pres. New Orleans Jewish Cmty. Ctr., 1973-75; active Nat. Jewish Welfare Bd., 1974-83; bd. dirs. New Orleans Jewish Welfare Fedn., Jewish Family and Children's Service, New Orleans, Communal Hebrew Sch.; v.p. New Orleans Home for Jewish Aged, 1978-80, Florence Heller Rsch. Found. With U.S Army, 1943-46. Mem. ABA, Fed. Bar Assn., La. Bar Assn., New Orleans Bar Assn. (exec. com. 1971-74), D.C. Bar Assn., Nat. Acad. Arbitrators. Home: 630 Burdette St New Orleans LA 70118-3937 Office: Texaco Bldg Ste 2050 400 Poydras St New Orleans LA 70130 Home Phone: 504-866-2929; Office Phone: 504-680-6045. Business E-Mail: bmarcus@lnmlaw.com.

MARCUS, BERNARD, foundation administrator, retired retail executive; b. Newark, 1929; married. BS, Rutgers U., 1954. V.p. Vornado Inc., 1952-68; pres. Odell Inc., 1968-70; v.p. Daylin Inc., 1970-73; with Handy Dan Home Improvement, LA, 1972-78; co-founder (ex. chmn. and CEO) Home Depot Inc., Atlanta, 1978—2002, ret., 2002. Exec. advisor Chief Exec. Leadership Inst., Yale U. Sch. Mgmt. Chmn., founder Marcus Found. Inc., Marcus Inst., 1991—; founder Ga. Aquarium, Marcus Devel. Resource Ctr., DC; bd. mem. City of Hope, Duarte, Calif., Shepherd Spinal Center, Atlanta, Am. Jewish Com., Atlanta Jewish Found. Named one of Forbes Richest Americans, 2006; recipient Golden Plate award, Acad. Achievement, 2006. *

MARCUS, CLAUDE, advertising executive; b. Paris, Aug. 28, 1924; s. Jacques and Louise (Bleustein) M.; m. Claudine Pohl, May 27, 1948; children: Michele, Pierre, Anne-Marie, Isabelle. Diploma in Econs., U. Paris, 1947; Lic., Paris Law Sch., 1947. Sec. gen. Publicis, Paris, 1948-55, dir. comml. to dir. gen. adjoint, 1961, dir. gen., 1962-68; mng. dir. Publicis Conseil, Paris, 1968-83; pres. Publicis Internat., Paris, 1984-88; vice-chmn. Publicis Comm., Paris, 1988—96. Decorated chevalier de la Legion d'Honneur. Mem. Bur. Verification de la Publicite (vice-chmn.), Racing Club (France). Home: 12 Rue Felicien David 75016 Paris France Office: Publicis 133 Champs Elysees 75008 Paris France Personal E-mail: claudius6@wanadoo.fr.

MARCUS, CRAIG HARLAN, ophthalmologist; b. NYC, Jan. 30, 1962; m. Robin Marcus; children: Aaron, Madeline. BA in English, U. Rochester, NY, 1983, BS in Biochemistry, 1983; MD, Chgo. Med. Sch., 1989. Bd. cert. Am. Bd. Ophthalmology. Intern internal medicine North Shore Cornell U., Meml. Sloan Kettering, NYC, 1990; resident ophthalmology Temple U., Phila., 1993; fellow Manhattan Eye, Ear and Throat, NYC, 1994; ophthalmologist Eye Care Ophthalmology, Bethpage, NY, Glaucoma Consultants LI, Lake Success, NY. Asst. clin. prof. Albert Einstein Coll. Medicine; attending North Shore U. Hosp., Manhasset and Syosset, NY, LI Jewish Med. Ctr., Albert Einstein Sch. Medicine, New Island Hosp., Winthrop U. Hosp.; asst. attending surgeon Manhattan Eye, Ear & Throat Hosp.; active voluntary staff Queens Hosp. Ctr., Jamaica, NY; chmn. quality assurance com. Nassau Ctr. for Ambulatory Surgery, 2005—, Nassau Surg. Ctr.; presenter in field. Article reviewer and referee: Exptl. Eye Rsch., 1987—88, Jour. Am. Soc. Cataract and Refractive Surgery, 1994, 1995; contbr. chapters to books, articles to profl. jours. Dir. Country Point Bd. Dirs., 2002—03. Named Eye Care Am. Vol., 2001; recipient Excellence in Rsch. award, Temple U. Hosp. Dept. Ophthalmology, 1990—93, Attending of Yr. award, North Shore U. Hosp., 1996, Most Dedicated Attending award, LI Jewish Med. Ctr., 1997; scholar, NY State Bd. Regents, 1979—83; Joseph C. Wilson scholar, U. Rochester, 1979—83. Fellow: ACS, Nassau Acad. Medicine, Am. Acad. Ophthalmology; mem.: AMA, LI Ophthal. Soc., Inc. (asst. sec. treas. 2004—), Am. Glaucoma Soc., Nassau County Med. Soc. (mem. edn. com. 2003—, trustee 2006), Assn. for Rsch. in Vision and Ophthalmology, NY State Ophthal. Soc., NY Soc. for Clin. Ophthalmology, Med. Soc. State NY. Avocations: fitness, sports, music, choir member. Office: Eye Care Ophthalmology 4212 Hempstead Turnpike Bethpage NY 11714

MARCUS, DONALD, lawyer; s. Samuel and Ida Marcus; m. Judith M. Maslow, Apr. 15, 1962; children: Ellen J. Azzolini, Susan H. LLB, Harvard U., Cambridge, Mass., 1958. Bar: NY Ct. Appeals 1961. Estate tax examiner, atty. US Treasury Dept., Bklyn. and NYC, 1963—95; pvt. practice voting rights lawyer Bklyn., 1990—. Cons. in field, NYC, 2002—. Editor-in-chief: legal jour. Mensa Juris. Rec. sec., chair NYCLU, Bklyn Chpt., 1985—90. Pvt. first class AUS, 1958—60, ETO. Recipient Hon. mention Sci. Talent Search, Westinghouse Corp., 1951. Mem.: Ams. for Dem. Action. Democrat. Avocations: puzzles, writing, travel, art, sports. Office: 1936 E 24 St Brooklyn NY 11229-2420 Office Phone: 718-375-5586. Business E-Mail: jdmar58@juno.com.

MARCUS, EDWARD, economist, educator; b. Bklyn., Apr. 29, 1918; s. Herman and Rose (Marayna) M.; m. Mildred Rendl, Aug. 10, 1956. BS, Harvard, 1939, MBA, 1941; student, King's Coll., Cambridge U., Eng., 1946-47; PhD, Princeton, 1950. Economist Fed. Res. Bd., 1950-52; prof. econs. Bklyn. Coll., 1952-81, chmn. dept., 1966-79. Cons. Nat. Acad. Scis., 1959, UN Conf. Trade and Devel., 1966; dir. Syracuse U. Maxwell Sch. Nigerian Project, 1961; participant Internat. Econometrics Assn., Amsterdam, Holland, 1968 Author: Canada and the International Business Cycle, 1927-1938, 1954, (with Mildred Rendl Marcus) Investment and Development Possibilities in Tropical Africa, 1960, International Trade and Finance, 1965, Monetary and Banking Theory, 1965, Economic Progress and the Developing World, 1971, Economics, 1978. Served with AUS, 1941-42, to comdr. USCGR, 1942-46. Grantee Merrill Found., 1953 Mem. AAUP, Am. Econ. Assn., Canadian Econ. Assn., N.Y. Met. Econ. Assn. (pres. 1966-67), Am. Fin Assn., Royal Econ. Soc., Econ. Soc. South Africa, New Canaan Hist. Soc. (treas. 1983—), Phi Beta Kappa.

MARCUS, EDWARD LEONARD, lawyer, political organization worker; b. Bklyn., June 14, 1927; s. Isaac Horatio and Dorothy (Kirchsten) M.; m. Phyllis Betzes, Sept. 19, 1948 (div. 1984); children: Shelley A., Susan E., Nicole Marie; m. Lisa E. Munson, 1984 (div. 1989); m. Lorraine Jill Surprenant, Aug. 9, 1989. BA, Yale Coll., 1948, LLB, LLD, 1950. Bar: Conn. 1950, U.S. Dist. Ct. Conn. 1952, U.S. Ct. Appeals (2d dist.) 1954, U.S. Supreme Ct. 1955. Sr. ptnr. Marcus Law Firm, New Haven, Conn., 1950—. Mem. Overseas Pvt. Invest Corp, Washington, 1978-81; bd. dirs. exec. com. Branford (Conn.) Savs. Bank, Boca Raton (Fla.) First Nat. Bank. Alderman City of New Haven, 1951-56; majority leader State Senate, Conn., 1958-70; chmn. Commn. Inter Govt. Rels., 1962-70, senate majority leader, 1966-70; chmn. Coun. State Govts., 1968-69; del. Dem. Nat. Conf., 1976, 92, 96; mem. Conn. Tourism Task Force, 1991—; mem. Dem. State Ctrl. Com., Conn., 1986—, chmn. fin. com., 1991-92; chmn. Conn. del. Dem. Nat. Conv., 1992, 96, 2000. Mem. ABA, Nat. Trial Lawyers Am. (bd. dirs., sec.), Conn. Bar Assn., New Haven Bar Assn. Democrat. Avocations: tennis, swimming. Home: 100 Stony Creek Rd Branford CT 06405-3236 Office: Marcus Law Firm 111 Whitney Ave Ste 2 New Haven CT 06510-1261 Business E-Mail: emarcus@marcuslawfirm.com.

MARCUS, ERIC PETER, lawyer; b. Newark, Aug. 31, 1950; s. John J. and Alice M. (Zeldin) M.; m. Terry R. Toll, Oct. 9, 1983. BA, Brown U., 1972; JD, Stanford U., 1976. Bar: N.Y. 1977, N.J. 1977. Assoc. Kaye, Scholer, Fierman, Hays & Handler LLP, NYC, 1976-84, ptnr., 1985—. Contbr. articles to profl. jours. Mem. Phi Beta Kappa. Office: Kaye Scholer LLP 425 Park Ave New York NY 10022-3506

MARCUS, ERIC ROBERT, psychiatrist; b. NYC, Feb. 16, 1944; s. Victor and Pearl (Maddow) M.; m. Eslee Samberg, Nov. 24, 1985; children: Max, Pia. AB, Columbia U., 1965; MD, U. Wis., 1969. Diplomate Am. Bd. Psychiatry and Neurology. Intern med. ctr. Bellevue hosp. NYU, 1969-70; resident NY state psychiat. inst. Columbia Presbyn. Med. Ctr.st., 1972-75; from dir. to dir. neuropsychiat//diagnostic treatment unit Columbia-Presbyn. Med. Ctr., NYC, 1975-84; dir. St. Marks Free Clinic, NYC, 1971-75; dir. med. student edn. in psychiatry coll. physicians and surgeons Columbia U., NYC, 1981—2007, bd. govs. student health, 1986—2003, supervising-tng. analyst ctr. psychoanalytic training and rsch., 1994—, clin. prof. psychiatry and social medicine coll. physicians and surgeons, 1995—, dir. psychoanalytic tng. and rsch., 2007—. Author: Psychosis and Near Psychosis, 1992, 2d edit., 2003; mem. editl. bd.: The Psychoanalytic Study of Society, 1989—94, Jour. Clin. Psychoanalysis, 1998—2002; co-editor: Psychiatry, 1998; contbr. articles to profl. jours. Recipient Weber Rsch. award Columbia U. Psychoanalytic Ctr., 1991, O'Connor Tchg. award, 1995, Columbia U. Presdl. award for Outstanding Tchg., 1999. Fellow: NY Acad. Medicine, Am. Coll. Psychoanalysts, Am. Psychiat. Assn. (pres. NY County Dist. 2002—03, Roeske award 1991); mem.: Assn. Psychoanalytic Medicine (pres. 1999—2001), Am. Psychoanalytic Assn. (chmn. com. on univ. and med. edn. 1999—2005, mem. editl. bd. Jour. 2000—03, Sabshin award 2003). Avocations: classical music, photography, swimming, reading. Office: Columbia U Dept Psychiatry 1051 Riverside Dr New York NY 10032-1013 Office Phone: 212-427-0543.

MARCUS, FRANK ISADORE, cardiologist, educator; b. Haverstraw, NY, Mar. 23, 1928; s. Samuel and Edith (Sattler) M.; m. Janet Geller, June 30, 1957; children: Ann, Steve, Lynn. BA, Columbia U., 1948; MS, Tufts U., 1951; MD cum laude, Boston U., 1953. Diplomate Am. Bd. Internal Medicine (subspecialty cardiovasc. diseases). Intern Peter Bent Brigham Hosp., Boston, 1953-54, asst. resident, 1956-57, research fellow in cardiology, 1957-58; clin. fellow in cardiology Georgetown U. Hosp., 1958-59, chief med. resident, 1959-60; chief of cardiology Georgetown U. Med. Service, D.C. Gen. Hosp., Washington, 1960-68; instr. medicine Georgetown U. Sch. Medicine, 1960-63, asst. prof., 1963-68, assoc. prof., 1968; prof. medicine, chief cardiology sect. U. Ariz. Coll. Medicine, Tucson, 1969-82, disting. prof. internal medicine (cardiology), 1982-99, emeritus prof., 1999—, dir. electrophysiology, 1982—2001; prin. investigator multidisciplinary study of right ventricular dysplasia Nat. Heart, Lung and Blood Inst., 2001—. Cons. cardiology VA Hosp., Tucson, 1969, USAF Regional Hosp., Davis-Monthan AFB, Tucson, 1969; mem. panel drug efficacy study, panel on cardiovascular drugs Nat. Acad. Scis.-NRC, 1967-68; chmn. undergrad. cardiovascular tng. grant com. HEW-NIH, 1970; dir. Arrhythmia Svcs., 1996-2001. Editor: Modern Concepts of Cardiovascular Disease, 1982—84; mem. editl. bd. Circulation, 1974—81, Current Problems in Cardiology, 1975—79, Cardiovascular Drugs and Therapy, 1986—2000, New Trends in Arrythmias, 1984—, Jour. Am. Coll. Cardiology, 1983—87, 1996—2000, Am. Jour. Cardiology, 1984—, Jour. Cardiovasc. Drugs and Therapy, 1991—2000, Pacing and Clin. Electrophysiology, 1995—, Annals of Noninvasive Electrocardiology, 1996—, Cardiology, 2000—, Jour. Electrocardiology, 2005—; contbr. articles to profl. jours. Chmn. Washington Heart Assn. High Sch. Heart Program, 1966-68. Capt. USAF, 1954-56. Recipient Career Devel. award NIH, 1965, Student AMA Golden Apple award Georgetown U. Sch. Medicine, 1968, Disting. Alumni award Boston U. Sch. Medicine, 2003, Master Clinician award Coun. Clin. Cardiology, 2005; Mass. Heart Assn. fellow, 1957-58; John and Mary Markle scholar, 1960-65; grantee Nat. Heart, Lung and Blood Inst., 2001—. Fellow Coun. on Clin. Cardiology Am. Heart Assn., ACP (Ariz. laureate award 1987), Am. Coll. Cardiology (bd. govs. Ariz. 1984-87, asst. sec. 1987-89, trustee); mem. Assn. Univ. Cardiologists, Inc. (v.p. 1989-90, pres. 1990-91), Ariz. Heart Assn. (dir. 1970, v.p. 1972-73, chmn. rsch. com. 1970-72), So. Ariz. Heart Assn. (dir. 1969), N.Am. Soc. Pacing and Electrophysiology, Alpha Omega Alpha. Home: 4949 E Glenn St Tucson AZ 85712-1212 Office: U Ariz Univ Med Ctr 1501 N Campbell Ave Tucson AZ 85724-0001 Home Phone: 520-327-1339; Office Phone: 502-626-1416. Business E-Mail: fmarcus@u.arizona.edu.

MARCUS, GREIL GERSTLEY, critic; b. San Francisco, June 19, 1945; s. Gerald Dodd and Eleanore (Hyman) M.; m. Jenelle Bernstein, June 26, 1966; children: Emily Rose, Cecily Helen. BA, U. Calif., Berkeley, 1967, MA, 1968. Record editor Rolling Stone mag., San Francisco and NYC, 1969-70, book columnist, 1975-80, Calif. Mag., LA, 1982-83, 88-90; pop music columnist Music Mag., Tokyo, 1978-94, New West mag., LA, 1978-82, Artforum mag., NYC, 1983—87, 1991—98, Village Voice newspaper, NYC, 1986—91, Interview Mag., NYC, 1992—; dir. Falter newspaper, Vienna, 1997-98; cultural columnist N.Y. Times, 1998, Esquire mag., 1998-99; music columnist Salon.com, 1999—2003, City Pages, 2003—04. Lectr. Princeton U., fall, 2000, 02, 06, U. Calif., Berkeley, spring, 2000, 06; presenter in field. Author: Mystery Train: Images of America in Rock 'n Roll Music, 1975, U.S. rev., 1982, 90, 97 (Brit., German, Greek, Dutch, Japanese, Italian and French edits.), Real Life Rock (Japanese), 1984, Lipstick Traces: A Secret History of the 20th Century, 1989 (Brit., Italian, Spanish, German, French, Turkish, and Greek edits.), Dead Elvis: A Chronicle of a Cultural Obsession, 1991 (Brit., French, Japanese and German edits., rev. 1999), Ranters and Crowd Pleasers: Punk in Pop Music, 1977-92, 93, In The Fascist Bathroom: Writings on Punk, 1999 (Brit., German and US edits.), The Dustbin of History (Brit. and German edits.), 1995, Invisible Republic: Bob Dylan's Basement Tapes, 1997 (Brit., Italian, German, Dutch, French, and Chinese edits.), Double Trouble: Bill Clinton and Elvis Presley in a Land of No Alternatives, 2000, rev. edit., 2001 (Brit. edit.), The Old, Weird America: The World of Bob Dylan's Basement Tapes, 2001, The Manchurian Candidate (Brit. edit.), 2002, Like a Rolling Stone: Bob Dylan at the Crossroads (Brit., German, French, Japanese, Italian edits.), 2005, The Shape of Things to Come: Prophecy and the American Voice (Brit., French edits.), 2006; editor: Stranded, 1979, rev. 1996, 2007, Psychotic Reactions and Carburetor Dung (Lester Bangs), 1987, (with Sean Wilentz) The Rose and the Briar: Death, Love and Liberty in The American Ballad, 2004; contbr. criticism to publs. including Creem, Express-Times, New Mus. Express, Another Room, RAW, Rock and Roll Confidential, Threepenny Rev., Representations, Common Knowledge, La Nouvelle Revue Francaise; curator Whitney Mus. Am. Art, N.Y., 1998.

MARCUS, GWEN ELLEN, sculptor; b. NYC; d. David Oscar and Doris (Sherman) M. BS, NYU, 1977. One-woman shows include Galeries Lafayette Trump Tower, NYC, 1994, exhibited in group shows at Catharine Lorillard Wolfe Art Club Inc., 2002, Wobun Abbey, Bedfordshire, Eng., 2002, Sudeley Castle, Gloucestershire, Eng., 2002, Stoneleigh Abbey, Warwickshire, Eng., 2002, Castle Howard, Yorkshire, Eng., 2002, Chi Mej Mus., Taiwan, 2002—07, Brookgreen Gardens Collection, S.C., 2006, Ind. U., 2003, Gallery North, Setauket, NY, 2003, Salmagundi Art Club Annual Exhbn., NYC, 2006 (Salmagundi Art Club award, 2006, Joseph Hartley Meml. Best in Show award, 2007), Salmagundi Exhbn., 2006, Represented in permanent collections Brookgreen Gardens, SC, Chi Mei Mus., Taiwan, Champs Hill, West Sussex, Eng. Recipient Elliot Liskin Meml. award, Salmagundi Photography & Sculpture Exhbn., N.Y., 1993, Excellence award, 1994, BBI award, 1995, Excellence award, Knickerbocker Artists, Washington, 1993, cert. Merit, Nat. Acad. Design Mus., N.Y., 1996, Elliot Liskin award, 2001, Coun. Am. Artists Soc. award, 1998, Michael Gressel Meml. award, 2001, Sculpture award, Art Students League NY, 2005. Fellow Nat. Sculpture Soc. (bd. dirs. 2001-07, Tallix Foundry Prize 69th annual exhibition, 2002); mem. Allied Artists Am. (Philip Eisenberg award 1990, Lindsey Morris Meml. award 1994, Gold Medal 1996, Josephine Beardsley Sander Meml. award 1999, 2001, Elliot Liskin Meml. award 2002, Mem. and Assocs. award, 2005), Catharine Lorillard Wofe Art Club (Medal of Honor 1993, Harriet W. Frishmuth Meml. award 1994, Anna Hyatt Huntington Bronze Medal 1995, CLWAC Centennial award 1996, Paul Manship Meml. award 2003-), Pen and Brush Club (sculpture soc., Solo Show award 1995, Leonard J. Meiselman Meml. award 1997, Charlotte Dunwiddie Meml. award 2001, Josephine B,. Sandor mem. award, 2002), Am. Medallic Sculpture Assn., Nat. Assn. Women Artists Inc., Hudson Valley Art Assn., Inc. (Agop Agopoff award 1998, Gold Medal honor 2000), Am. Artist Profl. League Inc. (Medal of Honor 1994, 95, 96, 2005, Pres.'s award 1995, Granville Carter Meml. award 1998, Frank C. Wright Meml. award 1999, Am. Artists Fund award 2001,

Kathryn Thayer Hobson Meml. award 2004, Helen G. Oehler Meml. award, 2006), Nat. Sculpture Soc. (Gloria medal 1990), Medallic Sculpture Assn. (bd. dir.), Audubon Artists, Inc. (Gold medal 1998, Renee and Chaim Mem. award 2002), Art Students League NY (Sculpture award, 2005), Am. Profl. League (Gold medal of honor 2005). Avocations: travel, theater, music, dance, volunteer work. Home and Office: 401 E 80th St Apt 19E New York NY 10075 Office Phone: 212-744-2114. Business E-Mail: marcustudio@aol.com.

MARCUS, HARRIS LEON, materials science educator; b. Ellenville, NY, July 5, 1931; s. David and Bertha (Messite) M.; m. Leona Gorker, Aug. 29, 1962; children: Leland, M'Risa. BS, Purdue U., 1963; PhD, Northwestern U., 1966. Registered profl. engr., Tex. Tech. staff Tex. Instruments, Attleboro, Mass., 1966—68, Rockwell Sci. Ctr., 1968—70, group leader, 1971—75; prof. mech. engring. U. Tex., Austin, 1975—79, Harry L. Kent Jr. prof. mech. engring., 1979—90, Cullen Found. prof., 1980—95, dir. ctr. for Materials Sci. and Engring., dir. program, 1979—95; prof. materials sci. and engring., dir. Inst. for Material Sci., U. Conn., 1995—. Cons. numerous orgns. Contbr. more than 300 articles to profl. publs. Recipient U. Tex. faculty U. Tex. Engring. Found., 1983; Krengel lectr. Technion, Israel, 1983; Alumni Merit medal Northwestern U., 1988, Disting. Purdue Univ. Engring. Alumnus award, 1994. Fellow Am. Soc. Metals; mem. ACS, AIME (bd. dirs. Metall. Soc. 1976-78, 84-86), Materials Rsch. Soc., Conn. Acad. Sci. and Engring. Achievements include 24 patents. Home: 78 Ellise Rd Storrs Mansfield CT 06268-1424 Office: Inst Materials Scis 97 N Eagleville Rd Unit U-3136 Storrs Mansfield CT 06269-3136 Office Phone: 860-486-4623. Personal E-mail: harrismarcus@charter.net. Business E-Mail: hmarcus@mail.ims.uconn.edu.

MARCUS, JAMES ELBERT, manufacturing executive; b. Helena, Ala., July 3, 1949; s. James Edward and Ora Dee (Shanks) M.; m. Willie Mae Murry, June 30, 1980; children: Charsie Latrice, Chareka Lenita, Carlisle Lamar. BS in Biology, Chemistry, Tuskegee U., 1971. Soft drink technician Custom Canners, Inc., Norcross, Ga., 1972-73; comml. inventory supr. Washington Inventory Svc., Inc., Atlanta, 1973-76; shipping and receiving specialist Norrell Temporary Svc., Atlanta, 1977-78; enology lab. technician Monarch Wine Co., Atlanta, 1978-80; R & D technician Pave-Mark Corp., Atlanta, 1980-82; mfg. tech. support specialist Dynatron Bondo Corp., Atlanta, 1982-85; equipment operator Circuit City, Inc., Atlanta, 1985-86; air filter technician Comml. Air Filter Co., Atlanta, 1987-88; owner, pres. Marcus Industries, Atlanta, 1989—, Group 38 Transp. Svcs., Inc., Atlanta, Group 38, Inc. Bus. Concerns, Atlanta. Sub-contractor, advt. distbr., investment profl., 1998. Prin. developer pavement marking material, 1981. Cub scout master Southeastern dist. Traveler's Rest Mt. Pleasant Bapt. Ch. Boy Scouts Am., 1988, 89, 90. Mem.: Nat. Hon. Soc. Pershing Rifles. Democrat. Baptist. Avocations: basketball, bowling, writing, electronics, billiards. Home: 2009 Rocking Ter Conley GA 30288-2109 Personal E-mail: mae7673@bellsouth.net.

MARCUS, JOHN RICHARD, lawyer; b. St. Helena, Calif., Apr. 28, 1930; s. Elias George Marcus and Dorothy Olive Jones; children: David, Debbie, Cathy, Nancy, Jonathan. BA, Walla Walla Coll., College Place, Wash., 1951; LLB, JD, UCLA, 1955. Bar: Calif. 1956, US Supreme Ct. 1963. Atty. Gen. Am. Ins., Panorama City, Calif., 1956—61; pvt. practice San Bernardino, Calif., 1961—. Pro-tem judge San Bernardion County, Riverside County. Past pres., bd. dirs. San Bernardion County Legal Aid Soc.; Rep. nominee Calif. State Senate, 1972. Recipient Achievement award, Calif. Supreme Ct., 2006, State Bar Calif., 2006. Mem.: Fed. Bar Assn., San Bernardino County Bar Assn., Lawyer Pilots Bar Assn., Law-Sci. Inst. Am., Am. Bd. Trial Adv. (pres. San Bernardino chpt. 1963—, bd. cert. 1963), Lake Arrowhead C. of C., Running Springs Area C. of C., Rotary. Avocations: hiking, cooking, travel, gardening, snow shoeing. Home: PO Box 1317 Running Springs CA 92382-1317 Office: 31564 Old City Creek Running Springs CA 92382-1317

MARCUS, KAREN JEAN, medical educator; m. Michael Marcus, Sept. 3, 1999; 1 child, Shoshana. BA, Yeshiva U., NY, 1975; MD, U. Md., Balt., 1980. Assoc. prof. med. sch. Harvard U., Boston, 2005—. Office: Childrens Hosp Boston Dfci 300 Longwood Ave Boston MA 02115 Home Phone: 617-566-1862; Office Phone: 617-355-8399. Business E-Mail: kmarcus@lroc.harvard.edu.

MARCUS, KENNETH L., federal official; m. Stephanie Marcus. Grad., Willams Coll.; JD, U. Calif., 1991. Litigation ptnr.; gen. dep. asst. sec. fair housing and equal oppty. U.S. Dept. HUD; dep. asst. sec. edn. for enforcement U.S. Dept. Edn., delegated the authority of asst. sec. edn. for civil rights, 2003—05; staff dir. U.S. Commn. on Civil Rights, 2004—. Office: US Commn Civil Rights 624 Ninth St NW Ste 700 Washington DC 20425 Home Phone: 703-669-0896; Office Phone: 202-376-7700. Office Fax: 202-376-7672. Business E-Mail: kmarcus@usccr.gov.

MARCUS, LARRY DAVID, broadcast executive; b. NYC, Jan. 27, 1949; s. Oscar Moses and Sylvia (Ackerman) Marcus; children from previous marriage: Julia Ilene, Barbara Maureen. BBA, CUNY, 1970, postgrad. studies Bus. Admistrn., 1970-72. Computer systems analyst Johnson & Johnson, 1972—73; acctg. mgr. Sta. WPLG-TV, Miami, Fla., 1974-75; v.p., bus. mgr. Sta. KPLR-TV-Koplar Comm., Inc., St. Louis, 1976-82; chief fin. officer Koplar Comm., Inc., St. Louis, 1982-88, River City Broadcasting Co., St. Louis, 1988-96; gen. ptnr. Marcus Investments, L.P., 1996—; CEO Peak Media Holdings LLC, St. Louis, 1997—. Computer design cons. PriceWaterhouse Coopers, Montgomery; ptnr. San Diego Social Venture. Bd. dirs. St. Louis Nat. Pub. Radio; pres. Del Mar TV Found. Mem.: Broadcast Cable Fin. Mgmt. Assn. (bd. dirs. 1976—89, treas. 1989—90, sec. 1990—91, v.p. 1991—92, pres. 1992—93). Jewish. Avocations: skiing, golf. Office: Peak Media LLC 13748 Pine Needles Dr Del Mar CA 92014 E-mail: ldmarcus@aol.com.

MARCUS, LINDA SUSAN, dermatologist; b. Bklyn. d. Nathaniel and Eugenia (Portnay) Marcus; m. Ronald Carlin, July 5, 1976; children: Robert Adam, Neal Marc. BS, Adelphi U., Garden City, NJ, 1970; MD, Downstate Med. Sch., Bklyn., 1975. Diplomate Am. Bd. Dermatology. Intern Long Island (N.Y.) Jewish Med. Ctr., 1975-76; resident in dermatology Columbia-St. Luke's, NYC, 1976-77, Boston U.-Tufts U., 1977-79; pvt. practice Wyckoff, NJ, 1980—. Dir. dermatology Valley Hosp., Ridgewood. Contbr. articles to profl. jours. Chair Nat. Psoriasis Found., NJ. Mem. Am. Acad. Dermatology (editor pamphlet editl. bd.), Am. Soc. Dermatol. Surgeons, Internat. Soc. Dermatol. Surgeons, N.J. Dermatol. Soc. (program dir.), N.J. North Dermatol. Soc. (co-chair), Dermatol. Soc. of NJ (pres.). Avocations: swimming, ice skating. Office: 271 Godwin Ave Wyckoff NJ 07481-2057 Office Phone: 201-891-4373. Personal E-mail: sexyderm@verizon.net.

MARCUS, MARIA LENHOFF, lawyer, educator; b. Vienna, June 23, 1933; came to U.S., 1938, naturalized, 1944; d. Arthur and Clara (Gruber) Lenhoff; m. Norman Marcus, Dec. 23, 1956; children: Valerie, Nicole, Eric. BA, Oberlin Coll., 1954; JD, Yale Law Sch., 1957. Bar: N.Y. 1961, U.S. Dist. Ct. (so. and ea. dists.) N.Y. 1962, U.S. Ct. Appeals (2d cir.) 1962, U.S. Supreme Ct. 1964. Assoc. counsel NAACP, NYC, 1961-67; asst. atty. gen. N.Y. State, NYC, 1967-78; chief litigation bur. Atty. Gen. N.Y. State, 1976-78; adj. assoc. prof. NYU Law Sch., 1976-78; assoc. prof. Fordham U. Law Sch., NYC, 1978-86, prof., 1986—, Joseph M. McLaughlin prof., 1997—. Arbitrator Nat. Assn. Securities Dealers; chair subcom. interrogatories U.S. Dist. Ct. (so. dist.) N.Y., 1983-85. Contbr. articles to profl. jours. Named Tchr. of Yr., Fordham Law School Students, 2001. Fellow N.Y. Bar Found.; mem. Assn. Bar City of N.Y. (v.p. 1995-96, long range planning com. 1996-2000, exec. com. 1976-80, com. audit 1988-95, labor com. 1981-84, judiciary com. 1975-76, chmn. civil rights com. 1972-75), N.Y. State Bar Assn. (exec. com. 1979-81, ho. dels. 1978-81, com. constitution and by-laws 1984-93), N.Y. Women's Bar Assn. (Pres.'s award 1999). Office: Fordham U Law Sch 140 W 62nd St New York NY 10023-7485

MARCUS, PAUL, law educator; b. NYC, Dec. 8, 1946; s. Edward and Lillian (Rubin) M.; m. Rebecca Nimmer, Dec. 22, 1968; children: Emily, Beth, Daniel. AB, UCLA, 1968, JD, 1971. Bar: Calif. 1971, U.S. Dist. Ct. (cen. dist.) Calif. 1972, U.S. Ct. Appeals (D.C. cir.) 1972, U.S. Ct. Appeals (7th cir.) 1976. Law clk. U.S. Ct. Appeals (D.C. cir.), 1971-72; assoc. Loeb & Loeb, LA, 1972-74; prof. law U. Ill., Urbana, 1974-83; dean Coll. Law U. Ariz., Tucson, 1983-88, prof., 1988-92; Haynes prof. law Coll. William and Mary, Williamsburg, Va., 1992—, Kelly prof. tchg. excellence, 1992—, interim dean, 1993-94, 97-98. Reporter, cons. Fed. Jud. Ctr. Commn., Nat. Com. on the Right to Counsel, 2004-07. Author: The Entrapment Defense, 1989, 3d edit., 2003, The Prosecution and Defense of Criminal Conspiracy, 1978, 6th edit., 2007, Gilbert Law Summary, 1982, 8th edit., 2004, Criminal Law: Cases and Materials, 1982, 6th edit., 2007, Criminal Procedure in Practice, 2001, 2d edit., 2003. Office: Coll William & Mary Law Sch PO Box 8795 Williamsburg VA 23187-8795 Home Phone: 757-253-0431; Office Phone: 757-221-3900. Business E-Mail: pxmarc@wm.edu.

MARCUS, PHILIP, dean; b. NYC, Nov. 26, 1946; s. Max and Rosaline Marcus; m. Rovena Shreck, Aug. 24, 1969; children: Mitchell Howard, Brian Seth, Alyssa Robyn. BS in Pharmacological Scis., Columbia U., NYC, 1969; MD, SUNY, Bklyn., 1973; MPH, Johns Hopkins U., Balt., 2001. Diplomate internal medicine Am. Bd. Internal Medicine, 1976, pulmonary diseases Am. Bd. Internal Medicine, 1978, critical care medicine Am. Bd. Internal Medicine, 1999. Assoc. dean, curriculum devel. NY Coll. Osteo. Medicine, Old Westbury, NY, 2001—; chief, divsn. pulmonary medicine St. Francis Hosp., Roslyn, NY, 2003—06. Contbr. articles various profl. jours. Fellow: ACP, Am. Coll. Chest Physicians (chair, practice mgmt. com. 2004—06). Avocation: travel. Office: NY Coll Osteo Medicine 233 E Shore Rd Great Neck NY 11023 Home Phone: 516-681-1912; Office Phone: 516-482-7810. Office Fax: 516-482-3760; Home Fax: 516-482-3760. Personal E-mail: pmarcus192@aol.com. E-mail: pmarcus@nyit.edu.

MARCUS, PHILIP IRVING, virology educator, researcher; b. Springfield, Mass., June 3, 1927; s. Julius and Marley Amelia (Speir) M.; m. Angela Joan Francis, Dec. 4, 1953; children: Craig F., Wendy L., Valerie L. BS, U. So. Calif., 1950; MS, U. Chgo., 1953; PhD, U. Colo., 1957. Asst. prof. biophysics U. Colo. Sch. Medicine, Denver, 1957-60; asso. prof. microbiology Albert Einstein Coll. Medicine, Bronx, NY, 1961-66, prof., 1967-69; prof. microbiology U. Conn., Storrs, 1969-75, head dept., 1969-75, prof. virology, 1969—, dir. Biotech. Ctr., 1990-95, 2002—, Bd. of Trustees Disting. prof., 2003—. Dir. Nat. Cancer Inst. Program Project, 1973-83; cons. NIH, NSF; mem. sci. adv. coun. Damon Runyon-Walter Winchell Cancer Fund, 1970-74, Am. Cancer Soc., 1986-88, Am. Found. for AIDS Rsch., 1990—. Editor Jour. Cellular Physiology, 1969-96; editor in chief Jour. Interferon Rsch., 1984-95, Jour. Interferon & Cytokine Rsch., 1995—2002, sr. cons. editor, 2003—; contbr. numerous articles to profl. jours.; patentee in field. Served with USAAC, 1945-47. Recipient USPHS rsch. career devel. award, 1960-70, excellence in rsch. award U. Conn. Alumni Assn., 1987; NIH grantee, 1960-94, NSF, USDA grantee. Mem. AAAS, Am. Soc. Microbiology, Am. Soc. Cell Biology, Am. Soc. Virology, Brit. Soc. Microbiology, Internat. Soc. Interferon and Cytokine Rsch. (hon.), Soc. In Vitro Biology, Harvey Soc., Conn. Acad. Sci. and Engring. Home: 24 Thompson Rd Storrs Mansfield CT 06268-1806 Office: U Conn Dept Molec & Cell Biol U-3044 Storrs Mansfield CT 06269 Office Phone: 860-486-4254. E-mail: philip.marcus@uconn.edu.

MARCUS, RICHARD GREENWALD, manufacturing executive; b. NYC, Sept. 24, 1947; s. Robert Greenwald and Natalie (Snider) M.; m. Beth Applebaum; children: Teri Applebaum, Todd Snider. SB, MIT, 1969, SM, 1971. Sales and mktg. assoc. Am. Biltrite Inc., Wellesley Hills, Mass., 1971-83, v.p., 1981-83, pres., 1983—. Office: Am Biltrite Inc 57 River St Wellesley MA 02481-2013

MARCUS, RICHARD SARGON, research scientist; AB, U. Pa., 1954, BSEE, 1955; MSEE, MIT, 1957, EE, 1958. Rsch. fellow MIT Rsch. Lab. for Electronics, 1955-58; prin. rsch. scientist MIT Lab. for Info. and Decision Systems, 1958-62, 67—; sr. systems engr. Itek Corp., 1962-67. Editl. bd. Info. Processing and Mgmt., Jour. of Intelligent Info. Systems; reviewer other jours. Mem. Am. Soc. for Info. Sci. (Best article of Yr. to Jour.), Assn. for Computing Machinery, Assn. for Computational Linguistics. Achievements include research on modeling of indexing and retrieval processes for bibliographic and textual databases and the application of those models in the development of expert search assistance systems. E-mail. Office: MIT LIDS 77 Mass Ave Rm 32D-558 Cambridge MA 02139-4307 Home Phone: 781-963-2792. Business E-Mail: rmarcus@mit.edu.

MARCUS, RUDOLPH ARTHUR, chemist, educator; b. Montreal, July 21, 1923; arrived in U.S., 1949, naturalized, 1958; s. Myer and Esther (Cohen) Marcus; m. Laura Hearne, Aug. 27, 1949 (dec. Jan. 2003); children: Alan Rudolph, Kenneth Hearne, Raymond Arthur. BS in Chemistry, McGill U., 1943, PhD in Chemistry, 1946, DSc (hon.), 1988, U. Chgo., 1983, Poly. U., 1986, U. Göteborg, Sweden, 1987, U. N.B., Can., 1993, Queens U., 1993, U. Oxford, Eng., 1995, Yokohama Nat. U., Japan, 1996, U. N.C., 1996, U. Ill., 1997, Technion-Israel Inst. Tech., 1998, Polytechnic U. Valencia, 1999, Northwestern U., 2000, U. Waterloo, Can., 2002. Rsch. staff RDX Project, Montreal, 1944—46; rsch. assoc. NRC of Can., Ottawa, Ont., 1946—49, U. N.C., 1949—51; asst. prof. Poly. Inst. Bklyn., 1951—54, assoc. prof., 1954—58, prof., 1958—64, acting head, div. phys. chem., 1961—62; prof. U. Ill., Urbana, 1964—78, head, div. phys. chem., 1967—68; Arthur Amos Noyes prof. chem. Calif. Inst. Tech., Pasadena, 1978—; vis. prof. theoretical chem. U. Oxford, 1975—76; Baker lectr. Cornell U., Ithaca, NY, 1991; Linnett vis. prof. chemistry Cambridge (Eng.) U., 1996; hon. prof. Fudan U., Shanghai, 1994—; hon prof. Inst. Chem. Chinese Acad. Scis., Beijing, 1995—; hon. fellow Univ. Coll., Oxford, 1995—; hon. prof. Tianjin U., China, 2002, China Ocean U., 2002, Dalian Inst. Chem. Physics, Dalian, China, 2005, Wenzhov Med. Coll., Wenzhov, China, 2005. Professorial fellow Univ. Coll., Oxford, 1975—76; mem. Courant Inst. Math. Scis., NYU, 1960—61; trustee Gordon Rsch. confs., 1966—69; assoc. mem. Ctr. Advanced Studies, U. Ill., Urbana, 1968—69; chmn. bd. dirs. Gordon Rsch. confs., 1968—69, mem. coun., 1965—68; mem. rev. panel Argonne Nat. Lab., 1966—72, chmn., 1967—68; mem. rev. panel Brookhaven Nat. Lab., 1971—74; mem. rev. com.Radiation Lab., U. Notre Dame Radiation Lab., U. Notre Dame, 1975—80; mem. panel on atmospheric chemistry climatic impact com. NAS-NRC, 1975—78, mem. com. kinetics of chem. reactions, 1973—77, chmn., 1975—77, mem. com. chem. scis., 1977—79; lectr. in field, 1982; mem. com. to survey opportunities in chem. scis., 1982—86; mem. math. panel Internat. Benchmarking of U.S. Rsch. Fields, 1996—97; mem. panel on accountability of federally funded rsch. Com. on Sci., Engring. and Pub. Policy, 2000—01; adv. com. for chemistry NSF, 1977—80; external adv. bd. NAS Ctr. Photoinduced Charge Transfer, 1990—; mem. presdl. chairs com., Chile, 1994—96; advisor, Ctr. for Molecular Scis. Chinese Acad. Scis. and State Key Lab. for Structural Chemistry of Unstable and Stable Species, Beijing, 1995—; co-hon. pres. 29th Internat. Chemistry Olympiad, 1997; hon. visitor Nat. Sci. Coun., China, 1999. Hon. editor Internat. Jour. Quantum Chemistry, 1996—, former mem. editl. bd. Jour. Chem. Physics, Ann. Rev. Phys. Chemistry, Jour. Phys. Chemistry, Accounts Chem. Rsch., Internat. Jour. Chem. Kinetics Molecular Physics, Theoretica Chimica Acta, Chem. Physics Letters, Faraday Trans., Jour. Chem. Soc., editl. bd. Laser Chemistry, 1982—, Advances in Chem. Physics, 1984—, World Sci. Pub., 1987—, Internat. Revs. in Phys. Chemistry, 1988—, Progress in Physics, Chemistry and Mechanics (China), 1989—, Perkins Transactions 2, Jour. Chem. Soc., 1992—, Chem. Physics Rsch. (India), 1992—, Trends in Chem. Physics Rsch. (India), 1992—, Internat. Jour. Molecular Chemistry, 2007—. Named Hon. Citizen, City of Winnipeg, 1994, Treasure of L.A., Ctrl. City Assn., 1995; recipient Anne Molson prize in chem., McGill U., 1943, Sr. U.S. Scientist award, Alexander von Humboldt-Stiftung, 1976, Electrochem. Soc. Lecture award, 1979, 1996, Robinson medal, Faraday divsn. Royal Soc. Chemistry, 1982, Centenary medal, 1988, Chandler medal, Columbia U., 1983, Wolf prize in chemistry, Wolf Found., Israel, 1985, Nat. medal of Sci., 1989, Evans award, Ohio State U., 1990, Nobel prize in Chem., 1992, Hirshfelder prize in Theoretical Chemistry, U. Wis., 1993, Golden Plate award, Am. Acad. Achievement, 1993, Lavoisier medal, French Chem. Soc., 1994, Oesper award, U. Cin., 1997, Key to City of Taipei, Taiwan, 1999, William Jost lectr. and medal, Deutsche Bunsenges and Acad. Sci., Göttingen, 1999, Susquicentennial medal, Polytech U., Bklyn.; fellow Alfred P. Sloan, 1960—61, NSF sr. postdoctoral, 1960—61; scholar Sr. Fulbright-Hays, 1972. Fellow: AAAS, Royal Soc. Can. (hon.), Internat. Acad. Quantum Molecular Sci. (hon.), Chinese Acad. Scis. (hon.), Internat. Soc. for Theoretical Chem. Physics (hon.), Internat. Soc. Electrochemistry (hon.), Royal Soc. Chemistry (hon.), Royal Soc. (London) (hon.), Am. Acad. Arts and Scis. (hon.; exec. com. western sect., co-chmn. 1981—84, rsch. and planning com. 1989—91); mem.: NAS (hon.), Am. Chem. Soc. (past divsn. chmn., mem. exec. com., mem. adv. bd. petroleum rsch. fund, Irving Langmuir award in chem. physics 1978, Peter Debye award in physic. chemistry 1988, Willard Gibbs medal Chgo. sect. 1988, S.C. Lind Lecture, East Tenn. sect. 1988, Theodore William Richards medal Northwestern sect. 1990, Edgar Fahs Smith award Phila. sect. 1991, Ira Remsen Meml. award Md. sect. 1991, Pauling medal Portland, Oreg., and Puget Sound sect. 1991, Auburn-Kosolapoff award 1996, Theoretical Chemistry award 1997, Top 75 Chem. & Engring. News award 1998), Am. Phys. Soc., Lit. and Hist. Soc., Univ. Coll. Dublin (hon.), European Acad. Scis. (hon.), Korean Chem. Soc. (hon.), Am. Philos. Soc. (hon.; coun. mem. 1990), Alpha Chi Sigma. Achievements include development of the Marcus Theory of electron transfer reactions in chemical systems and RRKM theory of unimolecular reactions. Home: 331 S Hill Ave Pasadena CA 91106-3405 Office Phone: 626-395-6566. Business E-Mail: ram@caltech.edu.

MARCUS, RUTH BARCAN, philosopher, educator, writer, lecturer; b. NYC; d. Samuel and Rose (Post) Barcan; divorced; children: James Spencer, Peter Webb, Katherine Hollister, Elizabeth Post. BA, NYU, 1941; MA, Yale U., 1942, PhD, 1946; DLH (hon.), U. Ill., 1995. Rsch. assoc. in anthropology Inst. for Human Relations, Yale U., New Haven, Conn., 1945-47; AAUW fellow U. Chgo., 1947-48; vis. prof. (intermittently) Northwestern U., 1950-57, Guggenheim fellow, 1953-54; asst. prof., assoc. prof. Roosevelt U., Chgo., 1957-63; NSF fellow, 1963-64; prof. philosophy U. Ill. at Chgo., 1963-70, head philosophy dept., 1963-69; fellow U. Ill. Center for Advanced Study, 1968-69; prof. philosophy Northwestern U., 1970-73; Reuben Post Halleck prof. philosophy Yale U., 1973-93; sr. rsch. scholar, 1994—. Fellow Ctr. Advanced Study in Behavioral Sci., Stanford, Calif., 1979; vis. fellow Inst. Advanced Study, U. Edinburgh, 1983, Wolfson Coll., Oxford U., 1985, 86; vis. fellow Clare Hall, Cambridge U., 1988, lifetime mem. coll. room, 1989—; past or present mem. adv. coms. Princeton U., MIT, Calif. Inst. Tech., Cornell U. Humanities Ctr., Columbia U., UCLA, Ohio State U., U. Calif. Santa Barbara, Carnegie Mellon, Brown U., U. Va., U. Tex., others; disting. vis. prof. U. Calif., Irvine, 1995—. Author: Modalities, 1993; editor: The Logical Enterprise, 1975, Logic Methodology and Philosophy of Science VII, 1986; mem. editorial bd. Past or Present Metaphilosophy, Monist, Philos. Studies, Signs, Jour. Symbolic Logic, The Philosophers Annual; editor, contbr. to profl. jours. and books. Recipient Machette prize for contbn. to profession; Medal, College de France, 1986, Wilbur Cross medal Yale U., 2000, Launer prize, Switzerland 2007—; Mellon sr. fellow Nat. Humanities Ctr., 1992-93; vis. disting. prof. U. Calif., Irvine, 1994, 96, 97, 98, 99, 2000; fellow Conn. Acad. Arts and Scis. Fellow Am. Acad. Arts and Scis.; mem. Coun. on Philos. Studies (pres. 1988-90), Assn. for Symbolic Logic (past exec. coun., exec. com. 1973-83, v.p. 1980-82, coun. 1980-85, pres. 1982-84), Am. Philos. Assn. (past sec., treas., nat. bd. dirs. 1977-83, pres. ctrl. divsn. 1975-78, chmn. nat. bd. officers 1977-85), Philosophy of Sci. Assn., Inst. Internat. Philosophie (past exec. com., v.p. 1983-86, pres. 1990-93, hon. pres. 1994—), Fedn. Internat. Philosophy (exec. com., steering com. 1985-99), Elizabethan Club (v.p. 1989, pres. 1989-90), Phi Beta Kappa. Office: Yale U Dept Philosophy PO Box 208306 New Haven CT 06520-8306 E-mail: ruth.marcus@yale.edu.

MARCUS, SHELDON, school policy and administration educator; b. NYC, Aug. 4, 1937; s. Manny and Sarah (Lande) M.; m. Phyllis Knight; children: Beth, Jonathan, Evan. BA, CCNY, 1959, MS, 1960; EdD, Yeshiva U., NYC, 1970. Tchr. NYC Pub. Schs., 1959—68; lectr. social sci. CUNY, 1965—68; mem. faculty Fordham U., NYC, 1968—70, chmn. divsn. urban edn., 1970—76, assoc. dean grad. edn. Tarrytown campus, 1976—93, prof., 1993—. Mem. exec. bd. tchr. corps program US Office Edn., 1974-82; trustee Doctoral Assn. NY, 1973-82; co-dir. Fordham Inst. for Rsch. on Supervision and Tchg., 1992-94, Fordham U./NYC Supts. Network, 1995—. Author or co-author: Conflicts in Urban Education, 1970, Urban Education: Crisis or Opportunity?, 1972; Father Coughlin: The Tumultuous Life of the Priest of the Little Flower, 1973, (nominated for Pulitzer Prize), The Urban In-Service Education Experience, 1977, Administrative Decision Making in Schools: A Case Study Approach to Strategic Planning, 1986, Strategic Planning: A Case Study Approach to Administrative Decision Making. Case Teaching Notes, 1987, Hot-Button Issues In Today's Schools, 2006, Hot-Button Issues For Teachers: What Every Educator Needs to Know, 2007; contbr. articles to profl. jours. Recipient Scanlon award for contbns. to edn., 1992, Adminstr. of Yr. award, Phi Delta Kappa, 1993. Mem. Am. Ednl. Rsch. Assn. (proposal reviewer 1992-97). Home: 36 Pocantico River Rd Pleasantville NY 10570-3510 Office: Fordham U Sch Educ Tarrytown NY 10591 Office Phone: 212-636-6432. Business E-Mail: marcus@fordham.edu.

MARCUS, STANLEY, federal judge; b. NYC, 1946; BA, CUNY, 1967; JD, Harvard U., 1971. Law clerk Hon. John Bartels, US Dist. Ct. (ea. dist.), NY; assoc. Botein, Hays, Sklar & Herzberg, NYC, 1974-75; asst. atty. US Dist. Ct. (ea. dist.)NY, 1975-78; spl. atty., dep. chief U.S. organized crime sect. Detroit Strike Force, 1978-79, chief U.S. organized crime sect., 1980-82; US atty. So. Dist. of Fla., Miami, 1982-85; judge US Dist. Ct. (so. dist.) Fla., Miami, 1985-97, US Ct. Appeals (11th cir.), 1997—. Mem. Fed. Bar Assn., Fla. Bar Assn, NY Bar Assn. Mem. US Army, 1968—74. Office: US Ct of Appeals 11th Cir 99 NE 4th St Rm 1262 Miami FL 33132-2185 *

MARCUS, STEPHEN HOWARD, lawyer; b. NYC, June 30, 1945; s. Jacob and Mildren (Cohen) M.; m. Carol Sylvia Beatrice, June 11, 1967; children: Joshua David, Rebecca Lynn, Daniel Benjamin. BME, MIT, 1967; JD, Harvard U., 1970. Bar: Calif. 1971, U.S. Dist. Ct. (cen. dist.) Calif. 1971, U.S. Dist. Ct. (so. dist.) Calif. 1974, U.S. Dist. Ct. (so. dist.) Calif. 1975, U.S. Ct. Appeals (9th cir.) 1980. Assoc. Mitchell, Silberberg & Knupp, LA, 1971-72, Greenberg, Bernhard, Weis & Karma, LA, 1972-76; ptnr. Greenberg, Bernhard, Weiss & Rosin, LA, 1976-85; assoc. Frandzel & Share, LA, 1985-87, ptnr., 1987-97, Gittler & Bradford, LA, 1997—; dir. Cerritos Valley Bancorp., 2001—02. Judge pro tem L.A. Mcpl. Ct., 1976-83. Editor Harvard Law Rev., 1970. Dir. legal com. Temple B'Nai Hayim, 1999-2003, bd. dirs., 1999-2003. Mem. Los Angeles County Bar Assn. (client rels. com. arbitrator 1982—, vice chair, 1996—), Century

City Bar Assn. (bd. govs. 1984-90), MIT Club So. Calif. (pres. 1978-79, bd. govs. 1979—), Sigma Xi, Tau Beta Pi. Democrat. Jewish. Avocations: senior soccer, square dancing. Office: Gittler & Bradford 10537 Santa Monica Blvd 3d Fl Los Angeles CA 90025-1793 E-mail: csmarcus@aol.com, smarcus@gblaw.net.

MARCUS, STEVEN IRL, electrical engineering educator; b. St. Louis, Apr. 2, 1949; s. Herbert A. and Peggy L. (Polishuk) M.; m. Jeanne M. Wilde, June 4, 1978; children: Jeremy A., Tobin L. BA, Rice U., 1971; SM, MIT, 1972, PhD, 1975. Research engr. The Analytic Scis. Corp., Reading, Mass., 1973; asst. prof. U. Tex., Austin, 1975-80, assoc. prof., 1980-84, prof., 1984-91, assoc. chmn., dept. elec. and computer engring., 1984-89, L.B. Meaders prof. engring., 1987-91; prof. elec. and computer engring. U. Md., College Park, 1991—, acting chair dept., 2000-01, chair, 2001—05, dir. Inst. for Sys. Rsch., 1991-96, acting chair, 2000-01. Cons. Tracor Inc., Austin, 1977, 90, ALPHATECH Inc., Arlington, 1999-02. Assoc. editor Math. of Control Signals and Systems, 1987-02, Jour. on Discrete Event Dynamic Systems, 1990-00, Acta Applicandae Mathematicae, 1983—. NSF fellow, 1971-74; Werner W. Dornberger Centennial Teaching fellowship in engring., U. Tex., Austin, 1982-84. Fellow IEEE (prize paper awards com. 1985-88, field awards com. 1989-90, assoc. editor Transactions Info. Theory 1990-92), IEEE Control Systems Soc. (bd. govs. 1985-90, chmn. conf. on decision and control program com. 1983, chmn. working group on stochastic control and estimation 1984-87, assoc. editor Transactions Automatic Control 1980-81); mem. Am. Math. Soc., Soc. Indsl. and Applied Math. (corr. editor Jour. Control and Optimization 1990—, editor-in-chief 2000-05), Acta Applicandae Math., 1983—, Eta Kappa Nu, Tau Beta Pi. Home: 9516 Thornhill Rd Silver Spring MD 20901-4836 Office: U Md Inst Sys Rsch 2219 Ave Williams Bldg 115 College Park MD 20742-0001

MARCUS, WILLIAM MICHAEL, rubber and vinyl products manufacturing company executive; b. Boston, Jan. 31, 1938; s. Richard and Diana (Litch) M.; m. Cynthia Steinman, Dec. 9, 1962; children: Melanie, Daniel, Richard. BS in Bus. Adminstrn., Babson Inst., 1959. With Am. Biltrite Inc., Wellesley Hills, Mass., 1960—, exec. v.p., treas., 1983—, also dir. Bd. dirs. Congoleum Corp., Aqua Bounty Tech. Served with US Army, 1960-61. Office: American Biltrite Inc 57 River St Wellesley Hills MA 02481-2013

MARCUSA, FRED HAYE, lawyer; b. Paterson, NJ, Jan. 31, 1946; s. Harry and Alice Marcusa; m. Andrea Disario, June 28, 1986; children; Michael, Daniel. AB, Dartmouth Coll., 1967; JD, U. Pa., 1970. Bar: N.Y. 1971. Assoc. Davis, Polk & Wardwell, NYC, 1970-79; v.p., gen. counsel The Coca-Cola Bottling Co. of NY, Inc., 1979-81; sr. ptnr. corp. & fin. dept. Kaye Scholer LLP, NYC, 1981—. Office: Kaye Scholer LLP 425 Park Ave New York NY 10022-3506 Office Phone: 212-836-8433. E-mail: fmarcusa@kayescholer.com.

MARCUSE, ADRIAN GREGORY, academic administrator; b. NYC, Mar. 25, 1922; s. Maxwell Frederick and Mildred Ann (Hitter) M.; m. Janet Constance Radlo, Oct. 28, 1945 (dec. Mar. 22, 1980); children: Nancy Ruth Marcuse Marshall, Sally Ann Marcuse Crawford, Elizabeth Susan Marcuse; m. Betty Jane Lieberman Rossman, Jan. 11, 1985; 1 stepchild, Amy Beth Rossman Schurtz. BS, MIT, 1942, MS, 1946; LLD (hon.), Lab Inst. Merchandising, 1992. Registered profl. engr. N.Y., Fla. Rsch. assoc. MIT, Cambridge, Mass., 1945-46; rsch. scientist United Aircraft Co., E. Hartford, Conn., 1946-47; application engr. Westinghouse Electric Corp., Boston, NYC, 1947-60; consulting engr. pvt. practice, NYC, 1955-62; v.p. mktg. and sales Corrosion Control Corp., NYC, 1960-62; sales and merchandising mgr. B. Altman & Co., NYC, 1962; v.p., COO Lab. Inst. of Merchandising, NYC, 1962-72, pres., CEO, 1972—2002, pres. emeritus, counsel to pres., 2002—, trustee, 1972—. Pres. LIM Fashion Edn. Found., N.Y.C., 1978—; chmn. Assn. Regionally Accredited Prvt. Colls. and Univs., Washington, 1990-93. Charter commr. City of Glen Cove, N.Y., 1964, chmn. bd. engrs., 1964-68, mem. planning bd., 1980-87; past treas. Community Concert Assn., Glen Cove; past trustee and budget chmn. North Country Reform Temple, Glen Cove; past mem. YMCA Fund-Raising Coun., Glen Cove; ranger, vol. JB McArthur State Park; v.p., bd. dirs. Gov.'s Pointe Condominium. 1st lt. USAAF, 1942-45, PTO. Mem.: Assn. Proprietary Colls. (pres. 1975—76), Sigma Beta Delta, Sigma Xi. Republican. Avocations: sailing, bicycling, travel, theater. Office: Lab Inst of Merchandising 12 E 53rd St Fl 2 New York NY 10022-5268 Home: 356 Golfview Rd #306 North Palm Beach FL 33408 Home Phone: 561-776-7420. Business E-Mail: amarcuse@limcollege.edu.

MARCUSE, DIETRICH, retired physicist; b. Koenigsberg, East Prussia, Germany, Feb. 27, 1929; arrived in US, 1957; s. Richard and Gertrud (Solty) M.; m. Haide Schwarz, Jan. 13, 1959; children: Christina, Mikel. Diplom Physiker, Freie Universität, Berlin, 1954; Doktor Ingenieur, Karlsruhe Universität, 1962. Mem. tech. staff Siemens and Halske, Berlin, 1954-57, AT&T Bell Labs., Holmdel, NJ, 1957-94, dist. mem. tech. staff, 1982-94; ret., 1994. Vis. rsch. prof. U. Md., Balt. County, 1995-99. Author: Principles of Quantum-Electronics, 2d edit., 1980, Light Transmission Optics, 2d edit., 1982, Theory of Dielectric Optical Wave-guides, 1972, 2nd edit.,1991, Principles of Optical Fiber Measurements, 1981; also over 200 articles. Fellow IEEE (Quantum Electronics award 1981), Optical Soc. Am. (Max Born award 1989). Personal E-mail: dmarcuse@optonline.net.

MARCUSS, ROSEMARY DALY, economist; b. Stamford, Conn., Aug. 27, 1945; d. Eugene Lawrence and Margaret Mary (Murphy) Daly; B.A. in Econs. cum laude, Newton (Mass.) Coll., 1967; M.S., U. Md., 1973, Ph.D., 1979; m. Stanley J. Marcuss, July 6, 1968; children— Elena Daly, Aidan Stanley. Jr. staff economist President's Council of Econ. Advisers, 1968-70; economist, asst. to pres. Am. Fedn. State, County and Mcpl. Employees, Washington, 1973; economist, mgmt. cons. Data Resources, Inc., Washington, 1974-78; dep. asst. dir. tax analysis Congressional Budget Office, Washington, 1980-83, asst. dir. tax analysis, 1983-98; dep. dir. Bur. Econ. Analysis, Washington, 1998—; pres. Nat. Assn Bus. Econ., 2005-. NSF fellow, 1970-73. Mem. Am. Econ. Assn., Nat. Tax Assn., Tax Inst. Am., So. Econ. Assn., Soc. Govt. Economists, Nat. Economists Club, Nat. Assn. Business Economists (v.p. 2003-), Washington Women Economists. Home: 4616 29th Pl NW Washington DC 20008-2105 Office: Congressional Budget Office 2nd & D Sts SW Washington DC 20515-0001

MARCUSS, STANLEY JOSEPH, lawyer; b. Hartford, Conn., Jan. 24, 1942; s. Stanley Joseph and Anne Sutton (Leone) M.; m. Rosemary Daly, July 6, 1968; children: Elena Daly, Aidan Stanley. BA, Trinity Coll., 1963, Cambridge U., 1965, MA, 1968; JD, Harvard U., 1968. Bar: D.C., N.Y., Conn., U.S. Supreme Ct. Staff atty. office of gen. counsel HUD, Washington, 1968; atty. firm Hogan and Hartson, Washington, 1968-73; counsel to internat. fin. subcom. U.S. Senate Com. on Banking, Housing and Urban Affairs, 1973-77; dep. asst. sec. for trade regulation Dept. Commerce, Washington, 1977-78, sr. dep. asst. sec. for industry and trade, 1978-79, acting asst. sec. for industry and trade, 1979-80, acting asst. sec. for trade regulation, 1980; mem. firm Milbank, Tweed, Hadley & McCloy, Washington, 1980-93, Bryan Cave, 1993—. Former adj. prof. Am. U. Law Sch. Author: Effective Washington Representation, 1983; mem. bd. overseers U. Calif. Berkeley Law Jour.; contbr. articles to profl. jours. Former trustee Trinity Coll., Hartford. Marshall scholar. Mem. ABA, D.C. Bar (former chmn., steering com. internat. law div.), Phi Beta Kappa. Home: 4616 29th Pl NW Washington DC 20008-2105

MARCY, GEOFFREY W., astronomer, physicist, educator; BA in Physics & Astronomy summa cum laude, UCLA, 1976; PhD in Astronomy & Astrophysics, U. Calif., Santa Cruz, 1982. Fellow Carnegie Inst., Wash., 1982—84; full prof. physics & astronomy San Francisco State U., 1984—96, disting. prof., 1997—99, adjunct prof. physics & astronomy, 1999—; prof. astronomy U. Calif., Berkeley, 1999—. Mem. Com. on the Status of Women in Astronomy, 1994—97, NASA Working Group: Origins of Solar Systems, 1998—2000, NASA Working Group: Terrestrial Planet Finder, 1998—2001; dir. Ctr. for Integrative Planetary Sci., 2000—; Bunyan lectr., physics dept. Stanford U., 1997; G. Darwin Lecture Royal Astronomical Soc., 2000; NSF Disting. Lectr., 00; prin. investigator NASA Space Interferometry Mission, 2001; Sackler Lectr. U. Leiden, 2001; Niels Bohr Lecture N.B. Inst., 2005. Author numerous scientific articles in peer-reviewed jours., newspapers, and mag.; appearances include ABC Nightline, CBS Nightly News, NBC Today Show, BBC Horizons, CNN News, PBS, Late Show with David Letterman. Named Person of Week, ABC News Hour, 1996, Alumnus Yr., U. Calif. Santa Cruz, 1997, Calif. Scientist of the Yr., 2000, Space Scientist Yr., Discover Mag., 2003; recipient Manne Siegbahn award, Swedish Acad., 1996, Internat. Assn. Universities Commn. 51 Bioastronomy Medal of Honor (First Ever Issued), 1997, Certificate of Recognition (First Ever Issued), Extrasolar Planetary Found., 1999, UCLA Alumni Profl. Achievement award, 1999, Carl Sagan award, Am. Astronautical & Planetary Soc., 2002, Exceptional Scientific Achievement medal, NASA, 2003, Shaw prize, 2005. Fellow: Calif. Acad. of Sci.; mem.: NAS (Henry Draper medal 2001), Astronomical Soc. of Pacific (bd. dirs. 1997—99, pub. bd. 1997—2002), Am. Astronomical Soc. (bd. of councilors 1998—2000, Beatrice M. Tinsley prize 2002). Made First Zeeman Measurements of Magnetic Fields for Solor-Type Stars; found Pauncity of Brown Dwarfs Orbiting Stars; developed the method of Precise Doppler Measurements; discovered 70 of the first 100 Extrasolor Planets known; found evidence that the Solar System maybe peculiar; discoverd the first system of planets around a sun-like star; discovered first transiting planet around another star; discovered the first candidate Saturn-Mass planets; discovered the first extrasolar planet orbiting beyond 5AU; co-discovered the first Neptune-Sized Planets: Gliese 436b and 55 Cancri e. Office: U Calif 417 Campbell Hall Berkeley CA 94720 Office Phone: 510-642-1952. Office Fax: 510-642-3411.

MARCY, KEVIN MICHAEL, film producer, lawyer; BS, U. Nev., Reno, 1974—78; JD, U. So. Calif., LA, 1978—81. Bar: Calif. 1981, DC 2006. Atty. Kinsella, Boesch, Fujikawa & Towle, LA, 1981—83; assoc. prodr. Paramount Pictures, LA, 1983—87, 1995; asst. to Dan Aykroyd Applied Action Rsch., LA, 1987—95, prodr., 2003—, Snake River Productions, Malibu, Calif., 1996—2003; assoc. prodr. Miramax Films, LA, 2003. V.p., guest rels. Ho. of Blues, LA, 1994; cons. Hitplay Media, LA, 2000. Prodr.: (films) The Testimony Of Taliesin Jones, 2000, (short film) Mr. Bill Goes To Law School; assoc. prodr. (films) The Naked Gun, 1988, The Coneheads, 1993, Scary Movie 3, 2003. Mem.: Ho. of Blues Found. (life), Dan Aykroyd Biker Gang (life), Phi Kappa Phi (life), Beta Gamma Sigma (life), Phi Alpa Delta (life), Delta Sigma Pi (life).

MARDEN, BRICE, artist; b. Bronxville, NY, Oct. 15, 1938; s. Nicholas Brice and Kathryn (Fox) Marden; m. Pauline Thalia Baez, 1960 (div. 1964); 1 child, Nicholas Brice; m. Helen Regina Harrington, Nov. 7, 1968; children: Maya Mirabelle Zahara, Melia Io Bricia. Student, Fla. So. Coll., 1957—58; BFA, Boston U., 1958—61; MFA, Yale U., 1961—63. Security guard Jewish Mus., NYC, 1963—64; gen. asst. to Robert Rauschenberg, 1966; inst. Sch. Visual Arts, NY, 1969—74. Pres. Plane Image, Inc. Exhibited in one man shows including Wilcox Gallery, Swarthmore, Pa., 1964, Bykert Gallery, NYC, 1966, 68-70, 72-74, Galerie Yvon Lambert, Paris, 1969, 73, Galleria Francoise Lambert, Milan, Italy, 1970, 73, Konrad Fischer, Dusseldorf, Fed. Republic of Germany, 1971-73, 75, 80, Gian Enzo Sperone, Turin, Italy, 1971, 77, Locksley-Shea Gallery, Mpls., 1972, 74, Jack Glenn Gallery, Corona del Mar, Calif., 1973, Cirrus Gallery, Los Angeles, 1974, Sable-Castelli Gallery, Toronto, Can., 1974, Contemporary Arts Mus., Houston, 1974, Loretto Hilton Gallery, St. Louis, 1974, Ft. Worth Art Mus., Tex., 1974, Mpls. Inst. Arts, 1975, D'Allesandro/Ferranti, Rome, 1975, Solomon R. Guggenheim Mus., NYC, 1975, Sperone Westwater Fischer, NYC, 1976, Max Protech Gallery, Washington, 1977, Bell Gallery, Providence, 1977, Jean and Karen Bernier, Athens, 1977, Pace Gallery, NYC, 1978, 80, 82, 84, Kunstraum, Munich, 1979, Inst. für Moderne Kunst, Nurnberg, Fed. Republic of Germany, 1979, Ink, Zurich, 1980, Stedelijk Mus., Amsterdam, 1981, Daniel Weinberg Gallery, Los Angeles, 1984, Mary Boone Gallery, NYC, 1987, Mary Boone/Michael Werner Gallery, NYC, 1988, 89, Gallery Montenay, Paris, 1988, Anthony d'Offay Gallery, London, 1988, Van Straaten Gallery, Chgo., 1989, Galerie Michael Werner, Cologne, 1990, Kunsthalle im Kulturhaus Palazzo, Baselland, Switzerland, 1991, Gagosian Gallery, NY, 1993, Mus. Fine Arts, Boston, 1993, Matthew Marks Gallery, NY, 1993, 95, 96, 98, Dia Ctr. for the Arts, NY, 1993, Walker Art Ctr., Mpls., 1993, Menil Collection, Houston, 1993, Mus. Nat. Ctr. de Arte, Madrid, 1993, Kunstmus., Bonn, Germany, 1993, Tate Gallery, London, 1993, Mus. d'Art Moderne de la Ville de Paris, 1993, Balt. Mus. Art, 1993, Curwen Gallery, London, 1993, Kunstmus. Basel, 1995, Mus. fur Gegenwartskunst, 1995, Mus. Fridericianum, Kassel, 1995, Kunsthalle, Bern, 1995, Vienna Secession, 1995, Stedelijk, Amsterdam, 1995, St. Louis Art Mus., 1995, Pace Gallery, NY, 1996, Thomas Ammann Fine Art AG, Zurich, Switzerland, 1997, Staatliche Graphisch Sammlung, Munchen, 1998, Kunstmus., Winterthur, Switzerland, 1998, Wexner Art Ctr., Ohio, 1999, Fogg Art Mus., Cambridge, Mass., 1999, Dallas Mus. Art, 1999, Etchings, Margo Leavin Gallery, LA, 2001, Serpentine Gallery, London, 2001, Drawing the Line: A Retrospective of Drawings, 2002, Alumni Gallery, Boston U., 2003, Attendants, Bears, and Rocks, Matthew Marks Gallery, NY, 2003, An Empty Space, Akira Ikeda Gallery, NY, 2005; represented in group shows including Lyman Allen Mus., New London, Conn., 1960, Leo Castelli Gallery, NYC, 1966, Park Place Gallery, NYC, 1966, Ithaca Coll. Mus. Art, NY, 1967, Krannert Art Mus., Champaign, Ill., 1967, Bykert Gallery, 1967-68, 70-71, 74, Inst. Contemporary Art, Phila., 1967, U. Omaha, 1967, Mus. Fine Arts, Houston, 1967, Clemson U. Sch. Architecture, 1968, Vassar Coll. Art Gallery, Poughkeepsie, NY, 1969, Stadtische Kunsthalle, Dusseldorf, 1969, Ft. Worth Art Mus., 1969, 74, Carmen Lamanna Gallery, Toronto, 1969, Whitney Mus. Am. Art, NYC, 1969, 71, 73, 77, 83, Locksley-Shea Gallery, 1970, Albright-Knox Gallery, Buffalo, 1970, Found. Maeght, St. Paul-de-Vence, France, 1970, Utah Mus. Fine Arts, Salt Lake City, 1970, Minn. Mus. Art, St. Paul, 1971, Henry Gallery, Seattle, 1972-73, Ariz. State U., Tempe, 1972, Ga. Mus. Art, Athens, 1972, Mus. Contemporary Art, Chgo., 1972, 86, Indpls. Mus. Art, 1972, Walker Art Ctr., Mpls., 1972, Univ. Art Mus., Berkeley, Calif., 1972, Art Inst. Chgo., 1972, Mus. Friderichianum and Neue Galerie, Kassel, Fed. Republic of Germany, 1972, Galerie Yvon Lambert, 1972, Yale U. Art Gallery, New Haven, 1973, Genthofte Kunstvenner and Genthofte Kommune, Denmark, 1973, Stadtisches Mus., Monchengladbach, Fed. Republic of Germany, 1973, I.C.C., Antwerp, Belgium, 1973, Centro Communitario di Brera, Milan, 1973, Royal Coll. Art, London, 1973, Parcheggio di Villa Borghese, Rome, 1974, Kathonah Gallery, NY, 1974, Nat. Gallery of Victoria, Australia, 1974, Art Gallery of New South Wales, Australia, 1974, Art Gallery of South Australia, Akelaide, 1974, West Australian Art Gallery, Perth, 1974, City of Auckland Art Gallery, Australia, 1974, Westfalischer Kunstverein, Munster, Fed. Republic of Germany, 1974, Scottish Arts Council, Edinburgh, 1974, Mus. Modern Art, NYC, 1974, 76, Rice Mus. and Sewall Gallery, 1975, Rijksmuseum Kroller-Muller, Otterlo, Holland, 1975, Basel (Switzerland) Kunstmuseum, 1975, Kunstahlle, Zurich, 1976, Staatliche Kunsthalle, Baden-Baden, Fed. Republic of Germany, 1976, Graphische Sammlung Albertina, Vienna, 1976, Sidney Janis Gallery, NYC, 1977, Wildenstein and Co., London, 1980, Bklyn. Mus., 1980, Mus. Contemporary Art, Los Angeles, 1983, Hayden Gallery, Cambridge, Mass., 1983, Pratt Inst. Gallery, NYC, 1983, Gallery Maeght Lelong, NYC, 1983, The Renaissance Soc., Chgo., 1984, Blum Helman Warehouse, NYC, 1984, Daniel Weinberg Gallery, Los Angeles, 1985, Guggenheim Mus., NYC, 1985, Condeso Lawler Gallery, NYC, 1985, Mary Boone Gallery, 1985, Carnegie Inst., Pitts., 1985, Ft. Lauderdale Mus. Art, Fla.,1986, P.S. 1, LI City, 1986, Charles Cowles Gallery, NYC, 1986, Musee d'Art Moderne, Paris, 1986, Los Angeles County Mus., 1986, Gemeentemuseum, The Hague, The Netherlands, 1986, Ludwig Mus., Kolm, Fed. Republic of Germany, 1986, Galerie Nachst St. Stephan, Vienna, 1986, CAPC Musee d'Art Contemporain de Bordeaux, France, 1986, Anthony d'Offay Gallery, London, 1987, The Sara Hilden Art Mus., Tampere, Finland, 1988, Carnegie Mus. Art, Pitts., 1988, Musee d'art contemporain, Lyon, 1988, Hirschl and Adler Modern, New York, 1989, Whitney Mus. Am. Art, NY, 1989, Albright Knox Art Gallery, Buffalo, Ctr. for the Fine Arts, Miami, Fla., Milwaukee Art Mus., Wis., Yale U. Art Gallery, New Haven, Conn., 1989, The Albertina, Vienna, 1990, Musee du Louvre, Paris, 1990, The Mus. of Modern Art, New York, 1992, Margo Leavin Gallery, LA, 1992, The Balt. Mus. Art, 1992, Kassel, Germany, 1992, The Aldrich Mus., Ridgefield, Conn., 1993, Luhring Augusting, NY, 1994, Nat. Gallery, Washington, 1994, The Art Inst. Chgo., 1995, Nat. Mus. Modern Art, Tokyo, 1995, Whitney Mus. Am. Art, NY, 1995, Musee national d'art modern, Centre Georges Pompidou, 1995, Mus. Contemporary Art, Chgo., 1996, La Biennale di Venizia, Venice, Italy, 1997, Mitchell-innes & Nash, NY, 1998, Hirshhorn Mus. and Sculpture Garden, Washington, Miami Art Mus., Fla., 1999-2000, Carnegie Mus. Art, Pitts., 2000, Serpentine Gallery, London, 2000, Kunst Mus., Luzern, Switzerland, 2000, Instituto Nazionale Per La Gradica, Rome, 2001, Archivio di Stato, Torino, Italy, 2002, Landesmuseum fur Kunst und Kulturgeschichte, Munster, Germany, 2002, Boston U. Gallery, 2002, Matthew Marks Gallery, NYC, 2002, Daros Collection, Zurich, Switzerland, 2003, Not Exactly Photographs, Fraenkel Gallery, San Francisco, 2004, A Minimal Future? Art as Object, Mus. Contemporary Art, LA, 2004, Singular Forms (Sometimes Repeated), Guggenheim Mus., NYC, 2004, Matisse to Freud: A Critic's Choice, Brit. Mus., London, 2005, Imageless Icons: Abstract Thoughts, Gagosian Gallery, London, 2005, Contemporary Voices, Mus. Modern Art, NYC, 2005. Fellow: Am. Acad. Arts and Sci. Office: 131 Varick St Rm 1003 New York NY 10013-1417 Home: Hydra Greece

MARDEN, KENNETH ALLEN, advertising executive; b. Dec. 12, 1928; s. Allen H. and Doris (Littlefield) M.; m. Julia Lee Black, June 11, 1949; children: Priscilla Anne, Emily Gage. BA, U. Maine, 1950. Hosp. salesman Johnson & Johnson, New Brunswick, NJ, 1959-61, product dir. hosp divsn., 1962-68, advt. and pub. rels. mgr. hosp. divsn., 1969-71, group product dir., patient care divsn., 1972-74, advt. dir. patient care divsn., 1974-78; v.p. E.J. Axelrod, Inc., NYC, 1978-80; v.p. account mgmt. Vicom/FCB, Phila., 1980-87; pres. Am. Kennel Club, NYC, 1987-90. Cons. on dog legislation, 1990—, also bd. dirs.; pres. Crossing Creek Comm., 1991—; bd. dirs. The Dog Mus., 1995—. 1st lt. U.S. Army, 1951-53; capt. Md. N.G., 1956-59. Mem. Dog Writers Assn. Am., German Shorthaired Pointer Am. Club (del. 1976—, v.p. 1985-86), Eastern German Shorthaired Pointer Club (pres. 1972-74, 94-98), Jersey Rag Racers (pres. 1994-96), Katahdin German Shorthaired Pointer Club of Greater Portland, Nat. Animal Interest Alliance (bd. dirs. 1994—), Nat. Breed Clubs Alliance (v.p. 1996-2000). Republican. Episcopalian. Home: 183 E River Rd Whitefield ME 04353 Office: Crossing Creek Communications 183 E River Rd Whitefield ME 04353 Office Phone: 207-549-4783. E-mail: kmarden@earthlink.net.

MARDER, BARBARA HERMLING, theater educator, department chairman; b. Peoria, Ill., Oct. 5, 1941; d. Harold Otha and Elizabeth Kendall Hermling; m. Stuart Charles Marder, Jan. 28, 1972; children: Joshua Gerold, Jody Elicia. MA, George Washington U., Washington, 1968. Cert. advanced profl. study in tech. Johns Hopkins U., 1980. Theatre arts faculty Anne Arundel C.C., Arnold, Md., 1978—2002, chair performing arts, 2002—. Dir.: (theatre) All My Sons (Cert. Merit, Am. Coll. Theatre Festival, 2000). Chair scholarship AAUW, Severna Park, Md., 2000—04. Mem.: Assn. for Theatre in Higher Edn. (2 yr. coll. conf. planner 2006—). Avocations: water sports, travel. Office: Anne Arundel Community College 101 College Pkwy Arnold MD 21012 Home Phone: 410-991-7114; Office Phone: 410-777-7030. Business E-Mail: bhmarder@aacc.edu.

MARDER, EVE ESTHER, neuroscientist, educator; b. NYC, May 30, 1948; d. Eric Marder and Dorothy Silverman. AB, Brandeis U., 1969; PhD, U. Calif., San Diego, 1974. Postdoctoral fellow U. Oreg., Eugene, 1975, Ecole Normale Superieure, Paris, 1976-78; from asst. prof. to assoc. prof. Brandeis U., Waltham, Mass., 1978-90, prof. neuroscience, dept. biology, 1990—; program dir. Sloan Swartz Ctr. for Theoretical Neurosci.; chief editor Jour. of Neurophysiology, 2002—. Forbes lectr., 2000. Founding editor: Jour. Computational Neurosci.; mem. editorial bd., Jour. Exptl. Biology, Jour. Neurobiology, curr. biol; jour. comp. physiol A; curr. opinion in Neurobiology; jour. of comp. neurology; contbr. papers and chpt. to sci. jour. Trustee Grass Found. Coun., 1999—2002. Recipient Javits award in neurosci. NINDS, 1987, Investigators award McKnight Found., 1994, NIMH Merit award, 1995; Alfred P. Sloan Found. fellow, 1978; McKnight scholar, 1978. Fellow AAAS, Am. Acad. Arts and Sci., Soc. for Neurosci (pres.-elect. 2007, Gerard prize 2005); mem. NAS. Office: Brandeis U Volen Ctr Waltham MA 02454 *

MARDER, JANET, rabbi; m. Sheldon Marder; children: Betsy, Rachel. BA, U. Calif Santa Cruz; grad. studies in Modern Hebrew and Yiddish, UCLA. Cert. ordained Rabbi Hebrew Union College-Jewish Institute of Religion, 1979. Rabbi Beth Chayim Chadashim, 1983—88; with Union of American Hebrew Congregations, 1988—99; sr. rabbi Congregation Beth Am, Los Altos Hills, Calif., 1999—. Contbr. articles to numerous profl. jours. incl. Reformed Judaism Mag., Reconstructionist, Sh'ma. Named one of The Top 50 Rabbis in America, Newsweek Mag., 2007. Mem.: Ctrl. Conf. Am. Rabbis (past v.p., pres.), Pacific Ocean Reform Rabbis (past pres.). Jewish. Office: Congreagtion Beth Am 26790 Arastradero Rd Los Altos CA 94022 *

MARDER, JOHN ADAM, lawyer; b. Fall River, Mass., Jan. 17, 1960; s. Everett Joseph and Brenda Joan (Leviss) M.; m. Bonnie Jane Webber, Nov. 11, 1989; 1 child, Max Phillip. BA, Bates Coll., 1982; JD, Calif. Western Sch. Law, 1985. Bar: Calif. 1986, U.S. Dist. Ct. (ctrl. dist.) Calif. 1989. Dep. dist. atty. San Bernardino D.A., 1985-87; atty. Home Ins. Co., LA, 1987; ptnr. Morris, Polich & Purdy LLP, LA, 1987-94; mng. ptnr. Manning & Marder Kass Ellrod Ramirez LLP (formerly Manning, Marder & Wolfe LLP), LA, 1994—. Gen. counsel Internat. Assn. Spl. Investigation Units, So. Calif. Chapter; bd. dirs. Athens Found. Named a Super Lawyer, Law & Politics, 2005; named Calif. Atty. of the Yr., Calif. Lawyer mag., 2005. Office: Manning & Marder Kass Ellrod Ramirez LLP 660 S Figueroa St 23rd Fl Los Angeles CA 90017

MARDER, MICHAEL ZACHARY, dental educator, researcher; b. NYC, Aug. 30, 1938; s. Jospeh Theodore and Rhea (Greenspun) M.; (widowed); children: Sherri Ellen, Robert Whitney. Student, Tufts U., 1959; DDS, Columbia U., 1963. Diplomate: Am. Bd. Oral Medicine. Practice dentistry, NYC, 1963-66, 68—; asst. Sch. Dental and Oral Surgery, Columbia U., NYC, 1963-66, instr., 1968, asst. clin. prof., 1968-72, assoc. clin. prof., 1972-76, NYC clin. prof. dentistry, 1976—, rschr., 1963—; dir. oral medicine, 1972-84; dir. clin. cancer tng., 1993—; attending dental surgeon Presbyn. Hosp., 1972-76; assoc. attending dentist, 1976-82; attending dentist, 1982—; cons. Good Samaritan Hosp., Suffern, NY. Lectr. field. Author 2 textbooks in dental medicine; contbr. chpts. to med. and dental textbooks, articles to profl. jours. Served to capt. US Army, 1966-68. Recipient Cert. Achievement US Army, 1968. Fellow NY Acad. Dentistry;

mem. ADA, Internat. Assn. Dental Rsch., Am. Acad. Oral Medicine, Frist Dist. Dental Soc. NY, Omicron Kappa Upsilon, Sigma Xi. Office: 119 W 57th St New York NY 10019-2303 Office Phone: 212-265-8291. Business E-Mail: mzm2@columbia.edu.

MARDILOVICH, IVAN P., education educator, researcher; b. Stolbtsy, Belarus, Sept. 21, 1952; s. Peter L and Elena I (Zvytsevich) Mardilovich; m. Galina A Semyonov, Apr. 23, 1977; children: Anastasia I, Katerina I. MSc, Belarus State U., 1975; PhD in phys. chemistry, Russian U. of Peoples' Friendship, 1982. Sr. rsch. scientist Nat. Acad. Sci. Belarus, Minsk, 1985—99; rsch. assoc. prof. Worcester Poly. Inst., Mass., 1999—. Sci. sec. of the divsn. of chem. and earth sciences NAS of Belarus, Minsk, Belarus, 1998—99. Sec.- gen. Internat. Fedn. of Chem. Societies, Minsk, Belarus, 1993—2000. Recipient Bronze medal, USSR Exhbn. of the Nat. Economy Achievements, 1985. Achievements include developed and characterized unique Pd and Pd-alloy membranes on porous supports for high temperature hydrogen separation and for a variety of hydrogen-related processes. Office: Worcester Poly Inst 100 Institute Rd Worcester MA 01609 Office Phone: 508-831-5474. Business E-Mail: ivanpm@wpi.edu.

MARDINLY, SUSAN J., musician, music educator; d. Ashe John Mardinly and Jane Elizabeth Fish; m. Fred Dale Shinkle, Feb. 21, 1998; children: Deborah Ruth Goodman, Sarah Nancy Goodman. MusB, New Eng. Conservatory of Music, 1969; MusM, U. Hartford, 1991; D in Musical Arts, U. Conn., 2004. Voice tchr., Seymour, 1979—84, Waterbury, Conn., 1985—91; voice tchr., dept. chair Hartford Conservatory, Hartford, Conn., 1992—99; voice tchr., arts adminstr. U. Conn., Storrs, 1992—96; voice tchr. The Hartt Sch. Cmty. Divsn., Hartford, Conn., 2005—. Lectr. recitals, 1978—; ch. soloist, choir dir., 1978—; dir. Chamber Musicians' Alliance, New Haven, 1979—83; operatic/oratorio soloist various cos., 1979—99; co-chair Ann. Concert of Music by Women Composers, Hartford, 2001—. Author (editor, arranger): (book) Barbara Strozzi and The Pleasures of Euterpe, 21 other publ. vocal works by Barbara Strozzi; musician (soprano soloist, chorister): Conn. Opera, 1986—92; contbr. articles to profl. jours. Benefit concerts Conn. Hospice, Branford/Litchfield, 1982—93, St. Vincent de Paul Shelter, Waterbury, Conn., 1992—99; dir. music St. Anthony Ch., Litchfield/Prospect, Conn., 1992—99; soprano soloist Ch. of Good Shepherd, Hartford, Conn., 1999—; mem. Musical Club Hartford, 1985—. Recipient Nine Dir. Music awards, Naugatuck Teen Theater, Conn., 1991; Doctoral fellow, U. Conn., 1993—96, Wagenlis scholar, 1994, Rsch. grantee, 1995. Mem.: Conn. Music Educators Assn. (cert. adjudicator 1995—), Conn. Nat. Assn. Tchrs. of Singing (judge 1981—, Conn. winner; New Eng. Regional Finalist Artist award 1982), AGMA (profl. liason 1986—92), Mu Phi Epsilon (life; two term sec. 1966—68), Pi Kappa Lambda (life). Avocations: travel, poetry, cooking. Office: Hartt Sch Bloomfield Ave Hartford CT 06117 Home Phone: 860-346-7171; Office Phone: 860-768-7768 ext 8562. Personal E-mail: susanmardinly@sbcglobal.net.

MARDIROSIAN, TOM, actor, playwright; b. Buffalo, Dec. 14, 1947; s. Matthew and Afro (Karahos) M. BA inTheatre, U. Buffalo, 1972. Tchr. U. Buffalo, 1972-75; drama coach Studio Arena Theater, Buffalo, 1972-75. Broadway performances include: The Magic Show, Cuba and His Teddy Bear, Happy Education, feature films include: Tootsie, 1982, Alphabet City, 1984, Trading Places, 1983, Power, 1986, The Rosary Murders, 1987, Shakedown, 1988, New York Stories, 1989, Betsy's Wedding, 1990, Presumed Innocent, 1990, The Dark Half, 1993, Don Juan DeMarco, 1995, On the Q.T., 1999, Razor's Edge, 1999, Lady in the Water, 2006, (TV films) Seizure: The Story of Kathy Morris, 1980, Muggable Mary, Street Cop, 1982, The Neighborhood, 1982, Rockabye, 1986, True Blue, 1989, Kojak: None So Blind, 1990, Quiet Killer, 1992, Miss Rose White, 1992, With Murder in Mind, 1992, If Looks Could Kill, 1996, Voice from the Grave, 1996; performer numerous off-Broadway plays; playwright: Saved from Obscurity, 1988 (Drama Desk nomination), Subfertile, 1990. With U.S. Army, 1967-69. Mem. SAG, AFTRA, Actors Equity Assn. Home: 210 W 16th St Apt 1C New York NY 10011-6132

MARDIS, HAL KENNEDY, urological surgeon, educator, researcher; b. Lincoln, Nebr., Apr. 4, 1934; s. Harold Corson and Marie (Swaim) M.; m. Janet Reimers Schenken, June 22, 1956; children: Michael Corson, Anne Lucille, Jeanne Marie. BS, U. Nebr., Lincoln, 1955; MD, U. Nebr., Omaha, 1958. Diplomate Am. Bd. Urology. Intern Nebr. Meth. Hosp., Omaha, 1958-59, med. dir. The Stone Ctr., 1966—; resident in urology Charity Hosp. La., New Orleans, 1959-62, chief resident in urology, 1962-63; pvt. practice Omaha, 1965—; instr., asst. prof. La. State U. Sch. Medicine, New Orleans, 1963-65; asst. prof., assoc. prof. surgery U. Nebr. Med. Ctr., 1965-85, prof., 1985—. Investigator North Cen. Cancer Treatment Group, Rochester, Minn., 1988—, Technomed Internat., Inc., Danvers, Mass., 1988—; cons. Boston Sci. Corp., Watertown, Mass., 1988—. Assoc. editor Jour. Stone Disease; contbr. articles to Jour. AMA, So. Med. Jour., Jour. Urology, Urology, Urol. Clinics N.Am., Seminars in Interventional Radiology. Sec., pres. Omaha Symphony Assn., 1973-76; advisor United Arts Omaha, 1983-88. Recipient Outstanding Contbn. award dept. surgery U. Nebr. Med. Ctr., 1990. Fellow ACS; mem. AMa (del. med. staff sect. 1983-86), Am. Urol. Assn. (pres. South Cen. chpt. 1990-91, 1st prize 1976, best clin. exhibit award 1977, Gold Cane achievement award 2001), Am. Lithotripsy Soc. (pres. 1989-90), Alpha Omega Alpha (pres. 1991-92). Republican. Achievements include development of guidewire techniques for angiography and endourology, thermoplastic internal ureteral stent; description of benefits of hydrophilic polymers for endourologic devices. Office: The Urology Ctr 111 S 90th St Omaha NE 68114-3907 Home Phone: 402-680-3553; Office Phone: 402-397-9800. Personal E-mail: hkmardis@cox.net.

MARDUEL, ALIX, venture capitalist; MD, U. Paris. Med. residency, Paris; postdoctoral fellowship U. Calif., San Francisco, Stanford U.; assoc. med. dir. ICI Pharma (now AstraZeneca), France, England; gen. ptnr. Sofinnova Ventures, 1990—97; mng. dir. Alta Partners, San Francisco, 1997—. Bd. dir. Cytos Biotechnology, 2000—, Corcept Therapeutics, 2001—, Syntonix, 2002—, NeurogesX, Metabolex, Inc., Genteric, Memory Pharm.; actively involved with the creation of several life sci. co. in the US and Europe, including Millennium Pharm., CV Therapeutics, Medicine Co., Genset & Aviaron. Office: Alta Partners One Embarcadero Ctr Ste 4050 San Francisco CA 94111

MARE, JENNIFER LE, medical technician; d. Jackie Mare. BS in Clin. Lab. Sci., SUNY, Stonybrook, 2002; M in Forensic Scis., Nat. U., San Diego, 2004. Cert. med. technologist Am. Soc. Clin. Pathology, 2003, lic. Fla., 2005. Med. technologist Boca Raton Cmty. Hosp., Fla., 2006—, point of care coord., 2006—. Mem.: Pi Delta Chi (assoc.). Achievements include research in inhibition of yeast growth by garlic. Home Phone: 954-918-2326. Personal E-mail: jmare868@yahoo.com.

MAREADY, WILLIAM FRANK, lawyer; b. Mullins, SC, Sept. 13, 1932; s. Jesse Frank and Vera (Sellers) M.; m. Brenda McCanless, Nov. 3, 1979. AB, U. N.C., 1955, JD with honors, 1958. Bar: N.C. 1958, U.S. Dist. Ct. N.C. 1960, U.S. Ct. Appeals (4th cir.) 1962, U.S. Supreme Ct. 1968. Assoc. Mudge, Stern, Baldwin & Todd, NYC, 1958-60, Hudson, Ferrell, Carter, Petree & Stockton, Winston-Salem, NC, 1960-65; ptnr. Petree, Stockton & Robinson, Winston-Salem, 1965-92, Robinson, Maready, Lawing & Comerford, 1992-97, Maready, Comerford & Britt, 1997-99; prin. Law Offices of William F. Maready, 1999—. N.C. chmn. Winston-Salem/Forsyth County Bd. Edn., 1968-70, chmn., bd. dirs. and mem. exec. com., N.C. State Port Authority, 1984-97. With Green Berets, U.S. Army, 1952-54. Recipient Disting. Svc. award N.C. Sch. Bds. Assn., Freedom award John Locke Soc., 2000. Fellow Am. Coll. Trial Lawyers, Am. Bar Found.; mem. ABA (chmn. standing com. on aero. law 1979-82, chmn. forum com. on air and space law 1982-86), N.C. Bar Assn. (chmn. litigation sect. 1981-82, adminstrn. of justice com. 1981-82), Nat. Parent Tchr. Assn. (life), Forsyth Country Club, Rotary (Winston-Salem), Order of Coif, Phi Delta Phi, Phi Beta Kappa. Republican. Methodist. Office Phone: 336-722-1027. Business E-Mail: billmaready@mareadylaw.com.

MARECEK, JEANNE, psychologist, educator; b. Berwyn, Ill., May 28, 1946; d. Frank J. and Josephine (Serio) M. BS, Loyola U., Chgo., 1968; MS, Yale U., 1971, PhD, 1973. From asst. prof. to prof. psychology Swarthmore (Pa.) Coll., 1972—, chmn. dept., 1986—91, 1994—95, 1998—99, head women's studies program, 1996—99. Fulbright sr. lectr., Sri Lanka, 1988. Co-author: Making a Difference: Psychology and the Construction of Gender; contbr. numerous articles to profl. jours. and chpts. to books. Bd. dirs. Women in Transition, Phila., 1980-86; vice patron Nest, Hendala, Sri Lanka, 1995—; bd. dirs. Women's Therapy Ctr., Phila., 1996-2004, CHOICE, Phila., 2006—. Fellow Swedish Collegium for Advanced Study in Social Scis., 1997; various fed. research grants. Mem. APA, Assn. for Asian Studies, Am. Inst. Sri Lanka Studies (sec. 1995-2000, pres. 2001—), Am. Overseas Rsch. Ctrs. (mem. exec. coun.). Office: Swarthmore Coll Dept Psychology 500 College Ave Swarthmore PA 19081-1306 Business E-Mail: jmarece1@swarthmore.edu.

MARÉE, KATHLEEN NANCY, retired language educator; b. Belleville, NJ, Nov. 8, 1942; d. Jacobus and Marie Theresa (Lilore) Marée. BA, Rutgers U., Newark, NJ, 1965; MA in Tchg. magna cum laude, Fairleigh Dickinson U., Rutherford, NJ, 1970. Elem. French tchr. Freehold (N.J.) Elem. Schs., 1965—66, River Edge (N.J.) Elem. Schs., 1966—71, dept. head and fgn. langs. in elem. sch. rep.; elem. French tchr. Hanahouli Elem. Sch., Honolulu, 1971—73; pub. rels. coord. Oceanic Cablevision, Honolulu, 1974—75; pub. rels. rep., adminstrv. asst. Hawaii State Legis., Honolulu, 1975; ESL instr., head tchr., asst. coord. New Intensive Course in English program U. Hawaii at Manoa, Honolulu, 1976—79; founder, pres., dir. Lang. Inst. Hawaii, Honolulu, 1979—86; advisor, coord. study cultural tours Internat. Pacific Asian Consortium, Honolulu, 1979—86; ESL instr. Fairleigh Dickinson U., Seton Hall U., Rutgers U., NJ, 1987—89; ESL lectr. and adj. Bergen CC, Paramus, NJ, 1989—2000. Pub. rels. Fgn. Lang. Elem. Sch., 1966—71; chairperson N.J. Assn. Tchrs. Fgn. Langs. Elem. Sch., 1970—71. ESL tchr., coord. employment Vietnamese Immigrant Vol. Assistance, Honolulu, 1975; mem., ESL sponsor CIVITAN, Honolulu, 1980—86; com. mem. Save Our Schs., Nutley, NJ, 2006—07. Grantee, East-West Ctr.-Culture Learning Inst., 1975—76. Avocations: reading, oil painting. Home: 11 Newman Ave Nutley NJ 07110-2125

MAREINISS, DARREN PETER, lawyer, physician; b. Hoboken, NJ, Nov. 15, 1972; s. Martin Charles Mareiniss and Jeanette Schwarz Young; m. Alexandra Morgan, Aug. 16, 1997. AB cum laude, Dartmouth Coll., Hanover, NH, 1994; MD, NYU Sch. Medicine, NYC, 1999; JD, U. Pa., Phila., 2005; Master of Bioethics, U. Pa. Sch. Medicine, Phila., 2005. Lic. medicine/surgery N.Y., 2000, N.J., 2003, instr. advanced trauma and life support ACS, 2005. Surg. intern NYU Med. Ctr./Bellevue Hosp., NYC, 1999—2000; surg. resident U. Tex. Southwestern Med. Ctr., Dallas, 2001—02; med. staff Gracie Sq. Hosp., NYC, 2002—03; cons. Woodcock Washburn, LLP, Phila., 2003; assoc. atty. Bickel & Brewer, Dallas, 2004—; sr. legal and med. policy cons. U. Md. Ctr. for Health and Homeland Security, 2006—. Lectr. Tex. Back Inst., Bioethics and Trauma. Contbr. articles to medical and legal jours. Recipient Letters Academic citation, Dartmouth Coll., 1991—93, N.Y. U. Sch. Medicine, 1996; Jaqua scholarship, Dartmouth Coll., 1993. Fellow: Am. Coll. Legal Medicine (mem. bioethics com 2004—, mem. grad. com. 2004—); mem.: AMA, Alpha Omega Alpha. Achievements include research in genetics and bioethics. Home: 3432 Mount Vernon Way Plano TX 75025 Office: Bickel & Brewer 4800 Bank One Ctr 1700 Main St Dallas TX 75201 Home Phone: 469-467-9052. Office Fax: 214-653-1015; Home Fax: 214-653-1015. Personal E-mail: dpmmd@sbcglobal.net. E-mail: dzm@bickelbrewer.com.

MAREK, JOYCELYN, publishing executive; m. Andrew Marek; children: Allison, Matthew. BBA, U. Houston, 1978; postgrad., Northwestern U., 1996, Hearst Mgmt. Inst., 1997-98. Rsch. analyst Houston Chronicle, 1978, chief analyst, 1978-84, asst. rsch. mgr., 1984-85, rsch. mgr., 1985-88, display advt. dir., 1988-90, mktg. dir., 1990-95, v.p. mktg. and electronic products, 1995—. Bd. dirs., exec. com. Sheltering Arms; mem. mktg. com. Houston Symphony; former bd. dirs. Houston Advt. Fedn. Mem. Am. Mktg. Assn. (edn./intern chair, past pres. Houston chpt.), Newspaper Assn. Am. (former chair market devel. and promotion coun.). Avocations: tennis, reading, golf. Office: Houston Chronicle PO Box 4260 Houston TX 77210-4260

MAREMONT, MARK, reporter; BA with honors, Brown Univ.; M in journalism, Columbia Univ. Telecom editor Bus. Week mag., NYC, 1983—86, corr. London, 1986—92, bureau chief Boston, 1992—97; sr. spl. writer Wall St. Journal, Boston, 1997—2000, dep. bureau chief, 2000—. Co-recipient Pulitzer Prize, explanatory reporting, 2003, Polk award for bus. reporting, 2006; recipient Gerald Loeb award, mag. category, 1997. Mem.: Phi Beta Kappa. Mailing: Wall St Journal 200 Liberty St New York NY 10281 Business E-Mail: mark.maremont@wsj.com. *

MARETT, LOUIS J., lawyer; b. NYC, Mar. 17, 1947; AB magna cum laude, Harvard U., 1968, JD cum laude, 1972. Bar: Mass. 1972, US Dist. Ct. Mass., US Tax Ct., US Ct Fed. Claims. With Nutter, McClennen & Fish, Boston; ptnr. Choate, Hall & Stewart. Chaired New England & Mass. Continuing Legal Edn. Trustee Mass. Taxpayers Found., Schepens Eye Rsch. Inst., St. Vincent de Paul Found. Named Best Lawyers Am. Mem.: ABA, Boston Bar Assn. Office: Choate Hall & Stewart 2 Internat Pl Boston MA 02110 Office Phone: 617-248-5091. Office Fax: 617-248-4000. Business E-Mail: lmarett@choate.com.

MARGALITH, HELEN MARGARET, retired librarian; b. NYC, Nov. 19, 1914; d. Louis and Caroline (Stern) Fleischer; m. Aaron Margalith, Jan. 26, 1947 (dec.); children: Carol Lenore, Joan Louise. BA, Hunter Coll., 1936, MA, 1944; MLS, Columbia U., 1958. Editl. corr. Book of the Month Club, 1936-47; rschr. libr. N.Y.C. Bd. Edn., 1955-80; prof. pibr. Touro Coll., NYC, 1980-90; mentor in libr. Empire State Coll., SUNY, 1991—. Cons. in field. Fellow Royal Soc. Medicine (libr. com., gerontology com., history of medicine com.); mem. Ch. and Synagogue Libr. Assn. (book reviewer), Internat. Honor Soc. Women in Edn., Am. Geolinguistic Assn. (bd. dirs. 2003—), Am. Soc. Geolinguistics, Delta Kappa Gamma Democrat. Avocations: reading, travel, research. Home: 205 W End Ave Apt 25S New York NY 10023-4804

MARGER, EDWIN, lawyer; b. NYC, Mar. 18, 1928; s. William and Fannie (Cohen) M.; m. Kaye Sanderson, Oct. 1, 1951; children: Shari Ann, Diane Elaine, Sandy Ben; m. L. Suzanne Smyth, July 5, 1968; 1 child, George Phinney; m. Mary Susan Hamel, May 6, 1987; 1 child, Charleston Faye. BA, U. Miami, 1951, JD, 1953. Bar: Fla. 1953, Ga. 1971, D.C. 1978. Pvt. practice, Miami Beach, Fla., 1953—67, Atlanta, 1971—90, Jasper, Ga., 1990—. Gen. counsel Physicians Nat. Risk Retention Group, 1988-91, Physicians Reliance Assn., 1988-91, Physicians Nat. Legal Def. Corp., 1988-91; spl. asst. atty. gen. Fla., 1960-61; atty., agt. Republic of Haiti, 1962-67, City of Port-au-Prince for Transp. and Housing, 1962, Dominican Republic for Trade and Industry, 1964-65; of counsel Richard Burns, Miami, 1967—. Contbr. articles to profl. jours. Tchr. Nat. Inst. Trial Advocacy; mem. Miami Beach Social Svc. Commn., 1957; chmn. Fulton County Aviation Adv. Com., 1980—; chmn. Pickens County Airport Adv. Com., 2004-06; trustee Forensic Scis. Found., 1984-88, v.p., 1986-88; lt. col., a.d.c. Gov. Ga., 1971-74, 80-84; col., a.d.c. Gov. La., 1977-87; Khan Bahador and mem. exiled King of Afghanistan Privy Coun., 1980—. With USAAF, 1946-47. Fellow Am. Acad. Forensic Scis. (chmn. jurisprudence sect. 1977-78, sec. 1976-77, bd. dirs. 1978-79, exec. com. 1983-86); mem. ATLA, ABA, Fla. Bar Assn. (aerospace com. 1971-83, bd. govs. 1983-87, 90-94, exec. com. 1993-94), State Bar Ga. (chmn. sect. environ. law 1974-75, aviation law sect. 1978, bd. govs. 1999-2005, stds. of the profession com.), Ga. Trial Lawyers Assn., Nat. Assn. Criminal Def. Lawyers, Ga. Assn. Criminal Def. Lawyers, Am. Judicature Soc., Am. Arbitration Assn. (commn. panel 1978), Inter-Am. Bar Assn. (sr.), World Assn. Lawyers (founding), Lawyer-Pilots Bar Assn. (founding, v.p. 1959-62), VFW, Am. Legion, Rotary, Lions, Navy League, U.S. Naval Inst., Advocates Club, Lawyers Club Atlanta. Office: 44 N Main St Jasper GA 30143-1501 Office Phone: 706-253-3060. Personal E-mail: admin@edmarger.com.

MARGESON, THEODORE EARL, judge; b. New Glasgow, NS, Can., Aug. 15, 1938; children: Theodore Jason, Mark Andrew Earl. BA, Mt. Allison U., Sackville, NB, Can., 1959, BEd, 1960; LLB, Dalhousie U., Halifax, NS, 1965. Barrister, solicitor, notary pub. Tchr. Shelburne HS, NS, 1960—61, New Glasgow HS, 1961-62; barrister, solicitor New Glasgow and Toronto, Ont., 1965-90; judge Tax Ct. of Can., Ottawa, 1990—. Bd. dirs. NS Legal Aid. Recipient Confedn. medal Govt. of Can., 1992; Jubilee medal, 2003. Mem. Can. Judges Conf., NS Barrister's Soc. (mem. of coun.), Continuing Legal Edn. Soc. (dir.). Avocations: golf, hockey, squash. Office: Tax Ct of Can 200 Kent St 3d Fl Ottawa ON Canada K1A OM1 Office Phone: 613-943-2915.

MARGETON, STEPHEN GEORGE, law librarian; b. Elizabeth, NJ, Mar. 22, 1945; s. Louis George and Josephine A. (Bednarik) M.; m. Margaret Mary Salter, May 14, 1977; children: Catherine Ann, Elizabeth Ann. AB, Mt. St. Mary's Coll., 1967; JD, George Washington U., 1970; MSLS, Cath. U., 1973. Reference librarian Am.-Brit. law div. Library of Congress, Washington, 1968-72; law libr. Steptoe & Johnson, Washington, 1972-85; librarian Supreme Ct. of U.S., Washington, 1985-88; dir. Judge Kathryn J. DuFour Law Libr. The Cath. Univ. Am., 1988—. Instr. George Mason Law Sch., Arlington, Va., 1977-80. Mem. Am. Assn. Law Libraries, Internat. Assn. Law Libraries., Am. Soc. Internat. Law. Office: Cath U Am Judge Kathryn J DuFour Law Libr 3600 John Mccormack Rd NE Washington DC 20064-0001

MARGIOTTA, MARY-LOU ANN, application developer; b. Waterbury, Conn., June 14, 1956; d. Rocco Donato and Louise Antoinette (Carosella) M. AS Gen. Edn., Mattatuck C.C., Waterbury, 1982; BSBA, Teikyo Post U., 1983; MS Computer Sci., Rensselaer Polytech. Inst., 1989. Programmer analyst Travelers Ins. Co., Hartford, Conn., 1985-87; sr. programmer analyst Conn. Bank and Trust Co., East Hartford, Conn., 1987-88; programmer analyst Ingersoll-Rand Corp., Torrington, Conn., 1990-91; sr. programmer analyst Orion Capital Cos. Inc., Farmington, Conn., 1991-92; pres., prin., software engr. A.M. Consultants, New Britain, Conn., 1992—. Pres. C++ Spl. Interest Group, 1995-96; bd. dirs. Conn. Object Oriented Users Group, 1995-96; tech. team leader Computer Scis. Corp., East Hartford, Conn., 1998-, Asnuntuck C. C., Enfield, Conn., 2003; adj. prof. Ctrl. Conn. State U., New Britain, 2000, New Eng. Tech. Inst., New Britain, Conn., 2002. Mem. social action com. St. Helena's Parish, West Hartford, Conn., 1988-95; advisor Jr. Achievement, Waterbury, 1981-83; tutor Traveler's Ins. Co. Tutorial Program, West Hartford, 1986-87; trainer CPR, ARC, Hartford, 1986-87; mem. Lang. and Cultural Adoptation Programs, Conn. and Mass., 1998— Clayborn Pell grantee Post Coll., 1982-83, State of Conn. grantee, 1982-83; recipient Citation, Jr. Achievement, 1982; Bd. Trustees scholar Post Coll., 1982-83. Mem. IEEE (chairwoman membership devel., Conn. chpt.), Am. Aculturation Assocs. (bd. dirs.), Toastmasters Internat., Tau Alpha, Beta Gamma. Roman Catholic. Avocations: european travel, gourmet cooking, reading, tennis, golf. Home: 210 Brittany Farms Rd Ste E New Britain CT 06053-1282 Office Phone: 860-229-3496. E-mail: raebedet@aol.com.

MARGO, KATHERINE LANE, family physician, educator; d. Warren Wilson and Virginia (Penney) Lane; m. Geoffrey Myles Margo, Apr. 20, 1980; 1 child, Benjamin stepchildren: Jenny, Judy. BA, Swarthmore Coll., 1974; MD, SUNY Health Sci. Ctr., Syracuse, 1978. Cert. in family medicine. Resident physician St. Joseph's Hosp., Syracuse, 1979-82; attending physician Health Svcs. Assn., Syracuse, 1982-90, asst. med. dir. for quality assurance, 1985-90, asst. prof. family medicine SUNY-HSC at Syracuse, 1990-94; mem. residency faculty Harrisburg (Pa.) Hosp., 1994-2000; med. dir. Harrisburg Kline Family Practice Ctr., 1996-2000; assoc. residency dir. Harrisburg Family Practice Residency, 1997-2000; predoctoral dir. Dept. Family Practice Cmty. Medicine U. Pa., 2000—, asst. prof., assoc. dir. family practice residency, 2000—. Clin. assoc. prof. Allegheny Med. Sch., 1997—2000. Contbr. articles to profl. jours. Bd. trustees Pt. Choice, Syracuse, 1993—94; chair med. com. Planned Parenthood, Syracuse, 1984—94; bd. dirs. Planned Parenthood Susquehanna Valley, 1996—2000; active Friends of Chamber Music, Syracuse, 1985—94; keyboard player Old World folk Band. Recipient Exemplary Tchg. award, Pa. Acad. of Family Practice, 2003, Penn Pearls Tchg. award, U. Pa. Sch. Medicine, 2004. Mem.: Am. Acad. Family Practitioners (v.p. Syracuse chpt.), Soc. Tchrs. of Family Medicine (chair group on predoctoral edn. 2003—04). Democrat. Avocations: music, theater, gardening, birdwatching. Home: 426 Carpenter Ln Philadelphia PA 19119-3040 Office: Univ Pa Dept Family Practice Community Medicine 2 Gates 3400 Spruce St Philadelphia PA 19104 Office Phone: 215-662-8941. E-mail: margok@uphs.upenn.edu.

MARGO, ROD DAVID, lawyer; b. Johannesburg, Republic of South Africa, Feb. 14, 1950; came to US, 1978; s. Cecil Stanley and Marguerite Giselle (Polné) M. BCom, U. Witwatersrand, Johannesburg, South Africa, 1970, LLB cum laude, 1973; D Civil Laws, McGill U., Montreal, Que., Can., 1979. Bar: Ga. 1979, Calif. 1981, DC 1996, Us Supreme Ct., 2005; solicitor, NSW, Australia, 2004. From assoc. to ptnr. Condon & Forsyth, LA, 1980—. Lectr. aviation law UCLA, 1981-98; adj. prof. law Inst. Air and Space Law, Montreal, Can. Author: Aviation Ins. 3d edit., 2000; co-author: Shawcross & Beaumont on Air Law, 4th rev. edit., 2006. Fellow: Royal Aero. Soc.; mem.: LA County Bar Assn. Office: Condon & Forsyth 1901 Avenue Of The Stars Ste 850 Los Angeles CA 90067-6010 Office Phone: 310-557-2030. Business E-Mail: rmargo@condonlaw.com.

MARGOLIASH, EMANUEL, biochemist, educator; b. Cairo, Feb. 10, 1920; s. Wolf and Bertha (Kotler) M.; m. Sima Beshkin, Aug. 22, 1944; children: Reuben, Daniel. BA, Am. U., Beirut, 1940, MA, 1942, MD, 1945. Rsch. fellow, lectr., acting head cancer rsch. labs. Hebrew U., Jerusalem, 1945-58; rsch. fellow Molteno Inst. Cambridge (Eng.) U., 1951-53; Dazian fellow Nobel Inst., 1958; rsch. assoc. U. Utah, Salt Lake City, 1958-60, McGill U., Montreal, Que., Canada, 1960-62; rsch. fellow Abbott Labs., North Chicago, Ill., 1962-69, sr. rsch. fellow, 1969-71, head protein sect., 1962-71; prof. biochemistry and molecular biology Northwestern U., Evanston, Ill., 1971-90, prof. chemistry, 1985-90, Owen L. Coon prof. molecular biology, 1988-90, Owen L. Coon prof. molecular biology emeritus, 1990—; prof. biol. scis. U. Ill., Chgo., 1989—, coord. lab. for molecular biology, 1990-93. Mem. com. on cytochrome nomenclature Internat. Union Biochemistry, 1962-75; mem. adv. com. Plant Research Lab., Mich. State U./AEC, 1967-72; co-chmn. Gordon Research Conf. on Proteins, 1967 Editl. bd. Jour. Biol. Chemistry, 1966-72, Biochem. Genetics, 1966-80, Jour. Molecular Evolution, 1971-82, Biochemistry and Molecular Biology Internat., 1981-99, Jour. Protein Chemistry, 1982-86, Chemtracts, Biochem. Molecular Biology, 1990-99; contbr. over 280 articles and revs. to sci. jours. Rudi Lemberg fellow Australian Acad. Sci., 1981; Guggenheim fellow, 1983 Fellow Am. Acad. Arts and Scis., Am. Acad. Microbiology, Am. Inst. Chemists; mem. Nat. Acad. Scis., Biochem. Soc. (Keilin Meml. lectr. 1970), Harvey Soc. (lectr. 1970-71), Am. Soc. Biochem. Molecular Biology (publs. com. 1973-76), Am. Chem. Soc., Am. Soc. Microbiology, Can. Biochem. Soc., Soc. Devel. Biology, Biophys. Soc. (exec. com. U.S. bioenergetics group 1980-83), N.Y. Acad. Sci., Ill. Acad. Sci., Am. Soc. Naturalists, Sigma Xi (nat. lectr. 1972-73, 74-77). Home: 353 Madison Ave Glencoe IL 60022-1809 Office: Biochemistry Molecular & Cell Biology Hogan Hall 2-100 Northwestern U Evanston IL 60208-3500 Office Phone: 847-491-5620.

MARGOLIN, BRUCE M., lawyer; LLB, U. So. Calif., 1963, JD, 1966. Bar: Calif. 1967, U.S. Dist. Ct. 1967, Ctrl. Dist. Calif. 1967. Pvt. practice, W. Hollywood, Calif. Dir. Nat. Orgn. Reform Marijuana Laws. Contbr. articles to profl. jours. Elected to State Calif. Dem. Com. Recipient Cert. Appreciation, ACLU. Mem.: Nat. Assn. Criminal Def. Lawyers (co-chmn. ethics com.), Criminal Cts. Bar Assn., Century City Bar Assn. (Criminal Def. Atty of Yr. 1999). Ran for governor of California in the 2003 recall election; contributed to the development of the California Prop 215 Medical Marijuana Initiative. Office: 8749 Holloway Dr West Hollywood CA 90069 Office Phone: 310-276-2231. Office Fax: 310-652-1501. E-mail: bmargolin@aol.com. *

MARGOLIN, ERIC MITCHELL, lawyer; b. NYC, Mar. 31, 1953; s. Benjamin and Muriel (Leibowitz) Margolin BA, SUNY, Buffalo, 1974; JD, Georgetown U., 1977. Bar: NY 1978. Staff atty. Met. Life Ins. Co., NYC, 1977-79; atty. Chesebrough-Pond's Inc., Greenwich, Conn., 1979—81, sr. atty., 1982—85; v.p., gen. counsel, sec., dir. Health-Tex Inc., NYC, 1985—92; sr. v.p., gen. counsel, sec. The He-Ro Group Ltd., NYC, 1992—93; v.p., gen. counsel, sec. Tire Kingdom Inc. (now TBC Corp.), West Palm Beach, Fla., 1993—2000; sr. v.p., gen. counsel, sec. Advance Auto Parts Inc., Roanoke, Va., 2001—. Mem.: ABA. Office: Advance Auto Parts Inc 5673 Airport Rd Roanoke VA 24012 Office Phone: 540-561-3225. Business E-Mail: emargolin@advanceautoparts.com. *

MARGOLIN, HAROLD, metallurgical educator; b. Hartford, Conn., July 12, 1922; s. Aaron David and Sonia (Krupnikoff) M.; m. Elaine Marjorie Rose, July 4, 1946; children: Shelley, Deborah, Amy. B in Engring., Yale U., 1943; M in Engring., Yale Univ., 1947, DEng, 1950. Rsch. assoc./scientist divsn. rsch. NYU, NYC, 1949-56, assoc. prof. metall. engring., 1956-62, prof., 1962-73; prof. phys. metallurgy Poly. U. N.Y., Bklyn., 1973-93, disting. rsch. prof., 1993—2003, 2004—05, emeritus prof., 2006. Theodore W. Krengel vis. prof. Technion, Haifa, Israel, 1983; cons. in field. Contbg. author books; contbr. articles to profl. publs.; patentee in field. With USNR, 1944-46. Fellow Am. Soc. Metals (edn. award N.Y. chpt. 1967); mem. Metall. Soc. (honoree symposium in his name San Francisco 1994), ASM Internat., TMS. Democrat. Jewish. Home: 81 Stony Run New Rochelle NY 10804-3415 Personal E-mail: hmemxox@aol.com. *Achievement, work, and refusal to accept defeat are intimately intertwined.*

MARGOLIN, KIM ALLYSON, internist, hematologist, oncologist; b. LA, Oct. 27, 1953; BS in Biochemistry (summa cum laude), U. Calif., LA, 1974; MD, Stanford U. Sch. Medicine, Calif., 1979. Diplomate Am. Bd. Internal Medicine with subspecialty in hematology/med. oncology; cert. Nat. Bd. Med. Examiners. Intern Yale-New Haven Hosp., 1979-80, resident, internal medicine, 1979—82; fellow, hematology/oncology U. Calif. San Diego Sch. Medicine, 1982-83; fellow, med. oncology and therapeutics rsch. City of Hope Nat. Med. Ctr., Duarte, Calif., 1983—84, fellow, hematology and bone marrow transplantation, 1984—85, staff physician, med. oncology and therapeutics rsch./hematology and bone marrow transplantation, 1985—, assoc. dir., clin. rsch., dept. med. oncology and therapeutics rsch., 1996—, prof., divsn. hematology & hematopoietic cell transplantation. Mem., Oncologic Drugs Adv. Com. FDA, 1994—2000; mem., Germ Cell and Renal Cancer Guidelines Com. Nat. Comprehensive Cancer Network, 1997—; mem. subcommittee on med. oncology Am. Bd. Internal Medicine, 2003—; invited lectr. in field. Contbr. articles to profl. jours., chapters to books; mem. editl. bd. Jour. Cancer Rsch. and Clin. Oncology, 1990—, mem. editl. adv. bd. cancer Am. Cancer Soc., 2003—. Fellow ACP; mem. Am. Soc. Clin. Oncology, Am. Soc. Hematologists, Am. Assn. Clin. Rsch. Office: City of Hope 1500 E Duarte Rd Duarte CA 91010 *

MARGOLIN, ROBERT JEREMY, lawyer; b. Kansas City, Mo., Mar. 21, 1935; s. Abraham Eugene and Florence Margolin; m. Dorothy Ann Macy, Sept. 20, 1959; 1 child, Kathryn R. Margolin Richter. AB, Dartmouth Coll., 1957; JD, LLB, U. Mich., 1960. Bar: Mo., U.S. Ct. Appeals (8th cir.). Ptnr. Margolin and Kirwan, Kansas City, 1960—. Bd. dirs. Kansas City Kings, Feld Leasing. Asst. editor Mich. Law Rev. Bd. dirs. Menorah Med. Ctr., Kansas City, Kansas City Philharm. Assn.; exec. com. Jewish Vocat. Svc., Kansas City. Mem. ABA, Nat. Basketball Assn. (bd. govs.), Mo. Bar Assn., Kansas City Bar Assn. Avocations: golf, skiing. Home: 1628 River Ridge Williamsburg VA 23185-7546 E-mail: bobj757@aol.com.

MARGOLIN, STUART, actor, director; b. Davenport, Iowa, Jan. 31, 1940; married. Actor (TV films): Perilous Voyage, 1976, Intruders, 1970, The California Kid, 1974, This is the West that Was, 1974, Lanigan's Rabbi, 1976, The Glitter Dome, 1984, Vendetta: Secrets of a Mafia Bride, 1991, To Grandmother's House We Go, 1992, others, (films) Limbo, 1972, The Stone Killer, 1973, Death Wish, 1974, Futureworld, 1976, Class, 1983, Running Hot, 1984, A Fine Mess, 1986, Iron Eagle II, 1988, Bye Bye Blues, 1989, Deep Sleep, 1990, Guilty by Suspicion, 1991, Impolite, 1992, The Lay of the Land, 1997, The Hi-Line, 1999, The Hoax, 2006; regular on TV series The Rockford Files, Nichols; other TV appearances include: Rhoda, He and She, Bewitched, It Takes a Thief, That Girl, MASH, Partridge Family, Gunsmoke, Mary Tyler Moore Show, My World and Welcome to It, Love, American Style, Bret Maverick, 1981; dir. TV movies Suddenly Love, 1979, Texas Wheelers, The Glitter Dome, 1983, A Shining Season; scored movies and TV shows; writer film Ballad of Andy Crocker. Recipient Emmy award Nat. Acad. TV Arts and Scis., 1979 Office: care ICM 321 Westminster Ave Los Angeles CA 90020-4652 *

MARGOLIS, BERNARD ALLEN, library administrator; b. Greenwich, Conn., Oct. 2, 1948; s. Sidney S. and Rose (Birkenfeld) M.; m. Amanda Batey, Nov. 2, 1973. BA in Polit. Sci., U. Denver, 1970, MA in Librarianship, 1973; D of Tech. (hon.), Wentworth Inst. Tech., 1999. Cert. libr., Mich. Asst. shelving supr. Denver Pub. Libr., 1968—70, libr. asst. I hist. divsn. lit. and hist. dept., 1970—72, br. head Va. Village Libr., 1972—73; dep. dir. Monroe County Libr. Sys., Mich., 1973—75, dir., 1976—88; dep. dir. SE Mich. Regional Film Libr., 1974—75, dir., 1976—88; asst. dir. Raisin Valley Libr. Sys., 1974—75, dir., 1976—78, Pikes Peak Libr. Dist., Colorado Springs, Colo., 1988—97; pres. Colo. Ctr. Books, 1989—92, Colo. Ctr. for the Book, 1993—97, Boston Pub. Libr., 1997—. Cons. in libr. pub. rels., 1976—; founding trustee United Colo. Investment Trust, 1993-95; chmn. Colo. Gov.'s Conf. on Libr. and Info. Svcs., 1990; lectr. Western Mich. U., Kalamazoo, 1978-81; appraiser rare books, Monroe, Colorado Springs, 1970—. Contbr. articles to profl. jours.; mem. editl. bd. Bottom Line Mag. Fin. Mgmt. for Librs., 1986—, Jour. Libr. Adminstrn., 1997-. Bd. dirs. Mass. Ctr. for Book, Back Bay Assn., Monroe Sr. Citizens Ctr., 1976-80, Monroe Fine Arts Coun., 1978-81, Am. the Beautiful Centennial Celebration, Inc., 1993, Boston Libr. Consortium, 1993-97, Downtown Colorado Springs, Inc., 1994-97, Friends of Copley Sq., Care & Share, Inc., sec., 1994-95, vice chmn., 1995, chmn., 1995-97, Blue Cross-Blue Shield Consumer Coun., Detroit, 1984-88; adv. bd. Access Colo. Libr. and Info. Network, 1991-97, Mercy Meml. Hosp., Monroe, 1984-86, 5th Congl. Art Competition Com., 1992-97; Dem. candidate Mich. Senate, 1986; allocations com. Pikes Peak United Way, 1988-91, bd. dirs., 1990-91, 94-97, chmn., 1990-91, Great Pikes Peak Cowboy Poetry Gathering, 1990-92, 94-96; del. White House Conf. Libr. and Info. Scis.; mem. El Paso County Retirement Bd., Colo., 1995-97, sec., 1996-97; fellow Boston Found., 1998—; overseer Hancock Shaker Village, Pittsfield, Mass., 1999—; leadership mgmt. com. Assn. Rsch. Librs., 2003—; bd. mem. Boston Pub. Libr. Found., Assocs. Boston Pub. Libr. Bd. Recipient Mayoral Cert. Commendation award Denver, 1972, 73, Commendation John F. Kennedy Ctr. Performing Arts, 1993, Frank Waters award Pikes Peak Writer's Conf., 1996; named Mich. Libr. of Yr., 1985, Colo. Libr. of Yr., 1990. Fellow: Mass. Hist. Soc.; mem.: ALA (cons. ann. swap and shop 1979—84, governing coun. 1985—2000, endowment trustee 1989—93, chmn. resolutions com. 1991—92, sr. endowment trustee 1993—2001, governing coun. 2007—, John Cotton Dana award 1977, 1991, Libr. Awareness Idea Search award Washington 1982), Am. Acad. Arts & Scis., Assn. Ednl. Comm. and Tech., Pub. Libr. Assn., Libr. Adminstrv. Mgmt. Assn., Internat. Fedn. Libr. Assns. and Instns. (ofcl. US del. pub. libr. sect. 1997—), New Eng. Libr. Assn., Mass. Libr. Assn. Democrat. Jewish. Office: Boston Pub Libr Copley Sq 700 Boylston St Boston MA 02116 Office Phone: 617-536-5400 ext. 4475. E-mail: bmargolis@bpl.org. *

MARGOLIS, BRUCE LEWIS, human resources executive; b. Bklyn., Nov. 16, 1944; s. Laurance Nathan and Augusta Margolis; m. Simone Braipson, Aug. 11, 1974; children: Mathew, Jessie Lara. BS, Bklyn. Coll., 1965; MA, Western Res. U., 1967; PhD, Case Western Res. U., 1970. Human resource dir. Jewel Food Stores, Melrose Park, Ill., 1978-80; v.p. human resources Jewel Cos., Chgo., 1980-84; dir. human resources devel. Household Merchandising, Des Plaines, Ill., 1984-86; v.p. human resources TJ Maxx, Framingham, Mass., 1986-95; sr. v.p. human resources The Marmaxx Group, Framingham, 1995; exec. v.p., chief human resources officer TJX Cos., Inc., 2002—. Corp. psychologist Jewel Cos. Inc., Chgo., 1974-78; sect. chief NIOSH, Cin., 1971-74; psychophysiologist Bur. of Occpl. Safety and Health, USPHS, 1970-71; staff psychologist Psychol. Resource Svcs., Cleve., 1968-70. Co-author: Managers Guide to Developing Subordinate Managers, 1980; editor: The Human Side of Accident Prevention, 1975. Bd. dirs. Metro West YMCA, Framingham, 1997-98, Employers Against Domestic Violence, 1997-2000. Avocation: tennis. Office: TJX Cos Inc 770 Cochituate Rd Framingham MA 01701 Office Phone: 508-390-1000.

MARGOLIS, DANIEL HERBERT, lawyer; b. 1926; s. Morris Abraham and Miriam M.; m. Anabel Tendler, Dec. 23, 1951 (dec.); children: Peter, Beth, Laura, James; m. Sidney Millman Moore, Feb. 5, 1983. BA, Johns Hopkins U., Balt., 1948; LLB, Harvard U., Cambridge, Mass., 1951. Bar: DC 1951, US Supreme Ct. 1959. Atty. adv. Office Price Stblzn., Washington, 1951-52; trial atty. Antitrust divsn. Dept. Justice, Washington, 1952-56; sr. ptnr. Bergson, Borkland, Margolis & Adler, Washington, 1962—86, McGuire, Woods, Battle & Boothe, Washington, 1986-89, Patton, Boggs LLP, Washington, 1989—2001; sr. counsel DC Office of Corp. Counsel, 2001—03; prin. Law Offices of Daniel H. Margolis, 2003—. With USN, 1945—46. Fellow: ABA, Coll. Comml. Arbitrators; mem.: Chartered Inst. Arbitrators. Avocations: sailing, skiing, cooking.

MARGOLIS, DORIS MAY ROSENBERG, editor, writer; b. Washington, May 10, 1936; d. Samuel Jacob and Eva (Mendelsohn) Rosenberg; m. Lawrence S. Margolis, Jan. 30, 1960; children: Mary Aleta, Paul Oliver. BA, George Wash. U., 1958. Founder, v.p., CEO Editorial Assocs., Washington, 1963-82, founder, pres., CEO, 1982—. Founder, pub., exec. editor Margolis Health Report, 1999—; bd. govs. Nat. Press Club, 1991-94; mem. adv. bd. Washington Journalism Conf., 1991-96; judge Biomedical Writing awards Am. Med. Writers Assn.-Mid-Atlantic, 1987-91, Blue Pencil Writing awards Nat. Assn. Govt. Contractors, 1992, 94, Rose Kushner Breast Cancer Writing award Am. Med. Writers Assn., 1992, Nat. Essay competition Pres.'s Com. on Employment of the Handicapped, Nat. Worker of Yr. competition Goodwill Industries of Am., Nat. Essay Competition Hospitalized Vets. Assn., others. Author: This Is Goodwill, 1968; editor-in-chief Jour. Rehab., 1960-67, (newsletters) Nat. Assn. Sheltered Workshops and Homebound Programs News, 1964-68, Jewish Occupational Coun. News, 1968-70, Aspen Update, 1976-80; contbg. editor (newspapers) Pediatric News, 1968-69, Ob-Gyn News, 1968-69, Internal Medicine News, 1968-69; columnist Jour. Rehab., 1960-67, Washington Jewish Week, 1968-73, Sports Medicine Monthly, 1984-85, Gazette Newspapers, 1999-2000; radio news corr. Physicians Radio News Network, 1969, 1976; contbr. articles to profl. jours.; editor: Concrete Facts Magazine, 1960, Rehabilitation of the Mentally Ill, 1961, Rehabilitation International, 1962, Rehabilitation of the Mentally Retarded, 1962, To Aid the Disabled, 1963, The Stroke Spectrum: Prevention, Treatment, and Rehabilitation, 1963, Workshops at the Crossroads, 1964, Sheltered Workshops: The Road Ahead, 1965, Sheltered Workshops, 1965, The Coronary Spectrum: Prevention, Treatment, and Rehabilitation, 1966, Medical Rehabilitation Model Delivery Systems, 1978; asst. editor NEA News, 1958-59. Singer, dancer Montgomery Light Opera Co., 1970's, Washington Civic Opera, 1978-84; singer, dancer, actress Hexagon Players, 1970-72; bd. dirs. Jewish Social Svcs. Agy., 1970-72; bd. govs. Am. Newspaper Women's Club, 1982-84, Woman's Nat. Dem. Club, 1983-88; exec. com. bd. dirs. People-to-People Com. on Disability, 1992-2000, vice-chmn., 1995-2000; pres. Inner Wheel Club of Washington, 1993-94. Recipient Ellen Woodhull scholastic scholarship George Washington U., 1957, Disting. Alumni Achievement award George Washington U., 1978, Nat. Press Club Vivian award, 1997, 99; personal commendations Pres. John F. Kennedy, 1963, Pres. Lyndon B. Johnson, 1966; Paul Harris fellow Rotary Internat., 1996. Fellow Am. Med. Writers Assn. (bd. dirs. 1989-94, nominating com. 1990-91, chair pub. rels., advt. and mktg. sect. 1989-90, pres. Mid-Atlantic chpt. 1990-91, exec. com. bd. dirs. 1993-94); mem. Nat. Assn. Sci. Writers, Rotary (bd. dirs. Wash. chpt. 1999-2001, 2002-06, v.p., pres. elect 2003-2004, pres. 2004-05, zone pub. rels. coord. Rotary Internat., 2006-07, rep. to OAS, 2006-07, rep. to World Bank, 2006-07, v.p. Rotary Found. D.C., 2007-, pres. elect), Cosmos Club, Alpha Epsilon Phi Alumni Assn. (pres. 1959-60), Mortar Bd. (treas. 1957-58), Phi Delta Epsilon (v.p. 1957-58), Psi Chi, Alpha Theta Nu. Office: Editorial Assocs Nat Press Bldg Washington DC 20045

MARGOLIS, EMANUEL, lawyer, educator; b. Bklyn., Mar. 18, 1926; s. Abraham and Esther (Levin) Margolis; m. Edith Cushing (div.); m. Estelle Thompson, Mar. 1, 1959; children: Elizabeth Margolis-Pineo, Catherine, Abby Margolis Newman, Joshua, Sarah Margolis Marsh. BA, U. N.C., 1947; MA, Harvard U., 1948, PhD, 1951; JD, Yale U., 1956. Bar: Conn. 1957, U.S. Dist. Ct. Conn. 1958, U.S. Supreme Ct. 1969. Instr. dept. govt. U. Conn., 1951-53; assoc. Silberberg & Silverstein, Ansonia, Conn., 1956-60, Wofsey Rosen Kweskin & Kuriansky, Stamford, Conn., 1960-66, ptnr., 1966-96, of counsel, 1996—. Arbitrator State of Conn., 1984—85; adj. prof. Quinnipiac U. Sch. Law, 1986—. Sr. editor: Conn. Bar Jour., 1971—80, 1983—, editor-in-chief:, 1980—83, human rights columnist: Conn. Law Tribune, 2005—; contbr. articles to profl. jours. Nat. bd. dirs. ACLU, 1975—79; mem. Westport (Conn.) Planning and Zoning Commn., 1971—75; chmn. Conn. CLU, 1988—95, legal advisor, 1995—; mem. exec. com. Yale Law Sch., 2000—04. With US Army, 1944—46. Decorated Purple Heart; recipient 1st award for Disting. Svc. to Conn. Bar, Conn. Law Tribune, 1987, Champion of Liberty award, Conn. Def. Lawyers Assn, 2004. Fellow: Conn. Bar Found. (James W. Cooper fellow 1996); mem.: ABA, Am. Arbitration Assn. (arbitrator 1998—, trial referee 1985—), Nat. Assn. Criminal Def. Lawyers, Conn. Bar Assn. (chmn. human rigts sect. 1970—73). Home: 72 Myrtle Ave Westport CT 06880-3512 Office Phone: 203-327-2300. Personal E-mail: emesq@optonline.net.

MARGOLIS, GERALD JOSEPH, psychiatrist, psychoanalyst; b. Bronx, NY, May 7, 1935; s. Max and Sophie (Siegel) M.; m. June Edelman Greenspan, July 13, 1976; children: David J., Peter S., Steven J. AB, U. Rochester, 1957; MD, U. Chgo., 1960; postgrad., Inst. Phila. Assn. Psychoa., 1972. Diplomate in psychiatry Am. Bd. Psychiatry and Neurology. Intern to resident in psychiatry Upstate Med. Ctr. SUNY, Syracuse, 1960-64, instr. psychiatry, 1966-67; from instr. to clin. prof. psychiatry Med. Sch. U. Pa., Phila., 1967—. Practice medicine specializing in psychiatry and psychoanalysis, Cherry Hill, NJ; tng. and supervising analyst Inst. of the Psychoanalytic Ctr. Phila. Contbr. articles to profl. jours. Served with M.C., USAF, 1964-66. Mem.: AMA, Med. Socl N.J., Camden County Med. Soc., Psychoanalytic Ctr. Phila. (tng. and supervising analyst), Am. Psychiat. Assn., Am. Psychoanalytic Assn. (cert.), B'nai B'rith, Phi Beta Kappa. Office: One Mall Dr Ste 930 Cherry Hill NJ 08002-2194 Home Phone: 856-234-7470; Office Phone: 856-667-1055.

MARGOLIS, JAY M., clothing executive; b. NYC, Feb. 11, 1949; s. Mac and Sarah Margolis; m. Donna Brenda Polsky, June 12, 1972; children: Jared Michael, Stacey Allyse. BA, Queens Coll., NYC, 1971. Asst. mdse. mgr. Manhattan Shirt Co., NYC, 1972-74; mdse. mgr. Arrow Shirt Co., NYC, 1974-78; pres. Yves St. Laurent-Biderman Inc., NYC, 1978-81, Ron Chereskin div. Cluett Peabody, NYC, 1981-83, Claiborne Mens-Liz Claiborne Inc., NYC, 1983-86; group pres., exec. v.p. corp. Liz Claiborne Inc., NYC, 1986-88, vice chmn., 1988—92; pres., vice chmn. Tommy Hilfiger, 1992—95; chmn., CEO Esprit de Corp., 1995—99, E7th.com, 1999—2001; pres. splty. bus. group Reebok Internat. Ltd., 2001, pres., COO, 2001—04; group pres. apparel Limited Brands, Inc., 2005—. Mem. bd. Fathers Day/Mothers Day Coun. Mem. City Athletic Club. Avocations: skiing, swimming, tennis, environmental studies. Office: Limited Brands Inc 3 Limited Pkwy Columbus OH 43216 *

MARGOLIS, JULIUS, economics professor; b. NYC, Sept. 26, 1920; s. Sam and Fannie (Weiner) Margolis; m. Doris Lubetsky, Oct. 30, 1942; children: Jane S., Carl W. BSS, CCNY, 1941; PhM in Econs, U. Wis., 1943; MPA in Econs, Harvard, 1947, PhD, 1949. Instr. econs. Tufts Coll., 1947-48; asst. prof. econs. and planning U. Chgo., 1948-51; asst. prof. econs. Stanford (Calif.) U., 1951-54, prof. econs. and engring. econ. systems, 1964-69; prof. bus adminstrn. U. Calif., Berkeley, 1954-64, prof. econs. Irvine, 1976—; prof., dir. Fels Ctr. Govt. U. Pa., 1969-76. Cons. govt. and industry, 1958—; dir. Ctr. Global Peace and Conflict Studies, 1985—. Author (with others): The Public Economy of Urban Communities, 1965, The Northern California's Water Industry, 1966, Public Economics, 1969, Public Expenditure and Policy Analysis, 1984; contbr. articles to profl. jours. With US Army, 1943—46. Mem.: Royal Econ. Soc., Am. Econ. Assn. Home: 45 Whitman Ct Irvine CA 92617-4059 Office: U Calif Dept Econ Irvine CA 92697-0001 Office Phone: 949-854-3911. Business E-Mail: jmargoli@uci.edu.

MARGOLIS, LAWRENCE STANLEY, federal judge; b. Phila., Mar. 13, 1935; m. Doris May Rosenberg, Jan. 30, 1960; children: Mary Aleta, Paul Oliver. BSME, Drexel U., 1957; JD, George Washington U., 1961. Bar: DC 1963. Patent examiner US Patent Office, Washington, 1957-62; patent counsel Naval Ordnance Lab., White Oak, Md., 1962-63; asst. corp. counsel Washington, 1963-66; atty. criminal divsn., spl. asst. US atty. US Dept. Justice, Washington, 1966-68, asst. US atty. DC, 1968-71; US magistrate judge US Dist. Ct., Washington, 1971-82; judge US Ct. Fed. Claims, Washington, 1982—97, sr. judge, 1997—; chmn. task force on discovery reform US Claims Ct., Washington, chmn. alt. dispute resolution; asst. atty. gen. Washington. Chmn. Space and Bldg. com., chmn. Ct. Security Com., mem. mgmt. com., mem. faculty Fed. Jud. Ctr. Editor-in-chief The Young Lawyer, 1965-66, DC Bar Jour., 1967-73; bd. editors The Dist. Lawyer, 1978-82. Trustee Drexel U., 1983-89; bd. govs. George Washington U. Alumni Assn., 1978-85, 93-96. Recipient Contbn. award DC Jaycees, 1966, Svc. award Boy Scouts Am., 1970, Alumni Svc. award George Washington U., 1976, Disting. Alumni Achievement award George Washington U., 1985, Disting. Alumni Achievement award Drexel U., 1988, Drexel 100 award, 1992, Alternative Dispute Resolution award Ctr. for Pub. Resources, 1988, Alternative Dispute Resolution Svc. award Ct. of Fed. Claims, 1996, Alumni Recognition award George Washington U., 1996. Fellow Inst. Jud. Adminstrn., Am. Bar Found.; mem. ABA (chmn. jud. adminstrn. divsn., Disting. Svc. award 1981), ABA Nat. Conf. Spl. Ct. Judges (chmn., Disting. Svc. award 1978), DC Jud. Conf., Bar Assn. DC (bd. dirs. 1970-72, jour. editor-in-chief, Chmn. of Yr. award, Contbn. award young lawyers sect. 1983), Fed. Bar Assn., George Washington U. Nat. Law Assn. (pres. DC chpt. 1974-76, nat. pres. 1983-84), Univ. Club., Rotary (bd. dirs. Washington 1984-90, pres. 1988-89, dist. gov. 1991-92, Rotarian of Yr. 1984, Rotary Internat. Rep. to the World Bank and Orgn. of Am. States, 1998-99, pres. Rotary Found. 1999-00, Rotarian of the Decade 2005), Charles Fahy Am. Inn of Ct. (Nat. Prog. award, 1997), Phila. Ctrl. HS Alumni (bd. mgrs. 2001-05). Office: US Ct Fed Claims 717 Madison Pl NW Ste 703 Washington DC 20005

MARGOLIS, MARK NEAL, actor; b. Phila., Nov. 26, 1939; s. Isidore and Fanya (Fried) M.; m. Jacqueline Petcove, June 3, 1962; 1 child, Morgan. Studied with, Stella Adler, Lee Strasberg, Bill Hickey, Barbara Loden. Actor: (films) Short Eyes, 1977, Going in Style, 1979, Dressed to Kill, 1980, You Better Watch Out, 1980, The Avenging, 1982, Diner, 1982, Eddie Macon's Run, 1983, Scarface, 1983, Far From Poland, 1984, The Cotton Club, 1984, The Bedroom Window, 1987, The Secret of My Success, 1987, The Rosary Murders, 1987, White Hot, 1989, Glory, 1989, Tales from the Darkside: The Movie, 1990, Delta Force: The Colombian Connection, 1990, 1492: Conquest of Paradise, 1992, Where the Rivers Flow North, 1994, Ace Ventura: Pet Detective, 1994, Squanto: A Warrior's Tale, 1994, I Shot Andy Warhol, 1996, The Pallbearer, 1996, Absolute Power, 1997, Trouble on the Corner, 1997, Above Freezing, 1998, Pants on Fire, 1998, 18 Shades of Dust, 1999, The Thomas Crown Affair, 1999, Mickey Blue Eyes, 1999, End of Days, 1999, Flawless, 1999, Angela, 2000, Requiem for a Dream, 2000, Dinner Rush, 2000, Hannibal, 2001, The Tailor of Panama, 2001, Hard Ball, 2001, Bridget, 2002, Infested, 2002, Particles of Truth, 2003, 2BPerfectlyHonest, 2004, House of D, 2004, Stay, 2005, The Fountain, 2006, Daredevil, others; (TV series) The Guiding Light, 1994, Santa Barbara, 1990, Oz, 1998-99, Brotherhood, 2006, The Black Donnellys, 2007; (TV films) Muggable Mary, Street Cop, 1982, Rage of Angels, 1983, Doubletake, 1985, Almost Partners, 1987, Lady Mobster, 1988, Columbo: Columbo Cries Wolf, 1990, Descending Angel, 1990, Boss of Bosses, 2001; (broadway prodns.) The World of Sholom Aleichem, Infidel Caesar); (off-broadway prodns.) Three Americanisms, My Uncle Sam, Balm in Gilead, Hospitality, Child of the Clay Country, The Big Knife, others; (regional theatre) The Substance of Fire, Ghosts, Love Me or Leave Me, Once in a Lifetime, The Boys Next Door, A Shayna Maidel, Hunting Cockroaches, The Seagull, Split Decision, The Front Page, Broken Glass, Quills; TV guest appearances include Kojak, 1977, The Equalizer, 1986-88, Crime Story, 1987, Quantum Leap, 1989, Mancuso, FBI, 1990, Star Trek: The Next Generation, 1990, Jake and the Fatman, 1990, The Antagonists, 1991, Law & Order, 1992, 97, 2001, New York Undercover, 1994, Prince Street, 1997, 2000, Now and Again, 1999, 100 Centre Street, 2001, The Practice, 2002, Hack, 2002, Ed, 2003-04, Sex and the City, 2004, Law & Order: Criminal Intent, 2004, Crossing Jordan, 2005. Office: HWA Talent Reps 220 E 23d St Ste 400 New York NY 10010 E-mail: markmargolis1@mac.com.

MARGOLIS, NADIA, language educator, translator, medievalist; b. Neuilly-sur-Seine, France, Apr. 27, 1949; came to U.S., 1950; d. Morton Margolis and Diane Seyfort-Ruegg Kensler; m. Peter Kenneth Marshall, May 23, 1984. BA, U. N.H., 1971; PhD, Stanford U., 1977. Lectr. in French Stanford (Calif.) U., 1976-77; editorial asst. Medieval Acad. of Am., Cambridge, Mass., 1977-78; asst. prof. in French Amherst (Mass.) Coll., 1978-85; assoc. prof. French U. Utah, Salt Lake City, 1985-89; rsch. assoc. Inst. Advanced Study in Humanities/U. Mass., Amherst, 1993—. Asst. coord. Jr. World Cycling Championships, Trexlertown, Pa., 1978; adj. instr. French, U. Mass., 1992-93, vis. lectr. in comparative lit., 1993; panelist NEH, Washington, 1984, 86-87; cons. Garland Medieval Series, N.Y.C., 1992—, for composer Richard Einhorn, 1994, for Capella Films, 1994; rsch. profl. Ctr. Nat. Sci. Rsch., Paris, 1973—; vis. assoc. prof. French U. Calif., Santa Barbara, 2002, UCLA, 2003, U. Mass., 2005; vis. prof French Mt. Holyoke Coll., 2006; disting. prof. medieval French lit. Ariz. State U., 2007. Author: Joan of Arc in History, Literature and Film; co-author, co-editor: Christine de Pizan, 2000, Women in the Middle Ages: An Encyclopedia, 2004, co-translator: Book of the Duke of True Lovers, 1991. Author, panel mem. Bicycle Safety/Bike Path com., Amherst, 1984. Miner Crary fellow Amherst Coll., 1979, NEH Ind. fellow, 1981; Rsch. grant Am. Philos. Soc., 1982. Mem. Modern Lang. Assn., Soc. Rencesvals, Medieval Acad. of Am., Christine de Pizan Soc. (sec. 1991—, editor newsletter 1991-96), Internat. Courtly Lit. Soc. Democrat. Jewish. Avocations: bicycling, gardening, drawing, painting. Home: 75 Amherst Rd Leverett MA 01054-5402 Office Phone: 413-548-9721. Personal E-mail: margolis@rcn.com.

MARGOLIS, PHILIP MARCUS, psychiatrist, educator; b. Lima, Ohio, July 7, 1925; s. Harry Sterling and Clara (Brunner) M.; m. Nancy Nupuf, July 26, 1959; children: Cynthia, Marc, David, Laurence. BA magna cum laude, U. Minn., 1945, MD, 1948. Diplomate Am. Bd. Psychiatry and Neurology, 1966 (examiner 1973—1999, 2003-), recert. com., 1998-2004. Intern Milw. County Hosp., 1948-49; resident VA Hosp. and U. Minn., 1949-52, Mass. Gen. Hosp. and Harvard U., Boston, 1952-54; instr. U. Minn., Milw., 1953-55; asst. prof. dept. psychiatry Med. Sch., U. Chgo., 1955-60, assoc. prof., 1960-66; prof. psychiatry Med. Sch. U. Mich., 1966—, prof. cmty. mental health, 1968—; prof. psychiatry emeritus L.S.A., 1997—, instr., 1977-97; chief psychiat. inpatient service U. Chgo. Hosps. and Clinics, 1956-66; dir. Civil Forensic Tng. Program, 1997—. Cons. Forensic Psychiat. Ctr., State of Mich., 1972—, coord. med. student edn. program, 1975-78, dir., 1978-82; cons. Turner Geriatric Clin., 1978-86, cons. Breast Cancer Clinic, 1988, Powertrain subs. Gen. Motors, 1984—, Dept. Mental Health, U.S. Dept. Justice; assoc. chief clin. affairs U. Mich. Hosps., 1981-85, chair legis. govt. com., 1996—, chmn. ethics com.; profl. rev. com. PSRO Area VII, 1982-86, PROM, 2003—; mem. Mich. State Bd. Medicine, 1986-94, chmn. 1992-94, senate adv. com. Univ. Affairs., 1986-89; spl. com. on profl. conduct and ethics Fedn. of State Med. Bds., 1998—, Mich. del., 1988-96, FLEX Com. Nat. Bd. Med. Examiners, 1988-98; civil liberties bd. U. Mich., 1995-2004, chmn., 1996-2002, gen counsel adv. com., 2002—; dir. Civil Forensic Tng. Program, 1997—. Author: Guide for Mental Health Workers, 1970, Patient Power: The Development of a Therapeutic Community in a General Hospital, 1974; also articles.; cons. editor: Community Mental Health jour, 1967—. Recipient Commonwealth Fund fellow award, 1964, Career Svc. award, 1992, Resident Appreciation award, 1991. Fellow: Am. Coll. Psychiatrists (chmn. bylaws com. 1997—, newsletter editor, Lifers 2003—), Am. Psychiat. Assn. (life; chmn. membership com. 1979—83, cons. ethics com. 1983—86, trustee 1985—88, sec. 1989—91, chmn. ethics appeals bd. 1989—, cons. steering com. on practical guidelines 1991—, budget com. 1991—, mem. assembly 1992, coun. med. edn. and career devel. 1993—, pres. Lifers 1994—, recertification com. 1998—, mem. pub. funding com. 2001—, assembly rep. 2003—, newsletter editor 2003—, cons. mem. com. 2004—, mem. audit com. 2004—, annual Lifers award 1999); mem.: Am. Acad. Psychiatry and Law (com. on psychoanalytic edn. 1995—, edn. com. 1998, treas. midwest chpt. 1998—2000, forensic tng. com. 2000—, pres. 2001—02), Am. Acad. Psychoanalysis, Mich. State Med. Soc. (bioethics com. 1989—, com. on med. licensure and discipline 1995—, legis. and regulations com. 1995—, mental health liaison com. 1995—, liaison com. Gen. Motors 1998—, chair 2000—, chair com. on med. licensure and discipline 2000—), Mich. Psychiat. Soc. (pres. 1980—81, chmn. ethics com. 1983—86, resolutions officer student rights responsibilities 1996—, chmn. legislation and govt. com. 1996—2005, v.p. 2000—, chmn. mem. com. 2004, 2004—, Career Achievement award 2000), Washtenaw County Med. Soc. (exec. coun. 1982—, chmn. ethics com. 1983—87, pres. 1987—88, editl. bd. 1995—, chair legis. commn. 1999—). Home: 228 Riverview Dr Ann Arbor MI 48104-1846 Office: 4250 Plymouth Rd Ann Arbor MI 48109 Office Phone: 734-647-8762. Business E-Mail: margolis@umich.edu.

MARGOLIS, SHERRY, newscaster; m. Jeffrey Zaslow, 1987; children: Jordan, Alexandra, Eden. BA in English, SUNY, Buffalo. Anchor and reporter WKBW-TV, Buffalo; reporter WJBK-TV, Detroit, 1984—, anchor "In the News", co-anchor 5am and noon news, anchor "Live at 11am", anchor "Fox-2 news at 5:30pm". Named Best Newscast in Mich., AP, 1990; recipient Best News Anchor Emmys, NATAS, 1993, 1999, Cmty. Involvement award, U. Mich., 2002, Emmy Reporting, NATAS, 2002, 2006, Pub. Affairs Emmy, 2004, Award of Excellence, Mich. Assn. Broadcasters, 2004, Edward R. Murrow award, 2006. Office: WJBK-TV Fox 2 PO Box 2000 Southfield MI 48037-2000

MARGOLIS, THOMAS IRA, vitreoretinal ophthalmologist; s. Herbert and Barbara M.; m. Robin Deborah Small, Mar. 12, 1989; children: Rebecca, Joshua, Jennifer. BA summa cum laude, U. Pa., 1984; MD magna cum laude, Harvard U., 1989. Cert. Am. Bd. Ophthalmology. Intern Cedars Sinai Med. Ctr., LA, 1989-90; resident Wills Eye Hosp., Phila., 1990-93; fellowship (vitreoretinal) Tufts U.-New Eng. Eye Ctr., Boston, 1993-95. Instr. ophthalmology Tufts U. Med. Sch., Boston, 1993-96; hosp. staff AtlantiCare Regional Med. Ctr., Shore Meml. Hosp., Somers Point, N.J. Contbr. sci. articles to profl. jours. and chpt. to book. Pres. Atlantic County Med. Soc., 2007—. Recipient Benjamin Franklin scholar U. Pa., 1980-84, Laurence B. Ellis scholar Harvard Med. Sch., 1987; named one of Top Docs, NJ Monthly, 2003, 05, Phila. Mag., 2004, 05, 06, NJ Life, 2005. Mem. AMA, Am. Acad. Ophthalmology, N.J. Acad. Ophthalmology, N.J. Med. Soc., Wills Eye Hosp. Soc., N.J. Retina Soc., Am. Soc. Retina Specialists, Phi Beta Kappa. Jewish. Avocations: running, skiing, golf, tennis, travel. Office: Retinal and Ophthalmic Cons PC 1500 Tilton Rd Northfield NJ 08225-1827 also: 2466 E Chestnut Ave Vineland NJ 08360 also: Ste 102 211 S Main St Cape May Court House NJ 08210 Office Phone: 609-646-5200. Business E-Mail: vitrector@aol.com.

MARGOLIUS, HARRY STEPHEN, pharmacologist, physician; b. Albany, NY, Jan. 29, 1938; s. Irving Robert and Betty (Zweig) M.; m. Francine Rockwood, May 22, 1964; children: Elizabeth Anne, Craig Matthew. BS, Union U., 1959, PhD, 1963; MD, U. Cin., 1968. Diplomate Nat. Bd. Med. Examiners, 1969, chmn. pharmacology test com., 1990-94. Intern, resident Harvard Med. Svc. Boston City Hosp., 1968-70, pharmcology rsch. assoc., 1970-72; sr. clin. investigator NHLBI NIH, Bethesda, 1972-74; assoc. prof. pharmacology, asst. prof. medicine Med. U. S.C., Charleston, 1974-77, prof. pharmacology, assoc. prof. medicine, 1977-80, prof. pharmacology, prof. medicine, 1980—, chmn. pharmacology, 1989—. Cons. NIH, FDA, VA, NSF, Washington, Bethesda, 1975—; mem. editorial bd. Am. Heart Assn., Dallas, 1980—. Editor: Kinins IV, 1986, Renal Function, Hypertension and Kallikrein-Kinin System, 1988; contbr. numerous articles to profl. jours. Commdr. USPHS, 1967-74. Recipient S.C. Gov.'s award for sci. S.C. Acad. Scis., 1988, Frey-Werle Commemorative medal for biomed. rsch., 1997; Burroughs-Wellcome scholar, 1976; vis. scholar U. Cambridge, Eng., 1980-81; sr. fellow Fitzwilliam Coll., 1996; NIH grantee, 1975—; named Theodore Cooper Meml. Lectr., 1995. Fellow Coun. for High Blood Pressure Rsch., Am. Heart Assn.; mem. Am. Soc. for Pharmacology and Exptl. Therapeutics, Am. Soc. for Clin. Investigation and 10 additional med., sci. socs. Jewish. Achievements include studies of the role of kallikreins and kinins in human and animal forms of hypertension; discovery of abnormalities which signify roles in causing high blood pressure. Office: Medical Univ SC Coll Medicine 171 Ashley Ave Charleston SC 29425-0001

MARGON, BRUCE HENRY, astrophysicist, educator; b. NYC, Jan. 7, 1948; 1 child Pamela. AB, Columbia U., 1968; MA, U. Calif.-Berkeley, 1971, PhD, 1973. Asst. rsch. astronomer U. Calif.-Berkeley, 1973—76; assoc. prof. astronomy UCLA, 1976—80; prof. astronomy U. Wash., Seattle, 1980—2001, chmn., 1981—87, 1990—95, sci. dir. Sloan Digital Sky Survey, 1998—99; assoc. dir. Space Telescope Sci. Inst., Balt., 2001—06; vice chancellor rsch., prof. astronomy and astrophysics U. Calif., Santa Cruz, 2006—. Bd. govs. Astrophys. Rsch. Consortium, Inc., Seattle; chmn. bd. dirs. AURA, Inc., Washington; co-investigator Hubble space telescope NASA, Washington, 1977—. NATO postdoctoral fellow, 1973-74; Sloan Found. rsch. fellow, 1979-83 Fellow AAAS, Am. Phys. Soc.; mem. Internat. Astron. Union, Am. Astron. Soc. (Pierce Prize 1981), Royal Astron. Soc. Office: Univ Calif Chacellors Office 1156 High St Santa Cruz CA 95064 Office Phone: 831-459-2425.

MARGOSHES, MIRIAM KAGAN, information specialist; b. Cambridge, Mass., Feb. 10, 1932; d. Baruch and Raizl (Rozinko) Kagan; m. Marvin Margoshes, Aug. 7, 1955; children: Bethia Anne, Sara Amy, Jessa Abi, Dan Raphael. BS, Simmons Coll., 1953; MS, CUNY, 1976. Cert. libr. media specialist NY. Libr. aide Harvard U. Librs., Cambridge, 1947-53; asst. libr. Wheelock Coll., Boston, 1954-57; libr., cons. Combined Book Exhibit, Briarcliff Manor, N.Y., 1971-73; instrnl. svcs. libr. Westchester C.C., Valhalla, N.Y., 1974-77; libr. dir., editor Pergamon Press, Inc., Elmsford, N.Y., 1978-83; libr. supr. Joseph E. Seagram & Sons, NYC, 1984-87; sr. rsch. assoc. House of Seagram, NYC, 1987-92; database specialist Towers Perrin, Valhalla, 1992—2004, ret., 2004; sr. database specialist IC/KM; part-time libr. Hastings Pub. Libr., 2005—. Cons. D.C. Welfare Dept., Washington, 1965-70; libr. cons. Pocantico Hills (N.Y.) Sch., 1973-74. Contbr. articles to profl. jours. Trustee Bethesda-Chevy Chase Libr. Bd., Md., 1968-71; dist. leader Tarrytown Dem. Com., 1972-74; trustee Temple Beth Abraham, Tarrytown, NY, 1980-89, 100th Anniversary publicity com., 1999-2000; chmn., sec. Warner Libr. Bd., Tarrytown, 1982, 84-94; trustee, sec. Westchester Libr. Sys. Bd., Elmsford, 1984-89, v.p. adv. com.; active Kerry/Edwards office, NYC, 2004; libr. vol. Anti-Defamation League, 2004-05; vol. Mus. Modern Art, 2005-. Recipient Luminary award Westchester Libr. Sys., 1999. Mem. Spl. Librs. Assn., Hadassah. Avocations: travel, cultural anthropology, aerobics. Personal E-mail: mirkamar@verizon.net.

MARGRAF, FRANCIS JOSEPH, JR., marine biologist, educator; b. Atlantic City, Oct. 17, 1947; s. Francis J. and Henrietta K. Margraf; m. Wennona A. Brown, Apr. 17, 1982; children: Jason Dirk, Marissa Leigh. BS, Cornell U., 1970; MS, PhD, Tex. A&M U., 1978. Unit leader, prof. fisheries Ohio Coop. Fish and Wildlife Rsch. Unit Ohio State U., Columbus, Ohio, 1980—87; unit leader, prof. fisheries W.Va. Coop. Fish and Wildlife Rsch. unit W.Va. U., Morgantown, 1987—95; unit leader, prof. fisheries Md. Coop. Fish and Wildlife Rsch. Unit U. Md. Ea. Shore, Princess Ann, Md., 1995—99; unit leader, prof. fisheries Alaska Coop. Fish and Wildlife Rsch. Unit U. Alaska, Fairbanks, Alaska, 1999—. Presenter in field. Contbr. over 100 articles to profl. jours. Fellow: Am. Inst. Fisheries Rsch. Biologists (dist. dir. 2003—); mem.: Am. Fisheries Soc. (life; v.p. we. divsn. 2003—04, pres. we divsn. 2005—06, Disting. Svc. award 2001), Mastiff Club of Am. (pres. 1997—99). Office: AK-CFWRU Univ Alaska Fairbanks 210A Irving I Fairbanks AK 99775-7020 Home Phone: 907-456-7059; Office Phone: 904-474-7661. Business E-Mail: joe.margraf@uaf.edu.

MARGULES, CECELIA, composer, poet; b. Stockholm, Apr. 11, 1947; d. Morris Berkowitz; m. Rubin Margules, June 5, 1971; children: Julie, Rachyl, Adam. BA, Bklyn. Coll., 1970; Interior Design Degree, N.Y. Sch. Interior Design. Design cons. ARM Mgmt. Co., Bklyn., 1985—. Composer N.Y.C. Parks Dept., Emma Lazarus tribute, 2004, Celebration '350'. Contbr. articles and poetry to profl. jours.; contbg. editor: Harmony, 1987; composer: (songs) Guiliani, 1987, New Sinai Sound, 2005. Chmn. Yossi Berger Holocaust Study Ctr., 1990—; cultural chmn. Jewish Heritage, NYC; bd. dirs. Jewish Cmty. Rels. Coun., NYC, 2000—. Recipient State of Israel Bonds award, 1996, Woman of Valor award, Coun. Jewish Orgns., 2003, 1st prize Zionist nat. song contest, Am. Zionist Movement, 1998. Mem.: Emunah of Am. (v.p., Kristallnacht Commemoration chmn. 2006, Woman of the Yr. 1991). Jewish. Office Phone: 718-648-2828. Personal E-mail: ceceliaproductions@yahoo.com.

MARGULIES, BETH ZELDES, state attorney general; b. Hartford, Conn., Apr. 24, 1954; d. Benjamin and Edith Rose (Herrmann) Zeldes; m. Martin B. Margulies, July 26, 1981; children: Max, Adam. BA in Anthropology, McGill U., Montreal, 1976; JD summa cum laude, U. Bridgeport, 1983; LLM, Yale U., 1985. Bar: Conn. 1983, US Dist. Ct. Conn. 1983, US Ct. Appeals (DC cir.) 1988, US Supreme Ct., 1989, US Ct. Appeals (2d cir.) 1992. Asst. atty. gen. Atty. Gen.'s Office State of Conn., Hartford, 1985—. Contbr. articles to profl. jours. Office: Atty Gen Office State of Conn 55 Elm St Hartford CT 06106-1746 Home Phone: 203-270-9255; Office Phone: 860-808-5340. Business E-Mail: beth.margulies@po.state.ct.us.

MARGULIES, JAMES HOWARD, editorial cartoonist; b. Bklyn., Oct. 8, 1951; s. Henry Norman and Miriam Margulies; m. Martha Anne Golub, May 21, 1978; children: Elana, David. BFA, Carnegie-Mellon U., 1973. Editorial cartoonist Jour. Newspapers, Springfield, Va., 1980-84, Houston Post, 1984-90, The Record, Hackensack, NJ, 1990—. Syndicated cartoonist various newspapers, 1985—. Author: My Husband Is Not a Wimp, 1988, Hitting Below the Beltway, 1998; contbr. columns to profl. jours.; cartoons featured on TV programs. Mem. leadership com. Jewish Community Ctr., Houston, 1987, 88. Recipient Best Cartoon award Population Inst., 1985, Global Media award, 1985, 2d Place Editl. award Pavillion of Humor, 1985, Judges award World Hunger Media awards, 1986, Katie award Press Club of Dallas, 1989, Best Black and White Illustration in Advt. and Graphic Arts Addy award Houston Advt. Fedn., 1990, John Peter Zenger award N.Y. State Bar Assn., 1992, Nat. Headliner award for editl. cartoons Press Club of Atlantic City, 1996, 1st prize Fischetti Editl. Cartoon Competition, Columbia Coll., Chgo., 1996, Deadline Club award for editl. cartoons N.Y. chpt. Soc. Profl. Journalists, 1998, 1st pl. for editl. cartoons Garden State Assn. of Black Journalists, 1999-2003, 3d Pl. Nat. Headliner awards for Editl. Cartoons. Press Club of Atlantic City, 2003, 04; named One of Texans Who Made the Eighties Winter, Ultra mag., 1990, Cartoonist of the Yr. Nat. Press Found., 2005, Berryman Cartoonist of Yr. Nat. Press Found., DC, 2005. Mem. Assn. Am. Editl. Cartoonists. Avocation: running. Office: The Record 150 River St Hackensack NJ 07601-7155 Office Phone: 201-646-4468. E-mail: jimmarg@aol.com.

MARGULIES, JULIANNA, actress; b. Spring Valley, NY, June 8, 1966; BA, Sarah Lawrence Coll., 1989. Actor (films) Out for Justice, 1991, Traveller, 1997, Paradise Road, 1997, A Price Above Rubies, 1997, The Newton Boys, 1998, The Big Day, 1999, What's Cooking, 2000, (voice only) Dinosaur, 2000, Ten Unknowns, 2001 (Lucille Lortel Award for outstanding featured actress, 2001), The Man From Elysian Fields, 2001, (voice only) Love Gets You Twisted, 2002, Ghost Ship, 2002, Evelyn, 2002, Slingshot, 2005, The Darwin Awrds, 2006, Snakes on a Plane, 2006; (TV series) Philly Heat, 1994, ER, 1994-2000 (Emmy award for supporting actress Drama, 1995, Golden Globe award winner, 1998, SAG award winner 1997, 98, 99); (TV mini-series) The Grid, 2004; (TV movies) The Mists of Avalon, 2001, Jenifer, 2001, Hitler: The Rise of Evil, 2003; (TV appearances) Law & Order, 1993, Murder, She Wrote, 1993, Homicide: Life on the Street, 1994, Scrubs, 2004, The Sopranos, 2006; (theater appearances) The Substance of Fire, At Home, Fefu and Her Friends, The Substance of Fire, Living Expenses, Dan Drift, Book of Names, Balm in Gilead, In the Boom Boom Room, The Vagina Monologues, 2000, Festen, 2006. Office: c/o William Morris Agency 151 S El Camino Dr Beverly Hills CA 90212

MARGULIES, MARTIN B., lawyer, educator; b. NYC, Oct. 6, 1940; s. Max N. and Mae (Cohen) M.; m. Beth Ellen Zeldes, July 26, 1981; children: Max Zeldes, Adam Zeldes. AB, Columbia Coll., 1961; LLB, Harvard U., 1964; LLM, NYU, 1966. Bar: N.D. 1968, N.Y. 1974, Mass. 1977, Conn. 1988, U.S. Dist. Ct. Mass. 1977, U.S. Ct. Appeals (2d cir.) 1984, U.S. Supreme Ct. 1995. Asst. prof. law U. N.D., Grand Forks, 1966-69; editor-in-chief Columbia Coll. Today, Columbia U., NYC, 1969-71; assoc. editor Parade Mag., NYC, 1971-72; assoc. prof. law Western New Eng. Law Sch., Springfield, Mass., 1973-76; Bernard Hersher prof. law U. Bridgeport, Conn., 1977-92; Neil H. Cogan Pub. Svc. prof. law Quinnipiac U., 1997-99, prof. law, 1992—2005, prof. emeritus, 2005—. Author: The Early Life of Sean O'Casey, 1970, The Battle of Prestonpans 1745, 2007; contbr. articles to profl. jours. Cooperating atty. Conn. Civil Liberties Union, Hartford, 1979—, bd. dirs., 1982-94; bd. dirs. Conn. Attys. for Progressive Legislature, New Haven, 1982; bd. dirs. ACLU, 1987-94, mem. free speech-assn. and poverty constl. rights com., 1988-94; chmn. bd. dirs. Fairfield County Civil Liberties Union, 1982-87, Hampden County Civil Liberties Union, 1976-78; bd. dirs. Civil Liberties Union Mass., Boston, 1975-78, Greater Springfield Urban League, 1976-78, Conn. Civil Liberties Union, 1982-94, ACLU, 1987-94, Ctr. for First Amendment Rights, Inc., 1993—. Recipient Media award, NY State Bar Assn., 1972, Gavel award, ABA, 1973, Outstanding Tchr. award, U. Bridgeport Law Sch., 1986, 1987. Mem. Mass. Bar Assn., N.Y. State Bar Assn. Jewish. Home: 79 High Rock Rd Sandy Hook CT 06482-1623 Office: Quinnipiac Univ Sch Law 275 Mt Carmel Ave Hamden CT 06518-1947 Home Phone: 203-270-9255; Office Phone: 203-582-3252. Personal E-mail: mmargulies023@earthlink.net.

MARGULIES, ALEXANDER RAFAILO, physician, educator; b. Belgrade, Yugoslavia, Mar. 21, 1921; arrived in U.S., 1946; s. Rafailo and Olga (Weiss-Belic) Margulis; m. Hedvig Hricak, Feb. 26, 1983; 1 child, Peter Hricak. Student, U. Belgrade, 1939—41, student, 1945—46; MD, Harvard U., 1950; Doctorate (hon.), Aix-Marseille U., 1980, Med. Coll. Wis., 1986, Cath. U. Louvain, 1986, Karolinska Inst., Stockholm, 1986, U. Munich, 1987, U. Toulouse, 1987, U. Montpellier, 1993, U. Novi Sad, 2005. Diplomate Am. Bd. Radiology. Intern Henry Ford Hosp., Detroit, 1950—51; resident in radiology U. Mich. Hosps., 1951—53; jr. clin. instr. U. Mich., 1953—54; instr., then asst. prof. U. Minn., 1954—59; asst. prof. sch. medicine Washington U., St. Louis, 1959—60, assoc. prof. to prof., 1960—63; prof. radiology, chmn. dept. U. Calif., San Francisco, 1963—89, dir. magnetic resonance Sci. Ctr., assoc. chancellor spl. projects, 1989—93, spl. cons. to vice chancellor, 1993—2000; clin. prof. radiology Cornell U. Weill Med. Coll., NYC, 2000—; radiologist N.Y.-Presbyn. Med. Ctr., 2000—. Radiologist in chief U. Calif. Hosps., 1963—89; cons. VA Hosp., Letterman Gen. Hosp., San Francisco, U.S. Naval Hosp., Oakland, Calif.; cons. in radiology Office Surgeon Gen., 1967—71. Author (with others): Roentgen Diagnosis of Abdominal Tumors in Childhood, 1957; editor: Modern Alimentary Tract Radiology, Opinion in Radiology, 1988—91; co-editor: Alimentary Tract Roentgenology; editl. bd. Calif. Medicine, 1964—74, Radiology, 1975—93, assoc. editor Investigative Radiology, 1980—89; author: Be in Charge: A Leadership Manual, 2002, The Road to Success (How to get to the top of your profession), 2006. Capt. US Army, 1957—59. Named to Hall of Honor, U. Mich. Med. Sch., 2006; recipient Cannon medal, Soc. Radiol., 1977, Gold medal, Am. Roentgen Ray Soc., 1988, J.P. Allyn medal, P. Roberts Rsch. Inst., 1989, Gold medal, Am. Coll. Radiology, 1999, UCSF medal, 2000. Fellow: Royal Coll. Radiologists (hon.); mem.: AMA (cons. drugs 1961—), Internat. Soc. Strategic Studies in Radiology (founding pres. 1995—99), Royal Coll. Radiologists of Thailand, Polish Soc. Radiology, Thai Coll. Radiology, Chinese Radiol. Soc., Russian Radiol. Soc., Royal Coll. Surgeons Ireland, French Radiol. Soc., Swiss Radiol. Soc., Italian Radiol. Soc., Russian Acad. Scis. (fgn.), Serbian Acad. Scis. (fgn.), Soc. Magnetic Resonance in Medicine (pres. 1983), Calif. Acad. Medicine (pres. 1978), San Francisco Radiol. Soc. (pres. 1973—74), Radiol. Soc. N.Am. (Gold medal 1983), Soc. Chmn. Acad. Radiology Depts. (pres. 1968—69), Am. Gastroenterology Assn., Assn. Univ. Radiologists (pres. 1966—67, chmn. adv. com. acad. radiology 1971, pres. 1971), Roentgen Ray Soc., NAS-Inst. Medicine, Japan Radiol. Soc. (hon.), German Radiol. Soc. (hon.), Rocky Mountain Radiol. Soc. (hon.), U. Mich. Med. Sch. Hall Honor. Office: NY Presbyn Hosp Rm N-09 Box 141 525 E 68th St New York NY 10021-4870 Business E-Mail: arm2001@med.cornell.edu.

MARGULIS, GREGORY A., mathematics and science professor, researcher; b. Moscow, Feb. 24, 1946; came to U.S., 1991; s. Alexander Y. Margulis and Tsilya M. Osherenko; m. Raisa T. Kristal, Aug. 30, 1972; 1 child, Boris. Diploma, Moscow U., 1967, PhD, 1970; DSc, Belorrussian Acad. Scis., Minsk, 1983. Rschr. Inst. Problems in Info. Transmission, Soviet Acad. Scis., Moscow, 1970-91; prof. math. Yale U., New Haven, 1991—. Mem. sci. adv. coun. Math. Scis. Rsch. Inst., Berkeley, Calif., 1993-97; mem. sci. adv. bd. Clay Math. Inst., Cambridge, Mass., 2003—. Author: Discrete Subgroups of Semisimple Lie Groups, 1991; mem. editl. bd. math. jours. Recipient prize for young mathematicians Moscow Math. Soc., 1968, Fields medal Internat. Math. Union, 1978, Humboldt Found. prize, 1995, Lobachevski prize Russian Acad. Scis., 1996, Wolf prize in math. Wolf Found., Israel, 2005. Mem. AAAS (fgn. hon.), NAS. Avocations: chess, jogging, swimming. Home: 20 Vista Ter New Haven CT 06515-2402 Office: Yale U Dept Math 10 Hillhouse Ave Dept Math New Haven CT 06511-6814

MARGULIS, HEIDI, health products executive; Licensure analyst Humana, Inc., 1985—95, v.p. govt. affairs, 1995—2000, sr. v.p. govt. affairs, 2000—. Mem. fed. adv. com. to streamline regulations to ensure quality health care svcs., 2002; mem. com. on Medicare edn. HFCA. Mem.: Women's Polit. Forum (bd. dirs.), Bus. and Profl. Women (pres. 1978—79), Bus. Roundtable, Health Care Leadership Coun., Am. Assn. Health Plans (policy, legis., advocacy and strategic planning coms.). Office: Humana Inc 500 W Main St Louisville KY 40202

MARGULIS, LYNN (LYNN ALEXANDER), evolutionist, educator; b. Chgo., Mar. 5, 1938; d. Morris and Leone Alexander; m. Carl Sagan, June 16, 1957; children: Dorion Sagan, Jeremy Sagan; m. Thomas N. Margulis, Jan. 18, 1967; children: Zachary Margulis-Ohnuma, Jennifer Margulis di Properzio. AB, U. Chgo., 1957; MS in Zoology and Genetics, U. Wis., 1960; PhD in Genetics, U. Calif., Berkeley, 1965; D (hon.), U. Montreal, Can., 1987, U. Valencia, Spain, 2001; DSc (hon.), Southeastern Mass. U., North Dartmouth, 1989, Westfield State Coll., Mass., 1989, Plymouth State Coll., NH, 1991, Tulane U., New Orleans, 1996, U. Montreal, 1997, Autonomous U. Madrid, 1998, Union Coll., Schenectady, NY, 2001, San Francisco U., Quito, Ecuador, 2001, Rutgers U., New Brunswick, 2004, Bates Coll., Lewiston, Maine, 2005, Tufts U., Medford, Mass., 2006, NC State U., Raleigh, 2006; Dr.rer.nat (hon.), U. Oldenburg, Germany, 1999. Mem. faculty Boston U., 1966—68, asst. prof. biology, 1967—71, assoc. prof., 1971—77, prof., 1977—88, Univ. prof., 1986—88; Disting. Univ.

prof. U. Mass., Amherst, 1988—. Sherman Fairchild Disting. scholar Calif. Inst. Tech., 1976—77; vis. prof. dept. microbiology U. Autónoma de Barcelona, Spain, 1986, Spain, 88; Disting. univ. prof. U. Mass.; mem. com. NASA, NYNEX Awards, Nat. Sci. Resource Ctr.; mem. OEB vis. com. Harvard Coll. Author: Origin of Eukaryotic Cells, 1970, Symbiosis in Cell Evolution, 1981, Early Life, 1982, 2d edit., 2002, Symbiosis in Cell Evolution, 2d edit., 1993, Microcosmos Videos, 1999; editor (with Mitchell Rambler and René Fester): Global Ecology, 1989; editor: (with others) Handbook of Protoctista, 1990; co-editor (with René Fester): Symbiosis as a Source of Evolutionary Innovation: Speciation and Morphogenesis, 1991; co-editor: Concepts of Symbiogenesis: A Historical and Critical Study of the Research of Russian Botanists, 1992, Environmental Evolution: Effects of the Origin and Evolution of Life on Planet Earth, 1992, Environmental Evolution: Effects of the Origin and Evolution of Life on Planet Earth, 2d edit., 2000, Glossary of Protoctista, 1993, What is Life?, 1995, Slanted Truths: Essays on Gaia, Evolution and Symbiosis, 1997; co-editor: (with Dorion Sagan) What Is Sex?, 1998; co-editor: Diversity of Life: The Illustrated Guide to the Five Kingdoms, 2d edit., 1999, Conversations with Ian McHary: Dwelling in Nature, 2006; co-author: Five Kingdoms, 1982, 3d edit., 1998, Microcosmos, 1986; co-author: (with Dorion Sagan) Origins of Sex, 1986; co-author: Garden of Microbial Delights, 1988, 2d edit., 1998, Biospheres From Earth To Space, 1988, Mystery Dance: On the Evolution of Human Sexuality, 1991, What Happens to Trash and Garbage: An Introduction to the Carbon Cycle, 1993, Living Sands: Mapping Time and Space with Forams, 2000, Early Life, 2d edit., 2002, Acquiring Genomes: A Theory of the Origins of Species, 2002, Peces Luminosos: Historias de Ciencia y Amor, 2002, Una Revolucion en la Evolucion, 2002; co-author: (with Andrew Wier) Vol. I Cells and Reproduction, Vol. II Evolution and Diversity; co-author: (with Lorraine Olendzenski) (videos) Looking at Microbes, An Introduction to the Microbiology Laboratory for Students, Symbiotic Planet. A New Look at Evolution, 1997; contbr. chapters to books, articles to profl. jours. Recipient Nat. Medal Sci., 1999, Humboldt Prize, 2002, Commonwealth of Mass. award; Guggenheim fellow, 1979. Fellow: AAAS; mem.: NAS, Internat. Soc. Study of Life, Soc. Sci. Rsch., Soc. Evolutionary Protistology (co-founder), Sigma Xi (pres. 2005—06). Office: U Mass Dept Geosci 611 No Pleasant St Amherst MA 01003-9297 Mailing: PO Box 671 Amherst MA 01004-0671 Office Phone: 413-545-3244. *We must, as E. M. Forster admonished, "only connect" and lower our population's growth rate. The sciences, the quest for knowledge about the universe and life are intrinsically unified. Like all other species ever to have lived on Earth, ours too will be replaced. The quality of that demise depends directly on preservation of habitat of our planetmates directly on our own population growth rates by presentation of habitat of our planetmates.*

MARIA, BERNARD L., pediatric neurologist; b. Montreal, Que., Can., Jan. 23, 1958; s. Maurice A. and Margaret Maria; m. Barbara E. Maria, Nov. 28, 1983; 1 child, Alexander. DEC, Coll. Marguerite-Bourgeois, Montreal, 1976; MD, U. Sherbrooke, Can., 1981; MBA, U. Fla., 1995. Diplomate Am. Bd. Pediatrics, Am. Bd. Neurology and Psychiatry. Resident in pediatrics McGill U., Montreal, 1981-83; resident in neurology Johns Hopkins U., Balt., 1983-86; fellow in neuro-oncology M.D. Anderson, Houston, 1986-88; asst. prof. U. Toronto, Ont., Can., 1988-90; assoc. prof. U. Fla., Gainesville, 1990-98, prof., 1998—, divsn. chief, 1990—. Founding dir. neuro-oncology group Johns Hopkins Hosp., 1984-86; founding dir. neuro-oncology program U. Fla., 1990—; lectr. in field. Editor consensus in Child Neurology, 1997—; Current Mgmt. in Child Neurology, 1999, 2002, 05; guest-editor Seminar in Child Neurology, 1997; guest editor Jour. Child Neurology, 2002-; mem. editl. bd. Jour. Child Neurology, 1995—, Pediat. Neurology, 1997—; reviewer jours. in field; contbr. articles to med. jours., chpt. to book; author monographs in field. Grantee NSC Found., 1988-90, Brain Rsch. Found., 1988-90, U. Fla., 1990, ORDCR Found., 1990, 91-97, Sigma-Tau Pharms., 1992, Stop! Children's Cancer, Inc., 1991-92, 96-97, Abbot Pharms., 1992, Parke Davis Pharms., 1992, Nat. Cancer Inst., 1992, 93, Children's Miracle Network, 1995, Depotech, Inc., 1994, Glaxo, Inc., 1995, Genetic Therapy, Inc., 1995, 96, Sturge-Weber Found., 1995, LAVFW, 1997-98, Glaxo Wellcome, 1997, Parke Davis, 1997, State of Fla., 1997-99, NINDS, 1999—, Medeva, 1998-99. Mem. AMA, Child Neurology Soc. (bylaws com. 1990-95, fin. com. 1995—), Soc. for Pediat. Rsch., Soc. for Neurosci., Pediat. Oncology Group, Profs. of Child Neurology, Internat. Child Neurology Assn., Am. Acad. Pediat., Am. Acad. Neurology, Am. Soc. Clin. Oncology, Am. Pediat. Soc., Soc. Neuro-Oncology. Office: MUSC PO Box 250514 173 Ashly Ave Ste 409 Charleston SC 29425 Home Phone: 843-884-8329; Office Phone: 843-792-7715. Business E-Mail: mariabl@musc.edu.

MARIAM, THOMAS FRED, public relations executive, radio producer; b. NYC, Feb. 26, 1957; s. Rudolph Karl and Lisa Gertrud (Silbermann) Mariam; m. Alyce Beth Appleman, Aug. 20, 2000; children: Michael Reese, Madison Leah. BA in Polit. Sci., Columbia U., 1978; MS in Broadcast Journalism, Boston U., 1980. News dir. Sta. WNBP, Newburyport, Mass., 1979-80; sports dir. Sta. WKCR-FM, NYC, 1976-78; editor, writer The Wall St. Jour. Report, NYC, 1980-84; nat. copy editor Dow Jones News Svc., NYC, 1984; dir. news svcs. Am. Stock Exch., NYC, 1984-95; sr. v.p. Rubenstein Assoc. Pub. Rels., NYC, 1995-96; sr. mgr. pub. rels. Booz-Allen & Hamilton, NYC, 1996-99; dir. mktg. and comm. Cadwalader, Wickersham & Taft, NYC, 1999-2000; dir. global comm. Clifford Chance Rogers & Wells LLP, 2000—02; pres. Mariam Comms. LLC, 2002—; prodr., co-host The Metro Golf Show, 2003—. Radio sports reporter Sports Final Radio Network, 1987—; NY corr. The Sports File, 1989-93. Producer, host (radio program) Amex Business Talk, 1985-94; freelance radio sports reporter, 1986—. Voting mem. Self-Help, Inc., N.Y.C., 1985-92; trustee Congregation Habonim. Mem. ABA, Legal Mktg. Assn., N.Y. Fin. Writers Assn. (bd. dirs. 1992-99), Radio-TV News Dirs. Assn., Pub. Rels. Soc. Am. (v.p. Westchester-Fairfield chpt. 2002—), Deadline Club N.Y., Nat. Assn. Broadcasters, Nat. Assn. Sportscasters and Sportswriters, Columbia Club N.Y. (dir.-at-large 1984-96, activities chmn. 1986-94, 1st v.p. 1988-96). Democrat. Jewish. Home and Office: 89 Country Ridge Dr Rye Brook NY 10573-1046 Office Phone: 914-939-4294. Business E-Mail: tom@mariam.biz.

MARIANELLA, VINCENZO, bartender; b. Italy; arrived in US, 1999; Attended, Australian Bartending Acad., Dimension Bar Freestyle Team Assn. Sch., Cerviniano Del Friuli, Italy. Bartender Smollensky's on the Strand, London, 7 MOMA, NYC, Valentino, LA; bar chef Providence, LA. Named one of LA's Rising Stars, StarChefs.com, 2006. Office: Providence Restaurant 5955 Melrose Ave Los Angeles CA 90038 Office Phone: 323-460-4170.

MARIANI, MICHAEL MATTHEW, lawyer; b. West Pittston, Pa., Sept. 25, 1950; s. Stephen Francis and Tulia Felicia (DelCorso) M.; m. Patricia Mary Leptak, June 26, 1976; children: Kathryn Elizabeth, Michael Joseph. BS with honors, Wilkes Coll., 1972; JD, St. John's U., Jamaica, NY, 1975; LLM, NYU, 1980. Bar: NY 1976, US Dist. Ct. (so. and ea. dists.) NY 1976, US Tax Ct. 1980. Law sec. to presiding judge Surrogate's Ct., New City, NY, 1976-80; assoc. Law offices of Edward S. Schlesinger P.C., NYC, 1981-97; sr. v.p., dep. trust counsel, dir. trust and estate svcs. Fiduciary Trust Co. Internat., NYC, 1997—. Adj. prof. law St. John's Univ. Sch. Law, Jamaica, NY, 2005—. Co-author: New York Probate, 1986, supplements 1987-2007; contbr. articles to profl. jours. Trustee Cath. Charities, Diocese of Bklyn., 1981—2005, treas., 1985—87, v.p., 1987—89, pres., 1989—91; bd. dirs. Mercy Home for Children, Bklyn., 1989—97, mem. adv. bd., 1997—; mem. profl. adv. bd. Calvary Hosp., 2002—; mem. Heritage bd. dirs. Am. Heart Assn., 2004—. Recipient Benemerenti medal Pope John Paul II, 1997. Mem. ABA (real property, probate and trust law sects.), NY State Bar Assn. (trusts and estates sects.), Assn. Bar City NY. Democrat. Home: 53-32 215th St Bayside NY 11364-1835 Office: 600 Fifth Ave New York NY 10020-2302 Office Phone: 212-632-3255. Business E-Mail: mmariani@ftci.com.

MARIANO, ANA VIRGINIA, retired pathologist; b. Baguio City, The Philippines, Nov. 20, 1938; came to US, 1963; d. Celestino Chuongco and Ana (Tanseco) Juan; m. Gregorio Torres Mariano, June 4, 1966; children: Joel, Eric, Greg, Anita. AA, U. St. Tomas, Manila, 1957, MD, 1962. Bd. cert. in anatomic pathology and clin. pathology Am. Bd. Pathology; lic. physician, NY, Pa. Med. intern Youngstown Hosp., Ohio, 1963; pathology resident I RI Hosp., Providence, 1964; pathology resident II-IV Wayne State U. Med. Sch., Detroit, 1965-68; assoc. pathologist Newark-Wayne Cmty. Hosp., Newark, NY, 1979-83; interim pathologist Clifton Springs Hosp., NY, 1983; lab. dir. and acting lab. dir. VA Med. Ctr., Altoona, Pa., 1995—97, staff pathologist, 1997-99. Locum tenens Altoona Hosp., Pa., 1999-2001; mem. courtesy med. staff Newark-Wayne Cmty. Hosp., 1983-92, Clifton Springs Hosp., NY, 1983-89; mem. adv. bd. Cath. Physicians Guild, Rochester, NY, 1991-92; cons. in pathology VA Med. Ctr., Altoona, 1993-96. Tchr. religious edn. St. Michael's Ch., Newark, 1978-80, 82-84. Fellow Am. Soc. Clin. Pathologists, Coll. Am. Pathologists. Roman Catholic. Avocations: swimming, aerobics, gardening.

MARIANO, ROBERT A., retail executive; BS, Univ. Ill., Chgo.; MBA, Univ. Chgo., 1987. V.p. dairy ops., mfg., retail ops. Dominick's Finer Foods, sr. v.p. mktg., perishable mdse., pres., COO, 1995—96, pres., CEO, 1996—98; commr. Ill. Gaming Bd., 2001—02; chmn., CEO, pres. Roundy's Supermarkets Inc., Milw., 2002—. Office: Roundy's Supermarkets Ste 100 875 E Wisconsin Ave Milwaukee WI 53202 Mailing: Roundy's Supermarkets PO Box 473 Milwaukee WI 53201-0473

MARICK, MICHAEL MIRON, lawyer; b. Chgo., Nov. 20, 1957; s. Miron Michael and Geraldyne Marilyn (Lid) M.; m. LIsa Amy Gelman, May 17, 1986. BA, Denison U., 1979; JD, Ill. Inst. Tech., 1982. Bar: Ill. 1982, US Dist. Ct. (no. dist.) Ill. 1982, Fla. 1983, US Ct. Appeals (3rd cir.) 1987, US Ct. Appeals (6th cir.) 1992, US Supreme Ct., 1992 US Ct. Appeals (5th cir.) 1998, US Ct. Appeals (11th Cir.) 2000, US Ct. Appeals (10th cir.) 2002. Assoc. Hinshaw, Culbertson, Moelmann, Hoban & Fuller, Chgo., 1982-85, Phelan, Pope & John, Chgo., 1985-90; ptnr. Pope & John, Chgo., 1990-94, Meckler Bulger & Tilson, Chgo., 1994—. Adj. prof. Ill. Inst. Tech./Chgo.-Kent Coll. Law, 1983-84, 87-99; comml. arbitrator Am. Arbitration Assn., Chgo., 1983—. Mem. Ill. Inst. Tech./Chgo.-Kent Law Rev., 1980-82; contbr. articles on ins. law and litigation to profl. jours. Denison U. Econs. fellow, 1978, State of Ill. Gov.'s fellow, 1978; recipient Disting. Svc. award Ill. Inst. Tech./Chgo. Kent Coll. Law, 1996. Mem. ABA (mem. exec. com., com. legis. action young lawyers divsn. 1983-84, vice chmn. TIPS excess surplus lines and reins. com. 1990-92), Ill. Bar Assn. (ins. law sect. coun. 1991-96, chair 1994-95, assembly rep. 1993-96), Fla. Bar Assn., Chgo. Bar Assn., Def. Rsch. Inst., Internat. Assn. Def. Counsel, Ill. Inst. Tech./Chgo.-Kent Coll. Law Alumni Assn. (v.p. 1990-94, pres. 1994-95, mem. bd. overseers, 2005-), Omicron Delta Upsilon, Pi Sigma Alpha, Alpha Tau Omega. Presbyterian. Home: 3605 Pebble Beach Rd Northbrook IL 60062-3109 Office: Meckler Bulger & Tilson 123 North Wacker Dr Ste 1800 Chicago IL 60606-6339 Business E-Mail: michael.marick@mbtlaw.com.

MARIENTHAL, GEORGE, telecommunications industry executive; b. Kansas City, Mo., Nov. 15, 1938; s. George and Sadie (James) M.; children: Shawn Ann Capon, Patrick James, Shannon Lee Van Winter. BS, U.S. Naval Acad., 1962; MS, Stanford U., 1963; MBA, Am. U., 1974. Sr. rsch. assoc. Logistics Mgmt. Inst., Washington, 1967-71; dir. regional ops. EPA, 1971-75, dir. water policy, 1984-85; dep. asst. sec. def. Dept. Def., Washington, 1975-81; v.p. Survival Tech., Inc., Bethesda, Md., 1981-84; dep. asst. sec. agr. Dept. Agr., Washington, 1985-86; dep. adv. programs Titan Systems, Inc., 1986-87; mgr. mktg. Computer Scis. Corp., Falls Church, Va., 1987-89; v.p. Verizon Business, Vienna, 1989—. Bd. dirs. Home Security Title Ins. Co. Served with USAF, 1962-67. Mem.: Nat. Def. Indsl. Assn., Internat. Telephone Pioneers Assn., Armed Forces Comms. and Electronics Assn., Masons. Republican. Episcopalian. Home: 1280 10th Ave N Naples FL 34102-5428

MARIER, ROBERT L., dean, hospital administrator; b. Mar. 29, 1943; m. Joanne Cain Marier; 2 children. AB, Boston Coll., 1965; MD, Yale U., 1969; MHA, Tulane U., 1990. Diplomate Am. Bd. Internal Medicine and Infectious Diseases. Intern in internal medicine Mass. Gen. Hosp., Boston, 1969-70, asst. resident in medicine, 1970-71; epidemic intelligence svc. officer Nat. Ctr. Disease Control USPHS, Atlanta, 1971-73; clin. rsch. fellow in inflammatory disease Yale U., New Haven, 1973-75, asst. prof. medicine, 1975-78; assoc. prof. medicine La. State U., New Orleans, 1978-83, acting head sect. infectious disease, 1982-83, dir. intro. to clin. medicine, 1982-85, dir. residency program, 1982-86, prof. medicine, 1983—, dir. office infection control, 1982—91; med. dir. Med. Ctr. La., 1982—92; chmn. Dept. Pub. Health La. State U. Sch. Medicine, New Orleans, 1993—95, dean, 1995—2002; acting dean La. State U. Sch. Pub. Health, New Orleans, 2003—04, dir. Health Policy and Systems Mgmt. Program; CEO La. Pub. Hosp. Sys., 1997—99. Vis. physician Yale-New Haven Hosp., 1975-78. Fellow ACP, Infectious Disease Soc. Am.; mem. AMA, La. State Med. Soc., Orleans Parish Med. Soc., Alpha Omega Alpha. Office Phone: 504-599-1396. Office Fax: 504-568-6905. E-mail: rmarier@lsuhsc.edu.

MARIL, DAVID C., editor; b. Balt., Apr. 2, 1950; s. Herman and Esta Cook Maril. BA in English, Clark U., 1972. Sports editor News Recorder, Worcester, Mass., 1972-75, Milford (Mass.) Daily News, 1975-2000; news copy editor, Sunday columnist Brockton (Mass.) Enterprise, 2000—, mem. contract negotiative bd., 2006—. V.p. Herman Maril Paintings, Balt., 1995—; sports editor AP Assn. Editor, writer Baseball Odyssey supplements, 1977-98 (award UPI 1988); columnist Off the Field, 1999. Bd. dirs. Highwood Condo Assn., Franklin, Mass., 1995—; mem. cable adv. com. Town of Franklin, 1988-91; mem. art adv. bd. Univ. Coll. of Univ. Md., 2001—. Recipient sports column awards UPI, 1986, 87, New Eng. Newspaper Assn., Boston, 1999, Cmty. Newspapers, Needham, Mass., 1999. Mem. Baseball Writers Assn. (Hall of Fame voter), Soc. Baseball Rsch., Boston Baseball Writers (bd. dirs.). Avocations: reading, cinema history, baseball history. Home: 37 Highwood Dr Franklin MA 02038 Office Phone: 774-571-2130. Personal E-mail: dmoriole13@yahoo.com.

MARIMOW, WILLIAM K. (BILL MARIMOW), editor; b. Phila., Aug. 4, 1947; s. Jay and Helen Alma (Gitnig) M.; m. Diane K. Macomb, Oct. 18, 1969; children: Ann Esther, Scott Macomb. BA, Trinity Coll., Conn., 1969. Asst. editor Comml. Car Jour., Chilton Co., Bala Cynwyd, Pa., 1969-70; asst. to econ. columnist Phila. Bull., 1970-72; staff writer Phila. Inquirer, 1972—, city hall bur. chief, 1979-81, editor Main Line Neighbors, 1986-87, NJ editor, 1987-89, city editor, 1989-91; city editor, asst. to pub. Phila. Inquirer & Daily News, 1991-93; met. editor Balt. Sun, 1993, assoc. mng. editor, 1993—95, mng. editor, 1995—2000, editor, sr. v.p., 2000—04; mng. editor Nat. Pub. Radio, Washington, 2004—05, v.p. news & info., 2006, ombudsman, 2006; editor Phila. Inquirer, 2006—. Instr. urban studies U. Pa., 1979; instr. English Rutgers U., Camden, NJ, 1981; nominating jury Pulitzer Prize, 1991—92, 1996—97, 2002—03; bd. fellows Trinity Coll., 1998—2000; mem. adv. bd. Knight Ctr. for Specialized Journalism at U. Md., 1999—2000; bd. visitors U. Md. Sch. Journalism, 2000—; mem. nat. adv. bd. Poynter Inst., 2004—. Recipient 1st place award for team reporting, Phila. Press Assn., 1977, 1st place award for deadline reporting, AP Mng. Editors Pa., 1977, 1st place award for best news story, Sigma Delta Chi Phila., 1977, 2nd place award for deadline reporting, 1980, 2nd place award for investigative reporting, Keystone Press Assn., 1978, 1985, 1st place award for best news story, 1982, Pulitzer Prize for disting pub. svc., 1978, Nat. Pub. Svc. award, Sigma Delta Chi, 1978, Robert F. Kennedy Journalism award, 1978, Roy W. Howard Pub. Svc. award, Scripps-Howard Found., 1978, Silver Gavel award, ABA, 1978, 1982, Media Achievement award, Phila. Bar. Assn., 1982, William Schnader award, Pa. Bar Assn., 1982, Alumni Achievement award, Trinity Coll., 1984, Nat. Headliners award, 1985, Pulitzer Prize for investigative reporting, 1985; Nieman fellow, Harvard U., 1982—83. Mem. Am. Soc. Newspaper Editors, Pen & Pencil Club, Investigative Reporters & Editors, Inc. (1st place for radio reporting, 2004). Office: Phila Inquirer PO Box 8263 Philadelphia PA 19101 Office Phone: 215-854-4141.

MARIN, DEBORAH B., psychiatrist, educator; b. Cleve., Oct. 9, 1957; d. Emanuel and Klara Blumenthal; m. Michael Marin; children: Lea, Max. BA, Wellesley Coll., 1979; MD, Mt. Sinai Med. Sch., 1984. Resident Mt. Sinai Med. Ctr., NYC, 1984—88; fellowship Cornell U., 1988—92; vice chair, prof. psychiatry Mt. Sinai Med. Ctr., NYC, 1992—, exec. v.p. for strategic devel., chief med. officer, 2004—; dean clin. rsch. Mt. Sinai Med. Sch., NYC, 2003—. Office: Mt Sinai Med Ctr 1425 Madison Ave New York NY 10029 E-mail: deborah.marin@mssm.edu.

MARIN, ROSARIO, state agency administrator, former federal agency administrator; b. Mexico City, Mex., Aug. 4, 1958; m. Alex Marin; children: Eric, Carmen, Alvaro. BS bus. adminstrn., Calif. State U., LA, 1983, LLD (hon.), 2002; grad., Harvard U., 1998. With City Nat. Bank, Beverly Hills, 1981—86; chief legis. affairs Calif. Dept. Devel. Svcs., 1992—93; chair Calif. State Coun. Developmental Disabilities, 1994—96; asst. dep. dir. Calif. State Dept. Social Svcs., 1996—97; dep. dir. Gov.'s Office Cmty. Rels., LA, 1997—98; mayor City of Huntington Park, Calif., 1999—2000; 41st U.S. treas. U.S. Dept. Treasury, Washington, 2001—03. Mem. Calif. Integrated Waste Mgmt. Bd., Sacramento, 2004—, chmn., 2004—. Recipient Rose Fitzgerald Kennedy award, U.N., 1995, Excellence in Pub. Svc. award, Latino Perspective Conf., 2000, Alumna of the Year, Calif. State U., 2002. Address: State and Consumer Svcs Agy 915 Capitol Mall #200 Sacramento CA 95814

MARINACCIO, JESSICA, dean; BA, Harvard U., 1991, MEd, 1994. Dir. admission ops Columbia U., NYC, dir. admissions Columbia Coll. and the Fu Found. Sch. Engring. and Applied Sci., 2004, exec. dir. undergraduate admissions, assoc. dean student affairs. Office: Columbia U 212 Hamilton Hall Mail Code: 2807 New York NY 10027 Office Phone: 212-854-1222. E-mail: jm996@columbia.edu. *

MARINCOLA, ELIZABETH MARK, nonprofit executive; b. New Haven, Conn., Aug. 31, 1959; d. James B.D. and Jean M. (Rambar) Mark; m. Francesco M. Marincola, Jan. 1, 1982; children: James Paul, Paula Rambar, Rachel Angela. AB, Stanford U., 1981, MBA, 1986. Dir. devel. Stanford (Calif.) U. Hosp., 1987-90; dep. dir. policy rsch. analysis NIMH, Rockville, Md., 1990-91; exec. dir. The Am. Soc. Cell Biology, Bethesda, Md., 1991—2005; pres. Science Service, 2005—; pub. Science News, Wash., DC. Mem. cell biology com. of visitors NSF, 2001; com. for divsn. on earth and life studies Nat. Acad. Sci., 2001—; mem. PubMed Ctrl. Nat. adv. com. Nat. Libr. of Medicine Nat. Inst. Health, 2000-03; 20th Annual Fae Golden Kass lectr. Harvard Med. Sch., 1999; mem. adv. bd. Krasnow Inst. for Advanced Study, George Mason U., 2002—; elected first citizen mem. Am. Soc. Cell Biology, 2003; mem. Joint Steering Com. for Pub. Policy, 1991—, exec. dir., 1991-2005. Mem. stratetic adv. bd. Thomson Sci., 2005; bd. dirs., mem. fin. com. Pub. Libr. Sci., 2005—. Home: 10110 Chapel Rd Potomac MD 20854-4143 Office: Science Service 1719 N St NW Washington DC 20036 Office Phone: 202-785-2255. Business E-Mail: emarincola@sciserv.org.

MARINE, CLYDE LOCKWOOD, agricultural products supplier, consultant; b. Knoxville, Tenn., Dec. 25, 1936; s. Harry H. and Idelle (Larue) M.; m. Eleanor Harb, Aug. 9, 1958; children: Cathleen, Sharon. BS in Agr., U. Tenn., 1958; MS in Agrl. Econs., U. Ill., 1959; PhD in Agrl. Econs., Mich. State U., 1963. Sr. market analyst Pet Milk Co., St. Louis, 1963-64; mgr. market planning agr. chems. div. Mobile Chem. Co., Richmond, Va., 1964-67; mgr. ingredient purchasing Central Soya Co., Ft. Wayne, Ind., 1970-73, corp. economist, 1967-70, v.p. ingredient purchasing, 1973-75, sr. v.p., 1975-90; pres. Marine Assocs., Ft. Wayne, 1991—; bd. dirs. SCAN, 1992—. Mem. agrl. policy adv. com. U.S.D.A. Bd. dirs. Ft. Wayne Fine Arts Found., 1976-79, Ft. Wayne Pub. Transp. Corp., 1975-83, Libr. Found.; commr. Metro Human Rels. Commn.; v.p. Ft. Wayne Philharm., 1974-76. Served with U.S. Army, 1959-60. Mem. Nat. Soybean Processors Assn. (chmn.), U.S. C. of C., Am. Agrl. Econs. Assn., Am. Feed Mfrs. Assn. (chmn. purchasing coun.). Clubs: Ft. Wayne Country. Episcopalian. Office: Marine Assocs 4646 W Jefferson Blvd Fort Wayne IN 46804-6842 Office Phone: 260-436-4180. E-mail: lmarine@proparkwest.com.

MARINE, MICHAEL W., ambassador; b. NYC, 1947; married; 2 children. BA summa cum laude in Chinese Hist., U. Calif., Santa Barbara, 1974. With US Dept. State, Washington, 1985—, various positions, 1985—91; dep. chief of mission US Embassy, Suva, Fiji, 1991—93, charge d' affaires, 1993—94, min. counselor for consular affairs Bonn, 1994—95, Moscow, 1995—97, dep. chief of mission Nairobi, Kenya, 1997—2000, charge d' affaires, 1999, dep. chief of mission Beijing, 2000—04; US amb. to Vietnam US Dept. State, Hanoi, 2004—. Joined Fgn. Svc., 1975, consular officer, 1979—81, polit. officer, Hong Kong, 1982—85. Advanced through grades to capt. USMC, 1967—71. Office: DOS Amb 4550 Hanoi Pl Washington DC 20521 *

MARINE, SUSAN SONCHIK, analytical chemist, educator; b. Maple Heights, Ohio, Mar. 10, 1954; d. Stephen Robert and Gloria Ann (Hach) Sonchik; m. Michael David Marine; 1 child, Matthew Robert Marine. BS in Chemistry magna cum laude, John Carroll U., Cleve., 1975; MS in Analytical Chemistry, Case Western Res. U., Cleve., 1978; PhD in Phys. Chemistry, Case Western Res. U., 1980. Asst. chemist Horizons Research Inc., Beachwood, Ohio, 1974-75; chemist specialist Standard Oil of Ohio, Warrensville Heights, Ohio, 1975-79; organic chemistry br. mgr. Versar, Inc., Springfield, Va., 1980-83; mgr. gas chromatography program IBM Instruments Inc., Danbury, Conn., 1983-87, radiation safety officer, 1985-87; expert witness, cons. Martin, Craig, Chester & Sonnenschein, Chgo., 1981-83; adv. engr. in advanced lithography IBM Corp., Essex Junction, Vt., 1987-95; vis. assoc. prof. chemistry Centre Coll., Danville, Ky., 1995-98; asst. prof. chemistry and biochemistry, coord. tech. program Miami U., Middletown, Ohio, 1998—2004; spl. term appointment energy sys. divsn. Argonne Nat. Lab., Ill., 2003—05; assoc. prof. chemistry and biochemistry, coord. tech. program Miami U., Middletown, Ohio, 2004—. Vis. asst. prof. chemistry and math. Heritage Coll., 1991—92; spkr. in field. Author: African Walking Safari, 1985; editl. adv. bd. Jour. Chromatographic Sci., 1977-93, guest editor, 1987. Active Danbury Conservation Commn., 1986-87, tchr. and tutor chemistry, 1985-89, 91-92, 94; troop leader Lake Erie coun. Girl Scouts U.S.A., 1971-80, Southwestern Conn., 1983-87; leader explorer post Cleve. coun. Boy Scouts Am., 1977-78, venture crew co-leader Dan Beard coun., 2006—; managerial advisor Jr. Achievement, Warrensville Heights, Ohio, 1977-78; judge State or Regional Sci. Fair, 1977, 80, 89-91, 99-2000, Odyssey of the Mind, 1994; asst. leader Internat. Folk Dancers, Newtown, Conn., 1985-87; tchr. religion, 1981-84, 87-90, 93-94; sch. bd. John XXIII Elem. Sch., 2004-07. Recipient Overall Best Paper award Eastern Analytical Symposium, 1984, First Gas Chromatograph award IBM Instruments Inc., 1985, contbn. award (tech. paper) 10th Internat. Congress of Essential Oils, Flavors, Fragrances, Washington, 1986. Mem. Am. Chem. Soc. (chmn. membership com. Green Mountain sect. 1988-89, chmn. 1990-91, local coord. Nat.

Chemistry Week 1991, 93-98, 2002-04, nat. com. on technician affairs 2005—, nat. com. on cmty. activities 2005, subcom. chmn. 2007, chmn. edn. com. nat. tech. divsn. 2007, Phoenix award 1994, 97, Salute to Excellence award 2004), Iota Sigma Pi (pres. N.E. Ohio chpt. 1978-79, mem.-at-large fin. mgr. 1993-97, nat. v.p. 1996-99, nat. pres. 1999-2002, immediate past pres. 2002-05), No. Vt. Canoe Cruisers (treas. 1990-92), Green Mountain Steppers (sec. 1993-95), Centre Coll. Outdoors Club (faculty advisor 1996-98), Miami U. Middletown Chemistry Club (faculty advisor 2003-04), Miami U. Middletown Ski and Snowboard Club (faculty advisor 2004-06), Phi Theta Kappa (faculty advisor Miami U. Middletown 2004—). Roman Catholic. Avocations: camping, dance, travel. Home: 4667 Sebald Dr Franklin OH 45005-5328 Office: Miami U Middletown 4200 E University Blvd Middletown OH 45042-3458

MARINELLI, JANICE, broadcast executive; b. NY, 1958; m. Thomas Mazza; 3 children. BS in Comm., St. John's U., NY. Rsch. analyst TeleRep; sr. rschr. Lorimar TV, Katz TV Group; acct. exec. Buena Vista TV, 1985, dir. sales western divsn., exec. v.p., 1996—99, pres. Burbank, Calif., 1999—. Named one of 100 Most Powerful Women in Entertainment, Hollywood Reporter, 2006. Office: Buena Vista TV 500 S Buena Vista St Burbank CA 91521 *

MARINELLI, ROD, professional football coach; b. Rosemead, Calif., July 13, 1949; m. Barbara Marinelli; children: Chris, Gina. Attended, Univ. Utah, 1968, Calif. Lutheran, 1970—72. Asst. coach Rosemead Highschool, Calif., 1973—75; defensive line coach Utah St. U., 1976—81, offensive line/spl. teams coach, 1982; defensive line coach U. Calif., 1983—91; asst. coach, defensive line coach Ariz. State U., 1993—95; defensive line coach U.S.C., 1995—96, Tampa Bay Bucaneers, 1996—2006; head coach Detroit Lions, 2006—. Served in US Army, 1969, Vietnam. Recipient All-Am. honors, NAIA, 1972. Office: Detroit Lions 222 Republic Drive Allen Park MI 48101

MARINELLO, KATHRYN V., information technology executive; b. 1956; married; 3 children. BS, SUNY, Albany; MBA, Hofstra U. Mgmt. positions with Barclay's, Citibank, Chemical Bank; pres. U.S. Bank Card Services; pres. electronic payments group First Data Corp.; mgmt. positions with Gen. Electric, 1997—2006, exec. v.p GE card services, pres. GE Capital cons. fin. services, pres., CEO GE Fin. Assurance Mktg. group, pres., CEO GE Fleet Services, 2002—06; pres., CEO Ceridian Corp., Mpls., 2006—. Bd. dirs. GM Corp., 2007—. Bd. dir. Greater Twin Cities United Way, Minn. Bus. Partnership. Named an Industry Leader, Mpls./St. Paul Bus. Journal, 2006. Office: Ceridian Corp 3311 E Old Shakopee Rd Minneapolis MN 55425 *

MARINER, JONATHAN D., major league baseball executive; m. Mildred Mariner; children: Brian, Phillip, Matthew. BS in Acctg., U. Va.; MBA, Harvard U. CPA. Sr. fin. analyst to sr. mgr. MCI Comm., Washington; various positions including sr. mgr. mergers and acquisitions, strategic planning and budgets, and controller insurance ops. Ryder Truck Rental, Fla.; v.p. fin. and adminstrn. Greater Miami Convention and Visitors Bur.; v.p., CFO Fla. Panthers Hockey Club, 1993—94; CFO Pro Player Stadium; pres. Marlins Ballpark Devel. Corp.; exec. v.p., CFO Fla. Marlins Baseball Club, 1992—2000; COO, CFO Charter Schs. USA, 2000—02; exec. v.p., CFO Major League Baseball, 2002—. Bd. dirs. Charter Schs. USA, BankAtlantic Bancorp, Ryan, Beck and Co., Steiner Leisure Ltd. Chmn. Broward Cmty. Coll. Found. Bd.; mem. advisory bd. U. Va. McIntire Sch. Commerce, Pine Crest Sch., Ft. Lauderdale, Fla. Named one of 101 Most Influential Minorities in Sports, Sports Illustrated mag. Avocation: martial arts. Office: Major League Baseball 245 Park Ave 31st Fl New York NY 10167

MARINESCU, DAN CRISTIAN, computer sciences educator, consultant; b. Craiova, Dolj, Romania, Mar. 4, 1942; s. Nicolae and Aurelia Marinescu; m. Gabriela Magdalena Sezon; 1 child, Andrei. PhD in EECS, Polytechnic Inst., Bucharest, Romania, 1972—75. Prof. computer sci. Purdue U., West Lafayette, Ind., 1984—2001, U. Ctrl. Florida, Orlando, 2001—02; sr. rschr. GSI, Darmstadt, Fla., Germany, 1980—84, Inst. Atomic Physics, Bucharest, Romania, 1965—79; assoc. prof. Polytechnic Inst., Bucharest, 1970—79. Vis. prof. INRIA Rocquencourt, Paris, 2000—00, Paris, 1999—99, IBM Rsch., Yorktown Heights, NY, 1985—85, Intel Supercomputer Sys., Portland, 1992—92. Author: Internet-Based Workflow Management, 2002; contbr. articles to profl. jours., 1987. Recipient Grand Challenge, National Science Foundation, 1995-2002, Virtual Lab for Computational Biology, Nat. Sci. Found., 2001—, Workflow Management, 2001—, 3D Reconstruction of Viruses, 2000—. Greek Orthodox. Avocations: skiing, photography, travel. Home: 14449 Dover Forest Dr Orlando FL 32828 Office: Computer Sci Dept UCF 4000 Central Florida Blvd Orlando FL 32816 E-mail: danc.marinescu@gmail.com.

MARINETTI, GUIDO V., biochemistry professor; b. Rochester, NY, June 26, 1918; s. Michael and Nancy (Lippa) M.; m. Antoinette Francione, Sept. 19, 1942; children: Timothy D., Hope L. BS, U. Rochester, 1950, PhD, 1953. Research biochemist Western Regional Lab., Albany, Calif., 1953-54; instr. U. Rochester, NY, 1954-57, asst. prof., 1957-60, assoc. prof., 1960-66, prof. sch. medicine and dentistry, 1966—97; prof. emeritus dept biochemistry and biophysics, 1997—. Cons. Eastman Kodak, 1978, Rochester Gas & Electric, 1979 Author: Disorders of Lipid Metabolism, 1990, I Beat Heart Disease, So Can You; editor: Lipid Chromatographic Analysis, 3 vols., 1969, 2nd edit., 1976; contbr. over 165 pub. articles in sci. jours. Served with USAAF, 1942-46. Recipient Nat. Infantile Paralysis award, 1952; recipient Glycerine Research award, 1957; NSF grantee, 1953; recipient Lederle Med. Faculty award, 1955, 56 Mem. Am. Soc. Biol. Chemists, Am. Chem. Soc., AAAS, Sigma Xi, Phi Beta Kappa Achievements include research in membrane structure and function, biochemistry of phospholipids, phosphatidylinositiol metabolism in isolated synaptosomes, membrane hormone receptors. Personal E-mail: gmarn19@frontiernet.net.

MARING, DONALD GEORGE, JR., electrical engineer; s. Donald Maring Sr. and Ruth Maring; m. Margery Leader, Aug. 6, 1982; 1 stepchild, Chris Barnes. AS, Monroe CC, Rochester, NY, 1970; BS in Physics, Rensselaer Poly. Inst., Troy, NY, 1976; BSEE, Rochester Inst. Tech., NY, 1982, MSEE, 1989. Registered profl. engr., NY. R&D technician Lehigh Design, Xerox, Rochester, 1976—77; telecomm. sr. field svc. engr. Wescom/Rockwell-Wescom, Rochester, 1977—81; cir. devel. engr., sr. network engr. Rochester Telephone, Frontier Telephone, 1981—. Pilot Angel Flight Northeast, Rochester, 2002—06. Sgt. USAF, 1970—74. Mem.: Artisan Flying Club.

MARING, MARY MUEHLEN, state supreme court justice; b. Devils Lake, ND, July 27, 1951; d. Joseph Edward and Charlotte Rose (Schorr) Muehlen: m. David Scott Maring, Aug. 30, 1975; children: Christopher David, Andrew Joseph. BA in Polit. Sci. summa cum laude, Moorhead State U., 1972; JD, U. N.D., 1975. Bar: Minn., N.D. Law clk. Hon. Bruce Stone, Mpls., 1975—76; assoc. Stefanson, Landberg & Alm, Ltd., Moorhead, Minn., 1976—82, Ohnstad, Twichell, Breitling, Rosenvold, Wanner, Nelson, Neugebauer & Maring, West Fargo, ND, 1982—88, Lee Hagan Law Office, Fargo, ND, 1988—91; pvt. practice Maring Law Office, Fargo, 1991—96; justice ND Supreme Ct., Bismarck, ND, 1996—. Women's bd. mem. 1st Nat. Bank, Fargo, 1977-82; career day speaker Moorhead Rotarians, 1980-83; mem. Court Svcs. Com., 1996-, Jud. Compensation, subcom. of Jud. Conf., 1998-, Five-State Jud. Conf. Planning Com., 1997-98, 99-2000; chmn. Gender Fairness Implementation Com., 1997-, Jud. Conf. Exec. Bd., 1998-, chair-elect, 2004-05, chair, 2005, Juvenile Drug Ct. Study, planning and Implementation Com., 1998-2000, Juvenile Drug Ct. Adv. Com., 2000-, Personnel Policy bd., 1999-2004, Govs. Drug and Alcohol Policy Adv. Bd., 1999-2001, N.Dak. Commn. on Drug and Alcohol Abuse, 2002-, No. Plains Ethics Inst., 2000-, Juvenile Policy Bd., 2001-, Jud. Edn. Com., 2005-, Jud. Planning Com., 2001-, Harold Schafer Leadership Ctr. Com. Contbr. note to legal rev.; note editor N.D. Law Rev., 1975. Mem. ABA (del. ann. conv. young lawyers sect. 1981-82, bd. govs. 1982-83), Minn. Women Lawyers, N.D. State Bar Assn. (bd. govs. 1991-93), Clay County Bar Assn. (v.p. 1983-84), N.D. Trial Lawyers Assn. (pres. 1992-93), Internat. Soc. of Barristers, Nat. Assn. of Women Judges (dist. 10 dir. 2001-03). Roman Catholic. Office: ND Supreme Ct 600 E Boulevard Ave Dept 180 Bismarck ND 58505-0530 *

MARINI, ALEX P., manufacturing executive; BS, MBA, Gannon Univ. Mgmt. positions through v.p., group controller Zurn Plumbing, Jacuzzi Brands Inc., West Palm Beach, Fla., 1969—84, v.p. sales, mktg. & adminstrn., 1984—87, pres. Wilkins div., 1987—96, pres., 1996—2005; pres., COO Jacuzzi Brands Inc., West Palm Beach, Fla., 2005—, bd. dir., CEO, 2006—. Past. pres. Fin. Executives Inst. Office: Jacuzzi Brands Inc Ste 1100 W 777 Flagler Dr West Palm Beach FL 33401

MARINI, ANN MARIE, medical researcher, educator; b. Stamford, Conn., May 27, 1949; d. Alfred Francis and Theresa Maryann Marini; m. Robert Henry Lipsky, Sept. 6, 1990; 1 child, Sarah. BA, Erskine Coll., 1971; PhD, Georgetown U., 1978, MD, 1980. Diplomate Am. Bd. Internal Medicine, Am. Bd. Psychiatry and Neurology. Med. resident U. Mass., Worcester, 1980-83; neurology resident Albert Einstein Coll. Medicine, Bronx, N.Y., 1983-86; post-doctoral fellow NIH, Bethesda, Md., 1986-93; staff neurologist Dept. Vet. Affairs, Washington, 1993-94; asst. prof. Uniformed Svcs. U. Health Scis., Bethesda, 1994-2001, assoc. prof., 2001—. Mem. Am. Acad. Neurology (tech. and therapeutics subcom. 1994-99), Soc. for Neurosci., Sigma Xi. Office: Uniformed Svcs U Health Scis 4301 Jones Bridge Rd Bethesda MD 20814-4712 Office Phone: 301-295-9686. Business E-Mail: amarini@usuhs.mil.

MARINI, FRANK NICHOLAS, political science and public administration educator; b. Melrose Park, Ill., June 18, 1935; s. Joseph and Lillian Lee (Stuart) M.; m. Elsie McKaskle Marini; children: Lisa M., Katherine D. BA, Ariz. State U., 1960, MA, 1961; PhD, U. Calif., Berkeley, 1966. Instr. U. Mo., Columbia, 1963-64; asst. prof. polit. sci. U. Ky., 1966-67; asst. prof. Syracuse U., 1967-70; assoc. prof., assoc. dean Syracuse U. (Maxwell Sch.), dir. public adminstrn. programs, 1970-73; dean Coll. Arts and Letters, San Diego State U., 1973-80; provost, v.p. acad. affairs Calif. State U., Fullerton, 1980-84, sr. adviser chancellor's office, 1984-85; sr. v.p., provost U. Akron, Ohio, 1985-90, prof. pub. adminstrn., urban studies, polit. sci. Ohio, 1990-96, prof. emeritus Ohio, 1996—. Author pamphlets; contbr. numerous articles to profl. jours.; editor: Toward a New Public Administration, 1971; mng. editor: Public Administrn. Rev, 1967-77; editor-in-chief Jour. Pub. Adminstrn. Edn., 1994-96. Served with USAF, 1954-58. Mem. Am. Soc. Pub. Adminstrn.

MARINI, ROBERT CHARLES, environmental engineering executive; b. Quincy, Mass., Sept. 29, 1931; s. Larry and Millie (Cirillo) M.; m. Myrna Lydia Pellegrini, June 26, 1955 (dec. June 1994); children: Debra, Robert Charles, Larry; m. B. Anne Jones, May 27, 1995. BSCE (hon.), Northeastern U., 1954, doctorate (hon.), 1997; SMSE, Harvard U., 1955, postgrad. in advanced mgmt., 1985. Registered profl. engr., Mass., N.Y., Calif., Mich., Va. Jr. engr. Camp Dresser & McKee Inc., Boston, 1955-56, project engr., 1958-64, assoc., 1964-67, ptnr., sr. v.p., 1967-77, pres. environ. engring. div., 1977-82, exec. v.p., 1982-84, pres., 1984-90, CEO, 1989-98, chmn. bd. dirs., 1998—99, vice chmn. bd. dirs., 1999-2001, chmn. emeritus, 2001—. Mem. civil engring. adv. com. Worcester (Mass.) Poly. Inst. 1985-90, U. Mass., 1986-90, U. Tex., Austin, 1989-91, chmn., 1991-92, mem. engring. found. adv. coun., 1991-98; trustee South Shore Savs. Bank, 1990—, audit com., 2001-. Contbr. articles to profl. jours. Dir. nat. coun. Northeastern U., Boston, 1983-2004, mem. corp. bd., 1983-2004, bd. overseers, 1985-89, trustee, 1989-2004; chmn. Leadership Phase Century II Fund, 1989-91, chmn. devel. com., 1991-98, vice chmn. bd. trustees, 1997-2004, vice chmn. emeritus, 2004-; bd. dirs. Mass. Bus. Round Table, 1991-99, vice chmn., 1995-97, chmn., 1997-99. Recipient Disting. Eagle Scout award Boy Scouts Am., 1986, Mass. Patriots award Old Colony Coun., 1998, W. Erwin Story award, 1991, Outstanding Civil Engring. Alumni award Northeastern U., 1992, Outstanding Alumni award, 1993; named Man of Yr., Don Orione, 1999. Fellow ASCE (hon., Opal award 2003), NAE, Boston Soc. Civil Engrs. (hon.); mem. Am. Pub. Works Assn. (Man of Yr. award New Eng. chpt. 1981), Am. Water Works Assn., Mass. Soc. Profl. Engrs. (Young Engr. of Yr. award 1966), Am. Acad. Environ. Engrs. (diplomate, trustee at large 1989-92, v.p. 1992-93, pres.-elect 1993-94, pres. 1994-95, Stanley E. Kappe award 1992, Gordon Maskew Fair award, 2005), Water Environment Fedn. (hon., N.E. chpt., Founders award 1999), Internat. Assn. Water Pollution Rsch. and Control, Engring. Soc. New Eng. (New Eng. award 1994), Greater Boston C. of C. (bd. dirs. 1997-99), Water Environ. Rsch. Found. (bd. dirs. 1998-2001), Tau Beta Pi, Phi Kappa Phi. Roman Catholic. Home: 1 Nevin Rd Weymouth MA 02190-1610 Office: Camp Dresser & McKee Inc 50 Hampshire St Cambridge MA 02139 Home Phone: 781-337-0068; Office Phone: 617-452-6000. Business E-Mail: marinirc@cdm.com.

MARINIS, THOMAS PAUL, JR., lawyer; b. Jacksonville, Tex., May 31, 1943; s. Thomas Paul and Betty Sue (Garner) M.; m. Lucinda Cruse, June 25, 1969; children: Courtney, Kathryn, Megan. BA, Yale U., 1965; LLB, U. Tex., 1968. Bar: Tex. 1968. Assoc. Vinson & Elkins, Houston, 1969-76, ptnr., 1977—. Bd. dirs. Phoenix House of Tex., Inc. Fellow Tex. Bar Found.; mem. ABA (sec. taxation sect. 1986-87), Houston Country Club, Houston Ctr. Club, Coronado Club. E-mail: tmarinis@velaw.com.

MARINKOVIC, SERGE PETER, urologist, educator, surgeon; s. Sergio Fabian and Elsa Salvadora Marinkovic; m. Christina Mallusack Plymale, May 23, 2003. BA in Biology, NYU, 1985; MD, Wayne State U., Detroit, 1991. Diplomate Am. Bd. Urology, 2005. Gen. surgery internship Providence Hosp., Southfield, Mich., 1991—92; urology internship Brown Sch. Medicine, Providence, 1992—94, Geisinger Med. Ctr., Danville, Pa., 1995—95; female urology & prosthetics fellowship Smith Inst. Urology, LI Jewish Hosp., New Hyde Pk., NY, 1998—99; urogynecology fellowship Stuart L. Stanton Urogynecology Unit, St. George's Hosp., London, 1999—2001; assoc. prof. female urologist/female reconstructive surgery So. Ill. U. Sch. Medicine, Springfield, 2001—. Attending female reconstructive surgeon Women's & Children's Hosp., Lafayette, La., 2005—. Contbr. articles to med. jours. Recipient Thirlby award, Am. Urol. Assn., 2004, 2005; Basic Sci. grantee, LI Jewish Hosp., 1999. Fellow: Am. Urogynecology Assn. (assoc.); mem.: Soc. Female Urology and Urodynamics. Republican. Roman Catholic. Avocations: piano, rare books. Office: Suite A220 4540 Ambassador Pkwy Lafayette LA 70508 Office Phone: 337-504-2671. Office Fax: 337-504-2673. Personal E-mail: urourogyn@yahoo.com.

MARINO, DAN (DANIEL CONSTANTINO MARINO JR.), sportscaster, retired professional football player; b. Pitts., Sept. 15, 1961; s. Daniel and Veronica Marino; m. Claire Veazey, Jan. 30, 1985; adopted children: Niki Lin, Lia children: Daniel Charles, Michael Joseph, Joseph Donald, Alexandra Claire. BA in Comm., U. Pitts., 1983. Quarterback Miami Dolphins, 1983—99; co-host Inside the NFL, HBO, 2000—, NFL Today, CBS, 2002—. Actor: (films) Ace Ventura: Pet Detective, 1994; co-author (with David Hyde): Dan Marino: My Life in Football, 2005. Founder Dan Marino Found., 1991—, Dan Marino Ctr., 1998—. Named All-Am. team quarterback, The Sporting News, 1981, Rookie of Yr., 1983, All-Pro, 1984—86; named to Am. Pro Bowl Team, 1983—87, Pro Bowl Team, 1991—92, 1994—95; recipient Bert Bell Most Valuable Player award, Maxwell Club, 1984, NFL MVP award, AP, 1984, NFL Comeback Player of Yr., 1994, Walter Payton Man of Yr. award, 1998. Achievements include holding the NFL record for career passing yards (61,361), passing attempts (8,358), touchdown passes (420), single season passing yards, (5,084), 1984; NFL record for most games (12) with 400 or more yards passing; NFL records for most seasons (6) with 4,000 or more yards passing, most seasons (9) with 3,000 or more yards passing, 1984-92; most games (17) with four or more touchdown passes, 1984; most consecutive games (4) with four or more touchdown passes, 1984; lowest percentage (2.03) of passes interecepted by a rookie, 1983; inducted into the Coll. Football Hall of Fame, 2003, Pro Football Hall of Fame, 2005. Office: Dan Marino Found PO Box 267640 Weston FL 33326 *

MARINO, EUGENE LOUIS, publishing executive, director; b. NYC, Jan. 7, 1929; s. Salvatore A. and Florence M. (Casabona) M.; m. Patricia Ryan, Mar. 11, 1948; children: Jeanette, Anthony, John, Eugene III. Student, Columbia U., 1945-48. Credit mgr. Sears, Roebuck Inc., LI, NY, 1951-60; gen. credit mgr. Davison-Paxon div. R.H. Macy, Inc., Atlanta, 1960-63, Grand-Way div. Grand Union Co., NYC, 1963-66; v.p., gen. credit mgr. Consumer Products div. Singer Co., NYC, 1966-75, Grolier, Inc., Danbury, Conn., 1975-90; ret. Officer, v.p., gen. credit mgr., dir. numerous subsidiaries. Recipient Quarter Century cert. Internat. Consumer Credit Assn., 1981. Mem. Mchts. Rsch. Coun., Internat. Consumer Credit Assn., Nat. Assn. Credit Mgmt., Alpha Sigma Phi. Home: 4858 Tivoli Ct Sarasota FL 34235-3653 E-mail: elmarino@comcast.net.

MARINO, GIOVANNI, surgeon; b. Catania, Italy, Dec. 23, 1969; s. Salvatore and Rosetta (Rapisarda) Marino. MD with honors, U. Catania, 1993, PhD, 2001. Cert. in Medicine 1993, in General Surgery with honors Italian Bd. Surgery, 2001. Internship U. Catania, Dept. Plastic Surgery, 1992—93; chief med. officer Italian Air Force, Rieti Mil. Base, Italy, 1994—95; fellow Dept. of Surg. Oncology, San Luigi Hosp., Catania, 1999—2001; primary care physician Italian Health Sys., Vizzini, Italy, 2001. Vis. fellow U. Pisa (Italy) Dept Surg. Endoscopy, 1996—97; vis. fellow Great Ormond St. Hosp., London, 1999; instr. surgery Thomas E. Starzl Transplantation Inst., U. Pitts., 2003—05. Author: Experimental Models of Liver Transplantation, 1998, Abdominal Surgery Today, 1999, Laparoscopic Approach to the Essential Varicocele, 2000, Surgery in Old Age, 2000; contbr. articles to profl. jours. Chief med. officer Italian Air Force, 1994—95, Rieti, Italy. Recipient S.I.S.M Scholarship, Italian Soc. of Med. Students, 1992, Fulbright Scholarship, Thomas E. Starzl Transplantation Inst., Fulbright Commn., 2001-2002. Mem.: Surg. Soc. Catania, European Assn. for Endoscopic Surgery, Internat. Liver Transplantation Soc., Italian Soc. Young Surgeons, Italian Soc. Endoscopic Surgery, Sicilian Soc. Surgery, Med. Soc. Catania. Achievements include first to perform laparoscopic robot assisted andrenalectomy; use a robot AESOP to perform endoscopy operations. Personal E-mail: marinog2312@yahoo.it.

MARINO, IGNAZIO ROBERTO, transplant surgeon, educator, researcher; b. Genoa, Italy, Mar. 10, 1955; s. Pietro Rosario and Valeria (Mazzanti) M.; m. Rossana Parisen-Toldin, Sept. 15, 1990; 1 child, Stefania Valeria. Maturità-Classica, Coll. of Merode, Rome, 1973; MD, Cath. U., Rome, 1979. Diplomate Nat. Bd. Gen. Surgery, Nat. Bd. Vascular Surgery. Intern, then resident Gemelli U. Hosp., Rome, 1979-84; temp. asst. dept. surgery Cath. U., Rome, 1981, asst. prof. surgery, 1983-92; asst. prof. surgery Transplantation Inst. U. Pitts., 1991-95, assoc. prof. surgery Transplantation Inst./, 1995-99; prof. surgery postgrad. Sch. Microsurgery, Exptl. Surgery U. Milan, 1994—; prof. surgery Sch. Medicine U. Perugia, 1994—; attending surgeon U. Pitts. Med. Ctr., Pitts., 1991—2002; assoc. dir. transplant divsn. VA Med. Ctr., Pitts., 1992—2002; attending surgeon Children's Hosp. Pitts., 1993—; prof. surgery Transplantation Inst., U. Pitts., 1999—2002, Thomas Jefferson Med. Coll., Phila., 2002—; dir. divsn. transplantation Thomas Jefferson U. Hosp., Phila., 2004—06; sen. Repub. of Italy, 2006—. Mem. surg. team 1st and 2d baboon to human liver transplants U. Pitts. Med. Ctr., 1992-93, dir. European med. divsn., 1995-02; sci. journalist Agenzia Nazionale Stampa Associata, 1992—; nat. ad hoc donations com. United Network for Organ Sharing, 1995—; cons. Nat. Transplant Com. Italy, 1999—; regional com. Organ Procurement Orgn. for Sicily, 1999—; mem. Nat. Tech. Commn. for Informative Campaign on Organ Donation of Italy, 1999—, Nat. Ctr. Transplantation of Italy, 2000—; co-founder, pres. Imagine ONLUS, 2005-; chmn. standing health com. Italian Senate, 2006-. Author: New Technique to Avoid the Revascularization Syndrome in Liver Transplantation, 1985 (Ann. prize Italian Soc. Surgery, 86), New Technique in Liver Transplantation, 1996 (De Angelis award, 86); mem. editl. bd.: Clin. Transplantation, Leadership Medica, Transplantation, Jour. Investigative Surgery; contbr. more then 600 sci. articles to profl. jours. Co-founder, pres. Imagine, 2005-. Grantee Italian Nat. Coun. Rsch., 1979, 86-93, Gastroenterology Soc., 1988; recipient award Inst. Nazionale Previdenza Dirigenti Aziende Industriali, 1982. Mem. ACS, Am. Soc. Transplantation Surgeons, Am. Soc. Transplant Physicians, Italian Soc. Surgery, Transplantation Soc. (grant 1988), European Soc. for Organ Transplantation, Soc. Surgeons Under 40 (ann. prize 1986), Cell Transplant Soc. (founding mem.), Acad. Surg. Rsch., Soc. Critical Care Medicine, Internat. Liver Transplantation Soc., Italian Order Journalists, Assn. Italian Corrs. in N.Am. (assoc.), Xenotransplantation Club (founding mem.), Internat. Coll. Surgeons, Assn. for Acad. Surgery, Nat. Assn. VA Physicians, Univ. Physician Practice Assn., Xenotransplantation Assn., Am. Assn. for the Study of Liver Diseases. Avocations: reading (history books), sailing, scuba diving, yoga. Home: Corso Italia 29 Rome 00198 Italy Office: Thomas Jefferson U Ste 605 Coll Bldg 1025 Walnut St Philadelphia PA 19107-5083 Office Phone: 215-955-8920. Business E-Mail: ignazio.marino@jefferson.edu.

MARINO, JANE B., library director; m. Jim Marino; 3 children. BA, LeMoyne Coll.; MLS, Long Island U., 1989. Dir. Bronxville Pub. Libr., White Plains, NY. Author: Sing Us a Story: Using Music in Preschool and Family Storytime, 1992, Babies in the Library, 2003. Mem.: NY Libr. Assn., Assn. Libr. Svc. to Children (chair early childhood and parent edn. com. 2000—01, mem. bd. dirs., mem. preconference planning com., mem. Caldecott award com., mem. publications com., v.p./pres.-elect 2006—07, pres. 2007—), ALA. Office: Bronxville Public Library 60 Woodcrest Ave White Plains NY 10604 Office Phone: 914-337-7680. Office Fax: 914-337-0332. E-mail: jbmarino@optonline.net.

MARINO, JOSEPH PAUL, SR., dean, chemist, researcher; s. Paul M. and Anella Marino; m. Yolanda Lucia Lizardi, Dec. 7, 1967; children: Joseph Paul Jr., Yolanda Maria Marino Swartz, Sylvia Maria Marino Chapman. BS, Pa. State U., State College, 1963; AM, Harvard U., Cambridge, Mass., 1965, PhD, 1967. Prof. chemistry U. Mich., Ann Arbor, 1969—2002, assoc. dean, 1994—97, chair dept. chemistry, 1997—2002; dean sci., prof. chemistry U. Notre Dame, Ind., 2002—. Fellow, NIH, 1967—69, US Govt., 1985. Mem.: Am. Chem. Soc. Home: 52219 Farmington Sq Rd Granger IN 46530 Office: U Notre Dame Coll Sci Notre Dame IN 46556 Home Phone: 574-631-6456; Office Phone: 574-631-6456. Office Fax: 574-631-8149; Home Fax: 574-631-8149. Business E-Mail: marino.12@nd.edu.

MARINO, LOUIS J(OHN), mathematics educator; b. Whitestone, NY, May 3, 1949; s. Lewis F. and Lillian (Sheilds) M.; m. Sheila Burris, Dec. 19, 1969; children: Sheila Noelle, Heather Michelle. BS, U. Tenn., 1971, MS, 1975; MA in Teaching, U. S.C., 1977; AS in Engring., Piedmont Tech. Coll., 1981. Cert. tchr., S.C., learning disabled, 2002-, elem. edn., 2001-, nat. bd. candidate, 2004. Salesman Harper Bros., Inc., Greenwood, S.C., 1971-72; tchr. Orangeburg County (S.C.) Sch. Dist. 5, 1975-76, Greenwood County (S.C.) Sch. Dist. 50, 1976-77; mgr. Burger King, Greenwood, 1977-79; tchr. Laurens County (S.C.) Sch. Dist. 55, 1980-94; math. tchr. Long Cane Acad., McCormick, SC, 1994-95, math tchr., 2000—01; entrepreneur, 1995-98; security agent Omnisec, Greenville, SC, 1998-99; math tchr. McCormick Mid. Sch., SC, 2001—02, Greenville County Sch. Dist., 2002—; math and sci. tchr. Woodmont Mid. Sch., 2002—05; spl. edn. tchr. Calhoun Falls H.S., 2005—. Adj. prof. Limestone Coll., Spartanburg, S.C., 1978-79, Piedmont Tech. Coll., Greenwood, 1979-81. S.C. Dept. Edn. grantee, 1986. Mem. Laurens County Edn. Assn. (pres. 1991-92, sec. 1980-83, 90-91, assn. rep. 1984-94, mem. svcs. 1984-86, chmn. membership com. 1988-89), Nat. Model Railroad Assn., 2001—, Phi Delta Kappa. Democrat. Presbyterian. Avocations: astronomy, model trains, coin collecting/numismatics. Home: 103 Essex Ct Greenwood SC 29649-9561

MARINO, MIGUEL ANGEL, engineering educator; b. Cienfuegos, Cuba, Nov. 10, 1940; arrived in US, 1957; s. Ramon and Julia Marino; m. Irma Padovani, July 27, 1968; 1 child, Raquel Christina. AA, Andrew Coll., 1959; BS, N.Mex. Inst. Mining and Tech., 1962, MS, 1965; PhD, UCLA, 1972. Asst. geohydrologist N.Mex. State Engrs. Office, Santa Fe, 1964; asst. hydrologist Ill. State Water Survey, Champaign, 1965-69; from asst. prof. to assoc. prof. U. Calif., Davis, 1972—80, prof., 1980-99, dir. hydrology program, 1996-98, prof. above-scale, 1999—2003, disting. prof., 2003—. Author: Groundwater and Seepage, 1982, Regional Management of Water Resources, 2001, Integrated Water Resources Management, 2001, (monograph) Subsurface Flow and Contamination, 1987; contbr. articles to profl. jours. Pres./elect Am. Inst. of Hydrology, 2003—05; v.p. Internat. Commn. Water Resources Sys.; bd. dirs. Univs. Coun. Water Resources. Recipient Warren A. Hall medal, Univs. Coun. Water Resources. Fellow: Am. Geophys. Union, Am. Water Resources Assn. (hon.); mem.: ASCE (hon. Outstanding Jour. Paper awards 1986, 1990, Julian Hinds award 1996, Richard R. Torrens award 1986), Internat. Assn. Hydrol. Scis. (Best Paper award), Am. Inst. Hydrology (pres.-elect, cert.), Am. Water Resources Assn., N.Y. Acad. Scis., Sigma Xi, Tau Beta Pi. Home: 813 Harrier Pl Davis CA 95616-0173 Office: Univ Calif 139 Veihmeyer Hall Davis CA 95616 Office Phone: 530-752-0684. Business E-Mail: MAMarino@ucdavis.edu.

MARINO, NANCY A., marketing professional; b. NYC, Aug. 11; d. Thomas and Ruth Firriolo; m. J. Richard Marino. BA in Mktg., Hunter Coll., 1971. Exec. v.p. AMC, NYC, 1990—97; pres., CEO Frederick Atkins, NYC, 1997—99; pres. Linmark, NYC, 1999—2002, SVP Brand Devel. Worldwide Sourcing, 2002—04; exec. dir. NMG Consulting Corp., NYC, 2004—05; sr. v.p. global sourcing Hanes Branded Apparel, 2005—. Bd. dirs. Cotton Inc., NYC. Mem. found. bd. Fashion Inst. Tech., NYC, 1999—. Mem.: Retail Mktg. Soc. (bd. dirs. 1998—). Office: 1000 E Hanes Mill Rd Winston Salem NC 27105 Office Phone: 336-519-4439. Personal E-mail: nancymarino@earthlink.net.

MARINO, PETER, architect; Grad. in Architecture, Cornell U., Ithaca, NY. With Skidmore Owings & Merrill, George Nelson, I.M. Pei/Cossutta & Ponte; founder, prin. Peter Marino Arch., PLLC, NYC, 1978—. Prin. works include Giorgio Armani NY (Excellence in Design award, AIA, 1997), Estée Lauder Plaza NY (Excellence in Design award, AIA, 1999), Chanel Osaka (Excellence in Design award, AIA, 2001), Private London Residence (Nat. Honor award, AIA, 2005), Chanel, rue Cambon (Merit in Design award, AIA, 2004, Nat. Honor award, AIA, 2005), Nassau County Mus. Art, NY (Merit in Design award, 2006). Chmn. bd. Young Concert Artists; bd. mem. NY Found. Architecture, Venetian Heritage Found. Fellow: AIA. Office: Peter Marino Arch PLLC 150 E 58th St New York NY 10022 Office Phone: 212-752-5444. Office Fax: 212-759-3727. *

MARINO, SHEILA BURRIS, education educator; b. Knoxville, Nov. 24, 1947; d. David Paul and Lucille Cora (Maupin) Burris; m. Louis John Marino, Dec. 19, 1969; children: Sheila Noelle, Heather Michelle. BS, U. Tenn., 1969, MS, 1971, EdD, 1976; postgrad., W.Va. U., Europe, Clemson U. Elem./early childhood tchr. Knoxville City Schs., 1969-71; cooperating tchr. U. Tenn., Knoxville, 1969-71; dir. early childhood edn./tchr. Glenville (W.Va.) State Coll., 1971-72, Colo. Women's Coll., Denver, 1972-73; asst. prof. edn. Lander U., Greenwood, SC, 1973-75; instr., spl. asst. to coord. elem./early childhood edn. U. Tenn., 1975-76; prof. edn., dir. clin. experiences, asst. dean Lander U. Sch. Edn., 1976—93, dean, 1993-94, dir. sci. discovery program, 1995—, prof. edn., dir. tchg. fellows program, 1995—. Cons. in field; dir. Creative Activities Prog. for Children, Lander U., 1979—; mem. W.Va. Gov.'s Early Childhood Adv. Bd., 1971-72, Gov.'s Team of Higher Edn. Profls. on Comprehensive Plan for S.C. Early Childhood Edn., 1982. Contbr. articles to profl. jours. and books; author: International Children's Literature, 1989. Bd. dirs. Greenwood Lit. Coun., v.p., 1990, pres., 1991; bd. dirs. St. Nicholas Speech and Hearing Ctr., Greenwood, pres., 1992; bd. dirs. Old Ninety-Six coun. Girl Scouts U.S.A., 1987-92; vol. March of Dimes Program, Greenwood, 1987; vice chair Greenwood County First Steps, 2004—. Mem. AAUW (pres. 1990-92), AAUP, SNEA (state advisor 1981-88, 98-99), S.C. Student Edn. Assn., Piedmont Assn. Children and Adults with Learning Disabilities (pres. 1986-93, exec. bd.), Learning Disabilities Assn. S.C. (pres. 1990-94), S.C. Edn. Assn., S. C. Assn. for Children Under Six, So. Assn. for Children under Six, S.C. Assn. Tchr. Educators, Piedmont Reading Coun. (v.p. 1985-86, 90-91, pres. 1986-88, 91-92, 96-97), S.C. Coun. Internat. Reading Assn. (exec. bd. 1986-88, 91-96), Delta Kappa Gamma (pres. Epsilon chpt. 1984-88, 92-94, mem. exec. bd.), Pi Lambda Theta, Kappa Delta Pi (pres. U. Tenn. chpt. 1974-75), Phi Delta Kappa (v.p. 1988-90, pres. Lander U. chpt. 1990-91, 94-96, 2005—). Democrat. Presbyterian. Avocations: reading, gardening, swimming, music, arts and crafts. Home: 103 Essex Ct Greenwood SC 29649-9561 Office: Lander U Stanley Avenue Greenwood SC 29649

MARINO, THOMAS A., prosecutor, lawyer; b. 1952; AA, Williamsport Area C.C., 1983; BA, Lycoming Coll.; JD, Dickinson U. Assoc. McNerney, Page, Vanderlin & Hall, Williamsport, Pa., 1988—96; dist. atty. Lycoming County, Pa., 1996—2002; US atty. (mid. dist.) Pa. US Dept. Justice, 2002—. Office: US Atty's Office PO Box 309 Scranton PA 18501 *

MARINO, V. JAMES, consumer products company executive; Group v.p. mktg. Alberto-Culver No. Am., 2000—02; pres. personal care worldwide Alberto-Culver Co., Melrose Park, Ill., 2002—04, pres. consumer products worldwide, 2004—06, pres., CEO, bd. dir., 2006—. Office: Alberto-Culver Co 2525 Armitage Ave Melrose Park IL 60160 *

MARINO, WILLIAM FRANCIS, telecommunications industry executive, consultant; b. Phila., Dec. 28, 1948; s. William F. and Edith Ellen (Dougherty) M.; m. Mary Ellen Klems, Sept. 29, 1979; children: Kiersten Leigh, Meghan Lyn. Student, Ohio State U., 1967; BS in Fin. and Acctg., Widener U., 1970. Sr. acctg., fin. positions U.S. Steel Corp., Pitts., 1970-83; v.p. U.S. Steel Credit Corp., Pitts., 1983-85; dir. fin. programs CIS Corp., Syracuse, N.Y., 1985, v.p. instl. sales, 1986; pres. CIS Credit Corp., Syracuse, N.Y., 1987, v.p. fin., 1988; v.p., chmn. reorganization com. Continental Info. Systems Corp., Syracuse, N.Y., 1989; v.p. fin., CFO ITEC Corp., Lake Bluff, Ill., 1990-91, pres., CEO, 1991—, Global Telecom Svcs. Corp., 2000—. Advisor, cons. Chong & Assocs., N.Y.C., 1989. Advisor Hiawatha coun. Boy Scouts Am., Syracuse, 1987; dir. Cystic Fibrosis Found., Syracuse, 1987-88. Recipient Century award Boy Scouts Am., Syracuse, 1988. Mem. Am. Assn. Equipment Lessors, Am. Mgmt. Assn., Fin. Execs. Inst., Aircraft, Owners & Pilots Assn. Republican. Avocations: flying, cross country skiing. Home: 8763 Muirfield Dr Naples FL 34109-4352 Office: Global Telecom Svcs Corp 8763 Muirfield Dr Naples FL 34109-4352 Personal E-mail: billmarino@comcast.net.

MARINO, WILLIAM J., insurance executive; Various positions Prudential Ins. Co. Am., 1968-91, Horizon Blue Cross & Blue Shield of N.J., Inc., Newark, 1991-94; pres., CEO Horizon Blue Cross & Blue Shield of NJ Inc, Newark, 1994—. Mem. exec. com. Blue Cross/Blue Shield Assn. (BCBSA), chair Inter-Plan Operating Com. and Emerging Issues of BCBSA, bd. dirs. of Health Insurance Assn. of America, Nat. Inst. for Health Care Mgmt. Trustee, chmn. United Way of Essex and West Hudson, N.J., campaign chmn., 1993-94; chmn., bd. dirs., mem. exec. com. Regional Bus. Partnership; trustee N.J. Network Found., St. Peter's Coll., Newark Mus.; bd. pres. advisors Fairleigh Dickinson U.; mem. chief justice com. on efficiency N.J. Jud. Sys.; past trustee Kessler Inst. for Rehab., Inc. Mem. N.J. State C. of C., past chmn. bd. dirs., exec. com. Blue Cross/Blue Shield Assn. (BCBSA), Inter-Plan Operating Com., mem. Emerging Issues Com. of BCBSA, bd. dirs. Health Insurance Assn. of Amer., Nat. Inst. for Health Care Mgmt. Office: Horizon Blue Cross/Blue Shield NJ Inc 3 Penn Plz E Newark NJ 07105-2245

MARION, ANNE WINDFOHR, rancher, museum administrator; b. Fort Worth, Tex., Nov. 10, 1938; d. James Goodwin Hall and Anne (Burnett) Hall Tandy; m. John Louis Marion, 1988; 1 child, Anne Phillips Grimes. Attended, Univ. Tex., Austin, Univ. Geneva, Switzerland. Chmn. Burnett Oil Co.; pres. Burnett Ranches Ltd., 6666 Ranch, Guthrie, Tex., Burnett Found., Forth Worth, Tex. Chmn. Georgia O'Keeffe Mus., Santa Fe; trustee Kimbell Art Mus., Forth Worth, Tex.; trustee, former chmn. & pres., chmn. acquisition com. Modern Art Mus., Forth Worth, Tex.; past trustee Mus. Modern Art, NYC; mem. bd. regents Texas Tech. Univ.; dir. emeritus Nat. Cowboy Hall of Fame; mem. exec. com. Forth Worth Stock Show; honorary bd. mem. Nat. Cowgirl Hall of Fame, West. Heritage Ctr. Named Great Woman of Texas, Fort Worth Bus. Press, 1993; named one of Top 200 Collectors, ARTNews Mag., 2003—, Forbes Richest Americans, 2006; recipient Charles Goodnight award, 1993, Golden Deed honoree, Fort Worth Exchange Club, 1993, Fern Sawyer award, Nat. Cowgirl Hall of Fame, 1994, Gov. award for excellence in the arts, New Mex., 1996, Boss of the Plains award, Ranching Heritage Ctr., 2003. Mem.: Tex. & S.W. Cattle Raisers Assn. (honorary v.p.), Am. Quarter Horse Assn. (honorary v.p., Merle Wood Humanitarian award 1999). Mailing: Burnett Ranches Ltd PO Box 130 Guthrie TX 79236

MARION, JOHN LOUIS, former fine arts auctioneer and appraiser; b. NYC, Nov. 27, 1933; s. Louis John and Florence Adelaide (Winters) Marion; m. Anne Burnett Windfohr, May 26, 1988; children from previous marriage: John L., Deborah Mary, Therese Marie, Michelle Marie. BS, Fordham U., 1956; postgrad., Columbia U., 1960—61. With Sotheby Parke Bernet Inc., NYC, 1960—, dir., 1965—, v.p., 1966—70, exec. v.p., 1970—72, pres., 1972—87; chmn. bd. Sotheby's Inc., NYC, 1975—, now hon. chmn. Bd. dirs. Sotheby Holdings Inc., London, Mus. N.Mex. Sys. Chmn. fine arts NYC divsn. Am. Cancer Soc., 1983—; vice chmn. bldg. steering com. Dobbs Ferry (NY) Hosp., 1975; bd. dirs. Internat. Found. Art Rsch.; Ctr. for Hope. Lt. (j.g.) USN, 1956—60. Named one of Top 200 Collectors, ARTnews Mag., 2004—. Mem.: Appraisers Assn. Am., Vintage Club, Shady Oaks Club, Eldorado Club, Lotos Club. Avocation: Collector of 17th and 18th century European art; modern and contemporary art.

MARION, JOHN MARTIN, instructional technology educator; b. Fitchburg, Mass., Jan. 11, 1947; s. Don Louis and Violet Pearl Marion; m. Joann Elizabeth Marion, Aug. 8, 1970; children: Benjamin Andrew, Jessica Noelle. BS in Edn., Fitchburg State Coll., 1969, MEd, 1971; doctoral candidate in ednl. tech., Pepperdine U. Tchr. Groton Dunstable Regional Schs., Mass., 1969—84; computer tchr. Littleton Pub. Schs., Mass., 1985—86; computer coord. K-12th grades Newburyport Pub. Schs., Mass., 1986—90; assoc. dean Acad. Computing Endicott Coll., Beverly, Mass., 1990—98; dir. tech. Reading Pub. Schs., Mass., 1998—2000; media tech. specialist Dracut Pub. Schs., Mass., 2000—03; tech. edn. specialist Jefferson County Pub. Sch., Colo., 2003—. Instr. Merrimack Edn. Ctr., Chelmsford, Mass., 1980-90; trainer, cons. Logo Computer Sys., Inc., NYC, 1984-90; tchr. trainer Lego-Decta, Lego Sys., Inc., Enfield, Conn., 1987-90; mem. adv. bd. Claris Software Co.; bd. dirs. Mass. Computer Using Educator, 1989-90; master tchr. trainer Intel-Teach to the Future program Jefferson Pub. Schs., 2004—, info. literacy adv. com., 2004—. Bd. dirs. Reading Cmty. TV, Inc., 1998-99. Fulbright scholar tchr. exch., Southampton, Eng., 1973-74. Mem.: ASCD, Internat. Tech. Edn. Assn., Phi Delta Kappa. Office: Jeffco Schs 9201 W Columbine Dr Littleton CO 80128-4140 Home: 29191 Shadow Mountain Dr Conifer CO 80433-8612 Office Phone: 303-982-4130. Personal E-mail: jmarion@aol.com.

MARION, MARJORIE ANNE, English language educator, educational consultant; b. Winterset, Iowa, May 6, 1935; d. Virgil Arthur and Marilyn Ruth (Sandy) Hammon; m. Robert H. Marion, Dec. 20, 1964; 1 child, Kathryn Ruth BA, Colo. Coll., 1958; MA, Purdue U., 1969; postgrad., Inst. Mgmt. Lifelong Edn. Harvard U., 1981. Chairperson English dept. Lincoln-Way H.S., New Lenox, Ill., 1964—68; dir. pub. rels. U. St. Francis, Joliet, Ill., 1968—70, chairperson English dept., 1971—75, chairperson humanities and fine arts divsn., 1975—79, coord. instrnl. devel., 1979—80, dir. continuing edn., 1980—84, acting v.p. acad. affairs, 1984—85, dean faculty, 1985—89, assoc. prof. English, 1989—97, dir. Freshman Core Program, 1993—95, dir. Writing Ctr., 1996, prof. emeritus, 1997—. Cons. to presdl. search U. St. Francis, 2001—02; mem. vis. team North Ctrl. Assn., Joliet and Lockport, Ill., 1975—79; lectr. at ednl. workshops and instns.; condr. writing workshops for adults returning to coll., 1995—; TV and radio appearances regarding lifelong edn., Chgo., St. Louis, Albuquerque, Phoenix, 1982—85; lit. presenter in field, 2004—; lectr. writing workshops. Author: A Guide to Writing for the Faint at Heart, 1996; author monograph; drama critic Joliet Herald News, 1970-82 Chmn. Cath. Franciscan Charism Coun., 2005—06. Recipient Pres.'s award Coll. St. Francis, 1975 Mem. Am. Assn. Higher Edn., Nat. Coun. Tchrs. English, Nat. Acad. Advising Assn. Roman Catholic. E-mail: mamarion1@msn.com.

MARION, SHAWN, professional basketball player; b. Waukegan, IL, May 7, 1978; Student, Vincennes U., Ind., UNLV. Player Phoenix Suns, 1999—. Mem. Team USA, Goodwill Games, Brisbane, Australia, 2001, Team USA, World Championships, Indpls., 2002, US Olympic Basketball Team, Athens, Greece, 2004. Named to All-Rookie second team, 2000, Western Conf. All-Star Team, NBA, 2003, 2005, 2007, All-NBA Second team, 2005. Achievements include winning the Gold medal with team USA, Goodwill Games, 2001. Office: c/o Phoenix Suns 201 E Jefferson St Phoenix AZ 85004 *

MARIOTTI, JAY ANTHONY, journalist; b. Ellwood City, Pa., June 22, 1959; s. Geno Anthony and Dolores Virginia (Lordi) M.; m. Dana Lynne Barnard, Apr. 19, 1985; children: Karina, Allison. Student, Ohio U., 1976-80. Sports writer The Detroit News, 1980-85; sports columnist The Cin. Post, 1985-87, The Rocky Mountain News, Denver, 1987-89, The Denver Post, 1989-90, The Nat. Sports Daily, NYC, 1990-91, The Chgo. Sun-Times, 1991—. Recipient AP Sports Editors award, 1987, 1993, Crain's Forty under 40 award Crain's Chgo. Bus., 1992, Peter Lisagor award Chgo. Headline Club, 1992. Avocations: reading, tennis, golf, travel. Office: Chicago Sun Times 350 N Orleans St Ste 1270 Chicago IL 60654-2148

MARIOTTO, MARCO JEROME, dean, psychology educator, researcher; b. Ill., Oct. 21, 1946; s. Marco Anibele and Sally (Hughes) M.; m. Danita Irene Czyzewski, May 4, 1985; children: Ana-Sofia Antonia, Marco Luca. BS, U. Ill., 1968, PhD, 1974. Diplomate Am. Bd. Sexology, Am. Bd. Forensic Examiners; lic. psychologist; cert. sex therapist, cert. health svcs. provider. Asst. rsch. dir. Adolf Meyer Ctr. Rsch. Units, Decatur, Ill., 1972-74; psychologist U.S. Army Acad. Health Scis., San Antonio, 1974; asst. prof. Purdue U., West Lafayette, Ind., 1975-79; assoc. prof. U. Houston, 1979-90, supervisory psychologist, 1979—, prof., 1990—, dept. chmn., 1994—99, founding dean grad. and profl. studies, 1999—. Cons. NIMH, Bethesda, Md., 1977—, NSF, Washington, 1980-84, Nat. Inst. Drug Abuse, Bethesda, 1986-89; adj. prof. U. Tex. Health Scis., Houston, 1980—. Contbr. chpts. to books and articles to profl. jours.; also rsch. monographs and tech. reports. Forensic cons. Harris County Dist. Atty.'s Office, Houston, 1988—, ABA, 1989—; founding mem. Gulf Coast Consortium on Mental Health, Houston and Galveston, Tex., 1989. Capt. U.S. Army, 1968-74. Named one of top 35 Young Scientist Profls. Jour. Cons. and Clin. Psychology, 1988; David Ross fellow Purdue U., 1977. Mem. APA, Am. Psychol. Soc.; mem. AAAS, Midwestern Psychol. Assn. (local rep. 1979—), Sigma Xi. Achievements include co-devel. of TSBC/SRIC planned access infosystem for rsch. and svc. for patients in residential treatment settings; rsch. in observational measurement in mental health, schizophrenia, chronic mental patients. Office: U Houston Office of the Dean Grad and Profl Studies Houston TX 77204-2012 Home Phone: 713-748-2783; Office Phone: 713-743-9088. Business E-Mail: mmariotto@uh.edu.

MARIS, STEPHEN S., lawyer, educator; b. Dallas, Dec. 19, 1949; children: Shane, Kara. BS, Stephen F. Austin State, Nacogdoches, Tex., 1971; JD, So. Meth. U., Dallas, 1975. Bar: US Dist. Ct. (no. dist.) Tex. 1975, US Dist. Ct. (ea. dist.) Tex. 1986, US Dist. Ct. (so. dist.) Tex. 1992, US Ct. Appeals (5th cir.) 1980, US Ct. Appeals (11th cir.) 1981, US Supreme Ct. Tex. 1975. Assoc. Passman & Jones, Dallas, 1975-80, ptnr., 1980-87, Fulbright & Jaworski, Dallas, 1987-97, Jenkens & Gilchrist, Dallas, 1997—. Prof. So. Ill. U., 1979-80, So. Meth. U., Dallas, 1980—; mem. faculty Nat. Inst. Trial Advocacy, 1980—. Editor: Southwest Law Journal, 1973-75. Mem. ABA, State Bar Tex., Dallas Bar Assn., Barristers, Order Coif, Phi Delta Phi. Office: Hunton & Williams 1445 Ross Ave Ste 3700 Dallas TX 75202-2785 Office Phone: 214-468-3352. Business E-Mail: smaris@hunton.com.

MARISTUEN, KEITH A., lawyer; b. Malta, Mont., 1953; BA with high honors, U. Mont., 1975, JD with honors, 1978. Bar: Mont. 1978, US Tax Ct. 1980, US Ct. Appeals (9th Cir.). Mem. Bosch, Kuhr, Dugdale, Martin & Kaze PLLP, Havre, Mont. Mem.: ABA (mem. gen. practice sect. and small bus. sect.), Mont. State Bar Assn. (pres. 2004—05, chmn. bd. 2002—03, trustee 1992—, chmn. ethics com. 1995—2000, chmn. bankruptcy sect. legis. com. 1990—2002). Office: Bosch Kuhr Dugdale Martin & Kaze PLLP 335 Fourth Ave PO Box 7152 Havre MT 59501 Office Phone: 406-265-6706. Office Fax: 406-265-7578. Business E-Mail: kmaristuen@bkdlaw.org. *

MARITZ, W. STEPHEN, marketing professional, service executive; b. St. Louis; BS, Princeton U., 1980. With Maritz Inc., Fenton, Mo., 1983—, dir. sales, 1993—95, vice chmn. bd., 1994—, sr. v.p., 1995—97, pres., COO, 1997—98, CEO, pres., 1998—2001, chmn., CEO, 2001—. Bd. dir. Laclede Group Inc. Bd. dir. St. Louis Regional Chamber and Growth Assn. Office: Maritz 1375 N Highway Dr Fenton MO 63099

MARIUCCI, STEVE, professional football coach, former college football coach; b. Iron Mountain, Mich., Nov. 4, 1955; m. Gayle Mariucci; 4 children. Football coach No. Mich. U., 1978-79, Calif. State U., Fullerton, 1980-82; asst. head coach U. Louisville, 1983-84; receivers coach Orlando Renegades U.S. Football League, 1985; quality control coach L.A. Rams, 1985; receivers/spl. teams coach U. So. Calif. Trojans, LA, 1986, wide receivers/spl. teams coach, 1987-89, quarterbacks coach, offensive coord., 1990-91; quarterbacks coach Green Bay (Wis.) Packers, 1992-95; head coach U. Calif. Golden Bears, 1996-98, San Francisco 49ers, 1996—2003, Detroit Lions, 2003—05.

MARIYA, DEBORAH LUETHJE, minister; b. Long Beach, Calif., Feb. 26, 1953; d. Betty and Keith Luethje; m. Sam John Tangredi, May 21, 1994. BA, Augustana Coll., Sioux Falls, SD, 1977; MDiv, Garrett-Evangelical Theol. Sem., Evanston, Ill., 1984; D in Ministry, Wesley Theol. Sem., Washington, 2003. Ordained United Meth. Ch., 1983. Assoc. pastor Wesley United Meth. Ch., Muscatine, Iowa, 1982—83; pastor Danbury United Meth. Ch. and Oto United Ch. of Christ, Iowa, 1984—86, Dawson-Cooper-Greenbrier United Meth. Chs., Iowa, 1986—90; commd. lt. j.g. USN, 1988, advanced through grades to lt. comdr.; comd. chaplain USS Cape Cod, San Diego, 1990—93; hosp. chaplain, Protestant chapel pastor Nat. Naval Med. Ctr., Bethesda, Md., 1993—95; Protestant chaplain USNS Comfort, Balt., 1993—95; squadron chaplain Amphibious Squadron Five, San Diego, 1995—96; supr. chaplain Command Chaplains Assistance Team, Comdr. Naval Surface Force, U.S. Pacific Fleet, San Diego, 1996—98; comd. chaplain, chapel pastor Naval Security Sta., Washington, 1998—2000; ret. USN, 2000; pastor Chicamuxen (Md.) United Meth. Ch., 2001—04; with Joint Mil. Attaché Sch., 2004—05. Chaplain CAP, U.S. Air Force, Forest Glen, Md., 1994—2004. Author: Holy Places: Sacred Sites in Washington, DC and the Surrounding Region. County election ofcl. Bd. Elections, Arlington, Va., 2001—03; elder Iowa ann. conf. United Meth. Ch., 1986; deacon Iowa annual conf., 1983. Decorated Navy and Marine Corps Commendation Medal (five awards) Sec. of the Navy, Armed Forces Expeditionary Medal Sec. of Def., South West Asia Svc. Medal-three awards, Kuwait Liberation Medal Govt. of Saudi Arabia, Kuwaiti Freedom Medal Govt. of Kuwait, Navy and Marine Corps Achievement Medal Sec. of the Navy, Nat. Def. Medal Sec. of Def. Mem.: Balt.-Washington Ann. Conf. of United Meth. Ch., Navy Mut. Aid Assn. (resident dir. 1994—99), Mil. Chaplains Assn., Navy League, Women in Mil. Svc. for Am. Meml. Methodist. Achievements include first woman to serve aboard a US Navy Carrier in a combat zone. Home: USDAO Athens PSC 108 Box 21 Apo AE 09842 Mailing: 835 D Ave #1 Coronado CA 92118 Office: St Pauls United Meth Ch 700 D Ave Coronado CA 92118

MARJANCZYK, JOSEPH ANICETUS, priest; b. Elizabeth, NJ, Apr. 17, 1921; s. Joseph John and Catherine Frances (Cwik) M. BA, Seton Hall U., 1941; MDiv, Darlington Sem., 1975. Ordained priest Roman Cath. Ch., 1945; named monsignor, 1979. Asst. pastor St. Valentine's Ch., Bloomfield, NJ, 1945-72; pastor St. Adalbert's Ch., Elizabeth, 1972-83, Our Lady of Mt. Carmel Ch., Bayonne, NJ, 1983-96; named protonotary apostolic, 1988; vicar episcopal South Hudson Vicariate, 1991—96; prof. Polish Master Sch. Fgn. Langs., Seton Hall U., 1948-60; pastor emeritus Our Lady of Mt. Carmel Ch., Bayonne, 1996—. Chmn. pers. bd. Archdiocese of Newark, 1972-74, mem. pastoral coun., 1972-83, archdiocesan trustee 1975-86; chmn. adminstrv. com., mem. exec. bd. Archdiocesan Pastoral Coun., 1972-84; dean Union County East Deanery, 1975-83; Polish Apostolate rep. Nat. Conf. Cath. Bishops Com. on Migration, 1989-96, chmn. Polish adv. bd. to conf. office for pastoral care of migrants and refugees, 1989-96. Chmn. bd. dirs. Polish Cultural Found., 1974-90, 92-97, 98-2000; trustee Seton Hall U., 1978-96, Immaculate Conception Sem., South Orange, N.J., 1979-86; commr. bd. edn. City of Elizabeth, 1979-83; nat. chaplain Polish Army Vets. Assn. Am., 1980-98; founder, pres. emeritus N.J. chpt. John Paul II Found., 1986-2000; chmn. exec. bd. Polish chapel renovation and rededication Nat. Shrine of Immaculate Conception, Washington, 1986-89. Decorated Gold Order of Merit (Republic of Poland), 1988; recipient Polish Apostolate Pride of Polonia award, 1996, Nat. Polish Priests' Assn. award, 2006; named Canon of Cathedral chpt. Archdiocese Warsaw, Poland, 1995. Mem. Archdiocesan Polish Clergy Soc. (hon. pres. 1979—), Polish Am. Priests Assn. (exec. com. 1991-99, Nat. award 2006), Polish Am. Congress, Polish Am. Hist. Assn., N.J. Hist. Soc., Polish Am. Numis. Assn., Polonians Club, KC. Home: 1177 Edgewood Pkwy Union NJ 07083-8005

MARJORAM, PAUL, medical educator, researcher; b. Bishop's Stortford, Eng., Sept. 17, 1962; s. Lloyd Victor Marjoram and Daphne Jean Younger. BSc, Warwick U., Eng., 1984; diploma, Cambridge U., Eng., 1986; PhD, Quen Mary Coll., London, 1989. Postdoctoral rsch. fellow Queen Mary Coll., 1989—92, Monash U., Melbourne, Australia, 1992—95; rsch. asst. prof. U. So. Calif., LA, 1995—98, asst. prof., 1999—. Office: U So Calif Dept Preventive Medicine 1540 Alcazar St CHP-220 Los Angeles CA 90089-9011 Office Phone: 323-442-0111.

MARK, DANIEL BENJAMIN, cardiologist; b. Boston, Aug. 1, 1953; s. Vernon H. and Alexandra M.; m. M. Lee Cheney. BA, Hampshire Coll., 1974; MD, Tufts U., 1978; MPH, Harvard Sch. of Pub. Health, 1979. Intern U. Va. Hosp., Charlottesville, 1979-80, resident, 1980-82; fellow Duke U. Med. Ctr., Durham, N.C., 1982-85, assoc. in medicine, 1985-86, asst. prof. of medicine, 1987-92, assoc. prof. of medicine, 1993-98, prof. of medicine, 1998—, dir. Outcomes Rsch. and Assessment Group, 1994—. Editor: Am. Heart Jour., 1996—; author: (book) Acute Coronary Care; contbr. articles to numerous profl. jours. and publs. Recipient Rsch. Excellence award Assn. of Pharmacoecons. and Outcomes Rsch., 1997. Fellow: ACP, AHA (rsch. com. 2002—), Am. Soc. Clin. Investigation, Am. Coll. Cardiology (guideline com. AHCPR-NIH Unstable Angina Guideline 1994, database R&D com. 1998—2001, Coronary Stent Consensus Guidelines 2001—02, Exercise Testing Guidelines 2002); mem.: European Soc. Cardiology, Assn. Am. Physicians, Assn. Health Svcs. Rsch., Soc. for Med. Decision Making. Office: Duke Clin Rsch Inst 2400 Pratt Ave Rm 311 Durham NC 27705-3976 E-mail: daniel.mark@duke.edu.

MARK, HANS MICHAEL, physicist, former federal agency administrator; b. Mannheim, Germany, June 17, 1929; arrived in U.S., 1940, naturalized, 1945; s. Herman Francis and Maria (Schramek) M.; m. Marion G. Thorpe, Jan. 28, 1951; children: Jane H., Rufus J. AB in Physics, U. Calif., Berkeley, 1951; PhD, MIT, 1954; ScD (hon.), Fla. Inst. Tech., 1978; DEng (hon.), Poly. U. NY, 1982, Milw. Sch. Engring., 1991; LHD (hon.), St. Edward's U., 1993; ScD (hon.), Royal Mil. Coll. Sci., UK, 2004; DEng (hon.), Tri-State U., 2005. Rsch. assoc. MIT, Cambridge, 1954-55, asst. prof., 1958-60; rsch. physicist Lawrence Radiation Lab. U. Calif., Livermore, 1955-58, 60-69, exptl. physics divsn. leader, 1960-64, assoc. prof. nuc. engring. Berkeley, 1960-66, prof., 1966-69, chmn. dept. nuc. engring., 1964-69, lectr. dept. applied sci. Davis, 1969-73; cons. prof. engring. Stanford (Calif.) U., 1973-84; dir. NASA-Ames Rsch. Ctr., 1969-77; undersec. Air Force, dir. Nat. Reconnaissance Office USAF, Washington, 1977-79, sec. Air Force, 1979-81; dep. adminstr. NASA, Washington, 1981-84; chancellor U. Tex. Sys., Austin, 1984-92; prof. aerospace engring. and engring. mechanics U. Tex., Austin, 1988—; dir. defense rsch. and engring. Dept. Def., Washington, 1998-2001. Mem. Pres.'s Adv. Group Sci. and Tech., 1975-76; bd. dirs. Astronautics Corp. Am.; trustee Poly. U., 1984—. Author: (with N.T. Olson) Experiments in Modern Physics, 1966; (with E. Teller and J.S. Foster, Jr.) Power and Security, 1976; (with A. Levine) The Management of Research Institutions, 1983, The Space Station-A Personal Journey, 1987, (with Victor G. Szebehely) Adventures in Celestial Mechanics, 1998; also numerous articles; editor: (with S. Fernbach) Properties of Matter Under Unusual Conditions, 1969; (with Lowell Wood) Energy in Physics, War and Peace, 1988. Recipient Disting. Svc. medal NASA, 1972, 77, medal for exceptional engring. achievement, 1984, Exceptional Civilian Svc. award USAF, 1979, Disting. Pub. Svc. medal, Dept. Def., 1981, 2001, Sec.'s Gold medal Dept. Energy, 2001. Fellow AIAA (hon., Von Karman lectr. astronautics 1992), Am. Phys. Soc.; mem. NAE, Am. Nuc. Soc., Am. Geophys. Union, Coun. Fgn. Rels., Cosmos Club. Achievements include research on nuclear energy levels, nuclear reactions, applications, nuclear energy for practical purposes, atomic flourescence yields, measurement X-rays above atmosphere, spacecraft and experimental aircraft design. Office: U Tex Dept Aerospace Engring/Engr Austin TX 78712 Home Phone: 512-477-2753; Office Phone: 512-471-5077. Business E-Mail: hmark@mail.utexas.edu.

MARK, HON FONG LOUIE, cytogeneticist; m. Roger Mark; children: Yvonne, Roger Jr., Seamus. PhD, Brown U. Diplomate Am. Bd. Med. Genetics. Postdoctoral fellow in med. genetics R.I. Hosp., Providence, asst., assoc. dir. cytogenetics, fellow molecular biology, dir. cytogenetics, 1990-99, clin. cytogeneticist Cancer & Leukemia Group B, 1990—99; pres., CEO KRAM Corp., 1994—; dir. human genetics RIDOH, 1999—2001; exec. dir. RIACA, 2001—02; dir. cytogenetics dept. Presbyn. Lab. Svcs., Charlotte, NC, 2002—04; dir. cytogenetics Boston U. Sch. Medicine, 2004—, clin. prof., 2004—. Instr. pathology Brown U., Providence, asst. prof. pathology; clin. prof. Brown Med. Sch., 1998—; assoc. mem. Maine Toxicology Inst., 1993-96; chair grants rev. com. mem., prenatal diagnosis com., chair cancer genetics com., steering com.; grant reviewer NIH, U.S. Army Breast Cancer Rsch. Program, U.S. Army Prostate Cancer Rsch. Program; reviewer numerous other panels. Author: Medical Cytogenetics, 2000; mem. editl. rev. bd. Applied Cytogenetics, Pathobiology, Exptl. and Molecular Pathology, Cancer Genetics and Cytogenetics; contbr. 200 articles to profl. jours. Recipient award Time Mag. Essay Writing Contest, Balfour award, Award R.I. Found.; NSF rsch. grantee Brown U., co-grantee Dept. Energy; Florence Seibert postdoctoral fellowship AAUW Ednl. Found.; North Providence Citizens scholar, Fruithill Jr. Women's Club scholar; others. Fellow Am. Coll. Med. Genetics; mem. AAAS, Am. Soc. Human Genetics, Assn. Genetic Technologists, Sigma Xi.

MARK, JAMES B. D., surgeon, educator; b. Nashville, June 26, 1929; s. Julius and Margaret (Baer) M.; m. Jean Rambar, Feb. 5, 1957; children: Jonathan, Michael, Margaret, Elizabeth, Katherine. BA, Vanderbilt U., 1950, MD, 1953. Intern, resident in gen. and thoracic surgery Yale-New Haven Hosp., 1953-60; instr. to asst. prof. surgery Yale U., 1960-65; assoc. prof. surgery Stanford U., 1965-69, prof., 1969-97, prof. emeritus, 1997—, Johnson and Johnson prof. surgery, 1978—97, head div. thoracic surgery, 1972-97, assoc. dean clin. affairs, 1988-92; chief staff Stanford U. Hosp., 1988-92. Governing bd. Health Systems Agy., Santa Clara County, 1978-80; sr. Fulbright-Hays fellow, vis. prof. surgery U. Dar es Salaam, Tanzania, 1972-73 Mem. editl. bd.: Jour. Thoracic and Cardiovasc. Surgery, 1986-94, World Jour. Surgery, 1995-2003, The Pharos, 2002-; contbr. numerous articles to sci. jours. Bd. dirs. Stanford U. Hosp., 1992-94. With USPHS, 1955-57. Fellow ACS (pres. No. Calif. chpt. 1980-81), Am. Coll. Chest Physicians (pres. 1994-95); mem. Am. Assn. Thoracic Surgery, Am. Surg. Assn., Western Surg. Assn., Pacific Coast Surg. Assn., Halsted Soc. (pres. 1984), Western Thoracic Surg. Assn. (pres. 1992-93), Calif. Acad. Medicine (pres. 1978), Santa Clara County Med. Soc. (pres. 1976-77). Home: 921 Casanueva Pl Stanford CA 94305-1001 Office: Stanford U Med Ctr CVRB Stanford CA 94305 Office Phone: 650-723-6649. E-mail: jbdm@stanford.edu.

MARK, KELLY S., telecommunications industry executive, investment advisor; b. 1972; BS, U. Ill., 1994; MBA, Harvard Bus. Sch., 1999. With Davis Industries, Ford Motor Co., Motorola Future Bus. Group, 1999; investment mgr. Motorola Ventures, Schaumberg, Ill.; dir. bus. devel. Motorola, Inc., Schaumberg, Ill., 2004—. Named one of 40 Under 40, Crain's Chgo. Bus., 2006. Office: Motorola Inc 1303 E Algonquin Rd Schaumburg IL 60196

MARK, LAURENCE MAURICE, film producer; b. NYC, Nov. 22; s. James Mark and Marion Lorraine (Huebner) Green. BA, Wesleyan U., 1971; MA, NYU, 1973. Exec. dir., publicity Paramount Pictures, NYC, 1978-80, v.p., West Coast mktg. LA, 1980-82, v.p., prodn., 1982-84; exec. v.p., prodn. Twentieth Century Fox, LA, 1984-86; pres. Laurence Mark Prodns., LA, 1986—. Exec. prodr.: (films) Black Widow, 1987, My Stepmother is an Alien, 1988, Working Girl, 1988, Mr. Destiny, 1990, Sister Act 2: Back in the Habit, 1993, As Good As It Gets, 1997, (TV) Sweet Bird of Youth, 1989, Oliver Twist, 1997, The Last Laugh, 2000, These Old Broads, 2001; prodr.: (films) Cookie, 1989, True Colors, 1991, One Good Cop, 1991, The Adventures of Huck Finn, 1993, Cutthroat Island, 1995, Tom and Huck, 1995, Jerry Maguire, 1996, Romy and Michele's High School Reunion, 1997, Deep Rising, 1998, The Object of My Affection, 1998, Simon Birch, 1998, Anywhere But Here, 1999, Bicentennial Man, 1999, Hanging Up, 2000, Center Stage, 2000, Finding Forrester, 2000, Glitter, 2001, Riding In Cars With Boys, 2001, I, Robot, 2004, Last Holiday, 2006, Dreamgirls, 2006, The Lookout, 2007; prodr. (theatre) Brooklyn Laundry, 1991, (Broadway) Big, 1996. Mem. Acad. Motion Pictures Arts and Scis. Office: Columbia Pictures Sony Studios 10202 Washington Blvd Culver City CA 90232-3119 Home: 12437 Mulholland Dr Beverly Hills CA 90210-1336

MARK, MELVIN, mechanical engineering educator, consultant; b. St. Paul, Nov. 15, 1922; s. Isadore William and Fannye (Abrahamson) M.; m. Elizabeth J. Wyner, Sept. 9, 1951; children: Jonathan S., David W., Peter B. B.M.E., U. Minn., 1943, MS, 1946; Sc.D. (Teaching, Research fellow), Harvard, 1950. Registered profl. engr., Mass., Minn. Instr. N.D. State U., 1943-44, U. Minn., 1945-47; project mgr. Gen. Electric Co., Lynn., Mass., 1950-52; mgr. Raytheon Co., Wayland, Mass., 1952-56; cons. engr., 1956—; prof. Lowell Technol. Inst., 1957-59, dean faculty, 1959-62; prof. mech. engring. Northeastern U., Boston, 1963-84, dean engring., 1968-79, provost, sr. v.p. for acad. affairs, 1979-84. Vis. lectr. Mass. Inst. Tech., 1955, Brandeis U., 1958; vis. prof. U. Mass., 1984-86; mem. Mass. Bd. Registration of Profl. Engrs. and Land Surveyors, 1990-2001. Author: Thermodynamics: An Auto-Instructional Text, 1967, Concepts of Thermodynamics, 1975, Thermodynamics: Principles and Applications, 1979, Engineering Thermodynamics, 1985; contbr. articles to profl. jours. Served with USAAF, 1944-45. Recipient prize Lincoln Arc Welding Found., 1947. Hon. fellow ASME (fellow 1948-50); mem. Am. Soc. Engring. Edn., Sigma Xi, Tau Beta Pi, Pi Tau Sigma, Phi Kappa Phi. Achievements include patents in field. Home: 17 Larch Rd Waban MA 02468-1413

MARK, MICHAEL DAVID, lawyer; b. Bklyn., Sept. 16, 1944; s. Irving and Mildred Mark; children: Dana Lynne, Stephanie Lauren. BA, Rutgers U., 1966; JD, U. Tenn., 1969. Bar: Tenn. 1969, N.J. 1970, U.S. Dist. Ct. N.J. 1970, U.S. Supreme Ct. 1973; cert. civil trial atty., N.J. Supreme Ct. 1992. House counsel Liberty Mut. Ins. Co., East Orange, N.J., 1969-71; assoc. Skoloff & Wolfe, Newark, 1971-73; pvt. practice, Union, N.J., 1973—. Past assoc. bd. dirs. United Jersey Bank, Union; Police Benevolent Assn. lawyer City of Linden, N.J., 1980—, Clark Twp., Clark, N.J., 1986; mem. Union-Essex County Early Settlement Panels, Elizabeth and Newark. Mem. Am. Acad. Matrimonial Lawyers (bd. mgrs. 1982—), N.J. Bar Assn., Union County Bar Assn., Union Lawyers Club (past pub. defender). Republican. Avocation: private pilot. Office: 2444 Morris Ave Union NJ 07083-5711

MARK, MICHAEL LAURENCE, retired music educator; b. Schenectady, NY, Dec. 1, 1936; s. David and Ruth (Garbowitz) M.; m. Lois Nitekman, Jan. 28, 1942; children: Michelle, Diana. BM, The Cath. U. of Am., 1958, DMA, 1969; MA, George Washington U., 1960; M in Music Edn., U. Mich., 1962. Tchr. Prince George's County, Md. Pub. Schs., 1958-60, 61-66; assoc. prof. music Morgan State U., Balt., 1966-70; supr. music Auburn (N.Y.) Enlarged Sch. Dist., 1970-72; dir. music Elmira (N.Y.) Enlarged Sch. Dist., 1972-73; assoc. prof., sch. music Cath. U. Am., Washington, 1973-81; dean grad. sch., prof. music Towson (Md.) U., 1981-95, prof. music, 1995-98, prof. emeritus, 1998; pres. Spectrum Assocs., Inc. Mem editl. com. five jours. in field. Author: Contemporary Music Education, 1978, 3rd rev. edit., 1996, Source Readings in Music Education History, 1982, 2nd edit., 2002; co-author: A History of American Music Education, 1992, 3d edit., 2007. Pres. Balt. Neighborhood, Inc. Mem. Music Educators Nat. Conf. (numerous coms., Music Educators Hall of Fame), Coll. Music Soc., Md. Music Educators Assn. (pres. 1999-2003, Hall of Fame), Mich.Sch. Music Alumni Soc. (bd. govs.). Avocations: travel, woodworking. E-mail: mimark@comcast.net.

MARK, PETER, performing company executive, conductor; b. NYC, Oct. 31, 1940; s. Irving and Edna M.; m. Thea Musgrave, Oct. 2, 1971. BA (Woodrow Wilson fellow), Columbia U., NYC, 1961; MS, Juilliard Sch. Music, NYC, 1963. Prof. music and dramatic art U. Calif., Santa Barbara, 1965-94. Fellow Creative Arts Inst., U. Calif., 1968-69, 71-72; guest condr. Wolf Trap Orch., 1979, NYC Opera, 1981, L.A. Opera Theater, 1981, Royal Opera House, London, 1982, Hong Kong Philharm. Orch., 1984, Jerusalem Symphony Orch., 1988, Tulsa Opera, 1988, Compania Nacional de Opera, Mexico City, 1989, 92, NY Pops, Carnegie Hall, 1991, Shanghai Opera, 2005. Concert violist US, S.Am., Europe, 1961-67; artistic dir., condr. Va. Opera, Norfolk, 1975—, art dir., 1978—; condr.: Am. premier of Mary, Queen of Scots (Musgrave), 1978; World premier of A Christmas Carol (Musgrave), 1979, of Harriet, the Woman Called Moses (Musgrave), 1985, of Simon Bolivar (Musgrave), 1984, Porgy and Bess, Buenos Aires, Mexico City and São Paulo, 1992, Orlando Opera co., 1993, Richmond Symphony, 1993, Va. Premieres, 1993, Krakow Opera, 1995, Pacific Opera Victoria (Can.), 1996, Salome, 1996, Cleve. Opera, 1996, Festival Pucciniano-Torre del Lago, Italy, 1996, The Flying Dutchman, 1996, Orfeo et Euridice, 1999, Rodelinda, 2000, Elektra, 2002, Die Walkure, 2002, Andrea Chenier, 2003, Fidelio, 2004, Tristan und Isolde, 2005, Agrippina, 2007. Recipient Elias Lifchey viola award Juilliard Sch. Music, 1963; named hon. citizen of Norfolk, Va. Mem. Musicians Union, Phi Beta Kappa. Office: Va Opera PO Box 2580 Norfolk VA 23501-2580 Office Phone: 757-627-9545 x 3337. Business E-Mail: pmark@vaopera.com.

MARK, REUBEN, consumer products company executive; b. Jersey City, Jan. 21, 1939; s. Edward and Libbie (Berman) M.; m. Arlene Slobzian, Jan. 10, 1964; children: Lisa, Peter, Stephen. AB, Middlebury Coll., 1960; MBA, Harvard U., 1963. With Colgate-Palmolive Co., NYC, 1963—, pres., gen. mgr. Venezuela, 1972-73, Can., 1973-74, v.p., gen. mgr. Far East div., 1974-75, v.p., gen. mgr. household products div., 1975-79, group v.p. domestic ops., 1979-81, exec. v.p., 1981-83, COO, 1983-84, pres., 1983-86, CEO, 1984—2007, chmn., 1986—. Lectr. Sch. Bus. Adminstrn. U. Conn., 1977; bd. dirs. Time Warner, 1993—, Cabela's Inc., Colgate-Palmolive Co., Pearson PLC. Served with U.S. Army, 1961. Mem. Soap and Detergent Assn. (bd. dirs.), Grocery Mfrs. Am. (dir.), Nat. Exec. Service Corp. Office: Colgate-Palmolive Co 300 Park Ave Fl 8 New York NY 10022-7499 *

MARK, WAYNE JOSEPH, lawyer; b. Humphrey, Nebr., Aug. 29, 1947; s. Gilbert Joseph and Evelyn Adelaide (Schroeder) M.; m. Mary Alice Kessler, June 7, 1969; children: Michaella, Christopher, Jeffrey, Marissa. BS in Bus., U. Nebr., 1969, JD with distinction, 1972. Bar: Nebr., 1972, US Dist. Ct. (Dist. Nebr.), US Ct. Appeals (8th Cir.). Mem. Fraser, Stryker, Vaughn, Meusey, Olson, Boyer & Bloch PC, Omaha, 1972—, ptnr. Dir. Nebr. Continuing Legal Edn., Lincoln, 1991-94. Fellow Am. Coll. Trial Lawyers (state chmn. 2000-02, mem. Alternative dispute resolution com.), Nebr. State Bar Found.; mem. ABA, Nebr. Bar Assn. (mem. ho. of dels. 1987-93, pres.-elect 2006-07), Nebr. Def. Counsel Assn. (pres. 1990-92), Omaha Bar Assn., Def. Rsch. Inst. and Trial Lawyers Assn. (state chmn. 1992-95), Nebr. Assn. Trial Lawyers (dir. 86-88); US Supreme Ct. Historical Soc. (state chmn. 2002-04); Knights of Columbus; Delta Theta Phi. Office: Fraser Stryker PC 500 Energy Pl 409 S 17th St Omaha NE 68102-2609 Office Phone: 402-978-5223. E-mail: wmark@fraserstryker.com.

MARKEE, KATHERINE MADIGAN, librarian, educator; b. Cleve., Feb. 24, 1931; d. Arthur Alexis and Margaret Elizabeth (Madigan) M. AB, Trinity Coll., Washington, 1953; MA, Columbia U., 1962; MLS, Case Western Res. U., 1968. Employment mgr., br. store tng. supr. The May Co., Cleve., 1965-67; assoc. prof. libr. sci., data bases libr. Purdue U. Libr., West Lafayette, Ind., 1968—96, libr. spl. collections, 1996—2006, oral history libr., 2006—. Contbr. articles to profl. jours. Mem. ALA, AAUP, Spl. Librs. Assn., Ind. Online Users Group, Sigma Xi (Rsch. Support award 1986), Oral History Assn., Soc. Am. Archivists. Avocations: photography, sailing, gardening. Office: Purdue U Libr 504 W State St West Lafayette IN 47907-2058 Office Phone: 765-496-1323. Business E-Mail: kmarkee@purdue.edu.

MARKEE, RICHARD L., retail executive; BS in Econ., U. Wis. Buyer Famous-Barr May Co.; v.p., divisional mdse. mgr. Target Stores Dayton Hudson Corp.; from v.p., gen. mdse. mgr. Kids "R" Us Divsn. to vice chmn. Toys "R" Us, Inc., Wayne, NJ, 1990—2003, vice chmn., 2003—, pres. U.S. Toy Stores, 2003—06, interim CEO, 2005—06; pres. Babies "R" Us, 2004—. Chmn. bd. Kids in Distressed Situations, Inc., bd. dir. Office: Toys R Us Inc 1 Geoffrey Way Wayne NJ 07470-2030

MARKEL, GREGORY ARTHUR, lawyer; b. NYC, Aug. 6, 1945; s. Edward and Ann (Larkin) M.; m. Dorothy Flanagan (div. 1979); 1 child, Kimberly; m. Belinda Elizabeth Heym, May 3, 1981; children: Alexis, Amy, William. BA in Econs., Columbia U., 1967; MBA in Fin. and Acctg., U. Mich., 1968; JD, Yale U., 1972. Bar: N.Y. 1972, U.S. Dist. Ct. (so. and ea. dists.) N.Y. 1974, U.S. Ct. Appeals (2nd cir.) 1975, U.S. Ct. Appeals (3rd cir.) 1978, U.S Dist. Ct. (no. dist.) Calif. 1984, U.S. Ct. Appeals (9th cirs.) 1984, U.S. Ct. Appeals (11th cir) 1987. Assoc. Cravath, Swaine & Moore, NYC, 1972-80; ptnr. Davis, Markel & Edwards, 1980-93, Brobeck Phleger & Harrison LLP, NYC; ptnr., chmn. litig. dept., mem. mgmt. com. Cadwalader Wickersham & Taft LLP, NYC, 2002—. Tv, radio commentator on legal issues; mem. securities litig. panel Ann. Inst. Securities Regulation, 1999, 2000, 01, 02, 03, 04, 05, 06, 07; bank commentator, instr., 2004—05. Contbr. articles to profl. jours. and chpts. to publs. in field. Named to Leading Securities Litig. Def. Attys., Chambers USA, Top Litigators for Comml. Litig., Best Lawyers in Am., Best Lawyers in NY, NY Super Lawyers, LawDragon 500 Top Lawyers in US. Fellow NY Bar Found.; Mem. ABA (mem. litig. and antitrust sects., litig. co-chair subcom. on fed. rules rev. of the pretrial practices and discovery com.), NY State Bar Assn. (mem. comml. litig. sect.), Fed. Bar Coun., Bar Assn. of City of NY, Bond Mkt. Assn. (due diligence com.), Securities Industry Assn. (compliance and legal divsn.). Office: Cadwalader Wickersham & Taft LLP 1 World Fin Ctr New York NY 10281 Home Phone: 212-759-4351; Office Phone: 212-504-6112. Office Fax: 212-504-6666. Business E-Mail: greg.markel@cwt.com.

MARKEL, HOWARD, physician, educator; b. Detroit, Apr. 23, 1960; s. Samuel and Bernice Markel; m. Marcia Deborah Gordin, Sept. 20, 1987 (dec. Oct. 1988); m. Kate Gelya Levin, Aug. 17, 1997; children: Bess Rachel, Samantha Louise. AB in English Lit. summa cum laude, U. Mich., 1982, MD cum laude, 1986; PhD in History of Sci., Medicine & Tech., Johns Hopkins U., 1994. Diplomate Am. Bd. Pediat., 1989. Intern, resident Johns Hopkins Hosp. & Sch. Medicine, Balt., 1986-89, fellow, gen. pediat. and adolescent medicine, 1989—91, fellow, history medicine, 1989—93; asst. prof. pediatrics, communicable diseases U. Mich., Ann Arbor, 1993-98, assoc. prof. pedicatrics, communicable diseases, 1998—2002, George E. Wantz prof. history medicine, 2000—, prof. pediat. and communicable diseases, prof. history, 2002—, prof. pub. health, psychiatry, 2004—. Dir. Ctr. for History of Medicine, U. Mich., 1996—. Author: The H.L. Mencken Baby Book, 1990, The Portable Pediatrician, 1992, The Portable Pediatrician, 2nd edit., 2000, The Practical Pediatrician, 1996 (Child Mag. Book of Yr., 1997), Quarantine! East European Jewish Immigrants and the New York City, 1997 (Arthur Viseltear prize, APHA, 2003), When Germs Travel, 2004. Recipient Nat. Rsch. Svc. award, NIH, 1991, James A. Shannon Dirs. award, 1996, Burroughs Wellcome Fund 40th Ann. History Medicine award, 1996, History of Medicine award, Nat. Libr. Medicine, NIH, 2005—; scholar Robert Wood Johnson Found., 1996—2000. Fellow: Am. Acad. Pediat.; mem.: Am. Pediat. Soc., Soc. Pediat. Rsch., Am. Assn. History Medicine (exec. coun. 1994—97). Democrat. Jewish. Office: U Mich Ctr for History of Medicine 100 Simpson Meml Inst 102 Observatory Ann Arbor MI 48109-0725 Office Phone: 734-647-6914. Business E-Mail: howard@umich.edu.

MARKELL, JACK A., state official; b. Newark, 1961; m. Carla Markell. Degree in economics, degree in devel. studies, Brown U.; MBA, U. Chgo., 1985. Sr. v.p. corp. devel. Nextel; sr. mgr. Comcast Corp.; cons. McKinsey and Co., Inc.; banker First Chgo. Corp.; state treas. Del., 1999—. Chmn. Del. Coll. Investment Plan, 1999—, Info. Svcs. Task Force, 2001; founder Del. Money Sch. Named one of Rising Stars of Democratic Party, Democratic Nat. Convention, 2000, 10 Innovative Leaders from Around the Country under Age 40, New Democrat Mag., 10 Most Influential Tech. Leaders in Phila. Region, Philly Tech. Mag., 2001. Office: State Treas Office 540 S DuPont Hwy Ste 4 Dover DE 19901 Office Phone: 302-744-1000. Office Fax: 302-739-5635. E-mail: statetreasurer@state.de.us. *

MARKEN, WILLIAM RILEY, editor-in-chief; b. San Jose, Calif., Sept. 2, 1942; s. Harry L. and Emma Catherine (Kraus) M.; m. Marilyn Tonascia, Aug. 30, 1964; children— Catherine, Elizabeth, Michael, Paul Student, Occidental Coll., 1960-62; BA, U. Calif., Berkeley, 1964. Editor-in-chief Sunset Mag., Menlo Park, Calif., 1981-96, eHow.com, 1999-2001, Garden Design Mag., 2001—. Bd. dirs. Calif. Tomorrow, 1979-83; pres. League to Save Lake Tahoe, 1994-97. Avocations: tennis, skiing, basketball.

MARKER, MARC LINTHACUM, lawyer, investor, entrepreneur; b. LA, July 19, 1941; s. Clifford Harry and Voris (Linthacum) M.; m. Sandra Vocom. Aug. 29, 1965; children: Victor, Gwendolyn. BA in Econs. and Geography, U. Calif.-Riverside, 1964; JD, U. So. Calif., 1967. Asst. v.p., asst. sec. Security Pacific Nat. Bank, LA, 1970-73; sr. v.p., chief counsel, sec. Security Pacific Leasing Corp., San Francisco, 1973-92; pres. Security Pacific Leasing Svcs. Corp., San Francisco, 1977-85, dir., 1977-92. Bd. dirs., sec. Voris, Inc., 1973-86; bd. dirs. Refiners Petroleum Corp., 1977-81, Security Pacific Leasing Singapore Ltd., 1983-85, Security Pacific Leasing Can. Ltd., 1989-92; lectr. in field. Served to comdr., USCGR. Mem. ABA, D.C. Bar Assn; Club: Army and Navy. Republican. Lutheran.

MARKERT, CYNTHIA ALLIN, artist; b. Oak Ridge, Tenn., Apr. 7, 1954; d. George Wilbur and Barbara Anderson Allin. BFA, U. Tenn., 1977. Exhibitions include So. Living Mag. Dream House, Atlanta, Bennett Gallery, Alexis Georges, New Orleans, Circa Gallery, Setting the Stage Artspace, Alexandria, Va., DC Space, Washington, Veni Vidi Vici, Zenith Gallery, Fla. Design Mag., Susan Key Gallery, Knoxville, Tenn., Vetrum Gallery, Asheville, NC, Michael B. Tusing Gallery, Staunton, Va., Impeccable Art, Winston Salem, NC, Kress Emporium, Asheville, Hanson Gallery, Knoxville, Studio E Gallery, Jupiter, Fla., Raiford Gallery, Roswell, Ga., C.J. Varnum Gallery, Palm Beach, Fla., Louis Aronow Gallery, San Francisco, Through the Lens Gallery, Knoxville, Tenn., World Grotto Marketplace, Vagabondia, Skirt Mag., Knoxville Mag., archives, Nat. Mus. Women in the Arts, Washington, exhibitions include Three Flights Up Gallery, Knoxville, So. Lady Mag., commns. include, Stanford U. Dept. Lively Arts, No. Ky. U. Dept. Dance, U. Tenn. Dept. Theatre, Pandora's Books, Knoxville, Tenn. Festival Ballet, Tressa'a Jazz Club, Asheville, New Millennium Writings, Image Conscious of San Francisco, Spiral Licensing of Cherre, France. Office: Markert Du Jour PO box 724 Knoxville TN 37901 Home Phone: 865-523-8696. Business E-Mail: cynthia@cynthiamarkert.com.

MARKESSINI, JOAN, research scientist, psychologist; b. NYC, Aug. 14, 1942; d. John Demetrios and Diana (Vlahos) M.; m. Peter John Georges, Jan. 28, 1981. BA in English and French, U. Del., 1964, PhD in Cognitive Psychology, 1979; MA in Linguistics, U. Wash., 1966. Tng. analyst U.S. Dept. State, Washington, 1967-70; writer, editor-in-chief Edcom Systems, Inc., Princeton, N.J., 1970-72; ednl. psychologist U. Del., Newark, 1972-78; dir. corp. and found. rels. Cath. U. Am., Washington, 1978-84; asst. dir. resources devel. Nat. Trust for Hist. Preservation, Washington, 1984-85; sr. staff psychologist BDM Internat., Inc., McLean, Va., 1985-87; dir. publs. and communications Maxwell Communication Corp., McLean, 1987-90; psychologist Allen Corp., Alexandria, Va., 1990—95; dir. R&D, dep. dir. med. systems and distance learning L-3 Comm., Inc.: LINK Simulation and Tng., NYC, 1995—2002; founder, pres. WELLTrek Internat., LLC, 1995—. Author: The First Year of Life (13 vols.), 1971, The First Twelve Months of Life, 1973, Effects of Listener Familiarity and Topic Knowledge on Speech Communication, 1979, TeleMedicine Art and Practice: An Instructional Program Series, 1995, A Taxonomy of Cognitive Capabilities for Executives, (film) Meeting the Challenge, 2000; editor: Perspectives on Leadership, Vols. 1-5, 1993; contb. articles to profl. jours.; prodr. (film) Death of a Giant, 1967; numerous reports. U. Wash. grad. fellow, 1965-66, U. Mich. fellow, 1965, U. Del. fellow, 1977-79. Mem. Am. Psychol. Assn., Assn. Psychol. Type (gen.), N.Y. Acad. Scis., Nat. Mus. Women in Arts (charter), Am. Film Inst. Club. Avocations: theater, opera, interior decorating, gardening. Home: PO Box 4218 Arlington VA 22204-0218

MARKEY, BRIAN MICHAEL, lawyer; b. Teaneck, NJ, Feb. 10, 1956; s. Raymond Joseph and Sheila (Barry) M.; m. Virginia M. Lincoln, Oct. 26, 1986. BA cum laude, Rider Coll., 1978; JD, Suffolk U., 1985. Bar: N.J. 1985, U.S. Dist. Ct. N.J. 1985, N.Y. 1988. Assoc. Kohler & Clinch, Hackensack, NJ, 1985—90, Law Office J. Dennis Kohler, Hackensack, NJ, 1990—91; pvt. practice law Glen Rock, NJ, 1991—94; ptnr. Lincoln & Markey, Glen Rock, 1995—. Dir. Glen Rock Savs. Bank. Chmn. Glen Rock Planning Bd. Mem. ABA, N.J. Bar Assn., Glen Rock Independence Day Assn. Office: 126 Valley Rd Glen Rock NJ 07452-1796

MARKEY, EDWARD JOHN, congressman; b. Malden, Mass., July 11, 1946; s. John E. and Christine M. Markey; m. Susan Blumenthal. BA, Boston Coll., 1968, JD, 1972. Bar: Mass. Mem. Mass. Ho. of Reps., 1973-76, U.S. Congress from 7th Mass. dist., 1976—, New Eng. Congl. Caucus, N.E.-Midwest Econ. Advancement Coalition, Dem. Study Group; mem. energy and commerce com. Mem. editorial staff: Boston Coll. Law Rev. Served with USAR, 1968-73. Mem. Mass. Bar Assn. (Mass. Legislator of Year 1975) Clubs: K.C. Democrat. Roman Catholic. Home: 7 Townsend St Malden MA 02148-6322 Office: US Ho of Reps 2108 Rayburn House Office Bldg Washington DC 20515-2107 Office Phone: 202-225-2836. Office Fax: 202-226-0092. *

MARKEY, JAMES KEVIN, lawyer; b. Springfield, Ill., July 15, 1956; s. James Owen and Marjorie Jean (Diesness) M.; m. Allison Markey; children: Lauren, Katherine. BBA with highest honors, U. Notre Dame, 1977; JD cum laude, U. Mich., 1980; MBA, U. Chgo., 1987; LLM in Taxation, DePaul U., 1993. CPA Ill., lic. Mich., 2002; bar: Ill. 1980. Assoc. Chapman & Cutler, Chgo., 1980-81; atty. Quaker Oats Co., Chgo., 1981-84; corp. counsel Baxter Healthcare Corp., Deerfield, Ill., 1984-90; v.p. law and other positions Motorola, Inc., Schaumburg, Ill., 1990-2000; v.p., chief counsel-securities and internat. Kellogg Co., Battle Creek, Mich., 2000—06; v.p., sec., gen. counsel MAG Industrial Automation Sys., LLC, Sterling Heights, Mich., 2006—. Mem. ABA, Beta Alpha Psi, Beta Gamma Sigma. Avocations: racquetball, running, bridge. Office: 13900 Lakeside Cir Sterling Heights MI 48313 Home: 1290 Grandview Rochester Hills MI 48306 Business E-Mail: james.markey@mag-ias.com.

MARKEY, JOHN K., lawyer; b. Melrose, Mass., Aug. 1, 1947; BS cum laude, Boston Coll., 1969, JD, 1973. Bar: Mass. 1974. Asst. dist. atty. Middlesex County, 1974-77; asst. US atty. Dist. Mass., 1978; mem. Mintz, Levin, Cohn, Ferris, Glovsky and Popeo PC, ptnr., Litig., chmn., pro bono com. Mem.: Boston Bar Assn. (task force on drugs & the cts., com. on state cts.study, chmn. criminal law sect. 1990—92), Mass. Bar Assn., ABA. Address: Mintz Levin Cohn Ferris Glovsky & Popeo PC 1 Financial Ctr Fl 39 Boston MA 02111-2621 Office Phone: 617-348-1686. Office Fax: 617-542-2241. Business E-Mail: jmarkey@mintz.com.

MARKEY, MAURICE, food products executive; b. 1966; MBA, Ind. U., 1994. With Goodyear Tire & Rubber Co., Kraft Foods, Inc., 1994, mktg. dir., spoonables divsn. Chgo. Mktg. expert New Schools for Chgo., Ill., 2005. Named one of 40 Under 40, Crain's Chgo. Bus., 2005. Office: Kraft Foods Inc 3 Lakes Dr Winnetka IL 60093 Office Fax: 847-646-6005. *

MARKEY, RANDOLPH DAVID, marketing professional; s. Robert Guy and Carol Sogg Markey; m. Molly Clare Sindelar; children: Max, Isabel. MBA, Weatherhead Sch. At Case Western Res. U. Nat. sales mgr. Matrix Essentials, Inc., Cleve., 1990—94; dir., mktg. Bristol-Myers Squibb, 1994—2000; mng. dir. Parkland Group, 2000—03; mng. ptnr. Capital Acceleration Ptnrs., 2003—. Bd. dirs. Sogg Found., Corp. Bd., OEM Labeling, Inc., LaVar Holdings, Inc.; chmn. bd. dirs. Phylogy, Inc., Geotrac, Inc. Contbr. chapters to books. Mem.: Social Venture Ptnrs. (bd. dirs.), Assn. for Corp. Growth, Turnaround Mgmt. Assn.

MARKEY, WILLIAM ALAN, health facility administrator, consultant; b. Cleve., Dec. 29, 1927; s. Oscar Bennett and Claire (Feldman) M.; m. Irene Nelson, Oct. 31, 1954; children: Janet Ellen Markey-Hisakawa, Suzanne Katherine Markey-Johnson. Student, Case Inst. Tech., 1945—48; BA, U. Mich., 1950; MS, Yale U., 1954. Resident in hosp. adminstrn. Beth Israel Hosp., Boston, 1953-54; asst. dir. Montefiore Hosp., Pitts., 1954-56; asst. adminstr. City of Hope Med. Ctr., Duarte, Calif., 1956-57, adminstrv. dir., 1957-66; assoc. dir. cancer hosp. project, instr. pub. health U. So. Calif. Sch. Medicine, 1966-67, asst. clin. prof. pub. health and cmty. medicine, 1968-70, asst. prof., 1970-75, dep. dir. regional med. programs, 1967-71; adminstr. Health Care Agy., County of San Diego, 1971-74, health svcs. cons., 1974-75; dir. Maricopa County Dept. Health Svcs., Phoenix, 1975-79, cons., 1979-80; adminstr. Sonoma Valley Hosp., Calif., 1980—83. Lectr. pub. health Sch. Pub. Health, UCLA, 1969-74; lectr. cmty. medicine Sch. Medicine, U. Calif., San Diego, 1973-75; cons. LA County Dept. Hosps., 1966-71, cons. Hosp./Health Svcs., 1983—; CEO Chinese Hosp., San Francisco, 1985-86, 90-91; adj. instr. Golden Gate U., 1992-96. Mem. bd. edn. Duarte Unified Sch. Dist., 1967-72, pres., 1970-72; bd. dir. Hosp. Coun. So. Calif., 1963-67, sec., 1966-67, Duarte Pub. Libr. Assn., 1965-72, Duarte-Bradbury chpt. Am. Field Svc., 1965-72, Duarte-Bradbury Cmty. Chest, 1961-68, Ctrl. Ariz. Health Svcs. Agy., 1975-80, Vis. Nurse Assn. The Redwoods, Santa Rosa, Calif., 1985-86, Sonoma Greens Homeowners Assn., 1990-95, 2002-05, Sonoma City Opera, 1987, 93, United Way, Sonoma, 1996—; com. chmn. Sonoma County Bd. Realtors, 1990-92; active Sonoma County Multiple Listing Svc., 1987-97; mem. Sonoma County Human Svcs. Commn., 2003-. With USN, 1950-52. Fellow Am. Coll. Health Care Execs. (life); mem. Am. Hosp. Assn. (life), APHA, Royal Soc. Health, Calif. Hosp. Assn. (trustee 1966-69, dir. 1966-69), Internat. Fedn. Hosps., Hosp. Coun. No. Calif. (dir. 1981-83), Kiwanis, Rotary (past pres. Duarte). Home: 866 Princeton Dr Sonoma CA 95476-4186

MARKEY, WINSTON ROSCOE, aeronautical engineering educator; b. Buffalo, Sept. 20, 1929; s. Roscoe Irvin and Catherine L. (Higgins) M.; m. Phoebe Anne Sproule, Sept. 10, 1955; children: Karl Richard, Katherine Ilse, Kristina Anne. BS, MIT, 1951, Sc.D., 1956. Engr. MIT, 1951-57, asst. prof., 1957-62, assoc. prof., 1962-66, prof., 1966—, undergrad. officer, 1988-2000, dir. Measurement Systems Lab., 1961-89. Chief scientist USAF, 1964-65, mem. sci. adv. bd., 1966-69 Author: (with J. Hovorka) The Mechanics of Inertial Position and Heading Indication, 1961; Assoc. editor: AIAA Jour, 1963-66. Recipient Exceptional Civilian Service award, USAF, 1965. Mem. Sigma Xi, Tau Beta Pi, Gamma Alpha Rho. Home: 11 Edgewood Rd Lexington MA 02420-3501 Office: MIT Bldg 33-208 Cambridge MA 02139 Office Phone: 617-253-2921. Personal E-mail: wrmarkey@earthlink.net. Business E-Mail: wrmarkey@mit.edu.

MARKEZICH, RON, information technology executive; BA in Mgmt. Info. Sys., U. Notre Dame. With electronics and high tech. group Accenture (formerly Andersen Consulting); joined Microsoft, 1998; gen. mgr. fin. and adminstrn. info. tech. Microsoft Info. Tech., gen. mgr. info. tech. client svcs., gen. mgr. global tech. svcs.; CIO, v.p. managed solutions Microsoft Corp., Redmond, Wash., 2004—. Office: Microsoft Corp 1 Microsoft Way Redmond WA 98052-6399

MARKGRAF, J(OHN) HODGE, chemist, educator; b. Cin., Mar. 16, 1930; s. Carl A. and Elizabeth (Hodge) M.; m. Nancy Hart, Apr. 4, 1957; children: Carrie G., Sarah T. AB, Williams Coll., 1952; M.Sc., Yale U., 1954, PhD, 1957; postgrad., U. Munich, W. Ger., 1956-57. Research chemist Procter & Gamble Co., Cin., 1958-59; asst. prof. chemistry Williams Coll., Williamstown, Mass., 1959-65, assoc. prof., 1965-69, prof., 1969-98, Ebenezer Fitch prof. chemistry, 1977-85, 94-98, prof. emeritus, 1998—, provost, 1980-83, v.p. for alumni relations and devel., 1985-94, coll. marshal, 1995-98. Vis. prof. U. Calif., Berkeley, 1964—65, 1968—69, 1976—77, Duke U., 1983—84, 2001, U. Houston, 1999, Williams Coll., 2002—04, 2006, Mass. Coll. Liberal Arts, 2005—06. Contbr. articles to profl. jours.; patentee in field. NSF sci. faculty fellow, 1964-65; NSF grantee, 1961-63, Am. Chem. Soc.-Petroleum Rsch. Fund grantee, 1965-68, 70-72, 93-95, Merck & Co. grantee, 1967, Rsch. Corp. grantee, 1963, 75, 90-92, Pfizer Inc. grantee, 1996, 97, 98, Camille and Henry Dreyfus Found. grantee, 2000-01, 04-05 Mem.: Am. Chem. Soc., Phi Beta Kappa, Sigma Xi. Home: 104 Forest Rd Williamstown MA 01267-2029 Office: Williams College Dept Chemistry Williamstown MA 01267-2692 E-mail: j.hodge.markgraf@williams.edu.

MARKHAM, CHARLES HENRY, neurologist; b. Pasadena, Calif., Dec. 24, 1923; s. Fred Smith and Maziebelle Valeta (Glover) M.; m. Kathleen Tiernan, Sept. 29, 1945 (div. 1971); children: Charles H., Arthur Tiernan, Daphne, James Daniel; m. Lisa Wells Overly, July 10, 1971; children: John Wells, Sara Brennan. Student, Colo. Sch. Mines, 1941-43; AB, Stanford U., 1947, MD, 1951. Intern, med. asst. resident Lane Hosp., San Francisco, 1950-52; fellow in neurology Children's Med. Ctr., Boston, 1952-53; asst. resident Boston City Hosp., 1953-54, chief resident, 1954-55; asst. prof. neurology UCLA Sch. Medicine, 1958-65, assoc. prof., 1965-70, assoc. prof. neurology, 1970-71, prof. neurology, 1971-94, prof. emeritus, 1994—; rsch. prof. dept. psychology U. Calif., Santa Barbara, 1995—. Sci. dir. Dystonia Med. Rsch. Found., Chgo., 1985-94, mem. bd. trustees, 1994—; sci. dir. Hereditary Disease Found., L.A., 1979-81; mem. adv. bd. Am. Parkinson Disease Assn., N.Y.C., 1976-83; attending physician UCLA Sch. Medicine, 1957—, cons. in neurology St. John's Hosp., Santa Monica, Calif., 1960-94. Contbr. articles to profl. jours.; author numerous books and abstracts. Trustee Westlake Sch. for Girls, L.A., 1965-74, St. Matthews Parish Sch., L.A., 1985-87; bd. dirs. Jubilee Christian Acad., 1996-99, Wildling Mus., 1997-2005, Las Positas Park Found., 1998-2000. With U.S. Army, 1943-45, ETO. Grantee NIH, NASA. Mem. Am. Acad. Neurology, AAAS, Am. Bd. Psychiatry and Neurology, Am. Epilepsy Soc., Am. Neurol. Assn., Am. Pain Soc., Am. Soc. for Gravitational and Space Biology, Bárány Soc. (Hallpike-Nylen prize 1990), Internat. Brain Rsch. Orgn., Internat. League Against Epilepsy, L.A. Soc. Neurology and Psychiatry, N.Y. Acad. Scis., Soc. for Neurosci., Western Inst. on Epilepsy, Rsch. Soc. for Parkinson Disease and Movement Disorders (pres. 1984-2000). Republican. Achievements include research in L-dopa and medical and surgical therapy for Parkinson's disease, dystonia, brain stem mechanisms for vestibular and quick and slow eye movements, long-term exposure to microgravity, space motion sickness, vestibular response to gravity, alcohol. Personal E-mail: cmarkham1@cox.net.

MARKHAM, CLAIRE AGNES (M. CLARE MARKHAM), retired chemistry educator, consultant; b. New Haven, Aug. 12, 1919; d. James J. and Agnes V. (Manning) M. BA, St. Joseph Coll., West Hartford, Conn., 1940, DHL (hon.), 1989; PhD, Cath. U. Am., 1952. Joined Sisters of Mercy, Roman Cath. Ch., 1940. Tchr. chemistry and math. Sacred Heart H.S., Waterbury, Conn., 1945-49; mem. faculty chemistry St. Joseph Coll., 1952-97, cons. instl. advancement, 1996—, prof. emeritus in chemistry, 1997—. Dept. chair St. Joseph Coll., 1959-70, dean Grad. Sch., 1979-87, asst. to pres. acad. affairs, 1987-95; dir. numerous tchr. insts., 1959-89; mem. vis. faculty Calvin's Lab., NSF, U. Calif., Berkeley, 1967-68. dir. CT Talent Prog., 2002-03. Contbr. articles to profl. jours.; editor sci. series McGraw Hill, 1956-60. Undersec. for Energy, Office of Policy and Mgmt., State of Conn., Hartford, 1977—79; mem. adv. com. Permanent Commn. Status of Women, Hartford, 1995—; mem. adv. coun. Dept. Higher Edn., State of Conn., Hartford, 1970—80; energy advisor Nat. Gov.'s Assn., 1977—79; bd. dirs. Conn. Energy Co-op, 2000—03. Recipient Equity award AAUW, 1992, Sci. Advocacy award, CSTA, 2002, award for outstanding sci. adv. Conn. Sci. Tchrs. Assn., 2002; Faculty fellow NSF, Trondheim, Norway, 1967, Travel grantee, cons., Madras, India, 1974-77. Fellow Conn. Acad. for Edn.; mem. AAAS, Am. Chem. Soc. (councilor 1968-88, chair Conn. Valley sect. 1955-67, 20 Yr. award 1988), Conn. Acad. Sci. and Engring. (founding mem., chair tech. bd. 1994-98), Sigma Xi (sect. chair 1993-95). Democrat. Avocations: photography, music, literature. Home: 1678 Asylum Ave West Hartford CT 06117-2791 Office: St Joseph Coll West Hartford CT 06117 Home Phone: 860-232-6730; Office Phone: 860-231-5501. Business E-Mail: cmarkham@sjc.edu.

MARKHAM, IAN STEPHEN, theology studies educator, dean; b. Crediton, England, Sept. 19, 1962; arrived in U.S., 2001; s. Stephen Keith Markham and Beryl Evelyn Walker; m. Lesley Patricia Dunn, July 4, 1987; 1 child, Luke Stephen Austin. BTh, Kings Coll., London, Eng., 1985; MLitt, Cambridge univ., Cambridge, Eng., 1990; PhD ethics, Exeter Devon, Exeter, Eng., 1994. Lectr. in theology Univ. Exeter, Devon, England, 1989—96; prof. of theology and pub. life Liverpool Hope Univ., Liverpool, England, 1996—2001; dean of the seminary, prof. of theology and ethics Hartford Seminary, Conn., 2001—. Coun. mem. and dir. Advt. Stds. Authority, London, 1993—99; Teape lectr., India, 2004; vis. prof. Leeds Metro. U., 2005. Author: Plurality and Christian Ethics, 1994, Truth and the Reality of God, 1999, Why Bother With Ethics, 2006; editor: September 11: Religious Perspectives on the causes and Consequences, 2002, Theology of Engagement, 2003, Globalization, Ethics and Islam: The Case of Bediuzzaman Said Nursi, 2005, Do Morals Matter?, 2007. Mem.: Am. Acad. of Religion. Home and Office: Hartford Seminary 77 Sherman St Hartford CT 06105 Office Phone: 860-509-9536. Business E-Mail: markham@hartsem.edu.

MARKHAM, J. DAVID, secondary school educator, writer, historical consultant; b. Austin, Tex., Dec. 26, 1945; s. James Walter and Myrtle (Sturges) M.; m. Barbara Ann Munson, May 14, 1983. BS, U. Iowa, 1971; MA, U. No. Iowa, 1972; postgrad., So. Ill. U., 1972-74, U. Wis., 1981-82; MEd, Ariz. State U., 1991; postgrad., Fla. State U., 1996—97, Oxford U., Eng., 1996. Instr. sociology U. Wis., Fond du Lac/Stevens Point, 1974-76; dir. Vietnam edn. grants Wis. Dept. Vet. Affairs, Madison, 1979-83; coordinator internat. edn. AFSCME, Phoenix, 1983-84; vets. svc. officer Ariz. Vets. Service Commn., Phoenix, 1984-86; asst. to dir. Commn. on Ariz. Environ., Phoenix, 1986-88; div. supr. Ariz. Dept. Liquor Lics. and Control, Phoenix, 1988-89; world history and English tchr. Tolleson Union H.S. Dist., 1990-92; world history tchr. Lake Worth H.S., Palm Beach, Fla., 1992-2000; history tchr. Tumwater H.S., 2000—01, Centralia H.S., 2001—02, Orting H.S., 2002—07. Instr. sociology and polit. sci., Maricopa C.C. Dist., Phoenix, 1985-91; instr. Palm Beach C.C., 1993-95. Author: Napoleon's Road to Glory: Triumphs, Defeats and Immortality, 2003, Imperial Glory: The Bulletins of Napoleon's Grande Armée, 2003, Napoleon and Dr. Verling on St. Helena, 2005, Napoleon for Dummies, 2005; co-author: Napoleon: The Final Verdict, 1996; contbg. author: Ency. World History, 2005, Ency. Leadership, 2005, Ency. Am. Revolution, 2005, Ency. French Revolutionary and Napoleonic Wars, 2005; contbr. articles to profl. jours. Bd. dirs. World Affairs Coun. Ariz., 1987-90; v.p. Ariz. Com. for Bicentennial of the French Revolution, 1988-89; pres. Olympia World Affairs Coun., 2003—. With U.S. Army, 1968-69, Vietnam. Decorated Bronze Star; recipient medal of Landtag of Badden-Württemberg, Germany, 1987, Spl. Svc. award Alliance Francaise of Phoenix, 1992, Marengo medal Province of Alessandria, Italy, 1997, medal City of Ajaccio, Corsica, France, 1997. Fellow Internat. Napoleonic Soc. (exec. v.p. and editor-in-chief 1995—, Legion of Merit 1996); mem. Napoleonic Alliance (exec. v.p. 1992—2004, pres. 2004-07, editor conf. procs., editor bull., Pres. medal 1998), Inst. on Napoleon and the French Revolution, Western Soc. for French History, Sierra Club, Population Connection, Alpha Kappa Delta, Phi Kappa Phi, Phi Alpha Theta. Democrat. Avocations: collecting Napoleonic items, writing history, outdoor activities, travel, music. Home: 1841 52nd Way SE Olympia WA 98501-8000 E-mail: imperialgloryof@comcast.net.

MARKHAM, JESSE WILLIAM, economist, educator; b. Richmond, Va., Apr. 21, 1916; s. John James and Edith (Luttrell) M.; m. Penelope Jane Anton, Oct. 15, 1944; children: Elizabeth Anton Markham McLean, John James, Jesse William. AB, U. Richmond, 1941; postgrad., Johns Hopkins U., 1941-42, U.S. Fgn. Svc. Sch., 1945; MA, Harvard U., 1947, PhD, 1949. Acct. E.I. duPont de Nemours Co., Richmond, 1935-38; tchg. fellow Harvard U., 1946-48; asst. prof. Vanderbilt U., 1948-52, assoc. prof., 1952-53; chief economist FTC, Washington, 1953-55; assoc. prof. Princeton U., 1955-57, prof. econs., 1957-68; prof. Harvard Grad. Sch. Bus. Adminstrn., 1968-72, Charles Edward Wilson prof., 1972-82, prof. emeritus, 1982—; prof. Harvard U. Ext. Svcs., 1984—. Vis. prof. Columbia U., 1958; Ford Found. vis. prof. Harvard Grad. Sch. Bus. ADminstrn., 1965-66; rsch. prof. Law and Econs. Ctr., Emory U., 1982-84; rsch. staff, mem. bd. editors Patent Trademark Copyright Rsch. Inst., George Washington U., 1955-70; econs. editor Houghton Mifflin Co., 1961-71; U.S. del. commn. experts on bus. practices European Productivity Agy., OEEC, 1956, 57, 58, 59, 61; vis. prof. Harvard U., 1961-62; dir. Ford Found. Seminar Region II, 1961; adv. com. mktg. to sec. commerce, 1967-71; mem. Am. Bar Assn. Commn. to study FTC, 1969. Author: Competition in the Rayon Industry, 1952, The Fertilizer Industry: Study of an Imperfect Market, 1958, The American Economy, 1963, (with Charles Fiero and Howard Piquet) The European Common Market: Friend or Competitor, 1964, (with Gustav Papnek) Industrial Organization and Economic Development, 1970, Conglomerate Enterprise and Public Policy, 1973, (with Paul Teplitz) Baseball Economics and Public Policy, 1982; sect. on oligopoly Internat. Ency. Social Scis.; contbr. articles to econ. jours. Del. People to People Diplomacy Mission to USSR, 1989; active Boy Scouts Am.; chmn. Harvard Parents Com., 1969-72. Served as lt. USNR, World War II. Ford Found. rsch. prof., 1958-59. Mem. Am. Econ. Assn., U.S. C. of C. (econ. policy com.), Harvard Club (N.Y.C., Sarasota, Fla.), The Cedars Club, Phi Beta Kappa. Episcopalian. Office: Harvard U Grad Sch Bus Adminstrn 300 Cumnock Boston MA 02163

MARKHAM, REED B., education educator, consultant; b. Alhambra, Calif., Feb. 14, 1957; s. John F. and Reeda (Bjarason) M. BA, MA, Brigham Young U., 1982; BS, Regents Coll., 1981, MA, 1982; MPA, U. So. Calif., 1983; MA, UCLA, 1989; PhD, Columbia Pacific U., 1991. Mem. faculty Brigham Young U., Provo, Utah, 1984, Calif. State U., Fullerton and Long Beach, 1984, Northridge, 1985, El Camino Coll., Torrance, Calif., 1986, Orange Coast Coll., Costa Mesa, Calif., 1986, Pasadena (Calif.) Coll., 1986, Fullerton (Calif.) Community Coll., 1986; instr., mem. pub. rels. com. Chaffey (Calif.) Coll., 1986-87; prof., CARES dir. Calif. State Poly. U., Pomona, 1987-98; adj. prof. Calif. State U., LA, 1992-93, dir. Ctr. for Student Retention, 1995—; prof. East LA Coll., 1996—98, Salt Lake CC, 1998—99, Daytona Coll., 2005—06, Daytona Beach CC, 2006—. Speechwriter US Supreme Ct., Washington, 1980; rsch. asst. to pres. Ctr. Study of Cmty. Coll., 1985; cons. gifted children program Johns Hopkins U./Scripps Coll., Claremont, Calif., 1987-88; mem. faculty Riverside (Calif.) Coll., 1989-90, Rio Hondo (Calif.) Coll., 1989-90, English Lang. Inst., 1994, Calif. Poly Summer Bridge, 1989-95; PACE Program East LA, 1995-96; adj. prof. Citrus Coll., 1998—, U. So. Calif., 1998—, Fla. CC, Jacksonville, 2004-05; mem. Pres.'s Coalition Am. Reads Challenge, 1999; mem. Olympic News Svc. 2002, 2001-; mem. governing bd. Coll. of Caribbean, 2005. Author: Power Speechwriting, 1983, Power Speaking, 1990, Public Opinion, 1990, Advances in Public Speaking, 1991, Leadership 2000: Success Skills for University Students, 1995, Excellence in Public Speaking, 1997; co-author: Student Retention: Success Models in Higher Education, 1996, Upward Bound Program Grant Proposal, 1996, Making Marriage Magnificent, 1998; editor Trojan in Govt., U. So. Calif., 1983; editl. bd. mem. Edn. Digest, Speaker and Gavel, Innovative Higher End., Pub. Rels. Rev., Nat. Forensic Jour., The Forensic Educator, Clearinghouse for the Contemporary Educator, Hispanic Am. Family Mag.; writer NY Times, Christian Sci. Monitor; ednl. columnist San Bernardino (Calif.) Sun., 1992-98. VOICE, 2000-01; contbg. editor Great Lives, 2002, American Lives, 2004. Pres. bd. trustees Regents Coll., 1986; appointed to Pres.'s Coalition for Am. Reads Challenge; mem. Olympic News Svc., 2001—; mem. Coun. Study of Cmty. Colls., 2002—; torchbearer Olympic Winter Games, 2002; unit commr. Boy Scouts of Am., 2002—; bd. govs. Univ. Coll. of Caribbean, 2005. Mem. Am. Comm. Assn. (Jour. editl. bd. 2007), Doctorate Assn. NY Scholars, Nat. Assn. Pvt. Nontraditional Colls. (accrediting com. 1989—), Pub. Rels. Soc. Am. (dir.-at-large inland empire 1992-93, faculty advisor), Ctr. Study Cmty. Colls. Mem. Lds Ch. Office Phone: 386-785-2035. Personal E-mail: rljmarkham@comcast.net, reed_markham@hotmail.com. Business E-Mail: markham@dbcc.edu.

MARKIDES, KYRIAKOS SOCRATES, gerontology educator; b. Nicosia, Cyprus, Mar. 21, 1948; arrived in U.S., 1968; s. Socrates and Persoulla Markides; m. Evelyn A. Stanton, Dec. 18, 1971; 1 child, Michael. BA, Bowling Green State U., 1972; MA, La. State U., 1973, PhD, 1976. Asst. prof. U. Tex. Health Sci. Ctr., San Antonio, 1976—82, assoc. prof., 1982—87; prof. U. Tex. Med. Br., Galveston, 1987—, Annie and John Gnitzinger Endowed prof., 1999—. Author (with others): Older Mexican Americans, 1983, Aging and Ethnicity, 1987, Retirement in Industrialized Societies, 1987, Aging and Health, 1989, Aging, Stress and Health, 1989, Minorities, Aging and Health, 1997, Encyclopedia of Health and Aging, 2007; mem. editl. bd. The Gerontologist Jour., 1980—, founding editor Jour. of Aging and Health, 1989—. Grantee Rsch. grantee, Nat. Inst. Aging, 1980—, Hogg Found., 1984—, Rockefeller Found. Fellow: Am. Coll. Epidemiology, Gerontol. Soc. Am.; mem.: APHA, Population Assn. Am., Am. Sociol. Assn. Office: Univ Tex Med Branch Galveston TX 77550 Office Phone: 409-772-2551. E-mail: kmarkide@utmb.edu.

MARKIN, KAREN MARY, research scientist, journalist; b. Hartford, Conn., Jan. 20, 1957; d. Walter Anthony Markin, Katherine Irene Markin; m. Benjamin Adams Cray, June 6, 1987; 1 child, Colleen Cray. BA, Clark U., 1979; MA, Ohio State U., 1986; PhD, U. NC, 1993. Reporter The Day, New London, Conn., 1975—85; dir. rsch. devel. U. R.I., Kingston, RI, 1999—. Head law divsn. Assn. for Edn. in Journalism and Mass Comm.,

Columbia, SC, 2004—05; dir. Ctr. for Humanities U. R.I., Kingston, 2001; proposal reviewer NSF, Arlington, 1999—2004, U.S. Dept. Edn., Washington, 1998—2001. Author (govt. publ.): Ballot Access, volumes 2-4, 1995. V.p. program AAUW, Middletown, RI, 1997—99, pres. Westerly, RI; program panelist AAUW Ednl. Found., 2002—. Mem.: Nat. Coun. Univ. Rsch. Adminstrs., Internat. Comm. Assn., Phi Beta Kappa (treas. RI chpt.). Office: Univ Rhode Island Rsch Office 70 Lower College Rd Kingston RI 02881

MARKISON, BRIAN A., pharmaceutical executive; BS, Iona Coll., 1982. Various mktg. and sales positions Bristol-Myers Squibb, 1982—98, sr. v.p., neuroscience/infectious disease, pres. neuroscience/infectious disease/dermatology, v.p., operational excellence and productivity, 1998—2001; pres. Bristol-Myers Squibb's Oncology, Virology and Oncology Therapeutics, 2001—04; COO King Pharm., Inc., Bristol, Tenn., 2004, pres. & CEO, 2004—. Bd. dir. King Pharm., Inc., Bristol, Tenn., 2004—. Office: King Pharmaceuticals Inc 501 Fifth St Bristol TN 37620 *

MARKLAND, FRANCIS SWABY, JR., biochemist, educator; b. Phila., Jan. 15, 1936; s. Francis Swaby Sr. and Willie Lawrence (Averritt) M.; m. Barbara Blake, Jun. 27, 1959 - April 5, 1996; children: Cathleen Blake, Francis Swaby IV. BS, Pa. State U., 1957; PhD, Johns Hopkins U., 1964. Postdoctoral fellow UCLA, 1964-66, asst. prof. biochemistry, 1966-73; vis. asst. prof. U. So. Calif., Los Angeles, 1973-74, assoc. prof., 1974-83, prof., 1983—, acting chmn. dept. biochemistry, 1986-88, vice-chmn., 1988-92, assoc. dean for sci. affairs, 2004—. Cons. Clin. Lab. Med. Group, LA, 1977-88, Cortech, Inc., Denver, 1983-88, Maret Corp., Wayne, Pa., 1996-2000; co-founder Pivotal BioScis., Inc., 2003-; mem. biochem., endocrinology study sect. NIH, 1986-90, mem FLAIR prog., rev. NIH NCI, 2002-2003, Contbg. editor: Toxicon, Jour. Natural Toxins; contbr. articles to profl. jours.:. Mem. Angeles Choral, L.A. Capt. USNR, 1957-59, ret. Recipient NIH rsch. career devel. award USPHS, NIH, 1968-73; rsch. grantee Nat. Cancer Inst., 1979-86, 91-93, Nat. Heart Lung and Blood Inst., 1984-88, 95-2002, State of Calif. Breast Cancer Rsch. Program, 1995-2002, State Calif. Cancer Rsch. Program, 2000-03, U.S. Army Prostate Cancer Rsch. Program, 2004—, Komen Found., 2004—; study sect. reviewer Western region Am. Heart Assn., 2003-06. Mem. AAAS, Am. Soc. Biochem. and Molecular Biology, Am. Chem. Soc., Internat. Soc. on Toxinology, Internat. Soc. on Thrombosis and Haemostasis (subcom. exogenous hemostatic factors, chair 1994-96, co-chair 1999—), Am. Assn. Cancer Rsch., Am. Soc. Hematology, Sigma Xi, Alpha Zeta. Avocations: singing, aerobics, bicycling. Office: U So Calif Keck Sch Medicine Cancer Rsch Lab Rm 106 1303 N Mission Rd Los Angeles CA 90033-1020 Business E-Mail: markland@usc.edu.

MARKLE, DAVID A., optical engineer; Sr. v.p., chief tech. officer Ultratech Stepper, San Jose, Calif. Recipient David Richardson medal Optical Soc. Am., 1994. Mem.: NAE. Office: 3050 Zanker Rd San Jose CA 95134-2126

MARKLEY, WILLIAM C., lawyer; b. Salina, Kans., Dec. 21, 1945; m. Marcia A. Markley. BS, US Naval Acad., 1967; JD, Hastings Coll. Law, 1974. Sr. v.p., gen. counsel, sec. Jacobs Engring. Group Inc., Pasadena, Calif. Mem.: Am. Corp. Counsel Assn., State Bar Calif., ABA, LA County Bar Assn. Office: Jacobs Engring Group Inc 1111 S Arroyo Pky PO Box 7084 Pasadena CA 91109-7084 Office Phone: 626-578-6855. Office Fax: 626-578-6990. Business E-Mail: Bill.Markley@Jacobs.com. *

MARKMAN, RONALD, artist, educator; b. Bronx, NY, May 29, 1931; s. Julius and Mildred (Berkowitz) M.; m. Barbara Miller, Sept. 12, 1959; 1 dau., Ericka Elizabeth. B.F.A., Yale U., 1957, M.F.A., 1959. Instr. Art Inst. Chgo., 1960-64; prof. fine arts Ind. U., 1964—. Color cons. Hallmark Card Co., 1959-60 One-man shows Kanegis Gallery, 1959, Reed Coll., 1966, Terry Dintenfass Gallery, 1965, 66, 68, 70, 76, 79, 82, 85, The Gallery, Bloomington, Ind., 1972, 79, Indpls. Mus., 1974, Tyler Sch. Art, Phila., 1976, Franklin Coll., 1980, Dart Gallery, Chgo., 1981, Patrick King Gallery, Indpls., 1983, 86, John Heron Gallery, Indpls., 1985, New Harmony Gallery, 1985, Mitchell Gallery, St. John's Coll., Annapolis, Md., 2005; two-man show Dintenfass Gallery, 1984; group shows include Kanegis Gallery, Boston, 1958, 60, 61, Boston Arts Festival, 1959, 60, Mus. Modern Art, 1959, 66, Whitney Mus., N.Y.C., 1960, Art Inst. Chgo., 1964, Gallery 99, Miami, Fla., 1966, Ball State Coll., 1966, Butler Inst., 1967, Indpls. Mus., 1968, 69, 72, 74, Phoenix Gallery, N.Y.C., 1970, Harvard U., 1974, Skidmore Coll., 1975, Am. Acad. Arts and Letters, 1977, 89, Tuthill-Gimprich Gallery, N.Y.C., 1980, Patrick King Gallery, 1988, numerous others; represented in permanent collections Met. Mus. Art, Mus. Modern Art, Art Inst. Chgo., Library of Congress, Cin. Art Mus., Bklyn. Mus., Ark. Art Center, others; commns. include 5 murals Riley Children's Hosp., Indpls., 1986; installation Evanston (Ill.) Art Ctr., 1989, 2-part installation Ortho Child Care Ctr., Raritan, N.J., 1991; illustrator Acid and Basics-A Guide to Acid-Base Physiology, 1992. Served with U.S. Army, 1952-54. Recipient Ind. Arts Commn. award, 1990, 93; Fulbright grantee, Italy, 1962, grantee Ctr. for New TV, Chgo., 1992; Lilly Endowment fellow, 1989, honorable mention, Ohio Film Festival, 1995. Home and Office: 1623 Saint Margarets Rd Annapolis MD 21401-5540

MARKMAN, STEPHEN J., state supreme court justice; b. Detroit, June 4, 1949; s. Julius and Pauline Markman; m. Mary Kathleen Sites, Aug. 25, 1974; children: James, Charles. BA, Duke U., 1971; JD, U. Cin., 1974. Legis. asst. to Rep. Edward Hutchinson, Mich., 1975, Rep. Tom Hagedorn, Minn., 1976—78; chief counsel, staff dir. subcom. on constn. Senate Com. on Judiciary, 1978—85, dep. chief counsel, 1983; asst. atty. gen. Office Legal Policy, Dept. Justice, Washington, 1985-89; U.S. atty. U.S. Dept. Justice, Detroit, 1989-93; mem. Miller, Canfield, Paddock & Stone, Detroit, 1993—95; judge Mich. Ct. Appeals, 1995—99; justice Mich. Supreme Ct., Lansing, Mich., 1999—. Prof. constitutional law Hillsdale Coll. Author numerous articles appearing in Stanford Law Review, U. Chicago Law Review, U. Mich. Jour. of Law Reform, Am. Criminal Justice Law Review, Barrister's Law Jour., Harvard Jour. of Law & Public Policy, Detroit Coll. of Law Review. Fellow: Mich. Bar Found.; mem.: ABA, One Hundred Club, Am. Inns of Ct. Office: Mich Supreme Ct Hall of Justice 925 W Ottawa St Fl 6 Lansing MI 48915 Office Phone: 517-373-9449.

MARKOE, FRANK, JR., lawyer, health facility administrator; b. Balt., Sept. 5, 1923; s. Frank and Margaret (Smith) M.; m. Margaret McCormack (div.); children: Andrée Markoe Caldwell, Ritchie Harrison Markoe Scribner. AB, Washington and Lee U., 1947; LLB, U. Md., 1950. Bar: Md. 1950. Pntr. Karl F. Steinmann, Balt., 1948-50, 50-53, Cable & McDaniel, Balt., 1954-55; gen. counsel, dir. Emerson Drug Co., Balt., 1955-56, adminstrv. v.p., 1957-58; v.p., sec., dir., gen. counsel Warner-Lambert Pharm. Co., 1958-67, exec. com., sr. v.p., dir., gen. counsel, sec., 1967-69, exec. asst. chmn. bd., 1970-71, sr. v.p., 1971-73; exec. v.p. Warner-Lambert Co., Morris Plains, NJ, 1973-77, vice chmn. bd., 1977-81; vice chmn. adv. bd. NY Hosp.-Cornell Med. Ctr., 1987—, also chmn. major gifts com. Capital Campaign; hon. holder Alfred E. Driscoll chair Fairleigh Dickinson U. Bd. dirs. NJ Coll. Medicine and Dentistry, Bd. Internat. Broadcasting, Radio Free Europe/Radio Liberty, Kips Bay Boys; bd. dirs., exec. com., pres. NJ Ballet. With USAAF, 1942-45, PTO. Mem. US C. of C., Proprietary Assn. (chmn., bd. dir., exec. com.), Pharm. Mfrs. Assn. (bd. dir., exec. com.), NJ State C. of C. (bd. dir.), Phi Beta Kappa. Home and Office: 201 Grenville Rd Hobe Sound FL 33455-2414

MARKOFF, BRAD STEVEN, lawyer; b. NYC, July 29, 1957; s. Daniel and Geri (Skitol) M.; m. Danna Kay Schmidt, May 17, 1980; children: Andrew David, Paul Steven, Samuel Joseph. AB, Duke U., 1979; JD, Washington U., St. Louis, 1982. Bar: Mo. 1982, U.S. Tax Ct. 1984, N.C. 1985. Assoc. Stolar Partnership, St. Louis, 1982-84; assoc., ptnr. Moore & Van Allen, Raleigh, NC, 1984-92; ptnr. Smith Helms Mulliss & Moore, Raleigh, NC, 1992-97, Alston & Bird LLP, Raleigh, NC, 1997—2005, ptnr. in charge Research Triangle Park, NC, 1997—2005, DLA Piper Rudnick Gray Cary US LLP, Raleigh, NC, 2005—; co-chair nat. REIT practice, mng. ptnr. Raleigh office. Bd. dirs. Coun. for Entrepreneurial Devel., Research Triangle Park, NC; spl. coun. apptd. by NC Gov. NC. R.R. Study Group, 1992-93; practice group head Alston & Bird's NC Bus. Practice, 1997—2005. Contbr. articles to profl. jours. Mem. ABA, Nat. Assn. Bond Lawyers, Nat. Assn. Real Estate Investment Trusts (mem. bd. advisors), Mo. Bar Assn., N.C. Bar Assn. Avocations: golf, skiing. Office: DLA Piper US LLP 4141 Parklake Ave Ste 300 Raleigh NC 27612-2350 Home Phone: 919-787-5021; Office Phone: 919-786-2000. Office Fax: 919-786-2200. Business E-Mail: brad.markoff@dlapiper.com.

MARKOFF, JOHN, reporter; b. Oakland, Calif., Oct. 24, 1949; m. Leslie Terzian. Bachelors, Whitman Coll., Walla Walla, Washington, 1971; Masters, U. Oreg., 1976. Covered tech. and def. industry Pacific News Svc., San Francisco, 1977—81; reporter, editor Infoworld, 1981—83; wrote column on personal computers San Jose Mercury, 1983—85; west coast editor Byte Mag., 1984—85; reporter San Francisco Examiner, 1985—88; reporter, bus. sect., computer and tech. NY Times, 1988—. Adj. faculty Stanford U., 2002—; lectr. U. Calif. Berkeley Sch. Journalism. Co-author (with Lennie Siegel): The High Cost of High Tech, 1985; co-author: (with Katie Hafner) Cyberpunk: Outlaws and Hackers on the Computer Frontier, 1991; co-author: (with Tsutomu Shimomura) Takedown: The Pursuit and Capture of America's Most Wanted Computer Outlaw, 1996. Recipient award for best new reporting, Software Pub. Assn., 1988, Gerald Loeb award, UCLA Anderson Sch. Mgmt. Office: NY Times 201 Spear St San Francisco CA 94105 Office Phone: 415-836-6700. Business E-Mail: markoff@nytimes.com.

MARKOFF, STEVEN C., finance company executive; CEO, pres., founder A. Mark Fin., Santa Monica, Calif., 1965—. Co-chmn. A. Mark Entertainment Film Prodn. Co., 2004; dir. Goldline Internat.; chmn. Careside Inc. Dir. ACLU Found. Southern Calif., 1979—; dir. Mgmt. Edn. Associates UCLA, 1986—92, dir. bd. visitors Grad. Sch. Mgmt., 1986; dir. Hollywood Cmty. Hosp., 1982—91. Office: A Mark Financial Corporation 233 Wilshire Blvd Ste 200 Santa Monica CA 90401-1227

MARKOS, CHRIS, retired real estate company executive; b. Cleve., Nov. 25, 1926; s. George and Bessie (Papathatou) Markos; m. Alice Zaharopoulos, Dec. 11, 1949 (dec.); children: Marilyn Martin, Irene Matthews, Betsy Feierabend; m. Marilyn Gardanier, Nov. 8, 2002; children: Kathleen Mitchell, Patricia Hickle. BA, Case Western Res. U., Cleve., 1960; LLB, LaSalle U., Chgo., 1964. Cert. gen. real estate appraiser Ohio. Pres. Brooklyn Realty Co., Cleve., 1953—63; vice-pres. Herbert Laronge Inc., Cleve., 1963-76; v.p. Calabrese, Racek and Markos Inc., Cleve., 1976-83, Herbert Laronge Inc., Cleve., 1983-87, pres., 1987-88; v.p. Cragin Lang, Inc., Cleve., 1989-91; sr. cons. Grubb & Ellis, Cleve., 1991-93; sr. v.p. Realty One Appraisal Divsn., Independence, Ohio, 1993-98. Pres. Alcrimar Inc., 1989—98. Co-author: Ohio Supplement to Modern Real Estate Practice, 5th-7th edits.; cons. editor, co-author: Modern Real Estate Practice in Ohio, 1st-3rd edits. Bd. dirs. Meyers U., Cleve., 1984-97. With US Army, 1945-46. Mem. Am. Soc. Appraisers (sr., pres. 1973, state dir. 1976), Cleve. Bd. Realtors (hon. life mem., pres. 1974, Realtor of Yr. award 1976). Republican. Greek Orthodox. Home: Corinthian Condominium 936 Intracoastal Dr Apt 6-H Fort Lauderdale FL 33304 Personal E-mail: alcrimar@bellsouth.net. *Everyone's life has a beginning and an ending. It is what happens between these two points that makes up the essence of a person.*

MARKOSKI, JOSEPH PETER, lawyer; b. Floral Park, NY, Nov. 7, 1948; s. Stephen Nicolas and Josephine Veronica (Lapkofsky) Markoski; m. Julie Ann Angus, June 30, 1979; children: Katherine, Caroline, Peter. BSFS, Georgetown U., 1970, JD, 1973. Bar: DC 1973. Law clk. Hon. Thomas A. Flannery US Dist. Ct., Washington, 1973-74; assoc. Wilkinson, Cragun & Barker, Washington, 1975-80, ptnr., 1980-82, Squire, Sanders & Dempsey, Washington, 1982-96, mng. ptnr., 1991-96, mng. ptnr. Europe London, 1996—, mng. ptnr. DC & Tysons Corner, Va. Offices, chmn., Comm. Practice Group. Co-chmn. task force on open network initiatives Strategic Planning Group of U.S. CCITT Nat. Com., 1988-92; bd. dirs. Cmty. Lodgings, Inc. Co-author: Internat. Telecommunications Handbook, 1986; contbr. articles to profl. jours. Capt. USAR, 1970—78. Mem. ABA (vice-chmn. common carrier com. sci. and tech. sect. 1986-88, internat. common carrier project 1980-86), Fed. Commn. Bar Assn. (com. common carrier practice and procedure 1980—), Computer Law Assn. (bd. dirs., chmn. telecomm. bar liaison com. 1994-96), Internat. Bar Assn. (mem. comm. and internat. computer and tech. law coms.), Am. C. of C. (Eng.). Democrat. Roman Catholic. Office: Squire Sanders & Dempsey LLP 1201 Pennsylvania Ave NW Washington DC 20044 also: Squire Sanders & Dempsey LLP 8000 Towers Crescent Dr 14th Floor Vienna VA 22182-2700 Office Fax: 703-720-7801, 202-626-6780. Business E-Mail: jmarkoski@ssd.com.

MARKOVICH, ALEXANDRIA, assistant principal; b. NYC, Jan. 18, 1954; d. Alexander and Mary Markovich; m. Robert Steven Young, Nov. 15, 1987; children: Anastasia Nicole Young, Christopher Robert Alexander Young. BA, SUNY, Stony Brook, NY, 1976; M Profl. Studies in Creativity Devel., Pratt Inst., Bklyn., 1978; MEd, Coll. New Rochelle, NY, 2002. Cert. art tchr. NY State Bd. Edn., 1979, tchr. nursery, kindergarten, grades 1-6 NY State Bd. Edn., 1979, spl. edn. tchr. NY State Bd. Edn., 1982, specialization in staff devel. NY State Bd. Edn., 2001, asst. prin. spl. edn. day HS NYC Bd. Edn., 2003, health conservation tchr. NYC Bd. Edn., 1982, fine arts jr. HS tchr. NYC Bd. Edn., 1982, fine arts Day HS tchr. NYC Bd. Edn., 1982, spl. edn. tchr. NYC Bd. Edn., 1996, asst. prin. spl. edn. schs. NYC Bd. Edn., 2003, asst. prin. elem., intermediate, and jr. HS NYC Bd. Edn., 2003, asst. prin. in Fine Arts Day H.S. NYC Bd. Edn., 2003, supr. spl. edn. NYC Bd. Edn., 2003, sch. dist. adminstr. NY State Dept. Edn., 2002, cert. nat. official US Luge Assn., 2000. Spl. edn. tchr. Pub. Sch. 23 at Elmhurst Hosp., NY, 1980—82; spl. edn. tchr., art therapist Pub. Sch. 177 Queens, Fresh Meadows, 1982—2003; asst. prin. Pub. Sch. 4 at 179 Queens, Fresh Meadows, 2003—; asst. to prin., adminstrv. intern Saw Mill Elem. Sch., Bellmore, 2000—01. Contbr. articles to profl. jours.; actor: (plays) Little Shop of Horrors, Bye, Bye Birdie, Hello Out There, Plaza Suite;. Nominee N.Y. State Tchr. of Yr. award, N.Y. State Dept. Edn., 1985, 1986, 1987; named Tchr. of Yr., Coun. Exceptional Children, 1985, 1986; recipient Outstanding Spl. Educators award, 1982, Outstanding Performance as an Art Educator award, N.Y.C. Bd. Edn., 1984, Superior Art Instrn. award, A.A.A., Nat. Traffic Safety Program, 1986. Mem.: ASCD, Coun. Sch. Supervisors and Adminstrs., NYC Art Tchrs. Assn. (fin. sec. 1988—89, sec. 1987—88), NY State Alliance for Arts Edn., NY State Art Tchrs. Assn. (ad hoc com. mem. 1986—87), Girl Scouts Nassau County (del. 2001—05), Girl Scouts Merrick Assn. (treas. 2000—06, recruiter registrar 1995—2000). Home Phone: 516-223-1937; Office Phone: 718-264-0916. Personal E-mail: alexandria11566@yahoo.com.

MARKOVICH, PATRICIA H., economist; b. Oakland, Calif. MS in Econs., U. Calif., Berkeley; postgrad., Stanford U. Cert. emergency mgmt. planner. Pvt. practice polit. and econs. cons.; former aide to majority whip Oreg. Ho. of Reps.; lectr., instr. various Calif. instns., Chemeketa (Oreg.) Coll., Portland (Oreg.) State U.; commr. City of Oakland, Calif. Chairperson, bd. dirs. Cable Sta. KCOM; econ. and emergency mgmt. cons. Mem. Piedmont (Calif.) Gen. Plan Commn. NSF grant Oreg. Grad. Rsch. Ctr., Lilly Found. grant. Mem.: Nat. Coordinating Coun. Emergency Mgmt., San Francisco Bay Area Rug Soc., Mensa.

MARKOVICH, VOYA R., information technology executive; arrived in US, 1969; s. Rista A. and Draga S. Markovic; m. Anita M. Sica, Jan. 9, 1951; children: Michael children: Steven. BS in Chemistry, U. Belgrade, Serbia, 1966; MS in Chemistry, Poly. Inst. N.Y., 1981. Analytical chemist Commodity Labs., Inc., NYC, 1969—81; devel. project mgr. IBM, Endicott, NY, 1981—2002; sr. v.p., chief tech. officer, gen. mgr. R&D and IP, Endicott Interconnect Techs., Inc., Endicott. Sr. tech. staff mem. IBM, Endicott, 1996—2002, mem. Acad. of Tech., 1997—2002. Contbr. chapters to books. Mem.: IEEE (assoc.), Electronic Components Tech. Conf. (assoc.), Internat. Printed Circuits (assoc.), Integrated Electronics Engring. Ctr. (assoc.), Internat. Microelectronics Packaging Soc. (assoc.). Achievements include 168 US patents in field; some of the patents include Direct Chip Attach on Laminate Packaging; Full Additive Process - Copper Bondable Surface (CBS); Z Interconnection for Organic Packaging; High Performance Core Board Technology; invention of High Speed Board design. Avocations: travel, technology, politics. Home: 3611 Joel Dr Endicott NY 13760 Office: Endicott Interconnect Technologies Inc 1701 North Street Endicott NY 13760 Home Phone: 607-754-9593; Office Phone: 607-755-1978. Personal E-mail: markovichv@yahoo.com, voyarm@aol.com. Business E-Mail: v.markovich@eitny.com. E-mail: voya.markovich@eitny.com.

MARKOVITS, ANDREI STEVEN, political science professor; b. Timisoara, Romania, Oct. 6, 1948; came to U.S., 1960, naturalized, 1971; s. Ludwig and Ida (Ritter) M. BA, Columbia U., NYC, 1969, MBA, 1971, MA, 1973, MPhil, 1974, PhD, 1976; PhD (hon.), Leuphana U., Lüneburg, Germany, 2007. Mem. faculty NYU, 1974, John Jay Coll. Criminal Justice, CUNY, 1974, Columbia U., 1975; rsch. assoc. Inst. Advanced Studies, Vienna, 1973—74, Wirtschafts und Sozialwissenschaftliches Inst., German Trade U. Fedn., Düsseldorf, Germany, 1979, Internat. Inst. Comparative Social Rsch., Sci. Ctr. Berlin, 1980; asst. prof. govt. Wesleyan U., Middletown, Conn., 1977—83; assoc. prof. polit. sci. Boston U., 1983—92; prof., chair dept. politics U. Calif., Santa Cruz, 1995—99; prof. dept. Germanic langs. and lit., dept. polit. sci., dept. sociology U. Mich., Ann Arbor, 1999—2003, Karl W. Deutsch Collegiate prof. comparative politics and German studies, 2003—. Sr. rsch. assoc. Ctrl. European Studies Harvard U., 1975—99; vis. prof. Tel Aviv U., 1986, Osnabruck U., 1987, Bochum U., 1991; Fulbright prof. U. Innsbruck, Austria, 1996; vis. prof. Harvard U., 2002—03, St. Gallen (Switzerland) U., 2004, Hebrew U., 2005, Dortmund U., 2006. Author, editor books and papers in field; TV and radio commentator. Univ. Pres.'s fellow Columbia U., 1969, B'nai B'rith Found. fellow, 1976-77, Kalmus Found. fellow, 1976-77, Ford Found. fellow, 1979, Hans Boeckler Found. fellow, 1982 Inst. for Advanced Study Berlin fellow, 1998-99; N.Y. State scholar Columbia U., 1969; Winner Golden Apple award Best Tchr. U. Mich., 2007. Mem. N.Y. Acad. Scis., Am. Polit. Sci. Assn., Internat. Polit. Sci. Assn., AAUP. Home: 718 Onondaga St Ann Arbor MI 48104-2611 Office: Univ Mich 3110 Modern Lang Bldg 812 E Washington St Ann Arbor MI 48109-1275 Office Phone: 734-764-8018. Personal E-mail: andreimarkovits@cs.com. Business E-Mail: andymark@umich.edu.

MARKOWITZ, DEBORAH LYNN, state official; b. Tarrytown, NY, Sept. 14, 1961; d. Gerald Harvey and Sandra Lee (Schulner) Markowitz; m. Paul William Markowitz, June 19, 1988; children: Aviva Lee, Sandra Rose, Ari David. BA with honors, U. Vt., 1982; JD magna cum laude, Georgetown U., 1987. Bar: Vt. 1988, US Dist. Ct. Vt. 1989. Assoc. Covington & Burling, Washington, summer 1986; jud. law clk. to Justice Peck Vt. Supreme Ct., Montpelier, 1987-88; assoc. Langrack, Sperry & Wool, Burlington, Vt., 1988-90; dir. Law Ctr. Vt. League Cities and Towns, Montpelier, Vt., 1990—97; devel. cons. Vt. Law Sch., South Royalton, 1997—; sec. state State of Vt., 1998—. Adj. faculty Vt. Law Sch., South Royalton, 1992; examiner Vt. Bd. Bar Examiners, Montpelier, 1994-98. Contbr. articles to profl. jours. Bd. dirs. Ctrl. Vt. Cmty. Action Agy., Vt. Hist. Soc.; trustee Woodbury Coll. Mem. ABA (state and local govt. sect.), Vt. Bar Assn. (mcpl. com.), Internat. Mcpl. Lawyers Assn. (chair pers. sect. 1993—), Nat. Assn. Secs. of State (pres.), Nat. Mus. Women in the Arts (bd. dirs. Vt. chpt.), Order of Coif. Democrat. Avocations: cross country skiing, singing, sketching, gardening. Office: Office Sec State Redstone Bldg 26 Terrace Street, PO Box 9 Montpelier VT 05609-0001 Office Phone: 802-828-2148. Office Fax: 802-828-2496. E-mail: dmarkowitz@sec.state.vt.us. *

MARKOWITZ, GERALD E., historian, educator; b. NYC, July 12, 1944; s. Irving and Esther Wittes Markowitz; m. Andrea Ades, Nov. 25, 1994; children: William, Tobias, Elena Kennedy, Isa Vasquez, Anton Vasquez. BA, Earlham Coll., Richmond, Ind., 1965; PhD, U. of Wis., 1971. Disting. prof. history John Jay Coll., CUNY, NYC, 1970—, Grad. Ctr., CUNY, NYC, 1990—; adj. prof. sociomed. sci. Mailman Sch. of Pub. Health, Columbia U., NYC, 2002—. Mem., bd. of dirs. Am. Social History Project, NYC, 2002—. Author (with David Rosner): (book) Deceit and Denial: The Deadly Politics of Industrial Pollution, Are We Ready? Public Health Since 9/11, Deceit and Denial: The Deadly Politics of Industrial Pollution, Deadly Dust: Silicosis and the Politics of Industrial Disease in Twentieth Century America (Outstanding Academic Book of 1991 by Choice, 1991); author: (with Marlene Park) Democratic Vistas: Post Offices and Public Art in the New Deal; author: Are We Ready: Public Health Since 9/11; editor (with David Rosner): Slaves of the Depression: Workers Letters About Life on the Job, Dying for Work: Workers' Safety and Health in Twentieth Century America; contbr. articles to profl. jours. Recipient Arthur Viseltear Award for Outstanding Contribns. to the History of Pub. Health, Med. Care Sect., APHA, 2000, Award for Disting. Work in Occupl. and Environ. Health, N.Y. Com. for Occupl. Health; grantee Power and Pollution: The Politics of Indsl. Disease, NSF, 2001—02, Interpretative Rsch. grantee, NEH, 1992—94, 1987—89, History of Occupl. Safety and Health grantee, Milbank Meml. Fund, 1985—86, The Un-Natural History of Pub. Health grantee, Robert Wood Johnson Investigator Awards in Health Policy Rsch., 2002—. Mem.: Am. Soc. for Environ. History, Orgn. of Am. History, Am. Hist. Assn. Office: John Jay College 899 Tenth Ave New York NY 10019 Office Phone: 212-237-8458. E-mail: gmarkowitz@jjay.cuny.edu.

MARKOWITZ, HARRY MAX, finance and economics educator; b. Chgo., Aug. 24, 1927; s. Morris and Mildred (Gruber) M.; m. Barbara Gay. PhB, U. Chgo., 1947, MA, 1950, PhD, 1954. With research staff Rand Corp., Santa Monica, Calif., 1952-60, 61-63; chmn. bd., tech. dir. Consol. Analysis Ctrs., Inc., Santa Monica, 1963-68; prof. UCLA, Westwood, 1968-69; pres. Arbitrage Mgmt. Co., NYC, 1969-72; pvt. practice cons. NYC, 1972-74; prof. Wharton Sch Bus., U. Pa., 1972—74; with research staff T.J. Watson Research Ctr. IBM, Yorktown Hills, NY, 1974-83; prof. Rutgers U., 1980—82; Marvin Speiser Disting. Prof. of Fin. and Econs. Baruch Coll. CUNY, NYC, 1982-93; dir. rsch. Daiwa Securities Trust Co, Jersey City, 1990-2000; prin., owner Harry Markowitz Co., 1993—; rsch. prof. dept. econs. U. Calif. San Diego. V.p. Inst. Mgmt. Sci., 1960-62. adv. bd. Jour. Investment Mgmt. Author: Portfolio Selection: Efficient Diversification of Investments, 1959, Mean-Variance Analysis in Portfolio Choice, 1987; co-author: SIMSCRIPT Simulation Programming Language, 1963; co-editor: Process Analysis of Economic Capabilities, 1963. Recipient John von Neumann Theory prize Ops. Rsch. Soc. Am. and Inst. Mgmt. Sci., 1989, Nobel Prize in Econs., 1990. Fellow Econometric Soc., Am. Acad. Arts and Scis., Am. Fin. Assn. Office: Ste 245 1010 Turquoise St San Diego CA 92109 *

MARKOWITZ, JOHN C., psychiatrist; b. NYC, Oct. 11, 1954; s. Joel and Elizabeth Jane (Rich) M.; m. Kathleen F. Clougherty, Mar. 28, 1980; 1 child, Caitlin Clougherty Markowitz. BA, Columbia Coll., NYC, 1976; MA, Columbia U. GSAS, NYC, 1978; MD, Columbia Coll. of Physicians and Surgeons, NYC, 1982. Intern. Payne Whitney Clin., N.Y. Hosp., NYC, 1982-83, Psychiatric res., 1983-86, chief res., 1986-87; instr. in psychiatry Cornell U. Med. Coll., NYC, 1986-89, asst. prof. of psychiatry, 1989-94, assoc. prof. clin. psychiatry, 1994—; lectr. psychiatry Columbia U. Coll. Physicians and Surgeons, NYC, 1993—. Edit. cons. Psychiat. Svcs., Jour. of Psychotherapy Practice and Rsch., Washington; cons. Commn. on Psychotherapy, 1996—. Author: Interpersonal Psychotherapy for Dysthymic Disorder, 1997, also numerous psychiatric chpts. and articles, 1984—. Recipient Individual Faculty Scholar Award, Nat. Inst. of Mental Health, Rockville, Md., 1988-91, APA/Burroughs Wellcome Fellowship, Washington, 1984-86; NIMH grantee, 1993-96. Fellow Am. Psychiat. Assn. (sci. program com. 1984-95, legis. rep. N.Y. County Dist. br. 1987-93, mem. com. on AIDS 1986—). Office: Payne Whitney Clinic NY Hosp 445 E 68th St New York NY 10021-6330

MARKOWITZ, MARTIN H., biomedical researcher; b. NYC, Nov. 22, 1953; BA in Biology, SUNY, Buffalo, NY, 1974; MD, Stanford U., 1978. Cert. internal medicine 1981, med. oncology 1983, hematology 1984. Intern, medicine Mt. Zion Hosp. and Med. Ctr., U. Calif., San Francisco, 1978—79, resident, medicine, 1979—81; clin. fellow, hematology/oncology Cornell Med. Coll., NY, 1981—82, rsch. fellow, hematology/oncology NY, 1982—83, chief clin. fellow, instr., dept. medicine, divsn. hematology/oncology, 1983—84; asst. attending physician Hosp. for Spl. Surgery, 1985; attending adult hematologist Regional Comprehensive Hemophilia Diagnostic and Treatment Ctr., Cornell Med. Coll., 1986; attending hematologist/oncologist Spellman Ctr. for the Treatment of HIV Related Disease, St. Clare's Hosp., NY, 1985—89; acting dir. Spellman Ctr., St. Clare's Hosp., NY, 1989; attending staff, dept. of medicine, divsn. hematology/oncology Lenox Hill Hosp., NY, 1985—90; vis. assoc. physician Rockefeller Univ. Hosp., NY, 1995—96; clin. fellow, divsn. infectious diseases NYU/Bellevue, NY, 1991—92; rsch. fellow Aaron Diamond AIDS Rsch. Ctr., NY, 1992—94, staff investigator NY, 1994—, clin. dir., 1998—; adj. assoc. physician, divsn. infectious diseases Cornell Med. Coll., 1996—; assoc. physician Rockefeller Univ. Hosp., NY, 1996—; assoc. prof. Rockefeller U., NYC, 2000. Instr., dept. medicine/div. hematology/oncology Cornell Med. Coll., 1984—85; instr., dept. medicine NYU, 1994—95; asst. prof., dept. medicine, divsn. infectious diseases NY Med. Sch., NY, 1995—96; assoc. prof. clin. investigation Rockefeller Univ., NY, 2000—. Editor: Journal of AIDS; review assignments Journal of American Med. Assn., Journal of Virology, Lancet, Journal of Infectious Diseases, AIDS and Human Retroviruses, PNAS, AIDS after PNAS. Named 10th Annual Mothers' Voices, 2001; recipient AMFAR award of Courage, NY, 2001. Mem.: Infectious Disease Soc. of Am., Am. Soc. Microbiology, Phi Beta Kappa. Achievements include research in HIV therapeutics and pathogenesis. Office: Aaron Diamond AIDS Rsch Ctr 455 First Ave 7th Fl New York NY 10016 E-mail: mmarkowitz@adarc.org.

MARKOWITZ, MARTY (MARTIN MARKOWITZ), city manager; b. Bklyn., Feb. 14, 1945; m. Jamie Markowitz, 1999. BA, Bklyn. Coll., 1970. Organizer Flatbush Tenants Coun., 1971; elected to NY State Senate, Albany, 1979—2002, past mem. aging com., civil svc. and pensions com., health com., housing and cmty. devel. com., labor com.; borough pres. Brooklyn, 2002—. Chair Initiative for a Competitive Brooklyn; creator Seaside Summer Concert Series, Coney Island, Martin Luther King, Jr. Concert Series, Flatbush. Mem. NAACP (life), Midwood Jewish Ctr., City Urban League. Office: 209 Joralemon St Brooklyn NY 11201 Office Phone: 718-802-3700.

MARKOWITZ, SAMUEL SOLOMON, chemistry professor; b. Bklyn., Oct. 31, 1931; s. Max and Florence Ethel (Goldman) M.; children: Michael, Daniel, Jonah; m. 2d Lydia de Antonis, Oct. 31, 1993. BS in Chemistry, Rensselaer Poly. Inst., 1953; MA, Princeton U., 1955, PhD, 1957; postgrad., Brookhaven Nat. Lab., 1955-57. Asst. prof. chemistry U. Calif., Berkeley, 1958-64, assoc. prof., 1964-72, prof., 1972—. Faculty sr. scientist Lawrence Berkeley Lab., 1958—; vis. prof. nuclear physics Weizmann Inst. Sci., Rehovot, Israel, 1973-74. Mem. Bd. Edn. of Berkeley Unified Sch. Dist., 1969-73, pres. bd., 1971-72. Recipient Elizabeth McFeely D'Urso Meml. Pub. Ofcl. award Alameda County Edn. Assn., 1973; LeRoy McKay fellow Princeton U., 1955, Charlotte Elizabeth Proctor fellow Princeton U., 1956, NSF postdoctoral fellow U. Birmingham, Eng., 1957-58, NSF sr. postdoctoral fellow Faculte des Scis. U. Paris a Orsay, Laboratoire Joliot-Curie de Physique Nucleaire, 1964-65. Fellow AAAS; mem. Am. Chem. Soc. (bd. dirs. Calif. sect., chmn. 1991, 93-94, Nat, Councilor, 1990-, Walter Petersen award 2003), Am. Phys. Soc., Am. Inst. chemists, N.Y. Acad. Scis., Calif. Inst. Chemists, Sigma Xi. Home: 555 Pierce St # 245 Albany CA 94706 Office: U Calif Dept Chemistry Berkeley CA 94720-1460 Office Phone: 510-642-2922. Business E-Mail: markowit@cchem.berkeley.edu.

MARKOWSKI, ELIZABETH M., lawyer; JD cum laude, NYU, 1978. Law clk. to Hon. Edward Weinfeld US Dist. Ct. (so. dist.) NY, 1978—79; sr. ptnr. Baker Botts LLP, NYC, 1992—2000; sr. v.p. legal Liberty Media Corp., Englewood, Colo., 2000—04; with Liberty Media Internat., Englewood, Colo., 2004—05; sr. v.p., gen. counsel, sec. Liberty Global Inc., Englewood, Colo., 2005—. Mem.: ABA, Assn. of Bar of City of NY. Office: Liberty Global, Inc 12300 Liberty Blvd Englewood CO 80112 Office Phone: 303-220-6600. Office Fax: 303-220-6601. *

MARKOWSKI, JAMES JOSEPH, lawyer; b. NYC, Sept. 28, 1956; s. Joseph Edward and Theresea Markowski; m. Dale Diane Dreps, June 17, 2006; children: Katerine Alexandra, Alexander James; stepchildren: Philp James Nacron, Risa Marie Nacron. JD, Georgetown U., Washington, 1981. Bar: NY 1982. Atty. Skadden, Arps, Slate, Meagher & Flom, NYC, 1981—83, Tory's, NYC, 1983—86, Shea & Gould, NYC, 1986—94; mng. dir., group counsel fin. svcs. BearingPoint, Inc., NYC, 1994—. Editor: Georgetown Law Jour., 1980—81. Trustee Bedford Ctrl. Sch. Dist., NY, 1993—99; com. mem. Bedford Rep. Town Com., 1990—2000; vestry mem. St. Matthew's Ch., Bedford, 1994—2000. Recipient Founder's Day award, NYU, 1978; Regent's scholar, NY State Bd. Regents, 1974—78, U. Honors scholar, NYU, 1978. Home: 7 Kitchawan Rd Pound Ridge NY 10576 Office: BearingPoint Inc 200 Vesey St 3 World Fin Ctr New York NY 10281 Office Phone: 212-698-6280.

MARKS, AARON H., lawyer; b. Washington, May 16, 1968; BA, BS, U. Pa., 1990; JD, Emory U. Sch. Law, 1993. Bar: NJ 1993, NY 1996, admitted to: US Dist. Ct., Dist. NJ 1993, US Ct. of Appeals, Fifth Cir. 1996, US Ct. of Appeals, Fourth Cir. 1997, US Dist. Ct., Eastern Dist. NY 1998, US Dist. Ct., Southern Dist. NY 1998. Ptnr. Kasowitz, Benson, Torres & Friedman LLP, NYC. Named one of Litigation's Rising Stars, The Am. Lawyer, 2007. Office: Kasowitz Benson Torres & Friedman LLP 1633 Broadway New York NY 10019 Office Phone: 212-506-1700. Office Fax: 212-506-1800. *

MARKS, ANDREW ROBERT, molecular biologist; b. NYC, Feb. 22, 1955; s. Paul Alan and Joan Harriet (Rosen) M.; m. Margaret Foster, Jan. 14, 1984; children: Joshua, Daniel, Sarah. BA (magna cum laude), Amherst Coll., 1976; MD, Harvard Med. Sch., 1980. Diplomate Am. Bd. Internal Medicine; cert. in cardiovascular diseases. Intern, resident Mass. Gen. Hosp., Boston, 1980-83, cardiology fellow, 1985-87; fellow genetics Harvard Med. Sch., Boston, 1983-85, instr. medicine, 1987-90; asst. prof. molecular biology Mt. Sinai Sch. Medicine, NYC, 1990-93; assoc. prof. molecular biology and medicine, 1993-97; Fishberg prof. medicine in cardiology Mt. Sinai Sch. Medicine, NYC, 1995-97; Wu prof. medicine, prof. pharmacology Coll. Physicians and Surgeons Columbia U., 1997—, dir. molecular cardiology, 1997—. Contbr. articles to profl. jours. Mem. editl. bd. Jour. Biol. Chemistry. Established investigatorship, Am. Heart Assn., 1993. Recipient Clinician-Scientist award Am. Heart Assn., 1986, Excellence in Rsch. award Am. Fedn. for Clin. Rsch., 1990, Syntex Scholars award, 1991. Mem. Am. Assn. Biol. Chemistry and Molecular Biology, Am. Assn. Cell Biology, Am. Soc. Clin. Investigation (nat. coun. 1997-2000), Inst. Medicine (2004), Biophys. Soc., Harvey Soc., NAS, Sierra Club. Achievements include research on the calcium release channel in cardiac and skeletal muscle; characterization of smooth muscle calcium release channel. Office: Columbia U PYS Bldg 630 W 168th St Bldg 9-401 New York NY 10032-3795

MARKS, BRUCE, performing company executive, choreographer; b. NYC, Jan. 23, 1937; s. Albert and Helen (Kosersky) M.; m. Toni Pihl Petersen, Jan. 27, 1966 (dec. May 1985); children: Erik Antony, Adam Christopher, Kenneth Rikard. Student, Brandeis U., 1954—55, Juilliard Sch., 1955—56; DFA, D, Northeastern U., 1997. Prof. U. Utah, 1981, 1984—86; artistic dir. Boston Ballet Co., 1985—97, artistic dir. emeritus, 1998—. Mem. dance adv. panel Nat. Endowment for Arts, 1979, chmn. internat. selection com., 1979, chmn. dance adv. panel, 1981, mem. nat. adv. bd. on arts and edn., 1989; bd. dirs., mem. exec. com., Dance/USA 1989, 92—, chmn., 1990-92, chmn. govt. affairs, 1992—; mem. U.S.-USSR Commn. on Dance and Theatre Studies, Am. Coun. Learned Socs./IREX; mem. jury Internat. Moscow Internat. Ballet Competition, 1989; mem. arts in edn. adv. coun. Harvard U., 1997; chmn. 3d Japan Internat. Ballet and Modern Dance competition, 1999; jury mem. Prague Internat. Ballet Competition, 2001; artistic advisor Ft. Worth/Dallas Ballet, 2000-01; tchr. 1st Seoul (Korea) Internat. Dance Competition, 2004. Prin. dancer Met. Opera, 1956-61, Am. Ballet Theatre, 1961-72, Royal Swedish Ballet, 1963, Festival Ballet, London, 1965, Royal Danish Ballet, 1971-76; artistic dir. Ballet West, Salt Lake City, 1976-85; choreographer Eliot Feld Ballet Co., 1970, Royal Danish Ballet, 1971-76, Netherlands Dance Theatre, 1974, Ballet West, 1976-85; artistic fellow Aspen Inst. for Humanistic Studies, 1979—. Bd. dirs. Am. Arts Alliance, 1983-85, Am. Coun. for Arts, 1985—, Dance U.S.A., 1988-94, chmn., 1990-92; chmn. U.S.A. Internat. Ballet Competition, Jackson, Micc., 1990—, vice chair jury Helsinki, Finland, 1991, judge Helsinki Ballet Competition 1995; mem. nat. adv. bd. on arts and edn. NEA, 1989-91; mem. internat. jury 1st and 2d Japan Internat. Ballet Competition, Nagoya, Japan, 1993, 96, 2005, Am. jury for Prix de Lausanne, 1994, 98; mem. Brandeis Creative Arts Awards Commn., 1993, chmn. Brandeis Creative Arts Awards Dance, 1994; chair Grants to Dance Cos. panel NEA, 1993, overview panel, 1994; chmn. 3d Japan Internat. Ballet Competition, Nagoya, 1999; artistic advisor Ft. Worth/Dallas Ballet, 2000-2001; mem. Princess Grace Awards panel, 2005. Recipient Disting. Svc. award for artistic prodn. Nat. Govs. Assn., 1994, Capezio award Balletmakers, Inc., 1995, Dance Mag. award, 1997, Honors award Dance/USA, 1998, Proscenium award, Boston, 2001, Juilliard medal Svc. to Arts, 2005

MARKS, CHARLES, surgeon, educator; b. Kiev, Ukraine, Jan. 28, 1922; came to U.S., 1963; s. Abe and Sonia (Beck) M.; m. Joyce Wernick, Dec. 11, 1949; children: Malcolm, Peter, Ian, Anthony. MD, U. Cape Town, South Africa, 1945; MS, Marquette U., 1966; PhD, Tulane U., 1973. Intern and surg. resident Groote Schuur Hosp., Cape Town, 1946-49; surg. resident Royal Coll. Surgeons Affiliated Hosps., London, 1950-53; cons. surgeon Salisbury (Rhodesia) Gen. Hosp., 1953-63; assoc. prof. surgery Marquette U. Med. Sch., Milw., 1963-67; dir. dept. surgery Mt. Sinai Hosp., Cleve., 1967-71; assoc. clin. prof. surgery Case Western Res. U. Sch. Medicine, Cleve., 1967-71; prof. surgery La. State U. Sch. Medicine, New Orleans, 1971-88; sr. attending surgeon Charity, VA, Touro and Hotel Dieu Hosps., New Orleans, 1971—88; med. exec. dir. Fla. Dept. Corrections, Charlotte, Fla., 1994-97. Cons. cardiothoracic surgeon Ministry of Health, Govt. Zimbabwe, Harare, 1989-94; Hunterian prof. Royal Coll. Surgeons, 1956. Mem. bd. govs. Drs. Hosp. Sarasota, 1997-2004, chmn. bd. govs., 2001—; mem. inner senatorial com. Rep. Party, Washington, 1997—. Recipient Schlieder Rsch. award, 1975. Fellow ACS, Royal Coll. Physicians Edinburgh, Am. Coll. Cardiology; mem. Internat. Cardiovasc. Soc., Am. Transplantation Soc., New Orleans Surg. Soc. (pres.). Republican. Avocations: tennis, golf, travel. Home: # 1517 988 Blvd of the Arts Sarasota FL 34236

MARKS, CHARLES CALDWELL, retired banker, manufacturing executive; b. Birmingham, Ala., June 1, 1921; s. Charles Pollard and Isabel (Caldwell) M.; m. Jeanne Vigeant, Jan. 12, 1945 (dec.); children: Randolph C., Margaret Marks Porter, Charles P.; m. Alice V. Scott, Sept. 18, 1999. Student, Birmingham U., 1930-38; BS in Physics, U. of South, 1942; grad. mgmt. seminar, Harvard U., 1957; DCL (hon.), U. of the South, 1989; LLD (hon.), U. Ala., Birmingham, 1990. With Owen-Richards Co. (name changed to Motion Industries, Inc. 1970), Birmingham, 1946—, chmn. bd., 1952-73, pres., 1973-83; vice chmn. bd. Porter White & Yardley Cos., Inc., 1984-92, ret., 1992. Bd. dirs. emeritus Genuine Parts Co., BE & K Inc., emeritus; bd. dirs., chmn. Birmingham br. Fed. Res. Bank of Atlanta. Bd. dirs. So. Rsch. Inst., exec. com., 1987-95, dir. emeritus, 1995—2001; bd. govs. Indian Springs Sch., dir. emeritus, 1995—; pres., bd. dirs. Workshop for Blind, Birmingham, 1958-61, Children's Aid Soc. Birmingham, 1962; chmn. Com. of 100, Birmingham, 1963; co-chmn. United Appeals of Jefferson County, 1963; trustee, regent U. of South; chmn. St. Vincent's Found., 1980-81, pres., 1987; bd. dirs. U. Ala.-Birmingham Rsch. Found., Exec. Svcs. Corps. of Birmingham, 1984-96. Lt. USNR, WWII, ATO, MTO. Named to Ala. Bus. Hall of Fame, 2005. Mem. The Club, Redstone Club, John's Island Club, Mountain Brook Club, Ala., Blue Key, Phi Beta Kappa, Sigma Alpha Epsilon. Episcopalian. Home: 500 Olde English Ln Apt 516 Birmingham AL 35223-1078 Office: Ste 104 402 Office Park Dr Birmingham AL 35223

MARKS, CHARLES DENNERY, insurance consultant; b. New Orleans, Nov. 22, 1935; s. Sidney Leroy Marks and Melanie Dennery; m. Gillian E. Otter, Sept. 1, 1963; children: Elizabeth Dennery, Richard Dennery. BA, Yale U., 1957. CLU; ChFC; accredited estate planner; cert. long term care, cert. sr. advisor; chartered advisor for sr. living. With Charles Dennery, Inc., 1959-63; sales rep. Prudential Ins. Co., New Orleans, 1964-97. Past bd. dirs. Boys Club Greater New Orleans, Big Bros. Greater New Orleans, United Way; past pres. Goodwill Rehab. Ctr.; vice-chmn. Jr. Achievement; active Temple Sinai Synagogue; bd. dirs. Am. Coll., 2000-2003, 2005, exec. com., 2001-2003; bd. dirs. Am. Coll. Found., 2001-05. 1st lt. U.S. Army, 1957-59. Recipient award Volunteer Activist, 1983. Mem.: Nat. Assn. Ins. and Fin. Advisors (vice chmn. fin. com. 1993—99, mem. audit com. 2003—, pres. Greater New Orleans chpt. 1983, Man of Yr. 1981), Million Dollar Round Table (exec. com. 1990—94, pres. 1993, Top of the Table 1986—89), New Orleans Estate Planning Coun. (pres. 1986—87), La. Assn. Ins. and Fin. Advisors (pres. 1986—87, Advisor of Yr. 1985, Advisor or Yr. 1987, Advisor of Yr. 2002), Soc. Fin. Svc. Profls. (pres. New Orleans chpt. 1984—85), Life and Health Found. for Edn. (life; chmn. 1996—98). Republican. Home and Office: 1525 Eleonore St New Orleans LA 70115-4242 Personal E-mail: cdmdrt@msn.com.

MARKS, DAVID HUNTER, civil engineering educator; b. White Plains, NY, Feb. 22, 1939; s. Sidney M. and Jean (Berger) M.; div.; 1 child, Joanna; m. Lilian Kemp, Dec. 17, 1998. BCE, Cornell U., 1962, MS in Environ. Engring., 1964; PhD, Johns Hopkins U., 1969. Registered profl. engr., N.Y., Mass.; registered hydrologist, Am. Inst. Hydrology. Sr. sanitary engr. USPHS, Phila., 1964-66; asst. prof. civil engring. MIT, Cambridge, Mass., 1969-72, assoc. prof., 1972-75, prof., 1975—, head dept., 1985-92, dir. program in environ. edn. and rsch., 1991-2000, James Mason Crafts prof., 1992-2000, Goulder Family prof., 2001—; coord. Alliance for Global Sustainability, 1996—; dir. Ctr. Environ. Initiatives, 1997-2001, Lab. for Energy and the Environment, 2001—. Office: Mit 1 Amherst St Rm E40-455 Cambridge MA 02139-4307 Home Phone: 617-864-4424; Office Phone: 617-253-1992. E-mail: dhmarks@mit.edu.

MARKS, DEBRA JANE, special education educator; b. Rockville Centre, NY, Aug. 22, 1948; d. Warren Godfrey and Beth Hyman; m. Michael Joel Marks, Aug. 23, 1969; children: Melissa, Stephanie, Karen. BS in Elem. Edn., U. Cin., 1970; M in Elem. Edn., LI U., 1973; cert. in spl. edn., Hofstra U., 1998. Tchr. 6th grade Hillside Grade Sch., New Hyde Park, NY, 1970—74; HS tchr. Jericho (NY) Jewish Ctr., 1978—80; owner Happily Ever After, Plainview, NY, 1985—89; from spl. edn. tchr. asst. to spl. edn. tchr. Nassau BOCES, Wantagh, NY, 1994—2000; spl. edn. tchr. W.T. Clarke Mid. Sch., East Meadow, NY, 2000—. Presenter in field; participant Nat. Svcs. Learning Conf., Phila., 2006; facilitator parallel report card devel. for spl. edn. W.T. Clarke Mid. Sch., 2005; coord., pres. Penny Harvest Exec. Svc. Learning Club, 2000—06. Contbr. chpts. to sch. dist. curriculum books. Named Founder's Day Honoree, East Meadow Sch. Dist., 2004—06; recipient, Nat. Wall of Tolerance Recognition, 2006; grantee, Common Cents NY, 2001—06, Future Corps, Newsday, 2004—06. Mem.: Spl. Edn. PTA (tchr. rep. 2004—06), Penny Harvest Exec. Svc. Learning Club, Martin Luther King Racial/Cultural Awareness Club (awareness com. 2004—05), Kappa Delta Pi. Avocations: travel, reading, golf. Office: WT Clarke Mid Sch 740 Edgewood Dr Westbury NY 11590

MARKS, DENNIS, music educator, musician, composer; b. North Miami, Fla., Aug. 1, 1967; s. Howard and Harriet Marks. MusB, U. Miami, Coral Gables, Fla., 1989, MusM, 1992. Lectr. Fla. Internat. U., Miami, 1996—2005, U. Miami, Coral Gables, 2003—05; asst. prof. U. North Fla., Jacksonville, 2005—. Bassist Maynard Ferguson, 1992—93, Arturo Sandoval, 1997—2005; performer Newport Jazz Festival, Playboy Jazz Festival, LA, Northsea Festival, Netherlands. Composer, musician: audio recording Images. Svc. to jazz edn. Internat. Assn. Jazz Educators, Miami, 1992, NYC, 1997. Named Best Coll. Instrumental Small Group, Downbeat Mag., 1986, 1989, Best Coll. Big Band, 1989. Mem.: BMI, Nat. Assn. Rec. Artists, Coll. Music Soc., Am. Fedn. Musicians. Office: University of North Florida 4567 St Johns Bluff Rd Jacksonville FL Home Phone: 904-223-8070; Office Phone: 904-620-3843. Personal E-mail: demarks1@aol.com. Business E-Mail: dmarks@unf.edu.

MARKS, GERALD, surgeon, educator; b. Bklyn., Apr. 14, 1925; s. Maurice and Lee (Leib) M.; m. Barbara Ann Hendershot, Nov. 25, 1950; children: Richard M., James M., John H. Grad., Villanova U., 1945; MD, Jefferson Med. Coll., 1949. Diplomate: Am. Bd. Surgery, Am. Bd. Colon and Rectal Surgery (examiner). Intern Jefferson Med. Coll. Hosp., Phila., 1949-51, resident in surgery, 1952-57, resident in proctology, 1953-54, asst. dir. Tumor Clinic, 1959-68; practice medicine specializing in gen. and colorectal surgery Phila., 1957—; asst. chief surgery Phila. Gen. Hosp., 1957-70, chief Proctology Clinic, 1968-70, coordinator student surg. edn. Jefferson Surg. Service, 1960-70; attending physician in surgery Thomas Jefferson U. Hosp., 1957-95, sec. med. staff, 1974-77, dir. Comprehensive Rectal Cancer Ctr., Colorectal Surgery Residency Program, exec. dir. Colorectal Surgical Found., 1984-95, co-dir. Colorectal Cancer Genetics Ctr.; dir. div. internat. surg. edn. and practice Ctr. for Research in Med. Edn. and Health Care; instr. surgery Jefferson Med. Coll., 1958-67, assoc. in clin. surgery, 1967-68, clin. assoc. prof. surgery, 1974-78, prof., 1978-95; chief sect. colorectal surgery, cons. in colon-rectal surgery Pa. Hosp.; cons. in colon-rectal surgery VA Hosp., Coatesville, Pa., 1959—, San Juan, P.R., 1968—, Wilmington, Del., 1977—; cons in colon-rectal surgery USN Regional Med. Ctr., Phila., 1977—; Edgar Deissler prof. surgery Allegheny U. Health Scis., 1995—2001, dir. comprehensive rectal cancer ctr., 1995—98, dir. GI surg. endoscopy, 1995. Adj. prof. surgery U. Pa. Sch. Medicine; sr. investigator, Lankenan Inst. for Med. Rsch.; dir. Internat. Network Comprehensive Rectal Cancer Ctrs., 1997-; chmn. Marks Colorectal Surg. Found.; clin. prof. surgery Drexel U. Sch. Medicine, 2001; Deissler prof. surgery and founding dir. divsn. colorectal surgery Hahnemann Med. Coll. of Allegheny U., 1995-2000 Sr. editor Surg. Endoscopy, Ultrasound and Interventional Techniques Jour.; assoc. editor Diseases of the Colon and Rectum Jour., 1977—; cons. editor Pa. Medicine; editl. cons. bd. mem. Gen. Surgery News, 1991, Jour. Surg. Techn.; contbr. articles to profl. jours.; developed colonscopic colon teaching model; solo artist exhbn. in watercolor painting in Italy and U.S Chmn. Marks Colorectal Surg. Rsch. Found. Served with USN, 1943-46; served to capt. M.C. USAF, 1951-52. Recipient 7th Ann. Jonathan M. Wainwright award, Moses Taylor Hosp., Scranton, Pa., 1989; Ann. Alumni Achievement award, Jefferson Med. Coll.; named Man of the Yr., Jewish Nat. Fund, Lifetime Achievement award Northeast Soc. of Colon and Rectal Surgeons, 2004 Mem. ACS (rep. to bd. govs. 1983, council Met. Phila. chpt.), AMA, Pa. Soc. Colon and Rectal Surgery (pres. 1981-82), Am. Soc. Colon and Rectal Surgeons (v.p. 1989), Am. Soc. Clin. Oncology, Internat. Soc. Univ. Colon and Rectal Surgeons, Coll. Physicians Phila., Internat. Fedn. Socs. Endoscopic Surgeons (founding pres. 1991-2000), Royal Soc. Medicine (affiliate), Ea. Surg. Soc., Phila. Acad. Surgery (mem. council), Pa. Med. Soc., Phila. County Med. Soc. (bd. dirs., v.p., chmn. publs. com., pub. affairs com., v.p. 1986—), Soc. Surgery Alimentary Tract, Am. Soc. Gastrointestinal Endoscopy, Italian Soc. Gastrointestinal Endoscopy (hon.), Soc. Am. Gastrointestinal Endoscopic Surgeons (founder, pres. 1980, bd. govs., honoree Annual Gerald Marks Lectureship, former chmn. internat. rels. com., Dist. Svc. award, 1997, Lifetime Achievement award, 2004), Italian Soc. Surgery (hon.), Northeastern Soc. Colon and Rectal Surgeons (past pres.), Jefferson Vol. Faculty Assn. (pres. 1973-74, Brady Cancer Rsch. Inst. award, 1997), Am. Soc. Colon and Rectal Surgeons (v.p. 1989—), Abruzzi Surg. Soc. (hon.), European Assn. Endoscopic Surgeons, Endolaparoscopic Surgeons of Asia, Puerto Rico Chpt. Am. Coll. Surgeons, Alpha Omega Alpha Home: 45 Fairview Rd Narberth PA 19072-1328 Office: 100 Lancaster Ave # 3-west Wynnewood PA 19096-3411 Home Phone: 610-896-5900; Office Phone: 610-645-9093. E-mail: marksg@mlhs.org.

MARKS, HERBERT EDWARD, lawyer; b. Dayton, Ohio, Nov. 3, 1935; s. I.M. and Sarah S. M.; m. Marcia Frager; children: Jennifer L., Susan E. AB with high distinction, U. Mich., 1957; JD, Yale U., 1960; postgrad., George Washington U. Law Sch., 1965-67. Bar: Ohio 1960, D.C. 1964, U.S. Supreme Ct. 1965. Law clk. to chief judge U.S. Ct. Claims, 1964-65; assoc. Wilkinson, Cragun & Barker, Washington, 1965-69, ptnr., 1969-82, Squire, Sanders & Dempsey, Washington, 1982—2003, sr. counsel, 2004—. Assoc. gen. counsel Presdl. Inaugural Coms., 1969, 73, 81; chmn. U.S. State Dept. Adv. Panel on Internat. Telecom. Law, 1987—91; mem. adv. com. on internat. comm. and info. policy U.S. State Dept., 1988—91, 2002—; mem. U.S. del. ITU European Telecom. Devel. Conf., 1991, ITU Plenipotentiary Conf., 1998, ITU Coun., 2000, 04; mem. ITU Sec. Gen.'s Expert Group, 1999—2002; vice chmn. ITU Treaty Working Group, 2004—; bd. dirs. Vet. Legal Svc. Program, 2004—. Contbr. articles to legal jours. Served to capt. JAG USAF, 1960-64. Mem. ABA (chair sci. and tech. sect. 1990-91), Computer Law Assn. (pres. 1975-77, bd. dirs. 1972-85, adv. bd. 1985—), Fed. Comms. Bar Assn., Cosmos Club, Kenwood Golf and Country Club, Phi Beta Kappa. Office: Squire Sanders & Dempsey 1201 Pennsylvania Ave NW PO Box 407 Washington DC 20044-0407 also: 5317 Cardinal Ct Bethesda MD 20816-2908 Home Phone: 301-229-6466; Office Phone: 202-626-6624.

MARKS, JAMES GARFIELD, JR., dermatologist; b. Trenton, NJ, May 19, 1945; s. James Garfield and Lavinia May (Ellis) M.; m. Joyce Lynne Turner, Aug. 9, 1969; 1 child, Shannon. BA, Wilkes Coll., 1967; MD,

Temple U., Phila., 1971. Intern Geisinger Med. Ctr., Danville, Pa., 1971-72; resident Wilford Hall USAF Med. Ctr., San Antonio, 1975-78; clin. instr. dermatology U. Tex. Health Sci. Ctr., San Antonio, 1978-80; staff dermatologist Pa. State U. Coll. Medicine, Hershey, 1980—, asst. prof., 1980-85, assoc. prof., 1985-91, prof. dermatology, 1991—; chair dept. dermatology Hershey Med. Ctr. Team leader Cosmic Ingredient Rev. Expert Panel; co-dir. Caribbean and Coastal Dermatology Symposia. Author: Atlas of Differential Diagnosis in Dermatology, 1998, Principles of Dermatology, 2006, Handbook of Contact Dermatitis, 2000, Contact and Occupational Dermatology, 2002, Principles and Practice of Dermatology, 1990, 2d edit., 1996, Occupational Skin Diseases, 1999, Conn's Current Therapy, 1988, 2d edit., 1989; author: (with others) Principles of Clinical Diagnosis, 1992, Dermatology, 2003; contbr. articles to profl. jours. Bd. dirs. Braun Sta. East Cmty., 1976. Maj. USAF, 1972-80. Decorated Meritorious Svc. Commendation meadl; Am. Acad. Dermatology Exch. fellow, 1984; recipient Roerig Pharms. Challenges in Dermatology Ednl. award, 1982. Mem. Am. Acad. Dermatology, Am. Contact Dermatitis Soc. (v.p. 1993, pres. 2001), N.Am. Contact Dermatitis Group, Pa. Acad. Dermatology, Phila. Dermatology Soc., European Soc. Contact Dermatitis, Soc. Investigative Dermatology, Assn. Mil. Dermatologists, Dermatology Found., Lions (v.p. 1982, pres. 1983). Office: Hershey Med Ctr 500 University Dr # 850 Hershey PA 17033-2360 Office Phone: 717-531-8307. Business E-Mail: jmarks@psu.edu.

MARKS, JAMES S., public health service administrator; b. May 13, 1948; AB cum laude, Williams Coll., 1969; MD, SUNY, Buffalo, 1973; MPH, Yale U., 1980. Diplomate Am. Bd. Pediatrics. Intern in pediat. U. Calif., San Francisco, 1973-74, resident in pediat., 1974-75, chief resident pediatric outpatient dept., 1975-76; fellow Robert Wood Johnson Clin. Scholars Program Yale U., New Haven, 1978-80; resident in preventive medicine Ctrs. for Disease Control, Atlanta, 1977-78, 1981-82, chief epidemiology and rsch. br., nutrition divsn., 1982-84, asst. dir. preventive medicine residency program, 1985-87, dir. divsn. reproductive health, 1987, coord. for chronic disease control activities, 1987-88, acting dir. divsn. diabetes transl., 1988-89, acting dir. divsn. chronic disease control, 1990-91, dir. divsn. reproductive health, 1992-95, dir. Nat. Ctr. Chronic Disease Prevention/Health Promotion, 1995—2004, acting dir., 2004; adj. assoc. prof. Emory U. Sch. Pub. Health, Atlanta, 1990—; sr. v.p., dir. health group Robert Wood Johnson Found., 2004—. Asst. surgeon general, 1996—; editor Chronic Disease Notes and Reports, 1989-92; clinic physician Planned Parenthood of San Francisco Teen Clinic, San Francisco, 1975-76; cons. physician Ohio Dept. Health Bur. Preventive Medicine, 1978-79; cons. PAHO Consultative Group on Perinatal Care, Washington, 1982, WHO Malaysia Ministry of Health, 1982, 83, WHO Maternal and Child Health Unit Geneva, 1983, World Bank China Program Third Health Project, 1988, 1991, World Bank Poland, Health Promotion/Chronic Disease Prevention, 1992, World Bank China, Seventh Health Project, 1993. Contbr. articles to profl. jours, chpts. to books. Exec. sec. Diabetes Tech. Adv. com., 1989-92; liaison mem. Nat. Diabetes Adv. Bd., 1988-89; mem. Diabetes Mellitus Interagy. Coording. com., 1988-89; mem. subcom. adult edn., Am. Cancer Soc., 1987-92; staff White House Task Force on Infant Mortality, 1989; presenter in field. Epidemic Intelligence Svc. Officer USPHS Field Svcs. Divsn., 1976-78. Recipient Alexander D. Langmuir award, 1978, CDC Group award, 1984, Commendation Medal USPHS, 1984, and many other awards and citations. Fellow Am. Coll. Epidemiology; mem. APHA (active in com. work), Inst. Medicine, Am. Epidemiol. Soc., Soc. Epidemiol. Rsch., Am. Acad. Pediat. (com. pediatric rsch. 1994-95), Internat. Epidemiol. Assn., Physicians for Social Responsibility, Soc. on Med. Decision Making, Epidemic Intelligence Svc. Alumni Assn., Sigma Xi. Home: 15 Houghton Rd Princeton NJ 08540-3300 Office: Robert Wood Johnson Found PO Box 2316 College Rd East and Rte 1 Princeton NJ 08543

MARKS, JOHN, engineer, consultant; adopted s. Cyril Bernard Marks and Laura Mary Kings. BS, U. Sussex, 1974. High Voltage Switching, C.e.g.b. Uk, 1990. Owners engr. Croatin Power Authority, Zagreb, Croatia, 2001—03; cons. engr. Tampa Electric Co, Tampa. Tech. dir. Cts (Uk) Ltd, Southampton, England, 1990—95. Sr. cons. (power) T.P.C., Taipei, Taiwan, 1979—84. Flt.lt. Brit. Mil., 1963—68. Mem.: ASME, IEEE. Conservative. Church Of England. Avocations: travel, swimming, rugby, music, reading. Office Phone: 34-680398351. Home Fax: 34-96676165. Personal E-mail: johnmarks4@aol.com.

MARKS, LAWRENCE EDWARD, psychologist, educator; b. NYC, Dec. 28, 1941; s. Milton and Anne (Parnes) M.; m. Joya Ellen Cazes, Dec. 24, 1963; children: Liza, Laura. AB, Hunter Coll., NYC, 1962; PhD, Harvard U., Cambridge, Mass., 1965; PhD honoris causa, Stockholm U., 1994. Rsch.-assoc. prof. Yale U., New Haven, 1966-84; asst.-assoc. fellow John B. Pierce Lab., New Haven, 1966-84; prof. epidemiology and psychology Yale U., New Haven, 1984—; fellow John B. Pierce Lab., New Haven, 1984—, dir., 1999—. Author: Sensory Processes: The New Psychophysics, 1974, The Unity of the Senses, 1978. Named to Hall of Fame, Hunter Coll., N.Y.C., 1985; recipient Jacob Javits award NIH, Washington, 1987. Fellow AAAS, Am. Psychol. Assn., Am. Psychol. Soc., N.Y. Acad. Sci. Democrat. Jewish. Achievements include elucidation of common principles underlying sensory processes in various sense modalities; development of validational scheme for quantifying magnitudes of sensory experience; indication of role of cross-modal (synesthetic) perception in relation to language and literature. Home: 48 Maplevale Dr Woodbridge CT 06525-1118 Office: John B Pierce Lab 290 Congress Ave New Haven CT 06519-1403 Home Phone: 203-393-1565; Office Phone: 203-562-9901. Business E-Mail: marks@jbpierce.org.

MARKS, LILLIAN SHAPIRO, retired secretarial studies educator, writer, editor; b. Bklyn., Mar. 16, 1907; d. Hayman and Celia (Merowitz) Shapiro; m. Joseph Marks, Feb. 21, 1932; children: Daniel, Sheila Blake, Jonathan. BS, NYU, 1928. High sch. tchr., NYC, 1929-30; tchr. Evalina de Rothschild Sch., Jerusalem, 1930-31; social worker United Jewish Aid Bklyn., 1931-32; tchr. Richmond Hill High Sch., 1932-40, Andrew Jackson High Sch., Cambria Heights, NY, 1940-71; staff Vassar Summer Inst., 1946; mem. faculty New Sch. Social Rsch., NYC, 1977-87; ret., 2006. Vol. tchr. English Israel schs., 1987—2000. Am. editor: Teeline, A System of Fast Writing, 1970; author: College Teeline, 1977, College Teeline Self Taught, 1988, Touch Typing Made Simple, 1985; contbr. articles to profl. lit. jours. Mem. Am. Fedn. Tchrs. Democrat. Home and Office: 300 E46 St 17J New York NY 10017

MARKS, MARTHA ALFORD, writer; b. Oxford, Miss., July 27, 1946; d. Truman and Margaret Alford; m. Bernard L. Marks, Jan. 27, 1968. BA, Centenary Coll., 1968; MA, Northwestern U., 1972, PhD, 1978. Tchr. Notre Dame High Sch. for Boys, Niles, Ill., 1969-74; teaching asst. Northwestern U., Evanston, Ill., 1974-78, lectr., lang. coord., 1978-83; asst. prof. Kalamazoo (Mich.) Coll., 1983-85; writer Riverwoods, Ill., 1985—2002. Cons. WGBH Edn. Found., Boston, 1988-91, Am. Coun. on the Tchg. of Fgn. Langs., 1981-92, Ednl. Testing Svcs., 1988-90, Peace Corps., 1993. Co-author: Destinos: An Introduction to Spanish, 1991, 96, Al corriente, 1989, 93, 97, Que tal?, 1986, 90; author: (workbook) Al corriente, 1989, 93; contbr. articles to profl. jours. Mem. Lake County (Ill.) Bd., Forest Preserve Commn., 1992-2002; co-founder Lake County Conservation Alliance; co-founder Reps. for Environ. Protection, 1995, pres. Reps. for Environ. Protection. Office Phone: 505-889-4544.

MARKS, MERTON ELEAZER, lawyer, international arbitrator, mediator, consultant; b. Chgo., Oct. 16, 1932; s. Alfred Tobias and Helene Fannie (Rosner) M.; m. Radee Maiden Feiler, May 20, 1966 (dec.); children: Sheldon, Elise Marks Vazelakis, Alan, Elaine Marks Ianchiou (dec.). BS, Northwestern U., 1954, JD, 1956. Bar: Ill. 1956, U.S. Ct. Mil. Appeals 1957, Ariz. 1958, U.S. Dist. Ct. Ariz. 1960, U.S. Ct. Appeals (9th cir.) 1962, U.S. Supreme Ct. 1970; cert. arbitrator U.S. Dist. Ct. Ariz. Assoc. Moser, Compere & Emerson, Chgo., 1956-57; ptnr. Morgan, Marks & Rogers, Tucson, 1960-62; asst. atty. gen. State of Ariz., Phoenix, 1962-64, counsel indsl. commn., 1964-65; from assoc. to ptnr. Shimmel, Hill, Bishop & Gruender, Phoenix, 1965-74; ptnr. Lewis & Roca, Phoenix, 1974—2001; prin. Merton E. Marks, PC, 2001—. Judge Pro Tempore Ariz. Ct. Appeals, 1994; CPR Inst. Dispute Resolution Inter-Insurer Arb. Panel; spl. master Ariz. Superior Ct., 2001—; U.S. and internat. alternative dispute resolution cons.; lectr. in field. Contbr. articles to profl. jours., columns. Past trustee Ariz. Opera Co., past chmn. endowment commn.; past mem. U.S. Olympic Com. for Ariz. Capt. JAGC, USAR, 1957-64. Fellow Chartered Inst. Arbitrators (London); mem. ABA (trial, tort and ins. practice sect., chmn. spl. com. on fed. asbestos legis. 1987-89, chmn. workers compensation and employers liability law com. 1983-84, dispute resolution sect.), Am. Bd. Trial Advs., Am. Coll. Legal Medicine, Am. Arbitration Assn. (panelist, mediator), Internat. Bar Assn. (sect. dispute resolution, arbitration com.), State Bar Ariz. (chmn. workers compensation sect. 1969-73), Fedn. Def. and Corp. Counsel (chmn. pharm. litig. sect. 1989-91, chmn. workers compensation sect. 1977-79, v.p. 1978-79, 81, bd. dirs. 1981-89, mem. products liability sect., mem. reinsurance sect., chmn. alternative dispute resolution sect. 2005-06), Internat. Assn. Def. Counsel, Ariz. Assn. Def. Counsel (pres. 1976-77), Maricopa County Bar Assn., Pima County Bar Assn., Def. Rsch. Inst. (drug and device com., chmn. workers compensation com. 1977-78), Reinsurance and Ins. Arbitration Soc., Nat. Assn. Securities Dealers Dispute Resolution (bd. arbitrators), Internat. C. of C. Office: Scottsdale Exec Office Pk 8655 E Via De Ventura Ste G200 Scottsdale AZ 85258-3321 also: 850 N Kolb Rd Tucson AZ 85710-1333 Office Phone: 602-840-0808. Personal E-mail: memarkspc@earthlink.net.

MARKS, MICHAEL E., electronics executive; BA, MA, Oberlin Coll.; MBA, Harvard U. Pres., CEO Metcal Inc., Menlo Park, Calif.; CEO Flextronics Internat. Ltd., Singapore, 1994—2005, chmn., 2006—; mem. Kohlberg Kravis Roberts & Co., Menlo Park, Calif., 2005—. Bd. dir. SanDisk Corp. Office: KKR Ste 200 2800 Sand Hill Rd Menlo Park CA 94025

MARKS, MICHAEL J., lawyer; b. 1938; AB, Cornell U., 1960; JD, U. Chgo., 1963. Assoc. Stroock & Lavan, 1964—70, Chun, Kerr & Dodd, 1970—72; counsel Kelso, Spencer, Snyder & Stirling, 1972—75; asst. gen. counsel Alexander & Baldwin Inc., Honolulu, 1975—80, v.p., gen. counsel, 1980—84, v.p., gen. counsel, sec., 1984—85, sr. v.p., gen. counsel, sec., 1985—. Office: Alexander & Baldwin Inc 822 Bishop St Honolulu HI 96813-3925

MARKS, MURRY AARON, lawyer; b. Carbondale, Ill., July 14, 1933; Student, Northwestern U., 1951-52; BA, Washington U., 1954; attended, U. So. Calif., 1956; JD, Washington U., 1963. Bar: Mo. 1963, U.S. Dist. Ct. (ea. and we. dists.) Mo. 1969, U.S. Ct. Appeals (8th cir.) 1969, (so. dist.) Ill. 2003, U.S. Supreme Ct. 1972, U.S. Tax Ct. 1984. Asst. county counsellor County of St. Louis, 1963-67; ptnr. Elliott, Marks & Freeman, St. Louis, 1967-1971; pvt. practice St. Louis, 1972. With U.S. Army, 1954-56. Fellow Mo. Bar Found., St. Louis Bar Found.; mem. ABA, ATLA, Nat. Assn. Criminal Def. Lawyers (life), St. Louis County Bar Assn., Mo. Bar Assn. (vice chmn. criminal law sect.), Am. Coll. Legal Medicine, Mo. Assn. Trial Attys., Mo. Assn. Criminal Def. Attys. (bd. dirs. 1986-90), First Amendment Lawyers Assn., Met. Bar Assn. St. Louis (chmn. criminal law sect. 2006-07, bd. govs., Golden Ann. fellow), Trial Lawyers for Pub. Justice, The Roscoe Pound Found. Office: Four Cityplace Dr Ste 497 Saint Louis MO 63141 Home Phone: 314-434-0848; Office Phone: 314-993-6300. Business E-Mail: mam@themarkslawfirm.com.

MARKS, PAUL ALAN, oncologist, cell biologist, educator; b. NYC, Aug. 16, 1926; s. Robert R. and Sarah (Bohorad) Marks; m. Joan Harriet Rosen, Nov. 28, 1953; children: Andrew Robert, Elizabeth Susan Marks Ostrer, Matthew Stuart. AB with gen. honors, Columbia U., 1945, MD, 1949, DSc (hon.), 2000; D in Biol. Sci. (hon.), U. Urbino, Italy, 1982; PhD (hon.), Hebrew U., Jerusalem, Israel, 1987, U. Tel Aviv, 1992; DSc (hon.), Ben Gurion U., Beer Sheva, Israel, 2003. From fellow to prof. Coll. Physicians and Surgeons Columbia U., NYC, 1952—67, prof. medicine Coll. Physicians and Surgeons, 1967—82, dean faculty of medicine, v.p. med. affairs Coll. Physicians and Surgeons, 1970—73, dir. Comprehensive Cancer Ctr. Coll. Physicians and Surgeons, 1972—80, v.p. health scis. Coll. Physicians and Surgeons, 1973—80; prof. cell biology and genetics Coll. Medicine Cornell U., NYC, 1980—, prof. medicine Grad. Sch. Med. Scis., 1983—; pres., CEO Meml. Sloan-Kettering Cancer Ctr., NYC, 1980—99, pres. emeritus, 2000—. Instr. Sch. Medicine George Washington U., 1954—55; cons. VA Hosp., NYC, 1962—66; attending physician Presbyn. Hosp., NYC, 1967—82, Meml. Hosp. for Cancer and Allied Diseases, 1980—; prin. investigator, Devel. Cell Biology Sloan-Kettering Inst. for Cancer Rsch., 1980—; adj. prof. Rockefeller U., 1980—; vis. physician Rockefeller U. Hosp., 1980—; bd. sci. counselors divsn. cancer treatment Nat. Cancer Inst., 1980—83; hon. staff N.Y. Hosp., 1981—; steering com. Frederick Cancer Rsch. Facility Nat. Cancer Inst., 1982—86; chmn. program adv. com. Robert Wood Johnson Found., 1983—89; adv. com. on NIH to Sec. HHS, 1989—90, 1993—98; external adv. com. Intramural Rsch. Program Rev. NIH; gov. com. NYPRHA, 1996; tech. adv. group UN Assn. U.S.; coun. biol. scis. Pritzker Sch. Medicine U. Chgo., 1977—88; William Dameshek vis. prof. hematology Mt. Sinai Med. Ctr., 1985; nat. vis. com. CUNY Med. Sch., 1986—89; trustee Feinberg Grad. Sch. Weizmann Inst. Sci., Rehovot, Israel, 1986—; vis. prof. Coll. de France, 1988; Alpha Omega Alpha vis. prof. N.Y. Med. Coll., 1990; Mario A. Baldini vis. prof. Med. Sch. Harvard U., 1991; sci. adv. bd. City Hope Nat. Med. Ctr., Duarte, Calif., 1987—92, Raymond and Beverly Sackler Found., Inc., 1989, Jefferson Cancer Inst., Phila., 1989, PTC Biotech., Inc., 2002—, Ikonysis, 2004—, Merck, Inc., 2004—05; mem. Found. Biomed. Rsch., 1989—; sci. adv. com. Imperial Cancer Rsch. Fund, 1994—2003; sr. adv. Lazard Freres, 2000—; co-founder, sec. and vice chmn. Aton Pharma, Tarrytown, NY, 2001—04; internat. adv. coun. Singapore Econ. Devel. Bd., 2000—03; dir. Dreyfus Mutual Funds, NC, 1998—2005; lectr. Nobel Forum, Karolinska Inst., Sweden, 2004. Author: 11 books; mem. editl. bd.: Blood, 1964—76, editor-in-chief:, 1978—82, mem. editl. bd.: Jour. Clin Investigation, 1970—71, editor-in-chief:, mem. editl. bd.: Cancer Treatment Revs., 1981—, Japanese Jour. Cancer Rsch., 1985—, Molecular Reprodn. and Devel., 1988—, Cancer Preventions, 1989, Sci., 1990, Current Opinion Oncologic Endocrine and Metabolic Drugs, 1998, expert analyst: Chemistry and Molecular Biology edit. of Chemtracts, 1990—92, mem. adv. bd.: Internat. Jour. Hematology, 1992, Stem Cells, bd. contbg. editors: Blood Cells, Molecules and Diseases, 1994, Comité des Sages, 1994; contbr. over 400 articles to profl. jours. Trustee St. Luke's Hosp., 1970—80, Roosevelt Hosp., 1970—80, Presbyn. Hosp., 1972—80, Metpath Inst. Med. Edn., 1977—79, Hadassah Med. Ctr., Jerusalem, 1996; mem. jury Albert Lasker Awards, 1974—82; bd. dirs. Revson Found., 1976—91, Am. Found. for Basic Rsch. Israel, Israel Acad. Scis., 1991; mem. tech. bd. Milbank Meml. Fund, 1978—85; bd. govs. Friends of Sheba Med. Ctr., Tel Hashomer; mem. commn. sci. and tech. Mayor, NYC, 1984—87; mem. commn. Shoreham Nuc. Plant Gov., NYC, 1983; mem. task force biomed. rsch. and tech. Mayor, NYC, 1999. Recipient Stevens Triennial prize, 1960, Swiss-Am. Found. award, 1965, Centenary medal, Inst. Pasteur, 1987, Found. for Promotion of Cancer Rsch. medal, Japan, 1984, DSM, Robert Wood Johnson Found., 1989, Outstanding Achievement award, U. Innsbruck, 1991, Pres.'s Nat. Medal Sci., 1991, Japan Found. for Cancer Rsch. award, 1995, Lifetime Achievement award, Greater N.Y. Hosp. Assn., 1997, Am. Italian Cancer Found., 1999, Humanitarian award, Breast Cancer Rsch. Found., 2000, Disting. Lifetime Achievement award, Healthcare Chaplaincy, NY, 2001, John Stearns award, NY Acad. Medicine, 2002, Annie Blount Storrs Humanitarian award, Calvary Hosp., NY, 2002; fellow Commonwealth Fund fellow, Pasteur Inst., 1961—62; Ayrey fellow, 1985. Master: ACP, Coll. Physicians and Surgeons (Gold medal 1994); fellow: AAAS, Pasteur Inst. Paris (Commonwealth Fund fellow 1961—62), Am. Acad. Arts and Scis., Royal Soc. Medicine; mem.: NAS (chmn. Acad. Forum Adv. Com. 1980—81, chmn. sect. med. genetics, hematology and oncology 1980—83, coun. 1984—87, del. biol. warfare com. Internat. Security and Arms Control 1986—89, bd. dirs. 2002), Am. Philos. Soc., N.Y. Acad. Sci. (bd. dirs. 2002—), European Acad. Scis., UN Assn. U.S.A. (tech. adv. group), Weizmann Inst. Sci. (bd. govs. 1976—, gov. emeritus, Israel), Third World Acad. Scis. (advisor), Soc. Study Devel. and Growth, Japan Soc. Hematology (Disting. lectr. 1989, Disting. lectr. 1989), Soc. Devel. Biology, Internat. Soc. Devel. Biologists, Harvey Soc. (pres. 1973—74), Assn. Am. Physicians, Am. Soc. Hematology (pres.-elect 1983, pres. 1984, chmn. adv. bd. 1985), Soc. Cell Biology, Assn. Am. Cancer Insts. (bd. dirs. 1983—88), Am. Assn. Cancer Rsch., Am. Soc. Human Genetics (past mem. program com.), Italian Assn. Cell Biology and Differentiation (hon.), Chinese Anti-Cancer Assn. (hon.), Japanese Cancer Assn. (hon.), Am. Soc. Biol. Chemists, Am. Soc. Clin. Investigation (pres. 1972—73), Am. Fedn. Clin. Rsch. (past councillor Ea. dist.), Red Cell Club (past chmn.), Inst. Medicine (coun. 1973—76, chmn. com. study resources clin. investigation with NAS 1988), Univ. Club, Soc. Interurban Clin. Club, Century Assn., Alpha Omega Alpha. Office: Meml Sloan-Kettering Cancer Ctr 1275 York Ave New York NY 10021-6094 Home Phone: 860-868-1659; Office Phone: 212-639-6568. Business E-Mail: paula_marks@mskcc.org.

MARKS, RAMON PAUL, lawyer; b. Washington, Dec. 9, 1948; s. Matthew J. and Simone V. (Van de Meulebroeke) M.; m. Susan Eleanor MacCarthy; children: Robert Justin, Timothy Matthew, Fletcher MacCarthy. AB magna cum laude, Dartmouth Coll., 1971; MA in Internat. Rels. with high distinction, Johns Hopkins U., 1973; JD, U. Va., 1976. Bar: NY 1977, Tex. 1983, US Dist. Ct. (so. dist.) Tex. 1984, US Ct. Appeals (5th cir.) 1984, US Ct. Internat. Trade 1988, US Dist. Ct. (so. dist.) NY 1989, US Ct Appeals (fed. cir.) 1989. Assoc., Alexander & Green, NYC, 1976-77; corp. atty. Schlumberger Ltd., NYC, 1978; asst. legal counsel svcs., techniques Schlumberger Paris, 1978-80; gen. counsel Schlumberger Well Svcs., Houston, 1980-84; sec., gen. counsel Dowell Schlumberger, Inc., Houston, 1984-85; asst. gen. counsel Schlumberger Ltd., Houston, 1986-87; ptnr. Marks & Murase, NYC, 1987,; ptnr., Dorsey & Whitney, NYC, 1997; ptnr., internat. litig., Arnold & Porter, NYC, 2005—. Mem. dean's coun. John F. Kennedy Sch. Govt., Harvard U. Mem. Assn. Bar City NY, Bus. Execs. Nat. Security (bd. dirs., co-chmn. policy com.), Phi Beta Kappa. Office: Arnold & Porter 399 Park Ave New York NY 10022-4690 Office Phone: 212-715-1145. Office Fax: 212-715-1399. Business E-Mail: ramon.marks@aporter.com.

MARKS, RICHARD DANIEL, lawyer; b. NYC, June 21, 1944; s. Morris Andrew and Dorothy (Schill) M.; m. Cheryl L. Hoffman, Nov. 13, 1971. BA, U. Va., 1966; JD, Yale U., 1969. Bar: D.C., U.S. Ct. Appeals (3rd, 4th, 8th, 11th and D.C. cir.), U.S. Supreme Ct. Assoc. Dow, Lohnes & Albertson, Washington, 1972-78, ptnr., 1978-97, Vinson & Elkins, Washington, 1997-2000, Davis Wright Tremaine, Washington, 2000—. Co-author: Legal Problems in Broadcasting, 1974. Trustee U. Va. Coll. Found., 2001-03. Capt. U.S. Army, 1970-72. Mem. ABA (chmn. contracting for computer com., sect. for sci. and tech., computer law div., chmn. computer law divsn. 1994-2002, chmn. HIPAA task force 2002—), chmn. program cmte. (2003-2004), Fed. Comms. Bar Assn., Am. Law Inst., Computer Law Assn. (dir. 1999-2002), Capital Area Assn. Flight Instrs. (pres. 1989-90), UVA Club of Washington (pres. 1991-92). Avocations: aviation, skiing. Office: Davis Wright Tremaine LLP 1500 K St NW Ste 450 Washington DC 20005-1272 Business E-Mail: richardmarks@dwt.com.

MARKS, ROBERTA BARBARA, artist, educator; b. Savannah, Ga.; d. Philip W. and Eleanore (Margolis) Dilner; children: Jeffery Allen, Steven Craig. BFA, U. Miami, Coral Gables, Fla., 1980; MFA, U. South Fla., Tampa, 1981. Instr., lectr. multi-media, lectr., vis. artist to numerous art schs., including U. South Fla., Tampa, 1998-05, Custom House Mus., Armory Art Ctr., Palm Beach, Fla., 2002, Key West, Fla., 2003, Galerie Jonas, Neuchatel, Switzerland, 2003, Chgo. Anderson Ranch Art Sch., Colo., 2004, U. South Fla., U. Miami Lowe Art Mus., Fla., Armory Art Ctr., Palm Beach, Fla., Valparaiso U., Ind., Rochester Inst. Tech. Am. Sch. of Crafts, NY, Galerie de Koull, Murten, Switzerland, Santa Fe Community Coll., Gainesville, Brookfield Craft Ctr., Conn., Fla. Keys Community Coll., U. Wis.-Milw., Parson Sch. Design, Key West C.C., Fla., 1991, Am. Embassy, Bern, Switzerland, 1993; juror Riverside Avondale Preservation Art Festival, Jacksonville, Fla., 1981, Ybor Square Art Festival, Tampa, 1980, Miami Lakes Art Festival, Fla., 1975. One woman shows include Brevard Community Coll., Melbourne, Fla., 1982, Cocoa, Fla., 1982, Coventry Galleries, Ltd., Tampa, 1983, Barbara Gillman Gallery, Miami, 1984, 87, Tennessee Williams Fine Arts Ctr., Key West, 1985, Garth Clark Gallery, NYC, 1985, Fred Gros Gallery, Key West, 1985, Key West Art and Historical Soc. East Martello Mus. and Gallery, 1985, U. Miami New Gallery, Fla., 1987, Katie Gingrass Gallery, Milw., 1987, Zimmerman Saturn Gallery, Nashville, 1987, Bern, Zurich Switzerland, 1988, Galerie Alte Krone, Altstadt, Biel, Switzerland, 1990, Helander Gallery, NYC, 1990, Gump's Gallery, San Francisco, 1990, Helander Gallery, NYC, 1991, LeMieux Gallery, New Orleans, 1991, Helander Gallery, Palm Beach, 1992, Galerie Etc., Bern, 1992, Galerie Bel Arte, Lengnau, Switzerland, 1992, Lucky Street Gallery, Key West, 1994-05, Barbara Gillman Gallery, Miami, 1994-05, Galerie Vinelz, Switzerland, 1994, Galerie Quattro, Zurich, 1994, many others; exhibited in group shows at Netsky Gallery, Miami, 1982, The Craftsman's Gallery, Scarsdale, NY, 1982, Garth Clark Gallery, Los Angeles, 1983, Nelson-Atkins Mus. Art, Kansas City, Mo., 1983, Am. Craft Mus., NYC, 1984, N. Miami Mus. and Art Ctr., 1985, Joanne Lyon Gallery, Aspen, Colo., 1984, Key West Art and Hist. Soc. East Martello Mus. and Gallery, 1985, Garth Clark Gallery, NYC and Los Angeles, 1985, 24X24, Ruth Siegel Ltd., NYC, 1987, Artforms Gallery, Louisville, 1986, The Pvt. Collection Women Artists, Ohio, 1987, East Martello Mus., Key West, Fla., 1990, East Martello Mus., Key West, Fla., 1990, Philharmonic Ctr. for Arts, Naples, Fla., 1993, Ctr. for Arts, Vero Beach, Fla., 1993, Helander Gallery, Palm Beach, 1993, Gingrass Gallery, Milw., 1993, many others; represented in permanent collections Mint Mus., Charlotte, NC, N.Mex Mus. Fine Arts, Sante Fe, Smithsonian Instn., Renwick Gallery, Rochester Inst. Tech. Fine Arts Dept., U. Utah Mus., U. South Fla. Fine Arts Dept., Galerie du Manoir, La Chaux-de-Fonds, Switzerland, Valencia Community Coll., Okum Gallery, Victoria and Albert Mus., London, IBM, Jacksonville, Fla., AT&T, NYC, Custom Ho. Mus., Key West, Fla., 2002, U. South Fla., Galerie Jonas, Neuchatel, Switzerland, 2003, Lucky St. Gallery, 2005, Mint Mus., Charlotte, NMex. Mus. Fine Arts, Sante Fe, others. Recipient Regional Visual Artist fellow, Miami, Fla., 1990, also numerous awards. Mem. World Craft Council, Artists Equity Assn., Internat. Sculpture Ctr.

MARKS, STEPHEN J., neurologist, educator; b. Bklyn., Aug. 30, 1953; s. Ansel R. Marks and Frances L. Carpenter; m. Cindy G. Marks, Mar. 27, 1994; children: Jordan, Avery. BA, Colgate U., 1979. Diplomate Am. Bd. Neurology & Psychiatry. Intern Lenox Hill Hosp., NYC; resident Mt. Sinai Hosp., NYC; assoc. prof. N.Y. Med. Coll., Valhalla, 1987—. Team neurologist N.Y. Jets, Hempstead, 1986. Co-author: (chapter) Principle & Practice of Emergency Medicine, 1992, (book), 1997. Fellow: Am. Heart Assn. (mem. stroke coun.); mem.: Soc. Neuroscience, Nat. Stroke Assn., Am. Acad. Neurology. Avocations: skiing, windsurfing. Office: Dept Neurology Munger Pavilion, NYMC Valhalla NY 10595

MARKS, THEODORE LEE, lawyer; b. NYC, Oct. 18, 1935; s. Irving Edward and Isabel (Goodman) M.; m. Benita Cooper, July 13, 1958; children: Eric, Robert, Jennifer BS, NYU, 1956, LLB, 1958. Bar: N.Y. 1959, U.S. Dist. Ct. (so. dist.) N.Y. 1963, U.S. Supreme Ct. 1964, U.S. Ct. Appeals (2d cir.) 1975, U.S. Dist. Ct. (ea. dist.) N.Y. 1978. Assoc. Silver, Bernstein, Seawell & Kaplan, NYC, 1959-65; pvt. practice NYC, 1965-70; ptnr. Lee, Cash & Marks, NYC, 1970-76, Vogel, Marks & Rosenberg, NYC, 1976-79, Bromberg, Gloger, Lifschultz & Marks, NYC, 1979-85, Epstein Becker Borsody & Green, P.C., NYC, 1985-86, Gelberg & Abrams, 1986-87, Morrison Cohen Singer & Weinstein, 1987—2004; counsel Morrison Cohen LLP, NYC, 2004—. Speaker at meetings of profl. assns. Contbr. articles to profl. jours. Served with Army N.G., 1958-61. Mem. NY State Bar Assn. (mem. real property, banking, corp. and bus. law sects.), NY County Lawyers Assn., T&M. Office: Morrison Cohen LLP 909 Third Ave New York NY 10022 E-mail: tmarks@morrisoncohen.com.

MARKS, TOBIN JAY, chemistry educator; b. Washington, Nov. 25, 1944; s. Eli Sidney and Miriam (Heller) M.; m. Indrani Mukharji, May 19, 1985 BS in Chemistry, U. Md., 1966; PhD in Chemistry, MIT, 1970. Asst. prof., chemistry Northwestern U., Evanston, Ill., 1970-74, assoc. prof., chemistry, 1974-78, Charles E. and Emma H. Morrison prof. chemistry, 1985—99, prof. materials sci. and engring., 1987—, Vladimir N. Ipatieff prof. catalytic chemistry, 1999—. Invited lectr. in field; cons. or advisor for several major corporations and start-ups. Editor: Organometallics of the F-Elements, 1979; assoc. editor Organometallics, 1986—; editor: Fundamental and Technological Aspects of Organo-F-Element Chemistry, 1985; mem. several editl. boards; contbr. articles to profl. jours. Sloan Found. fellow, 1974, Guggenheim fellow, 1989-1990; Dreyfus Found. scholar, 1975; recipient Nat. Fesenius award Phi Lambda Upsilon, 1979, Mack award Ohio State U., 1987, Francis Clifford Phillips award, U. Pitts., 1998, Paolo Chini award, Italian Chem. Soc., 1999, Burwell award, N.Am. Catalysis Soc., 2001., Am. Inst. Chemists Gold medal, 2002, Evans medal, Ohio State U., 2003, Karl Ziegler medal, German Chem. Soc., 2003, 2005 Nat. Medal Sci., NSF, 2007; named to U. Md. Alumni Hall of Fame, 2005; named U. Pierre et Marie Curie Institut U. de France prof., 2005. Fellow Am. Acad. Arts and Scis., Royal Soc. Chemistry (Centenary medal, 1997, Sir Edward Frankland medal, Royal Soc. Chemistry (UK), 2003); mem. NAS, Am. Chem. Soc. (A.K. Doolittle award 1984, award in Polymeric Materials, 1983, award in Organometallic Chemistry 1989, award in Inorganic Chemistry 1994, Cotton medal Tex. A&M sect., 2000, Williard Gibbs medal, Chgo. sect., 2001, Linus Pauling medal, Oreg.-Washington sections, 2001, award in Chemistry of Materials, 2001, John C. Bailar medal, Urbana-Champaign sect., 2005), Soc. for Applied Spectroscopy, Materials Rsch. Soc., Leopoldina German Nat. Acad. Natural Scis., Phi Beta Kappa. Achievements include patents in field. Home: 2300 Central Park Ave Evanston IL 60201-1810 Office Phone: 708-491-5658. Office Fax: 847-491-2990. Business E-Mail: t-marks@northwestern.edu. *

MARKSTEIN, DANIEL H., III, lawyer; b. Birmingham, Ala., Feb. 5, 1941; s. D. Harry Markstein Jr. and Elaine Adler; m. Rosalind Weil, Mar. 18, 1972; children: Daniel H IV, Virginia W. AB, Washington and Lee U., Lexington, Va., 1963; LLB, U. Ala., Tuscaloosa, 1966; LLM, Harvard U., Cambridge, Mass., 1969. Ptnr. Markstein, Morris and Liles PC, B'ham, Ala., 1969—87; shareholder Maynard, Cooper and Gale PC, B'ham, 1987—. Presenter in field. Contbr. articles to profl. jours. Pres. Estate Planning Coun., Birmingham, 1986; bd. dirs. U. Ala. Fed. Tax Clinic, Birmingham, 1989—92, Lex Mundi Ltd., 1994—2000. Capt. US Army, 1966—68, Vietnam. Fellow: Am. Coll. Tax. Coun., Am. Coll. Trust Estate Coun. (pres.); mem.: Am. Inst. Fed. Taxation (trustee). Office: Maynard Cooper and Gale PC 1901 6th Ave N Ste 2400 Birmingham AL 35203

MARKULIS, HENRYK JOHN, career military officer; b. Columbia, SC, July 10, 1945; s. Henryk F. Markulis and Judith E. (Taylor) Kassman; children: Mark C., Melinda L. BA, U. Buffalo, 1968; MA, Ctrl. Mich. U., 1977. Commd. USAF, 1969; advanced through ranks to col.; aircraft cmdr. 53d Weather Recon Squadron Ramey AFB, PR, 1970-74; gunship aircraft cmdr. 16th Spl. Ops. Squadron Korat RTAB, Thailand, 1974-75; cmdr. 437th Field Maintenance Squadron Sect. Charleston AFB, SC, 1975-78; exercise and contingency support 1701st Mobility Support Shaw AFB, SC, 1978-82; air staff action officer Joint Chiefs of Staff Pentagon, 1982-84; chief internat. programs Singapore, Malaysia & Brunei, 1984-93; dep. cmdr., chief staff Iceland Def. Force NATO, 1993-95, ret., 1995; pres., CEO Internat. Security and Mktg. Cons., 1996—. Cons. Nissan Motor Acceptance Corp., 1996—, Infiniti Fin. Svcs., 1996-, Project Boreas, 2006-. Mem. Am. Legion, VFW, Mil. Officers Assn. Am., Aircraft Owners and Pilots Assn., Army Navy Country Club, Order of Daedalians, Kiwanis, KC (4th degree). Avocation: golf. Office: 52 Union St Hamburg NY 14075 Home: 56 Union St Hamburg NY 14075-4910 Office Phone: 716-646-1589. E-mail: colonelm@adelphia.net.

MARKUS, LAWRENCE, retired mathematics professor; b. Hibbing, Minn., Oct. 13, 1922; s. Benjamin and Ruby (Friedman) M.; m. Lois Shoemaker, Dec. 9, 1950; children: Sylvia, Andrew. BS, U. Chgo., 1942, MS, 1946; PhD, Harvard U., Cambridge, Mass., 1951. Instr. meteorology U. Chgo., 1942-44; rsch. meteorologist Atomic Project, Hanford, 1944; instr. math. Harvard U., 1951-52; instr. Yale U., 1952-55; lectr. Princeton U., 1955-57; asst. prof. U. Minn., Mpls., 1957-58, assoc. prof., 1958-60, prof. math., 1960-93, assoc. chmn. dept. math., 1961-63, dir. control scis., 1964-73, Regents' prof. math., 1980-93, Regents' prof. emeritus, 1993—, dir. Control Sci. and Dynamical Sys. Ctr., 1980-89. Leverhulme prof. control theory, dir. control theory ctr. U. Warwick, Eng., 1970-73, Nuffield prof. math., 1970-85, hon. prof., 1985—; regional conf. lectr. NSF, 1969; vis. prof. Yale U., Columbia U., U. Calif., U. Warsaw, 1980, Tech. Inst. Zurich, 1983, Peking U. (China), 1983; dir. conf. Internat. Ctr. Math., Trieste, 1974; lectr. Internat. Math. Congress, 1974, Iranian Math. Soc., 1975, Brit. Math. Soc., 1976, Japan Soc. for Promotion Sci., 1976, Royal Instn., London, 1982, U. Beer Sheva, Israel, 1983; vis. prof. U. Tokyo, 1976, Tech. U., Denmark, 1979; mem. panel Internat. Congress Mathematicians, Helsinki, 1978; sr. vis. fellow Sci. Rsch. Coun., Imperial Coll., London, 1978; mem. UNESCO sci. adv. com. Control Symposium, U. Strasbourg, France, 1980; IEEE Plenary lectr., Orlando, Fla., 1982; Sci. and Engring. Rsch. Coun. vis. prof. U. Warwick, Eng., 1982-90; Neustadt Meml. lectr. U. So. Calif., 1985, prin. lectr. symposium U. Minn., 1988, dir. NSF workshop, 1989, prin. lectr. symposium in honor of his 75th birthday, 1997; Tate lectr. U. Cin., 1998; chmn. Conf. Markus-80, 2002; adv. bd. Office Naval Rsch., Air Force Office Sci. Rsch. Author: Flat Lorentz Manifolds, 1959, Flows on Homogeneous Spaces, 1963, Foundations of Optimal Control Theory, 1967, rev. edit., 1985, Lectures on Differentiable Dynamics, 1971, rev. edit., 1980, Generic Hamiltonian Dynamical Systems, 1974, Distributed Parameter Control Systems, 1991, Boundary Value Problems and Symplectic Algebra, 1998, Multi-Interval Linear Ordinary Boundary Value Problems and Complex Symplectic Algebra, 2001, Elliptic Partial Differential Operators and Symplectic Algebra, 2003, Infinite Dimensional Complex Symplectic Spaces, 2004; editor Internat. Jour. Nonlinear Mechanics, 1965-73, Jour. Control, 1963-67; mem. editl. bd. Proc. Georgian Acad. Sci. Math., 1993—; contbr. articles to profl. jours Lt. (j.g.) USNR, 1944-46. Recipient Rsch. prize Internat. Conf. Nonlinear Oscillations, Ukrainian Acad. Sci., Kiev, 1969, Festschrift volume, 1993; Fulbright fellow Paris, 1950; Guggenheim fellow Lausanne, Switzerland, 1963. Fellow Royal Soc. Edinburgh (hon.); mem. Am. Math. Soc. (past mem. nat. coun.), Am. Geophys. Soc., Soc. Indsl. and Applied Math. (past nat. lectr.), Phi Beta Kappa, Sigma Xi. Office: 109 Vincent Hall 206 Church St S Minneapolis MN 55455 Business E-Mail: markus@math.umn.edu.

MARKUS, MAURA, bank executive; BA summa cum laude, Boston Coll., Mass.; MBA, Harvard U. Joined Citibank, NYC, 1987, pres. North Am. Retail Distbr. Group, 2000—. Office: CBNA One Court Sq 49th Fl Long Island City NY 11120

MARKUS, RICHARD M., judge, arbitrator; b. Evanston, Ill., Apr. 16, 1930; s. Benjamin and Ruby M.; m. Carol Joanne Slater, July 26, 1952; children: Linda, Scott, Kent. BS magna cum laude, Northwestern U., 1951; JD cum laude, Harvard U., 1954. Bar: D.C. 1954, Ohio 1956, Fla. 1994. Appellate atty., civil div. Dept. Justice, Washington, 1954-56; ptnr. civil litigation law firms Cleve., 1956-76, 89-98; judge Cuyahoga County (Ohio) Common Pleas Ct., 1976-80, Ohio Ct. Appeals, 1981-88. Instr. M.I.T., 1952-54; adj. prof. Case Western Res. U. Law Sch., 1972-78, 84-87, Cleve. State U. Law Sch., 1960-80, prof. 1999-2000; prof. Harvard Law Sch., 1980-81; mem. Nat. Commn. on Med. Malpractice, 1971-73; chmn. Nat. Inst. Trial Advocacy, 1978-81, trustee 1971—. Author: Trial Handbook for Ohio Lawyers, all edits., 1971—, Ohio Evidence Rules with Commentary, 1999; contbr. articles to profl. jours.; editor Harvard U. Law Rev, 1952-54. Republican nominee Justice of Ohio Supreme Ct., 1978; bd. dirs. Luth. Metro Ministry, 1988—, Fairview Luth. Hosp., 1985—. Mem. Ohio State Bar Assn. (pres. 1991-92), Cuyahoga County Bar Assn., Greater Cleve. Bar Assn. (trustee 1967-70, 85-90), Assn. Trial Lawyers Am. (nat. pres. 1970-71), Ohio Acad. Trial Lawyers (pres. 1965-66), Phi Beta Kappa, Pi Mu Epsilon, Delta Sigma Rho, Phi Alpha Delta. Home and Office: Pvt Judicial Svcs Inc 3903 N Valley Dr Cleveland OH 44126-1716 E-mail: judgemarkus1@cs.com.

MARKUS, ROBERT MICHAEL, retired journalist; b. Chgo., Jan. 30, 1934; s. David White and Anna (Tonkonogy) M.; m. Leslie Winnifred Ator, Aug. 25, 1962; children— Catherine Mary, Patricia Anne, Michael Hughes. B.J., U. Mo., 1955. Gen. assignment reporter Moline (Ill.) Dispatch, 1955-59; successively copy editor, sports columnist, feature writer, baseball writer, coll. sports writer, hockey writer Chgo. Tribune, 1959-96, ret., 1996. Mem. Northbrook (Ill.) Caucus, 1967. Served with U.S. Army, 1956-58. Recipient Nat. Headliner award as best columnist, 1973; named Ill. Sports Writer of Year, 1970, 71, 72 Mem. Football Writers Assn. Am., Baseball Writers Assn. Am., Am. Auto Racing Writers and Broadcasters Assn. Home: 3000 Holiday Dr 1501 Fort Lauderdale FL 33316 Personal E-mail: bobmarkus34@gmail.com.

MARKWOOD, STEPHEN ERNEST, educator, college president; b. Glasgow, Ky., Nov. 26, 1942; s. Chester Ray and Mary (Tandy) M.; m. Susan Hendee, Dec. 26, 1965; children: Christopher M., Kathryn M. BS in Edn., Bowling Green U., 1964, MA, 1968; EdD, Pa. State U., 1983. Asst. dean student life Waynesburg Coll., Pa., 1968-70; assoc. dean students Dickinson Coll., Carlisle, Pa., 1970-77; dean student devel. Rio Grande Coll., Ohio, 1977-80; v.p. Marietta Coll., Ohio, 1980—92; provost Ottawa U., 1992-95; pres. Alderson-Broaddus Coll., 1995—. Academic vice chair W.Va. Ind. Colls., 2000-03; chair Appalachian Coll. Assn. 2003-05. Contbr. articles to prof. jours. Served to capt. U.S. Army, 1964-66. Recipient Disting. Leadership award Pa. State U., 2005. Mem. Nat. Assn. Student Personnel Adminstrs., Am. Coll. Personnel Assn. (commn. 1983-84), Ohio Coll. Personnel Assn. (pres. 1983-84, outstanding leadership 1984, 87), Am. Coll. Personnel Assn. (mem. com. 1983-87), Ohio C. of C. (v.p.), Marietta C. of C. (pres.), Ohio Assn. Student Personnel Adminstrs, Ottawa C. of C. (treas.), W.Va. Intercoll. Assn. (chair 2002-04), Philip/Barboud C. of C. (dir.), Kiwanis (bd. dirs.). Avocations: golf, running. Office: Alderson-Broaddus Coll PO Box 2035 Philippi WV 26416 Business E-Mail: markwoodse@mail.ab.edu.

MARLAND, ALKIS JOSEPH, leasing company executive, computer scientist, educator, financial planner; b. Athens, Greece, Mar. 8, 1943; arrived in U.S., 1961, naturalized, 1974; s. Basil and Maria (Pervanides) Mouradoglou; m. Anita Louise Malone, Dec. 19, 1970 (dec. Mar. 27, 2003); children: Andrea Weber, Alyssa. BS, Southwestern U., 1963; MA, U. Tex., Austin, 1967; MS in Engring. Adminstrn., So. Meth. U., 1971. CLU; cert. data processing, enrolled agt., fund specialist, ChFC, CFP, accredited tax advisor, accredited tax preparer. With Sun Co., Richardson, Tex., 1968-71, Phila., 1971-76; mgr. planning and acquisitions Sun Info. Svcs. subs. Sun Co., Dallas, 1976-78; v.p. Helios Capital Corp. subs. Sun Co., Radnor, Pa., 1978-83; pres. ALKAN Leasing Corp., Wayne, Pa., 1983—, also bd. dirs. Prof. dept. computer scis. and bus. adminstrn. Ea. Coll., St. Davids, Pa., 1985—87; prof. math. Villanova (Pa.) U., 1987—89. Contr. Christian Counseling and Ednl. Found., 2003—05; bd. dirs. Radnor Twp. Sch. Dist., 1987—91, Delaware County Intermediate Unit, 1988—91. Mem.: IEEE, Assn. Investment Mgmt. and Rsch., Phila. Union League, World Affairs Coun. Phila., Fgn. Policy Rsch. Inst., Phila. Fin. Assn. (mem. award 1988, sec. 1989—92, bd. dirs. 1989—92), Fin. Planning Assn. (treas. 2000—01, bd. dirs. Phila. Tri-State Area 2000—04, pres.-elect 2002, pres. 2003, chmn. 2004), Fin. Analysts Phila., Nat. Assn. Pub. Accts., Nat. Assn. Tax Practitioners, Nat. Assn. Enrolled Agts., Inst. Cert. Fin. Planners (bd. dirs. Phila. Tri-State Area 1993—99, v.p. membership 1994—95, treas. 1995—99), Am. Assn. Equipment Lessors, Fin. Svc. Profls., Data Processing Mgmt. Assn., Assn. Computing Machinery, Main Line C. of C., Wayne Club, Masons, Rotary (pres. 1989—90, asst. gov. 1990—92, 1993—94, treas. dist. 7450 2002—07). Republican. Home and Office: 4 Starling Ct Phoenixville PA 19460 Office: PO Box 1063 Oaks PA 19456-1063 Office Phone: 610-659-1279. Personal E-mail: almarland@aol.com.

MARLAND, MELISSA KAYE, judge; b. Beckley, W.Va., Feb. 16, 1955; d. James Robert and Fannie Evelyn (Cook) M. BA in Polit. Sci., W.Va U., 1976, JD, 1979. Bar: W.Va. 1979, U.S. Dist. Ct. (so. dist.) W.Va. 1979, U.S. Supreme Ct. 1983. Law clk. Pub. Svc. Commn. W.Va., Charleston, 1979-82, hearing examiner, 1982-87, dep. chief adminstrv. law judge, 1987-89, chief adminstrv. law judge, 1989—. Faculty mem. ann. regulatory studies program Nat. Assn. Regulatory Commrs./Inst. Pub. Utilities, Mich. State U., 1994-2004; mem. com. rule for adminstrv. appeals W.Va. Supreme Ct., 2005-07. Co-author: W.Va. Code of Conduct for Administrative Law Judges, 2004-05; assoc. editor: West Virginia Digest of Public Utility Decisions, vols. 1-7, 1986-91; contbr. articles to profl. jours. Mem. ABA, NAFE, W.Va. State Bar (com. on corp., banking and bus. law 1987—, adminstrv. law com. 1995—), Nat. Assn. Regulatory Commrs. (chmn. subcom. on adminstrv. law judges 1991-95), W.Va. Assn. Adminstrv. Law Judges (pres. 2007), Phi Beta Kappa, Phi Alpha Delta, Pi Sigma Alpha. Democrat. Avocations: music, reading. Office: Pub Svc Commn WVa 201 Brooks St Charleston WV 25301-1803 Office Phone: 304-340-0400. E-mail: mmarland@psc.state.wv.us.

MARLAR, DONALD FLOYD, lawyer; b. Little Rock, Jan. 15, 1944; s. Floyd Howard and Ruth May (Lawson) M.; m. Janet Jeanne Clark, Mar. 29, 1963; children: Jennifer Clark, Christopher Decker. BA, Ark. State U., 1966; JD, U. Tulsa, 1969; Masters in Taxation, George Washington U., 1972. Bar: Okla. 1969. Ptnr. Pray, Walker, Jackman, Williamson & Marlar, Tulsa, Okla., 1973-96, pres., 1996—. Chmn. Okla. Bar Tax Section, 1979-80. Dir. Tulsa Ballet Theatre, 1987—, pres., 1991-92; gen. coun., v.p. Gilcrease Mus., Tulsa, 1989—, pres., 2000-01, chmn. bd. dirs., 2001—; trustee Grace and Franklin Bernsen Found., Tulsa, 1992—, Tulsa C.C. Found.; dir. Tulsa Hist. Soc. Capt. U.S. Army, 1969-73. Mem. Am. Bar Assn., Tulsa Bar Assn., The Summit Club (bd. govs. 1986-92, pres. 1992). Home: 3517 E 70th Pl Tulsa OK 74136-2647 Office: Pray Walker Jackman Williamson & Marlar 900 Oneok Plz 100 W 5th St Tulsa OK 74103 Office Phone: 918-581-5500. E-mail: DFM@praywalker.com.

MARLAS, JAMES CONSTANTINE, diversified financial services company executive; b. Chgo., Aug. 22, 1937; s. Constantine J. and Helen (Cotsirilos) M.; m. Kendra S. Graham, 1968 (div. 1971); m. Glenn Close, 1984 (div. 1987); m. Marie Nugent-Head, 1993. AB cum laude, Harvard U., 1959; MA in Jurisprudence, Oxford U., Eng., 1961; JD, U. Chgo., 1963. Bar: Ill. 1963, N.Y. 1966. Assoc. firm Baker & McKenzie, London and NYC, 1963-66; exec. v.p. South East Commodity Corp., NYC, 1967-68; chmn. bd. Union Capital Corp., NYC, 1968—; vice chmn. bd. Mickelberry's Food Products Co., NYC, 1970-71; pres., dir. Mickelberry Comm. Corp., NYC, 1972—, chief exec. officer, 1973—, chmn. bd., 1984—; chmn. bd., CEO Newcourt Industries, Inc., 1976—. Chmn. bd. dirs. Bowmar Instrument Corp., chmn. exec. com., 1983-92. Co-editor: Univ. Chgo. Law Rev, 1962-63; Contbr. articles to profl. jours. Bd. dirs. N.Y.C. Opera, Commanderie de Bordeaux, Brasenose Coll. Charitable Found. Mem. Am. Fgn. Law Assn., Young Pres.'s Orgn. Clubs: Boodle's (London); Knickerbocker (N.Y.C.), Racquet and Tennis (N.Y.C.). Office: Union Capital Corp 405 Park Ave New York NY 10022-4405 Office Phone: 212-832-0944.

MARLATT, MICHAEL JAMES, lawyer; b. LA, Jan. 15, 1957; s. James Raymond and Norma Jean (Greenfield) M.; m. Donna Marie Healey, Apr. 13, 1985. BA, U. So. Calif., Calif. Poly., Pomona, 1981; JD, Pepperdine U., 1984. Bar: Calif. 1984, U.S. Dist. Ct. (ctrl. dist.) Calif. 1985, U.S. Supreme Ct. 1990. Project liaison U. So. Calif., Sch. Medicine, LA, 1975-78; documentation rschr. NASA-Jet Propulsion Lab., Pasadena, Calif., 1978-81; ptnr. Thompson & Colegate, Riverside, Calif., 1984—. Bd. dirs. Assn. So. Calif. Def. Counsel, L.A., U. Calif., Riverside; lectr. Calif. Trial Lawyers Assn., 1991-94, Princeton U., 1993, U. Amsterdam Law Sch., 1994, Loma Linda (Calif.) U. Sch. Medicine, 1991-94, 99, 2001-03, Boston Coll. Law Sch., 1997, U. London, 1998; chair Am. Legal Sys. Internat. Law Program Civil Litigation U. of Calif., 1997; lectr., spkr. to ins. cos. on health care, 1988—; radio commentator Stas. KCKC, KCAL, KMEN and KPRO. Pres. U. Calif., Riverside, 1996—2000, mem. steering com.NCAA/ Big West Athletic Assn., 2003; v.p. Mission Inn Found., 1996—98, pres., 1999—2001; mem. bioethics com. Riverside Cmty. Hosp., 1999—; bd. dirs. Humane Soc.; bd. visitors Calif. Bapt. U., 2003—06; Mem. ctr. com. Calif. Rep. Party, Sacramento, 1990—93; bd. dirs. U. Calif., Riverside, Mission Inn Found., Riverside County Regional Med. Ctr., ARC, 2002—; bd. regents La Salle Cath. Pasadena, 2002—; bd. visitors Calif. Bapt. U., 2003—; chair Riverside County Regional Med. Ctr., 2005—; bd. regents Pasadena LaSalle, 2004—; bd. trustees Riverside Med. Found., 2007—. Mem. Am. Bd. Trial Advocates, So. Calif. Assn. Hosp. (bylaws com. 1996-99), Victoria Country Club, Lincoln Club Riverside County, Phi Alpha Delta. Roman Catholic. Avocations: rare book collecting, collegiate athletics, travel. Office: Thompson & Colegate PO Box 1299 3610 14th St Riverside CA 92501-3843 Office Phone: 951-682-5550. Business E-Mail: mmarlatt@tclaw.net.

MARLEAU, PATRICK, professional hockey player; b. Aneroid, Sask., Can., Sept. 15, 1979; m. Christina Marleau. Center San Jose Sharks, 1997—, capt., 2003—. Mem. Team Can., World Cup of Hockey, 2004; player NHL All-Star Game, 2004, 07. Named San Jose Mercury News South Bay Sportsperson of Yr., 2006. Achievements include being a member of World Cup Champion Team Canada, 2004. Office: San Jose Sharks 525 W Santa Clara St San Jose CA 95113 *

MARLEN, JAMES S., chemical, plastics and building materials manufacturing company executive; b. Santiago, Chile, Mar. 14, 1941; came to U.S., 1961; m. Carolyn S. Shields, Jan. 23, 1965; children: James, Andrew, John. BSChemE, U. Ala., 1965; MBA, U. Akron, 1971. With GenCorp., Akron, Ohio, 1965-93, engring., mktg. and gen. mgmt. positions domestic and internat. ops., 1977—80; group pres. fabricated plastics GTR Coated Fabrics Co., 1980-87; pres. consumer and indsl. sects. GenCorp Polymer Products, Akron, Ohio, 1988—; v.p. and officer GenCorp, Akron, 1988-93; pres., CEO Ameron Internat. Corp., Pasadena, Calif., 1993—. Bd. dirs., Ameron, Inc., chmn. bd. dirs., pres. and CEO, 1995—; dir. A. Schulman, Inc., Tamco Steel, Parsons Corp.; gen. and hon. chmn. Nat. Inventors Hall of Fame Induction, 1993. Bd. dirs. YMCA Met. L.A., The Employers Group of Calif., Town Hall of L.A., gov.; mem. the Beavers; dir. L.A. Sports Coun.; mem. bd. visitors Anderson Sch. Bus., UCLA, 1999-2001. Mem. Chem. Mfrs. Assn. (past pres.), Assocs. Caltech, Calif. C. of C., L.A. C. of C. (dir.), Portage Country Club (Akron, Ohio), Calif. Club (L.A.), Annandale Golf Club (Pasadena), L.A. Country Club, Valley Hunt Club (Pasadena), Soc. Fellows of Huntington Libr. (L.A.), Birnam Wood Golf Club (Santa Barbara, Calif.). Office: Ameron Internat Corp 245 S Los Robles Ave Pasadena CA 91101-2820

MARLER, B. EVONNE, not-for-profit fundraiser; d. Larry Ralph and Brenda Fay Marler. BA, U. of South, Sewanee, Tenn., 1997. Asst. dir. ann. giving U. of South, 1997—99; dir. ann. giving Baylor Sch., Chattanooga, 1999—2003; dir. devel. YMCA Met. Chattanooga, 2003—. Chmn. 4 Bridges Arts Festival, Chattanooga, 2002, Go Red for Women Luncheon, Chattanooga, 2005; bd. dirs. SE affiliate Am. Heart Assn., Chattanooga, 2002—06; bd. dirs. St. Andrew's Ctr., Chattanooga, 2007. Wilkins scholar, U. of South, 1993—97. Mem.: North Am. YMCA Devel. Orgn., Coun. Advancement and Support Edn., Assn. Fundraising Profls., Leadership Chattanooga Alumni Assn. (sec. 2003—06), Assn. Visual Arts (chmn. membership 2002), Scenic City Women's Network (sec. 2007), Chattanooga/Lafayette Emmaus, Mountain City Club, Charlotte Manigault Soc. (life), Heritage Soc. (life), YMCA Heritage Club (life), Alpha Delta Theta (pres. 1996—97, alumni adv.). Office: YMCA Met Chattanooga 301 W Sixth St Chattanooga TN 37402 Office Phone: 423-265-8834.

MARLER, JOAN, writer, educator; b. Chico, Calif., June 6, 1947; d. William Thomas Marler and Grace Elizabeth Paddock; m. Dan Dimitrov Smith, Jan. 1, 1975; 1 child, Sorrel Smith. BA in Dance, Mills Coll., Oakland, CA, 1969; MA in Archaeomythology, Sonoma State U., Rohnert Park, Calif., 1998. Instr. folk and ethnic dance Santa Rosa (Calif.) Jr. Coll., 1975—; prof. archaeomythology Calif. Inst. Integral Studies, San Francisco, 1996—. Radio prodr. KPFA, Berkeley, 1982—96; vis. prof. art history Sonoma State U., Rohnert Park, 1998; adj. faculty New Coll. Calif., San Francisco, 1998—2001; founder, dir. Inst. Archaeomythology. Editor: From the Realm of the Ancestors: An Anthology in Honor of Marija Gimbutas, 1997; author: (article in anthology) Treasures: Studies in Honor of Ivan Marazov, 1998, In Le radici prime dellÆEuropa: Gli intrecci genetici, linguistici, storici, 2002, In Women in Transition: Voices, 2001, Il Mito e il Cueto della grande Dea, 2003, Die Diskriminierung der Matriarchatsforschung, 2003, Notable American Women, 2003; editor: (jour.) ReVision Jour., (by Marija Gimbutas) Civilization of the Goddess, 1991, Jour. of Archaeomythology. Founding mem. Monastery Project. Grantee, Calif. Inst. Integral Studies, 2000. Mem.: Anthrop. Assn. Am. (assoc.). Office: Institute of Archaeomythology PO Box 1902 Sebastopol CA 95473 Office Phone: 707-823-7727. Business E-Mail: jmarler@archaeomythology.org.

MARLETT, JUDITH ANN, nutritional sciences educator, researcher; b. Toledo; BS, Miami U., Oxford, Ohio, 1965; PhD, U. Minn., 1972; postgrad., Harvard U., 1973-74. Registered dietitian. Therapeutic and metabolic unit dietitian VA Hosp., Mpls., 1966-67; spl. instr. in nutrition Simmons Coll., Boston, 1973-74; asst. prof. U. Wis., Madison, 1975-80, assoc. prof. dept. nutritional scis., 1981-84, prof. dept. nutritional scis., 1984—. Cons. U.S. AID, Leyte, Philippines, 1983, Makerere U., Kampala, Uganda, 2005; acting dir. dietetic program dept. Nutritional Scis. U. Wis., 1977-78, dir., 1985-89; cons. grain, drug and food cos., 1985—, adv. bd. U. Ariz. Clin. Cancer Ctr., 1987-95; sci. bd. advisors Am. Health Found., 1988—; reviewer NIH, 1982-2004; vis. prof. Makerere U., Kampala, Uganada, 2005; spkr. in field. Mem. editl. bd. Jour. Sci. of Food and Agrl., 1989—, Jour. Food Composition and Analysis, 1994-2000, Jour. of

Nutrition, 2002—; contbr. articles to profl. jours. Mem. NIH (Diabetes amd Digestive and Kidney Disease spl. grant rev. com. 1992-96), Am. Soc. Nutrition, Am. Dietetic Assn. Achievements include research on human nutrition and disease, dietary fiber and gastrointestinal function. Office: U Wis Dept Nutritional Sci 1415 Linden Dr Madison WI 53706-1527 Home Phone: 623-972-5221; Office Phone: 623-972-5221. Business E-Mail: jmarlett@nutrisci.wisc.edu.

MARLETTA, MICHAEL A., biochemistry educator, researcher; b. Rochester, NY, Feb. 12, 1951; m. Margaret Gutowski, 1991. BA, SUNY, 1973; PhD in Pharm. Chemistry, U. Calif., San Francisco, 1978. NIH postdoctoral fellow, Dept. Chem. MIT, Cambridge, 1978-80, from asst. prof. to assoc. prof. toxicology, 1980-87; assoc. prof. med. chemistry U. Mich., Ann Arbor, 1987-91, assoc. prof. biol. chemistry, 1989-91, John G. Searle prof. med. chemistry, prof. biol. chemistry, 1991—2001; Miller vis. rsch. prof. Univ. Calif., Berkeley, 2000, prof., chem., prof. biochemistry and molecular biology, 2001—, Aldo DeBenedictis disting. prof., chmn. chem. dept., 2005—, Joel Hildebrand disting. prof. chem., 2005—. Investigator Howard Hughes Med. Inst., 1997—2001. Recipient George H. Hitchings award for innovative methods in drug discovery & design, 1991, Outstanding Achievement award, SUNY at Fredonia, 1993, State of Mich. Scientist of Yr., 2000; MacArthur fellow, John D. and Catherine T. MacArthur Found., 1995. Fellow: AAAS, Mich. Soc. Fellows (sr.); mem.: NAS, Inst. Medicine, Am. Chem. Soc., Am. Soc. Biochem. and Molecular Biology. Achievements include research in protein/structure function with a particular interest in enzyme reaction mechanisms and molecular mechanisms of signal transduction, study of nitric oxide synthase, guanylate cyclase and related enzymes in this signaling system. Office: Univ Calif Chemistry Dept 420 Latimer Hall Berkeley CA 94720-1460 Office Phone: 510-643-9325. Office Fax: 570-643-9358. E-mail: marletta@berkeley.edu.

MARLETTE, CYNTHIA, lawyer; Joined Fed. Energy Regulatory Commn., Washington, 1979—, dep. gen. counsel, 1979, assoc. gen. counsel, hydroelectric and electric, acting gen. counsel, 2001, gen. counsel, 2001—05, prin. dep. gen. counsel. Office: Fed Energy Regulatory Commn Rm 10A01 888 First St NE Washington DC 20426-0001 Office Phone: 202-502-6000. Office Fax: 202-208-2115.

MARLEY, DAMIAN ROBERT NESTA (JR. GONG), reggae artist; b. Kingston, Jamaica, July 21, 1978; s. Bob Marley and Cindy Breakspeare. Performer: (albums) Mr. Marley, 1996, Halfway Tree, 2001 (Grammy award, Best Reggae Album, 2002), Welcome to Jamrock, 2005 (Vibe mag. Boomshot award, 2005, Grammy award, Best Reggae Album, 2006, Grammy award, Best Urban/Alternative Performance, 2006, Best Album, Internat. Reggae & World Music Awards, 2006); performer: (with Stephen & Julian Marley) Educated Fool, 2001; performer: (songs) There for You, 2005, Welcome to Jamrock, 2005 (Music of Black Origin award, Best Song, Internat. Reggae & World Music Awards, 2006, Best Music Video, Internat. Reggae & World Music Awards, 2006). Co-recipient Songwriter of Yr. (with Stephen Marley), Internat. Reggae & World Music Awards, 2006; recipient Bob Marley award for Entertainer of Yr., 2006, Recording Artist of Yr., 2006. Rastafarian.

MARLING, KARAL ANN, art history educator, social sciences educator, curator; b. Rochester, NY, Nov. 5, 1943; d. Raymond J. and Marjorie (Karal) M. PhD, Bryn Mawr Coll., 1971. Prof. art history and Am. studies U. Minn., Mpls., 1977—. Author: Federal Art in Cleveland, 1933-1943: An Exhibition, 1974, Wall-to-Wall America: A Cultural History of Post-Office Murals in the Great Depression, 1982, 2d edit., 2001, The Colossus of the Roads: Myth and Symbol Along the American Highway, 1984, 2d edit., 2000, Tom Benton and His Drawings: A Biographical Essay and a Collection of His Sketches, Studies and Mural Cartoons, 1985, Frederick C. Knight (1898-1797), 1987, George Washington Slept Here: Colonial Revivals and American Culture, 1876-1986, 1988, Looking Back: A Perspective on the 1913 Inaugural Exhibition, 1988, Blue Ribbon: A Social and Pictorial History of the Minnesota State Fair, 1990; author: (with John Wetenhall) Iwo Jima: Monuments, Memories, and the American Hero, 1991; author: Edward Hopper, 1992, As Seen on T.V.: The Visual Culture of Everyday Life in the 1950's, 1994, Graceland: Going Home with Elvis, 1995; editor (with Jessica H. Foy): The Arts and the American Home, 1890-1930, 1994; editor: Norman Rockwell, 1997, Designing the Disney Theme Parks: The Architecture of Reassurance, 1997, Merry Christmas! Celebrating America's Greatest Holiday, 2000, Looking North, 2003, Debutante, 2004, Old Glory Unfurled, 2004, Norman Rockwell: America's Favorite Painter, 2005, Behind The Magic: 50 Years of Disneyland, 2005, Designs on The Heart: The Homemade Art of Grandma Moses, 2006; contbr. essays to catalogs. Recipient award Minn. Humanities Commn., 1986, Book History award Minn., 1994, Robert C. Smith award Decorative Arts Soc., 1994, award Internat. Assn. Art Critics, 1998; Woodrow Wilson fellow, fellow Luce Found. Office: 1920 S 1st St Ste 1301 Minneapolis MN 55454-1190 Office Phone: 612-339-6172. Personal E-mail: kmarling@comcast.net. Business E-Mail: marli001@umn.edu.

MARLON, ANTHONY M., healthcare company executive, cardiologist; m. Renee Marlon. Graduate, Coll. of Holy Cross, Mass., 1963; internship, residency in cardiology, Stanford Univ., 1967—72. Intern, resident, cardiology fellow Stanford (Calif.) U., 1967-72; chief cardiology U. Med. Ctr. So. Nev., 1972-85; pvt. practice cardiology, from 1972; founder, chmn. bd., CEO Sierra Health Svcs., Inc., Las Vegas, Nev., 1984—. Office: Sierra Health Svcs Inc 2724 N Tenaya Way Las Vegas NV 89128 *

MARLOW, EDWARD A., former army officer; b. Cleve., Nov. 22, 1946; m. Gari Ann Dill, Sept. 20, 1975. AA, Long Beach City Coll., 1971; cert., Officer Candidate Sch., Ft. Benning, 1974, Basic Infantry Officer Course, 1976; student, Am. Law Inst., NYC, 1979-80; cert., Advance Armor Officer Course, Ft. Knox, 1982, U.S. Army Command and Gen. Staff Coll., 1986; BS in Bus. Mgmt. and Polit. Sci., SUNY, 1987; MPA, U. So. Calif., 1990; cert., Advance Intelligence Officer Course, Ft. Huachuca, 1991. Registered investment adv. with SEC, 1978-90. Commd. 2d lt. inf. US Army, 1974, advanced through grades to maj., 1988, ret., 1998; chief real property br. Mil. Dept., Sacramento, 1968—2004; pres. and dir. TEAM Mgmt. Corp., 1978—2006; pres. Western Res. Corp., Goldfield, Nev., 2000—, bd. dir.; CEO TEAM Internat., LLC, Sacramento, 2004—06; pres. and CEO TEAM Profl. Svcs., LLC, 2004—; team leader Real Property Acquisition Program US Army Corps Engrs., LA, 2005—06; CEO Edward A. Marlow, LLC, 2005—. Del. Korean Svc. Vets. Revisit Program, Seoul, Republic of Korea, 1975. Mng. sr. ptnr. Caribbean Basin Latin Am. Devel. Orgn., Sacramento, 1988-98; trustee Hosp. Relief Fund Caribbean, Inc., Washington, 1989-92; mem. Caribbean Pvt. Sector Disaster Coord. subcom. White House Internat. Disaster Adv. Com., 1991-92; sr. ptnr. Caribbean Basin Latin Am. Devel. Orgn. Endowment Group, Sacramento, 1992-2003; chair bd. trustees CABALADO Relief Fund, Inc., 1993-99; provided disaster assistance and med. equipment to Glendon Hosp., Plymouth, Montserrat, West Indies, 1994-95; with Park and Recreation Com. Found., Santa Barbara, Calif., mem. steering com., 2004—; pres., Checkered Flag 200 mem. Petersen Automotive Mus., 2005-06; supporter Santa Barbara County Sheriff's Coun., 2005-06. Mem.: Euclid City Schs. Alumni Assn., U. So. Calif. Gen. Alumni Assn., Am. Assn. Retired Persons, DAV (life). Avocations: sailing, fishing. Office Phone: 916-961-9382. E-mail: emarlowe_teamwrc@yahoo.com.

MARLOW, JAMES ALLEN, lawyer; b. Crossville, Tenn., May 23, 1955; s. Dewey Harold and Anna Marie (Hinch) M.; m. Sabine Klein, June 9, 1987; children: Lucas Allen, Eric Justin. BA, U. Tenn., 1976, JD, 1979; postgrad., Air War Coll., Maxwell AFB, Ala., 1990-91, Internat. Studienzentrum, Heidelberg, Germany, 1985-86. Bar: Ga. 1979, D.C. 1980, Tenn. 1980, U.S. Dist. Ct. (mid. dist.) Tenn. 1984, U.S. Ct. Fed. Claims 1987, U.S. Ct. Internat. Trade 1988, U.S. Tax Ct. 1987, U.S. Ct. Mil. Appeals 1980, U.S. Ct. Appeals (fed. cir.) 1987, U.S. Supreme Ct. 1987. Assoc. Carter & Assocs., Frankfurt, Fed. Republic Germany, 1984-85; chief internat. law USAF, Sembach AFB, Germany, 1986-96; pvt. practice Crossville, 1997—. Instr. Ctrl. Tex. Coll., 1997-2005; asst. prof. Embry-Riddle Aero. U., Kaiserslauten, Fed. Republic Germany, 1985-1999 Capt. USAF, 1980-84, Col. USAFR. Mem. Phi Beta Kappa. Avocations: genealogy, german and spanish languages. Home and Office: 5746 Highway 127 S Crossville TN 38572

MARLOW, ORVAL LEE, II, lawyer; b. Denver, May 1, 1956; s. Jack Conger and Barbara A. (Stolzenburg) M.; m. Paige Wood, June 8, 1985; children: Lorri Wood, Orval Lee III. BA, U. Nebr., Lincoln, 1978, JD, 1981. Bar: Tex. 1981, U.S. Dist. Ct. (so. dist.) Tex. 1984, U.S. Ct. Appeals (5th cir.) 1984. Assoc. Krist & Scott, Houston, 1981-82; prin. Marlow & Assocs., Houston, 1982-83; ptnr. Lendais & Assocs., Houston, 1983-91; dir. Morris, Lendais, Hollrah & Snowden, 1992—. Mem. ABA, Internat. Bar Assn., Tex. Bar Assn., Houston Bar Assn., Phi Delta Phi. Lutheran. Avocations: golf, skiing, chess. Office: Morris Lendais Hollrah & Snowden 1980 Post Oak Blvd Ste 700 Houston TX 77056-3881 Office Phone: 713-966-7222. Business E-Mail: omarlow@mlhs.net.

MARLOW, PATRICIA BAIR BOND, realtor; b. Altoona, Pa., Dec. 3, 1932; d. John Lesley and Gladys Marie Bair; m. Neal Nelson Jensen Bond, Aug. 7, 1953 (dec. July 1963); children: John Scott Bond, Lisa Suzanne Moody, Lesley Ann Stephen; m. Laurin Purcell Marlow, Apr. 4, 1967. Student, Mary Washington Coll., 1950-52. Realtor Everitt/Luby, Dallas, 1971-80; with Merrill Lynch, Dallas, 1980-89; realtor Adleta Fine Properties, 1989—. Contbr. poetry to anthologies. Recipient Diamond Summit. Mem. Dallas Mus. Art, Dallas Arboretum, Les Femmes du Monde, Dallas Mus. Art League, Tex. Kidney Found., Salvation Army (women's aux.). Avocation: watercolor painting. Home: 5336 Mission Cir Granbury TX 76049 Office: Adleta Fine Properties 5950 Berkshire Ln Dallas TX 75225 Home Phone: 817-326-3263. Personal E-mail: patti@pattimarlow.com.

MARLOWE, WILLIE, artist, fine arts educator; b. Whiteville, NC, Jan. 17, 1943; d. John David and Tessie Ernestine (McLawhorn) M.; m. Thomas Blakeslee Speight, July 11, 1980. Student, Pa. Acad. Fine Arts, Phila., 1964; BS, East Carolina U., 1965; MFA, U. Idaho, 1969; postgrad., Peace Coll., 1993. Instr. dept. art Skidmore Coll., Saratoga Springs, NY, 1970-74, mentor univ. without walls, 1972-74; instr. dept. art Columbia-Greene C.C., Hudson, NY, 1973-74; instr. Empire State Coll. SUNY, Albany, 1974; prof. Dept. Visual Arts Sage Coll., Albany, 1977—; chmn. The Sage Colls., Albany, 1979-81. Co-founder, tchr. Saratoga Arts Workshop, Saratoga Springs, N.Y., 1970-74; watercolor tchr. abroad Sage Colls., Scotland, Ireland, 2001; tchr. Somerville Coll., Oxford U., Eng., 1992; vis. artist U. Ga. studies abroad program, Cortona, Italy, 1989; vis. artist, Wexford Arts Ctr., Ireland, 1998, Tula State Lev Tolstoy Pedagogica L U., Tula, Russia, artist-in-residence for Ptnrs. of the Americas, Barbados, W.I., 1986, The Millay Colony for the Arts, Austerlitz, N.Y., 1999; artist selection com. Albany Ctr. Gallery, 1998; internat. artists' residency Cill Rialaig Project, Ballinskelligs, Ireland, 2005, Emily Harvey Found., Venice, 2006; del. to Russia with Albany Tula Alliance; lectr. in field. One-woman shows include The Mint Mus. Art, Charlotte, NC, 1971, Schenectady Mus., NY, 1975, Marist Coll., Poughkeepsie, NY, 1976, Stockton State Coll., Pomono, NJ, 1977, Greenville Mus. Art, NC, 1982, 97, Ann Grey Gallery The Casino, Saratoga Springs, NY, 1985, The Barrett Art Gallery Utica Coll. Syracuse U., NY, 1986, The Atrium Gen. Electric Corp. R&D Ctr., Schenectady, 1988, Forum Gallery, Gütersloh, Germany, 1992, Albany Ctr. Gallery, 1992, 97, McHenry County Coll., Crystal Lake, Ill., Main St. Gallery, Dobbs Ferry, 1995, The Wexford Arts Ctr., Ireland, 1998, The Saratoga Arts Ctr., Saratoga Springs, NY, 2000, Fondo del Sol Gallery and Visual Arts Ctr., Washington, 2002, Barrett Arts Ctr., Poughkeepsie, NY, 2002, Gallery C, Raleigh, 2003, Color and Space traveling solo show, NC, 2006; exhibited in group shows Art Upstairs, Wexford, Ireland, 2007, Adirondack CC, Queensbury, NY, 2006, Gallery Neptune, Bethesda, Md., 2005, Wexford (Ireland) Arts Ctr., 2004, Art Ctr. for the Capital Region, Troy, NY, 2002, Reprize Internat. Invitational Show, Wexford Arts Ctr., Ireland, 2002, Martinez Gallery, Troy, NY, 2002, Artemisia Gallery, Chgo., 2000, 03, Nexus Gallery, NYC, 1997-99, Gang Gallery, NYC, Eng. & Co., London, 1993, Steinbaum-Krauss Gallery, NYC, 1990, Stux Gallery, Boston, 1987, Nat. Mus. Women Arts, Washington, 1987, Westbeth Gallery, NYC, 1994, Clocktower, NYC, 1986, Rice Gallery The Albany Inst. History & Art, 1986, Deborah Davis Fine Arts, Hudson, 2003-04, 06, Firlefanz Gallery, Albany, 2004, Gallery 100, Saratoga Springs, 2004, U. West Eng., Bristol, 2004, Nat. Coll. Art and Design, Dublin, Ireland, 2004; represented in pvt. collections; represented in permanent collections Legis, Nat. Orgn. Women in th Arts, Zimmerili Art Museum, Rutgers U., NJ. Offices Empire State Plz., Albany, First Albany Corp., Md. Dept. Econ. & Cmty. Devel., Balt., Quad Graphics, Boston, SUNY Albany, NC Nat. Bank, Charlotte, Greenville Mus. Art, East Carolina U., Greenville, NC, Boston Pub. Libr., Budapest Gallery, Russell Sage Coll., Troy, Mint Mus. Art, Charlotte, NC, Four Winds Ctr., Saratoga Springs, U. Mus. SUNY Albany, Bullard and McLeod & Assocs., Inc., Albany, NY, Rocky Mount Art Ctr., NC, Adirondack CC, NY, represented by Art Upstairs, Wexford, Ireland, Gallery C, Raleigh, NC, Martinez Gallery, Troy, NY, Denorah Davis Fine Art, Hudson, NY, Gallery Neptune, Bethesda, Md., Art Forms, Guiderland, NY, Art Gallery Ltd., New Bern, NJ; co-curator and curator for mail art shows. Recipient Purchase award in painting Hudson Mohawk Regional Ann., SUNY Albany, 1977, 95, 97, medal Internat. Art Competition Metro Arts, Inc., Scarsdale, N.Y., 1986, honorable mention in painting Third Ann. Nat. C.C. Miniature Painting Show, Lexington, 1987, Sywer award, 1995, and numerous others; N.Y. State Coun. on the Arts grantee Barrett Art Gallery Syracuse U., 1986, grantee Artists' Space, 1988, Spl. Opportunity grant N.Y. Found. Arts. Mem.: Nat. Assn. Women Artists, Albany Inst. History and Art, Fulton St. Gallery, Albany Ctr. Gallery, Woman's Caucus For Art. Avocations: painting, visual poetry, mail art. Personal E-mail: info@williemarlowe.com.

MARMARELIS, VASILIS ZISSIS, engineering educator, writer, consultant; b. Mytilini, Greece, Nov. 16, 1949; arrived in US, 1972; s. Zissis P. and Elpis V. (Galinos) M.; m. Melissa Emily Orme, Mar. 12, 1989; children: Zissis Eugene and Myrl Galinos. Diploma in elec. and mech. engring., Nat. Tech. U. Athens, 1972; MS in Info. Sci., Calif. Inst. Tech., 1973, PhD in Engring. Sci., 1976. Rsch. fellow Calif. Inst. Tech., Pasadena, 1976—78; asst. prof. U. So. Calif., LA, 1978—83, assoc. prof., 1983—88, prof., 1988—, also dir. biomed. simulations resource, 1985—, chmn. dept. biomed. engring., 1990—96; pres. Multispec Corp., LA, 1986—2000. Author: Analysis of Physiological Systems, 1978, translated in Russian 1981, translated in Chinese 1990; Advanced Methods of Physiological Systems Modeling, vol. I, 1987, vol. II, 1989, vol. III, 1994, Nonlinear Dynamic Modeling of Physiological Systems, 2004; contbr. numerous articles to profl. jours. Fellow: IEEE, Am. Inst. for Med. and Biol. Engring.; mem.: N.Y. Acad. Scis., Biomed. Engring. Soc., Neural Networks Soc. Achievements include invention of Artemis mammography system. Office: Univ So Calif DRB160 Los Angeles CA 90089-1111

MARMER, ELLEN LUCILLE, pediatrician, cardiologist; b. Bronx, NY, June 29, 1939; d. Benjamin and Diane (Goldstein) M.; m. Harold O. Shapiro, June 5, 1960; children: Cheri, Brenda. BS in Chemistry, U. Ala., 1960; MD, U. Ala., Birmingham, 1964. Cert. Nat. Bd. Med. Examiners; diplomate Am. Bd. Sports Medicine, Bd. Pediat., Bd. Qualified and Eligible Pediatric Cardiology, Bd. cert. sports medicine. Intern Upstate Med. Ctr., Syracuse, NY, 1964-65, resident, 1965-66; fellow in pediatric cardiology Columbia Presbyn. Med. Ctr.-Babies Hosp., NYC, 1967-69; pvt. practice Hartford, Vernon, Conn., 1969—. Examining pediatrician child devel. program Columbia Presbyn. Med. Ctr.-Babies Hosp., N.Y.C., 1967, instr. pediat., 1967-69; dir. pediatric cardiology clinic St. Francis Hosp., Hartford, 1970-80; asst. state med. examiner, Tolland County, Conn., 1974-79; sports physician Rockville (Conn.) High Sch., 1976—; advisor Cardiac Rehab. com., Rockville, 1984-90; mem. bd. examiners Am. Bd. Sports Medicine, 1991—, chmn. credentials com., 1991-93. Mem. Vernon Town Coun., 1985-89; bd. dirs. Child Guidance Clinic, Manchester, Conn., 1970—; life mem. Tolland County chpt. Hadassah, v.p., 1969-70, pres., 1970-72, bd. dirs., 1973-74; mem. B'nai Israel Congregation and Sisterhood, Vernon, 1969—, chmn. youth commn., 1970-72; mayor Town of Vernon, 2003-05, 05-. Recipient Outstanding Svc. award Indian Valley YMCA, 1985. Fellow Am. Acad. Pediat., Am. Coll. Cardiology, Am. Coll. Sports Medicine; mem. Conn. Med. Soc., Am. Heart Assn. (mem. coun. cardiovasc. disease in young 1969—, chmn. elect New Eng. regional heart com. 1990-91, mem. Heritage affiliate 1998—), Conn. Heart Assn. (bd. dirs. 1974-75, 83-84, pres. 1986-88), Heart Assn. Greater Hartford (bd. dirs. 1970-89, mem. exec. com. 1972-73, 79-84, pres. 1982-84), Tolland County Med. Assn. (sec. 1971-72), Vis. Nurse and Cmty. Care Tolland County, LWV (state program chairperson Vernon chpt. 1971-73). Democrat. Jewish. Avocation: sports. Office: 520 Hartford Tpke Vernon Rockville CT 06066 Office Phone: 860-870-9366.

MARMER, NANCY, editor; b. NYC, Nov. 19, 1932; d. Carl and Frances Marmer; m. Gerald Jay Goldberg, Jan. 23, 1954; 1 child, Robert. BA magna cum laude, Queens Coll., 1954; postgrad., U. Minn., 1954-57, UCLA, 1968-71. L.A. corr. Art Internat., 1965-67; West Coast editor Artforum, 1976-77; sr. editor Art in America, NYC, 1979-81, exec. editor, 1981-83, book rev. editor, 1983-97, mng. editor, 1983-97, editor-at-large, 1997-98, contbg. editor, 1998—. Lectr. Mellon seminar R.I. Sch. Design, 1983; lectr. art criticism Visual Arts dept. U. Calif., San Diego, 1978; faculty expository writing Dept. English, U. Minn., 1954-57. Author: The Modern Critical Spectrum, 1962; contbr. numerous articles to profl. jours.; art critic/reviewer for Art in America, Art Internat., Artforum, L.A. Times. Recipient Samuel Kress Found. Award in Art History; Nat. endowment for the Arts fellow in art criticism. Mem. Phi Beta Kappa. E-mail: 102424.711@compuserve.com.

MARMET, GOTTLIEB JOHN, lawyer; b. Chgo., Mar. 24, 1946; s. Gottlieb John and Margaret Ann (Saylor) M.; m. Jane Marie Borkowski, Sept. 12, 1970; children: Gottlieb John, Philip Stanley, Thomas Jacob. BS with distinction in Acctg., San Diego State U., 1967; JD, Northwestern U., 1970. Bar: Ill. 1970, U.S. Dist. Ct. (no. dist.) Ill. 1970, U.S. Tax Ct. 1981; CPA, Calif., Ill., Minn. Tax acct. Touche Ross & Co., Chgo., 1970-75; assoc. atty. Howington, Elworth, Osswald & Hough, Chgo., 1975-79; tax mgr. Peat, Marwick, Mitchell & Co., Mpls., 1979-81; assoc. Shefsky, Saitlin & Froelich, Ltd., Chgo., 1981-83; prin. G. John Marmet, Glenview, Ill., 1983—. Lectr. corp. law William Rainey Harper Coll., Arlington Heights, Ill., 1984; instr. Ill. Soc. CPAs, 1976, 77, Minn. Soc. CPAs, 1980. Author: Farm Corporations and Their Income Tax Treatment, 1970, 74; contbr. articles to jours., pubs. Active Northeast Ill. Coun. Boy Scouts Am., 1984—, dist. chmn. Skokie Valley, 1988, mem. exec. bd., 1989-91, 99-2006; bd. dirs. North Shore Sr. Ctr., 1995-99. Recipient Hon. Mention Chgo. Bar Assn. Art Show, 1972, Boy Scouts Am. Dist. award of merit, 1990, Silver Beaver award, 1997. Mem. AICPA, ABA, Ill. Bar Assn., Chgo. Bar Assn., Rotary (Service Above Self award 1986, 96, bd. dirs. 1988-90, v.p. 1990-91, pres. 1991-92, 2004—05), Internat. Fellowship Scouting Rotarians (life, chmn. Inter-Am. region 2005—7, Silver Wheel award 2005, Cliff Dochterman award 2006), Beta Gamma Sigma, Beta Alpha Psi, Phi Alpha Delta. Office: 950 Milwaukee Ave Ste 318 Glenview IL 60025-3779 Home Phone: 847-724-5196; Office Phone: 847-298-9428. Personal E-mail: gmarmet@aol.com.

MARMION, DANIEL KEITH, school librarian; b. Colo. m. Diana Mary Manttan; 1 child, Jennifer Lynn. Assoc. dir. librs. U. Notre Dame, 2000—; asst. dean librs. Western Mich. U. Office: Univ Notre Dame 221 Hesburgh Library Notre Dame IN 46556 Office Phone: 574-631-3811.

MARMOR, MICHAEL FRANKLIN, ophthalmologist, educator; b. NYC, Aug. 10, 1941; s. Judd and Katherine (Stern) M.; m. C. Jane Breeden, Dec. 20, 1968; children: Andrea K., David J. AB, Harvard U., Cambridge, Mass., 1962, MD, 1966. Diplomate Am. Bd. Ophthalmology. Med. intern UCLA Med. Ctr., 1967; fellow neurophysiology NIMH, 1967-70; resident in ophthalmology Mass. Eye and Ear Infirmary, Boston, 1970-73; asst. prof. ophthalmology U. Calif. Sch. Medicine, San Francisco, 1973-74; asst. prof. surgery (ophthalmology) Stanford U. Sch. Medicine, Calif., 1974-80, assoc. prof. Calif., 1980-86, prof. Calif., 1986—, head. div. ophthalmology Calif., 1984-88, chmn. dept. Calif., 1988-92, dir. Basic Sci. Course Ophthalmology Calif., 1993—2005. Faculty mem. program in human biology Stanford U., 1982—; chief ophthalmology sect. VA Med. Ctr., Palo Alto, Calif., 1974-84; mem. sci. adv. bd. No. Calif. Soc. to Prevent Blindness, 1984-92, Calif. Med. Assn., 1984-92, Nat. Retinitis Pigmentosa Found., 1985-95. Author: The Eye of the Artist, 1997, Degas Through his own Eyes, 2002; editor: The Retinal Pigment Epithelium, 1975, The Effects of Aging and Environment on Vision, 1991, The Retinal Pigment Epithelium: Function and Disease, 1998; editor-in-chief Doc. Ophthalmologica, 1995-99; history editor: Survey of Ophthalmology, TimeOph; contbr. more than 250 articles to peer-reviewed jours., 50 chpts. to books. Mem. affirmative action com. Stanford U. Sch. Medicine, 1984-92. Sr. asst. surgeon USPHS, 1967-70. Recipient Svc. award Nat. Retinitis Pigmentosa Found., Balt., 1981, Rsch. award Alcon Rsch. Found., Houston, 1989; rsch. grantee Nat. Eye. Inst., Bethesda, Md., 1974-94. Fellow Am. Acad. Ophthalmology (bd. councillors 1982-85, pub. health com. 1990-93, rep. to NAS com. on vision 1991-93, mus. com. 2004—, Honor award 1984, Sr. Honor award 1996), Cogan Ophthalmology Hist. Soc. (pres. 2003—); mem. Internat. Soc. Clin. Electrophysiology of Vision (v.p. 1990-98, dir. stds.), Assn. Rsch. in Vision and Ophthalmology, Internat. Soc. for Eye Rsch., Retina Soc., Macula Soc. (Green lectr. 2007). Democrat. Avocations: tennis, bicycling, chamber music (clarinet), art, history. Office: Stanford U Sch Medcine Dept Ophthalmology Stanford CA 94305-5308

MARMOR, THEODORE RICHARD, political science professor, writer; b. Bklyn., Feb. 24, 1939; s. James and Mira Bernice (Karpf) M.; m. Jan Schmidt, Oct. 20, 1961 (dec. 2003); children: Laura Carleton, Sarah Rogers; m. Kieke G.H. Okma, May 11, 2007. BA, Harvard U., 1960, PhD, 1966; postgrad., Wadham Coll., Oxford U., Eng., 1961-62. Asst. and assoc. prof. polit. sci. U. Wis.-Madison, 1967-69; assoc. prof. pub. affairs U. Minn.-Mpls., 1970-73; prof. U. Chgo., 1973-79; prof. polit. sci. Yale U., New Haven, 1979—, chmn. Ctr. Health Studies, 1979-85, prof. pub. mgmt. Sch. Orgn. and Mgmt., 1983—2007. Vis. fellow Russell Sage Found., 1987-88; cons., lectr. in field. Author: The Politics of Medicare, 1973, 2d edit., 2000, Political Analysis and American Medical Care, 1983, Understanding Health Care Reform, 1994, Fads, Fallacies and Foolishness: Medical Care Management and Policy, 2007; co-author: Health Care Policy, 1982, America's Misunderstood Welfare State, 1992; editor: Poverty Policy, 1971, National Health Insurance, 1980, Social Security: Beyond the Rhetoric of Crisis, 1988, Why Some People Are Healthy and Others Not, 1994, Jour. Health Politics Policy and Law, 1980-84, Jour. Health Politics and Law Policy; contbr. articles to profl. jours. Mem. Coun. Fgn. Rels., NYC, 1979-85, Pres.' Commn. on 1980s, 1980; social policy adviser Walter Mondale Presdl. Campaign, 1984. Can. Inst. Advanced Rsch. fellow, 1987-1994; fellow Adlai Stevenson Inst., J.F.K. Inst. Politics. Fellow Inst. Medicine, Nat. Acad. Social Ins.; mem. U.S. Squash Racquets

Assn. (bd. dirs. 1983-93), Century Assn., United Oxford and Cambridge Club, Lawn Club, Univ. Club. NY. Democrat. Jewish. Office: Yale U Sch Mgmt 135 Prospect St New Haven CT 06520-8200 Home: 434 E 52 St 6G New York NY 10022

MARMORSTEIN, VICTORIA E., lawyer; BA with distinction, U. Okla., 1973; JD, Am. U., 1977; LLM, U. Va., 1978. Bar: DC 1977, NY 1980, Calif. 1989. Ptnr., global chair, fin. and real estate dept. Latham & Watkins, LA. Adj. prof., UCLA Sch. of Law. Editor: Va. Jour. of Internat. Law; author: numerous articles in profl. publications. Named in Chambers & Partners Guide to America's Leading Lawyers for Bus., 2004, in Euromoney's Legal Group Guide to the World's Leading Securitization Lawyers; named one of Top Women Lawyers in LA, LA mag., 2004. Mem.: Phi Beta Kappa. Fluent in Spanish. Office: Latham & Watkins Ste 4000 633 W Fifth St Los Angeles CA 90071-2007

MARNELL, ANTHONY AUSTIN, II, architect; b. Riverside, Calif., Mar. 30, 1949; s. Anthony Austin and Ida Marie (Comforti) M.; m. Sandra Jean Graf, June 24, 1972 (div.); children: Anthony, Alisa. BArch, U. So. Calif., 1972. Architect, draftsman firms in Calif. and Nev., 1969-72; project coordinator Zuni Constrn. Co., Las Vegas, Nev., 1973-74; office mgr., architect Corrao Constrn. Co., Inc., Las Vegas, Nev., 1973-74, 1974-82; founder, CEO, chmn. bd. Marnell Corrao Assocs., Las Vegas, Nev., 1982—; pres. Marinelli Internat., Inc., Las Vegas, Nev., 1978—, A.A. Marnell II, Architect, Las Vegas, Nev., 1978—, Air Continental Jet Charter, Inc., Las Vegas, Nev., 1980-99; chmn., CEO Rio Hotel & Casino (acquired by Harrah's), 1986—99. Mem. ethics com. Nev. Bd. Architects, 1974; chmn. bd. Rio Hotel & Casino, Inc., 1986—, Focus 2000, Inc., 1989—. Prin. works include Mirage, Rio, Maxim Hotel, Treasure Island, Boulder Station, Sundance Hotel, Sam's Town, Excalibur; additions to Caesar's Palace, Desert Inn, Sands, Stardust, California, Frontier and Dunes Hotels (all Las Vegas), Caesar's, Atlantic City, others. Mem. Founders Bd. U. Nev., Las Vegas. Mem. Nat. Council Archtl. Registration Bds., Post Tensioning Inst. YPO (Nev. chmn. 1990). Roman Catholic. Office: Marnell Corrao Assoc Inc 222 Via Marnell Way Las Vegas NV 89119 Office Phone: 702-739-2000. Office Fax: 702-739-2005.

MARNEY, SAMUEL ROWE, JR., allergist, immunologist, educator; b. Bristol, Va., Feb. 15, 1934; m. Elizabeth Ann Bingham, Oct. 1, 1966; children: Samuel Rowe III, Annis Morison. BA in Chemistry, U. Va., 1955, MD, 1960. Diplomate Am. Bd. Internal Medicine, Am. Bd. Allergy and Immunology; cert. in Diagnostic Lab. Immunology, 1988. Staff physician VA Hosp., Nashville, 1968—69, clin. assoc., 1969—71, clin. investigator, 1971—74, staff physician, infectious disease and allergy cons., 1974—; asst. prof. medicine Med. Ctr. Vanderbilt U., Nashville, 1971—76, assoc. prof., 1976—, dir. allergy and immunology, 1974—. Vis. investigator Scripps Clinic and Rsch. Found., La Jolla, Calif., 1973-74. Capt. USAF, 1962—64, Korea. Fellow ACP, Am. Acad. Allergy and Immunology, Am. Coll. Allergy and Immunology; mem. Southeastern Allergy Assn. (pres. 1986-87, Hal M. Davison Meml. award, 1981, 99), Tenn. Soc. Allergy and Immunology. Home: 4340 Sneed Rd Nashville TN 37215-3242 Office: Vanderbilt U Med Ctr Allergy & Immunology 2611 W End Ave Nashville TN 37203-6013 Home Phone: 615-297-1251; Office Phone: 615-936-2727. Business E-Mail: samuel.marney@vanderbilt.edu.

MAROHN, WILLIAM D., consumer products company executive; BSME, Univ. Toledo, 1964. With Whirlpool Corp., 1964—98, division v.p., 1979—84, v.p., 1984—87, pres. Kenmore appliance group, 1987—89, exec. v.p. No. Am. ops., 1989—91, pres. Whirlpool Europe, 1992, pres., COO, 1992—97, vice chmn., 1997—98; dir. Newell Rubbermaid, Atlanta, 1999—, chmn., 2004—. Bd. dir. Cooper Tire & Rubber, Hanson Cold Storage. Dir. Mich. Jobs Commn.; chmn. Whirlpool Found., Lake Mich. Coll. Found.; mem. vis. com. Univ. Mich. Sch. Bus. Served USAF, Ohio & Mich. Air Nat. Guard. Recipient Gold T award, Univ. Toledo, 1997. Office: Newell Rubbermaid Ste 600 10 B Glendale Pkwy Atlanta GA 30328 *

MARON, DAVID JOEL, cardiologist, educator; b. Nov. 1, 1920; Undergraduate degree, Stanford Univ.; MD, Keck Sch. Medicine, Univ. Southern Calif. Sch. Medicine, 1981. Cert. Internal Medicine, Cardiovascular Disease. Intern, internal medicine UCLA Med. Ctr., 1981—82, resident, medicine, 1982—94; fellow, cardiology Stanford Univ., fellow; staff mem. St. John's Hosp., Santa Monica, 1991—93, Santa Monica Hosp., 1991—93, Vanderbilt Univ. Hosp., Nashville, 1993, Nashville VA Hosp.; clin. instr. Stanford U., 1984—89, UCLA, LA, 1992—93; asst. prof. medicine Vanderbilt Univ. Med. Ctr., Nashville, 1993—2002, assoc. prof. medicine, 2002—; med. dir. Kim Dayani Ctr. for Health Promotion. Mem. scientific adv. bd. Physician Nutrceutical Co., 2002; co-founder Cardiovascular Services of Am. Contbr. articles to profl. jours. Office: Vanderbilt Univ Med Ctr 2311 Pierce Ave Nashville TN 37232 *

MARON, MARC, comedian, actor, writer; b. 1963; m. Mishna Wolf. Stand-up comic, 1986—; host Short Attention Span Theater, Comedy Central; co-host (with Mark Riley) Morning Sedition, Air Am. Radio, 2004—05. Performer: (one-man show) Jerusalem Syndrome, 2000; author: (book) Jerusalem Syndrome: My Life as a Reluctant Messiah, 2001; actor: (films) Los Enchiladas!, 1999, Almost Famous, 2000; guest appearances (comedian) Late Show with David Letterman, Late Night with Conan O'Brian, (documentaries) Left of the Dial, 2005. Jewish.

MARONDE, ROBERT FRANCIS, internist, pharmacologist; b. Monterey Park, Calif., Jan. 13, 1920; s. John August and Emma Florence (Palmer) M.; m. Yolanda Cerda, Apr. 15, 1970; children: Robert George, Donna F. Maronde Varnau, James Augustus, Craig DeWald. BA, U. So. Calif., 1941, MD, 1944. Diplomate: Am. Bd. Internal Medicine. Intern L.A. County-U. So. Calif. Med. Ctr., 1943-44, resident, 1944-45, 47-48; asst. prof. physiology U. So. Calif., LA, 1948-49, asst. clin. prof. medicine, 1949-60, assoc. clin. prof. medicine, 1960-65, assoc. prof. medicine and pharmacology, 1965-67, prof. medicine and pharmacology, 1968-90, emeritus, 1990—, prof. emeritus, 1990—; spl. asst. v.p. for health affairs, 1990—. Cons. FDA, 1973, Medco Containment Co. Inc., 1991-97, State of Calif. Dept. Health Svcs., 1993; mem. adv. panel State of Calif., 1997—. Served to lt. (j.g.) USNR, 1945-47. Fellow ACP; mem. Am. Soc. Clin. Pharmacology and Therapeutics, Alpha Omega Alpha. Home: 785 Ridgecrest St Monterey Park CA 91754-3759 Business E-Mail: maronde@usc.edu. *Scientific integrity, objectivity, concern for the quality of life and adherence to the ethics of Nuremberg are ingredients for the evaluation of therapy for human illness. This is the ultimate objective of the practice of medicine.*

MARONE, ANTHONY F., JR., quality assurance professional; b. Framingham, Mass., Aug. 9, 1982; s. Anthony and Denise Marone. BS, Rutgers U., New Brunswick, NJ, 2000—04; MS in Bus. Adminstrn., Rutgers U., Newark, NJ, 2004—05. CPA NJ Bd. Accountancy, 2007. Assurance assoc. PricewaterhouseCoopers, LLP, NYC, 2005—. Editor: (internet newsletter) Tomorrow's CPA Newsletter; actor: (promotional video) Take The Next Step; contbr. articles to mags. Mem.: Am. Inst. CPAs, NJ Soc. CPA's (Merit scholarship 2000), Mensa, Nat. Soc. Collegiate Scholars, Tau Kappa Epsilon (pres. 1998—99). Office: Pricewaterhouse-Coopers LLP 300 Madison Ave New York NY 10017 Home Phone: 908-507-2469. Business E-Mail: anthony.f.marone@us.pwc.com.

MARONEY, SHARON A, special education educator; b. Naugatuck, Conn., Dec. 18, 1953; d. John G. and Doris M. Maroney; m. David G. Smith. PhD, U. Minn., Mpls., 1989. Prof. spl. edn. Buena Vista U., Storm Lake, Iowa, 1988—94, Western Ill. U. QuadCities, Moline, 1994—. Office: Western Ill Univ -Quad Cities 3561 60th St Moline IL 61265 Office Phone: 309-762-9481. Office Fax: 309-762-6989. Business E-Mail: sa-maroney1@wiu.edu.

MARONI, DONNA FAROLINO, biologist, researcher; b. Buffalo, Feb. 27, 1938; d. Enrico Victor and Eleanor (Redlinska) Farolino; m. Gustavo Primo Maroni, Dec. 16, 1974. BS, U. Wis., 1960, PhD, 1969. Project assoc. U. Wis., Madison, 1960-63, 68-74; Alexander von Humboldt fellow Inst. Genetics U. Cologne, Fed. Republic Germany, 1974-75; Hargitt fellow Duke U., Durham, NC, 1975-76, rsch. assoc., 1976-83, rsch. assoc. prof., 1983-87; sr. program specialist N.C. Biotech. Ctr., Research Triangle Park, 1987-88, dir. sci. programs div., 1988-92, v.p. for sci. programs, 1992-94, ret., 1995. Mem. adv. com. MICROMED at Bowman Gray Sch. Medicine, Winston-Salem, NC, 1988—94; mem. sci. adv. bd. NC Biosci. Fund, LLC, 1998—99, Minority Sci. Improvement Alliance for Instrn. and Rsch. in Biotech, Ala. A&M U., Normal, 1990—91. Contbr. articles to profl. jours. Grantee NSF, 1977-79, NIH, 1979-82, 79-83, 82-87. Mem. Genetics Soc. Am., N.C. Acad. Sci., Inc. (bd. dirs. 1983-86), Sigma Xi (mem. exec. com. Duke U. chpt. 1989-90). Achievements include research in electron microscopy, evolution of chromosomes, chromosome structure, evolution of mitosis, and mitosis and fungal phylogeny. Personal E-mail: dmaroni@email.unc.du.

MAROONE, MICHAEL E., automotive executive; b. 1962; CEO Maroone Car & Truck Sales, Pembroke Pines, Fla.; COO, pres. AutoNation Inc., Ft. Lauderdale, Fla., 1999—. Bd. dir. Intercontinental Bank; chmn. South Fla. Internat. Auto Show, 1995. Bd. dir. Dan Marino Found., Boys and Girls Club of Broward County, Children Cancer Caring Ctr., Police Athletic League. Named Humanitarian of Yr., Transflorida Bank; recipient Chmn.'s award, Ford Motor Co., Quality Dealer award, Time mag. Mem.: Fla. Automotive Dealers Assn. (bd. dir.), South Fla. Chevrolet Dealers Mktg. Assn. (pres. 1994), South Fla. Auto Truck Dealers Assn. (pres. 1994). Office: AutoNation Inc 110 S E 6th St Fort Lauderdale FL 33301 *

MAROONEY, RICHARD T., lawyer; b. Garden City, NY; BS, BA cum laude, Boston Col., 1991; JD with distinction, Hofstra Univ., 1994. Bar: N.Y. 1995, US Dist. Ct. So. & Ea. Dist. N.Y. 1996, US Dist. Ct. We. & No. Dist. N.Y. 1998. Ptnr., Litigation Practice Group King & Spalding LLP, New York. Editor (assoc.): Hofstra Law Rev. Office: King & Spalding LLP 1185 Ave of the Americas New York NY 10036 Office Phone: 212-556-2242. Office Fax: 212-556-2222. Business E-Mail: rmarooney@kslaw.com.

MAROSAN, GEORGE, plastic surgeon; b. Oradea, Romania, Apr. 20, 1955; s. Bela and Irene Marosan; m. Boglarka Hagya, June 1, 1986; children: Zoltan George, Nandor Christopher. BA, SUNY at Buffalo, 1978; MA, Roswell Pk. Cancer Inst., Buffalo, 1981; MD, Rush Med. Coll., Chgo., 1983. Diplomate Am. Bd. of Plastic Surgery, 1994. Gen. surgery resident Rush Univ. Hosp., 1983—84, Jersey City Med. Ctr., 1984—85, David Grant USAF Med. Ctr., Calif., 1986—89; plastic surgery resident Walter Reed Army Med. Ctr., Washington, 1990—92; plastic surgeon Bellevue Plastic Surgeons, Bellevue, Wash., 1996—. Lt. col. USAF, 1985—95. Decorated Air Force Commendation medal. Fellow: ACS; mem.: Am. Soc. for Laser Medicine and Surgery, Hungarian Med. Assn. of Am., Wash. Soc. of Plastic Surgeons, N.W. Soc. of Plastic Surgeons, Am. Soc. for Aesthetic Plastic Surgery, Am. Soc. of Plastic Surgeons. R-Consevative. Avocations: Tae Kwon Do, hiking, soccer. Office: Bellevue Plastic Surgeons 11820 Northup Way E-190 Bellevue WA 98005 Home Phone: 425-228-0822; Office Phone: 425-450-1994. Office Fax: 425-284-1803. E-mail: gmarosan@hotmail.com.

MAROTTA, JOSEPH THOMAS, medical educator; b. Niagara Falls, NY, May 28, 1926; emigrated to Can., 1930; s. Alfred and Mary (Montemuro) M.; m. Margaret Hughes, Aug. 31, 1953; children: Maureen, Patricia, Margaret, Fred, Thomas, Jo Anne, Michael, Martha, John, Virginia. MD, U. Toronto, 1949. Trainee in internal medicine U. Toronto, 1949-52; trainee in neurology Presbyn. Hosp., NYC, 1952-55, U. London, Eng., 1955-56; mem. faculty U. Toronto, 1956—, prof. medicine, 1969—; former assoc. dean clin. affairs U. Toronto Faculty of Medicine, 1981-89; hon. prof. of neurology U. Western Ont., 1990—. Fellow Royal Coll. Physicians (Can.); mem. Alpha Omega Alpha, Phi Chi. Home and Office: 46 Carnforth Rd London ON Canada N6G 4P6 Office Phone: 519-642-4698. Business E-Mail: jtmarotta@rogers.com.

MAROVITZ, SANFORD EARL, English language and literature educator; b. Chgo., May 10, 1933; s. Harold and Gertrude (Luster) M.; m. Eleonora Dimitsa, Sept. 1, 1964. BA with honors, Lake Forest Coll., 1960; MA, Duke U., 1961, PhD, 1968. Instr. English Temple U., 1963-65; Fulbright instr. U. Athens, Greece, 1965-67; from asst. prof. English to prof. Kent State U., Ohio, 1967-96, prof. emeritus, 1996—. Vis. prof. English, Shimane U., Matsue, Japan, 1976-77, chair, 1987-92; co-dir. Melville Among the Nations, Greece, 1997. Co-editor: Artful Thunder: Versions of Romanticism in American Literature in Honor of Howard P. Vincent, 1975, Melville Among the Nations: Proceedings, 2001; co-author: Bibliographical Guide to the Study of the Literature of the U.S.A., 5th edit., 1984; author: Abraham Cahan, 1996; contbr. articles to profl. jours. Nat. trustee Lake Forest Coll., 1990-98. With USAF, 1953-57. Woodrow Wilson fellow, 1960-61; recipient Disting. Svc. Citation Lake Forest Coll., 1985, Disting. Tchg. award Kent State U., 1985, Presdl. Citation Shimane U., 1998. Mem.: MLA, Jack London Soc., Coll. English Assn. (Robert Miller award for best article in CEA Critic 2000), R.W. Emerson Soc., Saul Bellow Soc., W.D. Howells Soc. (v.p. 2000—01, pres. 2002—03, editor The Howellsian 2004—07), Aldous Huxley Soc. (curator 1998—), Nathaniel Hawthorne Soc., Melville Soc. (sec. 1994—96, pres. 1998), Phi Beta Kappa, Phi Beta Delta, Omicron Delta Kappa. Democrat. Jewish. Home: 1155 Norwood St Kent OH 44240-3342 Office: Kent State U Dept English Kent OH 44242-0001 E-mail: smarovit@kent.edu.

MAROZSAN, JOHN ROBERT, retired publishing company executive; b. Trenton, NJ, Oct. 25, 1941; s. John Nichols and Anna Mary (Lacko) M.; m. Anne Marie Gousha, Mar. 18, 1983; children— Andre J., Marc J., Carl B. A.S., Trenton Jr. Coll., 1965; BA, Trenton State Coll., 1967; MA, Harvard U., 1969. Tchr. Princeton Pub. Sch., N.J., 1967-68; coordinator secondary pub. Ginn and Co., Boston, 1969-72, program mgr. Lexington, Mass., 1972-75; v.p., editor-in-chief Aspen Publishers, Inc., Rockville, Md., 1975-80, sr. v.p. pub., 1980-85; pres. Aspen Pubs., Inc., Gaithersburg, 1986-96; COO Commerce Clearing House, Riverwoods, Ill., 1996-97; pres., CEO Commerce Clearinghouse, Riverwoods, Ill.; ret., 1999. Bd. dirs. Innodata. Bd. dirs. Hospice Caring, Wolters Klumen, U.S. Bd.; bd. examiners Henry B. Betts Found.; bd. govs. WUSA One and Only Award. With USAF, 1959-63. Recipient Sci. award NSF, 1968. Mem. Newsletter Assn. Am., Rotary, North Star Owners Assn. (pres. 1998-2001). Home: 220 E Prospect Ave Lake Bluff IL 60044 E-mail: jmarozsan@sbcglobal.net.

MARPLE, DOROTHY JANE, retired church executive; b. Abington, Pa., Nov. 24, 1926; d. John Stanley and Jennie (Stetler) M. AB, Ursinus Coll., 1948; MA, Syracuse U., 1950; Ed.D., Columbia U. Tchrs. Coll., 1969; L.H.D., Thiel Coll., 1965, Gettysburg Coll., 1979, Ursinus Coll., 1981; D. Humanitarian Services, Newberry Coll., 1977; DD, Trinity Luth. Sem., 1987. Counselor, asst., office dean undergrad. women Women's Coll., Duke, 1950-53; dean women, fgn. student adv. Thiel Coll., 1953-61; asst. social dir. Whittier Hall, Columbia Tchrs. Coll., 1961-62; exec. dir. Luth. Ch. Women, Luth. Ch. Am., Phila., 1962-75; asst. to bishop Luth. Ch. Am., 1975-85; coord. Transition Office Evang. Luth. Ch. Am., 1986-87; asst. gen. sec. ops. Nat. Coun. Chs. of Christ in U.S., NYC, 1987-89. Coord. Luth. Ch. in Am. commn. on function and structure, 1970-72; chairperson Luth. World Fedn. Commn. Ch. Cooperation, 1983-90; mem. bd. dirs. Luth. Theol. Sem., Gettysburg, 1989-98; bd. trustees United Bd. Christian Higher Edn. in Asia, 1989-98. Home: 8018 Anderson St Philadelphia PA 19118-2936

MARPLE, THOMAS FRANKLIN, columnist, reporter; b. Winchester, Va., June 24, 1956; s. Thomas Franklin Marple Jr. and Mary Ellen Marple. BS in Mgmt., Shenandoah U., 1980. Reporter The Journal, Martinsburg, W.Va., 1997—2001; writer Mid-Atlantic Thoroughbred, Timonium, Md., 2001—, Horsemen's Jour., Austin, Tex., 2000—, Md. Jockey Club and Preakness Media Rels., 2002—. With US Army, 1980—82. Named Best Sports Columnist, W.Va. Press Assn., 2001. Mem.: W.Va. Sports Writers Assn., W.Va. Breeders Assn. (publicity dir. 2001—). Avocations: fishing, bicycling, weightlifting, basketball, gardening. Home: 1801 Sam Mason Rd Bunker Hill WV 25413 Office Phone: 304-229-5370. E-mail: hallowedhaha@aol.com.

MARQUAND, JEAN MACMURTRY, educational association administrator; b. Schenectady, NY, Feb. 1, 1947; d. Louis Frederick, Jr. and Eleanore Jean (Noyes) McMurtry. BA in Edn. with honors, Simmons Coll., Boston, 1969; MEd, U. Vt., Burlington, 1975; cert. advanced studies in mgmt., Harvard U., Cambridge, Mass., 1993. Elem. tchr., Pittsford, 1969-70; reading specialist Lincoln, Vt., 1971-73, Pembroke, Mass., 1976; grad. teaching asst U. Vt., 1975; elem tchr. Chatham, Mass., 1977-80; with Arthur D. Little, Cambridge, Mass., 1981-82; exec. sec. Meredith & Grew, Inc., Boston, 1982—2003; prin. On Holiday, LLC, 2003—. Bd. mgrs. Jr. League, Boston, 1990—92, v.p., 1993—94, sustaining com., 1997—, dir. sustainer mem., 2006—07; active Philanthropic Ednl. Orgn., Orleans, Mass., 1983—, treas., 2005—, chair Mass. state bylaws com., 1998. Recipient Vol. Recognition award, Jr. League Boston, 1989, 2006. Mem.: Internat. Alliance, PEO, Chowder Soc., Coll. Club (pres. 1994—98, chair bylaws com. 1998—2003, parliamentarian 2001—03). Personal E-mail: jean@onholidaydresswear.com.

MARQUARDT, CHRISTEL ELISABETH, judge; b. Chgo., Aug. 26, 1935; d. Herman Albert and Christine Marie (Geringer) Trolenberg; children: Eric, Philip, Andrew, Joel. BS in Edn., Mo. Western Coll., 1970; JD with honors, Washburn U., 1974. Bar: Kans. 1974, Mo. 1992, U.S. Dist. Ct. Kans. 1974, U.S. Dist. Ct. (we. dist.) Mo. 1992. Tchr. St. John's Ch., Tigerton, Wis., 1955-56; pers. asst. Columbia Records, LA, 1958-59; ptnr. Cosgrove, Webb & Oman, Topeka, 1974-86, Palmer & Marquardt, Topeka, 1986-91, Levy and Craig P.C., Overland Park, Kans., 1991-94; sr. ptnr. Marquardt and Assocs., L.L.C., Fairway, Kans., 1994-95; judge Kans. Ct. Appeals, 1995—. Mem. atty. bd. discipline Kans. Supreme Ct., 1984—86; mem. Kans. Sentencing Commn., 2004—, Kans. Criminal Justice Recodification, Rehab. and Restoration Com., 2004—; bd. regents Washburn U. Tokeka, 2007—. Mem. editorial adv. bd. Kans. Lawyers Weekly, 1992-96; contbr. articles to legal jours. Bd. dirs. Topeka Symphony, 1983-92, 96-, Arts and Humanities Assn. Johnson County, 1992-95, Brown Found., 1988-90; hearing examiner Human Rels. Com., Topeka, 1974-76; local advisor Boy Scouts Am., 1973-74; bd. dirs., mem. nominating com. YWCA, Topeka, 1979-81; bd. govs. Washburn U. Law Sch., 1987-2002, v.p., 1996-98, pres., 1998-2000, disting. alumni, 2004; mem. dist. bd. adjudication Mo. Synod Luth. Ch., Kans., 1982-88. Named Woman of Yr., Mayor, City of Topeka, 1982; Obee scholar Washburn U., 1972-74; recipient Jennie Mitchell Kellogg Atty. of Achievement award, 1999, Phil Lewis medal of Distinction, 2000, Atty. of Achievement award Kans. Women Attys. Assn., Disting. Svc. award Washburn U. Law Sch., 2002, 04; named Disting. Alumni, Washburn U. Fellow: Kans. Bar Found. (trustee 1987—89), Am. Bar Found.; mem.: ABA (mem. ho. dels. 1988—, chmn. specialization com. 1991—93, lawyer referral com. 1993—95, state del. 1995—99, bar svcs. and activities 1995—99, bd. govs., program and planning com. 1999—2002, bd. govs. 1999—2002, ctrl. and ea. European law initiative 2001—02, African law coun. 2002—04, del-at-large ho. of dels. 2002—, standing com. on jud. independence 2004—, SCOPE com. 2001—, SCOPE com. chair 2006—07), Scape and Correlation of Work (chair 2006—), Law and Organizational Econ. Ctr. (bd. dirs. 2000—02), Am. Bus. Women's Assn. (lectr., corr. sec. 1983—84, pres. career chpt. 1986—87, named one of Top 10 Bus. Women of Yr. 1985), Topeka Bar Assn., Kans. Trial Lawyers Assn. (bd. govs. 1982—86, lectr.), Kans. Bar Assn. (sec., treas. 1981—85, bd. dirs. 1983—, v.p. 1985—86, pres. 1987—88, mem., lawyer referral com. 1999—). Home: 3408 SW Alameda Dr Topeka KS 66614-5108 Office: 301 SW 10th Ave Topeka KS 66612-1502 Business E-Mail: marquardtc@kscourts.org.

MARQUARDT, DAVID F., venture capitalist; BSME, Columbia U., 1973; MBA, Stanford U., 1979. Design engr., devel. mgr. Diablo Systems; assoc. Instl. Venture Associates, 1979—80; founding ptnr. Tech. Venture Investors, 1980—95; founding gen. ptnr. August Capital, Menlo Park, Calif., 1995—. Founding mem. bd. dirs. Microsoft Corp., 1981—; bd. dirs. Alibre Inc., AutoTradeCenter Inc., NetCell Corp., Seagate Tech. Inc., Westbridge Tech. Inc., Netopia Inc., 1990—, Tumbleweed Comm. Corp. Inc., 1997—, Six Apart Ltd., 2004—. Mem.: Nat. Venture Capital Assn. (past dir.), We. Assn. Venture Capitalists (past pres.). Office: August Capital 2480 Sand Hill Rd Ste 101 Menlo Park CA 94025

MARQUARDT, MICHELE C., lawyer; b. Detroit, May 4, 1951; AB summa cum laude, Albion Coll., 1972; MA in Ednl. Psych., U. Mich., 1977; JD cum laude, Wayne State U., 1986. Bar: Mich. 1986, US Dist. Ct. (ea. dist. Mich.) 1986. Atty. DeMent & Marquardt, PLC, Kalamazoo. Named one of Top 100 Attys., Worth mag., 2006. Mem.: State Bar Mich. (mem. estate planning and real property sects.), ABA, Kalamazoo Bar Assn., Phi Beta Kappa. Office: DeMent & Marquardt 211 E Water St Ste 401 Kalamazoo MI 49007-5806 Office Phone: 269-343-2106. Office Fax: 269-343-2107. E-mail: michele@dementandmarquardt.com. *

MARQUARDT, SHIRLEY MARIE, retired management consultant; b. Orlando, Okla., Aug. 20, 1941; d. Arthur Theodore Jack and Eleanor Lou Hurst; m. Donald Lee Marquardt, June 7, 1960; 1 child, Shirley Marie. Diploma, Army Mgmt. Staff Coll., 1994; A in Gen. Studies, Ctrl. Tex. Coll., 1983; BS in Gen. Studies, Am. Technol. U., 1987; MS in Human Resource Develop., U. Ctrl. Tex., 1988; diploma in Orgnl. Effectiveness, US Army Orgnl. Effectiveness Ctr. and Sch., 1985. Cert. Journeyman Mgmt. Analyst Civilian Career Intern Program, Dept. Army, Info. Mapping Course Instr. Info. Mapping, Inc., Prevention Sexual Harassment Course Instr. III Corps, Ft. Hood, Number Skills Course Instr. Mc-Graw Hill Book Co., Investment in Excellence Course Facilitator Pacific Inst. Mil. personnel clerk III Corps., Ft. Hood, Tex., 1968—70, sec. computer sys. command, 1970—72, adminstrv. specialist, sec. stenographer, 1978, pers. clk., Civilian Pers. Dir., 1980—81, mgmt. analyst, Directorate of Resource Mgmt., 1981—84, asst. dir., Dir. Program Integration, Leadership, 1984—94, divsn. chief, Dir. Info. Mgmt., 1994—98; sec. First Meth. Ch., Perry, Okla., 1959—60; exec. sec. YMCA, El Paso, Tex., 1960—62; clk. typist Hdqs., US Army Ryukyu Islands, Okinawa, Japan, 1963—66; mil. pers. clk., adj. gen. office, hdqrs. Berlin Brigade, 1966—68; sec. U.S. Army Corps Engrs., Frankfurt, Germany, 1976—78; clk. stenographer VII Corps Arty., Aschafffenburg, Germany, 1975; pers. clk. Test, Evaluation Command Civilian Pers. Office, Aberdeen Proving Ground, Md., 1978—79; supr. mgmt. asst. U.S. Army Toxic, Hazardous Materials Agy., Aberdeen Proving Ground, 1979—80; office svcs. supr. Facilities Engring. Divsn., Aberdeen Proving Ground, 1979; ret., 1998. Prodr.: (30 minute TV film) Waverley Historic District; editor: Enid Oklahoma Waverley Wind. Mem. City Spl. Tax Oversight Com., Enid, 1999—2005, City Enid Comprehensive Planning Com., 2000—05, City Enid Cmty. Rels. Bd., 2003—06, Enid A.M. Too Am. Bus.

Club, 2004—06, City Enid Hist. Preservation Commn., 2005—06, Garfield County Rep. Women's Club, Enid, 2004—06; pres. Waverley Hist. Neighborhood Assn., Enid, Okla., 1999—2005; bd. mem. Horn of Plenty, Enid, 2004—06; bd. mem., edn. com. chair Sons and Daughters Cherokee Strip, Enid, 2005—06; mem. Am. Bus. Club. Decorated Achievement medal for Civilian Svc. US Army, III Corps, Ft. Hood, Army Individual Superior Civilian Svc. award with two oak leaf clusters United States Army, III Corps, Ft. Hood; recipient Employee of Yr., III Corps, Ft. Hood, 1987. Mem.: Nat. Trust Hist. Preservation, Okla. Hist. Soc. Conservative-R. Avocations: historic preservation, cmty. volunteerism. Home: 1323 W Broadway Ave Enid OK 73703-5720 Home Phone: 580-234-2197.

MARQUARDT, STEVE ROBERT, advocate; b. St. Paul, Sept. 7, 1943; s. Robert Thomas and Dorothy Jean (Kane) M.; m. Judy G. Brown, Aug. 4, 1968; 1 child, Sarah. BA in History, Macalester Coll., 1966; MA in History, U. Minn., 1970, MLS, 1973, PhD in History, 1978. History instr. Macalester Coll., St. Paul, 1968—69; cataloger N.Mex. State U. Libr., Las Cruces, 1973—75; acting univ. archivist, acting dir. Rio Grande Hist. Collections N. Mex. State U. Libr., Las Cruces, 1973—74; acquisitions librarian Western Ill. U. Libr., Macomb, 1976—77, head cataloger, Online Computer Libr. Ctr. coord., 1977—79; asst. dir. resources & tech. svcs. Ohio U. Libr., Athens, 1979—81; dir. librs. U. Wis., Eau Claire, 1981—89; dir. univ. librs. No. Ill. U., DeKalb, 1989—90; dir. librs. U. Wis., Eau Claire, 1990—96; dean of librs. S.D. State U., Brookings, 1996—2006. Editor Jour. Rio Grande History, 1974; contbg. editor: Library Issues, 1994-2003; contbr. articles to profl. jours. Coord., adoption group 275 Amnesty Internat., Eau Claire, 1985—88, legis. coord. Minn., 2007—, freadom co-chair, 2006—; pres. Chippewa Valley Free-net, 1994—96. Mem.: ALA. Lutheran. Avocation: bicycling. Home and Office: Rancho Mosquito 9383 123rd Ave SE Lake Lillian MN 56253-4700 Home Phone: 605-690-6113; Office Phone: 605-688-5106, 320-664-4231. E-mail: marquardt.steve@gmail.com.

MARQUESS, LAWRENCE WADE, lawyer; b. Bloomington, Ind., Mar. 2, 1950; s. Earl Lawrence and Mary Louise (Coberly) M.; m. Barbara Ann Bailey, June 17, 1978; children: Alexander Lawrence, Michael Wade. BSEE, Purdue U., 1973; JD, W.Va. U., 1977. Bar: W.Va. 1977, Tex. 1977, U.S. Dist. Ct. (so. dist.) W.Va. 1977, U.S. Dist. Ct. (no. dist.) Tex. 1977, Colo. 1980, U.S. Dist. Ct. Colo. 1980, U.S. Ct. Appeals (10th cir.) 1980, U.S. Supreme Ct. 1984, U.S. Dist. Ct. (no. dist.) Ohio 1988, U.S. Ct. Appeals (DC cir.) 1997, U.S. Dist. Ct. Nebr. 1999. Assoc. Johnson, Bromberg, Leeds & Riggs, Dallas, 1977-79, Bradley, Campbell & Carney, Golden, Colo., 1979-82, ptnr., 1983-84, Stettner, Miller & Cohn P.C., 1984-87, Nelson & Harding, Denver, 1987-88, Heron, Burchette, Ruckert & Rothwell, 1989-90, Harding & Ogborn, 1990-94, Otten, Johnson, Robinson, Neff & Ragonetti, Denver, 1994-2001, Littler Mendelson, P.C., Denver, 2001—, mng. shareholder, 2001—. Mem. faculty Am. Law Inst. - ABA Advanced Labor and Employment Law Course, 1986, 87. Mem.: ACLU, ABA (labor, antitrust and litig. sects.), Hist. Soc. 10th Jud. Circuit (founding mem.), Colo. Bar Found., Coll. Labor and Employment Lawyers, 1st Jud. Dist. Bar Assn., Denver Bar Assn., Colo. Bar Assn. (co-chmn. labor law com. 1989—92), Nat. Rlwy. Hist. Soc., Sierra Club. Democrat. Methodist. Home: 11883 W 27th Dr Lakewood CO 80215-7000 Office: Littler Mendelson PC 1200 17th St Ste 1000 Denver CO 80202 Office Phone: 303-362-2840. Business E-Mail: lmarquess@littler.com.

MARQUETTE, I. EDWARD, lawyer; b. Hannibal, Mo., Oct. 15, 1950; s. Clifford M. and Doris Elizabeth (McLane) M.; m. Ansie S. Goodrich, May 20, 1972; children: Brandeis, Brooks. BA in Econs., U. Mo., 1973; JD cum laude, Harvard U., 1976. Bar: Mo. 1976. Ptnr. Spencer, Fane, Britt & Browne LLP, 1976, Sonnenschein Nath & Rosenthal LLP. Contbr. articles to profl. jours., chpts. to books. Bd. dirs. Midwest Christian Counseling Combined Health Appeal, Kansas City, 1988-95. Named Best Lawyers Am. Mem. ABA (new info. tech. com.), Mo. Bar Assn. (tech. com.), Kansas City Bar Assn. (chmn. antitrust study grp. 1984, chmn. computer law com. 1989, 90, 95, 99), Silicon Prairie Tech. Assn., Phi Beta Kappa, Phi Kappa Phi & Delta Psi Omega. Democrat. Baptist. Avocation: computer programming. Office: Sonnenschein Nath & Rosenthal LLP 4520 Main St Ste 1100 Kansas City MO 64111 Office Phone: 816-460-2405. Office Fax: 816-531-7545. Business E-Mail: emarquette@sonnenschein.com.

MARQUEZ, ALFREDO C., federal judge; b. 1922; m. Linda Nowobilsky. BS, U. Ariz., 1948, JD, 1950. Bar: Ariz. Practice law Mesch Marquez & Rothschild, 1957-80; asst. atty. gen. State of Ariz., 1951-52; asst. county atty. Pima County, Ariz., 1953-54; adminstrv. asst. to Congressman Stewart Udall, 1955; judge U.S. Dist. Ct. Ariz., Tucson, 1980-91, sr. judge, 1991—. Served with USN, 1942-45 Office: US Dist Ct US Courthouse Rm 327 405 W Congress Ste 6180 Tucson AZ 85701-5060

MARQUEZ, VICTOR E., medical researcher; naturalized, US, 1987; BS in pharmacy, Ctrl. U. of Venezuela, Caracas, 1966; MS in medicinal chemistry, U. Mich., Ann Arbor, 1968, PhD, 1970. Postdoctoral training Nat. Cancer Inst., 1970—71; positions in pvt. industry Venezuela, 1971—76; vis. scientist Nat. Cancer Inst., 1977—87, granted tenure, 1987, now chief Lab. Medicinal Chemistry, head Organic Chemistry Sect., Lab. Medicinal Chemistry. Achievements include holding over 20 US patents. Office: Lab Medicinal Chemistry Nat Cancer Inst at Frederick 376 Boyles St PO Box B Frederick MD 21702-1201 Office Phone: 301-846-5954. Office Fax: 301-846-6033. E-mail: marquezv@dc37a.nci.nih.gov.

MÁRQUEZ-MAGAÑA, LETICIA MARIA, biology professor; b. Sacramento, Aug. 15, 1963; d. Jesús José and Guadalupe María Márquez; married; children: Joaquín, Elías. BS,MS in Biol. Scis., Stanford U., 1986; PhD in Biochemistry, U. Calif., Berkeley, 1991. Postdoctoral fellow Stanford (Calif.) U., 1991—94; asst. prof. biology San Francisco State U., 1994—99, assoc. prof. biology, 1999—2004, prof. biology, 2004—, microbial geneticist, 1994—. Contbr. articles to profl. jours., including Jour. Bacteriology and Jour. Biol. Chemistry. Motivational spkr. to minority students, No. Calif., 1994—; mem. task force Hispanic-Serving Inst. Hispanic Assn. Colls. and Univs.; mentor to UC San Fransico Tchg. postdoctoral fellows, 2002—. Named Hispanic Powerhitter, Hispanic Engr. mag., 2003; named one of 100 Most Influential Hispanics, Hispanic Bus. mag., 1998; NSF grant. Mem.: AAAS (Mentor award 2001), Soc. Advancement of Chicanos and Native Americans in Sci. (sci. ptnr. K-12 educators 2001—, bd. dirs. 1989—91), Am. Soc. Microbiology. Office: San Francisco State U Dept Biology 1600 Holloway Ave San Francisco CA 94132 E-mail: marquez@sfsu.edu.

MÁRQUEZ-PETERSON, LEA, business broker; b. 1970; m. Daniel Harold Peterson. B in Mktg. and Entrepreneurship, U. Ariz., 1992; MBA, Pepperdine, 1996. Franchise and bus. devel. Shell Oil Co., LA; founder Am. Retail Corp., Am. Fuel, Marquez-Peterson Grp., Marquez-Peterson II, Valle Verde Partners; exec. dir. Greater Tucson Leadership; owner TucsonBizForSale.com; bus. broker Bus. Source. Founder, former chairperson Pima County Small Bus. Commn.; former chairperson City of Tucson Small Bus. Commn. Mem., Dean of Students adv. bd. U. Ariz., mem., Pres. Bus. Adv. Coun.; mem. YWCA, Regional Transportation Authority Com., Tucson Convention Ctr. Commn. Named Tucson Small Bus. of Yr., Small Bus. Devel. Coun., 2000, Tucson Minority Small Bus. Retailer of Yr., 2002, Small Bus. Leader of Yr., Tucson Metro. Chamber of Commerce, Wells Fargo Bank, 2003; named one of 40 Under 40, Tucson Bus. Edge, 2006. Mem.: Nat. Fedn. Ind. Bus., Nat. Assn. Women Bus. Owners (former pres., Woman Bus. Owner of Yr. 2001). Office: Greater Tucson Leadership 5151 E Broadway Blvd Ste 1600 Tucson AZ 85711 Office Phone: 520-512-5485. Office Fax: 520-512-5401.

MARQUIS, WILLIAM OSCAR, lawyer; b. Fort Wayne, Ind., Feb. 26, 1944; s. William Oscar and Lenor Mae (Gaffney) M.; m. Mary Frances Funderburk, May 11, 1976; children: Lenor, Kathryn, Timothy Patrick, Daniel, Ann. BS, U. Wis., Madison, 1973; JD, South Tex. Coll. Law, 1977. Bar: Wis. 1979, U.S. Dist. Ct. (we. dist.) Wis. 1979, U.S. Dist. Ct. (ea. dist.) Wis. 1982, U.S. Tax Ct. 1983, U.S. Ct. Appeals (7th cir. 1985). With Wis. Dept. Vet. Affairs, Madison, 1977-79; corp. counsel Barron County, Wis., 1979-80; assoc. Riley, Bruns & Riley, Madison, 1980-81, Jastroch & LaBarge, S.C., Waukesha, Wis., 1981-84; ptnr. Groh, Hackbart & Marquis, 1984-93. Mem. ATLA, Wis. Trial Lawyers Assn. Office: 230 W Wells St Ste 327 Milwaukee WI 53203-1866 Home Phone: 414-962-3210; Office Phone: 414-276-4766. Personal E-mail: william.marquis@sbcglobal.net.

MARR, DANIEL G., food products executive; Divsn. v.p., N. Tex. Coca-Cola Enterprises, 1988—92, divsn. v.p., gen. mgr., E. Tex., 1992—96, v.p., mktg., 1996—2000, sr. v.p., chief customer officer, 2000—03, pres., N.Am. sales, 2003—. Office: Coca-Cola Enterprises 2500 Windy Ridge Pkwy Atlanta GA 30339

MARR, DAVID E., lawyer; BA, Colby Coll.; MA, Wesleyan U.; JD with honors, U. Conn. Bar: Conn. 1970, Mass. 1974, U.S. Dist. Ct. Conn. 1971, U.S. Dist. Ct. Mass. 1975, U.S. Ct. Appeals (2d cir.) 1971, U.S. Supreme Ct. 1974, U.S. Tax Ct. 1992. Assoc. Day, Berry & Howard, Hartford, Conn., 1970-73; counsel Honeywell Info. Sys., Inc., Waltham, Mass., 1973-75; pvt. practice Boston, 1975—79, Natick, Mass., 1980—. Editor-in-Chief Conn. Law Review, 1970. Author: Employment Law in Connecticut; opinion editor Mass. Lawyers Weekly, 1976-86. Rep. Regional Vocat. Sch.; chmn. Hist. Dist. Com.; bd. dirs. Hist. Soc. and Mus. Mem.: ATLA, Mass. Bar Assn. Office: 199 Union St Natick MA 01760-4759 Office Phone: 508-655-5522. E-mail: marrlaw@yahoo.com.

MARR, PHEBE ANN, retired historian, educator; b. Mt. Vernon, NY, Sept. 21, 1931; d. John Joseph and Lillian Victoria (Henningsen) Marr. BA, Barnard Coll., NYC, 1953; PhD, Harvard U., Cambridge, Mass., 1967. Rsch. assoc. ARAMCO, Dhahran, Saudi Arabia, 1960-62; dir. mid. east program Fgn. Svc. Inst., 1963-66; asst. prof. Stanislaus State Coll., Turlock, Calif., 1970-71, assoc. prof., 1971-74; assoc. prof. history U. Tenn., Knoxville, 1974—85, chmn. Asian studies program, 1977—79. Cons. ARAMCO, 1979-83. Author: The Modern History of Iraq, 1985, 2d edit., 2003; co-editor: Riding the Tiger: Middle East Challenge After the Cold War, 1993; contbr. articles to profl. jours. Bd. dirs. Mid. East Policy Coun., 2004. Rsch. fellow Mid. East Ctr., Harvard U., Cambridge, Mass., 1968-70, sr. fellow Nat. Def. U., Washington, 1985-97, Woodrow Wilson Ctr. fellow, 1998-99, Coun. on Fgn. Rels., U.S. Inst. Peace fellow, 2004-06. Mem. Mid. East Inst., Mid. East Studies Assn. Home and Office: 3637 Upton St NW Washington DC 20008-3126 Home Phone: 202-462-3580; Office Phone: 202-462-3580. Personal E-mail: marrphebe@aol.com.

MARR, ROBERT BRUCE, physicist, researcher; b. Quincy, Mass., Mar. 25, 1932; s. Ralph George and Ethel (Beals) M.; m. Nancy Rosa Parkes, June 12, 1954; children: Richard, Jonathan, Rebecca. BS, MIT, 1953; MA, Harvard U., 1955, PhD, 1959. Research asso. Brookhaven Nat. Lab., Upton, NY, 1959-61, asso. physicist, 1961-64, physicist, 1964-68, sr. physicist, 1968-95, assoc. chmn. applied math. dept., 1974-75, 83-88, chmn., 1975-78; ret., 1995. Adj. assoc. prof. Columbia U., 1969; lectr. SUNY at Stony Brook, 1969-70, vis. prof. dept. computer sci., 1979; guest mathematician U. Colo., 1970; vis. mathematician Lawrence Berkeley Lab., 1978; cons. NSF, NIH, 1969— Contbr. articles to profl. jours. Served with U.S. Army, 1958-59. NSF grantee, 1974 Mem. Soc. for Magnetic Resonance in Medicine (trustee 1982-87, sec.-treas. 1984-86, treas. 1986-87). Home: 368 Private Rd Patchogue NY 11772-5827

MARRA, ANTHONY TULLIO, audio visual specialist; b. Newark, June 26, 1947; s. John and Christine (Sapparito) M.; m. Erica Jane Curci, Nov. 25, 1987; children: Becky Michelle George, Antonio Tullio, Becky Lynn George, Crystal Marra, Heather Leigh Marra, Megan Marra. Advisor Govt. Liason for Ednl. Insts., Washington, 1978-91; media specialist, advisor Washington & Lee U., Lexington, Va., 1978-91; media specialist Longwood Coll., Farmville, Va., 1978-91, Hollins Coll., Salem, Va., 1978-91, Lynchburg (Va.) Coll., 1978-91, Randolph Macon Women's Coll., Lynchburg, Va., 1978-91; dir. audio-visual Sweet Briar (Va.) Coll., 1978-91; media cons. Africa Global Perspectives, 1994—; pres., owner Audio/Visual Advisors, 1997—; agt. bus. comms. sys. divsn. Lucent Techs./Bell Labs, 1997—. Acoustic expert rsch. and devel. NASA Langley Field, Hampton, Va., 1971-78; quality engr. Tyco-M/A-Com; ESD/MSD coord. Lynchburg facilities M/A-Com. Author: (books) Poetry in LIfe To Be in Death I Am, 1972, The Holy Quran-The Hereafter, 1989; inventor: overhead copy stand for ch.-sch. system, 1991, marking device for NASA Test Flights, 1972; designer TV studio and control room, 1994. Bd. dirs. S.W. Va. Free Clinic. With USMC, 1964-68, Vietnam. Recipient cert. appreciation NASA fors rsch. 1976, 78. Avocations: photography, videography, building computers, community work. Office: 3421 Plymouth Pl Lynchburg VA 24503-1300

MARRA, THOMAS M., investment company executive; Grad., St. Bonaventure U. Assoc. actuary Hartford Fin. Svcs. Group, 1980, v.p., dir. of individual annuities, 1990—94, head, individual life and annuities divsn., 1994—98, exec. v.p., 1996—2000, sr. v.p., 1994—96, dir. investment products divsn., 1998—2000, exec. v.p., 2000—, COO, Hartford Life, 2000—, pres., Hartford Life, 2002—07, pres., COO, 2007—. Mem., office of the chmn. Hartford Fin. Svcs. Group, 2000—; past chmn. Nat. Assn. of variable annuities. Mem. Bushnell Ctr. for the Performing Arts. Fellow: Soc. of Actuaries; mem.: Am. Acad. of Actuaries. Office: Hartford Financial Services Group Hartford Plaza 690 Asylum Ave Hartford CT 06115 *

MARRACK, PHILIPPA CHARLOTTE, immunologist, researcher; b. Ewell, Eng., June 28, 1945; m. John Kappler, 1974; children: Kate, Jim. BA, U. Cambridge, 1967, PhD in Biology, 1970. Post-doctoral fellow, lab. rschr. U. Calif., San Diego, 1971-73; post-doctoral rschr. fellow U. Rochester, NY, 1973-79, assoc. rschr. NY, 1974-75, asst. prof. immunology NY, 1975-79, assoc. prof. NY, 1980-85; prof. dept. microbiology and immunology U. Colo. Health Scis. Ctr., Denver, 1988—94, prof. integrated dept. of Immunology, 1994—, prof., dept. biochemistry and molecular biology, prof. medicine; head, div. of basic immunology Nat. Jewish Ctr. for Immunology and Respiratory Medicine, Denver, 1988—90; prof. dept. biophysics, biochemistry and genetics U. Colo. Health Scis. Ctr., Denver, 1985-88; head, div. of Basic Immunology Nat. Jewish Medical and Rsch. Ctr., Denver, 1998—99, sr. faculty mem., Integrated Dept. of Immunology; investigator Kappler and Marrack Rsch. Lab. Howard Hughes Med. Inst., Chevy Chase, Md., 1986—. Mem. dept. medicine Nat. Jewish Hosp. and Rsch. Ctr., Denver, 1979—. Contbr. articles to profl. jours.; mem. editl. bds. Cell, Science, and Journal of Immunology. Served on panels for Am. Cancer Soc., US NIH, Burroughs Wellcome Fund. Recipient Feodor Lynen medal, 1990, William B. Coley award Cancer Rsch. Inst., 1991, Wellcome Found. lecturer Royal Soc., 1990, Paul Ehrlich and Ludwig Darmstädter prize, 1993, Louisa Gross Horwitz prize, 1994, Women's Excellence Scis. award Fedn. Am. Socs. Exptl. Biology, 1995, Women in Sci. award, L'Oreal-UNESCO, 2004. Mem. NAS, Royal Soc., Am. Assn. Immunologists (pres. 2000-2001, Lifetime Achievement award, 2003), Brit. Soc. Immunology, Internat. Union of Immunological Societies (past pres.). Office: Howard Hughes Med Inst Natl Jewish Med and Rsch Ctr 1400 Jackson St 5th fl Goodman Bldg Denver CO 80206

MARRERO, VICTOR, federal judge, lawyer; b. Santurce, PR, Sept. 1, 1941; s. Ezequiel Marrero and Josefina (Sanabria) Santos M.; m. Veronica M. White, Dec. 1987. BA, NYU, 1964; LLB, Yale U., 1968; postgrad. (Fulbright scholar), U. Sheffield, Eng., 1966-67. Bar: N.Y. 1982. Exec. dir. NYC Dept. City Planning, 1973-74; spl. counsel to comptroller City of N.Y., 1974-75; 1st asst. counsel to gov. State of N.Y., Albany, 1975-76; chmn. NYC City Planning Commn., 1976-77; commr. N.Y. State Divsn. Housing and Cmty. Renewal, NYC, 1977-79; under-sec. HUD, Washington, 1979-81; ptnr. Tufo & Zuccotti, NYC, 1982-85, Brown & Wood, NYC, 1986-93; amb., U.S. rep. UN Econ. and Social Coun., NYC, 1993-97; amb., permanent U.S. rep. OAS, Dept. State, Washington, 1998-99; judge U.S. Dist. Ct. (So. Dist.), NYC, 1999—. Vis. lectr. Yale U. Law Sch., New Haven, 1986, Columbia U. Law Sch., 1991-93. Trustee N.Y. Pub. Libr., 1989—, SUNY, Albany, 1985-93, Cooper Union, 1989-93, Consolidated Edison Co., 1988-93; bd. dirs. P.R. Legal Def. and Edn. Fund., N.Y.C., 1972-86, N.Y. Telephone Co., 1987-93; chmn. N.Y. State Chief Judge's Com. to Improve Availability of Legal Svcs., 1988-90. Mem. ABA (Pro Bono Publico award 1993), N.Y. State Bar Assn. (Root/Stimson Pub. Svc. award 1992), Assn. Bar City N.Y. (mem. com. modern cts. 1980-93, exec. com. 1986-89, judiciary com. 1991-92, v.p. 1992-93). Office: US Courthouse 500 Pearl St Rm 660 New York NY 10007-1502 Office Phone: 212-805-6374.

MARRETT, CAROLINE DENISE, special education educator; b. Queens, NY, Jan. 15, 1962; d. Cyril Pratt, Sr. and Jennie Pratt; m. Phillip Marston Marrett, Oct. 10, 1987; children: Phillip Charles, Dwayne Anthony, Sylvia Nicole. BS in Elem. Edn., SUNY, Buffalo, 1984; MA in Learning Disabilities, Columbia U., NYC, 1986, MA in Spl. Edn., 1986; diploma in sch. adminstrn. & supervision, St. John's U., Queens, 2003; student in Spl. Edn., U. Ctrl. Fla., Orlando, 2004—. Tchr., borough transition coord. office of supt. of Manhattan high schs. HS of Graphic Communication Arts, NYC, 1982—93; tchr. trainer specialist Spl. Edn. Tchr. Resource Ctr., Queens, 1993—98; adminstrator Law, Govt. & Cmty. Svc. HS, Queens, NY, 1998—99; spl. edn. tchr. Volusia County Sch. Bd., Deltona, Fla., 2000—02, Volusia County Pub. Sch. Bd., Deltona, Fla., 2003—04. Student mem. Coun. for Exceptional Children, Arlington, Va. Scholar Project Lead, U. Ctrl. Fla., 2004—, The Holmes Partnership, 2004—. Mem.: Phi Delta Kappa Internat., Am. Ednl. Rsch. Assn., Coun. Exceptional Children. Home: 1631 N Normandy Blvd Deltona FL 32725 Home Phone: 386-532-5642. Personal E-mail: cmarrett@mail.ucf.edu.

MARRETT, CORA B., science educator; b. Richmond, Va., June 15, 1942; d. Horace Sterling and Clora Ann (Boswell) Bagley; m. Louis Everard Marrett, Dec. 24, 1968. BA, Va. Union U., 1963; MS, U. Wis., 1965, PhD, 1968. Asst. prof. U. N.C., Chapel Hill, 1968-69; from asst. to assoc. prof. Western Mich. U., Kalamazoo, 1969-73; from assoc. prof. to full prof. U. Wis., Madison, 1973-97; asst. dir. NSF, Arlington, Va., 1992-96; provost, vice chancellor for acad. affairs U. Mass., Amherst, 1997—2001; sr. v.p. for acad. affairs U. Wis. System, 2001—. Mem. sci. adv. panel U.S. Army, Washington, 1976-77; mem. Naval Rsch. Adv. Com., Washington, 1978-81, Pres. Commn. on the Accident at Three Mile Island, 1979; bd. govs. Argonne (Ill.) Nat. Lab., 1983-90, 96-99. Editor: Research in Race and Ethnic Relations, 1988, Gender and Classroom Interaction, 1990. Resident fellow NAS, 1973-74; fellow Ctr. for Advanced Study in Behavioral Scis., 1976-77. Mem. AAAS, ASA, Phi Kappa Phi. Avocations: reading, travel, film appreciation. Home: 7517 Farmington Way Madison WI 53717 Office: Office Acad Affairs U of Wisconsin System 1620 Van Hise Hall Madison WI 53706 Office Phone: 608-262-3826. E-mail: cmarrett@uwsa.edu.

MARRETT, MICHAEL MCFARLENE, chaplain; b. Greenwich Town, Surrey, Jamaica, Oct. 7, 1935; s. Kenneth Louis and Ivy Lynmae (McFarlane) M.; m. Margery Eva Mugford, Jan. 29, 1984. Cert. gen. ordination, Oxford U., Eng., 1961; cert. edn. in English lang., London U., 1967; MDiv, Gen. Theol. Sem., 1969, STM, 1970, N.Y. Theol. Sem., 1972; postgrad., Princeton Theol. Sem., 1972-73, Columbia U., 1973-75; BA, Fordham U., 1974; postgrad., The Coll. of Preachers, 1979, Yale U., 1979-81; PhD, NYU, 1980; MS, So. Conn. State U., 1982. Lic. pastoral counselor, Md.; cert. profl. mental health clergy, chaplain and fellow of Coll. Chaplains; nat. cert. bereavement facilitator Am. Acad. Bereavement; diplomate Am. Psychotherapy Assn. Staff chaplain St. Elizabeths Hosp., Washington, 1986-99; ret., 1999. Author: The Lambeth Conferences and Women Priests, 1981. Appointed commissary Diocese of Akoko, West Africa, 1984, appointed hon. canon St. Stephens Cathedral, 1987. Mem. Assn. Clin. Pastoral Edn. (clin.), Am. Assn. Christian Counselors, Am. Assn. Family Counselors. Home: PO Box 48232 1902 C St NE Washington DC 20002-6714

MARRIN, CHARLES AINSWORTH STAVELEY, cardiovascular and thoracic surgeon, educator; b. Santa Monica, Calif., Dec. 19, 1947; s. Charles Ainsworth and Cecilia Margaret (Staveley) M.; m. Marian Anthon Bruen, Apr. 19, 1976; 1 child, Minet A. B. MB, BS, U. London, Royal Free Hosp. Sch. Medicine, London, 1971. Ho. physician Willesden Gen. Hosp., London, 1971, Royal Free Hosp., London, 1972; resident in gen. surgery St. Luke's Hosp. Ctr., NYC, 1973-76, chief resident, 1976-77, fellow in cardiovasc. surgery, asst. physician, 1977; fellow in cardiovasc. surg. rsch. Coll. Physicians and Surgeons, Columbia U., NYC, 1978; resident in cardiovasc. and thoracic surgery Columbia-Presbyn. Med. Ctr., NYC, 1979-80, chief resident, 1980; staff surgeon Hitchcock Clinic and Dartmouth-Hitchcock Med. Ctr., Lebanon, N.H., 1981—; prof. surgery Dartmouth (N.H.) U. Med. Sch., 2000—. Author chpts. to books; contbr. articles to profl. jours. Co-prin. investigator Am. Heart Assn., 1993—; co-investigator U.S. Agy. for Health Care Policy and Rsch., 1993—. Fellow ACS, Am. Coll. Cardiology, Am. Coll. Chest Physicians; mem. AMA, Am. Assn. Thoracic Surgery, Soc. Thoracic Surgeons.

MARRINAN, MICHAEL JOSEPH, art historian, educator; b. St. Paul, Mar. 12, 1949; s. Michael Joseph and Margaret Mary Marrinan. D, NYU, NYC, 1983. Asst. prof. art history Columbia U., NYC, 1980—88, assoc. prof. art history, 1988—89; prof. art history Stanford U., Calif., 1990—. Author: Painting Politics for Louis-Philippe, 1988; editor: (collection scholarly essays) Mapping Benjamin: The Work of Art in the Digital Age, 2003, Regimes of Description: In the Archive of the 18th Century, 2005. Rsch. fellow, Am. Coun. Learned Socs., 1984, John Simon Guggenheim Meml. Found., 1989. Mem.: Am. Soc. 18th Century Studies, Am. Hist. Assn., Coll. Art Assn. Home: 172 Dolores St San Francisco CA 94103 Office: Stanford U Dept Art 435 Lasuen Mall Rm 101 Stanford CA 94305-2018 Office Phone: 650-723-4275. Office Fax: 650-725-0140. Business E-Mail: mmsfo@stanford.edu.

MARRINAN, SUSAN FAYE, lawyer; b. Vermillion, SD, May 29, 1948; BA, U. Minn., 1969, JD, 1973. Bar: Minn. 1973, Wis. 1973. Atty. Carlson Cos., Plymouth, Minn., 1973-74, Prudential Ins. Co., Mpls., 1974-75; v.p., gen. counsel, corp. sec. H.B. Fuller Co., St. Paul, 1977—90; gen. counsel, sec. Snap-On, Inc., Kenosha, Wis., 1990—92, v.p., gen. counsel, sec., 1992—2004, v.p., sec., chief legal officer, 2004—. Fundraiser Am. Cancer Soc.; bd. dirs. Family Svcs. St. Paul, Childrens Theatre Co. Mem. Am. Corp. Counsel (bd. dirs. Minn. chpt. 1986—), Am. Corp. Counsel Assn. (bd. dirs. 1997-02). Republican. Avocation: running. Office: Snap-On Inc 2801 80th St Kenosha WI 53141 *

MARRIOTT, DAVID R., lawyer; b. Salt Lake City, June 10, 1967; BA magna cum laude, Brigham Young Univ., 1991; JD, NYU, 1994. Bar: NY 1995. Law clk., Hon. Albert J. Engel US Ct. of Appeals, 6th Cir.; law clk., Hon. Eugene F. Lynch US Dist. Ct., No. Dist. Calif.; assoc. Cravath Swaine & Moore LLP, NYC, 1996—2003, ptnr., litig., 2003—. Staff editor NYU Jour. Internat. Law and Politics. Office: Cravath Swaine & Moore LLP Worldwide Plz 825 Eighth Ave New York NY 10019-7475 Office Phone: 212-474-1000. Office Fax: 212-474-3700. Business E-Mail: dmarriott@cravath.com.

MARRIOTT, JOHN W., III, hotel executive; BS, Univ. Utah, 1985. With Marriott Internat. Inc., Washington, 1976—, sr. v.p. mid-Atlantic region, exec. v.p. global sales & mktg., bd. dir., 2002—, exec. v.p. lodging, 2003—05, vice chmn., 2005—. CEO J.W.M. Family Enterprises, 2006. Named one of Forbes Richest Americans, 2006. Office: Marriott internat Inc Marriott Dr Washington DC 20058 *

MARRIOTT, JOHN WILLARD, JR., lodging and senior living executive; b. Washington, Mar. 25, 1932; s. John Willard and Alice (Sheets) M.; m. Donna Garff, June 29, 1955; children: Deborah, Stephen Garff, John Willard, David Sheets. BS in Banking and Fin., U. Utah, 1954. V.p. Marriott Hot Shoppes Inc., 1959-64, exec. v.p., bd. dirs., 1964; pres. Marriott Corp., 1964—, CEO, 1972—; chmn. bd. Marriott Internat., Inc. (formerly Marriott Corp.), 1985—. Bd. dirs. GM, U.S.-Russia Bus. Coun., Host Marriott Svcs. Corp., Naval Acad. Endowment Trust. Trustee Nat. Geog. Soc.; mem. nat. adv. bd. Boy Scouts Am.; mem. Bus. Coun., Bus. Roundtable.; exec. com. World Travel and Tourism Coun. Lt. USNR, 1954-56. Recipient Bus. Leader of Yr. award, Georgetown U. Sch. Bus. Adminstrn., 1984, Svc. Above Self award, Rotary Club at JFK Internat. Airport, 1985, Am. Mgr. of Yr. award, Nat. Mgmt. Assn., 1985, Golden Chain award, Nation's Restaurant News, 1985, Hall of Fame award, Consumer Digest Mag., 1985, Citizen of Yr. award, Boy Scouts of Am., 1986, Restaurant Bus. Leadership award, Restaurant Bus. Mag., 1986, Gold Plate award, Am. Acad. Achievement, 1986, Hall of Fame, Am. Hotel and Motel Assn., 1986, Hall of Fame award, Culinary Inst. of Am., 1987, Hospitality Exec. of Yr. award, Pa. State U., 1987, Bronze winner in Fin. World's Chief Exec. Officers award, 1988, Silver Plate award Lodging Hospitality Mag., 1988, Chief Exec. Officer of Yr. Chief Exec. Officer Mag., 1988, Signature award CA chpt. Nat. Multiple Scelerosis, 1988, Excellence Cmty. award Suburban Hosp., 1993, Silver Plate award Internat. Foodsvc. Mfrs. Assn., 1993, Good Scout award Boy Scouts Am. Greater N.Y. Coun., 1990, Trendsetter award Foodsvc. Cons. Soc., 1989 Mem. Conf. Bd., U.S. C. of C., Bald Peak C.C. (N.J.), Avenel Golf Club, Sigma Chi. Mem. LDS Ch. Clubs: Burning Tree (Washington), Met. (Washington). Office: Marriott Intl Inc 1 Marriott Dr Washington DC 20058-0001 *

MARRIOTT, MARCIA ANN, business, economics professor, health facility administrator; b. Rochester, NY, Mar. 21, 1947; d. Coyne and Alice (Schleper) M.; children: Brian, Jonathan. AA, Monroe C.C., Rochester, 1967; BS, SUNY, Brockport, 1970, MA, 1975; PhD, S.W. U. La., 1985. Program adminstr. N.Y. Dept. of Labor, NYC, 1970-75; employment mgr. Rochester Gen. Hosp., 1975-77, salary adminstr., 1982-98, compensation mgr., 1996—; corp. dir. wage and salary dept. Gannett Newspapers, Rochester, 1977-80; compensation and benefits adminstr. Sybron Corp., Rochester, 1980-82; compensation mgr. Rochester Gen. Hosp., 1996—; dir. compensation Via Health, Rochester, 1995-98; pres. Compensation Link, 1997—; prof. Grad. Sch. Bus. Rochester Inst. Tech., 1998—2003, SUNY, Brockport, 1998—2003. Instr. N.Y. State Sch. Indsl. Rels., Cornell U., N.Y.C., 1976-79; assoc. prof. Rochester Inst. Tech., 1978—, Monroe C.C., 1981—, dir. career adv. coun., 1989—; assoc. prof. SUNY, Brockport; assoc. prof. Nazareth Coll., 1998; dir. Rochester Presbyn. Home, 1987-91, 96—, v.p. bd. dirs., 1997-98, pres. bd. dirs., 1998—; dir. area hosp. coun. Kidney Svc. Ctrs., Rochester, 1988-91; cons. in field. Author: (pamphlets) Guideline for Writing Job Descriptions, 1983, (manual) Career Planning Manual, 1985, (booklet) Guideline for Writing Criteria-Based Job Descriptions, 1988, Skill-based Job Descriptions: A Quality Approach, 1994, Redesigning the Performance Appraisal Process, 1996. Campaign mgr. Carter Campaign Commn., Rochester, 1975; mem. coun. Messiah Luth. Ch., Rochester, 1991-94. Davenport-Hatch Found. grantee, 1973, Wegman Found. grantee, 1975. Mem. Am. Compensation Assn., Single Adopted Parents Group (pres. 1988-93). Avocations: tennis, hiking, reading, swimming, skiing. Office: Rochester Gen Hosp 1425 Portland Ave Rochester NY 14621-3095 Office Phone: 585-292-3241. Business E-Mail: mmarriott@monroecc.edu.

MARRIOTT, MICHEL, reporter; married; 3 children. BA in Philosophy and Journalism, Morehead State U., 1976; MA in Journalism, Northwestern U., 1977. Reporter Marion Chronicle-Tribune, Ind., 1977, Courier-Jour., Louisville, Washington Post, Phila. Daily News; gen. editor Newsweek mag., NY, 1994—95; reporter NY Times, 1987—94, reporter, Style Dept., 1995—98, tech. reporter Circuits Sect., 1998—. Adj. prof. Grad. Sch. Journalism Columbia U.; prof., Dept. Communication, Film & Video City Coll. NY; frequent contbr. Ann. Men's Issue Essence mag.; contbr. Esquire mag.; prof. Antioch Writer's Workshop. Author: Hedz; co-author: (screenplays) (based on his NY Times series) New Jersey Drive, 1995 (Pulitzer prize nominee). Recipient Outstanding Achievement award, Nat. Assn. Black Journalists, 1981; Nieman fellow, Harvard U., 2002. Office: Circuits Sect NY Times 229 West 43rd St New York NY 10036 Office Phone: 212-556-7803. Office Fax: 212-556-1448. E-mail: marr@nytimes.com.

MARRIOTT, RICHARD EDWIN, hotel and contract services executive; b. Washington, Jan. 9, 1939; s. John Willard and Alice Taylor (Sheets) M.; m. Nancy Peery, Mar. 20, 1962; children: Julie Ann, Sandra, Karen, Mary Alice. BS, U. Utah, 1963; MBA, Harvard U., 1965. With Marriott Corp., Washington, 1965—, group v.p. restaurant ops., 1976-78, corp. group v.p. restaurant and theme park ops., 1979-84, exec. v.p., 1984, vice chmn., 1986—92; chmn. Host Hotels & Resorts, Bethesda, Md., 1992—. Chmn. bd. dirs. Media Corp., 1973—; bd. dirs. Riggs Nat. Bank of Washington. Mem. Nat. Commn. Against Drunk Driving; trustee Boys Clubs Am., Dole Found. for Employemnt of Persons with Disabilities; chmn. Marriott Found. People with Disabilities. Named one of Forbes Richest Americans, 2006. Mem. Nat. Restaurant Assn., Sigma Chi. Mem. Lds Ch. Office: Host Hotels & Resorts Suite 1500 6903 Rockledge Dr Bethesda MD 20817 *

MARRIS, ROY O., agriculturist, consultant; b. Bogata, Tex., Oct. 6, 1922; s. Dick and Clara E. Marris; m. Myrle A. Marris, May 7, 1927; children: Dicky O., Donna, Dwight. MS, Sam Houston State U., Huntsville, Tex., 1951. Cert. real estate appraiser, Tex. Tech., 1953, Tex. A & M, 1966. Technician soil conservation USDA, Palestine, Tex., 1953—64, supr. Farmers Home Adminstrn. Nacogdoches, Tex., 1964—65, Ft. Worth, 1965—72; advisor to young farmers and ranchers Bogata, 1972—. Mem. Civil Def. Orgn., Ft. Worth, 1965—72; former membership chmn. Farm Bur. Tex.; former county chmn. Dem. Primary, Red River, Tex., former election judge; deacon First Bapt. Ch., 1954—. With US Army, 1942—45. Mem.: Agr. Workers. Democrat. Baptist. Achievements include research in program on animal breeding to determine the sex of animal at breeding time. Avocations: riding and training spotted horses, cow dogs. Home: 13614 Farm Rd 410 S Bogata TX 75417-3652

MARRISON, BENJAMIN J., editor-in-chief; b. Ashtabula, Ohio; BA, Bowling Green State U. With Toledo Blade, Cleve. Plain Dealer, 1990—99, Columbus bur. chief, 1996—99; mng. editor news Columbus (Ohio) Dispatch, 1999, editor, 1999—. Named to Bowling Green State U. Hall of Fame. Mem.: AP Soc. Ohio, Columbus Met. Club. Office: Columbus Dispatch 34 S 3rd St Columbus OH 43215 Office Phone: 614-461-5200. E-mail: bmarrison@dispatch.com. *

MARRO, ANTHONY JAMES, retired newspaper editor; b. Middlebury, Vt., Feb. 10, 1942; s. Francis James and Esther Martha (Butterfield) M.; m. Jacqueline Helen Cleary, June 5, 1965; 1 child, Alexandria. BA in History, U. Vt., 1965; MS in Journalism, Columbia U., 1968. Reporter Rutland (Vt.) Herald, 1964-67, Newsday, LI, NY, 1968-74, chief Washington bur., 1979-81, mng. editor, 1981-86, exec. editor, 1986-87, editor, 1987—2003; reporter Newsweek, Washington, 1974-76, N.Y. Times, Washington, 1976-79. Co-recipient Pulitzer prizes for Pub. Service Reporting, 1970, 74.

MARRON, DONALD BAIRD, venture capitalist; b. Goshen, NY, July 21, 1934; m. Catherine D. Calligar. Student, Baruch Sch. Bus., 1949-51, 55-57. Investment analyst NY Trust Co., NYC, 1951-56, Lionel D. Edie Co., NYC, 1956-58; mgr. research dept. George O'Neill & Co., 1958-59; pres. D.B. Marron & Co. Inc., NYC, 1959-65, Mitchell Hutchins & Co. Inc. (merger with D.B. Marron & Co. Inc. 1965), NYC, 1965-69, pres., chief exec. officer, 1969-77; pres. PaineWebber Inc. (merger with Mitchell Hutchins & Co. Inc. 1977), NYC, 1977—80, CEO, 1980—2000, chmn. bd., 1981—2000; co-founder, former chmn. Data Resources, Inc., 1969—79; chmn. UBS Am., 2000—03; chmn., CEO, founder Lightyear Capital, LLC, NYC, 2000—. Dir. NYSE 1974-81; bd. mem. Fannie Mae 2001-06, Shinsei Bank 1999-2005; chmn. Collegiate Funding Svcs. 2004-06; gov., vice chmn. Securities Industry Assn. 1974-77; gov. NASD 1997-2001. Chmn. Ctr. for Study of the Presidency; vice chmn. & former pres. bd. trustees Mus. of Modern Art, N.Y.C; mem. adv. bd. UBS Art Collection; mem. bd. overseers and mgrs. Meml. Sloan-Kettering Cancer Ctr.; trustee Charles A. Dana Found., Ctr. for Strategic & Internat. Studies (private sector co-chmn. Nat. Commn. on Retirement Policy); bd. dirs. NYC Partnership; mem. Govs.'s Sch. and Bus. Alliance Task Force, NY; former mem. Pres. Commn. on The Arts and The Humanities; former vice chmn. Calif. Inst. for the Arts. Named one of Top 200 Collectors, ARTnews Mag., 2004—. Mem.: Council on Fgn. Rels. Avocation: collector of 19th century European, modern & contemporary art. Office: Lightyear Capital LLC 11th Fl 375 Park Ave New York NY 10152 Business E-Mail: dbmarron@lycap.com.

MARRON, PAMELA ANNE, artist; b. Hackensack, NJ, Nov. 16, 1945; d. Chester Charles and Edith Anne Marron. AA, Parsons Sch. Design, NYC, 1968; postgrad., Stanford U., Calif., 1970. Mem. art com. Stratton Art Festival, Stratton Mountain, Vt.; founder, art com. Elm St. Arts, Manchester, Vt. Archtl. Digest, 1998, Women Artists Calendar, 1999, one-woman shows include Stratton Arts Festival, 1974—94, Park McCullough House, Bennington, Vt., 1976, The Hoosac Sch., N.Y., 1978, Garden Gallery, Londonderry, Vt., 1980, AVA Gallery, Hanover, N.H., 1984, Castleton State Coll., Vt., 1986, Pindar Gallery, N.Y.C., 1987, Northstar Gallery Show, Stratton Mountain, 1989—2002, Avanti Gallery, Lambertville, N.J., 1990, Nicholas Roeruch Mus., N.Y.C., 1990, Lotus Gallery, Cambridge, Mass., 1990, Vt. State House, Montpelier, 1992, Chaffee Art Ctr., Rutland, Vt., 1994, Elm St. Arts, Manchester Center, Vt., 1994, 95, 1994, 1995, Gallery Two, Woodstock, Vt., 1995, Olde Moon Gallery, Breckenridge, Colo., 1998, Grayson Gallery, Woodstock, 1999, Gardner Colby Gallery, Naples, Fla., 2001, Schenectady Mus., 2004, Haddad Lascano Gallery, Greater Barrington, Mass., 2005, Redux Gallery, Dorset, Vt., 2005, Nancy Price Gallery, Jamaica, Vt., 2005, Dorset Theater Festival, 2005, So. Vt. Art Ctr., 2006, Vt. Art Gallery, Brattleboro, 2006, So. Vt. Coll., Manchester Center, 1975, 79, 2006, Beside Myself Gallery, Arlington, Vt., 1982, 86, 90, Cove Gallery, Wellfleet, Mass., 1991, 97, The Artisans Gallery, Brattleboro, Vt., 2007, Brattleboro Mus., 2007, Represented in permanent collections Lotus Corp., Omni Corp., N.Y.C., Yoder Bros. Internat., Barberton, Ohio, numerous group exhbns. Recipient Max Beckman scholarship, 1967, 1968, Jurors award, Berkshire Mus., 1978, Stratton Art Festival, 1983, 1988, Jay Conaway award, 1987, 1990. Mem.: Vt. Coun. on Arts, So. Vt. Art Ctr. (art com., numerous art exhbns., Jurors award 1998). Avocations: singing, swimming, walking. Home: Box 563 Dorset VT 05251 Office Phone: 802-867-2246.

MARRONE, PHILIP A., chemical engineer; b. Everett, Mass., Jan. 9, 1968; s. Robert F. and Carol A. Marrone. BS, Columbia U., NYC, 1990; MS, MIT, Cambridge, Mass., 1992, PhD, 1998. Mgr. Arthur D. Little, Inc., Cambridge, 1998—2002, FOCIS Assocs. (a Geo-Centers Co.), Newton, Mass., 2002—05; chem. engr. Sci. Applications Internat. Corp. (SAIC), Newton, 2005—. Contbr. chapters to books; editor: (workshop procs.) Supercritical Water Oxidation — Achievements and Challenges in Commercial Applications; contbr. articles to profl. jours. Named Class Valedictorian, Sch. Engring. and Applied Sci., Columbia U., 1990; recipient Charles F. Bonilla medal for Outstanding Academic Merit, 1990, Illig medal for high GPA and commendable proficiency in studies, 1990. Mem.: AIChE (mem. career and profl. svcs. com. Boston sect. 2005—), Sigma Xi. Avocations: road biking, hiking, kayaking, travel, skiing. Home: 20 Ship Ave #21 Medford MA 02155 Office: SAIC 7 Wells Ave Newton MA 02459 Home Phone: 781-393-4948; Office Phone: 617-618-4686. Office Fax: 617-618-4697. Business E-Mail: philip.a.marrone@saic.com.

MARROW, DEBORAH, foundation administrator; d. Seymour Arthur and Adele M.; m. Michael J. McGuire; children: David Marrow McGuire, Anna Marrow McGuire. BA cum laude, U. Pa., PhD; MA, Johns Hopkins U. With Phila. Mus. of Art, 1974-75, Chrysalis Mag., LA, 1978-80, The J. Paul Getty Trust, LA, 1983—. Various positions including program officer Getty Grant Program; interim dir., The Getty Rsch. Inst.; dean for extern relations, The J. Paul Getty Trust; interim pres. and CEO, dir. The Getty Found. Mem. Save Am.'s Treas. com., Nat. Trust for Historic Preservation (in partnership with White House Millenium Coun.), 1998-2001; bd. govs. U. Calif Humanities Rsch. Inst., 2000-05; mem. US and internat. com. for History of Art; mem. bd. trustees U. Pa., 2003-. Office: The Getty Found 1200 Getty Center Dr Ste 800 Los Angeles CA 90049-1600 Office Phone: 310-440-7320.

MARROW, TRACY See ICE-T

MARRS, CAROL FAYE, performing arts educator, writer; b. Fairbanks, Alaska, Sept. 22, 1955; d. Morris Elton Robinson and Mary Emogene Hall; m. Gregory Evan Marrs; children: Matthew, Haley. BSc, West Tex. State U., Canyon, 1977. Tchr. English/Speech Hereford Ind. Sch. Dist., Tex., 1979—81; tchr. speech/drama/English River Rd. Ind. Sch. Dist., Amarillo, Tex., 1981—82, Canyon Ind. Sch. Dist., Tex., 1982—90; tchr. grade 1 Lewisville Ind. Sch. Dist., Carrollton, Tex., 1996—98, tchr. creative dramatics, 1998—2005, Flower Mound, 2005—. Workshop presenter Tex. Educators Theatre Assn., Austin, 2005; author, pub. spkr. Tex. Panhandle Penwomen, Amarillo, 1988—; dir. summer music theatre camp for children; tchr. music class for toddlers. Author: (children's poetry) Pet Cobwebs, 1988, (speech textbook) The Complete Book of Speech Communication, 1991. Mem. Grace Cmty. Assembly of God, Flower Mound, 2005—. Finalist Tchr. of Yr., LISD, 2003, 2004; named Elem. Tchr. of Yr., Indian Creek Ind. Elem. Sch., Lewisville Ind. Sch. Dist., 2003—04; grantee, Lewisville Edn. Found., 2003—04; 3 nominations Tchr. of Yr., Disney. Mem.: PTA, Tex. Educators Theatre Assn., Mothers In Touch (campus coord. 2005—06). Home: 420 Moran Dr Highland Village TX 79070 Office: Wellington Elem Flower Mound TX Office Phone: 469-713-5989.

MARS, FORREST E., JR., candy company executive; s. Forrest Mars Sr.; m. Virginia Cretella, Oct. 20, 1955 (div. Jan. 1990); children: Victoria B., Valerie A., Pamela D., Marijke E. BA, Yale U., 1953, BS. Chmn. bd. dirs., former CEO Mars Inc., Mc Lean, Va. Named one of World's Richest People, Forbes mag., 1999—, Forbes Richest Ams., 1999—. Office: Mars Inc 6885 Elm St Mc Lean VA 22101-3810 *

MARS, JACQUELINE BADGER, food products executive; b. 1939; m. David Badger, 1961 (div.); 3 children; m. Harold Vogel, 1986 (div.). Degree in anthropology, Bryn Mawr Coll., 1961. Co-owner Mars, Inc., McLean, Va., 1973—, corp. v.p., 1990—. Trustee Bryn Mawr Coll.; bd. trustee mem.-at-large Washington Nat. Opera. Named one of World's Richest People, Forbes mag., 2000—, Forbes Richest Ams., 1999—. Office: Mars Inc 6885 Elm St Mc Lean VA 22101 *

MARS, JOHN FRANKLYN, candy company executive; b. 1935; m. Adrienne Mars; 2 children. BA, Yale U., 1957, BS. Chmn. Kal Kan Foods Inc.; co-pres. Mars Inc., 1973—, CEO, 2000—, chmn. Named one of Forbes Richest Ams., 1999—, World's Richest People, Forbes mag, 1999—. Office: Mars Inc 6885 Elm St Mc Lean VA 22101 *

MARSALIS, WYNTON, musician; b. New Orleans, Oct. 18, 1961; s. Ellis and Dolores Marsalis. Studied with John Longo; student, New Orleans Ctr. for Performing Arts, Berkshire Music Ctr., Juilliard Sch. Music, 1979-81. Music dir. Lincoln Ctr. Jazz Orch. Trumpet soloist with New Orleans Philharm. Orch., 1975, recitalist with New Orleans Ctr. for Creative Arts, 1979, played with various New Orleans and NYC orchs., with Art Blakey's Jazz Messengers, 1980—81, Herbie Hancock's V.S.O.P. quartet, formed own group, 1981, albums Fathers and Sons, 1982, Hummel/Haydn/L. Mozart Trumpet Concertos, 1983 (Grammy award, 1983), Wynton Marsalis (Best Jazz Record, Downbeat readers' poll, 1982), Think of One, 1983 (Grammy award), Handel, purcell, Torelli, Fasch, Moler, Trumpet Concertos, 1983, Hot House Flowers, 1984, Black Codes from the Underground, 1985 (2 Grammy awards), J Mood, 1986, Carnaval, Marsalis Standard Time, Vol. 1, 1987 (Grammy award), Majesty of the Blues, 1989, Standard Time, Vol. 3, 1990, Intimacy Calling Standard Time, Soul Gestures in Southern Blue, Vols. 1, 2, 3, 1991, Blue Interlude, 1992, Citi Movement, 1993, In This House, On This Morning, 1994, Wynton Marsalis, 1995, Popular Songs: The Best Of Wynton Marsalis, 2001, All Rise, 2002, Unforgivable Blackness, 2004, The Magic Hour, 2004, Baroque Music For Trumpets, 2005, Trumpet Concertos, 2005, Live At The House Of Tribes, 2005, (with others) The All-American Hero, Live at Bubba's, In Gabriel's Garden, Sound of Jazz, All American Hero, 1996, Blood on the Fields, Jump Start and Jazz, Crescent City Xmas Card, 1997, Standard Time, Vol. 5: The Midnight Blues, One by One, Gold Collection, 1998. Named Jazz Musician of Yr., Downbeat readers' poll, 1982, 1984—86, 1989, Best Trumpet Player, Downbeat critics' poll, 1984, Acoustic Jazz Group of Yr., 1984, Best Trumpet Player, Downbeat readers' poll, 1985; named one of America's 25 Most Influential People, Time mag., 1996, 100 Most Influential People, Time Mag., 2006; recipient Grammy award for best solo jazz instrumental, 1983—85, Grammy award for best solo classical performance with orch., 1984—85, Grammy award for best jazz instrumental performance with group, 1985, 1987, musician of the Year, Down Beat Readers, 1992, Pulitzer prize for music, 1997, Algur H. Meadows award, Southern Meth. Univ., 1997, Nat. Medal of Arts, Nat. Endowment for the Arts, 2005, Most Influential Black Americans, Ebony mag., 2006.

MARSCHALL, NICOLE, music educator; d. Rickie and Julene Stiklestad. BA in Music Edn., U. Minn., Morris, 2002. Voice and piano tchr., Twin Cities, Minn., 2002—; vocal coach for mus. theater prodns. Burnsville H.S., Minn., 2002—. Avocations: piano, musical theater, concerts. Personal E-mail: nicole.marschall@yahoo.com.

MARSCIARELLI, GARRY KENT See MARSHALL, GARRY

MARSDEN, BRIAN GEOFFREY, astronomer; b. Cambridge, Eng., Aug. 5, 1937; arrived in US, 1959; s. Thomas and Eileen (West) M.; m. Nancy Lou Zissell, Dec. 26, 1964; children: Cynthia Louise, Jonathan Brian. BA, Oxford U., UK, 1959, MA, 1963; PhD, Yale U., 1965. Rsch. asst. Yale U., New Haven, 1959-65; lectr. astronomy Harvard U., Cambridge, Mass., 1966-83; astronomer Smithsonian Astrophys. Obs., Cambridge, 1965—; assoc. dir. planetary scis. Harvard-Smithsonian Ctr. for Astrophysics, Cambridge, 1987—2002. Dir. Ctrl. Bur. Astron. Telegrams, 1968-2000, Minor Planet Ctr. Internat. Astron. Union, 1978-2006. Editor: The Earth-Moon System, 1966, The Motion, Evolution of Orbits and Origin of Comets, 1972, Catalogue of Orbits of Unnumbered Minor Planets, 1996, Catalogue of Cometary Orbits, 2003. Recipient Merlin medal Brit. Astron. Assn., 1965, Goodacre medal, 1979, Alcock lectureship, 2003; Van Biesbroeck award U. Ariz., 1989, Camus-Waitz prize Societé astronomique de France, 1993, Dirk Brouwer award Am. Astron. Soc., 1995, Lacchini prize Unione Astrofili Italiani, 2001. Fellow Royal Astron. Soc. (Svc. award astronomy and geophysics 2006); mem. Am. Astron. Soc. (chmn. div. on dynamical astronomy 1976-78), Internat. Astron. Union (pres. commn. 1976-79, 2000-03), Astron. Soc. Pacific, Sigma Xi. Office: Harvard-Smithsonian Ctr Astrophysics 60 Garden St Cambridge MA 02138-1516 Home Phone: 781-862-6549. Business E-Mail: bmarsden@cfa.harvard.edu.

MARSDEN, HERCI IVANA, classical ballet artistic director; b. Omis-Split, Croatia, Dec. 2, 1937; d. Ante and Magda (Smith) Munitic; m. Myles Marsden, Aug. 10, 1957 (div. 1976); children: Ana, Richard, Mark.; m. Dujko Radovnikovic, Aug. 27, 1977; 1 child, Dujko. Student, Internat. Ballet Sch., 1955. Mem. corps de ballet Nat. Theatre, Split, 1954-58; founder Braecrest Sch. Ballet, Lincoln, RI, 1958—, State Ballet of R.I., Lincoln, 1960—, artistic dir., 1976—. Artistic dir. U. R.I. Classical Ballet, Kingston, 1966—, lectr., 1966—. Office: Brae Crest School of Ballet 52 Sherman Ave Lincoln RI 02865-3809 Office Phone: 401-334-2560. Business E-Mail: hmarsden@stateballet.com.

MARSDEN, JAMES (JAMES PAUL MARSDEN), actor; b. Stillwater, Okla., Sept. 18, 1973; m. Lisa Linde Marsden, July 22, 2000; children: Jack, Mary James. Student, Okla. State U. Actor: (films) No Dessert Dad, Til You Mow the Lawn, 1994, Public Enemies, 1996, Campfire Tales, 1997, Disturbing Behavior, 1998, Gossip, 2000, X-Men, 2000, Sugar & Spice, 2001, Zoolander, 2001, Interstate 60, 2002, X2, 2003, The 24th Day, 2004, The Notebook, 2004, Heights, 2004, The Alibi, 2006, 10th & Wolf, 2006, X-Men: The Last Stand, 2006, Superman Returns, 2006, Hairspray, 2007; (TV films) In the Line of Duty: Ambush in Waco, 1993, Search and Resume, 1994, 919 Fifth Avenue, 1995, Gone in a Heartbeat, 1996, One the Edge of Innocence, 1997, Bella Mafia, 1997; (TV series) Boogies Diner, 1994, Second Noah, 1996—97, Ally McBeal, 2001—02. Office: BWR Pub Rels 9100 Wilshire Blvd Sixth Fl W Tower Beverly Hills CA 90212 *

MARSE, MELISSA J., music educator, concert pianist; d. John Pat and Linda Marse. MusB, U. of Tex., Austin, 1996; MusM, Yale U., New Haven, Conn., 1998; PhD in Music in Collaborative Piano, New Eng. Conservatory, Boston, 2002; postgrad, Juilliard Sch., NYC, 1999. Prof. Houston Bapt. U., 2006—; artist in residence Kinkaid Sch., Houston; tchg. fellow Harvard U., Boston; adj. prof. Tex. State U., San Marcos. Pres. U. Tex. Fine Arts Coun., Austin. Musician (soloist): (Breckenridge Music Festival) Beethoven Emperor Concerto; piano soloist Aspen Music Festival, vocal coach faculty Mannes Art Song Inst., orchestral pianist (film music prodns.), soloist/chamber musician (worldwide). Mem. Mark O'Connor Trio; v.p., mem. bd. America's Dream Chamber Artists, NYC, 2003—06. Mem.: Tex. Music Educators Assn., Nat. Guild of Piano Tchrs. (assoc.), Music Tchres. Nat. Assn. (assoc.).

MARSEE, SUSANNE IRENE, vocalist; b. San Diego, Nov. 26, 1941; d. Warren Jefferson and Irene Rose (Wills) Dowell; m. Mark J. Weinstein, May, 1987; 1 child, Zachary. Student, Santa Monica City Coll., 1961; BA in History, UCLA, 1964; postgrad., Juilliard, 1969, La. State U., 1991—92. Mem. voice faculty Am. Mus. and Dramatic Acad., NYC, 1994-97, Pitts. Civic Light Opera Acad., 1997—2000, Duquesne U., 1998-2000; artist's lectr. Carnegie Mellon U., 2000—. Appeared with numerous U.S. opera cos., 1970—, including N.Y.C. Opera, San Francisco Opera, Boston Opera, Houston Grand Opera; appeared with fgn. cos., festivals, Mexico City Bellas Artes, 1973, 78, Canary Islands Co., 1976, Opera Metropolitana, Caracas, Venezuela, 1977, Spoleto (Italy) Festival, 1977, Aix en Provence Festival, France, 1977, Calgary, Alta., Can., 1986; recorded Tales of Hoffmann, ABC/Dunhill Records; TV appearances include Live from Lincoln Center, Turk in Italy, Cenerentola, 1989, Live from Wolftrap Roberto Devereux, 1975, Rigoletto, 1988, A Little Night Music, 1990, Marriage of Figaro, 1991, (PBS TV) Rachel, La Cubana; recs. and CDs Anna Bolena with Ramey, Scotto, Roberto Devereux with Beverly Sills, Roberto Devereux with Monserat Caballé Carreras, Tales of Hoffmann with Beverly Sills, Rigoletto with Quilico and Carreras; videotape Roberto Devereux with Beverly Sills. Recipient 2d place award Met. Opera Regional Auditions, 1968, San Francisco Opera Regional Auditions 1968; named winner Liederkranz Club Contest, 1970; Gladys Turk Found. grantee, 1968-69; Corbett Found. grantee, 1969-73; Martha Baird Rockefeller grantee, 1969-70, 71-72 Mem. AFTRA, Am. Guild Mus. Artists (past bd. dirs.), Nat. Assn. Tchrs. of Singing (past bd. dirs. for N.Y.). Democrat.

MARSH, BENJAMIN FRANKLIN, lawyer; b. Toledo, Apr. 30, 1927; s. Lester Randall and Alice (Smith) M.; m. Martha Kirkpatrick, July 12, 1952; children: Samuel, Elizabeth. BA, Ohio Wesleyan U., 1950; JD, George Washington U., 1954. Bar: Ohio 1955. Pvt. practice law, Toledo, 1955—88; assoc., ptnr. Doyle, Lewis & Warner, Toledo, 1955—71; ptnr. Ritter, Boesel, Robinson & Marsh, Toledo, 1971—88; mem. Marsh & McAdams, Maumee, 1988—98; pers. officer AEC, 1950—54; asst. atty. gen. State of Ohio, 1969—71; asst. solicitor City of Maumee, 1959—63, solicitor, 1963—92; mem. Marsh McAdams, Ltd., Maumee, 1999—. Mem. U.S. Fgn. Claims Settlement Commn., Washington, 1990-94; counsel N.W. Ohio Mayors and Mgrs. Assn., 1990-2000; regional bd. rev. Indsl. Commn. Ohio, Toledo, 1993-94; mem. Ohio Dental Bd., 1995-2000; trustee Corp. for Effective Govt., 1998-2003; mem. Ohio Elections Commn., 2001-07, chmn. 2003-04 U.S. rep. with rank spl. amb. to 10th Anniversary Independence of Botswana, 1976; past pres. Toledo and Lucas County Tb Soc.; co-chmn. citizens for metro pks.; past mem. Judges Com. Notaries Pub.; former mem. Lucas County Bd. Elections; former chmn. bldg. commn. Riverside Hosp., Toledo; past trustee Com. on Rels. with Toledo, Spain; past chmn. bd. trustee Med. Coll., Ohio; past treas. Coglin Meml. Inst.; chmn. Lucas County Rep. Exec. Com., 1973-74; precinct committeeman, Maumee, 1959-73; legal counsel, bd. dirs. Nat. Coun. Rep. Workshops, 1960-65; pres. Rep. Workshops, Ohio, 1960-64; alt. del. Rep. Nat. Conv., 1964; candidate 9th dist. U.S. Ho. of Reps., 1968; adminstrv. asst. to Rep. state chmn. Ray C. Bliss, 1954; chmn. Lucas County Bush for Pres., 1980; co-chmn. Reagan-Bush Com. for Northwestern Ohio, 1980, vice chmn. fin. com. Bush-Quayle, 1992; co-chmn. Ohio steering com. Bush for Pres., mem. nat. steering com., 1988; del. Rep. Nat. Conv., 1988; past bd. dirs. Ohio Tb and Respiratory Disease Assn.; apptd. Ohio chmn. UN Day, 1980, 81, 82; adminstrv. asst. Legis. Svc. Commn., Columbus, 1954-55; mem. Lucas County Charter Commn., Toledo, 1959-60; vice-chmn. U.S. Nat. Commn. for UNESCO, mem. legal com., del. 17th gen. conf., Paris, 1972, U.S. observer meeting of nat. commns., Africa, 1974, Addis Ababa, Ethiopia; past mem. industry functional adv. com. on stds. trade policy matters; mem. nat. def. exec. res. Dept. Commerce; active Am. Bicentennial Presdl. Inauguration, Diplomatic Adv. Com. With USNR, 1945-46. Named Outstanding Young Man of Toledo, 1962. Mem. ABA, Maumee C. of C. (past pres.), UN Assn., Ohio State Bar Assn., Toledo Bar Assn., Ohio Mpcl. League (past pres.), Am. Legion (comdr. Toledo Post), Lucas County Maumee Valley Hist. Soc. (past pres.), Internat. Inst. Toledo, Ohio Mcpl. Attys. Assn. (past pres.), Orgn. Security and Cooperation in Europe (registration supr., adjudicator, elections supr. in Bosnia), Western Lake Erie Hist. Soc., Ohio Hist. Soc., Canal Soc. Ohio, Toledo Mus. Art, Ohio Wesleyan U. Alumni Assn. (past pres.), Ohio State Bar Found., Toledo Bar Found., Rotary, Toledo Country Club, Torch Club Toledo, Navy League, Omicron Delta Kappa, Delta Sigma Rho, Theta Alpha Phi, Phi Delta Phi. Presbyterian. Home: 1624 Swan Creek Ln Toledo OH 43614 Office: 204 W Wayne St Maumee OH 43537-2125 Office Phone: 419-893-4880. Personal E-mail: bmarsh124@aol.com.

MARSH, BRUCE DAVID, geologist, educator; b. Munising, Mich., Jan. 4, 1947; s. William Roland and Audrey Jane (Steinhoff) M.; m. Judith Anne Congdon, Jan. 24, 1970; children: Hannah Eyre, William Noah. BS, Mich. State U., East Lansing, 1969; MS, U. Ariz., Tucson, 1971; PhD, U. Calif., Berkeley, 1974. Geologist, geophysicist Anaconda Co., Tucson, 1969-71; asst. prof. dept. earth/planet sci. Johns Hopkins U., Balt., 1974-78, assoc. prof., 1978-81, prof., 1981—. Chmn., 1989-93; vis. prof. Calif. Inst. Tech., Pasadena, 1985, U. Maine, 1992-93; co-chmn. Gordon Rsch. Conf. on Inorganic Geochemistry, Holderness, N.H., 1983-84; advisor NASA, Washington, 1975-84, NSF, Washington, 1978-90, NRC, 1985-91; Hallimond lectr. Mineral. Soc. Great Britain and Ireland, 1995. Assoc. editor Geology, 1981-83, Jour. Volcanology and Geothermal Rsch., 1978—, Jour. Petrology, 1986—; editor Jour. Volcanology and Geothermal Rsch., 1985—. Fellow Geol. Soc. Am. (assoc. editor Bulletin 1986-92), Royal Astron. Soc., Mineral. Soc. Am., Am. Geophys. Union (sec. sect. on volcanology, geochemistry and petrology 1984-86, pres. elect 1988-90, pres. 1990-92, Bowen award 1993, Daly lecture 2000); mem. Model A Ford Club Am. Achievements include being named in honor of research in Antarctica, Marsh Cirque, a glacial valley in the Olympus Mountains. Office: Johns Hopkins U Dept Earth-Planetary Scis 322 Olin Hall Baltimore MD 21218 Office Phone: 410-516-4652. Business E-Mail: bmarsh@jhu.edu.

MARSH, CARYL AMSTERDAM, retired curator, psychologist; b. NYC, Mar. 9, 1923; d. Louis and Kitty (Weitz) Amsterdam; m. Michael Marsh, Sept. 3, 1942 (dec. 1993); children: Susan E., Anna L. BA, Bklyn. Coll., 1942; MA, Columbia U., NYC, 1946; PhD, George Washington U., 1978. Lic. psychologist DC. Asst. cultural attache Am. Embassy, Paris, 1946-48; psychologist D.C. Recreation Dept., 1957-69; spl. asst. Smithsonian Instn., Washington, 1966-73; curator exhbns. Nat. Archives, Washington, 1978-85, sr. exhbns. specialist, 1985-86; dir. traveling psychology exhbn. Am. Psychol. Assn., 1986-93, sr. advisor, 1993-95; chair humanities seminars in sci. mus. Assn. Sci. Tech. Ctrs., 1994—2001; ret., 2003. Rsch. fellow exptl. gallery Smithsonian Instn., 1992; rsch. cons. Nat. Zoo, 1981-92, Smithsonian Folk Life Festival, Nat. Mus. Am. History, 1977-78; organizer Discovery Room Nat. Mus. Natural History, 1969-73; cons. Meyer Found., 1964-66; advisor Lemelson Ctr. for Study of Invention and Innovation, Nat. Mus. Am. History, 1999-2000. Editor: Exhibition: The American Image, 1979. Organizer Anacostia Neighborhood Mus., Washington, 1967, bd. dirs., 1974—, v.p. 1993—; sec. D.C. Commn. on Arts and Humanities, 1969-72; pres. Pre-Sch. Parents Coun., Washington, 1956-57; adv. bd. Youth Alive, 1977-99. Fellow Nat. Mus. Am. Art, 1975-77; vis. scholar Nat. Mus. Am. Art, 1978—; grad. fellow CUNY, 1945-46; scholar George Washington U.; noted for Disting. Contbn. to Pub. Understanding of Psychology, APA, 1993. Mem. AAAS, APA (Outstanding Svc. award 1992, Disting. Contbn. to Pub. Understanding of Psychology award 1993), D.C. Psychol. Assn., Am. Assn. Mus., Mus. Edn. Roundtable (bd. dirs. 1983-87). Home and Office: 10450 Lottsford Rd # 3011 Mitchellville MD 20721-2734

MARSH, DON ERMAL, supermarket executive; b. Muncie, Ind., Feb. 2, 1938; s. Ermal W. and Garnet (Gibson) M.; m. Marilyn Faust, Mar. 28, 1959; children: Don Ermal, Jr., Arthur Andrew, David Alan, Anne Elizabeth, Alexander Elliott. BA, Mich. State U., 1961. With Marsh Supermarkets, Inc., Indpls., 1961—2006, pres., 1968—2006, chmn. CEO; ret. Chmn. FoodPAC, Washington, 1991; bd. dirs. Nat. City Bank, Indpls., Ind. Energy, Inc., Indpls.; gov. World Econ. Forum—Food & Agro, Geneva. Bd. dirs. Corp. Community Coun., Culver Fathers Assn., Food Industry Crusade Against Hunger, Charlene S. Lugar Birth Defects Grant Fund, Am. Arbitration Assn, Ctrl. Ind. Corp., Econ. Club Indpls., Hanover Coll., other; bd. mem. Ind. Assn. Cities and Towns; mem. adv. com. on food distbn. Western Mich. U.; mem. Conner Prairie Pioneer Settlement Adv. Coun.; mem. Indpls. Mus. Art.; mgmt. coun. Am. Mgmt. Assn. Mem. Am. Mgmt. Assn., Mgmt. Execs. Soc., Gen. Mgmt. Coun., Internat. Food Congress, Assn. of Publicly Traded Cos. (bd. dirs., past chmn.), Food Mktg. Inst. (bd. dirs.), Indpls. C. of C., Ind. State C. of C. (bd. dirs.), Ind. Retail Coun. (bd. dirs.), Ind. Soc. Chgo., Chief Execs. Orgn., World Bus. Coun., Newcomen Soc. N.Am., Internat. Ctr. for Cos. of Food Trade and Industry (past chmn., bd. dirs.), Food Merchandisers Edn. Coun., Nat. Assn. Convenience Stores, Nat. Assn. Food Rsch., World Pres. Orgn., Young Pres. Orgn. Alumni, Nat. Soc. Fund Raising Execs., Well House Soc., Am. Bus. Club, Ind. Fiscal Policy Inst., Ind. Soc. Chgo., Ind. U. Varsity Club, Crooked Stick Golf Club, Columbia Club, Delaware Country Club, The Hundred Club Indpls., Indpls. Athletic Club, Marco Polo Club, Meridian Hills Country Club, Skyline Club, Masons, Elks, Pi Sigma Epsilon, Lambda Chi Alpha Found., Sigma Phi Omega. Republican. Presbyterian.

MARSH, DONNA M., sales executive, consultant; d. William Edward Marsh and Ethel Louise Hawkes Marsh Arventos. BA in Psychology, U. Rochester, NY, 1977. Sales mgr. BancTec, various locations, 1983—96; sales mgr. Mid. East Seagate Tech., Marlow, Eng. and Dubai, United Arab Emirates, 1996—2001; sales mgr. Far East Computer Network Tech., Langley, England, 2001—04; sales mgr. Nordic Spectralogic, Oxford, England, 2005; CEO Donna Marsh Cross Cultural Counseling, Old Windsor, England, 2006—. Mem.: Sietar, Mensa, Circumnavigators Club, Traveler's Century Club. Avocations: travel, scuba diving, wine, Asian cooking. Office: 4 White Hermitage Church Rd Old Windsor SL4 2JX England

MARSH, JACK, JR., (JOHN OTHO MARSH), lawyer, former federal agency administrator, congressman; b. Winchester, Va., Aug. 7, 1926; s. John Otho and Nell Virginia (Wayl) M.; m. Glenn Ann Patterson, July 22, 1950; children: John O., Rebecca Patterson, Scot Wayland. LLB, Washington and Lee U., 1951; degree (hon.), The Citadel, James Madison U., Shenandoah U., Hampden-Sydney Coll. Bar: Va. 1952, D.C. 1970. Pvt. practice, Strasburg, 1952; town judge, 1954-62; town atty. New Market, Va., 1954-62; mem. US Congress from 7th Va. dist., 1963—71; asst. sec. for legis. affairs US Dept. Def., Washington, 1972-73; asst. to the v.p. for nat. security affairs The White House, Washington, 1973-74, counselor to Pres., 1974-77; ptnr. Mays, Valentine, Davenport & Moore LLP, Washington, 1977-81; sec. Dept. Army, Washington, 1981-89; asst. sec. for spl. ops./low intensity conflict US Dept. Def., Washington, 1987-88, legis. counsel to sec., 1989-90; mem. Hazel & Thomas, P.C., Winchester and Falls Ch., Va., 1990-94, of counsel Winchester, Va., 1995—96; chmn., interim CEO Novavax, Inc., Rockville, Md., 1996—97. Mem. Shenandoah County (Va.) Sch. Bd., 1958-60; chmn. Res. Forces Policy Bd., 1989-94; chmn. Sec. Def.'s Panel on Quality of Life, 1995-; vis. prof. ethics, Va. Mil. Inst., 1998-99, adj. prof. law, Coll. William & Mary, 1999-2000, disting. adj. prof. law, George Mason U., 2005- Mem. Am. Revolution Bicentennial Commn., 1966-70. Served with AUS, 1944-47; lt. col. Va. N.G., ret. Recipient Disting. Pub. Svc. medal US Dept. Def. (5), Presdl. Citizen's medal, 1989, Outstanding Virginian award Va. Press Assn., 1990; named to Outstanding Young Man of Yr., 1959. Mem. Va. State Bar, Va. Jaycees (life), Am. Legion, VFW, N.G. Assn. U.S., Va. N.G. Assn., Masons, Phi Kappa Psi, Phi Delta Phi, Omicron Delta Kappa. Presbyterian (past elder). *

MARSH, JOAN KNIGHT, educational film company executive, video company executive, publishing executive; b. Apr. 8, 1934; d. E. Lyle and Ruth (Hopkins) Knight; m. Alan Reid Marsh, Sept. 27, 1958; children: Alan Reid, Clayton Knight. BA, Tex. Tech U., 1956. Owner, pres. MarshMedia, Kansas City, Mo., 1969—. Mem. ctrl. governing bd. Children's Mercy Hosp., 1996-05; mem. coun. Family Study Ctr., U. Mo., Kansas City, 1983-89, Children's Relief Assn. Mercy Hosp., Kansas City, 1984—, pres., 1989-91; chmn., hon. co-chmn. Rose Brooks Ctr. Cabaret, 1995, 2000; pres. Friends of Children's Mercy Hosp., 1996-98; chmn. The Jewel Ball, 1997, Nelson-Atkins Mus. Art: Great Ball of China II, 1999, An Asymmetrical Evening GAla Opening of Bloch Bldg., 2007; Genevieve Byrne spkr. Series ARC Kansas City chpt., 2004. Mem. Jr. League (sustaining chmn. 1982-84, Cmty. Svc. award 1999), Gamma Phi Beta. Republican. Presbyterian. Avocations: egyptology, filmology. Office Phone: 816-523-1059.

MARSH, JOSEPH FRANKLIN, JR., retired academic administrator; b. Charleston, W.Va., Feb. 24, 1925; s. Joseph Franklin and Florence (Keller) M. Student, Concord Coll., 1941-42, W.Va. U., 1942-43; AB, Dartmouth Coll., 1947; student, Nat. Inst. Pub. Affairs, Washington, 1947-48; M.P.A., Harvard U., 1949; LL.D., Davis and Elkins Coll., 1968; L.H.D., Alderson-Broaddus Coll., 1982. Cons. Hoover Commn., Washington, 1948; instr. in gt. issues Dartmouth, 1952—54, instr. econs., 1953—55, asst. prof., 1955—59; pres. Concord Coll., Athens, W.Va., 1959—73, pres. emeritus, 1985—; ednl. cons., 1973—74; pres. Waynesburg (Pa.) Coll., 1974—83, pres. emeritus, 1983—; v.p. The Armand Hammer United World Coll. of the Am. West, Montezuma, N.Mex., 1984—85; pres. Marsh Edn Cons., Athens, W.Va., 1985—. Dir. One Valley Bank of Mercer County, 1987-98, hon. dir., 1998-2000. Contbr. articles to profl. jours. Mem. State Dept. Ednl. Mission to U.A.R., 1964, Mercer County (W.Va.) Planning Commn., 1964-74, 83-94, hon., 1994—; vice chmn. W.Va. Com. for Constl. Amendments, 1966; mem. regional coun. Internat. Edn. Study Mission to Europe, 1970; bd. dirs. Am. Assn. State Colls. and Univs., 1972-73, Regional Coun. for Internat. Edn., 1973, Hospice Care Mercer County, W.Va., 1987-91, Faculty Merit Found. W.Va., 1990—, Greater Mercer County Charitable Found., Inc., W.Va., 1998-02, exec. com. 2001-02, chmn., pres., 1998-2001; bd. dirs. Charitable Found. of the Virginians, Inc., 2002-05, Pa. Assn. Colls. and Univs., 1974-83, exec. com., 1980-82; bd. dirs. Pa. Commn. for Ind. Colls. and Univs., 1974-83, sec.-treas., 1976-77, vice chmn., 1977-80, chmn., 1980-82; trustee Found. Ind. Colls. Pa., 1974-83, mem. exec. com., 1979-82; bd. visitors Midway Coll., Ky., 1979-93; adv. com. Pa. State Coun. Higher Edn., 1980-82; trustee Concord U. Found., 1986, bd. dirs., 1987—; active Town of Athens Planning Commn., 1986-94, pres. commn. 1987-94; bd. trustees, Princeton (W.Va.) Cmty. Hosp. Found., 1989-98, vice chmn., 1989-97; Gov.'s appointee to bd. dirs. State Coll. System W.Va., 1989-96, chmn. adminstrv. com., 1990-91, vice chmn. of bd., 1991-95, chmn., 1995-96; gov.'s appointee to the W.Va. Parkways, Econ. Devel. and Tourism Authority, 1998—2006, asst. sec., 2001-02, sec., 2002-03, vice chmn., 2003-04; gov.'s appointee Edn. Commn. of the States, 1998-2002. Served as gunnery officer USNR, 1943-46. Named Outstanding Young Man, W.Va. Jr. C. of C., 1960; recipient Alumnus of Yr. award Concord U., 1973, Golden Alumnus award, 1992, Outstanding Alumnus award for Career Achievement, 1996; Outstanding Citizen award Athens Woman's Club, 1992, Total Community Involvement Award, Town of Athens, WV, 2001; Rotary fellow Oxford (Eng.) U., 1950-52. Mem. AAUP, Am. Assn. Univ. Adminstrs., Am. Econ. Assn., Royal Inst. Pub. Adminstrn., Oxford Union Debating Soc. (life), Oxford Soc. (life), Pa. Soc., Duquesne Club (Pitts.), Univ. Club (Bluefield), Masons, Rotary (dist. gov. 1992-93), The Guild of Carillonneurs N.Am. (hon.), Phi Beta Kappa, Phi Tau, Phi Delta Pi, Phi Sigma Kappa, Alpha Kappa Psi (hon.). Methodist. Home: 106 First Ave Athens WV 24712 Office: PO Box 734 Athens WV 24712-0734 Home Phone: 304-384-9816; Office Phone: 304-384-9816.

MARSH, JOSEPH VIRGIL, real estate broker, retired investment advisor; b. Winston-Salem, NC, Apr. 28, 1952; s. Gilliam Hughes and Dovie Elizabeth (Watson) Marsh. Student, Surry CC, 1970-72, US Govt. Schs., Md., SC, Washington, 1972-74; BSEE, U. Md., 1976; diploma, NY Inst. Fin., 1978, NYU, 1978, MBA, 1980. Cert. comml. real estate broker NC. With Joint Armed Svcs. Tech. Liaison, Washington, 1974-75; cons. US Govt., 1975-76; corr., cons. individuals, bus. on tech. matters Ararat, NC, 1977—. Registered advisor SEC, 1981—2000. Active U.S. Presdl. Task Force, 1981—2000; founder Marsh Found., 1989; tech. liaison NASA, 1992. Recipient Presdl. medal of merit, Pres. of US, 1988, 1990. Mem.: VFW (hon.), Coun. Civilian Tech. Advisers, Internat. Assn. Sci. Devel., Ind. Cons. Assn., Internat. Entrepreneurs Assn., Armed Forces Assn. Republican. Office: Hwy 2019/2026 Ararat NC 27007-0178 Office Phone: 336-374-4405.

MARSH, MARIAN E., voice educator; b. San Mateo, Calif., Apr. 5, 1936; d. Richard Harding and Helen McGregor (Grant) Marsh; m. David Wade, Sept. 18, 1955. Voice tchr. Sonoma State U., Rohnert Park, Calif., 1965—70, U. Calif., Santa Cruz, 1974—88, Dominican U., San Rafael, Calif., 1975—; pvt. practice Calif., 1962—. Cruise ship entertainer, 1970—82, 1993, 95. Singer: San Francisco Symphony, LA Philharmonic, Oakland Symphony, Sinfonia Nat.; singer: (soloist) Schola Cantorum, De Anza Coll., San Francisco Civic Chorale, Winifred Baker Chorale, Coll. Marin, Diablo Valley Coll., San Mateo Masterworks Chorale, Contra Costa Chorale, Peninsula Singers, Coll. Marin Cmty. Chorus. Organist various chs., Calif., 1950—60, soloist San Francisco, 1964—97, Temple Emanuel, San Francisco, 1960—96; organist dir. Ch. of Nativity, San Rafael, Calif., 2002—. Recipient Met. Opera award, 1963, 1965, East Bay Opera League award, 1964. Mem.: Music Tchrs. Assn. (scholarship chair), Nat. Assn. Tchrs. Singing, Womens Musicians Club (pres., v.p., recital chair). Episcopalian. Home: 91 Grande Paseo San Rafael CA 94903 Office: Dominican Univ 50 Acacia San Rafael CA 94901 Personal E-mail: davidmarionsong@aol.com.

MARSH, MARTHA H., hospital administrator; BS, U. Rochester; MPH, MBA, Columbia U. Pres. and CEO Matthew Thornton Health Plan, Dartmouth-Hitchcock Med. Ctr., 1986—94; sr. v.p., profl. svcs. and managed care and v.p, managed care U. Pa. Health Sys., 1994—98; COO U. Calif.-Davis Health Care Sys., 1999—2002; dir., Hosp. and Clinics U. Calif.-Davis Medical Ctr., 1999—2002; pres. and CEO Stanford (Conn.) Hosp. and Clinics, 2002—. Apptd. by Pres. Bush Nat. Infrastructure Adv. Coun., 2003; bd. dirs. Calif. Healthcare Assoc., Integrated Healthcare Assoc., Blue Cross of Calif. Hosp. Relations Com. Office: Stanford Hosp 300 Pasteur Dr Ste H3200 Stanford CA 94305 Office Phone: 650-723-4000.

MARSH, MERRILYN DELANO, sculptor, artist, painter; b. Larchmont, NY, Dec. 26, 1923; d. Merrill Potter and Hazel (Holmes) Delano; m. George Estabrook Marsh, Sept. 18, 1954; children: Merrill Delano, George Estabrook Jr., Robert Houston. Diploma, Sch. of Mus. of Fine Arts, Boston, 1946, cert., 1947; postgrad., Acad. Grande Chaumière, Paris, 1947-48; student, Bennett Jr. Coll., Millbrook, NY, 1941—42. Art tchr. Choate Sch., Brookline, Mass., 1948, 49, Brookline Cmty. Ctr., 1948, 49; pvt. art tchr. Newton, Mass., 1948-49; comml. sculptor for display and mfg. cos., 1948-55; sculpture tchr. De Cordova Mus., Lincoln, Mass., 1950-54. Juror for numerous art exhbns., New Eng. area, 1954-55, 72-74. One-woman show at Copley Soc. of Boston, 1996, Wellesley Libr., Mass., 2006; commd. 7 reliefs for Sch. for Environ., Levine Sci. Ctr., Duke U., Durham, N.C., 1994, bronze statue for cloister garden St. Andrew's Episcopal Ch., Wellesley, Mass., 1995, bronze portrait reliefs for Houston and Sargent Athletic awards Tufts U., Medford, Mass., 1997, 2 bronze reliefs, Ellis Oval Athletic Field Tufts U., 2001, bronze portrait relief of Clarence P. "Pop" Houston, Houston Hall, Tufts U., 1965, bronze portrait relief for Rocco J. Carzo Cage, Cousens Gymnasium, Tufts U., 2002, others; profiled in Wellesley Weston Mag., 2006. Mrs. David Hunt Sculpture scholar Mus. Fine Arts, 1947; recipient Katherine Thayer Hobson award Pen and Brush Soc., 1991, Best in Show award Juliani Gallery, 1991, Pres.'s Cup award for golf Wellesley (Mass.) Country Club, 1998, 2d Pl. award Wellesley Soc. Artists, 2003, Hon. mention Wellesley Soc. Artists Spring Show, 2004, Margaret E. Fearnside Meml. award Wellesley Soc. Artists Fall Show, 2004. Mem. Copley Soc. Boston (Copley master, Maria Maravigna award 1988, 1st prize in sculpture and large works 1994, other awards, 1983, 89), New Eng. Sculptors Assn. (bd. dirs. 1986, award 1988), Wellesley Soc. Artists (awards 1985, 87, 89, 91-92, 95, 2001-02, 2d pl. award 2003, bd. dirs. 1970, 88—, Hon. Mention award 2004, Margaret E. Fearnside Meml. award 2004), Cambridge Art Assn. (Jack Schultz award, 2000, other awards 1993-94). Republican. Episcopalian.

MARSH, MILTON R.W., composer; b. Hamilton, Bermuda, Sept. 29, 1945; arrived in U.S., 1964; s. Milton Murray and Gwendolyn Isadora Marsh; children: Tanya, Jonathan Milton, Milton Andre. Cert. in Edn., London U., 1964; MB, Berklee Coll. Music, Boston, 1969; MusM, New Eng. Conservatory, Boston, 1971. Cert. tchr., adminstr. Calif. Music cons. Nat. Ctr. for Afro-Am. Artists, Boston, 1970—71; vis. prof. SUNY, Oneonta, 1972—73, prof., dir. Afro-Am. music studies Buffalo, 1973—77. Cons. Nat. Ctr. for Afro-Am. Artists, Boston, 1970—71. Author: (music) Monism, 1975, Continuum, 1985, We Are Not Separate, 2003. Recipient grant, Artist Found. Office: Alankara Records PO Box 230635 Boston MA 02123-0635 Office Phone: 781-979-2417. Office Fax: 781-324-4922. E-mail: mmarsh8113@aol.com, alankara@msn.com.

MARSH, PATRICIA GUYTON, humanities educator; b. Columbus, Miss., Mar. 17, 1947; d. Rickman Keith and Dora Hankins Guyton; m. Robert Tate Marsh, May 13, 1973; 1 child, Erin Tate. BA in Speech, Miss. State U., Starkville, 1968; MA in Theatre, U. Miss., Oxford, 1972, postgrad., 1972, postgrad., 2005, U. South Ala., Mobile, Miss. U. for Women, Columbus. Cert. English, speech and theatre tchr. Miss., Ala., Ga., Fla. Instr. Sidney Lanier Jr. HS for Boys, Macon, Ga., 1969, Warner Robins Sr. HS, 1969—71, U. Miss., Oxford, 1971—72, East Miss. Jr. Coll., Scooba, 1973, Pasco Comprehensive HS, Dade City, Fla., 1973—74, Pasco C.C., Dade City, Fla., 1974—75, Ala. Christian Coll., Mobile, 1975—76, St. Paul's Episcopal Sch., Mobile, 1976—2003, Columbus HS, 2003—04, East Miss. CC, Mayhew, 2004—. Adjudicator song writing divsn. Hank Williams Internat. Music Festival; adjudicator State 4H Oratorical Contest; guest lectr. Ala. Pub. Rels. Coun.; moderator Evenings with Ala. Writers series Spring Hill Coll.; actress Manhattan Theatre Co., NYC; actress, dir. Entertainer Dinner Theatre, Mobile, Ala.; dir. Granada Little Theatre, Miss., Warner Robins Little Theatre, Ga.; choreographer music and theatre depts. U. Miss.; dir. winning prodns. Southeastern Theatre Conf., Secondary Sch. Divsn., Crystal City, Va., Louisville. Dir., featured performer An Evening with Tennessee's Ladies Tennessee Williams Tribute, Columbus, 2005; mem. com. Roast and Boast, Columbus, 2005; dir. An Army of Stars benefit Salvation Army; site dir. Kaleidoscope benefit festival United Cerebral Palsy. Named Ala. Speech/Theatre Tchr. of Yr.; recipient Disting. Tchr. award, White House Commn. on Presdl. Scholars, Best Actress award, Southeastern Theatre Conf., Cmty. Theatre Divsn., Miss. State U., Joe Jefferson Playhouse, Mobile, Mobile Theatre Guild, Azalea City News and Review, Mobile; Pres. scholar, Miss. State U. Mem.: Ala. Speech Assn. (sec.), Ala. Theatre Assn. (sec.), Ala. Coun. Theatre/Speech, Southeastern

Theatre Conf. Republican. Methodist. Avocations: travel, gardening, antiques, theater, football. Home: 509 7th St South Columbus MS 39701 Office: East Miss CC PO Box 100 Mayhew MS 39753-0100

MARSH, RICHARD H., energy executive; BA, Kent State U.; MA in Clinical Psychology, U. Akron, MBA. CFA. Joined Ohio Edison, 1980, various financial positions, 1980—91; treasurer Ohio Edison (merged with Centerior Energy to form FirstEnergy), 1991—97; v.p. finance FirstEnergy Corp., Akron, Ohio, 1997, v.p., CFO, 1998—2001, sr. v.p., CFO, 2001—. Chmn. Utility Pension Fund Study Group; mem. fin. adv. com. Edison Elec. Inst. Mem. advancement coun. Coll. Bus. Admin. U. Akron, v.p. alumni coun.; chair We. Reserve Girl Scout Coun.; trustee FirstEnergy Found., H.M. Life Opportunity Services; mem. advisory com. for Master of Sci. in Fin. Engring. prog. Kent State U. Mem.: Cleve. Soc. Security Analysts. Office: First Energy Corp 76 S Main St Akron OH 44308-1890 *

MARSH, ROBERT HARRY, chemicals executive; b. Camden, NJ, Sept. 6, 1946; s. Harry Louis and Margaret Charlotte (Starke) M. BA, BSME, Rutgers U., 1969; MBA in Mgmt. and Fin., Temple U., 1980. Lic. profl. engr., NJ, Pa., Del. From mech. engr. to mech. specialist and project engr. Rohm & Haas Engring., Bristol, Pa., 1967—76; from staff engr. to sr. engring. specialist Hercules, Inc., Wilmington, Del., 1976—80, sr. fin. analyst for corp. strategic planning, 1980—81, sr. bus. analyst bus. group, 1982—83; mgr. bus. analysis Himont, Inc., 1983—86, dir. strategy and planning, 1986—88, dir. bus. mgmt., 1988—91, mng. dir. China, 1991—95, dir. strategy, 1991—95; founder R.H. Marsh & Assoc. Internat. Mgmt., Bethlehem, Pa., 1995—; pres., prin., CEO, chmn. bd. dirs. Internat. Bus. and Mktg. Mgmt., 1996—. Founder, bd. dirs. various cos., 1995—. Contbr. articles to profl. jours. Active Haddonfield (N.J.) Civic Affairs, Bethlehem (Pa.) Civic Affairs, Wesley Meth. Ch., Bethlehem, Pa., 2001—. Mem.: NSPE, ASME (vice chmn. awards com. 1980, membership chmn. 1982, nat. power com. 1977—84), Engrs. Club Phila., Pyramid Club Phila., Beta Gamma Sigma. Home and Office: 225 Flagstone Dr Bethlehem PA 18017 Office Phone: 856-986-4484. Personal E-mail: rbtmarsh@verizon.net, rbtmarsh@aol.com.

MARSH, ROBERT MORTIMER, sociologist, educator; b. Everett, Mass., Jan. 22, 1931; s. Henry Warren and Ruth (Dunbar) M.; children: Eleanor L., Christopher S.H., Diana E. Student, Boston U., 1948-50; AB, U. Chgo., 1952; MA, Columbia, 1953, PhD, 1959. Fellow Ford Found., Japan, Taiwan, Hong Kong, 1956-58; instr. sociology U. Mich., 1958-61; asst. prof. sociology Cornell U., 1961-65; asso. prof. Duke, 1965-67; mem. faculty Brown U., 1967—, prof. sociology, 1968—, chmn. dept., 1971-75. Manpower personnel and tng. rsch. prof. U.S. Naval Acad., Annapolis, 1987-88; vis. prof. Nat. Tsing Hua U., Taiwan, 1991. Author: The Mandarins: The Circulation of Elites in China, 1961, Comparative Sociology: A Codification of Cross-Societal Analysis, 1967; (with H. Mannari) Modernization and the Japanese Factory, 1976, Organizational Change in Japanese Factories, 1988, The Great Transformation: Social Change in Taipei, Taiwan Since the 1960s, 1996; also articles; assoc. editor Adminstrv. Sci. Quar., 1963-67, Jour. Comparative Family Studies, 1970-74; co-editor: (with J. Michael Armer) Comparative Sociological Research in the 1960s and 1970s. East Asian Inst. summer fellow Chinese Columbia, 1955; Ford Found. and Guggenheim Found. fellow Japan, 1969-70; Japan Soc. Promotion Sci. fellow, 1976, 83; Chiang Ching Kuo Found. and Nat. Sci. Coun. fellow (Taiwan, Republic of China). 1991-93. Mem. Am. Sociol. Assn., Ea. Sociol. Assn., Assn. Asian Studies, Internat. Studies Assn. (exec. com. comparative interdisciplinary studies sect. 1971-76), Japan Human Rels. Assn. (councilor 1970—). Office: Dept Sociology Brown Univ Providence RI 02912-0001 Business E-Mail: robert_marsh@brown.edu.

MARSH, WILLIAM ANDREW, III, lawyer; b. Durham, NC, Mar. 6, 1958; s. William Andrew Jr. and Bernice (Sawyer) M.; m. Sonja Denalli, July 20, 1991; 1 child, William Andrew IV. BA, Hampton Inst., 1979; JD, U. N.C., 1982. Bar: DC 1983, NC 1984, admitted to practice: US Dist. Ct. (DC) 1987, US Ct. Appeals (4th Cir.) 1995, US Supreme Ct. 1998. Assoc. Marsh & Banks, Durham, 1982-83, 85-86; asst. legal counsel Gov. of N.C., Raleigh, 1983-85; assoc. Hyatt Legal Svcs., Washington, 1987; asst. corp. counsel Govt. of D.C., 1987-92; gen. ptnr. Marsh & Marsh, Durham, 1993—. Interim dir. Land Loss Prevention, Durham, 1985. Mem. ABA, N.C. Assn. Black Lawyers, N.C. Bar Assn., D.C. Bar Assn., Durham County Bar Assn. (bd. dirs. 1994—), Kappa Alpha Psi. Democrat. African Methodist Episcopalian. Office: AME Church 120 E Parrish St Ste 310 Durham NC 27701-3346 Office Phone: 919-688-2374. Office Fax: 919-688-2376. E-mail: d2470@mindspring.com.

MARSHAK, ALAN HOWARD, electrical engineer, educator; b. Miami Beach, Fla., Mar. 21, 1938; s. Jerome and Yetta (Feiner) M.; children: Jerry Brian; m. Joan Grode Milner, May 25, 1997. BScEE, U. Miami, 1960; MS, La. State U., 1962; PhD, U. Ariz., 1969. Asst. prof. elec. engring. La. State U., Baton Rouge, 1969-73, assoc. prof., 1973-78, prof., 1978—2002, chmn. dept. elec. and computer engring., 1983—2002, prof. emeritus, 2002—. Vis. prof. Electron Device Rsch. Ctr., U. Fla., Gainesville, 1979-80; tech. reviewer NSF, 1976—, panelist, 1993-96; panelist NRC, 1993, 2001, 04; mem. Southeastern Ctr. Elec. Engring. Edn., 1984-2002, life mem., 2002—, chmn., CEO, 1992-2001, trustee, 1994—; spkr. profl. confs. Tech. referee various jours. including Solid-State Electronics, Jour. Applied Physics; editor: Device and Process Modeling, IEEE Trans. Electron Devices, 1991-2001; author: (with D. J. Hamilton and F. A. Lindholm) Principles and Applications of Semiconductor Device Modeling, 1971, Basic Experiments in Electronics: A Laboratory Manual, 1978, also 56 tech. papers. NSF grad. trainee, 1967-69; grantee, 1970, 73, 75, 78; named F.H. Coughlin/CLECO prof. of elec. engring., 1993. Fellow IEEE (life); mem. Electron Devices Soc., Sigma Xi, Eta Kappa Nu. Home: 113 Clipper Cove Lafayette LA 70508-7023

MARSHAK, HARRY, plastic surgeon; b. LA, Oct. 1, 1961; s. Herbert and Pearl (Engelson) M. BS, U. Calif., Riverside, 1981; MD, UCLA, 1984. Diplomate Am. Bd. Surgery, Am. Bd. Plastic Surgery. Pvt. practice, Beverly Hills, Calif., 1991—. Fellow ACS (hon.), Internat. Coll. Surgeons; mem. Am. Soc. Plastic and Reconstructive Surgeons, Calif. Soc. Plastic Surgery, Am. Soc. for Aesthetic Plastic Surgery. Republican. Avocation: sports. Office: 120 S Spalding Dr Ste 300 Beverly Hills CA 90212-1841 Office Phone: 310-657-7600. Personal E-mail: drharrymarshak@aol.com.

MARSHAK, MARVIN LLOYD, physicist, researcher; b. Mar. 11, 1946; s. Kalman and Goldie (Hait) M.; m. Anita Sue Kolman, Sept. 24, 1972; children: Rachel Kolman, Adam Kolman. AB in Physics, Cornell U., 1967; MS in Physics, U. Mich., PhD in Physics, 1970. Rsch. assoc. U. Minn., Mpls., 1970-74, from asst. prof. to assoc. prof., 1974-83, prof. physics, 1983-96, dir. grad. studies in physics, 1983-86, prin. investigator high energy physics, 1982-86, head Sch. Physics and Astronomy, 1986-96, sr. v.p. for acad. affairs, 1996-97, Morse-Alumni disting. tchg. prof. physics, 1996—, Inst. of Tech. prof., 2004—, dir. residential coll., 1997—2005, faculty legis. liason, 1997—2001, chair univ. senate consultative exec. com., 2004—05, dir. undergrad. rsch., 2007—. Contbr. articles to profl. jours. Trustee Children's Theater Co., 1989-94. Fellow: Am. Phys. Soc. Home: 2855 Ottawa Ave S Minneapolis MN 55416-1946 Office Phone: 612-624-1312. Business E-Mail: marshak@umn.edu.

MARSHAK, ROBERT REUBEN, retired dean, medical educator, veterinarian; b. NYC, Feb. 23, 1923; s. David and Edith (Youselovsky) Marshak; m. Ruth Emilie Lyons, Dec. 4, 1948 (div. 1983); children: William Lyons, John Ball, Richard Best; m. Margo Post Marshall, June 25, 1983. Student, U. Wis., 1940—41; DVM, Cornell U., 1945; DVM (hon.), U. Bern, 1968; MA (hon.), U. Pa., 1971. Diplomate Am. Coll. Vet. Internal Medicine (charter). Practice vet. medicine, Springfield, Vt., 1945—56; prof., chmn. dept. medicine Sch. Vet. Medicine, U. Pa., Phila., 1956—58; prof. medicine Grad. Sch. Medicine, 1957—64; chmn. dept. clin. studies Sch. Vet. Medicine, 1958—73; dir. Bovine Leukemia Research Center, 1965—73; dean Sch. Vet. Medicine, 1973—87; co-dir. Center on Interactions Animals and Soc., 1975—79, also mem. grad. group com. in comparative med. scis.; prof. medicine, chief sect. epidemiology and pub. health Sch. Vet. Medicine U. Pa., 1990—93, prof. medicine emeritus, 1993—, dean emeritus, 1987—. Adv. bd. Pa. Dept. Agr., 1973—87; chmn. Gov.'s STudy Group on Horse Racing Industry in Pa., 1979; del. to evaluate vet. med. and rsch. Chinese Ministry Agr.; adv. com. Stround Water Rsch. Ctr., 1992; adv. coun. Coll. Vet. Medicine, Cornell U., 1993—; animal use and care com. Calif. Inst. Tech., 2003—. Contbr. articles to profl. jours. Sci. adv. bd. Sch. Vet. Medicine The Hebrew U., Jerusalem, 1984—, rev. com., 1997—; trustee Upland Country Day Sch., 1988—91; animal adv. com. City of Phila., 1989—93; pres. rev. com. Koret Sch. Vet. Medicine Hebrew U. Jerusalem, 1997—98; bd. dirs. Humane Soc. U.S., 1978—82, Bide-a-wee Home Assn., 1980—85. With US Army, 1943—44. Recipient Disting. Vet. award, Pa. Vet. Med. Assn., 1984, Barnraiser award, Pa. Farmers Assn., 1987. Fellow: Phila. Coll. Physicians; mem.: Pa. Vet. Med. Assn., Am. Vet. Med. Assn., Nat. Acad. Inst. Medicine (sr.), John Morgan Soc. (pres. 1967—68), Phila. Zool. Soc. (bd. dirs. 1986—87), James A. Baker Inst. for Animal Health (mem. adv. coun. 1977—), Westminster Kennel Club, Phi Zeta, Sigma Xi. Personal E-mail: rmarshak@caltech.edu.

MARSHALL, ALAN GEORGE, chemistry and biochemistry educator; b. Bluffton, Ohio, May 26, 1944; s. Herbert Boyle Marshall and Cecil (Mogil) Rosser; m. Marilyn Gard, June 13, 1965; children: Gwendolyn Scott, Brian George. BA in Chemistry with honors, Northwestern U., 1965; PhD in Phys. Chemistry, Stanford U., 1970. Instr. II U. B.C., Vancouver, Can., 1969-71, asst. prof., 1971-76, assoc. prof., 1976-80; prof. chemistry and biochemistry, dir. Chem. Instrument Ctr. Ohio State U., Columbus, 1980—93; prof. chemistry and biochemistry Fla. State U., Tallahassee, 1993—, disting. rsch. prof., 1999, Kasha prof., 2000—06, Robert O. Lawton prof., 2006—. Dir. Ion Cyclotron Resonance Program Nat. High Magnetic Field Lab., 1993. Author: Biophysical Chemistry, 1978, Fourier Transforms in NMR, Optical and Mass Spectroscopy, 1990; editor: Nat. High Magnetic Field Lab. ICR/ION Trap newsletter, 1986—92, Rapid Comm. in Mass Spectrometry, 1998—2005; mem. editl. bd. Rapid Comm. in Mass Spectrometry, 2005—; mem. editl. adv. bd.: Analytical Chemistry, 1990—92, mem. editl. bd.: Internat. Jour. Mass Ion Procs., 1987—, Mass Spectrometry Rev., 1994—, Jour. Magnetic Resonance, 1996—2000, Chemometrics and Intelligent Lab. Systems, 1986—89, Ency. of Mass Spectrometry, 2000—, mem. internat. editl adv. bd.: ACS Ency. of Chem. Instrumentation, 1992—95; contbr. 450 articles to profl. jours. Recipient Disting. Scholar award, Ohio State U., 1988, award in analytical chemistry, Ea. Analytical Symposium, 1991, Maurice F. Hasler award, Spectroscopy Soc. Pitts., 1997, Two-Yr. Creativity award, NSF, 1997, gold medal, N.Y. Soc. Applied Spectroscopy, 1998, Pitts. Spectroscopy award, Spectroscopy Soc. Pitts., 2002; grad. fellow, NSF, 1965—69, Alfred P. Sloan rsch. fellow, 1976. Fellow: AAAS, Soc. Applied Spectroscopy, Am. Phys. Soc.; mem.: Am. Inst. Chemists (Chem. Pioneer award 2007), Am. Soc. Mass Spectroscopy (bd. dirs. 1991—93, 2003—, pres. 2004—06, mem. jour. editl. bd. 1987—89, 1999—2004, Disting. Contbn. award 1999), Soc. Applied Spectroscopy (hon.; chmn. local sect. 1990—93), Am. Chem. Soc. (Akron Sect. award 1988, award in chem. instrumentation 1990, Frank H. Field and Joe L. Franklin award in mass spectrometry 1995, award in analytical chemistry 2002, Herty medal (Ga. sect.) 2003, Fla. sect. award 2003, So. Chemist award (Memphis sect.) 2004), Internat. Mass Spectrum Soc. (Thomson medal 2000). Office: Fla State U Nat High Magnetic Field Lab 1800 E Paul Dirac Dr Tallahassee FL 32310-4005 Office Phone: 850-644-0529. Business E-Mail: marshall@magnet.fsu.edu.

MARSHALL, ALISON BUELL, lawyer; b. Poughkeepsie, NY, Aug. 6, 1959; d. Howard Drake and Natalie (Junemann) Marshall; m. Allen Lee Schirm, July 27, 1985; 2 children: Karen Anne, Janet Lynn. AB, Princeton U., NJ, 1981; JD, U. Pa., 1984. Bar: Pa. 1984, U.S. Dist. Ct. (ea. dist.) Pa. 1986, Mich. 1986, U.S. Ct. Appeals (2d cir.) 1988, (6th cir.) 1989, D.C. 1990. Law clk. to judge U.S. Dist. Ct. (ea. dist.) Pa., Phila., 1984-86; assoc. Miller, Canfield, Paddock & Stone, Detroit, 1986-91, ptnr. Washington, 1991—98, resident dir., 1998—; ptnr. Jones Day, 1998—. Chair diversity task force Jones Day, Washington, 2003—. Editl. adv. bd. mem.: Employee Rels. Law Jour., 2000—. Mem. ABA (labor and employment law sect., EEO com.), Mich. Bar Assn., Pa. Bar Assn., D.C. Bar Assn., Nat. Assn. for Perinatal Addiction Rsch. and Edn. (chair bd. dirs. 1990-95). Democrat. Home: 6500 Monique Ct Mc Lean VA 22101-1648 Office: Jones Day 51 Louisiana Ave NW Washington DC 20001-2105 Office Phone: 202-879-7611. Fax: 202-626-1700. Business E-Mail: abmarshall@jonesday.com.

MARSHALL, ALTON GARWOOD, real estate agent, consultant; b. Flint, Mich., Sept. 19, 1921; s. William Robert and Lela Christine (Brabon) M.; m. Mary Lee Golden, June 22, 1945 (div. July 1971); children: William A., Stephen B., Bruce S., Mary Ann Marshall Trebian, John L.; m. Sarah Elizabeth DeLand, Sept. 4, 1971; 1 child, Sarah Graham. BA, Hillsdale Coll., 1942; MS, Syracuse U., 1948, LLD (hon.), 1974; D Pub. Service & Bus. Adminstrn. (hon.), Hillsdale Coll., 1980. Sec. utility regulations pub. svc. commn. N.Y. State, Albany, 1953-61, dep. dir. div. budget, 1961-65, exec. officer, then sec. to gov., Office of Gov., 1965-70; pres., bd. dirs. Rockefeller Ctr., NYC, 1971-81; pres. A.G. Marshall Assocs., NYC, 1981—; chmn., pres., chief exec. officer Lincoln Savs. Bank, NYC, 1984-88, chmn., chief exec. officer, 1988-91, also bd. dirs. Mem. exec. com. Nat. Realty Com., Washington, 1970-99; bd. dirs. N.Y. State Electric & Gas Corp., 1971-98; ind. gen. ptnr. Equitable Capital Ptnrs. and Equitable Capital Ptnrs. Retirement Fund, 1989-99; trustee Hudson River Trust, 1991-97. Mem. exec. com., steering com. Assn. for a Better N.Y., 1971—; mem. exec., landmarks and polit. action coms. Real Estate Bd. N.Y.; chmn. Nat. Assn. on Drug Abuse Problems, 1990-92. Sr. fellow The Nelson A. Rockefeller Inst. Govt., 1991-94. Mem. Am. Soc. Real Estate Counselors. Office: Alton G Marshall Assocs Inc 136 E 79th St New York NY 10021-0328 Office Phone: 212-407-2514.

MARSHALL, BARRY JAMES, gastroenterologist; b. Kalgoorlie, Western Australia, Australia, Sept. 30, 1951; came to U.S., 1986; s. Robert William and Marjory Jean (Donald) M.; m. Adrienne Joyce Feldman, Dec. 27, 1972; children: Luke, Bronwyn, Caroline, Jessica. MBBS, U. Western Australia, Perth, 1974, postgrad., 1986. Intern Sir Charles Gairdner Hosp., Western Australia, 1975-76, resident Western Australia, 1976-77, registrar medicine, 1977-78, Royal Perth Hosp., 1979-82, Fremantle Hosp., 1983-84, microbiology register Western Australia, 1984; Nat. Health and Med. Rsch. Coun. (NHMRC) rsch. fellow, Gastroenterology Royal Perth Hosp., 1985-86; research fellow, prof. medicine U. Va. Sch. Med., Charlottesville, 1986—94; chief med. officer TRI-MED Distributors Pty Ltd, Australia, 1990—; prof. rsch. in internal medicine Univ. Va., 1996; clin. prof. medicine Univ. Western Australia, 1997, clin. prof. microbiology, 1999, Nat. Health and Med. Rsch. Coun. sr. rsch. fellow, 2003. Cons. Procter and Gamble Co., Cin., 1984—, Delta West Perth, 1985—; founder, Helicobacter Found., 1994-; bd. dirs. JARM Pty. Ltd., Perth, 1987—. Edited Helicobacter Pioneers Firsthand accounts from the scientists who discovered helicobacters, 1892-1982, 2002 Named one of Outstanding West Australians, Perth Jaycees, 1985; research grantee Australian Nat. Health and Med. Rsch. Coun., 1985-86; recipient Albert Lasker Clin. Med.Rsch. award, Albert and Mary Lasker Found., 1995, Gairdner Found. Internat. award, 1996, DR AH Heineken prize for Medicine, Amsterdam, 1998, Florey medal, Canberra, 1998, Buchanan medal, Brit. Soc. Medicine, 1998, Benjamin Franklin medal for Life Sciences, Phila., 1999, Keio Med. Sci. prize, 2002, Australian Centenary medal, 2003; co-recipient (with J. Robin Warren) Warren Alpert prize, 1994, Australian Med. Assn. award, 1995, Paul Ehrlich prize, 1997, Nobel prize for Physiology or Medicine, 2005. Fellow Royal Australian Coll. Physicians, Am. Coll. Gastroenterolgy; mem. Australian Med. Assn., Australian Gastroent. Soc. Achievements include Inventor Clotest (rapid urease test), 1985, Carbon-14 Urea Breath Test, 1985; co-discoverer Helicobacter Pylori bacilli in stomach of patients with gastritis and peptic ulcers, 1982; first person to culture Helicobacter Pylori bacilli. Avocations: computer hardware and software, photography, skin diving, american cuisine. Office: Nat Health and Med Rsch Coun Helicobacter pylori Rsch Lab Rm 1 11 L Block QEII Med Centre Nedlands 6009 Australia also: TRI-MED Distributors Pty Ltd 105 Hay St Subiaco 6008 Australia Mailing: TRI-MED Distributors Pty Ltd Locked Bag 15 Subiaco 6904 Australia

MARSHALL, BRIAN LAURENCE, federal official; b. Kingston-on-Thames, Eng., Apr. 6, 1941; arrived in US, 1949; s. John and Marguerite Elizabeth (Sandele) Marshall. BA in European History, U. N.C., 1963; MS in Internat. Mgmt., Am. Grad. Sch. Internat. Mgmt., Glendale, Ariz., 1973. Commd. 2d lt. USAF, 1964, advanced through grades to capt., 1972; instr. Armed Forces Air Intelligence Tng. Ctr., Denver, 1965-68; intelligence analyst Task Force Alpha, Nakhon Phanom, Thailand, 1968-69; intelligence systems analyst Hdqs. Tactical Air Command, Langley AFB, Va., 1969-72, resigned, 1972; sr. analyst Computer Scis. Corp., Falls Church, Va., 1974-87; dir. U.S. membership and pubs. U.S.-Mexico C. of C., Washington, 1987-91; v.p. pub. affairs, bd. dirs. N.Am. Free Trade Assn., Washington, 1991-96; v.p., bd. dirs. N.Am. Trade and Investment Group, Washington, 1991-97; with U.S. Dept. State, 2005—; dept. state adviser Govt. of Iraq, US Embassy, Baghdad, 2005—. Contract team leader strategic planning studies and analyses U.S. Dept. Def., Joint Chiefs Staff, Washington, 1976—82; regional oper. supr. elections in Bosnia Orgn. Security and Coop. in Europe (OSCE), 1997, election supr., Bosnia and Kosovo, 1997—98, Bosnia and Kosovo, 2000; internat. trade cons., 1998—2005; long and short term observer, Belarus, 2001, Belarus, 04, Azerbaijan, 03, Ukraine, 04. Contbr. articles to booklets and newsletters. Bd. dirs. Columbia Plz. Tenants Assn., Washington, 1981—84; vol. Pres. Ford Com., Washington, 1976. Mem.: VFW, Washington Mgmt. and Bus. Assn. (vice chmn. 1981—83, treas. 1987—91), Thunderbird Alumni Assn. (pres. Washington chpt. 1980—87), Fgn. Policy Assn. (group leader discussion program), World Affairs Coun., Assn. Former Intelligence Officers, Has House Harriers. Republican. Avocations: jogging, tennis, travel, discussion groups, reading. Home: 5304 Albemarle St Bethesda MD 20816-1827 Office: US Embassy Baghdad Irmo/Moi APO AE 09316 Personal E-mail: brnmarsh@hotmail.com.

MARSHALL, CHARLES, communications company executive; b. Vandalia, Ill., Apr. 21, 1929; s. William Forman and Ruth (Corson) M.; m. Millicent Bruner, Jan. 2, 1953; children: Ruth Ann, Marcia Marshall Rinek, William Forman, Charles Tedrick. BS in Agr, U. Ill., 1951. With Ill. Bell Telephone Co., 1953-59, 61-64, 65-70, 71-72, 77-81, pres., chief exec. officer Chgo., 1977-81; with AT&T, 1959-61, 64-65, 70-71, 76-77, 81-89; chmn., chief exec. officer Am. Bell, Morristown, N.J., 1983-84, AT&T Info. Systems, 1984-85; vice chmn. AT&T, NYC, 1985-89. Bd. dirs. Moorings Park, Naples; trustee U. Ill. Found., Naples Philharm. Soc. for the Arts. Served to 1st lt. USAF, 1951-53. Mem.: Chgo. Club, Club of Pelican Bay, Comml. Club Chgo., Econ. Club Chgo. Avocations: fishing, golf, reading. Home: 6001 Pelican Bay Blvd Ph B Naples FL 34108-8168 E-mail: cmmbaerie@earthlink.net.

MARSHALL, CHARLES NOBLE, rail transportation executive; b. Phila., Feb. 18, 1942; s. Donnell and Cornelia Lansdale (Brooke) M.; m. Ann Shaw Donovan, Jan. 12, 1971; children— Elizabeth, Caroline, Cornelia, Edward BS in Engring., Princeton U., 1963; JD, U. Mich., 1967. Bar: Md. 1967, D.C. 1975, Pa. 1978. Atty. Balt. & Ohio R.R., Balt. and Cleve., 1967-73; gen. atty. So. Ry., Washington, 1973-78; gen. counsel commerce Conrail, Phila., 1978-83, v.p. mktg., 1983-85, sr. v.p. mktg. and sales, 1985-89, sr. v.p. devel., 1989-95; pres., COO Genesee & Wyoming Inc., 1997—2005, vice chmn., 2005—06; sr. v.p. industry affairs Farmrail Sys., Inc., 2006—. Bd. dirs. Rails to Trails Conservancy.

MARSHALL, CHRISTOPHER G., bank executive; m. Leigh Ann Marshall; 3 children. BA, Univ. Fla.; MBA, Pepperdine Univ. CFO Allied Signal Corp.; COO, CFO glob. bus. services Honeywell Internat.; CFO Tech. & ops. Bank of Am., Charlotte, NC, 2001—02, COO & CFO tech. & ops., then CFO consumer products, then sr. exec. consumer & small bus., 2002—06; exec. v.p., CFO Fifth Third Bancorp, Cin., 2006—. Mem. adv. bd. Falfurrias Capital Partners. Trustee Mint Mus., Charlotte, NC. Office: Fifth Third Bancorp Fifth Third Ctr 38 Fountain Sq Plz Cincinnati OH 45263 *

MARSHALL, CODY, bishop; Bishop Ch. of God in Christ, No. Ill. Mem. Ch. Of God In Christ. Office: Freedom Temple Church of God in Christ 1459 W 74th St Chicago IL 60636-4027 Office Phone: 773-483-1140.

MARSHALL, CONRAD JOSEPH, entrepreneur; b. Detroit, Dec. 23, 1934; s. Edward Louis Fedak and Maria Magdalena Berzsenyi; m. Dorothy Genieve Karnafil, Dec. 1, 1956 (div. 1963); children: Conrad Joseph Jr., Kevin Conrad, Lisa Marie; m. Beryle Elizabeth Callahan, June 15, 1965 (div. 1972); children: Brent Jasmer, Farah Elizabeth. Diploma, Naval Air Tech. Tng. Ctr., Norman, Okla., 1952; student, Wayne State U., 1956-59; Diploma, L.A. Police Acad., 1961. Dir. mktg. Gulf Devel., Torrance, Calif., 1980-83; sales mgr. Baldwin Piano Co., Santa Monica, Calif., 1977-80; dir. mktg., v.p. Western Hose, Inc., LA, 1971-76; city letter carrier U.S. Post Office, LA, 1969-71; writer freelance LA, 1966—; police officer L.A. Police Dept., 1961-66; asst. sales mgr. Wesson Oil Co., Detroit, 1958-60; agt. Life Ins. Co. of Va., Wayne, Mich., 1956-58; pres. Am. Vision Mktg., LA, 1990—, Con-Mar Prodns., LA, 1983—; sr. v.p. Pacific Acquisition Group, 1992—, Invest. Admin. HealthCom., Int., 1993—; pres. Midway TV Co., 1994—. Tech. advisor Lion's Gate Films, Westwood, Calif., 1970-74, Medicine Wheel Prodns., Hollywood, Calif., 1965-75; mng. gen. ptnr. Encino Wireless #1, 1994—; CEO Midway TV Inc., 1995; v.p. nat. bus. affairs MMA Internat., 1997; v.p. mktg. Kidkritter, Inc., 1998; sr. prodn. exec. Alpine Pictures Inc., 1999, GigaPix Studios, Inc., 2005. Author: (series) Dial Hot Line, 1967, (screenplays) Heads Across the Border, 1968, The Fool Card, 1970, Probable Cause, 1972; author, sr. prodn. exec. (screenplays) The Home, 2003; co-author: The Fedak File, 1995; albums include: Conrad Marshall Quintet, 1991, Song Shark, 1992. Campaign vol. Dem. Ctrl. Com., L.A., 1976, Rep. Ctrl. Com., 1994. Mem. Screen Actors Guild, Internat. Platform Assn. Avocations: poetry, song writing, club singing, philosophy, theology.

MARSHALL, CONSUELO BLAND, federal judge; b. Knoxville, Tenn., Sept. 28, 1936; d. Clyde Theodore and Annie (Brown) Arnold; m. George Edward Marshall, Aug. 30, 1959; children: Michael Edward, Laurie Ann. AA, L.A. City Coll., 1956; BA, Howard U., 1958, LLB, 1961. Bar: Calif. 1962. Dep. atty., City of LA, 1962-67; assoc. Cochran & Atkins, LA, 1968-70; commr. LA Superior Ct., 1971-76; judge Inglewood Mcpl. Ct., 1976-77, LA Superior Ct., 1977-80, US Dist. Ct. (ctrl dist.) Calif., LA, 1980—, chief judge, 2001—. Lectr. U.S. Information Agy. in Yugoslavia, Greece and Italy, 1984, in Nigera and Ghana, 1991, in Ghana, 1992. Contbr. articles to profl. jours.; notes editor Law Jour. Howard U. Mem. adv. bd. Richstone Child Abuse Center. Recipient Judicial Excellence award Criminal Cts. Bar Assn., 1992, Ernestine Stalhut award; named

Criminal Ct. Judge of Yr., U.S. Dist. Ct., 1997; inducted into Langston Hall of Fame, 2000, Outstanding Jurist Award, LA County Bar Assn., 2005; rsch. fellow Howard U. Law Sch., 1959-60. Mem. State Bar Calif., Century City Bar Assn., Calif. Women Lawyers Assn., Calif. Assn. Black Lawyers, Calif. Judges Assn., Black Women Lawyers Assn., Los Angeles County Bar Assn., Nat. Assn. Women Judges, NAACP, Urban League, Beta Phi Sigma. Office: US Dist Ct 312 N Spring St Los Angeles CA 90012-4701

MARSHALL, DALE ROGERS, former academic administrator, political scientist, educator; b. Mar. 22, 1937; m. Donald J. Marshall; children: Jessica, Cynthia, Clayton. BA in Govt., Cornell U., 1959; MA in Polit. Sci., U. Calif., Berkeley, 1960; PhD in Polit. Sci. with distinction, UCLA, 1969. Lectr. in polit. sci. UCLA, 1969-70, U. Calif., Berkeley, 1970-72, from asst. prof. to prof. Davis, 1972-86, faculty asst. to vice chancellor acad. affairs, 1980-82, assoc. dean Coll. Letters and Scis., 1983-86; acting pres. Wellesley (Mass.) Coll., 1987-88, dean of coll., prof. polit. sci., 1986-92; pres. Wheaton (Mass.) Coll., 1992—2004; Fulbright scholar Kalmyk State U., Russia, 2006. Mem. exec. bd. Calif. Assembly Fellowship Program, 1980-86; bd. trustees, bd. overseers Newton-Wellesley Hosp., 1989-93; bd. trustees Cornell U., Ithaca, N.Y., 1983-93, chair Cornell Fund, co-chair Coll. Arts and Scis. Capital Campaign, 1990-93; bd. trustees New Eng. Zenith Fund, New Eng. Mut. Life Ins. Co., 1995—; bd. dirs. Am. Student Assistance Guarantor, Am. Student Assistance Corp, 1994-2001. Author: (with John C. Bollens) Guide to Participation: Field Work, Role Playing Cases and Other Forms, 1973, (with Roger Montgomery) Housing Policy for the 80's, 1980, (with Rufus P. Browning and David H. Tabb) Protest is Not Enough: The Struggle of Blacks and Hispanics for Equality in Urban Politics, 1984 (APSA Ralph J. Bunche award for best book on ethnic rels. 1985, Gladys Kammerer award for best book in Am. policy 1985); editor: Urban Policy Making, 1979, (with David K. Leonard) Institutions of Rural Development for the Poor: Decentralization and Organizatonal Linkages, 1982, (with Rufus P. Browning and David H. Tabb, co-editor), Racial Politics in American Cities, 1990, 3d edit., 2003; mem. editl. bd. Am. Polit. Sci. Rev., 1972-76, Pub. Adminstrn. Rev., 1985-86; contbr. articles to profl. jours. Woodrow Wilson fellow, 1959-60, Calif. Regents fellow, 1966-67, 67-68; NSF grantee, 1976-78, 79-80; recipient Disting. Teaching award Significant Contbn. to Status of Women citation Chancellor's Com. on Status of Women at U. Calif. at Davis, 1978. Mem. Am. Polit. Sci. Assn. (mem. exec. coun. 1974-76, v.p. 1985-86, mem. nominating com. 1988-90), Western Polit. Sci. Assn. (mem. exec. coun. 1973-75, pres. 1984-85), Nat. Acad. Pub. Adminstrn., Nat. Assn. Ind. Colls. and Univs. (bd. dirs.), Assn. Ind. Colls. and Univs. Mass. (exec. com.), Mortar Bd., Phi Beta Kappa, Phi Kappa Phi. *

MARSHALL, DANTE, lawyer; JD, Ohio State U., Columbus, 2003. Law clk. Law Firm Byron L. Potts & Co., LPA, Columbus, Ohio, 2001—03; atty. Law Firm of DMEG, Atlanta, 2003—. Mem.: ABA, Cobb County Bar Assn., Black Entertainment and Sports Law Assn., Atlanta Bar Assn., Ga. State Bar Assn. Office Phone: 404-320-5212. Office Fax: 404-320-5214. E-mail: info@dmeglaw.com.

MARSHALL, DAVID B., structural ceramics professional; BSc, Monash U., Melbourne, Australia, 1971, PhD, 1975. Rsch. fellow dept. applied physics U. NSW, Australia, 1975—79; assoc. rsch. engr. dept. materials sci. and mineral engrng. U. Calif., Berkeley, 1979—83; mgr. structural ceramics dept. Teledyne Sci. and Imaging (formerly Rockwell Sci. Co.), 1983—. Adj. prof. materials dept. U. Calif., Santa Barbara, 1988-. Contbr. articles to profl. jours. Fellow Am. Ceramic Soc. (editor jour., Ross Coffin Purdy award 1989, Fulrath award 1991, J.J. Jeppson award 1996, Sosman award 1998); mem. NAE. Achievements include patents in field. Office: Materials Divsn Teledyne Sci and Imaging 1049 Camino Dos Rios Thousand Oaks CA 91360-2362 Office Phone: 805-373-4170. Office Fax: 805-373-4017. E-mail: dmarshall@rwsc.com. *

MARSHALL, DEBORAH JILL, immunologist; b. Manhasset, NY, June 17, 1970; d. Gary Everett and Gary Everett Marshall; m. Jonathan Henry Alt, May 26, 2001; children: Jordyn Elizabeth Alt, Hailey Samantha Alt. PhD, U. Pa., Phila., 1997. Postdoctoral fellow Harvard U., Boston, 1997—2000; dir. immunotherapy Cytomatrix, Woburn, Mass., 2000—02; sr. rsch. scientist Centocor, Inc., Radnor, Pa., 2002—. Contbr. articles to sci. jours. Mem.: AACR. Democrat. Jewish. Home Phone: 215-628-8038; Office Phone: 610-240-8477. Personal E-mail: dmarshall670@hotmail.com.

MARSHALL, DEBRA LYNN, secondary school educator; b. Charleston, W.Va., July 7, 1956; d. James L. Marshall and Lena B. Bailey. BA in English cum laude, Ohio State U., Columbus, 1998; MEd in English, Ohio State U., 1999. Tchr. H.S. English Piqua (Ohio) City Sch., 1999—2003, Moreno Valley (Calif.) Unified Schs., 2003—. Adj. faculty Edison C.C., Piqua, 2001—03; coord. Ohio Writing Project, Piqua, 2000—02. Author: (short stories) Super Boy, 2003 (Hon. Mention award Sinclair C.C., 2003). Mem. pub. rels. team Spring Arts Show The Piqua (Ohio) Arts Coun., 2003. Mem.: NEA, Nat. Coun. Tchrs. English, Calif. Assn. Tchrs. English, Calif. Tchrs. Assn. Avocations: dog training, painting, cello. Office: CanyonSprings High School 23100 Cougar Canyon Dr Moreno Valley CA 92557 Office Phone: 951-571-4760. E-mail: marshalld4@adelphia.net.

MARSHALL, DONALD E., mathematics professor; s. Donald and Jeanne Cawley Marshall; m. Marianne Jensen, Sept. 2, 1972; children: Hans-Peter, Kristen Jensen, Bjorn. PhD, UCLA, LA, 1976. Prof. math. U. Wash., Seattle, 1976—, chair, dept math., 1998—2001; vis. prof. Mittag-Leffler Inst., Royal Swedish Acad. of Scis., Djursholm, Sweden, 1982—83, U. Bergen, Norway, 2003—04. Cons. Jet Propulsion Lab, Pasadena, Calif., 1975. Contbr. scientific papers. Recipient Disting. Svc. Award, UCLA, 1976; grantee Royalty Rsch. Fund, U. Wash., 1995—96, 2002—03; scholar Nat. Merit Scholarship, 1966; NATO Postdoctoral Fellowship, NSF, Principal Investigator grant, 1977—, Thord-Gray Fellowship, American-Scandinavian Found., 1982-1983. Mem.: Am. Math. Soc. Avocations: sailing, hiking, soccer. Office: Univ Wash Box 354350 Dept Math Seattle WA 98195-4350 Home Phone: 206-365-3767; Office Phone: 206-543-9352. Office Fax: 206-543-0397. Business E-Mail: marshall@math.washington.edu.

MARSHALL, DONALD GLENN, English language and literature educator; b. Long Beach, Calif., Sept. 9, 1943; s. Albert Louis and Margaret Corinne (Morrison) M.; m. Kathleen Bonann, June 21, 1975; children: Stephanie Deborah, Zachary Louis AB summa cum laude, Harvard U., 1965; MPhil, Yale U., 1969, PhD, 1971. Asst. prof. English UCLA, 1969-75; from assoc. prof. to prof. English U. Iowa, Iowa City, 1975-90; honors dir. U. Iowa Coll Liberal Arts, 1981-85; prof. English dept. U. Ill., Chgo., 1990—2003, head dept., 1990—2000; prof. Great Books Pepperdine U., Malibu, Calif., 2003—. Editor: Philosophy as Literature/Literature as Philosophy, 1986, The Force of Tradition: Response and Resistance in Literature, Religion, and Cultural Studies, 2005; compiler: Contemporary Critical Theory: A Selective Bibliography, 1993; translator: (with Joel Weinsheimer) Truth and Method by Hans-Georg Gadamer, 1989; contbr. articles and revs. to profl. jours. Recipient Bell prize Harvard U., 1965, Webster prize Yale U., 1967; NEH Younger Humanist fellow, 1973-74; grantee UCLA, U. Iowa Mem.: MLA, Ill. Humanities Coun. (bd. dirs. 1994—2000, Chgo. Humanities Festival bd. dir. 1997—2003), The Poetry Found. (trustee 1996—, pres. 1998—2000), Conf. Christianity and Lit. (bd. dirs. 2000—03). Democrat. Roman Catholic. Office: Pepperdine U Divsn Humanities and Tchr Edn 24255 Pacific Coast Hwy Malibu CA 90263 Office Phone: 310-506-7654. Business E-Mail: Donald.Marshall@pepperdine.edu.

MARSHALL, DOUGLAS WILLIAM, health research administrator, educator; b. Indpls., July 1, 1943; s. William Pryor and Virginia (Guthrie) M.; m. Heidi Christina Amenda, May 30, 1985; 1 child, W. Parker. BA, Denison U., Granville, Ohio, 1965; AM, U. Mich., 1967, PhD, 1976. Western field mgr. U. Mich. Alumni Assn., San Francisco, 1967-69; assoc. curator W.L. Clements Libr. Am. History U. Mich., Ann Arbor, 1970-82; project dir. Campbell-Ewald Co., Warren, Mich., 1982-83; sr. account exec. N.W. Ayer, Inc., Detroit, 1984; mgr. strategic planning GM, Detroit, 1985-91; program mgr. GM Internat., Detroit, 1991-96; CEO Onkoservices, Detroit, 1996-97; v.p. new bus. devel. Innovative Solutions in Healthcare, Detroit, 1997-99; prin. Blitz and Assoc. LLC, 2000—05; v.p. bus. devel. Idetix Inc., 2005—06; dir. vehicle mktg. Al-Ahel Co., 2006—. Adj. assoc. prof. radiation oncology Sch. Medicine, Wayne State U., Detroit, 1996-2000; coord. program in history of discovery U. Mich., Ann Arbor, 1973-81. Co-author: (with H.H. Peckham) Campaigns of the American Revolution: An Atlas Manuscript Maps, 1976; exec. editor Terrae Incognitae: Annals of the Soc. for the History of Discoveries, 1975-82; editor: Research Catalog of Maps of America to 1860, 4 vols., 1972; writer, narrator: (ednl. TV series) Maps: Horizons to Knowledge, 1981. Dir. Gt. Lakes region Am. Cancer Soc. Found., 1996-05; mem. dean's adv. bd. Rackham Grad. Sch., U. Mich., 1999-06; mem. S.E. Mich. strategic planning bd. United Found., Detroit, 1982-83; trustee City of Grosse Pointe Found., 2004—; mem. recruiting bd. USN, Great Lakes, 2007-. Rsch. fellow Nat. Geog. Soc., 1977; recipient Bicentennial award Bicentennial Commn., State of Mich., 1974; Fulbright lectr. U.S. Fulbright Commn., Helsinki U., 1980-81; William Andrews Clark postdoctoral fellow UCLA, 1979. Mem. Mich. Map Soc. (pres. 1984-85), Soc. for the History of Discoveries (coun. 1979-81), Bohemian Club Calif. Episcopalian. Home: 545 University Pl Grosse Pointe MI 48230-1639 also: 7090 Windemere PO Box 152 Harbor Springs MI 49740 Office: 21 Kercheval Ave Ste 270 Grosse Pointe MI 48236 Personal E-mail: dwmarshall652003@yahoo.com.

MARSHALL, EDITH, veterinarian; d. J. Markham and Cheryl C. Marshall. BS in Animal Sci., Cornell U., Ithaca, NY, 1996; DVM, Wash. State U., Pullman, 2000; MS in Preventive Vet. Medicine, U. Calif., Davis, 2004. Lic. vet. Calif., 2003, accredited vet. US Dept. Agr., 2000. Analyst, rsch. mgr. ctr. animal disease modeling and surveillance U. Calif., Davis, 2004—; emergency vet. Ohlone Vet. Emergency Clinic, Fremont, Calif., 2005—. Cons. in field. Vol. rural area vet. svc. Humane Soc. US, Guatemala, 2004—05. Recipient Outstanding Student award, Am. Soc. Animal Sci., 1994, 1995, 1996; scholar, Pfizer, 1999; Frontiers in Vet. Medicine fellowship, Geraldine R. Dodge Found., 1997, Morrison scholarship, Cornell U., 1994, 1995, 1996. Mem.: AVMA, Calif. Vet. Med. Assn. Democrat. Episcopalian. Avocations: hiking, backpacking, travel, dance, fly fishing. Home Phone: 530-753-1635; Office Phone: 530-297-4621. Business E-Mail: edie.marshall@gmail.com.

MARSHALL, ELAINE FOLK, state official; b. Lineboro, Md., Nov. 18, 1945; d. Donald and Pauline Folk; m. Bill Holdford; 5 stepchildren. BS in Textiles and Clothing, U. Md., 1968; JD, Campbell U., 1981; D (hon.), Meredith Coll., 2004, Lees McRae Coll., 2004. Bar: N.C., U.S. Dist. Ct. (ea. and mid. dists.), U.S. Ct. Appeals (4th cir.), U.S. Supreme Ct. Tchr., 1968—75; owner retail bus., 1968-79; assoc. Bain Law Firm, Lillington, NC, 1981-84; ptnr. Bain & Marshall, Lillington, 1985-92, Marshall & Marshall, Lillington, 1993-96; sec. state State of N.C., Raleigh, 1997—. Legal advisor Bus. and Profl. Women, N.C., 1982-90; mem., N.C.State Senate from 15th dist., 1993-94, N.C. Capital Planning Commn., 1993-94, 1997-, N.C. Cts. Commn., 1993-94, bd. mem. Nat. Electronic Commerce Coord. Coun., 2001-03, 2005—, v.p., 2005-06, bd. mem. Nat. Assn. Secretaries of State, 2001-04. Bd. dirs. Harnett County United Way, 1987-97, N.C. 4-H Devel. Fund, Inc., 1990—, N.C. Rural Econ. Devel. Fund, 1993-95, N.C. Bd. Econ. Devel., 1993-94, 97—, N.C. Ctr. Pub. Policy Rsch., 1994-99, N.C. Justice Acad. Found., 1994-98; mem. Divine St. United Meth. Ch.; founding chmn., hon. chmn. Harnett HelpNet Children, 1992—; trustee Meredith Coll., 1997-2002. Recipient N.C. Friends Ext. award, 1992, Spl. Achievement award, N.C. Acad. Trial Lawyers, 2000, Alumni of Yr. award, N.C. 4-H Found., Lifetime Achievement award, 2003, Best of Breed, In the Arena awards, Ctr. Digital Govt., 2002, Top 25 award, Govt. Tech. Mag., 2003, Atty. of Yr. award, N.C. Assn. Women Attorneys, 2004, Women in Bus. award RBC Centura Bank and Triangle Bus. Jour., 2005, Hon. Gold Record award Recording Industry Am., 2005, U.L. Lab. award, 2005, Get Real award Internat. Anti Counterfeit Coalition, 2005. Fellow N.C. Inst. Polit. Leadership (bd. dirs. 1996—); mem. Women's Forum N.C., Gamma Sigma Delta, Delta Kappa Gamma. Democrat. Office: 2 S Salisbury St Raleigh NC 27601 Office Phone: 919-807-2005. Business E-Mail: emarshall@sosnc.com. *

MARSHALL, ELLEN RUTH, lawyer; b. NYC, Apr. 23, 1949; d. Louis and Faith (Gladstone) M. AB, Yale U., 1971; JD, Harvard U., 1974. Bar: Calif. 1975, D.C. 1981, N.Y. 1989. Assoc. McKenna & Fitting, LA, 1975-80; ptnr. McKenna, Conner & Cuneo, LA and Orange County, Calif., 1980-88, Morrison & Foerster, LLP, Orange County, 1988—2003, Manatt, Phelps & Phillips LLP, Orange County, 2003—. Mem. ABA (bus. law sect., mem. savs. inst. com., mem. asset securitization com., tax sect., mem. employee benefits com.), Orange County Bar Assn., Center Club (Costa Mesa, Calif.), Yale Club (N.Y.C.). Office: Manatt Phelps & Phillips LLP 695 Town Ctr Dr Costa Mesa CA 92626

MARSHALL, FRANCIS JOSEPH, aerospace engineer; b. NYC, Sept. 5, 1923; s. Francis Joseph and Mary Gertrude (Leary) M.; m. Joan Eager, June 14, 1952; children— Peter, Colin, Stephen, Dana. BS in Mech. Engring, CCNY, 1948; MS, Rensselaer Poly. Inst., 1950; Dr. Eng. Sci., N.Y. U., 1955. Engr. Western Union Co., NYC, 1948, Gen. Electric Co., Schenectady, 1948-50; engr. Wright-Aero Corp., Woodridge, NJ, 1950-52; group leader Lab. for Applied Scis., U. Chgo., 1955-60; instr. Ill. Inst. Tech., 1957-59; prof. Sch. Aeros. and Astronautics, Purdue U., West Lafayette, Ind., 1960—. Engr. U.S. Naval Underseas Warfare Center, Pasadena, Calif., 1966-68; faculty fellow NASA-Langley, 1969-70; vis. prof. Inst. Tech. Mara-Midwest Univs. Consortium for Internat. Activities, Malayasia, 1989. Contbr. articles to profl. jours. Served with U.S. Army, 1943-46. Decorated Combat Inf. badge.; Rsch. grantee NASA, 1970-76; Fulbright scholar, Turkey, 1988-89. Assoc. fellow AIAA; mem. Am. Soc. Engring. Edn., AAUP. Home: 120 Leslie Ave West Lafayette IN 47906-2410 Office: Sch Aeros and Astronautics Purdue U West Lafayette IN 47907

MARSHALL, FRANK W., film producer, director; b. LA, Sept. 13, 1946; m. Kathleen Kennedy. Student, UCLA. Location mgr.: The Last Picture Show, 1971, What's Up Doc?, 1972; assoc. prodr.: Paper Moon, 1973, Daisy Miller, 1974, At Long Last Love, 1975. Nickelodeon, 1976, The Driver, 1978; line prodr.: Orson Welles' The Other Side of the Wind (unreleased), Marin Scorsese's The Last Waltz, 1977; prodr.: (films) Raiders of the Lost Ark, 1981 (Academy award nomination for best picture 1981), Noises Off, 1992; (with Steven Spielberg) Poltergeist, 1982; (with Spielberg, Quincy Jones, and Kathleen Kennedy) The Color Purple, 1985 (Academy award nomination for best picture 1985), (with Kathleen Kennedy and Kane Startz) Indian in a Cupboard, 1995; (with Spielberg and Kennedy) Empire of the Sun, 1987, Always, 1989; (with Robert Watts) Who Framed Roger Rabbit, 1988; (with Kennedy and Gerald R. Molen) Hook, 1991; (with Kennedy) Milk Money, 1994, The Sixth Sense, 1999, Snow Falling on Cedars, 1999, A Map of the World, 1999, Signs, 2002, The Young Black Stallion, 2003, The Bourne Supremacy, 2004, Roving Mars, 2006; exec. prodr.: (films) The Warriors, 1979, Twilight Zone-The Movie, 1983; (with George Lucas) Indiana Jones and the Temple of Doom, 1984; (with Kennedy and Spielberg) Gremlins, 1984, The Goonies, 1985, Back to the Future, 1985, Young Sherlock Holmes, 1985, *batteries not included, 1987, Dad, 1989, Back to the Future Part II, 1989, Gremlins 2: The New Batch, 1990, Back to the Future Part III, 1990, Joe Versus the Volcano, 1990, Cape Fear, 1991, We're Back! A Dinosaur's Story, 1993; (with Kennedy) Fandango, 1985; (with Kennedy, Spielberg, and David Kirschner) An American Tail, 1986; (with Kennedy and Art Levinson) The Money Pit, 1986; (with Kennedy, Spielberg, Peter Guber, and Jon Peters) Innerspace, 1987; (with Kennedy, Lucas, and Spielberg) The Land Before Time, 1988; (with Kennedy and Lucas) Indiana Jones and the Last Crusade, 1989; (with Kennedy and Kirschner) An American Tail: Fievel Goes West, 1991; (with Chris Meledandri) Swing Kids, 1993; (with Kennedy and Molen) A Far Off Place, 1993, Swing Kids, 1993, Congo, 1995, The Sports Pages, 2001, The Bourne Identity, 2002, Mr. 3000, 2004; exec. prodr. (with Spielberg, Robert W. Cort, and Ted Field), dir.: Arachnophobia, 1990; dir.: Alive, 1993, Congo, 1995, Eight Below, 2006; exec. producer: TV Roger Rabbit and the Secret of Toontown; prodr., dir. TV Johnny Bago.

MARSHALL, GAILEN DAUGHERTY, JR., allergist, educator; b. Houston, Sept. 9, 1950; s. Gailen D. and Evelyn C. (Gresham) M.; m. Elizabeth M. Marek, Nov. 5, 1978; children: Sarah Elizabeth, Jonathan David, Rebecca Marie. BS, U. Houston, 1972; MS, Tex. A&M U., 1975; PhD, U. Tex., 1979, MD, 1984. Rsch. sci. U. Tex., Galveston, 1981-84; rsch. fellow U. Iowa, Iowa City, 1985-86; lab. dir. Biotherapeutics Inc., Memphis, 1986-88; chief med. resident Bapt. Meml. Hosp., Memphis, 1988-89; assoc. dir. Rsch. for Health Inc., Houston, 1989-90; dir. divsn. allergy and immunology U. Tex., Houston, 1990—2004, clin. asst. prof. medicine, 1990-91, asst. prof. medicine, 1991—98, assoc. prof. medicine and pathology, 1998—2003, prof., 2003—04; vice chair medicine, dir. divsn. clin. immunology and allergy U. Miss. Med. Ctr., Jackson, Miss., 2004—, prof. medicine and pediatrics. Mem. sci. adv. com. Carrington Labs., Dallas, 1992-94; mem. Merck Rhinitis Adv. Bd., 2002-05, Genentech/Novartis Adv. Bd., 2003—. Mem. editl. bd. Molecular Biotherapy, 1992-93, Cancer Biotherapy, 1994-96, Allergy Procs., 1994-2003, Annals Allergy, Asthma and Immunology, 1995-99, Jour. Interferon Cytokin Rsch., 1999-2005, Clin. Immunology, 2001-05, Jour. Clin. Immunology, 2002-05, Cellular Molecular Allergy, 2003-05; editor-in-chief Annals of Allergy, Asthma and Immunology, 2006—; contbr. articles to profl. jours. Judge Greater Houston Sci. Fair, 1992—; adv. bd. Merck Rhinitis, 2002-04, Grenentech Worch's, 2003-05. Fellow ACP, Am. Coll. Allergy and Immunology, Am. Acad. Allergy-Immunology (chair com.); mem. Tex. Allergy-Immunology Soc. (chair com., bd. dirs. 1999-2002), Greater Houston Allergy Soc. Republican. Baptists. Avocations: classical music, fishing. Office: U Miss Med Ctr 2500 N State St Jackson MS 39216 Home Phone: 601-853-9872; Office Phone: 601-815-5527. Business E-Mail: gmarshall@umsmed.edu.

MARSHALL, GARRY K. (GARRY KENT MARSCIARELLI), film producer, director, writer; b. NYC, Nov. 13, 1934; m. Barbara Marshall, Mar. 1963; children: Lori, Kathleen, Scott. BS, Northwestern U. Writer Jack Paar Show, Joey Bishop Show, Danny Thomas Show; writer (TV series) Make Room For Daddy, 1953, The Dick Van Dyke Show, 1961, The Lucy Show, 1962, Gomer Pyle, USMC, 1964, I Spy, 1965, Barefoot in the Park, 1970, Love, American Style, 1969; writer (TV films) Sheriff Who, 1967 (also prodr.), The Murdocks and the McClays, 1970; writer, creator, prodr. (TV series) Hey Landlord, 1966; writer, creator (TV film) Wednesday Night Out, 1972; dir., exec. prodr. (TV series) The Odd Couple, 1970; creator, dir., prodr. Evil Roy Slade, 1972; creator, writer, exec. prodr., dir. Happy Days, 1974, Laverne and Shirley, 1976 (co-creator), Mork and Mindy, 1978; writer, prodr.(films) How Sweet It Is, 1968, The Grasshopper, 1970; screenwriter, dir. (films) Flamingo Kid, 1984, The Other Sister, 1999; dir. (films) Young Doctors in Love, 1982 (also exec. prodr.), Nothing in Common, 1987 (also prodr.), The Lottery, 1987, Overboard, 1987, Beaches, 1988, Pretty Woman, 1990, Frankie & Johnny, 1991 (also prodr.), Exit to Eden, 1994 (also prodr.), Dear God, 1996, Runaway Bride, 1999, The Princess Diaries, 2001, Raising Helen, 2004, The Princess Diaries 2:Royal Engagement, 2004; dir. (TV series) Me and the Chimp, 1972 (also creator, exec. prodr.), Blansky's Beauties, 1977 (also prodr.), Herndon, 1983 (also exec. prodr.), Murphy Brown, 1988; creator, dir., exec. prodr. (TV films) Dominic's Dream, 1974; actor (film) The Phony American, 1961, Maryjane, 1968, Psych-Out, 1968, Grand Theft Auto, 1977, Lost In America, 1985, Jumpin' Jack Flash, 1986, Secret Agent OO Soul, 1990, Soapdish, 1991, A League of Their Own, 1992, Statistically Speaking, 1995, With Friends Like These, 1998, Never Been Kissed, 1999, This Space Between Us, 2000, It's a Shame About Ray, 2000, Can't Be Heaven, 2000, Tomcats, 2001, The Hollywood Sign, 2001, (voice) The Majestic, 2001, Orange County, 2002, Mother Ghost, 2002, Devil's Knight, 2003, The Long Ride Home, 2003, They Call Him Sasquatch, 2003, Lucky 13, 2005, (voice) Chicken Little, 2005; actor (TV films) But Seriously, Folks, 1986, The Last Shot, 1993, The Twilight of the Golds, 1997 (also exec. prodr.), Frank Capra's American Dream, 1997, CHiPs '99, 1998; exec. prodr. (TV series) Who's Watching the Kids, 1978, Angie, 1979, Joanie Loves Chachi, 1982; (TV films) Beanes of Boston, 1979; guest appearances include Dick Van Dyke Show, 1965, 1966, Hey Landlord, 1967, The Odd Couple, 1974, Happy Days, 1975, Laverne & Shirley, 1976, Vega$, 1980, Murphy Brown, 1994-1997 (several episodes), The Naked Truth, 1997, The Simpsons (voice) 1999, Mad TV, 2000, Three Sisters, 2001, 2002, Monk, 2002, Sabrina, The Teenage Witch, 2002, Father of the Pride (voice), 2004, Unscripted, 2005, and several others. Office: Pkwy Prodns 10202 Washington Blvd Culver City CA 90232-3119

MARSHALL, GARY S., lawyer; b. Charlottesville, Va., 1952; AB magna cum laude, Princeton U., 1974; JD, Coll. William and Mary, Williamsburg, Va., 1979. Bar: Va. 1979, US Dist. Ct. Ea. Dist. Va. 1979, US Dist. Ct. We. Dist. Va. 1980, US Ct. Appeals 4th Cir. 1979, US Ct. Appeals 8th Cir. 1988, US Ct. Appeals 7th Cir. 1997. Ptnr. McGuireWoods LLP, Richmond, Va., 1987—, chair firm labor & employment dept. Adj. prof. labor law U. Richmond, 1984—87. Mem.: ABA (mem. sect. labor & employment 1994—). Office: McGuireWoods LLP One James Ctr 901 E Cary St Richmond VA 23219-4030 Office Phone: 804-775-1013. Office Fax: 804-698-2104. Business E-Mail: gmarshall@mcguirewoods.com.

MARSHALL, GERALD FRANCIS, optical engineer, consultant, physicist; b. Seven Kings, Eng., Feb. 26, 1929; BSc in Physics, London U., 1952. Physicist Morganite Internat., London, 1954—59; sr. rsch. devel. engr. Ferranti Ltd., Edinburgh, Scotland, 1959—67; project mgr. Diffraction Limited Inc., Bedford, Mass., 1967—69; dir. engrng. Medical Lasers, Inc., Burlington, Mass., 1969—71; staff cons. Speedring Systems, Troy, Mich., 1971—76; dir. optical engrng. Energy Conversion Devices, Inc., Troy, Mich., 1976—87; sr. tech. staff specialist Kaiser Electronics, San Jose, Calif., 1987—89; cons. in optics design and engring., 1989—. Editor, contbg. author: Laser Beam Scanning, 1985, Optical Scanning, 1991, Handbook of Optical and Laser Scanning, 2004. Fellow: Inst. Physics, SPIE - Internat. Soc. Optical Engrng. (bd. dirs. 1991—93), Optical Soc. Am. Achievements include patents in field. Home and Office: 410 Dusenbury St Niles MI 49120-1468 Office Phone: 269-687-1692.

MARSHALL, GERALD LEE, mathematician, educator; b. Franklin County, NC, June 27, 1947; s. George Eugene Marshall and Roberta Odell Perry; m. Judy Faye Beck, Nov. 24, 1991; 1 child, Kera Beck; m. Karen Louise Gebhart, June 19, 1971 (div.); children: Katharine Elizabeth, Katrina Marie. BSChE, N.C. State U., 1969; ThM in Christian Theology, Luther Rice Sem., 1975; MLS, Fla. State U., 1977; MDiv in New Testament Greek, Luther Rice Sem., 1976, DMin Theol. Libr., 1979; AA, C.C. Chgo., Wiesbaden, Germany, 1985; MA in Math., U. Ala., 1997; PhD in Math. Edn., Ill. State U., 2000. Ordained Christian min. So. Bapt. Conv.,

1985. Pastor Aschaffenburg Bapt. Ch., Germany, 1985—87; adj. lectr. C.C. Chgo., Wiesbaden, Germany, 1984—87; min. edn. Hillsboro Heights Bapt. Ch., Huntsville, Ala., 1987—89; supr. environ. svcs. Huntsville Hosp. Sys., 1989—98; adj. instr. Calhoun C.C., Decatur, Ala., 1989—98, Heartland C.C., Bloomington, Ill., 1998—2000; head dept. math. Tri-County Tech. Coll., Pendleton, SC, 2001—02, v.p., 2002—04, pres., 2007—. V.p. Tri-County Tech. Edn. Assn., Pendleton, SC, 2002—04; master presenter Nat. Inst. for Staff and Orgnl. Devel., Austin, Tex., 2002; presenter S.C. Tech. Edn. Assn., Myrtle Beach, SC, 2002—07. Contbr. articles to profl. jours. Capt. USAF, 1969—72, U.S. and Thailand. Grantee NSF, 2000—02, Sustainable Univs. Initiatives, 2002. Mem.: S.C. Math. Assn. Two-Yr. Colls. (pres. 2004—07), S.C. Coun. Tchrs. Math., Assn. Math. Tchr. Educators, Am. Math. Assn. Two-Year Colls., Nat. Coun. Tchrs. Math., Math. Assn. Am. Southern Baptist. Avocations: travel, mathematics history. Home: 2701 Bellview Rd Anderson SC 29621 Office: Tri-County Tech Coll P O Box 587 Pendleton SC 29670 Office Phone: 864-646-1368. Business E-Mail: gmarshal@tctc.edu.

MARSHALL, GRAYSON WILLIAM, JR., materials scientist, biomedical engineer, health sciences educator, dentist; b. Balt., Feb. 12, 1943; s. Grayson William and Muriel Marie Marshall; m. Sally Jean Rimkus, July 4, 1970; children: Grayson W. III, Jonathan Charles. BS in Metall. Engring., Va. Poly. Inst., 1965; PhD in Materials Sci., Northwestern U., 1972, DDS, 1986; MPH, U. Calif., Berkeley, 1992. Cert. dentist. Rsch. assoc., design and devel. ctr. Northwestern U., Evanston, Ill., 1972-73, NIH fellow, 1973, instr. Dental and Med. Schs. Chgo., 1973-74, asst. prof. Dental Sch., 1974-78, assoc. prof. Dental Sch. and Grad. Sch., 1978-87; prof. preventive and restorative dental scis. U. Calif., San Francisco, 1987—, chief biomaterials sect., 1988-92, chmn. biomaterials and bioengring. divsn., 1992—, vice chmn. rsch., 2005—. Chmn. oral and craniaofacial scis. program U. Calif., San Francisco, 2002—, UCSF Grad. Coun., 2003-05; guest scientist Lawrence Livermore Nat. Lab., 1989-2000, Lawrence Berkeley Nat. Lab., 1989—; cons. oral biology and medicine study sect. NIH, 1988-92; dir. Clin. Rsch. Unit, 1992-96, Dentist-Sci. Award Program, 1996-2004, Integrated DDS-PhD Program, 1996—, Comprehensive Oral Health Rsch. Tng. Program, 2001—. Contbr. articles to profl. jours. and books. Mem. City of Larkspur Heritage Preservation Bd., 1998—, chmn., 2006—, mem. centennial com., 2007—. Recipient Spl. Dental Rsch. award Nat. Inst. Dental Rsch., 1975, Rsch. Lectr. award U. Calif., San Francisco, 1994, Wilmer Souder Disting. Scientist award, 2007; vis. fellow U. Melbourne, Australia, 1981. Fellow: AAAS, Acad. Dental Materials (exec. sec. 1983—85, chmn. credentials 1984—91, bd. dirs. 1985—93, mem. editl. bd. Scanning Microscopy 1987—93, sec. 1988—91, pres. 1991—93, Cells and Materials 1992—2000, sect. editor 1993—2000, Jour. Oral Rehab. 1994—, Dent Mater 1998—, Am. Jour. Dentistry 2004—), Am. Coll. Dentists, Internat. Coll. Dentists; mem.: AIME, APHA, ADA (assoc. editor Jour. ADA 2002—05), U.S. Power Squadrons, U.S. Naval Inst., Calif. Pub. Health Assn.-North, Calif. Acad. Scis., N.Y. Acad. Scis., Am. Assn. Dental Rsch. (bd. dirs. 1996—98, San Francisco coun. 1997—2007, v.p. 2007—), Microscopy Soc. Am., Am. Soc. Metals, Am. Coll. Sports Medicine, Internat. Assn. Dental Rsch. (Chgo. sect. officer 1978—80, dental materials coun. 1990—96, pres. 1998—99, Wilmer Souder Disting. Scientist award 2007), Soc. Biomaterials, Am. Dental Edn. Assn. (sect. officer 1981—83), Omicron Kappa Upsilon, Sigma Gamma Epsilon, Sigma Xi, Alpha Sigma Mu. Avocations: swimming, sailing, hiking, travel. Office: U Calif Dept Preven & Restor Dental Scis San Francisco CA 94143-0758 Office Phone: 415-476-9119. Business E-Mail: gw.marshall@ucsf.edu, gwmarshall@lbl.gov.

MARSHALL, GREGG, men's college basketball coach; b. Greenwood, SC; m. Lynn Munday; children: Kellen, Maggie. BA in Econs./Bus., Randolph-Macon Coll., 1985; M in Sport Mgmt., U. Richmond, 1987. Asst. coach Randolph-Macon Coll., Ashland, Va., 1985—87, Belmont Abbey Coll., 1987—88, Coll. Charleston, 1988—96, Marshall U., 1996—98; head coach Winthrop U., Rock Hill, SC, 1998—2007, Wichita St. U., Kans., 2007—. Named Big South Conf. Coach of Yr., 1999, 2003, 2005. Office: Wichita State U Mens Basketball 1845 Fairmount St Wichita KS 67260 *

MARSHALL, HELEN M., county official; b. NYC, Sept. 30, 1929; m. Donald E. Marshall; children: Donald Jr., Agnes Marie. BA, Queens Coll.; student, L.I. U. Dir. Langston Hughes Libr., 1969, Elmcor Testing Assessment and Placement Program; mem. NY State Assembly, Dist. 35, 1983—91; city councilwoman Dist. 21, NYC, 1992—2001; borough pres. Queens, 2001—. Chmn. stds. and ethics com., mem. edn., housing and bldg. and environ. protection coms. Dem. nat. committeewoman, N.Y., 1975; del. Dem. Nat. Conv., 1980; mem. Nat. Dem. Exec. Com., N.Y. State assemblywoman, Dist. 35, 1983-91, past mem. cities, election law, higher edn., labor and transp. coms., chairwoman airport devel. subcom., 1985; vice chairwoman Women's Legis. Caucus, 1985, past chairwoman standing com. on state-fed. rels. Office: 120-55 Queens Blvd Kew Gardens NY 11424 Office Phone: 718-286-2870. E-mail: Marshall4Queens@aol.com, info@queensbp.org.

MARSHALL, HEMAN ALEXANDER, III, lawyer; b. Roanoke, Va., Feb. 15, 1950; s. Heman Alexander Jr. and Jeanne (Martin) M.; children: Alexander Tevis, Claiborne Henebry, Courtney Littlepaige; m. Judith Skaff, July 6, 1996. BA, U. Va., 1972, JD, 1975. Bar: Va. Assoc. Woods, Rogers, Muse, Walker & Thornton, Roanoke, Va., 1975-80, ptnr., 1981-85, Woods, Rogers & Hazlegrove, P.L.C., Roanoke, Va., 1985-93, prin., 1994—, pres., 1995—2001, chmn., 1997—2002. Contbr. articles to profl. jours. Bd. dirs. Binaba Found., 2003—06, Nat. Conf. Cmty. and Justice, Roanoke, 2000—04, Art Mus. Western Va., 2000—04. Fellow Va. Law Found., Am. Bar Found.; mem. ABA, Va. State Bar (chmn. health law sect. 1988-89, antitrust law sect. 1989-90), Va. Bar Assn. (chmn. health law sect. 1991-92, bd. govs. 2000-04, chmn. law practice mgmt. divsn. 2002-04), Health Law Sect. Governing Coun., Roanoke Bar Assn., Am. Health Lawyers Assn. Home: 6629 Cotton Hill Rd Roanoke VA 24018-6915 Office: Woods Rogers PLC 10 S Jefferson St Ste 1400 Roanoke VA 24011-1331 Home Phone: 540-989-0811; Office Phone: 540-983-7654. Business E-Mail: marshall@woodsrogers.com.

MARSHALL, HOWARD LOWEN, musicologist, retired music educator; b. Nokesville, Va., July 21, 1931; s. Howard Hampton and Florence Annie (Nash) Marshall; m. Doris Mae Rosencranz, July 14, 1962. B in Music Edn., Shenandoah U., Winchester, Va., 1952; MusM, U. Cin., 1958; PhD, U. Rochester, NY, 1968. Asst. prof. music Lake Forest Coll., Ill., 1966-73; Charles B. Thompson prof. music Mercer U., Macon, Ga., 1974—98, Charles B. Thompson emeritus prof. music, 1998—, chmn. dept. music, 1974-97. Author: The Four-Voice Motets of Thomas Crecquillon, Symbolism in Schubert's Winterreise in Studies in Romanticism, The Motets of Georg Prenner. Lt. comdr. USNR. Mem.: Am. Musicological Soc., Phi Kappa Lambda, Phi Mu Alpha. Avocation: photography. Home and Office: 7 W Harbor Pond Rd West Boothbay Harbor ME 04575 Personal E-mail: seaspray2@verizon.net.

MARSHALL, JAMES ARTHUR, chemistry professor; b. Oshkosh, Wis., Aug. 7, 1935; s. Claude Wendal and Alice (Rodat) M.; m. Elizabeth Binder, Aug. 3, 1983; children: Amy Sue, Andrew Robert, Samantha Leigh. BS, U. Wis., 1957; PhD, U. Mich., 1960; postdoctoral rsch., Stanford U., 1962. Mem. faculty Northwestern U., 1962-80, prof. chemistry, 1968-80; faculty, prof. chemistry U. S.C., 1980-95, Guy Lipscomb prof., 1984-95; prof. associaté Univ. Paris, 1991; prof. associaté U. Jos Fourier, Grenoble, 1994; faculty, Thomas Jefferson prof. chemistry U. Va., 1995—. Cons. to industry; mem. com. phys. scis. NRC, 1969; mem. U.S.-Brazil grad. edn. in chemistry study group, 1971—; lectr. Am. Swiss Found., 1972; Mobay lectr., 1981; Merck-Frosst lectr., 1989, 90; Monsanto lectr., 1989; FACS lectr., 1990, 94; mem. NIH Study Sect. on Fertility and Human Welfare, 1972-75; chmn. U.S.-Japan Conf. on Organic Synthesis, 1973; mem. medicinal chemistry study sect. USPHS, 1977-81; mem. adv. com. chemistry NSF, 1981-84; mem. devel. therapeutics rev. com. USPHS; chmn. Gordon Rsch. Conf. on Stereochemistry, 1990. Author papers in field; mem. editl. bd. Organic Reactions, 1970-77, adv. bd., 1977—; editl. bd. Jour. Organic Chemistry, 1972-76, assoc. editor, 1993—; editor Synthetic Communications, 1972-93. Named Depth Charger of Yr., 1978; Alfred P. Sloan fellow, 1967-68 Fellow AAAS, ACS (lectr. 1989), Japan Soc. Promotion of Sci.; mem. Am. Chem. Soc. (mem. exec. com. organic divsn. 1978—, chmn. organic divsn. 1992, Ernest Guenther award 1979, Russell award 1985, Stone award Piedmont sect. 1986, com. on nomenclature 1979—, Govs. award 1991, Arthur C. Cope Scholar award, 2007), Chem. Soc. (London), Brazilian Acad. Scis. (corr.). Office: Univ Va Dept Chem McCormick Rd PO Box 400319 Charlottesville VA 22904-4319 Office Phone: 434-924-7997. Office Fax: 434-924-3710. Business E-Mail: jam5x@virginia.edu. *

MARSHALL, JASON P., lawyer; b. Arlington Heights, Ill., June 19, 1966; BA, U. Ill., 1988; JD, Chgo.-Kent Coll. Law, 1994. Bar: Ill. 1994, RI 1999, Conn. 2001. Acct. LaSalle Ptnrs.; assoc. Edwards, Angell, Palmer & Dodge, LLP, Providence. Named one of Top 100 Attys., Worth mag., 2005—06. Mem.: Conn. Bar Assn., RI Bar Assn. Avocation: fishing. Office: Edwards Angell Palmer & Dodge LLP 2800 Financial Plz Providence RI 02903 Office Phone: 401-276-6623. Office Fax: 401-276-6611. E-mail: jmarshall@eapdlaw.com. *

MARSHALL, JEFFREY SCOTT, mechanical engineer, educator; b. Cin., Feb. 10, 1961; s. James C. and Norma E. (Everett) M.; m. Marilyn Jane Patterson, July 16, 1983; children: Judith K., Eric G., Emily J., Paul E. BS summa cum laude, UCLA, 1983, MS, 1984; PhD, U. Calif., Berkeley, 1987. Asst. rsch. engr. U. Calif., Berkeley, 1988; engr. Creare, Inc., Hanover, NH, 1988-89; from asst. to assoc. prof. dept. ocean engring. Fla. Atlantic U., 1989-93; from assoc. prof. to prof. dept. mech. engring. U. Iowa, Iowa City, 1993—2001, prof., 2001—06, chair dept. mech. and indsl. engring., 2001—06; prof. U. Vt., Burlington, Vt., 2006—, dir. Sch. Engring., 2006—. Assoc. editor Jour. Fluids Engring.; contbr. articles to profl. jours.; textbook author. Recipient Young Investigator award, 1992-95. Fellow ASME (assoc. editor jour. Fluids Engring. 2001-04, Henry Hess award 1992); mem. Am. Phys. Soc., Tau Beta Pi. Achievements include research in fluid mechanics, three-dimensional vortex dynamics and vortex-structure interaction, particulate flows, and thin film flows. Office: Vt Sch Engring Burlington VT 05405 Office Phone: 802-656-3826. Business E-Mail: jeffm@cems.uvm.edu.

MARSHALL, JIM (JAMES CREEL MARSHALL), congressman; b. Ithaca, NY, Mar. 31, 1948; s. Robert Creel and Mary Elizabeth (Pie) M.; m. Camille Hope, Mar. 17, 1976; children: Elizabeth, Robert Creel III. AB, Princeton Univ., 1972; JD, Boston Univ., 1977. Bar: Ga. 1977. Mayor City of Macon, 1995—99; mem. US Congress from 3rd Ga. dist., 2003—06, US Congress from 8th Ga. dist., 2006—, mem. Agrl. and Armed Svcs. Coms. Contbr. articles to profl. jours. Pres. Macon Heritage Assn., 1989-90, Leadership Macon, 1988-90; commn. Macon Housing Authority, 1989-95; mem. bd. govs. State Bar Ga., 1995—, mem. adv. bd. US Conf. of Mayors, 1997—; co-chair econ. devel. Nat. Conf. of Dem. Mayors, 1996—, chair criminal justice com. Ga. Mcpl. Assn., 1997—. With US Army, 1968-70, Vietnam. Mem. Macon Bar Assn. (pres. 1992-93), Palaver Club of Macon, League of Women Voters. Democrat. Roman Catholic. Avocations: reading, sports, hunting, piddling. Office: US Ho Reps 502 Cannon Ho Office Bldg Washington DC 20515-1003 also: 682 Cherry St, Ste 300 Macon GA 31201 *

MARSHALL, JO TAYLOR, social worker; b. NYC; BA, Sarah Lawrence Coll., Bronxville, NY, 1957; MSW, Columbia U., NYC, 1959. Cert. clin. social worker, NY, NJ; bd. cert. diplomate. Caseworker Youth Cons. Svcs., 1960-62; program cons. Social Work Recruiting Ctr., 1962-63; casework supr. Louise Wise Svcs., 1963-68; faculty field instr. sch. social work Columbia U., NYC, 1968-70; coord. social work vol. and student tng. programs St. Lukes/Roosevelt Hosp. Ctr., 1970-75; asst. dir. fieldwork, faculty lectr. in health care Columbia U., NYC, 1975-78; dir. social work and psychiat. emergency svcs. Morristown Meml. Hosp., 1978—95; social worker pvt. practice, 1995—2002; ret., 2002. Adj. prof. Columbia U.; adv. bd., faculty Nat. Discharge Planning Inst. SUNY, Buffalo; prin. speaker, cons. Hosp. Assn. Pa., 1983, Mid-Atlantic Health Congress, 1985, VA, East Orange, N.J., 1986, Hosp. Assn. Tenn., 1987; adv. com. Rutgers GGrad. Sch. Social Work; mem. multidisciplinary state rev. com. for discharge planning standards in NJ. Contbr. articles to profl. jours.; produced and cons. on numerous film and TV prodns. Named Dir. of Yr., NJ Hosp. Social Work, 1989-90. Mem.: NASW, Acad. Cert. Social Workers, Soc. Hosp. Social Work Dirs. (pres. NJ chpt. 1988—89, exec. bd., chmn. nat. media task force). Achievements include The New Welcome Terrace at Columbia Grad. Sch. of Social Work named in her honor. Home (Winter): 1230 Hillsboro Mile Hillsboro Beach FL 33062-1344 Home (Summer): PO Box 40 Far Hills NJ 07931-0040 Office Phone: 908-553-5444. Personal E-mail: jomase@msn.com.

MARSHALL, JOAN See HELPERN, JOAN

MARSHALL, JOHN CROOK, internal medicine educator, researcher; b. Blackburn, Lancashire, Eng., Feb. 28, 1941; came to US, 1976; s. Albert Acey and Marion Miller (Crook) M.; m. Marilyn Dallas Parry, Sept. 20, 1969; children: Samantha Jane, Susannah Crook. BS, Victoria U., Manchester, Eng., 1962, MB, ChB, 1965, MD, 1973. Diplomate Am. Bd. Internal Medicine, Am. Bd. Endocrinology and Metabolism. Intern Manchester Royal Infirmary, 1965-66; resident Brompton Hosp., Nat. Heart Hosp., Nat Hosp. Queen Sq., London, 1966-69, Hammersmith Hosp., London, 1966-69, rsch. fellow, 1969-72; lectr. U. Birmingham, Eng., 1972-76; assoc. prof. internal medicine U. Mich., Ann Arbor, 1976-79, prof., 1979-91, chief endocrinology and metabolism, 1987-91; prof. U. Va., Charlottesville, 1991—, dir. Ctr. for Rsch. in Reprod., 1996—. Sci. counselor NIH, Bethesda, Md., 1983-84. Editor: Endocrinology Jour., 1979-84, Endocrinology Text, 1990—; contbr. articles to profl. jour. Grantee NIH, 1977-, Fellow ACP, Royal Coll. Physicians, Royal Soc. Medicine; mem. Ctrl. Soc. for Clin. Rsch. (coun. 1983—), Assn. Am. Physicians, Am. Soc. for Clin. Investigation, Am. Clin. and Climatological Soc. Anglican. Avocations: vintage racing cars, golf. Office: U Va Sch Medicine Dept Internal Medicine Charlottesville VA 22908-0001 Business E-Mail: jcm9h@virginia.edu.

MARSHALL, JOHN DAVID, lawyer; b. Chgo., May 19, 1940; s. John Howard and Sophie (Brezenk) M.; m. Marcia A. Podlasinski, Aug. 26, 1961; children: Jacquelyn, David, Jason, Patricia, Brian, Denise, Michael, Catherine. BS in Acctg., U. Ill., 1961; JD, Ill. Inst. Tech., 1965. CPA Ill.; bar: Ill. 1965, U.S. Tax Ct. 1968, U.S. Dist. Ct. (no. dist.) Ill. 1971. Ptnr. Mayer, Brown & Platt, Chgo., 1961—2006. Bd. dirs. Levinson Ctr. for Handicapped Children, Chgo., 1970—75. Mem. Ill. Bar Assn., Chgo. Bar Assn. (agribus. com. 1978—, trust law com. 1969-95, probate practice com. 1969—, com. on coms. 1983-00, vice chmn. 1988-89, chmn. 1989-90, legis. com. of probate practice com. 1983—, chmn. and vice chmn. legis. com. of probate practice com. 1983-84, rules and forms com., 1996—, chmn. exec. com. probate practice com. 1982-83, vice chmn. exec. com. 1981-82, sec. exec. com. 1980-81, div. chmn. 78-79, div. vice chmn. 1977-78, div. sec. 1976-77, Appreciation award 1982-83), Union League Club (Chgo.). Roman Catholic. Home: 429 N Willow Wood Dr Palatine IL 60074-3831 Office: Attorney at Law 1300 E Woodfield Rd Schaumburg IL 60173 Business E-Mail: jmarshall@ncc-cpa.com.

MARSHALL, JOHN HARRIS, JR., geologist, oil industry executive; b. Dallas, Mar. 12, 1924; s. John Harris and Jessie Elizabeth (Mosley) Marshall; m. Betty Eugenia Zarecor, Aug. 9, 1947 (dec. 2003); children: John Harris III, George Z., Jacqueline Anne. BA in Geology, U. Mo., Columbia, 1949, MA in Geology, 1950; LHD, Garrett Evang. Theolgical, Chgo., 1996. Registered geologist Calif., Wyo., Ky., Tex. Geologist Magnolia Oil Co., Jackson, Miss., 1950-59; assoc. geologist Magnolia/Mobil Oil, Okla. City, Okla., 1959-63; from dist. and divsn. geologist to chief geologist worldwide Mobil Oil Corp., various, 1963-81, gen. mgr. exploration for Western Hemisphere NYC, 1981-82; chief geologist Ambrex, 1982—84; prin., owner Marshall Energetics, Inc., Dallas, 1982—. Dir. exploration Anschutz, 1985-91; pres. Summit Oil and Gas Worldwide, 1993-99, Madera Prodn. Co., 1992—; adv. bd. Salvation Army, Manhattan, 1980-82; trustee Sci. Place, Dallas, 1995-2002, pres. adv. coun. U. Mo., plan giving com., 2004— Geology devel. bd. U. Mo., past pres., 1982-, pres. Coll. Arts and Sci. devel. program, 1996—, devel. coun., 1996-2000, arts and scis. strategic devel. bd., 2000—; councilman, City of Warr Acres Okla., 1962-63; active United Meth. Ch., 1951—, Boy Scouts Am., 1960-68; trustee Found. of Evangelism, United Meth. Ch., 1984-, chair, 1988-96, AAPG Found., 2004—. With US Army, 1943—46. Decorated 3 Battle Stars US Army; recipient Curator's medal, U. Mo., 1949, Disting. Alumni Svc. award, 1996, Arts and Sci. award, The Mosaic Soc., U. Mo., 2000, Faculty-Alumni award, U. Mo., 2001, Hon. Life Mem., Geology Devel. Bd., U. Mo., 2004. Mem. Am. Assn. Petroleum Geologists (trustee AAPG Found. 2004—, Pub. Svc. award 2000), Am. Geol. Inst., Am. Geol. Soc. (Dallas, Alaska, Oklahoma City; LA Basin pres. 1969-70, trustee), Rocky Mountain Assn. Geologists, NY Acad. Sci., Pacific Petroleum Geologists, Am. Sci. Affiliation, Assn. Christian Geologists, United Meth. Gen. Bd. of Discipleship (nat. hispanic evangelization com., 2003-), Meth. Men Club, Denver Petroleum Club, Sigma Xi. Democrat. Office: 9526 Moss Haven Dr Dallas TX 75231-2608

MARSHALL, JOHN HENRY, lawyer; b. Paterson, NJ, July 31, 1949; s. Henry Leland and Elizabeth Marion (Bates) M.; m. Jan (Eastman), May 4, 1979. BA, Dartmouth Coll., 1971, Cambridge U., Eng., 1973; JD, Yale U., 1977. Bar: Vt. 1977, U.S. Dist. Ct. Vt., 1978. Assoc. Downs Rachlin Martin, St. Johnsbury, Vt., 1977—82, ptnr., 1982—, mng. ptnr., 2003—. Mem. Vt. Health Care Authority Adv. Com. Universal Access Plan, 1992. Chmn. Dist. Environ. Commn., St. Johnsbury, 1981-90; mem. Governor's Blue Ribbon Commn. on Health Care, 1991; chmn. Vt. Cmty. Found., 2000-02; chmn. Vt. Pub. TV, 2002-04. Capt. U.S. Army, 1973-74. Mem. Vt. Bar Assn. (chmn. environ. law com. 1987-92, chmn. health law com. 1994-96). Office: Downs Rachlin Martin PLLC 90 Prospect St Saint Johnsbury VT 05819-0099 Home: PO Box 19 Peacham VT 05862-0019 Business E-Mail: jmarshall@drm.com.

MARSHALL, JOHN PAUL, broadcast engineer; came to U.S., 1967. Degree, U. Grenoble, 1963; student, U. Munich, 1964—65, San Francisco State U., 1969—71, John O'Connell Tech. Inst., 1973—74. Cert. Novell adminstr., cert. broadcast technologist, A+ computer svc. technician Microsoft Cert. Profl.; cert. Networkplus Tech., Microsoft Cert. Profl., Microsoft Cert. Sys. Engr. Mem. faculty law and econ. scis. U. Grenoble, France, 1963—64; mem. Expo '67 staff City of Montreal, Que., Canada, 1967; filmmaker Cinemalab, San Francisco, 1970; engr. film and TV Able Studios, San Francisco, 1971—73; engr. radio and TV Sta. KALW-FM (Nat. Pub. Radio), San Francisco, 1973—74; broadcast engr. Sta. KRON-TV (NBC), San Francisco, 1974—91; intern Centre d'Informatique et de Maintenance Automatisme, 1993; founder Marshall U.S.A., San Francisco, 1994; freelance broadcast engr. KPIX-TV (CBS), KGO-Radio (ABC), KSFO-Radio (ABC), KPST-TV, San Francisco, 1995—2001; adminstr. Thomson Prometric, San Francisco, 2003—. Freelance audio visual tech. advisor, San Francisco area, 1975—, lectr. radio, TV, motion pictures, 1975—, cons. customized electronic effects; tech. advisor, assoc. Broadkast Skills Bank. Translator tech. pubs. and manuals, 1975—. Mus. dir., participant in theater prodns., 1950-59; active Boy Scouts Am. Govt. of France scholar, 1960-63. Mem. Rolls Royce Owners Club Found. (life), Internet Soc., Soc. Broadcast Engrs. (cert. broadcast networking technologist), Elec. Tech. Assn. Avocations: classical pianist, polyglot, world traveler. Personal E-mail: jpm1221@sbcglobal.net. *Personal philosophy: (French proverb) Aide toi, le ciel t'aidera--Use your own resources and you will always receive a helping hand from heaven.*

MARSHALL, JOHN TREUTLEN, lawyer, educator; b. Macon, Ga., Nov. 1, 1934; s. Hubert and Gladys (Lucas) Marshall; m. Katrine White, May 1, 1959; children: Allison, Rebecca, Paul, Mary Anne. BA, Vanderbilt U., 1956; LLB, Yale U., 1962. Bar: Ga. 1962, US Dist. Ct. (no., mid. and so. dists.) Ga. 1962, US Ct. Appeals (5th cir.) 1962, US Supreme Ct. 1978, US Ct. Appeals (11th cir.) 1982. Ptnr. Powell Goldstein LLP, Atlanta, 1962—. Chmn. bd. visitors Ga. State U. Law Sch., 2005—; chmn. No. Dist. Ga. Bar Coun., 1989, Ga. State Bar Commn. Continuing Lawyer Competency, 1991—93, Ga. State Commn. Stds. Profession, 1996—; bd. dirs. Ga. Eye Bank, Inc., Atlanta Bar Found. Bd. editor Yale Law Jour. Trustee Ga. Inst. Continuing Legal Edn., 1983—90; chmn. adv. bd. Atlanta Vol. Lawyers Found.; bd. dirs. Atlanta Legal Aid, 1972—73. Capt. USMC, 1959—62. Recipient S. Phillip Heiner award, Atlanta Vol. Lawyers Assn., 1992, A. Gus Cleveland award, Ga. Commn. Continuing Legal Edn., Tradition of Excellence award, State Bar Ga., 1995, Disting. Svc. award, Ga. State Bar, 2006, Professionalism award, Am. Inns of Ct. (11th Jud. Cir.), 2005, Ben F. Johnson, Jr. award for Pub. Svc., 2007. Fellow: Ga. Bar Found., Atlanta Bar Found. (bd. dirs.), Am. Acad. Appellate Lawyers, Am. Coll. Trial Lawyers (state chmn. 1985—86); mem.: ABA (ho. of dels. 1976—86, Harrison Tweed award 1986), Ga. Inst. Trial Advocacy (chmn. 1982—83), Atlanta Bar Assn. (pres. 1974—75, Charles E. Watkins Jr. award 1988, Leadership award 1996), Atlanta Bar Found. (bd. dirs.), State Bar Ga. (chmn. stds. profession com., Disting. Svc. award 2005), Am. Arbitration Assn., Lawyers Club. Office: Powell Goldstein LLP One Atlantic Ctr Fl 14 1201 W Peachtree St NW Atlanta GA 30309-3488 Office Phone: 404-572-6615. Business E-Mail: jmarshall@pogolaw.com.

MARSHALL, JONATHAN, foundation administrator, journalist; b. NYC, Jan. 20, 1924; s. James and Lenore (Guinzburg) M.; m. Maxine Besser, Apr. 6, 1955; children: Lucinda, Laura, Robert Louis, Jonathan Herbert. BA in Econs., U. Colo., 1946; postgrad., U. N.C., 1947—49; MS in Journalism, U. Oreg., 1962; LHD (hon.), Ariz. State U., 1994. Program assoc. Planning Dept., West Chester County, NY, 1949—52; editor, pub. Arts mag., NYC, 1953-58, Scottsdale Daily Progress, Ariz., 1963-87; program assoc. Ford Found., NYC, 1958-59; pres. New Hope Found., NYC, 1985-98, Marshall Fund, Scottsdale, Ariz., 1987—92. Pulitzer prize juror, 1983, 84; Ruhl fellow lectr. U. Oreg., 1986, Allen lectr., 91. Author: Reunion in Norway, 2005; former mem. editl. bd. Amicus Jour.; contbr. articles to various publs., including Masthead, ASNE Bull., Quill, Amicus Jour. Chmn. Oreg. Vols. for Stevenson, 1960, Ariz. Grandparents Day, 1972, 73; bd. dirs. Ariz. Theatre Co., Phoenix Art Mus., Nat. Com. for Effective Congress; former mem. bd. dirs. Am. Jewish Com., Camelback Hosp., Phoenix Urban League, Phoenix Symphony Assn. Recipient Nat. Phys. Fitness Leadership award U.S. Jaycees, 1973, Ariz. Newspapers' Master Editor-Pub. award, 1978, Disting. Svc. award Ariz. Press Club, 1988, Ariz. Philanthropist award Nat. Soc. Fundraising Execs., 1997, Ariz. State U. Coll. Liberal Arts, 1988, Pub. Interest award Ariz. Ctr. for Law in Pub. Interest, 1998, John W. Creasman award for excellence Ariz. State U., 1999, Martin Luther King, Jr. Diversity Champion award, 2001; named Ariz. Civil Libertarian of Yr., 1996; inducted into Ariz. Newspapers Hall of

Fame, 1996; named to U. Oreg. Journalism Sch. Hall of Achievement, 2001. Mem. Nat. Conf. Editl. Writers, Am. Soc. Newspapers Editors (past mem. editl. bd. Bull.), Soc. Profl. Journalists (1st Amendment award 1979). Democrat. Jewish.

MARSHALL, JOSHUA MICAH, publisher, blog writer, columnist, editor, political journalist; b. St. Louis, Mo., Feb. 15, 1969; m. Millet Israeli, 2005. Grad., Princeton U., 1991; PhD in American History, Brown U. Assoc. editor to Washington editor The American Prospect, 1998—2001; founder, editor, publisher talkingpointsmemo.com; editor, publisher TPMCafe.com, 2005—; contbg. editor The Washington Monthly, Washington; contbg. writer, columnist The Hill, Washington; columnist Time.com. Blog writer TPMmuckraker.com. Contbg. writer Salon.com; contbr. articles to the Atlantic Monthly, Boston Globe, Financial Times, Foreign Affairs, LA Times, NY Republic, New Yorker, NY Post, NY Times and Slate; guest appearances CNN, CNBC, C-Span, Fox and MSNBC. Office: The Hill 1625 K St NW Ste 900 Washington DC 20006 Address: The Washington Monthly 1319 F St NW Ste 710 Washington DC 20004

MARSHALL, JOSIE, secondary school educator; b. American, Idaho, Dec. 26, 1942; BS, U. Idaho, MS in Edn. Nat. bd. cert. tchr. 1999. Tchr. Sacajawea Jr. H.S., Lewiston, Idaho. Recipient Idaho Middle Sch. Tchr. of the Yr. award, 1997—98; Tom Wright fellow. Mem.: Idaho Edn. Assn. (bd. mem.), Nat. Bd. for Profl. Tchg. Stds. (bd. mem.). Office: Sacajawea Jr HS 3610 12th St Lewiston ID 83501

MARSHALL, KATE, state official; b. San Francisco, July 22, 1959; m. John Marshall; 2 children. Student, Calif. State Univ.; BA, Univ. Calif., Berkeley, 1982, JD. Law intern Laxalt, Washington, Perito & Debuc, Washington; tchr., English, Commerce Peace Corps, Kenya; with field offices Dept. Justice, Washington, San Francisco; in-house counsel ATG, Inc., 2000; pvt. practice atty.; sr. dep. atty. gen. State of Nev., 1997—2000, state treas., 2007—. Named Woman of Achievement, Nevada Women's Fund, 2001. Democrat. Office: State Treas Capitol Bldg 101 N Carson #4 Carson City NV 89701 Office Phone: 775-684-5600. Office Fax: 775-684-5623. Business E-Mail: statetreasurer@nevadatreasurer.gov. *

MARSHALL, KATHLEEN, choreographer, theater director; Mem. exec. bd. Soc. Stage Dirs. and Choreographers. Asst. choreographer (Broadway plays) Kiss of the Spider Woman, 1993—95, She Loves Me, 1993—94, Damn Yankees, 1994—95, choreographer Swinging on a Star, 1996 (Drama Desk nomination), 1776, 1997—98, Ring Round the Moon, 1999, Kiss Me, Kate, 1999—2001 (Tony nom. best choreography, 2001, Laurence Olivier nom. best choreography, 2002, Drama Desk nomination, Outer Critics Circle nomination, Astaire Award nomination), Seussical, 2000—01, Follies, 2001 (Outer Critics Circle award nomination), Little Shop of Horrors, 2003; dir.: (Broadway plays) Wonderful Town, 2003 (Tony nom. best dir. musical, 2004, Drama Desk award best choreography, 2004); choreographer (Broadway plays) Wonderful Town, 2003 (Tony award best choreography, 2004), The Pajama Game, 2005 (Outer Critics' Cir. award, outstanding choreography, 2006, Drama Desk award outstanding choreography, 2006, Tony award, best choreography, 2006), (TV films) The Music Man, 2003. Recipient Mr. Abbott Award, Stage Directors & Choreographers Found., 2005. Office: Ste 702 311 W 43rd St New York NY 10036

MARSHALL, KATHLEEN ANN, elementary school educator; b. Winchester, Conn., Dec. 18, 1951; d. Richard Bartholomew and Jeannine Rose Marshall. AA with honors, Bay Path Jr. Coll., 1978; BS with honors, U. Hartford, 1980, MEd with honors, 1988; Sixth Yr. Degree with honors, So. Conn. State U., 1998. Tchr. Riverside Sch., Torrington, Conn., 1980—81, Oliver Wolcott Sch., Torrington, 1981—84, 1986—87, Litchfield HS, Conn., 1984—86; tchr. elem. sch. Archdiocese Hartford, Bloomfield, Conn., 1987—2004; freelance sub. tchr. Conn., 2004—. Tchr. catacism St. Francis Assisi Ch., Torrington, 1981—89, 1999—2002; pvt. tutor, Torrington, 2004—. Vol. Big Bros. Big Sisters, Conn., 1997—. Mem.: ASCD. Avocations: reading, walking, doll collecting, gardening.

MARSHALL, KATHRYN SUE, lawyer; b. Decatur, Ill., Sept. 12, 1942; d. Edward Elda and Frances M. (Minor) Lahniers; m. Robert S. Marshall, Sept. 5, 1964 (div. Apr. 1984); children: Stephen Edward, Christine Elizabeth; m. Robert J. Arndt, June 25, 1988 (dec. 1999). BA, Lake Forest Coll., 1964; JD, John Marshall Law Sch., Chgo., 1976. Intern U.S. Atty.'s Office, Chgo., 1974—76; mng. ptnr. Marshall and Marshall Ltd., Waukegan, Ill., 1976—84; pvt. practice Waukegan, 1984—93, Preemptive Solutions, Wash. Contbr. articles to profl. jours. Bd. dirs., v.p. Lake Forest (Ill.) Fine Arts Ensemble; bd. dirs. Island Hosp. Health Found.; mem. steering com. Equal Justice Coalition; cert. jud. Dem. candidate Lake County, Ill.; bd. dirs. Camerata Soc., Lake Forest. Fellow: ABA (gov. 1993—96), Coll. Law Practice Mgmt., Ill. Bar Assn.; mem.: Navy League (life). Avocations: boating, reading, travel.

MARSHALL, KENNETH ROBERT, retired music educator; b. Aurora, Ill., May 18, 1939; s. John Redman and Gladys Marie Marshall. MusB, U. Ill., 1961, BS in Music Edn., 1962, MusM, 1963; BS in Hospitality Mgmt., Fla. Internat. U., 1980. Cert. evaluator Fla. Dept. Revenue. Choral dir. various high schs., Ill., Fla., 1963—68; dir. choral activities Brevard C.C., Cocoa, Fla., 1968—75; dir. choral activities, tchr. English Internat. Sch. Bangkok/Thai U., 1975—79; U.S. customs product clearance/tangible personal property Sunbelt Internat. Shoppers/Osceola Co. Property Dep. Appraiser, Orlando and Kissimmee, Fla., 1979—90; full time ch. musician, organist, dir. 1st United Meth. Ch., Sanford, Fla., 1990—92; med. records transcriptionist Leesburg (Fla.) Regional Med. Ctr., 1992—95; assoc. prof. humanities Valencia C.C., Orlando, Fla., 1995—2003; organist, dir. music Faith Viera (Fla.) Luth. Ch., 2004—. Tchr., counselor various high schs. and coll.s, Fla., 1963—2003; part-time ch. musician, 1975—95. Named Prof. of the Semester, Phi Theta Kappa, 1999—2000. Mem.: Am. Guild Organists (assoc.; regional officer 1968—75), Am. Choral Dirs. Assn. (life; state and conv. planning positions 1965—75), Phi Mu Alpha. Republican. Methodist/Lutheran. Avocations: animals, stamp collecting/philately. Home Phone: 321-242-1017; Office Phone: 321-636-5504. Personal E-mail: jsbach2@gmail.com.

MARSHALL, KERRY JAMES, artist; b. Birmingham, Ala., Oct. 17, 1955; BFA, Otis Art Inst., LA, 1978. Prodn. designer Praise House & Sankofa, 1991; assoc. prof. U. Ill., Chgo. Art instr. L.A. City Coll., 1980-83; art faculty L.A. S.W. Coll., 1981-85; adj. asst. prof. Sch. Art and Design, U. Ill., Chgo., 1993-94. One man exhibits include James Turcotte Gallery, L.A., 1983, Pepperdine U., Malibu, 1984, Koplin Gallery, 1985, 91, Studio Mus. Harlem, 1986, Terra Incognito, Chgo. Cultural Ctr., 1992, Jack Shainmen Gallery, N.Y.C., 1993, 95, Koplin Gallery, Santa Monica, Calif., 1993, Cleveland Ctr. Contemporary ARts, 1994, Drawings III, Koplin Gallery, Santa Monica, 1993, Markts of Resistance, White Columns Gallery, N.Y.C. 1993, 43rd Biennial of Contemporary Am. Painting, Corcoran Gallery Art, Washington, 1993, Document X, Kassel, Germany, 1997, Whitney Biennial Whitney Mus. Am. Art, N.Y.C., 1997, Saddlebrook Coll. Art Gallery, Mission Viejo, Calif., 1994, Addison Gallery Am. Art, 1997; contbr. articles to profl. jours. Recipient Herb Alpert award Cal Arts, 1997; fellow Nat. Endowment Arts Visual Art, 1991, John D. and Catherine T. MacArthur Found., 1997; visual arts grantee Ill. Arts Coun., 1992; grantee Tiffany Found., 1993, Disting. Artist Fellowship and Stillwater Found. grant, Coll. Fine Arts, U. Tex., Austin, 2004. Mem. Ill. Arts Coun. Office: 4122 S Calumet Ave Chicago IL 60653-2649

MARSHALL, KEVIN A., director; b. Bronx, NY, June 9, 1950; s. Aldon Eddie and Winifred Ann Marshall; m. Marlene Ann Cassella, Dec. 30, 1972; children: Jeffrey Aldon, Bryan Matthew. BA, William Paterson U., Wayne, NJ, 1972; MFA, Ohio U., Athens, 1974. Head grad. program in theatre mgmt. and arts adminstrn. U. Ala./Ala. Shakespeare Festival, Tuscaloosa, 1982—98; dir. Sch. Theatre and Dance U. Fla., Gainesville, 1998—. Bus. mgr. Festival Players, Chattanooga, 1979—82; house mgr. Manhattan Theatre Club, NYC, 1979; exec. dir. Johnson City Area Arts Coun., Tenn., 1982; ho. mgr. Ala. Shakespeare Festival, Anniston, Ala., 1983—84. Co-author: Theatre Management: A Successful Guide to Producing Plays on Commercial and Non-Profit Stages; editor: Theatre Mgmt. Jour. V.p. Chattanooga Wine Tasters, 1981—82; active Assn. Arts Adminstrn. Educators, Pitts., 1991—92, Tenn. Theatre Assn., Nashville, 1981—82, Appalachian Coun. for the Arts, Bristol, Tenn., 1982. Recipient Druid Arts award, Arts Coun. Tuscaloosa County, 1992. Mem.: Southeastern Theatre Conf., Assn. for Theatre in Higher Edn. (treas. 1990—95). Roman Catholic. Avocation: travel. Home: 4064 SW 98th Ter Gainesville FL 32608 Office: Univ Fla PO Box 115900 Gainesville FL 32611 Home Phone: 352-333-8459; Office Phone: 352-273-0501. Office Fax: 352-392-5114. Business E-Mail: kmarshall@arts.ufl.edu.

MARSHALL, LAWRENCE C., law educator; b. Jan. 10, 1959; m. Michelle Oberman, Mar. 17, 1996; children: Rachel, Steven, Jonathan, Hanna, Noa. BA, Beth Hatalmud Coll., Jerusalem, 1979; JD summa cum laude, Northwestern U., 1985; LHD (hon.), Nat.-Louis U., 2003. Bar: Ill. 1987. Law clk. to Chief Judge Patricia M. Wald US Ct. Appeals DC Cir., 1985-86; law clk. to Assoc. Justice John Paul Stevens US Supreme Ct., Washington, 1986-87; of counsel Mayer, Brown & Platt, 1989—93; assoc. prof. Northwestern U. Sch. Law, Chgo., 1987—99, prof. law, 1989—2005, co-founder, legal dir. Ctr. on Wrongful Convictions, 1999—2005; prof. law Stanford Law Sch., 2005—, David and Stephanie Mills dir. clin. edn., 2005—. Exec. dir. ROFEH, Inc., Boston, 1979-81; field rep. Devel. Corp. for Israel, Boston, 1981-82. Co-recipient Pro Bono Award, ABA, 1996, Cmty. Svc. Award, Mexican Legal Def. Fund, 1996; named Illinoisan of Yr., Ill. Newsbroadcasters' Assn., 2003; recipient Robert H. Childres Award for Tchg. Excellence, Northwestern U. Sch. Law, 1989, 2003, Mario Cuomo Act of Courage Award, Death Penalty Focus of Calif., 1999. Mem. Chgo. Inns of Ct. (barrister). Office: Stanford Law Sch Crown Quadrangle 559 Nathan Abbott Way Stanford CA 94305-8610 Office Phone: 650-723-7572. E-mail: lmarshall@stanford.edu.

MARSHALL, LINDA MURPHY, linguist, government official; b. St. Louis, Aug. 6, 1950; d. Samuel Baldwin and Barbara Anne (Chivvis) Murphy; m. Joseph A. Kelley, Aug. 31, 1974 (div. Sept. 1987); children: Alex, Mia; m. William Peyton Marshall, July 8, 1989. BA, U. Denver, 1972; MA, St. Louis U., 1974, PhD, 1978; postgrad., Washington U., 1981-85, Georgetown U., 1997-98. Translator Aerospace Ctr., Def. Mapping Agy., St. Louis, 1978-81; multi-linguist U.S. Fed. Govt., Washington, 1985—. Cons. Sotho Newspaper Reader, Reference Grammar and Lexicon, 1998. Contbr. articles to profl. jours.; co-author: Xhosa Newspaper Reader and Lexicon, 2002. Mem. Phi Beta Kappa. Episcopalian. Avocations: classical piano, poetry, travel, foreign languages. Home: 10391 Green Mountain Cir Columbia MD 21044-2455

MARSHALL, LUCILLE RUTH, retired mathematics professor; b. Waukegan, Ill., Mar. 20, 1941; d. James Arthur and Emily Ruth Cunnington; AA, Santa Rosa Jr. Coll., 1990; BA, Sonoma State U., 1994; MS, Mo. State U., 2000; post grad. in math., U. Mo., 2003. Tchg. asst. Mo. State U., Springfield, Mo., 1998—2000; grad. tchg. asst. U. Mo., Rolla, 2000—03; ret., 2004. Adj. faculty Ozarks Tech. Coll., Springfield. Vol. South Ctrl. Mo. Cmty. Action Agy., Winona. Mem.: Order Eastern Star. Home: PO Box 8 Winona MO 65588

MARSHALL, MARGARET HILARY, state supreme court chief justice; b. Newcastle, Natal, South Africa, Sept. 1, 1944; came to U.S., 1968; d. Bernard Charles and Hilary A.D. (Anderton) M; m. Samuel Shapiro, Dec. 14, 1968 (div. Apr. 1982); m. Anthony Lewis, Sept. 23, 1984. BA, Witwatersrand U., Johannesburg, 1966; MEd, Harvard U., 1969; JD, Yale U., 1976; LHD (hon.), Regis Coll., 1993. Bar: Mass. 1977, U.S. Dist. Ct. Mass., U.S. Dist. Ct. N.H., U.S. Dist. Ct. D.C., U.S. Dist. Ct. (ea. dist.) Mich., U.S. Tax Ct., U.S. Ct. Appeals (1st, 11th and D.C. cirs.), U.S. Supreme Ct. Assoc. Csaplar & Bok, Boston, 1976-83, ptnr., 1983-89, Choate, Hall & Stewart, Boston, 1989-92; v.p., gen. counsel Harvard U., Cambridge, Mass., 1992-96; justice Mass. Supreme Jud. Ct., 1996-99, chief justice, 1999—. Mem. jud. nominating coun., 1987-90, 92; chairperson ct. rules subcom. Alternative Dispute Resolution Working Group, 1985-87; mem. fed. appts. commn., 1993; mem. adv. com. Supreme Judicial Ct., 1989-92, mem. gender equality com., 1989-94; mem. civil justice adv. group U.S. Dist. Ct. Mass., 1991-93; spl. counsel Jud. Conduct Commn., 1988-92; trustee Mass. Continuing Legal Edn., Inc., 1990-92. Trustee Regis Coll., 1993-95; bd. dirs. Internat. Design Conf., Aspen, 1986-92, Boston Mcpl. Res. Bur., 1990-94, Supreme Judicial Ct. Hist. Soc., 1990-94, sec., 1990-94. Fellow Am. Bar Found. (Mass. state chair); mem. Boston Bar Assn. (treas. 1988-89, v.p. 1989-90, pres.-elect 1990-91, pres. 1991-92), Internat. Women's Forum, Mass. Women's Forum, Boston Club, Phi Beta Kappa (hon.). Office: Supreme Judicial Court 1 Pemberton Sq Ste 2-500 Boston MA 02108-1717 *

MARSHALL, MARILYN JOSEPHINE, retired lawyer; b. Dayton, Ohio, May 31, 1945; d. Foy Wylie and Inez Virginia (Smith) Gard; m. Alan George Marshall, June 13, 1965; children: Gwendolyn Scott, Brian George. Student, Northwestern U., 1963—65; BA, Stanford U., 1967; cert. in teaching, U. B.C., Vancouver, 1977; JD, Capital Law Sch., Columbus, Ohio, 1985. Bar: Ohio 1985, Fla. 1993, U.S Dist. Ct. (so. dist.) Ohio 1986, U.S. Dist. Ct. (no. dist., mid. dist. and so. dist.) Fla. 1994, U.S. Ct. Appeals (6th cir.) 1986, U.S. Ct. Appeals (11th cir.) 1994. Tchr. Sutherland Secondary Sch., North Vancouver, B.C., 1977-79; instr. Brit. Coll. Inst. Tech., Burnaby, B.C., 1979-80; assoc. Crabbe, Brown, Jones, Potts & Schmidt, Columbus, Ohio, 1985-86; clk. to judge U.S. Dist. Ct. (so. dist.) Ohio, Columbus, 1986-88; clk. to justice Ohio Supreme Ct., 1988-89; assoc. Squire, Sanders & Dempsey, 1989-92; with Columbus City Atty.'s Office, Columbus, Ohio, 1992-93; asst. atty. gen. civil divsn. State of Fla., Tallahassee, 1994-96; pvt. practice Tallahassee, 1996—2004; asst. atty. gen., child support and enforcement divsn. State of Fla., 2004—07; ret., 2007. Bd. dirs. Tallahassee Symphony. Mem. ABA, Ohio Bar Assn., Fla. Bar Assn., Tallahassee Bar Assn., Tallahassee Women Lawyers Assn., Capital U. Law Sch. Alumni Assn. Republican. Avocations: tennis, gardening, music. Personal E-mail: marilynjmarshall@earthlink.net.

MARSHALL, MARK F., lawyer; b. 1954; BS, U. SD, 1977, JD, 1981. Bar: SD 1981, US Dist. Ct. SD 1981, US Ct. Appeals (8th cir.) 1981, US Supreme Ct. 1984. Law clk. hon. Fred J. Nichol, 1981-83; ptnr. Bangs, McCullen, Butler, Foye & Simmons, Rapid City, SD, 1983-96; of counsel Johnson, Heidepriem, Miner, Marlow & Janklow, Sioux Falls, SD, 1996—2000; magistrate judge U.S. Dist. Ct. S.D., Sioux Falls, 1996-2000; ptnr. Davenport Law Firm, Sioux Falls, 2000—. Office: 206 W 14th St Sioux Falls SD 57105 Office Phone: 605-336-2880. Business E-Mail: mmarshall@dehs.com.

MARSHALL, MARTIN VIVAN, business administration educator, consultant; b. Kansas City, July 22, 1922; s. Vivan Dean and Marie (Church) M.; m. Rosanne Borden, Sept. 5, 1951 (dec. Feb. 8, 1986); children: Martin Dean, Michael Borden, Neil McNair; m. Hildegard Meyer, June 24, 1988. AB, U. Mo., 1943; MBA, Harvard U., 1947, D.C.S., 1953. Instr. mktg. and advt. U. Kans., 1947-48; mem. faculty Harvard U., 1948—, Henry R. Byers prof. bus. adminstrn., 1960—, chmn. mktg. area faculty, 1962-66, chmn. Smaller Co. Mgmt. Program, 1981-84, chmn. Owner/Pres. Mgmt. Program, 1985-94, mem. faculty Inst. Ednl. Mgmt., 1981-90, endowed chair, Martin Marshall prof. bus. adminstrn., 1999. Cons. U.S. and internat. bus., 1950—; dir. ann. seminar mktg. and advt. Am. Advt. Fedn., 1958-78; vis. prof. mktg. IMEDE Mgmt. Inst., Lausanne, 1965-66; sr. prof., ednl. dir. Internat. Mktg. Inst., 1967-71; vis. prof. Indian Inst. Mgmt., Agra, 1968, IPADE, Mexico City, 1969, U. Melbourne, Australia, 1977, 79; bd. dirs. Western Stone & Metal.; lectr. Templeton Coll., Oxford, summer 1998. Author: Automatic Merchandising, 1954, (with N.H. Borden) Advertising Management, 1960, Notes on Marketing, 1983, 88, 90, 92, 93, 2002, 2004. Bd. dirs. Youth Svcs. Internat., Inc., 1994-97, Moclean Co., 1998-99. Served to lt. (s.g.) USNR, 1943-46. Home: 130 Mount Auburn St Apt 309 Cambridge MA 02138-5779 Office: Harvard U Cumnock Hall Boston MA 02163

MARSHALL, MICHAEL BORDEN, marketing executive; b. Boston, Mar. 16, 1957; s. Martin Vivan and Rosanne (Borden) M.; m. Susan Diane (Parks), June 15, 1991; children: Samantha Rosanne, Brenton Alexander. BA, Oberlin Coll., Ohio, 1979; MBA, Harvard U., Cambridge, Mass., 1983. Analyst Benton and Bowles, Inc., NYC, 1977—80; mktg. mgr. Thor Metal Works, Ltd., Syracuse, NY, 1980—81; asst. mgr. Am. Express Co., NYC, 1982; sr. analyst Bank of Boston Corp., 1983—85; cons. John Hancock Mut. Life Ins. Co., Boston, 1985—89; corp. v.p. N.Y. Life Ins. Co., NYC, 1989—. Cons. assoc., Bank Mktg. Assn., Boston, 1983-89, N.Y., 1991—; advisor bus. analysis, Arthur D. Little, Inc., Cambridge, Mass., 1985-93. Contbr. articles to profl. journals. Mem. adv. bd. Youth Enrichment Svc. Boston, 1984-90; treas. St. James Episcopal Ch., North Salem, N.Y., 1996-99, jr. warden, 2005-06, sr. warden, 2007—. Recipient Jerome Davis Award Oberlin Coll., 1979, Copeland Sect. Award Harvard Bus. Sch., 1982, Corp. Spl. Award John Hancock Exec. Com., 1986. Mem. Am. Mktg. Assn. (sr. v.p. 1984-93), Mktg. Sci. Inst. (bd. dir. 1985-89), Life Ins. Mktg. and Rsch. Assn. (devel. bd. 1991-98, market rsch. com. 1995—, chmn. 2002-03, market rsch. conf. com. 2004-), Coun. on Fin. Competition (adv. bd. 1991—, market rsch. conf. com. 2004—), Soc. Ins. Strategists (founding mem.), Fin. Industry Rsch. Study Team (founding mem.), Am. Coun. on Life Ins. (rsch. advisor 1994-2003), N.Y. Mktg. Coun., Harvard Club. Office: NY Life Ins Co 1 Rockwood Rd Sleepy Hollow NY 10591 Business E-Mail: mmarshal@newyorklife.com.

MARSHALL, NATALIE JUNEMANN, economics professor; b. Milw., June 13, 1929; d. Harold E. and Myrtle (Findlay) Junemann; m. Howard D. Marshall, Aug. 7, 1954 (dec. 1972); children: Frederick S., Alison B.; m. Phillip Shatz, May 27, 1988. AB, Vassar Coll., 1951; MA, Columbia U., 1952, PhD, 1963, JD, 1994. Instr. Vassar Coll., Poughkeepsie, NY, 1952-54, 59, 59-60, 63, dean studies, prof. econs., 1973-75, v.p. for student affairs, 1975-80, v.p. for adminstrn. and student services and prof. econs., 1980-91, prof. econs., 1991-94; teaching fellow Wesleyan U., Middletown, Conn., 1955-56; from asst. prof. to prof. SUNY, New Paltz, 1964-73; prof. econs. Vassar Coll., Poughkeepsie, NY, 1973-94; of counsel Donoghue, Thomas, Auslander & Drohan, Hopewell Junction, NY, 1997—. Editor (with Howard Marshall): The History of Economic Thought, 1968; editor: Keynes, Updated or Outdated, 1970; author (with Howard Marshall): Collective Bargaining, 1971. Trustee St. Francis Hosp., 1979-88, Area Fund Dutchess County, 1981-87, Coll. New Rochelle, 1994-2000, Hudson Valley Philharm., 1985-92, pres., 1989-91. Mem. AAUP, Am. Assn. Higher Edn., Am. Econ. Assn., AAUW (v.p. N.Y. State div. 1964-66), Poughkeepsie Vassar Club (pres. 1965-67). Home: 157 Skidmore Rd Pleasant Valley NY 12569-5001

MARSHALL, PATRICK C., lawyer; b. San Francisco, Aug. 8, 1954; BA, Whitman Coll., 1976; JD with honors, U. Wash., 1979. Bar: Wash. 1979, Calif. 1984. Ptnr. Pillsbury Winthrop Shaw Pittman, San Francisco, 1984—, office mng. ptnr., 2004, co-leader Litigation sect., leader San Francisco Litigation sect. Mem.: San Francisco Bar Assn. Office: Pillsbury Winthrop Shaw Pittman 50 Fremont St San Francisco CA 94105 Office Phone: 415-983-7233. Office Fax: 415-983-1200. Business E-Mail: patrick.marshall@pillsburylaw.com.

MARSHALL, RAYMOND CHARLES, lawyer; b. Aquadilia, PR, July 23, 1953; 1 child, Kyle. BA summa cum laude, Coll. Idaho, 1975; JD, Harvard U., 1978. Bar: Calif. 1978, D.C. 1989. Ptnr. Bingham McCutchen LLP, San Francisco, co-chmn. white-collar crime & bus. regulation practice group. Chmn. Calif. Supreme Ct. Adv. Multi-Jurisdictional Practice, 2004. Co-author: Environmental Crimes, 1992; contbr. chpt. to manual; contbr. articles to profl. jours. Bd. dirs. Nat. Multiple Sclerosis Soc. Northern Calif. chpt., 1992—; adv. bd. United Negro Coll. Fund Northern Bay Area Chpt., 1992—; bd. trustees Alta Bates Found., 1994—; adv. coun. mem. San Francisco Sports Coun. Recipient San Francisco Neighborhood Legal Assistance Found. award, 1989, Earl Warren Legal Svcs. award NAACP Legal Def. & Ednl. Found., 1990, Unity award Minority Bar Coalition, 1992, Cmty. Svc. award Wiley Manuel Law Found., 1994, Disting. Jesuit award Anti-Defamation League, 2001. Mem. ABA (met. bar caucus exec. com. 1992-94, vice-chmn. natural resources & energy litigation com. 1989-93, environmental crimes com. 1990-92, nominating com. conf. of minority ptnrs. in maj. corp. law firms 1991, commn. on women in the profession 1994-95, co-chmn. environmental crimes subcom. of white collar crime com. 1994-95), Nat. Bar Assn., Calif. State Bar (bd. govs. 1995—, pres. 1998-99), Charles Houston Bar Assn. Avocations: travel, sports. Office: Bingham McCutchen LLP Three Embarcadero Ctr San Francisco CA 94111 Office Phone: 415-393-2348. Business E-Mail: raymond.marshall@bingham.com.

MARSHALL, RICHARD PAUL, JR., lawyer; b. Lincoln, Nebr., June 7, 1949; s. Richard P. and Betty Jean (Schleuning) M.; m. Mary Elizabeth Van Bloom, Jan. 28, 1970; 1 child, Sydna Suzanne. BA, U. Nebr., 1974; JD cum laude, Creighton U., 1979. Bar: Tex. 1979, U.S. Dist. Ct. (so. dist.) Tex. 1979, U.S. Ct Appeals (5th cir.) 1979, U.S. Dist. Ct. (we. dist.) Tex. 1988. Briefing atty., law clk. to presiding justice U.S. Ct. Appeals (5th cir.), Houston, 1979-80; assoc. Scott, Douglass & Keeton, Austin, Tex., 1980-83; ptnr. Scott, Douglass & Luton, Austin, 1984—. Editor-in-chief Creighton Law Rev., 1978-79. Bd. dirs. Swim-A-Long fundraiser Juvenile Diabetes Found., Austin, 1987-89; commr. Travis County Rural Fire Prevention Dist. 1, 1990-96. Mem. Tex. Bar Assn. (oil, gas and mineral law sect., litigation sect.), Travis County Bar Assn., Phi Alpha Delta (Scholastic Achievement award 1979). Democrat. Presbyterian. Avocations: golf, swimming, music, motorcycles, sport shooting. Office: Scott Douglass & Luton One American Ctr 600 Congress Ave Ste 1500 Austin TX 78701-2589 Home: 103 Coyote Trl Round Mountain TX 78663-6006

MARSHALL, RICHARD TREEGER, lawyer; b. NYC, May 17, 1925; s. Edward and Sydney (Treeger) M.; m. Dorothy M. Goodman, June 4, 1950; children: Abigail Ruth Marshall, Stanley Marshall; m. 2d Sylvia J. Kelley, June 10, 1979. BS, Cornell U., 1948; JD, Yale U., 1951. Bar: Tex. 1952, U.S. Ct. Appeals (5th cir.) 1966, U.S. Ct. Appeals (10th cir.) 1980, U.S. Supreme Ct. 1959; lic. Tex. Dept. Ins. Pvt. practice, El Paso, Tex., 1952-59, 61-79; assoc. Fryer & Milstead, El Paso, 1952; sr. ptnr. Marshall & Wendorf, El Paso, 1959-61, Marshall & Volk, El Paso, 1979-81; sr. atty. Richard T. Marshall & Assocs., PC, El Paso, 1981-85; sr. ptnr. Marshall, Thomas & Winters, El Paso, 1985-87; sr. atty. Marshall & Winters, 1987-88, Marshall, Sherrod & Winters, 1988-90; pvt. practice El Paso, 1990—. Instr. polit. sci. U. Tex., El Paso, 1961-62; instr. ins. law C.L.U. tng. course Am. Coll.; officer, dir. Advance Funding, Inc., El Paso; mem. El Paso Estate Planning Coun. Editor El Paso Trial Lawyers Rev., 1973-80; contbr. articles to profl. jours. Mem. ABA, ATLA (sec. personal injury law sect. 1967-68, nat. sec. 1969-70, sec.-treas. environ. law sect. 1970-71, vice chmn. family law litigation sec. 1971-72), El Paso Bar Assn., El Paso Trial

Lawyers Assn. (pres. 1965-66), Roscoe Pound-Am. Trial Lawyers Found. (commn. on profl. responsibility 1979-82), Soc. Cert. Sr. Advisors. Office: 423 Executive Ctr Blvd El Paso TX 79902-1003 Office Phone: 915-779-6627. Business E-Mail: rtmlaw@gmail.com.

MARSHALL, ROBERT, film, television and theater director, choreographer; b. Madison, Wis., Oct. 17, 1960; Grad., Carnegie Mellon U., 1982. Broadway dancer, NYC. Dir.: (plays) Chicago, 1992; co-choreographer (Broadway plays) Kiss of the Spider Woman, 1993; choreographer (Broadway plays) Damn Yankees (revival), 1994, Victor/Victoria, 1995, A Funny Thing Happened On the Way to the Forum (revival), 1996; overseer of dance sequences (TV films) Mrs. Santa Claus (CBS), 1996; choreographer (TV films) Rogers and Hammerstein's Cinderella (ABC), 1997, (films) The Cradle Will Rock, 1998; dir.(with Sam Mendes): (Broadway plays) Cabaret (revival), 1998 (Dora Mavor Moore award),: (TV films) Annie, 1999 (Emmy award, Am. Choreography award), (uncredited): (Broadway plays) Suessical, 2000,: (films) Chicago, 2002 (Nat. Bd. Rev. award, Outstanding Directorial Achievement in Feature Film, Dirs. Guild of Am., 2002, nominated for Oscar award), Memoirs of a Geisha, 2005, (TV specials) Tony Bennett: An American Classic, 2006 (Outstanding Directorial Achievement in Musical Variety, Dirs. Guild Am., 2007). Recipient Mr. Abbott award, Stage Dirs. & Choreographers Found., 2005. Mailing: c/o ICM 825 8th Ave New York NY 10019 *

MARSHALL, ROBERT CHARLES, computer company executive; b. Berwyn, Ill., June 19, 1931; s. Joseph H. and Rose M.; m. Sarane Virruso, Aug. 1, 1954; children— Joseph, Lisa, Jim. BSE.E., Heald Engring. Coll., 1956; MBA, Pepperdine U., 1976. Engr. Lawrence Radiation Lab., Livermore, Calif., 1956-64; systems engr. Electronics Assos., Palo Alto, Calif., 1964-69; v.p. mfg. Diablo Systems, Hayward, Calif., 1969-75; with Tandem Computers, Inc., Cupertino, Calif., 1975—, sr. v.p., chief operating officer, dir., 1979-96; pres., CEO Info Gear, 1996-97; gen. ptnr. Selby Venture Ptnrs., 1998—. Served with U.S. Army, 1952-54. E-mail: Bob@selbyventures.com.

MARSHALL, ROBERT LEWIS, musicologist, educator; b. NYC, Oct. 12, 1939; s. Saul and Pearl (Shapiro) M.; m. Traute Maass, Sept. 9, 1966; children— Eric, Brenda. AB, Columbia U., 1960; M.F.A., Princeton U., 1962, PhD, 1968; postgrad., U. Hamburg, W. Ger., 1965. Instr. dept. music U. Chgo., 1966-68, asst. prof., 1968-71, assoc. prof., chmn. dept., 1972-78, prof., 1978-83, Brandeis U., 1983-2000, chmn. dept., 1985-93, incumbent endowed chair Louis, Frances and Jeffrey Sachar prof. music, 1986-2000; emeritus, 2000—. Vis. assoc. prof. Princeton U., 1971-72; endowed prof. Univ. Ala., 1994; mem. rev. bd. rsch. materials program NEH, 1982, rev. bd. edits., 1991. Author: The Compositional Process of J.S. Bach, 2 vols., 1972, The Music of Johann Sebastian Bach: The Sources; The Style; The Significance, 1989, Mozart Speaks: Views on Music, Musicians and the World, 1991, Dennis Brain on Record: A Comprehensive Discography of His Solo, Chamber, and Orchestral Recordings, 1996; editor New Bach Edit., Eighteenth Century Keyboard Music, 1994, 2d edit., 2003; contbr. articles to musical jours. in U.S., Gt. Brit., Germany. Mem. music adv. bd. Ill. Arts Council, 1977-79. Recipient Deems Taylor award ASCAP, 1990; NEH fellow, 1978-79; Hon. Harold Spivacke consultantship Library of Congress. Mem. Am. Musicol. Soc. (bd. dirs. 1974-75, v.p. 1985-86, editl. bd. jour. 1975-80, rev. editor 1986-89, chmn. publs. com. 1991-94, Otto Kinkeldey prize 1974, hon. 2003), New Bach Soc. (chmn. Am. chpt. 1977-80), Phi Beta Kappa. Home: 100 Chestnut St Newton MA 02465-2538 E-mail: rmarshal@brandeis.edu.

MARSHALL, RUSSELL FRANK, consulting company executive; b. Fort Madison, Iowa, Sept. 10, 1941; s. William Frank and Dorothy Eleanor (Mikels) M.; m. Mary Jean Bailey, June 19, 1966; children: William Russell, Robert Scott (dec.), Gregory Howard. AB, Monmouth Coll., 1963; MS, U. Ill., 1965, PhD, 1971. Rsch. engr. Materials Rsch. Lab, Urbana, Ill., 1970-75; mgr. acad. computing Drake U., Des Moines, 1975-80; v.p. GMI Ltd., Des Moines, 1980-83; sr. v.p., treas. Communication Devel. Co., West Des Moines, 1983-96; pres. Marshall Assocs., West Des Moines, Iowa, 1996—; dir. info. svcs. Grand View Coll., Des Moines, 1996—. Contbr. articles to profl. jours. Active Boy Scouts Am., 1982—; mem. Des Moines Cmty. Theatre. Grantee AEC, 1964-71. Mem. Assn. Computing Machinery, Am. Phys. Soc., Assn. Info. Tech. Mgrs., Des Moines Symphony Assn. Presbyterian. Avocations: music, reading. Home: 1625 19th St West Des Moines IA 50265-1622 Home Phone: 515-225-0473. Business E-Mail: rmarshall@gvc.edu.

MARSHALL, SANDRA LEE, historian, writer; d. James Monroe and Virginia Elizabeth Marshall; m. George Ronald Matthews, Aug. 31, 2005. BA in Anthropology, U. Tex., Austin, 1978; MA in Anthropology, U. N.Mex., Albuquerque, 1986; MA in Pub. History, N.Mex. State U., Las Cruces, 2000. Archaeologist various locations, 1978—86, N.Mex. Dept. Transp., Santa Fe, 1987—98; editor Inst. for Hist. Survey Found., Las Cruces, N.Mex., 2000—01; historian Tex. Hist. Commn., Austin, 2001; archtl. historian Mo. Dept. Transp., Jefferson City, Mo., 2001—02, Nat. Pk. Svc., Omaha, 2003—05; owner, prin. investigator Marshall Hist. Consulting, Carson City, Nev., 2005—. Mem. N.Mex. Heritage Preservation Alliance, Santa Fe, 1995—2001; cons. historian Marjorie Russel Clothing and Textile Rsch. Ctr., Nev. State Mus., Carson City, Nev., 2005—07. Co-author: Historical Architectural Styles, Las Cruces, N.Mex., 2000 (Pasajero del Camino Real award, 2000), The Saint Louis Olympics, 1904, 2003; editor, compiler: A Short Story of War in France and Germany 1944-1945, 2001; exhibitions include Dua Sorella Gallery, Carson City, Nev., 2006—. Recipient Ira G. Clark award, N.Mex. State U., 1999—2000. Fellow: Phi Alpha Theta (v.p. local chpt. 1999—2000, Scholastic honors 2000); mem.: Soc. Archtl. Historians, Am. Assn. for State and Local History, Nat. Trust for Hist. Preservation. Avocations: reading, photography, travel, writing. Home and Office: 306 W Colorado Ave Trinidad CO 81082 Office Phone: 719-846-2127. E-mail: sand-marsh@hotmail.com.

MARSHALL, SHEILA HERMES, lawyer; b. NYC, Jan. 17, 1934; d. Paul Milton and Julia Angela (Meagher) Hermes; m. James Josiah Marshall, Sept. 30, 1967; 1 child, James J.H. BA, St. John's U., NYC, 1959; JD, NYU, 1963. Bar: N.Y. 1964, U.S. Ct. Appeals (2d, 3d, 5th and D.C. cirs.), U.S. Supreme Ct. 1970. Assoc. LeBoeuf, Lamb, Greene & MacRae, NYC, 1963-72, ptnr., 1973—95, of counsel, 1996—. Specialist in field. Mem. ABA, N.Y. State Bar Assn., Assn. of Bar of City of N.Y. Republican. Home: 325 E 72nd St New York NY 10021 Office: LeBoeuf Lamb Greene & MacRae 125 W 55th St New York NY 10019-5369 Home Phone: 212-628-3447; Office Phone: 212-424-8624. Business E-Mail: shmarsha@llgm.com.

MARSHALL, SIMONE VERNIERE, psychologist, psychoanalyst; b. Paris; came to U.S., 1951; d. Urbain and Gabrielle (Cadiergues) Verniere; m. Robert J. Marshall, Sept. 13, 1953; childrren: Gabrielle, Annette. Lic. psychology, Sorbonne U., 1948; MA in Devel. Psychology, Columbia U., 1951, PhD in Clin. Psychology, 1959. Cert. in psychoanalysis, White Inst., N.Y.C., 1970. Rsch. sch. psychologist Nat. Bd. of Edn., Paris, 1948-51; child clin. psychologist Children's Hosp., Buffalo, N.Y., 1953-54; clin. psychologist N.J. Dept. of Instns., Trenton, N.J., 1956-58; clin. instr. Rutgers Univ. Psychology Clinic, New Brunswick, N.J., 1958-59; part-time cons. Bd. of Edn., Ossining, N.Y., 1960-64; child therapist Rockland Mental Health Ctr., Monsey, N.Y., 1961-65; pvt. practice psychologist, psychoanalyst Westchester, N.Y., 1960-90, NYC, 1966—. Tng. analyst Blanton Peale Inst. Religion & Health, N.Y.C., 1984-90; supr. Inst. for Contemporary Psychotherapy, N.Y.C., 1974-97; faculty Nassau County Med. Ctr., L.I. Inst. for Psychoanalysis, 1980-94; lectr. Union Theol. Sem., N.Y.C., 1983-8 6. Co-authnor: (with R.J. Marshall) The Transference-Countertransference Matrix, 1988. Coord., founder Croton-Cortlandt Women's Ctr., Croton-on-Hudson, N.Y., 1976-81. Recipient Fullbright scholarship Columbia Univ., 1951-52. Mem. Am. Psychol. Assn., Am. Group Psychotherapy Assn., White Psychoanalytic Soc. Avocations: photography, painting. Home and Office: 300 E 74th St Apt 33D New York NY 10021-3746 Office Phone: 212-988-0634.

MARSHALL, SIRI SWENSON, lawyer, consumer products company executive; BA, Harvard U., 1970; JD, Yale U., 1974. Bar: NY 1975. Assoc. Debevoise & Plimpton, 1974-79; atty., sr. atty., asst. gen. counsel Avon Products, Inc., NYC, 1979-85, v.p. legal affairs, 1985-89, sr. v.p., gen. counsel, 1990-94, Gen. Mills, Inc., Mpls., 1994—. Bd. dirs. CPR Internat. Inst. Dispute Resolution, Internat. Inst. for Conflict Prevention and Resolution, Ameriprise Fin., Equifax. Trustee Mpls. Inst. Arts. Office: Gen Mills Inc Number One Gen Mills Blvd Minneapolis MN 55426

MARSHALL, THOMAS CARLISLE, retired applied physics professor; b. Cleve., Jan. 29, 1935; s. Stephen Irby and Bertha Marie (Bieger) M.; children— Julian, John B.Sc., Case Inst. Tech., 1957; M.Sc., U. Ill., 1958, PhD, 1960. Asst. prof. elec. engring. U. Ill., 1961-62; mem. faculty Columbia U., 1962—2006, asst. prof. elec. engring., 1962-65, assoc. prof., 1965-70, prof. engring. sci., 1970-78, prof. applied physics, 1978—2006, prof. emeritus, 2007—. Author: Free Electron Lasers, 1985, Book of the Toade, 1992; contbr. more than 170 articles to profl. jours. Research grantee Dept. Energy, Office Naval Research, NSF. Fellow: Am. Phys. Soc. (study group on directed energy weapons 1985—87); mem.: Free Election Lasers and Advanced Concepts in Accelerator Physics. Office: Columbia U 213 Mudd Bldg New York NY 10027 Office Phone: 212-854-3116. E-mail: tcm2@columbia.edu.

MARSHALL, TOBY, lawyer; BA cum laude, Calif. State U., 1996; JD, U. Wash., Seattle, 2002. Bar: Wash. 2002. Assoc. atty.; complex civil litig. Tousley Brain Stephens, P.L.L.C., 2001—. Contbr. articles to numerous profl. jours. Mem.: ABA, William L. Dwyer Inn of Ct., King Co. Bar Assn. Office: Tousley Brain Stephens PLLC Ste 2200 1700 Seventh Ave Seattle WA 98101-1332

MARSHALL, TOM, publishing executive; b. Shreveport, La., 1954; With Lousiana Life; pub. Alaska mag., 1987—89; gen. mgr. Cooking Light, 1991—98; v.p. mktg. So. Living, 1998—2003; v.p., pub. Sunset, NYC, 2003—. Recipient Gen. Excellence Nat. Mag. award, 1983. Office: Sunset Time and Life Bldg 20th Fl 1271 Avenue of the Americas New York NY 10020 Office Phone: 212-522-9058. Business E-Mail: marshallt@sunset.com.

MARSHALL, VINCENT DE PAUL, industrial microbiologist, researcher; b. Washington, Apr. 5, 1943; s. Vincent de Paul Sr. and Mary Frances (Bach) M.; m. Sylvia Ann Kieffer, Nov. 15, 1986; children from previous marriage: Vincent de Paul III, Amy. BS, Northeastern State Coll., Tahlequah, Okla., 1965; MS, U. Okla. Health Sci. Ctr., Oklahoma City, 1967, PhD, 1970. Rsch. assoc. U. Ill., Urbana, 1970, postdoctoral fellow, 1971-73; rsch. scientist The Upjohn Co., Kalamazoo, Mich., 1973-74, rsch. head, 1975, sr. rsch. scientist, 1976-91, sr. scientist, 1991-2000; cons., 2000—. Mem. editl. bd. Jour. of Antibiotics, 1990-2001, Jour. Indsl. Microbiology, 1989-2001, Devels. in Indsl. Microbiology, 1990; contbr. numerous articles to profl. jours., chpts. to books; patentee in field. Served with U.S. Army Nat. Guard, 1960-65. NIH predoctoral fellow, 1967-70; NIH postdoctoral fellow, 1971-73. Fellow Am. Acad. Microbiology; mem. Soc. for Indsl. Microbiology (membership com. 1988-90, co-chair edn. com. 1989-93, local sects. com. 1991-96, chair nominating com. 1993-94, mem. nominating com. 1999-2000, co-chair program com. 1993-94, dir. 1994-96, pres. So. Great Lakes sect. 1992-95), Am. Soc. Microbiology, Am. Soc. Biochemistry and Molecular Biology, Internat. Soc. for Antimicrobial Activity of Non-Antibiotics (sci. adv. bd.), Sigma Xi. Republican. Lutheran. Home and Office: 203 Paisley Ct Kalamazoo MI 49006-4359 Home Phone: 269-349-3795; Office Phone: 269-349-3795. E-mail: vince3795@aol.com.

MARSHALL, WAYNE KEITH, anesthesiology educator; b. Richmond, Va., Feb. 9, 1948; s. Chester Truman and Lois Ann (Tiller) M.; m. Dale Claire Reynolds, June 18, 1977; children: Meredith Reynolds, Catherine Truman, Whitney Wood. BS in Biology, Va. Poly. Inst. and State U., 1970; MD, Va. Commonwealth U., 1974. Diplomate Am. Bd. Anesthesiology, Nat. Bd. Med. Examiners; bd. cert. in pain mgmt. Surg. intern U. Cin., 1974-75, resident in surgery, 1975-77; resident in anesthesiology U. Va. Coll. Medicine, Charlottesville, 1977-79, rsch. fellow, 1979-80; asst. prof. anesthesia Pa. State U. Coll. Medicine, Hershey, 1980-86, assoc. prof., 1986-95, assoc. clin. dir. oper. rm., 1982-95, dir. pain mgmt. svc., 1984-95, chief divsn. pain mgmt., 1992-95; prof., chmn. dept. anesthesiology Med. Coll. Va., Richmond, 1995-99; med. dir. operating rms. MCV Hosp., 1995-99; prof. anesthesiology Coll. Medicine Pa. State U., Hershey, 1999—2004; pvt. practice, 2004—. Moderator nat. meetings. Mem. editorial bd. Am. Jour. Anesthesiology, 1987-99, Jour. Neurosurg. Anesthesiology, 1988—2004; contbr. articles and abstracts to med. jours. Recipient Antarctic Svc. medal NSF, 1980. Mem. AMA, Soc. Neurosurg. Anesthesia and Critical Care (sec.-treas. 1985-87, v.p. 1987-88, pres. 1989-90, bd. dirs. 1985-91), Assn. Univ. Anesthetists, Am. Soc. Anesthesiologists (del. ASA ho. of dels. 1990-92), Internat. Anesthesia Rsch. Soc., Pa. Soc. Anesthesiology. Republican. Baptist. Office Phone: 717-766-1127. Personal E-mail: wmarsh2723@aol.com.

MARSHALL, WILLIAM TAYLOR, lawyer; b. Dallas; s. Willis A. and Jane T. Marshall; m. Peggy Taylor, May 18, 1973; 1 child, Taylor. BSPA with honors, U. Ark., 1973, MBA with honors, 1975; JD with honors, U. Ark., Little Rock, 1981. Bar: Ark. 1981, U.S. Dist. Ct. (fed. dist.) 1982, U.S. Ct. Appeals (8th cir.) 1982, U.S. Supreme Ct. 1984; CPA, Ark. Fin. analyst Hosp. Affiliates Internat., Nashville, 1975-76, sr. fin. analyst, 1976-78; CFO Hosp. Affiliates Internat./Doctor's Hosp., Little Rock, 1978-81; assoc. House Holmes & Jewell, Little Rock, 1981-83, ptnr., 1983-85, Robinson, Staley, Marshall & Duke, Little Rock, 1985—. Lectr. in field. Contbr. articles to profl. jours. Mem. ABA, AICPAs, Ark. Bar Assn. (cert. tax specialist, health law sect. 1985—), Am. Health Lawyers Assn. Home: 1900 Beechwood St Little Rock AR 72207-2004 Office: Robinson Staley Marshall & Duke PA 400 W Capitol Ave Ste 2891 Little Rock AR 72201-3463 E-mail: bmarshall@rsmd.com.

MARSHALL, WILLIS HENRY, psychiatrist; b. Covington, Ky., Nov. 28, 1936; s. Willis Henry Sr. and Pauline Elizabeth (Murphy) M.; m. Carolyn Mae Kowalski; children: Louann Lorinda Marshall Johnson, John Willis. AB cum laude, U. Evansville, Ind., 1958; MD, Ind. U., Bloomington, 1961. Cert. psychiatry Am. Assn. Psychiat. Medicine, 2005. Intern Detroit Meml. Hosp., 1961-62; resident psychiatry Mental Health Inst., Cherokee, Iowa, 1965-67, 69-70, staff psychiatrist, 1967-69, Mental Health Ctr., Muskegon, Mich., 1970-71; pvt. practice psychiatry Madison, Tenn., 1974-85, Bowling Green, Ky., 1987-98; staff psychiatrist chief admission svc., staff psychiatrist treatment unit Mid. Tenn. Mental Health Inst., Nashville, 1981—85, staff psychiatrist evaluation unit forensic svcs. div., 1985—87, chief of staff, 1986-87; forensic psychiatrist State of Tenn., 1981—87; staff psychiatrist Moccasin Bend Mental Health Inst., Chattanooga, 1998—2003; staff psychiatrist, med. dir. Crisis Stabilization Unit Vol. Behavioral Health Svcs. Ctr., Chattanooga, 2003—05, outpatient psychiatrist, 2005—. Part-time staff psychiatrist Ottawa County Mental Health Ctr., Grand Haven, Mich., 1971-73, Tenn. Dept. Mental Health and Mental Retardation Mid. Tenn. Mental Health Inst., Nashville, 1981-87, Lifeskills, Inc., Glasgow, Ky., Franklin, Ky., 1987-89; psychiat. cons. Allegan County Mental Health Ctr., Allegen, Mich., 1973; med. svcs. cons. dept. of forensic svcs. Mid. Tenn. Mental Health Inst., Nashville, 1983-84; clin. asst. prof. psychiatry dept. allied health Trevecca Nazaraene Coll., Nashville, 1985-87; part-time pvt. practice psychiatry, Muskegon, Mich., 1970-74, Madison, Tenn., 1974-87; assoc. clin. dir. mental health unit Med. Ctr., Bowling Green, Ky., 1987-91; preceptor, asst. clin. prof. physician asst. program U. Ky., 1988-91; acting med. dir. Rivendell Children's Psychiat. Hosp., Bowling Green, 1989; med. dir. adult mental health unit Rivendell of Ky., 1992-94. Commd. officer, surgeon USPHS, 1962-65. Recipient AMA Physicians Recognition award, 1969, 79, 83, 86, 89, 92, Exemplary Psychiatrist award Nat. Alliance for Mentally Ill, 1993. Mem. Am. Psychiat. Assn. (life, art assn. 1976—), Ky. Med. Assn., Warren County Med. Soc., Am. Profl. Practice Assn., Am. Acad. Clin. Psychiatrists, Am. Assn. of Psychiat. Medicine, Am. Physicians Art Assn., NRA, Nat. Geog. Soc., AAA Automobile Club, Gallatin Gun Club, Alpha Omega Alpha. Republican. Avocations: sculpture, photography, painting, hunting, fixing old guns. Home: 5115 Silver Ln Apison TN 37302-9594 Office: 420 Bell Ave Chattanooga TN 37405 Personal E-mail: willishmarshall@aol.com.

MARSHALL-BEASLEY, ELIZABETH, landscape architect; b. Wilton, Conn., Mar. 14, 1959; d. Hamilton West Marshall, Jr. and Mary Barno Marshall; m. James W. Beasley, Jr., Nov. 28, 1986. BA, Princeton U., 1981; M in Landscape Arch., Fla. Internat. U., 1998. Policy analyst N.J. Legislature, 1981; field devel. dir. The Rouse Co., 1984; devel. mgr. Disney Devel. Co., Orlando, Fla., 1988; devel. dir. Norton Mus. Art, West Palm Beach, Fla., 1995; state orgn. dir. Jeb Bush for Gov., Tallahassee, 1996; project mgr., apprentice Morgan Wheelock Inc., West Palm Beach, 1999—2001; cons. Elizabeth Marshall-Beasley, West Palm Beach, 2001—02; pres. Elizabeth Marshall-Beasley, MLA, West Palm Beach, 2003—. Pres. coun. Nat. Pub. Radio, Washington, 2001—; gov. apptd. Bd. Landscape Arch., Tallahassee, 2002—; bd. dirs. Habitat for Humanity, West Palm Beach, New Horizon Svc. Dogs, Orlando. Sponsor Nantucket Conservation Found.; mem. curriculum com. Fla. A&M U. Grad. Sch. Arch.; active US VA Task Force Health and Rehab. Gardens; apptd. mem. City West Palm Beach Art in Pub. Places Commn.; mayor Art in Pub. Places Commn., 2006—. Recipient, ADDY, 1987, Comml. Project of 1989, Architecture Record, 1989; Fairchild Tropical Gardens: Off Site Collection Grad. scholar, 1997. Mem.: Am. Soc. Landscape Arch. (cert.), Sigma Alpha Lambda, Phi Kappa Phi. Episcopalian. Avocations: travel, theater. Office: Ste 1500 505 S Flagler Dr West Palm Beach FL 33401 E-mail: emb@landplandesign.com.

MARSHALL-DANIELS, MERYL, mediator, executive coach; b. LA, Oct. 16, 1949; d. Jack and Nita Corinblit; m. Raymond Daniels, Aug. 19, 2000. BA, UCLA, 1971; JD, Loyola Marymount U., LA, 1974. Bar: Calif. 1974. Dep. pub. defender County of L.A., 1975—77; sole practice LA, 1977—78; ptnr. Markman and Marshall, LA, 1978—79; sr. atty. NBC, Burbank, Calif., 1979—80, dir. programs, talent contracts bus. affairs, 1980, asst. gen. atty. NYC, 1980—82, v.p., compliance and practices Burbank, 1982; v.p. program affairs Group W Prodns., 1987—89, sr. v.p. future images, 1989—91, TV prodr., Meryl Marshall Prodns., 1991—93; pres. Mediation Ptnrs. and Two Oceans Entertainment Group, 1991—. Chmn., Nat. Women's Polit. Caucus, Westside, Calif., 1978-80; mem. Calif. Dem. Ctrl. Com., 1978-79; mem. Hollywood Women's Polit. Com., 1988; chmn. George Foster Peabody Awards. Mem.: Women in Film, Acad. TV Arts and Scis. (treas. 1985, bd. govs. 1989—2001, treas. 1993—97, chmn. bd., CEO 1997—2001). Democrat. Jewish. Office: Two Oceans Consulting Group 2017 Lemoyne St Los Angeles CA 90026 E-mail: twooceans@mac.com.

MARSTON, EDGAR JEAN, III, lawyer; b. Houston, July 5, 1939; s. Edgar Jr. and Jean (White) M.; m. Graeme Meyers, June 21, 1961; children: Christopher Graham, Jonathan Andrew. BA, Brown U., 1961; JD, U. Tex., 1964. Bar: Tex. 1964. Law clk. to presiding justice Supreme Ct. Tex., Austin, 1964-65; assoc. Baker & Botts, Houston, 1965-71; ptnr. Bracewell & Patterson, L.L.P., Houston, 1971-89, 96—, of counsel, 1990-96; exec. v.p., gen. counsel Southdown, Inc., Houston, 1987-95, also bd. dirs. Mem. ABA, Tex. Bar Assn., Tex. Bar Found., Houston Bar Assn., Houston Country Club, Coronado Club. Episcopalian. Avocations: hunting, fishing, stamp collecting/philately, reading. Office: Bracewell & Giuliani LLP 711 Louisiana St Ste 2300 Houston TX 77002-2770 Office Phone: 713-221-1315. E-mail: edgar.marston@bgllc.com.

MARSTON, MICHAEL, economist, consultant; b. Oakland, Calif., Dec. 4, 1936; s. Lester Woodbury and Josephine (Janovic) Marston; m. Alexandra Lynn Geyer, Apr. 30, 1966; children: John, Elizabeh. BA, U. Calif., Berkeley, 1959; postgrad., London Sch. Econs., 1961—63. Cert. rev. appraiser Nat. Assn. Rev. Appraisers and Mortgage Underwriters, 1984. V.p. Larry Smith & Co., San Francisco, 1969—72, exec. v.p. urban econ. divsn., 1969—72; chmn. bd. Keyser Marston Assocs., Inc., San Francisco, 1973—87; gen. ptnr. The Sequoia Partnership, 1979—91; pres. Marston Vineyard and Winery, 1982—, Marston Assocs., Inc., 1982—. Pres. The Ctr. Individual and Instnl. Renewal, 1996—. Contbr. articles to profl. jours. Mem. spkr. bus. Am. Embassy, London, 1961—63; mem. Gov.'s Issue Anlysis Com. and Spkr. Bur., 1966; v.p., bd. dirs. Dem. Forum, 1968—72; chmn. San Francisco Waterfront Com., 1969—86; v.p. People for Open Space, 1972—87, mem. exec. com., 1972—87; chmn. fin. com. San Francisco Planning and Urban Rsch. Assn., 1976—87, bd. dirs., 1976—87, mem. exec. com., 1976—87, treas., 1976—87; bd. trustees Cathedral Sch. Boys, 1981—82, Marin Country Day Sch., 1984—90; pres. Presidio Heights Assn. Neighbors, 1983—84; mem. Napa Valley Vintners, 1986—, mem. gov. affairs com.; v.p. St. Luke's Sch., 1986—91; chmn. Presidio Com., 1991—; v.p., trustee Youth for Svc. Served to lt. USNR. Mem.: Napa Valley Vintners, Calif. Vintage Wine Soc., World Congress Land Policy, Urban Land Inst., Pacific Union Club, Bohemian Club, Order of Golden Bear, Chevalier du Tastevin, Lambda Alpha. Home: 3375 Jackson St San Francisco CA 94118-2018 Personal E-mail: marstonmichael@yahoo.com. *Personal philosophy: Success is what you do with what you have not what others think or what is in vogue.*

MARTAN, JOSEPH RUDOLF, lawyer; b. Mar. 28, 1949; s. Joseph John and Margarete Paula (Rothenbock) M. BA with honors, U. Ill., 1971; JD with honors, Ill. Inst. Tech., 1977; cert., Masaryk U., Brno Czech Republic, 1993, 94, 95. Bar: Ill. 1977, U.S. Dist. Ct. (no. dist.) Ill. 1977. Assoc. V.C. Lopez, Chgo., 1978-80; corp. counsel Goldblatt Bros., Inc., Chgo., 1980-81; br. counsel Ill. br. Am. Family Ins. Group, Schaumburg, Ill., 1981-87; atty. Judge & Knight Ltd., Park Ridge, Ill., 1987-91, Judge & James, Ltd., Park Ridge, 1991-92; staff counsel Alliance of Am. Insurers Liability Ins. Rsch. Bur., Downers Grove, 1992—. Mem. Czech Republic program adv. bd. John Marshall law Sch., 1996—; mem. West Suburban Concert Band, Inc., Western Springs, Ill., 1975—, pres., 1979-81, v.p. 1989-90. with U.S. Army, 1972-74; capt. USAR, 1974-85. Mem. Ill. State Bar Assn., West Suburban Bar Assn., DuPage County Bar Assn., Bohemian Lawyer's Assn. Chgo. (pres. 1990), Windjammers Unltd. Inc., Chgo. Coun. Fgn. Rels., Czech-Am. C. of C., Res. Officer's Assn., Assn. U.S. Army, Met. Opera Guild, Pi Sigma Alpha. Home: 4056 Gilbert Ave Western Springs IL 60558-1235 Office: Alliance Of American Insurers 2600 S River Rd Des Plaines IL 60018-3203 E-mail: hundd44@hotmail.com.

MARTE-BAUTISTA, HELEN I., retired performing arts educator; d. Diosdado and Modesta Inocencio Marte; 1 child, Andreliz Marte Bautista. MA, San Francisco State U., 1970. Cert. Calif. State credential. Educator, staff devel. San Francisco Unified Sch. Dist., 1968—98. Commr. San Francisco Pub. Libr., 2000—; trustee Am. Libr. Trustee Assn., Chgo., 2002—. Choreographer (prodn.) dance drama, Santa Cruzan (Dance-in-

Residence award, 1968). Pres. City Celebration, Inc. Ethnic Dance Festival, San Francisco, 1984—88; sec., bd. mem. Kearny St. Housing Corp., Inc., San Francisco, 1986; pres. Friends of the San Francisco Commn. and Status of Women, 1986—88; treas. YWCA - San Francisco, Marin and San Mateo County, 1990—96; treas. Mayor's Protocol Office San Francisco/Manila Sister City Com., 1996; citizen adv. mem. Presidio Redevel. U.S. Dept. of Interior, San Francisco, 1997—99; sec., mem. bd. Internat. Hotel Sr. Housing Corp., Inc., San Francisco, 1998. Recipient Summer/Residence Citizenship award, Ethical Union Soc., Philippine Scouts Assn., U. Calif., Berkeley, 1961, Merit award outstanding pub. svc., San Francisco Mayor's Office Diane Feinstein, 1984, Human Rights award, San Francisco, Human Rights Commn., 1985; grantee Spl. Edn. program bilingual tchrs., U. San Francisco, 1979; Melvin Jones fellow, Lion's Found., 2005. Mem.: Delta Kappa Gamma (assoc.; pres. 1982—84, Beta Chi chpt.), Am. Fedn. of Teachers (assoc.; mem. of the bd. 1971—76), Fil-Am. Lions Club San Francisco (pres.), Am. Lions Club San Francisco (assoc.; mem. of the bd. 1988, Presdl. award 1996). Avocations: travel, art, music, literature, dance. Office Phone: 415-557-4233.

MARTEL, EVA LEONA, accountant; b. Bristol, Conn., Feb. 14, 1945; d. Samuel L. and Irene A. (Beaulieu) Martel. BS in Acctg., N.H. Coll., 1986; MBA, Plymouth State U., 1990. Cert. mgmt. acct.; cert. continuing edn. educator. Accts. payable Elliot Hosp., Manchester, N.H., 1971-79, bookkeeper, 1979-84, dir. acctg., 1984-94; portfolio mgr. Optima Health Inc., Manchester, N.H., 1994-97, mgr. managed care contracting, 1997-98, dir. managed care, 1998-2000; exec. dir. managed care Elliot Hosp., 2000—. Adj. faculty N.H. Coll., 1991—; speaker Daniel Webster coun. Boy Scouts Am., Manchester, 1988, Med. Assts. Workshop, 1997; mem. supervisory com. of bd. Telephone Credit Union, 2004—; panel mem. ednl. seminar, 1993. Treas. N.H. Indian Coun., 1980-84; vol. United Way, Manchester, 1988—, accountexec., 1990, 91; mem. adv. coun. health care adminstrn. N.H. Coll., 1990, faculty advisor weekend program, 1990-91; vol. N.H. Heart Assn., 1990-92; bd. dirs. N.H. chpt. Am. Cancer Soc., 1991—; road race com. Elliot Hosp.; mem. scholarship com. Jewett Sch. Recipient Excellence in Tchg. award N.H. Coll., 2000. Mem. NAFE, Hosp. Fin. Mgmt. Assn., Speaker's Bur. (smoke free com., recycling com. 1991), IMA, Healthcare Fin. Mgmt. Assn, Telephone Credit Union, (supr. com., 2004—). Roman Catholic. Avocations: physical fitness, reading, music, writing, teaching, coin collecting/numismatics. Home: 129 Riverledge Dr Goffstown NH 03045-6203 Office Phone: 603-663-6181. Business E-Mail: emartel@elliot-hs.org.

MARTEL, JOHN SHELDON, lawyer, writer; b. Stockton, Calif., Jan. 1, 1931; s. Henry T. and Alice L. M.; m. Bonnie Martel; children: John Sheldon, Melissa Ann. BS, U. Calif.-Berkeley, 1956, JD, 1959. Bar: Calif. 1959. Dep. dist. atty., Alameda County, 1960-61; assoc. trial atty. firm Bronson, Bronson & McKinnon, San Francisco, 1961-64; ptnr. firm Farella, Braun & Martel, San Francisco, 1964—. Lectr., mem. adv. bd. Hastings Ctr. for Trial and Appellate Adv., 1983—. Author: (novels) Partners, 1988, Conflicts of Interest, 1994, The Alternate, 1999, Billy Strobe, 2001; author, editor legal publs.; composer-writer popular songs; profl. musician. Pilot USAF, 1951-54. Winner Am. Song Festival awards, 1978-80, 82, 85, 87. Fellow Am. Coll. Trial Lawyers (state chmn. 1985-87, bd. regents 1993-98); mem. ABA (litigation, antitrust, tort and ins. sects.), Calif. Bar Assn., San Francisco Bar Assn. (former chair litigation sect.), Am. Bd. Trial Advocates (bd. dirs. 1991-93), Am. Fedn. Musicians, Phi Delta Phi, Kappa Sigma. Office: Farella Braun & Martel 235 Montgomery St Ste 3100 San Francisco CA 94104-2902 Home Phone: 831-336-3114; Office Phone: 415-954-4422. E-mail: jmartel@fbm.com.

MARTEL, ROLAND M., engineering executive; BA in Math., Colby Coll., Waterville, Maine, 1976; MBA in Ops. Mgmt., Cornell U., Ithaca, NY, 1982. Gen. mgr. Anchor Stampings Ill. Tool Works Inc. (ITW), Glenview, Ill., 1994, various v.p. and pres. positions Metal Components divsn., pres. Global Automotive Divsn., 2005—06, exec. v.p. global automotive components businesses, 2006—. Office: Ill Tool Works 3600 W Lake Ave Glenview IL 60026-1215 Office Phone: 847-724-7500. Office Fax: 847-657-4572. *

MARTELET, FRANCOIS R., pharmaceutical executive; b. Dijon, France, Feb. 17, 1960; m. Marie Santiard, July 9, 1991; children: Marie-Alix, Alexandre, Astrid-Marie. M in Bus., Dijon U., MD. Degree in med. law: France; cert. Advanced Gen. Mgmt. Program. Internat. mktg. trainee F. Hoffmann-La Roche, 1991—92, product mgr. Stockholm, 1992—94, group product mgr., 1994—95, internat. product mgr. Basel, Switzerland, 1996—96; head regional oncology, Europe, Middle East, Africa Eli Lilly Corp., London, 1996—99; bus. unit head Benelux Schering-Plough, Brussels, 1999—2000; v.p. pharma oncology intercontinental region, Latam, Asia-Pacific, CEE, Middle East, Africa) Novartis Pharma, East Hanover, NJ, 2001—03; regional head, Cen. and Ea. Europe, Mid. East, Africa Novartis, Munich, 2003—, Basel, Switzerland, 2003—05; v.p. oncology worldwide, human health divsn. Merck & Co., Inc., Whitehouse Station, NJ, 2005—06; French instr. US Mil. Acad., West Point, NY, 2006—. Lt. col. French Army Res., 2005—. Decorated Military Svcs. medal France. Mem.: Chem. Pharm. Assn., Internat. Execs. Resource Group, INSEAD Alumni, Greater Phila. Execs. Club, NJ Execs. Club. Roman Catholic. Avocations: skiing, horseback riding, jumping. Home: 25 Deer Chase Rd Morristown NJ 07960 Personal E-mail: francoismartelet@yahoo.com.

MARTELLA, ROGER ROMULUS, JR., federal agency administrator, lawyer; b. 1970; m. Ann Martella; 3 children. BA, Cornell U., 1992; JD, Vanderbilt U., 1995. Law clk. to Hon. David Ebel US Ct. Appeals (10 Cir.); atty. Sidley & Austin LLP; prin. counsel Complex Litig. Natural Resources Sect. US Dept. Justice; prin. dep. gen. counsel EPA, Washington, 2005—06, acting gen. counsel, 2006—07, asst. adminstr., gen. counsel, 2007—. Mem. Warrenton Town Coun. Office: Office of General Counsel Environmental Protection Agy 1200 Pennsylvania Ave NW Ste 2310A Washington DC 20460 Office Phone: 202-564-8040. Office Fax: 202-564-1778.

MARTEN, GORDON CORNELIUS, agronomist, educator, federal agency administrator; b. Wittenberg, Wis., Sept. 14, 1935; s. Clarence George and Cora Levina (Verpoorten) M.; m. Lynette Joy Hanson, Sept. 9, 1961; 1 dau., Kimberly Joy. BS, U. Wis., 1957; MS, U. Minn., 1959, PhD, 1961; postgrad., Purdue U., 1962; DSc (hon.), U. Minn., 2006. Rsch. agronomist U.S. Dept. Agr., U. Minn., St. Paul, 1961-72, supervisory rsch. agronomist, rsch. leader, 1972-89; adj. prof. agronomy U. Minn., St. Paul, 1971-96; assoc. dir. USDA-Agr. Rsch. Svc., Beltsville, Md., 1989-96; prof. emeritus U. Minn., St. Paul, 1996—. Mem. governing body and U.S. rep. to OECD Biol. Resource Mgmt. Program, Paris, 1990-96; adminstrv. coun. USDA Sustainable Agrl. Rsch. and Edn. Program, 1993-95. Assoc. editor: Crop Sci., 1972-74; sr. editor USDA Handbook Near Infrared Reflectance Spectroscopy: Analysis of Forage Quality, 1985, rev. edit., 1989; mem. edit. bd. Sci. of Food and Agriculture, 1985-90; contbr. numerous articles to profl. jours. NSF grad. fellow, 1959-61; recipient Merit award Am. Forage and Grassland Coun., 1976, Outstanding Svc. award, 1981, Civil Servant of Yr. award Twin Cities, Minn., 1976, Cert. of Merits, USDA Agrl. Rsch. Svc., Northrup King Faculty Outstanding Performance award U. Minn., 1986, Superior Svc. award USDA, 1987; named to Hall of Fame, Wausau Wis. Sch. Dist., 1998. Fellow: Crop Sci. Soc. Am. (bd. dirs. 1975—77), Am. Soc. Agronomy; mem.: Agronomic Sci. Found. (trustee 1984—89), Coun. Agr. Sci. and Tech. (bd. dirs. 1985—90), Am. Forage and Grassland Coun. (bd. dirs. 1977—80), North Suburban St. Paul Golden K Kiwanis (bd. dirs. 1998—2001), Biol. Club, Sigma Xi, Phi Kappa Phi, Delta Theta Sigma, Alpha Zeta, Gamma Sigma Delta (Adminstrn. award of merit Nat. Capital Area 1994). Lutheran. Home: 1312 Willow Cir Roseville MN 55113-3235

MARTENS, HARVEY ARTHUR, retired government worker, academic administrator; b. Bancroft, SD, Mar. 19, 1928; s. Henry Martens and Anna Naeve; m. Barbara Colwell, Oct. 7, 1956 (div. Jan. 0, 1979); children: Craig Colwell, Eric Harvey, Douglas Henry. BS in Polit. sci., S.D. State U., 1951; MPA, Maxwell Sch., Syracuse U., NYC, 1952, PhD, 1973. Asst. to dir. Navy Adminstrv. Office, Washington, 1952—58; head, mgmt. devel. staff Navy Mgmt. Office, Washington, 1958—62; mgmt. analyst U.S. Dept. of Agr., Washington, 1962—64; dir. spl. projects ASPA, Washington, 1964—65; dir. pub. adminstrn. programs, lectr. in pub. adminstrn. Maxwell Sch., Syracuse U., NY, 1965—73; project dir. Nat. Acad. of Pub. Adminstrn., Washington, 1970—71; dir. rsch. & planning, prof. pub. adminstrn. U. of Nebr., Omaha, 1973—77; dir. grants, prof. pub. adminstrn. Drake U., Des Moines, 1978—86; dir. grants Des Moines U., 1986—93. Editor: Navy Mgmt. Rev., 1960—62, ASPA News, 1962—64; author: (study report) The Orgn. and Adminstrn. of Federally Funded Cmty. Mental Health Ctrs. Pres. Ea. Nebr. Nutrition for Elderly, Omaha, 1974—77, Neighborhood Housing Svcs., Des Moines, 1985—89; chpt. pres. AARP, West Des Moines, Iowa; adv. com. of Polk County sr. svcs. Area Agy. on Aging, Des Moines, 1996—2006; mem. Older Iowans Legislature, Des Moines, 1998—2007; north am. adv. com. Internat. Coun. of Unitarian and Universalists, Prague, Czech Republic, 1999—2003; moderator, summer patio ch. First Unitarian Ch., Des Moines, 1985—2000. Lt. col. USAR, 1951—88, cpl. US Army, 1953—55. Decorated Nat. Def. Svc. medal U.S. Army, Meritorious Svc. medal 103d Corps Command; Scholarship, Syracuse U., 1951—52, Hixson Fellow, Kiwanis Internat., 1997. Mem.: Coun. Fgn. Rels. (Omaha), Am. Humanist Assn. (life), Torch Club Internat. (club pres. 1999—2000), Kiwanis Internat., Mason, Scottish Rite, Shriner. Liberal. Unitarian Universalist. Avocations: travel, genealogy. Home: 2935 Rutland Ave Des Moines IA 50311-3916 Personal E-mail: hmartens4@mchsi.com.

MARTI, KURT, chemistry professor; b. Berne, Switzerland, Aug. 18, 1936; came to U.S., 1965; s. Werner Marti and Emma H. (Habegger) M.; children: Andres Niklaus, Stefan Kurt, Lorenz Roman. MS, U. Berne, 1963, PhD, 1965. Postgrad. research chemist U. Calif.-San Diego, La Jolla, 1965-68, asst. prof., 1969-74, assoc. prof., 1974-80, prof., 1980—; vis. prof. phys. rsch. lab. Ahmedabad, India, 1977, U. Berne, Switzerland, 1977, 95. Vis. prof. U. Bordeaux, France, 1983, 94; mem. rev. panel Lunar Sci. Inst., Houston, 1971-74, 91-93; lunar sample analysis planning team mem. Johnson Space Ctr., Houston, 1975-78; lectr. in field. Assoc. editor Geochim. Cosmochim. Acta, 1985-95. Grantee NASA, 1971—; Guggenheim fellow, 1976. Fellow Meteoritical Soc.; mem. AAAS, Am. Geophys. Union, Am. Chem Soc. Home: 13424 Calais Dr Del Mar CA 92014-3524 Office: U Calif San Diego Dept Chemistry La Jolla CA 92093-0317 E-mail: kmarti@ucsd.edu.

MARTI, PAUL EDGAR, JR., architect, educator; b. Wichita, Sept. 7, 1929; s. Paul Edgar and Edna Clareen (Conley) M.; m. Audrey Lee Marti, Mar. 15, 1933; children: Dane Eric, Kara Lynn. BArch, Kans. State U., 1953; MA, U. Calif., Berkeley, 1958. Architect Murphy-Mackey, St. Louis, 1955—57, Hellmuth-Obata-K, St. Louis, 1958—62; v.p. Smith-Entzeroth, Clayton, Mo., 1962—88, Paul Marti Assocs. Architects, St. Louis, 1988—. Juror Am. Plywood Assn. awards, Seattle, 1973; instr. archtl. tech. Washington U., St. Louis, 1979—85. Contbr. articles in field to profl. jours. Alderman, 1986—; chmn. bd. St. Louis U. Cupples Hist. Mansion, 1995-2000; mayor, City of Oakland, Mo., 2001-; pres. Mayors Small Cities of St. Louis, 2004. Served with USAF, 1953-55. Citation of merit Am. Plywood Assn., 1978; Honor award, landmarks Assocs., 1996. Mem. AIA (award of merit St. Louis 1970, bd. dirs.), Alpha Tau Omega, Clayton Mo. Optimists (pres. 1968). Home: 105 Minturn Ave Saint Louis MO 63122-4842 Office: Paul Marti Architects 34 N Brentwood Blvd Ste 1 Saint Louis MO 63105-3746 Office Phone: 314-725-9006. Business E-Mail: martiarchitect@mailstation.com.

MARTIKAINEN, A(UNE) HELEN, retired health specialist educator; b. Harrison, Maine, May 11, 1916; d. Sylvester and Emma (Heikkinen) M. AB, Bates Coll., 1939, DSc (hon.), 1957; MPH, Yale U., 1941; DSc, Harvard U., 1964; DSc (hon.), Smith Coll., 1969. Health edn. sec. Hartford (Conn.) Tb and Pub. Health Assn., 1941; cons. USPHS, 1942—49; chief health edn. WHO, Geneva, 1949—74; ret., 1974; chair internat. affairs AAUW-NC, 1986—94, rep. to NC Coalition on Aging, 2001—, bd. dirs., 2001—; mem. NC Health Adv. Bd. Aging, 2001—. Hon. trustee Bridgton Acad., North Bridgton, Maine; mem. NC Women's Forum, 1984—; bd. dirs. NC Ctr. of Laws Affecting Women, Inc.; bd. dirs. West Triangle chpt. UNA-USA; chair residents health and social svcs. com., residents coun., residents com. for cmty. rels. Carol Woods. Recipient Delta Omega award Yale U., Nat. Adminstrv. award Am. Acad. Phys. Edn., Key award Bates Coll., Internat. Svc. award, France, 1953, Prentiss medal, 1956, Spl. medal, cert. for internat. health edn. svc. Nat. Acad. Medicine for France, 1959, Profl. award Soc. Pub. Health Educators, 1963, Benjamin Elijah Mays award Bates Coll. Alumni Assn., 1989, Legacy of Leadership honoree Pines of Carolina coun. Girl Scouts U.S., 2002; named to Bridgeton Acad. Hall of Fame, Maine, 2003. Fellow APHA (chmn. health edn. sect., Excellence award 1969); mem. AAUW, LWV, Women's Internat. League for Peace and Freedom, U.S. Soc. Pub. Health Educators, Internat. Union Health Edn. (Parisot medal, tech. adviser), Acad. Phys. Edn. (assoc.), NC Coun. Women's Orgns. (mem. coun. assembly 1988-92, Women of Distinction award 1989), Phi Beta Kappa. Home: 3113 Carol Woods 750 Weaver Dairy Rd Chapel Hill NC 27514-1443 Personal E-mail: ahm3113@hotmail.com.

MARTIN, ALBERT CHARLES, manufacturing executive, lawyer; b. San Lucido, Italy, Sept. 20, 1928; s. Joseph and Carmela M.; m. Jean Perrin, Aug. 22, 1953 (dec.); children: Lynne, Ken; m. Frances Doughty, June, 1996. BS, Mich. State U., 1952; MS, U. Mich., 1953; JD, Detroit Coll. Law, 1962. Bar: Mich. 1962. Corp. counsel, sec. Udylite Corp., Detroit, 1963-68; corp. counsel Hooker Chem. Corp., NYC, 1968-70, Grow Chem. Co., NYC, 1970-71; group v.p. Leeds & Northrup Internat., North Wales, Pa., 1971-79, pres., 1979—. Served with U.S. Army, 1946-48. Mem. Mich. Bar Assn. E-mail: franal8@aol.com.

MARTIN, ALICE HOWZE, prosecutor; b. Memphis, Apr. 25, 1956; married; 3 children. BSN, Vanderbilt U., 1978; JD, U. Miss., 1981. Bar: Tenn. 1981, Miss. 1981, Ala. 1989. Asst. US atty. US Attys. Office, Memphis, 1983-89; ptnr. Harris Harris & Martin, Florence, Ala., 1992—94; dist. mcpl. judge City of Florence, Ala., 1993—97; judge Cir. Ct. State of Ala., 1997—99; US atty. (no. dist.) Ala. US Dept. Justice, 2001—. Avocations: travel, skeet shooting. Office Phone: 205-244-2001. E-mail: Alice.Martin@usdoj.gov. *

MARTIN, ALLEN, retired lawyer; b. Manchester, Conn., Aug. 12, 1937; s. Richard and Ruth Palmer (Smith) M.; m. Bonnie Reid, Sept. 8, 1979; children: Elizabeth Palmer, Samuel Bates. BA, Williams Coll., 1960, Oxford U., 1962; LLB, Harvard U., 1965. Ptnr. Downs, Rachlin and Martin, Burlington, Vt., 1971—2002. Chmn. bd. dirs. Wicor Ams., 1991-2007; bd. dirs., chmn. compensation com. IDX Systems Corp., 1999-2006; bd. dirs., chm. fin. com. Union Mut. Ins. Co., New Eng. Guaranty Ins. Co.; mem. Vt. Jud. Responsibility Bd., vice-chmn., 1978-80; trustee Vt. Law Sch., 2000-04. Chmn. Vt. Bd. Edn., 1978-83; chmn. Vt. Rep. Party, 1991-95; mem. Rep. Nat. Com., 1991-95, 97-99. Mem.: ABA, Am. Law Inst. (life). Republican. Home: PO Box B Six Chimneys Orford NH 03777 Office Phone: 603-640-6100. E-mail: amartin@valley.net.

MARTIN, ANDREA LOUISE, actress, comedienne, writer; b. Portland, Maine, Jan. 15, 1947; m. Bob Dolman, 1980 (div.); children: Joe, Jack. Grad., Emerson Coll. Appearances include (plays) Hard Shell, 1980 (off-Broadway debut), Sorrows of Stephen, 1980, What's a Nice Country Like You Doing in a State Like This?, 1974, She Loves Me, My Favorite Year, 1993 (Tony award, Featured Actress in a Musical), (films) Cannibal Girls, 1973, Black Christmas, 1974, Wholly Moses!, 1980, Soup for One, 1982, Club Paradise, 1986, Innerspace, 1987, Martha Ruth and Eddie, 1988, Worth Winning, 1989, Boris and Natasha, 1989, Rude Awakening, 1989, Too Much Sun, 1991, Stepping Out, 1991, All I Want for Christmas, 1991, (voice) The Itsy Bitsy Spider, 1992, Striking Distance, 1993, Bogus, 1996, (voice) Anastasia, 1997, Wag the Dog, 1997, The Rugrats Movie (voice), 1998, Bartok the Magnificent, 1999, Believe, 2000, Loser, 2000, Recess: Schools Out (voice), 2001, All Over the Guy, 2000, Jimmy Neutron: Boy Genius, 2001, My Big Fat Greek Wedding, 2002, New York Minute, 2004, The Producers, 2005, The TV Set, 2006, How to Eat Fried Worms, 2006, Young Triffie's Been Made Away With, 2006, Black Christmas, 2006, (TV) Second City TV, 1977-81, That Thing on ABC, 1978, Torn Between Two Lovers, 1979, The Robert Klein Show, 1981, Kate and Allie, 1982, The Comedy Zone, 1984, Late Night Film Festival, 1985, Second City Twenty-Fifth Anniversary, 1985, Martin Short Concert for the North Americas, 1985, The Smothers Brothers Comedy Hour, 1988, Poison, 1988, The Martin Short Show, 1994, Earthworm Jim, 1995, Life...and Stuff, 1997, Damon, 1998, Committed, 2001, My Big Fat Greek Life, 2003, others; (TV movie) Charles Dickens' David Copperfield, 1993, Gypsy, 1993, In Search of Dr. Seuss, 1994, Harrison Bergeron, 1995, My Funny Valentine, 2000, The Kid, 2001, Sick in the Head, 2003, Kim Possible: A Sitch in Time, 2003, (voice) Jimmy Neutron: Attack of the Twonkies, 2005; TV host Women of the Night II, 1988, Second City Fifteen Anniversary Special, 1988, Andrea Martin: Together Again, 1989; actress/writer: TV series SCTV Network 90, 1981-83 (2 Emmy awards 1982, 83), SCTV Channel, 1983-84, TV pilot From Cleveland, 1980; also The Completely Mental Misadventures of Ed Grimley, 1988-90 (voice of Mrs. Freebus). *

MARTIN, ANDREW AYERS, lawyer, physician, educator; b. Toccoa, Ga., Aug. 18, 1958; s. Wallace Ford and Dorothy LaTranquil (Ayers) M.; children: William Ayers, Malorie Ayers. BA, Emory U., Atlanta, 1980, MD, 1984; JD, Duke U., 1988. Bar: Calif. 1989, La. 1990, D.C. 1991; diplomate Am. Bd. Pathology, Nat. Bd. Med. Examiners; lic. physician, La., Miss., Ark. Intern in pediatrics Emory U./Grady Meml. Hosp., Atlanta, 1984; intern Tulane U./Charity Hosp., New Orleans, 1989-90, resident in anatomic and clin. pathology, 1990-94; surg. pathology fellow Baylor Coll. Medicine, Houston, 1994-95; law clk. Ogletree, Deakins, Smoak, Stewart, Greenville, SC, summer 1986, Thelen Marrin Johnson Bridges, LA, summer 1987, Duke Hosp. Risk Mgmt., 1987-88; assoc. Haight Brown Bonesteel, Santa Monica, Calif., 1988; pvt. practice LA, 1989; physician/atty. Tulane Med. Ctr./Charity Hosp., New Orleans, 1989-94, Baylor Coll. Medicine/Tex. Med. Ctr., Houston, 1994-95; lab. dir. King's Daus. Hosp., Greenville, Miss., 1995—; asst. clin. prof. pathology Tulane U.; lab. dir., owner Vicksburg Pathology Lab., Bolivar Med. Ctr., Cleveland, Miss.; staff pathologist Delta Regional Ctr., Greenville, Miss., N.W. Miss. Regional Medical Ctr., Clarksdale, Miss., No. Sunflower County Hosp., Ruteville, Miss., Tallahatchie County Hosp., Charleston, Miss. Sr. ptnr. Mid-South Pathology Assocs.; med. dir. of labs. Vicksburg Pathology Lab., N.W. Miss. Regional Med. Ctr., Bolivar Med. Ctr., Delta Regional Med. Ctr., North Sunflower County Hosp., 1997—, Tallahatchie (Miss.) County Hosp., N.W. Miss. Regional Med. Ctr., Clarksdale, Lab Corp., Southaven, Miss., Tallahatchie County Hosp.; adj. faculty Moorhead U.; bd. dirs. Martin Bldrs., Inc., Toccoa; mem. AIDS Legis. Task Force for La.; case cons. Office of Tech. Assessment, Washington; tech. cons. and autopsy extra Oliver Stone's "JFK"; adj. clin. faculty Moorhead Coll. Contbr. articles to profl. jours.; author: Reflections on Rusted Chrome (book of poetry). Fellow Coll. Am. Pathologists, Coll. Legal Medicine, La. State Med. Soc. (del. meeting 1992-93). Home: 935 Lakehall Rd Lake Village AR 71653-6096 also: 4104 Alabama Ave Kenner LA 70065-5603 also: 3850 Old Highway 27 Vicksburg MS 39180-8829 Office: Mid-South Pathology Assocs PO Box 5880 Greenville MS 38704-5880

MARTIN, ANN MCCARTHY, library-media specialist, library association executive; b. Bklyn., Nov. 26, 1948; d. John G. and Cornelia (Dinneen) McCarthy; m. Charles S. Martin Jr., Aug. 23, 1969; children: Elizabeth Ann, Andrew Charles BS, Radford U., 1969; MA, George Washington U., 1995. Tchr. history, media specialist, Orono, Maine; libr.-media specialist Chesterfield County, Va.; ednl. specialist, Libr. Info. Svcs. Henrico County Schs., Richmond, Va. Mem. ALA, AASL (rep. to ALA Coun., mem. bd. dirs., exec. com., pres.-elect, 2007-), Va. Ednl. Media Assn. Home: 5039 Bonnie Brae Rd Richmond VA 23234-3765 Office: PO Box 23120 3820 Nine Mile Rd Richmond VA 23222

MARTIN, ARTHUR MEAD, lawyer; b. Cleve. Heights, Mar. 29, 1942; s. Bernard P. and Winifred (Mead) M. AB, Princeton U., 1963; LLB, Harvard U., 1966. Bar: Ill. 1966, U.S. Dist. Ct. (no. dist. Ill.) 1969, U.S. Ct. Appeals (7th cir.) 1970, U.S. Supreme Ct. 1980, U.S. Ct. Appeals (fed. cir.) 2000. Instr. law U. Wis., Madison, 1966-68; assoc. Jenner & Block, Chgo., 1968-74, ptnr., 1975—2003. Co-trustee Dille Family Trust, 1982—. Author: Historical and Practice Notes to the Illinois Civil Practice Act and Illinois Supreme Court Rules, 1968-88. Trustee 4th Presbyn. Ch., Chgo., 1996-99, sec. 1997-99, exec. com. 1997-99, mem. nominating com., 2006-07; bd. dirs. Stop Colon/Rectal Cancer Found., 1998—; founding bd. mem. Alliance for the Great Lakes, 2005—, chair nominating com., 2005—. Mem. ABA, Am. Law Inst. (mem. consultative group principles of law nonprofit orgns. 2004-), Ill. Bar Assn., Chgo. Bar Assn. (bd. editors 1972-86), Ill. State Hist. Soc. (adv. bd. 1998-99, bd. dirs. 1999—, exec. com. 1999—, fin. com. 1999—, treas. 2002—), Ill. Centennial Bus. Com., Lake Mich. Fedn. (bd. dirs. 1993-02, 03-, exec. com. 1994-02, treas. 1994-99, 01-02, sec. 1999-01), Law Club Chgo., Legal Club Chgo. Office: Jenner & Block 330 N Wabash Ave FL 4400 Chicago IL 60611 Business E-Mail: amartin@jenner.com.

MARTIN, BENJAMIN GAUFMAN, ophthalmologist; b. Louisville, Aug. 18, 1937; s. Benjamin and Catherine L. Martin; m. Caroline Sue Martin, May 25, 1975; children: Benjamin, Lori, Tamara, Farrell, Steven, David. BME, U. Louisville, 1954, M. Engring., 1973; MD, U. So. Calif., 1964. Design engr. Philco/Ford, Palo Alto, Calif., 1957-60; rsch. engr. N.Am./Rockwell, Inglewood, Calif., 1961-63; intern Wright-Patterson Med. Ctr., Dayton, Ohio, 1964-65; ophthalmology resident Wilford Hall Med. Ctr., San Antonio, 1968-71; commd. USAF, 1963, advanced through grades to col., ret., 1980; CEO Cape Coral (Fla.) Eye Ctr., 1980—. With USN, 1954-57. Decorated Legion of Merit, DFC, Bronze Star, Air medal. Mem.: DFC Soc., Daedalions, Elks, Shriners, Masons. Republican. Lutheran. Office: Cape Coral Eye Ctr 4120 Del Prado Blvd S Cape Coral FL 33904-7165 Office Phone: 239-542-2020.

MARTIN, BILLY (WILLIAM R. MARTIN), lawyer; b. Pitts., 1949; m. Michel Martin; children from previous marriage: Nikki, Erica. BA, Howard U., 1973; JD, U. Cin., 1976. Bar: Ohio 1976, DC 2000, admitted to practice: US Supreme Ct., US Ct. Appeals, DC Cir., US Ct. Appeals, 4th Cir., US Ct. Appeals, 6th Cir., US Ct. Appeals, 9th Cir., US Dist. Ct. DC, US Dist. Ct. Md., US Dist. Ct., So. Dist. Ohio. Asst. city prosecutor City Cin., Ohio, 1976—78; asst. US Atty., So. Dist. Ohio US Dept. Justice, Ohio, 1978—80, spl. atty., organized crime strike force San Francisco,

1980—84, asst. US Atty. Washington, 1984—88, exec. asst. US atty., 1988—90; ptnr., litig. dept. Eckert Seamans Cherin & Mellott, LLC, Washington, 1990—94; ptnr., principal William R. Martin & Assocs., Washington, 1994—97; ptnr., litigation dept. Manatt Phelps & Phillips, LLP, Washington, 1997—2000, Dyer Ellis & Joseph (merged with Blank Rome LLP, 2003), Washington, 2000—03; ptnr., commercial litigation group Blank Rome LLP, 2003—. Lead atty. for critical witness Office Independent Counsel (Starr) investigation of Pres. William Jefferson Clinton; instr. Trial Advocacy Inst., Justice Dept.; advisor NBA and NFL Players Assn. Offers commentary and legal analysis on major TV networks such as: CNN, NBC, CNBC, Court TV and BET. Named one of 75 Best Lawyers in Washington, Washingtonian Mag., 2002, and several others. Mem.: Washington Bar Assn., Nat. Bar Assn., DC Bar Assn., ABA. Achievements include defended Jayson Williams, Allen Iverson, Juwan Howard, Rod Strickland, Riddick Bowe, and Michael Vick; represented the family of Chandra Levy and the Lewinsky family. Office: Blank Rome LLP Watergate 11th Fl 600 New Hampshire Ave NW Washington DC 20037 Office Phone: 202-944-3000, 202-772-5939. Office Fax: 202-944-3068, 202-572-8380. Business E-Mail: martin-w@blankrome.com. *

MARTIN, BOE WILLIS, lawyer; b. Texarkana, Ark., Oct. 6, 1940; s. E.H. and Dorothy Annette (Willis) M.; m. Carol J. Edwards, June 12, 1965; children: Stephanie Diane, Scott Andrew. BA, Tex. A&M U., 1962; LLB, U. Tex., 1964; LLM, George Washington U., 1970. Bar: (Tex.) 1964. Law clk. Tex. Supreme Ct., 1966-67; assoc. Snakard, Brown & Gambill, Ft. Worth, 1967-69, assoc., ptnr., 1971-72; asst. counsel US Senate Labor and Pub. Welfare Com., 1969; legal asst. U.S. Senator Ralph W. Yarborough, 1969-71; assoc., ptnr. Stalcup & Johnson, Dallas, 1972-77; assoc. ptnr. Coke & Coke, Dallas, 1977-80; ptnr., shareholder Johnson & Gibbs, Dallas, 1981—95, Bell, Nunnally & Martin, Dallas, 1996—. Vis. prof. law So. Meth. U. Sch. Law, 1972-73, 75, 88-89, 95, 99-2000, 02-07, U. Tex. Sch. Law, 1977, 79, U. Houston Law Ctr., 2005. Contbr. articles to profl. jours. Staff Carter-Mondale Campaign, 1976, 80; cons. to v.p. of US, 1977-80; cons. Mondale for Pres. Campaign, 1983-84, Dukakis for Pres. Campaign, 1988; dep. coord. of visit of Pres. Mikhail Gorbachev to State of Minn., 1990. Capt. US Army, 1964-69. Mem. ABA, Tex. Bar Assn., Dallas Bar Assn. Democrat. Episcopalian. Home: 4055 Sweetwater Dr College Station TX 77845-964 Office: Bell & Nunnally & Martin 3232 Mckinney Ave Ste 1400 Dallas TX 75204-2426 Business E-Mail: boem@bellnunnally.com.

MARTIN, BOSTON FAUST, neurosurgeon; b. Tampa, fla., June 1, 1927; s. Boston Francis and Catharin Heidi Martin; m. Roselle Bayot, May 26, 1988; children: Sandrine, Nathalie, Samantha, Arielle. BS, Howard U., 1949; BMS, U. Fribourg, Switzerland, 1954; MD, U. Geneva, 1958. Diplomate Am. Bd. Neurological and Orthopedic Surgeons, Am. Bd. Minimally Invasive Spinal Surgery. Intern in gen. surgery Danbury (Conn.) Hosp., 1959-60; resident in gen. surgery Stamford (Conn.) Hosp.-Yale U. Affiliate, 1960-61; resident in neurology Met. Hosp., NYC, 1961-62; resident in neurosurgery NYU Bellevue Med. Ctr., NYC, 1962-65; chief resident in neurosurgery NYU Med. Ctr., NYC, 1965-66, fellow in neurosurgery, 1966-67; interim chief neurol. surgery sect. Sch. Medicine and Univ. Hosp., U. P.R., San Juan, 1969-70, asst. prof. neurosurgery, 1969-75; clin. instr. in neurol. surgery NYU, 1966-67; clin. instr. in rehab. medicine U. Medicine and Dentistry N.J./N.J. Med. Sch., Newark, 1978-86, clin. instr. surgery, 1996—; attending neurosurgeon Hosp. Ctr. at Orange, NJ, 1976—. Meadowlands Hosp. Med. Ctr., Secaucus, NJ, 1981—, chief neurol. surgery, 1998—; attending neurosurgeon Christ Hosp., Jersey City, 1987—. Pvt. practice, West Orange, 1976—; attending neurosurgeon Doctors Hosp., Santuce, 1970-75, Matilde Brenes Hosp., Bayamon, P.R., 1970-75, San Jorge Hosp., Santice, P.R., 1970-75, Tchrs. Hosp., Haty Rey, P.R., 1971-75, Auxilio Muto Hosp., Hato Rey, 1971-75, Presbyn. Hosp., Santuce, 1972-75; asst. attending neurosurgeon Knud-Hansen Meml. Hosp., St. Thomas, V.I., 1967-69, U. P.R. Univ. Hosp., 1969-75; attending neurosurgeon East Orange Gen. Hosp., 1976-86, chief neurol. surgery, 1990-2000; chief spinal cord injury svc. VA Med. Ctr., East Orange, 1975-84; active attending neurosurgeon Newark Beth Israel Med. Ctr., 1998—; presenter in field. Co-author: the Conus Medullaris: Physiological Anatomy and Clinical Considerations. 1987; contbr. articles to profl. jours. Lt. col., flight surgeon USAF, 1984-90. Recipient Cert. of Merit Lions Club Internat., 1969, Disting. citation DAV, 1977, spl. trophy for disting. svc. DAV, 1979. Mem. ACS, AAUP, Internat. Coll. Surgeons, Acad. Medicine N.J., Congress Neurol. Surgeons (mem. internat. com. 1974, socio-econ. com. 1974-76, med. legal subcom. 1978-84), Societe de Neuro-Cirurgie De Langue Francaise, N.J. Neurosurg. Soc., Assn. Mil. Surgeons U.S., Am. Acad. Neurol. and Orthopedic Surgeons, Air Force Assn., Orange Mountain Med. Soc., Alpha Phi Alpha. Office: 81 Northfield Ave West Orange NJ 07052-5338

MARTIN, BOYCE FICKLEN, JR., federal judge; b. Boston, Oct. 23, 1935; s. Boyce Ficklen and Helen Artt Martin; children: Mary V.H., Julia H.C., Boyce Ficklen III, Robert C.G. II; m. Anne B. Ogden, Jan. 6, 2000. AB, Davidson Coll., 1957; JD, U. Va., 1963; D of Laws, Hanover Coll., Ind., 2006. Bar: Ky. 1963. Law clk. to Hon. Shackelford Miller, Jr. US Ct. Appeals (6th cir.), Cin., 1963—64; asst. to US atty (we. dist.) Ky US Dept. Justice, Louisville, 1964, U.S. atty. (we dist.) Ky., 1965; instructor Louisville Law school, 1965—67; pvt. practice Louisville, 1966—74; 1st asst. Office of the County Attorney, Jefferson County, 1970—74; judge Jefferson Circuit Ct., Louisville, 1974—76; chief judge Ky. Ct. Appeals, Louisville, 1976—79; judge US Ct. Appeals (6th cir.), Cin. and Louisville, 1979—. Jud. coun. US Ct. Appeals (6th cir.), 1979—96, chmn., 1996—; mem. Jud. Conf. of US, 1996—, exec. com., 1998—2003. Chmn. Isaac W. Bernheim Found., Louisville, 1982—95; trustee Blackacre Found., Inc., Louiville, 1983—94, chmn., 1986—94; trustee Hanover Coll., Ind., 1982—, vice-chmn. Ind., 1992—97, chmn. Ind., 1998—2006; exec. bd. Old Ky. Home coun. Boy Scouts of Am., 1968—72; pres. Louisville Zool. Commn., 1971—74; trustee Isaac W. Bernheim Found., Louisville, 1981—97, 2006—; vestry mem. St. Francis in the Fields Episcopal Ch., Harrods Creek, Ky., 1979—83; bd. vis. Davidson Coll., NC, 1980—86, trustee NC, 1994—98. Capt. JAGC US Army, 1958—66. Fellow: Am. Bar Found.; mem.: ABA (com. effective appellate advocacy Conf. Appellate Judges), Nat. Assn. Criminal Def. (Lawyers award 2007), Metro. Louisville Ky. Bar Assn. (Judge Yr. 2001), Louisville Bar Assn., Ky. Bar Assn. (Judge Yr. 2007), Fed Bar Assn., Am. Judicature Soc., Inst. Jud. Adminstrn. Office: US Ct Appeals 209 US Courthouse 601 W Broadway Louisville KY 40202-2227 *

MARTIN, BRIAN, Olympic athlete; b. Palo Alto, Calif., Jan. 19, 1974; Student, Denver U. Luge racer with 2 man team, back driver, 1988—; mem. U.S. 1st Olympic Team; named to devel. team, 1989. Named winner, World Cup Races (4), 1997—98, All-Japan Championships, Nagano; recipient Bronze medal Luge Men's Doubles, Nagano Olympics, Japan, 1998, World Cup, 1998, Silver medal, Bell Atlantic Nat. champion, 1998, Silver medal, Luge Challenge Cup, 2000, Bronze medal, World Championship, 2000, 2005. Address: US Luge Association 35 Church St Lake Placid NY 12946-1805

MARTIN, BRUCE J., elementary school educator; b. Sarnia, Ontario, Can., Nov. 11, 1966; s. Keith Ray Martin and Patricia Ann Stothers Martin. BA in English, Brigham Young U., Provo, Utah, 1988—90; BA in Psychology, U. Houston, 2004; MA in Tchg., Western Govs. U., Salt Lake City, 2006. Cert. tchr. Tex., 2004. Tech. analysist Custom Tech. Solutions, Houston, 1990—2003; tchr. Klein Ind. Sch. Dist., Spring, Tex., 2004—. Scout leader Boy Scouts Am., Spring, Tex., 1998—2003. Independent. Church Of Jesus Christ Of Latter-Day Saints. Avocations: genealogy, outdoor recreation. Home Phone: 281-651-0419.

MARTIN, CAROL JACQUELYN, artist, educator; b. Ft. Worth, Tex., Oct. 6, 1943; d. John Warren and Dorothy Lorene (Coffman) Edwards; m. Boe Willis Martin, Oct. 6, 1940; children: Stephanie Diane, Scott Andrew. BA summa cum laude, U. North Tex., 1965; MA, U. Tex., El Paso, 1967; studied at, Art Students League NY, 2007. Tchr. English Edgemere Elem. Sch., El Paso, 1965—66; tchr. Fulmore Jr. H.S., Austin, Tex., 1966—67, Monnig Jr. H.S., Ft. Worth, 1967—68, Paschal H.S., Ft. Worth, 1968—69; instr. English Tarrant County Jr. Coll., Ft. Worth, 1968—69, 1971—72, Eastfield C.C., Dallas, 1981, Richland C.C. Dist., 1982; instr. art Meml. Student Ctr. UPlus Tex. A&M U., 2002—03; instr. art Brenham Fine Arts League, 2006. Artist Vt. Studio Ctr., 1998; press sec. Senator Gaylord Nelson, Washington, 1969—71. Editor The Avesta Mag., 1964-65; various art exhbns Mem. Nat. Mus. Women in Arts; mem. Brenham Fine Arts League, Friends of Meml. Student Ctr.-OPAS (Opera and Performing Arts Soc.), The Woman's Club. Mem. Lone Star Art Guild (sec. 2006-07), Brazos Valley Art League, Brazos Valley Symphony Soc., Mortar Board, Opera and Performing Arts Soc. Guild, Alpha Chi, Sigma Tau Delta, Kappa Delta Pi, Delta Gamma Democrat. Episcopalian. Avocations: travel, photography, skiing, painting. Address: 4055 Sweetwater Dr College Station TX 77845-9650

MARTIN, CHARLES NEIL, JR., health care management company executive; b. Florence, Ala., Dec. 11, 1942; s. Charles Neil Sr. and Hazel Lucy (Hawkins) M. BS, So. Coll., Chattanooga, 1964. Adminstr. El Reposo Nursing Home, Florence, 1964-66, Parkwood Convalescent Ctr., Chattanooga, 1966-67; project dir. Tenn. Hosp. Assn., Nashville, 1967-68, asst. dir., 1968-69; v.p. Gen. Care Corp., Nashville, 1969-76, exec. v.p., 1976-79, pres., COO, 1979-80; sr. v.p. HCA, Nashville, 1980-85, exec. v.p., 1985-87, also bd. dirs.; pres., chief operating officer HealthTrust, Inc., Nashville, 1987—92; chmn., pres., CEO OrNda HealthCorp., 1992—97; chmn., CEO Vanguard Health Sys., Nashville, 1997—. Bd. dirs. Equicor, Nashville, 1986—. Bd. dirs. Cystic Fibrosis Found., Nashville, 1987. Office: Vanguard Healthcare 20 Burton Hills Blvd Nashville TN 37215 *

MARTIN, CHESTER Y., sculptor, painter; b. Chattanooga, Nov. 2, 1934; s. Woodfin Ballenger and Mabel Willett (Young) M.; m. Patricia Ann Parnell, Aug. 15, 1963; 1 child, Sharon Elizabeth (Mrs. Christopher Pruitt). Student, U. Chattanooga, 1952-55, 60-61, Internat. Medallic Workshop-Pa. State U., 1984. Freelance artist, Chattanooga, 1967-86; sculptor, engraver U.S. Mint, Phila., 1986-92. One-man shows include Hunter Mus. Art, Chattanooga, 1979; group shows: Kottler Galleries, N.Y.C., 1966; Internat. Exposition Contemporary Medals, Italy, 1983, Sweden, 1985, Finland, 1990; U.S. Dept. State, 1984, Nat. Sculpture Soc., N.Y.C., 1984, 85, 99, Cast Iron Gallery, N.Y.C., 1992, Internat. Exhbn. of Contemporary Medals, Brit. Mus., London, 1992, Hungarian Nat. Gallery, Budapest, 1994, Neuchatel, 1996, Nat. Sculpture Soc., N.Y.C., 1999, Weimar, 2000, Paris Mint, 2002, Lisbon, 2004, numerous others; permanent collections: British Mus., London; Smithsonian Instn.; Food and Agrl. Orgn., Rome; Am. Numismatic Soc., N.Y.C.; Julius Wile Sons and Co., N.Y.C.; Brookgreen Gardens, S.C., U.S. Mint, Phila., Belmont U., Nashville; major comms.: World Food Day Medal, UN, 1984, others; other major works: History of Chattanooga Mural, 1974; theme painting of Br. Colonial Ft. Loudon, 1975; Centennial Mural for Chattem Inc., Chattanooga, 1980; sculptured Congl. Bicentennial Silver Dollar, 1989, Eisenhower Centennial Dollar reverse, Mt. Rushmore Dollar obverse, 1991; designer Andrew Wyeth Congl. medal, 1989, George H.W. Bush Presdl. medal reverse; designer Yosemite Nat. Park Centennial Congressional Medal, 1991, Gen. Colin L. Powell Congressional Medal, 1992, White House Bicentennial Dollar reverse, 1992; designer mural Chattanooga Met. Airport, 1999. Served with USAF, 1956-60. Recipient numerous art awards, most recent being Purchase award Benedictine Art Competition, 1975, Medallic Sculpture award Am. Numismatic Assn., 1993. Mem. Fedn. Internationale de la Medaille (Am. del.), Am. Medallic Sculpture Assn. (v.p. 1987). Methodist. Avocation: modern languages. Mailing: 4110 Sunbury Ave Chattanooga TN 37411-5232 Office Phone: 423-698-3561. E-mail: cymppm@comcast.net.

MARTIN, CHRIS, vocalist; b. Devon, England, Mar. 2, 1977; m. Gwenyth Paltrow, 2003; children: Apple Blythe Alison, Moses. Student in Ancient World Studies, U. Coll. London. Sign painter; vocalist, pianist, rhythm guitarist Coldplay, 1998—. Singer: (albums) Parachutes, 2000 (Grammy award: Best Alternative Music Album, 2001), A Rush of Blood to the Head, 2002 (Grammy awards: Best Alternative Music Album, 2002, Best Rock Performance By A Duo Or Group With Vocal for song "In My Place", 2002, Record Of The Yr. for song "Clocks", 2003), Live 2003, 2003, X&Y, 2005, Love, Actually, 2006. Recipient Favorite Alternative Artist (Coldplay), Am. Music Awards, 2005. Office: Capital Records 1750 North Vine St 10th Fl Hollywood CA 90028

MARTIN, CLAUDE RAYMOND, JR., marketing consultant, educator; b. Harrisburg, May 11, 1932; s. Claude R. and Marie Teresa (Stapf) M.; m. Marie Frances Culkin, Nov. 16, 1957; children: Elizabeth Ann, David Jude, Nancy Marie, William Jude, Patrick Jude, Cecelia Marie. BS, U. Scranton, Pa., 1954, MBA, 1963; PhD, Columbia U., NYC, 1969. Newsman Sta. WILK-TV, Wilkes-Barre, Pa., 1953-55; news dir. Sta. WNEP-TV, Scranton, Pa., 1955-60; dir. systems Blue Cross & Blue Shield Ins., Wilkes-Barre, 1960-63; lectr. mktg. St. Francis Coll., Bklyn., 1964, U. Mich., Ann Arbor, 1965-68, asst. prof., 1968-73, asso. prof., 1973-77, prof., 1977-80, Isadore and Leon Winkelman prof. retail mktg., 1980—92, chmn. mktg. dept., 1986-90, prof. retail mktg. Isadore and Loen Winkerman, 1992—. Bd. dirs. Perry Drug Stores, cons. mktg., 1983-89; spl. cons. on rsch. changes in U.S. currency Fed. Res. Sys., 1978—; pub. mem. Nat. Advt. Rev. Bd., 1989-94. Contbr. articles to profl. jours. Trustee U. Scranton, 1996—. Served with USNR, 1955-57. Mem. Acad. Mktg. Sci., Am. Mktg. Assn., SW Mktg. Assn., Bank Mktg. Assn., Assn. Consumer Rsch., Am. Collegiate Retailing Assn., Am. Acad. Advt. (Disting. Fellow). Roman Catholic. Home: 1116 Aberdeen Dr Ann Arbor MI 48104-2812 Personal E-mail: claudemartinjr@hotmail.com.

MARTIN, CLYDE F., engineering educator; b. Wichita, Kans., Nov. 6, 1943; BSE, Kans. State Tchr. Coll., 1965; PhD, U. Wyo., Laramie, 1971; D (hon.), Royal Inst. Tech. Sweden, 1998. With NASA, 1971—73, 1976—77; asst. prof. Utah State U., 1973—76; assoc. prof. Case Western Reserve U., 1978—83; P.W. Horn prof. Tex. Tech U., Lubbock, 1983—. Office: Texas Tech U 1400 Boston Ave Lubbock TX 79409 Office Phone: 806-742-1511.

MARTIN, CLYDE VERNE, psychiatrist; b. Coffeyville, Kans., Apr. 7, 1933; s. Howard Verne and Elfrieda Louise (Moehn) Martin; m. Barbara Jean McNeilly, June 24, 1956; children: Kent Clyde, Kristin Claire, Kerry Constance, Kyle Curtis. Student, Coffeyville Coll., 1951—52; AB, U. Kans., Lawrence, 1955, MD, 1958; MA, Webster Coll., St. Louis, 1977; JD, Thomas Jefferson Coll. Law, LA, 1985. Diplomate Am. Bd. Psychiatry and Neurology. Intern Lewis Gale Hosp., Roanoke, Va., 1958—59; resident in psychiatry U. Kans. Med. Ctr., Kansas City, 1959—62, Fresno br. U. Calif.-San Francisco, 1978; staff psychiatrist Neurol. Hosp., Kansas City, 1962; practice medicine specializing in psychiatry Kansas City, Mo., 1964—84; founder, med. dir., pres. bd. dirs. Mid-Continent Psychiat. Hosp., Olathe, Kans., 1972—84; adj. prof. psychology Baker U., Baldwin City, Kans., 1969—84; staff psychiatrist Atascadero State Hosp., Calif., 1984—85; clin. prof. psychiatry U. Calif., San Francisco, 1985—; chief psychiatrist Calif. Med. Facility, Vacaville, 1985—87. Pres., editor Corrective and Social Psychiatry, Olathe, 1970—84, Atascadero, 1984—85, Fairfield, Calif., 1985—97; cons. psychiatrist Brit. Health Svc. Plymouth (Eng.) Trust, 1999—2001. Contbr. articles to profl. jours. Bd. dirs. Meth. Youthville, Newton, Kans., 1965—75, Spofford Home, Kansas City, 1974—78; del. Kans. East Conf. Meth. Ch., 1972—80, bd. global ministries, 1974—80. Served to capt. USAF, 1962—64, ret. col. USAF. Scholar Oxford Law and Soc., 1993. Fellow: Am. Orthopsychiat. Assn., World Assn. Social Psychiatry, Royal Soc. Health (London), Am. Assn. Mental Health Profls. in Corrections, Am. Psychiat. Assn.; mem.: AMA, Assn. Mental Health Adminstrs. (cert.), Am. Assn. Sex Educators, Counselors and Therapists (cert.), Assn. for Advancement Psychotherapy, St. James Club (London), Capitol Hill Club (Washington), Marines Meml. Club (San Francisco), Pi Kappa Alpha, Phi Beta Pi. Office Phone: 707-688-3790. Personal E-mail: cvkcmartin@msn.com.

MARTIN, CRAIG LEE, engineering company executive; b. Dodge City, Kans., Nov. 23, 1949; s. Ray N. and Nadia C. Martin; m. Diane E. Hensley, Mar. 19, 1977. BSCE, U. Kans., 1971; MBA, U. Denver, 1982. Project mgr. Martin K. Eby Constrn. Co., Wichita, Kans., 1972-83; exec. v.p., COO CRSS Constructors, Inc., Denver, 1983-89; exec. v.p. CRSS Comml. Group, Houston, 1989-90; sr. v.p. CRSS Capital, Houston, 1990-92, CRSS Inc., Houston, 1992-94; pres. CRSS Architects, Inc., Houston, 1992-94; sr. v.p. ops. Jacobs Engring. Group Inc., 1994-95; pres. Jacobs Constructors, Inc., 1994-95; sr. v.p. gen. sales and mktg. to pres. Jacobs Engring. Group, Inc., Pasadena, Calif., 1995—2000, exec. v.p. global sales, 2000—02, pres., 2002—06, CEO, pres., 2006—. Adv. bd. Constrn. Bus. Rev., 1993—. Bd. govs. Woodbury U. Sch. Bus. Mem. ASCE. Avocations: golf, clay shooting. Home: 930 S El Molino Ave Pasadena CA 91106-4414 Office: Jacobs Engring Group Inc 1111 S Arroyo Pkwy Pasadena CA 91105-3254 Office Phone: 626-578-6813. Business E-Mail: craig.martin@jacobs.com.

MARTIN, DANIEL C., surgeon, gynecologist, educator; b. St. Louis, Apr. 7, 1946; s. Dan Allen and Ruth Keel (Fields) M.; m. Glenn Ann Blakemore, July 7, 1970; children: Josh, Adam. BS in Physics, Emory U., Atlanta, 1968, MD, 1972. Diplomate Am. Bd. Ob-Gyn. Rsch. asst. physics and radiology Emory U., Atlanta, 1968-69; intern, resident, fellow, instr. The Johns Hopkins Med. Instns., Balt., 1972-77; from asst. prof. to clin. asst. prof. U. Tenn., Memphis, 1977-90, clin. assoc. prof., 1990—2005, clin. prof., 2005—06, prof., 2006—; surgeon Reproductive Surgery, P.C., Memphis, 1977—2006, U. Tenn. Med. Group, Memphis, 2006—. Gynecologist, reproductive surgeon Bapt. Meml. Hosp., 1977—; Axel Munthe presenter, Naples, Italy, 1992; guest spkr.Annual Japanese Endometreosis Symposium, Osaka, 1994, 2004; dir. gynecologic laser and endoscopy workshops, 1982-93. Editor: (textbooks) Lasers in Endoscopy, 1990, Laparoscopic Appearance of Endometriosis, 1990, Manual of Endoscopy, 1990, Atlas of Endometriosis, 1993, Endoscopic Management of Gynecologic Disease, 1996. Picker Found. fellow Emory U., 1969; Tex. Assn. Ob-Gyn. hon. fellow, 1989; recipient Bridges trophy for athletics Emory U., 1968, Codman surg. award, 1982, 83, Video award Am. Fertility Soc., 1992, Physician Recognition awrd Endometriosis Assn., 1995; named one of Best Drs. Am. Woodward and White Inc., 1992, 94, 96, 98, 00,02, 04, Hon. mem. Australian Gynecol. Endoscopy Soc., 1993, named to Sports Hall of Fame, Emory Coll., 2002. Mem. ACOG (sect. chair jr. fellows Md.), Tenn. Med. Assn., Memphis and Shelby County Med. Soc. (comm. com.), Am. Nat. Std. Inst. (subcom. on laser safety in med. facility), Am. Assn. Gynecol. Laparoscopists (pres. 1990-91, Videoendoscopy award 1993), Gynecologic Surgery Soc. (pres. 1994-96, chmn. bd. 1996-98), Australian Gynecol. Endoscopy Soc. (hon.), Argentinian Ob-Gyn. Soc. (hon.). Office Phone: 901-347-8331.

MARTIN, DANIEL RICHARD, pharmaceutical executive; b. Lima, Peru, June 9, 1937; s. James Marion and Clementine Caroline (Valencia) M.; m. Barbara Artemis Cyrus, June 23, 1962; children: Daniel Richard Jr., John Alexander, Christopher Andrew. BA, Cornell U., 1958; MS, Columbia U., NYC, 1959. Area sales supr. Schering Corp., Bloomfield, NJ, 1960-64; assoc. McKinsey & Co., NYC, 1964-69; treas. Harper & Row, Pubs., NYC, 1969-72; mng. dir. Merck & Co., Rahway, NJ, 1972-77; group v.p. Bell & Howell Co., Chgo., 1977-80; pres. Howland Martin Corp., NYC, 1980-85; pres. Sterling Europe, Middle East, Africa Sterling Drug, Inc., NYC, 1986-89; pres., CEO, also bd. dirs. E-Z-EM, Inc., Westbury, NY, 1990-97; pres., also bd. dirs. Milestone Scientific, Inc., Livingston, NJ, 1998-99. Adj. prof. mgmt. Pace U., NYC, 1996—; bd. mgrs. Country Life LLC, 2005; bd. dir. DelMonte Ltd., Asia. Co-chmn. Accion Internat., Cambridge, Mass., 1988-98; trustee Bangor (Maine) Theol. Sem., 1991-2000, Key and Candle Found., 2006-; dir. Americas Found., 1995-; bd. dirs., fin. com. White Plains Hosp., NY, 1997-. Decorated Order of Merit (Ecuador). Mem. Coun. on Fgn. Rels., Americas Found., Cornell Club NYC Independent. Congregationalist. Home: 31 Rochambeau Dr Hartsdale NY 10530-3017 E-mail: drm1937@aol.com.

MARTIN, DAVID ALAN, law educator; b. Indpls., July 23, 1948; s. C. Wendell and Elizabeth Bowman (Meeker) M.; m. Cynthia Jo Lorman, June 13, 1970; children: Amy Lynn, Jeffrey David. BA, DePauw U., 1970; JD, Yale U., 1975. Bar: D.C. Law clk. to Hon. J. Skelly Wright U.S. Ct. Appeals (D.C. cir.), 1975—76; law clk. to Hon. Lewis F. Powell U.S. Supreme Ct., Washington, 1976—77; assoc. Rogovin, Stern & Huge, Washington, 1977—78; spl. asst. bur. human rights and humanitarian affairs U.S. State Dept., Washington, 1978—80; from asst. prof. to assoc. prof. U. Va. Sch. Law, Charlottesville, 1980—86, prof., 1986—91, Henry L. & Grace Doherty prof. law, 1991—2003, F. Palmer Weber Rsch. prof. civil liberties and human rights, 1992—95, 2000—03, Warner-Booker disting. prof. internat. law, 2003—, Class of 1963 rsch. prof., 2004—07. Cons. Adminstrv. Conf. U.S., Washington, 1988-89, 91-92, U.S. Dept. Justice, 1993-95, U.S. Dept. of State, 2003-04; gen. counsel U.S. Immigration and Naturalization Svc., 1995-98. Author: Forced Migration: Law and Policy, 2007, Immigration: Process and Policy, 1985, 5th edit., 2003, Asylum Case Law Sourcebook, 1994, 6th edit., 2006, The Endless Quest: Helping America's Farm Workers, 1994, The United States Refugee Admissions Program: Reforms for a New Era of Refugee Resettlement, 2005; editor: The New Asylum Seekers, 1988, Immigration Admissions, 1998, Immigration Controls, 1998, Rights and Duties of Dual Nationals: Evolution and Prospects, 2002, Immigration Stories, 2005; bd. editors Am. Jour. Internat. Law, 2004-; contbr. articles to profl. jours. Nat. governing bd. Common Cause, Washington, 1972-75; elder Westminster Presbyn. Ch., Charlottesville, 1982-84, 89-92; bd. dirs. Internat. Rescue Com., 2000-03. German Marshall Fund Rsch. fellow, Geneva, 1984-85. Mem. Am. Soc. Internat. Law (v.p. 2003-05, Book award 1986), Internat. Law Assn. Democrat. Office: U Va Sch Law 580 Massie Rd Charlottesville VA 22903-1738 Office Phone: 434-924-3144.

MARTIN, DAVID ALLEN, application developer, computer scientist; b. Louisville, Oct. 27, 1953; s. Philip Allen and Finas Ellen Martin; m. Rhonda Faye Martin, Apr. 12, 1998; children: Benjamin Lloyd, Sarah Beth Richert, Patricia Ellen, Bradley Alan Richert. BS in Computer Sci., U. Louisville, 1975, MS in Computer Sci., 1977. Field rep. Compugraphic Corp., Wilmington, Mass., 1977—80; chief tech. officer A. L. Sewell Co., Inc., Louisville, 1980—92, Computer Contractors Internat., Dana Point, Calif., 1992—97, e-PULSETrak.com, Louisville, 1997—. Cons. software bus. solutions Computer Contractors Internat., Dana Point, Calif., 1992—97. Author: (software) Traker; co-author: e-PULSETrak.com. Deacon Midlane Pk. Bapt. Ch., Louisville, 2004—06. Bapt. Avocations: travel, computers, reading, investments. Office: e-PULSETrakcom 4220 Bardstown Road Louisville KY 40218 Home Phone: 502-244-7894; Office Phone: 502-371-3106. Office Fax: 502-459-2955; Home Fax: 502-459-2955. Business E-Mail: davidm@e-pulsetrak.com.

MARTIN, DAVID BRITON HADDEN, JR., lawyer; b. Beverly, Mass., Dec. 9, 1946; s. David Briton Hadden and Mary Louise (Ward) Martin; m. Martha Bacon, June 21, 1969; children: Charlotte, Jessica, Benjamin Ward. BA, Yale U., 1969; JD, U. Va., 1976. Bar: Va. 1976, DC 1977. Assoc.

Dunnells, Duvall, Bennett & Porter, Washington, 1976—79, Dickstein, Shapiro & Morin, Washington, 1979—80; spl. counsel SEC, Washington, 1980—84, spl. counsel to chmn., 1984—85, dir., divsn. corp. fin., 2000—02; assoc. Hogan & Hartson, Washington, 1985—87, ptnr., 1987—99, Covington & Burling, Washington, 2002—, co-head, securities practice group, co-head corp. practice area. Mng. editor: U. Va. Law Rev., 1975—76. Bd. dirs. Jubilee Jobs, 1998—; trustee Westover Sch., 1998—, SEC Hist. Soc., 2004—. Mem.: Metro. Club. Office: Covington & Burling LLP 1201 Pennsylvania Ave Washington DC 20004-2401 Home Phone: 703-836-4915; Office Phone: 202-662-5128. Office Fax: 202-778-5128. Business E-Mail: dmartin@cov.com.

MARTIN, DAVID EDWARD, health sciences educator; b. Green Bay, Wis., Oct. 1, 1939; s. Edward Henry and Lillie (Luckman) M. BS, U. Wis., 1961, MS, 1963, PhD, 1970. Ford Found. research trainee Wis. Regional Primate Ctr., Madison, 1967-70; asst. prof. health scis. Ga. State U., Atlanta, 1970-74, assoc. prof., 1974-80, prof., 1980-91, regents prof., 1992—2000, regents prof. emeritus, 2000—. Affiliate scientist Yerkes Primate Rsch. Ctr., Emory U., Atlanta, 1970—98; US rep to Internat. Olympic Acad., 1978; sport medicine rsch. assoc. US Olympic Com., 1981—84; chmn. sports scis. USA Track and Field; mem. coaching staff US teams to world championships in distance running, Rome, 1982, Gateshead, England, 83, Budapest, Hungary, 94, Vilamoura, Portugal, 2000, Fukuoka, Japan, 06, head coach, Paris, 1980, Madrid, 84, Hiroshima, Japan, 85, Warsaw, 87, Antwerp, Belgium, 91; mem. Olympic med. support group Atlanta Olympic Games. Author: Laboratory Experiments in Human Physiology, 4th edit., 1980, The Marathon Footrace, 1979, La Corsa Di Maratona, 1982, The High Jump Book, 1982, The High Jump Book, 2d edit., 1987, Respiratory Anatomy and Physiology, 1987, Training Distance Runners, 1991, Training Distance Runners, 2d edit., 1997, Training Distance Runners, German edit., 1992, Training Distance Runners, Spanish edit., 1995, Training Distance Runners, Japanese edit., 2001, The Olympic Marathon, 2000. Trustee Ga. Found. for Athletic Excellence. Named Disting. prof. Ga. State U., 1975, 81, 85 Fellow Am. Coll. Sports Medicine; mem. Internat. Soc. Olympic Historians, Am. Physiol. Soc., Atlanta Track Club. Home: 510 Coventry Rd Apt 13A Decatur GA 30030-5038 Office: Ga State U Dept Cardiopul Care Atlanta GA 30303 Office Phone: 404-413-1272. Business E-Mail: drdave@gsu.edu.

MARTIN, DAVID HUBERT, internist, epidemiologist, educator; b. Detroit, Mar. 24, 1943; s. Hubert Cillis and Mable Anita (Stewart) M.; m. Jane Ellen Schlichtemeier, Nov. 22, 1970; children: Jennifer, Jason. BA with distinction, U. Kans., 1965; MD cum laude, Harvard Coll., 1969. Diplomate Nat. Bd. Med. Examiners, Am. Bd. Internal Medicine, Infectious Disease Subspecialty Bd. Am. Bd. Internal Medicine. Intern Bronx (N.Y.) Mcpl. Hosp. Ctr., 1969-70; staff assoc. Nat. Inst. Allergy and Infectious Diseases, Mid. Am. Rsch. Unit, NIH, Panama Canal Zone, 1970-73; med. resident U. Wash. Affiliated Hosps., 1973-75; sr. fellow in infectious diseases U. Wash., 1976-78; chief resident in medicine USPHS Hosp., Seattle, 1975-76, staff internal medicine clinic, 1975, attending physician internal medicine, 1976-78, staff dept. internal medicine New Orleans, 1979-81; staff Hotel Dieu Hosp., New Orleans, 1982-94; clin. asst. prof. medicine La. State U. Med. Sch., New Orleans, 1979-81, asst. prof. medicine divsn. infectious diseases, 1981-82, assoc. prof. medicine divsn. infectious diseases, 1982-88, assoc. prof. microbiology, 1986-88, prof. internal medicine and microbiology, 1988, asst. chief sect. infectious diseases, 1988-89, chief sect. infectious diseases, 1990—, Harry E. Dascomb M.D. prof. of medicine, 1990—. Instr. dept. medicine U. Wash. Sch. Medicine, Seattle, 1975-78, acting asst. prof. medicine, 1978-79; chmn. infection control com., chmn. instnl. rev. bd. human rsch. com., chmn. antibiotic utilization com., sec. rsch. and editl. com., sec. animal welfare com. USPHS Hosp., New Orleans, 1979-81, dep. chief clin. rsch. dept., 1979-81, chmn. credentials com., 1980-81; mem. infection control com. Hotel Dieu Hosp., New Orleans, 1983-84, chmn. pharmacy and therapeutics com., 1988-94, mem. infection control com., 1990-94; vis. physician Charity Hosp. (now Med. Ctr. of La. at New Orleans), New Orleans, 1982—, chmn. antiobiotics com., 1982—, dir. infection control program, 1993—, chmn. infection control com., 1993—, vice chmn. pharmacy and therapeutics com., 1995—; chmn. comprehensive medicine head search com. La. State U. Med. Sch., 1989-90, dept. medicine faculty promotion com., 1988—, AIDS policy com., 1992; adv. bd. La. State Labs., 1993—, State La. Pub. Health Lab. Adv. Com., 1994—, U.S. Pub. Health Region 6 Infertility Prevention Adv. Com., 1995—; mem. nat. STD treatment guidelines com. Ctrs. Disease Control, 1993, 98, nat. Chlamydia and gonorrheadiagnosis guidelines com., 1997—; dir. La. STD/HIV rsch. ctr., 2001-04, Gulf South STI/TM Collaborative Rsch. Ctr., 2004—. Peer reviewer various jours. including Sexually Transmitted Diseases, The Jour. of Infectious Diseases, The Am. Jour. of the Med. Scis., Archives of Internal Medicine, Clin. Infectious Diseases, New Eng. Jour. Medicine, Annals Internal Medicine, Jour. AMA; contbr. chpts. to books and articles to profl. jours. Dir. La. STD/HIV Rsch. Ctr., 2002—. With USPHS, 1970-82. Fellow ACP (La. chpt. program chmn. 1994-95), Infectious Diseases Soc. Am.; mem. Internat. Soc. for Sexually Transmitted Disease Rsch. (bd. dirs. 1991-99, chmn. 1995 meeting organizing com., pres. 1993-95, sec.-treas. 1999—), Am. Fedn. for Clin. Rsch., Am. Sexually Transmitted Diseases Assn. (v.p. 1992-94, pres. 1994-96), Am. Soc. for Microbiology, European Soc. for Clin. Microbiology and Infectious Diseases, So. Soc. for Clin. Investigation, La./Miss. Infectious Diseases Soc. (bd. dirs., sci. program chmn. 1993, pres. 1997-99), Phi Beta Kappa. Achievements include research in the effect of sexually transmitted microorganisms on pregnancy outcome, antibiotic treatment of sexually transmitted diseases and in particular C. trachomatis, epidemiology of C. trachomatis in normal populations, chancroid and other genital ulcer diseases; establishment of first chlamydia laboratory in the Gulf South. Office: La State U Med Sch 1542 Tulane Ave New Orleans LA 70112-2825 Office Phone: 504-568-5031.

MARTIN, DAVID S., retired secondary school educator, administrator; b. NYC, May 14, 1941; s. Perry Johnson and Polly Edith (Shedlov) M.; m. Florence E. Martin, Jan. 14, 1989; children: Drew Michael, Amy Davida. BA, Adelphi Coll., 1962, MA, 1966; profl. cert., Hofstra U., 1969. Cert. secondary tchr., sch. dist. adminstr., N.Y. Adj. assoc. prof. Pace U., White Plains, N.Y., 1978-92; tchr., computer coord. Jericho (N.Y.) Pub. Schs., 1962-99. Author: Teachers Manual for Introduction to Pascal; co-author: How To Prepare for SAT II: Physics, 6th edit.; also author other books; contbr. articles to profl. jours. Fulbright-Hays grantee, 1967-68; recipient Grand award L.I. Sci. Congress, 1958, Disting Achievement award Electronic Learning, 1983, Outstanding Accomplishment award RITEC, 1984. Mem.: IEEE (sr.), N.Y. State United Tchrs., Assn. Computing Machinery, Am. Assn. Physics Tchrs., Jericho Retirees Assn., Flambeau, Sigma Pi Sigma, Phi Delta Kappa, Omicron Delta Kappa. Home: 25 Cedar Ln N Glen Head NY 11545-1703

MARTIN, DAVID STANDISH, education educator; b. New Bedford, Mass., Aug. 24, 1937; s. Theodore Tripp and Elinor Louise (Raymond) M.; m. Susan Katherine Orowan, June 30, 1962. BA, Yale U., 1959; MEd, Harvard U., 1961, CAS, 1968; PhD, Boston Coll., 1971. Cert. tchr., prin. Tchr. Newton (Mass.) Pub. Schs., 1961-68, asst. prin., 1969-70; teaching asst. Boston Coll., Chestnut Hill, Mass., 1968-69; curriculum dir. Beverly (Mass.) Pub. Schs., 1970-73; prin. Mill Valley (Calif.) Pub. Schs., 1973-75, curriculum dir., 1975-80; chmn. dept. edn. Dominican Coll., San Rafael, Calif., 1978-80; coordinator undergrad. tchr. edn. Gallaudet U., Washington, 1980-85, dean sch. edn. and human svcs., 1985-95, prof. edn., 1995—2001, prof., dean emeritus, 2002—. Cons. Curriculum Devel. Assocs., Washington, 1975-2001; mem. bd. examiners Nat. Coun. Accreditation Tchr. Education; bd. dirs. USA-SINO Tchr. Education Consortium, Western Pa. Sch. for the Deaf; Fulbright fellow U. Witwatersrand, South Africa, 2003, 04, Open U., 2005, vis. rsch. prof. Author: Case Studies in Curriculum, 1989; editor: Cognition, Education and Deafness, 1985, Advances in Cognition Education and Deafness, 1991; co-editor, author: Assessing Deaf Adults, Curriculum for Deaf Learners; contbr. articles to profl. jours. Grantee Dept. Edn., 1970, 85, Knight Found., 1995-2001, Ford Found., 1998-2001. Mem. D.C. Assn. Colls. Tchr. Edn. (pres. 1989-92), Assn. for Supervision and Curricum Devel., Nat. Coun. for Social Studies, Am. Ednl. Rsch. Assn., Am. Assn. Colls. for Tchr. Edn. (bd. dirs.), Coun. for Exceptional Children, Phi Delta Kappa, Kappa Delta Pi (chair publ.), Ednl. Consulting Schs. and Univs. (prof., dean emeritus 2002-), Cape Cod Geneal. Soc. (co-pres. 2006-). Democrat. Unitarian Universalist. Avocations: genealogy, sailing, classical organ, astronomy. Home and Office: 10 Colonial Farm Cir Marstons Mills MA 02648 Home Phone: 508-420-0224. Personal E-mail: davidchina_2000@yahoo.com.

MARTIN, DONALD WALTER, editor, writer, publisher; b. Grants Pass, Oreg., Apr. 22, 1934; s. George E. and Irma Ann (Dallas) M.; m. Kathleen Elizabeth Murphy, July, 1970 (div. May 1979); children: Daniel Clayton, Kimberly Ann, Tory Lynn; m. Betty Woo, Mar. 18, 1985. Enlisted USMC, 1952, advanced through grades to staff sgt. Japan, Republic of Korea, Republic of China, 1956-61; reporter Blade-Tribune, Oceanside, Calif., 1961-65; entertainment editor Press-Courier, Oxnard, Calif., 1965-69; mng. editor Argus-Courier, Petaluma, Calif., 1969-70; assoc. editor Motorland mag., San Francisco, 1970-88; founder, prin., CEO Discover-Guides, Henderson, Nev., 1988—. Author: Best of the Gold Country, 1992, San Francisco's Ultimate Dining Guide, 1988, Inside Francisco, 1991, Oregon Discovery Guide, 1999, Northern California Discovery Guide, 1993, The Ultimate Wine Book, 2000, Washington Discovery Guide, 2000, Utah Discovery Guide, 1995, Adventure Cruising, 1996, Arizona Discovery Guide, 1996, Arizona in Your Future, 2003, The Toll-Free Traveler, 1997, Las Vegas: The Best of Glitter City, New Mexico Discovery Guide, 1998, California-Nevada Roads Less Traveled, 1999, San Diego: The Best of Sunshine City, 2000 (Lowell Thomas Travel Journalism Gold medal), Nevada in Your Future, 2004, Seattle: The Best of Emerald City, 2000, The Best of Phoenix and Tucson, 2004, The Best of Denver and the Rockies, 2001, Hawaii: The Best of Paradise, 2003, Undiscovered America, 2006. Recipient Diane Seely awards Ventura County Theatre Council, 1968, Lowell Thomas Travel Writing competition Gold medal, 2000. Mem. Soc. Am. Travel Writers, N.Am. Travel Journalists Assn. Democrat. Avocations: travel, hiking, white water rafting, biking.

MARTIN, DONNA LEE, retired publishing company executive; b. Detroit, Aug. 7, 1935; d. David M. Paul and Lillian (Paul); m. Rex Martin, June 5, 1956; children: Justin, Andrew. BA, Rice U., 1957. Mng. editor trade dept. Appleton-Century-Crofts Co., NYC, 1961-62; dir. publs. Lycoming Coll., Williamsport, Pa., 1966-68; editor Univ. Press of Kans., Lawrence, 1971-74; mng. editor Andrews McMeel Publ., Kansas City, Mo., 1974-80, v.p., editorial dir., 1980-95; v.p., editor-at-large, 1995-98; v.p. Universal Press Syndicate, Kansas City, 1980-98. Lectr. U. Mo., Kansas City, Johnson County Cmty. Coll., Kans.; free-lance writer, editor; cons. editor Kans. City Star Books. Author: (adaptation) Charles Dickens' A Christmas Carol: Adapted for Theatre; co-author (with Melissa Hayden) The Nutcracker Ballet; contbr. articles to profl. jours. Named Disting. Alumna Rice U., 1990. Mem. Ctrl. Exchange (Kansas City), The Groucho Club (London), Phi Beta Kappa. Home: 6810 W 66th Ter Shawnee Mission KS 66202-4147 Business E-Mail: donnamartin@kc.rr.com.

MARTIN, EDWARD BRIAN, electrical engineer; b. Lawrence, Kans., Feb. 9, 1936; s. Edward Brian and Dorothy Irene (Dowers) M.; m. Sharon Anne Zimmerman, Dec. 21, 1955; children: Terry Brian, Ricky Lynn, Mindy Anne, Timothy Alan. BSEE, U. Kans., 1958; MSEE, St. Louis U., 1969. Registered profl. engr., Mo. Program mgr. McDonnell Douglas, St. Louis, 1980-85, mgr. avionics, 1985-86, dir. engring., 1986-88, dir. electronics, 1988-89, sr. dir. tech. processes, 1989-91, sr. dir. avionics tech., 1991-92, dir. advanced missile systems, 1992-95, dir. advanced weapon systems, 1995-97; dir. advanced tactical missiles The Boeing Co., 1997—2000. Pres., chmn. bd. dirs. Martin Internat., Ltd.; ptnr, v.p. The Waverly Group, 2007—. Contbr. numerous articles to profl. jours. Pres. PTA, St. Louis, 1972; founder Martin Family Found. Mem. AIAA. Avocations: running, mountain climbing, writing. Home and Office: 5335 Lancelot Dr Saint Charles MO 63304-5742 Business E-Mail: emartin@waverlygroup.com.

MARTIN, EDWARD CURTIS, JR., landscape architect, educator; b. Albany, Ga., Aug. 21, 1928; s. Edward Curtis and Mildred Lee (Tyler) M.; m. Roberta Inman Parker, Mar. 18, 1967; children: Edward Curtis III, Andrew Parker. BFA, U. Ga., 1950, M of Landscape Architecture, 1969. Landscape arch. Norman C. Butts Landscape Contractor, Atlanta, 1950, M.T. Brooks Office of Landscape Architecture, Birmingham, Ala., 1950-56; Univ. landscape arch., horticulturist Miss. State U., 1956-70, prof. landscape architecture, 1970-92, Disting. prof., 1988, prof. emeritus, 1993—. Originator, chmn., lectr. Miss. Landscape Design Symposium, 1957-2005, Edward C. Martin Jr. Landscape Design Symposium, 2006—; guest lectr. U. San Luis Potosi, Mex., 1990, U. Mex. Sch. Architecture, Mexico City, 1991, La. State U., 1990-92, 94, 96, Biendenharn Found., Monroe, La., 1991, Longue Vue Found., New Orleans, 1991; prof. Miss. State U., 1992-93; guest instr. in field; originator, lectr. Garden Design Workshops, Miss. State U., 1988-2001; host numerous flower and garden shows and tours abroad; So. hist. gardens lectr. Miss. U. for Women, 1997-2000; photog. landscape archtl. rsch. study: Europe, 1958, 66, 74, 85, S.Am., 1960, Israel, 1993, 95, Greece, Turkey, 1998; vis. prof. La. State U., 1990-94, 97; instr. landscape design Bot. Gardens, Huntsville, Ala., 1996; instr. ecology tour Copper Canyon, Mex., 1994; spkr. and lectr. in field. Author: Landscape Plants in Design, A Photographic Guide, 1983; co-author: Home Landscapes, Planting Design and Management, 1994; invited to participate in Attingham Summer Program in Hist. Preservation (English country houses and gardens) Eng., 1985; author/photographer of 80-captioned slide series, one on Home Landscapes, another on Urban Landscape Design for use by Nat. Coun. State Garden Clubs, Inc., 1994. Mem. Miss. State Bd. Landscape Archs. for Profl. Registration, 1973-74; mem. Starkville Park and Recreation Bd., Miss., 1973-79; civic beautification com. Black Mountain, NC, 2002—; bd. visitors Warren Wilson Coll., Asheville, NC, 2002—; elder Trinity Presbyn. Ch., Starkville, Miss., Warren Wilson Presbyn. Ch. and Coll. Chapel, Asheville; garden tour guide Biltmore Estate, Asheville, 2003— Recipient Silver Seal award Nat. Coun. State Garden Clubs 1969, honoree 1995, Landscape Heritage award Fraser Found. Calif. 1986, Helent S. Hull Lit. award, 1996; Paul Harris fellow Rotary Internat., 1998; reception area (lobby) of Miss. State U. Dept. Landscape Architecture donated in his honor by Garden Clubs Miss. Inc., 2003. Fellow Am. Soc. Landscape Archs. (chmn. edn. com. 1960-61, pres. Miss. sect. S.W. chpt. 1975, chmn. S.W. chpt. ann. awards com. 1976, trustee Miss. chpt. 1977-81, nominated Jot Carpenter Tchg. medal Miss. chpt. 2006); mem. So. Garden History Soc., Nat. Coun. State Garden Clubs (chmn. landscape design 1993-97, Appreciation cert. 2005), Garden Clubs Miss. (bd. dirs. 1958—, Silver Trophy 1961, Spl. Silver award 1980, Gold trophy 1993, Appreciation citation 2005). Presbyterian. Home: 464 Chapel Rd Black Mountain NC 28711-2640 Office: Dept Landscape Architecture Box 9725 Mississippi State MS 39762-9725 Personal E-mail: edonthemountain@bellsouth.net.

MARTIN, EDWIN WILSON, corporate director, columnist, educational consultant, webmaster; b. Oceanside, NY, Sept. 3, 1931; s. Edwin Wilson and Jean (Carbone) Martin; m. Peggy Smith, Sept. 5, 1953; children: Scott Andrew, Bruce Leslie. AB, Muhlenberg Coll., Pa., 1953; MA, U. Ala., 1955; PhD, U. Pitts., 1961; D of Sci. Edn. (hon.), Muhlenberg Coll., Pa., 1981; DHL (hon.), Emerson Coll., Boston, 1984, LI U., 1995. From asst. to assoc. prof. speech pathology U. Ala., 1960—66; dir. sub-com. on handicapped US Ho. Reps., 1966—67; dep. assoc. commr. edn. US Office of Edn., 1967—69; assoc. commr., dir. Bur. Edn. Handicapped, 1969—79; dep. commr. edn. US Dept. HEW, 1979—80; asst. sec. edn. US Dept. Edn., 1980—81; lectr. in edn. Harvard U., 1979—81; adj. prof. edn. Columbia U., 1982—91; pres., CEO Nat. Disability Svcs., NY, 1981—94, pres. emeritus NY, 1994—; ret., 1994. Bd. dirs. Pall Corp., NY, Roslyn Savs. Bank, 1993—2003; adv. bd. Roslyn Bank divsn. NY Cmty. Bank, 2004—. Columnist: Venice Gondolier Sun, 2003—; contbr. articles to profl. jours., chapters to books. Active Mayor's Adv. Com. on Spl. Edn., NYC, 1987—89, Govs. Adv. Com. on Rehab., NY, 1990—94, Bd. Zoning Appeals, Venice, 2004—05; bd. mem. Golden Beach Assn., Inc., Venice, 1995—98, 2007—. Recipient Alexander Graham Bell award, Alexander Graham Bell Assn. for the Deaf, 1978, Disting. Leadership award, US Dept. Edn., 1986. Fellow: Am. Speech, Lang. and Hearing Assn.; mem.: Coun. for Exceptional Children (v.p., pres.-elect, pres., past pres. divsn. learning disabilities 1996—2000, Wallin award 1979), Jacaranda West Country Club (mem. nominating com. 2005, mem. green com. 2006, mem. bylaws and planning com. 2007). Business E-Mail: ed@insidevenicefiorida.com.

MARTIN, ELLIOT EDWARDS, theatrical producer; b. Denver, Feb. 25, 1924; m. Marjorie Cuesta, Oct. 7, 1949; children: Richard, Linda Lisa. Student, U. Denver, 1943-46. Actor, singer, stage mgr., assoc. producer Theatre Guild, NYC and London, 1947-53; prodn. stage mgr. 20 Broadway plays and musicals, 1953-61; theatrical producer Never Too Late, Nobody Loves an Albatross, NYC, 1962-66; theatre producer London, 1963; mng. dir. Center Theatre Group, Music Ctr., Los Angeles, 1966-71; producer Elliot Martin Prodns., NYC, 1972—. Mem. exec. bd. Nat. Theatre of the Deaf, Chester, Conn., 1981-, Westport-Weston Arts Council, 1976- Prodns. on Broadway include: Dinner at Eight, 1966, More Stately Mansions, 1967, Abelard and Heloise, 1971, Emperor Henry IV, 1973, A Moon for the Misbegotten, 1973 (spl. Tony award), When You Comin' Back, Red Rider, 1974 (Outer Critics award), Of Mice and Men, 1975, Touch of the Poet, 1976, Dirty Linen and New Found Land, 1977, Caesar and Cleopatra, 1977, Kingfisher, 1979, Clothes for a Summer Hotel, 1980, Kingdoms, 1981, American Buffalo, 1981, Angels Fall, 1983, Glengarry Glen Ross, 1984 (Pulitzer prize), Woza Albert, 1984, American Buffalo, 1984, Harrigan 'n' Hart, 1985, Arsenic and Old Lace (Broadway and nat. tour), 1986-87, Joe Turner's Come and Gone (7 Tony nominations, NY Drama Critic's award best play), 1988, Steel Magnolias (nat. tour), 1989, The Circle, 1989-90, Shadowlands, 1990-91, Breaking Legs, 1991-92, She Loves Me (9 Tony noms.), 1993-94, Death of a Salesman, 1995-96, A Moon For the Misbegotten, 2000, Down the Gaden Paths, 2001, I'm Not Rappaport, 2002, The Oldest Living Confederate Widow Tells All, 2003, (London) Moon for the Misbegotten at the Old Vic, 2006. Mem. bd. assocs. U. Bridgeport, 1978-83. Recipient Tony award for most innovative revival, 1977-78, Larry Tajiri award for outstanding contbn. to arts Denver Post, 1970, Congl. commendation, 1970, Profl. Achievement award U. Denver, 1987. Mem. Platform Speakers Am., League NY Theatres and Prodrs. (gov.), Am. Friends of Theatre (pres.), Players Club, NY Athletic Club (NYC). Republican. Home Phone: 212-245-4177; Office Phone: 212-245-4176. E-mail: eemmar@vevito.net.

MARTIN, FLOYD W., art educator; b. Gainesville, Ga., June 30, 1951; s. Raymond J. and Lois Jean Martin; m. Rebecca Jane Edge, Nov. 30, 1985; 1 child, Mary Rebecca. BA cum laude, Carleton Coll., Northfield, Minn., 1973; MA, U. Iowa, Iowa City, 1975; PhD, U. Ill., Urbana Champaign, 1982. Lectr. U. Ill., Urbana Champaign, 1981—82; prof. art history U. Ark., Little Rock, 1982—, chair dept. art, 1994—95, 2005. Inaugural prof. UA Clinton Sch. of Pub. Svc., Little Rock, 2003—06; bd. dirs. Southeastern Coll. Art Conf., 1986—89, 2001—07, editor, 1991—98, 2007. Flutist: U. Ark. Little Rock Cmty. Orch. Vestry mem. Christ Episcopal Ch., Little Rock, 2000—03, 2007—; bd. dirs. Friends of KLRE-KUAR Pub. Radio, Little Rock, 1990—96. Recipient Sir George Trevelyan scholarship, Attingham Trust Summer Sch., 1982, AHAS! Spl. award of Distinction, Little Rock Arts and Humanities Promotion Commn., 1996, Exemplary Achievement award, Southeastern Coll. Art Conf., 1999, Pres. award for Svc. in the Arts, 2005; fellow U. Fellowship in Art and Design, U. Ill., 1978-81, Nat. Endowment for the Humanities, 1985; scholar, Victorian Soc. Am., 1980. Mem.: Victorian Soc. in Am., Midwest Art History Assn., Coll. Art Assn., Southeastern Coll. Art Conf., Phi Kappa Phi (pres. U. Ark. Little Rock chpt. 1985—86). Episcopalian. Avocations: opera, gardening, dogs. Office: Univ Ark 2801 S University Ave Little Rock AR 72204-1099 Office Phone: 501-569-3182.

MARTIN, FRANK (FRANCISCO J. MARTIN), men's college basketball coach; m. Anya Martin; children: Brandon, Amalia. B in Phys. Edn., Fla. Internat. U., Miami, 1993. Asst. varsity coach, head jr. varsity coach Miami Sr. HS, Fla., 1985—93, head coach, 1995—99, North Miami Sr. HS, 1993—95, Booker T. Washington HS, 1999—2000; asst. coach Northeastern U., Boston, 2000—04, recruiting coord., 2002—04; asst. coach U. Cin., 2004—06, Kans. State U., Manhattan, 2006—07, head coach, 2007—. Office: Kans State U Mens Basketball Bramlage Coliseum 1800 College Ave Manhattan KS 66502 Office Phone: 785-532-6531. E-mail: fjm@ksu.edu. *

MARTIN, FRED, artist, academic administrator; b. San Francisco, June 13, 1927; s. Ernest Thomas and Leona (Richey) M.; m. Genevieve Catherine Fisette, Jan. 29, 1950 (dec.); children: T. Demian, Fredericka C., Anthony J.; m. Stephanie Zuperko Dudek, 1992. BA, U. Calif., Berkeley, 1949, MA, 1954; postgrad., Calif. Sch. Fine Arts, 1949—50. Registrar Oakland (Calif.) Art Mus., 1955-58; dir. exhbn. San Francisco Art Inst., 1958-65, 1965-75, dir. coll., 1983-92, dean acad. affairs. Exhibited one man shows, Zoe Dusanne Gallery, Seattle, 1952, M.H. deYoung Meml. Mus., San Francisco, 1954, 64, Oakland Mus. Calif., 1958, 2003, San Francisco Mus. Modern Art, 1958, 73, Dilexi Gallery, San Francisco, 1961, Minami Gallery, Tokyo, 1963, Royal Marks Gallery, NYC, 1965-70, Hansen Fuller Gallery, San Francisco, 1974, 75, 76, Quay Gallery, San Francisco, 1979, 81, 84, Natsoulas Gallery, Davis, Calif., 1991, Belcher Studios Gallery, San Francisco, 1994, Frederick Spratt Gallery, San Jose, 1996, Ebert Gallery, San Francisco, 1997, 98, 99, 2001, 2003, Art and Consciousness Gallery/John F. Kennedy U., Berkeley, 1997, Shasta Coll., 1998, Han Art Contemporaine, Montreal, 1999, Sanchez Art Ctr., 2003, Collector's Gallery of Oakland Mus., 2004, Paul Sunderholm Gallery, 2004, Gallery Denovo, Sun Valley, Idaho; represented in permanent collections, Mus. Modern Art, NYC, San Francisco Mus. Modern Art, Oakland Art Mus., Whitney Mus., Fogg Mus.; author: Beulah Land, 1966, Log of the Sun Ship, 1969, Liber Studiorum, 1973, A Travel Book, 1976, From an Antique Land, 1979; Bay area corr.: Art Internat., 1967-69, 75-76; contbg. editor Art Week, 1976-93. Recipient prizes Oakland Art Mus., 1951, 58, prizes San Francisco Mus. Art, 1957, 58, prizes Richmond (Calif.) Art Ctr., 1962, prizes Nat. Found. for Arts, 1970. Home: 232 Monte Vista Ave Oakland CA 94611-4922 Office: San Francisco Art Inst 800 Chestnut St San Francisco CA 94133-2206

MARTIN, FREDERICK NICHOLS, school system administrator; s. Frederick Wight and Elizabeth Foltz Martin. BA., Princeton U., NJ, 1994; MEd, Harvard U, Cambridge, 2000. Tchr. Arthur Morgan Sch., Burnsville, NC, 1995—99, clk. sch., 2001—03; admissions dir. The Meeting Sch., Rindge, NH, 2003—. Bd. dir. Pendle Hill, Wallingford, Pa., 2002—, Kestrel Ednl. Adventures, Gloucester, Mass., 2005—. Mem. Soc. Friends. Home: 120 Thomas Rd Rindge NH 03461 Office: The Meeting Sch 120 Thomas Rd Rindge NH 03461 Home Phone: 603-899-6689; Office Phone: 603-899-3366. Personal E-mail: frederick@meetingschool.org.

MARTIN, GARY JOSEPH, medical educator; b. Chgo., Mar. 12, 1952; m. Helen Gartner; children: Daniel T., David G. BA in Psychology, U. Ill., 1974, MD, 1978. Diplomate Am. Bd. Internal Medicine, Am. Bd. Cardiovascular Disease, Nat. Bd. Med. Examiners; lic. physician, Ill. Intern, resident internal medicine Northwestern U. Med. Sch., Chgo., 1978-81, instr. medicine, 1981-82, asst. prof. medicine, 1984-90, assoc. prof., 1990-96, prof., 1996—, divsn. chief, divsn. gen. internal medicine, 1988-2001, assoc. chmn. dept. medicine, 1998-2000, vice chmn. dept. medicine, 2001—; cardiology fellow Loyola U. Med. Ctr., 1982-84; attending physician Northwestern Meml. Hosp./Northwestern Med. Faculty Found., Chgo., 1984—; chief med. resident, attending physician Northwestern Meml. Hosp., Chgo., 1981-82; dir. primary care clerkship Nat. Ctr. for Advanced Med. Edn., 1984—. Chmn. outpatient utilization rev. and quality assurance com., 1985-93; chmn. Northwestern Meml. Hosp./Lakeside VA Rsch. Com., 1988-91; dir. tng. gen. internal medicine residency program, 1985-95; bd. dirs. com. Northwestern Med. Faculty Found., 1993—; cons. health care divsn. Ernst & Young, 1991—; peer reviewer Faculty Devel. Rev. Com. Panel 1, 1994. Contbr. articles to profl. jours. Fellow Buehler Ctr. on Aging. Fellow Am. Coll. Cardiology; mem. ACP, Soc. Gen. Internal Medicine, Am. Heart Assn. Office: Northwestern U Med Sch Divsn Gen Internal Medicine 675 N Saint Clair St Ste 18-200 Chicago IL 60611-5929

MARTIN, GARY WAYNE, lawyer; b. Cin., Feb. 14, 1946; s. Elmer DeForrest and Nellie May (Hughes) M.; m. Debra Lynn Goldsmith, June 25, 1982; children: Christopher, Jeremy, Joie, Casey. BA, Wilmington Coll., 1967; JD, U. Cin., 1974. Bar: Fla. 1974. With Fowler White Boggs Banker, Tampa, Fla., 1974—. Lt. USNR, 1967-71. Mem. Harbour Island Athletic Club. Republican. Presbyterian. Avocation: tennis. Office: Fowler White Gillen Boggs Villareal & Banker 501 E Kennedy Blvd Ste 1600 Tampa FL 33602-5240 Home Phone: 813-287-0079; Office Phone: 813-228-7411. Business E-Mail: gmartin@fowlerwhite.com.

MARTIN, GEORGE (WHITNEY), writer; b. NYC, Jan. 25, 1926; s. George Whitney and Agnes Wharton (Hutchinson) M. BA, Harvard U., 1948; student, Trinity Coll., Cambridge U., Eng., 1950; LL.B., U. Va., 1953. Bar: N.Y. 1955. With firm Emmet, Marvin & Martin, NYC, 1955-59; engaged in writing, 1959—. Author: The Opera Companion, A Guide for the Casual Operagoer, 1961, 5th edit., 1999, The Battle of the Frogs and Mice, An Homeric Fable, 1962, 2d edit., 1987, Verdi, His Music, Life and Times, 1963, 4th edit., 2001, The Red Shirt and The Cross of Savoy, The Story of Italy's Risorgimento, 1748-1871, 1969, Causes and Conflicts, The Centennial History of the Association of the Bar of the City of New York, 1870-1970, 1970, 2d edit., 1997, Madam Secretary: Frances Perkins, 1976, The Damrosch Dynasty, America's First Family of Music, 1983, Aspects of Verdi, 1988, 2nd edit., 1993, Verdi at the Golden Gate, San Francisco in the Golden Years, 1993, Twentieth Century Opera, A Guide, 1999, CCB: The Life and Century of Charles C. Burlingham, New York's First Citizen, 1858-1959 (Erwin N. Griswold award US Supreme Ct. Hist. Soc., 2006), 2005; contbr. articles to profl. jours., mags. Home: 53 Crosslands Dr Kennett Square PA 19348-2010 Office Phone: 610-388-0529.

MARTIN, GEORGE J., JR., lawyer; b. Port Chester, NY, June 7, 1942; s. George J. and Eileen Ann (Buckley) Martin; m. Joanne L. Frost, Aug. 21, 1965 (div. May 1986); children: Amy Anne, Ryan Frost; m. Anna Marie Cipriati, June 21, 1986; stepchildren: Marissa McCreay, Jill McCreay. BA, Georgetown U., 1964, JD, 1967. Bar: N.Y. 1969, conseil juridique: France 1977. From assoc. to ptnr. Mudge Rose Guthrie Alexander & Ferdon, NYC, 1967-95; ptnr. Coudert Bros., NYC, 1995—2004; of counsel Greenberg Traurig, LLP, NYC, 2005—. Mem.: French Heritage Soc. (gen. counsel dir.). Roman Catholic. Office: Greenberg Traurig LLP Met Life Bldg 200 Park Ave New York NY 10166 Office Phone: 212-801-2101. Personal E-mail: george0607@nyc.rr.com. Business E-Mail: marting@gtlaw.com.

MARTIN, GEORGE MONROE, pathologist, gerontologist, educator; m. Julaine Ruth Miller, Dec. 2, 1952 (dec. Apr. 2005); children: Peter C., Kelsey C., Thomas M., Andrew C. BS, U. Wash., 1949, MD, 1953. Diplomate Am. Bd. Pathology, Am. Bd. Med. Genetics. Intern Montreal Gen. Hosp., Que., Canada, 1953-54; resident, instr. U. Chgo., 1954-57; instr., prof. U. Wash., Seattle, 1957—2003, prof. emeritus, 2003—. Vis. scientist dept. genetics Albert Einstein Coll., NYC, 1964, Rockefeller U., 1998-99, UCLA, 2006; chmn. Gordon Confs. Molecular Pathology, Biology of Aging, 1974-79; chmn., nat. res. Plan on Aging Nat. Inst. on Aging, Bethesda, Md., 1985-89; dir. Alzheimer's Disease Rsch. Ctr. U. Wash., 1985—, assoc. dir., 1999—, dir. emeritus, 2003—; mem. bd. sci. counselors Nat. Inst. on Aging, 1994-98; mem. sci. adv. bd. Ellison Med. Found., 2998—, Benaroya Rsch. Inst., 2004—, Buck Inst. Aging Rsch., 2000-04. Editor Werner's Syndrome and Human Aging, 1985, Molecular Aspects of Aging, 1995; editor-in-chief: Science of Aging Knowledge Environment, 2000-06; contbr. articles in field to profl jours. Active Fedn. Am. Scientists, Human Rights Comm., Inst. Medicine. With USN, 1945—46. Recipient Allied Signal award in Aging, 1991, Rsch. medal Am. Aging Assn., 1992, Kleemeier award, 1994, Paul Glenn award for aging rsch., 1998, Longevity Prize, IPSEN Found., 2002, Irving Wright award of distinction Am. Fedn. Aging Rsch., 1996, Disting. Scientist award U. Urbino, 1998, others; named Disting. Alumnus, U. Wash. Sch. Medicine, 1987; USPHS rsch. fellow dept. genetics, Glasgow U., 1961-62; Eleanor Roosevelt Inst. Cancer Rsch. fellow Inst. de Biologie, Physiologie, Chimie, Paris, 1968-69; Josiah Macy faculty scholar Sir William Din Sch. Pathology, Oxford (Eng.) U., 1978-79, Humboldt Disting. scientist dept. genetics U. Wurzburg, Germany, 1991; Paul Harris fellow Rotary Internat., 1998. Fellow: AAAS, Tissue Culture Assn. (pres. 1986—88), Gerontol. Soc. Am. (chmn. Biol. Sci. 1979, pres. 2003, Brookdale award 1981, Lifetime Acheivement award for rsch. in alzheimer's disease World Alzheimer's Congress 2000); mem.: Am. Fedn. Aging Rsch. (pres. 1999—2001, sci. dir. 2003—), Am. Soc. Investigative Pathology, Am. Soc. Human Genetics, Am. Assn. Univ. Pathologists (emeritus), Inst. Medicine. Democrat. Avocations: travel, jazz, reading. Office Phone: 206-543-5088. Business E-Mail: gmmartin@u.washington.edu.

MARTIN, GEORGE RAYMOND RICHARD, writer; b. Bayonne, NJ, Sept. 20, 1948; s. Raymond and Margaret (Brady) M.; m. Gale Burnick, Nov. 15, 1975 (div. Dec. 1979). BS summa cum laude, Northwestern U., 1970; MS cum laude, 1971. Journalism intern Medill News Service, Washington, 1971; sportswriter, pub. relations officer N.J. Dept. Parks, Bayonne, 1971; coordinator communications and edn. Cook County (Ill.) Legal Assistance Found., Chgo., 1972-74; instr. journalism Clarke Coll., Dubuque, Iowa, 1976-78, writer-in-residence, 1978-79. Founder, chmn. Windy City Sci. Fiction Writers' Workshop, Chgo., 1972-76 Author sci. fiction: A Song for Lya, 1976, Songs of Stars and Shadows, 1977, Sandkings, 1981, Dying of the Light, 1977, Windhaven, 1981, Fevre Dream, 1982, The Armageddon Rag, 1983, Songs the Deadmen Sing, 1983, Nightflyers, 1985, Tuf Voyaging, 1986, Portraits of His Children, 1987, A Game of Throngs, 1996, A Clash of Kings, 1999, A Storm of Swords, 2000, A Feast for Crows, 2005 (No. 1 on Publishers Weekly hardcover bestseller list); editor: New Voices I, 1977, New Voices II, 1979, New Voices III, 1980, New Voices IV, 1981, John W. Campbell Awards vol. 5, 1984, Night Visions 3, 1987, Wild Cards, 1987, Aces High, 1987, Jokers Wild, 1987, Aces Abroad, 1988, Down & Dirty, 1988, Ace in the Hole, 1990, Dead Man's Hand, 1990, One-Eyed Jacks, 1991, Jokertown Shuffle, 1991, Double Solitaire, 1992, Dealer's Choice, 1992, Turn of the Cards, 1993, Card Sharks, 1993, Marked Cards, 1994, Black Trump, 1995, Deuces Down, 2002, Death Draws Five, 2006; story editor The Twilight Zone, CBS-TV, 1987; prodr. Beauty and the Beast, CBS-TV, 1987-88; exec. prodr. Doorways, (ABC-TV), 1992-93; contbr. short stories to mags. Mem. Sci. Fiction Writers Am. (dir. Central region 1977-79, v.p. 1996-97), Writers Guild Am. West. E-mail: georr@aol.com.

MARTIN, GINA LYNN, lawyer; BS cum laude, St. Michael's Coll., 1992; JD, Fordham U., 1995. Bar: NY 1996, Mass. 1999. Assoc. Fried, Frank, Harris, Shriver & Jacobson, NYC; ptnr. Bus. Law Dept. Goodwin Procter LLP, Boston. Mem.: Am. Bankruptcy Inst., ABA, Boston Bar Assn. Office: Goodwin Procter LLP Exchange Place 53 State St Boston MA 02109 Office Phone: 617-570-1330. E-mail: gmartin@goodwinprocter.com.

MARTIN, GRACE BURKETT, psychologist; b. Sumter, S.C., Aug. 27, 1939; d. John Hazel and Grace Thomasine (Briggs) Burkett; BA magna cum laude, Armstrong State Coll., 1976; MS, Fla. State U., 1979, PhD, 1980; m. H. Russell Martin, Jr., Oct. 9, 1957; children— H. Russell, Carolyne, Melinda. Lic. psychologist. Hist. preservationist, 1962—; dir. Christian edn. St. Thomas Parish, Savannah, Ga., 1970-74; prof. psychology Armstrong State Coll., Savannah, 1980-2001, prof. emeritus, 2002-, dept. head psychology, dir. gen. studies degree program; head. divsn. social and behavioral scis., interim dean arts and scis.; pres. Orgn. Cons.; lectr.; radio and TV appearances. Author, collaborator nat. and cross-nat. studies of women and work; co-author UNESCO manual for nat. leaders and policy makers; cons. editor Jour. Supplementary Abstract Svc., 1980, 81. Bd. dirs. Coastal Empire YMCA, 1972-75; mem. Savannah Symphony Soc.; mem. commn. on mission Episcopal Diocese of Ga., 1972-74, mem. liturg. commn., 1972-74, also lic. lay reader; pres. Operation Return, 1972-76. Named Mrs. Ga., 1962. Mem. Am. Psychol. Assn., Am. Psychol. Soc. (charter), Southeastern Psychol. Assn., Soc. Indsl. Organizational Psychology, Am. Mgmt. Assn., Nat. Assn. Women Deans and Administrators, Ga. Assn. Women Deans and Adminstrators, Commerce Club Savannah (charter), Ga. Ednl. Research Assn. Home: 50 Shipwatch Rd Savannah GA 31410-2950 Personal E-mail: martingrace@comcast.net.

MARTIN, GREGORY KEITH, lawyer, mayor; b. Conway, SC, Nov. 7, 1956; s. George Henry Martin and Julia Ann (Johnson) M. Land. BS in Fin. Mgmt., Clemson U., 1979; JD, U. S.C., 1983. Bar: S.C. 1983. Intern U.S. Senate, 1980; law clk. to presiding judge 15th Jud. Cir. Ct., Conway, 1983; assoc. Johnson & Martin, Conway, 1983-88, ptnr., 1988-93, Martin & Smith, Conway, 1993-98; mayor City of Conway, 1995—; sole practice Gregory K. Martin, PC, Conway, 1998—. Mem. Conway Planning Commn., 1986-89, chmn., 1989; bd. dirs. Conway-Main St. U.S.A., 1986-90, chmn., 1988; mem. Conway Bd. Appeals, 1987-89, Horry County Bd. Archtl. Rev., 1987-90; mem. Conway City Coun., 1991-94; pres., Horry County Hist. Soc., 1988, 90, mayor pro tem, 1994; mem. adv. bd. Pee Dee Heritage Ctr., 1988-2003. Mem. ABA, S.C. Bar Assn., Horry County Bar Assn., Sigma Nu, Phi Delta Phi. Methodist. Avocations: tennis, coin collecting/numismatics. Home: 706 Elm St Conway SC 29526-4373 Office: PO Box 736 Conway SC 29528-0736 Office Phone: 843-248-2089. Business E-Mail: gkm1law@sccoast.net.

MARTIN, GUY, lawyer; b. LA, Jan. 22, 1911; s. I.G. and Mary Pearl (Howe) M.; m. Edith Kingdon Gould, Oct. 12, 1946; children— Guy III, Jason Gould, Christopher Kingdon, Edith Maria Theodosia Burr. AB, Occidental Coll., 1931; BA (1st class hons.), Oxford U., 1934, MA, 1944; LL.B., Yale, 1937. Bar: N.Y. 1938, D.C. 1947. Practiced with Donovan, Leisure, Newton & Lumbard, NYC, 1938-41; gen. counsel All Am. Aviation, Inc., 1942, Am. Mexican Claims Commn., U.S. Dept. State, 1945-47; ptnr. Martin, Whitfield, Smith & Bebchick (and predecessors), Washington, 1952-80; counsel Martin and Smith (and predecessors), 1981-86; pres., vice chmn. bd., dep. chief exec. officer Internat. Bank, 1981-86; with Law Office of Saltzstein & Martin, 1988-99. Served with USN; sea duty 1942-45. Mem. ABA, Assn. of Bar of City of N.Y., Bar Assn. D.C, Phi Beta Kappa, Sigma Alpha Epsilon. Clubs: Yale, Brook, Knickerbocker (N.Y.C.); Metropolitan, City Tavern (Washington). Episcopalian. Home: 3300 O St NW Washington DC 20007-2813

MARTIN, HAROLD G., engineering consultant; b. Scotland, Pa. s. Abram Earl and Eula Mae Martin; m. Christina Shipley Martin, June 5, 1948; children: Susan (dec.), Judith Krieger, Bruce. BSCE, Pa. State U., 1944. Stress analyst, chief structures Fairchild Republic Co., Hagerstown, Md., 1967-70, mgr. tech. engring., 1970-71, chief problem analysis and corrective action A10 Program, 1977-81, chief quality engring., 1981, project engr. F14, FAA airworthiness coord., 1981-84; engring. cons., FAA designated engring. rep. Waynesboro, Pa., 1984—. Mem. sch. bd. Waynesboro Area Sch. Bd., 1978-84. Staff sgt. U.S. Army, 1944-46. Mem.: Mid Atlantic Air Mus., Am. Aviation Hist. Soc., Soc. of Automotive Engineers. Avocations: auto restoration, travel, writing, boating, fishing. Home and Office: 833 Anthony Ave Waynesboro PA 17268

MARTIN, HARRY C., lawyer; Grad., U. Va.; JD with honors, George Washington U. Ptnr. Fletcher, Heald, Hildreth PLC, Arlington, Va. Columnist Broadcast Engring. mag., 1981—, Radio mag., 1997—, frequent spkr. NAB, state broadcast industry conventions, regular panelist Kagan Radio Summit seminars. Bd. dir. Univ. Va. Club of Washington. Mem.: Fed. Comm. Bar Assn. (asst. secy-secy. 1997—99, asst. treas.-treas. 2000—02, pres.-elect 2003—04, pres. 2004—05, exec. com. 1994—2002). Office: Fletcher Heald & Hildreth 11th Fl 1300 N 17th St Arlington VA 22209 Office Phone: 703-812-0415. Office Fax: 703-812-0486. Business E-Mail: martin@fhhlaw.com.

MARTIN, HARRY CORPENING, lawyer, retired state supreme court justice; b. Lenoir, NC, Jan. 13, 1920; s. Hal C. and Johnsie Harshaw (Nelson) M.; m. Nancy Robiou Dallam, Apr. 16, 1955; children: John, Matthew, Mary. AB, U. N.C., 1942; LLB, Harvard U., 1948; LLM, U. Va., 1982. Bar: N.C. 1948. Pvt. practice, Asheville, NC, 1948-62; judge NC Superior Ct., Asheville, 1962-78, NC Ct. Appeals, Raleigh, 1978-82; justice NC Supreme Ct., 1982-92; ptnr. Martin & Martin, Attys., Hillsborough, 1992—. Adj. prof. U. N.C. Law Sch., 1983-92, Duke U., 1990-91, Dan K. Moore disting. vis. prof., U. N.C. Law Sch., 1992-94; sr. conf. atty. U.S. Ct. Appeals for 4th Cir., 1994-99; chief justice Supreme Ct. ea. bd. of Cherokee Indians, 2000—, ret. With U.S. Army, 1942-45, South Pacific. Mem. U.S. Supreme Ct. Hist. Soc., N.C. Supreme Ct. Hist. Soc. (pres.). Democrat. Episcopalian. Home: 1 Hilltop Rd Asheville NC 28803-3017 Office: Cherokee Supreme Ct PO Box 1629 Cherokee NC 28719 Home Phone: 828-274-4633; Office Phone: 828-497-1077. E-mail: judgemartin@bellsouth.net.

MARTIN, HARRY STRATTON, III, law librarian, educator; b. Hartford, Conn., Jan. 22, 1943; AB in History, Harvard U., 1965; JD, U. Minn., 1968; MLS, U. Pitts., 1971. Bar: Minn. 1968. Instr. U. Liberia, Monrovia, 1969—71; asst. libr. U. Tex., 1972—74, assoc. libr., 1975—76; libr. and asst. prof. Georgetown U., Washington, 1976—81; libr., prof. Harvard Law Sch., Cambridge, Mass., 1981—2002, Henry N. Ess III libr., prof., 2002—. Editl. bd. Computer Law Jour., 1979—, Westlaw, 1989—91. Contbr. articles to profl. jours. Mem.: Am. Libr. Assn., Am. Assn. Law Libr., New England Law Libr. Consortium (pres. 1995—97), Beta Phi Mu. Office: Harvard Law Sch Areeda 511 1563 Massachusetts Ave Cambridge MA 02138 Office Phone: 617-495-3700. Office Fax: 617-495-4449. Business E-Mail: martin@law.harvard.edu. *

MARTIN, HENRY ALAN, public defender; b. Nashville, Sept. 5, 1949; s. James Alvin and Mary Elizabeth (Long) M.; m. Gloria B. Ballard, May 9, 1975; children: Nathan Daniel, Anna Elizabeth. BA, Vanderbilt U., 1971, JD, 1974. Bar: Tenn. 1975, U.S. Dist. Ct. (mid. dist.) Tenn. 1975, U.S. Ct. Appeals (6th cir.) 1976, U.S. Supreme Ct. 1979. Pvt. practice, Nashville, 1975-76; ptnr. Haile & Martin, P.A., Nashville, 1976-82; assoc. firm Barrett & Ray, P.C., Nashville, 1982-85; fed. pub. defender U.S. Dist. Ct. (mid. dist.) Tenn., Nashville, 1985—. Mem. adv. com. on rules criminal procedure U.S. Judicial Conf., 1994-99. CO-author, co-editor trial manual, Tools for the Ultimate Trial, 1985, 2d edit., 1988; contbr. articles to profl. jours. Del., Witness for Peace, Managua, Nicaragua, 1987. Mem. ABA (coun. criminal justice sect. 1993-96), NACDL, Assn. Fed. Defenders (pres. 1995-98), Nashville Bar Assn., Napier Looby Bar Assn., Tenn. Assn. Criminal Def. Lawyers (bd. dirs. 1978-94, pres. 1984-85, Pres.'s award 1984). Democrat. Avocations: jogging, swimming. Home: 3802 Whitland Ave Nashville TN 37205-2432 Office: Fed Pub Defender 810 Broadway Ste 200 Nashville TN 37203-3861 Office Phone: 615-736-5047. Business E-Mail: henry_martin@fd.org.

MARTIN, HOWARD W., JR., lawyer; b. Norfolk, Va., Mar. 10, 1942; BS in Bus. Adminstrn., Washington & Lee U., 1964; LLB, U. Va., 1967. Sr. ptnr. Crenshaw Ware & Martin PLC, Norfolk, Va., mng. ptnr. Mem. Tidewater Estate Planning Coun.; mem. Norfolk Divsn. Bd. Hampton Roads C. of C., 2001—05; adminstrv. bd. mem. Ghent United Methodist Church, Norfolk, Va., 1978—, chmn., 1984—86; bd. dirs. Tidewater YMCA, 1978—84. Line officer USN, navy lawyer Judge Advocate General's Corp. USN. Mem.: Va. Law Found. (bd. mem. 1990—97, sec. 1993—94, pres. 1995—96, fellow 1997—), Norfolk & Portsmouth Bar Assn. (treas. 1994—96, pres. 1997), Va. Bar Assn. (exec. com. mem. 1987—90, sec. 1989—90), Va. State Bar (coun. mem. 2000—, exec. com. mem. 2003—, pres.-elect 2006—07), ABA. Office: Crenshaw Ware & Martin PLC Once Commercial Pl 1200 Bank of America Ctr Norfolk VA 23510-2111 Office Phone: 757-623-3000. Office Fax: 757-623-5735. E-mail: hmartin@cwm-law.com.

MARTIN, IONIS BRACY, artist, educator; b. Chgo., 1936; d. Francis Wright and Hattie Robinson Bracy; m. Allyn Aubrey Martin; 1 child, Allyn Bracy-Fletcher. BS, Fisk U., 1957; MEd, U. Hartford, 1968; MFA, Pratt Inst., Bklyn., 1987. Y-teen assoc. dir. YWCA of Greater Hartford, 1957—59; homefinder Conn. Child Welfare Assn, New Haven, 1959—61; art tchr. Arsenal elem sch. Hartford Bd. Edn., Conn., 1961, art tchr. Weaver H.S., 1961—67; lectr., adj. prof. Ctrl. Conn. State U., New Britain, 1985—2003; h.s. art tchr. Bloomfield Bd. Edn., Conn., 1971—2001. Co-founder, sec. treas., v.p. bd. dirs. Artist Collective, Hartford, 1972—2006; trustee Wadsworth Athenaeum Mus. Art, Hartford, 1978—97; corporator Hartford Art Sch., U. Hartford, West Hartford, 2001—06. Author: A Curriculum Sampler. Co-trustee Ella Burr McManus Trust, Hartford, 1985—2006; bd. dirs. Ancient Burial Ground, Hartford, 1998—2005, Huntington House Mus., Windsor, Conn., 2001—05., DuBois Inst. fellow Harvard U., 1994, Through Young Black Eyes grantee, Conn. Commn. on the Arts, Artist fellow, Skidmore Coll. Mem.: Canton Gallery on the Green, The Links, Art Works Gallery, Delta Sigma Theta. Home: 3120 S Indiana Ave Unit 404 Chicago IL 60616-3762 Office Phone: 860-202-4017. Personal E-mail: ionismartin@mac.com.

MARTIN, J. CLARK, lawyer; b. Washington, May 10, 1940; BSEE, La. State U., 1963, JD, 1966. Bar: La. 1966, Tex. 1970. Ptnr., co-head Intellectual Property / Technical Litig. Sect. Vinson & Elkins LLP, Houston. Fellow: Tex. Bar Found. Office: Vinson & Elkins LLP First City Tower 1001 Fannin St, Ste 2300 Houston TX 77002 Office Phone: 713-758-2400. E-mail: cmartin@velaw.com.

MARTIN, JACK, physician; b. Northport, Ala., Aug. 11, 1927; s. Marvin Oscar and Glenavis (Rice) M.; m. Ann Inman, Apr. 7, 1957; children: Sarah, Richard, Charles Randall, Robert. BS, U. Ala., 1949; MD, Vanderbilt U., 1953. Intern Charity Hosp., New Orleans, 1953-54; resident in adult and child psychiatry Cin. Gen. Hosp., 1954-58; dir. child psychiatry U. Tex. Health Scis. Ctr., Dallas, 1958-67, clin. prof. child psychiatry, 1967—; med. dir. Shady Brook Rsch. Ctr., Richardson, Tex., 1963-81; physician pvt. practice, Dallas, 1981—. With USNR, 1945-47. Independent. Episcopalian. Avocations: bridge, golf. Office: 5927 Club Hll Pl Dallas TX 75248 Personal E-mail: jam4757@aol.com.

MARTIN, JACK, educational services company executive, former federal agency administrator; b. Frendale, Mich. m. Bettye Martin; children: Randy, Ingrid. BS, MBA, Wayne State U.; postgrad., U. Minn. CPA. With GM Corp., Detroit; various mgmt. positions Control Data; cons. acct. Touche Ross & Co. (now Deloitte and Touche); mng. dir., CEO, founder Jack Martin and Co. P.C., CPAs, 1975—2002; chmn., acting CEO Home Fed. Savings Bank, Detroit, 1995—2002; chmn. Provider Reimbursement Rev. Bd. US Dept. Health & Human Services, 1991—94; CFO US Dept. Edn., Washington, 2002—05; acting dir. Selective Svc. System, Arlington, Va., 2004; exec. v.p. White Hat Mgmt., Akron, Ohio, 2005—. Chmn. of bd. Health Alliance Plan; mem. investment com. Mercy Health Sys. (now Trinity Health); chair Mich. adv. com. U.S. Civil Rights Commn.; v.p. Merrill Palmer Inst. Wayne State U. Treas. Alzheimer's Assn. Recipient Pres. Quality award for Improved Fin. Performance, US Dept. Edn., Certificate of Excellence in Accountability Reporting, Assn. Govt. Accountants, Alexander Hamilton award for Tech., Treasury & Risk Mgmt. mag. Mem.: AICPA (mem. practice stds. subcom.), Det. Athletic Club (bd. dirs.). Office: White Hat Mgmt 159 S Main St Ste 600 Akron OH 44308 *

MARTIN, JACQUELINE BRIGGS, writer; b. Maine; m. Rich Martin; children: Sarah, Justin. Author: Bizzy Bones and Moosemouse, 1986, Bizzy Bones and the Lost Quilt, 1988, Bizzy Bones and Uncle Ezra, 1984, Button, Bucket, Sky, 1998, The Finest Horse in Town, 1992, Grandmother Bryant's Pocket, 1996 (Lupine award 1996), The Green Truck Garden Giveaway: A Neighborhood Story and Almanac, 1997, Good Times on Grandfather Mountain, 1992, Higgins Bend Song and Dance, 1997, Snowflake Bentley, 1998 (Caldecott Award 1999, Lupine Award 1998), Washing the Willow Tree Loon, 1995, The Lamp, The Ice and The Boat Called Fish, 2001, The Water Gift and the Pig of the Pig (Lupine award 2003), 2003, On Sand Island, 2003, (with Sarah Martin Bosse) Banjo Granny, 2006, Chicken Joy on Redbean Road, 2007.

MARTIN, JACQUES, professional hockey coach and sports team executive; b. St. Pascal, Ont., Can., Oct. 1, 1952; Coach St. Louis Blues, 1986-88; asst. coach Chgo. Blackhawks, 1988-96; head coach Ottawa Senators, 1996—2004, Fla. Panthers, 2004—, gen. mgr., 2006—. Recipient Jack Adams award, 1999. Office: c/o Florida Panthers 1 Panther Pkwy Miami FL 33323

MARTIN, JAMES CHARLES, physician; b. Coleman, Tex., 1948; MD, U. Tex., San Antonio, 1973. Resident Bexar County Hosp., San Antonio, 1973-76; clin. prof. U. Tex. Health Sci. Ctr., San Antonio; physician pvt. practice, San Antonio, 1976—96; dir. residency program Santa Rosa Family Medicine, San Antonio, 1996—. V.p. med. affairs Christus Santa Rosa, San Antonio, 2004—; rev. com. family medicine Accreditation Coun. Grad. Med. Edn., 2005—. Mem. Am. Acad. Family Physicians (pres. 2002-03), Am. Bd. Family Practice (pres. 1997-98), Tex. Med. Assn. Office: Ste 4703 333 N Santa Rosa San Antonio TX 78207-3108 Office Phone: 210-704-2551. E-mail: james.martin@christushealth.org.

MARTIN, JAMES HANLEY, state attorney general; b. NYC, Dec. 22, 1960; s. James Patrick and Josephine Anne (Hanley) M. AB, Georgetown U., 1983; JD, Fordham U., 1986. Bar: N.J. 1986, U.S. Dist. Ct. N.J. 1986, N.Y. 1987, D.C. 1988, U.S. Dist. Ct. (so. and ea. dists.) N.Y. 1991, U.S. Ct. Appeals (D.C. and 3d cirs.) 1991, U.S. Supreme Ct. 1991. Dep. atty. gen. State of N.J., Newark, 1987—2003, dep. atty. gen. Litig. sect., 2003—04, asst. atty. gen. Litig. Trenton, 2004—. Mem. ABA, Am. Judicature Soc., Mercer County Bar Assn., N.J. State Bar Assn., D.C. Bar Assn. Roman Catholic. Office: State of NJ Divsn Law PO Box 112 25 Market St Trenton NJ 08625-0112

MARTIN, JAMES JOHN, JR., systems analyst, retired research and development company executive; b. Paterson, NJ, Feb. 3, 1936; s. James John and Lillian M.; m. Lydia Elizabeth Bent, June 11, 1954; children: David, Peter, Laura, Daniel, Lucas. BA, U. Wis.-Madison, 1955; postgrad., Div. Sch., Harvard U., 1955-57; MS, Navy Postgrad. Sch., 1963; PhD, MIT, 1965. Commd. ensign USN, 1957, advanced through grades to comdr., 1971, ret., 1977; sector v.p. Sci. Applications Internat. Corp., La Jolla, Calif., 1977-95. Author: Bayesian Decision Problems and Markov Chains, 1967; editor: On Not Confusing Ourselves, 1991; contbr. articles to profl. jours. Bd. dirs. Mil. Conflict Inst., 1986-92. Decorated Legion of Merit. Mem. Internat. Inst. Strategic Studies, Ops. Research Soc. Am., Mil. Ops. Research Soc. (bd. dirs. 1974-77) Democrat. Avocation: cooking. Home: 6603 Aranda Ave La Jolla CA 92037-6216

MARTIN, JAMES KAY, management consultant; b. Montreal, Que., Sept. 20, 1948; s. Douglas and Margaret Martin; m. Emma Lim Abrenica, Sept. 12, 1986. B of Math., U. Waterloo, Ont., 1970; PhD, U. Toronto, 1974. Sr. analyst Health & Welfare, Ottawa, 1974-79; asst. dir. transfer payments Social Devel. Ministry, Ottawa, 1980-84; exec. dir. planning Dept. Agr., Ottawa, 1984-90; exec dir. regulatory affairs Treasury bd. Can., Ottawa, 1990-96; dir. gen. Internal Audit and Risk Mgmt. Human Resources Can., Ottawa, 1997—2004; dir. gen. audit and evaluation Human Resources and Skills Devel., Ottawa, 2004—05; pres. JK & E Martin Cons., Inc., Ottawa, 2005—. Chmn. regulatory mgmt. group OECD, Paris, 1993-96. Contbr. articles to profl. jours. Chmn. grad. students union U. Toronto, 1973, mem. bd. govs., 1974. Fellow Nat. Rsch. Coun., 1970, Ont. Inst. for Edn., 1971, Can. Coun., 1972, 73. Mem. Ottawa Humane Soc. Roman Catholic. Avocations: running, canoeing, skiing, swimming. Office Phone: 613-614-3012. E-mail: martin.jk@rogers.com.

MARTIN, J(AMES) KENNETH, music educator; b. Washington, Jan. 20, 1947; s. Samuel M. Jr. and Georgia Irene (O'Dell) Martin; m. Nancy Gravley; children: Sara L., Susan I. Yancey. BA, Wake Forest U., 1969; postgrad., Vanderbilt Div. Sch., 1971; M Ch. Music, So. Bapt. Theol. Sem., 1981, D Mus. Arts, 1983. Pres., gen. mgr. Martin Asphalt Paving, Inc., Clinton, Md., 1972—77; min. music and edn. Hillandale Bapt. Ch., Adelphi, Md., 1977—79; prof. of music Campbellsville (Ky.) U., 1985—, chmn. faculty, 1989—90, 2004—05. Tchr. Russian Bapt. Pastors Sch., St. Petersburg, 1994, Siberian Bapt. Pastors Sch., Irkutsk, Russia, 1997, Irkutsk, 98; prof. of music Campbellsville U. Brazil Program, Recife, Brazil, 2002—; part-time or interim min. of music various chs., 1974—2004. Composer: (choral arrangement) My Old Kentucky Home, 1989; singer, actor: solo voice recitals in U.S. and Brazil; actor: (outdoor hist. music drama) Hoofprints on the Stairs, 1999—; contbr. revs., articles to profl. publs. Dir. choir, founder Capital Bapt. Chorale, 1976—79; mem. Lebanon Cmty. Choir, Ky., Mid-Ky. Chorus St. Catharine; deacon Pa. Ave. Bapt. Ch., Washington, 1972—75, Campbellsville Bapt. Ch., 1991—94; mem. Louisville Bach Soc.; organizer and dir. Martin Family Reunion, Mayodan, NC, 1972—. Named Hon. Chaplain, USN Chief of Chaplains, 1983; recipient Honors award cert. in Ministry, So. Bapt. Theol. Sem. Sch. of Ch. Music, 1981; Garrett fellow, So. Bapt. Theol. Sem., 1981—83. Mem.: Bapt. Ch. Music Conf., Nat. Assn. Tchrs. of Singing, Am. Choral Directors Assn., Phi Mu Alpha Sinfonia. Baptist. Avocation: genealogy. Home: 624 North Central Ave Campbellsville KY 42718 Home Phone: 270-465-2093; Office Phone: 270-789-5340. Office Fax: 270-789-5524. E-mail: jkmartin@campbellsville.edu.

MARTIN, JAMES KIRBY, historian, educator; b. Akron, Ohio, May 26, 1943; s. Paul Elmo and Dorothy Marie (Garrett) M.; m. Karen Wierwille, Aug. 7, 1965; children: Darcy Elizabeth, Sarah Marie, Joelle Kathryn Garrett. BA summa cum laude, Hiram Coll., 1965; MA, U. Wis., 1967, PhD, 1969. Asst. prof. history Rutgers U., New Brunswick, NJ, 1969-73, assoc. prof., 1973-79, prof., 1979-80, asst. provost, 1972-74, v.p. acad. affairs, 1977-79; vis. prof. Rutgers Ctr. of Alcohol Studies, 1978-88; prof. history U. Houston, 1980-97, disting. univ. prof., 1997—, chmn. dept., 1980-83; vis. prof. history Rice U., Houston, 1992. Chmn. bd. sponsors Papers of Thomas Edison Project, 1977-80; founding ptnr. PastQuest Rsch. Svcs., 1999. Author: Men in Rebellion, 1973, In the Course of Human Events, 1979, (with M.E. Lender) A Respectable Army: The Military Origins of the Republic, 1982, 2d edit., 2006, (contemporary mil. reading list), Drinking in America: A History, 1982, rev. edit. 1987, (with others) America and Its Peoples, 1989, 5th edit. 2004, concise edit. 1995, Benedict Arnold: Revolutionary Hero, 1997 (Homer D. Babbidge, Jr. award), audio edit., 2001,(with J.T. Glatthaar) Forgotten Allies: Oneida Indians and the American Revolution, 2006; editor: Interpreting Colonial America, 1973, 2d edit. 1978, The Human Dimensions of Nation Making, 1976, (with K. Stubaus) The American Revolution, Whose Revolution?, 1977, 81, (with M.E. Lender) Citizen-Soldier: The Revolutionary War Journal of Joseph Bloomfield, 1982 (R.P. McCormick prize), Ordinary Courage: The Revolutionary War Adventures of Joseph Plumb Martin, 1993, 2d edit., 1999; mem. editl. bd. Papers of William Livingston Project, 1973-80, Houston Rev., 1981-2003, N.J. History, 1986—, Conversations with the Past Series, 1993-95; gen. editor Am. Social Experience Series, 1983-2002. Recipient N.J. Soc. of the Cin. prize for Disting. Achievement in Am. History, 1995, Hiram Coll. Alumni Achievement award, 1996. Mem. Tex. Assn. for Advancement History (bd. dirs. 1981-93, v.p. 1986-90), Inst. for Internat. Bus. Analysis (adv. coun. 1982-86), Am. Hist. Assn. (Beveridge-Dunning prize com. 1990-93), Orgn. Am. Historians, So. Hist. Assn., Soc. Historians Early Am. Republic (adv. coun. 1985-88), Soc. for Mil. History, Phi Beta Kappa, Phi Kappa Phi, Pi Gamma Mu, Omicron Delta Kappa, Phi Alpha Theta. Office: U Houston Dept History 524 Arnold Hall Houston TX 77204-3003

MARTIN, JAMES LARENCE, dentist, educator; b. Dubuque, Iowa, Sept. 3, 1940; s. James Larence and Ada Virginia (Boone) M.; m. Willie Mae Walker, Jan. 23, 1941; children: Linda Gail, James Larence III, John Lance. BS, Loras Coll., Dubuque, 1959, LittD, 1982; MS, Tenn. State U., 1960; DDS, Meharry Med. Coll., 1966; MPH, U. Mich., 1975. Dental dir. children and youth Meharry Med. Coll., Nashville, 1967-72, acting dir. children and youth program, 1972-73, dir. primary dental svcs., 1973-75, coord. dental component Ctr. for Health Care Rsch., 1975-77, prof., 1981—; owner Martin Dental, Nashville, 1980—. Dental cons. Medically Dedicated, Washington, 1992—; pres. faculty senate Meharry Med. Coll., 1989-93, mem. pres.'s exec. mgmt. team, 1989-93, dir. divsn. dental public health 1999—, chmn. dept. dental pub. health, 1999—. Contbr. articles to profl. jours., chpts. to books. Bd. regents Loras Coll., 1997—. Recipient Meritorious Svc. award Acad. Oral Medicine, 1977. Mem. ADA, Am. Pub. Health Assn. (med. com.), Am. Assn. Pub. Health Dentistry, Nat. Assn. Cmty. Health Ctrs., Am. Acad. Goil Foil Operators, Soc. of the Upper 10th, Nashville Area C. of C., Beta Kappa Chi, Phi Sigma. Avocations: reading, swimming, photography. Home: 3515 Geneva Cir Nashville TN 37209-2524 Office: 908 34th Ave N Nashville TN 37209-2502 Office Phone: 615-327-4499. Personal E-mail: jmarti3817@aol.com.

MARTIN, JAMES ROBERT, identification company executive; b. Indpls., Mar. 31, 1943; s. Walter and Helen (Snider) M.; m. Jan. 24, 1970 (div. Dec. 1990); children: Julia, Justin; m. Tamara Hicks, Dec. 21, 1991; stepchildren: Hunter Hoskins, Laura Hoskins. BA, DePauw U., 1965; MBA, Ind. U., 1967. Bus. analyst TRW, Inc., Redondo Beach, Calif., 1967-70; fin. analyst Internat. Industries, Beverly Hills, Calif., 1970; v.p. fin., treas. A & E Plastik Pak Co., Inc., Industry, Calif., 1970-75; pres. Plasti-Line, Inc., Knoxville, Tenn., 1975-92, chmn., CEO, 1992—. Bd. dirs. 1st Am. Corp., Nashville, Signal Thread Co., Chattanooga, Tenn. Bd. dirs. Knoxville Symphony Soc., 1976, Knoxville United Way, 1986, Knoxville Mus. Art; bd. dirs., chmn. fin. com. Thompson Cancer Survival Ctr., Knoxville, 1985. Mem. Chief Execs. Orgn., Club LeConte (bd. dirs.), East Tenn. Automobile Club (bd. dirs.), St. Francis Yacht Club, Cherokee Country Club. Aspen Mountain Club. Republican. Episcopalian. Home: 1029 Scenic Dr Knoxville TN 37919 Office: ImagePoint PO Box 59043 Knoxville TN 37950-9043

MARTIN, JAMES RUSSELL, lawyer; b. Columbus, Ohio, June 24, 1947; s. Robert Wells and Gwendolyn (Collins) M.; m. Susan Virginia Jarman, Aug. 4, 1973; children: James Russell Jr., Elizabeth Collins. BA in History, Denison U., Granville, Ohio, 1969; JD, U. Denver, 1972. Bar: Colo. 1972, U.S. Dist. Ct. Colo. 1972. Assoc. Brundage & Yates, Denver, 1973; asst. atty. gen. State of Colo., Denver, 1974-76; assoc. Thomas & Esperti PC, 1976—78; v.p. Butterwick Enterprises Ltd., Denver, 1978-81, pres., 1981-83; ptnr. Baker & Hostetler LLP, Denver, 1985—2004; sr. v.p., gen. counsel, clerk Bluegreen Corp., Boca Raton, Fla., 2004—. Mem.: ABA, Assn. Corp. Counsel, Denver Bar Assn., Colo. Bar Assn., Am. Resort Devel. Assn. Avocations: skiing, tennis, bicycling. Office: Bluegreen Corp 4960 Conference Way N Ste 100 Boca Raton FL 33431 Office Phone: 561-443-8660. Business E-Mail: jim.martin@bluegreencorp.com.

MARTIN, JAMES WILLIAM, lawyer; b. Turlock, Calif., Dec. 20, 1949; Student, Ga. Inst. Tech., Atlanta, 1967—69; BS, Stetson U., DeLand, Fla., 1971, JD, 1974. Bar: Fla. 1974, US Dist. Ct. (mid. dist.) Fla. 1974, US Ct. Appeals (5th cir.) 1974, US Supreme Ct. 1978, US Ct. Appeals (11th cir.) 1987. Ptnr. Brickley & Martin, St. Petersburg, Fla., 1974-79; pres. James W. Martin, P.A., St. Petersburg, 1979—. Presenter in field. Author: West's Florida Corporation System, 1984, West's Legal Forms, 3d edit., Non-Profit Corporations, 1991, 92, 93, 94, 96, 97, 98, 99, 2000, 01, 02, 03, 04, West's Florida Legal Forms, Business Organizations, Real Estate, Specialized Forms, 1990, 91, 92, 93, 94, 95; supplement editor Fla. Jur. Forms, Legal and Bus., 1998, 99; contbr. articles to profl. jours. including Word Perfect mag., ALI-ABA Practical Lawyer, Fla. Bar News, Fla. Bar Jour. City councilman, St. Petersburg, 1982-83; active Leadership St. Petersburg; active charter class Leadership Tampa Bay; founding trustee, sec., counsel Salvador Dali Mus., 1980-2007; founding dir., sec., counsel Fla. Internat. Mus., 1992-94. Recipient Outstanding Young Man award Jaycees, 1982, Outstanding Contbn. to City award St. Petersburg C. of C., 1980. Mem.: St. Petersburg C. of C. (arts task force 1987, gen. counsel 1991—92, chmn. urban solutions com. 1992—93, chmn. downtown com. 1993—94, chmn. parking com.), St. Petersburg Bar Assn. (chair probate sect. 1999—2000, chair tech. sect. 2003—04, chair probate sect. 2006—07, 2006—), Fla. Bar (chair coordinating com. tech. 1992—93, probate rules com. 1994—2000), Fla. Trust for Hist. Preservation (bd. dirs. 2002—03), Pinellas County Arts Coun. (councilman 1997—2001), Pres. Club (hon. bd. dirs. 1985—91, founder). Office Phone: 727-821-0904. Office Fax: 727-823-3479. Business E-Mail: jim@jamesmartinpa.com.

MARTIN, JAY GRIFFITH, lawyer; b. Washington, Oct. 13, 1951; s. Drexel Reese and Joyce (Towne) M.; m. Jackie Wendt; children: Trevor, Jaclyn. BBA, So. Meth. U., 1973, MPA, JD, So. Meth. U., 1976. Bar: Tex., D.C., U.S. Ct. Appeals (5th cir.), U.S. Dist. Ct. (so. dist.) Tex., U.S. Dist. Ct. D.C., U.S. Supreme Ct. Counsel Pennzoil Co., Houston, 1976-78, sr. counsel, 1978-81; divsn. counsel The Superior Oil Co., Houston, 1981-85; sr. counsel Mobil Natural Gas, Houston, 1985-87, gen. counsel, 1987-91; asst. gen. counsel Mobil Oil Corp., Fairfax, Va., 1991-96; ptnr. Andrews & Kurth LLP, Washington, 1996-2000, Phelps Dunbar LLP, Houston, 2000—01, Winstead Sechrest & Minick, Houston, 2001—04; v.p., chief compliance officer, sr. deputy Gen. Coun. Baker Hughes, Inc., Houston, 2004—. Mem. sr. adv. bd. Bus. Laws Inc., Chesterland, Ohio, 1997—; mem. adv. bd. Inst. Transnat. Arbitration, Southwestern Legal Found., 1996—, Oil and Gas sect. of Inst. Am. and Internat. Law. Author: Environmental Management Systems, 1998, Dispute Resolution for Oil and Gas Practitioners, 2000, Environmental Dispute Resolution, 2002; mem. editl. bd.: Natural Gas Contracts, 1991—; contbr. over 60 articles on energy and environ. topics to profl. jours. Chmn. fundraising com. So. Meth. U., Washington, 1996—97, mem. dean's adv. coun. Sch. Law, 1995—; trustee Rocky Mountain Mineral Law Found., 2003—. Named Tex. Super Atty., Tex. Monthly Mag., 2004; named one of World's Outstanding Energy Lawyers, Euromoney, 1997, 1999, 2001, 2003. Fellow: State Bar Coll. of Tex., Tex. Bar Found., State Bar Tex. (life; adv. bd. 1985—, chmn. corp. counsel sect. 1990—91, mem. corp. counsel sect. adv. bd. 2003—06, mem. coun. for oil, gas and resources sect. 2003—06, coun. oil and gas sect. 2003—, dir. Tex. C-Bar); mem.: Instit. Am. and Internat. Law (adv. bd. 2004), Fed. Bar Assn. (chmn. 1986—87, bd. dirs. 1990—92, antitrust sect. 1991—98, chmn. internat. energy com. 1997—), Delta Theta Phi, Am. Soc. Internat. Law, Assn. Internat. Petroleum Negotiators, Houston Bar Assn. (mem. internat. com. 2006—), ABA (litig. sect. rep. on ABA coord. com. on energy law 1991—97, sect. pub. utility law 1991—, chmn. natural resources, energy and environ law internat. energy com. 1996—98, exec. coun., budget chmn. sect. on environment, energy and law 1996—, liaison to Fed. Energy Bar Assn. 1997—, ad hoc mem. of com. 1997—, sr. liaison oversight responsibility for all energy and resource coms. 1998—, vice chmn. sect. on environment, energy and resources' natural gas and), Energy Bar Assn. (chmn. antitrust sect. 1986—87, chmn. internat. energy com. 1998—99, chmn. internat. com.), Internat. Bar Assn. (sect. energy and natural resources 1994—), D.C. Bar Assn. (internat.sect.), Tex. Bar Assn. (dir. Tex.). Avocations: history, current events and politics, tennis, golf, jogging, rugby. Home: 10623 Gawain Houston TX 77024-1828 Office: Gen Coun Baker Hughes Inc 2929 Allen Pkwy Ste 2100 Houston TX 77019 Office Phone: 713-439-8439. Business E-Mail: jay.martin@bakerhughes.com.

MARTIN, JAY HERBERT, psychoanalyst, language professor, political science professor; b. Newark, Oct. 30, 1935; s. Sylvester K. and Ada M. (Smith) M.; m. Helen Bernadette Saldini, June 9, 1956; children: Helen E., Laura A., Jay Herbert. AB with honors, Columbia U., 1956; MA, Ohio State U., 1957, PhD, 1960; PhD in Psychoanalysis, So. Calif. Psychoanalytic Inst., 1983. Instr. English Pa. State U., 1957-58; instr., then asst. to assoc. prof. English and Am. Studies Yale U., New Haven, 1960-68; prof. English and comparative culture U. Calif., Irvine, 1968-79; asst. prof. psychiatry and human behavior, clin. supr. residency program Calif. Coll. Medicine Calif. Coll. Medicine U. Calif.-Irvine, 1978—96; Leo S. Bing prof. English and Am. lit. U. So. Calif., LA, 1979-96, dir. undergrad. program in Am. studies, 1968-69, dir. program in comparative culture, 1969-71, dir. edn. abroad program, 1971-75; prof. govt., Edward S. Gould prof. humanities Claremont McKenna Coll., 1996—; dir. civilization program Claremont (Calif.) McKenna Coll., 1996—2000, acting dir. Gould Ctr. for Humanistic Studies, 1998-2000, prof., English, grad. sch., 2004—. Instr. psychoanalysis So. Calif. Psychoanalytic Inst., 1984-96; Bicentennial prof. Am. lit. and culture Moscow State U., USSR, 1976, Dai Ho Chun (Wisdom) chair Prof. U. Hawaii, 2000-01; dir. NEH summer sems., 1976, 77; mem. evaluation com. dept. pvt. post-secondary edn. State of Calif., 1986; lectr. in field; cons. in field Author: (criticism and biography) Conrad Aiken: A Life of His Art, 1962, Harvests of Change: American Literature 1865-1914, 1967, Nathanael West: The Art of His Life, 1970 (U. Calif. Friends Libr. award), Robert Lowell, 1970, Always Merry and Bright. The Life of Henry Miller, 1978, (U. Calif. Friends of Libr. award, Phi Kappa Phi Best Faculty Publ. prize U. So. Calif., transl. in French, Japanese and German), (fiction) Winter Dreams: An American in Moscow, 1979, Who Am I This Time, Uncovering the Fictive Personality, 1988 (trans. Portuguese), Burlington No. Found. award 1989); Swallowing Tigers Whole, 1996, A Corresponding Leap of Love: Henry Miller, 1996, Henry Miller's Dream Song, 1996, Journey to Heavenly Mountain, 2002 (ForeWord mag. Book of Yr. prize), The Education of John Dewey, 2003; author one hour radio drama, William Faulkner. Sound Portraits of Twentieth-Century Humanists, starring Tennessee Williams, Glenn Close, Colleen Dewhurst, Nat. Pub. Radio, 1980; author one-act docudrama Trial Days in Coyocoan, Antioch Rev., 2001; author sects. 24 books including most recently American Writing Today, vol. I, 1982, The Haunted Dusk: American Supernatural Fiction, 1820-1902, 1983, Frontiers of Infant Psychiatry, vol.II, 1986, Centenary Essays on Huckleberry Finn, 1985, Robert Lowell: Essays on the Poetry, 1987, William Faulkner: The Best from American Literature, 1989, The Homosexualities: Reality, Fantasy and the Arts, 1991, Life Guidance Through Literature, 1992, Biography and Source Studies, 1995, William Faulkner and Psychology, 1995, Psychotherapy East and West, 1996, Readings on Huckleberry Finn, 1999, John Fante: A Critical Gathering, 2000, Uncollected Works By...Paul Laurence Dunbar, 2000, American Literature of the Civil War, 2004, Blackwell Companion to Modernist Literature and Culture, 2004,Cases as Catalysts, 2005, Only God: A Biography of Ramsuratkumar, 2005, International Research on Global Affairs, 2005; editor: Winfield Townley Scott (Yale series recorded poets), 1962, Twentieth Century Interpretations of the Waste Land: A Collection of Critical Essays, 1968, Twentieth Century Views of Nathanael West, 1972, A Singer in the Dawn: Reinterpretations of Paul Laurence Dunbar (with intro.), 1975, Economic Depression and American Humor (with intro.), 1986; mem. editl. bd. Am. Lit., 1978-81, Humanities in Society, 1979-1983; editor-in-chief Psychoanalytic Edn., 1984-89; editor Humanitas/Communitas, 1998-2000; appearances on TV and radio including Connie Martinson Talks Books, Barbara Brunner Nightline, Sonya Live in LA, Oprah Winfrey Show, C-SPAN, 1988-89; contbr. numerous articles and revs. to profl. jours., bulls. Pres. Friends of Irvine Pub. Libr., 1974-75; mem. Com. for Freud Mus. Recipient Fritz Schmidl Meml. prize for rsch. applied psychoanalysis Seattle Assn. Psychoanalysis, 1982, Marie H. Briehl prize for child psychoanalysis, 1982, Franz Alexander prize in psychoanalysis, 1984, Disting. Writers award Antioch Rev., 2004; Morse rsch. fellow, 1963-64, Am. Philos. Soc. fellow, 1966, J.S. Guggenheim fellow, 1966-67, Rockefeller Found.humanities sr. fellow, 1975-76, Rsch. Clin. fellow So. Calif. Psychoanalytic Soc. 1977-81, Rockefeller fellow, Bellagio, Italy, 1983, NEH sr. fellow, 1983-84; Durfee Found. fellow to China, 2004; fellow Bogliasco Found. Liguria Ctr. for Arts and Humanities, 2004. Mem. So. Calif. Am. Studies Assn. (pres. 1969-71), Am. Studies Assn. (exec. bd. 1969-71, del. to MLA Assembly 1974, chmn. Ralph Gabriel prize com. 1975-77), MLA (chmn. prize com. Jay B. Hubbell Silver medal in Am. lit. 1978-84), Nat. Assn. Arts and Letters (prize com. 1987-88), Nat. Humanities Faculty (advisor to Valhalla High Sch., El Cajon, Calif. 1979-81), Nat. Am. Studies Faculty, Internat. Psychoanalytic Assn., Internat. Assn. Empirical Aesthetics, Internat. Assn. U. Profs. English, Internat. Karen Horney Soc., Newport Psychoanalytical Inst., Phi Beta Kappa. Home: 748 Via Santo Tomas Claremont CA 91711-1569 Office Phone: 909-398-0193. Personal E-mail: helenjay@comcast.net. Business E-Mail: jmartin@mckenna.edu.

MARTIN, JERRY LEE, organization executive, educator; b. Turkey, Tex., Oct. 16, 1941; m. Abigail L. Rosenthal, 1998. Student, San Diego State Coll., 1961; BA in Polit. Sci., U. Calif., Riverside, 1963; MA in Philosophy and Polit. Sci., U. Chgo., 1966; PhD in Philosophy, Northwestern U., 1970; DHL (hon.), Thomas More Coll. Liberal Arts, 2003. Asst. prof. U. Colo., Boulder, 1967-74, chmn. dept. philosophy, 1979-81, assoc. prof., 1974-84, adjunct prof., 1984—; rsch. analyst House Rep. Rsch. Com., 1982-87; legis. asst. Congressman Hank Brown, 1982-87; dir. divsn. edn. programs NEH, Washington, 1987-88, asst. chmn. studies and evaluation, 1988-89, asst. chmn. programs and policy, 1989-95, acting chmn., 1993. Adj. prof. Georgetown U., 1993-95; adj. scholar Am. Enterprise Inst., 1993—; dir. Ctr. Study Values and Social Policy, U. Colo., Boulder, 1981-82; founding mem. organized rsch. program State of Colo., 1981-82; mem. exec. com. faculty adv. coun. Colo. Commn. Higher Edn., 1980-82; pres. Am. Coun. Trustees and Alumni, 1995-2004, chmn., 2004—; spkr. in field, frequent guest on radio and TV. Contbr. articles to profl. jours. Mem. Gov.'s Blue Ribbon Commn. on Higher Edn., 1998—2000. Andrew W. Mellon Found. Congl. fellow, 1992-93. Mem. AAUP (state pres. 1977-79), Am. Philos. Assn., Soc. Historians Early Am. Republic, Am. Polit. Sci. Assn., Soc. Social, Polit. and Legal Philosophy. Avocations: tennis, baseball, history. Home: 145 C Selner Ln Doylestown PA 18901 Office: Am Coun Trustees and Alumni 1726 M Street NW # 800 Washington DC 20036

MARTIN, JOANNE, social sciences educator; b. Salem, Mass., Sept. 25, 1946; d. Richard Drake and Nathalie (Ashton) M.; m. Beaumont A. Sheil, July 9, 1977; 1 child, Beaumont Martin Sheil. BA, Smith Coll., 1968; PhD in Social Psychology, Harvard U., 1977; PhD in Econs. and Bus. Adminstrn. (hon.), Copenhagen Bus. Sch., 2001; PhD (hon.), Vrije U., Amsterdam, 2005. Assoc. cons. McBer & Co. (formerly Behavior Sci. Ctr. of Sterling Inst.), 1968-70, dir. govt. mktg., 1970-72; asst. prof. orgnl. behavior Grad. Sch. Bus., Stanford (Calif.) U., 1977-80; assoc. prof. grad. sch. bus. Stanford U., 1980-91, prof. grad. sch. bus., 1991—, dir. doctoral programs, grad. sch. bus., 1991-95, Fred H. Merrill prof. orgn. behavior and, by courtesy, sociology, 1996—. Sec. univ. adv. bd. Stanford U., 1995—96, vice chair adv. bd., 1996—97; vis. scholar Australian Grad. Sch. Mgmt. U. N.S.W., 1989—90, Copenhagen Bus. Sch., 1998, 2004; vis. scholar dept. psychology Sydney (Australia) U., 1989—90; Ruffin fellow bus. ethics Darden Grad. Sch. Bus. Adminstrn. U. Va., 1990; mem. bd. advisors iMahal, 1990—; bd. dirs. C.P.P., Inc., 1993—2003; mem. internat. adv. bd. Internat. Ctr. for Rsch. in Orgnl. Discourse, Strategy and Change; Bus. Sch. rep. Stanford U., 1995—; vis. scholar U. Tech. Sydney, 2004—05. Mem. editl. bd. Adminstrv. Sci. Qtrly., 1984—88, Jour. Social Issues, 1981—83, Acad. Mgmt. Jour., 1984—85, Social Justice Rsch., 1985—90, Jour. Mgmt. Inquiry, 1991—, Orgn., 1994—, Jour. Mgmt. Studies, 1996—2004, Gender, Work and Organization, 1998—, Orgn. Studies, 2003—, Scandinavian Jour. Mgmt., 2003—, consulting editor Internat. Jour. Mgmt. Reviews, 1998—; co-author: five books; contbr. over 60 articles to profl. jours. and edited books. Recipient Centennial medal for contbns. to soc. Harvard U. Grad. Sch. Arts and Scis., 2002; Lena Lake Forrest Rsch. fellowship Bus. and Profl. Women's Found., 1978, James and Doris McNamara Faculty fellowship Grad. Sch. of Bus., Stanford U., 1990-91, Grad. Sch. Bus. Trust Faculty fellow, 2005-06. Fellow: APA, Am. Psychol. Soc., Acad. Mgmt. (nat. rep.-at-large 1983—85, divsn. program chair 1985—87, divsn. chair 1987—89, nat. bd. govs. 1992—95, we. divsn. Promising Young Scholar award 1982, Nat. Disting. Educator award 2000, We. Divsn. Disting. Scholar award 2003, Nat. Orgn. and Mgmt. Divsn. Disting. Scholar career achievement award 2005); mem.: Nat. Assn. Corp. Dirs. (adv. bd. 2000—04). Office: Stanford U Grad Sch Bus Littlefield Ctr 353 Stanford CA 94305 Business E-Mail: martin_joanne@gsb.stanford.edu.

MARTIN, JOEL W., curator, biology professor; BS in Zoology, U. Ky., 1978; MS in Biology, U. Southwestern La., 1981; PhD in Biol. Sci., Fla. State U., 1986. Vis. rsch. assoc. Fla. State U., 1986—88; rsch. assoc. San Diego Natural Hist. Mus., 1988—; asst. curator invertebrates Natural Hist. Mus. LA County, 1988—89, assoc. curator, 1989—93, full curator, 1993—. Adj. prof. biology U. So. Calif., 1988—, UCLA, 1933—. Contbr. articles to sci. jours.; co-editor: Crustacean Sexual Biology, 1991; assoc. editor: Jour. Crustacean Biology, 1992—97, Zoologica Scripta, 1992—99. Grantee, NSF, 1984—2004, Nat. Geog. Soc., 1992—94. Mem.: Soc. Systematic Biology, Crustacean Soc. (pres. 1998—2000, Outstanding Paper award 1984), Soc. Integrative and Comparative Biology, Sigma Xi (James. R. Fisher award 1985). Office: Rsch and Collections Crustacea Natural Hist Mus LA County 900 Exposition Blvd Los Angeles CA 90007 E-mail: jmartin@nhm.org. *

MARTIN, JOHN BRUCE, chemical engineer; b. Auburn, Ala., Feb. 2, 1922; s. Herbert Marshall and Lannie (Steadham) M.; m. Mildred Jane Foster, Aug. 7, 1943 (dec. Nov. 1960); children— Shirlie Martin Briggs, John Bruce; m. 2d, Phyllis Barbara Rodgers, June 25, 1963; 1 child, Richard Kipp BS, Ala. Poly. Inst., 1943; M.Sc., Ohio State U., 1947, PhD, 1949. With Procter & Gamble Co., Cin., 1949-82, coordinator orgn. devel., research and devel., 1967-77, mgr. indsl. chem. market research, 1977-82; sr. assoc. Indumar Inc., Cin., 1982-86, sr. v.p., 1986-87. Lectr. U. Cin., 1982-88; adj. assoc. prof. Auburn U., 1983-88. Author: Martin's Mini Mysteries, 1998, Killing is Murder, Pseudonym Pleiades, 2003, Defending Donald Harvey, 2005; contbr. articles to profl. jours.; patentee in field Served with AUS, 1943-46 Decorated Air Medal, Bronze Star with oak leaf cluster; recipient Disting. Alumnus award Coll. Engring., Ohio State U., 1970, Disting. Engr. award Tech. Socs. Council Cin., 1982 Fellow AIChE (bd. dirs. 1968-70, chmn. mktg. divsn. 1985, Mktg. Hall of Fame 1988, Chem. Engr. of Yr. award Ohio Valley 1971); mem. Am. Chem. Soc., Am. Soc. Engring. Edn., Engring. Soc. Cin. (pres. 1972-73), Tech. and Sci. Socs. Cin. (pres. 1972-73), Comml. Devel. and Mktg. Assn., Barbershop Harmony Soc., Mystery Writers Am., Sisters in Crime, Sigma Xi, Tau Beta Pi, Phi Kappa Phi, Phi Lambda Upsilon. Republican. Presbyterian. Home: 5513 Evergreen Ridge Dr Cincinnati OH 45215 E-mail: jmartin660@cinci.rr.com.

MARTIN, JOHN C., pharmaceutical company executive; b. 1952; MBA in Mktg., Golden Gate U.; PhD in Organic Chemistry, U. Chgo. With Syntex Corp., 1978-84; dir. antiviral chemistry Bristol-Myers Squibb, 1984-90; v.p. R&D Gilead Sciences Inc., Foster City, Calif., 1990-95, COO, 1995-96, pres., CEO, 1996—. Mem. Ctrs. for Disease Control/Health Resources and Svcs. Adminstrn. Advisory Com. on HIV and STD Prevention and Treatment, Nat. Inst. Allergy & Infectious Diseases Coun., 2000—03; chmn. Bay Area Bioscience Ctr., 1999—2001, Calif. Healthcare Inst. Bd. trustee U. Chgo., Golden Gate U. Recipient Isbell award, Am. Chemical Soc., Gertrude B. Elion award for Scientific Excellence, Internat. Soc. for Antiviral Rsch. Mem.: Internat. Soc. for Antiviral Rsch. (pres. 1998—2000). Achievements include invention of of the drug ganciclovir. Office: Gilead Scis Inc 333 Lakeside Dr Foster City CA 94404 *

MARTIN, JOHN CHARLES, judge; b. Durham, NC, Nov. 9, 1943; s. Chester Barton and Mary Blackwell (Pridgen) Martin; m. Margaret Rand; children: Lauren M. Smith, Sarah, Susan M. Prince stepchildren: Louise Short, Carl (Trip) Short. BA, Wake Forest U., 1965, JD, 1967; postgrad., Nat. Judicial Coll., Reno, 1979; cert. justice execs. program, U. NC, 1982. Bar: NC 1967, US Dist. Ct. (mid. dist.) NC 1967, US Dist. Ct. (ea. dist.) NC 1972, US Dist. Ct. (we. dist.) NC 1975, US Ct. Appeals (4th cir.) 1976, US Supreme Ct. 2002. Assoc. Haywood, Denny & Miller, Durham, N.C., 1969-72, ptnr., 1973-77; resident judge Superior Ct. 14th Jud. Dist. N.C., Durham, 1977-84; judge N.C. Ct. Appeals, Raleigh, 1985—88, 1993—2004, chief judge, 2004—; ptnr. Maxwell & Hutson, P.A., Durham, 1988-92; arbitrator U.S. Dist. Ct. (mid. dist.) N.C., 1988-92. Study com. rules of evidence and comparative negligence N.C. Legis. Research Commn., 1980; mem. N.C. Pattern Jury Instrn. drafting com., 1978-84, N.C. Trial Judge's Bench Book Drafting Com., 1984-87, N.C. News Media-Adminstrn. of Justice Coun., 1987, state/fed. Jud. Coun. N.C., 1985-87, chmn., 1987; bd. visitors Wake Forest U. Sch. Law, 1986—; mem. alumni coun. Wake Forest U., 1993-96, 2001—04; mem. N.C. Jud. Coun.; mem. N.C. State Jud. Edn. Study Com., 2000-2003; chmn. N.C. Jud. Stds. Commn., 2001—; exec. com. mem. Chief Justice's Commn. Professionalism. Mem. Durham City Coun., 1975—77, chair pub. works com.; panel of arbitrators Duke U. Pvt. Adjudication Ctr., 1988—92; mem. parent adv. bd. Chatham Hall Sch., 2003—05; mem. parent coun. Wake Forest U., 2006—. With Mil. Police Corps USAR, 1967—69. Recipient Disting. Svc. award Durham Jaycees, 1976. Mem. ABA, Appellate Judges Conf., Coun. of Chief Judges, N.C. Bar Assn. (chmn. adminstrn. of justice study com. 1990-92, bench, bar and law sch. com. 1987-91, jud. campaign oversight com. 1990, Lit. Sect. Coun. 1991-94, conv. planning com. 1995-98, adminstrn. justice task force 1996-98, appellate rules study com. 1999-2001, strategic planning/emerging trends com. 2002-04, endowment com. 2004—, v.p. 1997-98), Durham County Bar Assn. (bd. dirs. 1991-92), Wake County Bar Assn., 10th Jud. Dist. Bar Assn., NC Jud. Conf. (v.p. 1999-00), Hope Valley Country Club, Appalachian State U. Parents Assn. (bd. dirs. 1997-01), Phi Delta Phi. Democrat. Methodist. Office: PO Box 888 Raleigh NC 27602-0888 Office Phone: 919-733-4293. Business E-Mail: mnj@coa.state.nc.us.

MARTIN, JOHN CHARLES, lawyer; b. Sheridan, Wyo., Apr. 17, 1953; s. Charles S. and M. Louise (Ago) M.; m. Michele Pacifico, Dec. 9, 1989; children: Laura, Travis John, Hallie Jane. BS with high honors, U. Wyo., 1974; JD, Georgetown U., 1979. Bar: D.C., Wyo. Lawyer Hettinger & Leedy, Riverton, Wyo., 1979-80, Dept. of Interior, Washington, 1981-82, Dept. of Justice, Washington, 1982-85; ptnr., Environ. Health & Safety, Natural Resources, Litigation & Dispute Resolution practices Patton Boggs LLP, Washington, 1985—, mem. exec. com. Co-author: The Corporate Counsel's Guide to Environmental Law, 1989, Handbook on Environmental Law, 1989, Clean Water Handbook, 1990, Handbook of Environmental Law, 1994; contbr. articles to profl. jours. Mem. Wyo. Bar Assn., D.C. Bar Assn. Roman Catholic. Office: Patton Boggs LLP 2550 M St NW Washington DC 20037-1350 Office Phone: 202-457-6032. Office Fax: 202-457-6315. Business E-Mail: jmartin@pattonboggs.com.

MARTIN, JOHN E, psychologist, educator; b. Wyandotte, Mich., Apr. 24, 1949; s. John E and Eileen E Martin; m. Mary Lois Horton, Sept. 8, 1972; children: Valerie, Matthew, Andrew, Alison. BA, Sacred Heart Coll., 1971; specialist in sch. psychology, Eastern Mich. U., 1975; PhD in clin. psychology, U. Detroit, 1995. Cert. National School Psychologist Nat. Assn. of Sch. Psychologists, 1976, lic. Psychologist Mich. Dept. Commerce, 1995. Sch. psychologist Wayne Westland Schools, Westland, Mich., 1975—88, adminstr., 1988—93; adj. prof. Eastern Mich. U., 1984—86; clin. psychologist Lifespan Cmty. Ctr., Garden City, Mich., 1995—97; test cons. Wide Range Inc., Wilmington, Del., 1994—; adj. prof. U. Detroit, 1993—, assoc. prof., 2005—; sch. psychologist Wayne Westland Schools, 1993—. Cons. psychologist Psychological Corp., Chgo.; psychology intern Hawthorne Ctr., 1991—92; cons. psychologist Tchg. Resources, Chgo., 1990—95. Editor: (crisis manual) Addressing Crises, 2004. Mem.: Mich. Assn. Sch. Psychologists, Nat. Assn. Sch. Psychologists, Knights of Columbus. Avocations: golf, hiking, baseball. Home: 25309 Bridlepath Farmington MI 48335 Office: Univ Detroit Mercy Psychology Dept 4001 W McNichols Detroit MI 48221 Personal E-mail: schoolpsych424@yahoo.com.

MARTIN, JOHN F., academic administrator; b. Chico, Calif., June 20, 1959; s. Ernest Milo Martin and Esther Mildred Foster Martin; m. Karen LaNelle Beeman, June 11, 1982; 1 child, Kristen. BA in Bus., So. Nazarene U., Bethany, Okla., 1982; MA, Fuller Theol. Sem., Pasadena, Calif., 1999. Sales rep. Met. Life Ins. Co., Oklahoma City, 1982—85; mgr. Enterprise Rent A Car, Shreveport, La., 1985—90; dir. devel. Le Tourneau U., Longview, Tex., 1990—99; exec. dir. devel. So. Nazarene U., 1999—. Devel. officer So. Nazarene U., 1999—; instr. philanthropy Southwestern Christian U., Bethany, 2007—; presenter in field. Chmn. Northwest C. of C., Bethany, 2005—06; pres. Hospice Longview, Inc., 1999. Mem.: Assn. Fundraising Profls. (past pres. 2006—07), Kiwanis (pres. elect 2006—07, Outstanding Kiwanian of Yr. 2005).

MARTIN, JOHN JOSEPH, journalist; b. NYC, Dec. 3, 1938; s. John and Marie Agnes (Jacobsen) M.; children from previous marriage: Sophie Suzanne, Claire Catherine; m. Katherine Fitzhugh, Feb. 14, 1987. BA in Journalism, San Diego State U., 1995. Copy editor, reporter San Diego Union, 1958-62; copy editor Augusta (Ga.) Chronicle, 1963, N.Y. Times Internat. Edit., Paris, 1964-65; editorial asst. Temple Fielding Publs., Mallorca, Spain, 1965-66; reporter, producer Sta. KCRA-TV News, Sacramento, 1966-75; corr. ABC-TV News, 1975—2002. Adj. prof. Columbia U. Grad. Sch. of Journalism, 2002—. Editor, pub. Aztec Tennis Reporter, 1999—; contbg. writer Tennisone.com, 2000-02. Juror DuPont-Columbia Awards, 2005-. Served with U.S. Army, 1962-64. Recipient Nat. Headliner awards, 1980, 89, Emmy award, 1993, George Polk award, 1994, DuPont-Columbia U. Gold baton, 1994, Nat. Assn. Black Journalists award, 2002, Peabody award, 2002. Mem. AFTRA, U.S. Tennis Assn., Coffee House Club N.Y.C., Nat. Press Club, Overseas Press Club, U.S. Tennis Writers Assn.

MARTIN, JOHN K., communications executive; b. 1968; married; 1 child. BS in Econ., Wharton Sch. of Bus., U. Pa., 1989; MBA Fin. and Orgnl. Behavior, Grad. Sch. of Bus., Columbia U., 1994. CPA Ernst and Young LLP, NY; mgr., SEC fin. reporting Time Warner Inc., 1993, dir., Fin. Special Projects, dir., Office of Pres., v.p., Investor Rels., 1999—2000; dir., Equity Rsch. Grp. ABN AMRO Securities LLC, 2000—02; CFO Time Warner Cable, exec. v.p., CFO. Client adv. bd. Thomson Fin. Services; mem. Conf. Bd. Global Coun. of Investor Rels. Executives. Named Next Generation analyst for cable TV industy, Institutional Investor, 2001; named one of 40 Executives Under 40, Multichannel News, 2006. Mem.: Mus. TV & Radio, Nat. Investor Rels. Inst. Office: Time Warner Cable Inc 290 Harbor Dr Stamford CT 06902-6732 Office Phone: 203-328-0600. Office Fax: 203-328-0690.

MARTIN, JOHN LEWIS, state legislator; b. Eagle Lake, Maine, June 5, 1941; s. Frank and Edwidge (Raymond) M. BA in History and Govt., U. Maine, 1963, postgrad., 1963-64. Tchr. Am. govt. and history Ft. Kent (Maine) Community High Sch., 1966-72; instr. U. Maine, Ft. Kent, 1972-89, asst. prof., 1989—; mem. from Eagle Lake and St. Francis dist. Maine Ho. of Reps., 1964-94, minority fl. leader, 1970-74, speaker of ho., 1975-94, chmn. com. on energy & natural resources, 1994-95, mem. from dist. 151, 1998-2000. Mem. Maine Senate, Dist. 1, 2000—, chmn. com. natural resources, 1999-2004, human svcs., chmn. rules com.; adj. lectr.; mem. intergovtl. rels. com. Nat. Legis. Conf., 1970-74; chmn. Maine Land Use Regulation Commn., 1972-73, Maine Bur. Human Rels., 1972, State Legis. Leaders Found., 1979-83; mem. exec. bd. Nat. Conf. State Legislatures, chmn. state-fed. assembly, 1985-86, chair task force on reapportionment, 1987-88, vice chmn. budget, fiscal and rules com., 1986-87, v.p., 1988-89, pres.-elect, 1989-90, pres., 1990-91, immediate past pres., 1991-92; mem. exec. com. New Eng. Caucus of State Legislatures, 1978-95, chmn., 1982; mem. regional exec. com. Nat. Dem. State Legis. Leaders Assn., 1991-95, chmn., 1987-89; bd. dirs. Found. for State Legislatures, 1988-94; mem. exec. com. Dem. Nat. Com., 1991-94; pres. Ambulance Svc. Inc., 1975—. Trustee Eagle Lake Water and Sewer Dist., 1966—, No. Maine Gen. Hosp., Eagle Lake, Ea. Maine Health Care, 1991-92, No. Maine Med. Ctr., 1966—; mem. rural health steering com. Nat. Acad. for State Health Policy; advisor White House Task Force on Health Care Reform; dir. intergovtl. affairs Nat. Health Care Campaign, 1994; trustee Maine Med. Ctr., Ft. Kent. Mem. New Eng. Polit. Sci. Assn. Democrat. Home: PO Box 250 Eagle Lake ME 04739-0250 Office: Maine Senate State House Augusta ME 04333-0003 Office Phone: 207-287-1585.

MARTIN, JOHN RANDOLPH, judge; b. Lexington, Ky., May 26, 1948; s. Harry and Geraldine (Gray) M.; m. Jacqueline Lauren Snyder, Apr. 24, 1976; 1 child, Lauren Elizabeth. BA, U. Okla., 1973, MA, 1976, JD, 1980. Bar: Okla. 1981, U.S. Ct. Mil. Appeals 1981, U.S. Dist. Ct. (we. dist.) Okla. 1982, S.C. 1983, U.S. Ct. Appeals (10th cir.) 1983, U.S. Dist. Ct. S.C. 1984, U.S. Ct. Appeals (4th cir.) 1984, U.S. Supreme Ct. 1995. Assoc. Finkel, Georgaklis et al, Columbia, SC, 1984-86; ptnr. Mumford, Wishart & Martin, North Myrtle Beach, SC, 1986-87, Gertz, Kastanes, Moore & Martin, North Myrtle Beach, SC, 1987-91; with Office of Hearings and Appeals Social Security Adminstrn., Columbia, SC, 1991—. Lt. col. ret. U.S. Army, 1967-70, Vietnam, 1975-78, with Res. 1970-74, 78-81, 84-97, Desert Storm, JAGC, 1981-84. Mem. NRA, Masons, Shriners, Elks, Phi Delta Phi, Pi Kappa Alpha. Republican. Episcopalian. Avocations: singing, shooting. Office: Office of Hearing and Appeals 1927 Thurmond Mall Blvd Ste 200 Columbia SC 29201-2375

MARTIN, JOHN WILLIAM, JR., retired lawyer, automotive executive; b. Evergreen Park, Ill., Sept. 1, 1936; s. John William and Frances (Hayes) M.; m. Joanne Cross, July 2, 1966; children: Amanda Hayes, Bartholomew McGuire. AB in History, DePaul U., 1958, JD, 1961. Bar: Ill. 1961, D.C. 1962, N.Y. 1964, Mich. 1970. Antitrust trial atty. Dept. Justice, Washington, 1961-62; assoc. Donovan, Leisure, Newton & Irvine, NYC, 1962-70; sr. atty. Ford Motor Co., Dearborn, Mich., 1970-72, assoc. counsel, 1972-74, counsel, 1974-76, asst. gen. counsel, 1976-77, assoc. gen. counsel, 1977-89, v.p., gen. counsel, 1989-99; ret., 1999. Contbr. articles to profl. jours. Trustee DePaul U., 1998—2007, life trustee, 2007—; bd. dirs. Ctr. Social Gerontology, Inc., Nat. Women's Law Ctr., Friends of Legal Svcs. Corp. Mem.: Am. Law Inst., Assn. Gen. Counsel, Little Traverse Yacht Club (commodore 2006—). Republican. Roman Catholic. Personal E-mail: jwmartinjr@gmail.com.

MARTIN, JOHNNY BENJAMIN, accountant; b. Gainesville, Ga., June 9, 1947; s. John Daniel and Helen Amanda (Meeks) M.; m. Mary Sue West, June 8, 1969; 1 child, Tammy Michelle. BBA, U. Ga., Athens, 1969, MA, 1971. CPA, Ga. Tchr. high sch. Hall County Sch. Systems, Gainesville, 1969-70; instr. acctg. Austin Peay State U., Clarksville, Tenn., 1972-76; instr. bus. Gainesville Jr. Coll., 1976-77; contr. Home Fed. Savs. and Loan, Gainesville, 1977-83; ptnr. Kendrick & Jessup, CPA's, Gainesville, 1983-92; pvt. practice, Gainesville, 1992—. Mem. AICPA, Ga. Soc. CPAs, Civitan (bd. dirs., treas. 1981-82, treas. 1986-87), Phi Kappa Phi, Beta Gamma Sigma. Democrat. Baptist. Office Phone: 770-536-0318. Personal E-mail: johnnybmartin@netzero.com.

MARTIN, JOSEPH BOYD, neurologist, educator, retired dean; b. Bassano, Alta., Can., Oct. 20, 1938; s. Joseph Bruce and Ruth Elizabeth (Ramer) Martin; m. Rachel Ann Wenger, June 18, 1960; children: Bradley, Melanie, Douglas, Neil. BSc, Eastern Mennonite Coll., Harrisonburg, Va., 1959; MD, U. Alta., 1962; PhD in Anatomy, U. Rochester, NY, 1971; MA (hon.), Harvard U., 1978; ScD (hon.), McGill U., 1994, U. Rochester, 1996, U. Wis., 1997, U. Alta., 1998. Resident in internal medicine Univ. Hosp., Edmonton, Alta., 1962—64; resident in neurology, fellow in neuropathology Case-Western Res. U., Cleveland, Ohio, 1964—67; rsch. fellow U. Rochester, NY, 1967—70; mem. faculty McGill U. Faculty Medicine, Montreal, Canada, 1970—78, chair, dept. neurology and neurosurgery, 1977—78; prof. medicine and neurology, neurologist-in-chief Montreal Neurol. Inst., 1976—78; Bullard prof. neurology, chief dept. neurology svc. Mass. Gen. Hosp., Boston, 1978—89; Julieanne Dorn prof. neurology Harvard U. Med. Sch., 1984; dean Sch. Medicine U. Calif., San Francisco, 1989—93; chancellor U. Calif., San Francisco, 1993—97; dean faculty medicine Harvard U. Med. Sch., Boston, 1997—2007, Caroline Shields Walker prof. neurobiology and clinical neuroscience. Mem. med. adv. bd. Gairdner Found., Toronto, 1978—83, 1997—2005; adv. coun. neurol. disorders program Nat. Inst. Neurol., Communicative Disorders and Stroke, 1979—82; mem. scientific adv. bd. Encyclopedia of Neuroscience, 1993—, Alzheimer Rsch. Forum, 1998—; internat. adv. bd. Neuroscience, Neurology & Psychaitry, 1993—; bd. dir. Baxter, 2002—, Cytyc Corp., Scientific Learning Corp; chmn. bd. dirs. New England Healthcare Inst., 2006—. Co-author: Clinical Neuroendocrinology, 1977, The Hypothalamus, 1978, Clinical Neuroendocrinology: A Pathophysiological Approach, 1979, Neurosecretion and Brain Peptides: Implications for Brain Functions and Neurological Disease, 1981, Brain Peptides, 1983; editor: Harrison's Principles of Internal Medicine, 1980—99; mem. editl. bd. Human Brain Mapping, 1993—, Neuroreport, 1993—99, The Neuroscientist, 1994—, New England Journal of Medicine, Annual of Neurology and Science, mem. search com. for editor Archives of Neurology, 1995—; contbr. articles to profl. jours. Recipient Moshier Meml. gold medal, U. Alta. Faculty Medicine, 1962, John W. Scott gold med. award, 1962, Abraham Flexner award, AAMC, 1999; scholar, Med. Rsch. Coun. Can., 1970—75. Fellow: Am. Acad. Arts and Scis.; mem.: NAS, Inst. of Medicine, Assn. Am. Physicians, Soc. Neurosci., Royal Coll. Phys. and Surg. Can., Am. Physiol. Soc. (Bowditch lectr. 1978), Am. Neurol. Assn. (pres. 1990). Office: Dean Faculty Medicine Harvard U 25 Shattuck St Boston MA 02115-6027 Office Phone: 617-432-1501. E-mail: joseph_martin@hms.harvard.edu.

MARTIN, JOSEPH BRYAN, application developer; b. Tarrytown, NY, July 7, 1972; s. William Joseph and Brenda Marion Martin; m. Melissa Joy Helmbrecht, May 3, 2003. MS in Sys. Sci., SUNY Binghamton, Vestal, NY, 1996. Prin. software engr. BAE Sys., Arlington, Va., 1997—2005; pres., CEO Trinidyne Sys., LLC, Linden, Va., 2000—. Composer, prodr., sound engineer (jazz fusion CD) Algorythm. Achievements include patents pending for universal messaging interface emulator; development of Mimic, a software application that serves as an engineering test tool. Office: Trinidyne Sys LLC PO Box 576 Linden VA 22642

MARTIN, J(OSEPH) PATRICK, lawyer, judge; b. Detroit, Apr. 19, 1938; s. Joseph A. and Kathleen G. (Rich) Martin; m. Denise Taylor, June 27, 1964; children: Timothy J., Julie D. AB magna cum laude, U. Notre Dame, 1960; JD with distinction, U. Mich., 1963; postgrad., London Sch. Econs., 1964. Bar: Mich. 1963, U.S. Dist. Ct. (ea. dist.) Mich. 1963, U.S. Ct. Appeals (6th cir.) 1967, U.S. Supreme Ct. 1979, U.S. Dist. Ct. (we. dist.) Mich. 1981, U.S. Ct. Fed. Claims 1999. Spl. asst. to gen. counsel Ford Motor Co., Dearborn, Mich., 1962; assoc. Dykema, Wheat, Spencer et al, Detroit, 1963-66; from assoc. to ptnr. Poole Littell Sutherland, Detroit, 1966-76; sr. atty., ptnr., shareholder Butzel Long, Detroit and Birmingham, Mich., 1976-94; sr. atty., shareholder Vlcko, Lane, Payne & Broder PC, Bingham Farms, Mich., 1994-96; sr. atty. Gourwitz and Barr PC, Southfield, Mich., 1996-99; pvt. practice, 2000—; adminstrv. law judge State of Mich., 2002—. Arbitrator Am. Arbitration Assn., Southfield, Mich., 1968—, Nat. Assn. Security Dealers, 1988—, NY Stock Exch., 1991—, Constrn. Arbitration Svcs., Mt. Clemens, 2005—; adj. prof. remedies and alternative dispute resolution U. Detroit Law Sch., 1989—, Wayne State U. Law Sch., 1996—, Cooley Law Sch., 2001—; state ct. adminstrv. office approved mediator all Mich. cts. under new ADR rules; case evaluator, mediator, discovery master Oak County Cir. Ct., Pontiac, Mich., 1985—; mediator Lex Mundi, Coll. Mediators, 1992—; case evaluator, mediator Mediation Tribunal Assn. Wayne County Cir. Ct., 1992—, Oakland County Dist. Cts., 1998—, Wayne County Dist. Cts., 1998—, Wayne County Probate Ct., 2002—; moderator Mich. State Ct. Appeals, 1995—. Author, editor: Laches-Oak County Bar Assn. Legal Jour., 1984, 1992, 1996, Real Property Rev., 1989—90, Mich. Law Weekly, 1990, ADR Newsletter, 2000. Scholar, Cook Found., Ford Found., London, 1963—64. Mem.: ABA, Oakland County Bar Found., Mich. State Bar Found., Oakland County Bar Assn. (chair fed. ct. com., chair Mich. dist. ct. com., mem. ADR com., bd. dirs.), State Bar Mich. (chair alternative dispute sect.). Roman Catholic. Avocations: gardening, golf, walking. Home and Office: 1663 Hoit Tower Dr Bloomfield Hills MI 48302-2630 Fax: 248-932-0368. Personal E-mail: jpatrickmartin@comcast.net.

MARTIN, JOSEPH ROBERT, retired corporate financial executive; b. Phila., Dec. 9, 1947; s. Robert and Elva Ruth (Griffin) M.; m. Catherine Marie Kelly, Sept. 5, 1970; children: Joseph Robert Jr., Jennifer H., Patrick F., Kathleen K., Mariah E. BS, Embry Riddle U., 1974; MBA, U. Maine, 1976. Sr. corp. fin. analyst Keyes Fibre Co., Waterville, Maine, 1976—80; mgr. fin. analysis and planning Schlumberger, Fairchild, South Portland, Maine, 1980—83; divsn. contr. Schlumberger, Factron, Clifton Park, NY, 1983—84; corp. contr. VTC, Inc., Bloomington, Minn., 1984—87, v.p. fin., CFO, 1987—88, sr. v.p., CFO, 1989—90; dir. fin. Nat. Semiconductor, South Portland, Maine, 1990—91; v.p. fin. std. products group Nat. Semicondr., Santa Clara, Calif., 1991—95; v.p. fin. worldwide ops. Nat. Semiconductor, Santa Clara, Calif., 1995—96; exec. v.p., CFO, vice chmn. bd. dirs. Fairchild Semiconductor, South Portland, Maine, 1996—2006; ret., 2006. Bd. visitors U. So. Maine, 1998—2001; pres.'s bd. advisors Embry-Riddle Aero. U., 2000—04, trustee, 2004—; chmn. bd. dirs. Brooks Automation LLC, Chelmsford, Mass.; bd. dirs. Synqor, Inc., Hudston, Mass., Soitec, Inc., Bernin, France. Served to capt. U.S. Army, 1967-72, Vietnam. Decorated D.F.C., Purple Heart, Bronze Star medal, Air medal, Vietnamese Cross of Gallantry, Army Commendation medal. Home: 17 Stornoway Rd Cumberland Foreside ME 04110 Office: JR Martin Co 14 Lantern Ln Cumberland Foreside ME 04110 Office Phone: 207-781-2825. E-mail: joe@jrmandco.com.

MARTIN, JOSEPH VINSON, neuroscientist, educator; b. Boston, Sept. 17, 1952; s. James Cullen and Mary Louise (Echols) M.; m. Jean Ann Rusteberg, Apr. 27, 1989; 1 child, Lara Jean. BA, Northwestern U., Evanston, Ill., 1973; PhD, U. So. Calif., 1987. Rsch. asst. LA Harbor Commn., 1978—79; chemist NIMH, Bethesda, Md., 1982—87; postdoctoral rsch. assoc. SUNY, Stony Brook, 1987—88, rsch. instr.; asst. prof. Biology Dept., Rutgers U., Camden, NJ, 1989—95, assoc. prof., 1995—2004, prof., 2004—, chair, 2006—. Manuscript reviewer European Jour. Pharmacology, Hormones and Behavior, Pharmacology Biochemistry and Behavior, Sleep; lectr. in field. Contbr. articles to profl. jours. Recipient Nat. Merit Letter of Commendation, 1969; NSF Undergrad. Summer Rsch. fellowship, 1972, NIMH Predoctoral Rsch. fellowship, 1977-78, Rutgers U. Acad. Svc. Increment award, 1991, 93, 98, 2000-06, NSF grantee, 1994-97, 98-2001, 2002-04, 2004—, Dean's Citation, UMDNJ. Mem. AAAS, Assn. Profl. Sleep Socs., Internat. Brain Rsch. Orgn., NJ Acad. Sci., NY Acad. Scis., Sleep Rsch. Soc., Soc. for Neuroscience. Business E-Mail: jomartin@camden.rutgers.edu.

MARTIN, JUDITH MORAN, lawyer; b. Ann Arbor, Mich., Feb. 10, 1943; d. D. Lawrence and Donna E. (Webb) Moran; children: Laura M. Buford, Paul M. Martin, A. Lindsay McGill. BA, U. Mich., Ann Arbor, 1963; postgrad., U. Jean Moulin, Inst. du Droit, Lyon, France, 1981; JD, U. Minn., Mpls., 1982. Bar: Minn. 1982, Fla. 1991, Colo. 1994, U.S. Tax Ct. 1989, U.S. Dist. Ct. Minn. 1989, U.S. Ct. Appeals (8th cir.) 1989. Tax supr., dir. fin. planning, asst. nat. dir. Coopers & Lybrand, Mpls., 1981-84; dir. fin. planning Investors Diversified Services subs. Am. Express, Mpls. and NYC, 1984-85; sr. tax mgr., dir. fin. planning KPMG Peat Marwick Main & Co., Mpls., 1985-89; prin. Gray Plant Mooty Mooty & Bennett, P.A., Mpls., 2000—02; owner, mng. ptnr. Martin & Assoc., PA, Mpls., 1989—2000, 2002—. Faculty Minn. CLE, 1994; adv. bd. Nicollet/Ebenezer, 1996; instr. continuing profl. edn., Minn. Soc. CPAs, 1982-86, continuing legal edn., 1983-84, individual, trust and estate provisions Tax Reform Act 1986, continuing legal edn. estate planning 1994 Mem. Mpls. C. of C. Campaign, Downtown Coun. Coms., Mpls., 1982-84, Metro Tax Planning Group, 1984-86, Mpls. Estate Planning Coun., 1985-99, Planned Giving Coun.; class chmn. fundraising campaign U. Minn. Law Sch., Mpls., 1985, 98; bd. dirs. Ensemble Capriccio, chmn. fundraising com., 1998-2002; usher Christ Presbyn. Ch., Edina, Minn., 1983—; mem. adv. coun. on planned giving ARC. Mem. ABA (task force on legal fin. planning), Minn. Bar Assn., Hennepin County Bar Assn., Fla. Bar Assn., Colo. Bar Assn., Minn. Planned Giving Coun., Am. Assn. Ind. Investors (speaker), Am. Soc. CLUs, Minn. Soc. CLUs, Minn. Women Lawyers, Fla. Women Lawyers, Lex Alumnae, U. Mich. Alumni Assn. (coun. govs. 1989-2003, scholarship chmn.), U. Minn. Alumni Club (bd.

dirs. 1996, coun. govs. 1988-96, pres., treas. mem. com.), Interlachen Club, Lafayette Club, Montana Club, U. Minn. Alumni Assn. (mem. univ. issues com., nat. bd. dirs. 1996-99), The Woman's Club Mpls. Home: 5232 West 70th St Edina MN 55439 Office: Martin & Assoc PA 3800 American Blvd W #270 Minneapolis MN 55431 Home Phone: 952-944-4224; Office Phone: 952-857-2424. Business E-Mail: judith@martinandassociates.com.

MARTIN, JUDITH SYLVIA, journalist; b. Washington, Sept. 13, 1938; d. Jacob and Helen (Aronson) Perlman; m. Robert Martin, Jan. 30, 1960; children: Nicholas Ivor, Jacobina Helen. BA, Wellesley Coll., 1959; DHL (hon.), York Coll., 1985, Adelphi U., 1991. Reporter-critic, columnist Washington Post, 1960—83; syndicated columnist United Feature Syndicate, NYC, 1978—; columnist Microsoft, 1996—. Critic-at-large Vanity Fair, 1983—84. Author: The Name on the White House Floor, 1972, Miss Manners' Guide to Excruciatingly Correct Behavior, 1982, Gilbert, 1982, Miss Manners' Guide to Rearing Perfect Children, 1984, Common Courtesy, 1985, Style and Substance, 1986, Miss Manners' Guide for the Turn-of-the-Millennium, 1989, Miss Manners on (Painfully Proper) Weddings, 1996, Miss Manners Rescues Civilization, 1996, Miss Manners' Basic Training: Communications, 1997, Miss Manners' Basic Training: Eating, 1997, Miss Manners' Basic Training: The Right Thing to Say, 1998, Miss Manners' Guide to Domestic Tranquility, 1999, Star-Spangled Manners, 2002, Miss Manners Guide to Excruciatingly Correct Behavior (Freshly Updated), 2005, No Vulgar Hotel, The Desire and Pursuit of Venice, 2007. Bd. dirs. Friends of Scuola San Rocco. Recipient Nat. Humanities medal, 2005, Alumni Achievement award, Wellesley Coll., 2007. Mem. Cosmos Club, Literary Soc. Office: United Feature Syndicate 200 Madison Ave Fl 4 New York NY 10016-3911 Business E-Mail: MissManners@unitedmedia.com.

MARTIN, JULIE A., retired insurance company executive; BS, Tex. Tech. U.; MS in Fgn. Svc., George Washington U., MBA in Fin. Dir. investment missions program Overseas Pvt. Investment Corp., investment ins. officer, regional mgr. ins. dept., mng. dir. L.Am. and Caribbean ins. dept., mng. dir. policy and underwriting, chief underwriter polit. risk ins. dept., dep. v.p. ins., v.p. ins., 1997—. Office: Overseas Pvt Investment Corp 1100 New York Ave NW Washington DC 20527-0001

MARTIN, JUNE JOHNSON CALDWELL, journalist; b. Toledo, Oct. 06; d. John Franklin and Eunice Imogene (Fish) Johnson; m. Erskine Caldwell, Dec. 21, 1942 (div. Dec. 1955); 1 child, Jay Erskine; m. Keith Martin, May 5, 1966. AA, Phoenix Jr. Coll., 1941; BA, U. Ariz., 1943-59; postgrad., Ariz. State U., 1939-40. Freelance writer, 1944—; columnist Ariz. Daily Star, Tucson, 1956-59, 70-94, book reviewer, 1970-94, co-founder Ann. Book and Author Event; editor Ariz. Alumnus mag., Tucson, 1959-70; ind. book reviewer, audio tape columnist Tucson, 1994—; coord. S.W. Books of Yr. sponsored by Pima Pub. Libr., Ariz., 2000—06; columnist So. Ariz. Authors, Ariz., 2005—. Panelist, co-producer TV news show Tucson Press Club, 1954-55, pres., 1958. Contbg. author: Rocky Mountain Cities, 1949; contbr. articles to World Book Ency., and various mags. Mem. Tucson CD Com., 1961; vol. campaigns of Samuel Goddard, U.S. Rep. Morris Udall, U.S. amb. and Ariz. gov. Raul. Castro. Recipient award Nat. Headliners Club, 1959, Ariz. Press Club award, 1957-59, 96, Am. Alumni Coun., 1966, 70. Mem. Nat. Book Critics Circle, Ariz. Press Women, Jr. League of Tucson, Tucson Urban League, PEN U.S.A. West, Planned Parenthood So. Ariz., Tucson Press, Pi Beta Phi. Democrat. Methodist. Home: Desert Foothills Sta PO Box 65388 Tucson AZ 85728-5388

MARTIN, KAREN SIEBENTHAL, community health nurse; b. Bloomington, Ill., Sept. 15, 1942; d. Arthur A. and Evelyn R. (Ehresman) Siebenthal; m. Stanley A. Martin, Mar. 31, 1963; children: Steven, Kathleen, Kelly. Diploma, Meth. Hosp. Sch. Nursing, 1963; BSN, U. Iowa Coll. Nursing, 1969; MS in Nursing, U. Nebr. Coll. Nursing, 1977. Staff nurse, dir. nursing Champaign (Ill.)-Urbana Pub. Health, 1966-67, 69-73; dir. rsch. Vis. Nurse Assn. Omaha, 1978—93. Prin. investigator Nat. Ctr. Nursing Rsch., 1989—93; adj. prof. Midland Luth. Coll. Divsn. Nursing, Fremont, Nebr., 1994—; vis. prof. Japan and Taiwan, 1998, U.K., 2000—01, Ireland, 2001; co-chair Omaha Sys. Internat. Conf., St. Paul, 2001, Milw., 03, Minn., 05, Eagan, Minn., 07; bank of nurse experts Internat. Coun. Nurses, 2002; cons., presenter, spkr. in field. Author: 5 books, 1 translated into Japanese; editor: Home Health Focus, 1994—2000; mem. editl. adv. bd.: Pub. Health Nursing, 1990—, mem. editl. bd.: Outcomes Mgmt. for Nursing, 1997—2003, Home Care Provider, 1996—2001, bd. of review: Nursing Outlook, 1990—; contbr. articles to Australian, Japanese and Dutch profl. jours. Recipient Alumnus of Yr. award Meth. Med. Ctr. of Cen. Ill. Sch. Nursing, Peoria, Ill., 1995; named Disting. Alumus, U. Iowa Coll. Nursing, Iowa City, 2006. Mem.: APHA, ANA (Congress of Nursing Practice 1994—98, dist. bd. dirs. 1999—2001), Nat. Assn. County and City Health Officials, Am. Med. Informatics Assn., Internat. Coun. Nurses (internat. classification of nursing practice adv. com. 1994—), Midwest Nursing Rsch. Soc. (Disting. Nursing Informatics Rshr. award 2007), N.Am. Nursing Diagnosis Assn., Am. Acad. Nursing (expert panel on electronic networks 1995—97, expert panel on informatics 2002—), Sigma Theta Tau.

MARTIN, KEITH, lawyer; b. Mpls., May 5, 1953; s. L. John and Lois Ann (Henze) M. BA, Wesleyan U., 1974; JD, George Washington U., 1977; MSc, London Sch. Economics, 1978. Bar: DC 1978, NY 1985. Legis. asst. to Sen. Henry M. Jackson, Washington, 1974-77; legis. counsel to Sen. Daniel Patrick Moynihan, 1979-82; ptnr. Chadbourne & Parke LLP, Washington, 1983—, mng. ptnr., 1989-93. Democrat. Office: Chadbourne & Parke LLP 1200 New Hampshire Ave NW Washington DC 20036 Office Phone: 202-974-5674. E-mail: kmartin@chadbourne.com.

MARTIN, KEVIN J., federal agency administrator; b. Charlotte, NC, 1966; m. Catherine Jurgensmeyer Martin. BA, U. N.C., Chapel Hill; M Pub. Policy, Duke U.; JD, Harvard U. Bar: Fla., D.C. Law clk. to Hon. William M. Hoeveler U.S. Dist. Ct., Miami; assoc. Wileu, Rein & Fielding, Washington; with Office Ind. Counsel; legal advisor to commr. Harold Furchtgott-Roth FCC, 1997—99; deputy gen. counsel Bush Campaign, 1999—2000; with transition team Bush-Cheney; spl. asst. to the Pres. for econ. policy The White House, Washington, 2000—01; commr. FCC, 2001—, chmn., 2005—. Named one of Top 40 Lawyers Under 40, Nat. Law Jour., 2005, 50 Who Matter Now, CNNMoney.com Bus. 2.0, 2006. Mem.: D.C. Bar Assn., Fla. Bar Assn., Fed. Comm. Bar Assn. Republican. Office: FCC 445 12th St SW Rm 8B201 Washington DC 20554 Fax: 202-418-0982. *

MARTIN, KEVIN JOHN, nephrologist, educator; b. Dublin, Jan. 18, 1948; came to U.S., 1973; s. John Martin and Maura Martin; m. Grania E. O'Connor, Nov. 16, 1972; children: Alan, John, Ciara, Audrey. MB BCh, Univ. Coll. Dublin, 1971. Diplomate Am. Bd. Internal Medicine, Am. Bd. Nephrology. Intern St. Vincent's Hosp., Dublin, 1971-72, resident, 1972-73, Barnes Hosp., St. Louis, 1973-74, fellow, 1974-77; asst. prof. Washington U., St. Louis, 1977-84, assoc. prof., 1984-89; prof., dir. div. nephrology St. Louis U., 1989—. Contbr. numerous articles to med. jours. Office: Saint Louis Univ Med Ctr 3635 Vista Ave Saint Louis MO 63110-2539

MARTIN, LAURA KEIDAN, lawyer; b. Detroit, Oct. 8, 1964; BA, U. Mich., 1986; JD, Harvard U., 1989. Bar: Ill. 1989. Ptnr. Katten Muchin Rosenman LLP, Chgo. Mem.: ABA, Nat. Health Lawyers Assn., Ill. Assn. Healthcare Attys. (bd. dirs., pres.), Chgo. Bar Assn. (chair antitrust law com. 2004—05). Office: Katten Muchin Rosenman LLP 525 W Monroe St Chicago IL 60661 Office Fax: 312-902-5487, 312-577-8951. E-mail: laura.martin@kattenlaw.com.

MARTIN, LAURABELLE, property manager; b. Jackson County, Minn., Nov. 3, 1915; d. Eugene Wellington and Mary Christina (Hansen) M. BS, Mankato State U., 1968. Tchr. rural schs., Renville County, Minn., 1936-41, 45-50, Wabasso (Minn.) Pub. Sch., 1963-81; pres. Renville Farms and Feed Lots, 1982-86. Author: Hist. Biography of Joseph Renville, 1996; poet: Nat. Libr. Poetry (Silver Cup award, 2003). Pres. Wabasso (Minn.) Edn. Assn., 1974-75, publicity chmn., 1968-74; sec. and publicity agt. Hist. Renville Preservation Com., 1978-86; publicity chmn., sec. Town and Country Boosters, Renville, 1982-83. Recipient Outstanding Achievement in Poetry Award, Internat. Soc. Poets. Mem. Genealogy Soc. Renville County, Am. Legion Aux. Democrat. Lutheran. Avocations: antique furniture, travel, sewing, poetry. Home and Office: 334 NW 1201st Rd Holden MO 64040-9378

MARTIN, LAURALEE, real estate company executive; b. 1951; BA, Oregon State U.; MBA, U. Conn. Certain sr. mgmt. positions GE Credit Corp.; joined Heller Fin. Inc., 1986, mem. bd. dirs., 1991—98, pres. real estate grp., sr. grp. pres., exec v.p., CFO, 1996—2001; CFO Jones Lang LaSalle Inc., 2002—, COO, 2005—. Mem. bd. dirs. KeyCorp, 2003, Jones Lang LaSalle Inc., 2005. Named a Woman to Watch, Crain's Chgo. Bus., 2007. Office: Jones Lang LaSalle Inc 200 E Randolph Dr Chicago IL 60601 Office Phone: 312-782-5800. *

MARTIN, LAWRENCE B., academic administrator, anthropologist, educator; PhD in Anthropology, Univ. Coll. London, 1983. Postdoctoral fellow anatomy Univ. Coll. London, 1983—85; asst. prof. depts. anthropology and anat. scis. SUNY, Stony Brook, 1985—90, assoc. prof., 1990—96, dir. undergraduate studies, dir. doctoral prog. anthrop. scis., dean grad. sch., 1993—, prof., 1996—, dir. internat. progs., 1996—2003, assoc. provost analysis and planning, 2001—; founder Acad. Analytics. Mem. Task Force on Outcomes Assessment and Instl. Effectiveness NY State Dept. Edn.; mem. exec. com. Northeastern Assn. Grad. Schs. Contbr. articles to sci. jours., chapters to books. Office: Grad Sch SUNY Stony Brook 2401 Computer Sci Bldg Stony Brook NY 11794-4433 Office Phone: 631-632-7035. E-mail: lawrence.martin@stonybrook.edu. *

MARTIN, LELAND MORRIS (PAPPY), historian, educator; b. Patrick Springs, Va., Aug. 8, 1930; s. Rufus Wesley and Mary Hilda (Biggs) M.; m. Mildred Greer, May 12, 1956 (dec. June 2007); children: Lee Ann Geneve, Mitzi Jo. AB, Berea Coll., 1953; MS, U. Tenn., 1954; grad., Air War Coll., Maxwelll AFB, Ala., 1978; MA in History, U Tex. Pan-Am., 1993; cert. machinist, Tex. State Tech. Coll., 1997, AAS in Machining Technology-Tool and Die Making, 1999. Enlisted USAF, 1954, advanced through grades to col., 1977; comdr. RAF, Greenham Common, Welford, 1974-76; comdt., comdr. Noncommd. Officers Acad., McGuire AFB, NJ, 1976—79; vice comdr., comdr. RAF Mildenhall and RAF Chicksands, England, 1979-83; chief of staff 21st Air Force, McGuire AFB, 1983-84; pres. Air Force Phys. Evaluation Bd., Randolph AFB, NJ, 1984-86; ret., 1986; dep. exec. dir. Confederate Air Force, Harlingen, Tex., 1986-88; exec. dir. Am. Airpower Heritage Found., Harlingen, 1986-88; tchg. asst., lectr. in history U. Tex. Pan Am., Edinburg, 1989-93; adj. prof. history Tex. State Tech. Coll., Harlingen, 1994—2001. Co-chair (with Sir Douglas Bader) 1976 Internat. Air Tatoo at RAF Greenham Common; chair Air Fete 80 and 81, RAF Mildenhall, Eng. Co-editor: History of Military Assistance Command, Vietnam, 1970. Decorated Legion of Merit with two oak leaf clusters, Bronze Star; Cross of Gallantry (Vietnam); recipient Amb.'s award Ct. St. James, London, 1974, 83. Mem. Air Force Assn., Am. Watchmakers and Clockmakers Inst., Nat. Assn. Watch and Clock Collectors, Brit. Officers Club Phila. (hon.), Rotary (gov. internat. dist. 5930 1995-96), Phi Alpha Theta, Phi Kappa Phi. Republican. Presbyterian. Avocations: clock repairs, photography, golf, fishing. Home: 3001 Emerald Lake Dr Harlingen TX 78550-8621

MARTIN, LINDA GAYE, demographer, economist; b. Paris, Ark., Dec. 17, 1947; d. Leslie Paul and Margie La Verne (Thomas) Martin. BA in Math., Harvard U., 1970; MPA, Princeton U., 1972, PhD in Econs., 1978; DHL (hon.), Marlboro Coll., 2002; D in Pub. Policy (hon.), Rand Grad. Sch., 2006. Dir. mgmt. info. sr. ctrs. bur. purchased social svcs. for adults City of N.Y., 1972—74; rsch. assoc., rsch. dir. U.S. Ho. of Reps. Select Com. on Population, Washington, 1977—79; rsch. assoc. East-West Population Inst., Honolulu, 1979—89, asst. dir., 1982—84; asst. prof. econs. U. Hawaii, Honolulu, 1979—81, assoc. prof., 1981—89, prof., 1989; dir. com. on population Nat. Acad. Scis., Washington, 1989—93; dir. domestic rsch. divsn., v.p. RAND, Santa Monica, Calif., 1993—95, v.p. for rsch. devel., 1995—99; pres. Population Coun., NYC, 1999—2004; scholar in residence Inst. Medicine, 2004—. Neurosci. behavior and sociology of aging rev. com. Nat. Inst. on Aging, Bethesda, 1991—95; chair panel on aging in developing countries NAS, Washington, 1987, com. on population, 1993—99, panel on internat. aging data, 1999—2001; peer rev. oversight group NIH, 1998—2004. Editor: The ASEAN Success Story, 1987; co-editor: Demographic Change in Sub-Saharan Africa, 1993, The Demography of Aging, 1994, Racial and Ethnic Differences in the Health of Older Americans, 1997; contbr. articles to profl. jours. Mem. adv. coun. Woodrow Wilson Sch. Pub. and Internat. Affairs, Princeton U., NJ, 2000—. Recipient Fulbright Faculty Rsch. award, Coun. for Internat. Exch. of Scholars, 1988. Mem.: AAAS (adv. coun. 2003—06, chair social, econ. and polit. scis. sect. 2007—), Population Assn. Am. (bd. dir. 1991—93), Internat. Union for Sci. Study Population, Gerontol. Soc. Am. Democrat. Office: Inst of Medicine 500 5th St NW Rm 863 Washington DC 20001 Home: 3419 Mansfield Rd Falls Church VA 22041

MARTIN, LISA DEMET, lawyer; b. Pa., 1959; BA with honors, Wellesley Coll., 1980; JD, U. Pa., 1984. Bar: Mo. 1984. Ptnr., mem. exec. com. Bryan Cave LLP, St. Louis. Durant scholar Wellesley Coll. Mem. Phi Beta Kappa. Office: Bryan Cave LLP One Metropolitan Sq, Ste 3600 211 N Broadway Saint Louis MO 63102 Office Phone: 314-259-2125. E-mail: lmartin@bryancave.com.

MARTIN, LOREN WINSTON, allergist; b. Albertsville, Ala., Apr. 20, 1938; s. Loren d. and Byrda G. (Crotwell) M.; m. Vivian Elizabeth Sanger Martin, Dec. 29, 1960; children: Lori Ann, Karen Lynn, James Winston. BA in Chemistry, Duke U., 1959; MD, U. Tenn., 1962. Lic. physician, Ariz. Rotating internship Fitzsimons Army Hosp., Denver, 1963; med. residency Honolulu, 1964-67; med. officer U.S. Army, 1962-70; fellowship allergy U. Colo., Denver, 1970-71; pvt. practice Tucson, 1971—. Decorated Bronze Star. Fellow Am. Acad. Allergy & Immunology, Am. Coll. Allergy & Immunology; mem. Pima County Med. Soc. Republican. Office: 1661 N Swan Rd Ste 300 Tucson AZ 85712-4053 Home Phone: 520-760-0225; Office Phone: 520-795-1185.

MARTIN, LOUIS FRANK, surgery and healthcare outcomes analyst; b. Troy, NY, Nov. 7, 1951; s. Eugene Lavern and Lois Jane (Perkins) Martin; m. Deborah Lynn Tjarnberg, Mar. 12, 1977; children: Jesse Tjarnberg, James Casey, Tyler Gene. BA, Brown U., 1973, MD, 1976; MS in Health Adminstrn., U. Louisville, 1993. Diplomate Am. Bd. Surgery, Am. Bd. Med. Mgmt. Resident in gen. surgery U. Wash. Affiliated Hosps., Seattle, 1977-78, U. Louisville, 1978-83, rsch. fellow trauma rsch. and health care ednl. adminstrn., 1980-82; asst. prof. surgery Pa. State U., Hershey, 1983-88, asst. prof. physiology, 1986-88, assoc. prof. surgery and cellular and molecular physiology, 1988-92; prof. surgery La. State U., New Orleans, 1992—, prof. preventative medicine and pub. health, 1994—2003, prof. neurosci., 1995—, med. dir. St. Charles Weight Mgmt. Ctr., 1995—2004, med. dir. Touro Weight Mgmt. Ctr., 2005—; prof. healthcare quality and patient safety La. State U. Sch. Pub. Health, 2004—. Vis. scientist INSERM, Poste Orange, France, 1990-91; cons. TENET Health Care Corp. Med. Affairs Dept., 1995-04, Ethicon Endo-Surgery, Inc., 2000—, La. State Employees Office Group Benefits, 2003—. Mem. editl. bd. Shock, 1994-97, Obesity Surgery, 1997—, Jour. Surgical Outcomes, 1997-99, Surgery for Obesity and Related Diseases, 2004—; author med. books; contbr. articles to newspapers and profl. jours. Loyal Davis Traveling Surg. scholar ACS, 1990; recipient Clin. Investigator award NIH, 1985-90; named to Guide to America's Top Surgeons Gen. Surgery So. Region, Consumer's Rsch. Coun., 2004. Mem.: ACS, Shape Up Am., New Orleans Surg. Soc. (pres. 1999), Soc. Univ. Surgeons, Soc. Internat. Chirurgie, Collegium Internat. Chirurgiae Digestivae, Assn. for Acad. Surgery (councilman 1988—90), Am. Physiol. Soc., Am. Coll. Critical Care Medicine, Am. Soc. Bariatric Surgery (program chmn. 1997, 1998, mem. exec. coun. 1997—2000). Home: 3005 Palm Vista Dr Kenner LA 70065-1560 Office: La State U Dept Surgery 1542 Tulane Ave New Orleans LA 70112-2825 Home Phone: 504-885-2576; Office Phone: 504-568-4750. Business E-Mail: lmarti1@lsuhsc.edu.

MARTIN, MALCOLM ELLIOT, lawyer; b. Buffalo, Dec. 11, 1935; s. Carl Edward and Pearl Maude (Elliot) M.; m. Judith Hill Harley, June 27, 1964; children: Jennifer, Elizabeth, Christina, Katherine. BA, U. Mich., Ann Arbor, 1958, JD, 1962. Bar: N.Y. 1963, U.S. Ct. Appeals (2nd Cir.) 1966, U.S. Supreme Ct. 1967. Assoc. Chadbourne & Parke LLP (formerly Chadbourne Parke Whiteside & Wolff), NYC, 1962-73, ptnr., trusts, estates, pvt. clients practice groups, 1974—2006, of counsel, 2007—. Dir., sec. Carl and Dorothy Bennett Found., Inc.; sec., counsel Copper Devel. Assn., Inc. With US Army, 1958—60. Mem. ABA, NY State Bar Assn., Assn. Bar City NY, St. Andrew's Soc. NY, Rockefeller Ctr. Club, Copper Club (NYC). Office: Chadbourne & Parke LLP 30 Rockefeller Plz Fl 31 New York NY 10112-0129 Office Phone: 212-408-1040. Office Fax: 212-541-5369. Business E-Mail: mmartin@chadbourne.com.

MARTIN, MARCELLA EDRIC, retired community health nurse; b. Rosedale, Miss., Jan. 25, 1930; d. Amos and Alma Allen; m. Reuben Clifton Martin, Jan. 25, 1969; children: Brunetta, Jacqueline, Cornell, Constance. Student, Marygrove Coll., Detroit, 1971; ADN, Highland Park Sch. Nursing, Mich., 1979; ThB, Cmty. Bible Coll., Detroit, 1968. Lic. LPN. Nurse VA Hosp., Ann Arbor, Mich., Crittendon Hosp., Detroit, Vis. Nurses Assn., Detroit. Instr. Charles H. Mason Bible Sch., Detroit, 1991—95; mem. C.O.G.I.C. Bus. owners Assn., 1982—. Author: Women Who Struggle, 2001; prodr.: (plays) And Didn't Those Knees Bow, 2004. Founder Prime of Life Adult Foster Care Home, 1979, Somebody's Got To Care Min., 2003; mem. Nat. Campaign Tolerance-The Wall of Tolerance, 2003; missionary over women Chs. of God in Christ, 1986—2002; vol. Redford Geriatric Home, Mich., 1999—. Named to Wall of Tolerance, New Civil Rights Meml. Ctr., Montgomery, Ala., 2003; recipient Spirit of Detroit award, City of Detroit, 1978, 2000, 2002, Disting. Citizen of Detroit award, 1980, Testimonial Resolution award, 1985. Mem.: Detroit Writers Guild. Democrat. Pentecostal Ch. Avocations: reading, writing. Home: 25332 Shiawassee Cir Apt 106 Southfield MI 48034 Personal E-mail: reumarone@comcast.net.

MARTIN, MARCI, writer, former advertising specialist; b. Corsicana, Tex., Oct. 20, 1927; d. Roy Rhoston McNutt and Maggie Mae Price; m. Harold Durward Martin, May 31, 1947 (dec. Dec. 15, 1998); children: Jennifer Ann Martin Svihus, Gary(dec.). Student, North Tex. State U., Denton, 1945—46, So. Meth. U., Dallas, 1946, Miracosta Coll., Oceanside, Calif., 1990—91. Bus. rep. Southwestern Bell, Dallas, 1946—55; advt. rep. Christian Sci. Monitor, San Diego, 1982—89. Author: Go To Hell and Make a U-Turn, 1996, rev. edit., 2000, Secrets and Lies, 2000, License To Steal, 2001, (short stories, essays, articles) The Muse on My Shoulder, 2001, Tangled Webs, 2004, Out of Bounds - and Dead, 2005, Dirty Genes, 2006; co-editor: A Way With Murder, An Anthology by Arizona Mystery Writers, 2004; editor, ghost writer: Much Ado About Something, 2003. Vol. prison chaplain, San Diego, 1989—95. Recipient 1st pl. for poetry, Nat. U., 1991, 3d pl. for essay, Writer's Jour., 2d pl. and hon. mention, Ann. Showcase Writers Club, 1994, Tangled Webs 2d pl., Jim Woods prize, 2002. Mem.: Ariz. Mystery Writers (coord./pres. 1998—), Soc. Southwestern Authors (mentor 1998—). Avocation: golf. Home: 3011 W Sawmill Spring Trail Tucson AZ 85742

MARTIN, MARCIA D., science educator; d. James David Davis and Mary Louise Merriman; m. Francis P. Martin (div.); children: Marc Jon, Scott Anthony. Grad., U. So. Miss., Hattiesburg, 1986. Cert. tchr. Miss., Ark. Tchr. asst. remedial reading Pascagoula Sch. Dist., Miss., 1983—85; tchr. remedial reading Moss Point H.S., Miss., 1986—88; tchr. TLC program Pulaski County Sch. Dist., Little Rock, 1989—92, tchr. math., sci., 1992—95, 1995—97, tchr. 6th grade sci., 1997—. Sci. fair sponsor Daisy Bates Elem., Little Rock, 1989—93; tchr., curriculum writer MAST Program, Daisy Bates Elem., Little Rock, 1992—94; mem. West Nile Virus study County Sch. Dist., 2003. Recipient Disting. Leadership award, Ark. Leadership Acad., 1986; grantee, Pulaski County Sch. Dist., 2003. Mem.: Pulaski Assn. Classroom Tchrs. Avocations: classical piano, needlecrafts. E-mail: marcia_martin2002@yahoo.com.

MARTIN, MARCIA GRAY, retired architecture educator, artist, designer; b. Chgo., May 18, 1932; d. Harry Gray and Emma Bernstein; children: Elizabeth Anne, Charles Brandon. BArch, Ill. Inst. Tech., 1956; attended, De Paul Law Sch., 1957—58, U. Chgo., 1948—50; MA in Liberal Studies, North Ctrl. Coll., 1997. Freelance architect designer, Chgo., 1956—79; instr. architecture Coll. Dupage, Glen Ellyn, Ill., 1980—88, prof. architecture, 1989—2004, coord. architectural programs, 2000—04, prof. emeritis, 2004—; asst. art gallery Inspire Fine Art, Chgo., 2004—. Head traveling exhibition Coll. Dupage, 2001—; illustrator, artist Wheaton History Ctr., Ill., 1985—. Author: (books) Wheaton, USA, 1991, Architectural Drafting, 1997. Sec. Wheaton Historic Preservation Coun.; mem. City Wheaton Historic Com., Ill., 1992—93, Landmark Preservation Coun., Wheaton, 1990—2004; pres. Waterford Condominium Assn., Wheaton, 2005—; mem., bd. dirs. Dupage Art League, Wheaton, 1980—85; pres. bd. dirs. Wheaton Historic Preservation Coun.; bd. dirs. Waterford Condominium Assn., Wheaton. Recipient Wisdom and Counsel award, Wheaton Youth Outreach, 1990, Julia Beverage award, Ill. Inst. Tech., 2007. Achievements include created one of the few undergraduate historic preservation education programs. Home: 455 W Front St #302 Wheaton IL 60187 Personal E-mail: marciagraymartin@yahoo.com.

MARTIN, MARGARET M., artist, educator; b. Buffalo, Aug. 15, 1940; d. Earl and Margaret L. (Milley) M. BFA, Boston U., 1962; student, John Pike, Rex Brandt, Robert E. Wood, John Pellew, Milford Zornes; DFA (hon.), D'Youville Coll., Buffalo, NY, 2004. Graphic designer Wagner Folding Box, Buffalo, 1962-64; art director Manhardt Alexander Inc., Buffalo, 1964-77; freelance designer MMMartin Design, Buffalo, 1977-79; artist, tchr. Buffalo, 1979—. Cons. Niagara Frontier Watercolor Soc., Buffalo, 1986—. One-woman shows include Performing Arts Ctr., Buffalo, 1996, Kenan Gallery, Lockport, NY, 1997, D'Youville Coll., Buffalo, 2001, Garret Club, Buffalo, 2003, Buffalo Club, 2005; exhibited in group shows at Taiwan Art Inst., Taipei, 1994, Catharine Lorillard Wolfe Art Club, 1996-97, 03, 05, Balt. Watercolor Soc., 1996, Burchfield Penney Art Ctr. Buffalo, 2004, Am. Watercolor Soc., NYC, 2002, F.G Burroughs-S.B. Chapin Art Mus., Myrtle Beach SC, 2007; author: No More Wishy-Washy Watercolor, 1999; featured painting in the Movie "Bruce Almighty", Universal Studios, 2003. Recipient Morrison award Adirondacks Nat.

Exhbn. Am. Watercolor, 1991, Adriana R. Zahn award Catharine Lorillard Wolfe Art Club, 1992, Cynthia Shipp Goodgal Meml. Watercolor award Catharine Lorillard Wolfe Art Club, 2003, Best of Show award Internat. Plein Air Painters Worldwide Paintout, Niagara Falls, Ont., Can., 2004, Frank and Mary Anderson Cassidy Meml. award Catharine Lorillard Wolfe Art Assn., 2005, Mary LaGreca Meml. award Hudson Valley Art Assn. 75th Ann. Exhbn., 2006; featured painting in the Movie "Bruce Almighty", Universal Studios, 2003. Mem. Met. Mus. Art, Albright-Knox Art Gallery, Met. Opera Guild, Nat. Trust, Niagara Buffalo Partnership, Midwest Watercolor Soc. (bd. dirs. 1985-87, Grumbacher Gold Medal 1988), Nat. League Am. Pen Women, (exhbn. chmn. 1980-82, Biennial Award Excellence 1988), Salmagundi Club (Ogden Pleissner Meml. award), Nat. Arts Club (exhbn. com. award solo exhbn. 1985), Catharine Lorillard Wolfe Art Club (Anna Hyatt Huntington award painting 1985). Presbyterian. Avocations: horticulture, music. Studio: 69 Elmwood Ave Buffalo NY 14201-2018

MARTIN, MARIE ANN, art association administrator; b. Winthrop, Mass., July 13, 1963; d. Charles and Ann Marie-Kelly Murray; m. Harold Glen Martin; children: Garrison Cash, Carson Carter, Grace Elane. AA, Nat. Pk. C.C., Hot Springs, Ark., 2005; postgrad., Henderson State U., Arkadelphia, Ark., 2005—. Banking Principles, New Eng. Banking Inst./Boston, MA, 1983; Mass Marketing New Eng. Banking Inst./Boston, MA, 1984. Founder Elberta Arts Coun. and Humanities, Nashville, Ark., 2000—; exec. dir. Fine Arts Ctr. Hot Springs, 2002—04. Music dir. Maranatha Bapt. Ch., Nashville, 1996—99. Juror/judge/curator Elberta Arts Juried Art Exhibit, curator Fine Arts Center Exhibitions, Elberta Arts Center Exhibits. Mem. Literacy Coun. Howard County, Nashville, Ark., 2001—02. Recipient Svc. to Arts, Fine Arts Ctr. Hot Springs, 2004; Mid Am. Singers scholar, Nat. Pk. C.C., 2004—05, Tuition scholar, Henderson State U., 2005—. Mem.: Alpha Chi Omega. Avocations: president's list-national park comm. coll. -2005, dean's list-henderson state university -2006. Office: Elberta Arts Council & Humanities 109 S Main St Nashville AR 71901 Home Phone: 903-794-3808; Office Phone: 870-451-9966.

MARTIN, MARILYN MANN, retired media specialist; b. Greencastle, Ind., July 14, 1939; d. Emil Albert and Edith Costa Mann; m. Max Lee Martin; children: Michael Lee, Melanie Sue Martin Boesen. BS, Ind. State U., 1960, MS, 1970, MS, 1988. Tchr. Latin, sch. libr. Danville H.S., Ind., 1960; libr., media specialist Greencastle H.S., 1971—2002, ret., 2002. Mem. tech. connections com. Greencastle H.S., 1997-98; mem. exec. bd. Stone Hills Libr. Svcs., Bloomington, Ind., 1990-96. Mem.: NEA, ASCD, Putnam County Ret. Tchrs. Assn., Greencastle Classroom Tchrs. (scholarship chmn. 1985—2002), Assn. Ind. Media Educators (dist. advocacy chmn. 1998), Ind. Coop. Libr. Svcs., Ind. Libr. Found., Ind. Ret. Tchrs. Assn., Ret. Sr. Vol. Program, Nat. Home Gardening Club, Down-to-Earth Garden Club, Phi Kappa Phi. Avocations: gardening, reading, volunteering.

MARTIN, MARK, race car driver; b. Batesville, Ark., Jan. 9, 1959; m. Arlene Martin; children: Heather, Rachel, Stacy, Matthew Clyde. Profl. race car driver, 1978—; driver Winston Cup, 1981—; part-time racer with MB2 Motorsports, 2006—. Named winner, ASA Championship, 1978, 1979, 1980, 1986, AC Delco 500, 1989, Pontiac 500, 1989, Pontiac Excitement 400, 1990, Tyson/Holly Farms 400, 1990, Hardee's 500, 1991, Hanes 500, 1992, Mello Yello 500, 1992, Bud 500, 1993, Montain Dew So. 500, 1993, Slick 50 500, 1993, The But at the Glen, 1993, 1994, 1995, Hooters 500, 1994, Winston 500, 1995—97, Tyson 400, 1995, VAW-GM 500, 1995, Savemart 300, 1997, MENA 400, 1997, Las Vegas 400, 1998, Tex. 500, 1998, Calif. 500, 1998, Miller Lite 400, 1997, Goody's Headache Powder 500, 1998, VAW-GM Quality 500, 1998, MBNA Gold 400, 1998, 1999, Dura-Lube/Big KMart 400, 1999, IROC Championship, 1999, Goody's Body Pain 500, 2000, Coca-Cola 600, 2002, MBNA America 400 Dover International Speedway, 2004, Calif. 200, 2006, Daytona 250, 2006. Office: Roush Racing 122 Knob Hill Rd Mooresville NC 28117-6847 also: care NASCAR 1801 W Internat Speedway Bd Daytona Beach FL 32114 *

MARTIN, MARK D., State Supreme Court Justice; b. Apr. 29, 1963; s. M. Dean and Ann Martin. Student, U. Dayton, 1981; BS summa cum laude, Western Carolina U., 1985; JD (hon.), U. NC, 1988; grad., Nat. Jud. Coll., 1993; LLM, U. Va., 1998. Bar: N.C., U.S. Dist. Ct. (ea. and mid. dists.) N.C., U.S. Ct. Appeals (4th cir.), U.S. Supreme Ct. Law clk. to Hon. Clyde H. Hamilton US Dist. Ct., Columbia, SC, 1988-90; pvt. practice McNair Law Firm, Raleigh, NC, 1990-91; legal counsel to gov. Office of Gov., Raleigh, NC, 1991-92; superior ct. judge Jud. Dist. 3A, Greenville, NC, 1992-94; judge NC Ct. Appeals, 1994-99; assoc. justice NC Supreme Ct., 1999—. Mem. legis. and law reform com. Conf. Superior Ct. Judges, 1993—94; sec. NC Jud. Conf., 1997—99, co-chair legis. liaison com.; adj. prof. law U. NC, Chapel Hill; adj. faculty NC Ctrl. U. Sch. Law; sr. lecturing fellow Duke U. Law Sch., 2005—; chair Chief Justice's Commn. Future NC Bus. Ct., 2003—05. Editor-in-chief: Jour Internat. Law and Comml. Regulation. Office coord. United Way Ann. Combined Campaign, 1991, 1992; mem. master plan adv. com. N.C. Dept. Correction, 1992; mem. N.C. Coun. Women, 1992. Recipient Order Long Leaf Pine, 1992, Disting. Alumnus award, Western Carolina U., 1995, Svc. award, City of Raleigh Cmty. Svc. Dept., Book award, Sci. Methods for Lawyers; Lloyd C. Balfour fellow, N.C. Inst. Polit. Leadership fellow, 1992, Coun. State Govt. Toll fellow, 2001. Mem.: ABA (editl. bd. Judges' Jour., coalition justice com., commn. state ct. funding, John Marshall award rev. com., nominating com., exec. com., edn. chair appellate judges conf., com. to develop nat. issues forum programs on Am. jury, coalition for justice rep., com. to develop nat. issues forum programs on separation of powers, chair, rep. jud. divsn., adv. commn. World Justice Project), Appellate Judges Ednl. Inst. (chair, program planning com., bd. dirs.), Mortar Bd., Wake County Bar Assn. (bd. dirs., continuing legal edn. presenter 2003—), Assn. NC Women Attys., NC Assn. Black Lawyers, NC Bar Assn. (minorities profession com. 1995—2001, multidisciplinary practice task force 1999—2001, v.p. 2000—01, litig. sect. coun. 2000—03, strategic planning emerging trends com. 2001—, program com. 2004 Brown v. Bd. Edn. 50th anniversary), Carolina Law Alumni Assn. (bd. dirs.), U. NC Law Davis Soc., Rotary, Internat. Hon. Soc., Beta Gamma Sigma, Delta Sigma Phi (scholar 1986), Phi Alpha Delta, Omicron Delta Epsilon, Pi Gamma Mu, Phi Kappa Phi, Alpha Lambda Delta. Office: NC Supreme Ct PO Box 1841 Raleigh NC 27602-2170 Office Phone: 919-831-5712. Business E-Mail: maj@sc.state.nc.us, mmartin@sc.state.nc.us.

MARTIN, MARTHA ANN, secondary school educator; b. Oakland, Calif., Apr. 12, 1948; d. Joseph Francis Madeo Jr. and Mildred Ruth Curley; m. Charles Hamilton Martin II, May 16, 1970; children: Charles H. III, Christopher S., Susan E. BA in Edn., Madison Coll., Harrisonburg, Va., 1969; MA in Secondary Edn., William and Mary Coll., Williamsburgh, Va., 1989. 7th grade tchr. St. Hugh's Cath. Sch., Huntington Station, Va., 1969—70; asst. mgr. Pierce Goods Shop, Newport News, Va., 1972—73; homebound instr. New Kent HS, Va., 1976—. Dir., tchr. Sunshine Nursery Sch., Providence Forge, Va., 1977—78; tchr. New Kent HS, Va., 1978—2004, forensics coach, 1984—2004, cheering coach, 1994—2004. Co-author: (plays) Christmas Presence, 2005, (book) History Making Women of New Kent, 2006, (plays) On the Banks of Schminoe Creek, 2007. Co-founder, prodr. New Kent Stage Hands, 2004—; dist. rep. New Kent Hist. Commn., 2006—; dist. forensics champioin coach; mem. Providence Forge Presbyn. Ch., Providence, 1975—, Sunday sch. tchr., 1976—. Mem.: Va. Edn. Assn., New Kent Edn. Assn., Va. Assn. Speech and Debate. Avocations: travel, swimming, reading.

MARTIN, MARY-ANNE, art gallery owner; b. Hoboken, NJ, Apr. 26, 1943; d. Thomas Philipp and Ruth (Kelley) Martin; m. Henry S. Berman, June 9, 1963 (div. 1976); 1 child, Julia Coyote. Student, Smith Coll., 1961—63; BA, Barnard Coll., 1965. Head dept. painting Sotheby Parke Bernet, NYC, 1971-78; founder Latin Am. dept. Sotheby's, NYC, 1977, sr. v.p., 1978-82; pres. Mary Anne Martin, Fine Art, NYC, 1982—. Mem.: Art Dealers Assn. Am. (sr. v.p.). Avocations: art collecting, scuba diving. Office: 23 E 73rd St New York NY 10021-3522 Business E-Mail: mail@mamfa.com.

MARTIN, MELISSA CAROL, radiological physicist; b. Muskogee, Okla., Feb. 7, 1951; d. Carl Leroy and Helen Shirley (Hicks) Paden; m. Donald Ray Martin, Feb. 14, 1970; 1 child, Christina Gail. BS, Okla. State U., Stillwater, 1971; MS, UCLA, 1975. Cert. radiol. physicist Am. Bd. Radiology, radiation oncology Am. Bd. Med. Physics. Asst. radiation physicist Hosp. of the Good Samaritan, LA, 1975-80; radiol. physicist Meml. Med. Ctr., Long Beach, Calif., 1980-83, St. Joseph Hosp., Orange, Calif., 1983-92, Therapy Physics, Inc., Bellflower, Calif., 1993—. Cons. in field. Editor: (book) Current Regulatory Issues in Medical Physics, 1992. Fund raising campaign divsn. mgr. YMCA, Torrance, Calif., 1988-92; dir. AWANA Youth Club-Guards Group, Manhattan Beach, Calif., 1984—. Named Dir. of Symposium, Am. Coll. Med. Physics, 1992. Fellow Am. Coll. Med. Physics (chancellor western region 1992-95, treas. 2004-05), Am. Assn. Physicists in Medicine (profl. coun. 1990-95, 2006—, treas. 1998-2003, bd. dirs. 1994-2003, co-dir. summer sch. 2007, pres.-elect, 2008), Am. Coll. Radiology (econs. com. 1992-95, govt. rels. com. 1998—, councilor at large 2001-06, commn. on med. physics 2002-); mem. Calif. Med. Physics Soc. (treas. 1991-98), Am. Soc. for Therapeutic Radiology and Oncology, Health Physics Soc. (pres. So. Calif. chpt. 1992-93), Am. Brachytherapy Soc. Baptist. Avocation: christian youth group dir. Home: 507 Susana Ave Redondo Beach CA 90277-3953 Office: Therapy Physics Inc 879 W 190th St Ste 419 Gardena CA 90248 Office Phone: 310-217-4114. Personal E-mail: melissamartin@compuserve.com. Business E-Mail: melissa@therapyphysics.com.

MARTIN, MICHAEL JOHN, journalist, editor; b. Reno, Mar. 9, 1962; m. Alison Marie Tharp. BS in Chemistry, Gonzaga U., Spokane, 1984; MS in Physics, U. Wash., Seattle, 1997, MBA, 1997. Founder, pres. Orion Environ. Inc., Seattle, 1984—94; sr. sci. writer UPI, Washington, 2001—02; chief rsch. corr. Newsfactor, LA, 2002—06. Sr. writer, editor Helen Dwight Reid Ednl. Found., Washington, 2002—07; freelance writer. Bd. dirs. arts and culture City of Fed. Way, 1994—96; chairperson city fin. City of Columbia, Mo., 2002—05; bd. dirs. Hist. Preservation Commn., Columbia, 2004—07, Weyerhauser Ctr., Seattle, 1991—95. With USN, 1984—87. Mem.: Nat. Assn. Sci. Writers, Nat. Press Club. Avocations: travel, exercise.

MARTIN, MICHAEL TOWNSEND, sports association executive, marketing professional, consultant; b. NYC, Nov. 21, 1941; s. Townsend Bradley and Irene (Redmond) M.; m. Jennifer Johnston, Nov. 7, 1964 (div. Jan. 1977); children: Ryan Bradley, Christopher Townsend; m. Jean Kathleen Meyer, Mar. 1, 1980 Grad., The Choate Sch., 1960; student, Rutgers U., 1961-62. Asst. gen. mgr. N.Y. Jets Football Club, NYC, 1968-74; v.p. NAMANCO Prodns., NYC, 1975-76; v.p., gen. mgr. Cosmos Soccer Club, NYC, 1976-77; exec. asst. Warner Communications, NYC, 1978-84; owner, operator Martin Racing Stable, NYC, 1983—; pres. Sports Mark, Inc., NYC, 1990—2003. Bd. dirs. Mote Marine Lab., Sarasota, Fla., Animal Rescue Coalition, Coun. of Visitors, Woods Hole Marine Biol. Lab., Nat. Lighthouse Ctr. and Mus., Lemur Conservation Found., chmn. Ringling Sch. Art and Design; program com. WNET Channel 13; bd. advisors The Pennington Sch., Dir.'s Cir., Scripps Instn. Oceanography Mem. Athletics Congress (life, cert. official 1984—), U.S. Tennis Assn. (life), Internat. Oceanographic Found. (Miami life mem.), Fla. Thoroughbred Breeders Assn., Quogue Field Club, The Union Club. Republican. Episcopalian. Avocation: collecting inuit (eskimo) art. Home: 131 E 69th St Apt 11A New York NY 10021-5158 Office: 575 Madison Ave Ste 1006 New York NY 10022-2511 Office Phone: 212-980-9525. Personal E-mail: mmarti1237@aol.com.

MARTIN, MICHAEL V., academic administrator, economics professor; b. Crosby, Minn., Jan. 29, 1947; s. Ben F. and Dorothy A. Martin; m. Janis R. Roeglin, Aug. 15, 1970; children: Amanda C., Samuel J. BS in Econs., Mankato State Coll., 1969, MA in Econs., 1971; PhD in Applied Econs., U. Minn., 1977. Instr. in econs. U. Wis., Eau Claire, 1972-74; from asst. prof. to prof. Oreg. State U., Corvallis, 1977-92; assoc. dean U. Minn., St. Paul, 1992-95, dean, v.p., 1995-98; v.p. U. Fla., Gainesville, 1998—2004; pres. N.Mex. State Univ., Las Cruces, 2004—. Recipient Diversity Recognition award USDA-NRCS, 1997, Agrl. Achievement award Oreg. Dept. Agr., 1992, Minn. Forest Preserve, 1998, Social Justice award, N.MEx. State U., 2005; named Weekly Power Broker, N.Mex. Bus., 2006. Mem. Am. Econs. Assn., Am. Agrl. Econ. Assn., Internat. Assn. Agrl. Economists, Internat. Agrl. Trade Rsch. Consortium, Econ. Hist. Assn., Sigma Xi. Democrat. Avocations: reading, golf. Mailing: New Mexico State Univ Office of the President PO Box 30001 Las Cruces NM 88003 *

MARTIN, MICHIKO JEANNETTE, oceanographer, meteorologist, educational association administrator; d. Edgar and Masako Martin. BS in Oceanography, US Naval Acad., Md., 1987—91; MA in Ednl. Leadership, Troy State U., Ala., 1994—96; MA in Oceanography Engring., MIT, 1996—98. Oceanographer, meteorologist USN, 1991—2004; edn. dir. NOAA Nat. Marine Sanctuary Program, Silver Spring, Md., 2003—. Lt. comdr. USN, 1987—2004. Decorated Commendation medal USN. Mem.: NSTA, Am. Meteorol. Soc., Oceanography Soc., Nat. Marine Educators Assn., Am. Geophys. Union, Sigma Xi, Phi Kappa Phi. Office: Nat Oceanic & Atmospheric Admin 1305 East-West Hwy Silver Spring MD 20910 Home Phone: 301-713-7254. Business E-Mail: michiko.martin@noaa.gov.

MARTIN, MURRAY D., manufacturing executive; b. Hawkesville, Ontario; s. John and Melissa Martin. Studied computer sci. and mathematics, U. Waterloo. Joined Litton Industries; various positions to v.p., gen. mgr. Monroe Office Systems; pres. Dictaphone Canada subs. of Pitney Bowes, 1987—90; pres. Pitney Bowes copier systems, 1990—98, Pitney Bowes Internat., 1998—2001; group pres. global mailstream solutions Pitney Bowes Inc., Stamford, Conn., 2001—04, exec. v.p., 2003—04, pres., COO, 2004—07, pres., CEO, 2007—. Bd. dir. Brink's Co., 2005—. Bd. dir. United Way Internat., Forum of World Affairs. Named first disting. fellow, Waterloo U. Centre for Applied Cryptographic, 2001. Office: Pitney Bowes Inc 1 Elmcroft Rd Stamford CT 06926-0700 *

MARTIN, NOEL, graphics designer, educator; b. Syracuse, Ohio, Apr. 19, 1922; s. Harry Ross and Lula (Van Meter) M.; m. Coletta Ruchty, Aug. 29, 1942; children— Dana, Reid Cert. in Fine Arts, Art Acad. Cin., Doctorate (hon.), 1994. Designer Cin. Art Mus., 1947-93, asst. to dir., 1947-55; freelance designer for various ednl., cultural and indsl. orgns., 1947—; instr. Art Acad. Cin., 1951-57, artist-in-residence, 1993—. Design cons. Champion Internat., 1959-82, Xomox Corp., 1961—, Federated Dept. Stores, 1962-83, Hebrew Union Coll., 1969—; designer-in-residence U. Cin., 1968-71, adj. prof., 1968-73; mem. adv. bd. Carnegie-Mellon U., R.I. Sch. Design, Cin. Symphony Orch., Am. Inst. Graphic Arts; lectr. Smithsonian Instn., Libr. of Congress, Am. Inst. Graphic Arts, Aspen Design Conf., various additional schs. and orgns. nationally. One man shows include Contemporary Arts Ctr., Cin., 1954, 71, Addison Gallery Am. Art, 1955, R.I. Sch. Design, 1955, Soc. Typographic Arts, Chgo., 1956, White Mus. of Cornell U., 1956, Cooper & Beatty, Toronto, Ont., Can., 1958, Am. Inst. Graphic Arts, 1958, Ind. U., 1958, Ohio State U., 1971; exhibited in group shows at Mus. Modern Art, N.Y.C., Library of Congress, Musee d'Art Moderne, Paris, Grafiska Inst., Stockholm, Carpenter Ctr., Cambridge, Gutenberg Mus., Mainz, U.S. info. exhbns. In Europe, South America and USSR; represented in permanent collections Mus. Modern Art, Stedelijk Mus., Amsterdam, Cin. Art Mus., Boston Mus. Fine Arts, Cin. Hist. Soc., Library of Congress; contbr. to various publs. Served to sgt. U.S. Air Force, 1942-45 Recipient Art Directors medal, Phila., 1957, Sachs award, Cin., 1973, Lifetime Achievement award Cin. Art Dirs., 1989. Home Phone: 513-731-5519; Office Phone: 513-731-1287.

MARTIN, OLIVIA JEAN, social studies educator; b. LA, Nov. 08; d. Henry and Stella Martin. BA in Clin./Physiol. Psychology, U. So. Calif., 1990; MA in Edn. Adminstrn., Azusa Pacific U., 2005. Mgr. Eastman West, Montebello/Buena Park, Calif.; asst. mgr. Hortman Jewelers; peer coll. tutor East LA Coll., Monterey Park, Calif., 1985—86; facilitator U. So. Calif.-Biomed. Rsch. Program, LA, 1987—91; behavioral counselor, nutritional specialist Nutri Sys., West Covina, Calif.; tchr. asst. Franklin Adult H.S., LA; elem. tchr. L.A. Unified Sch. Dist., 1994—2001; asst. dir. curriculum L.A. Archdiocese/San Gabriel Mission H.S., 2001—02, sci. tchr., 2000—01; mid. sch. social studies and sci. tchr. Azusa (Calif.) Unified Sch. Dist., 2002—06, dist. mgmt. trainee, 2004—06. Participant Olive Crest Cruise for Kids, LA, 2004; hon. mem. exec. bd. Azusa PTA Coun., 2004—06; fundraiser Corvettes United Spl. Wish Found., LA, 1999—2005. Recipient Merit award, Gov. of Calif., 1998—2000, Congl. award, Rep. Edward Roybal, L.A., 1986, Best Facilitator AP Biology award, U. So. Calif., 1989. Mem.: ASCD, NEA, Calif. Assn. Bilingual Edn. (pres. Azusa Canyon chpt. 2006—07), Nat. Coun. Social Studies, Assn. Calif. Supts. and Adminstrs., Corvettes Ltd. Club, Pi Lambda Theta. Republican. Roman Catholic. Avocations: racquetball, auto shows, auto racing. Home: PO Box 80892 San Marino CA 91118-9982

MARTIN, PATRICK J., technology company executive; b. 1941; BS in math., Iona Coll.; MS in Elec. Engring., Doctorate in Elec. Engring., George Washington U.; grad. exec. edn. program, Harvard U. With US Dept. Agriculture; exec. Xerox Corp., pres. N.Am. solutions group; chmn., pres., CEO StorageTek, Louisville, Colo., 2000—. Past mem. bd. dirs. US C. of C., US/China Bus. Coun.; bd. trustees George Washington U.; adv. bd. com. George Washington U. Sch. Engring.; adv. com. Ohio State U. Fisher Sch. Bus. Recipient Jonas Bronck award, Bronx Hist. Soc., 2001, Ellis Island Medal Honor, 2003. Office: Storage Tech 1 Storage Tek Dr Louisville CO 80028

MARTIN, PATRICK MICHAEL, physicist, director; s. Anthony E. Lichamer; m. Julie Anne Wenc, May 29, 1989. MS in Applied Physics, U. Ill., Chgo., 1987. Worldwide tech. mgr. Tex. Instruments Inc., Dallas, 1988—99; exec. dir. core tech. devel. Photronics, Inc., Allen, Tex., 1999—. Contbr. articles to profl. jours. Mem.: Bay Area Chrome Users Soc. (pres. 2005—), Internat. Soc. Optical Engring. (assoc.; pres. Bacus tech. group 2005—07). Achievements include patents for semiconductor; photomask technology. Avocations: travel, scuba diving, golf, cooking, art. Office: Photronics Inc 601 Millennium Dr Allen TX 75013 Home Phone: 214-503-0529; Office Phone: 972-889-6231. Office Fax: 972-889-6471. E-mail: pmartin@photronics.com.

MARTIN, PAUL, former Prime Minister of Canada; b. Windsor, Ont., Can., Aug. 28, 1938; s. Paul Joseph and Eleanor (Adams) M.; m. Sheila Ann Cowan, Sept. 11, 1965; children: Paul William, Robert James, David Patrick. BA in Philosophy and History, U. Toronto, Can., 1962, LLB, 1965. Bar: Ont. 1966. Exec. asst. to pres. Power Corp. Can. Ltd., 1966-69, v.p., 1969-71; v.p. spl. projects Consol.-Bathurst Ltd., 1971-73; v.p. planning and devel. Power Corp., Can., 1973-74; pres. Can. S.S. Lines Ltd., Montreal, 1974-80, CEO, 1976-80; pres., CEO CSL Group Inc., 1980-88; M.P. Ho. of Commons, 1988—; min. for fed. office of regional devel. Govt. of Can., Ottawa, 1993-95, min. fin., 1993—2002, prime min., 2003—06; leader Liberal Party Can., 2003—06. Co-chair Nat. Platform Com. of Liberal Party of Can. Author: Making History: The Politics of Achievement; co-author (with Chaviva Hosek): Creating Opportunity: The Liberal Plan for Canada. Former mem. C.D. Howe Inst. Policy Analysis Com., Birt, N.Am. Com., Ctr. Rsch. Action on Race Rels.; former bd. dirs. Can. Coun. Christians and Jews; founding dir. emeritus North-South Inst., Can., Coun. Native Bus.; bd. govs. Concordia U., coun., v.p., past mem. bd. advisors; inaugural chair G-20, 1999. Liberal. Avocations: sports, reading.

MARTIN, PAUL CECIL, physicist, researcher; b. Bklyn., Jan. 31, 1931; s. Harry and Helen (Salzberger) M.; m. Ann Wallace Bradley, Aug. 7, 1957; children: Peter, Stephanie Glennon, Daniel. AB, Harvard U., 1952, PhD, 1954. Mem. faculty Harvard U., Cambridge, Mass., 1957—, prof. physics, 1964-82, J. H. VanVleck prof. pure and applied physics, 1982—, chmn. dept. physics, 1972-75, dean divsn. engring. and applied scis., 1977-98, assoc. dean Faculty Arts and Scis., 1981-98, dean rsch. and info. tech., 1998—2004. Vis. prof. Ecole Normale Superieure, Paris, 1963, 66, U. Paris, Orsay, 1971. Bd. editors: Jour. Math Physics, 1965-68, Annals of Physics, 1968-82, Jour. Statis. Physics, 1975-80, Proc. Nat. Acad. Scis., 2000—. Bd. dirs. Assoc. Univs. for Rsch. in Astronomy, 1979-85, Mass. Tech. Pk. Corp., 1900-, exec. com., 1992-; bd. dirs. Assoc. Univs., Inc., 1981—, exec. com., 1986-90, 92-94, chmn. bd. dirs., 1996-2000. NSF postdoctoral fellow, 1955; Sloan Found. fellow, 1959-62; Guggenheim fellow, 1966, 71 Fellow: AAAS (chair physics sect. 1986), Am. Phys. Soc. (councillor-at-large 1982—84, panel on pub. affairs 1983—86, chmn. nominating com. 1994), Am. Acad. Arts and Scis., NAS. Office: Harvard U Dept Physics Cambridge MA 02138 Business E-Mail: martin@harvard.edu.

MARTIN, PAUL EDWARD, lawyer; b. Atchison, Kans., Feb. 5, 1928; s. Harres C. and Thelma F. (Wilson) M.; m. Betty Lou Crawford, Aug. 28, 1954; children: Cherry G., Paul A., Marylou. BBA, Baylor U., 1955, LLB, 1956; LLM, Harvard U., 1957. Bar: Tex. 1956, Pa. 1958. Assoc. Ballard, Spahr, Andrews & Ingersoll, Phila., 1957-58; ptnr. Fulbright & Jaworski, Houston, 1959-77; shareholder Chamberlain, Hrdlicka, White, Williams & Martin, 1977—; instr. in estate planning U. Houston. Exec. com. Met. Houston March of Dimes, 1980-82; chmn. deacons West Meml. Bapt. Ch., 1979-80; trustee Baylor U., 1970-89, Meml. Hosp. Sys., 1975—, Fgn. Mission Bd., So. Bapt. Conv.; pres. Baylor U. Devel. Coun., 1973-74. Lt. comdr. USN, 1947-53. Fellow Am. Coll. Trust and Estate Coun.; mem. ABA (sect. real property, probate and trust law and sect. taxation), State Bar Tex., Houston Bar Assn., Houston Estate and Fin. Forum (pres. 1965-66), Houston Bus. and Estate Planning Coun., Houston Club, Phi Delta Phi. Republican. Co-author: How to Live and Die with Texas Probate. Home: 126 Lakeside Dr Montgomery TX 77356 Office: Chamberlin Hrdlicka Et Al 1200 Smith St Ste 1400 Houston TX 77002-4401 Office Phone: 713-622-9455. Office Fax: 713-658-2553. Business E-Mail: paul.martin@chamberlainlaw.com.

MARTIN, PAUL ROSS, editor; b. Lancaster, Pa., May 14, 1932; s. Paul Rupp and Amanda (Minnich) M.; m. Julia Ibbotson, June 5, 1954 (div. Apr. 1979); children: Monica Martin Goble, Julia, Paul Jr., Barbara, Drew, Eric. BA, Dartmouth Coll., 1954. Reporter, wire editor Lancaster New Era, Lancaster Newspapers Inc., 1954-60; copyreader, makeup editor Wall St. Jour. divsn. Dow Jones & Co., NYC, 1960-63, copy editor nat. news, 1963-69, editor bus. and fin. column, 1969-72, nat. copydesk chief, 1972-75, page one sr. spl. writer, 1975-90, asst. to mng. editor, 1990-93, asst. mng. editor, 1993—2002. Editor: The Possible Dream, 1978, Retirement Without Fear, 1981, Wall Street Journal Style Book, 1981, 4th edit., 1995, The Wall Street Journal Guide to Business Style and Usage, 2002; co-author, editor: American Dynasties Today, 1983. Bd. dirs. Cmty. Bd. 1, S.I., N.Y., 1976-80. Mem. N.Y. Fin. Writers Assn. (past officer). Avocations: basketball, tennis, travel. Office: Wall St Jour 200 Liberty St New York NY 10281-1003 E-mail: paul.martin-sr@wsj.com.

MARTIN, PETER GERARD, computer technician, consultant, secondary school educator; b. Weymouth, Mass., May 2, 1952; s. John Augustine and Jean Anita (Murphy) M.; m. Elizabeth Anne Collins, Aug. 24, 1974; children: Derek Grant, Erin Jean. BA, Nasson Coll., 1974; MS, U. R.I., 1979; postgrad., Boston Coll., U. So. Maine, 1977-79; MA, Columbia Pacific U., 1991; PhD, U. Heriseau, 2000. Computer programmer Baybank Data Services, Waltham, Mass., 1975-76; mathematician Factory Mut. Engring., Norwood, Mass., 1976-78; tchr. Kennebunk (Maine) High Sch., 1978-79; v.p. strategic planning The Foxboro (Mass.) Co., 1979-84, systems cons., 1984-85, mgr. system product planning, 1986-88, v.p. market strategies and comm., 1996-99, v.p. corp. mktg., 1999—; v.p. mktg. Intec Controls Corp., 1993-94; v.p. Automation Rsch. Corp., 1996. Instr. Dean Jr. Coll., Franklin, Mass. 1980-96; tech. cons. Balance Inc., Wiscassett, Maine, 1985-89. Author: Dynamic Performance Management: A Path to World Class Manufacturing, 1992, Bottom-Line Automation, 2001; contbr. articles to profl. jours. Pres. East Woonsocket Sch. Parent Council, R.I., 1983-85; mem. Parents Involvement Com., Woonsocket, 1985; Cub Scout den leader, Woonsocket, 1985-86; instr. religious edn. Our Lady of Lourdes Ch. Mem. Soc. Mfg. Engrs., Mfrs. Automation Protocol Users Group, Inst. Soc. of Am. Roman Catholic. Avocations: camping, tennis, boating. Office: The Foxboro Co Bristol Park 351-2C Bristol Park Foxboro MA 02035 E-mail: pmartin@foxboro.com.

MARTIN, PETER ROBERT, psychiatrist, pharmacologist; b. Budapest, Hungary, Sept. 6, 1949; came to U.S., 1980; s. Nicholas M. and Eva (Horvat) M.; m. Barbara Bradford, Dec. 23, 1985; 1 child, Alexander Bradford. BSc with honors, McGill U., Montreal, Que., Can., 1971, MD, CM, 1975; MSc, U. Toronto, Ont., Can., 1978. Diplomate Am. Bd. Psychiatry and Neurology, Psychiatry, Addiction Psychiatry. Resident in internal medicine U. Toronto, Can., 1975-76, resident in psychiatry, 1978-80; fellow clin. pharmacology Addiction Rsch. Found., Toronto, 1976-78; chief sect. clin. sci. Nat. Inst. on Alcohol Abuse & Alcoholism, Bethesda, 1983-86; assoc. prof. Vanderbilt U. Sch. Medicine, Nashville, 1986-92, prof., 1992—, dir. divsn. addiction medicine, 1986—, dir. addiction ctr., 1994—; dir. Vanderbilt Inst. for Coffee Studies, 1999—. Vis. scientist Lab. of Clin. Sci., NIMH, Bethesda, Md., 1980-83; investigator John F. Kennedy Ctr. for Rsch. on Human Devel., Nashville, 1993—. Fellow Royal Coll. Physicians (Can.), Am. Psychiat. Assn. (disting.); mem. AAAS, Am. Soc. Clin. Pharmacology and Therapeutics, Am. Acad. Addiction Psychiatry, Rsch. Soc. on Alcoholism, Internat. Soc. Biomed. Rsch. in Alcoholism. Office: Vanderbilt Psychiat Hosp Ste 3068 1601 23rd Ave South Nashville TN 37232-8650 Office Phone: 615-322-3527. E-mail: peter.martin@vanderbilt.edu.

MARTIN, PHILLIP DWIGHT, bank consulting company executive, mayor; b. Nevada, Mo., Jan. 4, 1943; s. E. Dwight and Berniece E. (Leedy) M. BS, U. Mo., 1964, MBA, 1965, cert. math. and bus. edn., 1966. Tchr. Warsaw (Mo.) Pub. Schs., 1966—68; investment analyst Bus. Men's Assurance Co. Am., Kansas City, Mo., 1968—70; exec. v.p. Farmer's Bank Walker, Mo., 1970—71; banking cons. Howard J. Blender Co., Dallas, 1971—84; chmn. Profit Motivators Internat., Inc., Boulder, Colo., 1984—2002; mayor City of Walker, 1986—2000, 2002—; math. tchr. El Dorado Springs, Mo., 2002—. Chair technology com. NRMC. Bd. dirs. Nev. Regional Med. Ctr., 2004—. Mem. Walker R-4 Alumni Assn. (co-founder, life mem. scholarship com., pres. 1994-96). Home: 214 E Marvin Ave Walker MO 64790-9106 E-mail: pdm19@neighborlink.us.

MARTIN, PHILLIP HAMMOND, lawyer; b. Tucson, Jan. 4, 1940; s. William P. and Harriet (Hammond) M.; m. Sandra S. Chandler, June 17, 1961 (div. Mar. 1989); children: Lisa, Craig, Wade, Ryan; m. Erika Zetty, May 9, 1990. BA, U. Minn., 1961, JD, 1964. Bar: Minn. 1964, U.S. Tax Ct. 1967, U.S. Dist. Ct. Minn. 1968, U.S. Ct. Appeals (8th cir.) 1973, U.S. Supreme Ct. 1981, U.S. Claims Ct. 1983, U.S. Ct. Appeals (fed. cir.) 1988, U.S. Ct. Appeals (7th cir.) 1989. Assoc. Dorsey & Whitney, Mpls., 1964-69, ptnr., 1970—. Home: 487 Portland Ave Saint Paul MN 55102-2216 Office: Dorsey & Whitney LLP Ste 1500 50 S 6th St Minneapolis MN 55402-1498 Home Phone: 651-291-1933; Office Phone: 612-340-2845. Business E-Mail: martin.phil@dorsey.com.

MARTIN, R. KEITH, business and information systems educator, consultant; b. Seattle, Sept. 5, 1933; s. Jerome Milton and Winifred (Gifford) M.; m. Carolyn Joanne Carosella, June 15, 1957; children: Jefferson, Sean, Jennifer, Katherine. AB, Whitman Coll., 1955; MBA with high honors, CCNY, 1965; PhD, U. Wash., 1973. Registered, lic. profl. engr.; cert. data processing, cert. systems profl., cert. computer profl. Div. mgr. Campus Merchandising Bur., Inc., NYC, 1955-56; sales rep. IBM, Seattle, 1956, Svc. Bur. Corp. subs. IBM, NYC, 1957-58; specialist mgmt. adv. svcs. Price Waterhouse & Co., NYC, 1959-65, Seattle, 1965-66, mgr., 1966-67; dir. mgmt. systems dept. U. Wash., 1967-71, lectr. dept. acctg. Sch. Bus. Adminstrn., 1971-73; asst. prof. dept. accountancy Baruch Coll., CUNY, 1973-76, assoc. prof., 1977-79; prof. acctg. Fairfield U., 1979-84, prof. acctg. and info. systems, 1984-94, assoc. dean Sch. Bus., 1980-82, dean, 1982-93, acting dean grad. Sch. of Communications, 1988-90, prof. info. systems, 1994-2001, prof. info. systems and ops. mgmt., 2001—05, prof. emeritus, 2005—, dept. chmn., 1999—2002, holder Stephen and Camille Schramm chair in bus., 2000—04. V.p. Eastalco Systems, 1971-72; faculty fin. div. Am. Mgmt. Assn., 1963-64; part-time lectr. Bellevue C.C., 1967-69, Shoreline Community Coll., 1968-72, Seattle U., 1971-72; program dir., summer program at Heslier (Rotterdam) 2000, 2001, Nat. Univ. Galway, 2003. Author: Management Information Systems in Higher Education: Case Studies at Three Universities, 1973, Effective Business Communications, 1976, 79, 91, Systems Development and Computer Concepts, 1977; Co-author: Management Control of Electronic Data Processing, 1965; assoc. editor: Industry Guides for Accountants and Auditors, 2 vols., 1980; mem. editorial rev. bd. Dickenson Pub. Co., 1974-75, Prentice-Hall, Inc., 1977-78, 87-88, 90-91, Reston Pub. Co., 1977-78, Jour. Acctg. Edn., 1981-83; featured roles (Amateur Comedy Club prodns.) Guys and Dolls, Our Town, The Fantastics, The Night of the Iguana, The Rainmaker, My Fair Lady; stage mgr. Some Assembly Required, Arcadia, Murder by the Book, Night Watch; house mgr.(plays) The Real Thing, The Tempest, play com., 2004—07, chmn., 2005-06; Footloose: The Musical, On Golden Pond; author numerous monographs; contbr. numerous articles to profl. jours. Mem. Mendelssohn Choir of Conn., Amateur Comedy Club, Westchester Chordsmen, Litchfield Norwestones; trustee Westchester County Hist. Soc. Recipient cert. of appreciation Am. Mgmt. Assn., 1966, cert. of merit for disting. service to Mgmt. Scis., 1969, for disting. service to info. systems profession, 1973; Merit award Assn. Systems Mgmt., 1971, Achievement award, 1972, Internat. award World Assn. for Case Method Rsch. and Application, 1996, 2002; cert. for service City of Seattle, 1973; named Outstanding Young Man Am., 1970, One of 300 Outstanding Alumni, Whitman Coll., 1979; Kellogg fellow, 1971-72, Price Waterhouse faculty fellow, 1976. Mem.: NSPE, AAUP, Am. Acctg. Assn., Soc. Mgmt. Info. Systems, NY Soc. Profl. Engrs., Soc. Cert. Data Processors, Assn. Computing Machinery, Data Processing Mgmt. Assn., Assn. Systems Mgmt. (sec. 1968—69, v.p. 1969—70, pres. Pacific NW chpt. 1970—71), Inst. Mgmt. Accts. (assoc. dir. NY chpt. 1963—64, Seattle chpt. 1967—70, assoc. dir. NY chpt. 1975—85), Acad. Creative Tchg. (exec. bd. 1998—), World Assn. Case Method Rsch. and Application (adv. bd. 1996—99, exec. bd. dirs. 1999—, vice-chair internat. case stds. setting com. 2001—), Am. Inst. Indsl. Engrs. (dir. Seattle chpt. 1967—70, chmn. regional conf. 1969), Westchester County Hist. Soc. (trustee 2005—), Amateur Comedy Club, Bronxville Field Club, Beta Alpha Psi, Phi Delta Kappa, Mu Gamma Tau, Beta Gamma Sigma, Phi Delta Theta (province pres. 1986—87, chpt. adv. com. 2006—, chpt. adv. bd. 2006—). Avocations: theater, singing. Home: 39 Sheldon Ln Litchfield CT 06759 Personal E-mail: rkmartin6221@msn.com.

MARTIN, RENWICK D., lawyer; b. 1947; AB, Stanford U., 1969; JD, Harvard U., 1972. Bar: NY 1975. With Sidley Austin LLP, NYC, 1972—, specialist asset-backed securities area, 1977—, mem. mgmt. and exec. coms. Mem.: ABA. Office: Sidley Austin LLP 787 Seventh Ave New York NY 10019 Office Phone: 212-839-5319. Office Fax: 212-839-5599. Business E-Mail: rmartin@sidley.com.

MARTIN, RICHARD J., food wholesale executive; Exec. v.p., CFO Rykoff-Sexton, Wilkes-Barre, Pa.; sr. v.p. fin. & adminstrn., CFO Cert. Grocers Calif., 1998-2000; CFO, exec. v.p. fin. & adminstrn. Unified Western Grocers, Inc., Commerce, Calif., 2000—. Office: Unified Western Grocers Inc 5200 Sheila St City Of Commerce CA 90040

MARTIN, RICHARD JAY, medical educator; b. Detroit, May 16, 1946; s. Peter Aaron and Tillie Jean (Munch) M.; m. Helene Iris Horowitz, Dec. 23, 1967; children: Elizabeth Hope, David Evan. BS, U. Mich., 1967, MD, 1971. Diplomate Am. Bd. Internal Medicine and Pulmonary Disease. Intern, Ariz., 1971-72; resident Tulane U., New Orleans, 1974-76; pulmonary fellow, 1976-78; asst. prof. medicine U. Okla., Okla. City, 1978-80, U. Colo., Denver, 1980-85, assoc. prof., 1985-92, prof., 1992—. Dir. Cardiorespiratory Sleep Rsch., Nat. Jewish Med. and Rsch. Ctr., Denver, 1980-89, staff physician, 1980-, head divsn. pulmonary medicine, 1993-2005, vice-chair dept. medicine, 1997-2004, acting chair dept. medicine, 2004-2005, chair dept. medicine, 2006—. Author: Cardiorespiratory Disorders During Sleep, 1984, 2d edit., 1990, (with others) Current Therapy in Internal Medicine, 1984, Clinical Pharmacology and Therapeutics in Nursing, 1985, Interdisciplinary Rehabilitation of Multiple Sclerosis and Neuromuscular Disorders, 1984, Drugs for the Respiratory System, 1985, Current Therapy in Pulmonary Medicine, 1985, Abnormalities of Respiration During Sleep, 1986, Mitchell's Synopis of Pulmonary Medicine, 1987, Pulmonary Grand Rounds, 1990, Asthma and Rhinitis, 1994, The High Risk Patient: Management of the Critically Ill, 1995, Manual of Asthma Management, 1995, 2000, Severe Asthma: Pathogenesis and Clinical Management, 1995, Curret Pulmonology, 1995, Pulmonary and Respiratory Therapy Secrets, 1996, (book chpts.) Lung Biology in Health and Disease, 1995, 3d edit., 2000, Allergy, 1997, Asthma, 1997, Emergency Asthma, 1999, Difficult Asthma, 1999, Asthma and Rhinitis, 1999, Imaging of Diffuse Lung Disease, 2000, Manual of Asthma Management, 2000, Severe Asthma, 2001, Asthma Critical Debates, 2002, Inhaled Steroids in Asthma, 2002, The Merck Manual, 2002, Current Review of Asthma, 2003; editor: Nocturnal Asthma: Mechanisms and Interventions, 1993, Cardiothoracic Interrelationships in Clinical Practice, 1997; author, editor: Nocturnal Asthma: Mechanisms and Treatment, 1993, Combination Therapy for Asthma and Chronic Obstructive Pulmonary Disease, 2000; mem. editl. bd. Chronobiology Internat., 1997—, Am. Jour. Respiratory and Critical Care Medicine, 1994-98, Bronchial Asthma: Index and Review, 1996-97; assoc. editor: Clinical Care for Asthma, 1995-97; contbr. articles to profl. jours. Pres. Congregation Rodef Shalom, Denver, 1984-85; regional v.p. United Synagogues of Am., Denver, 1988-89. Named Disting. Lectr., Royal Coll. Physicians and Surgeons Can., 1998, Cardio-Pulmonary Congress, Argentina, 1998, Assn. Argentina Allergy and Immunology, 2001; recipient Best Paper in Internal Medicine award, Okla. Soc. Interna. Medicine, 1977—78, U. Okla. Gastroenterology sect. 1977, Amb. award, Nat. Jewish Med. and Rsch. Ctr., 2002; grantee Am. Lung Assn., Va., U. Okla. Lung Assn., NIH, Parker B. Francis Found.; Pulmonary fellow, Am. Lung Assn., 1977—79, James F. Hammarsten Outstanding fellow, U. Okla. Health Scis. Ctr., 1978. Mem. ACP, Am. Thoracic Soc., Am. Fedn. for Clin. Rsch., Am. Coll. Chest Physicians (Disting. scholar in respiratory health 2003—, Disting Schoalr award, 2004—), Colo. Trudeau Soc., Western Soc. Clin. Investigation. Avocations: biking, golf, Karate. Office: Nat Jewish Med Rsch Ctr 1400 Jackson St Denver CO 80206-2761 Office Phone: 303-398-1847, 303-398-1095. Business E-Mail: martinr@njc.org.

MARTIN, RICHARD KELLEY, lawyer; b. Tulsa, June 30, 1952; s. Richard Loye and Maxine (Kelley) M.; m. Reba Lawson, June 12, 1993; children from previous marriage: R. Kyle, Andrew J. BA, Westminster Coll., 1974; JD, So. Meth. U., 1977. Bar: Tex. 1977, U.S. Tax Ct. 1979. Ptnr. Akin, Gump, Strauss, Hauer & Feld, LLP, Dallas, 1977-95, Haynes and Boone LLP, Dallas, 1995—. Bd. dirs. Goodwill Industries, Dallas, 1986-2000, v.p., 1986-91; bd. dirs. Greater Dallas Youth Orchs., 1987-90; bd. dirs., v.p., pres. Big Bros. and Sisters Met. Dallas, 1988-91; bd. dirs. Tejas coun. Girl Scouts U.S., 1997-2001, Salvation Army, Dallas, 2003--. Mem. Tex. Bar Assn., Salesmanship Club Dallas. Republican. Methodist. Office: Haynes and Boone LLP 2505 N Plano Rd Ste 4000 Richardson TX 75082-4101 Office Phone: 972-739-8634. Business E-Mail: rick.martin@haynesboone.com.

MARTIN, RICHARD L., retired insurance executive; b. Franklin, NJ, Feb. 2, 1932; s. Richard Lewis and Elizabeth (Roe) M.; m. Susan Mazuy, June 20, 1970; children: David Cory, Scott Mazuy; m. Victoria Lee Morton, May 30, 1998; 1 stepchild, Robert M. Ferguson. BEd, U. Miami, 1958; MA, Columbia U., 1963. Chartered Property Casualty Underwriter. Educator Franklin (N.J.) Sch. Dist., 1958-60; mng. dir. Sparta (N.J.) Sch. Dist., 1960-66; adminstr. Orange (N.J.) Sch. System, 1966-71; chief exec. officer Montague (N.J.) Sch. Dist., 1971-72, Stanhope (N.J.) Sch. System, 1972-73; v.p. Selective Ins. Group, Branchville, N.J., 1973-87; pres., chief exec. officer Med. Malpractice Ins. Assn., NYC, 1987-98; ret., 1998. Chmn. N.J. Anti-Car Theft Com., Trenton, 1980-87; treas. N.J. Ins. News Svc., Newark, 1982-87; chmn. AIA-N.J. State Conf., Trenton, 1983-87. Contbr. several articles to mags. With USMC, 1952-54. Mem. CPCU, Am. Mgmt. Assn., Soc. Ins. Research, Soc. for Corp. Planning, City Midday, Newton Country, Branchville Rotary, Sons of Am. Revolution, Mayflower Soc. Presbyterian. Avocations: golf, hunting. Home: Two Plains Rd Augusta NJ 07822

MARTIN, RICHARD PETER, classics educator, consultant; b. Boston, May 19, 1954; s. Nicholas Richard and Marie Eileen (Daly) M.; children: Catherine, Thomas. AB, Harvard U., 1976, AM, 1978, PhD, 1981. Teaching fellow Harvard U., Cambridge, Mass., 1978-81; from asst. to assoc. prof. Princeton (N.J.) U., 1981-94, prof., 1994—99; Antony and Isabelle Raubitschek Prof. of Classics Stanford U., 2000—. Author: Healing, Sacrifice and Battle, 1983, The Language of Heroes, 1989, Myths of the Ancient Greeks, 2003; editor: Bulfinch, Mythology, 1991. Class of 1936 preceptor Princeton U., 1984-87. Devel. grantee Apple Computer Co., 1989. Fellow Onassis Found.; mem. Am. Philol. Assn., Celtic Studies Assn. of N.Am., Irish Texts Soc. Democrat. Roman Catholic. Office: Stanford Univ Bldg 20 Main Quad Stanford CA 94305-2080 Home Phone: 650-823-4771; Office Phone: 650-723-0479. Business E-Mail: rpmartin@stanford.edu.

MARTIN, RICKY (ENRIQUE MARTIN MORALES IV), vocalist, actor, producer, composer; b. San Juan, Dec. 24, 1971; Mem. Menudo, 1984—89; solo artist, 1991—. Singer: (albums) Ricky Martin (Spanish), 1991, Me Amaras, 1993, A Medio Vivir, 1995, Vuelve, 1998 (Grammy award for Best Latin Pop Album, two Billboard Latin Music awards), Ricky Martin, 1999 (two MTV Video Music awards, Teen Choice award Favorite Male Artist, two Billboard Music awards, Am. Latino Media Arts award for Male Entertainer of Yr., two World Music awards, two Latin MTV Video Music awards, two Latin Billboard awards, People's Choice award, five Grammy nominations), Sound Loaded, 2000 (Latin Grammy Award, three World Music awards, Blockbuster award, Radio Music award, MTV Europe award, two ACE awards, Alma award), La Historia, 2001, The Best of Ricky Martin, 2001, Almas del Silencio, 2003 (Am. Music award, Premio Lo Nuestro award); singer, songwriter, producer (albums) Life, 2005, Ricky Martin MTV Unplugged, 2006; actor: (TV series) General Hospital, 1994—95; (Broadway plays) Les Miserables, 1996. Founded Ricky Martin Found., San Juan, 2000, launched People for Children Initiative, 2004; Goodwill Ambassador UNICEF, 2004—. Recipient Hispanic Heritage award, Hispanic Heritage Found., 2002, Lifetime Achievement award, Univision Premios Lo Nuestro, 2004, Latin Billboard Spirit of Hope award, 2002, Alma Awards Lifetime Achievement award, 2003, Internat. Humanitarian award, Internat. Ctr. Missing & Exploited Children, 2005, State Dept. Internat. Hero, 2005, The Others prize for social svc., Salvation Army, 2006, Person of Yr., Latin Recording Acad., 2006. Mem.: Latin Acad. Recording Arts and Scis., Nat. Acad. Recording Arts and Scis. Office: Ricky Martin Enterprises Santurce Sta PO Box 13534 San Juan PR 00908-3534 also: Ricky Martin Found PO Box 13534 San Juan PR 00908

MARTIN, ROBERT BRUCE, chemistry professor; b. Chgo., Apr. 29, 1929; s. Robert Frank and Helen (Woelffer) M.; m. Frances May Young, June 7, 1953. BS, Northwestern U., 1950; PhD, U. Rochester, 1953. Asst. prof. chemistry Am. U., Beirut, Lebanon, 1953-56; research fellow Calif. Inst. Tech., 1956-57, Harvard U., 1957-59; asst. prof. chemistry U. Va., Charlottesville, 1959-61, assoc. prof., 1961-65, prof., 1965—, chmn. dept., 1968-71. Spl. fellow Oxford U., 1961-62; Program dir. Molecular Biology Sect., NSF, 1965-66 Author: Introduction to Biophysical Chemistry, 1964. Fellow AAAS; mem. Am. Chem. Soc. Home: 620 Sand Hill Rd #314D Palo Alto CA 94304

MARTIN, ROBERT DALE, lawyer; b. Canton, Ohio, Oct. 1, 1937; s. Charles Leroy and Edith Ruby (Turnbull) M.; m. Carla Jean Kibler, Dec. 27, 1966; 1 child, Kendall Dalene. BA, Ohio U., 1960; JD, U. Akron, 1969, M in Taxation, 1989; MBA, Ashland U., NC, 1995; postgrad., Kent State U., 1998. Bar: Ohio 1969, U.S. Dist. Ct. (no. dist.) Ohio 1984, U.S. Ct. Appeals (6th cir.) 1984, Ohio 1969, U.S. Dist. Ct. (no. dist.) 1984, U.S. Ct. Appeals (6th cir.) 1984. Pers. adminstr. Hoover Co., North Canton, Ohio, 1966-67; atty. Allmon and Benson, Carrollton, Ohio, 1967-69; legal staff asst. Republic Steel Corp., Canton, 1969-71, indsl. rels. counsel, 1971-73, supr. labor rels., 1973-78, asst. supt. indsl. rels., 1978-85; mgr. human resources Republic Engineered Steel Corp., Canton, 1985-91; gen. counsel, dir. adminstrn. Office of Summit County Engr., Akron, Ohio, 1991-95; adminstr. bus. and human svcs. Ohio Dept. Transp., New Philadelphia, Ohio, 1995—2006. Adj. prof. bus. law Ashland (Ohio) U., 1988; gen. counsel mgmt. consulting Labor Rels. Assocs., Dayton, Ohio, 1991-93; gen. counsel human resource consulting Human Resources Assocs., Dayton, 1993-95. Sgt. US Army, 1960. Mem. Ohio State Bar Assn. (gen. sect. 1970-97, labor/employment law sect. 1995-99, probate/trust sect. 1996-99, corp. law 1996-99), Nat. Assn. Cert. Govt. Fin. Mgmt. Avocations: walking, fishing, reading, exercise. Home and Office: 850 Mcdaniel Ave Minerva OH 44657-1240 Office Phone: 330-868-6161. Office Fax: 330-868-6161. Personal E-mail: roblaw3@verizon.com.

MARTIN, ROBERT DAVID, judge, educator; b. Iowa City, Oct. 7, 1944; s. Murray and G'Ann (Holmgren) Martin; m. Ruth A. Haberman, Aug. 21, 1966; children: Jacob, Matthew, David. AB, Cornell Coll., Mt. Vernon, Iowa, 1966; JD, U. Chgo., 1969. Bar: Wis. 1969, US Dist. Ct. (we. dist.) Wis. 1969, US Supreme Ct. 1973, US Dist. Ct. (ea. dist.) Wis. 1974. Assoc. Ross & Stevens, S.C., Madison, Wis., 1969-72, ptnr., 1973-78; chief judge U.S. Bankruptcy Ct. We. Dist. Wis., 1978—. Instr. gen. practice course U. Wis. Law Sch., 1974, 76, 77, 80, lectr. debtor/creditor course, 1981-82, 83, 85, 87, 2001, 07, farm credit seminar, 1985, advanced bankruptcy problems, 1989, 91, 96; co-chmn. faculty Am. Law Inst.-ABA Fin. and Bus. Planning for Agr., Stanford U., 1979; faculty mem. Fed. Jud. Ctr. Schs. for New Bankruptcy Judges, 1985-96; chmn. Ann. Continuing Legal Edn. Wis. Debtor Creditor Conf., 1981—. Author: (book) Bankruptcy: Annotated Forms, 1989; co-author: Secured Transactions Handbook for Wisconsin Lawyers and Lenders, Bankruptcy-Text Statutes Rules and Forms, 1992, Ginsberg and Martin on Bankruptcy, 4th edit, 1996. Chmn., bd. dirs., mem. exec. com. Luth. Social Svc. Wis. and Upper Mich.; bd. dirs., mem. exec. com. Turnaround Mgmt. Assn., 1997—2007. Mem.: Wis. State Bar, Nat. Bankruptcy Conf., Nat. Conf. Bankruptcy Judges (bd. govs. 1989—91, sec. 1993—94, v.p. 1994—95, pres. 1995—96), Am. Coll. Bankruptcy. Office: 120 N Henry Rm 340 PO Box 548 Madison WI 53701-0548 Office Phone: 608-264-5188.

MARTIN, ROBERT EDWARD, architect; b. Dodge City, Kans., Mar. 17, 1928; s. Emry and Alice Jane (Boyce) M.; m. Billie Jo Lange, Aug. 16, 1952 (div. Feb. 1970); m. Kathryn M. Arvanitis, June 26, 1971; children: Lynn, Amy, Blaine. Student, McPherson Coll., 1946-48; BArch, U. Cin., 1954. Registered architect, Ohio. Architect Samborn, Steketee, Otis & Evans, Inc., Toledo, 1956-58; prin. Schauder & Martin, Toledo, 1958-72, The Collaborative, Inc., Toledo, 1972-93. Mem. Bd. Examiners Archs., Ohio, 1985-95, pres., 1989-94; bd. examiners Nat. Coun. Archtl. Registration Bds., 1986-95, edn. com., 1992; chmn. site design divsn. Archtl. Registration Exam., 1989, 90, 91; mem. Nat. Coun. Archtl. Registration Bds. Grading, 1987-94; chmn. study of Toledo Fire & Rescue Dept., Corp. for Effective Govt., 1994. Artist numerous paintings. Mem. Toledo Planning Commn., 1971-74, Toledo Zoning Appeals Bd., 1973, Toledo Bd. Bldg. Stds., 1967-84, Citizens Fire Adv. Commn., 1974-80, Citizens Urban Area Adv. Commn., 1962, Toledo Area Coun. Govts., 1977-80, Com. of 100, Toledo, 1987-89, Spectrum Friends Fine Arts, Inc., Toledo; chmn. bd. Toledo Area Govtl. Rsch. Assn., 1981-90; chmn. Corp. for Effective Govt., Study of Toledo Fire and Rescue Dept., 1994; chmn. Cystic Fibrosis, Toledo. 1985. Served to capt. USAF, 1954-56. Recipient numerous watercolor awards. Fellow AIA (pres. Toledo chpt. 1966, Arch. of Yr. 1993), Archs. Soc. Ohio (pres. 1975), Ohio Watercolor Soc. (trustee 1999—), N.W. Ohio Watercolor Soc., Toledo Fedn. Art Socs. (pres. 1989, 90), Spectrum, Tile Club (pres. 2006—), Toledo Artists Club, Sylvania Country Club, Toledo Club, Rotary, Masons, Shriners, Jesters. Mem. Ch. of Brethren. Avocation: painting. Home: 5119 Regency Dr Toledo OH 43615-2946 Office: 1700 N Reynolds Rd Toledo OH 43615-3628 Home Phone: 419-531-9777; Office Phone: 419-531-5753.

MARTIN, ROBERT SIDNEY, librarian, educator; b. Houston, Aug. 13, 1949; s. Sidney A. and Elizabeth Ann Martin. BA, Rice U., 1971; MLS, U. N. Tex., 1979; PhD, U. N.C., 1988; LHD (hon.), Dominican U., 2006. Libr. assoc. U. Tex., Austin, 1972-76, libr. Arlington, 1977-80; debt claims adjustor US Gen. Acctg. Office, Washington, 1977; instr. Sch. Libr. and Info. Sci. U. Wis., Madison, 1984; assoc. dean Librs. La. State U., Baton Rouge, 1985-95; dir., libr. Tex. State Libr. and Archives Commn., Austin, 1995—99; prof., interim dir. Sch. Library and Info. Studies, Texas Women's U., 1999—2001, Lillian Bradshaw endowed chair, 2005—; dir. The Inst. Mus. & Library Services, Washington, 2001—05. Co-author: Contours of Discovery, 1982, Maps of Texas and the Southwest, 1513-1900, 1984 (Kate Broock Bates award 1985); editor: Scholarly Communication in an Electronic Environment: Issues for Research, 1993, Carnegie Denied: Communities Rejecting Carnegie Library Construction Grants, 1993; mem. editl. bd. Am. Archivist, 1994-01, Libr. Quar., 1995-01, Libraries and Culture, 1999-01, Libraries and the Cultural Record, 2005-, Encyclopedia of Library and Information Sciences, 2005-. Exec. bd. Urban Libraries Coun., 2006—; bd. dirs. Inst. Learning Innovation, 2006—; mem. Nat. Coun. Humanities, 2006—, US Nat. Commn. UNESCO, 2004—, exec. com., 2005—. Mem. ALA (councilor 1998-01), Nat. Assn. Govt. Archivists and Records Adminstrs. (mem. exec. bd. 1996—), Tex. Map Soc. (v.p. 1996-00), Book Club Tex. (v.p. 1996-00). Avocations: hiking, photography, music.

MARTIN, ROBERT WILLIAM, retired utilities executive; b. Toronto, Ont., Can., June 7, 1936; s. William George and Evelyn Irene (Phillips) M.; m. Patricia Lorraine Norris, June 27, 1959; children: Stephen Gregory, Robert Scott, Adrienne Christine Teron. BASc., U. Toronto, 1958. Pres., CEO, Consumers Gas, Toronto, 1980—92. Bd. dirs. Enbridge Inc., HSBC Bank Can., Allied Properties Income Trust. Hon. gov. York U.; bd. dir. York U. Found.; past chmn. Toronto Symphony Orch. Recipient Meritorious Svc. award, U. Toronto, 1983, Arbor award, U. Ontario, Queen's Jubilee medal, 125 Yrs. Confederators medal, Govt. of Can., 1992. Mem.: Assn. Profl. Engrs. Ont., Toronto Club, Mad River Golf Club. Home: 118 Farnham Ave Toronto ON Canada M4V 1H4 Office Phone: 416-972-0970.

MARTIN, ROBERT WILLIAM, econometrician; b. Elizabeth, NJ, Nov. 14, 1961; s. Edward Robert Martin and Vivienne Angela Schaul; m. Nancy Leigh Lannan, Sept. 16, 2006. BA in English, U. N.C., 1984, BA in Econs., 1985; MA in Econs., Clemson U., 1989. Rsch. asst. dept. econs. Clemson (S.C.) U., 1988-89, lectr., policy analyst Ctr. Policy Studies, 1989-90; econometrician, exec. mgr. Bd. Econ. Advisors, Columbia, S.C., 1990—. Cons. Clemson U., 1990; adj. instr. Midlands Tech. Coll., Columbia; adj. faculty mem. of the yr. Sch. of Social & Behavioral Sciences, 1997; mem. S.C. budget and control bd. Grad. Leadership Acad., 2003. Contbr. articles to profl. jours. Mem. Am. Econ. Assn., Nat. Assn. Bus. Economists (Carolinas chpt. regional v.p. and sec.), Western Econ. Assn. Internat., Omicron Delta Epsilon, Sigma Tau Delta. Avocations: golf, woodworking. Home: 6503 Christie Rd Columbia SC 29209-2049 Office: Bd Econ Advisors Rembert Dennis Bldg 1000 Assembly St Ste 446 Columbia SC 29201 Office Phone: 803-734-4637. Business E-Mail: robert.martin@ors.sc.gov.

MARTIN, ROBLEE BOETTCHER, retired cement manufacturing executive; b. St. Louis, Apr. 21, 1922; s. Henry W. and Esther (Boettcher) M.; m. Lillian Segraves, July 15, 1940; children: Mary Katherine (dec.), Bruce Daniel, Amy Lee. BS in Chem. Engring., Columbia U., 1943, MS in Chem. Engring., 1947; D.Sc. in Bus. Adminstrn. (hon.), Cleary Coll., 1962. Prodn. supr. Monsanto Chem. Co., St. Louis, 1946-49; dir. research and devel. Miss. Lime Co., Ste. Genevieve, Mo., 1949-59; pres. Dundee Cement Co., Mich., 1959-69; v.p. Fruehauf Corp.; gen. mgr. (Fruehauf Bldgs. div.), Detroit, 1969-72; pres. Presidents Assn. div. Am. Mgmt. Assn., NYC, 1972-74; pres. insulation div. Keene Corp., Princeton, NJ, 1974-76; chmn., chief exec. officer Keystone Cement Co., Bath, Pa., 1976-89, Giant Cement Co., Harleyville, SC, 1985-89; sr. v.p., dir. Giant Group Ltd., Beverly Hills, Calif., 1985-89. Served to lt. (j.g.) USNR, 1944-46, PTO. Mem.: Phi Lambda Upsilon, Tau Beta Pi, Sigma Xi. Baptist. Home: 2590 Elms Plantation Blvd Charleston SC 29406

MARTIN, ROGER BOND, landscape architect; b. Virginia, Minn., Nov. 23, 1936; s. Thomas George and Audrey (Bond) M.; m. Janis Ann Kloss, Aug. 11, 1962; children: Thomas, Stephen, Jonathan. BS with high distinction, U. Minn., 1958; M. Landscape Arch., Harvard U., 1961. Asst. prof. U. Calif.-Berkeley, 1964-66; from assoc. prof. to prof. emeritus U. Minn., Mpls., 1966—99, prof. emeritus, 1999—; owner Roger Martin & Assoc., Mpls., 1966—68, 1999—; prin. InterDesign, Inc., Mpls., 1968-84, Martin & Pitz Assocs., Inc., Mpls., 1984-98. Vis. prof. U. Melbourne, Australia, 1979—80; vis. prof. coll. architecture U. Minn., Mpls., 2000—; sr. rsch. fellow Ctr. for Changing Landscapes, Mpls., 2003—. Prin. works include Minn. Zool. Gardens, 1978 (merit award Am. Soc. Landscape Archs., 1978), Mpls. Pkwy. Restorations, 1972—87 (merit award, 1978, Minn. Classic award Am. Soc. Landscape Archs., 1994), South St. Paul Ctrl. Sq., 1978 (merit award, 1978), Festival Park, Chisholm, Minn., 1986 (merit award, 1986), Miss. Wildlife Refuge Visual Image assessment (merit award, 1989), Nicollet Island Park, Hennepin Avenue Master Plan, 1995 (merit award, 1995), North Shore Scenic Byway Plan, 2005 (Honor award, 2005), Gitchi Gammi Trail Master Plan, 2005 (Honor award, 2006), Red Lake River Access Master Plan, 2007 (Honor award, 2007). Recipient Fredrick Mann award for svc. to edn. U. Minn., 1990, Disting. Educator award Sigma Lambda Alpha, 1990, Bradford Williams medals for outstanding articles in landscape Architecture mag., 1968, 69, Minn. chpt. Lob Pine award for outstanding svc. to Landscape architecture, 1988, Mpls. Com. on Urban Environ. award for design of Whittier Park, 1997; fellow Am. Acad. in Rome, 1962-64. Mem. Am. Soc. Landscape Archs. (pres. Minn. chpt. 1970-72, trustee 1980-84, nat. pres. 1987, chmn.-elect coun. fellows 1991, chmn. 1992-94, past chmn. 1994-96, Pub. Svc. award 1985, Minn. chpt. Classic award 1994, 1st Valued Places award 2005), Nat. Coun. Instrs. Landscape Architecture (pres. 1973-74), Can. Soc. Landscape Archs. (hon.). Home and Office: 2912 45th Ave S Minneapolis MN 55406-1829 Business E-Mail: marti009@umn.edu.

MARTIN, ROGER HARRY, retired college president; b. NYC, June 26, 1943; s. Edwin Diller and Emma (Neuenburg) M.; m. Susan Bradford, Aug. 29, 1970; children: Katherine R., Emily G. BA, Drew U., 1965; BD, Yale U., 1968, STM, 1969; DPhil, Oxford U., Eng., 1974. Program officer Edn. Incentive Program, NYC, 1969-70; devel. officer NYU, 1970-71, 75-76; asst. dir. devel. Rensselaer Polytech Inst., Troy, NY, 1974-75; asst. prof. history, exec. asst. to pres. Middlebury (Vt.) Coll., 1976-80; assoc. dean Harvard Div. Sch., Cambridge, Mass., 1980-86; prof. history, pres. Moravian Coll., Bethlehem, Pa., 1986-97; pres. Randolph-Macon Coll., 1997—2006, ret., 2006. Pres. Academic Collaborations, Inc. Author: Evangelicals United: Ecumenical Stirrings in Pre-Victorian Britain, 1795-1830, 1983. Bd. dirs. Brit. Schs. and Univs. Found., NYC. Mem. Harvard Club (N.Y.C.). Mem. Soc. Of Friends. Avocations: skiing, running. Home: 1321 Crown Ct Mamaroneck NY 10543

MARTIN, ROGER HEMENWAY, artist, educator; b. Sept. 3, 1925; s. Roger Hemenway and Ellie Emelia (Oker) M.; m. Joan Catherine Fertig, June 19, 1954; children: Christopher, Rachel, Mari; m. Ann O'Grady, Sept. 23, 1990. Diploma with honors, Boston Mus. Sch., 1950; DFA (hon.), Montserrat Coll., 1998. Tchr. New Eng. Sch. Art, Boston, 1966-70; founding mem., assoc. prof. Montserrat Coll. Art, Beverly, Mass., 1970—91, prof. ameritus, 1991—; mem. faculty Gordon Coll., Wenham, Mass., 1976-84. One-man shows include Carl Siembab Gallery, Boston, 1969, Eugenics Gallery, Magnolia, Mass., 1969, Manchester (Mass.) Art Assn., 1970, 83, Marion (Mass.) Art Ctr., 1975, Galleria Roseanna, Boston, 1976, Stagecoach Ho. Gallery, Gloucester, Mass., 1977, Montserrat Sch. Visual Art Gallery, Beverly, 1979, Retrospective, 1990, Pingree Sch. Gallery, South Hamilton, Mass., 1980, Orphanos Gallery, Boston, 1987-88; exhibited in group shows at Rockport Art Assn., 1954-75, 80—, De Cordova and Dana Mus., 1965, Inst. Contemporary Art, Boston, 1964, Carl Siembab Gallery, Boston, 1968, 69, Eugenics Gallery, Magnolia, 1969, Phoenix Gallery, 1969, Montserrat Sch. Visual Art, 1970-83, Doll and Richards Gallery, Boston, 1973-75, Sch. St. Gallery, Rockport, 1983, 85, Orphanos Gallery, Boston, 1987-88, Judi Rotenberg Gallery, Boston, 1988-89; commns. include Prose and Poetry, Child Life Mag.; contbr. articles to profl. jours.; illustrator Beacon Press, New Yorker Mag., N.Y. Times, Atlantic Monthly; woodcuts and paintings United Ch. Christ; case designer and carvings Fisk pipe organs Harvard U., Cambridge, Mass., Ho. Hope Presbyn. Ch., St. Paul, Pohick Ch., Lorton, Va., Stanford (Calif.) U., New Bern, N.C.; author: Rockport Remembered, 1997, A Rockport Album, 1998, Rockport Recollected, 2001. Mem. Rockport Fire Dept., 1960-83, capt. 1970-83; mem. Planning Bd. and Appeals Bd., Rockport. With USCG, 1942-46. Democrat. Home: 29 Penryn Way Rockport MA 01966

MARTIN, ROGER JOHN, computer scientist; b. Ft. Atkinson, Iowa, Sept. 11, 1947; s. Raymond Charles and Linda R. (Kuennen) M.; m. Jane Degnan, Nov. 21, 1970; children: John, Kathryn, Susan, Jacquelyn. BS in Computer Sci., Iowa State U., 1969, MS in Computer Sci., 1971. Computer specialist Naval Ship R & D Ctr., Bethesda, Md., 1971-76; supervisory sys. analyst Exec. Office of Pres., Washington, 1976-82; computer scientist, mgr. software engrng. group Inst. Computer Scis. and Tech., Nat. Inst. Stds. and Tech., Washington, 1982-92, chief sys. and software tech. divsn., 1993-95, mgr. software methods, 1995-96; mgr. stds. strategy. Sun Microsys., Palo Alto, Calif., 1996—2002; dir. stds. AOL, LLC, Dulles, Va., 2002—. Program co-chmn. Conf. on Software Maintenance, 1985, gen. mgr., 1987; gen. chmn. Computer Stds. Comf., 1988. Soccer coach Montgomery Country Recreation Dept., Rockville, Md., 1979-83; treas., del. Mill Creek Towne Elem. Sch. PTA, Rockville, 1981-84, pres., 1986-87; Magruder clustr PTA coord., 1984-856; leader Cub Scouts Am., Rockville, 1983-84, asst. troop scoutmaster, 1984-92. Recipient award for tech. excellence Interagy. Com. on Info. Resources Mgmt., 1989, Fed. Computer Week 100 award, 1992, cert. of recognition Nat. Bur. Stds., 1983, bronze medal Dept. Commerce, 1984, silver medal, 1989, Hans Karlsson award IEEE, 1995, Standards Medallion, 1992. Mem. Assn. for Computing Machinery, IEEE Computer Soc. (chmn. working group on test methods for POSIX 1986-93, tech. com. on conformance testing 1989-94, mem. tech. com. on operating sys. project mgmt. com. 1991-93, cert. of recognition 1987, Meritorious Svc. award 1991, Stds. medal 1992). Home: 1102 Round Pebble Ln Reston VA 20194-1002 Office: AOL 44900 Prentice Dr Sterling VA 20166 Office Phone: 703-265-6203. E-mail: roger.martin@corp.aol.com.

MARTIN, RUSSELL NATHAN COLTRANE JEANSON, JR., professional baseball player; b. East York, Ont., Feb. 15, 1983; s. Russell Martin, Sr. Student, Chipola Jr. Coll., Marianna, Fla. Draft pick LA Dodgers, 2002, catcher, 2006—. Named to Nat. League All-Star Team, Maj. League Baseball, 2007. Mailing: LA Dodgers 1000 Elysian Park Ave Los Angeles CA 90012 *

MARTIN, SALLY, singer, voice educator; d. Peter G. Mero and Sarah Charlotte Sabow; m. Fowler W. Martin, June 25, 1978 (div. 1994); children: Sophie C., Trevor E.; m. Carl Stephen O'Briant, July 25, 1998. BA in English and German Lit., Stanford U., Calif., 1974; MA, The Fletcher Sch., Tufts U., Medford, Mass., 1976. Freelance writer & editor, 1990—2000; pres. All Aboard Music, DC, 1998—; writer, editor Kiplinger Wash. Editors, DC, 2000—02. Tchr./coach Sally Martin Studios, DC, 2004—. Singer, recording artist (solo concert) CD Journeys. Mem.: Actors Equity, DC Cabaret Network (v.p. 2001—06). D-Liberal. Avocations: languages, travel, bicycling. Business E-Mail: sallymartin@sallymartinmusic.com.

MARTIN, SARAH MICHAEL, pharmacist, educator; b. Stillwater, Okla., Sept. 8, 1976; d. Michael Dwight and Jan LaVerne Figart; m. Chad Timothy Martin, July 21, 1995; children: Mathew, Alexis, Alexander, Steven, Mikayla. PharmD, Southwestern Okla. State U., Weatherford, 2003. Clin. staff pharmacist St. Francis Hosp., Tulsa, Okla., 2004, pharmacy practice resident, 2004—05; clin. pharmacist internal medicine St. John Med. Ctr., Tulsa, 2005—; prof. pharmacology Rogers State U., Claremore, Okla., 2005—. Asst. prof. pharmacy practice Southwestern Okla. State U., Weatherford, 2005—; asst. prof. pharmacy U. Okla., Tulsa, 2005—; prestige clin. instr. U. Toledo, 2007—. Contbr. articles to profl. jours. Mem.: Am. Soc. Health-System Pharmacists, Okla. Soc. Health-System Pharmacists, Am. Coll. Clin. Pharmacy. Home Phone: 918-396-9039; Office Phone: 918-744-3131 16492.

MARTIN, SHANE PATRICK, education educator, consultant; b. LA, Aug. 7, 1958; s. Robert Curtis and Lucille Catherine (Koch) M. BA in History, Loyola Marymount U., 1980; MDiv, Jesuit Sch. Theology, Berkeley, Calif., 1991, ThM, 1992; PhD, U. So. Calif., 1995. Cert. secondary tchr., Calif. Mem. faculty Bellarmine Coll. Prep. Sch., San Jose, Calif., 1984, 85-88, dir. campus ministry, 1987-88; grad. tchg. asst. Jesuit Sch. Theology, 1990-92; lectr. Loyola Marymount U., LA, 1994-95, assoc. prof. edn., 1995—2004, coord. secondary edn., 2000—02, acting coord. bilingual and multicultural edn. programs, 1999-2000, assoc. dean edn., 2002—04, acting dean edn., 2004—05, dean, 2005—, prof., 2005—. Adj. prof. U. San Francisco, 1996—; cons., sr. assoc. Karadenes & Assocs., L.A., 1998—; sr. rsch. cons. Imoyase Group, Inc., 2001-. Author: Cultural Diversity in Catholic Schools, 1996, Equity, Advocacy and Diversity: New Directions for Catholic Schools, 2004. Pres. Assn. Jesuit Colls. and Univs. Edn. Coun., 2003—; trustee Loyola H.S., LA, 1997—98; bd. dirs. Greendot Pub. Charter Schs., 2000—; bd. dirs., chmn. com. Coun. on Anthropology and Edn., 1998—2004; bd. dirs. Teach for Am., LA, Calif. Charter Schs. Assn. Grantee, Loyola Marymount U., 1996, 1998—99, 2001—04. Mem. Am. Anthrop. Assn., Am. Ednl. Rsch. Assn., Am. Assn. for Colls. Tchr. Edn., Assn. Tchr. Educators, Nat. Assn. for Multicultural Edn., Nat. Cath. Edn. Assn. (McGivney Meml. Fund grantee 1993), Nat. Coun. for Accreditation Tchr. Edn. (bd. examiners 2004—). Avocations: travel, cultural events, music, technology, mentoring. Office: Loyola Marymount U Sch Edn 1 LMU Dr UH Ste 2100 Los Angeles CA 90045-2659 Home Phone: 310-745-3015; Office Phone: 310-338-7301. Business E-Mail: smartin@lmu.edu.

MARTIN, SPENCER L., musician, educator; b. Goshen, Ind., Jan. 10, 1973; s. John A. and Leona M. Martin. MusB, Butler U., 1995; MusM, Wichita State U., 1999; DMA, U. Minn., Mpls., 2003. Asst. prof. viola U. Ala., Tuscaloosa, 2000—02; assoc. prof. music Luther Coll., Decorah, Iowa, 2002—. Recipient 3-month stipend for rsch. in Germany, Evang. Luth. Ch. Germany, 2006. Mem.: Pi Kappa Lambda (pres. 2004—06). Democrat. Lutheran. Avocations: travel, jogging, films. Office: Luther Coll Music Dept 700 College Dr Decorah IA 52101 Home Phone: 563-382-4288; Office Phone: 563-387-2424. Office Fax: 563-387-1076. Business E-Mail: martsp01@luther.edu.

MARTIN, STANLEY ALLEN, lawyer; b. Logansport, Ind., Apr. 9, 1955; s. Richard James and Helen Elizabeth M.; m. Kellie Lea McCabe, Aug. 14, 1988. BS, MIT, 1977; JD, Boston Coll., 1984. Bar: Mass. 1985, U.S. Dist. Ct. Mass. 1985, U.S. Ct. Appeals (1st cir.) 1985, N.H. 1986, U.S. Dist. Ct. N.H. 1987. Prin. Stan Martin, Designer/Builder, Andover, Mass., 1977-84; assoc. Gadsby & Hannah LLP, Boston, 1984-91, ptnr., 1992—2001, Holland & Knight LLP, Boston, 2001—. Lectr. Northeastern U., Boston, 1989—95, MIT, 2000—01. Author: Mechanic's Liens, Performance and Payment Bonds under Massachusetts Law, 1989, 7th rev. edit., 1996; co-author: Architect-Engineer Liability Under Massachusetts Law, 1985, 5th rev. edit., 1990; contbg. author ann. Aspen Construction Law Update, 1995—; contbr. articles to profl. jours. Bd. dirs. Andover Com./A Better Chance-ABC, 1981—84, Associated Gen. Contractors of Mass., 1999—2001, Boston Archtl. Ctr., 2000—04, Edgewood Retirement Cmty., 2001—. Mem. ABA (pub. contract sect., chair region I 1990-96), Am. Arbitration Assn. Constrn. Industry Panel, Mass. Bar Assn. (chair pub. law sect. 1993-94), Internat. Bar Assn., N.H. Bar Assn. Home: 7 Pendant Ct Andover MA 01810-6305 Office: Holland & Knight LLP 10 St James Ave Boston MA 02116 E-mail: stan.martin@hklaw.com.

MARTIN, STEPHEN F., chemist, educator, researcher; BS, U. N.Mex., 1968; PhD, Princeton U., 1972. Alexander von Humboldt stipendiat Inst. fur Organische Chemie U. Munich, 1972-73; NIH postdoctoral fellow MIT, 1973-74; M. June and J. Virgil Waggoner Regents Chair in chemistry U. Tex., Austin. Contbr. articles to profl. jours. Recipient Rsch. Career Devel. award NIH, 1980-85, Arthur C. Cope Scholar award Am. Chem. Soc., 1996, Alexander von Humboldt Sr. Scientist award, 1995-97, Japan Soc. for Promotion of Sci. award, 2001, Wyeth Rsch. award, 2003. Fellow: AAAS. Office: Chem & Biochem Dept Univ Texas 1 University Sta A5300 Austin TX 78712-1095 Office Phone: 512-471-3915. E-mail: sfmartin@mail.utexas.edu.

MARTIN, STEVE, actor, comedian; b. Waco, Tex., Aug. 14, 1945; s. Glenn and Mary Lee Martin; m. Victoria Tennant, Nov. 20, 1986 (div. 1994); m. Anne Stringfield, July 28, 2007 Student, Long Beach State Coll., UCLA. Exec. prodr. TV show Domestic Life, 1984. TV writer for Smothers Bros. (co-winner Emmy award 1969), Sonny and Cher, Pat Paulsen, Ray Stevens, Dick Van Dyke, John Denver, Glen Campbell; nightclub comedian; guest and host appearances NBC's Saturday Night Live, Tonight Show; appeared on Carol Burnett Show; starred in TV spls. Steve Martin: A Wild and Crazy Guy, 1978, Comedy is Not Pretty, 1980, Steve Martin's Best Show Ever, 1981; rec. comedy albums Let's Get Small, 1977 (Grammy award 1977), A Wild and Crazy Guy, 1978 (Grammy award 1978), Comedy is Not Pretty, 1979, The Steve Martin Brothers, 1982; actor, screenwriter (films) The Absent Minded Waiter, 1977 (Academy award nomination best short film 1977), The Jerk, 1979, Pennies From Heaven, 1981, Dead Men Don't Wear Plaid, 1982, The Man With Two Brains, 1983, All of Me, 1984 (Nat. Soc. Film Critics award best actor 1984, New York Film Critics' Circle award best actor 1984), Three Amigos, 1986 (also exec. prodr.), Roxanne, 1987 (also exec. prodr.), (Nat. Soc. Film Critics award best actor 1988, Los Angeles Film Critics' award best actor 1988), L.A. Story, 1991; actor (films) Sergeant Pepper's Lonely Hearts Club Band, 1978, The Muppet Movie, 1979, The Kids Are Alright, 1979, The Lonely Guy, 1984, Little Shop of Horrors, 1986, Planes, Trains and Automobiles, 1987, Dirty Rotten Scoundrels, 1988, Parenthood, 1989, My Blue Heaven, 1990, Father of the Bride, 1991, Grand Canyon, 1991, Housesitter, 1992, Leap of Faith, 1993, Mixed Nuts, 1994, Twist of Fate, 1994, Sgt. Bilko, 1995, The Spanish Prisoner, 1998, Bowfinger, 1999, Joe Gould's Secret, 2000, Novocaine, 2001, Bringing Down the House, 2003, Looney Tunes: Back in Action, 2003, Cheaper by the Dozen, 2003, Jiminy Glick in La La Wood, 2004, Shopgirl, 2005 (also writer, prodr.), Cheaper by the Dozen 2, 2005, The Pink Panther, 2006 (also writer); (theatre) Waiting For Godot, 1988; (television) And the Band Played On, 1993, Rutles 2: Can't Buy Me Lunch, 2002; screenwriter (films) Easy Money, 1983, Bowfinger, 1999; author: Cruel Shoes, 1977, Pure Drivel, 1998, Shopgirl, 2001; playwright Picasso at the Lapin Agile, 1993. Trustee L.A. Mus. Art. Named one of 50 Most Powerful People in Hollywood, Premiere mag., 2006; recipient Georgie award, Am. Guild Variety Artists, 1977, 1978, Grammy award, 1978, Mark Twain prize for Am. Humor, 2005. Office: PO Box 929 Beverly Hills CA 90213

MARTIN, SUSAN KATHERINE, librarian; b. Cambridge, Eng., Nov. 14, 1942; came to U.S., 1950, naturalized, 1961; d. Egon and Jolan (Schonfeld) Orowan; m. David S. Martin, June 30, 1962. BA with honors, Tufts U., 1963; MS, Simmons Coll., 1965; PhD, U. Calif., Berkeley, 1983. Intern libr. Harvard U., Cambridge, Mass., 1963-65, systems libr., 1965-73; head systems office gen. libr. U. Calif., Berkeley, 1973-79; dir. Milton S. Eisenhower Libr. Johns Hopkins U., Balt., 1979-88, exec. dir. Nat. Commn. on Libraries and Info. Sci., 1988-90; univ. libr. Georgetown U., Washington, 1990-2001, tchr., cons., 2001—; pres. SKM Assocs., 2001—; cons. dir. Marstons Mills Pub. Libr., 2003—05, dir., 2005—. Mem. libr. com. Princeton (N.J.) U., 1987—95; mem. vis. com. Harvard U. Libr., 1987—93, 1994—2000; bd. overseers for univ. libr. Tufts U., 1986—2001, Tufts U. Sch. Arts and Scis., 2001—06; cons. various librs. and info. cos., 1975—; mem. libr. adv. com. Hong Kong U. Sci. Tech., 1988—95; mem. acad. libr. adv. group U. Md. Sch. Librs. and Info. Scis., 1994—96; mem. adv. bd. ERIC, 1990—92; mem. Chadwyck-Healey N.Am. Adv. Com. on Lit. Online, 1997—99; vice chair, chair Chesapeake Info. and Rsch. Libr. Alliance, 1996—98; cons. libr. devel. & fundraising, 1998—; spkr. in field; mem. adv. bd. Georgetown U. Libr., 2001—. Author: Library Networks: Libraries in Partnership, 1986—87; editor: Jour. Libr. Automation, 1972—77; co-editor: Portal: Libraries and the Academy, 2000—04; mem. editl. bd. Portal: Libraries and the Academy, 2005—; mem. editl. bd.: Advanced Tech./Librs., 1973—93, Jour. Libr. Adminstrn., 1986—2000, Libr. Hi-Tech., 1989—93, Jour. Acad. Librarianship, 1994—99; contbr. articles to profl. jours. Trustee Phila. Area Libr. Network, 1980—81; bd. dirs. Universal Serials and Book Exch., 1981—82, v.p., 1983, pres., 1984; trustee Capital Consortium, 1992—95; mem. bd. Potomac Internet, 1995—96; pres., trustee Marstons Mills Pub. Libr., 2002—03. Named Samuel Lazerow disting. lectr., Drexel U., 1984, L.I. U., 2002; recipient Simmons Coll. Disting. Alumni award, 1977; Coun. on Libr. Resources fellow, 1973. Mem.: ALA (coun. 1988—92, structure revision TF 1995—97, chair task force on external accrediting body 1999—2002), Assn. Coll. and Rsch. Librs. (pres. 1994—95, vis. program officer for scholarly com. 2002—03), Coalition for Networked Info. (leader working group 1990—92), Assn. Jesuit Colls. and Univ. Librs. (chair 1997—98), Libr. of Congress (optical disk pilot project adv. com. 1985—89), Assn. Rsch. Librs. (info. policy com. 1995—97, stats. com. 1998—2000), Libr. and Info. Tech. Assn. (pres. 1978—79, chair Frederick Kilgour award com. 2006—07), Rsch. Librs. Group (bd. govs. 1981—88, exec. com. 1985—87), Internat. Fedn. Libr. Assns. Commn. on Access to Info. and Freedom of Expression, Cranberry Shores Chorus (publicity coord. 2002—05, webmaster 2004—, pres. 2005—07), Sweet Adelines Internat. (region 1 mgmt. team 2005—), Cosmos Club (libr. com. 1988—2005), Phi Beta Kappa (chair Georgetown U. chpt. 2000—01). Home: 10 Colonial Farm Cir Marstons Mills MA 02648 Office: Marston Mills Pub Library PO Box 9 2160 Main St Marstons Mills MA 02648 Office Phone: 508-428-5175. Business E-Mail: martin@skmassociates.net.

MARTIN, SYLVIA S., special education educator, psychology educator; 1 child, Kurt H. McGuire. BA, Salve Regina, Newport, RI, 1968; EdD, U. Houston, Houston. Cert. spl. edn. tchr. birth-22 yrs. Tex., English, lang. arts tchr. NJ, autism tchr. Tex., severely, profoundly handicapped tchr. Tex., severe emotional disturbance, behavior disorders tchr. Tex. Asst. prof. U. Houston-Clear Lake, 1999—2002; assoc. prof. Monmouth U., West Long Branch, NJ, 2002—. Legal adv. for persons with disabilities, Houston. Grantee, NJ and US Depts. Edn., 2004-2005. Mem.: Coun. for Exceptional Children, Assn. Tchr. Educators (mem. Leadership Acad. 2005—), Delta Kappa Gamma (mem. Internat. Leadership Soc. 2005—). Office: Monmouth U Cedar Ave West Long Branch NJ 07764-1898 Office Phone: 732-263-5761. Business E-Mail: smartin@monmouth.edu.

MARTIN, THEODORE KRINN, former university administrator; b. Blue Mountain, Miss., Jan. 2, 1915; s. Thomas Theodore and Ivy (Manning) M.; m. Lorene Garrison, Sept. 6, 1947; children: Glenn Krinn, Mary Ann, Janet Kay. AB, Georgetown Coll., Ky., 1935; MA, La. State U., 1941; PhD, George Peabody Coll., 1949. Tchr. Consol. Sch., Dumas, Miss., 1935-36; prin. Mississippi Heights Acad., 1936-39; tchr. Murphy High Sch., Mobile, Ala., 1940-41; registrar Miss. State U., 1949-53, registrar, adminstrv. asst. to pres., 1953-56, dean Sch. Edn., 1956-61, exec. asst. to pres., 1961-66, v.p., 1966-85, dir. Summer Sch., 1956-70, ret., 1985. Served as capt. AUS, 1941-46. T.K. Martin Ctr. for Tech. and Disability on Miss. State U. Campus named in his honor. Mem. Masons, Kappa Alpha, Phi Kappa Phi, Omicron Delta Kappa, Kappa Delta Pi, Phi Delta Kappa. Home: 1151 East Dr Starkville MS 39759-9491

MARTIN, THOMAS BROOKS, JR., computer company executive; b. Camden, NJ, Feb. 4, 1955; s. Thomas Brooks Sr. and Helen (Spicer) Martin; m. Mary Louise Kivlin, May 21, 1983; children: Catherine, Thomas Brooks III. AB, ScB, Brown U., 1977; MS, MIT, 1981. Engr. Westinghouse Corp., Detroit, 1977-79; sr. engagement mgr. McKinsey & Co., Chgo., 1981-86; asst. v.p. NEC Techs., Wood Dale, Ill., 1986-88; v.p. NEC Home Elecs., 1988-90; v.p. mktg. Tosiba Am. Info. Systems, Irvine, Calif., 1990-91, Dell Computer Corp., Austin, Tex., 1991—2000; gen. ptnr. Convergence Equity, Austin, 2000—. Chmn., bd. trustees Austin Lyric Opera, 2004—. Mem. Phi Beta Kappa, Tau Beta Pi. Roman Catholic. Avocations: history, music, golf. Office: Convergence Equity 4544 S Lamar Bldg G300 Austin TX 78745

MARTIN, THOMAS JOHN, pediatrician, sports medicine physician; b. Greensburg, Pa., July 4, 1934; s. John William and Mary DeTar Martin; m. Lois Darlene Miller, June 20, 1992; children: Jack T., Susan L. O'Malley, James S., David S. BS, Franklin and Marshall Coll., Lancaster, Pa., 1956; MD, U. Pitts., 1960. Diplomate Am. Bd. Pediats. Gen. practice medicine, Slippery Rock, Pa., 1961—62, 1964—65; pediat. resident Children's Hosp. of Pitts., 1965—67; assoc. in pediats. Geisinger Med. Ctr., Danville, Pa., 1967—75, chmn. pediats., 1975—95; dir. inpatient pediats. Aultman Hosp., Canton, Ohio, 1995—97; team physician, prof. Pa. State U., University Park, 1997—2004, clin. prof. pediats., Milton S. Hershey Med. Ctr., 2005—; assoc. program dir. family practice residency The Williamsport (Pa.) Hosp., 2004—; prof. emeritus dept. orthop. and rehab. Hershey Med. Ctr., 2005—. Adj. clin. assoc. prof. Jefferson Med. Coll., Phila.; team physician football, wrestling Pa. State U., University Park, 1997—2004; courtesy staff Lewistown (Pa.) Hosp., 1999—2004; active staff Centre Cmty. Hosp., State College, Pa., 1997—2004, Children's Hosp. Med. Ctr. of Akron, Ohio, 1995—97; lectr. in field. Contbr. articles to profl. jours. Pres. Riverside Home and Sch., Pa., 1968—69; coach, organizer Danville H.S. Swim Team, 1974; pres. Riverside Home and Sch. Assn., 1968—69; mem. global mission com. Upper Susquehanna Synod Coun., 1999—; fin. com. Pine St. Luth. Ch., Danville, 1994—96, coun. mem., 1993—95, chmn. religious com., 1993—95; bd. dirs. Sunbury Area YMCA, Pa., 1976—84. Capt. US Army, 1962—64. Named Citizen of the Yr., Elks, 1995; named to Geisinger's Pediat. Wall of Fame, 2005; recipient Honors for Exceptional Svc. to Children and Youth, Nat. Child Labor Com., N.Y.C., 1995. Mem.: AMA, Nat. Wrestling Coaches Assn., Pa. Med. Soc. (continuing med. edn. accreditation surveyor 1988—93), Am. Coll. Sports Medicine, Am. Acad. Pediats. (com. on sports medicine and fitness 1998—2004, exec. com. sect. on sports medicine 1997—2003, chpt. chmn. 1980—82), Lycoming County Med. Soc., Am. Bd. Pediats. Lutheran. Avocations: running, skiing, swimming, concerts. Home: 23 E Hayes Crossing Belleville PA 17004 Office: Susquehanna Health System 777 Rural Ave Williamsport PA 17701 Office Phone: 570-321-1000. Business E-Mail: tmartin@susquehannahealth.com.

MARTIN, THOMAS LYLE, JR., academic administrator; b. Memphis, Sept. 26, 1921; s. Thomas Lyle and Malvina (Rucks) M.; m. Helene Hartley, June 12, 1943 (dec. Sept. 1983); children: Michele Marie, Thomas Lyle; m. Mildred L. Moore, June 5, 1984. B.E.E., Rensselaer Poly. Inst., 1942, M.E.E., 1948, D.Eng., 1967; PhD, Stanford U., 1951; DSc (hon.), So. Meth. U., 2004. Prof. elec. engring. U. N.Mex., 1948-53; prof. engring. U. Ariz., 1953-63, dean engring., 1958-63, U. Fla., Gainesville, 1963-66, So. Meth. U., Dallas, 1966-74; pres. Ill. Inst. Tech., Chgo., 1974-87, pres. emeritus. Capt. Signal Corps AUS, 1943-46. Mem. ASEE Hall of Fame. Fellow IEEE; mem. Nat. Acad. Engring. Achievements include being one of the founders of Dallas-Ft. Worth Internat. Airport. Home and Office: PO Box 167845 Irving TX 75016-7845

MARTIN, THOMAS RHODES, communications executive, writer, educator; b. Memphis, July 10, 1953; s. Otis Knox and Joe Anne Coggin Martin; m. Wanda C. Benderman, Dec. 1, 1984; children: Seth Knox, Cyrus Rhodes. BA, Vanderbilt U., Tenn., 1975. Sales communication writer Schering and Plough Corp., Memphis, 1976-78; media devel. specialist, Fed. Express Corp., Memphis, 1978-81, sr. media devel. specialist, 1981-82, mgr. of mgmt. comm., 1982-84, mng. dir. employee comm., 1984-92, mng. dir. pub. rels., 1992-95, v.p. corp. comm., 1995-96; v.p. corp. rels., ITT Industries, White Plains, NY, 1996-99, sr. v.p., dir. corp. rels., 1999—2007; sr. counselor Feldman & Ptnrs., LA, 2007—; co-chair Adv. Coun. Dept. Comm., Coll. of Charleston, SC. Exec.-in-residence Dept. Comm. Coll. Charleston, 2007—. Contbg. editor Memphis mag., 1984—94, contbr. PR Week mag.; contbr. articles to profl. jours. Bd. dirs. Big Bros. and Big Sisters, Memphis, 1983—87, Memphis Oral Sch. for the Deaf, 1985—91, Leadership Memphis, 1986—87, 1992—96, Pub. Rels. Soc. Am. Found, 1999—2001; trustee Inst. for Pub. Rels., 1999—; bd. govs. Josephson Inst. Ethics. Named to PR News Hall of Fame, 2006; recipient Journalism award, Sigma Delta Phi, 1983, Mobius Advt. award, 1998, NY ADDY Award, 2001. Mem.: Pub. Rels. Seminar, Arthur W. Page Soc. (bd. dirs. 2001—, pres. 2004—05), Pub. Rels. Soc. Am. (Silver Anvil award 1995, Bronze Anvil award 1996), Internat. Assn. Bus. Communicators, The Wisemen. Avocations: writing, backpacking, sailing, skiing, running. Office: Coll Charleston Dept Comm 66 George St Charleston SC 29424 also: Feldman & Ptnrs Ste 2000 8491 Sunset Blvd Los Angeles CA 90069 Office Phone: 310-360-0211. E-mail: tom@feldmanandpartners.com, martintr@cofc.edu. *

MARTIN, THOMAS STEPHEN, lawyer; b. NYC, Aug. 31, 1946; s. Stephen Paul and Kathleen Mary (Redmond) M.; m. Lynne Kathryn Mallory, Oct. 2, 1968; children: Laura Kathryn, Mallory Anne. BA maxima cum laude, King's Coll., 1968; JD, U. Chgo., 1972. Bar: DC 1973. Assoc. Steptoe & Johnson, Washington, 1972-75; spl. asst. to asst. atty. gen., civil div. Dept. Justice, Washington, 1975-76, asst. to solicitor gen., 1976-78, dep. asst. atty. gen. civil div., 1978-80, acting asst. atty. gen. civil div., 1981-82; ptnr. Venable, Baetjer, Howard & Civiletti, Washington, 1982-83, Jenner & Block, Washington, 1983-90; ptnr. litigation group Shearman & Sterling LLP, Washington, 1990—, mng. ptnr., dir. Appellate and Supreme Ct. Practice Group; mem. adv. com. fed. rules of civil procedure, 1980-84. Chmn. com. admissions and grievances US Ct. Appeals (DC cir.), 1991—. Comment editor: U. Chgo. Law Rev, 1971-72. Mem. ABA, DC Bar Assn., Am. Law Inst. Office: Shearman & Sterling LLP 801 Pennsylvania Ave NW Ste 900 Washington DC 20004-2604 Office Phone: 202-508-8040. Office Fax: 202-508-8100. Business E-Mail: tmartin@shearman.com.

MARTIN, TONY, humanities educator; b. Port of Spain, Trinidad and Tobago, Feb. 21, 1942; arrived in U.S., 1969, naturalized; s. Claude G. and Vida Beryl M. BSc in econ. with honors, U. Hull, 1968; MA, Mich. State U., 1970, PhD, 1973. Bar: England 1966, Trinidad 1968. Barrister-at-law Hon. Soc. Gray's Inn, London, 1965; asst. prof. history, African-Afro Am. studies U. Mich., Flint, 1971—73; assoc. prof. history and Africana studies Wellesley Coll., 1973—75, assoc. prof. Africana studies, 1975—79, prof. Africana studies, 1979—. Vis. prof. history U. Minn., 1975, The Colo. Coll., Colo. Springs, 1985-86; vis. prof. African-Am. Studies, Brown U., Providence, R.I., 1991, Brandeis U., Waltham, Mass., 1974, 81; hon. rsch. fellow U. of West Indies, Trinidad, 1986-87; lectr. DuBois-Padmore-Nkrumah, Ghana, 1990; cons. founds.; expert witness Congl. Hearings, 1987; guest lectr. numerous univs., U.S., Can., Caribbean, Australia, Africa, Eng.; featured spkr. Conf. of Intellectuals of Africa and its Diaspora, Dakar, Senegal, 2004; mem. editl. bd. Jour. African American History, Jour. Black Studies, Afro-Americans in NY Life and History. Author: Race First, 1976, Literary Garveyism, 1983, The Pan-African Connection, 1983, Amy Ashwood Garvey, 2007, Marcus Garvey, Hero, 1983, Rare Afro-Americana (with Wendy Ball), 1981, The Jewish Onslaught, 1993; editor or compiler: Poetical Works of Marcus Garvey, 1983, African Fundamentalism, 1991, Message to the People, 1986, In Nobody's Backyard:The Grenada Revolution in its Own Words 1985;reviewer articles for profl. jours.; contbr. articles to profl. jours., encys., and other ref. books, intro. to E. Franklin Frazier and Eric Williams, eds, The Economic Future of the Caribbean, 2004; contbg. editor profl. jours.; reviewer of manuscripts for various publishers. Pres. Union of West Indian Students in Gt. Britain and No. Ireland, 1966—68. Recipient Rsch. award Am. Philos. Soc., Phila., 1990, Cmty. award Henry Sylvester Williams award from the Emancipation Support Com., Trinidad; disting. historian award, African American Inst., Northeastern U. Mem. Assn. of Caribbean Historians (exec. bd. mem. 1985-87), African Heritage Studies Assn., Assn. for the Study of Classical African Civilizations (John Henrik Clarke Living Legacy award), Organ. Am. Historians, Nat. Coun. Black Studies (v.p. New Eng. region, 1984-86), Caribbean Cultural Ctr., NY (bd. dir. 1988-90). Office: Wellesley Coll Africana Studies Dept Wellesley MA 02481 Office Phone: 781-283-2564. Personal E-mail: amartin@wellesley.edu, info@tonymartin.net.tt.

MARTIN, TRISA, education and human development educator; d. Heber and Edna Jensen; m. Keith Martin, Sept. 4, 1970; children: David, Jonathan, Michelle, Steven, Deborah, Joseph. BS in Elem. Edn., Brigham Young U., 1970; MEd, U. Utah, 1973. Elem. tchr. Davis Sch. Dist., Farmington, Utah, 1970—73, substitute tchr. k-12, 1989—98; adj. prof. edn. and human devel. Salt Lake C.C., Salt Lake City, 1998—. Contbr. articles to mags. Edn. leader Women's Orgn., Bountiful (Utah) 30th Ward, 2000—03. Mem.: League of Utah Writers (pres. Bountiful chpt. 1995—96). Home Phone: 801-292-8771.

MARTIN, VICKI JOAN, biology professor; BS, U. N.C., Charlotte, 1970—74; MS, Wake Forest U., NC, 1974—76, PhD, 1977—80. Postdoctoral fellow U. Alta., Edmonton, Canada, 1980—81; asst. prof. U. Louisville, Ky., 1981—83; asst. to assoc. prof. U. Notre Dame, Ind., 1983—99; prof. biology Appalachian State U., Boone, NC, 1999—, chair, dept. biology, 1999—2004. Dir., optical lab. U. Notre Dame, Notre Dame, 1983—99, dir. grad. studies, dept. biology, 1990—92; cons. Earth and Sky NPR, 1999—. Contbr. chapters to books, articles to profl. jours. and pubs. Recipient Career Advancement award, NSF, 1987—90, Frank O'Malley Undergraduate Tchg. award, U. Notre Dame, 1995—96, 100 Scholar's Rsch. award, Appalachian State U., 2004. Mem.: Nat. Coun. on Undergraduate Rsch. (elected councilor 2005—). Achievements include research in demonstration of visual pigments in primitive eyes of invertebrates. Office: Appalachian State Univ 572 Rivers St Boone NC 28608 Home Phone: 828-262-6923; Office Phone: 828-262-6923.

MARTIN, WILFRED WESLEY FINNY, psychologist, property owner and manager; b. Rock Lake, ND, Dec. 3, 1917; s. William Isaac and Anna Liisa (Hendrickson-Juntunen) M.; m. Stella Helland, Sept. 25, 1943; children: Sydney Wayne, William Allan. BA, Jamestown Coll., 1940; army specialized tng. program, Hamilton Coll., 1944; MS, EdD, U. So. Calif., 1956. Highsch. prin., coach pub. sch., Nekoma, ND, 1940—42; contact rep., psychologist VA, LA, 1946—49, psychologist, chief rehab., 1972—77; guidance dir. Moorhead (Minn.) Pub. Schs., 1951—53; instr. Concordia Coll., Moorhead, 1952—53; from intern to resident Fargo VA Hosp., ND, 1953—58; psychologist VA, Fargo, 1953—58; assoc. Sci. Rsch. Assoc./IBM, Boulder, Colo., 1958—65, regional dir. LA, 1966—72; owner, mgr. Martin Investments, Huntington Beach, Calif., 1977—. Adjutant U. Miss., Oxford, 1942; trustee Wilfred W. and Stella Martin Trust, Huntington Beach, 1991. Author: Veterans Administration Work Simplification, 1948, 57. Charter mem. Rep. Presdl. Task Force, 1980; adv. sr. ptnrs. bd. dirs. U. Calif. Med. Sch., Irvine, 1990; donor Dr. and Mrs. W.W. Martin Endowment, Jamestown Coll., N.D., 1985; mem. Assocs. of James Ford Bell Libr., U. Minn., Pres.'s Cir. Finlandia U. With U.S. Army, 1942-45. Mem. Am. Psychol. Assn., Cardinal & Gold U. So. Calif., Jamestown Coll. Heritage Circle (charter, Pres.'s Cir.), Finlandia U. Suomi Coll. Second Century Soc., Elks. Republican. Lutheran. Avocations: reading, Finnish heritage, swimming, sports, card playing. Home: PO Box 5445 Huntington Beach CA 92615-5445 *The dominant force in my life is described by the Finnish word SISU, which means perseverence, determination, competitiveness, and tenacity toward goal-oriented achievements. Due to SISU, faith, and hard work I enjoy an active successful life.*

MARTIN, WILLIAM C., social studies educator, writer; b. San Antonio, Dec. 31, 1937; s. Lowell Curtis and Joe Bailey (Brite) M.; m. Patricia Dale Summerlin, Dec. 31, 1957; children: Rex Martin, Jeff Martin, Elisabeth Dale Martin Thomas. BA, Abilene Christian U., 1958, MA, 1960; BD, Harvard Divinity Sch., 1963; PhD, Harvard U., 1969. Instr. history Dana Hall Sch., Wellesley, Mass., 1965-68; instr. sociology Rice U., Houston, 1968-69, asst. prof. sociology, 1969-73, assoc. prof. sociology, 1973-79, prof. sociology, 1979—, Chavanne prof. religion and pub. policy, 1996—, emeritus, 2005—, master Sid W. Richardson Coll., 1976-81, chair dept. sociology, 1983—86, 1989—94, 2003—04. Cons., spkr. in field. Author: These Were God's People, 1966, Christians in Conflict, 1972, A Prophet With Honor: Billy Graham Story, 1991 (Christianity Today's Critic's Choice award 1992), My Prostate and Me: Dealing With Prostate Cancer, 1994, With God on our Side: The Rise of the Religious Right in America, 1996; contbg. editor Tex. Monthly (Nat. Headliner award 1982); contbr. articles to profl. jours. and pop mags.; radio and TV appearances. Dir. House of the Carpenter, Inc., inner-city youth program, Boston, 1963-66, pres. and bd. dirs. non-profit housing corp.; bd. dirs. Fellowship Racial and Econ. Equality, 1970-71; mem. exec. com. Houston Coun. Human Rels. Sr. scholar James A. Baker III Inst. Pub. Policy, 1996-2005; Chavenne Sr. fellow for religion and pub. policy; grantee Am. Coun. Learned Socs. and Am. Philos. Soc., 1974; recipient Nicholas Salgo Outstanding Tchr. award Rice U., 1971, 93, Brown Coll. award for Tchg. in the Humanities Rice U., 1974, 76, George R. Brown Award for Superior Tchg., alumni Rice U., 1974, 76-77, 84, for Excellence in Tchg., 1975, 82, Life Honor award, 1985. Mem. Am. Sociol. Assn., Soc. Scientific Study Religion, Religious Rsch. Assn., Tex. Inst. Letters (J. Frank Dobie/Paisano fellowship 1980). Democrat. Avocation: bicycling. Home: 2929 Buffalo Speedway 312 Houston TX 77098 Office: Rice U Baker Inst MS40 6100 Main St Houston TX 77005-1892 Home Phone: 713-599-0369; Office Phone: 713-348-3481. Business E-Mail: wcm@rice.edu.

MARTIN, WILLIAM COLLIER, hospital administrator; b. Atlanta, Aug. 16, 1926; s. William Henry and Lillian (Collier) M.; m. Alice Elizabeth Nickle, Jan. 12, 1952 (dec.); children: Mary Anne, Patricia Jean, William Collier, Nancy Lee; m. Carol J. Sullivan, July 25, 1998. BS, U. Ga., 1950; diploma, Charlotte Meml. Hosp., 1952; postgrad., U. Okla., 1969. Operating room technician Athens Gen. Hosp., Ga., 1949-50; hosp. adminstrn. intern/resident Charlotte Meml. Hosp., NC, 1950-52; hosp. adminstr. Rockmart-Aragon Hosp., Rockmart, Ga., 1952-54; asst. hosp. adminstr. St. Agnes Hosp., Raleigh, NC, 1954-56; hosp. adminstr. Florence-Darlington Tb. Sanitorium, Florence, SC, 1956-58; commd. 1st lt., MSC US Army, 1959; advanced through grades to lt. col.; adj. US Army Hosp. Ft. Campbell, Ky., 1959; comdg. officer med. co. US Army Hosp., 1959-61; comdg. officer US Army Med. Svc. Detachment Ft. Gulick, Canal Zone, Panama, 1961-64; exec. officer 5th Evacuation Hosp. Ft. Bragg, NC, 1964; comdg. officer, 1964-65; adj. personnel officer 55th Med. Group Ft. Bragg, NC, 1965-66, Qui Nhon, Vietnam, 1966-67; comdg. officer 47th Gen. Hosp., Fitzsimons Gen. Hosp. Denver, 1967-68; exec. officer Evans Health Care Facility Ft. Buckner, Okinawa, Japan, 1968-69; dir. security plans and ops. U.S. Army Med. Ctr., Camp Kue, Okinawa, Japan, 1969-71; med. ops. officer VII Corps Moehringen, Germany, 1971-73; chief tng., exercise and readiness US Army Med. Command Heidelberg, Germany, 1973-74; dir. security plans and tng. Fitzsimons Army Med. Ctr., 1974-77; ret., 1977—. Guest lectr. healthcare adminstr. US Army Med. Command in Europe, 1973-74; exec. dir. Thoms Rehab. Hosp., Asheville, NC, 1977-78; pres./chair Escambia County Pub. Health Trust, 1978-86; founder Hospice of Northwest Fla. and Exec. Dir., 1979-86. Mem. Pres.'s Com. on Employment of the Handicapped, 1978; sec. United Meth. Bd. Pastoral Care and Counseling, 1988-90; mem., v.p., bd. ministries Pensacola Dist. United Meth. Ch., Inc., 1988-98; dir. lay speaking, bd. laity, coun. on ministries Pensacola Dist. United Meth. Ch., Inc., 1988-98; dir. lay speaking, bd. laity Ala.-West Fla. Conf. United Meth. Ch., 1988-97; mem. Health and Human Svcs. task force citizens goals for Pensacoloa, 1981-86; vice chmn. adminstrv. bd. Pine Forest United Meth. Ch., Pensacola, 1979-86; mem. fin. com., 1979-86; dir. lay speaking Pensacola Dist. United Meth. Ch., 1985-88; bd. dirs. Hispanic Ministries, Inc., 1986-93, Meth. Homes for the Aging, Inc., 1990—2006. Served with USN, 1944-46. Decorated Legion of Merit, Bronze Star, Meritorious Svc. medal (3); Vietnam Royal Cross of Gallantry with bronze palm; cert. lay speaker United Meth. Ch. Fellow Am. Acad. Med. Adminstrs.; mem. Am. soc. Tng. and Devel. (dir. 1977-78), Ret. Officers Assn., Assn. US Army (dir. Denver-Centennial chpt. 1974-77, Greater Gulf Coast chpt. 1979-86), US Power Squadrons, Ret. Officers Assn. (bd. dirs. Bob Sikes chpt. 1996-2000, bd. dirs. Escarosa chpt. 1985-99, pres. ESCAROSA chpt. 1989-90), VFW, Masons, Phi Delta Theta. Republican.

MARTIN, WILLIAM EDWIN, lawyer; b. Bowling Green, Ky., Oct. 16, 1943; s. John Edwin and Bess Carolyn (Matherly) M.; children: Anne Whitson, William Whitson; m. Jean Clinton Nelson, Aug. 1, 1981. BA, Vanderbilt U., 1965, JD, 1968. Bar: Tenn. 1968. Ptnr. Waller Lansden Dortch & Davis, Nashville, 1968-75; sr. ptnr. Harwell Martin & Stegall, Nashville, 1975-93; dep. asst. sec. for internat. affairs U.S. Dept. Commerce-NOAA, Washington, 1993-98; chmn. Will Martin Co., 1998—; sr. v.p. Pvt. Bus. Inc., Brentwood, Tenn., 1999; vice chmn. Tecniflex, Inc., Nashville, 2000—01; chmn. Imagic Corp., Nashville, 2000—01. Sr. fellow WWF, 1999—; chmn. Marine Stewardship Coun., London, 2005—; bd. dirs. Board Mem. Inc., Brentwood. Contbr. articles to profl. jours. and law revs. Dir. polar programs Wilderness Soc., Washington, 1990—92. Democrat. Episcopalian. Avocations: mountain climbing, photography, running, tennis, biking.

MARTIN, WILLIAM FRANCIS, JR., lawyer; b. Lowell, Mass., 1961; s. William F. and Patricia A. Martin; m. Martha Doherty, 1988; children: William F. III, Daniel J., Jacqueline E. BA in English, Coll. of Holy Cross, Worcester, Mass., 1983; JD, Boston Coll., 1986. Bar: Mass. 1986, N.H. 1991. Law clk. to Hon. Joseph R. Nolan Mass. Supreme Jud. Ct., Boston, 1986-87; assoc. Hale and Dorr, Boston and Manchester, 1987-93; ptnr. Eno, Boulay, Martin Donahue, LLP (and predecessor firm), Lowell, 1994—. Bd. dirs. Lowell Parks and Conservation Trust, Lowell, 1991—; mem. Lowell Conservation Commn., 1993-94, chmn., 1994-99. Articles editor Boston Coll. Law Review, 1985-86. Mem. Lowell City Coun., 2000-2005; mayor City of Lowell, 2006—; bd. dirs. D'Youville Sr. Care, 1997—. Mem. Omicron Delta Epsilon, Order of the Coif. Home: 173 Clark Rd Lowell MA 01852 Office: Eno Boulay Martin & Donahue LLP 21 George St Lowell MA 01852 Home Phone: 978-441-2203; Office Phone: 978-452-8902. Business E-Mail: b.martin@ebmdattorneys.com.

MARTIN, WILLIAM RAYMOND, retired financial manager; b. Phila., Oct. 16, 1939; s. Clyde Davis and Mary Anna (Coates) M.; m. Michaela Roberta Smink, Sept. 8, 1962 (div. 1969, dec. 2002); 1 child, James; m. Margaret Scouten, Oct. 16, 1970 (div. 1983); children: Mary Frances, Susanna; m. Joan Friedman Kennedy, Jan. 29, 1988 (div. 1999). BSME, Lehigh U., 1960; MBA, U. Pa., 1973. Mem. engring. staff Pa. R.R., 1960-65; asst. gen. mgr. Excelsior Truck Leasing, Phila., 1965-71; sr. policy analyst Assn. Am. R.R.s, Washington, 1973-76, mgr. engring. econ., 1976-78; mgr. fin. analysis So. Ry., Washington, 1978-83; dir. fin. planning Norfolk (Va.) So. Corp., 1984-92, asst. v.p. fin., 1992-95. Contbr. articles to profl. jours. Bd. dirs. Williams Sch., Norfolk, 1988—96, pres., 1992—96; bd. dirs. Va. Stage Co., Norfolk, 1995—2001, Feldman Chamber Music Soc., 2001—05, Norfolk Chamber Consort, 1998—2004, treas., 2001—04. Mem. ASME, Soc. Automotive Engrs., Mid Atlantic Roadracing Club. Home: 118 Woody's Ln Weems VA 22576

MARTIN, WILLIAM ROYALL, JR., retired professional society administrator; b. Raleigh, NC, Sept. 3, 1926; s. William Royall and Edith Ruth (Crocker) M.; m. Betty Anne Rader, June 14, 1952; children: Sallie Rader Martin Busby, Amy Kemp Martin Lewis. AB, U. N.C., 1948, MBA, 1964; BS, N.C. State U., 1952. Chemist Stamford (Conn.) rsch. labs. Am. Cyanamid Co., 1952—54; chemist Dan River Mills, Danville, Va., 1954—56, Union Carbide Corp., South Charleston, W.Va., 1956—59; rsch. assoc. Sch. Textiles N.C. State U., 1959—63; tech. dir. Am. Assn. Textile Chemists and Colorists, Research Triangle Park, NC, 1963—73, exec. dir., 1974—96. Adj. asst. prof. Coll. Textiles, N.C. State U., 1966-88, adj. assoc. prof., 1989-97; del. Internat. Orgn. Standardization, Pan Am. Standards Commn. With USNR, 1944—46. Fellow Am. Inst. Chemists, Soc. Dyers and Colourists, Textile Inst.; mem. Am. Chem. Soc., Coun. Engring. and Sci. Soc. Execs. (past pres. 1992-93), Fiber Soc., Am. Assn. Textile Chemists and Colorists, Masons, Rotary, Phi Kappa Phi, Phi Gamma Delta. Methodist. Home and Office: 224 Briarcliff Ln Cary NC 27511-3901 Office Phone: 919-467-9946. Personal E-mail: wrbrm@bellsouth.net.

MARTIN, WILLIAM RUSSELL, nuclear engineering educator; b. Flint, Mich., June 2, 1945; s. Carl Marcus and Audrey Winifred (Rosene) M.; m. Patricia Ann Williams, Aug. 13, 1967; children: Amy Leigh, Jonathan William. BSE in Engring. Physics, U. Mich., 1967; MS in Physics, U. Wis., 1968; MSE in Nuclear Engring., U. Mich., 1975, PhD in Nuclear Engring., 1976. Prin. physicist Combustion Engring., Inc., Windsor, Conn., 1976-77; asst. prof. nuclear engring. U. Mich., Ann Arbor, 1977-81, assoc. prof. nuclear engring., 1981-88, prof. nuclear engring., 1988—, dir. lab. for sci. computation, 1986—2001, chmn. nuclear engring., 1990-94, assoc. dean for acad. affairs Coll. Engring., 1994-99, dir. Ctr. for Advanced Computing, 2002—04; acting dir. Mich. Grid Ctr., 2002—04, chmn. nuclear engring., 2004—. Cons. Lawrence Livermore Nat. Lab., Livermore, Calif., 1982—, Los Alamos (N.Mex.) Nat. Lab., 1980-89, 2001—, IBM, Inc., Kingston, N.Y., 1984, Rockwell Internat., Pitts., 1985. Author: Transport Theory, 1979; author tech. and conf. papers. Recipient Glenn Murphy award Am. Soc. for Engring. Edn., 1993; Disting. scholar U. Mich. Coll. Engring., 1967; vis. fellow Royal Soc., London, 1989. Fellow Am. Nuclear Soc.; mem. Am. Phys. Soc., Soc. for Indsl. and Applied Math., IEEE. Avocations: running, reading, skiing, sailing. Home: 420 Huntington Dr Ann Arbor MI 48104 Office: U Mich Dept Nuclear Engring Ann Arbor MI 48109 Home Phone: 734-665-3776; Office Phone: 734-764-5534. Business E-Mail: wrm@umich.edu.

MARTINA, CARLO JACK, lawyer; b. Wyandotte, Mich., Jan. 1, 1954; s. Carlo and Matilda M.; m. Marie A. Pulte; children: Raphael, Ariel. BS with high distinction, U. Mich., 1976; JD, Wayne State U., 1979. Bar: Mich. 1979, U.S. Dist. Ct. (ea. dist.) Mich. 1980. Assoc. Provisor, Eisenberg et al, Southfield, Mich., 1979-81, Auslander, Babcock & Weiss, Southfield, Mich., 1981-83; atty. pvt. practice, Southfield, Mich., 1983—. Mem. adv. bd. Legal Alternatives for Women, Southfield, 1985-87; co-founder Mich. br. Justice for Children, 1995-97; co-founder, co-publisher, co-owner MetroParent Mag., Southfield, 1987-95;; mem. task force Oakland County Family Ct., 2001-03; lectr. in field. Legal expert (video) Latchkey Kids: Home Alone & Safe, 1994; author: Effective Discovery in Domestic Violence Litigation, 2002; contbr. chpts. to books, articles pub. to profl. jour. Mem. adv. bd. Gov.'s Internat. Yr. of Family Coun., Lansing, Mich., 1994-95, Roundtable of Christians, Muslims & Jews, Detroit, 1989-91, Anti-Defamation League, Southfield, 1988-90, Coalition Against Domestic Violence; scoutmaster Cub Scout Pack 1016, Birmingham, Mich., 1993-97. James P. Angel scholar U. Mich., 1977-79. Mem. Mich. Trial Lawyers Assn., Mich. Bar Assn. (bd. dirs., family law coun. 2001—, chmn. child support, alimony and friend of ct. com. 2002—, exec. bd. mem. state bar family law coun. 2003--, lectr.), Oakland County Bar Assn. (co-chair family support com., friend of ct. subcom. 2000-03), Wayne County Bar Assn. (family law divsn., liaison to Mich. Bar Assn., family law coun. 2001—, pres. 2004-05). Avocations: reading, fishing, furniture refinishing and home remodeling, model building. Office: 1158 S Main St Plymouth MI 48170-2214 Business E-Mail: MartinaLawOffice@aol.com.

MARTIN-BOWEN, LINDSEY, freelance writer; b. Kansas City, Kans., Aug. 4, 1959; d. Lawrence Richard and V. Marie Pickett; m. Frederick E.

Nicholson (div.); 1 child, Aaron Frederick; m. Edwin L. Martin (div.); 1 child, Ki Elise; m. Michael L. Bowen (div.). BA in English Lit., U. Mo., Kansas City, 1972, MA in English and Creative Writing, 1988, postgrad., 1991-94; JD, U. Mo. Kansas City Sch. Law, Kansas City, 2000. Bar: Mo. 2001. Tech. editor Office Hearings and Appeals, U.S. Dept. Interior, Washington, 1976-77; reporter, photographer Louisville Times, 1982-83; reporter, features editor Sun Newspapers, Overland Park, Kans., 1983-84; assoc. editor Modern Jeweler, Overland Park and NYC, 1984-85; writer Coll. Blvd. News, Overland Park, 1985-89, KC View, Kansas City, Mo., 1988-89; editor Number One, Kansas City, Mo., 1986-88, cons., 1988-89; copywriter Sta KXEO/KWWR Radio, Mexico, Mo., 1989; editorial asst. New Letters, 1985—; features writer, columnist The Squire, Prairie Village, Kans., 1990-95. Instr. lit., fiction writing, intro. to journalism, reporting, English, cultural studies, tech. writing, acad. writing and lit. U. Mo., Kansas City, 1986-88, 97-, Johnson County CC, 1988-95; fiction writer, 2002—; instr. world lit., writing Rockhurst U., 2002-03; tchr. English and fiction Longview CC, 1988-95, 97-98, 2004-05; instr. writing and mass comm. Webster U., 1990; instr. world lit., Am. lit., women in lit., creative writing Penn Valley CC, 1993-97, faculty sponsor The Penn; owner, writer Paladin Freelance Writing Svc., Kansas City, 1988—; prodn. editor Nat. Paralegal Reporter, 1992-95, editor 1994-97, columnist; staff writer, columnist NPR, 1992-05; writing contest judge New Letters, 1987-; judge poetry contest BkMk Press, U. Mo., Kansas City, 1998—; writing assessment coord. U. Mo., Kans. City, 2005-. Author: (novel) The Dark Horse Waits in Boulder, 1985, Deep City, 2005, Harvest, 2002, Denvie USA, 2003, Deep City, 2005, (poetry book) Second Touch, 1990, Standing on the Edge of the World, 2006, (fiction) Cicada Grove and Other Stories, 1992; author numerous poems; contbr. articles to profl. jours.; lead actress prodns. Coach House Players, 1969-70; extra HBO film Truman, 1995; staff mem., contbr. UMKC Law Rev., 1997-99. Campaigner McGovern for Pres. Campaign, Kansas City, 1971-72. Regents scholar, 1967; GAF fellow, 1986. Mem. U. Mo.-Kansas City Alumni Assn. (media com. 1983-84), Phi Kappa Phi. Roman Catholic. Avocations: acrylic and oil painting, downhill skiing, music, Greek cooking, paralegal work. Office: U Mo Kansas City English Dept Cockefair Hall Rm 111 5100 Rockhill Rd Kansas City MO 64110-2481 Home: 1129 SE 7th St Lees Summit MO 64063-6442

MARTINDALE, CARLA JOY, retired librarian; b. Ladysmith, Wis., Sept. 9, 1947; d. Howard Walter and Audrey Elizabeth (Stanton) Martindale. BA, Mt. Senario Coll., 1970; MLIS, U. South Fla., 1990. Libr. Blackhawk Schs., South Wayne, Ind., 1975-79, Osceola County Libr., Kissimee, Fla., 1989-90, Fla. Tech. Coll., Orlando, 1991-92, Orlando Coll. South, 1993-98; ret., 1998; libr. U. of Ctrl. Fla., 2003—. Vis. prof. distance learning libr. St. Leo (Fla.) U., 1999—2002; chair libr. 21st curriculum Phillips Coll., Orlando, 1995, acad. com., 1993—98, accreditation steering com., 1996. Named libr. in her honor, Orlando Coll. South, 1995. Avocations: reading, pets, stock investing. Home: 450 Narrows Dr Greers Ferry AR 72067 Personal E-mail: carlajoy52@yahoo.com.

MARTINEAU, ROBERT JOHN, retired law educator; b. Oconto, Wis., May 18, 1934; s. Francis Joseph and Gertrude (Schauer) Martineau; m. Constance Ann Zimmerman, Dec. 21, 1957; children: Robert John, Renee, Anne, Jeanne. BS, Coll. Holy Cross, 1956; JD, U. Chgo., 1959. Bar: Md. 1960, U.S. Supreme Ct. 1964, Iowa 1969, Wis. 1974. Law clk. to chief judge Md. Ct. Appeals, 1959-60; pvt. practice Md., 1960-68; asst. atty. gen. Md., 1964-65; assoc. prof. U. Iowa, 1968-71; prof., 1971-72; cir. exec. U.S. Ct. Appeals (8th cir.), Mo., 1972-74; exec. officer Wis. Supreme Ct., 1974-78; prof. U. Dayton, Ohio, 1978-80; prof. law U. Cin., 1980-88, disting. rsch. prof., 1988-93, emeritus, 1994—, assoc. dean, 1980—83, acting dean, 1985—86. Cons. Inst. Jud. Adminstrn., 1970—72, Fed. Jud. Ctr., 1978, Nat. Ctr. State Cts., 1978—79, 1987, Inst. Jud. Adminstrn., 1987—88, UN Devel. Program, Bhutan, 1999; spl. prof. U. Birmingham, England, 1987. Author: Wisconsin Appellate Practice, 1978, Judicial Reform in Wisconsin, in Court Reform in Seven States, 1980, Modern Appellate Practice-Federal and State Civil Appeals, 1983, Fundamentals of Modern Appellate Advocacy, 1985, Cases and Materials on Appellate Practice and Procedure, 1987; author: (with others) 2d edit., 2005; author: Appellate Justice in England and the United States: A Comparative Analysis, 1990, Drafting Legislation and Rules in Plain English, 1991; author: (with M. Salerno) Legal, Legislative, and Rule Drafting in Plain English, 2005. Reporter Wis. Supreme Ct. Com. Discipline Attys., 1975—77, Wis. Jud. Coun. Com. Appellate Practice and Procedure, 1976—78, Com. Contempt and Extraordinary Remedies, 1979—80; sec. Md. Constl. Conv. Commn., 1965—67, Md. Constl. Conv., 1967—68, Wis. Supreme Ct. Com. Study State Bar, 1975—77; mem. Iowa Mcpl. Laws Study Com., 1970—71, Wis. Legis. Coun. Com. Ct. Reorganization, 1977, Ohio Supreme Ct. Adv. Com. Rules, 1988—91; mem., reporter ABA Appellate Judges Conf. Com. Appellate Skills Tng., 1984—85, Com. Appellate Skills Tng., 1984—85; co-chair Com. Appellate Practice, 1986—88. Mem.: Am. Jud. Soc. (bd. dirs. 1966—68), Md. Bar Assn. (reporter com. jud. selection 1962—64, v.p. 1967), Assn. Am. Law Schs. (ho. reps. 1982—87). Democrat. Roman Catholic. Home Phone: 941-488-0455; Office Phone: 941-488-0455, Personal E-mail: r.j.martineau@gmail.com.

MARTINEN, JOHN A., travel company executive; b. Sault Ste Marie, Mich., June 26, 1938; s. John Albert and Ina Helia (Jarvi) M. BS with highest honors, Mich. State U., 1960; JD, NYU, 1963. Asst. purser Grace Line, NYC, 1963—65, chief purser, 1965—69; cons. Empresa Turistica Internat., Galapagos Cruises, Quito, Ecuador, 1969—70; regional mgr. Globus & Cosmos (Group Voyagers Inc.), NYC, 1970—73, v.p., 1974—76, exec. v.p., 1977—78, pres., CEO, 1979—92, Littleton, Colo., 1993—98, chmn., 1998; pres., CEO Vista Travel Ventures, Inc., Denver, 1999—2001; pres. Trafalgar Tours, Long Island City, NY, 2002; prin. Safe Passage Internat., Lakewood, Colo., 2003—. Bd. dirs. 366 Broadway Homeowners Assn., NYC, 1983—92, sec., 1987—92; bd. dirs. Edbrooke Homeowners Assn., Denver, 1992—2002, sec., 1994—97, pres., 1997—2002. Root-Tilden Scholar, N.Y.U. Law Sch., 1960—63. Mem. Am. Soc. Travel Agts. (chmn. tour operating program 1995-99), U.S. Tour Operators Assn. (bd. dirs. 1993-99, treas. 1996-97, sec. 1998-99, chmn. travel automation com., 1990-1998), Acad. Travel and Tourism (bd. advisors 1987-92, NY, 1992-01, Denver), Lotos Club NY, Wings Club (N.Y.), Columbine Country Club, Denver Athletic Club. Democrat. Home: 915 W End Ave Apt 7 A New York NY 10025 Office: Safe Passage Internat 3609 S Wadsworth Blvd Ste 565 Lakewood CO 80235 Office Phone: 800-777-7665. E-mail: JohnMartinen@TravelStrategies.net.

MARTINETTI, RONALD ANTHONY, lawyer; b. NYC, Aug. 13, 1945; s. Alfred Nathan and Frances Ann (Battipaglia) M.; m. Ky Le Du, June, 2002. Student, Columbia U., NYC, 1966—68, U. Chgo., 1981-82; JD, U. So. Calif., LA, 1982. Bar: Calif. 1982; U.S. Dist. Ct. (cen. and no. dists.) Calif. 1982, U.S. Dist. Ct. Ariz., 1992; U.S. Ct. Appeals (9th cir.) 1982. Ptnr. Kazanjian & Martinetti, Glendale, Calif., 1986—. Co-founder Am. Legends Website, 1995, Am. Legends Pub., 1996. Author: Nine Easy Ways to Strengthen Your Bad Faith Case in Discovery, 1991; co-author: (with M. Slattery) Rights of Owners of Lost, Stolen or Destroyed Instruments Under UCC Section 3-804: Can They Be Holders in Due Course?, 1993, James Dean Story, 1995; contbr. articles to profl. jours. and popular mags. Mem. Calif. Bar Assn. Office: 520 E Wilson Ave Glendale CA 91206-4374 Office Phone: 818-241-1011. Office Fax: 818-241-2193. Personal E-mail: amlegends@aol.com.

MARTINETTO, JOSEPH R., investment company executive; BA, Claremont McKenna Coll.; MBA, Univ. Calif., Berkeley. Fin. mgmt. positions through sr. v.p. asset & liability mgmt. First Interstate Bank, 1984—96; sr. asst. treas. Transamerica Corp., 1996—97; sr. v.p. Transamerica Fin. Corp., 1996—97; sr. v.p., treas. Charles Schwab Corp., San Francisco, 1997—2001, sr. v.p. retail fin., 2001—07, exec. v.p., CFO, 2007—. Office: Charles Schwab Corp 101 Montgomery St San Francisco CA 94104 *

MARTINEZ, ADRIANA, photographer; Student, U. Nev., Las Vegas; BA, Brooks Inst. Photography. Photography instr. C.C. So. Nev.; wedding photographer So. Nev. News Bur.; chair Nev. State Dem. Party, Las Vegas, 2003—06. Mem.: PTA. Mailing: 1499 Sunair Cir Las Vegas NV 89110 *

MARTINEZ, ALEX J., state supreme court justice; b. Denver, Apr. 1, 1951; m. Kathy Carter; children: Julia, Maggie. Diploma, Phillips Exeter Acad., NH, 1969; student, Reed Coll., 1969-72; BA, U. Colo., 1973, JD, 1976. Bar: Colo. 1976. Dep. state pub. defender, Pueblo and Denver, 1976-83; county ct. judge Pueblo, 1983-88; dist. ct. judge, 1988-97; justice Colo. Supreme Ct., Denver, 1997—. Supreme Ct. liaison Colo. Criminal Rules Com., Colo. Criminal Jury Instns.; chmn. Pub. Access Com., Jud. Edn. Com.; bd. dirs. Servicios de la Raza. Chmn. Pueblo adv. bd. Packard Found., 1993-96; chmn. site-based governing com. Pueblo Sch. Arts and Scis., 1994-95; mem. site-based governing coun. Roncalli Mid. Sch., 1993-94; bd. dirs. Colo. U. Law Alumni. Mem. Colo. Bar Assn. (regional v.p. 1995-96), Colo. Hispanic Bar Assn., Pueblo Bar Assn. (mem. exec. coun. 1994-96), Pueblo Hispanic Bar Assn. Office: Colo Supreme Ct 2 E 14th Ave Denver CO 80203-2115 *

MARTINEZ, ANTONIO, choir director, art director; b. Odessa, Tex., Dec. 15, 1972; s. Esmeralda Romero. Student, U. of Houston, 1996—2001. Chorister Houston Grand Opera, 1997—; dir. music Epworth-Parker United Meth. Ch., Houston, 1999—2000; dir. arts and worship St. Martin's Luth. Ch., Sugar Land, Tex., 2001—. Composer choral music. Sun. sch. tchr. St. Martin's Luth. Ch., Sugar Land, Tex., 2004—06. Mem.: Tex. Choral Dirs. Assn., Am. Choral Dirs. Assn. (Semi-Finalist, Student Conducting Awards 2001). Conservative. Lutheran. Avocation: computer building. Office: St Martin's Lutheran Church 1123 Burney Rd Sugar Land TX 77478 Office Phone: 281-980-0695. Office Fax: 281-980-0895. Personal E-mail: choirmaster@phmoscape.net.

MARTINEZ, ARTHUR C., bank executive, retired retail executive; b. NYC, Sept. 25, 1939; s. Arthur F. and Agnes (Caulfield) M.; m. Elizabeth Rusch, July 30, 1966; children: Lauren, Gregory. BSME, Polytech. U., 1960; MBA, Harvard U., 1965; LLD (hon.), U. Notre Dame, 1997. Dir. planning Internat. Paper Co., NYC, 1967-69; asst. to pres. Talley Industries, Mesa, Ariz., 1969-70; dir. fin. RCA Corp., NYC, 1970-73, v.p., 1973-80; sr. v.p., CFO Saks Fifth Ave. Inc., NYC, 1980-84, exec. v.p., 1984-87, vice chmn., 1990-92; sr. v.p. & group chief exec. Batus Inc., Louisville, 1987-90; chmn., CEO Sears Merchandise Group, Chgo., 1992-95, Sears, Roebuck and Co., 1995—2000, chmn., CEO emeritus, 2000—; interim chmn., CEO Internat. Flavors & Fragrances Inc., NYC, 2006; mem. supervisory bd. ABN AMRO Holdings N.V., 2002—, chmn., 2006—. Bd. dirs. PepsiCo, Inc., 1999-, Internat. Flavors & Fragrances, 2000-, IAC/InterActiveCorp., 2005-, Martha Stewart Living Omimedia, Inc., 2001-04; dep. chmn. Fed. Res. Bank, Chgo.; former chmn. Nat. Minority Supplier Devel. Coun., Inc. Bd. dirs. Defenders of Wildlife, 1992—, Nat. Urban League; chmn. bd. trustees Polytech. U., 1990—; trustee Art Inst., Orch. Assn. Chgo. Symphony Orch.; bd. dirs. Northestern Meml. Hosp., Chgo. 1st lt. U.S. Army, 1961-63. Named CEO of Yr., Fin. World Mag., 1996; recipient T.C. and Elizabeth Clarke medallion Sch. of Bus., Coll. William and Mary, 1997, Olin Sch. of Bus. Excellence in Bus. award, Washington U., St. Louis, 1997. Mem. Nat. Retail Fedn. (chmn. bd. dirs.). Avocations: tennis, golf, gardening. Office: ABN AMRO Holdings NV Gustav Mahlerlaan 10 1082 PP Amsterdam Netherlands *

MARTINEZ, BELINDA, health insurance company executive; MBA, U. So. Calif.; MPH, Loma Linda U. With Delta Ins.Co., 1988—, dir. acct. svcs. Delta Dental; v.p. profl. svcs. PMI Dental Health Plan Delta Ins.Co., v.p. underwriting and fin., 1999—2001, sr. v.p., COO, 2001—; COO Delta Ins.Co., 2003—. Named one of Top 10 Latinos in Healthcare, LatinoLeaders mag., 2004. Office: Delta Dental Calif 100 1st St San Francisco CA 94105

MARTINEZ, BENJAMIN RAY, security officer, retired military non-commissioned officer; b. Bakersfield, Calif., Apr. 13, 1955; s. Raymond Dominguez and Reba Lori Martinez; m. Carmencita Bugtong Adriatico, Dec. 6, 1986. Tech. cert., CC of Air Force, Gunther AFB, Ala., 1986, US Army Ordnance, Camp Roberts, Calf., 1999; tech. instr. cert., U. Calif., Long Beach, 2004. Security policeman USAF, San Antonio, 1973—86; wheel and track vehicle repairer Calif. Army N.G., Gardena, Calif., 1994—2002. Mentor North HS Army JROTC, Torrance, Calif.; mem. Easter Seals, USO; life mem. Rep. Nat. Party, San Bernardino, Calif., 1986—2004; mem. Rep. Presdl. Task Force. Staff sgt. USAF, 1973—86. Decorated Jts. Svcs. Commendation medal Supreme Hdqs. NATO, US Army 94th Engrs. Divsn. Coin; named Honor recipient, Eisenhower Commn., Rep. Nat. Party, 2006, Nat. Rep. Senatorial Com. Commn.; recipient letter of commendation and coin, US Dep. Sec. of Def. Hon. Rudy De Leon, 2000. Mem.: AARP, VFW, World Fedn. of UN, World Heritage Ctr., Paralyzed Vets. of Am., Nat. Space Soc., Planetary Soc., Nat. Inventors Hall of Fame, Inventors Workshop Internat. (assoc.), Air Force Assn. (life), Air Force Sgts. Assn. (life), US Army 9th/10th Cavalry (assoc.; sustaining mem. 1998—2004), Disabled Am. Vets., Nat. Geog. Soc., The Cousteau Soc., The Heritage Found., UN Assn. of the USA, Am. Legion. Republican. Achievements include invention and patent for object retrieving device; contributor to the US Forces Coalition during Operation Iraqi Freedom. Avocations: world travel, ancient military histories, archaeology, paleontology-geology, arts and humanities. Home: 1250 Kendall Dr D-305 San Bernardino CA 92407-5832 Personal E-mail: rangerthree@hotmail.com.

MARTINEZ, BOB, former federal official, governor; b. Tampa, Fla., Dec. 25, 1934; s. Serafin and Ida (Carreno) Martinez. BS, U. Tampa, 1957; MA in Labor and Industrial Rels., U. Ill., 1964. Tchr. Hillsborough County, 1957-62, 63-66; exec. dir. Hillsborough County Tchrs. Assn., 1966-75; pres. Cafe Sevilla Spanish Restaurant, 1975-83; mayor City of Tampa, 1979-86; gov. State of Fla., 1987-91; dir. Office Nat. Drug Control Policy, Washington, 1991—93; mng. dir. govt. cons. Carlton Fields, PA; sr. policy adv. Holland & Knight LLP, Tampa, 2007—. Lead gov. on drug trafficking and substance abuse, chmn. so. states energy bd. Nat. Govs. Assn., 1989; dir. Hillsborough Edn. Found.; hon. dir. Fla. Coun. on Econ. Edn. Pres. Fla. League of Cities, 1985—86; dir. Harmony Inst., Greater Tampa C. of C.; dir. emeritus The Collins Ctr.; bd. advisors Moffitt Cancer Ctr. & Rsch. Inst.; dir., chmn. devel. com. Tampa Bay History Ctr.; trustee emeritus U. Tampa. Mem.: Rotary Club of Tampa, Tampa's Lowry Park Zoological Soc. (dir., exec. com. mem.), Fla. Coun. of 100 (hon.). Office: Holland & Knight LLP 100 N Tampa St, Ste 4100 Tampa FL 33602-3644 Office Phone: 813-227-6308. Office Fax: 813-229-0134. E-mail: bob.martinez@hklaw.com.

MARTINEZ, CARMEN LORENA, library director; Dir. brs. LA Pub. Libr.; dir. libr. svcs. Oakland Pub. Libr., Calif., 2000—. Mem. com. on recruitment of pub. librs. Pub. Libr. Assn., 2000, mem. bylaws and orgn. com.; mem. Spl. Presdl. Task Force on Status of Librs. Bd. mem. Calif. Cultural and Hist. Endowment. Office: Oakland Pub Libr 125 14th St Oakland CA 94612 Office Phone: 510-238-3281. E-mail: cmartinez@oaklandnet.com.

MARTINEZ, CARMEN MARIA, ambassador; b. Pensacola, Fla., July 1950; married; 1 child. MA in Medieval Hist., MS in Nat. Security and Strategic Resources. Various positions US Fgn. Svc., Sao Paulo, Brazil, 1981; chief of the consular sect. Quito, Ecuador, 1989—93; prin. officer US consulate, Barranquilla, Colombia, 1993—94; dep. chief of mission US Dept. State, Maputo, Mozambique, 1997—99; prin. officer US consulate, San Paolo, Brazil, 1999—2000; charge d'affaires to Burma US Dept. State, Rangoon, 2002—05, US amb. to Zambia Lusaka, 2005—. Office: US Dept State 2310 Lusaka Pl Washington DC 20521

MARTINEZ, DAVID ROGER, chemist, researcher; b. Toledo, Jan. 22, 1954; s. Daniel and Herlinda (Ramirez) M. BS, U. Toledo, Ohio, 1978. Rsch. chemist S.W. Rsch. Inst., Houston, 1978-80; lab. tech. Shilstone Engrng. Testing Lab., Houston, 1981-82; quality control technician Pepsi-Cola Bottling Group, Houston, 1982-83, Chardonol divsn. Freeman Chem. Co., Houston, 1985-86; rsch. asst. U. Tex. Health Sci. Ctr., Houston, 1987—91, 1996—2004, Baylor Coll. Medicine, Houston, 1991-93; rsch. technician Howard Hughes Med. Inst., Houston, 1993—96, 1997—98; rsch. assoc. II, U. Tex. Med. Br., Galveston, Tex., 2005—07; assoc. scientist II, Cogenics, Divsn. Clin. Data, Houston, 2007—. Active Harris County Tejano Dems. Mem. Am. Chem. Soc. Democrat. Roman Catholic. Avocations: radio-electronics, computers, science fiction. Office: Cogenics divsn Clin Data Ste 103 9441 W Sam Houston Pky S Houston TX 77099 Personal E-mail: genescreen@aol.com. Business E-Mail: dmartinez@cogenics.com.

MARTINEZ, DENNIS J., art educator; b. Trinidad, Colo., May 23, 1964; BA, Princeton U., NJ, 1986; MA, U. N.Mex, Albuquerque, 1990; MFA, U. Colo., Boulder, 1995. Assoc. prof. art Dixie State Coll. Utah, St. George, 1995—. Mem. visual arts com. Utah Arts Coun., Salt Lake City, 2004—. Fellow, U. Colo., Boulder, 1992—95. Achievements include design of art and healing installation. Home: 15 W 500 N Veyo UT 84782 Office: Dixie State Coll Utah 225 S 700 E Saint George UT 84770 Home Phone: 435-574-2128; Office Phone: 435-652-7794. E-mail: martinez@dixie.edu.

MARTINEZ, FERNANDO V., civil engineer; b. Blewett, Tex., July 2, 1927; s. Catarino G. and Refugia V. M.; m. Dora Garza, Sept. 27, 1953; children: Fernando G., Karen Martinez Solano, Edward A. BS in Civil Engrng, Tex A&M U., 1951. Registered profl. engr., Tex. Field engr. Farnsworth & Chambers Co, Houston, Tex., 1953-54; design engr. Link Belt Co., Houston, 1954, Anderson Clayton & Co., Houston, 1954-59; project engr. Olin Mathieson Chem. Corp., Pasadena, Tex., 1959-80; project mgr. Mobil Oil Corp., Pasadena, 1980—. 1st lt. U.S. Army, 1951-53, Korea. Republican. Roman Catholic. Home: 710 Skylark Rd Pasadena TX 77502-4560 Office: Mobil Oil Corp 2001 Jackson Rd Pasadena TX 77501

MARTINEZ, GUSTAVE See SOLOMONS, GUS JR.

MARTINEZ, HERIBERTO, human resources professional; m. Migdalia Centeno. BA in Mgmt., Inter Am. U., PR, 1983. Cert. accountant tech., Dept. Labor, PR, 1979. Labor law cons. Dept. Labor, Arecibo, 1979—83; human resources mgr. Casera Foods Inc., Barceloneta, PR, 1983—93, Cardinal Health, Manati, PR, 1996—2006. Cons. in field. Mem. Century Soc. St. Labre Indian Sch.; dir. Coop. Ahorro y Credito de Manati, 1996—2003. Nominee Manuel A. Perez award, Dept. of Labor, 1983; named Dir. of Yr., Coop. Ahorro y. Credito, Manati, PR, 1998; recipient Recognition award for work performance, Adminstrn. Accion Juvenil, 1976, Recognition award, Ideas Program, 1981, Chmn. award, Cardinal Health, 1997. Mem.: Soc. Human Resource Mgmt. (assoc.), Century Soc., Mustang Club Am., PR Mustang Club (former sec. 2002—04). Democrat. Roman Catholic. Avocations: guitar, electrical bass, writing, cars. Home: 222 Montecarlo St Monaco 3 Manati PR 00674 Personal E-mail: martiger@atenas.com.

MARTINEZ, HERMINIA S., economist, banker; b. Havana, Cuba; came to U.S., 1960, naturalized, 1972; d. Carlos and Amelia (Santana) Martinez Sanchez; m. Mario Aguilar, 1982; children: Mario Aguilar, Carlos Aguilar. BA in Econs. cum laude, Am. U., 1965; MS in Fgn. Svc. (Univ. fellow); MS in Econs., Georgetown U., 1967, PhD in Econs., 1969; postgrad., Nat. U. Mex. Instr. econs. George Mason Coll., U. Va., Fairfax, 1967-68; researcher World Bank, 1967-69, indsl. economist, devel. econs. dept., 1969-71; economist World Bank Latin Am. (Ctrl. Am., Mex., Venezuala, Equador, Panama and Dominican Republic, Washington, 1971-79; sr. loan officer for Middle East and North Africa World Bank, 1977—84, sr. loan officer, sr. economist Africa Region, 1988-91, prin. ops. officer pvt. sector fin. group Africa region, 1992-96, lead specialist, regional mgr., 1996-2000; pvt. practice fin., econ. devel. Africa and Latin Am., 2000—. Contbg. author: The Economic Growth of Colombia: Problems and Prospects, 1973, Central American Financial Integration, 1975. Mid-Career fellow Princeton U., 1988-89. Mem. Am. Econ. Assn., Soc. Internat. Devel., Brookings Inst. Latin Am. Study Group. Roman Catholic. Home: 5145 Yuma St NW Washington DC 20016-4336 Office: World Bank 1818 H St NW Washington DC 20433-0001

MARTINEZ, IRIS, state senator; b. Chgo. 1 child. Grad., Northeastern U., U. Ill., Chgo. Mem. Ill. State Senate, Springfield, 2003—, mem. approprtions II com., health and human svcs. com. and sbucom. on health care, vice chhair com. on ins. and pensions, mem. subcom. on mandates. Liaison to Hispanic Ministry. Committeewoman Ill. Dem. State Com.; mem. Dem. Nat. Com. Democrat. Catholic. Office: Capitol M-106 Capitol Bldg Springfield IL 62706 also: District 3024 N Pulaski Rd Chicago IL 60641 Home: 3154 W Grace St # 1 Chicago IL 60618-4529

MARTÍNEZ, IVÁN DAVID, language educator, translator; MA, Western Mich. U., Kalamazoo, 1997. Lectr. U. Mich., Ann Arbor, 1998—2002; instr. Spanish, Ball State U., Muncie, Ind., 2004—. Avocation: accordion. Home: PO Box 2016 Muncie IN 47307 Office: Ball State U 2000 W University Ave Muncie IN 47306 Office Phone: 765-285-7545. Business E-Mail: idmartinez@bsu.edu.

MARTINEZ, JENNY S., lawyer; b. 1974; BA cum laude, Yale U., 1993; JD magna cum laude, Harvard Law Sch., 1997. Bar: Va., DC. Law clk. to Honorable Guido Calabresi, US Ct. Appeals Second Circuit, 1997—98, Chambers of Justice Stephen Breyer, US Supreme Ct., 1998—99; assoc. legal officer to Judge Patricia Walk, UN Internat. Criminal Tribunal for Former Yugoslavia, 1999—2000; assoc. Jenner & Block LLC, 2000—03; sr. rsch. fellow, vis. lectr. Yale U., 2002—03; asst. prof. law Stanford Law Sch., 2003—. Mng. editor Harvard Law Review; cons. Internat. Ctr. Transitional Justice, 2003—. Contbr. articles to profl. jours. Vol. tutor Thurgood Marshall Acad. Charter HS, Washington, 2001; vol. atty. DC Bar Law Firm Pro Bono Project, 2001; vol. cons. atty. Human Rights First, 2003—. Named one of Top 40 Lawyers Under 40, Nat. Law Jour., 2005, Litigation's Rising Stars, The Am. Lawyer, 2007; recipient Sears prize, Harvard Law, Temple Bar Scholar, Am. Inns Ct., 1999. Mem.: Hispanic Bar Assn. DC (v.p. internal affairs 2003—). Office: Stanford Law Sch 559 Nathan Abbott Way Stanford CA 94305-8610 Office Phone: 650-725-2749. Business E-Mail: jmartinez@law.stanford.edu. *

MARTINEZ, KATHRYN MARIE, music educator; b. St. Paul, Dec. 20, 1957; d. Lloyd Gerald and Patricia Anne Schleusner; m. Michael David Martinez, Feb. 27, 1982 (div. Aug. 22, 1994); children: Kristin Marie, Kelly Anne. BA in Elem. Edn., Coll. St. Catherine, St. Paul, 1979. Tchr. grade 2 South Pk. Consol. Sch., Mpls., 1979—80, St. Peters Sch., North St. Paul, Minn., 1980—81; tchr. pre-sch. St. Marks Ch., Independence, Mo.,

1985—86; ind. piano tchr. Independence, Mo., 1985, Geneva, Ill., 1986, St. Paul, 1987—. Accompanist St. Mary of the Lake, White Bear Lake, 1999—. Mem. pageant comm. Vadnais Heights Heritage Days, Minn., 1994, pageant co-dir., 1995—96. Recipient 1st Runner-up Miss Minn., 1978. Mem.: St. Paul Piano Tchr. Assoc. (3d v.p. 2002—), Minn. Music Tchr. Assoc. (mem. 1991—), Ea. Suburban Fed. Music Club (co-chair 2002—04, pres. 2005—). Catholic. Avocations: gardening, playing piano, travel, rubber stamping. Home and Office: 4309 Greenhaven Court Vadnais Heights MN 55127

MARTINEZ, LUCY, lawyer; b. Townsville, Queensland, Australia, Aug. 18, 1977; arrived in US, 2001; BA, LLB, U. Queensland, Brisbane, Australia, 1998; LLM, Columbia U., 2003. Bar: Supreme Ct. Queensland, Australia (Solicitor) 2001, N.Y. 2004. Assoc., judge's clk. Queensland Ct. of Appeal, Brisbane, 1999—2000, High Ct. of Australia, Sydney, NSW, 2000—01; lectr. U. NSW, Sydney, 2001—01; assoc. Columbia Law Sch., NYC, 2001—03; atty. White & Case LLP, NYC, 2003—07, Freshfields Bruckhaus Deringer LLP, 2007—. Contbr. articles to profl. jours. Mem.: ABA, Bar Assn. NY, Am. Soc. Internat. Law. Office: Freshfields Bruckhaus Deringer LLP 520 Madison Ave 34th Fl New York NY 10022 Office Phone: 212-284-4964. Business E-Mail: lucy.martinez@freshfields.com.

MARTINEZ, MARIA, computer software company executive; BA in elec. engring., U. PR; MA in computer engring, Ohio State U. Various mgmt. and engring. positions AT&T Bell Labs.; v.p., gen. mgr. Internet Connectivity Solutions Divsn. Motorola Inc.; CEO Embrace Network, Inc.; corp. v.p. comm. and mobile solutions unit Microsoft Corp., corp. v.p. worldwide services, 2007—. Named an Elite Woman, Hispanic mag., 2004; recipient several process and quality awards. Achievements include led Motorola's launching of first CDMA comml. sys. in world; played a leadership role in Bell Lab's devel. of UNIX sys. for symmetrics multiprocessing and high availability; patents for devel. and disk storage sys; launched first software platform and developed customer base for Embrace Networks, Inc; first female Hispanic named v.p. at Microsoft. Office: Microsoft Corp One Microsoft Way Redmond WA 98052-6399 Office Phone: 425-882-8080. Office Fax: 425-706-7329. *

MARTINEZ, MATTHEW GILBERT, former congressman; b. Walsenburg, Colo., Feb. 14, 1929; children: Matthew, Diane, Susan, Michael, Carol Ann. Cert of competence, Los Angeles Trade Tech. Sch., 1959. Small businessman and bldg. contractor; mem. 97th-106th Congresses from 31st Calif. dist., 1982-2001; mem. edn. and labor com., fgn. affairs com. Mem. Monterey Park Planning Commn., 1971-74; mayor City of Monterey Park, 1974-75; mem. Monterey Park City Council, 1974-80, Calif. State Assembly, 1980-82; bd. dirs. San Gabriel Valley YMCA. Served with USMC, 1947-50. Mem. Congl. Hispanic Caucus, Hispanic Am. Democrats, Nat. Assn. Latino Elected and Apptd. Ofcls., Communications Workers Am., VFW, Am. Legion, Latin Bus. Assn., Monterey Park C. of C., Navy League (dir.) Lodges: Rotary. Democrat.

MARTINEZ, MEL(QUIADES) (RAFAEL), senator, political organization administrator, former secretary of housing and urban development; b. Sagua La Grande, Cuba, Oct. 23, 1946; arrived in US, 1962, naturalized, 1971; s. Melquiades C. and Gladys V. (Ruiz) M.; m. Kathryn Tindal, June 13, 1970; children: Lauren Elizabeth, John Melquiades, Andrew Tindal. AA, Orlando Jr. Coll., 1967; BA in Internat. Affairs, Fla. State U., 1969, JD, 1973. Bar: Fla. 1973, US Dist. Ct. (mid. dist.) Fla. 1973, US Supreme Ct. 1979, US Dist. Ct. (so. dist.) Fla. 1986; cert. Nat. Bd. Trial Advocacy. Civil trial atty., ptnr. Martinez, Dalton, Dellecker and Wilson, Orlando, Fla., 1973-85; ptnr. Martinez, Dalton, Dellecker, Wilson and King, 1985-98; chmn. Orange County, Fla., 1998-2001; sec. US Dept. Housing & Urban Devel., Washington, 2001—03; US senator from Fla., 2005—; gen. chmn. Rep Nat Com., 2007—. Mem. Fla. Utilities Commn., 1994—97, pres., 1995—97; chmn. Fla. Growth Mgmt. Study Commn.; mem. com. banking, housing and urban affairs US Senate, com. energy and natural resources, com. fgn. relations, congressional-exec. commn. China, spl. com. aging. Bd. dirs. Cath. Social Svcs. Orlando, 1978-86; founder, chmn. Mayor's Hispanic Adv. Com., Orlando, 1981-82; chmn. bd. commrs. Orlando Housing Authority, 1983-86. Named one of 25 Most Influential Hispanics, Time Mag., 2005 Mem. Fla. Bar (bd. govs. young lawyers sect. 1980-81), Acad. Fla. Trial Lawyers (dir. 1981-85, treas. 1986-87, pres. 1988-89), 9th Jud. Cir. (jud. nomination commn. 1986), Congressional Hispanic Leadership Inst. Republican. Roman Catholic. Office: US Senate 317 Hart Senate Office Bldg Washington DC 20510 also: Landmark Ctr One Ste 475 315 East Robinson St Orlando FL 32801-4343 Office Phone: 202-224-3041, 407-254-2573. Office Fax: 202-228-5171. *

MARTINEZ, MIGUEL ACEVEDO, urologist, consultant, lecturer; b. Chihuahua, Mex., Aug. 18, 1953; came to US, 1956; s. Miguel Nuñez and Velia (Acevedo) M. AB, Stanford U., 1976; MD, Yale U., 1983. Diplomate Am. Bd. Urology. Intern U. S.C. Med. Ctr., 1983-84; resident in urology White Meml. Med. Ctr., LA, 1984-89, urologist, 1989—. Cons., lectr. physician asst. program U. So. Calif., L.A., 1990—, clin. instr.; patient edn. cons. ICI Pharm., Del., 1991—, Zeneca's Speaker Forum; patient edn. and med. cons., lectr. Abbott Labs., 1991—; mem. edn.cons. several radio/TV stas., 1991—; mem. subcom. for diseases on kidney and transplantation NIH, Washington, 1991; mem. nat. Hispanic adv. bd. Pfizer Pharms., Inc., 1998—; mem. adv. bd. Glaxo Smith Kline, 2002—; cons. spkrs. bur. Pfizer, Bayer/ESK. Author: Intercellular Pathways, 1981. Polit. cons. Xavier Becerra, US Congress, 1992, Martin Gallegos, Gil Cedillo, Calif. State Assembly, 1993, others; bd. dirs. Latino Ctr. for Prevention and Action in Health, Orange County, calif.; bd. govs., sec., rep. Zeneca Urology Econ. Summit, Washington, 1993; mem. Pfizer Nat. Hispanic Adv. Bd. Named Nat. Male Outstanding Teenage of Am., 1971, One of Outstanding Young Men of Am., 1981, Philanthropic Leadership award Philanthropic Svc. Instns., 2006; Nat. Hispanic Med. Assn. Pub. Policy fellow, 2000-01. Mem. AMA, Nat. Hispanic Med. Assn. (public policy fellow), Am. Urological Assn., Calif. Med. Assn. (polit. action com. bd. dirs. 1997—, del.), LA Med. Assn. (polit. action com. 1992—), LA County Med. Assn., Yale Alumni Assn., Stanford Alumni Assn., LA Athletic Club. Office: White Meml Med Ctr Rm 500 1701 Cesar Chavez Ave Los Angeles CA 90033-2438 Office Phone: 323-224-6202. Personal E-mail: uromd@earthlink.net.

MARTINEZ, NATALIE, newscaster; b. Buffalo; Degree, SUNY, Buffalo. Anchor, reporter, prodr. at upstate N.Y. radio and TV stations; reporter and weekend anchor WXAA-TV, Albany, NY, primary anchor; co-anchor weekend morning news and reporter WMAQ-TV, Chgo., 2001—. Mem.: Nat. League Female Execs., Nat. Assn. of Hispanic Journalists, One Voice. Office: WMAQ-TV NBC Tower 454 N Columbus Dr Chicago IL 60611-5555 Office Phone: 312-836-5830.

MARTINEZ, PEDRO JAIME, professional baseball player; b. Manoquayabo, Dominican Republic, July 25, 1971; With LA Dodgers, 1992—93; pitcher Montreal Expos, 1994—97, Boston Red Sox, 1998—2004, NY Mets, 2005—. Named Minor League Player of Yr., Sporting News, 1991, Nat. League Earned Runs Average (ERA) Leader, 1997, Am. League Earned Runs Average (ERA) Leader, 1999—2003, Am. League Wins Leader, 1999, Am. League Strikeouts Leader, 1999, 2000, 2002, All-Star MVP, 1999; named to Am. League All-Star Team, 1998—2000, 2002, Nat. League All-Star Team, 1996—97, 2005; recipient Nat. League Cy Young award, 1997, Am. League Cy Young award, 1999, 2000. Achievements include being a member of the World Series Champion Boston Red Sox, 2004; having over 200 career wins, 2006; becoming the 15th pitcher in history with 3,000 strikeouts in 2007. Office: NY Mets 123 01 Roosevelt Ave Flushing NY 11368 *

MARTINEZ, RICARDO, emergency medicine company executive; m. Robin Rosser. MD, La. State U. Sch. Medicine, 1980. Intern Lafayette (La.) Charity Hosp., 1980-81; resident Charity Hosp., New Orleans, 1983-85; vis. fellow accident rsch. unit Ctr. Automotive Engring./U. Birmingham, U.K., 1989; adminstr. Nat. Hwy. Traffic Safety Adminstrn, Washington, 1994—99; sr. v.p. health affairs Healtheon Web MD Corp., Atlanta, 1999—2000; pres., CEO Safety Intelligence Sys., Atlanta, 2000—04; exec. v.p. for med. affairs Schumacher Group, 2005—. Clin. prof. emergency medicine Emory U. Sch. Medicine, Atlanta. Mem.: Inst. Medicine. Home: 1254 Spring Creek Way Decatur GA 30033-2643 Office: 1275 Shiloh Rd NW Ste 2710 Kennesaw GA 30144 *

MARTINEZ, ROSE MARIE, health science association administrator; PhD, Johns Hopkins Sch. Hygiene and Pub. Health. Former asst. dir. health fin. and policy U.S. Gen. Acctg. Office; sr. health rschr. Mathematica Policy Rsch.; dir. IOM Bd. Health Promotion and Disease Prevention, 1999—. Office: Inst of Med 500 Fifth St NW Washington DC 20001

MARTINEZ, RUEBEN, entrepreneur; b. Miami, Ariz., 1940; Profl. barber; owner, founder Libreria Martinez Books and Art Gallery, 1993—. Co-founder Latino Book Festival; founding mem. Santa Ana's Reading com.; spkr. in field. Named MacArthur Fellow, John D. and Catherine T. MacArthur Found., 2004. Office: Libreria Martinez 1110 N Main St Santa Ana CA 92701 Office Phone: 714-973-7900.

MARTINEZ, TINO, professional baseball player; b. Tampa, Fla., Dec. 7, 1967; Baseball player Seattle Mariners, 1988-95, N.Y. Yankees, 1996—2001, 2005—, St. Louis Cardinals, 2002—03, Tampa Bay Devil Rays, 2004. Mem. U.S. Olympic baseball team, 1988. Named to Am. League All-Star game, 1995, 1997. Achievements include mem. World Series Champions N.Y. Yankees, 1996, 1998-2000. Office: NY Yankees Yankee Stadium E 161 St and River Ave Bronx NY 10451

MARTINEZ, TODD J., chemistry professor; BS, Calvin Coll., 1989; PhD, U. Calif., 1994. Fulbright fellow Fritz Haber Inst. Molecular Dynamics, Jerusalem; presdl. postdoctoral fellow U. Calif., LA, 1994—96; prof. U. Ill., Urbana-Champaign, 1996—. Faculty affiliate theoretical and computational biophysics group Beckman Inst. Advanced Sci. and Tech. Named a MacArthur fellow, John D. and Catherine T. MacArthur Found., 2005; recipient Beckman Young Investigator award, Beckman Found., 1999, Camille Dreyfuss Teacher-Scholar award, Camille & Henry Dreyfus Found., 2000, Rsch. Innovation award. Office: U Ill Dept Chemistry MC 712 600 S Mathews Urbana IL 61801 E-mail: tmartine@uiuc.edu.

MARTÍNEZ, TOMÁS ELOY, writer, journalist; b. Tucumán, Argentina, 1934; BA Spanish & Latin Am. Studies, U. Tucumán; MA, U. Paris; doctorates (hon.). Exec. editor Primera Plana, Buenos Aires, Panorama, Buenos Aires; editor La Opinión, Buenos Aires, Página 12, Buenos Aires, El Nacional, Caracas, Argentina; founder, exec. editor El Diario de Caracas; prof. Latin Am. Lit. U. Maryland, 1984—87; prof. Rutgers U., 1995—, dir. Latin Am. Studies Program, 1995—; syndicated columnist, 1995—. Dir. Ctr. Hemispheric Studies Rutgers U., 2000—, writer in residence, 2000—. Author: (essays) Structures of the Argentine Cinema, 1961, The Poetry of Ramos Sucre, 1981, The Argentine Dream, 1999, Requiem for a Lost Country, 2003, (short stories) The Commonplace Death, 1998, (novels) Sagrado, 1967, The Peron Novel, 1988, The Hand of the Master, 1991, Santa Evita, 1995, The Flight of the Queen, 2002 (Alfaguara Internat. Novel award), The Tango Singer, 2004. Woodrow Wilson Ctr. for Scholars fellowship, 1983, Guggenheim fellowship, 1987. Mem.: Com. to Protect Journalists. Office: RULAS Douglass Campus 105 George St New Brunswick NJ 08901-1414 also: NY Times Syndication Sales Corp 14th Fl 122 E 42nd St New York NY 10168 Office Phone: 732-932-0534, 732-932-9323 27, 212-499-3337. Office Fax: 212-499-3382. E-mail: eloy@rci.rutgers.edu.

MARTINEZ, VICTOR JESUS, professional baseball player; b. Ciudad Bolivar, Venezuela, Dec. 23, 1978; s. Margot Martinez; m. Margret Martinez; 1 child, Victor Jesus Jr. Catcher Cleve. Indians, 2004—. Co-chmn. Esperanza Fiesta of Hope Program, 2004; active Tribe Loving & Care Hosp. Visits. Named Man of Yr., Cleve. Chpt., Baseball Writer's Assn. Am., 2004; named to Am. League All-Star Game, 2004; recipient Silver Slugger award, 2004, 2005. Achievements include setting a new Indian's franchise record for a catcher with 101 RBIs in 2004; being the first catcher in Indian's franchise history to win a Silver Slugger award, 2004. Mailing: Jacobs Field 2401 Ontario St Cleveland OH 44115 Office Phone: 216-420-4200. *

MARTINEZ, VILMA SOCORRO, lawyer; b. San Antonio, Oct. 17, 1943; d. Salvador and Marina (Pina) M.; m. Stuart R. Singer, Nov. 1968; children: Carlos, Ricardo. B.A., U. Tex., 1964; LL.B., Columbia U., 1967. Bar: NY 1968, Calif. 1975. Staff atty. gen. civil rights litigation NAACP Legal Defense and Edn. Fund, 1967-70; EEO counsel NY State Div. Human Rights, 1970-71; litigation assoc. Cahill, Gordon & Reindel, 1971-73; pres., gen. counsel Mexican-Am. Legal Def. & Ednl. Fund, Inc., 1973-82; ptnr. Munger, Tolles & Olson LLP, Los Angeles, 1982—; dir. Anheuser-Busch Cos., Inc.; cons. US Commn. on Civil Rights, 1969-74, US Census Bur., 1975-81, US Treasury Dept., 1976, Calif. Fed. Jud. Selection Com., 1977-80, Presidential Adv. Bd. on Ambassadorial Appointments, 1977-81, US Hispanic-Mexican Govt. Internat. Commn., 1980-82. Regent U. Calif., 1976-90, chmn. 1984—86, mem. corp. bd. Shell Oil Co., 1997-2005, Sanwa Bank Calif., 1990-2005; trustee Edward W. Hazen Found. Recipient Lex award Mexican-Am. Bar Assn., 1983, Jefferson award Am. Idst. Pub. Service, 1976, John D. Rockefeller III Youth award Rockefeller Found., 1977, Univ. medal of excellence, Columbia U., 1978, Valerie Kantor award Mex. Am. Legal Defense Edn. Fund, Inc., 1982, Excellence medal Columbia U. Law Sch., 1992, Maynard Toll award, Legal Aid Found; named one of Boardroom Elite, Hispanic Bus. Mag., 2007; John Hay Whitney fellow, 1964, Samuel Rubin fellow Columbia U. Sch. Law, 1983. Office: Munger Tolles & Olson LLP 355 S Grand Ave Fl 35 Los Angeles CA 90071-1560 *

MARTÍNEZ, YOLANDA R., social services administrator; b. Feb. 11, 1936; d. Eduardo R. and Consuelo (Rincon) Martínez; m. William Edward Hawkins, Mar. 27, 1963 (dec. May 11, 1996); children: Ricardo, Eduardo, William T. AA, San Bernardino Valley Coll., 1959; BA, U. Wash., 1974. Tchr. pub. schs., Calif., 1958—59; parole adviser, project dir., counselor Active Mexicanos, Seattle, 1972—76; instr. Everett (Wash.) C.C., 1975—76; rschr., translator Wash. State Coun. Crime and Delinquency, Seattle, 1977; program asst., minority affairs Seattle Ctrl. C.C.; cons. to cmty. offenders programs, 1977—81; sr. cmty. svc. rep. Seattle Dept. Human Resources, 1981—, ret., 2003; bus. owner Neighborhood Solutions, 2003—. Cons. in field. Author: Usted y La Ley, 1977. Translator ARC Lang. Bank, 1975—; chmn. Region 10 Chicago Task Force on Drug Abuse, 1977—79; mem. Seattle Cable Citizens Adv. Bd., 1988—90; v.p. Concilio for Spanish Speaking; state dir., mem. nat. exec. bd. League United L.Am. Citizens, 1980—82; chmn. Hispanic adv. bd. Seattle Cmty. Coll. Dist. 6, 1981—83; chmn. Seattle/Mazatlan Sister City Assn., 1981—83; v.p. Neighborhoods U.S.A., 1987—92, 1995—, bd. dirs., 1986, United Way of King County; dist. adv. com. group health Northgate Clinic; del. White House Conf. on Families, LA, 1980; bd. dirs. N.W. Kidney Ctr. Regional Coun., 2002; bd. mem. Northgate Chamber, 2002; Dem. precinct committeeman, 1968, 1970, 1988—2002; vol. worker various local and state polit. campaigns. Named One of 100 Women Role Models for Pub. Schs., State Office Pub. Instrn., Lake City Citizen of Yr., 2000; recipient Gov.'s citation, 1974, award for committment to higher edn., Seattle C.C. Dist., 1983, One of 10 Unsung Heroes in Seattle, Radical Women, 1983, Cmty. Svc. award, Am. G.I. Forum, 1984, Golden Maple Leaf award, Maple Leaf Cmty. Coun., 1991, Commn. award, Seattle Commn. on Children and Youth, 1991, 1993, assoc. mem., Eastern Washington U. Found., Seattle Works award, Cmty. Ambassador, 2001, Seattle Works Award, 2002. Mem.: Northgate C. of C. (founding mem.), Rotary. Home: 12018 17th Ave NE Seattle WA 98125-5116 Home Phone: 206-365-8558. Personal E-mail: ymart@earthlink.net.

MARTINEZ-CANAS, MARIA, photography educator; d. Jose Martinez-Canas and Elena Mendez. BFA, Phila. Coll. Art, 1982; MFA, The Art Inst. Chgo., 1984. Adj. prof. photography U. Miami, 1988—93, New World Sch. The Arts, Miami, 1996—. One-woman shows include Sol Mednick Gallery, Phila., De Santos Gallery, Houston, Fredric Snitzer Gallery, Miami, Catherine Edelman Gallery, Chgo., Julie Saul Gallery, NYC, Mus. Art, Ft. Lauderdale. Recipient Artist-In-Residence award, Light Work, Syracuse, 1990, Island Gardens Pub. Art Commn. award, Flagstone Properties, 2003, Artist-In-Residence award, Mus. Contemporary Art, N. Miami, 2005, Frost Art Mus., FIU, 2006; fellow Individual Artist Fellowship, Divsn. Cultural Affairs, Fla. Dept. State, 1987; Fulbright-Hays Grant, Inst. Internat. Edn., 1986, Fellowship, Cintas Found., Inst. Internat. Edn., 1988, Photography Fellowship, Nat. Endowment for the Arts, 1988, Cultural Consortium Fellowship, Md. Cultural Affairs Coun., 1992. Office: 2011 SW 10 St Miami FL 33135 Office Phone: 305-643-1201. Business E-Mail: mfoto@aol.com.

MARTINEZ-FRAGA, PEDRO J., lawyer; b. Havana, Cuba, Sept. 9, 1960; BA with high honors, St. John's Coll., 1984; JD, Columbia U., 1987. Bar: Fla. 1988, DC 1988, US Dist. Ct. (so., mid. districts) Fla. 1988, US Ct. Appeals (11th cir.) 1989, US Dist. Ct. (Colo. dist.) 1991, US Supreme Ct. 1999. Adj. prof. law U. Miami, 2002—04; mem. com. Fla. Bar Rules of Civil Procedure, 1990—97, Fla. Bar Rules of Judicial Adminstrn., 1996—97; chair com. Fla. Bar Code & Rules of Evidence, 1996; mem. ad hoc com. on rules and procedures US Dist. Ct., So. Dist. Fla. Author, editor Florida Civil Procedure, 2000, 2001, (chapters to books); contbr. articles to profl. journals. Dir. Cuban-Am. Endowment for Arts; bd. dirs. Miami Lighthouse for Blind, New World Sch. Arts; bd. mem. bd. visitors and governors St. John's Coll. Named 2001 Lawyer of the Americas, U. Miami Inter-Am. Law Review; named one of Top Lawyers in So. Fla., So. Fla. Legal Guide, 2001—05, Fla. Legal Elite, Fla. Trend Mag., 2004—05, Top Lawyers in Fla., Fla. Monthly Mag., 2004, Best Lawyers in Am., 2005—07; named to, Am. Law Inst., 1999, Best of the Bar, So. Fla. Bus. Jour., 2003—05; recipient Harlan Fiske Stone scholarship, 1987. Fellow: Am. Bar Found.; mem.: Hispanic Bar Assn., Am. Trial Lawyers Assn., Cuban-Am. Bar Assn., Dade County Bar Assn. (chair internat. law com. 2001—02, chair fed. ct. com. 1996), Internat. Bar Assn. Office: Greenberg Traurig LLP 1221 Brickell Ave Miami FL 33131 Office Phone: 305-579-0595. Office Fax: 305-579-0717. Business E-Mail: martinezp@gtlaw.com.

MARTÍNEZ-LÓPEZ, CARMEN LEONOR, management consultant, educator; b. Aracataca, Magdalena, Colombia, Oct. 13, 1956; d. Domingo Ramón Martínez and Alicia Esther Acosta de Martínez; m. Iván R. López, May 26, 2000. Licenciate in Ednl. Adminstrn., U. San Buenaventura, Medellín, Colombia, 1980; M in Ednl. Adminstrn., U. Antioquia, Medellín, 1989; specialist in Pub. Adminstrn., U. Escuela de Adminstrn. Publica, Medellín, 1995; specialist in Indsl. Rels., U. Escuela de Adminstrn. and Fin., Medellín, 1983, MBA, 2003; PhD in Internat. Bus., U. Tex.-Pan Am., Edinburg, 2003. Bd. dirs. Inst. Polictectico Jaime Isaza Cadavid, Medellín, 1980—82; dep. and bd. dirs. budget commn. Dept. de Antioquia, Medellín, 1982—84; regional mgr. Nat. Agy. Social Security, Medellín, 1983—86; pres. External Orgnl. Cons., Medellín, 1987—93; prof., rsch. and cons. U. Escuela de Adminstrn. and Fin., Medellín, 1989—92; adminstrv. mgr. Am. Med. Holding, Medellín, 1992—93; dept. chair Inst. Colombiano de Edn. Superior de Incolda, Cali, Colombia, 1993—96; rschr. and tchr. asst. U. Tex.-Pan Am., Edinburg, 1998—2003; asst. prof. CUNY, 2004—. Strategic planning cons. Am. Med. Holding, Medellín, 1989—92; strategic mgmt. cons. U. ICESI, Cali, 1995—96; strategic planning cons. Ednl. Cooperative Uraba, Apartadó, Antioquia, Colombia, 1999—2001; vis. prof. U. Monterrey, Mexico, 1999—2000. Dep. Dept. of Antioquia, Medellín, 1982—84; v.p. Colombian Conservative Party, Medellín, 1981—83; active Poly. Inst. Jaime Isaza, Medellín, 1980—82. Fellow: Ptnrs. of the Ams. (assoc.); mem.: Acad. Internat. Bus., Bus. Assn. L.Am. Studies, Acad. Mgmt. Conservative. Roman Catholic. Avocations: golf, soccer, travel. Office: CUNY S661 199 Chambers St New York NY 10007-1097 Home: Apt 3A 450 Pelham Rd New Rochelle NY 10805 Office Phone: 212-220-8389. Home Fax: 914-637-9305. Personal E-mail: carleo13@aol.com.

MARTINEZ-MALDONADO, MANUEL, academic administrator, dean, medical and science educator; b. Yauco, PR, Aug. 25, 1937; s. Manuel and Josefa Maldonado (Josefa Maldonado) Martinez; m. Nivia Elena Rivera, Dec. 18, 1959; children: Manuel, David, Ricardo, Pablo. BS, U. PR, 1957; MD, Temple U., 1961. Diplomate Am. Bd. Internal Medicine, Am. Bd. Nephrology. Intern St. Charles Hosp., Toledo, 1961—62; resident VA Hosp., San Juan, 1962—65, chief resident, 1964—65, chief med. svcs., 1973—90, co-dir. renal metabolic lab., 1973—90; instr. U. Tex. Southwestern Med. Sch., Dallas, 1967—68; from asst. prof. to prof. medicine, co-dir. renal sect. Baylor Coll. Medicine, Houston, 1968—73; prof. medicine U. PR Sch. Medicine, 1973—90, prof. physiology, 1974—90; prof. medicine U. Caribbean, Bayamon, PR, 1980—90; prof., vice chmn. dept. medicine Emory U. Sch. Medicine, 1990—98; chief med. svcs. and clin. affairs Atlanta VA Med. Ctr., 1990—98; v.p. for rsch., prof. medicine Oreg. Health Scis. U., Portland, 1998—99, v.p. rsch., 1999—2000; pres., dean, prof. medicine and physiology Ponce Sch. Medicine, 2000—06; prof. medicine, pharmacology, toxicology U. Louisville, 2007, exec. v.p. rsch., 2007—. Assoc. mem. nephrology com. Am. Bd. Internal Medicine, 1982—86; nat. adv. bd. gen. medicine B study sect. Nat. Inst. Arthritis, Metabolism and Digestive Diseases NIH; bd. sci. counselors, sci. advisors com. Nat. Heart, Lung and Blood Inst., NIH. Author: La Voz Sostenida, 1984, Palm Beach Blues, 1986, Por Amor al Arte, 1989, Hotel Maria, 1989, Isla Verde, 1999, Novela de Mediodia, 2003; film critic: El Reportero, 1983—86, El Mundo, 1987—90, editor/co-editor: in field, mem. editl. bd.: U. P.R. Press; editor: Am. Jour. of Med. Scis., 1994—98, Am. Jour. Kidney Disease, 1997—2002; contbr. over 200 articles to profl. jours. Com. mem. 500th Anniversary of Discovery Am., PR, 1987—92; pres. bd. trustees Inst. Puerto Rican Culture and Performing Arts Ctr., 2001—05; trustee Corp. Musical Arts, 2001—05, Inst. Puerto Rican Lit., 2001—05; chair culture and recreation panel PR 2025; health com. Popular Dem. Com., PR, 1982—84; bd. dirs. Alliance for PR, Inc., bd. sec., 2004—06. Named one of Outstanding Young Men, PR C. of C., 1976; recipient Lederle Internat. award, Lederle Corp., 1966—67, Macy Faculty Scholar award, Ther Josiah Macy Jr. Found., 1979—80, Grand Mobil prize medicine, Mobil Oil Corp., 1981, Disting. Alumnus award, Temple Med. Sch., 1988, Presdl. award, Nat. Kidney Found., 1988, Donald W. Seldin award, 1994, Disting. Physician award, PR Hosps. Assn., 1988, Orden del Cafetal award, Municipality of Yauco, 1989, Abelardo Díaz Alfaro award, Medicine & Humanites Acad. of Family Medicine, 2002, Svc. Exec. award, PR Mfrs. Assn., 2005, Svc. Exec. of Yr. award, PR Mfrs. Assn. (So. region), 2006. Master: ACP; fellow: AAAS, Am. Heart Assn. (hypertension rsch. coun.), Coun. for High Blood Pressure Rsch.; mem.: Am. Acad. Arts and Scis. (hon. fgn.), Nat. Kidney Found. (chmn. pub. policy com. 1992—94), Consortium Southeastern Hypertension Ctrs. (bd. dirs.), Assn. Am. Physicians, Inter-Am. Soc. Hypertension Assn. (bd. govs., chmn. 8th Sci. Congress 1989, U.S. Pharmacopeial Conv. Cardio Renal Drugs com. 1990—96), L.Am. Soc. Nephrology (v.p. 1987—91, pres.-elect 1991—94, pres. 1994—96, Miatello award 1999), Am. Soc. for Clin. Investigation, So. Soc. Clin. Investigation (sec.-treas. 1983—85, pres. 1985—86,

Founders medal 1990, Pub. Svc. medal, Donald W. Seldin award), Am. Soc. Nephrology (legis. liaison com., chmn. audit com. 1988), Inst. Medicine of NAS (com. on human rights 1987—92), Alpha Omega Alpha. Roman Catholic. Achievements include research in kidney physiology and pathophysiology, treatment of clinical disturbances of blood composition, clinical use of diuretics, mechanisms of the devel. of hypertension. Avocations: theater, art, music, poetry, films. Office: U Louisville Rm 200 Jouett Hall 2310 S Third St Louisville KY 40292 Home Phone: 502-749-0339; Office Phone: 502-852-8373. Personal E-mail: martinem_pms@hotmail.com. Business E-Mail: m0mart10@louisville.edu.

MARTINEZ-MIER, ESPERANZA ANGELES, dental educator, researcher; b. Veracruz, Mex., Feb. 17, 1967; d. Gustavo Humberto Martinez Amilpa and Angela Mier Vidal; m. Juan Salvador Gudino, Dec. 1, 1990; children: Diego Gudino-Martinez, Pablo Gudino-Martinez. DDS, Autonomous U. Mex., 1990; MS in Dentistry, Ind. U., 1995, PhD, 2000. Lic. dentist Mex., 1990. Vis. prof. Ind. U. Sch. Dentistry, Indpls., 2000—01, asst. prof., 2001—. Dir, fluoride rsch. program Ind. U. Sch. Dentistry, 2002—. Contbr. articles to profl. jours. Pres. Hispanic Dental Assn., Indpls., 2001. Recipient Johnson award in pub. svc., Ind. U. Sch. Dentistry, 2002; grantee, NIH, 2002—. Mem.: Am. Assn. Dental Rsch. Achievements include development of gold standard techniques for fluoride analysis. Office: Ind U Sch Dentistry Oral Health Rsch Inst 415 Lansing St Indianapolis IN 46202 Office Phone: 317-274-8822.

MARTINEZ MYERS, FRANCES, real estate company executive; m. Jon Martinez Myers. Mem. PHH/Cendant; sr. v.p. bus. develop. Fox & Roach/Trident, LP; sr. v.p. Employee Transfer Corp.; chair Nat. Assn. Hispanic Real Estate Professionals, 2005—. Bd. dirs. Nat. Assn. Realtors; nat. adv. coun. Fannie Mae; affordable housing adv. coun. Freddie Mac; nat. adv. coun. Bank of Am. Named a Women of Distinction, Phila. Bus. Jour., 2006; named one of Top 100 Most Influential Hispanics in the Nation, Hispanic Bus. mag., 2005, Real Estate's 25 Most Influential Thought Leaders, Realtor Mag., 2006. Mem.: Worldwide Employee Relocation Coun. (Meritorious Svc. Award). Mailing: National Assn Hispanic Real Estate Professionals 1150 17th St NW Ste 504 Washington DC 20036 E-mail: Frances.MartinezMyers@prufoxroach.com. *

MARTINEZ TUCKER, SARA (SARA ALICIA TUCKER), federal agency and former educational association administrator; b. Laredo, Tex. BA in Journalism, U. Tex., Austin, 1976, MBA with high honors, 1979. Reporter San Antonio Express-News; various positions through regional v.p. AT&T, 1981—97; pres., CEO Hispanic Scholarship Fund, San Francisco, 1997—2006; under sec. US Dept. Edn., Washington, 2006—. Bd. dir. Student Loan Mktg. Assn. (Sallie Mae), 2001—; mem. No. Am. diversity adv. bd. Toyota Motor Corp.; founding mem. Nat. Ctr. for Edn. Accountability; mem. steering com. Council for Aid to Edn., RAND Corp.; mem. Sec. of Edn.'s Commn. on Future of Edn., 2005. Mem. Chancellor's Council Univ. Tex., Austin, mem. adv. council, Coll. of Nat. Sci.; mem. adv. bd. Oxygen Media / Markle Found. Named Hispanic of the Year, Hispanic mag., 2000; named one of 80 Elite Hispanic Women, Hispanic Bus. mag., 2003, 25 Most Influential Hispanics, Time Mag., 2005; recipient Disting. Alumnus award, U. Tex., 2005. Office: US Dept Edn 400 Maryland Ave SW Rm 7W310 Washington DC 20202 *

MARTING, MICHAEL G., lawyer; b. Cleve., Nov. 5, 1948; BA summa cum laude, Yale U., 1971, JD, 1974. Bar: Ohio 1974. Assoc. Jones Day, Cleve., 1974-83, ptnr., 1984—. Mem.: Chagrin Valley Hunt Club, Tavern Club (trustee local chpt. 1985—88, 2004—06, treas., sec.), Cleve. Racquet Club. Avocations: fly fishing, hunting, squash. Office: Jones Day N Point 901 Lakeside Ave E Cleveland OH 44114-1190 Home Phone: 216-371-5185; Office Phone: 216-586-7194. Business E-Mail: mgmarting@jonesday.com.

MARTINI, RICHARD K., theatrical producer; b. Bergenfield, NJ, Mar. 11, 1952; s. John F. and June L. (Fenton) M.; m. Susan C. Weaving, Aug. 1, 1981. BA, St. Francis Coll., Loretto, Pa., 1974; MEd, U. S.C., 1975. V.p. Am. Theatre Prodns., NYC, 1975-81; pres. Edgewood Orgn., NYC, 1981-86; pres., owner KL Mgmt., NYC, 1986—; owner, operator Martini Entertainment, Inc., NYC, 1991—. Home: 201 E 37th St New York NY 10016-3159 Office: Martini Entertainment Co 1501 Broadway Ste 1401 New York NY 10036-5601

MARTIN-LOWRY, BEVERLY ANNE, writer, columnist; b. Washington, Oct. 25, 1948; d. James Aubrey and Gertha Mae Martin; m. Courtland Alan Milner, Apr. 20, 1968 (div. Oct. 17, 1989); children: Jennifer Anne Litton, Martin Alan Milner; m. Peter Hans Lowry, Dec. 29, 1999. CEO Pen 2 Paper, Ink, Live Oak, Tex., 2003—. Author: In October, I Turn Fifty! A Satirical Look Back on Life, 2000, Memoirs and Confessions: From Europe to the USA, 2001, (novels) Strong Appetites, 2004, Can't Cook Anonymous, 2004, The Most Unlikely Angel: A Trilogy of Love, Life, and Laughter, 2005, The Reel Thing; editorial columnist: Sounding Off; contbr. articles to local newspapers. Mem.: Am. Legion (life). Republican. Presbyterian. Avocations: swimming, reading, travel. Home Phone: 210-646-9877; Office Phone: 210-646-9877. Personal E-mail: n2books@satx.rr.com.

MARTINO, JOSEPH PAUL, research scientist, researcher; b. Warren, Ohio, July 16, 1931; s. Joseph and Anna Elizabeth (Kubina) M.; m. Mary Lou Bouquot, May 18, 1957 (dec. Jan. 1988); children: Theresa, Anthony, Michael; m. Nancy McCoy, Dec. 28, 2000. AB in Physics, Miami U., Ohio, 1953; MSEE, Purdue U., 1955; PhD in Stats., Ohio State U., 1961; grad., Air War Coll., 1972. Commd. 2d lt. USAF, 1953, advanced through grades to col., 1973, project engr. armament lab. Wright-Patterson AFB, Ohio, 1955-58, mathematician Office Sci. Rsch. Washington, 1961-62, staff scientist Avionics Lab. Wright-Patterson AFB, 1972-73, dir. engring. standardization Def. Electronics Supply Ctr. Dayton, Ohio, 1973-75, ret., 1975; sr. scientist, rsch. inst. U. Dayton, 1975-93. Author: Technological Forecasting for Decisionmaking, 1972, rev. edit., 1983, 3d edit., 1992, A Fighting Chance-The Moral Use of Nuclear Weapons, 1988, Science Funding: Politics and Porkbarrel, 1992, Research and Development Project Selection, 1995, (novel) The Justice Cooperative, 2004; assoc. editor: Tech. Forecasting and Social Change Jour., 1968—. With USAF, 1953—75, col., 1973—75. Fellow IEEE (Centennial medal 1984), AAAS, AIAA (assoc.); mem. Inst. for Ops. Rsch. and Mgmt. Sci., Am. Soc. Engring. Mgmt., Engrs. Club of Dayton. Roman Catholic. Office Phone: 937-492-4729. Business E-Mail: j.p.martino@ieee.org.

MARTINO, MICHAEL CHARLES, entertainer, musician, actor; b. Phila., Sept. 10, 1950; s. Salvatore Joseph and Marie Angela (Langone) M. Grad. high sch., Upper Darby, Pa. Spokesperson/rep. Petosa Accordion Co., Seattle, 1979—; featured TV entertainer Mike Martino Show, Delaware County, Pa., 1987-89; accordion tchr. Drexel Hill, Pa., 1989—; featured artist Am. Accordion Soc. Conv., King of Prussia, Pa., 2003; actor TV series Hack, Channel 3, 2003. Entertainer, host, prodr. St. Jude's Children's Hosp. Marathon, King of Prussia, Pa., 1973; opening act comedian Morty Gunty, 1973, Pat Cooper, Phila., 1981; guest artist, entertainer Internat. Platform Assn. Conv., Washington, 1979, Am. Accordion Musicological Soc. Festival and symposium, King of Prussia, 2003; nite club performer Glen Mills, Pa., 1989; actor TV commls., Elkton, Md., 1979, Halloween Spl. KYW-TV, Phila., 1986, TV show Hack, 2003; performed radio contest jingle Sta. KISS 100 radio, Media, Pa., 1992; featured soloist Am. Accordian Festival, King of Prussia, Pa., 2003; opening act for Donna Theodore Fundraiser for Joe Theodore, Glassboro, NJ, 2005, Charlie Graci Rock and Roll Pioneer, Del. County, Pa., 2004. Author: (movie) Forever Fiftys, 1990; composer, dir., prodr., actor: (video) Forever Fiftys; composer: (movie) That First September; creator, performer Suspended Triple Bellows Shake Technique for the Accordion, 1994; composer (ballad) Through the Music, Through the Words I Sing, 1995, (sung by Donna Theodore) Through the Music Through the Words I Sing, 1998; actor: (movie) Jesus' Son, 1999, (TV show) Hack, 2003; guest performer Accordion Conv., King of Prussia, 2003; featured in various articles. Recipient citation U.S. Ho. Reps., 1989, Proclamation Mike Martino Day Mayor Ward, Del. County, 1988, Danny Thomas Hon. award St. Jude's Hosp., Del. County, 1973, Mayor's Svc. award Upper Darby, Pa., 1994. Roman Catholic. Avocations: antique cars, dogs. Home: 2530 Stoneybrook Ln Drexel Hill PA 19026-1610 Office Phone: 610-789-5753.

MARTINO, PETER DOMINIC, lawyer, financial software company executive, real estate developer, real estate broker, federal agency administrator, consultant, management consultant; b. NYC, Sept. 21, 1963; s. Rocco Leonard and Barbara Italia (D'Iorio) Martino; m. Manelle Victoria Nuñez, July 31, 2004; children: Elizabeth Marie, Arden Victoria, Willem Ludowyk. BS, U.S. Naval Acad., 1985; postgrad., Georgetown U., 2004—07. Cert. cash mgr.; cert. Treasury profl. Commd. ensign USN, 1985, advanced through grades to lt., 1989, resigned, 1990; with USNR, 1990-99; from v.p. mktg. to exec. v.p., COO XRT, Inc., Wayne, Pa., 1990-93, pres., 1993-98, CEO, 1996-98; pres., CEO XRT-CERG Am., Inc., 1998-2000; exec. v.p. XRT-CERG S.A., Paris, 1998-2000; pres., CEO, chmn., founder CharitEx, Inc., NYC, 2000—01; real estate broker Corcoran Group, NYC, 2001—03; real estate developer, 2001—03; COO dept. homeland security Infrastructure Protection, U.S. Govt. Sr. Exec. Svc., Washington, 2003—04; pres., CEO, founder The Develop. Coun., LLC, Washington, 2004—05; legal rsch. asst. Law Ctr. Georgetown U., 2005; summer law assoc. Morgan Lewis & Bockius, LLP, 2006; assoc. Quinn Emanuel Urquhart Oliver & Hedges, NYC, 2007—. Founder, dir. XRT Europe, Ltd., 1994-98; founder, dir., pres Four Star Software, Inc., Wayne, 1994-98; bd. dirs. Nat. Kidney Found. Delaware Valley; founder internet e-commerce bus. for charitable giving; mem. alternative dispute resolution divsn. Georgetown Law Barristers Coun., 2005-07; mem. Georgetown Jour. Law and Pub. Policy. News editor: Georgetown Law Weekly, 2005. Mem. Kennedy Ctr. for Performing Arts; trustee Annapolis Symphony Orch., 2007—; bd. mem. Md. Hall for the Creative Arts, 2007—; mem. Phoenixville Borough Coun., 1993—94; Rep. committeeman, 1995—97; mem. coun. Nat. Italian Am. Found., 2003—; bd. dir. Nat. Kidney Found. Delaware Valley, 1997—2001, Martino Found., 1998—2003, World Affairs Coun. Phila., 1999—2001; adv. bd. Pres.'s Cir. Naval Acad. Found. 2002—03. Mem. ABA, Federalist Soc. Law and Pub. Policy Studies, Am. Constitution Soc., Cato Inst., Treasury Mgmt. Assn., Naval Acad. Alumni Assn., Naval Acad. Athletic Assn., Naval Acad. Sailing Squadron, Nat. Italian Am. Found. (coun. mem.), N.Y. Athletic Club, Pyramid Club (Phila.), Avalon Yacht Club, Army-Navy Club. Roman Catholic. Avocations: sailing, real estate, fine wine, architecture, study of history/biography. Home: 168 W Lake Dr Annapolis MD 21403 Office Phone: 410-991-5280. Personal E-mail: peter332@gmail.com.

MARTINO, ROBERT SALVATORE, orthopedic surgeon; b. Clarksburg, W.Va., May 31, 1931; s. Leonard L. and Sarafina (Foglia) M.; m. Lenora Cappellanti, May 22, 1954; children: Robert S. Jr., Leslie L. Reckziegel. AB, W.Va. U., 1953, postgrad., 1955-56, BS in Medicine, 1958; MD, Northwestern U., 1960. Diplomate Am. Bd. Orthop. Surgery; lic. Ill., Calif., Ind. Intern Chgo. Wesley, 1960-61; resident dept. orthopaedic surgery Northwestern U., 1961-65, Chgo. Wesley Meml., 1961-62, Am. Legion Hosp. for Crippled Children, 1962-63, Cook County Hosp., Chgo., 1964, 64-65; orthopeadic surgeon Gary, Ind., 1965-67; orthopaedic surgeon Merrillville, Ind., 1967—. Fellow Nat. Found. Infantile Paralysis, 1956, Office of Vocat. Rehab., Hand Surgery, 1965; chief of staff St. Mary Med. Ctr., 1976, chief of surgery, 1974-85; chief of staff Gary Treatment Ctr./Ind. Crippled Children's Svcs., 1974-84; adj. asst. prof. anatomy Ind. U., 1978, clin. asst. prof. orthop. surgery, 1980, emeritus asst. prof. anatomy and cell biology Ind. U., 2003, emeritus clin. asst. prof. orthop. surgery, 2003; mem. Zoning Bd., 1989-90. Chmn. Planning Bd. Town of Dune Acres, 1992-96; bd. dirs. United Steel Workers Union Health Plan, 1994—, St. Mary's Med. Ctr., Hobart, Ind.; com. on Health Care Reform. Capt. infantry US Army, 1953—55, active duty USAR, 1955—58. Fellow ACS (emeritus), Am. Acad. Orthop. Surgery (emeritus); mem. AMA, NRA, Ind. Med. Soc., Ill. Med. Soc., Chgo. Med. Soc., Ill. Orthop. Soc., Ind. Orthop. Soc., Mid-Am. Orthop. Assn., Tri-State Orthop. Soc., Clin. Orthop. Soc. Republican. Roman Catholic. Home: 22 Oak Dr Chesterton IN 46304-1016 Personal E-mail: indorth@aol.com, brutabobm@aol.com.

MARTIN PATTERSON, CONNIE RUTH, retired lawyer; b. Clovis, N.Mex., Sept. 9, 1955; d. Lynn Latimer and Marian Ruth (Pierce) M.; m. Daniel A. Patterson, Nov. 21, 1987; step-children: David Patterson, Dana Patterson. B in Univ. Studies, Ea. N.Mex. U., 1976, MEd, 1977; JD, U. Mo., Kansas City, 1981. Bar: N.Mex. 1981, U.S. Dist. Ct. N.Mex. 1981, Colo. 2002. Asst. dist. atty. State of N.Mex., Farmington, 1981-84; ptnr. Tansey, Rosebrough, Gerding & Strother, PC, Farmington, 1984-93; pvt. practice Connie R. Martin, P.C., Farmington, 1993-94; domestic violence commr. 11th Judicial Dist. Ct., State of N.Mex., 1993-94; with Jeffrey B. Diamond Law Firm, Carlsbad, N. Mex., 1994-96; assoc. Sager, Curran, Sturges and Tepper PC, Las Cruces, N. Mex., 1996-97, Holt & Babington PC, Las Cruces, 1997-2000; ret., 2000. Dep. med. investigator State of N.Mex., Farmington, 1981—84; instr. San Juan Coll., 1987, N.Mex. State U., 1995; spkr. N.Mex. Jud. Edn. Ctr., 1993—94; chair paralegal program adv. com., 1988; adv. com. St. Francis Clin., Presbyn. Med. Svcs., 1994—96; bd. Bar Examiners State of N.Mex., 1989—2005, vice-chair, 1995—97, chair, 1997—99; asst. bar counsel Disciplinary Bd.; mem. profl. adv. com. Meml. Med. Ctr. Found., 1997—2000, trustee, 2000; mem. So. N.Mex. Estate Planning Coun., 1997—2000; mem. character and fitness com. Nat. Conf. Bar Examiners, 2002—03. Bd. dirs., exec. com. San Juan County Econ. Opportunity Coun., Farmington, 1982-83; bd. dirs. Four Corners Substance Abuse Coun., Farmington, 1984, N.Mex. Newspapers, Inc.; chmn. Cmty. Corrections-Intensive Supervision Panel, Farmington, 1987-88; jud. selection com. mem. San Juan County, 1991, Chavez County, 1995; nominating com. Supreme Ct./Ct of Appeals, 1991-96; treas. Ft. Morgan United Meth. Ch., 2001-03, mem. fin. com., 2001-06, chmn. fin. com., 2001-04. Recipient Distinguished Svcs. award for Outstanding Young Woman San Juan County Jaycees, 1984. Mem.: Farmington C. of C. (bd. dirs. 1991—93), San Juan County Bar Assn. (treas. 1985—87, v.p. 1987, pres. 1988), N.Mex. Bar Assn. (asst. new lawyers com. 1986—87, local bar com. 1988, bd. dirs. young lawyers divsn. 1989—91, bd. dirs. elder law sect. 1993—96, peer rev. task force 1994—95, bd. dirs. real property probate and trust sect. 1994—97), Keeshond Club Am. (bd. dirs. 2005—, sweepstakes judge 2006, 2d v.p. 2006—), Rocky Mountain Keeshond Club (bd. dirs. 2004—06). Methodist. Avocations: health, exercise, reading, dog show and therapy dog vol.

MARTINS, ALEX, professional sports team executive; m. Julia Martins; 1 child, Sophia. BSBA, Villanova U., 1986; MBA, U. Ctrl. Fla. Asst. pub. rels. dept. NBA Phila. 76ers, 1986—88; asst. sports info. dir. Georgetown U., 1988—89; dir. publicity/media rels. NBA Orlando Magic, 1989—96, sr. dir. comm., 1996—98, exec. v.p. mktg. and franchise rels., 2005—06, COO, 2006—; sr. v.p. mktg. and branding NBA New Orleans Hornets; v.p. comm. and pub. affairs NFL Cleve. Browns; v.p. sports ventures Tavistock Grp., 2003—05. Former chmn. bd. Magic Action Team Cmty. Fund (now Orlando Magic Youth Fund). Office: Orlando Magic 8701 Maitland Summit Blvd Orlando FL 32810 *

MARTINS, HEITOR MIRANDA, foreign language educator; b. Belo Horizonte, Brazil, July 22, 1933; came to U.S., 1960; s. Joaquim Pedro and Emilia (Miranda) M.; m. Teresomja Alves Pereira, Nov. 1, 1958 (div. 1977); children— Luzia Pereira, Emilia Pereira; m. Marlene Andrade, Jan. 11, 1984 AB, U. Federal de Minas Gerais, 1959; PhD, U. Federal de Minas Gerais, 1962. Instr. U. N.M., Albuquerque, 1960-62; asst. prof. Tulane U., New Orleans, 1962-66, assoc. prof., 1966-68; prof. dept. Spanish and Portuguese Ind. U., Bloomington, 1968—, chmn. dept., 1972-76. Vis. prof. U. Tex., Austin, 1963, Stanford U., 1968. Author: poetry Sirgo nos Cabelos, 1961; essay Manuel de Galhegos, 1964; essays Oswald de Andrade e Outros, 1973; critical anthology Neoclassicismo, 1982; Essays Do Barroco a Guimarães Rosa, 1983; editor: essays Luso-Brazilian Literary Studies. Social Sci. Research Council grantee, 1965; Fulbright-Hays Commn. grantee, 1966; Ford Found. grantee, 1970, 71 Mem. MLA, Renaissance Soc. Am., Am. Comparative Lit. Assn., Am. Assn. for 18th Century Studies. Home: 1316 S Nancy St Bloomington IN 47401-6050 Office: Indiana U Dept Spanish and Portuguese Bloomington IN 47405 E-mail: martins@indiana.edu.

MARTINS, NELSON, physics professor; b. Santos, Brazil, Oct. 18, 1930; s. Aniceto and Angelica Martins; m. Maria Lucia, Jan. 8, 1959 (div. Sept. 1983); children: Flavia, Paulo. BS in Physics, Mackenzie U., São Paulo, Brazil, 1958; D in Physics, Pontifica U., Campinas, Brazil, 1977. Cert. physicist. Dir. engring. Mackenzie U., 1971-73, dir. Exact Sci., 1983-90; gen. dir. Ednl. Found., Barretos, Brazil, 1973-76; chief physics dep. Engring. Sch., Araraquara, Brazil, 1991; chief physics dept. U. Santo Amaro, São Paulo, 1990-92; dir. CCET Ctr. Exact Scis. and Tech., São Paulo, 1992-95. Author: (with others) Electriciy and Magnetism, 1973, Dimensional Analysis, 1980, Dynamics, 1982. Mem. Am. Assn. Physics Tcrhs., Brazil Soc. Physics. Office: Sorocaba Engring Sch Rod Sen Jose Ermirio Moraes Sorocaba 18001970 Brazil Personal E-mail: nelson_martins30@yahoo.com.br.

MARTINS, PETER, ballet master, choreographer, dancer; b. Copenhagen, Oct. 27, 1946; arrived in U.S., 1967, naturalized, 1970; m. Lisa LaCour (div.); 1 child, Nilas; m. Darci Kistler. Pupil of Vera Volkova and Stanley Williams with Royal Danish Ballet. With NYC Ballet, 1967—, tchr., 1975, ballet master, 1981-83, co-ballet master-in-chief, 1983-89, ballet master-in-chief, 1990—. Tchr. Sch. Am. Ballet, NYC, 1975, chmn., 1983—; artistic advisor Pa. Ballet, 1982—; co-founder & artistic dir. NY Choreographic Inst., 2000—; participant, Voices of the Arts Kennedy Ctr. for Performing Arts, Washington, 2006. Mem. Royal Danish Ballet, 1965—67, prin. dancer including Bournonville repertory, 1967, guest artist NYC Ballet, 1967—70, prin. dancer, 1970—83, guest artist regional ballet cos. U.S., guest artist Nat. Ballet Can., Royal Ballet London, Grand Theatre Geneva, Paris Opera, Vienna State Opera, Munich State Opera, London Festival Ballet, Ballet Internat., Royal Danish Ballet, TV appearances in series of Balanchine works, 1974, appeared on PBS Dance in Am. series A Choreographer's Notebook: Stravinsky Piano Ballets by Peter Martins, 1984; choreographer Broadway musicals Dream of the Twins, 1982, On Your Toes, 1982, Song and Dance, 1985, Calcium Light Night, 1977, Tricolore-Pas de Basque sect., 1978, Rossini Pas de Deaux, 1978, ice ballet Tango-Tango, 1978, Dido and Aeneas, 1979, Sonate di Scarlatti, 1979, Eight Easy Pieces, 1980, Lille Suite, 1980, Suite from Histoire du Soldat, 1981, Capricio Italien, 1981, The Magic Flute, 1981, Symphony No. 1, 1981, Delibes Divertissement, 1982, Piano-Rag-Music, 1982, Concerto for Two Solo Pianos, 1982, Waltzes, 1983, Rossini Quartets, 1983, Tango, 1983, A Schubertiad, 1984, Mozart Violin Concerto, 1984, Poulenc Sonata, 1985, La Sylphide, 1985, Valse Triste, 1985, Eight More, 1985, We Are the World, 1985, Eight Miniatures, 1985, Ecstatic Orange, Tanzspiel, 1988, Jazz, 1993, Symphonic Dances, 1994, Barber Violin Concerto, 1994, Mozart Piano Concerto No. 17, 1994, X-Ray, 1995; author (autobiography): Far From Denmark, 1982. Named Knight of Order of Danneborg, Denmark, 1983; recipient Dance Mag. award, 1977, Golden Apple award, Cue, 1977, Merit award, Phila. Art Alliance, 1985, Liberty award, NYC, 1986, H.C. Andersen Ballet prize, Royal Danish Theatre, 1988. Office: NY State Theater NYC Ballet 20 Lincoln Center Plz New York NY 10023-6913 *

MARTINSON, BRADLEY JAMES, lawyer; b. Ortonville, Minn., Oct. 16, 1945; s. Edwin James and Helen Eleanor (Christenson) M.; m. Beth Louise Nelson, June 24, 1967; children: Sara, Timothy. BA, Concordia Coll., Moorhead, Minn., 1967; JD, U. Minn., 1973. Assoc. Robert Hillstrom & Assocs., Mpls., 1973-80; shareholder Hillstrom, Bale & Martinson, Mpls., 1980-85, Martinson, Schwartz & Corey, Mpls., 1985-87, Salmen, Brinkman & Martinson, St. Paul, 1987-90; shareholder, mng. ptnr. Tews, Squires, Martin & Martinson, Mpls., 1990-97; shareholder Law Offices of Bradley J. Martinson, Mpls., 1998—. 1st lt. U.S. Army, 1968-71. Mem. Midland Hills Country Club (pres. 1997-98). Home: 1928 29th Ave NW New Brighton MN 55112-1737 Office: 333 S 7th St Ste 1170 Minneapolis MN 55402 Office Phone: 612-335-9300. Business E-Mail: bmartinson@martinsonlaw.com.

MARTINSON, CONSTANCE FRYE, television personality and producer; b. Boston, Apr. 11, 1932; d. Edward and Rosalind Helen (Sperber) Frye; m. Leslie Herbert Martinson, Sept. 24, 1955; 1 child, Julianna Martinson Carner. BA in English Lit., Wellesley Coll., 1953. Dir. pub. rels. Coro Found., LA, 1974-79; prodr., host KHJ Dimensions, LA, 1979-81, Connie Martinson Talks Books, LA, 1981—. Instr. dept. humanities UCLA, 1981—, bd. dirs. Friends of English; moderator, instr. U. Judaism; celebrity advisor Book Fair-Music Ctr., LA, 1986; advisor, moderator LA Times Festival Books, 1996; TV rep. LA Pub. Libr. LA Cityview, Sta. WNYE-TV. Author: Dramatization of Wellesley After Images, 1974; book editor, columnist: Calif. Press Bur. Syndicate, 1986—, columnist: Beverly Hills Courier, 1997—. Pres. Mayor's Adv. Coun. Volunteerism, LA, 1981—82; chmn. cmty. affairs dept. Town Hall of Calif., LA, 1981—85; bd. dirs. legal def. fund NAACP, LA, 1981—84. Mem.: Nat. Book Critics Assn., PEN, Am. Film Inst., Women in Cable, Jewish TV Network (bd. dirs. 1985—87), Mulholland Tennis Club, Wellesley Coll. Club (pres. 1979—81). Democrat. Jewish. Avocations: tennis, theater, reading. Home and Office: 2288 Coldwater Canyon Dr Beverly Hills CA 90210-1756 Personal E-mail: conniemartinson@qmail.com. Business E-Mail: talksbooks@lycos.com.

MARTINSON, ELMER JAMES, retired surgeon; b. Hinsdale, Ill., Nov. 16, 1917; s. Carl Jerome and Alma Ingebord (Berglin) Martinson; m. Peggy Jo Guy, Nov. 24, 1946; children: Thomas James, Carl John, Bruce Jeffrey, William Jay. BA, Union Coll., Lincoln, Nebr., 1937; MD, Loma Linda U., Calif., 1942; MS in Surgery, U. Minn., 1950. Diplomate Am. Bd. Surgery, 1956. Intern Mpls. Gen. Hosp., 1941—42, resident, 1946—49; surgeon Martinson Clinic, Wayzata, Minn., 1950—92; staff examiner Cancer Detection Ctr. U. Minn., Mpls., 1992—97; med. expert Social Secaurity, Mpls., 1998—2005; ret., 2005. Maj. USAF, 1942—46. Fellow: ACS. Avocations: golf, painting, stamp collecting/philately, gardening. Home: 2799 Pheasant Rd Excelsior MN 55331

MARTINSON, IDA MARIE, retired medical/surgical nurse, physiologist; b. Mentor, Minn., Nov. 8, 1936; d. Oscar and Marvel (Nelson) Sather; m. Paul Varo Martinson, Mar. 31, 1962; children: Anna Marie, Peter. Diploma, St. Luke's Hosp. Sch. Nursing, 1957; BS, U. Minn., 1960, M.N.A., 1962; PhD, U. Ill., Chgo., 1972. Instr. Coll. St. Scholastica and St. Luke's Sch. Nursing, 1957—58, Thornton Jr. Coll., 1967—69; lab. asst. U. Ill. at Med. Ctr., 1970—72; lectr. dept. physiology U. Minn., St. Paul, 1972—82, asst. prof. Sch. Nursing, 1972—74, assoc. prof. rsch., 1974—77, prof., dir. rsch., 1977—82; prof. dept. family health care U. Calif., San Francisco, 1982—2003, chmn. dept., 1982—90. Vis. rsch. prof. Nat. Taiwan U., Def.

Med. Ctr., 1981; vis. prof. nursing Sun Yat-Sen U. Med. Scis., Guang Zhou, China, Ewha Women's U., Seoul, Republic of Korea, Frances Payne Bolton Sch. Nursing, Case Western Res. U., Cleve., 1994—96; chair, prof. dept. health scis. Hong Kong Poly. U., 1996—2000. Author: Mathematics for the Health Science Student, 1977; editor: Home Care for the Dying Child, 1976, Women in Stress, 1979, Women in Health and Illness, 1986, The Child and Family Facing Life Threatening Illness, 1987, Family Nursing, 1989, Home Health Care Nursing, 1989, Home Health Care Nursing, 2d edit., 2002; contbr. chapters to books, articles to profl. jours. Active Am. Cancer Soc. Recipient Book of Yr. award, Am. Jour. Nursing, 1977, 1980, 1987, 1990, Humanitarian award for pediat. nursing, 1993; fellow, Fulbright Found., 1991. Mem.: ANA, Inst. Medicine, Am. Acad. Nursing, Coun. Nurse Rschrs., Sigma Theta Tau, Sigma Xi. Lutheran. Address: 12149 E Movil Lake Rd NE Bemidji MN 56601 *The challenge of quality health care to all of society and the critical role nursing has to play in order to achieve this goal has motivated me throughout my professional life. The richness of talent in this country spurs me on.*

MARTINSON, JACOB CHRISTIAN, JR., academic administrator; b. Menomonie, Wis., Apr. 15, 1933; s. Jacob Christian and Matilda Kate (Wisner) M.; m. Elizabeth Smathers, Apr. 29, 1962; children— Elizabeth Anne, Kirsten Kate. BA, Huntingdon Coll., Ala., 1954, LLD (hon.), 1993; MDiv, Duke U., 1957; DDiv, Vanderbilt U., 1972; grad., Inst. Ednl. Mgmt., Harvard U., 1981. Ordained elder United Methodist Ch. Minister Trinity United Meth. Ch., Lighthouse Point, Fla., 1960-67; sr. minister First United Meth. Ch., Winter Park, Fla., 1967-71; supervising instr. Vanderbilt U. Div. Sch., Nashville, 1971-72; pres. Andrew Coll., Cuthbert, Ga., 1972-76, Brevard Coll., NC, 1976-85, High Point (N.C.) U., 1985—2005, hon. chancellor, 2005—; interim pres. Garrett-Evang. Theol. Sem., Evanston, Ill., 2006. Chmn. bd. dirs. First Union Nat. Bank (now Wachovia), High Point, 1989; lectr. St. Mary's Theol. Soc., U. St. Andrews, Scotland. Chmn. N.C. Friends of Higher Edn., 1986; mem. W.I.H. and Lula E. Pitts Found., Atlanta, 1972-76. Recipient Hickman Preaching award Duke U. Div. Sch.; Glen Slough scholar Vanderbilt U., 1971; hon. fellow Westminster Coll., Oxford, Eng., 1994; Rotary Paul Harris fellow. Mem. Brevard C. of C. (pres. 1979), High Point C. of C. (chmn. 1992), Piedmont Ind. Coll. Assn. (chmn. 1991-93), Carolinas Intercollegiate Athletic Conf. (pres. 1991-93), Phi Theta Kappa. Methodist. Avocation: mountain hiking. Home: 556 Crum Dr Lake Junaluska NC 28745 Office Phone: 828-456-5457. Personal E-mail: jmartinson@bellsouth.net.

MARTINUZZI, LEO SERGIO, JR., banker; b. Newton, Mass., Aug. 1, 1928; s. Leo Sergio and Jessica (Stewart) Martinuzzi; m. Helen Renfrew Gibson, Oct. 26, 1957 (dec. Oct. 1995); children: John James, Georgiana Gibson, Samuel Stewart; m. Sandra Stetson, Nov. 18, 2004. BA, Harvard U., 1950; B.Litt., Oxford U., 1952. With Chase Manhattan Bank, NYC, 1956-81, asst. treas., 1960, asst. v.p. Japanese brs., 1961-64, v.p. Japanese brs., 1964-68, marketing exec. internat. staff, 1968-72, sr. v.p., 1971-81; corporate devel. officer Chase Manhattan Corp., 1972-75, group exec. info. services, 1975-81; chmn. Chase Econometric Assocs. Inc., 1975-80; sr. v.p. strategic planning Squibb Corp., NY, 1981-87, cons., 1988-91. Chmn. Strategic Dimensions, Inc., 1990—; adj. prof. econs. Edison CC, 1993—97. Lt. (j.g.) USNR, 1952—56. Home: 336 Galleon Dr Naples FL 34102-7638

MARTOCCI, LEWIS NICHOLAS, III, writer; b. Forrigga, Italy, July 10, 1960; s. Lewis Nicholas Martocci, Jr. and Maria Laub. AA in World History, Malone Coll. Naval Base Br., Sassabo, Japan, 1988; AA in Specialized Bus. Criminal Justice, Lehigh Valley Coll., Ctr. Valley, Pa., 2005. With USMC, 1978—99; dep. chief field agt. A&M Fugitive Recovery Agy., 2000—05. Author: (poetry books) From Within, 2001, Doodles of the Mind, 2002. Recipient Pres.'s Award for Lit. Excellence, Nat. Authors Registry, 2000. Mem.: Grange. Republican. Presbyterian. Avocations: reading, fishing, music, book collecting, antiques. Home and Office: 722 W Pennsylvania Ave Pen Argyl PA 18072 Office Phone: 610-657-0110. E-mail: max1887@nni.com.

MARTONE, ERIC ANTHONY DOMENIC, history educator; b. Nuremberg, Bavaria, Germany, Sept. 29, 1978; s. Maria and Robert Cordery (Stepfather), Anthony Martone; m. Nicole Martone. BA in History cum laude, Pace U., Pleasantville, NY, 2000; MA in Global History, Iona Coll., New Rochelle, NY, 2003; tchr. cert., Western Conn. State U., Danbury, 2003, MA in European History, 2007; French cert., U. Toronto, Canada, 2006. Cert. provisional educator history/social studies grades 7-12 Conn., 2006. Rsch. analyst Pitney Bowes, Stamford, Conn., 1999—2002; tchr. Enlightenment Sch., Waterbury, 2004; history tchr. John F. Kennedy HS, Waterbury, 2004—. Creative cons. Teacher's Discovery, Auburn Hills, Mich., 2005—; vis. scholar Dickinson Coll., Carlisle, Pa., 2005, U. Mass. Dartmouth, North Dartmouth, 2006. Author: (book) With a Little Help From My German Friend: Leopold II of Belgium and the Berlin Conference, 1884-85, 2003; translator: (drama) The Vampire/Catilina: Two Plays by Alexandre Dumas, 2003; contbr. encys. in field. Named Outstanding History Maj., History Dept., Pace U., 2000; grantee, Freeman Found., Wesleyan U., 2005, NEH, 2005—06; Presdl. scholar, Pace U., 1996—2000, All-American scholar, US Achievement Acad., 1999, All-Academic Team scholar, Tau Kappa Epsilon, 1999. Mem.: Western Soc. for French History, Conn. Educators' Assn., Waterbury Tchrs.' Assn., Nat. Educators' Assn., French Hist. Soc., Societe des Amis d'Alexandre Dumas, Alpha Chi, Pi Gamma Mu, Phi Alpha Theta, Tau Kappa Epsilon. Office: John F Kennedy HS 422 Highland Ave Waterbury CT 06708 Business E-Mail: emartone@waterbury.k12.ct.us.

MARTONE, FREDERICK J., judge; b. Fall River, Mass., 1943; BS, Coll. Holy Cross, 1965; JD, U. Notre Dame, 1972; LLM, Harvard U., 1975. Bar: Mass. 1972, Ariz. 1974, U.S. Dist. Ct. Mass. 1973, U.S. Dist. Ct. Ariz. 1974, U.S. Ct. Appeals (1st cir.) 1973, U.S. Ct. Appeals (9th cir.) 1974, U.S. Supreme Ct. 1977. Law clk. to Hon. Edward F. Hennessey Mass. Supreme Judicial Ct., 1972-73; pvt. practice Phoenix, 1973-85; assoc. presiding judge Superior Ct. Ariz., Maricopa County, judge Phoenix, 1985-92; justice Supreme Ct. Ariz., Phoenix, 1992—2002; U.S. dist. judge Dist. of Ariz., 2002—. Editor notes and comments Notre Dame Law Rev., 1970-72; contbr. articles to profl. jours. Capt. USAF, 1965-69. Mem. Am. Judicature Soc., State Bar Ariz., Horace Rumpole Inn of Ct. Office: US Dist Ct Sandra Day O'Conner US Courthouse 401 W Washington St Spc 62 Ste 526 Phoenix AZ 85003-2158 E-mail: Frederick_Martone@azd.uscourts.gov.

MARTONE, PATRICIA ANN, lawyer; b. Bklyn., Apr. 28, 1947; d. David Andrew and Rita Mary (Dullmeyer) Martone; m. Barbara Ann Rosen, Sept. 2, 2006. BA in Chemistry, NYU, 1968, JD, 1973; MA in Phys. Chemistry, Johns Hopkins U., Balt., 1969. Bar: NY 1974, US Dist. Ct. (so. and ea. dists.) NY 1975, US Ct. Appeals (2d cir.) 1975, US Ct. Appeals (1st cir.) 1981, US Patent and Trademark Office 1983, US Ct. Appeals (fed. cir.) 1984, US Supreme Ct. 1984, US Dist. Ct. (ea. dist.) Mich. 1985, US Dist. Ct. (no. dist.) Calif. 1995, US Dist. Ct. Colo. 2004. Tech. rep. computer timesharing On-Line Sys., Inc., NYC, 1969-70; assoc. Kelley Drye & Warren, NYC, 1973-77, Fish & Neave, NYC, 1977-82, ptnr., 1983—2004, Ropes & Gray LLP, NYC, 2005—. Adj. prof. NYU Sch. Law, 1990—; mem. adv. coun. Engelberg Ctr. Innovation Law & Policy, 1996—; participating atty. Cmty. Law Offices, NYC, 1974—78; atty. Pro Bono Panel US Dist. Ct. (so. dist.) NY, 1982—84; lectr. Practising Law Inst., NYC, 1995—, Aspen Law & Bus., 1990—95, Franklin Pierce Law Sch., 1992—97, Lic. Exec. Soc.; chair, bd. dirs. NY Lawyers for the Pub. Interest, 1996—98, vice chair, 1998—2000, 2002—06, emeritus bd., 2006—. Mng. editor NYU Law Sch. Rev. Law and Social Change, 1972-73; contbr. articles to profl. jours. Bd. mem. Nat. Orgn. Italian Am. Women. Recipient Founder's Day award NYU Sch. Law, 1973, award NY Lawyers for Pub. Interest, 2006; NSF grad. trainee Johns Hopkins U., 1968-69; NYU scholar, 1964-68; fellow Litig. Counsel Am., 2007. Fellow Litigation Counsel of Am.; mem. ABA, Am. Intellectual Property Law Assn., Assn. Bar City NY (mem. environ. law com. 1978-83, trademarks, unfair competition com. 1983-86), Fed. Bar Coun., Fed. Cir. Bar Assn., Copyright Soc., Am. Chem. Soc., Licensing Execs. Soc., NY Intellectual Property Law Assn., Univ. Club. Office: Ropes & Gray LLP 1211 Ave of the Americas Fl 35 New York NY 10036-8704 Office Phone: 212-596-9021. Business E-Mail: patricia.martone@ropesgray.com.

MARTONOSI, ANTHONY NICHOLAS, retired biochemistry professor; b. Szeged, Hungary, Nov. 7, 1928; came to U.S., 1957; s. Antal and Anna (Zsoter) M.; m. Mary Alice Gouvea, May 2, 1959; children: Mary Anne, Anthony, Margaret, Susan. MD, U. Med. Sch., Szeged, 1953. Asst. prof. dept. physiology Med. Sch., Szeged, 1955-57; rsch. fellow Mass. Gen. Hosp., Boston, 1957-59; rsch. assoc. Retina Found., Boston, 1959-62, asst. dir. dept. muscle rsch., 1962-65; assoc. prof. biochemistry St. Louis U. Sch. Medicine, 1965-69, prof., 1969-79; prof. biochemistry SUNY Health Sci. Ctr., Syracuse, 1979-98; ret., 1998. Albert Szent-Gyorgyi prof. U. Med. Sch., Szeged, Hungary, 1994; adj. prof. Kwangju Inst. f Sci. and Tech., Korea, 1995—; vis. scientist dept. biochemistry U. Birmingham, Eng., 1963-64. Author: The Development of Sarcoplasmic Reticulum, 2000; editor: The Enzymes of Biological Membranes, Vols. 1-4, 1976, 2d edit., 1985; Membranes and Transport, Vols. 1-2, 1982; contbr. over 180 articles to profl. jours.; mem. editl. bd. Biochimica et Biophysica Acta, 1988-96. Recipient Established Investigator award Am. Heart Assn., 1961-66; Rsch. grantee USPHS, NIH, 1959-89, NSF, 1963-96, Muscular Dystrophy Assn., 1975-89. Mem. Am. Soc. Biochemists and Molecular Biologists. Roman Catholic. Home: 110 Stanwood Ln Manlius NY 13104-1412

MÁRTONYI, CSABA LÁSZLO, retired ophthalmic photographer; b. Budapest, Hungary, Mar. 23, 1941; came to U.S., 1951; s. Louis Péter and Magda (Gyürky) M.; m. Elnajean Beyst, Sept. 4, 1976; 1 child, Erika Lyn. Cert. retinal angiographer. Chief photographer U. Mich. Photog. Svcs., Ann Arbor, 1967—71; dir. ophthalmic photography, dept. ophthalmology U. Mich., Ann Arbor, 1971—75, instr. dept. ophthalmic photography, 1975—80, asst. prof., 1980—83, assoc. prof., 1983—2000, assoc. prof. emeritus, 2000—. First author: Clinical Slit-Lamp Biomicroscopy and Photo Slit-Lamp Biomicrography, 1985; author, artist exhibit of eye images Landscapes of the Eye, 1993; author sci. exhibits. With U.S. Naval Air Res., 1965-67. Recipient Disting. Tchg. award Joint Commn. on Allied Health Pers. in Ophthalmology, 1997. Fellow Ophthalmic Photographers Soc. (parliamentarian 1988—, chair hon. life membership com. 1991—, fellowship com., pres. 1978-80, chair bd. certification 1978-84, chmn. editl. com. 1987-89, awards including top award for outstanding contbns. to ophthalmic photography), Am. Acad. Ophthalmology (assoc., Honor award 1984, Sr. Honor award 2001). Personal E-mail: martonyi1@msn.com.

MARTORANA, BARBARA JOAN, secondary school educator; b. NYC, Oct. 18, 1942; d. Samuel and Joan Renee (Costello) M. BA, St. John's U., Jamaica, NY, 1970, MS in English Edn., 1972; advanced cert. computers in edn., LI U., 1988, profl. diploma in edn. adminstrn., 1990. Cert. sch. dist. adminstr., sch. adminstr. and supr., tchr. English grades 7-12, NY, Ed.D, Lit. Studies, Hofstra U., Hempstead, NY, 2003. Exec. sec. Am. Petroleum Inst., NYC, 1960-65; exec. asst. to v.p. Goldring, Inc., 1965-67; exec. asst. Rsch. Inst. for Cath. Edn., 1967-69; English tchr. St. Martin of Tours Sch., Amityville, 1970-77, Oceanside Jr. HS, 1977-78, Freeport HS, 1979—. Rec. sec. Freeport Tchr. Ctr. Policy Bd., NY, 1986-89; co-chair Middle States Steering Com., Freeport, 1988-90; chair Freeport H.S. Shared Decision Team, 1992-93, site-based mgmt. team, 2005—; adv. bd. LI Writing Project, Garden City, N.Y., 1993—, co-leader Summer Insts.; adj. prof. literacy studies dept. Hofstra U., NY, 1999—. Co-author: (textbooks) Writing Competency Practice, 1980, rev., expanded edit., 1989, 3d edit., 2007. With Seaford Rep. Club, NY, 1975—. Mem. Nat. Coun. Tchrs. English (conf. on English edn.), NY State English Coun., LI Writing Project. Avocations: reading, writing, travel. Office: Freeport HS 50 S Brookside Ave Freeport NY 11520-3144 Office Phone: 516-867-5300. Personal E-mail: engteech@aol.com.

MARTORE, GRACIA, publishing company executive; b. 1951; m. Joseph Martore; 2 children. BA, Wellesley Coll. Asst. treas. Gannett Co., Inc., Mc Lean, Va., 1985—93, v.p. Treasury Svcs., 1993, head Investor Rels., 1996—98, treas., v.p. Investor Rels., 1998—2001, sr. v.p., 2001—06, CFO, 2003—06, exec. v.p., CFO, 2006—. Office: Gannett Co Inc 7950 Jones Branch Dr Mc Lean VA 22107-0910

MARTORI, JOSEPH PETER, lawyer; b. NYC, Aug. 19, 1941; s. Joseph and Teresa Susan (Fezza) M. BS summa cum laude, NYU, 1964, MBA, 1968; JD cum laude, U. Notre Dame, 1967. Bar: DC 1968, U.S. Dist. Ct. DC 1968, U.S. Dist. Ct. Ariz. 1968, U.S. Ct. Appeals (9th cir.) 1969, U.S. Supreme Ct. 1977. Assoc. Sullivan & Cromwell, NYC, 1967-68, Snell & Wilmer, Phoenix, 1968-69; pres. Goldmar Inc., Phoenix, 1969-71; ptnr. Martori, Meyer, Hendricks & Victor, P.A., Phoenix, 1971-85, Brown & Bain, P.A., Phoenix, 1985-94, chmn. corp. banking & real estate dept., 1994—; chmn. bd. ILX Resorts, Inc., Phoenix. Chmn. ILX Inc., Varsity Clubs Am. Inc. Author: Street Fights, 1987; also articles. Trustee Boys' Clubs Met. Phoenix, 1974-99; consul for Govt. of Italy, State of Ariz., 1987-97. Mem. ABA, State Bar Ariz., Maricopa County Bar Assn., Lawyers Com.for Civil Rights Under Law (trustee 1976—), Phoenix Country Club, Plaza Club (founding bd. govs. 1979-90). Republican. Roman Catholic. Office: ILX Resorts Inc 2111 E Highland Ave Ste 200 Phoenix AZ 85016-4786 Business E-Mail: jmartorisr@IXLresorts.com.

MARTUCCI, VINCENT JAMES, composer, pianist; b. Medford, Mass., Oct. 21, 1954; s. Vincent James Sr. and Grace Alice (Giorgio) M.; m. Elizabeth Nicoll Lawrence, Sept. 20, 1981; children: Katharine Amalia, James Lawrence. Student, Berklee Coll. Music, 1974—75; BA in Music, Colby Coll., 1977; studied with Hal Galper, NYC, 1978—80; studied with Dave Holland, Woodstock, NY, 1982—84; MusM, SUNY Purchase, 2001. Lectr. music Alfred U., NY, 1978—80; registrar, instr. Creative Music Studio, Woodstock, 1980—82; owner, composer, performer Vinnie Martucci Prodns., West Hurley, NY, 1987—; prof. jazz studies SUNY, New Paltz, 1991—. Performer, composer, 1977—; free-lance composer, prodr. recs. and TV, 1986—; cons. synthesis and audio technique, 1985—; mem. U.S. Embassy tour concert series, Bogota, Colombia, 1991; participant conf. Internat. Assn. Jazz Educators, Boston, 1994; instr. music theory and piano Ashokan Fiddle & Dance, 1996—. Composer, performer, corporate spl. events The Dolphins, N.Am., S.Am., Europe, Can., including Newport Jazz at Saratoga, North Sea Jazz Festival, JVC Jazz Festival at Nice, France, The Hague, Holland, Jazz Mecca Festival, Holland, Pori Jazz Festival, Finland, Levercusen Jazz Festival Germany, Brubeck Family Project Tours, and many others, 1987—; performed with Hubert Laws, Nick Brignola, Livingston Taylor, Rory Block, Don Mclean; arranger radio concert series Karl Berger Composer, 1985; co-author, arranger Adventures of Comander Crumbcake - TV series, 1987; composer: (rec.) Malayan Breeze, 1991, network theme redesign package lifetime med. TV, 1988; travel channel, 1990, CNN-Daily Menus, 1991; composer, performer, arranger underscore CBS's As the World Turns, 1993—, NBC's Another World, 1993—, Guiding Light; co-composer: (rec.) Old World/New World, 1991, Ain't I a Woman, 1992; author instrnl. tape series Arranging and Recording Electronic Instruments, 1987—; co-prodr., performer, engr. music for theatrical prodns. McCarter Theatre (1 Tony award), Princeton, Asolo Theatre, Sarasota, Fla.; co-prodr., music for theatre prodn. Having Our Say, 1995—; performer, music dir. numerous live TV and radio performances; music dir. for Eileen Fulton star of As the World Turns, 1990-, music dir. Laurel Massé, 1997-; author: (book series) Introduction to Jazz Keyboards, Introduction to Blues Keyboards, Introduction to Rock Keyboards, 1997. Recipient 2d pl. jazz composition Billboard Mag., 1988. Mem. ASCAP, AFTRA, Am. Fedn. Musicians. Avocations: photography, bicycling, swimming. Home and Office: Vinnie Martucci Prodn 29 Pleasant Ridge Dr West Hurley NY 12491-5441 E-mail: tuchitune@aol.com.

MARTUCCI, WILLIAM CHRISTOPHER, lawyer; b. Asbury Park, NJ, Mar. 10, 1952; s. Frank and Evelyn (Gerrity) M.; children: Daniel Robert, William Sessions, John Andrew, James Christopher, Andrew Michael, Matthew Peter. AB magna cum laude, Rutgers U., 1974; JD with honors, U. Ark., 1977; LLM with honors, Georgetown U., 1981. Bar: Mo. 1977. Law clk. to presiding justice Mo. Ct. Appeals, Kansas City, 1977-78; assoc. Spencer, Fane, Britt & Browne, Kansas City, 1981-86, ptnr., 1987-99, Shook, Hardy & Bacon LLP, Kansas City, 2000—, leader Nat. Employment Litig. & Policy Group. Mem. practice and procedure com. Nat. Labor Relations Act; charter mem. Am. Employment Coun., 1993—; adj. prof. employment law U. Mo. Law Sch., Kansas City, 1988-95, chair minority affairs com. 1992-2002. Editor-in-chief Ark. Law Rev., 1976-77; contbr. articles to profl. jours. Chmn. adv. coun. Urban League Greater Kansas City Tng. Ctr., chmn. mentor program, 1988-2005; mem. Kansas City Civic Coun.; mem. Kansas City Tomorrow Leadership Program, 1992-93; adv. bd. Boys and Girls Club Kansas City, Reviving Baseball in the Inner City. Served to lt. JAGC, USN, 1978-81. Decorated Navy Commendation medal. Mem. ABA (employment and labor rels. com., EEO litigation com.), Mo. Bar Assn. (exec. com. continuing legal edn. 1987—, chair 1993-2000), Kansas City Bar Assn. (chmn. continuing legal edn. 1984-86, mem. exec. com. 1985-98, leadership award 1985, chmn. labor and employment law com. 1988-90, Pres. award 1992, 97), Lawyers Assn. Kansas City (mem. exec. com. young lawyers sect. 1981-82), Kansas City Club, Homestead Country Club, Rotary. Clubs: Kansas City. Republican. Roman Catholic. Office: Shook Hardy and Bacon 2555 Grand Blvd Kansas City MO 64105-2613 Home: 6429 Overbrook Rd Mission Hills KS 66208-1939 Home Phone: 913-403-0555; Office Phone: 816-474-6550. Business E-Mail: wmartucci@shb.com.

MARTY, MARTIN EMIL, theology studies educator; b. West Point, Nebr., Feb. 5, 1928; s. Emil A. and Anne Louise (Wuerdemann) Marty; m. Elsa Schumacher Marty, 1952 (dec. 1981); children: Frances, Joel, John, Peter, James, Micah, Ursula; m. Harriet Lindemann Marty, 1982. MDiv, Concordia Sem., 1952; STM, Luth. Sch. Theology, Chgo., 1954; PhD in Am. Religious and Intellectual History, U. Chgo., 1956; LittD (hon.), Thiel Coll., 1964; LHD (hon.), W.Va. Wesleyan Coll., 1967, Marian Coll., 1967, Providence Coll., 1967; DD (hon.), Muhlenberg Coll., 1967; LittD (hon.), Thomas More Coll., 1968; DD (hon.), Bethany Sem., 1969; LLD (hon.), Keuka Coll., 1972; LHD (hon.), Willamette U., 1974; DD (hon.), Wabash Coll., 1977; LLD (hon.), U. So. Calif., 1977, Valparaiso U., 1978; LHD (hon.), St. Olaf Coll., 1978, De Paul U., 1979; DD (hon.), Christ Sem.-Seminex, 1979, Capital U., 1980; LHD (hon.), Colo. Coll., 1980; DD (hon.), Maryville Coll., 1980, North Park Coll. Sem., 1982; LittD (hon.), Wittenberg U., 1983; LHD, Rosary Coll., 1984; LHD (hon.), Rockford Coll., 1984; DD (hon.), Va. Theol. Sem., 1984; LHD (hon.), Hamilton Coll., 1985, Loyola U., 1986; LLD (hon.), U. Notre Dame, 1987; LHD (hon.), Roanoke Coll., 1987, Mercer U., 1987, Ill. Wesleyan Coll., 1987, Roosevelt U., 1988, Aquinas Coll., 1988; LittD (hon.), Franklin Coll., 1988, U. Nebr., 1993; LHD (hon.), No. Mich. U., 1989, Muskingum Coll., Coe Coll., Lehigh U., 1989, Hebrew Union Coll. and Governors State U., 1990, Whittier Coll., 1991, Calif. Luth. U., 1993; DD (hon.), St. Xavier Coll. and Colgate U., 1990, Mt. Union Coll., 1991, Tex. Luth. Coll., 1991, Aurora U., 1991, Baker U., 1992; LHD (hon.), Luth. U., 1993; LHD, Calif. Luth. U., 1993, Midland Luth. Coll., 1995; DD, Hope Coll., 1993, Northwestern Coll., 1993; LHD (hon.), George Fox Coll., 1994, Drake U., 1994, Centre Coll., 1994, Fontbonne Coll., 1996; DD, Yale U., 1995; LHD (hon.), Otterbein Coll., 1996; ThD (hon.), Lycoming Coll., 1997; LHD, Dana Coll., 1998; LittD (hon.), Alma Coll., 1998, Concordia U. Portland, 1998, Niagara U., 1998; LHD (hon.), Kalamazoo Coll., 1999, William Jewell Coll., 1999; LittD, LittD, Lynchburg Coll., 2003; DD (hon.), Trinity Coll., 2001, Wake Forest U., 2003; DHum (hon.), Westminster Choir Coll., 2001; LHD (hon.), U. Scranton, 2001; DD (hon.), Wake Forest U., 2003; LHD (hon.), Ea. Mennonite U., 2003, Iona Coll.; LLD (hon.), Fordham U., 2005; LHD (hon.), Ill. Coll., 2007, Augsburg Coll., 2007. Ordained to ministry Luth. Ch., 1952. Pastor, Washington, 1950—51; asst. pastor River Forest, Ill., 1952—56; pastor Elk Grove Village, Ill., 1956—63; prof. history of modern Christianity Div. Sch. U. Chgo., 1963—, Fairfax M. Cone Disting. Svc. prof., 1978—98, prof. emeritus, 1998—; assoc. editor Christian Century mag., Chgo., 1956—85, sr. editor, 1985—98; co-editor Ch. History mag., 1963—97. Pres. Park Ridge Ctr. for Study of Health Faith and Ethics, Ill., 1985—89, sr. scholar-in-residence, 1989—98; pres. Am. Inst. for Study of Health, Faith and Ethics, 1985—89; dir. The Pub. Religion Project, 1996—99; interim pres. St. Olaf Coll., 2000—01. Author: A Short History of Christianity, 1959, The New Shape of American Religion, 1959, The Improper Opinion, 1961, The Infidel, 1961, Baptism, 1962, The Hidden Discipline, 1963, Second Chance for American Protestants, 1963, Church Unity and Church Mission, 1964, Varieties of Unbelief, 1964, The Search for a Usable Future, 1969, The Modern Schism, 1969, Righteous Empire, 1970, Protestantism, 1972, You Are Promise, 1973, The Fire We Can Light, 1973, The Pro and Con Book of Religious America, 1975, A Nation of Behavers, 1976, Religion, Awakening and Revolution, 1978, Friendship, 1980, By Way of Response, 1981, The Public Church, 1981, A Cry of Absence, 1983, Health and Medicine in the Lutheran Tradition, 1983, Pilgrims in Their Own Land, 1984, Protestantism in the United States, 1985, Modern American Religion, The Irony of it All, Vol. 1, 1986, An Invitation to American Catholic History, 1986, Religion and Republic, 1987, Modern American Religion: The Noise of Conflict, Vol. 2, 1991, Lutheran Questions, Lutheran Answers, 2007, The Mystery of the Child, 2004; author: (with R. Scott Appleby) The Glory and the Power, 1992; editor (with Jerald C. Brauer): The Unrelieved Paradox: Studies in the Theology of Franz Bibfeldt, 1994; editor: (with Micah Marty) Places Along the Way, 1994; editor: Our Hope for Years to Come, 1995, Modern American Religion, Under God, Indivisible, Vol. 3, 1996, The One and the Many, 1997, The Promise of Winter, 1997, When True Simplicity is Gained, 1998, Politics, Religion, and the Common Good, 2000, Education, Religion, and the Common Good, 2001, Speaking of Trust, 2003, Vision of Utopia, 2003;: When Faiths Collide, 2004, Protestant Voice in American Pluralism, 2004, Martin Luther, 2004; editor: (jours.) Context, 1969—; editor: Second Opinion; sr. editor: The Christian Century, 1956—98; contbr. articles to religious publs. Chmn. bd. regents St. Olaf Coll., 1996—2001, sr. regent, 2002—; dir. The Pub. Religion Project, 1996—2000. Recipient Nat. Medal Humanities, 1997, Alumni medal, U. Chgo., 1998. Fellow: Am. Acad. Political and Social Scis. (Mohandas K. Gandhi Fellow, Mohandas K. Gandhi fellow), Soc. Am. Historians, Am. Acad. Arts and Scis. (dir. fundamentalism project 1988—94); mem.: Am. Antiquarian Soc., Am. Acad. Religion (pres. 1987—88), Am. Cath. Hist. Assn. (pres. 1981), Am. Soc. Ch. History (pres. 1971), Am. Philos. Soc. Lutheran. Personal E-mail: memarty@aol.com.

MARTYL, (MRS. ALEXANDER LANGSDORF JR.), artist; b. St. Louis, Mar. 16, 1917; d. Martin and Aimee (Goldstone) Schweig; m. Alexander Langsdorf, Jr., Dec. 31, 1941; children: Suzanne, Alexandra. AB, Washington U., St. Louis, 1938. Instr. art dept. U. Chgo.; artist in residence Tamarind Inst., U. N.Mex., Albuquerque, 1974 Solo shows include, Calif. Palace of Legion of Honor, 1956, Chgo. Art Inst., 1949, 76, Feingarten Galleries, NYC, Beverly Hills and Chgo., 1961, 62, 63, St. Louis, 1962, Feingarten Gallery, NYC, 1963, LA, 1964, Kovler Gallery, Chgo., 1967, Washington U., St. Louis, 1967, U. Chgo. Oriental Inst. Mus.,

1970, Deson&Zaks Gallery, 1973, Fairweather-Hardin Gallery, 1977, 81, 83, Ill. State Mus., 1978, Fermilab, 1985, 91, Bklyn. Mus., 1986, Oriental Inst. Mus., 1987, Gibbes Art Mus., Charleston, SC, 1988, Fairweather-Hardin Gallery, 1988, Tokyo Internat. Art Expo, 1990, State of Ill. Art Gallery, Chgo., 1990, Expo Navy Pier, Chgo., 1993, Printworks Gallery Ltd., Chgo., 1995, 97, 99, 2002, 04, 07, Navy Pier, Chgo., 2003, 04, Oriental Inst. Mus., Chgo., Martyl: Nature/Artifice Ft. Wayne Mus. Art, 2000; represented in permanent collections Chgo. Art Inst., Pa. Acad. Fine Arts, Ill. State Mus., Bklyn. Mus., DuSable Mus., Chgo., LA County Mus., Whitney Mus. Am. Art, Davenport Mcpl. Mus., Iowa, St. Louis Art Mus., Washington U., U. Ariz., Arnot Gallery, Elmira, NY, Greenville Mus., SC, Nat. Coll. Fine Arts, Hirshhorn Mus. and Sculpture Gallery, Rockford Mus., Ill. Mem. Chgo. Network, Arts Club (Chgo.). Unitarian Universalist. *To be an artist means devoting a lifetime to an intensely difficult activity—one that requires concentration and skill. I've spent my time learning the power of color, line, shape and meaning. I like to think that I have opened out experiences people cannot reveal by themselves.*

MARTYN, EVI, music educator, musician; b. Athens, Greece, Nov. 12, 1941; arrived in U.S., 1965; d. Anastasios and Sophia (Alivizatos) Giannatos; BA, Royal Conservatory Athens, 1959; MA, Royal Conservatory Athens, Greece, 1959; PhD Music, Hochschule fur Musik, Munich, Germany, 1963. Owner, founder Martyn Sch. Music, Los Alamitos, Calif., 1973—, chair keyboard dept., 1973—. Lectr., adjudicator, demonstrator numerous competitions, seminars, workshops etc. Author: Art of Piano Playing, 1988, The Root of Evil, 2005; contbg. author: Hellenic Voice; contbr. articles to profl. mags.; internat. performances include Wigmore Hall, London, Playel Hall, Paris, Merkin Hall, NYC, soloist SW Symphony of Utah, St. George, 2006. Performer at numerous benefit concerts including: D.C. Performing Arts Ctr., 1983, KLON Pub. Radio, Long Beach, Calif., Rotary Club Benefit for Needy, Huntington Beach, Calif., 1985, Hellenic U. Club, Loyola Marymount U., Calif., 1996. Recipient Excellent Artistic Evaluation, Internat. Comm. Agy., Washington, 1980, Award of Merit, Rotary Club of So. Calif., 1986, Knights of Pythias, 1993, The Andreas Sygros Gold medal, Greece Minister of Culture, First prize with gold medal, Royal Conservatory, Athens, 1959. Mem.: Internat. Assn. Music Competitions, Nat. Assn. Music Tchrs., Nat. Guild Piano Tchrs. (Named to Hall of Fame 1989). Avocation: swimming. Office Phone: 714-995-5699. Personal E-mail: evimartyn@aol.com.

MARTZ, CLYDE OLLEN, lawyer, educator; b. Lincoln, Nebr., Aug. 14, 1920; s. Clyde O. and Elizabeth Mary (Anderson) M.; m. Ann Spieker, May 29, 1947; children: Robert Graham, Nancy. AB, U. Nebr., 1941; LLB, Harvard U., 1947. Bar: Colo. 1948, U.S. Ct. Appeals (D.C. cir.) 1968, U.S. Supreme Ct. 1969. Prof. U. Colo., Boulder, 1947-58, 60-62; jud. adminstr. State of Colo., Denver, 1959-60; ptnr. Davis, Graham & Stubbs, Denver, 1962-67, 69-80, 81-87, of counsel, 1988—; asst. atty. gen. U.S. Dept. Justice, Washington, 1967-69; solicitor U.S Dept. Interior, Washington, 1980-81; exec. dir. dept. natural resources State of Colo., 1987. Adj. prof. U. Denver, 1961-79, U. Colo., Boulder, 1988-96; cons. Pres. Materials Policy Commn., 1951; mem. Colo. Adv. Bd. Bur. Land Mgmt., 1967-69; bd. dirs., adv. bd. Natural Resources Law Ctr., 1982-2003. Author: Cases and Materials on Natural Resources Law, 1951, Water for Mushrooming Populations, 1954; co-author: American Law of Property, 1953, Water and Water Rights, 1963; editor, co-author: American Law of Mining, 1960. Co-chmn. Jud. Reorganization Commn., 1961-63; elder Presbyn. Ch., Boulder; pres. Rocky Mountain Mineral Law Found., 1961-62, others. Comdr. USN, 1942-58, PTO, with Res. Decorated Silver Star, Bronze Star, Letter of Commendation, Disting. Svc. award; honored by creation of Clyde O. Martz Natural Resources Scholarship Fund, 2002. Mem. ABA (chmn. natural resources sect. 1985-86), Fed. Bar Assn., Am. Health Lawyers Assn., Colo. Bar Assn. (chmn. water sect. 1957, chmn. mineral sect. 1961, award of merit 1962), Nat. Mining Assn. (Disting. Svc. award 1997), Order of Coif, Phi Beta Kappa. Democrat. Avocations: horticulture, woodworking, mountain climbing, skiing. Office: Davis Graham & Stubbs PO Box 185 Denver CO 80201-0185 Home: 970 Aurora Ave Apt A101 Boulder CO 80302-7239

MARTZ, GARY R., lawyer; BA, U. Toledo, 1979; JD, Ohio State U., 1982. Bar: Ohio 1982. Ptnr. Baker & Hostetler, LLP, 1982—2001; sr. v.p., gen. counsel, sec. Greif, Inc., 2002—; pres. Soterra LLC, 2005—. Office: Greif Inc 425 Winter Rd Delaware OH 43015 Office Phone: 740-549-6188. E-mail: garymartz@greif.com.

MARTZ, MIKE, former professional football coach; b. Sioux Falls, SD, May 13, 1951; BS summa cum laude, Fresno State. Asst. coach Los Angeles Rams, 1992—99, Washington Redskins, 1997-98; offensive coord. St. Louis Rams, 1999—2000, head coach, 2000—05; offensive coord. Detroit Lions, 2006—. Office: Detroit Lions Ford Field Ste 200 2000 Brush St Detroit MI 48226

MARUOKA, JO ANN ELIZABETH, retired information systems manager; b. Monrovia, Calif., Jan. 1, 1945; d. John Constantine and Pearl (Macovei) Gotsinas; m. Lester Hideo Maruoka, Nov. 8, 1973 (div. Aug. 1992); 1 child, John Nicholas Reyes-Burke; stepchildren: Les Scott Kaleohano, Lee Stuart Keola. BA with honors, UCLA, 1966; MBA, U. Hawaii, 1971. Office mgr. and asst. R. Wenkam, Photographer, Honolulu, 1966-69; computer mgmt. intern and sys. analyst Army Computer Sys. Command, Honolulu, 1969-78; reservations mgr. Hale Koa Hotel, Honolulu, 1978-79; equal employment opportunity specialist U.S. Army Pacific Hdqs., Honolulu, 1979-80, computer specialist, 1980-87, supervisory info. sys. mgr., chief info. tech. plans and programs, 1987-2001; ret., 2001. Bd. dirs. High Performance Computing and Comm. Coun., Tiverton, RI; Pacific v.p. Fedn. Govt. Info. Processing Couns., Washington, 1992-95. Active Nat. and Hawaii Women's Polit. Caucus, Honolulu, 1987—; pres. Fed. Women's Coun. Hawaii, Honolulu, 1976-77, advisor, 1977—. Recipient Svc. award Fed. Women's Coun. Hawaii, 1986, EEO Excellence award Sec. of Army, 1989, Pacific Fed. Mgr. award Honolulu-Pacific Fed. Exec. Bd., 1990, Info. Resources Mgmt. Interagy. Com. on Info. Resources Mgmt., 1991, Lead Dog Leadership award Fedn. Govt. Info. Processing Couns., 1993; named One of Fed. 100 (Execs.) of Yr., Fed. Computer Week, 1996. Mem. AAUW, Hawaii State LWV (officer 2003-05, dir. 2005-), NAFE, Nat. Women's Polit. Caucus, Armed Forces Comm.-Electronics Assn. (Hawaii chpt., Internat. award for Info. Resources Mgmt. Excellence 1992), Assn. US Army (Pacific Fed. Mgr. award 1990), Federally Employed Women (advisor Aloha and Rainbow chpts. 1977—), Army Signal Corps Regtl. Assn. (Bronze Order of Mercury 1997, Silver Order of Mercury, 2001), Hawaii Intergovt. Info. Processing Coun. (pres. 1988-89, Svc. award 1989), Beta Gamma Sigma. Avocations: travel, reading, tai chi, theater. Personal E-mail: maruokaj@hawaii.rr.com.

MARUPUDI, SAMBASIVA RAO, surgeon, educator; b. Chintalapudi, India, July 1, 1952; arrived in US, 1976; s. Venkateswarlu and Nagendramma (Gaddipati) M.; m. Usha Nandipati, Mar. 25, 1976; children: Neena, Neelima. MB, BS, Guntur Med. Coll., India, 1974. Diplomate Am. Bd. Surgery, Am. Bd. Colon and Rectal Surgery. Rotating internship St. Clare's Hosp., Schenectady, NY, 1976-77; resident in gen. surgery St. Agnes Hosp., Balt., 1977-78, Franklin Sq. Hosp., Balt., 1978-82; fellow in colon and rectal surgery U. Tex. Health Scis. Ctr., Houston, 1982-83; pvt. practice Amarillo, Tex., 1983—. Clin. asst. prof. dept. surgery Tex. Tech. U. Health Scis. Ctr., Amarillo, 1984—. Fellow ACS, Am. Soc. Colon and Rectal Surgeons, Internat. Coll. Surgeons; mem. AMA, Tex. Med. Assn., Potter-Randall County Med. Soc. (past pres.), Tex. Soc. Colon and Rectal Surgeons (past pres.). Republican. Hindu. Office: 800 Quail Creek Dr # 103 Amarillo TX 79124-1634 Office Phone: 806-358-7911. Personal E-mail: smarupudi@aol.com, drmarupudi@hotmail.com.

MARUYAMA, MAGOROH, business educator, researcher, consultant; b. Tokyo, Apr. 2, 1929; came to U.S., 1950; s. Shinsaku and Toyoko (Takashima) M.; m. Pierrette Duriez, Apr. 1966 (div. 1974); 1 child, Yukon; m. Kuniko Sakakibara, July 28, 1976; 1 child, Yuki. BA in Math., U. Calif., Berkeley, 1951; postgrad., U. Munich, U. Heidelberg, Fed. Republic of Germany, 1954-55, U. Copenhagen, 1955-57; PhD, U. Lund, Sweden, 1959. Asst. prof. human devel. U. Calif., Berkeley, 1960-62; rsch. assoc. psychology Stanford U., Calif., 1962-64; assoc. prof. psychology San Francisco State U., 1965-70; prof. computer sci. Antioch Coll., 1971-72; prof. systems sci. Portland (Oreg.) State U., 1973-76; vis. prof. anthropology and architecture U. Ill., Urbana, 1976-77; vis. prof. anthropology U. Uppsala, Sweden, 1982; vis. prof. mgmt. UCLA, 1983, Nat. U., Singapore, 1983-84; vis. prof. bus. administrn. U. Hawaii, Honolulu, 1984-86; prof. internat. bus. Aoyama Gakuin U., Tokyo, 1987-96, Aomori (Japan) Koritsu Daigaku, 1996—. Vis. prof. U. Oreg., U. Montpellier, France, 1986; cons. U.S. Dept. Commerce 1971, Can. Fed. Ministry Urban Affairs, 1974, NASA, 1975, Monsanto Chems., 1980, Volvo, Sweden, 1982, Fed. Motors of Indonesia, 1984, Technopolises Japan, 1984, MITI of Japan, 1985, Fujitsu, Japan, 1985, Hakuhodo, Japan, 1985, Gadelius, Sweden, 1988, Michelin, France, 1989, NEC, Japan, 1989-90, C. Itoh, Japan, 1990, OECD, France, 1990, Ministry of Rsch. and Tech., France, 1992. Author: The Second Cybernetics, 1963, Mindscapes and Science Theories, 1980, Mindscapes in Management, 1994, Heterogram Analysis, 1999, Interactive Heterogeneity, 2003. Sgt. USMC, 1952-54. Grantee NSF, NIMH, 1965-76. Fellow AAAS, APA; mem. Acad. Mgmt., Internat. Sociol. Assn., Sigma Xi, Pi Mu Epsilon Avocations: architecture, art design, music composition theory. Office Phone: 858-452-3826. Office Fax: 858-452-3826. Personal E-mail: kuniko_maruyama@sbcglobal.net.

MARVEL, JONATHAN J., architect; BA in Fine Arts, Dartmouth Coll., Hanover, NH, 1982; MArch, Harvard Grad. Sch. Design, Cambridge, Mass., 1986. With Richard Meier + Ptnrs.; pvt. practice arch.; prin. Rogers Marvel Archs., PLLC, NYC, 1992—. Faculty mem. architecture Parsons Sch. Design; archtl. cons. NY Pub. Libr. Sys. Mem. preservation com. Mcpl. Art Soc.; mem. streetscape com. NYC Art Commn.; mem. architecture, planning and design panel NY State Coun. on Arts. Office: Rogers Marvel Archs PLLC 145 Hudson St 3rd Fl New York NY 10013 Office Phone: 212-941-6718. Office Fax: 212-941-7573. *

MARVEL, L. PAIGE, federal judge; b. Easton, Md., Dec. 6, 1949; d. E. Warner Marvel and Louise H. Harrison; m. Robert H. Dyer, Jr., Aug. 9, 1975; children: Alex W. Dyer, Kelly E. Dyer. BA magna cum laude, Notre Dame Coll., 1971; JD with honors, U. Md., 1974. Bar: Md. 1974, US Dist. Ct. Md. 1974, US Tax Ct. 1975, US Ct. Appeals (4th cir.) 1977, US Supreme Ct. 1980, US Ct. Claims 1981, DC 1985. Assoc. Garbis & Schwait, P.A., Balt., 1974-76, shareholder, 1976-85, Garbis, Marvel & Junghans, P.A., Balt., 1985-86; mem. Melnicove, Kaufman, Weiner, Smouse & Garbis, P.A., Balt., 1986-88; ptnr. Venable, Baetjer and Howard LLP, Balt., 1988-98; judge US Tax Ct., Washington, 1998—. Mem. U. Md. Law Sch. Bd. Vis., 1995—2001; mem. adv. com. U.S. Dist. Ct. Md., 1991—93; mem. Commr.'s Rev. Panel on IRS Integrity, 1989—91. Co-editor procedure dept. Jour. Taxation, 1989-98; contbr. chpts. to books, articles to profl. jours. Active Women's Law Ctr., 1974-85, Md. Dept. Econ. and Cmty. Devel. Adv. Com., 1978-80; trustee Loyola-Notre Dame Libr., Inc., 1996-2003. Recipient Recognition award Balt. Is Best Prog., 1981, MSBA Taxation sect.'s Tax Excellence award, 2002, Pres. medal Coll. Notre Dame, 2006; named One of Md.'s Top 100 Women, The Daily Record, 1998. Fellow Am. Bar Found., Md. Bar Found., Am. Coll. Tax Counsel (regent 1995-98); mem. ABA (sect. taxation coun. dir. 1989-92, vice-chair com. ops. 1993-95, Disting. Svc. award, Jules Ritholz award 2004), Am. Law Inst. (adv. restatement of law third, law governing lawyers), Md. Bar Assn. (chmn. taxation sect. 1982-83, bd. dirs. 1988-90, 96-98, Disting. Svc. award), Balt. Bar Assn. (at-large exec. coun.), Am. Tax Policy Inst. (trustee 1997-98), Serjeant's Inn. Avocations: golf, music, travel. Office: US Tax Ct 400 2nd St NW Washington DC 20217-0001 Home Phone: 410-296-3851; Office Phone: 202-521-0740.

MARVEL, THOMAS STAHL, architect; b. Newburgh, NY, Mar. 15, 1935; s. Gordon Simis and Madelyn Emigh (Jova) M.; m. Lucilla Wellington Fuller, Apr. 19, 1958; children— Deacon Simis, Jonathan Jova, Thomas Stahl AB, Dartmouth Coll., Hanover, NH, 1956; MArch, Harvard U., Cambridge, Mass., 1962. Registered architect, NC, PR, Mass., NY. Designer Synergetics, Inc., Raleigh, NC, 1958; designer IBEC Housing, NYC, 1959; ptnr., architect Torres-Beauchamp-Marvel, San Juan, 1960-85, Marvel-Flores-Cobian, San Juan, 1985-97; ptnr. Thomas S. Marvel Architects, San Juan, 1997—. Prof. Sch. Architecture, U. PR, Rio Piedras, 1967-89. Author: Antonin Nechodoma, Architect, 1994; co-author: Parish Churches of Puerto Rico, 1984. Works include Am. Embassy, Guatemala, 1973, U.S. Courthouse and Fed. Office Bldg., V.I., 1976, City Hall, Bayamon, P.R., 1978, Mcpl. Baseball Stadium, Bayamon, 1975, Am. Embassy, Costa Rica, 1986. Bd. dirs. St. John's Sch., San Juan, 1976-93. Recipient 1st award for regional coll. design U. PR, Utuado, 1983; Harvard Grad. Sch. Design Julia Amory Appleton travelling fellow, 1962, Henry Klumb prize, 1991. Fellow AIA (bd. dirs. 1993-96, Design award for Fla. Caribbean region 1981, 84-85, 90-91); mem. PR Coll. Architects, Acad. Arts and Scis. Clubs: Harvard (NYC). Roman Catholic. Home: 450 Ave De La Constitucion San Juan PR 00915-3315 Office: Marvel & Marchand Architects 161 Calle San Jorge Santurce San Juan PR 00911-2018 Office Phone: 787-289-9494. Business E-Mail: tsmarvel@marvelarch.com.

MARVENTANO, DAVID, engineering and construction management company executive; B, SUNY, Oswego; law degree, Union U., Albany, NY. With Staff of Assemblyman Michael F. Nozzolio, Albany; with legis. counsel's office Staff of Assembly Minority Leader Clarence Rappleyea; v.p., sr. dir. govt. affairs Securities Industry Assn.; leadership position Staff of US Rep. Bill Paxon, Staff of US Rep. Billy Tauzin; staff dir. Energy & Commerce Com. US House Reps.; sr. v.p. govt. rels. Fluor Corp., 2003—. Office: Fluor Corp 403 E Capitol St SE Washington DC 20003 Office Phone: 202-548-5800. Office Fax: 202-548-5810. *

MARVIN, CHARLES ARTHUR, law educator; b. July 14, 1942; s. Burton Wright and Margaret Fiske (Medlar) Marvin; m. Elizabeth Maureen Woodrow, July 4, 1970 (div. July 1987); children: Colin, Kristin; m. Elizabeth Dale Wilson, Mar. 20, 1999. BA, U. Kans., Lawrence, 1964; postgrad., U. Toulouse, France, 1964-65; JD, U. Chgo., 1968, M of Comparative Law, 1970. Bar: Ill. 1969. Legal intern EEC, Brussels, 1970; lectr. law U. Kent, Canterbury, England, 1970-71; asst. prof. law Laval U., Quebec City, Que., Canada, 1971-73; legal adv. Constnl., internat. and adminstrv. law sect. Can. Dept. Justice, Ottawa, Ont., 1973-76, dir. Adminstrv. Law Reform Project, 1983-85; assoc. prof. law U. Man., Winnipeg, Canada, 1976-77; dir. adminstrv. law project Law Reform Commn., Ottawa, 1977-80; prof. law Villanova U., Pa., 1980-83, Ga. State U., 1985—, assoc. dean, 1987-89. Legal advisor on adminstrv. code revision Govt. of Kazakhstan, 1993; law faculty devel. adviser, Bulgaria, 93; dir. internat. human rights law summer program Regent U. Sch. Law., 1998; USIS lectr., Ivory Coast, 98; Fulbright prof. Riga Grad. Sch. Law, Latvia, 2000—03; vis. prof. law Vytautas Magnus U., Lithuania, 2004—. Fulbright scholar, U. Toulouse, 1964—65, Summerfield scholar, U. Kans., 1961—64, Ford Found. Comparative Law fellow, 1968—70. Fellow: Am. Bar Found.; mem.: ABA, Can. Coun. Internat. Law, Internat. Law Assn., Internat. Bar Assn., Am. Fgn. Law Assn., Am. Soc. Internat. Law, Chgo. Bar Assn., Ill. Bar Assn., Phi Beta Kappa, Phi Delta Phi, Phi Beta Delta, Omicron Delta Kappa. Office: Ga State U Coll Law PO Box 4037 Atlanta GA 30302-4037 Office Phone: 404-651-2436. Business E-Mail: cmarvin@gsu.edu.

MARVIN, CHARLES RODNEY, JR., lawyer; b. Elizabeth, NJ, Feb. 26, 1953; s. Charles Rodney and Doris Marie (Richards) Marvin; m. Carol Ann Welteroth, Aug. 30, 1975 (dec.); children: Kathryn, Kristin, Cynthia, Gregory; m. Nancy Agnes Ruggiero, Mar. 24, 2001; 1 stepchild, Susanna Myirski. BA in Econs., Mich. State U., 1975; JD, Boston U., 1978; LLM in Mil. Law, Judge Advocate Gen. Sch., 1987; LLM in Govt. Contracts, George Washington U., 1995. Bar: N.J. 1982, U.S. Dist. Ct. N.J. 1982, U.S. Ct. Mil. Appeals 1982, U.S. Ct. Appeals (fed. cir.) 1994, D.C. 1996, U.S. Ct. Fed. Claims 1996. Commd. 2nd lt. U.S. Army, 1975, advanced through grades to major, 1994, nuclear missile officer Schwaebisch Gmund, Germany, 1979-82, mil. prosecutor Fort Sill, Okla., 1983-86; sr. def. counsel U.S. Army Trial Def. Svc., Ft. Polk, La., 1987-89; trial counsel, chief protest br. U.S. Army Contract Appeals Divsn., Arlington, Va., 1990-94; ptnr., gov. contracts litig. Venable LLP (formerly Venable, Baetjer, Howard & Civiletti), Washington, 1994—. Mem. ABA (vice-chair, bid protest com., pub. contract law sect. 1992-93), FBA, Bd. Contract Appeals Bar Assn. (bd. govs. 1993-96), Fed. Cir. Bar Assn., John Carroll Soc., Nat. Contract Mgmt. Assn., Bishop McNamara High School (bd. dirs.), Forestville, MD. Roman Catholic. Office: Venable LLP 575 7th St Washington DC 20004-1601 Office Phone: 202-344-4963. Office Fax: 202-344-8300.

MARVIN, DAVID EDWARD SHREVE, lawyer; b. Jan. 6, 1950; s. George Charles Marvin and Shirley Mae (Martin) Schaible; m. Mary Anne Kennedy, Sept. 16, 1972; 1 child, John. BS cum laude, Mich. State U., East Lansing, 1972; JD cum laude, Wayne State U., Detroit, 1976. Bar: Mich. 1976, U.S. Dist. Ct. (ea. dist.) Mich. 1976, U.S. Dist. Ct. (we. dist.) Mich. 1978, U.S. Ct. Appeals (7th cir.) 1977, U.S. Ct. Appeals (6th cir.) 1979, U.S. Supreme Ct. 1979, U.S. Ct. Appeals (D.C. cir.) 1982, D.C. 1982. Asst. mgr. Alta Supply Co., Lansing, 1972-73; rsch. asst. Wayne State U., Detroit, fall 1975; jud. intern U.S. Dist. Ct., Detroit, summer 1975; shareholder Fraser Trebilcock Davis & Dunlap, P.C., Lansing, 1976—, v.p., 1997—2005, also bd. dirs. Pres. Red Rock Prodns., Inc., 1990-94; lectr. Inst. CLE, 1989; mem. qualifications rev. com. U.S. Dist. Ct. (we. dist.) Mich., 2001—. Exec. editor Wayne Law Rev., 1975-76; contbr. articles to law jours. Commr. Mich. Solar Resource Adv. Panel, Lansing, 1978-81, Mich. Commn. Profl. and Occupl. Licensure, 1981-83; chmn. Ingham County Energy Commn., Mason, Mich., 1978-80 (state bar rep. assembly 1985-88); dir., corp. sec. Friends Mich. Hist. Ctr., Inc., 1988-92; treas. Lansing Lawyer Referral Svc., 1981; state del. Nat. Solar Congress, Washington, 1978; hearing officer City of East Lansing, 1985; Tri-County Coun. of Bar Leaders (chmn. 1986); bd. dirs. East Lansing Edn. Found., 1990-92, Impression Five Sci. Mus., 1991-97; regional fin. chmn. Abraham for U.S. Senate, 1993-94, Abraham Senate 2000, 1995-2000; mem. transition team, Gov. Engler, 2000—03, Atty. Gen. Cox, 2002-03; exec. bd. chief Okemos coun. Boy Scouts Am., 1996—, pres., 2001-03. Recipient Disting. Vol. award Tri-County Voluntary Action Ctr., 1990, Gov.'s Minuteman award, 1990, John W. Cummiskey award State Bar Mich., 1990, George Washington Honor medal Freedoms Found., 1990; named Outstandin Young Man Am., 1984, The Outstanding Young Lawyer in Mich., 1985-86, Small Bus. Adv. Yr., C. of C., 1991, Silver Beaver award Boy Scouts Am., 2003, Disting. Citizen, Boy Scouts Am., 2005; Wm. D. Traitel scholar, 1975. Fellow ABA, Am. Bar Found., Mich. State Bar Found. (life); mem. ABA, State Bar Mich. (com. chmn., sect. coun. 1982—, state chmn. 1988-89), Energy Bar Assn., Mich. Soc. Assoc. Execs., Energy Bar Assn., Ingham County Bar Assn. (pres. 1985-86), Pro Bono Lawyers Svc. (pres. 1982-83), Lansing Regional C. of C. (v.p. 1987), Mich. Audubon Soc. (bd. dirs. 1991-93), Mich. State Univ. Alumni Assn. (nat. bd. dirs. 1992—), State Capital Law Firm Group (nat. bd. dirs. 1989—, chmn. com. Can. 1990-93, chair pub. utility, energy and comm. sect. 1994—, nat. sec. 1996-97, vice-chmn. 1997-98, chmn. 1998-99), Downtown Coaches Club (bd. dirs., pres. 1987), Nat. Resource Ctr. on State Laws and Regulations (nat. bd. dirs. 1993-99, chmn. 1998-99), Mich. State U. Pres.'s Club, Rotary (bd. dirs. 1995-97, pres. 2004-05, Paul Harris fellow), Phi Alpha Delta, Phi Eta Sigma, Theta Delta Chi (pres. 1972). Republican. Home: 1959 Groton Way East Lansing MI 48823-1347 Office: Fraser Trebilcock Davis & Dunlap PC Boji Tower Fl 10 124 West Allegan Street Lansing MI 48933 Office Phone: 517-377-0830. Business E-Mail: dmarvin@fraserlawfirm.com.

MARVIN, LAURA LYNN, art educator; b. Balt., Jan. 30, 1975; d. Donald Elbert and Esther Mae Head; m. Brian Marvin, July 6, 2002 (div. Mar. 4, 2006); 1 child, Kyle Everett. Assoc., Balt. County C.C., 1996; Bachelors, Towson U., 2002; Masters, Goucher Coll., Balt., 2002. Cert. elem., reading tchr. Md. Art/tech. tchr. Colgate Elem. Sch., Balt. County Pub. Schs., 2002—. Mentor tchr. Balt. County Pub. Schs., 2005—06. Meml. scholarship, Vietnam Vets. of Am. Chpt. 451, 1997. Mem.: NEA (life), Tchrs. Assn. of Balt. County (life), Md. State Tchrs. Assn. (life). Avocations: painting, drawing, decorating, sculpting. Home Phone: 410-288-2662; Office Phone: 410-887-7010.

MARVIN, MONICA LOUISE WOLF, lawyer; b. San Francisco, Feb. 3, 1947; d. Andrew John and Hazel Louise Wolf; children: Brett Lewis, Elizabeth Louise. Student, Pacific U., 1964—66, Sonoma State U., 1966—67; BA in Psychology, Chico State U., 1969; JD, Empire Coll., 1982. Bar: Calif. 1982, U.S. Dist. Ct. Calif. 1982, D.C. Bar Assn. Assoc. Fitzgerald Fitzgerald and Gowen, Santa Rosa, Calif., 1982—83, Gowen and Marvin, Santa Rosa, 1983—85, Rodeno Robertson & Assocs., Napa, Calif., 1985—86; pvt. practice St Helena, Calif., 1986—2004; of counsel Herdell & Yost LLP, 2000—04; sr. cons., counsel Brazile & Assocs. LLC, Washington, 2004—07; gen. coun. Pacific U., Forest Grove, Oreg., 2007—. Judge pro tempore Napa County Consol. Cts., Small Claims Divsn., 1991-04. Bd. dirs., v.p. Cmty. Resources for Children, Napa, 1991-94; mem. Napa County Commn. on Children, Youth and Families, 1994-97; mem. Napa County Dem. Ctrl. Com., 1994-98; mem. adv. bd. Napa County Vol. Ctr. Ombudsman Program, 1994-95; founder, chair St. Helena C. of C. Jumelage Com., Sister Chamber affiliation with Libourne C. of C. and Industry, France. Mem. State Bar Calif., Napa County Bar Assn. (bd. dirs. 1982-04), D.C. Bar Assn., Napa Women Lawyers (past pres., sec. 1987-92). Office: Pacific Univ 2043 College Way Forest Grove OR 97116 Personal E-mail: mwmarvin@comcast.net.

MARWEDEL, WARREN JOHN, lawyer; b. Chgo., July 3, 1944; s. August Frank and Eleanor (Wolgamot) M.; m. Marilyn Baran, Apr. 12, 1975. BS in Marine Engring., U.S. Merchant Marine Acad., 1966; JD, Loyola U., Chgo., 1972. Bar: Ill. 1972, U.S. Dist. Ct. (no. dist.) Ill. 1972, U.S. Supreme Ct. 1974. Pres. Marwedel Minichello & Reeb, P.C., Chgo. With U.S. Merchant Marines, 1966-70. Mem. ABA (Ho. of Dels. 1989-96), Ill. Bar Assn., Chgo. Bar Assn., Maritime Law Assn.(1st v.p.), Propeller Club (Chgo. pres. 1982). Avocations: boating, reading, history. Office: Marwedel Minichello & Reeb PC President 10 S Riverside Plz Ste 720 Chicago IL 60606-3708 Office Phone: 312-902-1600. Personal E-mail: wjmmmandr@aol.com. Business E-Mail: wmarwedel@mmr-law.com.

MARX, ANTHONY W., academic administrator; b. NYC, Feb. 28, 1959; s. Peter and Marion E. (Mankin) M.; m. Karen Barkey, Sept. 7, 1993; children: Joshua, Anna-Claire. Student, Wesleyan U., Middletown, Conn., 1977-79; BA, Yale U., 1981; MPA, Princeton U., 1986, MA, 1987, PhD, 1990. Adminstrv. aide to the pres. U. Pa., Phila., 1981-84; cons. SACHED Trust, Johannesburg, 1984, 86; vis. scholar Community Agy. for Social Enquiry, Johannesburg, 1988, 90; prof. polit. sci. Columbia U., NYC, 1990—2003; pres. Amherst Coll., 2003—. Rsch. asst. Ctr. for Ednl. Rsch. and Devel., Santiago, Chile, 1985; cons. UNDP, N.Y.C., 1991; vis. scholar Ctr. for Afro-Asian Studies, Rio de Janeiro, Brazil, 1993. Author: Lessons of Struggle, 1992, Making Race and Nation: A Comparison of the United States, South Africa and Brazil, 1998 (Ralph J. Bunche award Am. Polit.

Sci. Assn., 1999, Barrington Moore prize Am. Sociol. Assn., 2000), Faith in Nation: Exclusionary Origins of Nationalism, 2003; contbr. articles to profl. jours. Trustee, treas. Fund for Edn. in South Africa, N.Y.C., 1991—94. Grantee J. D. and C.T. MacArthur Found., Chgo., 1989-90, Social Sci. Rsch. Coun., N.Y.C., 1992-93, U.S. Inst. Peace, Washington, 1992-93; named fellow H.F. Guggenheim Found., N.Y.C., 1994.; John Simon Guggenheim fellow, 1997. Office: Office of Pres 103 Converse Hall PO Box 5000 Amherst MA 01002-5000 Office Phone: 413-542-2234. E-mail: marx@amherst.edu.

MARX, DARRELYN MADONNA, music and drama educator; b. Sauk Center, Minn., Apr. 19, 1951; d. Darrell and Jeanne Brawders; m. Kenneth Robert Marx, Apr. 2, 1991. BS in Edn., Speech/Theatre and Vocal Music, Minn. State U., Moorhead, 1974; MFA in Theatre, U. Ill., Champaign/Urbana, 1985. English, vocal music and drama instr. R.D. Parker Collegiate, Thompson, Man., Canada, 1974—82; grad. asst. U. Ill., Champaign/Urbana, 1982—85; vocal music and drama instr. New Trier H.S., Winnetka, Ill., 1985—2006. Bd. dirs. Stephen M. Hoenig Meml. Fund, Glencoe, Ill., 2005—. Recipient Jeff award for best supporting actress in a musical, Joseph Jefferson Com., Chgo., 2005; Sch. of Speech Summer fellow, Northwestern U., Evanston, Ill., 1988. Mem.: NEA, Ill. Theatre Assn., Ill. Edn. Assn. Achievements include development of Northern Illinois Theatre Educators. Avocations: acting, singing, theatre directing, choreography, dialect coaching. Home Phone: 847-692-4750.

MARX, GARY DEAN, educational consultant, futurist, think-tank executive; b. Manchester, SD, Nov. 28, 1938; s. Harvey Frederick and Lucille (Stemple) Marx; m. Judy Rae Marx, June 18, 1961; children: John Fredrick, Daniel Winston. BA, U. S.D., 1960. CAE, ASPR, APR. Newscaster, announcer, dir. KSOO radio and TV sta., Sioux Falls, SD, 1958-61; newscaster, announcer WOW radio and TV sta., Omaha, 1961-71; dir. comms. Westside Cmty. Schs., Omaha, 1971-77; exec. dir. comms. Jefferson County Pub. Schs., Denver, 1977-79; sr. assoc. exec. Am. Assn. Sch. Adminstrs., Arlington, Va., 1979-96, exec. dir. Leadership for Learning Found., 1996-98; pres. Ctr. for Pub. Outreach, Inc., Vienna, Va., 1998—. Sr. rsch. fellow Health, Energy and Productivity in Sch. project, Bethesda, Md., 2000-02; pub. rels. cons. Nat. Sch. Pub. Rels. Assn., Rockville, Md., 1972—; v.p., owner Sta. KOAK Radio, Red Oak, Iowa, 1977-82; v.p. Comms. Devel. Inc., Denver, 1974-76; chief evaluator CIVITAS Internat. Exch. Program, Calabasas, Calif., 2000—; cons., internat. spkr. in field. Author: Radio...Your Publics are Listening, 1976; Radio...Get the Message, 1977; Excellence in Our Schools...Making it Happen, 1984; Public Relations for Administrators, 1984, 88; Working with the News Media, 1993; Preparing Students for the 21st Century, 1996, 99; The Future of Cmty., 1999; Preparing Schools and School Systems for the 21st Century, 1999; Ten Trends...Educating Children for a Profoundly Different Future, 2000, Future Focused Leadership...Preparing Schools, Students and Communities for Tomorrow's Realities, 2006, 16 Trends...Their Profound Impact on Our Future, 2006; contbr. articles to profl. jours. Founder, chmn. Keystone Cmty. Task Force, Omaha, 1970-77; mem. Omaha Parks and Recreation Bd., City of Omaha, 1975-77; mem. urban growth policy bd., 1976; mem. nat. edn. adv. com. for restoration Statue of Liberty-Ellis Island Found,. NYC, 1984-86; mem. Horace Mann League, 1985-, bd. dirs. 2005—; mem. exec. com. edn. Commn. of Bicentennial of the US Constitution, Washington, 1986-92,; bd. dir. Campaign for New Priorities, Washington, 1992-93, Manchester Monument Adv. Coun., SD, 2006-07, Laura Ingalls Wilder Meml. Soc., 2007—; bd. dir., founder Coalition for America's Children, Washington, 1992-98; mem. steering com. Libr. of Congress, Ctr. for the Book, Washington, 1992-99, Goals 2000 Arts Edn. Partnership NEA, Washington, 1993-98, Civitas Internat., Brussels, Belgium, 1996—, Fulbright Scholars, selection com., 1998-; mem. design arts program steering com. NEA, Washington, 1993-94; mem. grants selection com. Alliance for Arts Edn., John F. Kennedy Ctr. for the Performing Arts, Washington, 1993-96, Nat. Tchr. of Yr. Program, Washington, 1979-99; mem. steering com., mem. selection com., judge Disney Salute to the Am. Tchr., Burbank, Calif., 1993-97; Emmy awards judge NATAS, NYC, 1995-97; mem. adv. bd. NBC The More You Know campaign, NYC, 1992-98; mem. nat. adv. bd. PBS, 1990-98; judge USA Today All USA Acad. Team, Arlington, Va., 1995-2000, Nat. History Day, 2002-; internat. cons., spkr., Ctr. Civic Edn., Calabasas, Calif., 1996—, USIA, US Dept. State, Washington, 1996—; mem. steering com., facilitator Nat. Ctr. Energy Mgmt. and Bldg. Techs., 2004—, mem. adv. coun., Manchester Monument Project, 2006-07. Recipient Radio Advertising Bureau Commercial award, 1967. Mem. Nat. Sch. Pub. Rels. Assn. (numerous offices and coms. 1971—, accredited, Pres.'s award 1999), Pub. Rels. Soc. Am. (accredited), Am. Soc. Assn. Exec. (cert.), Edn. Writers Assn. (bd. dir. 1979—), Am. Assn. Sch. Adminstrs. (Disting. Svc. award 2000), World Future Soc. (profl. member.)Horace Mann League (bd. dirs., 2005—). Avocations: folk art, travel, reading, writing, photography. Office: Ctr for Pub Outreach 1831 Toyon Way Vienna VA 22182-3355 Office Phone: 703-938-8725. Personal E-mail: gmarxcpo@aol.com.

MARX, JEFF, composer, lyricist, lawyer, writer; JD, Cardozo Sch. Law, 1996. Author, pub. How to Win a High School Election, 1999, creator, co-writer (Broadway plays) Avenue Q, 2003 (Lucille Lortel award for best musical, 2003, Tony award best original score, 2004, Tony award best musical, 2004); co-writer: musical episode of TV series Scrubs. Mem.: BMI Lehman Engel Musical Theater Workshop. Personal E-mail: jeffmarx@mac.com.

MARX, MICHAEL WILLIAM, language educator, writer; b. Phila., Nov. 1, 1951; s. Elmer Edward and Katharine Scott Marx. Student, Loyola U.; BA in Polit. Sci., Hobart Coll., 1973; MFA in Film Making, NYU, 1976; MA in English, Ind. State U., Terre Haute, 2001. Freelance writer, Calif., 1976-90; owner, head chef Freelandville Novelist Cafe, Ind., 1990—95; pub. Marx & Marx Writers & Pubs., 1998—99; instr. English lang. and lit. Ind. State U., Terre Haute, 1999—2001; instr. Lakeland Coll., Danville, Ill., 2000—01, Ivy Tech State Coll., Terra Haute & Greenfield, Ind., 2000—01, Mira Costa Coll., Oceanside, Calif., 2001—03, Southwestern Coll., Chula Vista, Calif., 2001—02, San Diego City Coll., 2001—, Palomar Coll., San Marcos, Calif., 2001—03, Miramar Coll., San Diego, 2001—03, Cuyumaca Coll., El Cajon, Calif., 2001—03, Inter-Am. Coll., National City, Calif., 2001—03, San Diego State U., 2002—04, Nat. U., 2002—04; instr. lit., film Webster U., 2004—; instr. Chapman U., 2004—05; instr. humanities, English composition, English lit., effective speaking Art Inst. Calif., San Diego, 2004—, chair libr. com., 2006—. Tchr. Vincennes U., Ind., 1991—93, Ind. Bus. Coll., 1995. Author: (book) A War Ends, 1977, A War Ends, 2d edit., 1985 (Artisan award Acad. Fine Arts and Friends), Eric Greenfield: Middle American, 1987, Justus: A Utopia, 1999; columnist: North Knox Leader, 1997—98, Knox County Daily News, Wabash Weekly News, 1991—92; movie reviewer Cine-Marx. Office Phone: 858-705-4882. Personal E-mail: michael@michaelmarx.com.

MARX, NICKI DIANE, sculptor, painter, jeweler; b. LA, Oct. 3, 1943; d. Donald F. and Ruth H. (Ungar) M. Student, U. Calif., Riverside, 1965, U. Calif., Santa Cruz, 1973. Represented by Nicki Marx Studio, Taos, N.Mex., Fred Kline Gallery, Santa Fe, N.Mex. One-woman shows include Palm Springs Desert Mus., 1977, Julie Artisans Gallery, NYC, 1975, Phoenix Art Mus., 1975, Weston Gallery, Carmel, Calif, 1981, Kirk de Gooyer Gallery, LA, 1982, Rocklands Gallery, Monterey, Calif., 1983, Fetish Gallery, Taos, 1988, Fenix Gallery, Taos, 1991, Earthworks, 1993, Lamberts, 1994, Stables Gallery, Taos, 1995, Fred Kline, 1995, Sun Cities Mus. Art, Ariz., 1996, Harwood Mus. Art, Taos, 1999, others; group exhbns. include E.P. Smith Gallery, Santa Cruz, 1994, Lumina Gallery, Taos, 1994, Cafe Gallery, Albuquerque, 1991, Bareiss Gallery, Taos, 1990, Ctr. for Contemporary Art, Santa Fe, 1989, Jordan Gallery, Taos, 1988-89, Stables Art Gallery, Taos, 1988, 94, Albuquerque State Fair Grounds, 1986, San Francisco Mus. Modern Art, 1977-78, Elements Gallery, Greenwich, Conn., 1977, Pacific Design Ctr., LA, 1976, Lesser Gallery, Inverness, Calif., 1976, others; represented in pub. collections IBM, Milford, Conn., NYC, San Jose, Calif., Bank of Am., San Francisco, The Continental Group, Inc., Stamford, Conn., Cedars-Sinai Hosp., LA, Farm Bur. Fedn., Sacramento, Calif., Sherman Fairchild Sci. Ctr., Stanford, Calif., Palm Springs Desert Mus., Calif., U. Mus., Ariz. State U. at Tempe, Mills Coll. Art Gallery, Berkeley, Calif.; exhibited in pvt. collections of Estate of Eugene Klein, Estate of Louise Nevelson, Estate of Georgia O'Keeffe, Fritz Scholder, Ray Graham, Bunny Horowitz, Sue and Otto Meyer, Burt Sugarman, Craig Moody, Paul Pletka, others; subject of numerous articles in jours. and mags. MacDowell Colony fellow, 1975; recipient Adolph and Esther Gottleib Found. grant, 1985. Studio: PO Box 128 Penasco NM 87553 Office Phone: 505-587-2383.

MARX, OWEN COX, lawyer; b. Grosse Pointe, Mich., Oct. 17, 1947; s. Leo A. and Anne (Cox) M.; m. Patricia Windschill, Aug. 14, 1971; children: Patrick Cox, Molly Simser, Anne Windschill. BA, Coll. of St. Thomas, St. Paul, 1969; JD, Cath. U., Washington, 1972. Bar: Minn. 1972, N.Y. 1973. Law clk. to presiding justice Minn. Supreme Ct., St. Paul, 1972-73; assoc. Mudge, Rose, Guthrie & Alexander, NYC, 1973-75, Dorsey & Whitney, Mpls., 1975-78, ptnr., 1979-86, ptnr., head London office, 1986-90, ptnr., corp. fin., internat. practice groups NYC, 1990—, and co-chmn., project devel. and fin. Bd. dirs. Bush Mfg. Co., Detroit, Off Site Tech. Inc., Detroit, OFLA Receivables Corp., San Diego, Hercules (Cayman) Ltd., Cayman Islands. Mem. Internat. Bar Assn., Minn. Bar Assn., N.Y. Athletic Club. Republican. Roman Catholic. Office: Dorsey & Whitney 250 Park Ave New York NY 10177-1500 Office Phone: 212-415-9285. Office Fax: 212-953-7201. Business E-Mail: marx.owen@dorsey.com.

MARX, PETER A., lawyer; b. NYC, June 14, 1942; s. Robert L. and Helen (Sohn) M.; m. Barbara K. Marx, Dec. 21, 1974; children: Laura, Lisa. BA, Cornell U., 1965, MBA, JD, 1968. Bar: N.Y. 1969, D.C. 1970, Mass. 1980. Atty., advisor U.S. SEC, Washington, 1968-71; assoc. Shaw Pittman, Washington, 1971-74; v.p., gen. counsel Interactive Data Corp., Waltham, Mass., 1975-85; ptnr. Goulston & Storrs, Boston, 1985-87; prin. The Marx Group, Wellesley, Mass., 1987—; pres. Legal Insight Media, Inc., 2003—. Dir. Info. Industry Assn., Washington, 1980—84, hon. counsel to bd., 1993—; chmn. Electronic Bus. Forum, 2002—04, N.E. Computer Law Forum, 1982—89; mem. adv. bd. CNC Interactive, 1998, LifetecNet.com, 1999—2001, ForPower.com, 1999—2002, Eye on Interactive, 1999, WebMediate.com, 2000—03; host Venture Capital Quest, 1998—2000; vice-chmn. bd. dirs. Internet Alliance, 1999—2000; exec.-in-residence Babon Coll., 2002—04; chmn. Electronic Bus. Form, 2002—03, Wellesley Cable Access Corp., 2002—06. Editor: Contracts in the Information Industry, 1988, II, 1990, III, 1995, IV, 2003; mem. bd. advisors Computer Law Strategist, 1987—99, info. law editor Info. Mgmt. Rev., 1987—90, host program Bus. Insight, Sta. WCAB-TV, 1991—, coord. editor The Info. Industry Deal Making Directory, 1994. Mem. ALI-ABA Computer Law Inst. (chmn. 1980-88), New Eng. Corp. Counsel Assn. (chmn. 1981-82), Cornell Club Boston (dir. 2002-07). Office: Legal Insight Media Inc 60 Valley Rd Wellesley MA 02481-1448 Office Phone: 781-235-3550. Business E-Mail: pmarx@legalinsight.com.

MARX, THOMAS GEORGE, economist; b. Trenton, NJ, Oct. 25, 1943; s. George Thomas and Ann (Szymanski) Marx; m. Arlene May Varga, Aug. 23, 1969; children: Melissa Ann, Thomas Jeffrey, Jeffrey Alan. BS summa cum laude, Rider Coll., 1969; PhD, U. Pa., Phila., 1973. Fin. analyst Am. Cyanamid Co., Trenton, 1968; economist FTC, Washington, 1973; econ. cons. Foster Assocs. Inc., Washington, 1974-77; sr. economist GM, Detroit, 1977-79, mgr. indsl. econs., 1980-81, dir. econs. policy studies, 1981-83, dir. corp. strategic planning group, 1984-86, gen. dir. market analysis and forecasting, 1986-88, gen. dir. econ. analysis, 1988-90, gen. dir. issues mgmt. on industry govt. rels. staff, 1990-96, dir. econ. issues and analysis corp. affairs staff, 1996-97, dir. global climate issue, 1997—2005; prof., dir. bus. adminstrn. doctorate program Coll. Mgmt. Lawrence Technol. U., 2005—. Mem. faculty Temple U., Phila., 1972—73, U. Pa., Phila., 1972—73; adj. prof. Wayne State U., 1981—89, U. Detroit, 1988—2005; prof., dir. bus. adminstrn. doctorate program Lawrence Technol. U., 2005—. Assoc. editor: Bus. Econs., 1980—98, mem. editl. bd.: Akron Jour. Bus. and Econs., 1981—90; contbr. articles to profl. jours. With USAF, 1961—65. Mem.: Assn. Pub. Policy Analysts, Planning Forum, Western Econ. Assn., So. Econ. Assn., Econ. Soc. Mich., Detroit Area Bus. Economists (v.p.), Nat. Assn. Bus. Economists, Am. Econ. Assn., Nat. Econs. Club, Beta Gamma Sigma, Pi Gamma Mu. Roman Catholic. Home: 3312 Bloomfield Park Dr West Bloomfield MI 48323-3514 Office Phone: 248-204-3081. Business E-Mail: tmarx@ltu.edu.

MARY, DIANE BRADLEY, elementary school educator, secondary school educator; d. William Joseph and Mary Ann Bradley; children: William Bradley, James Corbett, Megan Shannon Mary. Degree, Stanford U., Calif.; MA in Edn., U. Calif., Berkeley, 1965. Cert. counselor U. Calif. Berkley; tchr. San Francisco State U. Tchr. 7th grade sci., biology Sullivan Mid. Sch., Fairfield, 1989—2007, counselor, 2007—. Mentor tchr. U. Calif., Davis. Recipient Tchr. Yr., Sullivan Middle Sch., Disting. Alumni award, Stanford U. Home: 2889 St Andrews Rd Fairfield CA 94534 Office: Sullivan Middle Sch 2195 Union Ave Fairfield CA 94533 Office Phone: 707-421-4115. Office Fax: 707-421-3964. Personal E-mail: dmscience@aol.com.

MARYA, MANUEL PAUL CLAUDE, metallurgical and materials engineer; b. Nantes, France, July 1, 1972; s. Surendar Kumar and Annie Jeanne Suzanne (Crouau) Marya; m. Noriko Yao, Nov. 3, 2003. DUT in Mech. & Mfg. Engring., Inst. U. Nantes, France, 1990—92; BEng in Mech. Engring., U. Quebec, Can., 1992—95; MS in Metall. & Materials Engring., Colo. Sch. Mines, Golden, 1996—99, PhD in Metall. & Materials Engring., 1999—2001. Rsch. asst. Colo. Sch. Mines, Golden, Colo., 1996—2001, postdoctoral fellow, 2002, rsch. asst. prof., 2002—04; vis. scientist Gen. Motors Rsch. & Devel., Warren, Mich., 2002—04; sr. mem., tech. staff Nanocoolers Inc., Austin, Tex., 2004—. Engring. trainee ECN Centre LASER, Nantes, France, 1990—94; rsch. asst. U. Nottingham, England, 1995; material & welding rsch. cons. Ecole Centrale Nantes, France, 1996—. Contbr. over 40 articles to profl. jours. and internat. conf. proceedings, chapters to books. Recipient Henry Granjon award, Internat. Inst. Welding, 2002; grantee, Ford, Visteon, Gen. Motors, 1999—2004. Fellow: Am. Welding Soc.; mem.: Am. Soc. for Materials. Achievements include research in Magnesium Joining, Laser Processing Research, Alloy and Liquid Metal Development, Materials Processing, Coatings and Corrosion, etc; patents pending for Liquid Alloys, Product Development. Avocations: travel, art, reading. Office: Materials Engrng Dept Bldg 45 Office 1227 14910 Airline Rd Rosharon TX 77583 Office Phone: 281-285-6565. Office Fax: 281-285-5177. Personal E-mail: mpmarya@hotmail.com.

MARYANSKI, FRED J., academic administrator; BA in Math., Providence Coll.; MA in Computer Sci., Stevens Inst. Tech.; PhD in Computer Sci., U. Conn. Affiliate prof. Worcester Poly. Inst.; faculty Kans. State U., U. Conn., Storrs, 1983—, vice chancellor academic adminstrn., interim chancellor, provost U. affairs, 1999—2000, sr. vice provost academic affairs, provost, exec. v.p. academic affairs, 1999—2004; pres. Nev. State Coll., Henderson, 2005—. With Digital Equipment Corp., 1986—89. Office: Nev State Coll 1125 Nevada State Dr Henderson NV 89015 *

MARYKS, ROBERT A., history professor; b. Torun, Poland, Nov. 9, 1967; s. Zbigniew Antoni Maryks and Leokadia Antoniewicz. MA, U. Warsaw, 1992; BA in Theology, Pontificia Facoltà Teologica, Naples, 2001; PhD, Fordham U., 2005. State dipl. Spanish Ministry Of Edn. Spain, 1993, state dipl. Italian Inst. Italian Lang. and Culture, 2002. Prof. Latin, Italian and religion H.S., Warsaw, 1989—91; prof. religion Coll., Naples, 1994—96; prof. Italian Italian Embassy, Sarajevo, Bosnia-Herzegovina, 1996—97; tchg. asst. Fordham U., New York, 2003—04, tchg. fellow, 2004—05; adj. prof. Yeshiva U., New York, 2005—06; asst. prof. CUNY, 2006—. Dir.: (festival) Internat. Ignatian Youth Festival and Miriam Makeba's Concert, Children Mine Victims Aid Program; co-organizer Princess Diana's visit to Sarajevo; translator: John W. O'Malley's Trent And All That; author: St. Cicero and the Jesuits. Fellow Presdl. scholarship, Fordham U., 2002—05; grantee, 2005; Rsch. grant, CUNY, 2007. Mem.: Am. Hist. Assn., Sixteenth Century Soc. and Conf., Renaissance Soc. Am. Office Phone: 718-289-5248. Personal E-mail: rmaryks@yahoo.com. Business E-Mail: robert.maryks@bcc.cuny.edu.

MARZETTA, DANTE R., II, air transportation executive; Sr. dir. Cleve. Hub Continental Airlines, Inc., 1999—2001, staff v.p. Cleve. Hub, 2001—02, v.p. airport svcs., 2002—03, sr. v.p. airport svcs., 2003—04, sr. v.p. tech. ops. and purchasing, 2004—. Office: Continental Airlines Inc PO Box 4607 Houston TX 77210 Office Phone: 713-324-5000. Office Fax: 713-324-2637. *

MARZEWSKI, JANEEN LYNETTE, elementary school educator; d. Wanda Jay; m. Donald Joseph Marzewski, July 14, 1984; children: Bethany, Skyler. Med, Cabrini Coll., Radnor, PA, 2001—02; BS, Northwestern U., Evanston, IL, 1978—81. Cert. tchr. Pa., 2002, prin. cert. Pa., 2005. Kid's kare coord. Harleysville YMCA, Pa., 1989—92; enrichment coord./ supr. Plymouth/Canton Cmty. Schs., Mich., 1992—95; parks and recreation dir. Upper Gwynedd Twp., West Point, Pa., 1996—97, Towamencin Twp., 1997—99; activities dir./tchr. Methacton Sch. Dist., Norristown, Pa., 1999—. Cons. Internat. Festival; adv. bd. dir. Towamencin Twp.; dir. North Penn Recreation Coun., Lansdale, Pa.; chmn. Cmty. Edn. Adv. Bd., Norristown. Flute performer: Montgomery County Cmty. Band. Recipient St. Catherine medal, Kappa Gamma Pi, Cabrini Coll., 2002, 3 Best Program awards for Parks & Recreation, Pa. Parks & Recreation Soc., 1998. Mem.: Pa. Sch. Bd. Assn. (assoc.), Northwestern Alumni Assn., Am. Assn. of Am. Women. Democrat. Protestant. Avocations: music, travel, creative arts. Office: Methacton Sch Dist 1001 Kriebel Mill Rd Norristown PA 19408 Home Phone: 610-584-3096; Office Phone: 610-489-5000. Personal E-mail: marzewski1@comcast.net.

MARZIO, PETER CORT, museum director; b. Governor's Island, NY, May 8, 1943; s. Francis and Katherine (Mastroberte) M.; m. Frances Ann Parker, July 2, 1979; children: Sara Lon, Steven Arnold. BA, Juniata Coll., 1965; MA, U. Chgo., 1966, PhD, 1969. Rsch. asst. to dir., then historian Nat. Mus. History and Tech., Smithsonian Instn., 1969-73, assoc. curator prints, 1977-78, chmn. dept. cultural history, 1978; dir., CEO Corcoran Gallery Art, Washington, 1978-82; dir. Mus. Fine Arts, Houston, 1982—. Instr. Roosevelt U., Chgo., 1966-68; assoc. prof. U. Md., 1967-77; chmn. Fed. Coun. on Arts and Humanities, 1997-2000. Author: Rube Goldberg: His Life and Works, 1973, The Art Crusade, 1976, The Democratic Art: An Introduction to the History of Chromolithography in America, 1979; editor: A Nation of Nations, 1976. Bd. dirs. Wallace Found. Sr. Fulbright fellow, Italy, 1973-74. Mem. Cosmos Club (Washington), Coronado Club (Houston), Assn. of Art Museum Directors (pres. 1988-89). Office: Mus Fine Arts 1001 Bissonet St PO Box 6826 Houston TX 77265-6826 Office Phone: 713-639-7300. E-mail: pmarzio@mfah.org.

MARZORATI, GERALD, editor; b. Patterson, NJ, Feb. 8, 1953; BA, Villanova U., 1975. Editor SoHo (NY) News, Harper's Mag., NY, New Yorker Mag., 1994—98; editl. dir. NY Times Mag., NYC, 1998—2003, editor, 2003—; asst. mng. editor NY Times, NYC, 2006—. Author: A Painter of Darkness: Leon Golub and Our Times, 1990 (PEN/Martha Albrand award). Office: The New York Times 229 W 43rd St New York NY 10036-3959 *

MASA, GEORGE JOHN, retired bank executive; b. Chgo., Apr. 29, 1947; s. George John Sr. and Barbara Ann (Kos) M.; m. Judy Ann Martin, Apr. 24, 1971; children: Kimberly Janine, Kristin Marie. BS in Commerce, De Paul U., 1969; cert. banking, Rutgers U., 1979; cert. mgmt., Pa. State U., 1987. Field bank examiner FDIC, Chgo., 1969-77, rev. examiner, 1977-82, asst. regional dir. Dallas, 1982-85, asst. dir. policy Washington, 1985-86, asst. dir. ops., 1986-89, regional dir. Chgo., 1989-91, San Francisco, 1991—2002; ret., 2002; dir. Gateway Bank, 2003. With USAR, 1970-76. Personal E-mail: gjmasa@aol.com.

MASAGUTOV, VAKHID ERKINJONOVICH, application developer; s. Erkinjon G Nazarov and Rumiya V Masagutova. BS in math. and computer sci., N.Mex State U., 1998—2002; Math Advanced Study, Pa. State U., 2000. Tester/ programmer IBM, Durham, NC, 2001; intern Charles River Analytics, Cambridge, 2003—04. Programmer Phys. Sci. Lab., Las Cruces, N.Mex., 1999—2002. VIGRE Grad fellowship, Purdue U., 2003. Achievements include development of algorithms for network reliability analysis. Home Phone: 765-409-3985. Personal E-mail: vmasagut@math.purdue.edu.

MASAND, PRAKASH S., psychiatrist, researcher; b. Bombay; US, 1984; s. Sham Masand; m. Sonia Masand; 1 child, Natasha. MD, Topiwala Nat. Med. Coll., Bombay, 1982. Cert. Am. Bd. Psychiatry and Neurology, 1990. Resident in psychiatry SUNY Upstate Med. U., Syracuse, 1985—88, prof. psychiatry, 1989—2001; fellowship in consultation liaison psychiatry Mass. Gen. Hosp., Harvard Med. Sch., 1988—89; consulting prof. psychiatry Duke U. Med. Ctr., Durham, NC, 2001—. Sect. editor Current Psychiatry Reports, Phila., 2002—. Contbr. chapters to books, articles to profl. jours. Local candidate fund raiser, Chapel Hill, NC. Named Tchr. of Yr., Dept. Psychiatry SUNY Upstate Med. U., 1990, 1996; named one of Americas Top Psychiatrists, 2004—05, Best Doctors in Am., 2005—06. Fellow: Am. Psychiat. Assn. Office: DUMC Dept Psychiatry 2218 Elder St 2B STe 202 Durham NC 27705

MASAOKA, JAN, not-for-profit executive; BA, San Francisco State U. Regional dir. US.-China Friendship Assn., 1978—80; bus. mgr. Cognos Assocs., 1982—83; fin. dir. Advocates for Women, 1983—85; dir. cons. svcs. Support Ctr. for Nonprofit Mgmt., 1988—90; exec. dir. Compass-Point Nonprofit Svcs., San Francisco, 1993—. Lectr. Grad. Sch. of Pub. Adminstrn. Golden Gate U., 1987—96. Writer, editor Board Café, 1999—, mem. nat. editl. adv. com. BoardSource, 1999—; contbr. articles to profl. jours. Chair bd. dirs. Asian & Pacific Islander Wellness Ctr.; founding pres., mem. bd. dirs. San Francisco Found. Cmty. Initiative Funds. Named Nonprofit Exec. of Yr., NonProfit Times, 2002; recipient Robert E. Kantor Medal, Pacific Grad. Sch. Psychology, 2000, Woman Warrior, Pacific Asian Am. Women's Bay Area Coalition, 2002; grantee Gerbode Fellowship, Sch. of Social Work, U. Calif., Berkeley, 2001. Office: CompassPoint Nonprofit Svcs Ste 200 731 Market St San Francisco CA 94103 Office Phone: 415-541-9000. Office Fax: 415-541-7780.

MASCETTA, JOSEPH ANTHONY, principal; b. Canonsburg, Pa., Sept. 2, 1931; s. Joseph Alphonso and Amalia (Ciavarra) M.; m. Jean Verrone, June 18, 1960; children: Lisa Marie, Linda Jo, Lori Jean. BS, U. Pitts., 1954; MS, U. Pa., 1963; cert. advanced study, Harvard U., 1970. Cert. tchr. math., phys. scis., adminstr. secondary sch., Pa. Tchr. chemistry Canonsburg High Sch., 1956-59, Mt. Lebanon High Sch., Pitts., 1959-75, chair sci.

dept., 1967-75; coord. secondary curriculum Mt. Lebanon Sch. Dist., Pitts., 1975-81; prin. Mt. Lebanon Sr. High Sch., Pitts., 1981-91; ret., 1991; ednl. cons., 1991—. Vis. team Mid. States Assn. Colls. and Schs., Phila., 1967-78, chair vis. teams, 1981-96, Pa. state adv. com., 1988-91; sch. bd. and edn. commn. St. Patrick Sch., Canonsburg, 1972-85, 95-2002; tchr. undergrad. and grad. courses Duquesne U., Pitts., 1975-81; regional dir. Pa. Jr. Acad. Sci., Pitts., 1976-82; ednl. cons. Pitts. area schs., 1992—; quality edn. com. Pitts. Diocese, 1995-97. Author: Modern Chemistry Review, 1968, Chemistry the Easy Way, 1989, rev. edit., 2003, Barron's SAT II, Chemistry, 1994, 8th rev. edit., 2006; contbg. author: (ency.) Barron's Student Concise Ency., 1988, rev. 1994, Barron's New Student's Concise Ency., 1993, Perry Como Commemorative Booklet, 1998. Recipient Outstanding Tchr. award Spectroscopy Soc., 1973; grantee NSF, 1961, 62-63, 63, 67, 69-70, 73; sci. fellow GE, 1959. Mem. ASCD, Nat. Assn. Secondary Sch. Prins. (cert. recognition 1991), Pa. Assn. Curriculum & Supervision (exec. bd. dirs. 1985-87, regional pres. 1987), Western Pa. Assn. Curriculum and Supervision (v.p. 1983-85, pres. 1985-87, exec. bd. dirs. 1989-2001), Greater Canonsburg Heritage Soc., Italian-Am. Heritage and Cultural Soc. Washington County (chair scholarship com. 1992—, Man of Yr. award 2006), Phi Delta Kappa. Roman Catholic. Avocations: painting, writing. Home: 451 McClelland Rd Canonsburg PA 15317-2258 E-mail: jmascett@bellatlantic.net.

MASCHERIN, TERRI LYNN, lawyer; b. Trenton, NJ, July 9, 1959; d. Anthony Americus and Kathryn Eleanor Mascherin; m. Thomas Warren Abendroth, Aug. 31, 1985. AB, Duke U., 1981; JD, Northwestern U., 1984. Bar: Ill. 1984, U.S. Dist. Ct. (Ariz.) 1999, U.S. Dist. Ct. (no. dist. Calif.) 1991, U.S. Dist. Ct. (Colo.) 1999, U.S. Dist. Ct. (no. dist. Ill.) 1984, U.S. Dist. Ct. (ea. dist. Mich.) 1998, U.S. Dist. Ct. (we. dist. Mich.) 1998, U.S. Dist. Ct. (ea. dist. Wis.) 1998, U.S. Ct. Appeals (6th cir.) 1999, U.S. Ct. Appeals (7th cir.) 1987, U.S. Ct. Appeals (9th cir.) 1999, U.S. Ct. Appeals (10th cir.) 2000, U.S. Supreme Ct. 1995. Assoc. Jenner & Block, Chgo., 1984—92, ptnr., 1992—. Chair law bd. Nothwestern U., 2006—. Vice chair Law Bd. Northwestern U., 2004—06. Named one of The 50 Most Influential Women Lawyers in Am., Nat. Law Jour., 2007; recipient Charles A. Duke award, Duke U., 1996, Outstanding Legal Svc. award, Nat. Coalition to Abolish Death Penalty, 2002, Cunningham-Carey award, Ill. Coalition to Abolish Death Penalty, 2004. Fellow: Am. Bar Found.; mem.: ABA (chair Death Penalty Representation Project 2003—06), Women's Bar Assn. Ill., Ill. Bar Assn., Chgo. Bar Assn. (bd. mgrs. 2002—04, chair strategic planning com. 2005—06, treas. 2006—). Office: Jenner & Block 330 N Wabash Chicago IL 60611 Office Phone: 312-923-2799. Office Fax: 312-840-7799. Business E-Mail: tmascherin@jenner.com.

MASCHERONI, ELEANOR EARLE, marketing communications executive; b. Boston, June 6, 1955; d. Ralph II and Eleanor Forbes (Owens) Earle; m. Mark Mascheroni, May 30, 1981; children: Olivia Forbes, Isabella Starbuck, Rex Owens. AB, Brown U., 1977. Dept. adminstr. Sotheby Parke Bernet, NYC, 1978-79; asst. dir. devel. Inst. Architecture and Urban Studies, NYC, 1979-81; assoc. in pub. rels. Prudential Securities Inc., NYC, 1981-84, asst. v.p., 1984-86, assoc. v.p., 1986-87, v.p., mgr., 1987—89, 1st v.p., dir. corp. commns., 1989—91; v.p. corp. comms. Zurich Scudder Investments, Inc., NYC, 1991-95, prin., sr. v.p., dir. corp. comms., 1996-99, mng. dir., 1999—2001; CMO Ogilvy & Mather, 2001—. N.Y. Alumnae bd. govs. St. Timothy's Sch., Stevenson, Md., 1994—; trustee Hartley House, 2000—. Avocations: running, yoga, photography. Office Phone: 212-237-7239. Business E-Mail: eleanor.mascheroni@ogilvy.com.

MASCI, JOSEPH RICHARD, medical educator; b. New Brunswick, NJ, Nov. 27, 1950; s. Joseph Nicholas and Delfina (Musa) M.; m. Elizabeth Bass, May 21, 1993; 1 child, Jonathan Samuel. BA, Cornell U., 1972; MD, NYU, 1976. Diplomate Am. Bd. Internal Medicine, Am. Bd. Infectious Diseases. Instr. medicine Boston U. Sch. Medicine, 1979—80, Mt. Sinai Sch. Medicine, NYC, 1982—84, asst. prof. clin. medicine, 1984—88, asst. prof. medicine, 1988—90, assoc. prof. medicine, 1990—2003, prof. medicine, 2003—, chief infectious diseases, 1999—2002; assoc. dir. medicine Elmhurst (NY) Hosp. Ctr., 1987—2002, dir. medicine, 2002—. Peer reviewer NIH, 1994—. Author: Primary and Ambulatory Care of the HIV-Infected Adult, 1992, Outpatient Management of HIV-Infection, 2d edit., 1996, 3d edit., 2001, Bioterrorism: A Guide for Hospital Preparedness, 2005. Recipient Dr Linda Laubenstien award for Excellence in AIDS Care, 2002. Fellow Am. Coll. Chest Physicians; mem. ACP, Am. Soc. Microbiology, Assn. Program Dirs. Internal Medicine, Assn. Profs. of Medicine. Office: Elmhurst Hosp Ctr 79-01 Broadway Elmhurst NY 11373-1329

MASDEU, JOSE CRUZ, neurologist, health facility administrator; b. Madrid, Sept. 15, 1946; arrived in U.S., 1972; s. Jose and Maria Luisa Masdeu. MD, U. Madrid, 1969. Diplomate Am. Bd. Psychiatry and Neurology. Resident neurology Chgo. Med. Sch., 1972—75; fellow neuropathology Peter Bent Brigham Hosp., 1976—77; sect. chief neurology Hines VA Hosp., Ill., 1978—82; asst. prof. neurology Loyola U., 1978—82; head neurology sect. North Ctrl. Bronx (N.Y.) Hosp., 1982—87; assoc. attending staff Montefiore Med. Ctr., Bronx, 1982—87; assoc. prof. neurology Einstein, 1982—87; dir. neurology St. Vincent's Hosp./Med. Ctr., NYC, 1987—; attending staff, clin. prof. neurology Bellevue Hosp./NYU Med. Ctr., NYC, 1987—; prof., chmn. neurology dept. N.Y. Med. Coll./West County Med. Ctr., Valhalla, 1991—. Author (with C. Gonzalez, C.B. Grossman): Head and Spine Imaging, 1985; author: (with P. Brazis, J. Biller) Localization in Neurology, 4 edits., 1985—2001; author: (with L. Sudarsky, L. Wolfson) Gait Disturbances of Aging, 1997; editor-in-chief The HyperText Neurological Knowledgebase, 1999; co-editor: Encyclopedia of the Neurological Sciences, 2003; contbr. Named Outstanding New Citizen of Yr., Chgo. Citizenship Coun., 1977, Among Best Neurologists in N.Y., N.Y. Mag., 1991, 1996, Among 22 Best Neurologists in U.S., Am. Health Mag., 1996. Mem.: World Fedn. Neurology (chmn. neuroimaging rsch. group 1997—), Am. Soc. Neuroimaging (pres. 1994—96), Am. Acad. Neurology (chmn. neuroimaging sect. 1996—, chmn. subcom. practice com. 1990—, bd. dirs.). Roman Catholic. Avocation: Avocations: tennis, golf. Address: Neurology CUN Avda Pio XII 31008 Pamplona Spain Home Phone: 34 948 239 244; Office Phone: +34 948 255 400.

MASEKELA, BARBARA JOYCE MOSIMA, ambassador; 2 children. B, U. Ohio. Chief of staff to Nelson Mandela, 1990—94; exec. dir. for pub. and corp. affairs De Beers Consol. Mines (ret. 2003); South African amb. to France and UNESCO, 1995—99; South African amb. to the US Washington, 2003—. Asst. prof. English lit. Staten Island CC, NY, Rutgers U., NJ; trustee Nelson Mandela Children's Fund, Nelson Mandela Found.; various exec. and non-exec. directorships including Standard Bank of South Africa, South African Broadcasting Corp., and Internat. Mktg. Coun., 1999—2003. Achievements include founding African Nat. Congress Office of Arts and Culture. Office: Embassy of South Africa 3051 Mass Ave NW Washington DC 20008

MASELLI, JOHN ANTHONY, food products executive; b. NYC, Feb. 18, 1928; s. Anthony and Livia M.; m. Brigitta Degenkolb, Dec. 26, 1948; children: Elisa, John A. Jr. BS in Chemistry, CCNY, 1947; MS in Chemistry, Fordham U., 1949, PhD in Chemistry, 1952. Dir. research and devel. Standard Brands, Stamford, Conn., 1952-64; mgr. product devel. M&M/Mars, Hackettstown, NJ, 1964-67; pres. OZ Food Corp., Chgo., 1967-79; v.p. tech. Nabisco Brands, East Hanover, NJ, 1979-85; v.p. corp. research and devel. RJR Nabisco, Winston-Salem, NC, 1985-87; sr. v.p. tech. Planters LifeSavers Co., Winston-Salem, 1987-91, cons., 1991—. Bd. dirs. Cultor Food Scis. (Finland), NC Biotech. Ctr., Sci-Works, Winston Salem, Winston Salem Symphony. Patentee in field. Bd. dirs. Chgo. Boy's Club, 1975-79, YMCA, Wilton, Conn, 1980-84. Mem. AAAS, ACS, Inst. Food Tech., Am. Soc. Bakery Engrs., Indsl. Biotechnology Assn., Indsl. Research Inst. Republican. Avocations: sailing, photography, music. Home: 529 Knob View Pl Winston Salem NC 27104-5107

MASERITZ, GUY B., lawyer; b. Balt., June 5, 1937; m. Sally Jane Sugar, Mar. 30, 1961; children: Marjorie Ellen, Michael Louis. BA, Johns Hopkins U., Balt., 1959, MA in Econs., 1961; LLB, U. Md., 1966. Bar: Md. 1966, DC 1968, US Supreme Ct. 1975, US Dist. Ct. Md. 1979. Atty. SEC, Washington, 1966-70; asst. gen. counsel securities Am. Life Ins. Assn., Washington, 1971-74; atty. eval. sect., chief legis. unit antitrust divsn. U.S. Dept. Justice, Washington, 1974-78, spl. asst. U.S. atty. Alexandria, Va., 1978; pvt. practice Columbia, Md., 1978—. Author: U.S. Department of Justice Antitrust Report on Property-Liability Insurance Industry, 1977; contbr. articles to profl. jours. Mem. Howard County Charter Revision Commn., Md., 1979, Am. Inn of Ct., 2005-06; bd. dirs. Howard County YMCA, 1997-99, disting. bd. mem., 1999. With USAR, 1960—66. Mem. Md. Bar Assn., Howard County Bar Assn., Greater Howard County C. of C. (dir., gen. counsel 1981-84). Office: Hobbits Glen 5040 Rushlight Path Columbia MD 21044-1295 Office Phone: 410-997-9400. Business E-Mail: consult@maseritzlaw.com.

MASERU, NOBLE A.W., city health department administrator; b. Detroit; BS, Wayne State U.; MPH, Emory U. Sch. Medicine; PhD in Health Policy, Atlanta U. Founding dir., master of pub. health program Morehouse Sch. Medicine, Atlanta; health policy scientist Morehouse Coll., Pub. Health Scis. Inst.; v.p., cmty. health Greater Detroit Area Health Coun. Inc., 1998—2000; dir. and health officer Detroit Dept. Health and Wellness Promotion, 2003—. Office: Detroit Dept Health & Wellness Promotion Herman Kiefer Health Complex 1151 Taylor Detroit MI 48202 Office Phone: 313-876-4300.

MASEY, JACK, exhibition designer; b. NYC, June 10, 1924; s. Max and Anna Masey; m. Beverly Payeff-Masey, March 20, 2003. Student, Cooper Union, 1941-43; BFA, Yale U., 1950. Pres. MetaForm LLC, NYC, 1979—; co. project mgr. for design of La. Pavilion, World Expo., New Orleans, 1984, Statue of Liberty Exhibit, NYC, 1986; project mgr. for design Johnstown (Pa.) Flood Mus., 1988, Ellis Island Immigration Mus., NYC, 1990; co. project mgr. for design of Nat. D-Day Mus., New Orleans, 1994, designer D-Day Invasion, Pacific Exhbn., 2000; co. project mgr. for design of Harry S. Truman Mus., Independence, Mo., 2001. Lectr. Sch. Art and Arch., Yale U., 1968—69; design cons. State Hermitage Mus., St. Petersburg, Russia, 1998; project mgr. design Fly-Girls of WWII exhibn. The Mighty Eighth Air Force Mus., Savannah, Ga., 2005. Cartoonist Esquire mag, 1946; exhibits officer, USIS, New Delhi, 1951-55; designer U.S. Pavilion, Kabul Internat. Fair, 1956; dir. design Am. Nat. Exhbn., Moscow, 1959, chief, East-West exhibits br. USIA, Washington, 1960-67; chief design U.S. Pavilion, Montreal (Que., Can.) World Expo, 1967, dep. commr. gen. for planning and design Osaka (Japan) World Expn., 1970; dir. design Am. Revolution Bicentennial Commn., Washington, 1971-73; dir. design and exhbns. Am. Revolution Bicentennial Adminstrn., 1974-77, design dir. Internat. Communication Agy., Washington, 1977—; designer: Medicine-U.S.A. exhbn. for, USSR exchange program, 1962, Tech.-Books exhbns., 1963; co-designer Visitor Center, UN, 2001. Served with AUS, 1943-45, ETO. Recipient Meritorious Service award USIA, 1959, Superior Service award, 1964, Superior Honor award, 1967, 75; award of excellence Fed. Design Council, 1975; Outstanding Achievement award, 1979; award of excellence Soc. Fed. Artists and Designers, 1971; Gold medal Art Dirs. Club, 1965; cert. of excellence Am. Inst. Graphic Arts, 1964; two Fed. Design Achievement awards for Contributions to Excellence in Design, U.S. Govt., 1984, Presdl. awards for Statue of Liberty Mus., 1986, for Ellis Island Immigration Mus., 1990. Home: 131 E 66th St Apt 3A New York NY 10021-6129 also: 137 E 25th St New York NY 10010-2314 Office Phone: 212-532-8580. E-mail: jackmasey@cs.com.

MASH, DONALD J., college president; b. Oct. 12, 1942; children: Maria, Christina, Donnie (dec.). BS in Edn., Ind. U. Pa., 1960; MA in Geography, U. Pitts., 1966; PhD, Ohio State U., 1974. Teaching fellow U. Pitts., 1964-65; instr. geography U. Pitts.-Bradford, 1965-68; dean for student svcs. Ohio Dominican Coll., 1968-75; v.p. for student affairs George Mason U., Fairfax, Va., 1975-85, exec. v.p. adminstrn., 1985-88; pres. Wayne (Nebr.) State Coll., 1988-98; chancellor U. Wis.-Eau Claire, 1998—2005; exec. sr. v.p. U. Wis. Sys. Office: U Wis 1730 Van Hise Hall 1220 Linden Dr Madison WI 53706-4004 Office Phone: 608-262-4049. Business E-Mail: dmash@uwsa.edu.

MASHAGBEH, WASSEL KHALAF, economist; s. Khalaf Ghass and Fadieh Suliman Mashagbeh; m. Nesreen Y. Matarneh, Nov. 1, 2004. BA in Econs., Yarmouk U., Jordan, 1987; MA in Econs., Bowling Green State U., 1989, Wayne State U., 2003; M in Polit. Sci. and Pub. Adminstrn., Bowling Green State U., 1990; PhD in Econs., Wayne State U., Detroit, 2003. Economist US Dept. Transp., 2002—04, chief economist, policy advisor, 2004—05, sr. economist, dir. data and econ. analysis, 2005—. Recipient Inst. Scholar award, Am. Inst. Econ. Rsch., Great Barrington, Mass., 1991; fellow, Bowling Green State U., 1988, 1989, 1990, Wayne State U., 1992, 1993, 1994; scholar, Student Aid Assn., 1988, 1989. Mem.: Am. Econ. Assn. (assoc.). Office: United State Dept Transp 400 7th St SW Ste 8107 Washington DC 20590 Office Phone: 202-366-1715. Office Fax: 202-366-3890; Home Fax: 202-366-3890. Personal E-mail: mashagbeh@hotmail.com. Business E-Mail: wassel.mashagbeh@dot.gov.

MASHARIKI, ZOLA B., film company executive; b. Bklyn., Jan. 4, 1974; Grad., Dartmouth Coll., Hanover, NH, 1994; JD, Harvard Law Sch. Corp. atty. Manatt, Phelps & Phillips, L.L.P., LA, Proskauer Rose, L.L.P., NYC; prodn. intern Fox Searchlight, LA, 2000—01, creative exec., 2001—03, dir., 2003—06, v.p. prodn., 2006—. Prodr.: (films) Mboutoukou, 2002. Avocation: Tae Kwon Do. Office: Fox Searchlight 10201 W Pico Blvd Bldg 38 Los Angeles CA 90035 *

MASHBERN, WILLIAM ALLEN, minister, retired religious organization administrator; b. Sept. 15, 1947; MusB, Carson-Newman Coll., Jefferson City, Tenn., 1969; M in Ch. Music, So. Bapt. Theol. Sem., Louisville, 1972, D of Musical Arts, 1988; MusM, Memphis State U., 1980. Min. of music and youth East Hill Bapt. Ch., Pensacola, Fla., 1972—74; min. of music Aubudon Park Bapt. Ch., Memphis, 1974—81; min. of music and youth Evergreen Bapt. Ch., Frankfort, Ky., 1981—86; dir. worship and ch. music Ill. Bapt. State Assn., Springfield, Ill., 1986—2007; retired, 2007. Mem. (men's choir) The Century Men, 1987— (Grammy nominees, 2000). Mem.: Nat. Assn. Tchrs. of Singing, State Music Leaders Fellowship (treas. 2003—06). Home: 25 Merlin Dr Rochester IL 62563

MASHBURN, JAMAL, professional basketball player; b. NYC, Nov. 29, 1972; Grad., Ky. Coll. Forward Dallas Mavericks, 1993-97, Miami Heat, 1997-99, Charlotte Hornets, 1999—2004, Phila. 76ers, 2004—. Named to NBA All-Rookie First Team, 1994. Office: New Jersey Nets Continental Airlines Arena 50 Rte 120 East Rutherford NJ 07073

MASHECK, JOSEPH DANIEL, art critic, educator; b. NYC, Jan. 19, 1942; s. Joseph Anthony and Dorothy Anna (Cahill) M. AB, Columbia U., 1963, MA, 1965, PhD, 1973; MLitt, U. Dublin, 2001. Editorial researcher Bollingen Found.-Princeton U. Press, 1967-69; lectr. liberal studies Maidstone Coll. Art, Kent, England, 1968-69; preceptor in art history Columbia U., 1970-71; instr. art history Barnard Coll., 1971-73, asst. prof., 1973-82; lectr. visual and environ. studies Harvard U., Cambridge, Mass., 1983-86; assoc. prof. art history Hofstra U., Hempstead, NY, 1987-94, prof., 1994—. Coord. grad. program in humanities Hofstra Mus., Hempstead, 1991—99, curatorial cons., 1991—; centenary fellow, visiting prof. art history Edinburgh Coll. Art, Scotland, 2006—. Author: Historical Present: Essays of the 1970s, 1984, Smart Art (Point 1), 1984, Modernites: Art-Matters in the Present, 1993, Building-Art: Modern Architecture Under Cultural Construction, 1993, C's Aesthetics: Philosophy in the Painting, 2004; editor: Marcel Duchamp in Perspective 1975, reprint, 2002, Van Gogh 100, 1996, A.W. Dow's Composition, 1997; editor-in-chief Artforum mag., 1977-80. Bd. dirs. Crosby St. Project, N.Y., 1995-96; mem. adv. bd. Annals of Scholarship, 1998—. Samuel H. Kress Found. fellow, 1968-69, Nat. Endowment Arts fellow, 1972-73, 75-76, Guggenheim fellow, 1977-78; grantee Malevich Soc., 2003; Hon. Armiger, Coll. Arms, London Fellow Royal Soc. Arts, Soc. Antiquaries of Scotland; mem. AAUP, Coll. Art Assn., Internat. Assn. Art Critics, United Arts Club (Dublin). Roman Catholic. Democrat. Office: Hofstra U Dept Fine Arts and Art History Calkins Hall Hempstead NY 11549

MASHELKAR, RAGHUNATH ANANT, chemical engineer; b. Jan. 1, 1943; children: Shruti R., Shubra R., Amey R. BChemE, PhD in Chem. Engring., U Bombay, 1969. Rsch. fellow dept. chem. engring. U. Salford, U.K., 1969-70, lectr. chem. engring., 1970-76; asst. dir. Nat. Chem. Lab., Pune, India, 1976-78, head chem. engring. div., 1978-89, dir., 1989-95, Coun. Scientific & Indsl. Rsch., India, 1995—. Bd. dirs. Tech. Devel. and Info. Co., India, Indsl. Credit and Investments Corp, India; vis. prof. chem. engring. U. Del., 1975-76, 88, U. Denmark, 1982; hon. vis. prof. U. Salford, 1985-86, U. Pune, 1985-86; hon. prof. Jawaharlal Nehru Centre Advancement of Sci. Rsch., 1990—; G.P. Kane prof. U. Bombay, 1990; lectr. in field. Tech. assessor Bhopal Inquiry Commn., India, 1984; chmn. high and powered tech. com. IPCL's Petrochem. Complex at Nagothane, 1990-91. Recipient Bhatnagar prize, 1982, Nehru award on technology 1990, Padmashri Civilian Honor, Govt. of India, 1991. Fellow NAS, NAE, Indian Acad. Scis., Indian Nat. Sci. Acad., Maharashtra Acad. Scis., Third World Acad. Sci., Royal Soc. London. Avocations: reading, music. Home: DG's Flat CSIR Sci Ctr Lodi Gardens Gate # 2 Lodi Estate New Delhi 110003 India Office: CSIR Anusandhan Bhawan 2 Rafi Marg New Delhi 110001 India

MASHHOON, BAHRAM, physicist, researcher; b. Tehran, Iran, Sept. 9, 1947; s. Hassan Mashhoon and Nosrat Dargahi; 1 child, Yasmin. BA, U. Calif., 1969; PhD, Princeton U., 1972. Assoc. prof. U. Mo., physics dept., Columbia, 1985—95; prof. U. Mo., 1995—. Author: (nonlocal theory of accelerated observers) Physical Review A, 1993. Home: 404 Victoria Dr Columbia MO 65201 Office: Department of Physics and Astronomy University of Missouri-Columbia Columbia MO 65211 Office Phone: 573-882-6526. E-mail: mashhoonb@missouri.edu.

MASHNIK, STEPAN G., physicist; b. Brinzeni, Moldova, June 1, 1952; arrived in U.S., 1996, naturalized, 2004; s. George I. and Natalia G. Mashnik; m. Nadejda I. Sukhlova; children: Polina, Daria. BS, Kishinev State U., 1972; MS, Moscow State U., 1974; PhD, Joint Inst. Nuc. Rsch., Dubna, Russia, 1981; sr. rsch. diploma, Presidium Acad. Sci. USSR, Moscow, 1989. Jr. rsch. scientist Joint Inst. Nuc. Rsch., Dubna, 1975—82, sr. rsch. scientist, 1991—97; sr./jr. rschr. Acad. Sci. Moldova, Kishinev, 1982—91, leading rsch. scientist, 1991—2004; long term vis. staff mem. Los Alamos Nat. Lab., N.Mex., 1997—2001, staff mem., 2001—. Country coord. XXVIII Internat. Conf. High Energy Physics, Hamburg, 1996—97; mem. internat. sci. coun. Joint Inst. Nuc. Rsch., Dubna, 1992—95; mem. intermediate energy data group NEA/OECD, Paris, 1994—, liaison officer between Paris, and JINR, Dubna, 1996—97; vis. rschr. Oak Ridge Nat. Lab., Tenn., 1995—96, Centre d'Etudes de Bruyers-le-Chatel, France, 1996. Contbr. articles to profl. jours. Recipient Several Excellent Work and Dubna County awards, Joint Inst. Nuc. Rsch., 1975—82, Investigations in Theoretical Physics award, Inst. Applied Physics, Acad. Sci. Moldova, 1983, Moldova Award for Young Scientists, Am. Medal of Honor, 2003, Svc. award, Los Alamos Nat. Lab., 2007; CRDF Grant, Devel. of a Universal Intranuclear Cascade Type Model for Heavy Ion and Nucleon Induced Reactions at Intermediate Energies, 2001—, NASA Grant, Propagation Model for Cosmic Ray Species in the Galaxy, 2002—. Mem.: Phys. Soc. Republic of Moldova, Internat. Nuc. Soc., Am. Nuc. Soc., Am. Phys. Soc. Avocations: swimming, travel, skiing, jogging. Office Phone: 505-667-9946. Office Fax: 505-665-4479. Personal E-mail: mashniks@qwest.net. Business E-Mail: mashnik@lanl.gov.

MASHOUF, MANNY, apparel executive; b. Iran; m. Neda Mashouf; 1 child, Karim. BA in Polit. Sci., San Francisco State U., 1966. Founder & chmn. Bebe Stores Inc., San Francisco, 1976—. Mem. bus. adv. bd. San Francisco State U. Coll. Creative Arts. Named one of 400 Richest Americans, Forbes, 2006; named to San Francisco State U. Hall of Fame, 2003; recipient Alumnus of Yr. award, San Francisco State U., 2005. Office: Bebe Stores Inc 400 Valley Dr Brisbane CA 94005 Office Phone: 415-715-3900. Office Fax: 415-715-3939.

MASI, DALE A., project director, social sciences educator, research and development company executive; b. NYC; d. Alphonse E. and Vera Avella; children: Eric, Renee, Robin. BS, Coll. Mt. St. Vincent; MSW, U. Ill.; PhD Social Work, Cath. U. Lectr. Sch. Social Svcs., Ipswitch, Eng., 1970-72; project dir. occupational substance abuse program, asso. prof. Boston Coll. Grad. Sch. Social Work, 1972-79; dir. Office Employee Counseling Svc., Dept. Health/Human Svcs., Washington, 1979-84; pres. Masi Research Cons., Inc., 1984—2005; prof. emeritus U. Md. Grad. Sch. Social Work, 1980—2004; adj. prof. U. Md. Coll. Bus. and Mgmt., 1980—2004, prof. emeritus, 2004—; lectr. Bacconi U., Milan, 2004—; project dir. NIH Rsch. grantee coll. bingo drinking Northeastern U., 2005—. Mem. IBM Mental Health Adv. Bd., 1990-95; cons. IBM, Toyota, Mobil Chm., The Washington Post, U.S. Ho. Reps., U.S. Postal Svc., White House, WHO, Bechtel Corp., other orgns. in pub. and pvt. sector; bd. advisors Nat. Security Inst., Wayside Youth and Family Support Network; USIA Ampart lectr. on alcohol, drugs and AIDS in the workplace; chair CMHS Joint Industry Alliance, 2002—; acad. advisor Northwestern U. Author: Human Services in Industry, Organizing for Women, Designing Employee Assistance Programs, Drug Free Workplace, AIDS Issues in the Workplace: A Response Model for Human Resource Management, The AMA Handbook for Developing Employee Assistance and Counseling Programs, Evaluating Your Employee Assistance and Managed Behavioral Care Program, Internat. Employee Assistance Anthology, I, II and III edits., Productivity Lost: Alcohol and Drugs in the Workplace; co-author: Shrink to Fit: Answers to Your Questions About Therapy; also over 40 articles. Named Disting. Scholar, Nat. Acad. Practice, 2001—; named to Employee Assistance Program Hall of Fame; recipient award, Employee Assistance Program Digest; fellow Fulbright fellow, 1969—70, 1994, AAUW postdoctoral fellow, NIMH, 1962—64; Fulbright Sr. Specialist Canidate, 2002. Mem. AAUW, NASW (Internat. Rhoda G. Sarnat award 1993), Acad. Cert. Social Workers, Employee Assistance Profls. Assn. (nat. individual achievement award 1983), Fulbright Assn. (nat. bd.). Democrat. Roman Catholic. Office: 4 Copley Pl Suite 145 Boston MA 02116

MASI, JANE VIRGINIA, marketing and sales consultant; b. June 6, 1947; d. Vincent Joseph and Virginia Marie (Beddow) Masi; m. Charles Walter Friedman, Feb. 14, 1976 (div. Sept. 1998); m. Charles W. Friedman, July 29, 2006 (dec. Sept. 2006). BA in Comms. and Psychology, Mercy Coll., NYC, 1969; MA, New Sch. Social Rsch., 1979, postgrad., 1994. Asst. sales mgr. Chevron Chem., NYC, 1969-71; writer, 1973-75; ptnr. Masi-D'Angelo Constrn. and Devel. Assocs., NYC, 1979-83; pres., founder Beddow Mills Inc., NYC, 1982-85, Beddow Mfg. Inc., NYC,

1983-85; co-pres. TRS Mktg. Inc., NYC, 1985—. Founder Energy Works, 1985, Did You Know, 1989, Range Burgers, 1989, Terramor, 1989, In the Pink!, 1991, The Profl. Salon, 1991, Terramor Foods, 1991, Terramor Catering, 2003; founder, dir. TRS Inc. Profl. Suite, 1986—; pub. The Planetary Gazette, 2002-Happy Healing Hours cmty. svc. events concert, 2001-. N.Y. Regents scholar, 1965-69. Mem. Soc. Ethical Treatment of Animals. Avocations: woodworking, carpentry, advocating animal rights, design psychology. Office: TRS Mktg Inc 44 E 32nd St Fl 11 New York NY 10016-5508 Office Phone: 212-685-2848. E-mail: terramor@earthlink.net.

MASI, JULIA A., elementary school educator; d. Ralph Michel and Frances Marie Masi. MS, Adelphi U., 1987; MA, Adlephi U., 1991; cert. in Chinese, NYU, 1994; cert. in non-profit mgmt., U. Ill., Chgo., 2005. Cert. diamond appraiser Gemological Inst. Am. Tchr. Pub. Sch. 169, NYC Dept. Edn., Bklyn., 1988—97; sci. tchr. Pub. Sch. 24, NYC Dept. Edn., Bklyn., 1997—. Mng. editor: Fanzeen Mag., contbr.: Dance Pages; exhibitions include Brooklyn Hist. Soc., 2002. Vol. editor newsletter, website Magic Hosp.; vol. www.GourmetSoupKitchens.org; mem. Jane Godall Inst.; bd. dirs. Children of the City, Bklyn., 2005—; jr. assoc. Mus. of Modern Art, NYC, 1996—; mem. young collectors coun., aquisitons com. Guggenheim Mus., NYC, 1993—; vol. NY Cares, NYC, 2005—. Mem.: APA (assoc.). Democrat. Roman Catholic. Avocations: writing, ballet, mentoring, drawing, languages. Home Phone: 718-748-7848.

MASIELLO, ROCCO JOSEPH, air transportation executive, consultant; b. NYC, Jan. 9, 1922; s. Joseph and Armanda (Mansueti) M.; m. Rita Elizabeth Amoruso, Feb. 11, 1945; children: Richard, Robin, Janet. Student, CCNY, 1946-48, Hofstra U., 1951-54. Registered profl. engr., Maine. With Pan. Am. World Airways, NYC, 1950-59; v.p. maintenance and engring. U.S. Air Group, Pitts., 1959—73, Am. Airlines, Tulsa, 1973-82, sr. v.p. ops. Dallas, 1982-86; co-founder, exec. v.p. USAfrica Airways, 1990—94, also bd. dirs; founder The Reston Group; aerospace cons., prin. R.J. Masiello and Assoc. Mem. Soc. Aerospace Engr., Royal Aero. Soc. Roman Catholic. Home Phone: 207-594-5223; Office Phone: 207-594-5223.

MASIELLO, THOMAS PHILIP, JR., lawyer, risk management consultant; b. Medford, Mass., Oct. 13, 1961; s. Thomas Philip and Diane Marie (Traina) M.; m. Stephanie Hope Sadwin, Sept. 24, 1994; 1 child, Andrew Joseph. BA, Johnson State Coll., Vt., 1982, BFA, 1983; ARM, Bentley Coll., Waltham, Mass., 1986; JD, New Eng. Sch. Law, Boston, 1992. Bar: Mass. 1993, U.S. Supreme Ct. 1998. With Parker, Colter, Daley & White, 1986-88, Am. Internat. Group Ins. Com., 1988-91, McDonald & Wallace, 1991-92, Boston Housing Authority, 1992-95, Cumberland Farms-Gulf Oil, Canton, Mass., 1995—. Exec. dir. Mass. Mcpl. Workers Compensation Group. Author Workers Comp Bull., 1996. Mem. ABA, ATLA, Internat. Risk Mgmt. Inst. (self-insurers and risk mgr. law com.), Boston Bar Assn., Norfolk County Bar Assn., Risk Ins. Mgmt. Soc. (nat. governance com., nat. nominating com.), Mass. Acad. Trial Atty., Quality Ins. Congress, Nat. Assoc. of Convenence Sues (NACS), Mass Acad. Trial Atty.,(MATA). Avocation: travel. Home: 3 Grantland Rd Wellesley Hills MA 02481-7606 Office: Cumberland Farms/Gulf Oil 777 Dedham St Canton MA 02021-1402

MASIN, MICHAEL TERRY, lawyer; came to US, 1954; BA, Dartmouth U., 1966; JD, UCLA, 1969. Bar: Calif. 1969, D.C. 1970. Assoc. O'Melveny & Myers, LA, 1969-76, ptnr. Washington, 1976-91, mng. ptnr. NYC, 1991-93; vice chair, pres. GTE, Irving, Tex., 1993—2000; vice chmn., pres. Verizon Comms., NYC, 2000—02; vice chmn., COO Citigroup, NYC, 2002—03; ptnr. O'Melveny & Myers, LLP, NYC, 2004—. Trustee Carnegie Hall, W.M. Keck Found.; mem. dean's coun. UCLA Sch. Law Mem. Coun. on Fgn. Rels., The Brook. Republican. Methodist. Office: O'Melveny & Meyers 7 Times Sq 30th Fl New York NY 10036 E-mail: mmasin@omm.com.

MASINTER, PAUL JAMES, lawyer; b. New Orleans, June 28, 1961; s. Milton Paul Masinter and Shirley Mae (Rabé) Bradley; m. Audrey Renee Williams, Oct. 10, 1992. BA in Polit. Sci., La. State U., 1984, JD, 1987. Bar: La. 1987, U.S. Dist. Ct. (ea., mid. and we. dists.) La. 1987, U.S. Ct. Appeals (5th cir.) 1990, U.S. Supreme Ct. 1994. Law clk. to assoc. justice Hon. James L. Dennis La. Supreme Ct., New Orleans, 1987-88; assoc. McGlinchey, Stafford, New Orleans, 1988-90, Stone Pigman Walther Wittmann LLC, New Orleans, 1990-95; ptnr. Stone Pigman Walther Wittmann, LLC, New Orleans, 1996—. Assoc. editor La. Law Rev., 1986-87. Bd. dirs. Save Our Cemeteries, New Orleans, 1993—, treas., 1998, pres., 1999; mem. bd. commrs. New Orleans City Park Improvement Assn., Inc., 2003—; former mem. fin. com. Trinity Episcopal Sch. Mem. ABA (former chair newsletter subcom., co-chair bus. and corp. litigation com., bus. law sect.), La. State Bar Assn., New Orleans Bar Assn. Democrat. Roman Catholic. Office: Stone Pigman Walther & Wittmann LLC 546 Carondelet St Ste 100 New Orleans LA 70130-3588 Office Phone: 504-581-3200. Business E-Mail: PMasinter@stonepigman.com.

MASKAS, AUBA SUE, elementary school educator; b. Heidelburg, Germany, Mar. 6, 1952; arrived in US, 1952; d. Louis Leo Jacobs, Jr. and Auba Evelyn (Wilcox) Jacobs; m. Stephen Maskas (div.); children: Stephanie Biddle, Charles Stephen. BS in History, U. Houston, Clear Lake, Tex., 1989, MA in Edn., 1990. Cert. tchr. Tenn. Tchr. Henry County, Paris, Tenn., 1992—95, Paris Spl. Sch., 1995—. Office: Inman Middle Sch 400 Harrison Paris TN 38242

MASKET, EDWARD SEYMOUR, television executive; b. NYC, Mar. 3, 1923; s. Isadore and Jennie (Bernstein) M.; m. Frances Ellen Rees, June 11, 1958 (div.); children: Joel Daniel, Johanna Rees Bettaeib, Kate Isobel Smiley. BS, CCNY, 1942; LLB, JD, Harvard U., 1949. Bar: N.Y. 1949. Atty., dir. bus. affairs, v.p. bus. affairs ABC, 1951-68; v.p. to exec. v.p. Columbia Pictures TV, Burbank, Calif., 1968-81; sr. v.p. adminstrn. Universal TV, 1982-86, exec. v.p. adminstrn., 1986-90, MCA TV Group, 1990-93; TV cons., 1994—98; ret., 1998. Served as 2d lt. AUS, 1942-46, PTO. Mem. Motion Picture Pioneers, Phi Beta Kappa. E-mail: telemogul@aol.com.

MASKET, SAMUEL, medical association administrator; b. NYC, 1943; MD, N.Y. Med. Coll., 1968. Diplomate Am. Bd. Ophthalmology. Intern Bronx Mcpl. Hosp.-Einstein, NYC, 1968—69; resident Metro Hosp. Ctr.-N.Y. Med., 1969—73; fellow Columbia-Presbyn. Med. Ctr., NYC; asst. clin. prof. ophthalmology UCLA; mem. staff West Hills Hosp., Canoga Park, Calif.; chmn. Am. Bd. Ophthalmology, Bala Cynwyd, Pa.; clinical prof. Jules Stein Eye Inst., Los Angeles, Calif. Fellow: Am. Acad. Ophthalmology; mem.: PAAO, ASCRS, AMA. Office: Am Bd Ophthalmology 111 Presidential Blvd Ste 241 Bala Cynwyd PA 19004-1012 also: 7230 Med Ctr Dr Ste 204 Canoga Park CA 91307 Office: Jules Stein Eye Inst 100 Stein Plaza UCLA Los Angeles CA 90095

MASKIN, ERIC STARK, economics professor; b. NYC, Dec. 12, 1950; m. Gayle Sawtelle; children: Joseph, Charlotte. AB in Maths., Harvard U., 1972, AM in Applied maths., 1974, PhD in Applied Maths., 1976. Rsch. fellow Jesus Coll. Cambridge (Eng.) U., 1976-77; asst. prof. econs. MIT, Cambridge, Mass., 1977-80, assoc. prof. econs., 1980-81, prof. econs., 1981-84, Harvard U., Cambridge, 1985—2000; prof. social sci. Inst. for Advanced Study, Princeton, NJ, 2000—. Am. editor Rev. Econ. Studies, 1977—82; assoc. editor: Social Choice and Welfare, 1983—, Games and Econ. Behavior, 1988—; editor Quar. Jour. Econs., 1984—90, Econs. Letters, 1992—. Churchill Coll. fellow, 1980—81, Guggenheim fellow, 1980—81, Sloan fellow, 1983—85, St. John's Coll. fellow, 1987—88, hon. fellow, 2004—. Fellow: Am. Acad. Arts and Sci., Brit. Acad. (corr.), Econometric Soc. (hon.; pres. 2003). Office: Inst for Advanced Study Einstein Drive Princeton NJ 08540 Office Phone: 609-734-8309.

MASLACH, CHRISTINA, psychology professor; b. San Francisco, Jan. 21, 1946; d. George James and Doris Ann (Cuneo) M.; m. Philip George Zimbardo, Aug. 10, 1972; children: Zara, Tanya. BA, Harvard-Radcliffe Coll., 1967; PhD, Stanford U., 1971. Prof. psychology U. Calif.-Berkeley, 1971—, vice provost for undergrad. edn., 2001—. Author: Burnout: The Cost of Caring, 1982; co-author: Influencing Attitudes and Changing Behavior, 1977, Maslach Burnout Inventory (rsch. scale), 1981, 2d edit., 1986, 3d edit., 1996, Experiencing Social Psychology, 1979, 4th edit., 2001, Professional Burnout, 1993, The Truth About Burnout, 1997, Preventing Burnout and Building Engagement, 2000, Banishing Burnout, 2005. Recipient Disting. Teaching award, 1987, Best Paper award Jour. Orgnl. Behavior, 1994, Prof. of Yr. award Carnegie/CASE, 1997. Fellow AAAS, APA, Am. Psychol. Soc., Soc. Clin. and Exptl. Hypnosis (Henry Guze rsch. award 1980), We. Psychol. Assn. (pres. 1989); mem. Soc. Exptl. Social Psychology. Democrat. Office: U Calif Office of Chancellor 200 California Hall # 1500 Berkeley CA 94720-1500 Office Phone: 510-642-9594. Business E-Mail: maslach@berkeley.edu.

MASLANKA, DANIEL CHESTER, percussionist and music educator; b. Highland Park, Mich., Apr. 20, 1955; s. Chester J. and Irene F. (Baranski) M. MusB in Instrumental Edn. and Percussion Performance, Wayne State U., 1980. Cert. secondary tchr., Mich. Ind. percussion instr., 1971—; asst. dir. band L' Anse Creuse High and Mid. Schs., Mt. Clemens, Mich., 1979; head percussion dept. Ctr. Creative Studies div. Inst. Music and Dance, Detroit, 1985—; staff percussionist Birmingham (Mich.) Theater, 1984-95; co-owner Pro Percussion Ctr., Plymouth, Mich., 1996—2001. Mem. applied faculty Oakland U., Rochester, Mich., Macomb Cmty. Coll., Mt. Clemens; staff percussionist Church of Today weekly show, Sta. WKBD-TV, Detroit. Percussionist with nat. touring cos. of Cats, Wicked, White Christmas, Phantom of the Opera, King and I, Am. Ballet Theater, (bus. and truck prodns.) Dancin', Fiddler on the Roof, A Chorus Line, Joseph and the Amazing Technicolor Dream Coat, various entertainers including Danny Thomas, Johnny Mathis, Dionne Warwick, Luciano Pavarotti, Marvin Hamlisch, with many groups including Brookside Jazz Ensemble, Detroit Symphony Orch., Golden Rain Percussion Ensemble, Mich. Opera Theatre; numerous TV and radio commls. and live jazz broadcasts. Mem. Percussive Arts Soc. (v.p. Mich. chpt.), Mich. Music Assn., Am. Guild Music.

MASLIN, JANET, critic; b. NYC, Aug. 12, 1949; d. Paul and Lucille (Becker) M.; m. Benjamin Cheever; children: John, Andrew. BA in Math., U. Rochester, 1970. Film and music critic The Boston Phoenix, 1972-76; film critic Newsweek, NYC, 1976-77; dep. film critic NY Times, NYC, 1977-93, chief film critic, 1993-99, now book critic. Office: NY Times 229 W 43rd St New York NY 10036-3959 Office Phone: 212-556-5801. Office Fax: 212-556-1516.

MASNARI, NINO ANTONIO, electrical engineer, educator; b. Three Rivers, Mich., Sept. 20, 1935; s. Antonio and Giovanna (Lupato) M.; m. Judy E. Guild, June 29, 1957; children: Michael A., Jeffrey P., Maria L. BSEE, U. Mich., 1958, MSEE, 1959, PhD, 1964. Electronics engr. R & D ctr. GE, Schenectady, NY, 1967-69; lectr., rsch. assoc. U. Mich., Ann Arbor, 1964-67, assoc. prof. elec. engring., 1969-76, prof., 1976-79, dir. elec. physics lab., 1975-79; disting. prof. elec. and computer engring. NC State U., Raleigh, 1979—, head dept. elec. and computer engring., 1979-88, dir., Advanced Electronic Materials Processing Ctr., 1988-96, dean, Coll. Engring., 1996—2006. Cons. in field. Raytheon predoctoral fellow 1962. Fellow IEEE; mem. Am. Soc. Engring. Edn., Materials Rsch. Soc., Sigma Xi, Phi Kappa Phi, Tau Beta Pi, Eta Kappa Nu. Achievements include patent for Process for Manufacturing Inertial Confinement Fusion Targets and Resulting Product. Office: North Carolina State Univ ECE Dept Campus Box 7911 Raleigh NC 27695-7911 Office Phone: 919-515-5108. Business E-Mail: masnari@ncsu.edu.

MASNYJ, YURI, painter, sculptor; b. Washington, 1976; BFA, Cooper Union, 1998. One-man shows include On Our Black Rainbow, Sutton Lane, London, 2004, A World of Interiors, Metro Pictures, NY, 2004, exhibitions include 126a, Bklyn. Front Gallery, 2001, Ballpoint Inklings, Geoffrey Young Gallery, Mass., 2002, New Topography, 2003, Radical Vaudeville, 2005, Shallow Interiors, Rivington Arms Gallery, NY, 2002, From Here On, Guild & Greyskhul, NY, 2003, The Night Has a Thousand Eyes, 2005, Drawings, Metro Pictures, NY, 2003, International Paper, Hammer Mus., Univ. Calif., LA, 2003, Happy Days Are Here Again, David Zwirner, 2004, Greater New York, PS 1 Mus. Modern Art, Long Island City, NY, 2005, Landings, Susan Inglett Gallery, NY, 2005, Square Dance, Galerie Jacky Strenz, Frankfurt, 2005, Whitney Biennial: Day for Night, Whitney Mus. Am. Art, NY, 2006, New York Drawings, Travesia Cautro, Madrid, 2006. Mailing: c/o Metro Pictures 519 West 24th St New York NY 10011

MASON, AIMEE HUNNICUTT ROMBERGER, retired philosophy and humanities educator; b. Atlanta, Nov. 3, 1918; d. Edwin William and Aimee Greenleaf (Hunnicutt) Romberger; m. Samuel Venable Mason, Aug. 16, 1941 (dec. 1988); children: Olivia Elizabeth (Mrs. Mason Butcher), Christopher Leeds. BA, Conn. Coll., 1940; postgrad., Emory U., 1946-48; MA, U. Fla., 1979, PhD, 1980; MA, Stetson U., 1968. Model, coll. shop Saks Fifth Ave., NYC; jr. exec. merchandising G. Fox & Co., Hartford, Conn., 1940-41; air traffic contr. CAA, Atlanta, 1942; ptnr. Coronado Concrete Products, New Smyrna Beach, Fla., 1953-81; adj. faculty Valencia Jr. Coll., Orlando, Fla., 1969; instr. philosophy and Humanities Seminole C.C., Sanford, Fla., 1969. Area cons. ARC, 1947-50; del. Nat. Red Cross, Washington, 1949; founding mem. St. Joseph Hosp. Aux., Atlanta, 1950-53; v.p., treas. Nw Smyrna Beach PTA, 1955-60; bd. dirs. Atlanta Symphony Orch., Fla. Symphony Orch., 1954-59; mem Code Enforcement Bd., Edgewater, Fla., 1992-94. Lt. USCGR, 1943-46. Recipient award in graphics Nat. Assn. Women Artists, 1939, 41. Mem. AAUP, AAUW (founding mem. New Smyrna Beach, exec. bd. 1984-85, chmn. scholarship com. 1984-87, coll./univ. liaison 1987-91, citizens code enforcement bd. Edgewater 1992-94), DAV, Am. Philos. Assn., Fla. Philos. Assn. (exec. coun. 1978-79), Collegium Phenomenologicum, Soc. Existencial and Phenomenological Philosophy, Soc. Phenomenology in Human Scis., Merleau-Ponty Circle, Fla. Assn. Cmty. Colls., Univ. Club Winter Park. Home: B216/218 1620 Mayflower Court Winter Park FL 32792

MASON, ANDREW S., lawyer; b. Worcester, Mass., 1956; BA, Yale U., 1978, JD, 1981. Bar: NY 1982. Mem. Sullivan & Cromwell, NYC, 1981—89, ptnr., 1989—. Mem.: Assn. Bar City of NY (chmn. com.). Office: Sullivan & Cromwell 125 Broad St Fl 28 New York NY 10004-2489 Office Phone: 212-558-4000. Office Fax: 212-558-3588. Business E-Mail: masona@sullcrom.com.

MASON, ARDIS J.P., elementary school educator; m. Daniel Mason; children: Abigail, Damian, Margaret. BS, Mansfield U., Pa., 1985; MS, Lynchburg Coll., Va., 2000. Tchr. Lynchburg Sch. Dist., 1999—2001, Williamsport Area Sch. Dist., Pa., 2001—. Mem.: Internat. Reading Assn. Office: Curtin Middle School 85 Elred St Williamsport PA 17701 Home Phone: 570-323-7760; Office Phone: 570-323-4785 121.

MASON, BOBBIE ANN, writer; b. Mayfield, Ky., May 1, 1940; d. Wilburn A. and Christianna (Lee) M.; m. Roger B. Rawlings, Apr. 12, 1969. BA, U. Ky., 1962; MA, SUNY, Binghamton, 1966; PhD, U. Conn., 1972. Asst. prof. English Mansfield (Pa.) State Coll., 1972-79. Writer-in-residence, U. Ky., Lexington, 2001—. Author: Nabokov's Garden, 1974, The Girl Sleuth: A Feminist Guide to the Bobbsey Twins, Nancy Drew and Their Sisters, 1975, 2d edit., 1995, Shiloh and Other Stories, 1982 (PEN Hemingway award, Nat. Book Critics Circle award nominee, Am. Book award nominee, PEN Faulkner award nominee), 2d edit., 2001, In Country, 1985, 2d edit., 2005, Spence + Lila, 1988, 2d edit., 1998, Love Life, 1989, Feather Crowns, 1993 (Nat. Book award nominee Critics Cir., So. Book award Critics Cir.), Midnight Magic, 1998, Clear Springs, 1999 (Pulitzer prize finalist), Zigzagging Down a Wild Trail, 2001 (So. Book award Critics Cir.), Elvis Presley, 2003 (Ky. Literary award), An Atomic Romance, 2005; editor: Missing Mountains, 2005, Nancy Culpepper, 2006; contbr. New Yorker, 1980—, The Atlantic, Redbook, Paris Rev., Mother Jones, Harpers, N.Am. Rev., Va. Quar. Rev., Story, Ploughshares, So. Rev., Crazyhorse, DoubleTake; contbr. works Best American Short Stories, 1981, 83, The Pushcart Prize, Best of the Small Presses, 1983, 86, 97. Recipient O. Henry Anthology awards, 1986, 88, Hillsdale prize, 1999; grantee Pa. Arts Coun., 1983, 89, Nat. Endowment Arts, 1983, Am. Acad. and Inst. Arts and Letters, 1984; Guggenheim fellow, 1984. Mem.: PEN, Author's Guild, Fellowship of So. Writers. Office: Internat Creative Mgmt care Amanda Urban Agt 825 8th Ave New York NY 10128 Business E-Mail: aurban@icmtalent.com.

MASON, CHRISTOPHER MAY, lawyer; b. Orange County, NC, Nov. 4, 1957; s. Julian Dewey and Elsie (May) M. BA summa cum laude, U. N.C., 1979; JD magna cum laude, Duke U., 1983. Bar: N.Y. 1985, D.C. 1985, U.S. Dist. Ct. (so. and ea. dists.) N.Y. 1985, U.S. Dist. Ct. (no. and we. dists.) N.Y., 1989, U.S. Dist. Ct. D.C., 1995, U.S. Ct. Internat. Trade 1985, U.S. Temporary Emergency Ct. of Appeals 1985, U.S. Ct. Appeals (4th, 6th, 8th cirs.) 1985, U.S. Ct. Appeals (2d, 3d, 5th, 7th and 9th cirs.) 1988, U.S. Ct. Appeals (D.C. cir.) 1991, U. S. Supreme Ct. 1988. Law clk. to judge J. Clifford Wallace U.S. Ct. Appeals (9th cir.), San Diego, 1983-84; assoc. Cravath, Swaine & Moore, NYC, 1984-89, Hunton & Williams, NYC, 1989-91, ptnr., 1992-2000, Nixon Peabody LLP, NYC, 2000—. Contbr. articles to profl. jours. Mem. ABA, Assn. of Bar of City of N.Y., N.Y. State Bar Assn., Fed. Bar Coun., Phi Beta Kappa, Order of Coif. Presbyterian. Office: Nixon Peabody LLP 437 Madison Ave New York NY 10022-7001 E-mail: cmason@nixonpeabody.com.

MASON, CONNIE JEANNE, writer; b. Niles, Mich., Apr. 22, 1930; d. Frank G. and Frances (Coda) Roti; m. Lewis Gerald Mason, July 1, 1950; children: Jeri A. Vlasicak, Michelle A. Osborn, Mark. Author: Promise Me Forever, 1990, Brave Land, Brave Love, 1990, Surrender to The Fury, 1990, Ice @ Rapture, 1991, A Promise of Thunder, 1991, Lord Of The Night, 1991, Treasures Of The Heart, 1992, Tears Like Rain, 1993, Wind Rider, 1993, Sierra, 1994, The Lion's Bride, 1994, Taken By You, 1995, pure Temptation, 1995, Flame, 1996, A Love To Cherish, 1996, Shadow Walker, 1997, To Love A Stranger, 1997, Sheik, 1997, Viking!, 1998, The Black Knight, 1999 (NY Times Extended Bestseller List), Pirate, 1998, Gunslinger, 1999, To Tempt a Rogue, 1999, The Black Knight, 1999 (NY Times Extended List 1999), The Outlaws: Rafe, 2000, A Taste of Sin, 2000, The Outlaws: Jess, 2000, A Breath of Scandal, 2001, The Outlaws: Sam, 2001, The Dragon Lord, 2001, The Rogue and the Bastion, 2002, Lionheart, 2002, Seduced by a Rogue, 2003, The Laird of Stonehaven, 2003, The Last Rogue, 2004, The Pirate Prince, 2004, Gypsy Lover, 2005, A Knight's Honor, 2005, A Taste of Paradise, 2006, Highland Warrior, 2007, also novellas. Named Story Teller of Yr., Romantic Times, 1990; recipient Career Achievement award, 1994. Mem. Romance Writers Am., Novelists, Inc. Avocations: reading, travel.

MASON, CRAIG ALAN, clinician; b. Madison, Wis., Aug. 1, 1964; life ptnr. Carole Mary DeGroot; children: Jeff Alan, Nick. MusB, U. Wis., Platteville, 1982—88. Clinician, Stoughton, Wis., 1985—. Arranger (musical compositions). Grantee Kohl fellowship, State Wis., 1989. Office: Stoughton HS 600 Lincoln Ave Stoughton WI 53589 Home Phone: 608-513-4511. Office Fax: 608-877-5619. Business E-Mail: masoncr@stoughton.k12.wi.us.

MASON, DAN, broadcast executive; b. Louisville, Ky. 2 children. BS in Broadcasting, Ea. Ky. U. Joined WZGC-FM, Atlanta, 1975, program dir. Washington, 1977; nat. program dir. First Media, 1977; v.p., gen. mgr. KTSA/KTFM, San Antonio, 1979; exec. v.p. First Media; pres. Cook Inlet Radio Partners (formerly First Media), 1988; pres. Group W Radio Westinghouse, 1993—95; pres. CBS Radio Grp. (renamed Infinity Radio), 1995—2002, pres., CEO, 2007—; advisor and consultant to companies in the radio broadcasting industry, 2002—07. Bd. dirs. Spanish Broadcasting System, Inc. Named Outstanding Alumnus of the Year, Ea. Ky. U., 1995, Radio Executive of the Year, Radio and Records Mag., 2002. Office: CBS Radio 1515 Broadway New York NY 10036 *

MASON, DEAN TOWLE, cardiologist; b. Berkeley, Calif., Sept. 20, 1932; s. Ira Jenckes and Florence Mabel (Towle) M.; m. Maureen O'Brien, June 22, 1957; children: Kathleen, Alison. BA in Chemistry, Duke U., Durham, NC, 1954; MD, Duke U., 1958. Diplomate Am. Bd. Internal Medicine, Am. Bd. Cardiovasc. Diseases, Nat. Bd. Med. Examiners. Intern, then resident in medicine Johns Hopkins Hosp., 1958-61; clin. assoc. cardiology br., sr. asst. surgeon USPHS, Nat. Heart Inst., NIH, 1961-63, asst. sect. dir. cardiovascular diagnosis, attending physician, sr. investigator cardiology br., 1963-68; prof. medicine, prof. physiology, chief cardiovascular medicine U. Calif. Med. Sch., Davis-Sacramento Med. Center, 1968-82; dir. cardiac ctr. Cedars Med. Ctr., Miami, Fla., 1982-83; physician-in chief Western Heart Inst., San Francisco, 1983—2000; chmn. dept. cardiovascular medicine St. Mary's Med. Ctr., San Francisco, 1986-99, hon. med. staff, 2000—. Co-chmn. cardiovascular-renal drugs U.S. Pharmacopeia Com. Revision, 1970—75; mem. life scis. com. NASA; med. rsch. rev. bd. VA, NIH; prof. medicine (hon.) Peking Med. U., China, 1987; vis. prof. numerous univs.; cons. in field. Editor-in-chief Am. Heart Jour., 1980—96; contbr. chapters to books, articles. Recipient rsch. award, Am. Therapeutic Soc., 1965, Theodore and Susan B. Cummings Humanitarian award, Dept. State-Am. Coll. Cardiology, 1972, 1973, 1975, 1978, Skylab Achievement award, NASA, 1974, U. Calif. Faculty Rsch. award, 1978, Symbol of Excellence, Tex. Heart Inst., 1979, Disting. Alumnus award, Duke U. Sch. Medicine, 1979, award of Honor, Wisdom Soc., 1997, Medal of Honor, Winston Churchill Soc., 1998, Armand Hammer Creative Genius award, 1998, Dwight D. Eisenhower Admirable Am. of Achievement award, 1998, Eternal Jesus Christ award, 1998, Blessed Lord's Prayer award, 1998, Dean Towle Mason Eminent Physician of Wisdom award, 1998, Dean Towle Mason, M.D. Medal of Wisdom award, 2001, Cardiologist of the Century Wisdom award, 2001, Albert Schweitzer world Humanitarian of Wisdom award, 2002, Jonas Salk award for med. rsch., 2003, Albert Einstein Sci. Rsch. award, 2003, John Wayne Pioneer of Am. award, 2003, Ernest Hemingway award for maj. contbns. to med. lit., 2003, Will Durant Philosopher-Physician award, 2004, Paul Dudley White award for disting. svc. in cardiovasc. medicine, 2004, Newton Kugelmass Children's Cardiology Crusader award, 2004, Norman Vincent Peale Healing Power of Prayer award, 2005. Master Am. Coll. Cardiology (pres. 1977-78); fellow ACP, Am. Heart Assn., Am. Coll. Chest Physicians, Royal Soc. Medicine; mem. Am. Soc. Clin. Investigation, Am. Physiol. Soc., Am. Soc. Pharmacology and Exptl. Therapeutics (Exptl. Therapeutics award 1973), Am. Fedn. Clin. Research, NY Acad. Scis., Am. Assn. U. Cardiologists, Am. Soc. Clin. Pharmacology and Therapeutics, We. Assn. Physicians, AAUP, We. Soc. Clin. Rsch. (past pres.), El Macero Country Club, Phi Beta Kappa, Alpha Omega Alpha. Republican. Methodist. Home: 44725 Country Club Dr El Macero CA 95618-1047 Office: Western Heart Inst St Marys Med Ctr 450 Stanyan St San Francisco CA 94117-1079 Office Phone: 415-750-5598.

MASON, DEIRDRE DIANNE, secondary school educator; b. Cleve., Feb. 12, 1958; d. Richard Whiting and Ruth Elizabeth (Moody) M. BS, Ashland Coll., 1981; MS, Ohio State U., 1986. Cert. home economist. Grad. asst. Ohio State U., Columbus; adult regional cons./home econs. coord. Mansfield (Ohio) City Schs., home econs. tchr. Mem. Am. Home Econs. Assn., Ohio Home Econs. Assn., NEA, Ohio Edn. Assn., Mansfield Edn. Assn. (bldg. rep.), AAUW, ASCD, Nat. Mid. Sch. Assn., Ohio Mid. Sch. Assn., Am. Coun. on Consumer Interest, Kappa Omicron Phi.

MASON, DWAYNE L., lawyer; s. Leroy and Tillie Mason. BSChemE, Purdue U., 1984; JD, U. Houston, 1993. Bar: Tex. Supreme Ct. 1993, U.S. Patent & Trademark Office 1995. Ptnr. Matthew Joseph Shaddox & Mason, Houston, 1995—99, Winstead Secrest & Minick, Houston, 1999—2001, Akin Gump Strauss Hauer & Feld, Houston, 2001—. Dir. Harris Coutny MUD 222, Houston, 1995—2006. Editl. bd.: Nanotechnology Law and Bus. Mem. Greater Houston Ptnrship., 2001—; bd. mem. Houston Strategic Forum, 2005—, Kiwanis Club. Named Top Minority IP Ptnr., AIPLA/MCCA, 2003, Top Lawyer, Tex. mag., 2004. Mem.: Kiwanis (chair legal com. 2001—, bd.). Office: Akin Gump Strauss Hauer & Feld LLP 1111 Louisiana St 44th Fl Houston TX 77002 Office Phone: 713-220-8186. Office Fax: 713-236-0822. Business E-Mail: dmason@akingump.com.

MASON, EDWARD EATON, surgeon; b. Boise, Idaho, Oct. 16, 1920; s. Edward Files and Dora Bell (Eaton) M.; m. Dordana Fairman, June 18, 1944; children— Daniel Edward, Rose Mary, Richard Eaton, Charles Henry. BA, U. Iowa, 1943, MD, 1945; PhD in Surgery, U. Minn., 1953. Intern, resident in surgery Univ. Hosps., Mpls., 1945-52; asst. prof. surgery U. Iowa, 1953-55, asso. prof., 1956-60, prof., 1961-91, prof. emeritus, 1991—, chmn. gen. surgery, 1978-91. Cons. VA Hosp.; trainee Nat. Cancer Inst., 1949-52 Author: Computer Applications in Medicine, 1964, Fluid, Electrolyte and Nutrient Therapy in Surgery, 1974, Surgical Treatment of Obesity, 1981; developer gastric bypass and gastroplasty for treatment of obesity; contbr. articles profl. jours. Served to lt. (j.g.) USNR, 1945-47. Fellow ACS; mem. AMA, Am. Surg. Assn., Western Surg. Assn., Soc. Univ. Surgeons, Internat. Soc. Surgery, Ctrl. Surg. Assn., Soc. Surgery Alimentary Tract, Am. Thyroid Assn., Am. Soc. Bariatric Surgery, Sigma Xi, Alpha Omega Alpha. Republican. Presbyterian. Home: 5 Melrose Cir Iowa City IA 52246-2013 Office: Univ Hosp Dept Surgery Iowa City IA 52242 Business E-Mail: edward-mason@uiowa.edu. *Continuity of interest and planning weaves the daily decisions into a whole cloth that does more than cover one's imperfections.*

MASON, ELLSWORTH GOODWIN, retired librarian; b. Waterbury, Conn., Aug. 25, 1917; s. Frederick William and Kathryn Loretta (Watkins) Mason; m. Rose Ellen Maloy, May 13, 1951 (div. Oct. 1961); children: Kay Iris Morice, Joyce Iris Lande; m. Joan Lou Shinew, Aug. 16, 1964; 1 child, Sean David. BA, Yale U., 1938, MA, 1942, PhD, 1948; LHD, Hofstra U., 1973; diploma, Inst. Children's Lit., 1996. Cert. Christian Writer's Guild. Reference asst. Yale Library, 1938-42; export license officer Bd. Econ. Warfare, 1942-43; instr. English Williams Coll., 1948-50; instr. humanities Marlboro (Vt.) Coll., 1951-52; serials libr. U. Wyo. Libr., 1952-54; reference libr. Colo. Coll. Libr., Colorado Springs, 1954-58; lectr., libr. Colo. Coll., 1958-63; prof., dir. libr. svcs. Hofstra U., Hempstead, NY, 1963-72; prof., dir. U. Colo. Librs., Boulder, 1972-76; freelance writer children's lit., 1995—. Libr. cons., 1958—; vis. lectr. Northwestern U., 1961, Colo. Coll., 1965, Syracuse U., 1965—68, Elmira Coll., 1966, Columbia U., 1966—68, Lincoln U., 1969, U. BC, Canada, 1969, U. Toronto, 1970, U. Tulsa, 1971, 76, U. Rutgers, 1971, U. Ill., 1972, Colgate U., 1972, Simmons Coll., 1972, U. Oreg., 1973, Hofstra U., 1974, U. N.C., 1976, U. Ala., 1976, Ball State U., 1977, U. Lethbridge, Canada, 1977, U. Ariz., 1981, Ariz. State U., 1981, Victoria U., New Zealand, 1983, U. Canterbury, New Zealand, 1983, U. Nev., Las Vegas, 1992, Remember Pearl Harbor Assn., 1993, 94; rsch. assoc. U. Calif., Berkeley, 1965; adj. prof. U. Ill., Urbana, 1968; pres. Mason Assocs., Ltd., 1977—; libr. value engr., 1992—. Author (with Walter and Jean Shine): A MacDonald Potpourri, 1988, The University of Colorado Library and Its Makers, 1876-1972, 1994; editor (with Stanislaus Joyce): The Early Joyce, 1955; editor Xerox U.M. edit., 1964, Norwood: Norwood Editions, 1977, Philadelphia (R. West), 1978, editor with Richard Ellmann The Critical Writings of James Joyce, 1959, 2d edit., 1989, editor Colorado College Studies, 1959—62, Critical Commentary on a Portrait of the Artist as a Young Man, 1966, The Bookover's Bounty, 1977—82; translator: Recollections of James Joyce (S. Joyce), 1950, Essais de J. Joyce, 1966, Escritos Criticos de James Joyce, Portuguese edit., 1967, Spanish edit., 1973, 1975, James Joyce's Ulysses and Vico's Cycle, 1973, Krittische Schriften v. James Joyce, 1975, Mason on Library Buildings, 1980; editor, compiler: Focus on Robert Graves, 1972—88, adv. editor: Focus on Robert Graves and His Contemporaries, 1988—; mem. editl. bd. Serial Slants, 1957—59, Choice, 1962—65, Coll. and Rsch. Librs., 1969—72, Serials Libr., 1977—98; contbr. articles to profl. jours. Mem. chancellor's coun. U. Tex., Austin, 1982—; exec. bd. U. Ky. Libr. Assocs., 1991—94, Concerned Christians in Ky., 1993—98, Littlefield Soc. U. Tex., Austin, 2004—. With USN, 1943—46. Named Ky. Col., 1993; recipient Harry Bailly Spkr.'s award, Assn. Colls. Midwest, 1975; fellow, Coun. Libr. Resources, 1969—70; grantee, Am. Coun. Learned Socs., Edn. Facilities Labs., Hofstra U., U. Colo. Mem.: ALA (councilor-at-large 1961—65), Am. Christian Writers, Nat. Assn. Scholars, James Joyce Found. (chmn. sect. translation from Joyce 2d Internat. James Joyce Symposium 1969), Inst. Vico Studies, New Zealand Royal Forest and Bird Protection Soc., Conf. Editors Learned Jours., Alcuin Soc. Vancouver, Pvt. Librs. Assn., New Zealand Libr. Assn., Libr. Assn. (London), Bibliog. Soc. Am., Colo. Libr. Assn. (pres. so. dist. 1960—61), Black Am.'s PAC, Colo. Book Collectors (founder, pres. 1975—86), Ghost Town Club, Caxton Club, Archons of Colophon, Sigma Kappa Alpha (pres. 1969—70), Alpha Sigma Lambda. Home: 736 Providence Rd Lexington KY 40502-2267 also: 39 Discovery Dr Whitby New Zealand

MASON, FRANK HENRY, III, automotive and rental company executive; b. Paris, Tenn., Nov. 16, 1936; s. Frank H. and Dorothy (Carter) M.; children: Robert C., William C. B of Elec. Engring., Vanderbilt U., 1958; MS in Indsl. Mgmt., MIT, 1965. With Ford Motor Co., 1965-71; asst. controller Ford Brazil, Sao Paulo, 1971-74; mgr. overseas fin. dept. Ford Motor Co., Dearborn, Mich., 1974-76, asst. controller engine divsn., 1976-78, mgr. facilities and mgmt. svcs., 1978-81; controller Ford Motor Credit Co., Dearborn, Mich., 1981-87; dir. fin. Ford Fin. Svcs. Group, Dearborn, Mich., 1987-89; exec. v.p., chief fin. officer U.S. Leasing, Internat., San Francisco, 1989-92; retired, 1992. Lt. USN, 1958-63.

MASON, FRANK HERBERT, artist, educator; b. Cleve., Feb. 20, 1921; s. Walter Harrison and Mildred Mary (Corbin) M.; m. Anne Cary Crosby, Mar. 12, 1966; 1 son, Arden Harriman. Student, Nat. Acad. Design, 1937-38, Art Students League, NYC, 1938-51. Instr. fine arts Art Students League, 1951—. Represented in permanent collections: Ch. of San Giovanni di Malta, Venice, Italy (Cross of Merit for eight canvas murals on life of St. Anthony of Padua Sovereign Mil. Order of Malta), Am. Embassy, London, Duke U., Butler Inst. Am. Art, Eureka Coll., Phoenix Mus. Fine Arts, Mus. City of NY, St. Patrick's Old Cathedral, NY, San Antonio Mus. Art; 3 murals on naval history of Saudi Arabia, King Faisal Naval Base, Jiddah; (mural) And the Gods Smiled on These, Houston. Served with AUS, 1945-46. Recipient North Am. Continent award Expn. Intercontinentale, Monaco, 1968, Purchase prize, Am. Acad. Arts and Letters, Arthus Ross award, Newington-Cropsey award for Excellence. Mem. NAD (past treas.), Nat. Mural Soc., Allied Artist Am., Auduson Artists, Hudson Valley Artist Assn., Royal Soc. Arts, Salamagundi Club. Studio: 385 Broome St New York NY 10013-3961 Office Phone: 212-226-7033.

MASON, GEORGE HENRY, retired business educator; b. Chgo., Sept. 11, 1929; s. Robert De Main and Dorothy Wills (Belden) M.; m. Constance Eleanor Wolcott, May 14, 1960. AB, Kenyon Coll., Gambier, Ohio, 1955; MBA, Cornell U., Ithaca, NY, 1957; MF, Duke U., Durham, NC, 1983. CFA. Investment officer Travelers Ins. Co., Hartford, Conn., 1957-88; exec.-in-residence U. Hartford, West Hartford, 1989—98. Vis. prof. Jagiellonian U., Cracow, Poland, 1996, Yang-En U., Quanzhou, Fujian, China, 1997. Co-author: Timberland Investments, 1992. Investment adv. coun. State of Conn., 1999—2003, 2006—. Mem.: CFA Inst., Hartford Soc. Fin. Analysts, Farmington Hist. Soc. (bd. dirs. 2004—06), Dataw Island Club, Mill Reef Club, Country Club of Farmington. Republican. Avocations: skiing, golf, writing.

MASON, GREGG CLAUDE, orthopedic surgeon, researcher; b. Schenectady, NY, July 28, 1958; s. George and Maureen (Murphy) M.; m. Dina Marie Sokolowski, June 16, 1990. BS in Chemistry magna cum laude, Allegheny Coll., 1980; MD, U. Pitts., 1984. Diplomate Am. Bd. Orthop. Surgery, Nat. Bd. Med. Examiners. Gen. surgery intern U. Colo./U. Colo. Med. Ctrs., Denver, 1984-85; orthopaedic rsch. fellow U. Pitts., 1985-86, resident in orthopaedic surgery, 1986-89; orthopedic surgeon U.S. Naval Hosp., Okinawa, Japan, 1989-92; pvt. practice, Erie, 1992—. Active staff St. Vincent Med. Ctr., St. Vincent Surgery Ctr., Hamot Med. Ctr., Union City Meml. Hosp.; lectr. in field. Contbr. articles to profl. jours. Comdr. M.C. USNR, 1980—. Recipient Outstanding Student Rsch. award U. Pitt. Sch. Medicine, 1984, Harold Henderson Sankey Orthop. award, 1984; rsch. grantee Competitive Med. Rsch. Fund., Presbyn.-Univ. Hosp. of Pitts., 1986-87, U. Pitts. Rsch. Devel. Fund, 1986-87. Disting. Alden scholar 1977, 78, 79, 80, Sandra Doane Turk scholar, 1979, Armed Svcs. Health Professions scholar, 1981-84. Fellow ACS, Internat. Coll. Surgeons, Mil. Soc. Orthop. Surgeons, Am. Acad. Orthop. Surgeons (tchg. seal 1993); mem. AMA, Pa. Orthop. Soc. (Best Rsch. Paper 1987, 88), Erie Orthop. Soc., U. Pitts. Med. Ctr. Orthop. Alumni., Am. Orthop. Soc. of Sports Medicine (Cabaud award 1988), Ea. Orthop. Assn. (Founders award 1988), Phi Beta Kappa. Office: Orthopaedic Surgeons Inc 204 W 26th St Erie PA 16508-1898 Office Phone: 814-454-2401.

MASON, HERBERT WARREN, JR., religion and history educator, author; b. Wilmington, Del., Apr. 20, 1932; s. Herbert Warren and Mildred Jane (Noyes) M.; m. Jeanine Young, June 25, 1982; children from previous marriage: Cathleen, Paul, Sarah. AB, Harvard U., Cambridge, Mass., 1955, AM, 1965, PhD, 1969. English tchr. Am. Sch. Paris, 1959-60; asst. prof. St. Joseph's Coll., Gorham, Maine, 1960-62; vis. lectr. Simmons Coll., Boston, 1962-63; vis. lectr. in Islamic Hist. Tufts U., Medford, Mass., 1965-66; teaching fellow in English Harvard U., Cambridge, Mass., 1962-66, teaching fellow in Islamic Hist., 1966-67; translator Bollingen Found., NYC, 1968-72; prof. History and Religion Boston U., 1972-2000, William Goodwin Aurelio prof. history and religious thought, 2000—. U.K. cons. editor Banipal; dir. inst. study muslim socs. and civilians Boston U., 2006—. Author: Reflections on the Middle East Crisis, 1970, Two Statesmen of Medieval Islam, 1971, Gilgamesh, 1971, 2d edit., 2003, The Death of al-Hallaj, 1979, Moments in Passage, 1979, (novel) Summer Light, 1980; translator: La Passion d'al-Hallaj, 4 vols., Bollingen Series (Louis Massignon), 1983, abridged 1 vol., 1994, A Legend of Alexander, 1986, Memoir of a Friend: Louis Massignon, 1988, Testimonies and Reflections, 1989, al-Hallaj, 1995, Haythu Taltaqi al-Anhar (novel in Arabic "Where the Rivers Meet"), 1999, English edit., 2003, (poems) Disappearances, 1999; co-editor: Humaniora Islamica; cons. editor Banipal, London; contbr. articles, essays, revs., fiction and poetry to popular fiction mags. Sec. Inter-racial Riverside Assn., Cambridge, Mass., 1965-67; trustee Bd. Charity of Edward Hopkins, Boston Athenaeum. Fellow Soc. for Values in Higher Edn.; mem. PEN (bd. dirs. Delos chpt.), Medieval Acad. Am., Am. Oriental Soc., Am. Acad. Religion, Mark Twain Soc., Inst. Internat. des Recherches Louis Massignon in Paris (dir. edn., v.p.), Am. Acad. Poetry, Japan Poetry Mus. (Iwate-Ken). Home: 9 Seaview Lane Newbury MA 01951 Office: Boston U 745 Commonwealth Ave Boston MA 02215-1401 Office Phone: 617-358-1777. Personal E-mail: herbertwmason@comcast.net.

MASON, J. CHENEY, lawyer; b. Jacksonville, Fla., Dec. 12, 1943; BA, U. Fla., 1968, JD, 1970. Bar: Fla. 1971, U.S. Dist. Ct. (mid. dist. Fla.) 1972, U.S. Supreme Ct. 1975, U.S. Ct. Appeals (5th cir.) 1976, U.S. Dist. Ct. (so. dist. Fla. including trial bar) 1978, U.S. Ct. Appeals (11th cir.) 1984, bd. cert. Criminal Trial Lawyer: Fla. Bar Bd. Legal Specialization and Edn., cert.: Nat. Bd. Trial Advocacy (Criminal Trial Advocate). Pvt. practice, Orlando, Fla. Delegate internat. conf. criminal justice UN; lectr. in field. Contbr. articles to profl. jours. Mem.: NACDL (bd. dirs.), ABA, Fla. Assn. Criminal Def. Lawyers (treas. 1993, sec. 1994, v.p. 1995, pres.-elect 1996, pres. 1997—98), Fla. Bar Assn. (mem. legis. com. 1978—80, mem. ethics com. 1979—81, chmn. criminal law cert. com. 1984—86, mem. exec. coun. criminal law sect. 1984—94, chmn. 1992—93), Ninth Jud. Cir. (mem. grievance com. 1978—81, vice chmn. 1981), Orange County Bar Assn. (chmn. criminal law sect. 1978—79, mem. exec. coun. 1979—83, chmn. family law sect. 1982—84), Phi Alpha Delta (justice 1969). Office: J Cheney Mason PA Bank of Am Ctr 390 N Orange Ave Ste 2100 Orlando FL 32801 Office Phone: 407-843-5786. Office Fax: 407-422-6858.

MASON, JAMES HAMILTON, surgeon; b. Kokomo, Ind., June 5, 1930; d. Lorne Wilfred and Alice Hamilton Mason; m. Anabel Russell, Dec. 22, 1951; children: James Russell, Daniel Hamilton, John Lorne, Seth Gordon, Amy Alice. BA, DePauw U., Greencastle, Inc., 1952; MD, Cornell U., Ithica, NY, 1956. Diplomate Am. Bd. Surgery. Intern U. Ill, Chgo., 1956, resident, 1959—63; attending surgeon St. Francis Hosp., Evanston, Ill., 1963—, chief surgery, 1967—, dir. edn., 1967—. Assoc. prof. surgery U. Ill., Coll. Medicine, Chgo., 1967—; clin. assoc. prof. surgery Loyola U., Stritch Sch. Medicine, Ill., clin. prof. surgery, Ill., 1970—. Lt. USN, 1957—59. Mem.: AMA, Ill. State Med. Inter-Ins. Exch. (bd. govs.), Chgo. Inst. Medicine, Pan Pacific Surg. Assn., Ill. Surg. Soc. (2d v.p. 1978, counselor), We. Surg. Soc., Soc. Surgery of Alimentary Tract, Chgo. Surg. Soc. (recorder 1971—74, v.p. 1981—82), Chgo. Med. Soc., Ill. State Med. Soc. (pres. 1981—82), Am. Cancer Soc. (pres. N. Shore br. 1970—71, 1971—72), Warren H. Cole Soc. (sec. 1967—69, pres. 1972), Midwest Surg. Assn., Am. Coll. Surgeons (v.p. Chgo. met. chpt. 1973—74, pres. Chgo. met. chpt. 1976—77). Protestant. Home: 4620 N Catamount Tr NE Ada MI 49301

MASON, JEREMY R., lawyer; b. Cin., Aug. 1, 1974; BS, Cornell U., 1997; JD, Ohio State U., 2000. Bar: Ohio 2000, US Dist. Ct. Southern Dist. Ohio 2001, Ky. 2006, US Dist. Ct. Northern Dist. Ohio 2006, US Dist. Ct. Eastern Dist. Ky. 2006, US Dist. Ct. Western Dist. Ky. 2006. Named one of Ohio's Rising Stars, Super Lawyers, 2006. Mem.: Am. Bankruptcy Inst. (Medal of Excellence 2000), Comml. Law League, Ky. Bar Assn., Ohio State Assn., Cin. Bar Assn., Bus. Assn. (CALI award 1998), Delta Kappa Epsilon (Scholar award). Office: Mason Schilling & Mason Co LPA 11340 Montgomery Rd Ste 210 Cincinnati OH 45249-2313 Office Phone: 513-489-0829. Office Fax: 513-489-0834.

MASON, JOAN ELLEN, nurse; b. Reading, Pa., June 29, 1947; d. Richard Lenhart and Mary Jane (Miller) Fritz; m. W. Davis Mason, Feb. 12, 1977 (dec. Jan. 2002). RN, Temple U. Hosp. Sch. Nursing, 1968; BS in Nursing Edn., Temple U., 1971, EdM in Health Edn., 1981; postgrad., U. Pa. Staff nurse Temple U. Hosp., Phila., 1968-71; nursing instr. Phila. Gen. Hosp. Sch. Nursing, 1971-76; coord. staff devel. Meml. Hosp., Roxborough, Pa., 1976-84; clin. editor Springhouse Corp., Pa., 1984-94; nurse cons. Kelly Sci. Resources, 1995-98; adminstrn., profl. nurse Bed and Breakfast Inn, Cape May, NJ, 1982—2003; nurse cons. Reading, 1999—2003, Orwigsburg, 2003—05. Mem. exhibit com. Mus. Nursing History, Inc., 1988-2001. Editor Congl. Free Ch. of Chirst newsletter; contbr. articles to profl. jours. Vol. Reading Mus., Berks Arts Coun. Mem. Mid-Atlantic Ctr. for Arts, Orwigsburg Women's Libr. Soc. Republican. Home: 225 Eisenhower Dr Orwigsburg PA 17961-1605

MASON, JOHN LATIMER, engineering executive; b. LA, Nov. 8, 1923; s. Zene Upham and Edna Ella (Watkins) Mason; m. Frances Howe Draeger, Sept. 1, 1950 (dec. June 1951); m. Mary Josephine Schulte, Nov. 26, 1954; children: Andrew, Peter, Mary Anne, John Edward. BS in Meteorology, U. Chgo., 1944; BS in Applied Chemistry, Calif. Inst. Tech., 1947, MS in Chem. Engring., 1948, PhD, 1950. Registered profl. engr., Calif. Engr. AiResearch Mfg. Co., Los Angeles, 1950-60; dir. engring. AiResearch Mfg. Co. div. Garrett Corp., Los Angeles, 1960-72; v.p. engring. Garrett Corp., Los Angeles, 1972-87; v.p. engring. and tech. Allied-Signal Aerospace Co., Los Angeles, 1987-88, cons., 1989-96; chmn. tech. adv. com. Indsl. Turbines Internat., Inc., Los Angeles, 1972-81, bd. dirs., 1980-88; adj. prof. engring. Calif. State U., Long Beach, 1992-96. Tech. adv. bd. Tex. Ctr. for Superconductivity, U. Houston, 1989-02, Ceryx Inc., 1998-2001; chair Calif. Coun. Sci. and Tech. Panel on Transp. R&D Ctr., 1993-94; bd. dirs. Planetary Sci. Inst., sec., 1998—; cons. Capstone Turbine Corp., 1994-98; workshop com. Transp. Rsch. Bd., 1998.; cons. Cleaire, Inc., 2001-03, Applied Rsch. and Tech., 2001-; ptnr. Applied Rsch. and Tech., 2001-06. Patentee in field. Chmn. energy and environment com. FISITA Coun., 1990-94. 1st lt. USAAF, 1943-46, PTO. With USAF, 1946—57. Fellow AIAA, assoc. Soc. Automotive Engrs., bd. dirs. 1984-87, 90-93, pres.-elect 1989-90, pres. 1990-91, Performance Rev. Inst. chmn. 1990-91, bd. dirs. 1992-93; mem. AAAS, NRC of NAS, com. on alternative energy R&D strategies 1989-90, Office Sci. and Tech. Policy, Nat. Critical Techs. panel 1992-93, Inst. Medicine of NAS, com. on health effects of indoor allergens 1992-93, Nat. Acad. Engring., US Advanced Ceramics Assn. chmn. tech. com., bd. dirs. 1985-88, Am. Chem. Soc., Am. Ceramic Soc., Caltech Assocs., Sigma Xi assoc., Am. Soc. Mech. Engrs., Engrg. Adv. Bd., Univ. of So. Calif. Office Phone: 310-375-5161. Personal E-mail: JL-Mason@cox.net.

MASON, JOHN OLIVER, freelance journalist, community activist, poet; b. Kingston, Pa., Aug. 1, 1957; s. Oliver B. and Dorothy Mae (Hunter) Mason. BA, Temple U., 1984. Editl. writer Temple News, Phila., 1983—85; writer Phila. Tribune, 1989—95, Irish Edition, Phila., 1990—95, Northeast Breeze, Rockledge, Pa., 1993—95, Germantown Courier, Phila., 1996—, Phila. Sunday Sun, 1996—, Chestnut Hill Local, 2000—, Milestones, 2000—, The Progressive, 2005—. Sec. Concerned Citizens of Delaware Valley, 1990; rec. sec. A. Philip Randolph Inst., Phila., 2001; mem. Jewish Labor Com., Phila., 1985. Avocations: stamp collecting/philately, reading, cultural activities. E-mail: jomason97@verizon.net.

MASON, JOHN WAYNE, psychoneuroendocrinologist, retired medical educator; b. Chgo., Feb. 9, 1924; s. John Ralph and Frances Elsie (Swedman) Mason; m. Joyce Ann Towne; children: John Mark, Victoria Joyce, Peter Brooke. AB, Ind. U., Bloomington, 1944; MD, Ind. U., Indpls., 1947; MA (hon.), Yale U., New Haven, 1977. Diplomate in pathol. anatomy Am. Bd. Pathology. Surg. intern NY Hosp.-Cornell Med. Ctr., NYC, 1947—48, resident in pathology, 1948—50; chief dept. neuroendocrinology Walter Reed Army Inst. Rsch., Washington, 1953—74; prof. emeritus psychiatry Yale U. Sch. Medicine, New Haven, 1977—. Cons. and dir. psychoendocrine lab. Adult Psychiatry br. NIMH, Bethesda, Md., 1960—65; sci. advisor, neuropsychiatry br. Walter Reed Army Inst. of Rsch., Washington, 1974—77; dir. psychoendocrine lab. Nat. Ctr. for PTSD, VA Med. Ctr., West Haven, Conn., 1977—2000; lectr. and invited lectr. in field. Contbr. more than 170 sci. rsch. publs. to profl. jours., 24 chpts. to books, also revs. in field; author: (monograph) Organization of Psychoendocrine Mechanisms, 1968 (Med. Lit. Citation Classic award). Faculty sponsor, Campus Crusade for Christ ministry Yale U., 1983; Bible tchr. Trinity Evang. Free Ch., Woodbridge, Conn., 1978—. Served to maj. M.C. US Army, 1948—53. Recipient Rsch. Scientist Career award, NIMH, 1981-1991, medal, Pavlovian Soc., 1985, Meritorius Civilian Svc. award, Dept. of Army, 1960, Sustained Superior Performance Civil Svc. awards, 1960, 1966, 1969, Lifetime Achievement award, 21st Century Traumatology Conf., Georgetown U. Med. Ctr. Founds., 1996; grantee, NIMH, 1989-2000. Mem.: Assn. Psychosomatic Medicine (editl. bd. mem. 1963—91), Internat. Soc. Psychoneuroendocrinology (Lifetime Achievement award 2005), Endocrine Soc., Am. Psychosomatic Soc. (pres. 1969—70, Pres.'s award 2000), Alpha Omega Alpha, Phi Beta Kappa. Achievements include long term systematic basic and clinical research on the importance of psychosocial influences upon a wide range of endocrine systems in relation to stress and stress-related clinical disorders; major pioneering contributions to the development of the field of psychoneuroendocrinology and to exploring its far-reaching clinical implications for psychiatry and medicine; development of psychoendocrine strategies using concurrent hormonal and psychological measurements providing new leverage for the interdisciplinary study of; intrapsychic processes including emotional states, psychological defenses and coping styles; established that psychosocial and physical stress stimuli produce broadly organized multihormonal patterns of change involving many interdependent endocrine systems; received national and international recognition as a leader providing landmark experimental and conceptual contributions in the fields of psychoendocrinology and stress research; development of an unusual profile of thyroid hormonal alterations in PTSD patients, which provides compelling leads concerning the pathogenesis and possible treatment of this disorder. Home: 32 Maple Vale Dr Woodbridge CT 06525 Home Phone: 203-393-2448. Personal E-mail: jwmason@pol.net.

MASON, JOSEPH See BUSHINSKY, JAY

MASON, KAROL V., lawyer; b. Amityville, NY, Aug. 20, 1957; AB, Univ. NC, Chapel Hill, 1979; JD, Univ. Mich., 1982. Bar: Ga. 1983. Ptnr., chair, pub. fin. group Alston & Bird LLP, Atlanta. Notes editor Univ. Mich. Jour. Law Reform. Named Distinguished Young Alumna, Univ. NC, Chapel Hill, 1991. Mem.: Ga. Assn. Black Women Attys., Nat. Assn. Bond Lawyers. Office: Alston & Bird LLP One Atlantic Ctr 1201 W Peachtree St NW Atlanta GA 30309-3424 Office Phone: 404-881-7494. Office Fax: 404-881-7777. Business E-Mail: kmason@alston.com.

MASON, KEVIN GEORGE, military analyst and officer; b. Queens, NY, Oct. 24, 1955; s. David Park Mason and Gisela Margarete Elsa Herbst; m. Sana Marie Francis, Aug. 7, 1991; 1 child, Katherine Elizabeth. BA, Mich. State U., 1974; MA, Boston U., 1992, U. Tenn., 1997, MS, 1998. Cert. tchr. Tenn., 2003. Commd. 2d lt. US Army, 1977, advanced through grades to maj., 1989; mil. analyst Northrop-Grumman Info. Techs., Kaiserslautern, Rheinland-Pfalz, Germany, 1999—2003, Dept. of Army, Grafenwoehr, Bavaria, 2003—. Decorated Meritorious Svc. medal US Army, Army Commendation medal, Army Achievement award. Mem.: VFW, Assn. US Army, Mil. Officers Assn. Am., Infantrymen Assn., Am. Hist. Assn. (life), Masons. Presbyterian. Avocations: history, hunting, fishing, travel. Office: Joint Mulitnational Training Center CMR 415 Box 3077 APO AE 09114 Home Phone: 499644860661; Office Phone: 496641836730. Personal E-mail: manchu19@aol.com. E-mail: kevin.mason1@us.army.mil.

MASON, LINDA, physical education educator, coach; b. Indpls., Jan. 29, 1946; d. Harrison Linn and Hazel Marie (Bledsoe) Crouch; divorced; children: Cassandra, Andrew. BS, Ind. U., 1968, MS, 1977. Cert. phys. edn. tchr., K-12, Ind. Tchr. phys. edn. Woodview Jr. H.S., Indpls., 1968—71; tchr. phys. edn., coach Ind. U.-Purdue U. Indpls., 1972—76; basketball coach Butler U., Indpls., 1976—84; head softball coach, asst. basketball coach Westfield Washington High Sch., Westfield, Ind., 1985; tchr. phys.

edn., basketball coach Orchard Park Elem. Sch., Carmel, Ind., 1985—; tchr. elem. physical edn. Carmel-Clay Schs., Carmel, 1985—; asst. varsity coach softball Carmel H.S., 1993—95, head varsity softball coach, 1996—99. Head coach Ind. Girls' H.S. All-Stars Basketball Team, Indpls., 1998. Named Coach of Yr. Dist. 4, Nat. Collegiate Athletic Assn., 1983, Coach of Yr. for softball ICGSA, 1997, coach ICGSA Girls All Stars, 1998. Mem. Delta Psi Kappa. Personal E-mail: peteacherl@msn.com. Business E-Mail: lmason@ccs.k12.in.us. E-mail: peteacherl@indy.rr.com.

MASON, LOIS E. (J. DAY MASON), painter, poet, actress, educator; b. Boston, May 4, 1919; d. Harold Monroe and Orpah Cecil (Smith) Scheibe; m. Lucien Bunce Day, June 21, 1941 (div. 1954); children: Felicity, Christopher, Sarah; m. Frederick Dike Mason, Apr. 27, 1964 (dec.); children: Frederick Dike III, Victoria, Johanna. Student, U. Leiden, Netherlands, 1939; BA, Oberlin U., Ohio, 1940; postgrad., Cranbrook Acad. Art, Bloomfield Hills, Mich., 1941. Set-up and tchr. art dept. Pingree Sch., Hamilton Mass.; TV, lectr. creative arts and writing, Mass. and Conn., 1949-58. Actress appearing in Alien Corn, Twelfth Night, Crucible, George Washington Slept Here, Philadelphia Story, Auntie Mame, Skin of our Teeth, Spoon River, Anything Goes, Call Me Madame, Seven Keys to Baldpate, Other People's Money, Quilters, Golden Pond, Cat on a Hot Tin Roof, Little Foxes, Lettice and Lovage, Close Ties, Grace and Glorie, others; set designer, decorator Auntie Mame, See How They Run, Tea House of the August Moon, Spoon River, Archie and Mehitable; author: Speaking to Strangers, 1987-88; one-woman shows include New Britain (Conn.) Mus., Am. Ballet, N.Y., Green Mountain Gallery, N.Y.C., Essex (Mass.) Inst., Marblehead Arts, Quadrom, Mast Cove, 6 Deering, Miles Hosp., Atty. Gen.'s Office, Kennebec Valley Art Assn., Chocolate Ch. Art Ctr., Maine Gallery, Kristina's, Oliver's, Islesboro Historic Soc., West Island Gallery, Bath, Maine. Ch. ladies com. Hamilton Hall, Salem, Mass., 1975—78; set designer Cmty. Theater, Swampscott, Mass., 1973—78. Recipient C. Law/Watkins fellowship Phillips Gallery, Mus., Washington, 1944-46. Mem. Nat. Assn. Women Painters, Conn. Acad., Silvermine, Maine Gallery, Kennebec Valley Arts, Chocolate Ch. Art Ctr., Marblehead Arts, Conn. Acad., Maine Writers and Publs. Avocations: cooking, sailing, gardening.

MASON, MARILYN GELL, library administrator, writer, consultant; b. Chickasha, Okla., Aug. 23, 1944; d. Emmett D. and Dorothy (O'Bar) Killebrew; m. Carl L. Gell, Dec. 29 1965 (div. Oct. 1978); 1 son, Charles E.; m. Robert M. Mason, July 17, 1981. BA, U. Dallas, 1966; M.L.S., N. Tex. State U., Denton, 1968; M.P.A., Harvard U., 1978. Libr. N.J. State Libr., Trenton, 1968-69; head dept. Arlington County Pub. Libr., Va., 1969-73; chief libr. program Metro Washington Coun. Govts., 1973-77; dir. White House Conf. on Librs. and Info. Svcs., Washington, 1979-80; exec. v.p. Metrics Rsch. Corp., Atlanta, 1981-82; dir. Atlanta-Fulton Pub. Libr., Atlanta, 1982-86, Cleve. Pub. Libr., 1986-99; writer, cons., 1999—. Trustee Online Computer Library Ctr., 1984-97; Evalene Parsons Jackson lectr. divsn. librarianship Emory U., 1981; commr. Nat. Commn. Libr. Info. Svcs., 2001-02; book project dir. Information for the 1980's, 1980 Author: The Federal Role in Library and Information Services, 1983, Strategic Management for Today's Libraries, 1999; editor: Survey of Library Automation in the Washington Area, 1977 Bd. visitors Sch. Info. Studies, Syracuse U., 1981-85, Sch. of Libr. and Info. Sci., U. Tenn.-Knoxville, 1983-85; trustee Coun. on Libr. Resources, Washington, 1992-2000. Recipient Disting. Alumna award, N. Tex. State U., 1979, Herbert and Virginia White award, ALA, 1999; inducted into Ohio Libr. Coun. Hall of Fame, 1999. Mem. ALA (mem. council 1986—90), Am. Assn. Info. Sci., Ohio Library Assn., D.C. Library Assn. (pres. 1976-77) Home and Office: 2929 First Ave 1122 Seattle WA 98121 Office Phone: 206-714-3009. Personal E-mail: marilyngmason@earthlink.net. Business E-Mail: mgmason@oclc.org.

MASON, MARK D., lawyer; BA, Columbia U., 1980; JD, Boston U., 1984. Bar: Mass., US Dist. Ct. (Dist. Conn.), US Bankruptcy Ct. Mass. Ptnr. Litig. Dept. Cooley Shrair, Springfield, Mass. Mem. standing com. dispute resolution Supreme Judicial Ct. Pres. March Dimes of Western Mass.; co-founder and pres. Gay & Lesbian Civic Assn. Greater Springfield; chmn. and commr. Springfield Cultural Coun.; bd. dirs. Holyoke St. Sch., Cmty. Music Sch., Springfield, Mass., Mass. Gay & Lesbian Bar Assn. Named one of 10 Outstanding Lawyers of 2001, Mass. Lawyers Weekly; recipient Spirit of Justice award, Gay & Lesbian Advocates, 2004. Mem.: Hampden County Bar Assn. (chmn. young lawyers sect.), Mass. Bar Assn. (pres. 2006—07, treas., sec., v.p., sec. judicial adminstrn. com., chmn. alternat. dispurte resolution com., co-chair anniversary fee task force, chmn. same gender marriage task force). Office: Cooley Shrair 1380 Main St Springfield MA 01103-1616 Office Phone: 413-735-8040. E-mail: mmason@cooleyshrair.com.

MASON, MARSHA, actress, theater director, writer; b. St. Louis, Apr. 3, 1942; d. James and Jacqueline M.; m. Gary Campbell, 1965 (div.); m. Neil Simon, Oct. 25, 1973 (div.). Grad., Webster Coll., Mo. Performances include cast broadway and nat. tour cactus Flower, 1968; other stage appearances include The Deer Park, 1967, The Indian Wants the Bronx, 1968, Happy Birthday, Wanda June, 1970, Private Lives, 1971, You Can't Take It With You, 1972, Cyrano de Bergerac, 1972, A Doll's House, 1972, The Crucible, 1972, The Good Doctor, 1973, King Richard III, 1974, The Heiress, 1975, Mary Stuart, 1982, Amazing Grace, 1995, Night of the Iguana, 1996; one-woman show off-Broadway, The Big Love, Perry St. Theatre, 1988, Lake No Bottom, Second Stage, 1990, Escape From Happiness, With Naked Angels, 1994, Amazing Grace, 1998, House, 1998, (London) Prisoner of Second Avenue, 1999, Steel Magnolias, 2005; film appearances include Hot Rod Hullabaloo, 1966, Beyond the Law, 1968, Blume in Love, 1973, Cinderella Liberty, 1973 (recipient Golden Globe award 1974, Acad. award nominee), Audrey Rose, 1977, The Goodbye Girl, 1977 (recipient Golden Globe award 1978, Acad. award nominee), The Cheap Detective, 1978, Promises in the Dark, 1979, Chapter Two, 1979 (Acad. award nominee), Only When I Laugh, 1981 (Acad. award nominee), Max Dugan Returns, 1982, Heartbreak Ridge, 1986, Stella, 1988, Drop Dead Fred, 1990, I Love Trouble, 1994, Nick of Time, 1995, Two Days in the Valley, 1996, Bride & Prejudice, 2004, Bereft, 2004; (TV films) PBS series Cyrano de Bergerac, 1972, The Good Doctor, 1978, Lois Gibbs and the Love Canal, 1981, Surviving, 1985, Trapped in Silence, 1986, The Clinic, 1987, Dinner at Eight, 1989, The Image, 1990, Broken Trust, 1994, Dead Aviators, 1999, Life with Judy Garland:Me and My Shadows, 2001, The Long Shot: Believe in Courage, 2004; (TV series) Where the Heart Is, 1971, Love of Life, 1971-72, Young Dr. Kildare, 1972, Sibs, 1991; dir. (plays) Juno's Swans, 1987, Heaven Can Wait; dir. ABC Afternoon Spl. Little Miss Perfect, 1988; guest appearances include One Life to Live, 1993, Frasier, 1997, 1998 (Emmy Nom.), The Education of Max Bickford, 2002; author: Journey: A Personal Odyssey (Simon & Schuster), 2000. E-mail: douhlem@newmexico.com.

MASON, MARSHALL W., theater director, educator, author; b. Amarillo, Tex., Feb. 24, 1940; s. Marvin Marshall and Lorine (Chrisman) M. BS in Speech, Northwestern U., 1961. Prof. Ariz. State U., 1994-2005, prof. emeritus, 2005; chief drama critic New Times, Phoenix, 1994-96. Founder, artistic dir. Circle Repertory Co., 1969-87, guest artistic dir., Ctr. Theater Group, 1988; dir. Broadway prodns. Redwood Curtain, 1993, The Seagull, 1992, Solitary Confinement, 1992, Burn This, 1987, As Is, 1985 (Drama Desk award, Tony nomination), Passion, 1983, Angels Fall, 1983 (Tony nomination), Fifth of July, 1981 (Tony nomination), Talley's Folly, 1980, (Pulitzer Prize, N.Y. Drama Critics Circle award, Tony nomination), Murder at the Howard Johnsons, 1979, Gemini, 1977, Knock Knock, 1976 (Tony nomination); Off-Broadway prodns. Book of Days, 2002, Sympathetic Magic, 1997, Robbers, 1997, Cakewalk, 1996, A Poster of the Cosmos/The Moonshot Tape, 1994, The Destiny of Me, 1992, Sunshine, 1989, Talley and Son, 1985, Childe Byron, 1980, Hamlet, 1979, Serenading Louie, 1976 (Obie award), Knock Knock, 1976 (Obie award), The Mound Builders, 1975 (Obie award), Battle of Angeles, 1974 (Obie award), The Sea Horse, 1974, The Hot L Baltimore, 1973 (Obie award); dir. numerous prodns. including Who's Afraid of Virginia Woolf?, Tokyo, 1985, Talley's Folly, 1982, London, Home Free! and The Madness of Lady Bright, 1968, Nat. Tour Sleuth, 1988, Regional Summer and Smoke, 1988, Whisper in the Mind, 1990, King Lear, 1998 (Anzoni award), The Elephant Man, London, 1998, Long Day's Journey into Night, 1998 (Anzoni award), Riga, 1999, Ginger, 2000; transl. Pirandello's Enrico IV, 2001; dir. Ghosts, 2001, Private Lives, 2002, The Drawer Boy, 2003, The Cherry Orchard, 2004, The Cripple of Inishman, 2004, The Member of the Wedding, 2005, Cat on a Hot Tin Roof, 2005, The Goat, 2006 (Anzoni award); dir. TV prodns. including Picnic, 1986, Kennedy's Children, 1982, Fifth of July, 1983, The Mound Builders, 1975; author: Creating Life on Stage, 2006. Recipient Vernon Rice award, 1975, Drama Desk award, 1977, Margo Jones award, 1977, Outer Critics Circle award, 1978, Theatre World award, 1979, Shubert's Vaughan award, 1980, Obie award for Sustained Achievement, 1983, Inge Festival award for lifetime achievement, 1990, Last Frontier award, 1994, award Ariz. Press Club, 1995, Erwin Piscator award, 1996, Millennium Mr. Abbott award, 1999, Creative Achievement award Ariz. State U., 2001. Mem. Soc. Stage Dirs. and Choreographers (pres. 1983-85), Dirs. Guild Am., Actors Equity Assn., Coll. Fellow of Am. Theater. Address: 165 Christopher St 5I New York NY 10014 Office Phone: 213-446-4144. E-mail: mwm@asu.edu.

MASON, MATTHEW THOMAS, robotics researcher; b. Oklahoma City, Aug. 24, 1952; s. Robert Allen and Patricia Jean Mason; m. Mary Lynn Wilson, Aug. 19, 1972; children: Timm, Kate. BS in Computer Sci., MIT, 1976, MS in Artificial Intelligence, 1978, PhD in Artificial Intelligence, 1982. Rsch. visitor IBM Thomas J. Watson Rsch. Ctr., 1978, Sandia Nat. Labs, 1994, 1995; prof., computer sci. dept. and robotics inst. Carnegie Mellon U., Pitts., 1982—, chmn. robotics doctoral program, 1995—2004, dir., Robotics Inst., 2004—. Invited lectr. in field; mem. design review bd., Skywalker Project Carnegie Mellon U., 1999; mem. internat. steering com. Workshop on Control Problems in Robotics and Automation, 2002; mem. organizing com. NSF Robotics and Computer Vision PI Workshop, 2003; mem. NRC review panel Robotic Access and Human Plantary Landing Systems, 2005; founding coord. Assn. PhD Programs in Robotics, 2005—; mem. adv. bd. RoboBusiness, 2006; mem. sr. programm com. EUROS-06, 2006; mem. program com. Robotics: Sci. and Systems, 2006; juror Robot Hall of Fame, 2006. Co-author: Robot Motion: Planning and Control, 1982, Robot Hands and the Mechanics of Manipulation, 1985, Robotics: the Algorithmic Perspective: 1998 Workshop on Algorithmic Foundations of Robotics, 1998; Author: Mechanics of Robotic Manipulation, 2001; N.Am. editor, butterworths Series in Computer Automation, 1988-1994; mem. bd. editors, Robotic Review, MIT Press, 1988-1992; mem. editl. bd., International Journal of Robotics Research, 1998-2005contbr. articles to profl. jours. Fellow, NSF. 1976-1980; recipient Sys. Devel. Found. prize, 1983, Robotics Grad. Student Organization's Coll Person award, 1999, 2005. Fellow IEEE(mem. internat. adv. com., Internat. Conf. on Indsl. Technology, 2002, fellow nomination com., IEEE Robotics and Automation Soc., 2006), Am. Assn. for Artificial Intelligence Office: Robotics Inst Carnegie Mellon U 5000 Forbes Ave Pittsburgh PA 15213 Office Phone: 412-268-8804. Office Fax: 412-268-7350. E-mail: matt.mason@cs.cmu.edu. *

MASON, MICHAEL LAMOTT, librarian, researcher, writer; b. McKeesport, Pa., Apr. 29, 1954; s. Rugh Albert Mason and Mary Ann Halas; m. Phyllis Jean Lipka, May 1, 1987 (div. 1995). BA in English & Philosophy, Ind. U. Pa., 1973—76, MA in English Lang. & Lit., Rhetoric & Linguistics, 1980—81; MS in Libr. & Info. Sci., U. N.C., Chapel Hill, 1984—87. Cert. libr. Commonwealth of Mass. Bd. Libr. Commrs., 1988, State of N.J. Dept. Edn., 1988. Geology dept. map curator U. N.C., Chapel Hill, 1984—86; libr. dir., asst. dir., reference libr. Ocean City Free Pub. Libr., NJ, 1987—92; document delivery libr. Holme Roberts & Owen LLP, Denver, 1993—97; legal dept. libr., loose-leaf filer & site libr. liaison Hewlett-Packard Co., Inc., Fort Collins, Colo., 1997—99; reference libr. & rsch. asst. to the dean Colo. State U. Librs., Fort Collins, 1997—99; head libr. Ungaretti & Harris LLP, Chgo., 1999—. Presenter, vol. FortNet Cmty. Internet Festivals, Fort Collins, Colo., 1997—99. Contbr. articles to profl. jours. Member-at-large FortNet Cmty. Info. Network, Fort Collins, Colo., 1997—98; vol. Poudre RiverFest, Fort Collins, Colo.; environmentalist, media spot pub. figure, campus departmental program participation coord. SmartTrips, Fort Collins, Colo. Recipient Svc. Above Self, Rotary Club, 1991, Civic Contbn. Recognition, Lion's Club, 1991. Mem.: Colo. Assn. Law Librs. (assoc.; sec., member-at-large 1994—96), Chgo. Assn. Law Librs. (assoc.), Am. Indian Libr. Assn. (assoc.), Am. Assn. Law Librs. (assoc.). Avocations: baseball, softball, art. Mailing: One Renaissance Sq 2 N Central Ave Ste 170-179 Phoenix AZ 85004 Home Phone: 708-386-1876. Personal E-mail: lamott@usa.net.

MASON, PATRICK SAMUAL, manufacturing engineer; s. Landon Clay Mason and Charmazelle Kathy Jenkins, Jo Ann Colgan (Stepmother); m. Amanda Rae Howes, May 24, 2003. BS, Morehead State U., KY, 1995, Master, 2002. Cert. mfg. technologist Mich., 1994, sr. indsl. technologist Mich., 2003. Supr. and robotic tech. Arvin North Am. Automotive, Franklin, Ind., 1996—97; mfg. and robotic engr. Toyo Seat Corp, Flemingsburg, Ky., 1997—2000; tech. cons. Morehead State U., 2000—02, mfg. and robotic instr., 2002—05, mfg., robotic instr., 2005—; maintenance engring. instr. Mazak Corp., Florence, Ky., 2005—05. Mem. at large Morehead Theatre Guild, 2003—07; sec. Rowan County Christmas, Morehead, 2004—07; chairman-elect Soc. Mfg. Engrs., Lexington, 2007—; mem. Ea. Ky. Tech. Educators Assn., Ky., 2002—07. Named Most Outstanding Grad. Student, Morehead State U., Coll. Sci. and Tech., 2002. Mem.: Nat. Assn. Indsl. Tech. (assoc.), Soc. Mfg. Engrs. (assoc.; sec. 2005—06). Home: 115 Pine Tree Lane Morehead KY 40351 Office: Morehead State U 105A Lloyd Cassity Morehead KY 40351 Home Phone: 606-783-9441; Office Phone: 606-783-9441. Business E-Mail: s.mason@moreheadstate.edu.

MASON, RACHEL J., lawyer; b. Cin., Dec. 8, 1977; BA, Lehigh U., 2000; JD, Dickinson Sch. of Law, Pa. State U., 2003. Bar: Ohio 2003. Named one of Ohio's Rising Stars, Super Lawyers, 2006. Mem.: Assn. Credit and Collection Professionals, Nat. Assn. Retail Collection Attorneys, Comml. Law League Am. (award of Excellence), ABA, Ohio State Bar Assn., Cin. Bar Assn. Office: Mason Schilling & Mason Co LPA 11340 Cincinnati OH 45249-2313 Office Phone: 513-489-0829. Office Fax: 513-489-0834.

MASON, RAYMOND ADAMS (CHIP), diversified financial services company executive; b. Lynchburg, Va., Sept. 28, 1936; s. Raymond Watsi and Marion (Adams) M.; married; children: Paige Adams, Pamela Ann, Carter Meade, Morgan Rand. BA in Econs., Coll. William and Mary, 1959. Rep. Mason & Lee Inc., Richmond, Va., 1960-62; founder, pres. Mason & Co. Inc., Newport News, Va., 1962-70; pres. Legg, Mason & Co., Inc., Washington, 1970-73, Legg, Mason Wood Walker, Inc., Balt., 1978—81, chmn.; chmn., pres., CEO Legg Mason, Inc., Balt., 1981—. Chmn. regional firms com. N.Y. Stock Exchange, 1978-81. Trustee emeritus Endowment Assn., Coll. William and Mary; bd. dirs. emeritus William and Mary Sch. Bus. Adminstrn. Sponsors, Inc.; former trustee Balt. Mus. Art; former bd. dirs. Nat. Aquarium, Balt.; bd. dirs., exec. com., chair fin. com. Johns Hopkins Hosp.; chmn. bd., exec. com. Johns Hopkins U.; former chmn. bd. sponsors Sch. Bus. & Mgmt. Loyola Coll., Balt., 1980-88; bd. dirs. Greater Balt. Com., 1982-84, chmn., 1987-89; chmn. United Way Ctrl. Md. Mem. Nat. Assn. Securities Dealers (bd. govs. 1971-75, chmn. bd. govs. 1974-75), Securities Industry Assn. (bd. dirs. 1982—, chmn. 1985-86, bd. govs. 1984-88, chmn. bd. govs. 1987). Clubs: Ctr., Md., Balt. Country, L'Hirondelle, Elkridge Club, Balt. Country Club, New Orleans Country Club. Office: Legg Mason Inc Bldg 100 Light St Baltimore MD 21202-6189 *

MASON, RAYMOND E., JR., distributing company executive; b. Columbus, Ohio, Mar. 20, 1920; s. Raymond E. and Lula Estella (Potter) Mason; m. Margaret E. Edwards, Feb. 6, 1942; children: Raymond E. III, Michael D., Bruce R. BS, Ohio State U., 1941; grad., U.S. Command and Gen. Staff, 1962, U.S. Army War Coll., 1965; D of Bus. Sci. (hon.), Ohio State U., 2001; D (hon.), Franklin U., 2004; D of laws (hon.), Cumberland Coll., 2003. Ops. mgr. Suburban Motor Freight, Columbus, 1946-47; pres., gen. mgr. CFL Lines, Columbus, 1947-48; pres., chmn. Columbus Truck & Equipment Co., 1949—. Pres., chmn. REM Realty, Columbus, 1962—, Bode-Finn Co., Cin., 1966—99; chmn. Ford Bros. Inc., Ironton, Ohio, 1975—79; mem. distbr. adv. coun. Mack Trucks; mng. dir. J. D. Ranch, Myakka City, Fla. Active Boy Scouts Am.; former trustee Freedoms Found. Valley Forge, Ohio Hist. Found.; vice-chmn. New Coll. Found.; dir. Mote Marine Lab. Ohio State U. Found.; chmn. bd. trustees emeritus Franklin U. With US Army, 1941—45, maj. gen. USAR. Decorated Bronze Star medal with V for Valor, Legion of Merit, Silver Star; named State of Ohio Vet. Hall of Fame, 1997, Buckeye Boys State Hall of Fame, 1999, Ohio State U. ROTC Hall of Fame, Jr. Achievement Ctrl. Ohio Bus. Hall of Fame, 2000; recipient Pres. Unit citation, Truck Dealer of the Yr. award, Time mag., 1972, Good Scout award, Ctrl. Ohio Coun. Boy Scouts Am., Silver Beaver award, Boy Scouts Am., Silver Antelope award, Disting. Citizen of Yr. award, Centennial medal, Ohio State U., Pacesetters award, Coll. Bus. ISU, 1996, Virginia Steckler Internat. Svc. award, ARC, 1998, Lifetime Achievement award, Ohio State U., 1999, Harrison Sayre award, 2001, Philanthropist of the Yr., Columbus Found., 2001; Baden-Powell fellow, World Scout Found. Mem.: Ohio Truck Assn., Am. Truck Dealers, Ohio State U. Alumni Assn., Army War Coll. Alumni Assn., Armor Assn., U.S. Army Arty. Assn., Columbus Club, Rotary (past dist. gov., Man of Yr., Paul Harris fellow), Masons. Office: Columbus Truck Equipment Co PO Box 83250 Columbus OH 43203-0250 Home: 85 Sugar Mill Dr Osprey FL 34229-9067 Office Phone: 614-252-3111.

MASON, RICHARD J., lawyer; b. Syracuse, NY, June 16, 1951; BA with high honors, U. Ill., 1973; MBA, U. Chgo., 1980; JD, U. Notre Dame, 1977. Bar: Ill. 1977. Ptnr., mem. exec. com. Ross & Hardies, Chgo., 1990—2003; ptnr. McGuireWoods, Chgo., 2003—. Adj. prof. law Kent Coll. Law, Ill. Inst. Tech., Chgo., 1984—. Bd. dirs. Ill. Farm Legal Assistance Found., 1985-88. Fellow Am. Coll. Bankruptcy; mem. ABA (chmn. bus. bankruptcy subcom. on use and disposition of property under the bankruptcy code 1989—), Am. Bankruptcy Inst., Ill. State Bar Assn. (mem. banking and bankruptcy law sect. coun. 1986-88), Chgo. Bar Assn. (mem. bankrupcty and reorgn. com. 1978—). Office: McGuireWoods LLP 77 W Wacker Dr Ste 4100 Chicago IL 60601

MASON, ROBERT MCSPADDEN, information scientist, educator, dean; b. Sweetwater, Tenn., Jan. 16, 1941; s. Paul Rankin and Ruby May (McSpadden) M.; m. Betty Ann Durrence (div. 1980); children: Michael Dean, Donald Robert; m. Marilyn Killebrew Gell, July 17, 1981. SB, MIT, Cambridge, 1963, SM, 1965; PhD, Ga. Inst. Tech., Atlanta, 1973. Tech. staff mem. Sandia Labs., Livermore, Calif., 1965-68; rsch. scientist Ga. Inst. Tech., Atlanta, 1971-75, sr. rsch. scientist, 1975; prin. Metrics, Inc., Atlanta, 1975-80; pres. Metrics Rsch. Corp., Atlanta, 1980-86, Cleve., 1986-98, Tallahassee, 1998—2005, Seattle, 2005—; adj. prof. Weatherhead Sch. Mgmt. Case Western U., 1987-88, vis. prof., 1988-91, prof. for practice of tech. mgmt., 1991-98; dir. Ctr. Mgmt. Sci. and Tech., 1988-96; Sprint prof. mgmt. and prof. mgmt. info. sys. Coll. Bus. Fla. State U., Tallahassee, 1998—2005, chair mgmt. info. sys., 1998—2002; prof. info. sch. U. Wash., Seattle, 2006—, assoc. dean rsch., 2006—. Co-author: The Impact of Office Automation on Clerical Employment, 1985-00, 1985, Library Micro Consumer, 1986; co-editor: Information Services: Economics, Management, and Technology, 1981, Management of Technology V: Technology Management in a Changing World, 1996, Management of Technology, Sustainable Development, and Eco-Efficiency, 1998, Management of Technology: The Key to Prosperity in the Third Millenium, 2001; Am. editor Technovation, 1994-2005, sr. editl. bd., 2005—; contbr. articles to profl. jours. Mem. Internat. Assn. for Tech. Mgmt. (newsletter editor 1992-93, program chair internat. conf., 1996, pres. 1996-98, mem. exec. com. 1998—, Disting. Achievement award 2007). Republican. Presbyterian. Avocations: flying, skiing, sailing, scuba diving, photography. Home: 2929 1st Ave Unit 1122 Seattle WA 98121 Office: Info Sch U Wash Seattle WA 98195-2840

MASON, SALLY KAY FROST, academic administrator, biology professor; b. NYC, May 29, 1950; d. Michael and Alberta Viparina; m. John S. Frost, Aug. 1975 (div. Feb. 1982); m. Kenneth Andrew Mason, Mar. 17, 1990. BA in Zoology, U. Ky., 1972; MS in Cell/Devel. Biology, Purdue U., 1974; PhD in Cell/Devel. Biology, U. Ariz., 1978. Rsch. assoc. Ind. U., Bloomington, 1978-80; asst. prof. biology U. Kans., Lawrence, 1981-86, assoc. prof. biology, 1986-91, prof. biology, 1991-2001, chair dept. physiology and cell biology, 1986-89, assoc. dean scis., 1990-95, dean arts and scis., 1995-2001; provost, prof. biology Purdue U., West Lafayette, Ind., 2001—07; pres. U. Iowa, 2007—. Chmn. bd. Inproteo, 2003—; chmn. EHR adv. bd. NSF, 2005—; mem. exec. com. Nat. Assn. State U. and Land Grant Colls., 2002—; mem. Pres.'s Nat. Medal of Sci. Selection Com., 2006—. Mem. editl. bd. Pigment Cell Rsch., 1988-99; contbr. chpts. to books and articles to profl. jours. Dissertation fellow AAUW, 1977-78, Kemper Tchg. fellow U. Kans., Lawrence, 1997; grantee NSF, NIH, Washington, 1981—; Wesley Found. grantee Welsey Health Found., Wichita, Kans., 1991-93. Mem. Internat. Fedn. Pigment Cell Scis. (coun. mem. 1997-2000), Pan Am. Soc. for Pigment Cell Rsch. (coun. mem. 1988-98, pres. 1996-98), Coun. Colls. Arts and Scis. (bd. mem. 1997-99, pres. elect 1999-2000, pres. 2000-2001). Avocations: travel, reading, writing. Office: U Iowa Office of Pres 101 Jessup Hall Iowa City IA 52242-1316 *

MASON, SCOTT MACGREGOR, entrepreneur, inventor, consultant; b. NYC, Feb. 11, 1923; s. Gregory Mason and Mary Louise Turner; m. Mildred Davidson, Mar. 13, 1949 (div. 1970); children: Alan Gregory, Phoebe Louise, Caleb; m. Virginia Frances Perkins, May 5, 1970 (dec. 1990). AB, Princeton U., 1943; MS, NYU, 1947. Control chemist Firestone Tire & Rubber Co., Akron, Ohio, 1943-44; R & D chemist Am. Cyanamid Co. Rsch. Labs., Stamford, Conn., 1948-52; mgr. stearate dept. Warwick Chem. div. Sun Chem. Corp., Wood River Junction, R.I., 1952-58; cons., Stonington, Conn., 1958-59; instr. Williams Meml. Inst., New London, Conn., 1959-63; NSF fellow Brown U., Providence, 1963-64; tchr. Moses Brown Sch., Providence, 1964-70; owner, mgr. Innoventures, Wakefield, R.I., 1970—. Cons. Greene Plastics Corp., Canonchet, R.I., 1972-80, Dorette Inc., Pawtucket, R.I., 1982-83. Trustee Pine Point Sch., Stonington, 1956-62, pres. bd., 1959-61. With AUS, 1944-46, ETO. Named Tchr. of Week, Sta. WICE, Providence, 1967; summer rsch. fellow NSF, U. R.I., 1960. Mem. AAAS, N.Y. Acad. Scis. Achievements include patents in field. Avocations: tennis, fishing, snorkeling, photography, music. Office: Innoventures PO Box 369 Wakefield RI 02880-0369

MASON, STEPHEN OLIN, not-for-profit developer; b. Fresno, Calif., July 11, 1952; s. Olin James and Mary Edna (Moyer) Mason. BA, Bridgewater Coll., Va., 1974; MEd, James Madison U., 1979; PhD, Loyola U., Chgo., 1991. Asst. to the dir. student ctr. Bridgewater Coll., 1974-76; guidance counselor Woodlawn Elem. Sch., Sebring, Fla., 1976-77; asst.

dean for student devel. Bridgewater Coll., 1977-81; dir. student life Roger Williams Coll., Bristol, R.I., 1981-83; assoc. dean for residential svcs. Dickinson Coll., Carlisle, Pa., 1983-84; v.p., dean student affairs Westmar Coll., LeMars, Iowa, 1984; rsch. assoc. to pres. Elmhurst (Ill.) Coll., 1986-87; v.p. student affairs Felician Coll., Chgo., 1987-88; dean students Huntingdon Coll., Montgomery, Ala., 1988-90; dir. devel. McPherson (Kans.) Coll., 1990-94, v.p. fin. svcs., 1994-97; exec. dir. Assn. of Brethren Caregivers, Elgin, Ill., 1997—2003; v.p. coll. adv. Manchester Coll., No. Manchester, Ind., 2004—05; exec. dir. Cmty. Found. Wabash County, No. Manchester, Ind., 2005—06; dir. Brethren Found., Elgin, 2006—. Participant ARC Blood Drive, 1978—79; mem. allocations com. United Way, Carlisle, 1984; adv. bd. mem. LeMars chpt. Siouxland Coun. for Alcoholism and Drug Abuse, 1984; site coord. for coat drive Mental Health Greater Chgo., 1985; dir.-at-large Alumni Bd. Bridgewater Coll., 1987—93; v.p. McPherson Habitat for Humanity, 1993, 1994, bd. dirs., 1993—96, pres., 1994; bd. dirs. McPherson Mus. and Arts Found., 1992—94, Assn. Brethren Caregivers, 1993—97, Assn. Anabaptist Risk Mgmt., 2000—03; governing coun., mem. adv. Bethany Hosp., 2001—02. Mem.: Brethren Benefit Trust (bd. dirs. 2002—06). Avocations: calligraphy, theater, barbershop quartets, spelunking. Home: 106 S Merkle St North Manchester IN 46962 Home Phone: 260-982-1923; Office Phone: 847-695-0200. Business E-Mail: smason_bbt@brethren.org.

MASON, TERRY, city health department administrator, urologist; BS, Loyola U., 1974; MD, U. of Ill. Abraham Lincoln Sch. Medicine, 1978. Pres., ptnr. Prairie Med. Associates; chief Urology Mercy Hosp., Chgo.; assistant prof. surgery Abraham Lincoln Sch. Medicine U. of Ill.; commr. dept. public health City of Chgo., 2006—. Host radio prog. Doctor in the House WVON, Chgo. Author: Making Love Again, Renewing Intimacy & Helping Your Man Overcome Impotence, 1988. Recipient Physician of the Year, Nat. Med. Assn., 1999, Black Enterprise Best in Medicine award, 2001. Fellow: Am. Coll. Surgeons; mem.: World Impotence Assn. (regional dir.), Am. Urological Assn., Nat. Med. Assn. (nat. chmn.), AMA, Saltpond Redevelopment Inst., Ghana West Africa, NAACP. Office: City of Chgo Dept Health 333 S State St Ste 200 Chicago IL 60604 also: Prairie Med Assocs Ltd 2600 S Michigan Ste 303 Chicago IL 60616

MASON, THOMAS ALBERT, retired lawyer; b. Cleve., May 4, 1936; s. Victor Lewis and Frances (Speidel) M.; m. Elisabeth Gun Sward, Sept. 25, 1965; children: Thomas Lewis, Robert Albert. AB, Kenyon Coll., 1958; LLB, Case-Western Res. U., 1961. Bar: Ohio 1962. Assoc. Thompson, Hine and Flory, Cleve., 1965-73, ptnr., 1973—2001, ret., 2002—. Trustee Cleve. YMCA, 1975-94. Capt. USMCR, 1962-65. Mem. Am. Coll. Real Estate Lawyers, Ohio Bar Assn., Cleve. Bar Assn., The Country Club. Republican. Episcopalian. Avocations: tennis, golf. Office: Thompson Hine LLP 3900 Key Ctr 127 Public Sq Cleveland OH 44114-1291 Office Phone: 216-566-5519. E-mail: tom.mason@thompsonhine.com.

MASON, THOMAS ALEXANDER, historian, educator, author; b. Port Huron, Mich., Oct. 29, 1944; s. Frank Hallgren and Charlotte (Hamilton) M.; m. Christine Huguette Guyonneau, Aug. 11, 1984; 1 child, Charlotte Guyonneau. BA in History with highest honors, Kenyon Coll., 1966; MA, U. Va., 1970, PhD, 1975. Asst. prof. history Pembroke (N.C.) State U., 1976-79; assoc. editor Papers of James Madison, U. Va., 1979-86, acting editor, 1986-87; dir. publs. Ind. Hist. Soc., 1987—2001, v.p. publs., 2001—02; v.p. Ind. Hist. Soc. Press, 2002—. Author: Serving God and Mammon: William Juxon, 1582-1663, 1985; exec. editor: Traces of Indiana and Midwestern History, 1989—; editor: Documentary Editing, 1989-93, Mag. of Albermarle County History, 1984-86; co-editor: Papers of James Madison, congl. series, vols. 14-16, 1983-89, presdl. series, vol. 1, 1984; project dir.: Papers of Lew Wallace, 1992—; mem. editl. bd. Jour. of the Early Republic, 1991-95, Ency. of Indpls., 1990-94, Documentary Editing, 2002—; contbr. articles to encys. and scholarly jours. Served with USMC, 1966-68. Mem. Am. Assn. for State and Local History, Am. Hist. Assn., N.Am. Conf. on Brit. Studies, So. Hist. Assn., Assn. Documentary Editing (councillor-at-large 1999-2002, dir. publs. 1995-98, Disting. Svc. award 1993), Hist. Soc. of the Episcopal Ch. (sec. 1995—, bd. dirs. 1993—), English-Speaking Union U.S. (chmn. region VI 1996-2002, bd. dirs. 1995-2002, pres. Indpls. br. 1989-96, Lily Dabney scholar 1972, Merit award 2002), Raven Soc., Rotary (Indpls., bd. dirs. 1998-2000), Colonnade Club (Charlottesville), Royal Commonwealth Soc. (London), Omicron Delta Kappa (faculty sec. Va. Cir. 1984-86), Alpha Delta Phi. Episcopalian. Home: PO Box 20331 Indianapolis IN 46220-0331 Office: Ind Hist Soc 450 W Ohio St Indianapolis IN 46202-3269 E-mail: tmason@indianahistory.org.

MASON, THOMAS P., lawyer; BA with high distinction, U. Nebr., 1978; JD with honors, U. Tex., 1981. Bar: Tex. 1981. Ptnr. Andrews & Kurth, Houston; sr. energy and securities ptnr. Vinson & Elkins, Houston, 2001—07; gen. counsel Energy Transfer Partners, LP, Dallas, 2007—. Office: Energy Transfer Ptnrs, LP 2838 Woodside St Dallas TX 75204 Office Phone: 214-981-0700. *

MASON, THOMAS R., utilities executive; BEE, Purdue U.; MBA, U. Chgo. Pres., COO CalEnergy Operating Svcs., Inc., 1995—99; sr. v.p. Calpine Power Co., San Jose, Calif., 1999, exec. v.p., pres., 1999—. Office: Calpine Power Co 50 W San Fernando St 5th Fl San Jose CA 95113 Office Phone: 408-995-5115. Office Fax: 408-995-0505.

MASON, THOMASINE GRAYSON, judge; b. Summerton, SC, Nov. 7, 1918; d. James Fulton Grayson and Martha Anne Gentry; m. Edgar Fleming Mason, June 30, 1939 (dec.). BA, U. S.C., Columbia, 1938, LLB, 1942, JD, 1970. Certificate in cotton classing N.C. State Coll., 1956. Tchr., West Columbia, SC, 1938—39; civil svc. rep. during World War II Atlanta, Athens and Charleston Navy Yard; gen. practice of law Manning, SC; trial atty. Dept. Justice, Washington, 1969—71; fed. adminstrv. law judge Office of Hearings and Appeals, 1971—; hearing office chief adminstrv. law judge, 1985—2002. Bd. trustees Clarendon Meml. Hosp., Manning, SC; state senator SC; del. Nat. Dem. Conv., 1960. Mem.: Richland County Bar Assn., S.C. Bar Assn., ABA, DAR, Am. Legion Aux., Alpha Delta Pi. Republican. Baptist. Avocation: jet-skiing. Office: Office of Disability Adjudication and Review 1927 Thurmond Mall Blvd Ste 200 Columbia SC 29201 Business E-Mail: thomasine.g.mason@ssa.gov.

MASON, WILLIAM, opera company director; b. Chgo. m. Diana Davis; 2 children. MusB, Roosevelt U. Asst. to co-artistic dir. Pino Donati, 1962—66; asst. stage mgr. Lyric Opera Chgo., 1968—70; asst. to Felix Popper N.Y.C Opera, 1971; prod. stage mgr. Cin. Opera, 1972; stage mgr., asst. in musical preparation Light Opera of Manhattan, 1972; prod. mgr., asst. dir. Ohio-based Corbett Found., 1973; prod. dir. Lyric Opera Chgo., 1974—78, gen. dir., 1997—; artistic adminstr. San Francisco Opera, 1979—80. Mem. Lyric Children's Chorus, 1954—56. Office: Lyric Opera Chgo 20 N Wacker Dr Chicago IL 60606-2806 *

MASON, WILLIAM A(LVIN), psychologist, educator, researcher; b. Mountain View, Calif., Mar. 28, 1926; s. Alvin Frank and Ruth Sabina (Erwin) M.; m. Virginia Joan Carmichael, June 27, 1948; children: Todd, Paula, Nicole, Hunter. BA, Stanford U., 1950, MS, 1952, PhD, 1954. Asst. prof. U. Wis.-Madison, 1954-59; research assoc. Yerkes Labs. Primate Biology, Orange Park, Fla., 1959-63; head dept. behavioral sci. Delta Primate Research Ctr., Tulane U., Covington, La., 1963-71; prof. psychology, research psychologist U. Calif., Davis, 1971-91, leader behavioral biology unit Calif. Primate Rsch. Ctr., 1972-96, prof. emeritus, 1991. Bd. dirs. Jane Goodall Inst., 1978-92, Karisoke Rsch. Ctr., 1980-86. Mem. Editorial bd. Animal Learning and Behavior, 1973-76, Internat. Jour. Devel. Psychobiology, 1980-92, Internat. Jour. Primatology, 1980-90; contbr. numerous articles to profl. jours., chpts. to books. With USMC, 1944-46. USPHS spl. fellow, 1963-64. Fellow AAAS, APA (pres. divsn. 6 1982, disting. sci. contbn. award 1995), Am. Psychol. Soc., Animal Behavior Soc.; mem. Internat. Primatological Soc. (pres. 1976-80, 81-84), Am. Soc. Primatologists (pres. 1988-90, disting. primatologist award), Internat. Soc. Devel. Psychobiology (pres. 1971-72, Best Paper of Yr. award 1976), Sigma Xi. Home: 2809 Anza Ave Davis CA 95616-0257 Office: U Calif Regl Primate Rsch Ctr 1 Shields Ave Davis CA 95616 Home Phone: 530-756-2479. Business E-Mail: wamason@ucdavis.edu.

MASON-CHANEY, LISA, curator; b. Paducah, Ky., Apr. 18, 1962; d. Billy C. and Doris Ann Mason; m. Kevin Chaney, Nov. 20, 1994; stepchildren: Kevin Chaney Jr., Christina Chaney; children: Courtney Ann Jones, Robert Wesley Jones. BFA, MA, We. Ky. U., Bowling Green, 1989. Curatorial asst. Nat. Portrait Gallery, SI, Washington, 1990—93; collections mgr. Soc. Cin. at Anderson House Mus., Washington, 1992—99; mus. dir. Ellicott City B&O RR Sta. Mus., Ellicott City, Md., 2000—04; curator, asst. dir. Hammond-Harwood House, Annapolis, Md., 2004—. Mem.: Am. Assn. Mus. (mid-atlantic rep. small museums com. 2003—), Mid-Atlantic Assn. Mus. (profl. com. coun. chair 2005—), Md. Assn. History Mus. (v.p. 2005—06, pres. 2006—), Small Mus. Assn. (pres. 2005). Democrat. Avocations: travel, reading. Home: 313 Crandell Rd Severna Park MD 21146 Office: Hammond-Harwood House 19 Maryland Ave Annapolis MD 21401 Office Phone: 410-263-4683 x 12. Business E-Mail: lmchaney@hammondharwoodhouse.org.

MASON-HIPKINS, PATRICIA, minister; b. Pitts., Pa. d. Oliver Ellwood and Clarice Jane Hipkins; widowed; children: Rodney Williams Jr., Rhonda Haynes, Gregory Williams. MDiv, Interdenominational Theol. Sem., 1984, D in Ministry, 1990. Assoc. minister Ch. of God in Christ, Atlanta, 1981—90; dir. enlistment Interdenominational Theol. Sem., Atlanta, 1990—93; ch. devel. pastor Presbyn. of Atlanta, 1994—2000; pastor Hazelwood Presbyn., Pitts., 2001—. Grief counselor Arlington Cemetery, Atlanta, 1998—2000; therapist Auberle Ctr. Dep. and Delinquent Youth, 2000; grief counselor Anegheny Cemetery, Pitts., 2000—01. Commr. Gen. Assembly PC USA, Louisville, 2004—; mem. Com. Racial and Social Justice, Pitts., 2001—05, Com. on Ministry; commr. New Ch. Devel. Mem.: Nat. Black Presbyn. Caucus, Theta Phi. Presbyterian. Avocation: interior decorating. Office: Hazelwood Presbyn Ch 5000 2nd Ave Pittsburgh PA 15207 Office Phone: 412-421-0947. Personal E-mail: drpatmason@aol.com.

MASOTTI, LOUIS HENRY, real estate educator, consultant; b. NYC, May 16, 1934; s. Henry and Angela Catherine (Turi) Masotti; m. Iris Patricia Leonard, Aug. 28, 1958 (div. 1981); children: Laura Lynn, Andrea Anne; m. Ann Randel Humm, Mar. 5, 1988. AB, Princeton U., 1956; MA, Northwestern U., 1961, PhD, 1964. Fellow Nat. Ctr. Edn. in Politics, 1962; asst. prof. polit. sci. Case Western Res. U., Cleve., 1963-67, assoc. prof., 1967-69, dir. Civil Violence Rsch. Ctr., 1968-69; sr. Fulbright lectr. Johns Hopkins U. Ctr. Advanced Internat. Studies, Bologna, Italy, 1969-70; assoc. prof. Northwestern U., Evanston, Ill., 1970-72, prof. polit. sci. and urban affairs, 1972-83, dir. Ctr. Urban Affairs, 1971-80, dir. Program in Pub. and Not-for-Profit Mgmt., Kellogg Sch. Mgmt., 1979-80, prof. mgmt. and urban devel. Kellogg Sch. Mgmt., 1983-94, dir. Real Estate Research Ctr. Kellogg Sch. Mgmt., 1986-88. Cons. in field; vis. assoc. prof. U. Wash., 1969; exec. dir. Mayor Jane Byrne Transition Com., Chgo., 1979; vis. prof. Stanford Sch. Bus., 1989—92, UCLA Sch. Mgmt., 1989—92; prof., dir. real estate mgmt. program U. Calif. Grad. Sch. Mgmt., Irvine, 1992—98; bd. dirs. Mfd. Home Cmtys., Inc., Facilities Mgmt. Internat., S. Calif. Physicans Ins. Co. Author: (book) Educaiton and Politics in Suburbia, 1967, Shootout in Cleveland, 1969, A Time to Burn?, 1969, Suburbia in Transition, 1973, The New Urban Politics, 1976, The City in Comparative Perspective, 1976; co-editor: Metropolis in Crisis, 1968, Metropolis in Crisis, 2d edit., 1971, Riots and Rebellion, 1968, The Urbanization of the Suburbs, 1973, After Daley: Chicago Politics in Transition, 1981, Downtown Development, 1985, Downtown Development, 2d edit., 1987; editor: Edn. and Urban Soc., 1968—71, Urban Affairs Quar., 1973—80; sr. editor: Econ. Devel. Quar., 1986—92, vice chmn. bd.: Ill. Issues Jour., 1986—92, BOMA Office Mag., 1990—95. Mem. Cleveland Heights Bd. Edn., 1967—69; devel. coord. high tech. State of Ill. - City of Chgo., 1982—83; Rsch. dir. Carl Stokes for Mayor Cleve., 1967; advisor to various congl., gubernatorial and mayoral campaigns Ohio, Ill., NJ, Calif. Lt. USNR, 1956—59. Recipient Disting. Svc. award, Cleve. Jaycees, 1967; fellow, Homer Hoyt Inst. Advanced Real Estate Studies; numerous rsch. grants, 1963—2000. Mem.: Internat. Econ. Devel. Coun., Nat. Assn. Indsl. Office Properties, Internat. Devel. Rsch. Coun., Internat. Assn. Corp. Real Estate Execs., Nat. Trust Hist. Preservation, Habitat, Urban Land Inst., Lambda Alpha Internat. Address: 2010 W Twinoaks Dr Prescott AZ 86305 Office Phone: 619-750-1703. Personal E-mail: louismasotti@cableone.net.

MASOVER, GERALD KENNETH, microbiologist; b. Chgo., May 12, 1935; s. Morris H. and Lillian (Perelgut) M.; m. Bonnie Blumenthal, Mar. 30, 1958 (dec. 1992); children: Steven, Laurie, David; m. Lee H. Tower, Mar. 25, 1995. BS, U. Ill., Chgo., 1957, MS, 1970; PhD, Stanford U., 1973. Registered pharmacist Calif., Ill. Owner, operator Ropert Pharmacy, Chgo., 1960-68; rsch. assoc. Stanford U. Med. Sch., Palo Alto, Calif., 1974-80; assoc. rsch. cell biologist Children's Hosp., Oakland, Calif., 1980-83; rsch. microbiologist Hana Biologics, Berkeley, Calif., 1983-86; pharmacist various locations, 1958—98; quality control sect. head Genentech, Inc., South San Francisco, 1986-90, quality control sr. microbiologist, 1990—2004; ret., 2004. Cons. Genentech, Inc., South San Francisco, 2004—. Contbr. articles to profl. jours., chpts. to books. 1st Lt. USAR, 1957-66. NSF predoctoral fellow, 1970-73; Rsch. grant NIH, 1974-78. Mem. Internat. Orgn. for Mycoplasmology, Parenteral Drug Assn., Am. Soc. Microbiology, Sigma Xi. Jewish. Achievements include patents for triphasic mycoplasmatales detection method, triphasic mycoplasmatales detection device. Home: 6214 Acacia Ave Oakland CA 94618-1821

MASRANI, BHARAT B., bank executive; Grad., York U., Canada, 1978; MBA, 1979. Vice chair, pres., CEO TD Waterhouse Europe; sr. v.p. Toronto-Dominion Bank; pres., CEO TD Waterhouse Internat., 2002, e.Bank, 2002; exec. v.p., Toronto-Dominion Bank, 2002—03; vice chair Credit Asset Mgmt. TD Securities LLC, 2002—03; exec. v.p. risk mgmt. Toronto-Dominion Bank, 2003—05, vice chmn., chief risk officer, 2005—06; dir. TD Banknorth Inc., 2005—06, pres., 2006—07, pres., CEO, 2007—. Office: TD Banknorth Inc Two Portland Square 7th Fl Portland ME 04101 Office Phone: 207-761-8541. Office Fax: 207-761-6673. *

MASRI, MERLE SID, biochemist, consultant; b. Jerusalem, Palestine, Sept. 12, 1927; came to U.S., 1947; s. Sid Rajab and Fatima M.; m. Maryjean Loretta Anderson, June 28, 1952 (div. 1974); children: Kristin Corinne, Allan Eric, Wendy Joan, Heather Anderson. BA in Physiology, U. Calif., Berkeley, 1950; PhD in Mammalian Physiology and Biochemistry, U. Calif. Berkeley, 1953. Rsch. asst. Dept. Physiology, Univ. Calif., Berkeley, 1950-53; predoctoral fellow Baxter Labs., Berkeley, 1952-53; rsch. assoc. hematology Med. Rsch. Inst., Michael Reese Hosp., Chgo., 1954-56; sr. rsch. biochemist Agrl. Rsch. Svc., USDA, Berkeley, 1956-87; supervisory rsch. scientist Agrl. Rsch. Svc., USDA, N.D. State U. Sta., Fargo, ND, 1987-89; pvt. practice as cons. Emeryville, Calif., 1989—. Lectr. in field. Contbr. articles to profl. jours.; chpts. to books. Recipient Spl. Svc. and Merit awards USDA, 1966, 76, 77, Superior Svc. award USDA, 1977. Mem. AAAS, Am. Chem. Soc., Am. Oil Chemists Soc., Am. Assn. Cereal Chemists, N.Y. Acad. Scis., Inst. Food Technologists, Commonwealth Club Calif., Internat. Platform Assn., World Affairs Coun. of No. Calif., Sigma Xi. Achievements include patents for detoxification of aflatoxins in agricultural crops and aflatoxin contaminated milk, improved dyeability of cotton fabrics and reduced dye and electrolyte discharge in plant effluent, new closed-circuit raw wool scouring technology to conserve water and energy and control pollution, synthesis and use of polymers and modification of biopolymers for wastewater treatment, and for encapsulation, enzyme immobilization, toxic heavy metals removal and textile finishing treatment, non-polluting new technology for scouring raw wool in a closed circuit with water recycling and re-use and waste effluent control; studied chlorination of water in food processing operations and water re-use and recycle and the generation of mutagens and means of improving disinfection efficiency and reducing mutagen formation, pharmacology, metabolism, and toxicology of natural and synthetic compounds, cereal and baking technology and wheat and durum quality, carbohydrate chemistry, fermentation and enology, confectionery, ceramic chemistry and digital graphic art image production; discovery of new methods and reagents for protein and amino acid residue modification and analysis, new mammalian metabolic pathways; development of other non-polluting textile finishing treatments (shrink, wrinkle, insect and fire resistance). Home: 9 Commodore Dr Emeryville CA 94608-1652

MASRI, SAFWAN MALEK, industrial engineer, educator; BS in Industrial Engring., Purdue U., 1982, MS in Industrial Engring., 1984; PhD in Industrial Engring. & Mgmt., Stanford U., 1988. Former prof. Stanford U., Santa Clara U.; prof. Columbia U., 1988—, vice dean, dir., MBA program, grad. sch. of bus., 1993—. Bd. dirs. ARAMEX Internat., Nuqul Group, Aregon, Sage Ventures; consultant Merrill Lynch, PaineWebber, Salomon Brothers, Deutsche Bank, Bankers Trust, Citibank, Ford Motor Co., Pfizer, IBM, Bahrain Inst. of Banking and Fin., UN; advisor to Queen Rania Al-Abdullah of Jordan; mem. adv. bd. UN Develop. Programme Project for Assessment of Arab Universities. Bd. dirs. Colbert Found., Friends for Life. Office: Columbia Bus Sch Uris Hall 3022 Broadway New York NY 10027

MASS, M. F., allergist, immunologist; b. Phila., Feb. 24, 1945; m. Marilyn Halpern, June 12, 1966; children: Ellis, David. Student, U. Fla., 1963; BA, Brandeis U., 1966; MD, U. Fla., 1970; postgrad., U. Colo., Albany, NY, 1972, U. Colo., Denver, 1975. Intern Albany Med. Ctr., NY, 1970-71, residency, 1971-72; sr. residency U. Colo. Med. Ctr., Denver, 1972-73, postgrad. fellow/allergy-immunology, 1973-75; assoc. clin. prof. medicine U. Fla., Jacksonville, 1977—. Past chmn. dept. medicine Meml. Med. Ctr., Jacksonville; prin. investigator Jacksonville Ctr. for Clin. Rsch. Inventor skin chamber. Chmn. Duval County Environ. Protection Bd.; trustee Fla. CC at Jacksonville, 1999—, also bd. trustees. Maj. USAF, 1975-77. Health Professions scholar U. Fla. Fellow ACP, Am. Acad. Allergy and Immunology, Am. Coll. Allergy; mem. Duval County Med. Soc. (v.p., pres.-elect, pres.). Office: 3636 University Blvd S Ste B2 Jacksonville FL 32216-4223 Office Phone: 904-733-8200. E-mail: massjax@comcast.net.

MASS, MICHAEL DON, state legislator; b. McAlester, Okla., Oct. 29, 1951; s. Fred Jr. and Lois M.; m. Suzanne Kline; children: Elena, Angie, Micah, Lucas. Student, Grayson C.C., Sherman, Tex., Ea. Okla. State Coll. Mem. Ho. of Reps., 1991—. Dist. mgr. Pittsburg County Conservation Dist.; chair Okla. Dem. Party. Mem. McAlester C. of C. (exec. dir.), Latimer and Pittsburg County Cattlemen's Assn., Hartshorne C. of C. (v.p.). Democrat. Office: State Capitol Bldg Rm 501 2300 N Lincoln Blvd Oklahoma City OK 73105

MASSA, CONRAD HARRY, retired religious studies educator; b. Bklyn., Oct. 27, 1927; s. Harry Frederick and Josephine W. (Lepold) M.; m. Anna W. Rossi, Aug. 19, 1951; children: Stephen Mark, Barbara Ann. AB with honors, Columbia U., 1951; M.Div., Princeton Theol. Sem., 1954, PhD, 1960; HHD, Lafayette Coll., 1987. Ordained to ministry Presbyn. Ch., 1954. Pastor Elmwood Presbyn. Ch., East Orange, NJ, 1954-57; asst. prof. homiletics Princeton Theol. Sem., 1957-61; sr. pastor Old First Ch., Newark, 1961-66, Third Presbyn. Ch., Rochester, NY, 1966-78; dean acad. affairs Princeton Theol. Sem., 1978-94, dean emeritus, 1994—, Charlotte W. Newcombe prof., 1978-95, Charlotte W. Newcombe prof. emeritus, 1995—. 1st moderator Synod of the Northeast, United Presbyn. Ch.; vis. prof. St. Bernard's Roman Cath. Sem., Rochester, 1968-70; keynote speaker 11th ann. conf. Inst. Theology, Yonsei U., Seoul, Republic of Korea, 1991. Author articles and book revs. Trustee Lafayette Coll., Easton, Pa., 1982-93. Served with U.S. Army, 1946-47. Mem. Acad. Homiletics, Am. Acad. Religion, Internat. John Bunyan Soc. Home: 9583 SW 90th St Ocala FL 34481-7495 E-mail: chm1@sprynet.com. *I have learned to try to understand all events and persons in terms of their relationships to other things, persons and events. While it is sometimes fruitful to isolate a particular and study it in its solitude, nothing and no one really exists in such isolation. This has become a guiding principle in my continued research and growth in those areas of greatest interest - religion, education and society.*

MASSA, DAVID J., lawyer; b. Ill., 1955; Student, Princeton U.; BA magna cum laude, Washington U., 1975; JD, Yale U., 1978. Bar: Ill. 1978, Mo. 1979, US Dist. Ct. (ea. and we. dists.) Mo., US Dist. Ct. (so. dist.) Ill., US Ct. of Appeals (8th, 11th, Fed., and 7th cirs.). Ptnr. Bryan Cave, St. Louis; atty. Gallop, Johnson & Neuman, St. Louis. Mem.: ABA, Ill. State Bar Assn., Mo. Bar Assn., Met. St. Louis Bar Assn. Office: Gallop Johnson & Neuman 101 S Hanley Ste 1700 Saint Louis MO 63105 Office Phone: 314-615-6207. Office Fax: 314-615-6001.

MASSA, RICHARD WAYNE, retired communications educator; b. Carona, Kans., May 2, 1932; s. Columbo and Ella (Whitehead) M.; m. Mary Lou Marshall, May 29, 1960 (div. 1969); m. Teresa Rose Ramirez, Mar. 19, 1971; children: Tod, Daphne, Sara. B in Journalism, U. Mo., 1954, MA, 1955; postgrad., U. Ark., 1964-65. Instr. U. Mo., Columbia, 1955, Miss. State Coll. for Women, Columbus, 1957-58; from instr. to assoc.prof. comm. Okla. Coll. for Women/Okla. Coll. Liberal Arts, Chickasha, 1958-69; assoc. prof. Mo. So. State Coll., Joplin, 1972-87, prof., 1987-99, head dept. comm., 1980-99, dir. Inst. Internat. Studies, 1996-99, acting head dept. lang. and lit., 1979-80; ret., 1999. V.p. Interpersonal Comm. Consultants, Oklahoma City, 1969-72. Co-author: Principal Ideas of Medieval and Renaissance Man, 1967, Contemporary Man in World Society, 1969; co-editor: Classical Readings for Contemporary Man, 1967, Inquisitive Man; His Quest for Truth, 1970. With U.S. Army, 1955-57. Recipient Gov.'s award for Excellence in Tchg., Mo. Dept. Higher Edn., Jefferson City, 1996. Home: 25399 Demott Dr Joplin MO 64801-6309 Personal E-mail: massa727@aol.com.

MASSAD, STEPHEN ALBERT, lawyer; b. Wewoka, Okla., Dec. 20, 1950; s. Alexander Hamilton and Delores Jean (Razook) Massad; children: Caroline, Sarah, Margaret. AB, Princeton U., 1972; JD, Harvard U., 1975. Bar: Tex. 1975. Assoc. Baker Botts LLP, Houston, 1975-82, ptnr., 1983—, corporate dept. chair, 1994—2002, mem. exec. com., 1995—2001. Office: Baker Botts LLP 3000 One Shell Plz 910 Louisiana St Houston TX 77002 Office Phone: 713-229-1475. Business E-Mail: stephen.massad@bakerbotts.com.

MASSAD, TIMOTHY G., lawyer; b. New Orleans, July 30, 1956; s. Alexander H. and Delores Massad. AB magna cum laude, Harvard U., 1978, JD magna cum laude, 1984. Bar: NY 1985. Assoc. Cravath Swaine & Moore LLP, NYC, 1984—92, ptnr., corp., 1992—, resident ptnr. Hong Kong, 1998—2002. Corp. counsel Covenant House; vice chmn. Norwalk Redevel. Agy.; v.p. Norwalk CC Found.; bd. dirs. US-India Bus. Coun. Mem.: ABA, Internat. Bar Assn., NYC Bar Assn., NY State Bar Assn., Phi

Beta Kappa. Office: Cravath Swaine & Moore LLP Worldwide Plz 825 Eighth Ave New York NY 10019-7475 Office Phone: 212-474-1154. Office Fax: 212-474-3700. Business E-Mail: tmassad@cravath.com.

MASSAH, CHERILYN, retired auditor; b. Dallas, Jan. 31, 1951; d. Herman Hiram and Mary Charleene (Thomas) Hill; m. Fathollah Massah, June 30, 1979. AA with highest honors, Tarrant County Jr. Coll., Hurst, Tex., 1982; BBA, U. Tex., Arlington, 1987. CPA, Tex. Sr. auditor Def. Contract Audit Agy., Dallas, 1987—2006. Spl. Interest grantee Tarrant County Jr. Coll., 1982; nominated to Nat. Dean's List U. Tex.-Arlington, 1986-87. Mem. Assn. Govt. Accts., Beta Alpha Psi. Avocation: stamp collecting/philately. Home: 4708 Michelle Dr Arlington TX 76016-5339 Personal E-mail: chmassah@tx.rr.com.

MASSALSKI, THADDEUS BRONISLAW, materials scientist, educator; b. Warsaw, June 29, 1926; came to U.S., 1959; s. Piotr and Stanislawa (Andrukaniec) M.; m. Sheila Joan Harris, Sept. 19, 1953; children: Irena, Peter, Christopher. B.Sc., Birmingham U., Eng., 1952, PhD, 1954, D.Sc., 1964; fellow, Inst. Study Metals, U. Chgo., 1954-56; D.Sc. (h.c.), Warsaw U., 1973. Lectr. Birmingham U., 1956-59; head. metal physics dir. Mellon Inst., Pitts., 1959-75, 1961—69; prof. metal physics and materials sci. Carnegie-Mellon U., 1968—. Vis. prof. U. Buenos Aires, 1962, Calif. Inst. Tech., 1962, Stanford, 1963, U. Calif., 1964, 66, Inst. Physics, Bariloche Argentina, 1966, 70, Harvard, 1969; exchange prof. Krakow (Poland) U., 1968; vis. scientist Nat. Bur. Standards, 1980-81; NAVSEA prof. Naval Postgrad. Sch., Monterey, Calif; chmn. bd. govs. Acta Metallurgica, Inc., 1992—96. Co-author: Structure of Metals, 3d edit, 1966, Advanced Physical Metallurgy, 1965; co-editor Progress in Materials Science, 1969—, Metall. Transactions, 1991—; editor-in-chief ASM/NIST Phase Diagram Program, 1980-2000; author papers and articles on alloy theory, crystallography, metal physics, meteorites. Guggenheim fellow Oxford U., 1965-66; recipient Alexander von Humboldt prize, 1991, Sendzimir prize Polish Inst. Arts and Scis. in Am., 1998. Fellow Am. Soc. Metals (gold medal 1993), Am. Phys. Soc., The Metals Soc. (gold medal 1995), Brit. Inst. Materials (hon.), Brit. Inst. Physics, AIME (Hume-Rotherly prize 1989); mem. Polish Acad. Sci. (fgn.), German Acad. Sci. (fgn.), Phys. Soc., Associazione Italiana di Metallurgia (Losana gold medal). Home: 900 Field Club Rd Pittsburgh PA 15238-2127 Office: Carnegie Mellon U 3303 Wean Hall Pittsburgh PA 15213

MASSARO, TONI MARIE, dean, law educator; BS highest distinction, Northwestern U., 1977; JD, Coll. William and Mary, 1980. Assoc. Vedder, Price, Kaufman and Kammholz, Chgo., 1980—82; asst. prof. Washington and Lee U., U. Fla., 1982—84; prof. law U. Ariz., Tucson, 1989—, regents prof., Milton O. Riepe chair constl. law James E. Rogers Coll. Law, 1997—, dean James E. Rogers Coll. Law, 1999—. Vis. asst. prof. law U. Fla., 1984—85; vis. prof. Johann Goethe U., Frankfurt, Germany, 1988, U. NC, 1989, Stanford U., 1989. Author: Constitutional Literacy: A Core Curriculum for a Multi-Cultural Nation; co-author: Civil Procedure: Cases and Problems, 3d edit., 2006; contbr. articles to law revs. Recipient Women on the Move award, YWCA, 2002, Leslie F. and Patricia Bell Faculty Award, 1998. Fellow: Am. Bar Found.; mem.: Ariz. State Bar (Access to Justice com. 2003—04, Professionalism com. 2002—), Am. Law Inst., Am. Assn. Law Schs. (Academic Freedom and Tenure com. 2000—04), Order of the Coif. Office: U Ariz Coll Law 1201 E Speedway PO Box 210176 Tucson AZ 85721-0176 Office Phone: 520-621-1498. Office Fax: 520-621-9140. Business E-Mail: massaro@law.arizona.edu.

MASSE, WILLIAM BRUCE, archaeologist; b. San Diego, July 10, 1948; s. Gerald John Masse and Viola Hope Bumgarner; m. Judith Lee Peters, Sept. 12, 1971; 1 child, Jeffrey Alan. BA in Anthropology, Stanford U., 1971; MA in Anthropology, U. Ariz., 1977; PhD in Anthropology, So. Ill. U., 1990. Archeologist Nat. Park Svc., Tucson, 1977-79, Ariz. State Mus., Tucson, 1985-86; field archaeologist State Historic Preservation Office, Honolulu, 1988-89; pacific area archaeologist Dept. of Navy, Pearl Harbor, Hawaii, 1990-94; archaeologist Dept. Air Force, Luke Air Force Base, Ariz., 1995-98, Los Alamos (N.Mex.) Nat. Lab., 1999—. Editor: The Protohistoric Period in the North American Southwest, 1981; contbr.: Chaco and Hohokam: Prehistoric Regional Systems in the North American Southwest, 1991, Natural Catastrophes During Bronze Age Civilizations: Archaeological, Geological, Astronomical, and Cultural Perspectives, 1998; editor (spl. issue) Jour. S.W., 1996; contbr. articles to profl. jours. Mem.: AAAS, Soc. Am. Archaeology (repatriation com. 1998—2001), Am. Anthrop. Assn., Sigma Xi. Office: Los Alamos Nat Lab RRES-ECO Ecology Group Mail Stop M887 Los Alamos NM 87545 Fax: (505)667-0731. E-mail: wbmasse@lanl.gov.

MASSENGALE, MARTIN ANDREW, agronomist, educator, university president; b. Monticello, Ky., Oct. 25, 1933; s. Elbert G. and Orpha (Conn) M.; m. Ruth Audrey Klingelhofer, July 11, 1959; children: Alan Ross, Jennifer Lynn. BS, Western Ky. U., 1952; MS, U. Wis., 1954, PhD, 1956; LHD (hon.), Nebr. Wesleyan U., 1987; DS (hon.), Senshu U., Tokyo, 1995. Cert. profl. agronomist, profl. crop scientist. Research asst. agronomy U. Wis., 1952-56; asst. prof., asst. agronomist U. Ariz., 1958-62, assoc. prof., assoc. agronomist, 1962-65, prof., agronomist, 1965-76, head dept., 1966-74, assoc. dean Coll. Agr. assoc. dir. Ariz. Agr. Expt. Sta., 1974-76; vice chancellor for agr. and natural resources U. Nebr., 1976-81; chancellor U. Nebr.-Lincoln, 1981-91, interim pres., 1989-91; pres. U. Nebr., 1991-94, pres. emeritus, 1994, found. disting. prof. and dir., 1994—. Chmn. pure seed adv. com. Ariz. Agrl. Expt. Sta.; past chmn. bd., pres. Mid-Am. Internat. Agrl. Consortium; coord. com. environ. quality EPA-Dept. Agrl. Land Grand U.; past chmn. bd. dir. Am. Registry Cert. Profls. in Agronomy, Crops and Soils; bd. dir. Ctr. for Human Nutrition, Lincoln Ins. Group., Woodmen Accident & Life Co., LIG, Inc., Am. First, LLC, All Am. Enterprises, LLC; chair bd. dir. Agronomic Sci. Found., chmn. selection com; dir. devel. Secretariat, Filippo Maseri Florio World Prize Disting. Rsch. in Agr.; exec. com. U. Nebr. Tech. Park, LLC; mem. adv. bd. Nat. Agrl. Rsch., Ext., Edn. and Econs., 1998—, chair secs. nat. adv. bd., exec. com.; nat. adv. bd. Trees Am., 1998—. Chmn. NCAA Pres.'s Commn., 1988-91; distbn. revenue com., standing com. on appointments North Ctrl. Assn. Commn. on Insts. Higher Edn., 1991; trustee Nebr. Hist. Soc. Found.; bd. dir. Nebr. Hist. Soc.; bd. govs. Nebr. Sci. and Math. Initiative; mem. Knight Found. Commn. on Intercollegiate Athletics; bd. dir. Great Plains Funds, IBP, AGR Ednl. Found., 2004—; hon. life trustee Nebr. Coun. on Econ. Edn.; hon. lifetime trustee Nebr. Coun. on Econ. Edn.; bd. dir., trustee U. Nebr. Found. With U.S. Army, 1956-58. Named Midlands Man of Yr., 1982, to We. Ky. U. Hall of Disting. Alumni, 1992, DeKalb Crop Sci. Disting. Career award, 1996, Outstanding Educator Am., 1970, Wayne County H.S., Monticello, Ky., Charter Hall of Fame, 2002; recipient faculty recognition award Tucson Trade Bur., 1971, Ak-Sar-Ben Agrl. Achievement award, 1986, Agrl. Builders Nebr. award, 1986, Walter K. Beggs award, 1986, Vol. of Yr. award for disting. svc. Nebr. Coun. on Econ. Edn., IANR Team Initiation award, Agri award Triumph of Agr. Expn., 1999, Exemplary Svc. to Agr. award Nebr. AgRels. Coun., 2000, Friend of LEAD award Nat. LEAD Alumni Assn., 2001, Outstanding Pres. award All-Am. Football Found., 2001, Wagonmaster award Nebraskaland Found., 2006; named to Charter Hall of Fame, USDA, 2004; hon. state farmer degrees Ky., Ariz., Nebr. Future Farmers Am. Assn. Fellow AAAS (sect. chmn.), Crop Sci. Soc. Am. (past dir., pres. 1972-73, past assoc. editor, pres. western soc., Disting. Career award 1996), Am. Soc. Agronomy (past dir., vis. scientist program, past assoc. editor Agronomy Jour., Disting. Svc. award 1984); mem. Am. Grassland Coun., Ariz. Crop Improvement Assn. (bd. dir.), Am. Soc. Plant Physiology, Nat. Assn. Colls. and Tchrs. Agr., Soil and Water Conservation Soc. Am., Ariz. Acad. Sci., Nebr. Acad. Sci., Agrl. Coun. Am. (bd. dirs., issues com.), Coun. Agrl. Sci. and Tech. (bd. dir. budget and fin. 1979-82, 94-2005, treas., exec. com. 1997-2005), Nat. Assn. State Colls. and Land Grant Univs. (chmn. com. on info. tech. 1987-94, exec. com. 1990-92, bd. dir. 1992-94), Edn. Engring. Professions (mem. commn.), Coll. Football Assn. (chmn., bd. dir. 1986-88), Am. Assn. State Coll. and Univs. (task force instl. resource allocation), AAFL Enterprises LLC (bd. dir., 2004—), Assn. Am. Univs. Rsch. Librs. (steering com. 1992-94), Nebr. Crop Improvement Assn. (Disting. Svc. award), Grazing Lands Forum (pres.), Nebr. C. of C. and Industry, Nebr. Diplomats Inc. (hon. diplomate), Nebr. Vet. Med. Assn. (hon.), Sigma Xi, Phi Kappa Phi, Gamma Sigma Delta (Merit award), Alpha Zeta, Phi Sigma, Gamma Alpha, Alpha Gamma Rho (bd. dir. ednl. found. 2004—, Bros. of the Century award), Phi Beta Delta, Golden Key, Innocents Soc., AGR Ednl. Found. (bd. dir., 2004—). Office: U Nebr 220 Keim Hall Lincoln NE 68583-0953 Office Phone: 402-472-4101. Business E-Mail: mmassengale1@unl.edu.

MASSENGILL, DAVID E., lawyer; b. Albuquerque, Jan. 29, 1953; BS summa cum laude (in Psychology) (hon.), Tulane U., 1975; JD magna cum laude (hon.), Harvard U., 1978. Bar: NY 1979. Atty. Simpson Thacher & Bartlett, NYC, Simpson Thacher, NYC, 1981, ptnr., 1986—. Mem.: Phi Beta Kappa. Office: Simpson Thacher 425 Lexington Ave New York NY 10017-3954 Office Phone: 212-455-3555. Office Fax: 212-455-2502. Business E-Mail: dmassengill@stblaw.com.

MASSENGILL, MATTHEW H., computer company executive; BE, Purdue U., 1983. Rsch. engr., infra detectors and imaging sys. Ford Aerospace and Commn. Corp., 1982—85; product engr. Western Digital Corp., Irvine, Calif., 1985—86, v.p. mktg. personal storage divsn., 1993—97, sr. v.p., gen. mgr. enterprise storage group Rochester, Minn., 1997—98, chief operating officer Irvine, Calif., 1998—2000, CEO, 2000—05, chmn., 2001—. Launched a startup software co., 1986; mgr. of ranch, Oreg., 1990—91; bd. dir. ViewSonic Corp. Bd. dir. Orange County Technology Action Network, Calif., THINK Together, (Orange County), Calif.; vice-chmn. CEO Roundtable program, Univ. Calif., Irvine; chmn. TechNet So.Calif. Recipient Outstanding Elec. Engring. Alumni award, Purdue Univ., 1998, Disting. Engring Alumni award, 2002. Office: Western Digital Corp 20511 Lake Forest Dr Lake Forest CA 92630-7741 *

MASSEY, DOROTHY WILLIAMS, ophthalmologist, writer; b. Greenhills, NY, Nov. 1, 1933; d. Craig John Williams and Susan Sally Rutherford; m. Daniel Thomas Massey, Sept. 12, 1955. BS, SUNY, NYC, 1951, PhD, 1957. Prof. state sch., Amsterdam, Netherlands, 1958—67, Nice, France, 1968—85; pvt. practice, 1985—. Author: Green Bough, 1984, Woman of the City, 1991, Bone Mind, 2003. Fellow: Am. Ophthalmologists Assn. Avocations: writing, hunting, skiing. Mailing: 617 Arnold Ave Point Pleasant Beach NJ 08742-2502

MASSEY, ELEANOR NELSON, retired school librarian, media specialist; b. Apr. 1, 1930; d. Walter K. and Jeanette (Perlman) Nelson; m. Marvin Donald Massey, June 29, 1952; children: Henry, David, Michael, Jonathan. BA, Douglass Coll., New Brunswick, NJ, 1952; postgrad., Rutgers U. Cert. ednl. media specialist. Children's librarian Westfield (N.J.) Pub. Library, 1952-55; librarian Franklin Jr. High Sch., Metuchen, N.J., 1959-61; media specialist Campbell Sch., Metuchen, 1962—2006; coordinator libraries Metuchen Pub. Schs., 1982—2006; ret., 2006. Dir. Woodbridge-East Brunswick Area Coordination Council, 1982-85; mem. interim planning com. N.J. Library Network, 1984-85; cooperating tchr. Kean Coll. and Rutgers U., 1975—; speaker; bibliographer. V.p. Sisterhood Neve Shalom, Metuchen, 1960; dir. Neve Shalom, 1959-60; bd. dirs. Union-Middlesex Regional Library Cooperative, Region IV, Inc., 1985-89; active Metuchen Cable TV Adv. Commn., 1994—. Title II Demonstration Library grantee State of N.J., 1974-76, Sch.-Pub. Libr. Coop. grantee 1986, Metuchen Edn. Found grantee for AuthorsLive program, 1999. Recipient N.J. Gov.'s Tchr. Recognition award, 1991. Mem. Ednl. Media Assn. N.J. (exec. bd. 1976-78), ALA, N.J. Library Assn., Ednl. Media Assn. Middlesex County (treas. 1982-83). Home: 111 Clarendon Ct Metuchen NJ 08840 Personal E-mail: emassey@optonline.net.

MASSEY, HOWARD CLAYLAND, writer; b. Coolidge, Ga., Oct. 21, 1925; s. Paul Lester and Ruby Dell Massey; m. Hilda Dodson Schroer, June 17, 1966; 1 child, Sondra Gayle Siegel; m. Edna Ann Weller (div.); 1 child, Richard Clayton. M in Plumbing and Heating, Lindsey Hopkins Tech. Edn. Ctr., Miami, 1958. Owner Ctr. Plumbing & Heating Corp., Miami-Dade, 1958—73; plans examiner Met. Bldg. & Zoning Dept., Miami-Dade, 1974—88; author Craftsman Book Co., Hollywood, Fla., 1978—85, Vero Beach, Fla., 1986—. Designer plumbing isometrics State of Fla. Lic. Bd., 1982—84; creator exam. questions Constrn. Industry Lic. Bd., Fla., 1983—85. Author: (tech. book) Plumber's Handbook, 1978, Basic Plumbing With Illustrations, 1980, Estimating Plumbing Costs, 1982, Plumber's Exam Preparation Guide, 1985, Planning Drain, Waste & Vent Systems, 1990, International Plumbing & Fuel Gas Codes, 2003, America's Ragged Edge, 2005, Deep Woods, 2006. Seaman 3d class USN, 1943—45. Mem.: Gideons Internat., Authors Guild. Republican. Home and Office: 1240 Fifth St Vero Beach FL 32962 E-mail: hcmhcm@bellsouth.net.

MASSEY, JAMES EARL, retired clergyman, retired educator; b. Ferndale, Mich., Jan. 4, 1930; s. George Wilson and Elizabeth (Shelton) M.; m. Gwendolyn Inez Kilpatrick, Aug. 4, 1951. Student, U. Detroit, 1949-50, 55-57; BTh, BRE, Detroit Bible Coll., 1961; AM, Oberlin Grad Sch. Theology, 1964; postgrad., U. Mich., 1967-69; DD, Asbury Theol. Sem., 1972, Ashland Theol. Sem., 1991, Huntington Coll., 1994; HumD, Tuskegee U., 1995; DD, Warner Pacific Coll., 1995; LittD, Anderson U., 1995; DD, Wash. and Jefferson Coll., 1997, North Park Theol. Sem., 1999. Ordained to ministry Ch. of God, 1951. Assoc. min. Ch. of God, Detroit, 1951-53; sr. pastor Met. Ch. of God, Detroit, 1954-76, pastor-at-large, 1976; spkr. Christian Brotherhood Hour, 1977-82; prin. Jamaica Sch. Theology, Kingston, 1963-66; campus min. Anderson Coll., Ind., 1969-77, asst. prof. religious studies Ind., 1969-75, assoc. prof. Ind., 1975-80, prof. N.T. and homiletics Ind., 1981-84; dean of chapel and univ., prof. religion and society Tuskegee U., Ala., 1984-89; dean, prof. preaching and bibl. studies Anderson Sch. Theology, 1989-95, dean emeritus, prof. at large, 1995—; dean emeritus Tuskagee U. Chapel, 1998—; ret., 1998. Chmn. Comm. on Higher Edn. in the Ch. of God, 1968-71; vice chmn. bd. publs. Ch. of God, 1968-78; dir. Warner Press, Inc.; rsch. scholar Christianity Today Inst. Author: When Thou Prayest, 1960, The Worshipping Church, 1961, Raymond S. Jackson, A Portrait, 1967, The Soul Under Seige, 1970, The Church of God and the Negro, 1971, The Hidden Disciplines, 1972, The Responsible Pulpit, 1973, Temples of the Spirit, 1974, The Sermon in Perspective, 1976, Concerning Christian Unity, 1979; gen. editor: Christian Brotherhood Hour Study Bible, 1979, Designing the Sermon, 1980; co-editor: Interpreting God's Word for Today, 1982; editor: Educating for Service, 1984, The Spiritual Disciplines, 1985, The Bridge Between, 1988, Preaching From Hebrews, 1992, The Burdensome Joy of Preaching, 1996, Sundays at The Tuskegee Chapel, 1999, Aspects of My Pilgrimage: An Autobiography, 2002, Remembering William L. Dawson, 2004, African Americans and the Church of God, 2005, Stewards of the Story, 2005; mem. editl. bd. The Christian Scholar's Rev. Leadership mag.; mem. editl. bd., contbg. editor Vol I New Interpreter's Bible, 1990—; contbg. editor Preaching mag.; sr. editor Christianity Today mag. Mem. Corp. Inter-Vrsity Christian Fellowship; bd. dirs. World Vision. Served with AUS, 1951-53. Mem. Nat. Assn. Coll. and Univ. Chaplains, Nat. Com. Black Churchmen, Nat. Negro Evang. Assn. (bd. dirs. 1969-86). Office: 367 Beverly Rd Greensboro AL 36744-6034

MASSEY, JEANNE KELLY, performing company executive; b. Charleston, SC, Oct. 30, 1938; d. Lawrence Lees and Margaret Augusta (Montgomery) Kelly; m. William Massey III, June 25, 1960 (div. 1994); children: Kelly Massey-Carlier, John Gant Massey. BA, Duke U., 1960; advanced libr. cert., William and Mary Coll., 1976. Founding libr. Jamestown Acad., Williamsburg, Va., 1974-77; pres. Va. State Ballet, Newport News, Va., 1978-82; founder, pres. Arts Resale of Williamsburg, Va., 1978-88; pres., gen. mgr. Mid-Atlantic Chamber Orch., Washington, 1985-98; exec. prodr. Benedictinus 2000 Internat. Order of Benedictines, 1997—2000; prodr. Annual World Bank Mozart Festival, 1991—. Commr. Va. Commn. for the Arts, Richmond, 1979-84; nat. exec. com. Children of Am. Revolution, Washington, 1973-76; dir., pres. The Wyo. Condominium, Washington, 1988-91; mem. Arts Adv. Bd., Williamsburg, 1979-81. Recipient Platinum Violin award, Festival Williamsburg, 1984. Mem. DAR (pres. 1970-76), Jamestowne Soc., Jane Austen Soc. of N.Am., Phi Beta Kappa, Kappa Delta Pi, Sigma Delta Pi. Republican. Presbyterian. Avocations: walking, reading, concerts, museums, theater. Office: JKM Inc PO Box 21439 Washington DC 20009-0939 Home Phone: 202-837-3611. Fax: 202-337-1004. E-mail: jkminc@infionline.net.

MASSEY, MICHAEL J., lawyer, retail executive; b. St. Louis, Mo., May 5, 1964; BA with honors, Indiana U., 1985; JD, Wash. U., 1989. Bar: Mo. 1989, Kans. 1997. Atty. The May Dept. Stores Co., 1990—96; sr. counsel Payless ShoeSource Inc., Topeka, 1996—98, v.p. group counsel intellectual property, 1998—2000, v.p. contract manufacturing, 2000, v.p. internat. develop., 2001, sr. v.p., gen. counsel, corp. sec., 2003—. Recipient John W. Foster prize. Mem.: ABA, Am. Soc. of Corp. Counsel, Assn. of Corp. Counsel, Mo. Bar Assn., Kansas Bar Assn. Office: Payless ShoeSource Inc PO Box 1189 3231 SE Sixth St Topeka KS 66601

MASSEY, RAYMOND DAVID, lawyer; b. Goldsboro, NC, Oct. 13, 1946; s. Raymond L. and Dorris L. (Grant) Massey; m. Barbara A. Wamer, Aug. 16, 1967; children: Suzanne, Christine. BA, Wofford Coll., Spartanburg, SC, 1968; JD, U. S.C., Columbia, 1971; LLM in Taxation, Emory U., Atlanta, 1985. Bar: S.C. 1971, U.S. Dist. Ct. S.C. 1971, cert.: S.C. Supreme Ct. (specialist estate planning and probate law). Assoc. Perrin, Perrin & Mann, Spartanburg, Spartanburg, 1971—74; trust officer Bankers Trust of S.C., Columbia, SC, 1974—78; shareholder Brown, Massey, Evans, McLeod & Haynsworth, PA, Greenville, SC, 1978—. Pres. Greenville Estate Planning Coun., 1982; chair Cmty. Found. of Greater Greenville, 2001—02; dir. Greenville Hosp. Sys. Found., 2002—. Named to trusts and estates section, Best Lawyers in Am. Fellow: Am. Coll. Trust and Estate Counsel; mem.: S.C. Bar Assn. (chmn. probate, estate planning and trust sect. 1983), Greenville Bar Assn. (pres. tax sect. 1980—81), Poinsett Club, Greenville Country Club. Presbyterian. Office: PO Box 2464 Greenville SC 29602-2464 Office Phone: 864-271-7424.

MASSEY, RAYMOND LEE, lawyer; b. Macon, Ga., Sept. 25, 1948; s. Ford B. and Juanita (Sapp) M.; m. Lynn Ann Thielmeier, Aug. 23, 1967; children: Daniel, Caroline. BA, U. Mo., St. Louis, 1971; JD, U. Louisville, 1974. Bar: Mo. 1974, Ill. 1976, U.S. Dist. Ct. (ea. and we. dists.) Mo. 1974, U.S. Dist. Ct. (so. dist.) Ill. 1976, Tex. 1997. Assoc. Thompson & Mitchell, St. Louis, 1974-79; ptnr. Thompson & Mitchell (now Thompson & Coburn), St. Louis, 1979—. Mem. Maritime Law Assn. of U.S. (bd. dirs., chmn. ocean and river towing). Home: 3 Wild Rose Dr Saint Louis MO 63124-1465 Office: Thompson Coburn US Bank Ste 3400 Saint Louis MO 63101-1643 Home Phone: 314-991-1687; Office Phone: 314-552-6075. E-mail: rmassey@thompsoncoburn.com.

MASSEY, RICHARD N., lawyer, telecommunications industry executive; JD with honors, Univ. Ark. Ptnr. Kutak Rock, 1998—2000; mng. dir. Stephens Inc., Little Rock, 2000—05; exec. v.p., gen. counsel, corp. sec. Alltel Inc., 2005—. Office: Alltel Corp One Allied Dr Little Rock AR 72202 *

MASSEY, ROBERT UNRUH, internist, educator, dean; b. Detroit, Feb. 23, 1922; s. Emil Laverne and Esther Elisabeth (Unruh) M.; m. June Charlene Collins, May 28, 1943 (dec. July 2005); children: Robert Scott (dec.), Janet Charlene. Student, Oberlin Coll., 1939-42, U. Mich. Med. Sch., 1942-43; MD, Wayne State U., 1946. Intern, resident in internal medicine Henry Ford Hosp., Detroit, 1946-50; assoc. Lovelace Clinic, Albuquerque, 1950-68, chmn. dept. medicine, 1958-68, bd. govs., 1957-68; dir. med. edn. Lovelace Found. for Med. Edn. and Research, 1960-68; clin. assoc. U. N.Mex. Sch. Medicine, 1961-68; prof. medicine U. Conn. Sch. Medicine, Farmington, 1968-92, prof. emeritus, 1992—, assoc. dean for grad edn., 1968-71, dean Sch. Medicine, 1971-84, currently prof. emeritus dept. community medicine and health care, acting univ. v.p. for health affairs, 1975-76. Chief staff Newington VA Hosp., Conn., 1968-71; trustee Am. Assn. Med. Clinics, 1966-68; exec. com., regional adv. group Conn. Regional Med. Program, 1971-76; trustee, v.p. Capitol Area Health Consortium, 1974-78, pres., 1980-81. Editor-in-chief Conn. Medicine, 1986-99; editor Jour. of the History of Medicine and Allied Scis., 1987-91. Bd. dirs. Health Planning Coun., Inc., 1974-76; bd. dirs. Hartford Inst. for Criminal and Social Justice, 1976-80, Conn. Easter Seal Soc., 1977-85, Hospice Inst. Edn., Tng. and Rsch., 1979-81. With AUS, 1955-57; maj. Res. Fellow ACP; mem. Am. Group Practice Assn. (accreditation commn. 1968-78), Assn. Am. Med. Colls., Am. Assn. History of Medicine, Hartford County Med. Assn., AMA, Conn., Hartford med. socs., Am. Osler Soc., Beaumont Med. Club, Soc. Med. Adminstrs., Twilight Club (Hartford), Acorn Club, Sigma Xi, Alpha Omega Alpha. Roman Catholic.

MASSEY, STEPHEN CHARLES, rare book dealer, consultant; b. London, May 9, 1946; s. Charles Dudley and Sheila Florence (Browne) M.; divorced; 1 child, Sarah Louise. Grad. high sch., UK. Cataloguer books and manuscripts Christie's, London, 1964-75, sr. dir. rare books and manuscripts dept. NYC, 1975-96, sr. internat. cons., 1997-99. Fellow Pierpont Morgan Libr.; mem. The Grolier Club, The Old Book Table. Avocations: cinema, reading, running, music, forestry. Office Phone: 212-628-6850. Personal E-mail: scmassey@aol.com.

MASSEY, THOMAS BENJAMIN, retired university president; b. Charlotte, NC, Sept. 5, 1926; s. William Everard and Sarah (Corley) M.; m. Bylee Hunnicutt Massey, July 10, 1968; children: Pamela Ann, Caroline Forest. AB, Duke U., 1948; MS, N.C. State U., 1953; PhD, Cambridge U., 1968. Assoc. dean students Ga. Inst. Tech., Atlanta, 1950-58; lectr. U. Md. Univ. Coll., 1960-66, dir. London, 1966—69, dir. Toyko, 1969-71, dir. Heidelberg (Fed. Republic of Germany), 1971-76, vice chancellor, 1976-78, chancellor, 1978-88, pres., 1988-98, pres. emeritus, 1998—. Served with USN, 1943-46. Mem. APA, Univ. Continuing Edn. Assn., Am. Assn. Higher Edn., Internat. Confs. on Improving Learning and Tchg. at the Univ. (chair 1975—). Personal E-mail: benmassey@mac.com.

MASSEY, WALTER EUGENE, retired academic administrator, physicist; b. Hattiesburg, Miss., Apr. 5, 1938; s. Almor and Essie (Nelson) M.; m. Shirley Streeter, Oct. 25, 1969; children: Keith Anthony, Eric Eugene. BS, Morehouse Coll., 1958; MA, PhD, Washington U., St. Louis, 1966. Physicist Argonne Nat. Lab., Ill., 1966-68; asst. prof. physics U. Ill., Urbana, 1968-70; assoc. prof. Brown U., Providence, 1970-75, prof., dean of Coll., 1975-79; prof. physics U. Chgo., 1979-93; dir. Argonne Nat. Lab., 1979-84; v.p. for rsch. and for Argonne Nat. Lab. U. Chgo., 1984-91; dir. NSF, Washington, 1991-93; sr. v.p. acad. affairs U. Calif. System, 1993-95; pres. Morehouse Coll., Atlanta, 1995—2007. Cons. NAS, 1973-76; mem. NSB, 1978-84; chair Sec. Energy Adv. Bd., 1997-99; bd. dirs. Mellon Found, Bank Am. Corp. 1998-, McDonald's Corp., BP p.l.c.; mem. Gates Millennium Scholars Adv. Coun.; mem. coun. visitors Marine Biol. Lab.; mem. Pres.'s Coun. Advisors on Sci. and Tech., 1990-92, 01-. Contbr. articles on sci. edn. in secondary schs. and in theory of quantum fluids to profl. jours. Bd. fellows Brown U., 1980-90, Mus. Sci. and Industry, Chgo.,

1980-89, Ill. Math. and Sci. Acad., 1985-88; bd. dirs. Urban League RI, 1973-75; mem. Salzburg seminar, 1997—, Atlanta Symphony Orch., 1996—, Woodruf Art Ctr., 1995—, Atlanta Com. Pub. Edn., 1996-2004, Bd. Project GRAD, Gt. Schs. Atlanta Bd., 2004-; trustee U. Chgo; active Atalnta Com. for Progress, 2003—. Recipient over 25 hon. degrees; NAS fellow, 1961, NDEA fellow, 1959-60, AAAS fellow, 1962. Mem. AAAS (bd. dirs. 1981-85, pres.-elect 1987-88, pres. 1988-89, chmn. 1989-90), Am. Phys. Soc. (councillor-at-large 1980-83, v.p. 1990), Smithsonian Inst. (bd. regents), Sigma Xi. Office: Morehouse Coll 830 Westview Dr SW Atlanta GA 30314-3773 also: Bank of Am Corp 100 N Tryon St, 18th Fl Charlotte NC 28255

MASSEY, WILLIAM S., mathematician, educator; b. Granville, Ill., Aug. 23, 1920; s. Robert R. and Alma (Schumacher) M.; m. Ethel Heap, Mar. 14, 1953; children— Eleanor, Alexander, Joan. Student, Bradley U., 1937-39, MA (hon.), 2005; BS, U. Chgo., 1941, MS, 1942; PhD, Princeton, 1948. Mem. research dept. Princeton, 1948-50; from asst. prof. to prof. Brown U., 1950-60; prof. math. Yale, 1960—, Erastus L. Deforest prof. math, 1964-82, Eugene Higgins prof. math., 1983-91, Eugene Higgins prof. math. emeritus, 1991—, chmn. dept. math., 1968-71. Author: Algebraic Topology: An Introduction, 1967, Homology and Cohomology Theory, 1978, Singular Homology Theory, 1980, A Basic Course in Algebraic Topology, 1991; mem. editorial staff math. jours. Served as officer USNR, 1942-46. Fellow Am. Acad. Arts and Scis.; mem. Am. Math. Soc. Achievements include research in algebraic topology, differential topology, homotopy theory, fibre bundles. Home: 200 Leeder Hill Drive Hamden CT 06517-2729 Office: Yale U Math Dept PO Box 208283 New Haven CT 06520-8283

MASSEY, WILLIAM WALTER, JR., sales executive; b. Lawrenceburg, Tenn., Sept. 21, 1928; s. William Walter and Bess Ann (Brian) M.; m. Virginia Claire Smith, Aug. 16, 1952; children: William Walter III, Laura Ann, Lynn Smith, Lisa Claire. BBA, U. Miami, Fla., 1949; BFA, U. Fla., 1969. Co-owner Massey Motors, Inc., Jacksonville, Fla., 1950—; v.p., dir. Atlantic Discount Co. Inc., Jacksonville, 1954-64; pres. Owners Surety Corp., Jacksonville, 1959—, General Svcs. Corp., Jacksonville, 1960-69, Owners Guaranty Life, Phoenix, 1960-64, Securities Guaranty Life, Phoenix, 1961-64, Fla. Properties, Inc., Jacksonville, 1961-66, Chi-Cha, Inc., Jacksonville, 1965-70, Univ. Square Properties, Jacksonville, 1969-80; v.p., sec./treas. Spring Forest Properties, Cashiers, NC, 1978—2001. V.p., bd. dir. Southside Country Day School, Jacksonville, 1963-68; bd. dirs. Southside Atlantic Bank, Jacksonville, 1965-93. Exhibited in group shows at Internat., N.Y., 1970, Ball State U., 1972. Lt. USAF, 1950-1952. Mem. Ponte Vedra Club, River Club, Epping Forest Club, Deerwood Club, Sigma Chi. Methodist. Avocations: music, painting, writing. Office Phone: 904-398-6877. Office Fax: 904-642-8815.

MASSIE, CLIFFORD MICHAEL, music company executive; b. Bklyn., May 11, 1957; s. Michael and Jennifer Massie. BA cum laude with honors, Brandeis U., 1979. Pres. The Hit House, Levittown, NY, 1987—, Shoot No Blanks Music Publishing, Bethpage, NY, 1987—. Producer/remixer Teena Marie, Gloria Gaynor, David Hasselhoff, Evelyn Champagne King, Promoter Jay-Z, Ja Rule, DMX, Ludacris, Ashanti, Janet Jackson, Mariah Carey, Aaliyah, Snoop Dogg, Brian McKnight. Recipient Songwriter 1st Place Billboard Mag. contest, 1988. Mem.: NMPA, NARAS, ASCAP. Achievements include numerous Gold and Platinum singles/albums. Home: 3700 Mallard Rd Levittown NY 11756 Office: The Hit House 3700 Mallard Rd Levittown NY 11756 also: Shoot No Blanks Music Pub PO Box 102 Bethpage NY 11714 Office Phone: 516-735-3452. Office Fax: 516-735-3329. Personal E-mail: cliffmassie@optonline.net.

MASSIE, TAMMY JEANNE PARLIMENT, statistician; b. Suffern, NY, Jan. 4, 1972; d. Thomas Holden and Marjorie Eleanor (Wood) Parliment; m. Tristan Shaw Massie, Dec. 28, 1969. BS in Math., Stockton State Coll., 1994; MS in Stats., U. Ctrl. Fla., 1998; PhD in Biostatistics, Med. Coll. Va., Va. Commonwealth U., 2002. Grad. tchg. asst. U. Ctrl. Fla., Orlando, 1995—98; lfeguard, cast mem. Walt Disney World, Lake Buena Vista, Fla., 1996—98; statistician Whitehall Robins, Richmond, Va., 1999—2000; grad. rsch. asst. Med. Coll. Va., Va. Commonwealth U., 1998—2002; math. statistician Ctr. Vet. Medicine, FDA, Rockville, Md., 2002—04, Ctr. Drug Evaluation and Rsch., FDA, Rockville, 2004—. Statis. cons. U. Ctrl. Fla., 1995—98; statis. cons., biostatistical consulting lab student leader Med. Coll. Va., Va. Commonwealth U., 1998—2002. Contbr. to roundtable discussions, posters to sci. forums. Recipient Karl E. Peace award of Excellence, Med. Coll. Va., 2000—01; scholar Youth for Understanding Exch. Student award, Kraft Foods, 1990, Philip Morris Academic award, Philip Morris, 1992—94. Mem.: FDA Stats. Assn., Drug Info. Assn. (poster ann. meeting 2005), Soc. Clin. Trials (presenter ann. meeting 2005), Am. Statis. Assn., Assn. Women in Sci. Home: 171 Sharpstead Lane Gaithersburg MD 20878 Office: Food and Drug Administration-CDER 2901 Corporate Blvd Rockville MD 20850 Home Phone: 804-310-8745; Office Phone: 301-827-2549. Office Fax: 301-827-2577. Business E-Mail: tammy.massie@fda.gov.

MASSIER, PAUL FERDINAND, mechanical engineer; b. Pocatello, Idaho, July 22, 1923; s. John and Kathryn (Arki) M.; m. Miriam Parks, May 1, 1948 (dec. Aug. 1975); children: Marilyn Massier Schwegler, Paulette Massier Holden; m. Dorothy Hedlund Wright, Sept. 12, 1978. *Grandfather Ferdinand Massier pioneered the Baptist missionary movement in Bukovina and Galicia (Austria) during the late 1800's and early 1900's. Father John Massier, a cabinet maker, immigrated to the U.S. from Bukovina in 1903 and in 1951 was elected "Deacon for Life" by the First Baptist Church in Pocatello, Idaho. Mother Katie Arki immigrated from Croatia-Slavonia in 1906 and was an excellent cook and gardener. Daughter Marilyn, a flutist, was awarded "Musician of the Year" at Arcadia, California High School, where daughter Paulette, a violinist, was Concert Mistress of the orchestra. Both toured Europe with the American Youth Symphony Orchestra.* BSME, U. Colo., 1948; MSME, MIT, 1949. Cert. U. Idaho, So. Branch, 1943. Engr. Pan-Am. Refining Corp., Texas City, Tex., 1948; design engr. Maytag Co., Newton, Iowa, 1949-50; research engr. Boeing Co., Seattle, 1951-55; sr. research engr., supr. and dep. sect. mgr. Jet Propulsion Lab. Calif. Inst. Tech., Pasadena, 1955-84, task mgr., 1984-88, mem. tech. staff, 1989-94. *More than 40 years of engineering research and supervision led to: concepts and analysis of "far out" rocket propulsion systems such as antimatter, laser, nuclear, and metastable states; evaluation of rocket-engine fuel and oxidizer cooling capabilities including the upper limit of nucleate boiling for numerous liquid propellants such as hydrazine, nitrogen tetroxide, oxygen, alcohol, and many others; experimental determination of fluid mechanics and heat transfer phenomena for high-temperature compressible swirling flows in axisymmetric ducts and convergent-divergent nozzles; identification and evaluation of explanted heart valve prostheses; development of gas turbines for use as engines in trucks and boats and as air compressors.* Contbr. articles to profl. jours. Moderator Arcadia Congl. Ch., 1996-98; mem. Arcadia High Sch. Music Club, 1966-71. With U.S. Army, 1943-46. Recipient Apollo Achievement award NASA, 1969, Basic Noise Rsch. award NASA, 1980, Life Mem. Svc. award Calif. PTA, 1970, Layman of Yr. award Arcadia Congl. Ch., 1971, Mil. Unit Citation award, 1946. Fellow AIAA (assoc., Sustained Svc. award 1980-81); mem. AAAS, N.Y. Acad. Scis., Planetary Soc., Order of the Engr., Bukovina Soc. of the Ams., Sigma Xi, Tau Beta Pi, Pi Tau Sigma, Sigma Tau. Congregationalist. Achievements include 50% reduction of cooling requirements for rocket engines, experimental evaluation of heat transfer from thermally ionized gases at temperatures up to 13,000 degrees; experimental determination of starting characteristics, shock-wave structures, heat transfer and pressure distributions in supersonic diffusers led to the development of criteria for their design and their use as a means of simulating altitude conditions at ground level for static testing of rocket engines; experimental/analytical determination of the relationships of large-scale turbulent structures, density and temperature fluctuations, inverted velocity profiles, internally generated pure tones, twin jet shielding, and aircraft flight on noise emitted from aircraft supersonic jets; understanding of the formation of cenospheres during the combustion of heavy oils by analysis of electron microscope photo images of droplets, and stages of formed globules and cenospheres gathered on slides during combustion experiments. Home: 764 Lava Falls Dr Las Vegas NV 89110

MASSMAN, RICHARD ALLAN, lawyer; b. Beaumont, Tex., Aug. 19, 1943; s. Irwin Massman and Sylvia (Schmidt) Schwartz; m. Barbara Elaine Kessler; children: Jason Todd, Karen Faye. BS cum laude, U. Pa., 1965; JD cum laude, Harvard U., 1968. Bar: Tex. 1968; cert. in taxation, Tex. Bd. Legal Specialization. Assoc. Coke & Coke, Dallas, 1968-70, Johnson & Wortley, P.C. (formerly Johnson & Gibbs, P.C.), Dallas, 1970-71, ptnr., 1971-88, shareholder, 1988-94; of counsel Johnson & Wortley P.C., Dallas, 1994-95; sr. v.p., gen. counsel Hunt Consolidated, Inc., Dallas, 1994—. Lectr. So. Meth. U., Dallas, 1973; trustee Am. Beacon Funds, 2004—; bd. dirs. Retina Found. Southwest, 2004—. Chmn. Dallas Civil Svc. Bd., 1983; trustee Greenhill Sch., Dallas, 1985-92, vice chmn., 1990-92; trustee Dallas Opera, 1999—; chmn. Dallas Opera Found., 2007—; bd. dirs. Presbyn. Hosp. Found., 2007—; chmn. Temple Emanu-El Found., 2006—. Recipient Jurisprudence award Anti-Defamation League, 2000, Best Gen. Counsel award Dallas Bus. Jour., 2006. Mem. Am. Coll. Tax Coun., Tex. State Bar (chmn., sec. taxation 1983-84), Dallas Bar Assn. (chmn., sec. taxation 1978), Dallas Petroleum Club, Columbian Club, Trophy Club, Bent Tree Country Club. Office: Hunt Consolidated Inc Fountain Pl 20th Fl 1445 Ross at Field Dallas TX 75202-2785

MASSOF, ROBERT WILLIAM, neuroscientist, educator; b. Minn., Jan. 2, 1948; m. Patricia Massof; children: Eric, Allison. BA, Hamline U., 1970; PhD, Ind. U., 1975. Postdoctoral fellow in ophthalmology Johns Hopkins U. Sch. Medicine, Balt., 1975-76, instr. ophthalmology, 1976-78, from asst. prof. to assoc. prof., 1978-91, prof. ophthalmology, 1991—, prof. neurosci., 1994—, prof. computer sci., 1994—, mem. staff applied physics lab., 2000—. Lectr. in field. Mem. editl. bd. Clin. Vision Scis., N.Y.C., 1986-94, Eye Care Technology/Computers in Eye Care, Folsom, Calif., 1992-96; patentee in field (5); contbr. articles to profl. jours. Recipient Manpower award, 1989, Tech. Transfer award NASA, 1993, Popular Mechanics Design and Engring. award, 1994, EyeCare Tech. Lifetime Achievement award, 1995, Richard E. Hoover Svc. award, 1995, Humanitarian award Lions, 2000, Disting. Svc. in Vision award Am. Pub. Health Assn., William Feinbloom award Am. Acad. of Optometry, 2000, Alfred W. Bressler prize Jewish Guild for the Blind, 2004. Fellow Optical Soc. Am. (chmn. edn. coun. 1993-95, bd. dirs. 1993-95), Am. Acad. Optometry; mem. Assn. for Edn. and Rehab. of the Visually Impaired, Soc. for Info. Display, Am. Congress Rehab. Medicine, Assn. Rsch. in Vision and Ophthalmology. Office: Johns Hopkins Univ Lions Vision Ctr 550 N Broadway Fl 6 Baltimore MD 21205-2020 Home Phone: 410-439-2486; Office Phone: 410-502-6246. E-mail: rmassof@lions.med.jhu.edu.

MASSON, ROBERT HENRY, paper company executive; b. Boston, June 27, 1935; s. Robert Louis and Henrietta Hill (Worrell) M.; m. Virginia Lee Morton, Dec. 28, 1957; children: Linda Anne, Kenneth Morton, Robert Louis, II. BA in Econs. cum laude, Amherst Coll., 1957; MBA, Harvard U., 1964. Fin. staff Ford Motor Co., Dearborn, Mich., 1964-68, mktg. services div. controller, 1968-70; pres. Knutson Constrn. Co., Mpls., 1970-72; v.p. fin., treas. Ellerbe, Inc., Bloomington, Minn., 1972-77; fin. dir. CirTech, Inc., Mpls., 1973-77; v.p. fin. transp. div. PepsiCo., Inc., Tulsa, 1977, corp. v.p., treas. Purchase, N.Y., 1978-80; v.p., treas. Combustion Engring., Inc., Stamford, Conn., 1981-86, v.p. fin. and venture devel., 1986-87, v.p. venture fin. and internat. ops., 1988-90; v.p., CFO Parsons & Whittemore, Inc., Rye Brook, N.Y., 1990—. Mem. adv. bd. Fleet Bank, 1988—. Author: (with others) The Management of Racial Integration in Business, 1964. Pres. North Georgtown Homeowner's Assn., Birmingham, Mich., 1968-70, U.S. Presdl. Advance Man, 1972-76; trustee, chmn. fin. com. Naval Aviation Mus. Found., 1987—; trustee Hebron Acad., 1993-97; elder Presbyn. Ch. of Old Greenwich, 1992—. Served to lt. USN, 1957-62; lt. comdr. Res. Mem. Am. Forest and Paper Assn. (fin. com. 1991—), Fin. Execs. Inst. (com. on corp. fin. 1981—), Fairchester Treas. Group (pres. 1986), Lucas Point Homeowner's Assn. (pres. 1986-87), Theta Delta Chi. Clubs: Wayzata Yacht (dir.-treas. 1973-77), Riverside Yacht (asst. treas. 1985-87). Office: Parsons & Whittemore Inc 4 International Dr Ste 5 Rye Brook NY 10573-1064

MASSOUD, YEHIA, science educator; PhD, MIT, Cambridge, Mass., 1999. Prof. Rice U., Houston, 2003—. Contbr. articles to profl. jours. Recipient Career award, NSF, 2005. Office: Rice University 6100 Main St MS 380 Houston TX 77005 Office Phone: 713-348-6706.

MASSOUDI, BAHRAM BARRY, management consultant; b. Tehran, Iran, 1960; arrived in U.S., 1977; BS, Syracuse U., NYC, 1981; MEng, McGill U., Montreal, 1983; MBA, U. Wash., Seattle, 1992. Internat. compensation mgr. Schlumberger Ltd., Paris, 1984—90; principal Gemini Consulting, Morristown, NJ, 1992—99; founder, mng. ptnr. Cubicon LLC, Seattle, 1999—. Author: Do the Right Deal, Do the Deal Right: 35 Success Factors for Mergers and Acquisitions, 2006; contbr. articles to profl. jours. Chmn. Arts Commn., Mercer Island, Wash., 2004—06; commr. City of Mercer Island, 2006—. Avocations: jogging, photography, restoring old houses, gardening.

MASSY, WILLIAM FRANCIS, education educator, consultant; b. Milw., Mar. 26, 1934; s. Willard Francis and Ardys Dorothy (Digman) M.; m. Sally Vaughn Miller, July 21, 1984; children by previous marriage: Willard Francis, Elizabeth BS, Yale U., 1956; SM, MIT, 1958, PhD in Indsl. Econs., 1960. Asst. prof. indsl. mgmt. MIT, Cambridge, 1960-62; from asst. prof. to prof. edn. and bus. adminstrn. Stanford U., Calif., 1962-96, assoc. dean Grad. Sch. Bus. Calif., 1971, vice provost for rsch. Calif., 1971-77, v.p. for bus. and fin. Calif., 1977-88, v.p. fin. Calif., 1988-91, prof. emeritus, 1996—; prof. edn., dir. Stanford Inst. Higher Edn. Rsch., Calif., 1988-96; sr. v.p. P.R. Taylor Assocs., 1995-99; sr. rschr. Nat. Ctr. for Postsecondary Imrprovement, 1996—2002; pres. The Jackson Hole Higher Edn. Group, Inc., 1996—. Bd. dirs. MAC, Inc., 1969-84, Stanford Mgmt. Co., 1991-93; mem. u. grants com. Hong Kong, 1990-2003; mem. coun. Yale U., 1980-95; mgmt. cons. Stanford Mgmt. Co., 1991-93.bd. dirs. Diebold, Inc., chmn. audit com., 2003-07. Author: Stochastic Models of Buying Behavior, 1970, Marketing Management, 1972, Market Segmentation, 1972, Planning Models for Colleges and Universities, 1981, Endowment, 1991, Resource Allocation in Higher Education, 1996, Honoring The Trust, 2003, Remaking the American University, 2005, Academic Quality Work, 2007; mem. editl. bd. Jour. Mktg. Rsch., 1964-70, Harcourt, Brace Jovanovich, 1965-71; contbr. articles to profl. jours. Bd. dirs. Palo Alto-Stanford chpt. United Way, 1978-80, Stanford U. Hosp., 1980-91, EDUCOM, 1983-86. Ford Found. faculty rsch. fellow, 1966-67; recipient Frederick W. Lanchester prize, Operations Rsch. Soc., 1981; Outstanding Contributions to Coll. and Univ. Planning award, Soc. Coll. Univ. Planning., 1995. Mem. Am. Mktg. Assn. (bd. dirs. 1971-73, v.p. edn. 1976-77), Inst. Mgmt. Scis., Tau Beta Pi, Sigma Xi. Avocations: hiking, scuba diving, travel. Office: The Jackson Hole Higher Edn Group Inc PO Box 9849 Jackson WY 83002-9849 Personal E-mail: bill@jhheg.com.

MAST, GREGORY LEWIS, lawyer; b. Waterloo, Iowa, July 29, 1954; s. Kenneth Edgar and Shirley Louise (Crandall) M.; m. Jennifer Lynn East, Dec. 30, 1978; children: Millicent Ashley, William Robert. BA, De Pauw U., 1976; JD, Harvard U., 1979. Bar: Ariz. 1979, U.S. Dist. Ct. Ariz. 1979. Ptnr. Evans, Kitchel & Jenckes, P.C., Phoenix, 1979-85, Jones, Jury, Short & Mast, P.C., Phoenix, 1986-88, Gallagher & Kennedy, P.A., Phoenix, 1988, shareholder. Mem. Ariz. Town Hall, Phoenix C. of C. (spl. events com.), Ariz. Baseball Commn., Valley Partnership, White Mountain Country Club; bd. dir. Thunderbirds, Phoenix Country Club. Named Am's. Leading Bus. Lawyers, by Chambers USA, Best Lawyers Valley, by Phoenix mag., Best Lawyers Am., by Woodward/White, Inc., 2007. Mem.: DePauw U. Alumni Assn., Phi Beta Kappa, Maricopa County Bar Assn., State Bar Ariz. Office: Gallagher & Kennedy PA 2575 E Camelback Rd Ste 1100 Phoenix AZ 85016 Office Phone: 602-530-8310. Office Fax: 602-530-8500. Business E-Mail: glm@gknet.com.

MAST, KANDE WHITE, artist; b. St. Louis, Mar. 10, 1950; d. Elliott Maxwell and Mary (Barritt) W. Student, U. Mo., Kansas City, 1968-70, Longview C.C., Kansas City, Mo., 1970-71. Portrait painter, free-lance artist, Albany, NY, 1973-74, Kansas City, 1974—; dir., tchr. Studio Kande, Sch. Fine Arts, Kansas City, 1983-86; founder, exec. dir. Art Ctr. Kansas City, 1986-90; behavioral foster parent, 1989—2005; master foster parent, 1992—2005. Mem. psychiat. diversion team, mental health rev. team Jackson County Divsn. Family Svcs., 1992-95. Portrait painter and free-lance artist. Pres., bd. dirs. Advocates for Children, Inc., 1996—; vol. Ozanam Home for Boys, Kansas City, 1987—, mem. adv. bd., 1991—; mem. Cmty. Response Team, Jackson County, Divsn. Family Svcs.; founding mem. Nat. Campaign for Tolerance. Named Therapeutic Foster Parent of Yr., 1992. Mem.: Code Pink: Women for Peace, Nat. Campaign for Tolerance, Nat. Mus. of Women in Arts (charter). Home and Studio: 12406 Baltimore Ct Kansas City MO 64145 Personal E-mail: kande@kc.rr.com.

MAST, KENT E., lawyer; b. Bryn Mawr, Pa., July 12, 1943; s. John Earl and Jeanette (Skokowski) M.; m. Deborah Frieson Helmer, June 29, 1998; children: Roger, Grier, Jensen, Jeffrey. AB in Politics, Princeton U., NJ, 1965; JD, Duke U., Durham, NC, 1968. Bar: Ga. 1968, US Ct. Appeals (5th cir.) 1968, US Ct. Appeals (9th cir.) 1978, US Ct. Appeals (11th cir.) 1981, US Ct. Appeals (4th cir.) 1989. Assoc. Hansell & Post, Atlanta, 1968-73, ptnr., 1973-88, Hunton & Williams, Atlanta, 1988-90; sr. ptnr. Kilpatrick Stockton, Atlanta, 1990—2000; gen. counsel, corp. v.p. Equifax Inc., Atlanta, 2000—. Mem. ABA, Ga. Bar Assn., Atlanta Bar Assn., Consumer Data Industry Assn. (chmn. 2005), Highlands Falls Country Club, Oceanside Country Club. Office: Equifax Inc 1550 Peachtree St NW Atlanta GA 30309-2639 Office Phone: 404-885-8009.

MASTAGLIO, PETER JAMES, lawyer; b. Flushing, NY, Sept. 21, 1941; s. George Washington and Katherine (Clancy) M.; m. Deidre Mary Twomey, Apr. 3, 1971; children: James Peter, Elizabeth Clare. BA, Manhattan Coll., 1963; JD, NYU, 1968. Bar: NY, Mass., US Dist. Ct. (ea. and so. dists.) N. 1971, US Ct. Appeals (2d cir.) 1975, US Supreme Ct. 1977. Assoc. Cullen & Dykman Bleakley Platt LLP (formerly Cullen & Dykman), Garden City, NY, 1969-77, ptnr., 1977—. Chmn. bd. dirs., trustee YMCA of LI, Huntington, NY, 1981—; mem. com. on character and fitness 2d, 10th and 11th Jud. Dists., Bklyn., 1986—. Capt. USMC, 1966-69. Mem. NY State Bar Assn., Nassau County Bar Assn. Avocations: history, basketball. Home: 25 Kensington Rd Garden City NY 11530-4240 Office: Cullen & Dykman Bleakley Platt LLP 100 Quentin Roosevelt Blvd Garden City NY 11530-4850 Office Phone: 516-357-3751. Office Fax: 516-357-3792.

MASTANDREA, LINDA LEE, lawyer; b. Chgo., June 10, 1964; d. Robert Anthony and Dorothy Jean (Kilpatrick) M. BA in Speech Comm., U. Ill., 1986; JD, IIT, 1994. Bar: Ill. 1995. Account rep. Health Chgo. HMO, Lisle, Ill., 1986-87; peer counselor Peninsula Ctr. Ind. Living, Newport News, Va., 1988-89; program mgr. Progress Ctr. Ind. Living, Oak Park, Ill., 1990-91; atty. pvt. practice, Ill., 1995—. Pub. spkr., Ill., 1991—; sec. assoc. bd. Rehab. Inst. of Chgo. Athlete rep. Atlanta Paralympics, 1993-96; v.p. athlete's adv. com., assoc. bd. Rehab. Inst. Chgo., 1992—, sec., assoc. bd., 1997—, pub. policy com., vocat. action com.; athlete rep. on exec. com. Cerebral Palsy Internat. Sport and Recreation Assn. Named Athlete of Yr. Colo. Sports Coun., Denver, 1994, Outstanding Woman in Sports YWCA DuPage Dist., DuPage County, Ill., 1995, Outstanding Chgo. Women in Sports Crohn's and Colitis Found., 1997; recipient IOC Pres. Disabled Athlete award U.S. Sports Acad., Mobile, Ala., 1995, USCPAA Female Athlete of Yr., 1995; paralympics gold medalist 200m, 1996, silver medalist 100m, 1996. Mem. U.S. Cerebral Palsy Athletic Assn. (v.p. 1994—), Nat. Italian Bar Assn., Justinian Soc. Lawyers, Chgo. Bar Assn., ISBA. Avocation: wheelchair track world-record holder 100, 200, 400, 800 and 1500 meters.

MASTEN, BARBARA JEAN, education educator, department chairman; b. Toledo, Jan. 14, 1948; d. Joseph Anthony Czyzewski and Angela Rose Piorkowski; m. William Leonard Masten, Sept. 18, 1971; 1 child, Todd Michael. B in Edn., U. Toledo, 1970, M in Edn. Adminstrn., 1979. Sr. accountant and edn. and tchg. specialist Gen. Motors, Toledo, 1970—82; English instr. St. Ursula Acad., Toledo, 1983—89; instr. U. Toledo Cmty. Coll., 1989; assoc. prof./dept. chair Lourdes Coll., 1989—. Mem. adv. bd. Sch. Edn. Lourdes Coll., Sylvania, Ohio, 2003—, pres. faculty senate, 2005—06. Recipient Faculty Excellence award, Lourdes Coll., 1995, 1999, 2004. Mem.: Nat. Coun.Tchrs. English, Ohio Assn. Develop. Edn. Avocations: flower arranging, golf, reading. Office: Lourdes Coll 6832 Convent Blvd Sylvania OH 43560 Office Phone: 419-824-3758. Business E-Mail: bmasten@lourdes.edu.

MASTEN, JACQUELINE GWENDOLYN, small business owner; b. Brunswick, Maine, Oct. 24, 1941; d. Ralph Henry Bennet and Phyllis Estelle Crooker; children from previous marriage: Geraldine Frances Bullwinkel, Jennifer Lynn. Diploma in Bus., Pluss Sch. of Business, Portland, Maine, 1966. Shop owner Hudson Chair Caning Svcs., Hudson, NH, 1982; data entry operator Digital Corp., Nashua, NH, 1980; real estate landlady Hudson, NH, 1996—. Author: A Shaker Poetry Poetic History Book: A Tribute to My Aunt Eldress Gertrude Soule Shaker, 2003; contbr. poems to books. Named 1999 Poet of the Year, Famous Poets Soc., Nev., 1999, World Champion Amature, Internat. Soc. of Poets, 2001; recipient Shakespear medallion of Excellence, 2002. Mem.: New Eng. Saddlebred and Pony Assn., Quartzsite Roadrunner Gem and Mineral Club. Avocation: Shaker poetry writing, shaker tape chair seating, silversmith, gem faceting, lapidary. Personal E-mail: jgmas1025@aol.com.

MASTEN, SCOTT EDWARD, economics and public policy educator, consultant; s. Edward John and Helen Barbara Masten; m. Kathy Ann York, June 8, 1985; children: Meagan Callan, Edward James. AB, Dartmouth Coll., Hanover, NH, 1977; MA, PhD, U. Pa., Phila., 1982. Asst. prof. econs. U. Va., Charlottesville, 1982—84; asst. prof. U. Mich. Ross Sch. Bus., Ann Arbor, 1984—88, assoc. prof., 1988—95, prof. bus. econs. and pub. policy, 1995—, Louis and Myrtle Moskowitz rsch. prof. in bus. and law, 1998—99. Cons. US FTC, 1983—84, World Bank, 1997; academic advisor Princeton Economics Group, 2005—. John M. Olin Faculty Rsch. fellow, Ctr. Studies Law, Econs. and Pub. Policy, Yale Law Sch., 1990—91. Mem.: Internat. Indsl. Orgn. Soc., Am. Law and Econs. Assn., Am. Econ. Assn., Internat. Soc. New Instl. Econs. (v.p. 2006—07, pres.-elect 2007—). Office: U Mich Ross Sch Bus 701 Tappan St Ann Arbor MI 48109-1234 Office Phone: 734-764-1389.

MASTERN, DEAN SCOTT, personal growth and development consultant; b. Warren, Ohio, Aug. 26, 1961; s. Kenneth Richard and Joyce Eileen Mastern; m. Sheree Diane Grier, Aug. 21, 1987; children: Aaron Keith,

Rachel Colleen. PhD in Psychology, SW Acad. of Mental Health, 1987, PhD (hon.) in Quantum Biophysics, 1987; DD (hon.), World Christianship Ministries, 1987. Cons. Dean S. Mastern, PhD, Tyler, Tex., 1987—. Author: Theory of Quantum Biophysics, 1987. Mem.: Am. Assn. of Religious Counselors (life). Republican. Avocations: flying, sailing, sports cars, motorcycles. Office: Dean S Mastern PO Box 133012 Tyler TX 75713 Personal E-mail: dsmphd@yahoo.com.

MASTERNAK, MICHAL MATEUSZ, biotechnologist, educator, molecular biologist, researcher; arrived in US, 2002; s. Krzysztof and Danuta Masternak; m. Anna Idzinska, Aug. 14, 1999; children: Emilia, Adam. MS in Engring. and Biotechnology, August Cieszkowski Agrl. U. Poznan, Poland, 2000; PhD in Biol. Scis., Karol Marcinkowski U. Med. Scis., Poznan, 2002. Rschr. Inst. Human Genetics Polish Acad. of Scis., Poznan, 2000—02; vis. rsch. instr. So. Ill. U. Sch. Medicine, Springfield, 2002—04, rsch. asst. prof., 2004—. Recipient Samuel Goldstein Disting. Publ. award, Geron Corp., 2005. Office: So Ill Univ 801 N Rutledge Rm 4389 Springfield IL 62794-9628 Home Phone: 217-546-8915. Office Fax: 217-545-8006. Business E-Mail: mmasternak@siumed.edu.

MASTERS, ANNE, library director; Assoc. dir. system services and tng. Pioneer Libr. System, Okla., dir. Okla. Mem. Assistance League Cmty. Associates, Friendship Force of Okla.; mem. exec. bd. Norman Arts Coun., mem. writers com.; sec. Vestry of St. John's Episcopal Ch. Recipient Outstanding Alumni award, U. Okla. Sch. Libr. and Info. Studies, 2007. Mem.: Continuing Libr. Edn. and Networking Exchange Round Table (pres. 2006—07), Pub. Libr. Assn. (mem. trainer cadre), Urban Libraries Coun. (exec. leadership inst. sponsor, Joey Rodger Leadership award 2005), Okla. Libr. Assn. (Disting. Svc. award, Meritorious Svc. award, named Okla. Libr. Legend 2007), Norman Sooner Rotary. Office: Pioneer Libr System 225 N Webster Norman OK 73069 Office Phone: 405-701-2678. Office Fax: 405-701-2649. Business E-Mail: amsters@pls.lib.ok.us. *

MASTERS, ARLENE ELIZABETH, singer; b. Freeport, Ill., Oct. 6, 1960; d. Elmer and Mary (Green) Masters; m. Douglas Dewayne Burck (div.); 1 child, Douglas. Singer classic rock and blues, 2001—03; with A. Masters Entertainment and Publishing, 2001—03, 2004—. Singer: Ms. Arlene Masters and the Blues Transit Band, 2001—03, (albums), 2001. Mailing: PO Box 2832 Cottonwood AZ 86326-2537 Home Phone: 928-634-6167; Office Phone: 928-634-6167. Personal E-mail: arlene_masters@hotmail.com.

MASTERS, EDWARD EUGENE, association executive, former foreign service officer; b. Columbus, Ohio, June 21, 1924; s. George Henry and Ethel Verena (Shaw) M.; m. Allene Mary Roche, Apr. 2, 1956; children: Julie Allene, Edward Ralston. Student, Denison U., 1942—43; BA with distinction, George Washington U., 1948; MA, Fletcher Sch. Law and Diplomacy, 1949; grad., Nat. War Coll., 1964. Joined U.S. Fgn. Svc., 1950; intelligence rsch. analyst Near East Dept. State, 1949-50; resident officer Heidelberg, Germany, 1950-52; polit. officer embassy Karachi, Pakistan, 1952-54; Hindustani lang. and area tng. U. Pa., 1954-55; consul, polit. officer Madras, India, 1955-58; intelligence rsch. specialist South Asia Dept. State, 1958-60, chief Indonesia-Malaya br. Office Rsch. Asia, 1960-61, officer-in-charge Thailand affairs Bur. Far Eastern Affairs, 1961-63; counselor for polit. affairs Am. embassy, Djakarta, 1964-68; country dir. for Indonesia Dept. State, 1968-70; dir. Office East Asian Regional Affairs, 1970-71; minister Am. embassy, Bangkok, 1971-75; amb. to Bangladesh, 1976—77; amb. to Indonesia, 1977—81; adj. prof. diplomacy Fletcher Sch. Law and Diplomacy, 1981-82; sr. v.p. Natomas Co., 1982-84; pres. Nat. Planning Assn., 1985-92, Edward Masters & Assocs., Washington, 1992—, U.S.-Indonesia Soc., 1994-2000, chmn., 2000—. Adj. prof. Sch. Advanced Internat. Studies, 2000—02. Mem. Am. Fgn. Svc. Assn., Cosmos Club, Phi Beta Kappa, Omicron Delta Kappa, Pi Gamma Mu, Delta Phi Epsilon. Home: 4101 Cathedral Ave NW Apt 1001 Washington DC 20016-7500 Personal E-mail: mastersdc@att.net.

MASTERS, GEORGE WINDSOR, JR., electrical engineer, educator; b. Annapolis, Md., Mar. 11, 1930; s. George and Ruby Lena (Jess) Masters; m. Barbara Lyons Wilson; children: Barbara Anne, George W. III. BS, MIT, 1952, MS, 1954; PhD, U. Fla., 1966. Mem. tech. staff Instrument Lab., MIT, Cambridge, 1952-55; chief engr. Dynamic Instrument Co., Cambridge, 1955-58; sect. head Electromech. Rsch. Inc., Princeton, NJ, 1958-62; mem. sr. staff, sect. head flight control sect. The Aerospace Corp., El Segundo, Calif., 1962-75; chief engr. airborne sys. dept. USN Test Pilot Sch., Patuxent River, Md., 1975—2004; assoc. prof. elec. engring. Fla. Inst. Tech., Melbourne, 1984—2004; adj. assoc. prof. aviation sys. U. Tenn. Space Inst., Tullahoma, Tenn., 2004—. Recipient Meritorious Civilian Svc. award, Dept. of Navy, 2004. Mem. AIAA, IEEE, US Naval Inst., Elks, Kappa Sigma. Republican. Episcopalian. Personal E-mail: mastersgw@bellsouth.net.

MASTERS, JOHN CHRISTOPHER, psychologist, educator; b. Terre Haute, Ind., Oct. 25, 1941; s. Robert William and Lillian Virginia (Decker) M.; m. Mary Jayne Capps, June 6, 1970; children— Blair Christopher, Kyle Alexander. AB, Harvard Coll., 1963; PhD, Stanford U., 1967. Asst. prof. Ariz. State U., Tempe, 1968-69; from asst. prof. to prof. U. Minn., Mpls., 1969-79; assoc. dir. Inst. Child Devel., 1974-79; Luce prof. pub. policy and the family, prof. psychology Vanderbilt U., Nashville, 1979-87, interim chair dept. psychology, 1986-88; pres. Profl. Mgmt. Group, Inc., 1991—; dir. Master Ventures, 1989—, Master Travel, 1989—. Assoc. editor: Child Development, 1973-76, Behavior Therapy: Techniques and Empirical Findings, 1974, 79, 88; editor: Psychol. Bull., 1987-89. Home: 4923 Old Oakleaf Dr Sarasota FL 34233-3947 Office Phone: 800-767-6162.

MASTERS, JON JOSEPH, corporate governance specialist, management consultant; b. NYC, June 20, 1937; s. Arthur Edward and Esther (Shady) M.; m. Rosemary Dunaway Cox, June 16, 1962; children: Brooke Alison, Blake Edward. BA, Princeton U., 1958; JD, Harvard U., 1964. Bar: N.Y. 1965, U.S. Dist. Ct. (so. dist.) N.Y. 1965, U.S. Ct. Appeals (2d cir.) 1965. Cons. asst. to under sec. Dept. Army, 1961; mem. policy planning staff asst. sec. for internat. security affairs Dept. Def. Washington, 1962; mem. Pres. Johnson's Spl. Polit. Research Staff, Washington, 1964; assoc. Shearman & Sterling, NYC, 1965-68, 69; mem. staff Bedford-Stuyvesant D & S Corp., Bklyn., 1968-69; v.p., sec., gen. counsel, dir. Baker, Weeks & Co., Inc., NYC, 1969-76; co-founder, ptnr. Christy & Viener, NYC, 1976-96; Vice-chmn. Robb, Peck, McCooey Specialist Corp., NYC, 1996—98; prin. Lear, Yavitz & Assocs., NYC, 1996-2001, mng. prin., 1998—2001; prin. Mercer Delta Cons., NYC, 2001—02; chmn. Masters Governance Cons., LLC, NYC, 2002—05; co-founder, prin. Masters-Rudnick & Assocs., LLC, NYC, 2005—. SEC adv. com. broker-dealer compliance, 1972-74; legal advisor NACD Blue Ribbon Commn. on CEO and Dir. Performance Evaluation, 1994; chmn. bd. Clear and Present Prodns., 1992-93; dir. Harris & Harris Group, Inc., 1992-98. Mem. implementation com. Econ. Devel. Task Force of N.Y. Urban Coalition, 1968; mem. bd. Internat. Social Service, Am. Br., Inc., 1978-83, pres., 1979-83; bd. dirs. The Arts Connection, 1979-85; mem. steering com. N.Y. Lawyers Alliance for Nuclear Arms Control, 1983-96. Served with USN, 1958-61. Mem. ABA, Assn. Bar City N.Y. (com. mcpl. affairs 1977-80). Office: 350 E 82 St New York NY 10028 Office Phone: 212-879-0872. Business E-Mail: jjmasters@mastersrudnick.com.

MASTERS, JONATHAN EDWARD, clinical psychologist; b. Northport, NY, Sept. 27, 1962; s. Edward Joseph and Janet (Pendleton) Masters. BA, Marist Coll., Poughkeepsie, NY, 1985; grad., Gutter Inst. of Tech., 1986; MA, Pepperdine U., LA, 1991, PsyD, 1998; PhD candidate, Inst. Contemporary Psychoanalysis, LA, 2003—. Cert. psychologist Ariz. Bd. Psychologist Examiners, 1999. Part-time lectr. in astronomy Vanderbilt Planetarium, Centerport, NY, 1979—84; psychology trainee NY State Office Mental Health, Poughkeepsie, 1985; behavioral specialist Psychol. Support Svcs., Mission Hills, 1990—94, Prairie Group Home, Hawthorne, 1991—94, Only a Place to Start, Inglewood, 1991—94, John B. Kelley Residential Treatment Ctr. for Men, LA, 1992—94, John B. Kelley Residential Treatment Ctr. for Women, LA, 1992—94; psychology trainee Cath. Psychol. Svcs., LA, 1993, U. So. Calif. Med. Ctr., LA, 1994; predoctoral intern Pederson-Kraig Ctr., Huntington, NY, 1994—95; staff psychotherapist Advanced Ctr. Psychotherapy, Jamaica Estates, 1996—98; staff psychotherapist/psychologist New Hope Guild Ctr. for Children, Howard Beach, NY, 1996—99; clin. psychologist Paradise Valley Psychiat. Assocs., Phoenix, 2000—. Vol. Hurricane Katrina ARC, Phoenix, 2005. Mem.: APA (assoc.), SW Psychoanalytic Soc. (assoc.; practice com. mem. 2000, jour. group mem. 2000—01, chair program com. 2001—03, treas. 2004—05, bd. dirs. 2004—05). Office: Paradise Valley Psychiatric Assocs 4232 E Cactus Rd Ste 207 Phoenix AZ 85032 Home Phone: 480-767-7100; Office Phone: 602-494-8105. Personal E-mail: jmast99@cox.net.

MASTERS, JOSEPH, lawyer, construction executive; b. 1956; BSCE, Cleveland State U., 1979; JD, Case Western Reserve U., 1982. Bar: Ohio 1982. Pvt. practice; with URS Corp., San Francisco, 1992—, v.p., gen. counsel, 1997—2006, v.p., gen. counsel, corp. sec., 2006—. Mem.: ABA. Office: URS Corp 26th Fl 600 Montgomery St San Francisco CA 94111 Office Phone: 415-774-2700.

MASTERS, ROBERT EDWARD LEE, psychotherapist, sexologist; b. Jan. 4, 1927; s. Robert and Katherine (Leeper) Masters; m. Jean Houston, May 8, 1965. BA Philosophy, U. Mo., 1951; PhD Clin. Psychology, Humanistic Psychology Inst., 1974. Dir. Libr. Sex Rsch., NYC, 1962—66, Sensory Imagery Program, 1965—68; dir. rsch. Found. for Mind Rsch., NYC and Ashland, Oreg., 1965—. Dir. Zarathustra Project, Pomona, 1980—99; co-dir. Human Capacities Tng. Program, Ramapo, NJ, 1982—99; pvt. practice psychotherapy, neural re-edn., aging and geropsychology programs; prin. tchr. Hypnotherapist Tng., Pomona, 1982—99; pres. Human Capacities Corp., Ashland, 1982—. Author: Eros and Evil, 1962, Forbidden Sexual Behavior and Morality, 1964, Mind Games, 1972, Listening to the Body, 1978, Psychophysical Method Exercises, vols. I-VI, 1983, The Goddess Sekhmet, 1987, The Masters Technique, 1987, Neurospeak, 1994, The Way to Awaken, 1997, Swimming Where Madmen Drown, 2002, numerous poems, short fiction, Literary and Art Criticism, 1952—60; co-author (with J. Houston): Varieties of Psychedelic Experience, 1966, Psychedelic Art, 1968; contbr. articles to profl. jours. With USN, 1945—46, PTO. Grantee, Erickson Found., 1966, Kleiner Found., 1968, Babcock Found., 1970, Doris Duke Found., 1972. Fellow: Am. Psychotherapy Assn. (diplomate), Am. Acad. Clin. Sexologists (founder); mem.: AAAS, APA, NY Acad. Scis., Assn. Humanistic Psychology, Am. Assn. Sex Educators, Counselors and Therapists, Am. Bd. Sexology (clin. supr.). Office: Found Mind Rsch PMB 501 2305 Ashland St Ste C Ashland OR 97520-3777 Personal E-mail: hvhhbob@aol.com.

MASTERS, ROGER DAVIS, political scientist, educator, toxicologist; b. Boston, June 8, 1933; s. Maurice and S. Grace (Davis) M.; m. Judith Ann Rubin, June 6, 1956 (div. 1984); children— Seth J., William A., Katherine R.; m. Susanne R. Putnam, Aug. 25, 1984 (dec. 2006). BA, Harvard U., Cambridge, Mass., 1955; MA, U. Chgo., 1958, PhD, 1961; MA (hon.), Dartmouth Coll., Hanover, NH, 1974. Instr. dept. polit. sci. Yale U., 1961-62, asst. prof., 1962-67; assoc. prof. dept. govt. Dartmouth Coll., Hanover, NH, 1967-73, prof., 1973-98, John Sloan Dickey Third Century prof., 1980-85, chmn. dept., 1986-89, Nelson A. Rockefeller prof., 1991-98, prof. emeritus, 1998—, rsch. prof., 1999—. Cultural attache Am. Embassy, Paris, 1969—71; chmn. France-Am. Commn. Ednl. and Cultural Exch., 1969—71; vis. lectr. Yale U. Law Sch., 1988—89, Vt. Law Sch., 1993—94; sect. editor Social Sci. Info., 1971—; chmn. exec. com. Gruter Inst. Law and Behavioral Rsch., 1995—98; pres. Found. for Neurosci. and Soc., 1998—; mem. Get the Lead Out of Vt. Task Force, 2006. Author: The Nation Is Burdened, 1967, The Political Philosophy of Rousseau, 1968, The Nature of Politics, 1989, Beyond Relativism, 1993, Machiavelli, Leonardo, and the Science of Power, 1996, Fortune is a River, 1998; editor: Rousseau's Discourses, 1964, Rousseau's Social Contract, 1978; co-editor: Ostracism: A Social and Biological Phenomenon, 1986, Collected Writings of J.J. Rousseau, 1990—, Primate Politics, 1991, The Sense of Justice, 1992, The Neurotransmitter Revolution, 1994; editor Gruter Inst. Reader in Biology, Law, and Human Social Behavior, 1992. Served with AUS, 1955-57. Fulbright fellow Inst. d'Etudes Politiques, Paris, 1958-59, joint Yale U.-Social Sci. Rsch. Coun. fellow, 1964-65, Guggenheim fellow, 1967-68, Hastings Ctr. for Ethics and Life Scis. fellow, 1973-78. Mem. AAAS, Am. Polit. Sci. Assn., Assn. Polit. and Life Sci. (coun.), Am. Soc. for Legal and Polit. Philosophy, Internat. Soc. Human Ethology, Human Behavior Evolution Soc., Am. Acad. Environ. Medicine. Office: Dartmouth Coll Dept Govt Silsby Hall HB6108 Hanover NH 03755 Home: The Greens 53 Lyme Rd Unit #21 Hanover NH 03755 Office Phone: 603-646-1029. Business E-Mail: roger.d.masters@dartmouth.edu.

MASTERSON, CARLIN See GLYNN, CARLIN

MASTERSON, ELLEN HORNBERGER, accountant; b. Ft. Smith, Ark., Feb. 19, 1951; d. Evans Zacharias and Nancy Cravens (Eads) H.; m. Conrad J. Masterson, Jr., Sept. 26, 1987. BA, Emory U., 1973; MBA, So. Meth. U., 1978. CPA, Mass. Staff acct. Coopers & Lybrand, Boston, 1973, gen. practice ptnr. Dallas, 1985—97; CFO Am. Gen. Corp., Houston, 1997—99; ptnr. PricewaterhouseCoopers, NYC, 1999—. Instr. Sch. Mgmt. and Adminstrv. Scis., U. Tex., Dallas, 1980-81. Bd. dirs. Shakespeare Festival Dallas, 1983-86, Leadership Dallas, 1985-86, USA Film Festival, 1986-88, Dental Health Program, Inc., 1986-88; mem. Jr. League, The 500, Inc.; workshop leader, vol. Cmty. Bd. Inst.; cons. Ctr. for Non Profit Mgmt. Mem. AICPA, Mass. Soc. CPAs, Tex. CPAs, So. Meth. U. MBA Alumni Assn., Kappa Kappa Gamma, Alpha Iota Delta, Beta Gamma Sigma. Presbyterian. Office: PricewaterhouseCoopers 300 Madison Ave 24th fl New York NY 10017

MASTERSON, JAMES FRANCIS, psychiatrist; b. Phila., Mar. 25, 1926; s. James Francis and Evangeline (O'Boyle) M.; m. Patricia Cooke, Jan. 28, 1950; children: James F., Richard K., Nancy. BS, U. Notre Dame, 1947; MD, Jefferson Med. Sch., Phila., 1951. Diplomate Am. Bd. Psychiatry, Am. Bd. Neurology. Intern Phila. Gen. Hosp., 1951-52; resident in psychiatry Payne Whitney Clinic, N.Y. Hosp., N.Y.C., 1952-55, chief resident, 1955-56, dir. adolescent OPD, 1956-66, head adolescent program, 1968-75, asst. attending psychiatrist, 1956-60, assoc. attending psychiatrist, 1960-70, attending psychiatrist, 1970—, dir. The Symptomatic Adolescent Research Project, 1957-67; dir. Masterson Group, P.C. for Study and Treatment Personality Disorders, N.Y.C., 1977—. Author: Psychotherapy of the Borderline Adolescent, Psychotherapy of the Borderline Adult, Countertransference, Narcissistic Personality Disorder, The Real Self, The Psychiatric Dilemma of Adolescence, The Test of Time: From Borderline Adolescent to Functioning Adult, The Personality Disorders: As Seen Through the Lens of Attachment Theory and Neurobiology Development of the Self, 2005; contbr. articles to profl. jours. Fellow Am. Psychiat. Assn., Am. Coll. Psychoanalysts; mem. AMA, Am. Coll. Psychoanalysis, N.Y. Soc. Adolescent Psychiatry (founder, past pres.), N.Y. County Med. Soc. Office: 60 Sutton Pl S New York NY 10022-4168 Office Phone: 212-751-4992. Business E-Mail: mastersnin@aol.com.

MASTERSON, JOHN PATRICK, retired language educator; b. Chgo., Mar. 15, 1925; s. Michael Joseph and Delia Frances (Dolan) M.; m. Jean Frances Wegrzyn, Aug. 18, 1956; children: Mary Beth, Michael, Maureen, Laura. BA, St. Mary of the Lake, 1947; MA, De Paul U., 1952; PhD, U. Ill., 1961. Chmn. English dept. De Paul U., Chgo., 1964-67, head humanities div., 1967-70, prof. English, 1970, dean Coll. Liberal Arts and Scis., 1970-76, prof. mgmt., 1976-80, 82-87, prof. emeritus, 1988—, dean Grad. Sch., 1980-82. Cons. in field. Recipient award Shell Oil Co., 1968, Via Sapientiae award De Paul U., 1987; fellow adminstrn. program Am. Coun. Edn. Roman Catholic. Home: 1922 Belleview Ave Westchester IL 60154-4345

MASTERSON, JOSEPH D., lawyer, partner; b. Amirillo, Tex., Feb. 11, 1953; s. Thomas Murray and Elizabeth Francis (Leu) M.; m. Doris I. Touro, Aug. 8, 1981; children: Jeffrey S. Owen, Michele O. Ramirez. BS Bus. Adminstrn. summa cum laude, Culver-Stockton Coll., 1975; JD magna cum laude, Harvard U., 1978. Bar: Wis. 1978. Assoc. Quarles & Brady, Milw., 1978—, ptnr. Contbr. Mem.: ABA, State Bar Wis. United Methodist. mem. Harvard Law Rev. 1977-1978. Office: Quarles & Brady 411 E Wisconsin Ave Milwaukee WI 53202-4497 Office Phone: 414-277-5169. Office Fax: 414-978-8969. Business E-Mail: jdm@quarles.com.

MASTERSON, KENNETH RHODES, lawyer; b. Kennett, Mo., Feb. 22, 1944; s. H. Byron and Mary (Rhodes) M.; children— Michael K., Elizabeth Megel, Grace Megel BA, Westminster Coll., 1966; JD, Vanderbilt U., 1970. Bar: Mo. 1970, Tenn. 1976. Ptnr. Thomason, Crawford & Hendrix, Memphis, 1976-79; v.p. legal Federal Express, Memphis, 1980-81, sr. v.p., gen. counsel, 1981-93, sr. v.p., gen. counsel and sec., 1993-96, exec. v.p., gen. counsel and sec., 1996-98, FedEx Corp., Memphis, 1998—2005, cons., 2005—. Mem. ABA, Mo. Bar Assn., Am. Corp. Counsel Assn. Home: 8679 Classic Dr Memphis TN 38125-8824 Office: FedEx Corp 942 S Shady Grove Rd Memphis TN 38120-4117 Fax: 901-818-7590. *

MASTERSON, KLEBER SANLIN, JR., physicist; b. San Diego, Sept. 26, 1932; s. Kleber Sandlin and Charlotte Elizabeth (Parker) M.; m. Sara Ann Cooper, Dec. 21, 1957; children: Thomas Marshall, John Cooper. BS in Engring., U.S. Naval Acad., Annapolis, 1954; MS in Physics, US Naval Postgrad. Sch., Monterey, Calif., 1961; PhD in Physics, U. Calif., San Diego, 1963; student in Advanced Mgmt. Program, Harvard U., 1982. Commd. ensign USN, 1954, advanced through grades to rear adm., 1979, comdg. officer USS Preble Pearl Harbor, Hawaii, 1969-71, mgr. antiship missile def. project Washington, 1974-77, exec. asst. to sec. of Navy, 1977-79, asst. dep. comdr. Naval Sea Systems Command, 1979-81, chief Studies, Analyses and Gaming Agy., 1981-82, ret., 1982; prin. Booz, Allen and Hamilton, Inc., Arlington, Va., 1982-87, v.p. and ptnr., 1987-92; sr. v.p. Sci. Applications Internat. Corp., 1992-94; pres. The Riverside Group, Ltd., 1994—2005; ret. Bd. control U.S. Naval Inst., Annapolis, Md., 1971-82; bd. dirs. Mil. Ops. Rsch. Soc., 1984-90, pres., 1988-89; mem. divsn. rev. com. TSA divsn. Los Alamos Nat. Lab., 1996-2001, chmn. 1998-2001. Editor: Book of Navy Songs, 1954; contbr. articles on plasma and theoretical nuclear physics, computer science, radars, ops. rsch. to profl. publs. Active Historic Alexandria Resources Commn., 1998—, vice-chmn. 2001-02, chmn., 2002-04. Decorated Defense Superior Svc. medal, Legion of Merit with 2 gold stars, Navy Commendation medal with combat V and 2 gold stars. Mem. Am. Phys. Soc., US Naval Acad. Alumni Assn. (pres. Washington chpt. 1989-90), US Naval Acad. Found. (trustee 1991—), Soc. of Cin. (chmn. edn. com. 1997-2001, asst. sec. gen. 2001-04, editor Cin. Fourteen 2001-04, treas. gen. 2004-07, v.p. gen. 2007-), Mass. Soc. of Cin. (mem. standing com., v.p. 1999-2001, pres. 2001-04), Sigma Xi. Achievements include development of NELIAC computer program and strategic simulation methodology. Home and Office: 101 Pommander Walk Alexandria VA 22314-3844 Home Phone: 703-548-4464; Office Phone: 703-548-6183. Personal E-mail: skidmasterson@cs.com.

MASTERSON, MARY STUART, actress; b. NYC, June 28, 1966; d. Peter and Carlin Glynn Masterson. Theatre appearances include Alice in Wonderland, 1982, Been Taken, 1985, The Lucky Spot, 1987, Lily Dale, 1987, Three Sisters, 1991; TV movies include Love Lives On, 1985, City in Fear, 1980, Lily Dale, 1996, On the 2nd Day of Christmas, 1997; films: The Stepford Wives, 1975, Heaven Help Us, 1984, At Close Range, 1985, My Little Girl, 1986, Gardens of Stone, 1987, Some Kind of Wonderful, 1987, Mr. North, 1988, Chances Are, 1989, Immediate Family, 1989, Funny About Love, 1990, Married To It, 1990, Fried Green Tomatoes, 1991, Benny and Joon, 1993, Bad Girls, 1994, Radioland Murders, 1994, Heaven's Prisoners, 1996, Bed of Roses, 1996, Digging to China, 1997, Dogtown, 1997, The Postman, 1997, The Florentine, 1998, The Book of Stars, 1999, Black and Blue, 1999, The Book of Stars, 2000, Leo, 2002, West of Here, 2002; dir., writer for Showtime 2000; TV guest appearances include Amazing Stories, 1985, Inside the Actors Studio, 1994. Office: Creative Artists Agency 9830 Wilshire Blvd Beverly Hills CA 90212-1825

MASTERSON, PETER, actor, film producer; b. Houston, June 1, 1934; s. Carlos Bee and Josephine Yeager (Smith) M.; m. Carlin Glynn, Dec. 29, 1960; children: Carlin Alexandra, Mary Stuart, Peter Carlos. BA in History, Rice U., 1957. Appeared in Broadway plays Marathon '33, 1963, Blues for Mr. Charlies, 1964; title role in Trial of Lee Harvey Oswald, 1967; appeared in The Great White Hope, 1968, That Championship Season, 1974, The Poison Tree, 1975, (films) The Exorcist, 1972, Man on a Swing, 1973, The Stepford Wives, 1974; playwright The Best Little Whorehouse in Texas, 1978; dir. Broadway prodns. The Best Little Whorehouse in Texas, 1978 (Drama Desk award for Best Dir. of Musical 1978); co-dir., co-writer The Best Little Whorehouse Goes Public, 1994; dir. off-Broadway prodns. The Cover of Life, 1994, The Young Man from Atlanta (Pulitzer prize 1995); screenwriter The Best Little Whorehouse in Texas, 1980; prodr. (TV film) City in Fear, 1980; dir. films The Trip to Bountiful, 1985, Blood Red, 1986, Full Moon in Blue Water, 1987, Night Game, 1988, Convicts, 1989, Arctic Blue, 1993, Lily Dale, 1996, The Only Thrill, 1997, Mermaid, 1999, Lost Junction, 2001, Whiskey Sch., 2005. Mem. AFTRA, SAG, Actors Equity Assn., Soc. Stage Dirs. and Choreographers, Writers Guild Am., Actors Studio, Dirs. Guild Am., Seawanhaka Club, Corinthian Yacht Club, Tex. Corinthian Yacht Club.

MASTERSON, WILLIAM A., retired judge; b. NYC, June 25, 1931; s. John Patrick and Helen Audrey (O'Hara) M.; m. Julie Dohrmann Cosgrove; children: Mark, Mary, Timothy, Barbara. BA, UCLA, 1953, JD, 1958. Bar: Calif. 1959, U.S. Supreme Ct. 1965. Assoc. Sheppard, Mullin, Richter & Hampton, LA, 1952-62, ptnr., 1962-79; ptnr. Rogers & Wells, 1979-83, Skadden, Arps, Slate, Meagher & Flom, 1983-87; judge L.A. Superior Ct., 1987-92; justice Ct. Appeal, 1993-2000; ret., 2000. Author, editor: Civil Trial Practice: Strategies and Techniques, 1986. With inf. U.S. Army, 1953-55. Fellow Am. Coll. Trial Lawyers; mem. Order of Coif. Office: PO Box 190 Mendocino CA 95460

MASTERSON-SMITH, JULIE, librarian; BS in Elem. Edn., SUNY, 1991, MS in Reading, 1992; MLS, SUNY, Buffalo, 2003. Reading and math specialist Monticello Central School District, Monticello, NY, 1992—96, Honeoye Falls-Lima Central School District, Honeoye Falls, NY, 1996—2001, libr. media specialist, 2001—. Named one of the Movers and Shakers, Libr. Jour., 2007; recipient School Library Media Section

Scholarship Award, NY Libr. Assn., Teach award, Best Buy, 2004, Information Technology Pathfinder award, ALA/AASL, 2006. Office: Manor School- Honeoye School District 20 Church St Honeoye Falls NY 14472 Office Phone: 585-624-7000.

MASTIN, LYNN P., biology professor; d. Forest Lynn and Martha Hamilton Purdom; m. Nathan Edgar Mastin, Dec. 21, 1974; 1 child, E. Thomas. BA in Biology, U. West Ga., Carrollton, 1971, MS in Biology, 1973. Microbiologist Ctrs. for Disease Control, Atlanta, 1974—76; instr. Oklahoma City Schs., 1979—82, South Okla. City Jr. Coll., Oklahoma City, 1982—84, Mid-Del Christian Sch., Oklahoma City, 1984—89, Life Christian Sch., Oklahoma City, 1989—90, Lee County Schs., Tupelo, Miss., 1992—99, Itawamba C.C., Fulton, Miss., 1999—. Tchr., musician Union Christian Assembly, Tupelo, 1990—. Mem.: Miss. State Tchrs. Assn. Office: Itawamba Cmty Coll 601 N Hill St Fulton MS 38843 Office Phone: 662-862-8369. E-mail: lpmastin@iccms.edu.

MASTO, CATHERINE MARIE CORTEZ, state attorney general, former county official; b. Nev., Mar. 29, 1964; d. Manny and Joanna Cortez; m. Paul E. Masto. BS in Fin., U. Nev., Reno, 1986; JD cum laude, Gonzaga U. Sch. Law, Spokane, Wash., 1990. Bar: Nev. 1990, US Dist. Ct. (dist. Nev.) 1991, US Ct. Appeals (9th cir.) 1994. Law clk. to Judge Michael J. Wendell 8th Jud. Dist. Ct., 1990—91; assoc. Raleigh, Hunt & McGarry, P.C., Las Vegas, 1991—95; staff mem. to Gov. Bob Miller State of Nev., Carson City, 1995—98, chief of staff, 1998—2000; asst. US atty. Dist. Nev. US Dept. Justice, Las Vegas, 2000—02; asst. county mgr. Clark County, Nev., 2002—05; atty. gen. State of Nev., Carson City, 2007—. Mem. So. Nev. Domestic Violence Ct. Task Force, Supreme Ct. Nev. Ct. Funding Commn. Democrat. Office: Office of Atty Gen Nev Dept Justice 100 N Carson St Carson City NV 89701-4717 Office Phone: 775-684-1100. *

MASTRACCHIO, RICHARD A. (RICK), astronaut; b. Waterbury, Conn., Feb. 11, 1960; s. Ralph and Georgiana Mastracchio (Stepmother), Helen Cooke; m. Candace L. Stolfi; 3 children. BSEE and Computer Sci., U. Conn., 1982; MSEE, Rensselaer Poly. Inst., 1987; MS in Phys. Sci., U. Houston, Clear Lake, Tex., 1991. Engr. sys. design group Hamilton Std., Conn., 1982—87; with Rockwell Shuttle Ops. Co., Houston, 1987—90; engr. flight crew ops. directorate NASA, Houston, 1990—93, ascent/entry guidance and procedures officer in mission control, 1993—96; astronaut NASA, Johnson Space Ctr., Houston, 1996—. Mission specialist STS-106 Mission (Atlantis), 2000, STS-118 Mission (Endeavour) to Internat. Space Station, 2007. Mem.: IEEE. Achievements include 12 day mission aboard space shuttle Atlantis in Sept. 2000 to prepare International Space Station for arrival of first permanent crew; over 283 hours in space. Avocations: flying, baseball, basketball, swimming, woodworking. Office: Astronaut Office NASA Johnson Space Ctr Houston TX 77058 *

MASTRANTONIO, MARY ELIZABETH, actress; b. Lombard, Ill., Nov. 17, 1958; d. Frank A. and Mary D. (Pagone) M. m. Pat O' Conn0r; 2 children Jack, Declan Student, U. Ill., 1976-78. Actress: (stage prodns.) Copperfield, 1981, Oh, Brother, 1981, Amadeus, 1982, Sunday in the Park with George, 1983, The Human Comedy, 1984, Henry V, 1984, Measure for Measure, 1985, The Knife, 1987, Twelfth Night, (feature films) Scarface, 1983, The Color of Money, 1986 (Acad. award nomination 1986), Slam Dance, 1987, The January Man, 1989, The Abyss, 1989, Fools of Fortune, 1990, Class Action, 1991, Robin Hood: Prince of Thieves, 1991, Consenting Adults, 1992, White Sands, 1992, Three Wishes, 1995, Two Bits, 1995, My Life So Far, 1999, Limbo, 1999, The Perfect Storm, 2000, Tabloid, 2001; TV miniseries Mussolini: THe Untold Story, 1985; TV films Uncle Vanya, 1991, Witness Protection, 1999, The Brooke Ellison Story, 2004; TV guest appearance Frasier, 1993, Without a Trace, 2005-2006. Office: Internat Creative Mgmt 8942 Wilshire Blvd Beverly Hills CA 90211-1934

MASTRIAN, JAMES P., retail executive; BS in Pharmacy, U. Pitts., 1965. Lic. pharmacist Pa., Md., Ohio, Va. Pharmacist People's Drug Stores, Inc., 1965; pres., gen. mgr. Gray Drug Fair Stores Sherwin-Williams Co., 1983—89, sr. v.p. merchandising and mktg. Paint Stores Group, 1983—89; positions up to exec. v.p. mktg. Revco Drugstores, 1990—97; sr. exec. v.p. merchandising and mktg. OfficeMax; exec. v.p. category mgmt. Rite Aid Corp., Camp Hill, Pa., 1998-99, exec. v.p. mktg., 1999—2000, sr. exec. v.p. mktg., logistics and pharmacy svcs., 2000—05, COO, 2005—07, spl. advisor corp. strategy, 2007—. Office: Rite Aid Corp 30 Hunter Ln Camp Hill PA 17011-2410 Office Phone: 717-761-2633. *

MASTRIAN, STACEY LYNN, singer, educator; MusB in Vocal Performance, Cath. U. Am., Washington, 2000; MusM in Opera Performance, U. Md., College Park, 2002, D of Musical Arts in Voice Performance, 2007. Instr. U. Md., Coll. Pk., 2005—07. Pvt. studio tchr., Balt., 2001—; adj. faculty Peabody Conservatory, Balt., 2006—; lectr. in field. Singer: Vatican City, Georgian Radio, Susquehanna Orch., Blacksburg Orch., U. Md. Orch., Nova Amadeus Orch., Maxim Gorki Theater, 2003, Summer Opera Theatre Co., 2004—05, Opera Lafayette, 2005, 2007, Pisani Palace, 2005. Finalist, Palm Beach Opera Vocal Competition, 2005, Irma M. Cooper Opera Columbus Internat. Vocal Competition, 2005; named Disting. Tchg. Asst., U. Md., 2006; recipient Silver Medallion award, Rosa Ponselle Found., 1998, Benjamin T. Rome award, Cath. U., 2000, Discovery Series winner, Vocal Arts Soc., 2003, Hon. Mention award, Am. Bach Soc. Bethlehem Bach Choir Young Am. Singer Competition, 2004, Ulrich Grad. Competition winner, U. Md., 2004; fellow, Frank Huntington Beebe Fund for Musicians, 2002—03, U. Md., 2003—07; grantee, Fulbright Found., 2002—03; scholar, U. Md., 2000—02, Nat. Italian Am. Found., 2001, Mu Phi Epsilon, 2004; Archdiscesan scholar, Cath. U., 1996—2000, Max Kade scholar, Middlebury Coll., 2007, Songfest Profl. Program scholar, 2007, Richard F. Gold Career grant, Shoshana Found., 2005. Mem.: Nat. Assn. Tchrs. Singing (First Pl. winner Mid Atlantic Regionals 1998), Phi Eta Sigma, Pi Kappa Lambda (Music). Personal E-mail: stacey@staceymastrian.com.

MASTRO, CHRISTOPHER P., secondary school educator; b. Schenectady, NY, Oct. 17, 1946; s. George and Evelyn Mastro; m. Linda Mary Condon, June 27, 1981. BA in English, St. Michaels Coll., Winooski, Vt., 1968, MAT in English, 1969. English tchr. Mohonason H.S., Rotterdam, NY, 1969—71, Clayton Bouton H.S., Voorheesville, NY, 1971—98; edn. supr. St. Rose Coll., Albany, NY, 2001—02, SUNY, Albany, 2002—. H.S. basketball coach, 1971—86; spkr. in field; vol. writing/English instr. Hope House Residential Adolescent Facility, Colonie, NY, 2002—. Recipient Outstanding Tchr. award, Golub, 1990. Mem.: NY State United Tchrs.

MASTROENI, PABLO, professional soccer player; b. Mendoza, Argentina, Aug. 26, 1976; Attended, N.C. State Univ. Midfielder Miami Fusion, 1998—2002, Colorado Rapids, 2002—, capt., 2004—. 48 caps U.S. Nat. Soccer Team, 2001—; mem. U.S. World Cup Team, 2002, 06. Mailing: US Soccer Fedn 1801 S Prairie Ave Chicago IL 60616

MASTROIANNI, ANTHONY ROBERT, real estate company officer; b. Milford, Mass., Dec. 8, 1975; s. Ralph Anthony and Kathryn Ann Mastroianni. Chief tech. officer MLS Property Info. Network, Shrewsbury, Mass., 2003—. Mem.: Am. Mensa. Achievements include development of H3 MLS system. Office: MLS Property Info Network 904 Hartford Turnpike Shrewsbury MA 01545 Home Phone: 508-479-8186. Office Fax: 508-845-7820.

MASTROIANNI, LUIGI, JR., physician, educator; b. New Haven, Nov. 8, 1925; s. Marion (Dallas) Mastroianni; m. Elaine Catherine Pierson, Nov. 4, 1957; children: John James, Anna Catherine, Robert Luigi. AB, Yale U., 1946; MD, Boston U., 1950, DSc (hon.), 1973; MA (hon.), U. Pa., 1970. Diplomate Am. Bd. Ob-Gyn. and Reproductive Endocrinology and Infertility. Intern, then resident ob.-gyn. Met. Hosp. N.Y., 1950—54; fellow rsch. Harvard Med. Sch. and Free Hosp. for Women, Boston, 1954—55; instr. dept. ob-gyn. Yale U. Sch. Medicine, New Haven, 1955—56; asst. prof. ob.-gyn. dept. Yale U., New Haven, 1956—61; prof. U. Calif., LA, 1961—65; chief ob-gyn Harbor Gen. Hosp., LA, 1961—65; William Goodell prof. ob.-gyn., chmn. dept. U. Pa. Sch. of Medicine, Phila., 1965—87, William Goodell prof. ob.-gyn. dept., dir. human reproduction div., 1987—96. Contbr. articles to profl. jours. Recipient Squibb prize, Pacific Coast Fertility Soc., 1965, Christian R. and Mary Lindback award, 1969, Gold medal, Barren Found., 1977, King Faisal prize in medicine, 1989, Pub. Recognition award, Assn. Profls. of Gynecology and Obstetrics, 1990, Disting. Svc. award, Soc. Study Reprodn., 1992, Rector's medal, U. Chile, 1993, Axel Munthe award, 1996, Resolve Svc. award, 1997, medal, Coll. Physicians of Phila., 1998. Mem.: Soc. for Study of Reprodn. (Disting. Svc. award 1992), Endocrine Soc., Soc. for Exptl. Biology and Medicine, Soc. Gynecology Investigation (Disting. Scientist award 2004), Inst. of Medicine of NAS, Am. Physiol. Soc., Am. Soc. for Reproductive Medicine, Am. Gynecol. Club, Am. Gynecol. and Obstet. Soc., ACOG, ACS, Chilean Soc. Ob-Gyn. (hon.), Uruguan Soc. Sterility and Fertility (hon.), Israel Soc. Ob-Gyn. (hon.), Soc. Espanola de Fertilidad (hon.), Peruvian Fertility Soc. (hon.), Argentina Fertility Soc. (hon.), Italian Soc. Ob-Gyns. (hon.), Brazilian Fertility Soc. (hon.), Assn. Profs. Ob-Gyn. (hon.), N.C. Gynecol. Soc. (hon.), Tex. Assn. Ob-Gyns. (hon.), Ctrl. Assn. Ob-Gyns. (hon.), Pacific Coast Fertility Soc. (hon.), Alpha Omega Alpha, Sigma Xi. Home: 561 Ferndale Ln Haverford PA 19041-1614 Office: Pa Fertility Care 3701 Market St Fl 8 Philadelphia PA 19104-5509 Office Phone: 215-662-2970.

MASTROMARCO, DAN RALPH, lawyer, consultant; b. Saginaw, Mich., Jan. 18, 1958; s. Victor and Helen (Finkbeiner) M. Student, London Sch. of Econs., Eng., 1982; JD, U. Toledo, 1983; LLM, Georgetown U., 1985. Bar: Mich. 1983, DC 1984. Counsel US Senate, Permanent Subcom. on Investigations, Washington, 1983-85; trial atty. Tax div. US Dept. of Justice, Washington, 1985-86; asst. chief counsel for tax policy US SBA, Washington, 1986-92; dir. tax and fiscal policy Jefferson Group, Washington, 1992-94; pres., CEO The Argus Group, Washington, 1994—. Coord. Nat. Adv. Coun. for Small Bus., Tax Com., 1986-88; hon. mem. tax com. Small Bus. Legis. Coun., 1986-90; adj. prof. internat. mgmt. program U. Md.; exec. dir. Travel Coun. for Fair Competition; pres. The Prosperity Inst.; exec. dir. Small Bus. Regulators Coun. Author: The Art of Lobbying in Poland, 1995, Out by Its Roots, 1999, The Secret Chamber on the Public Square?, 2006; contbr. author, editor profl. jours., reports. Mem. Nat. Italian Am. Bar Assn. (trustee scholarship fund, counsel, v.p.), US C. of C. (tax policy com.). Roman Catholic. Office: 7764 Armistead Rd Lorton VA 22079 Office Phone: 703-521-3900. Personal E-mail: argusgroupdrm@aol.com.

MASUCCI, MICHAEL JAMES, artist; b. NYC, Nov. 24, 1952; s. Allen A. and Frances Masucci; life ptnr. Kate Johnson, Sept. 30, 1969. Student, Arts Students League of N.Y., Parsons Sch. of Design, CUNY, 1972—74, Columbia U., 1974—76. Studio mgr. Alan Kaplan Studios, NYC, 1978—79; master printer Modernage Photographics, NYC, 1979—2002; CEO/dir. EZTV, Santa Monica, Calif., 1983—; video artist Bethune Theaterdanse, LA, 1986—2002, Loretta Livingston and Dancers, LA, 2001—05. Co-creator, v.p. Rock Against Racism-USA, NYC, 1978—80; faculty Otis Coll. of Art and Design, LA, 2002—05; adv. bd. DV Expo, LA, 2003—05; curator Hacking the Timeline, Santa Monica, Calif., 2006—. Prodr.: (feature film) Exile in Paradise, 1989 (AFI Retrospective, 1999); dir.: Quantum Entanglement, 2003; contbr. book,; cinematographer (documentary film) The Sharpest Girl in Town, 1989 (commd. Mus. of Modern Art, NY, 1999); dir.: (documentary film) Zina Bethune in China, 1989 (AFI retrospective, 1999), Outside Looking In, 1996 (ICA-London Screening, 1996); contbr. articles to mags. and profl. jours. Judge for grants Roy Dean Film Awards, LA, 2002—06; adv. bd. LA Theater Ctr., 1990—92, West Hollywood Mktg. Corp., Calif., 1990—92; bd. mem. Avaz Internat. Dance Theater, LA, 2005—06; adv. bd. LA Free Clinic. Named one of Top 100 Prodrs., Prodr. Mag., 2000; recipient Artistic and Cmty. Svc. award, Dance Outreach/Bethune Theaterdanse, 1987, award, Changchun Film Studios, China, 1987, Artistic and Cmty. Svc. award, City of West Hollywood, 2001, Directing Award for Quantum Entanglement, Telly Awards, 2004, Curating award, James Irvine Found., 2005-6; Prodn. grant, Milken Found., 1989, Inst. of Contemporary Art, London, 1997, Exhbn. grant, West Hollywood Mktg. Com., 2000, Calif. Arts Coun., 2000, Online Exhbn. grant, Adobe Software, 2004-5, Artist grant, French Ministry of Culture, 2005-6, Prodn. grant, Santa Monica Cultural Affairs Dept., 2006, LA County Arts Commn., 2006. Mem.: L.A. Assn. of Ind. Video and Filmmakers (pres. 2006), Assn. of Ind. Video and Filmmakers, Assn. of Ind. Feature Film Prodrs., Assn. Computing Machinery Spl. Interest Group in Computer Graphics (chmn. digital video commitee 2002—03), Digital Video Expo (adv. bd. 2003—05). Achievements include invention of LiteCrane projection technology. Office: Eztv 1629 18th St #6 Santa Monica CA 90404 Home Phone: 323-459-3030; Office Phone: 310-829-3389. E-mail: mmasucci@eztvmedia.com.

MASUDA, MICHELE MICHI, statistician; d. Keiso and Marcella Masuda; life ptnr. Robert P. Stone. BA, U. Calif., Berkeley, 1987; MS, U. Wash., Seattle, 1996. Math. statistician Nat. Marine Fisheries Svc., Juneau, Alaska, 1987—. Mem. coho tech. com. Pacific Salmon Commn., Vancouver, BC, Canada, 1996—; mem. stock identification methods working group Internat. Coun. Exploration of Sea, Copenhagen, 2004—; mem. no. boundar tech. com. Pacific Salmon Commn., Vancouver, 2005—. Contbr. articles to profl. jours. Mem. Auke Bay Lab. Recycling Com.; treas. Aiding Women in Abuse and Rape Emergencies, Juneau, 2005—07; v.p. Juneau Fed. Employees Wellness Com., 2006—07. Recipient Cert. Recognition, U.S. Dept. Commerce, 1990, 1991, 1994, Bronze medal, NOAA, 2006. Mem.: Am. Statis. Assn., Juneau Cmty. Garden, Juneau Nordic Ski Club. Democrat. Avocations: nordic skiing, hiking, biking, travel, gardening, soccer.

MASUI, YOSHIO, zoology educator; b. Kyoto, Oct. 6, 1931; arrived in Can., 1969; s. Fusa and Toyo Masui; m. Yuriko Masui, May 9, 1959; children: Sayuri, Hitoshi. BSc, Kyoto U., 1953, MSc, 1955, PhD, 1961; DSc (hon.), U. Toronto, 1999. Asst. prof. Konan U., Kobe, Japan, 1965; rsch. staff biologist Yale U., New Haven, 1966-69, lectr., 1969; assoc. prof. U. Toronto, Ont., 1969-78, prof. Ont., 1978-97, prof. emeritus, 1997—, Konan U., 1999—. Recipient Manning award Manning Found., Calgary, Alta., 1991, Gairdner Internat. award Gairdner Found., Toronto, 1992, Albert Lasker Basic Med. Rsch. award, Lasker Found., 1998; named Officer, Order of Canada, 2003. Fellow Royal Soc. London., Royal Soc. Can. Achievements include discovery of Maturation Promoting Factor (MPF) and Cytostatic Factor (CSF) and their roles in cell divison control. Office: Univ Toronto Dept Cell and Sys Biology 25 Harbord St Toronto ON Canada M5S 3G5 Business E-Mail: masui@zoo.utoronto.ca.

MASULLO, ALFREDO SALVATORE, dermatologist; b. Weehawken, NJ, June 27, 1949; s. Gustavo and Natalina (Caridi) Masullo; m. Linda Bonura, 1983. BA, Rutgers U., 1971; MD, U. Medicine and Dentistry N.J., Newark, 1975. Diplomate Am. Bd. Dermatology. Intern in internal medicine U. Medicine and Dentistry N.J., 1975-76, resident, 1976-77; resident in dermatology St. Lukes, Roosevelt and Columbia-Presbyn. Med. Ctr., NYC, 1977-80; pvt. practice, Hackensack, NJ, 1980—. Attending physician Hackensack Univ. Med. Ctr., 1980—, Holy Name Hosp., Teaneck, N.J., 1980—. Fellow Am. Acad. Dermatology; mem. AMA. Office: 120 Prospect Ave Hackensack NJ 07601-2256 Office Phone: 201-488-0707.

MASUR, HENRY, internist; b. NYC, Mar. 8, 1946; s. Jack and Barbara (Forsch) Masur; m. Grace Steinacker, Jan. 14, 1979; children: Carrie, Jack, Julia. AB, Dartmouth Coll., 1968; MD, Cornell U., 1972. Diplomate Am. Bd. Internal Medicine, Am. Bd. Infectious Diseases. Intern, resident N.Y. Hosp., 1972—74; resident Johns Hopkins Hosp., Balt., 1974—75; asst. prof. Cornell Med. Coll., NYC, 1978—82; asst. chief critical care medicine NIH, Bethesda, Md., 1982—83, dep. chief critical care medicine, 1983—89, chief critical care medicine, 1989—. Clin. prof. George Washington U. Med. Sch., Washington. Mem.: Infectious Diseases Soc. Am. (pres. 2006—07), Assn. Am. Physicians, Am. Soc. Clin. Investigation. Office: NIH Rm 2C145 9000 Rockville Pike Bethesda MD 20892-1662 Home Phone: 301-229-1111. Business E-Mail: hmasur@nih.gov.

MASUR, JOSHUA MICHAEL, lawyer; b. Bronx, NY, July 19, 1968; s. Milton Leon and Sandra Kazahn Masur, Victor Schuster (Stepfather) and Prudence Emery (Stepmother); m. Shelly Kristine Millar, Nov. 28, 1993; children: Julia Astrid, Jacob Nelson, Noah Marshall. AB, Columbia Coll., 1990; JD, Columbia Law Sch., 1999. Bar: Calif. 1999. Mgr. computer graphics studio Sudler & Hennessey Advt., NYC, 1990—92; dir. consulting svcs. MESA Computer Sys., NYC, 1992—94; freelance computer cons. and graphic designer NYC, 1995—96; atty. Heller Ehrman White & McAuliffe, Menlo Park, Calif., 1999—2004, Mayer Brown Rowe & Maw LLP, Palo Alto, Calif., 2004—. Founder World Wide Web Artists' Consortium, NYC, 1994—96. Recipient Comment Competition 1st prize, Berkeley Tech. Law Jour., 1999; grantee, Columbia U. Law Sch. Pub. Interest Law Found., 1986—90; scholar, Nat. Merit Scholarship Corp., 1986—87; Chancellor James Kent scholar, Columbia U. Law Sch., 1997—98, Chief Justice Harlan Fiske Stone scholar, 1996—99. Mem.: San Francisco Bay Area Intellectual Property Inn Ct. (assoc.; sec. 2004—06, treas. 2004—06, v.p. 2006—). Democrat. Avocations: skiing, oenophile. Home: 440 Birch St Redwood City CA 94062 Office: Mayer Brown Rowe & Maw LLP 3000 El Camino Real Suite 2-300 Palo Alto CA 94306 Home Phone: 650-369-4101; Office Phone: 650-331-2053. Office Fax: 650-331-4553. Personal E-mail: josh@masur.us. Business E-Mail: jmasur@mayerbrownrowe.com.

MASUR, KURT, conductor, music director; b. Brieg, Silesia, Germany, July 18, 1927; Grad., Nat. Music Schule, Breslau, Germany, 1944, Leipzig Conservatory, 1946-48; degree (hon.), U. Mich., Cleve. Inst. Music, Leipzig U., Westminster Choir Coll., Hamilton Coll. Repetiteur and conductor Halle Nat. Theatre, 1948-51; conductor Erfurt City Theatre, 1951-53, Leipzig City Theatre, 1953-55, Dresden Philharm., 1955-58; gen. music dir. Mecklenburg Staatstheater, 1958-60; mus. dir. Komische Oper Berlin, 1960-64; chief conductor Dresden Philharm., 1967-72; conductor Leipzig Gewandhaus Orch., 1970-96; mus. dir. New York Philharmonic, NYC, 1991—2002; conductor London Philharm. Orch., 1989-92, 2000—; music dir. Orchestre National de France, Paris, 2002—; music dir. emeritus Philharmonic Soc. of NY, 2002—. Prof. Leipzig Acad. Music, 1975—; hon. guest condr. Israel Philharm. Orch., 1992. Musician (tours include): Europe, S.Am., Japan, U.S., Can., Mid. East; musician: (rec. artist) Symphonies by Mendelssohn, Symphonies by Brahms, Symphonies by Bruckner, Symphonies by Beethoven, Symphonies by Schumann, Symphonies by Tchaikovsky, Prokofiev's Piano Concertos, Beethoven's Missa Solemnis. Mailing: The London Philharmonic Orchestra 89 Albert Embankment London SE1 7TP England *

MASYR, JESSE JAMES, lawyer; b. Bklyn., Apr. 7, 1950; BA, SUNY Binghampton, 1971; JD, Tulane U., La., 1974. Bar: NY 1975. Counsel to pres. Manhattan Borough, 1978—79, dep. pres., 1979—82; faculty NYU Real Estate Inst., 1991; ptnr. Wachtel & Masyr, LLP, NYC, founder, Land Use Dept. Office: Wachtel & Masyr LLP 110 E 59th St New York NY 10022 Office Phone: 212-909-9513. Office Fax: 212-909-9429. *

MASYS, DANIEL RICHARD, medical educator, department chairman; b. Columbus, Ohio, Mar. 6, 1949; s. Paul John and Jane Marie (Mollenauer) M.; m. Linda Suzanne Bross, June 2, 1974; 1 child, Christopher. AB in Biochemistry, Princeton U., 1971; MD, Ohio State U., 1974. Diplomate Am. Bd. Internal Medicine. Staff hematologist, oncologist U.S. Naval Hosp., San Diego, 1980-84; chief ICRDB br. NIH, Bethesda, Md., 1984-86; dir. Lister Hill Nat. Ctr. Nat. Libr. Medicine, Bethesda, Md., 1986-94; dir. biomed. informatics, prof. Sch. Medicine U. Calif., San Diego, 1994—2004; prof., chair dept. biomedical informatics Vanderbilt U., 2005—. Assoc. editor Acad. Medicine jour., 1988-91, Jour. Am. Med. Informatics, Assn., 1994-2004. Mem. high performance computing White House Office of Sci., Washington, 1991-94; rep. Fed. Networking Coun., Washington, 1991-94. Capt. USPHS, 1984-94; NASA Adv. Aerospace Medicine, 2004-. Fellow: ACP, Am. Coll. Med. Informatics (exec. com. 1989—92, pres. 2006—); mem.: Nat. Acad. Scis., Inst. Medicine, Am. Med. Informatics Assn. (bd. dirs. 1992—95, assoc. editor jour. 1993—2004, Pres.'s award 1992), Alpha Omega Alpha. Office: Vanderbilt Univ 416 EBL 2209 Garland Ave Nashville TN 37232-8340

MATA, DAVID JOSEPH, physician; b. Houston, Feb. 3, 1956; s. José and Josephine M.; m. Patricia M. Mata; children: Daniel José, Timothy John. BA in Biology, Point Loma Coll., 1978; postgrad., Calif. State U., LA, 1978-80; MD, U. Minn., 1987. Diplomate Am. Bd. Family Practice, Nat. Bd. Med. Examiners. Resident in family medicine San Bernardino County Med. Ctr., Calif., 1987-90; med. dir. Salud Med. Ctr., Woodburn, Oreg., 1990-96; pvt. practice Hemet, Calif., 1996—. Adj. asst. prof. Oreg. Health Scis. U. Sch. Medicine, Portland, 1991—96; active staff mem. Salem Hosp., Oreg., 1992—96, Silverton Hosp., Oreg., 1992—96, Hemet Valley Med. Ctr., 1997—; vice-chair Family Medicine, 2000—02; cons., steering com. mem. Am. Lung Assn., Salem, 1992—94; med. dir. Birth Choice, Hemet, 2001—, Ramona Manor Convalescent Hosp., 2002—, Heartland Hospice, Hemet, 2005—06. Expert witness to U.S. Congress, Oreg. Supreme Ct., 1992; counselor East L.A. Task Force, 1979-80; chaplain Boy Scouts Am., Hemet, 1998—; adv. com. San Jacinto Head Start, 1998—; vol. physician 20th World Jamboree Boy Scouts Am., Thailand, 2002-03. Geriatric Medicine fellow U. Minn., 1985, Med. Student Rsch. tng. grantee NIH, 1985, scholar Nat. Hispanic Scholarship Found, 1987; named one of 10 Outstanding Young Ams., U.S. Jr. C. of C., 1993, Outstanding Young Person of World, 1993; recipient Golden Aztec award Oreg. Human Devel. Corp., 1993, Citation of Merit award Oreg./Pacific Dist. Ch. of Nazarene, 1993, Mentorship award Dept. Family Medicine Oreg. Health Scis. U., 1993, Disting. svc. award Ch. of the Nazarene, Woodburn, Oreg., 1996; named Family Doctor of the Yr., Oreg., 1995; recipient Congl. Tribute, U.S. Ho. of Reps., 1994. Fellow Am. Acad. Family Physicians; mem. Nazarene Health Care Fellowship, Am. Acad. Family Physicians, Northwest Regional Primary Care Assn. (clinicians com. 1990-93), Riverside County Med. Assn., Calif. Med. Assn. Democrat. Mem. Ch. Of The Nazarene. Avocations: drawing, camping, church activities, public speaking. Office: Bldg B, Ste A 255 N Gilbert St Hemet CA 92543-4066

MATA, ELIZABETH ADAMS, language educator, land investor; b. Raleigh, NC, Jan. 11, 1946; d. John Quincy Adams and Beulah Honeycutt; m. Juan Mata, June 21, 1968; children: Laura, Juan, Daniel. Student, Sweet Briar Coll., Paris, 1966-67; BA in French, Randolph-Macon Women's Coll., 1968; tchr. cert. in French and Spanish, N.C. State U., 1981; postgrad., U. Salamanca, Spain, 1983-86; MA in Spanish, NYU, 1986; cert. mentor tchr., N.C. State U., 1989; postgrad., Fordham U., 1994, U. N.C., 1995. Lic. real estate agt., N.C., 1991; cert. ESL tchr., 1999; Nat. Bd.

cert. in Spanish, 2003. Tchr. ESL, Am. Inst., Madrid, 1968-69; tchr. English, Ay J Garriques, Madrid, 1968-74, pvt. classes, Madrid, 1975-78; tchr. French, Wake County Sch., Cary, NC, 1982—83, tchr. Spanish, Apex, NC, 1982—; instr. ESL Wake Tech. Coll., Raleigh, NC, 1999—; Fulbright tchr. U. del Mar del Plata, Argentina, 2001—. Cons. ETS, 1999—. Named Tchr. of Yr., Apex HS, 1992-93. Mem. Am. Assn. Tchr. Spanish and Portuguese, Univ. Coun. on Edn., Alpha Kappa Delta (Beta Omicron chpt. hist. 1996-98, v.p. 1998-2000). Democrat. Avocations: sculpting, reading, gourmet cooking, restoring antiques, writing. Home: 643 Kings Fork Rd Cary NC 27511-5711 E-mail: elimata@aol.com.

MATA, LINDA SUE PROCTOR, writer, consultant; b. Topeka, Oct. 22, 1950; d. Frank Robert and Anabelle Simpson Proctor; m. Robert William Mata, Aug. 29, 1980; children: Adrian Robert-Proctor, Christiana Nicole. BA in Sociology, U. Ctrl. Okla., 1973; BA in Edn., Pacific Luth. U., 1983; MBA, City U., Renton, Wash., 1999; postgrad., Capella U. Tchr. North Thurston Sch. Dist., Olympia, Wash., 1986—88; cons. Dept. Social and Health Svcs., Olympia, 1988—. Tchr. Kid's Outreach, Olympia, 2001—. Author: Roads and Reminiscences, 2002; co-author (with Christiana Mata): Upon the Stars, 2004, Flowers in Bloom, 2005, Evening Shadows, 2006. Mem. Blacks in Govt., Olympia, 2001—03. With US Army, 1977—81. Recipient Diversity award, Dept. Soc. and Health Svcs., Diversity award for state employees, Washington State, 2004, Cert., South Sound Poets, 2004, Toastmaster Speakers award, 2005. Mem.: U. Okla. Alumni Assn. (assoc.), Toastmasters Internat. (sec.). Avocations: travel, doll collecting, reading, camping, poetry. Mailing: PO Box 5682 Lacey WA 98503 Personal E-mail: mata@comcast.net. E-mail: matals@dshs.wa.gov.

MATALIN, MARY, political consultant; b. Chgo., Aug. 19, 1953; d. Steven and Eileen Matalin; m. Artie Arnold (div.); m. James Carville, Nov. 25, 1993; 2 children. BA in Political Sci., Western Ill. Univ.; student, Hofstra Law Sch. With RNC, since the early 80's; voter contact dir. Reagan-Bush re-election campaign, 1984; chief staff to co-chmn. RNC, 1985; Midwest regional political dir. primary elections Bush-Quayle election campaign, 1988, dir. nat. victory '88 gen. election, 1988; polit. dir. George Bush's 1992 re-election campaign; co-host CNBC talk show, Equal Time, 1993—96; host radio show, CBS Talk Radio Network The Mary Matalin Show, 1996—98; co-host Crossfire, 1999—2001; asst. to Pres. & counselor to v.p. The White House, 2001—02. Author (with James Carville): All's Fair: Love, War and Running for President, 1992; author: Letters to My Daughters, 2004; appearance: (TV political series) K-Street. Office: The Office of Mary Matalin 424 S Wash St Lower Level Alexandria VA 22314 Office Phone: 703-739-6006. E-mail: mary@matalin.info. *

MATALLANA, LYNNE, medical association administrator; m. Richard Matallana. Former ptnr. advt. agy., Calif.; co-founder, pres. Nat. Fibromyalgia Assn., Calif., 1997—. Mem. FDA Ctr. for Drug Evaluation Rsch., Arthritis Adv. Com., Nat. Inst. Arthritis & Musculoskeletal & Skin Diseases Coalition. Pub., editor-in-chief Fibromyalgia AWARE mag, 2002—; co-author: The Complete Idiot's Guide: Fibromyalgia, 2005. Office: Nat Fibromyalgia Assn Ste A 2200 Glassell St Orange CA 92865 Office Phone: 714-321-0150. Office Fax: 714-921-6920.

MATALLY, M. GARSWA, minister; b. Dyede-dein, Grand Bassa, Liberia, Feb. 28, 1964; s. Garswa Zawodo-gbo and Martha Nyonon-Chean Garswa; m. Harriet Mamie Cooper, Aug. 25, 1992; children: Daneto Abba, Tojyea Garswa, Favor Jahnjay. BTh summa cum laude, Liberia Bapt. Theol. Sem., Paynesville, 1989; MDiv, So. Bapt. Theol. Sem., Louisville, 1993. Cert. Profl. Career Devel. Inst., 1999, A+ profl. CompTIA, 2001, computer tech. Ky. Cmty. and Tech. Coll. Sys., 2001, web page design I and II Ky. Cmty. and Tech. Coll. Sys., 2001; ordained Bapt. Ch., 1989. Pastor Grace Bapt. Ch., Monrovia, Liberia, 1987—90, Cedar St. Bapt. Ch., Owensboro, Ky., 1994—97, Wing Ave. Bapt. Ch., Owensboro, 1999—2004, Ch. for All, Inc., Owensboro, 2004—; assoc. min. Beargrass Bapt. Ch., Louisville, 1991—93. Summer missionary, ch. planter Christian County Bapt. Assn., Hopkinsville, Ky., 1992; co-founder, ch. planter Liberia Inter-Denominational Assembly, Buduburam, Ghana, 1990—91. Author: (book) Color Marriage: Mixed Couples of the Bible Uncovered; musician: (concerts, recordings on radio & tv) Glorious Harmony singing group. Organizer, cons. Helping Hand Owensboro, 2003—04, Fresh Start for Life, Inc., Owensboro, 2004—07; coord. relief supplies Liberian refugee camp, Buduburam, Ghana, 1990—91. Scholar, Am. Women Liberia, 1986—89, So. Bapt. Conv., 1991—93. Mem.: Am. Assn. Pastoral Counselors, Am. Assn. Christian Counselors. Achievements include founded churches in Liberia, Ghana and United States. Home: 3635 Legacy Run Owensboro KY 42301 Office: Church for All PO Box 1156 Owensboro KY 42302 Home Phone: 270-684-1827; Office Phone: 270-314-0942. Personal E-mail: mogama@gmail.com. Business E-Mail: attend@church4all.com.

MATALON, J. ROLANDO, rabbi; b. Buenos Aires, 1956; married; 2 children. BS in Chemistry, U. Montreal; grad. studies, Hebrew U., Jerusalem. Rabbi Congregation B'nai Jeshurun. Named one of The Top 50 Rabbis in America, Newsweek Mag., 2007. Mem.: Jewish Peace Fell., NY Bd. Rabbis, Rabbis For Human Rights No. Am., Am. Jewish World Svc. Conservative Jewish. Office: Congregation B'nai Jeshurun Ste 203 2901 Broadway New York NY 10023-2106 *

MATALON, VIVIAN, theatrical director; b. Manchester, Eng., Oct. 11, 1929; came to U.S., 1977; d. Moses and Rose (Tawil) M. Student, Munro Coll., Jamaica Coll., Neighborhood Playhouse, NYC. Prof. acting Brandeis U., 1977-78; prof. acting and direction SUNY, Stony Brook, 1985-86. Dir. Broadway prodns. After the Rain, Noel Coward in Two Keys, P.S. Your Cat is Dead, Morning's at Seven, 1980 (Tony award, Drama Desk award 1980), 2007, Brigadoon, The American Clock, The Corn is Green, The Tap Dance Kid (Tony nomination 1984); London West End Prodns. include Season of Goodwill, The Chinese Prime Minister, The Glass Menagerie, Suite in Three Keys, After the Rain, Two Cities, Girlfriend, I Never Sang for My Father, Small Craft Warnings, The Gingerbread Lady, Bus Stop, Morning's at Seven; dir. Ah Wilderness, Stratford (Ont., Can.) Festival, 1993, Our Town, Stratford, 1994, The Heiress, Chichester (Eng.) Festival, 1990; television prodns. Private Contentment, Am. Playhouse, Morning's at Seven, Showtime. Home: PO Box 242 Glenford NY 12433-0242 *

MATANKY, JAMES E., real estate developer; b. Chgo., Sept. 23, 1960; s. Eugene and Gertrude M. BS, U. Ill., 1982, JD, 1985; LLM, Cambridge U., 1991. Bar: Ill. Lawyer Epton, Mullin & Druth, Chgo., 1985-86, Much, Shelist, Freed et al, Chgo., 1986-90, Curschman, Schubel & Weiss, Hamburg, Germany, 1990; pres. Matanky Realty Group, Inc., Chgo., 1991—. V.p. JCCs Chgo., 2005—07; mentor retail devel. City Chgo., 1998; bd. dirs. Chgo. Assn. Neighborhood Devel. Corp., West Humboldt Park Devel. Coun., 2000—05, Mus. Contemporary Art-Chgo., 1995—2000; chair individual giving cir. Renaissance Soc. U. Chgo., 1995—2000; pres. Am. Friends Hebrew U. Jerusalem; mem. Ill. state com. Internat. Coun. Shopping Ctrs., 2007. Recipient Chgo. Neighborhood Devel. award, 2000, 06; Wexner fellow, 2006 Avocations: rowing, piano, architecture. Office: 200 N LaSalle St Ste 2350 Chicago IL 60601-1014 Office Phone: 312-337-1001. Office Fax: 312-337-5996.

MATARANGLO, ROBERT PATRICK, artist, educator; b. South Amboy, NJ, Mar. 17, 1947; s. Christopher Joseph and Kathleen Rita Mataranglo; m. Sabina Dougherty (div.); 1 child, Sabina. BS in Engring., Newark Coll. Engring., 1968; BS in Engring. Mgmt., NJ Inst. Tech., Newark, 1995; MA in Painting, Montclair Coll., NJ, 1999; MFA in Visual Arts, Vt. Coll., Montpelier, 2002. Sr. engr. John's Manville Corp., NJ, 1968—73, Interpace Corp., Parsippany, NJ, 1973—79; project engr. Ford Motor Co., Edison, NJ, 1979—81, Chanel Perfumes, Piscataway, NJ, 1981—85; sr. project engr. Sandoz Pharm., East Hanover, NJ, 1988—95. Adj. prof. Ocean County Coll., Toms River, NJ, 2000—03, Brookdale C.C., Lincroft, NJ, 2000—06, Monmouth U., Long Branch, NJ, 2003—05; artist-in-residence Health Farm, Middletown, NJ, 2004—06. Mem. Monmouth County Arts Coun., Art Alliance, 2006; co-founder, past v.p. Shore Inst. Contemporary Art; co-founder Black Box Asbury Pk.; founder, past pres. Chanel Employees Fed. Credit Union. Mem.: Mensa. Avocations: sculpting, movies. Home and Office: 335 Norwood Ln Avon By The Sea NJ 07717

MATARASSO, ALAN, plastic and reconstructive surgeon; b. NYC, Oct. 19, 1953; s. Daniel and Ethel M. BA magna cum laude, Boston U., 1975; MD, U. Miami, Miami, Fla., 1979. Diplomate Nat. Bd. Med. Examiners, 1980, Am. Bd. Plastic Surgery, 1986. Intern in dept. of gen. surgery Albert Einstein Coll. Med., Montefiore Med. Ctr., Bronx, NY, 1979-80, resident in dept. gen. surgery, 1980—83, chief resident dept. gen. surgery, 1982—83, resident and chief resident dept. of plastic surgery, 1983—85; fellow aesthetic surgery Manhattan Eye, Ear and Throat Hosp., Lenox Hill Hosp., 1985, asst. attending surgeon, 1985—. Surgeon St. Luke's/Roosevelt Hosp. Ctr., 1986—; attending surgeon NY Eye and Ear Infirmary, 1986—; asst. attending surgeon, Lenox Hill Hosp., 2000-; now assoc. clin. prof. plastic surgery Albert Einstein Coll. Medicine, 1996-; expert cons., State NY, Dept. Health, Office of Profl. Med. Conduct. Contbr. chpt. Encyclopedia of Flpas, Mastery in Plastic Surgery; instrnl. course vol. Plastic Surgery Ednl. Found.; editor Clinics in Plastic Surgery,; sr. sci. editor Aesthetic Surgery Jour.; numerous profl. presentations; contbr. 100 articles to profl. jours. Bd. dirs. Sephardic Home For The Aged, Bklyn.; NE reg. coord., Ultrasonic Assisted Lipoplasty Reg. Workshops, 1996-98. Recipient Physicians Recognition award AMA, 1994, 2004; named one of Best Drs. in Am. Am. Health Mag., 1996, Best Doctors in N.Y., N.Y. Mag., 1996, 98-2005, Castle-Connolly Guide to the Best Drs., NY Metro Area. Fellow ACS, NY Acad. Medicine, Internat. Coll. Surgeons (USA) in Plastic Surgery; mem. Am. Assn. Plastic Surgeons (chair videotape com., 1996-99, symposium com., 1997-99, mem. teaching course subcom., 1996-, vice chair, 1998-99, program com., 1996-, Strategic Planning com., 1999-, travelling prof., 1999-2001, edu. commn., 1999-2000, time and place com., 2000-, chair, corp. sponsorship com., 2000-, rep. to products/svcs. workshop, 2000, parliamentarian, 2001-2002); mem. Am. Soc. Aesthetic Plastic Surgery (bd. dirs.), Fla. Soc. Plastic and Reconstructive Surgeons, Internat. Soc. Aesthetic Plastic Surgeons (pub. edu. com., 2000), Lipoplasty Endowment for Plastic Surgery, Assn. for Academic Surgeons, Northeastern Soc. Plastic Surgeons (chmn., aesthetic symposium, 1998-99, bd. dirs.), NY Reg. Soc. of Plastic and Reconstructive Surgery (pres.), Soc. for Acad. Surgeons, Royal Soc. Medicine, England Oversee Fellow, Am. Cleft Palate Assn., Pan Am. Med. Soc. (mem., sect. on Plastic and Reconstructive Surgery), Pan Pacific Surgical Assn., NY County Med. Soc. (Young Physician's Com., 1992-94, peer review com. I & II, 1993-, grievance com., 1993-, media com., 1993-), Med. Soc. State NY (social discipline com., 1994-, state legis. com., 1994-96), NY Reg. Soc. Plastic Surgeons, (exec. com. 1988-, sci. com. med. program chair, 1988-), NY State Soc. Surgeons, Rhinoplasty Soc. (bd. dirs.), Soc. of Laparoendoscopic Surgeons, So. Med. Assn., AMA, Am. Soc. Plastic Surgeons (Young Plastic Surgeons, 1987-89, Plastic Surgery Product Assessment Commn., 1991-92, CPT/ICD 9 Coding Workshop, 1991-96, Ad Hoc Com. 1992, mktg. com, 2000), Plastic Surgery Edu. Found. (Computerized Exam, 1989, EF Teleplast, 1992-95, vis. scholar, 1993-94, Edu. Assessment, 1992, Internat. Symposia, 1993, chair, Resource Book Subcom. of Resident Information Com., 1995-98, rep. on Domsestic Clin. Symposia, 1997-, In-service Examination Com., Aesthetic and Breast Subcom., 2000, Device and Technique Assessment Com., 2000, Domestic Clin. Symposia Com., 2000), Aesthetic Surgery Edu. and Rsch. Found. (charter mem.), Skin Cancer Found. (med. adv. com., 1986-), Cancers and Careers.org (adv. bd. 2000). Developed a new technique of muscle tightening and liposuction for flattening the stomach. Office: 1009 Park Ave New York NY 10028-0936 Home Phone: 212-628-0900; Office Phone: 212-249-7500. Office Fax: 212-628-5000. Personal E-mail: matarasso@aol.com. *

MATARAZZO, JOSEPH DOMINIC, psychologist, educator; b. Caiazzo, Italy, Nov. 12, 1925; (parents Am. citizens); s. Nicholas and Adeline (Mastroianni) M.; m. Ruth Wood Gadbois, Mar. 26, 1949; children: Harris, Elizabeth, Sara. Student, Columbia U., 1944; BA, Brown U., 1946; MS, Northwestern U., 1950, PhD, 1952. Fellow in med. psychology Washington U. Sch. Medicine, 1950-51; instr. Washington U., 1951-53, asst. prof., 1953-55; rsch. assoc. Harvard Med. Sch., assoc. psychologist Mass. Gen. Hosp., 1955-57; prof., head med. psychol. dept. Oreg. Health Scis. U., Portland, 1957-96, prof. behavioral neurosci., 1996—. Mem. behavioral medicine study sect. NIH; nat. mental health adv. coun. NIMH; bd. regents Uniformed Svcs. U. Health Scis., 1974-80. Author: Wechsler's Measurement and Appraisal of Adult Intelligence, 5th edit., 1972, (with A.N. Wiens) The Interview: Research on its Anatomy and Structure, 1972, (with Harper and Wiens) Nonverbal Communication, 1978; editor: Behavioral Health: A Handbook of Health Enhancement and Disease Prevention, 1984; mem. editl. bd.: Jour. Clin. Psychology, 1962-96; cons. editor: Contemporary Psychology, 1962-70, 80-93, Intelligence: An Interdisciplinary Jour, 1976-90, Jour. Behavioral Medicine, 1977—, Profl. Psychology, 1978-94, Jour. Cons. and Clin. Psychology, 1978-85; editor: Psychology series Aldine Pub. Co, 1964-74; editor Williams & Wilkins Co, 1974-77; contbr. articles to profl. jours. With USNR, 1943-47; capt. Res. Recipient Hofheimer prize Am. Psychiat. Assn., 1962 Fellow AAAS, APA (pres. 1989-90, divsn. health psychology 1978-89, mem. coun. reps. 1982-91, bd. dirs. 1986-90, Ann. Disting. Profl. Contbn. award 1991, Ann. Gold Medal for Life Achievement in the Application of Psychology 2001); mem. Western Psychol. Assn. (pres. 1986-97), Am. Assn. State Psychology Bds. (pres. 1963-64), Nat. Assn. Mental Health (bd. dirs.), Oreg. Mental Health Assn. (bd. dirs., pres. 1962-63), Internat. Coun. Psychologists (bd. dirs. 1972-74, pres. 1976-77), Am. Psychol. Found. (pres. 1994-2000). Home: 1934 SW Vista Ave Portland OR 97201-2455 Office: Oreg Health Scis U Sch Medicine 3181 SW Sam Jackson Park Rd Portland OR 97239 Office Phone: 503-494-8644. Office Fax: 503-494-5972. Business E-Mail: matarazz@ohsu.edu.

MATARAZZO, MARIA C., finance educator, department chairman; b. Somerville, Mass., Nov. 9, 1945; d. Anthony Samuel and Rose Matarazzo. BS in Bus. Edn. cum laude, So. NH U., Manchester, 1974, MBA, 1983; postgrad., Nova Southeastern U., 1993—94. Instr. So. NH U., Manchester, 1980—84; prof. NH Cmty. Tech. Coll., Manchester, 1984—88; divsn. chair, assoc. prof. Rivier Coll., Nashua, NH, 1988—. Presenter in field. Named Bus. Tchr. of Yr., Dept. Edn., 2005. Mem.: Acad. Mgmt., Bus. and Profl. Women (bd. dirs. 2001—, legis. chair 2002—), Ea. Bus. Edn. Assn., Nat. Bus. Edn. Assn., NH Bus. Edn. Assn. (pres., v.p., bd. dirs., Achievement award 2004), Alpha Delta Kappa, Alpha Sigma Lambda, Pi Omega Pi. Office: Rivier Coll 420 Main St Nashua NH 03060

MATARAZZO, RUTH GADBOIS, retired psychology professor; b. New London, Conn., Nov. 9, 1926; d. John Stuart and Elizabeth (Wood) Gadbois; m. Joseph D. Matarazzo, Mar. 26, 1949; children: Harris, Elizabeth, Sara. AB, Brown U., 1948; MA, Washington U., St. Louis, 1952, PhD, 1955. Diplomate in clin. psychology and clin. neuropsychology Am. Bd. Examiners Profl. Psychology. Rsch. fellow pediat. Washington U. Med. Sch., 1954-55; rsch. fellow psychology Harvard U. Med. Sch., 1955-57; asst. prof. med. psychology Oreg. Health Scis. U., Portland, 1957-63, assoc. prof., 1963-68, prof. dept. med. psychology, 1968—, prof. emerita, 1997. Woman liaison officer Assn. Am. Med. Coll.s, 1979—90; cons. Tillamook Job Corps, Oreg. Bd. Med. Examiners, Social Security Adminstrn., Portland Ctr. Hearing and Speech. Author (E. Greif): (book) Behavioral Approaches to Rehabilitation: Coping with Change, 1982; contbr. chapters to books, articles to profl. jours., book reviews to jours. Bd. dirs. Portland Opera Assn., Morrison Child Guidance Clinic, Portland Chamber Orch., Neskowin Valley Sch., Hoover-Minthorn Mus. Fellow: APA (mem. policy and planning bd., mem. edn. and tng. bd., vice-chair accreditation bd., chair accreditation task force, mem. accreditation bd., site visitor APA accreditation of grad. programs, mem. coun. of reps.), Oreg. Psychol. Assn. (past pres.), We. Psychol. Assn. (bd. dirs.); mem.: AAAS, Portland Psychol. Assn. (past pres.), Sigma Xi. Home: 1934 SW Vista Ave Portland OR 97201-2455 Office Phone: 503-494-0279. Business E-Mail: matarazr@ohsu.edu.

MATARÉ, HERBERT F., physicist, consultant; b. Aachen, Germany, Sept. 22, 1912; came to U.S., 1953; s. Josef P. and Paula (Broicher) M.; m. Ursula Krenzien, Dec. 1939; children: Felicitas, Vitus; m. Elise Walbert, Dec. 1983; 1 child, Victor B. BS in Physics, Chemistry and Math., Aachen U. Geneva, 1933; MS in Tech. Physics, U. Aachen, 1939; PhD in Electronics, Tech. U. Berlin, 1942; PhD in Solid State Physics summa cum laude, Ecole Normale Supérieure, Paris, 1950. Asst. prof. physics & electronics Tech. U. Aachen, 1945—46; head of microwave receiver lab. Telefunken, A.G., Berlin, 1939—45; mgr. semicondr. lab. Westinghouse, Paris, 1946-52; founder, pres. Intermetall Corp., Düsseldorf, Fed. Republic Germany, 1952-56; head semicondr. R & D, corp. rsch. labs. Gen. Telephone & Electronics Co., NYC, 1956-59; dir. rsch. semicondr. dept. Tekade, Nürnberg, Fed. Republic Germany, 1959-61; head quantum physics dept. rsch. labs. Bendix Corp., Southfield, Mich., 1961—63; tech. dir., acting mgr. hybrid microelectronics rsch. labs. Lear Siegler, Santa Monica, Calif., 1963-64; asst. chief engr. advance electronics dept. Douglas Aircraft Co., Santa Monica, 1964-66; tech. dir. McDonnell Douglas Missile Divsn., 1965—69; sci. advisor to solid state electronics group Autonetics (Rockwell Internat.), Anaheim, Calif., 1966-69; pres. Internat. Solid State Electronics Cons., LA, 1973—. Prof. electronics U. Buenos Aires, 1953-54; vis. prof. UCLA, 1968-69, Calif. State U., Fullerton, 1969-70; dir. Compound Crystals Ltd., London, 1989—; cons. UN Indsl. Devel. Orgn.; presenter India Inst. Tech., New Delhi and Bombay, 1978. Author: Receiver Sensitivity in the UHF, 1951, Defect Electronics in Semiconductors, 1971, Conscientious Evolution, 1978, Energy, Facts and Future, 1989, (with P. Faber) Renewable Energies, 1993, Bioethics: The Ethics of Evolution and Genetic Interference, 1999; patentee of about 60 patents including first European transistor (1948), first vacuum growth of silicon crystals with levitation, growth of bicrystals, first low temperature transistor with bicrystals, optical heterodyning with bicrystals, first crystal TV transmission link, first color TV transmission over fiber with LEDs and bicrystals, liquid phase epitaxy for LEDs and batch process for III-V-solar cells; contbr. over 100 articles to profl. jours. Fellow IEEE (life); mem. AAAS, IEEE Nuclear Plasma Scis. Soc., IEEE Power Engring. Soc., Inst. for Advancement of Man (hon.), Am. Phys. Soc. (solid state div.), Electrochem. Soc., Am. Vacuum Soc. (thin film div.), Materials Rsch. Soc., N.Y. Acad. Scis. (emeritus). Avocations: astrophysics, biology, classical music, piano. Personal E-mail: hf.matare@verizon.net. Business E-Mail: hf.matare@gmx.de.

MATARIC, MAJA J., engineering educator; BS with honors in Computer Sci., U. Kans., 1987; SM in Computer Sci., MIT, Cambridge, 1990, PhD in Computer Sci. and Artificial Intelligence, 1994. Mem. tech. staff NASA Jet Propulsion Lab., Pasadena, Calif., 1988; cons. Advanced Rsch. and Devel. Grp. LEGO Futura, Cambridge, Mass., 1989—90; rsch. scientist Free U. Brussels, 1990, GTE Labs., Waltham, Mass., 1991; postdoctoral fellow MIT Artificial Intelligence Lab., 1994; asst. prof. computer sci. dept. and Volen Nat. Ctr. Complex Systems Brandeis U., Waltham, Mass., 1995—97; asst. prof. computer sci. dept. and neuroscience prog. U. So. Calif., LA, 1997—2001, assoc. prof., 2001—06, prof., 2006—. Vis. prof. Fed. Poly. Sch. Lausanne, Switzerland, 1994, Swedish Inst. Computer Sci., Stockholm, 1994; founding dir. Interaction Lab., 1995—; vis. rschr. ATR Human Info. Processing Rsch. Lab., Kyoto, 1996; dir. Robotics Rsch. Lab. U. So. Calif., LA, 1998—, assoc. dir. Inst. Robotics and Intelligent Systems, 1998—, founding dir. Ctr. Robotics and Embedded Systems, 2002—, sr. assoc. dean rsch. Viterbi Sch. Engring., 2006—; mem. sci. adv. bd. Evolution Robotics, Pasadena, Calif., 2002—; mem. academic adv. bd. Ctr. Neuromorphic Sys. Engring. Calif. Inst. Tech., 2002—05. Contbr. articles to profl. jours., chapters to books; assoc. editor: Adaptive Behavior Jour., 1995—, IEEE Transactions on Robotics and Automation, 2001—03, Internat. Jour. Humanoid Robotics, 2003—, mem. editl. bd.: Jour. Artificial Intelligence Rsch., 1999—2001, Internat. Jour. Autonomous Agents and Multi-Agent Systems, 2000—, mem. editl. adv. bd.: Internat. Jour. Advanced Robotic Systems, 2004—. Recipient Career award, NSF, 1996-2001, Paper award, Assn. Computing Machinery, 1999, TR100 Innovation award, MIT Tech. Rev., 1999, Early Career award, IEEE Robotics and Automation Soc., 2000, Best Paper award, Hawaii Internat. Conf. Sys. Scis., 2003, Okawa Found. award, 2004. Mem.: IEEE Robotics and Automation Soc., Sigma Xi, Internat. Soc. Adaptive Behavior, Am. Assn. Artificial Intelligence (exec. com.), IEEE (sr.), Phi Kappa Phi. Office: Computer Sci Dept U So Calif 941 W 37th Pl MC 0781 Los Angeles CA 90089-0781 E-mail: mataric@usc.edu.

MATASAR, ANN B., retired dean, finance educator; b. NYC, June 27, 1940; d. Harry and Tillie (Simon) Bergman; m. Robert Matasar, June 9, 1962; children— Seth Gideon, Toby Rachel AB, Vassar Coll., 1962; MA, Columbia U., 1964, PhD, 1968; M of Mgmt. in Fin., Northwestern U., 1977. Assoc. prof. Mundelein Coll., Chgo., 1965-78; prof., dir. Ctr. for Bus. and Econ. Elmhurst Coll., Elmhurst, Ill., 1978-84; dean Roosevelt U., Chgo., 1984-92; prof. Internat. Bus. and Fin. Walter E. Heller Coll. Bus. Adminstrn. Roosevelt U., 1992—2005, prof. bus. emerita, 2005—. Dir. Corp. Responsibility Group, Chgo., 1978-84; chmn. long range planning Ill. Bar Assn., 1982-83; mem. edn. com. Ill. Commn. on the Status of Women, 1978-81 Author: Corporate PACS and Federal Campaign Financing Laws: Use or Abuse of Power?, 1986; (with others) Research Guide to Women's Studies, 1974, (with others) The Impact of Geographic Deregulation on the American Banking Industry, 2002, Women of Wine: The Rise of Women in the Global Wine Industry, 2006; contbr. articles to profl. jours. Dem. candidate 1st legis. dist. Ill. State Senate, no. suburbs Chgo., 1972; mem. Dem. exec. com. New Trier Twp., Ill., 1972-76; rsch. dir., acad. advisor Congressman Abner Mikva, Ill., 1974-76; bd. dirs. Ctr. Ethics and Corp. Policy, 1985-90. Named Chgo. Woman of Achievement, Mayor of Chgo., 1978. Fellow AAUW (trustee ednl. found. 1992-97, v.p. fin. 1993-97); mem. Am. Polit. Sci. Assn., Midwest Bus. Adminstrn. Assn., Acad. Mgmt., Women's Caucus for Polit. Sci. (pres. 1980-81), John Howard Assn. (bd. dirs. 1986-90), Am. Assembly of Coll. Schs. of Bus. (bd. dirs. 1989-92, chair com. on diversity in mgmt. edn. 1991-92), North Ctrl. Assn. (commr. 1994-97), Beta Gamma Sigma. Democrat. Jewish. Avocations: walking, biking, opera, crosswords. Home Phone: 847-498-5959. E-mail: amatasar@roosevelt.edu.

MATASEJE, VERONICA JULIA, sales executive; b. St. Ann's, Ontario, Can., Apr. 5, 1949; came to U.S., 1985; d. John and Anna Veronica M. Grad. H.S., Smithville, Can. Clk. typist, typesetter Crown Life Ins. Co., Toronto, 1966-70; typesetter Toronto Life/Calendar Mag., 1970-71; typesetter, exec. sec. Cerebrus Prodns. Ltd., Toronto, 1971-74; pres. Veron Prodns. Ltd., Toronto, 1975-81, Acclaim Records Inc., Toronto, 1981-88; pvt. health care provider Las Vegas, 1989-94; retail sales mgr. Top Cats, Las Vegas, 1994-00; pres. Abracadabra Music Corp., 2000—. Campaign vol. Dist. Atty., Las Vegas, 1994; vol. pilot Angel Planes, Las Vegas, 1989. Avocations: gardening, interior decorating, travel, music. Home: 4326 Caliente St Las Vegas NV 89119-5801 Office: Top Cats PO Box 61173 Las Vegas NV 89160-1173 E-mail: vm@abracadabramusic.com.

MATCHAR, DAVID B., physician, researcher; b. Balt., Sept. 29, 1955; s. Joseph Charles and Evelyn M.; m. Barbara Fran Goldfinger, May 4, 1980; children: Emily Ruth, Benjamin Jacob, Daniel William. MD, U. Md., 1980. Diplomate Am. Bd. Internal Medicine. Prof. medicine Duke U. Med. Ctr., Durham, NC, 1985—, dir. Duke Ctr. Clin. Health Policy Rsch., 1985—. Fellow ACP, Soc. Gen. Internal Medicine (pres. so. sect. 1988), Am. Heart Assn., Soc. for Med. Decision Making (editl. bd., chair 1993 ann. meeting, trustee), Am. Acad. Neurology. Office: Duke Ctr Clin Health Policy Rsch 2200 W Main St Ste 220 Tower Durham NC 27705 Office Phone: 919-286-3399. Business E-Mail: match001@mc.duke.edu.

MATCHETT, WILLIAM H(ENRY), English literature educator; b. Chgo., Mar. 5, 1923; s. James Chapman and Lucy H. (Jipson) M.; m. Judith Wright, June 11, 1949; children: David H., Katherine C., Stephen C. BA with highest honors, Swarthmore Coll., 1949; MA, Harvard U., 1950, PhD, 1957. Teaching fellow Harvard U., Cambridge, Mass., 1953-54; instr. English lit. U. Wash., Seattle, 1954-56, asst. prof., 1956-61, assoc. prof., 1961-66, prof., 1966-82, prof. emeritus, 1982—. Author: Water Ouzel, 1955, The Phoenix and the Turtle, 1965, Fireweed, 1980, Shakespeare and Forgiveness, 2002, Elementary, 2004; numerous poems and articles; co-author: Poetry: From Statement to Meaning, 1965; editor: Modern Lang. Quar., Seattle, 1964-82. Mem. Soc. Friends. Home: 1017 Minor Ave Apt 702 Seattle WA 98104-1303

MATECKI, PAUL L., lawyer; b. 1955; BA, Grinnell Coll., 1978; JD, St. Louis U., 1981. Bar: Mo. 1981, Fla. 1987. Corp. counsel Raymond James Fin., Inc., St. Petersburg, Fla., 1989—97, sr. v.p., 1989—, gen. counsel, dir. compliance, 2004—, corp. sec., 2006—. Mem.: ABA, Assn. Corp. Counsel West Fla. Chpt. Office: Raymond James Fin Inc 880 Carillon Pky Saint Petersburg FL 33716 Office Phone: 727-567-1000. Office Fax: 727-567-8053. *

MATECZUN, JOHN MATTHEW, career military officer; b. Albuquerque, Aug. 29, 1946; s. Alfred Jospeh and Margaret Ellen Mateczun; m. Elizabeth Kathleen Holmes; children: Erin Johnson, Adam Johnson, Laura. MD, U. N.Mex., 1978; MPH, U. Calif., Berkeley, 1982; JD, Georgetown U., 1988. Diplomate Am. Bd. Psychiatry and Neurology, Am. Bd. Forensic Psychiatry, cert. physician exec. 1999. Asst. divsn. surgeon, divsn. psychiatrist 3rd Marine Divsn., Okinawa, Japan, 1982—83; med. staff Nat. Naval Med. Ctr., Bethesda, Md., 1983—85, intern advisor, dir. transitional internship, 1985—87, chmn. dept. psychiatry, 1989—90, dir. med. svcs., 1990—91; force surgeon U.S. Marine Corps Forces Pacific, Camp Smith, Hawaii, 1991—94; chmn. dept. psychiatry Naval Regional Med. Ctr., Portsmouth, Va., 1987—89; dir. TRICARE Region 1, Washington, 1994—95; prin. dir. clin. svcs. Office of the Asst. Sec. of Def. (Health Affairs), Washington, 1995—97; chief med. officer Tricare Mgmt. Activity, Washington, 1997—98; comdf. officer Naval Hosp., Charleston, SC, 1998—2000; asst. chief ops. US Navy Bur. of Medicine and Surgery, Washington, 2000—01, chief staff, 2003, dep. surgeon gen., vice chair, 2005—; med. advisor to Chmn. Joint Chiefs of Staff, Washington, 2001—03; comdr. Naval Med. Ctr., San Diego, 2003—05; dep. surgeon gen. USN, 2005—; vice chief Bur. Medicine and Surgery, 2005—. Assoc. prof. clin. psychiatry Uniformed Svcs. U. Health Sciences. Contbr. chapters to books. Rear adm. M.C. USN, 1978—2004. Decorated Navy Disting. Svc. medal, Def. Superior Svc. Medal with Oak Leaf Cluster, Legion Merit with two gold stars, Bronze Star, Def. Meritorious Svc. medal, Meritorious Svc. medal with gold star, Navy/Marine Corps Commendation medal, Army Commendation medal, Navy/Marine Corps Achievement medal. Fellow: APA (disting.); mem.: Am. Coll. Physician Execs., Am. Acad. Psychiatry and the Law, Assn. Mil. Surgeons of the U.S. (life). Office: Bureau Medicine and Surgery 2300 E St NW Washington DC 20372

MATEJKA, ROBERT, chemicals executive; BBA in Acctg., Cleve. State U. V.p. fin. Rockwell Automation Co.; v.p. RPM Internat., Medina, Calif., 2000—, controller, 2000—, CFO, 2001—. Office: RPM International 2628 Pearl Rd Medina OH 44258

MATELES, RICHARD ISAAC, biotechnologist; b. NYC, Sept. 11, 1935; s. Simon and Jean (Phillips) M.; m. Roslyn C. Fish, Sept. 2, 1956; children: Naomi, Susan, Sarah. BS, MIT, 1956, MS, 1957, DSc, 1959. USPHS fellow Laboratorium voor Microbiologie, Technische Hogeschool, Delft, The Netherlands, 1959-60; mem. faculty MIT, 1960-70, assoc. prof. biochem. engring., 1965-68; dir. fermentation unit Jerusalem, 1968-77; prof. applied microbiology Hebrew U., Hadassah Med. Sch., Jerusalem, 1968-80; vis. prof. dept. chem. engring. U. Pa., Phila., 1978-79; asst. dir. rsch. Stauffer Chem. Co., Westport, Conn., 1980, dir. rsch., 1980-81, v.p. rsch., 1981-88; sr. v.p. applied scis. IIT Rsch. Inst., Chgo., 1988-90; proprietor Candida Corp., Chgo., 1990—. Editor: Jour. Chem. Tech. and Biotech., 1972—; editor: (N.Am. edit.) Biotech., 2001—; editor: Penicillin: A Paradigm for Biotechnology, 1998, Directory of Toll Fermentation and Cell Culture Facilities, 2005; contbr. articles to profl. jours. Mem. Conn. Acad. Sci. Engring., 1981—; mem. vis. com., dept. applied biol. sci. MIT, 1980-88; mem. exec. com. Coun. on Chem. Rsch., 1981-85. Fellow Am. Inst. Med. and Biol. Engring.; mem. AICE, AAAS, SAR, Am. Chem. Soc., Am. Soc. Microbiology, Soc. for Gen. Microbiology U.K., Inst. Food Technologists, Soc. Chem. Ind. (U.K.) Union League, Sigma Xi. Home: 222 E Chestnut St Apt 10B Chicago IL 60611 Office: Candida Corp Ste 1310 220 S State St Chicago IL 60604 Office Phone: 312-431-1601. Business E-Mail: rmateles@candida.com.

MATELIC, CANDACE TANGORRA, museum director, educator; b. Detroit, Aug. 21, 1952; d. Paul Eugene and Madeline Marie (Tangora) M.; m. Steven Joseph Mrozek, Sept. 17, 1983 (div. Sept. 1987); 1 child, Madeline Rose. BA, U. Mich., 1974; MA, SUNY, Oneonta, 1977; PhD in Orgnl. Studies, SUNY, Albany, 2007. Interpretive specialist Living History Farms, Des Moines, 1978-80; mgr. adult edn. Henry Ford Mus./Greenfield Village, Dearborn, Mich., 1981-82, mgr. interpretive tng., 1982-84; dir., prof. mus. studies Cooperstown grad. program SUNY, Oneonta, 1985-94; exec. dir. Mission Houses Mus., Honolulu, 1994-96, Historic St. Mary's City, Md., 1997-98; pres./CEO CTM Profl. Svcs., Inc., 1999—; founder, prin. The Cherry Valley Group, 2002—04. Cons. history mus., 1979—; lectr., tchr. nat. and regional confs., workshops, seminars, 1979—; frequent keynote spkr.; grant reviewer NEH and Inst. for Mus. Svc., Washington, 1982—, PEW Charitable Trusts, 2003; mem. guest faculty U. Victoria, BC, 1993, 2000, 02, 03, 04, 06; faculty Distance Course, 2004, 05. Author: (with others) Exhibition Reader, 1992, Distance Learning Course, 2002-, Strategic Interpretation and Program Plan for the Mill and Anselma, 2005; co-author: A Pictorial History of Food in Iowa, 1980, Survey of 1200-Plus Museum Studies Graduates, 1988, Naper Settlement Strategic Interpretation and Program Plan, 2006; contbr. articles and videos on mus. interpretation, tng., orgnl. change and mentoring in mus., 1979—; author conf. procs. Trustee Motown Hist. Mus., 1985—2004; bd. dirs. Hawaii Youth Opera Chorus, 1996; project mgr. program plan for the Richard and Sarah Allen Ctr. for Faith, Freedom and Cmty, Mother Bethel Found., 2004-05. Mem. Am. Assn. State and Local History (sec., bd. dirs. 1988-93, program chmn. ann meeting 1988, mem. edn. com. 1996-99, co-chair task force on edn. and tng. 1994-96, faculty nat. workshop series 2001-04, Historic House Initiative), designed profl. tng. workshop series, 1999-00, Assn. Living Hist. Farms and Agrl. Mus. (bd. dirs. 1980-88, pres. 1985, John T. Schlebecker award Lifetime Disting. Svc. 1996), Midwest Open Air Mus. Coordinating Coun. (founder, bd. dirs., pres. 1978-80, Candace Tangorra Matelic essay award competition established by MOMCC 2002), Am. Assn. Museums (mus. studies com. 1986-94), Internat. Coun. Museums, Nat. Trust for Hist. Preservation, Hawaii Museums Assn. (bd. dirs. 1994-96), So. Md. Mus. Assn. (bd. dirs. 1997-98). Democrat. Roman Catholic. Home and Office: 338 Navigators Dr Pawleys Island SC 29585-7068 Office Phone: 843-237-5078. Personal E-mail: cmatelic@sc.rr.com.

MATEMA, ZSUN-NEE KIMBALL (ANNETTE K. MILLER), social sciences educator; b. Washington, Jan. 11, 1944; d. Emmett Robinson Miller and Annette Kimball Brooks; m. John Fitzgerald Payne, Aug. 31, 1963 (div.); children: Kellie Jon, Jaanai Kimball, Myya Machel, Robin Annette. BA, U. D.C., 1982; MMsc, U. Metaphysics. Cert. in clin. hypnosis Am. Hypnosis Tng. Acad.; lic. practitioner of religious sci. Ch. of Religious Sci.; ordained metaphysical min.; cert. in cmty. mediation Fed. Mediation Svcs.; cert. tchr. social studies. Artistic dir. Annette's Theatre of Dance, Inc., Washington, 1968-78; prodr., writer Nat. Broadcast Corp., Washington, 1971-74; ednl. counseling cons. Something Better/A.K. Millers & Assocs., Silver Spring, Md., 1979-86; dir. cmty. edn. Am. Digestive Disease Soc., Bethesda, Md., 1986-88; cmty. outreach/arena stage multicult. audience devel. assoc. Washington, 1989-92; founding dir. Intercultural Edn. Exch., Washington, 1991—; prof. behavioral scis. Washington Saturday Coll., 1997—; founder, pres. Brannum Robinson Hist. Soc., Inc., 2001—; tchr. social studies Prince Georges Pub. Schs. Native Am. storyteller The Painted Gourd: Red & Black Voices, Washington, 1991—; hist. interpreter Mt. Vernon; colonial and Civil War reenactor DC Ladies Contraband Relief Soc., Washington, 1991—; cmty. policing trainer Met. Police Dept., Washington, 1993-97; nat. dir. All Nations Drum, Washington, 1996; pub. rels. coord. The Walk to Can., Silver Spring, Md., 1996; underground railroad historian Nat. Pk. Svc., Washington, 1996—; cmty. mediator Montgomery County Md., 1996—; nat. adv. bd. Trail of Dreams Walk from North to South, Washington, 1999; founder, pres. Washington, Custis-Lee Enslaved Remembrance Soc., 2003; founder Red Women for Good Medicine, 2006; founder, artistic dir. Black History Mus. Players, Alexandria, Va. Contbg. poet: Gurus and Griots, 1986; prodr., writer (cable) Prejudice Picks on Children, 1988, Scripts, 1989, (radio drama) Underground Railroad Traveling Radio Show, 1998; playwright Tales from Tin Cup Alley, 1991; host, prodr. (radio) The Talking Feather, 2000—, Vital Signs, 2003—; author Elizabeth Keckley's Book of Good Measure; playwright Madame Elizabeth, 2001, Serpent Round My Tree, 2003; actor A Civil War Christmas, Discovery Channel, 2006; writer, rschr. (scripted permanent hist. markers) Maryland National Road Project, 2001-06. Pub. programs chair Afro-Asian Rels. Coun., Washington, 1989-96; past vice chair Com. for Ethnic Affairs, Silver Spring, 1990-96; AFRIASIA founding dir. Cultural Alliance Greater Washington, 1991-94; cmty. mediator Human Rights Commn., Rockville, Md., 1994—; adv. bd. mem. NAACP, Silver Spring, 1996-98, com. mem. multicultural group, 1996-98; Native Am. adv. rep. Montgomery County Sch. Bd., 1996-97; tng. devel. com. mem. Nat. Area Crisis Response Team, Washington, 1997-99; founder Red Women for Good Medicine, 2006. Grantee Nat. Endowment for the Arts, Washington, 1974-76, Hawaii Arts in the Sch., Inc., Owau, Hawaii, 1994. Mem. Zeta Phi Beta. Avocations: colonial reenactment, creative wall art, travel. Personal E-mail: zsunrise3@yahoo.com.

MATENAER, TEGWIN A., artist, retired educator, consultant; BA in Art, Calif. State U., Fresno, 1978. Cert. tchg. Calif. Dept. Edn., 1979, tchg. LH 1980, Resource SP 1982. Art tchr., grant participant Fresno City Elem. Dist., 1980; tchr. Fresno County Office of Edn., 1980—82, Shasta County Office of Edn., Redding, Calif., 1982—89; art tchr. Sequoia Mid. Sch., Redding Elem. Sch. Dist., 1989—95; art and photography tchr. Shasa Coll. Cmty. Edn., 1996—98; art. coord., artist in residence Redding Sch. of the Arts, K8 Visual and Performing Arts Charter Sch., 1999—2006. Mentor tchr. Shasta County Office of Edn., Redding, 1986—88; art grant coord. Calif. arts project Sequoia Mid. Sch., Redding Elem Sch. Dist., 1994—95; juror fine art, photgraphy numerous local and regional organizations and schools. One-woman shows include Funnel Follies (Category award pastel, 2006), exhibited in group shows at River Run (Best of Show, 2005), Summer Rains (Category award pastel, 2002), Acad. Scis., Moscow, Calif. Art Rev., Best of Photography Annual, Acad. of Sci., 1990, Redding City Hall Civic Ctr., 1998, 2001—05, Redding Airport, 2001, 2003—04, Whiskeytown Visitors Ctr., 2005—06, Internat. Ctr. Design, NYC. Mem.: AAUW (artist participant annual home tour scholarship fundraiser 1998—2007, past cultural coord.), Austin Pastel Soc., Sierra Pastel Soc., Pastel Soc. of the West Coast, Pastel Soc. of the SW, Pastel Soc. of N.Mex, Pastel Soc. of Colo., NW Pastel Soc. Office: Tegwin Matenaer Fine Arts PO Box 992538 Redding CA 96099-2538 Office Phone: 530-243-7694. Business E-Mail: tegsmail@tegwinart.com.

MATERA, FRANCES LORINE, retired elementary school educator; b. Eustis, Nebr., June 28, 1926; d. Frank Daniel and Marie Mathilda (Hess) Daiss; m. Daniel Matera, Dec. 27, 1973. Luth. tchrs. diploma, Concordia U., Seward, Nebr., 1947, BS in Edn., 1956; MEd, U. Oreg., Eugene, 1963. Elem. tchr. Our Savior's Luth. Ch., Colorado Springs, Colo., 1954—57; tchr. 5th grade Monterey Pub. Schs., Calif., 1957—59; tchr. 1st grade Roseburg Schs., Oreg., 1959—60; tchr. several schs. Palm Springs Unified Sch. Dist., Calif., 1960—93; tchr. 3rd grade Vista del Monte Sch., Palm Springs, Calif., 1973—93; ret., 1993. Named Tchr. of the Yr., Palm Springs Unified Schs. Mem. Kappa Kappa Iota (chpt. and state pres.). Personal E-mail: franmatera7@aol.com.

MATERIA, KATHLEEN PATRICIA AYLING, nurse; b. Jersey City, Nov. 7, 1954; d. Donald Anthony and Muriel Cecilia (Joyce) Ayling; m. Francis Peter Materia, June 5, 1983; children: Christopher Michael, Donna Nicole. BSN, Fairleigh Dickinson U., 1976. RN, N.J. Critical care nurse Palisades Gen. Hosp., North Bergen, N.J., 1976-87; grad. nurse, 1976-77; nurse critical care unit North Hudson Hosp., Weehawken, NJ, 1977-78. Mem. Alpha Sigma Tau. Democrat. Avocations: bowling, dance.

MATERNA, JOSEPH ANTHONY, lawyer; b. Passaic, NJ, June 13, 1947; s. Anthony E. and Peggy Ann (Popowich) Materna; m. Dolores Corio, Dec. 14, 1975; children: Jodi, Jennifer, Janine. BA, Columbia U., 1969, JD, 1973. Bar: N.Y. 1975, Fla. 1977, U.S. Dist. Ct. (ea. and so. dists.) N.Y. 1977, U.S. Supreme Ct. 1977, U.S. Tax Ct. 1978, U.S. Ct. of Claims 1978. Trusts and estates atty. Chadbourne Parke Whiteside & Wolff, NYC, 1973-76, Dreyer & Traub, NYC, 1976-80, Finley Kumble Wagner Heine Underberg & Casey, NYC, 1980-85; ptnr., head trusts and estates dept. Newman Tannenbaum Helpern Syracuse & Hirschtritt, NYC, 1985-90, Shapiro Beilly Rosenberg Aronowitz Levy & Fox LLP, NYC, 1990—2004, Solomon, Pearl, Blum, Heymann & Stich, LLP, NYC, 2004—. Lectr. in field; expert witness in trusts and estate field ct. litigations, N.Y., 1999—. Contbr. articles to profl. jours. Chmn. planned giving com., mem. bd. govs. Arthritis Found. N.Y. Chpt., N.Y.C., 1980—; mem. bd. trustees, corp. treas. Cath. Interracial Coun., N.Y.C., 1992—; mem. bequests and planned gifts com. Cath. Archdiocese of N.Y., N.Y.C., 1988—; corp. sec. Arthritis Found. N.Y. chpt., N.Y.C., 1997—, mem. budget and fin. com., 2001—; mem. Meml. Sloan-Kettering Nat. Trusts and Estates Assocs. Recipient Planned Giving award Arthritis Found.-N.Y. Chpt., N.Y.C., 1994, Discovery Alliance award Arthritis Found.-N.Y. Chpt., N.Y.C., 1995; named Accredited Estate Planner, Nat. Assn. Estate Planners, Marietta, Ga., 1995. Mem. ABA, Fla. Bar (trusts and estate com.), NY State Bar Assn. (com. on estates and trusts, com. on surrogate's ct.), Bar Assn. of NYC (mem. com. on surrogate's ct., mem. con. on estate taxation), NYC Estate Planning Coun. (lectr., author), NY County Lawyers Assn. (mem. com. on trusts and estates 1979—, com. on profl. ethics, com. on taxation 2000—, com. on surrogate's ct. 2007, con. on estates and trusts 2007), Queens County Bar Assn. (mem. com. trusts and estates 1990—, mem. com. on taxation, mem. com. on profl. ethics, com. on surrogate's ct.), Am. Judges Assn. (civil ct. arbitrator NYC), Am. Arbitration Assn. (panel of arbitrators), NY State Trial Lawyers Assn., Richmond County Bar Assn. (com. on surrogates ct., com. on estate taxation, com. on estates and trusts), Columbia Coll. Alumni Assn. of Columbia U. (class pres. 1969—), Columbia Law Sch. Assn., SI Richmondtown Hist. Soc., Archdiocese NY, Regina Coeli Legacy Soc. Republican. Roman Catholic. Avocations: music, history, theater, lecturing, European travel. Home: 155 Johanna Ln Staten Island NY 10309-3604 Office: Solomon Pearl Blum Heymann & Stich LLP 40 Wall Street 35th Fl New York NY 10005 Office Phone: 212-267-7600. Business E-Mail: jmaterna@solpearl.com.

MATERSON, RICHARD STEPHEN, physician, educator; b. Phila., Feb. 11, 1941; s. Alfred Lawrence and June Eileen (Slakoff) Materson; m. Rosa Maria Navarro, Aug. 22, 1964; children: Lisa Gail, Lawrence Mark. MD, U. Miami, Coral Gables, Fla., 1965. Diplomate Am. Bd. Phys. Medicine and Rehab. Intern Walter Reed Gen. Hosp., Washington, 1965; resident Letterman Gen. Hosp., San Francisco, 1966—68; chief phys. medicine and rehab. Tripler Gen. Hosp., Honolulu, 1968—72; asst. prof. phys. medicine and rehab. Ohio State U., Columbus, 1972—76; assoc. clin. prof. phys. medicine and rehab. Baylor Coll. Medicine, Houston, 1976—93, prof., 1997—; pres. Materson MD, PA, Houston, 1976—2005; sr. v.p. for med. affairs, med. dir. Nat. Rehab. Hosp., Washington, 1990—97; prof. neurology George Washington U. Med. Ctr., Washington, 1994—97; med. v.p. Meml. Healthcare Sys., Houston, 1997—2005; prof. phys. medicine and rehab. U. Tex. Health Sci. Ctr., Houston, 1997—; fellow Kaiser Inst., 1999, 2001; chief med. officer Meml. Hermann Continuing Care Corp., 2000—02; v.p. med. devel. Hermann Healthcare Sys., 2002—05; ret., 2005. Med. dir. dept. phys. medicine and rehab. Meml. Hosp. SE, Houston, 1978-90, Ctr. for Sports Medicine and Rehab., 1987-90, Electromyography Lab., 1978-90; faculty Kaiser Inst., 2000—. Co-author: Physical Medicine and Rehabilitation, 1977, 2d rev. edit., 1980, The Practice of Rehabilitation Medicine, 1982; co-editor: Management of Persons with Stroke, 1993; co-editor, author: The Non Surgical Management of Acute Low Back Pain, 1997, Pain Management, 1998; contbg. author: Practice of Medicine, 1978. Trustee Meml. Hosp. Sys., Houston, 1986—90, Nat. Rehab. Hosp., Washington, 1990—96; host family Experiment in Internat. Living, 1985—87; bd. dirs. Inst. for Religion and Health, Tex. Med. Ctr., 2002—, chmn. bd., 2006—. Served to maj. US Army, 1965—72. Fellow Am. Acad. Phys. Medicine and Rehab. (pres. 1986-87, Distng. Pub. Svc. award, 1992, Walter J. Zeiter lectr., 1994), Am. Assn. Electrodiagnostic Medicine; mem. AMA (del. 1978-93), Phys. Medicine and Rehab. Edn. and Rsch. Found. (founder, pres. 1982-90, bd. dirs. 1983-2001), Houston Acad. Phys. Medicine and Rehab. (pres. 1979-80), Am. Acad. Pain Mgmt. (chmn. bd. advisors 1989-90, bd. adv. 1990-2005), Internat. Wine and Food Soc., Knights of Vine (master comdr. 1982—), Confrerie des Chevaliers du Tastevin, Chaine des Rotisseurs Jewish. Personal E-mail: rmaterson@embarqmail.com.

MATES, BARBARA T., librarian, library association executive; MLS, Case Western Reserve U. Regional libr. Libr. for Blind and Physically Handicapped, Cleveland Pub. Libr. Mem.: Ohio Libr. Coun. (chair outreach and spl. services com.), Assn. Specialized and Coop. Libr. Services (pres.-elect 2006—07, pres. 2007—, Francis Joseph Campbell award 2001), ALA. Office: Cleveland Pub Libr 17121 Lake Shore Dr Cleveland OH 44110-4006 Office Phone: 216-623-2911. Office Fax: 216-623-7036. Business E-Mail: barbara.mates@cpl.org. *

MATES, LAWRENCE A., II, medical company executive, consultant; b. Toledo, Oct. 10, 1954; s. Lawrence A. and Phyllis A. (Thomas) M.; m. Ulrike D. Heermann, Dec. 23, 1977; children: Lawrence A. III, Jessica M. BS in Mktg. cum laude, Princeton U., 1976, MBA, 1977. Sales mgr. Technicare Corp., Cleve., 1977-80; dist. sales mgr. Siemens Med. Systems, Iselin, N.J., 1981-85; regional sales mgr. Digital Equipment Corp., Detroit, 1985-88; nat. sales mgr. Cemax, Inc., Fremont, Calif., 1988-92; exec. v.p. Philips Electronics, Cin., 1992-2000; sr. v.p. Siemens Med. Svcs., 2000—. Bd. dirs. Provident Nat. Bank. Bd. dirs. Cin. City Planners, 1994—, United Way, 1985-86, 92-96, Am. Cancer Soc., 1997-99; mem. Ea. Pa. Planning Commn., 2006—; v.p. West Chester Citizen's Bd., 2006—; mem. banker's bd., Malvern, Pa., 2006—. Mem. Med. Researchers Assn., Am. Hosp. Assn., Toledo Bus. Assn. (v.p. 1984-85), Ohio Young Men's Bus. Assn. (pres. 1985, chmn. 1992-93), Cin. Profl. Bus. Assn. (v.p. 1993—), Cin. Health Profls. (dir. 1994-95), Cin. Investors Ltd. (dir. 1994-98), Toledo Investors Ltd. (pres. 1986, 92), Cin. Bankers Club, Cin. Club, Univ. Club (v.p. 1993-96, pres. 1998-02), Sycamore Athletic Boosters (pres. 1996-98, bd. dirs. 1996—). Republican. Roman Catholic. Avocations: swimming, travel, wine collecting, automobiles, golf. Office Phone: 610-448-1517. E-mail: LMATES@aol.com.

MATES, ROBERT EDWARD, mechanical engineering educator; b. Buffalo, May 19, 1935; s. Cyril S. and Ruth Elizabeth Mates; m. Gail Paxson, June 4, 1960; children: Robert E., Elisabeth, Steven. BS, U. Rochester, 1957; MS, Cornell U., 1959, PhD, 1963. Lic. profl. engr., NY, 1962. Instr. Cornell U., Ithaca, NY, 1958-61; asst. prof. SUNY, Buffalo, 1962-65, assoc. prof., 1965-69, chmn. mech. and aero. engring., 1967-70, 79-82, prof. mech. engring., 1969-97, dir. Ctr. Biomed. Engring., 1989-96, prof. emeritus, 1997—. Editor various symposium proceedings; contbr. articles to profl. jours. Mem. supt. adv. com. vocat. edn. Buffalo Pub. Schs., 1990—98. NIH spl. rsch. fellow, 1970-71, 78-79, H.R. Lissner award Am. Soc of Mechanical Engineers, 1995. Fellow ASME (chmn. winter ann. meeting com. 1989-93, mem.-at-large bd. comm. 1988-93, v.p. bd. comm. 1994-98), Am. Inst. for Med. and Biol. Engring. (founding, chmn. acad. coun. 1996-97); mem. AAUP, Biomed. Engring. Soc. (bd. dirs. 1991-94, chmn. awards com. 1991-92, mem. pub. bd. 1992-94), Am. Soc. Engring. Edn. Democrat. Episcopalian. Avocations: woodworking, tennis, sailing, bridge. E-mail: matesr@asme.org.

MATESKY, NANCY LEE, music educator; b. West Point, Mo., Nov. 30, 1941; d. Enoch Ivy and Layla Nixon Miller; m. Michael Paul Matesky, Aug. 10, 1973; children: Angela Lynn, Michael Paul II. BS in Edn., U. Ark., 1963, MS in Edn., 1971. Piano tchr. self employed, Tex., Ark., Wash., 1960—90; music tchr. Rogers Ark. Sch., 1963—64, Fayetteville Sch., Ark., 1964—65, Springdale Sch., Ark., 1965—70; instr. U Ark., Fayetteville, 1971—72; asst. prof. West Tex. State U, Canyon, 1972—75; prof. Shoreline CC, Seattle, 1976—. Founder, first pres. Ark. Elem. Music Educators Assn., 1965—67. Performer: Shoreline CC, 1981—98, Seattle Art Mus., 2000, 2002, Matesky-Swisher Two Piano Duo. Named one of Outstanding Young Women in Am., 1968; recipient Outstanding Young Educator award, Jaycees, 1967. Mem.: Music Educators Nat. Conf., Music Tchr. Nat. Assn. (assoc.), Seattle Ladies Musical Club, Sigma Alpha Iota (Nat. Coll. Leadership award 1963, Nat. Alumnae Leadership award 2001). United Meth. Home: 23004 35th Ave S E Bothell WA 98021-8913 Office: Shoreline CC 16101 Greenwood Ave N Shoreline WA 98133 Office Phone: 206-546-4618. Personal E-mail: opus.four@gte.net.

MATHAS, THEODORE A., insurance company executive, lawyer; b. Apr. 4, 1967; m. Keryn Mathas; 3 children. AB, Stanford Univ., 1989; JD, Univ. Va., 1992. Atty. Debevoise & Plimpton; corp. v.p. NY Life Ins. Co., NYC, 1995—98, pres. Eagle Strategies Corp. subs., 1996—99, pres. NYLIFE Securities, 1997—99, sr. v.p., 1998—2004, COO agy. dept., 1999—2001, COO life & annuity, 2001—04, exec. v.p., co-head life & annuity, 2004—06, vice-chmn., COO, mem. exec. mgmt. com., 2006—07, pres., COO, 2007—. Bd. dir. Haier NY Life Ins. Ltd. Mem. Univ. Va. Law Review. Mem.: Order of the Coif. Office: NY Life Ins Co 51 Madison Ave New York NY 10010 *

MATHEE, KALAI, research scientist, educator; b. Kampar, Perak, Malaysia, Aug. 30, 1959; s. Loganayaki and Kaliaperumal; m. Giri Narasimhan, Apr. 12, 1993. BS, U. Malaya, Kuala Lumpur, 1984, MS,

1986; PhD, U. Tenn., 1992. Elem. sch. tchr., Sitiawan, Perak, Malaysia, 1980; tutor U. Malaya, Kuala Lumpur, Malaysia, 1984-86; postdoctoral fellow Tufts U., Boston, 1992-93, U. Tenn., Memphis, 1993-99; vis. scientist, vis. prof. Danish Tech. U., Lyngby, Denmark, 1997—; rsch. adj. faculty Copenhagen U., Lyngby, Denmark, 1999—; asst. prof. Fla. Internat. U., Miami, 1999—. Participant Genome Annotation Com. Project, Cystic Fibrosis Found., 1999—. Danish Med. Rsch. Coun. grantee, 1998—. Mem. AAAS, Am. Soc. Microbiology, Sigma Delta Epsilon. Avocations: reading, gardening, hiking, camping, travel. Office: Fla Internat U University Park Miami FL 33199-0001 Fax: 305 348-1986. E-mail: matheek@fiu.edu.

MATHENY, ADAM PENCE, JR., child psychologist, educator, consultant, researcher; b. Stanford, Ky., Sept. 6, 1932; s. Adam Pence and Dorotha (Steele) Matheny; m. Ute I. Debus, July 10, 1962 (div.); m. Mary P. Tolbert, June 24, 1967 (div.); children: Laura Steele, Jason Gaverick. BS, Columbia U., 1958; PhD, Vanderbilt U., 1962. Sr. human factors engr. Martin Aerospace divsn., Balt., 1962—63; instr. Johns Hopkins U. Med. Sch., Balt., 1963—65; staff fellow Nat. Inst. Child Health and Human Devel., 1965—67; from asst. prof. to prof. pediat. U. Louisville Med. Sch., 1967—75; assoc. dir. to dir. Louisville Twin Study, 1986—. Mem. rev. panel NIH, 1991—95. Co-author: Genetics and Counseling in Medical Practice, 1969; contbr. articles to profl. jours. With USN, 1951—55. Recipient Outstanding Rsch. medal, U. Louisville. Fellow: APA, Am. Psychol. Soc., Am. Assn. Applied and Preventive Psychology, Internat. Soc. Twin Studies; mem.: AAAS, Internat. Soc. Infant Study, Internat. Soc. Behavior Devel., Behavior Genetics Assn., Soc. Rsch. Child Devel., Sigma Xi, Phi Beta Kappa. Office Phone: 502-634-0050. Business E-Mail: apmathol@louisville.edu. E-mail: adammatheny@aol.com.

MATHENY, CHARLES WOODBURN, JR., former army officer, civil engineer, city official; b. Sarasota, Fla., Aug. 7, 1914; s. Charles Woodburn Sr. and Virginia (Yates) M.; m. Jeanne Felkel, July 12, 1942; children: Virginia Ann, Nancy Caroline, Charles Woodburn III. BSCE, U. Fla., 1936; grad., Army Command Gen. Staff Coll., 1944. Registered profl. engr., Ga., 1939; cert. surveyor Ga., 1939, lic. comml. pilot 1952. San. engr. Ga. State Dept. Health, 1937—39; civil engr. Fla. East Coast Rlwy., 1939—41; commd. 2d lt. F.A., USAR through ROTC U. Fla., 1936; 1st lt. F.A., USAR, 1939; vol. active army svc. F.A., US Army, 1941; commissioned 2d lt. F.A., US Army (Regular Army), 1942; advanced through grades to col. F.A., USAR, 1955; comdr. 351st Field Arty. Bn., 1944—45; commr. 33rd Field Arty. Bn., 1st Infantry Divsn., 1946; arty. staff officer 33rd Field Arty. Bn., 1st Inf. Divsn., 1947; gen. staff G-3 Plans Dept. Army, 1948—51; qualified Air Force liaison pilot, 1951; qualified Army aviator airplanes and helicopters, 1952; aviation officer 25th Infantry Divsn., Republic of Korea, 1952—53; sr. Army aviation advisor Korean Army, 1953; first dir. combat devel. dept. first dep. comdt. Army Aviation Sch., Ft. Sill, Okla., 1954—55; dep. dir. rsch., dep. dir. dept. tactics U.S. Army Field Arty. and Missile Sch., Ft. Sill, 1955—57; aviation officer 7th U.S. Army, Germany, 1957—58; Munich sub area comdr. So. Area Command, 1958—59; qualified sr. army aviator, 1959; dep. chief of staff for info. So. Area Command, 1960; Mich. sector comdr. VI Army Corps., 1961—62, ret., 1962; asst. dir. Tampa (Fla.) Dept. Pub. Works, 1963—81, ret., 1981. During World War II, Germany Commd., 351st field arty. Bn. in combat and occupation, 1945, also 33d field arty. bn., 1st Inf. Divsn., in occupation, 1946. Initiator and originator of tactical use of helicopters in Army, 1949, Army warrant officer helicopter aviator program and organization of first five Army Transp. Helicopter Co. move combat units battlefield authorized T.O. & E, 55-57, Oct. 24, 1950 by U.S. Army Chief of Staff Gen. J. Lawton Collins and establishment of a new U.S. Army pers. policy making U.S. Army helicopter pilots warrant officers instead of officers, 1950; 1st to envision army combat units and airphibious army divisions equipped with high performance helicopter mobility capable of land, sea or air warfare operations at 200 mph, 1950; initiated and prepared directive signed by Army chief of staff, Gen. J. Lawton Collins ordering first feasibility tests of Army super-mobile inf. and arty. units equipped with helicopter mobility, 1951; pilot 1st combat observation mission in army helicopter, Korea, 1952; organizer, comdr., helicopter pilot 1st Army combat ops. using helicopter mobility to support inf. and engr. front line combat units 25th Inf. Divsn., Korea, 1952 proving feasibility of Army helicopter mobility on the battlefield; 1st to advocate, rsch., prepare orgn. plans and design of super-mobile Army combat units equipped with armed and unarmed helicopter mobility, with model designs of helicopters armed with missiles, rockets, etc. to equip proposed combat units, 1955-56; proposed development reconnaissance helicopter 1957 similar to Army O/R Comanche, RAH-66 reconnaissance helicopter later developed by Army; U.S. Army first to exploit and develop helicopter mobility due to Matheny's devotion to its early begining; pilot 100 combat observation missions, Korea, 1952-53; author 1st state legis. to establish profl. sch. civil engring. filed in Fla. Legis. by Sen. Julian Lane, 1974; mem. U.S. Army's Strategic Planning Com., 1950-51. Contbr. articles to profl. jours., popular mags. Troop com. Boy Scouts Am., 1965-73; active various cmty. and ch. activities; patron Tampa Art Mus., 1965-83, Tampa Cmty. Concert Series, 1979-82; bd. dirs. Tampa YMCA, 1967-71, Fla. Easter Seal Soc., 1978, Easter Seal Soc. Hillsborough County, 1971-84, hon. bd. dirs., 1984-95, treas., 1973-76, pres., 1977. Decorated Bronze Star with oak leaf cluster, Air medal with three oak leaf clusters; recipient of the Eagle Scout award, 1928; Letterman football U.F., 1933, 35; named to U. Fla. Student Hall of Fame, 1936. Mem. ASCE (pres. West Coast br., dir. Fla. sect. 1973, Engr. of Yr. award West Coast br. Fla. sect. 1979, life mem. 1980), Am. Soc. Profl. Engrs., Fla. Engring. Soc., Am. Pub. Works Assn. (pres. West Coast br. Fla. chpt. 1972, exec. com. Fla. chpt. 1972-77, v.p. 1977, pres. 1978), Ret. Officers Assn., Army Aviation Assn., SAR, Fla. Blue Key, Alpha Tau Omega, Sigma Tau. Episcopalian. Achievements include research in tactical use of helicopter aerial vehicles. Home: 3501 Bayshore Blvd Apt 1402 Tampa FL 33629-8901 Office Phone: 813-835-3426.

MATHENY, EDWARD TAYLOR, JR., lawyer; b. Chgo., July 15, 1923; s. Edward Taylor and Lina (Pinnell) Matheny; m. Marion Elizabeth Shields, Sept. 10, 1947; children: Nancy Elizabeth, Edward Taylor III; m. Ann Spears, Jan. 14, 1984. BA, U. Mo., 1944; JD, Harvard, 1949. Bar: Mo. 1949. Pvt. practice, Kansas City, 1949-91; ptnr. firm Blackwell, Sanders, Matheny, Weary & Lombardi, 1954-91. Pres. St. Luke's Hosp., Kansas City, 1980-95; bd. dirs. Dunn Industries, Inc. Author: The Presence of Care (History of St. Luke's Hospital, Kansas City), 1997, A Long and Constant Courtship (The History of a Law Firm), 1998, The Rise and Fall of Excellence, 2000, The Pursuit of a Ruptured Duck (When Kansas Citians Went to War), 2001. Pres. Cmty. Svc. Broadcasting of Mid-Am., Inc., 1971—72; chmn. Citizens Assn. Kansas City, 1958; chmn. bd. dir. St. Luke's Found., 1989—95; trustee U. Kansas City, 1980—96, Kansas City Cmty. Found., 1983—94, Eye Found., 1990—2000, H&R Block Found., 1996—, Jacob L. and Ella C. Loose Found., 1996—2005. Mem. Kansas City Bar Assn., Mo. Bar, River Club, Mo. Acad. Squires, Mission Hills Country Club, Phi Beta Kappa, Sigma Chi (Balfour Nat. award 1944) Episcopalian (chancellor emeritus Diocese West Mo.). Home: 4900 Central St Kansas City MO 64112 Office: 4801 Main St Kansas City MO 64121-6777

MATHENY, KENNETH L., oil industry executive; b. Akron, Ohio; B in Acctg., U. Akron; MBA, Bowling Green State U. Dir. corp. fin. Marathon Oil Corp., Houston, 1988—89, dir. human resources, 1989—94, v.p. human resources and environment, 1994—97; v.p. contr. USX Corp., Pitts., 1997—2000, v.p. investor rels., 2000—02; v.p. investor rels. and pub. affairs Marathon Oil Corp., 2002—. Mem.: Petroleum Investor Rels. Assn., Nat. Investor Rels. Inst., Am. Inst. CPAs. Office: Marathon Oil Corp Corp Headquarters 5555 San Felipe Rd Houston TX 77056-2723

MATHENY, RUTH ANN, editor; b. Fargo, ND, Jan. 17, 1918; d. Jasper Gordon and Mary Elizabeth (Carey) Wheelock; m. Charles Edward Matheny, Oct. 24, 1960. BE, Mankato State Coll., 1938; MA, U. Minn., 1955; postgrad., Universidad Autonoma de Guadalajara, Mex., 1956, Georgetown U., 1960. Tchr., U.S. and S.Am., 1938-61; assoc. editor Charles E. Merrill Pub. Co., Columbus, Ohio, 1963-66; tchr. Confraternity Christian Doctrine, Washington Court House, Ohio, 1969-70; assoc. editor Jr. Cath. Messenger, Dayton, Ohio, 1966-68; editor Witness Intermediate, Dayton, 1968-70; editor in chief, assoc. pub. Today's Cath. Tchr., Dayton, 1970—2002, editor-in-chief emeritus, 2002—; editor in chief Catechist, Dayton, 1976-89, Ednl. Dealer, Dayton, 1976-80; v.p. Peter Li, Inc., Dayton, 1980—. Editl. collaborator: Dimensions of Personality series, 1969—; co-author: At Ease in the Classroom; author: Why a Catholic School?, Scripture Stories for Today: Why Religious Education?; freelance writer, 1943— Bd. dirs. Friends Ormond Beach Libr. Mem.: 3d Order St. Francis (eucharistic min. 1990—2006), Nat. Coun. Cath. Women. Home: 26 Reynolds Ave Ormond Beach FL 32174-7043 Office: Peter Li Ednl Group 2621 Dryden Rd Ste 300 Dayton OH 45439 Personal E-mail: chilermat@aol.com. *In a world that is constantly changing, a strong religious faith is a dependable compass through which we are able to stay on a positive, forward course.*

MATHER, ELIZABETH VIVIAN, healthcare executive; b. Richmond, Ind., Sept. 19, 1941; d. Willie Samuel and Lillie Mae (Harper) Fuqua; m. Roland Donald Mather, Dec. 26, 1966. BS, Maryville Coll., Tenn., 1963; postgrad., Columbia U., 1965-66. Tchr. Richmond Cmty. Schs., 1963-67, Indpls. Pub. Schs., 1967-68; systems analyst Ind. Blue Cross Blue Shield, Indpls., 1968-71, Ind. Nat. Bank, Indpls., 1971; med. cons. Ind. State Dept. Pub. Welfare, Indpls., 1971-78, cons. supr., 1978-86; systems analyst Ky. Blue Cross Blue Shield, Louisville, 1988-89; contracts specialist Humana Corp., Louisville, 1989—. Active Rep. Cen. Com. Montgomery County, Crawfordsville, 1976-86, Centenary Meth. Ch., adminstrv. bd., 1990. Mem. DAR (treas. 1963-66, sec. 1978-86). Avocation: designing and sewing clothes. Home: 6106 Partridge Pl Floyds Knobs IN 47119-9427 Office: 500 W Main St Fl 6 Louisville KY 40202-2946 Office Phone: 502-580-2519. Business E-Mail: emather@humana.com.

MATHER, JOHN CROMWELL, astrophysicist; b. Roanoke, Va., Aug. 7, 1946; s. Robert Eugene and Martha Belle (Cromwell) Mather; m. Jane Anne Hauser, Nov. 22, 1980. BA in Physics, Swarthmore Coll., Pa., 1968; PhD in Physics, U. Calif., Berkeley, 1974; DSc (hon.), Swarthmore Coll., 1994. NAS/NRC rsch. assoc. NASA/Goddard Inst. Space Studies, NYC, 1974—76; lectr. astronomy Columbia U., NYC, 1975—76; astrophysicist NASA/Goddard Space Flight Ctr., Greenbelt, Md., 1976—, prin. investigator FIRAS on COBE, 1976—, study scientist Cosmic Background Explorer Satellite, 1976—82, project scientist COBE, 1982—, head infrared astrophysics br., 1988—89, 1990—93, sr. scientist Greenbelt, Md., 1989—90, 1993—; head Office of Chief Scientist NASA, Washington, 2007—. Chmn. external adv. bd. U. Chgo. Ctr. Astrophys. Rsch. in the Antarctic, 1992—95; mem. lunar astrophysics mgmt. ops. working group NASA, Washington, 1992; study scientist Next Generation Space Telescope, 1995—2002; mem. NRC Bd. Physics and Astronomy, 1998—2001; sr. project scientist James Webb Space Telescope, 2002—; mem. astrophysics subcommittee NASA Adv. Coun., 2006—. Co-author (with John Boslough): The Very First Light: The True Inside Story of the Scientific Journey Back to the Dawn of the Universe, 1996; contbr. articles to profl. jours. Co-recipient Nobel Prize in Physics, Nobel Found., 2006; finalist Discover Mag. Tech. award, 1993; named one of The World's Most Influential People, TIME Mag., 2007; named to Hall of Fame, Aviation Week and Space Tech., 1997, Newton HS Hall of Fame, NJ, 2003; recipient Nat. Space Achievement award, Rotary, 1991, Nat. Air and Space Mus. Trophy, 1991, Laurels award for Space/Missles, Aviation Week and Space Tech., 1992, John Scott award, City of Phila., 1995, Marc Aaronson Meml. prize, 1998, Benjamin Franklin medal in Physics, Franklin Inst., 1999, Presdl. Rank award, NASA, 2003, Cosmology prize, Peter Gruber Found., 2006, 2006, Nobel prize in Physics, 2006; NSF Fellowship and hon. Woodrow Wilson Fellowship, 1968—70, Fellowship, Hertz Found., 1970—74, Goddard Fellow, 1994. Fellow: Am. Phys. Soc.; mem.: AIAA (Astronautics Space Sci. award 1993), NAS, Am. Acad. Arts & Scis. (Rumford prize 1996), Soc. Photo-Optical Instrumentation Engrs. (George W. Goddard award 2005), Internat. Astron. Union, Am. Astron. Soc. (councilor 1998—2001, Dannie Heineman prize astrophysics 1994), Phi Beta Kappa, Sigma Xi. Democrat. Unitarian Universalist. Achievements include proposing Cosmic Background Explorer Satellite, led team to successful launch in 1989; measured spectrum of cosmic microwave background radiation to unprecedented accuracy. Office: NASA/Goddard Space Flight Code 443 Observational Cosmology Greenbelt MD 20771 also: Office of Chief Scientist NASA 300 E St NW Washington DC 20546-0001 Office Phone: 301-286-8720, 301-286-6885. E-mail: john.c.mather@nasa.gov. *

MATHER, LYNN, law educator, political science professor; BA, U. Calif, LA; PhD, U. Calif., Irvine; postgrad., U. Calif., Berkeley, U. Wis. Nelson A. Rockefeller prof. govt. Dartmouth Coll., acting dir. Rockefeller Ctr. Social Sci.; prof. law & polit. sci. U. at Buffalo Law Sch., SUNY, 2002—, dir. Baldy Ctr. for Law & Social Policy, 2002—. Author: Plea Bargaining or Trial? The Process of Criminal Case Disposition; co-author: Divorce Lawyers at Work: Varieties of Professionalism in Practice (C. Herman Pritchett award, Am. Polit. Sci. Assn.); contbr. articles to prof. jour. Mem.: Am. Polit. Sci. Assn. (chair, Law & Ct. sect. 1993—94), Law & Soc. Assn. (pres. 2001—02). Office: U at Buffalo Law Sch 511 O'Brien Hall Buffalo NY 14260 Office Phone: 716-645-5541. Business E-Mail: lmather@buffalo.edu. *

MATHER, MILDRED EUNICE, retired archivist; b. Washington, Iowa, July 25, 1922; d. Hollis John and Delpha Irene (Cummings) Whiting; m. Stewart Elbert Mather, Aug. 7, 1955 (dec.); children: Julie Marie, Thomas Stewart(dec.). Cert., Burlington and Des Moines, 1941, 1947, Stenotype Inst., 1948. Typist Burlington Willow-Weave, 1941-42, Burlington Basket Co., 1942; clk. typist U.S. Dept. War, Washington, 1942-43; supr. internat. conf. U.S. Dept. State, Washington, 1949-52; bookkeeper Iowa Wesleyan Coll., Mt. Pleasant, 1952-55; clk. typist Herbert Hoover Presdl. Libr., West Branch, Iowa, 1964-69, archives technician, 1964-72, archivist, libr., 1972-92, ret., 1992. With WAC US Army, 1943—46. Mem.: Am. Legion, Order Ea. Star. Republican. Home: 1794 Garfield Ave West Branch IA 52358-9403

MATHER, RICHARD BURROUGHS, retired Chinese language and literature educator; b. Baoding, Hebei, China, Nov. 11, 1913; s. William Arnot and Grace (Burroughs) M.; m. Virginia Marjorie Temple, June 3, 1939; 1 dau., Elizabeth Temple. BA, Princeton U., 1935; B.Th., Princeton Theol. Sem., 1939; PhD in Oriental Langs, U. Calif., Berkeley, 1949. Ordained to ministry United Presbyterian Ch. U.S., 1939; pastor Belle Haven (Va.) Presbyterian Ch., 1939-41; asst. prof. Chinese U. Minn., Mpls., 1949-57, assoc. prof., 1957-64, prof., 1964-84. Mem. Am. Council Learned Socs. Com. on Study of Chinese Civilization, 1979-81 Author: Shih-shuo hsin-yu, A New Account of Tales of the World, 1976, rev. edit., 2002, The Poet Shen Yueh (441-513), the Reticent Marquis, 1988, The Age of Eternal Brilliance: Three Poets of the Yung-ming Era, 2003; contbr. articles to profl. jours. Guggenheim fellow, 1956-57; Fulbright Hays grantee, 1956-57, 63-64; Am. Council Learned Socs. grantee, 1963-64 Mem. Am. Oriental Soc. (pres. 1980-81), Assn. Asian Studies. Democrat. Achievements include research in medieval Chinese lit. and religion. Home: 1666 Coffman St Apt 108 Saint Paul MN 55108

MATHER, ROGER FREDERICK, retired music educator, writer; b. London, May 27, 1917; came to U.S., 1938; s. Richard and Marie Louise (Schultze) M.; m. Dorothea Meinen, Sept. 11, 1943 (div. Sept. 1971); children: Arielle Diane, Christopher Richard; m. Betty Louise Bang, Aug. 3, 1973. BA with honors, Cambridge U., 1938; MSc, MIT, Cambridge, 1940; MA in Metallurgy, U. Cambridge, 1941. Registered profl. engr., Ohio, Mich., Pa. Rsch. metallurgist Inland Steel Co., East Chicago, Ind., 1940-42; chief metallurgist Willys-Overland Motors, Toledo, 1942-46, Kaiser-Frazer Corp., Willow Run, Mich., 1946-50; project mgr. U.S. Steel Corp., Pitts., 1950-61; dir. rsch. engring. Mine Safety Appliances Co., Pitts., 1961-62; rsch. staff Du Pont Co., Wilmington, Del., 1962-63; chief nuclear power tech. br. NASA, Cleve., 1963-73; adj. prof. music U. Iowa, Iowa City, 1973-96; ret., 1996. Instr. pub. speaking and stage fright U. Iowa, 1983-85, Kirkwood C.C., Iowa City, 1983-85; cons. Miyazawa Flutes, U.S.A., Coralville, Iowa, 1985-90; lectr. U. Toledo; Mich. state examiner Registration of Profl. Engrs.; condr. numerous workshops, clinics, classes, and flute recitals regionally, nationally, Europe and Asia. Author: The Art of Playing the Flute, 1980, Vol. 2, 1981, Vol. 3, 1988; contbr. chpts. to several woodwind anthologies; pub., exec. editor The Romney Press, 1980—; contbr. poems to numerous poetry anthologies in US, Eng., numerous articles to sci. and music jours. Mem. Internat. Soc. Poets (Hall of Fame 1998, Poet of Merit 2002, Featured Artist 2005), Nat. Flute Assn. (life, coms.), The Pa. Assn., Mensa Episcopalian. Avocations: semi-professional photography, high fidelity sound reproduction contributions, alternative medicine. Home: 715 George St Iowa City IA 52246 Personal E-mail: bangmather@mchsi.com.

MATHER, STEPHANIE JUNE, lawyer; b. Kansas City, Mo., Dec. 5, 1952; d. Edward Wayne and H. June (Kunkel) M.; m. Miles Christopher Zimmerman, Sept. 23, 1988. BA magna cum laude, Okla. City U., 1975, JD with honors, 1980. Lawyer Pierce, Couch, Hendrickson, Johnston & Baysinger, Okla. City, Okla., 1980—88, Manchester, Hiltgen & Healy, P.C., Okla. City, 1989—90; sr. staff counsel Nat. Am. Ins. Co., Chandler, Okla., 1990—98; atty. Ctr. for Edn. Law, Oklahoma City, 1998—, v.p., shareholder, 2003—. Asst. v.p. Lagere & Walkingstick Ins. Agy., Inc., Chandler, Okla., 1993-98. Co-chair Lincoln County Dem. Party, 1991-92, 95-97; v.p. Lincoln County Dem. Women, 1992-95, pres., 1995-97; bd. dirs. Lincoln County Partnership for Children, 1994—. Gateway to Prevention and Recovery, 1996-97. Mem.: Lincoln County Profl. Women, Okla. State Sch. Bds. Assn. (coun. sch. attys. 1998—, bd. dirs. 2002—05, pres. 2005—06), Nat. Sch. Bds. Assn, (coun. sch. attys. 1998—), Lincoln County Bar Assn. (libr. bd. 1990—), Okla. Bar Assn. (editor, bd. editors 1992—99), Alpha Phi (treas. Ctrl. Okla. Alumnae 1997—99, Outstanding Okla. City Alumnae 2005, Panhellenic Woman of Yr. Oklahoma City 2005). Democrat. Avocations: reading, genealogy, ranching, cooking. Office: Center For Education Law 900 N Broadway Ave #300 Oklahoma City OK 73102-5828 Home: 808 Manvel Ave Chandler OK 74834-3858 also: 808 Marvel Ave Chandler OK 74834 Office Phone: 405-528-2800. E-mail: smather@cfel.com.

MATHERS, MARSHALL See EMINEM

MATHERS, PAULA JANECEK, lawyer; b. Zlin, Czech Republic, June 12, 1972; BA, Prairie View A&M U., 1994; JD, South Tex. Coll. Law, 1997. Bar: Tex. 1997, US Dist. Ct. (no., ea. and so. dists. Tex.) 1998. Atty. Hagans, Burdine, Montgomery, Rustay & Winchester, P.C., Houston, 1997—. Named a Rising Star, Tex. Super Lawyers mag., 2006. Mem.: Assn. Trial Lawyers of Am., Houston Young Lawyers Assn., Tex. Trial Lawyers Assn., Tex. Young Lawyers Assn., ABA, Houston Bar Assn. Office: Hagans Burdine Montgomery Rustay Winchester PC 3200 Travis 4th Fl Houston TX 77006 Office Phone: 713-222-2700. E-mail: pjmathers@hbb-law.com. *

MATHERS, WILLIAM HARRIS, lawyer; b. Newport, RI, Aug. 27, 1914; s. Howard and Margaret I. (Harris) M.; m. Myra T. Martin, Jan. 17, 1942; children: William Martin, Michael Harris, John Grinnell, Myra Tutt, Ursula Fraser. AB, Dartmouth Coll., 1935; JD, Yale U., 1938. Bar: NY 1940. With Milbank, Tweed & Hope, 1938-48; mem. Milbank, Tweed, Hope & Hadley, 1948-57; v.p., sec., dir. Yale & Towne Mfg. Co., Stamford, Conn., 1957-60; ptnr. Chadbourne & Parke, 1960-75, counsel, 1983—; exec. v.p., gen. counsel, sec., dir. United Brands Co., 1975-82. Mayor, trustee Village of Cove Neck, N.Y., 1950-82; trustee Barnard Coll., 1958-69. Served as pvt. to maj. U.S. Army, 1942-46. Mem. ABA, N.Y. State Bar Assn., Nassau County Bar Assn., Assn. of Bar of City of N.Y., New Eng. Soc. in City of N.Y., Casque and Gauntlet, Corbey Court, Piping Rock Club, Seminole Golf Club, N.Y. Yacht Club, Cold Spring Harbor Beach Club, Phi Beta Kappa, Psi Upsilon. Home: 1460 King George Farm Rd Sutton VT 05867 Office: 30 Rockefeller Plz New York NY 10112-0127 Office Phone: 212-408-5100.

MATHES, EDWARD CONRAD, architect; b. New Orleans, Mar. 10, 1943; s. Earl L. and Margaret (Gash) M.; m. Anne M. Ergenbright, Mar. 1, 1964 (div. June 2000); children: Margaret Elizabeth Hughes, Anne Catherine Aboud. BArch, U. Southwestern La., 1968. Registered arch., La., Miss., Fla., Tex., Ala., Ga., Tenn., Ky., N.C., S.C., W.Va., Conn. Tchr. U. Southwestern La., Lafayette, 1968-69; asst. to mng. arch. Rogers, Taliaferro, Kostritsky & Lamb, Balt., 1969; pres. Mathes, Bergman & Assocs., Inc., New Orleans, 1969-82, The Mathes Group, New Orleans, 1982—2000; chmn. MathesBrierre Architects, 2001—; bd. dirs. New Orleans Mus. Art, 2006—. Dean's adv. coun. U. La. Coll. of the Arts, Lafayette. Chmn. Orleans Svc. Ctr., ARC, 1993-94; bd. dirs. City Park Improvement Assn., 1996—, pres. Recipient Am. Sch. and Univ. award, 1983, 1985, Partnership award, ARC, 1998, CEO's award, S.E. La. chpt. ARC, People's Choice award for music., comms., theatre complex, Loyola New Orleans, 1989, People's Choice award for Univ. Libr., 2000, Cert. Recognition Design Excellence, Nat. Orgn. Minority Architects, 2002. Mem.: AIA (pres. New Orleans chpt. 1989, Inst. scholar 1968—69, Honor award New Orleans Chpt. 1982, 1989, 2000, Honor award La. 1982, 1986, 2001), Constrn. Industry Assn. (pres. 1984—85, Honor award 1993), City Energy Club, Metairie Country Club, Pickwick Club, Rotary (pres. New Orleans 1985—86). Republican. Presbyterian. Avocations: tennis, travel. Home: # 4 Park Island Dr New Orleans LA 70122 Office: MathesBrierre Architects 201 Saint Charles Ave Fl 41 New Orleans LA 70170-4100 Office Phone: 504-586-9303. Business E-Mail: emathes@mathesbrierre.com.

MATHES, JAMES R., bishop; b. Aug. 18, 1959; m. Teresa Yvette Sutton, Aug. 15, 1981; children: Rutherford Lee, Sarah Elizabeth Nam. BA magna cum laude, U. of the South, Sewanee, Tenn., 1982; MDiv, Va. Theol. Sem., Alexandria, 1991. Assoc. campaign dir. The Webb Sch., Bell Buckle, Tenn., 1983—85; math tchr. & coach St. Andrews-Sewanee Sch., St. Andrews, Tenn., 1985—86, dir. devel., 1986—89; asst. min. All Saints Episcopal Ch., Belmont, Mass., 1991—94; rector Church of St. James the Less, Northfield, Ill., 1994—2001; canon to the ordinary Episcopal Diocese of Chgo., 2001—05; bishop Episcopal Diocese of San Diego, 2005—. Episcopalian. Avocations: woodworking, backpacking, reading. Office: Episcopal Diocese of San Diego 2728 Sixth Ave San Diego CA 92103 Business E-Mail: jmathes@edsd.org.

MATHES, RACHEL CLARKE, voice educator, singer; b. Atlanta, Mar. 14, 1941; d. Frank Alfred and Jacqueline Woolfolk Mathes. MM, U. S.C., 1988, DMA, 1991. Leading soprano Stadttheater, Basel, Switzerland, 1966—66, Deutsche Opera Rhein, Duesseldorf, Germany, 1967—73, Met. Opera, NYC, 1974—77; prof. voice U. Ala., Birmingham, 1983—. Elder, tchr. bible South Highland Presbyn. Ch., Birmingham, 1999—. Recipient Birmingham News Obelisk award, 1979, 1981, Ala. Music Hall Fame

Contemporary award, 1987; scholar, Fulbright Found., 1962—63. Mem.: Nat. Fedn. Music Clubs, Nat. Assn Tchrs. Singing, Pi Kappa Alpha. Home Phone: 205-989-5838; Office Phone: 205-934-8781.

MATHES, STEPHEN JOHN, plastic and reconstructive surgeon, educator; b. New Orleans, Aug. 17, 1943; s. John Ernest and Norma (Deutsch) M.; children: David, Brian, Edward. BS, La. State U., 1964; MD, La. State U., New Orleans, 1968. Diplomate Am. Bd. Surgery, Am. Bd. Plastic Surgery (dir. 1993—). Asst. prof. surgery Wash. U., St. Louis, 1977-78; assoc. prof. U. Calif., San Francisco, 1978-84, prof. surgery, 1984, prof. surgery, anatomy and cell biology, 1984-85, also bd. dir. craniofacial anomalies; head plastic surgery sect. U. Mich., Ann Arbor, 1984-85, prof. surgery, 1984-85; prof. surgery, head plastic and reconstructive surgery div. U. Calif., San Francisco, 1985—2006, prof. growth and devel. Sch. Dentistry, 1985—2006. Chmn. residency rev. com. Accreditation Coun. Grad. Med. Edn., 2004—05. Author: (textbook) Clinical Applications for Muscle and Musculocutaneous Flaps, 1983 (Best Med. Book award Physician's category, Am. Med. Writer's Assn., 1983), Clinical Atlas of Muscle and Musculocutaneous Flaps, 1979, Plastic Surgery Principles and Practice, 1990, Reconstructive Surgery, 1996; editor: Plastic Surgery, 2d edit., 2006; mem. editl. bd. Jour. Plastic and Reconstructive Surgery, 1991-98; contbr. articles to profl. jours. Recipient 1st prize plastic surgery scholarship contest Plastic Surgery Edn. Found., 1981, 83, 84, 86, 93, 99, Spl. Achievement award Am. Soc. Plastic Surgery, 1980, Best Sci. Paper, Am. Soc. Aesthetic Plastic Surgery, 1981; grantee NIH, 1982-85, 86-90. Fellow ACS (chmn. adv. coun. on plastic and maxillofacial surgery 1999-02, gov. at large, mem. health policy steering com. 2000-06); mem. Am. Assn. Plastic Surgery (sec. 2005-06, Clinician of Yr. award 2001), Plastic Surgery Rsch. Coun. (pres. 1988), Am. Soc. Surgery of Hand, Soc. Univ. Surgeons, Am. Soc. Plastic Surgery (Spl. Achievement award 2005), Assn. Acad. Chairmen in Plastic Surgery (pres. 2001), Plastic Surgery Ednl. Found. (bd. dir. 1994-04, pres. 2002-03, Disting. Svc. award 2005). Republican. Episcopalian. Avocations: gardening, tennis. Home: 2730 Broderick St San Francisco CA 94123 Personal E-mail: sjmathes@pacbell.net. Business E-Mail: mathess@surgery.ucsf.edu.

MATHES, STEPHEN JON, lawyer; b. NYC, Mar. 18, 1945; s. Joseph and Beatrice M.; m. Michele Marshall, Oct. 22, 1972 (div. 1992); children: Aaron, Benjamin; m. Maria McGarry, Dec. 19, 1992; 1 child, Sara. BA, U. Pa., 1967, JD, 1970. Bar: NY 1971, Pa. 1972, U.S. Dist. Ct. (ea. dist.) Pa. 1971, U.S. Ct. Appeals (3d cir.) 1972, U.S. Supreme Ct. 1978, U.S. Ct. Appeals (5th cir.) 1985, U.S. Ct. Appeals (4th cir.) 1985, U.S. Ct. Appeals (9th cir.) 2000. Law clk. U.S. Ct. Appeals (3d cir.), Phila., 1970-71; asst. dist. atty. major felony unit, spl. investigation unit Office of Phila. Dist. Atty., 1975; assoc. Dilworth, Paxson, Kalish & Kauffman, Phila., 1971-74, 76-77, sr. ptnr., 1977-91, mem. exec. com., 1987-90, co-chmn. litig. dept., 1987-91; ptnr. Hoyle, Fickler, Herschel & Mathes (formerly Hoyle, Morris & Kerr), Phila., 1992—; bd. dirs. The Levitt Found., 1990—, sec., 1991—2006, pres., 2006—. Mgmt. com. Hoyle, Morris & Kerr, Phila., 1992-97, 2001—. Bd. dirs., exec. com. Acad. Vocal Arts, 1993-2000, mem. exec. com., chmn. student aid com.; mem. legal and compliance divsn. Securities Industry Assn., 1998—; trustee, Harvard Review of Philosophy, 2004-. Mem. ABA, Am. Law Inst., Securities Industries Assn., Pa. Bar Assn., Phila. Bar Assn. (mem. litig. divsn.), Thanatopsis Soc., Racquet Club, Germantown Cricket Club. Home: 199 Lynnebrook Ln Philadelphia PA 19118-2706 Office: Holye Fickler Herschel & Mathes Ste 1500 One S Broad St Philadelphia PA 19107 Office Phone: 215-981-5880. Business E-Mail: smathes@hoylelawfirm.com.

MATHESON, ALAN ADAMS, law educator; b. Cedar City, Utah, Feb. 2, 1932; s. Scott Milne and Adele (Adams) M.; m. Milicent Holbrook, Aug. 15, 1960; children: Alan, David Scott, John Robert. BA, U. Utah, 1953, MS, 1957, JD, 1959; postgrad., Columbia U. Bar: Utah 1960, Ariz. 1975. Asst. to pres. Utah State U., 1961-67; mem. faculty Ariz. State U., Tempe, 1967—, prof. law, 1970—, dean, 1972, 1978-84, 89, 97-98. Bd. dirs. Ariz. Found. for Legal Svcs. and Edn. Pres. Tri-City Mental Health Citizens Bd., 1973-74. With AUS, 1953-55. Mem. ABA, Utah Bar Assn., Ariz. Bar Assn., Maricopa County Bar Assn., Phi Beta Kappa, Order of Coif. Democrat. Mem. Lds Ch. Home: 720 E Geneva Dr Tempe AZ 85282-3737 Office: Ariz State U Coll Law Tempe AZ 85287 Office Phone: 480-965-6503.

MATHESON, JAMES DAVID (JIM), congressman; b. Salt Lake City, 1960; m. Amy Matheson; 2 children. BA in Govt., Harvard U., Cambridge, Mass., 1982; MBA, UCLA, 1987. Worked in energy industry, 12 yrs.; founder Matheson Grp., 1998; mem. US Congress from 2nd Utah dist., 2001—, mem. fin. svcs. com., mem. transp. and infrastructure com., mem. sci. com. Mem. Salt Lake Pub. Utilities bd., Scott M. Matheson Leadership Forum. Democrat. Mem. Lds Ch. Office: US Ho Reps 1222 Longworth Ho Office Bldg Washington DC 20515 Office Phone: 202-225-3011. *

MATHESON, LINDA, retired social worker; b. Martna, Estonia, Mar. 29, 1918; came to U.S., 1962, naturalized, 1969; d. Endrek and Leena Endrekson; m. Charles McLaren Matheson, Feb. 5, 1955. Diploma, Inst. Social Scis., Tallinn, Estonia, 1944; MS, Columbia U., 1966, D in Social Work, 1974. Diplomate clin. social work. Social work officer UN Rehab. and Resettlement Assn., Germany, 1946-48; social worker Victorian Mental Hygiene, Australia, 1955-62; rsch. assoc., social work project dir. Arthritis Midway House, NYC, 1966-68; rsch. Columbia Presbyn. Med. Ctr., NYC, 1971-75; field instr. Columbia U. Sch. Social Work, 1977-79, Columbia Presbyn. Med. Ctr., NYU Sch. Social Work, 1989-90; ret., 1992. Family Found. fellow, 1966, 89-90; grantee NIMH, 1969-72. Mem. Nat. Assn. Social Workers, Nat. Wildlife Fedn., Ctr. for Study of Presidency, Internat. Platform Assn., United Leaders, BATUN, Baltic-Am. Freedom League, Smithsonian Assn., English Spkg. Union, Alliance Francaise, Columbia U. Alumni Assn., Met. Mus. N.Y. Lutheran. Home: 30-95 29th St Astoria NY 11102-2735

MATHESON, NINA W., medical researcher; MLS, DSc. Libr. Ind. Univ. Libr., Bloomington, 1961—62; libr., asst. prof. Univ. Mo. Sch. Med., St. Louis, 1962—71; spl. asst. Nat. Libr. Med., Bethesda, Md., 1971—72, chief, office of prog. planning & evaluation, 1973—74, spl. expert cons., 1982—84; dir., asst. rsch. prof. Himmelfarb Health Sci. Libr., George Washington U., 1975—80; asst. dir. Assn. Am. Med. Coll., Washington, 1980—82; dir., assoc. prof. Welch Med. Libr., Johns Hopkins U., Balt., 1984—90, dir., prof. med. info., 1991—93, dir. emerita, prof. med info., 1994—. Named Disting. prof. nursing, Vanderbilt Sch. Nursing, 1976—82. Fellow: Am. Coll. Med. Informatics, Med. Libr. Assn. (bd. dir. 1977—80, 1982—84, pres. 1983, Ida & George Eliot prize 1995); mem.: Assn. Academic Health Sci. Libr. Dir. (pres. 1987—88), Phi Beta Kappa, Beta Phi Mu. Office: William H Welch Medical Library Johns Hopkins Univ 1900 E Monument St Baltimore MD 21205-2113

MATHESON, TIM, actor; b. Glendale, Calif., Dec. 31, 1947; m. Jennifer Leak, Sept. 28, 1968 (div. 1971); m. Megan Murphy Matheson, June 29, 1985; children: Molly, Emma, Cooper. Actor: (films) Divorce American Style, 1967, Yours, Mine and Ours, 1968, How to Commit Marriage, 1969, Magnum Force, 1973, Almost Summer, 1978, National Lampoon's Animal House, 1978, Dreamer, 1979, The Apple Dumpling Gang Rides Again, 1979, 1941, 1979, A Little Sex, 1982, To Be or Not to Be, 1983, Up the Creek, 1984, Impulse, 1984, Fletch, 1985, Speed Zone, 1989, Drop Dead Fred, 1991, Black Sheep, 1996, A Very Brady Sequel, 1996, A Very Unlucky Leprechaun, 1998, The Story of Us, 1999, She's All That, 1999, Chump Change, 2001, Van Wilder, 2002, Don't Come Knocking, 2005, Redline, 2007, (TV films) Lock, Stock and Barrel, 1970, Hitched, 1971, Owen Marshall, Counselor-at-Law, 1971, Remember When, 1974, The Last Day, 1975, The Runaway Barge, 1975, The Quest, 1976, Mary White, 1977, Bus Stop, 1982, Classmates, 1984, Obsessed with a Married Woman, 1986, Joshua's Heart, 1990, Fast Company, 1995, Twilight Man, 1996, An Unfinished Affair, 1996, Holiday for Love, 1996, Buried Secrets, 1996, Buried Alive 2, 1997, (voice) Legend of Calamity Jane, 1997, Sleeping with the Devil, 1997, Forever Love, 1998, Catch Me If You Can, 1998, At the Mercy of a Stranger, 1999, Sharing the Secret, 2000, Navigating the Heart, 2000, Hell Swam, 2000, Jackie Bouvier Kennedy Onassis, 2000, Mom's on Strike, 2002, Martha, Inc.: The Story of Martha Stewart, 2003, The King and Queen of Moonlight Bay, 2003, Augusta, Gone, 2006, (TV series) Window on Main Street, 1961-62, The Virginian, 1969-70, Bonanza, 1972-73, The Quest, 1976, Tucker's Witch, 1982-83, (TV episode) Amazing Stories, 1986, (stage prodn.) True West, 1984; dir. Tails You Live, Heads You're Dead, 1995, Buried Alive 2, 1997, In the Company of Spies, 1999; prodr. Rescuers: Stories of Courage: Two Families, 1997; dir., prodr. Breach of Conduct, 1994; TV guest appearances include Adam-12, Batman: The Animated Series, Night Gallery, Hawaii Five-O, Batman: Gotham Knights, others. Office: Creative Artists Agy care Steve Tellez 9830 Wilshire Blvd Beverly Hills CA 90212-1804 *

MATHEU, FEDERICO MANUEL, university chancellor; b. Humacao, PR, Mar. 17, 1941; s. Federico Matheu-Baez and Matilde Delgado-Vazquez; m. Myrna Delgado-Miranda, May 30, 1963; children: Federico Antonio, Rosa Myrna, Alfredo Javier, David Reinaldo. BS in Chem. Engring, U. P.R., 1962; PhD in Phys. Chemistry, U. Pitts., 1971. Chem. engr. Commonwealth Oil Refining Co., 1962-63; mem. adminstrv. staff and faculty U. P.R., 1963-78, dir. Humacao Coll., 1976-78; chancellor San German campus Inter Am. U. P.R., 1978-91; exec. dir., gen. coun. on edn. Commonwealth of P.R., Hato Rey, 1991-96; chancellor U. Metropolitana-Ana G. Méndez U. System, 1996—. Cons. in field. Author papers, reports in field. Named Disting. Educator P.R. Jaycees, 1974 Mem. Colegio de Quimicos P.R., Am. Chem. Soc., Sci. Tchrs. Assn. P.R. (pres. 1975-76), P.R. Acad. Arts and Scis., Phi Delta Kappa, Phi Tau Sigma. Home: Parque de Villa Caperra No 17 Zuania St Guaynabo PR 00966 Office: UMET PO Box 21150 San Juan PR 00928-1150 Office Phone: 787-766-1743. Business E-Mail: um_fmatheu@suagm.edu.

MATHEW, TRINI ANN, internist; MD with honors, Tver State Med. Acad., Russia, 1997; MPH, Harvard U., Boston, 2006. Diplomate Am. Bd. Internal Medicine. Rsch. fellow divsn. social medicine and health inequalities Brigham and Women's Hosp., Boston, 2004—06, mem. faculty, 2006—. Fellow infectious diseases Beth Israel Deaconess Med. Ctr., Boston, 2003—06. Vol. Missionaries of Xharity, Tomsk, Russia, 2005. Recipient cert. for disting. svc. in health, medicine and sci., Tver State Med. Acad., 1996; grantee, Internat. Rsch. and Exch. Bd., 2005, Whitman Meml. Found., Harvard Med. Sch., 2005. Mem.: ACP, HIV Med. Assn., Infectious Diseases Soc. Am. Achievements include research in effects of alcohol use disorders among TB patients in Tomsk; causes of death among TB patients in Tomsk Oblast, Russia.

MATHEWS, BARBARA EDITH, gynecologist; b. Oct. 5, 1946; d. Joseph Chesley and Pearl (Cieri) Mathews. AB, U. Calif., 1969; MD, Tufts U., 1972. Diplomate Am. Bd. Ob-Gyn. Intern Cottage Hosp., Santa Barbara, Calif., 1972-73, Santa Barbara Gen. Hosp., 1972-73; resident in ob-gyn Beth Israel Hosp., Boston, 1973-77; clin. fellow in ob-gyn Harvard U., Boston, 1973-76, instr., 1976-77; gynecologist Sansum Med. Clin., Santa Barbara, 1977-98; sr. scientist Sansum Med. Rsch. Inst., 1998—; med. dir., gynecologist Women's Health Svcs., Santa Barbara, 1998—. Faculty mem. ann. postgrad. course Harvard Med. Sch.; bd. dirs. Sansum Med. Clinic, 1989-96, vice chmn. bd. dirs., 1994-96; dir. ann. postgrad course UCLA Med. Sch. Bd. dirs. Meml. Rehab. Found., Santa Barbara, Channel City Club, Santa Barbara, Music Acad. of the West, Santa Barbara, St. Francis Med. Ctr., Santa Barbara; mem. citizen's contg. edn. adv. coun. Santa Barbara C.C.; moderator Santa Barbara Cottage Hosp. Cmty. Health Forum. Author: (with L. Burke) Colposcopy in Clinical Practice, 1977; contbg. author Manual of Ambulatory Surgery, 1982. Bd trustees Furman U., Greenville, SC, 2005—, bd. dirs., 2005—. Fellow ACOG, ACS; mem. AMA, Am. Soc. Colposcopy and Cervical Pathology (dir. 1982-84), Harvard U. Alumni Assn., Tri-counties Obstet. and Gynecol. Soc. (pres. 1981-82), Birnam Wood Golf Club (Santa Barbara), Phi Beta Kappa. Home: 2105 Anacapa St Santa Barbara CA 93105-3503 Office: 2235 De La Vina St Santa Barbara CA 93105-3815 Office Phone: 805-687-7778. Office Fax: 805-687-0012.

MATHEWS, BRIAN SCOTT, librarian; b. 1977; BA in English and History, U. Ctrl. Fla., Orlando, 1999; MA in Libr. and Info. Scis., U. Southern Fla., Tampa, 2001. Reference and instrn. libr. George Washington U., Va., 2002—04; info. svcs. libr., distance learning svcs. coord. Ga. Inst. Tech., 2004—. Interim web coord. George Washington U., 2004. Contbr. articles to numerous profl. jours. Named one of the Movers and Shakers, Libr. Jour., 2007. Mem.: ALA, Atlanta Interactive Mktg. Assn., Ga. Libr. Assn., Assn. Coll. and Rsch. Libraries. Office: Ga Inst Tech Library & Info Ctr 704 Cherry St Atlanta GA 30332 Office Phone: 404-894-4598. Business E-Mail: brian.mathews@library.gatech.edu.

MATHEWS, CHRISTOPHER KING, biochemist, educator; b. NYC, 1937; s. Frank Pelletreau and Alison Barstow (Murphy) M.; m. Catherine Anne Zitcer, June 19, 1960; children: Lawrence Stuart, Anne Catherine. BA in Chemistry, Reed Coll., 1958; PhD in Biochemistry (USPHS fellow), U. Wash., 1962. USPHS postdoctoral fellow in biochemistry U. Pa., 1962-63; asst. prof. biology Yale U., 1964-67; asso. prof. biochemistry U. Ariz. Coll. Medicine, 1967-73, prof. biochemistry, 1973-77; prof., chmn. dept. biochemistry and biophysics Oreg. State U., 1978—2002, Disting. prof., 1991, emeritus, 2002—. Mem. virology study sect. NIH, 1977-79, mem. microbial chemistry study sect., 1979-81; Tage Erlander guest prof. Swedish Nat. Sci. Rsch. Coun., 1994-95. Author: Bacteriophage Biochemistry, 1971, Bacteriophage T4, 1983; co-author: (with K.E. Van Holde) Biochemistry, 1990, 96, 2000; contbr. numerous articles on nucleotide and nucleic acid metabolism, biochemistry of virus replication, and regulation of cellular metabolism to profl. jours.; editl. bd. Jour. Virology, 1970-80, Archives Biochemistry and Biophysics, 1973-80, Jour. Biol. Chemistry, 1994—, Biochem. Molecular Biology Edn., 2000-, Faseb Jour., 2006-. Grantee US Army, 2003—; Am. Cancer Soc. scholar grantee, 1973-74; USPHS research grantee, 1964-2002; Am. Heart Assn. grantee, 1968-78; NSF research grantee, 1980-82, 83-86, 90-2006; Eleanor Roosevelt Internat. Cancer fellow, 1984-85; recipient Discovery award Med. Research Found. Oreg., 1986, Disting. prof. award Oreg. State U. Alumni Assn., 1988. Mem.: AAUP, AAAS, Am. Soc. Cell Biology, Am. Chem. Soc., Am. Soc. Microbiology, Am. Soc. Biochemistry and Molecular Biology. Home: 3336 SW Willamette Ave Corvallis OR 97333-1507 Office: Dept Biochemistry and Biophysics Oreg State U Corvallis OR 97331-7305 Home Phone: 541-754-1172; Office Phone: 541-737-1865. Personal E-mail: mathewsc2@comcast.net.

MATHEWS, HARRY BURCHELL, poet, writer, educator; b. NYC, Feb. 14, 1930; s. Edward James and Mary (Burchell) M.; m. Niki de Saint Phalle, June 6, 1949 (div. 1964); 2 children; m. Marie Chaix, July 29, 1992. BA cum laude, Harvard Coll., 1952. Faculty Bennington Coll., Vt., 1978-80; vis. lectr. Hamilton Coll., Clinton, NY, 1979, Columbia Coll., NYC, 1982-83; Musée du Louvre, Paris, 1992; French Inst., London, 1996; vis. writer Brown U., Providence, 1988, Temple U., Phila., 1990, Magdalene Coll., Cambridge, England, 1992, Berliner Literarisches Colloquium, Berlin, 1994, Duke U., 1996, New Coll. of Calif., Brown U., San Francisco Art Inst., 1997, Key West Literary Seminar, 1999, Key West Writers Workshops, 2000, New Sch. U., 2002—05; Regents lectr. U. Calif., San Diego, 2001. Founding dir. Shakespeare & Co., Lenox, Mass.; bd. dirs. Dalkey Archive Press; lectr. in field at nat., internat. colls, art ctrs. and instns. Author: The Conversions, 1962, Tlooth, 1964, The Sinking of the Odradek Stadium, 1975, Country Cooking and Other Stories, 1980, Cigarettes, 1987, 20 Lines A Day, 1988, The Orchard, 1988, The Way Home, 1988, The American Experience, 1991, Singular Pleasures, 1993, The Journalist, 1994, The Human Country, 2002, My Life in CIA, 2005, (with A. Brotchie) Oulipo Compendium, 1998, (in French) Sainte Catherine, 2000; (poetry) The Ring, Poems 1956-69, 1970, The Planisphere, 1974, Trial Impressions, 1977, Selected Declarations of Dependence, 1977, Armenian Papers: Poems 1954-84, 1987, Out of Bounds, 1989, A Mid-Season Sky: Poems 1954-89, 1991, (in French) Le savoir des rois: poèmes à perverbes, 1976, Ecrits français, 1990; (essays) Immeasurable Distances: The Collected Essays, 1981, The Case of the Persevering Maltese: Collected Essays, 2003; trans.: A Man in a Dream (Georges Perec) 1975, The Laurels of Lake Constance (Marie Chaix) 1977, The Life: Memoirs of a French Hooker (Jeanne Cordelier), 1978, Blue of Noon (Georges Bataille), 1978, Ellis Island (Georges Perec) 1996, The Dust of Suns (Raymond Roussel) 1991, various jour. articles; pub., co-editor Locus Solus, 1960-62; Paris editor The Paris Review, 1989-2003; contbr. poems, stories to anthologies, articles, criticisms, reviews to profl. jours. Decorated officer Ordre Arts et Lettres (France); recipient award Fiction Writing Am. Acad. Inst. Arts and Letters, NY, 1991, Am. award for lit., 1994; grantee Deutsche Akademische Austausch Dienst, Berlin, 1991; fiction writing grantee NEA, 1982. Mem. Ouvroir de Littérature Potentielle (Paris), Bielefelder Colloquium Neuer Poesie. Avocations: music making, back-country skiing, hiking, cooking. Home (Winter): Key West FL Home (Summer): Paris France E-mail: hmathews2@cs.com.

MATHEWS, JACK WAYNE, journalist, film critic; b. LA, Dec. 2, 1939; s. Walter Edwin and Dorothy Helen (Friley) M.; m. Lucinda Lucille Herbert, Nov. 5, 1971; children: Darren Brady, Shelby Kay. BA, San Jose Coll., Calif., 1965; MS, UCLA, 1966. Reporter Riverside (Calif.) Press, 1967-69; mktg. exec. Riverside Raceway, 1969-75; columnist, editor Rochester (N.Y.) Democrat & Chronicle, 1975-78; columnist, film critic Detroit Free Press, 1978-82, USA Today, LA, 1982-85; columnist L.A. Times, 1985-89, film editor, 1989-91; film critic Newsday, LI, 1991-99, N.Y. Daily News, 1999—, movie editor, 1999—2006. Co-host Cinema, PBS, 1995-98; juror Montreal World Film Festival, 1993. Author: The Battle of Brazil, 1987. Democrat. Office: 450 W 33rd St New York NY 10001-2681 Business E-Mail: jmathews@edit.nydailynews.com.

MATHEWS, JESSICA TUCHMAN, research executive, federal official, newswriter; b. NYC, July 4, 1946; d. Lester Reginald and Barbara (Wertheim) Tuchman; m. Colin D. Mathews, Feb. 25, 1978 (div.); children: Oliver Max Tuchman, Jordan Henry Morgenthau; m. Charles G. Boyd, Dec 31, 2005. AB magna cum laude, Radcliffe Coll., 1967; PhD, Calif. Inst. Tech., 1973. Congrl. sci. fellow AAAS, 1973-74; profl. staff mem. Energy and Environment subcom. House Com. on Interior and Insular Affairs, Washington, 1974-75; dir. issues and rsch. Udall Presdl. campaign, 1975-76; dir. Office of Global Issues NSC staff, Washington, 1977-79; mem. editorial bd. The Washington Post, 1980-82; v.p., dir. rsch. The World Resources Inst., Washington, 1982-92; dep. to undersec. for global affairs U.S. Dept. State, Washington, 1993; sr. fellow Coun. on Fgn. Rels., Washington, 1993-97; columnist Washington Post, 1991-97; pres. Carnegie Endowment Internat. Peace, Washington, 1997—. Mem. numerous adv. panels Office Tech. Assessment, NAS, AAAS, EPA; adv. com. Air Products Corp., 1995—99; bd. dirs. Somalogic Inc., Hanes Brands Inc. Trustee Rockefeller Found., Century Found., Nuc. Threat Initiative; mem. Coun. Fgn. Rels.; bd. dirs. Joyce Found., Chgo., 1984—91, Inter-Am. Dialogue, 1991—2000, Surface Transp. Policy Project, 1991—2003, Radcliffe Coll., 1992—96, Carnegie Endowment for Internat. Peace, Washington, 1992—, Rockefeller Bros. Fund, NYC, 1992—96, Brookings Instn., Washington, 1995—2001. Mem.: Inst. Internat. Econs. (adv. com.), Fedn. Am. Scientists (bd. dirs. 1985—87, 1988—92), Trilateral Commn. Democrat. Jewish. Office: Carnegie Endowment Internat Peace 1779 Massachusetts Ave NW Washington DC 20036-2109 Office Phone: 202-939-2210.

MATHEWS, JOAN HELENE, pediatrician; b. Manchester, NH, Feb. 3, 1940; d. John Barnaby and Helen A. Wlodkoski; m. Ernest Stephen Mathews, June 1, 1965; 3 children. BS, U. N.H., 1961; MD, Columbia U., 1965. Diplomate Am. Bd. Pediatrics. Med. intern Roosevelt Hosp., NYC, 1965-66; pediatric resident Babies Hosp. Columbia Presbyn. Med. Ctr., NYC, 1966-68, pediatric endocrine fellow Babies Hosp., 1968-70; instr. clin. pediat. Columbia U. Coll. Physicians and Surgeons, NYC, 1973-77; asst. prof. pediat. Cornell U. Med. Coll., NYC, 1977-81; clin. instr. pediat. Harvard Med. Sch., Boston, 1985—2003, clin. asst. prof. pediat., 2003—; clin. assoc. children's svc. Mass. Gen. Hosp., Boston, 1985—. Fellow: Am. Acad. Pediat.; mem.: Phi Beta Kappa. Office: 777 Concord Ave Cambridge MA 02138-1053 Office Phone: 617-876-6800. Office Fax: 617-876-5713. E-mail: joan.mathews@childrens.harvard.edu.

MATHEWS, LINDA MCVEIGH, newspaper editor; b. Redlands, Calif., Mar. 14, 1946; d. Glenard Ralph and Edith Lorene (Humphrey) McVeigh; m. Thomas Jay Mathews, June 15, 1967; children: Joseph, Peter, Katherine. BA, Radcliffe Coll., 1967; JD, Harvard U., 1972. Gen. assignment reporter L.A. Times, 1967-69, Supreme Ct. corr., 1972-76, corr. Hong Kong, 1977-79, China corr. Beijing, 1979-80, editor op-ed page, 1980-81, dep. nat. editor, 1981-84, dep. fgn. editor, 1985-88, editl. writer, 1988-89, editor L.A. Times Mag., 1989-92; corr. Wall Street Jour., Hong Kong, 1976-77; sr. prodr. ABC News, NYC, 1992-93; nat. editor N.Y. Times, NYC, 1993-96; editor USA Today, McLean, Va., 1997—. Lectr.; freelance writer. Author (with others): Journey into China, 1982, One Billion: A China Chronicle, 1983. Mem. Women's Legal Def. Fund, 1972-76; co-founder, pres. Hong Kong Montessori Sch., 1977-79; bd. dirs. Ctr. for Childhood. Mem.: Fgn. Corrs. Club Hong Kong. Office: USA Today 7950 Jones Branch Dr Mc Lean VA 22108 Office Phone: 703-854-5581. Personal E-mail: LiMathews@aol.com. Business E-Mail: lmathews@usatoday.com.

MATHEWS, LINNEA KOONS, science educator, librarian; b. Waterville, Maine, Jan. 27, 1957; d. Edwin Donaldson and Elizabeth (Ortquist) Koons; m. Thomas Joseph Mathews, Oct. 11, 1986. BA, Colby Coll., 1979. Cert. phys. sci. and life sci. Dept. of Edn., Maine, 1988. Science tchr. SAD 39, Buckfield, Maine, 1987—2002, Mt Blue HS, Farmington, Maine, 2002—. Digital libr. Math. and Sci. Tchg. Excellence Collaborative, Portland, Maine, 2001—. Educator (devel. assessment tasks) Maine Assessment Portfolio, Local Assessment Development (Maine Math. and Sci. Alliance Tchr. Leader, 2004). Grantee MMSTEC Digital Libr., Nat. Science Found. Mem.: NSTA, Nat. Coun. Tchrs. Math., US Eventing Assn., Am. Connemara Pony Soc. Democrat. Achievements include development of MMSTEC Digital Library. Avocations: horseback riding, cooking, gardening. Home: 230 Lovejoy Pond Rd Fayette ME 04349 Office: Mt Blue HS 129 Seamon Rd Farmington ME 04938 Home Phone: 207-685-9674; Office Phone: 207-778-3561. Home Fax: 207-685-4465. Personal E-mail: tayfarm@aol.com. Business E-Mail: lkoons@msad9.org.

MATHEWS, MARY KATHRYN, retired government official; b. Washington, Apr. 20, 1948; d. T. Odon and Kathryn (Augustine) M. Student, Pa. State U., 1966-68; BBA, Am. U., 1970, MBA, 1975. Personnel mgmt. specialist, coordinator coll. recruitment program, GSA, Washington, 1971-75, adminstrv. officer, 1975-78; personnel mgmt. specialist Office of Personnel Mgmt., Washington, 1978; employee devel. specialist Office Sec. Transp., Washington, 1978-80, asst. chief departmental services and spl. programs div., 1980-81; asst. dir. adminstrv. div. Farm Credit Adminstrn., Washington, 1981-84, dir. adminstrv. div. McLean, Va., 1984-86, chief adminstrv. services div., 1987-88; dep. staff dir. for mgmt. U.S. Commn. Civil Rights, Washington, 1988-90, asst. staff dir. for mgmt.,

1990-91, asst. staff dir. for congl. affairs, 1991-94, staff dir., 1994-97; ret., 1997. Chief spl. programs staff and homebound handicapped employment program GSA, Washington, 1973-74; mem. task force Presdl. mgmt. intern program U.S. Office Pers. Mgmt., Washington, 1977-78; coord. mgmt. devel. program for women Office Sec. Transp., Washington, 1979-81. Vol. mentor, speaker Alexandria Commn. on Women, 1991-93. Mem. Exec. Women in Govt. (treas. 1993-94, v.p. 1994-95, pres. 1995-96, bd. dirs.), Small Agy. Coun. (exec. com. 1990-91, 94-96, chmn. micro agy. group 1990-91), Internat. Alliance (bd. dirs. 1996-97), Nat. Trust Hist. Preservation, Nat. Assn. Mus. Women in Arts (charter), Delta Gamma (rush advisor 1971-73, pres. bd. dirs. local chpt. house corp. 1972-73).

MATHEWS, MICH, computer company executive; married; 2 children. Grad., U. Brighton, England. With Gen. Motors; pub. relations cons., U.K div. Microsoft Corp., head corp. pub. rels. group Redmond, Wash., 1993, v.p. corp. comms., 1993, mem., bus. leadership team, 1999—, sr. v.p. Ctrl. Mktg. Group. Office: Microsoft Corp Corp Mktg One Microsoft Way Redmond WA 98052-6399 *

MATHEWS, PEGGY ANNE, nurse, consultant; b. Oakdale, La., Sept. 10, 1941; d. Howard Douglas and Huldah Mary (Hicks) Tyler; children: Joseph, Mark, Debra. A.Nursing, La. State U., Alexandria, 1975; BSN Northwestern State U., La. Cert. legal nurse cons., Legal Nurse Cons. Inst., Houston. R.N., La. Nurse intensive care unit St. Frances Cabrini Hosp., Alexandria, 1975-78, 78-80, staff educator nurse edn. dept, 1978-80, dir. noninvasive cardiology dept, 1980-85, nurse edn. dept., 1979-80, dir. cardiology, 1980—, established cardiac rehab. program, 1982, dir. Cardiac Catheterization Lab.; med. dir. TRACE Detection Svcs. Mem. Am. Assn. Critical Care Nurses, Am. Heart Assn. Democrat. Roman Catholic. Avocations: dancing, fishing, horse back riding, gardening, hunting. Home: 122 Cedar Point Ln Boyce LA 71409-8798 Office: St Frances Cabrini Hosp 3330 Masonic Dr Alexandria LA 71301-3899 Personal E-mail: pmrn41@yahoo.com.

MATHEWS, RODERICK BELL, lawyer; b. Lawton, Okla., Mar. 12, 1941; s. James Malcolm and Sallie Lee (Bell) M.; m. Karla Kurbjin, Apr. 26, 1980; children: Roderick Bell Jr., Andrew Crittenden, Malcolm Timothy. BA, Hampden Syndey Coll., 1963; LLB, U. Richmond, 1966; postgrad., U. Mich., 1991. Bar: Va. 1966. Assoc. Christian, Barton, Parker, Epps & Brent, Richmond, Va., 1966-72; ptnr. Christian, Barton, Epps, Brent & Chappell, Richmond, 1972-88; sr. v.p., corp. legal and govt. affairs officer Trigon Blue Cross & Blue Shield, 1989-96. Trustee, mem. exec. com. Children's Hosp., Richmond, 1980—. Mem. ABA (ho. of dels. 1984-88, state del. Va. 1988-93, bd. govs. 1993-96, 2005-, exec. com. 1995-96), Am. Bar Found., Am. Bar Endowment (bd. dirs.), Am. Judicature Soc. (bd. dirs.), Va. Bar Found., Va. State Bar (pres. 1987-88). Avocations: travel, fly fishing, photography, skiing. Office: 700 East Main Richmond VA 23219 Office Phone: 804-377-0113.

MATHEWS, SHARON WALKER, performing company executive, secondary school educator; b. Shreveport, La., Feb. 1, 1947; d. Arthur Delmar and Nona (Frye) Walker; m. John William (Bill) Mathews, Aug. 14, 1971; children: Rebecca, Elizabeth, Anna. BS, La. State U., 1969, MS, 1971. Dance grad. asst. La. State U., Baton Rouge, 1969-71, choreographer, 1975-76; 6th grade tchr. East Baton Rouge Parish, 1971-72, health phys. edn. tchr., 1972-74; dance instr. Magnet High Sch., Baton Rouge, 1975—; artistic dir. Baton Rouge Ballet Theatre, 1975—; dance dir. Dancers' Workshop, Baton Rouge, 1971—; choreographer Baton Rouge Opera, 1989-94, Univ. H.S. Musical Theatre, 1998—; choreographer Baton Rouge Gilbert and Sullivan Soc. summer musical La. State U., 2000, 2001; choreographer Baton Rouge Little Theater, 2000, 2002. Author: East Baton Rouge Parish Dance Curriculum. Mem. La. Supts. Task Force Arts in Edn., 1999—2001, La. Content Stds. Com. Dance, 2001, East Baton Rouge Parish Curriculum Com. Dance, 1997, La. Arts Consortium, 2000—, La. Arts Content Stds. Com., 2002—, La. Arts Content Revision Com., 2002—03. Named Dance Educator of the Yr., La. Alliance Health, Phys. Edn., Recreation and Dance; named to Univ. HS Hall of Distinction, 2003, Baton Rouge Magnet HS Hall of Fame, 2003; recipient Stream award for Artistic Excellence, S.W. Regional Ballet Assn., 1991, Mayor's Pres.'s award for Excellence in the Arts, 1999, Creative Ticket award for excellence in the arts, Kennedy Ctr., 2005, John W. Barton Sr. Excellence in Nonprofit Mgmt. award, Baton Rouge Area Found. Mem.: La. Assn. Health, Phys. Edn., Recreation and Dance (dance chairperson 1995), Southwestern Regional Ballet Assn. (bd. dirs. 1981—, treas., exec. bd. dirs. 1989—92). Republican. Baptist. Office: Baton Rouge Ballet Theater 10745 Linkwood Ct Baton Rouge LA 70810 Office Phone: 225-767-5814.

MATHEWS, STANTON TERRY, lawyer; b. May 28, 1952; m. Lisa Diane Earls, Jan. 15, 1977; children: Amy Marie, Adriane Rene, Britton Lafe, Garret Tyler. BA, Brigham Young U., 1976; JD, Western State U. Coll. Law, 1981; cert. in aviation litig., Nat. Jud. Coll., Reno, Nev. Cert. ob-gyn. pediatric malpractice. Pvt. practice law, Laguna Hills, Calif., 1981—. Judge pro tem Orange County Superior Ct. Contbr. articles to profl. jours. Mem. ATLA, Orange County Bar Assn. (lectr. 1990—), Consumer Attys. of Calif., Diplomate Million Dollar Advocates Forum, Western Trial Lawyers Assn., Orange County Trial Lawyers. Office: 24012 Calle De La Plata Ste 320 Laguna Hills CA 92653-7624 Office Phone: 949-586-2235. Personal E-mail: tortlaw@pacbell.net.

MATHEWS, TIMOTHY NEWLYN, lawyer; b. Morristown, NJ, June 9, 1975; s. James Llewellyn and Kathleen Brown Mathews; m. Catherine Rebecca Krzyzanowski, Jan. 3, 2004; 1 child, Moses Luke. BA summa cum laude, Rutgers U., Camden, NJ, 2000; JD magna cum laude, Rutgers U., 2003. Bar: Pa. 2003, NJ 2003. Rsch. asst. Rutgers U. Sch. Law, Camden, 2001—02; assoc. Chimicles & Tikellis, LLP, Haverford, Pa., 2003—. Legal rsch. and writing tchg. asst. Rutgers U. Sch. of Law, Camden, NJ, 2001—02. Editor: Rutgers Jour. Law and Religion. Dean's Merit scholar, Rutgers Sch. Law - Camden, 2000—03. Mem.: ABA, Del. County Field and Stream. Independent. Presbyterian. Avocations: sailing, trap and skeet shooting. Home: 1518 Delmont Ave Havertown PA 19083 Office: Chimicles & Tikellis LLP 361 West Lancaster Ave Haverford PA 19041 Office Phone: 610-642-8500. Office Fax: 610-649-3633. Business E-Mail: timothymathews@chimicles.com.

MATHEWS, VALINDA GAIL, elementary school educator, theater educator, gifted and talented educator; b. Honolulu, Aug. 8, 1951; d. Harold Barr and Margarite Lillian Mathews. BS in Elem. Edn., Concordia U., Seward, Nebr., 1973; MS in Gifted Edn., Emporia State U., Kans., 1985. Cert. elem. tchr. Kans., K-12 gifted tchr. Kans., K-12 English lang. learning tchr. Kans., 6-12 speech/theater tchr. Kans. Head tchr. grades 4-8 Trinity Luth. Sch., Paola, Kans., 1974—77; tchr. grade 5, gifted tchr. grades 1-6 Louisburg Elem. Sch., Kans., 1977—82; gifted tchr. grades 7-9 Shawnee Mission Schs., Kans., 1982—94; gifted tchr. grades 6-9 Turner Schs., Kans., 1996—97; tchr. speech/theater Indian Trail Jr. HS, Olathe, Kans., 1997—2007; tchr. Salinas City Elem. Sch. Dist., Calif., 2007—. Publicist Film Soc. Greater Kansas City, Mo., 1992—94; mem. internat. studies design team Olathe Schs., Kans., 2001—03. Vol. Bradley Campaign, LA, 1969, McGovern Campaign, Seward, 1972, Moore Campaign, Shawnee Mission, 2000, 2002, 2004. Named Tchr. of Yr., Indian Trail Jr. H.S., 2001, Master Tchr. of Yr., 2001; named to Project Success, Emporia State U., 2003, Leadership Acad., Olathe Sch. Dist., 2003. Mem.: NEA, Ednl. Theatre Assn., Mensa, Phi Delta Kappa. Democrat. Avocations: travel, music, photography, theater. Office: Sherwood Elem Sch Grade 6 Salinas CA 93905 Office Phone: 831-751-3616.

MATHEWS, WILLIAM GREGORY, social services administrator; b. Louisville, Dec. 5, 1946; s. William Lee and Irma (Orgain) M.; m. Gwendolyn Alana Wilson, Feb. 14, 1975; children: Megan Nichole, Damon Andrew. BA, Ind. U., 1969; MS, U. Louisville, 1971. Lic. social worker. Substitute tchr. Clarksville (Ind.) Jr.-Sr. High Sch., 1969; probation officer, social worker Jefferson County Govt. Dept. for Human Svcs., Louisville, 1969-74; dir. Shively Social Control Program, Louisville, 1969-74; coord. Jefferson County Govt. Community Residential Group Homes, Louisville, 1974-79; adminstr., supt. Jefferson County Govt. Jefferson County Youth Ctr., Louisville, 1979-88; dep. dir. Jefferson County Govt. Program Planning & Strategic Planning, Louisville, 1988-90; exec. dir. Bellewood Presbyn. Children's Home, Anchorage, Ky., 1990—. Cons. Commn. on Accreditation for Corrections, Washington, 1985-88. Co-author: When Your Child is Arrested, 1973. Coach St. Leonard's Boys Basketball, Louisville, 1988-91, Lyndon (Ky.) Recreation Softball, 1984-91; committeeman Hillerich and Bradsby Project, Louisville, 1989-91; bd. dirs. L&N Hist. Soc., Louisville, 1987-88; den leader Boys Scouts Am., Pack 1, Louisville, 1988-91. Mem. Ky. Juvenile Detention Assn. (dir. 1984-88). Avocations: model trains, walking, reading, family, youth. Office: Bellewood Childrens Home PO Box 23309 Louisville KY 40223-0309

MATHEWSON, CHRISTOPHER COLVILLE, engineer, geologist, educator; b. Plainfield, NJ, Aug. 12, 1941; s. George Anderson and Elsa Rae (Shrimpton) M.; m. Janet Marie Olmsted, Nov. 2, 1968; children: Heather Alexis, Glenn George Anderson. BSCE, Case Inst. Tech., 1963; MS in Geol. Engring., U. Ariz., 1965, PhD in Geol. Engring., 1971. Registered profl. engr., Tex., Ariz.; profl. geologist Tex., Oreg., Alaska. Officer, lt. Nat. Ocean Survey, 1965-71; prof. Tex. A&M U., College Station, 1981—, Regents prof., 2005—. Mem. coun. of examiners Assn. State Bds. Geology, 1994—; cons., speaker in field. Author: Engineering Geology, 1981 (C.P. Holdredge award); contbr. articles to profl. publs. Chmn. College Station Planning and Zoning Commn., 1973—81; trustee Geol. Soc. Am. Found., 2001—03. Fellow Geol. Soc. Am. (chmn. engring. geology divsn. 1986-87, Meritorious Svc. award 1991), Soc. Am. Mil. Engrs.; mem. Assn. Engring. Geologists (editor bull. 1981-88, pres. 1988-89, C.P. Holdredge award 1981, F.T. Johnston Svc. award 1995, exec. dir. 1998-2002), Am. Geol. Inst. (pres. 1991-92), Nat. Coal Coun., Internat. Assn. Engring. Geologists (chmn. U.S. nat. com. 1995-98). Office: Tex A&M U Dept Geology And Geophysics College Station TX 77843-3115 Office Phone: 979-845-2488. E-mail: mathewson@geo.tamu.edu. *Commitment and dedication to the mission will lead to its successful completion regardless of the odds.*

MATHEWSON, GEORGE ATTERBURY, retired lawyer; b. Paterson, NJ, Mar. 31, 1935; s. Joseph B. and Christina A. (Atterbury) M.; m. Ann Elizabeth, July 31, 1975' 1 child, James Lemuel. AB cum laude, Amherst Coll., Mass., 1957; LLB, Cornell U., Ithaca, NY, 1960; LLM, U. Mich., 1961. Bar: NY 1963. Atty office spl. legal assts., trial atty. FTC, Washington, 1963-65; regional atty. NY State Dept. Environ. Conservation, Liverpool, 1972-73; pvt. practice Syracuse, 1967—72, 1973—2002; of counsel Banac and Mathewson, Manlius, NY, 2002—04; ret., 2004. Adj. instr. bus. law Onondaga C.C., Syracuse, 1979-84. Author: 1984 Arrives in America, 2005. Bd. dirs. South Side Businessmen, 1971-72, 88-91, v.p., 1992, pres. 1993; elder Onondaga Hill Presbyn. Ch., 1979, 82-85; dir. Manilus C. of C., 1995, v.p., 1997; trustee Steuben County Hist. Soc., 2002—05, v.p. 2005; bd. dirs. Yates County Arts Coun., Inc., 2003-06, sec., 2004; dir. Finger Lakes Chamber Music Festival, 2007. Mem. Fed. Bar Assn., NY State Bar Assn. (former mem. state and county bar assn. coms.), Onondaga County Bar Assn., Kiwanis (bd. dirs. Onondaga club 1988-89, v.p. 1989, pres. 1989-91). Patentee safety device for disabled airplanes. Home Phone: 315-536-4052.

MATHEWSON, MARK STUART, lawyer, editor; b. Pana, Ill., Mar. 6, 1955; s. Raymond Glenn and Frances (King) M.; m. Barbara Jean Siegert, Oct. 30, 1980; children: Margie, Molly. BA, U. Wis., Madison, 1978; JD, U. Ill., 1984; MA, U. Iowa, 1985. Bar: Ill. 1985. Reporter Ill. Times, Springfield, 1985; asst. prof. Culver Stockton Coll., Canton, Mo., 1986—87; pvt. practice Pana, Ill., 1987—2000; mng. editor Ill. Bar Jour., Ill. State Bar Assn., Springfield, dir. legal pub., 2000—. Home: RR 1 Box 2 Athens IL 62613-9787 Office: Ill State Bar Assn Ill Bar Journal Ill Bar Ctr Springfield IL 62701

MATHIAS, ALICE IRENE, business management consultant; b. NYC, Mar. 2, 1949; d. Murray and Charlotte (Kottle) Mathias. BS in Math., Western New Eng. Coll., 1972. Programmer Carnation Co., LA, 1973-78; programmer/analyst Cedars-Sinai Med. Ctr., LA, 1978-79, Union Bank, LA, 1979-81; group leader Kaiser Found. Health Plan, Pasadena, Calif., 1981-98; sr. cons. KPMG LLP, LA, 1998—99; prin. Info. Tech. Mgmt., LA, 1999—. Mem. NAFE, Am. Mgmt. Assn., L.A. County Mus. Art (sponsor), Smithsonian Inst., KCET Pub. TV, Choice In Dying, U.S. Holocaust Meml. Mus. (charter mem.), Caithness Collectors Club, Statue of Liberty Ellis Island Found. Home: 2031 Dracena Drive Apt 320 Los Angeles CA 90027 Office: Info Tech Mgmt 2031 Dracena Dr Ste 320 Los Angeles CA 90027

MATHIAS, ANDREW, real estate company executive; b. Buffalo, 1974; m. Tina Mathias. BS, U. Penn. Wharton Sch. With Bear Stearns & Co., Capital Trust/Victor Capital Group, NYC; chief investment officer SL Green Realty Corp., NYC, 1999—. Office: SL Green Realty Corp 420 Lexington Ave New York NY 10170 Office Phone: 212-594-2700. Office Fax: 212-216-1785. *

MATHIAS, EDWARD JOSEPH, merchant banker; b. Camden, NJ, Nov. 11, 1941; s. Edward Joseph and Zelma (Pollack) M.; 1 child, Ellen Susannah; m. Dale Lenzner, June 5, 2004. BA, U. Pa., 1964; MBA, Harvard U., 1971. Mng. dir., bd. dirs., mem. mgmt. com. T. Rowe Price Assocs., Inc., Balt., 1971-93; mng. dir. Carlyle Group Merchant Bank, Washington, 1994—. Bd. dirs. Victory Acquisition Corp., Nexcen Corp. Endeavor Acquisition Corp.; adv. bd. Diligence, Inc., Washington. Trustee U. Pa.; dean's adv. bd. Harvard Bus. Sch.; active Nat. Gallery Art, NAD and Gallery Art; trustee's coun., co-chmn. pres.'s cir. Nat. Gallery Art. Lt. USN, 1964—69. Mem. Coun. Fgn. Rels., Harvard Club, Univ. Club (NYC), Columbia Country Club (Chevy Chase, Md.), Robert Trent Jones Golf Club (Manassas, Va.), Coral Beach Club (Bermuda), Carnegie Abbey (Portsmouth, RI), The Brook (NYC), Met. Club (Washington), Georgetown Club (Washington), Country Club New Bedford (Mass.). Independent. Office: The Carlyle Group 1001 Pennsylvania Ave NW Washington DC 20004-2505 Office Phone: 202-626-1228. E-mail: edward.mathias@carlyle.com.

MATHIAS, JAMES D., lawyer; b. Washington, Mar. 6, 1961; BA magna cum laude, Amherst Coll., 1983; JD magna cum laude, Georgetown Univ., 1988. Bar: Md. 1988, DC 1996, US Dist. Ct. (Md., DC districts), US Ct. Appeals (4th cir.), US Tax Ct. Law clk. Hon. J. Frederick Motz US Dist. Ct. (Md. dist.); chair Balt. litig. dept., fin. svcs. group DLA Piper Rudnick Gray Cary, 1997—. Assoc. editor Georgetown Law Jour. Bd. dir. Babe Ruth Birthplace and Mus., 2003—; dir., fin. com. mem. Fund for Edul. Excellence, 2002—. Mem.: ABA, Balt. City Bar Assn., Fed. Bar Assn. (bd. gov., Md. chapter 2002—), Serjeants Inn Law Club, Order of Coif. Office: DLA Piper US LLP 6225 Smith Ave Baltimore MD 21209-3600 Office Phone: 410-580-4208. Office Fax: 410-580-3208. Business E-Mail: james.mathias@dlapiper.com.

MATHIAS, JOSEPH MARSHALL, lawyer, judge; b. Frankfort, Ky., Jan. 23, 1914; s. Harry L. and Catherine Snead (Marshall) M.; children: Mark Wellington, Marcia Ann Mathias Wilson, Marilyn Roberta. AB, U. Md., 1935; JD, Southeastern U., 1942. Bar: Md. 1942, U.S. Supreme Ct. 1949, U.S. Dist. Ct. Md. 1963. Ptnr. Moorman and Mathias, 1946-50, Jones, Mathias and O'Brien and predecessor firms, 1950-65; judge Md. Tax Ct., 1959-65; assoc. judge Circuit Ct. of Montgomery County (Md.), 1965-80; chief judge 6th Jud. Circuit of Md., 1980-81; spl. assignments, 1981-83; spl. counsel Beckett, Cromwell & Myers, P.A., 1983-88; of counsel Frank, Bernstein, Conaway and Goldman, 1988-92. Past dir. Nat. Bank Md., Bank So. Md.; former mem. adv. bd. Citizens Bank and Trust Co. Chmn. Bd. Property Rev., Montgomery, Md., 1992-2006. Served with USN, 1942-46. Recipient cert. of disting. citizenship Gov. of Md., 1981. Mem. ABA, Md. State Bar Assn., Md. Bar Found., Montgomery County Bar Assn., Am. Judicature Soc. Democrat. Roman Catholic. Home: 10011 Summit Ave Kensington MD 20895-3835 Personal E-mail: rwmjmm@erols.com.

MATHIAS, LESLIE MICHAEL, electronic manufacturing company executive; b. Bombay, Dec. 17, 1935; arrived in US, 1957; s. Paschal Lawrence and Dulcine M.; m. Vivian Mae Doolittle, Dec. 16, 1962. BSc, U. Bombay, 1957; BS, San Jose State U., Calif., 1961. Elec. engr. Indian Standard Metal, Bombay, 1957; sales engr. Bleisch Engring. and Tool, Mt. View, Calif., 1958-60; gen. mgr. Meadows Terminal Bds., Cupertino, Calif., 1961-63; prodn. mgr. Sharidon Corp., Menlo Park, Calif., 1963-67, Videx Corp., Sunnyvale, Calif., 1967-68, Data Tech. Corp., Mt. View, 1968-69; pres. L.G.M. Mfg., Inc., Mt. View, 1969-83; pvt. practice plating cons. Los Altos, Calif., 1983-87; materials mgr. Excel Cirs., Santa Clara, Calif., 1987-91, 93-98, acct. mgr., 1991-93, materials mgr., 1993-98, internat. materials mgr., 2000—03; buyer Planned Parenthood, San Jose, Calif., 1998-2000; acct. mgr. Streamline Circuits, Santa Clara, Calif., 2003—04. Social chmn. Internat. Students, San Jose, 1958—59. Mem. Nat. Fedn. Ind. Bus., Calif. Cirs. Assn., Better Bus. Bur., Purchasing Assn., U.S. C. of C. Roman Catholic. Avocations: electronics, reading. Home: 20664 Mapletree Pl Cupertino CA 95014-0449 Personal E-mail: hopalongles@netzero.net, hopalonges@earthlink.net.

MATHIAS, MARGARET GROSSMAN, manufacturing company executive, leasing company executive; b. Detroit; d. D. Ray and Lila May (Skinner) Grossman; children: Deborah, Robert, Lesley, Jennifer, Mary. BA, Mt. Holyoke Coll.; cert., Am. Acad. Art. Artist and co-mgr. Mary Chase Marionettes, NYC; exec. v.p. Star Five Corp., Elkhart, Ind., 1975-88, pres., treas., chmn. bd., 1985-90; sec., chmn. bd. L & J Press Corp., Elkhart, 1985-91, also chmn. bd. dirs.; chmn., pres., CEO Magland Co., Elkhart, 1986—, Magco Inc., Elkhart, 1986—; pres., chmn., CEO Tech Products, Inc., Elkhart, 1992—. Mem. fin. com. United Fund, Elkhart; mem. parents adv. bd. Furman U., Greenville, SC, 1978-83, mem. art adv. bd. Mt. Holyoke Coll., South Hadley, Mass., 1982—; pres. Tri Kappa Svc. Orgn., Elkhart, 1965-66; trustee Stanley Clark Sch., South Bend, Ind., 1977-87; bd. dirs. Bridgework Theatre, Goshen, Ind., also Balt., 1996—; mem. adv. bd. Ruthmere 1910 House Mus. designated one of Am.'s castles, 1999—; instr., spkr. etiquette Montessori Schs., Elkhart, 1998—; vol. Dept. Edn., 2003, Art Inst. Chgo., 2003; weekly vol. dept. edn. Art Inst. Chgo. Recipient Lawson Top Sculpture Purchase award Midwest Mus. Am. Art, 1990. Mem. Elkhart C. of C., Elcona Country Club (Elkhart), Woman's Athletic Club (Chgo.), Thursday Club (Elkhart, pres. 1976). Republican. Avocations: sculpting, travel, skiing. Home: 1077 Greenleaf Blvd Apt 101 Elkhart IN 46514-3562 Office: 429 S Main St Elkhart IN 46516-3210 Office Phone: 574-293-5941.

MATHIAS, REUBEN VICTOR (VIC MATHIAS), organization executive, real estate investor; b. Copperas Cove, Tex., Mar. 5, 1926; s. Alvin E. and Ella L. (Teinert) M.; m. Helen I. Thoresen, Jan. 28, 1950; children: Mona, Mark, Matt. BBA, U. Tex., 1950. Cert. Chamber Exec. Dist. mgr. W.A. Shaeffer Pen Co., Youngstown, Ohio, 1950-51; mgr. Cen-Tex Fair, Temple, Tex., 1951-52; dir. info. Tex. Assn. Soil Conservation Suprs., Temple, 1952-53; mgr. membership dept. Austin (Tex.) C. of C., 1953-56, chief exec. officer, 1956-82; dir. corp. devel. Hardin Corp., Austin, 1983-86; real estate and investments, 1987-92; pres. Tex. Travel Industry Assn., Austin, 1992-96. V.p. Austin Tours, Inc.; sec. Longhorn Caverns, Inc.; chmn. bd., instr. Inst. for Orgn. Mgmt., U. Houston; mgmt. cons. not-for-profit orgns., 1997-2003. Contbr. monthly editorial Thoughts While Thinking to Austin Mag., 1961-82. Pres. Austin USO Council, 1958-59; v.p. Beautify Tex. Council, 1975-77; founding pres. Discover Tex. Assn., 1969-71; chmn. Central Tex. Blood Donor Fund, 1979. Served with U.S. Army, 1944-46. Mem. Am. C. of C. Execs., Tex. C. of C. Execs. (pres. 1965), Rotary (pres. Austin 1985-86). Lutheran. Home: 3100 Mistywood Cir Austin TX 78746-7861 *You can find happiness only by giving it to others. Much of my life has been devoted to community building through voluntary action. The fact that my career has allowed me to stay in one community has made it possible for me to make and carry out long-term plans, both for the community and personally.*

MATHIAS, ROBERT JOSEPH, lawyer; b. Washington, Dec. 29, 1955; s. Wilbur J. and Elizabeth J. (Christenson) M.; m. Susan Joy Sawyer, Nov. 29, 1980; children: Christine Joy, Joan Castleton. BA, Yale U., 1977; JD, Harvard U., 1980. Bar: Md. 1980, D.C. 1993, U.S. Dist. Ct. Md. 1981, U.S. Ct. Appeals (4th cir.) 1981. Law clk. Hon. Joseph H. Young U.S. Dist. Ct., Balt., 1980-81; lawyer Piper & Marbury, L.L.P., Balt., 1981-83; asst. U.S. atty. U.S. Atty's. Office, Balt., 1983-88; ptnr. Piper & Marbury, then Piper Marbury Rudnick & Wolfe, Balt., 1988—2004; ptnr., joint global litig. leader, chmn. U.S. Litigation practice DLA Piper Rudnick Gray Cary, Balt., 2005—, mem. US exec. com., Global Bd. Faculty Md. Inst. for Continuing Legal Edn. Firm rep. Ctr. for Pub. Resources Inst. for Dispute Resolution; bd. dirs. Pub. Justice Ctr., Cmty. Mediation Prog. 1999-; trustee, mem. exec. com. Balt. Mus. Art 2001-; trustee 2000-, pres. 2001-03 Calvert Sch., chair United Way Leadership Campaign. Recipient Leadership in Law award, Daily Record, 2004. Fellow, Am. Bar Found., Am. Coll. Trial Lawyers; mem. Serjeant's Inn, Fed. Bar Assn. (bd. govs.), Md. State Bar Assn. (jud. adminstrn. sect. coun.), Harvard Law Sch. Assn. of Md. (treas.), Yale Alumni Assn. of Md. (pres. 1991-94). Office: DLA Piper Rudnick Gray Cary 6225 Smith Ave Baltimore MD 21209-3600 Office Phone: 410-580-4209. Office Fax: 410-580-3209. Business E-Mail: robert.mathias@dlapiper.com.

MATHIESON, GARRETT ALFRED, insurance brokerage executive; b. Bronxville, NY, June 12, 1952; s. William Frederick and Susan (Prager) M.; m. Doris King, June 21, 1980; children: Christine, William. BA, Hobart Coll., 1974; MBA, N.Y. U., 1980. Account rep. Marsh & McLennan, NYC, 1974-77; sr. broker Frank B. Hall & Co., NYC, 1977-78; risk mgmt. cons. Marsh & McLennan, NYC, 1978-80, cons. mgr.-asst. v.p., 1980-82, v.p., mgr. world consulting svcs., 1982-85; mng. cons. Towers Perrin Forster & Crosby, NYC, 1985-86; sr. v.p. Jardine Ins. Brokers, NYC, 1986-90; exec. v.p. Rollins Burdick Hunter, NYC, 1990-92; chmn., CEO, Rollins Hudig Hall Pa., Phila., 1992-94; vice chmn. Aon Risk Svcs., 1994—99; pres., CEO Willis Risk Solutions, NYC, 1999—2005; pres. Lockton Co. LLC, NYC, 2006—. Seminar mgr. World Trade Inst., 1982-84. Contbr. articles to profl. jour. Mem.: Univ. Glee Club, Kiawah Island Club, Shenorock Shore Club, Siwanoy Country Club. Presbyterian. Avocations: vocal music, theater, golf, tennis. Office: Lockton Co LLC 7 Times Sq New York NY 10036

MATHIEU, GAIL DENNISE, ambassador; b. NJ; m. Erick Mathieu; 1 child, Yuri. BA in Spanish and Latin Am. studies, Antioch Coll., 1973; JD, Rutgers U., 1976. Bar: N.J. 1976, D.C. 1977. Dep. chief of mission in Accra; U.S. observer UNESCO, 1991—95; dep. office dir. Pacific Island affairs US Dept. State, 1995—97, dep. office dir. of West African affairs, 1997—99, dep. chief of mission Accra, 1999—2002, U.S. amb. to Niger, 2002—. Asst. prosecutor City of Newark, NJ.

MATHIEU, GEORGES VICTOR ADOLPHE, artist; b. Boulogne, France, Jan. 27, 1921; s. Adolphe Mathieu d'Escaudoeuvres and Madeleine Dupre d'Ausque. Student, Facultés de droit et des lettres, Lille, France. Tchr. English; mgr. pub. rels. U.S. Lines. Exhbns. include Paris, 1950, N.Y.C., 1952, Japan, 1957, Scandinavia, 1958, Eng., Spain, Italy, Switzerland, Fed. Republic Germany, Austria and S.Am., 1959, Middle East, 1961-62, Can., 1963, Musée Municipal d'Art Moderne, Paris, 1963, Galerie Charpentier, Paris, 1965, Musée Nat. d'Art Moderne, Paris, 1967, Musée de la Manufacture Nat. des Gobelins, 1969, Antibes, 1976, Ostend, 1977, Grand Palais, Paris, 1978, Wildenstien Gallery, N.Y.C., Dominion Gallery, Montreal, Que., Can., 1979, Musée de la Poste, Paris, 1980, Palais des Papes, Avignon, 1985, Galerie Sapone, Nice, 1987, Galerie Protée, Paris, 1988, Abbaye de Chateautoux, France, 1990, Musée de Boulogne Sur Mer, St. Germain en Laye, 1994, Refectoize des Jacobins, Toulouse, 1995, Jeu De Paume, 2002, Liege (Belguim), 2003, Milano (Italia), 2003; prin. works include Hommage à la Mort, 1950, Hommage au Marechal de Turenne, 1952, Les Capetiens Partout, 1954, La Victoire de Denain, 1963, Hommage à Jean Cocteau, 1963, Paris, Capitale des Arts, 1965, Hommages aux Freres Boisseree, 1967, Hommages à Condillac, 1968, La prise de Berg op Zoom, 1969, Election de Charles Quint, 1971, Matta-Salums, 1978, La Liberation de Paris, 1980, La liberation d'Orleans par Jeanne d'Arc, 1982, Le Massacre des 269, 1985, Paradis des Orages, 1988, Les enfants de Bogota, 1989, Rumeurs de Paradis, 1991; designed gardens and bldgs. for B.C. transformer factory, Fontenay-le-comte, 1966; 16 posters for Air France; tapestries; 18 medals for Paris Mint, 1971, new 10 F coin, 1974; creater Tachism; author: Audela du Tachisme; Le privilege d'Etre; De la Revolté à Rénaissance; La Réponse de l'Abstraction lyrique; L'Abstraction Prophetique, Les Massacre de la Sensibilité, Desormais, Seul en Face de Dieu, Mathieu: 50 Years of Creation; represented in 90 museums and pub. collections. Mem. Acad. Fine Arts.

MATHIEU, HENRI DONAT See SAINT LAURENT, YVES

MATHIEU, MICHELE SUZANNE, grant writer, computer scientist, consultant; b. Chgo., Mar. 24, 1950; d. Joseph Edward Mathieu and Mary Ellen Fisher; m. Robert Steven Harris, May 1, 1988 (dec. Sept. 2000); life ptnr. Kathryn Ruth Huff, Aug. 16, 2002. BS in Mktg., Regents Coll., Albany, NY, 1998; cert. web site design, Columbia Coll., Chgo., 2000; cert. in Perl and CGI Scripting, San Diego C.C., 2003. Microsoft cert. profl. Broadcast coord. Grey-North Advt., Chgo., 1967-71; head drama dept. Patricia Stevens Coll., Chgo., 1972; instr. beginning acting Ted Liss Sch. Performing Arts, Chgo., 1973-75; project coord. grants and contracts Am. Dietetic Assn., Chgo., 1974-81, adminstr. govt. affairs, 1981-86, mgr. licensure comm., 1986-90, adminstr. nutrition svcs. payment systems, 1990-94, team leader, health care fin. team, 1994-97, dir. health care fin. team, 1998—2000, dir. mem. web, 2000—01, dir. applications devel., 2001—02; technician Networks Plus Tech. Group, San Diego, 2003—04; pc imaging technician Knowledge Info. Solutions, San Diego, 2004; dir. grants and contracts Virtual Reality Med. Ctr., San Diego, 2004—. Grant proposal cons. various performance arts, Chgo., 1978-2000; med. reporter, writer various internat. clients, 1994-; PC cons., Chgo., 1994-2002, San Diego, 2002—. Editor Legis. Newsletter, 1981-86; contbg. editor Nutrition Forum, 1986, Courier, 1987—2002; contbr. articles to profl. jours., mags., newspapers. Website project mgr. DigitalEve, Chgo., 2001. Ill. Arts Coun. grantee, 1981. Mem. Am. Med. Writers Assn., Am. Soc. Assn. Execs. (Excellence in Govt. award 1989), WebSanDiego. Avocations: reading, fitness walking, sailing.

MATHIEU, SUSAN LEIFER, recreational therapist, educator; b. Long Beach, Calif., Nov. 13, 1952; d. Sally and Oscar Solomon Leifer; m. Jeff Mathieu, Mar. 20, 1976; children: Joseph Gabriel Mathieu 18, Daniel Jacob Mathieu 16. BA, Calif. State U., Long Beach, 1975, MS, 1992; EdD, U. La Verne, 1999. Cert. therapeutic recreation specialist Nat. Coun. Therapeutic Recreation, 1984. Lectr. Calif. State U., Dominquez Hills, 1990—2002, asst. prof. Long Beach, 2002—. Therapeutic recreation tng., cons. Child-Net, Long Beach, 1989—. Contbr. articles to profl. jours. Recreation commr. City of Long Beach, Parks, Recreation and Harbor Recreation Commn., 1981—85; bd. dirs. Jr. League, Long Beach, 1983—2005, PTA, Rancho Palos Verdes, Calif., 1994—99; sisterhood bd. dirs. Congregation Ner Tamid, Rancho Palos Verdes, Calif., 2000—04. Recipient Spl. Recognition award, Cath. Charities Family Shelter for Homeless, 1996, Golden Rule award, JC Penny, 1998. Mem.: Nat. Recreation and Pk. Assn. (assoc.; spkr. 1996—2005, Profl. award Pacific S.W. region 1984, 1994), Long Beach Area Child and Domestic Violence Coun. (assoc.; spkr.), Calif. Pk. and Recreation Soc. (assoc.; com. chair 1998—99, Outstanding Therapeutic Recreation Educator award 1996), Calif. State U. Long Beach Alumni Assn. (bd. dirs. 2004—05), Guild for Infant Survival (assoc.; parent support 1990—95), Chi Kappa Rho Gamma (assoc.; scholarship com. 2002—04, mem. women in leisure svcs.). Jewish. Achievements include first to introduced reading to former gang members in a residential treatment facility. Avocations: kayaking, drums, international folk dancing, developing comedy routines as a teaching tool, guitar. Office: Calif State Univ Long Beach 1250 Bellflower Blvd Long Beach CA 90840 Home Phone: 310-995-8237; Office Phone: 562-985-8075. Office Fax: 562-985-8154. Business E-Mail: smathieu@csulb.edu.

MATHIEU BYERS, DEBORAH ANNE, performing company executive; d. Edward F. and Marjorie V. Mathieu; m. Stephen Paul Byers, June 29, 1996. Studied with, Nafe Katter, Jerry Rojo, 1976—77; BFA, U. Conn., 1978; studied at, A.C.T., San Francisco, 1978; studied with, Ray Burke, 1978, Charles Hampton and Stuart Chenoweth, 1979; MA, San Francisco State U., 1979; studied with, Michael Graves, NYC, 1984; master classes, Kate Collins, NYC, 1987; studied at, Video Assoc., 1990, Three of Us Studios, NYC, 1994, HB Studios, 1994. Exec. asst. to pres. and owner prodn. coord. Silver Blue Prodn., Ltd., NYC, 1982—86; freelance promoter and pub. rels. coord. Deborah Mathieu Consulting, Inc., 1984—90, designer makeup, hair and costume, 1987—90; assoc. casting dir. Stark Naked Prodn. Elsie Stark Casting, 1994—97; exec. asst. to owner R & V Internat. Inc., 1986—2002; chairperson acting technique dept. Sch. for Film and TV, 1995—2000; founder, president and producing artistic dir. Streetlight Prodn., Inc., 2000—. Pvt. acting coach, NYC, 1995—. Dir.: (plays) Chamber Music, 1979, Ghost Sonata, 1978, Your Carolyn Skiddoo Period, 1995, Communion, 2002, Cityscapes, 2002, Yearning for the Fourth Grade, 2002, Leavin' the Life & Hangin' at Joe's, 2003, Faith, Hope and Charity, 2004, The American Dream and Other Fractured Fairy Tales, 2005; actor: Bus Stop, 1978, A Midsummer's Night Dream, 1978, West Side Story, 1978, Anne of a Thousand Days, 1979, Macbeth, 1979, Chamber Music, 1980, A Faded Rose, 1980, Comedy Tonite!, 1982, All Ye Faithful, 1982, Reasonable Circulation, 1983, Lullaby Eve, 1986, Law School Suicide, 1990, Mary Tudor, 1993, Mary Stuart, 1994, The Knickerbockers, 1995, Nicola Sacco & Bartolomeo Vanezetti, 1999, Hamlet, 2001; dir., actor: (plays) Leaving My Apartment & Other Urban Adventures, 2003; (films) The Deadliest Season, 1976, U.H.F., 1988, Guess Who?, 1989, Dreamstreets, 1989, Funny About Love, 1989, State of Grace, 1989, Quiet on the Set!, 1990, Heidi Loves Missy, 1993, Annie, 1995; (TV series) The Days and Nights of Molly Dodd, 1988—90, Saturday Night Live, 1994, (commercials and industrial films); choreographer Jumpers, San Francisco, 1977, The Darkening of the Light, 1978; costumer: The Tempest, 1978. Mem.: AFTRA, SAG, Theatre Comm. Guild, Actors Equity Assn., The Drama League. Democrat. Office: Streetlight Prodns 110-64 Queens Blvd PMB 175 Forest Hills NY 11375

MATHILE, CLAYTON LEE, pet food company executive; b. Portage, Ohio, Jan. 11, 1941; s. Wilbert and Helen (Good) Mathile; m. Mary Ann Maas, July 7, 1962; children: Cathy, Tim, Mike, Tina, Jennie. BA, Ohio No. U., 1962; postgraduate studies, Bowling Green State U., 1964; DBA (hon.), Ohio No. U., 1991. Acct. GM, Napoleon, Ohio, 1962-63, Campbell Soup Co., Napoleon, 1963-65, buyer, 1965-67, purchasing agt., 1967-70; gen. mgr. The Iams Co., Dayton, Ohio, 1970-75, v.p., 1975-80, chief exec. officer, 1980-90, chmn., 1990-99, also dir.; ret., 1999. Mem. Pet Food Inst.; bd. dirs. Midwest Grp., Cin., Bush Bros. Co., Knoxville, Tenn., The Iams Co., 1999—. Author: A Bus. Owner's Perspective on Outside Bds. Trustee Chaminade-Julienne HS, Dayton, 1987—, U. Dayton; mem. adv. bd. coll. bus. Ohio No. U., Ada, 1987—, also trustee. Named Best of Best Ctr. for Values Rsch., Houston, 1987; named one of 400 Richest Ams. Forbes mag., 2006. Mem. Am. Mgmt. Assn., Am. Agt. Assn. Roman Catholic. Avocations: travel, swimming, golf. Office: The Iams Co PO Box 13615 Dayton OH 45413-0615

MATHIS, CATHERINE J., publishing executive; BS in Bus. Adminstrn., Univ. Minn., 1975, MBA in Mktg., Mgmt. Info. Sys., 1979. Mkt. rsch. analyst Internat. Paper Co., Purchase, NY, 1980—81, mgr. bus. sys., 1981—84, mgr. sales analysis, 1984—87, mgr. shareholder comm., 1987—92; former v.p. corp. rels. Overseas Shipholding Group Inc.; dir. investor rels NY Times Co., NYC, 1997—2000, v.p. corp. comm., 2000—; and spokesperson NY Times and The Times Co., 2000—. Dir. Nat. Investor Rels. Inst., 2005—. Office: Corp Comm NY Times Co 229 W 43rd St New York NY 10036 Office Phone: 212-556-1981. Business E-Mail: mathis@nytimes.com.

MATHIS, JAMES FORREST, retired petroleum company executive; b. Dallas, Sept. 28, 1925; s. Forrest and Martha (Godbold) M.; m. Frances Ellisor, Sept. 4, 1948; children: Alan Forrest (dec.), Lisa Lynn Lambeth. BSChE, Tex. A&M U., 1946; MS, U. Wis., 1951, PhD, 1953. Rsch. engr. Humble Oil & Refining Co., Baytown, Tex., 1946-49, 53-61, mgr. R & D, 1961-63, mgr. Splty. products planning, 1963-65; v.p. Exxon Rsch. & Engring. Co., Linden, NJ, 1966-68; sr. v.p., dir. Imperial Oil Ltd., Toronto, Ont., Canada, 1968-71; v.p. tech. Exxon Chem. Co., Florham Pk., NJ, 1971-80; v.p. sci. and tech. Exxon Corp., NYC, 1980-84; ret., 1984. Cons. Arthur D. Little, 1985-92, ChemShare Corp., 1989-92; chmn. N.J. Commn. Sci and Tech., 1988-96; dir. Laser Recording Systems, Inc., 1989-93, N L Industries, 1985-86, Hanlin Corp., 1989-99, Beaver Lake Realty Co., 1995-98. Bd. dirs. Chem. Industry Inst. Toxicology, 1975-83, treas., 1977-80, chmn., 1980-83; bd. dirs. Tex. Inst. for Advancement of Chem. Tech., 2001-; trustee Wis. Alumni Rsch. Found., 1984-2004, pres., 1993-97; bd. chem. sci. and tech. of Nat. Rsch. Coun., 1987-89, chem. weapon stockpile demilitarization comn., 1998-2001. Served with AC, USNR, 1944-45 Recipient Disting. Alumni award Coll. Engring. Tex. A&M U., 1982, Disting. Svc. citation Coll. Engring. U. Wis., 1969. Fellow Am. Inst. Chem. Engrs. (interim exec. dir., sec. 1987-88, Robert L. Jacks award in Mgmt. 1985, Van Antwerpen award for Svc. to Inst. 1989); mem. AAAS, NAE, Am. Chem. Soc. (Earle B. Barnes award for Chem. Rsch. Mgmt. 1984), Sigma Xi, Phi Lambda Upsilon, Tau Beta Pi. Presbyterian. Achievements include 2 patents in field. Home: 2714 S Southern Oaks Dr Houston TX 77068-2600 Office Phone: 281-587-0117. Personal E-mail: jfmathis@aol.com.

MATHIS, JOHN PRENTISS, lawyer; b. New Orleans, Feb. 10, 1944; s. Robert Prentess and Lena (Horton) M.; m. Karen Elizabeth McHugh, May 31, 1966; children: Lisa Lynne Mathis Kirkpatrick, Andrew P. BA magna cum laude, So. Meth. U., 1966; JD cum laude, Harvard U., 1969. Bar: Calif. 1970, D.C. 1975, U.S. Ct. Appeals (D.C. cir.) 1972, U.S. Ct. Appeals (5th cir.) 1975, U.S. Ct. Appeals (3d cir.) 1980, U.S. Supreme Ct. 1982. Assoc. Latham & Watkins, LA, 1969-71; spl. asst. to gen. counsel FPC, Washington, 1971-72; gen. counsel Calif. Pub. Utilities Commn., San Francisco, 1972-74; assoc. Baker & Botts, Washington, 1974-76, ptnr., 1976-92, Hogan & Hartson, Washington, 1992—2000; v.p., assoc. gen. counsel regulatory affairs Edison Mission Energy, Washington, 2000—06. Bd. dirs. Chesapeake Wildlife Heritage, Easton, Md., Talbot Preservation Alliance, Easton, Mid-Atlantic Symphony Orch., Ocean City, Md. Mem. ABA (litig. sect., chmn. energy litig. com. 1985-89, divsn. dir. 1989-90, chmn. legis. com. 1990-94, rep. to coord. group energy law 1992-97), Fed. Energy Bar Assn., Harvard U. Law Sch. Assn. D.C. (past pres.), Congl. Country Club, Met. Club (Washington), Talbot Country Club (Easton, Md.). Republican. Episcopalian. Home Phone: 410-822-4209. Personal E-mail: john.p.mathis@gmail.com.

MATHIS, KAREN J., lawyer, legal association administrator; b. Providence, Nov. 7, 1950; d. Charles H. Young and Elizabeth L. (Kriegal) Ballard; m. Stan A. Mathis, Sept. 7, 1970 (div. 1978). BA, U. Denver, 1972; JD, U. Colo., 1975; postgrad., U. Colo., Denver, 1975-76; LLD, Sienna Coll., 2003, Sturm Law Sch., U. Denver, 2005. Bar: Colo. Supreme Ct. 1975, U.S. Dist. Ct. 1975, U.S. Ct. Appeals (10th cir.) 1978, U.S. Tax Ct. 1980. Tax acct. Peat Marwick Mitchell, Denver, 1975-76; ptnr. Rothenberg & Mathis, Denver, 1976-79; sole practitioner Denver, 1979-80; assoc. Sterling & Simon PC, Denver, 1980-83; ptnr. Hughes & Dorsey, Denver, 1983-84; shareholder, dir. Sterling & Miller, Denver, 1984-86; pres. The Mathis Law Firm, Denver, 1986—2004; pres., CEO Mathis Asset Mgmt., Inc., Denver, 1989—2004; ptnr. McElroy, Deutsch, Mulvaney & Carpenter LLP, Denver, 2004—. Contbr. articles to profl. jours. Bd. dirs. CORRA, Denver, Planned Parenthood Rocky Mountains, Denver; bd. dirs., v.p. Rocky Mountain Meml. Soc., Denver; mem. adv. com. Colo. Dept. Social Svcs., Denver. Named Disting. Alumni U. Colo., 1992; recipient Order of the Coif (hon.) U. Colo., 2002; named one of The 50 Most Influential Women Lawyers in Am., Nat. Law Jour., 2007. Mem. ABA (ho. of dels. 1982-, interim Colo. state del. 1992-2000, chair standing com. on mem., 1994-97, chair commn. on women in the profession, 1997-2000, chair ho. dels., 2000-02, chair gen. practice, solo & small firm section, 2002-03, pres-elect, 2005-06, pres., 2006-), Colo. Bar Assn. (1st v.p. 1992-93, bd. govs. 1983-, outstanding young lawyer in Colo.), Denver Bar Assn. Office: McElroy Deutsch Mulvaney & Carpenter LLP Mile High Ctr 1700 Broadway Ste 1900 Denver CO 80290 *

MATHIS, LUSTER DOYLE, academic administrator, political scientist, educator; b. Gainesville, Ga., May 5, 1936; s. Luster and Fay Selena (Wingo) M.; m. Rheba Burch, June 5, 1958; children— Douglas James, Deborah Jane. AB, Berry Coll., 1958; MA, U. Ga., 1958, PhD (Univ. Alumni Rsch. fellow), 1966. Asst. prof. polit. sci. Brenau Coll., Gainesville, 1960-61; asso. prof. Calif. Baptist Coll., 1961-62, Belmont Coll., Nashville, 1962-64; asso. prof., head dept. polit. sci. W.Ga. Coll., Carrollton, 1965-68, prof., 1969-75, head dept., 1969-71, chmn. div. grad. studies, 1970-73; assoc. dean, 1972-75; research asso., asst. editor Papers of Thomas Jefferson Princeton U., 1968-69; v.p., dean of coll. Berry Coll., Mt. Berry, Ga., 1975-93, v.p. acad. affairs, 1993-99, provost, 1999-2000, coll. historian, prof. govt., 2000—03. Cons. Citizens Com. on Ga. Gen. Assembly. Co-author: Courts as Political Instruments, 1970. Mem. Ga. Democratic Charter Commn., 1974-75; mem. consumer adv. com. Floyd Med. Center, 1978-80. Fellow, Nat. Hist. Publs. Comm., 1968—69. Mem. Am. Assn. Higher Edn., Am. Conf. Acad. Deans, Ga. Polit. Sci. Assn. (pres. 1968-69). Democrat. Baptist. Office: 200 Salt Air Dr Unit 136 Saint Simons Island GA 31522 Business E-Mail: dmathis@berry.edu.

MATHIS, MARSHA DEBRA, customer service administrator; b. Detroit, Dec. 22, 1953; d. Marshall, Jr. and Anita Willene (Biggers) Mathis. BS, Fla. State U., 1978; MBA, Miss. Coll., 1982. With telecom. dept. Fla. State Dept. Safety, Tallahassee, 1973-76; asst. to chmn. Tallahassee Savs. and Loan Assn., 1976-78; sales engr. Prehler, Inc., Jackson, Miss., 1978-82; mktg. mgr. Norand Corp., Arlington, Tex., 1982-87; v.p. mktg. and sales Profl. Datasolutions, Inc., Irving, Tex., 1987-88; v.p. mktg. and sales, ptnr. Target Systems, Inc., Irving, 1988-89, also bd. dirs.; v.p. mktg. Profl. Datasolutions, Inc., Irving, 1990—2002, Onvance, Atlanta, 2002; v.p. bus. devel. Performance Retail, Austin, Tex., 2004—. Contbr. articles to profl. jours. Advisor Am. Diabetes Assn., Jackson, 1983—, Diabetes Found. Miss., Jackson, 1983—. Mem.: Network Exec. Women, Nat. Assn. Convenience Stores (mem. industry task force 1987—88, mem. supplier com. 2007—), Nat. Adv. Group, Internat. Platform Assn. Republican. Roman Catholic. Avocations: scuba diving, sailing, reading, coin collecting/numismatics. Home: 1615 Purple Sage Dr Cedar Park TX 78613 Office: Dresser Wayne Bldg 2 Ste 101 6500 River Place Blvd Austin TX 78730 Office Phone: 512-527-6623. Personal E-mail: marsha.mathis@wayne.com. Business E-Mail: marsha_mathis@performanceretail.com.

MATHIS, STEPHANIE CHARLOTTE, veterinarian; b. Merced, Calif., Feb. 11, 1974; d. Lewis Moulton and Christyn Errecarte Mathis. BS, U. Calif., Davis, 1996, DVM, 2001. Diplomate Am. Coll. Vet. Surgeons, 2007. Vet. intern Ariz. Equine Med. and Surg. Ctr., Gilbert, Ariz., 2001—02; fellow-large animal medicine and surgery coll. vet. medicine Oreg. State U., Corvallis, 2002—03; resident equine surgery Peterson & Smith Equine Hosp., Ocala, Fla., 2003—06, clin. assoc. equine emergency surgery and critical care, 2006—. Mem.: AVMA, Am. Coll. Vet. Surgeons, Am. Assn. Equine Practitioners. Home Phone: 352-817-4414. Personal E-mail: scmathis01@yahoo.com.

MATHISEN, DOUGLAS J., thoracic surgeon; b. Spring Valley, Ill., 1948; MD, U. Ill. Diplomate Am. Bd. Thoracic Surgery, Am. Bd. Surgery. Thoracic surgeon Mass. Gen. Hosp., Boston, 1995—; asst. prof. thoracic surgery Harvard U. Med. Sch., 1989—99, Hermes C. Grillo prof. thoracic surgery, 1999—; chief general thoracic surgery Mass. Gen. Hosp. Fellow Am. Coll. Surgeons; mem. AMA, ACCPA, Am. Assn. Thoracic Surgery, Soc. Thoracic Surgery (bd. mem.), Cardiothoracic Surgery Network, Thoracic Surgery Directors Assn., Thoracic Surgery Found. for Rsch. & Edn., Soc. Thoracic Surgeons (treas.). Office: Mass Gen Hosp Thoracic Surgery Blake 1570 55 Fruit St Boston MA 02114 Business E-Mail: dmathisen@partners.org.

MATHISEN, HOWARD, psychologist, educator, minister; b. Bklyn., June 3, 1938; s. Olaf and Hjordis K. (Skjaerum) Mathisen; m. Sue Jane Andrews, June 13, 1960 (div. 1975); m. Kathleen Ann Poce, Sept. 20, 1980 (dec. 1987); m. Carolynn Anne Burroughs, Aug. 22, 1992. BA in Psychology, Taylor U., Upland, IN, 1956—60; MDiv, Phila. Theol. Sem., 1960—63; postgrad. in Theology, Luth. Theol. Sem., 1964—65; MA in Religion, Concordia Sem., St. Louis, 1966—67; postgrad. Alcoholism studies, Rutgers U., 1975; postgrad. in Psycholody, Assumption Coll., Worcester, MA, 1971—76; DMin in Psychology, Andover Newton Theol. Sch., 1972—76. Lic. psychologist, Mass., marriage and family therapist, Mass.; cert. diplomate of sex therapy Am. Assn. Sexuality Educators, Counselors and Therapists; diplomate in marital and sex therapy Am. Bd. Family Psychology; diplomate Am. Bd. Sexology. Pastor Christ Meml. Ch., Phila., 1962-66, Zion Luth. Ch., Webster, Mass., 1967-73; dir. Human Svcs. Ctr. Hubbard Regional Hosp., Webster, 1973-81; pvt. practice psychology Boylston, Mass., 1976-81; co-dir. Counseling Affiliates, Worcester, Mass., 1981-97; dir. pastoral counseling Boston Road Clinic, Worcester, 1997—2001; dir. credentialing svcs. Capstan, Worcester, 1998-99; asst. pastor Concordia Luth. Ch., Worcester, 1976-98; dir. min. asst. program New Eng. Synod, Evangelical Luth. Ch., 1991—; psychologist Prescott Health Care, 2002—. Adj. instr. psychology Nichols Coll., Dudley, Mass., 1981, Assumption Coll., Worcester, 1983-86. Dean ctrl. Mass. conf. New Eng. Synod, Luth. Ch., 1988-90; bd. dirs. Luth. Svc. Assn. New Eng., 1973-87, vice chmn., 1983-85, chmn., 1985-87; bd. dirs. Luth. Home of Worcester, 1987-92, chmn., 1987-89; chmn. bldg. com. Luth. Nursing Home, Worcester, 1977-79; chmn. Family Svcs. Com., 1981-83; mem. Mass. Adv. Com. Continuing Edn. for Nursing, 1979-81; bd. dirs. Family Planning Svcs. Ctrl. Mass., 1975-81; mem. tech. adv. subcom. substance abuse Ctrl. Mass. Health Sys. Agy., 1979-80. Fellow Acad. Family Psychology, Am. Acad. Clin. Sexologists; mem. APA, Am. Assn. Marriage and Family Therapy, Mass. Psychol. Assn., Mass. Assn. Marriage and Family Therapy, Acad. Managed Care Providers. Lutheran. Avocations: travel, photography. Home: 6 Camelot Cir Dudley MA 01571-6110 Office: Prescott Health Care 95 Lincoln St Worcester MA 01605 Office Phone: 508-754-1803. E-mail: mathisen@charter.net.

MATHIS-THORTON, DIANNA DAWN, protective services official, writer, publishing executive, not-for-profit developer; b. Dallas, Tex., Nov. 16, 1967; d. Jimmie Lee and Billie Jo Mathis; m. Ryan Lee Thorton, Dec. 22, 2002. BS Home security, Fla. Met. Univ., 1989—. Cert. crime prevention inspector Tex., domestic violence counselor. Exec. sec. Sears logistic Svcs., Dallas, 1986—90; police officer Dallas police Depart., Dallas, 1991—; owner, pres. Mathis Pub. Co., Dallas, 1991—; founder, pres. Domestic Awareness, Dallas, 2003—. Instr. safety first Dallas after sch. program, 2004—, future writers of Am., 2005—. Author: Dianna'a poetry of Life, 2001, Safety First Children's Guide, 2004, Future Writers of Am., 2005. Mem. counselor Victim relief Ministries, Dallas, 2004—; mentor, counselor Speak Life Ministries, Dallas, 1999—. Recipient Officer of the Yr, Woman of Dallas Inc., 1998, Nat. Assn. ins. Woman of Dallas Inc., 1998, Life Saving award, Dallas police dept., 1997. Mem.: Intenat. Code Coun. Christian. Avocations: reading, writing, poetry, movie scripts. Office: Dallas Police Dept 725 N Jim Miller Dallas TX 75217

MATHOG, ROBERT HENRY, otolaryngologist, educator; b. New Haven, Apr. 13, 1939; s. William and Tiby (Gans) M.; m. Deena Jane Rabinowitz, June 14, 1964; children: Tiby, Heather, Lauren, Jason. AB, Dartmouth Coll., 1960; MD, NYU, 1964. Diplomate Am. Bd. Facial Plastic and Reconstructive Surgery. Intern Duke Hosp., Durham, NC, 1964-65, resident surgery, 1965-66, resident otolaryngology, 1966-69; practice medicine, specializing in otolaryngology Mpls., 1971-77, Detroit, 1977—; chief of otolaryngology Hennepin County Med. Center, Mpls., 1972-77; asst. prof. U. Minn., 1971-74, asso. prof., 1974-77; prof., chmn. dept. otolaryngology Wayne State U. Sch. Medicine, 1977—. Chief otolaryngology Hennepin County Hosp., Mpls., 1972-77, Harper-Grace Hosps., Detroit, 1977—, Detroit Receiving Hosp., 1977-92; cons. staff VA Hosp., Allen Park, Minn., 1977—, Children's Hosp., Detroit, 1977—, Hutzel Hosp., Detroit, 1966, St. Joseph Mercy Hosp., Oakland, Mich., 2001; mem. adv. coun. Nat. Inst. Deaf and Other Communicable Disorders NIH, 1992-96; chief otolaryngology, head and neck surgery June Hosp., 1994-95. Author: Otolaryngology Clinics of North America, 1976, Textbook of Maxillofacial Trauma, 1983; editor in chief Videomed. Edn. Systems, 1972-75; editor: Atlas of Craniofacial Trauma, 1992; contbr. articles to med. jours. Bd. dirs. Bexer County Hearing Soc., 1969-71; adv. coun. WIDCB, 1993; chmn. Lions Hearing Ctr. S.E. Mich. Maj. USAF, 1969-71. Recipient Valentine Mott medal for proficiency in anatomy, 1961, Recognition award Wayne State Bd. Govs. Faculty, 1993; Deafness Rsch. Found. grantee, 1979-81, NIH grantee, 1986, 92, 96, Lawrence M. Weiner Alumni award Wayne State U. Sch. Med., 1999. Fellow ACS, Am. Acad. Otolaryngology, Head and Neck Surgery (Cert. award 1976, Cert. of Appreciation 1978), Am. Soc. Head and Neck Surgery, Triological Soc. (v.p. 1995-96, mtg. guest of honor 2002, Vice Presdl. Citation award 2004), Am. Otol. Soc., Am. Acad. Facial Plastic and Reconstructive Surgery (v.p. 1980), Am. Neurotology Soc.; mem. AMA, Am. Laryngol. Soc. (coun. 1994—), Am. Laryngol. Assn., Mich. Med. Soc., Am. Head and Neck Soc., Soc. Univ. Otolaryngologists (pres. 1995), Assn. Acad. Depts. Otolaryngology, Assn. Rsch. Otolaryngology (pres. 1981). Home: 27115 Wellington Rd Franklin MI 48025-1329 Office: 43494 Woodward Ste 210 Bloomfield Hills MI 48312 Also: Wayne State U Sch Med 540 E Canfield St Detroit MI 48201-1928

MATHUR, BHAWNESH, electronics executive; B in Chem. Engring., U. Fla., Gainesville; MBA, U. Ariz., Tucson. Various exec. positions IBM, 1979—2000; exec. v.p. global supply chain mgmt. Sanmina-SCI, 2000—03, exec. v.p. Global Logistics and Svcs. divsn. and Server divsn., 2002—05; chief supply chain officer Arrow Electronics, Inc., Melville, NY, 2005—06, sr. v.p. supplier mktg. and asset mgmt. Global Components, 2006—. Office: Arrow Electronics Inc 50 Marcus Dr Melville NY 11747-4210 Office Phone: 631-847-2000. *

MATHUR, IKE, finance educator; b. Jamshedpur, India, Nov. 22, 1943; arrived in US, 1961; s. Robert William and Ivy (Phillips) Mathur; children: Rebecca Lynn, Jason Gabriel. BS, Eastern Mich. U., 1965, MBA, 1968; PhD, U. Cin., 1974. Editor Am. Math. Soc., Providence, 1965-69; rsch. asst. U. Cin., 1969-72; instr. U. Dayton, Ohio, 1972-73; asst. prof. U. Pitts., 1973-77; assoc. prof. fin. So. Ill. U., Carbondale, 1977-81, prof., 1981—, chmn. fin., 1979-92, 94-95, dean Coll. Bus., 1992-94. Mgmt. trainer AID, Washington, 1978—81; Fulbright prof., Turku, Finland, 1983—84, Lisbon, Portugal, 1993. Author: Introduction to Financial Management, 1979, Cases in Managerial Finance, 1984, Personal Finance, 1989, Wealth Creation in Eastern Europe, 1992, Financial Management in Post Europe, 1992. Mem.: Fin. Mgmt. Assn., Midwest Fin. Assn., Western Fin. Assn., French Fin. Assn., Am. Fin. Assn. Avocations: running, martial arts, travel. Home: 4 Oxford Ln Glen Carbon IL 62034-1531 Office: So Ill U Coll Bus Carbondale IL 62901 Office Phone: 618-453-1421. Personal E-mail: imathur@msn.com. Business E-Mail: imathur@cba.siu.edu.

MATHUR, SHISHIR, finance educator, researcher; b. Sept. 17, 1973; BArch, Regional Engring. Coll., Tiruchirrapalli, India, 1995; M in Urban Planning, Sch. Planning and Arch., New Delhi, 1997; PhD, U. Wash., Seattle, 2003. Cert. planner Inst. Town Planners, India, 1997. Acting asst. processor U. Wash., Seattle, 2003—04; dir., inst. met. studies San Jose State U., 2005—, asst. prof., 2004—. Contbr. articles to profl. jours., chapters to books. Grantee, Local Initiatives Support Corp., 2005, Mineta Transport Inst., 2005, 2006, Lincoln Inst. Land Policy, 2006. Office: San Jose State Univ Wsq 216 One Washington Sq San Jose CA 95192-0185 Office Phone: 408-924-5875. Business E-Mail: shishir.mathur@sjsu.edu.

MATIA, PAUL RAMON, lawyer; s. Leo Clemens and Irene Elizabeth (Linkert) M.; m. Nancy Arch Van Meter, Jan. 2, 1993. BA, Case Western Res. U., 1959; JD, Harvard U., 1962. Bar: Ohio 1962, US Dist. Ct. (no. dist.) Ohio 1969. Law clk. Common Pleas Ct. of Cuyahoga County, Cleve., 1963-66, judge, 1985-91; asst. atty. gen. State of Ohio, Cleve., 1966-69, adminstrv. ast. to atty. gen. Columbus, 1969-70; senator Ohio State Senate, Columbus, 1971-75, 79-83; ptnr. Hadley, Matia, Mills & MacLean Co., L.P.A., Cleve., 1975-84, Porter Wright Morris & Arthur LLP, Cleve., 2005—; judge U.S. Dist. Ct. (no. dist.) Ohio, 1991-99, chief dist. judge, 1999—2004, sr. judge, 2005; mem. 6th Cir. Jud. Coun., 1999—2004. Candidate Lt. Gov. Rep. Primary, 1982, Ohio Supreme Ct., 1988. Named Outstanding Legislator, Ohio Assn. for Retarded Citizens, 1974, Watchdog of Ohio Treasury, United Conservatives of Ohio, 1979; recipient Heritage award Polonia Found., 1988. Mem. Fed. Bar Assn., Ohio State Bar Assn., Cleve. Bar Assn., Cuyahoga County Bar Assn., Sixth Cir. (life), Judge John M. Manos Inn of Ct., Club at Key Ctr., Vineyards Country Club, Naples, Fla. Republican. Avocations: skiing, gardening, travel. Office: Porter Wright Morris & Arthur LLP 925 Euclid Ave Ste 1700 Cleveland OH 44115-1483 Office Phone: 216-443-2548. Business E-Mail: pmatia@porterwright.com.

MATIJEVIC, EGON, chemistry professor; b. Otocac, Croatia, Apr. 27, 1922; came to U.S., 1957; s. Grgur and Stefica (Spiegel) M.; m. Bozica Biscan, Feb. 27, 1947. Diploma in Chem. Engring., U. Zagreb, 1944, PhD in Chemistry, 1948, D Habilitation in Phys. Chemistry, 1952; DSc (hon.), Lehigh U., 1977, M. Curie-Sklodowska U., Lublin, Poland, 1990, Clarkson U., 1992, Zagreb U., Croatia, 1998, Nat. U. San Martin, Buenos Aires, 2003, U. Ljubljana, Slovenia, 2003. Instr. chemistry U. Zagreb, 1944-47, sr. instr. phys. chemistry, 1949-52, privat dozent in colloid chemistry, 1952-54, dozent in phys. and colloid chemistry, 1955-56, on leave, 1956-59; rsch. assoc. Inst. Cinematography, Zagreb, 1948; rsch. fellow dept. colloid sci. U. Cambridge, England, 1956-57; vis. prof. Clarkson Coll. Tech., Potsdam, NY, 1957-59, assoc. prof. chemistry Postdam, NY, 1960-62; prof. Clarkson U., Postdam, NY, 1962-86, disting. univ. prof., 1986-99, LaMer prof. colloid and surface sci., 2000—; assoc. dir. Inst. Colloid and Surface Sci. Clarkson Coll. Tech., 1966-68, dir. inst., 1968-81, chmn. dept. chemistry, 1981-87. Vis. prof. Japan Soc. for Promotion Sci., 1973, U. Melbourne, Australia, 1976, Sci. U. Tokyo, 1979, 84, fgn. guest Inst. Colloid and Interface Sci., 82; vis. scientist U. Leningrad, Russia, 1977; advisor IAEA, Buenos Aires, 1978, Buenos Aires, 80; lectr. in field. Author: (with M. Kesler) General and Inorganic Chemistry for Senior High Schools, 11 edits., including Croatian, Macedonian, Hungarian, Italian, 1943-63; translator: Einfuhrung in die Stochiometrie (Nylen and Wigern), 1948; editor: (with Alter J. Weber) Adsorption from Aqueous Solution, 1968, Surface and Colloid Science, vols. 1-17, 1969-2002; contbr. numerous articles to profl. pubs. Recipient Gold medal, Am. Electroplaters Soc., 1976, guest of honor 56th and 63d Colloid and Surface Sci. Symposia, Blacksburg, Va., 1982, Seattle, 1989, Boston, 2002, Egon Matijevic chair endowed in his name, Clarkson U., 1992. Mem. Am. Chem. Soc. (councilor divsn. colloid and surface chemistry 1982-87, chmn. 1969-70, Kendall award 1972, Langmuir Disting. Lectureship award 1985, Ralph K. Iler award 1993), Kolloid Gesellschaft (hon. life, Thomas Graham award 1985), Internat. Assn. Colloid Interface Sci. (pres. 1985-87), Chem. Soc. Japan, Inst. Colloid and Interface Sci. of Sci. U. of Tokyo (hon.), Phalanx Soc., Croatian Acad. Scis. and Arts (fgn.), Am. Ceramic Soc. (hon.), Materials Rsch. Soc. Japan (hon.), Acad. Ceramics (Italy), Croatian Chem. Soc. (hon., Bozo Tezak medal 1991), Sigma Xi (Clarkson Coll. Tech. chpt. award 1972, nat. lectr. 1987-89). Roman Catholic. Office: Ctr Advanced Materials Proc Clarkson U Dept Chem Potsdam NY 13699-5814 Home Phone: 315-265-2263. Business E-Mail: matiegon@clarkson.edu.

MATIS, NINA B., lawyer; b. NYC, June 23, 1947; AB cum laude, Smith Coll., 1969; JD, NYU, 1972. Bar: Ill. 1973. Ptnr. Katten Muchin Zavis Rosenman, Chgo. Adj. prof. law Northwestern U., 1984-87. Named one of 500 Leading Lawyer in Am., Lawdragon, 100 Most Influential Lawyers, Nat. Law Jour., 2006, The 50 Most Influential Women Lawyers in Am., 2007. Mem. Am. Bar Assn., Am. Coll. Real Estate Lawyers, Chicago Fin. Exchange, Chicago Real Estate Exec. Women, Chicago Real Estate Women, Econ. Club of Chicago, Lambda Alpha Internat. (Ely Chpt.), Internat. Coun. of Shopping Centers, Lakefront SRO, Pension Real Estate Assn., Real Estate Fin. Forum, The Chicago Network, Urban Land Inst. Office: Katten Muchin Zavis Rosenman 525 W Monroe St Ste 1600 Chicago IL 60661-3693 Office Fax: 312-577-8686. E-mail: nina.matis@kmzr.com. *

MATISE, JOHN J., investment company executive; s. Salvatore A. and Patricia M. Matise; m. Ann Hayden, 1994; 1 child, Anthony Joseph. BA with high honors, U. Calif., Davis, 1992; MBA, Anderson Sch. UCLA, 2000. Sr. consulant Andersen Cons., San Francisco, 1992—94; mgr. Deloitte Consulting, San Francisco, 1994—97, Accenture, San Francisco, 1997—99; v.p. Encore Venture Partners, LA, 1999—2001; v.p. pvt. equity Wedbush, Inc., LA, 2001—04; prin. Matise Capital, Playa Del Rey, Calif., 2004—; v.p. internat. and s7 Saleen, Inc., Irvine, Calif., 2004—05; COO Small World Kids, Inc., Culver City, 2006; mng. dir. Stone Canyon Venture Partners, L.P., Beverly Hills, 2007—. Mem. The Karma Found., Beverly Hills, Calif., 2005; chmn. UCLA Venture Capital and Pvt. Equity Alumni Assn., Los Angeles, Calif., 2001; mem. UCLA Anderson Sch. Alumni Rels. Bd., Los Angeles, Calif., 2001—05; bd. dir. Small World Kids, Inc., Culver City, Calif., 2004—06. Avocations: travel, outdoor activities. Office: Stone Canyon Venture Prtnrs LP Ste 302 301 N Canon Dr Beverly Hills CA 90210 Office Phone: 310-432-5182. Office Fax: 720-228-1848. Business E-Mail: jmatise@scvp.com.

MATKOWSKI, BETTE, academic administrator; m. Joe Matkowski; 1 child, Anne. BA in English, Mount Union Coll., Alliance, Ohio; MA in English, Ohio State U., Columbus. Tchr., English Ohio pub. schools; faculty Vt. Cmty. Coll., adv., equity officer, dir. western region, dean advancement and enrollment; pres. Lamar Cmty. Coll., Colo., 2000—05, Johnson & Wales U., Denver, 2005—. Named Communicator of Yr., Eastern Region, Nat. Coun. Mktg. and Pub. Rels., 2000; named to Salute to Women 2001, Lamar Daily News; recipient Sister Elizabeth Candon award for disting. svc., Vt. Women in Higher Edn., 2000. Office: Johnson and Wales University Office of Pres 7150 Montview Blvd Denver CO 80220 Office Phone: 303-256-9398. *

MATKOWSKY, BERNARD JUDAH, mathematician, educator; b. NYC, Aug. 19, 1939; s. Morris N. and Ethel H. M.; m. Florence Knobel, Apr. 11, 1965; children: David, Daniel, Devorah. BS, CCNY, 1960; M.E.E., NYU, 1961, MS, 1963, PhD, 1966. Fellow Courant Inst. Math. Scis., NYU, 1961-66; mem. faculty dept. math. Rensselaer Poly. Inst., 1966-77; John Evans prof. applied math., mech. engring. & math. Northwestern U., Evanston, Ill., 1977—, chmn. engring. sci. and applied math. dept., 1993-99. Vis. prof. Tel Aviv U., 1972-73; vis. scientist Weizmann Inst. Sci., Israel, summer 1976, summer 1980, Tel Aviv U., summer 1980; cons. Argonne Nat. Lab., Sandia Labs., Lawrence Livermore Nat. Lab., Exxon Research and Engring. Co. Editor Wave Motion—An Internat. Jour., 1979-99, Applied Math. Letters, 1987—, SIAM Jour. Applied Math., 1976-95, European Jour. Applied Math., 1990-96, Random and Computational Dynamics, 1991-97, Internat. Jour. SHS, 1992—, Jour. Materials Synthesis and Processing, 1992-2002, SIAM Mongraphs Math. Modeling and Computation, 2005—, Mathematical Modeling of Natural Phenomena, 2007—; mem. editl. adv. bd. Springer Verlag Applied Math. Scis. Series; contbr. chpts. to books, articles to profl. jours. Fulbright grantee, 1972-73; Guggenheim fellow, 1982-83 Fellow: AAAS, Am. Phys. Soc., Am. Acad. Mechs.; mem.: Soc. Natural Philosophy, Com. Concerned Scientists, Conf. Bd. Math. Scis. (coun., com. human rights math. scientists), Am. Assn. Combustion Synthesis, Combustion Inst., Am. Math. Soc., Soc. Indsl. and Applied Math., Eta Kappa Nu, Sigma Xi. Home: 3704 Davis St Skokie IL 60076-1745 Office: Northwestern U Technological Institute Evanston IL 60208-0001 Office Phone: 847-491-5396. Business E-Mail: b-matkowsky@northwestern.edu.

MATLINS, STUART M., management consultant, publisher; b. NYC, July 25, 1940; s. Louis Karl and Lillian M. m. Andrea Cines, June 20, 1960 (div.); children: Seth, Andrew; m. Antoinette Leonard, Oct. 9, 1977. Attended, London Sch. Econs., 1958—59; BS, U. Wis., Madison, 1960; AM, Princeton U., NJ, 1962; postgrad., Princeton U., 1962—63. Internat. economist Bur. Internat. Commerce, U.S. Dept. Commerce, Washington, 1963-66; cons. Booz Allen & Hamilton, Inc., NYC, 1966-67, asst. to pres. internat./adminstrv. dir., 1967-70, v.p. internat. ops., 1970-71, v.p./mng. officer, instl. and pub. mgmt. div., 1971-74; pres., mgmt. cons. Stuart Matlins Assocs., Inc., Woodstock, Vt., 1974—. Chmn. bd. dirs. LongHill Ptnrs., Inc.; publisher Gemstone Press, Jewish Lights Pub., SkyLight Paths Pub. Bd. dirs. Health Edn. Found., Woodstock Area Jewish Cmty., Vt.; former chmn. overseers NY Sch., Hebrew Union Coll.-Jewish Inst. Religion; bd. govs. Hebrew Union Coll.; trustee South Woodstock Fire Protection Assn., Inc., Mertens House, Woodstock; capital budget com. Town of Woodstock; adv. bd. Abraham Geiger Coll., Germany; dir. Jewish Book Coun. Woodrow Wilson fellow, 1960-61, Herbert O. Peet fellow, 1961-62, Phillip A. Rollins fellow, 1962-63; recipient Am. Jewish Disting. Svc. award Hebrew Union Coll., 2006. Mem. Princeton Club. Office: LongHill Ptnrs Inc PO Box 237 Woodstock VT 05091-0237 also: Sunset Farm Offices Rt 4 Woodstock VT 05091

MATLOCK, B. JANE, science educator; b. Kankakee, Ill., Jan. 31, 1953; d. Richard Lea Mann and Edith Lucille Joy-Mann; m. Michael Dean Matlock, July 15, 1972; 1 child, Leslie Joy Matlock-Starling. BS in Psychology and Elem. Ed., Olivet Nazarene U., 1989. Cert. K-9 Ill. State Bd. Edn., 1989, mid. sch. endorsements Ill. State Bd. Edn., 1991. Tchr. 3rd grade Bruning Elem. Sch., Wilmington, Ill., 1989—90; edn. coord. Ideal Computer Systems, Kankakee, Ill., 1990—91; social studies methods tchr. Olivet Nazarene U., Kankakee, 1991; sci. tchr. 7th grade L.J. Mid. Sch., Wilmington, 1991—92; sci. tchr. 7th gr. Oster-Oakview Jr. High, New Lenox, Ill., 1992—94, L.J. Stevens Mid. Sch., Wilmington, 1994—2005; tchr. 5th gr. Plainfield (Ill.) Sch. Dist. 202, 2005—. Sch. improvement team Oster-Oakview Jr. High, New Lenox, Ill., 1992—94; sch. leadership team Wilmington SD# 209-U, 1995—2002; Jjr. Beta Club sponsor L.J. Stevens Mid. Sch., 1997—2000, head volleyball coach, 1998—99, sci. club sponsor, 1999—2005; Challenger team trainer Will County Aerospace Team, 2000—; tchr. Jason Expdn., 2004—; MAD sci. tchr. River View Elem. Sch., 2006—; mem. Astronomy Resources Connecting Schs., 2005—, mem. sci. curriculum com., 2006—. Chancel choir and worship com. First United Meth. Ch., Wilmington, 1986—2006. Recipient Bright Idea award, Oster-Oakview PTO, 1993, Extra Mile award, L.J. Stevens Mid. Sch., 2005. Mem.: AAUW, NSTA, Space Exploration Educators Conf., Ill. Sci. Tchrs. Am., Kappa Delta Pi, Mensa (assoc.). Methodist. Home: 817 Mae St Wilmington IL 60481 Office: River View Elem Sch 2097 Bronk Rd Plainfield IL 60586 Home Phone: 815-476-5572; Office Phone: 815-439-4840. Personal E-mail: matlock817@msn.com. Business E-Mail: jmatlock@learningcommunity202.org.

MATLOCK, JACK FOUST, JR., diplomat; b. Greensboro, NC, Oct. 1, 1929; s. Jack Foust and Nellie (McSwain) M.; m. Rebecca Burrum, Sept. 2, 1949; children: James, Hugh, Nell, David, Joseph. AB summa cum laude, Duke U., 1950; MA, Columbia U., 1952; cert., Russian Inst., 1952; LLD (hon.), Greensboro Coll., 1989, Albright Coll., 1992, Conn. Coll., 1993; LLD (hon.), Latvian Acad. Scis., 2002. Instr. Dartmouth, 1953-56; fgn. service officer Dept. State, 1956-91; assigned Washington, 1956-58, Am. Embassy, Vienna, 1958-60; Am. consul. gen. Munich, 1960-61; assigned Am. Embassy, Moscow, 1961-63, Accra, Ghana, 1963-66, Am. Consulate, Zanzibar, 1967-69, Am. Embassy, Dar es Salaam, Tanzania, 1969-70, Sr. Seminar in Fgn. Policy, Dept. State, 1970-71; country dir. for USSR State Dept., 1971-74; minister-counselor, dep. chief mission Am. Embassy, Moscow, 1974-78; diplomat-in-residence Vanderbilt U., Nashville, 1978-79; dep. dir. Fgn. Service Inst., Washington, 1979-80; chargé d'affaires ad interim Am. Embassy, Moscow, 1981; ambassador to Czechoslovakia, 1981-83; spl. asst. to pres., sr. dir. European and Soviet Affairs Nat. Security Council, 1983-87; U.S. ambassador to the Soviet Union, Moscow, 1987-91; sr. rsch. fellow Columbia U., NYC, 1991-93, Kathryn and Shelby Collum Davis prof. Practice Internat. Diplomacy, 1993-96; George F. Kennan prof. Inst. for Advanced Study, Princeton, NJ, 1996-2001; John L. Weinberg/Goldman Sachs and Co. vis. prof. pub. and internat. affairs Princeton U., 2001—02; Sol Linowitz prof. internat. rels. Hamilton Coll., 2006. Author: Autopsy on an Empire: The American Ambassador's Account of the Collapse of the Soviet Union, 1995, Reagan and Gorbachev: How the Cold War Ended, 2004; compiler, editor: Index to J.V. Stalin's Works, 2d edit., 1971. Mem. Am. Acad. Diplomacy, Coun. on Fgn. Rels., Century Assn. N.Y., Am. Philos. Soc. Home: 940 Princeton Kingston Rd Princeton NJ 08540-4128 also: 32 Wagoner Hill Rd Fayetteville TN 37334 Office Phone: 609-252-1953. Personal E-mail: jfmatlock@patmedia.net. E-mail: matlock@ias.edu.

MATLOCK, JOHN HUDSON, science administrator, materials engineer; b. San Angelo, Tex., Nov. 23, 1944; s. Lee Hudson Jr. and Harriett (Kidder) M.; m. Kathe Lynne Reep, Sept. 3, 1966; children: Michelle, Joseph. B in Engring. Sci., U. Tex., 1967, MSME, 1969, PhD in Material Sci. and Engring., 1970; MBA, So. Ill. U., Edwardsville, 1976. Registered profl. engr., Mo., Wash., Oreg. Sr. rsch. engr. Monsanto Co., St. Peters, Mo., 1970-72, rsch. specialist, 1972-74, supt. tech. svcs., 1974-79; sr. staff engr. Mostek Corp., Carrollton, Tex., 1979-80, mgr. material tech. group, 1980-83; v.p. tech. SEH Am., Inc., Vancouver, Wash., 1983-90, exec. v.p., 1990-96, Komatsu Silicon Am., Hillsboro, Oreg., 1996, pres., CEO, 1997—2005; global officer Komatsu, Ltd., 1999—2003, sr. adv., 2006—; dir. Komatsu Electronic Metals, Ltd., 1999—2006. Adj. asst. prof. physics So. Ill. U., Edwardsville, 1973-76; mem. engring. adv. bd. Wash. State U., Pullman, 1984-96, adj. lectr., 1985; adj. prof. mech. engring., mem. grad. faculty Oreg. State U., Corvallis, 1985-90; mem. vis. com. Engring. Coll., U. Wash., Seattle, 1985-94, mem. indsl. adv. bd. Material Sci. and Engring., 1988-2000; bd. dirs. Wash. Tech. Ctr., 1990-96. Contbr. approximately 40 articles on silicon crystal growing and the effect of silicon properties on electronic device performance to profl. and trade jours. Bd. trustees 1st Ch. of God, Vancouver, 1988-91, tchr. adult ch. sch., 1986-91, 2001-02, spl. assignment missionary to Tanzania, 2006-; sch. bd. Kingsway Christian Sch., Vancouver, 1990-91; bd. dir., Wash. Tech. Ctr., 1990-96; elder Sonrise Ch., Hillsboro, 2004-. Mem. Electrochem. Soc., Metall. Soc., AIME, Am. Soc. for Materials, Soc., Tau Beta Pi, Pi Tau Sigma, Phi Kappa Phi, Beta Gamma Sigma. Office Phone: 503-640-7000. Business E-Mail: jmatlock@komsil.com.

MATLOCK, KENT, advertising and public relations executive; BS, Morehouse Coll. Chmn., CEO Matlock & Assocs. Inc., 1984—.

MATOS, CRUZ ALFONSO, environmental consultant; b. NYC, Mar. 6, 1929; s. José and Gertrudes (Manzanares) M.; m. Aurelia Santos, Dec. 13, 1963; children: Miguel, Veronica, Monica, Angélica. B Engring. Sci., Oxford U., 1957, M Engring. Sci., 1958; DSc (hon.), U. Met., PR, 1995. Pres., CEO Fischer & Porter de P.R., 1964—69; asst. sec. dept. pub. works Govt. of P.R., 1969—70, exec. dir. Environ. Quality Bd., 1970—73, sec. dept. natural resources, 1973—75, cabinet mem., 1970—75; UN chief tech., dir. Inst. Marine Affairs, Trinidad and Tobago, 1975—79; UN Devel. Program regional rep. Barbados, Surinam, Dutch W.I., Trinidad and Tobago, 1979—80; UN chief tech. adviser South Pacific, dir. Com. for Coordination of Offshore Prospecting in the South Pacific, Suva, Fiji, 1980—89; ret., 1989. Advisor to pres. P.R. Senate for natural resources, the environ. and energy, 1993-97; advisor to exec. dir. UN Environ. Program for L.Am. and Caribbean, 1994-98; mem. various adv. panels and overseas mission U.S. NAS; mem. U.S. Nat. Commn. on Environment, Consejo Consultive Recursos Naturales y Ambientales (apptd. Gov. P.R.), Com. Sobre Política Publica Energetica P.R., Consejo Asesor Sobre Energia. Contbr. articles to sci. jours. and mags. Bd. dirs. Caribbean Environment and Devel. Inst. With U.S. Army, 1952-54. Named Dept. Natural and Environ. Resources bldg. the Dr. Cruz A. Matos Bldg., Govt. P.R., 2005, ann. scholarship for post grad. environ. studies Dr. Cruz A. Matos Scholarship, 2005; recipient Boriquen Conservation award, 1971; scholarship and bldg. named in his honor, Govt. PR, 2005. Office: PO Box 7627-HC77 Playa Cerro Gordo Vega Alta PR 00692

MATROS, RICHARD K., insurance company executive; b. Queens, NY; m. Adrienne Matros; children: Carly, Chelsea, Alex. BA in Psychology, Alfred U.; MA in Gerontology, U. S.C. Facility adminstr. Extended Care Inc., Catered Living Inc.; regional adminstr., v.p. We. Ops. Beverly Enterprises Inc.; exec. v.p. ops. Care Enterprises, 1988—91, pres., COO, 1988—91, 1991—94, pres., CEO, 1994; pres., COO Regency Health Svcs. Inc., 1994—95, pres., CEO, 1995—97, Bright Now! Dental, 1998—2000; chmn., CEO Sun Healthcare Group, 2001—. Office: Sun Healthcare Group Ste 400 18831 Von Karman Ave Irvine CA 92612

MATSAKIS, ELIAS N., lawyer; b. 1951; BA with honors, U. Chgo., 1971; JD cum laude, Harvard Law Sch., 1974. Bar: Ill. 1974. Ptnr. Holland & Knight LLP, Chgo., mem. dir. com. Staff mem. Harvard Civil Rights and Civil Liberties Law Review, 1972, lead author Navigating the Changing Tides of Managed Care and Health Reform, AMA. Mem. sch. bd. Dist. 225, Northfield Twp. Mem.: Comml. Law League Am., ABA, Hellenic Bar Assn. (Ill.), Ill. State Bar Assn., Chgo. Bar Assn. (chmn. pro se ct. com., young lawyers sect. 1977, David C. Hilliard award). Office: Holland & Knight LLP 131 S Dearborn St 30th Fl Chicago IL 60603 Office Phone: 312-715-5731. Business E-Mail: elias.matsakis@hklaw.com.

MATSCHULLAT, DALE LEWIS, lawyer; b. Ft. Sill, Okla., May 1, 1945; s. Wayne Emil and Harriet Jane (Bowman) M.; m. Eileen Joanne Davidson, Aug. 26, 1967; children— Robert Charles, Stephen Francis. AB, Stanford U., 1967, JD, 1970. Bar: NY, Wis. Law clk. US Dist. Ct. (ea. dist. NY), Bklyn., 1970-71; assoc. firm Davis, Polk & Wardwell, NYC, 1972-77; sector counsel Allis Chalmers Corp., Milw., 1977, v.p., gen. counsel, Newell Rubbermaid Inc., Rockford, Ill., 1989—, corp. sec., 2003—. Roman Catholic. Office: Newell Rubbermaid 10B Glenlake Pky Ste 300 Atlanta GA 30328 *

MATSCHULLAT, ROBERT W., former consumer products company executive; b. Nov. 21, 1947; married. BA, Stanford U., 1969, MBA, 1972. CFO The Seagram Co. Ltd., 1995—99, vice chmn., 1995—2000; head worldwide investment banking Morgan Stanley & Co. Inc., 2000—04; non-exec. chmn. The Clorox Co., Oakland, Calif., 2004—05, interim chmn., CEO, 2006. Bd. dirs. The Clorox Co., 1999—, The Walt Disney Co., 2002—, McKesson Inc.

MATSEN, FREDERICK ALBERT, III, orthopedic educator; b. Austin, Tex., Feb. 5, 1944; s. Frederick Albert II and Cecilia (Kirkegaard) M.; m. Anne Lovell, Dec. 24, 1966; children: Susanna Lovell, Frederick A. IV, Laura Jane Megan. BA, U. Tex., Austin, 1964; MD, Baylor U., 1968. Intern Johns Hopkins U., Balt., 1971; resident in orthopaedics U. Wash., Seattle, 1971-74, acting instr. orthopaedics, 1974, asst. prof. orthopaedics, 1975-79, assoc. prof. orthopaedics, 1979-82, prof., 1982-85, 86—, adjunct prof. Ctr. Bioengring., 1985—, dir. residency program orthopaedics, 1978-81, vice chmn. dept. orthopaedics, 1982-85, acting chmn. dept. orthopaedics, 1983-84, prof., chmn. dept. orthopaedics, 1981—. Mem. Orthopaedic Residency Rev. Com., Chgo., 1981-86. Author: Compartmental Syndromes, 1980; editor: The Shoulder, 1990; contbr. articles to profl. jours., chpts. to textbooks; assoc. editor Clin. Orthopaedics, Jour. Orthopaedic Rsch., 1981—. Lt. comdr. USPHS, 1969-71. Recipient Traveling fellowship Am. Orthopaedic Assn., 1983, Nicholas Andry award Assn. Bone and Joint Surgery, 1979, Henry Meyerding Essay award Am. Fracture Assn., 1974. Mem. Am. Shoulder and Elbow Surgeons (founding, pres. 1991—), Am. Acad. Orthopaedic Surgeons (bd. dirs. 1984-85), Orthopaedic Rsch. Soc., Western Orthopaedic Assn., Phi Beta Kappa. Office: U Wash Dept Orthopaedics RK 10 1959 NE Pacific St Seattle WA 98195-0001 Office Phone: 206-543-3690. Business E-Mail: matsen@u.washington.edu.

MATSEN, JEFFREY ROBERT, lawyer; b. Salt Lake City, Nov. 24, 1939; s. John Martin and Bessie (Jackson) M.; m. Susan Davis, July 27, 1973; children: Gregory David, Melinda Kaye, Brian Robert, Jeffrey Lamont, Kristin Sue, Nicole, Brett Richard. BA cum laude, Brigham Young U., 1964; JD with honors, UCLA, 1967. Bar: Calif. 1968, US Dist. Ct. (ctrl.

dist. Calif.) 1968, US Tax Ct. 1972, DC 1974, US Supreme Ct. 1974. Atty., LA, 1968, Newport Beach, Calif., 1971—; mng. ptnr. Jeffrey R. Matsen & Assocs., Newport Beach, Calif., 1978—. Prof. law Western State U. Coll. Law, Fullerton, Calif., 1969-85; instr. Golden Gate U. Grad. Taxation Prog., 1978-84. Author: Business Planning for California Closely-Held Enterprises; contbr. articles to legal jours. Capt., USMCR, 1968-71. Decorated Navy Commendation medal; named one of Top 100 Attys., Worth mag., 2005—06. Mem. State Bar Calif., ABA, Order of Coif. Office: Jeffrey R Matsen and Assocs 695 Town Center Dr Ste 700 Costa Mesa CA 92626 Office Phone: 714-384-6500. Office Fax: 714-384-6501. E-mail: jeff@jrmatsen.com. *

MATSEN, JOHN MARTIN, academic administrator, pathologist; b. Salt Lake City, Feb. 7, 1933; s. John M. and Bessie (Jackson) M.; m. Joneen Johnson, June 6, 1959; children: Marilee, Sharon, Coleen, Sally, John H., Martin K., Maureen, Catherine, Carl, Jeri. BA, Brigham Young U., 1958; MD, UCLA, 1963; DSc (hon.), U. Utah, 2006. Diplomate Am. Bd. Pediatrics, Am. Bd. Pathology, Spl. Competence in Med. Microbiology. Intern UCLA, 1963-65; resident in pediat. LA County Harbor/UCLA Med. Ctr., Torrance, Calif., 1965—66; USPHS fellow U. Minn., Mpls., 1966-68, asst. prof., 1968-70, assoc. prof., 1971-74, prof., 1974, U. Utah, Salt Lake City, 1974—, assoc. dean, 1979-81, chmn. dept. pathology, 1981-93, univ. sr. v.p. health scis., dean Sch. Medicine, 1993-98. Pres. Associated Regional and Univ. Pathologists, Inc., Salt Lake City, 1983-93, chmn. bd. dirs., 1993-99. Author over 200 publs. in field. Recipient Becton Dickenson award Am. Soc. Microbiology, bioMèrieux Sonnenwirth award 1993, Disting. Svc. award Collegium Aesculapium Found., 2006, Am. Soc. Clin. Pathology, 2006; grantee TREK Diagnostic Sys., 2007. Fellow: Am. Acad. Microbiology; mem.: Assn. Pathology Chmn. (pres. 1990—92), Acad. Clin. Lab. Physicians and Scientists (pres. 1978—79). Mem. Lds Ch.

MATSON, PAMELA ANNE, environmental scientist, science educator; b. Eau Claire, Wis., Aug. 3, 1953; BS, U. Wis., 1975; MS, Ind. U., 1980; PhD, Oreg. State U., 1983. Prof. U. Calif., Berkeley, 1993—97; Goldman prof. environ. studies Stanford U., Calif., 1997—, Naramore dean sch. earth sci., 2002—. Contbr. articles to profl. jours.; editor: Annual Rev. of Environment & Resources. Fellow MacArthur fellow, 1995. Fellow: Am. Acad. Arts & Scis.; mem.: Nat. Acad. Sci. Achievements include research in interactions between the biosphere and the atmosphere; land-use changes on atmospheric change, analyzing the effects of greenhouse gas emissions resulting from tropical deforestization; intensive agriculture on the atmosphere, especially the effects of tropical agriculture and cattle ranching; development of agricultural productivity can be expanded without causing off-site environmental consequences. Office: Stanford U Sch Earth Scis Stanford CA 94305-2210

MATSON, TIMOTHY C., lawyer; b. Mpls., May 10, 1966; BA cum laude, St. Olaf Coll., 1988; JD, U. Minn., 1991. Bar: Minn. 1992, US Dist. Ct. Minn. 1993. Law clk. to Hon. Thomas H. Carey Minn. Dist. Ct. (4th Jud. Dist.), 1992—93; assoc. Lommen, Abdo, Cole, King & Stageberg, P.A., Mpls. Instr. music bus. prog. McNally Smith Coll. Music, 1996—98. Named a Rising Star, Minn. Super Lawyers mag., 2006. Mem.: Minn. State Bar Assn. (chair arts & entertainment law sect. 2003—04), Hennepin County Bar Assn. Office: Lomen Abdo Cole King & Stageberg PA 2000 IDS Ctr 80 S 8th St Minneapolis MN 55402 Office Phone: 612-336-9331. E-mail: tim@lommen.com. *

MATSON, VIRGINIA MAE FREEBERG (MRS. EDWARD J. MATSON), retired special education educator, author; b. Chgo., Aug. 25, 1914; d. Axel George and Mae (Dalrymple) Freeberg; m. Edward John Matson, Oct. 18, 1941; children: Karin (Mrs. Donald H. Skadden), Sara M. Drake, Edward Robert, Laurence D., David O. BA, U. Ky., 1934; MA, Northwestern U., 1941. Spl. edn. tchr. area high schs., Chgo., 1934-42, Ridge Farm, 1944-45; tchr. h.s. Pub. Schs. Lake County, Ill., 1956-59; founder Grove Sch., Lake Forest, Ill., 1958-87, ret., 1987. Instr. evening sch. Carthage Coll., 1965-66. Author: Shadow on the Lost Rock, 1958, Saul, the King, 1968, Abba Father, 1970 (Friends Lit. Fiction award 1972), Buried Alive, 1970, A School for Peter, 1974, A Home for Peter, 1983, Letters to Lauren, A History of the Methodist Campgrounds, Des Plaines, 1985; contbr. many articles to profl. publs. Mem. Friends of Lit. Dem. Recipient Humanitarian award Ill. Med. Soc. Aux. Dem. Home: 4133 Mockingbird Ln Suffolk VA 23434-7186

MATSUDA, FUJIO, retired academic administrator; b. Honolulu, Oct. 18, 1924; s. Yoshio and Shimo (Iwasaki) M.; m. Amy M. Saiki, June 11, 1949; children: Bailey Koki, Thomas Junji, Sherry Noriko, Joan Yuuko, Ann Mitsuyo, Richard Hideo. BSCE, Rose Poly. Inst., 1949; DSc, MIT, 1952; DEng (hon.), Rose Hulman Inst. Tech., 1975. Rsch. engr. MIT, 1952—54; rsch. asst. prof. engring. U. Ill., Urbana, 1954—55; asst. prof. to prof. engring. U. Hawaii, Honolulu, 1955—62, chmn. dept. civil engring., 1962—63, v.p. bus. affairs, 1973-74, pres., 1974-84, exec. dir. Rsch. Corp., 1984-94; pres. Japan-Am. Inst. Mgmt. Sci., Honolulu, 1994-96. Bd. dirs. First Hawaiian Bank, Jalms, Uresenke Fedn. Hawaii, Pacific Internat. Ctr. High Tech. Rsch. Chmn. Pacific Buddhist Acad., 2004. With US Army, 1943—45. Recipient Honor Alumnus award Rose Poly. Inst., 1971, Disting. Svc. award Airport Ops. Coun. Internat., 1973; named Disting. Alumnus U. Hawaii, 1974, 91, Hawaii Engr. of Yr., 1972. Mem. NAE, NSPE, ASCE (Parcel-Sverdrup Engring. Mgmt. award 1986), Social Sci. Assn., Japan-Am. Soc. Hawaii (trustee 1976-84, adv. coun. 1984—), Japan-Hawaii Econ. Coun., Sigma Xi, Tau Beta Pi. Personal E-mail: fmatsuda@hawaii.rr.com.

MATSUDA, MASATAKE, rail transportation executive; b. Hokkaido, Japan, 1936; Student, Hokkaido U. Chmn. E. Japan Rlwy. Co., Tokyo; joined Japan Nat. Rlwy., 1961, formerly Planning Mgr. of Office of Planning Mgmt., Planning Mgr. Hokkaido Hdqs., Dir.-Gen. Reconstruction Promotion Hdqs.; Mgmt. Dir. Corpn. Planning Hdqs. E Japan Rlwy Co. (Japan Rlwy. East-co. created after privatization of JNR 1987), Gen.-Mgr., V.P., Pres., 1993; current Chmn. Japan Rlwy. East. Dir. Mizuho Holdings Inc.; Pres. World Exec. Coun., Internat. Union of Railways (UIC); V.P. UIC, 2003—04; mem. Prime Min. Adv. Panel to oversee Privatization of Semi Governmental Expressway Corporations, 2003, resigned in protest of privatization scheme. Office: East Japan Railway 2-2-2 Yoyogi Shibuya-ku Tokyo 151-8578 Japan Office Phone: (3) 5334-1310. Office Fax: (3) 5334-1297.

MATSUDA, PAUL KEI, literature and language professor; PhD in English, Purdue U., West Lafayette, Ind., 2000. Asst. prof. English Miami U., Oxford, Ohio, 2000—01; assoc. prof. English U. NH, Durham, 2001—. Founding chair Symposium on Second Lang. Writing, 1988—. Editor: (book) On Second Language Writing, Landmark Essays on ESL Writing, Second Language Writing Research: Perspectives on the Process of Knowledge Construction, The Politics of Second Language Writing, Second-Language Writing in the Composition Classroom. Recipient TOEFL Outstanding Young Scholar award, Ednl. Testing Svc., 2004, Richard Ohmann award, Nat. Coun. Tchrs. English, 2006. Mem.: TESOL (nonnative English spkrs. caucus chair), Am. Assn. for Applied Linguistics, Conf. on Coll. Composition and Commn. (exec. com. mem., second lang. writing com. chair). Office Phone: 603-862-0292.

MATSUDA, TAKAYOSHI, surgeon, educator, biomedical researcher; b. Tonan, Japan, 1937; came to U.S., 1965; *Takayoshi Matsuda's father, Shinyu Matsuda, MD, PhD, started a 20-bed hospital that he continued to expand creating Kyorin University Medical School in 1971 in Tokyo, Japan (the first medical school in Japan after WWII). He added colleges of Nursing, Medical Technology, Social Science, and Linguistics. He received a second degree Medal of Honor from the Japanese Government. His brother, Hiroharu Matsuda, MD, PhD, a professor of traumatology and critical care medicine, has been Chairman of the Board of Kyorin University since their father's death. He has two sisters, Shigemi Matsuda, MD, PhD, an ophthalmologist, and Hiroye Asanuma, MD, PhD, a dermatologist.* MD, Keio Gijuku U., Tokyo, 1963. Diplomate Am. Bd. Surgery. Rotating intern Cook County Hosp., Chgo., 1965-66, resident in surgery, 1966-71, dir. burn ctr., 1975-93; asst. prof. surgery Kyorin U., Tokyo, 1971-75; asst. prof. U. Ill., Chgo., 1977—; pres. TM & Assocs., Oak Park, Ill., 1994—. Cons. alternative medicine, cons. leadership devel., fin. freedom; investigator renewable energy; spkr. in field. *Takayoshi Matsuda accumulated broad knowledge in the field of alternative and complimentary medicine through his extensive research in free radical and antioxidant therapy for burns. He invented mechanical devices to elevate patient's limbs in order to perform surgical operations and dressing changes rapidly and safely.* Editl. bd. Jour. Burn Care Rehab., 1987-93; contbr. articles to profl. publ., chpt. to books. Recipient Jerry and Thelma Stergios award for Excellence in Basic Rsch., U. Ill. at Chgo., 1979, The Superior Pub. Serv. award, County of Cook, State of Ill., 1993. Fellow ACS; mem. Internat. Soc. Surgery, Internat. Soc. Burn Injuries, Am. Burn Assn., Am. Assn. Surgery Trauma, Soc. Critical Care Medicine, Chgo. Surg. Soc. Achievements include research in and devel. of a novel approach for the production of electricity without pollution; established the first human skin bank in the State of Illinois at the Burn Unit of Cook County Hospital, 1977. Office: TM & Assocs Alternative Medicine Cons 103 Bishop Quarter Ln Oak Park IL 60302-2672 Office Phone: 708-386-2522. Personal E-mail: takimatsuda@hotmail.com.

MATSUHISA, NOBUYUKI, chef, restaurant owner; b. Saitama, Japan; Chef, owner Matsuhisa, Beverly Hills, 1987—, Aspen, Colo., 1997—, Nobu, NYC, 1994—, London, 1997—, Tokyo, 1998—, Malibu, Calif., 1999—, Las Vegas, 1999—, Nobu Next Door, NYC, 1998—, Ubon, LA, 1999—. Author: Nobu: The Cookbook, Nobu Now, 2005. Named one of Am.'s 10 Best New Chefs, Food & Wine Mag., 1989, So. Calif.'s Rising Stars, LA Times Mag., 1998. Office: Nobu 105 Hudson St New York NY 10013-2331 *

MATSUI, CONNIE L., pharmaceutical executive; b. Piedmont, Calif. m. William Beckman; 2 children. BA, Stanford U., MBA, 1977. Various positions Wells Fargo Bank, 1977—91; sr. dir., planning and resource devel. IDEC Pharm., 1992—94, v.p., planning and resource devel., 1994—2000, sr. v.p., planning and resource devel., 2000—03; exec. v.p. corp. strategy and communication Biogen Idec Inc., 2003—. Bd. dirs. Halozyme Therapeutics, Inc., 2006—. Nat. pres. Girl Scouts Am., 1999—2002. Office: Biogen Inc 14 Cambridge Ctr Cambridge MA 02142

MATSUI, DORIS OKADA, congresswoman; b. Poston, Ariz., Sept. 25, 1944; m. Robert Takeo Matsui (dec. Jan. 1, 2005), Sept. 17, 1966; 1 child. BA in Psychology, U. Calif., Berkeley, 1966. Dep. dir. pub. liaison The White House, Washington, 1993—94, 1996—99, dep. asst. to the Pres. for pub. liaison, 1994—96; dir. govt. rels. Collier, Shannon & Scott PLLC, Washington, 1999—2005; mem. US Congress from 5th Calif. dist., 2005—. Mem. Clinton-Gore Transition Team, 1992—93; bd. trustees Woodrow Wilson Internat. Ctr. Scholars, Meridian Internat. Ctr., Calif. Inst. Bd., Arena Stage. Recipient Action for Breast Cancer Awareness award, Advocates award, Nat. Assn. Mental Health, Mentor award, U. So. Calif. -Sacramento Sch. Pub. Adminstrn., Newmyer award, Sidwell Friends Sch., Rosalie Stern award, U. Calif. Alumni Assn. Democrat. Methodist. Office: US Ho Reps 2310 Ho Office Bldg Washington DC 20515-0505 also: Robert T Matsui Fed Courthouse Ste 12-600 501 I St Sacramento CA 95814 *

MATSUI, HIDEKI, professional baseball player; b. Kanazawa, Japan, June 12, 1974; Player Yomiuri Giants (Central League), Japan, 1992—2002, NY Yankees, 2003—. Major donor Japanese Red Cross Society for Tsunami Relief, 2004. Named MVP, Central League (Japan), 1998, 2000, 2002; recipient Golden Spirit Award, 1999, 2000. Achievements include being a member of Japan Series Championship team, 1994, 2000, 2002; recognized nine times as Japanese League All-Star; being a member of American League All-Star Team 2003; being the runner-up American League Rookie of the Year 2003. Office: c/o New York Yankees 161st St and River Ave Bronx NY 10452 Office Phone: 718-293-4300. Office Fax: 718-293-8431.

MATSUMORI, DOUGLAS, lawyer; b. Salt Lake City, Oct. 22, 1947; BS, U. Utah, 1973; JD, Harvard U., 1976. Ptnr. Ray, Quinney & Nebeker PC, Salt Lake City. Mem. Utah State Bar, Phi Beta Kappa. Office: Ray Quinney & Nebeker PO Box 45385 Salt Lake City UT 84145-0385

MATSUMOTO, CAROLEE SETSUKO, researcher, education developer and administrator; b. Denver, Feb. 13, 1943; d. Harry Katsumi and Pearl Shizuho (Nakamura) M.; m. David Luther Gilbertson, Oct. 20, 1990. BA, Ea. Mich. U., 1965; MEd, Wayne State U., 1968; EdD, Harvard Univ., 1991. Cert. biology, sci. tchr., adminstr., Mass. Sci. tchr. Greenburgh Sch. Dist. #8, Hartsdale, NY, 1965-67; sci. dept., head tchr. Nagoya Internat. Sch., Japan, 1968-70; tchr. sci. grades 7-8 Brookline HS, Mass., 1970—73, tchr. biology, 1976—79, sci. supr., 1979-81; sci. dept. head Graded Am. Sch., Sao Paulo, Brazil, 1973-76; asst. supt. curriculum, instrn. Concord and Concord/Carlisle Pub. Schs., Mass., 1981-87; teaching fellow Harvard U., Cambridge, Mass., 1984-85; curriculum dir., prin. investigator Edn. Devel. Ctr., Newton, Mass., 1987-93, sr. project dir., sr. scientist, 1993—. Bd. dir. New Eng. & Islands Reg. Lab., Andover, Mass., 1985-96, Lloyd Environ. Ctr., S. Dartmouth, Mass., 1990-97; mem. adv. coun. Collaboration Equity, Am. Assn. for Advancement Sci., Washington, 1994-96; mem. Mass Dept. Edn. Cultural Proficiency Steering Com., 2006-; vis. scholar Stanford U., Palo Alto, 1993; rep. Carpe Vitam Found., Sweden; co-dir. U. Mass., Dartmouth, K-12 Rsch. Devel. Dissemination Ctr. Bd. dir. Tchrs. 21, Wellesley, Mass., 1993—; bd. govs. New Bedford Oceanarium. Mem.: ASCD, Nat. Sch. Devel. Coun., Am. Ednl. Rsch. Assn., Nat. Sci. Tchrs. Assn. Avocations: travel, photography. Home: 17 Arnold Pl New Bedford MA 02740-3634

MATSUMOTO, HIROYUKI, biochemistry professor, researcher; b. Izuhara, Nagasaki, Japan, May 5, 1948; arrived in US, 1977; s. Masayuki and Yuriko (Heima) M.; m. Makiko Ohnishi; 1 child, Masaomi. BS, Kyoto U., Japan, 1972, PhD, 1977. Jr. rschr. U. Hawaii, Honolulu, 1977-79; ass. rsch. scientist Purdue U., West Lafayette, Ind., 1980-85; from asst. asst. prof. to assoc. prof. U. Okla. Health Sci. Ctr., Oklahoma City, 1985-97; prof. Health Sci. Ctr., U. Okla., Oklahoma City, 1997—. Mem. study sect. NIH, 1998—; dir. Epscor Okla. biotech. network laser mass spectrometry facility NSF. Contbr. articles to profl. jours. including Nature, Science. Rsch. grantee NSF, 1980-88, NIH, 1985—. Mem. Assn. Rsch. Vision and Ophthalmology, Am. Soc. Biol. Chemists, Protein Soc., Am. Soc. for Mass Spectrometry, Am. Soc. for Photobiology, Japanese Soc. Zoology, Sigma Xi. Achievements include prediction of beta-ionone ring binding pocket in rhodopsin; discovery of phosphorylated homologs of arrestin; research in molecular mechanism of vision, biological mass spectrometry, and ocular proteomics. Office: U Okla Health Sci Ctr 940 Stanton L Young Blvd Oklahoma City OK 73104-5020 Home: 1821 Danfield Dr Norman OK 73072-3000 Office Phone: 405-271-2227. Business E-Mail: hiro-matsumoto@ouhsc.edu.

MATSUSHIMA, AKIRA PAUL, manufacturing executive; b. Tokyo, July 7, 1937; arrived in U.S., 1970; s. Hiromasa and Tomiko (Watanabe) Matsushima; m. Kathleen Sue Rowland, Aug. 18, 1968; children: John Hikaru, Karen Emi, Amy Kathryn. BS, Waseda U., Tokyo, 1961, MS in Mech. Engring., 1964; M in Mgmt., Northwestern U., 1981. Registered profl. engr., Calif. With NOK Corp., Tokyo, 1961—85, mgr. rsch. planning, 1968-70, dep. gen. mgr. engring. divsn., 1983-85; dir. engring. NOK-USA, Inc., LA, 1970-72, v.p., 1973-74, exec. v.p. Chgo., 1975-83, sec., 1979-82, dir., 1971-85; with Chgo. Rawhide Mfg. Co. (SKF), Elgin, 1985—98, sr. v.p., 1995-98; pres. Matsushima Mgmt., Palatine, 1999—. Japanese govt. del. Internat. Standardization Orgn., 1973—78; chmn. K. C. Engring. Ltd., Yokohama, Japan, 1989—95, pres., 1991—95; del. Internat. Standardization Org. Internat., 1990, 92, 94; exec. dir. US ops. Yaguchi Seisakusho Co. Ltd., 1999—; bd. dirs. PLACO Co., Ltd., Saitama, Japan, 1999—, Hi-Tech Arai, Inc., Madurai, India, 2000—06; bd. dirs., pres., sec., treas. ARAI Ams. Inc., Virginia Beach, Va., 2001—06; v.p., bd. dirs. Nihon Clin. Co., Inc., Virginia Beach, 2002—04; comisario PT Arai Rubber Seal Indonesia, Jakarta, 2002—04; mem. Exec. Ptnrs., Coll. William and Mary, Grad. Sch. Bus., Williamsburg, Va., 2005—; sr. advisor Azuma Forestry Rsch. Assn., Gumma, Japan, 2006—. Contbr. articles to profl. jours. Fund dr. chair western divsn. Jr. Achievement, Chgo., 1988—89, mem. governing bd., 1990—98, United Way Elgin, 1988—96, v.p. planning, 1991—92; pres. Oak Crest Residence, Elgin, 1993—95; commr. to gen. assembly Presbyn. Ch. U.S.A., 2001. Mem.: NSPE, Soc. Automotive Engrs. (adv. bd. seals com., cert. of Appreciation 1986), Internat. House Japan. Achievements include patents in field. Office Phone: 847-705-9130. Personal E-mail: apmatsu@aol.com.

MATSUURA, KENNETH RAY, counseling administrator; b. Urbana, Ill., July 17, 1954; s. George Shigeo and Sally Sueko (Kawasaki) M.; m. Peggy Ai Iwata, May 27, 1995; 1 child, Claire Miya Sara. BA, U. Calif., Santa Barbara, 1976; MA, UCLA, 1978, PhD, 1996. Career counselor Calif. State U. Dominguez Hills, Carson, 1984-85; grad. recruitment coord. U. Calif., Irvine, 1985-90; counselor/articulation officer Cerritos Coll., Norwalk, Calif., 1990—. Mem. accreditation teams Western Assn. Schs. and Colls., L.A., 1994, Alameda, 1999, mem. accreditation task force Project Renewal; chair South Coast Higher Edn. Coun.; co-chair region 8 articulation officers and transfer ctre. dirs.; program reviewer Am. Coll. Pers. Assn. Ann. conf., Washington, 1988; presenter to confs. UCLA grad. advancement program fellow, 1977—78. Avocations: singing, music. Home: 101 Santa Ynez Dr Arcadia CA 91007 Office Phone: 562-860-2451 2141. Business E-Mail: matsuura@cerritos.edu.

MATSUZAKA, DAISUKE, professional baseball player; b. Tokyo, Sept. 13, 1980; Pitcher Seibu Lions, 1999—2006, Team Japan, World Baseball Classic, 2006, Boston Red Sox, 2006—. Named MVP, Mem. All-Tourney Team, World Baseball Classic, 2006; recipient Rookie of the Year, Pacific League, 1998, Sawamura award, 2001. Achievements include leading Japan past Mexico in elimination game in World Baseball Classic, 2006; winning one Japan Series Title (2004); signing biggest deal ever offered for an initial contract for Japanes player coming to MLB, 2006. Office: Boston Red Sox 4 Yawkey Way Boston MA 02215-3496 Fax: 617-375-0944. *

MATTA, CHÉRIF FARID, chemistry professor; b. Alexandria, Egypt, Sept. 8, 1963; arrived in Can., 1995, naturalized; s. Farid Alphonse Matta and Nabila Nassif Abdel Nour. BSc in Pharm. Sci., Alexandria U., 1987; PhD in Theoretical, Computational Chemistry, McMaster U., Hamilton, Ont., Can., 2002. Registered pharmacist 1987, cert. in health and hosp. adminstrn. Sadat Acad., Nat. Inst. Higher Mgmt., Alexandria, 1994. Pharmacist Matta Pharmacy, Alexandria, 1987—91; asst. to chief pharmacist Naval Forces HQ, Egypt, 1988—90; med. supplies specialist World Health Orgn., 1991—94; post-doctoral fellow U. Toronto, 2002—04; I.W. Killam post-doctoral fellow Dalhousie U., Halifax, 2004—06; asst. prof. Mt. St. Vincent U., Halifax, 2006—. Adj. prof. Dalhousie U., Halifax, 2006—, McMaster U., Hamilton, Ont., 2004—05; invited asst. and assoc. prof. U. Henri Poincare, Nancy, France, 2007, Nat. Ctr. Scientific Rsch., 2007. Author: The Quantum Theory of Atoms in Molecules: From Solid State to DNA and Drug Design, 2007; mem. editl. bd.: Internat. Jour. Applied Chemistry, 2005—, reviewer for profl. jours.:; contbr. scientific papers, chapters to books. Mem. academic rev. bd. Internat. Jour. Computational Sci., 2007—; mem. adv. bd. Scientific Jours. Internat., 2007—; mem. bd. gov. McMaster U., 2000—01; mem. bd. trustees Dalhousie Legal Aids, 2007—. 1st lt. Naval Med. Corps., 1988—90. Recipient John C. Polanyi Prize, Can., 2004, Chemistry Tchg. award, U. Toronto, 2003—04; fellow, World Biol. Forum, 2003—05. Mem.: Scientific Rsch. Soc., European Soc. Computational Methods in Sci. and Engring., Am. Chem. Soc., Can. Chem. Soc., Ont. Pub. Health Assn., Chem. Inst. Can., Sigma Xi. Avocations: astronomy, philosophy, painting, politics, exercise. Office: Mt St Vincent U Dept Chemistry and Physics Halifax NS B3M 2J6 Canada Office Phone: 902-457-6142. Home Fax: 902-457-6134. Personal E-mail: quantumjazz@hotmail.com.

MATTA, MARK W., human resources specialist, manufacturing executive; BS, MA, St. Francis Coll. Employee rels. coord. Morgan Engring. Alliance, Ohio; labor rels. supr. Wiley Mfg., Port Deposit, Md.; employee rels. mgr. Frito-Lay, Kirkwood, NY; v.p. human resources Sherwin-Williams Co.; sr. v.p. human resources OfficeMax, Inc., Shaker Heights, Ohio, Winn-Dixie Stores, Inc., Jacksonville, Fla., 2003—. Bd. dirs. Students in Free Enterprise. Office: Winn-Dixie Stores Inc 5050 Edgewood Ct Jacksonville FL 32254

MATTA, THAD MICHAEL, men's college basketball coach; b. Hoopeston, Ill., July 11, 1967; s. Jim Matta; m. Barbara Matta; children: Ali, Emily. Student, So. Ill. U.; BS, Butler U., 1990. Grad. asst. coach Ind. State U., 1990—91; academic coord., adminstrv. asst. Butler U., Indpls., 1991—94, asst. coach, 1997—2000, head coach, 2000—01; asst. coach Miami U., Ohio, 1994—95, 1996—97, Western Carolina U., 1995—96; head coach Xavier U., Cin., 2001—04, Ohio State U., Columbus, 2004—. Named Nat. Rookie Coach of Yr., CBS SportsLine.com and Coll. Insider.com, 2001, Coach of Yr., Midwestern Collegiate Conf., 2001, Atlantic 10 Conf., 2002, Columbus Dispatch, 2004, Big Ten Conf. and US Basketball Writers Assn. Dist. V, 2006. Office: Men's Basketball Ohio State U Jerome Schottenstein Ctr 555 Borror Dr Columbus OH 43210 Office Phone: 614-292-0505. E-mail: matta@osu.edu. *

MATTAR, LAWRENCE JOSEPH, lawyer; b. Buffalo, Apr. 17, 1934; s. Joseph and Anne (Abraham) M.; m. Elaine Kolbe, Aug. 1, 1959; children: Lorraine, Brenda, Anne, Deborah. Grad., Canisius Coll., Buffalo, 1956; JD, SUNY, Buffalo, 1959. Bar: NY 1959, Fla. 1977, US Supreme Ct. 1972. Sole practice, Buffalo, 1959-62; sr. ptnr. Mattar & D'Agostino and predecessors, Buffalo, 1962—. Asst. to county ct. judge, 1961-66; counsel NY State Senate Pub. Utilities Com., 1969-71. Bd. dirs. Better Bus. Bur. Western NY; exec. com. pres.'s coun. Canisius Coll.; mem. ho. of dels. United Way of Buffalo and Erie County; active Nat. Maronite Bishops' Adv. Coun., US Congl. Adv. Bd.; Selective Svc. Bd., Western NY Rep. Presdl. Task Force; del. Rep. Jud. Conv. 8th Dist., 1985. Decorated Knight of St. Charbiel, highest honor available to a Maronite Cath.; recipient award for outstanding svc. Buffalo Eye Bank, 1962, Leadership award Lions Club Buffalo, 1963, Citizen's award Erie C.C., 1982, Nat. Tree of Life award Bd. dirs. Jewish Nat. Fund Am., 1987. Mem. Erie County Bar Assn., Erie County Trial Lawyers Assn., NY State Bar Assn., Fla. Bar Assn., NY State Trial Lawyers Assn., Buffalo C. of C., NFL Players Alumni Assn. (assoc.), Di Gamma (life), Rotary Club (sec. 1978-79, dir. 1978-80, trustee, sec., mem. exec. com. Buffalo Rotary Found.), Buffalo Club (Buffalo), Transit Valley Country Club (East Amherst, NY). Roman

Catholic. Avocations: golf, skiing. Home: 386 Woodbridge Ave Buffalo NY 14214-1530 Office: Mattar & D'Agostino LLP 17 Court St Ste 600 Buffalo NY 14202-3294 Office Phone: 716-856-4022. Business E-Mail: lmattar@mdg-law.com.

MATTAR, PHILIP, writer; b. Haifa, Palestine, Jan. 21, 1944; came to U.S. 1961; m. Evelyn Ann Keith, June 20, 1971; 1 child, Christina. MPhil, Columbia U., 1977, PhD, 1981. Exec. dir. Inst. for Palestine Studies, Washington, 1984-2001; assoc. editor Jour. Palestine Studies, Washington, 1985-2001; fellow Woodrow Wilson Ctr., 2001—02; sr. fellow U.S. Inst. Peace, 2002—03; guest scholar U.S. Inst. of Peace, 2003—04. Adj. lectr. history Yale U., 1981; adj. prof. history Georgetown U., 1990, 91, 94. Author: Mufti of Jerusalem, 1988, 2d edit., 1991; editor: Encyclopedia of the Modern Middle East and North Africa, 2004, Encyclopedia of the Palentinians, 2005; contbr. articles to profl. jours., including Fgn. Policy, Middle East Jour., Middle Ea. Studies. Mem. adv. com. Human Rights Watch/Middle East. Vis. scholar Columbia U., 1984; Fulbright-Hays Rsch. fellow, 1978. Mem. Middle East Studies Assn., Middle East Inst. Avocations: jogging, chess, reading, travel. E-mail: pjmattar@aol.com.

MATTAR, WISSAM ELIAS, physician; b. Strasbourg, France, Sept. 15, 1979; arrived in US, 2005; s. Elias Nassib Mattar and Charlotte Youssef Gemayel. MD, St. Joseph U., Beirut, Lebanon, 2004. Resident in surgery St. Joseph U., 2004—05; medicine resident Ind. U., Indpls., 2005—. Contbr. articles to med. jours., chpt. to book. Mem. Lebanese Sports Fedn., Beirut, 1999—2000. Mem.: AMA, ACP (assoc. 3d prize for med. abstract 2006). Avocations: tennis, skiing, travel. Home: 5715 Maplewood Dr Apt C Indianapolis IN 46224 Office: Ind U Medicine 1001 W 10th St Indianapolis IN 46202 Home Phone: 317-777-0691; Office Phone: 317-656-4276. Office Fax: 317-630-2667. Personal E-mail: wissamat@hotmail.com.

MATTAUCH, ROBERT JOSEPH, retired electrical engineering educator, retired dean; b. Rochester, Pa., May 30, 1940; s. Henry Paul and Anna Marie (Mlinarcik) M.; m. Frances Sabo, Dec. 29, 1962; children: Lori Ann, Thomas J. BS, Carnegie Inst. Tech., Pitts., 1962; MEE, N.C. State U., Raleigh, 1963, PhD, 1967. Asst. prof. elec. engring. U. Va., Charlottesville, 1966-70, assoc. prof. elec. engring., 1970-76, prof. elec. engring., 1976-83, Wilson prof. elec. engring., 1983-86, Standard Oil Co. prof. sci. and tech., 1986-89, chmn. dept. elect. engring., 1987-95, BP Am. prof. sci. and tech., 1989-95; Commonwealth prof., founding chair dept. elec. engring. Va. Commonwealth U., Richmond, 1995-99, dean engring., Commonwealth prof., 1999—2006, dean emeritus, Commonwealth prof., 2006—. Cons. The Rochester Corp., Culpepper, Va., 1983—88, Milltech Corp., Deerfield, Mass., 1985. Patentee: infrared detector; solid state switching capacitor; thin wire pointing method, whiskerless Schottky diode, controlled in-situ etch back growth technique. Bd. dirs. U. Va. Patent Found., 1989-95, Greater Richmond Tech. Coun., 2001—, Va. Bioscis. Devel. Ctr., 2000—06, Richmond Symphony Orch., 2003-. Recipient Excellence in Instruction of Engring. Students award Western Electric, 1980, Greater Richmond Tech. Coun. Leadership award, 2006; named one of Top Ten Talents of 1990 Wash. Tech. Fellow IEEE (Centennial medal 1984); mem. Eta Kappa Nu (recipient Oustanding Prof. in Elec. Engring. 1975), Sigma Xi, Tau Beta Pi, Sigma Pi Sigma, Phi Kappa Phi. Office: Va Commonwealth U PO Box 843072 Richmond VA 23284-3072 Office Phone: 804-334-8245. Business E-Mail: rjmattau@vcu.edu.

MATTEI, IVAN E., lawyer; b. Dec. 13, 1955; BS summa cum laude, Georgetown U., 1979; JD magna cum laude, Harvard U., 1985. Bar: NY 1987. Mem. Debevoise & Plimpton LLP, NYC, 1987—. Adj. prof. Columbia Law Sch., 1994—97. Mem.: ABA, Assn. Bar of City NY. Office: Debevoise & Plimpton LLP 919 Third Ave New York NY 10022 Office Phone: 212-909-6060. Fax: 212-909-6836. E-mail: iemattei@debevoise.com.

MATTEO, CHRISTINE E., librarian; b. Jersey City, May 26, 1952; d. Peter J. G. and Doris Ella (Stoffel) Dirschauer; m. Joseph A. Matteo, Sept. 9, 1978. BA in Psychology, Washington Coll., Chestertown, Md., 1974; MLS, Rutgers U., New Brunswick, NJ, 1977; cert. in Computer Aided Drafting and Design, Brookdale C.C., 2007. Cert. CADD Brookdale CC, 2007; libr. N.J. Sr. libr., br. mgr. Ocean County Libr., Beachwood, NJ, 1976-78, prin. libr., br. mgr. Jackson, NJ, 1978-86, automation implementation mgr. Toms River, NJ, 1986-89, supervising libr. ctrl. svcs., 1989-91, chief libr. pub. svcs., 1991-95, chief libr. tech., 1995—2003, chief libr. adminstrn., 2003—. Mem. exec. bd., treas. Customers Dynix, Inc., Provo, Utah, 1989—91, Ctrl. Jersey Regional Libr., Freehold, 1994—96; editor, mem. steering com. Ocean County Libr. Master Plan, Toms River, 1984—85, 1991—92, 1997—98; mem. exec. bd. One Ease-E-Link, Toms River, 1998—2002; presenter in field, 2005—06. Mem.: NAACP, ASPCA, ALA, NJ Libr. Assn. (info. techs. sect., mem. LGBT Roundtable), World Future Soc., World Wildlife Fund, Environ. Def. Fund, Tuckerton Seaport Soc. (charter), Earthwatch, Humane Soc. U.S., Greenpeace, Toms River Seaport Soc., Monmouth County SPCA, Animal Birth Control Inc., Humane Soc. U.S., Associated Humane Socs., Toms River Yacht Club. Avocations: sailing, gardening, dog obedience, kayaking, science fiction. Office: Ocean County Libr 101 Washington St Toms River NJ 08753-7688 Office Phone: 732-349-6200. Business E-Mail: cmatteo@oceancountylibrary.org.

MATTERN, DOUGLAS JAMES, think-tank executive; b. Creede, Colo., May 19, 1933; s. John A. and Ethel (Franklin) Mattern; m. Noemi E. Del Cioppo, May 4, 1963. Student, San Jose State U., 1956-58. Reliability engr. Intersil, Sunnyvale, Calif., 1973-80; sr. engr. Data Gen. Corp., Sunnyvale, 1981-87; staff engr. Apple Computer, Cupertino, Calif., 1987-97; sr. engr. Trimble Navigation, Sunnyvale, 1998-2000. Sec. Gen. World Citizens Assembly, San Francisco, 1975—86; dir. World Citizens Diplomats, Palo Alto, Calif., 1988—90; pres. Assn. World Citizens, San Francisco, 1989—; CEO World Citizens Found., San Francisco, 1979—; chmn. World Citizens Assembly, San Francisco, 1995, Taipei, Taiwan, 2001, Internat. Peace Conf., San Francisco, 2005. Author: Resolution to End the Arms Race, 1982, Looking for Square Two-Moving from War and Violence to Global Community, 2006; contbg. author: Building a More Democratic United Nations, 1991; editor: World Citizen Newsmag., 1973—; contbr. Bd. dirs. San Francisco chpt. UN Assn.; bd. dirs. War/Peace Found. With USN, 1951—55. Recipient Albert Einstein Peace award, Internat. World Educators for World Peace, 2001, Lifetime Achievement award for Love and Peace, Fowpal, 2005. Home: 2671 South Ct Palo Alto CA 94306-2462 Office: 55 New Montgomery St Ste 224 San Francisco CA 94105-3421 Office Phone: 415-541-9610. E-mail: worldcit@best.com.

MATTERSON, JOAN MCDEVITT, physical therapist; b. Bryn Mawr, Pa., Feb. 24, 1949; d. William J. and Wanda Jean (Edwards) McD.; children: Brian, Jennie, Kira. BS in Biology, St. Joseph's U., Phila., 1973; cert. in Phys. Therapy, U. Pa., 1974. Assoc. pharmacologist, rschr. immunology and arthritis Prog. Phys. Therapy, P.A., Wilmington, Del., 1976-93, pediatric phys. therapist, 1974-81, pres., 1976-95; rehab. dir. Achievement Rehab.; phys. therapist Liberty Home Health, 1995—; rehab. dir. Office of Joan Matterson, 1995—, Integrated Health Svcs.- Kent, Smyrna, Del., 1996—; dir. rehab. Keystone Care Therapies, Media, Pa., 1997—, with Pain Mgmt. Ctr. Chester, Pa., 1999; with Hands on Health, Wilmington, 1999—2000; phys. therapist Hickory House Nursing and Rehab. Ctr., Honeybrook, Pa., 2000—; pvt. practice Wilmington, 2000—. Lectr. in field of low level laser therapy. Dep. gov. Am. Biog. Rsch. Inst.; mem. adv. bd. Internat. Biog. Rsch. Inst., Cambridge, Eng. Mem. NAFE, Am. Soc. Laser Medicine and Surgery, Internat. Platform Assn., Am. Acad. Pain (assoc.), Inst. Noetic Sci., Am. Bd. Forensic Examiners, N.Am. Assn. Laser Therapy, Internat. Exec. Service Corp. Avocations: dance, skiing, cooking. Office Phone: 610-457-9158. Personal E-mail: jnmttrsn711@aol.com.

MATTES, MARTIN ANTHONY, lawyer; b. San Francisco, June 18, 1946; s. Hans Adam and Marion Jane (Burge) M.; m. Catherine Elvira Garzio, May 26, 1984; children: Nicholas Anthony, Daniel Joseph, Thomas George. BA, Stanford U., 1968; postgrad., U. Chgo., 1968-69, U. Bonn, Germany, 1971; JD, U. Calif., Berkeley, 1974. Bar: Calif. 1974, U.S. Ct. Appeals (D.C., 5th and 9th cirs.) 1978, U.S. Dist. Ct. (no. dist.) Calif. 1979, U.S. Dist. Ct. (ea. dist.) Calif. 1991. Asst. legal officer Internat. Union Conservation of Nature and Natural Resources, Bonn, 1974-76; staff counsel Calif. Pub. Utilities Commn., San Francisco, 1976-79, legal advisor to pres., 1979-82, adminstrv. law judge, 1983, asst. chief adminstrv. law judge, 1983-86; ptnr. Graham & James, San Francisco, 1986-98, Nossaman Guthner Knox and Elliott, LLP, San Francisco, 1998—. Adv. group. Calif. Senate Subcom. on Pub. Utilities Commn. Procedural Reform, 1994. Mng. editor Ecology Law Quar., 1973-74; contbr. articles to profl. jours. Mem. Conf. Calif. Pub. Utility Counsel (treas. 1988-90, v.p. 1990-91, pres. 1991-92), Internat. Coun. Environ. Law, San Francisco Bar Assn., Fed. Comms. Bar Assn., Power Assn. No. Calif. Office: Nossaman Guthner Knox Elliott LLP 50 California St Fl 34 San Francisco CA 94111-4624 Office Phone: 415-398-3600. Business E-Mail: mmattes@nossaman.com.

MATTESON, CAROL J., academic administrator; BS in Health Edn., Slippery Rock U. of Pa.; MS in Psychomotor Learning, U. Oreg.; PhD in Bus. Adminstrn., U. Pitts. Faculty Sturt Coll. of Edn., South Australia, Slippery Rock U., U. Maine, Augusta, Rowan U., NJ; asst. to pres. Slippery Rock U. of Pa.; dean coll. of bus. Bloomsburg U., Pa., provost and v.p. academic affairs Pa., 1992—95; exec. v.p. and provost Rowan U., NJ, 1995—2000; pres. Mt. Ida Coll., Newton, Mass., 2000—. Office: Mt Ida Coll 777 Dedham St Newton MA 02459 Office Phone: 617-928-4502. E-mail: cmatteson@mountida.edu.

MATTESON, KARLA J., health science association administrator; BS in Chemistry, Beloit Coll., Wis., 1969; MS in Chemistry, Marquette U., 1976; PhD, Med. Coll. Wis., 1981. Postdoctoral fellow Baylor Coll. Medicine, Houston, 1981—83; former asst. dir. U. Tenn Devel. and Genetic Ctr., Knoxville; assoc. prof. med. genetics and pathology U. Tenn., Knoxville, 1986—, dir. biochem. and molecular genetics lab., 1986—; bd. dirs. Am. Bd. Med. Genetics, 1998—2001, exec. dir., 2001—. Fellow: Am. Coll. Med. Genetics; mem.: AAAS, Soc. for Inborn Metabolic Disorders. Office: U Tenn Grad Sch Medicine Ste 435 1924 Alcoa Hwy Knoxville TN 37920-6999 also: Am Bd Med Genetics 9650 Rockville Pike Bethesda MD 20814-3998

MATTESON, WILLIAM BLEECKER, lawyer; b. NYC, Oct. 20, 1928; s. Leonard Jerome and Mary Jo (Harwell) M.; m. Marilee Brill, Aug. 26, 1950; children: Lynn, Sandra, Holly. BA, Yale U., 1950; JD, Harvard U., 1953. Bar: N.Y. 1954. Clk. to judge Augustus N. Hand U.S. Ct. Appeals, 1953-54; clk. to U.S. Supreme Ct. Justice Harold H. Burton, 1954-55; assoc. firm Debevoise & Plimpton (and predecessors), NYC, 1955-61, ptnr., 1961—98, Debevoise & Plimpton (European office), Paris, 1973-78; presiding ptnr. Debevoise & Plimpton, 1988-93. Lectr. Columbia U. Law Sch., 1972-73, 78-80. Trustee Peddie Sch., Hightstown, N.J., 1968-73, Kalamazoo Coll., 1972-77, Miss Porter's Sch., Farmington, Conn., 1977-83, N.Y. Inst. Spl. Edn., 1981-2004, Salk Inst., La Jolla, Calif., 1993-96, vice-chair, 1994-96, Statue of Liberty Ellis Island Found., 1996—. Hartford Found., 1996-2004; active USA Bus. and Industry Adv. Com. to the Orgn. for Econ. Coop. and Devel., Paris, 1986-2000; chmn. Worldwide Bus. and Industry Adv. Com., 1994-96; vice chmn. U.S. Coun. for Internat. Bus., 1990-2000, hon. trustee. Mem. ABA, FBA, Internat. Bar Assn., N.Y. State Bar Assn., Assn. Bar City of N.Y. (chmn. securities regulation com. 1968-71), Harvard U. Law Sch. Assn. N.Y.C. (trustee 1968-73), Coun. Fgn. Rels., Union Club, Sky Club, Sankaty Head Club, John's Island and Windsor Clubs. Office: Debevoise & Plimpton 919 3d Ave 47th Fl New York NY 10022 E-mail: wbmatteson@debevoise.com.

MATTESSICH, RICHARD VICTOR (ALVARUS), business administration researcher; b. Trieste, Venezia-Julia, Italy, Aug. 9, 1922; s. Victor and Gertrude M.; m. Hermine Auguste Mattessich, Apr. 12, 1952. Mech. engr., Engring. Coll., Vienna, Austria, 1940; Diplomkaufmann, Hochschule für Welthandel, Vienna, 1944; Dr.rer.pol., Hochschule für Welthandel, 1945; Accademico Ordinario, Accademia Italiana di Economia Aziendale, Bologna, 1980—; D honoris causa, U. Complutense, Madrid, 1998, U. Montesquieux, Bordeaux, 2006, U. Malaga, 2006. Rsch. fellow Austrian Inst. Econ. Rsch., Vienna, 1945-47; instr. Rosenberg Coll., St. Gallen, 1947-52; dep. head Mt. Allison U., Sackville, Canada, 1953-59; assoc. prof. U. Calif., Berkeley, 1958-67; prof. econs. Ruhr U., Bochum, Germany, 1966-67; prof. indsl. adminstrn. U. Tech., Vienna, 1976-78; prof. bus. adminstrn. U. B.C., Vancouver, Canada, 1967-87, prof. emeritus, 1988—, Arthur Andersen & Co. Disting. chair, 1980-87. Vis. prof. Free U., Berlin, 1965, U. Social Scis., St. Gallen, Switzerland, 1965-66, U. Canterbury, 1970, Austrian Acad. Mgmt., 1971, 73, City Univ. Hong Kong, 1992, Chuo U., Tokyo, 1992; hon. prof. Centro Univ. Francesco de Vitoria, Madrid; mem. bd. nominations Acctg. Hall of Fame, Columbus, Ohio, 1978-87, 2004—; bd. govs. Sch. Chartered Accountancy, Vancouver, 1981-82; bd. dirs. Can. Cert. Gen. Accts. Rsch. Found., 1984-90, internat. adv. bd., 1993—. Author: Accounting and Analytical Methods, 1964, in German, 1970, in Japanese, 1972, in Spanish, 2002, Simulation of the Firm Through a Budget Computer Program, 1964, Instrumental Reasoning and Systems Methodology, 1978, Critique of Accounting: Foundational Research in Accounting, 1995, Professional Memoirs and Beyond, 1995, The Beginnings of Accounting and Accounting Thought, 2000; editor: Modern Accounting Research History, Survey and Guide, 1984, 89, 92, Accounting Research in the 1980s and Its Future Influence, 1991, French transl., 1993, others; mem. editl. bd. Theory and Decision Libr., Jour. Bus. Adminstrn., Economia Aziendale, Praxiology, Acctg., Bus. and Fin. History. Sec.-treas. Internat. House, U. B.C., 1969-70. Served to lt. Orgn. Todt., 1944-45. Recipient Lit. award AICPA, 1972, Haim Falk award Can. Acad. Acctg. Assn., 1991, highest rsch. award Acad. Accounting Historians, 2003, Hourglass award; Ford Found. fellow, 1961-62; Disting. Erskine fellow U. Canterbury, 1970; Killam sr. fellow U. B.C., 1971-72; nominated Nobel Meml. prize in Econs., 2002. Fellow Accademia Italiana di Economia Aziendale (accademico ordinario 1980—); mem. Am. Acctg. Assn. (lit. award 1972), Schmalenbach Gesellschaft, Verb. d. Hochschullehrer für Betriebswirtschaft (exec. adv. coun. 1976-78), Inst. Chartered Accts. of B.C. (bd. of govs. 1981-82), Austrian Acad. Scis. (corr.), Acad. Acctg. Historians (life). Achievements include pioneering analytical methods in accounting and the computerized spreadsheet. Office: U BC Sauder Sch Bus Vancouver BC Canada V6T 1Z2 Business E-Mail: richard.mattessich@sauder.ubc.ca. *Cautious optimism is the best long-run strategy.*

MATTHAEI, GAY HUMPHREY, interior designer; b. NYC, Mar. 13, 1931; d. Robert Louis and Ethel Gladys Humphrey; m. Konrad Henry Matthaei, Nov. 16, 1956; children: Marcella, Leslie, Konrad. BA, Mt. Holyoke Coll., 1952; MIA, Columbia U., 1954, MA, cert. Russian Inst., 1954; grad., Parsons Sch. Design, 1970. Lectr., cons. NBC, 1956; dir. Radrick Prodns., Where Time Is a River, 1966—67; cons. N.Y.C. Parks Recreation and Cultural Adminstrn., 1970—72; assoc. Pearl R. Mitchell A.S.I.D., 1972—74, owner, 1974—97; owner, mgr. Gay Matthaei Interiors, NYC, 1975—2003. Ptnr. Two Fold Graphics, 1992—96. Restorations include Town Farms Inn, 1978, State Capital of Conn., 1977-78, Pres.'s House, Mt. Holyoke Coll., 1982, Samuel Russell House, Wesleyan Coll., 1984, Courtly Manor, Greenwich, Conn., 1987 Buhl Family Found., 1993; author: The Ledgerbook of Thomas Blue Eagle, 1994, 1995, (CD-Rom) The Journey of Thomas Blue Eagle, 1995, Sketchbook of Thomas Blue Eagle (Best Books for Teenagers NY Pub. Libr. 2002). Trustee Mt. Holyoke Coll.; mem. Commn. on State Capital Preservation and Restoration, Conn., 1997-82, Greenwich Bd. Realtors, Nat. Bd. Realtors; literacy vol., Greenich, Conn., 2005. Recipient Christopher award, 1994, Internat. Readers Assn. award, 1995, EMMA award, best CD-Rom award Multimedia Asia, others. Mem.: Nat. Mus. Am. Indian (charter), Mt. Holyoke Club, Phi Beta Kappa. Home: 710 Riverbank Rd Stamford CT 06903-3514 Office: Capital Properties and Estates Weichert Realtors 25 Field Point Rd Greenwich CT 06830-5335 Office Phone: 203-249-1459. Personal E-mail: tphq@optonline.net.

MATTHEI, EDWARD HODGE, architect; b. Chgo., Dec. 21, 1927; s. Henry Reinhard and Myra Beth (Hodge) M.; m. Mary Nina Hoffmann, June 30, 1951; children: Edward Hodge, Suzanne Marie, Christie Ann, Laura Jean, John William. BS in Archtl. Engring, U. Ill., 1951. Registered arch. 17 states, including Ariz., Fla., Ill., Mich., N.Y., Wis., Calif.; cert. NCARB. Dir. health facilities planning and constrn. Child & Smith (architects and engrs.), Chgo., 1951-60; sr. v.p. health facilities planning Perkins & Will, Chgo., 1960-74; ptnr. firm Matthei & Colin Assoc., Chgo., 1974-96; planning and archtl. design cons. Chgo., 1996—. Com. chmn. Am. Nat. Standards Inst., 1983-89; lectr. 1st Internat. Conf. on Rehab. of Handicapped, Beijing, 1986, Design USA, Novosbirsk and Moscow, USSR, 1990. Editor: Inland Architect, 1956-58; prin. works health facilities projects, med. ctr. master plans including Akron (Ohio) Gen. Hosp., Heritage Hosp., Taylor, Mich., Rose Meml., Denver, Silver Cross Hosp., Joliet, Ill., Shands Tchg. Hosp. & Med. Sch., U. Fla., Gainesville, Mercy Hosp., Davenport, Iowa, Westlake Cmty. Hosp., Chgo., Highland Park (Ill.) Hosp., Ctrl. DuPage Hosp., Winfield, Ill., Nebr. Meth. Hosp., Omaha, Rockford (Ill.) Meml. Hosp., U. Ala. Med. Ctr., Birmingham, U. Calif. Sch. Medicine, Irvine, Kent Hall, U. Chgo., Holy Cross Hosp., Md., West Mich. Cancer Ctr. Mem. profl. adv. com. Nat. Easter Seal Soc., 1965-1970, chair, 1988-89, second v.p., 1978; mem. bd. dirs. St. Scholastica H.S., Chgo., 1973-83, 86-96; mem. Welfare Coun. Greater Met. Chgo., 1965-72. With AUS, 1946-47. Recipient Leon Chatelain award for barrier-free environ. Nat. Easter Seals Soc., 1979, Disting. Svc. award, 1990, 99, Meritorious Svc. award Am. Nat. Standards Inst., 1987, Speedy award Paralyzed Vets. Am., 1993. Fellow: AIA (chmn. com. on arch. for health 1963—74, chmn. AMA joint com. on environ. health 1967—70, chmn. bldg. affairs com. Chgo. chpt. 1959—66, Disting. Svc. award Chgo. chpt. 1988); mem.: Builders Assn. Chgo., Nat. Center Barrier Free Environment (dir.), Internat. Hosp. Fedn., Am. Assn. Hosp. Planning, Am. Hosp. Assn., Chgo. Assn. Commerce and Industry. Home: 1437 W Glenlake Ave Chicago IL 60660-1801 Office: Matthei & Colin Assocs 332 S Michigan Ave Chicago IL 60604-4434

MATTHEW, LYN, sales executive, consultant, marketing professional; b. Long Beach, Calif., Dec. 15, 1936; d. Harold G. and Beatrice (Hunt) Matthew; m. Wayne Thomas Castleberry, Aug. 12, 1961 (div. Jan. 1976); children: Melanie Castleberry, Cheryl Castleberry, Nicole Castleberry, Matthew Castleberry. BS, U. Calif., Davis, 1958; MA, Ariz. State U., 1979. Cert. hotel sales exec., meeting profl., hospitality mktg. exec., hospitality mgmt. exec. Pres. Davlyn Cons. Found., Scottsdale, Ariz., 1979-82; cons., vis. prof. Art Bus., Scottsdale, 1982—; pres., dir. sales and mktg. Embassy Stes., Scottsdale, 1987-98; pres. Matthew Enterprises, Inc., Scottsdale, 1998—. Vis. prof. Maricopa CC, Phoenix, 1979—, Ariz. State U., Tempe, 1980—83; cons. Women's Caucus Art, Phoenix, 1983—88; coun. adminstr. Lynn Andrews Prodns., 2001—. Author: The Business Aspects of Art, Book I, 1979, Book II, 1989, Marketing Strategies for the Creative Artist, 1985, Moxibustion Manual, 1999. Bd. dirs. Rossom Ho. and Heritage Sq. Found., Phoenix, 1987—88; trustee Hotel Sales and Mktg. Assn. Internat. Found., 1988—90, chmn., 1991—93, mem. exec. com., 1993—95. Recipient Cmty. Bldg. award, 2000. Mem.: Am. Orgn. Bodywork Therapies Asia (pres., state dir. 1999—2003), Ariz. Acad. Performing Arts (v.p. bd. dir. 1987—88, pres. 1988—89), Soc. Govt. Meeting Planners (charter bd. dir. 1987, nat. conf. co-chair 1993—94, Sam Gilmer award 1992), Meeting Planners Internat. (v.p. Ariz. Sunbelt chpt. 1989—91, pres. 1991—92, CMP cert. trainer 1995—, Supplier of the Yr. award 1988), Cert. Hospitality Mktg. Execs. (profl. designation tng. chair 1995), Hotels Sales and Mktg. Assn. Internat. (bd. dir. 1985—90, pres. Great Phoenix chpt. 1988—89, regional dir. 1989—90, mktg. exec. 1998—), Ariz. Vocat. Edn. Assn. (sec. 1978—80), Ariz. Women's Caucus Art (pres. 1980—82, hon. advisor 1986—87), Nat. Women's Caucus Art (v.p. 1981—83), Women in Higher Edn., Ariz. Visionary Artists (treas. 1987—88), Women Image Now (Achievement and Contbn. in Visual Arts award 1983), Coun. Whistling Elk (worldwide coun. adminstr. 2001—06). Personal E-mail: lynmatthew@aol.com.

MATTHEW, NEIL EDWARD, artist, educator; b. Anderson, Ind., Jan. 19, 1925; s. Mark Neil and Mary Bertha (Clifford) Matthew; m. Jeannette Morrow, Dec. 22, 1963 (dec. Aug. 30, 2000). BA in Edn., Ariz. State U., 1949; MFA, Ind. U., 1955; postgrad., U. Iowa, 1957-58, State Acad. of Fine Arts, Stuttgart, Germany, 1959-60. Tchr., art Covington (Ind.) Jr. HS, 1949-50, Clay HS, South Bend, Ind., 1955-57; instr. art Ind. U., Kokomo, 1960-64, from instr. to asst. prof. art. Indpls., 1964-71; from asst. to assoc. prof. Herron Sch. Art/Ind. U. Purdue U., Indpls., 1971-87, assoc. prof. emeritus, 1987—. Art exhibit judge Kokomo Art Assn., 1970; rschr. salary studies AAUP, Ind. U. Purdue U., others. One-man shows include Lieber's Gallery, Indpls., 1962, 1968, Purdue U. Gallery, 1962, Ind. U. Med. Ctr., Indpls., 1966, Ind. U., Kokomo, 1967, Ind. U. Purdue U., Indpls., 1996, 1998, Lyman-Snodgrass Gallery, 1984, others, exhibited in group shows at Libr. Congress, 1956, 1958, 1959, Purdue U., 1966, 1969, Ind. Arts Competition, 1988, U. Ariz. Mus. Art, Tucson, 2005, Represented in permanent collections Ctr. Creative Photography, U. Ariz. Mus. Art, Ind. U. Purdue U., Indpls., Indpls. Mus. Art, Ind. U. Art Mus., Bloomington, Ind., Ind. State Mus., Indpls., Ind., Ctr. Creative Photography, 2003. With US Army, 1950—52. Scholar, U. Iowa, 1957—58; Fulbright grantee, Stuttgart, 1959—60. Mem.: Coll. Art Assn., Fulbright Assn., Ctr. Creative Photography, Soc. Ind. Pioneers. Independent. Presbyterian. Avocations: travel, reading, history, fiction. Home: The Forum #353 A 2500 N Rosemont Blvd Tucson AZ 85712-2132

MATTHEWS, ALEXANDER, health facility administrator; b. NYC, Sept. 8, 1924; s. Matthew and Helen (Tertis) Fotopoulos; m. Ann Koutsatsa Matthews (dec.); m. Linda Kay Warren, Dec. 30, 1999; children: Andrew Philip, Lydia Ann. BA, Boston U., 1948; MD, SUNY, 1952. Diplomate Am. Bd. Surgery, Bd. Thoracic Surgery. Pvt. practice, 1960—90; med. dir. Des Moines Med. Exchange Program, Stavropal, Russia, 1990—95; chief med. officer Mil. Entrance Processing Sta., Des Moines, 1995—. Chief surgery, med. staff, bd. dirs. Iowa Luth. Hosp., Des Moines, 1962—90. Comdr. USPHS, 1952—59. Fellow: ACS, Am. Coll. Chest Physicians; mem.: Soc. Thoracic Surgeons. Home: 505 Glenview Dr Des Moines IA 50312 Office: Mil Entrance Processing Sta Dept Defense 2500 U Ave West Des Moines IA 50266-1480

MATTHEWS, ALLAN FREEMAN, geologist; b. Wakefield, Mass., May 27, 1916; s. Ralph Freeman Matthews and Mary (Morrill) Hill; m. Shirley Jean Spencer, Dec. 23, 1937 (div. Oct. 1955, dec. 1989); children: David Allan, Kim; m. Mary Cerantonio Thomas, Feb. 24, 1956, (div. Jan. 5, 1962); m. Doris Olive Haignere, June 26, 1962 (Dec. 2003). BA, Carleton Coll., Northfield, Minn., 1937; MS, Antioch Coll., Yellow Springs, Ohio, 1939; postgrad., Johns Hopkins U., Balt., 1939-40. Tech. editor Ceramic Industry Jour., Chgo., 1940-41; editor, sect. chief U.S. Bur. of Mines, Washington, 1941-51; asst. dir., staff Pres.'s Materials Policy Commn.,

Washington, 1951-52; materials cons. Nat. Security Resources Bd., Washington, 1952-53; ops. analyst Johns Hopkins Ops. Rsch. Office, Chevy Chase, Md., 1953-54; program officer U.S. Agy. for Internat. Devel., Washington, 1954-75; editor, pub. Developing Country Courier, McLean, Va., 1978-85. Del. UN Global Modeling Conf., Paris, 1982; initiated citizens transnat. constl. conv., The Hague, Netherlands, 1998; chmn. constn. action group Alliance for Democracy, Waltham, Mass., 1997-99; minerals cons. Global 2000 Project, 1978-80; cons. and presenter in field. Author: Sovereigns Peacefully Take Charge, 1997, 2nd edit., 2005; editor: Minerals Yearbook, 1947-50; contbr. articles to profl. jours. and chpts. to books Dir. Streit Council for a Union of Democracies, Washington, 1957—; core planner 20/20 Vision, Washington, 1991-97; a founder The Reston Forum, 1990-92; pres. Waterford Sq. Condominium Assn., Reston, 1992; apptd. adv. bd. Phila. Two Orgn. Direct Democracy, 2001, Signatory of Natl. Initiative for Democracy, 2002. Lt. (j.g.) USN, 1944-46. Recipient Meritorious award U.S. Agy. for Internat. Devel., 1955, Commendation for Devel. Analysis, 1957; named Fellow in Geology, 1937-39. Mem. AAAS, ACLU, Democratic Socialists Am., Natural Resources Def. Coun., U N Assn., World Federalist Movement, Unitarian Universalist Assn., Fed. Am. Scientists, Phila. Two Direct Democracy, Soc. for Internat. Devel. (proposer continental fed. unions at N.Am. regional conf. 2000), Ctr. Def. Info, Initiative and Referendum Inst. Green Party. Achievements include evaluation of mineral resources adequacy and advancement of transnational constitutions. Home: Apt 624 900 N Taylor St Arlington VA 22203-1863 Personal E-mail: allan_matthews@comcast.net.

MATTHEWS, BRIAN W., molecular biology educator; b. Mount Barker, Australia, May 25, 1938; came to U.S., 1967; s. Lionel A. and Ethlinda L. (Harris) M.; m. Helen F. Denley, Sept. 7, 1963; children: Susan, Kristine. BS, U. Adelaide, Australia, 1959, BS with honors, 1960, PhD, 1964, DSc, 1986. Mem. staff Med. Rsch. Coun., Cambridge, Eng., 1963-66; vis. assoc. NIH, Bethesda, Md., 1967-69; prof. molecular biology U. Oreg., Eugene, 1969—, chmn. dept. physics, 1985-86, dir. Inst. Molecular Biology, 1980-83, 90-92; Drummond lectr. U. Calgary (Can.), 1995. Advisor NSF, Washington, 1975-77; investigator Howard Hughes Med. Inst., 1989—; mem. U.S. Nat. Commn. for Crystallography, Washington, 1980-86, 88-90. Editor: Protein Science, 2007—. Rsch. fellow Alfred P. Sloan Found., 1971, Guggenheim fellow, 1977; recipient Career Devel. award NIH, 1973, Faculty Excellence award Oreg. Bd. Edn., 1984, Discovery award Med. Rsch. Found. Oreg., 1987, Reed Coll. Vollum award, 1994, Stein and Moore award Protein Soc., 2000. Mem. NAS, AAAS, Crystallographic Assn., Am. Chem. Soc., Protein Soc. (pres. 1995-97), Biophysical Soc. (nat. lectr. 2001). Office: U Oreg HHMI Inst Molecular Biology Eugene OR 97403 Office Phone: 541-346-2572. E-mail: brian@uoxray.uoregon.edu.

MATTHEWS, CHARLES SEDWICK, petroleum engineer, consultant; b. Houston, Mar. 27, 1920; s. Charles James and Zadoc Coleman (Sedwick) M.; m. Miriam Loraine Ormerod, June 2, 1945; children— Joan Gail, Wendy Loraine BSChemE, Rice U., 1941, MSChemE, 1943, PhD in Chemistry, 1944. Registered profl. engr., Tex. Engr. Shell Devel. Co., San Francisco, 1944-48, rsch. engr. Houston, 1948-56, dir. rsch., 1967-72; chief reservoir engr. Shell Oil Co., Houston, 1965, mgr. engring., 1972-73, sr. petroleum engring. cons., 1973-89. Engring. adv. com. Rice U., Houston, 1973-77; cons. Dept. Energy, Washington, 1974-78, adv. com., 1975-79; spl. asst. Nat. Petroleum Council, Washington, 1981-83; reserves com. Am. Petroleum Inst. Author: Pressure Buildup and Flow Tests in Wells, 1967; contbr. articles to profl. jours.; patentee in field. Chmn. Tex. Engrs. for Conservation, Houston, 1973 Recipient Disting. Alumnus award Rice U., 1994. Mem. NAE, Soc. Petroleum Engrs. (hon. mem., Lester Uren award 1975, disting. author, disting. lectr. 1968, Disting. lectr. emeritus 1986), Phi Beta Kappa, Sigma Xi, Tau Beta Pi, Phi Lambda Upsilon. Clubs: Houston, Meyerland (treas. 1982-85). Republican. Methodist. Avocations: swimming, fishing. Home: 5307 S Braeswood Blvd Houston TX 77096-4149 Office Phone: 713-729-4140.

MATTHEWS, CHARLES W., JR., oil industry executive, lawyer; b. Houston, Feb. 27, 1945; BA, U. Tex., 1967; JD, U. Houston, 1970. Bar: Tex. 1970, Tenn. 1980, admitted to: U.S. Dist. Ct., So. Dist. Tex. 1975, U.S. Supreme Ct., U.S. Ct. Appeals, Dist. Columbia Circuit, U.S. Ct. Appeals, Fifth and Eleventh Circuits 1981. Trial atty. law dept. Exxon Corp., 1971-78, region atty. southeastern and southern region mktg. offices, 1978-81, assoc. gen. atty. litigation sect., gen. counsel & dir. Petroleum Casualty Co. and Exxon Risk Mgmt. Svcs., 1981-92; from assoc. gen. counsel law dept. to gen. counsel law dept. Exxon U.S.A., 1992; v.p., gen. counsel Exxon Mobil Corp., 1995—. Instr. State Bar Tex. Profl. Develop. Program, Litigating the Oil and Gas Case, 1988, U. Houston Law Found., mem. bd. trustees. Author: Recent Developments in Liability for Oil and Gas Operations, 1987. Nat. trustee Southwest Region Boys and Girls Club Am.; chair U. Tex. Chancellor's Coun., 2002; mem. bd. overseers Rand Inst. Civil Justice; mem. develop. bd. U. Tex. Recipient Alumnus of the Yr., Univ. of Houston, 2000. Fellow: Tex. Bar Found.; mem.: ABA (fellow, mem. com. corp. gen. counsel), Tex. Access Justice Commn. (commr. 2004—), Chief Legal Officers Roundtable, Am. Inns Ct. Found. (trustee, mem. leadership coun.), Nat. Ctr. State Courts (co-chair gen. counsel com. 2002—), Defense Rsch. Inst., State Bar Tex. (vice chmn. adminstrn. justice com. 1988, corp. counsel liaison to litigation section 1988—89), Ctr. Am. and Internat. Law (chmn. exec. com. 2002—, trustee), Internat. Assn. Def. Counsel Found. (chmn. corp. counsel com. 1991, v.p. 1993—95, bd. dirs.), Assn. Gen. Counsel, Dallas Bar Assn., Dallas Bar Found. (fellow, v.p., gen. counsel), Houston Bar Assn. (bd. dirs. 1994—95, fellow), Order Barons. Office: Exxon Mobil Corp Law Dept 5959 Las Colinas Blvd Irving TX 75039-2298 *

MATTHEWS, CHRISTIAN WILLIAM, JR., minister; b. Jersey City, Oct. 12, 1934; s. Christian William and Lydia Louise (Weller) M.; m. Elaine Louise Ochs, June 18, 1955; children: Christian William III, Patricia Louise, Judith Ann, Barbara Jean. BA, King's Coll., 1956; MRE, Ea. Theol. Sem., 1960, MDiv, 1962; MEd, U. Del., 1961; ThM, Princeton Theol. Sem., 1965; DD, Grove City Coll., 1988. Ordained to ministry Presbyn. Ch. (U.S.A.), 1962. Intern Bklyn. Jewish Hosp., NY, 1961—62, resident, 1962—64, resident endocrinology, 1964—65; dir. Christian edn. United Presbyn. Ch. of Manoa, Havertown, Pa., 1959-62; asst. min. 1st Presbyn. Ch., Norristown, Pa., 1962-65; assoc. min. Marble Collegiate Ch., NYC, 1965-68; sr. min. Fox Chapel Presbyn. Ch., Pitts., 1968-79, Christ Presbyn. Ch., Toledo, 1979-2000, 2d Presbyn. Ch., Balt., 2000—04, 1st Presbyn. Ch., Grand Haven, Mich., 2004—. Mem. The Fellowship, Washington, Synod Gen. Coun. Presbyn. Ch. U.S.A.; chmn. Synod Evangelism; leader marriage and family seminars; mem. alumni fund bd. Princeton Theol. Sem.; mem. Kirk coun., Alma Coll.; cons. Presbyn. Ch. in U.S.A., Nat. Com. for Prison Reform, County Human Svc. Commn. Author: Lingering with Luke—A Study of the Life of Christ, 1976, Marriage and Family Study Course, 1983; developer (nat. program for Presbyn. chs.) Risk Evangelism; signer Lausanne Covenant of Internat. Congress on World Evangelization. Chmn. Com. for Ecol. Instrn.; founding pres. Samaritan Counseling Ctr.; sec. The Ability Ctr.; bd. dirs. area coun. Boy Scouts Am., Toledo Rotary Club, James C. Caldwell Cmty. Ctr., Met. Toledo Chs. United, AASK-Mid Am., Toledo Leadership Found.; mem. Coun. for Religion and Psychiatry. Mem.: Rotary Club of Toledo. Home and Office: 337 Sawgrass Ct Holland OH 43528-9210 Office Phone: 443-418-5593. Business E-Mail: drcwmatthews@aol.com. *As I reflect upon life, I believe that God is at work in our world bringing together people of faith to meet the complex challenges confronting us at this time of history. Working together, we are able to encourage, strengthen, and support one another in meeting the needs of our world.*

MATTHEWS, CHRISTOPHER JOHN, political commentator, writer; b. Phila., Dec. 17, 1945; s. Herbert Charles and Mary Teresa (Shields) Matthews; m. Kathleen Ann Cunningham, 1980; children: Michael, Thomas, Caroline. BA in Economics, Coll. Holy Cross, 1967, LLD (hon.), 2003; grad. studies, U. NC; doctorate (hon.), St. Leo U., Loyola Coll., Md., Niagara U., Fontbonne Coll., Beaver Coll., New England Sch. Law, Anna Maria Coll., Chesnut Hill Coll. Legis. asst. to US Senator Frank Moss of Utah, 1971—73; staff mem. US Senator Edward Muskie of Maine; staff asst. US Senate Budget Com., 1974—77; speechwriter for Pres. Jimmy Carter, 1977—79; aide to Speaker of House Tip O'Neill US Ho. of Reps., 1981—87; polit. analyst CBS This Morning, 1987; bur. chief, columnist San Francisco Examiner, Washington, 1987—2000; past nat. syndicated columnist San Francisco Chronicle; past pres., CEO govt. rsch. corp., Washington; host Hardball with Chris Matthews CNBC, 1997—2002, MSNBC, 1999—; host syndicated program, The Chris Matthews Show, 2002—. Author: Hardball: How Politics is Really Played- Told By One Who Knows the Game, 1988, Kennedy & Nixon: The Rivalry That Shaped PostWar America, 1996, Now, Let Me Tell You What I Really Think, 2001, American: Beyond Our Grandest Notions, 2002, articles for The New Republic, US News and World Report, The NY Times, Christian Sci. Monitor, Am. Politics; actor: (films) Man of the Year, 2006. Trade devel. advisor US Peace Corps, Swaziland, 1968—70. Recipient Lincoln Award, Union League of Phila. Democrat. Office: Hardball With Chris Matthews 30 Rockefeller Plz New York NY 10112 *

MATTHEWS, CRAIG GERARD, retired energy executive; b. Bklyn., Mar. 8, 1943; m. Carol O. Olsen, Sept. 10, 1971; children: Kenneth C., Bradford P., Melinda M. BCE, Rutgers U., 1965; MS in Indsl. Mgmt., Polytech. Inst. Bklyn., 1971. Vice chmn., COO, KeySpan Corp. (formerly Bklyn. Union Gas Co.), 1965—2002, ret., 2002; pres., CEO NUI Corp., 2004; ret., 2004—. Bd. dirs. Hess Corp., Nat. Fuel Gas; mem. adv. bd. Republic Fin. Chmn. nat. bd. dirs. Salvation Army, chmn. bd. dirs. NY; bd. dirs. Bklyn. Philharm.; chmn. Poly. U., Bklyn. Republican. Presbyterian. Home: 132 Canterbury Way Basking Ridge NJ 07920 Office Phone: 908-719-4290. E-mail: craiggmatthews@aol.com.

MATTHEWS, DANIEL B., air transportation executive; BA in Bus. Adminstrn. and Econs., Lewis U., Romeoville, Ill., 1976; MBA, Loyola U., Chgo., 1977. Various comml. lending and tax-oriented lease financing positions Borg-Warner Leasing, Chgo., Sears Bank & Trust Co.; various corp. fin. and treasury-related positions Ea. Air Lines, Inc., 1982—90, staff v.p., treas.; asst. treas. Ryder Sys., Inc., 1990—93; with NW Airlines Corp., Minn., 1993—, v.p. aircraft transactions, v.p., asst. treas., 1999—2000, sr. v.p., treas. Bd. mem. DARTS, Mpls. Mem. spl. adv. coun. Lewis U. Office: NW Airlines Corp 2700 Lone Oak Pky Eagan MN 55121 Office Phone: 612-726-2111. *

MATTHEWS, DARRYL R., SR., not-for-profit fundraiser; m. Allison Paige Stinson; children: Julian, Blake, Darryl Jr. BSc in Polit. Sci. and Sociology, Ctrl. Mo. State Univ., 1977. Claims adjuster USF&G, Kansas City, Mo., 1977—78; asst. exec. sec. Alpha Phi Alpha Fraternity, Inc., Chgo., 1978—81, dir. mktg., membership Balt., 1983—93, dep. exec. dir., 1993—94, interim exec. dir., 1994—95, exec. dir., COO, 1995—96, sr. gen. pres. Baltimore, Md., 2005—; account exec. AT&T, Southwestern Bell, Am. Bell, Kansas City, 1981—83; exec. dir. mktg. Bingwa Software Co., Norcross, Ga., 1996—97; ind. cons. White House Presdl. Advance Office, 1997—98; exec. dir., COO Nat. Assn. of Black Accts., Inc., Greenbelt, Md., 1998—. Vice-chmn. bd. dirs. Martin Luther King Jr. Nat. Meml., Washington. Named one of Most Influential Black Americans, Ebony mag., 2006. Office: Nat Assn Black Accountants Inc 7249 A Hanover Pkwy Greenbelt MD 20770 Office Phone: 410-554-0040, 301-474-6222. Office Fax: 410-554-0054, 301-474-3114.

MATTHEWS, DAVE, singer, musician; b. Johannesburg, Jan. 9, 1967; s. John and Val Matthews; m. Jennifer Ashley Harper, Aug. 10, 2000; children: Grace Anne, Stella Busina, August Oliver. Vocalist, guitarist The Dave Matthews Band, 1991—; founder ATO Records, 2000—. Bd. dirs. Farm Aid, 2001—. Musician: (albums) Remember Two Things, 1993, Under the Table and Dreaming, 1994, Crash, 1996 (Grammy award Best Rock Performance by A Duo Or Group, 1996), Live at Red Rocks, 9-15-95, 1997, Before These Crowded Streets, 1998, Live at Luther College, 1999, Listener Supported, 1999, Live in Chicago 12-19-98, 2001, Everyday, 2001, Live at Folsom Field, Boulder Colorado, 2002, Busted Stuff, 2002, The Central Park Concert, 2003, The Gorge, 2004, Stand Up, 2005, Live at Radio City Music Hall, 2007, (solo albums) Some Devil, 2003 (Grammy award Best Male Rock Vocal Performance, 2003); actor: (films) Where the Red Fern Grows, 2003, Because of Winn-Dixie, 2005, I Now Pronounce You Chuck and Larry, 2007. Office: ATO Records 157 Chambers St New York NY 10007 *

MATTHEWS, DAVID, clergyman; b. Indianola, Miss., Jan. 29, 1920; s. Albert and Bertha (Henderson) M.; m. Lillian Pearl Banks, Aug. 28, 1951; 1 dau., Denise. AB, Morehouse Coll., Atlanta, 1950; student, Atlanta U., 1950, Memphis Theol. Sem., 1965, Delta State U., Cleveland, Miss., 1969, 71, 72; D.D. (hon.), Natchez Jr. Coll., Miss., 1973, Morris Booker Meml. Coll., 1988. Ordained minister Nat. Baptist Conv. U.S.A., 1946; pastor chs. in Miss., 1951—, Bell Grove Baptist Ch., Indianola, 1951—, Strangers Home, Greenwood, 1958—. Tchr., chmn. dept. social sci. Gentry H.S., Indianola, 1958-83; moderator Sunflower Bapt. Assn., 1957—; v.p. Gen. Bapt. Conv. Miss., 1958—, former lectr., conv. congress religious edn.; v.p. Nat. Bapt. Conv. U.S.A., 1971-94; del. to Nat. Coun. Chs., 1960, supr. oratorial contest, 1976; pres. Gen. Missionary Bapt. State Conv. Miss., 1974-98. Mem. Sunflower County Anti-Poverty Bd., 1965-71, Indianola Bi-Racial Com., 1965—; mem. Gov.'s Advisory Com.; col. on staff Gov. Finch, 1976-80; mem. budget com. Indianola United Fund, 1971—; chmn. bd. Indianola FHA, 1971—; trustee Natchez Jr. Coll.; mem. Miss. Gov.'s Research and Devel. Council, 1984—; apptd. mem. So. Govs. Ecumenical Coun. Infant Mortality, 1987. Served with U.S. Army, 1942-45, PTO. Recipient citation Morehouse Coll., 1950, citation Miss. Valley State Coll., 1956, J.H. Jackson Preaching award Midwestern Baptist Laymen Fellowship, 1974, Gov.'s Merit award, 1975, Human Svc. award Miss. Valley State U., 2004. Mem. NEA, Miss., Indianola Tchrs. Assns., Am. Bible Soc. (adv. coun. 1991-2000, student reform theol. sem. centennial edn. 1990—). Democrat. Baptist. Home: PO Box 627 Indianola MS 38751-0627 Fax: 662-887-9078. Personal E-mail: matthews3463@bills.net. *I have learned not to seek honors and success but to become so involved in worthwhile works that I lose myself and by such actions success and honors have come.*

MATTHEWS, DAVID FORT, career officer; b. Lancaster, NH, Sept. 25, 1944; s. Clinton Fort and Mabel Sawin (Oaks) M.; m. Eva Mae Horton, Nov. 10, 1990. BA, Vanderbilt U., 1966; MA, Mid. Tenn. U., 1973. Cert. acquisition mgr. Rsch. and devel. officer U.S. Army Rsch. Inst., Washington, 1974-77; exec. officer 194th Maintenence Battalion-Camp Humphreys, Korea, 1978-79; career program mgr. U.S. Army Mil. Pers. Ctr., Washington, 1979-82; logistics staff officer Dep. Chief of Staff Logistics, Washington, 1982-83; team chief Chief of Staff Army Study Group, Washington, 1983-85; logistics div. chief Multiple Launch Rocket System Project Office, Huntsville, Ala., 1985-88; comdr. Ordnance Program Div., Riyadh, Saudi Arabia, 1988-90; project mgr. Army Tactical Missile System, Huntsville, 1990-94; sr. lectr. weapon systems acquisition Naval Postgrad. Sch., Monterey, Calif., 1994—. Decorated Legion of Merit, Bronze Star; recipient award as project mgr. of yr. Sec. of Army, 1991. Mem. Nat. Def. Indsl. Assn., Assn. U.S. Army. Avocations: sports, water-skiing, reading, scuba diving. Home: 83 High Meadow Ln Carmel CA 93923 Office: Naval Postgrad Sch Monterey CA 93943 Office Phone: 831-656-2360. Business E-Mail: DMatthews@nps.navy.mil.

MATTHEWS, EDWIN SPENCER, JR., lawyer; b. Spokane, Wash., May 31, 1934; s. Edwin Spencer and Dorothy Chace (Ehrhardt) M.; m. Marie-Claude Paris, Dec. 19, 1959 (div. 1982); children: Nadia, Sylvie, Clarissa; m. Patricia L. Sills Barnes, Dec. 22, 1983; children: Paxton, Gillian. AB magna cum laude, Harvard U., Cambridge, Mass., 1956; Diplome d'Etudes Francaises, Inst. de Touraine, Tours, France, 1958; LLB, Yale U., New Haven, Conn., 1962. Bar: NY 1963, Calif. 1979, US Supreme Ct. 1992; Conseil Juridique (France) 1965-79. Assoc. Coudert Bros., NYC, 1962-65, Coudert Freres, Paris, 1965-69, ptnr., 1969-79, Coudert Bros., San Francisco, 1979-80, NYC, 1980—2003, of counsel, 2003—05, Baker & McKenzie LLP, 2005—. Trustee Earthjustice Legal Def. Fund, San Francisco, 1984-2006, Steep Rock Assn., Washington, Conn., 1998-2004; bd. dirs. Friends of Earth Found., NYC, 1979-85; bd. dirs. Friends of Earth Inc., Washington, Conn., 1970-85, pres., 1979-80; bd. dirs. Shepang River Assn., pres., 1995—. With US Army, 1957-58. Mem. Assn. of Bar of City of NY (com. on housing and urban devel. 1964-65, com. on capital representation, 1995-2003), Harvard Club, NY Athletic Club. Democrat. Avocations: ocean sailing, carpentry, sculling, wilderness canoeing, photography. Home: 11 Harrison St New York NY 10013-2837 also: PO Box 493 Washington Depot CT 06794-0493 Office: Baker & McKenzie LLP 1114 Avenue Of The Americas New York NY 10036-7703

MATTHEWS, EUGENE EDWARD, artist; b. Davenport, Iowa, Mar. 22, 1931; s. Nickolas Arthur and Velma (Schroeder) M.; m. Wanda Lee Miller, Sept. 14, 1952; children: Anthony Lee, Daniel Nickolas. Student, Bradley U., 1948-51; BFA, U. Iowa, 1953, MFA, 1957. Prof. fine arts grad. faculty U. Colo., Boulder, 1961-96, prof. fine arts emeritus, 1996—, dir. vis. artists program, 1985-96. Vis. artist Am. Acad. Rome, 1989. One-man shows include U. Wis., Milw., 1960, Brena Gallery, Denver, 1963, 65, 67, 70, 74, 76, 78, 80, 83, 88, Colorado Springs Fine Arts Ctr., 1967, Sheldon Art Gallery, U. Nebr., 1968, Denver Art Mus., 1972, James Yu Gallery, N.Y.C., 1973, 77, Dubins Gallery, L.A., 1981, Galeria Rysunku, Poznan, 1983, CU. Art Galleries, U. Colo., Boulder, 1996, Rule Art Gallery, Denver, 1998; exhibited in numerous group shows U.S., Europe, Africa, Asia; internat. watercolor exhbn. New Orleans, 1983, Louvre, Paris, Met. Mus. of Art, N.Y.C., Internat. Art Ctr., Kyoto, Japan, Mus. of Modern Art, Rijeka, Yugoslavia, Taipei Fine Arts Mus., Taiwan, Republic of China, Internat. Watercolor Biennial-East/West, Champaign, Ill., 1997; represented in permanent collections Nat. Mus. Am. Art, Washington, Denver Art Mus., Butler Inst. Am. Art, Chrysler Art Mus., others. Recipient Penello d'Argento award Acitrezza Internazionale, 1958, S.P.Q.R. Cup of Rome, Roma Olimpionica Internazionale, 1959, Gold medal of honor Nat. Arts Club, N.Y.C., 1969, Bicentennial award Rocky Mountain Nat. Watercolor Exhbn., 1976, Am. Drawings IV Purchase award, 1982, others; fellow in painting Am. Acad. Rome, 1957-60, U. Colo. Creative Rsch. fellow, 1966-67. Mem. Watercolor U.S.A. Honor Soc. (charter). Home: 2865 Jay Rd Boulder CO 80301-1605

MATTHEWS, GILBERT ELLIOTT, investment banker; b. Brookline, Mass., Apr. 24, 1930; s. Martin W. and Charlotte (Cohen) M.; m. Anne Lisbeth Barnett, Apr. 20, 1958 (div. 1975); children: Lisa Joan, Diana Kory (dec. 1995); m. Elaine Rita Siegal Pulitzer, Jan. 2, 1978 (div. 1999); 1 child, Jennifer Rachel. AB, Harvard U., 1951; MBA, Columbia U., 1953. Chartered fin. analyst. Dept. mgr. Bloomingdale's, NYC, 1953, 56-60; security analyst Merrill Lynch, NYC, 1960; investment banker Bear, Stearns & Co., NYC, 1960-95, gen. ptnr., 1979-85; mng. dir. Bear, Stearns & Co. Inc., 1985-86, sr. mng. dir., 1986-95, Sutter Securities Inc., San Francisco, 1995—, chmn. bd. dirs., 1997—. Served as lt. (j.g.) USN, 1953-56. Mem. N.Y. Soc. Security Analysts. Democrat. Jewish. Office: Sutter Securities Inc 555 California St Ste 3330 San Francisco CA 94104 Office Phone: 415-352-6336. Business E-Mail: gil@suttersf.com.

MATTHEWS, JACK (JOHN HAROLD MATTHEWS), language educator, writer; b. Columbus, Ohio, July 22, 1925; s. John Harold and Lulu Emma (Grover) M.; m. Barbara Jane Reese, Sept. 16, 1947; children: Cynthia Ann Matthews Warnock, Barbara Ellen Matthews Saunders, John Harold. BA, Ohio State U., 1949, MA, 1954. Clk. U.S. Post Office, Columbus, 1950-59; prof. English Urbana Coll., Ohio, 1959-64, Ohio U., Athens, 1964-77, disting. prof., 1977—2003, disting. prof. emeritus, 2003—. Author: Bitter Knowledge, 1964 (Ohioana fiction award 1964), Hanger Stout, Awake!, 1967, The Charisma Campaigns, 1972, Collecting Rare Bodies For Pleasure and Profit, 1977, Sassafras, 1983, Crazy Women, 1985, Booking in the Heartland, 1986 (Ohioana Non-fiction award 1986), Ghostly Populations, 1986, Memoirs of a Bookman, 1989, Dirty Tricks, 1990, On The Shore of That Beautiful Shore (play), 1991, An Interview with the Sphinx (play), 1992, Storyhood As We Know It and Other Tales (stories), 1993, Booking Pleasures, 1996, (essays) Reading Matter, 2000, Schopenhauerova Vule, 2002, others. Served with USCG, 1943-45. Recipient numerous ind. artist awards Ohio Art Council, Major Artist award, 1989-90, Ohioana Career award, 2005; Guggenheim fellow, 1974-75 Mem. Phi Beta Kappa Home: 4314 Fisher Rd Athens OH 45701-9333 Office: Ohio U Dept English Athens OH 45701 Business E-Mail: matthej1@ohio.edu.

MATTHEWS, JAMES SHADLEY, lawyer; b. Omaha, Nov. 24, 1951; s. Donald E. and Lois Jean (Shadley) M.; m. Mary Kvaal, May 3, 1991; 1 child, Katherine. BA cum laude, St. Olaf Coll., 1973; JD, U. Ill., 1976; MBA, U. Denver, 1977. Bar: Minn. 1976, U.S. Dist. Ct. Minn. 1978. With Northwestern Nat. Life Ins. Co., Mpls., 1978-89, v.p., asst. gen. counsel, 1985-89; ptnr. Lindquist & Venum, Mpls., 1990—. Sr. v.p., gen. counsel Washington Square Capital, Inc., 1989; sec. NWNL Health Network, Inc., St. Paul, 1987-89; pub. dir. Minn. Health Reins. Assn., 1992-94; bd. dirs. Northstar Life Ins. Co., 2001-03; spkr. in field. Mem. ABA, Am. Health Lawyers Assn., Minn. Bar Assn. (chmn. health law sect. 1986-87). Office: Lindquist & Vennum IDS Ctr 80 S 8th St Ste 4200 Minneapolis MN 55402-2274 Office Phone: 612-371-3211. Business E-Mail: jmatthews@lindquist.com.

MATTHEWS, JOHN, human resources specialist, wholesale distribution executive; M in Finance. Various positions in human resources Costo Wholesale Corp., Issaquah, Wash., 1990—, sr. v.p., human resources and risk mgmt. Former comdr., logistics expert USN. Office: Costco Wholesale Corp 999 Lake Dr Issaquah WA 98027 Office Phone: 425-313-8100. Office Fax: 425-313-8103.

MATTHEWS, KATHLEEN SHIVE, biochemistry educator; b. Austin, Tex., Aug. 30, 1945; d. William and Gwyn Shive; m. Randall Matthews. BS in Chemistry, U. Tex., 1966; PhD in Biochemistry, U. Calif., Berkeley, 1970. Post doctoral fellow Stanford (Calif.) U., 1970-72; mem. faculty Rice U., Houston, 1972—, chair dept., 1987-95, Wiess prof., 1989-96, Stewart Meml. chair, 1996—, dean natural scis., 1998—. Mem. BBCB study sect. NIH, Bethesda, Md., 1980-84, 86-88, BRSG adv. com., 1992-94; mem. adv. com. on rsch. programs Tex. Higher Edn. Coord. Bd., Austin, 1987-92; mem. undergrad. edn. initiative rev. panel Howard Hughes Rsch. Inst., Bethesda, 1991, mem. rsch. resources rev. panel, 1995, mem. predoctoral fellowships rev. panel, 2001, trustee S.W. Rsch. Inst., 2003—, steering com. adv. bd. Vinson & Elkins Women's Initiative, 2001-06. Mem. editl. bd. Jour. Biol. Chemistry, 1988-93, assoc. editor, 1994-99; contbr. 150 reviewed papers. Fellow AAAS; mem. Am. Soc. Biochemistry and Molecular Biology (nominating com. 1993-94, 96-97, fin. com. 2001-2002), Protein Soc., Biophys. Soc. (pub. affairs com. 2002-05), Am. Chem. Soc., Phi Beta Kappa. Office: Rice Univ PO Box 1892 6100 Main St MS102 Houston TX 77005-1892 E-mail: ksm@rice.edu.

MATTHEWS, LEONARD SARVER, advertising and marketing executive; b. Glendean, Ky., Jan. 6, 1922; s. Clell and Zetta Price (Sarver) M.; m. Dorothy Lucille Fessler; children: Nancy, James, Douglas. BS summa cum laude, Northwestern U., 1948. With Leo Burnett Co., Inc., Chgo., 1948-75, v.p., dir., 1958-59, exec. v.p. charge mktg. services, 1959-61, exec. v.p. client svc., 1961-69, pres., 1970-75; asst. sec. commerce for domestic and internat. bus., 1976; pres., exec. com., dir. Young and Rubicam, 1977-78; pres. Am. Assn. Advt. Agys., 1979-89; co-founder Matthews & Johnston, Stamford, Conn., 1989-92; chmn. Next Century Media, 1992—99. Mem. adv. bd. Scripps Capital, San Diego. Ensign USCGR, 1942-46. Named to Advt. Hall of Fame, 1999. Mem. Advt. Coun. (life bd. dirs.), Sky Club (N.Y.C.), Pine Valley Golf Club (N.J.), Rancho Santa Fe Golf (Calif.), Georgetown Club (Washington), Delta Sigma Pi, Beta Gamma Sigma. Republican. Lutheran. Office: PO Box 2629 Rancho Santa Fe CA 92067-2629

MATTHEWS, MILDRED SHAPLEY, freelance/self-employed editor; b. Pasadena, Calif., Feb. 15, 1915; d. Harlow and Martha (Betz) Shapley; m. Ralph Vernon Matthews, Sept. 25, 1937; children: June Lorrain, Bruce Shapley, Melvin Lloyd, Martha Alys. AB, U. Mich., 1936. Rsch. asst. Calif. Inst. Tech., Pasadena, 1950—61; bilingual editor, rsch. asst. Astron. Obs. Merate-Milan and Trieste, Italy, 1960—70; rsch. asst. Lunar-Planetary Lab., editor space sci. series U. Ariz., Tucson, 1970—96; ret., 1996. Contbr. articles to Sky and Telescope, Astronomia. Recipient Masursky Meritorious Svc. award div. planetary sci. Am. Astron. Soc., 1993. Avocations: classical music concerts, especially opera, travel. Home: 3154 Del Vina St Pasadena CA 91107

MATTHEWS, NORMAN STUART, retail executive; b. Boston, Jan. 13, 1933; s. Martin W. and Charlotte (Cohen) M.; m. Joanne Banks, June 11, 1956; children: Gary S., Jeffrey B., Patricia A. BA, Princeton U.; MBA, Harvard U. Ptnr. Beacon Mktg. and Advt. Assocs., NYC, 1956-71; sr. v.p. Broyhill Furniture Co., Lenoir, NC, 1971-73, E.J. Korvettes, NYC, 1973-78; chmn., chief exec. officer Gold Circle Stores, Columbus, Ohio, 1978-82; vice chmn. Federated Dept. Stores, Cin., from 1982, pres., chief oper. officer, 1987-88, retail cons., 1988—. Dir. Progressive Corp., Finlay Fine Jewelry, NYC, Henry Schein, Inc., Melville, NY. Office Phone: 212-308-5605. Personal E-mail: normanmatthews@yahoo.com.

MATTHEWS, PAUL AARON, lawyer; b. Memphis, May 7, 1952; s. Joseph Curtis and Sarah Rebecca M.; m. Roberta, July 29, 1978. AB, Duke U., Durham, NC, 1974; JD, Vanderbilt U., Nashville, 1977. Bar: Tenn. 1977, US Dist. Ct. (we. dist.) Tenn. 1977, US Dist. Ct. (ea. dist.) Mich. 1987, US Dist. Ct. (ea. dist.) Tenn. 1991, US Ct. Appeals (6th cir.) 1991, US Dist. Ct. (ea. and we. dists.) Ark. 1995, US Dist. Ct. (mid. dist.) Tenn. 1998, US Dist. Ct. (no. and so. dists.) Miss. 2000, US Supreme Ct. 1998; cert. in bus. bankruptcy law and consumer bankruptcy law, Am. Bd. Certification and Tenn. Comm. on Cont. Legal Edn. and Specialization, 1999. Assoc. Armstrong Allen, PLLC, Memphis, 1977-82, mem., 1982—2006, Bourland Heflin Alvarez Minor & Matthews PLC, 2006—. Chief Justice Vanderbilt Law Sch. Moot Ct. Bd., Nashville, 1976—77. Co-author: Passport to Tennessee History, 1996; contbg. editor: Martindale-Hubbell Tenn. Law Digest, 1994—99; contbr. articles to profl. publs. Com. chmn. Memphis-in-May Internat. Festival, 1977—79; mem. Leadership Memphis Class of 1987, alumni adv. coun., 2000—06; trustee Tenn. Hist. Commn. Found., 1998—2005; commr. Shelby County Hist. Commn., 1997—2004, vice-chmn., 1999, chmn., 2000—01; commr. Tenn. Hist. Commn., 1987—97, 2005—, Tenn. Wars Commn., 1994—97; vestry Episcopal Ch. of the Holy Communion, 1995—98; trustee St. Mary's Episcopal Sch., 2001—07; bd. dirs. Davies Manor Assn., Brunswick, Tenn., 1994—99, pres., 1996—97. Recipient Newman award Memphis Heritage, Inc., 1992; named one of Top 100 Lawyers in Tenn. Mid-South Super Lawyers, 2006. Fellow Tenn. Bar Found.; mem. ABA, SAR (Isaac Shelby chpt.), Am. Bankruptcy Inst., Tenn. Bar Assn., Memphis Bar Assn. (publs. coun. 1990-98, bd. dirs. 1999-2001, jud. practice and procedures com. 2000-02, vice chmn. professionalism com. 2003, chmn. 2004, task force on local rules of ct. 2004-05), Memphis and Shelby County Mental Health Assn. (pres. 1984-85), Duke U. Alumni Assn. (pres. Memphis chpt. 1986-88), Descs. of Early Settlers of Shelby County (v.p. 1999-2003, pres. 2004-05), Sigma Alpha Epsilon. Episcopalian.

MATTHEWS, ROGER HARDIN, lawyer; b. Greensboro, NC, Sept. 16, 1948; s. Shuford Roger and Jacqueline (Hardin) M.; m. Jane Elizabeth Dougan, Aug. 7, 1982; children: Christopher Hardin, Marielle Aimée. AB, Harvard U., 1970, JD, 1974. Bar: Mass. 1974, US Tax Ct. 1992. Assoc. Ropes & Gray, Boston, 1974-84, ptnr., 1984—. Mem. Northeast IRS Pension Liaison Grp., Wash. Update Prog. Planning New Eng. Employee Benefits Coun., Boston ERISA Discussion Grp. Recipient Best Lawyers in Am., 1997—2007. Mem. ABA (employee benefits com., tax sect.), Boston Bar Assn. (co-chmn. Employee Retirement Income Security Act com. 1985-88), former co-chmn. ERISA Com. Boston Bar Assn. Avocation: piano. Office: Ropes & Gray 1 International Pl Boston MA 02110-2624 Office Phone: 617-951-7259. Office Fax: 617-235-0071. Business E-Mail: hardin.matthews@ropesgray.com.

MATTHEWS, RONDRA J., publishing executive; b. Inglewood, Calif., July 13, 1955; d. Nedra Plummer; m. Keith Matthews. BS in Behavioral Sci., High Point U.; MBA, Rollins Coll. Former pres. Better Bus. Bur, Ctrl. Fla.; various mgmt. positions Orlando (Fla.) Sentinel Comms., 1980—99, v.p., gen. mgr., 1999—2000; pres., pub., CEO Daily Press, Newport News, Va., 2000—06; publisher, CEO Baltimore Sun Co., 2006—07. Bd. dirs. Peninsula Alliance for Econ. Devel., Hampton Roads Partnership, Greater Peninsula NOW; bd. advisors Christopher Newport U. Sch. Bus.; chair-elect bd. dirs. United Way of the Va. Peninsula.

MATTHEWS, ROWENA GREEN, biological chemistry educator; b. Cambridge, Eng., Aug. 20, 1938; (father Am. citizen); d. David E. and Doris (Cribb) Green; m. Larry Stanford Matthews, June 18, 1960; children: Brian Stanford, Keith David. BA, Radcliffe Coll., 1960; PhD, U. Mich., 1969. Instr. U. S.C., Columbia, 1964-65; postdoctoral fellow U. Mich., Ann Arbor, 1970-75, asst. prof., 1975-81, assoc. prof. biol. chemistry, 1981-86, prof., 1986—, assoc. chmn., 1988-92, G. Robert Greenberg disting. univ. prof., 1995—, chair biophysics rsch. divsn., 1996—2001. Mem. phys. biochemistry study sect. NIH, 1982-86; mem. adv. coun. Nat. Inst. Gen. Med. Scis., NIH, 1991-94; adv. bd. NATO, 1994-96; mem. Commn. on Advancement of Women and Minorities in Sci., Engring. and Tech. Devel., 1999; mem. faculty Life Scis. Inst., 2002—. Mem. editl. adv. bd. Biochem. Jour., 1984-92, Arch. Biochemistry, Biophysics, 1992-97, Biochemistry, 1993—, Jour. Bacteriology, 1995-2003; contbr. articles to profl. jours. Recipient Merit award Nat. Inst. Gen. Med. Scis., 1991-2001; NIH grantee, 1978—, NSF grantee, 1992-2003. Fellow AAAS, NAS, Am. Acad. Arts & Scis, Inst. Medicine; mem. Am. Soc. Biochem. and Molecular Biology (program chair 1995, chair human resources 1996-98, William C. Rose award 2000), Am. Chem. Soc. (program chair biochemistry divsn. 1985, sec. biochemistry divsn. 1990-92, chair 1994-96, Repligen award 2001), Inst. Medicine (2004), Phi Beta Kappa, Sigma Xi. Office: Life Sci Inst U Mich 210 Washtenaw Ave Ann Arbor MI 48109-2216 Home: 1609 S University Ann Arbor MI 48104 Business E-Mail: rmatthew@umich.edu.

MATTHEWS, ROY S., management consultant; b. 1945; BS, Lewis U., 1967; MBA, No. Ill. U., 1971. With Regis Paper Co., Chgo., 1967-68, Continental Ill. Nat. Bank, Chgo., 1968-69; instr. acctg. Marquette U., Milw., 1971-72; asst. dean Lewis U. Coll. Bus., Romeoville, Ill., 1972-78; mgr. Peat, Marwick, Mitchell & Co., Chgo., 1978-84; with George S. May Internat. Co., Park Ridge, Ill., 1984—, now v.p. fin., sec.-treas. With USAR, 1968-74. Office: George S May Internat Co 303 S Northwest Hwy Park Ridge IL 60068-4232

MATTHEWS, STEVE ALLEN, lawyer; b. Columbia, SC, Oct. 11, 1955; s. Philip Garland and Vernecia Neely (Wilson) M.; m. Caroline Elizabeth FitzSimons, Sept. 26, 1987; children: Philip Garland II, Nathalie FitzSimons, Caroline Salley. BA in History, U. S.C., 1977; JD, Yale U., 1980. Bar: S.C. 1980, D.C. 1982. Assoc. Boyd, Knowlton, Tate & Finlay, Columbia, 1980—81, Dewey, Ballantine, Bushby, Palmer & Wood, Washington, 1981—85; spl. counsel to asst. atty. gen. Civil Rights Divsn. U.S. Dept. Justice, Washington, 1985—86, dep. asst. atty. gen. for jud. selection, Office of Legal Policy, 1986—88; exec. asst. to U.S. Atty. Gen., 1988; mem. Haynsworth Sinkler Boyd, PA, Columbia, 1988—, mng. ptnr., 2001—. Sec. Landmark Legal Found.; chair Gov.'s Edn. Reform Coun., SC, 2005—06. Mem. Federalist Soc., Nat. Assn. Bond Lawyers (bd. dirs. 1995-96), Am. Coll. Bond Counsel (bd. dirs. 1995-99), Collegiate Network, Inc. (chmn. bd. dirs.), Am. Intellectual Property Lawyers Assn., SC Ind. Colls. and Univs. (bd. dirs.), Phila. Soc., St. Andrews Soc. Columbia, Jr. Achievement (bd. dirs.). Office: Haynsworth Sinkler Boyd PA 1201 Main St Fl 22 Columbia SC 29201-3226 Office Phone: 803-779-3080. Business E-Mail: smatthews@hsblawfirm.com.

MATTHEWS, THOMAS J., game company executive; BS in Fin., U. So. Calif., 1986. From pres. to pres., CEO, COO Global Gaming Distributors Inc. (acquired by Anchor Gaming), Reno; pres., CEO, chmn. Anchor Gaming (acquired by Internat. Game. Tech.), 1994—2001; COO Internat. Game Tech., 2001—03, pres., CEO, COO, 2003—05, chmn., pres., CEO, COO, 2005—. Office: International Game Technology 9295 Prototype Dr Reno NV 89521-8986 *

MATTHEWS, WARREN WAYNE, state supreme court justice; b. Santa Cruz, Calif., Apr. 5, 1939; s. Warren Wayne and Ruth Ann (Maginnis) M.; m. Donna Stearns, Aug. 17, 1963; children: Holly Maginnis, Meredith Sample. BA, Stanford U., 1961; JD, Harvard U., 1964. Bar: Alaska 1965. Assoc. firm Burr, Boney & Pease, Anchorage, 1964-69, Matthews & Dunn, Matthews, Dunn and Baily, Anchorage, 1969-77; justice Alaska Supreme Ct., Anchorage, 1977—, chief justice, 1987—90, 1997—2000. Mem. Alaska Bar Ethics & Unauthorized Practices Com., Supreme Ct. Criminal Rules Revision Com., Alaska Sentencing Commn., 1990-93; former bd. mem., second v.p. Conference Chief Justices; chmn. Alaska Judicial Council, 1987-90, 1997-2000. Bd. dirs. Alaska Legal Services Corp., 1969-70. Mem. Alaska Bar Assn. (bd. govs. 1974-77), ABA, Anchorage Bar Assn. Office: Alaska Supreme Ct 303 K St Anchorage AK 99501-2013 *

MATTHEWS, WILLIAM R., JR., (BILL MATTHEWS), headmaster; Former dir. of development St. Paul's Sch., Concord, NH, former vice rector, interim rector, 2005—06, rector, 2006—. Office: St Paul's Sch 325 Pleasant St Concord NH 03301 *

MATTHEWS, WYHOMME S., retired music educator, academic administrator; b. Battle Creek, Mich., July 22, 1948; d. Woodrow R. and LouLease (Graham) Sellers; m. Edward L. Matthews, Apr. 29, 1972; children: Channing DuVall, Triston Curran, Landon Edward, Brandon Graham. AA, Kellogg C.C., 1968; MusB, Mich. State U., 1970, MA, MusM, Mich. State U., 1972. Cert. elem. and secondary tchr., Mich. Tchr., vocal music dir. Benton Harbor (Mich.) Pub. Schs., 1971-72, dir. vocal music, 1972; dir. edn. head start program Burlington (N.J.) County, 1972-73; pvt. music tchr., 1973-89; tchr. Southeastern Jr. H.S., 1986-87, W.K. Kellogg Jr. H.S., 1987-89; chair visual and performing arts dept. Kellogg C.C., Battle Creek, Mich., 1989-99, dir. Eastern acad. Ctr., 1999—2003, ret., 2003. Part-time instr. Kellogg C.C., 1973—, dir. Eclectic Chorale, 1973-2005, dir., organizer Kellogg C.C. Eclectic Chorale Sacred Cultural Festival, 1979—, judge various contests; artistic dir. Battle Creek Sojourner Truth Monument Presentation Day, 1999; presenter in field. Pres. Dudley Elem. Sch., 1981-85; active Battle Creek Pub. Schs. PTA, Pennfield Pub. Schs. PTA, Mt. Zion African Meth. Episc. Ch.; v.p. Life Care Amb. Bd., 1990-2003; bd. dirs. Leila Aboretum Soc.; mem. Battle Creek Cmty. Found., Glen Cross Arts and Infrasture Fund; founder Echoes of Grace, Inc., 2005, dir. cmty. choir. Recipient Outstanding Cmty. Svc. award, 1975, Sojourner Truth award, 2000, George award, City of Battle Creek, 2000; fellow, Mich. State U., 1971. Mem. Mich. Music Tchr. Assn., Nat. Music Tchrs. Assn., Battle Creek Music Tchrs. Assn., Battle Creek Morning Music Club (bd. dirs.), Nat. Leadership Acad., Battle Creek Cmty. Concert Assn. Home: 466 Alton Ave Battle Creek MI 49017-3212 Home Phone: 269-964-2228. Personal E-mail: wmatth5278@aol.com.

MATTHIAS, JOHN EDWARD, English literature educator; b. Columbus, Ohio, Sept. 5, 1941; s. John Marshall and Lois (Kirkpatrick) M.; m. Diana Clare Jocelyn, Dec. 27, 1967; children— Cynouai, Laura. BA, Ohio State U., 1963; MA, Stanford U., 1966; postgrad., U. London, 1967. Asst. prof. dept. English U. Notre Dame, Ind., 1966-73, assoc. prof. Ind., 1973-80, prof. Ind., 1980—. Vis. fellow Clare Hall, Cambridge U., 1966-77, assoc., 1977—; vis. prof. dept. English, Skidmore Coll., Saratoga Springs, N.Y., 1975, U. Chgo., 1980. Author: Bucyrus, 1971, Turns, 1975, Crossing, 1979, Five American Poets, 1980, Introducing David Jones, 1980, Contemporary Swedish Poetry, 1980, Bathory and Lermontov, 1980, Northern Summer, New and Selected Poems, 1984, The Battle of Kosovo, 1987, David Jones: Man and Poet: A Gathering of Ways, 1991, Reading Old Friends, 1991, Swimming at Midnight, 1995, Beltane at Aphelion, 1995, Pages: New Poems and Cuttings, 2000, Working Progress, 2002, Three-Toed Gull: Selected Poems of Jesper Svenbro, 2003, New Selected Poems, 2004. Recipient Columbia U. Transl. award, 1978, Swedish Inst. award, 1981, Poetry award Soc. Midland Authors, 1984, Ingram Merrill Found. award, 1984, 90; Woodrow Wilson fellow, 1963, Lily Endowment fellow, 1993; Fulbright grantee, 1966. Mem. AAUP, PEN, Poets and Writers, Poetry Soc. Am. (George Bogin Meml. award 1990). Office: U Notre Dame Dept English Notre Dame IN 46556

MATTHIES, FREDERICK JOHN, civil and environmental engineer; b. Omaha, Oct. 4, 1925; s. Fred. J. and Charlotte Leota (Metz) M.; m. Carol Mae Dean, Sept. 14, 1947; children: John Frederick, Jane Carolyn Matthies Golding BSCE, Cornell U., 1947; postgrad., U. Nebr., 1952-53. Bd. cert. Am. Acad. Environ. Engrs.; registered profl. engr., Nebr. Civil engr. Henningson, Durham & Richardson, Omaha, 1947-50, 52-54; sr. v.p. devel. Leo A. Daly Co., Omaha, 1954-90; cons. engr., 1990—. Lectr. in field; mem. dist. export coun. U.S. Dept. Commerce, 1981-83. Contbr. articles to profl. jours. Mem. Douglas County Rep. Cen. Com., Nebr., 1968-72; bd. regents Augustana Coll., Sioux Falls., S.D., 1976-89; bd. dirs. Orange County Luth. Hosp. Assn., Anaheim, Calif., 1961-62, Nebr. Humanities Coun., 1988-94, Omaha-Shizuoka City (Japan) Sister City Orgn.; trustee Luth. Med. Ctr., Omaha, 1978-82; mem. adv. bd. Marine Mil. Acad., Harlingen, Tex. 1st lt. USMCR, 1943-46, 50-52, Korea. Fellow ASCE, Instn. Civil Engrs. (London), Euro Engr. European Econ. Commn.; mem. NSPE, Am. Water Works Assn. (life), Air Force Assn., Am. Legion, VFW. Home: 950 Southridge Greens Blvd # 15 Fort Collins CO 80525-6726

MATTHIES, MARY CONSTANCE T., lawyer; b. Baton Rouge, Mar. 22, 1948; d. Allen Douglas and Mazie (Poche) Tillman. BS, Okla. State, 1969; JD, U. Tulsa, 1972. Bar: Okla. 1973, U.S. Ct. Appeals (10th cir.) 1974, U.S. Ct. Appeals (8th and D.C. cirs.) 1975, U.S. Supreme Ct. 1976. Assoc. ptnr. Kothe, Nichols & Wolfe, Inc., Tulsa, Okla., 1972—78; pvt. practice Tulsa, 1978—. Guest lectr. U. Tulsa Coll. Law, U. Okla. Sch. Law, Oral Roberts U. Sch.; mem. staff Tulsa Law Jour., 1971—72. Contbr. articles to profl. jours. Fellow: Am. Coll. of Labor and Employment Lawyers; mem.: ABA (mgmt. co-chmn. equal employment law subcoms. nat. origin discriminatio 1974—75, spl. subcom. for liaison with EEOC 1974—, class actions and remedies 1975—80, spl. subcom. for liaison with OFCCP 1979—), Okla. Bar Assn. (coun. mem. labor law sect. 1974—80, chmn. 1978—79), Women's Law Caucus, Phi Delta Phi. Presbyterian. Office: PO Box 700876 Tulsa OK 74170-0876 Office Phone: 918-582-4400. Personal E-mail: mattlawfrm@aol.com.

MATTICE, DEBORA J., special education educator, consultant; b. Concord, Calif., June 21, 1959; d. Fred Alexander and Sarah Elizabeth Elder; m. Galen Donald Mattice, July 24, 1993; 1 child, Paul Daniel Reininger. AS, Monroe C.C., 1990; BS, SUNY, Brockport, 1990; MS, Nazareth Coll., 1995; postgrad., Cumberland U., 2002. Cert. profl. tchg. State Dept. Edn., Tenn., permanent tchg. State of N.Y. Tchr. Rochester City Sch., 1993—94, spl. edn. tchr., 1995—96, Dede Wallace Sch., Nashville, 1996, Stones River Acad., Murfreesboro, Tenn., 1996—97, Metro Nashville Sch., 1997—. Notary pub., Tenn. Foster parent Dept. Children's Svcs., Davidson County. Mem.: Assn. Supr. and Curriculum Design, Christian Educators Assn., Nat. Geographic, Smithsonian Instn., Davison County Foster and Adoptive Care Assn. (sec. 2000—06), Am. Civil Liberties Union, Kappa Delta Epsilon Phi, Kappi Delta Pi. Democrat. Presbyterian. Avocations: reading, crafts, writing. Home: 5020 Sunshine Dr Antioch TN 37013 Office: John F Kennedy Mid Sch 5832 Pettus Rd Antioch TN 37013 Office Phone: 615-941-7515 ext. 1216.

MATTICE, HARRY SANDLIN, JR., federal judge, former prosecutor; b. Chattanooga, Tenn., Mar. 10, 1954; s. Harry Sandlin Sr. and Kathryn (McCoy) M.; m. Janet Lynn LeVan, Jan 4, 1975; children: Harry Sandlin III, Bryan Christopher, Kevin LeVan. BS, U. Tenn., Chattanooga, 1976; JD, U. Tenn., 1981. Bar: Tenn. 1981, US Dist. Ct. (ea. dist.) Tenn. 1981, US Ct. Appeals (6th cir.) 1984, US Tax Ct. 1984, US Claims Ct. 1984, US Dist. Ct. (we. dist.) Tenn. 1989. Staff acct. Deloitte, Haskins & Sells, Chattanooga, 1976-78; from assoc. to ptnr. Miller & Martin, Chattanooga, 1981—2000; shareholder Baker, Donelson, Bearman & Caldwell, Chattanooga, 2000—01; U.S. atty. (ea. dist.) Tenn. US Dept. Justice, 2001—05; judge US Dist. Ct. (ea. dist.) Tenn., Chattanooga, 2005—. Pres. Chattanooga Tax Practitioners, 1987-88; sr. counsel U.S. Senate Com. on Govtl. Affairs, Spl. Investigation, 1997. Asst. to pres. Chattanooga Goodwill Industries, 1988-92; chmn. Hamilton County Rep. Party, 1993-95. Mem. Order of Coif, Signal Mountain Golf and Country Club, Phi Kappa Phi. Republican. Episcopalian. Home: 609 Marr Dr Signal Mountain TN 37377-2280 Office: US Dist Ct Rm 104 900 Georgia Ave Chattanooga TN 37402

MATTICE, HOWARD LEROY, education educator; b. Roxbury, NY, Sept. 23, 1935; s. Charles Pierce and Loretta Jane (Ellis) M.; m. Elaine Grace Potts, Feb. 4, 1956 (dec. Jan. 2002); children: Kevin, Stephen. BA, King's Coll., 1960; MA, L.I. U., 1965, NYU, 1969; cert., CUNY, 1972; EdD, NYU, 1978. Cert. tchr. N.Y., clin. educators trainer, Fla. Dept. Edn. Social studies tchr. N.Y.C. Bd. Edn., 1961-90, mid. and jr. H.S. asst. prin., 1970-72, 73-75; assoc. prof. edn. and history Clearwater (Fla.) Christian Coll., 1990-92, chmn. divsn. edn., prof. edn. and history, 1992-99, prof. edn. and history, 2002—; social studies curriculum writer Accelerated Christian Edn., 2003. Adj. lectr. history S.I. CC, CUNY, 1969-75; curriculum writer NYC Bd. Edn., 1985, Accelerated Christian Edn., Largo, Fla., 2003—; program reviewer Fla. Dept. Edn., Tallahassee, 1994—; item writer GED Testing Svc., Washington, 1988-92; mem. So. Assn. Colls. and Schs. Accreditation Team H.S., 1995—; adj. prof. DeVry U., Chengda, China, 2004-06; adj. prof. Derry U., 2004-2006; conversational Englis tchr., Chengdu, China. Chmn. bd. New Dorp Christian Acad., S.I., 1973-90; chmn. bd. deacons New Dorp. Bapt. Ch., S.I., 1981-90. Mem. ASCD, Assn. Tchr. Educators, Nat. Coun. Social Studies, So. Assn. Colls. and Schs. (h.s. accreditation review team 1995—). Avocations: reading, travel, gardening. Office Phone: 727-726-1153 ext. 259. Business E-Mail: howardmattice@clearwater.edu.

MATTILA, EDWARD CHARLES, music educator; b. Duluth, Minn., Nov. 30, 1927; s. Edward H. and Ellen M. (Matson) M.; m. Nancy Ann Norton, Oct. 12, 1956; children: Amy Lara, Edward Norton. BA in Music, U. Minn., 1950, PhD in Music Theory and Composition, 1963; MMus, New Eng. Conservatory, 1956. Instr. Concordia Coll., St. Paul, 1958-62; asst. prof. Bishop Coll., Dallas, 1962-64; faculty U. Kans., Lawrence, 1964—, prof. music, 1975—, producer, host program contemporary music Sta. KANU, 1971—. Served with Signal Corps, U.S. Army, 1952-53. Grantee in field. Mem. Am. Soc. Univ. Composers, Coll. Music Soc., Am. Music Ctr. Composer: Symphony No. 1, Theme and Variations for 2 pianos, Partitions for String Orch., 6 arrays for piano, Repercussions for Tape, Movements for Computer and Dancers, Six by Six, Seaborne for Solo Dancer & Tape, Pelagos, Caracole, Primordius, Dreaming up the Cosmos, Proa, (cd recordings) View from the Keyboard, Extended Resources, Electrophonic Means. Office: U Kans Sch Fine Arts Lawrence KS 66045-0001 Personal E-mail: emattila@cybertrails.com.

MATTILA, MARY JO KALSEM, elementary school educator, special education educator, art educator; b. Canton, Ill., Oct. 26, 1944; d. Joseph Nelson and Bernice Nora (Milbauer) Kalsem; m. John Peter Mattila, Jan. 27, 1968. BS in Art, U. Wis., Madison, 1966; postgrad., Ohio State U., Columbus, 1972, Drake U., Des Moines, Iowa, 1981; MS in Ednl. Adminstrn., Iowa State U., Ames, 1988. Cert. tchr., prin., supr., adminstr., art tchr., secondary tchr., Iowa. Tchr. 2d grade McHenry Pub. Schs., Ill., 1966-67, Wisconsin Hts. Schs., Black Earth, Wis., 1967-69; substitute tchr. Columbus City Schs., Ohio, 1969-70; elem. art tchr. Southwestern City Schs., Columbus, 1972-73; adminstrv. intern Ames, Iowa, 1984-86; lead tchr. at Roosevelt Sch. Ames Cmty. Schs., 1986-87, art vertical curriculum chair, 1983-89, art educator, elem. and spl. edn., 1973—2003. Contbr. articles to profl. jours. Mem. human rels. commn. City of Ames, prevention policy bd. youth and shelter svcs., Breaking Down Barriers, Ames, Iowa, 2004—. Recipient Very Spl. Svc. award for Disting. Svc. in Very Spl. Arts, Gov. of Iowa, 1984. Mem.: LWV, Ctrl. Iowa Orchid Soc., Questers, Am. Orchid Soc. Avocations: collecting old stoneware jugs, growing orchids, reading. Home: 2822 Duff Ave Ames IA 50010-4710 Office: Ames Cmty Schs 415 Stanton Ave Ames IA 50014-7331

MATTINGLY, MACK FRANCIS, former ambassador, senator, entrepreneur; b. Anderson, Ind., Jan. 7, 1931; m. Carolyn Longcamp, 1957 (dec.); children: Jane, Anne; m. Leslie Ann Davisson, 1998. BS, Ind. U., 1957. Acct. supr. IND, Arvin, Ind., 1957-59; mktg. rep. IBM, Ga., 1959-79; owner, pres. M's Inc., Ga., 1975-80; U.S. senator from Ga., 1981-87; asst. sec. gen. def. support NATO, Brussels, 1987-90; amb. to Seychelles Dept. State, 1992-93. Spkr./author econ., def., fgn. policy, entrepreneur, 1993—; mem. U.S. Senate Com. Appropriations, chmn. legis. and mil. constrn. subcoms.; mem. energy and water devel., agt. rural devel., treasury, postal svc. and gen. govt., mil. constrn. legis. subcoms., U.S. Senate com. Banking, Housing and Urban Affairs, chmn. rural housing, econ. policy subcoms.; mem. select com. ethics, 1981-83, joint econ. com., 1983-87; chmn. Rep. Com. on Coms., mem. Rep. Senate Leadership, 1985-87, Holocaust Commn.; U.S. del. GATT, Geneva, 1982; bd. dirs. CompuCredit Corp.; hon. co-chmn. GMACC, Hemisphere, Inc. Author 40 U.S. Sen. Bills, Amendments and Resolutions. Sgt.-at-arms, Rep. Nat. Convs., del. Georgian Rep. Party Convs., 1964-90; chmn. 8th Dist. Goldwater for Pres., 1964, Ga. 8th Congl. Dist., Cand. U.S. Congress, 8th Dist., 1966; mem. Ga. Rep. Ctrl. Com.; mem. Ga. Exec. Com., vice chmn., 1968-75; chmn. Ga. Rep. Party, 1975-77; elected 1st Rep. U.S. Senator from Ga. since 1871, 1980; bd. dirs. NOVECON, Cumberland Preservation Soc., Inst. for Global

Econ. Growth, Ga. Ports Authority; hon. bd. dirs. M.L. King Jr. Fed. Holiday Commn., Brunswick Golden Isles C. of C. Staff sgt. USAF, 1951-55. Recipient S.E. Father of Yr. award 1984, Ga. Wildlife Fed. Conservationist of Yr. award 1985, Selective Svc. System Dist. Svc. Gold medal 1985, Watchdog of Treasury award 1981-86, Nat. Taxpayers Union Taxpayers Best Friend award 1981-86, NFIB's Guardian of Small Bus. award 1981-86, Am. Security Coun. award 1981-86, Sec. Def. medal for Outstanding Pub. Svc. 1988. Episcopalian.

MATTIODA, ANDREW LIGE, chemist, researcher, space scientist; b. Hartshorne, Okla., Jan. 20, 1967; s. Tony and Gloria (Ranallo) Mattioda. AS, Ea. Okla. State Coll., Wilburton, 1987; BSc, East Ctrl. U., Ada, Okla., 1989; MSc in Chemistry, U. Okla., Norman, 1993, DSc in Chemistry, 1995. Cert. open water diver Profl. Assn. Diving Instrs., 1994, lic. pvt. pilot FAA, 2004. Environ. chemist US Army Corps. Engrs., Tulsa, Okla., 1995—99; vis. prof. U. Tulsa, 1999—2000, Rogers State U., Tulsa, 1999—2000; NRC fellow Ames Rsrch. Ctr. NASA, Moffett Field, Calif., 2000—03; rsch. scientist, prin. investigator Ames Astrochemistry Lab. SETI Inst. NASA, Mountain View, Calif., 2003—07; rsch. scientist, space scientist NASA, Moffett Field, 2007—. Spkr. in field; lectr. in field. Contbr. articles to profl. jours. Coord. Mountain View Cath. Singles, Calif., 2000—02. Recipient Superior Performance Award, U.S. Army Corps. Engrs., 1996, Spl. Svc. Achievement award, 1997, Performance Evaluation award, 1997, 1998, Ark. Traveler award, Gov. Mike Huckabee, Ark., 2004; fellow Karcher Fellowship, U. of Okla., 1989, Nat. Rsch. Coun., 2000—03. Mem.: AAAS, Am. Chem. Soc. (chmn. organizing annual chemistry day Tulsa chpt. 1997—98, co-chmn. environ. chemistry symposia), Profl. Assn. Diving Instrs., Nat. Italian Am. Found., Planetary Soc., Nat. Space Soc., Aircraft Owners and Pilots Assn. Roman Catholic. Achievements include identifying the possibility that polycyclic aromatic nitrogen heterocycles are present in interstellar space; research in molecular spectroscopy of interstellar polycyclic aromatic hydrocarbons and lunar dust. Avocations: hiking, travel, scuba diving, flying, cooking. Office: NASA MS245-6 Moffett Field CA 94035 Home Phone: 650-283-3198; Office Phone: 650-604-1075. Personal E-mail: andrew@mattioda.com. Business E-Mail: amattioda@mail.arc.nasa.gov.

MATTIS, DANIEL CHARLES, physicist, researcher; b. Brussels, Sept. 8, 1932; came to US, 1941; s. Joseph and Lucie (Applebaum) M. BS, MIT, Cambridge, 1953; MS, U. Ill., Urbana, 1954, PhD, 1957. Mem. rsch. staff IBM, NYC, 1959—65; prof. Belfer Grad. Sch. Yeshiva U., NYC, 1965—78; Thomas Potts prof. Polytech. U., NYC, 1978—80; prof. U. Utah, Salt Lake City, 1980—. Wei-Lun vis. prof. Chinese U. Hong Kong, 1997. Author: Theory of Magnetism, Vol. 1, 1981, Vol. 2, 1985, Many Body Theory, 1994, Statistical Mechanics Made Simple, 2003, Theory of Magnetism Made Simple, 2006; mem. editl. bd. Internat. Jour. Modern Physics; contbr. articles to profl. jours. Fellow: Am. Phys. Soc. Achievements include 4 patents. Office: U Utah Dept Physics Salt Lake City UT 84112 Office Phone: 801-581-3690. Business E-Mail: mattis@physics.utah.edu.

MATTISON, DONALD ROGER, gynecologist, toxicologist, educator, medical association administrator, public health service officer; b. Mpls., Apr. 28, 1944; s. Milford Zachary and Elizabeth Ruth (Davey) M.; m. Margaret Rose Libby, Jan. 28, 1967; children: Jon, Amy. BA cum laude in Chemistry and Math., Augsburg Coll., Mpls., 1966; MS in Chemistry, MIT, 1968; MD, Columbia U., 1973. Resident in ob-gyn Presbyn. Hosp., NYC, 1973-75, 77-78; commd. officer, rsch. assoc. USPHS, 1975, advanced through grades to comdr., 1984; rsch. assoc. Nat. Inst. Child Health and Human Devel., NIH, Bethesda, Md., 1975-77, med. officer, 1978-84; assoc. prof. ob-gyn. U. Ark., Little Rock, 1984-87; prof. U. Pitts., 1987-90, assoc. prof. toxicology, 1984-88, prof., 1988-90, dean Grad. Sch. Pub. Health, prof., 1990-99; med. dir. March of Dimes, 1998—2002; sr. advisor to dirs. NICHD and CRMC, 2002—. Contbr. articles, astracts, letters and editls. to profl. publs. Recipient Am. Chem. Soc. medal Minn. sect. Am. Chem. Soc., 1966, Assn. Am. Publs. award, 1983. Fellow AAAS; mem. APHA, Inst. of Medicine NAS, Soc. Risk Analysis (editl. bd. jour. 1988—), Pitts. chpt. Soc. Risk Analysis, Am. Assn. Cancer Rsch., N.Y. Acad. Sci., Am. Coll. Toxicology, Am. Fertility Soc., Soc. Gynecologic Investigation, Soc. Toxicology. Avocations: photography, computer sciences, fly fishing, cross country skiing. Office: NICHD/NIH 6100 Executive Blvd MSC 7510 Bethesda MD 20892 E-mail: mattisod@mail.nih.gov.

MATTISON, PRISCILLA JANE, lawyer; d. Verne Sylvester and Virginia M.; m. Bernard M. Resnick, Aug. 4, 1995. BA, Yale U., 1982; cert. in producing, Am. Film Inst., LA, 1987; JD, U. Pa., 1997. Bar: Pa. 1997, D.C. 1999. Distbn. dir. Michael Blackwood Prodns., NYC, 1985-86; dir. devel., head of casting/head of overseas prodn. Concorde Pictures, LA, 1987-90; ind. filmmaker LA, 1990-94; assoc. Harkins Cunningham, Phila., 1997—2000; staff atty. Clean Air Coun., Phila., 2000—02; atty. Bernard M. Resnick Esq. PC, 2000—. Dir., assoc. prodr. numerous films, 1987-90; screenwriter, 1988-94; songwriter, 1983—; photographer; author numerous poems. Sec. Penn Valley Civic Assn., Pa., 1998-2006. Named Pa. Rising Star, Super Lawyers Mag., 2005, 06; Fulbright grantee, 1982-83. Mem. Phila. Bar Assn., Fulbright Alumni Assn. (bd. dirs. Delaware Valley chpt. 1997-2002), BMI, NY Women in Film and T.V., Rec. Acad. (assoc.), Internat. Assn. Entertainment Lawyers, Nature Conservancy, Earthjustice, World Wildlife Fund, Nat. Wildlife Fedn., Lowre Merion Conservancy, Bridlewild Trails Assn., Pa. Horticultural Soc. Avocations: travel, photography, writing, songwriting, hiking. Office: Bernard M Resnick Esq PC Two Bala Plaza Ste 300 Bala Cynwyd PA 19004 Office Phone: 610-660-7774. Personal E-mail: smattison@aol.com.

MATTOON, PETER MILLS, lawyer; b. Bryn Mawr, Pa., Oct. 22, 1931; s. Harold Gleason and Marguerite Jeanette (Mills) M.; m. Mary Joan Henley, June 27, 1953; children: Pamela M. Zisselman, R. Stephen, Peter H., Philip P. AB, Dartmouth Coll., 1953; LLB, Harvard U., 1959; LLD (hon.), Widener U., 2001. Bar: Pa. 1960. Assoc. Ballard Spahr Andrews & Ingersoll, Phila., 1959-67; ptnr. Ballard Spahr Andrews & Ingersoll, LLP, Phila., 1967—2001, sr. counsel, 2002—. Emeritus trustee Episcopal Acad., Merion, Pa., 1970—, past chmn.; trustee, v.p. Widener Meml. Found., Lafayette Hill, Pa., 1972—; trustee, vice-chmn. Thomas Jefferson U., Phila., 1989—; overseer Widener U. Law Sch., Wilmington, 1979—. Lt. USN, 1953-56. Office: Ballard Spahr Andrews & Ingersoll LLP 1735 Market St Fl 51 Philadelphia PA 19103-7599 Business E-Mail: mattoon@ballardspahr.com.

MATTOON, ROBERT H., JR., (SKIP), headmaster; m. Carolyn Orr; children: Danielle, Ashley. BA, Dartmouth Coll.; MA, PhD, Yale U. Former assoc. headmaster and dean of faculty Deerfield Acad.; head of sch. Hotchkiss Sch., Lakeville, Conn., 1996—. Former prof. Latin Am. history U. Ariz., U. Michigan. Trustee Bement Sch., Deerfield, Mass.; bd. chmn. Green Fields Country Day Sch., Tucson; bd. mem. Conn. Assn. of Independent Schools; mem. bd. dirs. Am. Secondary Schools for Internat. Students and Teachers. Grantee Fulbright-Hays Fellowship. Mem.: Assn. of Boarding Schools. Office: Hotchkiss School PO Box 800 Lakeville CT 06039-0800 *

MATTOON, SCOTT ALEXANDER, private school educator; b. NYC, May 12, 1969; s. David Scott and Diana Mattoon; m. Dawn Rachel Gray, July 6, 1996; children: Ryland David, Avery Rachel. BA, Trinity Coll., 1991; MA, UCLA, 1994. Tchr. St. Mark's Sch. Tex., Dallas, 1991—92, UCLA, 1992—94, Collegiate Sch., NYC, 1997—2000; tchr., head lang. dept. Webb Sch. Calif., Claremont, 1994—97; tchr. Choate Rosemary Hall, Wallingford, Conn., 2000—, head lang. dept., 2006—. Vis. evaluator Chase Collegiate Acad., Waterbury, Conn., 2004; mem. evaluation com. New Eng. Assn. Schs. and Colls., 2006. Recipient Excellence in Tchg. award, Webb Sch., 1996, Collegiate Sch., 1998—99; NEH ind. study grantee, Coun. Basic Edn., 1996. Mem.: Alliance Francaise, Am. Assn. Tchrs. French (chmn. nat. French contest 1997—2000). Office Phone: 203-697-2357. Business E-Mail: smattoon@choate.edu.

MATTOX, JOHNNY LYNN, biologist, educator; b. Corinth, Miss., Apr. 13, 1951; s. Oliver Lee Mattox Jr. and Margaret Joyce Mills; m. Glenda Jean Eaton, Aug. 11, 1973; children: Jason Lynn, Jenny Amanda, Julia Elizabeth. AA, NE Miss. C.C., Booneville, 1971; BA Edn., U. Miss., Jackson, 1973, MCS, 1974, PhD, 1979. Tchr. sci. Kossuth HS., Miss., 1973—74; instr. sci. Itawamba CC, Fulton, Miss., 1975—80; instr. Biology NE Miss. CC, Booneville, 1981—2005; assoc. prof. Biology Blue Mountain Coll., Miss., 2005—. Adj. asst. prof. Miss. U. Women, Columbus, 1984—2000, U. Miss., University, 1991—93, 1996—, U. Tenn. Martin, Selmer, 2000—; chair dept. math. and natural scis. Blue Mountain Coll., 2007—. Chmn. Sci. Edn. divsn. Miss. Acad. Sci., 1980—81; deacon Union Bapt. Ch., Kossuth, 1963—, treas., 1963—, organist, 1963—. Mem.: NSTA, SAR (Booneville chpt.), Assn. Southeastern Biologists, Miss. Acad. Scis., Miss. Sci. Tchrs. Assn., Nat. Assn. Biology Tchrs., Alcorn County Hist. Soc. (pres. 1982—83), Kossuth Hist. Soc. (pres. 1996—98), Kappa Delta Pi, Phi Theta kappa (advisor 1979—2005), Phi Kappa Phi. Baptist. Office Phone: 662-685-4771 ext. 164. E-mail: jmattox@bmc.edu.

MATTOX, SHARON M., lawyer; b. Wichita Falls, Tex., Oct. 4, 1952; BA, Emporia State U., 1974; JD, U. Tex., 1974, PhD, 1978. Ptnr. Vinson & Elkins LLP, Houston, co-head adminstrv., environ. law sect. Fellow: Tex. Bar Found. Office: Vinson & Elkins LLP First City Tower 1001 Fannin St, Ste 2300 Houston TX 77002 Office Phone: 713-758-4598. E-mail: smattox@velaw.com.

MATTRAN, DONALD ALBERT, management consultant, educator; b. Chgo., July 8, 1934; s. George Charles and Lucille Alice (Boule) M.; m. Betty Elena Flores, July 18, 1953 (div. Mar. 1988); children: Donald, Julie, Kimberly, Guy, Christy; m. Rose Lynn Castellano, May, 1988. B.Mus., U. Mich., 1957, M.Mus., 1960. Tchr. Van Buren Schs., Belleville, Mich., 1957-61; asst. prof. U. N.H., Durham, 1961-65, Boston U., 1965-66; assoc. prof. Hartt Sch. Music, West Hartford, Conn., 1966-82, dean, 1971-80; dir. Syracuse U. Sch. Music, NY, 1982-83; dean Sch. Fine and Performing Arts Montclair State Coll, Upper Montclair, NJ, 1983-87; pres. Sales Consultants of Sarasota (Fla.) Inc., 1987—. Cons. Music div. Kaman Corp., Bloomfield, Conn.; cons., evaluator Nat. Assn. Schs. of Music and Joint Commn. Theater and Dance Accreditation; guest condr. Hartford Symphony Orch., Hartt Opera Theatre, All-State Festivals, 1976-83, Soc. New Music, Syracuse, N.J. Sch. Arts Orch., 1985-87. Co-author: (with Mary Rasmussen) A Teacher's Guide to the Literature of Woodwind Instruments, 1966; condr.: rec. Concerto for Cello and Jazz Band, 1972. Chmn. adv. com. Prodigy Inc., Syracuse, 1982-86; trustee Conn. Opera Assn., 1977-80; bd. advs. Watkinson Sch. Creative Arts Program, Hartford, 1977-80; mem. humanities adv. com. N.J. Dept. Higher Edn., 1984—; mem. multidisciplinary panel N.J. State Council on Arts, 1985-87; mem. adv. com. on auditions Met. Opera Nat. Council, 1984-87; mem. adv. com. Frank and Lydia Bergen Found., 1986-87; grants panelist, Sarasota County Arts Coun., 2005-; bd. mem. WUSF Ptnrs., 2006-; pres. Condo on the Bay Tower 1 Assn., 2007-; v.p. Condo on the Bay Mgmt. Corp., 2007-. Mem. Nat. Assn. Schs. Music (exec. bd., sec. 1978-81). Avocations: yachting, auto racing. Home: Apt 204 888 Boulevard Of The Arts Sarasota FL 34236-4827 Office: 1343 Main St Ste 600 Sarasota FL 34236-5630 Home Phone: 941-952-0639; Office Phone: 941-365-5151. Business E-Mail: dmattran@scsarasota.com.

MATTRICK, DONALD A., interactive entertainment software company executive; Founder, chmn. Distinctive Software Inc. (acquired by Electronic Arts in 1991), 1982—91; sr. v.p. N.Am. Studios, exec. v.p., gen. mgr. EA Canada, v.p. Electronic Arts, Inc., 1991—96, exec. v.p. N.Am. Studios, 1996—97, pres. Worldwide Studios, 1997—2006; external adv., entertainment & devices divsn. Microsoft Corp., 2007, corp. v.p., interactive entertainment bus., entertainment & devices divsn., 2007—. Office: Microsoft Corp One Microsoft Way Redmond WA 98052-7329 *

MATTSON, INGRID, theology studies educator, religious organization administrator; married; 2 children. BA, U. Waterloo, 1987; PhD in Islamic Studies, U Chgo., 1999. Tchg. asst. Dept. Near Eastern Languages and Civilizations U. Chgo., 1994—95, lectr. Oriental Inst., 1997; prof. Islamic studies, dir. Islamic chaplaincy Macdonald Ctr for Islamic Studies and Christian-Muslim Relations, Hartford Seminary, Conn., 1998—. Dir. Projects for Afghan Refugee Women, 1987—98; advisor to Afghan delegation UN Commn. on the Status of Women, 1995; vis. prof. Osgoode Law Sch., Toronto, 2003; spkr. in field. Advisor to PBS film project Muhammad: Legacy of a Prophet, 2001—02, assoc. editor The Muslim World; contbr. articles to profl. jours. Bd. dirs. Nawawi Found., Chgo., 2000—. Mem.: Am. Acad. Religion, Middle East Studies Assn., Islamic Soc. N.Am. (v.p. 2001—06, pres. 2006—), Middle East Medievalists. Office: Hartford Seminary Duncan Black Macdonald Ctr 77 Sherman St Hartford CT 06105 also: Islamic Soc NAm PO Box 38 Plainfield IN 46168 Office Phone: 860-509-9531, 317-204-0935. Office Fax: 860-509-9539. E-mail: imattson@hartsem.edu, isnapresident@isna.net. *

MATTSON, JAMES STEWART, lawyer, environmental scientist, educator; b. Providence, July 22, 1945; s. Irving Carl and Virginia (Lutey) M.; m. Carol Sandry, Aug. 15, 1964 (div. 1979); children: James, Birgitta; m. Rana A. Fine, Jan. 5, 1983. BS in Chemistry, U. Mich., 1966, MS in Environ. Health Scis., 1969, PhD in Water Resources Scis., 1970; JD with honors, George Washington U., 1979. Bar: D.C. 1979, Fla. 1983, U.S. Dist. Ct. D.C. 1979, U.S. Dist. Ct. (so. dist.) Fla. 1984, U.S. Ct. Appeals (D.C. cir.) 1979, U.S. Ct. Claims 1985, U.S. Supreme Ct. 1985, U.S. Ct. Appeals (11th cir.) 1985, U.S. Ct. Appeals (5th cir.) 1987, U.S. Ct. Appeals (fed. cir.) 1990. Staff scientist Gulf Gen. Atomic Co., San Diego, 1970-71; dir. R & D Ouachita Industries, Inc., Monroe, La., 1971-72; asst. prof. chem. oceanography Rosenstiel Sch. Marine & Atmospheric Sci., U. Miami, Fla., 1972-76; phys. scientist NOAA, Washington, 1976-78; mem. profl. staff & congl. liaison Nat. Adv. Commn. on Oceans and Atmosphere, 1978-80; ptnr. Mattson & Pave, Washington, Miami, Key Largo, 1980-86, Mattson & Tobin, Key Largo, 1987-2000; founder/CEO Great House of Wine, Inc, Ft. Lauderdale, Fla. and Napa, Calif., 1997—2003; sole practitioner Key Largo, Fla., 2000—. Adj. prof. law U. Miami, 1983-93; cons. Alaska Dept. Environ. Conservation, 1981-91, cons. oil and hazardous material spills, natural res. damage assessment. Author: (with H.B. Mark) Activated Carbon: Surface Chemistry and Adsorption from Solution, 1971; editor (with others): Computers in Chemistry and Instrumentation, 8 vols., 1972-76; (with P.L. Grose) The Argo Merchant Oil Spill: A Preliminary Scientific Report, 1977, (with H.B. Mark) Water Quality Measurement: Modern Analytical Techniques, 1981; contbr. articles to profl. jours. Candidate dist. 120 Fla. Ho. of Reps., 1994. Fellow Fed. Water Pollution Control Adminstrn., 1967-68; recipient Spl. Achievement award U.S. Dept. Commerce, 1976-77; Regents Alumni scholar U. Mich., 1963. Mem. ABA, Am. Chem. Soc. (chmn. Symposium on Oil Spill Indentification 1971), Order of Coif. Avocations: photography, hiking, sailing, scuba diving, fishing. Address: PO Box 586 Key Largo FL 33037-0586 Home Phone: 305-451-3951; Office Phone: 305-451-3951. Personal E-mail: mattsonj@bellsouth.net. Business E-Mail: jmattson@mattsonlaw.com.

MATTSON, JOE, sports marketing executive; b. Cashmere, Wash. BA English & Am. Lit., Harvard U.; MBA, James H. Warsaw Sports Mktg. Ctr., U. of Oreg., 2007. On-air sponsorship supervisor ESPN/ABC Sports Customer Mktg. & Sales; MBA Intern Mktg. Partnerships and Mktg. Properties NBA; joined Relay Worldwide, 2007—. Named one of 40 Under 40, Advt. Age, 2007. Avocations: bookstores, football, microbrews, travel. Office: Relay Worldwide NYC Office 233 Broadway 20th Fl New York NY 10007 Office Phone: 212-699-9210. *

MATTSON, MARLIN ROY ALBIN, health facility administrator, psychiatry educator; b. Bellingham, Wash., Apr. 25, 1939; s. Conrad Roy and Ruth Viola (Thompson) M. BA, U. Wash., 1961, MD, 1965. Diplomate Am. Bd. Psychiatry and Neurology. Intern and resident in medicine Cornell U. program at Bellevue and Meml. Hosps., NYC, 1965-67; resident in psychiatry Payne Whitney Clin. The N.Y. Hosp., NYC, 1969-72, chief resident in psychiatry, 1972-73, asst. med. dir., 1973-89, assoc. med. dir., 1989-99; asst. med. dir. quality assurance Westchester Divsn. N.Y. Hosp., White Plains, 1979-89, assoc. med. dir. quality assurance, 1989-93, head quality assurance program dept. psychiatry NYC, 1979-94; assoc. med. dir. for quality mgmt. Dept. Psychiatry N.Y. Presbyn. Hosp., Payne Whitney Clinic and Westchester divsn., 1999—2001, assoc. vice chmn. quality mgmt., 2002—03, assoc. vice chmn. compliance, 2003—. Asst. prof. psychiatry Cornell U. Med. Coll., N.Y.C., 1973-79, assoc. prof. clin. psychiatry, 1979-2005, prof. clin. psychiatry, 2005—, sec. gen. faculty coun., 1999-2001, vice chmn. gen. faculty coun., 2001-03, chmn. gen. faculty coun., 2003—05, sr. coun. gen. faculty coun., 2005-; bd. visitors Manhattan Psychiat. Ctr., 1991—; bd. dirs. N.Y. County Health Svcs. Rev. Orgn., N.Y.C., 1983-95; mem. stds. com. URAC, 1996-2000, bd. dirs., 2000—, mem. exec. com., 2005—, sec., 2006—. Editor Manual of Psychiat. Quality Assurance, 1992; contbr. numerous articles to profl. jours. Capt. U.S. Army Med. Corp., 1967-69, Korea. Fellow Am. Psychiat. Assn. (disting.,life mem. nat. com. on quality assurance 1988-95, chmn. 1992-95, mem. com. champus peer rev. program 1984-86, sec. N.Y. County dist. br. 1987-91, pres.-elect 1991-92, pres. 1992-93, co-pres. 1995-96, assembly rep. 1996-2003, cons. or mem. nat. com. on stds. and survey procedures 1996—), N.Y. Acad. Medicine (com. pub. health 1984-92, sec. sect. on psychiatry 1993-94, chmn. 1994-95); mem. N.Y. State Psychiat. Assn. (chmn. peer rev. com. 1982-95, mem. com. econ. affairs 1995—), N.Y. County Med. Soc. (bd. dirs. 2002—), Republican. Episcopalian. Avocations: piano, european travel, theater, swedish-american organizations. Office: NY Presbyterian Hosp Payne Whitney 525 E 68th St Box 140 New York NY 10021-4885 Home Phone: 212-879-5168; Office Phone: 212-746-3775. E-mail: mmattson@med.cornell.edu.

MATTSON, ROBERT MARVIN, JR., lawyer; b. Phila., May 13, 1948; s. Robert Marvin and Rillie Lee (Wright) M.; m. Carlene Kay Anderson; children: Michael Tyler, Jeffery David. AB, Stanford U., 1971; M in Mgmt., Northwestern U., 1975, JD, 1975. Bar: Calif. 1975. Assoc. Morrison & Foerster, San Francisco, 1975-81, ptnr., 1981—, co-chair corp. practice, 2004—06. Mem. State Bar Calif. (exec. com. Bus. Law Sect. 1994-98, vice-chmn. 1997-98). Avocations: reading, travel, sports. Office: Morrison & Foerster LLP 19900 MacArthur Blvd Irvine CA 92612-2445 Office Phone: 949-251-7138. Office Fax: 949-251-0900. Business E-Mail: rmattson@mofo.com.

MATTSON, STEPHEN JOSEPH, retired lawyer; b. Abilene, Tex., Oct. 11, 1943; s. Joseph Martin and Dorothy Irene (Doyle) M.; m. Lynn Louise Mitchell, Mar. 13, 1965; children: Eric, Laura. BA (hon.), U. Ill., 1965, JD (hon.), 1970. Bar: Ill., 1970, U.S. Dist. Ct. (no. dist.) Ill. 1970. Assoc. Mayer, Brown, Rowe & Maw, Chgo., 1970—77, ptnr., 1978—2003, ret., 2003. Mem. ABA, Order of Coif.

MATTSSON, AKE, psychiatrist, physician; b. Stockholm, May 30, 1929; came to U.S., 1956, naturalized, 1964; s. Erik H. and Thyra (Bergtsson) M.; m. Margareta Fürst, Jan. 5, 1953; children: Erik, Peter, Nicholas; m. Judith Whitley Powell, Nov. 25, 2000. MB, Karolinska Inst., Stockholm, 1950, MD, 1955. Intern Vanderbilt U. Med. Sch., Nashville, 1955-56; resident in pediat. and child psychiatry Karolinska Hosp., Stockholm, 1958-60; fellow in child devel. Case Western Res. U. Med. Sch., 1957-58, resident in psychiatry and child psychiatry, 1960-64, asst. prof. psychiatry, 1964-70; prof. psychiatry and pediat. U. Va. Med. Sch., 1970-77, U. Pitts Med. Sch., 1977-78; prof. psychiatry and pediat., dir. divsn. child and adolescent psychiatry NYU Med. Sch., 1978-85, rsch. prof. psychiatry, 1985—; prof. psychiatry U. Va. Med. Sch., 1985-91; prof. psychiatry and pediat., dir. divsn. child and adolescent psychiatry Med. Sch., East Carolina U., Greenville, NC, 1991-97; med. dir. divsn. mental health V.I. Dept. Health, St. Thomas, 1997—2003; med. dir. New Dimension, Inc., Washington, 2005—. Clin. prof. psychiatry Med. Sch. George Washington U., 2004—. Contbr. numerous articles to med. jours. Served with Swedish Navy, 1948-59. Fulbright-Hays grantee, 1975. Mem. Am. Psychiat. Assn., Am. Psychoanalytical Assn., N.Y. Psychiat. Soc., Am. Acad. Child Adolescent Psychiatry, N.Y. Acad. Scis., Soc. Biol. Psychiatry, Am. Acad. Psychiatry and the Law. Office: 700 New Hampshire Ave NW Apt 1409 Washington DC 20037 Office Phone: 202-744-0177.

MATUANO, TONY, chef; Chef Spiaggia, 1984. Author: (books) The Spiaggia Cookbook: Eleganza Italiana Cucina. Named one of Best New Chefs, Food & Wine, 1984; recipient Best Chef: Midwest award, The James Beard Found., 2005. Office: c/o Levy Restaurants 980 N Michigan Ave Chicago IL 60611 Office Phone: 312-664-8200.

MATUS, KRISTI ANN, insurance company executive; B, U. Wis., Oshkosh. Product devel. actuary Thrivent Fin. Bank, Wis., Medicare supplement actuary, product mgr. Wis., exec. v.p., COO Wis.; with USAA (United Svcs. Automobile Assn.), San Antonio, 2002—, v.p. products and regulatory mgmt. Life Ins. Co., pres. Life Ins. Co., 2004—. Bd. dirs. Am. Coun. Life Insurers. Fellow: Soc. Actuaries; mem.: Am. Acad. Actuaries. Office: USAA 9800 Fredericksburg Rd San Antonio TX 78288 Office Phone: 210-498-8222. *

MATUS, WAYNE CHARLES, lawyer; b. NYC, Mar. 10, 1950; s. Eli and Alma (Platt) M.; children: Marshall Scott, Scott Adam. BA, Johns Hopkins U., 1972; JD, NYU, 1975. Law clk. Superior Ct. D.C., 1975-76; assoc. Marshall, Bratter, Greene, Allison and Tucker, NYC, 1976-79, Christy & Viener, NYC, 1979-83, ptnr., 1984—98, Salans Hertzfeld Heilbronn Christy & Viener, NYC, 1999—2001, Leboeuf Lamb Greene & MacRae, NYC, 2001—04, Mayer, Brown, Rowe & Maw LLP, NYC, 2004—. Faculty ABA-Am. Law Inst., 1988; neutral mediator comml. divsn. 1st jud. dist. Supreme Ct. State of NY Unified Ct. Sys., 1997—. Assoc. editor Nanotechnology Law and Bus. Jour., mem. editl. bd. ABA Model Jury Instructions for Trademarks, Trade Dress and Copyright; contbg. editor: Commercial Corporate Strategies for Drafting and Negotiating. Mem. Assn. Bar City of NY (com. on computer law 1985-88, chmn. com. on state cts., subcom. on motion practice 1982-84, com. product liability 1994-97, com. on privacy 2003—), NY State Bar Assn. (com. on class actions and complex civil litigation comml. fed. litigation sect. 1990-99, com. on Internet and litigation 2000-02, lectr.), N.Y. Litigators Club (steering com. 1985—), Johns Hopkins U. Alumni Assn. (bd. dirs. met. NY chpt., v.p. 1988—2002, nat. alumni counsel 1996-2002, pres. 2002-06, mem. The Sedona Conf. 2003-). Office: Mayer Brown Rowe & Maw 1675 Broadway New York NY 10019 Office Phone: 212-506-2122.

MATUSCHAK, MARK G., lawyer; b. 1959; AB cum laude, Dartmouth Coll., 1981; JD, Columbia U., 1984. Bar: Mass., US Dist. Ct. (Mass. dist.), US Ct. Appeals (1st, 2d, 3d & Fed. cir.). Law clk. Judge Neil L. Lynch, Supreme Judicial Ct. Mass., 1984—85; assoc. to sr. ptnr. Wilmer Cutler Pickering Hale & Dorr, Boston, 1985—, vice chmn. Litigation dept. & mem. Intellectual Property Litigation group. Mem.: Dartmouth Lawyers Assn., Boston Coll. Law Sch. Intellectual Property Am. Inn of Ct., Boston

Bar Assn., Am. Intellectual Property Law Assn. Office: Wilmer Cutler Pickering Hale & Dorr 60 State St Boston MA 02109 Office Fax: 617-526-6559, 617-526-5000. Business E-Mail: mark.matuschak@wilmerhale.com.

MATUSH, WILLIAM JOE, educational association administrator; b. Temple, Tex., Aug. 31, 1926; s. Frank Joe and Janie Bravenec Matush; m. Lynda Lou Feild, July 4, 1976; children: Marily, Michael, Mona, Lori. AA, Temple Coll., Tex., 1947; BS, Tex. A&M Coll., Coll. Sta., 1950. Ptnr. Auto Dealter and Parts Bus., Temple, Tex., 1953—68; coll. adminstrn. Temple Coll., 1968—88; ranching Branet City, Tex., 1988—2007. Roundup com. Temple Chamber Com., 1954—68; pres. Temple Kiwanis Club, 1957, Dawson Class, Temple, 1958. Lt. Combat Engrs., 1951—53, Korea. Decorated Bronze Star medal US Army; named Outstanding New Resident Rancher award, Lake Victor, 1995. Mem.: VFW, Am. Legion Post 133, Temple A&M Ex-Student Club. Meth. Avocations: woodworking, golf, ranching. Home: 606 W Shell Temple TX 76501

MATUSIAK, KRYSTYNA K., school librarian, translator; b. Wolborz, Poland, May 6, 1959; d. Lucjan Kornacki and Teresa Kornacka; m. Brian C. Matusiak, Feb. 24, 1987; children: Alexander L., Thomas E. MA Polish Lit. and Theater History, Jagiellonian U., Crakow, Poland, 1985; MLS in Libr. and Info. Sci., U. Wis., Milw., 1999. Polish lang. instr. U. Wis., Milw., 1997—2004, academic libr., 1999—. Digitization cons. Press Inst. Mongolia, Ulan-Baatar, 2005—. Mem.: ALA, Polish Women's Cultural Club. Achievements include design of digital collections at University of Wisconsin-Milwaukee Libraries. Office: Univ Wis 2311 E Hartford Ave Milwaukee WI 53211 Home Phone: 262-512-1014.

MATUSZEK, JOHN MICHAEL, JR., environmental scientist, educator, consultant; b. Worcester, Mass., Apr. 16, 1935; s. John Michael and Felicia Martha (Shandruk) M.; m. Roberta Eva Coonan, Nov. 30, 1957; children: Debra-Jane Y., John Michael III, Kevin P., Jennifer R. BS in Chemistry with distinction, Worcester Poly. Inst., 1957; PhD in Nuclear Chemistry, Clark U., 1962. Dept. mgr. Teledyne Isotopes, Westwood, NJ, 1964-71; rsch. scientist in nuclear chemistry, radioactive waste mgmt., radiological health, environ. radioactivity and radiation N.Y. State Health Dept., Albany, 1971-2000; cons., owner JMM Cons. Svcs., Delmar, NY, 1992—. Adj. prof. Rensselaer Poly. Inst., Troy, N.Y., 1977-2003; prof. SUNY, Albany, 1996-99. Lt. comdr. USPHS, 1962-64. Mem.: Internat. Commn. Radionuclide Metrology. Avocations: skiing, music. Home and Office: JMM Cons Svcs 10 Fieldstone Dr Delmar NY 12054 E-mail: jmatuszek@verizon.net.

MATUSZKO, ANTHONY JOSEPH, research chemist, administrator; b. Hadley, Mass., Jan. 31, 1926; s. Joseph Anthony and Katherine (Narog) M.; m. Anita Colley, Oct. 26, 1956; children— Martha, Mary, Stephen, Richard. BA, Amherst Coll., 1946; MS in Chemistry, U. Mass., 1951; PhD in Chemistry, McGill U., 1953. Demonstrator in chemistry McGill U., Montreal, Que., Can., 1950-52; from instr. to assoc. prof. chemistry Lafayette Coll., Easton, Pa., 1952-58; head fundamental process div. Naval Propellant Lab., Indian Head, Md., 1958-62; program mgr. in chemistry Air Force Office Sci. Research, Washington, 1962-89; rsch. steering com. Dept. Def. Biotech., 1986-89; cons., Annandale, Va., 1989—. Contbr. articles to tech. jours. Patentee in field. Pres. Forest Heights PTA, Md., 1967. Served with U.S. Army, 1946-48. Named Hon. Fellow in Chemistry, U. Wis.-Madison, 1967-68, recipient Superior Performance award USAF, Outstanding Career Svc. award U.S. Govt. Fellow AAAS, Am. Inst. Chemists (life); mem. Am. Chem. Soc., Cosmos Club, Sigma Xi. Home: 4210 Elizabeth Ln Annandale VA 22003-3654

MATYJASZEWSKI, KRZYSZTOF, chemist, educator; b. Konstantynow, Poland, Apr. 8, 1950; arrived in U.S., 1985; s. Henryk and Antonina (Styss) M.; m. Malgorzata Kowalska, July 15, 1972; children: Antoni, Maria. BS, MS, Tech. U., Moscow, 1972; PhD, Polish Acad. Scis., Lodz, 1976; DSc, Lodz Poly., 1985; degree (hon.), U. Ghent, Belgium, 2002, Russian Acad. Sci., 2006. Postdoctoral fellow U. Fla., 1977-78; rsch. assoc. Polish Acad. Scis., 1978-84, CNRS, France, 1984-85; asst. prof. chemistry Carnegie Mellon U., Pitts., 1985-89, assoc. prof., 1989-93, prof., 1993—, head dept. chemistry, 1994-98, J.C. Warner prof., 1998—, univ. prof., 2004—. Invited prof. U. Paris, 1985; vis. prof. U. Freiburg, 1988, U. Paris, 1990, 97, 98, 06, U. Bayreuth, 1991, U. Strasbourg, 1992, U. Bordeaux, 1996, 04, U. Ulm, 1999, U. Pisa, 2000; adj. prof., U. Pitts., 2000-, Polish Acad. Sci., 2000-; cons. Dow Corning, Midland, Mich., 1988-89, Arco, Phila., 1990-92, GE, Schenectady, 1992-00, Amoco, Naperville, Ill., 1994-97, Reilly Ind., Indpls., 1994—, Air Products, Allentown, Pa., 1994-97. Author 10 books; mem. editorial bd. Macromolecules, Macromolecular Synthesis, Jour. Polymer Sci., Jour. Macromolecular Sci.-Pure and Applied Chemistry, Jour. Inorganic and Organometallic Polymers, Polymer, others; editor Progress Polymer Sci., Ctrl. European Jour. Chemistry; contbr. chpts. to books, more than 600 articles to profl. jours.; 31 U.S. and 78 internat. patents in field. Recipient award Polish Chem. Soc., 1980, Polish Acad. Sci., 1981, Presdl. Young Investigator award NSF, 1989, Humboldt award for Sr. US Scientists, 1999, Pitts. award, 2001, Polish Sci. Found. prize, 2004, UK Macro Group medal, 2005. Fellow: Internat. Union Pure and Applied Chemistry (corr. mem. polymer nomenclature), Polymer Materials Sci. Engring., Am. Chem. Soc. (Carl S. Marvel award 1995, Polymer Chemistry award 2002, Coop. Rsch. award 2004, Hermann F. Mark Sr. Scholar award 2007); mem.: NAE, Russian Acad. Scis., Polish Acad. Scis. (fgn. mem. 2005), French Acad. Sci. (Elf chair 1998). Achievements include research in synthesis of well defined macromolecules via living and controlled polymerizations; organometallic polymers. Home: 9 Queens Ct Pittsburgh PA 15238-1519 Office: Carnegie Mellon U 4400 5th Ave Pittsburgh PA 15213-2617 Business E-Mail: matyjaszewski@yahoo.com.

MATZ, JAMES RICHARD, municipal official; BA with honors, U. Tex., 1961; postgrad., Mexico city Coll., 1961-62. Mktg. exec. Fluor Corp.; mem. diplomatic corps Dept. of State; commr. City of Harlingen, Tex., Cameron County. Mem. Pres.'s Exec. Interchange Program, Bank of Am.; mayor Palm Valley, Tex. Contbr. articles to profl. jours. Founder Harlingen Proud; founder, chmn. Valley Proud Environ. Coun., 1990; mem. citizen's exec. adv. coun. Rio Grande State Mental Health and Retardation Ctr.; bd. dirs. Harlingen, South Padre Island, San Benito Emergency Med. Svcs.; chmn. Tex. Reg. Cmty. Devel. Grant Rev. Com.; mem. Met. Planning Orgn., Cameron County; mem. exploration com. World Birding Ctr.; bd. dirs. Tex. Urban Forestry Coun.; mem. Tex. Energy Coord. Coun., Govt. Adv. Com. to U.S. Rep. to N.Am. Commn. for Environ. Coop.; past vice chmn. legis. policy com. on utility regulation and environment Tex. Mcpl. League; past chmn. City of Harlingen Utility Rate Rev. Bd., pub. works com. Harlingen Capital Improvement Adv. Bd.; past. bd. dirs. Rio Grande basin Sustainable Devel. Initiative, Border Trade Alliance, Area Health Edn. Ctr. South Tex., Keep Tex. Beautiful; former commr. Cameron County; past exec. com. Rio Grande Valley Emergency Mgmt. Coord. Coun., numerous others. Recipient Dist. Svc. award Rotary Found., 1990, Svc. Above Self award Harlingen Rotary, 1991, Tex. Urban Forestry Individual Accomplishment award, 1992, Harlingen Proud, Chairman's award, 1992, Outstanding Dist. Gov., Keep Tex. Beautiful, 1995, Leadership award, 1995, Pres.'s Nat. Svc. award, 1995, Outstanding tex. Urban Forester award, 1996, State of Tex. Senate Resolution #989, 1995, Joint Resolution of Appreciation, San Benito City Commn. and San Benito Area C. of C., 1997, Tex. Environ. Excellence award Tex. Commn. Environ. Quality, 2004, Gulf Guardian award, 2004, Tex. Gov.'s Lonestar Cmty. Svc. award, 2005, Lone Star Land Steward award Tex. Parks and Wildlife Dept., 2006, Frederick Law Olmsted award Nat. Arbor Day Found., 2006, One Nation award Vails Morning Star Newspaper. Mem. Harlingen Area C. of C. (past dir.), Assn. for Local Control of Utility Rates (past officer, dir.). Office: 900 Palm Valley Dr W Harlingen TX 78552

MATZ, SEAN CORMICK, electrical engineer; b. Fullerton, Calif., July 31, 1959; s. Joseph Albert and Audrey Margaret Matz. BS in Math., U. Calif., Irvine, 1981, MS in Math., 1983, PhD in Elec. Engring., 2000; MSEE, Calif. Poly. U., Pomona, 1985. Mem. of the tech. staff Hughes Aircraft Co., Fullerton, Calif., 1986—88; staff engr. Walter Dorwin Teague Assoc., Pomona, Calif., 1989—92; engr./scientist The Boeing Co., Seal Beach, Calif., 2000—. Fellow Calif. Microelectronics and Computer Sci. fellow, U. of Calif., Irvine, 1993—94, Regents' fellow, 1996. Mem.: Math. Assn. of Am., IEEE. Independent-Republican. Roman Catholic. Avocations: reading, music, mathematics, computers. Home: 313 South Poinsettia Ave Brea CA 92821 Office: The Boeing Company 2800 Westminster Blvd Seal Beach CA 90740 Home Phone: 714-529-1444; Office Phone: 562-797-2839. Personal E-mail: smatz@cyberhotline.com. Business E-Mail: sean.c.matz@boeing.com.

MATZDORFF, JAMES ARTHUR, investment banker, internet marketing professional; BS, U. So. Calif.; MBA, Loyola U., LA. Comml. loan officer Bank Am., LA, 1976—78; mng. dir. James A. Matzdorff and Co., Beverly Hills, Calif., 1978—. Mem. Rep. Nat. Com., 1980-. Mem. Am. Fin. Assn., Phi Delta Theta. Avocations: tennis, sailing, Karate, skiing. Home and Office: 537 Newport Ctr Dr #144 Newport Beach CA 92660 Office Phone: 800-348-4212. Business E-Mail: James@premierelender.com.

MATZIORINIS, KENNETH N., economist; b. NYC, May 4, 1954; s. Neocles N. and Popi (Gregoratos) Matziorinis; m. Catherine Marina Astrakianakis, July 27, 1985; children: Anna Maria, Angela Ellen Fylitsa. BA, McGill U., 1976, MA, 1979, PhD, 1988. Cert. mgmt. cons. Asst. economist Nat. Bank Greece (Can.), Montreal, 1978-81; lectr. econs. McGill U., Montreal, 1977—; prof. econs. John Abbott Coll., Montreal, 1981—. Pres. Canbek Econ. Cons., Inc., Montreal, 1983—; econs. adviser to bd. dirs. Internat. Orgn. Psychophysiology, 1982-89; bd. dirs. Nat. Bank Greece, Can., 1991-2006; dir. Hellas Capital, Inc., Can., 2001—. Author: Introduction to Macro Economics: An Applied Approach, 1988, 4th edit., 2005, Business Economics: Theory and Practice, 4th edit., 2006; editor: Vital Graphs of Canadian Economy, 1984; contbr. articles to profl. jours. V.p. Westmount Liberal Riding Assn., Montreal, 1975-77; bd. govs. McGill U., 1978-81, John Abbott Coll., 1988-91; chmn. bd. dirs. Cmty. Svc. Ctr. St. Louis, Montreal, 1978-80; bd. trustees Trafalgar Sch. for Girls, 2002—. Recipient Distinguished Tchg. award McGill U., 1993, 2006. Mem. Am. Econ. Assn., Am. Hellenic Ednl. and Progressive Assn., Can. Assn. Bus. Economists, Can. Econ. Assn., Que. Inst. Cert. Mgmt. Cons., Nat. Assn. Bus. Economists. Greek Orthodox. Home: Laval 615 67th Ave Montreal PQ Canada H7V 3N9 Business E-Mail: canbekeconomics@videotron.ca.

MAU, BOB, statistician; b. Sheboygan, Wis., Sept. 1, 1950; s. Robert W. Mau and Lydia Welsch; m. Lynn Ellen Deschler, Sept. 29, 1979. BA, Lawrence U., Appleton, Wis., 1973; PhD, U. Wis., Madison, 1996. Mgr. rsch. program Wis. Survey Rsch. Lab., Madison, 1980—90; sr. scientist U. Wis., Madison, 1996—. Contbr. articles to profl. jours. Postdoctoral fellow Computational Molecular Biology, Sloan Found. / DOE, 1999—2001. Fellow: Royal Statis. Soc.; mem.: Soc. Molecular Biol. Evolution, Inst. Math. Stats., Am. Statis. Soc. Achievements include research in the identification of genomic rearrangements using Markov chain Monte Carlo; Bayesian phylogenetic inference using Markov chain Monte Carlo; genome-wide detection of allelic substitution. Home: 207 E Racine Jefferson WI 53549 Office: U Wis Madison 425 Henry Mall Madison WI 53706 Office Phone: 608-890-0172. Business E-Mail: bobmau@biotech.wisc.edu.

MAU, LISA ANNE, special education educator; b. Niskayuna, NY, Jan. 13, 1966; d. Joanne Elizabeth and William DiCaprio; m. Matthew Walter Mau, July 1, 1989; 1 child, Joshua Matthew. AA in Early Childhood Edn. with high honors, SUNY, Cobleskill, 1986; BS in Spl. Edn. magna cum laude, Coll. St. Rose, Albany, 1988, M with honors, 1993. Cert. Tchr. NY Dept. Edn., 1993. Spl. edn. tchr. grades 3-5 Middleburgh Elem., NY, 1988—. Wilson reading tchr. Middleburgh Elem., 2002—. Home: 405 Glen Ave Scotia NY 12302 Office: Middleburgh Elem Sch 245 Main St Middleburgh NY 12122 Home Phone: 518-372-7043; Office Phone: 518-827-3600.

MAUCH, ROBERT CARL, energy and financial services executive; b. Cleve., Dec. 7, 1939; AMP, Harvard U., 1983; MS, U. Calif., Berkeley, 1965; BSChemE, Cleve. State U., 1962. V.p., gen. mgr., LP gas divsn. Amerigas Inc., Valley Forge, Pa., 1978-83; v.p. UGI Corp., Valley Forge, 1978-87, sr. v.p., 1987-90; dir. Ansutech, Inc., Valley Forge, 1981-82, Matheson Gas Products, Inc., Valley Forge, 1981-82; pres., dir. AP Propane Inc., Valley Forge, 1983-90, Amerigas Propane, Valley Forge, 1983-96; pres., CEO, dir. AmeriGas Inc., Valley Forge, 1991-96, Petrolane, Inc., Valley Forge, 1993-96, Amerigas, Inc. subs. UGI Corp., Valley Forge, 1990-96, AmeriGas Propane Inc. (gen. ptnr. AmeriGas Ptnrs. L.P.); chmn., CEO Anthem Holdings Corp., Valley Forge, 1997-98, AllianceOne Inc., Exton, 1998—2006. Bd. govs. Pa. Economy League, Phila., 1985-91; mem. World Affairs Coun., Phila., 1980-95. Mem.: Propane Vehicle Coun. (chmn. 1994—), Waynesborough C. of C., Nat. Propane Gas Assn. (pres. 1978—, bd. dirs., exec. com.). Lutheran. Avocations: tennis, reading, yoga, opera, weight training.

MAUCKER, EARL ROBERT, editor, publishing executive; b. St. Louis, Sept. 20, 1947; s. Robert Buffem and Linette (Meloy) M.; m. Betsy Ann Johnson, May 21, 1977; children: Eric Robert, Michael Earl. BA in Mass Communications, So. Ill. U., 1972. Reporter Alton (Ill.) Telegraph, 1969-73; reporter, city editor, news editor, asst. mng. editor Rockford (Ill.) Morning Star, 1973-79; mng. editor Springfield (Mo.) Daily News, 1979-80, Ft. Lauderdale (Fla.) Sun-Sentinel, 1990-95, v.p. editorial, 1995—2001, editor & sr. v.p., 2001—. Sgt. SUAF, 1966-69. Named Editor of Yr., Editor & Pub., 2007. Mem. Am. Soc. Newspapers Editors, Fla. Soc. Newspapers Editors, Associated Press Mng. Editors Assn. (bd. dirs. 1989-93). Office: Sun-Sentinel 200 E Las Olas Blvd Fort Lauderdale FL 33301-2293 Office Phone: 954-356-4600. E-mail: emaucker@sun-sentinel.com. *

MAUDERLY, JOE LLOYD, pulmonary toxicologist; b. Strong City, Kans., Aug. 31, 1943; s. Joseph Park and Violet May (Cox) M.; m. Cheryl Gaines, Jan. 31, 1965; children: Laurie Jean, Jameson Lynn. BS, Kans. State U., 1965, DVM, 1967. Respiratory physiologist Inhalation Toxicology Rsch. Inst., Albuquerque, 1967-89, supr. pathophysiology group, 1976-89, dir., 1989-96; rsch. prof. medicine U. N.Mex., Albuquerque, 1988—, clin. prof. pharmacy, 1990—; sr. scientist, dir. external affairs Lovelace Respiratory Rsch. Inst., Albuquerque, 1997-99; v.p., dir. Nat. Environ. Respiratory Ctr., 1999—. Cons. in field; mem. EPA Clean Air Scientific Adv. Com., 1992-96, chair, 1997-2000. Assoc. editor Fundamental Applied Toxicology, 1989-94, editl. bd. exptl. lung rsch., 1983-2003; mem. editl. bd. Inhalation Toxicology, 2004—; contbr. articles to profl. jours., chpts. to books. Served to capt. USAF, 1967-69. Mem. Am. Thoracic Soc. (chmn. assembly of environ. and occupational health 1991-93, long-range planning com. 1991-94, sci. adv. com. 1993-96), Am. Physiol. Soc., Am. Vet. Med. Assn., N.Mex. Vet. Med. Assn., Soc. Toxicology (pres. inhalation specialty sect. 1994-95, career achievement award 1999). Republican. Home: 4517 Banff Dr NE Albuquerque NM 87111-2829 Home Phone: 505-296-7246; Office Phone: 505-348-9432. Business E-Mail: jmauderl@lrri.org.

MAUDLIN, ROBERT V., economics and government affairs consultant; b. Wash., June 8, 1927; s. Cecil V. and Eva Jane (Wright) M.; m. Carole M. Jackson, Sept. 3, 1949; children: Lynda C., David V., Tim W.E. Student, MIT, 1945; BS, Am. U., 1951. Ptnr. C.V. & R.V. Maudlin, Washington, 1952-72, owner, 1972—. Mng. dir. Bur. Applied Econs., Washington, 1960—; sec. Nat. Assn. Scissors and Shears Mfrs., 1970-97; exec. dir. Joint Govt. Liaison Com., 1973-81; mem. Industry Sector Adv. Com. U.S. Dept. Commerce and U.S. Trade Rep., Washington, 1975-97; commr. Adv. Neighborhood Commn. of D.C., 1999-2007. Author econ. and statis. reports. Pres. Forest Hills Citizens Assn., Washington, 1964; chmn. Boy Scouts Am., Washington, 1972, amateur radio operator KC3LI. 1st lt. C.E., AUS, 1945-47, USAR, 1947-55. Republican. Avocation: amateur radio. E-mail: maudlin@alum.mit.edu.

MAUER, JOE, professional baseball player; b. St. Paul, Minn., Apr. 19, 1983; Drafted first round Minn. Twins, 2001, catcher, 2004—. Named to Am. League All-Star Team, MLB All-Star Game, 2006. Achievements include becoming first Am. League Catcher ever to win batting title for highest avg. (.347), 2006. Office: Minn Twins 34 Kirby Puckett Pl Minneapolis MN 55415 *

MAUGER, THOMAS F., ophthalmologist, department chairman; s. Eugene D. Mauger; m. Leah C. Laxson, May 20, 1989; 1 child, Nathaniel Scott. MD, Ohio State U., Columbus, 1984. Diplomate Am. Bd. Ophthalmology, 1990. Chmn. dept. ophthalmology Ohio State U., 2004—. Fellow: Am. Acad. Ophthalmology. Office Phone: 614-293-5635.

MAUGERE, DENNIS PAUL, historian, educator; b. Newark, Sept. 3, 1946; s. William John and Virginia Webb Maugere; m. Joanne Maria Cella, Sept. 21, 1974; children: Lisa Marie, Anthony Paul, Lauren Michelle. AS cum laude in History and Polit. Sci., Broward Jr. Coll., 1966; BA in hist., polit. sci., U. Fla., 1969, MA in tchg., am. hist., polit. sci., social founds. of edn., 1976. Cert. profl. social studies educator State Dept. Edn., Fla and NY. Human rels. specialist Broward County Commn. Govt., Ft. Lauderdale, Fla., 1977—80, Broward Employ. Tng. Admin., 1981—82; adj. prof., hist. govt. Broward CC, Pembroke Pines, Fla., 1984—99; hist. prof. Cooper City (Fla.) HS, 1984—. Chmn. Broward County Adv. Bd. for Disabled, Ft. Lauderdale, 1979—81; keynote spkr. South Fla Second Conf. on Handicapped, Hollywood, Fla., 1979. Author: (social studies course) The Warren Commission Report and The Assassination of President John F. Kennedy, 1998; performer: (talk show host) Concerns of the Disabled, Sta. WAVC-TV, 1977, Hotline for the Disabled, Sta. WKID-TV, 1978. Guest spkr. various comm. functions for handicapped issues. Named Leadership Coun. Wall of Tolerance Honoree, So. Poverty Law Ctr., 2005; recipient Citation of Merit award, Muscular Dystrophy Assn., Inc., 1978, Physically Handicapped, Inc., 1978, Award of Excellence, Nat. Assn. County Organ., 1978, Three Presdl. Invitations for Ann. Meeting Pres.'s Com. Employment of Handicapped, Pres. Carter Adminstrn., 1978—80, US Citizen Ambassador, Hist. Edn. Del. to Russia and Latvia selectee, Ariz. State U., 1993, honoree, Cmty. Leader's Banquet, Tamarac, Fla., 1993, Tchrs. Making a Difference award in the Lives of Fla. Children, Fla. Devel. Disabilities Coun., 2005. Mem.: Southern Poverty Law Ctr., Am. Hist. Assn., Phi Alpha Theta, Internat. Roman Catholic. Achievements include co-founder South Florida's 1st annual conference on the handicapped; development of numerous county ordinances for the rights of the handicapped. Office: Cooper City HS Wendy Doll Principle 9401 Stirling Rd Cooper City FL 33328 Office Phone: 754-323-0200. Office Fax: 754-323-0330. Personal E-mail: maugered@aol.com.

MAUKE, OTTO RUSSELL, retired college president; b. Webster, Mass., Jan. 26, 1924; s. Otto G. and Florence (Giroux) M.; m. Leah Louison, June 18, 1950. AB, Clark U., 1947, A.M., 1948; PhD (Kellogg fellow), U. Tex., 1965. Tchr. history, acad. dean Endicott Jr. Coll., Beverly, Mass., 1948-65; acad. dean Cumberland County Coll., Vineland, NJ, 1966-67; pres. Camden County Coll., Blackwood, NJ, 1967-87, pres. emeritus. Served with U.S. Army, 1943-46, PTO. Home: 2119 E Lakeview Dr Sebastian FL 32958-8519

MAUL, RONALD ALLEN, surgeon; b. Holyoke, Colo., Dec. 30, 1948; s. Clemens John and LaVerne Anna Maul; m. Norma Jean Curfman, June 7, 1980; children: Debbra Sue Piert, Kristen Lynn Anders, Michael Terry Anders. BS, Colo. State U., Fort Collins, 1971, MS, 1972; DO, Kans. City U., 1976; M inStrategic Studies, US Army War Coll., Carlisle, Pa., 2003. Diplomate Nat. Bd. Med. Examiners Osteo. Phys. and Surgeons, Am. Osteo. Bd. Family Practice, 1988, lic. physician Oreg. Bd. Med. Examiners, 1979, Colo. Bd. Med. Examiners, 1977, Fla. Bd. Med. Examiners, 2004. Commd. officer physician USPHS US Army, Sterling, Colo., 1977—80, advanced through grades to col.; pvt. practice physician Davies Clinic, PC, Canby, Oreg., 1980—88; commd. officer Oreg. Army N.G., Portland, Oreg., 1983—88; chief family medicine svc. Tripler army med. ctr. US Army, Honolulu, 1988—91, commd. surgeon, sr. med. adviser 25th inf. divsn. Schofield Barracks, Hawaii, 1991—93, chief dept. primary care Ireland army cmty. hosp. Fort Knox, Ky., 1993—95, commdg. officer mobile army surg. hosp. Camp Humphreys, Republic of Korea, 1995—97, commdg. officer Guthrie army cmty. hosp. Fort Drum, NY, 1997—99, surgeon, sr. med. adviser Fort McPherson, Ga., 1999—2001, surgeon, sr. med. adviser ctrl. commd. MacDill Air Force Base, Fla., 2001—04, commdg. officer Womack army med. ctr. Fort Bragg, NC, 2004—06, asst. surgeon gen., exec. v.p. sustainment med. commd. Fort Sam Houston, Tex., 2006—. Decorated Army Svc. ribbon US Army, Army Achievement Medal, Oreg. Meritorious Svc. medal Mil. Dept., State of Oreg., Army Commendation medal US Army, Armed Forces Res. medal, Res. Component Achievement medal, Nat. Def. medal, Korea Def. Svc. medal, Legion of Merit medal, Armed Forces Expeditionary medal, Global War on Terrorism Svc. medal, Joint Svc. Commendatoin medal, Afghanistan Campaign medal, Def. Superior Svc. medal, Def. Meritorious Svc. medal, Overseas Svc. ribbon, Meritorious Svc. medal, Global War on Terrorism Expeditionary medal, Joint Meritorious Unit award, Iraq Campaign medal; recipient Order Mil. Med. merit, Office of the Surgeon Gen. US Army, 1995. Mem.: VFW, Am. Coll. Osteo. Physicians, Assn. US Army, Army Med. Dept. Rgt., Am. Coll. Physician Execs., Assn. Mil. Osteo. Physicians and Surgeons (pres. 2001—02), Am. Osteo. Assn., Assn. Mil. Surgeons US (life), Rho Sigma Chi, Phi Kappa Tau, Iota Tau Sigma. Republican. Lutheran. Home Phone: 813-785-6366; Office Phone: 210-221-7896. Office Fax: 210-221-6896. Business E-Mail: ronald.maul@us.army.mil.

MAULDIN, BARBARA BARIEAU, curator; d. William Eugene and Kathryn Beck Barieau. BA in Art History, U. Calif., Santa Barbara, 1971; MA in Art History, U. N.Mex., Albuquerque, 1989, PhD in Art History, 2001. Curator Native Am. art Lab. Anthropology, Santa Fe, 1976—84; asst. curator Mus. Internat. Folk Art, Santa Fe, 1987—90, curator Latin Am. folk art, 1990—. Author: Carnaval, Masks of Mexico, The Revival of Puebla Mayolica in the Twentieth Century, In Ceramic y Cultura: the Story of Spanish and Mexican Mayolica., Lightbulbs, Watchbands, and Plastic Baby Dolls: Industrial Appropriations in Corpus Christi Festival Headdresses of Highland Ecuador, In Recycled, Re-Seen: Folk Art from the Global Scrap Heap.; curator (exhibitions) Carnaval. Bd. mem. Southwestern Assn. Indian Affairs, Santa Fe, 1981—83; com. mem. Art and Environment Com. for the Archdiocese of Santa Fe Commn. for the Preservation of Hist. N.Mex Churches, 1989—91; treas. All the Worlds Children UNICEF store, Santa Fe, 1995—98; chmn. evaluation com. Santa

Fe Internat. Folk Art Market, 2004—07. Grantee, Nat. Endowment for the Arts, 1984—85, NEH, 1999—2004, Rockefeller Found., 2002—05. Avocations: travel, tennis, swimming, skiing. Office: Museum of International Folk Art PO Box 2087 Santa Fe NM 87504 Home Phone: 505-984-2951; Office Phone: 505-476-1222. Office Fax: 505-476-1300. Personal E-mail: bmauldinsf@msn.org. Business E-Mail: barbara.mauldin@state.nm.us.

MAULDIN, JOHN INGLIS, public defender; b. Atlanta, Nov. 6, 1947; s. Earle and Isabel (Inglis) M.; m. Cynthia Ann Balchin, Apr. 15, 1967 (div. Dec. 1985); children: Tracy Rutherford, Abigail Inglis; m. Linda W. Farmer, Nov. 7, 1998. BA, Wofford Coll., 1970; JD, Emory U., 1973. Bar: S.C. 1974, U.S. Ct. Appeals (4th cir.) 1974, U.S. Dist. Ct. S.C. 1975, U.S. Supreme Ct. 1978. Asst. pub. def. Defender Corp. Greenville County, S.C., 1974-76; ptnr. Mauldin & Allison, Greenville, 1977-92; pub. defender Greenville County, S.C., 1992—. Chair S.C. Commn. on Indigent Def., 1993-96. Bd. dirs. Speech Hearing and Learning Ctr., Greenville, 1977-90, pres., 1982; bd. dirs. Def. Corp. Greenville County, 1979-92, Save Our Sons, 1995-2006, Palmetto Innocence Project, 2002—. Named SC Atty. Yr. ACLU, SC, 1986. Mem.: SC Pub. Defender Assn. (bd. dirs. 1992—2006, SC Atty. of Yr. 2006), SC Assn. Criminal Def. Lawyers (bd. dirs. 1997—99), SC Trial Lawyers Assn., Nat. Legal Aid and Defender Assn. (defender policy group 1999—, bd. dirs. 2002—), Nat. Assn. Criminal Def. Attys., Rotary, Sigma Delta Phi. Democrat. Methodist. Office: PO Box 10264fs Greenville SC 29603 Office Phone: 864-467-8522.

MAULE, JAMES EDWARD, law educator; b. Phila., Nov. 26, 1951; s. Edward Randolph George and Jennie Elisabeth (Zappone) M.; m. Susan Margaret Noonan, June 26, 1982 (div. May 1988); children: Charles Edward, Sarah Margaret; m. Susan K. Garrison, Apr. 7, 1990 (div. 1991). BS cum laude, U. Pa. Wharton Sch., 1973; JD cum laude, Villanova U., 1976; LLM with highest honors, George Washington U., 1979. Bar: Pa. 1976, US Tax Ct. 1986. Atty.-adv. Office Chief Counsel to IRS Legis. and Regulations Divsn., Washington, 1976-78; atty.-adv. judge US Tax Ct., Washington, 1978-80; asst. prof. law Dickinson Sch. Law, 1981-83, lectr. and tax program chmn. continuing legal edn., 1981-83; assoc. prof. Villanova Sch. Law, 1983-86, prof., 1986—. Lectr. continuing legal edn. Pa. Bar Inst., Harrisburg, Continuing Legal Edn. Satellite Network, Inc., 1988; lectr. state and local taxes Georgetown U. Law Ctr. Inst., 1992; sr. tax and tech. ptnr. Ctr. Info. Law and Policy, 1993—99; owner JEMBook Pub. Co., TaxJEM Inc.; co-owner Starjem LLC, 2001—04; lectr. continuing legal edn. Phila. Tax Conf., 1996, 2001. Author: Cases and Materials in Federal Income Taxation, 1981, 26th edit., 2006, Materials in Partnership Law and Taxation, 1985, 6th edit., 1991, Materials in Partnership Taxation, 1987, 29th edit., 2007, Materials in Introduction to Taxation, 1987, Cases and Materials in Introduction to the Taxation of Business Entities, 1992, 15th edit., 2007, Materials in Taxation of Fundamental Wealth Transfers, 1986;: 2d edit., 1988, Materials in Tax Consequences of Disposition of Property, 1983, Materials and Problems in Taxation of Property Disposition I, 1987, Materials in Tax Planning for Real Estate, 1986, Materials in Estate and Gift Tax, 1983;: 3d edit., 1985, Materials in Taxation of Real Estate Transactions, 1986, 3d edit., 1992, Taxation of Residence Transactions, 1985, S Corporations: State Law and Taxation, 1989, (supplemental edits.), 1989, 1990, 1991, 1992, 1993, Materials and Problems in Computer Applications in the Law, 1990, 6th edit., 1995, Materials in Tax Policy, 1990, Materials in Digital Legal Practice Skills, 1996, Materials and Problems in Computer Applications in Tax Law, 1991, 8th edit., 1998, Better That 100 Witches Should Live, 1995, Materials in Decedents Estates and Trusts, 1997, 10th edit., 2006; co-author (with A. Clay): Preparing the 1065 Return, 1992, 1993; author: Continuing Legal Edn. Publs., 1981—; contbg. author: Federal Tax Service, 1989, Tax Practice Series, 1989—, Center for Computer-Assisted Legal Instruction, 2005—07; contbr. articles to profl. jours., chapters to books, monographs; author, developer: Computer Assisted Legal Edn. Programs in Taxation, owner, author, editor: computer assisted tax law instruction TaxJEM Inc., cons., prin. author: ABA Section of Taxation Model S Corporation Income Tax Act and Commentary, 1989, author, editor: Report of the Subcommittee on Comparison of S Corporations and Partnerships, 1990, 1991, case and comment editor: Villanova Law Rev., 1975—76, columnist, mem. editl. bd.: S Corps. Jour., 1987—91, Jour. of Ltd. Liability Cos., 1994—98, BNA Tax Mgmt., 1994—. Recipient Disting. Author award, BNA Tax Mgmt., 1993; Nat. Merit scholar, 1969—73. Mem. ABA (chair and reporter phaseout Elimination Project, Tax Simplification and Restructuring Com., sect. of taxation, cons., ex-officio mem. subcom. on state law, S Corp. com., chmn. subcom. on comparison of partnerships, mem. task force on pass-through entities, tax sect., former chmn. subcom. manuscripts and unpublished tchg. material, com. tchg. tax), Phila. Bar Assn. (lectr. tax sect. state and local tax CLE program 1991, fed. income taxes 1992—), Ctr. Info. Law and Policy, Order of Coif, Friars Sr. Soc. (Phila), Beta Alpha Psi. Home: 219 Comrie Dr Villanova PA 19085-1402 Office: Villanova U Sch Law Rm 12 299 N Spring Mill Rd Villanova PA 19085 Home Phone: 610-527-5144. Business E-Mail: maule@law.villanova.edu.

MAULION, RICHARD PETER, psychiatrist, physician, neurolinguist; b. Rosario, Argentina, Sept. 2, 1949; s. Peter Henry and Vivien Ormsby (Gough) M.; divorced; 1 child, Maximillian. BS, Colegio Salesiano San Jose, Rosario, ARgentina, 1967; MD, U. Nacional de Rosario, 1980. Diplomate Am. Bd. Psychiatry and Neurology, Am. Acad. Psychoanalysis, Am. Acad. Addiction Medicine, Am. Acad. Pain Mgmt., Am. Bd. Forensic Examiners, Am. Bd. Quality Assurance and Utilization Rev. Physicians, Am. Bd. Disability Analysts, Am. Acad. Experts in Traumatic Stress; cert. neurolinguistic programming (NLP) master practitioner and trainer. Intern Kans. U., Kansas City, 1981-82; resident in psychiatry Tulane U., New Orleans, 1983-86, fellow in psychoanalytic medicine, 1984-87; pvt. practice gen. psychiatry Covington, La., 1986-87; pvt. practice psychiatry Ft. Lauderdale, 1987—; founder, med. dir. The Rose Inst., Ft. Lauderdale, Fla., 1988—; founder Integrative Medicine Sch. of Thought, 1999; neurolinguistic programming master practitioner and trainer, 2000—. Sec. med. exec. com., chmn. quality assurance com. The Retreat Hosp., Sunrise, Fla., 1994-95; med. dir. Anxiety and Depression prog., CPC Ft. Lauderdale Hosp., 1989-90; med. dir. Acad. Medicine and Psychology, Ft. Lauderdale, 1988-89, CEPHAS Prog., HSA Greenbrier Neuropsychiat. Hosp., Covington, La., 1986-87, chief med. staff, 1987; clin. instr. psychiatry Tulane U. Med. Ctr., 1986-87; pres. med. exec. com., chief med. staff, chmn. quality assurance com. Retreat Hosp., 1992-96; workshop speaker; radio program host The Rose Institute Hour; lectr. in field; cons. in field. Host ednl.-cmty. svc. radio program The Rose Inst. Hour, 1995-97. Mem. pub. health com. for the Health and Human Svcs. Bd., Dist. 10; mem. alcohol, drugs and mental health com. Fellow Am. Acad. Psychoanalysis, Am. Bd. Forensic Examiners, Interam. Coll. Physicians and Surgeons; mem. AMA, Am. Psychiat. Assn., Am. Acad. Psychoanalysis, Am. Soc. Clin. Hypnosis, Am. Acad. Anti-Aging Medicine, Fla. Med. Assn. (Med. Speaker of Yr. award, 1st pl. radio, 2nd pl. TV, 1990, del. 1993—), Fla. Psychiat. Soc. (coun. mem. 1993-94), Broward County Psychiat. Soc. (med. exec. com., pres. 1994-95), Broward County Med. Assn. (chmn. physicians recovery network com., bd. dirs.), Broward County Psychiat. Soc. (pres. 1993-96), M.I.N.D. Home and Office: 1521 Alton Rd # 332 Miami FL 33139 E-mail: richardmaulion@yahoo.com.

MAULL, GEORGE MARRINER, conductor, educator; b. Phila., Oct. 14, 1947; s. Frederick Dunlap and Helen Norbury (Jordan) M.; m. Marcia Eileen Korn, Aug. 13, 1984. MusB, U. Louisville, Ky., 1970, MusM, 1972; postgrad., Juilliard Sch. Music, 1976-78. Condr. Louisville Ballet Co., 1971-75; asst. condr. Opera Orch. NY, NYC, 1976-78, NJ Symphony Orch., Newark, 1979-80; music dir., condr. Bloomingdale Chamber Orch., NYC, 1980-83, NJ Youth Symphony, Summit, 1979—97, Philharm. Orch. NJ, Warren, 1987—2006; Condr. Laureate NJ Youth Symphony, 1997; founder, artistic dir. The Discovery Orch., 2006—. Conductor: Carnegie Hall, NYC, 1989, Lincoln Ctr., NYC, writer, host, condr.: Philharmonic Orch. of NJ, Discovery Concert Bach to the Future, Am. Pub. TV, 2003 (Emmy nomination, 2004), Polish Nat. Radio Symphony Orch., 2001—02; writer, host, condr. (CD recs. with) Sono Lumina, 2006; featured in WNET mini-documentary: Art Effects: Young and Noteworthy, 1988. Named Disting. Alumnus, U. Louisville, 1994. Mem. Am. Fedn. Musicians, Am. Symphony Orch. League (conducting fellow 1978, Nat. Cert. Merit 1980), Condr's. Guild. Episcopalian. Office: The Discovery Orch PO Box 4064 Warren NJ 07059-0064

MAUN, MARY ELLEN, computer consultant; b. NYC, Dec. 18, 1951; d. Emmet Joseph and Mary Alice (McMahon) M. BA, CUNY, 1977, MBA, 1988. Sales rep. N.Y. Telephone Co., NYC, 1970-76, comml. rep., 1977-83, programmer, 1984-86; systems analyst Telesector Resources Group, NYC, 1987-89, sr. systems analyst, 1990-95; pres. Sleepy Hollow (N.Y.) Techs., Inc., N.Y., 1995—. Corp. chmn. United Way of Tri-State Area, N.Y.C., 1985; recreation activities vol. Pioneers Am., N.Y.C., 1982—; founder Mary Ellen Maun Philanthropic Found., 1998; dist. leader for Dem. Party Tarrytown. Recipient Outstanding Cmty. Svc. award, Calvary Hosp., Bronx, N.Y., 1984. Mem. N.Y. Health and Racquet Club, Road Runners. Avocations: antique restoration, classical music, skiing, running. Office: Sleepy Hollow Techs Inc 539 Martling Ave Tarrytown NY 10591-4719 Personal E-mail: mauningnews@msn.com.

MAUNDER, ADDISON BRUCE, agronomic research company executive; b. Holdrege, Nebr., May 13, 1934; s. Addison Haynes and Marie Sophia (Luebs) M.; m. Katherina Marlene Blum, Sept. 8, 1978; children: Lynda Diane, Christopher Allen. B.Sc., U. Nebr., 1956; M.Sc., Purdue U., 1958, PhD, 1960; DSc (hon.), U. Nebr., 1991; DAgr (hon.), Purdue U., 2003. With DeKalb AgResearch, Inc., Lubbock, Tex., 1960-96, sorghum breeder, 1960-61, dir. sorghum research, 1961-76, v.p. sorghum research, 1976-78, v.p. rsch., 1978-82; v.p. DeKalb-Pfizer Genetics, DeKalb, Ill., 1982-89; v.p. agronomic research DeKalb Plant Genetics, DeKalb, Ill., 1989-91; sr. v.p. DeKalb Genetics Corp., DeKalb, Ill., 1991-96; rsch. advisor Nat. Grain Sorghum Prodrs. Assn., 1997—. Bd. dirs. Diversity Mag., Washington, 1984-95; adj. prof. Tex. Tech. U., 1992—; pres. Nat. Grain Sorghum Prodrs. Found., 2004— Contbr. articles to profl. jours., chapters to books. Mem. deans adv. com. Tex. Tech. U., Lubbock, 1983-86; chmn. external rev. INTSORMIL of U.S. AID, Lincoln, Nebr., 1980-2001; bd. dirs. Tex. Tech. U. Rsch. Found., 1986-92; mem. Nat. Plant Genetic Resources Bd., 1991-92, Nat. Plant Variety Protection Bd., 1991-94; mem. World Food Prize Com., 1997-2003. Recipient Gerald Thomas award Tex. Tech. U., 1974, Prodn. award Grain Sorghum Producers Assn., 1985, Genetics and Plant Breeding award for Industry, 1987, Indsl. Agronomy award, 1988, Purdue Disting. Alumni award, 1997, Monsanto Crop Sci. Disting. Career award, 2000, Pres.'s Disting Svc. award Am. Seed Trade Assn., 2001. Fellow AAAS, Am. Soc. Agronomy (bd. dirs. 1991-92), Crop Sci. Soc. Am. (bd. dirs. 1991-92, pres. 1995-96); mem. Am. Seed Trade Assn., Sigma Xi, Alpha Zeta. Republican. Achievements include development of plant products (150 hybrids) emphasizing yield, improved drought and insect resistance as well as nutritional quality. Office Phone: 806-749-3478. Personal E-mail: texasgreenbug@aol.com.

MAUNEY, BRANDI SAVAGE, special education diagnostician; b. Miami, Mar. 5, 1976; d. Victor Martin and Yvonne Marie Savage; m. John David Mauney, Mar. 30, 1975. B in Psychology, Ga. Coll. and State U., 1999, M in Spl. Edn., 2004; student in Child, Youth and Human Svcs., Nova Southeastern U., 2005—. Cert. tchr. Profl. Stds. Commn. in Ga. Spl. edn. tchr. Henry County Bd. of Edn., McDonough, Ga., 2002—04, spl. edn. liason/diagnostician, 2004—. Spl. edn. homebound tchr. for medically fragile Henry Count Bd. of Edn., McDounough, 2004—. Mem.: Collaboration Team: Direct On-going Tng. of Adminstrn. and Staff, State Monitoring Com. (assoc.), Continuous Improvement Monitoring Com. (assoc.), Interagency Child Coun. (assoc.; com. chair 2005—05), Sigma Alpha Iota (life; v.p. 1995—97). Republican. Baptist. Achievements include research in effects of Child-Find and Early Intervention. Avocations: music, swimming, yoga, travel, bicycling. Office: Henry County Bd Edn 33 N Zack Hinton Pkwy Mcdonough GA 30253 Home Phone: 770-385-0431; Office Phone: 770-316-5830. Personal E-mail: brandisavage@yahoo.com. E-mail: bmauney@henry.k12.ga.us.

MAUPIN, A. WILLIAM, state supreme court justice; children: Allison, Michael. BA, U. Nev., 1968; JD, U. Ariz., 1971. Atty., ptnr. Thorndal, Backus, Maupin and Armstrong, Las Vegas, 1976—93; judge 8th Jud. Dist. Clark County, 1993—97; assoc. justice Nev. Supreme Ct., 1997—, chief justice, 2001—02, 2007—. Bd. govs. Nev. State Bar, 1991—95. Mem.: Nev. Supreme Ct. (study com. to review jud. elections, chmn. 1995, alternate dispute resolution implementation com. chmn. 1992—96). Office: Nev Supreme Ct 201 S Carson St Carson City NV 89701-4702

MAUPIN, ALAN RODGER, science educator; b. Fayette, Mo., July 8, 1953; s. George Worth and Donna Jean (Wright) Maupin; m. Karen Ann Peterman, Dec. 18, 1993; children: Emily L., Gabriel E. BS, Southeast Mo. State U., Cape Girardeau, 1975; BA, Washington U., St. Louis, 1992; MA, U. Tex., Brownsville, 2001. Tech. instr. flightline supr. USN, Whidbey Island, Wash., 1976—80; materials and distbn. supr. Union Carbide Agrl. Products Co., St. Louis, 1980—89; ground svc. supr. Trans World Airlines, St. Louis, 1989—91; sci. educator Harlingen Consolidated Ind. Schs., Tex., 1992—. Chess club coach Harlingen Consolidated Ind. Sch. Dist., 1992—, supr. adv. com., 1994—97, edn. improvement coun., 1995—2007, swimming and diving coach, 1998—. Mem.: Intertel, Tex. Interscholastic Swim Coaches Assn., Rio Grande Valley Swim Coaches Assn. (Diving Coach Yr. 2005—06), Am. Mensa (proctor 1987—). Libertarian. Methodist. Achievements include design of Energy Star energy efficient home. Avocations: swimming, diving, chess. Home: 2609 Louann Ln Harlingen TX 78550 Office: Harlingen Consolidated Ind Sch Dist 1201 E Marshall St Harlingen TX 78550

MAUPIN, ARMISTEAD JONES, JR., writer; b. Washington, May 13, 1944; s. Armistead Jones and Diana Jane (Barton) M. BA, U. N.C., 1966. Reporter News and Courier, Charleston, S.C., 1970-71, AP, San Francisco, 1971-72; account exec. Lowry Russom and Leeper, Pub. Rels., San Francisco, 1973; columnist Pacific Sun mag., San Francisco, 1974; publicist San Francisco Opera, 1975; serialist San Francisco Chronicle, 1976-77, 81, 83; commentator Sta. KRON-TV, San Francisco, 1979; serialist San Francisco Examiner, 1986. Author: (novels) Tales of the City, 1978, More Tales of the City, 1980, Further Tales of the City, 1982, Babycakes, 1984, Significant Others, 1987, Sure of You, 1989, (omnibus) 28 Barbary Lane, 1990, (omnibus) Back to Barbary Lane, 1991, Maybe the Moon, 1992, The Night Listener, 2000; co-author: The Essential Clive Barker, 1999; librettist musical Heart's Desire, 1990; exec. prodr. (TV program) Armistead Maupin's Tales of the City, 1993; contbr. articles to N.Y. Times, L.A. Times, others. Lt. (j.g.) USN, 1967-70, Vietnam. Recipient Freedom Leadership award Freedoms Found., Valley Forge, Pa., 1972, Comms. award Met. Elections Com. L.A., 1989, Exceptional Achievement award ALA, 1990, Best Dramatic Serial award Royal TV Soc., 1994, Peabody award 1994, Outstanding Miniseries award, Gay and Lesbian Alliance Against Defamation, 1994, Best Miniseries award Nat. Bd. of Rev., 1994. Office: ICM Care Amanda Urban 40 W 57th St Fl 16 New York NY 10019-4098 Address: c/o Literary Bent PO Box 4109990 Ste 528 San Francisco CA 94141 E-mail: inquiries@literarybent.com.

MAUPIN, ELIZABETH THATCHER, theater critic; b. Cleve., Oct. 21, 1951; d. Addison and Margaret (Thatcher) M.; m. Jay Yellen, Dec. 29, 1995. BA in English, Wellesley Coll., Mass., 1973; M in Journalism, U. Calif., Berkeley, 1976. Editorial asst. Houghton Mifflin Co., Boston, 1973-74; reporter, movie critic Times-Standard, Eureka, Calif., 1976-78; theater and movie critic Chronicle-Telegram, Elyria, Ohio, 1978-79; movie critic Ledger-Star, Norfolk, Va., 1979-82; feature writer Va.-Pilot and Ledger-Star, Norfolk, 1982-83; sr. theater critic Orlando (Fla.) Sentinel, 1983—. Fellow Nat. Arts Journalism program Columbia U., 1995-96. Fellow Nat. Critics Inst.; mem. Am. Theatre Critics Assn. (exec. com. 1993-99, 05-06, chair 1996-99). Office: Orlando Sentinel 633 N Orange Ave Orlando FL 32801-1349

MAUPIN, KARIN LOUISE, secondary school educator; d. Alfred Bertil and Kathryn Louise (Snapp) Swanson; m. Bernard Kent Fredrick Maupin, Aug. 11, 1973; children: Kristin Louise, Kevin Alfred. BA in Anthropology, Northwestern U., 1970, tchg. cert., 1972; postgrad., U. Ill., 1972—73, Aquinas Coll., 1994—95; M in Spl. Edn. and Learning Disabilities, Calvin Coll., 1998. Commodities trading asst. E.F. Hutton & Co., Chgo., 1972—73; comml. paper trader Montgomery Ward Credit Corp., Chgo., 1973—77; tchr. Creative Learning Ctr., Grand Rapids, Mich., 1982—83; program dir. Alternative Methods for Internat. Stability/Trees Corps., 1989—; tutor SLD Ctr., Grand Rapids, 1995—98; substitute tchr. Forest Hills Pub. Schs., Grand Rapids, 1996—97, tchr., 1997—. Odyssey of the Mind coach Forest Hills No. Middle Sch., Grand Rapids, 1995; adult sponsor F.O.M.E. Environ. Club Forest Hills No. H.S., 1995—98. Contbg. editor: mag. Our Children, 1991—93. Tutor Head Start Program, Grand Rapids, Mich., 1966, James Taylor Sch., Chgo., 1971, Cabrini Green Housing Project, 1976—77; vol. curator Field Mus. Natural History, Chgo., 1978—80; vol. curator, docent Grand Rapids Pub. Mus., 1981—83; bd. mem. Summerfest Ballet Sch., 1983—85; pres. Kent County Med. Soc. Aux., 1984—85; coord. Citizens Liability Action Com., 1984—87; legis. chmn. Mich. State Med. Soc. Aux., 1985—87; pres. Coffinberry Archaeol. Soc., 1988; bd. mem. Children's Inter-active Sci. Ctr., 1995—99, SLD Learning Ctr. Western Mich., 1995—99; rep. Northwestern U. Alumni, 1996—; mem. edn. com. Frederik Meijer Gardens, 1997—2001. Recipient Cert. Appreciation, Mich. State Med. Soc., 1987, AMA, 1987, Letter Appreciation for environ. stewardship, Former Pres. Gerald R. Ford, 1989, Achievement award, Global Releaf, 1990, Letter Appreciation for environ. stewardship, Pres. George Bush, 1992, Cert. Appreciation, Gov. Engler, Mich. Office of Governor, 1992, Cmty. Svc. award, Mich. Forestry & Park Assn., 1992, State Winner, Pres. Bush's Take Pride in Am., 1992, Nongovtl. Agy. award for environ. stewardship, Mich. Audubon Soc., 1993, Letter Appreciation, Kent County Commrs., 1994, Cert. Appreciation, Grand Rapids Pub. Schs., 1994, Pres. Clinton's Coun. on Sustainable Development, 1997. Avocations: travel, gardening, tennis, bicycling, golf. Office: Forest Hills Pub Schs 6590 Cascade Rd SE Grand Rapids MI 49506 E-mail: amistrees@aol.com.

MAUPIN, MICHAEL DENNIS, quality assurance professional; Cert. in Aviation Maintenance Technician, Sacramento City Coll., 1975. Inspector aviation components E.F. Felt Co., San Leandro, Calif., 1977—88; supr. Turbine Engine Shop Associated Aerospace Activities, Inc., San Leandro, 1983—87; dir. quality assurance WECO Aerospace Sys., Inc., Lincoln, Calif., 1988—. Achievements include electrical generator installation for helicopters for law enforcement and emergency medical ships. Avocations: home brewing, gardening, fishing, hiking, camping. Office: WECO Aerospace Systems Inc 1501 Aviation Blvd L-1 Lincoln CA 95648 Home Phone: 530-476-2352.

MAURER, DAVID LEO, lawyer; b. Evansville, Ind., Oct. 31, 1945; s. John G. Jr. and Mildred M. (Lintzenich) M.; m. Diane M. Kaput, Aug. 11, 1973; children: Eric W., Kathryn A. BA magna cum laude, U. Detroit, 1967, Cert. in Teaching, 1971; JD, Wayne State U., 1975. Bar: Mich., U.S. Dist. Ct. (ea. and we. dist.) Mich., U.S. Ct. Appeals (6th cir.) Cin. Law clk. Mich. Ct. Appeals, Detroit, 1976, Supreme Ct. Mich., Lansing, 1977-78; asst. U.S. atty. civil div. U.S. Dept. Justice, Detroit, 1978-81; assoc. to ptnr. Butzel, Long, Gust, Klein & Van Zile, Detroit, 1981-85; ptnr. Pepper, Hamilton & Scheetz (now Pepper Hamilton LLP), Detroit, 1985—. Guest lectr. Practicing Law Inst., 1988—, Nat. Bus. Inst., 1989—, U. Mich. Law Sch., U. Detroit Law Sch., 1990, Hazardous Waste Super Conf., 1986-87. Co-author: Michigan Environmental Law Deskbook, 1992; contbr. articles to profl. jours. and chpts. in books. Mem. Energy & Environ. Policy Com., 1988—, chairperson, 1989-90; mem. Great Lakes Water Resources Commn., 1986. Mem. State Bar Mich. (environ. couns. 1986-91, sec., treas., chairperson-elect, chairperson 1991-93). Office: Pepper Hamilton LLP 100 Renaissance Ctr Ste 3600 Detroit MI 48243-1157 Office Phone: 313-393-7448. Business E-Mail: maurerd@pepperlaw.com.

MAURER, FRANK W, JR., land trust administrator; b. Boston, Aug. 25, 1941; s. Frank W Sr. and Elizabeth M. Maurer; m. Lenora Ann Timm, Apr. 19, 1985; children from previous marriage: Pierre Crispin, Basil Gavin. *Father and namesake, Frank W Maurer, Sr., having a background in both engineering and physiology, was asked to work in secret at the beginning of WWII to design and produce high-altitude breathing equipment for Allied pilots to over-fly the Axis pilots with their then superior equipment. At the conclusion of the war, he returned all patents to the federal government, saying he could not profit from such a horrible event. For the rest of his life he was an inventor and designer. The family likes to think that his creative and social sensibilities live on in his children and grandchildren. Mother, Elizabeth M. Maurer, was always a free thinker, having voted for socialist, Norman Thomas, in her first presidential election. During my childhood, she was open minded in her approach to raising me and my siblings. Her role modeling allowed me to be the free thinker I became.* BA in Biology, Antioch Coll., Yellow Springs, Ohio, 1964; PhD in Vertebrate Zoology and Ecology, Cornell U., Ithaca, NY, 1968. Lic. vessel operator Calif. Asst. prof. biology U. Bosphorus, Istanbul, Turkey, 1968—71; lectr. zoology Nat. U. Lesotho, 1971—76; rsch. assoc. Swedish U. Agrl. Scis., Uppsala, 1977; interviewer 13 countries in Asia, 1978; owner, operator, dir. Rsch. Farm, Davis, Calif., 1978—; organic farmers' market prodr., 1978—; exec. dir., pres. Quail Ridge Wilderness Conservancy, Davis, 1989—, Environ. Edn. Farm Found., Davis, 1993—. Lectr. in field; cons. on openspace and conservation models for small landowners, Wyo., 2004—07, Nev., 2007—; owner Deer Canyon Preserve, N.Mex. *Always among his goals are human rights, education, promoting environmental and open space programs, interwoven with artistic expression. In addition to starting an educational teaching farm in Davis, CA in 1978, he and his wife worked over 24 years to create a 2000 acre native habitat and wildlife reserve in Napa County by purchasing, via innovative fundraising strategies, land destined for development. He led the initiative to incorporate this reserve into the University of California's Natural Reserve System. Today's activities focus on public speaking, voting reform, habitat restoration, creating openspace and conservation models for small landowners, and using the art of hand-carved petroglyphs for teaching and commemorations.* Author: (legislation) Calif. State Grass Bill, 2004; author: (facilitator) Wyo. State Grass Bill, 2007; petroglyphs, Calif. State Archives, 2000, 2004, Wash. State Archives, 2002, 2003, Assembly of Wales, 2003, Coun. of Cornwall, 2003, Parliament of Scotland, 2004, Oreg. State Archives, 2004, Nev. State Libr. and Archives, 2005, Utah State Archives, 2005, Wyo. State Archives, 2005; prodr.: (CD) Scottish Poetry, 2003, (ednl. videos) Quail Ridge Reserve, 1998, Reflections, 2000, (photobook) Portraits of a Vanishing Landscape A Pictorial Interpretation of the Western Sagebrush Steppe, 2006; contbr. articles to profl. publs. Registered pacifist US Draft Bd., 1966; activist Ctr. for Voting and Democracy, Takoma Park, Md., 2004—, Californians for Electoral Reform, Sacramento, 2004—. Recipient John Muir award, Davis Farmers Market, 1989, Conservation Achievement recognition, Napa County Land Trust, 1990. Mem.: Soc. Conservation Biology (life), Soc. Study of Evolution (life), Am. Soc. Mammalogy (life), Dixon Scottish Cultural Assn., Sacramento Caledonian Club. Green Party. Avocations: travel, hiking, birdwatching. Home: 25344 County Rd 95 Davis CA 95616 Office: Quail Ridge Wilderness Conservancy/ Environ Edn Farm Found 25344 County Rd 95 Davis CA 95616 Office Phone: 530-758-1387. Office Fax: 530-758-1316.

MAURER, FREDERIC GEORGE, III, bank executive; b. Grand Rapids, Mich., May 15, 1952; s. Frederic George and Rhea Marie (Annesser) Maurer. BA, St. Louis U., 1974, MBA, 1977. Dir. residence Marguerite Hall St. Louis U., 1977-79; internat. banking analyst Merc. Trust Co., St. Louis, 1979-80, banking rep. Latin Am., 1980-81, internat. officer, 1981-83, asst. v.p., 1983, Union Bank, LA, 1983-86; asst. v.p. internat. sect. Centerre Bank, N.A., St. Louis, 1986-87, asst. v.p. portfolio mgmt. sect., 1987-88; with pvt. banking dept. Boatmen's Nat. Bank, St. Louis, 1988-90, v.p., 1990-97, Nations Bank, St. Louis, 1997-99, Bank Am., St. Louis, 1999-2001, Commerce Trust Co., St. Louis, 2001—06, Bank Midwest, N.A., St. Louis, 2006—. Bd. dirs. Assocs. St. Louis U. Librs., 1975—79, NCCJ, 1992—, Food Outreach, Inc., 2001—, Downtown/Marquette YMCA, 2003—; mem. dir.'s assn. Mo. Bot. Garden, 1986—; bd. dirs. Franciscan Missionary Union, 1996—2001. Internat. Bus. fellow, 1975—77. Mem.: DuBourg Soc., LA English-Speaking Union, Performing Arts Coun.-In the Wings, Opera Guild, Robert Morris Assocs., Ctr. Internat. Banking Studies, U. Va., Alumni Coun. St. Louis U., Mo. Athletic Club (St. Louis), Noonday Club. Home: 849 Aldan Dr Saint Louis MO 63132-3501 Office: 1 N Brentwood Blvd Ste 100 Saint Louis MO 63105 Office Phone: 314-862-4953. Business E-Mail: maurerfg@dfckc.com.

MAURER, GILBERT CHARLES, media specialist; b. NYC, May 24, 1928; s. Charles and Mildred (Petite) M.; m. Ann D'Espinosa. AB, St. Lawrence U., 1950; MBA, Harvard U., 1952. With Cowles Communications, Inc., NYC, 1952-71, Look Mag., 1952-62; pub. Venture mag., 1963-67; pres. Family Circle mag., 1967-69, v.p., dir. corporate planning, exec. com., 1969-71; sr. v.p., dir. F.A.S. Internat., Inc., 1971-73; v.p. mag. div. Hearst Corp., 1973-74, exec. v.p., 1974-76, pres. mag. div., 1976-90, also dir.; exec. v.p. The Hearst Corp., 1985-98, chief operating officer, 1990-98, cons. Mem. NY adv. bd. Salvation Army, 1979—; trustee Whitney Mus. Am. Art, 1983—, pres., 1994-98, trustee Norton Mus. of Art, 1998—; mem. vis. com. Medill Sch. Journalism Northwestern U., 1985-94, chmn., 1989-94; bd. dirs. Boys and Girls Club Am., 1986—, William Randolph Hearst Found., The Hearst Found.; mem. bd. mgrs. NY Bot. Garden, 1989. Mem. Mag. Pubs. Assn. (bd. dirs., chmn. 1979-81) Clubs: Harvard (NYC), Metropolitan (NYC). Office: Hearst 300 W 57th St New York NY 10019

MAURER, HAROLD MAURICE, pediatrician; b. NYC, Sept. 10, 1936; s. Isador and Sarah (Rothkowitz) M.; m. Beverly Bennett, June 12, 1960; children: Ann Maurer Rosenbach, Wendy Maurer Linsky. AB, NYU, 1957; MD, SUNY, Bklyn., 1961. Diplomate Am. Bd. Pediatrics, Am. Bd. Pediatric Hematology-Oncology. Intern pediatrics Kings County Hosp., NYC, 1961-62; resident in pediatrics Babies Hosp., Columbia-Presbyn. Med. Center, NYC, 1962-64; fellow in pediatric hematology/oncology Columbia-Presbyn. Med. Center, 1966-68; asst. prof. pediatrics Med. Coll. Va., Richmond, 1968-71, asso. prof., 1971-75, prof., 1975—, chmn. dept. pediatrics, 1976-93; dean U. Nebr. Coll. Medicine, Omaha, 1993-98; chancellor U. Nebr. Med. Ctr., Omaha, 1998—. Chmn. Intergroup Rhabdomyosarcoma Study, 1972-98; exec. com. Pediatric Oncology Group. Editor: pediatrics, 1983, Rhabdomyosarcoma and Related Tumors in Children and Adolescence, 1991; mem. editorial bd. Am. Jour. Hematology, Journal Pediatric Hematology and Oncology, Medical and Pediatric Oncology, 1984-99; contbr. articles to profl. jours. Mem. Youth Health Task Force, City of Richmond., Gov.'s Adv. Com. on Handicapped., Gov.'s Homeland Security Policy Group, Nebr., 2002-; mem. coun. biodefense Assn. Academic Health Ctr., 2003—, coun. global health, 2003—, gov.'s homeland security policy group 2002—; mem. nat. com. on childhood cancer Am. Cancer Soc., bd. dirs. Va. divsn.; bd. dirs. Nebr. Med. Ctr., 1997—, Friends of Nat. Inst. Nursing Rsch., 2004-05; adv. com. Lisstratcom, 2004—. Served to lt. comdr. USPHS, 1964-66. Named Ak-Sar-Ben King C IX, 2005; recipient Midlander of Yr., Omaha World Herald Newspaper, 2004, Face on the Barroom Floor award, Omaha Press Club, 2007; grantee, NIH, 1974—98. Mem. Am. Acad. Pediatrics (com. oncology-hematology), Am. Soc. Hematology, Soc. Pediatric Rsch., Am. Pediatric Soc., Va. Pediatric Sic. (exec. com.), Assn. Med. Sch. Pediatric Dept. Chmn., Internat. Soc. Pediatric Oncology, Am. Soc. Clin. Oncology, Va. Hematology Soc., Am. Assn. Cancer Rsch., Am. Cancer Soc., Am. Soc. Pediatric Hematology-Oncology (v.p. 1990-91, pres. 1991-93, Lifetime Achievement award children's oncology group 2003), Sigma Xi, Coun. Deans AAMC, Gov.'s Blue Ribbon Commn., Alpha Omega Alpha. Republican. Jewish. Home: 9822 Ascot Dr Omaha NE 68114-3848 Office: U Nebr Med Ctr 986605 Nebraska Med Ctr Omaha NE 68198-6605 Business E-Mail: hmmaurer@unmc.edu.

MAURER, JEFFREY STUART, trust company executive; b. NYC, July 9, 1947; s. Herbert and Phoebe Maurer; m. Wendy S. Nemerov. BA, Alfred U., 1969; MBA, NYU, 1975; JD, St. John's U., 1976. With US Trust Co. NY, NYC, 1970—, pres., 1990, COO, 1994-2001, CEO, 2001—02, chmn., CEO, 2002—03; CEO Lehman Bros. Trust Co., N.A., NYC, 2003—05, chmn., 2006—. Trustee Alfred (N.Y.) U., 1984, North Shore L.I. Jewish Health Sys.; bd. dirs., treas. Children's Health Fund, N.Y.C., 1988; chmn. Hebrew Home Aged, Riverdale, NY. Mem. ABA, N.Y. State Bar Assn., Glen Head Country Club, Harmonie Club. Jewish. Office: Lehman Bros Trust Co NA 399 Park Ave Fl 5 New York NY 10022 Office Phone: 212-526-8503. Business E-Mail: jeffrey.maurer@lehman.com.

MAURER, KATHLEEN MARIE, music educator, vocalist; b. Pitts. MusB in Vocal Performance, Butler U., Indpls., 1977; MusM in Vocal Performance, Bowling Green State U., Bowling Green, Ohio, 1979; DMA in Vocal Performance, U Cincinnati Coll.-Conservatory of Music, 2007. Profl. opera singer Städtische Bühne Hagen, Hagen, Rheinland-Pfalz, Germany, 1983—85, Nationaltheater Mannheim, Mannheim, Baden-Württemberg, Germany, 1985—98; faculty assoc. in voice Wright State U., Dayton, Ohio, 1998—2003; asst. prof. of voice performance Ball State U. Sch. of Music, Muncie, Ind., 2003—. Singer (orchestra concerts) Beethoven's Symphony No. 9, "Happy (Belated) Birthday, Richard Rodgers", "A Richard Rodgers Centennial Celebration," (oratorios) Handel's Messiah, Mozart Requiem Mass, Mozart Coronation Mass, Saint Saens Christmas Oratorio, (chamber music world premiers) "Wildpeace" (Deborah Netanel, 2002), "Within My Garden" (Eleanor Trawick, 2005), "As Lady from her Door: A song cycle of escape" (Anthony Amstutz, 2007, (recitals) Gesichte der Liebe (Faces of Love), All About Love: A Romantic Recital, All in the Family: Music of Related Composers, (operas) The Ballad of Baby Doe, Suor Angelica, (lecture recital) Poems of Love and the Rain (Ned Rorem). Mem.: Coll. Music Soc. (campus rep. 2005—), Nat. Assn. Tchrs. of Singing, Ball State U. Women's Club, Phi Kappa Phi, Pi Kappa Lambda. Avocations: attending concerts, handcrafts, reading. Office: Ball State University School of Music Muncie IN 47306 Office Phone: 765-285-5408. Business E-Mail: kmmaurer@bsu.edu.

MAURER, RICHARD HORNSBY, physicist; b. Reading, Pa., Apr. 27, 1942; s. Samuel Forest and Marian E. (Hornsby) M.; m. Marian Ross Harvey, May 3, 1975; children: Jonathan, Andrew. BS, L.I. U., 1964; PhD, U. Pitts., 1970. Postdoctoral fellow Bartol Rsch. Found., Swarthmore, Pa., 1970-73; environ. engr. AMP Inc., Harrisburg, Pa., 1973-81; physicist Applied Physics Lab. Johns Hopkins U., Laurel, Md., 1981—, reliability group supr. test and evaluation sect., 1986-94, instr. Whiting Sch. Engring., 1988—. Contbr. chpt. to: Space Systems Reliability and Survivability, 1994; contbr. articles to Jour. IEEE Transactions Nuclear Sci., Jour. Spacecraft and Rockets, Internat. Reliability Physics Symposium. Baseball mgr. Howard County Youth Program, Ellicott City, Md., 1985-97; lector St. John's Episcopal Ch., 1994-98. Mem. IEEE, Am. Soc. Quality Control, Am. Phys. Soc., Sigma Xi. Achievements include patent for fabrication of thermal batteries by multi-layer ceramic of organic printed circuit board methods; research on effects of radiation on electronic devices, on reliability of electronic packaging designs and gallium arsenide devices; development of portable neutron spectrometer. Office: Johns Hopkins U Applied Physics Lab 11100 Johns Hopkins Rd Laurel MD 20723-6005 Office Phone: 443-778-6482. Personal E-mail: ecmd@aol.com.

MAURER, RICHARD MICHAEL, investment company executive; b. Bethlehem, Pa., June 4, 1948; s. Richard Thomas and Anna Theresa (Bold) M.; m. Karen Coe, June 13, 1970; children: Christopher Coe, Mark Emerson. Student, Pa. State U., 1966-68; BS, Point Park Coll., 1971; MBA, U. Pitts., 1982. CPA Pa. Staff acct. Price Waterhouse, Pitts., 1972-74, tax acct., 1974, sr. tax acct., 1974-77, tax mgr., 1977-78; dir. taxes The Hillman Co., Pitts., 1978-85; pres. Maurer Ross & Co., Inc., Pitts., 1985—; co-mng. ptnr. Wesmar Ptnrs., Pitts., 1985—; mng. dir. Source Cos., LLC, Pitts., 2006; pres. Arrow Capital Advisors, LLC, Pitts., 2007—. Bd. dirs. Women's Golf Unltd., Inc., Maurer Ross & Co., Inc., Maurer & Ross, Inc. Mem. AICPA, Assn. Corp. Growth, Pa. Inst. CPAs, Rotary (past dir., past pres.), Oakmont Country Club, Duquesne Club. Office: 1606 Carmody Ct Ste 300 Sewickley PA 15143 E-mail: maurer.rick@gmail.com.

MAURER, ROBERT DISTLER, retired industrial physicist; b. St. Louis, July 20, 1924; s. John and Elizabeth J. (Distler) M.; m. Barbara A. Mansfield, June 9, 1951; children: Robert M., James B., Janet L. BS, U. Ark., 1948, LLD, 1980; PhD, MIT, 1951. Mem. staff MIT, 1951-52; with Corning Glass Works, NY, 1952-89, mgr. physics research, 1963-78, research fellow, 1978-89. Contbr. articles to profl. jours., chpts. to books; patentee in field. Served with U.S. Army, 1943-46. Recipient Indsl. Physics prize Am. Inst. Physics, 1978, L.M. Ericsson Internat. prize in telecommunications, 1979, Indsl. Rsch. Inst. Achievement award, 1988, Optical Soc. Am./IEEE Leos Tyndall award, 1987, Disting. Alumni award U. Ark, 1994, Am. Innovator award U.S. Dept. Commerce, 1995, Nat. Medal of Technology, 2000; decorated Purple Heart. Fellow IEEE (Morris N. Liebmann award 1978), Am. Ceramic Soc. (George W. Morey award 1976), Am. Phys. Soc. (New Materials prize 1989); mem. NAE (Charles Draper prize 1999), Nat. Inventors Hall of Fame. Home: 2572 W 28th Ave Eugene OR 97405

MAURER, STEPHEN MARK, academic program director; BA summa cum laude, Yale U., New Haven, 1979; JD, Harvard Law Sch., 1982. Bar: Calif. Assoc. Brown & Bain, Phoenix, 1982—87; sr. assoc. Lasky, Haas, Cohler & Munter, San Francisco, 1988—92, Ritchey, Fisher, Whitman & Klein, Palo Alto, Calif., 1994—96, Fliesler, Dubb, Meyer & Lovejoy, San Francisco, 1998; contract atty. San Francisco and Palo Alto, Calif., 1992—94; lectr. U. Calif. Goldman Sch. Pub. Policy, Berkeley, 1999—2004, acting dir. Info. Tech. and Homeland Security Project, 2005. Cons. Diversified Risk Mgmt., Mutations Database Initiative, Virtual Physics Assocs.; mem. com. geophys. data NAS, 2003—04; adj. assoc. prof. U. Calif., Berkeley; co-founder Tropical Disease Initiative. Contbr. articles to profl. jours., to popular sci. publs. Named one of 50 Who Matter Now, CNNMoney.com Bus. 2.0, 2006. Achievements include writing a proposal to impose a code of conduct on the field of synthetic biology. Office: U Calif Berkeley 2607 Hearst Ave MC 7320 Berkeley CA 94720 Office Phone: 510-643-6990. E-mail: smaurer@berkeley.edu. *

MAURER, TRENT W., humanities educator; s. John and Brenda Maurer. BA, U. Notre Dame, Ind., 1998; MS, U. Ill., Urbana-Champaign, 1999, PhD, 2003. Asst. prof. child and family devel. Ga. So. U., Statesboro, 2003—. Mem.: Phi Upsilon Omicron, Phi Kappa Phi, Phi Beta Kappa.

MAURER, VIRGINIA GALLAHER, law educator; b. Shawnee, Okla., Nov. 7, 1946; d. Paul Clark Gallaher and Virginia Ruth (Watson) Abernathy; m. Ralph Gerald Maurer, July 31, 1971; children: Ralph Emmett, William Edward. BA, Northwestern U., 1968; MA, Stanford U., 1969, JD, 1975. Bar: Iowa 1976. Tchr. social studies San Mateo H.S. Dist., Calif., 1969—71; spl. asst. to pres. U. Iowa, Iowa City, 1976—80, adj. asst. prof. law, 1979—80; affiliate asst. prof. law U. Fla., Gainesville, 1981, asst. prof. bus. law, 1980—85, assoc. prof., 1985—93, prof., 1993—, Huber Hurst prof., 1997—. Dir. Poe Bus. Ethics Ctr., 1998—, MBA program U. Fla., 1987, chair dept. mgmt., 1994-2003; vis. scholar Wolfson Coll., Cambridge, 1994; vis. prof. SDA Bocconi U., Milan, 1994-96, Helsinki Sch. Econs. and Bus., 1998, U. Catania, Sicily, 1999, 2002-03; cons. Gov.'s Com. on Iowa 2000, Iowa City, 1976-77, Fla. Banker's Assn., Gainesville, 1982, various law firms, 1995—. Contbr. articles to profl. jours.; jr. editor Am. Bus. Law Jour., 1989-90, mng. editor, 1990-91, editor-in-chief, 1992-94 Bd. dirs. Gainesville Chamber Orch., 1990-93; fundraising com. Pro Arte Musica, Gainesville, 1980-84; sr. warden, vestry Holy Trinity Episc. Ch., 1991-93, 99-2004, jr. warden, 2000-02; bd. dirs. Holy Trinity Found., Gainesville, 1991-93; com. charter and canon law Episc. Diocese Fla., 1994-96; bd. dirs. Samaritan Ctrs. of North Ctrl. Fla., Inc., 1995-97, Early Childhood Learning Coalition Alachea County, Fla., 2007—. Named Fla. Bluekey Disting. Faculty mem., 2004, Woman of Distinction, Alachua County, 2005. Fellow Soc. Advanced Legal Studies (UK); mem. ABA, AAUW, Acad. Legal Studies in Bus. (ho. of dels. 1989-90, exec. com. 1992, 98—, sec.-treas. 1998-99, v.p. 1999-2000, pres-elect 2000-01, pres. 2001-02, exec. com. 2002-), Southeastern Bus. Law Assn. (proc. editor 1984-87, treas. 1985-86, v.p. 1986-87, pres.-elect 1987-88, pres. 1988-89), Iowa Bar Assn., LWV, U. Fla. Athletic Assn. (bd. dirs. 2004-, v.p. chmn. fin. com. 1982-88), Gainesville Womens' Forum (bd. dirs. 1988-91), Fla. Women' Network (bd. dirs. 1995-99), Univ. Woman's Club (Gainesville, Fla.), Rotary (bd. dirs. 1989-91, dist. scholarship com. 1997-99, regional scholarship com. 2000, chair 2001), Beta Gamma Sigma, Kappa Alpha Theta, Delta Sigma Pi Home: 2210 NW 6th Pl Gainesville FL 32603-1409 Office: U Fla Grad Sch Bus Gainesville FL 32611 Office Phone: 352-392-1048. Business E-Mail: virginia.maurer@cba.ufl.edu.

MAURICE, PATRICIA ANN, geochemist, educator; b. Manchester, Conn., Sept. 3, 1960; d. Robert Aime and Helen M.; m. Gregory Richard Madey; 1 child, Alexander Gregory. BA, Johns Hopkins U., Balt., 1982; MS, Dartmouth Coll., 1985; PhD, Stanford U., 1994. Project chief hydrogeochemistry US Geol. Survey, 1985-89; asst. prof. geochemistry Kent State U., Ohio, 1994-99, assoc. prof., 1999-2000, U. Notre Dame, Ind., 2000—03; prof., dir. Ctr. for Environ. Sci. and Tech., 2003—. Contbr. numerous articles to profl. jours. Recipient Pres. award, U. Notre Dame. Mem. Am. Geophys. Union, Am. Chem. Soc., Clay Minerals Soc. Avocations: Tae Kwon Do, quilting. Office: Univ of Notre Dame Dept Civil Eng/Geol Sci Notre Dame IN 46556

MAURICE, PAUL, professional hockey coach; b. Sault Ste. Marie, Ont., Canada, Jan. 30, 1967; m. Michelle; 1 child, Sydney. Asst. coach Detroit Jr. Red Wings, 1988-93, head coach, 1993-94, Hartford Whalers, 1995—97, Carolina Hurricanes, 1997—2003, Toronto Marlies, 2005—06, Toronto Maple Leafs, 2006—. Asst. coach NHL All-Star Game, 1997. Named runner up Coach of Yr. nominamtion OHL, 1995. Mem. Compuware Hockey Orgn. Office: Toronto Maple Leafs Air Canada Ctr 40 Bay St Ste 300 Toronto ON Canada

MAURIN, JAMES E., real estate executive; Grad. in aerospace engring., La. State U., 1970; MBA, Tulane U., 1972. Acct. Ernst and Ernst, New Orleans; mng. ptnr. Maurin-Ogden Properties, Covington, La., 1975—; chmn. Stirling Properties, Covington, La., 1975—. Mem. bus. sch. coun. Tulane U., La. State U.; bd. dirs. Ochsner Found. Hosp. Mem.: Internat. Coun. Shopping Ctrs. (chmn. 2004—05), World Pres.'s Orgn. (chmn. La. chpt. 2005), Urban Land Inst. (chmn. La. dist. coun. 2002—04). Office: Stirling Properties 109 Northpark Blvd Covington LA 70433-5005 Office Phone: 985-898-2022. Business E-Mail: jmau@stirlingprop.com.

MAURO, MICHAEL ANTHONY, state official; b. Sept. 29, 1948; m. Dorothy Fischer; children: Steven, Nick, Michael. Grad., Drake U., Des Moines, 1970. Lic. real estate broker, cert. elections/registration adminstr. 2003. HS govt. tchr., coach, referee; election dir. Polk County, Iowa, 1984—96, auditor Iowa, 1997—2007; sec. state State of Iowa, Des Moines, 2007—. Mem. I-VOTERS Standards com. Polk County, mem. HAVA State Plan Adv. Com., mem. Voting Equipment Users Grp., mem. Deferred Compensation Bd. Democrat. Office: Office Sec State State Capitol Rm 105 1007 E Grand Ave Des Moines IA 50319 *

MAURY, RICHARD, painter; b. Washington, Nov. 6, 1935; Attended, U. Md., College Park, 1954—55, Corcoran Art Sch., 1956, The Art Students League, 1957—59, L'Academia delle belle Arti, Florence, Italy, 1960—62. Exhibitions include Capricorn Gallery Bethesda Md, 1968, Nat. Press Club Washington, 1971, Medici Gallery London, 1972, Gerold Wunderlich & Co. NYC, 1986-95, Forum Gallery NYC, 2001-03, Forum Gallery LA, 2003; represented in collections of Am. Express Co., Arnot Art Mus. Elmira NY, Art Students League NYC, Flint Inst. Arts, Mich., Met. Mus. Art NYC, New Britain Mus. Art, Conn., Fogg Mus. Cambridge Mass., Uffizi Gallery Florence Italy. Mem.: NAD (academician). Mailing: c/o Forum Gallery 5th Fl 745 Fifth Ave New York NY 10151

MAU-SHIMIZU, PATRICIA ANN, lawyer; b. Jan. 17, 1953; d. Herbert G. K. and Leilani (Yuen) Mau; 1 child, Melissa Rose. BS, U. San Francisco, 1975; JD, Golden Gate U., 1979. Bar: Hawaii 1979. Law clk. State Supreme Ct., Honolulu, 1979-80; atty. Bendet, Fidell & Sakai, Honolulu, 1980-81; legis. atty. Honolulu City Coun., 1981-83, House Majority Staff Office, Honolulu, 1983-84, dir., 1984-93; chief clk. Hawaii Ho. of Reps., 1993—. Mem. Hawaii Bar Assn., Hawaii Women Lawyers, Jr. League Hawaii. Democrat. Roman Catholic. Home: 7187 Hawaii Kai Dr Honolulu HI 96825-3115 Office: State House Reps 415 S Beretania St Rm 027 Honolulu HI 96813-2407 Home Phone: 808-395-2428; Office Phone: 808-586-6127. Business E-Mail: pat@capital.hawaii.gov.

MAUSKOPF, ROSLYNN R., prosecutor; b. Washington, 1957; d. Barry and Regina Mauskopf. BA, Brandeis U., 1979; JD, Georgetown U., 1982. Asst. dist. atty. NY County Dist. Atty.'s Office, 1982—95, dep. chief spl. prosecution bur., 1992, chief frauds bur., 1993; insp. gen. State of NY, 1995—2002; US atty. (ea. dist.) NY US Dept. Justice, Bklyn., 2002—. Chair Moreland Commn. N.Y.C. Schs., 1999. Office: US Attys Office 147 Pierrepont St Brooklyn NY 11201 *

MAUSKOPF, SEYMOUR HAROLD, history professor; b. Cleve., Nov. 11, 1938; s. Philip and Dora (Trompeter) M.; m. Josephine Mary Album, Aug. 9, 1964; children: Deborah, Philip, Alice. AB, Cornell U., 1960; PhD, Princeton U., 1966. Instr. history Duke U., Durham, NC, 1964-66, asst. prof., 1966-72, assoc. prof., 1972-80, prof., 1980—, dir. program in sci. tech. and human values, 1979-84, dir. Focus Interdisciplinary programs, 1995—2003. Author: Crystals and Compounds, Molecular Structure and Composition in Nineteenth Century French Science, 1976, (with M.R. McVaugh) The Elusive Science; Origins of Experimental Physical Research, 1915-1940, 1980; editor: The Reception of Unconventional Science by the Scientific Community, 1979, Chemical Sciences in the Modern World, 1993. Recipient Dexter award for outstanding achievement in history of chemistry, 1998, award Sci. and Religion Course Program, Ctr. Theology and the Natural Scis., 2002, Alumni Disting. Undergraduate Tchg. award Duke U., 2006; NSF postdoctoral fellow, 1971-72, Charles Price fellow Chem. Heritage Found., 2000; NSF grantee, 1974, 92-93; Am. Philos. Soc. travel grantee, 1979; Nat. Endowment for Humanities summer stipend, 1982; Edelstein internat. fellow in history chem. scis. and tech. Beckman Ctr. U. Pa. and Hebrew Univ., Jerusalem, 1988-89. Mem. History Sci. Soc. (exec. com. treas. 1979-83, coun. 1993-95). Jewish. Office Phone: 919-684-2581. E-mail: shmaus@duke.edu.

MAVILIO, DOMENICO, medical researcher, physician; b. Brindisi, Brindisi, Italy, May 22, 1975; s. Angelo Nicolo' Mavilio and Rosa Capitanio; m. Ivana Matera, Dec. 18, 2005; 1 child, Francesco Angelo. MD, PhD, U. Genova, Italy, 2006. Lic. Italian Bd. Med. Drs. Italy, 1998. Resident U. Genova, 1998—2002; rsch. fellow LIR/NIAID/NIH, Bethesda, 2002—. Achievements include research in clinical immunology. Home Phone: 301-654-6466; Office Phone: 301-496-8043.

MAVRIDES, ELAINE, retired mental health services professional, retired social worker; b. Akron, Ohio, July 24, 1936; d. Paul A. and Clara Regas Mavrides; children: Kimberly Ann Morgan, Patty Blower, Denise M. Riegler. BA, U. Akron, Ohio, 1970, MEd, 1980. Elem. tchr. Cath. Diocese Cleve., 1966—76; psychiat. social worker Western Res. Human Svcs., Stow, Ohio, 1976—88; counselor, case mgr. Cmty. Support Svcs., Akron, 1988—2003; psychiat. screener Psychiat. ER Svcs., 1988—98; ret., 2003. Family therapist Barberton Citizens Hosp., Ohio, 1988; adv. bd. Summit County Homeless, 1989—90; organizer First Link Family Support Group Families Emotionally Ill Summit County, 1980—88. Citizens adv. bd. Summit County Bd. Mental Retardation, Akron, 1990; treas., pres. Ohio Mental Health Counselors, Columbus, 1990—91. Recipient Excellence cert., Ohio Dept. Mental Health, 1988, Case Mgr. of Yr. award, 1989, award, Summit County Mental Health Assn., 1990, Past Pres.'s award, Ohio Mental Health Counselor's Assn., 1992, award, Am. Mental Inst. Mem.: Nat. Health and Wellness Club, Nat. Gerontology Honor Soc., Sigma Phi Omega. Democrat. Avocations: reading, walking, bicycling, movies, swimming. Home: 76 Emerald Woods Dr L9 Naples FL 34108

MAVROUDI, MARIA, philologist, educator; BA, U. Thessaloniki, 1990; MA, Harvard U., 1992, PhD, 1998. Postdoctoral fellow Byzantine studies Dumbarton Oaks, 2000—01; postdoctoral tchg. fellow Hellenic studies Princeton U., 2001—02; asst. prof. U. Calif., Berkeley, 2002—05, assoc. prof., 2005. Author: A Bzyantine Book on Dream Interpretation: The Oneirocriticon of Achmet and its Arabic Sources, 2002. MacArthur fellow, 2004. Office: U Calif Berkeley 2223 Dwinelle Hall Berkeley CA 94720 Office Phone: 510-643-4413. E-mail: mavroudi@berkeley.edu.

MAVROUDIS, JOHN M., lawyer; b. NYC, July 24, 1947; s. Michael and Anna (Hariton) Mavroudis; m. Anne Drogaris; children: Michael, Lauren. JD cum laude, Syracuse Coll. Law, 1972. Bar: Fla. 1972, N.Y. 1973, N.J. 1975. Assoc. Patterson, Belknap & Webb, NYC, 1972—74; sole practice NYC, 1974—77; sr. ptnr. Nicolette & Mavroudis, P.A., Hackensack, NJ, 1978—83, Klinger, Nicolette, Mavroudis & Honig, P.A., 1984—89, Mavroudis & Rizzo, 1990—. Editor: Syracuse Law Rev., 1972. Trustee The Greek Orthodox Cathedral of St. John the Theologian, NJ, Hellenic Coll. and Holy Cross Greek Orthodox Sch. Theology, Brookline, Mass., 1987—91; gen. counsel Greek Orthodox Archdiocese Am., 1997—2000; bd. advisors Syracuse Coll. Law, 2005—. Served to capt. USAR. Recipient Ellis Island Medal of Honor, 1999; Archon of the Ecumenical Patriarchate Constantinople. Mem.: Bar Assn. City N.Y., Justinian Soc. Office: 690 Kinderkamack Rd # 300 Oradell NJ 07649-1524 Office Phone: 201-262-3000.

MAVROVIC, PAUL J., information technology executive; s. Ivo and Erna Mavrovic. BS in Bus. Mgmt., U. Hartford, Conn., 1987—91. Cert. Info. Sys. Security Profl. Internet Info. Sys. Security Certification Consortium,

2005. Dir., info. tech. svcs. Urea Technologies Inc., Hackensack, NJ, 1991—99; pres. Pm Tech Inc, Hackensack, 1999—. 2nd v.p. Edgewater Apts Inc., New York, NY, 2000—04. Mem.: ISC2. Office: Pm Tech Inc 1 University Plz Ste 304 Hackensack NJ 07601 Home Phone: 212-570-4883; Office Phone: 201-488-0700. Office Fax: 201-488-1062. Business E-Mail: paul@pmtechinc.net, mavrovic@pmtechinc.net.

MAWARDI, OSMAN KAMEL, retired plasma physicist; b. Cairo, Dec. 12, 1917; arrived in U.S., 1946, naturalized, 1952; s. Kamel Ibrahim and Marie (Wiennig) M.; m. Betty Louise Hosmer, Nov. 23, 1950. BS, Cairo U., 1940, MS, 1945; A.M., Harvard U., 1947, PhD, 1948. Lectr. physics Cairo U., 1940-45; asst. prof. Mass Inst. Tech., 1951-56, assoc. prof., 1956-60; prof. engring., dir. plasma research program Case Inst. Tech., Cleve., 1960-88; dir. Energy Research Office, Case Western Res. U., 1977-82; ret., 1988. Pres. Collaborative Planners, Inc.; mem. Inst. Advanced Study, 1969-70; also cons. Contbr. articles to profl. jours. Past trustee Print Club Cleve., Cleve. Inst. Art. Recipient Biennial award Acoustical Soc. Am., 1952; CECON medal of achievement, 1979 Fellow AAAS, Acoustical Soc. Am., IEEE (Edison lectr. 1968-69, Centennial award 1984, Cleve. sect. Engr. of Yr. 1994); mem. N.Y. Acad. Scis., Sigma Xi, Eta Kappa Nu. Home: 15 Mornington Ln Cleveland OH 44106 Office: 2490 Lee Rd Cleveland OH 44118-4125 Home Phone: 216-321-1809; Office Phone: 216-932-9550. Business E-Mail: okm@case.edu. *I never cease to be amazed that the goals I really believe in invariably materialize.*

MAWHINNEY, THOMAS STEPHEN, education educator, educational consultant; b. Pittsfield, Mass., Sept. 20, 1949; s. William Lawrence Mawhinney and Dorothy Frances Hickman; life ptnr. Laura Lynn Starr; children: Daniel Foster, Katharine Elizabeth. BS, YS Coast Guard Acad., New London, Conn., 1971; EdM, Westfield State Coll., Mass., 1978; Cert. in Advanced Grad. Study, U. Mass., Amherst, 1992; EdD, St. John's U., Jamaica, NY, 2002. Cert. ednl. adminstrn. NY State Bd. Regents, 1993. Head tchr. Hibbard Alternative Sch., Pittsfield, Mass., 1973—87; asst. prin. Hoosac Valley H.S., Cheshire, Mass., 1987—92, Behlehem Ctrl. H.S., Delmar, NY, 1992—93; prin. Rhinebeck H.S., NY, 1993—2003; assoc. prof. Touro Coll., NYC, 2003—. Ednl. cons. Leading for Learning, Inc., Poughkeepsie, NY, 2003—. Contbr. chapters to books, articles to profl. jours. Divsn. 2-3 coll. football ofcl. Mem.: ASCD, Harvard Prins. Ctr., Nat. Assn. Secondary Sch. Prins., Nat. Staff Devel. Coun., Phi Delta Kappa. Independent. Avocations: walking, hiking. Home: 35 N Grand Ave Poughkeepsie NY 12603-4401 Office: Touro College 43 W 23rd St New York NY 10010 Home Phone: 914-388-2582. Home Fax: 845-625-1456. Personal E-mail: moonmoon@aol.com.

MAWHOOD, ARISTIDE ROSCOE, mechanical engineer; b. Darjeeling, India, Nov. 18, 1933; parents Brit. citizens; s. Charles Timothy and Thelma Quida (Hollow) M.; m. Mary Bridget McManamon, Dec. 1, 1962; children: Sean Ross, Anton Morgan. BSME, Brit. Inst. Engring. Tech., 1955; postgrad., Imperial Coll. Sci. and Tech. Registered profl. engr., U.S.; profl. engr., U.K. Apprentice engr. Cen. Electricity Generating Bd., 1951-55; dist. engr., mgr., adv. and field engr. Worthington Corp., 1956-63; sr. maintenance engr., maintenance project engr. Hess Oil Virgin Islands Corp., 1970-73; mgr. field engring. svcs. Sam P. Wallace, Internat., 1973; chief engr., chief planning engr., sr. constrn. engr. C.E. Lummus Corp., 1973-75; chief field and resident engr. Pritchard Internat., Inc., 1976-77; engr. 1 mech. (project mgmt. team) Arabian Am. Oil Co., 1977-82; sr. sys. engr. ITT-Fed. Electric Corp., 1985; sr. engr.-cum-cons. Mawhood & Assocs., 1983, 84, 86; sr. mech. engr.-cum-cons. Brown & Root Internat., Inc., 1987-88; sr. engr.-cum-cons. Allis Chalmers Compressor Corp., Appleton, Wis., 1988-89; tech. asst. specialist Corporacion Venezolana de Guayana, S.A., 1989-90, M&H Engring., Inc., Houston, 1990-91; project mgr., engr. Am. Samoa Govt., Pago Pago, American Samoa, 1991-94; sr. program officer, cons. Fed. Emergency Mgmt. Agy. (Pacific), 1994-95; mech. engr., cons. Saudi Arabian Oil Co., Dammam, Saudi Arabia, 1995-96; mech. engr. Dow Chem. Co., Houston, 1996-97; cons. electronic data processing, 1997—. Mech. engr., cons. Saudi Arabian Oil Co., Damman, Saudi Arabia, 1995-96; mech. engr. tech. support unit, engring. and constrn. divsn. Dow Chem. USA, Inc., 1996-97, Engring. and Constrn. Venezuela (Petrozuata) Extra Heavy Crude Oil Engring. Project, Brown & Root USA, Inc., 1997-98; semi-ret. project mgr., engr., tech. cons., 1998—; condr. seminars and revs. Tex. Employment Commn., Houston, 1983-84. Author: Value Engineering, 1975, Role of Gas Turbines, 1978 (IGTI award 1980), Machinery Diseases, 1982 (Vibration Inst. award 1983), Saline Water Conversion, 1987 (Water Inst. award 1988). Active various ch. groups, Houston. Recipient Safety at Constrn. Sites award Constrn. Assn. Can., 1974, Tech. Transfer award Operaciones al Sur del Orinoco, Puerto Ordaz, Venezuela, Value Engring. award Refineria Isla, Curacao, 1987. Fellow Instn. Plant Engrs., India Soc. Mech Engrs., Japan Soc. Mech. Engrs.; mem. ASME (corp.), NSPE, Am. Soc. Metals, Soc. Am. Mil. Engrs., Am. Inst. Plant Engrs., Instn. Mech. Engrs. (assoc.). Republican. Christian Scientist. Achievements include development of solutions for erosion/corrosion problems on pump casings; findings on excess stiffness characteristics in Bendex Diaphragm Couplings for high-speed gas compressors. Home: West Univ PO Box 272562 Houston TX 77277-2562

MAWS, TONY, chef; b. Boston, 1970; m. Karolyn Maws. BA in Psych., U. Mich. Chef Restaurant Clio, Blue Room, La Rivore, Lyon, France, La Folie, Postrio, San Francisco, Coyote Café, Santa Fe; owner, exec. chef Cragie Street Bistrot, Boston, 2002—. Featured in Travel & Leisure mag., Gourmet mag., Boston Globe. Named Boston's Best Up-and-Coming Chef, Boston mag., 2005; named one of Am. Top 10 New Chefs, Food & Wine mag., 2005, Boston's Rising Stars, StarChefs.com, 2006. Avocations: Red Sox, skiing, travel, reading cookbooks. Office: Craigie Street Bistrot 5 Craigie Cir Cambridge MA 02138 Office Phone: 617-497-5511.

MAX, BUDDY (BORIS MAX PASTUCH), musician; b. Jan. 25; m. Freda Max; 1 child, John. Musician, performer as America's Singing Flea Market Cowboy: albums include: Many Styles and Sounds of Buddy Max, 1980, The Great Nashville Star, 1984, The Story of Freda and Bud, 1985, Cowboy Junction Stars, 1985, Tribute to Challenger's Crew of 7, 1986, With Our Friends at Cowboy Junction, 1989, Little Circle B, 1990, Together-Our Masterpiece, 1991, The Life to Fame and Fortune, 1992, Orange Blossom Special, 1996, Hall of Fame, Gold Record Award Winning Buddy Max, 1996, Hall of Fame, Tribute to Bing Crosby, 2004, Tribute to Jimmy Rodgers, Meridian, Mo., 2005, A Tribute to Al Dexter, 2005, Hospice Ctirus County, 2005; composer songs include When the Magnolia Tree Blooms in Lecanto, The Story of Barney Clark, Hang My Guitar on the Wall, John F. Kennedy, The Challenger, Where the Maple Syrups Flow, Little Circle B, Way Up on the Mountain, Desert Storm, When Do I Love You, The Pretty Girl on TV. Recipient World Hall of Fame award and gold medalion, 1997, numerous trophies, awards for benefit and non-profit shows Am. Heart Assn., Am. Lung Assn., Girl Scouts Am., Citizens of Citrus County Fla., Deaf Svcs. of Citrus County, Statue of Liberty trophy and coin award Cowboy Junction Opry Country Music Show, 2000 for song I Love Miss America, cert. Young Marines of Citrus County, 2002; named Ky. Col., Gov. Paul E. Patton, 2001. Address: care Cowboy Junction 3949 W Hwy 44 & Jct 490 Lecanto FL 34461-9232 Office Phone: 352-746-4754.

MAX, ELIZABETH, retired language educator; b. Ft. Worth, Oct. 9, 1924; d. Frederick Ward and Alice Louise (Matthews) Maxwell; m. Herbert Jones McCorkle, Sept. 22, 1945 (div. Oct., 1969); children: Anne McCorkle Moore, Louise Kate McCorkle, Bruce Ward McCorkle, Sallie Matthews McCorkle. BS, Tex. Woman's U., 1944; MSLS, U. North Tex., 1966; EdD, Okla. State U., 1974. Cert. secondary, elementary tchr., Tex., Okla.; cert. sch. librarian, Tex., Okla. Copy clerk, beginning writer UPI, NBC, NYC, 1944—45; tchr. elem. and secondary various schs., Tex., 1950—69; instr. libr. sci. We. Ill. U., Macomb, 1969—70; asst. prof., fine arts libr. Okla. State U., Stillwater, 1970—72, asst. prof., coord. Libr. Sci. Dept., 1972—76, assoc. prof., 1976—82, prof. emerita, 1990—, supr. English Edn., 1982—90. Cons. Skelly Oil Co., Tulsa, Okla., 1976, The Ctr. for Local Govt. Tech., 1983-84, Stillwater Library Sys. Bd., 1985, media reviewer Previews; book revs. Sch. Libr. Jour., 1976-77. Author (with others): Teaching the Short Story, 1996; mem. reader panel New York Times, 1996—2001, mem. New York Times Online Panel, 2002—; contbr. articles to profl. jours. Pres. Meml. Soc. Central Pa., 1994, 96-99; vol. Nat. Disaster Relief, ARC, 1991-96; mem. Dem. Nat. Com.; women's rights activist. Mem. NEA, ALA, Nat. Women's Studies Assn. (founder), Okla State U. Women's Coun. (founder, 2d chair), Okla. Adult and Continuing Edn., Nat. Collegiate Players, Stillwater Okla. Writer's Club (pres., 1985-89), Greek Sabbatical, Nat. Coun. Tchrs. of English (comparative and world lit. com. 1990-97), Gen. Soc. Mayflower Descs., Parents and Friends of Lesbians and Gays, Emily's List, NARAL, ACLU, Phi Delta Kappa, Phi Kappa Phi, Beta Phi Mu. Home and Office: 2414 North Glenwood Dr Stillwater OK 74075 Personal E-mail: elizabethmax@earthlink.net.

MAX, ERNEST, surgeon; b. Vienna, Mar. 3, 1936; m. Silvia Neger, Mar. 18, 1964; children: Yvette Rosa, Oliver Fredrick. MD, U. Chile, 1961. Diplomate Am. Bd. Surgery, Am. Bd. Colon and Rectal Surgeons, Am. Bd. Laser Surgery. Intern Hosp. San Borja, Santiago, Chile, 1960-61, resident, 1962-63; fellow in gen. surgery, colon and rectal surgery Lahey Clinic Found., Boston, 1969-70; resident Sinai Hosp., Balt., 1971-72, The Western Pa. Hosp., Pitts., 1972-74; resident in colon and rectal surgery Hermann Hosp., Houston, 1974-75, staff, 1975—, Park Plz. Hosp., 1975—, Meml. Hosp. Southwest, 1975—, Meml. NW Hosp., 1975—, Diagnostic Ctr. Hosp., 1975—, The Methodist Hosp., 1976—, Meml. City Hosp., 1976—, Houston NW Med. Ctr., 1976—, St. Luke's Episcopal Hosp., 1981—, Cypress Fairbanks, 1983—; chief of staff Meml. Hosp., 1983; staff HCA Med. Ctr., 1986—; CEO Colon and Rectal Clinic PA, 1989—. Clin. assoc. prof. surgery Baylor Coll. Medicine; clin. instr. surgery U. Tex. Med. Sch., Houston. Author: (with others) Current Diagnosis, 1971. Recipient Walter A. Fansler Travel Edn. award Am. Soc. Colon and Rectal Surgeons, 1974, Harriet Cunningham award Tex. Med. Assn., 1988, Best of the Best award Tex. Med. Assc., 1989; The Purdue Fredrick fellow Am. Soc. Colon and Rectal Surgeons, 1974. Mem. Am. Coll. Surgeons, Tex. Med. Soc., Harris County Med. Soc., Tex. Soc. Colon and Rectal Surgeons (pres. 1982-83), Am. Soc. Laser Medicine and Surgery, Internat. Soc. Univ. Colon and Rectal Surgeons, Lahey Clinic Alumni Assn., Am. Soc. Colon and Rectal Surgeons, Tex. Gulf Coast Colon and Rectal Surgical Soc. (sec. treas. 1992—), Colombian Soc. Colo-Proctology (hon. mem.). Office: Colon & Rectal Clinic PA 6550 Fannin St Ste 2307 Houston TX 77030-2723 Home Phone: 713-721-8047; Office Phone: 713-790-9250. Business E-Mail: emax@crchouston.com.

MAXEY, JOSEPH T., marriage and family therapist, educator, hospital administrator; s. Theodore and Pauline Maxey; m. Margaret A. Klimcheck, Aug. 19, 1961; children: Lee Gordon, Susan Jeanette, Christine Marie. BA, Am. U., Washington, 1961—61; MSW, Cath. U., Washington, 1963. Group worker Hillcrest Children's Ctr., Washington, 1958—61; family therapist, adminstr. Children's Convalescent Hosp., Washington, 1963—65, hosp. adminstr., 1965—67; clin. dir. UK Family Children's Ctr., Lakenheath, England, 1967—72, U. Rochester, NY, 1972—98; pres., individual and family therapist Mercy OUtreach Ctr., Rochester, NY, 1998—. Pres. Partial Hospitalization Study Group, 1978—80, RCCA, Pittsford, NY, 1996—2001. Editor: Bibliography on Partial Hospitalization from 1937-1979. Vol. Rochester Philharm., NY; mem. RCCA, Pittsford; pres. Am. Assn. Partial Hospitalization, 1981—84; bd. dirs. Hist. Pittsford, 2003—, pres., 2004—; bd. dirs. Huther Doyle, Rochester, 2000—04. Home: 5 Sutherland St Pittsford NY 14534 Office: Historic Pittsford 18 Monroe Ave Pittsford NY 14534 Home Phone: 585-586-3079.

MAXEY, KEVIN, chef; Degree in Mktg., Tex. Christian U., 1994. Chef The Riviera, Tex., Gramercy Tavern, NYC; exec. chef Craft, Dallas, 2005—. Named one of Dallas' Rising Stars, StarChefs.com, 2007. Office: Craft W Hotel 2440 Victory Park Ln Dallas TX 75219 Office Phone: 214-397-4111. *

MAXFIELD, GUY BUDD, lawyer, educator; b. Galesburg, Ill., May 4, 1933; s. Guy W. and Isabelle B. Maxfield; m. Carol Tunick, Dec. 27, 1970; children: Susan, Stephen, Karen. AB summa cum laude, Augustana Coll., 1955; JD, U. Mich., 1958. Bar: NY 1959. Assoc. White & Case, NYC, 1958—63; prof. law NYU Sch. Law, NYC, 1963—; sr. counsel Fox Rothschild LLP. Author: Tennessee Will and Trust Manual, 1982, Federal Estate and Gift Taxation, 8th edit., 2002, Florida Will and Trust Manual, 1984, Tax Planning for Professionals, 1986; contbr. articles to law jours. Trustee Acomb Found., Newark, 1974—. With U.S. Army, 1958-64. Fellow Am. Coll. Tax Counsel; mem. ABA, Am. Law Inst., NY State Bar Assn., Order of Coif, Phi Beta Kappa. Office: NYU Sch Law 40 Washington Sq S New York NY 10012-1099 Office Phone: 561-835-9600, 561-804-4406. Business E-Mail: gmaxfield@foxrothschild.com.

MAXFIELD, JOHN EDWARD, retired university dean; b. LA, Mar. 17, 1927; s. Chauncey George and Rena Lucile (Cain) M.; m. Margaret Alice Waugh, Nov. 24, 1948; children— Frederick George (dec.), David Glen, Elaine Rebecca, Nancy Catherine, Daniel John. BS, Mass. Inst. Tech., 1947; MS, U. Wis., 1949; PhD, U. Oreg., 1951. Instr. U. Oreg., 1950-51; mathmatician U.S. Naval Ordnance Test Sta., China Lake, Calif., 1949-56, head computing br., 1956-57, head math. div., 1957-60; lectr. UCLA, 1951-60; head prof. dept. math. U. Fla., 1960-67; prof., chmn. dept. math. Kans. State U., 1967-81; dean Grad. Sch. and univ. research La. Tech. U., 1981-92, dean emeritus, 1992—; ret. La. Tech. U., 1992. Mem. Am. Math. Soc., Math. Assn. Am., Soc. Indsl. and Applied Math., Sigma Xi. Home: 209 E Louisiana Ave Ruston LA 71270-4417

MAXFIELD, LORI ROCHELLE, education educator; b. Denver, Jan. 16, 1959; d. Lawrence Wesley and Caroline Kay (Gideon) M. BS, U. Nebr., 1983, MEd, 1991; PhD, U. Conn., 2000. Recreation aide Lincoln (Nebr.) Parks and Recreation, 1976-84; tchr. Harding County Pub. Schs., Reva, Buffalo, S.D., 1984-89; rsch. assoc. U. Nebr., Lincoln, 1990-91, asst. project coord., 1991-92; sch. enrichment coord. Sch. Dist. 145, Waverly/Eagle, Nebr., 1992-94, also future problem solving coach, Invent America! coord., 1992-94; rsch. assoc. U. Conn., Storrs, 1994-96, lectr., 1995-97, instr. CONFRATUTE, 1995-97; asst. prof. Mankato State U., Minn., 1997—98; state staff develop coord. Minn. Dept. Children, Families, Learning, 1998—99; asst. prof. edn. Coll. St. Catherine, 2000—05, assoc. prof. edn., 2005—, program dir. undergraduate edn. programs, 2005—07. Adv., coach Nat. History Day Harding County Pub. Schs., Reva, 1987-89; coach Odyssey of the Mind, 1986, 93; head coach Jr. High Sch. girls basketball, 1988; asst. coach varsity track, 1989. Field reviewer: Gifted Child Today, 2003—. Youth advisor Slim Buttes Luther League, Reva, 1988-89; ptnr. Spl. Olympics, 1992-94. Recipient Outstanding Youth award Nebr. Coun. for Youth and Children, 1977, Outstanding Leadership award Elks, 1977, Golden Apple award Harding County Tchrs., Buffalo, S.D., 1988, Nebr. Ednl. Tech. Assn. grant, 1993. Mem. ASCD, Am. Ednl. Rsch. Assn., Northeastern Ednl. Rsch. Assn. (Lorne H. Wollatt Disting. Paper of Yr. award 1995), Nebr. Assn. for Gifted (adv. bd. 1991-93, bd. dirs. 1993-94, mem. editl. bd. 1992-94, Disting. Svc. award 1994), Nebr. U. Alumni Assn. (life), Wilson Ctr. Assocs., Nat. Assn. for Gifted Children Outstanding Doctoral Student award 1997), Nat. Mid. Sch. Assn., Nat. Coun. Social Studies, Nat. Sci. Tchrs. Assn., Am. Assn. Univ. Women Profs., Am. Soc. Engring. Edn., Am. Assn. Colls. and Univs. (assoc.), So. Poverty Law Ctr. (leadership counsel, named to Wall Tolerance 2007), Nat. Women's History Mus., Phi Delta Kappa, Phi Lambda Theta. Democrat. Lutheran. Avocations: gardening, hiking. Home: 766 Curfew St Saint Paul MN 55114-1045 Office Phone: 651-690-8898. Business E-Mail: lrmaxfield@stkate.edu.

MAXFIELD, LOUISE FONDA GRIBBLE, executive secretary; b. Waco, Tex., Sept. 27, 1924; d. Theodore Miles and Louise Irwin Gribble; m. Jack G.S. Maxfield, July 21, 1951 (dec.); children: Martha Woodson Maxfield Cottingham, Elizabeth Fonda. BA, Randolph-Macon Woman's Coll., Lynchburg,Va., 1945; M Liberal Arts, So. Meth. U., Dallas, 1982. Editor, indsl. house organ Gen. Tire & Rubber Co., Waco, Tex., 1945—51; bus. mgr. Maxfield Clin./Hosp., Dallas, 1976—84, Covenant Presbyn. ch., Carrollton, Tex., 1984—99. Named Woman of Yr., Carrollton, Tex., 2004; Paul Harris fellow, Rotary Internat.

MAXFIELD, MAX R., state official; b. Wis., 1945; m. Gayla Y. Maxfield; 4 children. Student, U. Wis. Dir. Wyo. Recreation Commn., 1987—89, Wyo. Dept. Commerce, 1989—94; state auditor State of Wyo., Cheyenne, 1995—2006, sec. state, 2007—. Mem. state loan and investment bd. State of Wyo., mem. bd. land commrs., mem. state bldg. commn., mem. state canvassing bd., chmn. state fin. adv. com. Dir. YMCA. Republican. Office: Office of State Auditor State Capitol Bldg Rm 114 Cheyenne WY 82002 Office Phone: 307-777-7831. Office Fax: 307-777-6983. E-mail: mmaxfi@state.wy.us. *

MAXFIELD, PETER CHARLES, state legislator, lawyer, educator; b. 1941; AB, Regis Coll., 1963; JD, U. Denver, 1966; LLM, Harvard U., 1968. Bar: Colo. 1966, Wyo. 1969. Trial atty. Dept. Justice, 1966-67; assoc. Hindry, Erickson & Meyer, Denver, 1968-69; asst. prof. U. Wyo. Coll. Law, 1969-72, assoc. prof., 1972-76, prof., 1976-96, dean, 1979-87, prof. emeritus, 1996—. Vis. assoc. prof. U. N.Mex., 1972-73; Raymond F. Rice Disting. prof. U. Kans., 1984; Chapman Vis. Disting. prof. U. Tulsa, 1987; vis. prof. U. Utah, 1992. Author: (with Garr Houghton) Cases and Materials on the Taxation of Oil and Gas and Natural Resources Transactions, 1990, (with Allen and Houghton) Taxation of Mining Operation, 1981, 97, 2002; (with Trelease and Dietrich) Natural Resources Law on American Indian Lands, 1977. Coord. Wyo. State Planning 1988-89; spl. asst. Gov. Wyo. 1989-90; Dem. nominee U.S. Ho. Reps., 1990; mem. Wyo. Environ. Quality Coun., 1991-93; mem. Wyo. Senate, Laramie, 1993-97; counsel Gov. Wyo., 2006. Mem. Omicron Delta Kappa, Pi Delta Phi, Order of the Coif (faculty). Home: 1159 Escalera St Laramie WY 82072-5020 Office: U Wyo Coll Law PO Box 3035 Laramie WY 82071-3035 Business E-Mail: petemaxfield@earthlink.net.

MAXFIELD, ROSE MARY, retired government official; b. Shelbyville, Ill., Mar. 23, 1918; d. Claude Fielding Stiarwalt and Nina Eugenia Whitlock; m. Orville Eldred Maxfield, June 6, 1941; children: Mary Patricia, Mary Constance, Marilyn Joan. BS, U. Ill., Champaign-Urbana, 1939. Adminstrv. asst. U.S. Treasury Dept., Washington, 1942—73; ret., 1973. Author: (chpt.) Amy White of the Old 300, 1986, Biography for New Texas Handbook, 1996. Mem. Sam Houston Regional Libr. and Rsch. Ctr., Tex., Va. Ctr. Civil War Studies, Atascocito Hist. Soc., Liberty, Tex. Recipient Meritorious Svc. award, U.S. Treasury Dept., 1967, Sec.'s Cert., 1969, Albert Gallatin award, 1973, Spl. Achievement award, 1973. Mem.: Nat. Soc. DAR, Wharton County Hist. Mus., Glover Park Citizens Assn., Swiss Club Washington, Nat. Mus. Women in Arts (charter mem.), Nat. Soc. Daus. of Colonial Wars, Daus. of Republic of Tex., United Daus. Confederacy, Nat. Soc. U.S. Daus. of 1812, Flagon and Trencher (life), Assn. for Preservation of Va. Antiquities (life), Soc. Descs. of Colonial Clergy (life), U. Ill. Alumni Assn. (life), Treasury Hist. Assn. (charter mem. 1968), Nat. Soc. Col. Dames 17th Century, Soc. Descs. of Austin's Old 300, Nat. Soc. Sons. and Daus. of the Pilgrims, So. Relief Soc. D.C., Friends of Folger Libr., Shelby County Hist. and Geneal. Soc., Delta Zeta. Avocations: reading, genealogy, needlecrafts, travel, musical performances. Home: 218 Mayfair Cir Wharton TX 77488 Personal E-mail: msmaxfield@sbcglobal.net.

MAXMAN, SUSAN ABEL, architect; b. Columbus, Ohio, Dec. 30, 1938; d. Richard Jack Abel and Gussie (Brenner) Seiden; m. Rolf Sauer; children: Andrew Frankel, Thomas Frankel, Elizabeth Frankel, Melissa, Abby, William Jr., Madeleine Sauer. Student, Smith Coll., 1960; MArch., U. Pa., 1977; HHD, Ball State U., 1993, U. Detroit Mercy, 1997. Registered profl. arch. Pa., Mich., NH, Nat. Coun. Archtl. Registration Bds. Project designer Kopple Sheward & Day, Phila., 1978-80; ptnr. Maxman & Sutphin, Phila., 1980-83; prin. Susan Maxman & Ptnrs., Phila., 1984—. Mem. bd. overseers Grad. Sch. Fine Arts U. Pa., mem. corp. vis. com. MIT; mem. Planning and Design Commn., Ga. Inst. Tech. Works include design of Women's Humane Soc. Animal Shelter, Bensalem, Pa. (Northeastern Sustainable Energy Assn.'s Comml. Bldg. award, 1994, Metal Constrn. Assn. award 1995, Gov.'s Award for Environ. Excellence 1997, AIA Pa. Hon. award 1997), Camp Tweedale-Freedom Valley Girl Scouts USA (AIA Honor award, 1991), Cusano Environ. Edn. Ctr. at John Heinz Nat. Wildlife Refuge at Tinicum, Phila. (US Dept. Energy Fed. Energy Saver Showcase award, US Dept. Interior Environ. Achievement award, Top Ten Green Bldg. award AIA 2003, AIA Cote Top Ten Green Buildings award, 2003), Robert Lewis House (McArthur award 1985), Phila., Restoration Pennock Farmstead (Grand Prize Nat. Trust Hist. Preservation 1995), Canaan Valley Inst. Hdqs., Renovation of Second Bank of US, Phila., Navy Yard Bldg. 10 (Honor award, AIA, Phila. chpt., 2004, citation of merit, PA Historic Presercation award), Natural Lands Trust Hdqs. Expansion, Media, Pa. (N.E. Sustainable Energy Assn. Bldg. award 2004, Exemplary Sustainable Bldgs. Industry Coun. award 2005), Kutztown U., Pa. Sisters Servants of the Immaculate Heart of Mary Renovation of the Motherhouse (Mich. Hist. Preservation Network Bldg. award 2003, Top Ten Green Bldg. award AIA 2006), Renovation of U. Pa. Nursing Edn. Bldg., Phila., Barbara C. Harris Camp and Conf. Ctr., Greenfield, NH, Chestnut Hill Nat. Bank, Phila., Somerset (Pa.) Hist. Ctr., Seneca Rocks Visitor Ctr., Seneca Rocks, W.Va., Fort Necessity/Nat. Rd. Interpretive Edn. Ctr., Farmington, Pa., The Woods Residence Hall at Pa. State-Berks, Reading, Roberts Hall Renovation and Addition U. Pa. Law Sch., others. Mem. Eco-Efficiency Task Force Pres. Coun. Sustainable Devel.; past chair Environ. Coun., Urban Land Inst.; mem. trustee's coun. for Pa. Women, U. Pa. Recipient Disting. Dau. Pa. award Gov. Tom Ridge, 1995, Excellence citation Engring. News Record, Shattering the Glass Ceiling award Women's Nat. Dem. Club, Mayor's commendation City Phila., citation Pa. Ho. Reps., Gov.'s award Environ. Excellence, 1997, Pa. Hist. and Mus. Commn. Preservation Achievement award Preservation Alliance Greater Phila.; named to Pa. Honor Roll of Women, Pa. Commn. for Women, 1996, named 1 of Pa.'s Best 50 Women in Bus. 1996. Mem. AIA (nat. pres. 1993), Pa. Women's Forum, Forum Exec. Women, Carpenter's Co. Phila. Avocation: sailing. Office: 1600 Walnut St Fl 2D Philadelphia PA 19103-5405 Office Phone: 215-985-4410. Business E-Mail: sam@maxmanpartners.com.

MAX NIKIAS, See NIKIAS, CHRYSOSTOMOS

MAXON, DON CARLTON, mining and construction executive, consultant; b. Downers Grove, Ill., Dec. 23, 1914; s. Norman T. and Agnes M. (Matteson) Maxon; m. Mary T. Quirk, June 14, 1941; children: Maureen, Don, Paul, Anne, Lee; m. Ella Luanne Roy, Dec. 10, 1971; 1 stepchild, Tom Roy. Founder and pres. Maxon Constrn. Co., Barrington, Ill., 1936, Gen. Mining & Devel. Co., Santa Fe, 1967—, U.S. Communities S.A., Panama, 1974, Taipei, Taiwan, 1986, Carson City, Nev., 1989—, Bonanza Mines Internat., 1987. Rancher; builder U.S. Gypsum Co. Rsch. Village, Barrington; founder City of Streamwood, 1954, City of Green Valley, Ariz., 1963; internat. fin. cons. Mem. pres.'s club Pres. Johnson and Kennedy; mem. Pockets of Poverty Commn. With Seabees USN, 1942—45. Named a Tenn. Squire; recipient design awards for family communities of Streamwood, Barrington Woods, Trout Valley, Ill., Parents Mag., 1953, 1959, 1960. Mem.: Nat. Assn. Home Builders (Pres.'s Land Planning first place award 1954), Gov.'s Club Ariz. Democrat. Roman Catholic. Achievements include research in methods for testing and extracting gold from complex ores; finest possible environment for quality of life and sci. applications of all disciplines needed for a self contained city of 150,000 population. Home: 2586 E Ave De Maria Tucson AZ 85718-3056

MAXSON, LINDA ELLEN, biologist, educator; b. NYC, Apr. 24, 1943; d. Albert and Ruth (Rosenfeld) Resnick; m. Richard Dey Maxson, June 13, 1964; 1 child, Kevin. BS in Zoology, San Diego State U., 1964, MA in Biology, 1966; PhD in Genetics, San Diego State U./U. Calif., Berkeley, 1973. Instr. biology San Diego State U., 1966-68; tchr. gen. sci. San Diego Unified Sch. Dist., 1968-69; instr. biochemistry U. Calif., Berkeley, 1974; asst. prof. zoology, dept. genetics and devel. U. Ill., Urbana-Champaign, 1974-76, asst. prof. dept. genetics, devel. and ecology, ethology & evolution, 1976-79, assoc. prof., 1979-84, prof., 1984-87, prof. ecology, ethology and evolution, 1987-88; prof., head dept. biology Pa. State U., State College, 1988-94; assoc. vice-chancellor acad. affairs/dean undergrad. acad. affairs, prof. ecology and evolutionary biology U. Tenn., Knoxville, 1995-97; dean Coll. Liberal Arts & Scis., prof. biol. scis. U. Iowa, Iowa City, 1997—. Exec. officer biology programs Sch. Life Scis., U. Ill., 1981-86, assoc. dir. acad. affairs, 1984-86, dir. campus honors program, 1985-88; vis. prof. ecology and evolutionary biology U. Calif., Irvine, 1988; mem. adv. panel rsch. tng. groups behavioral biol. scis. NSF, 1990-94; rsch. assoc. Smithsonian Instn. Author: Genetics: A Human Perspective, 3d edit., 1992; mem. editl. bd. Molecular Biology Evolution; exec. editor Biochem. Sys. & Ecology, 1993-2001; contbr. numerous articles to scientific jours. Recipient Disting. Alumni award, San Diego State U., 1989, Disting. Herpetologist award, Herpetologists' League, 1993. Fellow: AAAS; mem.: Soc. Molecular Biology and Evolution (treas. 1992—94, sec. 1992—95), Soc. Study Evolution, Soc. for Study of Amphibians and Reptiles (pres. 1991), Am. Men and Women in Sci., Phi Beta Kappa. Office: U Iowa 240 Schaeffer Hall Iowa City IA 52242-1409 Business E-Mail: linda-maxson@uiowa.edu.

MAXWELL, ANDERS JOHN, investment banker; b. San Francisco, Oct. 3, 1946; s. John L. and Deborah A. Maxwell; m. Carlene S. Maxwell, 2000; children from previous marriage: Lauren A., Colin A., Ian W., Erin C., Ryan N. BArch, U. Calif., Berkeley, 1969; MBA, U. Pa., 1971. Analyst GE, 1971-73; v.p. GE Credit Corp., Stamford, Conn., 1973-83; mng. dir. Dean Witter Reynolds Inc., NYC, 1983-87; v.p. Kidder Peabody & Co., Inc., NYC, 1987-88; prin. L.F. Rothschild & Co., NYC, 1988; v.p. Smith Barney, Harris Upham & Co., Inc., 1989-91, Lazard Frères & Co., NYC, 1991-92; ptnr. Benedetto, Gartland & Greene, NYC, 1992-94; v.p., gen. mgr. GE Capital Corp., Stamford, Conn., 1994-96; dir. Salomon Smith Barney Inc., NYC, 1997-98; mng. dir. Barington Capital Group, NYC, 1998; mng. dir., ptnr. Peter J. Solomon Co., NYC, 1999—. Capt. US Army, 1971. Office: Peter J Solomon Co 520 Madison Ave New York NY 10022 Home Phone: 201-612-0744; Office Phone: 212-508-1683. Business E-Mail: amaxwell@pjsolomon.com.

MAXWELL, CARLA LENA, dancer, choreographer, educator; b. Glendale, Calif., Oct. 25, 1945; d. Robert and Victoria (Carbone) Maxwell. Student, Bennington Coll., 1963-64; BS, Juilliard Sch. Music, 1967. Mem. Jose Limón Dance Co., NYC, 1965, prin. dancer, 1969—, acting artistic dir., 1977-78, artistic dir., 1978—. Lectr., tchr. in field. Dancer soloist Louis Falco Dance Co., 1967—71, Harkness Festival at Delacorte Theater, N.Y.C., 1964—, artist-in-residence Gettysburg Coll., 1970—, Luther Coll., Decorah, Iowa, 1971—, U. Idaho, 1973—; guest tchr., performer Centre Internat. de la Danse, Vichy, France, 1976—; choreographer Function, 1970—, Improvisations on a Dream, 1970—, A Suite of Psalms, 1973—, Homage to José Linón, Place Spirit, 1975, Aadvark Brothers: Schwartz and Columbo Present Please Don't Stone the Clowns, 1975, Blue Warrior, 1975, Sonata, 1980, Keeping Still Mountain, 1987; featured Carlota, Dances for Isadora, La Malinche, Comedy, The Moor's Pavane, The Winged, There is a Time, The Shakers, Brandenburg Concerto No. 4, Translucence, Caviar, Missa Brevis, Day on Earth, Two Ecstatic Themes, A Choreographic Offering, The Exiles, Sacred Conversations; dancer toured East and West Africa, 1969. Recipient Dance Mag. award, 1995; N.Y. State Cultural Coun. grantee, 1971. Home: 7 Great Jones St New York NY 10012-1135 Office: Jose Limon Dance Fedn 611 Broadway Fl 9 New York NY 10012-2608

MAXWELL, DAVID E., academic executive, educator; b. NYC, Dec. 2, 1944; s. James Kendrick and Gertrude Sarah (Bernstein) M.; children: Justin Kendrick, Stephen Edward. BA, Grinnell Coll., 1966; MA, Brown U., 1968, PhD, 1974. Instr. Tufts U., Medford, Mass., 1971-74, asst. prof., 1974-78, assoc. prof. Russian lang. and lit., 1978-89, dean undergrad. studies, 1981-89; pres. Whitman Coll., Walla Walla, Wash., 1989-93; dir. Nat. Fgn. Lang. Ctr., Washington, 1993-99; pres. Drake U., Des Moines, 1999—. Chmn. steering com. Coop. Russian Lang. Program, Leningrad, USSR, 1981-86, chmn. 1986-90; cons. Coun. Internat. Ednl. Exch., 1974-94, bd. dirs., 1988-92, 93-94, vice chair, 1991-92, cons. Internat. Rsch. Exchs., 1976-83; mem. adv. bd. Israeli Lang. Policy Inst. Contbr. articles to scholarly jours. Cmty. bd. dirs. Wells Fargo; bd. dirs. Iowa Wellness Coun.; bd. dirs. Greater Des Moines Partnership; pres. Des Moines Higher Edn. Collaborative, 2000—; bd. dirs. Downtown Cmty Alliance, Des Moines. Fulbright fellow, 1970-71, Brown U., 1966-67, NDEA Title IV, 1967-70; recipient Lillian Leibner award Tufts U., 1970; citation Grad. Sch. Arts and Scis., Brown U., 1991. Mem. MLA, Am. Coun. Edn. (commn. on internat. edn., pres.'s coun. on internat. edn.), Assn. Am. Colls., Am. Assn. Higher Edn., Brown U. Alumni Assn. (exec. com.), Bus. Higher Edn. Forum (bd. trustees, coun. econ. devel.), Phi Beta Kappa. Democrat. Avocations: tennis, running, music. Office: Drake Univ Office of the Pres 2507 University Ave Des Moines IA 50311-4505 Home Phone: 515-277-2822; Office Phone: 515-271-2191. Business E-Mail: david.maxwell@drake.edu.

MAXWELL, DAVID OGDEN, federal agency administrator, mortgage company executive; b. Phila., May 16, 1930; s. David Farrow and Emily Ogden (Nelson) M.; m. Joan Clark Paddock, Dec. 14, 1968. BA, Yale U., 1952; LLB, Harvard U., 1955. Bar: Pa. 1955, D.C. 1955. From assoc. to ptnr. Obermayer, Rebmann, Maxwell & Hippel, Phila., 1959-67; from ins. commr. to adminstrn. and budget sec. State of Pa., 1967-70; gen. counsel HUD, Washington, 1970-73; pres., CEO Ticor Mortgage Ins. Co., 1973-81; CEO Fannie Mae, Washington, 1981-91; dir. bus. and non-profit orgns. Bd. dirs. Centre Ptnrs., L.P. Bd. dirs. Sta. WETA-TV; trustee emeritus Nat. Gallery Art. With USNR, 1955-59. Office: 5335 Wisconsin Ave NW Ste 440 Washington DC 20015-2052

MAXWELL, DIANA KATHLEEN, education educator, primary school educator; b. Seminole, Okla., Dec. 16, 1949; d. William Hunter and ImoJean (Mahurin) Rivers; m. Clarence Estel Maxwell, Jly 3, 1969; children: Amanda Hunter, Alexandra Jane. BS, U. Md., 1972; M of Secondary Edn., Boston U., 1974; PhD, U. Md., 1980. Cert. tchr., counselor, Tex. Tchr. Child Garden Presch., Adelphi, Md., 1969-71; tchr., dir. PREP Edn. Ctr., Heidelberg, Germany, 1972-74; tchr. N.E. Ind. Schs. Larkspur, San Antonio, 1974-77, 89-90, Headstart, Boyds, Md., 1978; tchg. asst. Coll. Edn. U. Md., College Park, 1978—80; dir., founder First Bapt. Child Devel. Ctr., Bryan, Tex., 1982-84; instr. English lang. Yonsei Med. Ctr., Seoul, Republic of Korea, 1985-87; asst. prof. Incarnate Word Coll., San Antonio, 1987-89; tchr. kindergarten Fairfax County Pub. Schs., Kings Park, Va., 1990-94; tchr. Encino Park, San Antonio, 1994-95; lectr. U. Tex., San Antonio, 1995-96; multi-age tchr., theater arts tchr. Ft. Sam Houston Elem. Sch., San Antonio, 1996—. Cons. Sugar N'Spice Child Devel. Ctr., Kilgore, Tex., 1980—90; trainer region XX Tex. Edn. Assn., 2000—03. Contbr. articles to newspapers. Block chair March of Dimes, 1991-93, 2000-06, Am. Heart Assn., Fairfax, Va., 1991, 92, San Antonio, 2000-06, Am. Diabetes Assn., Fairfax, 1992; judge speaking com. Burke Optomists, 1992-93; judge writing competition N.E. Ind. Sch. Dist., 1996; judge speech/debate competition Tex. Forensics League, MacArthur HS, 2003—; sec. Cole H.S. Cougar Club, Ft. Sam Houston, San Antonio, 1996-97, v.p., 1997-2002, chair project graduation, 2002—; Bible tchr. 1st Bapt. Ch., Alexandria, Va., 1993-95; tchr. kindergarten Trinity Bapt. Ch., San Antonio, 1995-99, 2005, tchr. 1st grade, 2001-05; Region XX TEA TOPP trainer, 2001-03. Named one of Outstanding Young Women of Am., 1983; Md. fellow State of Md., 1978, 79; Tech. grantee Tex. Edn. Agy., San Antonio, 1990, State of Va. and Fairfax County, Springfield, 1991; recipient Yellow Rose of Tex. vol. award Gov. of Tex., 1996, Dean's Outstanding Tchg. award U. Tex., San Antonio, 1995-96, Ft. Sam Houston Hero award, 2001, 02. Mem. ASCD, Assn. Profl. Tchr. Educators. Avocations: oriental brush painting, singing, collecting butterflies, children/teacher advocate. Home: 2602 Country Square St San Antonio TX 78209-2235 Office: Ft Sam Houston Elem Sch 3370 Nursery Rd San Antonio TX 78234-1479 E-mail: kmaxwell@fshisd.net.

MAXWELL, GEORGE PATRICK, plastic surgeon; b. Selma, Ala., July 15, 1946; married; 1 child. MD, Vanderbilt U., Nashville, 1972. Cert. Am. Bd. Plastic Surgery, 1981. Intern gen. surgery Johns Hopkins Hosp., Balt., 1972—73, resident plastic surgery, 1973—76, resident microsurgery, 1976—79; fellow Davis Med. Ctr., San Francisco, 1975; with Baptist Hosp., Nashville; asst. clin. prof. Vanderbilt U.; founder Inst. Aesthetic and Reconstructive Surgery, Nashville, 1989; with Nashville Plastic Surgery. Med. advisor Inamed Corp., Santa Barbara, Calif.; founder, chmn. Inamed Acad.; co-founder, exec. v.p., chief surg. officer Diversified Specialty Insts.; founder, bd. mem. Aspen Ctr. Integrative Health. Contbr. articles to med. jours.; featured: newspapers New York Times, magazines Departures, 1997, Town & Country, 1999, Good Housekeeping, 1999, W, 2000, 2001, Redbook, 2001, New York Times Mag., 2005, More. Mem.: Southeastern Soc. Plastic Surgeons, Am. Soc. Aesthetic Plastic Surgery (Walter Scott Brown award), Am. Assn. Plastic Surgeons (James Barrett Brown award), Am. Soc. Plastic Surgeons (Presdl. award 2005, Robert H. Ivy Soc. award), Am. Coll. Surgeons, South African Soc. Plastic Surgery (hon.), Japanese Soc. Plastic Surgery (hon.), Can. Soc. Plastic Surgery (hon.). Achievements include patents in field. Office: Nashville Plastic Surgery Medical Plz II Ste 310 2021 Church St Nashville TN 37203 Office Phone: 615-284-8200.

MAXWELL, J. B., financial, marketing professional, consultant; b. Clarksburg, W.Va., Sept. 30, 1944; s. J. B. and Martha (Hornor) Maxwell; m. Valerie Ronson, Oct. 13, 1983; 1 child, Jennifer. BS, Salem Coll., W.Va., 1967; M in Mktg., Harvard U., 1970. Lic. real estate sales, ins., securities, registered commodity rep., accredited mgmt. cons. and fin. planner, registered fin. planner, investment advisor, accredited asset mgmt. specialist. Exec. v.p. Textron Inc., Providence, 1968-71; pres. Martech Inc. and 6 other cos., Portland, Maine, 1968—; v.p. E. F. Hutton Co., Portland, 1976-83; 1st v.p. fin. planning Dean Witter, Boston, 1983-90; pres. Planning Svcs. Corp., Boston, 1990-92; 1st v.p. Gruntal & Co., Inc., Boston, 1992—2003; with Ryan Beck & Co., Wellesley, Mass., 2003—. Author: handbooks, booklets; contbr. articles to profl. jours., Portland Coll. Art, 1980—93. Bd. dirs. Wellness Inst., Boston, 1990—91. Recipient Bronze award, Nat. Acad. Scis., 1962. Mem.: Nat. Assn. Security Dealers (former br. office mgr.), World Affairs Coun., Inst. Mgmt. Cons., Am. Mktg. Assn., Am. Mgmt. Assn., Internat. Assn. Fin. Planning, Boston C. of C., Rotary. Avocations: golf, woodworking, travel, literature. Home: 15 Bailey Road Arlington MA 02476 Office: Oppenheimer & Co 155 Federal St 14th Fl Boston MA 02110 Home Phone: 617-271-7757; Office Phone: 866-548-4763 x 4918. E-mail: j.b.maxwell@opco.com.

MAXWELL, JACK ERWIN, manufacturing executive; b. Cleve., July 17, 1926; s. Fred A. and Gertrude F. (Haug) M.; m. Martha Jane Miller, Dec. 28, 1966; children by previous marriage: Laura Jane, Fredric, Elizabeth Grant, Carla Moore, Linda Hanson. BS, Case Inst. Tech., 1949; MBA, Harvard U., 1952. Indsl. engr. Lincoln Electric Co., Cleve., 1952—53; mgr. purchase analysis Ford Motor Co., Dearborn, Mich., 1953—57; v.p. Booz, Allen & Hamilton, Inc., Detroit, 1957—69; v.p. corp. devel. Am. Motors Corp., Detroit, 1969—71, v.p. adminstrn., 1967—76, v.p. non-automotive subsidiaries, 1976—79, v.p. diversified ops., 1979—80; chmn., pres. Wheel Horse Products, Inc., South Bend, Ind., 1974—80; chmn., CEO Ingersoll Products Corp., Chgo., 1980—86; pres. Wellmax, Inc., 1976—. Served with USNR, 1944-46. Mem. Case Inst. Tech. Alumni Assn., Harvard Bus. Sch. Alumni Assn., Detroit Athletic Club, Detroit Econ. Club, Chgo. Club, Old Club, Tau Beta Pi, Theta Tau. Address: Ste 105-37 1000 S Old Woodward AVe Birmingham MI 48009 Home Phone: 248-669-5235; Office Phone: 248-646-3554. Personal E-mail: wellmaxx@earthlink.net.

MAXWELL, JEROME EUGENE, corporate executive; b. Princeton, Ill., June 2, 1944; s. Emmett Eugene and June (Erickson) M.; m. Cynthia Jane O'Connell, July 30, 1977; children: Eric Vaughn, Christina Dawn, Jeremy Emmett, Jason Daniel, Nicholas Mark. BSEE, So. Meth. U., 1967, MSEE, 1971. Maintainability engr. product support divsn. Collins Radio Co., Richardson, Tex., 1965-67, jr. engr. computer sys. divsn., 1967-70; sr. engr. TRW Electronics Products, Inc., Colorado Springs, Colo., 1970-73, mgr. engring., 1973-79, mgr. program mgmt. office, 1979-81, gen. mgr. space electronics mfg. divsn., 1981-86; pres., CEO G&S Sys., Inc., Bedford, Mass., 1986-87, Atec, Inc., Houston, 1987-91; v.p., divsn. dir. Nat. Sys. & Rsch. Co., Colorado Springs, 1992-94; pres., chmn. bd. dirs. Tech. Assocs. of Colo., Inc., Colorado Springs, 1994-96; pres., CEO Advanced Profl. Tng., Inc., Colorado Springs, 1996—. Patentee in field. Mem. adv. coun. U. Colo., Colorado Springs, 1973-86, U. So. Colo., Pueblo, 1974-78; Webelo leader, asst. pack leader Boy Scouts Am., 1976-77; fin. chmn. Ascension Luth. Ch., 1981-86; cons. to cmty. edn. coord. for computer sys. and equipment, 1980-86; mem. Soli Deo Gloria Choir, 1999—. Fellow: Nat. Assn. of Ch. Bus. Adminstr.; mem.: AIAA (sr.), Mesa Sertoma (charter, bd. dirs.), Assn. Old Crows (pres. space chpt.). Republican. Personal E-mail: president@yourtraining.net.

MAXWELL, JUDITH, think-tank executive, economist; b. Kingston, Ont., Can., July 21, 1943; d. James Ruffee and Marguerite Jane (Spanner) McMahon; m. Anthony Stirling Maxwell, May 8, 1970; 2 children. B in Commerce, Dalhousie U., 1963, LLD, 1991; postgrad., London Sch. Econs., 1965-66; LLD, Queen's U., 1992. Researcher Combines Investigation Br. Consumer and Corp. Affairs, Ottawa, Can., 1963-65; econs. writer, mem. editorial bd. Fin. Times, Montreal, Que., Can., 1966-72; dir. policy studies C.D. Howe Inst., Montreal, 1972-80; cons. Esso Europe Inc., London, Eng., 1980-82, Coopers & Lybrand, Montreal, Que., 1982-85; chmn. Econ. Council Can., Ottawa, Ont., 1985-92; exec. dir. Queen's-U. Ottawa Econ. Projects, 1992—. Dir. Can. Found. for Econ. Edn., 1985-88, Inst. for Rsch. on Pub. Policy, 1987-88. Author: Energy From the Arctic, 1973; (with C. Pestieau) Economic Realities of Contemporary Confederation, 1980; (with S. Currie) Partnership for Growth: Corporate University Education in Canada, 1984. Active Ont. Premier's Coun., 1988-90, Nfld. and Labrador Sci. and Tech. Adv. Coun., 1988-90. Mem. Can. Assn. Bus. Econs. (pres. 1976-77), Montreal Econs. Assn. (pres. 1975-76). Office: Canadian Policy Rsch Networks 600-250 Albert St Ottawa ON Canada K1P 6M1 Business E-Mail: jmaxwell@cprn.org.

MAXWELL, MAX ANTHONY, retired language educator; b. Duncans, Trelawny, Jamaica, Aug. 27, 1937; s. John William Maxwell and Zelma Cynthia Thelwell; m. Barbara M. Durham, Feb. 27, 1965; children: Megan Christine, Maritza Joan. BA, L.I. U., 1963; MA, Rutgers U., 1970. Asst. instr. Rutgers U., New Brunswick, NJ, 1964—68; instr. L.I. U., New York, NY, 1968—69; tchr. English, Henry C. Woods Family Disting. Tchg. chair The Lawrenceville Sch., Lawrenceville, NJ, 1969; ret., 2006. Faculty cons. Ednl. Testing Svcs., Princeton, NJ, 1970—. Avocations: writing, photography, coaching cricket & soccer, carpentry. Office: The Lawrenceville School Main Street Lawrenceville NJ 08648 Office Phone: 609-895-2028. E-mail: mamaxwel@lawrenceville.org.

MAXWELL, RICHARD ANTHONY, retail executive; b. NYC, Apr. 1, 1933; s. Arthur William and Mary Ellen (Winestock) M.; m. Jacqueline Ann Creamer, Oct. 27, 1962. Student, NYU, 1957-58, Acad. Advanced Traffic, 1959. Import ops. mgr. Associated Merchandising Corp., NYC, 1950-52, 56-65; v.p. Associated Dry Goods Corp., NYC, 1965-86, sr. v.p. mktg., 1980-82, exec. v.p. mktg., 1982-86; pres. A.D.G. Export Mktg., Florence, Italy, 1982-86, Associated Dry Goods Ltd., Hong Kong, 1983-86, Inter Textyle Corp., 1987-89; with Matol Botanical Internat. Ltd.; exec. v.p. Matol World Corp., Montreal, Que., Canada, 1992-94; dir. Matol Botanical New Zealand, 1994-96; v.p. internat. ops. L'Aprina Internat. Inc., 1994-96; chief internat. officer Camelot Concept Co., Montreal, 1995-96; CFO Showcase Prodns., Phoenix, 1996; exec. v.p. Harmony House Internat., Phoenix, 1996-97, IGW Trust, Phoenix, 1997-99, Pre-Paid Legal Svcs., Inc., 1999—; pres. Team 39, Inc., Dunedin, Fla., 2000-2001; dir. Presley Promotions Inc., Memphis, 2001—02; pres., COO Home Farms Techs. Inc., Brandon, Man., Canada, 2002—. Mem. industry sector adv. com. Dept. Commerce, 1984-93; mem. shippers adv. com. Nat. Maritime Coun. Served with USAF, 1952-56. Recipient Silver medal for contbns. to trade expansion, Republic of China, 1980; appt. to rank of comdr. in Order of Merit in recognition of improvement of trade between Italy and U.S., Republic of Italy, 1985. Mem. Am. Assn. Exporters and Importers (past pres., dir.), Shippers Conf. Greater N.Y. (past pres., dir.), Nat. Retail Mchts. Assn. (vice chmn. fgn. trade com.), Nat. Com. Internat. Trade Documentation (past vice chmn. gen. bus. com.), Transp. Assn. Am., Italy-Am. C. of C. (past pres., dir.), Am. Soc. of Italian Legion of Merit (dir.). Home: 2408 Stag Run Blvd Clearwater FL 33765-1832

MAXWELL, RICHARD CALLENDER, retired lawyer, educator; b. Mpls., Oct. 7, 1919; s. Bertram Wayburn and Blossom (Callender) M.; m. Frances Lida McKay, Jan 27, 1942; children: Richard Callender, John McKay. BSL, U. Minn., 1941, LLB, 1947; LLD (hon.), Calif. Western U., 1983; LLD, Southwestern U., 1993. Assoc. prof. U. ND, 1947-49, U. Tex., 1949-51, prof., 1951-53; counsel Amerada Petroleum Corp., 1952-53; prof. UCLA, 1953-81; dean UCLA Sch. Law, 1959-69, Connell prof., 1979-81, Connell prof. emeritus, 1981—; Chadwick prof. Duke U. Sch. Law, 1981-89, Chadwick prof. emeritus, 1989—. Vis. prof. Columbia U., 1955; vis. Alumni prof. U. Minn., 1970-71; Fulbright lectr. Queen's U., No. Ireland, 1970; vis. Ford Found. prof. U. Singapore, 1971; Thompson prof. U. Colo., 1982; vis. prof. Hastings Coll. Law, 1976, Duke U., 1979-80, U. Tex., 1985; pres. Minn. Law Rev., 1946; chmn. Coun. Legal Edn. Opportunity, 1971-72; pres. Assn. Am. Law Schs., 1972; chmn. adv. com. law Fulbright Program, 1971-74, chmn. adv. com. U.K., 1974-77; mem. com. on gas prodn. opportunities NRC, 1977-78; mem. law sch. editl. and adv. bd. West Pub. Co., 1971-94. Author: (with S. A. Riesenfeld) Cases and Materials on Modern Social Legislation, 1950, (with H.R. Williams and C.J. Meyers) Cases on Oil and Gas Law, 1956, 8th edit., (with Patrick H. Martin, Bruce M. Kramer), 2007, (with S.A. Riesenfeld) California Cases on Security Transactions, 1957, 4th edit. (with S.A. Riesenfeld, J.R. Hetland, W.D. Warren), 1991; West Coast editor Oil and Gas Reporter, 1953-. Mem. LA Employee Rels. Bd., 1971-74; bd. dirs. Constl. Rights Found., 1963-81; trustee Calif. Western U., 1979-81; bd. visitors Duke U. Sch. Law, 1973-79, chmn. bd. Pvt. Adjudication Ctr., 1984-89; bd. visitors Southwestern U. Sch. Law, 1981-90. Served to lt. comdr. USNR, 1941-46. Recipient Clyde O. Martz Tchg. award Rocky Mountain Mineral Law Found., 1994, Disting. Tchg. award, UCLA, 1977, Duke Law Sch., 1986, UCLA medal, 1982. Mem. ABA (com. on youth edn. for citizenship 1975-79, spl. com. on pub. understanding about the law 1979-84), Order of Coif. (nat. exec. com. 1980-86). Office: Duke U Sch Law Durham NC 27708-0362 Office Phone: 919-613-7045. Personal E-mail: rcmaxwell@mindspring.com.

MAXWELL, ROBERT EARL, federal judge; b. Elkins, W.Va., Mar. 15, 1924; s. Earl L. and Nellie E. (Rexstrew) M.; m. Ann Marie Grabowski, Mar. 29, 1948; children— Mary Ann, Carol Lynn, Ellen Lindsay, Earl Wilson. LLD (hon.), Davis and Elkins Coll., 1984; LLB, W.Va. U., 1949. Bar: W.Va. 1949. Practiced in, Randolph County, 1949; pros. atty., 1952-61; U.S. atty. for No. Dist. W.Va., 1961-64; judge U.S. Dist. Ct. (no. dist.) W.Va., Elkins, 1965—94, sr. judge, 1994—; judge Temp. Emergency Ct. of Appeals, 1980-89. Past chmn. budget com. Jud. Conf. U.S.; former mem. exec. com. Nat. Conf. Fed. Trial Judges; former mem. adv. bd. W.Va. U. Mem. bd. advisors W.Va. U., past chmn.; bd. advisors Mary Babb Randolph Cancer Ctr. Recipient Alumni Disting. Svc. award Davis and Elkins Coll., 1969, Religious Heritage Am. award, 1979, Outstanding Trial Judge award W.Va. Trail Lawyers Assn., 1988, Order of Vandalia award W.Va. U., Outstanding Alumnus award, 1992, Tenured Faculty Mem. Recognition award Bd. Govs., Def. Trail Coun., W.Va., 1992, Cert. of Merit, W.Va. State Bar, 1994, Justitia Officium award Coll. of Law, W.Va. U., 1994, award of merit W.Va. Bar Assn., 2004, Lawyer Citizen of Yr. award, 2005, Humanitarian award Odd Fellows, 2005; fellow W.Va. Bar Found., 1999; Melvin Jones fellow Lions Internat. Found., 2001. Mem. Nat. Conf. Federal Trial Judges, Dist. Judges Assn. 4th Cir. (past pres.), Moose (life), Lions (life), Beta Alpha Beta (merit award), Elkins-Randolph County C. of C. (citizen of yr. 1994). Office: US Dist Ct No Dist PO Box 1275 Elkins WV 26241-1275 E-mail: judge_maxwell@wvnd.uscourts.gov.

MAXWELL, ROBERT WALLACE, II, lawyer; b. Sept. 6, 1943; s. Robert Wallace and Margaret Maxwell; m. Mamie Lee Payne, June 18, 1966; children: Virginia, Robert, William. BS magna cum laude, Hampden-Sydney Coll., 1965; JD with honors, Duke U., 1968. Bar: Ohio 1968. Assoc. Taft, Stettinius & Hollister, Cin., 1968—75, ptnr., 1975—88, Keating, Muething & Klekamp, Cin., 1988—. Instr. U. Cin. Sch. Law, 1975—76. Elder Knox Presbyn. Ch.; bd. dir. Contemporary Arts Ctr. of Cin., Cin. Ballet Co. Mem.: ABA, Am. Assn. Mus. Trustees. Republican. Home: 535 Larchmont Dr Cincinnati OH 45215-4215 Office: Keating Muething & Klekamp 1 E 4th St Ste 1400 Cincinnati OH 45202-3752 Office Phone: 513-579-6594. E-mail: rmaxwell@kmklaw.com.

MAXWELL, ROBERT WILLIAM, investment banker, financial analyst; b. Brentwood, Essex, Eng., June 19, 1948; s. William and Dilys Maxwell; m. Vanessa Vorman; children: Duncan, Spencer, Kennon. BA in Econs., Manchester, Eng., 1970; MBA, Harvard U., 1977. Registered NASD Series 7 & 24. Lending officer Bank of Montreal Internat., Que., Canada, 1970—75; mgr. new ventures Freeport-McMoRan, New Orleans, 1977—87; pres., CEO Financing for Sci. Internat., Farmington, 1987—97; sr. v.p., CFO ProHealth Physicians, Farmington, 1997—99; mng. dir., founder Ironwood Capital Ltd., Avon, Conn., 1999—2001; prin. Brentwood Capital, LLC, Farmington, Conn., 2001—05; mng. dir. Westbury Group LLC, Southport, Conn., 2005—. Trustee Mooreland Hill Sch., Kensington, 1996—99; pres. Farmington Field Club, 2002—. Mem.: Harvard Club NY. Business E-Mail: rmaxwell@brentwoodsecurties.com.

MAXWELL, SARA ELIZABETH (SALLY), psychologist, educator, speech pathology/audiology services professional, recording industry executive, director; b. DuQuoin, Ill., Jan. 23; d. Jean A. (Patterson) Green; m. David Lowell Maxwell, Dec. 27, 1960 (div. Mar. 1990); children: Lisa Marina, David Scott; m. James F. Manning, July 19, 1997 (div. Aug. 1998). BS, So. Ill. U., 1963, MS, 1964, MS in Edn., 1965; MEd, Boston Coll.,

1982, PhD, 1992; postgrad., Harvard U., 1983. Cert. and lic. speech.-lang. pathologist, early childhood specialist, guidance counselor, sch. adjustment counselor, behavior specialist, EMT. Clin. supr. Clin. Ctr. So. Ill. U., Carbondale, 1964-65, grad. clin. instr., 1965-66; speech/lang. pathologist, sch. adjustment counselor Westwood (Mass.) Pub. Schs., 1967-93; grad. faculty Emerson Coll., Boston, 1979-81; cons. Mass. Dept. Mental Health, Boston, 1979-82; grad. clin. supr. Robbins Speech/Hearing Ctr., Emerson Coll., Boston, 1979-82; predoctoral intern in clin. psychology South Shore Mental Health Ctr., Quincy, Mass., 1985-86, devel. and clin. staff psychologist Hingham and Quincy, 1989-93, emergency svcs. team and respite house manager Quincy, 1990-93; cons. Westwood Nursery Preschs., 1986-93; pvt. practice Twin Oaks Clin. Assocs., Westwood, 1986-88, South Coast Counseling Assocs., Quincy, 1989-93, South Shore Clin. Assocs., Ft. Lauderdale, Fla., 1993—2005; CEO Morpheus Music, 2005—. Cons. local collaboratives and preschs., Westwood, 1980-83; profl. workshops presenter Head Start, 1980; program specialist speech, lang., learning Broward County (Fla.) Schs., 1993-96, exceptional student edn. specialist, 1996-98; behavior specialist, 1999-2005; adj. prof. grad. sch. of psychology Nova Southeastern U., 1995-2005; chmn Broward County Action Rsch. Grant Project 2002-03; presenter Head Start, ASHA, CEC, APSC, IALP and other profl., nat. and state confs., 1980-99; invited del. to Sino-Am. Conf. on Exceptionality, Beijing Normal U., China, 1995. Contbr. articles to profl. jours., chpts. to textbooks. Mem. adv. coun. Westwood Bd. Health, 1977-80; emergency med. technician Westwood Pub. Schs. Athletic Dept., 1981. Vocat. Rehab. fellow So. Ill. U., 1964; Merit scholar Perry County, Ill., 1959-64, Credi meml. scholar So. Ill. U., 1964. Mem. Am. Speech & Hearing Assn. (nat. schs. com., nat. chairperson Pub. Sch. Caucus 1985-87), Am. Psychol. Assn., Assn. Psychiat. Svcs. for Children, Coun. Exceptional Children, Internat. Assn. of Logopedics, Rio Vista Civic Assn., Boston Coll. Alumni Assn., Harvard Club. Episcopalian. Avocations: squash, sailing, skiing.

MAXWELL, W(ILBUR) RICHARD, retired management consultant; b. Troy, Ohio, June 20, 1920; s. Wilbur D. and Gertrude (McDowell) M.; m. Roberta Mae Kennedy, June 29, 1942 (dec.); children: Douglas R., Jean Ann. Student, Ohio Wesleyan U., 1938-41; BS, Richmond Profl. Inst. of Coll. William and Mary, 1955. Sec. Troy C. of C., 1948-50, Va. C. of C., 1950-55; asst. to pres./chmn. bd. Reynolds Metals Co., 1955-64; v.p., dir. Reynolds Fgn. Sales Inc., 1964-68; pres. Nat. Better Bus. Bur., 1968-70; pres., chief exec. officer Jr. Achievement, Inc., Stamford, Conn., 1970-82. Instr. Richmond Profl. Inst., part-time 1955-57; sponsor-trustee U. Va. Grad. Bus. Sch., 1963-72. Pres. Lancaster County Libr., 1984-85, Rappahannock Gen. Hosp. Found., 1988-90, Northern Neck Vocat.-Tech. Edn. Ctr., 1991-93; bd. dirs. Rappahannock Gen. Hosp., 1988-90, Richmond (Va.) Cmty. H.S., 1989-91; chmn. Northumberland County (Va.) Econ. Devel. Commn., 1994-97. Civilian specialist USAAC, USN, 1942-46. Recipient Albert Schweitzer award Hugh O'Brien Youth Fedn., 1982; named to Jr. Achievement Profl. Hall of Fame, 1986. Mem. Indian Creek Yacht and Country Club (v.p., 1991-93, bd. dirs. 1991-93). Home: 13715 Richmond Pk Dr N #1203 Jacksonville FL 32224

MAXWELL, WILLIAM HALL CHRISTIE, civil, environmental engineer, educator; b. Coleraine, No. Ireland, Jan. 25, 1936; came to U.S., 1958, naturalized, 1967; s. William Robert and Catherine Dempsey (Christie) M.; m. Mary Carolyn McLaughlin, Sept. 28, 1960; children: Katrina, Kevin, Wendy, Liam. BSc, Queen's U., Belfast, No. Ireland, 1956; MSc, Queen's U., Kingston, Ont., Can., 1958; PhD, U. Minn., 1964. Registered profl. engr., Ill. Site engr. Motor Columbus AG, Baden, Switzerland, 1956; tchg. asst. Queen's U., Kingston, 1956-58; from rsch. asst. to instr. U. Minn., Mpls., 1959-64; asst. prof. civil engring. U. Ill., Urbana, 1964-70, assoc. prof., 1970-82, prof., 1982-96, prof. emeritus civil and environ. engring., 1997—. Chmn. program com. 1st Internat. Conf. on New/Emerging Concepts for Rivers, Chgo., 1996. Editor: Water Resources Management in Industrial Areas, 1982, Water for Human Consumption, Man and His Environment, 1983, Frontiers in Hydrology, 1984, New/Emerging Concepts for Rivers, 1996. Vestryman Emmanuel Meml. Episcopal Ch., Champaign, Ill., 1977-80; state exhibitor Ministry Edn., Stormont, No. Ireland, 1953-56. Queen's U. Found. scholar, Belfast, 1954-56, R.S. McLaughlin travel fellow Queen's U., Kingston, 1958-59. Fellow ASCE (com. chmn. 1982-83), Internat. Water Resources Assn. (editor-in-chief Water Internat. 1986-93, sr. editor 1994-98, mem. publs. com. 1980-98, v.p. U.S. geog. com. 1986-91, chmn. awards com. 1995-97, bd. dirs. 1995-97, Editl. award 1994); mem. Am. Geophys. Union, Internat. Assn. for Hydraulic Rsch., Nat. Assn. Scholars. Avocations: home construction, painting. Home: 1210 Devonshire Dr Champaign IL 61821-6527 Office: U Ill Dept Civil and Environ Engring 205 N Mathews Ave Urbana IL 61801-2350 Business E-Mail: wmaxwell@uiuc.edu.

MAXWELL, WILLIAM LAUGHLIN, retired industrial engineering educator; b. Phila., July 11, 1934; s. William Henry and Elizabeth (Laughlin) M.; m. Judith Behrens, July 5, 1969; children: Deborah, William, Judith, Keely BMechE, Cornell U., 1957, PhD, 1961. Andrew Schultz Jr. prof. dept. indsl. engring. Cornell U., Ithaca, NY, 1961-98. Author: Theory of Scheduling, 1967. Recipient Disting. Teaching award Cornell Soc. Engrs., 1968, Ralph S. Watts Tchg. award, 1997. Fellow Informs, Inst. Indsl. Engrs.; mem. Nat. Acad. Engring. Home: 106 Lake Ave Ithaca NY 14850-3537

MAXWELL, WILLIAM STIRLING, retired lawyer; b. Chgo., May 2, 1922; s. W. Stirling and Ethel (Bowes) Maxwell Reineke. AB with distinction, U. Mich., 1947, postgrad., 1946-49, JD, 1949. Bar: Ill. 1949, U.S. Ct. Mil. Appeals 1951, U.S. Supreme Ct. 1952. Assoc. Sidley & Austin, Chgo., 1949-60, 61, ptnr., 1962-84; now ret.; sr. legis. counsel U.S. Treasury, Washington, 1960-61. Trustee Mid-North Animal Shelter Found., Chgo., 1971—. Mem. Order of Coif, Phi Beta Kappa Clubs: Lawyers Club. Republican. Episcopalian. Home: PO Box 1839 Brookings OR 97415-0048

MAXWELL DIAL, ELEANORE, foreign language educator; b. Norwich, Connecticut, Feb. 21, 1929; d. Joseph Walter and Irene (Beetham) Maxwell; m. John E. Dial, Aug. 27, 1959. BA, U. Bridgeport, Conn., 1951; MA in Spanish, Mexico City Coll., 1955; PhD, U. Mo., 1968. Mem. faculty U. Wis., Milw., 1968—75, Ind. State U., Terre Haute, 1975—78, Bowling Green State U., Ohio, 1978—79; asst. prof. dept. fgn. lang. and lit. Iowa State U., Ames, 1979—85, assoc. prof., 1985—96, emerita assoc. prof., 1996—. Cons. pub. companies; participant workshops; del. First World Congress Women Journalists and Writers, Mex., 1975, mem. edn. commn. Contbr. articles, anthologies, and reviews to scholarly journals. Active governor's commn. on fgn. lang. and internat. studies, 1988-95. NDEA grantee, 1967, Ctr. Latin Am. grantee, 1972, NEH summer seminar UCLA, 1981, U. Calif., Santa Barbara, 1984. Mem. MLA, Am. Assn. Teachers Spanish and Portuguese, Midwest MLA, N. Ctrl. Coun. Latin Americanists, Midwest Assn. Latin Am. Studies, Clermont County Geneal. Soc., Ohio Geneal. Soc., Story County Iowa Geneal. Soc., Caribbean Studies Assn., P.G. Wodehouse Soc., Phi Beta Delta, Phi Sigma Iota, Sigma Delta Pi. Home: 190 North St Batavia OH 45103-2911 Office: Iowa State U Ames IA 50011-0001

MAXWORTHY, TONY, mechanical and aerospace engineering educator; b. London, May 21, 1933; came to U.S., 1954, naturalized, 1961; s. Ernest Charles and Gladys May (Butson) M.; m. Emily Jean Parkinson, June 20, 1956 (div. 1974); children: Kirsten, Kara; m. Anna Barbara Parks, May 21, 1979 BS in Engring. with honors, U. London, 1954; MSE, Princeton U., 1955; PhD, Harvard U., 1959. Rsch. asst. Harvard U., Cambridge, Mass., 1955-59; sr. scientist, group supr. Jet Propulsion Lab., Pasadena, Calif., 1960-67; assoc. prof. U. So. Calif., LA, 1967-70, prof., 1970—, Smith Internat. prof. mech. and aero. engring., 1988—, chmn. dept. mech. engring., 1979-89; cons. BBC Rsch. Ctr., Baden, Switzerland, 1972-82, J.P.L., Pasadena, Calif., 1968-80; lectr. Woods Hole Oceanographic Inst., Mass., summers 1965, 70, 72, 83. Forman vis. prof. aeronautics Technion Haifa, 1986; vis. prof. U. Poly., Madrid, 1988, Inst. Superiore Tech., Lisbon, 1988, Swiss Fed. Inst. Tech., Lausanne, 1989-95; assoc. prof. IMG, U. Joseph Fourier, Grenoble, 1980—, Ecole Superieure Physics and Indsl. Chemistry, Paris, 1995—; Shimizu vis. prof. Stanford U., 1996—, U. Canterbury, New Zealand, 2005—. Mem. editorial bd. Geophys. Fluid Dynamics, 1973-79, 88-96, Dynamic Atmospheric Oceans, 1976-83, Phys. Fluids, 1978-81, Zeitschrift fuer Angewandte Mathematik und Physik, 1987-96; contbr. articles to profl. jours. Recipient Humboldt Sr. Scientist award, 1981-93, G.I. Taylor medal Soc. Engring. Sci., 2003; life fellow Clare Hall, Cambridge U., 1974, 93—, Australian Nat. U., 1978, Nat. Ctr. Atmospheric Rsch., 1976, Glennon fellow U. Western Australia, 1990, F.W. Mosey fellow, 1993, Sr. Queen's fellow in marine scis. Commonwealth of Australia, 1984; sr. visitor DAMTP, Cambridge U., 1975—. Fellow: Am. Phys. Soc. (chmn. exec. com. fluid dynamics divsn. 1974—79, Otto Laporte award 1990), Am. Acad. Arts and Scis.; mem.: NAE, Oceanography Soc., European Geophys. Soc., Am. Geophys. Union. Office: U So Calif Dept Aerospace & Mech Engr Exposition Park Los Angeles CA 90089-1191 Business E-Mail: maxworth@usc.edu.

MAY, ALAN ALFRED, lawyer; b. Detroit, Apr. 7, 1942; s. Alfred Albert and Sylvia (Sheer) M.; m. Elizabeth Miller; children: Stacy Ann, Julie Beth. BA, U. Mich., 1963, JD cum laude, 1966. Bar: Mich. 1967, D.C. 1976; former reg. nursing home adminstr., Mich. Ptnr. May and May PC, Detroit, 1979—2001; ptnr., shareholder, v.p. Kemp Klein, Umphrey and May, P.C., Troy, Mich., 2001—05; CEO NCCJ, 2005. Spl. asst. atty. gen. State of Mich., 1970—; pres., instr. Med-Leg Seminars, Inc., 1978; lectr. Wayne State U., 1974; instr. Oakland U., 1969. Chmn. Rep. 18th Congrl. Dist. Com., 1983-87, now chmn. emeritus; chmn. 19th Congrl. Dist. Com., 1981-83; mem. Mich. Rep. Com., 1976-84; del. Rep. Nat. Conv., 1984, rules com., 1984; del. Rep. Nat. Conv., 1988, platform com., 1988; former chmn. Mich. Civil Rights Commn.; mem., vice chair Mich. Civil Svc. Commn., 1984-88; former trustee, mem. exec. bd., vice chmn. nat conf. for cmty. and justice NCCJ; trustee Temple Beth El Birmingham, Mich., past pres. exec. bd.; mem. Electoral Coll.; former bd. dirs. ADL, Mich.; bd. dirs. exec. bd., past pres. Detroit Region/Nat. Conf. Cmty. and Justice, Charfoos Charitable Found. Mem. Nat. Conf. Cmty. and Justice (former exec. bd., vice chmn., pres., CEO 2005—, interim pres. 2005), Detroit Bar Assn., Oakland County Bar Assn., Victors Club, Franklin Hills Country Club (past pres., bd. dirs.), President's Club. Home: 4140 Echo Rd Bloomfield Hills MI 48302-1941 Office: Kemp Klein Umphrey Endelman & May PC 201 W Big Beaver Rd Ste 600 Troy MI 48084 Office Phone: 248-528-1111. Business E-Mail: alan.may@kkue.com.

MAY, ARTHUR W., retired academic administrator, educator; b. St. John's, Nfld., Can., June 29, 1937; s. William J. and Florence (Dawe), M.; m. Sonia Susan Streeter, Aug. 18, 1958; children: Stephen J., Heather E., Maria S., Douglas W. BSc with honors, Meml. U., St. John's, 1958; MSc, Meml. U., 1964; PhD, McGill U., Montreal, Que., Can., 1966; D of Univ. (hon.), U. Ottawa, 1988; DSc (hon.), Meml. U. Nfld., 1989; LLD (hon.), Brock U., 1992. Sci. adviser internat. fisheries Dept. Fisheries, Ottawa, Ont., Canada, 1971-73, dir. Nfld. biol. sta. St. John's, 1973-75, dir. gen. resource services Ottawa, 1975-78; asst. dep. minister Atlantic Dept. Fisheries and Oceans, Ottawa, 1978-82, dep. minister, 1982-86; pres. Natural Sci. and Engring. Rsch. Coun. Canada, 1986-90; pres., vice chancellor Meml. U. Nfld., St. Johns, 1990-99, ret., 1999—. V.p. Internat. Coun. for Exploration of Seas, Copenhagen, 1977-79; mem. Task Force on Atlantic Fisheries, Ottawa, 1982, Nat. Adv. Bd. Sci. and Tech., 1988-90, 94-95; Canadian rep. to NATO Sci. Com., 1990-97; bd. dirs. Canadian Millenium Scholarship Found., World Wildlife Can.; chmn. bd. One Ocean, 2001—. Contbr. articles to profl. jours. Served to sub. lt. Can. Navy, 1955-58 Decorated officer Order of Can.; recipient Gov.-Gen.'s medal Nfld. Dept. Edn., 1954, Meml. U. Nfld., 1958; named Alumnus of Yr., Meml. U. Nfld., 1983. Mem. N.W. Atlantic Fisheries Orgn. (pres. 1977-80) Anglican. Avocations: gardening, stamp collecting/philately. Office: Meml Univ Nfld 4003 Spencer Hall Saint John's NL Canada A1C 5S7 Home: St 303 25 Bonaventure Ave Saint John's NL Canada AIC 6N8

MAY, AVIVA RABINOWITZ, music educator, musician, linguist; b. Tel Aviv; naturalized, 1958; d. Samuel and Paula Pessia (Gordon) Rabinowitz; children: Chelley Mosoff, Alan May, Risa McPherson, Ellanna May/Gassman. AA, Oakton C.C., 1977; BA in Piano Pedagogy, Northeastern Ill. U., 1978. Folksinger, educator, musician Aviva May Studio/Piano and Guitar, 1948—; Sunday sch. dir. Canton (Ohio) Synagogue, 1952-54; nursery sch. tchr. Allentown (Pa.) Jewish Cmty. Ctr., 1954-56; Hebrew music tchr. Brith Shalom Cmty. Ctr., Bethlehem, Pa., 1954-62; Hebrew tchr. Beth Hillel Congregation, Wilmette, Ill., 1964-83; tchr. B'nai Mitzva, 1978—79; music dir. McCormick Health Ctrs., Chgo., 1978-79, Cove Sch. Perceptually Handicapped Children, Evanston, 1978-79; prof. Hebrew and Yiddish, Spertus Coll. Judaica, Chgo., 1980-89; Hebrew tchr. Anshe Emet Day Sch., 1989—, West Suburban Temple Har Zion, Oak Park, Ill., 1993—; music studio tchr. Cosmopolitan Sch., Chgo., 1992—. Tchr. continuing edn. Northeastern Ill. U., 1978-84, Niles Twp. Jewish Congregation, 1993—97, also Jewish Cmty. Ctrs., 1977-78; translator Office Spl. Investigations, Dept. Justice, Washington; music dir. Temple Emanuel Rosenwald Sch. Composer classical music for piano, choral work, folk songs; developer 8-hour system for learning piano or guitar; contbr. articles to profl. jours. Recipient Magen David Adom Pub. Svc. award 1973; grantee Ill. State, 1975-79, Ill. Congressman Woody Bowman, 1978-79. Mem. Music Tchrs. Nat. Assn., Ill. Music Tchrs. Assn., Organ and Piano Tchrs. Assn., Am. Coll. Musicians, Ill. Assn. Learning Disabilities, North Shore Music Tchrs. Assn. (charter mem., co-founder), Sherwood Sch. Music, Friends of Holocaust Survivers, Nat. Yiddish Book Exch., Nat. Ctr. for Jewish Films, Chgo. Jewish Hist. Soc., Oakton C.C. Alumni Assn., Northeastern Ill. U. Alumni Assn. Office: Aviva May Studio 410 S Michigan Ave Ste 920 Chicago IL 60605-1471 Office Phone: 773-348-8700.

MAY, BENJAMIN TALLMAN, securities specialist, administrator; b. NYC, Dec. 22, 1957; s. Joseph Leserman and Natalie Maria (McCuaig) M.; m. Kaaren Todd Clark, Sept. 1, 1985; children: Caroline Todd, Emily Applegate, Suzannah Tallman. BA, Yale U., 1980; MBA, NYU, 1985. Corp. bond trader, v.p. Drexel Burnham Lambert, NYC, 1980-84; high yield bond trader, sr. v.p. Dillon Read, Inc., NYC, 1984-95; mng. dir., head high yield bond dept. 1st Union Corp., Charlotte, NC, 1995-2000; mng. dir., head fixed income sales, trading and rsch. Wachovia Corp., Charlotte, NC, 2000—04; fin. advisor Merrill Lynch, 2005; mng. dir., head high yield and structured products Piper Jaffray, 2005—. Mem. Alexis de Toqueville Soc., United Way, Charlotte, 1997-2003; trustee Charlotte Arts and Sci. Coun. Mem. Yale Club N.Y. (Yale Alumni Recruiter), The Bond Market Assn. (bd. dirs. 2001-03), Montgomery Bell Acad. (adv. bd. 2004-). Republican. Jewish. Home: 2420 Lemon Tree Ln Charlotte NC 28211 Office: 1st Union Corp 301 S College St Charlotte NC 28202-6000 Office Phone: 704-562-3769. E-mail: benjamin.t.may@pjc.com.

MAY, BRUCE BARNETT, lawyer; b. Portland, Oreg., Apr. 16, 1948; s. Ralph Barnett May and Barbara (Newton) Evans; m. Deborah Sue Wright, Jan. 22, 1972; children: Alexander, Christopher, Elizabeth, Andrew. BA, Princeton U., 1971; JD, U. Oreg., 1978. Bar: Ariz. 1978. Ptnr. Jennings Strouss & Salmon, Phoenix, 2004—. Lectr. various bar and trade assns. Contbr. articles to profl. jours. Dir. Phoenix Mountain Preservation Coun., 1985-89; mem. Paradise Valley Urban Village Planning Com., Phoenix, 1985-87, Men's Art Coun., 1987-91, Phoenix Valley Partnership; mem. adv. bd. Corp. Supportive Housing; bd. Phoenix Revitalogation Coun.; mem. exec. bd. Phoenix Cmty. Alliance. Lt. (j.g.) USN, 1972-75. Mem. ABA (chmn. land sales regulation com., vice chair divsn. CLE, task force future of CLE, co-chmn. brokers and brokerage com.), Am. Coll. Real Estate Lawyers, Order of Coif. Republican. Episcopalian. Avocations: book collecting, running, boxing. Office: Jennings Strouss & Salmon 201 E Washington St Ste1100 Phoenix AZ 85004-2385 Office Phone: 602-262-5923. Business E-Mail: bmay@jsslaw.com.

MAY, CAROL LEE, mechanical engineer; b. Arlington, Va., May 10, 1961; d. Ralph Waldo Jr. and Jane Brownley (Moore) M. BS, Va. Poly. Inst. and State U., 1983; postgrad., U. Göttingen, Germany, 1984-85; MS, Stanford U., 1984. Registered profl. engr., Va. Engring. technician (co-op student) Nat. Park Svc., Wyo., Colo., Alaska, 1980-82; physics instr. Fairfax County Pub. Schs., Oakton, Va., 1985; sr. engr. Cortana Corp., Falls Church, Va., 1986—. Author, co-author over 50 corp. reports on submarine tech., 1986—; contbr. articles to profl. jours. and conf. procs. Stanford U. grad. fellow, 1983-84; Deutsche Akademische Austauschdienst postgrad. fellow in fluid mechs., 1984-85. Mem. AIAA, Naval Submarine League. Achievements include coordinating transfer and documentation of fluid mechanics technology from Russian and Ukrainian institutes; providing design recommendations for U.S. and foreign submarines; investigating influence of boundary layer control techniques on drag and flow noise; managing large software development and R&D programs in remote sensing, developing new and continuing business; 1 patent. Home: 7215 Janet Pl Falls Church VA 22046-3724 Office: Cortana Corp 520 N Washington St Ste 200 Falls Church VA 22046-3549 Home Phone: 703-207-0758. Business E-Mail: cmay@cortana.com.

MAY, CECIL RICHARD, JR., academic administrator; b. Memphis, June 13, 1932; BA in Biblical Langs. magna cum laude, Harding U., MA in New Testament, MTh; LLD (hon.), Freed-Hardeman U., 1984. Min., Holly Springs, Miss., 1954-57, Ripley, Miss., 1957-59, Pine Bluff Ch., Ctrl. Acad. Ch., Miss., 1959-60; dist. scout exec. Yocona Area Coun. Boy Scouts Am., Oxford, Miss., 1959-60; min. Ashland, Miss., 1961, Fulton, Miss., 1962-67, Eastside Campus Ch., Portland, Oreg., 1967-69; Bible tchr. Columbia Christian Coll., Portland, 1967-69; min. Vicksburg, Miss., 1969-76; dean Internat. Bible Coll., Florence, Ala., 1977-80; pres. Magnolia Bible Coll., Kosciusko, Miss., 1980-97; dean bibl. studies Faulkner U., Montgomery, Ala., 1998—, dir. annual Bible lectureship. Lectr. in field. Editor: Preacher Talk; assoc. editor: Magnolia Messenger; contbr. articles to profl. jours. Elder Vicksburg Ch., Miss., 1971-76, South Huntington St. Ch., Kosciusko, 1981-97, U. Ch., Montgomery, 2003—; active Boy Scouts Am., 1954-76; com. chair Kosciusko-Attala County C. of C., 1992; bd. dirs. Am. Cancer Soc., 1971-74, fin. campaign chmn., 1971; bd. dirs. Miss. Econ. Coun., 1985-86, 89-92, area vice-chmn., 1991-92; chmn. Attala County Med. Study Task Force, 1991-92; mem. Evang. Theol. Soc. Recipient Disting. Christian Svc. award, Harding U., 2003. Achievements include Classroom Building at Magnolia Bible College named Cecil May Jr. Classroom Building, 1997. Office: Faulkner Univ 5345 Atlanta Hwy Montgomery AL 36109-3390 Office Phone: 334-386-7154. Business E-Mail: cmay@faulkner.edu.

MAY, CHRISTOPHER N., retired law educator; b. Evanston, Ill., 1943; s. Robert L. May and Virginia Newton; m. Barbara C. McGraw. AB cum laude, Harvard U., Cambridge, Mass., 1961—65; LLB, Yale U., New Haven, Conn., 1965—68. Bar: Calif. 1971. Dir. rsch. Nat. Inst. Edn. Law & Poverty Nortwestern U., Chgo., 1968—69; staff atty. San Francisco Neighborhood Legal Assistance Found., Mission Law Office, San Francisco, 1970—73; prof. law Loyola Law Sch., LA, 1973—2006, assoc. dean, 1975—79, prof. law emeritus, 2006—. Mem. Met. Governance Rsch. Com., Resources for Future, DC, 1973—75; mem. adv. com. Calif. Small Claims Ct. Exptl. Project, Sacramento, 1977—79. Author: (books) A Manual on the Laws and Administrative Regulations of the General Assistance and AFDC Programs in the State of Illinois, 1967, In the Name of War: Judicial Review and the War Powers Since 1918, 1989 (Alpha Sigma Nu Nat. SJ Book award, 1989), Presidential Defiance of Unconstitutional Laws: Reviving the Royal Prerogative, 1998; co-author (with Allan Ides) (books) Constitutional Law: National Power and Federalism, 4th ed., 2007, Constitutional Law: Individual Rights, 2007, Civil Procedure: Cases and Problems, 2d ed., 2006. Bd. dirs. We. Ctr. Law & Poverty, LA, 1974—76, Calif. Rural Legal Assistance, Inc., Sacramento, 1978—82, Calif. Rural Legal Assistance Found., Sacramento, 1982—95, San Francisco, 1982—95.

MAY, DONALD ROBERT LEE, ophthalmologist, educator, academic administrator, farmer; b. Spring Valley, Ill., Nov. 26, 1945; BS in Liberal Arts and Scis. with high honors and distinction, U. Ill., 1968, MD, 1972. Diplomate Am. Bd. Ophthalmology, Nat. Bd. Med. Examiners. Rsch. fellow dept. ophthalmology U. Ill. Eye and Ear Infirmary, Chgo., 1971—72; intern Northwestern U. Sch. Medicine Meml. Hosps., Chgo., 1972—73; resident in ophthalmology U. Ill. Eye and Ear Infirmary, Chgo., 1973—76, instr. dept. ophthalmology, 1974—77, attending surgeon dept. ophthalmology, 1976—77, fellow in diabetic retinopathy study, diabetic retinopathy vitrectomy study, and retina and vitreous surgery, 1976—77; founder, dir. retina svc., dept. ophthalmology Wilford Hall USAF Med. Ctr., San Antonio, 1977—79; asst. prof. ophthalmology, founder, dir. Retina/Vitreous/Ocular Trauma Svc. U. Calif. Davis Sch. Medicine, Calif., 1979—81; assoc. prof., dir. retina, vitreous and ocular trauma svc. U. Calif. Sch. Medicine, Davis, 1981—84; prof. ophthalmology Tulane U. Sch. Medicine, New Orleans, 1984—89, dir. med. student edn. dept. ophthalmology, 1985—89, dir. ophthalmology Charity Hosp., 1985—89; prof. Tex. Tech U. Health Scis. Ctr., Lubbock, Tex., 1989—2001, chmn. dept. ophthalmology and visual scis., 1989—94, prof. dept. health orgn. mgmt., 1993—2001, assoc. dean Sch. Medicine, 1994—96. Co-investigator in the intraocular gentamicin prophylaxis study Govt. Erskine Hosp., Madurai, India, 1975, Dept. Ophthalmology, Audie Murphy VA Hosp., San Antonio, 1977—79, Martinez VA Hosp., Calif., 1979—84, VA Hosp., New Orleans, 1984—89, VA Med. Ctr., Big Spring, Tex., 1989—93, 1996—2001, VA Ctr., Lubbock, Tex., 1989—92, Lubbock, 1996—2001; vis. prof., Germany, 1984, Switzerland, 87; pres. US Eye Injury Registry, 1994—96; founder, med. dir. Tex. Eye Injury Registry, 1991—2001; cons. in field. Contbg. editor: Outcome/Fragmatome Newsletter, 1978—81; assoc. editor: Vitreoretinal Surgery and Tech., 1989—98, mem. editl. bd.: Jour. Eye Trauma, 1996—2001; contbr. articles to profl. jours.; appeared in numerous TV and radio programs. Com. mem. Sch. Medicine U. Calif., Davis, Tulane U. Sch. Medicine, New Orleans, Sch. Medicine Tex. Tech. U. Health Scis. Ctr.; bd. dirs. Lubbock Internat. Cultural Ctr., Inc., 1997—, pres. bd. dirs., 2005—07; planning com., chmn. medicine and history com., liaison Vatican Mus. Exhbn. Found., 2001—02; bd. trustees Nat. Exhibits Assn. Mus., Post, Tex., 2007—. Maj. USAF, 1973—80. Decorated Air Force Commendation medal. Mem.: AMA, ACS, Mil. Officers Assn. of Am., Mil. Officers Assn. Am. (bd. dirs. Greater Lubbock chpt. 2007—), Ill. Farm Bur., Ill. Agrl. Assn., Am. Farm Bur. Fedn., Soc. Med. Cons. Armed Forces, Vitreous Soc. (charter), Retina Soc., Schepens Internat. Soc., Tex. Tech. Rsch. Found. (bd. dirs. 1993—96), Tex. Ophthal. Assn. (chair edn. com. 1990—93, coun. 1990—93, nominating com. 1991—93), So. Retina Study Group, Tex. Med. Assn. (com. continuing edn. 1993—96, bd. dirs. TEXPAC 2000—02), So. Med. Assn. (vice-chmn. sec. ophthalmology 1995—96, chmn. sec. ophthalmology 1996—97), Christian Med. Assn., Assn. Rsch. Vision and Ophthalmology (pub. rels. com. 1997—2000), Am. Acad. Ophthalmology (bylaws and rules com. 1990—95, com. internat. ophthalmology 1991—95), Lubbock C. of C., Am. Legion, Sigma Xi (sec. Tex. Tech. chpt. 1990—91, v.p., pres.-elect 1999—2000, pres. 2000—01). Republican. Lutheran. Avocations: travel, photography, bicycling, hiking. Office: PO Box 1678 Lubbock TX 79408-1678 *If we are to survive as a* *free society, we must each accept responsibility. The individual must function on the premise that personal rewards come with the investment of hard, honest work and not as a right mediated by government at the expense of others. Our legislative bodies must enact laws for the common good and not for individual self-interest. Our judicial systems must provide for the just enforcement of our laws. Our leadership must be the watchdog to ensure the indivdual has the opportunity to life without unreasonable danger, the freedom to follow one's dreams, and the ability to pursue happiness through individual achievement. Security comes with the contribution of all who are able.*

MAY, EDGAR, former state legislator; b. Zurich, Switzerland, June 27, 1929; arrived in U.S., 1940, naturalized, 1954; s. Ferdinand and Renee (Bloch) May. B.J. with highest distinction, Northwestern U., 1957. Reporter, acting editor Bellows Falls (Vt.) Times, 1951-53; reporter Fitchburg (Mass.) Sentinel, 1953; part time reporter Chgo. Tribune, 1955-57; reporter Buffalo Evening News, 1958-61; dir. pub. welfare projects State Charities Aid Assn., 1962-64; mem. President's Task Force on War Against Poverty, 1964; spl. asst. to dir., asst. dir. Office Econ. Opportunity, 1964; spl. adviser to Ambassador Sargent Shriver, 1968-70; cons. Ford Found., 1970-75; mem. Vt. Ho. of Reps., 1975-82, Vt. Senate, 1983-91, chmn. com. appropriations; project dir. Vt. Jud. Mgmt. Study, 1992; COO Spl. Olympics Internat., Washington, 1993-96; cons. New Eng. Culinary Inst., 1996—2001; chmn. So. Vt. Recreation Ctr. Found., 1998—2006. Author: The Wasted Americans, 1964. With AUS, 1953-55. Recipient Page One award Buffalo Newspaper Guild, 1959, Walter O. Bingham award, 1959, Pulitzer prize for local reporting, 1961, Merit award Northwestern U. Alumni Assn., 1962. Cmty. Leader of Yr. award Vt. Coun. Rural Devel., 2006; named Citizen of Yr., C. of C., 2003.

MAY, ERNEST DEWEY, academic administrator, musician; b. Jersey City, May 8, 1942; s. Ernest Max and Harriet Elizabeth (Dewey) May; m. Eileen Marie Mayhew, Jan. 29, 1963 (div. 1984); children: Ernest Jr., Elizabeth May Goodell, Katherine May Waite, Caroline, Christopher, Abigail May Robies, Deirdre May Maitre; m. Mary L. Milkey, June 29, 1985. AB, Harvard U., Cambridge, Mass., 1964; MFA, Princeton U., NJ, 1968, PhD, 1975. Asst. prof. music Amherst Coll., Mass., 1969-75; from asst. prof. to prof. music dept. music and dance U. Mass., Amherst, 1976-88, prof. music, chmn. dept. music and dance, 1988-2000, presiding officer faculty senate, 1997-2000, sec. faculty senate, 2000—. Faculty rep. bd. trustees U. Mass., 1988-97; chair Intercampus Faculty Coun., 2001—; organist, dir. mus. South Congl. Ch., Springfield, Mass., 1983-05. Rec.: Music for Trumpet and Organ, 1979, 2001; co-editor: J.S. Bach: Neve Ausgabe Samtlicher Werke Vol. I/20, 1986, J.S. Bach as Organist, 1986; contbr. New Harvard Dictionary of Music, 1986. Mem.: Am. Musicological Soc. (pres. New Eng. chpt. 1988—90), Am. Guild Organists. Home: 44 Amherst Rd Pelham MA 01002-9700 Office: U Mass Faculty Senate Amherst MA 01003 Business E-Mail: secretary@senate.umass.edu.

MAY, GARY STEPHEN, electrical engineer; b. St. Louis, May 17, 1964; s. Warren and Gloria (Hunter) M.; m. LeShelle; c. Simone Imani, Jordan Amani May BEE, Ga. Inst. Tech., 1985; MEE and Computer Science, U. Calif., Berkeley, 1987, PhD in Electrical Engring. and Computer Sci., 1991. Tutor Ga. Inst. Tech., 1982-84, rsch. asst., 1985; joined Sch. Electrical and Computer Engring., the microelectronics group Ga. Inst. Tech, 1991, Motorola Found. prof., 2001—05, assoc. chair., sch. electrical and computer engring., 2001—05, exec. asst. to pres., 2002—05, prof., Steve W. Chaddick Sch. Electrical and Computer Engring. chair, 2005—; coop. edn. staff McDonnell-Douglas Corp., 1982-84; mem. tech. staff AT&T Bell Labs., summers 1985-86; rsch. asst. U. Calif., Berkeley, 1989-90, grad. student instr., 1988—91. Founder, dir. Summer Undergraduate Rsch. Engring./Sci. Prog. (SURE), Ga. Inst. Tech., 1992—, Facilitating Academic Careers in Engineering and Science (FACES), Ga. Inst. Tech., 1998—; served on Congl. Commn. on the Advancement of Women and Minorities in Sci., Engring., and Tech., NSF Com. on Equal Opportunity in Sci. and Engring., chair, 2000—01; spkr. in field. Editor-in-chief IEEE Transactions on Semiconductor Manufacturing, 1997—2001 (Oustanding Paper award, 1998, 2000); contbr. articles to profl. jours. NSF fellow, AT&T Bell Lab. Fellow; recipient Outstanding Young Alumnus, Ga. Inst. Tech., 1993, AT&T Info. Systems award, Eso-Systems award, GE Latimer Achievement award, Martin Luther King Jr. Svc. award., Giant of Sci. award, Quality Edn. for Minorities Network, 2002, Wickenden award for Outstanding Paper, Journal of Engring. Edn., 2003, Minorities in Engring. award, 2004, 2006 AAAS Mentor award, 2007; named Nat. Young Investigator, 1993-98; selected by the NAE to Participate in Frontiers of Engineering Conference as one of the nation's top 100 engineers between the ages of 30-45, 2000. Fellow IEEE; mem. Nat. Soc. Black Engrs. (nat. chmn. emeritus, nat. chmn. 1987-89, editorial bd. 1985-, mem. nat. adv. bd., Outstanding Leadership award, 1988, 89, Golden Torch Award: Janice A. Lumpkin Educator of Yr., 2006, Nat. Action Coun. for Minorities in Engring., NAACP, Ga. Inst. Tech. Exec. Roundtable, Phi Eta Sigma (Dorothy C. Yancy Incentive award), Lambda Sigma, Eta Kappa Nu, Briarean Soc., Eta Kappa Nu, Omicron Delta Kappa, Phi Kappa Phi, Tau Beta Pi, Anak. Avocations: art, reading, music, football, tennis. Office Phone: 404-894-2902. Office Fax: 404-894-4641. E-mail: gary.may@ece.gatech.edu.

MAY, GITA, literature educator; b. Brussels, Sept. 16, 1929; came to U.S., 1947, naturalized, 1950; d. Albert and Blima (Sieradska) Jochimek; m. Irving May, Dec. 21, 1947. BA magna cum laude, CUNY-Hunter Coll., 1953; MA, Columbia U., 1954, PhD, 1957. Lectr. French CUNY-Hunter Coll., 1953—56; from instr. to assoc. prof. Columbia U., NYC, 1956—68, prof., 1968—, chmn., 1983—93, mem. senate, 1979—83, 1986—88, chmn. Seminar on 18th Century Culture, 1986—89. Lecture tour English univs., 1965. Author: Diderot et Baudelaire, critiques d'art, 1957, De Jean-Jacques Rousseau à Madame Roland: essai sur la sensibilité préromantique et révolutionnaire, 1964, Madame Roland and the Age of Revolution, 1970 (Van Amringe Disting. Book award), Stendhal and the Age of Napoleon, 1977, French Women Writers, 1991, Encyclopedia of Aesthetics, 1998, Dictionnaire de Diderot, 1999, The Feminist Encyclopedia of French Literature, 1999, Elisabeth Vigée Le Brun: The Odyssey of an Artist in an Age of Revolution, 2005; co-editor: Diderot Studies III, 1961; mem. editl. bd. Romanic Rev., 1959—, 18th Century Studies, 1975—78, French Rev., 1975—86, 1998—, Women in French Studies, 2000—; contbg. editor: Oeuvres complètes de Diderot, 1984—, 1995—; gen. editor The Age of Revolution and Romanticism: Interdisciplinary Studies, 1990—, extensive essays on Diderot and George Sand in European Writers, 1984, 1985, and on Rebecca West, Anita Brookner and Graham Swift in British Writers, 1996, 1997, 1999, Bayle, Fontenelle and Fénelon in Dictionary of Literary Biography, 2003, Voltaire's Candide (in Barnes and Noble Classics), 2003; contbr. articles and revs. to profl. jours. Decorated chevalier and officier Ordre des Palmes Acad.; recipient award Am. Coun. Learned Socs., 1961, award for outstanding achievement CUNY-Hunter Coll., 1963; Fulbright rsch. grantee, 1964-65; Guggenheim fellow, 1964-65, NEH fellow, 1971-72. Mem. AAUP, MLA (del. assembly 1973-75, com. rsch. activities 1975-78, exec. coun. 1980-83), Am. Assn. Tchrs. French, Am. Soc. 18th Century Studies (pres. 1985-86, 2d v.p. 1983-84, 1st v.p. 1984-85, One of Gt. Tchrs. award 1999), Soc. Française d'Etude du Dix-Huitième Siècle, Soc. Diderot, Am. Soc. French Acad. Palms, Soc. des Etudes Staëliennes, N.Am. Soc. for Study of Jean-Jacques Rousseau, Soc. des Professeurs Français et Francophones d'Amérique, Phi Beta Kappa. Office: Columbia U Dept French/Romance Philol 516 Philosophy Hall MC4918 New York NY 10027 Business E-Mail: gm9@columbia.edu.

MAY, HAROLD LOUIS, retired surgeon, not-for-profit developer; s. Arthur Earnest and Margaret Jestina May; m. Agnes Martens, Apr. 26, 1960; children: Jeannette Elizabeth, Alison Gabrielle, Margaret May Jenkins. MD, Harvard U., Cambridge, Mass., 1951, MPH, 1974. Lic. physician Mass., 1959, diplomate Am. Bd. of Surgery, 1965. Med. intern U. Minn. Hosps., Mpls., 1951—52; med. asst. resident Boston City Hosp., 1952—53; surg. resident Mass. Gen. Hosp., Boston, 1953—59; chief of surgery Albert Schweitzer Hosp., Deschapelles, Haiti, 1960—70; dir. Divsn. Cmty. Health and Med. Care Peter Bent Brigham Hosp., Boston, 1970—75; assoc. surgery Peter Bent Brigham Hosp. and Brigham and Women's Hosp., Boston, 1970—94; asst. prof. surgery Harvard Med. Sch., 1970—94; dir. med. svcs. Wrentham (Mass.) Devel. Svcs., 1975—94, ret., 1994. Exec. com. Boston-Brookline (Mass.) Health Resources Orgn., 1970—73; chmn. Region VI Emergency Med. Svcs. Com., Mass., 1972—74. Editor (author): Emergency Medicine, 1984; editor: Emergency Procedures, 1984; editor in chief: Emergency Medicine, 2d edit., 1992. Founder and pres. FAMILY, Inc., Boston, 1997; co-founder Ecole La Providence Primary Sch., Deschapelles, Haiti, 1962. Aviation cadet US Army Air Corps, 1945. Recipient Excellence in Tchg. Faculty prize, Harvard Med. Sch., 1987, 1992. Fellow: ACS; mem.: Boston Surg. Soc. Avocations: music, painting. Home and Office: FAMILY Inc 80 Waban Hill Road Newton MA 02467 Business E-Mail: haroldmay@familysystem.net.

MAY, HENRY STRATFORD, JR., lawyer; b. Greensboro, NC, May 12, 1947; s. Henry Stratford and Doris (Richardson) May. BA, U. Tex., 1969, JD, 1971. Bar: Tex. 1972, US Ct. Appeals (DC cir.) 1974, US Supreme Ct. 1977, US Ct. Appeals (5th and 11th cirs.) 1981, US Dist. Ct. (so. dist.) Tex. 1985. Law clk. to judge U.S. Ct. Appeals (D.C. cir.), Washington, 1972-73; assoc. Vinson & Elkins LLP, Houston, 1973-79, ptnr., 1979—, head energy sect., 1990—. Mem. ABA, Tex. Bar Assn. E-mail: hmay@velaw.com.

MAY, INGRID BARBARA, elementary school educator; d. Pedro B. and Maria B. Luna; m. Fred L. May, Aug. 13, 1977; 1 child, Rebecca S. BA, Oklahoma City U., 1971; MA, So. Nazarene U., Bethany, Okla., 1975. Reading cert. Okla., 1975, nat. bd. cert. Nat. Bd. for Profl. Tchg. Stds., 2005. Educator, third grade Overholser Elementary Sch., Oklahoma City, 1972—; mem. Putnam City Sch. District Reading Com., 1974—, Putnam City Sch. Reading Coun., Oklahoma City, 1972—82, treas., 1974—79, pres., 1980—81; chmn. Overholser Reading Com., Bethany, 1980—, Overholser Social Studies Com., 1999—2005; mem. Title I, Bethany, 2004—, Overholser Prin.'s Adv. Comm., 2005—. Accompanist Silver Strings of Putnam City, Oklahoma City, 2000—05. Dir. Adopt-a-Grandparent Project, Bethany, 2004—. Named Tchr. of Yr., Overholser Elem. Sch., 1980—81, 2005—06; scholar Nat. Bd. Certification, Edn. Leadership Okla., 2005, Gt. Expectations, Okla. State Reading Orgn., 2006—. Mem.: NEA (assoc.), Putnam City Reading Coun., Internat. Reading Assn., Putnam City Assn. Classroom Tchrs. (assoc.), Okla. Edn. Assn. (assoc.). Republican. Nazarene. Avocations: handbell choir, piano, singing, gardening, sewing. Home Phone: 405-495-4539; Office Phone: 405-789-7913.

MAY, JAMES HARVEY, communications educator; s. Rhoudy and Ruby Mae May; m. Margit Röder, June 10, 1967; children: James Richard, Anika Nikol; 1 child, Tanja Babette Youngs. BS, Stanford U., 1958; MBA, Harvard U., 1964; certificate in radio and TV, NYU, 1966; DLS, Columbia U., 1973—78, advanced certificate in librarianship, 1977. Econ. engr. Gilbert Associates, Inc., NYC, 1964—67; v.p., treas. Pandex, Macmillan Info. Corp., NYC, 1967—72; dir., ctr. comm. and info. rsch. U. Denver, 1972—74; assoc. libr. dir., acting libr. dir. Sonoma State U., Rohnert Pk., Calif., 1974—83; vice provost info. resources Calif. State U., Chico, 1983—94; prof. comm. sci. and tech. Calif. State U. Monterey Bay, Seaside, 1994—, founding dean instrn., 1994—96, asst. to the pres., 1996—98. Ofcl. historian, bd. mem. Soc. Computer Simulation, 1991—97; panelist with US v.p. Al Gore Unity '99, Seattle, 1999; treas. Calif. Faculty Assn., 1999—2003, chpt. pres., 1998—2001, 2004—05; ednl. effectiveness panel Am. Distance Edn. Consortium, 2000—; keynote spkr. Open Learning 2000, Brisbane, Queensland, Australia, 2000; bd. dir. Am. Indian Sci. and Engring. Soc., 2002—; co-chair, vice chair, bd. mem. Native Am. Pub. Telecom.; chmn. bd. Native Am. TV. Contbr. articles to jour. and chpt. to books. Lt. JG USN, 1959—62, Las Vegas and No. Ireland. Recipient outstanding leadership in libr. services for Am. Indian People and founding the Am. Indian Libr. Assn., Am. Indian Libr. Assn., 1994, Svc. to Am. Indians in Field of Tech., Stanford U. Am. Indian Alumni Assn., 1995, Union Mem. Yr., Monterey Ctrl. Labor Coun., AFL-CIO, 2000, Trade Unionist Yr., Monterey Bay Ctrl. Labor Coun., AFL-CIO, 2002. Mem.: Am. Indian Sci. and Engring. Soc. (life; bd.dir. 2002—, Ely S. Parker Medal 2000), United Keetoowah Band of Cherokee Indians (life). Achievements include created first computerized bibliographic database. Office: Calif State Univ Monterey Bay 100 Campus Ctr Seaside CA Home: 3704 Clubside Ln Sacramento CA 95835 E-mail: jameshmay@yahoo.com.

MAY, JAMES M., medical educator, researcher; b. Oklahoma City, Aug. 20, 1947; married; 2 children. BS, Yale Coll., 1969; MD, Vanderbilt U., 1973. Diplomate Am. Bd. Internal Medicine, Am. Bd. Endocrinology and Metabolism. Intern Vanderbilt U., Nashville, 1973—74; resident in medicine Johns Hopkins Hosp., Balt., 1974—75; fellow in endocrinology U. Wash., Seattle, 1975—78; asst. prof. medicine Med. Coll. Va., Richmond, 1978—83, assoc. prof. medicine, 1983—86; assoc. prof. to prof. medicine Vanderbilt U., Nashville, 1986—, assoc. prof. to prof. molecular physiology and biophysics, 1993—. Mem. awards com. dept. medicine Vanderbilt U., 1992—; mem. awards com. Summer Diabetes Program Diabetes Rsch. and Tng. Ctr., 1994—. Mem. editl. bd.: Metabolism, 1996—; contbr. articles to profl. jours. Recipient Nat. Rsch. Svc. award, NIH, 1975—78, Poncin Fund award, 1975—78; grantee, NIH, 1993, 1995. Mem.: Southern Soc. Clin. Investigation, Am. Soc. Clin. Investigation, Am. Fedn. Clin. Rsch. (sec.-treas. Southern sect. 1983—86, nat. councilor 1983—88, pres.-elect and pres. 1986—88), Am. Diabetes Assn. (pres. Va. affiliate 1985—86, chmn. rsch. com. Tenn. affiliate 1990—92, Rsch. award 1996), Alpha Omega Alpha. Home: 44 Concord Park E Nashville TN 37205-4705 Office: Vanderbilt U Med Ctr Divsn Endocrinology & Diabetes 2220 Pierce Ave Bldg 2 Nashville TN 37232-0001

MAY, JAMES WARREN, JR., plastic surgeon, medical association executive; b. Lexington, Ky., 1943; MD, Northwestern U., 1969. Cert. Gen. Surgery, 1975, Plastic Surgery, 1977. Intern Mass. Gen. Hosp., Boston, 1969-70, resident, 1970-75, resident plastic surgeon, 1975—; fellow U. Louisville, 1975; assoc. prof. clin. surgery Harvard Med. Sch., Boston; chmn. Am. Bd. Plastic Surgery; chief, plastic, reconstructive surgery Mass. Gen. Hosp. Cancer Ctr., Boston. Named one of Top Cancer Specialists for Women, Good Houskeeping mag., 1999, Top Breast Cancer Doctors, Redbook mag., 2002, Boston's Top Doctor's, Boston mag., 2006. Mem.: Am. Assn. Plastic Surgeons (pres.-elect 2006, pres. 2007). Office: Divsn Plastic Surgery Mass Gen Hosp Cancer Ctr 55 Fruit St Boston MA 02114-3117 also: MGH Prof Office Bldg Ste 502 275 Cambridge St Boston MA 02114 Office Phone: 617-724-9922. *

MAY, JANET SUE, playwright, lyricist; b. Bloomington, Ill., Dec. 24, 1946; d. James Woolston and Josephine Elisabeth (Ferguson) Grubb; children: John, Darbi, Heather, Brandy. Student, Lincoln Coll., 1965, Wabash Coll., 1965, St. Joseph's Hosp., 1966, Indian River C.C., 1983, Bloomington Sch. Practical Nursing, 1984; cert. in food svc. sanitation, Ill. State U., 1988. Chem. lab. tech. Eureka Williams, Bloomington, 1966; histology tech. St. Joseph's Hosp., Bloomington, 1966—67; activity dir. McLean County Nursing Home, Normal, Ill., 1968—70; rsch. asst. U. Fla. Med. Entomology Lab., Vero Beach, Fla., 1984—85; asst. libr. condemned unit Pontiac Prison, Ill., 1974—75; activity dir., meal supr. Bloomington Housing Authority, 1987—89; pub. rels. mgr. Miracle Ear, Peoria, Ill., 1990—92. Author: (children's poetry books) Winston-Smythe Worm, Prissy Penelope Grasshopper Presents, (children's books) Four Little Creatures; co-author (with James Kitzmiller): Patronymics of Mosquitoes, 2d edit., 1986; playwright: More Than Just A Man, 2001; playwright: Abrahams House, 2005; playwright (musical) A Christmas Forgotten, 2007; songwriter: Ice Age; author: (musical) Abraham's House, 2005. Achievements include co-inventor, tissue vacuum pump; invention of jeweled perfumed hair tie; blinking hair tie. Avocations: art, poetry, singing. Personal E-mail: lgrubworm@aol.com.

MAY, JOSEPH LESERMAN (JACK MAY), retired lawyer; b. Nashville, May 27, 1929; s. Daniel and Dorothy (Fishel) M.; m. Natalie McCuaig, Apr. 12, 1957 (dec. May 1990); children: Benjamin, Andrew, Joshua, Maria; m. Lynn Hewes Lance, June 10, 1994. BA, Yale U., New Haven, Conn., 1951; JD, NYU, 1958; postgrad., Harvard Bus. Sch., Cambridge, Mass., 1969. Bar: Tenn. 1959. Prodr. Candied Yam Jackson Show, 1947-51; with CIA, 1951-55; pres. Nuweave Socks, Inc., NYC, 1955-59, May Hosiery Mills, Nashville, 1960-83, Athens Hosiery Mills, Tenn., 1966-83; v.p. Wayne-Gossard Corp., Chattanooga, 1972-83; dir. pvt. practice law Nashville, 1984—; ret., 2004. Dir. Merrill Lynch Investment Mgmt., 1987—2002; mem. adv. bd. Asian Strategies Group, 1994; chmn. Guardianship and Trust Corp., 1994—96; founding dir. Nashville Bank and Trust Co., 2003. Author: (book) Walking Around the House, 2007. Bd. dirs. Vanderbilt Cancer Ctr., 1994-99; pres. Jewish Cmty. Ctr., 1969; chmn. Campus for Human Devel., 2000-02; mem. Collectors Cir., Frist Art Mus., 2004—; With USN, 1947-53, US Army, 1954. Mem. Tenn. Bar Assn., Nashville Bar Assn., Am. Arbitration Assn. Panel of Neutrals, Tenn. Hist. Soc. (trustee, pres. 2000-02), Eagle Scout Assn., Belle Meade Country Club, Shamus Club, Old Oak Club, Old Goats, Zodiac, Group of Six, Yale Club NY, Rotary (pres. Nashville 1971). Republican. Jewish. Home: 133 Abbottsford Nashville TN 37215-2442

MAY, KENNETH AUSTIN, consumer products company executive; b. Memphis, Nov. 14, 1960; s. Forrest Sherman and Elizabeth (Austin) M. Degree in real estate, Memphis State U., 1983; MBA, U. Tenn., 1994. Supr. United Parcel Svc., Memphis, 1979-82; sr. mgr. Federal Express Corp., Memphis, 1982-90, mng. dir. Miami, 1990-96, v.p. Memphis, 1996—2004; exec. v.p., CEO FedEx Kinko's Inc., Dallas, 2004—06, pres., CEO, 2006—. Trustee March of Dimes Birth Defects Found., White Plains, NY. Republican. Baptist. Avocations: water-skiing, skiing, basketball, golf, fishing. Office: FedEx Kinkos Inc 3 Galleria Tower Ste 1600 13155 Noel Rd Dallas TX 75240 Office Phone: 214-550-7000. Office Fax: 214-550-7001.

MAY, KENNETH NATHANIEL, retired food industry consultant; b. Livingston, La., Dec. 24, 1930; s. Robert William and Mary Hulda (Caraway) M.; m. Patsy Jean Farr, Aug. 4, 1953; children: Sherry Alison (dec.), Nathan Elliott. BS in Poultry Sci., La. State U., 1952, MS in Poultry Sci., 1955; PhD in Food Tech., Purdue U., 1959, DAgr, 1988. Asst. prof. U. Ga., Athens, 1958-64, assoc. prof., 1964-67, prof., 1967-68, Miss. State U., State College, 1968-70; dir. rsch. Holly Farms Poultry, Wilkesboro, N.C., 1970-73, v.p., 1973-85, pres., 1985-88, chmn., CEO, 1989—89, ret., 2005. Adj. prof. N.C. State U., 1975. Contbr. over 60 articles to profl. jours.; patentee treatment of cooked poultry. Bd. trustees Appalachian State U., 1987-94, chmn., 1989-90. Recipient Industry Service award Poultry and Egg Inst. Am., 1971, Meritorious Service award, Ga. Egg Commn., 1964, Disting. Service award Agribus. N.C., 1986; named to Am. Poultry Hall of Fame, 1992. Fellow Poultry Sci. Assn. (Disting. Poultry Industry Career award 2007); mem. Nat. Poultry Hist. Soc. (bd. dirs. 1982-83), Inst. Food Technologists. Methodist. Avocations: reading, stained glass. Office: 113 La Maison Belle Dr Denham Springs LA 70726 Personal E-mail: drknmay@aol.com.

MAY, LAWRENCE EDWARD, lawyer; b. NYC, Aug. 7, 1947; s. Jack and Ann Marie (Schnell) M.; m. Rosalind Marsha Israel, Feb. 3, 1979; children: Jeremy, Lindsey. BA, UCLA, 1969, JD, 1972. Bar: Calif. 1972, NY 1973. Assoc. Paul, Weiss, Rifkind, Wharton & Garrison, NYC, 1972-76, Levine, Krom & Unger, Beverly Hills, Calif., 1976-79, Weissburg & Aronson, LA, 1979-81, Valensi & Rose, LA, 1981-83; prin. Lawrence E. May, P. C., LA, 1983—. Bd. dirs. Pub. Counsel, 1989-97; pres., 1995-96. Mem. editl. bd.: LA Jewish Jour., 1985—91. Exec. com. Pacific S.W. Region Anti-Defamation League, 1985—; bd. dirs. LA Youth, 1997-2002. Named a L.A. Super Lawyer Closely-Held Bus., 2005, 2006, 2007. Mem. State Bar Calif., Los Angeles County Bar Assn. (trustee 1987-88, pro bono coun. 1995-98), Beverly Hills Bar Assn. (bd. govs. 1981-90, pres. 1988-89, chmn. bus. law sect. 1984-85). Democrat. Avocations: current events, golf, family activities. Office: Ste 350 10350 Santa Monica Blvd Los Angeles CA 90025-5075 Office Phone: 310-203-0930. Business E-Mail: lmay@maylaw.com.

MAY, LINDA KAREN CARDIFF, occupational health nurse, safety engineer, consultant; b. San Mateo, Calif., Oct. 26, 1948; d. Leon Davis and Jane Vivian (Gallow) Cardiff; m. Donald William May, Dec. 7, 1969 (div. Feb. 1988); children: Charles David, Andrew William. At, So. Ill. U., 1969; post grad., Ill. Wesleyan U., 1989; AAS, Parkland Coll., 1977; BS in Pub. Health and Safety Engring. with honors, U. Ill., Urbana, 1987; BSN, Lakeview Coll., 1990. RN Ill., Ind., Mo., N.Mex., Tex., Wis., registered profl. nurse; nat. registered EMT Ill., accredited instr. constrn. safety and health OSHA. Indsl. nurse C.S. Johnson Co., Champaign, Ill., 1979—84; safety engr. Clinton Nuclear Power Plant Ill. Power Co., 1984—86; occupl. safety and health specialist Danville Vet.'s Med. Ctr., 1986—. With LKM Health and Safety Cons., Inc., Champaign, Ill. Active Mercy Hosp. Aux., Covenant Hosp Aux., 1977—, Champaign County Task Force on Arson, 1981—; alumni assn. liason Parkland Coll. Found. Bd., 1993; mem. Champaign County Crime Prevention Coun., 1978—83, bd. dir., 1980—82. Ill. State Gen. Assembly scholar, 1967. Mem.: APHA (occpl. health and safety sect.), AACN, Lakeview Coll. Nursing Alumni Assn., N.Y. Acad. Sci., Ill. EMTs Assn., Pre-Hosp. Care Providers Ill., Associated Ill. Milk, Food and Environ. Sanitarians, Ill. Soc. Pub. Health Educators, Ill. Environ. Health Assn., Nat. Registry EMT, Am. Assn. Occupational Health Nurses, Am. Nuc. Assn. (mem. biology and medicine divsn., mem. radiopharm. and isotope product stds. com.), Am. Soc. Safety Engrs. (vice chair Ctrl. Ill. sect. 1985—86), Ill. Wesleyan U. Alumni Assn., U. Ill. Alumni Assn. (life), Parkland Coll. Alumni Assn. (life; bd. dir. 1987—, v.p. 1992—), Eta Sigma Gamma. Methodist. Home: PO Box 3954 Champaign IL 61826-3954 Personal E-mail: lmay4111@aol.com.

MAY, MISTY, Olympic athlete; b. July 30, 1977; Majored in Kinesiology & Physical Ed., Long Beach State U. Mem. U.S. National Indoor Team, 1998, 1999; beach volleyball player Team USA, Sydney Olympic Games, 2000, Team USA, Athens Olympic Games, 2004. Named BVA Rookie of the Yr., 2000, AVP Team of the Yr. (with Kerri Walsh), 2003. Achievements include member of NCAA national championship team, 1998; one of only three players to be named a two-time AVCA National Player of the Year, 1997, 1998; winning FIVB Tour with teammate Kerri Walsh, 2002, 2003; winning a gold medal at Athens Olympic Games, beach volleyball, 2004. Office: c/o USOC One Olympic Plz Colorado Springs CO 80909

MAY, NICHOLAS G.B., lawyer; BA, U. Iowa, 1994; JD magna cum laude, William Mitchell Coll. Law, 1998. Bar: US Ct. Appeals (8th cir.), US Dist. Ct. (dist. Minn.), Minn. Supreme Ct. Ptnr. May & O'Brien, L.L.P., Hastings, Minn. Named a Rising Star, Minn. Super Lawyers mag., 2006. Mem.: Minn. Trial Lawyers Assn., Dakota County Bar Assn., Minn. Bar Assn. (mem. labor and employment sect.), ABA, Nat. Employment Lawyers Assn. (Minn. chpt.) (bd. mem., past pres.). Office: May & O'Brien

LLP 204 Sibley St Ste 202 Hastings MN 55033 Office Phone: 651-437-6300. E-mail: nmay@mayobrien.com. *

MAY, PETER WILLIAM, business executive; b. NYC, Dec. 11, 1942; s. Samuel D. and Isabel (Meyer) M.; m. Leni Finkelstein, Aug. 16, 1964; children: Jonathan Paul, Leslie Ann. AB, U. Chgo., 1964, MBA, 1965. CPA, N.Y. Mgr. Peat, Marwick, Mitchell & Co., NYC, 1965-72; exec. v.p. Flagstaff Corp., NYC, 1972-78; pres., chief operating officer Trian Group. L.P. (formerly Triangle Industries, Inc.), NYC, 1978—93, also bd. dirs.; pres., COO Triarc Cos., Inc., NYC, 1993—. Bd. dirs. Encore Capital Group Inc., 1998—. Trustee Mt. Sinai Hosp., N.Y.C., exec. com., founding mem. Laura Rosenberg Meml. Fund for Pediatric Leukemia Rsch.; alumni dir. U. Chgo. Grad. Sh. Bus.; bd. dirs. 92d St. YMCA, United Jewish Appeal, Operation Exodus campaign. Mem. Am. Inst. CPA's, N.Y. Soc. of CPA's. Office: Triarc 280 Park Ave New York NY 10017

MAY, PHILIP ALAN, sociologist, educator; b. Bethesda, Md., Nov. 6, 1947; s. Everette Lee and Marie (Lee) M.; m. Doreen Ann Garcia, Sept. 5, 1972; children: Katrina Ruth, Marie Ann. BA in Sociology, Catawba Coll., 1969; MA in Sociology, Wake Forest U., 1971; PhD in Sociology, U. Mont., 1976. NIMH predoctoral fellow U. Mont., Missoula, 1973-76; dir. health stats. and rsch. Navajo Health Authority, Window Rock, Ariz., 1976-78; from asst. prof. to prof. U. N.Mex., Albuquerque, 1978—89, prof., 1989—, from dir. Ctr. on Alcoholism, Substance abuse and Addictions to sr. rsch. scientist, 1990—2000, sr. rsch. scientist Ctr. on Alcoholism, Substance abuse and Addictions, 2000—, assoc. dir. Ctr. on Alcoholism, Substance abuse and Addictions, 2002—04, interim dir. Ctr. on Alcoholism, Substance abuse and Addictions, 2004. Fetal alcohol syndrome study com. Inst. Medicine of NAS, 1994-96; dir. Nat. Indian Fetal Alcohol Syndrome Prevention Program, Albuquerque, 1979-85; adv. bd. Nat. Orgn. on Fetal Alcohol Syndrome, Washington, 1990—; rsch. assoc. Nat. Ctr. for Am. Indian and Alaska Native Mental Health Rsch., 1986—; mem. U.S. Surgeon Gens. Task Force on Drunk Driving, 1988-89; prin. investigator fetal alcohol syndrome epidemiology rsch. in South Africa, 1997—; com. on pathophysiology and prevention of adolescent and adult suicide Inst. Medicine of NRC, NAS, 2000-02; cons. in field. Contbr. chpts. to books, articles to profl. jours. V.p. Bd. Edn., Laguna Pueblo, N.Mex., 1998—2002, pres., 2002—; mem. N.Mex. Indian Edn. Adv. Coun., 2006—, N.Mex. Gov.'s Commn. on Compulsive Gambling, 2006—. Lt. (s.g.) USPHS, 1970—73. Recipient Spl. Recognition award U.S. Indian Health Svc., 1992, award Navajo Tribe and U.S. Indian Health Svc., 1992, Human Rights Promotion award UN Assn., 1994, Program award for Contbns. to Mental Health of Am. Indians, U.S. Indian Health Svc., 1996, O.B. Michael Outstanding Alumnus award Catawba Coll., 2000. Mem. APHA, Am. Sociol. Assn., Am. Assn. Suicidology, Population Ref. Bur., Coll. on Problems of Drug Dependence, Rsch. Soc. Alcoholism. Methodist. Home: 4610 Idlewilde Ln SE Albuquerque NM 87108-3422 Office: U NMex CASAA 2650 Yale Blvd Albuquerque NM 87106-3202 Home Phone: 505-266-0781; Office Phone: 505-925-2307. Business E-Mail: pmay@unm.edu.

MAY, PHYLLIS JEAN, financial executive; b. Flint, Mich., May 31, 1932; d. Bert A. and Alice C. (Rushton) Irvine; m. John May, Apr. 24, 1971 (dec. 1997). Grad., Dorsey Sch. Bus., Detroit, 1957; cert., Internat. Corr. Schs., 1959; MBA, Mich. U., Ann Arbor, 1970; cert., Nat. Tax Inst., NYC, 1978. Registered real estate agt; lic. life, auto and home ins. agt. Office mgr. Comml. Constrn. Co., Flint, 1962-68; bus. mgr. new and used car dealership Flint, 1968-70; contr. various corps., 1970-75; fiscal dir. Rubicon Odyssey Inc., Detroit, 1976-87, Wayne County Treas.'s Office, 1987-93; exec. fin. office Grosse Pointe Meml. Ch., Mich., 1993—. Acad. cons. acctg. Detroit Inst. Commerce, 1980-81; pres. small bus. specializing in adminstrv. cons. and acctg., 1982—; supr. mobile svc. stat., upholstery and home improvement businesses; owner retail bus. Pieces and Things. Pres. PTA Westwood Heights Schs., 1972; vol. Fedn. of Blind, 1974-76, Probate Ct., 1974-76; mem. citizens adv. bd. Northville Regional Psychiat. Hosp., 1988, sec., 1989-90; pres. La Renaissance Condominium Assn., Atlantic City, 1996-2000, sec., 2000-02, treas., 2004—. Recipient Meritorious Svc. award Genesee County for Youth, 1976, Excellent Performance and High Achievement award Odyssey Inc., 1981. Mem. NAFE (bd. dirs.), Am. Bus. Women's Assn. (treas. 1981, rec. sec. 1982, v.p. 1982-83, Woman of Yr. 1982), Womens Assn. Dearborn Orch. Soc., Dearborn Cmty. Art Ctr., Mich. Mental Health Assn., Internat. Platform Assn., Guild of Carillonneurs in N.Am., Pi Omicron (officer 1984-85, treas. 2002-05, state treas. 2004-06, dist. treas. 2005-06, nat. treas. 2006). Presbyterian. Business E-Mail: pmay@gpmchurch.org.

MAY, RICHARD B., psychology professor; b. Seattle, Dec. 20, 1938; s. Louie B. and Ruby J. (Simmons) M.; m. Marjorie Ann Stevenson, Aug. 25, 1962; children: Robert Tobyn, Richard Forrest. BA, Whitman Coll., 1961; MA, Claremont Grad. Sch., 1963, PhD, 1966. Asst. prof. U. Victoria, B.C., Can., 1966-71, assoc. prof. B.C., 1971-81, prof. psychology, 1981-96, prof. emeritus, 1996—; rsch. assoc. Oxford U., England, 1972-73; vis. scholar U. Utah, Salt Lake City, 1995—96. Cons. Victoria Sch. Dist., 1971-72, Dept. Human Resources, Victoria, 1974-75. Author: Application of Statistics in Behavioral Research, 1990; contbr. articles to profl. jours., chpt. to book. Mem. foster care rev. bd. State of Utah, 1997-2001; gen. mgr. RMAY Investments LLC, 2001—. Fellow Social Scis. and Humanities Rsch. Coun., 1972-73, 79-80, 86-87, USPHS, 1962-66; rsch. grantee Nat. Sci. and Engrig. Coun. Rsch., 1969-71, 71-74, 74-77. Avocations: investing, reading, internet, card games. Home: 2072 S Parkwood Cir Spokane WA 99223-5037 Personal E-mail: rb.may@comcast.net.

MAY, RICHARD WARREN, writer; b. Marlboro, Mass., Mar. 1, 1944; s. Richard and Lavinia (Crane) M. BS in Psychology, U. Mass., 1968; MA in Humanities and Philosophy, Calif. State U., Dominguez Hills, 1991. Lic. real estate broker. Tchr. Boston Pub. Schs., 1970-89; pres., founder The Aleph (formerly Promethean Pastimes), Boston, 1975—. Adv. bd. mem. and rsch. assoc. Point One Adv. Group, Inc., Madisonville, Ky. Author: (games of strategy) Game of the Gods, 1984, Trihex, 1985, Aliens and Amazons, The Game of Tetra, 1994; contbr. (anthology) Thinking on the Edge, 1993; patentee game bd. and pieces TriHex, 1988. Mem. Assn. Advance Ethical Hypnosis, West Orange, NJ, 1974-75, Boston Tchrs. Union, 1984-89, Point One Adv. Group. Fellow Internat. Soc. Philos. Enquiry (asst. historian 1981-82, diplomate); mem. Nat. Coalition of Ind. Scholars, Prometheus Soc. (past first jour. editor, ombudsman 1984-94, pres. 1991-98), Hoeflin Rsch. Group, The Mega Soc., One-in-Million Soc., Triple Nine Soc. (membership officer 1983-84, regent 1987-90), Mensa, Intertel, Am. Acad. Religion, Internat. Acad. Philosophy (bd. dirs., founder Found.), The Jewish Geneal. Soc., Omega Soc. Office: Point One Adv Group PO Box 1111 Madisonville KY 42431-0022 Personal E-mail: ferdlilac@yahoo.com.

MAY, ROBERT GEORGE, dean, accounting educator; b. Detroit, Nov. 11, 1943; s. George Joseph and Winifred Marie (Donnelly) M.; m. Carol Ann Rogers, June 18, 1965; children: Gregory Charles, Lynn Marie. BBA, Mich. State U., 1965, PhD, 1970. Asst. prof. U. Wash., Seattle, 1970-73, assoc. prof., 1973-79; prof. acctg. U. Tex., Austin, 1979—, chmn. dept. acctg., 1988-92, assoc. dean, 1992-95, interim dean, 1995-2001, dean McCombs Sch. Bus., 2001—. Vis. asst. prof. Stanford U., 1972-73; dir. Fedn. Schs. Accountancy, Athens, Ga., 1982. Co-author: Accounting, 1995, Financial Accounting, 1995, Managerial Accounting, 1995, Corporate Financial Accounting, 1995; assoc. editor: the Accounting Review Recipient Notable Contbn. to Acctg. Lit. award AICPAs, 1976; named Outstanding Alumnus, Mich. State U. Dept. Acctg., 1995. Mem. Am. Acctg. Assn. (chmn. audit sect. 1988-89, pres., adminstrs. of acctg. programs 1993-94, Innovation in Acctg. Edn. award 1991, 93). Office: McCombs Sch Bus U Tex Deans Office 21st and Speedway GSB2 104 Austin TX 78712

MAY, ROBERT MCCREDIE (LORD MAY OF OXFORD), biology educator; b. Sydney, Jan. 8, 1936; s. Henry W. and Kathleen (McCredie) M.; m. Judith Feiner, Aug. 3, 1962; 1 child, Naomi Felicity. BSc, Sydney U., 1956, PhD, 1959; DSc (hon.), City U. London, 1989, Uppsala U., 1990, Yale U., 1993, Heriot-Watt U., 1994, U. Edinburgh, 1994; DSC (hon.), U. Sydney, 1995. Gordon Mackay lectr. applied math Harvard U., Cambridge, Mass., 1959—61, mem. vis. faculty, 1966; theoretical physics lectr. Sydney U., 1962—64, reader, 1964—69, personal chair, 1969—73; prof. biology Princeton U., NJ, 1973—88; Royal Soc. rsch. prof. U. Oxford, England, 1989—, fellow Merton Coll., 1989—. Vis. faculty Calif. Inst. Tech., 1967; vis. prof. UKAEA Culham Lab., 1971, Magdalen Coll., 1971, Imperial Coll., England, 1975—95; chief sci. adviser to U.K. Govt., head U.K. Office Sci. and Tech., 1995—2000. Editor: Stability and Complexity in Model Ecosystems, 1973, Population Biology of Infectious Diseases, 1982, Theoretical Ecology: Principles and Applications, 1976, Perspectives in Ecological Theory, 1989, Infectious Diseases of Humans: Dynamics and Control, 1991, Extinction Rates, 1995. Trustee Nuffield Found., Cambridge U. Gates Trust; chmn. emeritus bd. trustees Natural History Museum; bd. mem. UK Sport Institute. Decorated Order of Australia, Knighthood; recipient MacArthur award, 1984, Linnean Medal, Linnean Soc., 1991, Christian Marsh prize, 1992, Frink medal, 1995, Crafoord prize, Royal Swedish Acad. Scis., 1996, Balzan prize, 1998, Blue Planet prize, Asahi Glass Found., 2001, Life Peerage, Ho. of Lords Appointments Commn., 2001, Order of Merit, 2002. Fellow Royal Soc. (pres. 2000-2005), Am. Acad. Arts and Scis.; mem. NAS, Athenaeum Club. Office: The Royal Society 6-9 Carlton House Terrace SW1Y 5AG London England E-mail: robert.may@zoo.ox.ac.uk.

MAY, ROBERT P., energy executive; b. May 1949; married; 5 children. Student, Harvard U. Former CEO Intelogistics divsn. Intelligence Electronics; former COO Towne Air Freight; sr. exec. FedEx Corp., 1973—94; COO, dir. Cablevision Sys. Corp., 1997—99; pres., CEO PNV Inc., 1999—2000; pvt. investor, strategic cons. for telecom. and logistics cos.; interim CEO HealthSouth Corp., Birmingham, Ala., 2003—04, non exec. chmn., 2004—05; acting pres., CEO Charter Communications, Inc., St. Louis, 2005; CEO Calpine Corp., San Jose, Calif., 2005—. Bd. dirs. HealthSouth Corp., 2002—03, Charter Communications, Inc., 2004—. With USMC. Office: Calpine Corp 50 W San Fernando St San Jose CA 95113 *

MAY, RONALD ALAN, lawyer; b. Waterloo, Iowa, Sept. 8, 1928; s. John W. and Elsie (Finlayson) M.; m. Naomi Gray, Aug. 18, 1950 (div. Feb. 1974); children: Sarah, Jonathan, Andrew, Rachel; m. Susan East Gray, May 9, 1975. BA, U. Iowa, 1950; LL.B., Vanderbilt U., 1953. Bar: Ark. 1953. Atty. Daggett & Daggett, Marianna, 1953-57, Wright, Lindsey & Jennings LLP, Little Rock, 1957-84, sr. ptnr., 1984-96; of counsel Wright, Lindsey & Jennings, LLP, 1996—. Editor: Automated Law Research, 1972, Sense and Systems in Automated Law Research, 1975; contbg. editor Fifty State Construction Lien and Bond Law, 1992, Fifty State Public Construction Contracting, 1996; assoc. editor Jour. Irreproducible Results. Pres. Spl. Com. on Pub. Edn., Ark. Assn. for Mental Health, Friends of Library, Central Ark. Radiation Therapy Inst.; chmn. Ark. Cancer Research Ctr., 1990-92; bd. dirs. Nat. Assn. for Mental Health, Ark. State Hosp., Gaines House, State Bd. Architects; bd. dirs. State Bd. Bar Examiners, chmn. 1987-88, Ark. ethics com., 1991-93; trustee Mus. Sci. and Natural History, Little Rock, chmn., 1973; mem. profl. adv. bd. sch. architecture U. Ark., 1990-96, mem. profl. adv. bd. sch. urban studies and design, 1993—; mem. instl. rev. bd. U. Ark. for Med. Scis., 2000—. Served with AUS, 1946-47. Mem. ABA (chmn. sci. and tech. sect. 1975-76), Ark., Pulaski County Bar Assns., Internat. Assn. Def. Counsel, Am. Inns of Ct. (Master of the Bench), Assn. for Computing Machinery, Chamber Music Soc. (bd. Little Rock 2006-), Order of Coif, Phi Beta Kappa. Episcopalian. Home: 821 Ash St Little Rock AR 72205-2051 Office: Wright Lindsey & Jennings LLP 200 W Capitol Ave Ste 2300 Little Rock AR 72201-3699 Office Phone: 501-371-0808. Business E-Mail: rmay@wlj.com.

MAY, STEPHEN, writer, federal official, historian; b. Rochester, NY, July 30, 1931; s. Arthur J. and Hilda (Jones) M. Grad., Wesleyan U., 1953; LLB, Georgetown U., 1961. Bar: NY 1963. Exec. asst. to Rep. and Senator Kenneth B. Keating, 1955-64; assoc., mem., then ptnr. Branch, Turner & Wise, Rochester, 1965-81; city councilman-at-large Rochester, 1966-73; mayor, 1970-73; chmn. and commr. N.Y. State Bd. Elections, Albany, 1975-79; asst. sec. for legis. and Congl. rels. Dept. Housing and Urban Devel., 1981-88; ind. historian, writer, lectr. for mags. and newspapers, 1988—. Vice chmn. Temporary State Commn. on Powers of Local Govt., 1970-73; mem. 20th Century Fund Task Force on Future of N.Y.C., 1979, Nat. Adv. Commn. Higher Edn. for Police Officers, 1977-79, Joint Com. Assn. Bar City N.Y. and Drug Abuse Coun. on N.Y. Drug Law Evaluation, 1977-78; chmn. Rochester Interfaith Com. on Israel, 1973-81; del.-at-large Rep. Nat. Conv., 1972; mem. N.Y. State Crime Control Planning Bd., 1970-73; historian, writer and lectr. on art, culture, historic preservation and travels, 1988—. Bd. dirs. Police Found., 1970-81, Nat. Com. for Labor Israel, 1977-81, Empire State Report, 1974-81, Inst. Mediation and Conflict Resolution, 1973-81. Served with U.S. Army, 1953-55. Mem. Phi Beta Kappa. Home and Office: 4101 Cathedral Ave NW Washington DC 20016-3585 also: 270 Mt Pleasant Rd Union ME 04862-3003 Office Phone: 202-362-2399, 207-785-4178. Personal E-mail: stephenmay4@yahoo.com.

MAY, STEPHEN JAMES, communications educator, writer; b. Toronto, Ont., Can., Sept. 10, 1946; s. Thomas and Claire (Thompson) M.; m. Caroline Casteel, Sept. 27, 1947; children: Trevor, Brittany. BA, Calif. State U., Carson, 1975; MA, Calif. State U., LA, 1977; DLitt, Internat. U., London, 1990. Prof. and chair dept. of English and Lit. Pikes Peak C.C., Colorado Springs, Colo., 1980-91; prof. Colo. N.W. C.C., Craig, 1992-98; chair dept. of English and Lit. Pikes Peak C.C., Colorado Springs, Colo., 1998—2001; vis. prof. U. No. Colo., 2001—; prof. English Front Range C.C., 2001—06. Advisor Internat. Biog. Ctr., Cambridge, Eng., 1989-95; vis. prof. U. Colo., 2000—; spl. cons. James A. Michener Art Mus., 2006-, James A. Michener Libr. Author: Pilgrimage, 1987, Fire From the Skies, 1990, Footloose, 1993, Zane Grey, 1997, Maverick Heart, 2000, Rascals, 2002, Michener: A Writer's Journey, 2005; contbr. articles to profl. jours. including SouthWest Art, Ohio Review, Texas Highways. Mem. Western Writers Am., Colo. Authors League, Zane Grey Soc., Soc. S.W. Authors, C.C. Humanities, James A. Mitchener Soc. Avocations: travel, writing, drawing. Home: 731 Peregrine Run Fort Collins CO 80524 Personal E-mail: stepkm@msn.com.

MAY, THOMAS J., electric company executive; BS, Stonehill Coll.; MS in Fin., Bentley Coll. Various positions Boston Edison Co., 1976-90, exec. v.p., 1990-93, pres., CEO, 1993-94, chmn., CEO, 1994-99, NStar, Boston, 1999—2002, chmn., pres., CEO, 2002—. Office: NStar MSC P 1600 800 Boylston St Boston MA 02199 *

MAY, TIMOTHY JAMES, lawyer; b. Denver, Aug. 3, 1932; s. Thomas Henry and Helen Frances (O'Conner) M.; m. Monica Anita Gross, Aug. 24, 1957; children: Stephanie, Maureen, Cynthia, Timothy, Anthony. BA, Cath. U. Am., 1954; LLB, Georgetown U., 1957, LLM, 1960. Bar: D.C. 1957, US Ct. Appeals (Armed Forces, DC, 2d, 3d cir.), U.S. Supreme Ct. 1961. Law clk. to judge U.S. Ct. Appeals, D.C. Cir., 1957-58; assoc. Covington & Burling, Washington, 1958-61; cons. Exec. Office of Pres. U.S., Washington, 1961-62; chief counsel subcom. on stockpile Armed Svcs. Com., U.S. Senate, Washington, 1962-63; mng. dir. Fed. Maritime Commn., Washington, 1963-66; gen. counsel U.S. Post Office Dept., Washington, 1966-69; ptnr., Postal Policy & Regulation, Legis. Affairs practices, Patton Boggs LLP, Washington, 1969—, mem. exec. com. Bd. dirs. Legal Aid Soc. DC, 1984—; pres. Holy Family of Bethlehem Found., 1997-99, Coun. for Ct. Excellence, Washington, 1999-2005, Marine Corps Law Enforcement Found., 1996-2003; chmn. bd. regents Cath. U. Am., 1988-93, trustee, 1993-2005, trustee emeritus, 2005—. Recipient Servant of Justice award Legal Aid Soc. D.C., 1997, St. Elizabeth Ann Seton award SOAR!, 1998, Caritas award Archdiocese D.C., 1998, Presdl. Award for Pub. Adminstrn., Jump Mem. Award. Fellow Am. Bar Found. (life); mem. ABA (ho. of dels.), Fed. Bar Assn., Bar Assn. of DC (pres. 1991-92, Lawyer of Yr. award 1999), Congl. Country Club (bd. govs. 1992-98, sec. 1994-97), Nat. Christian Leadership Conf. for Israel (exec. com. 1992-2003), Met. Club, Indian Creek Country Club (bd. dirs. 1999—, pres. 2005—07), Fed. City Coun., Econ. Club DC (bd. dirs. 2001—), Knight of Malta, Constantinian Order St. George (knight). Democrat. Roman Catholic. Home: 3828 52nd St NW Washington DC 20016-1924 Office: Patton Boggs LLP 2550 M St NW Washington DC 20037-1350 Home (Winter): 286 Bal Bay Dr Miami FL 33154 Office Phone: 202-457-6050. Office Fax: 202-457-6315. Business E-Mail: tmay@pattonboggs.com.

MAY, WILLIAM FREDERICK, manufacturing executive; b. Chgo., Oct. 25, 1915; s. Arthur W. and Florence (Hartwick) M.; m. Kathleen Thompson, June 14, 1947; children: Katherine Hartwick (Mrs. Edward W. Bickford), Elizabeth Shaw. BS, U. Rochester, 1937; grad. Advanced Mgmt. Program, Harvard U., 1950; D in Engring., Clarkson U.; LLD, Okla. Christian Coll.; LHD, Livingstone U.; LLD, Lafayette U. Rsch. worker E.I. Du Pont de Nemours Co., 1937-38; with Am. Can Co., Greenwich, Conn., 1940-80, mgr., 1957-58, v.p., 1958-64, exec. v.p., 1964-65, vice chmn. bd. dirs., 1965, chmn. bd. dirs., CEO, 1965-80, mem. exec. com., 1960—. Dean Grad. Sch. Bus. Adminstrn., NYU, 1980-84; chmn. and CEO Statue of Liberty Found., 1984—. Bd. dirs. Lincoln Ctr.; trustee Am. Ditchley Found., Am. Mus. Natural History, Columbia-Presbyn. Hosp., U. Rochester; mem. corp. Poly. Inst. N.Y.; chmn. pub. policy coun. Advt. Coun. Mem. Nat. Order of Merit (France, officier), Econ. Club, Round Hill Club, Megunticook Golf Club, Indian Harbor Yacht Club, Camden Yacht Club, Phi Beta Kappa, Alpha Delta Phi. Episcopalian. Home: 84 Indian Harbor Dr Greenwich CT 06830-7148 Office: Statue of Liberty Found 292 Madison Ave New York NY 10017-7769 Personal E-mail: wkmay@aol.com.

MAYARAM, KARTIKEYA, electrical engineer, educator; arrived in U.S., 1981; m. Namita Gandhi. BS in Engring. with honors, Birla Inst. Tech. and Sci., 1981; MS, SUNY, 1982; PhD, U. Calif., Berkeley, 1988. Mem. tech. staff Tex. Instruments Inc., Dallas, 1988—92, Bell Labs., Allentown, Pa., 1992—96; assoc. prof. Wash. State U., Pullman, Wash., 1996—99, Oreg. State U., Corvallis, Oreg., 2000—03, prof., 2003—. Cons. Mentor Graphics Corp., Wilsonville, Oreg., 1998—2001, Lucent Bell Labs., Allentown, Pa., 1996—98, Fairchild Semiconductor, San Jose, Calif., 2000—01; tech. advisor Berkeley Design Automation, Santa Clara, Calif., 2003—. Co-author: Analog Integrated Circuits for Communication: Principles, Simulation and Design. Grantee Career award, NSF, 1997—2001. Fellow: IEEE (fellow 2005). Home Phone: 541-745-6490; Office Phone: 541-737-2972. Business E-Mail: karti@eecs.oregonstate.edu.

MAYDEN, BARBARA MENDEL, lawyer; b. Chattanooga, Sept. 18, 1951; d. Eugene Lester Mendel and Blanche (Krugman) Rosenberg; m. Martin Ted Mayden, Sept. 14, 1986. AB, Ind. U., 1973; JD, U. Ga., 1976. Bar: Ga. 1976, N.Y. 1980. Assoc. King & Spalding, Atlanta, 1976-79, Willkie Farr & Gallagher, NYC, 1980, Morgan Lewis & Bockius, NYC, 1980-82, White & Case, NYC, 1982-89; spl. counsel Skadden, Arps, Slate, Meagher & Flom, NYC, 1989-95; mem. Bass, Berry & Sims PLC, Nashville, 1996—2006; lectr. Vanderbilt U. Sch. Law, Nashville, 1995-97, of counsel, 2006—. Mem. editl. bd.: mag. Business Law Today; editor: Business Lawyer; chair sect. bus. law:, 2004—05. Mem. bd. visitors U. Ga. Sch. Law, Athens, 1986—89; mem. Leadership Nashville, 1999—2000; mem. adv. bd. Women's Fund of the Cmty. Found. of Mid. Tenn., 2001—; co-pres. Nashville sect. Nat. Coun. Jewish Women, 2007—; 1st v.p. West End Synagogue, 2007—; bd. dirs. YWCA, 2001—07, Jewish Cmty. Ctr., 2001—02. Fellow Am. Bar Found. (life); mem. ABA (chair young lawyers divsn. 1985-86, ho. of dels. 1986—2004, commn. on women 1987-91, commn. opportunities for minorities in profession 1986-87, select com. of the house 1989-91, chmn. assembly resolutions com. 1990-91, membership com. of the house 1991-92, bd. govs. 1991-94, chair com. on rules and calendar 1996-98, chair bd. govs. ops. com., exec. com. 1993-94, task force long range fin. planning 1993-94, com. scope correlation of work 1998-2003, chair 2001-02, sec. bus. law sect. 2001-02, vice-chair 2002-03, chair-elect 2003-04, chair 2004—05), Nat. Assn. Bond Lawyers (bd. dirs. 1985-86), Bond Attys.' Workshop (chmn. 1986), N.Y. State Bar Assn. (ho. of dels. 1993-95), Assn. Bar City N.Y. (internat. human rights com. 1986-89, 2d century com. 1986-90, com. women in the profession, 1989-92), N.Y. County Lawyers Assn. (com. spl. projects, chair com. rels with other bars), Am. Law Inst., Tenn. Bar Assn. (com. chair), Am. Bar Ins. Plans Cons., Inc. (bd. dirs., treas.). Democrat. Jewish. Home: 4414 Herbert Pl Nashville TN 37215-4544 Office: Bass Berry & Sims PLC AmSouth Center 315 Deaderick St Ste 2700 Nashville TN 37238-3001 Office Phone: 615-742-6208. Business E-Mail: bmayden@bassberry.com.

MAYDWELL, ROBERT MASON, JR., social sciences educator; b. Bronx, NY, July 6, 1962; s. Robert Mason Maydwell, Sr.; children: Kristy Lynn, Kelly Ann, Ethan Robert. M, Ft. Hays State U., Kans., 1999. Social sci. and human svcs. instr. Iowa Western C.C., Council Bluffs, 2005—. Grants mgmt. asst. Nat. Pk. Svc., Omaha, 2005. With USN, 1983—87. Decorated Expeditionary medal US Navy-Submarine Svc.; Viva Stimits Meml. scholar, Ft. Hays State U., 1997. Mem.: Am. Legion, Phi Alpha Theta (life; historian, pres. 1994—96). Home: 319 N Linn Ave Logan IA 51546 Office: Nat Pk Svc 601 Riverfront Dr Omaha NE 68102 Home Phone: 712-644-9031; Office Phone: 402-661-1546. Personal E-mail: rmaydwell@iwcc.edu. Business E-Mail: robert_maydwell@nps.gov.

MAYEAUX, ANNE RUSSELL, education educator; b. Meridian, Miss., Aug. 27, 1943; d. Constant Hyacinth and Laura Archer Mayeaux. BA, St. Xavier U., 1961—65; PhD, Emory U., 1968—75. Dir. World Peace Ctr., Chgo., 1967—68; postdoctoral fellow and adj. faculty Candler Sch. of Theology, Atlanta, 1975—81. Exec. dir. Ga. Endowment for the Humanities, 1979—81; faculty and pres. Aquinas Ctr. of Theology at Emory U., Atlanta, 1983—90; vis. scholar in ethics and soc. Harvard Div. Sch., Cambridge, Mass., 1990—91; assoc. prof. Siena Heights U., Adrian, Mich., 1991—96; rschr. Inst. for Social Rsch., U. of Mich., 1996—99; chair, theology dept., and faculty St. Joseph, Madison, Miss., 1999—; adj. faculty Hinds C.C., Jackson, Miss., 2000—. Contbr. articles to jours. Pres. Las Casas, Nat. Ministry among the Native Americans, Clinton, Okla., 1989—93; bd. dirs. Nat. Assembly of Religious Women, Chgo., 1991—94; sec./treas. Internat. Found. for Scholarly Exch., Atlanta, 1988—94. Recipient Human Rights Citation, Dominican Justice Promoters of N.Am., 1991, Outstanding Tchg. of the Yr., Siena Heights U., 1992—93, Internat. Del. of Scholars to Russia and the Ukraine, People to People and Am. Acad. of Religion, 1993, Outstanding Tchg., Archdiocese of Atlanta, 1983—84, Catharine of Siena award, St. Catharine's Dominican Congregation, 1990, Citation for Courage for Human Rights Work in Gulf War, U.S. Dominican Leadership Conf., 1991; Catherine McAuley scholar, St. Xavier U., 1965, Raskob Found. grant, Raskob Found., 1992—94, N.E.H. Landmarks of Am. History: Summer Inst., Nat. Endowment for the Humanities, 2004, grant, 2002, Fulbright Scholar, U. of Tuebingen, German, Fulbright

Commn., 1966—67. Mem.: AAUP (v.p., siena heights u. chpt. 1995), Am. Acad. of Religion (chair, program sect., s.e. region 1975—91). Democrat-Npl. Roman Catholic. Home: 217 Melrose Dr Jackson MS 39211 Home Phone: 601-206-8002.

MAYER, ALLAN, communications consultant, writer; b. NYC, Mar. 15, 1950; s. Theodore H. and Phyllis (Zwick) M. BA, Cornell U., 1971. Staff reporter Wall Street Jour., NYC, 1972-73; assoc. editor, gen. editor Newsweek mag., NYC, 1973-77, fgn. corr. London, 1977-80, sr. editor NYC, 1980-82; editl. dir. Arbor House Pub., NYC, 1986-88; sr. editor Simon & Schuster, NYC, 1988-89; editor-in-chief Buzz mag., LA, 1990-95, editor-in-chief, pub., 1996; sr. ptnr. Sitrick and Co., LA, 1997—2004, mng. dir., 2004—06; ptnr. 42 West LLC, LA, 2006—. Author: Madam Prime Minister, 1980, Gaston's War: A True Story of a Hero of the Resistance in World War II, 1987; co-author: (with Michael S. Sitrick) Spin: How to Turn the Power of the Press to Your Advantage, 1998. Recipient award Overseas Press Club, 1974, Nat. Mag. award Am. Soc. Mag. Editors, 1978, William Allen White award City and Regional Mag. Assn., 1995-96. Mem. Writers Guild Am. Personal E-mail: allan.mayer@42west.net.

MAYER, ANTHONY JOHN, investment company executive; b. Milw., Apr. 21, 1936; s. Anton J. and Mary (Plensk) Mayer. BS in Bus., Marquette U., 1958, advanced degree in Bus., 1965. Registered investment adv., 1994; cert. nutritionist 2000. Adminstrv. mgr. Marquette U., 1960—63; ins. claims exec., 1962—65; founder Fixed Income Mutual Fund, Milw., 1968—; motel exec., 1968—80; pvt. investor, 1968—; pres. Anthony J. Mayer, Inc., Milw., 1994—, Tunica Southern Belle Project, 1995—98; v.p. Banc One Investment Mgmt. Group, Chgo., 2001—07. Founder Fixed Income Fund, Milw., 1968—; chmn. Westridge Investors, 1998—2007, New Berlin Investors, 1998—2007, Millionaire Investor Entities Guidance.Com, 2000—07, Hungarian Investors Com., 2003; country music seminar host, 1995; reporter Election Ctrl., 1973. Anthony J. Mayer Investment Parables, 1995, Anthony J. Mayer Investment Advisory Book, 2003; author, editor, newsletter: Anthony J. Mayer Investment Bible, 1995;; columnist: Alaska newspapers, 1959—60; investment radio personality, 1990—93; prodr.: (plays) Surviving Without Love, 2001; contbr. articles to profl. jours. Vol. ARC, 1961—62; del. Adv. Coun. Nat. Rep. Congl. Com., 2001—; mem. Rep. Nat. Com., 2005—; chmn. adv. bd. Nat. Rep. Party, 2004—; hon. sponsor Pres. Bush victory dinner, 2001; grassroots leader Rep. Campaign, 2004; primary election candidate for gov. Wis., 2006; active Heritage Inner Cir., 1999—; bd. dirs. West Allis Food for Milw., 1997—2007, First Mcpl. Credit Union, 1996—2001, Mukwonago State Bank, Wis., 2006—; trustee Jesuit Ptnrs., 1998—; pres. Pub. Lands Decor Classics, 2000—07. With US Army, 1958—60. Named Successful Investor of Yr., Sta. WGN, 1996, Notable Pulaskian, Milw. Pub. Sch. Sys., 1999, Hon. Regional Chmn., Nat. Rep. Com., 2007; recipient VIP award, Speedway-Super Am., 1995, Cleve. Meadows Achievement award, 1998, VIP award, Speedway-Super Am., 2000, Commendation cert., State of Wis., 2002, Animal Stewardship award, 2002, Cmty. Svc. award, Jerusalem Christian, 2003. Mem.: N.Am. Investors Alliance (founder, chmn. 1993), Rep. Govs. Assn., Aircraft Owners Assn., Acad. Country Music, Country Music Assn., KC. Roman Catholic. Avocation: reading. Office Phone: 414-321-7126.

MAYER, CARL JOSEPH, prosecutor, lawyer, educator; b. Boston, Apr. 23, 1959; s. Arno Joseph and Nancy Sue (Grant) M. AB magna cum laude, Princeton U., 1981; JD, U. of Chgo., 1986; LLM, Harvard U., 1988. Bar: N.J. 1986, Mass. 1988, N.Y. 1989, D.C. 1989. Writer for Ralph Nader, Washington, 1981-83; law clk. to presiding justice U.S. Dist. Ct., Wilmington, Del., 1986-87; prof. law Hofstra Law Sch., Hempstead, NY, 1989-94; atty. Milberg, Weiss, Bershad, Hynes and Lerach, NYC, 1995-96; spl. counsel N.Y. State Atty. Gen.'s Office, NYC, 1999—2000; pvt. practice Mayer Law Group, LLC, 2000—. Cons. U.S. Senate Com., Washington, 1988-89. Author: Shakedown, 1998; co-author: Public Domain, Private Dominion, 1985; contbr. articles to profl. jours. Town committeeman, Princeton, N.J., 1995-98. NYU fellow, 1988-89. Mem. ABA, N.Y. Bar Assn., N.J. Bar Assn., Mass. Bar Assn. Avocations: running, squash, tennis. Home: 58 Battle Rd Princeton NJ 08540-4902 Office: Mayer Law Group LLC 1040 Ave of Americas Ste 2400 New York NY 10018 Office Phone: 212-382-4686. E-mail: cyberesquire@aol.com.

MAYER, CHRISTOPHER, lawyer; b. Phila., Feb. 21, 1946; BA, Princeton U., 1968; JD, Columbia U., 1974. Bar: N.Y. 1975. Assoc. Davis Polk & Wardell, NYC, 1974—82, ptnr., 1982—, mem. firm mgmt. com., 1992—2005. Mem. ABA, N.Y. State Bar Assn., Assn. of Bar of City of N.Y. Office: Davis Polk & Wardwell 450 Lexington Ave New York NY 10017-3982 Office Phone: 212-450-4338. Office Fax: 212-450-3338. Business E-Mail: chris.mayer@dpw.com.

MAYER, FREDERICK RICKARD, oil industry executive; b. Youngstown, Ohio, Jan. 25, 1928; s. Frederick Miller and Mildred Kathryn (Rickard) M.; m. Jan MacCasler Perry, Nov. 1, 1958; children: Frederick MacCasler, Anthony Rickard, Perry Ellen. BA, Yale U., 1950. Founder, pres. Exeter Drilling Co., Dallas and Denver, 1953-70, chmn. bd., chief exec. officer, 1970-80. Chmn. bd., dir. Exeter Drilling No., Inc., Denver, Exeter Drilling So., Inc., New Orleans, until 1982 Chmn. Wallace Village for Children, 1971-74; trustee Graland Country Day Sch., 1973-79; mem. arts adv. com. Phillips Exeter Acad., 1974—, trustee, 1980—; trustee Denver Art Museum, 1970-, v.p., 1971-75, chmn. bd. trustees, 1975-79, interim chmn. bd. trustees, 1980-81; trustee Am. Fedn. Arts, 1977-81, Nat. Gallery, 1983—; founder JFM Foundation, Denver. Served with U.S. Army, 1950-52. Named one of Top 200 Collectors, ARTnews Mag., 2004, 2006. Mem. Ind. Petroleum Assn. Am. (exec. com.), Chief Execs. Forum, Metro Denver Exec. Club, Am. Petroleum Inst. (bd. dirs.), Ind. Petroleum Assn. Mountain States (Rocky Mountain Wildcatter of Yr. award 1983), 25 Yr. Club of Petroleum Industry, Nat. Petroleum Council, Inst. Nautical Archaeology (bd. dirs. 1981-85, chmn. bd. 1985—). Clubs: Cherry Hills Country, Univ. of Denver, Garden of Gods, Castle Pines Golf, Denver and Dallas Petroleum, N.Y. Yacht. Avocation: Collector of Colonial and Latin American art. Home: PO Box 481150 Denver CO 80248-1150 Office: Exeter Drilling Co PO Box 5083 Denver CO 80217-5083 also: 1700 Lincoln St Suite 5000 Denver CO 80203

MAYER, GEORGE ROY, education educator; b. National City, Calif, Aug. 28, 1940; s. George Eberly and Helen Janet (Knight) M.; m. Barbara Ann Fife, Sept. 9, 1964 (div. June 1986); children: Kevin Roy, Debbie Rae Ann; m. Jocelyn Volk Finn, Aug. 3, 1986 (div. July 2003); m. Mary Rossetti, Sept. 22, 2005 BA, San Diego State U., 1962; MA, Ind. U., 1965, EdD, 1966. Cert. sch. psychologist; bd. cert. behavior analyst. Sch. counselor, psychologist Ind. U., Bloomington, 1964-66; asst. prof. guidance and ednl. psychology So. Ill. U., Carbondale, 1966-69; profl. edn. Calif. State U., LA, 1966—. Cons. in field; adv. bd. Dept. Spl. Edn., L.A., 1986-90, Jay Nolan Ctr. for Autism, Newhall, Calif., 1975-86; lectr. in field; study group on youth violence prevention Nat. Ctr. for Injury Prevention and Control, Divsn. Violence Prevention of the Ctrs. for Disease Control and Prevention, 1998. Author: Classroom Mgmt.: A Calif. Resource Guide, 2000, Teaching Alternative Behaviors Schoolwide: Preventing Schoolwide Behavior Problems, 2003; co-author: Behavior Analysis for Lasting Change, 1991, Gang Violence Prevention & Intervention Strategies for Schools, 2006; contbr. articles to profl. jour. Recipient Outstanding Prof. award Calif. State U.-L.A., 1988; U.S. Dept. Edn. grantee, 1996—. Mem. Assn. for Behavior Analysis, Nat. Assn. Sch. Psychologists, Calif. Assn. Behavior Analysis (hon. life, pres., conf. chmn., Outstanding Contbr. to Behavior Analysis award 1997), Cambridge Ctr. for Behavioral Studies (adv. bd.), Calif. Assn. Sch. Psychologists (chmn. practitioners conf. 1994—). Avocations: horseback riding, fishing, swimming. Home: 10735 Frank Daniels Way San Diego CA 92131- Office Phone: 858-361-1993. Personal E-mail: grmayer@aol.com.

MAYER, GERARD J., physician; b. Buenos Aires, Nov. 8, 1942; Came to the U.S., 1968. s. Ludwig and Yvonne (Moritz) M.; m. Nicole Paulette Wolf, July 23, 1971; children: Daniella, Marc. BA, Saint Andrews Scots Sch., Olivos, Argentina, 1960; MD, U. Buenos Aires, 1967. Diplomate Am. Bd. Pediatrics. Intern pediatrics Michael Reese Hosp., Chgo., 1968-69, resident in pediatrics, 1969-70, Montefiore Med. Ctr., Bronx, NY, 1970-71, Strong Meml. Hosp., U. of Rochester, NY, 1971-72; fellow in pediatrics St. Christopher's Hosp. for Children, Phila., 1972-74; attending physician Montefiore Hosp., Bronx, 1974—, North Central, Bronx, 1976-98; pvt. practice Yorktown Heights, NY, 1985—; head pediatric emergency Montefiore-NCB, Bronx, 1978-83; head pediatric primary care North Central Bronx Hosp., 1978-85; attending physician No. Westchester Hosp., Mount Kisco, NY, 1986—. Fellow Am. Acad. Pediatrics. Home: 60 Old Aspetong Rd Katonah NY 10536-3845 Office: 1880 Commerce St Yorktown Heights NY 10598 Office Phone: 914-962-5556.

MAYER, HALDANE ROBERT, federal judge; b. Buffalo, Feb. 21, 1941; s. Haldane Rupert and Myrtle Kathleen Mayer; m. Mary Anne McCurdy, Aug. 13, 1966; children: Anne Christian, Rebecca Paige. BS, US Mil. Acad., 1963; JD, Coll. William and Mary, 1971. Bar: Va. 1971, DC 1980, US Ct. Appeals (4th cir.) 1972, US Dist. Ct. (ea. dist.) Va. 1972, US Ct. Mil. Appeals 1973, US Supreme Ct. 1977, US Ct. Claims 1984. Law clk. US Ct. Appeals (4th cir.), Richmond, Va., 1971—72; atty. McGuire Woods & Battle, Charlottesville, Va., 1975—77; spl. asst. to chief justice US Supreme Ct., Washington, 1977—80; atty. Baker & McKenzie, Washington, 1980—81; acting spl. counsel US Merit Systems Protection Bd., Washington, 1981—82; judge US Claims Ct., Washington, 1982—87, US Ct. Appeals (Fed. cir.), Washington, 1987—, chief judge, 1997—2004. Adj. prof. U. Va. Sch. Law, 1975—77, 1992—94, George Washington U. Law Sch., 1992—96. Bd. dirs. William and Mary Law Sch. Assn., 1979—85. Maj. US Army, 1963—75, ret. lt. col. USAR. Decorated Bronze Star. Mem.: West Point Soc. DC, Army Athletic Assn., West Point Assn. Grads., Omicron Delta Kappa. Office: US Ct Appeals for Fed Cir 717 Madison Pl NW Washington DC 20439-0002 Office Phone: 202-633-6556. *

MAYER, IRA EDWARD, gastroenterologist; b. Bklyn., July 31, 1951; s. Elias M. and Mollie (Taxerman) M.; m. Celeste Ann Sivak, Mar. 13, 1976; children: Madelaine Rose, Amanda Beth. BS, Bklyn. Coll., 1972; MD, N.Y. Med. Coll., 1975. Diplomate Am. Bd. Internal Medicine, Am. Bd. Gastroenterology, Nat. Bd. Med. Examiners. Asst. resident in internal medicine N.Y. Med. Coll./Met. Hosp. Ctr., NYC, 1975-76, resident in internal medicine, 1976-78; fellow digestive diseases divsn. Emory U., Atlanta, 1978-80; attending gastroenterologist Maimonides Med. Ctr., Bklyn., 1980—, pres. med. staff, 2005—07; clin. instr. medicine SUNY Health Sci. Ctr., Bklyn., 1980-81, instr. medicine, 1981-83, clin. asst. prof. medicine, 1983—2002, chmn. patient care com., 1984-99; clin. asst. prof. medicine Mt. Sinai Sch. Medicine, 2003—. Author: (with others) Digestive Diseases, 1983, Medicine, 1983; contbr. articles to profl. jours. Fellow ACP, Am. Coll. Gastroenterology; mem. Am. Gastroent. Assn., Am. Soc. for Gastrointestinal Endoscopy, N.Y. Acad. Scis., N.Y. Acad. Gastroenterolgy, N.Y. Soc. for Gastrointestinal Endoscopy, Med. Soc. for the State of N.Y. Jewish. Office: 575 Kings Hwy Brooklyn NY 11223-2046 Office Phone: 718-891-0100.

MAYER, JAMES HOCK, lawyer, mediator; b. Neptune City, NJ, Nov. 1, 1935; s. J. Kenneth and Marie Ruth (Hock) M.; m. Carol I. Keating, Sept. 20, 1958 (div. Feb. 1981); children: Craig, Jeffrey; m. Patrisha Renk, Mar. 28, 1981 (div. July 2001); m. Judith Courtemanche, Mar. 23, 2004. AB with distinction, Dartmouth Coll., 1957; JD, Harvard U., 1964. Bar: Calif. 1965, U.S. Dist. Ct (no. dist., so. dist.) Calif. 1965, U.S. Ct. Appeals (9th cir.) 1965, U.S. Supreme Ct. 1974. Assoc. Pillsbury, Madison & Sutro, San Francisco, 1964—72, ptnr., 1973—; ind. mediator, 1992—. Rear adm. USNR, 1957-93. Rufus Choate scholar Dartmouth Coll., 1956-57. Mem. Newcomen Soc., Navy League, Naval Order of U.S., Naval War Coll. Found. (regional v.p.), Harvard Club, La Jolla Country Club, La Jolla Beach and Tennis Club. Office: Mayer Mediation Svcs 7924 Ivanhoe Ave Ste 3 La Jolla CA 92037 Home: 2370 Avenida de La Playa La Jolla CA 92037 Office Phone: 858-551-5525. Business E-Mail: just-results@msn.com.

MAYER, JAMES JOSEPH, retired corporate lawyer; b. Cin., Nov. 27, 1938; s. Cletus Joseph and Berna Mae (Schroeder) M.; m. Margaret Ann Hobbs, Oct. 24, 1964; children: Kimberly, Susanne, Terri. BEE, U. Cin., 1961; JD, No. Ky. U., 1969. Registered profl. engr., Ohio. Bar: Ohio 1969, Ky. 1975. Engr. Cin. Gas & Electric Co., 1961-69, atty., 1969-85, gen. counsel, 1986-91, v.p., gen. counsel, 1991-95, ret., 1995; of counsel Taft, Stetinius & Hollister, Cin., 1995—. With USAFR, 1961-64. Mem. Ohio Bar Assn., Ky. Bar Assn., Cin. Bar Assn., Terrace Park Country Club. Republican. Roman Catholic. Avocations: home remodeling, sports, golf. Office Phone: 513-381-2838. Business E-Mail: mayer@taftlaw.com.

MAYER, JOHN, musician; b. Bridgeport, Conn., Oct. 16, 1977; Student, Berklee Coll. Music. Singer: (albums) Inside Wants Out, 1999, Room for Squares, 2001, Any Given Thursday, 2003, Heavier Things, 2003, As/is, 2004, Continuum, 2006 (Best Pop Vocal Album, Grammy Awards, 2007); singer: (with John Mayer Trio) Try! John Mayer Trio Live In Concert, 2005; composer: (films) Serendipity, 2001, Vanilla Sky, 2001, How to Deal, 2003, Win a Date with Tad Hamilton!, 2004; exec. prodr.: (TV series) John Mayer Has a TV Show, 2004; monthly columnist Esquire mag., 2004—. Named one of The World's Most Influential People, TIME mag., 2007; recipient Best Male Pop Vocal Performance (Your Body is A Wonderland), Grammy Awards, 2002, Song of the Yr. (Daughters), 2005, Best Male Pop Vocal Performance (Waiting on the World To Change), 2007. Office: Creative Artists Agy c/o Scott Clayton 3310 West End Ave 5th Fl Nashville TN 37203 *

MAYER, JOYCE HARRIS, artist; b. NYC, May 7, 1935; d. Harold and Dorothy Harris; m. Bernard Charles Mayer, Mar. 15, 1969; 1 child, Robert Charles. AAS, Inst. of Applied Art and Sci., NYC, 1957. Sketcher Merrylen Cartooning Studio, 1952. Client contact, layout artist, Haire Publ., NYC, 1957-59; art dir., Real Estate Forum, NYC, 1959-60; Denhard and Stewart, NYC, 1960-67; Herb Lubalin Graphic Art Award, 1964; self employed NYC, 1967-71; co curator, New Orleans Mus. of Art, 1985. Among first women to have work pub. in Art Direction, 1964, exhibitions include NY Inst. of Applied Arts and Sci., New Orleans Mus. of Art, 2003, Horizon Gallery, Royal Typographers, NY, Nat. Arts Club, Tulane Univ., Dominican Coll., Robinson Gallery, Mario Villa and Arthur Roger, New Orleans, TWEED Gallery, Plainfield, N.J., Barbara Gillman Gallery, Miami, Contemporary Art Ctr., New Orleans, Bruce Mus., Conn., Historic New Orleans Collection, N.C. Mus. Art, LBI Found. Arts and Sci. NJ, Cheltenham Art Ctr., Pa., Long Beach Island Nat. Exhbn., 2004, NJ Print Coun. Traveling Internat. Competition, 2005, AIR Gallery, Chelsea, NY, 2006, Spring Bull Gallery, Newport, RI, 2006, Represented in permanent collections paintings, mono prints, and digital art in numerous collections in Europe and U.S., Digital La., Contemporary Art Ctr., New Orleans, 2002, Biennale Internazionale dell Arte Contemporanea, Florence, Italy, 2003, NC Mus. Art, numerous others. Mem. Bd. Edn., Greenwich, Conn., 1978; art advisor Freeport McMoRan Art Collection, New Orleans, 1985; curator Mario Villa Gallery, New Orleans, 1989; juror Arts Coun., New Orleans, 1990. Recipient Chiam Gross sculpture award, 1967, N.Y. Graphic Soc. award, 1976, medal in photography, Florence Biennale, 2003, Otis B. Morse Meml. award, Am. Coll., Pa., 2005, Silicon Gallery Fine Art award, 2006. Mem. Medici Coll. Art Assn., Am. Color Print Soc., The Print Ctr., Nat. Assn. Women Artists. Avocations: reading, theater, ballet, birdwatching. Studio: 8 Golfview Dr Medford NJ 08055 Office Phone: 609-953-2390. Personal E-mail: joycehmayer@aol.com.

MAYER, KENNETH HUGH, physician; b. NYC, Dec. 27, 1950; BA, U. Pa., 1972; MD, Northwestern U., 1977; postgrad., New Eng. Epidemiology Inst., 1991. Diplomate Am. Bd. Internal Medicine, Am. Bd. Infectious Diseases, lic. Rhode Island, 1983, Mass., 1978. Intern, jr. and sr. resident in internal medicine Beth Israel Hosp., Boston, 1977—80; clin. fellow in infectious diseases Brigham and Women's Hosp., Boston, 1980—81, rsch. fellow in infectious diseases, 1981—83; rsch. fellow dept. microbiology and molecular genetics Harvard Med. Sch., Boston, 1981—83; assoc. staff mem. Norwood Hosp., Mass., 1980—83; staff physician, rsch. med. dir. Fenway Cmty. Health, Boston, 1980; attending physician Beth Israel Hosp., 1981—; infectious disease specialist, staff physician Meml. Hosp., Pawtucket, RI, 1983—2001, assoc. microbiologist, 1983—2001, chief infectious disease divsn., 1984—2001; physician Miriam Hosp., Providence, 2001—. Clin. rsch. assoc. dept. cmty. medicine Northwestern U. Med. Sch., Chgo., 1974-77; adj. asst. prof. microbiology U. RI, Kingstown, 1988; adj. asst. prof. epidemiology U. Mass., Amherst, 1986-89, adj. assoc. prof., 1989; asst. prof. medicine divsn. biology and medicine Sch. Medicine Brown U., Providence, 1983-88, dir. AIDS Program, 1987, assoc. prof. medicine and cmty. health, 1989-93, prof., 1993—; lectr. continuing edn. Northeastern U., Boston, 1983; lab. instr. infectious disease pathophysiology Harvard Med. Sch., Boston, 1982, clin. instr. medicine, 1983; mem. Mayor's Ad Hoc Com. on AIDS, Boston, 1982-86; cons. RI State Dept. of Health Adv. Group on AIDS, 1983-87, Mass. Dept. Health, 1983-87, Health AIDS exec. task force NIH, 1986-87, Ctrs. for Disease Ctrl. and Prevention, 2006; bd. dirs. Internat. AIDS Prospective Epidemiology Network, 1985; mem. transfusion medicine curriculum rev. com. program in medicine Brown, 1985; mem. HIV program adv. com. RI Dept. Health, 1989-01; vis. scientist Clin. Rsch. Ctr., MIT, 1990; mem. sci. adv. com. Am. Found. for AIDS Rsch., 1990, bd. dirs.; Paul J. Galkin lectr., Brown U., Providence, 2001; cons. in field; mem. epidemiology and tech. transfer AIDS rsch. rev. com. NIAID, 1991-, internat. sci. com. 2d, 3d, 4th and 5th Internat. Confs. Prevention of Infection, Nice, France, 1992, 94, 96, 98, 1991-; chair Am. Found. AIDS Rsch., 1991-; co-chair Clin. Rsch. Com., 1991-; mem. AIDS com. Infectious Dsiease Soc. Am., 1998-; mem. steering com. HIV Medicine Assn., 1998-; mem. biomed. prevention track com. 4th IAS Conf. HIV Pathogenesis, Treatment and Prevention, Sydney, 2006; mem. program com. US Dept. Vets. Affairs, 2005, sci. program com. 1st Nat. Conf. AIDS Soc. India, 2005; mem. microbicides sci. adv. bd. Internat. Partnership, 2005; mem. health action AIDS adv. bd. exec. com. Physicians Human Rights, 2005; program com. mem. Track C, 2005; HIV/AIDS prevention sci. working group Office AIDS Rsch., NIH, 2005; mem., chair various other coms. Mem. editl. bd. Brown U. STD Report, 1987, Case and Consensus, 1988, AIDS Alert, 1990, Jour. Clin. Microbiology, 1991, Opportunistic Infections in HIV Infected Patients, 1992, AIDS Patient Care and STDs, 1996, 2006, LGBT Health Rsch., 2006; med. editor AIDS/HIV Treatment Directory, 1992; mem. internat. editl. adv. com. Actualizaciones en Sida, 1994, Atualizacao em AIDS, 1995; mem. editl. adv. com. Clin. Microbiology and Infection, 1995; reviewer various jours.; contbr. articles, abstracts to profl. publs., chpts. to books. Fellow Wayland Collegium, Brown U., 1991-;, ctr. alcohol and addiction studies Brown U., 1991-; recipient Cmty. Svc. award Search for A Cure, Boston, 1998, AIDS Leadership award, RI Cmty. Planning Group, 1998, Dean's Tchg. Excellence award Brown U., Providence, 2001, 04, Med. Achievement award AIDS Project RI Ann. Meeting, Warwick, 2002; Triannamed one of Best Doctors in Am. 2003-04, 2003; Grantee NIH, 1983, 87—. R.I. Found., 1983, 87-88, Schering Corp., 1984, Squibb Pharms., 1984, Miles Pharms., 1985, 86, Commonwealth of Mass., 1985, Ctrs. Disease Control, 1985, 91, Brown U., 1986, 91, Rhone-Poulenc Pharms., 1986, Warner-Lambert Pharms., 1987, 90, Nat. Inst. Allergy and Infectious Diseases, 1987, Genetic Systems, Inc., 1987-88, Cambridge Biosci. Corp., 1987-88, Searle, Inc., 1988, Health Resources and Svc. Adminstrn., 1988-91, 96-98, Ctrs. Disease Control, 1988-91, 96—, Abbott Labs., 1989, Bristol-Myers Pharm., 1989, Integra Inst./NIMH, 1989, World AIDS Found., 1990, Am. Found. AIDS Rsch., 1990, 91, Glaxo Pharm., 1993, Upjohn Pharm., 1993, Nat. Inst. Allergy and Infectious Diseases, 1995, 96-97, Immune Response Corp., 1996, Nat. Insts. Drug Abuse, 1997-98, Gilead Scis., 1997-98, Triangle Pharms., 1998, Nat. Insts. Allergy and Infectious Disease, 1999, 2000, 01, Ea. Va. Med. Sch., 2003, Fogarty Internat. Ctr. AIDS Internat. Rsch. and Tng. Program, 2005, Mass. Dept. Pub. Health Sexually Transmitted Diseases/HIV Prevention Tng. Ctr., 2006; recipient Gov.'s Recognition award for AIDS Rsch., Commonwealth of Mass., 1986, Cmty. Recognition award AIDS Action Com., Boston, 1990. Fellow ACP; mem. APHA, AAAS, Am. Fedn. for Clin. Rsch., Am. Soc. Microbiology, Assn. Practitioners in Infection Control, Am. Venereal Disease Assn., Infectious Disease Soc. Am. (AIDS com. 1993), Soc. Epidemiol. Rsch., Internat. AIDS Soc., Internat. Soc. Infectious Diseases, Internat. Acad. Sex Rsch., Soc. Hosp. Epidemiology, Immunocompromised Host Soc., Soc. Hosp. Epidemiologists Am. (AIDS/TB com. 1993), Indian Med. Assn. (hon. life mem. Chennai ctrl. br.). Jewish. Office: Miriam Hosp 164 Summit Ave Providence RI 02906 Home: 1313 Washington St Apt 713 Boston MA 02118 Office Phone: 401-793-4710. Business E-Mail: kenneth_mayer@brown.edu.

MAYER, MARGARET ELLEN, medical coding specialist; d. Theodore Robert and Doris Jane Mayer; children: J. Bradford Bellamy, Christian D. Bellamy, Stephen J. Bellamy. Student, Towson U., Md.; AA, Essex CC, Balt., 1990. Coding and data mgr. Union Hosp. Cecil County, Elkton, Md.; coding specialist Johns Hopkins Bayview Med. Ctr., Balt., Greater Balt. Med. Ctr., Towson. Cons. Receivables OutSourcing, Inc., Tominium, Md., FMAS Corp., Columbia, Md., Quadra Med. Corp., Bethlehem, Pa. Docent Md. Zoo, Balt., 2005; mem. gov.'s team Md. Rep. Party, 2006. Mem.: Am. Health Info. Mgmt. Assn. (cert. coding specialist), Phi Theta Kappa. Republican. Methodist. Avocations: equestrian events, painting, history, wildlife conservation, beekeeping. Office: Union Hosp Cecil County 106 Bow St Elkton MD 21921

MAYER, MARISSA ANN, information technology executive; b. Wausau, Wis., May 30, 1975; BS with honors in Symbolic Sys., Stanford U., MS in Computer Sci. With UBS rsch. lab, Zurich, Switzerland, SRI Internat., Menlo Park, Calif.; programmer, software engr. Google Inc., 1999, dir. consumer web products Mountain View, v.p. search products & user experience. Tchr. computer programming Stanford U. Named one of 25 Masters of Innovation, BusinessWeek, 2006, America 's Top Women in Bus.-Game Changers, Pink mag. & Forté Found., 2007; recipient Centennial Tchg. award, Stanford U., Forsythe award. Office: Google Inc 1600 Amphitheatre Pky Mountain View CA 94043 Office Phone: 650-253-0000. Office Fax: 650-253-0001. E-mail: marissa@google.com. *

MAYER, MARTIN PRAGER, writer; b. NYC, Jan. 14, 1928; s. Henry and Ruby (Prager) M.; m. Ellen Moers, June 23, 1949 (dec. Aug. 1979); children: Thomas, James; m. Karin Lissakers, Oct. 25, 1980; children: Fredrica, Henry. AB, Harvard U., 1947; D.Litt. (hon.), Wake Forest U., 1977, Adelphi U., 1981. Reporter, N.Y. Jour. Commerce, 1947-48; asst. editor Labor and Nation, 1948-49; editor Hillman Periodicals, 1949-51; assoc. editor Esquire mag., 1951-54, record critic, 1952-75; freelance writer, 1954—; N.Y. critic Opera Mag. (Eng.), 1985—2004; columnist American Banker, 1987-89. Rsch. dir. study of internat. secondary edn. Twentieth Century Fund, 1965-66; cons. Am. Council Learned Socs., 1961-63, Twentieth Century Fund, Carnegie Found., Ford Found., Sloan Found., Kettering Found. Author: (novel) The Experts, 1955, Wall Street, Men and Money, 2d edit., 1960, Madison Avenue, USA, 1958, A Voice

That Fills the House, 1959, The Schools, 1961, Where, When and Why, Social Studies in American Schools, 1963, The Lawyers, 1967, Emory Buckner, 1968, Diploma, 1968, (with Cornell Capa) New Breed on Wall Street, 1969, Bricks, Mortar and the Performing Arts, 1970, All You Know Is Facts, 1970, The Teachers Strike, 1970, About Television, 1972, The Bankers, 1975, Conflicts of Interest: Broker-Dealer Firms, 1975, Today and Tomorrow in America, 1976, The Builders, 1978, (novel) Trigger Points, 1979, The Fate of the Dollar, 1980, The Met: One Hundred Years of Grand Opera, 1983, The Diplomats, 1983, The Money Bazaars, 1984, (with G. Fitzgerald) Grandissimo Pavarotti, 1986, Making News, 1987, Markets, 1988, The Greatest Ever Bank Robbery, 1990, Whatever Happened to Madison Avenue?, 1991, Stealing the Market, 1992, Nightmare on Wall Street, 1993, (with Elizabeth Luessenshop) Risky Business, 1995, The Bankers: The Next Generation, 1997, Risk Reduction in the New Financial Architecture, 1999, The Fed, 2001, The Judges, 2007. Mem. Pres.'s Panel on Ednl. Research and Devel., 1961-66; mem. edn. com. Music Critics Assn., 1978-82; chmn. N.Y.C. Local Sch. Bd., 1962-67; commr. Nat. Commn. on Reform Secondary Edn., 1972-73; bd. visitors Wake Forest U., 1972-87; mem. Pres.'s Commn. on Housing, 1981-82. Guest scholar Brookings Instn., 1993—. Mem.: Century (N.Y.C.); Gardiner's Bay (Shelter Island, N.Y.). Democrat. Jewish. Address: PO Box 478 Shelter Island NY 11964-0478 Office Phone: 631-749-0610. Personal E-mail: mmayer2A1@netscape.net.

MAYER, MICHAEL, theater director; b. Washington, May 27, 1960; Ed., NYU. Dir.: (films) A Home at the End of the World, 2004, Flicka, 2006; (Broadway plays) Triumph of Love, 1997, A View from the Bridge, 1997 (Drama Desk award outstanding direction of play, 1998), Side Man, 1998 (Drama Desk award outstanding direction of play, 1998), You're a Good Man, Charlie Brown, 1999, The Lion in Winter, 1999, Uncle Vanya, 2000, An Almost Holy Picture, 2002, Thoroughly Modern Millie, 2002 (Drama Desk award outstanding direction of a musical, 2002), After the Fall, 2004, 'night Mother, 2004, Spring Awakening, 2006 (Outer Critics Cir. award Spring Awakening, 2007, Drama Desk award outstanding dir. of a musical, 2007, Tony award best direction of a musical, 2007), (off-Broadway) The Credeaux Canvas, Stupid Kids, Antigone in New York, Baby Anger, View of the Dome, Missing Persons, America Dreaming, Hundreds of Hats, (nat. tour) Angels in America. *

MAYER, MICHEL, computer company executive; b. France; Ingenieur, Ecole Superieure d'Electricite, Paris. Engring. & mgmt. positions through gen. mgr. IBM, 1984—2001, mem. worldwide mgmt. council; gen. mgr. IBM Microelectronics, 2001—04; chmn., CEO Freescale Semiconductor Inc., Austin, Tex., 2004—. Bd. dir. Semiconductor Ind. Assn. Office: Freescale Semiconductor 6501 William Cannon Dr W Austin TX 78735

MAYER, MORRIS LEHMAN, marketing educator; b. Demopolis, Ala., Dec. 14, 1925; s. Lehman M. and Anne (Rochotsh) M.; m. Judith Marian Morton, Dec. 22, 1957; children: Susan Morton, Elizabeth Anne. BS in Bus. Adminstrn, U. Ala., 1949, DHL (hon.), 1994; MS in Retailing, N.Y. U., 1950; PhD in Bus. Orgn, Ohio State U., 1961. Buyer Goldblatts Dept. Store, Chgo., 1951-55; mem. faculty U. Ala., 1955—, prof., 1960—, chmn. dept. mktg., 1969-74, dir. Hess Inst. Retailing, 1985-92, Bruno prof. mktg., 1986-92; Bruno prof. mktg. emeritus, 1992—; instr. Ohio State U., Columbus, 1956-60. Cons. Mgmt. Horizons Co., Columbus, 1966-70, N.C.R. Co., Dayton, Ohio, 1967-75. Co-author: Modern Retailing, 1978, 6th edit., 1993, Retailing, 1981, 5th edit., 1993. With AUS, 1944-46, 50-51. Recipient Teaching Excellence award Burlington No. Found., 1986, Distinctive Image award Jewish Childrens Regional Svc. Bd., 1997, Circle of Honor award Direct Selling Edn. Found., 1997; Ford Found. fellow, 1962-63, So. Mktg. fellow, 1986; named to U. Ala. Bus. Faculty Hall of Fame, 1995, Retail Patronage Acad. Hall of Fame, 1995; Morris Mayer Endowed scholarship established 1992; Morris L. Mayer award established U. Ala., 1993; Morris L. Mayer Outstanding Sutdent award established Sales and Mktg. Execs., 1993, others. Mem. Am. Mktg. Assn. (Morris L. Mayer Outstanding Mem. award estab. Birmingham chpt. 1993), So. Mktg. Assn. (pres.), Ala. Retail Assn. (bd. dirs.), Am. Coll. Retail Assn. (pres., Hall of Fame 1992, Mortar Bd., Beta Gamma Sigma, Eta Mu Pi, Pi Sigma Epsilon, Omicron Delta Kappa, Zeta Beta Tau (chpt. trustee). Jewish. Office: U Ala PO Box 870225 Tuscaloosa AL 35487-0154 Home: Capstone Village Traditions Way #14 601 5th Ave E Tuscaloosa AL 35401

MAYER, NEAL MICHAEL, lawyer; b. NYC, Dec. 4, 1941; s. Joseph Henry and Cele (Brodsky) M.; m. Jane Ellen Greenberg, Aug. 24, 1963; children: Andrew Warren, Amy Lynn, Rebecca Ann, Jenny Leigh. BA in History with honors, Kenyon Coll., Gambler, Ohio, 1963, LLD (hon.), 2007; JD, Georgetown U., Washington, 1966. Bar: DC 1967, US Dist. Ct. DC 1967, US Ct. Appeals (DC cir.) 1967, US Customs Ct. 1967, US Supreme Ct. 1970, US Ct. Appeals (5th cir.) 1975. Assoc. Coles & Goertner, Washington, 1966-71, ptnr., 1971-82; sr. ptnr. Hoppel, Mayer & Coleman, Washington, 1982—. Trustee Kenyon Coll., 1995-2002. Mem. ABA, DC Bar Assn., Maritime Adminstrv. Bar Assn. (pres. 1979), Assn. Transp. Profls., Propeller Club of US (Washington), Kenyon Coll. Alumni Assn. (pres. 1993-94). Office: Hoppel Mayer & Coleman 1050 Conn Ave NW Washington DC 20036 Business E-Mail: nmayer@hmc-law.com.

MAYER, SISTER PATRICIA E., elementary school educator; b. Union City, NJ, Dec. 20, 1929; d. Joseph Victor and Johanna Bruns Mayer. BA, Coll. St. Elizabeth, Convent Station, NJ, 1964. Joined Sisters of Charity Roman Cath. Ch., 1948; cert. tchr. Alaska. Tchr. 1st grade St. Aloysius Sch., Jersey City, 1949—50, St. Andrew's Sch., Westwood, NJ, 1950—51; tchr. 4th grade St. Rose of Lima Sch., Short Hills, NJ, 1951—53; tchr. 5-6th grade St. Michael's Sch., Union City, NJ, 1953—59; tchr. 4th grade St. Nicholas Sch., Passaic, NJ, 1959—60; tchr. 3rd, 6-7th grades St. Bridget Sch., Jersey City, 1960—70; tchr. 7-8th grade St. Paul of the Cross Sch., Jersey City, 1970—83, Immaculate Conception/Monroe Cath. HS, 1983—. Spkr. in field. Bd. dirs. Monroe Found., 2004—. Recipient Appreciation cert., Alaska Interagy. Coord. Ctr., 2004, Dir. Cath. Schs. Fairbanks. Avocations: bowling, tennis, cooking, baking, sewing. Office: Monroe Cath Jr/Sr High Sch 615 Monroe St Fairbanks AK 99701

MAYER, RAYMOND RICHARD, business administration educator; b. Chgo., Aug. 31, 1924; s. Adam and Mary (Bogdala) M.; m. Helen Lakowski, Jan. 30, 1954; children: Mark, John, Mary, Jane. BS, Ill. Inst. Tech., 1948, MS, 1954, PhD, 1957. Indsl. engr. Standard Oil Co., Whiting, Ind., 1948-51; orgn. analyst Ford Motor Co., Chgo., 1951-53; instr. Ill. Inst. Tech., Chgo., 1953-56, asso. prof., 1958-60; asst. prof. U. Chgo., 1956-58; Walter F. Mullady prof. bus. adminstrn. Loyola U., Chgo., 1960—. Author: Financial Analysis of Investment Alternatives, 1966, Production Management, 1962, rev. edit., 1968, Production and Operations Management, 1975, rev. edit., 1982, Capital Expenditure Analysis, 1978. Served with USNR, 1944-46. Ingersoll Found. fellow, 1955-56; Machinery and Allied Products Inst. fellow, 1954-55; Ford Found. fellow, 1962 Mem. Acad. Mgmt., Am. Econ. Assn., Am. Statis. Assn., Am. Inst. for Decision Scis., Nat. Assn. Purchasing Mgmt., Polish Inst. Arts and Scis. in Am., Alpha Iota Delta, Alpha Kappa Psi, Beta Gamma Sigma. Home: 730 Green Bay Rd Winnetka IL 60093-1912 Office: 820 N Michigan Ave Chicago IL 60611-2147

MAYER, RENEE G., lawyer; b. Elizabeth, NJ, Apr. 17, 1933; d. Harry and Bertha Sheinblatt Miller; m. Joseph C. Mayer, June 19, 1955; children: Douglas, Julia, Amy, Andrew. BS, Cornell U., 1955; JD, Hofstra U., 1978. Bar: N.Y. 1979, U.S. Dist. Ct. (ea. dist.) N.Y. 1979, U.S. Ct. Appeals (2d cir., fed. cir.) 1983, U.S. Supreme Ct. 1982. Assoc. atty. Meyer, English & Cianciulli, Mineola, N.Y., 1978-79; pvt. practice Mineola, N.Y., 1979-89; ptnr. Riebesehl, Mayer, Keegan & Horowitz, Garden City, N.Y., 1989-97; pvt. practice law Mineola, N.Y., 1997-2001, Port Washington, N.Y., 2001—. Mem. N.Y. State Bar Assn., Nassau Lawyers Assn. Long Island, Inc. (pres. 1996-97, first vice chancellor conf. of continuing legal edn. 1999-2006), Nassau County Women's Bar Assn. (pres. 1985-86), Nassau County Bar Assn. (dir. 1984-87, asst. dean acad. law 1987-91), Cornell Club (bd. govs. 1980-90), Democratic Com. (zone leader, Port. Washington, N.Y., 1980-93). Avocations: reading, theater, travel. Home and Office: 7 Leeds Dr Port Washington NY 11050-4116

MAYER, RICHARD EDWIN, psychology professor; b. Chgo., Feb. 8, 1947; s. James S. and Bernis (Lowy) M.; m. Beverly Linn Pastor, Dec. 19, 1971; children: Kenneth Michael, David Mark, Sarah Ann. BA with honors, Miami U., Oxford, Ohio, 1969; MS in Psychology, U. Mich., 1971, PhD in Psychology, 1973. Vis. asst. prof. Ind. U., Bloomington, 1973-75; asst. prof. psychology U. Calif., Santa Barbara, 1975-80, assoc. prof., 1980-85, prof., 1985—, pres., chmn. dept., 1987-90. Vis. scholar Learning Rsch. and Devel. Ctr., U. Pitts., 1979, Ctr. for Study of Reading, U. Ill., 1984. Author: Foundations of Learning and Memory, 1979, The Promise of Cognitive Psychology, 1981, Thinking, Problem Solving, Cognition, 1983, 2d edit., 1992, BASIC: A Short Course, 1985, Educational Psychology, 1987, The Critical Thinker, 1990, 2d edit., 1995, The Promise of Educational Psychology, Vol. I, 1999, Vol. II, 2002, Multimedia Learning, 2001, Learning and Instruction, 2003, (with R. Clark) E-Learning and the Science of Instruction, 2004, Cambridge Handbook of Multimedia Learning, 2005; editor: Human Reasoning, 1980, Teaching and Learning Computer Programming, 1988; editor jours. Instructional Sci., 1983-87, Educational Psychologist, 1983-89. Sch. bd. officer Goleta (Calif.) Union Sch. Dist., 1981—. Grantee, NSF, 1975—88, 1991—. Fellow APA (divsn. 15 officer 1987—, G. Stanley Hall lectr. 1988, E.L. Thorndike award 2000), Am. Psychol. Soc.; mem. Am. Ednl. Rsch. Assn. (divsn. C officer 1986-88), Psychonomic Soc. Democrat. Jewish. Avocations: computers, hiking, bicycling, reading, dogs. Office: U Calif Dept Of Psychology Santa Barbara CA 93106 Home Phone: 805-964-5936. Business E-Mail: mayer@psych.ucsb.edu.

MAYER, ROBERT ANTHONY, retired college president; b. NYC, Oct. 30, 1933; s. Ernest John and Theresa Margaret (Mazura) M.; m. Laura Wiley Christ, Apr. 30, 1960. BA magna cum laude, Fairleigh Dickinson U., 1955; MA, NYU, 1967. With N.J. Bank and Trust Co., Paterson, 1955-61, mgr. advt. dept., 1959-61; program supr. advt. dept. Mobil Oil Co., NYC, 1961-62; asst. to dir. Latin Am. program Ford Found., NYC, 1963-65, asst. rep. Brazil, 1965-67; asst. to v.p. adminstrn., 1967-73; officer in charge logistical services Ford Found., 1968-73; asst. dir. programs N.Y. Community Trust, NYC, 1973-76; exec. dir. N.Y. State Council on the Arts, NYC, 1976-79; mgmt. cons. NYC, 1979-80; dir. Internat. Mus. Photography, George Eastman House, Rochester, NY, 1980-89, mgmt. cons., 1989-90; pres. Cleve. Inst. of Art, 1990-97; ret., 1997. Author: (plays) La Borgia, 1971, Alijandru, 1971, They'll Grow No Roses, 1975; mem. editl. adv. bd. Grants mag., 1978—80, exhibited profl. photography, 1993—. Mem. state program adv. panel NEA, 1977—80; mem. Mayor's Com. Cultural Policy, NYC, 1974—75; mem. pres.'s adv. com. Bklyn. campus L.I. U., 1978—79; bd. dirs. Fedn. Protestant Welfare Agys., NYC, 1977—79, Arts Greater Rochester, 1981—83, Garth Fagan's Dance Theatre, 1982—86; trustee Internat. Mus. Photography, 1981—89, Lacoste Sch. Arts, France, 1991—96, sec., 1994—96; mem. dean's adv. com. Grad. Sch. Social Welfare, Fordham U., 1976; mem. N.Y. State Motion Picture, TV Devel. Adv. Bd., 1984—87, N.Y. State Martin Luther King Jr. Commn., 1985—90, Cleve. Coun. Cultural Affairs, 1992—94; chmn. Greater Cleve. Regional Transit Authority Arts in Transit Com., 1992—95; bd. dirs. Friends Ariz. State U. Ctr. Latin Am. Studies, 1997—99, Villa Solana Townhouse Assn., 2001—06, pres., 2000; bd. dirs. Mesa Art Ctr. Found., 2004—06; mem. nat. armed svcs. com. YMCA, 1976. Recipient Nat. award on advocacy for girls Girls Clubs Am., 1976 Mem. Nat. Assembly State Art Agys. (bd. dirs. 1977-79, 1st vice chmn. 1978-79), Alliance Ind. Colls. Art (bd. dirs. 1983-91, vice chmn. 1986-87, sec. 1987-89), N.Y. State Assn. Museums (bd. councilors 1983-86, pres. 1986-89), Assn. Ind. Colls. Art and Design (bd. dirs. 1991-97, exec. com. 1991-93, 96-97).

MAYER, ROSEMARY, artist; b. Ridgewood, NY, Feb. 27, 1943; d. Theodore Albert and Marie Anne (Stumpf) M. AB magna cum laude, U. Iowa, 1964; postgrad., Bklyn. Mus. Art Sch., 1964—65, Sch. Visual Arts, NYC, 1967—69. Model Raphael Soyer, NYC, 1968—74; writer Arts Mag., NYC, 1972—75, Art in Am., NYC, 1974—75. Vis. artist many schs. including Hartwick Coll., Oneonta, N.Y., 1976, Art Inst., Chgo., 1974; guest artist Nat. Endowment Workshop, Tyler Sch. Art, Phila., Mpls. Acad. Art and Design, 1981; adj. lectr. La Guardia C.C., CUNY, 1992—; adj. prof. L.I. U., 1988—; writer, speaker A.I.R. Gallery, N.Y.C., 1972-74. Translator: Pontormo's Diary 1983; author: Swatches, 1969, Surroundings, 1977. Grantee numerous orgns. including NEA, CAPS, 1976—. Democrat. Home: 55 Leonard St New York NY 10013-2928

MAYER, SUSAN MARTIN, art educator; b. Atlanta, Oct. 25, 1931; d. Paul McKeen and Ione (Garrett) Martin; m. Arthur James Mayer, Aug. 9, 1953; 1 child, Melinda Marilyn. Student, Am. U., 1949-50; BA, U. N.C., Greensboro, 1953; postgrad., U. Del., 1956-58; MA, Ariz. State U., 1966. Artist-in-residence Armed Forces Staff Coll., Norfolk, Va., 1968-69; mem. art faculty U. Tex., Austin, 1971—2003; ret., 2002. Co-editor: Museum Education: History, Theory and Practice, 1989; author various mus. publs.; contbr. articles to profl. jours. Recipient award Austin Ind. Sch. Bd., 1985. Mem. Nat. Art Edn. Assn. (bd. dirs. 1983-87, award 1987, 91), Tex. Art Edn. Assn. (mus. edn. chair 1982-83, Mus. Educator of Yr. 1986), Tex. Assn. Mus. (mus. edn. chair), Austin Visual Arts Assn., Am. Assn. Mus. Personal E-mail: susanm@mail.utexas.edu.

MAYER, THEODORE V.H., lawyer; b. Waltham, Mass., Sept. 30, 1952; s. Jean and Elizabeth (Van Huysen) M.; m. Margery Weil, Dec. 28, 1975; children: Lily, Henry. BA, Yale U., 1974; JD, Harvard U., 1977. Bar: NY 1978, Mass. 1989, US Ct. Appeals 2nd, 3rd, 7th, Fed. Circuits, US Dist. Ct. So., Ea., We. Districts NY, US Dist. Ct. Dist. Ariz. Assoc. Hughes, Hubbard & Reed LLP, NYC, 1978-85, ptnr., 1985—. Co-author (with Robb Patryk): Product Liability, 1998; contbr. articles to profl. jours. Bd. dirs. New Media Repertory Co., NYC, 1991—, chair, 1996-2006; bd. dirs. Inst. Global Leadership, Tufts U., 2005—. Mem. ABA (co-chair subcom. internat. environ. litig. of com. environ. litig. 1993-95), Assn. Bar City NY (chair com. product liability 2002-05). Office: Hughes Hubbard & Reed LLP One Battery Pk Plz New York NY 10004-1482 Office Phone: 212-837-6888. Office Fax: 212-422-4726. E-mail: mayer@hugheshubbard.com.

MAYER, VICTOR JAMES, geologist, educator; b. Mayville, Wis., Mar. 25, 1933; s. Victor Charles and Phyllis (Bachhuber) M.; m. Mary Jo Anne White, Nov. 25, 1965; children: Gregory, Maribeth. BS Geology, U. Wis., 1956; MS Geology, U. Colo., 1960, PhD Sci. Edn., 1966. Tchr. Colo. Pub. Schs., 1961—85; asst. prof. SUNY, Oneonta, 1965—67, Ohio State U., Columbus, 1967—70, assoc. prof., 1970—75, prof. ednl. studies, geol. scis. and natural resources, 1975—95, prof. emeritus, 1995—; affiliate prof. U. Northern Colo., 2005—. Co-organizer symposa 29th and 31st Internat. Geol. Congresses; internat. sci. edn. assistance to individuals and orgns. in Japan, Korea, Taiwan, Russia, and Venezuela; dir. NSF Insts., program leadership Earth Sys. Edn., 1990-95; dir. Korean Sci. Tchrs. Insts., 1986-88, 95, 2005-07; co-convenor Second Internat. conf. Geosci. Edn., Hilo, Hawaii, 1997; disting. vis. prof. SUNY, Plattsburg, 1994; vis. rsch. scholar Hyogo U., Japan, 1996; sr. Fulbright rschr. Shizuoka U., Japan, 1998; vis. prof. Korea Nat. U. Edn., 2000; Fulbright prof. Pusan Nat. U. Korea, 2003-04, spkr. in field. Contbr. articles to profl. jours. Served with USAR Recipient Lifetime Disting. Svc. award Internat. Earth Sci. Edn. Cmty., 1997; named Disting. Investigator Ohio Sea Grant Program, 1983 Fellow AAAS (chmn. edn. 1988-89), Ohio Acad. Sci. (v.p. 1978-79, exec. com. 1993-94, Outstanding univ. educator 1995); mem. NSTA (bd. dirs. 1984-86), Sci. Edn. Coun. Ohio (pres. 1987-88), Sigma Xi, Phi Delta Kappa Roman Catholic. Avocation: photography. Home and Office: 8483 Sand Dollar Dr Windsor CO 80528 E-mail: mayer.4@osu.edu.

MAYER, WILLIAM EMILIO, investor; b. NYC, May 7, 1940; s. Emilio and Marie Mayer; m. Katherine Mayer, May 16, 1964; children: Kristen Elizabeth, William Franz. BS, U. Md., 1966, MBA, 1967. Pres., CEO First Boston Corp., NYC, 1967-91; dean Coll. Bus. and Mgmt. U. Md., College Park, 1992-96; ptnr. Devel. Capital, 1996-99, Park Ave. Equity Ptnrs., 1999—. Bd. dirs. Lee Enterprises, Inc., Columbia Fund Group. Chmn. bd. U. Md.; chmn. bd. trustees Aspen Inst. 1st lt. USAF, 1961—65. Mem. Annapolis Yacht Club, Manhasset Bay Club (N.Y.), Wilson Cove Yacht Club, Univ. Club (N.Y.C.), Mashomack Fish and Game Club, Met. Club (Washington). Home: 172 Long Neck Point Rd Darien CT 06820-5816 Office: 399 Park Ave Ste 3204 New York NY 10022-1606 Office Phone: 212-430-0160.

MAYER, WILLIAM P., lawyer; AB summa cum laude, Dartmouth Coll., 1973; MS, U. Dar es Salaam, Tanzania, 1974; JD, U. Va. Law Sch., 1977. Bar: DC 1978, Mass. 1984. Law clerk, Hon. William H. Timbers US Ct. Appeals (2nd cir.), 1977—78; ptnr., bus. law dept., mem. fin. svcs. dept. Goodwin Procter LLP, Boston. Editor: Va. Law Rev.; lectr. in field. Bd. adv. Morin Ctr. Banking and Fin. Law Studies, Boston Univ. Office: Goodwin Procter LLP Exchange Pl 53 State St Boston MA 02109 Office Phone: 617-570-1534. Office Fax: 617-523-1231. Business E-Mail: wmayer@goodwinprocter.com.

MAYERS, DANIEL KRIEGSMAN, lawyer; b. Scarsdale, NY, July 10, 1934; s. Chauncey Maurice and Helen P. (Kriegsman) M.; m. Karen E. Silverman, Sept. 30, 1956, children: Peter D., Leslie H. Shroyer. AB, Harvard U., 1955, LLB, 1960. Bar: D.C. 1961, U.S. Supreme Ct. 1961. Law clk. to Justice Felix Frankfurter, U.S. Supreme Ct., Washington, 1960-61; spl. asst. U.S. Dept. Justice, Washington, 1961-62; assoc. Wilmer Cutler & Pickering, Washington, 1962-65, ptnr., 1967-99, of counsel, 2000—; exec. asst. to undersec. U.S. State Dept., Washington, 1965-66. Vis. com. Harvard Law Sch., Cambridge, Mass., 1982-89, chmn., 1986-89; chmn. Legal Action Ctr., N.Y.C., 1998—, Washington Ednl. TV Assn., 1993-97, Survivors Fund for Pentagon Victims, 2001--; bd. dirs. Hypres Corp., Netscan, Inc. Pres. Nat. Symphony Orch., Washington, 1987-89; chmn. Sidwell Friends Sch., Washington, 1979-81; mem. Ams. for Peace Now, 1991—, Fed. City Coun., Washington, 1981—; trustee Cmty. Found. for Nat. Capital Area, 1997—; dir. Internat. Sr. Lawyers' Program, 2004—, Higher Achievement, 2006—; counsel, dir. Ctr. for Nat. Policy, Washington, 1984-93. With U.S. Army, 1955-57. Recipient Sears prize Harvard Law Sch., 1959 Mem. ABA, Met. Club, Burning Tree Woodstock Country Club. Democrat. Jewish. Avocations: tennis, fishing. Home: 3222 Woodland Dr NW Washington DC 20008-3547

MAYERS, DAVID, political science professor, department chairman, history professor; b. El Paso, Tex., Nov. 30, 1951; s. Eugene David and Odette Margaret Julliette (Gilchriest) M.; m. Elizabeth Kirkland Jones, Dec. 4, 1982; 1 child, Peter. BA, Oberlin Coll., 1974; postgrad., Oxford U., Eng., 1974-75; MA, U. Chgo., 1976, PhD, 1979. Faculty Kenyon Coll., 1979-80, U. Calif., Santa Cruz, 1980-88; prof. polit. sci. and history Boston U., 1989—, 1999—, dir. undergrad. studies polit. sci., 1991-98, dir. grad. studies polit. sci., 1998-2000, chmn. dept. polit. sci., 2001—. Lectr. in field; active various profl. confs.; mem. numerous profl. panels. Author: Cracking the Monolith: US Policy against the Sino-Soviet Alliance, 1949-55, 1986, Reevaluating Eisenhower; American Foreign Policy in the 1950s, 1987, George Kennan and the Dilemmas of US Foreign Policy, 1988, The Ambassadors and America's Soviet Policy, 1995 (Book prize The Am. Acad. Diplomacy 1995), Wars and Peace: The Future Americans Envisioned, 1861-1991, 1998, Dissenting Voices in America's Rise to Power, 2007; contbr. articles to profl. jours., chpts. to books. Vol. ARC; bd. trustees Carnegie Coun. on Ethics and Internat. Affairs. Fellowships from Oberlin Coll., Oxford U., U. Chgo., U. Calif., Santa Cruz, Inst. on Global Conflict and Coop., 1983-89, Inst. for Study of World Politics, 1986, Boston U., Hoover Instn., Stanford U., 1990, Ctr. Internat. Studies at U. So. Calif., 1991, John M. Olin Found., 1991, Gilder Lehrman Inst. Am. History, 2000. Episcopalian. Democrat. Avocations: tennis, swimming, camping, skiing, sailing. Home: 173 Oliver Rd Waban MA 02468-2322 Office: Boston Univ Dept Polit Sci Boston MA 02215 Office Phone: 617-353-2543. Business E-Mail: dmayers@bu.edu.

MAYERS, STANLEY PENROSE, JR., public health service officer, educator; b. Phila., Nov. 9, 1926; s. Stanley Penrose and Margaret Amelia (Thorpe) M.; m. Virginia Lee Lytle, Aug. 25, 1951 (dec. Oct. 1990); children: Douglas Lytle, Kenneth Stanley, Daniel John, Andrew William; m. Patricia Ann Harne Hulsey, Mar. 6, 1993. BA, U. Pa., 1949, MD, 1953; MPH, Johns Hopkins U., 1958. Diplomate Am. Bd. Preventive Medicine. Intern Phila. Gen. Hosp., 1953-54; resident Arlington County Health Dept., Va., 1954-55; health dir. Henry-Martinsville-Patrick Health Dist., Martinsville, Va., 1955-57; regional dir. Va. State Health Dept., Richmond, 1958-59; dist. state health officer N.J. State Dept. of Health, Trenton, 1959-62; asst. prof. and asst. dean Johns Hopkins Sch. Hygiene and Pub. Health, Balt., 1962-65; dir. Arlington County Dept. of Human Resources, Arlington, Va., 1965-71; prof. health policy and adminstrn. Pa. State U., University Park, 1971-97, prof. emeritus, 1997—, chmn., 1979-88, assoc. dean undergrad. studies Coll. Health and Human Devel., 1989-92, assoc. dean acad. studies Coll. Health and Human Devel., 1992-95, assoc. dean emeritus, 1997—. Interim dir. internat. edn. programs and studies Pa. State U., 2000-2001; faculty assoc. Johns Hopkins U. Sch. Hygiene and Pub. Health, Balt., 1965-75; clin. assoc. prof. Georgetown U. Sch. Medicine, Washington, 1965-71; cons. VA, 1985—. Contbr. articles to profl. jours. Pres. Arlington Optimist Club, 1970-71; bd. dirs. Centre County Family Planning Svcs., Bellefonte, Pa., 1972-79, vice chmn., Ctr. County Hosp. Commn., 2005-; With USN, 1945-46. Recipient Outstanding Achievement award Dept. Community Medicine, Georgetown U. Sch. Medicine, 1968, Saubel award Coll. of Human Devel., Pa. State U., 1985, Pioneer Achievement award Frankford H.S., Phila., 1999. Fellow Am. Coll. Preventive Med., APHA (chmn. membership com. health officer's sect. 1968-70, mem. nominating com. health adminstrn. sect. 1970-72, chmn. com. to draft a statement on local health agy. responsibilities 1973-74); mem. AMA, Arlington County Med. Soc. (Wellborn award 1971), Centre County Med. Soc. (pres. 1978), Med. Soc. Va., Met. Washington Health Officers Assn. (sec. 1967-71), Am. Assn. Pub. Health Physicians (pres. Va. chpt. 1970-71), Pa. Med. Soc. (mem. Ho. of Dels. for Centre County 1974-76, 81-97, treas. 1973-74, 85—, sec. 1974-76, v.p. 1976, pres. elect 1977, pres. 1978), Mt. Nittany Soc., Univ. Club (State College, Pa.), Phi Beta Kappa. Episcopalian. Avocations: fishing, boating, hiking. Home: 648 Wiltshire Dr State College PA 16803-1450 Office: Pa State U Human Devel Bldg Rm 115 University Park PA 16802 Business E-Mail: spm1@psu.edu. *Never attempt to promote something or someone that you do not believe in yourself.*

MAYERSON, PHILIP, classics educator; b. NYC, May 20, 1918; s. Theodore and Clara (Fader) M.; m. Joy Gottesman Ungerleider, Nov. 25, 1976 (dec. Sept. 9, 1995); children: Miriam Mayerson, Clare Mayerson. AB, NYU, 1947, PhD, 1956. With Puritan Fed. Clothing Stores, NYC, 1935-42; instr. NYU, 1948-56, asst. prof., 1956-60, assoc. prof., 1960-66, prof. classics, 1966—, vice dean, 1969-71, acting dean, 1971-73, dean Washington Sq. and U. Coll. Arts and Scis., 1973-78. Author: The Ancient Agricultural Regime of Nessana and the Central Negeb, 1961, Classical Mythology in Literature, Art and Music, 1971, Monks, Martyrs, Soldiers and Saracens, 1994; contbr. articles in field of papyrology to profl. jours. Served with USN, 1942-45. Rockefeller Found. grantee, 1956-57; Am. Coun. of Learned Socs. fellow, 1961-62. Mem. Am. Philol. Assn., Am. Schs. of Oriental Rsch. Home: 720 Walton Ave Mamaroneck NY 10543-4437 Office: NYU Dept Classics 25 Waverly Pl New York NY 10003 Business E-Mail: pm2@nyu.edu.

MAYERSON, SANDRA ELAINE, lawyer; b. Dayton, Ohio, Feb. 8, 1952; d. Manuel David and Florence Louise (Tepper) M.; m. Scott Burns, May 29, 1977 (div. Oct. 1978); 1 child, Katy Joy. BA cum laude, Yale U., 1973; JD, Northwestern U., 1976. Bar: Ill. 1976, N.Y. 1997, U.S. Ct. Appeals (7th cir.) 1976, U.S. Dist. Ct. (no. dist.) Ill. 1977, U.S. Dist. Ct. Md. 1989, U.S. Ct. Appeals (5th cir.) 1994, U.S. Dist. Ct. (so. and ea. dists.) N.Y. 1997, U.S. Ct. Appeals (2nd Cir.) 1997, U.S. Dist. Ct. (ea. dist.) Mich. 2000. Assoc. gen. counsel JMB Realty Corp., Chgo., 1979-80; assoc. Chatz, Sugarman, Abrams et al, Chgo., 1980-81; ptnr. Pollack, Mayerson & Berman, Chgo., 1981-83; dep. gen. counsel AM Internat., Inc., Chgo., 1983-85; ptnr. Kirkland & Ellis, Chgo., 1985-87; ptnr., chmn. bankruptcy group Kelley Drye & Warren, NYC, 1987-93; ptnr., chmn. N.Y. bankruptcy group McDermott, Will & Emery, NYC, 1993-99; ptnr., bankruptcy nat. practice group leader Holland and Knight, NYC, 1999—. Examiner Interco chpt. 11, 1991. Contbr. articles to profl. jours. Bd. dirs. Jr. Med. Rsch. Inst. coun. Michael Reese Hosp., Chgo., 1981-86, Self Help Inc., 2000-; met. divsn. Jewish Guild for Blind, 1990-92; nat. legal afffairs com. Anti-Defamation League, 1990-91; lawyers' exec. com. United Jewish Appeal; chair Holland & Knight Nat. Bankruptcy & Creditors Rights Group, 2001-. Named one of Top 50 Women Litigators, Nat. Law Jour., 2001; assoc. fellow, Branford Coll., Yale U., 1993—. Mem. ABA (bus. bankruptcy com. 1976—, sec. 1990-93, chair avoiding powers subcom. 1993-96, chair claims trading subcom. 1997-2000, chair strategic planning subcom., 2000-), Ill. State Bar Assn. (governing council corp. and securities sect. 1983-86), Chgo. Bar Assn. (current events chmn. corp. sect. 1980-81), 7th Cir. Bar Assn., Yale Club (N.Y.C.). Democrat. Jewish. Office: Holland and Knight 195 Broadway Fl 24 New York NY 10007-3100 Business E-Mail: sandy.mayerson@hklaw.com.

MAYES, MICHELE COLEMAN, lawyer; b. LA, July 9, 1949; BA, U. Mich., 1971, JD, 1974. Bar: Mich. 1974, US Dist. Ct. 1974, Ea. Dist. Mich. 1976, Ill. 1980, US Supreme Ct. 1988, Pa. 1988. Adj. prof. Wayne State U., 1981—87; in-house counsel Colgate-Palmolive, 1992—2003; sr. v.p., gen. counsel Pitney Bowes Inc., 2003—. Mem.: ABA (mem. commn. on women in the profession 1992, co-chair, arbitration com. 1990—92). Office: Pitney Bowes Inc 1 Elmcroft Rd Stamford CT 06926-0700 Office Phone: 203-351-6480. E-mail: michele.mayes@pb.com. *

MAYES, WENDELL WISE, JR., former broadcasting company executive; b. San Antonio, Mar. 2, 1924; s. Wendell Wise and Dorothy Lydia (Evans) M.; m. Mary Jane King, May 11, 1946; children: Cathey, Sarah, Wendell Wise, III. Student, Schreiner Inst., 1941-42, U. Tex., 1942, Daniel Baker Coll., 1946; BS, Tex. Tech. Coll., 1949; BA summa cum laude, St. Edward's U., 2002, MLA, 2005, MBA, 2006. Program dir., sta. mgr. Sta. KBWD, Brownwood, Tex., 1949-57; mgr. Sta. KCRS, Midland, Tex., 1957-63, pres., 1965-84, chmn., 1984-96; pres. Sta. KNOW, Austin, Tex., 1970-81, Stas. KVIC and KAMG, Victoria, Tex., 1970-84, chmn., 1984-98, Sta. KCRS-FM, Midland, 1984-96; pres. Sta. KCSW, San Marcos, 1976-81; sec.-treas. Sta. KSNY-AM-FM, Snyder, 1952-94; mem. bd. mgrs. Sta. KLBJ/KHHT-AM-FM, Austin, 1991-97. Bd. advisors Patton Med. Devices, 2006—; lectr. Coll. Comm., U. Tex., Austin, 1978—81. Chmn. bd. Am. Diabetes Assn., 1974—77; mem. Nat. Diabetes Adv. Bd., 1977—84; v.p. Internat. Diabetes Fedn., 1980—88, pres.-elect, 1988—91, pres., 1991—94, hon. pres., 1997—; pres. Tex. Broadcast Edn. Found., 1973—76, dir., 2002—; mem. Tex. Diabetes Coun., 1983—86, chmn., 1983—86, exec. dir., 1999; bd. regents Tex. Tech U., 1985—91, chmn., 1987—88; bd. dirs., treas. Writer's League Tex., 2005—. With USNR, 1943—46. Named Disting. Alumnus, Tex. Tech U., 1981, Disting. Engr., 1985, Disting. Alumnus, Schreiner U., 2006; named to Tex. Tech. Mass Comm. Hall of Fame, 1978, Hall of Fame Tex. affiliate, Am. Diabetes Assn., 1994, Tex. Radio Hall of Fame, 2002; recipient Addison B. Scoville award, Am. Diabetes Assn., 1977, first Wendell Mayes Jr. award, 1986, Josiah K. Lilly award, 1991, Harold Rifkin award, 1994, Masaji Takeda medal, Kobe, Japan Colloquium Med. Sci., 1994. Mem. Tex. Assn. Broadcasters (pres. 1964, named Pioneer Broadcaster of Year 1978), Nat. Assn. Broadcasters (dir. 1969-72), Am. Council on Edn. in Journalism (dir. 1977-80), Broadcast Edn. Assn. (dir. 1973-77), AP Broadcasters (bd. dirs. 1988-91), Tex. Tech. Elec. Engring. Acad. Episcopalian (vestryman 1966-69, 86-88; sr. warden 1988). Home: 2834 Montebello Rd Apt 1 Austin TX 78746-6820 Office: 1907 N Lamar Blvd Austin TX 78705-4992 Home Phone: 512-329-9919; Office Phone: 512-477-6866. E-mail: wmayes@swbell.net.

MAYEUX, RICHARD, hospital administrator, neurologist; b. New Orleans, 1946; MD, U. Okla., 1972. Diplomate Am. Bd. Psychiatry and Neurology. Intern Boston City Hosp., 1972—73, resident in internal medicine, 1973—74; resident in neurology Columbia Presbyn. Med. Ctr., NYC, 1974—77; fellow in neurology Boston U., 1977—78; neurologist Sergievsky Ctr., NYC; staff neurologist Columbia Presbyn. Med. Ctr., NYC; prof. Columbia Coll. Physicians and Surgeons, NYC; dir. Taub Inst., NYC; Gertrude H. Sergievsky prof. neurology, psychiatry & epidemiology Columbia Univ., dir. Gertrude H. Sergievsky Ctr.; mem. Aging Rev. Com. NIH, mem. Epidemiology of Chronic Disorders Com.; med. & scientific adv. bd. Alzheimer's Assn. Robert Aird visiting prof. U. Calif. San Francisco; Emanuel Goldberg visiting prof. U. Rochester; J.L. Silversides visiting prof. U. Toronto. Recipient Leadership & Excellence in Alzheimer's Disease award, Nat. Inst. Aging, 1992, MERIT award, 2004, Dean's Disting. Clin. Scientist award, Columbia U., Rita Hayworth award, Alzheimer's Assn. Fellow: Am. Acad. Neurology (Potamkin prize 2007); mem.: AAP, Soc. for Neuroscience, Soc. Epidemiologic Rsch., Am. Neurological Assn., NY Acad. Sci., Am. Epidemiological Soc., Assn. Rsch. Nervous & Mental Disease (ARNMD), Inst. of Medicine of NAS. Office: Coll Physicians and Surgeons Columbia U 630 W 168th St New York NY 10032 Office Phone: 212-305-2391. Office Fax: 212-305-2518. E-mail: rpm2@columbia.edu. *

MAYFIELD, (BRITT) MAX, meteorologist; b. Okla. City, Sept. 19, 1948; m. Linda C. Mayfield; 3 children. BS in Math., U. Okla., 1970; MS in Meterology, Fla. St. U., 1987. With NOAA/Nat. Weather Svc., Miami, 1972—2007, hurricane forecaster, 1988—90, sr. forecaster, 1990—98, dep. dir. Nat. Hurricane Ctr., 1998—2000, acting dir., 2000, dir., 2000—07; hurricane specialist WPLG-TV Local 10, Miami, 2007—. Chmn. regional assn. IV hurricane com. World Meterological Orgn.; chmn. office of fed. coord. Meteorology Working Group on Hurricanes; spkr. in field. Contbr. articles to profl. jours. Recipient Francis W. Reichelderfer award, Am. Meterological Soc., 1996, Outstanding Achievement award, Nat. Hurricane Ctr., 2000, Richard Hagemeyer award, Interdepartmental Hurricane Conf., 2004, Emmy award, 2004, Presdl. Rank award for Meritorious Svc., 2005, NOAA Bronze medal, US Dept. Commerce. Mem.: Nat. Weather Assn., Am. Meteorological Soc. Office: WPLG-TV 3900 Biscayne Blvd Miami FL 33137 *

MAYFIELD, PEGGY LEE, counselor; d. Ralph Russel Horn and Dorothy Fae Roll; m. Jack Lynn Mayfield. AS in Biology, Richland C.C., Decatur, Ill., 1988; BA in Psychology, U. Ill., Springfield, 1993, MA in Counseling, 1996. Cert. nat. counselor Nat. Bd. Cert. Counselors. Child and adolescent therapist Decatur Mental Health Ctr., Ill., 1994—95, intensive family therapist, 1995—96; foster care supr., therapist Cath. Social Svcs., Bloomington, Ill., 1996—97, foster care supr., 1997—2000; lic. clin. profl. counselor Decatur, 2000—; adj. human devel. instr. U. Ill., Springfield, 1988—, accredition exhibit rm. coord., 2002—06, chair alumni coun. Coll. Edn. and Human Svcs., 2004—06, dir. accreditation documentation, 2006—, immediate past chair, 2006—, adj. instr., tchr. edn. program, 2007—. Compassion fatigue trainer, Decatur, 1996—; trainer Lips Are Sealed Syndrome, 1997—; comm. skills trainer, Decatur, 1998—2000. Named Alumni of Yr., Human Devel. Counseling Program, 1998. Mem.: U. Ill. Alumni Assn. (Loyalty award 2005), U. Ill. Coll. of Edn. Human Svcs. Alumni (chair 2004—06, Alumnist of Yr. 1998). Home: 2155 W Center St Decatur IL 62526 Office Phone: 217-206-7583. Personal E-mail: mayfield.peggy@uis.edu.

MAYFIELD, ROBERT CHARLES, academic administrator, geographer, educator; b. Abilene, Tex., Oct. 15, 1928; s. Percy Anderson and Fay (Hicks) M.; m. Loraine Poindexter, Sept. 3, 1952; children: Julie Barnes, Jennifer Manley, Mark Stanley, Malcolm Randall. BA, Tex. Christian U., 1952; MS, Ind. U., 1953; PhD, U. Wash., 1961. Chmn. geography dept. Tex. Christian U., Ft. Worth, 1960-64, U. Tex., Austin, 1968—71, Boston U., 1971—84, acad. v.p. external programs, 1977-83, provost, 1979-84. Cons. Coun. for Econ. Action, Boston, 1980—; adj. prof. U. Tex., Austin, 1987—; lectr. U.S. Info. Svc., Bangladesh, 1994; seminar dir. U. Tex. Seminars for Adult Growth and Enrichment, 1995—; mem. faculty rev. bd. Bangladesh U. Engring. and Tech., Dacca, 1996—. Editor, contbg. author: Man, Environment and Space, 1972. With USAF, 1946-49. Rsch. fellow Nat. Acad. Sci. No. India, 1957-58, Fulbright-Hays fellow Office Edn., Bangalore, Mysore, India, 1966-67; Rsch. grant Agrl. Devel. Coun., 1968. Mem. Assn. Am. Geographers. Business E-Mail: rmayfield@austin.rr.com.

MAYFIELD, T. BRIENT, IV, media and computer executive; b. Athens, Tenn., Mar. 31, 1947; s. Thomas Brient III and Alma Ruth (Bolton) M.; m. N. Katherine Rodgers, Dec. 7, 1974 (div. Mar. 1984); children: Brittany Alexander, Blair Ashton, Katherine Thomas; m. Margaret L. Reeves, Oct. 3, 1987 (div. Feb. 1998). BS, U. Tenn., 1969. Project mgr. Mayfield Dairy Farms, Athens, 1969-70; v.p. fin. 13-30 Corp., Knoxville, Tenn., 1970-72; exec. v.p. Computer Concepts Corp., Knoxville, 1970-77, pres., 1977-85, Resource Optimization Inc., Knoxville, 1986—; co-founder Whittle Communications LP, Knoxville, 1970, v.p., pub., 1987-92. Bd. dirs. Results Edn. Fund, Washington, 1990—. Republican. Avocations: flying, tennis, music. Address: PO Box 436 Knoxville TN 37901 Office: Resource Optimization PO Box 2747 Knoxville TN 37901-2747

MAYGARDEN, JERRY LOUIS, healthcare foundation executive; b. Pensacola, Fla., Dec. 22, 1948; s. Louis Ameal and Jean (Saxon) Maygarden; m. Rhonda Delene Fosha, June 25, 1977; children: Louis Ameal III, Morgan Lora. AA in Liberal Arts, Pensacola Jr. Coll., 1972; BA in Communications Arts, U. West Fla., 1974, MA in Communication, 1975. V.p. U. West Fla., Pensacola, 1980-83; exec. v.p. Sacred Heart Found., Pensacola, 1983-89; pres. Bapt. Health Care Found., Pensacola, 1989—. Bd. dirs. Bank of Pensacola; mem. Fla. House of Reps., 1994—. City councilman Pensacola City Coun., 1985-92, mayor pro tem, 1989-91, mayor, 1991-94; bd. dirs. C. of C. Com. 100, Pensacola, 1989—. With USN, 1968-74, Viet Nam. Recipient George Washington Honor medal, Freedoms Found. of Valley Forge, 1992, Paul Harris fellow, Rotary Found Internat., 1993; named Cmty. Leader of Yr. C. of C., Pensacola, 1988, Outstanding Young Man Am. U.S. Jaycees, 1977, Nat. Soc. Fund Raising Execs., Assn. for Health Care Philanthropy, Rotary Internat. Mem. Fla. League Cities, Nat. League Cities, Nat. Soc. Fund Raising Execs., Assn. for Health Care Philanthropy, Rotary Internat. Democrat. Methodist. Avocations: tennis, sailing, hiking, biking, fishing. Office: Bapt Health Care Found PO Box 17500 Pensacola FL 32522-7500 Home: 516 E Zarragossa St Pensacola FL 32502-6155

MAYHALL, CLIFFORD WESLEY, lawyer; b. Birmingham, Ala., Aug. 23, 1972; s. Clyde Wesley and Pamela Hayes Mayhall. BA in Govt. and English, Coll. William and Mary, Williamsburg, Va., 1994; MA in Polit. Sci., U. Fla., Gainesville, 1996; JD, Fla. State U., Tallahassee, 2000. Bar: Fla. 2000, US Dist Ct. (no. dist.) Fla. 2002, US Dist. Ct. (so. dist.) Fla. 2002, US Dist. Ct. (mid. dist.) Fla. 2005, US Ct. Appeals (11th cir.) 2005, US Supreme Ct. 2005. Rsch. asst. Reubin Askew Inst., Gainesville, 1994—96; staff aide US Senator Bob Graham, Tallahassee, 1995; rsch. specialist Legis. Com. on Intergovtl. Rels., Tallahassee, 1996—98; jud. clk. Sr. US Dist. Judge Maurice Paul, Gainesville, 2000—01; atty. Katz, Kutter, Alderman & Bryant, PA, Tallahassee, 2001—04, Akerman Senterfitt, Tallahassee, 2004—. Legis. editor Fla. State U. Law Rev., 2000. Sec., past pres. Tree Ho. Children's Shelter, Tallahassee, 2001—; mem. rector search com. St. John's Episcopal Ch., Tallahassee, 2006—; bd. dirs. So. Shakespeare Festival, Tallahassee, 1998—2002. Mem.: FBA, ABA, Fla. Bar, Emerge Tallahassee, Emerge Fla., Capital Tiger Bay Club, Order of Coif. Home: 1234 Waverly Rd Tallahassee FL 32312 Office: Akerman Senterfitt 106 E College Ave Ste 1200 Tallahassee FL 32301 Office Phone: 850-425-1647. Office Fax: 850-325-2547. Personal E-mail: cwmayhall@yahoo.com.

MAYHAR, ARDATH FRANCES (FRANK CANNON, JOHN KILLDEER, FRANCES HURST), writer; b. 1930; Ind. book cons., 1979—; dairyman, 1947—57; prin. East Tex. Bookstore, Nacogdoches, 1958—62; proofreader Capital Jour., Salem, Oreg., 1968—75; chicken farmer, 1976—78; proofreader Daily Sentinel, Nacogdoches, 1979—82; writer, 1982—; co-mgr. View From Orbit Bookstore, Nacogdoches, 1984—99; writing instr. Writer's Digest, 1982—2005. Author: How the Gods Wove in Kyrannon, 1979, The Seekers of Shar Nuhn, 1980, Soul Singer of Tyrnos, 1981, Warlock's Gift, 1982, Khi to Freedom, 1982, Runes of the Lyre, 1982, Golden Dream, 1983, Lords of the Triple Moons, 1983, Exile on Vlahil, 1984, The Saga of Grittel Sundotha, 1985, The World Ends in Hickory Hollow, 1985, Medicine Walk, 1985, Carrots and Miggle, 1986, The Wall, 1987, Makra Choria, 1987, Feud at Sweetwater Creek (as Frank Cannon), 1988, A Place of Silver Silence, 1988; (collaboration with Marylois Dunn) The Absolutely Perfect Horse, 1983; (collaboration with Ron Fortier) Trail of the Seahawks, 1987, Monkey Station, TSR, 1989; (as John Killdeer) Wild Country, The Untamed, Wilderness Rendezvous, Blood Kin, People of the Mesa, 1992, Island in the Lake, 1993, Towers of the Earth, 1994, Passage West, 1994, Far Horizons, 1994, Hunters of the Plains, 1995, (as Frances Hurst) High Mountain Winter, 1996, Riddles and Dreams, 2003, elec. edits., 2004-05, 30 out-of-print paperback reprints, 2007. Mem.: Sci. Fiction/Fantasy Writers Am. Home: 533 CR 486 Chireno TX 75937 Office Phone: 936-362-2913. E-mail: ardathm@netdot.com.

MAYHEW, AUBREY, music industry executive; b. Washington, Oct. 2, 1927; s. Aubrey and Verna June (Hall) M.; m. Carol de Onis, May 10, 1962 (div. 1971); children: Lawrence Aubrey, Michael Aubrey, Parris Mitchell, Casey Aran. Student, Wilson Tchs. Coll., 1948. Dir. WWVA, Wheeling, W.Va., 1947-54, WCOP, Boston, 1954-56; asst. to pres. MGM Records, NYC, 1957-58; v.p. mktg. Capitol Records, LA, 1958-60; prodr., dir. KCAM-TV Prodns., Nashville, 1981—. Pres., founder John F. Kennedy Meml. Ctr., 1968; authority on John F. Kennedy life and memorabilia. Author: (books) Commandants Marine Corps, 1953, World Tribute to John F. Kennedy, 1965; composer (music) Touch My Heart, 1966 (Broadcast Music, Inc. award, 1967); record producer, artist mgmt., 1947—; music pub., 1954—; developed careers numerous entertainers including Johnny Paycheck, Jeannie C. Riley, Bobby Helms. Served to cpl. U.S. Army Signal Corps, 1945-48. Named Govs. Aide, Nashville, 1978. Mem. Country Music Assn., Broadcast Music Inc., Manuscript Soc., N.Y. Numismatic Soc., Gospel Music Assn. Republican. Episcopalian. Avocations: collector, historian, author. Office: Amcorp Music Group 827 Meridian St Nashville TN 37207-5856

MAYHEW, DAVID RAYMOND, political science professor; b. Putnam, Conn., May 18, 1937; s. Raymond William and Jeanie (Nicholson) M. BA, Amherst Coll., 1958; PhD, Harvard U., 1964. Tchg. fellow Harvard U., 1961-63; from instr. to asst. prof. polit. sci. U. Mass., Amherst, 1963-67; vis. asst. prof. Amherst Coll., 1965-66; faculty Yale U., 1968-77, prof. polit. sci., 1977—, chmn. dept., 1979-82, Alfred Cowles prof. govt., 1982-98, Sterling prof. polit. sci., 1998—. Olin vis. prof. Am. govt. Nuffield Coll., Oxford (Eng.) U., 2000-01. Author: Party Loyalty Among Congressmen, 1966, Congress: The Electoral Connection, 1974 (Washington Monthly ann. polit. book award 1974), Placing Parties in American Politics, 1986, Divided We Govern, 1991, America's Congress, 2000, Electoral Realignments, 2002. Recipient Richard E. Neustadt prize 1992, James Madison award, 2002, Yale Grad. Student Mentor award, 2002, Samuel J. Eldersveld award, 2004; Woodrow Wilson fellow, 1958-59, vis. fellow Nuffield Coll., Oxford, 1978, Guggenheim fellow, 1978-79, Hoover Nat. fellow, 1978-79, Sherman Fairchild fellow, 1990-91, fellow Ctr. for Advanced Study in Behavioral Scis., 1995-96. Fellow Am. Acad. Arts and Scis.; mem. Am. Polit. Sci. Assn. (nat. council 1976-78, Congl. fellow 1967-68), Am. Philos. Soc., So. Polit. Sci. Assn., New Eng. Polit. Sci. Assn. Home: 100 York St Apt 5C New Haven CT 06511-5611 Office: Yale U Polit Sci Dept Box 208301 New Haven CT 06520-8301 Office Phone: 203-432-5237. Business E-Mail: david.mayhew@yale.edu.

MAYHEW, ERIC GEORGE, medical researcher, educator, consultant; b. London, June 22, 1938; came to U.S., 1964; s. George James and Doris Ivy (Tipping) M.; m. Barbara Doe, Sept. 28, 1966 (div. 1976); 1 child, Miles; m. Karen Caruana, Apr. 1, 1978 (div. 1994); children: Ian, Andrea; m. Ludmila Khatchatrian, June 29, 1995. BS, U. London, 1960, MS, 1963, PhD, 1967, DSc, 1993. Rsch. asst. Chester Beatty Rsch. Inst., London, 1960—64; cancer rsch. scientist Roswell Pk. Meml. Inst., Buffalo, 1964—68, sr. cancer rsch. scientist, 1968—72, assoc. cancer rsch. scientist, 1979—83, dep. dir. exptl. pathology, 1988—93; prin. scientist The Liposome Co., Princeton, NJ, 1993—99, May Pharm Consulting, 2000—. Assoc. rsch. prof. SUNY, Buffalo, 1979-93; ad-hoc mem. NIH study sects., 1982-94; cons. to industry, 2000-. Editor jour. Selective Cancer Therapeutics, 1989-91; contbr. articles to Jour. Nat. Cancer Inst., Cancer Rsch. and many other profl. jours. Grantee NIH, Am. Heart Assn., and pvt. industry, 1972-93. Mem. Am. Assn. Cancer Rsch., N.Y. Acad. Sci. Achievements include development of liposomes for drug delivery and patents for new chemical entities and liposome delivery. Office: May Pharm Consulting 1782 S Seaview Ave Coupeville WA 98239 Home Phone: 360-678-2175. Personal E-mail: eailkmay@aol.com.

MAYHEW, KARIN D., health and medical products executive; BA, Fordham U., NY; M, Wesleyan U., Middletown, Conn.; grad. Smith Coll. Mgmt. Program, U. Mich. Advanced Human Resources Exec. Program. Sr. v.p. orgn. devel. So. New Eng. Telecom. Corp.; with Health Net, Inc., Woodland Hills, Calif., 1999—, sr. v.p. orgn. effectiveness. Lectr. Babson Coll. Ctr. Exec. Edn., Wellesley, Mass. Office: Health Net Inc 21650 Oxnard St Woodland Hills CA 91367 Office Phone: 818-676-6000. *

MAYHEW, KENNETH EDWIN, JR., retired transportation executive; b. Shelby, NC, Sept. 27, 1934; s. Kenneth Edwin and Evelyn Lee (Dellinger) M.; m. Frances Elaine Craft, Apr. 7, 1957 (dec. 2005); m. Darlene Burgess Randall, Jan. 7, 2006; 1 dau., Catherine Lynn Prince. AB, Duke U., 1956. CPA NC. Sr. auditor Arthur Andersen & Co., Atlanta, 1956-58, 60-63; controller Trendline, Inc., Hickory, NC, 1963-66; with Carolina Freight Corp., Cherryville, 1966-93, treas., 1969-74; v.p. Carolina Freight Carriers Corp., Cherryville, 1971-72, exec. v.p., 1972-85, pres., COO, 1985-89, dir., 1968-93, chmn., pres., CEO, 1989-93; ret., 1993. Pres., dir. Robo Auto Wash Shelby Inc., 1967-73, Robo Auto Wash Cherryville, Inc., 1968-73; dir. Cherryville Nat. Bank, Kenmar Bus. Group, Inc. Mem. Bus. Adv. Bd., Fuqua Sch. Bus., Duke U.; bd. dirs., vice-chmn. Gaston Meml. Hosp.; trustee Pfeiffer U. With AUS, 1958-60. Mem. AICPA, Am. Trucking Assn. (dir., v.p.), N.C. Trucking Assn. (dir., chmn.), Gaston County C. of C. (v.p. pub. affairs), Lions (pres. Cherryville 1972-73), Phi Beta Kappa, Omicron Delta Kappa, Phi Eta Sigma. Methodist. Home: 507 Spring St Cherryville NC 28021-3540

MAYHUE, RICHARD LEE, dean, minister, writer; b. Takoma Park, Md., Aug. 31, 1944; s. J. Richard Mayhue and Myrtle Lorraine (Hartsell) Lee; m. Lois Elaine Nettleingham, June 18, 1966; children: Lee, Wade. BS, Ohio State U., 1966; MDiv, Grace Theol. Seminary, 1974, ThM, 1977; ThD, Grace Theol. Seminary, Winona Lake, Ind., 1981. Ordained pastor. Asst. pastor Grace Brethren Ch. of Columbus, Ohio, 1975—77; asst. prof. New Testament and Greek, Grace Theol. Seminary, Winona Lake, Ind., 1977—80; assoc. pastor Grace Cmty. Ch., Sun Valley, Calif., 1980—84, 1989—2004; sr. pastor Grace Brethren Ch., Long Beach, Calif., 1984—89; sr. v.p., dean, prof. systematic theology and pastoral mins. The Master's Seminary, Sun Valley, 1989—; sr. v.p., provost The Master's Coll., Santa Clarita, Calif., 2000—. Bd. dirs. Grace Theol. Sem., 1987-89. Author: The Biblical Pattern for Divine Healing, 1979, 2002, Snatched Before the Storm, 1980, 2002, Divine Healing Today, 1983, How to Interpret the Bible for Yourself, 1986, A Christian's Survival Guide, 1987, Unmasking Satan, 1988, 2d edit., 2001, Spiritual Intimacy, 1990, Spiritual Maturity, 1992, The Healing Promise, 1994, What Would Jesus Say About Your Church?, 1995, 2d edit., 2001, Fight the Good Fight, 1999, 2d edit., 2006, 1 and 2 Thessalonians, 1999, Seeking God, 2000, Practicing Proverbs, 2003; contbr., co-editor: Rediscovering Expository Preaching, 1992, rev. edit., 2005, Rediscovering Pastoral Ministry, 1994, rev. edit., 2005, The Master's Perspective on Pastoral Ministry, 2002, The Master's Perspective on Biblical Prophecy, 2002; contbr., assoc. editor MacArthur Study Bible, 1997, Think Biblically!, 2003; editor MacArthur Bible Commentary, 2005, assoc. editor: Counseling: How to Counsel Biblically, 2005; contbr. articles to profl. jours., chpts. to books. Bd. dirs. Capitol Ministries, 1996-2005, Slavic Gospel Assn, 1993-2002; bd. elders Grace Cmty. Ch., 1989-2004; mem. bd. of ref. Coun. on Bibl. Manhood and Womanhood, 1991—. Recipient Bronze Star with Combat V USN, 1969. Mem. Evang. Theol. Soc., Nat. Fellowship Grace Brethren Ministers (pres. 1988), Far West Region Evang. Theol. Soc. (pres. 1995), Evang. Homiletics Soc. Avocations: n-gauge model railroading, U.S. stamp collecting. Office: The Master's Seminary 13248 Roscoe Blvd Sun Valley CA 91352-3739 also: The Master's Coll 21726 Placerita Canyon Rd Santa Clarita CA 91321-1200 Business E-Mail: rmayhue@tms.edu.

MAYLAND, KENNETH THEODORE, economist; b. Miami, Fla., Nov. 17, 1951; s. Herbert and Vera (Bob) M; m. Gail Fern Bassok, Apr. 14, 1984. BS, MIT, Cambridge, Mass., 1973; MS, U. Pa., Phila., 1976, PhD, 1979. Cons. economist Data Resources, Inc., Lexington, Mass., 1973; economist, then chief economist First Pa. Bank, Phila., 1973-89; sr. v.p., chief economist Soc. Nat. Bank, Cleve., 1989-94; sr. v.p., chief fin. economist Key Corp., Cleve., 1994-96, sr. v.p., chief economist, 1996-2000; pres. ClearView Econs., LLC, 2000—. Econs. instr., Chartered Fin. Aanalysts Assn., Phila, 1984—; econ. adv. com. Phila. Econ. Devel. Coalition, 1984-86; chmn. econ. adv. com. Pa. Bankers Assn., Harrisburg, 1982-84; mem. Gov.'s Econ. Adv. Com., Ohio, 1989—. Contbr. semi-monthly periodical Money Markets, 1981-85, quar. periodical Regional Report, 1980-89, EconViewpoint/KeyViewpoint biweekly periodical, 1989-2000, Regional Rev. quar. periodical, 1989-94, ClearView on the Economy, 2000—. Mem. curriculum adv. com. Widener U., 1986-89. Named 2d Best Forecaster for 2003, USA Today survey panel, Top Forecaster mid-2003 to mid-2004, Bloomberg Mag., 2004, #1 Most Accurate Forecaster, BusinessWeek, 2006. Mem. Am. Bankers Assn. (econ. adv. com. 1990-93), Internat. Econ. Roundtable (vice chmn. 1987-88, chmn. 1988-90), Nat. Assn. Bus. Economists (New Face for the Eighties award 1979), Phila. Coun. Bus.

Economists (pres. 1982-84), Cleve. Bus. Economist Club (sec.-treas. 1990-91, v.p. 1991-92, pres. 1992-93). Avocations: fishing, badminton, gardening, camping. Office: 3237 Fox Hollow Dr Cleveland OH 44124-5426 Office Phone: 216-595-9931.

MAYNARD, CHARLES DOUGLAS, radiologist; b. Atlantic City, Sept. 11, 1934; m. Mary Anne Satterwhite; children: Charles D., Deanne, David. BS, Wake Forest U., 1955, MD, 1959. Diplomate Am. Bd. Radiology (trustee 1987-99, sec.-treas., v.p. 1992-94, pres. 1994-96, guest examiner). Intern U.S. Army Hosp., Honolulu, 1959—60; resident N.C. Baptist Hosp., 1963—66; dir. Nuclear Medicine Lab., 1966—77; asst. dean admissions Bowman Gray Sch. Medicine, 1966—71, asso. dean student affairs, 1971—75, prof. radiology, chmn. dept., 1977—2000. Mem. Am. Bd. Med. Specialists; acting dean Wake Forest U. Sch. Medicine, 2001—02. Author: Clinical Nuclear Medicine, 1969; mem. editl. bd.: Yearbook of Diagnostic Radiology, Contemporary Diagnostic Radiology. Mem. Leadership Winston-Salem, Triad Leadership Network; bd. dirs. Downtown Devel. Corp., 1995—2000, Winston-Salem Bus., Inc., 1995—99, Forsyth Tech. CC, 1997—2005, pres., 2004—05; bd. dirs. Va. Tech. Coll. Engring., 2002—06, Wake Forest U. Health Scis., 2003—. Mem.: AMA, Greater Winston-Salem C. of C. (bd. dirs.), Acad. Radiology Rsch. (pres. 1999—2001), Soc. Chairmen Radiology Depts. (past pres.), Assn. Univ. Radiologists, Radiol. Soc. N.Am. Rsch. and Edn. Found. (chmn. bd. 1999), Radiol. Soc. N.Am. (pres. 1999—2000), Am. Coll. Radiology (past bd. chancellors, past chmn. commn. on nuc. medicine), Soc. Nuc. Medicine (past pres.). Office: Wake Forest U Sch Medicine Dept Radiology Medical Center Blvd Winston Salem NC 27157-1088 Business E-Mail: dmaynard@wfubmc.edu.

MAYNARD, ELLIOTT E., state supreme court justice; b. Williamson, W.Va., Dec. 8, 1942; BS in Psychology, Fla. So. Coll., 1967; JD, W.Va. U., 1974. Atty. priv. practice, Williamson, W.Va., 1974—81; prosecuting atty. Mingo County, 1976—81; judge W.Va. Cir. Ct. 30th Jud. Cir., 1982-97; justice W.Va. Supreme Ct. Appeals, Charleston, 1997—, chief justice, 2000, 2004. Mng. dir. Tug Valley C. of C., 1968-70; active Boy Scouts Am.; dist. chmn. Mingo-Pike Dist., Chief Cornstalk Dist.; bd. dirs. Buckskin Coun. With USAF, 1961—66. Recipient Silver Beaver award Boy Scouts Am. Mem.: ABA, W.Va. Bar Assn., Am. Judicature Soc., Am. Judge's Assn. Office: State Capital State Ct Appeals Bldg 1 Rm E306 Charleston WV 25305 *

MAYNARD, HUGH M., lawyer; b. Bethesda, Md., Mar. 29, 1949; BA math., Carleton Coll., 1971; JD, Harvard U., 1975. Bar: Minn. 1975, Maine 1980. Ptnr. Leonard, Street and Deinard P.A., Mpls., shareholder. Mem. ABA (property sect.), Minn. Bar Assn., Hennepin County Bar Assn. (real property sect.), Phi Beta Kappa, Sigma Xi, Pi Mu Epsilon, Sensible Land Use Coalition. Staff mem., Civil Rights-Civil Liberties Law Review. Office: Leonard Street & Deinard PA 150 S 5th St Ste 2300 Minneapolis MN 55402-4223 Office Phone: 612-335-1562. Office Fax: 612-335-1657. Business E-Mail: hugh.maynard@leonard.com.

MAYNARD, JOHN RALPH, lawyer; b. Mar. 5, 1942; s. John R. Maynard and Frances Jane (Mitchell) Maynard Kendryk; m. Meridee J. Sagadin, Sept. 11, 1995; children: Bryce James, Pamela Ann. BA, U. Wash., 1964; JD, Calif. Western U., San Diego, 1972; LLM, Harvard U., 1973. Bar: Calif. 1972, Wis. 1973. Assoc. Whyte & Hirschboeck, Milw., 1973-78, Minahan & Peterson, Milw., 1979-91, Quarles & Brady, Milw., 1991-2000, Davis & Kuelthau, Milw., 2000—05, Maynard, McIlnay, Schmitt & Button, Grafton, Wis., 2005—. Bd. dirs. Transitional Living Svcs., Inc., 1999—2003; pres. Milw. Chamber Orch., 2000—02; mem. Wis. Adv. Coun. to U.S. SBA, 1987—89; bd. dirs. Am. Heart Assn., 1979—82, Found. Internal Medicine Exchange, 2004—, Bel Canto Chorus, 2004—. Mem.: ABA, Harvard Club (Wis.). Home: 809 E Lake Forest Ave Milwaukee WI 53217-5377 Office: Maynard McIlnay Schmitt & Button 1150 Washington St Grafton WI 53024 Office Phone: 262-387-4980. Business E-Mail: jmaynard@runbox.com.

MAYNARD, JOHN ROGERS, language educator; b. Williamsville, NY, Oct. 6, 1941; s. Atherton Rogers and Olive (Fisher) M.; m. Florence Michelson, July 1, 1967 (div. 1980); 1 child, Alex Stevens; m. Ursula Krammer, Oct. 17, 1992 (div. 1995). BA, Harvard U., 1963, PhD, 1970. Asst. prof. Harvard U., Cambridge, Mass., 1969-74, NYU, NYC, 1974-76, assoc. prof., 1976-84, prof. English, 1984—, chmn. English dept., 1983-89. Chmn. Faculty Council NYU, 1983-84; vis. prof. U. Venice, Italy, 1991; co-dir. Biography Seminar, 2004—. Author: Brownings Youth, 1977 (Wilson prize 1977), Charlotte Bronte and Sexuality, 1984, Victorian Discourses on Sexuality and Religion, 1993, Browning Re-Viewed, 1998; editor: Literature and Sexuality, 1991-2004; series of books on sexuality and lit.; co-editor: (with Lockridge and Stone) Nineteenth Century Lives, 1989, (with Bloom) Shankman's Anne Thackeray Ritchie: Journals and Letters, (with Munich) Victorian Literature and Culture, 1991—, Tennyson: Poetry for Young People, Blake: Poetry for Young People. Organizer Concord Sq. Assn., Boston, 1972—74. NEH grantee, 1972-73; Guggenheim fellow, 1979-80. Mem. IAUPE, MLA, PEN, Browning Inst. (bd. dirs.), Signet Soc., Fly Club, Andiron Club (pres. 1983-84), Brooklyn Heights Assn. Democrat. Avocation: bicycling. Office: NYU Dept of English 5th Fl 19 University Pl New York NY 10003-4556

MAYNARD, KENNETH DOUGLAS, architect; b. Hackensack, NJ, Aug. 16, 1931; s. Douglas Harry and Eva (Whiting) M.; m. Myrna Myrtle James, Feb. 4, 1956; children: Colin, Vivien Noll. Cert. in Architecture, U. Natal, Durban, Republic of South Africa, 1958. Registered arch. Alaska State Bd. Registration Archs., Engrs., and Land Surveyors, 2004. Draftsman Morrows & Graff, Johannesburg, Republic of South Africa, 1950-51, Anglo-Am. Corp., Johannesburg, Republic of South Africa, 1951-54, Moir & Llewellyn, Empangeni, Zululand, Republic of South Africa, 1955-57; architect Pearse Aneck-Hahn & Bristol, Johannesburg, 1957-60, Manley & Mayer, Anchorage, 1960-61, FAA, Anchorage, 1961-62, Crittenden Cassetta Wirum & Jacobs, Anchorage, 1962-65; prin. Schultz & Maynard, Anchorage, 1965-68, Kenneth Maynard Assocs., Anchorage, 1968-78; pres. Maynard & Partch, Anchorage, 1978-96; prin. USKH, Inc., Anchorage, 1996—. Active Western Alaska Coun. Boy Scouts. Am., Anchorage, 1965-84; bd. dirs. Salvation Army Adv. Bd., Anchorage, 1981-87, Anchorage Mus. Assn., 1969-86, Anchorage Opera Co., 1983-90; chmn. Mayor's Comprehensive Homeless Program Strategy Group, 1992-94. Fellow: AIA (pres. Alaska chpt. 1969, NW regional rep. for nat. com. on design 1976—89, nat. bd. 1999—2001); mem.: Constrn. Specification Inst. (pres. Cook Inlet chpt. 1993—94). Republican. Avocations: reading, travel. Home: 2237 Forest Park Dr Anchorage AK 99517-1324 Office: USKH 2515 A St Anchorage AK 99503-2776

MAYNARD, KENNETH IRWIN, pharmaceutical executive, medical educator, researcher; b. San Fernando, Trinidad, Jan. 17, 1963; Student, Howard U., 1982; BSc with honors, Univ. Coll., London, 1986, MSc, 1987, PhD, 1991. Cert. design and conduct of clin. trials. Postdoctoral rsch. assistantship Univ. Coll., London, 1991; postdoctoral rsch. fellow Stroke Rsch. Lab. Neurosurg. Svc. Mass. Gen. Hosp., Harvard Med. Sch., Boston, 1991—93, postdoctoral rsch. fellow neurophysiology lab. Neurosurg. Svc., 1993—97; tchg. fellow dept. neurobiology Harvard Med. Sch., Boston, 1992, instr. in surgery, 1995—98, asst. prof., 1998—2001; asst. neuroscientist Mass. Gen. Hosp., 1998—2001; section head, cerebrovascular disorders Aventis Pharms., Inc., 2000—02, prin. sci., 2002—04; project dir. Sanofi-Aventis, Inc., 2005—. Ad hoc reviewer Jour. Vascular Rsch., 1991, Neurosci. Letters, 1995, Vision Rsch., 1996, Neurosurgery, 1998, others; presenter in field; tutor dept. of neurobiology, 1998—2000; asst. prof. surgery, 1998; steering com. Boston Area Neurosci. Group, 1998—2000; ad hoc reviewer Ministry of Health, Internal Grant Agy., Czech Republic, 1998; med. rsch. grant program Jewish Hosp. Found., 2000; cons. neurosurgery Mass. Gen. Hosp., 2001—02; lectr. Harvard U. Med. Sch., 2001—02. Contbr. articles to med. jours. including Neurosci. Letters, articles to med. jours. including Stroke, articles to med. jours. including Exptl. Neurology, articles to med. jours. including Jour. Neurol. Rsch. Mem. parish pastoral coun. St. Joseph's Cath. Ch., Boston, 1992—95, chmn. stewardship commn., 1997; advisor regional com. ctrl. region on stewardship Archdiocese of Boston, 1995—97. Recipient Travel fellowship for minority neuroscientists, Nat. Inst. Neurol. Disease and Stroke, 1995, travel award, FASEB MARC, 1998; scholar, Autumn Sch. Caen France, 1996, Tokyo, 1998. Fellow: Am. Heart Assn. (minority scientist devel. award 1996, nat. affiliate brain/stroke study sect. 1999—, stroke coun. 2002, minority affairs com.); mem.: AAAS, Internat. Soc. Cerebral Blood Flow and Metabolism (Young Scientist Bursary award 1993), Congress of Neurosurg. Surgeons, Am. Assn. Neurosurg. Surgeons (adj. assoc. mem. joint sect. on cerebrovascular surgery 1995), Soc. for Neurosci. (minority neurosci. fellowship program 2000—02, minority edn., tng. and profl. advancement com. 2000—03, membership com. 2002—07, fin. com. 2007—), N.Y. Acad. Sci., Am. Stroke Assn. (affiliate brain rsch. peer rev. group 1999—2003). Roman Catholic. Office: Sanofi Aventis Inc 200 Crossing Blvd BX2-309A Bridgewater NJ 08807 Office Phone: 908-304-6352. Business E-Mail: kenneth.maynard@sanofi-aventis.com.

MAYNARD, MICHAEL, librarian; b. Yuma, Ariz., July 8, 1955; s. Ernest Ray and Refugio (Guerrero) M. AAS in Electronic Tech., Phoenix Coll., 1986; BA in German, Ariz. State U., 1989; postgrad., U. Leipzig, 1990, Eberhard-Karls U., Tubingen, Germany, 1990—91; MLS, U. Ariz., 1992; cert. in computer applications, Rio Salado Coll., 2004. Electronics technician USN, 1977-83; asst. libr. Chapel Libr., Venice, Fla., 1983-84; security officer Anderson Agy., Phoenix, 1984-89; grad. asst. U. Ariz., Tuscon, 1989-90, libr. asst. main libr. acquisitions dept., 1992; asst. libr. Internat. Bapt. Coll., Tempe, Ariz., 1992-94; head libr. Velda Rose Ch. Fitch Libr., Mesa, Ariz., 1994-97; libr. II Ariz. Dept. Corrections, Douglas, 1997-2000, Goodyear, 2000—, instr. Latin, Greek, Hebrew, Russian, German, French, and Spanish, 2003—06. Author: History of the Debate Over I John 5:7-8, 1995. With USN, 1977—83. Scholar U. Ariz., 1989-90, Herman Weinel scholar, 1990. Mem.: Am. Classical League. Baptist. Avocations: foreign languages, lexicology, philology, nutrition, New Testament studies. Home and Office: Comma Publs PO Box 1625 Tempe AZ 85280-1625 E-mail: receptus@sprynet.com.

MAYNARD, MICHELINE ANN, journalist, writer; b. Ann Arbor, Mich., Aug. 5, 1958; d. Frank Henry and Bernice Genevieve Maynard. BA in Humanities, Mich. State U., 1979; MA in Journalism, Columbia U., 1990. Legis. corr. United Press Internat., Lansing, Mich.; intern White House Press Office; assoc. editor US News & World Report, Washington, 1984-86; sr. bus. writer Newsday, NYC, 1986-88; bur. chief Reuters News Svc., Detroit, 1988-90; bus. journalist USA Today, Arlington, Va., 1999; freelance journalist, 1999—2003; bus. day reporter NY Times, Detroit, 2004—. Lectr. U. Mich. Sch. Bus. Adminstrn., 2000—03, U. Mich. Sch. Pub. Policy, 2004—. Author: Collision Course: Inside the Battle for General Motors, 1995, The Global Manufacturing Vanguard, 1998, The End of Detroit, 2003. Knight-Bagehot fellow, bus. and economics journalism, Columbia U., 1989—90, Knight Wallace fellow, U. Mich., 1999—2000, media fellow, Japan Soc. of NY, 2002. Mem.: Authors Guild, Univ. Musical Soc. Avocations: antiques, gardening, classical music, yoga, contemporary film. Office: NY Times 229 West 43rd St New York NY 10036 Office Phone: 212-556-1474. Office Fax: 212-556-1448. Business E-Mail: mickimay@nytimes.com. E-mail: Micheline@MichelineMaynard.com.

MAYNARD, NATALIE RYSHNA, pianist, educator; b. Phila., Aug. 21, 1930; d. George Thomas Hook and Helen Agatha Reese; m. Harry Edgar Maynard, Jan. 30, 1960; children: Melanie Dawn, Amie Anne. Degree in piano performance, Juilliard Graduate Sch. Music, NYC, 1952. Concert pianist Columbia Artists Mgmt., tours in U.S. and Europe, 1963-94; rec. artist Contemporary Records and Ambiphon Records, 1957-75; pvt. piano instr., 1985—; project dir. Title III and State Urban Edn. program N.Y.C. schs. Founder, chmn. edn. com. Sta. WNET/13-TV, NYC, 1973—77; pres. Performers Conn., Westport, 1985—91, bd. dirs., 1982—; exec. dir. R. B. Fisher Found. Composer Awards, 1986—96; v.p. ednl. outreach Friends of Music Fairfield County, 1995—99. Apptd. to arts adv. com. Town of Westport, 1998—2000, 2000—, co-chair town millenium edn. com., 1998; mem. adv. bd. Stamford Symphony Orch., 2004—07; bd. dir. Friends of Channel 13 Nat. Friends Pub. Broadcasting, 1971—82. Recipient Outstanding Women Conn. award, Lt. Gov. Conn., 2003. Mem.: Conn. State Music Tchrs. Assn., Nat. Music Tchrs. Assn., Schubert Club. Office Phone: 203-226-1394.

MAYNARD, SHIRLEY, educational association administrator; b. San Fernando, Trinidad, WI, Jan. 25, 1941; d. Charles Jacob Maynard and Josephine Anastasia Noriega-Maynard; m. Ambrose Charles McIntosh (div.); children: Charles Maynard McIntosh(dec.), Alex Maynard McIntosh(dec.). BA, Marygrove Coll., Detroit, 1965; MA, Fordham U., Bronx, NY, 1966. Sch. tchr. lit., Port of Spain, Trinidad and Tobago, 1966—68; sys. analyst NYC, 1968—69; sys. programmer, 1969—70; computer ctr. mgr. Port of Spain, Trinidad and Tobago, 1970—78; exec. adminstr., 1978—88; office mgr. Hialeah, Fla., 1997—2005; pres. Pembroke Pines, Fla., 2006—. Sec. bd. Family Humanity Inc., Hollywood, Fla., 2006—; pres. Schalex Inc., Pembroke Pines, 2006—. Guest editl. writer (cmty. newspaper), 2004. Sec. bd. River of Grass Unitarian Universalist Congregation, Plantation, Fla., 2005—06. Scholar, Cannon Max Murphy, Trinidad, 1962. Avocations: reading, gardening, writing, interior decorating. Home and Office: Schalex Inc 9613 NW 16th Ct Pembroke Pines FL 33024

MAYNARD, VIRGINIA MADDEN, foundation administrator; b. New London, Conn., Jan. 29, 1924; d. Raymond and Edna Sarah (Madden) Maynard. BS, U. Conn., 1945; postgrad., Am. Inst. Banking, 1964—66, Cornell U., 1975. With Nat. City Bank (now Citibank), NYC, 1954—79, asst. cashier, 1965—69, asst. v.p., 1969-74, v.p. internat. banking group, 1974-76, comptroller's div., 1976-79; v.p. First Women's Bank, NYC, 1979-80; rep. Internat. Fedn. Univ. Women UN, 1982—2003. Trustee fellowships endowment fund AAUW Ednl. Found., Washington, 1977—80, Va. Gildersleeve Internat. Fund Univ. Women, Inc., pres., 1987—93, bd. dirs., 1994—2000, rep. UN, 1997—; bd. dirs. Conf. Nongovtl. Orgns. Found., Inc., 1997—, treas., 1999—. Mem.: AAUW (fin. chmn. N.Y.C. br. 1976—79, bylaws chmn. 1979—83, adminstr. Meml. Fund 1983—92, 2000—, bd. dirs. 1992—94, 1996—99, Woman of Achievement 1976). Republican. Congregationalist. Home: 601 E 20th St New York NY 10010-7622

MAYNE, KENNY, sports anchor; b. Sept. 1, 1959; Student, Wenatchee Valley CC, Wash.; BA in Broadcasting, U. Nev.-Las Vegas, 1982. Reporter Sta. KLVX-TV, Las Vegas, 1982, Sta. KSTW-TV, Tacoma/Seattle, 1982-89, prodn. asst., 1982-83, news writer, 1983-86, weekend sports anchor, news reporter, 1986-89; freelance reporter, field prodr. SportsCenter ESPN, 1990-94, SportSmash anchor, 1994, SportsNight reporter, 1994, anchor SportsCenter, 1994—; host RPM 2Night ESPN2, 1994. Football player, free agt. Seattle Seahawks, 1982 Guest appearance Dancing with the Stars, ABC, 2006. Office: c/o ESPN ESPN Plaza Bristol CT 06010

MAYNE, LUCILLE STRINGER, finance educator; b. Washington, June 6, 1924; d. Henry Edmond and Hattie Benham (Benson) Stringer; children: Pat A., Christine Gail, Barbara Marie. BS, U. Md., College Park, 1946; MBA, Ohio State U., Columbus, 1949; PhD, Northwestern U., Evanston, Ill., 1966. Instr. fin. Utica Coll., 1949-50; lectr. fin. Roosevelt U., 1961-64, Pa. State U., 1965-66, asst. prof., 1966-69, assoc. prof., 1969-70; assoc. prof. banking and fin. Case-Western Res. U., 1971-76, prof., 1976-94, prof. emerita, 1994—, grad. dean Sch. Grad. Studies, 1980-84. Sr. economist, cons. FDIC, 1977-78; cons. Nat. Commn. Electronic Fund Transfer Sys., 1976; rsch. cons. Am. Bankers Assn., 1975, Fed. Res. Bank of Cleve., 1968-70, 73; cons. Pres.'s Commn. Fin. Structure and Regulation, 1971, staff economist, 1970-71; analytical statistician Air Materiel Command, Dayton, Ohio, 1950-52; asst. to promotion mgr. NBC, Washington, 1946-48; expert witness cases involving fin. instns. Assoc. editor: Jour. Money, Credit and Banking, 1980-83, Bus. Econs., 1980-85; contbr. articles to profl. jours. Vol. Cleve. Soc. for Blind, 1979-2004, Benjamin Rose Inst., 1995-2005; mem. policyholders nominating com. Tchrs. Ins. and Annuity Assn./Coll. Retirement Equities Fund, 1982-84, chair com., 1984; bd. dirs. Women's Cmty. Found., 1994-96. Grad. scholar, Ohio State U., 1949, doctoral fellow, Northwestern U., 1963—65. Mem. LWV (bd. dirs. Shaker Heights chpt. 1999--), Midwest Fin. Assn. (pres. 1991-92, bd. dirs. 1975-79, officer 1988-93), Phi Kappa Phi, Beta Gamma Sigma. Episcopalian. Home: 3723 Normandy Rd Cleveland OH 44120-5246 Office: Case Western Res U Weatherhead Sch Mgmt U Circle Cleveland OH 44106-7235 Business E-Mail: lucille.mayne@case.edu.

MAYNE, THOM, architect; b. Waterbury, Conn., Jan. 19, 1944; s. Walter and Bernice (Gornall) M.; m. Susan Burnham, Sept. 10, 1964 (div. 1970); 1 child, Richard; m. Blythe Alison Mayne, Aug. 8, 1981; children: Sam, Cooper. BArch, U. So. Calif., 1968; MArch, Harvard U., 1978. Mem. faculty UCLA Sch. Art and Architecture, Santa Monica, Calif., 1972—; bd. dirs. So. Calif. Inst. Architecture, Santa Monica, Calif., 1983—; architect Morphosis, Santa Monica, Calif. Adj. prof. UCLA, 1993; mem. vis. faculty Calif. State Coll., Pomona, 1971, Miami U., Ohio, 1982, Washington U., St. Louis, 1984, U. Tex., Austin, 1984, U. Pa., 1985, Columbia U., N.Y.C., 1986, Harvard U., 1988, Clemson U., 1991, Yale U., 1991, UCLA, 1986, 92, U. Ill., Urbana-Champaign, 1992-93, Tech. U., Vienna, Austria, 1993, Berlage Inst., Amsterdam, 1993, Hochschule für Andgewandt Kunst, Vienna, 1991, 93; lectr. in field; adjudicator numerous awards. Archtl. one-man exhbns. include 2 AES Gallery, San Francisco, 1988, Cheney Cowles Mus., Spokane, Wash., 1989, Walker Arts Ctr., Mpls., 1989, Gallery of Architecture, L.A., 1989, Contemporary Arts Ctr., Cin., 1989, San Francisco Mus. Modern Art, 1990, Graham Found., Chgo., 1990, Aedes Galerie and Architecture Forum, Berlin, 1990, Fenster Architekturgalerie, Frankfurt, Germany, 1990, Gallery MA, Toyko, 1990, Laguna (Calif.) Art Mus., 1991, G201 Gallery, Ohio, 1991, 1-Space Gallery, Chgo., 1992, Sadock & Uzzan Galerie, Paris, 1992, Diane Farris Gallery, 1993; group exhbns. include Umwelt Galerie, Stuttgart, Germany, 1978, The Archtl. Gallery, Venice, Calif., 1979, La Jolla (Calif.) Mus. of Contemporary Art, 1982, Inst. Contemporary Arts, London, 1983, Archtl. Assn., London, 1983, NAD, N.Y.C., 1983, 88, Mus. Modern Art, San Francisco, 1983, Calif. Mus. Sci. and Industry, 1984, G.A. Gallery, Tokyo, 1985, 87, 90, Max Protech Gallery, N.Y.C., 1985, 86, I.D.C., N.Y.C., 1986, Axis Gallery, Tokyo, Milan, Paris, 1988, Pacific Design Ctr., L.A., 1988, Australia Ctr. for Contemporary Arts, Victoria, 1988, Cooper-Hewitt Mus., N.Y.C., 1988, Aedes Galerie für Architektur und Raum, Berlin, 1988, Kirsten Kiser Gallery, 1988, 89, Visual Arts Ontario, Toronto, 1988, Gallery Functional Art, Santa Monica, Calif., 1989, Deutsches Architektur Mus., Frankfurt, 1989, USIA, Moscow, 1989-90, Lameier Sculpture Park, St. Louis, 1989, Gwenda Jay Gallery, Chgo., 1990, Sadock & Uzzan Galerie, 1991, Bannatyne Gallery, Santa Monica, 1991, ROM Galleri for Arkitektur, Oslo, 1992, 65 Thompson Street Gallery, N.Y.C., 1992; archtl. projects include Sequoyah Edn. and Rsch. Ctr., Santa Monica, 1977 (Progressive Architecture award 1974), Flores Residence, 1979 (Progressive Architecture award 1980), Sedlak Residence, 1980 (AIA award 1981), Western Melrose Office Bldg, 1981 (Progressive Architecture award 1982), Hermosa Beach Ctrl. Bus. Dist. (Progressive Architecture award 1984), 72 Market Street Restaurant, 1983 (AIA award 1985, CCAIA award 1986), Bergren Residence, 1984 (AIA award 1985, CCAIA award 1986, Nat. AIA award 1986), Cedar Sinai Comprehensive Cancer Ctr., L.A., 1988 (Progressive Architecture award 1987, AIA award 1988, CCAIA award 1989), Arts Park Performing Pavilion, 1988, (Progressive Architecture award 1989), Leon Max Showroom, L.A., 1988 (CCAIA award 1990, Archtl. Record Interior award 1990), Club Post Nuclear, Laguna Beach, Calif., 1988, Berlin Wall Competition, 1988, Expo '90 Folly, Osaka, Japan, 1989, The Emery Ctr. Performing Arts, 1989, Temple U. CCC, Phila., 1989, Politix, 1990 (AIA award 1990), Salick Health Care Corp. Hdqs., 1990 (AIA award 1992, CCAIA award 1993), Visual Performing Arts Sch. at Thomas More Coll., Crestview, N.Y., 1990, MTV Studios, L.A., 1990, Higashi Azabu Tower, Tokyo, 1991, Yuzen Vintage Car Mus., L.A., 1991 (AIA award 1993), Disney Inst. and Town Ctr. Competition, Orlando, Fla., 1991, Cranbrook Acad. Gatehouse Competition (Pilkington Planar prize 1993), Spreebogen Master Plan, Berlin, 1993, Check Point Charlie Office Bldg., Berlin, 1993; contbr. articles to profl. jours. Rome Prize fellow Am. Acad. Rome, 1987; recipient Architecture award Am. Acad. Arts and Letters, 1992, Pritzker Architecture prize Hyatt Found., 2005. Mem. AIA, Am. Acad. Design. Democrat. Avocations: skiing, travel. Office: Morphosis Architecture 2041 Colorado Ave Santa Monica CA 90404-3415 Office Phone: 310-570-0123. Business E-Mail: t.mayne@morphosis.net. *

MAYO, CLYDE CALVIN, psychologist, educator; b. Robstown, Tex., Feb. 2, 1940; s. Clyde Culberson and Velma (Oxford) Mayo; m. Jeanne Lynn McCain, Aug. 24, 1963; children: Brady Scott, Amber Camille. BA, Rice U., Houston, 1961; BS, U. Houston, 1964, PhD, 1972; MS, Trinity U., 1966. Lic. psychologist Tex., La. Mgmt. engr. LWFW, Inc., Houston, 1966-72, sr. cons., 1972-78, prin., 1978-81; ptnr. Mayo, Thompson, Bigby, Houston, 1981-83; founder Mgmt. and Pers. Systems, Houston, 1983—. Counselor Interface Counseling Ctr., Houston, 1976—79; dir. Mental Health HMO Group, 1985—87; instr. St. Thomas U., Houston, 1979—90, U. Houston Downtown Sch., 1972, 2002—06, U. Houston, Clear Lake, 1983—88, U. Houston-Ctrl. Campus, 1984—; dir. mgmt. devel. insts. U. Houston Woodlands and West Houston, 1986—91; adj. prof. U. Houston, 1991—. Author: LWFW Annual Survey of Manufacturers, 1966—81, Bi/Polar Inventory of Strengths, 1978. Coach, mgr. Meyerland Little League, 1974—78, So. Belles Softball, 1979—80, S.W. Colt Baseball, 1982—83, Friends of Fondren Libr. Rice U., 1988—; charter mem. Holocaust Mus. Mem.: APA, Houston Area Indsl. Orgnl. Psychologists (bd. dirs. 1989—92), Am. Psychol. Soc., Tex. Psychol. Assn., Houston Psychol. Assn. (membership dir. 1978, sec. 1984), Tex. Indsl. Orgnl. Psychologists (founder, bd. dirs. 1995—, pres. 1999—2002), Soc. Indsl. Orgn. Psychologists, Found. Contemporary Theology (bd. dirs. 2005—, chair youth recruitment com. 2006—), Meyerland Club (bd. dirs. 1988—92, pres. 1991), Forum Club. Home: 8723 Ferris Dr Houston TX 77096-1409 Office: Mgmt and Personnel Systems 4545 Bissonnet St Bellaire TX 77401-3121 Office Phone: 713-667-9251. Personal E-mail: mpsmayo@aol.com.

MAYO, CORA LOUISE, educator; b. Chgo., Oct. 31, 1925; d. Charles Amos and Mary (Elder) Scott; m. Marion Wesley Mayo, July 21, 1948; children: Lynne, Charles (dec.), Janice (dec.), Jo Ann, Thomas. BS, U. Ill.-Urbana, 1949, advanced degree in adminstrn. and supervision, 1973; MA, U. Chgo., 1961; PhD, Heed U., Fla., 1981. Program facilitator Chgo. Bd. Edn., 1955—; owner/pres. From the Black Experience, Inc., Chgo., 1979—; dir. pub. relations Afro-Am. Pub. Co., 1972-73; ednl. cons. Ednl. Leadership Inst., Chgo., 1976-78; cmty. prof. Govs. State U., Park Forest, Ill., 1975—83. Author: Developmental Skills Activities Guide, 1982; columnist Teaching Black Positively; editor Human Relations Digest; author/pub.: (early childhood learning kit) Mwenzi Compañeros, 1982. Bd. dirs. Woodson Delany Ednl. Fund, Chgo., 1975—77, House of the Black Madonna, Chgo., 1978—80; cons. Head Start, St. Stephen's Ch.,

Chgo., 1982-83; organizer Women for Washington, 1982-83, Women for Jackson, 1984; vol. instr. parenting House of the Black Madonna; proposals cons. Du Sable Mus. Afro-Am. History, Chgo. Recipient Leadership award Boy Scouts Am., 1971; named Outstanding Educator of Yr., Woodson-Delany Ednl. Fund, 1976, Sr. Citizen of Yr, Chgo. Dist., 1994; others. Mem. Assn. for Study of Ancient Classical African Civilizations (bd., elder), Nat. Assn. Media Women (pres., fin. sec. 1983—, sec. chpt. 1982—, v.p. 1973), Nat. Hook Up of Black Women, Women in Comm., Friends of Amistad (bd. dirs.), Alpha Gamma Pi (v.p., corres. sec.), Delta Sigma Theta, Phi Delta Kappa. Democrat. Congregationalist. Club: Debonnettes (pres. 1984) (Chgo.). Home: 1618 E 85th Pl Chicago IL 60617-2235 Fax: 773-374-6749.

MAYO, DOUGLAS BLAKE, computer scientist, application developer; b. Gloucester, Mass., Apr. 20, 1948; BS in Math. & Physics, U. Maine, Farmington, 1973; MS in Computer Sci., Farleigh-Dickinson U., Teaneck, NJ, 1983; MBA in Data Processing, Farleigh-Dickinson U., Florham, 1988. Cert. pub. adjuster NJ, 2005. Computer scientist Rdecom Cerdec Sed, Ft. Monmouth, NJ, 1975—. Home: 511 Wellington Pl Matawan NJ 07747 Personal E-mail: douglasmayo@optonline.net. Business E-Mail: douglas.mayo@us.army.mil.

MAYO, GEORGE WASHINGTON, JR., lawyer; b. Waycross, Ga., Dec. 23, 1946; s. George Washington and Perrie R. (Ling) M.; m. Katherine Louise Boland, Nov. 15, 1977; children: Regan L.B., Taylor L.B. BA, Emory U., 1967; JD, U. Va., 1973. Bar: Va. 1973, DC 1974. Assoc. Hogan & Hartson, Washington, 1973—80, ptnr., 1980—, mng. ptnr.-ops. Contbr. articles. Bd. dirs. Vietnam Vets Meml. Fund, Inc., 1978—, Earth Conservation Corps, 1990—; bd. dirs. coll. coun. advisors Emory U., 1994—; bd. dirs. Deafness Rsch. Found., 1997—2001. 1st lt. US Army, 1969—71, Vietnam. Mem.: ABA, DC Bar Assn., Congl. Country Club (Washington), City Club (Washington), Met. Club (Washington), Order of the Coif. Democrat. Methodist. Home: 26 Holly Leaf Ct Bethesda MD 20817-2652 Office: Hogan & Hartson 555 13th St NW Ste 800E Washington DC 20004-1161 Office Phone: 202-637-5679. Office Fax: 202-637-5910. Business E-Mail: gwmayo@hhlaw.com.

MAYO, HENRY P., surveyor; b. Bryan, Tex., June 18, 1963; s. David R. and Mary J. Mayo; m. Sandra K. Bruggman, Oct. 7, 1989; children: Sarah, John. Degree, Tex. A&M U., College Station. Registered land surveyor State of Tex. V.p. Joe Orr, Inc., College Station, 1993—. Pres. bd. Brazos Valley Mus., Bryan, 2004—06; co-chair Brazos County Hist. Commn., Brian, Tex., 2004—; pres. Brazos Valley Rep. Club, College Station, 2005. Mem.: Tex. Soc. Profl. Surveyors (pres. chpt. 20). Republican. Roman Catholic. Avocations: travel, history.

MAYO, JOHN W., finance educator; BA in Econs., Hendrix Coll.; MA in Econs., PhD in Econs., Washington U., St. Louis. Chief economist US Senate Small Bus. Com.; mem. faculty Washington U., U. Tenn., Va. Tech.; prof. McDonough Sch. Bus., Georgetown U., 1997—, sr. assoc. dean, 1999—2001, acting dean, 2002—04. Adv., cons. pub. and pvt. agys. including U.S. Dept. Justice, Fed. Trade Commn., Tenn. Valley Authority, U.S. Dept. Energy, Oak Ridge Nat. Lab.; former chief economist U.S. Senate Small Bus. Com. Co-author (with David L. Kaserman): Government and Business: The Economics of Antitrust and Regulation, 1995; contbr. numerous articles to profl. jours. Zaeslin Fellowship in law and econs., U. Basel, Switzerland. Mem.: Antitrust Law and Economics Assn., We. Econ. Assn., So. Econ. Assn., Am. Econ. Assn. Office: Georgetown U McDonough Sch Bus 37th and O Sts NW Washington DC 20057 Office Phone: 202-687-6972. Business E-Mail: mayoj@georgetown.edu.

MAYO, LOUIS ALLEN, diversified financial services company executive; b. Durham, NC, Nov. 27, 1928; s. Louis Allen and Amy Earl (Overton) M.; m. Emma Jean Minshew, Oct. 31, 1953 (div.); children: Louis Allen III, Robert Lawrence, Carolyn Jean; m. Myrna Ann Smith, Feb. 16, 1980 (div.). Student, Calif. State Poly. Coll., 1948—50; BA in Criminology, Calif. State Coll., Fresno, 1952; MA in Pub. Adminstrn., Am. U., 1960, PhD in Pub. Adminstrn., 1983; postgrad., U. So. Calif., 1960—62. Spl. agt. U.S. Secret Svc., Treasury Dept., LA, 1956-58, 60-63, White House, Washington, 1958-60, 63-66; program mgr. law enforcement Office Law Enforcement Assistance, Justice Dept., 1967-68; acting chief Rsch. Ctr., rsch. program mgr. Nat. Inst. Law Enforcement and Criminal Justice, 1968-74; alternate assoc. mem. Fed. Coun. on Sci. and Tech., White House, 1973-74; dir. tng. and testing divsn. Nat. Inst. Justice, 1975—87; pres. Mayo, Mayo & Assocs., Alexandria, Va., 1987—. Lectr. criminology Armed Forces Inst. Tech., 1954-55; professorial lectr. Am. U., 1974-82; adj. prof. August Vollmer U., 1990-95. 2d lt. to 1st lt. USAF, 1952-56. Mem. Police Assn. Coll. Edn. (exec. dir., founder), Internat. Assn. Chiefs of Police, ASPA (nat. chmn. sect. on criminal justice adminstrn. 1975-76), Am. Soc. for Law Enfocement Tng., Acad. Criminal Justice Scis., Police Exec. Rsch. Forum, Soc. Police Futurists Internat., Pi Sigma Alpha. Methodist. Home: 63 Lake Forest Dr Mineral VA 23117 Home Phone: 540-894-8781; Office Phone: 540-894-8781. Personal E-mail: loumayo@police-association.org.

MAYO, ROBERT N., computer science researcher; b. Washington, Aug. 23, 1959; s. Robert P. and Marian A. Mayo. BS in Computer Sci., Washington U., St. Louis, 1981; MS in Computer Sci., U. Calif., Berkeley, 1983, PhD of Computer Sci., 1987. Asst. prof. U. Wis., Madison, 1988; staff Digital Equipment Corp./Compaq Computer/Hewlett Packard, Palo Alto, Calif., 1989—2006; cons., 2007—. Mem. IEEE, Assn. Computer Machinery. Home: 2800 Elliott Ave Apt 630 Seattle WA 98121

MAYO, ROBERT RAYMOND (BOB MAYO), university librarian; AA, Acad. Aeronautics; BA, SUNY, Plattsburgh; MLS, SUNY, Geneseo. Worked with sys. test, cost engring., and market devel. IBM Corp.; adminstrv. libr. Rensselaer Poly. Inst., Troy, NY, 2001—06, acting dir. rsch. libraries, 2006—. Office: Research Libraries Rensselaer Poly Inst 110 8th St Troy NY 12180 Office Phone: 518-276-8300. Office Fax: 518-276-2044. Business E-Mail: mayor@rpi.edu.

MAYO, STEPHEN L., biochemist; BS in Chemistry, Pa. State U., 1983; PhD in Chemistry, Calif. Inst. Tech., 1987; postdoctoral study, U. Calif., Berkeley, 1988—89. Co-founder Molecular Simulations, Inc., 1984, v.p. bio. scis., 1989—90; sr. rsch. fellow Calif. Inst. Tech., 1991—92, asst. prof. biology, 1992—98, assoc. prof., 1998—2001, assoc. prof. biology and chemistry, 2001—; asst. investigator Howard Hughes Med. Inst., 1994—2000, assoc. investigator, 2000—. Adj. asst. prof. U. So. Calif. Sch. Medicine, 1994—. Recipient Scholar award, Rita Allen Found., 1993—98, Searle, 1994—97, prize, Johnson Found., 1997; fellow, Packard Found., 1993—98; Miller Rsch. fellowship, 1988—89. Mem.: NAS. Office: Calif Inst Tech Divsn Biology Mail Code 114-96 Pasadena CA 91125 Business E-Mail; steve@mayo.caltech.edu.

MAYO, THOMAS WILLIAM, law educator; b. Bangor, Maine, Sept. 7, 1949; s. Harvey William and Marilyn Louise (Chase) M.; m. Jane King Pollard, July 31, 1971; children: David William, Jeffrey Robert, Andrew Chase. BA Philosophy, Amherst Coll., 1971; JD magna cum laude, Syracuse U., 1977. Bar: N.Y. 1978, U.S. Ct. Appeals (D.C. cir.) 1979, D.C. 1980, U.S. Ct. Mil. Appeals 1980, U.S. Ct. Appeals (2nd cir.) 1981, U.S. Supreme Ct. 1981, U.S. Ct. Appeals (11th cir.) 1983. Assoc. Nixon, Hargrave, Devans & Doyle, Rochester, N.Y., 1977-79; law clk. U.S. Ct. Appeals (D.C. cir.), Washington, 1979-80; assoc. Covington & Burling, Washington, 1980-84; assoc. prof. Sch. Law So. Meth. U., Dallas, 1990—2004, asst. prof. Sch. Law, 1984-90, asst. prof., 2004—; assoc. dean acad. affairs, 1992-95; adj. assoc. prof., Dept. Internal Med. Univ. of Tex. So. Western Med. Sch., Dallas, 1994—; counsel Haynes & Boone LLP, Dallas, 1989—. Of counsel Haynes and Boone, Dallas, 1989—; adv. coun. Susan G. Komen Found., 1999—. Contbr. articles to profl. jours. Co-founder, advisor Dallas Legal Hospice, 1988. With U.S. Army, 1971-74.Member, Institutional Ethics Comm.; Parkland Mem. Hosp. Dallas, 1989, co-chair 1992—; Baylor Univ. Med. Ctr., 1991—; RHD Mem. Hosp. Dallas, 1994—, Children's Med. Ctr., Dallas, 2001-; Adv. Comm. Program in Ethics in Sci & Med. Univ. of Tex. Southwestern Med. Ctr., 1998; Community Oversight Comm. Xenotransplantation Proj. Baylor Inst. of Transplantation Sciences, 1997—; Poetry columnist, Dallas Morning News, 1998—. Mem. ABA (health law sect.), Am. Coll. Legal Medicine, Am. Soc. Law and Medicine, Am. Acad. Hosp. Attys., Am. Health Lawyers Assn. (bd. dirs. 1997—), Order of Coif., Maguire Ctr. Ethics & Pub. Responsibility, Tex. Bar Assoc., Am. Coll. Health Care Execs., Nat. Bd. of Advisors Bureau of Nat. Affairs (Health Law reporter), Bd of Editors Matthew Bender's Health Care Law Monthly, Healthcare Financial Mgmt. Assoc., Dallas-Ft Worth Hosp. Coun., State Bar Tex. (health law sect. coun.). Democrat. Episcopalian. Office: So Meth U PO Box 750116 Dallas TX 75275-0116 E-mail: tmayo@mail.smu.edu.

MAYO-JOHNSTON, JULIA A., psychiatry professor, psychotherapist; b. Phila., Aug. 16, 1926; d. Henry Mayo and Mamie Clark; 1 child, Wilvena Gordon. BA in Sociology with honors, U. Pa., Phila., 1947, PhD in Social Rsch., Social Work and Adminstrn., 1958; MS in Social Rsch., Bryn Mawr Coll., Pa., 1949. ACSW NY State Dept. Edn., bd. cert. diplomate clin. social work Am. Acad. Experts in Traumatic Stress, diplomate, master therapist Am. Psychotherapy Assn.; cert. in individual and group psychotherapy, supervision and adminstrn. Wash. Sch. Psychiatry, 1963. Probation officer Family Ct., Wilmington, Del., 1949—52; psychiatric social worker intern Embreeville State Hosp., Pa., 1952—53; psychiatric social worker Vets. Adminstrn. Hosp., Lyons, NJ, 1953—54, asst. chief, outpatient clinic Wilmington, 1954—61, chief social worker, dept. psychiatry, 1954—61; chief clin. social worker and psychosocial rsch. clin. studies CNRC, NIMH, NIH, Washington, 1961—66; chief clin. sociologist, rsch. divsn., dept. psychiatry St. Vincent's Hosp., NYC, 1966—72, chief evaluation unit/preventive treatment program, dept. psychiatry, 1972—75, chief clin. studies, dept. psychiatry, 1975—96, clin. supr. group and individual psychotherapy, chmn. clin. studies group, 1980—96, mem. various committees; assoc. prof. clin. psychiatry and behavioral sci. NY Med. Coll., Valhalla, 1978—92, clin. prof. psychiatry, 1993, clin. prof. psychiatry emeritus, 1996. Field work supr. for grad. students various schs., 1958—88; rsch. com. I.R.B. St. Vincent's Hosp. and Med. Ctr., 1974—76; adj. prof. med. anthropology New Sch. Social Rsch., 1978; mem. editl. bd. Comprehensive Psychiatry, 1975—, Group Psychotherapy Glossary, Clin. Sociology Review; cons. in field; pvt. practice, 1958—; alumni secondary sch. com. U. Pa. Undergraduate Admissions, 1981; bd. mem. Nat. Assn. D.M.D.A., 1992; lectr. and presenter in field. Contbr. articles to jour., chapters to books. Recipient Outstanding Performance award, Vets. Adminstrn. Hosp., Wilmington, 1959, Commendation/Meritorious Svc., 1961, Outstanding Tchr. of Yr. award, Dept. Psychiatry, St. Vincent's Hosp. and Med. Ctr., NY, 1989, 1992, Cert. of Commendation, John Templeton Spirituality and Medicine award, Award for Excellent Contbn., 2003; grantee, Karp Found., 1987, 1989; John F. Creed grant for rsch., 1985. Fellow: APPA, Am. Assn. Family and Marriage Counselors, Am. Group Psychotherapy Assn., Am. Psychopathological Assn. (life); mem.: AAAS, Nat. Inst. Healthcare Rsch., Am. Assn. Social Work and Rsch., Am. Assn. Profl. Hypnotherapists, Am. Assn. Behavioral Therapists, Internat. Soc. Psychologists, Internat. Acad. Counseling and Psychotheraphy, NY Acad. Scis., Internat. Coun. Sex Edn. and Parenthood, Assn. Profl. Responsibility in Medicine and Rsch., Am. Acad. Psychotherapists, Am. Personnel Guidance Assn., Met. Med. Anthropology Assn., Soc. Study Social Biology, Am. Assn. Clin. Psychosocial Rsch., Acad. Cert. Social Workers, Ea. Sociol. Assn., Clin. Sociology Assn. (bd. mem. at large, Disting. Career in Clin. Sociology award 1986), Am. Sociol. Assn. Democrat. Episcopalian. Avocations: travel, music, theater, dance. Home and Office: 205 W End Ave 24J New York NY 10023 Office Phone: 212-787-6524.

MAYOPOULOS, TIMOTHY J., lawyer, bank executive; b. Reading, Pa., Mar. 7, 1959; s. Harry B. and Eleanor Ida (Raifsnider) M.; m. Amy F. Lefkof, Apr. 28, 1990; 1 child, Philip Alexander. AB with distinction, Cornell U., 1980; JD cum laude, NYU, 1984. Bar: NY 1985, US Dist. Ct. (so. and ea. dists. NY) 1987, US Ct. Appeals (2nd cir.) 1993, Supreme Ct., 1993, US Dist. Ct. (ea. and we. dists. Ark.) 1994, US Ct. Appeals (8th cir.), 1995. Law clk. to Hon. William C. Conner US Dist. Ct. (so. dist. NY), NYC, 1984-86; assoc. Davis, Polk & Wardwell, NYC, 1986—94; assoc. ind. counsel Office Ind. Couns. Kenneth Starr, 1994—96; assoc. gen. counsel Donaldson, Lufkin & Jenrette, 1996; mng. dir., sr. dep. gen. counsel, Americas Credit Suisse First Boston; mng. dir., gen. counsel, corp. investment bank, Americas Deutsche Bank AG, 2002—04; exec. v.p., gen. counsel Bank of America, Charlotte, NC, 2004—. Mem. Fed. Bar Coun., Assn. of Bar of City of NY, NY State Bar Assn., Securities Industry Assn., Order of the Coif. Office: Bank of Am Bank of America Plz 101 S Tryon St NC1-002-29-01 Charlotte NC 28225 *

MAYORA-ALVARADO, EDUARDO RENE, lawyer, educator; b. Guatemala, Apr. 20, 1957; s. Eduardo Alfredo Mayora-Dawe and Adelaida (Alvarado) De Mayora; m. Alicia Bascunana, June 18, 1983; children: Javier Eduardo, Santiago, Jose Andres, Sebastian. JD, U. Rafael Landivar, Guatemala, 1980; LLM, Georgetown U., U.S.A., 1982; Diploma (2) in Principles Econ. Sci., U. Francisco Marroquin, Guatemala, 1991, LLD, 1997; D in Pluralist, Pub. and Pvt. Law, M in Pluralist, Pub. and Pvt. Law, U. Autonoma Barcelona, 2004. Bar: Guatemala, 1980; cert. notary. Assoc. Mayora & Mayora, Guatemala, 1980-81, ptnr., 1982—, mem. tax adminstrn. bd., 1998-2000; prof. bus. law and principles of law U. Francisco Marroquin, Guatemala, 1984-87, prof. bus. law and principles of law Sch. of Econs., 1986-88, prof. constitutional law, dean Sch. of Law, 1989-2000, prof. principles of pvt. and pub. law, 1993; bd. dirs. Financiera de Inversion, S.A., Guatemala, 1988-96. Alt. dir. Seguros Alianza S.A., Guatemala, 1988-94; trustee U. Francisco Marroquin, 1989—; vis. prof. Pontificia U. Catolica, Porto Alegre, Brazil, 1994, Montpellier U. Sch. Law, France, 1995. Co-author: El Desafio Neoliberal, 1992; author: Teoría Constitucional para una sociedad libre Fundación República para una nueva generación, 1997, El Imperio Del Derecho Y El Contencioso Administrativo En El Derecho Guatemalteco Comparado, 2005; (essay) El Drama De La Arena Movedisa, 1993 (Charles Stillman award 1993); contbr. to profl. jours. Mem. Guatemala Bar Assn. (author articles Bar Law Jour. 1990—m v.p. ethics bd. 1985-86), Assn. De Amigos Del Pais, Fundacion Para La Cultura (v.p. 1994), Inst. Guatemalteco De Derecho Notarial, Phi Delta Phi, Guatemala Country Club. Roman Catholic. Avocations: reading, sailing, golf. Office: Mayora & Mayora15 Calle 1-04 Plz Centrica 3er Nivel #301 Zona 10 Guatemala City Guatemala also: PO Box 661447 Miami FL 33266-1447 Home Phone: 502-369-7979; Office Phone: 502-236-625-31. Business E-Mail: emayora@mayora-mayora.com.

MAYORAS, DONALD EUGENE, corporate executive, writer, consultant, educator; b. Danville, Ill., Aug. 25, 1939; s. Andrew John and Katherine Ann (Shelato) M.; m. JoAnna Marie Kacmer, June 9, 1962; children: D. Tyler, Stacie J. BS in Edn., Purdue U., 1962; postgrad., Northwestern U., 1968-71; MBA, So. Ill. U., 1977. Regional mgr. Pacific Intermountain Express, Akron, Ohio, 1972-74; v.p. United Van Lines, Fenton, Mo., 1974-78; pres. Bekins Van Lines, LA, 1978-83; pres., CEO Sun Carriers, Inc., Holliston, Mass., 1983-90, chmn. bd. dirs.; vice-chmn., CEO Builders Transport, Camden, SC, 1990—91; chmn., CEO Truckload Holding, Inc., Chester, NY, 1995—2004, Cloverleaf Transp. Inc., Chester, 1997—2004; founder MDC Svcs. Inc., Gallatin, Tex., Goshen, NY. Spkr., cons. in field. Trustee Ross Ade Found., West Lafayette, Ind., 1962—. Capt. U.S. Army, 1962-68; Europe, Vietnam. Decorated Bronze Star. Mem. Am. Trucking Assn. (v.p. 1983—, trustee Found. 1983-91), Nat. Spkrs. Assn., Nat. Coun. Logistics, Nat. Pvt. Truck Coun., Purdue U. Alumni Assn., Nat. Def. Transp. Assn., Aronomink Golf Club, Orange County Golf Club Club at Fairvue Plantation, Delta Nu Alpha, Beta Gamma Sigma, Omicron Delta Kappa Republican. Roman Catholic. Avocations: golf, antiques, classic automobiles. Business E-Mail: demayoras@aol.com.

MAYORKAS, ALEJANDRO, lawyer, former prosecutor; b. Cuba; With Patterson, Belknap, Webb & Tyler, LA, 1986-89; asst. U.S. atty., 1989-99; chief office's gen. crimes sect., 1996-98; U.S. atty. cen. dist. Calif. U.S. Dept. Justice, 1999—2001; ptnr. O'Melveny & Myers, LA, 2001—. Tchr. trial advocacy Loyola Law Sch., 1997-98. Office: O'Melveny & Myers 400 S Hope St Los Angeles CA 90071-2899 Office Phone: 213-430-6363. Business E-Mail: amayorkas@omm.com.

MAYPOLE, JOHN FLOYD, real estate company executive; b. Chgo., May 17, 1939; s. John James and Althea Floyd M.; m. Anne White, 1961; children: Cynthia, John, Kimberly. BA in Econs, Yale U., 1961. With Arthur Andersen & Co., 1961-62, 65-66; mgr. corp. acctg. Interpace Corp., 1966, asst. treas., 1967-68, treas., 1968-70, treas., controller, 1970-73, v.p. fin., 1973-77, sr. v.p., 1977-80, exec. v.p., 1980-81, pres., 1981-83; pres., chief operating officer Clevepak Corp., 1983-84; mng. ptnr. Peach State Real Estate Holding Co., Toccoa, Ga., 1984—. Bd. dirs. Knoll, Inc., Mass. Mut. Fin. Group, Nat. Captioning Inst., Inc. Bd. adjustment Borough of Mountain Lakes, N.J., 1971-81, chmn., 1980-81. Served with USMC, 1962-65. Mem. Yale Club, Ivy League Club (Sarasota), Rockaway River Country Club, Laurel Oak Country Club. Republican. Office: PO Box 1223 Toccoa GA 30577-1421

MAYR, JAMES FRANCIS, physician; b. Milw., Dec. 23, 1945; s. Francis Joseph and Lucille Gladys Mayr. MD, Med. Coll. Wis., Milw., 1971. Cert. occupl. medicine Am. Bd. Preventive Medicine, 1979. Physician USN, Groton, Conn., 1972—79; occupl. medicine USN Civil Svc., Pensacola, Fla., 2000—06. Home: 4255 S 78th St Greenfield WI 53220-2806 Home Phone: 414-543-4976.

MAYRO, KARL R., realtor; b. Drexel Hill, Pa., Apr. 13, 1966; s. Allan Dale and Patricia Mayro. BA in Econs., St. Joseph's U., 1988. Realtor Prudential Fox & Roach, Newtown Square, Pa., 1988—. Bd. mgrs. The Episcopal Acad., Merion, Pa., 2002—. Mem.: Suburban West Realtors Assn., Pa. Assn. Realtors, Nat. Assn. Realtors, World Affairs Coun. Phila., Phila. Mus. Art, Pa. Hort. Soc. Avocations: gardening, classic Cadillacs, golf, photography.

MAYRON, LEWIS WALTER, clinical ecology consultant; b. Chgo., Sept. 20, 1932; s. Max and Florence Minette (Brody) M.; m. Sondra Mayron; children: Leslie Hope Mayron Coff, Eric Brian. BS in Chemistry, Roosevelt U., 1954; MS in Biol. Chemistry, U. Ill., 1955, PhD in Biol. Chemistry, 1959. Rsch. assoc. dept. biochemistry and nutrition U. So. Calif., LA, 1959-61; asst. biochemist dept. biochemistry Presbyn.-St. Luke's Hosp., Chgo., 1961-62; instr. dept. biol. chemistry U. Ill., Chgo., 1961-62; biochemistry group leader Tardanbek Labs., Chgo., 1962-63; sr. devel. chemist Abbott Labs., Chgo., 1963-64; asst. attending physician, mem. spl. staff Michael Reese Hosp. and Med. Ctr., Chgo., 1964-66, rsch. assoc. Dept. Allergy Rsch., 1964-66; asst. prof. in biochemistry and physiology Sch. Dentistry Loyola U., Chgo., 1968-71; guest investigator Argonne (Ill.) Nat. Lab., 1973-79; rsch. chemist V.A. Hosp., Hines, Ill., 1968-79; chief clin. radiobiochemist nuclear medicine svc. V.A. Wadsworth Hosp. Ctr., LA, 1979-83; cons. in clin. ecology, 1980—. Contbr. articles to profl. jours. Mem. AAAS, Am. Assn. Clin. Chemists, Soc. for Exptl. Biology and Medicine, Sigma Xi. Home: 823 S 1850 West Cedar City UT 84720-8237

MAYS, J. C., automotive executive; b. 1955; Grad., Art Ctr. Coll. of Design, 1980. Designer Audi AG, Ingolstad, Germany, 1980—83, BMW, Munich, 1983—84; sr. designer Audi AG, Ingolstad, Germany, 1984—89; chief designer Volkswagon of Am., Simi Valley, Calif., 1989—93; design dir. Audi AG, Ingolstad, Germany, 1993—95; v.p. design devel. SHR Perceptual Mgmt., Scottsdale, 1995—97; v.p. design Ford Motor Co., Dearborn, Mich., 1997—2003, group v.p. design, 2003—, chief creative officer, 2005—. Design (exhibitions) "Retrofuturism: The Car Design of J. Mays", Geffen Mus. Contemporary Art LA, 2002. Named a Master of Design, Fast Company mag., 2004; recipient Excellence in Design award, Harvard Design Sch., 2002, Don Kubly Profl. Attainment award, 2002. Office: Ford Motor Co One American Rd Dearborn MI 48126-1899

MAYS, JANICE ANN, lawyer; b. Waycross, Ga., Nov. 21, 1951; d. William H. and Jean (Bagley) M. AB (hon.), Wesleyan Coll., Macon, Ga., 1973; JD, U. Ga., 1975; LLM in Taxation, U. Georgetown, 1980. Bar: Ga. 1976. Tax counsel com. on ways and means U.S. Ho. Reps., Washington, 1975-88, chief tax counsel com. on ways and means, staff dir. subcom. select revenue measures, 1988-93, chief counsel, staff dir. com. on ways and means, 1993-95, minority chief counsel, staff dir. com. on ways and means, 1995—. Recipient Disting. Achievement in Profession Alumnae award Wesleyan Coll., 1998. Mem. Tax Coalition (past chair). Office: Ways & Means Com 1106 Longworth Office Bldg Washington DC 20515-0001

MAYS, JEFFERSON, actor; BA, Yale U.; MFA, UCSD. Actor: (TV series) Dynaman, 1988; (TV miniseries) Liberty! The American Revolution, 1997; (films) The Killing Box, 1993, Some Folks Call It a Sling Blade, 1994, The Low Life, 1995, Hudson River Blues, 1997, Cousin Bette, 1998, The Big Brass Ring, 1999, (regional theater) Rosencrantz & Guildenstern Are Dead, Misalliance, The Importance of Being Earnest, The Beauty Part, Not Suitable for Children, The Cherry Orchard, The Winter's Tale, She Stoops to Conquer, Servant of Two Masters, Macbeth, Miss Julie, Private Lives; (Broadway plays) I Am My Own Wife, 2003— (Theater World award, 2004, Drama Desk award outstanding solo performance, 2004, Obie award outstanding performance, 2004, Tony award best actor in a play, 2004, Joseph Jefferson award for actor in a principal role (play), 2005), Of Thee I Sing, 2006.

MAYS, JOHN E., lawyer; b. Richmond, Va., 1948; Grad., Birmingham Sch. Law, 1976, U. Va., Mercer U. Judge advocate gen. N.G.; pvt. practice, 1977—. Author: (books) Defending Death Penalty Cases In Alabama, Defending Child Sex Abuse Cases in Alabama, Defending Domestic Cases in Alabama/Crimes Against the Family, Drug Condemnations and Forfeitures in Alabama, Use of Computers in Criminal Trials. With U.S. Army. Mem.: Ala. Criminal Def. Lawyers Assn. (life Roderick Beddow Sr. Lifetime Achievement award 2004). Office: 414 E Moulton St PO Box 655 Decatur AL 35602 also: PO Box 655 Decatur AL 35602 E-mail: aquit13@aol.com.

MAYS, L(ESTER) LOWRY, broadcast executive; b. Houston, July 24, 1935; s. Lester T. and Virginia (Lowry) M.; m. Peggy Pitman, July 29, 1959; children: Kathryn Mays Johnson, Linda Mays McCaul, Mark P., Randall T. BS in Petroleum Engring., Tex. A&M U., 1959; MBA, Harvard U., 1962. Comml. recorder, San Antonio; with Sta. KTTU-TV, Tucson, Sta. KOKI/KTFO-TV, Tulsa, Sta. WMPI/WJTC-TV, Mobile and Pensacola, Okla., Sta. WAWS-TV, Jacksonville, Fla., Sta. KSAS-TV, Wichita, Kans., Sta. KLRT/KASN-TV, Little Rock, Sta. WFTC-TV, Mpls., Sta. WFTC-TV, WLMT/WMTU-TV, Memphis, Sta. WXXA, Albany, Sta. WQUE-AM-FM, New Orleans, Clear Channel Sports, Des Moines, Okla. News Network, Oklahoma City, Va. News Network, Stas. KJYO and KTOK,

Oklahoma City, Sta. KEBC, Oklahoma City, Sta. WELI, New Haven, Sta. WKCI-WAVZ, New Haven, Sta. KPEZ, Austin, Tex., Stas. KHYS, KALO, KBXX, KMJQ, KPRC, KSEV and KYOK, Houston and Point Arthur, Tex., KMOD & KAKC, Tulsa, KTAM & KORA, Bryan and College Station, Tex., WHAS & WAMZ, Louisville; with radio and TV broadcasting WOAI, KQXT, and KAJA, San Antonio; chmn., CEO Clear Channel Communications Inc., San Antonio, 1975—2004; chmn. C;ear Channel Communications Inc., San Antonio, 2004—. Past chmn. bd. CBS Radio Affiliates Bd. Bd. dirs., trustee Tex. Rsch. Pk.; bd. dirs., mem. exec. com. United Way; chmn. United Way San Antonio and Bexar County, 1995; regent emeritus Tex. A&M U. Sys.; trustee Tex. Rsch. and Tech. Found.; mem. deve. bd. U. Tex. Health Sci. Ctr.; adv. dir. Permanent Univ. Fund Tex. Mem. Nat. Assn. Broadcasters (past chmn. joint bd.), Greater San Antonio C. of C. (past chmn.), Rotary. Home: 400 Geneseo Rd San Antonio TX 78209-6127 Office: Clear Channel Comms Inc PO Box 659512 San Antonio TX 78265-9512 *

MAYS, MARK PITMAN, communication company executive; b. San Antonio, Aug. 2, 1963; BA in Econs. and Math., Vanderbilt U.; MBA, Columbia U. V.p., treas. Clear Channel Comms., San Antonio, sr. v.p. ops., 1993—96, pres., COO, 1996—2004, interim CEO, 2004, pres., CEO, 2004—06, CEO, 2006—. Bd. dirs. NAB Radio Bd. Bd. dirs. Jr. Achievement San Antonio Chap., Alamo Area Coun. Boy Scouts Am., United Way San Antonio, SW Found. Biomedical Rsch. Office: Clear Channel Comms 200 E Basse Rd San Antonio TX 78209-8328 Fax: 210-822-2299. *

MAYS, QUINCEY, art educator; b. Jinmachi, Japan, July 21, 1948; s. Joseph Roles and Edna Eilleen Mays; 1 child from previous marriage, Isaac Marshall. B in Mil. Sci., Cameron U., 1971, BA in Math., 1971, BS in Elem. Edn., 1981, BFA, 1984; MEd, U. Okla., 1979. Tchr. Indiahoma (Okla.) HS, 1974—75, Brockland Elem., Lawton, Okla., 1976—81; tchr. art Whittier Elem., Lawton, 1982—93, Pat Henry Elem., Lawton, 1994—97, Lawton HS, 1998—. Adj. prof. Cameron U., Lawton, 1984—96; coach cross country/tennis Lawton HS, 1998—, chmn. curriculum fine arts dept., 1999—; artist-in-residence kindergarten acad. Lawton Pub. Schs., 2002—; instr. Goddard Youth Camp Gifted/Talented, Lake of Arbuckles, Sulpher, 1981—2001; coach cross country MacArthur H.S., Lawton, 2005—. Mem. Arts and Humanities Coun., Lawton, 1995—. Capt. US Army, 1970—74. Named Cross Country Coach of Yr., Okla. Secondary Schs. Athletic Assn., 2006—07; recipient numerous Best of Show awards for Visual Art; grantee, Coll. Bd., 1999. Mem.: Okla. Secondary Schs. Activities Assn., Phi Theta Kappa. Republican. Avocations: running, fishing, art, guitar, tennis. Home: 1702 NW Liberty Lawton OK 73507 Office: Lawton HS 601 NW Fort Sill Blvd Lawton OK 73507

MAYS, RANDALL T., communications company executive; b. 1966; married. BA with honors, Univ. Tex., Austin, Tex.; MBA, Harvard Bus. Sch. With Trammell Crow Co. Real Estate Firm, Goldman, Sachs & Co., NY; v.p., treas. Clear Channel Comm., San Antonio, 1993—97, CFO, exec. v.p., 1997—2006, CFO, pres., 2006—; chmn. CCE SpinCo, Inc. Bd. dirs. XM Satellite Radio. Adv. coun. Univ. Tex McCombs Bus. Sch. Mem.: Broadcast Cable Fin. Mgmt. Assn. (CFO of the Yr. 2002), Nat. Assn. of Broadcasters. Office: CCE Spinco Inc 2000 W Loop South Ste 1300 Houston TX 77027 *

MAYS, WILLIAM G., chemical company executive; MBA, Ind. U. Test chemist Linkbelt Facility, Indpls.; acct. mgr. Procter & Gamble; market planning Eli Lilly and Co.; asst. to pres. Cummins Engine Co.; founder, pres. Mays Chem. Co., Indpls., 1980—. Bd. dirs. NBD-Inc. Mem. exec. com., bd. dirs. United Way Ctrl. Ind., Ind. Conv. and Visitors Assn.; bd. dirs. Associated Group, Corp. Cmty. Coun., Ind. Univ. Found., Cmty. Leaders Allied for Superior Schs.; mem. dean's adv. coun. Ind. U. Sch. Bus.; mem. pres.'s coun. Ind. U.; co-chmn. Coca-Cola Circle City Classic; elder Witherspoon Presbyn. Ch. Recipient Man of Yr. award B'Nai B'Rith Isidora Feibleman award, 1990, Elder Watson Diggs Achievement award Kappa Alpha Psi, 1991, Ind. Minority Small Bus. Advocate of Yr. award, 1991, Sagamore of Wabash award Gov. Ind., 1991, Ind. Enterprise award, 1992, Ind. Christian Leadership Conf. Businessman of Yr. award, 1992, Disting. Hooser, 1992, 13th in Black Enterprise Mag. Top 100 Indsl./Svc Cos., 'Above and Beyond' award Ind. Black Expo, 1992, Pres.'s award Black Pres.'s Roundtable Assn., 1992, Vol. Fund Raiser award, 1992, Anti-Defamation League Americanizm award, 1993, Charles Whistler award, 1993, Indpls. Edn. Assn.'s Human Rights award, 1994, Ind. State Conf. NAACP Labor and Industry award, 1994, Robert W. Briggs Humanitarian award, 1995, and numerous others; carried Olympic flame during trip through Indpls., 1995. Mem. Ind. C. of C. (bd. dirs.), Indpls. C. of C. (exec. com., bd. dirs.). Office: Mays Chemical Co Inc PO Box 50915 Indianapolis IN 46250-0915

MAYS, WILLIAM GAY, II, lawyer, real estate developer; b. Washington, Mo., Apr. 8, 1947; s. Frank G. and Geneva Pauline (Brookhart) M.; 1 son, Daniel Brookhart. AB, U. Mo., 1969, JD, 1972. Bar: Mo. 1972, U.S. Dist. Ct. (we. dist.) Mo. 1972. Legis. rschr. State of Mo., 1972; pub. defender 13th Jud. Cir. Mo., 1973-77; ptnr. Holt, Mays & Brady, Columbia, Mo., 1977-98; ptnr. and gen. counsel comml. real devel. firm. Mem. Jud. Planning Commn., Mo., 1977. Served to capt. USAFR, 1969-82. Named Outstanding Young Man of Am., 1974. Mem. Mo. Bar Assn., Boone and Callaway County Bar Assn., Mo. Trial Lawyers Assn., Mo. Pub. Defender Assn. (pres. 1976-77), Beta Theta Pi. Republican. Office: The Mays Bldg PO Box 10013 Columbia MO 65205-4001

MAYS, WILLIE HOWARD, JR., (SAY HEY KID), retired professional baseball player; b. Westfield, Ala., May 6, 1931; s. William Howard and Ann M.; m. Margherite Wendell Chapman, 1956 (div. 1961), 1 adopted son, Michael; m. Mae Louise Allen, Nov. 27, 1971 LHD (hon.), Yale Univ., 2004. Baseball player Birmingham Black Barons, 1948-50, Trenton Inter-State League, 1950-51, Mpls. Millers, Am. Assn., 1951, N.Y. Giants, 1951-57, San Francisco Giants, 1958-72, N.Y. Mets, 1972-73; with Bally's Park Place, Atlantic City, 1980—; pub. rels. exec. San Francisco Giants, 1986-98, retired, 1998. Author: Willie Mays: My Life In and Out of Baseball, 1966, Say Hey: The Autobiography of Willie Mays, 1988. Served with AUS, 1952-54. Named MVP Nat. League, 1954, 65, Player of Yr. Sporting News, 1954, Baseball Player of Decade Sporting News, 1970, Male Athlete of Yr. AP, 1954, NL Rookie of Yr., 1951, Sporting News Player of the Year award, 1954, All-Star Game, 1954-73; recipient Hickok belt, 1954, Golden Bat award to commemorate 600 home runs, Gold Glove award (12 times), 1st Commissioner's award, 1970, Golden Plate awarded to America's Captains of Achievement by Am. Acad. Achievement, 1976, Spirit of Life award City of Hope, 1988, Sportsman of Decade, Cong. Racial Equality, 1991, Legendary Star award HBO Video; inducted into Ala. Sports Hall of Fame, Baseball Hall of Fame, 1979, Black Hall of Fame, 1973, Calif. Sports Hall of Fame; named to All-Time Rawlings Gold Glove Team, 2007. Achievements include being the holder of 4th place in major league homeruns (660); lifetime batting average of .302; signed lifetime pub. rels. contract with San Francisco Giants, 1993. Office: Baseball Hall of Fame PO Box 590 Cooperstown NY 13326-0590

MAYSILLES, DANIEL BRUCE, pharmaceutical services executive; b. Hamilton, Ohio, May 26, 1952; s. Carl A. and Ella Jean (Thorpe) M.; m. Dawn M. Hamilton, Aug. 9, 1975 (div. May 1989); m. Nancy K. Cragg, Feb. 15, 1992; 1 child, Ryan. AA, U. South Fla., 1972; BS in Pharmacy, U. Fla., 1975. Registered pharmacist. Pharmacist Roscoe's Rexall Drugs, New Port Richey, Fla., 1975-77, Eckerd Drugs, Spring Hill, Fla., 1977-79; staff pharmacist Cmty. Hosp., New Port Richey, 1979-83; assoc. dir. pharmacy HCA New Port Richey Hosp., 1983-85; dir. pharmacy Cmty. Hosp. New Port Richey, 1985—. Pharmacy adv. com. Hosp. Corp. Am., Nashville, 1985—93, tech. adv. com., 1991—93, HPG/PACT adv. com., 2001—; care of the patient chairperson Columbia New Port Richey Hosp., 1994—2003, cons. pharmacist; assoc. prof. Pasco/Hernando C.C., New Port Richey, 1987—88; interim dir. pharmacy HCA Oak Hill Hosp., 2001, Regional Med. Ctr. of Bayonet Point, 2004. Chmn., mem. planning and zoning bd. City of New Port Richey, 1979—, hand devel. rev. bd., 2003-07; sect. chair Acad. Pharmacy Practice Fla. Pharmacy Assn.; mem. pastors coun. Ch. of God, Tarpon Springs, Fla., 1978-88. Regents scholar Bd. Regents, 1970. Mem. Pasco/Hernando Pharmacy Assn. (pres. 1995-96, historian 1993-94, John Dunwoody award 1996, Humanitarian award 1993), Am. Soc. of Health Systems, Rotary Internat., Kappa Psi (Pres. award 1975). Republican. Avocations: golf, tennis, fishing, reading, music. Home: 6134 Oak Ridge Ave New Port Richey FL 34653-4235 Office: Cmty Hosp New Port Richey 5637 Marine Pkwy New Port Richey FL 34652-4316 Office Phone: 727-845-9140. E-mail: gatorx1@msn.com, daniel.maysilles@hcahealthcare.com.

MAYSILLES, ELIZABETH, speech communication professional, educator; b. Sleepy Creek, W.Va. d. Evers and Rose (Scott) M. AB, W.Va. U., Morgantown; MA, Hunter Coll., NYC, 1963; PhD, NYU, 1980. Announcer Radio Sta. WAJR, Morgantown, W.Va.; broadcaster Radio Sta. WGHF-FM, Rural Radio Network, NYC; group leader GMAC, NYC; instr. NYU, NYC; adj. prof. speech comm. Pace U., NYC, 1978—2002; exec. adminstr. Am.-Scottish Found., NYC, 1980-90; adminstrv. asst. Brit. Schs. and Univs. Found., Inc. Numerous radio and television appearances; lectr. in field; personal investment portfolio mgmt.; cons. Vol. counselor Help Line, NYC, 1971-75. Recipient Disting. Svc. award NYU Grad. Orgn., 1970-71. Mem. Internat. Platform Assn. (bd. govs. 1980—), Nat. Inst. Social Scis. (sec. 2005—), NY Acad. Scis., Caledonian Club NY (bd. dirs. 1994-96, 04-06, chieftain 2001-02). Avocations: reading, swimming, gardening, travel in England and Scotland. Home and Office: 155 E 77th St Apt 6F New York NY 10021

MAYSLES, ALBERT H., filmmaker; b. Boston, Nov. 26, 1926; s. Philip and Ethel (Epstein) M.; m. Gillian Walker, Sept. 14, 1976; children: Rebekah, Philip, Sara. BA, Syracuse U., 1949; MA, Boston U., 1953. Rsch. fellow in anesthesia Mass. Gen. Hosp., Boston, 1951-52; instr. social rels. Boston U., 1953-55; pres. Maysles Films, Inc., NYC, 1962—. Filmmaker, prodr. Psychiatry in Russia, 1955, (with others) Primary, 1960, Showman, 1963, What's Happening: The Beatles in the USA, 1964, Salesman, 1967, Gimme Shelter, 1970, Christo's Valley Curtain, 1974, (Blue Ribbon award 1975, Acad. award nomination), Grey Gardens, 1976, Running Fence, 1978 (Blue Ribbon award 1978), Ozawa, 1985, Vladimir Horowitz: The Last Romantic, 1985, Islands, 1986 (Blue Ribbon award, Emmy award), Horowitz Plays Mozart, 1987, Christo in Paris, 1990, Soldiers of Music: Rostropovitch Returns to Russia, 1990 (Emmy award), Abortion: Desparate Choices, 1995 (Peabody award), Letting Go, A Hospice Journey, 1996 (Ace Cable award), Concert of Wills: The Making of the Getty Art Center, 1997; LaLee's Kin, 2000, The Reales of Grey Gardens, 2006. Served as pvt. U.S. Army, 1944-46. Named one of 100 World's Finest Cinematographers, Eastman Kodak, 1999; recipient Career Achievement award, Internat. Documentary Assn., 1994, John Grierson award for Documentary, SMPTE, 1997, Pres.'s award, Am. Soc. Cinematographers, 1998, Vision award, The Boston Film and Video Found., 1998, The Doubletake Career Achievement award, 1998, Lifetime Achievement award, Toronto's Hot Docs, 1999, Flaherty award, 1999, award for documentaries, Sundance Film Festival Cinematography, 2001, Dupont award, 2004, Medal of Honor for Theatre, Nat. Arts Club, 2007; Guggenheim fellow, 1965. Mem. The Reality Club. Home: 21 W 122nd St New York NY 10027-5602 Office: 343 Lenox Ave New York NY 10027 Office Phone: 212-582-6050. E-mail: amaysles@mayslesfilms.com.

MAYUGA, KENNETH A., physician; s. Ruperto D. and Amelita A. Mayuga. BA, Northwestern U., Evanston, Ill., 1996—99; MD, U. Ill., Chgo.-Rockford, 2001—05. Vis. predoctoral fellow Feinberg Cardiovasc. Rsch. Inst., Northwestern U., Chgo., 2001—02; physician in residency Cleve. Clinic Found., Ohio, 2005—. Rschr., cardiology/cardiac electrophysiology Northwestern U. Med. Sch., 1999—2002. Contbr. articles and papers to profl. jours. and pubs. Recipient Eagle Scout, Boy Scouts Am., 1996; grantee Nat. Merit scholarship, 1996. Achievements include research in evaluation of autonomic and non-autonomic components of cardiac repolarization. Home Phone: 216-691-3885.

MAYWEATHER, FLOYD, JR., professional boxer; b. Grand Rapids, Mich., Feb. 24, 1977; s. Floyd Mayweather, Sr.; 3 children. Profl. boxer, 1996—2006; emeritus lightweight champion World Boxing Coun., 2006—. Winner world title vs. Genaro Hernandez by tech. knockout, superfeatherweight divsn. World Boxing Coun., 1998, winner world title def. vs. Angel Manfredy by tech. knockout, superfeatherweight divsn., 98, winner world title def. vs. Carlos Rios by unanimous decision, superfeatherweight divsn., 99, winner world title def. vs. Justin Juuko, superfeatherweight divsn., 99, winner world title def. vs. Carlos Gerena by tech. knockout, superfeatherweight divsn., 99, winner world title def. vs. Goyo Vargas by unanimous decision, superfeatherweight divsn., 2000, winner world title def. vs. Diego Corrales by tech. knockout, superfeatherweight divsn., 01, winner world title def. vs. Carlos Hernandez by unanimous decision, superfeatherweight divsn., 01, winner world title def. vs. Jesus Chavez by tech. knockout, superfeatherweight divsn., 01, winner world title vs. Jose Luis Castillo by unanimous decision, lightweight divsn., 02, winner world title def. vs. Jose Luis Castillo by unanimous decision, lightweight divsn., 02, winner world title def. vs. Victoriano Sosa by unanimous decision, lightweight divsn., 03, winner world title def. vs. Phillip Ndou by tech. knockout, lightweight divsn., 03, winner world title eliminator vs. Demarcus Corley by unanimous decision, superlightweight divsn., 04, winner world title eliminator vs. Henry Bruseles by tech. knockout, superlightweight divsn., 05. Performer: Dancing With the Stars, 2007. Named Fighter of Yr., The Ring Mag., 1998; recipient Bronze medal for 125 pound divsn., US Olympics, Atlanta, 1996. Achievements include eight successful defenses of WBC Super Featherweight Title; five-time US Nat. Amateur Champion. Office: USA Boxing One Olympic Plz Colorado Springs CO 80909 *

MAYYAS, MOHAMMAD A., mechanical engineer, researcher; b. Al-Ramtha, Jordan, Mar. 1978; s. Abdullah Ayed Mayyas and Taraky Zubi. BS in Mech. Engring., Jordan U. Sci. & Tech., Irbid, 2001; MS in Mech. Engring., U. Tex., Arlington, 2004; PhD in Mech. Engring., U. Tex., 2007. Cert. mech. engr., Jordan Assn. Engring., 2001. Lectr. Jordan U. Sci. & Tech., 2001—03; tchg. asst. U. Tex., Arlington, 2003—04; rsch. assoc. Automation & Robotics Rsch. Inst., Ft. Worth, 2005—. Recipient Best Symposium Paper award, Nano & Micro-Smart Sys. Symposium, 2006. Mem.: Am. Soc. Mech. Engring. (corr.). Achievements include development of novel designs of electrothermal microgrippers; patents pending for bio-micropump, monolithic detethering structures; research in microrobotic self-assembly. Avocation: travel. Home: 2309 Stratton Ln Apt# 4104 Arlington TX 76006 Office: Univ Tex Arlington 7300 Jack Newell Blvd S Fort Worth TX 76118 Personal E-mail: mayyas@uta.edu. Business E-Mail: mohammad@arri.uta.edu.

MAZABEL, HECTOR ANTONIO, psychotherapist, guidance counselor, researcher, journalist, announcer; b. Palmira, Valle, Colombia, Sept. 9, 1947; arrived in U.S., 1992; s. Jose Antonio Mazabel and Amelia Buitrago; m. Tatiana Isabel Serbousek, Jan. 26, 2001. MDiv in Philosophy and Theology, Seminario Counciliar, Ibague, 1975; B in Philosophy and religious studies, U. Santo Tomas, Bogota, 1984, M (hon.) in Ednl. Evaluation and Rsch., 1990; MS in Edn., Fhordam U., NYC, 2002; M in Spl. Edn., Bkly. Coll., NYC, 2001. Pastor Ch. of San José of Nazareth Huila Families, 1985—91; tchr. Dioceses of Garzon U. Colombia, 1985—91; parochial vicar asst. Archdiocess of Newark (N.J.), 1992—93; parochial vicar St. Elizabeth Ch., NYC, 1993—95; parochial vicar, broadcaster St. Patrick's Old Cathedral, NYC, 1995—2000; spl. edn. tchr. Bd. of Edn. Dist. 75, NYC, 1998—2002; guidance counselor Dept. Edn., NYC, 2002—. Ednl. pastor, del., tchr. Diocesis Garzon (Colombia). Prodr.(dir.): (radio show) Impacto Hispano, 1995—2000; author: (book) En Los Umbrales del Terccer Milenio, 1995, jours. and newsletters. Journalist Assn. Journalists, Colombia, 1986—91; radio broadcaster Assn. Broadcaster, Colombia, 1986—91. Democrat. Roman Catholic. Achievements include research in methodology and strategies to evaluate learning group process. Avocations: basketball, running, reading, writing, researching. Home: 2014 Colden Ave Bronx NY 10462 Office Phone: 646-295-7747. Personal E-mail: mazab2@aol.com.

MAZAK, ARLENE PATRICIA, marriage and family therapist; d. John Andrew Mazak and Irene Kraszewski. BA in Liberal Arts, Sarah Lawrence Coll., Bronxville, NY, 1967; MA in Counselling, U. San Francisco, Calif., 1992; PhD in South Asian Langs. and Civilization, U. Chgo., Ill., 1994. Cert. orgnl. devel. and transformation specialist Calif. Inst. Integral Studies, 1993, lic. marriage and family therapist Calif. Core faculty Calif. Inst. Integral Studies, San Francisco, 1986—93; tng. dir. Spiritual Emergence Network, Menlo Park, Calif., 1990—91; core faculty Inst. Transpersonal Psychology, Palo Alto, Calif., 1993—2000; adj. faculty gerontology Coastline C.C., Fountain Valley, Calif., 2001—06; marriage and family therapist, life coach and spiritual dir. Innercall: Transpersonal Healing and Devel. Svcs., Fountain Valley and Encinitas, Calif., 2001—. Recipient Dean's prize, Calif. Inst. Integral Studies, 1993; Fulbright Hays fellow, India, 1971—72. Home: 1170 Saxony Rd Encinitas CA 92024-2225 Home Phone: 760-487-1080. Personal E-mail: arlene@innercall.net.

MAZANKOWSKI, DONALD FRANK, Canadian government official; b. Viking, Alta., Can., July 27, 1935; s. Frank and Dora (Lonowski) M.; m. Lorraine Poleschuk, Sept. 6, 1958; children: Gregory, Roger, Donald. Student, pub. schs., 1987; PhD in Engring (hon.), N.S. Inst. Tech.; LLD (hon.), U. Alta., 1993. MP Ho. of Commons, 1968—, chmn. com. transp., 1972-74, mem. com. govt. ops., 1976-77, mem. com. trans. and communication, 1977-79; min. of transp., min. responsible for Can. Wheat Bd. Govt. of Can., 1979-80, min. of transp. (re-drafted Nat. Transp. Act), 1984-86, dep. prime min., 1986—, govt. house leader, 1986-88, pres. Privy Coun., 1986-91, pres. Treas. Bd., 1987-88, min. responsible for privatization and regulatory affairs, 1988-91, min. of agriculture, 1988-91, min. of fin., 1991-93; former chmn. Inst. Health Econs. Former mem. bd. govs. U. Alta; bd. dirs. Power Corp. Can., Power Fin. Corp., Great West Life Assurance, The Investors Group, Shaw Comms. Inc., Weyerhauser Co., Can. Oilsands Trust, ATCO Ltd., London Life Ins., Yellow Pages Group; former chmn. Can. Genetic Diseases Network.; sr. advisor Gowlings Lafleur Henderson, LLP. Apptd. chmn. Premier's Adv. Coun. on Health. Decorated officer Order of Can., Alta. Order of Excellence; recipient Alta. Centennial medal, 2005; Paul Harris fellow Rotary Internat., 2002; honoree Pub. Policy Forum Can., 2003; named one of Alta.'s 50 Most Influential People, 2002. Mem. Royal Can. Legion (life). Clubs: Vegreville Rotary (past dir.). Lodges: KC. Roman Catholic. Office Phone: 780-410-0728. E-mail: donmaz@shaw.ca.

MAZER, MIKE, cardiologist, retired nephrologist, artist; b. Boston, May 17, 1936; s. Louis and Belle Mazer; m. Marilyn Wood, Feb. 26, 1987; children: Mark, Pamela. BS cum laude, Boston U., Mass., 1958; MD, U. Cin., 1962. Diplomate in internal medicine Am. Bd. Internal Medicine, 1970, in nephrology Am. Bd. Nephrology, 1978, in cardiology Am. Bd. Cardiology, 1979. Fellow gastrointestinal disease U. Cin., 1962—64; fellow renal and metabolic studies Med. Ctr. Boston U., 1964—65; fellow cardiovasc. disease West Roxbury VA Hosp., Boston, 1967—68; dir. acute hemodialysis Goddard Meml. Hosp., Stoughton, Mass., 1968—90, chief Echocardiography and Noninvasive Vascular Lab, 1977—94, chief cardiology, 1986—94; chief of nephrology Cardinal Cushing Hosp., Brockton, Mass., 1968—94; pvt. practice Bridgewater Goddard Pk. Med. Assocs., Mass., 1968—98; co-dir. Brockton- Goddard Hemodialysis Unit, Brockton, 1992—97; chief cardiology Good Samaritan Med. Ctr., Brockton, 1994—97, chief Echocardiography and Noninvasive Vascular Lab, 1994—97; med. dir. Pk. Cardiographics, Taunton, Mass.; dir. Cardiac Ultrasonography and Transtelephonic Monitoring Nat. Med. Co, Taunton; dir. Cardiac Rehab. Ctr. Striar Jewish Cmty. Ctr., Stoughton, 1994—97; artist Mattapoisett, Mass., 1997—. Splash 9: Watercolor Secrets, 2006, Contemporary American Marine Art, 2003—04; co-author: Principles of Interpretation in Echocardiography, 1985; editor: Jour. Diagnostic Med. Sonography, 1985—87; over 240 exhbns. Recipient Top Money Water Media award, Am. Artists Profl. League, Grand Nat. Exhibitions, 1999, 2004, Best in Show award, Stoughton Art Assn., 2002, 2004, Miss. Grand Nat. Exhbn., 2003. Fellow: Am. Artists Profl. League; mem.: Phila. Watercolor Soc., New Eng. Watercolor Soc. (pres. 2004—07), Canton (Mass.) Art Assn. (dir. edn. 1997—2007), Ea. Wash. Watercolor Soc., Coast Guard Artist Program, Cape Cod Art Assn., Audubon Artists, Inc, Allied Artists of Am., Academic Artists Assn., Am. Soc. of Marine Artists, R.I. Watercolor Soc. (Best in Show award 2004), North Shore Arts Assn., Phila. North East Watercolor Soc., Tex. Watercolor Soc., Pa. Watercolor Soc., Nat. Soc. of Artists, Mo. Watercolor Soc., Internat. Guild of Realism (assoc.), Miss. Watercolor Soc., Mont. Watercolor Soc., Internat. Soc. of Marine Painters, Hudson Valley Art Assn., Ga. Watercolor Soc., The Salmagundi Club, Alpha Omega Alpha, Watercolor U.S.A. Honor Soc. Achievements include development of the first acute hemodialysis on the South Shore of Massachusetts, 1968; discovery of a Left Ventricular Myxoma by ultra sonography, 1984. Home: 7 Holly Woods Rd Mattapoisett MA 02739 Home Phone: 508-758-6216.

MAZER, TOBY ROTMAN, adminstrative director; b. Phila., June 12, 1939; d. David and Fania Rotman; m. Howard Mazer, June 4, 1960; children: Ira, Renée. BS in Edn., Temple U., 1961, MPH, 1981. Adminstrv. dir. Stroke Network Devel. Thomas Jefferson U., Phila., 1994—. Exec. dir., founder, patient advocate Phila. Stroke Coun., 1995—. Recipient Congrl. Recognitive award Phila. Stroke Coun., 1997, Recognition award State of Pa., 1997, City of Phila., 1997. Mem. Nat. Stroke Assn. (bd. dirs. 1995—). Home: 1420 Locust St Apt 32I Philadelphia PA 19102-4219 Office: Thomas Jefferson U Hosp 925 Chestnut St Ste 200 Philadelphia PA 19107 E-mail: toby.mazer@mail.tju.edu.

MAZLEN, ROGER GEOFFREY, ophthalmologist, pharmacologist; b. Bklyn., Nov. 23, 1937; s. Henry Gershwin and Ann Kurland (Shapero) M.; m. Sandra Phyllis Kuritzky, Aug. 7, 1960; children: James Edward, Vivien Gayle. BS in Biology, Rensselaer Poly. Inst., 1959; MD, SUNY, Bklyn., 1963. Intern maimonides Med. Ctr., Bklyn., 1963-64, resident in medicine, 1964-65; rsch. assoc. NIH, Bethesda, Md., 1965-67; resident in med. ophthalmology Mt. Sinai Med. Ctr., NYC, 1967-69; assoc. med. dir. Pfizer Inc., NYC, 1970-71; asst. dir. clin. rsch. Ayerst Labs., NYC, 1971-75; assoc. dir. clin. rsch. Schering Corp., Bloomfield, NJ, 1975-78; adj. asst. prof. medicine N.Y. Med. Coll.; sr. clin. asst. prof. Mt Sinai Sch. Medicine; sr. faculty, sr. attending div. endocrinology and metabolism Mt. Sinai Med. Ctr. Mem. cons. Profl. Children's Sch.; cons. in clin. nutrition and metabolism South Oaks Hosp; chief sci. officer Biomelecular Sci., Inc., 2000-. Author: A New Manifesto for Middle America, 1972; author: (with others) Nutrition and Health Care; contbr. (chpt.) Quick Reference to Clinical Nutrition, mem. editl. staff Jour. of the Chiropractic Coun. on Nutrition. Founder, chmn. Queens County (N.Y.) Common Cause, 1972—75, vice chmn. for N.Y. State, 1974—75; bd. dirs. Bayside Hills Civic Assn., 1970—80; adv. mem. bd. dirs. U.S.A., Inc., 1970—72; chmn. hyperalimentation com. Astoria (N.Y.) Gen. Hosp.; former dir. Clin. Rsch.

N. Am. Immunatee Ltd., Montreal; nutrition dir. Cernitin Am. Nutritional, 1983—88, also mem. eating disorder adv. bd. With USPHS, 1965—67. Fellow: Am. Coll. Nutrition (chmn. coun. on nutrition and cardiovasc. diseases 1976—85, sec.-treas.); mem.: N.Y. State Soc. Internal Medicine, Soc. for Natural Immunity, Am. Coll. Cardiology (constituent mem. N.Y. State chpt.), Am. Soc. Clin. Pharmacology and Therapeutics, Muhammad Ali Internat. Sport Youth Athletic Found. Inc. (bd. dirs.). Republican. Office: 30 Middledeck Rd Roslyn NY 11576 Home Phone: 718-631-4908; Office Phone: 516-869-0717. E-mail: rgm1@aol.com.

MAZLISH, BRUCE, historian, educator; b. NYC, Sept. 15, 1923; s. Louis and Lee (Reuben) M.; m. Neva Goodwin, Nov. 22, 1988; children from previous marriage: Cordelia, Peter, Anthony, Jared. BA, Columbia U., 1944, MA, 1947, PhD, 1955. Instr. history U. Maine, 1946-48, Columbia U., 1949- 50, Mass. Inst. Tech., 1950-53; dir. Am. Sch. in Madrid, Spain, 1953-55; from mem. faculty to prof. emeritus Mass. Inst. Tech., 1955—2004, prof. emeritus, 2004—. Vis. prof. Harvard U., Cambridge, Mass., 2001—02; scholars coun. Libr. of Congress, 2001—04. Author: (with J. Bronowski) The Western Intellectual Tradition, 1960, The Riddle of History, 1966, In Search of Nixon, 1972, James and John Stuart Mill: Father and Son in the 19th Century, 1975, 2d edition, 1988, The Revolutionary Ascetic, 1976, Kissinger, The European Mind in American Policy, 1976, The Meaning of Karl Marx, 1984, A New Science: The Breakdown of Connections and the Birth of Sociology, 1989, The Leader, the Led and the Psyche, 1990, The Fourth Discontinuity: The Co-Evolution of Humans and Machines, 1993, The Uncertain Sciences, 1998, Civilization and Its Contents, 2004, (with Alfred Chandler) Leviathans, The Multinational Corporations and New Global History, 2005, (with Akira Iriya) The Global History Reader, 2005, The New Global History, 2006; Editor: Psychoanalysis and History, 1963, rev. edit., 1971, The Railroad and the Space Program: An Exploration in Historical Analogy, 1965, (with Ralph Buultjens) Conceptualizing Global History, 1993, (with Leo Marx) Progress: Fact or Illusion, 1996; contbr. articles to profl. jours. Bd. dirs. Rockefeller Family Fund, 1987-97; v.p. Mount Desert Festival of Chamber Music, 1985—; bd. dirs. Toynbee Prize Found., 1992—, pres., 1997—2006; mem. gov. bd. Rockefeller Archives Ctr., 1999-2005. Served with inf. and OSS, AUS, 1943-45. Recipient Toynbee prize, 1986-87. Fellow Am. Acad. Arts and Scis. Clubs: Cambridge Tennis, Badminton and Tennis; Harbor (Seal Harbor, Maine). Home: 11 Lowell St Cambridge MA 02138-4725 Office: MIT 77 Massachusetts Ave Cambridge MA 02139-4307 Business E-Mail: bmazlish@mit.edu.

MAZO, MARK ELLIOTT, lawyer; b. Phila., Jan. 12, 1950; s. Earl and Rita (Vane) M.; m. Fern Rosalyn Litman, Aug. 19, 1973; children: Samantha Lauren, Dana Suzanne, Ross Elliott, Courtney Litman. AB, Princeton U., 1971; JD, Harvard U., 1974. Bar: DC 1975, US Dist. Ct. DC 1975, US Claims Ct. 1975, US Ct. Appeals (DC cir.) 1976, US Supreme Ct. 1979. Ptnr. Hogan & Hartson, L.L.P., Washington and Paris, 1990—. Contbr. articles to profl. jours. White House intern Exec. Office of Pres., Washington, 1972. Capt. USAR, 1971-79. Mem. ABA, Harvard Law Sch. Assn., DC Bar Assn., Columbia Country Club, Princeton Club (NYC), Colonial Club, City Club, Nassau Club, Timbers Club, Phi Beta Kappa. Republican. Home: 3719 Cardiff Rd Chevy Chase MD 20815-5943 Office: Hogan & Hartson LLP 555 13th St NW Washington DC 20004 also: Hogan & Hartson MNP 69 Ave Franklin Roosevelt 75008 Paris France Office Phone: 202-637-5673, (33)(0)1 55 73 23 00. Business E-Mail: memazo@hhlaw.com.

MAZO, ROBERT MARC, retired chemistry professor; b. Bklyn., Oct. 3, 1930; s. Nathan and Rose Marion (Mazo) M.; m. Joan Ruth Spector, Sept. 5, 1954; children: Ruth, Jeffrey, Daniel. BA, Harvard U., 1952; MS, Yale U., 1953, PhD, 1955. Rsch. assoc. U. Chgo., 1956-58; asst. prof. Calif. Inst. Tech., 1958-62; assoc. prof. U. Oreg., Eugene, 1962-65, prof. chemistry, 1965-95, prof. emeritus, 1996, head chemistry dept., 1978-81, dir. Inst. Theoretical Sci., 1964-67, 84-87, assoc. dean Grad. Sch., 1967-71; program dir. NSF, 1977-78. Alfred P. Sloan fellow, NSF Sr. Postdoctoral fellow, vis. prof. U. Libre de Bruxelles, Belgium, 1968-69; vis. prof. Technische Hochschule Aachen, Weizmann Inst., Rehovoth, Israel, 1981-82, U. New South Wales, Australia, 1989. Author: Statistical Mechanical Theories of Transport Processes, 1967, Brownian Motion, 2002, also rsch. articles. NSF Postdoctoral fellow U. Amsterdam, Netherlands, 1955-56. Fellow Am. Phys. Soc. Home: 2460 Charnelton St Eugene OR 97405-3214 Office: U Oreg Inst Theoretical Sci Eugene OR 97403 Home Phone: 541-344-0807; Office Phone: 541-346-5224. Business E-Mail: mazo@uoregon.edu.

MAZON, MARGARET FAUSOLD, language educator; b. Windber, Pa., Dec. 26, 1946; d. George McLelland and Ann (Shank) Fausold; m. José Antonio Mazón, Apr. 21, 1973 (div. June 1985); children: David José Mazón, Daniel Eladio Fausold Mazón. Student, U. Valladolid, 1967; BS in Spanish Edn., Ind. U. Pa., 1968; MA in Spanish, W.Va. U., 1973, EdD, 1992. Permanent state tchg. cert., Spanish N-12 NY. Tchr. Spanish McGuffey St. Jr.-Sr. H.S., Claysville, Pa., 1968—70; tchr. ESL Briam Inst., Madrid, 1970—71; adj. prof., asst. prof. St. Bonaventure U., Olean, NY, 1979—2002, assoc. prof., Dept. Chair, 2002—06, assoc. prof., 2006—. Contbr. articles to profl. jours.; translator: Olean Gen. Hosp., 2000—. Vol. Interfaith Caregivers, Olean, 1999—. Recipient Fr. Joe Doino award. Mem.: Modern Lang. Assn. Democrat. Presbyterian. Avocations: swimming, bicycling, cooking, gardening. Office: Modern Lang Dept St Bonaventure Univ Saint Bonaventure NY 14778 Office Phone: 716-375-2468. Business E-Mail: mmazon@sbu.edu.

MAZRIA, EDWARD, architectural firm executive; BArch, Pratt Inst., 1963. With Edward Larabee Barnes, NY; tchr. architecture, rschr. U. N.Mex., 1973; founding mem. Mazria Inc. (formerly Mazria Assocs., Inc.), Santa Fe, 1978—. Tchr. architecture U. Oreg., U. Colo., Denver, UCLA, U. Nebr., Lincoln; mem. Design Arts Roundtable; lectr. in field. Contbr. articles to profl. jours., to mainstream mags.; author: The Passive Solar Energy Book, 1979; prin. works include Genoveva Chavez Cmty. Ctr., Santa Fe (Best Bldg. award, Albuquerque Bus. Jour., 2000, Best Bldg. Design award, Western Region Assn. Gen. Contractors), Mt. Airy Pub. Libr., NC (Instl. Bldg. Design award, Dept. Energy, AIA Honor award), Stockebrand Residence, Albuquerque (Design award, Am. Solar Energy Soc.), Woods Residence, Wintergreen, Va. (Design award, Am. Solar Energy Soc.), Tierra Contenta, Santa Fe, 1999 (Outstanding Planning award, Am. Planning Assn., 1999), Rio Grande Conservatory, Albuquerque Biol. Pk. (Landmark Designation award, Albuquerque Conservation Assn., Best Bldg. award, Albuquerque Bus. Jour., 1997), Bishops Lodge Resort ShaNah Spa and Wellness Ctr., Santa Fe (Most Outstanding Spa in N.Am., Condé Nast Johansens, 2003), Bishops Lodge Resort Cottonwood Lodge (Best Bldg. award, N.Mex. Br., Associated Gen. Contractors and N.Mex. Bus. Jour., 2004), U. N.Mex. Law Sch. Frederick M. Hart Addition, Albuquerque (Best Bldg. award, N.Mex. Bldg. Br., Associated Gen. Contractors and N.Mex. Bus. Jour., 2003, Merit award, AIA Santa Fe chpt., 2002), Agua Fria Elem. Sch. Addition, Santa Fe. Arch. Peace Corps, Arequipa, Peru. Recipient AIA Design award, Design Innovation award, AIA Santa Fe chpt., 1996, Comml. Bldg. award, Dept. Energy, Pioneer award, Am. Solar Energy Soc., 1996. Office: Mazria Inc 607 Cerrillos Rd Ste G Santa Fe NM 87501 Office Phone: 505-988-5309. E-mail: mazria@mazria.com. *

MAZRUI, ALI AL'AMIN, political science professor, researcher; b. Mombasa, Kenya, Feb. 24, 1933; came to U.S., 1960; s. Al'Amin Ali and Safia (Suleiman) M.; m. Molly Vickerman, 1962 (div. 1982); children: Jamal, Al'Amin, Kim Abubakar; m. Pauline Uti, Oct. 1991; children: Farid Chinedu, Harith Ekenechukwu. BA with distinction, U. Manchester, Eng., 1960; MA, Columbia U., 1961; DPhil, Oxford U., 1966. Lectr. Makerere U., Kampala, Uganda, 1963-65, prof. polit. sci., head dept. polit. sci., 1965-73; dean faculty social scis. Faculty Social Scis., Makerere U., Kampala, Uganda, 1967-69; prof. polit. sci. U. Mich., Ann Arbor, 1974-91, prof. Ctr. Afroam. and African Studies, dept. polit. sci., 1974-91; Andrew D. White prof.-at-large Cornell U., Ithaca, 1986-92; research prof. polit. sci. U. Jos, Nigeria, 1981-86; Albert Schweitzer prof. humanities SUNY, Binghamton, 1989—; Albert Luthuli prof.-at-large U. Jos (Nigeria), 1991—; sr. scholar, Andrew D. White prof.-at-large emeritus Cornell U, Ithaca, 1992—; dir. Inst. Global Cultural Studies SUNY, Binghamton, 1991—; chancellor Jomo Kenyatta Univ. Agrl. and Tech., Kenya, 2003—. Ibn Khaldun prof.-at-large Sch. Islamic and Social Scis., Leesburg, Va., 1997-2000; Reith lectr. BBC, London, 1979; vis. prof. various univs. including U. London, U. Chgo., Oxford U., U. Pa., Ohio State U., Manchester U., Harvard U., Nairobi U., UCLA, Northwestern U., U. Singapore, Colgate Coll., U. Australia, Stanford U., U. Cairo, Sussex U., U. Leeds, Internat. Islamic U., Malaysia, 1965—; mem. bank's coun. African advisers, World Bank, Washington, 1988-91; Walter Rodney disting. prof. U. Guyana, Georgetown, 1997-98. Author: Towards A Pax Africana: A Study of Ideology and Ambition, 1967, The Anglo-African Commonwealth: Political Friction and Cultural Fusion, 1967, On Heroes and Uhuru-Worship: Essays on Independent Africa, 1967, Violence and Thought: Essays on Social Tensions in Africa, 1969, Cultural Engineering and Nation-Building in East Africa, 1972, World Culture and the Black Experience, 1974, The Political Sociology of the English Language: An African Perspective, 1975, Soldiers and Kinsmen in Uganda: The Making of a Military Ethnocracy, 1975; co-editor: (with Robert I. Rotberg) Protest and Power in Black Africa, 1970, (with Hasu Patel) Africa in World Affairs: The Next Thirty Years, 1973; editor: The Warrior Tradition in Modern Africa, 1978, Africa since 1935 Volume III Unesco General History of Africa, 1973-93, (with Alamin M. Mazrui) The Political Culture of Language: Swahili, Society and the State, 1996—99, (with Alamin M. Mazrui) The Power of Babel: Language and Governance in Africa's Experience, 1998; sr. editor: (with T.K. Levine) The Africans: A Reader, 1986; author: The Trial of Christopher Okigbo, 1971, A World Federation of Cultures: An African Perspective, 1976; Africa's International Relations: The Diplomacy of Dependency and Change, 1977, Political Values and the Educated Class in Africa, 1978, The African Condition: A Political Diagnosis, 1980, (with Michael Tidy) Nationalism and New States in Africa, From About 1935 to the Present, 1984; narrator, presenter: The Africans: A Triple Heritage, 1986, Cultural Forces in World Politics, 1990, A Tale of Two Africas, 2006, Islam Between Globalization and Counterterrorism, 2006; mem. editl. bd. various profl. jours., 1963—; contbr. articles to profl. publs. Fellow Ctr for Advanced Study in Behavioral Scis., Palo Alto, Calif., 1972-73; sr. fellow Hoover Instn. on War, Revolution and Peace, Stanford, Calif., 1973-74, Mich. Soc. Fellows, 1978-82; Commander of the Burning Spear award, Kenya, 2005; ECOWAS award of Living Legend, 2007; South African award of Grand Companion of Oliver Tambo, 2007. Fellow Internat. Assn. Mid. Ea. Studies, Ghana Acad. Arts and Scis. (hon.); mem. African Studies Assn. (exec. bd. 1975-80, pres. 1978-79, Disting. Africans award 1995), Internat. Congress African Studies (v.p. 1978-85), Internat. Polit. Sci. Assn. (v.p. 1970-73), World Order Models Project (dir. African sect. 1968-83), Royal African Soc. (v.p.), Royal Commonwealth Soc., United Kenya Club (Nairobi), Athenaeum Club (London). Office: SUNY Inst Global Cultural Studies Off Schweitzer Chair PO Box 6000 Binghamton NY 13902-6000 Office Phone: 607-777-4494. E-mail: amazrui@binghamton.edu.

MAZUMDER, SANDIP, engineer, researcher; b. Calcutta, India, Feb. 23, 1969; came to U.S., 1991; s. Satya and Amita Mazumder; m. Srirupa Dhar, Nov. 25, 1998. BTech with honors, Indian Inst. Tech., 1991; MS, Pa. State U., 1993, PhD, 1997. Project engr. CFD Rsch. Corp., Huntsville, Ala., 1997-98, sr. engr., 1999-2000, group leader, 2000—. Reviewer NSF, Arlington, Va., 1999—, Jour. Heat Transfer, 1997—, Numerical Heat Transfer, 1999—. Contbr. over 20 articles to profl. jours. including Internat. Jour. Heat and Mass Transfer, Jour. Heat Transfer, Internat. Jour. Numerical Method Fluids, Numerical Heat Transfer, others. Grantee NSF, 1999—. Mem. ASME, AIAA. Avocations: piano, guitar. E-mail: sm@cfdrc.com.

MAZUR, BARRY CHARLES, mathematician, educator; b. NYC, Dec. 19, 1937; 1 child. PhD in Math., Princeton U., 1959; DSc (hon.), Colby Coll., 2004. Jr. fellow Harvard U., Cambridge, Mass., 1959—62, from asst. prof. to prof., 1962—82, William Petschek prof. math., 1982—98, Gerhardt Gade Univ. prof., 1998—. Author: Imagining Numbers, 2002. Recipient Veblen prize in Geometry, Am. Math. Soc., 1965, Cole prize in Number Theory, 1982, Steele Prize, 1999, Chauvenet prize, Math. Assn. Am., 1994. Mem.: AAAS, NAS, American Philol. Soc. Office: Harvard U FAS Math Dept / Sci Ctr 1 Oxford St Cambridge MA 02138-2901 E-mail: mazur@math.harvard.edu.

MAZUR, EDWARD JOHN, JR., financial planner; b. Lowell, Mass., Mar. 5, 1948; s. Edward John Sr. and Mary Annette (Terry) M.; m. Sheila MacDonald, Dec. 13, 1969 (div. Nov. 1984); 1 child, Kristen Leigh; m. Anna Maria Maia, May 18, 1985; children: Edward John III, Kara Maia Mazur. BA in History, U. Mass., 1969. CLU, Chartered Fin. Cons., Life Underwriters Tng. Coun. Fellow. From agt. to dir. agys. John Hancock Mut. Life Ins. Co., Boston, 1973—84, gen. agt. Hartford, 1984-89; founder Mazur Fin., Farmington, Conn., 1990—2000, Profl. Investors Exch., LLC, Farmington, 2000—05, Profl. Investor's Life and Annuity LLC, 2005—. Team coord. Team Conn., 1998—. Recipient Raymond T. Wilbur award, Mass. Jaycees, 1982-83; named President of Yr., Mass. Jaycees, 1982-83, Outstanding Young Men of Am., Mass. Jaycees, 1984. Mem. Million Dollar Round Table, Nat. Assn. Ins. and Fin. Advisors (pres. Conn. chpt. 2000-01), Hartford Life Underwriters Assn. (pres. 1995-97), US Racquetball Assn. (pres. jr. coun. 2005—), Conn. Racquetball Assn. (pres. 1985-94). Avocations: racquetball, coaching, hiking. Home: 48 Knollwood Ln Avon CT 06001-2701 Office Phone: 860-678-7806. E-mail: mazurfin@aol.com.

MAZUR, LEONARD L., pharmaceutical company executive; b. Ansbach, Germany, Jan. 23, 1945; came to U.S., 1949; s. Walter and Maria (Zatwarnitsky) M.; m. Helena Maria Olijnyk, Nov. 1966; children: Maria, Michael, Irene. BA, Temple U., 1968, MBA, 1975. Mktg. mgr. Cooper Labs., Inc., Fairfield, N.J. and Palo Alto, Calif., 1971—81; dir. product mgmt. Knoll Pharm. Corp. divsn. BASF, Whippany, NJ, 1981—84; v.p. ICN Pharm. Corp., Costa Mesa, Calif., 1984—88; pres., COO Chantal Pharm. Corp., LA, 1988—89; exec. v.p. Medicis Pharm. Corp., NYC, 1989—93; vice chmn. Cabot Labs., Inc., NYC, 1994—96; chmn., CEO Genesis Pharm., Inc., Parsippany, NJ, 1996—2006; COO Triax Pharms., LLC, Cranford, NJ, 2006—. Ptnr. Mazier Ptnrs. LLC, Morristown, NJ, 1995-05. Adv. bd. Manor Coll., Jenkintown, Pa., 1972-78, trustee, 2000-06; ind. observer Referendum for Independence, Ukraine, 1991; bd. visitors Coll. Liberal Arts Temple U., 2006—. Roman Catholic. Achievements include patents in field. Office: Triax Pharms LLC 20 Commerce Dr Cranford NJ 07016

MAZUR, MICHAEL, artist; b. NYC, Nov. 2, 1935; s. Burton Boris and Helen (Isaacs) M.; m. Gail Lewis Beckwith, Dec. 28, 1958; children: Daniel Isaac, Kathe Elizabeth. BA, Amherst Coll., 1958; BFA, Yale U., 1959, MFA, 1961; PhD in Fine Arts (hon.), Lesley Coll., Cambridge, Mass., 2002; DFA (hon.), Coll. Creative Studies, Detroit, 2006. Asst. prof. fine arts Brandeis U., Waltham, Mass., 1965-76; instr. RISD, 1962-65. Vis. prof. Yale U. Sch. Art and Arch., 1972, 81, Queens Coll., CUNY, 1973, U. Calif., Santa Barbara, 1974-75, Boston U., 1982, Mass. Coll. Art, 1994, 95; lectr. Mus. Fine Arts, Boston, Brown U., U. Calif., Berkeley, New Sch. for Social Rsch., Bennington Coll., U. Iowa, Boston U., 1994-95, Katonah Mus., N.Y. Studio Sch., 1994; vis. lectr. Carpenter Ctr., Harvard U., 1976, 78, 89, 92, 94, 95, 97, others; illustrator Fleur du Mal, 1984, The Inferno of Dante, Farrar, Strans & Giroux, 1994, Genesis, 1996; co-chair bd. Fine Arts Work Ctr., Provincetown, Mass., 1996—. Exhibited in one-man shows at Kornblee Gallery, N.Y.C., 1960, 63, 66, Boris Mirski, Boston, 1963, 65, Phila. Print Club, 1964, Silvermine Guild, 1964, Fla. State U., 1966, Shoemaker Gallery Juniata Coll., 1966, Alpha Gallery, Boston, 1967, 68, 74, OGL Gallery, LA, 1968, Rose Art Mus., Brandeis U., 1969, A.A.A. Gallery, 1969, Inst. Contemporary Art, Boston, 1970, Terry Dintenfass, NYC, 1974, 76, Picker Gallery, Colgate U., 1973, Trinity Coll., 1976, Ohio State U., 1975, Robert Miller Gallery, NYC, 1977, 80, Harkus-Krakow, Boston, 1977, 79-80, Pace Gallery, NYC, 1980, John Stoller, Mpls., 1981, 85, 88, 91, William and Mary Coll., 1981, Ronald Greenberg, St. Louis, 1981, Janus Gallery, LA, 1982, 84, 88, Barbara Mathes Gallery, NYC, 1984, 86, Barbara Krakow Gallery, Boston, 1984, 86, 89, 91, 93, 95, 97-98, 2000, Art Club Chgo., 1985, Beaver Coll., 1985, Joe Fawbush, NY, 1987-88, Jan Turner Gallery, LA, 1988, Butler Gallery, Houston, 1989, Mary Ryan Gallery, NYC, 1990, 94-2000, Mus. Fine Arts, Boston, 2000, Cantor Ctr.-Stanford U., 2000, Zimmerli Art Mus., New Brunswick, NJ, 2000, Mus. di Castelvecchio, Verona, Italy, 2000, Am. Acad. Rome, 2000-06, Flemming Gallery, Vt., 2006, Fisher Gallery U. So. Calif., LA, 2006; exhibited group shows at, Mus. Modern Art, 1964, 75, Bklyn. Mus., 1960, 62, 64, 66, 76, 80, 84, 86, Fogg Art Mus., 1966, 76, 94, Art. Inst. Chgo., 1964, Pa. Acad., 1966, 93, Phila. Mus., 1966, 88, Boston Mus. Fine Arts., 1967-68, 76-77, 80, 88, 90-92, DeCordova Mus., Lincoln, Mass., 1965-67, 75, 86, 87, Whitney Mus. Am. Art, 1965, 81, 90, 92, Nat. Inst. Arts and Letters, 1965, 74, 80, 86, Sivermine Guild, 1965, Print Biennial of Americas, Santiago, Chile, 1965, Paris Biennale, 1969, Venice Biennale, 1970, Finch Coll. Mus., 1971-72, 2d and 3d Biennial Graphic Art, Cali, Colombia, N.A.D. Ann., 1974, Butler Inst., Youngstown, Ohio, 1974, Ball State U., 1974, America-1976, Sense of Place, Met. Mus., NYC, 1979-80, Montreal Mus. Fine Arts, 1977, Palais Royale, Brussels, 1979, Claude Bernard, Paris, 1980, Alan Frumkin, NYC, 1981, 82, Madison Art Ctr., 1989, Nat. Gallery of Art, Washington, 1990, Pratt Mus., NYC, 1990, Nat. Mus. Am. Art, 1997; traveling exhbns. include, Bicentennial Exhbn., 1976, State Arts Councils, Iowa, Kans., Mo., Nebr., 1973, Am. Monotypes, Smithsonian Instn., 1977; represented in permanent collections, Met. Mus., NYC, Mus. Modern Art, Smith Coll. Art Mus., Library Congress, Fogg Art Mus., Art Inst. Chgo., Whitney Mus., LA County Art Mus., Mus. R.I. Sch. Design, Oreg. Art Mus., U. Maine, Mpls. Inst., Pa. State U., Toledo Art Mus., Phila. Art Mus., U. Ohio Westminster Found., Boston Mus. Fine Arts, Boston Pub. Library, Bklyn. Mus., Addison Gallery, Andover Acad., Yale Art Gallery, Montreal Mus. Fine Arts; commd. Fed. Res. Bank, Boston, 1998, USB-Warburg-Dillon, Stanford, Conn., 1999; (Recipient 2d prize Soc. Am. Graphic Artists 1963, Nat. Inst. Arts and Letters award 1965). Co-founder Artists Against Racism and the War, 1968; bd. dirs. Artists Found., co-chair, 1995—; bd. dirs. Fine Arts Work Ctr., Provincetown, Mass.; mem. Mass. Coun. on Arts and Humanities; mem. Pennell com. Libr. of Congress, 1983-93; founder, dir. Art for Nuc. Weapons Freeze, 1983-84, New Provincetown Print Project, 1990-95; chmn. bd. Provincetown Fine Arts Work Ctr.; overseer Mus. Fine Arts, Boston. Grantee Tiffany Found., 1964, Tamarind Lithography Workshop, 1968; Guggenheim Found. fellow, 1964-65; winner numerous purchase awards; recipient Disting. Svc. "Printworks Emeritus", So. Graphics Coun., 2005. Home: 5 Walnut Ave Cambridge MA 02140-2706 Personal E-mail: mbzur@comcast.net.

MAZUR, PETER, physiologist, cryobiologist; b. NYC, Mar. 3, 1928; s. Paul M. and Adolphia (Kaske) M.; m. Drusilla Stevens, May 28, 1953 (dec. May 1982); 1 child, Timothy Stevens; m. Sara Jo Bolling, June 16, 1984 (dec. Apr. 2003). AB magna cum laude, Harvard U., 1949, PhD, 1953; DSc (hon.), Wilson Coll., 1998. NSF postdoctoral fellow Princeton (N.J.) U., 1957-59; rsch. staff biology divsn. Oak Ridge Nat. Lab., 1959-98. Group leader fundamental and applied cryobiology Oak Ridge Nat. Lab., 1966-98, sci. dir. biophysics and cell physiology, biology div., 1974-75, corporate fellow, 1985; chmn. ORNL Corp. Fellows Coun., 1985-86; mem. vis. com. biology Harvard U. Bd. Overseers 1972-77; rsch. prof. dept. biochem. and cellular and molecular biology U. Tenn., 1998—; mem. Space Sci. Bd. of Nat. Acad., 1975-77; Sigma Xi nat. lectr., 1980. Trustee Wilson Coll., Pa., 1984-93, trustee emeritus, 2003; bd. dirs. Meth. Hosp. Found., Oak Ridge, 1997—2003. Capt. USAF, 1953-57. Recipient Author of Yr. award, Martin-Marietta Energy Sys., 1985, Disting. Svc. award, Am. Assn. Tissue Banks, 1993, R&D 100 award, R&D Mag., 1993, Disting. Achievement award, Am. Soc. Reproductive Medicine, 2000; Lalor fellow, Harvard U., 1952, John Harvard fellow, 1951. Fellow AAAS, Soc. Cryobiology (pres. 1973-74, bd. govs. 1979-96); mem. Rotary Club Oak Ridge, Phi Beta Kappa, Cosmos Club (Washington). Current work includes cryobiology and the mechanisms of freezing injury in living cells and tissues. Subspecialties are cell biology and biophysics. Home: 125 Westlook Cir Oak Ridge TN 37830-3856 Office: Dept Biochemistry and Cellular and Molecular Biology M407 Walters Life Sci Bldg Knoxville TN 37996-0001 Office Phone: 865-974-9960. Business E-Mail: pmazur@utk.edu.

MAZUR, RHODA HIMMEL, community volunteer; b. Bklyn., July 4, 1929; d. Morris and Gussie (Nadler) Himmel; m. Marvin Irwin Mazur, June 7, 1952; children: Jody, Amy, Leslie, Eric. Student, CCNY, CUNY. Bd. dirs. Newport News Social Svcs. Adv. Bd., 1979-84, Gov.'s Commn. Status Women, Richmond, 1981-84, Coun. Jewish Fedns., NYC, 1985-87, Nat. Coun. Christians and Jews, 1985-89, Rodef Sholom Endowment Com., 1996—, Peninsula Jewish Hist. Soc., 1998—; v.p. Anti-Defamation League Regional Bd., Richmond, 1983-85, bd. dirs., 1985-98; pres. Newport News Hadassah, 1984-85, United Jewish Cmty. Va. Peninsula Inc., Newport News, 1985-88, Rodef Sholom Sisterhood, 1997-98; active Newport News Task Force on Emergency Housing, 1984-85; chair fin. com. Peninsula Peace Edn. Ctr., Newport News, 1984-85; adv. bd. Friends of the Homeless, Inc., 1987-00, pres., 1993-98, v.p., 1998-99; adv. bd. Associated Marine Inst., 1988-92; mem. social svcs. com. United Jewish Cmty. Va. Peninsula, 1995—, mem. campaign coun., 1999-, Jewish Hist. Soc. Va. Peninsula, 1995-; chair social action com. Rodef Sholom Temple, 1993-96, endowment com., 1998—; cmty. activist; bd. dirs., Peninsula Camp Fund, 2001—, Fed. Emergency Mgmt. Agy., 2001. Recipient Young Leadership award Jewish Fedn. Newport News, 1968, Brotherhood citation Nat. Conf. Christians and Jews, 1984, Anti-Defamation Leadership award, 1997. Democrat. Avocations: hand crafts, reading, music, photography. Home: 114 James River Dr Newport News VA 23601-3604

MAZUR, THOMAS A., music educator; b. Newark, Nov. 10, 1945; s. Richard C. and Leocadia Mazur; m. Faith Frankel, Mar. 29, 1975; 1 child, Joy; m. Jacqueline Mazur, Dec. 30, 2004. BA in Music, Rutgers U., 1989; M in Music Edn., NJCU, 2004. Vocal music tchr. Long Branch (N.J.) H.S., 1990—95, Roosevelt Mid. Sch., West Orange, NJ, 1995—. Recipient Excellence in Tchg. award, N.J. Symphony Orch., Newark, 1996—97. Mem.: Kappa Delta Pi. Avocation: mountain climbing. Home: 708 Buckland Ct Denville NJ 07834 Office: Roosevelt Mid Sch 36 Gilbert Pl West Orange NJ 07052 Personal E-mail: tmazur@woboe.org.

MAZZA, DAVID S., pediatrician; b. Burlington, Vt., Dec. 10, 1947; s. Frank, Jr. and Margret Alice (Fuller) M. B.A., U. Vt., 1969, M.A. in Math., 1971, M.D., 1977. Diplomate Am. Bd. Pediatrics. Resident in pediatrics NYU-Bellevue Hosp., N.Y.C., 1977-80, fellow in ambulatory pediatrics, 1980-82; attending staff emergency service Bellevue Hosp., 1982—; dir. pediatric ambulatory services Booth Meml. Med. Ctr., N.Y.C., 1982—, dir. fellowship program, 1985; attending staff North Shore U. Hosp., N.Y., 1985—, Cornell U., 1985—; instr. NYU, 1982-84. City Council campaign vol., N.Y.C., 1985. Mem. Am. Acad. Pediatrics, AAAS, N.Y. Acad. Sci., Sierra Club, Defenders of Wildlife, Nature Conservancy Group. Democrat. Avocations: swimming; bicycling; travel.

MAZZAFERRI, ERNEST LOUIS, endocrinologist, educator; b. Cleve., Sept. 27, 1936; s. Joseph and Nanetta (Marinelli) M.; m. Florence Mildred Marolt, Nov. 23, 1957; children: Patricia Marie Atchison, Michael Louis, Sharon Lynne Brown, Ernest Louis. BS cum laude, John Carroll U., 1958; MD, Ohio State U., 1962. Diplomate Am. Bd. Internal Medicine. Intern Ohio State U. Hosps., Columbus, 1962-63, resident, 1963-64, 66-68; asst. prof. medicine Ohio State U., 1968-70, assoc. prof., 1973-76, prof., 1976-79, dir. div. endocrinology and metabolism, 1975-78; acting dean U. Nev., Reno, 1979-81, prof., chmn. dept. medicine, 1978-84, prof. physiology, 1982-84; prof., chmn. dept. medicine, prof. physiology Ohio State U., Columbus, 1984-99, prof. emeritus, 1999—; pres. Dept. of Medicine Found., 1986-99; chmn. bd. Ohio State Practice Group, 1996-99; clin. prof. medicine U. Fla., Gainesville, 2001—. Bd. dirs. The Ohio State U. Hosps., 1997—99; mem. com. on exposure of Am. people to I-131 from Nev. atomic bomb tests Nat. Acad. Sci. Inst. of Medicine, 1997—99, mem. com. on health effects assoc. with exposures experienced during the Gulf War, 1999—2000; mem. com. guidelines for thyroid cancer screening Inst. Medicine, 1997—99; chmn. Nat. Cancer Ctr. Network Com. on Thyroid Cancer Guidelines; mem. com. on health effects associated with exposures during the Gulf War Inst. of Medicine Nat. Academies of Sci., 1999—2000. Author: Endocrinology Case Studies, 3d edit., 1985, Internal Medicine Pearls, 1993; editor: Textbook of Endocrinology, 3d edit., 1986, Contemporary Internal Medicine, 1988, 3d edit., 1990, Advances in Endocrinology and Metabolism, Vol. 6, 1995, Endocrine Tumors, 1993, Morning Report, 1999, Yearbook of Endocrinology, 1999—; Endocrine editor Yearbook of Medicine, 1999—; editor: Practical Management of Thyroid Cancer: A Medical Disciplinary Approach, 2005, Essentials of Thyroid Cancer Management, Kluwer Acad. Publishers, 2005-; mem. sci. adv. bd. Western Jour. Medicine, 1993; mem. editl. bd. Jour. Lab. Clin. Medicine, 1987-97, Hosp. Practice, Jour. of Clin. Endocrinology and Metabolism, Thyroid, 1999—; contbr. articles to profl. jours. Chmn. Gov.'s Com. on Radiation Fallout in Nev., 1980-84, hosp. ethics com. Ohio State U., 1994-98; mem. Sec. of Energy Dose Assessment Adv. Com., 1980-84, Agy. for Health Care Policy, Rsch. Cataract Guideline Com., 1991-92, Inst. of Medicine Guideline for Thyroid Cancer Screening com., 1997-99; mem. rsch. coun. com. on expense of Am. People to I-131 from Nev. Atomic Bomb Tests: Implications for Public Health, 1997-99. Capt. USAF, 1964, maj. USAF, 1968, lt. col. USAF, 1968—73, col. USAR, 1984—91. Recipient Earl N. Metz Disting. Physician award, Ohio State U., 1998, Light of Life award, Light of Life Found. N.Y., 1999, Graves' award, Thyroid Soc. for Rsch. and Edn., 2001. Master: ACP (gov. for Nev. 1984—85, chmn. clin. efficacy assessment program com. 1992—95, edn. policy com. 1992—95, mem. health and pub. policy com.); mem.: AMA, Am. Coll. Clin. Endocrinology (bd. dis. 1995—96, Disting. Clinician award 2002), Ctrl. Soc. Clin. Rsch., Am. Clin. and Climatol. Assn., Endocrine Soc. (Disting. Educator award 2005), Am. Diabetes Assn. (pres. Ohio affiliate 1988—89), Am. Thyroid Assn. (pres.-elect 2004—05, pres. 2005—, Paul Star award), Am. Bd. Internal Medicine (chmn. Endocrinology and Metabolism 1999—2003, bd. dirs. 1999—2003, cert. in endocrinology and metabolism, gen. internal medicine, cert. in geriatrics, continuous profl. devel.), Alpha Omega Alpha. Roman Catholic. Achievements include research in thyroid cancer. Home: 4020 SW 93rd Dr Gainesville FL 32608-4653 Office Phone: 352-846-2749. Personal E-mail: mazz01@bellsouth.net. E-mail: emazzaferri@cox.net. *Success, like every other human experience, is relative, measured against shifting standards and subject to the scrutiny of time. One must strike a fine balance— self certainty against external review— that permits the full expression of new ideas enriched by the best and time-worn thoughts of others.*

MAZZAFERRO, JAMES JOSEPH, music educator; b. San Francisco, Calif., Apr. 19, 1956; s. James John and Marilyn Jean Mazzaferro; m. Anita Marie Piccone, Nov. 27, 1976; children: Cherylyn, Joseph, Jeanette. Bachelors Music Edn., San Francisco State U., San Francisco, CA, 1978; Masters in Music Conducting, Calif. State U., Sacramento, 1995. San Francisco Archdiocese Archbishop Riordan HS, San Francisco, 1979—89; tchr. music Florin H.S. Elk Grove Unified, Sacramento, 1989—97, Sacramento City Coll. Los Rios CC, Sacramento, 1997—2001, Sheldon HS Elk Grove Unified, Sacramento, 1997—, Cosumnes River Coll. Los Rios CC, Sacramento, 1999—. Bd. directors Cazadero Performing Arts, Cazadero, Calif., 1995—2001, Calif. Band Directors, Fresno, Calif., 1999—2001. Mem.: Calif. Music Educators Assn. (band rep. 1994—98), Musician's Union Local 6, Music Educators Nat. Conf., Phi Kappa Lambda (hon.), Phi Kappa Phi (hon.). Avocation: music performance. Home: 9068 Shetland Court Elk Grove CA 95624 Office: Sheldon High School 8333 Kingsbridge Drive Sacramento CA 95829 Home Phone: 916-685-3867; Office Phone: 916-681-7500. Personal E-mail: jmazz1@surewest.net.

MAZZAFERRO, KATHRYN E., statistician, researcher; d. Joseph R. and Elizabeth M. Mazzaferro. MA, U. Pitts., 2006. Rsch. coord. U. Pitts., Grad. Sch. Pub. Health, 2003—06; statistician U. Pitts., Ctr. Rsch. Health Care, 2006—. Contbr. scientific papers, articles to profl. jours. Vol. Pa. Dem. Party, Pitts., 2000—07, Moveon.org PAC, Pitts., 2004—07, Am. Coming Together, Pitts., 2004, Young Democrats Am., Pitts., 2004—07. Democrat-Npl. Avocations: running, travel, crossword puzzles. Office: Univ Pitts 200 Meyran Ave Ste 200 Pittsburgh PA 15213 Home Phone: 412-601-0836; Office Phone: 412-692-2018.

MAZZARELLA, DAVID, editor; b. 1938; With AP, Lisbon, NYC, Rome, 1962—70, Daily American, Rome, 1971—75, Gannett News, Washington, 1976—77, The Bridgewater, Bridgewater, NJ, 1977—83; editor USA Today, Arlington, Va., sr. v.p., 1999—. Office: USA Today 7950 Jones Branch Dr Mc Lean VA 22108-0001

MAZZE, EDWARD MARK, marketing educator, consultant; b. NYC, Feb. 14, 1941; s. Harry Alan and Mollie (Schneider) M.; m. Sharon Sue Hastings, Sept. 9, 1967; children: Candace, Thomas. BBA, City U. NY, 1961, MBA, 1962; PhD, Pa. State U., 1966. Lectr. bus. adminstrn. CCNY, 1961-62; bus. cons., 1961—; instr. bus. Pa. State U., 1963-66; assoc. prof. mktg. U. Detroit, 1966-68; assoc. prof., dir. spl. programs W.Va. U., 1968-70; prof. bus. adminstrn., coordinator mktg. program Va. Poly. Inst. and State U., Blacksburg, 1970-75; v.p. adminstrv. services, dean Sch. Bus., Seton Hall U., South Orange, NJ, 1975-79; dean sch. bus. adminstrn. Temple U., Phila., 1979-86, prof. mktg. and internat. bus., 1979-93; dean Belk Coll. Bus. Adminstrn., prof. mktg. U. NC, Charlotte, 1993-98, co.-dir. Frank Hawkins Kenan Inst. Pvt. Enterprise, 1997—98; dean Coll. Bus. Adminstrn., Alfred J. Verrecchia-Hasbro Inc. Leadership chair in bus. U. RI, Kingston, 1998—2006, disting. univ. prof. bus. adminstrn., 2006—. Chmn. bd. William Penn Bank, Phila., 1985-87; bd. dirs. Technitrol, Inc., Washington Trust Bancorp, Inc., Barrett Growth Fund, Ocean State Bus. Devel. Authority; mem. dist. export coun. US Dept. Commerce, 1978-80, 83-93; mem. panel chpt. 7 trustees US Dept. Justice, 1984-96, 2005; adv. bd. McGettigan Ptrns., 1997-99, Radiator Specialty Co., 1997-99, Piedmont Venture Ptrns., 1997-98; mem. faculty master liberal arts in mgmt. program Harvard U., 2003, 06-07. Author: International Business: Articles and Essays, 1963, Readings in Organization and Management, 1963, Marketing in Action, 1963, Case Histories in Sales Management, 1965, Sales Management: Theory and Practice, 1965, International Marketing Adminstration, 1967, Introduction to Marketing, 1970, Marketing in Turbulent Times: The Challenges and the Opportunities, 1975, Personal Selling: Choice Against Chance, 1976, The Food Marketing Wars: Marketing Triumphs and Blunders, 1998, Specialty Retailers: Marketing Triumphs and Blunders, 2001, Lifestyle Marketing: Reaching the New American Consumer, 2003, The Affluent Consumer: Marketing and Selling the Luxury Lifestyle, 2006; mem. editl. bd. Jour. Econs. and Bus., 1976-80, Indsl. Mktg. Mgmt., 1977-2006, Jour. Internat. Bus. Studies, 1978-82, Jour. Acad. Mktg. Sci., 1980-91, Jour. Mktg. Edn., 1985-94, Jour. Global Mktg., 1987-2006; contbr. articles to profl. jours. Trustee Phila. Home Care, 1984-89, Manor Coll., 1985-92, Thomas A. Edison State Coll. Found., 1987-89, Delaware Valley Coll. Sci. and Agr., 1991-97, Pa. Inst. Tech., 1992-93; chmn. econ. devel. adv. com. Village South Orange, 1977-80; mem., vice-chmn. Bd. Suprs. Doylestown Twp., 1980-81. Ford. Found. fellow, 1962-63 Mem. Am. Mktg. Assn., Acad. Internat. Bus., Nat. Assn. Corp. Dirs., Acad. Mktg. Sci., Beta Gamma Sigma, Pi Kappa Alpha. Home: 52 Horizon Dr Saunderstown RI 02874-2402 Office: U RI Coll Business 304 Ballentine Hall Kingston RI 02881 Home Phone: 401-295-5802; Office Phone: 401-874-4308. Personal E-mail: emazze@cox.net.

MAZZEO, ANTHONY R., chemist; b. Buffalo, May 2, 1958; s. George J. and Louise C. M.; m. Darlene Van Eseltine, May 21, 1988; children: Victoria, Seth. BS, SUNY, Brockport, 1980; PhD, Syracuse U., 1991. Chemist DuPont, Aiken, SC, 1980—84; rschr., tchg. asst. Syracuse U., NY, 1984—88; mgr. quality assurance/tech. support New Methods Rsch., Syracuse, 1988—93; quality assurance scientist Bayer Corp., Spokane, Wash., 1993—99; sr. quality assurance scientist Hollister-Stier Labs., Spokane, 1999—2000; mgr. R&D stability DuPont Pharm. Co., Wilmington, Del., 2000—02; sr. prin. scientist Pfizer Global R&D, Ann Arbor, Mich., 2002—06; prin. scientist Bristol-Myers Squibb Co. Pharm. Rsch. Inst., New Brunswick, NJ, 2006—. Contbr. articles to profl. jours. Mem. Am. Chem. Soc. (chair Inland N.W. sect. 1998-2000, sec. treas. 1996), Am. Assn. Pharm. Scientists, Pharm. Rsch. and Mfrs. Assn. (stability expert team). Home: 250 Norsam Dr Langhorne PA 19047 Office: Bristol-Myers Squibb Co 1 Squibb Dr New Brunswick NJ 08903

MAZZEO, DANIEL PATRICK, aerospace engineer, consultant; b. NYC, Apr. 18, 1949; s. Gennaro and Marie Grace (Mazzei) M.; m. Belva Faye Musick, Sept. 10, 1977; children: Gennaro, Jina Marie. BS in Aerospace Engring., Poly. U. NY, 1971; grad. in Aviation Safety, U.S. Naval Postgrad. Sch., Monterey, Calif., 1981. Commd. ensign USN, 1969, advanced through grades to comdr., 1982, aviator, 1969-91; aviation program mgr. BDI Engring., Pensacola, Fla., 1991-95; aviation project mgr. DH Engrs., Sarasota, Fla., 1995-99; pres., CEO Aerocomm Group, Pensacola, Fla., 1999—; sr. project mgr. Banks Engring., Naples, Fla., 2004—06. Airline transport pilot rating FAA, 1979; mem. State Aviation Planning Process, Fla., 1990—; completed over 150 major airport improvement projects; instr. civil engring. and engring. graphics Pensacola Tech. Acad., 2003-05; head Dept. Constrn. Tech. Triangle Tech. Inst., 2005—. Contbr. articles to profl. jours. Grad. Leadership Santa Rosa County, 1982; tech. advisor in aviation County Govt., Escambia, Fla., 1985, Santa Rosa, Fla., 1987, Tallahassee, Fla., 1994. Decorated Navy commendation medal, Navy expdn. medal, Navy Mertourous Citation Ribbon (four bronze stars), Navy Battle Ribbon (battle E), Navy Sea Svc. Ribbon (one bronze star), Navy Expert Pistol Ribbon, Def. Svc. medal with one bronze star; recipient Sci. grant N.Y.C., 1965, 68, Innovative Environmental award FAA, 1997, Airport of the Year award Fla. Dept. Transp., 1997. Mem. ASCE (section pres.), AIAA (sect. vice-chmn.), Soc. Am. Mil. Engrs., Aircraft Owners and Pilots Assn. (advisor 1997). Achievements include invention of electrophotographic imaging machine and invention of the respirograph employed in medical research. Home: PO Box 614 Gulf Breeze FL 32562-0614 Office: Aerocomm Group Pensacola FL 32502 Office Phone: 850-206-4213. Personal E-mail: onegoodengineer@aol.com.

MAZZEO-MERKLE, LINDA LOU, legal administrator; b. Washington, Apr. 6, 1947; d. Robert Clifton Shreeves II and Esther A. (Harrison) Shreeves; m. John T. Mazzeo; children: Christina L. Schneider, Regina L. Hodges; stepchildren: John T. Mazzeo Jr., Christina M. Mazzeo. Lic. real estate salesperson, Prince Georges C.C., Largo, Md., 1972. Various secretarial positions, 1964-65, 67-72; real estate saleswoman, 1973-74; divsn. sec. Prince Georges C.C., 1974-75; real estate saleswoman Harvest Realty Inc., Clinton, Md., 1974-75; legal adminstr., property mgr., investment mgr. Tucker, Flyer, Sanger, Reider & Lewis, P.C., Washington, 1975-84; legal adminstr. Anderson, Heibey, Nauheim & Blair, Washington, 1984-85; v.p. fin. and adminstrn. Barnes, Morris, Pardoe & Foster, Inc., Washington, 1985-93; former CFO, chief adminstrv. officer Barnes, Morris & Pardoe, Inc.; legal adminstr. Payne, Negroni & Winston, Washington, 1994-95, Buckmaster & Assocs., Washington, 1996-98; cert. NIA instr. Vicksburg, Miss., 1998—; designer, owner Instant Ancestor, Jewelry Co., 2000—. Cons. and spkr. in field. Mem. Assn. Legal Adminstrs. (chmn. new adminstrs. and gen. adminstrn. sect. 1984-85). Home: 100 Lakewood Hls Vicksburg MS 39180-5343

MAZZILLI, LEE, sportscaster, former professional baseball manager; b. Bklyn., Mar. 25, 1955; s. Libero Mazzilli; m. Dani Mazzilli; children: Jenna, Lee Jr., Lacey. Profl. baseball player NY Mets, 1976—81, 1986—89, Tex. Rangers, 1982, NY Yankees, 1982, Pitts. Pirates, 1983—86, Toronto Blue Jays, 1989; coach Tampa (Fla.) Yankees, 1997—98, Norwich (Conn.) Yankees, 1998—2000; first base & outfield coach NY Yankees, 2000—03, bench coach, 2006; mgr. Balt. Orioles, 2004—05; lead studio analyst SportsNet NY, 2006—. Named to Nat. League All Star Team, 1979. *

MAZZIO-MOORE, JOAN L., retired radiology educator, physician; b. Belmont, Mass., Oct. 26, 1935; d. Frank Joseph and Maria L. Mazzio; children: James Thomas Moore, Edwin Stuart Moore. BA in Chemistry and Theology, Emmanuel Coll., 1957; MA in Genetics and Physiology, Wellesley Coll., Mass., 1961; PhD in Genetics, Bryn Mawr Coll., Pa., 1964; MD, Phila. Coll. of Medicine, 1977, MSc in Radiology, 1981. Instr. organic chemistry Gwynedd Mercy Coll., 1962—63; instr. in genetics Holy Family Coll., Phila., 1965—66; instr. in anatomy Phila. Coll. of Medicine, 1971—77, instr., 1973—77, assoc. prof., 1977—84; prof. W.Va. Sch. of Medicine, 1984—2003, ret., 2004; rotating intern Phila. Coll. of Medicine Hosp., 1977—78, resident in radiology and radiation therapy, 1978—81, mem. hosp. staff, 1981—84. Author (with Dr. DiVirgilito): Essentials of Neuropathology, 1974. Treas. Hist. Soc. of Frankford, Phila., 1968—75, Sch. Mother's Assn., Devon, Pa., 1980—81; vol. mem. Ct. Appts. Spl. Adv. for Children; parlamentarian Greenbrier Com. on Aging; bd. trustees Lake Erie Coll. Medicine and Pharmacy, Erie, Pa.; organist Ch. of Incarnation, W.Va., St. Charles Borromeo Ch., White Sulphur Springs, W.Va., 2001—; lector St. Ann's Cath. Ch., Phoenixville, Pa., 1981—84. Lt. col. MC USAR, 1984—2003. Mem. AAUP, Am. Assn. Women Radiologists, Am. Med. Women's Assn., Am. Osteo. Coll. Radiology (life), Am. Soc. Clin. Oncology, Am. Soc. Therapeutic Radiologists, Hist. Soc. Lewisburg (life), Pa. Osteo. Med. Assn., Radiol. Soc. N.Am., Radiation Rsch. Soc., Res. Officers Assn. (life), W.Va. Soc. Osteo. Medicine, Greenbrier Valley Med. Soc., NRA (life). Home: PO Box 97 Frankford WV 24938 Home Fax: 304-497-2752. Personal E-mail: drjoanlmoore@yahoo.com.

MAZZO, KAY, ballet dancer, educator; b. Evanston, Ill., Jan. 17, 1946; d. Frank Alfred and Catherine M. (Hengel) M.; m. Albert C. Bellas, 1978; children: Andrew, Kathryn. Student, Sch. Am. Ballet, 1959-61. Co-chair faculty Sch. Am. Ballet. Profl. debut in ballets U.S.A. 1961, touring Europe with co., performing for Pres. Kennedy at White House, 1961, joined N.Y.C. Ballet, 1962-80, soloist, 1965-69, prin. ballerina, 1969-80, prin. roles in world premiere of ballets including Tschaikowsky Suite No. #3, 1970, PAMTGG, 1971, Stravinsky Violin Concerto, 1972, Scherzo A La Russe, 1972, Duo Concertant, 1972, Sheherazade, 1975, Union Jack, 1976, Vienna Waltzes, 1977, Davidsbundlertanze, 1980; ballet tchr. Sch. Am. Ballet, 1980—; appeared as guest artist in leading roles with numerous cos. including Boston Ballet, Washington Ballet, Berlin Ballet, Geneva Ballet; appeared on TV in U.S., Can., Fed. Republic Germany. Recipient Mademoiselle Merit award 1970 Office: Sch Am Ballet 70 Lincoln Center Plz New York NY 10023-6548

MAZZOLA, ANTHONY THOMAS, editor, graphics designer, consultant; b. Passaic, NJ, June 13, 1923; s. Thomas and Jennie (Failla) M.; m. Michele Morgan, Nov. 18, 1967; children: Anthony Thomas II, Marc Eden, Alisa Morgan. Grad., Cooper Union Art Sch., NYC, 1948. Art dir. Street & Smith Publs., NYC, 1948, Town and Country mag. (pub. by Hearst Corp.), NYC, 1948-65, editor-in-chief, 1965-72, Harpers Bazaar, 1972-92; editor-in-chief, pres. Anthony Mazzola Design Corp., NYC, 1963—; creative cons. Hearst Corp., 1992—. Editl. dir. 125 Great Moments of Harper's Bazaar, 1991—94, Town & Country 150th Anniversary, 1994—; curator fine arts Hearst Corp., 2001—; cons. designer UN Childrens' Fund, Assn. Jr. Leagues Am., Columbia Pictures Corp., Sells Spltys., Gen. Foods, Paramount Pictures, Princess Marcella Borghese, Inc., Huntington Hartford Ltd., NY World's Fair, 1965 Exhibited, Art Dirs. Club NY, ann. exhbns., 1948—. Exhibited, Art Dirs. Club. N.Y., ann. exhbns., 1948—. Served with AUS, 1943-46. Decorated Bronze Star, Knight Officer of Order of Merit Italy; recipient Cert. of Merit awards N.Y. Art Dirs. Club; medal Art Dirs. Club N.Y.C., 1955. Office: Hearst Corp 300 W 57th St New York NY 10019

MAZZOLA, JOHN WILLIAM, retired performing company executive, consultant; b. Bayonne, NJ, Jan. 20, 1928; s. Roy Stephen and Eleanor Burton (Davis) M.; m. Sylvia Drulie, Mar. 7, 1959; children: Alison, Amy. AB, Tufts U., 1949; LLD, Fordham U., 1952. Bar: N.Y. 1956. Mem. firm Milbank, Tweed, Hadley & McCloy, NYC, 1952-64; sec., exec. v.p. Lincoln Center for Performing Arts, NYC, 1964-68, gen. mgr., chief exec. officer, 1969-70, mng. dir., chief exec. officer, 1970-77, pres., chief exec. officer, 1977-84; exec. v.p. Embassy Pictures, 1984—86. Cons. performing arts ctrs. in U.S. and abroad, also motion pictures, non-profit orgns. Bd. dirs. various charitable orgns.; mem. adv. bd. Santa Fe Symphony. With CIC US Army, 1953—55. Decorated cavaliere ufficiale Ordine al Merito della Repubblica Italiana; Ordre des Arts et des Lettres France; Benjamin Franklin fellow Royal Soc. Arts. Mem. Watch Hill Yacht Club, Misquamicut Club (R.I.). Episcopalian. Home: 12 Beekman Pl New York NY 10022-8059 Office Phone: 212-755-5117. Personal E-mail: johnwmazzola@aol.com.

MAZZOTTA, GIUSEPPE FRANCESCO, literature and language professor; b. Curinga, Calabria, Italy, Jan. 1, 1942; s. Pasquale and Rosa (Anania) M.; m. Carol Carlson, Mar. 2, 1972; children: Rosanna, Antony, Paula. BA, U. Toronto, Can., 1965, MA, 1966; PhD, Cornell U., 1969. Asst. prof. dept. romance studies Cornell U., Ithaca, NY, 1969-70, assoc. prof. dept. romance studies, 1973-78, prof. romance langs., 1978-83; asst. prof. dept. romance studies Yale U., New Haven, 1970-72, prof. Italian lang. and lit., 1983—; assoc. prof. Medieval Inst. U. Toronto, 1972-73. Author: Dante, Poet of the Desert: History and Allegory in the Divine Comedy, 1979, 2d edit., 1987, The World of Play: A Study of Boccaccio's Decameron, 1986, Dante's Vision and the Circle of Knowledge, 1993, The Worlds of Petrarch, 1993, The New Map of the World: The Poetic Philosophy of G.B. Vico, 1999, Cosmopoiesis: The Renaissance Experiment, 2001; mem. editl. bd. Yale Italian Studies, Dante Studies, Yale Jour. Criticism, Yale Jour. Law and Humanities. NEH fellow Cornell U., 1977, Guggenheim Found. fellow Yale U., 1986-87. Fellow Am. Coun. Learned Soc., Soc. for the Humanities; mem. Dante Soc. Am. (pres., Silone prize). Roman Catholic. Avocation: basketball. Office: Yale U 82-90 Wall St Fl 4 New Haven CT 06520 Home: 148 Peck Hill Rd Woodbridge CT 06525-1009 Home Phone: 203-393-3336; Office Phone: 203-432-0595. Business E-Mail: giuseppemazzotta@yale.edu.

MAZZUCELLI, COLETTE GRACE CELIA, author, educator; b. Bklyn., Nov. 26, 1962; d. Silvio Anthony and Adeline Marie De Ponte. BA, U. Scranton, 1983; MALD in Law and Diplomacy, Fletcher Sch., Tufts U., 1987; PhD, Georgetown U., 1996; post grad., Columbia U., 2003—. Asst. ratification process Treaty European Union German Fgn. Ministry, 1992—93; lectr. U.S. Info. Svc. Spkrs. Program, Europe, 1994; dir. internat. programs and lectr. Budapest Inst. Grad. Internat. and Diplomatic Studies, 1995—97; instr. in-ho. tng. negotiations Hungarian Fgn. Ministry, 1996—97; del. to NATO accession talks Hungarian Ministry Def., 1997; advisor to bd. dirs. Transatlantic Info. Exch. Svc., 1997—98; founding dir., internat. peace and conflict resolution grad. program, asst. prof. polit. sci. Arcadia U., 1998—2000; chair Transatlantic internet multimedia seminar S.E. Europe (TIMSSE) ScPo, Paris, 2000—03; fellow EastWest Inst., 2001; program officer, edn. NGO rep. UN Carnegie Coun. Ethics and Internat. Affairs, 2001—02; program devel. assoc. Tchrs. Coll. Columbia U., 2002—04; faculty John C. Whitehead Sch. Diplomacy and Internat. Rels. Seton Hall U., 2005—06; asst. prof. dept. history and polit. sci. Molloy Coll., Rockville Centre, 2006—. Rsch. fellow Inst. Europaeische Politik, Deutsche Gesellschaft Auswaertige Politk, Bonn, Deutsch-Franzoesisches Inst., Ludwigsburg; instr. Georgetown U., Washington, 1990, 96; adj. asst. prof. MS program global affairs Sch. Continuing and Profl. Studies NYU, 2005—. Author: Monnet Case Studies in European Affairs, 1995, France and Germany at Maastricht Politics and Negotiations to Create the European Union, 1997, paperback 2d edit., 1999; asst. editor: The Evolution of an International Actor: Western Europe's New Assertiveness, 1990; co-editor: Ethics and Global Politics: The Active Learning Sourcebook, 2004, Leadership in the Big Bangs of European Integration, 2007; contbr. articles to profl. jours.; chpts. to books. Mem. founding cabinet World Peace and Diplomacy Forum, 2003—; adv. group UN Chronicle, 2006—; v.p. recognition bd. World Congress Arts, Scis. and Comm., 2007. Named Internat. Educator of Yr., 2003, Da Vinci Laureate, 2004, Pirate of Yr., 2006; recipient citation Nat. Women's Conf., 2006; grantee Swiss U., 1984-85, Profl. Devel. NYU, 2006, Fulbright Found., 2007; scholar Pi Gamma Mu, 1985, Rsury Grad. scholar, 1987-88, Fulbright scholar, 1991, 07; fellow Jean Monnet Coun., 1991, European Commn., 1992, Robert Bosch Found., 1992-93, Salzburg Seminar, 1997, 21st Century Trust fellow Merton Coll., Oxford U., Eng., 2001, Bosch Pub. Policy fellow Am. Acad., Berlin, Aspen Inst., Berlin, 2001, Wilton Park Conf. fellow, Poland, 2007. Mem.: AAUW, Wilton Park Internat. Assn., Carnegie Coun. Ethics and Internat. Affairs, Fgn. Policy Assn., Robert Bosch Found. Alumni Assn. (mem. exec. com. 1994—96, 1997—98, co-pres. 1999—2000), European Union Studies Assn., Am. Coun. Germany, Am. Assn. Advancement Slavic Studies, Am. Polit. Sci. Assn., Rotary Club Metro N.Y., The Fletcher Club of N.Y. (v.p. 1998), Delta Tau Kappa, Alpha Mu Gamma, Pi Sigma Alpha, Phi Alpha Theta, Phi Sigma Tau (founder Scranton chpt.), Pi Gamma Mu (chpt. sec. 1982—84, Frank C. Brown scholarship medal 1984), Alpha Sigma Nu (student pres. 1984). Avocations: chess, swimming, creative writing, astrology, Tae Kwon Do. Home: 1864 74th St Brooklyn NY 11204-5752 Office: Molloy Coll PO Box 5002 1000 Hempstead Ave Rockville Centre NY 11571 Office Phone: 646-372-4396. Business E-Mail: cmazzucelli@molloy.edu, cgm7@nyu.edu.

MBANEFO, ARTHUR CHRISTOPHER IZUEGBUNAN, diplomat; b. Onitsha, Nigeria, June 11, 1930; With Chater, Knight & Co., Brighton, England, 1955—61, Coopers & Lybrand, London, 1961—65, Lybrand, Ross Bros. & Montgomery, Detroit, 1965—66, Price Waterhouse & Co., London, 1970—71; ptnr. Akintola Williams & Co., Lagos, Nigeria, 1962—99; amb. from Nigeria UN, NYC, 1999—. Fellow: Inst. Chartered Accts. England, Inst. Chartered Accts. Nigeria; mem.: Nigerian Assn. Mgmt. Cons. (coun. 1976—86, pres. 1986—89), Assn. Accountancy Bodies (coun. 1983—91, pres. 1987). Office: NY Permanent Mission 828 2d Ave New York NY 10017

MCABEE, GARY, neurologist, lawyer; JD, St. John's Sch. Law, NY, 1992; DO, Coll. Osteo. Medicine and Surgery, Des Moines, Iowa, 1980. Diplomate child and adult neurology Am. Bd. Neurology and Psychiatry, 1989, Am. Bd. Pediat., 1989. Attending child neurologist Children's Regional Hosp., Camden, NJ, 1996—; chmn. pediat. UMDNJ, Stratford, NJ, 1996—2003; chief child neurology Nassau County Med. Ctr., East Meadow, NY. Named Top Dr. in Pediatric Neurology, South Jersey Mag., 2003, 2006; named one of Best Doctors in Am., Best Doctors, Inc., 2006; recipient Med. Aumni Assn. award, St. Joseph's U., 1975, Disting. Svc. award, Nassau County Med. Ctr., 1994, Outstanding Svc. Faculty award, Robert Wood Johnson Sch. Medicine, 1999. Fellow: Am. Coll. Osteo. Pediatricians, Am. Coll. Legal Medicine, Am. Acad. Pediat. (chmn. com. med. liability and risk mgmt.).

MCABEE, SONJA LOUISE, library administrator; b. Anniston, Ala., Mar. 17, 1955; d. Ralph J. and Thelma Louise Sherman; m. Kenneth Blair McAbee, July 15, 1978; children: Megan Elizabeth, Patrick Ryan. BA in Polit. Sci., Jacksonville State U., 1975; MLS, U. Ala., 1988. Acquisitions libr. Jacksonville (Ala.) State U., 1990-96, head libr. svcs., 1996—. Contbr. articles to profl. jours. Mem. Ala. Libr. Assn. Democrat. Avocations: gardening, reading, home improvement projects. Home: 1837 Noah Valley Rd Jacksonville AL 36265 Office: Jacksonville State U 700 Pelham Rd North Jacksonville AL 36265 Office Phone: 256-782-5757. Office Fax: 256-782-5872. Business E-Mail: smcabee@jsu.edu.

MCABEE, THOMAS ALLEN, psychologist; b. Spartanburg, SC, Mar. 31, 1949; s. Thomas Walker and Doris Lee (Gillespie) McA. Student, Ga. Inst. Tech., 1967-69; BA, Furman U., 1971; MA, U. S.C., 1975, PhD, 1979. Clin. counselor Adolescent Inpatient Svc. William S. Hall Psychiat. Inst., Columbia, S.C., 1971-73; counselor children's therapeutic camp Columbia Area Mental Health Ctr., 1974; co-dir. cmty. problems survey Eau Claire Cmty. Project, Columbia, 1975; asst. aging svcs. planner Ctrl. Midlands Regional Planning Coun., Columbia, 1976; instr. U. S.C., 1976; NSF intern S.C. State Legislature, 1978; rsch. dir. S.C. Legis. Gov.'s Com. Mental Health and Mental Retardation, Columbia, 1979-80; co-dir. TV project "Feelings Just Are" Columbia Area Mental Health Ctr., 1980-89; psychologist S.C. Dept. Mental Retardation, 1982-93, S.C. Dept. Disabilities and Spl. Needs, 1993—2003, S.C. Vocat. Rehab. Dept., 2004—. Cons. S.C. Protection and Advocacy System for Handicapped Citizens, 1980, 81, S.C. Dept. Mental Health, 1981; mem. deinstitutionalization task force S.C. Developmental Disabilities Coun., 1979-80; mem. subcom. State Commr.'s Ad Hoc Com. to Study and Develop Work/Lodge System for S.C., S.C. Dept. Mental Health, 1979-80; mem. Media Task Force of Gov.'s Adv. Com. on Early Childhood Devel. and Edn., 1980-81; chmn. primary prevention public media com. S.C. Dept. Mental Health, 1979-81; adj. faculty U. S.C., Spartanburg, 2003. Recipient Palmetto Pictures Photography award, 1977; NIMH fellow, 1976-77. Mem. APA, S.C. Psychol. Assn. Home: 310 Snow St Greer SC 29651-4006 Office Phone: 864-585-3693. Business E-Mail: tmcabee@scvrd.state.sc.us.

MCADAM, LOWELL C., telecommunications industry executive; b. May 28, 1954; B in Engring., Cornell U.; MBA, U. San Diego. EIT. With Pacific Bell, 1983—93, v.p., Bay Area Mktg., gen. mgr., South Bay customer services; exec. dir. internat. applications and ops. AirTouch Commn., 1993, v.p. internat. ops.; COO PrimeCo Personal Commn., pres., CEO; exec. v.p., COO Verizon Wireless, pres., CEO, 2007—. Vice chmn., bd. dirs. CTIA. Mem., Engr. USN. Office: Verizon Wireless 1 Verizon Way Basking Ridge NJ 07920 *

MCADAM, PAUL EDWARD, retired library administrator; b. Balt., Jan. 30, 1934; s. Joseph Francis Jr. and Irene Cecile (Heineck) McA. BA in Romance Langs., Johns Hopkins U., Balt., 1955, MA, 1956; MLS, Drexel U., Phila., 1970. Libr. Free Libr. Phila., 1969-81; br. mgr. Phila. City. Inst. Libr., 1974-81; dir. Am. Libr., Paris, 1981-85; libr. collection devel., libr. tech. svcs. Catonsville C.C., Md., 1986-89; assoc. v.p. learning resources Carroll C.C., Westminster, Md., 1989-99, assoc. v.p. emeritus, 1999—; adj. libr. C.C. of Baltimore County, Catonsville, Md., 1999—2002, instr. continuing edn., 2003—04; adj. libr. Balt. Internat. Coll., 2000—; rschr. Transform, Inc., Columbia, Md., 2003—04. Mem. adv. bd. Coop. Librs. Ctrl. Md., Annapolis, 1992-96, State Libr. Resource Ctr., Balt., 1994-95; bd. dirs. Renew, 1995-2003; del. Internat. Fedn. Libr. Assn, 1993, 95. Vol. MPT, 1989-2000, Walters Art Mus., 1991—, Md. Fine Arts Festival, 1991-97 AIRS, 1999-2005, Drexel U., 2002—, Johns Hopkins U., 2004-05. 1st lt. U.S. Army, 1956-58. Mem. ALA (membership com. 1996-98), Coll. Air Consortium, Congress Acad. Libr. Dirs. (treas. 1998-2000), Md. Libr. Assn. (hon. mem., chair 1993-96, awards chair 1996-97, 1999-2000, treas. 1997-99, chair fundraising task force 2001-02), Consortium Md. C.C. Libr. Dirs. (treas. 1998-2000), Beta Phi Mu. Democrat. Home: 524 Academy Rd Baltimore MD 21228-1814 Personal E-mail: paulmcad@verizon.net.

MCADAM, WILL, electronics executive, consultant; b. Wheeling, W.Va., Oct. 22, 1921; s. Will and Elizabeth Margaret (Wickham) McA.; m. Evelyn Virginia Warren, Sept. 22, 1945; children: Elizabeth Ruth, Margaret Evelyn. BSEE, Case Sch. Applied Sci., 1942; MSEE, U. Pa., 1959. Rsch. technologist Leeds & Northrup Co., Phila., 1945-57, head elec. sect. R&D dept. North Wales, Pa., 1957-68, assoc. dir. rsch. ops., 1968-76, mgr. devel. and engring. adv. devel., 1977-79, prin. scientist rsch. dept., 1979-82, ret., 1982; cons. in electronics, 1982—. Contbr. articles to profl. jours., chpts. to handbooks; 30 patents in field. 1st lt. AUS, 1942-45, ETO. Decorated Bronze Star. Fellow IEEE (life, chmn. subcom. on elec. and high frequency measurements 1957-59, com. indsl. electronic and control instruments 1961-65, Prize Paper award 1958), Eta Kappa Nu, Tau Beta Pi. Republican. Presbyterian. Avocations: amateur radio, woodworking/cabinetmaking. Home: 3321 Twin Silo Dr Blue Bell PA 19422

MCADAMS, FRANK JOSEPH, III, communications educator; b. Chgo., Nov. 18, 1940; s. Frank Joseph Jr. and Mary Irene (Geary) McA.; m. Patty Ann Rafferty, Dec. 27, 1966. BS, Loyola U., Chgo., 1967; MFA, UCLA, 1979. Instr. UCLA, 1981—, U. Calif., Irvine, 1989—. Adj. prof. Sch. Cinema, U. So. Calif., LA, 1991—; mem. judging panel Diane Thomas Awards, UCLA, 1986—2000; vis. lectr. screenplay structure U. Navarra, Pamplona, Spain, 1990; vis. lectr. Southampton Coll., LI U., 1997; mem. screenwriting adv. bd. U. Calif.-Irvine Extension, 1995-2001. Screenwriter California Rain, 1978, Stagecoach Bravo, 1979; author: The American War Film: History and Hollywood, 2002; co-author: Final Affair, 2002. Capt. USMC, 1966—72. Decorated Armed Forces Expeditionary medal, Laos, Vietnam Svc. medal, Rep. of Vietnam Campaign medal with four stars, Navy-Marine Corps medal, Navy Comm. medal with combat V, Presdl. Unit citation, Navy Unit citation, Meritorius Unit commendation; recipient award for best newspaper col. Orange County Press Club, 1974, HM for Best Series, 1974, Sam Goldwyn Screenwriting award Sam Goldwyn Found., 1978, 79. Mem. 1st Marine Divsn. Assn., VFW, Writers Guild Am. West, UCLA Theater Arts Alumni Assn., PEN Ctr. USA West. Democrat. Roman Catholic. Office: MAGLA PO Box 1511 Hollywood CA 90078-1511 Office Phone: 818-244-2144. Business E-Mail: rushact@cox.net.

MCADAMS, JOHN POPE, lawyer; b. Phila., June 5, 1949; s. Eugene P. and Mary (Miller) McA.; m. Anne Christina Connelly, Sept. 5, 1970; children: Emily Lane, Anne Connelly. BA, U. NC, 1971; JD, Wake Forest U., 1976. Bar: Fla. 1976, NC 1976, US Dist. Ct. (mid. dist.) Fla. 1977. Assoc. Carlton Fields, Tampa, Fla., 1976-82, ptnr., 1982—2007, of counsel, 2007—. Contbg. editor: The Developing Labor Law, 1983, Employee Duty of Loyalty, 1995; contbr. articles to profl. jours. Pres. Hillsborough Cmty. Mental Health Ctr., Tampa, 1983; trustee City of Temple Terrace Pension Plan, Fla., 1985-89; pres. Hyde Park Preservation, Inc., Tampa, 1993; bd. dir., pres. Child Abuse Coun., Inc., Tampa Lighthouse Blind. Mem. ABA, ABA Equal Rights & Responsibilities Com., Fla. Bar Assn. (exec. coun. labor sect. 1987-89). Republican. Episcopalian. Home: 820 S Delaware Ave Tampa FL 33606-2915 Office: Carlton Fields PO Box 3239 Tampa FL 33601-3239 Office Phone: 813-223-7000. Business E-Mail: jmcadams@carltonfields.com.

MCADAMS, RACHEL, actress; b. London, Ont., Can., Oct. 7, 1976; d. Lance and Sandy McAdams. BFA with honors, NYU. Actor: (films) My Name is Tanino, 2002, Perfect Pie, 2002, The Hot Chick, 2002, Mean Girls, 2004, The Notebook, 2004, Wedding Crashers, 2005, Red-Eye, 2005, The Family Stone, 2005; (TV films) Guilt by Association, 2002; (TV series) Shotgun Love Dolls, 2001, Slings and Arrows, 2003. Named Choice Movie Actress: Comedy, Teen Choice awards, 2006. Office: The Gersh Agy 232 N Canon Dr Beverly Hills CA 90210 Office Phone: 310-274-6611.

MCADARAGH, RAYMON MICHAEL, aerospace engineer, researcher; b. Springfield, Ohio, Feb. 19, 1951; s. Bernard E. and Joan Patricia McAdaragh; m. Carol Ann Reese, Jan. 23, 1988; children: Jeffrey, Eric; 1 child from previous marriage, Sandra. BS, Christopher New Port U., 1980; BS in Aerospace Tech., Thomas A. Edison State Coll., 1990; M in Aerospace, Embry/Riddle Aero. U., 1994; PhD, U. Fla., 1999. Electrician Newport News (Va.) Ship Bldg. Co., 1974—78; wastewater treatment plant operator Hampton Rds. Sanitation Dist., Williamsburg, Va., 1980, lab. technician, 1981; air traffic control specialist FAA, Williamsport, Pa., 1982—88, Gainesville, Fla., 1988—99, aero. engring. rsch. psychologist Hampton, Va., 1999—. Cons., rschr. NASA, Hampton, 1999—2004; initiator, dir. human factors rsch. coordination NASA/FAA, Hampton, 2002—04, mem. weather tech. integration team, Washington, 2005—, mem. vision team, 2005—. Writer, musician, singer: albums Midnight on the Water, 2001, East Virginia Bound, 2001, New World Destiny, 2005, Pleromatic Journey, 2006. Vol. curriculum devel. team Poquoson Sch. Bd., Va., 2001. With US Army, 1969—74. Recipient 1st degree black belt, Shorin-Ken Karate, brown belt, Shorin-Ryu Karate, orange belt, Judo, Outstanding Contbns. to Aviation Weather Info. Rsch. award, NASA, 2002, Avaiation Safety Program award, 2004. Mem.: Tidewater Human Factors and Ergonomic Soc., Aerospace Human Factors Assn., Aerospace Med. Assn., Theosophical Soc. Am., Masons (3d degree, 32d degree Scottish Rite). Avocations: fishing, boating. Home: 40 Lodge Rd Poquoson VA 23662 Office: FAA NASA Langley Rsch Ctr Hampton VA 23681 Office Phone: 757-864-1941. Business E-Mail: raymon.mcadaragh@nasa.gov.

MCAFEE, DIANA MAE, media specialist, music educator; b. Charlestown, Ind., Oct. 24, 1951; d. Robert E. and Dorothy N. Williams; m. John J. McAfee, May 27, 1972; children: Michelle Renee McAfee Logan, Jennifer Melynne. B in Music Edn., Evangel U., Springfield, Mo., 1973; MusM, Pittsburg State U., Kans., 1977. Libr. cert. Mo. Piano instr. Evangel U., Springfield, 1971—73; piano tchr., judge Nat. Piano Guild, Carthage, Mo., 1975—; tchr. Carthage R-9 Schs., 1986—94, libr. media coord., 1995—99, libr. media specialist, 1999—. Adj. prof. Crowder Coll., Neosho, Mo., 1995—97; chairperson Career Ladder Carthage Schs., 2003—05. Choir dir. 1st Assembly God, Carthage, 1974—94. Mem.: Mo. Assn. Sch. Librs., Mo. State Tchrs. Assn. Avocations: travel, reading, movies. Home: 17184 Hawthorne Rd Carthage MO 64836 Office: Fairview Elem Sch 1201 E Fairview Carthage MO 64836 Business E-Mail: mcafeed@carthage.k12.mo.us.

MCAFEE, LARRY W., chemistry educator; b. Oklahoma City, Okla., Oct. 20, 1946; s. Mv and Margaret McAfee; m. Donna Sigwart, Aug. 7, 1971; children: Joy Kiser, Hope Morgan. BA, U. N.C., Charlotte, 1965—69, MA, 1975—80. Chemistry tchr. South Cobb HS, Austell, Ga., 1969—71; sci. tchr. Coulwood Jr. HS, Charlotte, NC, 1971—74; chemistry tchr. East Mecklenburg HS, Charlotte, 1974—. Cross country/track coach South Cobb HS, 1969—71; track coach Coulwood Jr. HS, 1971—74; cross country/track coach East Mecklenburg HS, 1974—2003. State meet dir., cross country N.C. HS Athletic Assn., Charlotte, 1980—2001, state meet dir., indoor track Chapel Hill, 1990—2000; asst. regional coord. Foot Locker Cross Country Championships, Charlotte, 1982—2006; asst. coord. Foot Locker Nat. Cross Country Championships, San Diego, Calif., 1982—2006. Recipient County Achievement award, Nat. Assn. Counties, Wash. D.C., 1981, Outstanding Achievement, N.C. HS Athletic Assn., 1992, N.C. Chemistry Tchr. of Yr., Ciba Chem., N.C. State U., 1993, Star Tchr. award, Time-Warner, 1997, Oustanding Svc., N.C. HS Athletic Assn., 1999, Track Coach of Yr., 2000, Merit award, Foot Locker Cross Country Championships, 2005; grantee Summer Tchr. Rsch. Program, Hoechst Celanese, 1992, Sandoz Chem., 1994. Mem.: State Employees Assn. N.C. Avocations: photography, travel. Office: E Mecklenburg HS 6800 Monroe Rd Charlotte NC 28212 Home Phone: 704-366-5709; Office Phone: 980-343-6430.

MCAFEE, NOELLE CLAIRE, philosopher, educator; b. Tagiura, Libya, Nov. 25, 1960; d. Horatio Paul and Marika Chaniotakis McAfee; m. David G Armstrong, Aug. 8, 1992; children: Guthrie McAfee Armstrong, Eliza Dorothy Armstrong. BA in hist., U. of Tex. at Austin, 1986; MA in pub. policy, Duke U., 1987; MA in Philosophy, U. of Wis. at Madison, 1990; PhD, U. of Tex. at Austin, 1998. Lectr. in polit. theory U. Tex., Dept. of Govt., 1998—99; asst. prof. philosophy U. Mass., 1999—2003, assoc. prof. philosophy, 2003—. Dir. honors program U. Mass., 2004—; vis. prof. philosophy Brandeis U., Waltham, Mass., 2004. Assoc. editor Kettering Review, 1991—; author: Julia Kristeva, 2003, Habermas, Kristeva and Citizenship, 2000; editor: Standing with the Public, 1997; contbr. chapters to books, articles to profl. jours. Office: Dept of Philosophy, U Mass Lowell One University Ave Lowell MA 01854 Office Phone: 978-934-3912.

MCAFEE, R. PRESTON, economics professor; b. 1956; m. Kristin Familari; 2 children. BA (highest honors) in Economics, U. Fla., 1976; MS in Math., Purdue U., 1978, MS in Economics, 1978, PhD in Economics, 1980. Vis. asst. prof., economics Purdue U., 1980—81; asst. prof., economics U. Western Ont., 1981—87, assoc. prof. economics, 1987—89, prof. economics, 1989—90; vis. assoc. prof. economics Calif. Inst. Tech., 1988—89, vis. prof. economics, 1989—90, exec. officer for soc. sci., 2005—07, J. Stanley Johnson prof. (on leave to Yahoo!2007-2009), 2004—; vis. prof. economics MIT, 1994—95; Rex G. Baker, Jr. prof. polit. economy U. Tex., Austin, 1990—97, Murray S. Johnson chair, 1997—2003; vis. prof. bus. strategy U. Chgo. Grad. Sch. Bus., 2000—01; vp and rsch. fellow Yahoo! Rsch., Burbank, Calif., 2007—. Mem. adv. bd. EconJobSearch.org, 2007—; cons. in field. Contbr. articles to profl. jours.; referee (for several jours.); co-author (with John McMillan): Incentives in Government Contracting, 1988; author: Competitive Solutions: A Strategist's Toolkit, 2003; contbr. chapters to books; assoc. editor Journal of Economic Theory, 1992—96, 2002—04, American Economic Review, 1992—93, 2002—05, Theoretical Economics, 2005—; co-editor: American Economic Review, 1993—2002; program editor Latin Am. Econometric Soc., 2007. Fellow: Econometric Soc. (program com., N.Am. winter meetings 2005, mem. program com. summer meetings 2007); mem.: Soc. for Econ. Theory (mem. exec. bd. 2005—), Soc. for the Promotion Econ. Theory, ABA (assoc.), Am. Economics Assn. (nominating com. 2002, program com. 2004, editor search com. for Am. Econ. Jour.: Microeconomics 2006), Phi Beta Kappa. Achievements include patents in field. Mailing: Yahoo! Rsch 3333 Empire Blvd Burbank CA 91504 Office: Calif Inst Tech Divsn Humanities and Soc Scis MC 228-77 100 Baxter Hall Pasadena CA 91125 Office Phone: 818-524-3290, 626-395-3476. Office Fax: 626-793-4681. Business E-Mail: mcafee@hss.caltech.edu. E-mail: preston@mcafee.cc. *

MC AFEE, WILLIAM, government official; b. Port Royal, Jan. 25, 1910; s. French and Willietta (Anderson) McA. BA, Coll. of Wooster, 1932; MA in Am. History, Pa. State U., 1941; student, Oxford, Eng., summer 1937. Wooster in India rep. on faculty Ewing Christian Coll., Allahabad, India, 1932-35; tchr. pub. high schs. and prep. sch. Pa., 1935-42; joined State Dept., 1946; country specialist (Office Chinese Affairs), 1946-50; coordinator current intelligence (Bur. Intelligence and Research), 1950-56, spl. asst. to dir., 1956-60, dir. ops. staff, 1960-66, asst. dep. dir. coordination, 1966-72, dep. dir. coordination, 1972-80, dep. asst. sec. intelligence coordination, 1980—; dir. (Office of Intelligence Liaison), 1981-86, ret. Adviser Griffin Econ. Aid Mission to S.E. Asia, 1950 Served to lt. col. AUS, 1942-46, CBI. Decorated Legion of Merit; Order Brit. Empire; Precious Tripod Chinese Nationalist Govt.; recipient Superior Honor award State Dept., 1964, Disting. Honor award, 1980 Mem. Am. Fgn. Service Assn., Delta Sigma Rho. Home: 4433 Brandywine St NW Washington DC 20016-4419

MCAFEE, WILLIAM JAMES, lawyer; b. Bronx, NY, June 18, 1962; s. James J. and Marie A. (Theyson) McA.; m. Helen W. Wagner, Oct. 12, 1962; children: Rebecca A., Ryan P. BA, AA, U.C.F., 1984; JD, Stetson U., St. Petersburg, Fla., 1987. Bar: Fla. 1987, U.S. Dist. Ct. (so. dist.) Fla. 1988, U.S. Dist. Ct. (mid. dist.) Fla. 1989. Asst. states atty. County of Palm Beach, West Palm Beach, Fla., 1987-88; assoc. Schuler & Wilkerson, West Palm Beach, 1988-89, Slawson & Burman, West Palm Beach, 1989-90; ptnr. Wagner, Johnson & McAfee, West Palm Beach, 1990—2000, Ricci Hubaro Leopolo Frankel Farmer & McAfee, West Palm Beach, 2000—02, McAfee & Russo, 2002—. Contbr. articles to profl. jours. Mem. Fla. Acad. Trial Lawyers (pres. young lawyers sect. 1989-92, frequent lectr.). Avocations: family, fishing, exercise, yard work, Karate. Office: McAfee Russo 701 Northpoint Pkwy Ste 415 West Palm Beach FL 33407

MCALEENAN, DONALD F., lawyer, construction executive; BS, Georgetown U.; JD, NYU. Asst. gen. counsel AT&E Corp.; v.p., dep. gen. counsel Fibreboard Corp., 1992—97; sr. v.p., gen. counsel, co-founder Builders FirstSource, Inc., Dallas, 1997—. Office: Builders FirstSource Ste 1600 2001 Bryan St Dallas TX 75201 *

MCALEESE DUBE, EILEEN MARIE, retired secondary school educator; b. May 23, 1937; d. Patrick Leo and Hazel May (Dishon) McAleese; m. Darrell Eugene Dube, Sept. 17, 1960; 1 child, Brent Alexander. BA English, U. Akron, 1959. Tchr. Buchtel H.S. Akron Pub. Schs., Ohio, 1959—60, tchr. Ctrl.-Hower H.S., 1965—73, tchr. sr. advanced placement English East H.S., 1973—94; ret., 1994. Advisor Yr. Book East H.S., 1973—88. Contbr. Scholar, Jennings Found., 1982—83. Mem.: Ohio Coun. Tchrs. Eng. and Lang. Arts, Akron Edn. Assn., Greater Akron Tchrs. Eng., Nat. Coun.Tchrs. Eng., Ancient Order Hibernians Am., Friends Children's Hosp., Akron Fraternal Order Police Aux., Fairlawn City Women's Club, Phi Mu. Republican. Roman Catholic.

MCALHANY, TONI ANNE, lawyer; b. Decatur, Ind., May 1, 1951; d. Robert Keith and Evelyn L. (Fisher) McA. BA, Ind. U., 1973; JD, Valparaiso U., 1976. Bar: Mich. 1976, Ind. 1982, Ill. 1986, U.S. Dist. Ct. (no. dist.) Ind. 1989. Asst. prosecutor Ottawa County Prosecutor's Office, Grand Haven, Mich., 1976-81; assoc. Hann, Doss & Persinger, Holland, Mich., 1981-82, Romero & Thonert, Auburn, Ind., 1982-85; ptnr. Dahlgren & McAlhany, Berwyn, Ill., 1985-88, Colbeck, McAlhany & Stewart, Angola, Ind. & Coldwater, Mich., 1988-98; friend of the ct. for Branch County, domestic rels. referee, 1999—. Atty. Angola Housing Authority, 1989-98. Bd. dirs. Child and Family Svcs., Ft. Wayne, Ind., 1983, Fillmore Ctr., Berwyn, 1986-88, Altrusa, Coldwater, 1989-92. Mem. ATLA, State Bar Mich., State Bar Ind., State Bar Ill., Mich. Friend of the Ct. Assn., Referees Assn. Mich., Branch County Bar Assn., Steuben County Bar Assn. Avocations: travel, horseback riding. Mailing: 2241 US 6 Waterloo IN 46793 Office Phone: 517-279-4314. E-mail: tmcalhany@hotmail.com.

MCALISTER, HAROLD ALISTER, astronomer; b. Chattanooga, July 1, 1949; s. Harold Joy and Edna (Robbins) McA.; m. Susan Paulette Johnson, Aug. 5, 1972; 1 child, Merritt Ellen. BA in Physics, U. Tenn., Chattanooga, 1971; MA in Astronomy, U. Va., 1974, PhD in Astronomy, 1975. Grad. rsch. asst. dept. astronomy U. Va., Charlottesville, 1971-75; rsch. assoc. Kitt Peak Nat. Obs., Tucson, 1975-77; asst. prof. dept. physics and astronomy Ga. State U., Atlanta, 1977-82, assoc. prof., 1982-87, prof., 1987—98, founder, dir. Ctr. High Angular Resolution Astronomy, 1987—, regents' prof., 1998—; dir., CEO Mt. Wilson Inst., Pasadena, Calif., 2003—. Contbr. articles to profl. jours. Capt. US Army, 1971-78. Prin. investigator numerous grants NSF, AFOSR, NASA. Mem. Am. Astron. Soc., Astron. Soc. Pacific (Maria & Eric Muhlmann award 2007), Internat. Astron. Union (pres. Commn. 26 1988-91). Office: Ga State U Ctr for High Angular Resolution Atlanta GA 30303 *

MCALISTER, MICHAEL H., architect; b. Calif. s. Doyle R. and Mary E. McAlister. AA, Bakersfield Coll.; BArch, Calif. Poly. U. Planning technician Bakersfield (Calif.) City Hall, 1963; carpenter Del Webb Corp., Kern City, Calif., 1964; archtl. draftsman Goss & Choy Archs., Bakersfield, 1965-67; arch., v.p. D.G.C. & Assocs., Bakersfield, 1971-80; dir. architecture, v.p. N.B.A. & Assocs., Archs., Bakersfield, 1980-83; arch. Michael H. McAlister, A.I.A., Bakersfield, 1983—. Nepthrology design cons. for various treatment groups and hosps., 1987—. Commr., archtl. advisor Hist. Preservation Commn., Bakersfield, 1986-87; bd. dirs. Camp Fire Coun., Kern County, Calif., 1980-84 Recipient Archtl. Pub. Bldg. Hist. award Beautiful Bakersfield Com., City of Bakersfield's City Coun. and Hist. Preservation Commn., 1985, 87, Exterior Environ. Design Excellence Bakersfield C. of C., 1988, Comml. Design Excellence award, 1984, Design Excellence and Beautification award City of Taft, Calif., 1989, Design Excellence award State of Nev., 1992, Beautiful Bakersfield Archtl. Comml. Remodel award, 2003 Mem. AIA (Calif. Coun., Golden Empire chpt.). Avocation: religious architecture and art. Office: 1302 Ironstone Dr Studio 201 Bakersfield CA 93312-4668

MCALLISTER, BRUCE RICHARD, art educator; b. Stanford, Calif., Feb. 25, 1964; s. Mark Marion McAllister and Ruth Cannon Lee; m. Katherine Reed, Apr. 10, 1993; children: Cameron Dale, Eric Reed. BFA, U. Calif., Irvine, 1989; MFA, Calif. Coll. of the Arts, San Francisco, 1993—95. Art instr. Pacific Art League, Palo Alto, Calif., 1991; adj. art instr. City Coll. of San Francisco, 1998; art instr. Antelope Valley Coll., Lancaster, Calif., 2000—, LA Pierce Coll., Woodland Hills, Calif., 2001—; adj. art instr. Glendale C.C., Calif., 2003—; art instr. Moorpark Coll., Calif., 2004—. Muralist, prop designer, builder Ahrens Studios, Novato, Calif., 1995—97, Club Ed, Lancaster, 1999—2002; creator storyboard for film The Big E Oaf Prodns., Glendale, Calif., 1999; web site developer Strategic Internet Sollutions, Lancaster, 1999—2001, bkmdesign.com, Quartz Hill, Calif., 2001—; juror Antelope Valley Union HS Dist. Art Show, Lancaster City Gallery and Mus., 2001. One-man shows include Pamela Skinner Gallery, Sacramento, 2004, 2005 (Critic's Pick, Sacramento Bee, 2005), 2006, B. Sakata Garo Gallery, Sacramento, 2004 (Critic's Pick, Sacramento Bee, 2004), exhibited in group shows at Fed. Bldg. Towers, Oakland, Calif., 1994, Palo Alto Cmty. Ctr., 1995, Andrea Schwartz Gallery, San Francisco, 1995, Weintraub Thomas Gallery, Sacramento, 1997, Lancaster City Gallery and Mus., Calif., 2001, Julie Baker Fine Art Gallery, Grass Valley, Calif., 2003—04, O'Hanlon Ctr., Calif., 2004, Solaris Gallery, West Hollywood, Calif., 2005, Pierce Coll., Woodland Hills, Calif., 2005, contemporaryquarterly.com, 2006, Roshambo Winery Gallery, Healdsburg, Calif., 2006, Pamela Skinner Gallery, 2006, Calif. Coll. of Arts 100th Anniversary Exhbn., San Francisco, 2007, Calif. Coll. of the Arts Alumni Exhbn., 2007, represented in numerous pvt. collections. Recipient Gold Key Nat. Honor Soc., U. of Calif. at Irvine,

1988. Home: 4776 West Ave L-12 Quartz Hill CA 93536 Home Phone: 661-722-3060; Office Phone: 661-722-3060. Personal E-mail: bruce@brucemcallister.com.

MC ALLISTER, GERALD NICHOLAS, retired bishop, minister; b. San Antonio, Feb. 23, 1923; s. Walter Williams and Leonora Elizabeth (Alexander) McA.; m. Helen Earle Black, Oct. 2, 1953; children— Michael Lee, David Alexander, Stephen Williams, Elizabeth. Student, U. Tex., 1939-42, Va. Theol. Sem., 1948-51, DD (hon.), 1977. Ordained to ministry Episcopal Ch. as deacon, 1953, as priest, 1954. Rancher, 1946-48; deacon, priest Ch. of Epiphany, Raymondville, Ch. of Incarnation, Corpus Christi, St. Francis Ch., Victoria, Tex., 1951-63; 1st canon Diocese of West Tex., 1963-70; rector St. David's Ch., San Antonio, 1970-76; consecreated Episcopal bishop of Okla., Oklahoma City, 1977-89, ret., 1989; bishop-in-residence Episcopal Theol. Sem., Austin, Tex., 1990-93. Trustee Episcopal Theol. Sem. of S.W., 1961-2000, adv. bd., 1974—; mem. Case Commn. Bd. for Theol. Edn., 1981-82; pres. Tex. Council Chs., 1966-68, Okla. Conf. Chs., 1980-83; bd. dirs. Presiding Bishop's Fund for World Relief, 1972-77, Ch. Hist. Soc., 1976—; chmn. Nat. and World Mission Program Group, 1973-76; mem. Structure of Ch. Standing Commn., 1979, mem. standing com. on Stewardship/Devel., 1979-85; founder Chaplaincy Program, Bexar County Jail, 1968; mem. governing bd. nat. council Ch. of Christ, 1982-85; chmn. standing commn. on stewardship Episcopal Ch., 1983-85; v.p., trustee The Episc., Episc. Theol. Sem. of Southwest, 1987-93, chmn. bd. trustees, 1993-97. Author: What We Learned from What You Said, 1973, This Fragile Earth Our Island Home, 1980. Bd. dirs. Econ. Opportunity Devel. Corp., San Antonio, 1968-69; mem. exec. com. United Way, 1968-70, vice-chmn., 1970. With U.S. Mcht. Marines, 1942; to 1st lt. USAAF, 1942-45. Recipient Agudas Achim Brotherhood award, 1968. Mem.: Alumni Coun. Va. Theol. Sem. Episcopalian. Address: 507 Bluffestates San Antonio TX 78216-7930

MCALLISTER, KENNETH WAYNE, lawyer; b. High Point, NC, Jan. 3, 1949; s. John Calhoun and Ruth Welch (Buie) McA.; children: Katherine Owen, Kenneth Grey. BA, U. N.C., 1971; JD, Duke U., 1974. Bar: N.C. 1974, U.S. Dist. Ct. for Middle dist. N.C. 1974, U.S. Ct. Appeals for 4th circuit 1980, U.S. Supreme Ct. 1980. Ptnr. Fisher, Fisher & McAllister, High Point, 1974—81; U.S. atty. (middle dist.) N.C. U.S. Dept. Justice, Greensboro, 1981—86; sr. exec. v.p., gen. counsel Wachovia Corp., Winston-Salem, NC, 1988—2001; mem. McAllister & Hanks PLLC. Bd. dirs, Culp Inc., 2002-; bd. visitors Wake Forest U. Sch. of Law, 1988-96, U. N.C. at Chapel Hill, 1989-93, Duke U. Law Sch., 1996—; bd. advisors, U. N.C.Sch. Law Banking Inst., 1998-2002. Pres. High Point Drug Action Coun., 1977-78; chmn. High Point Rep.Com., 1976-78, 88-89; mem. adv. bd. Salvation Army, High Point, 197-79; bd. dirs. Sch. of Nursing Found., U. N.C., Chapel Hill, 1993-99; vice chair Attys. Gen. Adv. Com. U. S Atty., 1985-86; govs. commn. Bus. Laws and the Economy, 1994—; bd. govs. Presbyn. Homes, 1997—, chmn. 2000—; permanent mem. Fourth Cir. Jud. Conf. John Motley Morehead scholar Morehead Found., 1967; Arthur Priest scholar Phi Delta Theta, 1971 Fellow Am. Bar Found.; mem. N.C. Bar Assn. (bd. govs. 2000-03), Piedmont Triad Airport Authority (bd. dirs. 1998-2001), High Point Country Club, Phi Beta Kappa. Republican. Presbyterian. Office: McAllister & Hanks PLLC 201 Neal Pl PO Box 5006 High Point NC 27262 Home Phone: 336-841-0906; Office Phone: 336-882-4300. Business E-Mail: kmcallister@mcallisterhanks.com.

MCALLISTER, STEPHEN ROBERT, dean, law educator; b. Lawrence, Kans., Nov. 27, 1962; s. Stephen Ray and Rhoda Alice (Bening) McA.; m. Suzanne Carey McAllister, Feb. 26, 2004. BA in Econs., U. Kans., 1985, JD, 1988. Bar: Ill. 1989, U.S. Ct. Appeals (7th cir.) 1989. Law clk. to Hon. Richard Posner U.S. Ct. Appeals (7th cir.), Chgo., 1988-89; law clk. to Hon. Byron R. White U.S. Supreme Ct., Washington, 1989—91; assoc. Gibson, Dunn & Crutcher, Washington, 1992—93; vis. assoc. prof. U. Kans. Sch. Law, 1993—95, assoc. prof., 1995—98, prof., 1999—, assoc. dean Academic Affairs, 1999—2000, dean, 2000—05. Interim dir. Dole Inst. Politics, 2003—04. Recipient Dean Frederick J. Moreau Award, 1997; grantee W.T. Kemper Fellowship, 1999. Fellow: Am. Bar Found.; mem.: Supreme Ct. Hist. Soc. (trustee), Order of Coif. Office: U Kans Sch Law 1535 W 15th St Lawrence KS 66045 E-mail: stever@ku.edu.

MCALLISTER, WILLIAM HOWARD, III, newspaper reporter, columnist, public affairs consultant; b. Durham, NC, Nov. 6, 1941; s. William Howard, Jr. and Dorothy Fisk (Tillett) McA.; m. Rena Catherine Farrell, June 13, 1965; children: William Howard IV, Christopher F., Jonathan T., Benjamin J. BA in Polit. Sci, U. NC, Chapel Hill, 1964, MA in Journalism, 1966. Cecil Prince research asst. U. NC, 1965; reporter The Virginian-Pilot, Norfolk, 1964-67; reporter, city editor Virginian-Pilot, 1972-75; reporter Wall St. Jour., San Francisco, 1968-72, Washington Post, 1975-78, Va. editor, 1978-86, nat. reporter, 1986-99, columnist stamp and coin sect., 1987-99, lobbying columnist, 1997-99; Washington bur. chief Denver Post and MediaNews Newspapers, 1999—2003; Washington corr. Linn's Stamp News, 1997—. TV cons. Ford Found., 1969-72; cons. The Newseum, Arlington, Va., 2003—. Capt. USNR, 1966-93. Decorated Navy Commendation medal, Meritorous Svc. medal, Gold Star; recipient Lidman prize for philatelic writing, 1990. Mem. Am. Soc. Newspaper Editors, Kappa Tau Alpha, Nat. Press Club. Presbyterian. Home and Office: 10121 Ratcliffe Manor Dr Fairfax VA 22030-2427 Personal E-mail: bmcallister@cox.net.

MCALONIS, CHRISTOPHER M., engineer; b. Cleve., Sept. 29, 1977; s. Kenneth P. and Marilyn A. McAlonis. BS in Mech. Engring., U. Toledo, 2000. Cert. profl. engr., Ohio, 2007. Inside sales engr. Wadsworth Slawson NE, Cleve., 2001—06; inside sales mgr. Northrich Co., Garfield Heights, Ohio, 2006—. Mem.: ASHRAE (assoc.). Independent.

MCALPIN, KIRK MARTIN, lawyer; b. Newark, Sept. 14, 1923; s. Aaron Champion and Margaret (Martin) McAlpin; m. Sarah Frances Morgan, Dec. 14, 1951; children: Kirk Martin Jr., Philip Morgan, Margaret Champion Margeson. LLB, U. Ga., 1948; postgrad., Columbia U., 1949. Bar: Ga. 1949. Asst. solicitor gen. Ea. Jud. Cir. Ct. Ga., 1951; assoc. Bouhan, Lawrence, Williams, Levy & McAlpin, Savannah, Ga., 1952-53, ptnr., 1954-63; sr. ptnr. King & Spalding, Atlanta, 1963-86; pvt. practice Savannah, 1987—97, Atlanta, 1998—. Chmn. Inst. Continuing Legal Edn., 1980-81, Inst. Continuing Jud. Edn. in Ga., 1981-84, Jud. Council Ga., 1979-82. Pres. Atlanta Legal Aid Soc., 1971. Fellow Am. Bar Found., Am. Law Inst., Am. Coll. Trial Lawyers, Internat. Acad. Trial Lawyers, Internat. Soc. Barristers; mem. ABA (Jr. Bar Conf. chmn. 1958-59, chmn. gen. practice sect. 1972-73, chmn. sr. lawyers div. 1986-87, ho. of dels. 1960-90, state del. 1970-90, bd. govs. 1973-76), State Bar Ga. Assn. (chmn. Young Lawyers 1953-54, bd. govs. 1953-63, pres. 1979-80), Atlanta Bar Assn., Savannah Bar Assn. (v.p. 1960-61), Nat. Conf. Bar Pres. (exec. com. 1981-83), Ga. Def. Lawyers Assn., Fed. Bar Assn., Am. Judicature Soc., Assn. R.R. Trial Counsel, Soc. of Cin., Sons Colonial Wars, St. Andrews Soc., Capital City Club, Piedmont Driving Club, Oglethorpe Club, Phi Delta Phi, Sigma Alpha Epsilon. Episcopalian. Office: The Paces 352 77 E Andrews Dr NW Atlanta GA 30305-1392 Office Phone: 404-467-8307. Office Fax: 404-467-0619. Personal E-mail: kmcasratty@mindspring.com.

MCALPINE, DONALD EUGENE, physician; b. Milaca, Minn., Dec. 12, 1949; s. Donald Eugene and Katherine Elizabeth McAlpine; m. Mary Lois Dorr, Nov. 11, 1950; children: Megan Erin Osterlund, David Aaron. MD, U. Minn., Mpls., 1979. Diplomate Am. Bd. Psychiatry and Neurology, 1984; cert. in Addiction Psychiatry Am. Bd. Psychiatry and Neurology, in Psychosomatic Medicine Am. Bd. Psychiatry and Neurology, in Geriatric Psychiatry Am. Bd. Psychiatry and Neurology. Cons. in psychiatry Mayo Clinic Coll. Medicine, Rochester, Minn., 1983—. Avocations: fishing, hunting. Office: Mayo Clinic Coll Medicine 200 SW 1st St Rochester MN 55905 Office Phone: 507-284-2511. Office Fax: 507-284-4158. Business E-Mail: mcalpine.donald@mayo.edu.

MCALWEE, MARTIN FREDERICK, lawyer; b. Washington, Oct. 4, 1943; s. Robert Walter and Norma Jean McAlwee; m. Maryann Sharma Siuda, Apr. 21, 2000; children from previous marriage: Gerald Steven, Jennifer Anne, Geoffrey Patrick. BA in Govt. and Polit., U. Md., Coll. Pk., 1966; JD, Cath. U., Washington, 1969; MSc in Acquistion and Contract Mgmt., Fla. Inst. Tech., 1982. Bar: DC 1969, Fla. 1982, Fla. Supreme Ct., U.S. Ct. Appeals (D.C. cir.), U.S. Dist. Ct. D.C. Judge advocate USAF, 1970—74; trial atty. Fed. Maritime Commn., Washington, 1974—79; contract mgmt. position Harris Corp., 1979—88; atty. advisor Office Staff Advocate 45th Space Wing, Patrick AFB, Fla., 1988—. Adj. prof. AF Inst. Tech., Wright-Patterson AFB, Ohio. Leader Boy Scouts Am. Ret. col. USAFR, 1999. Decorated Legion of Merit medal USAF, Bronze Star medal, Civil Svc. Meritorious Svc. medal; recipient James O. Wrightson award, 2000, Outstanding Civilian Atty., USAF Space Command, 1994, AF Space Command, 1998. Fellow: Nat. Contract Mgmt. Assn.; mem.: ABA, DC Bar Assn., Fla. Bar Assn. Avocations: golf, fishing. Office: 45th Space Wing Office Staff Judge Advocate 642 O Malley Rd Patrick Afb FL 32925-3329

MCAMIS, EDWIN EARL, lawyer; b. Cape Girardeau, Mo., Aug. 8, 1934; s. Zenas Earl and Anna Louise (Miller) McAmis; m. Malin Eklof, May 31, 1959 (div. 1979); 1 child, Andrew Bruce; life ptnr. Gerson Gonzalez. AB magna cum laude, Harvard U., 1956, LLB, 1959. Bar: N.Y. 1960, U.S. Dist. Ct. (so. dist.) N.Y. 1962, U.S. Supreme Ct. 1965, U.S. Ct. Appeals (2d and 3d cirs.) 1964, U.S. Ct. Appeals (D.C. cir.) 1981. Assoc. law firm Webster, Sheffield & Chrystie, NYC, 1959-61, Regan Goldfarb Powell & Quinn, NYC, 1962-65, Lovejoy, Wasson, Lundgren & Ashton, NYC, 1965-69, ptnr., 1969-77, Skadden, Arps, Slate, Meagher & Flom, NYC, 1977-90, spl. ptnr., pro bono, 1990-93; adj. prof. law Fordham U., 1984-85, Benjamin N. Cardozo Sch. Law, NYC, 1985-90. Mem. Lambda Legal and Edn. Fund, 1991—95; bd. dirs. Aston Magna Found. Music, Inc., 1982—93, Cmty. Rsch. Initiative N.Y., 1988—89. With US Army, 1961—62. Mem.: ABA, Selden Soc. Personal E-mail: edwinmcamis@comcast.net.

MCANARNEY, ELIZABETH R., pediatrician, educator; b. NYC, May 7, 1940; d. Henry Kellers and Kathryn (Blaney) McA. AB, Vassar Coll., 1962; MD, SUNY, Syracuse, 1966. Diplomate Am. Bd. Pediatrics in pediatrics and adolescent medicine. Intern, resident SUNY Upstate Med. Ctr., Syracuse, NY, 1966-68; fellow in behavioral pediatrics U. Rochester (N.Y.) Med. Ctr., 1968-70, sr. instr. pediatrics, 1969-71, asst. prof. pediatrics, 1971-77, assoc. prof. pediatrics, 1977-85, prof. pediatrics, 1985—, chair pediatrics dept., 1993—. Adv. com. Fertility and Maternal Health FDA, Bethesda, Md, 1987-92; mem. program adv. bd. Robert Wood Johnson Clin. Scholars Program, Princeton, N.J., 1995—. Editor: (books) Premature Adolescent Pregnancy, 1983, Identifying Social/ Psychological Antecedents of Adolescent Pregnancy, 1984, Textbook of Adolescent Medicine, 1992; co-author of nearly 200 papers, chpts., and comm. Recipient McNeil Outstanding Achievement award Soc. for Adolescent Medicine, 1989, Job Lewis Smith award Cmty. Pediat., Am. Acad. Pediat., 1990; named to Alumni Honor Roll, SUNY, 1998. Fellow AAAS; mem. Soc. for Pediatric Rsch., Am. Pediatric Soc. (mem. exec. coun. 1998—, pres. 2004-2005), Assn. for Med. Sch. Pediatric Chairs (pres. 1999), Inst. Medicine, Nat. Acad. Sci. Achievements include determination of relationship between young maternal age and maternal/neonatal outcomes. Office: U Rochester Med Ctr Dept Pediatrics 601 Elmwood Ave Box 777 Rochester NY 14642-0001 E-mail: carole_berger@urmc.rochester.edu.

MCANDREW, MARK PHILIP, orthopaedic surgeon, educator, clinical researcher; b. Kalona, Iowa, Sept. 23, 1953; s. Paul Joseph and Virginia McAndrew; m. Paula Kay Link, May 25, 1974; children: Christopher, Patrick, Timothy. BSc in Biochemistry with honors, U. Iowa, 1975, MD, 1978. Diplomate Am. Bd. Orthopaedic Surgery. Resident in orthopaedics U. Iowa Hosps. and Clinics, 1978-83; fellow Basel (Switzerland) Kantonspital, 1984; assoc. prof. dept. orthopaedics and reehab. Vanderbilt U., Nashville, 1997—. Assoc. editor Clin. Orthopaedics and Related Rsch. Fellow Am. Acad. Orthopaedic Surgeons; mem. ACS, Orthopaedic Trauma Assn. (chmn. membership com. 1994-96, bylaws com. 1999-2002). Avocation: running. Office: Vanderbilt U Med Ctr 1611 21st Ave S D-4207 Nashville TN 37232-0001 Fax: 615-936-1566. E-mail: mark.p.mcandrew@mcmail.vanderbilt.

MCANDREW, MARK S., insurance company executive; Mgmt. positions with Torchmark Corp., McKinney, Tex., 1980—; pres. Globe Life & Accident Ins. Co., 1991—2005, CEO, 1999—2005; pres. United Am. Ins. Co., 1991—2004, CEO, 1999—2004; pres., CEO Am. Income Life Ins. Co., 1999—2003; bd. dir. Torchmark Corp., 1998—, exec. v.p., 1999—2003, chmn. ins. ops., 2003—05, CEO, 2005—06, chmn., CEO, 2006—. Office: Torchmark Corp 3700 S Stonebridge Dr PO Box 8080 Mc Kinney TX 75070-8080 *

MCANDREW, PAUL JOSEPH, JR., lawyer; b. Kalona, Iowa, Mar. 8, 1957; s. Paul Joseph and Virginia (Krowka) McA.; m. Lola Maxine Miller, Mar. 1, 1975; children: Stephanie, Susan, Rose, Paul Joseph III, Bridget. BA with honors, U. Iowa, 1979, JD with high distinction, 1983. Bar: Iowa 1983, U.S. Dist. Ct. Iowa 1985, U.S. Claim Ct. 1985, U.S. Ct. Appeals (8th cir.) 1999, U.S. Supreme Ct. 2000. Law clk. to chief judge U.S. Dist. Ct. (so. dist.) Iowa, Des Moines, 1983-85; ptnr. Meardon, Sueppel, Downer & Hayes, Iowa City, 1985-99, Paul J. McAndrew Law Firm, Coralville, 1999—. Claimant's counsel rep. Iowa Workers' Compensation Adv. Com., 2000—. Recipient Hancher-Finkbine award, 1979. Mem. ABA, ATLA (chair workers' compensation sect. 2003), Iowa Bar Assn. (chair workers' compensation sect. 1993-95), Iowa Trial Lawyers Assn. (rep. bd. govs. 1993—, workers' compensation sect. 1997—), Johnson County Bar Assn., Iowa Assn. Workers Compensation Attys. (rep. bd. govs. 1993—), Work Injury Litigation Group (Iowa rep. to nat. bd. govs. 1997—). Democrat. Roman Catholic. Avocations: jogging, biking, golf, travel. Home: 620 Scott Park Dr Iowa City IA 52245-5140 Office: Paul McAndrew Law Firm 2590 Holiday Rd Ste 100 Coralville IA 52241 Fax: 319 887 1693.

MCANDREW, THOMAS JOSEPH, lawyer; b. Providence, Oct. 19, 1945; s. Joseph L. and Amelia L. (Bonhotel) McA.; children: John Maxwell, Mercedes, Hope, Marya, Cornelia. BA, Providence Coll., 1968; JD, Georgetown U.-Am. U.-George Washington U., 1971; LLM, Georgetown U., 1973. Bar: R.I., 1971, US Dist. Ct. R.I., 1972, D.C. 1972, US Ct. Claims, 1972, US Tax Ct., 1971, US Custom and Patent Ct., 1971, US Ct. Mil. Appeals, 1971, US Ct. Appeals (1st cir.), 1971, US Ct. Appeals (DC), 1971, US Ct. Appeals (4th cir.), US Supreme Ct., 1974, Commonwealth Mass., 1985. Trial atty. Civil Aeros. Bd., Washington, 1971-72; legal asst. to John H. Fanning NLRB, Washington, 1972-73; labor rels. officer dept. edn. State of R.I., Providence, 1973-74, dep. asst. commr. edn., 1974-79, adminstr. labor rels., 1979-80; ptnr. Powers & McAndrew, Inc., Providence, 1980-87; pvt. practice Thomas J. McAndrew & Assocs., Providence, 1987—. Adj. prof. law U. R.I., Kingston, 1976; lectr. in field. Contbr. articles to profl. jours. Treas., trustee John E. Fogarty Found., Providence, 1974—; mem. Providence Com. on Fgn. Rels., Providence. Mem. ABA (com. on labor law) FBA, ATLA, Am. Arbitration Assn. (adv. coun.). Avocations: golf, tennis, walking. Home: 6 Wingate Rd Providence RI 02906-4910 Office: Ste 205 One Turks Head Place Providence RI 02903 Office Phone: 401-455-0350. Fax: 401-455-0882. Business E-Mail: tmcandrew@tjmcandrewlaw.com.

MCANDREWS, BRIAN, digital marketing executive; MBA, Stanford U., Calif.; BA, Harvard U., Cambridge, Mass. Product mgr. Gen. Mills, Inc., 1984—89; exec. positions at ABC Sports, ABC Entertainment and ABC TV Network including exec. v.p. and gen. mgr. of ABC Sports ABC, 1990—99; CEO, bd. dirs. aQuantive, Inc., Seattle, 1999—, pres., 2000—. Bd. dirs. Blue Nile, Inc., 2004—, Advt. Rsch. Found., Whitepages.com, Inc. Named one of 50 Who Matter Now, CNNMoney.com Bus. 2.0, 2006, 2007. Mem.: Nat. Assn. Corp. Dirs. (bd. dirs Seattle-N.W. chpt.). Office: aQuantive Inc 821 2nd Ave Ste 1800 Seattle WA 98104 *

MCANDREWS, JAMES PATRICK, retired lawyer; b. Carbondale, Pa., May 11, 1929; s. James Patrick and Mary Agnes (Walsh) McA.; m. Mona Marie Steinke, Sept. 4, 1954; children: James P., George A., Catherine McAndrews Hazel, Joseph M., Anne Marie, Michael P., Edward R., Daniel P. BS, U. Scranton, 1949; LL.B., Fordham U., 1952; grad., Real Estate Inst., NYU, 1972. Bar: N.Y. 1953, Ohio 1974. Assoc. James F. McManus, Levittown, NY, 1955; atty. Emigrant Savs. Bank, NYC, 1955-68; counsel Tchrs. Ins. and Annuity Assn., NYC, 1968-73; assoc. Thompson, Hine & Flory, 1973-74, ptnr. Cleve., 1974-84, Benesch, Friedlander, Coplan & Aronoff, Cleve., 1984-94. Mem. law faculty Am. Inst. Banking, N.Y.C., 1968-69; mem. faculty Lakeland C.C., 1995-97. Author: Commercial Real Estate Law Practice Manual with Forms, 2001. 1st lt. USAF, 1952-54. Fellow Am. Bar Found. (life); mem. Am. Coll. Real Estate Lawyers (gov. 1983-86, treas. 1986-88, chmn. membership devel. com. 1985-87), Ohio Land Title Assn. (life, trustee 1985-88), Bar Assn. Greater Cleve. (hon. life; past chmn. real estate sect.), Ohio State Bar Assn. (hon. life). Roman Catholic. Home: Marine Towers West 12540 Edgewater Dr Ste 311 Lakewood OH 44107-1614 Personal E-mail: jpmlake@sbcglobal.net.

MCANIFF, EDWARD JOHN, lawyer; b. NYC, June 29, 1934; s. John Edward and Josephine (Toomey); m. Jane Reiss, June 11, 1960; children: John E., Maura T., Anne T. Annick, Jane A., Peter J., Kathleen A. AB magna cum laude, Holy Cross Coll., 1956; LLB cum laude, NYU, 1961. Bar: N.Y. 1962, Calif. 1963, D.C. 1976. Law clk. to Justice A.T. Goodwin Supreme Ct. Oreg., Salem, 1961-62; ptnr., of counsel O'Melveny & Myers, LA, 1962—. Adj. prof. Sch. Law Stanford U., 1974-75, 94-98, Boalt Hall Law Sch., 1992-95, UCLA Law Sch., 1996—; vis. prof. U. Oreg. Law Sch., 1999—; fgn. law counsel Freehill, Hollingdale & Page, Sydney, 1981-82; bd. dirs. Mellon Fin. Corp. Bd. dirs. L.A. Master Chorale, 1979-81, 87—, chmn., 1996—; dir., exec. com. Perf. Art Ctr. Los Angeles County, 1992—; bd. dirs. Music Ctr. Found., 1992—. Capt. USNR, 1956-87. Republican. Office: O Melveny & Myers 400 S Hope St Ste 1717 Los Angeles CA 90071-2899 E-mail: tmcaniff@omm.com.

MCANIFF, NORA P., former publishing executive; b. NY, Oct. 14, 1958; BA, Baruch Coll., 1980. From mktg. info. mgr. to pres. People Mag. Time Inc., NYC, 1982—98, pub. Life Mag., 1992—93, pub. Teen People, 1997—98, pres. People Mag., 1998—2001, group pres. People Mag. Group, 2001—02, exec. v.p., women's entertainment & luxury group, 2002—05, co-COO, 2005—07. Pres. Advt. Women of NY, 1997—99; bd. dirs. Saks Inc., 2002—, Michael J. Fox Found. for Parkinson's Rsch.

MCANINCH, JACK WELDON, urological surgeon, educator; b. Merkel, Tex., Mar. 17, 1936; s. Weldon Thomas and Margaret (Canon) McA.; m. Barbara B. Buchanan, Dec. 29, 1960 (div. Aug. 1972); m. Burnet B. Sumner, Dec. 29, 1987; children: David A., Todd G., Brendan J. BS, Tex. Tech U., 1958; MS, U. Idaho, 1960; MD, U. Tex., 1964. Diplomate Am. Bd. Urology (trustee 1991-97, pres. 1996-97). Commd. capt. U.S. Army, 1964-66, advanced through grades to col., 1977, ret., 1977; col. USAR; intern then resident Letterman Army Med. Ctr., San Francisco, 1964-69; chief urol. surgery San Francisco Gen. Hosp., 1977—; prof. urol. surgery U. Calif., San Francisco, 1977—. Editor: Urogenital Trauma, 1985, Urologic Clinics of North America, 1989, Smith's General Urology, 1995; section editor: Early Care of the Injured Patient, 1990, Traumatic and Reconstructive Urology, 1996. Col. US Army, 1964-72. Recipient Disting. Alumnus award Tex. Tech U., 1994; named Disting. Alumnus U. Idaho, 1997. Fellow ACS (gov. 1992-97, regent 1998—); mem. Am. Urol. Assn. (pres. we. sect. 1992-93, bd. dirs. 1990—, pres. 1996-97), Genitourinary Reconstructive Surgeons (pres.), Am. Assn. Surgery Trauma (v.p.), Soc. Univ. Urologists, Am. Bd. Urology (pres. 1996-97). Office: San Francisco Gen Hosp Dept Urology 1001 Potrero Ave San Francisco CA 94110-3594 Home Phone: 415-282-1149; Office Phone: 415-476-3372.

MCANUFF, DES, artistic director; b. Princeton, Ill., June 19, 1952; s. John Nelson and Ellen Boyd; m. Susan Berman, Jan. 1, 1984; 1 child, Julia Violet. Artistic dir. La Jolla Playhouse, Calif., 1994—2007, artistic dir. emeritus Calif., 2007—. Founding mem. Dodger Prodns.; former faculty Julliard Sch.; now adj. prof. theatre U. Calif. San Diego. Dir.: (Broadway prodns.) Big River (Tony award 1985), A Walk in the Woods (San Diego Critics Circle award), Tommy (Tony award 1993), How to Succeed in Business Without Really Trying (Tony nomination 1995), 700 Sundays, 2004, Jersey Boys, 2005, Zhivago, 2006, The Wiz, 2006; (off-Broadway prodns.) Gimme Shelter (Soho Arts award 1979), The Crazy Locomotive, Chelsea Theatre Ctr., Mary Stuart, How It All Began, Henry IV Part One, The Death of Von Richthofen as Witnessed from Earth (Villager award 1982), NY Shakespeare Festival, A Mad World My Masters, Romeo & Juliet, As You Like It (San Diego Critics Circle award), The Sea Gull, Shout Up A Morning, Gillette, The Matchmaker, Two Rooms, 80 Days, Down The Road, Macbeth, The Three Sisters, A Funny Thing Happened on the Way to the Forum, Twelfth Night, La Jolla Playhouse, Macbeth, Stratford Festival Can., Palm Beach: The Screwball Musical, 2005; others; prodr.: A Walk in the Woods, My Children! My Africa!; playwright Leave it to Beaver is Dead (Soho Arts award), The Death of Von Richthofen as Witnessed from Earth (Villager and Bay Area Critics awards), Troll, A Lime in the Morning, Silent Edward; contbg. editor Am. Theatre Mag. Can. Council grantee, Rockefeller grantee. Mem. Theatre Communications Group (past bd. dirs.), Soc. of Stage Dirs. and Choreographers. *

MCANULTY, WILLIAM E., JR., state supreme court justice; m. Kristi W. McAnulty; 4 children. Grad., Ind. U.; MAT, JD, U. Louisville. With Jefferson County Juvenile Ct., Ind., 1975—83; judge Jefferson Dist. Ct., 1978—83, Jefferson Circuit Ct., 1984—90; atty., priv. practice Ind., 1990—93; judge Jefferson Circuit Ct., 1993—98, chief judge, 1998; judge Ky. Ct. of Appeals, 1998—2006; justice Ky. Supreme Ct., 2006—. Recipient Thomas C. Simons Disting. Leadership award, Leadership Louisville Foundation. Mem.: Ky. Trial Attorneys Assn. (Henry V. Pennington Outstanding Judge of Yr. 1997), Ky. Bar Assn., Louisville Bar Assn. Office: Ky Supreme Ct Jefferson Cty Judicial Ctr 700 W Jefferson St Ste 1000 Louisville KY 40202 Office Phone: 502-595-3199. *

MCARDLE, BARRY FRANCIS, dentist; b. Boston, Jan. 28, 1958; s. Joseph William and Brigitte Johanna Maria (Brock). BS, Boston U., 1980; DMD, Tufts U., 1985. Rsch. assoc. Naval Blood Rsch. Lab., Boston, 1980-81; dentist pvt. practice, Portsmouth, NH, 1985—. Cons. United Dental Systems, Portsmouth, 1996—2000; active med. staff in dentistry Concord Hosp., 1998—2002; mem. Seacoast Dental Adv. Bd., 2001—; spkr., lectr. in field; sr. dental advisor Digital Dental website, 2004—05. Reviewer Jour. the Am. Dental Assn., 2007. Mem.: ADA, Bus. Network Internat. (pres. Tri-State Seacoast chpt. 1998—99), Alliance for Optimal Dental Care, Seacoast Esthetic Dentistry Assn. (co-founder), N.H. Dental Soc. (editl. bd. Granite State Dentist newsletter 1999—2004), New Eng. Dental Soc., Boston U. Alumni Assn., Portsmouth C. of C., Rotary (Portsmouth, NH chpt.). Independent. Achievements include patents in field. Avocations: fine art, jazz, bodybuilding, hockey. Office: The Captain Moses House 118 Maplewood Ave Ste B-7 Portsmouth NH 03801-3787 Office Phone: 603-430-1010. Business E-Mail: drmcardle@mcardledmd.com.

MCARDLE, RICHARD JOSEPH, retired academic administrator; b. Omaha, Mar. 10, 1934; s. William James and Abby Marie (Menzies) McA.; m. Katherine Ann McAndrew, Dec. 27, 1958; children: Bernard, Constance, Nancy, Susan, Richard. BA, Creighton U., 1955, MA, 1961; PhD, U. Nebr., 1969. Tchr. pub. high schs., Nebr., 1955-65; grad. asst. romance langs. U. Nebr., 1965-66, instr. fgn. lang. methods, 1966-69; chmn. dept. edn. Cleve. State U., 1969-70; chmn. dept. elem. and secondary edn. U. North Fla., 1971-75; dean Coll. Edn. Cleve. State U., 1975-87, prof. edn., 1987-89, spl. asst. to pres. for campus planning, 1989-91, vice provost for strategic planning, 1991-92, acting provost, v.p. for acad. affairs, 1992-94, vice provost for strategic planning, 1994-96, prof. edn., 1996-2001, ret., 2001. Cons. in field. Author articles related to issues in tchr. edn. Mem. Am. Assn. Higher Edn. Office: CASAL Dept Cleve State U Cleveland OH 44115 Business E-Mail: r.mcardle@csuohio.edu.

MCARTHUR, ELDON DURANT, geneticist, researcher; b. Hurricane, Utah, Mar. 12, 1941; s. Eldon and Denise (Dalton) McA.; m. Virginia Johnson, Dec. 20, 1963; children: Curtis D., Monica McArthur Bennion, Denise McArthur Johnson, Ted O. AS with high honors, Dixie Coll., 1963; BS cum laude, U. Utah, 1965, MS, 1967, PhD, 1970. Postdoctoral rsch. fellow, dept. demonstrator Agrl. Rsch. Coun. Gt. Britain, Leeds, Eng., 1970-71; rsch. geneticist Intermountain Rsch. Sta. USDA Forest Svc., Ephraim, Utah, 1972-75, rsch. geneticist Shrub Scis. Lab., Intermountain Rsch. Sta. Provo, Utah, 1975-83, project leader, chief rsch. geneticist, 1983-97, Rocky Mountain Rsch. Sta., USDA Forest Svc., Provo, 1997—2006, program mgr., 2006—. Adj. prof. dept. plant and wildlife scis. Brigham Young U., Provo, 1976—. Author more than 425 rsch. papers; contbr. chpts. to books; editor symposium procs. Named USDA Forest Svc. Superior Scientist, 1990, Disting. Scientist, 1996; Sigma Xi grantee, 1970, NSF grantee, 1981, 85, 96, Coop. State Rsch., Svc. grantee, 1986, 91; recipient Eminent Sci. Publ. award Rocky Mtn. Rsch. Station, 2001, New Century of Svc. award 2002, USDI BLM Svc. 1st award USDA Forest Svc., 2007. Mem. Soc. Range Mgmt. (pres. Utah sect. 1987, Outstanding Achievement award 1992, Utah sect. Range Mgr. of Yr. 2004), Botan. Soc. Am., Soc. Study Evolution, Am. Genetic Assn., Shrub Rsch. Consortium (chmn. 1983—, Disting. Svc. award 2002), Intermountain Consortium for Aridlands Rsch. (pres. 1991—). Mem. Lds Ch. Avocations: hiking, bicycling, basketball. Home: 555 N 1200 E Orem UT 84097-4350 Office: USDA Forest Svc Shrub Scis Lab 735 N 500 E Provo UT 84606-1856 Office Phone: 801-356-5112. Personal E-mail: edmdixie@aol.com. Business E-Mail: dmcarthur@fs.fed.us.

MCARTHUR, JOHN HECTOR, business educator; b. Vancouver, BC, Can., Mar. 31, 1934; came to U.S., 1957; s. Hector and Elizabeth Lee (Whyte) McA.; m. Netilia Ewasiuk, Sept. 15, 1956; children: Jocelyn Natasha, Susan Patricia. B in Commerce, U. B.C., 1957, LLD (hon.), 1995; MBA, Harvard U., 1959, DBA, 1962; LLD (hon.), Simon Fraser U., 1982, Queens U., 1985, Middlebury Coll., 1988, U. Navarra, Spain, 1989, U. Western Ont., 1992. Prof. bus. adminstrn. Harvard U., Cambridge, Mass., 1962—79, Sylvan C. Coleman prof. fin. mgmt., 1972—80, George F. Baker prof. bus. adminstrn., 1980—96; dean Harvard Bus. Sch., 1980-96; sr. advisor to pres. World Bank Group, Washington, 1995—2005. Bd. dirs., chmn. Asia Pacific Found. Can., AES Corp., Bell Can., Bell Can. Enterprises, Inc., Cabot Corp., Duke U. Health System, KOC Holdings A.S., Nat. Healthcare Coalition, Reuters Founders Share Co. Ltd., Telsat Can., Devel. Gateway Found.; cons. numerous cos. and govt. agys. in Can., Europe, Asia and U.S. Named Hon. Citizen, Remauville, France, McArthur Hall in his honor, Harvard Bus. Sch., 1999, John H. McArthur Can. Fellowship program in his honor, 2002, Dir. of Yr., Nat. Assn. Corp. Dirs., 2007; recipient Harvard Statesman award, HBS Club, NYC, Mgmt. Achievement award, McGill U., Can. Bus. Leadership award, HBS Clubs of Can., Lifetime Achievement award, Nat. Assn. Corp. Dirs., 2007; John and Natty McArthur Univ. chair established at, Harvard U., 1997. Mem. Harvard Club, Links Club, Comml. Club, Somerset Club, Willowbend Club, Varsity Club. Home: 140 Old Connecticut Path Wayland MA 01778-3202 Office: Harvard Univ Sch Bus Adminstrn Boston MA 02163

MCARTHUR, JOHN R., utilities executive, lawyer; b. Rock Hill, SC, Jan. 5, 1956; BA cum laude, Davidson Coll., 1977; JD with honors, Univ. So. Carolina, 1981. Bar: NC 1982. Law clk. Judge Sam. J. Ervin III, US Ct. Appeals, 4th cir., 1981—82; assoc. to ptnr. Hunton & Williams, Raleigh, NC, 1982—92; chief counsel NC Atty. Gen. Office, NC, 1993—97; sr. advisor NC Gov., Mike Easley, NC, 1998—2001; v.p., pub. affairs Progress Energy Inc., Raleigh, NC, 2001—02, sr. v.p., corp. rels., 2002—, gen. counsel, corp. sec., 2004—. Editor Law Rev. U.S.C.; law clerk Hon. Sam J. Ervin III US Ct. Appeals Fourth Cir. Mem.: NC Bar Assn., Order of the Coif, Wig & Robe. Office: Progress Energy Inc 410 S Wilmington St Raleigh NC 27601-1551 Office Phone: 919-546-4070. Business E-Mail: john.mcarthur@pgnmail.com.

MCARTHUR, LISA R., music educator, musician; d. Tremaine James and Judith Hammon McArthur. PhD in Music Theory, U. of Ky., Lexington, Kentucky, 1995—99; MA in Music Theory, Kent State U., Kent, Ohio, 1990—94, MusM in performance, 1990—93; MusB in Music Edn., SUNY Potsdam Coll., Crane Sch. of Music, Potsdam, New York, 1986—90. Grad. asst. Kent State U., Kent, Ohio, 1990—92; orch. dir., grades 4-12 Akron Pub. Schools, Akron, Ohio, 1993—95; grad. tchg. asst. U. of Ky., Lexington, Ky., 1995—98; assoc. prof. Campbellsville U., Campbellsville, Ky., 1998—. Clinician Emerson Flutes, Elkhart, Ind., 2000—; dir. flute ensemble Campbellsville (Ky.) U., 1998—; presenter in field. Musician: (albums) Something Old, Something New, Something Borrowed, Something Blue, 2004; arranger: for flute ensemble Symphony No. 1, for flute solo and flute ensemble accompaniment Scherzino by Andersen and Concerto in D and G Maj. by Mozart. Named Coll./U. Educator of the Yr., Ky. Music Educators Assn., 2001; recipient Performer's cert., Crane Sch. of Music, 1990. Mem.: Nat. Assn. of Coll. Wind and Percussion Instructors, Nat. Flute Assn., Soc. for Music Theory, Coll. Music Soc., Music Educators Nat. Conf. (coll. chpt. advisor 1998—, state chpt. advisor 2003—05), Ky. Music Educators Assn., Flute Soc. of Ky. (pres. 2000—), Pi Kappa Lambda, Sigma Alpha Iota (life). Office: Campbellsville University UPO 922 Campbellsville KY 42718 E-mail: lrmcarthur@campbellsville.edu.

MCARTHUR, STEVEN FRANCIS, psychologist, educator; b. Grand Rapids, Mich., Aug. 12, 1954; s. George Harold and Evelyn Theresa McArthur; m. Barbara Louise Duch, Oct. 18, 1975; children: Ryan, Alan. BA in Psychology, Aquinas Coll., Grand Rapids, 1975; PhD in Psychology, So. Ill. U., 1990. Lic. psychologist, Mich. Staff psychologist St. John Hosp. and Med. Ctr., Detroit, 1990-95, Henry Ford Ctr. Human Sexuality, West Bloomfield, Mich., 1991-95; primary care provider VA Med. Ctr., Detroit, 1997—; asst. prof. dept. psychiatry and behavioral neurosci. Wayne State U. Sch. Medicine. Mem. rev. panel behavior and performance NASA, Washington. Mem. APA, Nat. Register Health Svc. Providers Psychology, Mich. Psychol. Assn., N.Y. Acad. Scis. Office: Detroit Receiving Hosp 3-P 4201 St Antoine Detroit MI 48201 Office Phone: 313-745-9263. Business E-Mail: smcarthu@med.wayne.edu.

MCARTHUR, WILLIAM SURLES, JR., astronaut, retired military officer; b. Laurinburg, NC, July 26, 1951; s. William S. and Edith P. (Avant) McArthur; m. Cynthia Catherine Lovin; 2 children. BS in Applied Scis. and Engring., U.S. Mil. Acad., West Point, NY, 1973; MS in Aerospace Engring., Ga. Inst. Tech., 1983; DSc (hon.), U.N.C., Pembroke. Commd. 2d lt. U.S. Army, 1973, advamced through grades to Col., retired, 2001; 2d lt. U.S. Airborne Divsn., Fort Bragg, 1973—75; student U.S. Army Aviation Sch., 1975—76; aeroscout team leader, brigade aviation sect. commdr. US Army 2nd Infantry Divsn, Republic of Korea, 1976—78; company commdr., platoon leader, ops. officer 24th Combat Aviation Battalion, Savanna, Ga.; asst. prof. dept. mechs. U.S. Mil. Acad., West Point, 1983—86; student pilot USN Test Pilot Sch., 1986—87; exptl. test pilot U.S. Army, 1987—91; space shuttle vehicle integration test engr. NASA Johnson Space Ctr., Houston, 1987—91, astronaut, 1991—, held various assignments in the astronaut office, 1991—. Crew mem. STS-58 Columbia launched from Kennedy Space Ctr., Fla.; landed at Edwards AFB, Calif., 1993; crew mem. STS-74 Atlantis Kennedy Space Ctr., Fla., 1995; crew mem. STS-92 Discovery launched from Kennedy Space Ctr., Fla.; landed Edwards Air Force Base, Calif., 2000; crew mem. ISS mission, 05. Named vis. Green Hons. Prof., Dept. Sci. and Engring. Tex. Christian U., 1997; recipient Order of the Long Leaf Pine, NC, Ellis Island Medal of Honor., DSM, Def. Superior Svc. medal, Def. Meritorious Svc. medal (First Oak Leaf Cluster), Meritorious Svc. Medal (First Oak Leaf Cluster), Army Commendation medal, NASA Space Flight medal, NASA Exceptional Svc. medal, Ga. Tech Acad. Disting. Alumni, Flight Achievement award, Am. Astronautical Soc., 1996, Korolev Diploma, Fedn. Aeronautique Internat., 2000. Mem.: MENSA, AIAA, Assn. Space Explorers, U.S. Mil. Acad. Assn. Grads., Assn. United States Army, Army Aviation Assn. Am. (Order of St. Michael (Silver award) 2000, Robert M. Leich award 2000), West Point Soc. Greater Houston, Phi Kappa Phi. Avocations: basketball, running, working with personal computers. Office: NASA Johnson Space Ctr Houston TX 77058

MCATEE, DARIN P., lawyer; b. Hays, Kans., Dec. 16, 1965; BA with highest distinction, Univ. Kans., 1988; JD magna cum laude, Harvard Univ., 1991. Bar: NY 1993. Law clk., Hon. Stanley F. Birch, Jr. US Ct. of Appeals, 11th Cir.; assoc. Cravath Swaine & Moore LLP, NYC, 1992—2004, ptnr., litig., 2004—. Articles editor Harvard Law Rev. Office: Cravath Swaine & Moore LLP Worldwide Plz 825 Eighth Ave New York NY 10019-7475 Office Phone: 212-474-1480. Office Fax: 212-474-3700. Business E-Mail: dmcatee@cravath.com.

MCATEE, DAVID RAY, lawyer; b. Rosebud, Tex., Nov. 20, 1941; s. Lee Ray and Florine (Davis) McAtee; m. Carole Kay Pendergraft, Jan. 28, 1967; children: David Ray, Kristin Carole. BBA with honors, Baylor U., 1964; LLB, U. Tex., 1967. Bar: Tex. 1967, US Dist. Ct. (no. dist.) Tex. 1968, US Dist. Ct. (so. dist.) Tex. 1994, US Dist. Ct. (ea. dist.) Tex. 1996, US Ct. Appeals (5th cir.) 1969, US Ct. Appeals (11th cir.) 1981, US Tax Ct. 1993. Briefing atty. Supreme Ct. Tex., Austin, 1967—68; ptnr. Thompson & Knight, Dallas, 1968—90, Gibson, Dunn & Crutcher, Dallas, 1990—95; with Akin Gump Strauss Hauer & Feld LLP, Dallas, 1995. Mem. City of Dallas Plan Commn., 1979—83, vice chmn., 1981—83; chmn. City of Dallas Thoroughfare Com., 1979—81; mem. City of Dallas Citizens Safety Adv. Com., Goals for Dallas Com.; founder, bd. dirs. No. Hills. Neighborhood Assn., 1974—76; pres., bd. dirs. Montessori Sch. of Park Cities, 1975—76; chmn. bd. dirs. Dallas Area Rapid Transit, 1992; bd. dirs. Friends of the Katy Trail, 2005—06. Mem.: Tex. Bar Found. (trustee 2005—), ABA (antitrust sect.), Tex. Bar Assn. (legal ethics com. 1975—81), Dallas Bar Assn., U. Tex. Law Alumni Assn. (exec. com. 2003—07). Democrat. Methodist. Office: Akin Gump Strauss Hauer & Feld LLP 1700 Pacific Ave Ste 4100 Dallas TX 75201-4675

MCAULEY, VAN ALFON, aerospace mathematician; b. Travelers Rest, SC, Aug. 28, 1926; s. Stephen Floyd and Emily Floree (Cox) McA. BA, U. N.C., Chapel Hill, 1951; postgrad., U. Ala., Huntsville, 1956-57, 60-63. Mathematician Army Ballistic Missile Agy., Huntsville, Ala., 1956-59; physicist NASA, Marshall Center, Huntsville, 1960-61, rsch. mathematician, 1962-70, mathematician, 1970-81. Contbr. articles to profl. jours.; patentee for aerospace control invention; publ. method for solution of polynomial equations; devised methods for numerical solution of heat flow using partial differential equations. Served with U.S. Army, 1944-46. Recipient Apollo achievement award NASA, 1969, cost savs. award, 1973, Skylab achievement award, 1974, Outstanding Performance award, 1976, NASA Cert. of Recognition, 1977. Mem. AAAS, Am. Math. Soc., N.Y. Acad. Scis., Phi Beta Kappa.

MCAULIFFE, DANIEL JOSEPH, lawyer; b. NYC, Mar. 27, 1945; s. Daniel Joseph and Ethel Louise (Dierks) McA.; m. J. Wyn Drake, May 20, 1972 (div. Sept. 1977); 1 child, Kelly Elizabeth McAuliffe; m. Ellen Ross, Sept. 16, 1987. BA, Fordham U., 1966; JD, Harvard U., 1969. Bar: DC 1969, Ariz. 1973, Supreme Ct. Ariz., Calif., Nev., Supreme jud. Ct. Mass., US Supreme Ct., US Cts. Appeals (9th & 10th cir.), US Dist. Ct., Dist. Ariz., US Dist. Ct. Dist. Nev. Trial atty. U.S. Dept. Justice, Washington, 1969-71, Dep. Asst. Atty. Gen., 1971-73; atty. Snell & Wilmer, Phoenix, 1973-77, ptnr., 1977—. Mem. Ariz. Commn. on Judicial Qualifications, Task Force Ariz. Commn. on Courts, Ariz. Bar Found. Fellows (vice chmn.). Author/editor: Arizona Legal Forms Vols. 1 and 2, 1988. Chmn. Phoenix Human Rels. Commn., 1974-79; bd. dirs. Phoenix Symphony Assn., 1989—, Phoenix Symphony Coun., 1987—. Mem. ABA, State Bar Calif., Fed. Bar Assn., Am. Judicature Soc., Am. Law Inst., Ariz. State Bar Assn. (chmn. civil practice & procedure com. 1984-91; bd. govs. 1991-1999 & 2002-2003; chmn. professionalism course com. 1994; exec. coun. appellate practice sect. 1995, task force tech. 1995; 2nd v.p. 2004, pres.-elect 2006-07). Avocations: tennis, reading. Office: Snell & Wilmer One Ariz Ctr Phoenix AZ 85004-0001 Office Phone: 602-382-6000. Office Fax: 602-382-6070. E-mail: daniel.mcauliffe@azbar.org.

MCAULIFFE, ROSEMARY, lawyer; b. New Rochelle, NY, May 24, 1927; d. William J. and Rose B. (Payne) McA. BA, Regis Coll., 1949; JD, New Eng. Sch. Law, 1954; MEd, Boston State Coll., 1971, Cert. advanced grad studies, 1981; LLD (hon.), New Eng. Sch. Law, Boston, 2002. Bar: Mass. 1956, U.S. Dist. Ct. Mass. 1957, U.S. Supreme Ct. 1961. Pvt. practice law, Boston, 1956—. Tchr. City of Boston, 1965-93. Prodr. (weekly TV show) The Legal Line, Boston Pub. Access Answer Channel. Active World Affairs Coun., Boston, 1980-95; sec. Italian Hist. Assn. Mass., 1988—. Mem. Mass. Bar Assn., Am. Acad. Trial Lawyers, Mass. Assn. Women Lawyers. Home and Office: 61 Prince St Boston MA 02113-1829

MCAULIFFE, STEVEN JAMES, federal judge; b. 1948; BA, Va. Mil. Inst., 1970; JD, Georgetown U., 1973. Capt. appellate coun. US Army JAGC, 1973-77; asst. atty. gen. Office NH Atty. Gen., 1977-80; ptnr. Gallagher, Callahan, Gartrell, P.A., Concord, NH, 1980-92; fed. judge US Dist. Ct. (NH dist.), Concord, 1992—2005, chief judge, 2005. Chair Rhodes Scholarship Selection Com. NH, 1998—2004. Trustee Univ. Sys. of NH, 1986-94; bd. dirs. NH Med. Malpractice Stabilization Res. Fund Trust, 1987-92, Office Pub. Guardian, 1980-92, Challenger Ctr. for Space Sci. Edn.; active NH Dem. Leadership Coun., 1988-92. Capt. US Army, 1970-77, USAR, 1977-80, NH Army NG, 1980-88. Decorated US Army Commendation medal. Fellow NH Bar Found.; mem. ABA, NH Bar Assn. (pres. 1991-92, pres.-elect 1990-91, v.p. 1989-90, mem. ex-officio NH Supreme Ct. com. profl. conduct 1989-90, mem. ethics com. 1984-86), Nat. Conf. Bar Pres., Merrimack County Bar Assn., DC Bar Assn., US Supreme Ct. Hist. Soc., NH Jud. Coun. (vice-chmn. 1991-92), Aircraft Owners and Pilots Assn., Concord Country Club. Office: US Dist Ct 55 Pleasant St Room 416 Concord NH 03301-3904

MCAULIFFE, TERRY (TERENCE RICHARD MCAULIFFE), former political organization administrator; b. Syracuse, NY, 1957; s. Jack and Millie McAuliffe; m. Dorothy Swann, 1988; children: Dori, Jack, Mary, Sally, Peter. BA in Polit. Sci., Cath. U., 1979; JD, Georgetown U., 1984. Fin. chmn. Gephardt for Pres. Campaign Com., 1988; amb., commr. gen. Internat. Expo., 1993; chmn. Dem. Bus. Coun., 1993; fin. chmn. Dem. Nat. Com., 1994, Bill Clinton/Al Gore Election Campaign, 1996; co-chair Presdl. Inaugural Com., 1997; chmn. Dem. Nat. Conv., LA, 2000, Dem. Nat. Com., 2001—05. Author: What A Party: My Life Among Democrats: Presidents, Candidates, Donors, Activists, Alligators, and Other Wild Animals, 2007.

MCAUSLAND, RANDOLPH MELVILLE NEAL, writer, art consultant; b. Phila., Oct. 9, 1934; s. John Randolph and Helen (Neal) McA.; m. Marilynn Kemp, July 10, 1965 (div. 1976); children: Andrew, Sean; m. Jan E. Tribbey, May 9, 1986 AB, Princeton U., 1957. Copy editor Wall Street Jour., NYC, 1960—61; editor, pub. Stowe Reporter, 1961—63; consulting editor Interpub. Group Cos., 1963—67; creative dir. The Progress Group, NYC, 1967—70, gen. mgr., 1970—75; dir. mktg. Billboard Pubs., NYC, 1975—77; asst. to pres. Macmillan Mag., Stamford, Conn., 1977—80; editor The New Satirist, New Canaan, Conn., 1980—82; pres. Design Pubs. Inc., NYC, 1983—89; dir. Design Arts Program, NEA, Washington, 1989—90; dep. chmn. NEA, Washington, 1990—93; writer, arts cons. Richmond, Va., 1993—94. Founder, dir. Design History Found., NYC, 1987—89. Author: Supermarkets: History of an American Institution, 1980; contbr. articles to profl. jours.; radio host WOBO FM, Cin., 2006—. Bd. dirs. Hand Workshop, Richmond, 1993-94, Richmond Choral Soc., 1994, Worldesign Found., 1994-97, Fla. Friends Librs., 1995-99, Cin. Chamber Orch., 2002-04, Fla. Ctr. for the Book, Broward County Vision Com., Catacoustic Consort, dep. exec. dir., 2002—. With U.S. Army, 1957-60. Recipient Commendation N.Y.C. Police Dept., 1971, Pres. Cup Am. Comedy Club N.Y., N.Y.C., 1974, Bronze Apple award Indsl. Design Soc., 1987, Disting. Svc. award NEA, 1991-92 Mem. Am. Ctr. For Design (hon.), Coalition Ind. Scholars, Ivy Club Home: 7405 Fair Oaks Dr Cincinnati OH 45237-2925 Home Phone: 513-351-4204; Office Phone: 513-315-9678. E-mail: RandyMCA@cinci.rr.com.

MCAVENEY, MARY SUSAN, marketing executive; b. Perth Amboy, NJ, Jan. 1, 1965; d. Catherine Geraldine and Charles Joseph McAveney; m. David Clifford Briggs, Sept. 27, 1997; children: Alexander Patrick Briggs, Colin Andrew Briggs. BA, Coll. of NJ., 1989. Writer The Herald, Wall Township, NJ, 1984—88; mktg. assoc. Graphis US, Inc., NYC, 1989—92; mktg. mgr. Harry N. Abrams, Inc., NYC, 1992—98; mktg. dir. HarperCollins Children's Books, NYC, 1998—. Spkr. Internat. Quality and Productivity Ctr. Kid Power XChange, Fla., 2003, Internat. Quality and Productivity Coun.; Kid Power XChange, Fla., 2005—. Contbr. poetry. Sec. Sch. Leadership Team Pub. Sch. 58, Bklyn., 2004—05; mem. Curriculum Com., Pub. Sch. 58, Bklyn., 2004—05, Women's Dem. Com., Washington, 2004—05; mem., fundraiser Nat. Dem. Com., Washington, 2004—05; mem. Families First, Family Ctr., Bklyn., 2000—03. Garden State scholarship, State of N.J., 1983. Mem.: Promotion, Advt., and Mktg. Assn., Children's Book Coun. Democrat-Npl. Avocations: travel, photography, writing, cooking. Office: HarperCollins Children's Books 1350 Avenue of Americas New York NY 10019 Home Phone: 718-855-7347; Office Phone: 212-307-3623. Office Fax: 212-261-6785. Business E-Mail: mary.mcaveney@harpercollins.com.

MCAVITY, JOHN GILLIS, museum director, association executive, museologist; b. St. John, NB, Can., Oct. 30, 1950; s. J. Patrick H. and Catharine A. (McNeill) McA. BA, U. N.B., 1972. Cert. assn. exec. Asst. curator Kings Landing Mus., Fredericton, N.B., Can., 1972-73; provincial mus. adviser N.B. Mus., St. John, Can., 1973-76; exec. dir. Ont. Mus. Assn., Toronto, Can., 1976-81, Can. Mus. Assn., Ottawa, Ont., Can., 1981—. Bd. dirs. internat. mus. Mgmt. Com., Internat. Coun. Mus., Can. Soc. of the Decorative Arts; sec. treas. Intercom, 2001—. Editor INTERCOM News, 1997—. V.p. St. John Heritage Trust, 1974-76; exec. com. Can. Club, St. John, 1975, English Speaking Union, St. John, 1974-76; vol. fundraiser Kidney Found., Can.; bd. dirs. Centretown Citizens Corp.; founding dir. Mus. Found. Can., 1994—. Recipient Queen's Jubilee medal, 2002. Mem.: Internat. Coun. Museums (task force, legal affairs com. 2002—), Shefford Heritage Co-op (membership chair 1992—95, 2000—), Can. Art Mus. Dirs. Orgn., Can. Soc. Assn. Execs. (bd. dirs. 1993—96, Long Svc. Achievement award 2002), Can. Soc. Copyright Consumers, Ont. Assn. Art Galleries (bd. dirs. 1986—90), Nat. Mus. Assn. (chair internat. com. 2000—), Assn. Museums N.B. (founding), Tourism Industry Assn. Can. (bd. dirs.), Quaco Hist. and Libr. Soc. (hon. life), Assn. Cultural Execs. (bd. dirs. 1988—92, appt. to senate 1995), Inst. Assn. Execs. (chmn. postal com., cert., bd. dirs. Ottawa chpt.), Mus. Found. Can. (founding dir. 1994—), Am. Assn. State and Local History (awards com. 1981—84, nominations com. 1985), Am. Assn. Museums. Anglican. Home: 300 Cooper St Apt 41 Ottawa ON Canada K2P 0G7 Home (Summer): 29 Kingshurst Ln Rothesay NB Canada E2H 1T3 E-mail: jmcavity@museums.ca.

MCAVOY, BRUCE RONALD, engineer, consultant; b. Jamestown, NY, Jan. 30, 1933; s. George Harold and Agda Amelia (Martinson) McA. BS in Physics, U. Rochester, 1954. Jr. engr. Westinghouse Air Arm Div., Balt., 1956-57, assoc. engr., 1957-58; rsch. engr. Westinghouse Rsch. Ctr., Pitts., 1958-69; sr. rsch. engr. Westinghouse R & D Ctr., Pitts., 1969-78, fellow engr., 1978-84, adv. scientist, 1984—. Mem. adv. bd. Nat. Ctr. Phys. Acoustics, U. Miss., 1987—88; lectr. elect. engring. dept. Carnegie Mellon U., 1968—70. Editor spl. issue IEEE Trans. Microwave Theory Tech., Ultrasonics Symposium procs., 1976-96; mem. editl. bd. jour. Microwave and Guided Wave Letters, 1990. With U.S. Army, 1954-56. Fellow IEEE (life, awards and recognition com. 1989—, def. R&D policy com. 1989-91, Centennial medal 1984, tech. program com. Internat. Microwave Symposium 1986-99); mem. DAV (life), Ultrasonic, Ferroelectric and Frequency Control Soc. of IEEE (pres. 1986-87, Disting. Svc. award 1999), Electromagnetics Acad., Microwave Theory and Techniques Soc. (chmn. microwave acoustics tech. com. 1988-99). Republican. Lutheran. Home: 926 Ivy St Pittsburgh PA 15232-2651 Home Phone: 412-621-2791; Office Phone: 412-621-2791. E-mail: brmcavoy@comcast.net.

MCAVOY, JOHN JOSEPH, lawyer; b. Worley, Idaho, June 28, 1933; s. Earl Francis and Florence Jewel (Mitchell) McA.; m. Joan Marjorie Zeldon, Sept. 20, 1964; children: Jason, Jon. BA, U. Idaho, 1954, LLB, 1958; LLM, Yale U., 1959. Bar: Idaho 1958, U.S. Supreme Ct. 1962, N.Y. 1963, U.S. Tax Ct. 1969, D.C. 1976. Asst. prof. law George Washington U., Washington, 1959-62; staff atty. stockpile investigating subcom. Armed Forces Com. U.S. Senate, Washington, 1962; assoc. White & Case, NYC, 1963-71, ptnr., 1972-95; of counsel Lukas, Nace, Gutierrez & Sachs, Washington, 1995—. Adj. prof. Washington Coll. Law, Am. U., Washington, 1990; mem. D.C. com. on grievances U.S. Dist. Ct., 2003-. Bd. dirs. N.Y. Civil Liberties Union, 1975-77, commr. Uniform State Laws, 2001—; chmn. due process com. ACLU, 1971-75. With U.S. Army, 1954-56. Mem. DC Bar Assn. (ethics com. 1982-88, vice chmn. 1986-87, chmn. 1987-88), Phi Beta Kappa, Phi Alpha Delta. Democrat. Avocations: swimming, bicycling, foreign travel. Personal E-mail: mcavoylaw@aol.com.

MCAVOY, JOHN MARTIN, plastic surgeon; b. White Plains, NY, Jan. 8, 1947; s. Joseph Patrick and Claire Margaret (Boucher) McAvoy; m. Laurel Ann Streeter, June 21, 1969; children: Holly, Ian. BS in Biology, Tufts U., Medford, Mass., 1968; MD, Tufts U., Boston, 1972. Cert. Am. Bd. Surgery, Am. Bd. Plastic Surgery, Nat. Bd. Med. Examiners, ACLS. Resident dept. surgery UCLA Med. Ctr., 1972—77, chief resident dept. surgery, 1976—77; resident plastic surgery U. Colo. Med. Ctr., Denver, 1977—79, chief resident plastic surgery, 1978—79; chief plastic surgery Santa Rosa Meml. Hosp., Calif., 1986—91; pvt. practice Santa Rosa, Calif., 1979—. Presenter in field. Contbg. editor: Hosp. Physician mag., 1976—81; contbr.

articles to profl. jours. Youth baseball coach Santa Rosa Babe Ruth Rincon Valley Little League, 1992—96. Reinach-Turnesia Caddie scholar, Westchester County, 1964. Fellow: ACS; mem.: Am. Soc. Plastic Surgeons (membership com.), Calif. Soc. Plastic Surgeons (ins. mediation com.), Am. Soc. for Aesthetic Plastic Surgery. Avocations: woodworking, gardening, poetry. Office: 4773 Hoen Ave Santa Rosa CA 95405

MCBANE, SARAH ELIZABETH, pharmacist, educator; b. Burlington, NC, Dec. 27, 1976; d. A. Scott and Linda G. McBane; m. John S. An. BS in Biology & Chemistry, Guilford Coll., Greensboro, NC, 1998; PharmD, U. NC, Chapel Hill, 2003. Cert. diabetes eduator Nat. Cert. Bd. Diabetes Educators, Ill., 2006. Asst. prof. pharmacy practice Campbell U., Buies Creek, NC, 2004—; clin. pharmacist Duke Family Medicine, Durham, NC, 2004—. Mem.: Rx for Change; Clinician Assisted Tobacco Cessation, NC Assn. Pharmacists, Am. Soc. Health Sys. Pharmacists, Am. Coll. Clin. Pharmacy. Office: Duke Univ Med Ctr Box 3886 2100 Erwin Rd Durham NC 27710 Office Phone: 919-684-6721.

MCBEE, CHRISTY DAWN, art educator, pre-school educator; b. Tullahomo, Tenn., Nov. 15, 1974; d. Larry Wayne and Dorothy Jean McInturff; m. Michael Scott McBee, June 26, 2004; children: Stacy Carol, Mitchell Larry. BSc, Mid. Tenn. State U., Murfreesboro, 1997. Art endorsement Arrowmont Sch. Arts & Crafts, 2002, registered visual arts tchr. Tenn., 2002. Tchr. 3rd grade Broadview Elem. Sch., Winchester, Tenn., 1997—98; Sparks grant tchr. Warren County Schs., McMinnville, Tenn., 1998—2000; tchr. art Woodland Elem. Sch., Woodbury, Tenn., 2000—03, Cascade H.S., Shelbyville, Tenn., 2003—04, Crab Orchard & Pineview Elem. Schs., Crossville, Tenn., 2004—. Head fine arts dept., mem. spl. concerns com. Cascade H.S., Crab Orchard, Pineview, Shelbyville, Crossville, 2003—06; chmn. flower com. Crab Orchard Elem. Sch., Crossville, 2006—. Author: (poem) Anthology of Am. Poetry, 1997. Sponsor Awana Internat. Worldwide Missions, 2005—06, Habitat for Humanity, Warren County, 1997—2006, Jesus Film Project Worldwide Missions, 2005—06. Nominee 10 Yr. Svc. award, Cumberland County Schs., Crossville, 2006; recipient Awana Achievement award, Morrison 1st Bapt. Ch., 2005; grantee Sparks grant, Warren County Schs., 1998—2000. Mem.: Tenn. Edn. Assn., Nat. Tchrs. Edn. Assn. Democrat. Southern Bapt. Achievements include leading a student to receive statewide recognition for winning My Home Is Tenessee Art Contest in Nashville. Avocations: reading, poetry, painting, music, birdwatching. Office: Crab Orchard Elem Sch 240 School Rd Crab Orchard TN 37723 Business E-Mail: mcbee@cumberlandcountyk-12.com.

MCBEE, MARY LOUISE, retired state legislator, academic administrator; b. Strawberry Plains, Tenn., June 15, 1924; d. John Wallace and Nina Aileen (Umbarger) McB. BS, East Tenn. State U., 1946; MA, Columbia U., 1951; PhD, Ohio State U., 1961. Tchr. East Tenn. State U., Johnson City, 1947-51; asst. dean of women, 1952-56, 57-60; dean of women, 1961-63, U. Ga., Athens, 1963-67; world campus afloat adminstr., 1966-67; assoc. dean of students, 1967-72; dean of students, 1972-74; asst. v.p. acad. affairs, 1974-76; assoc. v.p. acad. affairs, 1976-86; v.p. acad. affairs, 1986-88; ret., 1988; state rep. Clarke County Ga. Gen. Assembly, 1991—2004. Author: College Responsibility for Values, 1980; co-author: The American Woman: Who Will She Be?, 1974, Essays, 1979, 2d edit. 1981. Bd. dirs. Salvation Army, Athens, 1978—, United Way, Athens. Fulbright scholar, The Netherlands, 1956-57. Mem. Athens C. of C. (bd. dirs.). Democrat. Methodist. Avocations: gardening, tennis, hiking. Home: 145 Pine Valley Pl Athens GA 30606-4031 Personal E-mail: louisemcbee@charter.com.

MCBEE, SUSANNA BARNES, retired journalist; b. Santa Fe, N.Mex., Mar. 28, 1935; d. Jess Stephen and Sybil Elizabeth (Barnes) McBee; m. Paul H. Recer, July 2, 1983. AB, U. So. Calif., 1956; MA, U. Chgo., 1962. Staff writer Washington Post, 1957-65, 73-74, 77-79, asst. nat. editor, 1974-77; asst. sec. pub. affairs HEW, 1979; articles editor Washingtonian mag., 1980-81; assoc. editor U.S. News & World Report, 1981-86; news editor Washington Bur., Hearst Newspapers, 1987-89, asst. bur. chief, 1990—2003, ret., 2003; Washington corr. Life mag., 1965—69; Washington editor McCall's mag., 1970—72. Bd. dirs. Washington Press Club Found., 1992-95. Recipient Penney-Missouri mag. award, 1969, Hall of Fame award, Soc. Profl. Journalists, 1996, Sigma Delta Chi Pub. Svc. award, 1969, Hearst Eagle award, 1994. Mem. Nat. Press Club, Cosmos Club. Home: 5190 Watson St NW Washington DC 20016-5329

MCBRAYER, SANDRA L., educational director, homeless outreach educator; AA, San Diego Mesa Coll., 1981; BA in Applied Arts and Scis., San Diego State U., 1986, MA in Edn., 1990. Cert. presch.-kindergarten, grs. 1-12, adult edn., Calif. Tchr. asst. group homes Oz, The Bridge, Gatehouse, 1984-87; tchr. Hillcrest Receiving Home, 1987-88, Juvenile Hall, 1987-88, Comprehensive Adolescent Treatment Ctr., 1987-88; head tchr. the Monarch HS, 1988-96; CEO The Children's Initiative, San Diego. Lectr., cons. Ctrs. Careers Edn., Sch. Tchr. Edn. San Diego State U., 1990—; collaborator sch. dists. State Dept. Edn., Equity/Homeless Office, 1992—; staff devel. tng.; adj. prof. Coll. Edn., San Diego (Calif.) State U. Recipient award Exceptional Vols. Svc. Family Care Ctr., 1988, San Diego's 10 Leadership award Sta. KGTV, 1991, Celebrate Literacy award Internat. Reading Assn., 1992, Women of Vision in Edn. award LWV San Diego, 1992, Disting. Alumna of Yr.-Edn. award San Diego State U., 1992, Golden Bell award Calif. Sch. Bds. Found., 1992, Coun. of State Sch. Officers Nat. Tchr. of Yr. award 1994; named San Diego County Tchr. of Yr. by San Diego County Office of Edn., 1993, Calif. Tchr. of Yr. by State Dept. Edn., 1993, Nat. Tchr. of Yr., Pres. Clinton, 1994, Tech. Tchr. of Yr., Coun. on Tech. Tchr. Edn., 1994, Exceptional Svc. award Calif. State PTA, Humanitarian award Youth Advocacy Assn., Living Legacy award Internat. Women's Ctr.; recognized by local and nat. news media. Mem. NEA, Calif. Tchrs. Assn., Assn. Educators, Nat. Dropout Prevention Network, Calif. Homeless Coalition, Phi Kappa Phi. Office: The Childrens Initiative 4438 Ingraham St San Diego CA 92109 *

MCBRIDE, ANDREW GERALD, prosecutor; b. Paterson, NJ, June 26, 1960; s. Andrew Gerald and Patricia Ann (Millard) McB. BA, Holy Cross Coll., 1982; JD, Stanford U., 1987. Bar: N.Y., D.C., U.S. Dist. Ct. (2d, 4th, 5th and 9th cirs.) D.C. Law clk. to Hon. Robert H. Bork U.S. Ct. Appeals, Washington, 1987-88; law clk. to Justice Sandra Day O'Connor U.S. Supreme Ct., Washington, 1988-89; spl. asst. office of legal counsel U.S. Dept. Justice, Washington, 1989-90, assoc. dep. atty. gen., 1990-91, asst. to atty. gen., 1991-92, asst. U.S. atty., 1992-99; of counsel Cooper, Carvin & Rosenthal, P.C., Washington, 1999—. Recipient Rotary fellowship, 1983; named to Order of the Coif, 1987. Mem. ABA (mem. criminal justice sect. 1991—), N.Y. Bar Assn., D.C. Bar Assn., Federalist Soc. Republican. Roman Catholic. Avocation: bicycling. Home: 10932 Hunter Gate Way Reston VA 20194-1422

MCBRIDE, ANGELA BARRON, nursing educator; b. Balt., Jan. 16, 1941; d. John Stanley and Mary C. (Szczepanska) Barron; m. William Leon McBride, June 12, 1965; children: Catherine, Kara. BS in Nursing, Georgetown U., Washington, 1962; MS in Nursing, Yale U., New Haven, Conn., 1964; PhD, Purdue U., West Lafayette, Ind., 1978; doctorate of Pub. Svc. (hon.), U. Cin., 1983; LittD (hon.), Purdue U., 1998; LLD (hon.), Ea. Ky. U., 1991; LHD (hon.), Georgetown U., 1993; DSc (hon.), Med. Coll. Ohio, 1995; LHD (hon.), U. Akron, 1997. Asst. prof., rsch. asst. inst. Yale U., New Haven, 1964-73; assoc. prof., chairperson Ind. U. Sch. Nursing, Indpls., 1978-81, 80-84, prof., 1981-92, assoc. dean rsch., 1985—91, interim dean, 1991—92, univ. dean, 1992—2003, disting. prof., 1992—2005, disting. prof., univ. dean emerita, 2006—; sr. v.p. acad. affairs, nursing Clarian Health Ptnrs., 1997—2003; Am. Acad. Nursing, Am. Nurses Found. scholar-in-residence Inst. Medicine, 2003—04; Helene Denne Schulte vis. prof. U. Wis., Madison, 2006. Mem. Nat. Adv. Mental Health Coun., 1987—91; adv. com. NIH Office of Women's Health Rsch., 1997—2001, NIH Office of Women's Health Rsch. Specialized Ctrs. Rsch. on Sex and Gender Factors, 2003—06; coun. mem. Yale U. Coun., 1999—2005; ext. acad. advisor Sch. Nursing, Hong Kong Poly. U., 2000—06; adv. bd. Meth. Health Found., 2000—; advisor U. Hong Kong, 2004—, Hong Kong Acad. Nursing, 2004—. Author: The Growth and Development of Mothers, 1973 (Best Book award 1973), Living with Contradictions, A Married Feminist, 1976, How to Enjoy A Good Life With Your Teenager, 1987; editor: Psychiatric-Mental Health Nursing: Integrating the Behavioral and Biological Sciences, 1996 (Best Book award 1996); compiler: Nursing and Philanthropy, 2000. Adv. bd. Women's Fund Indpls., 2000—05; bd. dirs. United Way of Ctrl. Ind., 2002—06, Clarian Health Ptnrs., 2004—, chair quality and patient safety com.; mem. Yale U. Sch. Nursing Adv. Bd., 2006—, chair, 2007—. Recipient Disting. Alumna award Yale U., Disting. Alumna award Purdue U., Univ. Medallion, U. San Francisco, 1993, Hoosier Heritage award, 2000, Disting. Nurse Educator award Coll. Mt. St. Joseph, Cin., 2000, Ross Pioneering Spirit award Am. Assn. Critical-Care Nurses, 2004, Lifetime Achievement award Assn. Fundraising Profls., Ind., 2005, Woman of Achievement award, Ball State U., 2005 Torchbearer award Ind. Commn. for Women, 2005, Melva Jo Hendrix Leadership award Internat. Soc. Psychiat. Nursing, 2006; named Influential Woman in Indpls., Indpls. Bus. Jour./Ind. Lawyer, 1999, HealthCare Hero Indpls. Bus. Jour., 2003, Adele Herwitz Disting. scholar Commn. Fgn. Nursing Schs., 2005; Kellogg nat. fellow; Am. Nurses Found. scholar, Salute to Women award Indpls. YMCA, 1999, Sagamore of Wabash, 1999. Fellow: Nat. Acads. Practice, Am. Acad. Nursing (dir. leadership devel. bldg. acad. geriatric nursing capacity program 2000—, past pres., Living Legend 2006), APA (Nursing and Health Psychology award divsn. 38 1995); mem.: Soc. for Women's Health Rsch. (bd. mem. 2007—), Nat. Acad. Scis., Inst. of Medicine (mem. bd. health policy ednl. programs and fellowships 2006—), Soc. for Rsch. in Child Devel., Midwest Nursing Rsch. Soc. (Disting. Rsch. award 1985), Sigma Theta Tau (past pres., Mentor award 1993, disting. lectr 1995—99, Melanie Dreher award for contbns. as a dean 2001), Chi Eta Phi (hon.). Home: 744 Cherokee Ave Lafayette IN 47905-1872 Home Phone: 765-474-9187; Office Phone: 317-278-9076. Business E-Mail: amcbride@iupui.edu.

MCBRIDE, BRIAN, professional soccer player; b. Arlington Heights, Ill., June 19, 1972; m. Dina McBride; 2 children. Attended, St. Louis Univ. Forward Vfl Wolfsburg, Germany, 1994—95, Columbus Crew, 1996—2001, Preston North End, England, 2000—01, Columbus Crew, 2002, Everton FC, England, 2003, Columbus Crew, 2003—04, Fulham FC, England, 2004—. 92 caps, 30 goals U.S. Nat. Soccer Team, 1993—; mem. U.S. World Cup Team, 1998, 2002, 06. Spokesperson Ctrl. Ohio Diabetes Assn. Named to, Ea. Conf. All Star Team, 1996, 1997; recipient Gold Ball MVP award & Gold Boot top scorer award, CONCACAF Gold Cup, 2002.

MCBRIDE, BRIAN F., biomedical researcher, consultant; s. Francis J. and Maria C. McBride. PharmD, Phila. Coll. Pharmacy, 2002. Cardiology fellow Hartford Hosp., Conn., 2002—04; rsch. fellow Vanderbilt U. Med. Ctr., Nashville, 2004—. Mem.: KC (assoc.). Home Phone: 856-655-0418; Office Phone: 615-322-2959. Business E-Mail: brian.mcbride@vanderbilt.edu.

MCBRIDE, DENNIS RAY, curator, writer; b. Boulder City, Nev., Jan. 13, 1959; s. Ray McBride and Orpha Alveta Bowman. B, U. Nev., Las Vegas, 1977—2007, M, 1982. Editl. asst. US Bur. of Reclamation, Boulder City, 1973—84; libr. asst. III U. Nev., 1988—93; curator Boulder City Mus. and Hist. Assn., Nev., 1998—. Author: (book) Building Hoover Dam: An Oral History of the Great Depression, 1993, Hard Work and Far From Home: The Civilian Conservation Corps at Lake Mead, Nevada, 1995, Midnight on Arizona Street: The Secret Life of the Boulder Dam Hotel, 1993, In the Beginning: A History of Boulder City, Nevada, 1981. Recipient award, Las Vegas Bugle Found., 2004, Alice Isenberg Meml. award, Boulder City C. of C., 2005—06; Marjorie Barrick fellowship, U. Nev. Las Vegas, 1982. Socialist. Home: 607 Ave F Boulder City NV 89005 Office: Boulder City Mus and Historical Assn PO Box 60516 Boulder City NV 89005-0516 Home Phone: 702-293-4030; Office Phone: 702-294-1988. Personal E-mail: d_r_mcbride@yahoo.com. E-mail: bcmha@yahoo.com.

MCBRIDE, EARLE F., geologist, educator; PhD, John Hopkins, 1960. Prof. and J. Nalle Gregory Chair in sedimentary geology U. Tex., Austin. Recipient Pettijon Sedimentology medal Soc. Sedimentaty Geology, 1995. Office: U Tex at Austin Geol Sci Dept 1 University Station C1100 Office 4 138 Austin TX 78712-0254 Office Phone: 512-471-1905. Office Fax: 512-471-9425. Business E-Mail: efmcbride@mail.utexas.edu.

MCBRIDE, GERALD FRANCIS, lawyer; b. Albuquerque, N.Mex, Sept. 15, 1953; s. Myrrl William and Maria Elisa McBride. BA, U. N.Mex, Albuquerque, 1975, JD, 1982. Bar: N.Mex 1983. Internal revenue svc. tax auditor IRS, Santa Fe, 1977—79; mng. atty. So. N.Mex Legal Svcs, Las Cruces, 1983—85; child protective svcs. atty. Human Svcs. Dept., Albuquerque, 1985—92; adult and child protective svcs. atty. Children, Youth and Families, Albuquerque, 1992—2005; adult protective svcs. atty. Aging and Long-Term Svcs., Albuquerque, 2005—. Presenter Health Edn. Network, Albuquerque, 1998—. Musician (violinist): Symphony Orch. Albuquerque, 2000—02. Bd. dirs. Uniting New Mexicans Against Adult Abuse, Albuquerque, 1992—. Recipient 1st prize, Scholastic Mags., 1971. Mem.: State Bar N.Mex, Mensa. Avocations: writing, trivia. Office: Aging and Long-Term Svcs Dept 625 Silver SW # 400 Albuquerque NM 87102

MCBRIDE, GUY THORNTON, JR., college president emeritus; b. Austin, Tex., Dec. 12, 1919; s. Guy Thornton and Imogene (Thrasher) McB.; m. Rebekah Jane Bush, Sept. 2, 1942 (dec. Aug. 1998); children: Rebekah Ann, William Howard, Ellen M. Alsobrooks; m. Cordelia D. Rush, Aug. 7, 1999. BS in Chem. Engring., U. Tex., 1940; Sc.D., MIT, 1948; D.P.S. (hon.), Regis Coll., 1979; D.Engring. (hon.), Colo. Sch. Mines, 1984. Registered profl. engr., Tex. La., N.Y., Colo. Instr. chem. engring. Mass. Inst. Tech., 1942-44, research assoc., 1946-48; job engr. Standard Oil Co. Calif., 1944-46; asst. prof. chem. engring Rice Inst., 1948-55, assoc. dean students, 1950-57, dean, 1957-58, assoc. prof., 1955-58; cons. Tex. Gulf Sulphur Co., 1950-58, asst. mgr. research dept., 1958-59, mgr., 1959-60, v.p., mgr. research, 1960-63; v.p. Tex. Gulf Sulphur Co. (Phosphate div.), 1963-70, gen. mgr., 1966-70; pres. Colo. Sch. Mines, Golden, 1970-84; ret. Dir. Halliburton Co., Kerr-McGee Corp., Hercules, Inc.; hon. dir. Texasgulf Inc. Fellow Am. Inst. Chem. Engrs.; mem. Am. Chem. Soc., Nat. Soc. Profl. Engrs., Sigma Xi, Phi Lambda Upsilon, Tau Beta Pi. Clubs: Mile High (Denver). Home: 2615 Oak Dr Apt 13 Lakewood CO 80215-7182

MCBRIDE, JAMES M., school system administrator; m. Sandi McBride; children: Jim, Monique. MBA, La. Tech. U., 1981; EdD, U. NC, 1983. Tchr. Caesar Rodney Jr. HS, Dover, Del., Air Force Acad.; pres. CC of Air Force (CCAF), 1996—2001; supt. schs. Bennett, Colo., 2001—03; tech. adminstr. Wyo. Dept. Edn., 2003—05, supt. pub. instrn., 2005—. Mem. Coun. Chief State Sch. Officers, Mid-continent Rsch. for Edn. and Learning. Mem. Montgomery Trust Fund for Visually Impaired, Wyo. Higher Edn. Assistance Authority, Wyo. Early Childhood Coun., Wyo. Workforce Develop. Coun., Wyo. Edn. Planning and Coord. Coun. With USAF, 1975—2001. Office: Wyo Dept Edn Hathaway Bldg, 2nd Fl 2300 Capitol Ave Cheyenne WY 82002-0050 Office Phone: 303-777-7675. Business E-Mail: jmcbri@educ.state.wy.us. E-mail: supt@educ.state.wy.us. *

MCBRIDE, JANET MARIE, small business owner; b. Ft. Wayne, Ind., Nov. 21, 1948; d. Robert W and Helen F Plasterer; m. Joey W McBride, July 26, 1976; children: Kenneth Schortgen, Jr., Christian Schortgen, Dawna McBride Ross, Brand. Grad., Phoenix Coll., 1995. Feng Shui practitioner Western Sch. of Feng Shui, Calif., 2000. Dod ednl. exec asst DOD Schools-Europe, Madrid, 1979—82; engring. project adminstr. Honeywell, Inc., Tempe, 1987—95; cons., coach Young Living, Salt Lake City, 2000—. Singer (songwriter/producer): (spiritual songs) Irish Girl with the Heart of a Jew; singer: (musician/producer) (messianic hymns) Irish Girl with Heart of a Jew; author: Scriptural Essence; Radio Health Talk Personality. Address: 5388 Mountain Gate Cir Lakeside AZ 85929 Office Phone: 623-925-8994. E-mail: essentialvitality@cox.net.

MCBRIDE, JONATHAN EVANS, management consultant, director; b. Wash., June 16, 1942; s. Gordon Williams and Martha Alice (Evans) McBride; m. Emilie Evans Dean, Sept. 5, 1970; children: Webster Dean, Morley Evans. BA, Yale U., New Haven, Conn., 1964. Account exec. Merrill Lynch & Co., Washington, 1968—72; v.p. dept. mgr. Lionel D. Edie & Co., NYC, 1972—76; v.p. and exec. search cons. Simmons Assoc., Inc., Washington, 1976—79; pres. McBride Assoc., 1979—. Bd. dir. Yale U. Alumni Fund, 1974—79; trustee Sidwell Friends Sch., Washington, 1996—2004, vice chair, 2002—04. To lt. USNR, 1964—68. Mem.: Chevy Chase (Md.) Club, Met. Club (Washington), Yale Club (NYC). Office: 1700 Pennsylvania Ave NW Ste 400 Washington DC 20006 Office Phone: 202-349-3663. Personal E-mail: hearthunt@aol.com.

MCBRIDE, JONICA HELENE, mathematics professor; b. Charleston, Ill., July 16, 1977; d. John M. and Joyce H. Craft; m. Michael Lee McBride, July 31, 1999; children: Ethan Pierce children: Michaela Joy, Makenna Cait. BA in Math., Ea. Ill. U., Charleston, 2000, MA in Pure Math., 2005; postgrad., Ind. State U., 2006—. Math. instr. Lake Land Coll., Mattoon, Ill., 2002—, Ea. Ill. U., Charleston, 2005—. Deaconess Charleston Cmty. Ch., 2003—05. Recipient Dulgar Math Grad. Student-Assts. award, The Family of Lee Dulgar, 2004—05. Mem.: U. Profls. Ill. Home: 6867 Knollcrest Dr Charleston IL 61920 Office: Eastern Illinois Univ Math Dept 600 Lincoln Ave Charleston IL 61920 Office Fax: 217-581-6284.

MCBRIDE, MARTINA, vocalist; b. Medicine Lodge, Kans., July 29, 1966; d. Daryl and Jeanne Schiff; m. John McBride, May 15, 1988; children: Delaney Katherine, Emma Justine, Ava Rose Kathleen. Vocalist Schiffters, 1975-86, assorted bands, Wichita, Kans.; represented by RCA Records, 1991—; backup singer Garth Brooks, 1992—93, European tour, 1994. Singer: (albums) The Time Has Come, 1992, The Way That I Am, 1993 (Platinum), Wild Angels, 1995 (Platinum), Evolution, 1997 (Triple Platinum), Martina McBride Christmas, 1998, Emotion, 1999 (Platinum), White Christmas, 1999 (Platinum), (various artists) Girls Night Out, 1999, (Group recording) Safe In The Arms Of Love, 2000, Greatest Hits, 2001 (Dounble Platinum), Martina, 2003 (Gold), Timeless, 2005, Waking Up Laughing, 2007, (songs) (Runaway Bride soundtrack) I Love You, 1999, (Backstage at the Grand Ole Opry) Wrong Again, 2000, (Where The Heart Is soundtrack) There You Are, 2000, (The Mercy Project) You'll Get Through This, 2000; performer: (tv appearances co-star Pat Benatar) CMT Crossraods, 2003, (tv appearances) Stand By Your Man, 2003, (tv appearance) Nat. Anthem, NBA All Star Game, 2003, (presenter of award) CMT Flameworthy Awards, 2003, (tv biography) Lifetime Intimate portrait, 2002. Nominee Best Country Song for "Independence Day", Grammy, 1994, Video Yr. for "Independence Day", Acad. Country Music, 1994, Best Country Collaboration with Vocals for "Own My Own" with Reba McEntire, Linda Davis, and Trisha Yearwood, Grammy, 1995, Vocal Event Yr. for "On My Own" with Reba McEntire, Linda Davis, and Trisha Yearwood., Country Music Assn., 1996, Album Yr. for "Wild Angels", 1996, Best Country Female Vocal Performance for "Safe In The Arms of Love", Grammy, 1995, Vocal Event Yr. for "Still Holding On" with Clint Black, Country Music Assn., 1997, Best Country Collaboration with Vocals for "Still Holding You" with Clint Black, Grammy, 1997, Video Yr. for "A Broken Wing", Country Music Assn., 1998, Single Yr. for "A Broken Wing", 1998, Acad. Country Music, 1999, Song Yr. for "A Broken Wing", 1999, Video Yr. for "A Broken Wing", 1999, Best Country Female Vocal Performance for "I Love You", Grammy, 1999, Single Yr. for "Blessed", Country Music Assn., 2002, Best Female Country Vocal Performance for "Blessed", Grammy, 2002, Video Yr. for "Concrete Angel", Country Music Assn., 2003, Top Female Vocalist, Acad. Country Music, 1993, 1998, 2000, 2001, Horizon award, Country Music Assn., 1994, Female Vocalist Yr., 1996, 1998, 1999, 2001, Am. Music Awards, 2003; recipient Breakthrough Artist Video for "My Baby Loves Me", Music Row Ind. Summit Award, 1994, Music Video Yr. for "Independence Day", Country Music Assn. Awards, 1994, Best Video Yr. for "Independence Day", Gt. Brit. Music Awards, 1994, Video Yr. for "Independence Day", Nashville Music Awards, 1995, TNN Music City News Award, 1995, Gold Clio for Country Music Video Yr. for "Independence Day", Clio Awards, 1995, Best Southern Gospel, Country Gospel or Bluegrass Gospel for "Amazing Grace - A Country Salute To Gospel", Grammy Awards, 1995, Country Album Yr. for "Wild Angels", Nashville Music Awards, 1996, Video Yr. for "Safe In The Arms of Love", 1996, Female Video Yr. for "Blessed", CMT Flameworthy Awards, 2002, Female Video Yr. for "Concrete Angel", CMT Flameworthy Award, 2003, Top Female Vocalist, Acad. Country Music, 2002, Acad. Country Music award, 2003, 2004, Female Vocalist Yr., Country Music Assn. Award, 2002, Female Vocalist Yr. award, Country Music Assn., 2003, 2004, Country Female Artist Yr., Billboard Music Award, 2002, Best Female Artist, Country Radio Music Awards, 1996, Favorite Female Artist, Country, Am. Music Awards, 2003, Favorite Female Artist, Country Weekly, 2003. Address: RCA Records 1400 18th Ave S Nashville TN 37212-2809

MCBRIDE, MICHAEL FLYNN, lawyer; b. Milw., Mar. 27, 1951; s. Raymond Edward and Marian Dunne McBride; m. Kerin Ann (O'Brien), Mar. 23, 1991; children: Raymond Erin, Barbara Marian. BS in Chemistry and Biology, U. Wis., 1972, JD, 1976; MS in Environ. Engring. Sci., Calif. Inst. Tech., 1973. Bar: Wis. 1976, DC 1976. Assoc. LeBoeuf, Lamb, Greene, & MacRae LLP, Washington, 1976—84, ptnr., 1985—, chmn. Transp. Practice Group. Mem. Assn. Transp. Law Profls. (v.p., law inst. com. 1990, exec. com. 1990-, pres. 1994-95, 2004-, chmn. program com. 1998-99), Congl. Country Club. Avocations: golf, reading, travel. Office: LeBoeuf Lamb Greene & MacRae LLP 1101 New York Ave NW Washington DC 20005 Home Phone: 703-442-0149; Office Phone: 202-986-8050. Office Fax: 202-986-8102. Business E-Mail: michael.mcbride@llgm.com.

MCBRIDE, MILDRED MAYLEA, retired elementary school educator; b. Bowerston, Ohio, Oct. 7, 1922; d. Harry Scott and Mary McGary (Mowl) McB.; 1 adopted child, Marjorie Mi Sang McBride. BS in Music, Baldwin-Wallace Coll., 1944; MA, Columbia U., NYC, 1949. Cert. tchr., Ohio, Hawaii. Traveling music tchr. Tuscarawas County Sch., 1944-45; tchr. elem. music Parma (Ohio) Schs., 1945-48, tchr. jr. h.s. music, 1946-48; tchr. h.s. gen. music, chorus Kamehameha Sch. for Girls, Honolulu, 1949-59; tchr. elem. music Tempe (Ariz.) Schs., 1959-60, Hawaii Pub. Sch. Sys., 1960-86, ret., 1986. Co-founder Elem., Intermediate, Gen. Music Interest Group, Honolulu, 1969-79. Author, editor: Meg!, 1996, Three Women of Kintail, 2001, Lady Janet, Genny MacKenzie and Her Bairns, 2003, The Troubled Child, Angus and Margaret Moira, 2004, Two Brothers, 2006; writer mus. plays. Helper Bowerston Pub. Libr., 1939, 48, 97—; bd. dirs.; mem. Honolulu Symphony Chorus; soup kitchen, vol. Harris United Meth. Ch., Honolulu, 1990-96, mem. choir, 1975-96. Avocations: golf, travel, singing, cooking, enjoying daughter.

MCBRIDE, MILFORD LAWRENCE, JR., lawyer; b. Grove City, Pa., July 16, 1923; s. Milford Lawrence and Elizabeth B. (Douthett) McB.; m. Madeleine Coulter, Aug. 6, 1947; children: Marta, Brenda, Trip, Randy, Barry. AB, Grove City Coll., 1944; BS, NYU, 1944; JD, U. Pa., 1949. Bar: Pa. 1949, US Dist. Ct. (we. dist.) Pa. US Supreme Ct. Ptnr., McBride & McBride, Grove City, 1949-77, sr. ptnr., 1992—; ptnr. McBride and McNickle, Grove City, 1977-92; dir. Integra Fin. Corp., 1988-93; trustee Grove City Coll., 1995—. 1st lt. USAAF, 1943-46. Mem. Mercer County Bar Assn. (state treas. 1970-77), ABA, Am. Bar Found., Oakmont Country Club, Univ. Club (Pitts.). Republican Office: 211 S Center St Grove City PA 16127-1508 Office Phone: 724-458-6640.

MCBRIDE, ROBERT ALBERT, training services executive; b. Woonsocket, RI, Mar. 9, 1960; s. Albert and Leonora Anna McB.; m. Kathryn Moore, June 14, 1998; 1 child, Jordan. BA in Psychology, Providence Coll., 1982; MBA in Mgmt., Bryant Coll., 1994. Commd. ensign USN, 1985, advanced through grades to capt.; sales rep. Aventis Pharms., Providence, 1991—96, regional trainer New England region, 1996—99, area mgr. Pa., 1999—2002; dir. global tng. Genzyme Corp., 2002—. Mem. adv. bd. Boy's & Girl's Club, Cumberland, R.I., 1995-99; instr. Literacy Vols. Am., Woonsocket, R.I., 1997-99; vol. pvt. sch. basketball coach. Decorated Navy & Marine Corp Commendation medal, Navy Achievement medal; recipient Global War on Terrorism Svc. medal. Mem. World Affairs Coun., U.S. Naval Res. Assn., Naval Inst. Roman Catholic. Avocations: golf, biking, reading, basketball. Home: 10 Cathedral Ct Cumberland RI 02864 Office: Genzyme Corp 500 Kendall St Cambridge MA 02142 Office Phone: 401-658-5320. E-mail: bob.mcbride@genzyme.com.

MCBRIDE, TAMERA SHAWN DEW, geologist; d. Lawrence Bernard Dew, Jr. and Daris Virginia Hutchinson Dew; m. William Scott McBride, June 6, 1998; children: Alynaza Isabella, Rastus. BA cum laude, Rollins Coll., 1993; MS, U. So. Fla., 1995. Cert. radon measurement technician Fla. Dept. Health, Divsn. Environ. Health, 1997, profl. geologist Fla. Dept. Bus. and Profl. Regulation, 2002. Phys. sci. technician U.S. Geol. Survey, Ocala, Fla., 1991—94; scientist Environ. Resources Mgmt., Inc., Tampa, Fla., 1995—2000; planner S.W. Fla. Water Mgmt. Dist., Brooksville, Fla., 2000—04, profl. geologist, 2004—. Acting ex-officio mem. Ctrl. Fla. Regional Planning Coun., Bartow, Fla., 2000—04. Soloist St. Catherine (Fla.) United Meth. Ch., 1975—, mem. choir, 2001—, vice chair com. lay leadership, 2005; asst. sec. S.W. Fla. Water Mgmt. Dist. Employee Com., 2003—04, vice-chair, 2004—06, Fla., 2007—. Mem.: U. South Fla. Geology Alumni Soc. (bd. dirs. 1998—2000), Fla. Assn. Profl. Geologists, Chronic Fatigue and Immune Dysfunction Syndrome Assn. of Am., Phi Eta Sigma. Avocations: fishing, travel, dance. Home: PO Box 1223 Bushnell FL 33513 Office: Southwest Florida Water Mgmt Dist 2379 Broad St Brooksville FL 34604 Home Phone: 352-793-2664; Office Phone: 352-796-7211. Business E-Mail: tamera.mcbride@swfwmd.state.fl.us.

MCBRIDE, THOMAS DWAYNE, management consultant; b. Brownwood, Tex., Feb. 13, 1947; s. Thomas Alfred and Eula Faye (Harvey) McB.; m. Peggy Anne Kimbrough McBride, Oct. 14, 1967; children: Jeffery Dwayne, Stacy Anne. AS, Crowder Coll., Neosho, Mo., 1967; BS in Mech. Engring., U. Mo., Rolla, 1970; MBA in Mgmt., U. Akron, 1978. Registered profl. engr., Ohio. Engring. supr. Babcock & Wilcox, Barberton, Ohio, 1972-79; mgr. engring. Bendix Corp., South Beloit, Ill., 1979-83; mgr. sales engring. Bendix/Warner & Swasey, Worcester, Mass., 1983-84, mgr. Product Engring., 1984-86; program mgr. Design Tech. Corp., Billerica, Mass., 1986-87; mgr. engring. Netco, Inc., Haverhill, Mass., 1987-88; dir. engring. The Nelmor Co., North Uxbridge, Mass., 1988-95; tech. mgr. Lawrence (Mass.) Pumps Inc., 1995-96, ops. mgr., 1996-2000; pres. Ptnrs. for Creative Solutions, Inc., Shrewsbury, Mass., 2000—. Tech. and bus. cons. Micromation, Inc., Altoona, Pa., 1988-90. Inventor: Granulator Knife, 1991, 94, Bin Deflector, 1991; author: Society of Manufacturing Engineers, 1992, M&A Today, 2000. Mem. Trinity Ch. 1st lt. US Army, 1971—72. Recipient Curator's scholarship, U. Mo., 1967. Mem.: Am. Soc. for Quality, Soc. Mfg. Engrs., Corridor 9 C. of C., Phi Theta Kappa (chpt. pres. 1966—67). Avocations: golf, bicycling, genealogy, religious history, hiking. Personal E-mail: tmcbride@pcs-info.com.

MC BRIDE, WILLIAM LEON, philosopher, educator; b. NYC, Jan. 19, 1938; s. William Joseph and Irene May (Choffin) McB.; m. Angela Barron, July 12, 1965; children: Catherine, Kara. AB, Georgetown U., Washington, DC, 1959; postgrad. (Fulbright fellow), U. Lille, 1959-60; MA (Woodrow Wilson fellow), Yale U., New Haven, Conn., 1962, PhD (Social Sci. Rsch. Coun. fellow), 1964. Instr. philosophy Yale U., New Haven, 1964-66, asst. prof., 1966-70, assoc. prof., 1970-73; lectr. Northwestern U., Evanston, Ill., summer 1972; assoc. prof. Purdue U., West Lafayette, Ind., 1973-76, prof., 1976-2001, Arthur G. Hansen disting. prof., 2001—. Senate chmn. Purdue U., 2004-05; lectr. Korcula Summer Sch., Yugoslavia, 1971, 73; Fulbright lectr. Sofia U., Bulgaria, 1997. Author: Fundamental Change in Law and Society, 1970, The Philosophy of Marx, 1977, Social Theory at a Crossroads, 1980, (with R.A. Dahl) Demokrati og Autoritet, 1980, Sartre's Political Theory, 1991, Social and Political Philosophy, 1994, Philosophical Reflections on the Changes in Eastern Europe, 1999, From Yugoslav Praxis to Global Pathos, 2001; editor: (with C.O. Schrag) Phenomenology in a Pluralistic Context, 1983, Sartre and Existentialism, 8 vols., 1997, (with M.B. Matustik) Calvin O. Schrag and the Task of Philosophy after Postmodernity, 2002, The Idea of Values, 2003, Social and Political Philosophy, 2006. Decorated chevalier Ordre des Palmes Académiques. Mem. AAUP (pres. Purdue chpt. 1983-86, pres. Ind. conf. 1988-89), Am. Philos. Assn. (chmn. com. on internat. coop. 1992-95, bd. dirs. 1992-95), N.Am. Soc. for Social Philosophy (v.p. 1997-2000, pres. 2000-05), Am. Soc. Polit. and Legal Philosophy, Soc. Phenemonology and Existential Philosophy (exec. co-sec. 1977-80), Sartre Soc. N.Am. (chmn. bd. dirs. 1985-88, 91-93), Am. Soc. Philosophy in the French Lang. (pres. 1994-96), Fed. Internat. Soc. Philosophie (steering com. 1998—, sec. gen. 2003—). Home: 744 Cherokee Ave Lafayette IN 47905-1872 Office: Purdue U Dept Philosophy 100 N Univ St West Lafayette IN 47907-2098 Office Phone: 765-494-4285. Business E-Mail: wmcbride@purdue.edu.

MCBRYDE, JOHN HENRY, federal judge; b. Jackson, Oct. 9, 1931; m. Betty Vinson; children: Rebecca, Jennifer, John Blake. BS in Commerce, Tex. Christian U., 1953; LLB, U. Tex., 1956. Bar: Tex. 1956, U.S. Ct. Appeals (5th cir.) 1958, U.S. Dist. Ct. (no. dist.) 1958, U.S. Dist. Ct. (ea. dist.) 1989, U.S. Supreme Ct. 1972. Assoc. Cantey, Hanger, Johnson, Scarborough & Gooch, Ft. Worth, 1956-62; ptnr. Cantey & Hanger and predecessor firm, Ft. Worth, 1962-69, McBryde, Bennett and predecessor firms, Ft. Worth, 1969-90; judge U.S. Dist. Ct. (no. dist.) Tex., Ft. Worth, 1990—. Fellow Am. Bar Found. (life), Tex. Bar Found. (life), Am. Coll. Trial Lawyers. Office: US Dist Ct US Courthouse 501 W 10th St Ste 401 Fort Worth TX 76102-3642

MCBRYDE, NEILL GREGORY, lawyer; b. Durham, NC, Jan. 11, 1944; s. Angus M. and Priscilla (Gregory) McBryde; m. Margaret McPherson, Aug. 1, 1970; children: Margaret Courtauld McBryde Young, Neill Gregory Jr. AB cum laude, Davidson Coll., 1966; JD with high honors, U. N.C., 1969. Bar: N.C. 1969., Ga. 1972. Assoc. King & Spalding, Atlanta, 1971-76; ptnr. Fleming, Robinson, Bradshaw & Hinson, Charlotte, NC, 1977-81, Helms, Mulliss & Johnston, Charlotte, 1981-86, Smith Helms Mulliss & Moore, Charlotte, 1986-90, Moore & Van Allen PLLC, Charlotte, 1990—. Lectr. in field; condr. workshops in field. Author, editor: First Union National Bank of North Carolina Will Book, 1986; contbr. articles to profl. jours. Elder and Deacon Myers Park Presbyn. Ch., Charlotte, 1980-86, 92-95, 2001-04, 05—; bd. dirs., sec. Presbyn. Home for Aged, Charlotte, 1978-82; trustee Charlotte Latins Sch., Inc., 1980-86, 87-93; past chmn., past trustee Mint Mus. Charlotte. Fellow Am. Coll. Trust and Estate Counsel (past mem. bd. regents, past pres.), Am. Coll. Tax Counsel; mem. ABA, Ga. Bar Assn., NC Bar Assn. (probate and fiduciary law sect.), So. Fed. Tax Inst. (trustee 1999—, pres. 2005-06), Order of Coif, Phi Beta Kappa, Omicron Delta Kappa. Avocations: tennis, golf, fishing. Office: Moore & Van Allen PLLC Bank of Am Corp Ctr 100 N Tryon St Fl 47 Charlotte NC 28202-4003 Office Phone: 704-331-1094.

MCBURNEY, CHARLES WALKER, JR., lawyer; b. Orlando, Fla., June 6, 1957; s. Charles Walker McBurney and Jeane (Brown) Chappell. BA, U. Fla., 1979, JD, 1982. Bar: Fla. 1982, U.S. Dist. Ct. (mid. dist.) Fla. 1983, U.S. Ct. Appeals (11th cir.) 1984. Assoc. Mathews, Osborne, McNatt, Gobelman & Cobb, Jacksonville, Fla., 1982-84; asst. state's atty. State's Atty.'s Office, Jacksonville, 1984-90, civil atty., 1987-88, sr. trial atty., 1988-90; ptnr. Fischette, Owen, Held & McBurney, Jacksonville, 1990—2004; pvt. practice Law Office Charles W. McBurney Jr., Jacksonville, 2004—. Dir. Serious or Habitual Juvenile Offender Program, 1986. Mem. adv. coun. Mandarin Oaks Elem. Sch., vice chmn., 2003—04, chmn., 2004—06; mem. Mayor's Bicentennial Constnl. Commn., 1989—91; chmn. com. congl. campaigns Jacksonville, 1982, 1984, 1988; deacon South Jacksonville Presbyn. Ch., 2003—; bd. dirs. Civic Round Table, 1988—92, treas., 1988—89, pres., 1989—90; dir. Internat. Devel. Commn. for Jacksonville, 1993—2003, treas., 1995—97; chmn. S.E. Citizens Planning Adv. Com., 2005—07; bd. dirs. Am. Heart Assn. N.E. Fla., 1990—92. Mem.: ABA, Comml. Law League (So. region exec. coun. 1998—, treas. 2000—), Jacksonville Bankruptcy Bar Assn. (bd. dirs. 1999—2004, treas. 2003—04), Jacksonville Bar Assn. (chmn. bankruptcy sect. 1998—2000, 2002—03), Duval County Rep. Party (treas. 2002—), Jacksonville Hist. Soc., First Coast Tiger Bay Forum (bd. dirs. 2001—, Leadership award 2004), Jacksonville C. of C. (bd. govs. 1987, govtl. affairs com. 1998—), Fla. Jaycees (legal counsel 1987—88, Most Outstanding Local Pres. award 1987), Jacksonville Jaycees (pres. 1986, Jaycee of yr. 1984, Businessperson of Yr. 2006), Summit Civitan (judge adv. 1991—93, 2001—02), James Madison Inst., Southside Bus. Men's Club (v.p. 2003—04, parliamentarian 2006—), Bull Snort Club (pres. 1995—96, chmn. bd. 1996—99, pres. 1999—2000), Masons, N.E. Fla. Phi Beta Kappa Alumni Assn. (v.p. 1998—2000, 2003—04). Republican. Presbyterian. Home: 6326 Christopher Creek Rd E Jacksonville FL 32217-2485 Office: Ste 590 76 S Laura St Jacksonville FL 32202 Personal E-mail: cmcburney@bellsouth.net.

MCBURNEY, ELIZABETH INNES, dermatologist, physician, educator; b. Lake Charles, La., Dec. 24, 1944; d. Theodore John and Martha (Caldwell) Innes; divorced, 1980; children: Leanne Marie, Susan Eleanor. BS, U. Southwestern La., 1965; MD, La. State U., 1969. Diplomate Am. Bd. Internal Medicine, Am. Bd. Dermatology. Intern Pensacola (Fla.) Edn. Program, 1969-70; resident in internal medicine Boston U. and Carney Hosps., 1970-72; resident in dermatology Charity Hosp., New Orleans, 1972-74; staff physician Ochsner Hosp., New Orleans, 1974-80; assoc. head of dermatology Ochsner Clinic, New Orleans, 1974-80; clin. asst. prof. La. Health Scis., New Orleans, 1976-79, clin. assoc. prof., 1979-90, clin. prof., 1990—; clin. asst. prof. Tulane Health Scis., New Orleans, 1976-88, clin. assoc. prof., 1988-91, clin. prof., 1991—. Courtesy staff Northshore Regional Med. Ctr., Slidell, La., 1985—; staff Slidell Meml. Hosp., 1988—, chmn. CME courses, 1988—, pres.-elect med. staff, 2000-01, pres., 2001—02; regional dir. Mycosis Fungoides Study Group, Balt., 1974-94. Contbr. articles to profl. jours. Bd. dirs. Slidell Art Coun., 1988—, Camp Fire, New Orleans, 1979-83, Cancer Assn. New Orleans, 1978-83; juror Art in Pub. Places, Slidell, 1989; councilman St. Tammany Art Coun., 2003-06. Recipient Disting. Woman Physician award AMA, 1999, Thomas Pearson edn. meml. award, 2004. Fellow ACP; mem. Am. Soc. Dermatologic Surgery (treas. 1991-94, bd. dirs. 1988-91, pres. elect 1995-96, pres. 1996-97), Women's Dermatol. Soc. (pres. 2006—, Samuel Stegman award 2000, Pub. Svc. award, 2001), Am. Acad. Dermatology (bd. dirs. 1994-98), Am. Bd. Laser Medicine and Surgery (bd. dirs. 1991-96), La. Dermatologic Soc. (pres. 1989-90), St. Tammany Med. Soc. (pres. 1988), Phi Kappa Phi, Alpha Omega Alpha. Avocations: reading, gardening, fine art, music, films. Office: 1051 Gause Blvd Ste 460 Slidell LA 70458-2985 Office Phone: 985-649-5880.

MCBURNEY, MARGOT B., retired librarian; b. Lethbridge, Alta., Can. d. Ronald Laurence Maness and R. Blanche (Lott) Hart; children: Margot Elisabeth McBurney Lane, James Ronald Gordon. BA with honours, Principia Coll., 1953; M.Sc. in L.S, U. Ill., 1969. Sec. Marshall Brooks Library, Principia Coll., Elsah, Ill., 1966-69, reference librarian, 1969-70; systems analyst trainee in library systems U. Alta. Library, Edmonton, 1970-71, undergrad. reference librarian, 1971-72, editor periodicals holdings list, 1972-73, serials cataloguer, 1973-74, head acquisitions div., 1974-77; chief librarian Queen's U. Library, Kingston, Ont., Canada, 1977-90; distbr. Pharmanex, 2005—06. Editor: Am. Soc. Info. Sci. Western Can. chpt. Proceedings, 1975, 76. Mem. Am. Soc. Info. Sci. (councilor-at-large 1976-79, past chmn. chpt.), Assn. Research Libraries (dir. 1978-81, chmn. task force on library edn. 1980-83), Can. Assn. Info. Sci., Can. Assn. Research Libraries, Can. Library Assn., Council on Library Resources (PETREL com. 1981-84), Phi Alpha Eta, Beta Phi Mu. Home Phone: 613-267-4280. E-mail: mbm33@sympatico.ca.

MCCABE, BROOKS FLEMING, JR., state legislator; b. Charleston, W.Va., Jan. 19, 1949; s. Brooks F. Sr. and Jane (Mason) McC.; m. Barbara Given McCabe; 1 child, Katherine Jane. BS in Mgmt. Engring., MEd in Adminstrn., U. Vt., Burlington, 1972; EdD in Adminstrn., W.Va. U., 1975. Asst. to dir. Gov.'s Office Fed. and State Rels., Gov.'s Office Fed. and State Rels., Charleston, 1975-77; gov.'s housing coord. State of W.Va., Charleston, 1977-79; comml. real estate salesperson Home Finders, Inc., Charleston, 1979-80; comml. real estate brokerage and devel. McCabe Hanley LP, Charleston, 1980—; gen. ptnr. McCabe Land Co. LP, Charleston, 1987—; mem. W.Va. Senate, Charleston, 1998—. Bd. dirs. Charleston Renaissance Corp., 1995-02; pres., bd. dirs. Silver Creek Properties, Inc., Slaty Fork, W.Va., 1988-92. Pres. Cmty. Coun. of Kanawha Valley, Charleston, 1987-89; campaign chmn. United Way of Kanawha Valley, Charleston, 1988; trustee U. Vt., Burlington, 1976-82, The Gow Sch., South Wales, NY, 1988-97, W.Va. Wesleyan Coll., Buchanon, 2000-02; bd. dirs. Greater Kanawha Valley Found., 1988-91, Charleston Area Med. Ctr. Found., 1992-98, W.Va. State Coll. Found., Inc., 1994-98. Named Vol. of the Yr., United Way of Kanawha Valley, 1986-87. Mem. Am. Inst. Cert. Planners, W.Va. Planning Assn., Kanawha Valley Bd. Realtors, W.Va. Assn. Realtors, Urban Land Inst., Nat. Trust Hist. Preservation, W.Va. Roundtable. Democrat. Episcopalian. Avocations: reading, history, skiing. Office: McCabe Henley LP 107 Capitol St Charleston WV 25301-2609 Address: WVa State Senate 1900 Kanawha Blvd E Rm 441M Charleston WV 25305-0009 Office Phone: 304-347-7500.

MCCABE, DAVID J., lawyer; b. New Rochelle, NY, Aug. 16, 1958; BA, Iona Coll., 1980; JD, Fordham U., 1983. Bar: NY 1984. Sr. ptnr. Pvt. Clients Group Willkie Farr & Gallagher LLP, NYC. Mem. estate planning and taxation com. Trusts and Estates Mag.; lectr. in field. Co-author: New York Limited Liability Companies: A Guide to Law and Practice, 1995; contbr. articles for mags. Co-founder Huguenot Children's Libr., pres., 1993—98, dir., 1993—2002; mem. adv. bd City Harvest, Inc., 1989—93, bd. dirs., 1993—96, mem. exec. com., sec., 1994—96; mem. Profl. Adv. Com. Mus. Arts and Design, NYC, 2003—; mem. Profl. Adv. Coun. Lincoln Ctr. for Performing Arts, NYC, 2003—; bd. dirs., v.p., co-counsel Boys and Girls Club, New Rochelle, 2002—; bd. dirs. New Rochelle Humane Soc., New Rochelle, 2002—05, Ursuline Sch., 2004—; bd. legal trustees Iona Coll., New Rochelle, 2006—. Fellow: Am. Coll. Trusts and Estate Counsel; mem.: Assn. Bar City NY (chair com. trusts, estates and surrogate cts. 2005—, judiciary com. 2005—), NY State Bar Assn. (trusts and estates law sect., vice chmn. com. estate and trust adminstrn. 1996—99, ad hoc com. liaison to legis. adv. com.). Office: Willkie Farr & Gallagher LLP 787 Seventh Ave New York NY 10019 Office Phone: 212-728-8723. Office Fax: 212-728-9723. Business E-Mail: dmccabe@willkie.com.

MCCABE, EDWARD R. B., hospital administrator, educator, physician; b. Balt., Mar. 26, 1946; BA in Biology, Johns Hopkins U., 1967; PhD in Pharmacology, U. So. Calif., 1972, MD, 1974. Diplomate Am. Bd. Pediatrics. Resident in pediatrics U. Minn. Hosps., Mpls., 1974—76; pediatric metabolism fellow Sch. Medicine U. Colo., Denver, 1976—78, instr., asst. prof., assoc. prof. pediatrics Sch. Medicine, 1978—86; from assoc. prof. to prof. genetics, pediatrics Baylor Coll. Medicine, Houston, 1986—94; exec. prof., chmn. dept. pediatrics David Geffen Sch. Medicine UCLA, 1994—. Physician-in-chief Mattel Children's Hosp. UCLA, 1995—; mem. med. genetics residency rev. com. Accreditation Coun. Grad. MEd. Edn., 1993—97; chmn. conf. gaucher disease NIH, Bethesda, Md., 1994—96; mem. NICHD Coun., 1995—99. Editor: Biochem. and Molecular Medicine, 1990—97, Molecular Genetics and Metabolism, 1998—. Chair sci. adv. bd. HEreditary Disease Found., LA, 1998—99; chmn. Basil O'Connor award March Dimes, White Plains, NY, 1997—99. Mem.: Inst. Medicine, Soc. Pediatric Rsch. (E. Mead Johnson award 1993), Am. Coll. Med. Genetics (chair sec.'s adv. com. genetics, health and society 2002—, maternal and child health bur. 1999—2000, pres. 2001—02, co-chair newborn screening screening task force), Am. Soc. Biochem. and Molecular Biology, Am. Pediatric Soc., Am. Fedn. Clin. Rsch., Am. Soc. Human Genetics, Am. Bd. Med. Genetics (bd. dirs. 1992—97, pres. Bethesda 1995—96, diplomate), Am. Acad. Pediatrics (chmn. com. genetics Elk Grove Village, Ill. 1987—91, co-founder, chmn. sect. genetics Elk Grove Village 1990, 1993—95), Alpha Omega Alpha, Sigma Xi, Phi Kappa Phi. Achievements include First to describe the Continguous Gene Syndrome Complex Glyverol Kinase Deficiency; first to extract DNA from blood in newborn screening blotters; first to set up molecular genetic diagonosis for sickle cell disease as part of newborn screening; development of concept of molecular genetic triage of bacterial infection. Office: UCLA Pediatrics Box 951752 22-412 MDCC Los Angeles CA 90095 Office Phone: 310-825-5095. E-mail: emccabe@mednet.ucla.edu.

MCCABE, EUGENE, information technology executive; Various positions in network and sys. product design and field engring. support Digital Equipment Corp., v.p. mfg. Alpha Systems and Mfg. Tech.; with Compaq, Sun Microsystems, Inc., Santa Clara, Calif., 1999—, v.p. high end ops., exec. v.p. worldwide ops., 2006—. Office: Sun Microsystems Inc 4150 Network Cir Santa Clara CA 95054 Office Phone: 650-960-1300. *

MC CABE, GERARD BENEDICT, retired library administrator; b. NYC, Jan. 22, 1930; s. Patrick Joseph and Margaret Irene (McDonald) McC.; m. Jacqueline L. Maloney, Aug. 3, 1963 (dec. 1987); children: Theresa Marie, Rebecca Mary. BA in English, Manhattan Coll., 1952; A.M. in Library Sci. (scholar), U. Mich., 1954; MA in English, Mich. State U., 1959. Asst. acquisitions dept. U. Nebr. Library, Lincoln, 1954-56; chief bibliog. acquisitions dept. Mich. State U. Library, East Lansing, 1956-58; librarian Inst. Community Devel. and Service, Mich. State U., 1958-59; acquisitions librarian U. S. Fla., Tampa, 1959-66, asst. dir. planning and devel., 1967-70; assoc. dir. U. Ark. Library, Fayetteville, 1966-67; dir. univ. libraries Va. Commonwealth U., Richmond, 1970-82; dir. libraries Clarion U. of Pa., 1982-95; ret., 1995; libr. cons., Wilmington, NC, 1995—. Editor: The Smaller Academic Library: A Management Handbook, 1988, Operations Handbook for Small Academic Library, 1989, Academic Libraries in Urban and Metropolitan Areas, 1992; co-editor ann. pub. Advances in Libr. Adminstrn. and Orgn., vols. 1-12, Insider's Guide to Libr. Automation: Essays of Practical Experience, 1993, Acad. Librs.: Their Rationale and Role in Am. Higher Edn., 1995, Introducing and Managing Academic Library Automation Projects, 1996, Leadership for Academic Librarians, 1998, Planning for a New Generation of Public Library Buildings, 2000, Planning the Modern Public Library Building, 2003, It's All About Student Learning, 2006, Our New Public, A Changing Clientele: Bewildering Issues or New Challenges for Managing Libraries, 2007; contbr. articles to profl. jours. Mem. ALA, Southeastern Libr. Assn. Home and Office: 201 Crain Hwy N Apt 3B Glen Burnie MD 21061-3375 Home Phone: 410-302-5911; Office Phone: 410-302-5911. Personal E-mail: bldlib@comcast.net. *Consideration for others is a guiding principle for my personal and professional behavior. I, as a librarian, must have concern for those I serve. Their needs are my first and only interest, not success, not notoriety, only their service and their satisfaction.*

MCCABE, JAMES PATRICK, university librarian; b. Phila., May 24, 1937; s. Felix and Josephine (Murtaugh) McC. BA, Niagara U., 1963; MA, U. Mich., 1964, MA in LS, 1965, PhD, 1968. Libr. dir. Allentown Coll., Center Valley, Pa., 1968-89; acting libr. dir. Muhlenberg Cedar Crest Colls., Allentown, Pa., 1989-90; univ. libr. Fordham U., NYC, 1990—. Author: Critical Guide to Catholic Reference Books, 3d edit., 1989. Bd. dirs. Pa. Shakespeare Festival, Center Valley, 1990—. Office: Fordham U Univ Libr Rose Hill Campus Bronx NY 10458 Office Phone: 718-817-3570. *

MCCABE, JIM, publishing executive; BA in Polit. Sci., Hartwick Coll. Rsch. analyst Ogilvy & Mather Advertising; mgr. mktg. sales Forbes; with The New Republic; pub. Worth mag., Fast Company mag.; publ., v.p. Fast Company mag. and Inc. mag.; v.p., pub. PC mag., 2005—. Office: PC Mag 28 East 28th St New York NY 10016 Office Phone: 212-503-3500. Office Fax: 212-503-5799. E-mail: jim_mccabe@ziffdavis.com. *

MCCABE, JOHN L., lawyer; b. Chgo., Oct. 17, 1941; BA, U. Notre Dame, 1963; LLB, Harvard U., 1966. Bar: Ill. 1967, Colo. 1967. Ptnr. Davis Graham & Stubbs LLP, Denver. Office: Davis Graham & Stubbs LLP 1550 Seventeenth St Ste 500 Denver CO 80202 Office Phone: 303-892-9400. Business E-Mail: john.mccabe@dgslaw.com.

MCCABE, LINDA JEAN, elementary school educator; d. Francis E. and Virginia M. Brazes; m. Robert D. McCabe. BA, U. No. Colo., Greeley, 1969. Lic. profl. tchr. State of Colo., 1969, cert. tchr. Tex. Edn. Agy., 1981, profl. edn. State of Wash., 2000. Tchr. Pub. Schs., Colo., 1969—76, tchr., coach k-12 phys. edn., 1971—79, tchr. elem. sch. Tex., 1980—97, Colo., 1997—2001, Wash., 2001—. Com. mem. Develop Comprehensive Math Model OSPI, Wash., 2004—05; trainer and facilitator cert. Project Wild, PLT, WET, FLP, Colo.; math modules trainer Tex. Edn. Agy., Tex. Amateur radio operator lic.; fire fighter US Forest Svc.; vol. fire fighter Maybell Fire Dept., Colo., 1999—2001. Recipient Outstanding Rural Educator, Moffat County Edn. Assn., 1998, John Irwin award, Colo. Dept. Edn. Mem.: Nat. Sci. Tchr. Assn., Nat. Coun. Tchrs. Math., Internat. Reading Assn. Avocations: outdoor activities, travel, music.

MCCABE, LOUISE BEACHBOARD, language educator; b. NYC, Apr. 11, 1941; d. Walter William and Harriet Wood (Colby) Beachboard; m. James Laws McCabe, June 8, 1974; children: Sarah Beachboard, William Laws. BA, Smith Coll., 1963; MAT, Yale U., 1966; PhD, Harvard U., 1978. Instr. Italian, Harvard U., 1969-70, Harvard U., 1971-72, Yale U., New Haven, 1974-75, Tyler Art Sch. Temple U., Elkins Park, Pa., 1984-87, Villanova U., Pa., 1987-91; Latin tchr. Roxbury Latin Sch., Mass., 1970-71; tchr. ESOL, Sch. Dist. Phila., 1992-93, Inst. Italian and French Holy Family Coll., 1999-2002, Ctrl. HS, Phila., 2002-04; adj. prof. Italian, St. Joseph's U., Phila., 1993; instr. Pa. State U., 2003-05. Asst. editor Chilton Books, Phila., 1963-65. Contbr. articles to profl. jours. Founding mem. Somerville Police Cmty. Rels. Com., Mass., 1973. Mem. Colonial

Dames Am., Internat. Womens Club Phila., Acorn Club (Phila.), Smith Coll. Club (bd. dirs. 1989-91). Republican. Episcopalian. Avocation: genealogy Home: 701 Williamson Rd Bryn Mawr PA 19010-1830 E-mail: whatisthis@erols.com.

MCCABE, MARY F., marketing professional; d. Frank Camarda and Inez Cunningham; children: Vincent Joseph Papile, Kristin Julia Papile. BA, Smith Coll., 1982, MA, 1983; MFA, Yale U., 1994. Co-founder, mng. dir. Children's Theatre of Mass., Springfield, 1980—91; assoc. mng. dir. Yale Repertory Theatre; mng. dir. Nat. Playwrights Conf., O'Neill Ctr., 1994—2001; assoc. mktg. solution Lehman Bros., 2001—. Strategic planning com. O'Neill Theater Ctr., 1997—2000, transition com. to identify exec. dir., 1999—2000. Edn. task force Springfield Schs., 1987—99; liaison for Yale Repertory Theatre Spl. Olympic World Games, 1993; mem. Coast Guard Auxiliary, 1997—; bd. advisors Seven Devils Playwrights Festival, Boise, Idaho, 2000—. Recipient regional award for artistic achievement, New England Theater Conf. (NETC), 1990. Democrat. Roman Catholic. Home: 95 Cabrini Blvd Apt 3-L New York NY 10033 Office: Lehman Bros 745 7th Ave 30th Fl New York NY 10033 Home Phone: 212-927-0847; Office Phone: 212-526-8272. Personal E-mail: acthuman@aol.com. Business E-Mail: mmccabe@lehman.com.

MCCABE, MICHAEL J. (MICK), insurance executive, lawyer; b. Denver, June 19, 1945; s. Joseph J. and Mary J. (Kane) McC.; m. Catherine Corrine Marquette, July 21, 1978; children: Brian Michael, Shannon Marquette. BS, U. No. Colo., 1967; JD, Cath. U. Am., 1971. Bar: D.C. Air transport econ. analyst U.S. Civil Aeronautics Bd., Washington, 1967-71; Washington counsel Allstate Ins. Co., Northbrook, Ill., 1971-74, of counsel, law and regulation office, 1974-82, asst. v.p. bus. planning, 1982-84, v.p. corp. planning, 1984-89, group v.p., gen. atty., 1989-95, sr. v.p., property-casualty claim svc., 1995—97, sr. v.p., mktg., brand devel., 1997—99; v.p., gen. counsel Allstate Corp., Northbrook, Ill., 1999—; and sr. v.p., gen. counsel Allstate Ins. Co., Northbrook, Ill., 1999—. Bd. advisors No. Ill. U. Sch. Bus., DeKalb, 1986—. Chmn. Gateway Found. Mem. ABA, Fed. Bar Assn., D.C. Bar Assn., Planning Forum, Sigma Chi, Pi Alpha Delta. Democrat. Roman Catholic. Office: Allstate Ins Co 2775 Sanders Rd Northbrook IL 60062 Office Phone: 847-402-5000. *

MCCABE, ROBERT HOWARD, college president; b. Dec. 23, 1929; s. Joseph A. and Kathryn (Greer) McC.; m. Arva Moore Parks, June 1992. BEd, U. Miami, 1952, LLD (hon.), 1992; MS, Appalachian State U., Boone, NC, 1959; PhD, U. Tex., 1963; LLD (hon.), Barry U., 1986, Fla. Internat. U., 1990. Asst. to pres. Miami Dade C. of C., Fla., 1963-65, v.p. Fla., 1965-67, exec. v.p. Fla., 1967—80, pres. Fla., 1980—95, Essex County Coll., Newark, 1967-69; sr. fellow League for Innovation in the C.C., 1995—; Disting. fellow Edn. Commn. of the States, 2000—. Exec. com. So. Regional Edn. Bd., Atlanta, 1981-83; trustee Coll. Bd., chmn., 1988-90; vice chair The Miami Coalition for a Drug-Free Cmty., 1989-94, chair, 1991—; dir. The Bridge Partnership, 2002—; exec. dir. Nat. Alliance Cmty. and Tech. Colls., 2005—. Author: Man and Environment, 1971, No One to Waste, 2000, Yes We Can, 2002, several monographs; editor: Jour. Environ. Edn.; cons. editor Change Mag., 1980—; contbr. articles to profl. jours. Bd. dirs. Nat. Ctr. Pub. Policy and Higher Edn., 1998—. Recipient Disting. Svc. award Fla. Congl. Del., 1983, Spirit of Excellence award The Miami Herald, 1988, Harold W. McGraw Jr. prize in Edn., 1991, The Coll. Bd. medal, 1995; named Outstanding Grad., Coll. Edn., U. Tex., 1982, named one of the 18 Most Effective Chief Exec. Officers in Am. Higher Edn. Bowling Green U., 1988; Disting. Svc. award Dade County, Fla., 1983; Kellogg fellow, 1962-63, MacArthur sr. fellow John D. and Catherine T. MacArthur Found., 1992. Fellow League for Innovation in the C.C. (sr. fellow, dir. exec. com. 1985—, Disting. Svc. award 1995); mem. Am. Assn. C.C. (bd. dirs. 1991—, Disting Svc. award 1995), Am. Assn. Higher Edn. (dir. on Higher Edn. Issues, Higher Edn. Consortium), Am. Coun. Edn. (dir. 1973-75), Am. Assn. for Environ. Edn. (pres. 1970-73), Am. Coun. on Edn. (bd. dirs. 1983-85, 92—), Southeast Fla. Edn. Consortium (chmn. bd. 1981-83). Episcopalian. Home: 1601 S Miami Ave Miami FL 33129-1103 Office Phone: 305-854-4428. Personal E-mail: rmccabe@bellsouth.net.

MCCABE, THOMAS EDWARD, lawyer, financial software executive; b. Washington, Jan. 22, 1955; s. Edward Aeneas and Janet Isabel McCabe; m. Kelly Marie McCarthy; children: Edward Charles, Benjamin Patrick, Adrienne Marie, Therese Eileen, Luke Stevens, Nicholas Joseph, Maximilian Karol, Eva Christina. AB, Georgetown U., 1977; MBA, JD, U. Notre Dame, 1981. Bar: D.C. 1982, U.S. Dist. Ct. D.C. 1983, U.S. Ct. Appeals (D.C. cir.) 1983, Va. 1989, U.S. Supreme Ct. 1990. Law clk. U.S. Dist. Ct. Judge Hon. Charles R. Richey, Washington, 1981-82; assoc. Reavis & McGrath, Washington, 1982-84, Venable Baetjer Howard & Civiletti, Washington, 1984-85, McCarthy & Durrette, Washington, 1985-88; ptnr. McCarthy & Burke, Washington, 1988-91; sr. v.p., dir. corp. devel., gen. counsel, sec. GRC Internat., Inc., Vienna, Va., 1992—2000; pres., CEO COBIS Corp., Great Falls, Va., 2001—05; v.p., dep. gen. counsel XM Satellite Radio, 2005—. Republican. Roman Catholic. Business E-Mail: tom.mccabe@xmradio.com.

MCCAFFERTY, BARBARA JEAN (BJ MCCAFFERTY), sales executive; b. Lincoln, Nebr., Dec. 6, 1940; d. Russell Rowley and Ruth Alice (Williams) Wightman; m. Eriks Zeltins, Dec. 29, 1962 (div. Oct. 1976); 1 child, Brian K. Zeltins; m. Charles F. McCafferty Jr., Oct. 3, 1981 (div. July 1986). Student, Drexel U., 1958—61; BS magna cum laude, Del. Valley Coll. Sci. and Agri., Doylestown, Pa., 1984; MBA in Mktg., LaSalle U., 1998, MBA in Fin., 2002. Dept. mgr. Strawbridge & Clothier, Neshaminy, Pa., 1968-73, asst. buyer Phila., 1973-76; office adminstr. Am. Protein Products, Croydon, Pa., 1976-78; tech. librarian Honeywell Power Sources Ctr., Horsham, Pa., 1978-85; sales dir. Colonial Life and Accident Ins., Wayne, Pa., 1985-86; adminstrn. mgr. Mobi Systems, Inc., Ft. Washington, Pa., 1986-88; spl. rep. Universal Mktg. Corp., Southampton, Pa., 1988-89; ind. contractor McCafferty Ins. Svcs., Doylestown, Pa., 1989—; bus. rsch. asst. Merck & Co., Inc., West Point, Pa., 1993—. Alumni recruitment connection Delaware Valley Coll. Sci. and Agr Mem. NAFE, Nat. Assn. Profl. Saleswomen, Options, Inc., Franklin Mint Collectors Soc., Optomists, Lenox Collections Republican. Presbyterian. Avocations: aerobics, walking, reading, yoga, bicycling. Home: 224 Hastings Ct Doylestown PA 18901-2506 Business E-Mail: barbara_mccafferty@merck.com.

MCCAFFERTY, LEO RAYMOND, plastic surgeon; b. Pitts., Nov. 24, 1953; s. Leo Garvey and Virginia Catherine (Ballard) McC.; m. Susan Mary Kimball, July 31, 1992; children: Leo Thomas, Kristin Rae, Kimberly Lynn. BS, Pa. State U., 1975; MD, Temple U., 1981. Diplomate Am. Bd. Plastic Surgery. Resident in gen. surgery Cedars-Sinai Med. Ctr., LA, 1981-85; resident in plastic surgery Jackson Meml. Hosp. U. Miami (Fla.), 1985-87, asst. prof. plastic surgery, 1987-90; pvt. practice, vol. asst. prof. Plastic Surgery U. Pitts., Pitts., 1990—. Asst. clin. prof. Plastic Surgery U. Pitts. Sch. Medicine, Pitts., 1990—. Contbr. articles to profl. jours. Med. practitioner Govt. Jamaica, Jamaica, 1987. State Sen. scholar Temple U., 1977-78, Measey scholar Temple U., 1977-78. Mem. Am. Soc. Plastic Surgeons, Am. Soc. Maxillofacial Surgeons, Am. Cleft Palate Assn., Am. Burn Assn., Greater Pitts. Plastic Surgery Soc. Avocations: athletics, art, music. Office: Plastic Surgery 211532 S Aiken Ave Pittsburgh PA 15232

MCCAFFREY, BARRY RICHARD, retired military officer; b. Taunton, Mass., Nov. 17, 1942; s. William Joseph and Mary Veronica (Curtin) McC.; m. Jill Ann Faulkner, June 8, 1964; children: Sean, Tara, Amy. BS, U.S. Mil. Acad., 1964; MA, Am. U., 1971; postgrad., Command and Gen. Staff Coll., Ft. Leavenworth, Kans., 1976, Army War Coll., Carlisle Barracks, Pa., 1982. Commd. 2d lt. U.S. Army, 1964, advanced through grades to gen., 1994; ret., 1996; co. comdr. 7th Cav. Div., Vietnam, 1968-69; assoc. prof. dept. social sci. U.S. Mil. Acad., West Point, NY, 1972-75; from chief ops. br. to comdr. 2d battalion 3d Inf. Div., Germany, 1976-81; from chief staff to comdr. 3d brigade 9th Inf. Div., Ft. Lewis, Wash., 1982-86, comdr. 3d brigade, 1984-86; asst. comdt. U.S. Army Inf. Sch., Ft. Benning, Ga., 1986-88; dep. U.S. mil. rep. NATO, Brussels, 1988-89; div. comdr. 24th Inf. Div., Ft. Stewart, Ga., 1990-92; asst. to Chmn. Joint Chiefs of Staff The Pentagon, Washington, 1992-93; dir. strategic plans and policy directory The Joint Staff, Washington, 1993-94; comdr. in chief U.S. So. Commd., Quarry Heights, Panama, 1994-96; dir. White Ho. Office Nat. Drug Control Policy, Washington, 1996—2001; Olin disting. prof. nat. security studies U.S. Mil. Acad., 2001—05; pres. B.R. McCaffrey Assocs., LLC, Alexandria, Va., 2001—; mil. analyst NBC News. Contbr. articles to mil. publs. Decorated D.S.C. with oak leaf cluster, D.M.S. with oak leaf cluster, Silver Star with oak leaf cluster, Def. Superior Svc. medal, Purple Heart with two oak leaf clusters. Mem. NAACP, Assn. of U.S. Army, Coun. of Fgn. Rels., Inter-Am. Dialogue, Legion of Valor of U.S. Independent. Avocations: hunting, reading. Office: Br Mccaffrey Associates Llc 2900 S Quincy St Arlington VA 22206-2231

MCCAFFREY, CARLYN SUNDBERG, lawyer; b. NYC, Jan. 7, 1942; d. Carl Andrew Lawrence and Evelyn (Back) Sundberg; m. John P. McCaffrey, May 24, 1967; children: John C., Patrick, Jennifer, Kathleen. Student, Barnard Coll., 1963; AB in Econs., George Washington U., 1963; LLB cum laude, NYU, 1967, LLM in Taxation, 1970. Bar: NY 1974, US Tax Ct. 1975. Law clk. to C. J. Traynor Calif. Supreme Ct., 1967-68; teaching fellow law NYU, NYC, 1968-70, asst. prof. law, 1970-74; assoc. Weil, Gotshal & Manges LLP, NYC, 1974-80, ptnr., 1980—, co-head trust and estate dept. Prof. in residence Rubin Hall NYU, 1971-75; asst. prof. law 1970-74, adj. assoc. prof. law 1975-79, adj. prof. law 1979-, NYU Sch. Law; adj. prof. law U. Miami, 1979-81; lectr. in field; mem. adv. bd. Tax Analysts, mem. adv. com. Philip E. Heckerling Inst. on Estate Planning, U. Miami, 1978-. Co-author Structuring the Tax Consequences of Marriage and Divorce; Contbr. articles to profl. jours. Mem. bd. trustee Blythedale; bd. dir. Breast Cancer Rsch. Fund, Children's Hosp.; mem. NY Archdiocese Planned Gifts Bequests Com.; mem., sec. bd. dirs. Catholic Communal Fund; chair Central Park Profl. Adv. Com.; mem. planning giving adv. com. Mus. Modern Art; mem. profl. advisors coun. com. Lincoln Ctr. for the Performing Arts, Inc. Mem. ABA (chmn. and vice-chmn. com. on generation-skipping transfer tax com. 1979-81, 93—, mem. coun. real property probate and trust law sect.), NY State Bar Assn. (exec. com. tax sect. 1979-80, co-chmn. estate and gift taxation com. 1976-78, 85—88, chmn. life ins. com. trusts and estates and tax sects. 1983-85, former co-chair com. income taxation of trusts and estates 1988-89, co-chmn. estates and trusts com. 1995-), Assn. of Bar of City of NY (matrimonial law com., chmn. tax subcom. 1984-86, Am. College Trusts & Estates Counsel (fellow, bd. regents 1992-97, mem. exec. com. 1995-97, past pres. 2002), Internat. Acad. Trust & Estate Counsel (mem., v.p.); fellow Am. Coll. Tax Counsel. Home: PO Box 232 Waccabuc NY 10597-0232 Office: Weil Gotshal & Manges LLP 767 5th Ave New York NY 10153 Office Phone: 212-310-8136. Office Fax: 212-310-8007. E-mail: carlyn.mccaffrey@weil.com.

MCCAFFREY, JUDITH ELIZABETH, lawyer; b. Providence, Apr. 26, 1944; d. Charles V. and Isadore Frances (Langford) McC.; m. Martin D. Minsker, Dec. 31, 1969 (div. May 1981); children: Ethan Hart Minsker, Natasha Langford Minsker. BA, Tufts U., 1966; JD, Boston U., 1970; grad. in pastry arts, French Culinary Inst., 2004. Bar: Mass. 1970, D.C. 1972, Fla. 1991, NY, 2005. Assoc. Sullivan & Worcester, Washington, 1970-76; atty. FDIC, Washington, 1976-78; assoc. Dechert, Price & Rhoads, Washington, 1978-82, McKenna, Conner & Cuneo, Washington, 1982-83; gen. counsel, corp. sec. Perpetual Savs. Bank, FSB, Alexandria, Va., 1983-91; ptnr. Powell, Goldstein, Frazer & Murphy, Washington, 1991-92, McCaffrey P.A., 1992—2006, McCaffrey PLLC, 2006—. Contbr. articles to profl. jours. Mem. Leadership Collier, 1998. Mem. ABA (chair subcom. thrift instns. 1985-90), D.C. Bar Assn. (bd. govs. 1981-85), Fla. Bar Assn. (chmn. fin. svcs. com. 1999-2000, exec. coun. bus. law sect. 1998-2005), Women's Bar Assn. D.C. (pres. 1980-81), Collier County Women's Bar Assn. (pres. 1997-98), Gulf Coast Venture Forum (pres. 2001-03), Burleith Citizens Assn. (dir. 2006—). Episcopalian. Avocations: travel, reading, martial arts, Spanish. Home: 3801 Porter St NW #101 Washington DC 20016 Office: McCaffrey PLLC 3801 Porter St NW #101 Washington DC 20016-2947

MCCAFFREY, ROBERT HENRY, JR., retired manufacturing company executive; b. Syracuse, NY, Jan. 20, 1927; s. Robert Henry and May Ann (McGuire) McC.; m. Dorothy Anne Evers, Sept. 22, 1956; children: Michael Robert, Kathleen Mary. BS, Syracuse U., 1949. Sales asst. Sealright Corp., Fulton, NY, 1949-50; with TEK Hughes div. Johnson & Johnson, Metuchen, NJ, 1950-67, gen. sales mgr., 1958-59, v.p. sales, 1959-62, pres., 1962-67; gen. mgr. med. div. Howmet Corp., NYC, 1967-70; group v.p. Howmedica, Inc., 1970-73, sr. v.p., 1973-74, exec. v.p., also bd. dirs., 1974-76; pres., CEO C.R. Bard, Inc., Murray Hill, NJ, 1976-78, chmn. bd. dirs., CEO, 1978-89, chmn. bd., 1989-91, also bd. dirs., chmn. exec. com., 1991—99. Bd. dirs. Summit and Elizabeth Trust, Summit Bancorp, Thomas & Betts Corp. Trustee Found. for Univ. Medicine and Dentistry N.J., 1987-90, Syracuse U., 1979-04, chmn. corp. adv. council, 1974-75. With AUS, 1945-46. Mem. Orthopedic Surg. Mfrs. Assn., Health Industry Mfrs. Assn. (bd. dir., chmn. 1982-83), N.Y. Sales Execs. Club, Sigma Chi. Republican. Roman Catholic. Avocations: reading, skiing, golf. Office: C R Bard Inc 730 Central Ave New Providence NJ 07974

MCCAGHY, CHARLES HENRY, retired social sciences educator; b. Eau Claire, Wis., Apr. 29, 1934; s. Elmer and Anna Josephine (Soha) McC.; m. M. Dawn Ysebaert, June 10, 1961 BBA, U. Wis., 1956, MS, 1962, PhD, 1966. Instr. sociology U. Conn., 1964-66; asst. prof. sociology Case Western Res. U., Cleve., 1966-70; assoc. prof. sociology Bowling Green State U., Ohio, 1970-76, prof. Ohio, 1976-94, prof. emeritus Ohio, 1994—; ret., 1994. Vis. scholar Australian Inst. Criminology, 1984 Author: Deviant Behavior: Crime, Conflict and Interest Groups, 1976, 7th edit., 2006, Crime in American Society, 1980, 2d edit., 1987. Lt. (j.g.) USN, 1956-59 Mem. Am. Soc. Criminology (treas. 1978-82). Home: 221 Williams St Bowling Green OH 43402-3259

MCCAIN, BETTY LANDON RAY (MRS. JOHN LEWIS MCCAIN), political party and state official; b. Feb. 23, 1931; d. Horace Truman and Mary Howell (Perrett) Ray; m. John Lewis McCain, Nov. 19, 1955; children: Paul Pressly III, Mary Eloise. Student, St. Mary's Jr. Coll., Raleigh, NC, 1948—50; AB in Music, U. N.C., Chapel Hill, 1952, LLD (hon.), 1998; MA, Columbia U., NYC, 1953; LittD (hon.), U. N.C., Wilmington, 1997; LLD (hon.), Wake Forest U., Winston-Salem, NC, 1999, Barton Coll., Wilson, NC, 1999; DHL (hon.), U. NC, Greensboro, 2007. Courier, European tour guide Ednl. Travel Assocs., Plainfield, NJ, 1952-54; asst. dir. YWCA, U. N.C., Chapel Hill, 1953-55; chmn. N.C. Dem. Exec. Com., 1976-79; mem. Dem. Nat. Com., 1971-72, 76-79, 80-85, chmn. sustaining fund NC, 1981, 88-91, mem. com. on presdl. nominations (Hunt Commn.), 1981-82, mem. rules com., 1982-85, mem. cabinet Gov. James B. Hunt, Jr., 1993-2001, sec. dept. cultural resources, 1993-2001; mem. State Dem. Exec. Com., 1971—99, 2001—. Mem. Winograd Commn., 1977-78; pres. Dem. Women of N.C., 1971-72, dist. dir., 1969-72; pres. Wilson County Dem. Women, 1966-67; precinct chmn., 1972-76; del. Dem. Nat. Conv., 1972, 88; mem. Dem. Mid-Term Confs., 1974, 78, mem. jud. coun. Dem. Nat. Com., 1985-89; dir. Carolina Tel. & Tel. Co. (now Embarq), 1981-97 (1st woman); bd. trustees U. N.C.-TV, 2002—, vice chmn., 2006—; interim chair McCain Internat. Empowerment Project, 2001—. Contbg. editor: History of N.C. Med. Soc. Treas. Wilson on the Move, 1990—92; mem. Coun. on State Goals and Policy, 1970—72, Gov.'s Task Force on Child Advocacy, 1975—78; chmn. Wilson-Greene Morehead scholarship com., 1986—89; mem. career and personal counseling svc. adv. bd. St. Andrews Coll.; charter mem. Wilson Edn. Devel. Coun.; active Arts Coun. of Wilson, Inc.; pres. Wilson County Mental Health Assn., bd. dirs., legis. chmn.; bd. govs. U. N.C., 1975—81, 1985—93, pers. and tenure com., 1985—91, chmn. budget and fin. com., 1991—93; bd. regents Barium Springs Home for Children, chair Founds. com. Capital Campaign, 2003—; bd. dirs. N.C. Mus. History Assocs., 1982—83, pres., 1982—83, membership chair, 1987—88; co-chmn. Com. to Elect Jim Hunt Gov., 1976, 1980, co-chmn. senatorial campaign, 1984; mem. N.C. Adv. Budget Com. (1st woman), 1981—85; chmn. State Employees Combined Campaign N.C., 1993; bd. visitors Peace Coll., Wake Forest U. Sch. Law, 1980—83, U. N.C., Chapel Hill; co-chmn. fund dr. Wilson Cmty. Theater; v.p. Wilson County Hist. Assn., 2004—; chmn. devel. com., bd. visitors Lineberger Comprehensive Cancer Ctr., 2006—, vice chmn. bd. visitors, 2007—; chmn. centennial Am. Lung Assn., NC, hon. chmn. hist. observance centennial N.C., 2006—07; Sunday sch. tchr. 1st Presbyn. Ch., Wilson, 1970—71, 1986—88, 1990—92, mem. chancel choir, 1985—, deacon, 1986—92, chmn. fin. com., 1990—91, chair, 1992—93, elder, 1992—98, 2006—; N.C. state bd. dirs. Am. Lung Assn., state bd. dirs., 1985—88; bd. dirs. Roanoke Island Commn.; mem. battleship commn. USS/NC, 1993—2001; bd. dirs. Wilson Rose Garden, 2002—. Recipient state awards N.C. Heart Assn., 1967, Easter Seal Soc., 1967, Cmty. Svc. award Wilson Downtown Bus. Assocs., 1977, award N.C. Jaycees, 1979, 85, Women in Govt. award N.C. and U.S. Jaycettes, 1985, Alumni Disting. Svc. award U. N.C., Chapel Hill, 1993, Flora Mac Donald Scottish Heritage award, 1995, Carpathian award N.C. Equity, 1995, Pinnacle award, 1997, 1st winner Holderness-Weaver award U. N.C., Greensboro, 1999, Citizen of Yr. award Wilson C. of C., 2001, Ruth Coltrane Cannon award for hist. preservation Preservation N.C., 2000, N.C. State U. Sch. of Design award, 2000, The North Caroliniana award, 2006; named to Order of Old Well and Valkyries, U. N.C., 1952; named Dem. Woman of Yr., N.C., 1976, Internat. Founders award Eta State Delta Kappa Gamma Soc., 2005; named Outstanding Wilson Citizen of Yr., Wilson Red Cross, 2004. Mem.: DAR, UDC (historian John W. Dunham chpt.), Rotary Internat. (Paul Harris fellow 2003), N.C. Inst. Medicine (bd. dirs. 1993—2005), N.C. Sch. Arts (trustee 1993—2001), N.C. Equity (bd. dirs.), N.C. Soc. Internal Medicine Aux. (pres.), N.C. Symphony (trustee 1993—2001, 2002—05), Info. Resources Mgmt. Commn. N.C. (bd. dirs. 1993—2001), N.C. Agy. Pub. Telecom. (bd. dirs. 1993—2001), N.C. Found. for Nursing (bd. dirs. 1989—92), St. Mary's Alumni Assn. (regional v.p., Most Disting. Alumna 2005), U. N.C. Chapel Hill Alumni Assn. (chmn. 2001—02, bd dir.), Nat. Soc. Colonial Dames Am. NC (sec. local com., program co-chmn.), AMA Alliance (dir., nat. vol. health svcs. chmn., aux. liaison rep. AMA Coun. on Mental Health, aux. rep. Coun. on Vol. Health Orgns.), N.C. Art Soc., N.C. Lit. and Hist. Assn., Wilson Sertoma Club (Svc. to Mankind award 2006), Wilson Country Club, Little Book Club, The Book Club (pres.), Pi Beta Phi. Home: 1134 Woodland Dr NW Wilson NC 27893-2122 Office Phone: 252-243-4248.

MCCAIN, JOHN (JOHN SIDNEY MCCAIN III), senator; b. Canal Zone, Panama, Aug. 29, 1936; s. John Sidney and Roberta (Wright) McCain; m. Carol, 1965 (div. 1980); 1 child Sidney Ann; m. Cindy Hensley, May 17, 1980; children: Doug, Andrew, Sidney, Meghan, Jack, Jimmy, Bridget. Grad. U.S. Naval Acad., 1958; grad., Nat. War Coll., 1973-74; degree (hon.), Johns Hopkins U., 1999, Colgate U., 2000, U. Penn., 2001, Wake Forest U., 2002, U. So. Calif., 2004. Dir. Navy Senate Liaison Office, Washington, 1977-81; mem. US Congress from 1st Ariz. Dist., 1983—86; US Senator from Ariz., 1987—; mem. armed svcs. com. US Senate, chmn. commerce, sci. and transp. com., 1997—2001, 2001, 2003, chmn. Indian affairs com. Chmn. Internat. Republican Inst., 1993—; Republican candidate for presidential nomination, 2000; mem. Commn. on the Intelligence Capabilities of the US Regarding Weapons of Mass Destruction, 2004; speaker Republican Nat. Convention, NYC, 2004. Co-author (with Mark Salter): Faith of My Fathers, 1999, Worth the Fighting For: What I Learned from Mavericks, Heroes, and Politics, 2002, Why Courage Matters: The Way to a Braver Life, 2004, Character Is Destiny: Inspiring Stories Every Young Person Should Know and Every Adult Should Remember, 2005, Hard Call: Great Decisions and the Extraordinary People Who Made Them, 2007. Served in USN, 1958—81, prisoner of war, 1967—73, Vietnam, became captain USN, 1977. Excellence in Pub. Svc. award, Am. Acad. of Pediatrics, 1999, Friendship award, League of Latin Am. Citizens, 1999, Intrepid Freedom award, Intrepid Museum Found., 1999, Profile in Courage award, John F. Kennedy Library Found., 1999, Paul H. Douglas Ethics in Govt. award, Institute of Govt. & Pub. Affairs, U. Il, 2000, William Penn Mott Jr. Park Leadership award, Nat. Parks Conservation Assn., 2001, Citizen Patriot award Citizen Patriot Orgn., 2003, Arthur T. Marix Congresional Leadership award Mil. Officers Assn. Am., 2004, Cancer Survivor of Yr. Cancer Rsch. and Treatment Fund, 2004, Econ. Patriot award The Concord Coalition, 2004, Evelyn F. Burkey award Writers Guild Am. East, 2004, Disting. Leadership award Am. Ireland Fund, 2005; Decorated Legion of Merit, Silver Star, Bronze Star, Purple Heart, Disting. Flying Cross, Vietnamese Legion of Honor; named on of the 25 Most Influential People in Am., Time mag., 1997, 100 Most Influential People, TIME mag. 2006. Mem., Am. Legion, Society of the Cincinnati, VFW; bd. dirs. Community Assistance League, Phoenix, 1981-, Internat. Rep. Inst., 1993-, Nixon Ctr. for Peace and Freedom. Republican. Episcopalian. Office: US Senate 241 Russell Office Bldg Washington DC 20510 also: District Office Ste 105 5353 North 16th St Phoenix AZ 85016-3282 Office Phone: 202-224-2235, 602-952-2410. Office Fax: 202-228-2862, 602-952-8702. *

MCCALEB, ANNETTE WATTS, executive secretary; b. Darbfork, Ky., Dec. 11, 1931; d. Benjamin Taylor and Suzanna Elizabeth (White) Watts; m. John Henry McCaleb, Oct. 23, 1962; children: Jonathan Jeffrey, Suzanna Elizabeth McCaleb Woodhead, Sarah Leslie McCaleb Kaza. BS, U. Ky., 1954. Med. technologist Good Samaritan, Lexington, Ky., 1953-54; lab. supr. Charleston (W.Va.) Meml., 1954-58; chief med. technologist Meml. Hosp., Indpls., 1958-63; assoc. prof. UAMC, Little Rock, 1963-66; sec., treas., co-owner John H. McCaleb Constrn., Inc., Little Rock, 1966—. Justice of the peace Pulaski County Quorum Ct., Ark., 1989—; state bd. dirs. F.L.A.G., 1989-. Mem. S.W. Kiwanis (pres. 1997-99), Pulaski County Property Owners Assn. (pres. 1990-2000). Democrat. Baptist. Avocations: reading, crossword puzzles, gardening, sewing, swimming. Home and Office: 3900 Annette Ln Little Rock AR 72206-5357 Office Phone: 501-888-4253. Personal E-mail: annmccaleb@sbcglobal.net.

MCCALEB, GARY DAY, university official; b. Anson, Tex., Nov. 2, 1941; s. Victor Earl and Vivian (Day) McC.; m. Sylvia Ravanelli, June 5, 1964; children: Cara Lee Cranford, Bryan Day. BA, Abilene Christian Coll., 1964; MBA, Tex. A&M U., 1975, PhD, 1979. Asst. dir. alumni rels. Abilene (Tex.) Christian U., 1964-65, dir. alumni rels., 1965-69, dir. coll. rels., 1969-73, asst. acad. dean, 1978-80, v.p. pub. rels., 1980-83, v.p., dean campus life, 1983-91, v.p., 1991—, exec. dir. Ctr. for Bldg. Cmty., 1999—; asst. dir. devel. Tex. A&M U., Bryan, 1973-75. Leader internat. travel and goodwill groups; U.S. rep. to world exec. com. Internat. Union Local Authorities, 1996-99. Author: Community, The Gift of Community. Coun. mem. City of Abilene, 1985-90, mayor, 1990-99; bd. dirs. Taylor County Am. Cancer Soc., 1972-73; mem. adv. bd. United Way of Abilene, 1979-83, dir. pub. svc. divsn., 1987, chmn. consortium on drug and alcohol abuse, 1989; bd. dirs. Civic Abilene, Inc., 1981-83; treas. Abilene Task Force on Drug and Alcohol Abuse, 1984-86; active March of Dimes; mem. Tex. Sci. and Tech. Coun., 1997-2000. Recipient Polit. Courage award John

Ben Shepperd Pub. Leadership Forum, Austin, Tex., 1993, Tex. Urban Leadersip award U. Tex.-Arlington Sch. Urban and Pub. Affairs, 1995. Mem. Nat. League Cities (nat. steering com. on fin., adminstrn. and intergovtl. rels. 1989-90, adv. bd. 1994, bd. dirs. 1992-94), U.S. Conf. Mayors, Internat. Mcpl. Consortium (chmn. 1994-95), Tex. Mcpl. League (legis. policy com. Houston 1986, resolutions com. Dallas 1988, v.p. region 6 1988-89, bd. dirs. 1989-90, pres. 1992), Abilene C. of C. (aviation com. 1981, 94). Republican. Mem. Ch. of Christ. Avocations: art, baseball, jogging. Office: Abilene Christian Univ PO Box 29136 Abilene TX 79699-0001 E-mail: mccalebg@acu.edu.

MCCALEB, JOE WALLACE, lawyer; b. Nashville, Dec. 9, 1941; s. J.W. McCaleb and Majorie June (Hudson) DePriest; m. Glenda Jean Queen, June 26, 1965. BA, Union U., 1964; JD, Memphis State U., 1970; MSEL cum laude, Vt. Law Sch., 1995. Bar: Tenn. 1971, U.S. Dist. Ct. (mid. dist.), Tenn., 1977, U.S. Ct. Appeals (6th cir.) 1984, U.S. Supreme Ct. 1978, U.S. Dist. Ct. (ea. dist.) Tenn. 2001. Law clk. to presiding justice Tenn. Supreme Ct., Memphis, 1970-71; staff atty. Tenn. Dept. of Pub. Health Bur. Environ. Svcs., Nashville, 1971-77; pvt. practice Hendersonville, Tenn., 1977-94, 96—. Chmn. Hendersonville Recycling Com., 1990-91; adv. coun. Indian affairs State of Tenn., 2005— Mem.: Nashville Bar Assn., Tenn. Bar Assn., Native Am. Indian Assocs. Tenn. (Aniyaweya Nation Eagle award 2001), Alliance Native Am. Indian Rights, Tenn. Clean Water Network (pres. 2001—03), Tenn. Environ. Coun. (v.p. 1987—88, conservation advocate 1991—92), Sierra Club (chmn. local chpt. 1980—81, chmn. mid-Tenn. group 1989—90, 1993—94, chmn. water quality com., co-chmn. forestry com.). Democrat. Avocations: wilderness backpacking, photography, forestry, environmental protection. Home: 100 Colonial Dr Hendersonville TN 37075-3205 Office: 315 W Main St Ste 112 Hendersonville TN 37075 Office Phone: 615-826-7245. Personal E-mail: jeremyah@bellsouth.net.

MCCALEB, MALCOLM, JR., lawyer; b. Evanston, Ill., June 4, 1945; BA, Colgate U., 1967; JD, Northwestern U., 1971. Bar: Ill. 1971. Atty. McCaleb, Lucas & Brugman, Chgo., 1970—85; ptnr. Keck, Mahin & Cate, Chgo., 1985—95, Foley & Lardner, Chgo., 1995—2000, Barack Ferrazzano Kirschbaum Perlman & Nagelberg, LLP, Chgo., 2000—. Chmn. Northfield (Ill.) Village Caucus, 1981-82, active, 1977-82, Northfield Zoning Commn., 1985-88; pres. bd. dirs. Vols. Am., 1977-79; active Northfield Sch. and Park Bd. Caucus, 1980-87. Mem. Chgo. Bar Assn., Bar Assn. 7th Fed. Cir., Patent Law Assn. Chgo., Internat. Trademark Assn. Office: Barack Ferrazzano Kirschbaum Perlman & Nagelberg LLC 333 W Wacker Dr Chicago IL 60606 Office Phone: 312-984-3100. Business E-Mail: mac.mccaleb@bfkpn.com.

MCCALEB, NEAL A., former federal agency administrator; b. Oklahoma City; m. Georgann McCaleb; 4 children. BS in Civil Engring., Okla. State U. Sec. transp. Dept. Transp., Okla., 1987—91, Okla., 1995—2001; asst. sec. Bur. Indian Affairs, U.S. Dept. Interior, Washington, 2001—03. Mem. Okla. Ho. of Reps., minority floor leader, 1978.

MCCALIP, DAVID RAY, lawyer; b. Houston, Oct. 9, 1969; s. Ronald Wayne and Gloria Fern McCalip; m. Silvia Elena Dominguez, Dec. 14, 1995. JD, William Mitchell Coll. Law, St. Paul, 2001. Bar: Minn. 2001. Assoc. Abrams & Smith, PA, Mpls., 2001—04, Tomsche, Sonnesyn & Tomsche, PA, Golden Valley, Minn., 2004—06, Wilford & Geske, PA, Woodbury, Minn., 2006—. Mem.: Minn. Bar Assn. Office: Wilford & Geske PA 7650 Currell Blvd Woodbury MN 55125 Home Phone: 651-769-1720; Office Phone: 651-209-3300. Office Fax: 651-209-3339. Business E-Mail: dmccalip@wilfordgeske.com.

MCCALL, CHARLES BARNARD, health facility administrator, educator; b. Memphis, Nov. 2, 1928; s. John W. and Lizette (Kimbrough) McCall; m. Carolyn Jean Rosselot, June 9, 1951 (dec. Feb. 2002); children: Linda, Kim, Betsy, Cathy; m. Ernestine Mann, Jan. 5, 2004. BA, Vanderbilt U., 1950, MD, 1953. Diplomate Am. Bd. Internal Medicine, Am. Bd. Pulmonary Diseases. Intern Vanderbilt U. Hosp., Nashville, 1953-54; clin. assoc., sr. asst. surgeon USPHS, Nat. Cancer Inst., NIH, 1954-56; sr. asst. resident in medicine U. Ala. Hosp., 1956-57, chief resident, 1958-59; fellow chest diseases Nat. Acad. Scis.-NRC, 1957-58; instr. U. Ala. Med. Sch., 1958-59; from asst. prof. to assoc. prof. medicine U. Tenn. Med. Sch., 1959-69, chief pulmonary diseases, 1964-69; mem. faculty U. Tex. Sys., Galveston, 1969-75, prof. med. br., 1971-73; assoc. prof. medicine Health Sci. Ctr., Southwestern Med. Sch., Dallas, 1973-75, also assoc. dean clin. programs, 1973-75; dir. Office Grants Mgmt. and Devel., 1973-75; dean, prof. medicine U. Tenn. Coll. Medicine, 1975-77, Oral Roberts U. Sch. Medicine, Tulsa, 1977-78; interim assoc. dean U. Okla. Tulsa Med. Coll., 1978-79; clin. prof. medicine U. Colo. Med. Sch., Denver, 1979-80; prof. medicine, assoc. dean U. Okla. Med. Sch., 1980-82; exec. dean and dean U. Okla. Coll. Medicine, 1982-85; v.p. patient affairs, prof. medicine U. Tex. M. D. Anderson Cancer Ctr., 1985-94; chief of staff VA Med. Ctr., Oklahoma City, 1980-82; ret., 2004. Exec. dir. Worldwide Healthcare Svcs., Inc., Waco, Tex., 1998—2002; clinic dir. Claremore Family Medicine, 2002—04, cons., 2002; bd. dirs. Amigos Internacionales, Inc. Contbr. articles to med. jours. Fellow: ACP, Am. Coll. Chest Physicians; mem.: AMA, Am. Fedn. Clin. Rsch., So. Thoracic Soc. (pres. 1968—69), Am. Thoracic Soc., Sigma Xi, Alpha Omega Alpha. Baptist. Home: 225 Whitetail Dr Walnut Shade MO 65771 Personal E-mail: mccallcharles@centurytel.net.

MCCALL, GENE WILLIAM, conservator, sculptor, artist, furniture designer; s. Joseph Frederick and Verna Irene McCall; m. Sandra Ann Andreassi, Apr. 21, 1982; children: Kate, Taylor. Student, Keystone Coll., 1969—71, Elizabethtown Coll., 1971—73, Nat. Acad. Design/Sch. Fine Arts, 1981—82, SUNY, Purchase, 1983—84. Restorer/furniture maker Brumble's Antiques, Richmond, Va., 1973—75; owner McCall's Antiques, Richmond, 1975—78; conservator/furniture designer Reese's Antique Co., Richmond, 1978—79, Antique Furniture Workroom (formerly Stair & Co.), NYC, 1979—82; owner McCall & Co., Mahopac, NY, 1983—91; pres. Gene McCall Conservation & Restoration Inc., Englewood, Fla., 1991—. Instr. wood sculpture Ringling Sch. Art and Design, Sarasota, Fla., 1992—93; judge fine furniture competition Fla. State Fair, Tampa, 1995—2003; guest expert Antiques Roadshow (PBS), Tampa, 1999; spkr. in field; cons. in field. Author: Best of Fine Woodworking (Tables and Chairs), 1995; sculpture, City of Joy (Best of Show, 1993), exhibitions include Ringling Mus. Art, 1998, Kristofer Lindsay Gallery; prodr.: (video series (episode 1) The Art of Gold Leafing with Gene McCall, 2004. Co-founder/bd. mem. Englewood (Fla.) Cmty. Alliance, 2004—05; pres. bd. Olde Englewood Village Assn., 2005. Recipient Outstanding Achievement award, Tampa/Hillsborough Planning Commn., 1999; fellow Conservation grantee, Hillsborough County Pub. Arts Commn., 2004. Mem.: Nat. Sculpture Soc., Am. Inst. for Conservation Hist. and Artistic Works (assoc.). Achievements include patents for new type of extensible furniture. Avocations: photography, kayaking. Office: Conservation & Restoration Inc 860-D South River Rd Englewood FL 34223 Home Phone: 941-473-0345; Office Phone: 941-473-1348. Office Fax: 941-473-2444; Home Fax: 941-473-2444. Personal E-mail: gmccall@ewol.com.

MCCALL, H. CARL, financial services executive, former state comptroller; b. Boston, Oct. 17, 1935; m. Joyce Brown; 1 child, Marci. BA, Dartmouth Coll., 1958; student, Andover Newton Theol. Sch., U. Edinburgh. Senator upper Manhattan dist. N.Y. State Senate, 1975—79; v.p. Citicorp/Citibank, 1984—93; pres. N.Y.C. Bd Edn., 1991—93; comptroller State of N.Y., 1993—2003; vice chmn., mng. dir. HealthPoint, LLC, 2003—. Bd. dirs. NY Stock Exch., 1999—2003, Tyco Internat. Ltd., 2003—. Amb. to UN; commr. Port Authority N.Y. and N.J.; commr. N.Y. State Divsn. Human Rights, 1983-85; mem. Coun. Fgn. Rels., Coun. Am. Ambs.; past. bd. dirs. N.Y. State Commn. State and Local Fin., Harlem Internat. Trade Ctr. Corp. Recipient Nelson A. Rockefeller Disting. Public Service award, 2002. Office: Healthpoint LLC 505 Park Ave 12th Fl New York NY 10022

MCCALL, JACK HUMPHREYS, JR., lawyer; b. Nashville, Jan. 10, 1961; s. Jack Humphreys Sr. and Patricia Jean (Holmes) McC.; m. Jennifer Lynn Ashley, Oct. 4, 1992; 1 child, Margaret Ashley. BA, Vanderbilt U., 1983; JD, U. Tenn., 1991. Bar: Tenn. 1992, US Ct. Appeals (6th cir.) 1993. Clk. Hon. Gilbert S. Merritt, Chief Judge US Ct. Appeals 6th Cir., Nashville, 1991-92; assoc. Farris, Warfield & Kanaday, Nashville, 1992-94; counsel Hunton & Williams, Knoxville, Tenn., 1994—2003, Tenn. Valley Authority, Knoxville, 2006—; gen. counsel CTI Molecular Imaging, Inc., Knoxville, 2003—05, Siemens Med. Solutions USA, Knoxville, 2005. Adj. prof. U. Tenn. Coll. Law, Knoxville, 1997—; bd. dir. Legal Aid of East Tenn., 2001-03. Author: Pogiebait's War, 2001; contbr. chpt. to book and articles to profl. jour. Mem. alumni adv. coun. U. Tenn. Coll. Law, Knoxville, 1992-95. Capt. US Army, 1983-88. Recipient Loevinger prize ABA Sect. of Sci. and Tech., 1992, Bruno Bittker award ABA Standing Com. World Order Law, 1993, Pro Bono Lawyer award Knoxville Legal Aid Soc., 1999, 2000, 05. Mem.: Tenn. Bar Assn. (chair corp. counsel sect. 2004—05, bd. govs. 2004—), Nashville Bar Assn. (elder law com. chair young lawyers divsn. 1993—94, vice-chair internat. law and practice com. 1993—94), Knoxville Bar Assn. (com. chair young lawyers sect. 1995—97, bd. govs. 2001—03, corp. counsel section chair 2006—), Nat. Assn. Real Estate Investment Trusts, Rotary Club Knoxville. Methodist. Avocations: history, writing, genealogy, languages, travel. Office: Tenn Valley Authority 400 W Summit Hill Dr WT6A-K Knoxville TN 37901 Business E-Mail: jhmccall@tva.gov.

MCCALL, JENNIFER JORDAN, lawyer; b. NYC, Feb. 15, 1956; m. James W. McCall; children: Caroline, Hillary. BA cum laude in English Lit., Princeton U., 1978; JD, U. Va. Sch. Law, 1982; LLM in Taxation, NYU, 1988. Bar: N.Y. 1983, Calif. 2002. Assoc. Lord Day & Lord, NYC, 1982-92; ptnr. Lord Day & Lord, Barrett Smith, NYC, 1992-94; ptnr. Pvt. Client Group Cadwalader, Wickersham & Taft, NYC, 1994—2003; ptnr. Pillsbury Winthrop, LLP, NYC & Palo Alto, Calif., 2003—05; ptnr., co-chmn. Wealth Mgmt. & Individual Client practice Pillsbury Winthrop Shaw Pittman, NYC & Palo Alto, Calif., 2005—. Trustee Charitable Founds. and Trusts and advisor to numerous high net worth individuals; spkr. in field on estate and tax planning and adminstrn. Co-author: Estate Planning for Authors and Artists, 1998; contbr. chpt. to Estate Tax Techniques. Steering com., Planned Giving Adv. Com., The Mus. of Modern Art; mem. Profl. Advisor's Coun., Lincoln Ctr., Inc.; trustee League for the Hard of Hearing, N.Y.C., 1992-2003, East Side House Settlement, Bronx, N.Y., 1995-2002, Chapin Sch., N.Y.C., 1998-2001; chairperson Ethel Gray Stringfellow Art Case Com., N.Y.C.; bd. trustees San Francisco Ballet. Fellow Am. Coll. Trust and Estate Counsel; mem. ABA (real property, probate and trust law sects.), N.Y. State Bar Assn. (com. on trusts and estates adminstrn.; chairperson subcom. on proposed legislation on executor's commns.), Calif. State Bar Assn. Office: Pillsbury Winthrop Shaw Pittman 2470 Hanover St Palo Alto CA 94304-1114 also: Pillsbury Winthrop Shaw Pittman 1540 Broadway New York NY 10036 Office Phone: 650-233-4020. Office Fax: 650-233-4545. Business E-Mail: jenniferjordan.mccall@pillsburylaw.com.

MC CALL, JERRY CHALMERS, retired federal official; b. Oxford, Miss., June 30, 1927; s. E. Forrest and Mariada (Huffaker) McC.; m. Margaret Denton, Nov. 28, 1952; children: Betsy, Lynn, Kim. BA, MA, U. Miss., 1951; MS, U. Ill., 1956, PhD, 1959. Tchg. asst. dept. math. U. Miss., 1950-51, instr. math., 1952-53, prof. math., 1973-76, exec. vice chancellor, 1973-76; rsch. assoc. U. Ill., 1953-57; applied sci. rep. IBM, Springfield, Ill., 1957-58, mgr. Bethesda, Md., 1966-68, Huntsville, Ala., 1968-71, Owego, N.Y., 1971-72; exec. v.p. Midwest Computer Service, Inc., Decatur, Ill., 1958-59; mem. sci. staff computation lab. Army Ballistic Missile Agy., Huntsville, 1959-60; asst. to dir. Marshall Space Flight Ctr., NASA, Huntsville, 1960-63; dep. dir. rsch. and devel. ops. Marshall Space Flight Ctr. NASA, Huntsville, 1963-66, dir. info. rsch. NASA Miss. Test Facility Bay St. Louis, 1972-73; pres. 1st State Bank and Trust Co., Gulfport, Miss., 1976-77; dir. Nat. Data Buoy Ctr., Miss., 1977-99; pres. McKool, Inc., Gulfport, Miss., 1982-94, Am. Mini Storage, Gulfport, 1985—, Am Crane Rentals, Inc., 1985-89, Cool-Power, Inc., 1988-93; ret., 1999; cons. EG & G Corp., 1999—2000; pres. Greentree Apts., 1999—2005. Head math. dept. St. Bernard Coll., Cullman, Ala., part-time, 1960-65; asso. prof. math. U. Ala., Huntsville, 1960-62; pub. speaker, 1960-63; chmn. incorporators First State Bank & Trust Co., Gulfport, Miss., 1973-76; tech. cons. Gen. Electric Co., 1974-75 Editor: (with Ernst Stuhlinger) Astronautical Engineering and Science, 1963, From Peenemunde to Outer Space, 1963. Mem. Miss. Criminal Justice Standards Commn., 1974-75; mem. Miss. Marine Resources Council, 1974-76; bd. dirs. U. Miss. Found.; bd. advisers Sch. Engring., U. Miss., 1965-73; mem. indsl. advisors U. New Orleans; chmn. founders U. Ala. Research Inst., Huntsville, 1960-62. Mem. U.S. Dept. Commerce Sr. Exec. Assn. (bd. dirs.), Am. Judicature Soc. (lay mem.), U. Miss. Alumni Assn. (dir. 1966-73) Home: 19630Chanticleer Ct Baton Rouge LA 70809 Home Phone: 225-753-6705; Office Phone: 228-864-1004.

MCCALL, JOHN PATRICK, college president, educator; b. Yonkers, NY, July 17, 1927; s. Ambrose V. and Vera E. (Rush) McC.; m. Mary-Berenice Morris, June 15, 1957; children: Claire, Anne, Ambrose, Peter. AB, Coll. of Holy Cross, 1949; MA, Princeton U., 1952, PhD, 1955; DHL, Knox Coll., Galesburg, Ill., 1993. Instr. Georgetown U., 1955-57, asst. prof. English, 1957-62, assoc. prof., 1962-66; prof. U. Cin., 1966-82, head dept. English, 1970-76, sr. v.p., provost, 1976-82; pres. Knox Coll., 1982-93, pres. emeritus and prof. emeritus English, 1993—; vol. Peace Corps, Turkmenistan, 1993-95. Vis. prof. Turkmen State U., 1994-95; vice chmn. Gov.'s Task Force on Rural Ill., 1986; pres. Associated Colls. Ill., 1986-88; chmn. Associated Colls. of M.W., 1991-92; mem. edn. com. Ill. Bd. Higher Edn., 1985, 90; mem. rural libr. panel, State of Ill., 1992. Author: Chaucer Among the Gods: the Poetics of Classical Myth, 1979; contbr. articles to profl. jours.; research in medieval lit. and Chaucer's poetry. Exec.-in-residence Xavier U. La., 1997—. With Signal Corps, U.S. Army, 1952-54. Am. Coun. Learned Socs. fellow, 1962-63; John Simon Guggenheim Meml. Found. fellow, 1975; Fulbright grantee, 1962. Mem. Medieval Acad. Am. MLA, AAUP, World Affairs Coun. New Orleans, Order of St. Louis, Archdiocese of New Orleans. Democrat. Roman Catholic. Home: 1750 St Charles Ave #317 New Orleans LA 70130 Office Phone: 504-520-6795. Business E-Mail: jmccall@xula.edu.

MCCALL, JOHN RICHARD, lawyer; b. New Orleans, Sept. 18, 1943; s. Duke Kimbrough and Marguerite (Mullinnix) McC.; m. Sara Boykin Ferris, July 13, 1945; children: Sara Marguerite, Katherine Kimbrough, John Mathews. BA, Vanderbilt U., 1965, JD, 1967. Bar: Ky. 1967, U.S. Dist. Ct. (ea. and we. dists.) Ky. 1967, U.S. Dist. Ct. (so dist.) Ohio 1981, U.S. Dist. Ct. Colo. 1981, U.S. Ct. Appeals (6th and 10th cirs.) 1981. Assoc. Middleton, Seelbach, Wolford, Willis & Cochran, 1970-72; ptnr. Middleton & Reutlinger, Louisville, 1972-83, chmn. mgmt. com., 1979-82; ptnr. Brown, Todd & Heyburn, Louisville, 1983-99, chmn. litigation dept.; exec. v.p., gen. counsel and corp. sec. LG&E Energy Corp., Louisville, 1994—. Dir., sec. Ky. Wood Floors, Inc., Louisville. Mem. exec. com. So. Bapt. Conv.; chmn. Citizens for Better Judges; chmn. bd. Metro United Way, 1982-83. Served to lt. USNR, 1967-70. Mem. ABA, Def. Rsch. Inst., Ky. Def. Counsel, Louisville Bar Assn. Clubs: Country, Law Jefferson (Louisville). Democrat. Baptist. Office: LG & E Energy Corp 15th Fl 220 W Main St Louisville KY 40202-1377 E-mail: john.mccall@lgeenergy.com.

MC CALL, JULIEN LACHICOTTE, banker; b. Florence, SC, Apr. 1, 1921; s. Arthur M. and Julia (Lachicotte) McC.; m. Janet Jones, Sept. 30, 1950; children: Melissa, Alison Gregg, Julien Lachicotte Jr. BS, Davidson Coll., 1942, LLD (hon.), 1983; MBA, Harvard U., 1947. With First Nat. City Bank, NYC, 1948-71, asst. mgr. bond dept., 1952-53, asst. cashier, 1953-55, asst. v.p., 1955-57, v.p., 1957-71; 1st v.p. Nat. City Bank, Cleve., 1971-72, pres., 1972-79, chmn., 1979-85, chief exec. officer, from 1979, also bd. dirs.; pres. Nat. City Corp., 1973-80, chmn., chief exec. officer, 1980-86, also bd. dirs., cons. Mem. fed. adv. coun. Fed. Res. Bd., 1984-87. Trustee St. Luke's Found., United Way Services, Boy Scouts Am., Playhouse Sq. Found., Cleve. Mus. Natural History. To 1st lt. Ordinance Corps US Army, 1942—46, Aftrica, ETO. Mem. Pepper Pike Club, Chagrin Valley Hunt Club, Mountain Lake Club (Lake Wales, Fla.), Rolling Rock Club (Ligonier, Pa.). Episcopalian. Office: 30195 Chagrin Blvd Ste 104W Pepper Pike OH 44124-5703 Home: Mountain Lake PO Box 832 Lake Wales FL 33859

MCCALL, SHEDRICK DWIGHT, psychologist; b. Richmond, Va., Apr. 24, 1970; s. Roslyn Annette and Shedrick Dwight McCall; m. Nancy Adelle Swann, July 25, 1992. B, Maryville Coll., 1995; M, Liberty U., 2000; D, Argosy U., 2005. Ceo Youth Pathways, LLC, Richmond, Va., 2000—. Mem. NCAAP, Chesterfield, Va., 1997. Minority scholarship, Maryville Coll., 1989—95. Mem.: Kappa Alpha Psi (assoc.; asst. keeper of exchequer 2004—). Home: 6608 Gills gate Drive Chesterfield VA 23832 Office: Youth Pathways LLC PO Box 34003 Richmond VA 23234 Home Phone: 804-564-4173; Office Phone: 804-564-4173. Office Fax: 804-674-1021; Home Fax: 804-674-1021. Personal E-mail: shedrickmccall@verizon.net.

MCCALLIE, JOANNE P., women's college basketball coach; m. John McCallie; children: Madeline, John (Jack) Wyatt. BA in Polit. Sci., Northwestern U., 1987; MBA, Auburn U., 1990. Asst. basketball coach Auburn U., 1988—92; head women's basketball coach U. Maine, 1992—2000, Mich. State U., 2001—07, Duke U., 2007—. Named to Maine Sports Legends Hall of Fame, 2005; recipient Nat. Coach. of Yr., AP, 2005. Office: Duke Athletics 118 Cameron Indoor Stadium Durham NC 27708 *

MCCALLIE, SPENCER WYATT, lawyer; b. Ft. Benning, Ga., July 11, 1944; s. Thomas Hooke and Eleanor Augusta (Wyatt) McC.; m. Joan M. Schwartz, Nov. 13, 1971; children: Katherine Rachel, Allison Elyse. AB, U. N.C., 1966; JD, Yale U., 1974. Bar: Colo. 1974. Commd. ensign USN, 1966, advanced through grades to lt., 1970, resigned, 1971; assoc. Holland & Hart, Denver, 1974-77; assoc. corp. counsel Manville Corp., Denver, 1977-84; gen. counsel CH2M Hill Cos., Ltd., Englewood, Colo., 1984—. Bd. dirs. Iotech, Inc., Northglenn, Colo. Mem. ABA, Am. Corp. Counsel Assn., Colo. Bar Assn., Denver Bar Assn., Denver C. of C. (chmn. surface transp. task force 1982-88, hazardous waste action coalition, chmn. fed. action com. 1988—). Clubs: Eastmoor, Metropolitan (Denver). Presbyterian. Home: 4150 S Pontiac St Denver CO 80237-2059 Office: CH2M Hill 9191 S Jamaica St Englewood CO 80112 Office Phone: 303-771-0900.

MCCALLISTER, BEN D., internist, cardiologist, educator; b. Fort Worth, Tex., 1932; s. Clarence Dee and Agnes (Horton) McC.; m. Virginia McCallister, Aug. 20, 1956; children: Ben Jr., Scott, John, Tom, Katherine. BA, U. Kans., 1954; MD, U. Kans., Kansas City, 1957. Intern Tripler Army Hosp., Honolulu, 1957-58; resident cardiology and internal medicine Mayo Clinic, Rochester, Minn., 1960-65, cons., 1965-70, St. Lukes Hosp., Kansas City, 1970—; dir. cardiovasc. rsch., endowed chair Mid-Am. Heart Inst., Kansas City, 1996—; and prof. medicine Univ. Mo.-Kans. City Sch. Medicine. Prof. medicine U. Mo., Kansas City. Recipient Nobel award for leadership potential, Mayo Found., 1965, W.F. Yates Medallion for Disting. Svc. in Medicine, William Jewell Coll., 1989, named a Kans. City Super Doctor, Kans. City mag., 2007. Fellow ACP, Am. Coll. Cardiology (treas., bd. trustees), Clin. Coun. Cardiology, Soc. Cardiac Angiography & Intervention; mem. AMA., Am. Heart Assn., Kans. City Heart Assn., Mo. Heart Assn., Am. Fedn. Clin. Rsch., Ctrl. Soc. Clin. Investigation, Met. Med. Assn. Kans. City, SW Clin. Soc., Mo. Med. Assn., Phi Beta Kappa, Sigma Xi, Office: MidAm Heart Inst 4401 Wornall Rd Kansas City MO 64111-3220 *

MCCALLISTER, MICHAEL B., insurance company executive; b. Indianapolis, May 27, 1952; m. Charlene Gray, 1985; children: Megan, Ryan. BA, La. Tech. U., 1974; MBA, Pepperdine U., 1983. Fin. specialist Humana Inc., Louisville, 1974—75, exec. dir. fin. Cmty. Hosp. Springhill, La., 1975; exec. dir. Humana Hosps. in, Huntington and West Anaheim, Calif., 1978—85, Humana Hosp. West Hills, Canoga Park, Calif., 1985—88; pres. Humana Hosp. Phoenix, 1988—89; v.p. Humana Health Care Plans, Phoenix, 1989—92, San Antonio, 1992—96, pres. divsn. 1 with responsibility for Tex., Fla. and P.R., 1996—97; sr. v.p. health sys. mgmt. Humana Inc., Louisville, 1997—99, sr. v.p., office chmn., 1999—2000, pres., CEO, 2000—. Recipient Tower Medallian Award, La. Tech., 2003. Mem.: Am. Assn. Health Plans (bd. dirs.). Office: Humana Inc 500 W Main St Ste 300 Louisville KY 40202-4268 *

MCCALLISTER, MYRNA J., school librarian, administrator; MLS, U. Mich., 1981. Dir. Trexler Libr. Muhlenberg Coll., Allentown, Pa.; libr. dir. U. Balt.; dean of the libr. Ind. State U. Libr., Terre Haute, 2003—. Contbr. chapters to books; mem. editl. bd.: Libr. LiveWire. Recipient NY Times Libr. award, 2006. Office: Ind State U Cunningham Meml Libr 650 Sycamore St Rm 132D Terre Haute IN 47809 Office Phone: 812-237-3700. E-mail: mmccallist1@isugw.indstate.edu.

MCCALLISTER, RICHARD ANTHONY, business consulting company executive; b. Newark, Ohio, Apr. 10, 1937; s. Ward C. and LeDema Mc.; m. Trina D. Gordon, Sept. 1, 1979; children: Todd, Mark. BS, Ill. State U., 1960; postgrad., U. So. Calif., 1960-62. Indsl. cons. Sci. Rsch. Assocs., 1964-66; v.p. Mgmt. Psychologists, Inc., Chgo., 1966-68; dir. Price Waterhouse & Co., Chgo., 1968-75; pres. William H. Clark Assocs., Inc., Chgo., 1975-89; sr. v.p., dir. Boyden Internat., Chgo., 1989-91; mng. dir. Boyden Midwest, Chgo., 1991—. Chmn. bd. DH2O, 2004—; chmn. WHCA Ptnrs., 1986—; bd. dir. Spirian Techs., Boyden World Corp., mng. dir.; bd. dir. Mid Am., sec., treas.; mem. adv. bd. Fiduciary Management, Inc., Lionheart Trust Co., 1988—93; bd. dirs. Opencel, LLC, 2005—. Former pres. Dist. 113 Bd. Edn., Deerfield, Ill.; bd. dirs., exec. com. Grant Hosp., Chgo., House of Vision, 1975-82. Mem. Glen View Club, Racquet Club, Chgo. Club, Mid-Am. Club (bd. dirs., treas., pres. 1998—). Office: 180 N Stetson Ave Chicago IL 60601-6710 Office Phone: 312-565-1300.

MCCALL-RODRIGUEZ, LEONOR, healthcare services company executive, entrepreneur; b. Chgo., Feb. 21, 1958; d. Sixto Rodriguez Hernandez and Dolores Leonor Jimenez de Rodriguez; m. Dean W. McCall, July 14, 2002; stepchildren: Samantha Lynn McCall, Christopher Dean McCall. Licenciatura in Econs., Universidad Nacional Autónoma de México, Mexico City, 1982; MBA, Universidad de Las Americas, Mexico City, 1998. Lic. economist Secretaria de Educación Publica, Mexico. Mktg. mgr. Casa Pedro Domecq, Mexico City, 1984—90, Braun divsn. Gillette, Mexico City, 1990—91, PepsiCo-Frito Lay, Mexico City, 1991—97, La Opinion, LA, 1999—2000; pres. Bus. and Mktg. Solutions, Mexico City, 1997—99; v.p. Face to Face Mktg., Inc., Pasadena, Calif., 2000—03; gen. mgr. Walker Advt., Inc., San Pedro, Calif., 2000; pres., founder Mira Promo, Inc., Redondo Beach, Calif., 2003—04, Latino Speakers Bur., Redondo Beach, 2003—; v.p., emerging mkts. WellPoint Inc., Indianapolis, Ind., 2004—. Adj. prof. econs. Universidad Nacional Autónoma de México, Mexico City, 1982—84. Author: (short stories) Cuentos de Juanita

La Ranita, 2004; editor, translator: novel La Quileña, 2004. Vol. art tchr. 1736 Family Crisis Ctr., LA, 2000—03; nat. bus. adv. coun. Rainbow Push Coalition. Named Corp. Leader of the Yr., Nat. Latina Bus. Women Assn., 2006. Mem.: Mexican Am. Nat. Assn. (assoc.), Women's Bus. Entrepreneurs Nat. Coun. (assoc.), Nat. Assn. Women Bus. Owners (assoc.), Latin Bus. Assn. (assoc.). Democrat. Roman Catholic. Avocations: writing, reef aquaria, travel.

MCCALLUM, BENNETT TARLTON, economist, educator; b. Poteet, Tex., July 27, 1935; s. Henry DeRosset and Frances (Tarlton) McCallum; m. Sally Jo Hart, June 3, 1961. BA, Rice U., 1957, BSChemE, 1958, PhD, 1969; MBA, Harvard U., 1963. Chem. engr. Petro-Tex Chem. Corp., Houston, 1958-61; lectr. U. Sussex, England, 1965-66; asst. prof. to prof. U. Va., Charlottesville, 1967-80; prof. econs. Carnegie-Mellon U., Pitts., 1981-86, H. J. Heinz prof. econs., 1986—. Cons. Fed. Res. Bd., Washington, 1974—75; adviser Fed. Res. Bank, Richmond, Va., 1981—; rsch. assoc. Nat. Bur. Econ. Rsch., Cambridge, Mass., 1979—; mem. Shadow Open Market Com., 2000—; hon. advisor Inst. Monetary Econ. Studies, Bank Japan. Author: (book) Monetary Economics, 1989, International Monetary Economics, 1996; co-editor: Am. Econ. Rev., 1988—91, Carnegie-Rochester Conf. series pub. policy, 1995—; contbr. articles to profl. jours. Vis. scholar, IMF, Washington, 1989—90, Bank Japan, 1993, Victoria U. Wellington and Res. Bank New Zealand, 1995; NSF grantee, 1977—86. Fellow: Econometric Soc.; mem.: Am. Econ. Assn. Home: 219 Gladstone Rd Pittsburgh PA 15217-1111 Office: Carnegie-Mellon U Tepper Sch 256 Pittsburgh PA 15213

MC CALLUM, CHARLES ALEXANDER, academic administrator; b. North Adams, Mass., Nov. 1, 1925; s. Charles Alexander and Mabel Helen (Cassidy) McC.; m. Alice Rebecca Lasseter, Dec. 17, 1955; children: Scott Alan, Charles Alexander III, Philip Warren, Christopher Jay. Student, Dartmouth Coll., 1943-44, Wesleyan U., Middletown, Conn., 1946-47; DMD, Tufts U., 1951; MD, Med. Coll. Ala., 1957; DSc (hon.), U. Ala., 1975, Georgetown U., 1982, Tufts U., 1988, Chulalongkorn U., Thailand, 1993, U. Medicine and Dentistry, NJ, 1993. Diplomate Am. Bd. Oral Surgery (pres. 1970). Intern oral surgery Univ. Hosp., Birmingham, Ala., 1951-52, resident oral surgery, 1952-54, intern medicine, 1957-58; mem. faculty U. Ala. Sch. Dentistry, 1956-96, prof., chmn. dept. oral surgery, 1959-65, dean sch., 1962-77; prof., dept. surgery U. Ala. Sch. of Medicine, 1965-96; v.p. for health affairs, dir. U. Ala. Med. Center, Birmingham, 1977-87; pres. U. Ala., Birmingham, 1987-93, chief sect. oral surgery Sch. Dentistry, 1958-65, 68-69; prof., 1959-93; disting. prof., 1992-2000; disting. prof. emeritus, dean emeritus, 2000—. Mem. nat. adv. dental rsch. coun. NIH, 1968-72; mem. Joint Commn. on Accreditation of Hosps., 1980-91, vice chmn., 1985, chmn., 1986-88. Fellow Am. Coll. Dentists, Internat. Coll. Dentists; mem. ADA (council on dental edn. 1970-76), Am. Assn. Dental Schs. (pres. 1969), Ala. Acad. of Honor, AMA, Am. Soc. Oral Surgeons (trustee 1972-73, pres. 1975-76), Southeastern Soc. Oral Surgeons (pres. 1970), Inst. of Medicine of Nat. Acad. of Scis., Assn. Acad. Health Ctrs. (chmn. bd. dirs. 1984-85), Omicron Kappa Upsilon, Phi Beta Pi. Home: 2328 Garland Dr Birmingham AL 35216-3002

MCCALLUM, CHARLES EDWARD, lawyer; b. Memphis, Mar. 13, 1939; s. Edward Payson and India Raimelle (Musick) McC.; m. Lois Ann Gowell Temple, Nov. 30, 1985; children: Florence Andrea, Printha Kyle, Chandler Ward, Sabra Nicole Temple. BS in Math., MIT, 1960; JD, Vanderbilt U., 1964. Bar: Mich., Tenn. 1964. Assoc. Warner Norcross & Judd LLP, Grand Rapids, Mich., 1964-69, ptnr., 1969—, mng. ptnr., 1992-97. Rep. assemblyman State Bar Mich., 1973-78; chmn. Rsch. and Tech. Inst. West Mich., 1989-91; lectr. continuing legal edn. programs; mem. West Mich. World Trade Week Com., 1988-99, chmn., 1990-91; mem. Mich. Dist. Export Coun., 1990-99, chmn., 1992-97; chmn., CEO TerraLex, 2006-. Chmn. Grand Rapids Area Transit Authority, 1976-79, mem., 1972-79; regional v.p. Nat. Mcpl. League, 1978-86, mem. coun., 1971-78; pres. Grand Rapids Art Mus., 1979-81, 96-98, trustee, 1976-83, 94-99; chmn. Butterworth Hosp., 1979-87, trustee, 1977-87; chmn. Butterworth Health Corp., 1982-89, dir., 1982-97, vice chmn., 1989-91, sec., 1991-97; chmn. Priority Health, 1995-2004, bd. dirs., 1995-2006. Woodrow Wilson fellow, 1960-61; Fulbright scholar U. Manchester, Eng., 1960-61. Fellow Coll. Law Practice Mgmt.; mem. ABA (chair bus. law sect. 2007-, chair standing com. on ethics and profl. responsibility 2004-05, com. on multijurisdictional practice 2000-02, task force on corp. responsibility, 2001-03, task force on tax shelter ethical responsibilities, 2004-2005, editor-in-chief Bus. Lawyer 2005-06), Am. Bar Found., Am. Law Inst., Tenn. Bar Assn., Mich. Bar Assn. (mem. coun. bus. law sect., sect. chmn. 1988-89), Grand Rapids Bar Assn., Internat. Bar Assn., Grand Rapids C. of C. (pres. 1975, bd. dirs. 1970-76), Univ. Club, Order of Coif, Sigma Xi. Home: 5410 Forest Bend Dr SE Ada MI 49301 Office: Warner Norcross & Judd LLP 990 Fifth Third Ctr 111 Lyon St NW Grand Rapids MI 49503 Home (Summer): 265 Clear Ridge Dr Healdsburg CA 95448 Office Phone: 616-752-2104.

MCCALLUM, GERALD CHRISTOPHER, clinical psychologist; s. William Robert and Helen Frances (Kaullen) McCallum. BS in Psychology, U. Ill., Champaign, 1984; MS in Clin. Psychology, U. Memphis, 1991, PhD in Clin. Psychology, 1992. Lic. clin. psychologist Ill. Technician Forest Hosp., Des Plaines, Ill., 1983—86; clin. therapist, rschr., instr. U. Memphis, 1986—91; clin. intern Ark. Children's Hosp., U. Ark. Med. Scis., Little Rock, 1991—92; postdoctoral fellow U. Tenn., Memphis, 1992—93; clin. psychologist, program coord. Alexian Bros. Med. Ctr., Elk Grove, Ill., 1993—98; instr. Chgo. Sch. Profl. Psychology, 1995; clin. psychologist DuPage Psychol. Assocs., Naperville, Ill., 1995—. Mem.: APA, Ill. Psychol. Assn., Nat. Register Health Svc. Providers in Psychology. Roman Catholic. Avocations: reading, gardening, woodworking, travel, running. Home: PO Box 4345 Naperville IL 60567 Office: DuPage Psychol Assocs 1112 S Washington St Ste 217 Naperville IL 60540 Office Phone: 630-355-4070.

MCCALLUM, LAURIE RIACH, state government lawyer; b. Virginia, Minn., Aug. 19, 1950; d. Keith Kelvin and Maybelle Louella (Hanson) Riach; m. J. Scott McCallum, June 19, 1979; children: Zachary, Rory, Cara. BA, U. Ariz., Tucson, 1972; JD, So. Meth. U., Dallas, 1977. Bar: Wis. 1977. Consumer atty. Office of Commr. of Ins., Madison, Wis., 1977-79; asst. legal counsel Gov. of Wis., Madison, Wis., 1979-82; mng. ptnr. Petri and McCallum Law Firm, Fond du Lac, Wis., 1979-80; exec. dir. Wis. Coun. on Criminal Justice, Madison, 1981-82; commr. Wis. Pers. Commn., Madison, 1982—2002, chairperson, 1988—2002; commr. Wis. Labor and Industry Rev. Commn., 2002—03, sr. rev. atty., 2003—. Mem. gov.'s jud. selection com. Supreme Ct., 1993; dir. State Bar Labor Law Sect., Madison, 1988-91; faculty U. Wis. Law Sch., Madison, 1992-. Dir. Prevent Blindness Wis., Madison Symphony Orch., Wis. Women in Govt., Wis. Exec. Residence Found., Combat Blindness Found. Named Wis. Person of Vision, 2002, 1st Lady of Wis., 2001—03; recipient Disting. Svc. award, Wis. Coun. of the Blind, 2002. Mem.: State Bar Wis. Republican. Avocations: fabric art, piano. Office: LIRC PO Box 8126 Madison WI 53708-8126 Office Phone: 608-266-9850. Business E-Mail: mccalla@dwd.state.wi.us.

MCCALLUM, RICHARD WARWICK, medical researcher, clinician, educator; b. Brisbane, Australia, Jan. 21, 1945; came to U.S., 1969; MD, BS, Queensland U., Australia, 1968. Rotating intern Charity Hosp. La., New Orleans, 1969-70; resident in internal medicine Barnes Hosp., Washington, 1970-72; fellow in gastroenterology Wadsworth VA Hosp., LA, 1972-74, chief endoscopic unit, dept gastroenterology, 1974-76; dir. gastrointestinal diagnostic svcs. Yale-New Haven Med. Ctr., New Haven, 1979-85; asst. prof. medicine UCLA, 1974-76, Yale U., New Haven, 1977-82, assoc. prof., 1982-85; prof., chief div. gastroenterology, hepatology and nutrition U. Va., Charlottesville, 1985-95; dir. GI Motility Ctr. U. Va. Health Sci. Ctr., Charlottesville, 1990-96; Paul Janssen prof. medicine U. Va., Charlottesville, 1987-96; prof. medicine and physiology U. Kans. Med. Ctr., Kansas City, 1996—, chief div. gastroenterology and hepatology, 1996—, dir. Ctr. for Gastrointestinal, Nerve and Muscle Function and Motility Disorders, 1996—. Patentee catheter for espohageal perfusion, gastrointestinal pacemaker usingphased multipoint stimulation, esophageal protection by mastication. Fellow ACP, Am. Coll. Gastroenterology (gov. Kans. 1998—), Royal Australasian Coll. Physicians, Royal Australian Coll. Surgeons; mem. Australian Gastroenterology Soc., Am. Fedn. Clin. Rsch., Am. Assn. Study Liver Diseases, Am. Soc. Gastrointestinal Endoscopy, Am. Soc. for Clin. Investigation, Am. Gastroenterology Assn., Am. Motility Soc. (host-organizer 11th biennial meeting Kansas City 2000), So. Soc. for Clin. Investigation (pres. 1997-98), Internat. Electrogastrography Soc. (pres. 1998-2000), So. Med. Assn. (chmn. gastrointestinal 1996-97). Office: U Kans Med Ctr Dept Internal Medicine 3901 Rainbow Blvd Kansas City KS 66160-0001 Office Phone: 913-588-3842. Business E-Mail: rmccallu@kumc.edu.

MCCALLUM, ROBERT DAVIS, JR., ambassador, former federal agency administrator; b. Jan. 30, 1946; s. Robert D. McCallum Sr. and Virginia Blackwell Jett McCallum; m. Mary W. McCallum. BA, Yale U., 1968, JD, 1973; MA, Oxford U., 1971. Spl. asst. atty gen. State of GA, Atlanta, 1979—87; assoc. Alston & Bird LLP, Atlanta, 1973—79, ptnr., 1973—2001; asst. atty. gen. civil divsn. US Dept. Justice, Washington, 2001—03, assoc. atty. gen., 2003—06, acting dep. atty. gen., 2003—06; US amb. to Australia US Dept. State, Canberra, 2006—. Scholar Rhodes scholar, 1971. Office: DOS Amb 7800 Canberra Pl Washington DC 20521-7800 *

MCCALLY, CHARLES RICHARD, construction company executive, consultant, mathematician, educator; b. Dallas, Oct. 5, 1958; s. Richard Holt and Elizabeth Ann (Webster) McC.; m. Shirley Elizabeth Avant, Aug. 18, 1979 (div.); children: Charles Richard Jr., Meredith Holt; m. Judy Lynn Tackett, June 24, 1993. BSME, So. Meth. U., 1981; MS in Higher Edn. and Math. summa cum laude, Tex. A&M U., 2003. Engr. McCally Co., Dallas, 1977-83; owner, v.p. DRT Mech. Corp., Dallas, 1983-95; owner McCally Svc. Co., Inc., Dallas, 1995-97; pres. C.R. McCally & Assocs., Inc., Dallas, 1997—. Prof. math. Navarro Coll., Corsicana, Tex., 1999—; cons. McCally Group, Inc., Lewisville, Tex., 2002—05; mech. group mgr. Hidalgo Internat. Svcs., Inc., 2005—. Active Young Reps., Dallas, 1980—. Mem. NSPE, ASME, ASHRAE, Am. Soc. Plumbing Engrs. (membership com. 1983-89), Tex. Soc. Profl. Engrs., So. Meth. U. Alumni Assn., SMU Mustang Club, Bent Tree Country Club (Dallas), Oaktree Country Club (Garland, Tex.) (bd. dirs. 1986-89), Sigma Chi. Avocations: tennis, boating, travel, camping. Home: 203 Chinaberry Way Coppell TX 75019-2961 E-mail: rick@mccally.com, rmccally@hidalgointernational.com.

MCCAMBRIDGE, JOHN JAMES, retired civil engineer; b. Bklyn., Oct. 27, 1933; s. John Joseph and Florence Josita (McDonnell) McC.; m. Dorothy Antoinette Cook, Mar. 17, 1962; children: Sharon J., John S., Patrick J., Kathleen C. BCE, Manhattan Coll., 1955; MS, Vanderbilt U., 1958; postgrad., UCLA, 1963—66. Civil engr. Raymond Concrete Pile Co., NYC, 1955; commd. 2d lt. USAF, 1955, advanced through grades to col., 1972; exec. sec. Def. Com. On Rsch., Washington, 1971-73, DOD-NASA Supportive Rsch. Tech. Panel, Washington, 1972-74; asst. dir. Def. Rsch. and Engring. (for Environ. and Life Scis.) Office Sec. Def., Washington, 1974-75; dir. Air Force Life Support Systems Program Office, Wright Patterson AFB, Ohio, 1975-79; ret. USAF, 1979; prin. Booz, Allen & Hamilton, Inc., Bethesda, Md., 1979-86; v.p. Espey, Huston & Assoc., Inc., Falls Church, Va., 1986-90; mng. prin. JMC Cons. Group, McLean, Va., 1990—2005; ret., 2006. Chmn. air panel on NBC Def., NATO, Evere, Belgium, 1970-71; def. dept. rep. to physics survey com., NAS, Washington, 1971. Contbr. articles to profl. jours. Decorated Legion of Merit with oak leaf cluster; named John J. McCambridge Rsch. grant in his honor, Inst. Hazardous Materials Mgmt., 2006. Fellow Aerospace Med. Assn. (exec. coun. 1972-73), Inst. Hazardous Materials Mgmt. (Disting. Diplomate, dir. 1984—2005, chmn. 1988-94, Lifetime Achievement award 2005, Founding Father award 2005); mem. Coun. Engring. and Sci. Splty. Bds. (dir., exec. com. 1995—2005, v.p. 2000, pres. 2001), Acad. Cert. Hazardous Materials Mgrs. (pres. 1984-86), Survival and Flight Equipment Assn. (nat. sec. 1977-78), Air Force Ret. Officers' Cmty. (dir. 1997-2003), The Washington Assembly (treas. 2002-03, vice chmn. 2003-05, chmn. 2005-06), Black Tie Club (treas. 2002-03, v.p. 2003-04, pres. 2004-05), Dwight D. Eisenhower Soc. (trustee 2006-), Tower Club, KC, Sigma Xi, Chi Epsilon. Republican. Roman Catholic. Personal E-mail: jjmccambridge@earthlink.net.

MC CAMERON, FRITZ ALLEN, retired university administrator; b. Nacogdoches, Tex., Oct. 8, 1929; s. Leland Allen and Gladys (Turner) Mc C.; m. Jeannine Young, June 11, 1957; 1 child, Mary Hartley. BBA, Stephen F. Austin State Coll., 1950, MA, 1951; PhD, U. Ala., 1954. C.P.A., La. Asso. prof. La. State U., 1959-62, prof., 1962-67, chmn. dept. accounting, 1967-71, asst. vice chancellor, 1971-73, dean continuing edn., 1973-95; ret., 1995. Cons. in field. Author: FORTRAN Logic and Programming, 1968, Cobol Logic and Programming, rev. edit, 1970, 5th edit., 1985, FORTRAN IV, 1970, rev. edit., 1974, 3d edit., 1977. Mem. numerous civic and charitable bds. including Salvation Army, Womens Hosp., Computer Rehab. Tng. and others. Mem. Am. Inst. C.P.A.'s, La. Soc. C.P.A.'s, Am. Accounting Assn. Home: 930 Rodney Dr Baton Rouge LA 70808-5867

MCCAMMON, JAMES ANDREW, chemistry professor; b. Lafayette, Ind., Feb. 8, 1947; s. Lewis Brown and Jean Ann (McClintock) McC.; m. Anne Elizabeth Woltmann, June 6, 1969. BA magna cum laude, Pomona Coll., 1969; MA, Harvard U., 1970, PhD, 1976. NSF/NIH postdoctoral research fellow Harvard U., Cambridge, Mass., 1976-78; asst. prof. chemistry U. Houston, 1978-81, full prof., 1981, M.D. Anderson prof. chemistry, 1981-94, dir. Inst. for Molecular Design, 1987-94, prof. biochemistry, 1989-94; Joseph E. Mayer chair theoretical chemistry U. Calif. San Diego, 1995—; prof. pharmacology U. Calif. San Diego Sch. Medicine, 1995—; investigator Howard Hughes Med. Inst., 2000—. Adj. prof. molecular physiology and biophysics Baylor Coll. Medicine, Houston, 1986-94, adj. prof. biochemistry, 1992-94; cons. to Sterling-Winthrop Pharma., Stardent Computers, Rhone-Poulenc, Accelrys, Kimberly-Clark, DuPont-Merck Pharm., Merck — Co., and Bristol-Myers Squibb; mem. adv. bd. NAS, NSF, NIH and other agencies. Author: Dynamics of Proteins and Nucleic Acids, 1987; contbr. articles to profl. jours. Recipient Tchr.-scholar award Camille and Henry Dreyfus Found., 1982-87, NIH Rsch. Career Develop. award, 1980-85, George H. Hitchings award for Innovative Methods in Drug Design, Burroughs-Wellcome Fund, 1987, Smithsonian award for Breakthrough Computational Sci., 1995, Chancellor's Associates award for Rsch., 2002; named Alfred P. Sloan Rsch. fellow, 1980-84, Centennial lectr., U. Chgo., 1991 Fellow AAAS, Am. Phys. Soc., Biophys. Soc., Am. Acad. Arts & Sciences; mem. Am. Chem. Soc., Protein Soc., Phi Beta Kappa. Achievements include development of the molecular dynamics simulation method for proteins and nucleic acids, of the thermodynamic cycle perturbation method for studying molecular recognition, and of the Brownian dynamics method for simulating diffusion-controlled reactions. Office: U Calif San Diego Dept Chemistry La Jolla CA 92093-0365 E-mail: jmccammon@ucsd.edu.

MCCAMPBELL, EDWIN LEE, physician; b. Kansas City, Mo., Aug. 8, 1943; s. Ernest James and Kathryne Hall McCampbell; m. Vicki Rexrode, Aug. 9, 2003; children from previous marriage: Amy Baluzy, Beth, Edwin Scott. BA, Kenyon Coll., Gambier, Ohio, 1964; MD, Howard U., Washington, 1968. Diplomate Am. Bd. Family Practice, 1974. Intern VA Med. Ctr., 1968—69; resident in internal medicine Kaiser Found. Hosp., Oakland, Calif., 1969—71, chief resident, 1970—71; fellow in cardiology and family practice Howard U., 1971—72, dir. residency family practice, 1974—76, asst. prof. family practice, 1974—76; med. dir. Shaw Cmty. Health Ctr., Washington, 1976—78, Home Health Svcs. Metro DC, Washington, 1976—78, East Orange Family Health Ctr., NJ, 1982—92; pres. med. staff East Orange Gen. Hosp., 1991—92; dir. quality assurance Newark Cmty. Health Ctrs., 1992—98; pvt. practice. Med. dir. Seton Hall Geriatric Nurse Practitioner Program, South Orange, NJ, 1988—90; primary care cons. Abbott Labs. Author: The Pretoria Solution, 1985, A Rendezvous with Destiny, 1998. Maj. US Army, 1972—74. Named Top Dr. in NJ, NJ Monthly Mag., 1996, 2001, 2003, Top Dr. in US, Town and Country Mag., 2000, Top Dr. in NY Metro Area, NY Mag., 1999—2007. Mem.: North Jersey Med. Soc. (v.p. 1978). Avocations: writing, music, photography, travel. Office: 85 S Harrison St # 201 East Orange NJ 07018

MCCAMPBELL, ROBERT GARNER, lawyer, former prosecutor; b. Oklahoma City, Nov. 23, 1957; s. Stanley Reid and Joan Fontane (Garner) McC. BA in History with honors, Vanderbilt U., 1980; JD, Yale U., 1983. Bar: Okla. 1983. Assoc. Crowe & Dunlevy, Oklahoma City, 1983-87, dir., 1994—2001, 2005—; asst. US atty. (we. dist.) Okla. US Dept. Justice, 1987-94, chief fin. fraud unit (we. dist.) Okla., 1990-94, Us atty. (we. dist.) Okla., 2001—05. Dir. Ctr. for Advancement of Sci. and Tech., 1995, chmn., 1999—2001; chmn. sub-com. sentencing Atty. Gen., 2004—05. Mem. ABA, Nat. Assn. Former U.S. Attys., Phi Beta Kappa. Republican. Episcopalian. Office: Crowe & Dunlevy 20 N Broadway Ste 1800 Oklahoma City OK 73102 Office Phone: 405-235-7700. Business E-Mail: mccampbr@crowedunlevy.com.

MCCAMY, CALVIN SAMUEL, retired optics scientist; b. St. Joseph, Mo., Sept. 22, 1924; s. Benjamin Samuel and Della Emma (Cervenka) McC.; m. Mabel Alice Bellerud, Nov. 4, 1945; children: Susan, Nicholas, Carter. BSChemE, U. Minn., 1945, M in Physics, 1950. Instr. math. U. Minn., Mpls., 1947-50; instr. physics Clemson U., SC, 1950-52; chief image optics and photography Nat. Bur. Stds., Gaithersburg, Md., 1952-70; v.p. for rsch. Macbeth, Newburgh, NY, 1970-89; pvt. practice cons. in color sci. Edgewater, Md., 1990—. Leader in nat. and internat. standardization; adj. prof. chemistry Rensselaer Poly. Inst., Troy, NY, 1980-85; mem. adv. bd. Munsell Color Sci. Lab., Rochester (NY) Inst. Tech., 1985—; pres. Kollmorgen Found., Hartford, 1979-89; photog. analyst Ho. of Reps. investigation of shooting of Pres. John F. Kennedy, Washington, 1978. Editor: Papers on Image Optics from National Bureau of Standards, 1973; contbr. over 100 articles to profl. jours., books and encys. Lt. (j.g.) USN, 1943-47. Fellow Optical Soc. Am. (chmn. color com. 1978), Soc. Photographic Scientists and Engrs. (v.p. sci. 1968-72, vis. lectr. 1986), Royal Photographic Soc. Gt. Britain, Soc. Motion Picture and TV Engrs., Washington Acad. Scis., NY Acad. Scis., Inter-Soc. Color Coun. Achievements include improving Munsell color system; development of new principle of absolute radiometry, the compensated variable aperture; discovery of cause of redox blemishes threatening federal microfilm records; design of color test chart used internationally; discovery of visual effects of dotforms on colored grounds. Home: 617 Barton Rd Edgewater MD 21037 Personal E-mail: csmccamy@comcast.net.

MCCAMY, SHARON GROVE, English educator; b. Fredericksburg, Va., May 31, 1961; d. Howard E. and Vivian R. Grove; m. Michael D. McCamy, Jan. 10, 1986; 1 child, Katherine Howard. BA in English, U. Va., 1983; MA in English, George Mason U., 1994. Devel. asst. Corcoran Gallery of Art, Washington, 1983-84; coord. individual giving Nat. Parks Conservation Assn., Washington, 1984-87; dir. devel. Piedmont Environ. Coun., Warrenton, Va., 1991-94; lectr. in English Mary Washington Coll., Fredericksburg, Va., 1996-99; head Divsn Arts and Scis. No. Va. Campus ECPI Coll. Tech., 2005—, dir. edn. No. Va. Campus, 2006—, provost, No. Va. campus, 2006—. Mem. Fauquier County Bd. Suprs., 2000—03; mem. bd. Fauquier County Water and Sewer Authority, 2000—03; mem. Fauquier County Soc. Svcs.Bd., 2004—07; vice chair Fauquier County Social Svcs. Bd., 2007—; mem. com. Fauquier Rep. Com., 1997—; bd. dirs. Fauquier County Pub. Libr., Warrenton, 1996—2000, Libr. Va., 1998—2003, Libr. Va. Found., 1999—2003, Va. Ctr. Book, 2000—03. Mem.: Fauquier County Social Svcs. Bd. (vice chair 2007—), Piedmont Rep. Women's Club (sec. 1998—2000, v.p. 2004—06). Home: PO Box 10 Sumerduck VA 22742 Personal E-mail: sharonmccamy@hughes.net.

MCCAN, JAMES LAWTON, education educator; b. Plymouth, Ind., Aug. 10, 1952; s.Jean F. and Mildred P. (Hayn) McC.; m. Carolyn G. Splain, Jan. 16, 1971; children: Kendra, Brittany. B of Phys. Edn., Purdue U., 1974; MS in Edn., 1981, PhD, 1983. Tchr. reading and English Waynetown (Ind.) Mid. Sch., 1974-75, Yorkville (Ill.) H.S., 1979-80; reading specialist Purdue U., West Lafayette, Ind., 1983-89; program chair Basic Skills Advancement Ind. Voc-Tech. Coll., Lafayette, 1989-91; asst. prof., coord. student teaching Hillsdale (Mich.) Coll., 1991-95; dir. Student Achievement Zone, South Bend, Ind., 1995-96; assoc. prof. Nova Southeastern U., Ft. Lauderdale, Fla., 1996—. Contbr. articles and poetry to jours. Mem. Internat. Reading Assn., Fla. Reading Assn. Avocations: reading, music. Home: 1024 St Croix Ave Apopka FL 32703 Office: Nova Southeastern U Dept Edn Fort Lauderdale FL 33314

MC CANDLESS, BARBARA J., tax consultant; b. Cottonwood Falls, Kans., Oct. 25, 1931; d. Arch G. and Grace (Kittle) McCandless; m. Allyn O. Lockner, 1969. BS, Kans. State U., 1953; MS, Cornell U., 1959; postgrad. U. Minn., 1962-66, U. Calif., Berkeley, 1971-72. Enrolled agt. IRS. Home demonstration agt. Kans. State U., 1953-57; teaching asst. Cornell U., 1957-58, asst. extension home economist in marketing, 1958-59; consumer mktg. specialist, asst. prof. Oreg. State U., 1959-62; instr. home econs. U. Minn., 1962-63, research asst. agrl. econs., 1963-66; asst. prof. U. R.I., 1966-67; assoc. prof. family econs., mgmt., housing, equipment dept. head S.D. State U., 1967-73; asst. to sec. Dept. Commerce and Consumer Affairs, S.D., 1973-79, tax cons., 1980-91; revenue auditor Kans. Dept. Revenue, Topeka, 1991-2000; tax cons., 2001—. Mem. Am. Agrl. Econs. Assn., Am. Assn. Family and Consumer Scis., Am. Coun. Consumer Interests, Nat. Coun. on Family Rels., LWV, Kans. State U. Alumni Assn., Pi Gamma Mu, Sierra Club. Address: 2135 SW Potomac Dr Topeka KS 66611-1450 E-mail: bmccandless@cox.net.

MCCANDLESS, BRUCE, II, aerospace engineer, retired astronaut; b. Boston, June 8, 1937; s. Bruce and Sue McCandless; m. Alfreda Bernice Doyle, Aug. 6, 1960; children: Bruce III, Tracy. BS, U.S. Naval Acad., 1958; MSEE, Stanford U., 1965; MBA, U. Houston, Clear Lake, 1987. Commd. ensign USN, 1958, advanced through grades to capt., 1979, naval aviator, 1960, with Fighter Squadron 102, 1960-64; astronaut Johnson Space Ctr., NASA, Houston, 1966-90; mem. Skylab 1 backup crew Johnson Space Center, NASA, Houston, mem. STS-11 shuttle crew, mem. STS-31 Hubble Space Telescope deployment crew; ret. USN, 1990; prin. staff engr. Lockheed Martin Astronautics, Denver, 1990-97, chief scientist Advanced Space Transp. Sys. Co., 1997—2005, prin. staff scientist civil space, 2005—. Mem. Hubble salvage strategy panel NASA. Decorated Legion of Merit; recipient Def. Superior Service medal, NASA Exceptional Service medal, NASA Spaceflight medal, NASA Exceptional Engring. Achievement medal, Collier Trophy, 1985, Haley Space Flight award AIAA, 1991; named to Astronomy Hall Fame, 2005. Fellow Am. Astron. Soc.; mem. U.S. Naval Inst., Nat. Audubon Soc., Houston Audubon Soc. (past pres.) Episcopalian. Achievements include executing 1st untethered free flight in space using Manned Maneuvering Unit. Home: 21852

Pleasant Park Rd Conifer CO 80433-6802 Office: Lockheed Martin Space Sys Co Civil Space Product Area PO Box 179 Denver CO 80201-0179 Office Phone: 303-971-6308. Personal E-mail: bruce2mc@logcabin.com.

MCCANDLESS, CAROLYN KELLER, retired human resources specialist; b. Patuxent River, Md., June 6, 1945; d. Stevens Henry and Betty Jane (Bethune) Keller; m. Stephen Porter McCandless, Apr. 22, 1972; children: Peter Keller, Deborah Marion. BA, Stanford U., Calif., 1967; MBA, Harvard U., Cambridge, Mass., 1969. Fin. analyst Time Inc., NYC, 1969-72, mgr. budgets and fin. analysis, 1972-78, asst. sec., dir. internat. adminstrn., 1978-85, v.p., dir. employee benefits, 1985-90; v.p human resources and adminstrn. Time Warner, Inc., NYC, 1990—2001; ret., 2001. Bd. dirs., treas. Friends and Relatives Institutionalized Aged; bd. dirs., mem. exec. com. Svc. Program Older People, Inc.; bd. dirs., mem. exec. com., trustee Annie Eaton Soc.; bd. dirs. Time-Life Alumni Soc.; mem. pres.'s coun. Nat. Pub. Radio. Democrat. Unitarian.

MCCANLESS, ROSS WILLIAM, lawyer, retail executive; b. 1957; BS in Acctg., Univ. N.C., 1979; JD cum laude, Wake Forest Univ., 1982. CPA. Pvt. practice, 1982—89; various positions, CEO, vice chmn. FoodLion, Delhaize Am., Inc., 1989—2003; sr. v.p., gen. counsel, sec. Lowe's Cos. Inc., Mooresville, NC, 2003—. Mem.: Am. Corp. Counsel Assn., Rowan County Bar Assn., Am. Bar Assn., N.C. State Bar Assn. Office: SVP & General Counsel Lowe's Companies Inc 1000 Lowe's Blvd Mooresville NC 28117 Office Phone: 704-758-1000. *

MCCANN, BRIAN MICHAEL, professional baseball player; b. Athens, Ga., Feb. 20, 1984; s. Howard McCann. Catcher Atlanta Braves, 2005—. Named to Baseball Am. All-Rookie Team, 2005, Topps' All-Rookie Team, 2005, All-Star Team, 2006, 2007; recipient Silver Slugger award, 2006. Achievements include being the third catcher in Brave's franchise history to have 58 extra-base hits in 2006; having a five game home run streak in 2006, the longest streak by a catcher since Sandy Alomar in 1997. Office: Turner Field 755 Hank Aaron Dr Atlanta GA 30315 Office Phone: 404-522-7630. *

MCCANN, CLIFTON EVERETT, lawyer; b. Des Moines, July 11, 1950; s. George Lockhart and Evelyn Elizabeth (Miller) McC.; m. Marcia Ellen Morrow, Feb. 19, 1984; children: Gregory Lockhart, Jeanna Lauren. BA in Psychology, No. Ill. U., 1972; JD, Columbus Sch. Law, 1977; LLM in Intellectual Property, George Washington U., 1985. Bar: Va. 1978, U.S. Patent Office 1980, U.S. Ct. Appeals (fed. cir.) 1982, U.S. Supreme Ct. 1983, D.C. 1984. Assoc. Beveridge, DeGrandi & Kline, Washington, 1978-83; ptnr. Lane, Aitken & McCann, Washington, 1983-2000; ptnr., intellectual property litig. Venable LLP, Washington, 2000—. Counsel intellectual property Am. Mensa, Ltd., Fort Worth, 1984—. Mem.: Am. Intellectual Prperty Law Assn., Bar Assn. D.C. (mem. steering com. patent, trademark, copyright sect. 1984—, chair 1996—97), D.C. Bar Assn. (chmn. trademark com. of the patent, trademark and copyright sect. 1985—89), Va. Bar Assn., ABA (chair fed. litigation sub-com. on patent claim interpretation 1996—99, chair com. on intellectual property litigation 1999—2001), Patent Lawyers Club (Washington), Delta Theta Phi. Office: Venable LLP 575 7th St NW Washington DC 20004

MCCANN, DIANA RAE, secondary school educator; b. Huron, SD, Nov. 16, 1948; d. Ralph Henry and Rosina Agnes (Rowen) Yager; m. Gregory Charles McCann, 1974; children: Grant Christopher, Holly Ann. BS, S.D. State U., 1972. Tchr. Bon Homme 4-2, Tyndall, SD, 1972—74, 1976—; Avon (S.D.) Sch., 1975—76. Math. curriculum adv. bd., SD, 1992—; coord. Presdl. awards in math., SD, 1998—. Leader 4-H Club, 1986—; sec.-treas. 4-H Leaders Assn., 1992—2000; tournament coord. Bon Homme Youth Wrestling Club, 1986—93. Recipient Elem. Math. Presdl. award for Excellence in Math. Tchgs., NSF, 1993, Disting. Svc. award for Math. in S.D., 2003, Bon Homme Outstanding Tchr. award, 2005. Mem.: S.D. Coun. Tchrs. Math. (pres.-elect 1990—92, pres. 1992—94, treas. 1999—), Nat. Coun. Tchrs. Math. Avocation: gardening. Personal E-mail: dm57062@valyou.net.

MCCANN, ELIZABETH IRELAND, theater, television and film producer; b. NYC, Mar. 29, 1931; d. Patrick and Rebecca (Henry) McC. BA, Manhattanville Coll., 1952, PhD hon., 1983; MA, Columbia U., 1954; LLD, Fordham U., 1966; ArtsD (hon.), Manhattanville Coll., 1987; LitD (hon.), Marymount Coll., 1993. Bar: N.Y. 1966. Assoc. firm Paul, Weiss, Rifkind, Wharton & Garrison, NYC, 1965-66; assoc. numerous theater mgmts. Robert Joffrey, Hal Prince, Saint Suber, Maurice Evans, 1956-68; mng. dir. Nederlander Orgn., NYC, 1968-76; pres. McCann & Nugent Prodns., Inc., NYC, 1976-86; mng. prodr. Tony Awards, NYC, 2001—. Bd. dirs. City Ctr. Music and Dance, Marymount Coll. Prodr.: (play) My Fat Friend, 1975, Dracula (Tony award for most innovative prodn. revival, 1978), The Elephant Man, 1978 (Tony award for best play, 1979, Drama Critics award, 1978, Drama Desk award, 1978, Outer Critics Circle award 1978, Obie award 1978), Night and Day, 1979, Home, 1980 (Adelco award, 1980), Morning's at Seven, 1980 (Tony award for reproduction play/musical, 1980), Amadeus, 1980 (Tony award for best play, 1981, Drama Desk award, 1980), The Philadelphia Story, 1980, Piaf, 1981, Rose, 1981, The Dresser, 1981, Mass Appeal, 1981, Macbeth, 1981, The Floating Light Bulb, 1981, The Life and Adventures of Nicholas Nickleby, 1981 (Tony award for best play, 1982, Drama Critics Circle award, 1981), Good, 1982, All's Well That Ends Well, 1983, The Glass Menagerie, 1983, Total Abandon, 1983, Painting Churches, 1983, The Lady and the Clarinet, 1983, Cyrano de Bergerac/Much Ado About Nothing, 1984, Pacific Overtures, 1984, Leader of the Pack, 1985, Les Liaisons Dangereuses, 1987 (Drama Critics Circle award, 1987), Stepping Out, 1987, Orpheus Descending, 1989, Nick & Nora, 1991, Three Tall Women, 1995, A Midsummer Night's Dream, 1995, In the West End with Robert Fox, Ltd., 1996, Who's Afraid of Virginia Woolf?, 1996, A Delicate Balance, 1997, A View from the Bridge, 1998 (Tony award for best revival play, 1998), The Unexpected Man, 1998, A View from the Bridge (Tony award), 1999, Copenhagen, 2000 (Tony award for best play, 2000), Cobb, 2000, The Play About the Baby, 2001, Tuesdays with Morrie, 2002, The Goat, or Who is Sylvia?, 2002 (Tony award for best play, 2002), The Smell of the Kill, 2002, Beckee/Albee, 2003, Well-, 2005, Who's Afraid of Virginia Woolf?, 2005; Butley, 2006; The Lady from Dubuque, 2007; TV show Piaf, 1981, Morning's at Seven, 1982, Pilobolus Dance Theatre, 1982; assoc. prodr. Orpheus Descending, 1990. Recipient Entrepreneurial Woman award Women Bus. Owners of N.Y., 1981, 82, James J. and Jame Hoey award for Interracial Justice, 1981, Spl Drama League award for co-producing the Life and Adventures of Nicholas Nickleby on Broadway, 1982, Dr Louis M. Spadero award Fordham Grad. Sch. Bus., 1982

MCCANN, GAIL ELIZABETH, lawyer; b. Boston, Aug. 25, 1953; d. Joseph and Ruth E. (Lagerquist) McC.; m. Stanley J. Lukasiewicz. AB, Brown U., 1975; JD, U. Pa., Phila., 1978. Bar: RI 1978, Mass. 1984, US Dist. Ct. RI 1978, US Dist. Ct. Mass. 1990. Ptnr. Edwards Angell Palmer & Dodge LLP, Providence, 1978—. Bd. dirs. Caritas House, Inc.; mem. R.I. adv. coun. New Eng. Legal Found. Mem.: Am. Coll. Mortgage Attys. (RI state chair), RI Bar Assn., Brown U. Alumni Assn. (past pres.). Avocations: hiking, travel, yoga. Office: Edwards Angell Palmer & Dodge LLP 2800 Financial Plz Providence RI 02903 Office Phone: 401-274-9200.

MCCANN, JEAN FRIEDRICHS, artist, educator; b. NYC, Dec. 6, 1937; d. Herbert Joseph and Catherine Brady (Ward) Friedrichs; m. William Joseph McCann, May 14, 1960; children: Kevin, Brian, Maureen McCann Breslin, William, James, Denis Gerard, Kathleen. Student, Caton-Rose Inst. Fine Arts, 1955—57; AAS, SUNY, Farmingdale, 1959; BS, SUNY-Empire State Coll., Binghamton, 1986; MA summa cum laude, Marywood Coll., 1987, MFA in Art summa cum laude, 1989; completed Kellogg Leadership Program, Sch. Mgmt., SUNY, Binghamton, 1992; PhD, Nova Coll., 1995. Designer Patton Corp., NYC, 1959—66; sub. art tchr. Owego-Apalachin Sch. Dist., 1968—88; tutor, evaluator Empire State Coll. SUNY, 1987—; dir. ArtSpace Gallery, Owego, NY, 1992—94. V.p. bd. dirs. Tioga County Coun. on Arts, 1990—91, pres., 1992—95; demonstrator for various schs., ednl. TV and county museums. One-woman shows include IBM, Owego, 1972, Tioga Hist. Soc. Mus., 1975, Nat. Hist. Ct. House, 1982, Visual Arts Ctr., Scranton, Pa., 1989—90, ArtSpace, Owego, N.Y., 1991, MacDonald Art Gallery, Coll. Misericordia, Dallas, Pa., 1992, Plaza Gallery, Binghamton, 1992, Krembs Gallery, 1993, 2000, 2003, Wilson Gallery, Johnson City, N.Y., 1994, 2001, 2003, Countryside Gallery, Owego, N.Y., 1996, 2002, Meml. Gallery, SUNY, Farmingdale, 1998, juried groups show, Roberson Mus., Binghamton, N.Y., 1972, Arnot Art Mus., Elmira, N.Y., 1974, 1989, 1992, Arena Nat. Exhibits, Binghamton, 1974—76, Pennino's Gallery, Burlington, Vt., 1975—77, Riise Gallery, St. Thomas, 1975—78, Grand Concourse Gallery, Albany, 1987, Schweinfurth Meml. Art Ctr., Auburn, N.Y., 2002, numerous pvt. and pub. collections. Bd. dirs. Birthright of Owego, 1993—2003. Recipient N.Y. State Artisans award, 1982, Nat. Strathmore award, 1989, 1st pl. in Graphic Arts award Jericho Arts Coun., 1994. Mem. Nat. Mus. Women in Arts (charter), Kappa Pi (pres. Zeta Omicron chpt. 1987-89, life), Artists Guild. Avocations: travel, reading. Home (Winter): 1776 Atwater Ct Kissimmee FL 34746 Home: 6403 Roberts Dr Victor NY 14564

MCCANN, JIM (JAMES F. MCCANN), consumer products company executive; b. July 28, 1951; married; 3 children. BS in Psychology, John Jay Coll., 1974. Creator chain of 14 flower shops, NYC; chmn., CEO 1-800-FLOWERS.COM, 1987—. Bd. dirs. Gateway 2000, OfficeMax, Inc., PETCO, Inc., Nat. Retail Fedn., Very Spl. Arts., Gtech Holdings, Boyd's Bears, Nat. Retail Federation. Author: Stop and Sell the Roses, 1998. Bd. dirs. Hofstra U., Winthrop-Univ. Hosp. Named Entrepreneur of Yr., Merrill Lynch and Inc. Mag., Retailer of Yr., Ernst & Young and L.I. Assn., one of top 100 Bus. Men, Irish Am. Mag., Direct Marketer of Yr., Direct Mktg. Day N.Y., 1996, Outstanding Bus. Spkr., Toastmaster Internat., 1997.

MCCANN, JOHN JOSEPH, lawyer; b. NYC, Feb. 4, 1937; s. John and Katherine (McKeon) Mc C.; m. June M. Evangelist, Oct. 16, 1965; children: Catherine Anne, John Bernard, Robert Joseph, James Patrick. AB, Fordham U., 1958; LLB, Columbia U., 1961. Bar: N.Y. 1962, N.J. 1974, Fla. 1994. Exec. v.p., chief legal officer Orion Capital Corp., Farmington, Conn. Mem. legal adv. com. N.Y. Stock Exch., 1989-92. Mem. ABA (chair bus. law sect. 1992-93), Am. Law Inst., Am. Coll. Investment Counsel (pres. 1984-85), Am. Arbitration Assn. (bd. govs. 1985-96), Canoe Brook Golf and Country Club. Roman Catholic. Office: Orion Capital Corp 9 Farm Springs Rd Farmington CT 06032-2526

MCCANN, JOSEPH LEO, lawyer, former government official; b. Phila., Aug. 27, 1948; s. Joseph John and Christina Mary (Kirwan) McCann; m. Aida Laico Kabigting, Dec. 6, 1986; 1 child, Angela Kathleen. BA, St. Charles Sem., Phila., 1970, postgrad., 1970-71; MA, Temple U., 1975, JD, 1977. Bar: Pa. 1977, U.S. Dist. Ct. (ea. dist.) Pa. 1977, U.S. Dist. Ct. (mid. dist.) Pa. 1978, U.S. Ct. Appeals (3d cir.) 1978, D.C. 1986, U.S. Supreme Ct. 1986, Md. 1987, U.S. Ct. Appeals (Fed. cir.) 1988, U.S. Ct. Internat. Trade 1988. Law clk. to chief justice Pa. Supreme Ct., Phila., 1977-78; dep. atty. gen. Pa. Dept. Justice, Harrisburg, 1978-80; sr. atty. U.S. GAO, Washington, 1980-96; sr. asst. gen. counsel GSA, Washington, 1996-99; pres., counsel, headmaster The Kabigting-Kirwan Meml. Nonprofit Corp., 1997-2000; atty., 2001—. Mem. Pa. Bar Assn., Phila. Bar Assn., Md. State Bar Assn. Roman Catholic. Home and Office: 204 Bookham Ln Gaithersburg MD 20877-3789 Office Phone: 301-330-1585. Personal E-mail: ajmccann1@msn.com.

MCCANN, JUNE VIVIAN, retired physical education educator; b. Mpls., June 11, 1911; d. William H. and Lillian (Varco) McCann. BA in Edn., UCLA, 1932; MS, U. So. Calif., LA, 1952, EdD, 1954. Cert. secondary tchr., adminstr. Calif. Playground dir., evening sch. tchr. LA City Schs., 1932—37; tchr. Ctrl. Jr. HS, LA, 1937, San Pedro HS, LA, 1937—42, East LA Jr. Coll., 1947—54; prof. UCLA, 1954—57; prof., dept. chmn. San Jose State U., 1957—76, mem. bd. athletics, 1968—78. Com. mem. Calif. Commn. on Children and Youth, 1959—60. Co-author: Exploring Physical Education, 1962; contbr. articles to profl. jours. Charter mem. San Jose City Sports Commn., 1964—73; pres. women's golf assn. Villages Golf and Country Club, 1986—87, chmn. rules com., 1988—89, 1992—96, bd. dirs., 1989—90. Lt. USNR, 1942—46. Recipient Cert. of Recognition for Outstanding Svc., Villages Women's Golf Assn., 1999, 2001. Mem.: Calif. Tchrs. Assn. (life), Calif. Assn. Health, Phys. Edn., Recreation and Dance (life; pres. 1957, Verne Landreth award 1971, Honor award 1961), Western Soc. for Phys. Edn. of Coll. Women (life; bd. dirs., life honor award), US Golf Assn., US Tennis Assn., WAVES Nat., Soroptimist (life; pres. 1965, SW dist. scholarship chmn. 1970, pres. 1972). Congregationalist. Avocations: bridge, music, sports.

MCCANN, KIM LOU M., theater educator, director; b. Joplin, Mo., Dec. 8, 1954; d. James Cleland McCann and Mary Earline (Campbell) Kelley; m. Mark A. Lawson, Feb. 15, 2003; children: Mark Lawson Jr., Marcus Lawson, Arlene J. Lawson. AA in Drama, Diablo Valley Coll., 1974; BA in Theater, Calif. State U., 1976; MFA in Drama, U. Calif., Davis, 1981. Artist, instr., asst. program dir. Short Ctr. South, Sacramento, 1982—; theater, film lectr., resident dir. Sacramento City Coll., City Theatre and Sacramento Shakespeare Festival, 1984—; program dir. Short Ctr. South, 2006—. Chair bd. dirs. City Theatre Sacramento Shakespeare Festival, 1995—; mem. theatre alumni chpt. bd. Calif. State U., Sacramento, 2003—, pres., 2005—06. Dir. Twelfth Night, Love's Labour's Lost, Hamlet, Cyrano DeBergerac, Measure for Measure, Midsummer Night's Dream, Three Musketeers, Much Ado About Nothing, Twelfth Night, Shrew, Equus, As You Like It, Blood Wedding, Romeo & Juliet, Comic Potential, MacBeth and 60 others; actor in over 150 prodns. including Mother Courage, Top Girls, Dancing at Lughnasa, Our Town, Hay Fever, Midsummer Night's Dream, The Matchmaker, Merry Wives, Winter's Tale, others. Recipient 5 Elly awards, Sacramento Area Regional Theatre Alliance, Chesley award, Woodland Opera House. Mem.: Sacramento State U. Theatre, Dance Alumni Chpt., U. Calif. Davis Alumni Chpt. Avocations: pets, music, reading, films. Office: Sacramento City College ACTH 3 3835 Freeport Blvd Sacramento CA 95822-1386 Business E-Mail: mccannk@scc.losrios.edu.

MCCANN, LAWRENCE ALTON, music educator; b. Sikeston, Mo., Jan. 11, 1951; s. William Alton and Billie Sue (Thomas) McC.; m. Vickie Dean Brown, Apr. 14, 1979; children: Luke Adam, Mollie Elizabeth. B Music Edn., Southeast Mo. State U., 1976; M Ednl. Adminstrn., William Woods U., 2003. Cert. vocal music K-12 tchg. Interstate Sch. Leaders Licensure Consortium, k-8 sch. prin. Music/youth dir. First Bapt. Ch., Gideon, Mo., 1974-77, Red Star Bapt. Ch., Cape Girardeau, Mo., 1977-78; news dir., announcer KPBM-FM, Poplar Bluff, Mo., 1979; elem. music tchr. Doniphan (Mo.) Elem. Sch., 1979—; pvt. guitar tchr. Three Rivers C.C., Poplar Bluff, 1979-86; music/youth dir. Calvary Bapt. Ch., Dexter, Mo., 1982-87; music dir. Temple Bapt. Ch., Poplar Bluff, 1987—. Profl. devel. chmn. Doniphan R-I Sch. Dist., 1993-2005; owner Luke and Mollie Music. Composer, lyricist: Mo. Conservation Melodies, 1982, Opus One, 1988, Choral Praise, 1989, We Teach the Children, 1992, Sacred Music Quarterly/Hong Kong, 1993, Luke and Mollie Music, Dare to Live, 1993. Commr. planning and zoning, City of Poplar Bluff, 1982; team coach/youth soccer Optimist Soccer League, Poplar Bluff, 1988-96; team coach/youth baseball, Park and Recreation Dept., Poplar Bluff, 1993; bicentennial choir dir., Gideon (Mo.) Bicentennial Com., 1976. Recipient Cmty. Svc. award Mo. N.G., 1991; Outstanding Contbr. DARE and Drug Consortium, Ripley County, Mo., 1993. Mem. ASCAP, ASCD, Mo. State Tchrs. Assn. (state exec. bd. 1994-2000, pres. S.E. dist. 1992-93, CTA pres. 1984-85, 91-92, 2004-05, Medium Sized Sch. Outstanding Leadership award for state, dist. and local svc., SE Region meritorious svc. edn. award 2001), Music Educators Nat. Conf., Mo. Music Educators Assn., Nat. Staff Devel. Coun., Mo. Staff Devel. Coun., Nashville Songwriters Assn. Internat., Rec. Acad., Gospel Music Assn. Baptist. Avocations: photography, sports card collecting, record collecting, ornament collecting. Office: Doniphan Elem Sch 603 E Summit St Doniphan MO 63901-1142 also: Temple Baptist Ch 1813 Barron Rd Poplar Bluff MO 63901 Home Phone: 573-785-4836; Office Phone: 573-996-3523. Personal E-mail: mccannmusic69@netscape.net.

MCCANN, MAURICE JOSEPH, lawyer; b. St. Louis, July 26, 1950; s. James M. and Marie V. (Del Commune) M.; m. Suzanne Marie Grob, Dec. 29, 1990; 1 child, Mathew Maurice. BS, So. Ill. U., Carbondale, 1972, MA, 1974, PhD, 1976, JD, 1986. Bar: Ill. 1986, Mo. 1987, U.S. Dist. Ct. (ea. dist.) Mo. 1987, U.S. Dist. Ct. (so. dist.) Ill. 1988, U.S. Ct. Appeals (7th cir.) 1998. Teaching asst. So. Ill. U., Carbondale, 1972-76; asst. dir. Vermillion County Comprehensive Employment and Tng. Act, Danville, Ill., 1976; prof. John A. Logan Coll., Carterville, Ill., 1977; adj. prof. St. Louis U., 1977-78; exec. dir. Jackson County Comprehensive Employment and Tng. Act, Murphysboro, Ill., 1978-81, Jackson County YMCA, Carbondale, 1982-83; ptnr. McCann & Foley, Murphysboro, 1986-88; pvt. practice law Murphysboro, 1988—. Atty. Murphysboro Fire Protection Dist., Jackson County, 1988—; instr. dept. fin. So. Ill. U., 1988—, instr. dept. higher edn., 1994-96. Author: A Prelude to McCarthyism, 1974, Truman Administration and Federal Aid to Education, 1976, The Black Sox Scandal, 1986. Mem. Found. for Restoration of Ste. Genevieve, Mo., 1984; bd. dirs. So. Ill. Spl. Olympics, Carbondale, 1983-86; commr. Murphysboro Pk. Dist., 1990-92. Harry S. Truman scholar Truman Libr., Independence, Mo., 1975. Mem. ABA, Ill. Bar Assn., St. Louis Bar Assn., Mo. Bar Assn., Jackson County Bar Assn. Roman Catholic. Home: 42 Brian Ave Murphysboro IL 62966-6189 Office: 1331 Walnut St Murphysboro IL 62966-2026 Office Phone: 618-684-5242. Business E-Mail: mjmccann@globaleyes.net.

MCCANN, PETER PAUL, biology researcher, educator; s. Peter F. and Kathleen (Burnett) McC.; m. Danielle Soury, July 31, 1971. AB in Zoology, Columbia U., 1965; PhD, Syracuse U., 1970. Fellow NIH, Bethesda, Md., 1970-73; sr. scientist Ctr. of Rsch. Merrell Internat., Strasbourg, France, 1973-79; sr. biochemist Merrell Dow Rsch. Ctr., Cin., 1979-82; rsch. assoc. scientist Merrell Dow Rsch. Inst., Cin., 1982-84, dir. scientific and acad. liaison, 1984-90, dir. sci. adminstrn., 1988-90; prof. U. Cin. Coll. Medicine, 1981—; sr. dir., ctr. dir. Marion Merrell Dow Inc., Indpls., 1990-93; pres. Brit. Biotech Inc., Annapolis, Md., 1993-98; interim pres. U. Md. Biotech. Inst., College Park, Md., 1998-99; pres., CEO Oncostasis, Inc., 1999—2001, Mymetics Corp., 2001—03; GG; ptnr. Profl. Fin. Assoc., 2004—. Co-vice chmn. Gordon Rsch. Conf. on Polyamines, 1987, co-chmn., 1989. Chief editor, co-author Inhibition of Polyamine Metabolism, 1987; co-editor, co-author: Enzymes as Targets for Drug Design, 1989; contbr. articles to profl. jours. Mem. Am. Soc. Cell Biology, Am. Soc. Tropical Medicine and Hygiene, Am. Soc. Biochemistry and Molecular Biology, Biochem. Soc. (editl. adv. bd. 1986-92, editor 1992-99), Soc. Protozoologists (editl. bd. reviewers 1989-95), Am. Philat. Congress, Inc. (pres. 1990-95), Am. Philat. Soc. (v.p. 1995-99, pres. 1999-2003, Fédération Internat. De Philatélie (v.p. 2004—). Achievements include patents for method of inhibiting the growth of protozoa, method of controlling phytopathogenic fungus. Personal E-mail: p103226706@cs.com.

MCCANN, RENETTA, advertising executive; b. Chgo., Dec. 8, 1956; d. Aditha Lorraine Collymore Walker; married; 2 children. BS in Speech, Northwestern U., 1978. Client svc. trainee Starcom, 1978, v.p., 1988, media dir., 1989, sr. v.p., 1995; CEO Starcom N.Am., Chgo., 1999—2004; CEO Americas Starcom MediaVest Group, 2004—. Bd. mem. Audit Bur. Circulations Northwestern U., mem. adv. bd. Media Mgmt. Ctr.; bd. mem. Chgo. United. Spkr. in field. Named a Woman to Watch, Crain's Chgo. Bus., 2007; named Media Maven, Advt. Age, 2001, Corp. Exec. of Yr., Black Enterprise, 2002, Advt. Woman of Yr., Women's Advt. Club Chgo., 2002; named one of 50 Women Who Are Changing the World, Essence, 2003, 50 Women to Watch, Wall Street Journal, 2005, Most Influential Black Americans, Ebony mag., 2006, Next 20 Female CEOs, Pink Mag. & Forté Found., 2006; recipient Outstanding Women in Comm. award, Ebony, Vanguard award, Chgo. Mags. Assn., Media Strategies award, Bus. Week, Matrix award for advertising, NY Women in Comm. Inc., 2006. Mem.: Am. Advt. Fedn. (mem. multicultural bus. practices leadership coun.), Am. Assn. Advt. Agys. (chair media policy com.). Office: Starcom NAm 35 W Wacker Dr Chicago IL 60601 *

MCCANN, RICHARD EUGENE, lawyer; b. Billings, Mont., Aug. 14, 1939; s. Oakey O. and Edith May (Miller) McC.; children: Tami, Todd (dec.), Jennifer. BA magna cum laude, Rocky Mountain Coll., 1965; JD with highest honors, U. Mont., 1972. Bar: Mont. 1972, Washington 1977, Alaska 1982. Law clk. to Judge W. Jameson U.S. Dist. Ct., Billings, 1972-73; assoc. Crowley, Haughey, Hansen, Toole & Dietrich, Billings, 1973-77, Perkins Coie, Seattle, 1977-80, ptnr., 1981—2002, sr. counsel, 2003—. Contbr. articles to profl. jours. Trustee Rocky Mountain Coll., Billings., 1973-77. Served with USMC, 1957-61. Mem. ABA, Mont. Bar Assn., Wash. Bar Assn., Alaska Bar Assn. Office: Perkins Coie 1201 3rd Ave Fl 40 Seattle WA 98101-3029 Office Phone: 206-359-8616. Business E-Mail: rmccann@perkinscoie.com.

MCCANN, ROBERT J., investment company executive; m. Cindy McCann; 2 children. BA, Bethany Coll., 1980; MBA, Tex. Christian U., 1982; grad. from advanced mgmt. prog., Harvard Bus. Sch. Assoc. MBA sales and trading prog. Merrill Lynch & Co., Inc., 1982, head US Equities, 1995—98, COO corp. and instl. client group (now global markets and investment banking), 2000—01, head global securities rsch. and econs., 2001—03, exec. v.p., vice chmn. wealth mgmt. group, 2003—05, exec. v.p., vice chmn. and pres. global pvt. client grp., 2005—. Bd. dirs. Am. Ireland Fund. Recipient Annie Moore award, Irish Am. Cultural Inst. Office: Merrill Lynch & Co Inc 4 World Fin Ctr 250 Vesey St New York NY 10080 *

MCCANN, VONYA B., federal agency administrator, telecommunications industry executive; BA, U. Calif., LA, 1976; MA in Pub. Policy, U. Calif., Berkeley, 1979, JD, 1980. Bar: D.C., 1980. Law clk. Commr. Tyrone Brown, Fed. Comm. Commn.; policy analyst Nat. Telecommunications and Info. Adminstrn. Dept. Commerce; ptnr. Arent, Fox, Kintner, Plotkin and Kahn; amb., dep. asst. sec. internat. comm. & info. policy Dept. State, 1994—99, prin. dep. asst. sec. of state for econ. and bus. affairs, 1997—99; sr. v.p., fed. external affairs Sprint Corp., Overland, Kans., 1999—2005; v.p. govt. affairs Sprint Nextel Corp., Overland, 2005—. Office: Sprint World Hdqrs 6200 Sprint Pkwy Overland Park KS 66251

MCCARBERG, BILL HAROLD, physician; b. Seattle, Apr. 4, 1948; s. Harold Carl and Elizabeth Ann Mehlberg; m. Peggy J. McCarthy McCarberg. BA summa cum laude, U. Calif., Berkeley, 1972; MD, Northwestern U., 1976. Diplomate Am. Bd. Family Practice, Am. Coll. Pain Medicine; cert. in geriatrics. Residency Highland Hosp., Rochester, NY, 1979; physician in charge Kaiser Permanent, Escondido, Calif., 1982—2003; asst. clin. prof. U. Calif. Sch. Medicine, San Diego, 1983—; coord. pain svcs. Kaiser Permanent, San Diego, 1974—2002, dir. chronic pain mgmt.

program, 1984—2003; founding mem. managed care task force Am. Pain Soc., 1990—. Adv. bd. Knoll Pharma, Olive Mt., N.J., 1998—. Author: (monograph) Chronic Pain Management: Perspective for Primary Care Physicians, 1998, (book chpt.) A Sample of Existing Managed Care Organizations Pain Programs, 1999; contbr. articles to profl. jours. Recipient K Star for Outstanding Svc., Kaiser Permanente, San Diego, 1985, 92, Award of Excellence Southern Calif. Cancer Pain Initiative, L.A., 1999. Mem. Am. Acad. Pain Medicine, Am. Pain Soc. (chair managed care com. 2000—, bd. dirs., Elizabeth Narcessian award 2003), Western Pain Soc. (chair program 1999—, pres.), Appraisal Physician Svcs., Phi Beta Kappa. Avocations: running, guitar, golf. Office: Kaiser Permanente 732 N Broadway Escondido CA 92025

MCCARDELL, JAMES ELTON, retired naval officer; b. Daytona Beach, Fla., Jan. 22, 1931; s. J. Elton and Margaret Almira (Payne) McC.; m. Nancy Ann Chandler, July 9, 1955; children: Jenise, Patrick. Student, U. Fla., Gainesville, 1948-50; BA, US Naval Postgrad. Sch., 1965. Commd. ensign USN, 1952, advanced through grades to rear adm., 1980; exec. officer USS Forrestal, 1972-73; dep. chief of staff Air Readiness Staff, Chief Naval Res., New Orleans, 1973-76; comdg. officer NAS, Key West, Fla., 1976-78; chief of staff Staff of Chief Naval Res., New Orleans, 1978-80; def. and naval attache US Embassy, Brasilia, Brazil, 1981-83; dir. Inter-Am. Def. Coll., Fort L.J. McNair, Washington, 1983-85; ret., 1985. Decorated Legion of Merit with cluster, Bronze Star medal, Air medal with 12 clusters, Def. Disting. Service medal, Def. Superior Performance medal Republican. Roman Catholic. Home: PO Box 719 Pass Christian MS 39571-0719 *The absolute measure of successful leadership has always been reflected by performance of subordinates in the achievement of unit goals.*

MCCARDELL, JOHN MALCOLM, JR., history professor, academic administrator; b. Frederick, Md., June 17, 1949; s. John Malcolm and Susan (Lane) McCardell; m. Bonnie Greenwald, Dec. 30, 1976; children: John Malcolm III, James Benjamin Lee. AB, Washington and Lee U., 1971; postgrad., John Hopkins U., 1972-73; PhD, Harvard U., 1976; LittD (hon.), Washington and Lee U., 1997; LHD (hon.), St. Michael's Coll., 2004. From asst. prof. history to prof. Middlebury (Vt.) Coll., 1976—87, prof. history, 1987—, dean facuty, 1988-89, provost, v.p for academic affairs, 1989-91, acting pres., 1991-92, pres., 1992—2004, pres. emeritus, 2004—; sr. rsch fellow U. S.C., Columbia, 1980-81, 96. Bd. dirs. Nat. Bank Middlebury, Comm. fin. Svcs. Group; vice chmn. bd. trustees Episc. H.S., 2004—. Author: The Idea of a Southern Nation, 1979 (Allan Nevins award, 1977); editor: A Master's Due, 1985. Bd. trustees Am. Civil War Ctr., Tredegar, Va. Sgt. USAR, 1971—77. Recipient Algernon Sydney Sullivan prize, Washington and Lee U., 1971, Charles Eliot medal, Eliot House Harvard U., 1976; fellow, NEH, 1980, Am. Philosophical Soc., 1979. Mem.: Vt. Hist. Soc., S.C. History Soc., So. Hist. Assn., Orgn. Am. Historians, Am. Hist. Assn., Lambda Chi Alpha, Phi Beta Kappa, Omicron Delta Kappa.

MCCAREY, WILMA RUTH, retired lawyer; b. St. Louis, Dec. 7, 1943; d. Ferdinand Martin and Ruth Anna Cora Kisro; m. Michael Carl McCarey, Aug. 21, 1965; children: Darren Michael, David Brian. BS in Math. with honors, Valparaiso U., Ind., 1965; JD with honors, George Washington U., 1978. Bar: DC, Va., U.S. Dist. Ct. Md., U.S. Dist. Ct. DC, U.S. Ct. Appeals (DC cir.), U.S. Ct. Appeals (4th cir.). Computer sys. analyst Tech. Ops., Inc., Rosslyn, Va., 1965—66, Kroger Co., Cin., 1966—69; rsch. asst. govt. contracts George Washington Nat. Law Ctr., 1976—78; atty. C&P Telephone/Bell Atlantic (now Verizon), 1978—83; sr. atty. AT&T Corp. Mid Atlantic Region, 1983—85, gen. atty., 1985—95, v.p. govt. affairs, pres. comm. Va., Md., W.Va. and DC, 1995—2001; ret., 2001. Bd. dirs. Fairfax Edn. Found., Fairfax C. of C., Fairfax Symphony, Juvenile Diabetes Rsch. Found., No. Va. Luth. Campus Ministries, Va. Econ. Bridge, Vol. Fairfax, Character Counts; mem. adv. bd. Women Execs. in State Govt. Mem.: Va. Telephone Industry Assn. (sec., treas. exec. bd.). Lutheran. Avocations: sailing, golf, travel, exercise, volunteering.

MCCARL, HENRY NEWTON, economist, geologist, consultant, venture capitalist; b. Balt., Jan. 24, 1941; s. Fred Henderson and Mary Y. McCarl; m. Louise Becker Rys, June 8, 1963 (div. 1985); children: Katherine Lynne(dec.), Patricia Louise, Fredrick James; m. Mary Frederica Rhinelander, Jan. 31, 1987; 1 stepchild, Francesca C. Morgan. BS in Earth Sci., MIT, 1962; MS in Geology, Pa. State U., 1964, PhD in Mineral Econ., 1969. Lic. profl. geologist Ala., N.H. Market rsch. analyst Vulcan Materials Co., 1966-69; asst. prof. econ., asst. prof. geology U. Ala., Birmingham, 1969-72, assoc. prof. econ., 1973-77, assoc. prof. econ. and geology, 1978-91, prof. econs. and geology, 1991-95, prof. econ., edn. and geology, 1995-2001, prof. emeritus, 2001—, dir. Ctr. for Econ. Edn., Sch. Bus., 1987-2001; chief econ. div. Ala. Energy Mgmt. Bd., Montgomery, 1973-74; sr. lectr. in energy econs. Fulbright-Hays Program, Bucharest, Romania, 1977-78; ret., 2001. Mng. dir. McCarl & Assocs., Gloucester, Mass., 1969—; vis. fellow Grad. Sch. Arts and Scis. Harvard U., Cambridge, Mass., 1987; ptnr. Economagic, 1999—; dir. Pebble Creek Mining, Ltd., 1999—. Co-author: Energy Conservation Economics, 1986, Introduction to Energy Conservation, 1987; contbr. articles to profl. jours. Mem. Birmingham Planning Commn., 1974—86, chmn., 1980—86; dist. commr. Boy Scouts Am., Birmingham, 1988—94, asst. coun. Com. Greater Ala. Coun., 1999—2001; mem. Glouster Planning Bd., 2002—; mem. edn. coun. MIT, 1974—. Recipient George B. Morgan award, MIT Alumni Assn., 1999. Mem.: SAR (life; nat. trustee 1996—97, treas. gen. 2000—03, sec. gen. 2003—04, pres. gen. 2004—05, chmn. found. bd. 2004—05, nat. trustee 2004—07), Nat. Gavel Soc., Ala. Geol. Soc., Mineral Econ. and Mgmt. Soc. (pres. 1992—93), Am. Inst. Profl. Geologists (sect. pres. 1981—83, registered profl. geologist), Soc. Mining Engr. of AIME (bd. dirs. 1978—80, Disting. Mem. award 2000), St. Andrews Soc. Mid-South (life; sec. 1996—97), Sovereign Mil. Order the Temple Jerusalem. Republican. Episcopalian. Avocations: amateur radio, woodworking, beekeeping, model railroading. Home: 28 Old Nugent Farm Rd Gloucester MA 01930-3167 Office: 112 Eastern Ave Gloucester MA 01930 Office Phone: 978-283-6344. Business E-Mail: hmccarl@alum.mit.edu.

MCCARNEY, DAN, former college football coach; b. Iowa City, Iowa, July 28, 1953; m. Margy McCarney; children: Shane, Jillian, Melanie. BS, U. Iowa, 1975. Asst. coach Iowa U. Hawkeyes, 1977-89; defensive coord., defensive line coach U. Wis. Badgers, 1990-94; head coach Iowa State U. Cyclones, 1995—2006. Named Big-12 Coach of the Yr., Collegefootballnews.com, 2001. Mem. Am. Football Coaches Assn. *

MCCARRICK, EDWARD R., publishing executive; married; 2 children. Grad., Manhattan Coll., NY, 1971. Sales trainee to pub. Time Mag., NYC, 1973—99, pub., 1999—, worldwide pres., 2005—; sales dir. Life Mag., NYC, 1988—91, pub., 1993—99. Vol. Cath. Charities; bd. dirs. YMCA/YWCA. Avocations: golf, squash, tennis. Office: Time Inc 1271 Avenue of the Americas New York NY 10020-1300 Office Phone: 212-522-3273. E-mail: ed_mccarrick@timeinc.com. *

MCCARRICK, THEODORE CARDINAL, archbishop emeritus; b. NYC, July 7, 1930; s. Theodore Egan and Margaret (McLaughlin) McCarrick. AB, St. Joseph's Sem., 1954, AM, 1958; MA, Cath. U., 1960, PhD, 1963. Ordained priest Roman Cath. Ch., 1958, Episcopal ordination 1977. Asst. chaplain Cath. U. Am., Washington, 1959—61, dean students, 1961—63, asst. to rector, dir. devel., 1963—65, instr. dept. sociology, 1961—65; domestic prelate, 1965; pres. Cath. U. PR, 1965—69; assoc. dir. edn. Archdiocese of NY, 1969—71; sec. to Cardinal-Archbishop NY, 1971—77; aux. bishop, 1977—81; titular bishop of Rusibisir, 1977—81; apptd. first bishop Diocese of Metuchen, NJ, 1981, first bishop, 1982—86; archbishop Archdiocese of Newark, 1986—2000, Archdiocese of Washington, 2001—06, archbishop emeritus, 2006; created Cardinal titular ch. Saints Nereus e Archilleus, 2001. Mem. Fed. Commn. for Study of Migration and Econ. Devel., 1989; policy bd. Washington Consortium, Peace Corps, 1962—63, Pontifical Commn. for Migrants and Refugees, 1987; chmn. U.S. Bishops Com. on Migration, 1986—89, 1992—95, Gov.'s Commn. for Higher Edn. in P.R., 1968, P.R. Adv. Coun. on Tech. and Vocat. Edn., 1968—69; with US Sec. of State's Adv. Com. on Religious Freedom Abroad, 1996—99, US Com. Internat. Religious Freedom, 1999—2001, Synod for Am. and Post Synod Coun.; Episcopal promoter Apostleship of the Sea, 1989—92; chmn. Com. Aid to Ch. in Ctrl. and Ea. Europe, U.S. Conf. of Cath. Bishops, 1992—96, chmn. internat. policy com., 1996—99, chmn. domestic policy com., 2002—05. Sec.-treas. Papal Found., 1988—96, pres., 1997—. Decorated officer, knight grand cross Holy Sepulchre, Order of Cedars of Lebanon. Mem.: Knights Malta (chaplain 1978—82). Roman Catholic.

MCCARRON, DOUGLAS J., labor union administrator; b. LA, Sept. 23, 1950; V.p., sec.-treas. LA County Dist. Coun. of Carpenters, pres., 1983; mem. Local 1506 United Brotherhood of Carpenters, LA, 1968, v.p., 1994—95; pres. United Brotherhood of Carpenters and Joiners Am., Washington, 1995—. Former bd. mem. ULLICO Inc.; mem. S. Calif. Council of Carpenters; trustee S. Calif. Pension Fund; pres. So. Calif. Conf. Carpenters, 1982. Office: United Brotherhood of Carpenters and Joiners 101 Constitution Ave NW Washington DC 20001-2133 also: 1221 Massachusetts Ave Washington DC 20005 Office Phone: 202-546-6206. *

MCCARRON, JOHN FRANCIS, editor; b. Providence, Jan. 20, 1949; s. Hugh Francis and Katherine Anne (Brooks) McC.; m. Janet Ann Velsor, Sept. 3, 1971; children: Veronica, Catherine. BS in Journalism, Northwestern U., 1970, MS in Journalism, 1973. Gen. assignment reporter Chgo. Tribune, 1973-80, urban affairs writer, 1980-91, fin. editor, 1991-92, editorial bd. columnist, 1992-2000; v.p. strategy and comms. Met. Planning Coun. Chgo., 2000—02; adj. prof. Medill Sch. Journalism Northwestern U., 2002—. Contbr. to Planning mag., World Book Ency., Preservation mag. Lt. USNR, 1970-72. Recipient Editors award AP, 1983, 84, Ann. Journalism award Am. Planning Assn., 1983, Heywood Broun award Am. Newspaper Guild, Washington, 1989, Peter Lisagor award Soc. Profl. Journalists, 1994, Nat. Journalism award Lambda Alpha Internat., 2007. Home: 1425 Noyes St Evanston IL 60201-2639 E-mail: j.mccarron@att.net.

MC CARTAN, PATRICK FRANCIS, lawyer; b. Cleve., Aug. 3, 1934; s. Patrick Francis and Stella Mercedes (Ashton) Mc Cartan; m. Lois Ann Buchman, Aug. 30, 1958; children: M. Karen, Patrick Francis III. AB magna cum laude, U. Notre Dame, 1956, JD, 1959. Bar: Ohio 1960, U.S. Ct. Appeals (6th cir.) 1961, U.S. Ct. Appeals (3rd cir.) 1965, U.S. Ct. Appeals (DC cir.) 1980, U.S. Ct. Appeals (5th cir.) 1981, U.S. Ct. Appeals (4th cir.) 1989, U.S. Ct. Appeals (7th cir.) 1992, U.S. Supreme Ct. 1970. Law clk. to Hon. Charles Evans Whittaker, U.S. Supreme Ct., 1959; assoc. Jones Day, Cleve., 1961—65, ptnr., 1966—93, mng. ptnr., 1993—2002, sr. ptnr., 2003—. Trustee U. Notre Dame, 1989—, chair, 2000—07; trustee Cleve. Clinic Found.; standing com. on rules of practice and procedure Jud. Conf. of US. Fellow: Internat. Acad. Trial Lawyers, Am. Coll. Trial Lawyers; mem.: ABA, Bar Assn. Greater Cleve. (pres. 1977—78), Ohio Bar Assn., 6th Cir. Jud. Conf. (life), U.S.-Japan Bus. Coun., Coun. on Fgn. Rels., Greater Cleve. Growth Assn. (chmn. 1997—2000). Roman Catholic. Office: Jones Day North Point 901 Lakeside Ave E Cleveland OH 44114-1190 Office Phone: 216-586-3939, 216-586-7272. Business E-Mail: pmccartan@jonesday.com.

MCCARTER, CHARLES CHASE, lawyer; b. Pleasanton, Kans., Mar. 17, 1926; s. Charles Nelson and Donna (Chase) McC.; m. Clarice Blanchard, June 25, 1950; children: Charles Kevin, Cheryl Ann. BA, Principia Coll., 1950; JD, Washburn U., 1953; LLM, Yale U., 1954. Bar: Kans. 1953, U.S. Supreme Ct. 1962, Mo. 1968. Asst. atty. gen. State of Kans., 1954-57; lectr. law sch. Washburn U., 1956-57; appellate counsel FCC, Washington, 1957-58; assoc. Weigand, Curfman, Brainerd, Harris & Kaufman, Wichita, 1958-61; gen. counsel Kans. Corp. Commn., 1961-63; ptnr. McCarter, Frizzel & Wettig, Wichita, 1963-68, McCarter & Badger, Wichita, 1968-73; pvt. practice law St. Louis, 1968-76; ptnr. McCarter & Greenley, St. Louis, 1976-85; mng. ptnr. Gage & Tucker, St. Louis, 1985-87, Husch and Eppenberger, St. Louis, 1987-89, McCarter & Greenley, LLC, St. Louis, 1990—. Prof. law, assoc. dir. law sch. Nat. Energy Law and Policy Inst. Tulsa U., 1977-79; prof. law, coach nat. moot ct. coll. of law Stetson U. Coll., St. Petersburg, Fla., 1980-84; mem. govtl. adv. coun. Gulf Oil Corp., 1977-81; legal com. Interstate Oil Compact Commn.; mem. adv. bd. Allegiant Bank, 1997—. Co-author: Missouri Lawyers Guide; assoc. editor Washburn U. Law Rev., 1952-53; contbr. articles to profl. jours. Chmn. Wichita Human Rels. Devel. Adv. Bd., 1967-68; bd. dirs. Peace Haven Assn.; active St. Louis Estate Planning Coun., 1987—; mem. bequests and endowment com. Salvation Army, 1995—; mem. YMCA endowment com., 1996—; mem. gifts and endowment bd. TV Channel 9, KETC, St. Louis, 2004—. With USNR, 1944-46. Recipient Excellent Prof. award U. Tulsa, 1979; vis. scholar Yale U., 1980 Mem. ABA (sect. real property, probate and trust law, bus. law sect.), Kans. Bar Assn., Mo. Bar Assn. (probate and trust com., tax com.), Am. Legion, VFW, Native Sons and Daus. Kans (pres. 1957-58), Kappa Sigma, Delta Theta Phi, Principia Dads Club (bd. dirs.) Republican. Office: One Metropolitan Sq Ste 2100 Saint Louis MO 63102-2751 Office Phone: 314-436-2100 ext. 107. Business E-Mail: cmccarter@mccartergreenley.com.

MCCARTER, DAVID HAROLD, historian, volunteer; b. Franklin, Ind., Sept. 21, 1958; s. Harold Wilbur and Lois Lavoune (Banjamin) McCarter; m. L. Kristine Bennett, Sept. 26, 1981; children: Natasha Renee MaCarter, Nathan Eric. BA, Lincoln Christian Coll., Ill., 1980; MA, Lincoln Christian Sem., Ill., 1986, N.E. Mo. State U., Kirksville, 1989; PhD, U. Iowa, Iowa City, 2000. Ordination Christian ministry Southport Heights Christian Ch., Indpls., Ind., 1980. Houseparent, group home Shiloh Children's Christian Ranch, Clarence, Mo., 1985—87, Illini Children's Christian Home, Erie, IL, Ill., 1987—99, Oblong Children's Christian Home, Ill., 1999—; tchg. asst. U. Iowa, 1991—99; adjunt instr. Lincoln Christian Coll., 1994—95; adj. instr. Ind. State U., Terre Haute, 2000—. Youth worker Highland Ch. Christ, Robinson, Ill., 2000—. Elizabeth Bennett Ink Rsch. fellow, U. Iowa, 1993, Andrew Mellen Rsch. fellow, Mass. Hist. Soc., 1994, Resident Rsch. fellow, Francis C. Wood Inst. History Medicine, 1994, William Cordell Rsch. fellow, Ind. State U., 2004, 2006. Mem.: Dictionary Soc. N.Am., Soc. Social History Medicine, Orgn. Am. History, Am. Hist. Assn., Omohundro Inst. Early Am. History and Culture (assoc.). Home: 4086 E 1050th Ave Oblong IL 62449 Office: Ind State Univ Department of History Terre Haute IN 47809 Business E-Mail: dmccarter@indstate.edu.

MC CARTER, JOHN WILBUR, JR., museum executive; b. Oak Park, Ill., Mar. 2, 1938; s. John Wilbur and Ruth Rebecca McC.; m. Judith Field West, May 1, 1965; children: James Philip, Jeffrey John, Katherine Field. AB, Princeton U., 1960; postgrad., London Sch. Econs., 1961; MBA, Harvard U., 1963. Cons., assoc., v.p. Booz Allen and Hamilton, Inc., Chgo., 1963-69; White House fellow Washington, 1966-67; dir. Bur. Budget and Dept. Fin., State of Ill., Springfield, 1969-73; v.p. DeKalb AgResearch, Ill., 1973-78, dir. Ill., 1975-86, exec. v.p. Ill., 1978-80, pres. Ill., 1981-82; pres., chief exec. officer DeKalb-Pfizer Genetics, 1982-86; pres. DeKalb Corp., 1985-86; sr. v.p. Booz Allen & Hamilton Inc., 1987-97; pres., CEO Field Mus., Chgo., 1996—. Bd. dirs. Divergence Inc., W.W. Grainger, Inc., Janus. Trustee Chgo. Pub. Television, 1973—, chmn., 1989-96, trustee Princeton U., 1983-87, U. Chgo., 1993—. Office: Field Museum 1400 S Lake Shore Dr Chicago IL 60605-2496

MCCARTER, LOUIS EUGENE, lawyer; b. Enid, Okla., Mar. 15, 1940; s. Louis Eugene and Bertha Marguerite (Krittenbrink) McC.; m. Janet Ann Korn, May 25, 1968; children— Scott Louis, Kathryn Nicole. B.A., U. Okla., 1962; LL.M., U. Tex., 1965. Bar: Tex. 1965, U.S. Dist. Ct. (ea. and so. dists.) Tex. 1975, U.S. Ct. Mil. Appeals 1966. Assoc., Vinson & Elkins, Houston, 1968-75, ptnr., 1975—. Served to capt. JAGC, U.S. Army, 1965-68; Vietnam. Decorated Bronze Star, Army Commendation medal. Mem. ABA, Tex. Bar Assn., Tex. Bd. Legal Specialization, Am. Bd. Trial Advs., Internat. Assn. Def. Counsel, Ctr. Club, Houston Country Club. E-mail: lmccarter@velaw.com. Office: Vinson & Elkins 3300 First City Tower 1001 Fannin St Ste 3300 Houston TX 77002-6706 Home Phone: 713-782-6550; Office Phone: 713-758-2530. Business E-Mail: mccarter@velaw.com.

MCCARTER, NANCY R., graphics designer, educator, artist, small business owner; d. Robert and Anna McCarter. AA in Liberal Arts, Moorpark Coll., Calif., 1977—80. Cert. exotic animal care & handling Moorpark Coll., 1980. Freelance computer & art instr., Thousand Oaks, Calif., 1995—2006; owner, graphic designer, muralist, tech. writer World Peace Depot, Thousand Oaks, 2001—. Exhibitions include Fresco Reliefs. Co-founder Am. Youth Soccer Orgn., Thousand Oaks, 1969—, soccer coach, 1994—97. Achievements include design of world peace flag (Flag of All Nations). Avocations: travel, photography. Office: World Peace Depot 2861 Los Robles Rd Thousand Oaks CA 91362 Business E-Mail: nmccarter@worldpeacedepot.com.

MCCARTER, THOMAS NESBITT, III, investment company executive, consultant; b. NYC, Dec. 16, 1929; s. Thomas N. Jr. and Suzanne M. (Pierson) McCarter. Student, Princeton U., 1948-51. Chartered investment counselor. Sales exec. Mack Trucks, Inc., NYC, 1952—59; ptnr. Kelly, McCarter, D-Arcy Investment Counsel, NYC, 1959—62; v.p., sec., dir. D-Arcy McCarter & Chew, NYC, 1962—66; v.p., dir. Trainer, Wortham & Co., Inc., NYC, 1967—71, exec. v.p., 1971—75; chmn. bd., dir. Island Security Bank Ltd., 1976—78; pres. Knottingham Ltd., NYC, 1976—84; gen. ptnr. W.P. Miles Timber Properties, New Orleans, 1974—; exec. v.p. Yorke McCarter Owen & Bartles, Inc., NYC, 1985—89. Cons. Laidlaw Holdings, Inc., 1990—92; pres. Mentor Mgmt. Group, Inc., NYC, 1986—90; chmn. bd. dirs. Ramapo Land Co., Sloatsburg, NY, 1990—, Stillrock Mgmt., Inc., NYC, 1992—96, Pendragon Tech., 1996—98, Dir Anker Coal Group Inc., Hyseq, Inc., Nuvelo, Inc.; bd. advisors Knowledge Delivery Sys. Inc.; adv. dir. Runnymede Capital Mgmt., Inc.; bd. dirs. Inst. Scientific Investment and Governance KCK Tokyo, So. Union Co. Chmn. bd. trustees Christodora Found., Inc., NYC, 1970-93; charter trustee Dalton Sch., NYC, 1969-76, v.p., 1972-76; pres., trustee Civil War Libr. and Mus., Phila., 1985-92; chmn. bd. trustees ASPCA, 1984-95; chmn. loyal Legion Found., NYC; trustee Children's Aid Soc. NYC, 1973-94, Joffrey Ballet, Found. for Am. Dance, 1973-77; pres., trustee NYC Marble Cemetery Assn., 1990-2002; mem. Nat. Com. for Preservation of US Treasury Bldg., 1988-92; trustee Nat. Symphony Orch., Washington, 1990-94; chmn. Gibralter Am. Coun., 1998-2002; bd. assocs. Whitehead Inst., Cambridge, Mass., 2000—. Mem. Loyal Legion US (comdr. NY State 1964-66, nat. comdr. in chief 1977-81), Brook Club, Links Club, River Club, St. Nicholas Soc., Pilgrims of US (NYC), Meadow Club (Southampton, NY), Ivy Club (Princeton, NJ), Moorings Club (Vero Beach, Fla.), Everglades Club. Republican. Office: PO Box 2380 Palm Beach FL 33480

MCCARTHY, ANN PRICE, lawyer; b. LA, Jan. 30, 1947; d. Frank Judson and Marianna (Chase) Price; 1 child, Sundae Jan Cloe; m. Joseph Stephen McCarthy, Dec. 15, 1974; 1 child, Caitlin Price. BA, Old Coll., Reno, 1983; JD, Nev. Sch. Law, 1987. Bar: Nev. 1987, Calif. 1988, U.S. Dist. Ct. (no. dist.) Calif. 1988, U.S. Ct. Appeals (9th cir.) 1989. Legal asst. Aebi, FitzSimmons & Lambrose, Carson City, Nev., 1981-84; ind. legal researcher Reno, 1985; law clk. Martin H. Wiener, Esquire, Reno, 1985-87, Hon. Robin C. Wright, Reno, 1987-88, Hon. John C. Mowbray, Carson City, 1988; ptnr. Eck & McCarthy, Carson City, 1988-90; pvt. practice Ann Price McCarthy, Ltd., Carson City, 1990-91; ptnr. Aebi & McCarthy, Carson City, 1991—. Lectr. Nat. Bus. Inst., Reno, 1992, 93; instr. Juvenile Drug and Alcohol Edn. Program, Carson City, 1992. Bd. dirs., sec. Brewery Arts Ctr., Carson City, 1992, bd. dirs., pres., 1993-95. Mem. Am. Trial Lawyers Assn., Nev. Trial Lawyers Assn., Washoe County Bar Assn., First Jud. Dist. Bar Assn. (pres. 1991-92, 92-93), State Bar of Nev. (pres. 2004). Address: Ann Price McCarthy & Assoc 777 E William St Ste 201 Carson City NV 89701 Office: Aebi and McCarthy Ste 201 777 E William St Carson City NV 89701-4058

MCCARTHY, BERNARD FRANCIS, lawyer; b. Butte, Mont., Aug. 20, 1955; s. John Joseph and Helen Patricia (Ryan) McC.; m. Helen Jean Waldbillig, Sept. 1, 1990; children: Sean Michael, Patrick Nicholas. BA, Carroll Coll., 1977; JD, U. Mont., 1983. Bar: Mont. 1983, U.S. Dist. Ct. Mont. 1983. Mgmt. analyst Mont. Supreme Ct., Helena, 1978-79; ptnr. O'Leary & McCarthy, Helena, 1983-85; justice of peace Lewis and Clark County, Helena, 1984-89; clk. US Bankruptcy Ct. (Dist. Mont.), Butte, Mont., 1990—. Chair edn. com. Fed. Jud. Ctr., Washington, 1994—; mem. State Bar Mont., Helena, (law practice com. 1994, sec.-treas. 2000, pres-elect 2004); Nat. Conf. Bankruptcy Clks., Dayton, Ohio, (v.p., pres.-elect, 1996-98, pres., 1998-2000; mem. Nat. Integrated Bankruptcy System user group Adminstr. Office U.S. Cts., Washington, 1996—; sec., treas. State Bar Mont., 2001-04, pres.-elect, 2004-05, pres., 2005-06. Pres. bd. Big Bros. and Sisters, Helena, 1985-86. Mem. KC, Lions (pres./sec. 1992-94). Democrat. Roman Catholic. Avocations: horse riding, fishing, reading, travel, ranching. Home: PO Box 523 176 Paul Gulch Rd Whitehall MT 59759 Office: Us Bankruptcy Court 400 N Main St Rm 303 Butte MT 59701-8866 Office Phone: 406-497-1243. Business E-Mail: bernard-mccarthy@meb.uscaucts.gov.

MCCARTHY, BRIAN NELSON, real estate developer; b. Detroit, May 24, 1945; s. Andrew Nelson and Ruth Elizabeth (Hill) McC.; children: Amanda Lang, Kelly Elizabeth, Meghan Virginia, Connor Michael; m. Valerie Reiheld, 1997. BS in Engring. Sci., Oakland U., 1966; MBA, Harvard U., 1972. Engr. Gen. Motors Corp., Pontiac, Mich., 1965-67; co-owner Sound Wave Systems, Costa Mesa, Calif., 1971-78; CFO, controller A&W Gershenson Co., Farmington, Mich., 1972-75; pres. Devel. Group, Inc., Southfield, Mich., 1975—81; CEO Brichard & Co., San Francisco, 1982-87; pres. Watermark Corp., Sausalito, Calif., 1987—92, Indian Wells Water Co., Inc., Sausalito, 1993—2000; dir. Co-Investor Group, Sonoma, Calif., 2000—01; chmn., pres. Southfork Devel. Group, El Dorado Hills, Calif., 2002—. Rear adm. USNR, 1966-96, res. Recipient Navy Achievement medal, Navy Commendation medal with gold star, Joint Commendation medal, Navy Meritorious Svc. medal with 2 gold stars, Joint Meritorious Svc. medal with oak leaf cluster, others. Mem. Navy Supply Corps Assn. (bd. dirs. 1987-96). Republican. Office: Southfork Devel Group PO Box 778 Camino CA 95762

MCCARTHY, CAROLYN, congresswoman; b. Bklyn., Jan. 5, 1944; m. Dennis McCarthy (dec. Dec. 1993); 1 child. LPN, Glen Cove Nursing Sch., NY, 1964. LPN St. Francis and Winthrop Hosp., 1964—93; gun safety activist, 1994—97; mem. US Congress from 4th NY dist., 1997—. Mem. edn. and labor com., US Congress, mem. fin. svcs. com., chairwoman subcommittee on healthy families and communities. Recipient numerous awards, including being named one of Newsday's 100 LI Influentials, Congl. Quarterly's 50 Most Effective Legislators in Congress, one of nine Redbook Mag.'s "Mothers and Shakers", Ladies' Home Jour. list of

America's 100 Most Important Women, and Advertising Age's list of Most Impact by Women in 1999; also honored by US Women's Soccer Team and Oprah Winfrey. Mem.: New Yorkers Against Gun Violence, NYC Stop the Violence Campaign, Guns for Goods, Ams. Against Gun Violence (hon.). Democrat. Roman Catholic. Office: US House Reps 106 Cannon House Office Bldg Washington DC 20515-3204 Office Phone: 202-225-5516. *

MCCARTHY, CHARLES FRANCIS, JR., lawyer; b. Springfield, Mass., Dec. 9, 1926; s. Charles Francis and Maude Veronica (Clayton) McC.; m. Dorothy B. Sadosky, June 14, 1952 (dec. June 1987); children: Richard J., Linda A. Moylan, Robert P. AB, St. Michael's Coll., 1949; JD, Boston Coll., 1951. Bar: Mass. 1952, U.S. Dist. Ct. Mass. 1953. Assoc. Ganley, Crook & Smith, Springfield, Mass., 1954-67, Laming, Smith & Auchter, Springfield, 1967-80; of counsel Bacon & Wilson, P.C. and predecessor firms, Springfield, 1980-94; ret., 1994. Clk. Ellis Title Co., Inc., Springfield, 1988—94. Mem.: St. Thomas More Soc. Democrat. Roman Catholic. Home: 130 Plumtree Rd Springfield MA 01118

MCCARTHY, CHRISTINE M., museum director; b. Hartford, Conn., June 8, 1967; BA in Humanities, Providence Coll., 1985—89; MA in Mus. Studies, Syracuse U., NY, 1990—92. Dir. adminstrn. & planning Inst. Contemporary Art, Boston, 1994—2001; exec. dir. Provincetown Art Assn. & Mus., Mass., 2001—. Cultural econ. devel. com. mem. Campus Provincetown, 2001—. Mem.: Am. Assn. Museums. D-Liberal. Office: Provincetown Art Assn & Museum 460 Commercial St Provincetown MA 02657 Office Fax: 508-487-4372. Business E-Mail: cmccarthy@paam.org.

MCCARTHY, CONNIE KEARNS, university librarian; BA, Rosary Coll., Ill., 1968; MSLS, Catholic U., 1972. Past cataloger Folger U. Shakespeare Libr.; asst. univ. libr. for collections George Washingtn U.; assoc. univ. libr. William R. Perkins Libr. Duke U.; dean univ. libr. Coll. William and Mary, 1997—. Chair steering com. Virtual Libr. of Va.; chair edtl. bd. CHOICE jour. Mem.: ALA. Office: Earl Gregg Swem Libr Coll William and Mary PO Box 8794 Williamsburg VA 23187-8794 Office Phone: 757-221-3055. Office Fax: 757-221-2635. E-mail: ckmcca@wm.edu. *

MCCARTHY, CORMAC (CHARLES JOSEPH MCCARTHY), writer; b. Providence, July 20, 1933; s. Charles Joseph and Gladys (McGrail) McC.; m. Lee Holleman, 1961 (div.); 1 child, Cullen; m. Anne DeLisle, 1967 (div. 1981); m. Jennifer Winkley, 1 child, John. Author: (novels) The Orchard Keeper, 1965 (William Faulkner Found. award, 1965), Outer Dark, 1968, Child of God, 1974, Suttree, 1979, Blood Meridian, or The Evening Redness in the West, 1985, All the Pretty Horses, 1992 (Nat. Book award for fiction 1992, Nat. Book Critics Circle award for fiction 1993), The Crossing, 1994, Cities of the Plain, 1998, No Country for Old Men, 2005, The Road, 2006 (Pulitzer Prize for fiction, 2007); (teleplays) The Gardner's Son, 1977; (plays) The Stonemason: A Play in Five Acts, 1994. Served in USAF, 1953—57. Ingram-Merrill Found. creative writing grantee, 1960, Am. Acad. Arts and Letter traveling fellow, 1965-66, Rockefeller Found. grantee, 1966, Guggenheim fellow, 1976, MacArthur Found. grantee, 1981; recipient Jean Stein award Am. Acad. and Inst. Arts and Letters, 1991 Mailing: c/o Amanda Urban ICM 40 W 57th St New York NY 10019 *

MCCARTHY, DANIEL WILLIAM, management consultant; b. Syracuse, NY, Apr. 15, 1952; s. William Cornelius and Ruth Francis (Geller) McC.; m. Mary Coleen Kisil, Jan. 17, 1987; children: Katherine M., Kevin D., Patrick W. BA in Polit. Sci., SUNY, Geneseo, 1974; MBA, NYU, 1982. Asst. buyer Abraham & Straus, Bklyn., 1976—78; buyer Lord & Taylor, NYC, 1978—80; cons. Touche Ross, Newark, 1982—87; sr. mgr. Deloitte & Touche, NYC, 1987—93; dir. Coach Leatherware, NYC, 1993—94; prin. Greenvale Consulting Group, Poughkeepsie, NY, 1994—2000; pres. Retex Cons. Group, NYC, 2000—02, Greenvale Cons. Group, LLC, NY, 2002—03; dir. spl. projects Island Pacific, Inc., 2003—06; prin. Greenvale Cons. Group, 2006—07; ops. mgr. US Enabler-Wipro, 2007—. Author: Point of Sale - Current Trends and Beyond, 1986; contbr. articles to profl. jours. Mem. Town of Poughkeepsie Hist. Planning Commn. Named Open Foil Champion, North Atlantic Veterans, 2000, 2001, 2004. Mem. Nat. Retail Fedn., Inst. Mgmt. Cons. Roman Catholic. Avocations: wine collecting, ballet, fencing, architecture, investing. Personal E-mail: danmcd@msn.com.

MCCARTHY, DOROTHY A. (LANDERS), educator; d. Dorthy Landers; m. Philip Francis McCarthy; children: Colleen, Timothy, Kevin, Shawn. BA, Elms Coll., Chicopee, Mass., 1971; MEd, Nat. Louis U., Heidelberg, Germany, 1990. Tchr. Rochester Cath. Sch., NH, 1979—80, Dept. Defense Schs., Wuerzburg, Germany, 1980—83, Vogelweh, 1983—86, Ramstein, 1986—90, Naples, Italy, 1990—2004, Ft. Stewart, Ga., 2004—. Adv., students of Dept. Def. Schs. Nat. Honor Soc., Italy & Germany, 1980—2004; social studies task mem. Dept. Def. Schs.; visitation team mem. NCAA, coord. global svc. and humanitarian projects. Mem. Italia chpt. Phi Delta Kappa, 1992—. Mem.: Nat. Coun. Social Studies, Fed. Edn. Assn. Roman Catholic. Avocation: travel. Office: Brittin Elem Sch 2772 Hero Rd Fort Stewart GA 31313 Office Phone: 912-368-3324.

MC CARTHY, FRANK MARTIN, oral surgeon, educator; b. Olean, NY, Aug. 27, 1924; s. Frank Michael and Joan (Quinn) McC.; m. Julia Richmond, Nov. 24, 1949; children: Robert Lee, Joan Lee. BS, U. Pitts., 1943, DDS, 1945, MD, 1949; MS in Oral Surgery, Georgetown U., 1954; ScD (hon.), St. Bonaventure U., 1956. Med. intern Mercy Hosp., Pitts., 1949-50; practice oral surgery LA, 1954-75; tchg. fellow Georgetown U., 1952-53; rsch. fellow NIH, 1953-54; prof. oral surgery U. So. Calif. Sch. Dentistry, 1966-75, prof., chmn. sect. anesthesia and medicine, 1975-90, prof. emeritus, 1990—, chmn. dept. surg. scis., 1979-84, assoc. dean adminstrv. affairs, 1977-79, asst. dean hosp. affairs, 1979-84. Dir. anesthesiology U.So. Calif. oral surgery sect. L.A. County Hosp., 1958-89; clin. supr., lectr. dental hygiene program Pasadena City Coll., 1992—; v.p. Am. Dental Bd. Anesthesiology, 1984-89; lectr. in field; mem. adv. panel on dentistry sect. anesthesizing agts. Nat. Fire Protection Assn., 1971-79; mem. Am. Nat. Stds. Com., 1974-86, 95—; cons. in field. Author: Emergencies in Dental Practice, 1967, rev., 1972, 79, Medical Emergencies in Dentistry, 1982, Safe Treatment of the Medically Compromised Patient, 1987, Essentials of Safe Dentistry for the Medically Compromised Patient, 1989; mem. editorial bd.: Calif. Dental Assn. Jour; contbr. articles to profl. pubs. Bd. councilors Sch. Dentistry, U. So. Calif., 1972-75. Served as lt., M.C. USNR, 1950-52. Recipient Lifetime Achievement award, So. Calif. Orofacial Acad., Palm Springs, Calif., 2006. Fellow Internat. Assn. Oral Surgeons (founder), Am. Coll. Dentists, Internat. Coll. Dentists; mem. ADA (editl. bd. jour.), Am. Dental Soc. Anesthesiology (Heidbrink award 1977), Am. Assn. Oral-Max Surgeons (chmn. anesthesia com. 1971), So. Calif. Soc. Oral Surgeons (pres. 1974), Calif., L.A. County Dental Assns., Delta Tau Delta, Psi Omega, Phi Rho Sigma, Omicron Kappa Upsilon. Home and Office: 480 S Orange Grove Blvd Apt 11 Pasadena CA 91105-1720

MCCARTHY, G. DANIEL, lawyer; b. Butte, Mont., Mar. 23, 1949; s. George Denis and Mary Agnes (Kiely) McC.; m. Carolyn M. Scully, June 19, 1976; children: Brendan, Katie, Kelly, Sean. BA, U. Dayton, 1971; JD, U. Notre Dame, 1974; AMP, Harvard U., 1994. Bar: Md. 1974, D.C. 1975, U.S. Ct. Appeals (D.C. cir.) 1976, Pa. 1977, N.Y. 1985, U.S. Ct. Appeals (10th cir.) 1985. Assoc. Bilger & Blair, Washington, 1974-77, 79-80; asst. U.S. atty. U.S. Dist. Ct. (ea. dist.) Pa., Phila., 1977-78; assoc. Abourezk, Shack & Mendenhall, Washington, 1980-83; atty. AT&T, NYC, 1983-85; v.p., gen. counsel and sec. AT&T Credit Corp., Morristown, NJ, 1985-89; sr. v.p., gen. counsel, sec., chief risk mgmt. officer. AT&T Capital Corp., Morristown, NJ, 1990-96; v.p., gen. counsel, sec. Compaq Fin. Svcs. Corp., Murray Hill, NJ, 1996—2002; v.p. govt. affairs, dep. gen. counsel Compaq Computer Corp., Houston, 2001—02; v.p., gen. counsel, sec. Hewlett-Packard Fin. Svcs. Co., Murray Hill, NJ, 2002—. Vis. lectr. Marymount Coll., Arlington, Va., 1979-83; mem. adv. coun. U. Dayton, Coll. of Arts and Scis., 1993-97, chmn., 1994-96; bd. dirs. Hewlett-Packard Europe Fin., Ltd., HP Fin. Svcs. Internat. Holdings Co., Hewlett-Packard Internat. Bank PLC. Mem.: DC Bar Assn., Fairmount Country Club (Chatham, NJ) (bd. dirs. 2002—07). Avocations: golf, fly fishing. Office: HP Fin Svcs Co 420 Mountain Ave New Providence NJ 07974-0006 Office Phone: 908-898-4003. Business E-Mail: dan.mccarthy@hp.com.

MCCARTHY, HAROLD CHARLES, retired insurance company executive; b. Madelia, Minn., Dec. 5, 1926; s. Charles and Merle (Humphry) McC.; m. Barbara Kaercher, June 24, 1949; children: David, Susan. BA, Carleton Coll., Northfield, Minn., 1950; postgrad. With Federated Mut. Ins. Co., Owatonna, Minn., 1950-67; with Meridian Mut. Ins. Co., Indpls., 1967-91, exec. v.p., then exec. v.p., gen. mgr., 1972-75, pres., 1975-90, bd. dirs., past chmn. bd., 1990-91; past pres. North Meridian Bus. Group; past pres., chmn. bd. Meridian Ins. Group, Inc. Chmn. bd., dir. Meridian Life Ins. Co.; past chmn., exec. com., bd. dirs. Ind. Ins. Inst.; mem. adv. bd. Harbor Fed. Savs. Bank. Former mem. Met. Devel. Commn., Corp. Cmty. Coun.; bd. dirs. Meth. Health Found., Family Services Assn., Boy Scouts Am., Indian River Symphony Assn.; trustee Butler U. With USNR, 1944-46. Named Sagamore of the Wabash. Mem. Skyline Club (Indpls.), Indian River Golf Club. Republican.

MCCARTHY, IAN J., construction executive; BS, City U., London. Chartered civil engr. With Kier Ltd., 1980—81; pres., CEO Beazer Homes USA, Inc., Atlanta, 1989—, bd. dirs., 1994—. Dir. Beazer Far East, 1981—91; bd. dirs. Builder Homesite, Inc. Chmn. HomeAid's Nat. Adv. Bd.; trustee Woodruff Arts Ctr., Atlanta; bd. dirs. Metro Atlanta C. of C. Named to Calif. Bldg. Industry Hall of Fame, 2004. Office: Beazer Homes 1000 Abernathy Rd Ste 1200 Atlanta GA 30328-5606 Office Phone: 770-829-3700. Office Fax: 770-481-2808. *

MCCARTHY, J. THOMAS, lawyer, educator; b. Detroit, July 2, 1937; s. John E. and Virginia M. (Hanlon) McC.; m. Nancy Irene Orrell, July 10, 1976 BS, U. Detroit, 1960; JD, U. Mich., 1963. Bar: Calif. 1964. Assoc. Julian Caplan, San Francisco, 1963—66; prof. law U. San Francisco, 1966—; counsel Morrison and Foerster, 2001—. Founding dir. McCarthy Inst. Intellectual Property and Tech. Law; mem. Trademark Rev. Commn., 1986—88; cons. in field. Author: McCarthy on Trademarks and Unfair Competition, 7 vols., 4th edit., 1996, McCarthy on Rights of Publicity and Privacy, 1987, 2d edit., 2000, McCarthy's Desk Encyclopedia of Intellectual Property, 3d edit., 2004. Recipient Jefferson medal N.J. Intellectual Property Assn., 1994, Ladas award Brand Names Ednl. Found., 1997, Pattishall medal Brand Names Found., 2000, Pres.'s award Internat. Trademark Assn., 2003. Mem. IEEE, Am. Intellectual Property Law Assn. (Watson award 1965, Centennial award in Trademark law 1997), Internat. Assn. for Advancement of Tchg. and Rsch. in Intellectual Property, Am. Law Inst. (adv. com. on restatement of law of unfair competition).

MCCARTHY, JENNY, actress; b. Chgo., Nov. 1, 1972; m. John Mallory Asher, Sept. 11, 1999 (div. 2005); 1 child, Evan Joseph Asher. Student Sch. Nursing, So. Ill. U. Spokeswoman Jose Cuervo Tequilla. Appeared in films Things to Do in Denver When You're Dead, 1995, The Stupids, 1996, BASEketball, 1998, Diamonds, 1999, Scream 3, 2000, Dirty Love, 2005, John Tucker Must Die, 2006; TV shows The Jenny McCarthy Show, 1997, Jenny, 1997-98, The Bad Girl's Guide, 2005; host game show Singled Out, MTV, 1995-96, Party @ the Palms, 2005; featured photographs in Playboy mag., 1993-96, 98, 05, including as Miss Oct. 1993, then as Playmate of Yr., 1994; author Jen-X, 1997, Belly Laughs: The Naked Truth About Pregnancy and Childbirth, 2004 (NY Times Bestseller list, 2004), Baby Laughs: The Naked Truth About the First Year of Mommyhood, 2005 (NY Times Bestseller list, 2005). Named one of 50 Most Beautiful People in the World, People mag., 1996. Avocation: kickboxing. Address: c/o United Talent Agy 9560 Wilshire Blvd Ste 500 Beverly Hills CA 90212-2427

MCCARTHY, JOHN, computer scientist, educator; b. Boston, Sept. 4, 1927; s. Patrick Joseph and Ida McCarthy; children: Susan Joanne, Sarah Kathleen, Timothy Talcott. BS in Math., Calif. Inst. Tech., 1948; PhD in Math., Princeton U., 1951; Degree (hon.), Linkoping U., Sweden, Polytechnic U., Madrid, Colby Coll., Dublin and Concordia U., Montreal. Procter Fellow Princeton U., 1950—51, Higgins Rsch. instr. in math., 1951—53; acting asst. prof. math. Stanford U., 1953—55; asst. prof. math. Dartmouth Coll., 1955—58; asst. prof. comm. sciences MIT, Cambridge, 1958—61, assoc. prof. comm. sciences, 1961—62; prof. computer sci. Stanford U., 1962—2001, Charles M. Pigott prof. Sch. Engring., 1987—94, prof. emeritus computer scis., 2001—. Academic advisor Nat. Legal Ctr. for Pub. Info., 1976—80; fellow Ctr. for Advanced Study in the Behavioral Sciences, 1979—80; Bobby R. Inman prof. computer sci. U. Tex., 1987; bd. dir. Info. Internat., Inc., 1962—95, Inference Corp., 1983—91, Mad Intelligent Systems, 1987—91. Contbr. articles to profl. jours.; mem. editl. bd. Artificial Intelligence Jour., 1975—. Served with AUS, 1945-46. Named Disting. Alumnus, Calif. Inst. Tech.; recipient first Rsch. Excellence award, Internat. Joint Conf. on Artificial Intelligence, 1985, Kyoto prize, Inamori Found., 1988, Nat. Medal of Sci., NSF, 1990, Fellow award, Computer History Mus., 1999; Sloan Fellow in Phy. Sci., 1957—59. Fellow: Am. Assn. Artificial Intelligence (pres. 1983—84); mem.: Nat. Acad. Scis., NAE, NAS, AAAS, Am. Math. Soc., Assn. for Computing Machinery (A.M. Turing award 1971), Am. Acad. Arts and Scis., Sigma Xi. Achievements include invention of LISP programming language in 1958; circumscription method of non-monotonic reasoning in 1978; coined the term Artifical Intelligence in 1955. Home: 885 Allardice Way Stanford CA 94305-1050 Office: Stanford U Rm 208 Gates Bldg 2A Computer Sci Dept Stanford CA 94305-9020 Office Phone: 650-723-4430. Office Fax: 650-725-7411. Business E-Mail: jmc@cs.stanford.edu. E-mail: mccarthy@stanford.edu.

MC CARTHY, JOSEPH MICHAEL, historian, educator; b. Lynn, Mass., Oct. 2, 1940; s. Joseph Donald and Johanna (Downing) Mc C.; m. Kathleen Theresa Wright, July 30, 1966; children: Joanna, Kristenmarie, Erika, Joseph Michael. AB, St. Johns Sem., 1961, postgrad., 1961-63; AM, Boston Coll., 1968, PhD, 1972. Tchr. Bishop Fenwick H.S., Peabody, Mass., 1964-67; fin. adminstr. Boston Coll., 1967-71, lectr. edn., 1971-74; prof. edn., dir. leadership programs Suffolk U., Boston, 1973—2006, prof. emeritus, 2006—. Vis. prof. Boston Coll., 1990; adj. lectr. Merrimack Coll., 1975, Boston U., 1973; prin. Ednl. Mgmt. Svcs., 1976—; gen. editor Garland Pub., 1979-92; bd. dirs. Inst. for Study of Academia, 1992-94. Author: An International List of Articles on the History of Education, 1977, Guinea-Bissau and Cape Verde Islands, 1977, Humanistic Emphases in the Educational Thought of Vincent of Beauvais, 1976, Pierre Teilhard de Chardin, 1981; mem. editl. bd. The Urban and Social Chage Rev., 1969-72, The Bureaucrat, Inc., 1974-76; contbr. articles to profl. jours. Pres. N.E. region Popular Culture Assn./Am. Culture Assn., 1998-99. Hearn scholar, 1959-61, fellow, 1961-63. Mem. Am. Cath. Hist. Assn., Soc. for Medieval and Renaissance Philosophy, Soc. Romanian Historians, Soc. Mil. History, East European Rsch. Inst., Phi Alpha Theta, Phi Delta Kappa. Home: Knockglen Farm 103 Fuller St Middleboro MA 02346-1700 Office: Suffolk U Beacon Hill Boston MA 02108 Business E-Mail: jmccarth@suffolk.edu.

MCCARTHY, KAREN P., former congresswoman, former state legislator; b. Mass., Mar. 18, 1947; BS in English, Biology, U. Kans., 1969, MBA, 1985; MEd in English, U. Mo., Kansas City, 1976. Tchr. Shawnee Mission (Kans.) South High Sch., 1969-75, The Sunset Hill (Kans.) Sch., 1975-76; mem. Mo. House of Reps., Jefferson City, 1977-94; cons. govt. affairs Marion Labs., Kansas City, Mo., 1986-93; mem. U.S. Congress from 5th Mo. dist., Washington, 1995—2005; mem. commerce com.; mem. Ho. Select Com. on Homeland Security. Rsch. analyst pub. fin. dept. Stearn Bros. & Co., 1984-85, Kansas City, Mo.; rsch. analyst Midwest Rsch. Inst., econs. and mgmt. scis. dept., Kansas City, 1985-86. Del. Dem. Nat. Conv., 1992, Dem. Nat. Party Conf., 1982, Dem. Nat. Policy Com. Policy Commn., 1985-86; mem. Ho. Commerce Com. Energy and Power, Telecom., Trade and Consumer Protection; co-chair Dem. Caucus Task Health Care Reform. Recipient Outstanding Young Woman Am. award, 1977, Outstanding Woman Mo. award Phi Chi Theta, Woman of Achievement award Mid-Continent Coun. Girl Scouts U.S., 1983, 87, Annie Baxter Leadership award, 1993; named Conservation Legislator of Yr., Conservation Fed. Mo., 1987. Fellow Inst. of Politics; mem. Nat. Inst. of Politics; mem. Nat. Conf. on State Legis. (del. on trade and econ. devel. to Fed. Republic of Germany, Bulgaria, Japan, France and Italy, mem. energy com. 1978-84, fed. taxation, trade and econ. devel. com. 1986, chmn. fed. budget and taxation com. 1987, vice chmn. state fed. assembly 1988, pres.-elect 1993, pres. 1994), Nat. Dem. Inst. for Internat. Affairs (instr. No. Ireland 1988, Baltic Republics 1992, Hungary 1993). Democrat.

MCCARTHY, KATHY, actress, writer; B, Western Wash. U. Actress, LA, 1999—. Pres., founder Enviornmental & Conservation Coun. Group, LA; mem. Film Ind., LA. Actor: Meatloaf To Hell & Back, Dancing At The Harvest Moon; dir.: AmerAsian; prodr.: The Amoeba. Mem.: AFTRA, Am. Film Inst., Entertainment Industry Found., Women In Film, Screen Actor's Guild. Achievements include patents for cosmetic. Home Phone: 661-283-4960; Office Phone: 661-784-2246. Business E-Mail: kathymcc@kathymccarthy.com.

MCCARTHY, KEVIN, congressman, former state legislator; b. Bakersfield, Calif., Jan. 26, 1965; m. Judy McCarthy; children: Connor, Meghan. Student, Bakersfield Coll., 1984—85; BS in Bus. Adminstrn., Calif. State U., Bakersfield, 1989, MBA, 1994. Owner Bakersfield Batting Range, Kevin O's Deli; dist. dir. to Rep. Bill Thomas US Congress; mem. Calif. State Assembly, 2002—07, minority leader, 2004—06; mem. US Congress from 22nd Calif. dist., 2007—, mem. agrl com., house adminstrn. com., joint com. on printing. Chmn. Young Republican Nat. Fedn., 1999—2001; bd. dirs. Kern Econ. Opportunity Corp. Trustee dist. bd. Kern C.C., 2000—02; exec. dir. McCarthy Found., 2000—; coach YMCA, 1999—; mem. Kern County Rep. Ctrl. Com., 1992—; bd. dirs. First Book, 2001—, Head Start, Kern County Food Bank. Mem.: Rotary. Republican. Baptist. Office: 1523 Longworth House Office Bldg Washington DC 20515 also: 4100 Empire Dr Ste 150 Bakersfield CA 93309 *

MCCARTHY, KEVIN BART, lawyer; b. Washington, May 7, 1948; s. Frank Jeremiah and Frances Patricia (Bilderback) McC.; m. Patrice Borders, Apr. 3, 1971; children: Kevin Patrick, Charles Ryan, Molly Virginia, Bridget Louise, Moira Patrice. BBA, U. Notre Dame, 1970; JD, Ind. U., Indpls., 1973. Bar: Ind. 1973, U.S. Dist. Ct. (so. dist.) Ind. 1973, U.S. Ct. Appeals (7th cir.) 1974, Ill 1976, U.S. Dist. Ct. (cen. dist.) Ill. 1985, U.S. Ct. Appeals (6th cir.) 1985. Bail commr. Mcpl. Ct. Marion County, Indpls., 1972-73; asst. regional counsel Fed. Hwy. Adminstrn., Homewood, Ill., 1973-75; 1st asst., chief counsel Ill. Dept. Transp., Springfield, 1975-77; counsel com. on interstate and fgn. commerce, subcom. on transp. and commerce Ho. Reps., Washington, 1977-79, asst. counsel com. on pub. works and transp., 1979-82, counsel com. on pub. works and transp., 1982; pvt. practice law Springfield, 1982-87; acting U.S. trustee Dept. Justice, Springfield, 1987-88, U.S. trustee Indpls., 1988—. Pvt. practice Indpls. and Springfield. Mem. Ill. State Bd. Agrl. Advisors, 1987-88. Home: 5619 Surrey Hill Rd Indianapolis IN 46226-1561

MCCARTHY, KEVIN JOHN, lawyer; b. NYC, Apr. 8, 1941; s. Vincent Patrick and Mary (H.) McC.; m. Marianne Pitts, Nov. 5, 1966; children: Mary Rita, Kevin, Colin. BS, U. Md., 1963; JD, U. Md., Balt., 1966. Bar: Md. 1966, U.S. Dist. Ct. Md. 1966, U.S. Ct. Appeals (4th cir.) 1966, U.S. Supreme Ct. 1972, D.C. 1976, U.S. Dist. Ct. D.C. 1976, U.S. Ct. Appeals (D.C. cir.) 1976, Fla. 1998. Law clk. Cir. Ct. for P.G. County, Upper Marlboro, Md., 1964-66; assoc., ptnr. Sasscer, Clagett & Channing, Upper Marlboro, Md., 1966-76; ptnr. O'Malley, Miles & McCarthy, Upper Marlboro, Md., 1976-86, McCarthy, Bacon & Costello, Landover, Md., 1986—2005, McCarthy & Winkelman, LLP, Landover, Md., 2005—. Arbitrator Am. Arbitration Assn., Washington, 1972—. Contbg. author: Maryland Civil Patter Jury Instructions, 1975, 2d edit., 1984, 3d edit., 1993. Named one of The Best Lawyers in Am., Woodward/White, 1994-2006. Fellow Am. Bar Found., Md. Bar Found.; mem. ATLA, Am. Bd. Trial Advs., Md. Trial Lawyers Assn., Million Dollar Advs. Forum, Trial Lawyers for Pub. Justice, Acad. Catastrophic Injury Attys., Belle Soc. Avocations: golf, racquetball, coaching soccer and lacrosse. Office: One Town Center 4201 Northview Dr Ste 410 Bowie MD 20716-2668 Office Phone: 301-262-7422. Business E-Mail: Kevin@McCarthyWinkelman.com.

MCCARTHY, MARK FRANCIS, lawyer; b. Boston, July 8, 1951; s. William Alfred and Martha Louise (Blodgett) McC.; m. Karen Marie Umerley; children: Kevin Francis, Daniel Henry. AB in Theology, Georgetown U., 1973, JD, 1976. Bar: Ohio 1976. Assoc. Sweeney, Mahon, & Vlad, Cleve., 1976-80; ptnr. Arter & Hadden, 1980—2003, Tucker Ellis & West LLP, Cleve., 2003—. Atty. asst. to bd. pres. Bd. Cuyahoga County Commrs., Cleve., 1976-80; adj. prof. Case Western Reserve Law Ctr., Cleve., 1986-2004. Active Greater Cleve. Growth Assn. Leadership Cleve., 1979-80; trustee Parmadale, Parma, Ohio, Western Res. Hist. Soc., 1978-80, Cath. Charities Found.; chmn. Cath. Charities Svcs. Corp.; trustee, sec. Caritas Connection; founder, sec., gen. counsel St. Martin De Porres H.S., Cleve., Inc. Mem. Ohio Assn. Civil Trial Attys. (chmn. product liability sect. 1989—), Fedn. Ins. & Corp. Counsel, Ct. of Nisi Prius, Rowfant Club. Democrat. Roman Catholic. Avocations: book collecting, fly fishing, upland shooting. Home: 363 Britannia Pky Avon Lake OH 44012-2180 Office: Tucker Ellis & West LLP 1150 Huntington Bldg 925 Euclid Ave Cleveland OH 44115-1475 Home Phone: 440-930-2707; Office Phone: 216-696-3290. Business E-Mail: mfm@tuckerellis.com.

MCCARTHY, MICHAEL SHAWN, health care company executive, lawyer; b. Evergreen Park, Ill., May 16, 1953; s. Martin J. and Margaret Anne (McNeill) McC.; m. Jane F. Alberding, Oct. 28, 1988; children: Caroline Margaret, Nicholas Michael, Claire Patricia. BA, Georgetown U., 1975; MS, U. Ill., 1976; JD, Loyola U., 1980. Bar: Ill. 1980, U.S. Dist. Ct. (no. dist.) Ill. 1980. V.p., sec., gen. counsel Luth. Gen. Health Care System, Park Ridge, Ill., 1980-85, sr. v.p., sec., gen. counsel, 1985-91, sr. v.p. corp. svcs., sec., gen. counsel, 1990-93; chmn., CEO Parkside Sr. Svcs., LLC, Skokie, Ill., 1993—. Life trustee Lake Forest Acad.; mem. coun. of regents Loyola U., Chgo., Ill. Mem. ABA, ASHA (exec. bd.), Ill. Hosp. Assn., Ill. Pub. Health Assn., Chgo. Bar Assn., ALFA Leadership Coun. Roman Catholic. Avocations: golf, travel. Home: 1026 Pine St Winnetka IL 60093-2024 Office: Parkside Sr Svcs LLC 5215 Old Orchard Rd Skokie IL 60077-1035 E-mail: McCarthy@parkside-sr.com.

MCCARTHY, MIKE, professional football coach; b. Pitts., Oct. 10, 1963; Grad., Baker U., 1986. Grad. asst. Fort Hays State, 1987—88; quarterbacks, wide receivers coach U. Pitts., 1989—92; offensive asst. Kans. City Chiefs, 1993—94, quarterbacks coach, 1995—98, Green Bay

Packers, 1999, head coach, 2006—; offensive coord. New Orleans Saints, 2000—04, San Francisco 49ers, 2005. Recipient NFC Asst. Coach Yr., 2000. Office: Green Bay Packers Lambeau Field 1265 Lombardi Ave Green Bay WI 54307

MCCARTHY, PAMELA MAFFEI, magazine editor; b. NYC, May 28, 1952; d. Rudolph Paul Maffei and Mary Frances Maresca; m. Joseph Matthews McCarthy, Sept. 16, 1978; 2 children. Student, Trinity Coll., Dublin, Ireland, 1972-73; BA, Mt. Holyoke Coll., 1974. Copy staff Esquire mag., NYC, 1974-76, copy editor, 1976-79, exec. editor, 1978-84; mng. editor Vanity Fair mag., NYC, 1984-92, The New Yorker, NYC, 1992-95, 1995—, dep. editor. Mem. Am. Soc. Mag. Editors Office: The New Yorker Advance Publications Inc 4 Times Sq New York NY 10036-6561

MCCARTHY, PATRICIA ANNE, reading educator; d. John Donald and Ruth Catherine McCarthy; m. Moses Samuel Schanfield, Aug. 16, 1998; 1 stepchild, Amanda; 1 stepchild, Samantha children: Stephanie Anne Murdock, Karin Joann Plotkin. BS, Le Moyne Coll., 1969; MA, Marquette U., 1971, PhD, 1999. Adj. asst. prof. Cardinal Stritch U., Milw., 1988—98; dir. Early Literacy Intervention Program, Wauwatosa, Wis., 1988—98; asst. prof. SUNY, Geneseo, 1999—2002, Hood Coll., 2003—04, Loyola Coll. in Md., Balt., 2004—. Scholar Milw. Area Tchrs. Assn., 1988—98, Marquette U. Edn. Dept., 1994—95. Mem.: ASCD, Nat. Reading Conf., Internat. Reading Assn., Phi Delta Kappa. Avocations: travel, art collecting, reading, walking. Office: Loyola Coll in Md 4501 N Charles St Baltimore MD 21210 Office Phone: 401-617-2459. Business E-Mail: pamccarthy@loyola.edu.

MCCARTHY, PATRICK, publishing executive; Joined Women's Wear Daily, 1977, reporter Washington, bur. chief London, Paris, editor NYC, 1985-88, exec. editor, 1988-92; editor W, NYC, 1985-88, exec. editor, 1988-92; exec. v.p. Fairchild Publs., NYC, 1992-97; chmn., editl. dir., 1997—. Recipient Eugenia Sheppard award for fashion journalism CFDA, 1994. Office: Conde Nast Publs 750 Third Ave New York NY 10017

MCCARTHY, PATRICK M., surgeon; s. Martin Joseph and Margaret Anne McCarthy; m. Michelle M. Despres, June 20, 1978; children: Daniel, Elizabeth. MD, Loyola U., Maywood, Ill., 1980. Dir. heart transplantation Kaufman Ctr. Heart Failure Cleve. Clinic Found., 1990—2004; chief cardiothoracic surgery, co-dir. Bluhm Cardiovasc. Inst. Northwestern U., Chgo., 2004—. Cons. Edwards Lifescis., LLC, Irvine, Calif., AtriCure, West Chester, Ohio. Fellow: Am. Coll. Cardiology; mem.: AMA, Heart Failure Soc. Am., Flagship Healthcare Mgmt., Chgo. Cardiothoracic Surg. Soc. (dir.), Cardiac Surgery Biology Club, Am. Soc. Transplant Surgeons, Am. Heart Assn. (coun. mem.), Priestley Soc., Internat. Soc. Heart and Lung Transplant (com. mem.), Internat. Acad. Cardiology (internat. sci. adv. bd.), Heart Valve Soc. Am. (coun. mem.), Am. Assn. Thoracic Surgery. Independent. Achievements include invention of valve rings for mitral & tricuspid repair. Office: Northwestern University 201 E Huron Galter 10-105 Chicago IL 60611 Office Phone: 312-695-3114. Office Fax: 312-695-0178.

MCCARTHY, PAUL FENTON, aerospace transportation executive, retired military officer; b. Boston, Mar. 3, 1934; s. Paul Fenton and Jane Gertrude (O'Connor) McC.; m. Sandra Williams, June 20, 1959; children: Paul Fenton III, Susan Stacy. BS in Marine and Elec. Engring., Mass. Maritime Acad., 1954; MS in Mgmt., U.S. Naval Postgrad. Sch., 1964; D of Pub. Adminstrn. (hon.), Mass. Maritime Acad., 1987. Commd. ensign U.S. Navy, 1954, advanced through grades to vice adm., 1985; 7 command tours have included Aircraft Carrier USS Constellation, Carrier Group One, Task Force Seventy-seven; commdr. U.S. 7th Fleet, 1980-82; dir. R & D USN, Washington, 1980-83; negotiator Naval Air, Incidents at Sea Agreement, Moscow, 1980; ret., 1990; cons. in field Alexandria, Va., 1990-92; pres. McCarthy and McCarthy, Ltd.; v.p., chief engr., dep. gen.mgr. McDonnell Douglas Aerospace/Boeing, St. Louis, 1992-95; v.p. processes and sys. integration McDonnell Douglas Aerospace, St. Louis, 1995-97, dir. naval systems integration, 1997-2000; vis. disting. prof. Peter Conrad chair Naval Post Grad. Sch., 2000-02; sr. ptnr. McCarthy and McCarthy, LLC, 2002—; sr. lectr. grad studies U. San Diego, 2005—. Bd. visitors Mass. Maritime Acad., 1993. Decorated D.S.M., Legion of Merit, D.F.C., also by govts. of South Vietnam, Korea, Japan. Mem.: Mass. Maritime Acad. Alumni Assn. Episcopalian. Avocations: development and acquisition, aircraft and missile systems, financial management. Office Phone: 619-922-9494. E-mail: mcandmc@aol.com.

MCCARTHY, PETER B., federal agency administrator; m. Mary McCarthy; 3 children. BA Govt., Cornell U., 1972; MBA Fin., So. Meth. U. Sr. officer Bank One, Tokyo; v.p., divsn. head Chase Manhattan Bank; sr. v.p., area head Bank One; dep. mng. dir. Inst. Internat. Fin. (IIF), 2002—06; asst. sec. for mgmt., CFO US Dept. Treasury, 2007—. Office: US Dept Treasury 1500 Pennsylvania Ave NW Rm 2438 Washington DC 20220 Office Phone: 202-622-0410. Office Fax: 202-622-2337. E-mail: peter.mccarthy@do.treas.gov. *

MCCARTHY, RHODA ANN, retired nursing administrator, retired medical/surgical nurse; b. ND, Apr. 6, 1928; d. Roy Leavitt and Emma (Norby) Hall; m. James L. McCarthy, Oct. 1, 1949; children: Kathryn, Margaret, Shirley, John, Patrick. BS in Sociology, Valley City State Coll., 1979; B in Human Resources Adminstrn. and Mgmt., U. Valley City, 1986; BSN, U. Albuquerque, 1986; B in Psychology, Calif. Coast U., 1987, M in Psychology, 1998, D in Psychology, 2003. Cert. Human Resources Admin. and Mgmt. Valley City U., 1986, staff nurse, psych. U. of N. Mex. Staff nurse Jamestown and Trinity Hosps., ND, 1949—60; dir. nurses Trinity Hosp., Jamestown, ND, 1960—63; supr. Jamestown Hosp., Jamestown, 1963—66; staff nurse Hibbing Gen. Hosp., Minn., 1966—69, Victory Meml. Hosp., Waukegan, Ill., 1969—71; asst. dir. nurses N.D. State Hosp., Jamestown, 1971—83; staff nurse Vets. Hosp., Albuquerque, 1983—90, nurse mgr. orthopedics, 1990—91; staff nurse St. Joseph's Hosp., Albuquerque, 1991—2003; staff nurse psychiat. unit N.Mex. Med. Hosp., Albuquerque, 2003—04; ret., 2004.

MCCARTHY, ROBERT EMMETT, lawyer; b. Bklyn., May 26, 1951; s. John Joseph and Leona Mary (Hart) McC.; m. Elizabeth Anne Naumoff, May 20, 1978; children: John Philip, Emily Jane. BS in Fgn. Studies, Georgetown U., 1973, MS in Fgn. Studies, JD, 1978. Bar: N.J. 1978, U.S. Dist. Ct. (ea. and so. dists.) N.Y. 1979. Assoc. Patterson, Belknap et al, NYC, 1978-84; gen. counsel MTV Networks Inc., NYC, 1984-86; v.p., counsel/communications Viacom Internat., NYC, 1986-87; exec. v.p. Nelson Vending Tech., Ltd., NYC, 1987-89; exec. v.p., gen. counsel Cateret Savs. Bank FA, Morristown, N.J., 1989-91; cons. McCarthy Comms., Elizabeth, N.J., 1991-95; sr. v.p., gen. counsel Time, Inc., NYC, 1996—. Cons. UN Ctr. on Transnat. Corps., N.Y.C., 1979; exec. dir. Spl. Master Reapportionment of N.Y., 1982; term mem. Council Fgn. Relations, N.Y.C., 1980-84. Founder, pres. Elizabeth (N.J.) Dem. Assn., 1980; coordinator Florio for Gov., Union County, N.J., 1981. Mem. ABA, N.Y. State Bar Assn., N.J. State Bar Assn., Assn. Bar City N.Y. Roman Catholic. Home: 3 Woods Ln Chatham NJ 07928-1760 Office: Time Inc 33rd Fl 1271 Avenue Of The Americas New York NY 10020-1300 E-mail: RobertMcCarthy1@aol.com.

MCCARTHY, ROGER LEE, mechanical engineer; AB in Philosophy with high distinction, U. Mich., 1972, BS in Mech. Engring. summa cum laude, 1972; MS in Mech. Engring., MIT, 1973, D in Mech. Engring., 1975, PhD in Mech. Engring., 1977. Registered profl. engr., Calif., Ga., Ariz. Project engr. machine design and devel. engring. divsn. Proctor & Gamble, Inc., Cin., 1973-74; program mgr. Spl. Machinery Group Foster-Miller Assocs., Inc., Waltham, Mass., 1976-78; prin. design engr. Failure Analysis Assocs., Inc. (became Exponent Failure Analysis Assocs., Inc. in 1998), Menlo Park, Calif., 1978—, chmn. bd. dirs., 1988—; chmn. emeritus Failure Analysis Assocs., Inc., Menlo Park, 2005—; CEO The Failure Group, Inc., Menlo Park, 1988-96, chief tech. officer, 1996-98; chmn. Exponent Failure Analysis Assocs., Inc., Menlo Park, 1998—. Co-contbr. numerous articles to profl. jours. Mem. Pres.' Commn. on Nat. Medal of Sci., 1992-94. Recipient Outstanding Civilian Svc. Gold medal U.S. Army, 1998; NSF fellow, 1972-75. Mem. ASME, ASHRAE, ASTM, NAE, Am. Soc. Metals, Soc. Automotive Engrs., Am. Welding Soc., Human Factors Soc., Nat. Fire Protection Assn., Phi Beta Kappa, Sigma Xi (James B. Angell scholar). Office: Exponent Failure Analysis Assn Inc 149 Commonwealth Dr Menlo Park CA 94025 Home Phone: 650-330-1828; Office Phone: 650-688-7100. Office Fax: 650-688-7366. E-mail: sfrlm@exponent.com.

MCCARTHY, SHERRI NEVADA, psychologist, educator, educational consultant; b. Topeka, June 2, 1958; d. Wallace Gene and Lois Elaine (McDyson) McCarthy; m. Scott Newlin Tucker, Feb. 14, 1983 (div. Feb. 2001); children: Colin Apollo, Chrysallis Altair; m. Brian David Ewing, Feb. 5, 2006. AA in Liberal Arts, Phoenix Coll., 1981; BA in Psychology, Ariz. State U., 1984, BEd in English Lit., 1985, MA in Spl. Edn., 1987, PhD in Ednl. Psychology, 1995. Cert. kindergarten -12 spl. edn., ESL tchr., Ariz. Mng. editor Scottsdale (Ariz.) Free Press, 1977-78; instr. English Skills Ctr. Phoenix C.C., 1978-80; spl. instr. Title I Creighton Sch. Dist., Phoenix, 1980-81; lit. instr. CTY program Johns Hopkins U., 1985; gifted specialist Fountain Hills (Ariz.) Schs., 1985-87; writing instr. Ariz. State U. Ctr. Acad. Precocity, 1986; tchr. ESL Chandler-Gilbert C.C., Chandler, Ariz., 1986-87; tchr. of gifted Chandler (Ariz.) Unified Schs., 1987-90; psychology tchr., cons. Maricopa County C.C., Tempe, Ariz., 1988-96; prof. ednl. psychology No. Ariz. U., Yuma, 1993—. Freelance writer, 1974—; spl. edn. tchr. Hawaii Dept. Edn., 1990-91; faculty assoc. ednl. psychology Ariz. State U., Phoenix, 1992-96; tchr. English Mesa (Ariz.) C.C., 1993-96; advisor, asst. honors coord. Phi Theta Kappa, 1994-96; gifted ednl. specialist Kyrene Pub. Schs., Chandler, Ariz., 1995-96; vis. prof. adolescent psychology Fed. U., Porto Alegre, Brazil, 2002-03; sr. lectr., rschr. Vologola State U., Russia, 2003-2004. Author: Metamorphosis-A Collection of Poems, 1975, Speed Communication, 1979, A Matter of Time, 1980, A Death in the Family, 1988, Coping with Special Needs Classmates, 1993, Preventing Adolescent Aggression, 2005, International Teaching Practices in Psychology, 2006; staff writer: Ariz. Hwy. Patrolman mag., Phoenix, 1979-82; newsletter editor: Ednl. Opportunity Ctr., Tempe, Ariz., 1982-83; contbr. articles to profl. jours. Bd. dirs. Young Astronauts, Fountain Hills, 1985-87. US Fulbright scholar, US State Dept. to Russian Fedn., 2003—04, Rsch. scholar, U. Fed. Rio Grande do Sul, 2004—06. Fellow APA (CIRP liaison 1992—), Internat. Coun. Psychologists (bd. dirs. 1998—), Internat. Coun. Psychology Educators (conf. organizer 2000—); mem. Ariz. Ednl. Rsch. Orgn. (bd. dirs. 1997—), Ariz. English Tchrs. Assn. (bd. dirs. 1998—), Odyssey of the Mind (mem. bd. govs. 1987-89, Creativity award 1986, 87). Democrat. Roman Catholic. Avocations: writing, guitar, camping, travel, piano. Office: No Ariz U PO Box 6236 Yuma AZ 85366-6236 Business E-Mail: sherri.mccarthy@nau.edu.

MCCARTHY, THOMAS EDWARD, retired telecommunications executive; b. Sacramento, July 18, 1925; s. James Daniel and Lorene Margaret McCarthy; m. Joyce Elaine Reilly, June 28, 1952 (dec. Nov. 1987); children: Thomas E. Jr., Sharon E., Lisa A. McCarthy Harding; m. Gloria Adair Radford, Dec. 30, 1989. BS in Journalism with distinction, Northwestern U., Evanston, Ill., 1950. Cert. Pub. Rels. Soc. Am. Reporter UP, San Francisco, 1951-54, Wall St. Jour., NYC, 1954-56; pub. rels. project mgr. Sylvania Electric, NYC, 1956-62; mgr. pub. info. GTE Corp., NYC, 1962-72, dir. pub. info. Stamford, Conn., 1972-80, v.p. pub. affairs, 1980-86; ret., 1986. Cons. in field. Author: The History of GTE Corp., 1990 (Assn. Bus. Comms. award, 1991), Irish Jubilee, 1997. With USAAC, 1943—46. Mem.: Zeta Psi, Kappa Tau Alpha, Sigma Delta Chi. Roman Catholic. Avocations: reading, writing, travel, walking, history. Home: 9885 Mill Station Rd Sebastopol CA 95472-9662 Office Phone: 707-823-4151. Personal E-mail: tgmccart@comcast.net.

MCCARTHY, THOMAS JAMES, JR., lawyer; b. Pulaski, Va., Nov. 24, 1943; s. Thomas James and Jane (Osborne) McC.; m. Sally Stockdale, July 25, 1987. BA in Econs., Washington and Lee U., 1967; JD, U. Va., 1970. Bar: Va. 1970, U.S. Dist. Ct. (we. dist.) Va. 1974, U.S. Supreme Ct. 2000. Asoc. Gilmer, Sadler, Ingram Sutherland & Hutton, Pulaski, 1970-75, ptnr., 1975—; county atty. Pulaski County, Pulaski, 1983—. Adminstrv. hearings officer Commonwealth of Va., 1983—; commr. of accts. Pulaski County, 1989—. Bd. dirs. Coun. Sch. Attys., 2005—, New River CC, 1980—88, 1996—2004, vice-chair, 1981—88, 2000—02, chair, 2002—04, found. bd., 1989—91, 2004—05, chair, 2006—. Col. JAGC USAR, 1997, ret. Decorated Legion of Merit, Meritorious Svc. medal, Army Commendation medal. Mem. Va. Bar Assn., 27th Jud. Cir. Bar Assn. (pres. 1978-81), Pulaski County Bar Assn.; fellow Va. Law Found., Sigma Chi, Phi Alpha Delta. Democrat. Episcopalian. Home: PO Box 818 Pulaski VA 24301-0818 Office: Gilmer Sadler et al 65 E Main St Pulaski VA 24301-5013 Office Phone: 540-980-1360 x33.

MCCARTHY, VINCENT PAUL, lawyer; b. Boston, Sept. 25, 1940; s. John Patrick and Marion (Buckley) McC.; children: Vincent, Sybil, Hope. AB, Boston Coll., 1962; JD, Harvard U., 1965. Bar: Mass. 1965. Ptnr. Hale and Dorr LLP, Boston, 1965—; sr. ptnr. Hale and Dorr, Boston, 1976—2003; counsel Wilmer Cutler Pickering Hale & Dorr LLP, 2004—. Co-founder, bd. dirs., sec. Robert F. Kennedy Action Corps, Inc.; mem. Mass. Gov.'s Adv. Coun. on Alcoholism, Boston, 1984-94, Gov.'s Jud. Nominating Com., 1991-96; chmn. Mass. Housing Partnership Fund, 1991-2003; past chmn. Boston Ctr. for Arts; mem. adv. coun. Harvard Internat. AIDS Inst.; trustee, sec. Franklin Square House; past pres. Mass. Assn. for Mental Health; bd. dirs., past sec.-treas. Human Rights Campaign Found.; chmn. Gov.'s Commn. on Gay and Lesbian Youth, 2001-2003. Recipient Vols. of Am. Outstanding Svc. award, 1989. Mem.: ABA (Pro Bono Publico award 1987), Boston Bar Assn. (Pub. Svc. award 1995), Mass. Bar Assn. Home Phone: 617-783-2134; Office Phone: 617-526-6933. Business E-Mail: vincent.mccarthy@wilmerhale.com.

MC CARTHY, WALTER JOHN, JR., retired utilities executive; b. NYC, Apr. 20, 1925; s. Walter John and Irene McC.; m. Linda Lyon, May 6, 1988; children by previous marriage: Walter, David, Sharon, James, William. B.M.E., Cornell U., 1949; grad., Oak Ridge Sch. Reactor Tech., 1952; D.Eng. (hon.), Lawrence Inst. Tech., 1981; D.Sc. (hon.), Eastern Mich. U., 1983; LHD, Wayne State U., 1984; LLD, Alma Coll., Mich., 1985. Engr. Public Service Electric & Gas Co., Newark, 1949-56; sect. head Atomic Power Devel. Assos., Detroit, 1956-61; gen. mgr. Power Reactor Devel. Co., Detroit, 1961-68; with Detroit Edison Co., 1968-90, exec. v.p. ops., 1975-77, exec. v.p. divs., 1977-79, pres., chief operating officer, 1979-81, chmn., chief exec. officer, 1981-90. Author papers in field. Past chmn., bd. dirs. Inst. Nuclear Power Ops., Fed. Mogul Corp., Comerica Bank; past pres. Monterey County Symphony Orch., Detroit Symphony Orch.; past chmn. Detroit Econ. Growth Corp., Detroit Area Coun. Boy Scouts of Am. Fellow Am. Nuc. Soc., Engring. Soc. Detroit; mem. ASME, NAE. Methodist.

MCCARTHY-ALLEN, MARY FRANCES, medical foundation administrator, not-for-profit fundraiser, consultant; b. Washington, Apr. 16, 1937; d. Joseph Francis and Frances (Oddi) McGowan; m. Charles M. Sappenfield, Dec. 14, 1963 (div. June 1990); children: Charles Ross, Sarah Kathleen; m. Daniel Fendrich McCarthy, Jr., Aug. 25, 1990 (dec. Apr. 1999); m. Cary Walter Allen, Nov. 30, 2002. BA, Trinity Coll., Washington, 1958; cert. in bus. adminstrn., Harvard U.-Radcliffe Coll., 1959; MA, Ball State U., Muncie, Ind., 1984. Systems engr. IBM, Cambridge, Mass., 1959-61; editl. asst. Kiplinger Washington Editors, 1961-63; feature writer pub. info. dept. Ball State U., 1984-85, coll. editor Coll. Bus., 1985-86, coord. alumni and devel., 1986-88, dir. major gift clubs and donor rels., 1988-90; dir. devel. Sweet Briar (Va.) Coll., 1990-91; adminstr. St. Mary's Hosp. and Med. Ctr. Found., Grand Junction, Colo., 1991—. Editor: A History of Maxon Corporation, 1986, Managing Change, 1986, Indiana's Investment Banker, 1987; assoc. editor Mid-Am. Jour. Bus., 1985-86. Participant Leadership Lynchburg, 1990, Jr. League; regional dir. IX Assn. for Healthcare Philanthropy, 1996—98, found. bd., 1997—; bd. dirs. Sr. Companions, Grand Junction, 1992—; mem. steering com. Mesa County Health Cmtys., 1992—; bd. dirs. Grand Junction Musical Arts, 1997—; trustee Women's Found. of Colo., 2000—; bd. dirs. Grand Valley Hospice, 2002—; mem. Mesa County Health Assessment, 1994—. Recipient Golden Broom award Muncie Clean City, 1989; svc. of distinction award Ball State U. Coll. Bus., 1990. Mem. Coun. for Advancement and Support of Edn., Assn. of Healthcare Philanthropy (regional 9 cabinet 1992—, bd. dirs. 1997—), Nat. Soc. Fundraising Execs. (cert., Colo. chpt. bd. dirs. 1994—), Rotary. Republican. Avocations: biking, walking, cross country skiing, gardening.

MCCARTIN, JOSEPH T., bank executive; BSEE, Worcester Poly. Inst., Mass.; M in Sys. Tech., Naval Postgraduate Sch.; MBA, U. Notre Dame, Ind. Chief info. officer Banc One Mortgage, Indpls., 1993—97; v.p., chief info. officer GE Capital Mortgage Svcs., Cherry Hill, NJ, 1997—98; chief info. officer Fleet Mortgage Group, Columbia, SC, 1998—2002; cons. Feld Group, 2002—03; sr. v.p., chief info. officer Nat. City Corp., Cleve., 2003—. Served in USAF, 1984—93. Named one of Premier 100 Info. Tech. Leaders, Computerworld, 2006. Office: Nat City Corp Nat City Ctr 1900 E 9th St Cleveland OH 44114-3484 Office Phone: 216-222-2000. *

MCCARTNEY, DAVID FARNHAM, archivist, educator; b. Charles City, Iowa, May 29, 1956; s. Ralph Farnham and Rhoda Mae Huxsol McCartney; life ptnr. James Anthony Petersen. BA, U. Wis., 1979; MA, MLS, U. Md., 1998. Cert. Acad. Cert. Archivists, 2000. Archives technician Nat. Archives and Records Adminstrn., College Park, Md., 1994—98; records officer IMF, Washington, 1998—99; archives asst. Nat. Pub. Broadcasting Archives, College Park, 1995—2000; archives cons. History Assoc., Inc., Rockville, Md., 1999—2000; archivist U. Iowa, Iowa City, 2001—, adj. prof., 2002—. Nat. adv. bd. Iowa Broadcasting Archives, Waverly, Iowa, 2004—; bd. dirs. Nat. Collaborative for Women's History Sites, Chgo., 2004—07. Contbr. chapters to books. Donor, scholarship fund Midwest Archives Conf., Milw., 2005; donor, vol. web mgr. Floyd County Hist. Soc., Charles City, 1998—; donor Englert Civic Theater, Iowa City, 2002. Fellow, Richard Eaton Found., 1996—98; grantee, Nat. Film Preservation Found., 2002, 2003, 2005, Nat. TV and Video Preservation Found., 2004; scholar, H.W. Wilson Co., U. Md., 1996; Frank G. Burke fellow in Archives Studies, U. Md., 1998. Mem.: Soc. Am. Archivists (steering com. coll. and u. archives sect. 2004—06, donor scholarship fund), Midwest Archives Conf. (sec. 2007—), Iowa Conservation and Preservation Consortium, Consortium Iowa Archivists, Com. Instl. Coop. U. Archivists Group, Assn. Moving Image Archivists, Nat. 19th Amendment Soc. (adv. bd. 1991—), Nat. Collaborative for Women's History Sites, Beta Phi Mu. Avocations: reading, bicycling, hiking. Home: 1302 Muscatine Ave Iowa City IA 52240 Office: Dept Special Collections 100 Main Library Iowa City IA 52242-1420 Home Phone: 319-341-3597; Office Phone: 319-335-5921. Office Fax: 319-335-5900. Personal E-mail: dfmcc@yahoo.com. Business E-Mail: david-mccartney@uiowa.edu.

MCCARTNEY, KATHLEEN, dean, education educator; m. William Hagen; children: Pres, Sam, Kaitlin, Kimberly. BA summa cum laude, Tufts Univ.; MS psychology, PhD psychology, Yale Univ. Asst. prof. psychology dept. Harvard U., 1982—87, mem. faculty edn., 2000—, Gerald S. Lesser prof. early childhood edn., academic dean, 2004—05, acting dean Grad. Sch. Edn., 2005—06, dean Grad. Sch. Edn., 2006—; dir. Child Study and Development Ctr. U. NH; prin. investigator Nat. Inst. Child Health & Human Devel. Vis. rsch. scholar Ctr. for Rsch. on Women, Wellesley Coll. Editl. bd. Child Devel. Jour., Devel. Psychology; contbr. articles tp profl. jours. Grantee Am. Psychological Soc., Bush Fellow, Yale Univ. Fellow: Am. Psychological Soc.; mem.: Soc. Research Child Devel. (co-chmn.). Office: Harvard U Human Devel & Psychology 7th Fl Larsen Hall Cambridge MA 02138 Office Phone: 617-495-3401. Office Fax: 617-496-1182. E-mail: kathleen_mccartney@gse.harvard.edu.

MCCARTNEY, SIR PAUL (JAMES PAUL MCCARTNEY), musician; b. Liverpool, Eng., June 18, 1942; s. James and Mary Patricia (Mohin) McC.; m. Linda Eastman, Mar. 12, 1969 (dec. April 17, 1998); children, James, Stella, Mary, Heather; m. Heather Mills, June 11, 2002 (separated May 17, 2006); 1 child, Beatrice. Degree, Univ. Sussex, Brighton, 1988. With John Lennon and George Harrison in groups Quarrymen, Johnny and the Moondogs, Silver Beatles, 1956-62, with John Lennon, George Harrison and Ringo Starr in group The Beatles, 1962-70,with group Wings, 1970-80; solo performer, 1970-; (albums with The Beatles) Meet the Beatles, 1964, The Beatles '65, 1964, Hard Day's Night, 1964, Help!, 1965, Rubber Soul, 1965, Revolver, 1966, Sgt. Pepper's Lonely Hearts Club Band, 1967, Magical Mystery Tour, 1967, The Beatles (The White Album), 1968, Yellow Submarine, 1969, Abbey Road, 1969, Hey Jude, 1970, Let It Be, 1970; (solo albums) McCartney, 1970, Ram, 1971, Red Rose Speedway, 1973, Band on the Run, 1973, Venus and Mars, 1975, Wings Over America, 1975, Wings at the Speed of Sound, 1976, London Town, 1978, Wings Greatest, 1978, Back to the Egg, 1979, McCartney II, 1980, Tug of War, 1982, Press to Play, 1986, All the Best, 1987, Flowers in the Dirt, 1989, Jet, 1989, Tripping the Live Fantastic, 1990, Unplugged/The Official Bootleg, 1991, Off the Ground, 1993, Paul is Live, 1993, Flaming Pie, 1997, Run Devil Run, 1999, Driving Rain, 2001, Chaos and Creation in the Backyard, 2005, Memory Almost Full, 2007; composer numerous songs (with John Lennon) including Please Please Me, I Want To Hold Your Hand, All My Loving, Can't Buy Me Love, I Saw Her Standing There, Love Me Do, Yesterday, Michelle, She's a Woman, Here, There and Everywhere, Good Day Sunshine, Penny Lane, She's Leaving Home, Fool on the Hill, Back in the USSR, Martha My Dear, Blackbird, Helter Skelter, Hey Jude, Let It Be, The Long and Winding Road, Get Back; (solo) Maybe I'm Amazed, My Love, Live and Let Die, Band on the Run, Silly Love Songs, Another Day, No More Lonely Nights, With a Little Luck; composer The Liverpool Oratorio, 1991; animator, composer Paul McCartney: The Music and Animation Collection, 2004; film appearances include: A Hard Day's Night, 1964, Help!, 1965, Let It Be, 1970, Give My Regards to Broad Street, 1984, Get Back, 1991; TV appearances include Doctor Who, 1965, Magical Mystery Tour, 1967, The Morecambe & Wise Show, 1968, Frost on Sunday, 1968, James Paul McCartney, 1973, Wings Over the World, 1979, Bread, 1986, (voice) The Simpsons, 1995, Saturday Night Live, 1998, V.I.P., 2000; videos include The Beatles: The First U.S. Visit, 1994, Paul McCartney: In the World Tonight, 1997, Twentieth Century Blues: The Songs of Noel Coward, 1998; producer animated film The Oriental Nightfish, 1978; author, Each One Believing: Paul McCartney On Stage, Off Stage, and Backstage, 2004; (children's book) High in the Clouds, 2005. Decorated Order of Brit. Empire, 1965, Knight Comdr., 1997; recipient Acad. award (with Beatles) for Best Original Song Score, Let It Be, 1970, 5 Grammy awards with Beatles, 2 solo, 1 with Wings, Ivor Novello award for outstanding services to Brit. music, 1989, (with Linda McCartney) Lifetime Achievement award People for the Ethical Treatment of Animals, 1996; named to Rock and Roll Hall of Fame, 1988, Lifetime Achievement award, 1990. Fellow Royal Coll. Music. *

MC CARTNEY, RALPH FARNHAM, lawyer; b. Charles City, Iowa, Dec. 11, 1924; s. Ralph C. and Helen (Farnham) McC.; m. Rhoda Mae Huxsol, June 25, 1950; children: Ralph, Julia, David. JD, U. Mich., 1950; BSc, Iowa State U., 1972. Bar: Iowa 1950. Mem. firm Miller, Heuber & Miller, Des Moines, 1950-52, Frye & McCartney, Charles City, 1952-73, McCartney & Erb, Charles City, 1973-78; judge Dist. Ct. Iowa, Charles City, 1978-87; chief judge 2d Judicial Dist., 1987-92; sr. judge Ct. Appeals, 1992—. Mem. jud. coordinating com. Iowa Supreme Ct. Chmn. Supreme Ct. Adv. Com. on Adminstrn. of Clks. Offices; mem. Iowa Ho. of Reps., 1967-70, majority floor leader, 1969-70; mem. Iowa Senate, 1973-74. Bd. regents U. Iowa, Iowa State U., U. No. Iowa, Iowa Sch. for Deaf, Iowa Braille and Sight Saving Sch. Served with AUS, 1942-45. Mem.: Iowa Judges Assn. Home: 1828 Cedar View Dr Charles City IA 50616-9129 Home Phone: 641-228-2518.

MCCARTNEY, ROBERT CHARLES, retired lawyer; b. Pitts., May 3, 1934; s. Nathaniel Hugh and Esther Mary (Smith) McC.; m. Janet Carolyn Moore, June 16, 1956; children: Ronald K., Sharon S., Carole J. AB, Princeton U., 1956; JD, Harvard U., 1959. Bar: D.C. 1959, Pa. 1960, U.S. Dist. Ct. (we. dist.) Pa. 1960, U.S. Ct. Appeals (3d dist.) 1960, U.S. Supreme Ct. 1966. Assoc. Eckert Seamans Cherin & Mellott, LLC, Pitts., 1959—64, ptnr., 1965—93, mem. exec. com., 1991—93, of counsel, 1993—. Sec., gen. counsel Ryan Homes, Inc., 1969-93; bd. dirs. United Meth. Found. of Western Pa., 1971— v.p., 1981-85, chmn., 1985-86; sec., gen. counsel Rimoldi of Am., Inc., 1989-99. Solicitor North Pitts. Cmty. Devel. Corp., 1968-76, alt. dir., 1968-80; mem. McCandless Twp. Govt. Study Commn., 1973-74, Princeton U. Leadership Devel. Coun., 2002-06; solicitor, asst. sec. McCandless Indsl. Devel. Authority, 1972-98; exec. com. Princeton U. Alumni Coun., 1966-70, 76-85, vice-chmn., 1981-83, chmn., 1983-85, co-chair spl. com. 250th Anniversary Princeton U., 1994-97, nat chmn. class planned giving program, 2002—, mem. planned giving adv. com., 2002-, mem. steardship adv. coun., 2004—; trustee Otterbein Coll., 1975-83, Pa. S.W. Assn., 1992-96; bd. dirs. Pitts. Cultural Trust, 1992-99; chmn. conf.-wide endowment program United Meth. Conf. We. Pa., 1985-87; bd. dir. Pitts. Civic Light Opera Assn., 1984—, v.p., 1987-92, pres., 1992-99; dir. The Ireland Inst. Pitts., 1991-2004, vice-chmn., 1996-2004; mem. No. Ireland Partnership, 1991—; bd. dir. Pitts. Concert Chorale, 1997-2003, Pitts. Irish and Classical Theater, 2000-05. Princeton fellow Harvard U., 1956-59. Mem. Princeton U. Alumni Assn. West Pa. (pres. 1976-78), Duquesne Club, Princeton Club of NY, Nassau Club. Republican. Home: 9843 Woodland Rd N Pittsburgh PA 15237-4347 Office: Eckert Seamans 600 Grant St Ste 44th Fl Pittsburgh PA 15219-2703 Office Phone: 412-566-6025.

MCCARTY, DARREN, professional hockey player; b. British Columbia, Canada, Apr. 1, 1972; Mem. Detroit Red Wings, 1993—2005, Calgary Flames, 2005—. Achievements include member of Stanely Cup Champion Detroit Red Wings, 1997, 1998, 2002. Office: c/o Calgary Flames PO Box 1540 Stn M T2P 3B9 Calgary AL Canada

MCCARTY, DORAN CHESTER, religious organization administrator; b. Bolivar, Mo., Feb. 3, 1931; s. Bartie Lee and Donta Marian (Russell) McC.; m. Gloria Jean Laffoon, June 14, 1952; children: Gaye, Risë, Marletta, Leslie. AA, Southwest Bapt. Coll., 1950; AB, William Jewell Coll., 1952; BD, So. Bapt. Theol. Sem, 1956, PhD, 1963. Pastor 1st Bapt. Ch., Switz City, Ind., 1956-62, Pleasant Hill, Mo., 1962-65, Susquehanna Bapt. Ch., Independence, Mo., 1965-67; prof. Midwestern Bapt. Theol. Sem., Kansas City, Mo., 1967-81, Golden Gate Bapt. Theol. Sem., Mill Valley, Calif., 1981-87; coord. Northeastern Bapt. Sch. Ministry, NYC, 1987-94; exec. dir. Sem. Ext., Nashville, 1988-94; pres. McCarty Svcs., Nashville, 1994—. Cons. Bapt. Home Mission Bd., 1981—; assoc. dean So. Bapt. Theol. Sem., Louisville, 1989; pres. McCarty Svcs., St. Augustine. Author: Rightly Dividing trhe Word, 1973, Teilhard de Chardin, 1976, The Supervision of Ministry Students, 1978, The Supervision of Mission Personnel, 1983, The Inner Heart of Ministry, 1985, Working With People, 1987, Leading the Small Church, 1991, Supervision: Developing and Directing People on Mission, 1994, Making the Most of Your Time, 1996, Making the Most of Conflict, 1997, Making the Most of Change, 1998, Making the Most if Empowerment, 1999, Making the Most of Coping, 2000, Making the Most of Pastoral Leadership, 2002, Hallowed Be Thy Name, 2002; editor: Key Resources, 5 vols., Broadman Leadership Series, 16 vols., The Practice of Ministry: A Sourcebook, 1995. Recipient Life Service award Southwest Bapt. U., Bolivar, 1973, William Jewell Coll. Achievement citation, 1987. Mem. Assn. for Theol. Field Edn. (chairperson 1979-81), Inst. Theol. Reflection (exec. dir. 1978-86), Fellowship In Service Guidance Dirs. (pres. 1986-87, Lewis Newman award 1988). Home: 116 Village Del Lago Ln Saint Augustine FL 32080 E-mail: doranmccarty@bellsouth.net, doran@ang.com. *As I have experienced life, grace affords priviledge, priviledge calls forth duty, duty depends on transcendence, and transcendence provides enrichment.*

MCCARTY, FREDERICK BRIGGS, electrical engineer, consultant; b. Dilley, Tex., Aug. 11, 1926; s. John Frederick Briggs and Olive Ruth (Snell) Briggs McCarty; m. Doris Mary Cox, May 3, 1950 (div. 1970); children: Mark Frederick, David Lambuth, Jackson Clare; m. Nina Lucile Butman, Aug. 17, 1973. BSEE, U. Tex., 1949. Design engr. GE, Schenectady, NY, 1949-51; sr. design engr. Convair, Ft. Worth, 1951-55; sr. engr. Aerojet Gen., Azusa, Calif., 1955-61; sr. engring. specialist Garrett Corp., Torrance, Calif., 1961-91; v.p., founder Patio Pacific, Inc., Torrance, 1973-84; owner, operator Textiger Co., Torrance, 1980-91; cons., 1991—. With USNR, 1944—46, PTO. Mem.: IEEE (sr.), Eta Kappa Nu, Tau Beta Pi. Democrat. Achievements include patents in field; design of superconducting acyclic motor for USN and high speed elec. machines for aerospace and transp. Home and Office: 1366 Stonewood Ct San Pedro CA 90732-1550

MCCARTY, JOHN ALBERT, management educator; b. Nashville, May 28, 1951; s. Justin Hunter and Emily Lavinder (Lacy) McC. BA, Vanderbilt U., 1973; MA, U. Ill., 1979, PhD, 1986; MA, U. Chgo., 1981. Rsch. assoc. Needham Harper Worldwide Advt., Chgo., 1983-85; asst. prof. dept. advt. and bus. adminstrn. U. Ill., Urbana, 1986-93; asst. prof. dept. mktg. Am. U., Washington, 1993—98; asst. prof. sch. mgmt. George Mason U., Fairfax, Va., 1998—2001; from asst. prof. to assoc. prof. sch. bus. Coll. NJ, Ewing, 2001—. Vis. lectr. dept. advt. U. Ill., 1985-86. Contbr. chpts. in books: Advances in Non Profit Marketing, 1990, Global and Multi-National Advertising, 1994, Marketing and Consumer Research in the Public Interest, 1996, Integrated Communication: Synergy of Persuasive Voices, 1996, Values, Lifestyles and Psychographics, 1997, The Psychology of Entertainment Media, 2004, Marketing Communications: New Approaches, Technologies and Styles, 2005; contbr. articles to profl. jours.; reviewer Jour. of Advt., 1988—. Lt. (j.g.) USN, 1973-76. Mem. Am. Mktg. Assn. (workshop coord. 1987-88), Assn. for Consumer Rsch., Am. Acad. Advt., Am. Assn. Pub. Opinion Rsch. Office: Coll NJ 2000 Pennington Rd Ewing NJ 08628 Home Phone: 609-882-1236; Office Phone: 609-771-3220. Business E-Mail: mccarty@tcnj.edu.

MCCARTY, LOIS LEONE, retired sociologist; b. Oakland, Calif., Feb. 28, 1939; d. Richard Oliver McCarty and Nina Lea Wiley; m. Donald Greene (div. 1976). BA in Psychology, San Jose State U., Calif., 1960, MS in Sociology, 1962; postgrad. in Sociology, Psychology and Human Resource Mgmt., U. Calif., Berkeley, Santa Clara U., Calif. Cert. tchr. Calif. Prof. sociology Foothill Coll., Los Altos Hills, Calif., 1965—2000; juvenile probation officer Santa Cruz County, Calif., 1962—63; adult probation officer San Mateo County, Redwood City, Calif., 1963—67; prof. sociology Santa Rosa Jr. Coll., Calif., 1964—65; adminstrv. evaluator Foothill Coll., Los Altos Hills, Calif., 2000—05; ret., 2005. Recipient SALGO-NOREN Found. award for Tchg. Excellence, 1975, NIDSO Tchg. Excellence award, 1993, 1994, Pres.'s award for acad. excellence, Foothill Coll., 2000, Appreciation plaque, Foothill Coll. Faculty, Students and Staff of Women's Studies, 2000. Mem.: Am. Sociol. Assn., Lodi Women's Club. Avocations: travel, interior decorating, volunteerism, music. Home: 9303 N Hildreth Ln Stockton CA 95212 Office Phone: 209-931-3590. Personal E-mail: lomccr@aol.com.

MCCARTY, PERRY LEE, civil and environmental engineering educator; b. Grosse Pointe, Mich., Oct. 29, 1931; m. Martha Davis Collins, Sept. 5, 1953; children: Perry Lee, Cara L., Susan A., Kathleen R. BSCE, Wayne State U., Detroit, 1953; MS in San. Engring., MIT, Cambridge, 1957, ScD, 1959; DEng (hon.), Colo. Sch. Mines, Golden, 1992. Field engr. Edwin Orr Co., Dearborn, Mich., 1951-52; engr. Pate & Hirn, Detroit, 1952-53; field engr. Hubbell, Roth & Clark, Detroit, 1953; instr. civil engring. Wayne State U., 1953-54; field engr. George Jerome & Co., Detroit, 1954; engr. Civil Engrs., Inc., Detroit, 1956; assoc. Rolf Eliassen Assocs., Winchester, Mass., 1958-61; asst. prof. san. engring. MIT, 1958-62; faculty Stanford U., Calif., 1962—, prof. civil engring., 1967-75, Silas H. Palmer prof., 1975-99, Silas H. Palmer prof. emeritus, 1999—, chmn. dept. civil engring., 1980-85; chair prof. environ. sci. and engring. Tsinghua U., 2004—07. Chmn. Gordon Rsch. Conf. Environ. Scis., 1972; vice chmn. environ. studies bd. NRC-NAS, 1976-80, mem. com. on phys. scis., math. and resources, 1985-88, bd. on radioactive waste mgmt., 1989-96, mem. com. geoscis., environment, resources, 1994-97. Co-author: Chemistry for Environmental Engineering and Science, 5th edit., 2003, Environmental Biotechnology Principles and Applications, 2001. Served with AUS, 1954-56. Recipient Tyler Prize for Environ. Achievement, 1992, Clarke Prize Outstanding Achievement Water Sci. and Tech., 1997, Stockholm Water prize, 2007; NSF faculty fellow, 1968-69. Fellow AAAS, Am. Acad. Microbiology, Am. Acad. Arts and Scis.; mem. ASCE (Walter L. Huber Rsch. prize 1964, Simon W. Freese Environ. Engring. award 1979, James R. Croes medal 1995), NAE, Am. Water Works Assn. (hon., life, chmn. water quality divsn. 1972-73, trustee rsch. divsn. 1980-85, Best Paper award 1985, A.P. Black Rsch. award 1989), Am. Soc. for Microbiology, Water Environment Fedn. (hon. 1989, Harrison P. Eddy award 1962, 77, Thomas Camp award 1975), Assn. Environ. Engring. Sci. Profs. (Disting. Faculty award 1966, Oustanding Publ. award 1985, 88, 98, 2003, Founders award 1992), Am. Soc. Engring. Edn.(vice-chmn. environ. engring. divsn. 1968-69), Sigma Xi, Tau Beta Pi (fellow 1957-58). Home: 823 Sonoma Ter Stanford CA 94305-1024 Office: Stanford U Civil Environ Engring Dept Stanford CA 94305-4020 Office Phone: 650-723-4131. Business E-Mail: pmccarty@stanford.edu.

MCCARTY, RICHARD CHARLES, psychology professor, dean; b. Portsmouth, Va., July 12, 1947; s. Constantine Ambrose and Helen Marie (Householder) McC.; m. Sheila Adair Miltier, July 15, 1965; children: Christopher Charles, Lorraine Marie, Ryan Lester, Patrick James. BS in Biology, Old Dominion U., 1970, MS in Zoology, 1972; PhD in Pathobiology, Johns Hopkins U., 1976. Rsch. assoc. NIMH, Bethesda, Md., 1976-78; asst. prof. U. Va., Charlottesville, 1978-84, assoc. prof., 1984-88, prof., 1988-2001, chair psychology, 1990-98, chair Coun. of Grad. Depts. Psychology, 1996-97; exec. dir. sci. directorate APA, Washington, 1998-2001; dean arts and sci. Vanderbilt U., Nashville, 2001—. Mem. editl. bd. Behavioral and Neural Biology, 1985—90, Physiology and Behavior, 1989—, editor-in-chief Stress, 1995—99; editor: Am. Psychologist, 2000—01. Lt. comdr. USPHS, 1976—78. Recipient Rsch. Scientist Devel. award, NIMH, 1985—90; sr. fellow, Nat. Heart Lung Blood Inst., NIH, 1984—85. Fellow AAAS, APA, Assn. Psychol. Sci. Roman Catholic. Office: Office of the Dean Vanderbilt U Coll Arts and Sci 301 Kirkland Hall Nashville TN 37240 Business E-Mail: richard.mccarty@vanderbilt.edu.

MCCARTY, ROBERT CLARKE, mathematician; b. Mountain View, Calif., Apr. 29, 1922; s. John Emmet and Eldora Lydia (Freeman) McC.; m. Netta Cassen, July 29, 1945 (div. Oct. 1968) 1 child, Stephanie Ann; m. Rita Ransier, July 29, 1969; children: Michael Wayne, Teresa Kay, Kathleen Gail. BA in Math., San Jose Sate U., 1950; MS in Math. and Statistics, U. Wash., Seattle, 1957; PhD in Math., Pacific Western U., 1990. Staff mathematician Boeing Rsch. Labs., Seattle, 1952-59; rsch. mathematician Stanford Rsch. Inst., Menlo Park, Calif., 1959-70; pres., cons. McCarty and Assocs., Gilroy, Calif., 1976—; sr. staff scientist ESL-TRW Corp., Sunnyvale, Calif., 1984-87; prin. staff scientist ARGO Systems, Sunnyvale, 1987-93. Sci. advisor to Congresswoman Zoe Lofgren, sci. com. US Congress, 1994—; rsch. proxy for Prof. A.S. Paulraj, Dept. Elec. Engring., Info. Scis., Stanford U., 1993-95; sr. rsch. mathematician Ares Corp., Arlington, Va., 1994-96; cons. in field. Contbr. articles to profl. jours. Lt. USCGR, 1941—52, WWII, European and Pacific, ret. lt. USCGR, 1951—52, Korean War, Ctrl. and North Pacific. Mem. Sigma Xi. Avocations: amateur radio, rifle and pistol marksmanship, swimming. Home and Office: 9425 Marcella Ave Gilroy CA 95020-9085 Office Phone: 408-842-9880.

MCCARTY, SHIRLEY CAROLYN, retired aerospace executive; b. Minot, ND, May 2, 1934; d. Harry and Cecelia Marie (Engene) Wolhowe; m. John Myron McCarty, Apr. 3, 1958. BSBA, U. ND, Grand Forks, 1958. Mem. tech. staff Douglas Aircraft, El Segundo, Calif., 1960-62, The Aerospace Corp., El Segundo, 1962-72, mgr., 1972-73, dir., 1973-79, prin. dir., 1979-89, gen. mgr., 1989—96; ret., 1996; pres. Shamrock Consulting, 1996—. Mem. adv. coun. Calif. State U., Northridge, 1979-01, chmn., 1984-86; mem. indsl. adv. bd. Purdue U. Soc. Women Engrs., West Lafayette, Ind., 1979-82, 85-; mem. adv. bd. Calif. Acad. Math. and Sci., 1991-96; apptd. mem. aerospace safety adv. panel NASA, 1998, chair, 2002-03; spkr. in field. Named Woman of Yr. The Aerospace Corp., 1976, Pres.'s award, 1987; named to Hall of Fame Women in Tech. Internat., 2003; recipient Spl. Judges Award for Leadership, Los Angeles YWCA, 1977, Sioux Alumni Award, U. N.D, 1982, Achievement award Los Angeles County Commn. for Women, 1987. Fellow Soc. Women Engrs.; mem. IEEE, Assn. for Computing Machinery, Soc. Women Engrs., Bus. and Profl. Women (Woman of Achievement 1984, Golden Nike award 1985), Women in Bus.(corp. achievement award, 1987), Women in Computing (founding mem., bd. dirs.). Avocations: raising and training siberian huskies, travel, writing, architecture. Home: 357 Valley St El Segundo CA 90245-2932

MCCARTY, THOMAS JOSEPH, publishing executive; b. Waltham, Mass., June 10, 1938; s. Raymond Anthony and Mary Agatha (Riley) McC; m. Colette Ann Koechley, Aug. 3, 1963; children: Matthew Thomas, Brendan James, Sarah Katherine. BA, Holy Cross Coll., 1960; cert., Harvard U., 1961. Cert. Srs. Health Ins. Info. NC Dept. Ins., 2006. Various mgmt. positions Oxford U. Press, NYC, 1960-71, mgr. ops., 1971-79, dir. distbn., 1980-81, v.p. distbn., 1982-84, v.p. distbn. and info. systems, 1985-88, sr. v.p., 1988-90; sr. v.p., gen. mgr. Oxford U. Press, Cary, N.C. ops., 1990-98, spl. cons. to pres., 1998-2000. Chmn., bd. advs. Carolina Pub. Inst. U. N.C., Chapel Hill, 1995-98. Trustee N.C. Symphony Found., v.p., 1998—; mem. adv. bd. Sch. Info. and L.S., U. N.C., Chapel Hill; mem. City of Cary Unified Devel. Ordinance Adv. Commn., 1999—; mem. bd. advisors Open Mind Publ. Group, 2000; mem. N.C. Mus. Art; bd. dirs. Shakti for Children Found., 1994—98, English Speaking Union of Research Triangle, pres., 1998—2002. Mem.: Exec. Svc. Corps., Fine Arts League Cary, Am. Mgmt. Assn., Svc. Corps Ret. Execs., Am. Assn. Pubs., U. N.C. Faculty Club (Chapel Hill), McGregor Downs Country Club (Cary).

MCCARTY, TODD, retail executive; BBA, U. Minn. Positions including divsn. employment supr. Quaker Oats Co., 1989—92; positions including human resources mgr., dir. human resources North Am. ops. and v.p. human resources Frito-Lay Can. PepsiCo, Inc., 1992—2000; sr. v.p. human resources N.Am. Starwood Hotels and Resorts Worldwide, 2000—05; sr. v.p. human resources Rite Aid Corp., Camp Hill, Pa., 2005—. Office: Rite Aid Corp 30 Hunter Ln Camp Hill PA 17011 Office Phone: 717-761-2633. *

MCCARTY, V. K., publishing executive, chaplain, librarian; b. Boston, June 26, 1948; d. Charles Osner and Dorothy June (McAlister) Long. BM, Mich. State U., 1969; MM, U. Louisville, 1972; cert. in theatre arts, U. London, 1972; intern in clin. pastoral edn., St. Luke's Roosevelt Hosp., 1989, resident in clin. pastoral edn., 1995; student, Congl. Devel. Inst. Tng., Diocese of Newark, 2003. Advt. asst. Lansing (Mich.) State Jour., 1968-69; market rsch. cons. Sta. WKLO, Louisville, 1969-70; libr. Louisville Free Pub. Libr., 1970-72; v.p. assoc. pub. Gen. Media Inc., NYC, 1979-2000; acquisitions libr. Gen. Theol. Sem. St. Mark's Libr., NYC, 2000—; part-time acquisitions libr. Union Theol. Sem. Burke Libr., NYC, 2001—02; dir. Christian Formation, St. Paul's Ch., Chatham, NJ, 2002—03. Bd. dirs. B.F.T., Inc., NYC. Dance editor Saturday Review Mag. Online, 1993-95. Master of ceremonies St. Ignatius of Antioch, N.Y.C., 1984-98; chaplaincy coord. St. Luke's Roosevelt Hosp., N.Y.C. Mem. N.Y. Liturgical Music Found. (steering com. 1982-84), N.Y. Ch. Club. Avocations: Biblical languages, riding, ballet, preservation of Benedictine monasticism, Byzantine art. Office: Gen Theol Sem St Mark's Libr 175 9th Ave New York NY 10011-4977

MCCARTY-PUHL, J-PETRINA, chemistry educator; BS in Botany, Univ. Nev., Reno; MA in Curriculum and Instruction, Nova Southeastern Univ.; Crime Investigator Technician Degree, Kaplan Coll., 2005. Cert. Nat. Bd. Tchg. Standards, 2001. Tchr. Washoe County Sch. Dist., 1987—; chemistry, forensics tchr. Robert McQueen H.S., Reno. Named Nev. Tchr. of Yr., 2006; recipient Outstanding H.S. tchr. award, Ariz.-Nev. Acad. Sci., 2003, Presdl. Excellence award for Secondary Sci. Tchr., Best of Edn. award, Subaru Sci. award for Excellence in Tchg., We. Region, The I CAN Learn-NEA Found. awards for Tchg. Excellence, 2007; grantee Brandywine Fellowship. Office: Robert McQueen High Sch 6055 Lancer St Reno NV 89523 Business E-Mail: pmccarty@washoe.k12.nv.us. *

MCCARUS, ERNEST NASSEPH, retired language educator; b. Charleston, W.Va., Sept. 10, 1922; s. Nasseph Mitchell and Della (Saad) McC.; m. Adele Najib Haddad, Sept. 10, 1955; children: Peter Kevin, Carol Ann. Student, Morris Harvey Coll., 1939-40; AB, U. Mich., 1945, MA, 1949, PhD, 1956. Translation team capt. Allied Translators and Interpreters' Service, Allied Hqrs., Tokyo, 1946-47; mem. English Lang. Inst. staff U. Mich., 1948-52, mem. univ. expdn. to Near East, 1951, instr. univ., 1952-56, asst. prof. Arabic, 1956-61; dir. Fgn. Service Inst. Field Sch. Arabic Lang. and Area Study, U.S. Dept. State, Beirut, 1958-60; assoc. prof. Arabic and Kurdish, dept. Near Ea. studies U. Mich., 1961-67, prof., 1967-95, chmn. dept., 1969-77, dir. Ctr. for Arabic Study Abroad, 1974-83, dir. U. Mich. Center for Middle Eastern and North African Studies, 1983-92, prof. emeritus, 1995—. Author: Grammar of Kurdish of Sulaimania, Iraq, 1958, (with H. Hoenigswald, R. Noss, J. Yamagiwa) A Survey of Intensive Programs in the Uncommon Languages, 1962, (with A. Yacoub) Elements of Contemporary Arabic, 1962, 3d edn., 1966, (with Raji Rammuny) First Level Arabic: Elementary Literary Arabic for Secondary Schools, 1964, Teacher's Manual to Accompany First Level Arabic, 1964, (with Jamal J. Abdullah) Kurdish Basic Course - Dialect of Sulaimania, Iraq, 1967, Kurdish Readers, Vol. I Newspaper Kurdish, Vol. II. Kurdish Essays, Vol. III Kurdish Short Stories, 1967, A Kurdish-English Dictionary, 1967, (with P. Abboud) Elementary Modern Standard Arabic, 1983, (with R. Rammuny) Word Count of Elementary Modern Literary Arabic Textbooks, 1969, (with P. Abboud, E.T. Abdel-Massih, S. Altoma, W. Erwin, R. Rammuny) Modern Standard Arabic Intermediate Level, 1971, (with R. Rammuny) A Programmed Course in Modern Literary Arabic Phonology and Script, 1974; editor: Language Learning, Vol. VII, 1956-57, Language Learning, Vol. XIII, 1963, An-Nashra, 1967-74, Contemporary Arabic Readers, Vols. I-V, 1962-66, The Development of Arab-American Identity, 1994, English Grammar for Students of Arabic, 2006; contbr. articles to scholastic jours. Served with US Army, 1942-46. Recipient Lifetime Contbn. award CASA, 2004, Mesa/Bacharach Svc. award, 2005; Rockefeller fellow, 1951. Mem. Mich. Linguistic Soc. (pres. 1962-63), Am. Assn. Tchrs. Arabic (pres. 1973, exec. coun. 1979-81, 89-92), Middle East Studies Assn. (bd. dirs. 1973-75), Linguistic Soc. Am., Am. Oriental Soc., Linguistic Circle N.Y., Arabic Linguistic Soc. (pres. 1992). Home: 1400 Beechwood Dr Ann Arbor MI 48103-2940 E-mail: enm@umich.edu.

MCCASH, JUNE HALL, writer, retired language educator; b. Newberry, SC, June 8, 1938; d. James DeLeon and Williemaye Stone Hall; m. Marvin Hampton Martin (div. June 1971); children: Michael Hall Martin, Christopher Brenden Martin; m. William Barton McCash, July 3, 1974 (dec. Feb. 1991); m. Richard Douglas Gleaves, Jr., May 21, 1994. BA, Agnes Scott Coll., 1960; MA, Emory U., 1963, PhD, 1967. Instr. dept. romance langs. Emory U., Atlanta, 1964—66; from asst. to assoc. prof. Mid. Tenn. State U., Murfreesboro, 1967—70, from assoc prof. to prof., 1970—75, founding dir. honors program, 1973—80, prof. dept. fgn. langs., 1975—2004, chair dept. fgn. langs., 1980—92, grad. dir. dept. fgn. langs. and lits., 1996—2004, prof. emerita, 2004—. Presenter in field; fellow Am. Coun. Edn., 1986—87; elderhostel instr. W. Ga. Coll., Ga., 1992; interpreter for vis. French del. C. of C., Murfreesboro, 1992; exec. bd. Tenn. Humanities Coun., 1987—89, chair grant program com., 1987—88, vice-chair, 1988—89, chair, 1990—96, So. Humanities Media Fund, 1989—91, Tenn. Humanities Coun., 1989—91, exec. bd., 1991—92; local coord. ESL Inst. Tenn. Dept. Edn., 1992; coord. various profl. workshops. Author: Love's Fools: Aucassin, Troilus, Calisto and the Parody of the Courtly Lover, 1972, The Jekyll Island Cottage Colony, 1998, Jekyll Island's Early Years: From Prehistory through Reconstruction, 2005; co-author: Jekyll Island Club Historic District 100 Years, 1986, The Jekyll Island Club: Southern Haven for America's Millionaires, 1989, The Life of Saint Audrey: A Text by Marie de France, 2006; editor: The Cultural Patronage of Medieval Women, 1996; contbr. articles to profl. jours.; mem. editl. bd. Le Cygne: A Jour. on Marie de France. Hon. life mem. Jekyll Island Mus. Assocs., Friends of Linebaugh; trustee Jekyll Island Found., 2000—; layreader St. Paul's Episcopal Ch., Murfreesboro; chair adv. bd. So. Festival Books, 1988—92, mem. author's com., 1988—94. Recipient awrds for poetry, novel and juvenile fiction, Southeastern Writers Assn., 2006, Novel award, 2006, Smith Moseley Poetry award, 2006, Daphne Cantrell Chambless Juvenile Fiction award, 2006, Poetry award, By-Line Mag., 2007; fellow, Nat. Humanities Coun., 1975; Young Humanists fellow, NEH, 1975, Mellon grantee for workshop on medieval culture, Vanderbilt U., 1982, Am. Coun. Edn. fellow, 1986—87. Mem.: AAUP (chair com. on status of women 1969—70, sec. MTSU chpt. 1970—71, mem. exec. com. 1970—74, v.p. 1971—72), Medieval Acad. Am., Internat. Marie de France Soc. (mem. exec. bd. 1993—95, mem. adv. coun. 2001—), Southeastern Medieval Assn. (mem. exec. com. 1991—94, v.p. 1995—97, pres. 1997—99,), Internat. Courtly Lit. Soc. (internat. treas. 1980—86, v.p. N.Am. br. 1990—92, pres. N.Am. br. 1992—95, internat. v.p. 2001—04, internat. pres. 2004—07), Soc. Rencesvals, Phi Sigma Iota, Phi Kappa Phi (pres. elect 1997—98, pres. 1998—99, MTSU chpt.), Alpha Mu Gamma. Democrat. Avocations: painting, photography, reading.

MCCASKEY, MICHAEL B., professional football team executive; b. Lancaster, Pa., Dec. 11, 1943; s. Edward B. and Virginia (Halas) McCaskey; m. Nancy McCaskey; children: John, Kathryn. Grad., Yale U., 1965; PhD, Case Western Res. U. Tchr. UCLA, 1972-75, Harvard U. Sch. Bus., Cambridge, Mass., 1975-82; pres., chief exec. officer Chgo. Bears (NFL),

1983-99, chmn. bd., 1999—. Author: The Executive Challenge: Managing Change and Ambiguity. Named Exec. of Yr. Sporting News, 1985. Office: 1000 Football Dr Lake Forest IL 60045-4829

MCCASKEY, RAYMOND F., insurance company executive; b. 1944; m. Judy McCaskey. With Continental Assurance Co., Chgo., 1963-73; assist v.p. Health Care Service Corp., 1973—79, chief actuary, 1979—82, CFO, 1982—91, pres., COO, 1991—98, pres., CEO, 1998—. Former bd. chmn. Lincoln Found. for Bus. Excellence. Office: Health Care Service Corp 300 E Randolph St Chicago IL 60601-5014 Office Phone: 312-938-6000.

MCCASKILL, CLAIRE C., senator, former auditor; b. Houston, July 25, 1953; d. William Y. and Betty Anne McCaskill; m. David Exposito (div. 1995); children: Austin, Maddie, Lily; m. Joseph Shepard, 2002; stepchildren: Benjamin, Carl, Marilyn, Michael. BS in Polit. Sci., U. Mo., Columbia, 1975, JD, 1978. Law clk. Mo. Ct. Appeals (we. dist.), Kansas City, 1978—79; asst. prosecutor County of Jackson, Mo., county prosecutor Mo., 1993—99; mem. Mo. Ho. of Reps., 1982—88; auditor State of Mo., Jefferson City, 1999—2007; US Senator from Mo., 2007—. Democrat. Office: US Senate 825A Hart Senate Office Bldg Washington DC 20510 Office Phone: 202-224-3121. Fax: 573-751-6539. *

MCCASLIN, DAVID E., hotel executive; BS in Hotel Mgmt., U. Mo., 1979. Gen. mgr. Lincoln Hotels, Dallas; hotel gen. mgr. CapStar, 1987-88, v.p. ops., COO, 1988; pres. MeriStar Hotels & Resorts, Inc.

MCCASLIN, ELIZABETH ANN, athletic trainer; b. Murfreesboro, Tenn., May 12, 1979; d. James Donald and Edwina Hassell McCaslin. BS in Athletic Tng., East Tenn. State U., Johnson City, 2001; postgrad., U. SC, Columbia, 2006—. Cert. athletic trainer Nat. Athletic Trainers' Assn. Head camp mgr. Universal Cheerleaders Assn., Memphis, 2000—01; athletic tng. fellow Steadman Hawkins Clinic, Vail, Colo., 2002—03, clin. coord., 2003—05; athletic trainer, med. asst. Moore Orthopedic Clinic, Columbia, SC, 2006—. Contbr. articles to profl. jours. Mem.: US Tennis Assn. (vol. 2006), SE Athletic Trainers Assn., SC Athletic Trainers Assn., Nat. Athletic Trainers Assn. (cert.). Avocations: tennis, golf, skiing, travel. Home: 1100 Pulaski St # 524 Columbia SC 29201 Office: Moore Orthopedic Clinic 14 Medical Park Ste 200 Columbia SC 29203 Personal E-mail: lizatc01@msn.com.

MCCASLIN, LATANYA, art educator; d. Frank and Eloise McCaslin. Student, U. Ala., Birmingham, 1987—92. Art lectr., amb. Birmingham Mus. Art, 1992—; cultural arts dir. Sparkle Arts and Computers, Fairfield, Ala., 1992—. Mem. Friend of U. Ala. Art Dept.; active Dem. Nat. Com., Washington, Dem. Congl. Campaign Com., Washington. Mem.: Coll. Art Assn., Am. Assn. Mus., Amnesty Internat. Home: 113 60th St Fairfield AL 35064 Office Phone: 205-785-3636. Personal E-mail: dartagnan@wwisp.com.

MCCASLIN, RICHARD BRYAN, history educator; b. Atlanta, Feb. 21, 1961; s. Jerry L. and Ann Elizabeth (Sharman) McCaslin; m. Jana Dawn Maryovich, Apr. 5, 1979; 1 child, Christina Michele. BA, Delta State U., 1982; MA, La. State U., 1983; PhD, U. Tex., 1988. Tchg. asst. La. State U., 1982-83, grad. asst. La. Bus. Rev., 1983; tchg. asst. U. Tex., Austin, 1983-87, rsch. assoc., 1984-87; rsch. asst. prof. U. Tenn., Knoxville, 1988-90; asst. prof. history High Point U., 1990-94, assoc. prof., 1994-2000, prof., 2000—04; assoc. prof. U. N. Tex., Denton, 2004—07, prof., 2007—. Instr. Pellissippi State CC, 1988—89, Roane State CC, 1989; adj. prof. Corpus Christi State U., Tex., 1989, Hawaii Pacific U., 2003—; lectr. E. Tenn. Hist. Soc., 1990; rsch. cons. Tex. Senate, 1986—89, Nat. Pk. Svc., 1989—90, Tex. State Hist. Assn., 2000—; assoc. historian Futurepast: History Co., Spokane, Wash., 1987—89; presenter Southwestern Social Sci. Assn., AAAS, Soc. Mil. History. Author (with Earnest F. Gloyna): Commitment to Excellence: One Hundred Years of Engineering Education at the University of Texas at Austin, 1986; author: Andrew Johnson: A Bibliography, 1992, Portraits of Conflict: A Photographic History of South Carolina in the Civil War, 1994, Tainted Breeze: The Great Hanging at Gainesville, Texas, October 1862, 1994 (Tullis prize Tex. State Hist. Assn., commendation Am. Assn. State and Local History), Remembered Be Thy Blessings: High Point University - The College Years, 1924-1991, 1995, Portraits of Conflict: A Photographic History of North Carolina in the Civil War, 1997, Lee in the Shadow of Washington, 2001 (Slatten award Va. Hist. Soc., Laney prize Austin Civil War Roundtable), The Last Stronghold: The Fort Fisher Campaign, 2003, Portraits of Conflict: A Photographic History of Tennessee in the Civil War, 2007, At the Heart of Texas: One Hundred Years of the Texas State Historical Association, 2007; co-author: 100 Years of Science and Technology in Texas: A Sigma Xi Centennial Volume, 1986; columnist: Greensboro News and Record, 1993—94; referee Southwestern Hist. Quar., La. State U. Press, U. Nebr. Press, U. S.C. Press, Tex. A&M U. Press, U. N. Tex. Press,; from asst. editor to assoc. editor: Papers of Andrew Johnson, U. Tenn., 1988—90; contbr. articles and book revs. to profl. publs. Dissertation fellow, U. Tex., 1987—88, Clara H. Driscoll fellow, Daus. Republic of Tex., 1985—87, James H. and Minnie M. Edmonds Ednl. Found. scholar, 1983—85, Colonial Dames Am. grad. scholar, 1987. Fellow: Tex. State Hist. Assn. (presenter); mem.: E. Tex. Hist. Soc. (presenter), Soc. Civil War Historians (presenter), So. Hist. Assn. (presenter). Episcopalian. Home: 1321 East Windsor Dr Denton TX 76209 Office: Univ North Tex Dept History PO Box 310650 Denton TX 76203-0650 Office Phone: 940-565-4207. Business E-Mail: mccaslin@unt.edu.

MCCASLIN, TERESA EVE, human resources specialist; b. Jersey City, Nov. 22, 1949; d. Felix F. and Ann E. (Golaszewski) Hrynkiewicz; m. Gary A. McCue. BA, Marymount Coll., 1971; MBA, L.I. U., 1981. Adminstrv. officer Civil Service Commn., Fed. Republic Germany, 1972-76; personnel dir. Oceanroutes, Inc., Palo Alto, Calif., 1976-78; mgr., coll. relations Continental Grain Co., NYC, 1978-79, corp. personnel mgr., 1979-81, dir. bus. redesign, internal cons., 1981-84; dir., human resources Grow Group, Inc., NYC, 1984-85, v.p. human resources, 1985-86, v.p. adminstrn., 1986-89; corp. v.p. human resources Avery Dennison Corp., Pasadena, Calif., 1989-94; v.p. human resources Monsanto Co., St. Louis, 1994-97; sr. v.p. human resources, mem. mgmt. com. Conti Group Cos. (formerly Continental Grain Co.), NYC, 1997—, exec. v.p. human resources & info. tech., 1999. Mem. global adv. bd. Am. Grad. Sch. Internat. Mgmt.; bd. dirs. Am. Arbitrator Assn., 2005. Mem. Am. Mgmt. Assn. (chair bd. trustees, fin. and exec. com.), Human Resources Coun. Roman Catholic. Avocations: skiing, travel, golf. Office: Conti Group Cos 277 Park Ave New York NY 10172-0003 Business E-Mail: teri.mccaslin@conti.com.

MCCAUL, ELIZABETH, investment advisor, former state agency administrator; BA in econ., Boston U., 1985; postgrad., Georgetown U. Congl. intern, 1981; investment banker, v.p. Goldman, Sachs & Co., 1985—95; chief of staff N.Y. State Banking Dept., 1995—96, first dep. supt. banks, 1996—97, acting supt. banks, 1997-2000, supt. banks, 2000—03; ptnr. Promontory Fin. Group, 2003—. Dir. Empire State Devel. Corp., State N.Y. Mortgage Agy., N.Y. State Job Devel. Authority, Harlem Cmty. Devel. Corp.; statutory mem. Cmty. Facilities Project Guarantee Fund. Scholar European Econ. Cmty., Inst. European Studies, Freiburg, Germany. Mem. Conf. State Bank Suprs. (bd. dirs., supervisory chmn., 2001-02, internat. bankers adv. bd.), Fed. Fin. Inst. Examination Coun., 2002-03. Office: Promotory Fin Group 1201 Pennsylvania Ave NW Ste 617 Washington DC 20004

MCCAUL, JOSEPH PATRICK, chemical engineer; b. NYC, May 11, 1952; s. Joseph and Marion (Sheehan) McCaul; m. Kathleen Anne Crowley, Aug. 3, 1974 (div.); children: Kenneth, Christine; m. Nancy Marie Powell, May 28, 2000. BSChemE, Poly. Inst. Bklyn., 1973, M in Polymer Sci. and Engring., 1977; MBA, Case Western Res. U., 1987. Registered ofcl. baseball umpire Ill. H.S. Assn., cert. bus. intermediary 2005, master intermediary 2006. Prodn. supr. Mobay Chem. Corp., Bayonne, NJ, 1973—77; process engr. Borg Warner Chems., Parkersburg, W.Va., 1977—78, process control engr. Ottawa, Ill., 1978—79, process control mgr. Linmar plant, 1979—82; mgr. tech. svc. Std. Oil Co., Cleve., 1982—87; mgr. internat. sales and tech. svc. Barex Group BP Chems., Cleve., 1987—96, dir. sales and licensing, 1996—98; group v.p. sales and mktg. EVAL Co. Am., Lisle, Ill., 1998—2001, v.p. rsch. and bus. devel., 2001; founder, pres. Joseph Assoc. Internat., Inc., Chgo., 2002—. Contbr. articles to profl. jours., mags., ency. Exec. bd. dirs. Mentor Lake Area Baseball, Mentor on the Lake, Ohio, 1988—89; pres. Mentor McMinn Area Baseball League, 1989—91; trustee Pinegate Homeowners Assn., Mentor, Ohio, 1988—89. Recipient award, Soc. Plastics Engrs., 1987, Ann. award for bus. excellence, Bus. Ledger, 2006. Mem.: Midwest Bus. Brokers and Intermediaries (bd. dirs. 2005—06, Collaboration award 2005, 2006), Internat. Bus. Brokers Assn., DuPage Exec. Network (bd. dirs. 2004—06), Naperville C. of C. (com. chair, mem. spkrs. bur. 2004), Am. Mensa, Union League Club Chgo., World Trade Ctr. Ill. (bd. dirs. 2007—). Achievements include patents in field. Avocations: fishing, boating, exercise, baseball, travel. Office: Chgo Bd of Trade Bldg 141 W Jackson Blvd Ste 3420 Chicago IL 60604 Office Phone: 312-212-8046. Business E-Mail: jmccaul@brokerchicago.com.

MCCAUL, MICHAEL T., congressman; b. Dallas, Jan. 14, 1962; m. Linda McCaul; children: Caroline, Jewell, Lauren, Michael, Avery. BS, Trinity U., 1984; JD, St. Mary's U., 1987; sr. exec. fellow, Harvard U. John F. Kennedy Sch. Govt. Asst. atty. gen., Austin, Tex., 1987—90; atty. US Dept. Justice Criminal divsn., Washington, 1990—99; spl. asst. atty. gen. State of Tex., 1999—2000, dep. atty. gen. for criminal justice, 2000—02; chief Terrorism & Nat. Security sect. US Dept. Justice, U.S. Atty. we. dist. Tex., 2002; mem. US Congress from 10th Tex. dist., 2005—, mem. homeland security com., chmn. investigations subcommittee, mem. internat. rels. com., mem. sci. com. Mem. Com. Fgn. Affairs, Ho. Rep. Policy Com.; vice chmn. US-Mex. Inter-Parliamentary Group, 2005. Republican. Roman Catholic. Office: US Ho Reps 131 Cannon Ho Office Bldg Washington DC 20515-4310 Office Phone: 202-225-2401.

MCCAULEY, ANN, lawyer, retail executive; b. Washington, July 28, 1950; BA, Clark U., 1972; JD, Columbia U., 1978. Bar: NY 1979, US Dist. Ct. (so. dist. NY) 1979. Assoc. Cadwalader, Wickersham & Taft, NYC, 1978—80; atty. Port Authority of NY & NJ, 1980—83, TJX Cos., Framingham, Mass., 1985, v.p. legal, 1992—2004, sr. v.p. legal, 2004—07, chief corp. gen. counsel Framingham, Mass., 2005—07, exec. v.p., gen. counsel, sec., 2007—. Mem.: New Eng. Corp. Counsel Assn., NY State Bar Assn. Office: TJX Cos Inc 770 Cochituate Rd Framingham MA 01701 Office Phone: 508-390-1000. Office Fax: 508-390-2457. E-mail: ann_mccauley@tjx.com. *

MCCAULEY, BRUCE GORDON, financial consultant; b. St. Louis; s. William Maurice and Evylin Adele (Halbert) McC.; m. Barbara Allen Stevens, Mar. 16, 1945 (dec.); children: David S., Sharon; m. Gwen Crumpton Cummings, Nov. 25, 1967. Student, U. Mo., 1939-41, Yale U., 1944; BS in Engring., U. Calif., Berkeley, 1948, MBA, 1949, MS in Indsl. Engring., 1952. Registered profl. engr., N.Y., Calif., Hawaii. Asst. purchasing agt. Curtis Mfg. Co., St. Louis, 1941—43; teaching asst. U. Calif., Berkeley, 1948—49, asst. prof. mech. engring., 1950—56, chmn. indsl. engring. inst., 1954—55; design engr. Standard Oil Co. of Calif., 1949—50; sr. ptnr. McCauley & Dunmire, San Francisco, 1952—56; v.p. Shand & Jurs Co., Berkeley, 1956—58, exec. v.p., 1958—60; asst. to pres. Honolulu Star-Bulletin, 1960—62; gen. mgr. Christian Sci. Pub. Soc., Boston, 1962—69; gen. mgr., sec. N.Y. Daily News Inc., NYC, 1969—74, v.p., 1971—73, sr. v.p., 1973—75, asst. to pres., 1974—75, dir., 1971—75; v.p. Daseke & Co. Inc., Westport, Conn., 1975—77, sr. v.p., 1977—86, mgr. West Coast office, 1978—86; vis. scholar Principia Coll., Elsah, Ill., 1988—91; pres. Rossmoor Mut. 48 Corp., Walnut Creek, 1994—97. Bd. dirs. Better Bus. Bur., N.Y.C., 1973-77, N.Y.C. Conv. and Visitors Bur., 1974-77, Albert Baker Found., 1979-90, Asher Found., 1983-93, Sopac Energy Corp., 1986-92. Capt. USAAF, 1943-46, PTO. Mem. ASME (life), NSPE (life), Am. Inst. Indsl. Engrs. (life), Nat. Assn. Accts. (life), U. Calif. Alumni Assn., Principia Alumni Assn., Rossmoor Golf Club, Masons (32 degree), Kiwanis, Sigma Xi, Tau Beta Pi, Beta Gamma Sigma, Pi Mu Epsilon. Christian Scientist. Home: 3266 Ptarmigan Dr Apt 3B Walnut Creek CA 94595-3149

MCCAULEY, CLEYBURN LYCURGUS, lawyer; b. Houston, Feb. 8, 1929; s. Reese Stephens and Elizabeth Ann (Burleson) McC.; m. Elizabeth Kelton McKoy, June 7, 1950; children: Stephens Francis, Lillian Elizabeth, Cleyburn, Lucy Annette. BS, U.S. Mil. Acad., 1950; MS in Engring. Econ., Statistical Quality Control and Indsl. Engring., Stanford U., 1959; JD, Coll. William and Mary, 1970. Bar: D.C. 1971, Va. 1970, Tex. 1970, U.S. Ct. Claims 1971, U.S. Tax Ct. 1971, U.S. Supreme Ct. 1973. Commd. 2d lt. U.S. Air Force, 1950, advanced through grades to lt. col., 1971, ret., 1971; pvt. practice law, Washington, 1975—. Mem. Fed. Bar Assn., Va. Bar Assn., Tex. Bar Assn., D.C. Bar Assn., IEEE, AIAA, Am. Soc. Quality Control, Phi Alpha Delta. Home: 402 S 3rd St Wilmington NC 28401-5102

MCCAULEY, GERARD FRANCIS, literary agent; b. Pitts., Apr. 9, 1934; s. John Edward and Beatrice (McNally) McCauley; m. Kerstin E. Borg, Apr. 24, 1965; children: Peter, Brian. BA, U. Pitts., 1956. Editor Alfred A. Knopf Publishing, NYC, 1961—62, Little Brown, Boston, 1962—63; literary agt. Curtis Brown Ltd., NYC, 1964—70, Gerard McCauley Agy., Katonah, NY, 1970—2003. Editor: (book) Playing Around, 1973. Petty officer 3d class USN, 1956—58, Key West, Fla. Mem.: Orgn. of Am. Historians, Assn. of Authors Reps., Dutch Treat Club. Democrat. Episcopalian. Home: 7 Outpost Rd Katonah NY 10536

MCCAULEY, HAROLD HOMER, retired mechanical engineer; b. Stockton, Calif., Aug. 26, 1923; s. Homer Wilson and Hilda Lucile (Moore) McCauley; m. Patricia June Canfield, July 22, 1951; children: Carol, Barbara, Avis, Allan. BS in Mech. Engring., Kans. State U., Manhattan, 1949. Registered profl. engr., Kans. Civilian engr. Army Corps Engrs., Kansas City, 1949—54; mech., elec. engr. Servis, Van Dorn & Hazard, Topeka, 1954—59; supr. engr. ICMB Launcher Sites, Topeka, Salina and Wichita, Kans., 1959—63; mech. engr. Army Office Chief Engrs., Mil. Constrn. Directorate Engring. Divsn., Washington, 1963—70, chief facilities devel. sect., 1970—74, chief advance tech. br., 1974—77, chief mech., elec. sys. br., 1977—82; ret., 1982. Mem. evaluation team Israeli AFB, Washington, 1978. Treas. Cameron Sch. PTA, Fairfax County, Va., 1965—66, Woodlawn Sch. PTA, Fairfax County, 1968—71; pres. Woodlawn Civic Assn., Fairfax County, 1971; bd. dirs. Orange County Com. Affordable Housing, 1990—92; bd. dirs., chmn. site selection com. Rapidan Habitat for Humanity, 1992—95. With USN, 1945—46. Recipient Meritorious Civil Svc. award, US Army, 1982. Mem.: NSPE, Sigma Tau, Phi Tau Sigma. Republican. Presbyterian. Avocations: travel, singing, photography, handyman projects.

MCCAULEY, JOHN, music educator; b. Des Moines, Iowa, Nov. 16, 1937; s. Lester Francis and Elisabeth Coelestin McCauley. BS, U. Ill., Urbana, 1959, BMus cum laude, 1961; MSc, Jilliard Sch. Music, NY, 1964; studied piano, with Claire Richards, Carlo Zecchi, Friederich Wuehrer, Josef Raieff and Beveridge Webster, Tanglewood, Aspen, Mozarteum Summer Acad., Salzburg, Austria; studied conducting, with Jorge Mester and Jean Morel; master classes in conducting, with Hoerbert von Karajan. Cert. piano, chamber music, conducting Mozarteum Salzburg. Mem. piano faculty Riverdale Country Sch. and Sch. of Music, 1967—80; instr. Lehman Coll., CUNY, 1972—82; instr. piano, vocal coach, accompanist for student recitals and masterclasses 92d St. Y Music Dept., 1997—; adj. vocal coach Manhattan Sch. of Music, 1997—. Recital accompanist Columbia Artists Mgmt. Cmty. Concerts, various locations throughout US, 1980—84; piano recitals throughout US and Europe including Lincoln Ctr. and Julliard, 1978—91, NY Radio, The Listening Room with Robert Sherman (WQXR), 1983, 90; asst. condr., music coach Des Moines Metro Opera, 1984—94; guest condr. Bronx Symphony Orch., 1985, 97; asst. condr. Ariz. Opera, Tucson and Phoenix, 1984; music dir. Nev. Opera Studio, 1995; founder Music Dir. and Condr., Chamber Orch. of Sci. & Medicine, NYC, 2001—. Pianist (NY performance for narrator and chamber ensemble): The Night of the Murdered Poets by Morris Cotel, 1985, Am. Cathedral's Arts George V recital series, Paris, 2002, 03, (chamber music perfomances) 92d St. Y Tisch Ctr. for the Performing Arts Meet the Virtuoso Series, 2003, solo piano recital 2004; condr. Bel Canto Opera, NY, (east coast tours) Opera Northeast and Eastern Opera Theater, 1978-85; assoc. condr. Bkyln. Philharmonic, 1983; contbr. reviews of new music NOTES (Jour. of Music Libr. Assn.). Grad. fellowship, Juilliard Sch., 1964, scholarship, U. Ill., 1955—59, fellowship, Tanglewood Aspen, 1964, 1964. Achievements include debut Carnegie Hall 1975, Lincoln Center 1968; performed at Rockefeller University, Music at St. Paul's Series, Columbia University, Advent Lutheran Church, Good Shepherd Church at Lincoln Center with Chamber Orchestra of Science and Medicine. Personal E-mail: jmccaulster@gmail.com.

MCCAULEY, JOHN MICHAEL, real estate appraiser, consultant; b. Holyoke, Mass., Aug. 3, 1972; s. John P. and Jeanne F. Medina; m. Karen Lynn Broadway, Feb. 18, 2001; children: Jade Mckenzie, Dylan John. BS in Bus. Mgmt., U. Phoenix, 2007. Cert. residential appraiser Colo. Bd. Appraisers, 2003. Sr. appraiser, pres. Integrity Appraisal and Consulting, Inc., Parker, Colo., 2003—. With USN, 1990—94, with US Army, 1995—99. Decorated Army Commendation medal, Army Achievement medal, Army Good Conduct medal, Nat. Def. medal, Southwest Asian Svc. medal with bronze star, Army Svc. ribbon, Army Overseas Svc. ribbon, Navy Sea Svc. Deployment ribbon with 2 bronze stars, Saudi Arabian Liberation of Kuwait medal, others. Avocation: motorcycling. Home and Office: Integrity Appraisal and Consulting 11500 Whooping Crane Dr Parker CO 80134 Office Phone: 303-284-5527. Office Fax: 303-284-5528. Personal E-mail: jmc1972@comcast.net. Business E-Mail: jmccauley@integrityappraisal.net.

MCCAULEY, MATTHEW K., apparel executive; b. 1973; BBA, Brigham Young U. Planning mgr. GAP Inc., 2000—01, mgr. bus. solutions, 2001; dir. allocation Gymboree Corp., 2001—03, v.p. planning and allocation, 2003—05, sr. v.p., gen. mgr., 2005, pres., 2005—, CEO, 2006—, chmn., 2006—. Office: Gymboree Corp 500 Howard Street San Francisco CA 94105 Office Phone: 415-278-7000. Office Fax: 415-278-7100.

MC CAULEY, R. PAUL, criminologist, educator; b. Highspire, Pa., Jan. 13, 1943; s. Paul Herbert and Frances Vaden (Harper) McC.; m. Gail Lee Gummo, Jan. 30, 1965; 1 child, Brent Clayton. A.S., Harrisburg Area Community Coll., 1968; BS, Va. Commonwealth U., 1969; MS, Eastern Ky. U., 1971; PhD (fellow), Sam Houston U., 1973; certificate Home Office Detective Tng. Course, Eng., 1967. Diplomate Am. Coll. Forensic Examiners, Am. Bd. Law Enforcement Experts. Police officer Highspire Police, 1964-69; adminstr. Burns Internat. Security Services Inc., 1969-71; prof. police sci. and adminstrn., dir. grad. studies in adminstrn. of justice U. Louisville, 1973-82; prof., chmn. dept. criminology Indiana U. of Pa., 1982—; co-founder Sempas Security and Safety Technologies, 1980; advisor Reagan Presdl./Congressional Task Force on Criminal Justice, 1980; mem. staff So. Police Inst., 1973-82, Nat. Crime Prevention Inst., 1973-82. Researcher, ptnr. McShan Assocs., 1974-85; cons. U.S. Congress Com. on Emergency Communications, 1967. Co-author: The Criminal Justice System, 1976, 3d edit., 1984; co-founder, editor: Criminal Justice Policy Rev., 1984-86; contbr. chpts. to books, articles to profl. jours.; patents. Active Metro Child Abuse Program, Crime Clinic of Greater Harrisburg, 1965-74; mem. Lower Swatara Twp. Police Civil Service Commn., 1967-69. Served with USMC, 1962-66 Recipient Mayor's Citation, City of Louisville, 1982, Gold medal Educator of the 1980's; honoree Silliman Coll., Yale U., 1984; Fulbright scholar, lectr., Australia, 1987. Mem. Acad. Criminal Justice Scis. (exec. bd. 1980-83, pres. 1985), Navy League (award for disting. community service) Home: 4620 Lucerne Rd Indiana PA 15701-6003 Office: Indiana U of Pa G-1 McElhaney Hall Indiana PA 15705-0001 Office Phone: 724-349-9676. Business E-Mail: mccauley@iup.edu. *One's philosophy, spirit, and drive contributes more to his relative success than do economic resources, social position, planning, or timing.*

MCCAUSLAND, MARGARET A., lawyer, educator; b. Bryn Mawr, Pa., Feb. 2, 1950; d. Joseph Edward and Margaret Mary O'Donnell; m. Paul Joseph McCausland, June 22, 1968; children: Patricia, Joseph. BS summa cum laude, St. Joseph's U., Phila., 1984; JD cum laude, Villanova U., 1987. Bar: Pa. 1987, U.S. Dist. Ct. (ea. dist.) Pa. 1987, U.S. Dist. Ct. (we. dist.) Mich. 1995, U.S. Ct. Appeals (3d cir.) 1997, U.S. Supreme Ct. 2002. Sec. Bankers Life, Bala Cynwyd, Pa., 1968—70, 1975—77, Frederick Brown & Assoc., Newton Square, Pa., 1977—84; assoc. Dechert LLP, Phila., 1987—93, Blank Rome LLP, Phila., 1993—97, ptnr., 1997—2006; atty. Law Offices of Margaret A. McCausland, LLC, 2006—. Adj. faculty Villanova U. Law Sch., Pa., 1999—, bd. adv., 2001—04. Vol. atty. Support Ctr. Child Advs., Phila., 1987—; tutor Phila. Reads, 2001—06; mem. bd. advisors Archbishop Prendergast HS Girls, Phila., 2001—05; bd. dirs., v.p. Robin's Nest, Inc., Glassboro, NJ, 1995—; pres., bd. dirs. CeaseFire Pa., Phila., 2002—. Named Disting. Adv., Support Ctr. Child Advs., 1996, Woman of Distinction, Phila. Bus. Jour., 2001, Pa. Super Lawyer, Law and Politics Mag., 2004—07; recipient Citizens Pro Bono award, Phila. Bar Found., 2004. Mem.: ABA, AAUW, Pa. Bar Assn., J. Willard O'Brien Inn Ct., Phila. Bar Assn. (bd. dirs.), Forum Exec. Women, Order of the Coif. Office: 531 Plymouth Rd Ste 500 Plymouth Meeting PA 19462 Office Phone: 610-834-1720. Business E-Mail: mccausland@mccauslandlaw.com.

MCCAUSLAND, PETER, technology company executive; b. 1950; BA, U. S.C.; JD, Boston U. Bar: Pa. 1974. Gen. counsel MG Industries, Inc.; founder, chmn., CEO Airgas, Inc., Radnor, Pa., 1982—. Bd. dirs. Metrocall, Inc. Dir. Fox Chase Cancer Center, Independence Seaport Museum, Internat. Oxygen Manufacturers Assoc., Inc. Fax: 610-687-1052. *

MCCAUSLAND, THOMAS JAMES, JR., retired brokerage house executive; b. Cleve., Nov. 27, 1934; s. Thomas James and Jean Anna (Hanna) McC.; m. Kathryn Margaret Schacht, Feb. 9, 1957; children: Thomas James III, Andrew John, Theodore Scott. BA in Econs., Beloit Coll., Wis., 1956. V.p. A.G. Becker & Co., Inc., Chgo., 1959-74; v.p. The Chgo. Corp., 1974-76, sr. v.p., dir., 1976-83, exec. v.p., 1983-90, vice chmn., 1991-96; pres. The Chgo. Corp. Internat., 1990-96; ret., 2000. Treas. The LaSalle St. Coun., Chgo., 1990-95. V.p. Hospice the North Shore, Evanston, Ill., 1986-90; bd. dirs. McCormick Theol. Sem., Chgo., 1971-79, Presbyn. Home, Evanston, 1968-74; trustee Beloit Coll., 1987-90. Lt. USN, 1956-59. Mem. Union League, United Presbyn. Found. (trustee, vice-chmn. 1980-86), Skokie Country Club (bd. dirs. 1983-85, pres. 1993),

Pelican Bay Club (Naples, Fla.)(chmn. 2001-03), Forum Club of Naples (bd. dirs.), Royal Poinciana Golf Club (Naples), Old Elm Club (Ill.). Republican. Avocations: travel, golf, history.

MCCAW, CRAIG O., communications executive; b. Centralia, Wash., Aug. 11, 1949; s. John Elroy and Marion McCaw. Grad., Stanford U., 1973. Pilot; chmn., CEO McCaw Comm., 1968-88; chmn. bd. dirs., CEO McCaw Cellular Comm., Inc. (acquired MCI's cellular and paging ops. in 1986 sold to AT&T in 1994), Kirkland, Wash., 1982-94; chmn., CEO Lin Broadcasting Co., 1990—; founder, chief, co-exec. officer Teledesic Corp., Kirkland, 1990—; chmn., CEO NEXTLINK Comm. Inc. (now XO Comm.), 1994—2002, Eagle River Inc., Clearwire, 2003—, co-CEO, 2006—; acquired NextNet Wireless Inc, Minneapolis, 2004—. Bd. dirs. RadioFrame Networks, Inc., China Unicom Ltd., China, 2000—, non-exec. dir., 2002—; mem. Nat. Security Telecom. Adv. Com. Named one of 400 Richest Ams., Forbes mag., 2006; named to Gallery of Achievers Hall of Bus., 1989, Horatio Alger Assn. of Disting. Ams., 1999. Avocation: boating. Office: Clearwire 5808 Lake Washington Blvd NE Ste 300 Kirkland WA 98033

MCCAW, JOHN E., JR., investment company, professional sports team executive; s. John Elroy McCaw; married; 4 children. Grad., U. Wash. Co-founder McCaw Cable Vision, McCaw Cellular Comm., Orca Bay Ptnrs., Vancouver, BC; chmn. Orca Bay Sports and Entertainment, Orca Bay Capital Corp.; chmn., gov. Vancouver Canucks; owner, bd. dirs. Seattle Mariners, 1992; co-founder Tahoma Fund. Bd. dirs. Kistler Aerospace Corp. Bd. mem. Conservation Internat. Office: Vancouver Canucks 800 Griffiths Way Vancouver BC Canada V6B 6G1 also: Orca Bay Ptnrs 1301 First Ave Seattle WA 98101

MCCAW, ROBERT BRUCE, lawyer; b. Durham, NC, Dec. 24, 1943; s. Robert Hall and Patricia Louise (McKean) McC.; m. Susan Leland Wood, June 15, 1968 (dec. June 2002); children: Anne Meredith, Benjamin Hugo. BS in Math., Georgetown U., 1965; JD, U. Va., 1970. Bar: Va. 1970, U.S. Dist. Ct. D.C. 1971, U.S. Ct. Appeals (10th cir.) 1974, U.S. Supreme Ct. 1974, U.S. Ct. Appeals (7th cir.) 1987. Law clk. to assoc. justice Hugo L. Black U.S. Supreme Ct., Washington, 1970-71; assoc. Wilmer, Cutler & Pickering, Washington, 1971-78, ptnr., 1978—2004; ptnr., co-chmn. Securities dept., office sr. ptnr. Wilmer Cutler Pickering Hale & Dorr, NYC, 2004—. Adj. prof., lectr. securities regulation George Washington U., Washington, 1980-83. Editor-in-chief Va. U. Law Rev., 1969-70; contbr. articles to profl. jours. 1st lt. U.S. Army, 1965-67. Mem. Order of Coif. Presbyterian. Office: WIlmer Cutler Pickering Hale & Dorr LLP 399 Park Ave New York NY 10022 Office Phone: 212-230-8810. Office Fax: 212-230-8888. Business E-Mail: robert.mccaw@wilmerhale.com.

MCCAW, SUSAN RASINSKI, ambassador; b. Orange City, Calif. m. Craig McCaw; 3 children. BA, Stanford U.; MBA, Harvard U., 1988. Bus. analyst McKinsey & Co., NY, Hong Kong; assoc. Robertson Stephens' Venture Capital Group; principal Robertson Stephens & Co., San Francisco; pres. COM Investments, Wash.; mng. ptnr. Eagle Creek Capital; US amb. to Austria U.S. Dept. State, Vienna, 2005—. Mem. exec. bd. Stanford Alumni Assn. Office: US Dept State 9900 Vienna Pl Washington DC 20521-9900

MCCAW, WENDY PETRAK, publishing executive; b. 1952; m. Craig Oliver McCaw, Aug. 18, 1974 (div. 1997). BA, Stanford U., 1973. Co-owner Cellular One Comm., Wash.; founder, CEO Ampersand Holdings LLC, Santa Barbara, Calif., 1998—; owner & CEO Santa Barbara (Calif.) News-Press, 2000—, co-publisher, 2006—. Pres. Wendy P. McCaw Found. (formerly Craig & Wendy McCaw Found.), Santa Barbara, Calif. Named one of America's Richest People, Forbes, 1999, World's Richest People, 2000. Avocations: environmentalism, vegetarianism. Mailing: Santa Barbara News-Press PO Box 1359 Santa Barbara CA 93102 Office: Santa Barbara News-Press 715 Anacapa St Santa Barbara CA 93101 Office Phone: 805-564-5200. Office Fax: 805-966-6258. E-mail: wmccaw@newspress.com.

MCCAWLEY, AUSTIN, psychiatrist, educator; b. Greenock, Scotland, Jan. 17, 1925; arrived in U.S., 1954; s. Austin and Anna Theresa (McBride) McC.; m. Gloria Klein, Feb. 15, 1958; children: Joseph, Tessa. MBCHB, U. Glasgow, 1948. Diplomate Am. Bd. Psychiatry and Neurology; DPM Royal Coll. London. Intern Glasgow Royal Infirmary, Scotland, 1948; resident Inst. Living, Harford, Conn., 1954-57, clin. dir., 1960-66; med. dir. Westchestor br. St. Vincent's Hosp., NYC, 1966-72; dir. psychiatry St. Francis Hosp., Hartford, 1972-88; prof. psychiatry U. Conn. Med. Sch., Farmington, 1983-93; pvt. practice, West Hartford, Conn., 1988—. Dir. psychiatry Kaiser Permanente of Conn., 1996-99. Co-author: The Physician, 1983; contbr. articles to profl. jours. Chmn. Bd. Mental Health, State of Conn., 1981-84, Search Com. for Commr. Mental Health, Conn., 1981; mem. Gov.'s Spl. Task Force on Mental health Policy, Conn., 1982. With RAF, 1948-50. Fellow: Am. Coll. Psychiatry (charter fellow, founder), Am. Psychiat. Assn.; mem.: Conn. Psychiat. Soc. (pres. 1978—79, Disting. Life fellow). Democrat. Roman Catholic. Avocation: music. Home and Office: 20 Worthington Dr Farmington CT 06032 Home Phone: 860-677-0109; Office Phone: 860-677-0109.

MCCHESNEY, FRED S., law educator; b. Washington, Nov. 19, 1948; AB magna cum laude, Holy Cross Coll., 1970; JD cum laude, U. Miami, 1978; PhD in Econs., U. Va., 1982. Law clk. to Judge Alfred T. Goodwin US Ct. Appeals (9th cir.), 1978—79; assoc. Steptoe & Johnson, 1979—81; assoc. dir. policy and evaluation FTC, 1981—83; asst. prof. Emory U. Sch. Law, 1983—85, assoc. prof., 1985—87, Robert T. Thompson prof. law and bus., 1987—97; prof. econs. Emory U., 1987—97; prof. Cornell U. Law Sch., 1997—99; Class of 1967 James B. Haddad prof. law Northwestern U. Sch. Law, Chgo. Vis. prof. Centro di Formazione e Studi, Naples, Italy, 1992; lectr. Am. Law Ctr., Moscow, 1994; John M. Olin vis. fellow in law and econs. Cornell U. Law Sch., 1994. Co-author: Causes and Consequences of Antitrust: The Public Choice Perspective, 1995, Antitrust Law: Interpretation and Implementation, 1998, Property Rights: Cooperation, Conflict and Law, 2003; author: Teacher's Manual to Antitrust Law: Interpretation and Implementation, 1998, 2002; editor: Economic Inputs, Legal Outputs: The Role of Economists in Modern Antitrust, 1997; contbr. articles to profl. jours. Vis. scholar Internat. Centre for Econ. Rsch., Turin, Italy, 1994. Office: Northwestern U Sch Law 357 E Chicago Ave Chicago IL 60611 Office Phone: 312-503-2277. Office Fax: 312-503-5950. Business E-Mail: f-mcchesney@northwestern.edu.

MCCHESNEY, MICHAEL C., computer company executive; b. Atlanta; BSBA magna cum laude, Vanderbilt U.; MBA in Fin. and Multinat. Enterprise, U. Pa. Sr. assoc. Investments Orange Nassau, Boston; v.p. corp. devel Lantech Sys., Inc., Dallas; co-founder, CEO SecureWare, Security First Techs. (formerly Five Paces and SecureWare), Atlanta, 1995-2000; chmn. Security First Network Bank, Atlanta, 1995-96; founder Webtone, Atlanta, 2000—. Office: Webtone Technologies 3535 Piedmont Rd Ne #800 Atlanta GA 30305-4535

MCCHESNEY, ROBERT MICHAEL, SR., retired academic administrator; s. J.D. and Helen Grace (Russell) McC.; m. Laraine Freestone Freeman, Aug. 28, 1965; children: Robert M. Jr., Todd Patrick, Jennifer Laraine Turner, Grant Russell, Brent Steven. BA, U. La., Lafayette, 1964; MA, U. Va., 1967, PhD, 1969. Asst. instr. U. Va., Charlottesville, 1967-68; chmn. dept. polit. sci. U. Ctrl. Ark., Conway, 1971-76, dean coll. scis. and humanities, 1976-82, v.p. for acad. affairs, 1982-89, disting. prof., 1989-90; provost U. Montevallo, Ala., 1990-92, pres., 1992—2006. V.p. Survey Rsch., Inc., Conway, 1989-92; spl. cons. U. Ark. System, Little Rock, 1989. Mem. Carmichael Found., Conway, 1975-79; exec. bd. Quapaw coun. Boy Scouts Am., Little Rock, 1982-88; Greater Ala. Area Coun., 1995-2006; chair Ala. Univ. Coun. Pres., 1994-96, Ala. Higher Edn. Partnership, Pres. Adv. Coun., 1999-2001. Capt. med. svcs. US Army, 1969—71. Grantee, State Justice Inst./Adminstrv. Office of Cts., Ark., 1989. Mem. Ala. Coun. Univ. and Coll. Pres. (chmn. 1993-95, vice chmn. 2005-), So. Com. Colls. and Schs. (exec. coun. 1996-99), Birmingham C. of C., Montevall C. of C., Rotary (pres. Conway Club 1987-88, Paul Harris fellow 1986), Phi Beta Kappa, Phi Kappa Phi, Alpha Chi, Golden Key, Phi Alpha Theta, Phi Eta Sigma, Blue Key. Mem. Lds Ch. Avocations: hunting, fishing, golf. Home: 402 Norwick Cir Alabaster AL 35007 Personal E-mail: rmcchesney@prodigy.net.

MCCHESNEY, ROBERT PEARSON, artist; b. Marshall, Mo., Jan. 16, 1913; s. John and Ruby (Pearson) McC.; m. Mary Ellen Fuller, Dec. 17, 1949. Student, Sch. Fine Arts, Washington U., 1931-34, Otis Art Inst., Los Angeles, 1936-37. Represented by Annex Galleries, Santa Rosa, Calif., Robert Green Fine Arts, Mill Valley, Calif., Thomas McCormick Gallery, Chgo., Claire Carlevaro Art Exchange, San Francisco, Michael Rosenfeld Gallery, NYC, Quicksilver, Forestville, Calif. Instr. art Calif. Sch. Fine Arts, San Francisco, 1949-51, Santa Rosa Jr. Coll., 1957-58; trustee San Francisco Art Inst., 1965-67. One-man shows include San Francisco Mus. Modern Art, 1949, 53, San Francisco Art Inst., 1957, 20th Century West, 1965, Bolles Gallery, N.Y., 1962, Nev. Mus., 1994, San Jose Mus., Calif., 2005-06, Quicksilver Mine, Calif., 2005, others; one-man retrospective Fresno Mus. Art, Calif., 1996, 2006, Calif. State U., Fresno, 1999, City Visions Gallery, Santa Rosa, Calif., 2000, Art Exch., San Francisco, 2002; group shows include Art Inst. Chgo., 1947, 3d Biennial Sau Paulo, Brazil, 1955, Whitney Annual, 1955, Corcoran, 1957, Provincetown, 1957, Chgo., 1959, Osaka, Japan, 1970, Whitney, 1980, Robert Green Fine Arts, Mill Valley, Calif., others; represented in permanent collections, Fresno Art Mus., Art Inst. Chgo., Worcester (Mass.) Art Mus., Whitney Mus., NY, San Francisco Mus. Modern Art, Utah State Mus., Nev. Art Mus., Laguna Beach Art Mus., Cleve. Art Mus., San Jose Mus. Art, others; executed mural San Francisco Social Svcs. Bldg., 1978; (photo biography) Robert McChesney-An American Painter, 1996. Mailing: 2955 Sonoma Mountain Rd Petaluma CA 94954-9559 Address: c/o Dennis Calabi 7731 Elphick Rd Sebastopol CA 95462 Office Phone: 707-795-4612. *The desert wilderness, which I truly love to be in as much as possible, has influenced me a great deal. Of course, the artist is no different from anyone else in that he is influenced by everything around him visually and psychologically, but he has the ability to digest this, you might say, and then transform it into art.*

MCCHESNEY, S. ELAINE, lawyer; b. Bowling Green, Ky., Sept. 14, 1954; d. Kelsey H. McChesney and Lorraine (Carter) Durey; m. Paul Boylan; children: Michael, Jessica, Andrew. AB summa cum laude, Western Ky. U., 1975; JD, Harvard U., 1978. Bar Mass., Mass. Supreme Judicial Ct., We. Dist. Ky., US Cir. Ct. Appeals (1st, 6th cir.), US Dist. Ct. Dist. Mass., US Dist. Ct. (we. dist.) Ky., US Supreme Ct. With Bingham Dana, LLP, Boston, 1978—, ptnr., Litig. Area, 1985—, co-chair, Appellate Practice Group; ptnr. Bingham McCutchen LLP, Boston. Chair joint MBA/BBA bar com. on jud. appts., 1988-89, 90-91; trial practice advisor moot ct. exercises Harvard Law Sch.; panelist, speaker in field; moot ct. judge Harvard Law Sch., Boston U., Suffolk U. Author: (with Gordon and Rainer) Massachusetts Civil Practice: Discovery, 1996; (with Lauriat, Gordon and Rainer) Massachusetts Practice: Discovery, 2001; contbr. articles to profl. jours. Treas., bd. dirs. St. Paul's Nursery Sch., Dedham, Mass., 1990-95; parent rep., trustee Charles River Sch., Dover, Mass., 1997-2000, vol. numerous coms.; vol. Am. Heart Found., March of Dimes; vol. street canvassing on zoning issues. Recipient Top 50 Women Super Lawyers, Boston mag, 2005, 2006. Mem. ABA (labor law sect. subcom. individual rights in the workplace 1982—, comml. banking or fin. transactions litigation 1982), Mass. Bar Assn., Boston Bar Assn. (coun. 1994—, law sch. liaison com. 1984-85, IOLTA com., co-chair ann. mtg.), Women's Bar Assn. (editor calendar 1988-92, bd. dirs. 1999—). Bd. editors Mass. Lawyer's Weekly, 1987-88. Office: Bingham McCutchen LLP 150 Federal St Boston MA 02110 Office Phone: 617-951-8501, 617-951-8501. Office Fax: 617-951-8736. Business E-Mail: elaine.mcchesney@bingham.com. E-mail: semcchesney@bingham.com.

MCCLAIN, BRENDA C., pain management physician; b. Wilson, NC, July 17, 1954; MD, U. NC, Chapel Hill, 1984. Cert. Pain Mgmt., Am. Bd. Anesthesiology, diplomate Am. Bd. Pain Medicine. Intern, anesthesia John Hopkins Hosp., Baltimore, Md., 1984—85, resident, anesthesiology and critical care medicine, 1985—87; fellow pediatric anesthesiology Children's Hosp. Pitts., 1987—88; asst. prof. Med. Coll. Ga., Augusta; dir. pediatric pain Vanderbilt U.; dir., pediatric pain mgmt. services, attending physician pediatric anesthesiology Yale-New Haven Hosp.; assoc. prof., anesthesiology and pediatrics Yale U., 1998—. Chairperson Yale New Haven Hosp. Sedation Analgesia Coun.; mem. examination coun. Am. Bd. Pain Medicine; spkr. in field. Contbr. articles to profl. jours., chapters to books; mem. several editl. boards. Mem.: Am. Pain Soc. (mem. pediatric pain pre-conference prog. com.), Am. Cancer Soc., Am. Acad. Pain Medicine. Office: Yale U 333 Cedar St TMP3 PO Box 208051 New Haven CT 06520-8051 Office Fax: 203-785-2802, 203-785-6664. Business E-Mail: brenda.mcclain@yale.edu.

MCCLAIN, DAVID STANLEY, academic administrator, business and management professor; b. St. Joseph, Mo., Nov. 11, 1946; s. Stanley Russell and Veletta Mabel (Willis) McC.; m. Gayla Sue Webb, Dec. 30, 1967 (div. 1978); 1 child, Molly; m. Wendie Susan Kastler, Jan. 13, 1979; children: Emily, Jenna. BA, U. Kans., 1968; PhD, MIT, 1974. Dir. internat. econs. Data Resources, Inc., Lexington, Mass., 1974-78; sr. staff economist Coun. Econ. Advisers to Pres. Jimmy Carter, Washington, 1979—80; asst. prof. Sch. Mgmt. Boston U., 1978—83, assoc. prof., 1983—91, chmn. fin. and econs. dept., 1985—88; Henry A. Walker Jr. Disting. Prof. Univ. Hawaii, Manoa, 1991—99, dean Coll. Bus. & 1st Hawaiian Bank Disting. Prof. Mgmt., 2000—03; v.p. academic affairs Univ. Hawaii Sys., Honolulu, 2003—04, interim pres., 2004—06, pres., 2006—. Econ. advisor Babson-United, Boston, 1984—2002; lectr. Sloan Sch. Mgmt. MIT, Boston, U. Gabriela Mistral, Santiago, Chile; founding dir. Mgmt. Devel. Program-Japan Boston U.; vis. scholar Keio U., Japan, Meiji U., Japan; bd. dirs. ML Resources, Inc., First Ins. Co. Author Apocalypse on Wall Street; contbr. On the Money tv series, 1984-85, articles to profl. jours. Bd. dirs. non-profits. 1st lt. US Army, 1968—71, Vietnam. Fellow, Woodrow Wilson Ctr., NSF. Mem. Am. Econ. Assn., Phi Beta Kappa, Sigma Chi, Beta Gamma Sigma. Democrat. Avocations: golf, hiking. Office: University of Hawaii Bachman 204 2444 Dole St Honolulu HI 96822 Office Phone: 808-956-9704. Office Fax: 808-956-9943.

MCCLAIN, EDWARD FIFER, JR., retired physicist; b. Carrolton, Mo., Aug. 22, 1921; s. Edward Fifer and Corrine Carrie (Rahmoeller) McC.; m. Louise Cherry Shelby, Dec. 9, 1943; children: Deanna Louise, William Edward, Robert Jay. BSEE, George Washington U., 1950. With Naval Rsch. Lab., Washington, 1942-68, head radio astronomy br., 1956-68; ret., 1968. Past chmn. commn. radio astronomy Internat. Scientific Radio Union; past adv. com. Nat. Radio Astronomy Obs.; cons. Nat. Acad. Sci., Interdept. Radio Adv. Com., Nat. Radio Astronomy Obs.; astronomy panel NSF. Contbr. articles to profl. jours.; patentee in field. Fellow AAAS, Washington Acad. Scis.; mem. IEEE (sr., life), Internat. Astron. Union, Am. Astron. Soc., Scientific Rsch. Soc. Am., Sigma Tau. Achievements include conducting sea trials ST periscope radar in submarine; designed AN/APN67 self-contained doppler automatic navigator for aircraft; determined correct distance to radio source Cass A using galactic hydrogen absorption. Home: 4133 Maple Rd Suitland MD 20746-3514

MCCLAIN, GEORGE NELSON, economist, lawyer; b. New Haven, Aug. 20, 1962; s. James and Trina. BS in Econs., U. Conn., 1975; JD, Yale U., 1978. Pres. McClain Internat., Washington, 1990—. Office: 6923 Storck CIR Lanham MD 20706-2129

MCCLAIN, GREGORY DAVID, chaplain; b. Anderson, SC, June 6, 1957; s. Lemuel David and Mary Josephine (Hawkins) McC.; m. Anne Leigh (Blackwell), May 21, 1983; children: Jonathan David and Sean Gregory. AS, Anderson Coll., 1977; BA, Erskine Coll., 1979; MDiv, Southeastern Bapt. Theol. Sem., Wake Forrest, NC, 1982; D of Ministry, Wesley Theol. Sem., Washington, 1996. ordained Boulevard Bapt. Ch., 1983; bd. cert. chaplain, Assn. of Profl. Chaplains, 2006. Chaplain extern Bapt. Med. Ctr., Columbia, SC, 1982; assoc. pastor First Bapt. Ch., South Boston, Va., 1983-86; min. Corrottoman Bapt. Ch., Lancaster, Va., 1986-93, Colonial Beach Bapt. Ch., 1993-98, Neill's Creek Bapt. Ch., Angier, NC, 1998—2001; CCR tchr. Harnett Ctrl. Mid. Sch., 2001—02; chaplain Duke U. Med. Ctr., Durham, NC, 2002—03, Wake Med, Raleigh, NC, 2003—04, N.C. Dept. Corrections, Lillington, 2004—05, Johnston Meml. Hosp., Smithfield, NC, 2005—. Pres. Dan River Bapt. Pastors, Halifax, Va., 1984-85; preacher jr. high weekend Va. Bapt. Gen. Assn., 1986, faculty youth week, 1984-88; v.p. Lancaster Ministerial Assn., 1987-88; v.p. Little River Bapt. Pastor's Conf., Lillington, N.C., 2000. Active CROP walk, South Boston, Va., 1984-85; coach youth soccer, South Boston, 1985, Westmoreland County, Va., 1995-97, Buics Creek, N.C., 1998; merit badge counselor Boy Scouts Am., Lancaster, 1990-93; mem. Lancaster Ednl. Task Force, 1988. Mem. Ruritan Club (chaplain 1990-93). Office: Johnston Meml Hosp PO Box 1376 Smithfield NC 27577 Business E-Mail: gmcclain@johnstonmemorial.org. *The Kingdom of God exists wherever God is king.*

MCCLAIN, JOHN T., corporate financial executive; BS, Lehigh Univ. CPA NJ. Audit mgr. Arthur Andersen; asst. controller, dir. acctg. ITT Corp.; v.p., chief acctg. officer Sirius Satellite Radio, 1998—99; sr. v.p. fin., controller Cendant Corp., 1999—2006; sr. v.p., chief acctg. officer Avis Budget Group Inc., Parsippany, NJ, 2006—07; CFO Jones Apparel Group Inc., Bristol, Pa., 2007—. Office: Jones Apparel Group 250 Rittenhouse Cir Bristol PA 19007 *

MCCLAIN, LENA ALEXANDRIA, protective services official; b. Toledo, Ohio, Aug. 15, 1966; d. Lee Earl McClain, Mattie May Roberts-McClain; m. David Angelo Neyland, Aug. 4, 1990 (div. July 1995). AAS in Criminal Justice Adminstrn., Pikes Peak C.C., Colorado Springs, Colo., 1994; postgrad., U. Colo., 1994—95; BS in Criminology, U. So. Colo., 1996; postgrad., Spring Arbor U., Mich., 2001—02; postgrad. in Social Work, Lourdes Coll., Toledo, OH, 2003—. Corrections officer Colo. Dept. Corrections, Colorado Springs, 1994—96, sgt., 1996—97, case mgr./lt., 1997—99; sr. resident specialist coord. N.W. Cmty. Corrections Ctr., Bowling Green, Ohio, 1999—2000; shift supr. Lucas County Dept. Wk. Release, Toledo, 2000—. Employee counsel, bd. dirs. Delta Correctional Ctr., 1998—99. Mem. Colo. Grievance Team, 1998; trio mem. Townsend Learning Ctr.; bd. dirs. Pub. Arts Commn., Delta, Colo., 1999; bd. dirs., liaison Nat. Assn. Blacks in Criminal Justice, Delta, 1998. With US Army, 1987—90. Mem.: Am. Correctional Assn., Correctional Peace Officers Found., Social Work Nat. Honor Soc., Phi Theta Kappa. Democrat. Avocations: golf, basketball, softball, chess, writing. E-mail: brealis37@aol.com, brealis@toast.net.

MCCLAIN, PAULA DENICE, political scientist, educator; b. Louisville, Jan. 3, 1950; d. Robert Landis and Mabel (Molock) McC.; stepdau. of Annette Williams McClain; m. Paul C. Jacobson, Jan. 30, 1988; children: Kristina L., Jessica A. BA, Howard U., Washington, 1972; MA, Howard U., 1974, PhD, 1977; postgrad., U. Pa., 1981—82. Asst. prof. dept. polit. sci. U. Wis., Milw., 1977-82; assoc. prof. and prof. pub. affairs Ariz. State U., Tempe, 1982-91; prof. govt. and fgn. affairs U. Va., Charlottesville, 1991-2000, chair govt. and fgn. affairs, 1994-97; prof. dept. polit. sci. Duke U., Durham, NC, 2000—. Co-author: Can We All Get Along? Racial and Ethnic Minorities in American Politics, 1995, 4th edit. 2006, Race, Place and Risk: Black Homicide in Urban America, 1990; editor: Minority Group Influence, 1993; co-editor: Urban Minority Administrators, 1988. Mem. Nat. Conf. Black Polit. Scientists (pres. 1989-90), Am. Polit. Sci. Assn. (exec. coun. 1985-87, v.p. 1993-94), So. Polit. Sci. Assn. (exec. coun. 1992-95, v.p. 2002-03, pres. elect 2004, pres. 2005), Internat. Polit. Sci. Assn. (exec. com. 1997-2003, v.p. 1997-2003), Midwest Polit. Sci. Assn. (v.p. 2002-04). Office: Duke U Dept Polit Sci Perkins Libr PO Box 90204 Durham NC 27708-0204 Office Phone: 919-660-4303. E-mail: pmcclain@duke.edu.

MCCLAIN, SHAWN, chef; Grad., U. Miami Ohio, School of Culinary Arts Kendall Coll., 1988—90. Chef Les Plumes, Prairie Restaurant, Boulevard Restaurant, Hotel Intercontinental, Chgo., sous chef; line cook Trio, Evanston, Ill., 1993, sous chef, exec. chef; owner, exec. chef Spring Restaurant, Chgo., 2000—, Green Zebra, Chgo., 2002—, Custom House, Chgo., 2005—. Named Rising Star Chef of Yr., Jean Banchet Awards for Culinary Excellence, 2002, 40 Under 40, Crain's Chgo. Bus., 2002; recipient Chef of Yr. award, Esquire Mag., 2001, Best chef: Midwest award, James Beard Found., 2006. Office: Spring Restaurant 2039 W N Ave Chicago IL 60647

MCCLAIN, THOMAS EMERSON, retired communications executive; b. East Liverpool, Ohio, July 26, 1950; s. Thomas E. and Helen Marie (Polinski) McC. BA, Case Western Reserve, Cleve., 1972; MA, Kans. State U., 1973. With intergovtl. rels. Ohio EPA, Columbus, 1974-77; legis. liaison Ohio Consumers Counsel, Columbus, 1977-80, dep. dir., 1980-81; press sec. Ohio Atty. Gen., Columbus, 1982-83; asst. dir. Pub. Utilities Commn., Columbus, 1983; with instnl. rels. dept. Battelle Project Mgmt. Div., Chgo., 1983-84, mgr. instl. rels., 1984-86; mgr. comms. Battelle, Columbus, 1986-88, dir. corp. comm., 1989-95, v.p. corp. comms., 1995—2006; ret., 2006. Sec. devel. bd. Children's Hosp., Columbus, 1990-91; adj. prof. Franklin U., Columbus, Ohio, 2006—. Vol. Ohio Youth Commn., Columbus, 1975-76; active ARC-Cen. Ohio chpt., 1986-87; mem. design rev. com. Ohio State U. Sci. and Tech. Park. Mem. Rotary (chmn. program com. 1991-93, bd. dirs. 1994-95, 2d v.p. 1996-97). Roman Catholic. Avocations: basketball, golf. Home: 2607 Wexford Rd Columbus OH 43221-3215

MCCLAIN, TIM S., lawyer; b. 1948; m. Lynn Hollyfield; children: Scott, Brendan. Grad., U.S. Naval Acad., 1970; JD, Calif. We. Sch. Law, San Diego, 1978. Bar: Calif., DC, US Supreme Ct. Commd. Navy JAG Corps USN, ret., 1990, mil. def. counsel Navy Legal Svc. Office San Diego, head claims officer Navy Legal Svc. Office, head legal assistance officer Navy Legal Svc. Office, staff judge adv. for the commanding officer Naval Air Station Miramar, 1981—83, dept. head, instr. Naval Justice Sch. Newport, RI, 1981—86, gen. court-martial mil. judge Navy-Marine Trial Judiciary, S.W., 1986—90; with litigation law firm, San Diego, 1990—96; joined internat. mgmt. cons. firm, dir. opers., 1996—99; pvt. practice Principi and McClain, La Jolla, Calif., 1999—2001; gen. counsel US Dept. Vets. Affairs, Washington, 2001—06, acting asst. sec. for human resources & adminstrn., 2004; mem. Womble Carlyle Sandridge & Rice PLLC, Washington, 2007—. Office: Womble Carlyle Sandridge & Rice PLLC 1401 Eye St NW Seventh Fl Washington DC 20005

MCCLAIN, WILLIAM ANDREW, lawyer; b. Sanford, NC, Jan. 11, 1913; s. Frank and Blanche (Leslie) McClain; m. Roberta White, Nov. 11, 1944. AB, Wittenberg U., 1934; JD, U. Mich., 1937; LLD (hon.), Wilberforce U., 1963, U. Cin., 1971; LHD, Wittenberg U., 1972. Bar: Ohio

1938, U.S. Dist. Ct. (so. dist.) Ohio 1940, U.S. Ct. Appeals (6th cir.) 1946, U.S. Supreme Ct. 1946. Mem. Berry, McClain & White, 1937—58; dep. solicitor City of Cin., 1957—63, solicitor, 1963—72; mem. Keating, Muething & Klekamp, Cin., 1972—73; gen. counsel Cin. br. SBA, 1973—75; judge Hamilton County Common Pleas Ct., 1975—76, Mcpl. Ct., 1976—80; of counsel Manley, burke, Lipton & Cook, Cin., 1980—. Adj. prof. U. Cin., 1963—72, Salmon P. Chase Law Sch., 1965—72. Mem. exec. com. ARC, Cin., 1978—; bd. dirs. NCCJ, 1975—. 1st lt. JAG US Army, 1943—46. Decorated Army Commendation medal; recipient Nat. Layman award, A.M.E. Ch., 1963, Alumni award, Wittenberg U., 1966, Nat. Inst. Mcpl. Law Officers award, 1971, Ellis Island Medal of Honor, 1997. Fellow: Am. Bar Found.; mem.: ABA, Nat. Bar Assn., Ohio Bar Assn., Cin. Bar Assn., Am. Judicature Soc., Fed. Bar Assn., Bankers Club, Friendly Sons St. Patrick, Masons (32d degree), Sigma Pi Phi, Alpha Phi Alpha. Republican. Methodist. Home: 2101 Grandin Rd Apt 904 Cincinnati OH 45208-3346 Office Phone: 513-721-5525.

MCCLANAHAN, DAVID M., energy executive; B in Math., U. Tex.; MBA, U. Houston. Various exec. capacities Reliant Energy, 1986—; pres., COO electric utility divsn. Reliant Energy HL&P, 1997—99; pres., COO delivery group Reliant Energy, 1999—2000, vice-chmn., 2000—02; pres., CEO, dir. CenterPoint Energy, Houston, 2002—. Chmn. bd. dirs. ERCOT; bd. dirs. Edison Electric Inst., Am. Gas Assn., Interstate Natural Gas Assn. Am. Chmn. bd. Univ. St. Thomas. Office: CenterPoint Energy PO Box 4567 Houston TX 77210-4567 *

MCCLANAHAN, LELAND, university director; b. Hammond, Ind., Mar. 14, 1931; s. Alonzo Leland and Eva (Hermanson) McC.; m. Lavaughn Adell Meyrer, June 5, 1954; children: Lindel, Loren. Diploma, Ctrl. Bible Coll., Springfield, Mo., 1954; BA, Southwestern Coll., Chula Vista, Calif., 1973; MA, Fla. State Christian Coll., Kissimee, Fla., 1964; PhBB, Nat. Postgrad. Bible Acad., 1969; ThD, Fla. State Christian Coll., Kissimee, Fla., 1970; PhD, Faith Bible Coll. and Sem., Ft. Lauderdale, Fla. and Marina, Lagos, Nigeria, 1969; MA, Bapt. Christian U., Shreveport, La., 1988; PhD, Freedom U., 1989; ThD, Bapt. Christian U., Shreveport, La., 1989, DLitt (hon.), 1990, PsyD, 1981; PhD, Hawaii U., 1995; DEd, Bapt. Christian U., Shreveport, La., 1992, D in Bus. Adminstrn., 1993; DD (hon.), Internat. Evangelism Crusades, 1969, Trinity Union Coll., 1991; LLD, La. Bapt. U., 1994; StD, PhD, Trinity Internat. U., 1994; HHD (hon.), La. Bapt. U., 1995; LittD (hon.), Cambridge Theol. Sem., 1995; PhD, LittD, PsyD, DBA, LLD, EdD, U. Hawaii, 1995; LittD (hon.), Messianic Coll. Rabbinical Studies; MA, Am. Bible Coll. & Sem., 1998; MDiv, Chapel Christian U., 1991; PhD, Midwestern U., 1998; D in Min., Am. Bible Coll. and Sem., 1999; PhD, Gulf Coast Coll. and Seminary, 2005, Chapel Christian U., 2006. Diplomate Nat. Bd. Christian Clin. Therapists; ordained pastor, Christian Ch., 1950. Founder, pastor Evangel Temple, Griffith, Ind., 1954-73, Abundant Life Temple, Cocoa, Fla., 1974-77; mgr. ins. divsn. United Agys., Cocoa, Fla., 1979-81; assoc. pastor Merritt Assembly of God, Merritt Island, Fla., 1982-85, Palm Chapel, Merritt Island, 1987-89, 1990-93; founder Hawaii U., Merritt Island Offices, Merritt Island, Fla., 1990-97; chancellor Hawaii U. Merritt Island Offices, 1995-97; dir. Fla. Hawaii U. Schs., 1994-97; dir., founder Chapel Christian U., Merritt Island, Fla., 1990—; founder People's Ch. Internat., Inc., 2000—. Founder, dir. Griffith Youth Ctr., 1960-70, Todd Nursery Sch., Griffith, 1971-73; founder, chancellor Ind. Bible Coll., Griffith, 1971-73; dir. Chapel Counseling Ctr., Merritt Island, 1990-94; nat. accreditation com. Hawaii U.; founder, pres. Brevard Humanity Ctr., Inc., 2002; founder Mini Job Link, 2002, Adult Edn., 2003. Author: Is Divine Healing For Today?, 1989, Truths From the Gospel of St. John, 1991, An Outline of the Revelation, 1993, Numbers in the Bible, 1994, An Outline of the Acts of the Apostle, 1995, An Outline of the Book of Proverbs, 2000, How to Feel Better and Live Longer, 2006; author 144 coll. courses and books. Recipient Disting. Svc. award US Jaycees, 1966, Govs.'s Points of Light award, Fla., 2003, Congl. Order of Merit award, 2004, 06; named Hon. Lt. Col., Gov. Guy Hunt, 1988, Archbishop, Hierarchical Christ Ch., 2000, Rep. Presdl. Honor Roll, 2005, Nat. Congl. Com., 2005. Fellow Am. Biog. Inst. (life); mem. Internat. Platform Assn., Order of Internat. Fellowship (life), Am. Inst. Clin. Psychotherapists, Am. Assn. christian Counselors, Nat. Christian Counseling Assn. (assoc., lic.), Internat. Assn. Pastoral Psychologists (lic.), Order of St. John, Knight of Malta (comdr. 1990), Angel Soc. Republican. Avocations: reading, walking, watching sports, watching television adventures, weightlifting. Office: Chapel Christian Univ 870 Australian St Merritt Island FL 32953-4676 Office Phone: 321-452-0135. Personal E-mail: sxrlelpeopl@pc.com.

MCCLANAHAN, RUE (EDDI-RUE MCCLANAHAN), actress; b. Healdton, Okla., Feb. 21, 1934; d. William Edwin and Dreda Rheua-Nell (Medaris) McC.; m. Tom Bish, 1958; 1 child, Mark Thomas Bish; m. Norman Hartweg; m. Peter DeMaio; m. Gus Fisher, 1976; m. Tom Keel, 1984 (div. 1985); m. Morrow Wilson, 1997. BA in German & Theatre Arts cum laude, U. Tulsa, 1956. Appearances include (theatre) Lottice and Lovage, Vienna, 1993, Harvey (London); (Broadway) Jimmy Shine, 1968-69, Sticks and Bones, 1972, California Suite, 1977, After-Play, 1995, The Women, 2002, Wicked, 2005, My First Five Husbands, 2007; (TV series) Maude, 1973-78, Apple Pie, 1978, Mama's Family, 1982-84, Golden Girls, 1985-92, Golden Palace, 1992-93, Safe Harbor, 1999; (TV movies) Having Babies III, 1978, Sgt. Matlowch vs. the U.S. Air Force, 1978, Rainbow, 1978, Topper, 1979, The Great American Traffic Jam, 1980, Word of Honor, 1981, The Day the Bubble Burst, 1982, The Little Match Girl, 1987, Liberace, 1988, Take My Daughters Please, 1988, Let Me Hear You Whisper, 1988, To the Heroes, 1989, After the Shock, 1990, Children of the Bride, 1990, To My Daughter, 1990, The Dreamer of Oz, 1990, Baby of the Bride, 1991, Mother of the Bride, 1993, Danielle Steele's Message from Nam, 1993, Burning Passion: The Margaret Mitchell Story, 1994, Nunsense, 1995, A Holiday to Remember, 1995, Columbo: Ashes to Ashes, 1998; (films) The People Next Door, 1970, They Might Be Giants, 1971, The Pursuit of Happiness, 1971, Modern Love, 1990, This World, Then the Fireworks, 1996, Dear God, 1996, Out to Sea, 1997, Rusty: A Dog's Tale, 1997, Starship Troopers, 1997, Border to Border, 1998, Columbo: Ashes to Ashes, 1998, A Saintly Switch, 1999, The Moving of Sophia Miles, 2000, (off-Broadway prodn.) The Vagina Monologues, 2001, (mini-series) Innocent Victims, 1995. Recipient Obie award for leading off-Broadway role in Who's Happy Now, 1970; Emmy award Best Actress in a comedy, 1987; named Woman of Yr., Pasadena Playhouse, 1986; Spl. scholar Pasadena (Calif.) Playhouse, 1959, Phi Beta Gamma scholar, 1955. Mem. Actors Studio, Actors Equity Assn., AFTRA, Screen Actors Guild. Office Phone: 212-372-1270.

MCCLANE, ROBERT SANFORD, entrepreneur, bank executive; b. Kenedy, Tex., May 5, 1939; s. Norris Robert and Ella Addie (Stockton) McC.; m. Sue Nitschke, Mar. 31, 1968; children: Len Stokes McClane Brown, Norris Robert. BS in Bus. Adminstrn., Trinity U., San Antonio, 1961. With Ford Motor Co., Detroit, 1961-62; with Frost Nat. Bank, San Antonio, 1962-97; exec. v.p. Cullen/Frost Bankers, Inc., 1976—85, pres., 1985-97, dir., 1985—, Benefit Planners, Inc., 1997-2001; advisor, dir. Ellison Grandchildren Trust, 1996—; pres., owner McClane Ptnrs., LLC, 1997—; dir., vice chmn. Tobin Internat., 1998—2003. Bd. dirs. Frost Nat. Bank, San Antonio, Princeton eCom., CCI Telecom, Inc., CareNet, 2005—. Crusade chmn. Bexar County chpt. Am. Cancer Soc., 1974; bd. dirs. Bexar County ARC, 1969-72; sr. warden St. Luke's Episopal Ch., San Antonio, 1980; trustee Alamo Pub. Telecomms. Coun., San Antonio, 1981-88; chmn. San Antonio Econ. Devel. Found., 1987-89, exec. com. 1985-91; bd. trustees Trinity U., 1990—, chmn., 2001-04 Mem. Greater San Antonio C. of C. (chmn. leadership San Antonio 1975-76, bd. dirs. exec. com. 1994-97, chmn. 1996), Trinity U. Alumni Assn. (pres. 1968-69, disting. alumnus 1987), Free Trade Alliance San Antonio (bd. dirs., 1997—, chmn. 1998-2000), Southwest Rsch. Inst. (trustee 1997—), San Antonio German Club, Order Alamo, Tex. Cavaliers, Argyle Club, Club Giraud, Plaza Club (bd. dirs. 1973-92). Episcopalian. Office Phone: 210-220-5353.

MCCLARD, JACK EDWARD, lawyer; b. Lafayette, La., May 13, 1946; s. Lee Franklin and Mercedes Cecile (Landry) McClard; m. Marilyn Kay O'Gorman, June 3, 1972; 1 child, Lauren Minton. BA in History, Rice U., 1968; JD, U. Tex., 1974. Bar: Va. 1974, U.S. Dist. Ct. (ea. and we. dists.) Va. 1974, U.S. Ct. Appeals (4th cir.) 1978, DC 1981, U.S. Dist. Ct. DC 1981, U.S. Ct. Appeals (DC cir.) 1981, N.Y. 1985, U.S. Dist. Ct. (so. and ea. dists.) N.Y. 1985, U.S. Ct. Appeals (5th cir.) 1993, Tex. 1996, U.S. Dist. Ct. (ea. dist.) Tex. 1998, U.S. Ct. Appeals (7th cir.) 2001. Assoc. Hunton & Williams, Richmond, Va., 1974-81, ptnr., 1981—2006, sr. counsel, 2006—. Contbr. articles to profl. jours., chapters to books. Served to lt. (j.g.) USN, 1968—71. Mem.: Lewis F. Powell, Jr. Inns Ct. (exec. com. 2003—07), 5th Cir. Bar, Richmond Bar Assn. Democrat. Episcopalian. Avocations: bridge, gardening, wine. Home: 100 Trowbridge Rd Richmond VA 23238 Office: Hunton and Williams Riverfront Plz E Tower 951 E Byrd St Richmond VA 23219-4074 Home Phone: 804-740-0898; Office Phone: 804-788-8490. Business E-Mail: jmcclard@hunton.com.

MCCLASKEY, MICHAEL KEITH, information technology executive; b. Kirksville, Mo., June 8, 1963; s. Billy Keith and Martha Lee (Jones) McC.; m. Janet Sue Yearns, June 20, 1987. BA and BS in English, Truman State Univ., 1985; MA in English Lit., U. Mo., 1987. Teaching asst. U. Mo., Columbia, 1985-87; coord., tech. svcs. Mo. Sch. Bds. Assn., Columbia, 1987-90, dir., tech. svcs., 1990—95; leader US tech. svc. practice, bus. develop. group Perot Sys., Plano, Tex., 1995—2002, v.p. infrastructure solutions & chief info. officer, 2002—. Named one of Premier 100 IT Leaders, Computerworld, 2004. Baptist. Office: Perot Sys Corp 2300 W Plano Pkwy Plano TX 75075-8499

MCCLATCHY, KEVIN S., professional sports team executive; b. Sacramento, Jan. 13, 1963; Diploma in Polit. Sci., U. Calif., Santa Barbara. Sport prodr. WPLG-TV, Miami; mktg. profl. Knight-Ridder Newspapers; nat. sales mgr. Newspaper Network (subs. McClatchy Newspapers); bus. ops. mgr. Amador Ledger-Dispatch, Calif., 1990; CEO, mng. gen. ptnr., owner Pitts. Pirates, 1996—2007. Co-owner Modesto A's, Oakland Athletics. Trustee Trinity-Pawling H.S., Pawling, N.Y., U. Calif. Santa Barbara; active United Way, Roberto Clemente Found., Extra Mile Found., U. Pitts. Cancer Inst., also Catholic charities.

MCCLAUGHERTY, JOE L., lawyer, educator; b. June 1, 1951; s. Frank Lee and Elease (Terrell) McClaugherty. BBA with honors, U. Tex., 1973, JD with honors, 1976. Bar: Tex. 1976, N.Mex 1976, U.S. Dist. Ct. N.Mex 1976, U.S. Ct. Appeals (10th cir.) 1976, U.S. Supreme Ct. 1979, Colo. 1988. Assoc. Rodey, Dickason, Sloan, Akin & Robb, P.A., Albuquerque, 1976-81, ptnr., dir., 1981-87, resident ptnr. Santa Fe, 1983-87, mng. ptnr., 1985-87; ptnr. Kemp, Smith, Duncan & Hammond, P.C., 1987-92, mng. ptnr., 1987-92; ptnr. McClaugherty & Silver, P.C., Santa Fe, 1992—. Adj. prof. law U. N.Mex, Albuquerque, 1983—; faculty Nat. Inst. Trial Advocacy, So. Meth. U. Law Sch., 1983—, Hastings Ctr. Trial and Appellate Advocacy, 1985—, U. Denver Law Sch., 1986—, U. Colo. Law Sch., 1987; bd. dirs. MCM Corp., Brit.-Am. Ins. Co., Ltd., Nassau, 1985—91. Mem.: N.Mex Assn. Def. Lawyers (pres. 1982—83, bd. dirs. 1982—85), N.Mex Bar Assn. (bd. dirs. trial practice sect. 1976—85, chairperson 1983—84, dir. young lawyers divsn. 1978—80). Office: McClaugherty & Silver PC PO Box 8680 Santa Fe NM 87504-8680 Office Phone: 505-988-8804.

MCCLAVE, DONALD SILSBEE, academic administrator; b. Cleve., May 7, 1941; s. Charles Green and Anne Elizabeth (Oakley) McC.; m. Christine Phyllis Mary Tomkins, Feb. 19, 1966; children: Andrew Green, Susan Elizabeth (dec.). BA, Denison U., 1963. Mktg. rsch. officer Bank of Calif., San Francisco, 1968-70; v.p. Cen. Nat. Bank, Chgo., 1970-75, First Interstate Bank, Portland, Oreg., 1975-77, sr. v.p., 1977-79, exec. v.p., 1979-86; pres., CEO Portland Met. C. of C., 1987—2002; asst. to pres. Portland State U., 2002—. Instr. Pacific Coast Sch. Banking, Seattle, 1976-78, Grad. Sch. Mktg. and Strategic Planning, Athens, Ga., 1982-84; dir., mem. exec. com. Bank Mktg. Assn., 1976-82; bd. mem. Oreg. Nanosci. and Microtechs. Inst., 2003, dir. and chair fin. com. Pres. Oreg. Episc. Sch. Bd., Portland, 1983-84; pres. Assn. Oreg. Industries Found., Salem, 1984-85; pres., co-chmn. Japan-Am. Conf. Mayors and C. of C., Portland, 1985, trustee, 1991-98, exec. com., 1992-97; trustee YMCA of Columbia-Willamette, 1990-92, Portland Student Svcs. Corp., 1991-93; mem. METRO Urban Growth Mgmt. Adv. Com., 1989-92; mem. adv. com. Downtown Housing Preservation Partnership Adv. Com., 1989-94; mem. City of Portland Mayoral Transition Team, 1992, Mayor's Bus. Roundtable, 1993—; bd. dirs. Oreg. Trail chpt. ARC, 1994-95, Tri-Met, 1994—, chair fin. com., 1995—, United Way Columbia Willamette, 1978-83, 2000-01, Urban League Portland, 2000-01, Oreg. Nanoscience and Microtechnologies Inst., 2003-. Capt. USAF, 1963-68. Mem. Oreg. Chamber Execs. Assn. (pres. 1998). Avocations: reading, travel, golf, model building. Office: Portland State U PO Box 751 Portland OR 97207-0751

MCCLEAN, MURRAY R., metal products executive; Mng. dir. Commercial Metals Co., Sydney, Australia, 1985—93, pres. internat. div., 1993—99, pres. mktg. & dist. segment Irving, Tex., 1999—2004, exec. v.p., COO, 2004—06, pres., COO, 2006, pres., CEO, 2006—. Office: Commercial Metals Co Ste 800 6565 N MacArthur Blvd Irving TX 75039 *

MCCLEAN, PATRICK H., otolaryngologist; s. Hugh Patrick and Geraldine McClean; m. Michele McClean, Jan. 31, 1987; children: Megan, Christopher, Stephanie. BS, U. Wash., Seattle, 1978, MD, 1982. Diplomate Am. Bd. Otolaryngology. Resident UCLA, 1982—88; physician, owner South Seattle Otolaryngology, Burien, Wash., 1988—. Trustee Highline Hosp., Burien, 1997—2004; mem. St. Francis, Burien, 2001—, Highline Found., Burien, 2003—; pres. U. Wash. Med. Alumni, Seattle, 1991. Mem.: AMA, Am. Acad. Otolaryngology, Wash. State Med. Assn., King County Med. Soc. (trustee 2002—). Avocations: boating, fishing, skiing. Office: S Seattle Otolaryngology 16259 Sylvester Rd SW # 505 Burien WA 98166

MCCLEARY, BENJAMIN WARD, investment banker; b. Washington, July 9, 1944; s. George William and Nancy (Grim) McCleary; m. Dierdre Marsters, May 6, 1967 (div. 1977); children: Benjamin, Katherine; m. Jean Muchmore, Oct. 15, 1983. AB, Princeton U., 1966. With Chemical Bank, NYC, 1969-81, trainee, asst. sec., asst. v.p., v.p.; sr. v.p. Lehman Bros. Kuhn Loeb, NYC, 1981-83; mng. dir. Shearson Lehman Bros., 1983-87, Shearson Lehman Hutton Internat., London, 1987-88, Shearson Lehman Hutton, Inc., NYC, 1988-89; ptnr. McFarland Dewey & Co., LLC, NYC, 1989—2005. Bd. dirs. Detrex Corp., Harvel Plastics; mem. Seaview Capital LLC, Providence, 2005. Lt. (j.g.) USN, 1966—69. Office: Sea View Capital LLC 30 Kennedy Plaza Ste 400 Providence RI 02903 also: McFarland Dewey & Co LLC 420 Lexington Ave Ste 2650 New York NY 10170 Office Phone: 401-490-4845.

MCCLEARY, LLOYD E(VERALD), education educator; b. Bradley, Ill., May 10, 1924; s. Hal and Pearl McC.; m. Iva Dene Carter, June 13, 1971; children: Joan Kay, Victoria Lea, Karen Ann. Student, Kans. U., 1941—42; BS, U. Ill., 1948, MS, 1950, EdD, 1956; postgrad., Sorbonne U., Paris, 1946. Tchr., asst. prin. Portland (Oreg.) Pub. Schs., 1949-51; asst. prin. Univ. H.S., Urbana, Ill., 1951-52, prin., 1953-56; asst. supt. Evanston Twp. (Ill.) H.S., 1956-60; assoc. Roosevelt U., 1957-69; mem. faculty U. Mich., summers, 1958-59; prof. ednl. adminstrn. U. Utah, 1969—, chmn. dept., 1969-74. Assoc. CFK Ltd. Found., 1971-76; dir. projects in L.Am. for AID, World Bank, Ford Found., Bolivian Govt.; dir. Nat. Sch. Prin. Study, 1976-79, 86-89, res. project Families in Edn., 1992-94; edn. rep. to Utah People to People Program; keynoter Asian Conf. Edn., 1985; edn. adviser Office of the Queen, Jordan, 1985-86; advisor Nat. Commn. on Stds. in the Principalship; U.S. del. Conf. on Status Children, Senegal, 1992, Yr. of the Family, Malta, 1993; J. Lloyd Trump lectr., New Orleans, 1994. Author: Organizational Analysis X-Change, 1975, Politics and Power in Education, 1976, The Senior High School Principalship, 1980, Educational Administration, Today, 1984, High School Leaders and Their Schools, vols. 1 and 2, 1990, Leadership, 1996; editor Western Hemisphere Edn. Sch. Orgn., 1989—. Served with inf. AUS, 1941-46. Decorated Bronze Star with oak leaf cluster, Army Commendation medal; S.D. Shankland fellow, 1956; grantee Ford Found., 1968, 72, AID, 1966, 67, 70, 72, 74, 76, CFK Ltd., 1970-74, Rockefeller Family Found., 1979-80, U.S. Dept. State, 1981, 86-87, U.S. Dept. Def., 1986—; recipient Hatch Prize, 1988-89. Mem. Nat. Assn. Secondary Sch. Prins. (cert. of merit 1978, scholar-in-residence fall 1989, grantee 1969, 77, 86—), Assn. Supervision and Curriculum Devel., Nat. Assn. Elem. Sch. Prins., Phi Delta Kappa, Kappa Delta Pi. Methodist. Home: 1470 Wilton Way Salt Lake City UT 84108-2549 Office: U Utah 339 MBH Salt Lake City UT 84112 E-mail: www.birdsphoto@aol.com.

MCCLEARY, WILLIAM E(RNEST), retired school librarian, historian; b. Alexandria, Va., May 29, 1927; s. Ernest Earl and Laura Hearte (McGuire) McCleary. BA in Humanities, Centenary Coll., Shreveport, La., 1948; MA in Journalism, La. State U., Baton Rouge, 1950, MS in Libr. Sci., 1958. Tchr. Caddo Parish Schs., Shreveport, 1951—58; catalog libr. Shreveport Meml. Lab., 1958—61; libr. supr. Union Producing Co., United Gas Corp., Shreveport, 1961—67; sr. libr. La. State U., Shreveport, 1967—89; ret. Asst. prof. La. State U., Baton Rouge, 1972; founder, co-leader Auth. Writers Centenary Coll., Shreveport, 1993—. Contbr. articles to profl. jours. Co-pres. Self Help Hard of Hearing, Shreveport, 2000—06. Cpl. USMC Res, 1945—46, cpl. USMC Res., 1948—51. Mem.: Book Discussion Group, North La. Hist. Assn. (Bradbury award 2003), Spl. Librs. Assn. (chair 1987—88, 1988—89, Skaw award 1993), La. Libr. Assn. (treas. 1964—65, Foote award 1997). Democrat. Lutheran.

MCCLEERY, WINSTON THEODORE, information technology executive; b. Mobile, Ala., Sept. 6, 1935; s. Robert Alton and Theadora K. (Kiebel) McC.; m. Sandra Thoss, Dec. 28, 1958; children: Winston T., Jacqueline McCleery McNeely. BS, Springhill Coll., 1957; postgrad., U. Ala., 1957-58. Logic design engr. Autonetics N.Am. Aviation, Anaheim, Calif., 1960—65; dir. info. sys. Litton Industries, LA, 1965—69; founder, owner Winston T. McCleery, Cons., 1969—; pres., CEO Mgmt. Software Systems, Inc., Mobile, 1979—. Patentee in field. With U.S. Army, 1958-60. Recipient Cert. for Heroism, Boy Scouts Am., 1949, Collifontanum award, Spring Hill Coll., 2006. Mem. Data Processing Mgmt. Assn., Assn. Computer Machinery, Am. Mgmt. Assn., Ind. Computer Cons.'s Assn., Optimists (pres. 1972). Republican. Achievements include contributions to the design and development of the U.S. Army Field Artillery's first digital fire direction computer; member of design team of the centaur missile's guidance system that made the first soft landing on the moon; design and development of seamless, integrated, on-line and instant-time computer application system for main frame class computers; inventor computer power and temperature enviroment control system, development of automatic documentation system used to document computer programs written in the Cobol language. Home: 5213 Janekyn Dr Mobile AL 36693-4142 Office: PO Box 9365 Mobile AL 36691-0365 Office Phone: 251-345-9960.

MC CLELLAN, CATHARINE, anthropologist, educator; b. York, Pa., Mar. 1, 1921; d. William Smith and Josephine (Niles) McClellan; m. John Thayer Hitchcock, June 6, 1974. AB magna cum laude in Classical Archaeology, Bryn Mawr Coll., 1942; PhD (Anthropology fellow), U. Calif., Berkeley, 1950. Vis. asst. prof. U. Mo. at Columbia, 1952; asst. prof. anthropology U. Wash., Seattle, 1952-56; anthrop. cons. USPHS, Arctic Health Research Center, Alaska, 1956; asst. prof. anthropology, chmn. dept. anthropology Barnard Coll., Columbia U., 1956-61; asso. prof. anthropology U. Wis. at Madison, 1961-65, prof., 1965-83, prof. emeritus, 1983—, John Bascom prof., 1973. Vis. lectr. Bryn Mawr (Pa.) Coll., 1954; vis. prof. U. Alaska, 1973, 87. Assoc. editor: Arctic Anthropology, 1961; editor, 1975-82; assoc. editor: The Western Canadian Jour. of Anthropology, 1970-73. Served to lt. WAVES, 1942-46. Margaret Snell fellow AAUW, 1950-51; Am. Acad. Arts and Scis. grantee, 1963-64, Nat. Mus. Can. grantee, 1948-74 Fellow Am. Anthrop. Assn., Royal Anthrop. Inst. Gt. Britain and Ireland, AAAS, Arctic Inst. N.Am.; mem. Am. Ethnol. Soc. (sec.-treas. 1958-59, v.p. 1964, pres. 1965), Kroeber Anthrop. Soc., Am. Folklore Soc., Am. Soc. Ethnohistory (exec. com. 1968-71), Sigma Xi. Achievements include research in archaeological and ethnographic field investigations in Alaska and Yukon Territory in Canada.

MCCLELLAN, CRAIG RENE, lawyer; b. Portland, Oreg., June 28, 1947; s. Charles Russell and Annette Irene (Benedict) McC.; m. Susan Armistead Nash, June 7, 1975; children: Ryan Alexander, Shannon Lea. BS in Econs., U. Oreg., 1969; JD magna cum laude, Calif. We. U., 1976. Bar: Calif. 1976, U.S. Dist. Ct. (so. dist.) Calif. 1976, U.S. Dist. Ct. (ea., ctrl., no. dists.) Calif. 1991, U.S. Supreme Ct. 1991. Compliance specialist Cost of Living Coun. and Price Commn., Washington, 1972—73, dir. Oil Policy subcom., 1973; ptnr. Luce, Forward, Hamilton & Scripps, San Diego, 1976—87; owner McClellan Law Firm, San Diego, 1987—. Chmn. annual fundraising auction KPBS, 1984. Capt. USMC, 1969-72. Fellow Am. Coll. Trial Lawyers; mem. Inner Circle of Advs., Assn. Trial Lawyers Am., Am. Bd. Trial Advocates, Am. Inns of Ct. (master), Calif. State Bar Assn., San Diego County Bar Assn., Calif. Trial Lawyers Assn. (bd. govs. 1985-87), San Diego Trial Lawyers Assn. (bd. dirs. 1983-90), Nat. Forensics League, Phi Gamma Delta, Phi Alpha Delta. Presbyterian. Avocations: reading, running, tennis, chess, civic activities. Office: McClellan Law Firm 1144 State St San Diego CA 92101-3529 Office Phone: 619-231-0505. E-mail: craig@mcclellanlaw.com.

MCCLELLAN, EDWIN, literature educator; b. Kobe, Japan, Oct. 24, 1925; came to U.S., 1952; s. Andrew and Teru (Yokobori) McC.; m. Rachel Elizabeth Pott, May 28, 1955; children: Andrew Lockwood, Sarah Rose. MA, U. St. Andrews, Scotland, 1952; PhD, U. Chgo., 1957. Instr. English, U. Chgo., 1957-59, asst. prof. Japanese lang. and lit., 1959-63, assoc. prof., 1963-65, prof., 1965-70, Carl Darling Buck prof., 1970-72, chmn. dept. Far Eastern langs. and civilizations, 1966-72; prof. Japanese lit. Yale U., New Haven, 1972-79, Sumitomo prof. Japanese studies, 1979-98, Sterling prof. Japanese lit., 1998-2000, Sterling prof. emeritus Japanese lit., 2000—, chmn. dept. East Asian langs. and lits. New Haven, 1973-82, 88-91, chmn. council humanities, 1975-77, chmn. council East Asian studies, 1979-82. Vis. lectr. Far Eastern langs. Harvard U., spring 1965; mem. adv. coun. dept. Oriental studies Princeton U., 1966-71; mem. Com. to Visit East Asian Studies, Harvard U., 1982-88; mem. Am. adv. com. Japan Found., 1985-95; mem. bd. Coun. for Internat. Exch. Scholars, 1981-84. Translator: Kokoro (Natsume Soseki), 1957, Grass on the Wayside (Soseki), 1969, A Dark Night's Passing (Naoya Shiga), 1976, Fragments of a Past (Eiji Yoshikawa), 1992; author: Two Japanese Novelists: Soseki and Toson, 1969, Woman in the Crested Kimono, 1985; mem. bd. editors Jour. Japanese Studies, 1986-99; contbr. articles to profl. jours. Liason intelligence officer Royal Air Force, Washington, 1945-47; bd. trustees Society Japanese Studies U. Wash., 1992-99. With Royal Air Force, 1944—48. Recipient Kikuchi Kan prize for contbn. to study of Japanese lit., Tokyo, 1994, Noma Lit. Translation prize, 1995, Order of the Rising Sun, Gold

Rays with Neck Ribbon, Japanese Govt., 1998, Dist. Contributions to Asian Studies award Assn. Asian Studies, 2005 Fellow Am. Acad. Arts and Scis. Home: 641 Ridge Rd Hamden CT 06517-2516

MCCLELLAN, LARRY ALLEN, minister, educator; b. Buffalo, Nov. 3, 1944; s. Edward Lurelle McClellan and Helen (Denison) Greenlee; m. Diane Eunice Bonfoey, Aug. 19, 1973; children: Kara E., Seth C. Student, U. Ghana, 1964-65; BA in Psychology, Occidental Coll., 1966; MTh, U. Chgo., 1969, D Ministry, 1970. Ordained to ministry Presbyn. Ch. (U.S.A.), 1970. Prof. of sociology and community studies Govs. State U., University Park, Ill., 1970-86; interim pastor Presbyn. Ch. (U.S.A.), Chgo. area, 1980-86; sr. pastor St. Paul Community Ch., Homewood, Ill., 1986-96; adj. prof. Govs. State U., University Park, Ill., 1987-96; dir. South Met. Regional Leadership Ctr., Govs. State U., University Park, Ill., 1996—2001; cmty. rels. dir. Northeastern Ill. Planning Commn., 2001—05; pastor First Christian Ch. (Disciples), Chicago Heights, Ill., 2003—. Newspaper columnist Star Publs. Chgo., 1993-2004; trustee Internat. Coun. Community Chs., 1989-91, pres., 1991-93. Author: Local History South of Chicago, 1988; developer social simulation games; contbr. articles to profl. publs. Mayor Village of Park Forest South (name now University Park), Ill., 1975-79; co-organizer S. Region Habitat for Humanity, Chgo. area, 1989; pres. S. Suburban Heritage Assn., Chgo. area, 1988-91. Fellow Layne Found., 1966-70, NEH, 1979. Mem. Am. Assn. State and Local History, Ill. State Hist. Soc. (Spl. Achievement award 1989). Office Phone: 708-754-3792. E-mail: larryamcclel@msn.com.

MCCLELLAN, MARK B., former federal agency administrator; b. Austin, Tex., June 26, 1963; m. Stephanie McClellan; 2 children. BA, BS, U. Tex., Austin, 1985; MA, MPA, Harvard U., 1991, MD, 1992; PhD in economics, MIT, 1993. Resident in internal medicine Brigham and Women's Hosp., Boston; cons. The Rand Corp., Santa Monica, Calif., 1989—91; rsch. assoc. Harvard Med. Sch. Dept. of Health Care Policy, Boston, 1991—95; attending physician Stanford U. Health Services; assoc. prof. economics Stanford U., 1995—99; assoc. prof. medicine Stanford Med. Sch., dir. program on health outcomes rsch.; dep. asst. sec. for econ. policy US Dept. Treasury, Washington, 1998—99; mem. Coun. Econ. Advisors Exec. Office of the Pres., Washington, 2001—02; commr. FDA, Rockville, Md., 2002—04; adminstr. Centers for Medicare & Medicaid Services US Dept. Health & Human Services, Washington, 2004—06; sr. rsch. fellow Am. Enterprise Inst.-Brookings Joint Ctr. for Regulatory Studies, Washington, 2006—. Recipient Kenneth J. Arrow award for Outstanding Rsch. In Health Economics. Mem.: Inst. Medicine. Office: AEI Brookings Joint Ctr 1150 Seventeenth St NW Ste 1100 Washington DC 20036 *

MCCLELLAN, MARY ANN, pediatric nurse practitioner; b. Mar. 29, 1942; BS, Tex. Woman's U., 1964; MN, U. Wash., 1968-69; cert., U. Tex., Arlington, 1997. Cert. family life educator, CPNP, pediatric nurse practitioner; advanced RN practitioner, Okla. Charge nurse Baylor U. Med. Ctr., Dallas, 1964—65; pub. health staff nurse Dallas County Health Dept., Dallas, 1965—68; supervising nurse Okla. State Dept. Health, Oklahoma City, 1969—70, maternal-child health nurse cons., 1971; asst. prof. U. Okla. Coll. Nursing, Oklahoma City, 1971—72; from instr. to asst. prof. Harris Coll. Nursing Tex. Christian U., Ft. Worth, 1972—75; asst. prof. continuing edn. U. Okla. Coll. Nursing, Oklahoma City, 1976—79, asst. prof. baccalaureate program, 1979—96, mem. grad. faculty, 1991—. Cons. and lectr. in field. Contbr. chpts. to books, articles to profl. jours. Mem. Nat. Coun. on Family Rels., Okla. Family Resources Coalition, Nat. Assn. Pediatric Nurse Assocs. and Practitioners, Assn. Faculty of Pediat. Nurse Practitioner Programs, Okla. Coun. on Family Rels., Sigma Theta Tau., Phi Kappa Phi. Office: U Okla Coll Nursing PO Box 26901 Oklahoma City OK 73126-0901

MCCLELLAN, RICHARD AUGUSTUS, retired small business owner; b. Gainesville, Fla., Sept. 13, 1930; s. Marion Theodore Sr. and Cornelia (Hampton) McC.; m. Thelma Watson, May 19, 1947 (dec. Mar. 1980); children: Richard A., Wayne Theodore, Viola Patricia, Michael Ray; m. Betty Lee Snow, Dec. 12, 1980 (div. July 1991); children: Claranell Y., Juanita F., Johnnie C.; m. Geraldine C. Williams, Aug. 14, 1993. Diploma, Nat. Inst. Drycleaning, 0975, Napoleon Hill Found., 1994. Drycleaner S & S Cleaners, Gainesville, 1958-97; ret., 1997. Mem. Am. Soc. Notaries (govt. rels. com. 1984, pub. rels. com. 1989), Notary Pub. Assn. State Fla., Nat. Notary Assn., Internat. Order St. Luke the Physician. Democrat. Mem. United Methodist Ch. Avocations: reading, radio, jazz music. Home and Office: 625 SE 15th St Gainesville FL 32641-3123

MCCLELLAN, ROGER ORVILLE, toxicologist; b. Tracy, Minn., Jan. 5, 1937; s. Orville and Gladys (Paulson) McC.; m. Kathleen Mary Dunagan, June 23, 1962; children: Eric John, Elizabeth Christine, Katherine Ruth. DVM with highest honors, Wash. State U., 1960; M of Mgmt., U. N.Mex., 1980; DSc (hon.), Ohio State U., 2005. Diplomate Am. Bd. Vet. Toxicology, Am. Bd. Toxicology. From biol. scientist to sr. scientist Gen. Electric Co., Richland, Wash., 1957-64; sr. scientist biology dept. Pacific N.W. Labs., Richland, Wash., 1965; scientist med. rsch. br. divsn. biology and medicine AEC, Washington, 1965-66; asst. dir. rsch., dir. fission product inhalation program Lovelace Found. Med. Edn. and Rsch., Albuquerque, 1966-73; v.p., dir. rsch. adminstrn., dir. Lovelace Inhalation Toxicology Rsch. Inst., Albuquerque, 1973-76, pres., dir., 1976-88; chmn. bd. dirs. Lovelace Biomed. and Environ. Rsch. Inst., Albuquerque, 1988-96; pres., CEO Lovelace Respiratory Rsch. Inst., Triangle Park, NC, 1988-99; pres. emeritus Hamner Inst. Health Sci., Triangle Park, NC, 1999—; pvt. advisor Toxicology and Human Health Risk Analysis, 1999—. Mem. rsch. com. Health Effects Inst., 1981-92, mem. future techs. com., 2000—; bd. dir. Toxicology Lab. Accreditation Bd., 1982-90, treas., 1984-90; adj. prof. Wash. State U., 1980-95, U. Ark., 1970-88; clin. assoc. U. N.Mex., 1971-85, adj. prof. toxicology, 1985—; adj. prof. toxicology and occupl. and environ. medicine Duke U., 1988—; adj. prof. toxicology U. N.C., Chapel Hill, 1989-2000; adj. prof. toxicology N.C. State U., 1991—; cons. faculty Colo. State U., 2002—; regents lectr. UCLA, 1999-2000; mem. dose assessment adv. group U.S. Dept. Energy, 1980-87, mem. health and environ. rsch. adv. com., 1984-85, 1999-2004; mem. exec. com. sci. adv. bd. EPA, 1974-95, mem. environ. health com., 1980-83, chmn., 1982-83, chmn. radionuclide emissions rev. com., 1984-85, chmn. Clean Air Sci. Adv. Com., 1987-92, Diesel Exhaust Panel, 1996-2001, chmn. rsch. strategies adv. com., 1992-94, mem. Particulate Matter Panel, 1993-97, 99-2006; mem. com. toxicology NAS-NRC, 1979-87, chmn., 1980-87; mem. com. risk assessment methodology for hazardous air pollution NAS-NRC, 1991-94, com. biol. effects of Radon NAS NRC, 1994-98, com. rsch. priorities airborne particulate matter, 1998-2004; mem. Environ. Roundtable, Inst. Medicine, 1998-2002; mem. com. on environ. justice Inst. of Medicine, 1996-99, trustee toxicology excellence in risk assessment, 2000—, chmn. bd. trustees, 2002-04, mem. coord. com. strengthening sci.-based decision making, 2002—; pres. Am. Bd. Vet. Toxicology, 1970-73; mem. adv. coun. Ctr. for Risk Mgmt., Resources for the Future, 1987-2001; mem. Nat. Coun. for Radiation Protection, 1970-2001, hon. mem., 2002—; bd. dirs. N.C. Assn. Biomed. Rsch., 1989-91, N.C. Vet. Med. Found., 1990-95, pres., 1993-94; bd. govs. Rsch. Triangle Inst., 1994-2001; mem. adv. com. alternative toxicol. methods Interagy. Ctr. Evaluation Alternative Methods, Health and Human Svcs., 1998-2001, mem. sci. adv. com. on Alternative Toxic and Logical Methods Nat. Inst. Environ. Health Scis., 2006-; mem. sci. adv. bd. strategic environ. rsch. strategies program Dept. Def./Dept. Energy/EPA, 1997-99; mem. adv. com. Ctr. for Environ. Health, Agy. for Toxic Substances and Disease Registry, CDC, 2002-04, lunar dust toxicity panel NASA, 2005—; mem. bd. sci. counselors Ctr. for Environ. Health/Agy. Toxic Substances Disease Registry, 2004-06; mem. sci. adv. com. alternative toxicol. methods Nat. Inst. Environ. Health Scis., 2006—. Jour. Toxicology, 1984—89, assoc. dir., 1987—89; editor: Critical Revs. in Toxicology, 1987—; mem. editl bd.: Regulatory Toxicology and Pharmacology, 1993—, Risk Analysis, 1998—, Ullman's Ency. of Indsl. Chemistry, 1999—, Non-Linearity in Biology-Toxicology-Medicine, 2003—; contbr. articles to profl. jours. Trustee Wash. State U. Found., 2001—; mem. bd. of vis. Wash. State Univ., Coll. Sci., 2002—; mem. dean's adv. coun. Coll. Vet. Medicine Wash. State U., 2003—, chair dean's adv. coun., 2003—05. Recipient Herbert E. Stokinger award Am. Conf. Govtl. Indsl. Hygienists, 1985, Alumni Achievement award Wash. State U., 1987, Disting. Assoc. award Dept. Energy, 1987, 88, Arnold Lehman award Soc. Toxicology, 1992, N.Mex. Disting. Pub. Svc. award, 2006; co-recipient Frank R. Blood award Soc. Toxicology, 1989, Merit award Soc. Toxicology, 2005, Disting. Pub. Svc. award N.Mex., 2006,; named Disting. Vet. Medicine Alumnus Wash. State U., 1999, Robert Leader Meml. lectr. Mich. State U., 1999, H.M. Parker Meml. lectr. H.M. Parker Found., 1999; named to Hall of Fame Robert O. Anderson Schs. of Mgmt., U. N.Mex., 2002; fellow Internat. Aerosol Rsch. Assembly, 1998. Fellow: AAAS, Acad. Toxicol. Sci., Gesellschaft fur Zerosol Forschung, Health Physics Soc. (chmn. program com. 1972, Elda E. Anderson award 1974), Am. Acad. Vet. and Comparative Toxicology, Soc. Risk Analysis; mem.: Am. Vet. Med. Assn., Internat. Soc. Aerosols in Medicine (Thomas Mercer Joint prize for Aerosol Rsch. 1997), Am. Assn. Aerosol Rsch. (bd. dir. 1982—94, treas. 1986—90, v.p. to pres. 1990—93), Toxicology Edn. Found. (founding pres. 1990—91), Internat. Congress Toxicology VII (treas. 1995), Soc.Toxicology (chmn. 1983—85, inhalation splty. sect. v.p. to pres. 1983—86, bd. publs. 1983—86, v.p.-elect to pres. 1987—90, Amb.mid-Atlantic chpt. 1995, founding chair endowment fund bd. 2006—), Am. Conf. Govtl. Indsl. Hygienists, Internat. Regulatory Pharmacology and Toxicology (Internat. Achievement award 1999), Am. Assn. Cancer Rsch., Am. Thoracic Soc., Radiation Rsch. Soc. (chmn. fin. com. 1979—82, sec.-treas. 1982—84), Inst. Medicine (chair other health professions sect. 1999—2001), Am. Chem. Soc., Phi Zeta, Phi Kappa Phi, Sigma Xi. Republican. Lutheran. E-mail: roger.o.mcclellan@att.net.

MCCLELLAN, SCOTT K., former White House press secretary; b. Austin, Tex., Feb. 14, 1968; s. Barr McClellan and Carole Keeton Strayhorn; m. Jill Martinez, Nov. 2003. BA, U. Tex., Austin, 1991. Campaign mgr. for Carole Keeton Strayhorn Tex. Comptroller, 1998; dep. comm. dir. to Gov. George W. Bush State of Tex., 1999—2000; traveling press sec. Bush-Cheney Presdl. Campaign, 2000; dep. press sec. The White House, Washington, DC, 2001—03, asst. to Pres., press sec., 2003—06. Republican.

MC CLELLAN, WILLIAM MONSON, retired library director; b. Groton, Mass., Jan. 7, 1934; s. James Lewis and Ruth Caldwell (Monson) McC.; m. Jane Muir, Sept. 3, 1955; children— Jennifer, Anne, Margaret, Amy. BA, Colo. Coll., 1956, MA, 1961; A.M. in L.S, U. Mich., Ann Arbor, 1959. Music librarian U. Colo., Boulder, 1959-65; dir. Music Library, U. Ill., Urbana, 1965-97. Cons. music library resources and services to colls. and univs.; co-dir. Inst. Music Librarianship, Kent State U., 1969 Editor: Music Library Assn. Notes, 1977-82; Contbr. articles to profl. jours. Council on Library Resources fellow, 1976-77 Mem. Internat. Assn. Music Librs., Music. Libr. Assn. (pres. 1971-73, conf. panelist, chmn. stats. subcom. 1990-93). Home: 1212 Raintree Dr Apt I175 Fort Collins CO 80526 Home Phone: 970-266-0284. Personal E-mail: muirmack@frii.com. *To commit myself daily to giving and opening myself to others in all professional and other contexts.*

MCCLELLAND, FRANK, chef, restaurant owner; b. NH; m. Catherine McClelland; children: Keppler, Annie, James. Chef The Harvest, Cambridge, Mass., L'Espalier, Boston, exec. sous chef, 1986—, owner, 1988—; exec. chef The Country Inn, Princeton, Mass., 1984—86; owner, exec. chef Sel de la Terre, Boston, 2000—. Named Best Chef: Northeast, James Beard Found., 2007; named one of Top 25 New Chefs, Food & Wine Mag., 1985. Office: L'Espalier 30 Gloucester St Boston MA 02115 *

MCCLELLAND, JAMES LLOYD, psychologist, educator, cognitive neuroscientist; b. Cambridge, Mass., Dec. 1, 1948; s. Walter Moore and Frances (Shaffer) McClelland; m. Heidi Marsha Feldman, May 6, 1978; children: Mollie S., Heather Ann. BA in Psychology, Columbia U., 1970; PhD in Cognitive Psychology, U. Pa., 1975. Asst. prof. dept. psychology U. California, San Diego, 1974-80, assoc. prof., 1980-84, Carnegie-Mellon U., Pitts., 1984-85, prof. psychology, 1985—2006, co-dir. Ctr. for Neural Basis of Cognition, 1994—2006, univ. prof., 2001—06, Walter Van Dyke Bingham chair in psychology and cognitive neurosci., 2002—06; prof. psychology, dir. Ctr. Mind, Body and Computation Stanford U., Calif., 2006—. Rev. panel for cognition, emotion and personality NIMH, 1983-87, Cognitive Functional Neurosci., 1995-99, chair 1997-99; mem. Nat. Adv. Mental Health Coun., 2000-2003, Assoc. Neuroscience Rsch. Program. Author: (with others) Parallel Distributed Processing: Explorations in the Microstructure of Cognition, Vols. I, II, 1986; co-author: A Handbook of Models, Programs, and Exercises, 1988, Semantic Cognition: A Parallel-Distributed Processing Approach, 2004; contbr. numerous articles, reports, book chpts. to profl. publs.; sr. editor Cognitive Sci., 1988-91; sect. editor (Cognitive Neuroscience), Internat. Ency. of The Social and Behavioral Sciences; mem. numerous jour. edit. bds. Co-recipient Grawemeyer prize in psychology, 2002; recipient William W. Cumming prize, Columbia U., 1970, Rsch. Scientist Career Devel. award, NIMH, 1981—86, 1987—97; fellow, NSF, 1970—73; grantee, 1976—79, 1980—84, 1986—87, 1988—, Office Naval Rsch., 1982—87. Fellow: APA (Disting. Sci. Contbn. award 1996), AAAS, Am. Psychol. Soc. (William James Fellow award 2003—04); mem.: NAS, Soc. Exptl. Psychologists (Warren medal 1993), Internat. Assn. for Study Attention and Performance (lectr. 1986, governing bd. 1986—94), Psychonomics Soc., Cognitive Sci. Soc. (governing bd. 1988—93, chmn. 1991), Phi Beta Kappa. Office: Stanford Univ Dept Psychology Jordan Hall Bldg 420 450 Serra Mall Stanford CA 94305-2130 Business E-Mail: mcclelland@stanford.edu.

MCCLELLAND, KATE, librarian; Asst. dir., dir. youth svcs. Perrot Meml. Libr., Old Greenwich, Conn. Contbr. articles to profl. publs. Recipient NY Times Libr. award, 2006. Mem.: Assn. Libr. Svc. to Children (bd. dirs. 2005—, mem. Notable Books for Children (jointly with ALA)). Office: Perrot Meml Libr 90 Sound Beach Ave Old Greenwich CT 06870 Office Phone: 203-637-1066 ext. 27. Office Fax: 203-637-3876. E-mail: kmcclelland@perrotlibrary.org.

MCCLELLAND, RICHARD LEE, dentist; b. Pitts., May 18, 1927; s. William Noble and Pauline Elizabeth (Lee) McC.; m. Elizabeth Anne Michon, Dec. 6, I958; children: Richard Scott, William Alfred, Robert Craig. BA, Princeton U., 1950; DDS, U. Pa., 1954. Pvt. practice, Princeton, NJ, 1958-92. Clin. instr. U. Pa. Dental Sch., Phila., 1958-62; mem. exec. com. Med. Ctr. Princeton, 1971-72, past chmn. dental dept.; elected Nat. Dental Surgeon Res. Officers Assn. of U.S., 1972-73. With USN, 1945-46, WWII, lt. Dental Corps, USNR, 1954-57, capt., ret. Fellow: Acad. Gen. Dentistry, Internat. Coll. Dentists, Am. Coll. Dentists; mem.: ADA, Fedn. Dentaire Internat., Princeton Officers' Soc., Res. Officers Assn., Cedarwood Club Charlotte, Princeton Club (N.Y.C.), Princeton Nassau Club, Rotary (pres. Princeton 1978—79). Republican. Episcopalian. Avocations: sailing, photography. Home: 2606 Emmy Lane Charlotte NC 28226-3353

MC CLELLAND, ROBERT NELSON, surgeon, educator; b. Gilmer, Tex., Nov. 20, 1929; s. Robert Hilton and Verna Louise (Nelson) McC.; m. Connie Logan, May 5, 1958; children: Robert Christopher, Alison, Julie. BA, U. Tex., Austin, 1952; MD, U. Tex., Galveston, 1954. Diplomate Am. Bd. Surgery. Rotating intern U. Kans. Med. center, 1954-55; resident in gen. surgery Parkland Hosp., Dallas, 1957-59, 60-62; instr. surgery Southwestern Med. Sch., U. Tex., Dallas, 1962-63, asst. prof., 1963-67, asso. prof., 1967-71, prof., 1971—, Alvin Baldwin prof. surgery, 1977—. Examiner Nat. Bd. Med. Examiners Editor Audio Jour. Rev. Gen. Surgery, 1971-82, Selected Readings in Gen. Surgery, 1974—; contbr. numerous articles to profl. jours., chpts. to books. Served to capt. M.C. USAF, 1955-57. Fellow ACS (mem. grad. edn. com.); mem. AMA, Am. Surg. Assn., Western Surg. Assn., Soc. Surgery of Alimentary Tract, Am. Gastroent. Assn., Southwestern Surg. Soc., So. Surg. Assn., Dallas Soc. Gen. Surgeons (pres. 1987-88), Tex. Surg. Soc., Tex. Med. Assn., Dallas Country Med. Soc., Soc. Internatale de Chiurgie (bd. dirs. Am. chpt.), Phi Beta Kappa, Alpha Omega Alpha. Republican. Methodist. Home: 3601 Potomac Ave Dallas TX 75205-2110 Office: 5323 Harry Hines Blvd Dallas TX 75390-7208 Office Phone: 214-648-3540.

MCCLELLAND, SHEARWOOD JUNIOR, orthopaedic surgeon; s. Shearwood and Zenobia McClelland; m. Yvonne Shirley Thornton, 1974; children: Shearwood III, Kimberly. AB, Princeton U., 1969; MD, Columbia U., 1974, MPH, 1996. Diplomate Am. Bd. Orthopaedic Surgery. Intern St. Luke's Hosp., NYC, 1974—75; resident St. Luke;s Hosp., 1975—76; asst. resident in orthop. surgery N.Y. Orthop. Hosp., 1976—79; lt. comdr. USNR, 1979—82; staff orthop. surgeon Nat. Naval Med. Ctr., Bethesda, Md., 1979—82; asst. prof. surgery Uniformed Svcs. U. Health Scis., 1980—82; acting chief orthop. surgery Harlem Hosp. Ctr., 1983—84, assoc. dir. orthop. surgery, 1985—92, acting dir., 1992—94, dir., 1994—; asst. prof. clin. orthop. surgery Columbia U., 1983—94, assoc. prof. clinic, 1994—. Oral examiner Am. Bd. Othopaedic Surgery, 1993—; mem. N.Y. State Bd. of Profl. Med. Conduct, 1989-98. Annie C. Kane fellow in orthopaedic surgery, 1978-79; fellow in total joint implant surgery Ohio State U., 1982. Recipient Alumni Fedn. medal, Columbia U., 2005, P&S Gold medal, 2006; fellow, Nat. Assn. Pub. Hosps., 2005. Fellow ACS, AMA, Am. Acad. Orthop. Surgeons, N.Y. Acad. Medicine, Nat. Assn. Pub. Hosps.; mem. Assn. Mil. Surgeons U.S., Am. Coll. Phys. Execs., N.Y. Orthop. Hosp. Alumni Assn., Mensa, No. N.J. Princeton Alumni Assn., Columbia P&S Alumni Assoc. (pres. 2002-04, Alumni Fedn. medal 2005) Office: Harlem Hosp Ctr Dept Orthopaedic Surgery 506 Lenox Ave New York NY 10037-1802 Office Phone: 212-939-3510. E-mail: sjm2@columbia.edu.

MCCLENDON, AUBREY K., energy executive; m. Kathleen Byrns. Graduate, Trinity Coll. Duke Univ., 1981. Independent producer of oil & gas, 1982—89; co-founder, chmn., CEO Chesapeake Energy Corp., Okla. City, 1989—. Mem. bd. vis. Fuqua Sch. Bus., Duke Univ., Fuqua Sch. Bus. Duke Univ. Named one of Forbes' Richest Americans, 2006. Office: Chesapeake Energy Corp PO Box 18496 Oklahoma City OK 73154-0496 *

MCCLENDON, FRED VERNON, real estate professional, equity and realty appraiser, financial consultant; b. Vernon, Tex. s. Guy C. and Lexie M. (Johnson) Mc C.; m. Dorothy J. Seibert, June 1943 (div. 1953); children: Cathy, Kent, Tracy; m. Ethel R. Cherry, Sept. 15, 1959; children: Tess, Rob. J.T. Assoc. in Commerce, Hannibal La Grange Coll., 1947; BBA, Baylor U., 1949; MBA, Harvard U., 1951, postgrad. in law, 1951; postgrad. in banking, Colo. U., 1951—52; postgrad., Denver U., 1951—52. Lic. ins. agt., Tenn.; cert. real estate broker, Tenn.; cert. internat. financier. Asst. cashier U.S. Nat. Bank, Denver, 1951; gen. mgr. Nat. Paper Band Co., Denver, 1952—53; mgr. pers. Houston Fire & Casualty Co., Ft. Worth, 1954—56; mgr. gen. sales City Lincoln/Mercury, Dallas, 1957—58; owner INS-Bank Pers. Agy., Dallas, 1959—61; mng. ptnr. Allen & Mc Clendon Ins., Dallas, 1959—63; owner, broker Mc Clendon Real Estate, Dallas, 1959—63; pres. Mc Clendon Realty Co., Hampton, Tenn., 1961—2001; gen. mgr. Eagle Nest Ranch, Roan Mountain, Tenn., 1963—88, Mile High Ranch, Roan Mountain, 1988—99; pres. FMV Appraisal Co., Hampton, 1988—99, Amerifund Ventures, Internat., Tex., 2000—. Cons. Gen. Adjustments Bur., 1981—, Debourdieux Corp., 1985—, Wachesaw Corp., 1985—, Hidden Lakes Devel. Corp., various ins. cos. and law firms in U.S. and Can., IRS, U.S. Marshals Svc., U.S. Customs, 1993—, Heartland Presbyn. Ctr.; exec. cons. El Dorado Ranch, 1991-98; lectr. to lodges and assns.; gen. ptnr. Flexnet Investments, Ltd., Dallas, 1988-91; pres. Bus. Realty Internat. Cons., Hillsboro, Tex., 2000—; exec. v.p. OmniVue, Inc., S.C., 1992-95; chmn. AmeriFund Ventures, Internat., Tex., 1995-99, Tex., 2000—; pres. U.S. Med-Am. Bus. Svcs., 1995—. Contbr. articles to profl. jours. Recipient W.T. Grant fellow Harvard U., 1950-51. Mem. Am. Quarter Horse Assn. (life), Australian Appaloosa Assn., Appaloosa Horse Club U.S., Tenn. Walking Horse Breeders Assn., Am. Paint Horse Assn., Am. Soc. Equine Appraisers, Am. Horse Coun., Am. Soc. Appraisers (Accredited sr. appraiser, bd. examiners 1990—), Internat. Real Estate Inst., Nat. Assn. Real Estate Appraisers, Environ. Assessment Assoc. (cert. insp. 1991—), Appraisers Assn. Am. (cert. sr. appraiser), Internat. Soc. Financiers (cert. internat. financier). Republican. Mem. Seventh Day Adventists. Avocations: boating, travel, fishing, swimming. Office: Amerifund Ventures Internat PO 1209 Hillsboro TX 76645-1209 Office Phone: 254-632-4441. Personal E-mail: fredmcclendon@yahoo.com, fredmcclendoon@yahoo.com.

MCCLENDON, MICHELE ROSALIND, literature educator; BS in English Edn., Ind. U. Pa., 1970; M in Edn. Reading Specialist, Duquesne U., 1992. Cert. Elem. Edn. Duquesne U., Pa., 1994, Reading Supervision Edn. Duquesne U., Pa., 2005. Reading tchr. Hill Ho. Assn. Pitts. in Partnership with Parents, 1990—92, 1990—92, ednl. coord., 1992, 1992; reading specialist Pitts. Pub. Sch., 1992—95, 1992—95; English tchr. Pitts. Pub. Sch., Langley HS, 1995—2001; secondary literacy coach Pitts. Pub. Sch., Allderdice HS, Langley HS, 2001—05; secondary literacy coach, testing coord. Pitts. Pub. Sch., Allderdice HS, 2005—07; ret., 2007. Reading com. mem. Pa. Dept. Edn., Harrisburg; summer seminar participation profl. devel. Pitts. Health Career Initiative, 1997—2001; rep. Pitts. Tchrs. Inst., 1998—2001; tech. team Langley HS Pitts. Pub. Sch., 1998—2001; cons. Partners Edn. Consortium, 1999. Mem.: ASCD (assoc.), Nat. Coun. Tchrs.English (assoc.), Internat. Reading Assn. (assoc.). Avocations: piano, cooking. Office: Pitts Public Sch Allderdice HS 2409 Shady Ave Pittsburgh PA 15219 Home Phone: 412-471-5890.

MC CLENDON, WILLIAM HUTCHINSON, III, retired lawyer; b. New Orleans, Feb. 19, 1933; s. William H. and Eleanor (Eaton) McC.; m. Eugenia Mills Slaughter, Feb. 6, 1960; children: William Hutchinson, IV, Virginia Morris, Eleanor Eaton, Bryan Slaughter. BA, Tulane U., 1956, LLB, 1958. Bar: La. 1958, US Supreme Ct. 1964. Atty. Humble Oil & Refining Co., 1958-60; with firm Taylor, Porter, Brooks & Phillips, Baton Rouge, 1960—, ptnr., 1966-2001, mem. exec. com., 1987-2001; mediator, assoc. Mediation Arbitration Profl. Sys., Inc., 1999—2001. Instr. comml. law and negotiable instruments Am. Inst. Banking, 1963-74; lectr. movable Property La. Bar Assn. Bridging the Gap Inst., 1965; lectr. La. State U. LAw Sch. and Real Estate Seminar chmn., 1972, 74, 76, 80, 82, 85, 87, 95, La. Soc. of Profl. Surveying, 1989, La. Soc. CPA's, 1991, Banking Seminar, 1995; adj. prof. La. State U. Legal Negotiation, 1983—, U. Tenn., 2003-, Western Carolina U., 2003-; mem. faculty Profl. Edn. Group, Inc. Contbr. articles to legal jour. Bd. dir. Cancer Soc. Baton Rouge, 1968-71; trustee Episcopal HS, 1976-78; mem. Dean's council Tulane U. Law Sch., 1984-88. Served to capt. AUS. Recipient Preservation award Found. for Hist. La., 1997. Mem. ABA, Am. Judicature Soc., La. Bar Assn. (chmn. sect. trust estates, probate and immovable property law 1969-70, Meml. award article 1987), Baton Rouge Bar Assn. (chmn. title standards com. 1968-69), Tulane Alumni Assn. Greater Baton Rouge (pres. 1968-69), Baton Rouge Green (bd. dir. 1991-93), Hilltop Aboretum (bd. dir. 1993-95), La. Civil Svc. League (pres. 1992-94), La. Tulane Law Alumni (treas., 2d v.p. 1964-65), Baton Rouge Assembly (treas. 1983, ball chmn. 1997, chmn. 1999), Toastmasters (pres. 1970), Baton Rouge Country Club, Camelot Club, Pickwick Club, Rotary (bd. dir. Baton Rouge club 1972), Kappa Alpha, Baton Rouge Symphony (bd. dir. 2001-02). Republican. Episcopalian (vestry, sr. warden 1975, 81, 84, diocesan standing com. 1985-89). Personal E-mail: wh.mcclendon@gmail.com.

MCCLENNEN, MIRIAM J., former state official; b. Seattle, Sept. 16, 1923; d. Phillip and Frieda (Golub) Jacobs; m. Louis McClennen, Apr. 25, 1969; stepchildren: Adams Peter, James C.A., Helen, Persis, Crane, Emery. BA, U. Wash., 1945; MBA, Northwestern U., 1947. Exec. trainee Marshall Field & Co., Chgo., 1945-47; buyer Frederick & Nelson (subs. of Marshall Field), 1949-57, Goldwaters, Phoenix, 1963—67; adminstrv. asst. to pres. Ariz. State Senate, Phoenix, 1973-76; dir. publs. Office of Sec. of State, Phoenix, 1976-87. Chairwoman legis. subcom. adminstrv. procedure Ariz. State Legislature, Phoenix, 1984-85. Original compiler, codifier, editor publ. Ariz. Adminstrv. Code, 1973-87, Ariz. Adminstrv. Register, 1976-87. Mem. Cape Mus. Fine Arts, 1996—; commr. Ariz. Commn. on Arts, 1989—96; league bd. Phoenix Art Mus., 1966—; bd. dirs., mem. exec. bd. Phoenix Symphony Guild, 1969—88; bd. dirs., mem. Phoenix Art Mus. League, 1972—90; bd. dirs. Phoenix Art Coun., 1973—78; bd. dirs., sec. Combined Met. Phoenix Arts and Scis., 1974—90; bd. dirs. Master Apprentice Programs, 1980—83; bd. dirs., mem. exec. bd. Heard Mus., 1982—88, 1990—; mem. adv. bd. Ariz. State Hist. Records, 1987—90, Combined Met. Phoenix Arts and Scis., 1990—95; bd. dirs. Arizonans for Cultural Devel., 1996—2002; mem. Phoenix Symphony Bd. Overseers, 2007—. Recipient Disting. Svc. award Atty. Gen. Ariz., 1987, Outstanding Svc. to People, Ariz. State Senate, 1987, Nat. Assn. Secs. of State award, 1987. Mem.: Univ. Club, Ariz. Club, Phoenix Country Club, Charter 100 (bd. dirs. 1981—85). Personal E-mail: mjmlm@earthlink.net.

MC CLENNEY, BYRON NELSON, community college administrator; b. San Antonio, Dec. 14, 1939; s. Thomas B. and Lorene Holley McC.; children: Mark Nelson, Don Alan; m. Kay McCullough, May 17, 1986. BS, U. Tex., 1961, MEd, 1963, EdD, 1969. Asst. dean evening divsn. San Antonio Coll., 1966-68; dean instrn. McLennan C.C., Waco, Tex., 1968-70, Eastfield Coll., Dallas County, Tex., 1970-71, pres., 1971-78, Parkersburg (W.Va.) C.C., 1978-81, San Antonio C.C. Dist., 1981; chancellor Alamo C.C. Dist., 1982-86; pres. C.C. Denver, 1986-2000, Kingsborough C.C., 2000—. Author: Management for Productivity, 1980. Mem. steering com. Pres. Clinton's Am. Reads Challenge, 1997-2000. Recipient PBS O'Banion prize, 2002; NDEA fellow, 1965-66; recipient Disting. Alumni award U. Tex. Coll. Edn., 1982-83, Thomas J. Peters Nat. Leadership award League for Innovation, 1989. Mem. Am. Assn. Cmty. and Jr. Colls. (chmn. pres.'s acad. 1983-84, mem. urban commn. 1987-90), Commn. on Instns. of Higher Edn. Clubs: Rotary (past dist. gov.). Presbyterian. Office: 2001 Oriental Blvd Brooklyn NY 11235

MCCLENNY, PATSY See FAIRCHILD, MORGAN

MCCLENON, JOHN RAYMOND, retired chemistry professor; b. Grinnell, Iowa, May 1, 1937; s. Raymond Benedict and Erika (Weber) McC.; m. Mary Alice Thornton, June 7, 1959; children: Anne Jeanette, Marca Kay, Maureen. BA, Grinnell Coll., 1959; PhD, UCLA, 1964. Asst. prof. Milton Coll., Wis., 1963-65; asst. prof. chemistry Sweet Briar (Va.) Coll., 1965-72, assoc. prof., 1972-76, prof., 1976-82, Charles A. Dana prof., 1982—2002. Head FBN Microcomputing, Lynchburg, Va., 1980—, Johnny McClenon Big Band, Lynchburg, Va., 1978— Editor: (newsletter) Macintosh User's Group, Sweet Briar Coll. Chmn. ACLU local chpt., 1966-75; prin. clarinettist Lynchburg Symphony, Va., 1976—. Mem. AAUP (chmn. Sweet Briar chpt. 1982-83) Democrat. Unitarian Universalist. Home: 712 Riverside Dr Lynchburg VA 24503-1327 E-mail: mcclenon@cstone.net.

MCCLIMON, TIMOTHY JOHN, lawyer; b. Clinton, Iowa, July 17, 1953; s. Leonard James and Celeste Margaret (Borman) McC.; m. Suzanne Berman, Jan. 30, 1994. BA magna cum laude, Luther Coll., 1975; MS, St. Cloud State U., 1976; JD, Georgetown U., 1986. Bar: N.Y. 1987. Asst. dir. student activities St. Cloud State U., Minn., 1975-76; performing arts coordinator Western Ill. U., Macomb, 1976-79; program specialist Nat. Endowment for the Arts, Washington, 1979-82, program adminstr., 1982-86, law clk., 1985-86; assoc. Webster and Sheffield, NYC, 1986-88; v.p. AT&T Found., 1988-96, exec. dir., 1996—2003, Second Stage Theatre, 2003—06; pres. Am. Express Found., NYC, 2006—. Adj. prof. NYU, 1990—; bd. dirs. Second Stage Theatre, N.Y.C., BBB Found., N.Y.C., Times Square Alliance, N.Y.C., Field Papers, Inc., N.Y.C.; spkr. confs. on arts mgmt., fundraising and nonprofit mgmt., 1979—; cons. NEA, Washington, 1986—; mem. mayor's cultural affairs adv. commn. City of N.Y.C., 1992-94. Author: (textbook chpt.) Audiences and the Arts, 1981; contbr. articles to Jour. of Law and the Arts, 1986, other publs., 1989—. Recipient Eagle Scout award Boy Scouts Am., 1967, Faculty award Blue Key Nat. Honor Frat., 1979. Mem. N.Y.C. Bar Assn. (com. mem. 1987-92), ABA (com. mem. 1986-88), N.Y. State Bar Assn., Vol. Lawyers for the Arts. Avocations: photography, bicycling, travel, reading. Home: 222 Riverside Dr Apt 14A New York NY 10025-6809 Office: American Express 200 Vesey St New York NY 10284 Home Phone: 212-316-2219. Personal E-mail: mcclimon1@verizon.net. Business E-Mail: timothy.j.mcclimon@aexp.com.

MCCLINTOCK, DONALD WILLIAM, III, lawyer; b. Sapporo, Japan, Feb. 10, 1954; came to U.S., 1956; s. Donald William McClintock and Kazuko (Uchida) Inman; m. Barbara Joan Cleary, Aug. 9, 1980; children: Kime, Daniel. AB, Stanford U., 1976; JD, Harvard U., 1980. Bar: Calif. 1980, Alaska 1981, U.S. Dist. Ct. Alaska 1982, U.S. Ct. Appeals (9th cir.) 1987, U.S. Supreme Ct. 1988. Law clk. to justice Alaska Supreme Ct., Anchorage, 1980-81; asst. atty. gen. Alaska State Dept. Law, Anchorage, 1981-83; pres. Ashburn & Mason, Anchorage, 1983—2006. Bd. dirs. Family Resource Ctr. Anchorage, 1984-88, Alaska Youth and Parent Found., 1984-90; bd. dirs. Anchorage Cmty. Mental Health Assocs., 1994—, pres., 1996-98. Recipient Pro Bono award, Robert E. Hickerson, 2006. Mem.Alaska Bar Assn. Office: Ashburn & Mason 1227 W 9th Ave Ste 200 Anchorage AK 99501 Office Phone: 907-276-4331. Business E-Mail: dwm@anchorlaw.com.

MCCLINTOCK, JESSICA, fashion designer; b. Frenchville, Maine, June 19, 1930; d. Rene Gagnon and Verna Hedrich; m. Frank Staples (dec. 1964); 1 child Scott. BA, San Jose State U., 1963. Elem. sch. tchr., Marblehead, Mass., 1966-68, Long Island, N.Y., 1968, Sunnyvale, Calif., 1964-65, 68-69; fashion designer Jessica McClintock, Inc., San Francisco, 1969—. Active donor, AIDS and Homeless programs; scholarship sponsor Fashion Inst. Design and Merchandising. Recipient Merit award Design, 1989, Dallas Fashion award, 1988, Tommy award, 1986, Pres. Appreciation award, 1986, Best Interior Store Design, 1986, Calif. Designer award, 1985, Earnie award, 1981, numerous others. Mem. Coun. Fashion Designers of Am., Fashion Inst. Design & Merchandising (adv. bd. 1979—), San Francisco Fashion Industry (pres. 1976-78, bd. dirs. 1989). Office: Jessica McClintock Inc 1400 16th St San Francisco CA 94103-5181

MCCLINTOCK, RICHARD POLSON, dermatologist; b. Lancaster, NH, Dec. 16, 1933; s. Richard P. and Dorothy Grace McClintock; m. Barbara Wyatt, June 1959 (div. Mar. 1970); children: Peter, Pamela; m. Mary Joy Fitzgerald, Mar. 21, 1970; children: Wayne, Patrick. BA, Dartmouth Coll., 1956; MD, Harvard U., 1960. Diplomate Am. Bd. Dermatology, Am. Bd. Dermatopathology. Intern in medicine U. N.C., Chapel Hill, 1960-61; resident in dermatology Stanford U., Palo Alto, Calif., 1964-67; pvt. practice Ukiah, Calif., 1967—; clin. instr. dermatology Stanford U., Palo Alto, 1967-78, clin. asst. prof., 1978-86, assoc. clin. prof., 1986-92, lectr., 1992-98, assoc. clin. prof., 1998—. Mem. hosp. staff Ukiah Valley Med. Ctr., chief of staff, 1974; bd. dirs. IPA and Found. Med. Care Mendocino and Lake Counties. Contbr. articles to profl. jours. Trustee Found. for Med. Care for Mendocino and Lake Counties, 1990-94, pres., 1992-94. Lt. Med. Corps, USN, 1961-64. Mem. San Francisco Dermatol. Soc. (Practitioner of Yr. 2004), Pacific Dermatol. Assn., Am. Acad. Dermatology, Calif. Med. Soc., Mendocino Lake County Med. Soc., Internat. Soc. Dermatopathology. Office: 723 S Dora St Ukiah CA 95482-5335 E-mail: fitzmac@pacific.net.

MCCLINTOCK, WILLIAM THOMAS, healthcare consultant; b. Pittsfield, Mass., Oct. 23, 1934; s. Ernest William and Helen Elizabeth (Clum) M.; m. Wendolyn Hope Eckerman, June 22, 1963; children: Anne Elizabeth, Carol Jean, Thomas Daniel. BA, St. Lawrence U., Canton, NY, 1956; MBA, U. Chgo., 1959, MHA, 1962. Prodn. planner Corning Glass, NY, 1959-60; adminstrv. resident Alameda County Med. Instns., Oakland, Calif., 1961-62; adminstrv. asst. Univ. Hosps. of Cleve., 1962-65; asst. adminstr. Presbyn. Hosp., Whittier, Calif., 1965-68; regional asst. Kaiser Found. Hosps., Oakland, 1968-70; assoc. dir., exec. dir. Conn. Hosp. Planning Commn., New Haven, 1970-75; project dir., lectr. sch. health studies U. NH, Durham, 1975-77; regional mgr. Tex. Med. Found., Austin, 1977-81; adminstr. Schick Shadel Hosp., Ft. Worth, 1981-87; mgmt. cons. George S. May Internat. Co., Park Ridge, Ill., 1987-88; mgr. Nat. Ctr. Rsch. Programs Am. Heart Assn., Dallas, 1988-89; adminstr. Ambulatory Svcs. Health Care of Tex., Ft. Worth, 1990-92; CEO Boundary Cmty. Hosp., Bonners Ferry, Idaho, 1992-2000; healthcare cons., 2000—02; exec. dir. Oceanview Convalescent Ctr., Long Beach, Wash., 2002—06, Gilroy Healthcare and Rehab. Ctr., Calif., 2006. 1st lt. US Army, 1957. Fellow Am. Coll. Health Care Execs. (life, Sr.-Level Healthcare Exec. Regent's award 2000); mem. Am. Hosp. Assn. (life), Am. Heart Assn. (bd. dirs. Idaho/Mont. affiliate 1993-95), Idaho Hosp. Assn. (bd. dirs. 1995-2000, sec.-treas. 1998, chmn. bd. dirs. 1999, Recognition of Retirement award 2000), Masons, Rotary. Avocations: book collections, gardening, photography, fly fishing. Office Phone: 208-267-2570. Personal E-mail: wtmcclintock@earthlink.net.

MCCLINTON, DAVID ANTHONY, performing company executive; s. Tyrone McClinton and Dolores Marlene Rosebrook. BA, U. Denver, 1988. Data analyst Internat. Bus. Svc./Source One Mgmt., Lakewood/Denver, 1984—89; actor Denver Theatre & Media, 1991—; photographer, publicist Denver Theatre Venues, 1997—, dir., 1997—, playwright, 1997—; spl. places ops. supr. U.S. Census Bur., Denver, 1999—2000; artistic dir. Temple Events Ctr., Denver, 2001—, Brooks Ctr. Arts, Denver, 2006—. Founder, artistic dir. Temple Theatre Co., Denver, 2001—, Temple Arts Cmty., Denver, 2001, Temple Theatre Project, Denver, 2001, N.Y.C. Stage West Theatre Prodns., Denver, 2004—, Brooks Ctr. Arts' Play Showcase Festival, Denver, 2006. Author: (plays) Sybil's Others, 1998, (screenplays) Weirding Ways, 1998, (plays) Sisters in Blood, 2004, poetry. Named Semi Finalist Playwright, Moondance Internat. Film Festival, 2002, Quarter Finalist Screenwriter, The Writer's Network, 2003, 2004. Avocations: sailing, tennis, bicycling, hiking, dance. Office: Brooks Ctr Arts 1400 Williams St Denver CO 80210 E-mail: agogus1@yahoo.com.

MCCLINTON, DONALD GEORGE, retired diversified holding company executive; b. Pitts., June 30, 1933; s. Donald K. and Ethel M. McC.; m. Jane Ann Knoebel, Apr. 12, 1958; children: Catherine, D. Scott. BS, Miami U., Oxford, Ohio, 1955. Audit mgr. Arthur Andersen & Co., Cleve., 1955-62; mgr. accounting E. Ohio Gas Co., Cleve., 1962-66; exec. v.p. Nat. Industries, Inc., Louisville, 1966-79; pres. Yellow Cab Co., Louisville, 1979-94; owner, chmn. bd. Interlock Industries, Inc., 1982-94; pres. Skylight Thoroughbred Tng. Ctr., Inc., 1994—2002. Bd. dirs. Almost Framily, Clifton Ctr., MidAm. Bancorp, 1980—2002; trustee Jewish Hosp. Health Care Systems, Inc., 1983—2004, 2006—. Mem. Louisville-Jefferson County Bicentennial Commn., 1976-77; mem. coun., treas. Old Kentucky Home. coun. Boy Scouts Am., 1976-94; mem. Citizens at Large Jefferson County Budget Com., 1978-84; bd. overseers Bellarmine Coll., 1978-84; bd. dirs. Ky. Derby Festival, 1978—, Jewish Hosp., Louisville, 1978-83; trustee Spalding U., 1985-91. Mem.: Fin. Execs. Inst. E-mail: dmcclinton@insight.bb.com.

MCCLINTON, JAMES LEROY, city administrator; b. Longview, Wash., Oct. 14, 1949; s. James Delmer and Norma Jean (Ammons) McC.; m. Carmen Lassaphine Amador, Nov. 7, 1983; children: James Andrew, Ian Tyler, Kevin Riley. AA, SUNY, Albany, 1973; BA, Upper Iowa U., 1974; MA, Calif. State U., Carson, 1984; PhD, Calif. Coast U., 1985. Cert. mgr. Inst. Cert. Profl. Mgrs. With USCG, 1967-89, commd. officer, 1981-83, advanced through grades to comdr., 1987, ret., 1989; bur. mgr. adminstrv. svcs. Charleston (S.C.) County Sheriff's Office, 1989—2003; chief dep. clk. of ct. Berkeley County, SC, 2003—. Spkr. pro tem S.C. Criminal Justice Acad., Columbia, 1989—; mem. auditor selection com. Charleston County Govt., 1989—, computer users action com., 1989—; mem. various coms. County Govt. and Sheriff's Office, Charleston, 1989—; chief dep. clerk of ct. Berkeley County, S.C., 2003-. Editor: (newsletter) The Badge, 1989—; author: Pawprints in Heaven, —; contbr. articles to profl. jours. and mags.; newspaper columnist. Mem. Charleston Police Pipes and Drums, 1994—; grad. Leadership S.C., 1993, Leadership Charleston, 1997. Recipient Achievement award Nat. Assn. Counties, Washington, 1993, 96, Golden Pen award The Post and Courier Newspaper, Charleston, 1996. Mem. ASPA, SC Law Enforcement Officers Assn., Rotary Internat. (bd. dirs. North Charleston), Nat. Assn. Count Mgrs., SC Assn. Countywide Elected Execs., SC Assn. Clerks of Ct. Republican. Avocations: bagpipes, writing. Home Phone: 843-572-9264; Office Phone: 843-719-4508. Personal E-mail: ag4nm@comcast.net. Business E-Mail: jmcclinton@co.berkeley.sc.us.

MCCLISTER, MICHAEL, writer; b. Bristol, Va., July 9, 1941; s. Cecil McClister and Pauline McNeil; divorced; children: Porter, Jennifer. BA, U. N.C., Chapel Hill, 1962; MA, Rutgers U., New Brunswick, NJ, 1963. Author: Campaign Manual Series -- Democratic National Committee, 1976, Grassroots Campaigning -- National Education Association, 1981, Victim's Choice, 1999, Double Deal, 2000. Mem.: Phi Beta Kappa. Home: PO Box 3279 Placida FL 33946-3279 Office Phone: 941-716-0273. Home Fax: 941-697-1868. Personal E-mail: mcclister123@comcast.net.

MCCLOSKEY, DEIRDRE NANSEN, economics and history educator; b. Ann Arbor, Mich., Sept. 11, 1942; s. Robert Green and Helen (Stueland) McC.; m. J. Comi, June 19, 1965 (div. 1995); children: Daniel Robert, Margaret Anne. BA, Harvard U., 1964, PhD, 1970. Mem. faculty U. Chgo., 1968-80, assoc. prof. econs., 1973-80, assoc. prof. history, 1979-80; prof. econs. and history U. Iowa, Iowa City, 1980-99; Disting. Prof. Econs., History and English U. Ill., Chgo., 1999—. Vis. prof. Erasmus U. Rotterdam, Stanford U., Australian Nat. U., U. York, U. Manchester, U. London. Author: Economic Maturity and Entrepreneurial Decline, 1973, Enterprise and Trade in Victorian Britain, 1981, The Applied Theory of Price, 1986, The Rhetoric of Economics, 1986, If You're So Smart, 1990, Knowledge and Persuasion in Economics, 1994, The Vices of Economists, 1996, Crossing: A Memoir, 1999, How to Be Human Though an Economist, 2001; editor: Jour. Econ. History, 1980-85. Fellow Guggenheim, 1983, Inst. for Advanced Study-Princeton, N.J., 1983-84 Mem. Am. Econ. History Assn. (pres. 1996-97), Social Sci. History Assn. (pres.), Midwest Econ. Assn. (pres. 1992), Ea. Econ. Assn. (pres. 2003). Home: 720 S Dearborn St Apt 206 Chicago IL 60605-1820 Office: Dept Economics U Ill 601 S Morgan 210UH M/C 144 Chicago IL 60607 Office Phone: 312-996-3913. Office Fax: 312-996-3344. E-mail: deirdre2@uic.edu.

MCCLOSKEY, J(OHN) MICHAEL, retired environmental services administrator; b. Eugene, Oreg., Apr. 26, 1934; s. John Clement and Agnes Margaret (Studer) McC.; m. Maxine Mugg Johnson, June 17, 1965 (dec. 2006); stepchildren: Claire, Laura, James, Rosemary Johnson. BA, Harvard U., 1956; JD, U. Oreg., 1961. N.W. rep. Sierra Club, Eugene, 1961-65, asst. to pres. San Francisco, 1965-66, conservation dir., 1966-69, exec. dir., 1969-85, chmn. Washington, 1985-99, acting exec. dir., 1986-87; vice-chmn. Commn. on Environ. Law and Policy (Internat. Union for Conservation of Nature), Gland, Switzerland, 1978-88; mem. Pres.'s Commn. on Agenda for 1980's, Washington, 1979-80; co-chmn. OSHA-Environ. Conf., Washington, 1983-87; vice chmn. Am. Com. on Internat. Conservation, 1988-90; mem. Internat. Union Conservation of Nature World Commn. Protected Areas, 1988—; ret.; with urban forestry commn. City of Portland, 2005—. Mem. adj. faculty Sch. Natural Resources, U. Mich., 1988—2000; chmn. Mineral Policy Ctr., 1998-2001, Nat. Resources Coun. of Am., 1992-93; co-chmn. environ. policy task force Pres.'s Coun. Sustainable Devel., 1997-99; pres. Fedn. of Western Outdoor Clubs, 2000-03. Contbr. articles to profl. jours. Bd. dirs. Nat. Resources Coun. Am., 1988-94, vice chmn., 1989-91, chmn., 1992-93, chmn. Advocacy Forum, 1989-91; bd. dirs. Ind. Sector, 1990-96, Mineral Policy Ctr., 1988-2001, Coalition for Environmentally Responsible Economies, 1989-99, OMB Watch, 1998-2004; bd. trustees Sierra Club Found., 2000—; mem. steering com. Blueprint for Environ., 1987-88; nominated candidate Oreg. Ho. of Reps., 1962. Recipient award Calif. Conservation Coun., 1969, John Muir award Sierra Club, 1979, UN Environ. Program Global 500 award, 1992, Lifetime Achievement award Wild Found., 1998, Honor award Natural Resources Coun. Am., 1999, Packard award Internat. Union for Conservation of Nature Parks Commn., 2003, Conservation award Fedn. of Western Outdoor Clubs, 2004, Lifetime Achievement award Pub. Land Law Conf., 2006. Mem. Univ. Club (Portland, Oreg.), Explorers Club (N.Y.C.). Democrat. Office Phone: 503-245-9338. Personal E-mail: jmmccloskey@aol.com.

MCCLOSKEY, MICHAEL, social sciences, psychology, and sociology educator; AB with honors, U. Scranton, Pa., 1965; MA, Loyola U., Chgo., 1969, PhD, 1974; MDiv, Cath. Theol. Union Chgo., 1987. Ordained Roman Cath. deacon Holy Name Cathedral, Chgo. Asst. prof. Benedictine U., Lisle, Ill., 1970—74; prof. social sci., psychology, sociology Harry S. Truman City Coll., Chgo., 1974—. Recipient Grad. medal, Loyola U. Chgo., 1970, Centennial medallion, 1970; Arthur J. Schmitt scholar, Schmitt Found., 1969—70. Mem.: Religious Rsch. Assn. (mng. editor 1972—78), Assn. for Sociology Religion, Am. Sociol. Assn. Office: Harry S Truman City College 1145 W Wilson Ave Chicago IL 60640-6063

MCCLOUD, MELODY T., obstetrician-gynecologist, surgeon; BA, Boston U., 1977, MD, 1981. Intern Emory U. Affiliated Hosps., Atlanta, 1981-82, resident in ob-gyn., 1982-85; pres., founder, CEO Atlanta Women's Health Care, 1985—. Bd. dirs. Vis. Nurses Health Sys., Atlanta; med. cons. Greeley Co., Wis., 1994—; spkr. Nat. Dental Assn.-Atlanta Bus. League, 1995, Women-On-Tour Conf., Nat. Coalition 100 Black Women, Congl. Black Caucus-Women, others; cons. health WXIA-TV, Atlanta, 1995, 99. Author: Medical Bloopers!! Amusing, Amazing Stories, 1994, The Health Diary for Women, 1999, Blessed Health, 2003, Melodies of the Heart, 2004; med. advisor Body and Soul, 1994; health columnist: Women Looking Ahead, 1995—. Med. support group Com. Olympic Games, Atlanta, 1996; chair selection com. YWCA Acad., Atlanta, 1999 Inductee Leadership Atlanta, 1992, YWCA Acad. for Women Achievers, 1992; named Bus. Woman of Yr. Am. Bus. Women's Assn., 1994, Atlanta's Top 100 Black Women of Influence Atlanta Bus. League, 2003; recipient Cmty. Health Svc. award Black Pages. Mem. Med. Assn. Ga., Ga. Ob-Gyn Soc., Med. Assn. Atlanta, Atlanta Med. Assn., Soc. Laparoendoscopic Surgeons. Baptist. Avocations: tennis, bowling, water sports, theater, travel. Office: Melody T McCloud MD PO Box 344 Roswell GA 30077-0344 Office Phone: 770-921-6038. E-mail: mtm@drmccloud.com.

MCCLOW, ROGER JAMES, labor lawyer; b. St. Johns, Mich., July 23, 1947; s. Jack Gordon and Madalene V. (Mahaffy) McC.; m. Suzanne Terese Posler, July 13, 1978. BA in Polit. Sci. with distinction, U. Mich., 1969; JD magna cum laude, Wayne State U., 1976. Bar: Mich. 1977, U.S. Dist. Ct. (ea. dist.) Mich. 1977, U.S. Ct. Appeals (6th cir.) 1985, U.S. Ct. Appeals (8th cir.) 1987, U.S. Supreme Ct. 1988. Assoc. Miller, Cohen, Martens & Sugerman, Detroit, 1977-81, Klimist, McKnight & Sale, P.C., Southfield, Mich., 1981-83; ptnr. Klimist, McKnight, Sale, McClow & Canzano, P.C., Southfield, 1983—. Bd. dirs. Hemid (Sr. Citizen's Agy.), Detroit, 1982-2002; tutor Children's Ctr., Detroit, 1990-93; vol. Hospice Legal Aid, Detroit, 1991—, Patient Advocate Found., 1998—; mem. gun safety com. Alliance for Greater, Safer Detroit, 1993-95. Recipient Outstanding Vol. Svc. award Children's Ctr. Detroit, 1993. Mem. State Bar Mich. (coun. mem., labor law and employment sect. 1992-96), Detroit Bar Assn., Oakland County Bar Assn., Assn. Trial Lawyers Am., Mich. Trial Lawyers Assn., Indsl. Rels. Rsch. Assn., Phi Sigma Alpha. Democrat. Avocations: antiques, tennis, historic home restoration, landscaping. Office: Klimist McKnight Sale McClow & Canzano 400 Galleria Officentre Ste 117 Southfield MI 48034-2161 Home Phone: 248-857-8750; Office Phone: 248-354-9650. Business E-Mail: rmcclow@kmsmc.com.

MCCLOY, SHIRLEY, physical education educator; b. Riverton, Utah, May 30, 1972; d. Ronald J. and LaFawn Stepan; m. Scott Alexander McCloy, May 14, 1994; children: Makenna, Tamika. AA, Coll. So. Idaho, Twin Falls, 1993; BS, U. Utah, Salt Lake City, 2005, MS, 2006. Cert. tchr. Utah, adapted phys. educator 2006. Coach Globe Unified Sch. Dist., Ariz., 1995—96, Jordan Sch. Dist., Salt Lake City, 1997—98; claims processor Unibase, Salt Lake City, 1999—2000; referee Tooele Jr. Jazz, Utah, 2000; stocker/receiver Maceys Grocery, Tooele, 2000—02; coach Tooele Sch. Dist., 2000—03; asst. coord. UFIT U. Utah, Salt Lake City, 2006; tchr. health, phys. edn. Tooele Jr. High Sch., 2007—. Lic. foster care parent Utah Foster Care, Divsn. Child Family Svcs., 2002—. Mem.: AAHPERD, Nat. Fedn. State HS Assns., Utah Golf Assn. Mem. Lds Ch. Avocations: golf, camping, hiking, basketball, boating. E-mail: macnstep@comcast.net.

MCCLUGGAGE, KERRY, film and television executive; Studied broadcasting and film, U. So. Calif., 1976; MBA, Harvard U., 1978. With MCA/Universal, 1979—90; chmn. Paramount TV Group, Viacom, 1991—2002; founder, independent prodr., CEO Craftsman Films, 2002—; acquired with Jeff Sagansky, also co-chmn. Ardustry Home Entertainment, Woodland Hills, Calif., 2005—. Co-founder UPN Network, 1995. Supervised and developed programs such as: The A-Team, Coach, Deadwood, The Equalizer, Frasier, JAG, Northern Exposure, Law & Order, Miami Vice, Murder She Wrote, Quantum Leap and a few Star Trek Series. Address: Ardustry Home Entertainment 21250 Califa St Ste 102 Woodland Hills CA 91367

MCCLUNG, A(LEXANDER) KEITH, JR., retired lawyer; b. Gallipolis, Ohio, Sept. 13, 1934; s. Alexander Keith and Florence (Juhling) McC.; m. Sandra B. Foley, Aug. 17, 1957; children: Alexander Keith III, Martha E. AB, W.Va. U., 1956; JD, Harvard U., 1959. Bar: W.Va. 1959, Md. 1970, Mich. 1972. Assoc. Jackson, Kelly, Holt & O'Farrell, Charleston, W.Va., 1959-69; assoc. counsel Comml. Credit Corp., Balt., 1969-70; v.p., counsel McCullagh Leasing, Inc., Roseville, Mich., 1970-73, Comml. Credit Corp., Balt., 1973-82, gen. atty., 1982-85; sr. gen. atty. Comml. Credit Co., Balt., 1985-89, sr. v.p., gen. counsel, 1989-98. Bd. dirs. Travelers Bank; trustee Roland Park Found.; mem. adv. coun. Coll. Arts and Sci., W.Va. U. Capt. USAR. Mem. ABA (subcom. uniform comml. code, com. equipment leasing), Soc. Colonial Wars in the State of Md., St. George Soc. Md. Democrat. Home: 13 Devon Hill Rd Baltimore MD 21210-1044 E-mail: campussandy@aol.com.

MCCLUNG, GWENDOLYN, soil microbiologist; b. Takoma Park, Md., Sept. 5, 1956; d. Lowell Neal and Margaret May (Whaley) McC.; m. Guy Alan Athey; children: John Carl, Elaine Ashley Athey. BS in Agronomy, U. Md., 1977, MS in Soil Microbiology, 1981; PhD in Soil Microbiology, U. Calif., Riverside, 1986. Student lab. technician dept. agronomy U. Md., College Park, 1974-77, faculty rsch. asst., 1977-81; grad. rsch. and tchg. asst. dept. soil and environ. scis. U. Calif., Riverside, 1981-86; postdoctoral fellow dept. agronomy Ohio State U., Wooster, 1987-88; postdoctoral fellow Belts Agrl. Rsch. Ctr., USDA, Beltsville, Md., 1988-90; microbiologist, ecol. hazard assessor, risk assessor of genetically engineered microorganisms U.S. EPA, Washington, 1990—. Guest lectr. U. Md., College Park, 1991, 95. Contbr. articles to profl. jours. Pres. postdoctoral fellow Ohio State U., Wooster, 1986-87, Kinney postdoctoral fellow Beltsville Agrl. Rsch. Ctr., USDA, 1988-90. Mem. Am. Soc. Microbiology, Am. Soc. Agronomy, Soil Sci. Soc. Am. Achievements include research on plants and soil science and microbiology. Office: US EPA 1200 Pennsylvania Ave NW Washington DC 20460-0002 Office Phone: 202-564-8911. E-mail: mcclung.gwendolyn@epa.gov.

MCCLUNG, KENNETH AUSTIN, JR., training executive, performance consultant; b. Decatur, Ga., Apr. 11, 1947; s. Kenneth Austin Sr. and Marianne (Conklin) McC.; m. Christina June Palensar, Mar. 21, 1975. BA, North Ga. Coll., 1969; MS, EdD, U. So. Calif., 1976. Commd. 2d lt. U.S. Army, 1969, advanced through grades to maj., 1980—2000; col. USAR; sr. ptnr. Instrl. Design Group, Inc., Morristown, N.J., 1981-99; v.p., nat. learning dir. Jack Morton Worldwide, 1999-2000, nat. learning dir., 2000—02; ptnr. McClung, McClung & Assoc., Hertford, NC, 2002—. Bd. dirs. Nat. Productivity Ctr., Boulder, Colo., Price Waterhouse Learning Bd.; author/mgr. over 150 mgmt., sales, and tech. tng. programs; cons. in field. Author: Microcomputers for Medical Professionals, 1984, Microcomputers for Legal Professionals, 1984, Microcomputers for Investment Professionals, 1984, Microcomputers for Insurance Professionals, 1984, Personal Computers for Executives, 1984, French edit. 1985; co-author: Sales Training Handbook, 1989. Mem. ASTD, Internat. Soc. for Performance Improvement (pres. N.J. chpt. 1986-88, N.E. regional cons. 1989-90, nat. nomination chmn. 1990-91, nat. emerging tech. chmn. 1991-92). Avocations: sailing, tennis, bicycling, running, skiing. Home: 128 Back Creek Dr Hertford NC 27944 Office: McClung McClung & Assoc 128 Back Creek Dr Hertford NC 27944 E-mail: kenmcclung@earthlink.net.

MCCLUNG, MARY DENISE, psychology professor; b. Parkersburg, W.Va., Nov. 3, 1955; d. Bill and Nordeen Yearego; m. Phil McClung, 1979; children: Dustin, Donovan. BS, Marshall U., Huntington, 1978; MS, W.Va. U., Morgantown, 1980. LCSW W.Va., 1993. Dir. mktg. St. Joseph's Hosp., Parkersburg, W.Va., 1984—93; prof. W.Va. U., Parkersburg, 1993—. Chair Nat. Alliance Mentally Ill, Mid-Ohio Valley, 1996—. Office: WVa Univ 300 Campus Dr Parkersburg WV 26101

MCCLUNG, PHIL ORAN, psychology professor; s. Basil McClung Jesse and Virginia Pearl McClung; m. Mary Denise McClung, Sept. 14, 1979; children: Dustin Chad, Donovan Shane. BA in Psychology, W.Va. U., Morgantown, 1970, MS in Indsl. Rels., 1974, EdD, 1993. Cert. counselor NBCC, 1984, lic. practical counselor W.Va. Bd. Examiners Counseling, 1988. Dir. W.Va. U., 1970—90, prof., 1970—2007. Cons. W.Va. U. Mgmt. Inst., Parkersburg, 1975—2007; adj. prof. Marshall U. Grad. Sch., Charleston, W.Va., 2000—03. Author: (books) Desulfurization Technology, 1975, Potential Waste Products from Coal, 1975. Bd. mem. Sharpe Hosp., Weston, W.Va., 2000—07, W.Va. Alliance Mentally Ill, Charleston, 2000—07, Transitional Living Facility, Weston, 2007. Finalist W.Va. Prof. of Yr. award, Nat. Merit Found., 2006; recipient Outstanding Staff Support Person award, W.Va. UP Student Body, 1976—77, 1980, Prof. of Yr. award, 2006. Mem.: W.Va. Career Counseling Assn. (assoc.; pres. 1979—80), W.Va. Alliance Mentally Ill (assoc.; dir. 2000—07). Democrat-Npl. Achievements include development of an environmental psychology program. Avocations: tennis, volleyball, golf, badminton, table tennis. Home: 136 Whispering Pines Rd Davisville WV 26142 Office: WVa Univ 300 Campus Dr Parkersburg WV 26104 Office Fax: 304-424-8315; Home Fax: 304-424-8315. Business E-Mail: phil.mcclung@mail.wvu.edu.

MCCLURE, ANN CRAWFORD, judge, lawyer; b. Cin., Sept. 5, 1953; d. William Edward and Patricia Ann (Jewett) Crawford; m. David R. McClure, Nov. 12, 1983; children: Kinsey Tristen, Scott Crawford. BFA magna cum laude, Tex. Christian U., 1974; JD, U. Houston, 1979. Bd. cert. in family law and civil appellate law Tex. Bd. Legal Specialization. Assoc. Piro and Lilly, Houston, 1979-83; pvt. practice El Paso, Tex., 1983-92; ptnr. McClure and McClure, El Paso, 1992-94; justice 8th Ct. of Appeals, El Paso, 1995—. Past mem. Tex. Bd. Law Examiners, Bd. Disciplinary Appeals; mem. Family Law Specialization Exam Com., 1989—93; chair civil appellate law adv. com. Tex. Bd. Legal Specialization; past mem. Tex. Jud. Coun. Contbr. articles to profl. jours.; past editor The Family Law Forum; past contbg. editor: Texas Family Law Service; mem. editl. bd. Tex. Family Law Practice Manual, 1982-93; editl. cons. Matthew Bender Tex. Family Law Practice and Procedure. Mem.: El Paso Bar Assn. (sec. 2002—03, treas. 2003—04, v.p. 2004—05, pres.-elect 2005—06, pres. 2006—07), Tex. Acad. Family Law Specialists (past dir.), State Bar Tex. (family law sect. chair 1997—98, appellate law sect. chair 2000—01, appellate divsn. jud. sect. chair 2001—02). Democrat. Presbyterian. Office Phone: 915-546-2240.

MCCLURE, BROOKS, management consultant; b. NYC, Mar. 8, 1919; s. Walter Harsha and Angelica (Mendoza) McClure; m. Olga Beatrice Gallik, Oct. 15, 1949; 1 child, Karen (dec.). AB summa cum laude, U. Md.; disting. grad., U.S. Naval War Coll. N.Y. corr. Western Press Ltd., Australia, 1939-42; copy editor Washington Eve. Star, 1946-51; joined State Dept. Fgn. Service, 1951; information officer, attache embassy Copenhagen, 1951-53; press attache embassy Vienna, 1953-55; information officer, attache embassy Cairo, 1956—57, Seoul, 1957-60, Bonn, 1960-63; policy officer Europe USIA, 1963-66; pub. affairs officer 1st sec. embassy, Copenhagen, 1967-72; spl. asst. policy plans and nat. security council affairs, internat. security affairs Dept. Def., 1972-76; internat. security adviser USIA, 1976-77; program coordinator Crisis Assessment Staff, Dept. Commerce, 1977-78; dir. ops. Internat. Mgmt. Analysis and Resources Corp., 1978-81, v.p., 1982—; sec. Cross-Continent Assocs. Ltd., 1994-99. Various spl. assignments Europe, Mid. East, Asia, Africa; detailed to Vietnam, 1967; mem. working group Cabinet Com. to Combat Terrorism, 1973—77; lectr. FBI Acad., Fgn. Svc. Inst., Inter-Am. Def. Coll., Army War Coll., Navy War Coll., NJ Police Acad., NY State Police Acad. Contbg. author: book Modern Guerrilla Warfare, 1962, International Terrorism in Contemporary World, 1978, Corporate Vulnerability and How to Assess it: Political Terrorism and Business, 1979, Business and the Middle East, 1981, Political Terrorism and Energy, 1981; author (treatise) Dynamics of Terrorism, 1977; contbr. articles to profl. jours.; author: report to Senate Judiciary Com. on internat. terrorism and hostage def. measures; testifier on internat. security, hostage behavior, def. of Alaskan pipeline, FBI charter U.S. Senate, 1975—79. With AUS, 1942—46, ETO. Recipient Presdl. medal, Slovak Republic, 2002. Mem.: DACOR, Nat. Press Club, Assn. Diplomatic Studies, Am. Fgn. Svc. Assn., Alpha Sigma Lambda, Phi Kappa Phi. Home: 6204 Rockhurst Rd Bethesda MD 20817-1756 Office: IMAR Corp PO Box 34528 Bethesda MD 20827-0528 E-mail: imarmgtsvcs@mindspring.com, b-kmcclure@mindspring.com.

MCCLURE, CHARLES G., automotive executive; BS in Mech. Engring., Cornell U.; MBA, U. Mich. Heavy truck sales engr., product engr. Ford Motor Co.; v.p., gen. mgr. automotive sys. groups for the Ams. Johnson Controls, Inc., pres., Detroit Diesel Corp., 1997—2003, CEO, 1999—2003; CEO, pres. Federal-Mogul Corp., 2003—04; chmn., pres., CEO ArvinMeritor Inc., Troy, Mich., 2004—. Mem. Bus. Roundtable; bd. dir. NAM, R.L. Polk and Co., Intermet Corp., Motor & Equip. Mfr. Assn. Bd. dir. Detroit Renaissance, Detroit Regional C. of C., Horizons Upward Bound; mem. exec. com. A World in Motion. Lt. (j.g.) USN, 1975—79. Office: ArvinMeritor Inc 2135 W Maple Rd Troy MI 48084 *

MCCLURE, CHARLES ROBERT, library and information science educator, consultant; b. Syracuse, NY, May 24, 1949; s. Robert C. and Doris C. (Gordon) McC.; m. Victoria A. Jones, Dec. 30, 1971; 1 child, Gwendolyn A. BA in Spanish, Okla. State U., 1971, MA in History, 1972; MLS, U. Okla., 1973; PhD in Info. Studies, Rutgers U., 1977. Head govt.-history dept. U. Tex. Libr., El Paso, 1972-73; instr. Sch. Libr. and Info. Scis., Rutgers U., New Brunswick, NJ, 1974-76; prof. Sch. Libr. and Info. Scis., U. Okla., Norman, 1977-86, Sch. Info. Studies, Syracuse U., 1986—94, disting. prof., 1994—99; pres. Info. Mgmt. Cons. Svcs. Inc., 1986—; Francis Eppes prof. info. studies Coll. Info., Fla. State U., Tallahassee, 1999—, dir. Info. Use Mgmt. and Policy Inst. Cons. US Govt. Printing Office, Washington, 1989-90, US Congress Office Tech. Assessment, Washington, 1990-91. Author: Federal Information Policies in the 1980s, 1988 (Best Book of Yr. Am. Soc. Info. Sci.), Public Access to Government Information, 1989. Named Disting. Rschr. Nat. Commn. Librs. and Info. Sci., 1993. Mem. ALA (cons. 1986-88), Am. Soc. for Info. Sci., Assn. Libr. and Info. Sci. Educators. Office: Coll Info Fla State U Louis Shores Bldg, Rm 226 Tallahassee FL 32306-2100 Office Fax: 850-644-8109, 850-644-9763. E-mail: cmcclure@lis.fsu.edu. *

MCCLURE, D. ERIC, state agency administrator; m. Janet McClure; 3 children. Grad. in Fin. and Banking, U. Mo., Columbia, 1980; grad. with honors, Grad. Sch. Banking, Madison, Wis., 1992. Bank examiner Mo. Divsn. Fin., Springfield and St. Louis, dist. supr. Springfield office, 1989—98, dep. commr., 1998—99, acting commr., 1999—2003, commr., 2003—. Mem.: Conf. State Bank Suprs. (chmn. 2005—). Office: Mo Divsn Fin Truman Bldg North Wing Jefferson City MO 65101 Office Phone: 573-751-3242. Office Fax: 573-751-9192. E-mail: eric.mcclure@ded.mo.gov.

MCCLURE, DANIEL M., lawyer; b. Enid, Okla., Feb. 5, 1952; s. Larry M. and Marie Dolores (Sarver) McC.; m. Judy Lynn Pinson, Jan. 3, 1976; children: Andrew Mead, Mark William, Kathleen Claire. BA with highest hons., U. Okla., 1974; JD cum laude, Harvard U., 1978. Bar: Tex. 1978, U.S. Dist. Ct. (so. dist., ea. dist.) Tex. 1979, U.S. Ct. Appeals (5th cir., 10th cir., 11th cir.) 1981, U.S. Supreme Ct., 2003. Assoc. Fulbright & Jaworski, LLP, Houston, 1978-86, ptnr., 1986—. Mem. exec. com. Inst. Energy Law. Fellow Tex. Bar Found.; mem. ABA, Nat. Health Lawyers Assn., Nat. Assn. R.R. Trial Counsel, Tex. Bar Assn., Houston Bar Assn. (cert. civil trial law), Am. Inns of Ct., Harvard Law Sch. Assn. Avocations: tennis, bicycling. Home: 2 Long Timbers Ln Houston TX 77024-5445 Office: Fulbright & Jaworski LLP 1301 McKinney St Houston TX 77010-3031 Office Phone: 713-651-5151. E-mail: dmcclure@fulbright.com.

MCCLURE, DONALD STUART, physical chemist, educator; b. Yonkers, NY, Aug. 27, 1920; s. Robert Hirt and Helen (Campbell) McC.; m. Laura Lee Thompson, July 9, 1949; children: Edward, Katherine, Kevin. BChem, U. Minn., 1942; PhD, U. Calif., Berkeley, 1948. With war rsch. divsn. Columbia U., 1942-46; mem. faculty U. Calif., Berkeley, 1948-55; group leader, mem. profl. staff RCA Labs., 1955-62; prof. chemistry U. Chgo., 1962-67, Princeton (N.J.) U., 1967-91, prof. emeritus, 1991—, sr. rsch. assoc. Vis. lectr. various univs.; cons. to govt. and industry. Author: Electronic Spectra of Molecules and Ions in Crystals, 1959; co-author: Some Aspects of Crystal Field Theory, 1964; also articles. Guggenheim fellow Oxford (Eng.) U., 1972-73; Humboldt fellow, 1980; recipient Irving Langmuir prize, 1979 Fellow Am. Acad. Arts and Scis., Nat. Acad. Scis., Am. Phys. Soc.; mem. Am. Chem. Soc. Home: 23 Hemlock Cir Princeton NJ 08540-5405 Office Phone: 609-258-4980. Personal E-mail: d.s.mcclure@att.net. Business E-Mail: dmcclure@princeton.edu.

MCCLURE, FREDERICK DONALD, lawyer; b. Ft. Worth, Feb. 2, 1954; s. Foster Donald and Mayme Nell (Barnett) McClure; m. Harriet Elizabeth Jackson, Dec. 17, 1977; children: Lauren Elizabeth, Frederick Donald. BS in Agrl. Economics, summa cum laude, Tex. A&M U., 1976; JD, Baylor U., 1981. Bar: Tex., 1981, DC, US Dist. Ct. So. Dist. Tex., 1982, US Ct. Appeals 5th Cir., 1982. Agrl. asst. to US Senator John Tower, Washington, 1977-79, legis. dir., 1983-84; assoc. Reynolds, Allen & Cook, Houston, 1981-83; assoc. dep. atty. gen. US Dept. Justice, Washington, 1984-85; spl. asst. for legis. affairs to Pres. Ronald Reagan, Washington, 1985-86; v.p. govt. affairs Tex. Air. Corp., 1986—89; asst. for legis. affairs to Pres. George H.W. Bush, Washington, 1989-92; mng. dir. First S.W. Co., Dallas, 1992-94, Pub. Strategies, Inc., 1995—2001; mng. shareholder Winstead Sechrest & Minick, Washington, 2001—04; ptnr., pub. law & policy strategies group Sonnenschein Nath & Rosenthal LLP, Washington, 2004—. Mem. State of Tex. Inaugural Com., 1994, Bush-Cheney Transition Com., 2001; mem. transition com. Gov. Rick Perry, Tex., 2001; mem. Sec. Energy Adv. Bd.; bd. dirs. Alex Lee, Inc. Mem. bd. visitors US Naval Acad., 1992-95, chmn., 1994; bd regents Tex A&M U. Sys., 1995-2001. Named a Tex. A&M Disting. Alumni, Assn. Former Students & Tex. A&M U., 1991; named Disting. Alumnus, Baylor U., 1991; named one of Am.'s 50 most promising leaders age 40 and under, Time mag., 1994; recipient Jimmy Williams Disting. Svc. Award, Dallas A&M Club, 2002. Mem. State Bar Tex., Former Students Assn. of Tex. A&M (v.p. 1985-89, 93-95), Future Farmers Am. (nat. sec. 1973-74), Tex. Future Farmers Am. (state pres. 1972-73), Cotton Bowl Athletic Assn. (chmn. 1998—2002), Phi Alpha Delta, Phi Kappa Phi, Alpha Zeta (dir. 1985-93), Alpha Gamma Rho. Republican. Baptist. Office: Sonnenschein Nath & Rosenthal LLP Ste 600, E Tower 1301 K St NW Washington DC 20005 Office Phone: 202-408-3235. Office Fax: 202-408-6399. Business E-Mail: fmcclure@sonnenschein.com.

MCCLURE, HAL H., film producer; b. Indpls. s. Harold Alonzo and Betty (Zemah Hays) McClure; m. Dorothea Vernell Millar, Jan. 15, 1949 (dec. 1994). AA, L.A. City Coll., 1941. Journalist various newspapers, Calif., 1949-56; newsman AP, LA, 1956-58, NYC, 1959-60, fgn. corr. S.E. Asia and Mid. East, 1961-76, bur. chief N.J. Newark, 1976-77; prin., travel film prodr. Hal McClure Prodns., Laguna Woods, Calif., 1978—. Adj. asst. prof. journalism Seton Hall U., South Orange, NJ, 1976—77. Co-author: (book) Lighting Out of Israel, 1967; co-editor: Fire Over Suez, 1971; prodr.: (films) Istanbul-Travels in Turkey, 1990, Land of Legend-England Scotland and Wales, 1993, Adventure Holland, 1994, Mystery Tales of Europe, 1996, Dracula-Travels in Transylvania, 1997, Story Book England, 1999, Magic of Malaysia, 2001, Casablanca-Travels in Morocco, 2003, Echo of Hoofbeats - the Pony Express Story, 2005; editor, co-owner Travel Adventure Cinema mag., 1978—, leader in move to digital prodn. travel film field. Capt. USAFR, 1942—56. Named to Travelogue Hall of Fame, 1994; recipient Rising Star award, 1978; Ogden Reid Found. fellow, 1959. Mem.: Travel Adventure Cinema Soc. Home and Office: 686 Avenida Sevilla # C Laguna Woods CA 92637-3838

MCCLURE, HOWARD JEAN, JR., advocate; b. High Point, NC, June 15, 1959; s. Howard Jean McClure Sr. and Mary Elizabeth McClure. Author: Conflict Of Interest, 1999. Chmn. polit. action com. Carolina Advocates for Legal Reform, Charlotte, NC, 2001—02, v.p., 2001—02; mem. Charlotte Mecklenburg Cmty. Rels. Com., 2002—07; chmn. membership and cmty. rels. com. Western Region NC Black Leadership Caucus, 2003—05; active Black Polit. Caucus Charlotte-Mecklenburg, 1998—2004, Robert F. Kennedy Meml., 2005—07; founder Citizens Coun. for Equal Opportunity, 2003; mem. Nat. Campaign for Tolerance; vice chmn. 29th precinct Mecklenburg County Dem. Party, 2004—07. Recipient Outstanding Svc. award, Black Polit. Caucus of Charlotte Mecklenburg, 2003, Appreciation award, 2004, Chmn.'s Dem. of Month award, Mecklenburg County Dem. Party, 2004, Advocacy award, Nat. Assn. Human Rights Workers, 2005. Mem.: NAACP (mem. legal redress com. 1999—, edn. com. 2001—, labor and industry com. 2003—). Conservative. Avocations: music, writing, fishing, travel, football. Home: 3621 B Central Ave Charlotte NC 28205 Office: Citizens Coun Equal Opportunity PO Box 18812 Charlotte NC 28218 Office Phone: 704-531-3543. Personal E-mail: theebonysaint@webtv.net, theebonysaint2@msn.com.

MCCLURE, JAMES FOCHT, JR., federal judge; b. Danville, Pa., Apr. 6, 1931; s. James Focht and Florence Kathryn (Fowler) McC.; m. Elizabeth Louise Barber, June 14, 1952; children: Holly McClure Kerwin, Kimberly Ann Pacala, Jamee McClure Sealy, Mary Elizabeth Hudec, Margaret McClure Persing. AB, Amherst Coll., 1952; JD, U. Pa., 1957. Bar: D.C. 1957, Pa. 1958, U.S. Dist. Ct. D.C. 1957, U.S. Dist. Ct. (ea. and mid. dist.) Pa. 1958, U.S. Ct. Appeals (3d cir.) 1959. Atty., advisor Dept. State, Washington, 1957-58; assoc. Morgan, Lewis & Bockius, Phila., 1958-61; atty. Merck & Co., Inc., NYC, 1961-65; ptnr. McClure & McClure, Lewisburg, Pa., 1965-77, McClure & Light, Lewisburg, 1978-84; pres., judge Ct. Common Pleas, 17th Jud. Dist. Pa., Lewisburg, 1984-90; sr. dist. judge U.S. Dist. Ct. (mid. dist.) Pa., Williamsport, Pa., 1990—. Dist. atty. Union County, Lewisburg, 1974-75. Pres. bd. sch. dirs. Lewisburg Area Sch. Dist., 1969-74. Cpl. U.S. Army, 1952-54. Mem. Pa. Bar Assn., Union County Bar Assn., Bucknell U. Golf Club, Susquehanna Valley Chorale, Order of Coif, Phi Beta Kappa. Republican. Presbyterian. Office: US Dist Ct 240 W 3rd St Ste 320 Williamsport PA 17701-6466 Home Phone: 570-524-7341; Office Phone: 570-323-9772.

MCCLURE, JAMES JULIUS, JR., lawyer, former city official; b. Oak Park, Ill., Sept. 23, 1920; s. James J. and Ada Leslie (Baker) McC.; m. Margaret Carolyn Phelps, Apr. 9, 1949; children: John Phelps, Julia Jean, Donald Stewart. BA, U. Chgo., 1942, JD, 1949. Bar: Ill. 1950. Ptnr. Gardner, Carton & Douglas, Chgo., 1962-91, of counsel, 1991—; mem. Oak Park Plan Commn., 1966-73, Northeastern Ill. Planning Commn., 1973-77, pres., 1975-77, Village of Oak Park, 1973-81, Oak Park Exch. Congress Inc., 1978—2002. Mem. Bus. Leaders for Transp., 1998—. Pres. United Christian Cmty. Svcs., 1967-69, 71-73, Erie Neighborhood House, 1953-55, Oak Park-River Forest Cmty. Chest, 1967; moderator Presbytery Chgo., 1969; mem. Gov.'s Spl. Com. on MPO, 1978-79; bd. dirs. Leadership Coun. of Met. Open Cmtys., 1981-2002, sec., 1990-98; bd. dirs. Met. Planning Coun., 1982-93, hon. dir., 1993—; bd. dirs. Cmty. Renewal Soc., 1982-91, v.p., 1984-88, treas. 1988-91; bd. dirs. Christian Century Found., 1972—, chmn., 1981—; trustee McCormick Theol. Sem., 1981—, chmn. bd. 1987-90. hon. trustee, 1990—; mem. vocation agy., 1973-82; mem. ch. vocations unit, 1987-92, vice chair 1990; mem. gen. assembly coun. Presbyn. Ch. U.S.A., 1987-90, mem. gen. assembly Permanent Jud. Commn., 1997-2003; bd. dirs. Oak Park Edn. Found., 1991-96, Oak Park River Forest Cmty. Found., 1991-2002; mem. Vision 2000 (Oak Park) Coordinating Com., 1995. With USNR, 1942-46. Recipient Disting. Citizen award Oak Park, 1976; Silver Beaver award; Disting. Eagle Scout award Boy Scouts Am., Carl Winters Cmty. Svc. award Oak Park Rotary Club, 1996, William Staczak award Oak Park Edn. Found., 1997, Rita Johnson award Oak Park Family Svc. and Mental Health Ctr., 1997, Public Svc. award U. Chgo. Alumni Assn., 1997, Tradition of Excellence award Oak Pk. River Forest H.S., 1998, Alumni Svc. medal, Chgo. Alumni Assn., 2003, Gutenberg Award Chgo. Bible Soc., 2003; named one of 100 disting. Oak Parkers for Millenium, Wed Jour., 2002. Mem. ABA, Am. Coll. Trust and Estate Counsel, Ill. State Bar Assn., Chgo. Bar Assn., Am. Law Inst., Order of the Coif, Lambda Alpha. Clubs: Univ. (Chgo.). Office: Drinker Biddle Gardner Carton 191 N Wacker Dr Chicago IL 60606-4719 *Love of God, love of family, awareness of both the uniqueness and the contribution of every other human being, a sense of the wholeness of life with my religious faith, my profession of law, my family and my community service each playing an important part and complimenting each other.*

MCCLURE, JEFFREY B., lawyer; b. Columbus, Ohio, 1952; BA, Miami U., 1974; JD summa cum laude, Ohio State U., 1977. Bar: Tex. 1978, Calif. 1978, US Ct. Appeals (5th Cir.), US Dist. Ct. (No. Dist.) Tex., US Dist. Ct. (So. Dist.) Tex., US Dist. Ct. (Ea. Dist.) Tex., US Dist. Ct. (We. Dist.) Tex. Law clk. to Hon. John V. Singleton US Dist. Ct. (So. Dist.) Tex., 1977-78; atty. Butler & Binion, Houston; ptnr., Health Care Litig. Andrews Kurth LLP, Houston, mem. mgmt. com. Spkr. in field. Mem.: Def. Rsch. Inst., Nat. Health Lawyers Assn., Greater Houston Soc. Healthcare Risk Mgmt., Houston Bar Assn., State Bar Calif., Tex. Assn. Def. Counsel, State Bar Tex., Am. Soc. Healthcare Risk Mgmt., Order of Coif. Office: Andrews Kurth LLP 600 Travis St Ste 4200 Houston TX 77001-3090 Office Phone: 713-220-4772. Office Fax: 713-238-7403. Business E-Mail: jeffmcclure@andrewskurth.com.

MCCLURE, MATTHEW N., lawyer; BA, Loyola Coll., 1994; diploma in European Studies, Katholieke Universiteit Leuven, 1993; JD, Villanova U., 1999. Bar: Pa. 1999, NJ 1999. Head media rels. US Conf. of Mayors; assoc. Real Estate Dept. Ballard Spahr Andrews & Ingersoll, LLP, Phila., mem. Real Estate Devel Group, Zoning and Land Use Group, Eminent Domain and Valuation Group, Real Estate Fin. Group and Telecomm. Group. Bd. dirs. East Falls Devel. Corp., Blue Future PAC; mem. East Falls Schs. Com. Named one of 40 Under 40, Phila. Bus. Jour., 2006; named to Lamda Alpha Internat., 2006; recipient Pa. Rising Star Super Lawyer, Law & Politics Mag. and Phila. Mag. Mem.: ABA, Phila. Bar Assn., Pa. Bar Assn., NJ State Bar Assn. Office: Ballard Spahr Andrews & Ingersoll, LLP 51st FL 1735 Market St Philadelphia PA 19103-7599 Office Phone: 215-864-8771. Office Fax: 215-864-8272. E-mail: mcclure@ballardspahr.com.

MCCLURE, R. DALE, physician; b. Jan. 4, 1943; MD, U. Western Ontario, Can., 1968. Prof. urology U. Wash. Sch. Medicine, 1991—. Mem.: Pacific Coast Reproductive Soc. (pres. 1994), Am. Soc. Reproductive Medicine (mem. exec. bd. 2004—). Office: Virginia Mason Med Ctr 1100 9th Ave Seattle WA 98101-2756

MCCLURE, TERI PLUMMER, lawyer, delivery service executive; b. Kansas City, Dec. 31, 1963; m. Roderick McClure; 2 children. BS, BA, Washington U., 1985; JD, Emory U., 1988. Bar: Ga. 1988. Employment counsel United Parcel Svc. Inc., 1995—98, coord. labor and practice group, 1998—2003, mgr. ctrl. Fla. dist., 2003—05, gen. counsel, sr. v.p. legal, compliance and pub. affairs, corp. sec., mgmt. com. mem., 2005—. Bd. dirs. Jr. Achievement Ga., Anne E. Casey Found., UPS Found., Ctr. for Working Families. Mem.: Nat. Employment Law Counsel (mem. coord. com.), State Bar Ga. (mem. labor and employment law sect.), Am. Corp. Counsel Assn., Atlanta Bar Assn. Office: United Parcel Svc Inc 55 Glenlake Pkwy NE Atlanta GA 30328 *

MCCLURE, THOMAS EDWARD, lawyer; b. Urbana, Ill., Nov. 8, 1954; s. William Leslie McClure and Carolyn Jean (Hovey) McClure Byrnes; m. Karen Leah Zinn, Dec. 14, 1985. BS, Ill. State U., 1976; JD, DePaul U., 1979; MS, Ill. State U., 2001. Bar: Ill. 1979, U.S. Dist. Ct. (no. dist.) Ill. 1979, U.S. Ct. Appeals (7th cir.) 1980, U.S. Dist. Ct. (cen. dist.) Ill. 1983, U.S. Dist. Ct. (no. dist.) Ind. 1991, U.S. Supreme Ct. 1993. Law clk. to presiding justice Ill. Ct. Appeals (1st dist.), Chgo., 1979-81; assoc. Elliott & McClure, Bourbonnais and Momence, Ill., 1981-88; ptnr. Elliott & McClure P.C., Bourbonnais and Momence, Ill., 1988—2006, of counsel, 2007—. Legal counsel Ill. Jaycees, 1985-86, individual devel. v.p., 1987-88, regional dir., 1988-89; atty. Village of Bourbonnais, 1989-93, Village of Chebanse, 1993-97, Village of Manteno, 1999-2001; bd. mem.

Bourbonnais Elem. Sch. Dist., 2001-05, pres., 2003-2004; adj. instr. Ill. State U., 2003—. Editor DePaul Law Rev., 1978-79; contbr. articles to profl. jours. Recipient Outstanding Instrn. award Dale Carnegie & Assocs., 1982, 83, Dennis Hamilton Meml. award U.S. Jaycees, 1988. Mem. ABA, Ill. Bar Assn. (cert. of recognition 1983), 7th Cir. Bar Assn. (cert. of recognition 1994), Chgo. Bar Assn., Kankakee County Bar Assn., Appellate Lawyers Assn., Ill. Jaycees (individual devel. v.p. 1987-88, Outstanding Local Pres. 1985, Outstanding Local Dir. East Region 1984, Outstanding Portfolio V.P. 1987-88, Outstanding Regional Dir. 1988-89), Kankakee Jaycees (pres. 1984-85, bd. dirs. 1983-86), Ill. Jaycees Charitable Found., Inc. (bd. dirs., mem. and legal counsel 1986-89), Ill. Jaycees Charitable Camp, Inc. (bd. dirs., legal counsel 1989-91). Office: Elliott & McClure 18 Briarcliff Prof Ctr Bourbonnais IL 60914-1775

MCCLURE, WILLIAM PENDLETON, lawyer; b. Washington, May 25, 1925; s. John Elmer and Helen Newsome (Pendleton) McC.; children: Marilyn Alexander, Helen Pendleton, Elizabeth Ruffin, Melinda Geoghegan. BS, U. Pa., 1949; JD, George Washington U., 1951, LLM, 1954; postgrad., The Hague Acad. Internat. Law, Netherlands, 1952. Bar: D.C. 1951. Sr. ptnr. McClure & Trotter, Washington, 1952-91, McClure, Trotter & Mentz, Washington, 1991-93, McClure, Trotter & Mentz, chartered, Washington, 1993-95; of counsel White & Case, Washington, 1995—. Chmn. D.C. div. Crusade Against Cancer, Am. Cancer Soc., 1966, 67. Served from pvt. to 1st lt., inf. U.S. Army, 1943-46, PTO. Mem. Am. Bar Assn., Bar Assn. D.C., Am. Judicature Soc., Order of Coif, Phi Delta Phi, Phi Delta Theta. Clubs: Metropolitan (Washington), Columbia Country (Washington). Office: 701 13t St NW Washington DC 20005

MCCLUSKEY, CHARLES JAMES, JR., physician assistant; b. Rockville Center, NY, Oct. 16, 1947; s. Charles James McCluskey Sr. and Genevieve Ann (Reaves) Murphy; children: Charles James III, Christopher James, Katie Killam. Student, Broward Jr. Coll., 1967, Weber State Coll., 1971; cert. physician asst., Med. U. S.C., 1975. Cert. physician's asst., Fla., cert. procurement transplant coord. Am. Bd. Transplant Coords. Staff physician asst. George L. Timmons, MD, P.A., Hartsville, SC, 1975-76; physician asst. U.S. Dept. Justice, Washington, 1977-80, supervisory physician asst., health svc. adminstr., 1980-82; organ procurement coord. U. Fla., Jacksonville, 1982-86, exec. dir. organ procurement ops. Gainesville, 1986—2002; healthcare cons. in transplant, 2003—. Cons. Japanese Transplant Orgn., Kobe, Osaka, 1989—; transplant cons., 2002-; cons. in organ procurement Japan Kidney Transplant Network, 1997—; pres. bd. dirs. Nat. Coalition on Organ and Tissue Donation, 1999-2002, pres. 2001-2002. Contbr. articles to profl. jours. State dir. S.C. Jaycees, Hartsville, 1975—77; bd. dirs., v.p. Nat. Kidney Found., Jacksonville, 1983—87, bd. trustee, 1996—; pres. Nat. Coalition Donation, 2000—02; bd. dirs. Nielsen Organ Transplant Found., Jacksonville, 1983—; chairperson Fla. Coalition on Organ and Tissue Donation, 1998. Fellow Am. Acad. Physician's Assts. (liaison transplantation 1975—), N.Am. Transplant Coord. Orgn. (chair edn. 1982—, liaison to Japan 1986-88, Appreciation award 1986); mem. S.E. Organ Procurement Found. (chair procurement presentation 1982—, organ procurement orgn. com. 1997—, Appreciation award 1991), United Network for Organ Sharing, Coalition on Organ and Tissue Donation (chairperson Fla. 1998-99, bd. dirs. 1999). Avocations: skiing, diving, boating, golf. Home: 2401 Andalusia Way NE Saint Petersburg FL 33704 Office Phone: 727-820-7778. Personal E-mail: cjmcc@yahoo.com, transplantconsultant@yahoo.com.

MCCLUSKEY, FRANK BRYCE, director; b. Orange, NJ, July 28, 1949; s. Frank Bryce and Angela McCluskey; life ptnr. Marguerite Walker; children: Brandon Albert McCluskey, Kelly Bryce. BA in Philosophy, Bloomfield Coll., NJ, 1972; PhD in Philosophy, New Sch. U., NYC, 1977. Prof. philosophy Mercy Coll., Dobbs Ferry, NY, 1977—, dean of online learning, 2000—; postdoctoral fellow Yale U., New Haven, 1978. Cons. Am. Mgmt. Assn., NYC, 1994—2001; spkr. in field. Author: Thoughts on Fire; Life Lessons of a Volunteer Firefighter (Readers Choice award Writers Advantage, 2003), Burning for Success; contbr. articles to profl. jours. V.p. Putnam County Fire Chiefs, Carmel, NY, 1995—2004. Named Firefighter of Yr., Mahopac Falls (N.Y.) Vol. Fire Dept., 1990; fellow, NEH, 1978. Mem.: Internat. Assn. Fire Chiefs, Nat. Assn. Vol. Firefighters, N.Y. State Assn. Fire Chiefs. Republican. Roman Catholic. Avocation: travel. Home: 456 N Lake Blvd Mahopac NY 10541 Office: Mercy Coll 555 Broadway Mahopac NY 10522 E-mail: fmccluskey@mercy.edu.

MCCLUSKEY, LAURIE A., lawyer; b. Cin., Oct. 16, 1973; BSN, U. Cin., 1996; JD, Salmon P. Chase Coll. Law, 2002. Bar: Ohio 2002. Assoc. Undhorst & Dreidame Co., L.P.A., Cin. Named one of Ohio's Rising Stars, Super Lawyers, 2006. Mem.: Ohio State Bar Assn., ABA, Cin. Bar Assn. Office: Lindhorst & Dreidame Co LPA 312 Walnut St Ste 2300 Cincinnati OH 45202-4091 Office Phone: 513-421-6630. Office Fax: 513-421-0212.

MCCLUSKEY, NEIL GERARD, gerontologist, educator, literary agent; b. Seattle, Dec. 15, 1920; s. Patrick John and Mary Genevieve (Casey) McC.; m. Elaine Lituchy, June 5, 1977. AB, Gonzaga U., 1944, MA, 1945; Lic. in Sacred Theology, Gen. Theol. Union, Berkeley, 1952; PhD, Columbia U., 1957. Assoc. editor Am. (Nat. Cath. Weekly), NYC, 1955-60; dean sch. edn. Gonzaga U., Spokane, 1960-62, dir. hons. program, 1963-65, v.p. acad., 1963-66; prof. U. Notre Dame, South Bend, Ind., 1966-71, dean, dir. Inst. Studies in Edn., 1968-71; prof., dean profl. studies Lehman Coll. CUNY, 1971-75; dir. Ctr. Gerontol. Studies CUNY Grad. Sch., 1975-81; exec. dir. BHRAGS Social Svcs. Ctr., Bklyn., 1981-84; sr. cons. Retirement Advisors, Inc., NYC, 1985—. Pres. Westchester Lit. Agy., 1991—. Author: Public Schools and Moral Education, 1958, Catholic Viewpoint on Education, 1959, Catholic Education Faces Its Future, 1969; author, editor: Aging and Society, 1980, Aging and Retirement, 1981. Bd. dirs. Cath. Big Bros. N.Y., 1985—. Home: 5144 NE 18th Terr Fort Lauderdale FL 33308 Personal E-mail: neilagency@adelphia.net.

MCCOBB, JOHN BRADFORD, JR., lawyer; b. Oct. 14, 1939; s. John Bradford and Dorothea Joyce (Hoffman) M.; m. Maureen Kelly, Oct. 6, 1973; 1 child, Carrie Elizabeth. AB cum laude, Princeton U., 1961; JD, Stanford U., 1966; LLM, NYU, 1973. Bar: Calif. 1967. Assoc. IBM, Armonk, NY, 1966—74, gen. counsel Tokyo, 1974—77, lab. counsel Endicott, NY, 1977—79, sr. atty. White Plains, NY, 1979—81, regional counsel Dallas, 1981—83; counsel, sec. IBM Instruments, Inc., Danbury, Conn., 1983—87; area counsel European Labs., Hursley, England, 1987—90; counsel govtl. programs IBM, Washington, 1990—97. Princeton-in-Asia tchg. fellow Chinese U. Hong Kong, 1963—65. Contbr. articles to profl. jours. Trustee Princeton-in-Asia, Inc., 1970—86. Mem.: ABA, State Bar of Calif., Phi Beta Kappa.

MC COIN, JOHN MACK, social worker; b. Sparta, NC, Jan. 21, 1931; s. Robert Avery and Ollie (Osborne) McC. BS, Appalachian State Tchrs. Coll., Boone, NC, 1960; MS in Social Work, Richmond Profl. Inst., Va., 1962; postgrad., U. NC, 1959—60; PhD, U. Minn., 1977. Lic. master social worker; cert. social worker, N.Y. Social svc. worker Broughton State Hosp., Morganton, NC, 1958-59, John Unstead State Hosp., Butner, NC, 1960-61; clin. social worker Dorothea Dix State Hosp., Raleigh, NC, 1962-63; child welfare case worker Wake County Welfare Dept., Raleigh, 1963-64; psychiat. social worker Toledo Mental Hygiene Clinic, 1964-66; sr. psychiat. social worker N.Y. Hosp.-Cornell U. Med. Ctr. Westchester divsn., White Plains, 1966-68; social worker VA Hosp., Montrose, NY, 1968-73; also vol. mental health worker Westchester County Mental Health Assn. and Mental Health Bd., White Plains; seminar instr. Grad. Sch. Social Work U. Minn., Mpls., 1973-74; social worker F.D.R. VA Health Care Facility, Montrose, 1975-77; asst. prof. social work U. Wis., Oshkosh, 1977-79, chmn. dept. cmty. liaison com., 1978-79; assoc. prof. social work Grand Valley State Colls., Allendale, Mich., 1979-81; social worker VA Med. Ctr., Battle Creek, Mich., 1981-83, supr. social worker dept. Leavenworth, Kans., 1983-94. Cons. 44th Gen. Hosp., USAR, Menasha, Wis., 1978-79, 5540th Support Command, USAR, Grand Rapids, Mich., 1979-83; cons. in field; adj. faculty social scis. dept. Kansas City C.C., 1985-89, St. Mary Coll., 1984, Kellogg C.C., Battle Creek, 1981-83; adj. faculty sch. social welfare U. Kans., Lawrence, 1992; presenter in field. Author: Adult Foster Homes: Their Managers and Residents, 1983; founder (with Human Scis. Press), editor Adult Foster Care Jour., 1987-88, Adult Resdl. Care Jour., 1989-91, ind. jour., 1992-96; contbr. articles to profl. jours. With USMC, 1948-52, USMCR, 1957-72; lt. col. USAR, 1972-91. Recipient Outstanding Performance award VA, 1971, 83, Superior Performance award, 1982; grantee NIMH, 1974. Mem. NASW (social action com. West Mich. br. 1980-81), Alpha Delta Mu. Democrat. Baptist. Avocations: golf, jogging, genealogy, military history. Home and Office: 4913 Colonial Way Lawrence KS 66049-3599

MCCOLGAN, ELLYN A., diversified financial services company executive; b. Jersey City, Jan. 16, 1954; BA in Psychology, Montclair State Coll., NJ; MBA, Harvard Bus. Sch.; LLD, Babson Coll., 2005. With Shearson Lehman Bros., NYC, 1983, Bank of New Eng., Fidelity Investments, 1990—; pres. Fidelity Investments Tax-Exempt Svcs. Co., 1996—2000, Fidelity Investments Institutional Retirement Group, 2000—01, Fidelity Fin. Intermediary Svcs., 2001—02, Fidelity Brokerage Co., 2002—07; pres. distbn. & ops. Fidelity Investments, 2007. Mem. bd. dir. Securities Industry Assn. Trustee Babson Coll. Named one of 50 Most Powerful Women in Bus., Fortune mag., 2006. *

MCCOLLAM, CRAIG A., manufacturing executive; b. 1960; Dir. fin., corp. controller Dionex Corp, Sunnyvale, Calif., 1993-99, v.p. fin. & adminstrn., CFO, 1999—. Office: PO Box 3603 1228 Titan Way Sunnyvale CA 94085-4015 Office Phone: 408-481-4107. Business E-Mail: craig.mccollam@dionex.com.

MCCOLLAM, MARION ANDRUS, consulting firm executive, educator; b. New Orleans, Feb. 8, 1931; d. Gerald Louis and Lucile Gordon (Isacks) Andrus; m. Andrew McCollam, Jr., Jan. 29, 1955 (div. 1978); children: Andrew III, Gerald Andrus, Marion Cage. BA, Tulane U., 1952; M. Urban and Reg. Planning, U. New Orleans, 1978. Human affairs coord. Office of the Mayor, City of New Orleans, 1978, arts coord., 1978-80; dir. planning, prin. cons. Duncan Plaza Design Project, New Orleans, 1978-80; dir. planning Downtown Devel. Dist., New Orleans, 1980-81; pres. Andrus and Roberts Inc., Phoenix, New Orleans, 1980-84; exec. dir. Arts Coun. New Orleans, 1981-90, Cultural Arts Coun. of Houston and Harris County, 1991-98; pres. McCollam Cons., LLC, 1998—. Adj. lectr. in arts adminstrn. Goucher Coll., 1998—2004, mem. nat. adv. com., 2005—; cons. in field. Mem. nat. adv. com. Working Capital Fund, Mpls., 1995-99, Nat. Arts Stabilization, Balt., 1998—; adv. panel design Nat. Endowment for the Arts, Washington, 1995, adv. and chair local arts agencies, 1992-94; bd. dirs., sr. fellow Am. Leadership Forum, Houston, 1994—; mem. cmty. assessment com. United Way of Tex. Gulf Coast, 1995-99; bd. dirs. Urban League of New Orleans, 1984-89; pres. Jr. League of New Orleans, 1969-70. Recipient Arts Adminstr. of Yr. award Arts Mgmt. Inst./Nat. News Svc., 1987, Award for Sustained Mgmt. Excellence, Greater New Orleans Found., 1989. Mem. Am. Inst. Cert. Planners, AIA (hon.), U.S. Urban Arts Fedn. (pres. 1988), Nat. Assembly of Local Arts Agencies (vice chmn. bd. dirs. 1988-94, Chairman's award 1992). Avocations: music, art, reading, travel. Office: 1914 Bissonnet St Houston TX 77005-1645

MCCOLLAM, WILLIAM, JR., utilities executive; b. New Orleans, Mar. 15, 1925; s. William and Marie (Mason) McC.; m. Hope Flower Joffrion, Apr. 20, 1947; children: Ellendale McCollam Hoffman, William Cage, Stephen Mason. BS, La. State U., 1943; BS in Engring., U.S. Mil. Acad., 1946; MS in Civil Engring., MIT, 1954. Registered profl. engr., N.Y. Commd. 2d lt. U.S. Army, 1946; advanced through grades to lt. col. U.S Army; resigned U.S. Army, 1961; with Ark. Power and Light Co., Little Rock, 1961-70, exec. asst., 1961-64; v.p. Ark Power and Light Co., Little Rock, 1964-68; sr. v.p. Ark. Power and Light Co., Little Rock, 1968-70; exec. v.p. New Orleans Pub. Service, 1970-71, pres., 1971-78, Edison Electric Inst., Washington, 1978-90, pres. emeritus, 1990—. Cons. energy mgmt., Washington, 1990—; bd. dirs. Burns and Roe Group, Inc., Oradell, NJ; trustee Thomas Alva Edison Found., Detroit, 1978—89; past chmn. S.W. Power Pool, Little Rock, 1973—74, Nat. Elec. Reliability Coun., Princeton, NJ, 1975—78; bd. dirs., exec. com. U.S. Mem. Com., World Energy Coun., Washington, 1978—94; bd. dirs. McDermott Internat., Inc., 1990—99. Past pres. Greater New Orleans area C. of C., 1974-75; former dir. Loyola U., New Orleans, 1975-78; pres.'s council Tulane U., 1982-86. Named to La. State U. Alumni Hall of Distinction, 1985; recipient U.S. Energy award in recognition of outstanding contbn. to world energy coun., 1991. Mem. La. Soc. Profl. Engrs. (A.B. Paterson award 1975) Clubs: Chevy Chase, Metropolitan (Washington); Boston, New Orleans Country. Republican. Episcopalian. Office: Edison Electric Inst 701 Pennsylvania Ave NW Fl 3 Washington DC 20004-2696 Home: 4563 Powers Ferry Rd Nw Atlanta GA 30327-3424

MCCOLLEY, ROBERT MCNAIR, historian, educator; b. Salina, Kans., Feb. 2, 1933; s. Grant and Alice Elizabeth (McNair) McC.; m. Diane Laurene Kelsey, Aug. 30, 1958; children: Rebecca, Susanna, Teresa, Margaret, Carolyn, Robert Lauren. BA, Harvard U., 1954, MA, 1955; PhD, U Calif.-Berkeley, 1960. Instr. to prof. history U. Ill., Urbana, 1960—97. Mem. Com. for Advanced Placement Test in Am. History, 1987-90, chmn. 1988-90. Author: Slavery and Jeffersonian Virginia, 1964 (Dickerson award 1964); editor: Federalists, Republicans and Foreign Entanglements, 1969, Henry Adams, John Randolph, 1995, Jour. Early Ill. State Hist. Soc., 1998-2002, mem. editl. bd. 2002-07; co-editor: Refracting America, 1993; mem. editl. bd. Jour. Early Republic, 1981-85, Va. Mag. of History and Biography, 1994-98; classical recs. reviewer Fanfare mag., 1989-2006. Mem. Soc. Historians of Early Republic (pres. 1982), Orgn. Am. Historians, Va. Hist. Soc., Ill. Hist. Soc. (bd. dirs. 1978-81, 92-95, pres. 1997-99), Chgo. Hist. Soc., Cliff Dwellers. Home: 503 W Illinois St Urbana IL 61801-3927 E-mail: rmccolle@uiuc.edu.

MC COLLISTER, JOHN CHARLES, writer, minister, educator; b. Pitts., June 1, 1935; s. John Charles and Caroline Jesse (Hall) Mc C.; m. Beverly Ann Chase, Aug. 6, 1960; children: Beth Ann, Amy Susan, Michael John. BA, Capital U., 1957; MDiv, Luth. Theol. Sem., Columbus, Ohio, 1961; PhD, Mich. State U., 1969. Ordained to ministry Luth. Ch., 1961. Pastor Zion Luth. Ch., Freeland, Mich., 1961-65, Bethlehem Luth. Ch., Lansing, Mich., 1965-71; prof. religion and Greek Olivet (Mich.) Coll., 1970-74; prof. religion and philosophy Bethune-Cookman Coll., Daytona Beach, Fla., 1974-76, Embry-Riddle Aero. U., 1976-82, dir. profl. programs, 1979-80, cons. to pres., 1980-82. Pres. Wright Advt. Co., Daytona Beach, 1975-76; CEO New Arran Prodns., Inc., Daytona Beach, 1993—, Yongestreet Prodns., Ormond Beach, Fla., 1986; arbitrator Fed. Mediation and Conciliation Svc., 1978; spl. master Fla. Pub. Employees Rels. Commn., 1975—; mgmt. cons. Hoover Ball and Bearing, Charlotte, Mich.; pres. Am. Writers Inst., 1982—. Host Open Phone Forum, radio sta. WROD, Daytona Beach, 1974—76; author: A Philosophy of Flight, 1981, So Help Me, God, 1981, The Christian Book of Why, 1983; Problem Solving for Executives, 1984; author: The Sky is Home, 1986; co-author: The Sunshine Book, 1979, Day by Day, 1990; editor and compiler A Child is Born, 1972, Portraits of the Christ, 1974, Writing for Dollars, 1995, The Story of the Pittsburgh Pirates, 1998, The Tigers and Their Den, 1999, The Best Baseball Games Ever Played, 2002, Tales from the Pirates Dugout, 2003, Tales from the Cockpit, 2003, Echoes from the Smithsonian, 2004; editor and compiler: Tales From the 1979 Pittsburgh Pirates, 2005, God and the Oval Office, 2005; contbr. articles to various mags. Vol. probation officer, Mich., 1961-71, hearing officer, 1970-74; commr. Mich. Dept. Commerce, 1969-72; speaker Nat. Lincoln Day Observance, Washington, 1982; internat. adviser Han Nam U., Taejon, Republic of Korea, 1989. Recipient Outstanding Am. award Daytona Beach Jaycees, 1974. Mem. Am. Arbitration Assn. Home and Office: 26 Lazy Eight Dr Daytona Beach FL 32128-6775 Home Phone: 386-767-9999; Office Phone: 386-767-9999. E-mail: writerdoc@aol.com.

MCCOLLOUGH, JACK, apparel designer; b. Montclair, NJ; Attended, San Francisco Art Inst.; BA, Parsons Sch. of Design, 2002. Former intern Marc Jacobs; designer, co-founder, co-owner (with Lazaro Hernandez) Proenza Schouler, 2003—. Work featured in Women's Wear Daily, People, Town & Country and New York mag. Named Designers of the Yr., Parsons Benefit and Fashion Show; recipient Womenswear Designer of Yr. award (with Lazaro Hernandez), Coun. Fashion Designers Am., 2007. Office: c/o PR Consulting 42 Bond St 6 Fl New York NY 10012 *

MCCOLLOUGH, NEWTON CLARK, III, orthopaedic surgeon; b. Butler, Pa., July 17, 1934; s. Newton C. and Margaret Elizabeth (Mattocks) McC.; m. Mary Eva Semanski, Feb. 22, 1968; children: Peter Scott, Amy Marie. BA, Duke U., 1956; MD, U. Pa., 1959. Diplomate: Am. Bd. Orthopaedic Surgery. Intern Jackson Meml. Hosp., Miami, Fla., 1959-60, resident in orthopaedic surgery, 1960-64; dir. orthopaedic resident edn. Orange Meml. Hosp., Orlando, Fla., 1965-66; asst. prof. orthopaedics and rehab. U. Miami Sch. Medicine, 1968-72, assoc. prof., 1972-76, prof., vice chmn. dept., 1976-78, prof., chmn. dept., 1978-86; dir. rehab. Jackson Meml. Hosp., Miami, 1972-82, chief orthopedics and rehab., 1978-86; dir. med. affairs Internat. Shriners Hosps. Children, Tampa, Fla., 1986-2001, 2001—, mem. med. adv. bd., 2001—, dir. med. affairs emeritus, 2001—, med. adv. bd., 2001—. Dir. Am. Bd. for Certification in Prosthetics/Orthotics, 1974-77; mem. Health Planning Council So. Fla. Task Force on Long Term Patient Care, 1974-77; asst. med. dir. Div. of Children's Med. Services, State of Fla., 1975-86; chmn. Statewide Com. for Spinal Cord Injury, 1976-78 Trustee Jour. Bone and Joint Surgery, 1992-98, vice chmn., 1996-98; contbr. articles to med. jours. Served to lt. comdr. M.C. USNR, 1966-68. Decorated Legion of Merit. Mem. ACS, AMA, Am. Acad. Orthopaedic Surgeons (bd. dirs. 1978-79, 87-92, 2d v.p. 1987-88, 1st v.p. 1988-89, pres. 1989-90), Am. Burn Assn. (Disting. Achievement award 2001), Fla. Orthopaedic Soc. (mem. exec. com. 1978-79), Miami Orthopaedic Soc. (v.p. 1978-79), Am. Acad. Orthotists and Prosthetists (hon.), Fla. Med. Soc. Hillsborough County Med. Assn., Am. Congress Rehab. Medicine, Nat. Rehab. Assn., Scoliosos Rsch. Soc., Internat. Soc. Prosthetics and Orthotics, Am. Orthopaedic Assn., Orthopaedic Rsch. and Edn. Found. (trustee 1991-97, sec. 1995-97), Internat. Soc. Prosthetics and Orthotics (dir. 1980-83), Assn. Children's Prosthetic and Orthotic Clinics (pres. 1983-84), Rehab. Engring. Soc. N.Am. (dir. 1980-83), Am. Spinal Injury Assn., Internat. Med. Soc. Paraplegia, Pediatric Orthopaedic Soc. (dir. 1983-84, pres. 1984-85, Disting. Achievement award 2000), 20th Century Orthopaedic Assn. (treas. 1984-89), Am. Acad. Pediatrics, Phi Beta Kappa, Alpha Omega. Republican. Lutheran. Office: 602 Juan Anasco Dr Longboat Key FL 34228 Office Phone: 941-383-6146. Personal E-mail: newt3md@aol.com.

MCCOLLUM, ALVIN AUGUST, consultant, real estate company executive, real estate developer; b. LA, Jan. 20, 1920; s. Nile Clarkson and Ida Martha (Kuhlman) McC.; m. Maxine Eleanor Seeberg, July 29, 1944; children: Robert Michael, James Alan, Patricia Kathleen. BA, UCLA, 1941; postgrad., U.S. Naval Acad., 1946, Southwestern U., 1949-50. Exec. v.p., dir. Strout Realty, NYC, 1948-61, Del E. Webb Corp., Phoenix, 1961-67; pres., dir. Sahara Nev. Corp., Las Vegas, 1964-67, Devel. Svcs., Inc., Scottsdale, Ariz., 1967-69; pres., chmn. Recreation Leisure Land, Inc., Scottsdale, 1969-71; asst. pres., dir. A.J. Industries, Inc., LA, 1971-74; pres., dir. Carefree (Ariz.) Ranch, Inc., 1974-76; pres., bd. dir. Cons. Internat., Scottsdale, 1976—; chmn. CEO Greenway Environ. Svs., Inc., Gilbert, Ariz., 1992—. Pres., bd. dirs. Combined Assets, Inc., Westlake Village, Calif., First Realty Fin., Inc., L.A., Corp. Capital Resources, Inc., Westlake Village. Bd. dirs. Admiral Nimitz Found., Fredericksburg, Tex., 1970—, Boys Club Las Vegas, 1964-68, United Fund, Las Vegas, 1966; co-chmn. NCCJ, Las Vegas, 1966; elder Presbyn. Ch. USA, 1954—. Lt. USN, 1943-48, PTO. Mem. Masons, Shriners, Am. Legion, Mt. Shadows Country Club (bd. dirs. 1962-64). Republican. Avocations: golf, swimming, camping, sailing. Home: 8311 E Via de Ventura 1038 Scottsdale AZ 85258

MCCOLLUM, BETTY, congresswoman; b. Mpls., July 12, 1954; m. Douglas McCollum; 2 children. BS in Edn., Coll. St. Catherine, 1987. Retail store mgr., Minn.; mem. Minn. Ho. Reps., 1992-2000, mem. edn. com., environ. and natural resources com., mem. gen. legis. com., vet. affairs and elections com., mem. transportation and transit com., asst. majority leader, chair legis. commn. on econ. status of women, mem. rules and adminstrv. legis. com.; mem. U.S. Congress from Minn. 4th Dist., Washington, 2001—; mem. edn. and workforce com., resources com.; mem. Com. on Internat. Relations. Mem. St. Croix Valley Coun. Girl Scouts. Mem.: Am. Legion Aux., VFW Aux. Democrat. Office: US Ho Reps 1029 Longworth Ho Office Bldg Washington DC 20515-2304 *

MCCOLLUM, BILL (IRA WILLIAM MCCOLLUM JR.), state attorney general, former congressman; b. Brooksville, Fla., July 12, 1944; s. Ira William and Arline Gray (Lockhart) McCollum; m. Ingrid Mary Seebohm, Sept. 25, 1971; children: Douglas Michael, Justin Randolph, Andrew Lockhart. BA, U. Fla., 1965, JD, 1968. Bar: Fla. 1968, DC 2002. Ptnr. Pitts, Eubanks & Ross, P.A., Orlando, Fla., 1973-80; mem. US Congress from 5th Fla. dist., 1981-92, US Congress from 8th Fla. dist., 1993-2001, vice chmn. banking/fin. svcs. com., chmn. judiciary subcommittee on crime, mem. select com. on intelligence; ptnr. Baker & Hostetler, L.L.P., Orlando, Fla. and Washington, DC, 2001—06; atty. gen. State of Fla., 2007—. Vice chair House Rep. Conf. 101st-103d Congresses. Chmn. Rep. Exec. Com. Seminole County, Fla., 1976-80; county chmn.'s rep. 5th Dist. Fla. State Rep. Exec. Com., 1977-80; co-chmn. rep. platform com., 1992. Served in USN, 1969—72, comdr. Judge Adv. Gen.'s Corps USNR, 1973—92. Mem. Fla. Bar, Naval Res. Assn., Res. Officers Assn., Orange County Bar Assn. (exec. coun. 1975-79), Am. Legion, Mil. Order World Wars, Fla. Blue Key, Phi Delta Phi, Omicron Delta Kappa, Kiwanis. Republican. Episcopalian. Office: Office of Atty Gen The Capitol PL-01 Tallahassee FL 32399-1050 Office Phone: 850-245-0222.

MCCOLLUM, CLIFFORD GLENN, college dean emeritus; b. South Gifford, Mo., May 12, 1919; s. William Henry and Aultie V. (Westfall) McC.; m. Alice Elizabeth Erickson, Aug. 18, 1940; children: Eric Edward, Lisa Buren. Student, Central Coll., 1935-37; BS, U. Mo., 1939, MA, 1947, EdD, 1949. Tchr. pub. schs., Monett, Mo., 1938-39, Poplar Bluff, Mo., 1939-41, Boonville, Mo., 1941-42; asst. prof. sci. U. No. Iowa, 1949-55, assoc. prof., 1956-59, prof., 1959-84, prof. emeritus, 1984—, head dept. sci., 1957-68; dean U. No. Iowa (Coll. Natural Scis.), 1968-84, dean emeritus, 1984—. Prof. State U. N.Y. at Oneonta, 1955-56; Dir., instl. rep. Central States Univs., Inc.; cons. Coronet Instrnl. Films; cons. on sci. curricula to pub. schs. and colls.; speaker in field. Contbr. articles to profl. jours. Served with USAAF, 1943-46. Sci. Bldg. at U. Norther Iowa named in his honor, upon retirement. Fellow AAAS (nat. committeeman 1964-67), Iowa Acad. Sci. (pres. 1979-80); mem. Am. Inst. Biol. Scis., Nat. Assn. Biology Tchrs. (regional dir. 1963-65), Nat. Assn. Research in Sci. Teaching, Nat. Sci. Tchrs. Assn., Sigma Xi, Phi Delta Kappa. Home: 6511 N Revere Ave Kansas City MO 64151-3989 Personal E-mail: cmccollum1@kc.rr.com. *My personal response to the philosophical con-*

ditions in which we live today is one of preparing to live rather consistently with crises. It is my conviction that the mood of our time is toward a growing pessimism, and much of this is associated with the concomitants of a galloping technology. Yet we are not willing at this point to give up our human condition to the natural evolution that would result from basic environmental mechanisms. We will still try to condition that destiny.

MCCOLLUM, JAMES FOUNTAIN, lawyer; b. Reidsville, NC, Mar. 24, 1946; s. James F. and Dell (Frazier) McC.; m. Susan Shasek, Apr. 26, 1969; children: Audra Lynne, Amy Elizabeth. BS, Fla. Atlantic U., Boca Raton, 1968; JD, Fla. State U., Tallahassee, 1972. Bar: US Ct. Appeals (5th cir.) 1973, Fla. 1972, US Ct. Appeals (11th cir.) 1982, US Supreme Ct. 2006. Assoc. Kennedy & McCollum, 1972-73; prin. McCollum & Rinaldo, PA, 1973-77, McCollum & Oberhausen, PA, 1977-80, McCollum, Oberhausen & Tuck, LLP (and predecessor firm), Sebring, Fla., 1977—. Bd. dirs. Comml. Bancorp, Inc., Comml. Bank Highlands County; pres. Highlands Devel. Concepts, Inc., Sebring, 1982—; sec. Focus Broadcast Comm., Inc., Sebring, 1982-87; mng. ptnr. Highlands Investment Service; pres. Am. Svc. Title & Escrow, Inc., 2001— Treas. Highlands County chpt. ARC, 1973-76; vestryman St. Agnes Episcopal Ch., 1973—, chancellor, 1978—; mem. Fla. Sch. Bd. Atty.'s Assn., 1974-2001, bd. dirs., 1989-97, pres., 1995-96; mem. Com. 100 of Highlands County, 1975-83, bd. dirs., 1985-87, chmn., 1991-92; chmn. Highlands County High Speed Rail Task Force; chmn. bd., treas. Ctrl. Fla. Racing Assn., 1976-78; chmn. Leadership Sebring: life mem., past pres. Highlands Little Theatre, Inc.; bd. dirs. Palms of Sebring Nursing Home, 1988-90, Palms Estate Mobile Home Park, Sebring Airport Authority, 1988-90, treas., 1988, chmn. indsl. com., 1988, vice-chmn., 1989-90, chmn., 1990-91, Highlands County High Speed Rail Task Force, 1986-89, Highlands County Family YMCA, 1985-93, pres. Sebring br., 1992-93, chmn. bldg. com., 1992-94, Good Shepherd Hospice, Inc., v.p., 2000—, chmn. bd. dirs., 2003—, Primal Connection, Inc., 2006—; commr. Sebring Redevel. Agy., 2006—; campaign chmn. Jeb Bush for Gov., Highlands County, 1998, 2002, George W. Bush for President, 2000, 04. Recipient ARC citation, 1974, Presdl. award of appreciation Fla. Jaycees, 1980-82, 85, Outstanding Svc. award Highlands Coun. of 100, 1988, Most Valuable Player award Highlands Little Theatre, Inc., 1986, Zenon Significant Achievement award, 1991, Best Set award, 2002; named Jaycee of Year, Sebring Jaycees, 1981, Outstanding Local Chpt. Pres., US Jaycees, 1977, Citizen of Yr., United Way Ctrl. Fla., 2004, Highlands Counties Best Lawyer, Highlands Today and News Sun newspapers, 2003, 05, 06, 07. Mem. ABA, ATLA, Comml. Law League Am., Am. Arbitration Assn. (comml. arbitration panel), Nat. Assn. Retail Credit Attys., Fla. Bar (jour. com.), Highlands County Bar Assn. (past chmn. legal aid com.), Fla. Sch. Bd. Attys. Assn. (bd. dirs. 1989-97, v.p. 1993-94, pres. 1994-95), Greater Sebring C. of C. (dir. 1982-89, pres. 1986-87, chmn. transp. com. 1986—, Most Valuable Dir. award 1986-87), Fla. Jaycees (life, internat. senate 1977—), Lions (bd. dirs. 1972-73, v.p. 1994-95, Disting. award 1984). Republican. Episcopalian. Office: 129 S Commerce Ave Sebring FL 33870-3602 Office Phone: 863-385-5188. Personal E-mail: jim@jimmccollum.com.

MCCOLLUM, JOHN MORRIS, tenor; b. Coalinga, Calif., Feb. 21, 1922; s. Fay James and Ingabord Telette (Mason) McC.; m. Mary Margaret Wilson, Jan. 23, 1944; children: Kristi Elizabeth, Timothy James. Student, Coalinga Coll., 1939—40; BA in Journalism, U. Calif., Berkeley, 1947; student, Am. Theatre Wing, 1951—53. Reporter, city editor Coalinga Record, 1947-50; editor agrl. news U. Calif. Coll. Agr., 1950-51. Prof. music and chmn. voice faculty U. Mich.; dir. U. Mich. div. Nat. Music Camp; faculty Aspen Music Festival and School, 1963-76 Concert and opera singer, 1951—, soloist, Fifth Ave. Presbyn. Ch., NYC, 1953-56, debut, Town Hall, NYC, 1952, with, Boston Symphony Orchestra, Tanglewood, Mass., 1952, engagements with Symphony Orchestras in, N.Y.C., Chgo., Phila., San Francisco, Cleve., Washington, St. Louis, Detroit, New Orleans, Toronto, London, Mexico; with opera companies of, Boston, Washington, Toronto, Ft. Worth, Central City, Colo., NBC-TV, music festivals and oratorio societies, European debut, Festival of Two Worlds, Spoleto, Italy, summer 1958, Santa Fe Opera Co., leading tenor, NYC Opera Co., performing mem., Music Assos. of Aspen. (Recipient award Atwater Kent Auditions 1950, Am. Theatre Wing award 1952). Mem. Rep. Ctrl. Com., Fresno County, Calif., 1950; pres. Ann Arbor Civic Theatre, 1987-88; mem. Sarasota County Rep. exec. com.; mem., bd. dirs. Sarasota Concert Assn.; bd. dirs. Univ. Mich. Alumni Club. Served with U.S. Navy, 1942-49. Mem. U. Calif. Alumni Assn., Nat. Assn. Tchrs. Singing, Am. Acad. Tchrs. Singing, Alpha Tau Omega, Sigma Delta Chi, Pi Kappa Lambda. Episcopalian (lay reader). Clubs: Rotary (pres. 1977, Paul Harris fellow), Ann Arbor Golf and Outing (pres. 1979), The Meadows Country Club (Sarasota, Fla.). Home: 3380 W Chelmsford Ct Sarasota FL 34235-0947

MCCOLLUM, M. GREGORY, lawyer; b. Easley, SC; BA, Clemson U., 1982; JD, U. SC, 1985. Bar: S.C. 1988, U.S. Dist. Ct. S.C. 1992, cert.: U.S. Supreme Ct. SC (Lead Counsel Death Penalty Def.). Jud. clk. State Cir. Ct., SC, 1988; asst. pub. defender, 1988; asst. dist. atty. 15th jud. cir., 1989—94; DUI prosecutor Horry County, SC, 1994—95; pvt. practice Myrtle Beach, SC. Bd. dirs. Horry County Pub. Def. Corp. Mem.: SC Assn. Criminal Def. Lawyers, SC Bar Assn., Horry County Bar Assn., Nat. Assn. Criminal Def. Lawyers (life). Office: 516 29th Ave N Myrtle Beach SC 29577-3008 Office Phone: 846-626-5480. Office Fax: 843-626-2581. E-mail: gregorymccollum@sc.rr.com.

MCCOLLUM, MARIANNE, pharmacist, educator, medical researcher; d. Victor Joseph and Marianne McCollum. BA in Molecular, Cellular and Developmental Biology, U. Colo., Boulder, 1983; BS, in Pharmacy, U. Colo. Health Scis. Ctr., Denver, 1989, PhD in Pharm. Outcomes Rsch., 1999. Cert. pharmacotherapy specialist Am. Pharm. Assn., 1995, Board Certified Pharmacotherapy Specialist (Recertified) Am. Pharm. Assn., Wash., DC, 2002, Registered Pharmacist State of Colo., 1989. Asst. prof. Sch. Pharmacy U. Colo. Health Scis. Ctr., Denver, 2000—; asst. chief inpatient pharmacy mgr. Denver Vets. Affairs Med. Ctr., 2001—06. Pres. Symmetry Enterprises, Inc., Boulder, 2004—. Contbr. articles to profl. publs., chpt. to book. Vol. Boulder County AIDS Project, 1989—96; mem. friends of flock ATL Found., Denver, 2000—06. Pre-doctoral fellow, Am. Found. Pharm. Edn., 1998—99. Mem.: Am. Diabetes Assn., Internat. Soc. Pharmacoeconomics and Outcomes Rsch., Am. Assn. Colls. Pharmacy, Am. Coll. Clin. Pharmacy (chmn. outcomes and economics practice and rsch. network 2006—, Investigator Devel. award 2004—05, Career Devel. award 2005—), Phi Lambda Sigma (life), Rho Chi Soc. (life; pres. 1988—89). Avocations: golf, fishing, boating. Office: U Colo Health Scis Ctr 4200 East 9th Ave Box C-238 Denver CO 80262 Home Phone: 720-201-2340; Office Phone: 303-315-8952.

MCCOLLUM, PAMELA RAE, music educator; d. Donald L. and Mildred A. Swartz; m. Timothy James McCollum, June 10, 1972; children: Emily, Andrew. MusB, U. Mich., Ann Arbor, 1970, MusM, 1971. Cert. tchr. Mich., 1971, Wis., 1996. Cellist NC Symphony, Raleigh, 1971—72; Suzuki tchr. U. Wis., Stevens Point, 1974—98; educator Sch. Dist. Marshfield, Wis., 2000—. Cellist Marshfield Symphony, 1974—2000, Ctrl. Wis. Symphony, Stevens Point, 1995—2000. Altar guild local ch., Marshfield, 1974—, vestry mem., 2004—, Sunday sch. coord., 2005—. Recipient Crystal Apple award, Rotary Club, Marshfield, 2004; scholar, U. Mich., Ann Arbor, 1966—71. Mem.: Marshfield Tchrs. Assn., PEO Sisterhood Chpt. CL. Avocations: reading, gardening.

MCCOLLUM, ROBERT WAYNE, epidemiologist, educator; b. Waco, Tex., Jan. 29, 1925; s. Robert Wayne and Minnie (Brown) McC.; m. Audrey Talmage, Oct. 16, 1954; children: Cynthia, Douglas Scott. AB, Baylor U., 1945; MD, Johns Hopkins, 1948; DPH, London Sch. Hygiene and Tropical Medicine, 1958; MA (hon.), Yale U., 1965, Dartmouth Coll., 1985. Intern in pathology Columbia-Presbyn. Med. Center, NYC, 1948-49; intern in internal medicine Vanderbilt Hosp., Nashville, 1949-50; asst. resident in internal medicine Yale-New Haven Med. Center, 1950-51; faculty Yale Sch. Medicine, 1951-81, prof. epidemiology, 1965-81, chmn. dept. epidemiology and public health, 1969-81; dean Sch. Medicine Dartmouth Coll., Hanover, NH, 1982-90, prof. epidemiology, 1982-95, dean emeritus, 1990—; prof. emeritus, 1995—. Assoc. physician Yale-New Haven Hosp., from 1954; v.p. Dartmouth-Hitchcock Med. Ctr., 1983-90, acting v.p. for devel., 1999; cons. WHO, 1962-79; surgeon gen. U.S. Army, from 1960. Contbr. articles on epidemiology and control infectious diseases to profl. jours. Bd. sci. advisers Merck Inst., 1981-85; trustee Mary Hitchcock Meml. Hosp., Hanover, 1982-90. Capt. M.C., AUS, 1952-54. Mem. Assn. Tchrs. Preventive Medicine, Am. Epidemiological Soc., Internat. Epidemiological Assn., Infectious Diseases Soc. Am.; Conn. Acad. Sci. and Engring., Am. Coll. Epidemiology Office: Dartmouth Med Sch Dartmouth-Hitchcock Med Ctr Lebanon NH 03756

MCCOLLUM, W. LEE, chemical company executive; CFO SC Johnson & Son, Inc., Racine, Wis. Bd. dir. Sigma Aldrich Corp., Johnson Outdoors Inc., Johnson Bank, Cofresco. Office: SC Johnson & Son Inc 1525 Howe St Racine WI 53403 *

MCCOMAS, DAVID JOHN, science administrator, space physicist; b. Milw., May 22, 1958; s. Harrold James and Hazelyn (Melconian) McC.; m. Richelle Wolff, May 30, 1981; children: Random A., Koan I., Orion G. BS in Physics, MIT, Cambridge, 1980; MS in Geophysics and Space Physics, UCLA, 1985, PhD in Geophysics and Space Physics, 1986. Mem. staff Los Alamos Nat. Lab., N.Mex., 1980-91, sect. leader space plasma and planetary physics N.Mex., 1991-92, group leader for space and atmospheric scis. N.Mex., 1992-98, founding dir. Ctr. for Space Sci. and Exploration, NASA program N.Mex., 1998—2000; exec. dir. space sci. and engring. divsn. S.W. Rsch. Inst., San Antonio, 2000—03, sr. exec. dir., 2004—. Strategic planning com. earth and space scis. divsn. Los Alamos Nat. Lab, 1986; advanced composition explorer phase A study team NASA, 1988-89, space physics data system steering com., 1990-91, inner magnetosphere imaging study team, 1991-94, prin. investigator Interstellar Boundary Explorer, Ulysses Solar Wind Observations Over the Poles of the Sun Experiment, Two Wide-Angle Imaging Neutral-Atom Spectrometers, Explorer Mission-of-Opportunity, Solar Wind Electron Proton Alpha Monitor (instrument on the Advanced Composition Explorer, co-investigator Medium Energy Neutral Atom instrument on IMAGE Mid-sized Discovery Mission, plasma instrument for Cassini mission to Saturn, GENESIS Discovery mission, ISTP Polar Spacecraft's Thermal Ion Dynamics Experiment, Cluster plasma electron instrument, team New Millennium Plasma Experiment for Planetary Exploration, Space Sci. Adv. Com., chmn. Sun-Earth Connections Adv. Subcom., Solar Probe Sci. and Tech. Definition Team, NASA, 2004-05; com. solar-terrestrial rsch. Nat. Rsch. Coun., 1991-94, com. space sci. tech. planning Aeronautics and Space Engring. Bd./space studies bd., 1992, task group rsch. prioritization future space sci. space studies bd., 1994—; former prin. investigator series of 10 magnetospheric plasma analyzer instruments at geosynchronous orbit Dept. Energy; com. mem., panelist Nat. Acad. Sci.'s Nat. Rsch. Coun., U. Calif., State of N.Mex., others; adj. prof. dept. physics and astronomy U. Tex., San Antonio. Assoc. editor Jour. Geophys. Rsch.-Space Physics, 1993-94; contbr. articles to profl. jours. Grad. fellow Inst. Geophysics and Planetary Physics, 1983-84. Fellow AAAS, Am. Geophys. Union (James B. Macelwane award 1993). Achievements include patents in field. Office: SW Rsch Inst PO Drawer 28510 San Antonio TX 78228-0510

MCCOMB, DAVID GLENDINNING, history professor; b. Kokomo, Ind., Oct. 26, 1934; s. John Floyd and Jennie (Glendinning) McC.; m. Mary Alice Collier, Sept. 6, 1957; children: Katherine, Susan, Joseph. BA, So. Meth. U., 1956; MBA, Stanford U., 1958; MA, Rice U., 1962; PhD, U. Tex., 1968. Purchasing agt. McRan Co., Houston, 1958-60; instr. South Tex. Jr. Coll., Houston, 1962, U. Houston, 1966-68; asst. prof. San Antonio Coll., 1962-66; rsch. assoc. U. Tex., Austin, 1968-69; asst. prof. history Colo. State U., Ft. Collins, 1969-72, assoc. prof., 1972-77, prof., 1977—2002, chmn. dept., 1975—80, emeritus prof., 2002—. Interviewer, dir. Oral History of Colo. Project, 1973—77, Big Thompson Disaster Oral History, 1976—78, Olympic Tng. Ctr. Oral History, 1983—87. Author: Houston, a History, 1969, rev. edit., 1981 (Tullis award 1969), Galveston, a History, 1986 (Tex. history 1987), Texas, a Modern History, 1989, Texas, an Illustrated History, 1995, Historic Seacoast of Texas, 1999, Travels with Joe, 2001, Sports in World History, 2004, also others; editor: World History Ann. Edits., 1987, 89, 92, 96, 98, 2000, 01; contbr. articles to hist. jours. Recipient award of merit Am. Assn. for State and Local History, 1980, Disting. Svc. award Colo. State U., 1986; Danforth Found. grantee, 1978, Sigma Xi, 2001, also others, 1966-85. Fellow Tex. Hist. Assn.; mem. Oral History Assn. (program chmn. 1980), N.Am. Assn. for Sports History, World History Assn. (exec. coun. 1997-99), Western History Assn. (program chmn. 1979), Rocky Mountain World History Assn. (chmn. 1988-92). Democrat. Unitarian Universalist. Avocation: master swimming competition. Office: Colo State U Dept History Fort Collins CO 80523-0001 Office Phone: 970-491-6335. Business E-Mail: david.mccomb@colostate.edu.

MCCOMB, WILLIAM L., retail and former pharmaceutical executive; b. Columbia, Mo., Dec. 29, 1962; m. Marianne D. McComb; 3 children. BA in Economics, Miami U. of Ohio, 1984; MBA in Mktg. and Fin., U. Chgo., 1987. With Leo Burnett advertising firm, 1989—92; asst. product dir. consumer products Johnson & Johnson, 1992—93, product dir. consumer products, 1993—94, group product dir. consumer products, 1995, v.p. Johnson & Johnson Merck, 1996—97, v.p. new markets, Johnson & Johnson Professional Markets, 1997—98, v.p. mktg. McNeil Consumer Healthcare, 1999—2001, pres. McNeil Consumer & Specialty Pharmaceuticals, 2001—05, pres. Ortho Women's Health and Urology, 2004—05, group chmn. orthopaedics and neurologics, worldwide franchise chmn., mem. J&J medical device and diagnostics group operating com., 2005—06; CEO Liz Claiborne Inc., NYC, 2006—. Bd. dirs. Liz Claiborne Inc., 2006—. Office: Liz Claiborne Inc 1441 Broadway New York NY 10018 *

MCCOMBS, BILLY JOE (RED MCCOMBS), professional football team executive; m. Charlene McCombs; 3 daughters. Founder, dir. Clear Channel Communications, Inc, 1972—; former owner, chmn. bd. Denver Nuggets, 1982—86, San Antonio Spurs; chair. bd of trustees Southwestern Univ.; owner, chair., pres. Minnesota Vikings, Eden Prairie, 1998—2005. Film appearances: The Longest Yard, 2005. Chmn. bd. trustees Southwestern U.; former chmn. United Way of San Antonio, HemisFair World's Fair '68. Named to Bus. Hall of Fame; named one of Forbes Richest Americans, 2006. Mem. San Antonio C. of C. (former chmn.), Nat. Ford Dealers, U. Tex. Longhorn Club. Office: Winter Pk Admin Office 9520 Viking Dr Eden Prairie MN 55344-3898

MCCOMBS, DAVID LOUIS, lawyer; b. Gloucester, Mass., July 5, 1959; s. H.L. and Joan (Vasek) McCombs. BS in Physics, Denison U., 1981; JD, U. Miami, Fla., 1984. Bar: Tex. 1984, admitted to practice: US Dist. Ct. (No. Dist.) Tex. 1985, US Ct. Appeals (Fed. Cir.) 1985, US Ct. Appeals (5th Cir.) 1986, US Patent and Trademark Office. Assoc. Hubbard, Thurman, Turner & Tucker, Dallas, 1984—; ptnr. Haynes & Boone LLP, Dallas. Exec. bd. mem. Richardson Symphony Orchestra; rsch. adv. bd. U. Tex., Dallas; adv. bd. mem., Metroplex Tech. Bus. Council Richardson C. of C.; bd. mem. Trolley For Toys. Mem.: Computer Law Assn., Inst. Elec. and Electronics Engrings., Am. Electronics Assn., State Bar Tex., Dallas-Fort Worth Patent Law Assn. (pres. 1994), Nat. Assn. Mfrs., Assn. Trial Lawyers Am., Am. Intellectual Property Law Assn., ABA (antitrust, litig., patents trademarks and copyrights sects.), Sigma Pi Sigma. Office: Haynes & Boone LLP 901 Main St Ste 3100 Dallas TX 75202-3789 Office Phone: 214-651-5533. Office Fax: 214-651-5940. Business E-Mail: david.mccombs@haynesboone.com.

MCCOMBS, GILLIAN M., library director, dean; BA with honors, U. Warwick, 1968; MA in Librarianship, Leeds Sch. of Librarianship; MPA, SUNY, Albany. Head music libr. Huddersfield Pub. Libr., England, 1969—70; asst. libr. landscape architecture and hort. libr. Dumbarton Oaks Rsch. Libr. and Collection, Washington, 1976—78; cataloger TeleSec Libr. Contracting Svcs., Washington, 1981—82; head catalog Authority Files and Shelflist Maintenance Dept. Univ. Librs., SUNY, Albany, 1982—88, asst. dir. tech. svcs. and sys., 1988—98; dean, dir. Ctrl. Univ. Librs., So. Meth. U., Dallas, 1998—. Tchr. Sch. Info. Sci. and Policy, SUNY, Albany, 1988—94, Palmer Sch. Libr. and Info. Sci., LI U., 1995, Sch. Libr. and Info. Scis., U. North Tex., 1999, 2003, Sch. Libr. and Info. Studies, Tex. Woman's U., 1999, 2000; spkr. in field. Contbr. articles to profl. jours. Recipient Disting. Svc. Award, Hudson Mohawk Libr. Assn., 1997. Mem.: ALA, Tex. Libr. Assn., Internat. Fedn. Libr. Assns. and Insts., Libr. Adminstrn. and Mgmt. Assn., Assn. Coll. and Rsch. Librs. Office: So Meth U PO Box 750135 Dallas TX 75275-0135 Office Phone: 214-768-2401. Office Fax: 214-768-3815. E-mail: gmccombs@smu.edu. *

MCCONAUGHEY, MATTHEW, actor; b. Uvalde, Tex., Nov. 4, 1969; Grad., U. Tex., Austin, 1993. Represented by William Morris Agy., Beverly Hills, Calif., 1993—. Appearances in films include: My Boyfriend's Back, 1993, Dazed and Confused, 1993, The Return of the Chainsaw Massacre, 1994, Angels in the Outfield, 1994, Boys Submission, 1995, Judgement, 1995, Boys on the Side, 1995, Lone Star, 1996, A Time to Kill, 1996, Larger than Life, 1996, Glory Daze, 1996, Scorpion Spring, 1997, Amistad, 1997, Contact, 1997, The Rebel, 1998 (also writer, dir.), The Newton Boys, 1998, Making Sandwiches, 1998, South Beach, 1999, Last Flight of the Raven, 1999, Edtv, 1999, U-571, 2000, The Wedding Planner, 2001, Thirteen Conversations About One Thing, 2001, Frailty, 2001, Reign of Fire, 2002, How To Lose a Guy in 10 Days, 2003, Tiptoes, 2003, Two for the Money, 2005, Failure to Launch, 2006, We Are Marshall, 2006; actor, exec. prodr.: Sahara, 2005; TV films Absolute Evel: The Evel Knievel Story, 2005; TV appearances include Unsolved Mysteries, 1992, (voice) King of the Hill, 1999, Sex and the City, 2000. Named Sexiest Man Alive, People mag., 2005; recipient Favorite Male Action Star, People's Choice Award, 2006. *

MCCONKEY, JAMES RODNEY, literature and language educator, writer; b. Lakewood, Ohio, Sept. 2, 1921; s. Clayton Delano and Grace (Baird) McC.; m. Gladys Jean Voorhees, May 6, 1944; children: Lawrence Clark, John Crispin, James Clayton. BA, Cleve. Coll., 1943; MA, Western Res. U., 1946; PhD, U. Iowa, 1953. Teaching fellow, instr. Cleve. Coll., 1945-46; teaching asst. U. Iowa, Iowa City, 1949-50; asst. prof. Morehead State Coll., Ky., 1950-54, assoc. prof. Ky., 1954-56; asst. prof. Cornell U., Ithaca, N.Y., 1956-62, assoc. prof., 1962-67, prof., 1967-87, Goldwin Smith prof. English lit., 1987-92; Goldwin Smith prof. emeritus, 1992—. Dir. Morehead Writers Workshop, 1951-56, Antioch Seminar in Writing and Pub., Yellow Springs, Ohio, 1957-59 Author: The Novels of E.M. Forster, 1957, Night Stand, 1965, Crossroads, 1968, Journey to Sahalin, 1971, The Tree House Confessions, 1979, Court of Memory, 1983, To a Distant Island, 1984, Kayo: The Authentic and Annotated Autobiographical Novel From Outer Space, 1987, Rowan's Progress, 1992, Stories From My Life With the Other Animals, 1993, The Telescope in the Parlor, 2004; editor: The Structure of Prose, 1963, Chekhov and Our Age, 1984, The Anatomy of Memory, 1996. Served with U.S. Army, 1943-45. Guggenheim fellow, 1970; Eugene Saxton Meml. Trust Fund fellow, 1962; recipient Nat. Endowment of Arts essay award, 1968, Am. Acad. and Inst. Arts and Letters award in lit., 1979 Democrat. Home: 402 Aiken Rd Trumansburg NY 14886-9733 Office: Cornell Univ Goldwin Smith Hall Dept English Ithaca NY 14853 E-mail: jrm9@cornell.edu.

MCCONKIE, GEORGE WILSON, education educator; b. Holden, Utah, July 15, 1937; s. G. Wilson and Mabel (Stephenson) McC.; m. Orlene Carol Johnson, Sept. 6, 1962; children: Lynnette Mooth, Heather Usevitch, April Rhiner, Faline Coffelt, George Wilson, Bryce Johnson, Camille Howard, Elissa, Esther Ostler, Bryna Fisher, Ruth Olson, Anna May Cox, Cynthia, Thomas Oscar. AA, Dixie Jr. Coll., 1957; BS, Brigham Young U., 1960, MS, 1961; PhD, Stanford U., 1966. Missionary LDS Ch., 1957-59; asst. prof. edn. Cornell U., 1964-70, asso. prof., 1970-75, prof., 1975-78, chmn. dept. edn., 1977-78; prof. U. Ill., Champaign, 1978—2003, chmn. dept. ednl. psychology, 1993-94, 95-97, prof. emeritus, 2003—. Sr. scientist Ctr. for Study of Reading, 1978-95, Beckman Inst., 1989-2004; rsch. fellow Cath. U. Louvain, Belgium, 1991-92; vis. prof. Nat. Yang Ming U., Taiwan, 1998, Beijing Normal U., 1999. Contbr. articles to profl. jours. Recipient Outstanding Sci. Contbn. award Soc. for Sci. Study of Reading, 1995; NIMH spl. fellow, 1971-72, NIH Fogarty Internat. fellow, 1991-92; grantee U.S. Office Edn., 1970-73, Nat. Inst. Edn., 1974-77, NIMH, 1974-84, NICHHD, 1983-89, 91-95, AT&T, 1986-89, NSF, 1989-91, 2000-03, CIA, 1991-97, Army Rsch. Lab., 1996-2001, Yamaha Motor Corp., 1997-99, GM, 2002-04; Fulbright scholar, Taiwan, 1998, Sr. scholar Chiang Chung Kuo Found., 1998-99. Mem. Lds Ch. Home: 2605 Berniece Dr Champaign IL 61822-7225 Office: Coll Education Dept Educational Psych 1310 S Sixth St Champaign IL 61820 Business E-Mail: gmcconk@uiuc.edu.

MCCONNAUGHAY, PHILIP J., dean, law educator; BA, Ill. U., 1975, JD, 1982. Bar: Ill. 1978, Calif. 1979, DC 1983. Clk. to Hon. A.Y. Kirkland US Dist. Ct., No. Dist., Ill., 1978—79; assoc. Morrison & Foerster, San Francisco, 1979—83, ptnr. Washington, DC, Tokyo, Hong Kong, 1985—95; spl. dep. gen. counsel EEOC, Washington, DC, 1983—84; assoc. prof. U. Ill. Coll. Law, 1996—2001, prof., 2001—02; dean, Donald J. Farage Prof. Law Pa. State U., Dickinson Sch. Law, Carlisle, Pa., 2002—. Office: Dickinson Sch Law Pa State U 150 S Coll St Carlisle PA 17013 Office Phone: 717-240-5272. E-mail: pjm30@psu.edu.

MCCONNAUGHEY, GEORGE CARLTON, JR., retired lawyer; b. Hillsboro, Ohio, Aug. 9, 1925; s. George Carlton and Nelle (Morse) McC.; m. Carolyn Schlieper, June 16, 1951; children: Elizabeth, Susan, Nancy. BA, Denison U., 1949; LLB, Ohio State U., 1951, JD, 1967. Bar: Ohio 1951. Sole practice, Columbus; ptnr. McConnaughey & McConnaughey, 1954-57, McConnaughey, McConnaughey & Stradley, 1957-62, Laylin, McConnaughey & Stradley, 1962-67, George, Greek, King, McMahon & McConnaughey, 1967-79, McConnaughey, Stradley, Mone & Moul, 1979-81, Thompson, Hine & Flory (merger McConnaughey, Stradley, Mone & Moul with Thompson, Hine & Flory), 1981—92, ret. ptnr., 1992—. Bd. dirs. N.Am. Broadcasting Co. (Sta. WMNI, WBZX and WTDA Radio); asst. atty. gen. State of Ohio, 1951-54. Pres. Upper Arlington (Ohio) Bd. Edn., 1967-69, Columbus Town Meeting Assn., 1974-76; chmn. Ohio Young Reps., 1956; U.S. presdl. elector, 1956; trustee Buckeye Boys Ranch, Columbus, 1967-73, 75-81, Upper Arlington Edn. Found., 1987-93; elder Covenant Presbyn. Ch., Columbus. With U.S. Army, 1943-45, ETO. Fellow Am. Bar Found., Ohio Bar Found., Columbus Bar Found.; mem. ABA, Ohio State Bar Assn., Columbus Bar Assn., Am. Judicature Soc., Scioto Country Club, Athletic Club, Rotary, Masons. Home: 1993 Collingswood Rd Columbus OH 43221-3741 Office: Thompson Hine LLP One Columbus 10 W Broad St Ste 700 Columbus OH 43215-3435 Office Phone: 614-469-3224.

MCCONNAUGHEY, JAMES WALTER, economist; b. Washington, May 8, 1951; s. William Eugene and Eunice (Ensor) McC.; m. Rosemarie

Fuchs, June 23, 1984. BS in Econs. with high honors, U. Md., 1973; MA in Econs., George Washington U., 1979; MPA with high honors, Harvard U., 1992. Industry economist FCC Common Carrier Bur., Washington, 1973-80, sr. economist, 1981-83; sr. assoc. Bolter and Nilsson, Bethesda, Md., 1983; mgr. rsch. studies div. Bethesda Rsch. Inst., 1983-89; sr. economist office policy analysis and devel. U.S. Dept. Commerce Nat. Telecommunications and Info. Adminstrn., Washington, 1989—2005, sr. econ. advisor, 2005—. Mem. rsch. bd. advisors Am. Biographical Inst., 1994—; presenter in field of telecomms. policy. Author: (with others) Telecommunications Policy for the 1980's: The Transition to Competition, 1984, Telecommunications Policy for the 1990's and Beyond, 1990, U.S. Telecommunications in a Global Economy: Competitiveness at a Crossroads, 1990, Telecommunications in the Age of Information, 1991, NII Field Hearings on Universal Service and Open Access: America Speaks Out, 1994, Falling Through the Net and a Nation Online: Reports on the "Digital Divide," 1995, 1998-2004, (with others) Structure of American Industry, 2000, 3rd edit., 2007. Campaign worker, contbr. nat. and local elections; coach Bowie (Md.) Boy's Club; mem. Neighborhood Open Space Com.; worker, contbr. numerous environ. and consumer orgns.; awards evaluator Ford Found./Harvard U. Recipient certs. of appreciation for leadership Prince George's County (Md.) Pub. Sch. System, 1986, Nat. Found. Cancer Rsch., 1990, U.S. Dept. Commerce Gold medal, 1998, 2000, Silver medal for leadership/excellence, 2000, 2001; Robert Seamans tech. fellow, Lucius Littauer fellow John F. Kennedy Sch. Govt., Harvard U., 1991-92. Mem. Am. Econ. Assn. (pub. utilities group), Ea. Econ. Assn., So. Econ. Assn., Soc. Govt. Economists, Indsl. Orgn. Soc., DAV Comdrs. Club, Phi Eta Sigma, Omicron Delta Epsilon, Beta Gamma Sigma, Phi Kappa Phi. Avocations: hiking, reading. Home: 8380 Sweet Cherry Ln Laurel MD 20723-1062 Office Phone: 202-482-1880.

MCCONNEL, W. BRUCE, lawyer; b. Pitts., 1943; AB cum laude, Princeton Univ., 1965; JD, Univ. Pa., 1970. Bar: Pa. 1971. Atty., gen. counsel's office to legal asst. to Commr. Richard Smith SEC, 1970—73; assoc. Drinker Biddle & Reath LLP, Phila., 1973—77, ptnr., 1977—2002, mng. ptnr., 2002—, chmn., investment mgmt. group and mem., mgmt. com. Office: Drinker Biddle & Reath LLP One Logan Sq 18th & Cherry Sts Philadelphia PA 19103-6996 Office Phone: 215-988-2817. Office Fax: 215-988-2757. Business E-Mail: bruce.mcconnel@dbr.com.

MCCONNELL, ALBERT LYNN, director; b. Springfield, Ohio, Oct. 20, 1946; s. Jack Pershing and Betty Ann (Venema) McConnell; m. Rannette Oledge, Dec. 21, 2001; 1 child, Ciara Lynn 1 stepchild, Joshua Hooper. BA, Ctrl. State U., 1969; MA, Webster U., 1983; MS, USACGSC, 1984. Commd. 2d. lt. U.S. Army, 1969, advanced through grades. to maj., 1980; ret., 1989; served as inf. bn. intelligence officer Schofield Barracks, Hawaii, 1970-71; inf. co. comdr., asst. ops. officer, inf. bn., 1971; intelligence analyst and briefer U.S. Mil. Assistance Command, Schofield Barracks, 1972-73; instr. U.S. Army Intelligence Sch., Ft Huachuca, Ariz., 1973-77; served in 3rd Armored Divsn., Frankfurt, Germany, 1980-81; project officer Combined Arms Ctr., Ft. Leavenworth, Kans., 1981-83, comdr. spl. security detachment, 1981-83; dir. intelligence, asst. chief staff for intelligence U.S. Army South, Ft. Clayton, Panama, 1984-85, mng. exec. officer Ft. Davis, Panama, 1985-86; tactical intelligence officer, chief adminstrv. svcs. U.S. Army Air Def. Arty. Sch., Ft. Bliss, Tex., 1986-87, dep. directorate chief, 1987-88, sr. intelligence officer, dept. divsn. chief, 1988-89; ops. analyst RAM Inc., Sierra Vista, Ariz., 1989-92; prof. bus. adminstrn. and mgmt. So. Ohio Coll., Columbus, 1992, Bliss Coll., Columbus, 1993; store mgr. Circle K Corp., Yuma, Ariz., 1993-94; tchr. Glendale (Ariz.) Union HS, 1994-95; mgr. Dexter Book Store, 1995-96; dean students Ariz. Inst. Bus. and Tech., Phoenix, 1996-98, 2002—04, campus dir. Mesa, Ariz., 1998-2000, prof. Phoenix, 2002—03; dir. edn. High Tech Inst., Phoenix, 2000—02; dean students Internat. Inst. Ams., Phoenix, 2003—05, campus dir., 2005—. Met. Coll., Phoenix, 2005. Adj. prof. Chapman U., Sierra Vista, 1990—92; tax preparer H&R Block, Sierra Vista, 1990—92; br. mgr. Jackson Hewitt Tax Svc. Met. Ctr., Phoenix, 2002—. Voter registration ofcl. Maricopa County, Ariz., 2001—02; treas. Antioch Missionary Bapt. Ch., Huachuca City, Ariz., 1991—92. Decorated Bronze Star. Mem.: Assn. Old Crows, Ret. Officers Assn., Assn. U.S. Army, Air Force Assn., Scabbard and Blade, Iota Beta Sigma, Phi Alpha Theta. Republican. Baptist. Avocations: photography, reading, coaching youth football and baseball. Office: IIA 6049 N 43rd Ave Phoenix AZ 85019-1600 Office Phone: 602-242-6265 210. Personal E-mail: azlynnmac@hotmail.com. Business E-Mail: lmcconnell@iia.edu.

MCCONNELL, BRIGHT, III, orthopaedic surgeon; b. Augusta, Ga., Mar. 3, 1953; s. Bright McConnell, Jr. and Elizabeth Custer McConnell; m. Pam Hollings, Oct. 14, 1978; children: Elizabeth Anne, Bright McConnell, IV, Ian Deryck. BS, Davidson Coll., NC, 1971—75; MD, Med. Coll. Ga., Augusta, 1975—79. Lic. orthopaedic surgeon Am. Bd. Orthopaedic Surgery, 1987, cert. clin. densitometrist Internat. Soc. Clin. Densitometry, 2001. Residency in orthopaedic surgery U. Fla., 1984; fellowship in sports medicine Kerlan-Jobe Orthopaedic Clinic & Nat. Athletic Health Inst., 1985; orthopaedic surgeon, ptnr. Orthopaedic Specialists of Charleston, SC, 1985—2002; CEO Prevecare, Charleston, 2002—05; pvt. practice Daniel Island, SC, 2005—. Mem. Internat. Ctr. Birds of Prey, Awendaw, SC, 2000—. Named to Best Doctors in Am., 2006. Fellow: Am. Acad. Orthopaedic Surgery; mem.: Charleston County Med. Soc., Am. Orthopaedic Soc. Sports Medicine, Aircraft Owners & Pilots Assn. Avocations: aerobatics, fishing, flying. Home: 8863 Hwy 17N Mc Clellanville SC 29458 Office: 900 Island Park Dr Ste 105 Charleston SC 29492 Home Phone: 843-887-4055. Office Fax: 843-284-5201. Personal E-mail: makaira1@aol.com. Business E-Mail: drbrightmcconnell@yahoo.com.

MCCONNELL, CHARLES PRESCOTT, retired science educator; b. Wayne, Nebr., Mar. 3, 1942; s. Charlie Irving and Truma McConnell; m. Cathie Dianne Harris, Aug. 22, 1964; children: Stefanie Michele, John Edward. BS, U. Nebr., 1964, MS, 1967. Tchr. Fresno Unified Sch. Dist., Calif., 1967—2001. Active Boy Scouts Am. Recipient Silver Beaver award. Mem. NEA (life), Calif. Tchr. Assn., Fresno Tchr. Assn. (life), Calif. Retired Tchr. Assn., Quarter Century Wireless Assn. (life), Am. Radio Relay League (life, sect. mgr. 1976-89, 2002-, vice dir. Pacific div. 1988-90, dir. 1990-93), Sigma Xi (assoc.). Republican. Lutheran. Avocation: amateur radio. Home: 1658 W Mesa Ave Fresno CA 93711-1944 E-mail: w6dpd@arrl.org.

MCCONNELL, DAVID KELSO, lawyer; b. NYC, July 12, 1932; s. David and Caroline Hanna (Kelso) McC.; m. Alice Schmitt, Dec. 26, 1953; children: Elissa Anne McConnell Henebry, Kathleen Anne, David Willet. BCE, CCNY, 1954; LLB, Yale U., 1962. Bar: Conn. 1962, U.S. Dist. Ct. Conn. 1963, U.S. Ct. Appeals (2d cir.) 1964, U.S. Ct. Appeals (3d cir.) 1966, U.S. Sup. Ct. 1970, U.S. Dist. Ct. (ea. dist.) Pa. 1971, Pa. 1975, N.Y. 1986. Asst. counsel N.Y.N.H. & H. R.R., New Haven, 1962-65, counsel, 1966-68; asst. atty. gen. U.S. V.I., 1965-66; asst. gen. atty. Pa. Cen. Transp. Co., New Haven, 1969-70, asst. gen. counsel Phila., 1970-71, sr. reorganization atty., 1971, adminstrv. officer, spl. counsel to trustees, 1971-76, gen. atty., 1977-78; asst. to chmn., CEO The Penn Cen. Corp., NYC, 1979-80, corp. sec., 1980-82; v.p., gen. counsel Gen. Cable Co., Greenwich, Conn., 1982-85; pvt. practice Stamford, Conn., 1985-86, Pelham, N.Y., 1989-91, Greenwich, Conn., 1991-98. Of counsel McCarthy, Fingar, Donovan, Drazen & Smith, White Plains, N.Y., 1986-89. Dep. supr., councilman Town of Pelham, NY, 1986—90, budget officer; dep. mayor, trustee Village of Pelham, 1992—95, village atty., 1995—96; clk. of session, elder, trustee, deacon Huguenot Meml. Ch., Pelham; pres., bd. dirs. Newport Rotary Charities Fund, 2005—. With USN, 1954—59, with USNR, 1959—79. Mem.: Mil. Officers Assn., Navy League, Yale Law Sch. Assn. (exec. com. 1988—91, dir. New Eng. 2001—), Assn. Bar City NY, NY Bar Assn., Conn. Bar Assn., Quindecim, The Corinthians (mem. afterguard, dir. The Corinthians Assn., fleet capt. New Eng. fleet, trustee, pres., treas., sec. The Corinthians Endowment Fund), St. Andrews Soc. NY (bd. mgrs. 1986—89, chmn. bd. mgrs. 1988—89, bd. mgrs. 1996—99), Little Ship Club, Newport Sail and Power Squadron, Rotary Club of Newport RI (dir. 2001—06), Rotary Club of The Pelhams NY (pres. 1993—94). Home: 68 1/2 Roseneath Ave Newport RI 02840-3849 Business E-Mail: david.mcconnell.law.62@aya.yale.edu.

MCCONNELL, E. HOY, II, advertising and public policy executive; b. Syracuse, NY, May 14, 1941; s. E. Hoy and Dorothy R. (Schmitt) McC.; m. Patricia Irwin, June 26, 1965; children: E. Hoy, III, Courtney. BA in Am. Studies magna cum laude with high honors, Yale U., 1963; MBA in Mktg, Harvard Bus. Sch., 1965. With Foote, Cone & Belding, Chgo., 1965-76, v.p. account supr., 1971—76; with D'Arcy-MacManus & Masius, Chgo., 1976-85, sr. v.p., dir. client services, then vice chmn., 1978-80, pres., 1980-84, chmn., 1984-85; mng. dir. D'Arcy Masius Benton & Bowles, Chgo., 1986-96, also bd. dirs.; sr. v.p., account dir. Leo Burnett Co., Chgo., 1996-98; exec. dir. Bus. and Profl. People for the Pub. Interest, 1999—. Bd. dirs. Evanston (Ill.) United Way, 1980-83, Evanston Youth Hockey Assn., 1980-89, pres. 1981-83; bd. dirs. Off-the-Street Club, 1980-90, Bus. Profl. People for Pub. Interest, 1981-, v.p. 1984-89, pres. 1990-95; co-chair Housing Ill., 2002-; bd. dirs. Harvard Bus. Sch. Club, 1990-92; bd. dirs. The Cradle Soc., 2000-07, mem. exec com., 2004-07, sec, 2004-05, treas., 2005-07; mem. Chgo. Coun. on Fgn. Rels., 1989-95, Wayfarers Club, 2001-. Mem. Am. Assn. Advt. Agys. (gov.-at-large Chgo. coun. 1984, sec. 1986, vice chmn. 1987, chmn. 1988-89), Glen View Country Club (bd. dirs. 1992-96), Dairymen's Country Club, Yale Club Chgo. (bd. dirs. 1996-99). Democrat. Unitarian Universalist. Home: 2703 Colfax St Evanston IL 60201-2035 Office: BPI 25 E Washington St Ste 1515 Chicago IL 60602-1804 Office Phone: 312-759-8259. Business E-Mail: hmcconnell@bpichicago.org.

MCCONNELL, EDWARD BOSWORTH, legal association administrator, lawyer; b. Greenwich, Conn., Apr. 3, 1920; s. Raymond Arnott and Anna Bell (Lee) McC.; m. Jeanne M. Rotton (dec. 1984); children: Annalee, Marilyn, Edward (dec. 1994), Barbara, William; m. Florence M. Leonard, (dec. 1991); stepchildren: Susan L. Little, William R. Leonard, Molly M. Leonard. AB, U. Nebr., 1941, LLB, 1947; MBA with distinction, Harvard U., 1943. Bar: Nebr. 1947, NJ 1950. Mem. faculty Rutgers U. Sch. Bus. Adminstrn., Newark, 1947-53; assoc. firm Toner, Speakman and Crowley, Newark, 1949-50; adminstrv. asst. and law sec. to Chief Justice of NJ, 1950-53; adminstrv. dir. Cts. of NJ, Trenton, 1953-73; also standing master Supreme Ct., 1953-73; pres. Nat. Center for State Cts., Williamsburg, 1973-90, bd. dirs., 1980-90, pres. emeritus, 1990—, cons. on ct. mgmt., 1990—. Mem. US Dept. Justice Coun. on Role of Cts. in Am. Soc., 1978-83; mem. adv. com. Dispute Resolution Policy Study, Social Sci. Rsch. Inst., U. So. Calif., 1975-79, Civil Litigation Rsch. Project, U. Wis. and U. So. Calif., 1979-83, nat. judge edn. program to promote equality for men and women in the cts., 1980—; mem. Nat. Inst. Criminal Justice Task Force, Urban Consortium, 1979-83; participant Access To Justice Colloquium, European Univ. Inst., Florence, Italy, 1979; nat. adv. coun. Ctr. Adminstrn. Justice, Wayne State U., 1973-77; nat. project com. State Jud. Info. Sys. Project SEARCH Group, 1973-76; lectr. Inst. of Local and State Govt. Wharton Sch. U. Pa., 1955-65, Appellate Judges Seminar, Inst. Jud. Adminstrn., NYU, 1962-75; vis. expert UN Asia and Far East Inst., Tokyo, 1971; mem. Cts. Task Force Nat. Adv. Commn. Criminal Justice Standards and Goals, 1971-73; nat. adv. com. DC Ct. Mgmt. Project, 1966-70; trustee Inst. Ct. Mgmt., 1969-73, 84-86; chmn. Nat. Conf. Ct. Adminstrv. Officers, 1956; mem. nat. task force on gender bias in cts. Nat. Assn. Women Judge's 1985-90; mem. adv. bd. Nat. Ctr. for Citizen Participation in Adminstrn. of Justice, 1984-90; mem. Nat. Commn. Trial Ct. Performance Standards, 1991-95. Mem. adv. com. on article III Commn. on the Bicentennial of the Constitution, 1989-91; adv. com. Judicary Leadership Coun., 1990-95. Maj. C.E., AUS, 1943-46, European Theater, 1944-46. Decorated Bronze Star medal; recipient Warren E. Burger award for greatest contbn. to improvement of ct. adminstrn. Inst. for Ct. Mgmt., 1975, Herbert Lincoln Harley award for efficient adminstrn. justice Am. Judicature Soc., 1973, Glenn R. Winters award for outstanding service in jud. adminstrn. Am. Judges Assn., 1974, Tom C. Clark award for outstanding contbns. to field of ct. adminstrn. Nat. Conf. Met. Cts., 1983, Award of Merit Nat. Assn. Ct. Mgmt., 1987, Spl. award, Nat. Assn. Women Judges, 1989, Paul C. Reardon award for disting. svc. Nat. Ctr. for State Cts., 1991, Alumni Achievement award U. Nebr., 1991, Robert B. Yegge award ABA Jud. Divsn. Lawyers Conf., 1997. Fellow Nat. Acad. Pub. Adminstrn. (mem. panel on evaluation budget decentralization project of fed. cts. 1989-91, chmn. panel long range planning in fed. cts. 1991-92, mem. panel for study of fed. trial ct. adminstrv. structure 1995-96); mem. ABA (fellow-at-large, coun. mem. 1960-66, 71-80, house of dels., 1977-80, chmn. com. on oversight and goals 1975-76, chmn. com. on jud. compensation jud. adminstrn. div. 1984-89, chmn. jud. adminstrn. div. 1976-77, sect. of litigation task force on excess litigiousness in Am. 1986-88, task force on reduction of litigation cost and delay, jud. adminstrn. dir. 1984-94, chmn. 1991-94, mem. long range planning com. 1989-94), N.J. Bar Assn., Nebr. Bar Assn., Fellows of Am. Bar Found. (life), Warren E. Burger Soc., Kingsmill (Va.) Golf Club, Kingsmill Tennis Club (pres. 2001), Kingsmill Yacht Club, Order of Coif (hon.), Delta Upsilon, Sigma Delta Phi, Phi Delta Phi. Office Phone: 757-220-3012. Personal E-mail: ebm80@aol.com.

MCCONNELL, JACK BAYLOR, retired corporate executive, physician; b. Crumpler, W.Va., Feb. 1, 1925; s. Enoch L. and Mattie (Davidson) McC.; m. Mary Ellen Rhodes, Nov. 29, 1958; children: Steven Rhodes, Katherine Marie, Page Samuel. Student, U. Va., 1943-45, U. Miss., 1945-47; MD, U. Tenn., 1949; postgrad., Columbia U., 1963, Harvard U., 1972; DSc (hon.), Emory & Henry Coll., 1982; HHD (hon.), Presbyn. Coll. of SC, 1998. Dir. clin. investigation Lederle Labs., Pearl River, NY, 1953-61; v.p. comml. devel. McNeil Labs., Ft. Washington, Pa., 1961-68; corp. dir. advanced tech. Johnson & Johnson, New Brunseick, NJ, 1968—89. Trustee Morristown (N.J.) Meml. Hosp., 1977-87; bd. dirs. African Med. and Rsch. Found., NYC. Author: The Story of the Volunteers in Medicine Clinic, 1998. Mem. Bd. Health, Basking Ridge, N.J., 1972-74; cons. U.S. Senate, Washington, 1987—. With USN, 1943-46; founder, chmn. emeritus, Vols. in Medicine Clinic, Hilton Head, SC., 1994-, Vols. in Medicine Inst. Recipient Disting. Scientist award Tenn. Tech. Found., 1985, Disting. Svc. to State Govt. award Nat. Govs.' Assn., 1993, Outstanding Svc. award Hilton Head Chpt. NAACP, 1993, award of Achievement, Gleitsman Found., 1994, Cmty. Svc. award SC Hosp. Assn., 1994, Citizen of Yr. award Presbyn. Men's Club of Hilton Head, 1995, Nat. Assn. Cmty. Health Ctrs. award, 1997, Disting. Svc. Award, SC Rural Health, 1999, Humanitarian award Watson Clinic Found., Lakeland, Fla., 2000, Pride in Profession award AMA Found., 2004; named Humanitarian of Yr., Kidney Found. of NJ, 1988, Disting. Alumnus of Yr., U. Tenn. Coll. Medicine, 1990, Physician of Yr., Nat. Assn. Hospice and Home Care, 1995; named one of 200 Disting. Grads., U. Tenn., 1994; named to Order of the Palmetto, State of SC, 1999. Mem. AMA. Avocations: sports, jazz, travel, bridge.

MCCONNELL, JOHN, environmental activist, founder of Earth Day; b. Davis City, Iowa, Mar. 22, 1915; V.p. Nobell Rsch. Found., Calif., 1939; publisher Toe Valley View, NC, 1956, Mountain View, Calif., 1959; dir. No. Calif. Meals for Millions, 1962; founder Minute for Peace, 1963, World Equality Inc., 1968; proposed & organized Earth Day, 1969; founder Earth Soc., 1973. Author: Earth Charter, 1979, 77 Theses on the Care of Earth, 1985, Earth Magna Carta, 1995. Mailing: 4924 E Kentucky Cir Denver CO 80246 E-mail: trusteeone@aol.com.

MCCONNELL, JOHN DOWLING, urologist, educator; b. Independence, Kans., Oct. 16, 1953; m. Melinda Bohr, 1975; 1 child, Cara. BA with honors in Biochemistry, U. Kans., 1975; MD magna cum laude, Loyola U., 1978. Diplomate Am. Bd. Urology. Intern in surgery Parkland Meml. Hosp., Dallas, 1978-79, resident in surgery, 1979-80; resident in urology U. Tex. Southwestern Med. Sch. Affiliated Hosps., Dallas, 1980-84; asst. prof. divsn. urology U. Tex. Southwestern Med. Ctr., Dallas, 1984-91, assoc. prof. divsn. urology, 1991-94, dir. Prostate Disease Ctr., 1992—, prof., chmn. dept. urology, 1994—, S.T. Harris family chair in med. sci., exec. v.p. for health sys. affairs. Staff physician Parkland Meml. Hosp., Zale Lipshy U. Hosp., VA Med. Ctr., St. Paul, Children's Med. Ctr., 1984—; chief urology svc. VA Med. Ctr., Dallas, 1986-91; U. Tex. Southwestern Urology Clinic, Aston, 1993—; mem. coms., study sects. NIH, 1990—; mem. numerous hosp. coms.; cons., lectr in field. Author: (with others) Harrison's Principles of Internal Medicine, 13th edit., 1998, Infertility in the Male, 3d edit., 1996, Principles of Surgery, 7th edit., 1998; editor: Technical Report: Guidelines for the Diagnosis and Treatment of BPH, 1994, Clinical Guidelines for the Diagnosis and Treatment of BPH, 1994; asst. editor The Jour. of Urology, 1988-92, reviewer, 1986—; World Jour. of Urology, 1990—, Urology, 1992—; The Prostate, 1988—, Jour. Andrology, 1989—; contbr. articles to profl. jours. Recipient Edwin Beer award NY Acad. of Medicine, 1989-91; instl. grantee U. Tex. Southwestern Med. Ctr., 1985-86, Merit Rev. grantee VA, 1989-92, Clin. Investigation grantee Am. Cancer Soc., 1991-93, grantee Agy. Health Care Policy and Rsch., 1990-92, 92—, NIH, 1992—, 93—, Merck Rsch. Labs., 1987-91, 88—, Merck Sharp & Dohme Rsch. Labs., 1990-92, 90—, 92—, others. Fellow ACS, AAAS, Am. Urological Assn. (Gold Cystoscope award 1991), Am. Soc. Andrology, Am. Soc. Cell Biology, Am. Diabetes Assn., Am. Fertility Soc., Am. Fedn. Clin. Rsch., Tex. Med. Assn., Soc. for the Study of Reproduction, Soc. Univ. Urologists, Soc. Basic Urology Rsch., Urologic Rsch. Soc., Nat. Urologic Forum, Urol. Investigator's Forum, Inst. Medicine, Phi Beta Kappa, Alpha Omega Alpha. Home: 4326 Enfield Dr Dallas TX 75220-3810 Office: U Tex Southwestern Med Ctr Dept Urology 5323 Harry Hines Blvd Dallas TX 75390-9131 Office Phone: 214-648-2800.

MCCONNELL, JOHN EDWARD, retired electrical engineering company executive; b. Minot, ND, July 28, 1931; s. Lloyd Waldorf and Sarah McConnell; m. Carol Claire Myers, July 4, 1952 (dec. Feb. 1989); children: Kathleen Anne, James, Amy Lynn; m. Heidi Banziger, Sept. 29, 1990. BSME, U. Pitts., 1952; MS, Drexel Inst. Tech., 1958. Registered profl. engr., Pa. With mktg. and design depts. for turbomachinery Westinghouse Electric Corp., Lester, Pa., 1954-60, 63-67, Pitts., 1960-63; mgr. power generation equipment activities in U.S. ASEA, Inc., White Plains, NY, 1967-79, regional mgr. power equipment activities Middle Atlantic and Southeastern U.S. regions, 1967-79, mgr. turbine generator dept., 1979-83, mgr. internat. ops. Power Sys. divsn., 1983-84, mgr. transmission substas. dept., 1984-85; mgr. Ea. U.S. ops. ASEA Power Sys., Inc., 1985-86, mgr. ea. ops. measurement divsn. GEC, 1986-91; mgr. ea. region Protection and Control divsn. GEC Alsthom T&D Inc., 1991-98; prin. JEMTECH, 1998—2005; v.p. ATG Exodus, 2000—02. Adviser U.S. Congress 1968-74; spkr. in field Contbr. articles on energy and electric power to profl. jours. 1st lt. C.E., U.S. Army, 1952-54. Mem. IEEE (life, sr., energy com., past chmn. subcom. energy conservation and cogeneration, hon. mem. power sys. relay com.), IEEE Power Engring. Soc. (sr., past chmn. chpts. pub. affairs subcom.). Republican. Achievements include development of analytical techniques for power systems performance characteristics and economics of cogeneration sys. Home: 173 Remington Rd Ridgefield CT 06877-4324 Office: JEMTECH PO Box 229 Ridgefield CT 06877-0229 Personal E-mail: j.e.mcconnell@ieee.org. *1) If it doesn't produce revenue, is it worthwhile? 2) Problem solving begins with careful listening. 3) Keep people informed. If they don't know, they'll assume the worst. 4) The truth is the most credible explanation you'll find.*

MCCONNELL, JOHN HOWARD, personnel management consultant, writer; b. Highland Park, Mich., June 18, 1933; s. Melvin William and Dorothy Marie (Miller) McC.; m. Dolores Ann Cooper, Oct. 29, 1955; children: Keith Ernest, Brian Howard, Eric William. BS, Wayne State U., 1957, MEd, 1963. Tchr. Detroit Bd. Edn., 1957-59, Highland Park Bd. Edn., 1959-60; personnel mgr. Wolverine Tube Co., Allen Park, Mich., 1960-69; personnel dir. Garan, Inc., NYC, 1970-71; cons. Morristown, N.J., 1971-74; cons. human resource mgmt., pres. McConnell, Simmons & Co., Inc., Morristown, 1974—. Bd. dirs. Circus Royale, Inc., Morristown. Author: How To Audit, 8 vols., 1974-85, Introduction to Human Resources, 1982, A Ring, A Horse and A Clown, 1994, Shrine Circus, 1998, Hunting Heads, 1999, Auditing the Human Resources Department, 2000, How to Identify Training Needs, 2002, How to Design, Implement and Interpret an Employee Survey, 2003, How to Develop Essential HR Policies and Procedures, 2004; prodr. Player's Theater in Concert, 1989, 90, London Follies, 1994, 96; contbr. articles to various publs. Pres. Morristown Civic Assn., 1980. Mem. APA, ASTD, Soc. Human Resource Mgmt., Am. Mgmt. Assn., Acad. Magical Arts, Magic Castle Club (LA), Circus Hist. Soc. (bd. dirs.), Masons. Democrat. Methodist. Avocation: producing entertainment events. Home: 1 Skyline Dr Morristown NJ 07960-5146 Office: 73 E Hanover Ave Morristown NJ 07960-3161 Office Phone: 201-859-5514. Business E-Mail: john@mcconnell-simmons.com.

MCCONNELL, JOHN P., metal products executive; With Worthington Industries, Columbus, Ohio, 1975—, v.p., gen. mgr., 1985, dir., 1990—, vice chmn., 1992—96, CEO, 1993—, chmn., 1996—. Bd. dir. Alltel Corp., The Wilds. Office: Worthington Industries 200 Old Wilson Bridge Rd Columbus OH 43085 *

MCCONNELL, JOHN THOMAS, publishing executive; b. Peoria, Ill., May 1, 1945; s. Golden A. and Margaret (Lyon) McC.; 1 child, Justin. BA, U. Ariz., 1967. Mgr. Fast Printing Co., Peoria, 1970-71; mgmt. trainee Quad-Cities Times, Davenport, Iowa, 1972-73; asst. gen. mgr., then v.p., gen. mgr. Peoria Jour. Star, 1973-81, pub., 1981—, pres., 1987—; v.p. The Copley Press, Inc., Peoria, 1997—. Bd. dirs. Peoria Downtown Devel. Council, Peoria Devel. Corp.; past trustee Methodist Hosp., Peoria. Served with USAR, 1967-69. Named Young Man of Year Peoria Jaycees, 1979 Mem. Peoria Advt. and Selling Club, Peoria C. of C. Clubs: Peoria Country, Mt. Hawley C.C. Congregationalist. Office: Peoria Jour Star Inc 1 News Plz Peoria IL 61643-0001 Business E-Mail: mac@pjstar.com.

MCCONNELL, JOHN WILLIAM, JR., lawyer; b. Bessemer, Ala., Apr. 17, 1921; s. John W. and Elizabeth (Sheridan) McC.; m. Margaret B. Snider, Jan. 7, 1944; children— Margaret E. (Mrs. John Evans), Rebecca L. (Mrs. A.D. Braden), Catherine L., John W. III. AB, U. Ala., 1942, MA, 1946; LL.B., Yale, 1948. Bar: Ala. 1948, D.C. 1977. Atty. Inge, Twitty, Armbrecht & Jackson, Mobile, Ala., 1948-56, Armbrecht, Jackson, McConnell & DeMouy, 1956-65; dir. U.S. Peace Corps, Nigeria, 1965-68; v.p. legal Sea-Land Service, Inc., Menlo Park, NJ, 1968-76; also dir., of counsel Haight, Gardner, Poor & Havens, Washington, 1977-94. Atty. for Reynolds v. Sims on legislative reapportionment, U.S. Supreme Ct., 1963-64 Mem. Ala. Dem. Exec. Com., 1963-65. Served to capt. AUS, 1943-46, 50-52, maj. ret., 1957. Mem. ABA, Ala. Bar Assn., D.C. Bar Assn., Maritime Law Assn.

MCCONNELL, LORELEI CATHERINE, retired library director; b. Port Jefferson, NY, Dec. 5, 1938; d. Alvin and Mary (McConnell) Philibert; m. Thomas McConnell, Jan. 20, 1962; children: Catherine, Michael. BA, Drew U., 1960; MLS, Rutgers U., 1963. Reference libr. Irvington (N.J.) Pub. Libr., 1963-90, dir., 1990-99; founder Irvington Literacy Program, 1986, dir., 1986-90; ret., 1999; cons., 2000—. Mem. exec. bd. Infolink, 1998-99. Mem. ALA, N.J. Libr. Assn. (mem. exec. bd. 1990-93, N.J. Libr.

of Yr. 1993-94), Irvington (N.J.) C. of C. (exec. bd. 1992—, Civic award 1996), Beta Phi Mu. Home: 563 Park St Montclair NJ 07043-2027 *The world would be a better place if we could find ways to reward and honor every single person who works hard and does the right thing.*

MCCONNELL, MARY PATRICIA, lawyer; b. Mpls., Sept. 30, 1952; BS, U. Minn., 1978; JD, William Mitchell Coll. Law, St. Paul, 1984. Bar: Minn. 1988. Sr. biologist C.E., U.S. Army, St. Paul, 1979-84; asst. county atty. Dakota County, Hastings, Minn., 1985—92; ptnr. Lindquist & Vennum, Mpls., 1992—95; from v.p. environ. and regulatory affairs to sr. v.p., gen. counsel, sec. Genmar Holdings, Inc., 1995—2002; gen. counsel control products divsn. Honeywell, 2002—03; v.p., gen. counsel Polaris Industries, Inc., Medinia, Minn., 2003—. Master gardener U. Minn. Ext., St. Paul, 1992—. Contbr. articles to profl. jours. Dir. Wetlands Forum, Mpls., 1990—. Mem. Minn. Bar Assn. (governing coun. environ. and natural resources 1990—, law sect.), Mpls. C. of C. (Leadership Mpls. 1992). Office: Polaris Industries Inc 2100 Highway 55 Medina MN 55340 Office Phone: 763-542-0500. Office Fax: 763-542-0599. E-mail: mary.mcconnell@polarisind.com.

MCCONNELL, MATTHEW STEPHEN, composer, educator; b. North Adams, Mass., Dec. 1, 1980; s. Stephen Earl and Patricia Ann McConnell. BA in Music, Bennington Coll., 2003; MusM in Composition, New England Conservatory, 2005. Organist St. Andrew's Episcopal Chapel, North Adams, Mass., 1996—2003; organist, choir dir. 1st Bapt. Ch., Cheshire, 1998—99; asst. instr. composition Bennington Coll., Vt., 2002; music copyist Ricky Ian Gordon, 2002—04; tchg. fellow New Eng. Conservatory Music, 2006. Pvt. tutor, Boston, 2003—; freelance organist, 2003—; co-founder, performer The Toyland Band, Boston, 2004—. Composer: Sonata for Solo Viola, 2003, Piano Trio No. 1, 2004, Concerto for Toy Piano & Chamber Orch., 2004. Benefit concert organist Salvation Army, North Adams, Mass., 1999, Berkshire Food Project, 2000, C.O.D.Y. Youth Project, 2001. Grantee, Wolley Fund Composition, 2003; scholar, Berkshire AGO, 1993—94, The Conducting Inst., 2001. Mem.: Am. Guild Organists. Episcopalian. Home: 39 Williams St North Adams MA 01247

MCCONNELL, MICHAEL, art educator; b. 1944; Prof. art U. NH, chmn. art dept. Office: Dept Art & Art History University N H 30 College Rd Durham NH 03824-3538 Office Fax: 603-862-2190. E-mail: michael.mcconnell@unh.edu.

MCCONNELL, MICHAEL ARTHUR, lawyer; b. Ft. Worth, Jan. 15, 1947; BA, Loyola U., New Orleans, 1969; JD, U. Tex., 1975. Bar: Tex. 1976, U.S. Dist. Ct. (no. dist.) Tex. 1976, U.S. Dist. Ct. (ea. dist.) Tex. 1981, U.S. Dist. Ct. (we. dist.) Tex. 1982, U.S. Dist. Ct. (so. dist.) Tex. 1989, U.S. Ct. Appeals (5th cir.) Tex. 1980, U.S. Ct. Appeals (10th cir.) 1987. Briefing atty. U.S. Dist. Ct. Hon. Eldon B. Mahon, Ft. Worth, 1976-77; assoc. atty. Cantey, Hanger, Gooch, Munn and Collins, Ft. Worth, 1977-81, ptnr., 1981-83; judge no. dist. U.S. Bankruptcy Ct., Ft. Worth, 1983-86; ptnr. Jackson Walker LLP, Ft. Worth, 1988—95, McConnell & Assocs., Ft. Worth, 1995—2000, Winstead Sechrest & Miniak P.C., Ft. Worth, 2000—06, Kelly Hart & Hallman LLP, Ft. Worth, 2006—. Trustee Am. Inns of Ct. Nat. Found. Sgt. USAF, 1969—73. Fellow: Am. Coll. Bankruptcy; mem.: Am. Law Inst. Office: Kelly Hart & Hallman LLP 201 Main St Ste 2500 Fort Worth TX 76102 Office Phone: 817-332-2500. Business E-Mail: michael.mcconnell@khh.com.

MCCONNELL, MICHAEL THEODORE, lawyer; b. San Francisco, June 18, 1954; s. Lawrence V. and Ann McConnell. BS, U. Oreg., 1977; JD, U. Denver, 1980. Bar: Colo., Wyo., U.S. Dist. Ct. Colo., U.S. Ct. Appeals (10th cir.), U.S. Supreme Ct., U.S. Dist. Ct. Wyo. Ptnr. Long & Jaudon, Denver, 1980—2001; founding mem., CEO McConnell Siderius Fleischner Houghtaling & Craigmile, LLC, Denver, 2002—. Fellow Am. Coll. Trial Lawyers; mem. ABA, Colo. Bar Assn., Denver Bar Assn., Colo. Def. Lawyers Assn. Office: McConnell Siderius Fleischner Houghtaling & Craigmile, PC 4700 S Syracuse St, Ste 200 Denver CO 80237 Office Phone: 303-480-0400. Office Fax: 303-458-9520. Business E-Mail: mmcconnell@msfhc.com.

MCCONNELL, MICHAEL W., federal judge, law educator; b. Louisville, Ky., May 18, 1955; m. Mary Cargill Norton McConnell; 3 children. BA, Mich. State U., 1976; JD, U. Chgo., 1979. Bar: DC 1981. Law clk. to Hon. J. Skelly Wright US Ct. Appeals (DC cir.), 1979-80; law clk. to Hon. William J. Brennan Jr. US Supreme Ct., Washington, 1980-81; asst. gen. counsel US Office of Mgmt. and Budget, Washington, 1981-83; asst. to the solicitor gen. US Dept. Justice, Washington, 1983-85; asst. prof. U. Chgo., 1984-89, prof., 1989—92, William Graham prof. law, 1992—96; Presdl. prof. U. Utah Coll. Law, 1997—2002; vis. prof. Harvard Law School, 1999; special consultant Mayer, Brown & Platt, 1989—2002; judge US Ct. Appeals (10th cir.), 2002—. Mem. Am. Acad. Arts and Scis., Order of Coif, Phi Beta Kappa, Phi Kappa Phi. Office: 10th Circuit Ct Appeals 125 S State St # 6404 Salt Lake City UT 84138 *

MCCONNELL, MIKE (JOHN MICHAEL MCCONNELL), Director of National Intelligence, retired military officer; b. Greenville, SC, July 26, 1943; s. Harold Eddie and Dorothy Beatrice (Cassell) Mc.; children from previous marriage: Susan Erin McConnell, Jennifer Michelle McConnell; m. Mary Theresa Wagner, Jan. 29, 1988; children: Mark Richard Sentner, Christine Marie Sentner; 2 stepchildren BA in Econs., Furman U., 1966; MPA in Govt./Pub. Adminstrn., George Washington U., 1986; grad., Nat. Def. U., 1986; PhD in Strategic Intelligence (hon.), Def. Intelligence Coll., 1992. Advanced through ranks to vice admiral USN, 1992, ret., 1996; asst. engr., damage control officer USS Colleton, Mekong Delta, Vietnam, 1967-68; counterintelligence analyst Naval Investigative Svc., Yokosuka, Japan, 1968-70; analyst and supr. CNO Undersea Warfare Intelligence Watch, Washington, 1971-74; force intelligence officer Commdr. Middle East Force Persian Gulf, Indian Ocean, 1974-76; ops. officer Fleet Ocean Surveillance Info. Facility, Rota, Spain, 1976-79; intelligence analyst CNO Intelligence Staff, Washington, 1979-81; intelligence officer Commdr. in Chief Pacific Fleet, Honolulu, 1981-83; fleet intelligence officer Commdr. Seventh Fleet Western Pacific, 1983-85; exec. asst. to dir. Office Naval Intelligence, Washington, 1985-86; chief naval forces divsn. Nat. Security Agy., Ft. Meade, Md., 1987-88; asst. chief staff/intelligence Commdr. in Chief Pacific Fleet, Honolulu, 1988-90; dir. intelligence, The Joint Staff The Pentagon, Washington, 1990-92; dir. Nat. Security Agy., Ft. Meade, Md., 1992—96; sr. v.p. Booz Allen Hamilton, McLean, Va., 1996—2006; dir. Office Nat. Intelligence, 2007—. Bd. dirs. CompuDyne Corp., 2004—07. Recipient Navy Unit Commendation Sec. Navy, 1968, Presdl. Unit Citation Combat Action ribbon CINCPACFLT, Navy Achievement medal Sec. Navy, 1974, Navy Commendation medalw/Combat V, 1968, Navy E ribbon Sec. of the Navy, 1984, Nat. Defense Svc. medal with 1 Bronze star, Vietnam Svc. medal with 2 Bronze Stars, Humanitarian Svc. medal, Sea Svc. Deployment ribbon, Navy & Marine Corps Overseas Svc. ribbon, Rep. Vietnam Meritorious Unit Citation Civil Actions Color, Campaign medal Rep. Vietnam, Meritorious Svc. medal with 2 Gold Stars Sec. Navy, 1981, 85, Legion of Merit with 2 Gold Stars, 1985, 87, 90, Defense Superior Svc. medal, 1988, Defense Dist. Svc. medal, 1992. Avocations: world affairs, foreign policy, reading. Office: Office Nat Intelligence NEOB 725 17th St Washington DC 20500 *

MCCONNELL, (ADDISON) MITCHELL, JR., senator, lawyer; b. Tuscumbia, Ala., Feb. 20, 1942; s. Addison Mitchell and Julia (Shockley) McC.; m. Elaine Chao, Feb. 6, 1993; children: Eleanor Hayes, Claire Redmon, Marion Porter. BA with honors, U. Louisville, 1964; JD, U. Ky., 1967. Bar: Ky. 1967. Chief legis. asst. to Senator Marlow Cook, Washington, 1968-70; pvt. law practice Louisville, 1970-74; dep. asst. atty. gen. US Dept. Justice, Washington, 1974-75; judge Jefferson County, Louisville, 1978-85; US Senator from Ky., 1985—; majority whip, 2002—07; minority leader, 2007—. Com. agr., nutrition, and forestry US Senate, com. appropriations, com. rules and adminstrn. Chmn. Jefferson County Republican Com., 1973-74; co-chmn. Nat. Child Tragedies Coalition, 1981; chmn., founder Ky. Task Force on Exploited and Missing Children, 1982; mem. Pres.'s Partnership on Child Safety. Recipient commendation Nat. Trust on Hist. Preservation in U.S., 1982, Conservationist of Yr. award League Ky. Sportsmen, 1983, cert. of appreciation Am. Correctional Assn., 1985, Golden Plow award, Am. Farm Bur. Fedn., 1996, Freedom award Nat. Coun. Union Burma, 1999, Sam Rainsy Pary Freedom award, 2002, Ky. Warbler Migratory Songbird Conservation award US Fish and Wildlife Svc., Ky. Dept. Fish and Wildlife Resources, 2002, Defender of Freedom award James Madison Ctr. Freedom Speech, 2002, Disting. Svc. award Am. Farm Bur., 2002. Mem. Ky. Assn. County Judge Execs. (pres. 1982), Nat. Inst. Justice (adv. bd. 1982-84) Republican. Baptist. Avocations: fishing, cooking. Office: US Senate 361-A Russell Office Bldg Washington DC 20510-0001 also: Gene Snyder US Courthouse Rm 630 601 West Broadway Louisville KY 40202-2228 Office Phone: 202-224-2541, 502-582-6304. Office Fax: 202-224-2499, 502-582-5326. *

MCCONNELL, NICHOLAS STILLWELL, lawyer; b. Chgo., May 25, 1946; s. James Millholland and Emily (Robinson) McC.; m. Nancy Haines Fifield, Dec. 14, 1968; children: Abigail Haven, Rebecca Fifield. BA, Bowdoin Coll., 1968; JD, George Wash. U., 1972. Bar: Va. Supreme Ct. 1972, U.S. Supreme Ct. 1973, U.S. Ct. Appeals D.C. 1973, D.C. Ct. Appeals 1973, U.S. Dist. Ct. D.C. 1973, Md. Ct. Appeals 1978, US Ct. Claims, 1991, US Ct. Appeals (11th cir) 1996, US Dist. Ct., Md., 2001. Assoc. Jackson, Gray & Laskey, Washington, 1972-78; prin. Jackson & Campbell, P.C., Washington, 1978—. Mem. faculty Nat. Inst. Trial Advocacy, South Bend, Ind., 1984-95; dir. Sauls Lithograph Co., Inc., Washington, 1986—, Am. Hospice Found., 1997-2003. Pres., dir. Combined Health Appeal Nat. Capital Area, Washington, 1980-93; dir. Combined Health Appeal Am., Atlanta, 1993-94; pres. Albert L. and Elizabeth T. Tucker Found, 1996-; dir. Am. Hospice Found., 1997-2003. With U.S. Army, 1969-71. Recipient Young Lawyer of Yr. award Bar Assn. D.C., 1982. Fellow Am. Coll. Trial Lawyers; mem. Am. Health Lawyers Assn., D.C. Def. Lawyers, Def. Rsch. Inst., Barristers (pres. 1998), Counsellors, Bar Assn. D.C. (pres.-elect 2002-03, pres. 2003-04), Am. Bar Assn. (house of dels., 2003-2004)9+, Cosmos Club, Lawyers Club Congregationalist. Avocations: tennis, squash, golf, sailing. Home: 5004 Warren St NW Washington DC 20016-4370 Office: Jackson & Campbell PC 1 Lafayette Ctr 300 S Tower 1120 20th St NW Washington DC 20036-3437 Office Phone: 202-457-1628. E-mail: nmcconnell@jackscamp.com.

MCCONNELL, SUSAN K., neuroscientist; AB summa cum laude in Biology, Harvard and Radcliffe Colls., Mass., 1980; PhD in Neurobiology, Harvard U., Mass., 1987. Postdoctoral fellow dept. neurobiology Stanford U. Sch. Medicine, Calif., 1987—89, prof. neurology and neurol. scis., 2002—; asst. prof. biol. scis. Stanford U., 1989—95, assoc. prof., 1995—2000, prof., 2000—; Susan B. Ford prof. Stanford U. Sch. Humanities and Scis., 2003—. Mem. sci. adv. bd. Hereditary Disease Found., 1992—96, Cure Autism Now, 1997—2001, James S. McDonnell Found. Prog. in Brain Cancer Rsch., 2003—; mem. nat. adv. bd. Pew Scholars Prog. in Biomedical Scis., 1999—2005; mem. adv. com. Nat. Inst. Neurol. Disorders and Stroke Gene Expression Nervous Sys. Atlas, 2003—; mem. external adv. com. Rose F. Kennedy Ctr. Rsch. in Mental Retardation and Devel. Disabilities, Albert Einstein Coll. Medicine, 2004—; mem. external adv. bd. Alaskan Basic Neuroscience Prog. U. Alaska, Fairbanks, 2004—; mem. sci. adv. com. Studies to Advance Autism Rsch. and Treatment and Collaborative Progs. of Excellence in Autism Ctrs., 2004—. Contbr. articles to profl. jours.; ad hoc reviewer: Science, 1989—, mem. bd. reviewing editors:, 1996—2001, ad hoc reviewer: Neuron, 1989—, mem. editl. bd.:, 1995—, ad hoc reviewer: Cell, 1989—, Development, 1989—, mem. editl. adv. bd.:, 1999—2002, ad hoc reviewer: Devel. Biology, 1989—, European Jour. Neuroscience, 1989—, Jour. Neuroscience, 1989—, assoc. editor:, 1992—98, 2005—, mem. publs. com.: Soc. Neuroscience, 1993—96, mem. editl. bd.: Jour. Neurobiology, 1995—, Molecular and Cellular Biology, 1995—2002, reviewing editor: Molecular and Cellular Neuroscience, 2002—, mem. editl. com.: Ann. Rev. Cell and Devel. Biology, 1999—2004; co-editor: Fundamental Neuroscience, 2002. Named Pew Scholar, Biomedical Scis., 1989—94, McKnight Scholar, 1993—96, McKnight Investigator, 1997—99; recipient Nat. Rsch. Svc. award, Nat. Eye Inst., 1987—89, Searle Scholars award, 1989—92, Marcus Singer award, 1990, Presdl. Young Investigator award, NSF, 1991—93, Hoagland prize, Undergraduate Tchg., 1997; grantee Presdl. Faculty fellowship, NSF, 1993—96, Alfred P. Sloan Rsch. fellowship, 1991—93. Fellow: Am. Acad. Arts & Scis.; mem.: Soc. Devel. Biology, AAAS, Soc. Neuroscience (Young Investigator award 1995), Phi Beta Kappa. Office: Dept Biol Scis Stanford U Stanford CA 94305-5020 E-mail: suemcc@stanford.edu.

MCCONNELL, TED (THEODORE) F., not-for-profit fundraiser, director; b. Boise, Idaho, Oct. 10, 1955; s. H. Eldon and Frances Leek McConnell. Co-coord., congl. conf. civic edn. Ctr. Civic Edn. Alliance Rep. Democracy, Washington, 2003—; dir., Ctr. Civic Edn., Washington, 1999—. Congl. affairs asst. office sec. US Dept. Commerce, Washington, 1981—84; dir., pub. rels. and mktg. Commn. Bicentennial US Constn., 1985—89; pub. rels. cons., 1989—93; exec. v.p. Engring. and Mgmt. Execs, Inc, Alexandria, Va., 1993—99; exec. & steering com. Campaign Civic Mission Schs., 2004—. Campaign cons., campaign mgr., staff, rep. nat. com., 1975—81. Mem.: Nat. Coun. Social Studies. Office: Ctr Civic Edn 1743 Connecticut Ave NW Washington DC 20009 Office Phone: 202-861-8800. Business E-Mail: mcconnell@civiced.org.

MCCONNELL, WILLIAM F., JR., medical products executive; b. LaGrange, Ill. BS in sys. analysis, Miami U., Oxford, Ohio, 1971. CPA. Staff mem. Arthur Andersen LLP, Indpls., 1971—75, mgr., 1975—81, ptnr., 1981—83, mng. ptnr., bus. cons., 1983—89, rejoined, 1997; CFO Resort Condo. Internat., 1989—90, COO, 1990—96, info. officer, worldwide, 1996—97; v.p., COO Guidant Corp., Indpls., Ill., 1998—. Bd. dir. Global Healthcare Exchange, Vesalius Ventures. Former chmn. Children's Mus. of Indpls., Am. Red Cross of Greater Indpls., Red Cross of Conner Prairie; former bd. mem. Acordia Personal Ins. Svcs.; hon. trustee Children's Mus. of Indpls.; bd. gov. Nat. Am. Red Cross; chmn. bd. trustee Trustee Leadership Development; bd. mem., info. tech. com. Cmty. Hosp. of Indpls., Inc., Ind. U. Info. Tech. Advancement Coun. Office: Guidant Corp 111 Monument Cir 2900 Indianapolis IN 46204-5129 Mailing: Guidant Corp PO Box 44906 Indianapolis IN 46244

MCCONNELL, WILLIAM STEWART, application developer; b. Munich, June 30, 1955; s. William Marion and Mary Catherine McConnell; m. Lisa Ann Fuller, July 17, 2004; children: Elizabeth Ann Sammulia, Stephan Anthony, Margrette Catherine, Ashley Marie Fuller, Brian Daniel Fuller, Caleb Matthew Fuller Whiteside. AS in Aerospace Control Sys., C.C. USAF, 1983; AS in Computer Info. Sys., George C. Wallace State C.C., 1995; BS in Computer Info. Sys., Troy State U., 1998; MS in Computer Info. Sys., U. Phoenix, 2005. Commd. lt. USAF, 1974, advanced through grades to MSGT, 1974—87, non-commissioned officer various assignments, 1977—93, ret., 1994; warehouse mgr. The Barn, Ozark, Ala., 1993—98; software designer Grossman and Assocs., Savoy, Ill., 1998—. Dist. leader Boy Scouts Am., Del Rio, Tex., 1989—92. Decorated Commendation medal USAF, Meritorious Svc. medal, Achievement medal. Avocations: music, ballroom dancing. Home: 1353 Abram Dr Rantoul IL 61866 Office: Grossman and Assocs 5 Dunlap Ct Savoy IL 61840 Home Phone: 217-893-8023; Office Phone: 217-398-1986. Personal E-mail: stew_mcconnell@hotmail.com. Business E-Mail: smcconnell@gman.com.

MCCONNELL, WILLIAM THOMPSON, bank executive; b. Zanesville, Ohio, Aug. 8, 1933; s. William Gerald and Mary Gladys McC.; m. Jane Charlotte Cook, Aug. 25, 1956; children: Jennifer Wynne, William Gerald. BA, Denison U., 1955; MBA, Northwestern U., 1959. Pres. Park Nat. Bank, Newark, Ohio, 1979-83, pres., chief exec. officer, 1983-93, chmn., chief exec. officer, 1993-98, also bd. dirs., chmn., 1999—2004; pres., chief exec. officer Park Nat. Corp., Newark, 1987-94, chmn., CEO, 1994-98, chmn., 1999—2004, chmn. exec. com., 2005—. Mem. Newark Area C. of C. (past pres., dir. 1977-83), Ohio Bankers Assn. (pres., chmn. 1981-83), Am. Bankers Assn. (pres. 1997-98). Office: Park Nat Bank PO Box 3500 Newark OH 43058-3500

MCCONNELL-SERIO, SUZIE THERESA, women's college basketball coach, retired professional basketball player; b. Pitts., July 29, 1966; m. Pete McConnell-Serio; children: Peter, Jordan, Mandy, Madison. BA in Edn., Pa. State U., 1988. Head coach Oakland Cath. HS, Pitts., 1990—2003, Minn. Lynx, 2003—06, Duquesne U., 2007—; guard Cleve. Rockers, 1998—2000. Recipient Gold medal Olympic Games, Seoul, 1988, Bronze medal Olympic Games, Barcelona, 1992, Sportsmanship award WNBA, 1998, 2000, Newcomer award, 1998; named to All-WNBA 1st team, 1998, Western Pa. Sports Hall of Fame, 2001, Women's Basketball Hall of Fame, 2007; named Dapper Dan Sportswoman of Yr., 1999, WNBA Coach of Yr., 2004. Office: Duquesne U Womens Basketball AJ Palumbo Ctr 600 Forbes Ave Pittsburgh PA 15282 *

MCCONVILLE, EDWARD PATRICK, lawyer; b. Albany, NY, Nov. 5, 1932; s. Edward Patrick McConville and Anne Dolores Leonard; m. Lois Anne Bessette, June 30, 1956 (div. Aug. 1982); 1 child, Stephen Patrick; m. Michelle Cristin Coderre, Mar. 17, 1984; 1 child, Collin William. BA, U. Notre Dame, 1954; JD, Union U., 1956. Bar: N.Y., INd., D.C., U.S. Supreme Ct. Investigator U.S. Civil Svc. Commn., NYC, 1958—59; asst. divsn. counsel bowling divsn. Am. Machine and Foundry Co., NYC, 1959—63; asst. counsel Lincoln Nat. Life Ins. Co., Ft. Wayne, Ind., 1963—66; asst. chief counsel U.S. Dept. Commerce, Econ. Devel. Adminstrn., Portland, Maine, 1966—67, Washington, 1967—68; v.p. First Nat. Bank, Washington, 1968—70, sr. v.p., 1970—73, exec. v.p., 1973, Cmty. State Bank, Albany, NY, 1973—75, Union Nat. Bank, Albany, 1975—77; sr. v.p. Maney McConville & Liccardi, P.C., East Greenbush, NY, 1977—, ptnr. Valatie, NY, 1977—; pres. People Comml. Bank, Albany, 1984—86; hearing officer N.Y.S. Dept. Agr. and Markets, 2006—. Instr. Hudson Valley C.C., 1978—85, 1992; lectr. fin. Siena Coll., 1989; instr. bus. law and internat. bus. St. Rose Coll., 1991—98; chmn. bd. Evergreen Bank, Albany, NY, 1991—92. Vol. probation officer Albany County Probation Dept., 1981; dir. Cath. Youth Orgn., Washington, 1971—73; bd. dirs. Model Cities Econ. Devel. Corp., Washington, 1972—73. With US Army, 1956—58, with USAR, 1958—60. Mem.: N.Am. Curragh Assn. (pres. 1988—89), Old Chatham Hunt Club (pres. 1981—85), Albany Curragh Rowing Club (dir. 1987—), Ft. Orange Club. Democrat. Roman Catholic. Avocations: rowing, horseback riding. Home: 55 Fordham Rd Valatie NY 12184 Office: Maney McConville and Liccari 22 Troy Rd East Greenbush NY 12061 Office Phone: 518-477-7951. Business E-Mail: edmcconville@mmlesq.com.

MCCONVILLE, JUDY ALLEN, social studies educator; d. Edwin Frederick and Bertha Herdegen Allen; m. James McConville, June 25, 1978; children: Catherine Margarethe, Elizabeth Allen. BA in History, Randolph-Macon Woman's Coll., Lynchburg, Va., 1968; MA in Tchg. Govt., U. Va., Charlottesville, 1972. Tchr. Alexandria City Pub. Schools, Va., 1971—98, curriculum specialist for social studies, 1998—. Chmn. Va. Conf. for Social Studies Educators, Norfolk, 2004, World History Stds. of Learning Revision Com., Richmond, Va., 2000—01; mem. Mgmt. Com. History and Social Sci. Stds. of Learning, Richmond, Va., 2000—01. Edn. com., sub com. co-chair coll. student outreach Annandale United Meth. Ch., Va., 1998—2004. Mem.: NEA, Nat. Social Studies Suprs. Assn., Nat. Coun. for the Social Studies, Va. Conf. for Social Studies Educators (treas. 2005—), Va. Consortium of Social Studies Specialists and Coll. Educators (pres. 2003—04), Nat. Coun. for History Edn., Va. Edn. Assn., Edn. Assn. Alexandria, Alpha Delta Kappa (pres. 1988—90, pres. chpt. 1996—98). Methodist. Avocations: reading, needlecrafts. Office: Alexandria City Pub Schools 2000 N Beauregard St Alexandria VA Home Phone: 703-323-9275; Office Phone: 703-461-4043. Office Fax: 703-370-7704. E-mail: jmcconvi@acps.k12.va.us.

MCCOOEY, ROBERT H., JR., brokerage house executive; b. Rye, NY; 6 children. With NYSE, 1983—2006, floor trader, CEO, founder Griswald Co. floor brokerage firm, 1988—2006, mem. group's market performance com., chmn. tech. and planning oversight com., mem. exec. bd., 2003; sr. v.p. capital markets group Nasdaq Stock Market Inc., 2006—. Office: Nasdaq Stock Market Inc 1 Liberty Plz 165 Broadway 50th Fl New York NY 10006

MCCOOK, JACQUELINE K. HESLOP, food products executive; B in Internat. Rels., Stanford U., Calif.; MBA, Harvard Bus. Sch. Gen. mgr. Taco Bell Internat.; v.p. mktg. PepsiCo Restaurants Internat. (now YUM! Brands); sr. v.p. worldwide strategic planning & branding Burger King; pres., CEO McCook Group, 2000—06; chief growth officer, exec. v.p. internat. ConAgra Foods, Inc., Omaha, 2006—. Bd. dirs. Pasha's Restaurants, Inc. Office: ConAgra Foods Inc 1 ConAgra Dr Omaha NE 68102-5001 Office Phone: 402-595-4000. *

MCCOOK, KATHLEEN DE LA PEÑA, librarian, educator; b. Chgo. d. Frank Eugene and Margaret L. (de la Peña) McEntee; m. Philip G. Heim, Mar. 20, 1972 (div.); 1 child, Margaret Marie; m. William Woodrow Lee McCook, Oct. 12, 1991; stepchildren: Cecilia, Billie Jean, Nicole. BA, U. Ill., Chgo.; MA, Marquette U., Chgo.; PhD, U. Wis.-Madison. Reference librarian Elmhurst Coll. Libr., Ill.; dir. pub. svcs. Dominican U., River Forest, Ill.; lectr. U. Wis., Madison; asst. prof. library sci. U. Ill., Urbana; dean, prof. La. State U. Sch. Libr. and Info. Sci., Baton Rouge; dean grad. sch. La. State U.; dir. Sch. Libr. and Info. Sci., U. South Fla., 1993-99, prof., 1993—, coord. cmty. outreach, 2000—02, disting. univ. prof., 2002—; McCusker lectr. Dominican U., 2003—. Author: (wth K. Weibel) Role of Women in Librarianship, 1978, (with L. Estabrook) Career Profiles, 1983, (with William E. Moen) Occupational Entry, 1989, Adult Services, 1990, (with Gary O. Rolstad) Developing Readers' Advisory Services, 1993, Toward a Just and Productive Soc., 1994, Opportunities in Library and Information Science, 1997, (with B. Ford) Global Reach: Local Touch, 1998, Women of Color in Librarianship, 1998, (with B. Immroth) Library Services to Youth of Hispanic Heritage, 2000, A Place at the Table, 2000, Introduction To Public Libraries, 2004; mem. editl. bd. Cath. Lib. World Jour., 2005—; contbr. essays to books, articles to profl. jours. Chmn. Equal Rights Amendment Task Force, Ill., 1977-79, South Count Coalition for Cmty. Concerns, 1996-; active Eugene McCarthy campaign, U. Ill., Chgo., 1968, Bill Clinton campaign, 1992, 96, Al Gore campaign, 2000, Bill McBride campaign, Fla., 2002; Betty Castor campaign, 2004; John F. Kerry campaign, 2004; mem. La. Gov.'s Commn.for Women, 1985-88; bd. dirs. La. Endowment for Humanities, 1991-92; mem. exec. bd. Rural Social Svcs. Partnership, Hillsborough County, 1998-2001; mem. dem. exec. com., Hillsborough County, 2001-04; dem. del. Fla. State Convention, 2002-03; Ruskin Neigborhood Adv. Com., Fla., 2003-06, Hillsborough County, Citizen's Action Bd., 2004—; mem. collective bargaining com. United Faculty Fla., 2003-; mem. Cmty. Action Bd., 2004—.

Recipient Disting. Alumnus award U. Wis., 1991, award of merit Trejo Foster Found., 1999; named Bradshaw scholar Tex. Woman's Univ., 1994; named scholar in residence Chgo. Pub. Libr., 2003. Mem. ALA (com. chmn. 1980—, editor RQ jour. 1982-88, Pub. Librs. Jour. 1989-90, Am. Librs. adv. com. 1994-96, contbg. editor Am. Librs. 1999-2001, column editor RUSQ 2000-06, Notable Books Coun. 2001-06), Progressive Librs. Guild. (coord. com., editl. bd., 2005—), REFORMA (bd. dirs. 1997-98, Latino Libr. of Yr. 2002, Equality award 1987, Monroe Adult Svc. award 1991, Futas Catalyst for Change award 1998, Achievement in Diversity Rsch. award 2004), Assn. for Libr. and Info. Sci. Edn. (com. chmn. 1981—, pres. 1987-88, Pres. award 1997), Fla. Libr. Assn. (bd. dirs. 1995-98, Transformer award 1996), Tampa Bay Libr. Consortium (bd. dirs. 1994-97), Women Libr. Workers, Ruskin Civic Assn. (sec. 1997-99), Ill. Libr. Assn. (treas. 1981-83), Progressive LIbrarians Guild (coord. com. 2004-06), Beta Phi Mu (50th Anniversary Disting. Mem. 1999, Dist. Lectr. award 2002, Disting. Svc. to Edn. for Librarianship 2003), Cath. Libr. Assn. (Brubaker award for Outstanding Article 2003), prog. libr., editl. bd., 2005-. Democrat. Avocation: reading. Office: U South Fla Sch Libr and Info Sci 4202 E Fowler Ave Stop CIS1040 Tampa FL 33620-7800 Personal E-mail: kmccook@tampabay.rr.com.

MCCOOK, RICHARD PAUL, grocery chain financial executive; b. Miami, Fla., Mar. 15, 1953; s. Leon Ennis and Ruth Erminor (Davenport) McC.; m. Anne Thackerson, Mar. 22, 1975; children: Ryan Wesley, Kelly Lauren. BS in Acctg., Fla. State U., 1975, M in Accountancy, 1976. CPA, Fla. Sr. audit mgr. Peat, Marwick, Mitchell & Co., Jacksonville, Fla., 1976-84; fin. v.p., CFO Winn-Dixie Stores, Inc., 1984—, sr. v.p., CFO. Participant Leadership Jacksonville, 1986-87. Mem. Am. Inst. CPA's, Fla. Inst. CPA's, Fin. Execs. Inst. Clubs: River (Jacksonville). Democrat. Methodist. Avocations: hunting, fishing, tennis. Office: Winn-Dixie Stores Inc 5050 Edgewood Ct Jacksonville FL 32254-3601

MCCOOL, COURTNEY, Olympic athlete; b. Kansas City, Apr. 1, 1988; Mem. U.S. Nat. Gymnastics Team, 2002—; gymnast Team USA, Athens Olympic Games, 2004. Achievements include mem. U.S. Championship Team, Pan Am. Games, 2003; invention of Athens Test Event, 1st in all-around, 2004; Silver medal, Olympics. Office: c/o USOC One Olympic Plz Colorado Springs CO 80909

MCCORD, GUYTE PIERCE, JR., retired judge; b. Tallahassee, Sept. 23, 1914; s. Guyte Pierce and Jean (Patterson) McC.; m. Laura Elizabeth Mack, Dec. 1, 1939 (dec. Oct. 8, 2000); children: Florence Elizabeth, Guyte Pierce III, Edward LeRoy; m. Elizabeth Rogers Green, May 24, 2002. Student, Davidson Coll., 1933-34; BA, JD, U. Fla., 1940. Bar: Fla. 1940. Summer ranger Yosemite Nat. Park, 1936-39; rsch. aide Fla. Supreme Ct., summer 1940; pvt. practice Tallahassee, 1940-48; dep. commr. Fla. Indsl. Commn., 1946-47; pros. atty. Leon County, 1947-48; asst. gen. counsel Fla. Pub. Svc. Commn., 1949-60; judge 2d Jud. Cir. Fla., Tallahasee, 1960-74, Ct. Appeals 1st Dist. Fla., 1974-83, chief judge, 1977-79; ret., 1979. Mem. Fla. Senate Pres.'s Council on Criminal Justice 1972; mem. appellate ct. rules com. Fla. Supreme Ct., 1977-78, mem. appellate ct. structure commn. 1978-79. Pres. Murat House Assn., Inc., 1967-69; bd. dirs. Fla. Heritage Found., 1969-70, mem. exec. com., 1965-69; mem. Andrew Jackson staff of Springtime Tallahassee, 1973-74, 84-86, Andrew Jackson, 1987. Commdr. USNR, 1942—64, WWII, Korea. Mem. ABA, Mil. Officers Assn. Am., Fla. Bar, Fla. Conf. Cir. Judges (sec.-treas. 1970, chmn. 1972), Fla. State U. Pres. Club, Kiwanis (dir. 1958-59), Sigma Alpha Epsilon, Phi Delta Phi. Presbyterian (elder 1960—, ch. trustee 1981-86). Home: 2718 Timbertrail Cir Tallahassee FL 32308-5745

MCCOREY, WILLIAM E., JR., retail executive; Mgmt. positions Circuit City, Richmond, Va., 1991—2005; CIO 2nd Swing Inc., 2005; v.p. bus. applications Circuit City, Richmond, Va., 2005—06, sr. v.p., CIO, 2006—. Office: Circuit City 9950 Mayland Dr Richmond VA 23233 *

MCCORISON, MARCUS ALLEN, librarian, cultural organization administrator; b. Lancaster, Wis., July 17, 1926; s. Joseph Lyle and Ruth (Mink) McCorison; m. Janet Buckbee Knop, June 10, 1950 (dec. 1998); children: Marcus Allen II, Judith McCorison Gove, Andrew Buckbee, Mary McCorison Rosenbloom(dec.), James Rice, Peter Gardner; life ptnr. Carolyn K. Dik. AB, Ripon Coll., 1950; MA, U. Vt., 1951, LittD (hon.), 1992; MS, Columbia U., 1954; LHD (hon.), Assumption Coll., Worcester, Mass., 1987, Coll. of the Holy Cross, 1992; LittD (hon.), Clark U., 1992. Librarian Kellogg-Hubbard Library, Montpelier, Vt., 1954-55; chief of rare books dept. Dartmouth Coll. Library, Hanover, NH, 1955-59; head spl. collections dept. State U. Iowa Libraries, 1959-60; libr. Am. Antiquarian Soc., Worcester, Mass., 1960-91, editor Procs., 1960-67, dir., 1967-89, pres., 1989-92, pres. emeritus, 1993—; cons. Christie, Manson & Woods, Internat., 1993-96, N.Y. Hist. Soc., 1994-95, Libr. Congress, Hist. Soc. of Pa., 1996, U. Kans., 1998-99. Mem. N.Am. steering com. 18th Century Short Title Catalogue, 1977—; mem. Com. for a New Eng. Bibliography, 1968-90, treas., 1970-77; mem. adv. com. Eleutherian Mills-Hagley Found., 1971-74, 87-89; chmn. Ind. Rsch. Librs. Assn., 1972-73, 78-80; mem. adv. coun. Princeton U. Libr., 1988-92; bd. govs. Rsch. Librs. Group, 1980-91, chmn. preservation com., 1982-85, chmn. governance com., 1989-91, chmn. Writings of James Fenimore Cooper, 1991-2002. Author: Vermont Imprints 1778-1820, 1963, The 1764 Catalogue of the Redwood Library, 1965; contbr.: The Pursuit of Knowledge in the Early American Republic, 1976, Publishing and Readership in Revolutionary France and America, 1993; editor: History of Printing in America by Isaiah Thomas, 1970. Trustee Fruitlands Mus., 1978-89, Old Sturbridge Village, 1981-92, Hist. Deerfield, Inc., 1991-2002, Newberry Libr., 1995—; mem. bd. mgrs. Lewis Walpole Libr., Yale U., 1995—; mem. Cultural Commn. City Worcester, Mass., 1999-2004, Mass. Hist. Commn., 1999—; mem. com. mgmt. Wm. L. Clements Libr., U. Mich., 2001—. Recipient Samuel Pepys medal Ephemera Soc., London, 1980, Disting. Alumni award Ripon Coll., 1989, Columbia U. Sch. Libr. Svc., 1992. Rickards medal Ephemera Soc. Am., 2000. Mem. Am. Antiquarian Soc., Coll. and Rsch. Librs. Assn. (chmn. rare books sect. 1965-66), Bibliog. Soc. Am. (pres. 1980-84, del. to ACLS 1985—2002), Am. Printing Hist. Assn. (trustee 1998—2004, laureate 1998), Vt. Hist. Soc. (trustee 1956-66), Worcester Hist. Mus. (exec. com. 1967-80), Ctr. for Rsch. on Vt. (assoc.), N.E. Am. Soc. 18th Century Studies (pres. 1978-79), Colonial Soc. Mass., Club of Odd Vols., Grolier Club (councillor 1979-82, 83-84), Zamorano Club (hon.), Roxburghe Club, Century Assn. Democrat. Home and Office: 101 Greenwich Ct Worcester MA 01609-1159

MCCORKINDALE, DOUGLAS HAMILTON, publishing executive; b. NYC, June 14, 1939; s. William Douglas and Kathleen (Miles) McC.; m. Nancy Walsh, Dec. 24, 1991; children by previous marriage: Laura Ann, Heather Jean. BA, Columbia U., 1961, LLB cum laude (Harlan Fiske Stone scholar), 1964. Bar: N.Y. 1964. Assoc. Thacher Proffitt & Wood, NYC, 1964-70, ptnr., 1970-71; gen. counsel, sec. Gannett Co., Inc., Arlington, Va., 1971-72, v.p., gen. counsel, sec., 1972-77, sr. v.p. fin. and law, 1977-79, sr. v.p., chief fin. officer, 1979-83, pres. diversified media div., 1980-83, exec. v.p., 1983, vice chmn., 1985—2001, CFO, 1985—97, chief adminstrv. officer, 1986—97, pres., 1997—2005, CEO, 2000—05, chmn., 2005—06. Bd. dirs. AP, Continental Airlines Inc., Lockheed Martin Corp., Mut. Ins. Co. Ltd. Mem. ABA, Newspaper Assn. Am., Pine Valley Golf Club, Mid Ocean Club, Burning Tree Club. Office: Gannett Co Inc 7950 Jones Branch Dr Mc Lean VA 22102

MCCORKLE, LEON MARSHALL, JR., lawyer, educator; b. Alliance, Ohio, Mar. 2, 1941; s. Leon Marshall and Mary Carrington McC.; m. Patricia McCorkle Dec. 28, 1964 (div. Oct. 1982); children: Catherine Shapiro, Molly Carrington McCorkle; m. Virginia Marie Brotherton Trethewey, Nov. 28, 1986; children: Kyle, John Marshall. AB, Harvard Coll., Cambridge, Mass., 1964; JD, The Ohio State U. Coll. Law, Columbus, 1972. Bar: Supreme Ct. Ohio, 1972, U.S. Ct. (so. dist.), 1990. Sr. ptnr. Vorys, Sater, Seymour & Pease, LLP, Columbus, Ohio, 1972-98; adj. prof. Ohio State U. Coll. Law, Columbus, 1991-92, 95—; sr. v.p., gen. counsel Wendy's Internat., Inc., Dublin, Ohio, 1998, exec. v.p., gen. counsel, sec. Commr. Nat. Conf. Commissioners on Uniform State Laws, Chgo., 1988—. Editor in chief The Ohio State U. Law Jour., 1971-72. Lt. USN, 1963-69. Trustee Columbus Symphony Orchestra, Columbus, 1997-98, Columbus Bar Svcs., Inc., 1999; mem. bd. dirs. ACCA, Columbus, 1999. Fellow Columbus Bar Found.; mem. ABA, Ohio State Bar Found., Columbus Bar Found., Put-in-Bay Yacht Club, Am. Law Inst., Order of the Coif. Avocations: boating, weather instructor U.S. Power Squadrons, my children. Office: Wendys Internat Inc PO Box 256 Dublin OH 43017-0256 also: Wendy's International Inc One Dave Thomas Blvd Dublin OH 43017 *

MCCORKLE, RUTH, oncological nurse, educator, researcher; BS, U. Md., 1968; MA, U. Iowa, 1972, PhD, 1975. Staff nurse CCU Vanvouver (Wash.) Med. Hosp., 1968-69; oncological clin. nurse specialist U. Iowa Hosps. and Clinics, Iowa City, 1971-73; instr. psychiat. nursing and oncological nursing Sch. Nursing, U. Iowa, Iowa City, 1974-75; from asst. prof. to prof. dept. cmty. health care sys. U. Wash., Seattle, 1975-85; prof. adult health and illness divsn. Sch. Nursing, U. Pa., Phila., 1986—98, chairperson, 1988-89, dir. Ctr. Advancing Care in Serious Illness, 1989—98, dir. cancer control Cancer Comprehensive Ctr., 1990-98; prof. nursing, chmn. doc program, dir. Ctr. Chronic Illness Sch. Yale U., New Haven, 1998—. Mem. nursing sci. rev. com. Nat. Ctr. Nursing Rsch., 1988-92. Contbr. articles to profl. jours. Fellow Am. Acad. Nursing; mem. ANA, NAS, Internat. Soc. Nurses Cancer Care (dir.-at-large 1983-89), Am. Assn. Cancer Edn., Am. Psychosocial Oncology Soc. (charter mem., dir.-at-large 1998-), Oncology Nursing Soc. (charter mem., mem. rsch. com. 1981-82, dir.-at-large 1983-85). Office: Yale U 100 Church St S PO Box 9740 New Haven CT 06536-0740 Business E-Mail: ruth.mccorkle@yale.edu.

MC CORMAC, JOHN WAVERLY, judge; b. Zanesville, Ohio, Feb. 8, 1926; s. Samuel D. and Phyllis (Murray) McC.; m. Martha Ann Cunningham, June 22, 1952; children: Michael Paul, John Mark, James Samuel. BS, Muskingum Coll., 1951; JD, Capital U., 1961. Bar: Ohio 1961. Fire protection engr. Ohio Insp. Bur., 1951—60; pvt. practice Columbus, 1961—65; prof. law Capital U., Columbus, 1965-66, 71-74, dean Law Sch., 1966—71; judge 10th Dist. Ct. Appeals, 1975—92; prof. law Ohio State U., Columbus, 1993—2001. Mem. staff cons. rules adv. com. Supreme Ct. Ohio; chmn. adv. bd. Vols. in Probation, 1972-74; chmn. ohio Jud. Conf., 1982-84; commr. Ohio Dispute Resolution Com., 1989-96, chmn., 1993-95; chief justice Ohio Ct. Appeals Assn., 1989-91. Author: Ohio Civil Rules Practice, 1970, 2nd edit., 1992, Anderson's Ohio Civil Practice, Vol. 1, 1971, Vol. 2, 1976, Vol. 3, 1977, Wrongful Death in Ohio, 1982. Served with USNR, 1943-46. Fellow Ohio Bar Assn. Found.; mem. League Ohio Law Schs. (pres. 1969-70), ABA, Ohio Bar Assn. (council of dels. 1973-77), Columbus Bar Assn. (bd. govs. 1968-72, sec.-treas. 1973-74, pres. 1975-76), Am. Judicature Soc., Phi Alpha Delta. Clubs: Masons (33 deg.). Republican. Home: 395 Longfellow Ave Columbus OH 43085-3024 E-mail: johnmccormac46@hotmail.com.

MCCORMACK, DERMOT, communications executive; b. 1970; Creator, sponsorship models for iVillage; CFO, co-founder Flooz.com; v.p., consumer Web sites Cablevision Systems Corp., 2001—06, sr. v.p., Interactive Advt. and Devel., 2006—. Named one of Top 100 Irish Americans in Bus., Irish Am. Mag., 40 Executives Under 40, Multichannel News, 2006. Office: Cablevision Systems Corporations 1111 Stewart Ave Bethpage NY 11714 Office Phone: 516-803-2300. Office Fax: 516-803-3134.

MCCORMACK, DONALD PAUL, newspaper consultant; b. Brockton, Mass., Jan. 15, 1926; s. Everett G. and Esther (Lufkin) McC.; m. Petronella Ruth Seger, Apr. 28, 1951; 1 son, Christopher Paul. BA, U. Pitts., 1949. Corr. U.P.I., 1949-52; asst. city editor Pitts. Sun-Telegraph, 1952-56; pub. relations exec., 1956-64; copy reader N.Y. News, 1964-67, editorial writer, 1967-72, chief editorial writer, 1972-82; cons., 1982—. With USAAF, 1944-46, Pa. N.G., 1952-57. Home and Office: PO Box 3539 Westport CT 06880-8539

MCCORMACK, DOUGLAS P., lawyer; b. 1969; BA in Polit. Sci., U. So. Calif., 1992; JD, Am. U., 1998. Bar: Md. 2000. With Arent Fox Kintner Plotkin & Kahn, Washington; ptnr., pub. law & policy strategies group Sonnenschein Nath & Rosenthal LLP, Washington, 2002—.

MCCORMACK, ERIC, actor; b. Toronto, Ont., Can., Apr. 18, 1963; currently holds dual citizenship in Am. and Can. s. James Keith and Doris McCormack; m. Janet Holden, Aug. 1, 1997; 1 child, Finnigan Holden. Grad., Ryerson U. Sch. Theatre, Toronto. Mem. Stratford Shakespearean Festival, Canada, 1985—89. Actor: (plays) A Midsummer Night's Dream, Henry V, The Three Sisters, Some Girl(s), 2006; (TV films) The Boys From Syracuse, 1986, Much Ado About Nothing, 1987, Relentless: Mind of a Killer, 1993, Family of Strangers, 1993, Miracle on Interstate 880, 1993, Call of the Wild, 1993, Double, Double, Toil and Trouble, 1993, Island City, 1994, The Man Who Wouldn't Die, 1994, Townies, 1996, Night Visitors, 1996, Borrowed Hearts, 1997, The Audrey Hepburn Story, 2000, Dead Like Me, 2004, In From the Night, 2005; (TV series) Street Justice, 1992—93, Lonesome Dove: The Series, 1994, Lonesome Dove: The Outlaw Years, 1995, Will & Grace, 1998—2006 (Emmy award, outstanding lead actor in a comedy, 2001); (TV miniseries) A Will of Their Own, 1998; (films) The Lost World, 1992, Return to the Lost World, 1992, Giant Steps, 1992, Exception to the Rule, 1997, Free Enterprise, 1998, Holy Man, 1998, Here's to Life, 2000, Break a Leg, 2005, The Sisters, 2006; (Broadway plays) The Music Man, 2001; writer/dir. (films) Pirates, 2003. Mailing: Will & Grace NBC 100 Universal City Plaza Universal City CA 91608 also: c/o Hyler Mgmt 20 Ocean Park Blvd Ste 25 Santa Monica CA 90405

MC CORMACK, FRANCIS XAVIER, lawyer, former oil company executive; b. Bklyn., July 9, 1929; s. Joseph and Blanche V. (Dengel) Mc C.; m. Margaret V. Hynes, Apr. 24, 1954; children: Marguerite, Francis Xavier, Sean Michael, Keith John, Cecelia Blanche, Christopher Thomas. AB cum laude, St. Francis Coll., Bklyn., 1951; LLB, Columbia U., 1954. Bar: N.Y. 1955, Mich. 1963, Calif. 1974, Pa. 1975. Assoc. Cravath, Swaine & Moore, NYC, 1956-62; sr. atty. Ford Motor Co., 1962-64, asst. gen. counsel, 1970-72; v.p., gen. counsel, sec. Philco-Ford Corp., 1964-72; v.p., gen. counsel Atlantic Richfield Co., 1972-73, sr. v.p., gen. counsel, 1973-94. Editor Columbia U. Law Rev., 1954. Decorated commendatore Ordine al Merito (Italy); Stone scholar Columbia U., 1954. Mem. Calif. Club, Chancery Club, Annandale Golf Club.

MCCORMACK, JOHN JOSEPH, JR., insurance company executive; b. Morristown, NJ, Aug. 22, 1944; s. John Joseph and Marion Loretta (Smith) McC.; m. Judith Gail Harvey, July 20, 1968; children: Brendan, Matthew, Margaret. BBA, St. Bonaventure U., 1966. From group underwriter to exec. v.p. Tchrs. Ins. and Annuity Assn.-Coll. Retirement Equities Fund, NYC, 1966-98; pres. TIAA-CREF Enterprises, 1998-99, group pres., 1999-2001; chmn. McCormack's Retirement and Fin. Svcs. Cons., 2001—. Trustee Am. Psychol. Assn. Ins. Trust, Washington, 1980-90, chmn., 1985-86, trustee investment com., 1990-98, 2001—; trustee Employee Benefit Rsch. Inst., Washington, 1983—, treas., 1986-90, vice-chmn., 1997-98, chmn., 1999-2001; mem. adv. bd. Andrew W. Mellon Found., N.Y.C., 1997-2001. Pres.'s coun. St. Bonaventure U., 1986—, chmn., 1986-89, trustee, 1996—, chmn. investment com., 1999-2003, vice chmn. bd. trustees, 2003—; bd. visitors Ctr. for Study Future Mgmt. U. Md., 1987-92; trustee Coll. and Univ. Pers. Assn. Found., 1992-94; bd. govs. Investment Co. Inst., 1994-2000; trustee Fenimore Asset Mgmt. Funds, 2004-. Roman Catholic. Office: PO Box 432 New Vernon NJ 07976-0432 Office Phone: 908-415-0104. Personal E-mail: jmccsbu@aol.com.

MCCORMACK, JOHN ROBERT, lawyer; b. Middletown, Conn., Mar. 30, 1962; s. John Francis and Ann Jane (Monarca) McC.; m. Cristina Dorthea Dwyer, Sept. 27, 1986; children: Kevin, Cara. BS, Univ. Conn., 1984; JD, Stetson Univ., 1990. Assoc. Kelly & McKee, P.A., Tampa, Fla., 1990-92; ptnr. Wiggins & McCormack, Clearwater, Fla., 1992-94; sole practitioner J. Robert McCormack, P.A., Clearwater, Fla., 1994-00; ptnr. Persante & McCormack, P.A., 2000—. Editor: Labor and Employment in Florida, 1990, Critical Issues in Labor and Employment Labor, 1990. Mem. ABA (labor and employment law sect.), Fla. Bar Labor and Employment Law Sect., Barney Masterson Inn of Ct. (treas. 1998-99), Clearwater Bar Employment Law Com. (co-chair 1997-99). Office: Persante & McCormack P A 2555 Enterprise Rd Bldg 15 Clearwater FL 33763

MCCORMACK, LOWELL RAY, oil industry executive, corporate financial executive, consultant; b. Ladonia, Tex., Oct. 26, 1925; d. Lowell and Orianna (McDonnold) Coney; m. Paul H. McCormack, June 4, 1948; children: Sharron Ann, Lowell Henry. At, Rutherford Met. Coll., Dallas, 1962, U. Tex., Arlington and Dallas, Eastfield Coll., Dallas, Cooke County Coll., Gainesville, Tex., 1989—; AA, Wm. Alexander Art, 1991. Master graphoanalyst Internat. Graphoanalysis Soc. Bookeeper Jot-Em-Down Gin Corp., Pecan Gap, Tex., 1947, Shedd-Bartush Foods, Dallas, 1948—52; v.p. and sec.-treas. Safari Oil Co., 1954—88, pres., 1989—; acct. and credit mgr. J. P. Ashcraft Co., Inc., 1956—65; v.p., sec.-treas. and CFO Dallas Title Co., 1965—83; treas. First Nat. Bank, Cooper, Tex., 1986—87; pres. Scorpio Oil Co., 1987—. Treas. Butterfield Stage, Gainesville, Tex.; acctg. cons. to atty.; lectr. in field. Author: Stories of Growing Up in the Coney Family, 2005; featured writer Tex. State Hist. Assn. Web Site, 2005. Troop leader Girl Scouts USA, 1955—65; founder Yarn Spinners, Gainesville, Tex., 1988; mem. Newcomers Club, 1986—, pres., 1989—92; columnist Cooke County Leader, 1988; founding mem. Gainesville Area Visual Arts; mem. Baptist Choir, Centennial Cir. Mem.: Internat. Platform Assn., North Tex. Oil and Gas Assn., Internat. Graphoanalysis Soc. (life; v.p. Tex. chpt. 1978, pres. 1979, Graphoanalyst of Yr. 1987, keynote spkr. 1987, Okla. seminar leader 1990), Red Hat. Soc., Crosstimbers Geneal. Soc., Gainesville C. of C., Cooke County Heritage Soc., Kiwanis (one of 1st women mems. Gainesville chpt. 1988, v.p. 1990—91, pres. 1991—92), Zonta Club (co-chmn. fin. com. 1982, dir. and 2d v.p. 1983—84), Soroptimist Club, Toastmistress (pres. 1981, com. chmn. internat. conv 1984), Phi Theta Kappa (treas. Psi Iota chpt. 1990, acad. all-Am. 3d team for cmty. tech. and jr. colls. 1992). Baptist. Home: 631 S Lindsay St Gainesville TX 76240-5336 Personal E-mail: l.r.mccormack@sbcglobal.net.

MCCORMACK, MICHAEL, state supreme court justice; b. Omaha, July 20, 1939; JD, Creighton U., 1963. Asst. pub. defender, Douglas County, Nebr., 1963-66; pvt. practice Omaha, 1966-97; justice Nebr. Supreme Ct., 1997—. Fellow: Internat. Soc. Barristers; mem.: Sarpy County Bar Assn., Omaha Bar Assn., Colo. Bar Assn., Nebr. State Bar Assn. Office: State Capitol Bldg Rm 2218 Lincoln NE 68509 also: PO Box 98910 Lincoln NE 68509 *

MCCORMACK, PATRICIA LYNN, retired psychologist; b. Buffalo, Oct. 4, 1945; d. Michael James and Helen Lorraine McCormack; life ptnr. John F. Connor; 1 child, Seraphina Cabral Uludong. BS in Social Work, U. Buffalo, 1965; MA in Spl. Edn., U. Oreg., Eugene, 1975, MA in Sch. Psychology, 1981. Cert. tchr. K-12 Wash., 1975, Oreg., 1975, Nat. Bd. Cert. Counselors, 1981, Nat. Bd. Sch. Psychologists, 1983. Ednl. psychologist instr. U. Oreg., 1973—74; spl. edn. tchr. Springfield Sch. Dist., Eugene, 1974—80; sch. psychologist Portland Pub. Schs., 1980—86, Evergreen Sch. Dist., Vancouver, Wash., 1987—99; ret. Coord. suport svcs. Head Start, Eugene, 1971—72. Mem. Am. Frieds Svc. Com., Portland, 1989—98. Recipient Outstanding Young Women of Yr. award, 1978. Mem.: Nat. Bd. Counselors (life), Nat: Bd. Sch. Psychologist (life). Democrat-Npl. Avocations: travel, swimming, reading. Home: 349 Claremont Ave Buffalo NY 14223

MCCORMACK, RICHARD THOMAS FOX, diversified financial services company executive, former ambassador; b. Bradford, Pa., Mar. 6, 1941; s. C.H. and Ruth N. (Fox) McC.; m. Karen L. Hagstrom, Oct. 18, 1980; children: Charlotte Louise, Justin Randall, Elizabeth Caroline. BA, Georgetown U., 1963; PhD, U. Fribourg, Switzerland, 1966. With Peace Corps, 1966-67; sr. staff mem. Pres.' Adv. Council on Exec. Orgn., White House, Washington, 1969-71; with Am. Enterprise Inst., 1975-77; dep. asst. sec. for internat. econ. affairs US Dept. Treasury, 1974; mem. staff U.S. Senate, 1979-81; asst. sec. state for econ. and bus. affairs U.S. Dept. State, Washington, 1982-85, US amb. to OAS, 1985-89, under sec. for econ. affairs, 1989-91; sr. advisor Ctr. Strategic Internat. Studies, Washington, 2004—06; vice chmn. Merrill Lynch & Co., Inc., NYC, 2006—. Candidate in primary elections for U.S. Congress, 1972, 74; cons. Office Telecommunications Policy, 1971, Coun. on Internat. Econ. Policy, 1972, Office Spl. Trade Rep., 1975, Exec. Office of the Pres., White House, Washington; guest scholar Woodrow Wilson Ctr. Smithsonian Instn., Washington, 1991-92; bus. advisor Am. companies, cons. U.S. Govt. on Internat. Econ. Affairs, 1992-2005. Author: Asians in Kenya, 1971, The Twilight War, 1979, Microeconomic Reforms for Israel, 1991, Managing Japan's Financial Crisis, 1992, Vulnerabilities in the Global Economy: Looking Forward in War Time, 2005. Recipient Superior Honor award Dept. State, 1987, Sec. of State's Disting. Svc. award, 1991; decorated Legion of Honor (France). Mem. Econ. Club NY, Coun. Am. Ambs., Coun. Fgn. Rels. Republican. Office: Merrill Lynch & Co Inc 4 Financial World Ctr New York NY 10080 Office Phone: 212-449-9300.

MCCORMACK, ROBERT CORNELIUS, investment banker; b. NYC, Nov. 7, 1939; m. Mary Lester, Dec. 14, 1963; children: Robert Cornelius Jr., Walter, Scott. BA, U. N.C., 1962; MBA, U. Chgo., 1968. V.p. Dillon Read & Co. Inc., 1968-81; mng. dir. Morgan Stanley & Co., Inc., Chgo., 1981-87; dep. asst sec. def. prodn. support U.S. Dept. Def., Washington, 1987-88, dep. under sec. def. indsl. and internat. programs, 1988-89, acting dep. under sec. of def. acquisition, 1989-90, asst. sec. Navy fin. mgmt. Washington, 1990-93; founding ptnr. Trident Capital L.P., Chgo., 1993—. Served to lt. USNR, 1963-66. Office: 277 83RD St #B2 Burr Ridge IL 60527-5846

MCCORMACK, SEAN IAN, federal agency administrator; B in Econs., Colby Coll., 1986; MA, U. Md., 1990. Analyst Meridian Corp.; with Fgn. Svc., 1995—99; Farsi-speaking officer consular sect. U.S. Embassy, Ankara, 1996—98, econ. reporter on consular issues Algiers, 1998—99; with ops. ctr. US Dept. State, Washington, 1999, with exec. secretariat staff; dep. press sec. for fgn. policy The White House, Washington; spl. asst. to Pres., spokesman NSC, Washington, 2001—05; asst. sec. pub. affairs, dept. spokesman US Dept. State, Washington, 2005—. Office: US Dept State Harry S Truman Bldg 2201 C St NW Rm 6800 Washington DC 20520 Office Phone: 202-647-6607.

MCCORMACK, TERRY R., automotive executive; BS in Pyschology, Ball State U., Muncie, Ind. Sales trainee Dana Corp., 1973, pres. Aftermarket Group, 2000—04; pres., CEO Affinia Group Intermediate Holdings, 2004—. Bd. dirs. Motor & Equipment Mfrs. Assn. Bd. dirs. U. NC Charlotte Belk Coll. Sch. Bus. Mem.: Automotive Presidents' Group. Office: Affinia Group Inc 1101 Technology Dr Ann Arbor MI 48108 Office Phone: 734-827-5400. *

MCCORMACK, THOMAS JOSEPH, retired publishing executive, playwright; b. Boston, Jan. 5, 1932; s. Thomas Joseph and Lena Carolyn (Allen) McC.; m. Sandra Harriet Danenberg, Aug. 21, 1964; children: Daniel Aaron, Jed Charles (dec.), Jessie Ann. Student, U. Conn., 1950-51; AB summa cum laude (James Manning scholar), Brown U., 1954; postgrad. (G.H. Palmer scholar, Woodrow Wilson fellow), Harvard U., 1956. Writer radio news WSTC, Stamford, Conn., 1957-59; editor Doubleday & Co., Inc., NYC, 1959-64, Harper & Row, NYC, 1964-67; edn. editor New Am. Library, NYC, 1967-69; dir. trade dept. St. Martin's Press, NYC, 1969-70, pres., 1970-87, chief exec. officer, editorial dir., 1970-96, chmn., 1987-97. Pres., chmn. bd. St. James Press, Ltd., London, 1973-79; v.p., treas. Sandra D. McCormack, Inc. (Interior Designer.); chmn., chief exec. officer Tor Books, N.Y.C., 1987-96; exec. com. Holtzbrinck GmbH, Stuttgart, Germany, 1995-97. Author: Afterwords, Novelists on Their Novels, 1969, The Fiction Editor, the Novel and the Novelist, (plays) American Roulette, 1969, Endpapers, 2002; columnist: The Cheerful Skeptic, 1997—99. Mem. Play Devel. Coun., Manhattan Theater Club, 1995-2001, Dramatists Gild, 1997—. With AUS, 1954-56. Mem. Assn. Am. Pubs. (dir. 1973-76, freedom to read com. 1974-77, Curtis Benjamin award 1997, LMP Lifetime Achievement award 1997), Phi Beta Kappa. Clubs: The Players (N.Y.C.), Century Assn. (N.Y.C.). Home: 50 Central Park W New York NY 10023-6028 E-mail: cheerskep@aol.com.

MCCORMACK, WILLIAM ARTHUR, lawyer; b. Rochester, NY, Sept. 18, 1951; s. Austin Francis and June Ann (Doyle) McC. AB in Polit. Sci. magna cum laude, St. Louis U., 1973; cert., Sorbonne, Paris, 1974; JD, Georgetown U., Washington, DC, 1977; exec. tng., Harvard Bus. Sch., Cambridge, Mass. Bar: Tex. 1977, DC 1979. Assoc. Crutcher, Hull et al., Dallas, 1978—82, Hughes & Luce, Dallas, 1982—83, ptnr., 1983—2005, mem. mgmt. com., exec. com., sect. head, 1993—97, mng. ptnr., chmn., 1997—2003; ptnr. Fulbright & Jaworski, Dallas, NYC, London, 2005—. Bd. dirs. Engles Capital Corp., McCormack Corp.; adj. prof. U. Tex. Sch. of Law, 2007; spkr. and author on legal topics. Contbr. articles to profl. jours. Bd. dirs. Alliance Francaise Found., Dallas, Jesuit Found., St. Anthony Found., Dallas Epilepsy Found., pres., 1992, Dallas Citizens Coun.; bd. advisors Jesuit Prep., Bishop Dunne H.S., Bus. Com. for the Arts, Dallas; coun. mem., exec. comm. circle ten coun. Boy Scouts Am.; leadership coun. Dallas Chamber. Mem. ABA, State Bar Assn. Tex. (chmn. minority com.), Dallas Bar Assn. (chmn. legal ethics com., minority commn.), Pi Sigma Alpha, Alpha Sigma Nu. Roman Catholic. Office: Fulbright Jaworski 2200 Ross Ave Dallas TX 75201

MCCORMACK, WILLIAM F., lawyer; b. Washington, Dec. 27, 1946; BS, Va. Poly. Univ., 1968; JD, Catholic Univ., Washington, 1971; LLM, Univ. Va., 1972. Bar: Va. 1971, N.Y. 1973. Ptnr. Reboul MacMurray Hewitt & Maynard; ptnr. corp. dept. & co-head private equity practice group Ropes & Gray, NYC, 2003—. Mem.: ABA, N.Y. State Bar Assn., Va. Bar Assn. Office: Ropes & Gray 45 Rockefeller Plz New York NY 10111-0087 Office Phone: 212-841-0627. Office Fax: 212-841-5725. Business E-Mail: william.mccormack@ropesgray.com.

MCCORMALLY, KEVIN JAY, editor; b. Boston, Mar. 13, 1950; s. John Patrick and Marguerite Louise (Wichert) McC.; m. Anne Louise Long, May 27, 1972; children: Niamh Anna, Patrick Henry. BA with honors, U. Iowa, 1972. Area editor Burlington (Iowa) Hawk Eye, 1969-70; city editor Daily Iowan, Iowa City, 1971-72; press sec. U.S. Rep. Edward Mezvinsky, Washington, 1972-77; assoc. editor Changing Times Mag., Washington, 1977-85, sr. editor, 1985-90; exec. editor Kiplinger's Personal Fin. Mag. (formerly Changing Times), Washington, 1991-2000; editl. dir. Kiplinger's Personal Fin. mag., 2000—05, Kiplinger Washington Editors, 2005—. Commentator Nightly Bus. Report PBS and ABC Radio. Author: Successful Tax Planning, 1988, Sure Ways to Cut Your Taxes, 1989-94, Cut Your Taxes, 1996, 97, 98, 99; co-author: A Term to Remember, 1977; editor: Get More for Your Money, 1981. Mem. Nat. Press Club (best consumer journalism award 1986, 88), Sigma Delta Chi. Democrat. Roman Catholic. Avocation: photography. Home: 161 D St SE Washington DC 20003-1809 Office: Kiplingers Washington Editors 1729 H St NW Washington DC 20006-3925 Business E-Mail: kmccormally@kiplinger.com.

MCCORMICK, BARNES WARNOCK, aerospace engineering educator; b. Waycross, Ga., July 15, 1926; s. Barnes Warnock and Edwina (Brogdon) McC.; m. Emily Joan Hess, July 18, 1946; 1 dau., Cynthia Joan. BS in Aero. Engring, Pa. State U., 1948, MS, 1949, PhD, 1954. Research assoc. Pa. State U., University Park, 1949-54, assoc. prof., 1954-55, prof. aero. engring., 1959-92, Boeing prof. aero. engring., 1985-92, prof. emeritus, cons., 1992—, head dept. aerospace engring., 1969-85. Assoc. prof., chmn. aero. dept. Wichita U., 1958-59; chief aerodynamics Vertol Helicopter Co., 1955-58; mem. Congl. Adv. Com. Aeros., 1984-86; U.S. coord. flight vehicle integration panel Adv. Group for Aerospace R&D, 1988—; cons. to industry. Author: Aerodynamics of V/Stol Flight, 1967, Aerodynamics, Aeronautics and Flight Mechanics, 1979, 2d edit., 1995; co-author: (with M.P. Papadakis) Aircraft Accident Reconstruction and Litigation, 1996; contbr. articles to profl. jours.; patentee in field. Served with USNR, 1944-46. Recipient joint award for achievement in aerospace edn. Am. Soc. Engring. Edn.-Am. Inst. Aeros. and Astronautics, 1976 Fellow Am. Inst. Aeros. and Astronautics (F.E. Newbold award, 2002); mem. ASEE, Am. Helicopter Soc. (hon. fellow), Sigma Xi, Sigma Gamma Tau, Tau Beta Pi. Clubs: Masons. Home: 611 Glenn Rd State College PA 16803-3475 Office: Pa State U Coll Engring University Park PA 16802 Office Phone: 814-863-0602. Business E-Mail: bwmaer@engr.psu.edu.

MCCORMICK, CHAD DONALD, otolaryngologist; b. Sandpoint, Idaho, Apr. 19, 1972; BS, Washington State U., Pullman, 1994; MD, U. Utah, Salt Lake City, 1999. Diplomate Am. Acad. Otolaryngology, 2005. Otolaryngology head & neck surgeon Ohio State U., Columbus, 1999—2004, Ear, Nose and Throat, Coeur d'Alene, Idaho, 2004—. Mem.: Idaho Med. Assn., Am. Acad. Otolaryngic Surgery, Am. Acad. Otolaryngology Head & Neck Surgery. Cath. Avocations: fly fishing, hunting, skiing. Office: Ear Nose Throat of Coeur d'Alene 700 Ironwood Dr Ste 236 Coeur D' Alene ID 83815 Business E-Mail: cdaent@yahoo.com.

MCCORMICK, DALE, state official; b. NY, Jan. 17, 1947; BA, U. Iowa, 1970. Mem. Maine State Senate from 18th dist, 1991-96; treas. State of Maine, Augusta, 1997—2004; dir. State Housing Aithority, Maine, 2004—. Author: Against the Grain, a Carpentry Manual for Women, 1977. Office: Maine State Housing Authority 353 Water St Augusta ME 04330-4633

MCCORMICK, DAVID ARTHUR, lawyer; b. McKeesport, Pa., Oct. 26, 1946; s. Arthur Paul and Eleanor Irene (Gibson) McC. BA, Westminster Coll., 1967; JD, Duquesne U., 1973, U. Pa., 1975. Bar: Pa. 1973, D.C. 1978, U.S. Ct. Appeals (3d cir.) 1977, U.S. Ct. Appeals (4th and D.C. cirs.) 1980, U.S. Supreme Ct. 1980. Asst. commerce counsel Penn Ctrl. R.R., Phila., 1973—76; assoc. labor counsel Consol. Rail Corp., Phila., 1976—78; atty. Dept. Army, Washington, 1978—. Author: various geneal. and hist. works; contbr. articles to profl. jours. Mem. Pa. Bar Assn., Phila. Bar Assn., DC Bar Assn., Am. Assn. for Justice, Assn. Transp. Law Profls., Soc. Petroleum Engrs., Soc. Cin., SAR, Am. Legion, Res. Officers Assn., Masons, Phi Alpha Delta, Theta Chi. Presbyterian.

MCCORMICK, DAVID HAROLD, federal agency administrator; b. Washington, Pa., Aug. 17, 1965; s. James Harold and Maryan (Garner) McCormick; m. Amy Frances Richardson, May 30, 1999; children: Elizabeth Cora, Tess Ann, Ava Garner. BS in Mech. Engring., US Mil. Acad. West Point, 1987; MPA, Princeton U., 1994, PhD, 1996. Mgmt. cons. McKinsey & Co., Inc., 1996—99; gen. mgr. core bus. markets FreeMarkets, Inc., 1999—2001, v.p., 1999—2000, sr. v.p., 2000—01, exec. v.p., 2001—02, pres., 2002—04, CEO, 2003—04; pres. Ariba, Inc., 2004—05; under sec. for industry & security US Dept. Commerce, Washington, 2005—06; dep. asst. to Pres., dep. nat. security adv. for internat. econ. affairs NSC, Washington, 2006—07; under sec. for internat. affairs US Dept. Treasury, Washington, 2007—. Bd. mem. Pitts. Tech. Coun., 2004—05, Allegheny Conf. on Cmty. Devel., 2004—05. Author: (chapt.) From Peacekeeping to Peacebuilding: Restructuring Military and Policy Institutions in El Salvador in Keeping the Peace: Multidimensional UN Operations, (book) The Downsized Warrior: America's Army in Transition. Bd. mem. Pitts. Parks Conservancy, 2001—05, Manchester Bidwell Corp., Pitts., 2000—05. Served in US Army, 1987—92, Ft. Bragg, NC, 1st Gulf War. Decorated Bronze Star; recipient Young Leader award, French-Am. Found., 1999; fellow, Earhart Found., 1996; Henry Crown Fellow, Aspen Inst., 2003. Fellow: Henry Crown Fell. Peace Corps, 2003. Office: US Dept Treasury 1500 Pennsylvania Ave Rm 4440 Washington DC 20220 *

MCCORMICK, DONALD BRUCE, retired biochemist, educator; b. Front Royal, Va., July 15, 1932; s. Jesse Allen and Elizabeth (Hord) McC.; m. Norma Jean Dunn, June 6, 1955; children: Susan Lynn, Donald Bruce, Michael Allen. BA, Vanderbilt U., Nashville, Tenn., 1953, PhD, 1958. Postdoctoral fellow U. Calif., Berkeley, 1958—60; asst. prof. Cornell U., 1960-63, assoc. prof., 1963-69, prof. nutrition, biochemistry and molecular biology, biol. scis., 1969-79, Liberty Hyde Bailey prof. nutritional biochemistry, 1978-79; chmn. dept. biochemistry Emory U., Atlanta, 1979-94, Fuller E. Callaway prof. biochemistry, 1979-99, prof. emeritus, 1999—; exec. assoc. dean sci. Emory U. Sch. Medicine, 1985-89. Vis. lectr. U. Ill, 1963; Wellcome vis. prof. U. Fla., 1986, Med. Coll. Pa., 1989; Hurley lectr. U. Calif., Davis, 1992; O'Dell lectr. U. Mo., Columbia, 1993; biochem. cons. Interdepartmental Com. on Nutrition for Nat. Def., Spain, 1958; mem. and chmn. nutrition study sect. NIH, 1977-81; mem. diet and health com., dietary guidelines implementation com., vice chmn. food and nutrition bd. NRC, Inst. Medicine of NAS; exec. com., chmn. dept. med. biochemistry, Coun. Acad. Soc., Am. Assn. Med. Colls., 1984-87; mem. biology panel U.S. Civilian R&D Found., 1998-2001. Author: (with others) Spain: Nutrition Survey of the Armed Forces, 1958, Molecular Associations in Biology, 1968, Flavins and Flavin Enzymes, 1968, Flavins and Flavoproteins, 1980, 91, Comprehensive Biochemistry, Vol. 21, 1971, Riboflavin, 1974, Metal Ions in Biological Systems, Vol. 1, 1974, Present Knowledge in Nutrition, 1976, 2006, Natural Sulphur Compounds, 1979, Vitamin B6, Metabolism and Role in Growth, 1980, Ann. Rev. of Nutrition, Vol. 1, 1981, Vol. 9, 1989, Vol. 24, 2004, Mechanisms of Enzymatic Reactions: Stereochemistry, 1986, Chemical and Biological Aspects of Vitamin B6 Catalysis, Part A, 1984, Biochemistry of Vitamin B6, 1987, Biochemistry and Molecular Biology of Vitamin B6 and PQQ-Dependent Proteins, 2000, Tietz Textbook of Clinical Chemistry, 1986, 99, Fundamentals of Clinical Chemistry, 1987, 2000, Vitamins and Biofactors in Life Science, 1992, Encyclopedia of Food Science, 1993, 2003, Encyclopedia of Life Sciences, 1999, Encyclopedia of Molecular, Biology and Molecular Medicine, 1996, 2003, McGraw-Hill Encylopedia of Science and Technology, 2006, Modern Nutrition in Health and Disease, 1988, 2006, New Trends in Biological Chemistry, 1990, Chemistry and Biochemistry of Flavins, 1991, Encyclopedia of Human Biology, 1991, 97, Liver, 1994, Molecular Biology and Biotechnology, 1995, Biochemical and Physiological Bases of Human Nutrition, 2000, 2006, Nutrition in Space Flight and Weightlessness Models, 1999, Molecular Nutrition, 2003, Encyclopedia of Dietary Supplements, 2005; editor: Vitamins and Hormones, Vitamins and Coenzymes, Ann. Rev. of Nutrition, Handbook of Vitamins. Recipient award Bausch and Lomb, 1950, award Mead Johnson, 1970, award Osborne and Mendel, 1978, award Ga. Nutrition Coun., 1989, award Bristol-Myers Squibb/Mead Johnson, 1999; Westinghouse Sci. scholar, 1950; fellow NIH, 1957-58, 58-60; Guggenheim fellow, 1966-67. Fellow AAAS, Am. Inst. Nutrition (now Am. Soc. Nutrition, pres. 1991); mem. Am. Soc. Biochemistry and Molecular Biology, Soc. Exptl. Biology and Medicine, Am. Chem. Soc., Am. Inst. Biol. Sci., Biophysics Soc., Fedn. Am. Socs. Exptl. Biology (bd. dirs., LSRO sci. steering group), Microbiol. Soc., Photobiol. Soc., N.Y. Acad. Sci., Protein Soc., Sigma Xi. Office Phone: 770-270-5508. Business E-Mail: biocdbm@emory.edu.

MCCORMICK, FRANK, research scientist; BSc in biochemistry, U. Birmingham, 1972; PhD in biochemistry, U. Cambridge, 1975; postdoctoral fellow, SUNY, Stony Brook, 1975—78, Imperial Cancer Rsch. Fund, 1978—81. Dir. molecular biology Cetus Corp., 1981—90, v.p. rsch., 1990—91, Chiron Corp., 1991—92; founder and chief sci. officer Onyx Pharm., 1992—96; dir. Comprehensive Cancer Ctr. and Cancer Rsch. Inst. U. Calif., San Francisco, 1997—, mem. Biomedical Sci. Program, 1997—, mem. Herbert Boyer Program in Bio. Sci., 1997, David A. Wood endowed chair in tumor biology and cancer rsch., 1997—. Mem. sci. adv. bd. Iconix Pharm. Recipient AACR-GHA Clowes Meml. award, 2002; fellow, Royal Soc., 1996. Mem.: Inst. Medicine. Office: Comprehensive Cancer Ctr Univ Calif San Francisco 2340 Sutter St Box 0128 San Francisco CA 94143 also: Comprehensive Rsch Ctr Univ Calif San Francisco Box 0128 San Francisco CA 94143-0128

MCCORMICK, HEATHER N., mathematics educator; d. Thomas Leon and Teresa Jackson Nix; m. Lionel Barry McCormick, May 28, 2005. BS, Miss. Coll., Clnton, 1997; MS, U. Miss., Oxford, 1999. Legal rschr. Jones & Nix, Jackson, Miss., 1993—98; grad. asst. U. Miss., 1997—99; adj. instr. Hinds CC, Raymond, Miss., 1999—2001; math. tchr. Clinton HS, Miss., 1999—2001; math. instr. Holmes CC, Ridgeland, Miss., 2001—05, Itawamba CC, Fulton, Miss., 2005—. Children's Sunday sch. tchr. 1st Bapt. Ch. Jackson, 2001—04; children's choir worker, mem. choir, Bible study leader 1st Bapt. Ch. Fulton, 2006. Mem.: Miss. Coun. Tchrs. Math., Nat. Coun. Tchrs. Math., Faculty Assn. Itawamba CC (pres. 2007—, v.p. 2006—07). Avocations: reading, music.

MCCORMICK, HOMER L., JR., lawyer; b. Frederick, Md., Nov. 11, 1928; s. Homer Lee McCormick and Rosebelle Irene Biser; m. Jacquelyn R.; children: Deidre Ann and Thomas Lee. Student, George Washington U., 1946-48; AB, San Jose State U., 1951; JD, U. Calif., San Francisco, 1961. Bar: Calif. 1961, U.S. Dist. Ct. Ctrl. Dist. Calif. 1972, U.S. Dist. No. Calif. 1961, U.S. Dist. Ct., So. Dist. Calif. 1976, U.S. Dist. Ct. of Appeals (9th cir. 1961), U.S. Tax Ct. 1977, U.S. Ct. Claims 1977, U.S. Supreme Ct. 1977. Atty. Holiway Jones State of Calif., 1961-63; atty. assoc. Rutan & Tucker, Santa Ana, Calif., 1963-66, atty. ptnr., 1966-70, atty., sr. ptnr. Costa Mesa, Calif., 1970-88, dept. head pub. law, 1974-88, mng. ptnr., 1984-88; founding ptnr., sr. ptnr. McCormick, Kidman & Behrens, Costa Mesa, 1988—. Arbitrator Am. Arbitration Assn., 1966-88; judge pro tem Orange County Superior Ct., 1975, 81, 84; profl. designation Internat. Right of Way Assn.; elected mem. Calif. Condemnation Lawyers, 1994—; spkr., lectr. in field. Contbg. author: Real Property Remedies, 1982; contbr. articles to profl. jours. Bd. govs. Bus. Com. Arts, Orange County Philharm. Soc. Lt. USMCR, 1951—56, pilot, Korea. Named Alumnus of Year Hastings Law Sch., 1992. Mem. ABA (com. chair 1991), Am. Bd. Trial Adv. (pres. O.C. chpt. 1973), Orange City Atty. Assn. (pres. 1972), Fed. Bar Assoc., Consumer Attys. Calif., Am. Judicature Soc., Orange County Bar Assn. (com. chair 1991-92), Orange County Bus. Trial Lawyers, Order Coif, Thurston Soc., Hastings Alumni Assn. (pres. 1973), US Supreme Ct. Hist. Soc., 9th Cir. Hist. Soc., Hastings 1066 Found. (pres. 1974), Springs Country Club, Delta Theta Pi Republican. Episcopalian. Avocations: boating, fishing, flying, golf, foreign travel. Office Phone: 714-755-3100. Business E-Mail: mmccormick@mkblawyers.com.

MCCORMICK, HUGH THOMAS, lawyer; b. McAlester, Okla., Nov. 24, 1944; s. Hugh O. and Lois (McGucken) McC.; m. Suzanna G. Weingarten, Dec. 5, 1975; 1 child, John B. BA, U. Mich., 1968; JD, Rutgers U., 1977; LLM in Taxation, Georgetown U., 1980. Bar: N.Y. 1977, D.C. 1979, Maine 1981. Atty. office chief counsel interpretative divsn. IRS, Washington, 1977-81; assoc. Perkins, Thompson, Hinkley & Keddy, Portland, Maine, 1981-83, LeBoeuf, Lamb, Leiby & MacRae, NYC, 1983-88, counsel, 1989-91; ptnr. LeBoeuf, Lamb, Greene & MacRae, L.L.P., NYC, 1992—2005; exec. v.p. Scottish Re Group, Ltd., Hamilton, Bermuda, 2005—. Dir. Ins. Tax Conf., 1993-04, pres., 2002-04. Mem. bd. contbrs. and advisors Jour. of Taxation of Investments; contbr. articles to profl. jours. Trustee U.S. Team Handball Found., N.J., 1985-95. Fellow Am. Bar Found.; mem. ABA (chmn. com. on taxation of ins. cos. 1989, chmn. subcom. sect. of taxation 1989-96, mem. torts and ins. practice sect., sect. on taxation), D.C. Bar Assn. Democrat. Home: 7132 Seton House Ln Charlotte NC 28277 Office: Scottish Re Group Ltd Crown House 4 Par La Ville Rd 3rd Flr Hamilton HM MX Bermuda Office Phone: 441 298 4397. Business E-Mail: hugh.mccormick@scottishre.com.

MCCORMICK, JAMES HAROLD, academic administrator; b. Ind., Pa., Nov. 11, 1938; s. Harold Clark and Mary Blanche (Truby) McCormick; m. Maryan Kough Garner, June 7, 1963; children: David Harold, Douglas Paul. BS, Indiana U. of Pa., 1959; MEd, U. Pitts., 1961, EdD, 1963, postdoctoral, 1966, Columbia U., U. Mich., 1966-67, Harvard U., 1982. Tchr. Punxsutawney (Pa.) Area Joint Sch. Dist., 1959-61; adminstr. Baldwin-Whitehall Schs., Pitts., 1961-64; grad. asst. U. Pitts., 1962-63; asst. supt. instrn. Washington (Pa.) City Schs., 1964-65; prof. dept. edn. and psychology, asst. dean acad. affairs, acting dean acad. affairs, acting dean tchr. edn., asst. to pres., v.p. adminstrn. and fin. Shippensburg (Pa.) U., 1965-73; pres. Bloomsburg (Pa.) U., 1973-83, pres. emeritus, 1983—; founding chancellor Pa. State System Higher Edn., Harrisburg, 1983—2001; chancellor Minn. State Colls. and Univs., 2001—. Falk intern in politics, 1959; mem. adv. bd. Pa. Ednl. Policy Seminar; mem. Gov.'s Econ. Devel. Partnership Bd.; mem. higher edn. adv. coun. Pa. State Bd. Edn.; past commr. Edn. Commn. of the States; past chmn. Midwestern Higher Edn. Compact; bd. mem. Great North Alliance, Minn. Job Skills Partnership; founder, mem. Minn. P-16 Edn. Partnership; active Govs. Edn. Coun.; mem. postsecondary edn. and workforce devel. adv. com. Edn. Comm. States. Contbr. articles profl. jours. Named One of 10 Outstanding Young Men of Yr., Pa. Jr. C. of C.; recipient Young Leader in Edn. award Phi Delta Kappa, 1981, Disting. Alumnus award Indiana U. Pa., 1981, Outstanding Alumni award Bloomsburg U., 1984, Outstanding Alumnus award U. Pitts., 1985, Adler award Pa. Edn. Assn., 1992; selected CIVITAS Prague mission, 1995, Presdl. Lectures, Kuwait U., 1993, Svc. award Coll. and Univ. Pub. Rels., Assn. Pa., 1999, Disting. Svc. award Pa. Assn. Couns. of Trustees, 1998, Alumni Assn. Leadership award Bloomsburg U., 1999; McCormick Human Svcs. Ctr. named in his honor Bloomsburg U., 1983; McCormick House named in his honor Dixon U., 1994. Mem. Am. Assn. State Colls. and Univs. (Pa. state rep. 1988-93, former chmn. acad. and student pers. com., mem. com. on state rels. and task force on ednl. equity, chmn. policies and purposes com., mem. Internat. Edn.), Am. Coun. on Edn. (commn. on women in higher edn.), Nat. Assn. Sys. Heads, (exec. com., past pres.), Commn. State Colls. and Univs. (mem. and past chmn. govt. rels. and student rels. coms.), Assn. Governing Bds. (adv. coun.), Am. Assn. for Affirmative Action, Am. Assn. Higher Edn., Am. Assn. Sch. Adminstrs., Am. Assn. Univ. Adminstrs. (Tosney Leadership award 1993), Pa. Assn. Colls. and Univs. (bd. dirs., chair 1982), Natl. Ctr. for the Study of Sport in Soc., Pa. Black Conf. on Higher Edn., State Higher Edn. Exec. Ofcrs. (exec. com., chair Fed. Relations Com.), Pers. Assn., Bloomsburg Area C. of C. (pres. 1983), Harrisburg Rotary (bd. dirs. to 1992), St. Paul Rotary (bd. dir.), Phi Delta Kappa. Office: Wells Fargo Pl 30 7th St East Ste 350 Saint Paul MN 55101 Home: 10560 Pinnacle Way Woodbury MN 55129 Office Phone: 651-296-7971.

MCCORMICK, JOHN HOYLE, lawyer; b. Pensacola, Fla., July 30, 1933; s. Clyde Hoyle and Orrie Brooks (Frink) McC.; m. Patricia McCall, Dec. 27, 1974. BS, U. Fla., 1955; JD, Stetson U., 1958. Bar: Fla. 1958. Ptnr. McCormick, Drury & Scaff, Jasper, Fla., 1958-74; county atty., 1973—; sr. ptnr. McCormick, Drury & Scaff, Jasper, 1974-91; pvt. practice Jasper, 1991—. County judge, Hamilton County, Fla., 1960-72; local counsel So. Ry. System, 1968—, CSX, Ry., 1972—; atty. Hamilton County Devel. Authority, 1970-91; bd. dirs. 1st Fed. Savs. Bank Fla.; bd. dirs., v.p., atty. Hamilton County Bank. Mayor City of White Springs, Fla., 1959; pres. Hamilton County C. of C., Jasper, 1961. Mem.: Masons, Phi Delta Phi. Democrat. Methodist. Avocations: gardening, motorhome camping, college football. Home: 403 2nd Ave NW Jasper FL 32052-6687 Office: 215 2nd St NE Jasper FL 32052-6616 Address: PO Drawer O Jasper FL 32052-0695

MCCORMICK, JOHN OWEN, retired comparative literature educator; b. Thief River Falls, Minn., Sept. 20, 1918; s. Owen Charles and Marie Antoinette Beauchemin (Smith) McC.; m. Helen Manuel, 1942; m. Mairi Clare MacInnes, 1954; children: Jonathan, Peter, Antoinette, Fergus. BA magna cum laude, U. Minn., 1941; MA, Harvard U., 1947, PhD, 1951. Dean, lectr. Salzburg Seminar in Am. Studies, 1951-52; lectr., prof. Free U., Berlin, 1952-59; prof. comparative lit. Rutgers U., 1959-87, prof. emeritus, 1987—. Vis. prof. Nat. U. Mexico, 1961-62, Hachioji (Tokyo) seminar, 1979; Christian Gauss Seminar lectr. Princeton, 1969; resident fellow Sch. Letters of Ind. U., 1970 Author: The Middle Distance: A Comparative History of American Imaginative Literature, 1919-32, 1971, The Complete Aficionado, 1967, 2d edit., 1998, (with Mairi MacInnes McCormick) Versions of Censorship, 1962, Der moderne amerikanische Roman, 1960, Amerikanische Lyrik, 1957, Catastrophe and Imagination, 1957, 2d edit., 1998, Fiction as Knowledge, 1975, 2d edit., 1999, George Santayana: A Biography, 1987, 2003, Wolfe, Malraux, Hesse, 1987, American and European Literary Imagination: 1919-1932, 2000; editor: (with G. Core) Sallies of the Mind: Essays of Francis Fergusson, 1998, Seagoing: Essay-Memoirs, 2000. With USNR, 1941-46. Recipient prize for non-fiction Longview Found., 1960, Am. Acad. and Inst. Arts and Letters award, 1988; Gugenheim fellow, 1964-65, 79-80, Bruern fellow Leeds (Eng.) U., 1975-76, NEH fellow, 1983-84, hon. fellow U. York, 1992. Mem. Taurino Club (London), Harvard Club (NYC), Authors League

MCCORMICK, MARIE CLARE, pediatrician, educator; b. Winchester, Mass., Jan. 7, 1946; d. Richard John and Clare Bernadine (Keleher) McC.; m. Robert Jay Blendon, Dec. 30, 1977. BA magna cum laude, Emmanuel Coll., 1967, LHD (hon.), 2006; MD, Johns Hopkins U., 1971, ScD, 1978; MA, Harvard U., 1991; D of Humane Letters (hon.), Emmanuel Coll., Boston, 2006. Diplomate Am. Bd. Pediat. Pediatric resident, fellow Johns Hopkins Hosp., Balt., 1971-75, rsch. fellow, 1972-75; asst. prof. U. Ill. Schs. Medicine & Pub. Health, Chgo., 1975-76; pediat. instr. Johns Hopkins Med. Sch., Balt., 1976-78; asst. prof. healthcare orgn. Johns Hopkins Sch. Hygiene & Pub. Health, 1978-81; asst. prof. pediat. U. Pa., Phila., 1981-86, assoc. prof. pediat., 1986-87, Harvard Med. Sch., Boston, 1987-91, prof. pediat., 1992—, 1st Sumner and Esther Feldberg prof. maternal/child health, 1996—; prof. Harvard Sch. Pub. Health, Boston, 1992—2003, chair maternal and child health, 1992—2003, prof. Soc., Human Devel. and Health, 2003—. Adj. assoc. prof. pediat. U. Pa.,

1987-92; active attending physician, Johns Hopkins Hosp., 1976-81, asst. physician Children's Hosp. Phila., 1981-84, assoc. physician, 1984-86, sr. physician, 1986-87, assoc. pediatrician Brigham & Women's Hosp., 1987—; sr. assoc. in medicine Children's Hosp., 1987—; sr. assoc. in pediat. Beth Israel Deaconess Med. Ctr., 1987—; vis. prof. Wash. U., St. Louis, 1993; editl. bds. Health Svcs. Rsch., 1985-94, Pediat. in Rev., 1986-91, Pediat., 1993-99; assoc. editor Jour. Ambulatory Pediatric Assn., 1999—; adv. coun. Ctr. Perinatal & Family Health Brigham & Women's Hosp., 1991—; cons. to numerous coms., orgns. and bds. Contbr. articles to profl. jours. Adv. The David and Lucile Packard Found., 1993-95; bd. dirs. Family Planning Coun. S.E. Pa., 1984-87; chair com. child health Mayor's Commn. Phila., 1982-83. Named Henry Strong Denison scholar, Johns Hopkins Sch. Medicine, 1971, Leonard Davis Inst.; recipient Johns Hopkins U. Soc. Scholars award, 1995, award, Nat. Assn. of Nat. Acads., 2001, David Rall award, Inst. Medicine, 2005; Health Econs. fellow, U. Pa., 1984. Fellow Am. Acad. Pediat.; mem. AAAS, Inst. Medicine of NAS, Ambulatory Pediat. Assn. (Rsch. award 1996), Soc. Pediatric Rsch. (sr., Douglas K. Richardson award 2006), Am. Pediatric Soc., Am. Pub. Health Assn., Internat. Epidemiol. Assn., Assn. Health Svcs. Rsch., Ea. Soc. Pediatric Rsch., Soc. Pediatric Epidemiologic Rsch., Assn. Tchrs. Maternal and Child Health, Mass. Med. Soc., Norfolk Dist. Med. Soc., Mass. Pub. Health Assn., Johns Hopkins U. Soc. Scholars. Office: Harvard Sch Pub Health 677 Huntington Ave Boston MA 02115-6096 Business E-Mail: mmccormi@hsph.harvard.edu.

MCCORMICK, PAULA SHURLING, elementary school educator; b. Macon, Ga., Sept. 28, 1951; d. Harley Frank and Christine (Thaxton) Shurling; m. John Douglas McCormick, June 24, 1973; children: John, Jason, Josh, Justin. BSHE, U. Ga., 1973; MED, Ga. So. U., 1983, EdS, 1987. nat. bd. cert. tchr., Ga., 2003. Tchr. Blackwell Jr. High Sch., Elberton, Ga., 1973, Willow Hill, Portal, Ga., 1973—74, Southeast Bulloch Jr. High Sch., Brooklet, Ga., 1974-76, Brooklet Elem. Sch., 1986—. Life mem. supt.'s coun. Statesboro, Ga. Mem. Ga. Coun. Tchrs. Math., Profl. Assn. Ga. Educators. Methodist. Avocations: needlecrafts, crocheting, reading. Home: 902 Rushing Rd Brooklet GA 30415-6372 Office: Brooklet Elem Sch 600 West Lane St Brooklet GA 30415-6216

MCCORMICK, QUEEN ESTHER WILLIAMS, clergyman; b. Apr. 5, 1941; BA in Theology, Internat. Sem., 1986; MA in Theology, Logos Bible Coll., 1993, PhD in Ministry, 1996. Adj. prof. Internat. Sem., Plymouth, Fla., 1987,91,98; founder, pastor New Birth House of Prayer for All People, Ft. Lauderdale, Fla., 1980—; pres. CEO Compassionate Hearts-Serving Hands, 2000. Radio/TV min., 1974-97; gospel singer, 1946—. Author: The Elect Lady in Ministry, 3d edit., 1998. Office: PO Box 5712 Fort Lauderdale FL 33310-5712

MCCORMICK, RICHARD LEVIS, academic administrator; b. New Brunswick, NJ, Dec. 26, 1947; s. Richard Patrick and Katheryne Crook (Levis) McCormick; m. Joan C. Barry, July 22, 2006; children: Elizabeth, Michael. BA in Am. Studies, Amherst Coll., 1969; PhD in History, Yale U., 1976. From asst. prof. to prof. Rutgers U., New Brunswick, NJ, 1976—92, dean Faculty Arts and Scis., 1989—92; exec. vice chancellor, provost, vice chancellor acad. affair U. N.C., Chapel Hill, 1992—95; pres. U. Wash., Seattle, 1995—2002, Rutgers U., New Brunswick, NJ, 2002—. Author: From Realignment to Reform: Political Change in New York State 1893-1910, 1981, The Party Period and Public Policy: American Politics from the Age of Jackson to the Progressive Era, 1986. Fellow, Am. Coun. Learned Socs., 1978—79, John Simon Guggenheim Meml. Found., 1985. Mem.: Phi Beta Kappa. Office: Rutgers Univ New Brunswick NJ 08901 Office Phone: 732-932-7454. E-mail: rlm@rutgers.edu.

MCCORMICK, ROBERT JUNIOR, former federal agency administrator; b. Boone, Iowa, Aug. 1, 1929; s. Ivyl Robert and Darlene Adel (Bowes) McC.; m. Shirley May Zerbe, Dec. 24, 1950; children: Elaine McCormick Newland, Kathleen, Michael, Tara McCormick Wieting, Tammy McCormick Kirby. Grad., Flying Sch., Williams Field, Ariz., 1951, Parachute Jump Sch., 1964, Armed Forces Staff Coll., Norfolk, Va., 1966, Def. Systems Mgmt. Coll., Ft. Belvoir, Va., 1975; BS in Mech. Engring., Tex. Tech. U., 1963; cert., Harvard U. Def. Studies Program, 1984. Served as enlisted man USAF, 1948—51, commd. 2d lt., 1951, advanced through grades to col., 1971, pilot U.S., Japan, Europe, Vietnam, fighter pilot Korean War, 1951—52; exec. officer to Gen. George Brown 7th Air Force, Saigon, Vietnam, 1969—70; mil. asst. to asst. sec. of Air Force for research and devel. USAF, Washington, 1970—74, ret., 1975; exec. officer NASA, Washington, 1976—80; adminstrv. asst. to sec. of Air Force USAF, Washington, 1980—94; mem. U.S. Sr. Exec. Service, 1979—94; pres. McG, Ltd., Fairfax, Va. Mem. Pres.'s transition team Dept. of Def., 2001. Decorated Air Force Legion of Merit, Bronze star, Air medal, Meritorious Svc. medal, Air Force Exceptional Civilian Svc. medal, NASA Exceptional Svc. medal, 1980; recipient Presdl. Meritorious Rank, 1989, Disting. Civilian Svc. medal Dept. Def., 1994, Commendation medal State of Calif., 2001. Mem. ASME, DAV, Air Force Assn., Nat. Def. Indsl. Assn., Order of Daedalians, St. Andrews Soc. Washington, Mil. Order of Carabao, Chevaliers du Testevin. Clubs: Army-Navy Country (Fairfax, Va.). E-mail: mcgltd1@aol.com.

MCCORMICK, STEVEN D., lawyer; b. Waterloo, Iowa, Apr. 24, 1946; AB, U. Notre Dame, 1968; JD, Northwestern U., 1971. Bar: Ill. 1972, NY 1992. Ptnr. Kirkland & Ellis LLP, Chgo., 1977—, head in-house trial advocacy prog., 1993—. Lectr., demonstrator, instr. Nat. Inst. Trial Advocacy, Chgo. and Boulder, Colo., 1989—98; adj. prof. integrated trial advocacy course Northwestern U. Sch. Law, 1997—. Articles editor: Northwestern U. Law Rev., 1970—71. Named one of Top 10 Trial Lawyers in Am., Nat. Law Jour., 2006, Am.'s Leading Lawyers for Bus., Chambers USA, 2006. Office: Kirkland & Ellis LLP 200 E Randolph Dr Fl 54 Chicago IL 60601-6636 Office Phone: 312-861-2246. Office Fax: 312-861-2200. E-mail: smccormick@kirkland.com. *

MCCORMICK, STEVEN THOMAS, insurance company executive; b. Phila., Dec. 18, 1955; s. Howard C. and Ruth Marion (Stahl) McC.; m. Helene Mary Trommler, Nov. 21, 1981; children: Matthew Thomas, Bria Helene. BBA, U. Ky., 1978; gen. ins cert., Ins. Inst. Am., 1980; MBA, Sullivan U., 2006. Cert. adminstrv. mgr., purchasing mgr., ins. agt., Ky., 1980. Supr. trainee Ky. Farm Bur. Ins. Cos., Louisville, 1978-79, supr. micrographics dept., 1979-83, supr. adminstrv. svcs., 1983-85, mgr. adminstrv. svcs., 1985-89, asst. v.p. ops., 1989—, dir. adminstrv. svcs., 2005—. Bd. dirs. Ky. Athletic Hall of Fame, 2005—. Named to Hon. Order Ky. Cols., Outstanding Employee of Yr., Nat. Assn. of Mut. Ins. Cos., 1986; recipient Cert. of Excellence, Jefferson County Bd. Edn. Mem. Adminstrv. Mgmt. Soc. (internat. top recruiter 1985, chpt. pres. 1988, internat. dir. area 7 1990-91, internat. v.p. profl. devel. 1992-93), Acad. Adminstrv. Mgmt. (mem. bd. regents 1991-92, internat. v.p. 1992-93, internat. pres. 1993-94), U. Ky. Alumni Assn., Sigma Nu. Republican. Home: 706 Elsmere Cir Louisville KY 40223-2764 Office: Ky Farm Bur Ins Cos PO Box 20700 Louisville KY 40250-0700

MCCORMICK, WALTER BERNARD, JR., trade association administrator; b. Kansas City, Mo., Feb. 8, 1954; s. Walter Bernard and Dorothy Ann (Power) M.; m. Mary Lou Edelsen, Jan. 3, 1987; children: Walter Patrick, Megan Boutin. Student, Georgetown U., 1975; BJ, U. Mo., 1976, JD, 1979. Bar: Mo. 1979, D.C. 1980. Assoc. Leighton, Conklin, Lemov & Jacobs, Washington, 1980-81, Pepper, Hamilton & Scheetz, Washington, 1981-82; legis. asst. US Senate, Washington, 1982-84; gen. counsel US Senate Com. Commerce, Sci. and Transp., Washington, 1985-87, minority chief counsel, staff dir., 1988-92; gen. counsel US Dept. Transp., Washington, 1992-93; ptnr. Bryan Cave LLP, Washington, 1993—98; pres., CEO Am. Trucking Assns., 1998—2001, US Telecom Assn., 2001—. Mem. City Club, Washington, 1993—. Republican. Roman Catholic. Office: US Telecom Assn 607 14th St NW Ste 400 Washington DC 20005 Office Phone: 202-326-7300.

MCCORMICK, WILLIAM PAUL, ambassador; b. Providence, Aug. 18, 1939; m. Gail McCormick; 6 children. Attended, Roger Williams Jr. Coll., Boston U. With Conn. Gen. Life Ins. Co., San Francisco, 1963—65; co-owner Refectory Internat. Inc.; co-founder, pres. McCormick & Schmick's Seafood Restaurants, Inc., 1972—94, chmn., 2003—04, chmn. emeritus, 2004—05; U.S. amb. to New Zealand and Samoa US Dept. State, Wellington, 2005—. Served with Army Reserve Military Police. Recipient Secretary's award, US Dept. Veteran's Affairs. Office: 4360 Wellington Pl Washington DC 20521

MCCOTTER, THADDEUS GEORGE, congressman; b. Livonia, Mich., Aug. 22, 1965; s. Dennis and Joan McCotter; m. Rita Michel; children: George, Timothy, Emilia. BA in Polit. Sci., summa cum laude, U. Detroit, 1987, JD, 1990. Bar: Mich. 1991. Trustee Schoolcraft C.C., 1989; commr. Wayne County, Mich., 1992-98; mem. 9th dist. Mich. Senate, Lansing, 1998—2002; mem. US Congress from 3rd Mich. dist., 2003—. Mem. com. budget US Congress, com. internat. relations, com. small bus. Rep. precinct del., 1986; chair Wayne County Rep. com. Recipient Outstanding Michigander award, Mich. Jaycees, 2001, Legis. of Yr., Police Officers Assn. of Mich., 2002. Republican. Roman Catholic. Office: District Office 17197 N Laurel Pk Dr Ste 533 Livonia MI 48152-7908 also: US Congress 1632 LHOB Washington DC 20515-2211 Office Phone: 202-225-8171, 734-632-0314. Office Fax: 202-225-2667, 734-632-0373. *

MCCOURT, FRANK (FRANCIS MCCOURT), writer; b. Bklyn., Aug. 19, 1931; s. Malachy and Angela McCourt; m. Ellen McCourt. Bachelors, Masters, NYU. Tchr. McKee Vocat. and Tech. Sch., Peter Stuyvesant H.S., NYC. Author: Angela's Ashes, 1996 (National Book Critics Circle award 1997, Pulitzer prize 1997), Tis: A memoir, 2000, Through Irish Eyes: Visual Companion to Angela in Court's Ireland, 2001, Brotherhood, 2001, Teacher Man, 2005; (films) The McCourts of Limerick, 1998, The McCourts of NY, 1999. Address: Simon & Schuster Trade Division 1230 Avenue Of The Americas New York NY 10020-1513

MCCOWEN, ALEC, actor; b. Tunbridge Wells, May 26, 1925; s. Duncan and Mary (Walkden) McC., Ed. Skinners Sch., Tunbridge Wells, and Royal Acad. Dramatic Art. Appeared as Touchstone, Ford, Richard II, Mercutio, Malvolio, Oberon at Old Vic Theatre, 1959-60; appeared with R.S.C. as Fool in King Lear, 1964, Hadrian VII, 1968, The Philanthropist, 1970, The Misanthrope, 1972, as Dr. Dysart in Equus, 1972, as Henry Higgins in Pygmalion, 1974, as Ben in The Family Dance, 1976, Someone Who'll Watch Over Me, 1992, as Prospero in The Tempest, 1994, as Gaev in The Cherry Orchard, 1995; appeared with Prospect Co. as Antony in Antony and Cleopartra, 1977, in solo performance of St. Mark's Gospel, 1978, 81, as Frank in Tishoo, 1979, as Malvolio in Twelfth Night (TV), 1980, of Kipling, 1984, as Reilly in The Cocktail Party, 1986, as Nicolai in Fathers and Sons, 1987, as Vladimir in Waiting for Godot, 1987; appeared with Nat. Theatre and Abbey Dublin as Jack in Dancing at Cughnasa, 1990; appeared with Nat. Theatre as Crocker-Harris in The Browning Version, Arthur in Harlequinade, Capt. Corcoran in H.M.S. Pinafore, 1981, Adolf Hitler in The Portage to San Cristobal of AH, PTO, 1982, Reginald, in 2000 Quartet; films: Frenzy, 1971, Travels with My Aunt, 1973, Stevie, 1978, Personal Services, Cry Freedom, 1987, The Age of Innocence, 1992, Gangs of New York, 2000; TV: Private Lives, 1976; author: Young Gemini,1979, Double Bill, 1980, Personal Mark, 1984. Named Best Actor, Evening Standard (now New Standard), 1968, 73, 82, Variety Club Stage Actor, 1970. Office: care Conway Van Gelder 18-21 Jermyn St London SW1 Y6HB England

MCCOWN, LINDA JEAN, medical technology educator; d. William Ernest and Mary Elizabeth McC. BS, Pa. State U., 1975; MS, U. Pitts., 1979; ABD, U. Mo., St. Louis, 2007. Cert. med. technologist, clin. lab. scientist. Microbiology aide Pa. State U., University Park, 1973—74; med. technologist, asst. supr., rsch. technologist Children's Hosp. of Pitts., 1975—80; asst. prof. med. tech., assoc. program dir. Ctrl. Wash. U., Ellensburg, 1980—99; asst. prof. clinilab. sci. Jewish Hosp. Coll. of Nursing and Allied Health at Wash. Univ. Med. Ctr., 1999—2005; affiliate asst. prof. U. Mo., St. Louis, 2000—04; assoc. prof., program dir. clin. lab. sci. U. Ill., Springfield, 2005—. Critiquer, insp. Nat. Accreditation Agy. for Clin. Lab. Scis., Chgo., 1984—; test item writer Nat. Cert. Agy., Lenexa, Kans., 1989—; recruiter Am. Soc. Clin. Pathologists, Chgo., 1988-98; guest lectr. physician asst. program U. Wash., Seattle, 1996-99; presenter, spkr. in field. Contbr. articles to profl. jours. Stephen ministry, deacon First Presbyn. Ch., Yakima, Wash., 1992-98; bd. dirs. The Campbell Farm, Wapato, Wash., 1990-95; rally chmn. Heifer Project Internat., Wapato, 1991-94; profl. affairs com. chairperson Mo. Orgn. for Clin. Lab. Sci., 1999-01; host com. Clin. Lab. Educators' Conf., 2001; identity com. Second Bapt. Ch., St. Louis, 2001-03. Recipient Key to the Future award Mo. Orgn. Clin. Lab. Sci., 2000. Mem. Am. Soc. for Med. Tech. (mem. commn. on accreditation 1988-91), Am. Soc. Clin. Lab. Sci. (Ill. Springfield-So. br. pres.-elect 2006-07, pres. 2007-08), Wash. State Soc. for Clin. Lab. Sci. (conv. chair 1992, edn. chair 1986-94, 95-96, Pres.'s award 1992, convention hospitality chair and cons. 1998), Mo. orgn. for Clin. Lab Sci. (chmn. hematology sci. assembly 2001-2003), Columbia Basin Soc. Clin. Lab. Sci. (pres.-elect 1993, pres. 1994-95), Am. Assn. for Adult and Continuing Edn. (spkr., presenter internat. unit), Omicron Sigma, Phi Kappa Phi. Avocations: photography, tennis, travel, music. Office: U Ill - Springfield Mail Stop HSB 314 One University Plz Springfield IL 62703 E-mail: mccown.linda@uis.edu.

MCCOY, DOROTHY ELOISE, writer, educator; b. Houston, Sept. 4, 1916; d. Robert Major and Evie Letha (Grimes) Morgan; m. Roy McCoy, May 22, 1942; children: Roy Jr., Robert Nicholas (dec.). BA, Rice U., 1938; MA, Tex. A&I U., 1968; postgrad., Ind. U., 1971, U. Calif., Berkeley, 1972, U. Calif., Santa Cruz, 1977. Cert. secondary tchr. BA Corpus Christi (Tex.) Independent Schs., 1958-84, MA, 1985; freelance writer Corpus Christi, 1987—; co-owner United Iron and Machine Works, Corpus Christi, 1946-82. Freelance lectr.; master tchr. Nat. Coun. Tchrs. English, 1971, Nat. Humanities Faculty, Concord Mass., 1977-78; mem. steering com. Edn. Summit, Corpus Christi, 1990-91, mem. summit update, 1991. Author: A Teacher Talks Back, 1990, Let's Restructure the Schools, 1992; contbr. articles and columns to profl. jours. Sr. advisor to U.S. Congress, Washington, 1982-85; trustee Corpus Christi Librs., 1987-90; mem. Corpus Christi Mus.; mem. Friends Corpus Christi Librs., chmn. publicity com., 1988; participant Walk to Emmaus Group, 1990, UPDATE, U. Tex., 1978-92; cons. Libr. Bd. Democracy competition Am. 2000; sec. adminstrv. bd. First United Meth. Ch., 1992-93. Recipient Teacher of Yr. Paul Caplan Humanitarian award, 1981, Advanced Senior Option Program award, 1968. Mem. AAUW, LWV, Phi Beta Kappa. Avocations: gardening, writing. Home Phone: 361-852-0726; Office Phone: 361-852-0726.

MCCOY, DUSTAN ELWOOD, manufacturing executive, lawyer; b. Ashland, Ky., July 16, 1949; s. Elwood and Mary Anna (Mullins) McC.; m. Rebecca Lancashire, Feb. 28, 1970; children: Dustan Chad, Drew Christopher. BA, Eastern Ky. U., 1971; JD, No. Ky. U., 1978. Bar: Ky. 1978. Atty. Ashland Oil Inc., Ky., 1973-83, sr. atty. Ky., 1983-85, gen. atty. Ky., 1985, assoc. gen. counsel Ky.; sr. v.p., gen. counsel, corp. sec., exec. v.p. Witco Corp.; v.p., gen. counsel Brunswick Corp., 1999—2000, pres. Brunswick boat group, 2000—05, chmn., CEO, 2005—. Bd. dirs. La.-Pacific Corp. Local bd. mem. U.S. SSS, 1987; mem. law bd. visitors No. Ky. U. Mem. ABA, Ky. Bar Assn. Avocations: jogging, hunting, fishing. Office: Brunswick Corp 1 N Field Ct Lake Forest IL 60045-4811 Office Phone: 847-735-4700. Office Fax: 847-735-4765. *

MCCOY, JEANIE SHEARER, analytical chemist, consultant; b. Mancelona, Mich., May 27, 1921; d. Theophil R. and Goldie Margaret (Halladay) Schroeder; m. Theodore R. Shearer, June 14, 1958 (div. 1964); 1 child, Blair Barnett; m. George Altha McCoy, July 23, 1966. AA, North Park Coll., 1941; BS, Northwestern U., 1944; MS, No. Ill. U., 1970. Jr. analytical chemist Buick Motor divsn. GM, Melrose Park, Ill., 1944—45; asst. rsch. chemist Hodson Oil Corp., Chgo., 1945—47; asst. analytical chemist Internat. Harvester Co., Melrose Park, 1947—49, analytical chemist, 1949—60, prin. chemist, 1961—74, supr. metal process control, 1974—82; cons. cutting fluid mgmt. divsn. JMT, Inc., Lombard, Ill., 1983—2003; cons. Jeanie McCoy Cutting Fluid Mgmt., Lombard, 2004—. Editor: Lubrication Engring. Mag., 1979—2000; contbr. chapters to books. Recipient P. M. Ku award, 1991, Internat. award, 2000. Fellow: Soc. Tribologists and Lubrication Engrs. (Allan Mantafel award Chgo sect. 1987); mem.: AAUW, Soc. Mfg. Engrs., Abrasive Engring. Soc., Am. Chem. Soc., Soc. Automotive Engrs. Avocations: seashell collecting, stamp collecting/philately, fitness activities. Home and Office: 654 N West Rd Lombard IL 60148-1547 Office Phone: 630-627-2721. Personal E-mail: j10mccoy@aol.com.

MCCOY, JERRY JACK, lawyer; b. Pitts., Aug. 4, 1941; s. Norris and Martha (Jack) McC.; m. Alexandra Armstrong; children: MadeleineRena, Allison Norah, Jonathan Howard. BS, W.Va. U., 1963; LLB, Duke U., 1966; LLM in Taxation, N.Y.U., 1967. Bar: D.C. 1968, N.Y. 1967. Assoc. Silverstein & Mullens, Washington, 1968-72, ptnr., 1973-92; of counsel Reid and Priest, NYC, Washington, 1992-94; sole practitioner Washington, 1994—. Adj. law faculty U. Miami, Fla., 1983—, Law Ctr. Georgetown U., 1996—. Co-author: Family Foundation Handbook, 2007; exec. editor Tax Management, Estates Gifts and Trusts series, Washington, 1972—92, co-founder, co-editor Charitable Gift Planning News, Dallas, 1983—, Family Foundation Advisor, 2002—; contbr. articles to profl. jours. Mem. ABA, Am. Law Inst., Am. Coll. Trust and Estate Counsel (past chair com. on charitable planning and exempt orgns.), Am. Coll. Tax Counsel. Home: 3560 Winfield Ln NW Washington DC 20007-2368 Office: PO Box 66491 Washington DC 20035-6491 Business E-Mail: jjm@mccoylaw.com.

MCCOY, JOHN BONNET, retired bank executive; b. Columbus, Ohio, June 11, 1943; s. John Gardner and Jeanne Newlove (Bonnet) McC.; m. Jane Deborah Taylor, Apr. 21, 1968; children: Tracy Bonnet, Paige Taylor, John Taylor. BA, Williams Coll., Williamstown, Mass., 1965; MBA, Stanford U., Calif., 1967; LLD (hon.), Williams Coll., 1991; D of Bus. Adminstrn. (hon.), Ohio State U., 1993; LLD (hon.), Kenyon Coll., Gambier, Ohio, 1994. With Banc One Corp., Columbus NA, Columbus, Ohio, 1970—, banking officer, 1970-73, v.p., 1973-77, pres., 1977-83; pres., COO Banc One Corp., Columbus, Ohio, 1983-84, pres., CEO, 1984-87, chmn., CEO, 1987-99, also bd. dirs., past chmn., CEO Chgo., 1999. Pres., COO Banc One Corp., Columbus, Ohio, 1983-84, pres., CEO, 1984-87, chmn. CEO, 1987—, also bd. dirs.; pres. Bank One Trust Co., 1979-81; bd. dirs. Cardinal Health, Inc., Fed. Home Loan Mortgage Corp., 1990-2005, AT&T, Choice Point, Inc., InsLogic; fed. adv. coun. Fed. Res. Sys., 1991-93. Active Boy Scouts Am.; trustee, chmn. bd. dirs. Kenyon Coll., 1992-95; trustee Stanford U., 1986-96, Williams Coll., 1996-2001, Battelle Meml. Inst.; bd. dirs., chmn. bd. PGA Tour; past pres. Columbus Area Growth Found.; chmn. Capitol South Urban Redevel. Corp., 1975-2007. Capt. USAF, 1967-70. Recipient Ernest C. Arbuckle award Stanford U., 1994. Mem. Columbus C. of C. (past chmn., trustee), Am. Bankers Assn., Bankers Roundtable (bd. dirs. 1989-94), Assn. Bank Holding Cos., Young Pres. Orgn. (chmn. Columbus chpt. 1982-83), Cypress Point Club, Seminole Golf Club, Links Club N.Y.C. Episcopalian. Office: Banc One Corp 191 W Nationwide Blvd Ste 625 Columbus OH 43215

MCCOY, JOHN DENNY, artist; b. Columbus, Ohio, Dec. 13, 1945; s. Robert William and Dorothy Louise (Denny) McC.; children: Melinda Rene and Nathan Robert. Cert. of Grad., Columbus Coll. Art and Design, 1967; MFA, Washington U., St. Louis, 1969. Instr. Columbus Coll. Art and Design, Ohio, 1969—73; program dir. Presidio of Monterey, Calif., 1975—78; gallery dir. Richard Danskin Gallery, Carmel, Calif., 1978—79, Bleich Gallery West, Carmel, Calif., 1979—80. One-man shows include Brunswick Gallery, Columbus, 1973, Seaside, Calif. City Hall, 1978, Bleich Gallery, Carmel, Calif., 1980, Angles Gallery, Santa Monica, Calif., 1987, Hagger Gallery, Dallas, 1999, Flatbed Gallery, Austin, Tex., 2000, O2 Gallery, Austin, Tex., 2004, d. berman Gallery, Austin, Tex., 2005; exhibited in group shows at Columbus Mus. Art, 1965, Laclede Town Gallery, St. Louis, 1967, Merton Boyd Gallery, Columbus, 1970, Changing Scene Gallery, 1971-72, Gallery Five, Columbus, 1972, Monterey Peninsula Mus. Art, 1976-77, Angles Gallery, Santa Monica, 1989, Richard Bennett Gallery, L.A., 1991, Arlington Mus. Art, 1998, Meridian Internat. Ctr., Washington, Vietnam, China, Singapore, Indonesia, 1999-2000, Haggerty Gallery, Dallas, 2000, d. berman Gallery, Austin, Tex., 2002, 04. Columbus Coll. Art and Design scholar, 1963; Ford Found. grantee, 1966; Washington U. fellow, 1968-69. Home: PO Box 989 Wimberley TX 78676-0989

MCCOY, JOHN JOSEPH, lawyer; b. Cin., Mar. 15, 1952; s. Raymond F. and Margaret T. (Hohmann) McC. BS in Math. summa cum laude, Xavier U., 1974; JD, U. Chgo., 1977. Bar: Ohio 1977, D.C. 1980. Ptnr. Taft, Stettinius & Hollister, Cin., 1977—, exec. com., 2002—. Lectr. Greater Cin. C. of C., 1984. Pro bono rep. Jr. Achievement Greater Cin., 1978; fund raiser Dan Beard coun. Boy Scouts Am., 1983; fund raising team leader Cin. Regatta, Cin. Ctr. Devel. Disorders, 1983; account mgr. United Appeal, Cin., 1984; mem. green areas trust adv. com. Village of Indian Hill, 1994-98. Named to Ohio Super Lawyers, 2006, Best Lawyers in Am. Mem. ABA, Ohio State Bar Assn. (banking, comml. and bankruptcy law com., corp. law com., fed. ct. practice com.), Cin. Bar Assn. (fed. cts., common pleas cts. and negligence law coms., trustee Vol. Lawyers for the Poor Found. 1994-2007, chmn. 1996-97), Cin. Inn. of Ct. (barrister 1984-86), Cin. Athletic Club (pres. bd. trustees 1986-89, nominating com. 1989—), Rhodesian Ridgeback Club of the U.S. (bd. dirs. 2000—). Office Phone: 513-357-9348.

MCCOY, JOHN V., lawyer; b. Waukesha, Wis., June 7, 1958; BS, U. Wis., Oshkosh, 1980; JD, Drake U., 1984. Bar: Wis. 1988, Iowa 1984, US Dist. Ct. (Ea. & We. Dist.), Wis. Ptnr. McCoy & Hofbauer, Waukesha, Wis. Pres. Propane Gas Defense Assn., 1994—95; chair & founding mem. Self-Insurance Inst. of Am., Wis. div., 1998; mem. Civil Trial Counsel of Wis., Defense Rsch. Inst., Federation of Defense and Corp. Counsel. Pres. & founding mem. Wis. Clean Cities-Southeast Area, Inc., 1994—; bd. dirs. Ctr. for Deaf and Hard of Hearing, 1990—96, 1999—. Mem.: Waukesha County Bar Assn., Milwaukee County Bar Assn., Wis. Bar Assn. Office: McCoy & Hofbauer Riverwood Corp Ctr N19 W24200 Riverwood Dr Ste 125 Waukesha WI 53188 Office Phone: 252-522-7000. Office Fax: 252-522-7020. Business E-Mail: jmccoy@mh-law.us.

MCCOY, LILYS D., lawyer; b. San Diego, Sept. 23, 1967; d. Walter Lee, Jr. and Leoné Doris McCoy; children: Joshua Thomas Moses-McCoy, Jonathan Lee Moses-McCoy. BA with distinction, U. Calif., San Diego, 1987; JD, U. Ariz., Tucson, 1991. Of counsel Law Offices of Frederick Meiser, San Diego, 1992—94; assoc. Law Offices of Gregory Jon Anthony, San Diego, 1994—96; of counsel Barmick, Rutherford and Scott, San Diego, 1996—99; assoc. Rosner Law and Mansfield, San Diego, 1999—2003; shareholder McCoy, Turnage & Robertson APLC, San Diego, 2003—. Pres. Lawyers Club of San Diego, 2002—03, adv. bd., 2002—, judicial endorsements, 2002—, chair, 2005. Named one of Top Attys., San

Diego Daily Transcript, 2006. Mem.: Conf. of Delegates (bd. mem. 2004—), Tom Homann Law Assn. (co-pres. 2005—). Democrat. Episcopalian. Office: McCoy Turnage & Robertson APLC 5469 Kearny Village Rd #206 San Diego CA 92123 Office Phone: 858-300-1900. Business E-Mail: ldm@mtrlaw.com.

MCCOY, LOIS CLARK, retired social services administrator, retired county official, editor; b. New Haven, Oct. 1, 1920; m. Herbert Irving McCoy, Oct. 17, 1943; children: Whitney, Kevin, Marianne, Tori, Debra, Sally, Daniel. BS, Skidmore Coll., 1942; student, Nat. Search and Rescue Sch., 1974. Asst. buyer R.H. Macy & Co., NYC, 1942-44, assoc. buyer, 1944-48; instr. Mountain Medicine & Survival, U. Calif., San Diego, 1973-74; cons. editor Search & Rescue Mag., 1975, Rescue Mag., 1988-97, editor, 1992-94, Press On Newsletter, 1992—2000. Coord. San Diego Mountain Rescue Team, La Jolla, Calif., 1973-75; exec. sec. Nat. Assn. for Search and Rescue, Inc., Nashville, La Jolla, 1975-80, comptr., 1980-82; disaster officer San Diego County, 1980-86, Santa Barbara County, 1985-91, ret.; pres. Nat. Inst. Urban Search & Rescue, Inc., 1987—; assoc. dir. Armed Forces Commns. and Electronics Assn., 2003—; mem. project info. techs. to enhance disaster mgmt., NAS, 2005, group using info. tech. to enhance crisis preparedness and response, Nat. Rsch. Coun., 2005; lectr. in field. Author: Search and Rescue Glossary, 1974, The Last Desperado, 2005, Kiss, Shoot, Aim, 2006, Max's Story, 2006; contbr. editor Rescue Mag., 1989-97; editor-in-chief Response! mag., 1982-86; editor Press On! Electronic mag., 1994-2001; adv. bd. Hazard Monthly, 1991-99; contbr. articles to profl. jours. Cons. law enforcement divsn. Calif. Office Emergency Svcs., 1976-77; pres. San Diego Com. for LA Philharm. Orch., 1957-58; bd. dirs. Search and Rescue of the Californias, 1976-77, Nat. Assn. for Search and Rescue, Inc., 1980-87, pres., 1985-87, trustee, 1987-90, mem. Calif. OES strategic com., 1992-96; CEO Nat. Inst. for Urban Search, 1989—; mem. Gov.'s Task Force on Earthquakes, 1981-82, Earthquake Preparedness Task Force, Seismic Safety Commn., 1982-85, Army Sci. and Tech. Commn., 2003; mem. adv. coun. Nat. Meml. Inst. for the Protection from Terrorism; named to NSF Project "Info. Tech. to Enhance Disaster Mgmt.", 2005. Recipient Hal Foss Outstanding Svc. to Search and Rescue award, 1982, Diamond Safety award, 1996, Superior Performance award AFCEA, 2004, Rep. Senatorial Freedom medal, 2004, Congl. Order merit Rep. Congl. Del., 2005; named to The Fed. 100, 2002. Mem.: IEEE, Armed Forces Comm. and Electronics Assn. (named to Army Sci. and Tech. com. for Homeland Def. 2003—04, bd. dirs. 2003—), San Diego Mountain Rescue (life), Nat. Assn. Search and Rescue (life Svc. award 1985, 2002), Santa Barbara Amateur Radio Club. Episcopalian. Office: PO Box 91648 Santa Barbara CA 93190-1648 Office Phone: 800-767-0093. Personal E-mail: niusr@cox.net.

MCCOY, MARY JANE, retired principal; d. Albert Louis Haley and Della Muriel (Haley-Skinner) Smith; m. Edgar Allen McCoy, Aug. 31, 1957; children: Kim Michelle, Shelley Anne. AA, San Bernardino Valley Jr. Coll., Calif., 1965; BS, Calif. State U., San Bernardino, 1967; MS, Pepperdine U., 1976. Tchg. credential Calif., Wash., adminstrv. credential Calif., Wash. Tchr. San Bernardino Unified, 1968—76, resource reading specialist, 1972—76, elem. vice prin., 1976—78, elem. prin., 1978—92; tchr. Dist. 81, Spokane, Wash., 1992—95. Mem.: NAACP (life), Spokane Women's Coalition, The Links, Inc. (1st v.p. Spokane chpt. 2004—, pres. Spokane chpt. 2000—04, v.p.), Soroptimists, Delta Sigma Theta (sec. 2002—), Phi Delta Kappa (regional dir. far west 1994—95, pres. 1995—, pres. perpetual scholarship found. 1995—). Avocations: reading, crafts, sewing, cross stitch.

MCCOY, MICHAEL D., lawyer; b. Joliet, Ill., Apr. 8, 1950; BSEE with honors, U. Ill., 1972; JD with honors, Chgo.-Kent Coll. Law, 1975. Bar: Ill. 1975, N.C. 1983, U.S. Patent and Trademark Office. Ptnr. and coord. intellectual property law practice Alston & Bird LLP, Charlotte, NC. Mem. panel patent dispute arbitrators Am. Arbitration Assn., Internat. Anti-counterfeiting Coalition, 1984—. Contbr. articles to profl. jours. Named one of Best Lawyers in Am., 2005—. Mem.: ABA, Licensing Exec. Soc. Office: Alston & Bird LLP Bank of Am Plz Ste 4000 101 S Tryon St Charlotte NC 28280-4000 Office Phone: 704-444-1011. Office Fax: 704-444-1111. Business E-Mail: mike.mccoy@alston.com.

MCCOY, R. BURL, lawyer; b. Mansfield, Ohio, Apr. 13, 1948; AB, U. Ky., 1969, JD, 1972; LLM, U. Miami, 1973. Bar: Ky. 1972, Fla. 1974, U.S. Supreme Ct. 1977, U.S. Dist. Ct. Ky. (Ea. and We. Dist.) 1977, cert.: Nat. Bd. Trial Advocacy (criminal law specialist). Asst. U.S. atty., 1974—77; dir. litigation Lexington-Fayette Urban County Govt., 1977—78; ptnr. McCoy, Baker & West; mng. ptnr., criminal def. atty. McCoy, West, Franklin & Beal, Lexington, Ky., 2002—. Adj. prof. law U. Ky.; bd. dirs. Traditional Bank, Lexington, Ky. Maj. USAR. Mem.: ABA, Nat. Assn. Criminal Def. Lawyers, Assn. Trial Lawyers Am., Ky. Acad. Trial Attys., Fed. Bar Assn., Ky. Bar Assn., Fayette County Bar Assn., Delta Theta Phi. Office: McCoy West Franklin & Beal 309 N Broadway PO Box 1660 Lexington KY 40508 Office Phone: 859-254-6363. Office Fax: 859-233-4234. E-mail: mccoy@mccoyandwest.com.

MCCOY, R. WESLEY, biology educator; b. Augusta, Ga., Sept. 20, 1954; s. Roger and Frances (Amick) McC.; m. Deborah Stringer, June 16, 1984. BS in Biology, Ga. State U., 1975; MEd in Sci. Edn., U. Ga., 1977; PhD, Ga. State U. Tchr. North Cobb High Sch., Kennesaw, Ga., 1978-83, sci. dept. chmn., 1987—, tchr., Biology, Genetics, and Astronomy; edn. specialist NASA, Kennedy Space Ctr. (Fla.), 1983-87; tchr. Ga. Govs. Honors Program, Dahlonega, 1981-82. Adj. asst. prof. Okla. State U., Stillwater, 1983-87; mem. NSF DNA literacy program, Cold Spring Harbor Lab, NOAA Nat. Undersea Rsch. Program Marine Biology Workshop; del. leader People to People Youth Sci. Exch. to Soviet Union; Fulbright tchr. exch. to U.K.; vice-chair, Ga. Citizens for Integrity in Sci. Edn. Christa McAuliffe fellow, 1992, SCI-MAT fellow, NSF, 1992, Ga. Sci. Tchr. of Yr., GTE G.I.F.T. fellow, 1993, Tandy scholar 1994; recipient Presdl. Award for Excellence in Sci. and Math. Teaching, 1996, Outstanding Biology Tchr. for Ga., Evolution-Education award, Found. for the Furure, 2003, 2006 AAAS Award for Scientific Freedom and Responsibility, 2007. Mem. NSTA, Nat. Bd. Dirs. Presbyn. Assn. for Sci., Tech. and Christian Faith, Ga. Sci. Tchrs. Assn., Fulbright Assn., Phi Delta Kappa. Lutheran. Office: North Cobb High Sch 3400 Old Highway 41 Kennesaw GA 30144-1072 *

MCCOY, REAGAN SCOTT, oil industry executive, lawyer; b. Port Arthur, Tex., Nov. 25, 1945; s. William Murray and Elizabeth (Gilbert) McC.; m. Pat Kowalski, June 21, 1969; 1 child, Traci. BCE, Ga. Inst. Tech., 1968; JD, Loyola U., 1972. Bar: Tex. 1972, La. 1978; registered profl. engr., Tex., La. Structural engr. McDermott Inc., New Orleans, 1966-72, data processing mgr. London, 1972-76, cons. engr. New Orleans, 1976-79; adminstrv. mgr. Concord Oil Co., San Antonio, 1979-81, v.p., 1981—, also bd. dirs. Mem. World Affairs Coun., Tex. Luth. U. Bus. Sch. Adv. Com. Treas. Countryside San Pedro Recreation Club, 1981-82; bd. dirs. Countryside San Pedro Homeowners Assn., 1984-86; v.p. Bluffview Homeowners Assn., 1998-99, pres., 1999-2004; pres. San Antonio Baylor U. Parents League, 1995-96; mem. Tex. State Bd. Pub. Accountancy, 1997-2003, chair CPE com., 2002-03; bd. dirs. Consumer Credit Counseling Svc. Greater San Antonio, 2000—, treas., 2003-06, sec., 2006-, exec. com., 2003—. Fellow Tau Beta Pi; mem. ABA, NSPE, ASCE, Am. Assn. Profl. Landmen (San Antonio chpt. treas. 1990-91, v.p. 1991-93, 2004-05, pres. 1993-94, 2005-06, exec. bd. 2006-07), La. State Bar Assn., Tex. State Bar, San Antonio Bar Assn. (natural resources com. treas. 1986-87, vice chmn. 1987-88, chmn. 1988-89, bd. dirs. contrn. law sect. 2003-04), Tex. Soc. Profl. Engrs., La. Soc. Profl. Engrs., So. Tex. Assn. Divsn. Order Analysts (v.p. 1993, pres. 1994, 98, bd. dirs. 1999-04), Fin Execs. Inst. (treas. 1991-92, sec. 1992-93, v.p. 1993-94, pres. 1994-95, bd. dirs. 1995-97), Soc. Mining Engrs., Real Estate Fin. Soc. (bd. dirs. 1986-89, v.p. 1987-88, pres. 1988-89, 98-2000, pres. coun.), San Antonio Bus. and Econ. Soc. (bd. dirs. 2006—), Adminstrv. Mgmt. Soc. (pres. 1985-86, 89-90), Tex. Ind. Prodrs. and Royalty Owners Assn., Am. Petroleum Inst. (South Tex. chpt. pres. 1997-99), Assn. Corp. Counsel (treas. 2004-05, pres.-elect 2006, pres. 2007), Plaza Club, Sonterra Club. Presbyterian. Avocations: water sports, reading, woodworking. Home: 14103 Bluff Manor Dr San Antonio TX 78216-7976 Office: Concord Oil Co 100 W Houston Ste 1500 San Antonio TX 78205-1424

MCCOY, THOMAS M., information technology executive; BA in History, Stanford U.; JD, U. So. Calif. Law clk. US Ct. Appeals (9th cir.); assoc. to ptnr. O'Melveny and Meyers, 1977—95; gen. counsel Advanced Micro Devices, Sunnyvale, Calif., 1993—95, sec., 1995—2003, sr. v.p., gen. counsel, 1998—2003, exec. v.p. legal affairs, chief adminstrv. officer, 2003—. Office: Advanced Micro Devices One AMD Pl PO Box 3453 Sunnyvale CA 94088-3453 *

MC COY, TIDAL WINDHAM, former government official; b. Gainesville, Fla., Apr. 25, 1945; Grad., U.S. Mil. Acad., 1967; MA in Bus. Fin, George Washington U., 1975. Officer U.S. Army, 1967-72; mem. long-range planning and net assessment group Office of Sec. Def., Washington, 1972-73; mem. staff Nat. Security Council, 1973; staff asst. and then dep. asst. to Sec. Def., 1973-77; sci. asst. to asst. sec. for research, engring. and systems Dept. Navy, 1977-78; dir. policy research, office of under sec. for policy Dept. Def., 1978-79; asst. for nat. security affairs to Sen. Jake Garn, 1979-81; asst. sec. for manpower, res. affairs and installations Dept. Air Force, Washington, 1981-87; asst. sec. for readiness support USAF, Washington, 1987-88, acting sec. and undersec., 1981-88; sr. assoc. Hecht, Spencer & Assocs., 1988-89; v.p. govt. rels. Thiokol Corp., 1989—2002; chmn., CEO Washington Capital Ptnrs., 1998—. Chmn. Washington Capital Ptnrs., 1998—. Recipient DOD Outstanding Civil Svc. medal, USAF Exceptional Civilian Svc. medal. Mem. Space Transp. Assn. U.S.A. (dir., chmn. 1996—), Def. Forum Found. (vice-chmn.).

MCCOY, WESLEY LAWRENCE, musician, educator, conductor; b. Memphis, Jan. 27, 1935; s. Harlan Eftin and Gladys (Coggin) McC.; m. Carolyn June Noble, Aug. 26, 1960; children: Jill Laurene McCoy Kurtz, Scott Edward. B of Music Edn., La. State U., 1957, PhD, 1970; M of Music Edn., U. Louisville, 1958; M of Sacred Music, So. Bapt. Theol. Sem., 1960. Min. of music Beechmont Bapt. Ch., Louisville, 1959-62; also instr. music So. Bapt. Theol. Sem., Louisville; asst. prof. music, dir. bands Carson Newman Coll., Jefferson City, Tenn., 1962-67; asst. prof. music U. S.C., Columbia, 1969-72; assoc. prof. music U. Ark., Little Rock, 1972-77, prof., 1977-80, asst. dean for pub. svc. Coll. Fine Arts, 1978-79; condr. Wind Ensemble, River City Cmty. Band, 1972-80, Oklahoma City Youth Symphony, 1985—87; chmn. dept. music Phillips U., Enid, Okla., 1980-82, chmn. fine arts divsn., 1982-84; music tchr. Bishop Sullivan H.S., 2003—04; supr. Baton Rouge Recreation Dept., 2004—. Choral dir. 1st United Meth. Ch., Edmond, Okla., 1983-2000; owner WJ Travel, Oklahoma City, 1985-2002. French horn player, Knoxville (Tenn.) Symphony Orch., 1962-67, Columbia Philharm. Orch., 1969-72, Ark. Symphony Orch., 1972-80, Enid-Phillips Symphony, 1980-84; contbr. to Ch. Musician, 1974-76, 85-86. Co-chmn. Jefferson County (Tenn.) Com. for Goldwater for Pres., 1962; mem. Pulaski County (Ark.) Rep. Com., 1977-81; mem. Oklahoma County Rep. exec. Com., 1995-97; pres. Ctrl. Okla. La. State U. Alumni, 1997-98; choir dir. First United Meth. Ch., Hammond, La., 2004—. Mem. S.C. Music Educators Assn. (pres. coll. divsn. 1971-73), Ark. Music Edn. Assn. (chmn. rsch. 1975-80), Phi Mu Alpha, Pi Kappa Lambda, Phi Delta Kappa, Alpha Tau Omega. Republican. Baptist. Home and Office: 8548 Kaylynn Ave Baton Rouge LA 70810 Personal E-mail: wesleymccoy@yahoo.com.

MCCRABB, DONALD RAYMOND, pastoral field educator; m. Barbara Humphrey; children: Andrew Thomas, Jacob Creighton, Martin Joseph. BA in Religion, BA in Polit. Sci., Wright State U., 1975; MA in Theology, U. Dayton, 1978; DMin, United Theol. Sem., 1998. Cert. catechetical leader, Roman Cath. Ch. Campus min. Newman Ctr., Wright State U., Dayton, Ohio, 1975-76; grad. asst. U. Dayton, 1976-78; pastoral assoc. St. Raphael Cath. Ch., Springfield, Ohio, 1978-82; Cath. campus min. Cen. State U., Wilberforce U., 1982-85; exec. dir. Cath. Campus Ministry Assn., 1985-98; dir. devel. Sojourners, Washington, 1998-99; dir. pastoral field edn. Dominican House of Studies, Washington, 1999—, dir. adminstrn. Mem. planning com. Cath. Edn. Futures Project, 1985-88; bd. dirs., site visitor Commn. on Cert. and Accreditation, U.S. Cath. Conf., 1986-92. Office: Dominican House of Studies 487 Michigan Ave NE Washington DC 20017-1585 Office Phone: 202-529-5300. Business E-Mail: dmccrabb@dhs.edu.

MCCRACKEN, EDWARD R., electronics executive; b. Fairfield, Iowa, 1943; children: Kathi, David. BSEE, Iowa State U., 1966; MBA, Stanford U., 1968. With Hewlett Packard Co.; pres., CEO Silicon Graphics, Inc., 1984—98, chmn., CEO, 1994—98. Bd. dirs. Digital Rsch., Inc.; chmn. bd. The PRASAD Project, 1992—; dir. Nat. Semiconductor Corp., Tularik, Inc., Acumen Internat. Recipient Disting. Info. Scis. award, Data Processing Mgmt. Assn., 1994, Nat. Tech. medal, 1995, Exec. of Yr., R&D Mag., 1995, Disting. Achievement award, Iowa State Alumni Assn., 1995.

MCCRACKEN, EUGENE LUKE, lawyer; b. Savannah, Ga., Aug. 9, 1932; s. John and Estelle (Powers) M.; m. Helen Kelly Morekis, May 9, 1964; A.A., Armstrong State Coll., 1952; BA, Mercer U., Macon, Ga., 1954; LLB, U. Ga., Athens, 1957. Bar: Ga. 1958, U.S. Dist. Ct. (so. dist.) Ga. 1959, U.S. Ct. Appeals (11th cir.) 1961, U.S. Supreme Ct. 1978. Assoc. Brannen, Clark & Hester, Savannah, 1958-64; sole practice, Savannah, 1964—; asst. dist. atty. Chatham County, Ga., 1963-64; asst. city atty. City of Savannah, 1970-74; judge pro tem Juvenile Ct. of Chatham County, 1974-80. Bd. dirs. United Way of Savannah, 1973-74; mem. Chatham County Zoning Bd. Appeals, 1967-70; chmn. Chatham County Reps., 1985-87, chmn. 1st congl. dist. Ga. Rep. Party, 1987-89. Named Savannah's Outstanding Young Man of Yr., Jaycees, 1966; recipient Sword of Hope award Am. Cancer Soc., 1968. Mem. State Bar of Ga., Savannah (Ga.) Bar Assn., Armstrong State Coll. Alumni Assn. (pres. 1973, 83), Hibernian Soc. Savannah (pres. 2004-05), St. Andrews Soc. Savannah, First City Club. Roman Catholic. Home: 16 Brightwater Dr Savannah GA 31410-3301 Office: 223 W York St Savannah GA 31401-3636 Home Phone: 912-897-2373; Office Phone: 912-232-4106.

MCCRACKEN, HARRY, journalist; b. Boston; s. Samuel and Natalie (Jacobson) McC. BA in History, Boston U., 1986. Editor Animato Mag., Cambridge, Mass., 1987-91; sr. editor CorpTech, Woburn, Mass., 1987-91; reviews editor Computer Buying World Mag., Wakefield, Mass., 1991-92; features editor Infoworld Direct mag., Boston, 1992-94; sr. assoc. editor PC World mag. and pcworld.com, 1994—2000, exec. features editor, 2000—02, editor, 2002—04, editor-in-chief, 2004—, v.p, 2004—. Chmn. Jesse H. Neal award competition Am. Bus. Media, 2007—. Contbg. editor: Multimedia World Mag., San Francisco, 1994-96; mem. editl. bd. Am. Bus. Media; contbr. articles to profl. jours. Office: PC World Communications 501 Second Street San Francisco CA 94107

MCCRACKEN, PETER H., librarian; b. 1969; BA in English, Oberlin Coll.; MLS, U. N.C., Chapel Hill; MA in Maritime History, U. N.C. Reference libr. East Carolina U., Greenville, NC, 1999—2000; reference libr., coord. for collection devel. U. Wash., Seattle; co-founder, dir. electronic content mgmt. Serial Solutions, Seattle, 2000—. Mem. coun. advocates U. Wash. Libraries, Seattle; mem. bd. visitors Sch. Info. & Library Sci., U. N.C., Chapel Hill. Office: Serial Solutions 501 N 34th St #400 Seattle WA 98103

MC CRACKEN, PHILIP TRAFTON, sculptor; b. Bellingham, Wash., Nov. 14, 1928; s. William Franklin and Maude (Trafton) McC.; m. Anne MacFetridge, Aug. 14, 1954; children— Timothy, Robert, Daniel. BA in Sculpture, U. Wash., 1954. Asst. to Henry Moore, England, 1954. One-man shows: Willard Gallery, N.Y.C., 1960, 65, 68, 70, Seattle Art Mus., 1961, Wash. State Capitol Mus., Olympia, 1964, Art Gallery of Greater Victoria, B.C., 1964, LaJolla (Calif.) Mus. Art, 1970, Anchorage Hist. and Fine Arts Mus., 1970, Tacoma Art Mus., 1980, Kennedy Galleries, N.Y.C., 1985, Lynn McAllister Gallery, Seattle, 1986, 89, Valley Mus. N.W. Art, La Conner, Wash., 1993, Whatcom Mus., Bellingham, Wash., 1994, Schneider Mus. Art, 1994, So. Oreg. State Coll., 1994, Monterey Mus. Art, 1999, Mus. N.W. Art, La Conner, 2004, others; group shows include: Mus. Art, Ogunquit, Maine, 1957, Chgo. Art Inst., 1958, Detroit Inst. Arts, 1958, Pa. Acad. Fine Arts, 1958, Contemporary Art Gallery, Houston, 1958, DeYoung Meml. Mus., San Francisco, 1960, L.A. Mcpl. Art Mus., 1960, Galerie Claude Bernard, Paris, 1960, Phillips Gallery, Washington, 1966, Corcoran Gallery, 1966, Mus. Art, Akron, 1967, Finch Coll., N.Y.C., 1968, Rutgers U., 1968, Whitney Mus. Art, 1978, Portland Art Mus., 1976, Mont. State U., Bozeman, 1979, Brigham Young U., 1980, Bellevue (Wash.) Art Mus., 1986, Lynn McAllister Gallery, 1986, Am. Acad. Arts and Letters, N.Y.C., 1986, Schmidt Bingham Gallery, N.Y.C., 1987, Wash. State Capital Mus., 1987, 89, Cheney-Cowles Mus., Spokane, Wash., 1988, Smithsonian Instn., 1991—, Nat. Mus., Ottawa, Can., 1991-92, Gallery Three-Zero, N.Y.C., 1993, Seattle Art Mus., 1994, SA Gallery Christ Ch., New Zealand, 1996, Art and Cultural Ctr., Fallbrook, Calif., 2002, Port Angeles Fine Art Ctr., Wash., 2007, others; sculptures represented: Norton Bldg., Seattle, Kankakee (Ill.) State Hosp., Swinomish Indian Tribal Center, LaConner, UN Assn., N.Y.C., King County King Dome, Seattle, City Hall, Everett, Wash., Bartlett Square, Tulsa, 2005, others. Recipient numerous art awards. Address: 5029 Guemes Island Rd Anacortes WA 98221-9039

MCCRACKEN, STEVEN CARL, lawyer; b. Artesia, Calif., Oct. 29, 1950; s. Glenn A. and Helen V. (Fears) McCracken; m. Susan Lee Waggener, July 29, 1979; children: Casey James, Scott Kevin. BA magna cum laude, U. Calif., Irvine, 1972; JD, U. Va., 1975. Bar: Calif. 1975, U.S. Dist. Ct. (cen. dist.) Calif. 1975, U.S. Ct. Appeals (9th cir.) 1976, U.S. Dist. Ct. (no. dist.) Calif. 1977, D.C. 1979, U.S. Supreme Ct. 1985, U.S. Dist. Ct. (so. dist.) Calif. 1990. Assoc. Gibson, Dunn & Crutcher, LA, 1975-82, ptnr. Irvine, Calif., 1983-94; v.p., sec. and gen. counsel Callaway Golf Co., Carlsbad, Calif., 1994-96, exec. v.p., gen. counsel and sec., 1996-97, exec. v.p. licensing, chief legal officer, sec., 1997-2000, sr. exec. v.p., chief legal officer, sec., 2000—. Lawyer rep. Ninth Cir. Jud. Conf., 1989-91. Editor Va. Law Rev., 1973-75, mng. bd. 1974-75, bd. editors The Computer Lawyer, 1984-96. Mem. ABA (antitrust sect.), Orange County Bar Assn. (bd. dirs. 1988-90, chmn. fed. ct. com. 1988-89, chmn. bus. litigation sect. 1990, sec. 1991, treas. 1992, pres.-elect 1993, pres. 1994). Democrat. Office: Callaway Golf Co 2180 Rutherford Rd Carlsbad CA 92008-8815

MCCRACKEN, THOMAS JAMES, JR., lawyer; b. Chgo., Oct. 27, 1952; s. Thomas J. Sr. and Eileen (Brophy) McC.; children: Catherine, Michael, Amanda, Quinn. BA, Marquette U., 1974; JD, Loyola U., 1977. Bar: Ill. 1977, U.S. Dist. Ct. (no. dist.) Ill., U.S. Ct. Appeals (7th cir.) 1984. Asst. state's atty. DuPage County State's Atty.'s Office, Wheaton, Ill., 1977—81; assoc. atty. McCracken & Walsh, Chgo., 1981—84; ptnr. McCracken, Walsh & deLaVan, Chgo., 1984—. Commr. Nat. Conf. of Commns. on Uniform State Laws, 1989—; bd. dirs. DuPage Nat. Bank, West Chgo., 2007. Contbr. articles to profl. jours. State rep. Ill. Gen. Assembly, Springfield, Ill., 1983-93, state senator, 1993; chmn. Regional Trans. Authority, Chgo., 1993-2004; dir. United Republican Fund, 2005-, Civic. Fedn. Chgo., 2006-. Named Top Ten Legislators Chgo. Mag., 1990. Mem.: Chgo. Bar Assn., Ill. State Bar Assn. Avocations: skiing, hunting, golf. Office: McCracken Walsh & deLaVan 134 N La Salle St Ste 600 Chicago IL 60602-1079 Office Phone: 312-346-7700. Business E-Mail: tjm@mcc-w.com.

MCCRACKEN, WILLIAM HENRY, retired mining executive; b. Johnstown, Pa., Dec. 3, 1923; s. William Henry and Bernice (Johnson) McCracken; m. Juana Edelmira Pascarella, Oct. 3, 1959; children: William Henry, Derek James, David Andrew, Susan Linda. BS in Mining Engring., Pa. State U., 1944, MS in Mining Engring., 1947. Profl. engr., Pa. Field engr. Harbison-Walker Refractories Co., Pitts., 1947-57; mng. dir. Refractarios Peruanos SA, Lima, Peru, 1957-72; mgr. raw materials Harbison-Walker Refractories Co., Pitts., 1972—85; tech. dir. minerals and ores F&S Internat., Inc., Pitts., 1985-98; ret., 1998. Lt. (j.g.) USNR, 1944—46. Fellow: Am. Ceramic Soc.; mem.: AIME (legion of honor mem.), ALAFAR (hon.), UNITECR (life), Pa. Ceramic Assn. (dir. emeritus). Home: 2219 Alnwick Dr Duluth GA 30096-2212

MCCRADY, BARBARA SACHS, psychologist, educator; b. Evanston, Ill., May 7, 1949; d. James Frederick and Margaret Maxine (Miller) Sachs; m. Dennis D. McCrady, June 13, 1969; 1 child, Eric Paul. BS, Purdue U., 1969; PhD, U. R.I., 1975. Lic. clin. psychologist. Clin. project evaluator Butler Hosp., Providence, 1974-75, chief psychol. assessment program, 1975-76, chief problem drinkers' project, 1976-83; assoc. prof. psychology Rutgers U., Piscataway, NJ, 1983-89, prof. psychology, 1989-2000, prof. II, 2000—. From instr. to assoc. prof. psychiatry Brown U., Providence, 1975—83; reviewer Nat. Inst. on Alcohol Abuse and Alcoholism, Washington, 1979—82, extramural sci. adv. bd., 1989—93; cons. Inst. Medicine, Washington, 1988—89; acting dir. Rutgers Ctr. Alcohol Studies, Piscataway, 1990—92, dir. clin. tng. dept. psychology, 1993—2005, chair dept. psychology, 2005—07; dir. Ctr. on Alcoholism, Substance Abuse, and Addictions U. N. Mex., Albuquerque, 2007—, prof. dept. psychol., 2007—. Author: The Alcoholic Marriage, 1977; editor: Marriage and Marital Therapy, 1978, Directions in Alcohol Abuse Treatment Research, 1985, Research on Alcoholics Anonymous: Opportunities and Alternatives, 1993, Addictions: A Comprehensive Guidebook, 1999. Grantee Nat. Inst. on Alcohol Abuse and Alcoholism, 1979-83, 1988—. Fellow Am. Psychol. Assn. (past pres. divsn. addictions); mem. Assn. for Advancement Behavior Therapy, Rsch. Soc. on Alcoholism (bd. dirs., 1999-2003). Avocations: horseback riding, skiing, piano. Office: Univ N Mex CASAA 2560 Yale Blvd SE MSCII 6280 Albuquerque NM 87106 Home Phone: 505-856-1161; Office Phone: 505-925-2388. Business E-Mail: bmccrady@unm.edu.

MCCRADY, JAMES DAVID, veterinarian, educator; b. Beaumont, Tex., June 26, 1930; s. James Homer and Lucyle (Ward) McCrady; m. Mary Elizabeth McDougald, Sept. 8, 1951; children: David, Diane, Darla. BS, Tex. A&M U., 1952, DVM, 1958; PhD, Baylor U., 1965. From instr. to asst. prof. Tex. A&M U., 1958- 62, mem. faculty, 1964—, prof., head dept. vet. physiology and pharmacology, 1966-90, prof., dir. spl. programs, 1990—; dir. animal rsch., instr. Baylor U. Coll. Medicine, 1962-64. Dir. Russian-Am. Tng. Partnership, 1995—; adj. prof. Baylor Coll. Medicine, M.D. Anderson Hosp., Tumor Inst. With USAF, 1952—54. Mem.: AVMA, Am. Physiol. Soc., Tex. Acad. Sci., Sigma Xi, Phi Zeta, Phi Kappa Phi. Achievements include research in comparative cardiovascular and respiratory physiology. Home: 511 Olive St Bryan TX 77801-3506 Office: Tex A&M U College Station TX 77843-0001 Office Phone: 979-845-7261. Business E-Mail: jd-mccrady@tamu.edu.

MCCRAE, JOCELYN DIANE, psychologist; b. Elizabeth, NJ, Dec. 19, 1957; d. John Christopher and Edna Mae McCrae. BA, Temple U., 1980; MSc, Villanova U., 1987; PhD, Wayne State U., 1996. Lic. Psychologist

Mich., 2000. Clin. psychologist Children's Hosp. Mich., Detroit, 1993—. Bd. mem., cmty. mental health bd. Phila. Cmty. Coun., 1978—79. Contbr. articles to profl. jours. Tel. crisis counselor Contact Teleministries, Phila., 1986—87. Recipient Legion Honor award, Chapel Four Chaplains, 1983, Recognition cert., Contact Teleministries, 1986; fellow, Wayne State U., 1991—92; Thomas C. Rumble Grad. fellow, 1988—89, Rsch. grant, 1994, Martin Luther King, Jr.-Cesar Chavez-Rosa Parks fellow, 1991—92. Mem.: APA, Soc. Pediatric Psychology. Methodist. Achievements include facilitating the formation of a martial arts support group for children with sickle cell disease. Office: Childrens Hosp Michigan 3901 Beaubien Blvd Detroit MI 48201 Personal E-mail: jocelynmccrae@netscape.net.

MCCRANK, LAWRENCE J., dean, school librarian; b. Fargo, ND, Apr. 17, 1945; s. James F. McCrank and Florence Kloeckner; m. Ruth D. Madson; children: Kirstin L., Jaime L. BA, Minn. State U., Moorhead, 1967; MA, U. Kans., 1969; PhD, U. Va., 1974; MLS, U. Oregon, 1975. Asst. prof. libr. and info. sci. U. Md., College Park, 1976—82; dept. head rare books and spl. collections Ind. State U., Terre Haute, 1982—84; dean librs. Auburn U., Montgomery, Ala., 1984—88, Ferris State U., Big Rapids, Mich., 1988—95; dir. librs. ITT Tech. I, Grand Rapids, Mich., 1996—97, Davenport U., Grand Rapids, Mich., 1998—99; dean libr. and instrn. svcs. Chgo. State U., 2000—. Author: Historical Information Science, 2002, History Under Debate, 2004; contbr. articles to profl. jours. Fellow: Royal Archeol. Soc. Tarragona, Soc. Am. Archivists. Avocations: medieval history, Frontier studies. Office: Chgo State Univ 9501 S King Dr Chicago IL 60628-1598 Office Phone: 773-995-2253. Office Fax: 773-995-3772. Business E-Mail: lmccrank@csu.edu.

MCCRARY, CHARLES D., utilities executive; b. 1951; BS in Mech. Engring., Auburn U., Ala.; JD, Birmingham Sch. Law. Asst. project planning engr. Ala. Power Southern Co., 1973, various exec. positions Ala. Power and Southern Nuc., chief prodn. officer, exec. v.p. external affairs Ala. Power, 1994—98, pres. Southern Co. Generation and Energy Mktg., 1998—2001, v.p., 1998—2001, pres., COO Ala. Power, 2001, pres., CEO Ala. Power, 2001—, exec. v.p., 2002—. Bd. dirs. Amsouth Bancorporation, 2001—, Protective Life Corp., 2005—, Mercedes-Benz US Internat., Inc. Office: Southern Co 30 Ivan Allen Jr Blvd NW Atlanta GA 30308 Office Phone: 404-506-5000. *

MCCRARY, EUGENIA LESTER (MRS. DENNIS DAUGHTRY MCCRARY), civic worker, writer; b. Annapolis, Md., Mar. 23, 1929; d. John Campbell and Eugenia (Potts) Lester; m. John Campbell Howard, July 15, 1955 (dec. Sept. 1965); m. Dennis Daughtry McCrary, June 28, 1969; 1 child, Dennis Campbell. AB cum laude, Radcliffe Coll.-Harvard U., 1950; MA, Johns Hopkins U., 1952; postgrad., Harvard U., 1953, Pa. State U., 1953—54, Drew U., 1957—58, Inst. Study of USSR, Munich, 1964. Grad. asst. dept. Romance langs. Pa. State U., 1953—54; tchr. dept. math. The Brearley Sch., NYC, 1954—57; dir. Sch. Langs., Inc., Summit, NJ, 1958—69, trustee, 1960—69. Co-author: Nom de Plume: Eugenia Campbell Lester, (with Allegra Branson) Frontiers Aflame, 1987; film script adaptation (with John Gallagher) Frontier, 1998. Dist. dir. Ea. Pa. and NJ auditions Met. Opera Nat. Coun., NYC, 1960-66, dist. dir. publicity, 1966-67, nat. vice chmn. publicity, 1967-71, nat. chmn. public rels., 1972-75, hon. nat. chmn. pub. rels., 1976-99; bd. govs., chmn. Van Cortlandt House Mus., 1985-90 Mem. Nat. Soc. Colonial Dames Am. (bd. mgrs. NY 1985-90), Met. Opera Nat. Coun., Soc. Mayflower Descs. (former bd. dirs. NY soc., chmn. house com. 1986-89), Soc. Daus. Holland Dames (bd. dirs. 1982-87, 96—, 3d directress gen. 1987-92, directress gen. 1992-96), L'Eglise du St.-Esprit (vestry 1985-88, sr. warden 1988-90), Huguenot Soc. Am. (governing coun. 1984-90, 2000-03, 2004-05, asst. treas. 1990-91, sec. 1991-95, 2d v.p. 1995-2000), Colonial Dames Am., Daus. of Cin., Colony Club (bd. govs. 1988-96), Causeries du Lundi, The Hereditary Order Descendants of Colonial Govs. Republican. Episcopalian. Home: 24 Central Park S New York NY 10019-1629 Personal E-mail: d-emccrary@hotmail.com.

MCCRARY, JONATHAN MARK, mathematician, educator; b. Topkea, Kans., Dec. 13, 1979; s. Kelly and Kathy McCrary; m. Lorien Helene Riead, Oct. 2, 2004. BA in Math. and Computer Sci., Drury U., Springfield, Mo., 2003; student in Math., U. Ark., Fayetteville, 2003—. Tchg. asst. U. Ark., Fayetteville, 2003—. Mem.: Mensa. Home Phone: 479-283-4185.

MCCRARY, LISA HOOPER, secondary school educator; b. Greenville, SC, Jan. 27, 1960; d. Gerald Nelson Hooper and Janet Lee Holliday; m. Carmen Elbert McCrary, Dec. 20, 1980; children: Ryan Nelson, Logan Miller, Taylor Dallas. BS, Mary Washington Coll., Fredericksburg, Va., 1999. English tchr. Spotsylvania County Schs., Fredericksburg, 1999—. Pres., dir. Battlefield Driving Sch., Fredericksburg, 2005—. Children's facilitator RAACAP, Fredericksburg, 1998—99. Office: Spotsylvania County Schs 6300 Harrison Road Fredericksburg VA 22407 Home Phone: 540-785-8899; Office Phone: 540-786-2606. Office Fax: 540-786-1176. Business E-Mail: lhoop410@aol.com.

MCCRARY ANTHONY, CRYSTAL, writer, producer, lawyer; b. Oct. 1969; m. Greg Anthony (div.); children: Cole, Ella. BA cum laude, U. Mich., Ann Arbor, 1991; JD, NYU, 1995. Bar: NY. Assoc. entertainment law Paul, Weiss, Rifkind, Wharton and Garrison LLP, NYC, 1995—97. Co-author (with Rita Ewing): Homecourt Advantage, 1998; co-author: (with Tonya Lewis Lee) Gotham Diaries, 2004 (Blackboard Fiction Book of Yr., 2005); exec. prodr.: (TV series) My Model Looks Better Than Your Model, 2006, Real Life Divas, 2006; (films) Dirty Laundry, 2006 (Am. Black Film Festival Best Feature Film); guest appearance (TV series) The Big Idea with Donny Deutsch, 2006, guest host The View, 2006, co-host My 2 Cents, BET-J, pop culture critic CNN American Morning, legal analyst Fox News Channel, CNBC, Court TV; contbr. articles to Vibe, Glamour, Savoy, Tastemakers NYC; adv. com. mem. VOICE: A New Imprint for Women. Adv. bd. mem. Jumpstart. Named one of 40 Under 40, Crain's NY Bus., 2007. Office: c/o BET 1235 W St, NE Washington DC 20018-1211 E-mail: crystal@crystalmccraryanthony.com. *

MCCRAVEN, EVA STEWART MAPES, health service administrator; b. LA, Sept. 26, 1936; d. Paul Melvin and Wilma Zech (Ziegler) Stewart; m. Carl Clarke McCraven, Mar. 18, 1978; children: David Anthony, Lawrence James, Maria Lynn Mapes. ABS magna cum laude, Calif. State U., Northridge, 1974; MS, Cambridge Grad. Sch. Psycholoy, 1987, PhD, 1991. Dir. spl. projects Pacoima Meml. Hosp., 1969—71, dir. health edn., 1971—74; asst. exec. dir., v.p. Hillview Cmty. Mental Health Ctr., Lakeview Terrace, Calif., 1974—99, exec. dir., 1999—2004, CEO and pres., 2004—. Past dir. dept. consultation and edn. Hillview Ctr., developer, mgr. long-term residential program, 1986-90; former program mgr. crisis residential program, transitional residential program and day treatment program for mentally ill offenders, past dir. mentally ill offenders svcs.; former program dir. Valley Homeless Shelter Mental Health Counseling Program; dir. Integrated Svcs. Agy., Hillview Mental Health Ctr., Inc., 1993-98, dir. clin. programs, 1996-99, exec. dir. 1999— Former pres. San Fernando Valley Coordinating Coun. Area Assn., Sunland-Tujunga Coordinating Coun.; bd. advisors Pacoima Sr. Citizens Multi-Purpose Ctr.; bd. dirs. N.E. Valley Health Corp., 1970-73, Golden Gate Cmty. Mental Health Ctr., 1970-73 Recipient Resolution of Commendation State of Calif., 1988, Commendation award, 1988, Spl. Mayor's plaque, 1988, Cmty. Svcs. Commendation awards City of L.A., 1989, County of Los Angeles, 1989, Calif. Assembly, 1989, Calif. Senate, 1989, award Sunland-Tujunga Police Support Coun., 1989 Mem. Health Svcs. Adminstrn. Alumni Assn. (past v.p.), Sunland-Tujunga Bus. and Profl. Women (Women of Achievement award 1990), LWV, Valley Philharm. Soc Office: Hillview Cmty Mental Health Ctr 11500 Eldridge Ave Lake View Terrace CA 91342-6523 Business E-Mail: esm@hillviewmhc.org.

MCCRAW, THOMAS KINCAID, business history educator emeritus, editor, writer; b. Corinth, Miss., Sept. 11, 1940; s. John Carey and Eugenia Olive (Kincaid) McC.; m. Susan Morehead, Sept. 22, 1962; children: Elizabeth, Thomas Kincaid Jr. BA, U. Miss., 1962; MA, U. Wis., 1968, PhD, 1970; MA (hon.), Harvard U., 1978. Tchg. asst. U. Wis., Madison, 1968-69; asst. prof. U. Tex., Austin, 1970-74, assoc. prof., 1974-78; vis. assoc. prof. Harvard Bus. Sch., Boston, 1976-78, prof., 1978-89, Isidor Straus prof. bus. history, 1986—2006, Isidor Straus prof. bus. history, emeritus, 2006—, dir. research, 1984—86, chair and co-chmn. bus. govt. and internat. economy unit, 1986—97. Ednl. cons. to cos., U.S., Japan, 1977-95. Author: Morgan versus Lilienthal:The Feud Within the TVA, 1970 (William P. Lyons award), TVA and the Power Fight, 1971, Prophets of Regulation: Charles Francis Adams, Luis D. Brandeis, James M. Landis, Alfred E. Kahn, 1984(Pulitzer Prize for History, 1985, Thomas Newcomen Book award, 1986), American Business, 1920-2000: How it Worked, 2000, Prophet of Innovation: Joseph Schumpeter and Creative Destruction, 2007; co-author, editor: Management Past and Present, 1996, Creating Modern Capitalism: How Entrepreneurs, Companies, and Countries Triumphed in Three Industrial Revolutions, 1997, The Intellectual Venture Capitalist: John H. McArthur and the Work of the Harvard Business School, 1999; editor: Regulation in Perspective, 1981, America Versus Japan, 1986, The Essential Alfred Chandler, 1988; editor: Bus. History Rev., 1994—; co-editor: The Intellectual Venture Capitalist, 1999; assoc. editor The Encyclopedia of the United States in the Twentieth Century, 1996; mem. editl. bd. Reviews in American History; bd. dir. Syndics of Harvard U.; contbr. numerous articles to various publs., chpts. to books. Trustee Bus. History Conf., 1986-95, pres., 1989; mem. coun. Mass. Hist. Soc., 1989-92. Lt. USN, 1962-66. Recipient Lyons Master's Essay award Loyola U., Chgo., 1969, Younger Humanist award NEH, 1975; Woodrow Wilson fellow, 1966-67; named to Alumni Hall of Fame, U. Miss., 1986; Newcomen fellowship Harvard U., 1973-74. Mem. Orgn. Am. Historians, Econ. Hist. Assn., Am. Econ. Assn. Democrat. Roman Catholic. Office: Harvard Bus Sch Soldiers Field Boston MA 02163-1317 Office Phone: 617-495-6364. Business E-Mail: tmccraw@hbs.edu. *

MCCRAW, WILLIAM GARY, music educator, director, musician; b. Spartanburg, SC, July 7, 1955; s. William Charles and Annie Rollins McCraw; m. Julie Karen McAlhany, Apr. 17, 1982; 1 child, Collins William. AA, Spartanburg Meth. Coll., 1975; BSc, Wofford Coll., 1977; MusM, U. SC, 1996. Instr. piano Case Bros. and Brasington Ho. Music, 1977—86; dir. music ministry Westminster Presbyn. Ch., Spartanburg, SC, 1986—; asst. prof., dir. of music Wofford Coll., 2000—. Pianist: Spartanburg Little Theatre; musician: (cd recording) Hymns to Him, Christmas Memories; composer: Song of Dedication. Mem.: Alpha Psi Omega. R-Conservative. Presbyterian. Avocations: travel, reading. Home: 134 Mabry Rd Spartanburg SC 29307-4438 Office: Wofford Coll 429 N Church St Spartanburg SC 29303-3663 Home Phone: 864-579-3631; Office Phone: 864-597-4597. Office Fax: 864-597-4595. Personal E-mail: gmac1@charter.net. Business E-Mail: mccrawwg@wofford.edu.

MCCRAY, LORA, real estate developer; b. Donalsonville, Ga., Nov. 5, 1963; d. Robert and Eula Mae McCray. BA in Polit. Sci., U. Ga., 1985; JD, U. Wash., 1988; MA in Applied Anthropology, U. Memphis, 1998. Bar: Md. 1988. Sr. case supr. DSZ & Assocs., Arlington, Va., 1990—96; rsch. assoc. Ctr. Urban Rsch. and Ext., Memphis, 1996—98; bus. developer Fannie Mae, Washington, 1998—2002; sr. devel. assoc. McAuley Inst., Silver Spring, Md., 2002—. Dir. Lamont Productions, Washington, 1996—; leadership awards com. mem. Washington Area Womens Found., 2002—03. Literacy tutor Washington Literacy Coun., Washington, 1999—2002. Fellow, U. Wash., 1985—88; scholar, Nat. Merit Scholar Program, 1981—85. Mem.: ABA, Am. Anthrop. Assn., Md. State Bar Assn. (licentiate), Phi Kapp Phi. Avocations: travel, reading, literature. Office: Mcauley Institute 8380 Colesville Rd Ste 300 Silver Spring MD 20910-6264 Personal E-mail: java2jo@aol.com. E-mail: lmccray@mcauley.org.

MC CRAY, RONALD DAVID, lawyer, health products executive; b. Bronx, NY, July 2, 1957; s. Sylvester David and Vivian Marie (Bethea) McCray; m. Monica Ann Simon, Sept. 28, 1985; children: Morgan Marie, Adriane Michelle, Jordan Ellyse. BA, Cornell U., Ithaca, NY, 1979; JD, Harvard U., 1983. Bar: NY 1984, Tex. 1994. Assoc. Weil, Gotshal & Manges, NYC, 1983-85, Jones, Day, Reavis & Pogue, Dallas, 1985-87; sr. atty. Kimberly-Clark Corp., Dallas, 1987—93, sr. counsel, 1993—96, v.p., chief counsel, 1996—99, v.p., sec., 1999—2001, v.p., assoc. gen. counsel, sec., 2001—03, sr. v.p. law and govt. affairs, 2003—, chief compliance officer, 2004—. Bd. dirs. Knight-Ridder Inc., 2003—. Editor: Pattern Discovery: Anti-Trust, 1982, Harvard CR/CL Law Rev., 1981-82. Trustee The Hockaday Sch., Dallas. Mem. ABA (wire payment systems subcommittee 1988—), NY Bar Assn., Tex. Bar Assn. (comml. code com. 1989-93), Dallas Bar Assn., Tex. Bus. Law Found. (bd. dirs. 1990-93), Nat. Assn. Securities Profls., Am. Corp. Counsel Assn., Coun. Fgn. Rels. Roman Catholic. Avocations: reading, sports, music. Office: Kimberly-Clark Corp 351 Phelps Dr Irving TX 75038 *

MCCREA, DEREK DUANE, military officer, artist; b. Albany, Ga., Feb. 19, 1969; s. James Bernard and Barbara Ann McCrea; m. Sheila Leigh Duke; children: Devin Blake, Jeffrey Ryan. BBA, Franklin U., Ohio, 2007. Commd. officer US Army, 1987, advanced through grades to sgt. maj., ops. sgt. maj. 3-15 Inf. Ft. Stewart, Ga., 2001—03, first sgt. 1-64 Armor, 2003—06, sgt. maj. 2-87 Tng. Support Cocoa Beach, Fla., 2007—. Decorated Bronze Star medal Sec. of Army, 2nd Bronze Star medal; recipient 1st pl., Ga. States Arts Exhbn., 1984. Mem.: Sgt. Audie Murphy Club (life ARCOM 1992). Home and Office: Bzzzzzz Creative Expressions Gallery 4112 Bowens Mill Rd Douglas GA 31533 Home Phone: 912-384-7122. Personal E-mail: dereklovessheila@yahoo.com.

MCCREA, SHAUN S., lawyer; b. 1956; d. Robert McCrea. BA, U. Oreg.; JD, 1983. Bar: Oreg. Atty. McCrea P.C., Eugene, Oreg. Vice chmn. Oreg. Pub. Def. Svcs. Commn. Mem.: Nat. Assn. Criminal Def. Lawyers, Oreg. Criminal Def. Lawyers Assn. (past pres.). Avocation: mythology. Office: McCrea PC 1147 High St Eugene OR 97401 Office Phone: 541-485-1182. Office Fax: 541-485-6847. E-mail: smccrea@callatg.com. *

MCCREADY, KENNETH FRANK, former electric utility executive; b. Edmonton, Alta., Can., Oct. 9, 1939; s. Ralph and Lilian McCready; children: John, Janet, Brian. BSc, U. Alta., 1963. Supr. data processing and systems Calgary (Alta.) Power Ltd., 1965-67, supr. rates and contracts, 1967-68, adminstrv. asst. to exec. v.p., 1968-72, asst. mgr. mgmt. cons. div., 1972-75; mgr. mgmt. systems dept., gen. mgr. Montreal Engring. Co., Calgary, 1975-76; v.p. adminstrn. Calgary (Alta.) Power Ltd., 1976-80; sr. v.p. ops. TransAlta Utilities, Calgary, 1980-85, pres., COO, 1985-89, also bd. dirs., 1988-96; pres., CEO TransAlta Corp., 1989-96; CEO TransAlta Energy Corp., 1989-96; pres. K. F. McCready & Assocs. Ltd., Calgary, 1996—. Bd. dirs. Encana Corp., Calgary, Biosphere Technologies, Inc., Edmonton, Canada, Computer Modelling Group, Calgary, Can. Environ. Tech. Advancement Corp., Calgary, Nexterra Energy Corp., Vancouver, Naikun Wind Devel. Inc., Vancouver, Canada, NABEST, Innovest Strategic Value Advisors Inc., NYC, Minister's Adv. Coun. on Sci. and Tech., Ottawa; sr. policy advisor Energy Coun. Can., Ottawa; past chmn. Conf. Bd. Can.; past chmn. bd. Advanced Computing Techs., Inc.; past adv. bd. Tata Energy Rsch. Inst., Washington, Internat. Inst. for Sustainable Devel., Airborne Techs. Inc., Calgary; past moderator Premier's Forum, Govt. of Alta.; past environ. adv. bd. ABB Asea Brown Boveri, Zurich. Past dep. chmn. bd. govs. So. Alta. Inst. Tech.; past chair Alta. Round Table on Environment and Econ.; past mem. com. on trade and environment Govt. Can. Internat. Trade Adv.; past pres. Western Electric Power and Light Assn.; past chair environ. task force Bus. Coun. Nat. Issues. Mem. Assn. Profl. Engrs., Geologists and Geophysicists of Alta., Ranchmen's Club. Avocations: computers, bicycling, photography. E-mail: ken.mccready@telus.net.

MCCREADY, SAM, theater educator, actor, theater director; b. Belfast, No. Ireland, Nov. 22, 1936; s. David James and Sarah Elizabeth (Howlett) McC.; m. Joan Carslake, Mar. 16, 1962; children: Marcus Diarmuid Julian, Richard Alastair. MA, U. N. Wales, UK, 1976. Advt. mgr. Berkshire Internat., Ireland, 1961-63; head dept. theatre Orangefield Boys Sch., Belfast, Ireland, 1963-67, head English dept., 1967-69; lectr. U. North Wales, Bangor, England, 1969-78; artistic dir. Lyric Theatre, Belfast, Ireland, 1980-81; head dept. theatre Stranmillis Coll., Belfast, Ireland, 1978-83; assoc. prof. theatre U. Md., Catonsville, 1984-99, prof., 1999—2001; artistic dir. Shakespeare On Wheels, 1985-96. Examiner Guildhall Sch. Music and Drama, London, 1969—; trustee Lyric Theatre, Belfast, 1978-82; adjudicator Hong Kong Speech and Drama Festival, 1980, 84, 87, 93, 96, 2001, 04, 06; actor Tartuffe, Md. Stage Co., Ctr. Stage, Balt., 1997, 98, Serebriakov, Round House Theatre, Washington, 1997, Songs of Wandering Aengus, NYC, Sligo, Ireland, 1999, 2000, Krapp's Last Tape, Trinity Coll., Hartford, Conn., 1999, That Time, 2000, Early Memories, NY, 2001; The Great Yeats, 2002, Elizabeth the Queen, 2003, Folger Theatre, Washington, 2003; Heartbreak House, Roundhouse, DC, 2003; lectr. Yeats Internat. Summer Sch., Sligo, Ireland, 1998, 99, 2000, 03, 04, 05, 06, 07. Author: Theatre in the North of Ireland, 1969-99, 2000, Lucille Lortel: The Queen of Off-Broadway, 1993, Yeats Encyclopedia, 1997, Coole Lady, 2005, Baptism by Fire, 2007, New York State of Mind, 2007; adaptor, dir. play: Spring's Awakening, 1987 (Best Dir. award 1987), No Country for Old Men, 1985, Picture of Dorian Gray, 1988, Salome, 1989, The Tutor, 1992, The Widening Gyre, 1994, The Shadow of a Gunman, 1995, Diary of a Scoundrel, 1996 (Best Dir. award 1997), On the Verge, 1997, Deirdre, 1997, What the Butler Saw, 1998, Yerma, 2000, Macbeth, 2001, The Belfast Carmen, 2002, Death of Cuchulain, Sligo, 2003, Coole Lady (Irish tour), 2004, (off Broadway) Sword Against the Sea (Terre Haute and Irish tour), 2005, Two By Yeats, 2006, Philadelphia, Here I Come!, 2007; contbr. articles to profl. jours. Named Outstanding Dir. Am. Coll. Theatre Festival, 1986, 87, 93, 97. Mem. Brit. Actors Equity, Am. Actors Equity, East Ctrl. Theatre Conf., Am. Conf. Irish Studies, Phi Kappa Phi. Episcopalian. Avocations: painting, music, photography, reading, gardening. Personal E-mail: akwadux@yahoo.com.

MCCREARY, FRANK E., III, lawyer; b. Santa Monica, Calif., Mar. 25, 1943; s. Frank Elijah and Irma (Holland) McC.; m. Jacqueline Moehlman, Feb. 15, 1969; children: Jennifer Claire, Frank Ward. BA, Cornell U., 1965; LLB with honors, U. Tex., 1968. Bar: Tex. 1968. Ptnr. Vinson & Elkins, Houston, 1970—2006. Trustee United Way Tex. Gulf Coast, Houston, 1988-90; bd. dir. Vol. Ctr., Houston, 1987-99. Capt. US Army, 1968-70, Vietnam. Mem. Nat. Assn. Bond Lawyers, Tex. Law Rev. Assn., Houston Bar Found. Office: Vinson & Elkins Ste 2500 First City Tower 1001 Fannin St Houston TX 77002-6760 Office Phone: 713-758-2440. Office Fax: 713-615-5256. E-mail: fmccreary@velaw.com.

MC CREARY, JAMES FRANKLIN, lawyer, mediator; b. Farmington, Mo., June 15, 1942; s. Frank J. and Bernice E. (Dugal) McCreary; m. Martha Jean Tucker, June 30, 1962; children: James Franklin, III, Jason Tucker, Josh Adam. BSBA, U. Evansville, 1964; JD, Nashville Law Sch., 1969; MBA, Vanderbilt U., 1980. Bar: Tenn. 1969, rule 31 listed mediator: Tenn. With Old Nat. Bank, Evansville, Ind., 1960-64; with First Am. Corp., Nashville, 1972-80, exec. v.p., corp. sec., gen. counsel, 1974-80; with First Am. Nat. Bank Nashville (N.A.), 1964-72, 80-86, exec. v.p., 1980-86; ptnr. Borod & Huggins Attys., Memphis, 1986-87, Gerrish McCreary Smith PC, Memphis, 1988, of counsel, 1988—92, dir., 1993—. Pres. Met. Fed. Bank, 1988-91; vis. prof. bus. law David Lipscomb U., 1975-77; instr. law and banking Am. Inst. Banking, 1969-75. Mem. Am. Arbitration Assn., Beta Gamma Sigma Mem. Ch. of Christ. Office: Gerrish McCreary Smith PC 5214 Maryland Way Brentwood TN 37027 E-mail: fmccreary@gerrish.com.

MCCREARY, LORI L., entertainment business executive; b. Antioch, Calif., Feb. 14, 1961; d. Ronald Royce and Sharon A. (Rich) McC. BS in Computer Sci., UCLA, 1984. V.p. tech. svcs. CompuLaw Inc., Culver City, Calif., 1982-85; owner McCreary and Assocs., Santa Monica, Calif., 1985-95; CEO, pres. Revelations Entertainment, Santa Monica, 1996—. Named one of 100 Most Powerful Women in Entertainment, Hollywood Reporter, 2006. Office: Revelations Entertainment 1221 2nd St Fl 4 Santa Monica CA 90401-1150 *

MCCREDIE, JAMES ROBERT, fine arts educator; b. Chgo., Dec. 31, 1935; s. William and Mareta (Black) McC.; m. Marian Lucille Miles, Sept. 3, 1960; children: Miles William, Meredeth Black Winter. AB in History and Literature summa cum laude, Harvard U., 1958, AM, 1961, PhD, 1963; student, Am. Sch. Classical Studies, Athens, Greece, 1958-59, 61-62; LittD (hon.), U. Athens, 2004. Instr. NYU, 1963-64, asst. prof., 1965-66, assoc. prof., 1967-70, prof., 1970, 78-88, Sherman Fairchild prof. fine arts, 1988—2002, Sherman Fairchild prof. emeritus fine arts, 2002—, dep. dir. Inst. Fine Arts, 1967-69, acting dir., 1982-83, dir., 1983—2002, trustee, 2003—, asst. field dir. Excavations in Samothrace, 1962, field dir., 1963-65, dir. excavations, 1966—. Dir. Am. Sch. Classical Studies at Athens, Greece, 1969—77, chmn. mng. com., 1980—90, trustee, 1980—, pres., 2001—; vis. mem. Inst. Advanced Study, Princeton, NJ, 1977—78; mem. vis. com. dept. classical and Near Ea. archaeology Bryn Mawr Coll., 1982; mem. vis. com. dept. European paintings Met. Mus. Art, 1983—2003; mem. vis. com. Ctr. Old World Archaeology and Art Brown U., Providence, 1985; mem. adv. bd. Alexander S. Onassis Ctr. for Hellenic Studies NYU, 1990—97; cons. in field. Author: Fortified Military Camps in Attica, Hesperia, 1966, Samothrace, 7, The Rotunda of Arsinoe, 1992; mem. adv. bd. Am. Jour. Archaeology, 1969-81; contbr. articles to prof. jours. Bd. dirs. Hellenic-Am. Union, Athens, 1973-77, vice chmn., 1974-77, U.S. Ednl. Found., Greece, 1969-75; active Pres. Adv. Com. on Cultural Property, 1992-95. Charles Norton fellow, 1961-62; named hon. citizen Community of Samothrace, 1976. Mem. Am. Philos. Soc., Archaeol. Inst. Am. (life, trustee 1972-75, mem. exec. com. 1978-81), Archaeol. Soc. Athens (hon.), Deutsches archaeologisches Inst. (corr.). Home: 30 Battle Rd Princeton NJ 08540-4902 also: Palaiopolis GR-680 02 Samothrace Greece Office: NYU Inst Fine Arts 1 E 78th St New York NY 10021-0119 Business E-Mail: jrm1@nyu.edu.

MCCREE, DONALD HANNA, III, diversified financial services company executive; Grad., U. Vt. Co-head Investment Banking Europe J.P. Morgan Chase & Co., co-head North Am. Credit Markets Grp., mng. dir. Mem. exec. com. J.P. Morgan Chase & Co., mem. investment bank mgmt. com., mem. exec. risk com. Bd. trustees Westchester Arts Coun. Office: JP Morgan Chase & Co 270 Park Ave New York NY 10017-2070

MCCREE, PAUL WILLIAM, JR., systems design and engineering company executive; b. St. Louis, Oct. 27, 1926; s. Paul William and Hazel Elfrieda (Wilson) McC.; m. Carolyn Williams, Sept. 7, 1955; children: Brian, Paula, Ross. BS in Biochem. Scis., Harvard U., 1950. Mem. tech. staff System Devel. Corp., Santa Monica, Calif., 1956-62, Mitre Corp., Bedford, Mass., 1966-67; prin. engr. equipment divsn. Raytheon Co., Sudbury, Mass., 1963-66, 67-72; mem. tech. staff MIT Lincoln Labs., Lexington, Mass., 1972-76; mgr. Aerospace Systems divsn. Input Output,

Waltham, Mass., 1976-79, tech. dir., 1979-80; mem. tech. staff Mitre Corp., Bedford, Mass., 1980-82; founder, pres. BPR Co., Profl. Cons. Svcs., 1981—. Sr. mem. tech. staff, mgr. subsystem design and devel. dept. GTE Strategic Systems Divsn., 1982-84; tech. dir. HH Aerospace and Design Co. Inc., Bedford, 1984-85; prin. engr., mem. tech. staff Raytheon equipment divsn. Software Sys. Lab., Sudbury, 1985-86; v.p. HH Aerospace and Design Co. Inc., Bedford, 1986-91. Mem. NAACP, Urban League. Served with U.S. Army, 1944. Recipient Black Achiever award, Greater Boston YMCA, 1977. Mem. AAAS, IEEE, Math. Assn. Am., Am. Math. Soc., N.Y. Acad. Scis., Harvard Inst. Learning in Retirement. Democrat. Home: 173 Goodman's Hill Rd PO Box 77 Sudbury MA 01776-0077 Office Phone: 978-440-9268. Personal E-mail: pmccree@att.net.

MCCREEDY, EDWIN JAMES, lawyer; b. Atlanta, Dec. 29, 1939; m. Linda Jandora, Mar. 20, 1965; children: James M., Matthew B. BA, Columbia Coll., 1961; JD, Fordham U., 1968. Bar: N.J. 1968, U.S. Supreme Ct. 1982, cert. civil trial atty. N.J. Supreme Ct. 1982. Ptnr. McCreedy & Cox, Cranford, NJ, 1984—. Pres. Richard J. Hughes Inn of Court, 1991-92; mem. civil practice com. Supreme Ct. N.J., 1985-96. Capt. USMC, 1961—65. Fellow ABA, Internat. Soc. Barristers, Internat. Acad. Trial Lawyers, Am. Coll. Trial Lawyers (chair state com, 1995-97); mem. N.J. State Bar Assn. (trustee 1997-2001, chmn. jud. adminstrn. com. 1994-96, treas. 2001, 1st v.p. 2002, pres. elect 2002-03, pres. 2004-05), Trial Attys. N.J. (trustee), Union County Bar Assn. (pres. 1987). Avocations: golf, travel. Office: McCreedy & Cox 6 Commerce Dr Ste 13 Cranford NJ 07016-3551 Home Phone: 732-946-2693; Office Phone: 908-709-0400. Personal E-mail: edjmccr@aol.com. *

MCCREIGHT, JOANN OAKLEY, retired librarian; b. Suffern, NY, Sept. 3, 1937; d. Leslie S. and A. Mildred (Roland) Oakley; m. John C. McCreight Jr., June 25, 1961; children: JoMargaret, Jennifer C. Madlem, Leslie Ann. BS in Edn., SUNY, New Paltz, 1959; MLS, SUNY, Albany, 1983. Tchr. jr. high social studies Goshen Ctrl. Sch., NY, 1959-63; tchr. Hartford Ctrl. Sch., 1966-67; elem. tchr. Catskill Ctrl. Sch., 1973-75; clk. Pub. Libr., 1980-83; pub. libr. dir. Saugerties Pub. Libr., NY, 1983-85; evening libr. Columbia Greene C.C., Hudson, 1985—87; A-V libr. Marist Coll., Poughkeepsie, NY, 1986—88; reference libr. Hudson Valley C.C., Troy, 1989; libr. dir. Fulton Montgomery C.C., Johnstown, 1990-94; ret., 1994. Avocations: bird watching, travel, genealogy, needlecrafts. Home: 10 Orchard Dr Kinderhook NY 12106-1810

MCCRERY, JAMES (JIM MCCRERY), congressman; b. Shreveport, La., Sept. 18, 1949; m. Johnette Hawkins, Aug. 3, 1991; children: Claiborne Scott, Otis Clark. BA, La. Tech. U., 1971; JD, La. State U., 1975. Bar: La. 1975. Pvt. practice, Leesville, La., 1975-78; asst. city atty. City of Shreveport, 1979-80; staff U.S. Rep. Buddy Roemer, 1981-84; regional mgr. Ga.-Pacific Corp., 1984-88; mem. U.S. Congress from 4th La. dist., 1988-93, 97—, U.S. Congress from 5th La. dist., 1993-97; mem. ways and means com. Republican. Office: US Ho Reps 2104 Rayburn Ho Office Bldg Washington DC 20515-1804 *

MCCRIE, ROBERT DELBERT, editor, educator; b. Sarnia, Ont., Can., Oct. 8, 1938; s. Robert Newton and Evelyn May (Johnston) McC.; m. Fulvia Madia, Dec. 22, 1965; children: Carla Alexandra, Mara Elizabeth. BA, Ohio Wesleyan U., 1960; MS, U. Toledo, 1964; postgrad., U. Chgo., 1962-63; MA, Hunter Coll., 1994; MPhil, CUNY, 1994, PhD, 1995. Cert. protection profl. Researcher Connective Tissues Research Lab., Copenhagen, 1963; copywriter numerous advt. agys., 1965-70; owner, editor Security Letter, NYC, 1970—; editor, pub. HBJ Publs., NYC, 1973-76; pres. Mags. for Medicine, Inc., NYC, 1972-81. Faculty John Jay Coll. Criminal Justice, 1985—, adj. to full prof., chair Law, Police Sci. and Criminal Justice Adminstrn., 1997—2003; cons. in field; spkr. at numerous meetings. Author: Security Operations Management, 2001, rev. edit., 2007, Readings in Security Management, 2002; editor: Security Letter Source Book, 1983—, Behavioral Medicine, 1978—81, Security Jour., 1989—98; contbr. books and articles on security and urban crime and policing. Mem.: AAUP, Accolade, Internat. Assn. Profl. Security Cons. Disting. Svc., Internat. Security Mgmt. Assn. (Brennan award 1993), Nat. Coun. Investigation and Security Svcs. (Duffy Meml. Achievement award 1992), ASIS Internat. (pres.'s cert. of merit 1990), Correctional Edn. Assn., Urban History Assn. (life), Union League Club, Pi Delta Epsilon, Delta Sigma Rho, Alpha Tau Omega. Presbyterian. Home: 49 E 96th St New York NY 10128-0782 Office: 166 E 96th St New York NY 10128-2565 also: John Jay Coll Criminal Justice 899 10th Ave New York NY 10019-1069 Office Phone: 212-237-8386. Personal E-mail: rmccrie@verizon.net. Business E-Mail: rmccrie@jjay.cuny.edu.

MCCRIMMON, BARBARA SMITH, writer, librarian; b. Anoka, Minn., May 3, 1918; d. Webster Roy and Jessie (Sargeant) Smith; m. James McNab McCrimmon, June 10, 1939; Children: Kevin Mor, John Marshall. BA, U. Minn., Mpls., 1939; MSL.S., U. Ill., Champaign-Urbana, 1961; PhD, Fla. State U., Tallahassee, 1973. Asst. librarian Ill. State Nat. Hist. Survey, Champaign, Ill., 1961-62; research assoc. Bur. Community Planning, U. Ill., Champaign, 1962-63; librarian Ill. Water Survey, Champaign, 1964-65, Am. Meterol. Soc., Boston, 1965-67; edit. asst. Jour. Library History, Tallahassee, 1967-69, 73-74. Adj. asst. prof. Sch. Library Sci., Fla. State U., Tallahassee, 1976-77. Author: Power, Politics and Print, 1981, Richard Garnett: The Scholar as Librarian, 1989; editor: American Library Philosophy, 1975; contbr. articles to profl. jours. Mem. ALA, Pvt. Libraries Assn., Beta Phi Mu, Manuscript Soc. Democrat. Home: The Colonnades C30 2600 Barracks Rd Charlottesville VA 22901

MCCRODDEN, BRUCE A., bank executive; B in Engring., U. Del., Newark, 1969. With pub. and govt. sectors and various bus. lines BP, Cleve., NYC, London and Washington; with Nat. City Corp., Cleve., 1999—, sr. v.p. corp. pub. affairs. Bd. dirs. ARC, Ctr. for Families and Children, Ohio C. of C. Office: Nat City Corp Nat City Ctr 1900 E Ninth St Cleveland OH 44114-3484 Office Phone: 216-222-2000. *

MCCROHON, CRAIG, lawyer; b. Harvey, Ill., Oct. 17, 1961; s. Maxwell and Nancy McCrohon. BA, Harvard U., 1984; postgrad., London Sch. Econs., 1988; JD, MBA, U. Pa., 1989. Bar: Ill. 1989, U.S. Dist. Ct. (no. dist.) Ill. 1989. Ptnr. Burke, Warren, Chgo., 2001—. Editor: Let's Go: USA, 1983. Mem. Ill. Gov.'s Transition Team Tech., Venture Capital & Regulated Industries, 2002. Mem.: Tech. Execs. Roundtable (pres. 1996—2001), Ill. C. of C. (working group econ. devel. com.), Chgo. Bar Assn. (chmn. com. on consumer fin. svcs. 1991—92, chmn. com. on corp. law depts. 2004—). Home: 330 S Michigan Ave Apt 1701 Chicago IL 60604-4328 Office: 330 N Wabash Ave Chicago IL 60611

MCCRONE, ALISTAIR WILLIAM, retired academic administrator; b. Regina, Can., Oct. 7, 1931; BA, U. Sask., 1953; MSc, U. Nebr., 1955; PhD, U. Kans., 1961. Instr. geology NYU, 1959-61, asst. prof., 1961-64, assoc. prof., 1964-69, prof., 1969-70, supr. Rsch. Ship Sea Owl on L.I. Sound, 1959-64, asst. dir. univ. program at Sterling Forest, 1965-66, resident master Rubin Internat. Residence Hall, 1966-69, chmn. dept. geology, 1966-69, assoc. dean Grad. Sch. Arts and Scis., 1969-70; prof. geology, acad. v.p. U. Pacific, 1970-74, acting pres., 1971; prof. geology, pres. Calif. State U. Sys. Humboldt State U., Arcata, 1974—2002. Exec. coun. Calif. State U. Sys., 1974-2002, acad. senate Humboldt State U., 1974-2002, chancellor's com. on innovative programs, 1974-76, trustees' task force on off-campus instrn., 1975-76, exec. com. Chancellor's Coun. of Pres., 1976-79, Calif. state del. Am. Assn. State Coll. and Univ., 1977-80; mem. Commn. on Ednl. Telecomm., 1983-86; chair Calif. State U. Statewide Task Force on Earthquake and Emergency preparedness, 1985-88, 95-97; chmn., accreditation teams Western Assn. Sch. and Coll.; chair com. on energy and environ. Am. Assn. State Coll. and Univ., 1980-84; chair program com. Western Coll. Assn., 1983-84, panelist, 1983. Contbr. articles to profl. jour.; lectr. on geology Sunrise Semester program CBS Nat. Network, 1969-70; various appearances on local TV stas. Bd. trustees Presbyn. Hosp.-Pacific Med. Ctr., San Francisco, 1971-74; mem. Calif. Coun. for Humanities, 1977-82; mem. local campaign bd. United Way, 1977-83; mem. Am. Friends Wilton Park, 1980—; bd. dirs. Humboldt Convention and Visitors Bur., 1980-87, Redwood Empire Assn., 1983-87; bd. dirs. Calif. State Automobile Assn., 1988-2007, Am. Automobile Assn., 1990-93; bd. trustees Calif. State Parks Found., 1994-2000. Recipient Erasmus Haworth Disting. Alumnus award U. Kans., 2000; Shell fellow in geology U. Nebr., 1954-55; Danforth assoc. NYU, 1964. Fellow Calif. Acad. Sci.; mem. AAAS, Geol. Soc. Am., Am. Assn. U. Adminstrs. (nat. bd. 1986-89, 96-99, 2001-2002), Assn. Am. Coll. (bd. dir. 1989-92, chair 1991), St. Andrews Soc. NY (life), Rotary, Sigma Xi (pres. NYU chpt. 1967-69), Phi Kappa Phi. Avocation: golf. Office: Humboldt State U Univ Campus Arcata CA 95521 Office Phone: 707-826-5074. Business E-Mail: mccrone@humboldt.edu.

MCCRORY, JOHN BROOKS, retired lawyer; b. St. Cloud, Minn., Oct. 23, 1925; s. John Raymond and Mary Lee (Rutter) McC.; m. Margaret Joan Dickson, Sept. 4, 1954 (dec. Apr. 1957); 1 child, William B.; m. Elizabeth Ann Quick, June 27, 1959; children: John B., Ann Elizabeth. BA, Swarthmore Coll., Pa., 1948; JD, U. Pa., Phila., 1951. Bar: N.Y. 1952, D.C. 1985. Assoc. Donovan, Leisure, Newton, Lumbard & Irvine, NYC, 1951-52, Nixon, Hargrave, Devans & Doyle, Rochester, NY, 1952-62, ptnr., 1963-92; ret., 1992. Author: Constitutional Privilege in Libel Law, 1977-90. Served to lt. comdr. USNR, 1943—47, PTO. Fellow Am. Coll. Trial Lawyers; mem. ABA, Monroe County Bar Assn., N.Y. State Bar Assn., D.C. Bar Assn. Democrat. Mem. Soc. Of Friends. Address: 25 Kendal Dr Kennett Square PA 19348-2321 Office: Nixon Peabody LLP Clinton Sq PO Box 31051 Rochester NY 14603-1051

MCCRORY, PATRICK, mayor; b. Columbus, Oct. 17, 1956; m. Ann Gordon McCrory. BA in Polit. Sci. and Edn., Catawba Coll., 1978, doctorate (hon.), 2001. With Duke Energy Corp., NC, 1978—, now mgr. bus. rels. NC, Charlotte City Coun., NC, 1989—95, mayor protem NC, 1993-95, mayor NC, 1995—. Co-chmn. Charlotte's Fighting Back Commn.; mem. Children Svcs. Network; hon. chmn. Cystic Fibrosis Found., Arthritis Found.; former chmn. United Way Corp. Campaign; former mem. U. NC-Charlotte Bus. Adv. Com., Charlotte Bond Campaign, ARC Pers. Recruitment Com.; HS basketball ofcl.; former bd. dirs. Drug Free Workplace Alliance Com.; founder Uptown Crime Prevention Coun., Mayor's Mentoring Alliance, 1995; leader Homeland Security; mem. adv. coun. President's Homeland Security; pres. Republican Mayors and Local Ofcls.; bd. dir. US Conf. of Mayors, chair, Hosing and Cmty. Develop. Com.; chair NC Metropolitan Coalition; hon. chair Charlotte chpts., Alzheimer Found., Cystic Fibrosis Found., Arthritis Found. Recipient Governor's Outstanding Local Ofcl. award, 2001. Mem.: Mayor's Mentoring Alliance (founder 1995), Republican Mayors and Local Ofcls. Orgn. (pres.), U.S. Conf. Mayors. Office: Office of the Mayor Govt Ctr 600 E 4th St Charlotte NC 28202-2816 Business E-Mail: mayor@ci.charlotte.nc.us. *

MCCUAN, WILLIAM PATRICK, real estate company executive; b. Muskogee, Okla., Oct. 28, 1941; s. Lee L. and LaRee A. (Beverage) McC.; m. Jill Pamela Thomas, May 5, 1982; children: LaRee, Megan. Student, U. Tulsa, 1961—62; BA Psychology, Baylor U., 1965; MRE, So. Sem., Louisville, 1967; MS, U. Louisville, 1969; postgrad., U. Md., 1971—73. Prof., asst. dean grad. sch. U. Md., Balt., 1969—73; lobbyist and cons. Washington, 1973—76; CEO KMS Group, Inc., Columbia, Md., 1976—84, MDG Cos. Md., 1984—, MDG-Capital Corp., Naples, Fla., 1992—, MDG Cos. W.Va., Berkeley Springs, 1991—, McCuan Family Found., McCuan Farms, LLC, 2005—. Adj. prof. Cmty. Coll., Balt., 1969-72, U. Md. College Park, 1969-71; lectr. Univ. Coll.-U. Md., Balt., 1970-71, Howard C.C., Columbia, 1987-88; CEO Pet Holiday, Inc., Toledo, 1973-94; CEO Uniglobe Columbia Travel Ctr., 1986-94; non-lawyer mem. Md. Atty. Grievance Commn., 1990-96. Contbr. articles to numerous publs. Chmn., bd. dir. Concert Soc. Md., 1988-98; chmn. United Way, Howard County, Md., 1984, Am. Presdl. Inaugural Com., Md., 1988, 2004, Howard County Cmty. Partnerships; fin. chmn. Rep. Ctrl. Com., Howard County, 1988-92; trustee Columbia Found.; mem. Pres.'s Commn. on Food, Nutrition and Health, Washington, 1970, Howard County Environ. Affairs Bd.; mem. bus. adv. coun. Howard C.C.; bd. dir. Congl. Commn. on Mental Health of Children, Washington, 1973-75, Human Svcs. Inst. Children and Families; pres., chmn. & trustee McCuan Family Found., 1997—; active Nat. Rep. Com. Eagles, Team 100, 2002—; bd. govs. St. Margaret's Sch., 2003— Recipient Alumni Fellows award, U. Louisville, 1996. Mem. Nat. Assn. Home Builders (bd. dir. 1979-87, fed. govt. affairs com.), Md. Builders Assn. (pres. 1981-82), Home Builders Assn. Md. (bd. dir. 1977-82, Award of Honor 1979, Award of Excellence 1980, Presdl. award 1982), Howard County Home Builders Assn. (pres. 1978-80), Howard County C. of C. (pres. bd. dir. 1984-86) Home: 4256 Snowberry Ln Naples FL 34119-8513 Office: MDG Corp Ctr I Ste 400 8850 Columbia 100 Pky Columbia MD 21045 Office Phone: 410-730-9091. Business E-Mail: pmccuan@mdgcompanies.com.

MCCUBBIN, SHARON A., elementary school educator; children: Julie, Adrian, Matthew; m. Robert Patrick McCubbin BA, U. Calif., 1973; MEd, Cleve. State U., 1993. Cert. mid. childhood generalist Nat. Bd. for Profl. Tchg. Stds., 2000, early childhood generalist Nat. Bd. for Profl. Tchg. Stds., 2003, English as a new lang. Nat. Bd. for Profl. Tchg. Stds., 2002, literacy, reading and lang. arts Nat. Bd. for Profl. Tchg. Stds., 2005, Nat. Bd. Cert. Tchrs. Clear crosscultural, lang. and acad. devel. tchr. Primanti Montessori, Orange, Calif., 1977—81; tchr., adminstr. Montessori of Orange, 1981-83, Tustin Hills Montessori, Santa Ana, Calif., 1983-89; tchr., cons. for Montessori programs Irvine (Calif.) Unified Sch. Dist., 1990—; Montessori elem. mentor tchr., 1990—. Cons. title VII programs Irvine Unified Sch. Dist., 1990—; adv. bd. mem. GATE; corp. cons. early childhood; founding legacy ptnr. Irvine Pub. Sch. Found., 2004—. Asst. Jr. Disabled Programs, Orange, 1988—; bd. mem. Orange Co. Children's Therapeutic Arts Ctr., 2004—06. SBD fellow Johns Hopkins U., 1999. Mem. ASCD, AAUW, Assn. Montessori Internat., Assn. Montessori Internat./U.S.A., Assn. Montessori Internat. Elem. Alumni Assn., N.Am. Montessori Tchrs. Assn., Calif. Tchrs. Assn., Irvine Tchrs. Assn., Nat. Coun. Tchrs. Math., Nat. Assn. Edn. of Young Children, Educateurs sans Frontieres, U. Calif.-Irvine Alumni Assn., Pi Lamda Theta. Office: Irvine Unified Sch Dist 5050 Barranca Pkwy Irvine CA 92604-4698 also: Springbrook Elem Sch 655 N Springbrook Irvine CA 92614 Office Phone: 949-936-6077. Business E-Mail: smccubbi@iusd.org.

MCCUE, ARTHUR HARRY, artist, educator; b. NYC, Sept. 27, 1944; s. Raymond Noel and Alice (Cassidy) McC.; m. Lorraine Havel Bingham, Nov. 18, 1989. BFA, Pratt Inst., NYC, 1967; MFA, U. Colo., Boulder, 1969. Instr. art SUNY, Geneseo, 1969-72; instr. printmaking and drawing Ithaca Coll., NYC, 1973-77, assoc. prof., 1987-2001, chmn. dept. art, 1977—, prof., 2001—. Guest speaker sch. supt.'s seminar Ithaca Coll., 1990; guest artist N.Y. State Pastel Artists Assn., Cooperstown, 1990, 92, Schweinfurth Meml. Art Ctr., 1990; cons., interpreter on wheelwrighting Onondaga County Parks, Salt Mus., Liverpool, N.Y., 1989-90; guest lectr. dept. art Tompkins Cortland Community Coll., 1987. One-man shows include Univ. Club, Boulder, Colo., 1968, David Gallery, Rochester, NY, 1973, Ithaca Coll., 1977, 79, 97, Art Gallery Adelphi U., Garden City, NY, 1980, Ithaca House Gallery, 1984, 85, Schwein Furth Meml. Mus., Auburn, NY, 1986, Johnson Mus. Art, Ithaca, 1987, Upstairs Gallery, Ithaca, 1992, Lamoreaux Landing Wine Cellars Gallery, Lodi, NY, 1993, 97, 99, Trumanburg Conservatory Fine Arts, 1993, Wells Coll., Aurora, NY, 1995; exhibited in two-person shows at Harry McCue/David Smyth, Ithaca House, 1980, Hackworth/McCue, U. Pa., Edinboro, Grippi/McCue, Handwerker Gallery, Ithaca, McCue/Licht, Upstairs Gallery, Ithaca, McCue/Smith, CNYCAC Gallery, Utica, NY, 2002, McCue/Weisend, Handwerker Gallery, Ithaca 2004; exhibited in group shows at Internat. Gallery, Denver, 1969, Double U. Gallery, NYC, 1977, Handwerker Gallery, 1980, 82, 84-87, 89-95, 97-2000, 2003, Upstairs Gallery, 1983-2006, Everson Mus., Syracuse (2d prize printmaking 1987), New Visions Gallery, Ithaca, 1987-90, Elmira Coll., 1991, Cazenovia Coll., 1993, Cooperstown Nat., 1993, 96-97, 01, Old Forge Art Assn., 1992, West End Gallery, Corning, NY, 1996-97, 2001-07; nat. exhibitions: Galeria Mesa, Ariz., 1998, Wright State U., Dayton, Ohio, 2000, Wichita (Kans.) Ctr. for Arts, 2001, 04, Purdue U., Lafayette, Ind., 2004-07, U. Wis., Parkside, Wis., 2003-07; Fall River Art Show, Mass., 1973-74, 76, Marietta (Ohio) Coll., 1974, 76, Arnot Mus., Elmira, NY, 1977, 96, 2001, Ft. Hays State U., 1984, 2003, U. Maine, 1985, 92-93, 96-99, Everson Mus., 1985, 2006, Schweinfurth, Auburn, NY, 2007, Priebe Gallery, U. Wis., Oshkosh, 2007, Higgins Gallery, Cape Cod Cmty. Coll., Barnstble, Mass., 2007; included in book The American History Supply Catalogue, 1983, NY Art Rev., 3d edit.; invited spl. guest at Christie's Auction House, NYC, 1984, Roch Meml. Art Gallery, 1991; commd. by Cornell U./Statler Hotel to design art work for hotel, 1988; paintings on loan to Sen. Hillary Rodham Clinton for office in Senate Russell Office Bldg., Washington, 2004-07; represented in permanent collection at Wichita Ctr. for Arts. Lodestar grantee, 1984; recepient: Juror's award, Galleria Mesa, Mesa Art Ctr., Ariz., 1998, Made in New York honor award, Schweinfurth Mem. Art Ctr., Auburn, NY, 1999, merit purchase award, Maine Maritime Provinces Exhibition, U. Maine, 1996, purchase award, Wichita Art Ctr., Kans., 2004. Home: 2423 Skinner Rd Lodi NY 14860-9739 Office: Ithaca Coll Dept Art Danby Rd Ithaca NY 14850-5736 Business E-Mail: hmccue@ithaca.edu.

MCCUE, DAVID J., information systems specialist, entrepreneur; b. Phila., Mar. 28, 1956; s. Earl E. and A. Kathleen McCue; m. Nicole E. Schumacher, Aug. 16, 1981; 1 child, Christopher D. BSc, Rider U., 1978; MBA, NYU, 1980. Cons. Human Sys. Inc., New Vernon, NJ, 1980-81; from cons. to regional dir. tech. Andersen Consulting, NJ, 1981-93; chief info. and resource officer Am. Practice Mgmt., Inc., NYC, 1993-96; chief info. officer Computer Scis. Corp., NYC, 1996-2001; corp. dir. global applications Computer Scis. Corp. Worldwide, NYC, 2001—03; v.p. applications portfolio mgmt. Computer Scis. Corp., Falls Church, Va., 2003—06, chief info. officer, 2006—. Mem. adv. bd. Coll. Edn., Rider U., Lawrenceville, N.J., 1997-99. Mgr. Somerset County 4-H Fair, 1998—99; mem. Air Safety Found.; bd. dirs. Rider U. Alumni Assn., 1984—. Mem. Inst. Mgmt. Cons. (cert.), Assn. MBA Execs., Am. Prodn. and Inventory Control Soc. (cert. prodn. and inventory mgr.). Am. Soc. Indsl. Security, Aircraft Owners and Pilots Assn., Exptl. Aircraft Assn., NRA, NRCC (bus. adv. coun.). Republican. Roman Catholic. Avocations: aviation, horseback riding. Home: PO Box 909 21580 Lower Woodchuck Rd Florence MT 59833-0909 Office: CSC Corp Office VTC-C 630 MC 320 3170 Fairview Park Dr Falls Church VA 22042 Office Phone: 706-641-3076. Business E-Mail: djmccue@mccue.org.

MCCUE, DENNIS MICHAEL, management consultant; b. Pitts., July 28, 1952; s. Stephen J. and Mary (Maddalon) McC. BA, U. Dayton, 1974. Dist. exec. Allegheny Trails Coun., Boy Scouts Am., Pitts., 1974-77; area mgr. The Nestle Co., Pitts., 1977-79; account mgr. So. Pacific Communications, Pitts., 1979-82; dir. sales and mktg. Amertel Co., Pitts., 1982-84, ITT Bu. Communications, Newport Beach, Calif., 1985-86; dir. mktg. Damac Products, Santa Fe Springs, Calif., 1986-87; ptnr. Hunter-McCue Mgmt. Cons., Newport Beach, Calif., 1987-89; pres. Dynamic Firm Mgmt., Newport Beach, Calif., 1989—. Instr. computer info. sys. Cerritos Coll., Norwalk, Calif., 1996-2000. Contbr. articles to profl. jours. Grad. Leadership Tomorrow, 1988, program chmn., bd. dirs., 1993-95. Mem. Nat. Assn. Corp. Dirs., Nat. Bur. Profl. Mgmt. Cons. (cert.), Inst. Mgmt. Cons. (cert., bd. dirs., pres. 2004-06), Profl. Network Group (group leader), Assn. Profl. Cons., L.A. County Bar Assn. (exec. com. practice mgmt. sect. 2004—), Lew Epstein Men's Club (mgr. 1986-90). Avocations: travel, pc computing, dogs. Office: Dynamic Firm Mgmt 4570 Campus Dr Ste 60 Newport Beach CA 92660

MCCUE, HOWARD MCDOWELL, III, lawyer, educator; b. Sumter, SC, Jan. 4, 1946; s. Howard McDowell and Carolyn Hartwell (Moore) McC.; m. Judith Weiss, Apr. 3, 1971; children— Howard McDowell IV, Leigh AB, Princeton U., 1968; JD, Harvard U., 1971. Bar: Mass. 1971, Ill. 1975, U.S. Tax Ct. 1977. Assoc. Hale and Dorr, Boston, 1971-72, Mayer Brown Rowe & Maw LLP, Chgo., 1975-77, ptnr., 1977—. Adj. prof. law master in tax program Chgo. Kent Coll. Law, 1981— Author: (with others) Drafting Wills and Trust Agreements, 1979, 82, 85, 87, 90; mem. editorial adv. bd. Trusts and Estates mag., 1981-2000; contbr. articles to profl. jours. Bd. dirs. Art Inst. Chgo., Arts Club Chgo.; former chmn. bd. govs. Northwestern U. Libr. Coun.; past vice-chmn. Ravinia Festival Assn.; chmn. Lloyd A. Fry Found. Lt. USN, 1972-75. Princeton U. scholar, 1965 Mem. ABA, Chgo. Bar Assn. (fed. tax com., past chmn., exec. coun.), Chgo. Bar Found. (past pres.), Am. Coll. Tax Counsel, Am. Coll. Trust and Estate Counsel (regent, past chair charitable planning and exempt orgns. com.), Harvard Law Soc. Ill., Internat. Acad. Estate and Trust Law, Phi Beta Kappa.

MCCUE, JUDITH W., lawyer; b. Phila., Apr. 7, 1948; d. Emanuel Leo and Rebecca (Raffel) Weiss; m. Howard M. McCue III, Apr. 3, 1971; children: Howard, Leigh. BA cum laude, U. Pa., Phila., 1969; JD, Harvard U., Cambridge, Mass., 1972. Bar: Ill. 1972, U.S. Tax Ct. 1984. Ptnr. McDermott Will & Emery LLP, Chgo., 1995—. Dir. Schawk, Inc., Des Plaines, Ill.; past pres. Chgo. Estate Planning Coun. Trustee Chgo. Symphony Orch., 1995—, vice chmn., 1998—2001, 2005—. Mem.: Chgo. Bar Assn. (chmn. probate practice com. 1984—85, chmn. estate and gift tax divsn. of fed. tax com. 1988—89), Am. Coll. Trust and Estate Counsel (com. chmn. 1991—94, regent 1993—2000, com. chmn. 1998—2001, pres. 2005—06). Office: McDermott Will & Emery LLP 227 W Monroe St Ste 3100 Chicago IL 60606-5096 Business E-Mail: jmccue@mwe.com.

MCCUE, LEIGH SHAW, aerospace engineer, educator; BS in Mech. and Aerospace Engring., Princeton U., 2000; MS in Aerospace Engring., U. Mich., 2001; MS in Naval Arch. and Marine Engring., U. Mich., Ann Arbor, 2002, PhD in Naval Arch. and Marine Engring., 2004. Asst. prof. Va. Tech, Blacksburg, 2005—. Office: Va Tech Aerospace & Ocean Engring 215 Randolph Hall 0203 Blacksburg VA 24061

MCCUEN, JOHN, columnist, educator, consultant on counterinsurgency operations; b. Washington, Mar. 30, 1926; s. Joseph Raymond and Josephine (Joachim) McCuen; m. Gloria Joyce Seidel, June 16, 1949; children: John Joachim Jr., Les Seidel. BS, U.S. Mil. Acad., 1948; M of Internat. Affairs, Columbia U., 1961; grad., U.S. Army War Coll., 1968. Commd. 2d. lt. US Army, 1948, advanced through grades to col., 1969; dir. internal def. and devel. US Army War Coll., Carlisle Barracks, Pa., 1969—72; chief US Def. Liaison Group, Jakarta, Indonesia, 1972—74; chief field survey office US Army Tng. and Doctrine Command, Ft. Monroe, Va., 1974—76; ret. US Army, 1976; cons. to US Govt. on nuclear security, 1976—77; mgr. tng. Chrysler Def., Center Line, Mich., 1977—82; mgr. modification ctr. Land Sys. divsn. Gen. Dynamics, Sterling Heights, Mich., 1982—83; mgr. field ops. Warren, Mich., 1983—94; pres. Mich. Econ. Devel. Corp., Birmingham, Mich., 1994—, The Magic Christmas Tree, Inc., Birmingham, 1994—; pres., CEO Laminar, Inc.,

Southfield, Mich., 1996—; owner Adventure and Exotic Travel Outfitters, Inc., Birmingham, 1995—; past pres. First Internat. Corp., Birmingham, 1995—97; chmn., CEO Multi-Nat. Tooling LLC, Birmingham, 2005—; cons. to US Army on counter-insurgency ops., 2006—. Ptnr. East West Connection, Birmingham; past pres. Energy Resource Mgmt. Sys., Inc., Birmingham; armor advisor 3d Royal Thai Army, 1957—58; staff Dept. of Army, Washington, 1961—64; chief tng. U.S. Army Europe, Heidelberg, Germany, 1964—66; U.S. rep. users' com. NATO Missile Firing Installation Crete, Paris, 1964—66; squadron comdr. 8th Cavalry, Manheim, Germany, 1966—67; advisor Vietnamese Nat. Def. Coll., Saigon, 1968—69; spkr., writer terrorism and counter insurgency; lectr. in field. Author: The Art of Counter Revolutionary War-The Strategy of Counter Insurgency, Faber, 1966, Stackpole, 1967, Circulo Militar, 1967, Hailer, 2005 (Book now designated by Army and Marines as a "classic" on counterinsurgency); columnist: Army Times, 2002—. Bd. dirs. Troy and Mt. Clemens (Mich.) Cmty. Concert Assn., 1982—2006, pres., 1985—2006; past pres. Mich. Oriental Art Soc., Birmingham; pres. Grander View Found. Sr. Housing and Nursing, Milford, Mich., 1984—89; past chmn. region VI N.E. unit Detroit United Way Campaign; 1st reader First Ch. of Christ Scientist, Birmingham, 1989—92, chmn. bd. dirs., 2000—01. Mem.: Nat. Mgmt. Assn., Soc. Logistics Engrs., Oriental Art Soc., Assn. U.S. Army. Republican. Avocations: oriental antiques, writing. Home: 1530 Northlawn Blvd Birmingham MI 48009 Office: 999 Haynes Ste 235 Birmingham MI 48009 also: Consultancy on Counterinsurgency Ops 1530 Northlawn Blvd Birmingham MI 48009 Office Phone: 248-644-3485. Personal E-mail: jjmccuen@aol.com.

MCCUEN, JOHN FRANCIS, JR., lawyer; b. NYC, Mar. 11, 1944; s. John Francis and Elizabeth Agnes McCuen; m. Christine McCuen; children: Sarah, Mary, John. AB, U. Notre Dame, 1966; JD, U. Detroit, 1969. Bar: Mich. 1970, Fla. 1970, Ohio 1978. Legal counsel Kelsey-Hayes Co., Romulus, Mich., 1970-77; corp. counsel Sheller-Globe Corp., Toledo, 1977-79, v.p., gen. counsel, 1979-86, sec., 1982-87, sr. v.p. gen. counsel, 1986-89; ptnr. Marshall & Melhorn, Toledo, 1989-92; pvt. practice Law Offices John F. McCuen, Toledo, 1992-93; counsel Butzel Long, Ann Arbor, Mich., 1993—94; v.p. legal Kelsey Hayes Co., Livonia, Mich., 1994-98, v.p., gen. counsel, 1998-99; of counsel Butzel Long, 1999—2001. Trustee Kidney Found. N.W. Ohio, 1979-88, pres., 1984-86. Mem. Mich. Bar, Forest Lake Country Club. Home: 1668 Trading Post Ln Bloomfield Hills MI 48302-1868

MCCUEN, MAUREEN E., history educator; b. Fairfax, Va., July 24, 1972; d. John M. and Mary Anne McGovern; m. Jeffrey P. McCuen, Apr. 25, 1998; children: Elizabeth K., Patrick R. BA, James Madison U., Harrisonburg, Va., 1989—93. Cert. Secondary Composite Social Studies Tchr. Tex. Bd. Edn., 1998. Social studies tchr. Potomac Sr. HS, Prince William County Pub. Schs., Dumfries, Va., 1995—98, Travis Jr. HS, Paris Ind. Sch. Dist., Tex., 1998—2002; AP/honors. U.S. history tchr. Paris HS, Paris Ind. Sch. Dist., 2002—. Academic decathlon coach Paris HS, 2003—05, future problem solving coach, 2006—. Mem.: Nat. Coun. Social Studies, Assn. Supervision and Curriculum Devel. Avocations: camping, running, violin, theater. Office: Paris HS 2400 Jefferson Rd Paris TX 75462 Home Phone: 903-517-3802; Office Phone: 903-737-7400. Business E-Mail: mmccuen@parisisd.net.

MCCUISTION, PEG OREM, retired health facility administrator; b. Houston, July 28, 1930; d. William Darby and Dorothy Mildred (Beckett) Orem; m. Palmer Day McCuistion, Sept. 4, 1949 (div. 1960); 1 child, Leeanne E. BBA, Southwest Tex. State, 1963; MBA, George Washington U., 1968; EdD, Wayne State U., 1989. Patient care adminstr. Holy Cross Hosp., Silver Spring, Md., 1968-79; exec. dir. Hospice of S.E. Mich., Southfield, 1979-86, Hospice Austin, Tex., 1987-94; CEO EMBI, Inc., Arlington, Tex., 1994—98; gen. mgr. Hospice Home Care, San Antonio, 2001—04, ret., 2004. Bd. dirs. Cmty. Home for the Elderly, Austin, 1989-92. Fellow Am. Coll. Health Care Execs. (membership com.); mem. Internat. Hospice Inst. (assoc.), Nat. Hospice Orgn. (chair standards and accreditation com.), Tex. Hospice Orgn. (pres. 1993-94), exec. com., standards and ethics com., edn. com., chair legis. com.), Mich. Hospice Orgn. (chair edn. com., bd. dirs.). Personal E-mail: pegomc@wimberley-tx.com.

MCCUISTION, ROBERT WILEY, hospital administrator, management consultant, lawyer; b. Wilson, Ark., June 15, 1927; s. Ed Talmadge and Ruth Wiley (Bassett) McC.; m. Martha Virginia Golden, June 11, 1949 (dec. Nov. 1991); children: Beth, Dan, Jed.; m. Sudola M. Getz, Feb. 12, 1994. AB in History, Hendrix Coll., Conway, Ark., 1949; JD, U. Ark., 1952. Bar: Ark. 1952, U.S. Dist. Ct. (we. dist.) Ark. 1953. Practice in, Dermott, Ark., 1952-57; dep. pros. atty. 10th Jud. Dist. Ark., 1952-57; bus. mgr. St. Mary's Hosp., Dermott, 1953-56, asst. adminstr., 1956-57; adminstr. Stuttgart (Ark.) Meml. Hosp., 1957-60, Forrest Meml. Hosp., Forrest City, Ark., 1960-68; assoc. adminstr. St. Edward Mercy Hosp., Ft. Smith, Ark., 1968-70; pres. Meml. Med Center, Corpus Christi, Tex., 1970-79; adminstr. Methodist Hosp., Mitchell, SD, 1979-85, cons., 1985-86; mgmt. cons., owner Creative Leadership Concepts, Arlington, Tex., 1985—; adminstr. Cen. United Meth. Ch., Fayetteville, 1986-91. Sec. Ark. Hosp. Adminstrs. Forum, 1958-59, pres., 1959-60; pres. Ark. Hosp. Assn., 1964-65, Areawide Health Planning, 1970; pres. Ark. Conf. Cath. Hosps., 1970; chmn. Twin City Hosp. Coun. West Ark., 1968; v.p. Ark. Assn. Mental Health, 1966-70. Div. chmn. Forrest City United Cmty.Svcs., 1961, Corpus Christi United Way Cmty. Svcs., 1972, DeSoto coun. Boy Scouts Am., Explorer advisor, 1954-57; vice chmn., sec. ofcl. bd. Meth. Ch., 1957, lay del. S.D. ann. conf., 1980-85, cert. lay spkr., 1960—; trustee Midwest Hosp. Conf., Kansas City, Mo., 1964-1966. With USAAF, World War II. Recipient Eminent Leadership award DeSoto Area council Boy Scouts Am., 1956 Mem. Am. Assn. Hosp. Accts. (pres. Ark. chpt. 1957), S.D. Hosp. Assn. (dist. chmn. 1980-81), Mid-West Hosp. Assn. (trustee 1963-65), Am. Coll. Health Execs. (life), Rotary (pres. Forrest City 1964-65). Home and Office: 2401 St Gregory St Arlington TX 76013

MCCULLAGH, GRANT GIBSON, retired architect; b. Cleve., Apr. 18, 1951; s. Robert Ernest and Barbara Louise (Grant) McC.; m. Suzanne Dewar Folds, Sept. 13, 1975; children: Charles Weston Folds, Grant Gibson Jr. BArch, U. Ill., 1973; MArch, U. Pa., 1975; MBA, U. Chgo., 1979. Registered architect, Ill. Dir. mktg. The Austin Co., Chgo., 1977-83, asst. dist. mgr., 1983-84, dist. mgr., 1984-88, v.p., 1987-88; chmn., CEO McClier Corp., Chgo., 1988—98; chmn. Holmes & Narver, Orange, Calif., 1997-2001; exec. v.p. AECOM, LA, 2000—03, vice chmn., 2003—04; chmn., CEO Global Integrated Bus. Solutions, Inc., 2004—; CEO The Facility Group, 2005—07. Contbr. articles to various indsl. publs. Trustee Newberry Libr., Brookfield Zoo/Chgo. Zool. Soc., 2004—, Chgo. Pub. Libr. Found.; council trustee Nat. Trust for Historic Preservation. Fellow: AIA; mem.: Design/Build Inst. Am., Calif. Club, Comml. Club, Indian Hill Country Club, Univ. Club, Casino Club, Chgo. Club, Econ. Club. Republican. Episcopalian. Home: 43 Locust Rd Winnetka IL 60093-3725 Office: 181 W Madison St Ste 3900 Chicago IL 60602 E-mail: grant.mccullagh@gibscorp.com.

MCCULLAGH, JAMES CHARLES, publishing executive; b. London, Oct. 22, 1941; s. James Christopher and Violet Anne (Smith) McCullagh; children: Declan, Deidre. BS, Ind. U. Pa., 1968; MA, Lehigh U., 1970, PhD, 1974. Tchr. Holidaysburg (Pa.) Area H.S., 1968; teaching asst. Lehigh U., Bethlehem, Pa., 1968-71, doctoral fellow, 1971-73; vis. poet Pa. Coun. Arts Inc., Harrisburg, 1974-78; editor Rodale Press Inc., Emaus, Pa., 1979-83, pub., editor dir., group v.p., 1984—; pub. Novii Fermer, USSR, 1991—; pub. dir. Scuba Diving, 1992; sr. v.p. Internat. Mag. Devel.; mng. dir. Rodale Press, Inc., Russia, 1996—, DeSilva & Phillips, 1997—; dir. acquisitions Hachette Filipacchi Mags., NYC, 1998-99, v.p. corp. strategy, 1999—; mng. dir. Sci. Am., NYC, 2000—. Author: (book) Bicycle Fitness Book, 1984, Bicycling for Health and Fitness, 1995, Cycling for Health, Fitness and Well-Being, 1995, The Mad Cow Culture Book, 1999, (poetry) That Kingdom Coming Business, 1984, Magazines and Culture, 2005, The Gods of War, 2006; pub.: Mountain Bike, 1994; editor: Pedal Power, 1978, Ways to Play, 1978, The Solar Greenhouse Book, 2003. With USN, 1960—64. Recipient Man of the Yr. award, Bicycle Mfrs. Assn. Am., 1983. Mem.: Bicycle Inst. Am. (pres. 1993—), Bicycle Fedn. (bd. dirs. 1980—), Mag. Pubs. Assn. (sr. v.p. 2003—), Am. Assn. Mag. Editors. Democrat. Roman Catholic. Home: 16 Germonds Rd New City NY 10956-2857 Home Phone: 845-624-0860; Office Phone: 212-872-3770. Business E-Mail: cmccullagh@magazine.org.

MCCULLAGH, SUZANNE, curator; b. Jan. 30, 1951; AB, Smith Coll., Northampton, Mass., 1973; MA, Harvard U., Cambridge, Mass., 1974, PhD, 1981. Intern Met. Mus. Art, 1972; curatorial asst. in charge Harvard U., 1974—75; curatorial asst. Art Inst. Chgo., Dept. Prints and Drawings, 1975—79, asst. curator, 1979—84, coord. self study, long range planning, 1980—82, assoc. curator, 1985—87, Anne Vogt Fuller and Marion Titus Searle curator earlier prints and drawings, 1987—. Lectr. in field. Contbr. articles to profl. jours. Trustee Coll. Atlantic, Bar Harbor, Maine, 2000—01, 2001—, mem. exec. com., 2002—04; trustee Groton Sch., Mass., 2004—07, chmn. parents assn., 2004—07; trustee Northeast Harbor Libr., 2002—, North Shore Country Day Sch., Winnetka, Ill., 1988—99, chmn. art com., 1987—2001; vis. com. Snite Art Mus., Notre Dame U., 1985—2006; mem. vis. com. Smith Vis. Com., 2002—; bd. dirs. Print Coun. Am., 1982—85. Mem.: NEA (indemnification panel 2005—), Landmarks Preservation Coun. Ill., Harvard Club Chgo. (dir. 1995—), Arts Club Chgo. (dir. 2000—). Office: Art Inst Chgo 111 S Michigan Ave Chicago IL 60603 Office Phone: 312-443-3662. Business E-Mail: smccullagh@artic.edu.

MCCULLEY, TIMOTHY J., ophthalmologist, surgeon, educator; b. Boston, Sept. 26, 1968; s. James P. and Mary Ann McCulley; m. Lynda Van. BA, Pitzer Coll. of the Claremont (Calif.) Colls., 1991; MD, Washington U., St. Louis, 1995. Dir. ophthalmic plastic and reconstructive surgery U. Calif., Irvine, dir. ophthalmic plastic and reconstructive plastic surgery, 2000—03; dir. ophthalmic plastic and reconstructive surgery and neuro-ophthalmology Stanford U. Sch. Medicine, Calif., 2003—06; dir. ophthalmic plastic and reconstructive surgery U. Calif. Sch. Medicine, San Francisco, 2006—. Presenter in field; vis. prof. numerous profl. socs. and univ.-based continuing edn. courses, 2000—06. Contbr. articles to profl. jours. Named to Guide to Am.'s Top Ophthalmologists, Consumers Rsch. Coun. Am., 2006; recipient Carl F. and Gerty T. Cory awards for superior scholarship in biochemistry, Washington U. Sch. Medicine, 1996, award for best case series, TEI Pfizer, 2003, Ophthalmology Tchg. award, Joint Commn. of Allied Health Profls., 2004. Fellow: Am. Soc. Ophthalmic Plastic and Reconstructive Surgery, Am. Acad. Ophthalmology (editl. com. basic and clin. sci. course 2001—06); mem.: Peninsula Eye Soc. (incumbent pres. 2006—), N.Am. Neuro-Ophthalmology Soc. (patient edn. com. 2001—06), Assn. Rsch. in Vision and Ophthalmology. Avocations: scuba diving, surfing, hiking, soccer, travel. Office: U Calif San Francisco Sch Medicine 10 Koret Way Campus Box 0730 San Francisco CA 94143 Office Phone: 415-476-3321. Office Fax: 415-476-0336.

MC CULLOCH, ERNEST ARMSTRONG, internist, educator; b. Toronto, Ont., Can., Apr. 27, 1926; s. Albert E. and Letitia (Riddell) McC.; m. Ona Mary Morganty, 1953; children: James A., Michael E., Robert E., Cecelia E., Paul A. MD with honors, U. Toronto, 1948, DSc (hon.), 2004. Intern Toronto Gen. Hosp., 1949-50, sr. intern, 1951-52; NRC fellow dept. pathology U. Toronto, 1950-51; asst. resident Sunnybrook Hosp., Toronto, 1952-53; pvt. practice specializing in internal medicine Toronto, 1954-67; clin. tchr. dept. medicine U. Toronto, Toronto, 1954-60, asst. prof. dept. med. biophysics, 1959-64, assoc. prof., 1964-66, prof., 1966, asst. prof. dept. medicine, 1967-68, assoc. prof., 1968-70, prof., 1970—, Univ. prof., 1982-91, Univ. prof. emeritus, 1991—; mem. grad. faculty U. Toronto (Inst. Med. Sci.), 1968—, dir., 1975-79; asst. dean Sch. Grad. Studies U. Toronto, 1979-82. Physician Toronto Gen. Hosp., 1960-67; sr. scientist, sr. physician Ont. Cancer Inst., 1957-91, head divsn. biol. rsch., 1982-89, head divsn. cell and molecular biology, 1989-91, sr. scientist emeritus, 1991-93; vis. prof. U. Tex. Med. Ctr. Anderson Cancer Ctr., Houston, 1992-93, adj. prof., 1993-98; cons. Nat. Cancer Plan, 1972—; mem. standing com. on health rsch. and devel. Ont. Coun. Health, 1974-82. Author numerous articles on rsch. in hematology; mem. editl. bd.: Blood, 1969-80, Biomedicine, 1973, Clin. Immunology and Immunopathology, 1972-76; assoc. editor: Jour. Cellular Physiology, 1966-68; editor, 1968-91. Trustee Banting Rsch. Found., 1975-84, hon. sec.-treas., 1958-74, v.p., 1977-79. Decorated officer Order of Can., 1988; recipient William Goldie prize U. Toronto, 1964, Gairdner award Internat. Gairdner Found., 1969, Starr Medallist award Dept. Anatomy U. Toronto, 1957; Thomas W. Eadie Medal, 1991, Royal Soc. Canada, Nat. Cancer Inst. Can. fellow, 1954-57, Albert Lasker award for Basic Med. Rsch., Lasker Found., 2005; named to Can. Med. Hall of Fame, 2004. Fellow Royal Soc. Can. (pres. Nat. Acad. Sci. 1987-90, Thomas W. Eadie Medal 1991, Golden Jubilee Medal), Royal Coll. Physicians and Surgeons Can., Royal Soc. London, Can. Acad. Sci.; mem. Am. Soc. Exptl. Pathology, Am. Assn. Cancer Rsch., Can. Soc. Cell Biology, Can. Soc. Clin. Investigation, Am., Internat. Socs. Hematology, Internat. Soc. Exptl. Hematology, Inst. Acad. Medicine (charter mem.), Badminton Club, Racquet Club. Home: 480 Summerhill Ave Toronto ON Canada M4W 2E4 Office: Princess Margaret Hosp 9th Fl Rm 112 610 University Ave Toronto ON Canada M5G 2M9 Home Phone: 416-425-2564. E-mail: mcculloch@uhnres.utoronto.ca. *Research success depends on associating with agreeable and talented people.*

MCCULLOCH, LINDA, school system administrator; b. Mont., Dec. 21, 1954; m. Bill McCulloch, 1978. BA in Elem. Edn., U. Mont., 1982, MA in Elem. Edn., 1990. Tchr. Pub. Schs, Mont., Ashland, Missoula, Bonner, 1978—95; rep. Mont. Ho. of Reps., 1995—2001; supt. pub. instrn. Mont., 2002—. Faculty affiliate U. Mont., 1995—2000; mem. judiciary, highways & transportation, local govt. edn. and house rules committees Mont. Ho. Reps., 1997, interim com. assignments included juvenile justice & mental health, Indian Affairs, and edn. & local govt.; minority caucus leader Ho. Reps., Helena, Mont., 1999; vice chair edn. com. Mont. Ho. Reps., 1999. Mem., officer PTA Assn., Helena, 1985—; bd. dirs. Missoula Developmental Services. Corp.; mem. adv. com. Missoula Youth Homes Foster Care; bd. mem. Pub Edn., Bd. Reagents, Mont. Libr. Commn. and Land Board, N.W. Regional Ednl. Lab., Mont. Heritage Project, Profl. Tchg. Found. Recipient Mike and Maureen Mansfield Libr. scholaship, 1981, J.C. Penny Vol. Program award, 1998. Mem.: AAUW, LWV, Five Valleys Reading Assn., Mont. State Reading Coun., Mont. Fedn. Tchrs., Mont. Ednl. Assn., Mont. Libr. Assn. (Legislator of Yr. award 1997), Mont. Family Union, Mont. Dem. Womens Club. Office: Mont Office Pub Instruction PO Box 202501 Helena MT 59620-2501 Office Fax: 406-444-5658. Business E-Mail: opisupt@mt.gov. *

MCCULLOCH, RACHEL, economist, educator; b. 1942; m. Gary Edward Chamberlain; children: Laura Chamberlain Gehl, Neil Dudley Chamberlain. BA, U. Pa., 1962; MA in Teaching, U. Chgo., 1965, MA, 1971, PhD, 1973; student, MIT, 1966-67. Economist Cabinet Task Force on Oil Import Control, Washington, 1969; instr., then asst. prof. Grad. Sch. Bus. U. Chgo., 1971-73; asst. prof., then assoc. prof. econs. Harvard U., Cambridge, Mass., 1973-79; assoc. prof., then prof. econs. U. Wis., Madison, 1979-87; prof. Brandeis U., Waltham, Mass., 1987—, Rosen Family prof., 1989—, dir. Lemberg Program in Internat. Econs. and Fin., 1990-91, dir. PhD program Internat. Bus. Sch., 1994—2001, chair dept. econs., 2006—. Mem. Pres.'s Commn. on Indsl. Competitiveness, 1983-84; mem. adv. coun. Office Tech. Assessment, U.S. Congress, 1979-88; cons. World Bank, Washington, 1984-86, 2004-05; mem. com. on internat. rels. studies with People's Republic of China, 1984-91; rsch. assoc. Nat. Bur. Econ. Rsch., Cambridge, 1985-93; mem. adv. com. Inst. for Internat. Econs., Washington, 1987—; faculty Advanced Mgmt. Network, La Jolla, Calif., 1985-92; mem. com. examiners econs. test Grad. Record Exam. Ednl. Testing Svc., 1990-96, chair, 1992-96; mem. discipline adv. com. for Fulbright scholar awards in econs. Coun. Internat. Exch. Scholars, 1991-93, chair, 1992-93; mem. adv. com. for Fulbright Chairs Program, 1997; cons. Global Economy Project, Edn. Film Ctr., 1993-94; mem. study group on pvt. capital flows to developing and transitional economies Coun. Fgn. Rels., 1995-96, acad. adv. panel, Fed. Reserve Bank of Boston, 1999—; faculty assoc. Harvard Inst. for Internat. Devel., 1997-2000; fellow Internat. Leadership Forum, 2001-; AGIP prof. internat. econs. Sch. Advanced Internat. Studies, Bologna Ctr., Johns Hopkins U., 2004-05, cons. Asian Devel. Bank, 2007. Author: Research and Development as a Determinant of U.S. International Competitiveness, 1978; contbr. articles to profl. jours. and books. Grantee NSF, 1975-79, Hoover Inst., 1984-85, German Marshall Fund of U.S., 1985, Ford Found., 1985-88, U.S. Dept. Edn., 1990-91, Schulhof Found., 2001-02. Mem. Am. Econ. Assn. (dir. summer program for minority students 1983-84, mem. executive com., 1997-2000), Internat. Trade and Fin. Assn. (bd. dirs. 1993-95). Office: Brandeis U Dept Econs MS 021 PO Box 549110 Waltham MA 02454-9110 Business E-Mail: mcculloch@brandeis.edu.

MC CULLOCH, SAMUEL CLYDE, history professor; b. Ararat, Australia, Sept. 3, 1916; came to U.S., 1936, naturalized, 1944; s. Samuel and Agnes Almond (Clyde) McC.; m. Sara Ellen Rand, Feb. 19, 1944; children: Ellen (Mrs. William Henry Meyer III), David Rand, Malcolm Clyde. AB with highest honors in History, UCLA, 1940, MA (grad. fellow history), 1942; PhD, U. Calif. at Los Angeles, 1944. Asst. U. Calif. at Los Angeles, 1943-44; instr. Oberlin Coll., 1944-45; asst. prof. Amherst Coll., 1945-46; vis. asst. prof. U. Mich., 1946-47; mem. faculty Rutgers U., 1947-60, prof. history, assoc. dean arts and scis., 1958-60; dean coll., prof. history San Francisco State Coll., 1960-63; dean humanities, prof. history U. Calif. at Irvine, 1963-70, prof., 1970-87, prof. emeritus, 1987—, coordinator Edn. Abroad Program, 1975-85, dir. Australian Study Ctr., 1986, 87. Vis. summer prof. Oberlin Coll., 1945, 46, U. Calif. at Los Angeles, 1947, U. Del., 1949; Fulbright Research prof. Monash U., Melbourne (Australia) U., 1970; Am. Philos. Soc. grantee, 1970 Author: British Humanitarianism, 1950, George Gipps, 1966, River King: The Mc Culloch Carrying Company and Echura, 1865-1898, 1986, Instant University: A History of U.C.I., 1957-1993, 1995, William McCulloch, 1932-1909, 1997, A Collection of Book Reviews, 1948-93, 2000; contbr. numerous articles, revs. to profl. jours.; assoc. editor Jour. Brit. Studies, 1960-68, bd. advisors, 1968-70; bd. corrs. Hist. Studies: Australia and New Zealand, 1949-83. Mem. Calif. Curriculum Commn., 1961-67, Highland Park (N.J.) Bd. Edn., 1959-60. Grantee Am. Philos. Soc., Social Sci. Rsch. Coun. and Rutgers U. Rsch. Coun. to Australia, 1951; Fulbright rsch. fellow U. Sydney, Australia, 1954-55; grantee Social Sci. Rsch. Coun. to Eng., summer 1955 Fellow Royal Hist. Soc.; mem. Am. Hist. Assn., Church, Royal Australian Hist. Socs., A.A.U.P., N.Am. Conf. Brit. Studies (exec. sec. 1968-73, pres. 1975-77, Liftime Disting. Contbns. Brit. Studies award 1995), English Speaking Union (pres. New Brunswick 1957-59), Phi Beta Kappa, Pi Gamma Mu. Episcopalian (vestry). Home: 2121 Windward Ln Newport Beach CA 92660-3820

MCCULLOH, JUDITH MARIE, editor; b. Spring Valley, Ill., Aug. 16, 1935; d. Henry A. and Edna Mae (Traub) Binkele; m. Leon Royce McCulloh, Aug. 26, 1961. BA, Ohio Wesleyan U., 1956; MA, Ohio State U., 1957; PhD, Ind. U., 1970. Asst. to dir. Archives of Traditional Music, Bloomington, Ind., 1964-65; asst. editor U. Ill. Press, Champaign, 1972-77, assoc. editor, 1977-82, sr. editor, 1982-85, exec. editor, 1985—2007, dir. devel., 1992—2003; asst. dir., 1997—2007. Advisor John Edwards Meml. Forum, LA, 1973—. Mem. Editorial Bd. Am. Music, 1980-89, 2007—, Jour. Am. Folklore, Washington, 1986-90; co-editor Stars of Country Music, 1975; editor (LP) Green Fields of Ill., 1963, (LP) Hell-Bound Train, 1964, Ethnic Recordings in America, 1982; gen. editor Music in American Life series. Trustee Am. Folklife Ctr., Libr. of Congress, Washington, 1986—2004, chair, 1990—92, 1996—98, trustee emerita, 2004—. Fulbright grantee, 1958-59; NDEA grantee, 1961, 62-63; grantee Nat. Endowment for the Humanities, 1978; recipient Disting. Achievement citation Ohio Wesleyan U. Alumni Assn., Disting. Svc. award Soc. for Am. Music, Lifetime Achievement award Belmont U. Curb Music Industry, Disting. Achievement award Internat. Bluegrass Music Assn. Fellow: Am. Folklore Soc. (exec. bd. 1974—79, pres. 1986—87, exec. bd. 2001—03); mem.: Am. Musicological Soc. (mem. coun. 2005—07), Am. Anthropol. Assn., Soc. Ethnomusicology (hon.; treas. 1982—86), Soc. Am. Music (1st v.p. 1989—93, coun. 2005—). Democrat. Office: U Ill Press 1325 S Oak St Champaign IL 61820-6903 Business E-Mail: jmmccull@uillinois.edu.

MCCULLOH, THAYNE MARTIN, university administrator, consultant; b. LA, Aug. 20, 1964; m. Julie Ann Lopach, July 24, 1993; children: Kathryne Angela, Anne Elizabeth, Emily Clara. BA in Psychology, Gonzaga U., 1989; PhD in Exptl. Social Psychology, Oxford U., 1998. Test adminstr. Pearn Kandola Downs Occupl. Psychologists, Oxford, England, 1989—90; coord. residence life Gonzaga U., Spokane, 1990—92, dir. housing, 1993—95, asst. dean students, 1995—96, dean student acad. svcs., 1996—98, dean student fin. svcs., 1998—2002, assoc. acad. v.p., 2002—04, v.p. adminstrn. and planning, 2004—. Tutor in social psychology Oxford U., England, 1989—93; accreditation evaluator N.W. Commn. Coll. and U., Redmond, Wash., 1997—; cons. enrollment mgmt. and fin. aid, Spokane, 2000—. Mem. Human Rights Commn., Spokane, 2005—06. Sgt. US Army, 1983—86. Decorated Army Achievement medal U.S. Army, Army Commendation medal; recipient Sr. award, Gonzaga U. Alumni Assn., 1989; scholar, Chancellors and Prin., U.K., 1989—93. Mem.: APA, Citibank Ednl. Leadership Financing Coun., Nat. Assn. Student Fin. Aid Adminstrs., Nat. Assn. Student Pers. Adminstrs. (New Profl. of Yr., region V 1995). Roman Catholic. Achievements include research in mentoring and its relationship to leadership succession planning. Home: 1208 S Wall St Spokane WA 99204-3748 Office: Gonzaga Univ 502 E Boone Ave Spokane WA 99258-0086 Home Phone: 509-869-2957; Office Phone: 509-323-6289. Office Fax: 509-323-6288.

MCCULLOUGH, COLLEEN, author; b. Wellington, N.S.W., Australia, June 1, 1937; m. Ric Robinson, Apr. 13, 1984. Student, U. Sydney, Australia, London U.; LittD (hon.), Macquarie U., Sydney, 1993. Neurophysiologist Sydney, London, Yale U. Sch. Medicine, 1967-77. Author: Tim, 1974, The Thorn Birds, 1977, An Indecent Obsession, 1981, Cooking with Colleen McCullough and Jean Easthope, 1982, A Creed for the Third Millennium, 1985, The Ladies of Missalonghi, 1987, The First Man in Rome, 1990, The Grass Crown, 1991, Fortune's Favorites, 1993, Caesar's Women, 1996, Caesar, 1997, The Song of Troy, 1998, Roden Cutler, V.C. (The Biography), 1998, Morgan's Run, 2000, The October Horse, 2002, The Touch, 2003, Angel Puss, 2004. Office: PO Box 333 Norfolk Island Australia Fax: (6723) 23313.

MCCULLOUGH, DAVID, writer, educator; b. Pitts., July 7, 1933; s. Christian Hax and Ruth (Rankin) McC.; m. Rosalee Ingram Barnes, Dec. 18, 1954; children: Melissa, David, William Barnes, Geoffrey Barnes, Doreen Kane. BA, Yale U., 1955; LHD, Skidmore Coll., 1983, Rensselaer Poly. Inst., 1983; LHD (hon.), Wesleyan U., Middletown, Conn., 1984, Colo. Coll., 1985, U. N.H., 1993, Chatham Coll., 1994, Beloit Coll., 1996, Georgetown U., 1995, Coll. William and Mary, 1996, Grinnell Coll., 1997, Dickinson Coll., 1998, Northeastern U., 2002, Brandeis U., 2003, OH State

U., 2003; DEng (hon.), Villanova U., 1984; doctorate (hon.), Worcester Poly. Inst., 1984, U. Miami, 1996, Grand Valley State U., 1997, Yale U., 1998, Brown U., 2000, Tufts U., 2001, U. Del., 2001; LittD (hon.), Allegheny Coll., 1984, Middlebury Coll., 1986, Indiana U. at Pa., 1991, U. S.C., 1993, U. Pitts., 1994, Union Coll., 1994, Washington Coll., 1994, Hamilton Coll., 1996, SUNY, 1999, U. Conn., 1999, U. Vt., 2002, Dartmouth Coll., 2003; LLD (hon.), Lafayette Coll., 1995, U. Mass., 1998, Wheaton Coll., 2002. Writer, editor Time, Inc., NYC, 1956-61, USIA, Washington, 1961-64, Am. Heritage Pub. Co., NYC, 1964-70; sr. contbg. editor Am. Heritage mag.; free-lance author, 1970—. Newman vis. prof. American civilization, Cornell U., fall 1989; mem. Bennington (Vt.) Coll. Writers Workshop, 1978-79; scholar-in-residence U. N. Mex., 1979, Wesleyan U. Writers Conf., 1982, 83; mem. adv. bd. Ctr. for the Book, Libr. of Congress; past vis. prof. Dartmouth Coll., Wesleyan U.; spkr. and lectr. in field. Author: The Great Bridge, 1972, The Path Between the Seas, 1977, The Johnstown Flood, 1968, Mornings on Horseback, 1981, Brave Companions, 1992, Truman, 1992 (Pulitzer Prize for biography 1993), John Adams, 2001 (Pulitzer prize for biography 2002), 1776, 2005 (Quills award for best history/current events/politics, 2005, #1 on Publishers Weekly Bestseller list, 2005); host TV series: Smithsonian World, 1984-88, The American Experience, 1988—; narrator numerous TV documentaries including The Civil War, Napoleon, 2000, Abraham & Mary Lincoln: A House Divided, 2001. Mem. Harry S. Truman Centennial Commn.; trustee Nat. Trust Hist. Preservation, Harry S. Truman Libr. Inst., Hist. Soc. Western Pa., Jefferson Meml. Found., Boston Pub. Libr.; hon. trustee Carnegie Inst.; founding mem. Protect Hist. Am. Guggenheim fellow, 1976; recipient N.Y. Diamond Jubilee award, 1973, cert. of merit Mcpl. Art Soc. N.Y., 1973, Nat. Book award for history, 1978, Francis Parkman prize, 1978, 93, Samuel Eliot Morison award, 1978, Cornelius Ryan award, 1978, Civil Engring. History and Heritage award, 1978, L.A. Times prize for biography, 1981, Am. Book award for biography, 1982, Harry S. Truman Pub. Svc. award, 1993, St. Louis Lit. award, 1993, Pa. Gov.'s award for excellence, 1993, Pa. Soc. Gold Medal award, 1994, Charles Frankel prize contributions to humanities Endowment Humanities and U.S. Govt., 1995, Disting. Contbns. to Am. Letters award. Nat. Book Found., Lit. Lion award N.Y. Pub. Libr., 1981, Emmy award for work in pub. TV, 1985, Gold medal Pa. Soc., Carl Sandburg Lit. award, 2000, Am. Revolution Round Table Book award, 2001, LA Pub. Libr. Lit. award, 2002, William Bradford award, Pilgrim Soc., 2002, Christopher award, 2002, Robin Winks award, Nat. Pks. Conservation Assn., 2003, Presdl. Medal of Freedom, 2006. Fellow Soc. Am. Historians (pres.); mem. ASCE (hon.), Am. Acad. Arts and Scis., Am. Acad. Arts and Letters, Soc. Am. Historians (pres. 1991—). Avocations: travel, reader, landscape painter, sunday night spaghetti chef. Office: Janklow & Nesbit Associates 445 Park Ave # 13th New York NY 10022-2606 *

MCCULLOUGH, DAVID LEGARDE, urologist; b. Chattanooga, 1938; MD, Bowman Gray, 1964. Intern U. Hosps. Case Western Res. U., Cleve., 1964-65, resident in surgery, 1965-66; fellow urology Baylor U. Coll. Medicine, Houston, 1968-69; resident in urology Mass. Gen. Hosp., Boston, 1969-72; chief urologist N.C. Bapt. Hosp., Winston-Salem, 1983—; prof., former chmn. urology Wake Forest U. Coll. Medicine, Winston-Salem. Past pres. Am. Bd. Urology. Mem. ACS, AMA, Am. Urol. Assn. (past pres. southeastern sect., past pres., bd. dirs., chair for edn.), Am. Assn. Genitourinary Surgeons (past pres.), Clin. Soc. Urol. Surgeons, Halsted Soc. Office Phone: 336-716-4131.

MCCULLOUGH, EDWARD L., artist, educator; b. Danville, Ill., Sept. 18, 1934; s. Fred and Helen McCullough; m. Gale Carter, Dec. 15, 1954; children: Scott, Reggie Johnson, Allison McClendon. BS, Ill. State U., 1962, MA, 1966. Assoc. prof. of art Ill. Wesleyan U., Bloomington, 1966—80; adj. prof. of art Columbia Coll., Chgo., 1990—. Sculpture, Meridian III, Ea. Ill. U., 1997, VISION, Fed. Res. Bank Chgo., 1998, Meridian VII, Chgo. Pub. Art Program, 2001, Meridian VI, Ctrl. Ill. Regional Airport, Bloomington, Ill., 2001, sculptue, Meridian VIII, Dominican U., River Forest, Ill., 2005, Engima Variation #2, So. Ill. U. Sch. Medicine, Springfield, Ill., 2006. Petty officer 2nd class submarine svc. USN, 1955—59. Fellow Artist in Residence Program, Nat. Endowment of the Arts, 1980, 1981; Project Completion grant, Ill. Arts Coun., 1985. Mem.: Chgo. Sculpture Soc., Internat. Sculpture Soc., Chgo. Artists Coalition (assoc.). Home: 421 N First St Cissna Park IL 60924-9789 Home Phone: 815-457-2763. Home Fax: 815-457-3010.

MCCULLOUGH, EILEEN (EILEEN MCCULLOUGH LEPAGE, ELLI MCCULLOUGH), financial consultant, writer, editor, educator; b. Phila., Oct. 16, 1946; d. Charles Norman and Marie Teresa (Inglesby) McCullough; m. Clifford Bennett LePage Jr., Mar. 6, 1970; children: Clifford Bennett III, Alexander Pierce. BA in English and Secondary Edn., George Washington U., DC, 1969; MEd in Spl. Edn., Temple U., Phila., 1972. Cert. secondary sch. tchr.; registered securities rep. Record-keeper child growth and devel. program Children's Hosp. of Phila., 1965; with advt. dept. Phila. Inquirer, 1966-67; with ops. control U.S. Civil Svc. Commn., Washington, 1967-69; mgr. N.J. Bell Telephone, Trenton, 1969; rschr. Temple U., Phila., 1969-71; tchr. Wyomissing, Pa., 1972-77; fin. cons. various orgns., 1984-93; cons. EMLC, Reading, 1994—. Adj. instr. Reading (Pa.) Area C.C., 1978-81; lectr. English Albright Coll., Reading, 1981-84; founding mem. Common Cents Investment Club, 1983-93; founding and mng. ptnr. Klein LePage McCullough Partnership, Ocean City, N.J., 1982-96; presenter in field. Author: The Clue in the Snow, 1959; editor: 1st Complete Pocket Guide to Atlantic City Casinos, 1984, The Autobiography of Capt. Michael Kevolic, 1986; photographer Cherry Hill Mtg. Bd. dirs. Nat. Found. March of Dimes, Reading, 1969-75, chmn., 1974-75; bd. sch. dirs. Wyomissing Area Sch. Dist., 1984-92; bd. dirs. Wyomissing Pub. Libr., Reading, 1980-85; asst. chmn Region 8 Pa. Sch. Bds. Assn., 1989-91; dir. Saturday Morning Sch., Assn. for Children with Learning Disabilities, Reading, 1970; acting sec. Berks County Commn. for Women, Reading, 1993; active Reading Community Players, 1980; past bd. mem. Berks Ballet Theatre; past vol. Berks C. of C.; vol. mus. guide Reading Pub. Mus. and Art Gallery, 1999-2002, Berks County Chpt Am. Red Cross, 1997; presenter Green Circle, Reading Berks Human Rels. coun., Reading Pub. Schs., 1998-99. Fellow Pa. writing project; mem. AAUW (life; top chmn.), Am. Assn. Individual Investors (life), Internat. Platform Soc., Women's Internat. Fedn. for World Peace. Avocations: dance, singing. Home and Office: EMLC 10 Phoebe Dr Reading PA 19610-2857 E-mail: emlco@comcast.net.

MCCULLOUGH, FRANK WITCHER, III, lawyer; b. New Orleans, Dec. 13, 1945; s. Frank Witcher, Jr. and Kathleen Elizabeth (Van Pelt) McCullough; m. Barry Jean Bock, Mar. 7, 1981; children: William David Oat, Frank Witcher IV, Elizabeth Layton. BA, Stetson U., 1967; JD, W.Va. U., 1970. Bar: W.Va. 1970, Tex. 1970, US Dist. Ct. (so. dist.) W.Va. 1970, US Dist. Ct. (so. dist.) Tex. 1972, US Ct. Appeals (5th cir.) 1972, US Supreme Ct. 1980, US Dist. Ct. (no. dist.) Calif. 1983, US Dist. Ct. (we. dist.) Tex. 1987, US Dist. Ct. (ea. dist.) Tex. 1993, US Dist. Ct. (no. dist.) W.Va. 2007. Indsl. rels. specialist Continental Oil Co., Houston, 1970-72; asst. U.S. atty. U.S. Atty.'s Office, Houston, 1972-75; assoc. Baker & Botts, Houston, 1975-76, Austin, Tex., 1985-89; ptnr. Weiner Strother & Lamkin, Houston, 1983-85; regional counsel GATX Leasing Corp., Houston, 1976-78; ptnr. Walsh Squires Tompkins & McCullough, Houston, 1978-82; shareholder Sheinfeld, Maley & Kay, Austin, 1989-2001, Diamond McCarthy Taylor & Finley, Austin, 2001—04, Haynes and Boone, LLP, Austin, 2004—. Spl. commr. Harris County, Houston, 1982; mem. Bellaire (Tex.) Bd. Adjustments, 1982; bd. dirs. Big Bros. and Big Sisters Austin, 1991—94. Mem.: SAR, State Bar Tex. (mem. grievance com. 1979—87, chmn. unauthorized practice law com. 1984—87, mem. grievance com. 1995—2001, panel chair 2000—01), Stetson U. Alumni Assn. (bd. dirs. 2006—), Austin Country Club. Republican. Episcopalian. Home: 6707 Bridge Hill Cv Austin TX 78746-1338 Office: Haynes and Boone LLP 600 Congress Ave Ste 1300 Austin TX 78701 *Notable cases include: Univ. Savs. Assn. vs. Springwoods Shopping Ctr., 1982, in which the Tex. Supreme Ct. created significant exception to the rule of law that the terms and provisions of deed of trust must be strictly followed in foreclosure proceeding.*

MCCULLOUGH, GARY E., education company executive; BS, Wright State Univ.; MBA, Northwestern Univ. Mgmt. positions Procter & Gamble, 1987—95, mktg. dir., 1995—98, gen. mgr. No. Am. home care, 1998—2000; sr. v.p. Americas Wm. Wrigley Jr. Co., 2000—03; pres. Ross products div. Abbott Laboratories, 2003—07; pres., CEO Career Edn. Corp., Hoffman Estates, Ill., 2007—. Bd. dir. Sherwin Williams Co. Served 5 years to capt. US Army. Decorated Meritorious Service Medal; named one of 75 Most Powerful African Americans in bus., Black Enterprise Mag., 2005. Office: Career Edn Corp 2895 Greenspoint Pkwy Hoffman Estates IL 60169 *

MCCULLOUGH, GLENN L., JR., electric power industry executive; b. Tupelo, Miss. m. Laura White; children: Vance, Glenn Thomas. Degree in agrl. econ., Miss. State U., 1977. Dir. Appalachian Regional Commn. (ARC), Miss., 1992—97; mayor Tupelo, Miss., 1997—99; chmn., bd. dirs. Tenn. Valley Authority, 1999—. Mem. Nat. Electric Adv. Bd., Dept. Energy; mem. bd. Miss. Partnership Econ. Devel., Econ. Devel. Partnership, Ala.; mem. governing bd. Electric Power Rsch. Inst., Inst. Nuc. Power Ops., Nuc. Energy Inst. Governing bd. United Way; mem. Big Bros./Big Sisters Orgn.; governing bd. Cmty. Devel. Found., Commn. Future Northeast Miss. Recipient All-Am. City award, Nat. Civic League, 1999. Office: Tenn Valley Authority 400 W Summit Hill Dr Knoxville TN 37902-1499 Office Phone: 865-632-2600. Business E-Mail: tvaineot@va.gov.

MC CULLOUGH, J. LEE, industrial psychologist; b. Bryn Mawr, Pa., Oct. 3, 1945; s. Leo Francis and Margaret Mary (Hart) McC.; m. Bonnie R. Goldberg, Jan. 14, 1979. AB, Villanova U., 1967; MA, Ohio State U., 1968, PhD, 1971. Tchg. asst. Ohio State U., 1967-68, rsch. assoc., 1968-69; assoc. O.P.S. Assocs., Columbus, 1970-71; assoc., sr. assoc., sr. prin., v.p Hay Group, NYC, 1971-90, v.p., dir. fin. svcs. cons., 1990-94; prin. William M. Mercer, Inc., NYC, 1994—2006; sr. cons. Towers Perrin, Inc., NYC, 2006—. Adj. prof. Fordham U. Grad. Sch. Bus., 1984-89. Served with AUS, 1972. NSF fellow, 1969; NDEA Title IV fellow, 1970; Univ. Dissertation Year fellow, 1971. Mem. Am. Psychol. Soc., Met. Psychol. Assn. Home: 6 Hereford Dr Princeton Junction NJ 08550-1514 Office: Towers Perrin Inc 21st Fl 335 Madison Ave New York NY 10017-4605 Office Phone: 212-309-3712. Personal E-mail: LeeMcCullough@comcast.net. Business E-Mail: lee.mccullough@towersperrin.com.

MCCULLOUGH, JOHN PHILLIP, management consultant, educator; b. Lincoln, Ill., Feb. 2, 1945; s. Phillip and Lucile Ethel (Ornellas) McC.; m. Barbara Elaine Carley, Nov. 29, 1968; children: Carley Jo, Ryan Phillip. BS, Ill. State U., 1967, MS, 1968; PhD, U. N.D., 1971. Adminstrv. mgr. McCullough Ins. Agy., Atlanta, Ill., 1963-68; ops. supr. Stetson China Co., Lincoln, 1967; asst. mgr. Brandtville Svc., Inc., Bloomington, Ill., 1968; instr. in bus. Ill. Ctrl. Coll., 1968-69; rsch. asst. U. N.D., Grand Forks, 1969-71; assoc. prof. mgmt. West Liberty State Coll., 1971-74, prof., 1974—. Chmn. dept. mgmt., West Liberty State Coll., 1974-82, dir. Sch. Bus., 1982-86, dean, 1986—, provost, 1998—, interim pres., 2001, dir. Small Bus. Inst., 1978—; mgmt. cons., Triadelphia, W.Va., 1971—; instr. Am. Inst. Banking, 1971—; lectr. W.Va. U., 1971—; adj. prof. MBA program Wheeling Coll., 1972—, U. Steubenville, 1982—; lectr. Ohio U., 1982—; profl. assoc. Inst. Mgmt. and Human Behavior, 1975—; v.p. West Liberty State Coll. Fed. Credit Union, 1976—; rep. W.Va. Bd. Regents Adv. Coun. of Faculty. Author: (with Howard Fryette) Primer in Supervisory Management, 1973; contbr. articles to profl. jours. Team leader Wheeling divsn. Am. Cancer Soc.; coord. Upper Ohio Valley United Fund, 1972-74; instr. AFL-CIO Cmty. Svcs. Program, Wheeling; project dir. Ctr. for Edn. and Rsch. with Industry; bd. dirs. Family Svc.-Upper Ohio Valley, Ohio Valley Indsl. and Bus. Devel. Corp., Inc., Labor Mgmt. Inst. Wheeling Salvation Army, Progress, Inc., Ohio Valley Health Svcs. and Edn. Corp. Recipient Svc. award Bank Adminstrn. Inst., 1974, United Fund, 1973, Acad. Achievement award Harris-Casals Found., 1971. Mem. Soc. Humanistic Mgmt. (nat. chmn.), ORgn. Planning Mgmt. Assn. (exec. com.), Spl. Interest Group for Cert. Bus. Educators (nat. dir.), Soc. Advancement Mgmt. (chpt. advisor), Acad. Mgmt., Adminstrv. Mgmt. Soc. (cert.), Am. Soc. Pers. Adminstrn. (cert.), Nat. Bus. Honor Soc. (Excellence in Tchg. award 1976, dir. 1974—), Alpha Kappa Psi (Dist. Svc. award 1973, Civic award 1977, chpt. advisor 1971—), Merit Found. W.Va. (Edn. Excellence award), Delta Mu Delta, Delta Pi Epsilon, Delta Tau Kappa, Phi Gamma Nu, Phi Theta Pi, Pi Gamma Mu, Pi Omega Pi, Omicron Delta Epsilon. Home: 68 Elm Dr Triadelphia WV 26059-9620 Office Phone: 304-336-8004. Business E-Mail: mcculljp@wlsc.edu.

MCCULLOUGH, JOSEPH, retired academic administrator; b. Pitts., July 6, 1922; s. Joseph Phillip and Margaret (List) McC.; m. Elizabeth Cramer, Mar. 31, 1945; children— Marjorie Ann, Warren BFA, Yale U., 1949-50, MFA, 1951; Diploma, Cleve. Sch. Art, 1948; DFA (hon.), U. Evansville, Ind., 1980; DA (hon.), Cleve. Inst. Art, 1996. Instr. San Jose State Coll., Calif., 1948-49; asst. instr. Yale U., New Haven, 1949-51; asst. dir. Cleve. Inst. Art, 1952-54, dir., 1954-74, pres., 1974-88. Artist paintings, nat. regional and local exhbns., 1948— Chmn. Fine Arts Adv. Com., Cleve. Planning Commn., 1963-91; trustee Mpls. Coll. of Art and Design, 1988-98, Sculpture Ctr. Cleve., 1990-98; trustee, sec. Access to the Arts, Cleve., 1991-95. Capt. USAAF, 1943-46, ETO. Recipient Cleve. Arts prize Women's City Club, 1971, Centennial medal John Carroll U., 1987, medal for excellence Cleve. Inst. of Art, 1997. Mem.: Coll. Art Assn. ((past dir.)). Home: 20101 North Park Blvd Cleveland OH 44118-5006

MCCULLOUGH, LAURENCE BERNARD, medical educator, consultant; b. Phila., Aug. 2, 1947; s. Henry Joseph and Marie J. (Burns) McC.; m. Linda Jean Quintanilla, May 14, 1977. AB, Williams Coll., 1969; PhD, U. Tex., 1975. Postdoctoral fellow Hastings Ctr., Hastings-on-Hudson, N.Y., 1975-76; Asst. prof. med. humanities and philosophy Tex. A&M U., College Station, 1976-79; from asst. prof. to prof. cmty. and family medicine Georgetown U., Washington, 1979-88; prof. medicine and med. ethics Baylor Coll. Medicine, Houston, 1988—. Adj. prof. ethics in ob-gyn. and pub. health Weill Med. Coll., Cornell U., N.Y.C., 1988—. Co-author: Ethics in Obstetrics & Gynecology, 1994, Medical Ethics, 1984, Spanish transl., 1987, Japanese transl., 1992; author: Leibniz on Individuals and Individuation, 1996, John Gregory and the Invention of Professional Medical Ethics and the Profession of Medicine, 1998; co-editor: Surgical Ethics, 1998, Medical Ethics: Codes, Opinions, and Statements, 2000, Medical Ethics: Analysis of the Issues Raised by the Codes, Opinions, and Statements, 2001. Home Phone: 713-665-0556; Office Phone: 713-798-3505. Business E-Mail: mccullou@bcm.edu.

MCCULLOUGH, RALPH CLAYTON, II, law educator; b. Daytona Beach, Fla., Mar. 28, 1941; s. Ralph C. and Doris (Johnson) McCullough; m. Elizabeth Grier Henderson, Apr. 5, 1986; children: Melissa Wells, Clayton Baldwin. BA, Erskine Coll., 1962; JD, Tulane U., 1965. Bar: La. 1965, SC 1974. Assoc. Baldwin, Haspel, Maloney, Rainold and Meyer, New Orleans, 1965-68; from asst. prof. law to prof. U. SC, Columbia, 1968—2002, disting. prof., 2002—03; mng. dir., prof. Charleston Sch. Law, 2005—. Asst. dean U. SC Sch. Law 1970-75, Disting. prof. law, 2001, Disting. prof. law emeritus, 2003—; of counsel Finkel & Altman, 1978-; adj. prof. medicine Med. U. SC, 1984-, adj. prof. pathology, 1985—, mem. bd. vis.; mem. adv. com. rules and procedures US Ct. Appeals (4th cir.), 2001—, chair, 2006—. Author: (with J.L. Underwood) The Civil Trial Manual, 1974, 7th supplement, 1987, The Civil Trial Manual II, 1984, 87, (with Myers and Felix) New Directions in Legal Education, 1970, (with Finkel) S.C. Torts II, 1986, III, 1990, IV, 1995; co-reporter S.C. Criminal Code, 1977, S.C. Study Sentencing, 1977. Mem. bd. visitors Med. U. SC, 2006—. Mem. ATLA, ABA, La. Bar Assn., SC Bar (sec. 1975-76, exec. dir. 1972-76, award of service 1978), New Orleans Bar Assn., Am. Law Inst. (life), Am. Coll. Trial Lawyers, Southeastern Assn. Am. Law Schs. (pres.), SC Trial Lawyers Assn. (bd. govs. 1984-88), Forest Lake Club, Phi Alpha Delta. Republican. Episcopalian. Home: PO Box 939 Charleston SC 29402 Office: 440 King St Charleston SC 29402 Office Phone: 843-329-1000 ext. 2426. Business E-Mail: rmccullough@charlestonlaw.org.

MCCULLOUGH, RICHARD LAWRENCE, advertising executive; b. Chgo., Dec. 1, 1937; s. Francis John and Sadie Beatrice McCullough; m. Julia Louise Kreimer, May 6, 1961; children: Stephen, Jeffery, Julie. BS, Marquette U., 1959. Commd. U.S. Army, 1959, advance through grades to sgt., 1966; account exec. Edward H. Weiss Advt., Chgo., 1960-66; account supr. Doyle Dane Bernbach, NYC, 1966-68; sr. v.p. J. Walter Thompson Co., Chgo., 1969-86; pres. E.H. Brown Advt., Chgo., 1986-97; exec. v.p. Space-Time Media Mgmt., Chgo., 1997—; ptnr. Callahan Group, Chgo., 2000—05. Developer Mktg. with Country Music nat. seminar, 1996; chmn. J. L. McCullough Advertising and Pub. Rels., Evanston, Ill., 2004—. Author: Building Country Radio, 1986, A New Look at Country Music Audiences, 1988, (video) Country Music Marketing, 1989. Bd. dirs. Gateway Found., Chgo., 1976—, chmn., 1988-91; bd. dirs., chmn. mktg. com. Cath. Charities, Chgo. Recipient Nat. Cmty. Svc. award, Gateway Found., 2002, Dennis Kelly Honor award, Cath. Charities, 2002. Mem. Country Music Assn. (Nashville bd. dirs. 1979-2004, pres. 1983-85, Pres.'s award 1987, elector Country Music Hall of Fame), NARAS (Nashville chpt.), North Shore Country Club (Glenview, Ill.), Dairymen's Country Club (Boulder Junction, Wis.). Roman Catholic. Home: 2720 Lincoln St Evanston IL 60201-2043 Office: Space-Time Media Mgmt Inc 35 E Wacker Dr Chicago IL 60601-2103 Home: 2720 Lincoln St Evanston IL 60201-2043 E-mail: dick@spacetimemedia.com, relchar@aol.com.

MCCULLOUGH, ROBERT DALE, II, osteopath; b. Tulsa, June 2, 1937; s. Robert Dale and Roberta Maud (Purdy) McC.; m. Lindell Arlene Wilcox, Sept. 28, 1963; children: Robert Mark, Lori Lindell. Student, Wheaton Coll., Ill., 1955-57; BS, N.E. Mo. State U., 1958; DO, Kans. City Coll. Osteopathy, Mo., 1958-62. Diplomate in internal medicine and med. oncology Am. Osteo. Bd. Internal Medicine. Gen. practice McCullough Clinic, Tulsa, 1963-68; internal medicine resident Detroit Osteo. Hosp., 1968-71; internal medicine Baker-Todd-McCullough-Sutton, Tulsa, 1971-74; fellow med. oncology M.D. Anderson Hosp., Houston, 1974-75; internal medicine-med. oncology Baker-Todd-McCullough-Sutton, Tulsa, 1975-90; pvt. practice Tulsa, 1990-93; attending staff mem. VA Outpatient Clinic, Tulsa, 1993-94; assoc. med. dir. Blue Cross/Blue Shield of Okla., Tulsa, 1994—2005. Trustee Tulsa Regional Med. Cttr., 1983-88, 90-93; bd. dirs. Okla. Blue Cross Blue Shield, Tulsa, 1983-92, vice chmn., 1991-92; mem. adv. coun. Okla. State U. Coll. Osteo. Medicine, 1988-94, chmn., 1988-90; part-time worker VA and Indian Health Svc. Mem. bd. editors Patient Care Magazine, Montvale, N.J., 1988-93. Mem. Okla. State Bd. Health, Oklahoma City, 1983—87, Tulsa City/County Bd. Health, 1988—95, chmn., 1993; bd. mem. Cmty. Health Found., 1997—, chmn., 2003—05. Mem. Nat. Osteo. Found. (trustee 1993-00, treas. 1998-00), Am. Osteo. Assn. (vice speaker Ho. of Dels. 1986-92, trustee 1993-00), Am. Coll. Osteo. Internists, Okla. Osteo. Assn. (pres. 1982-83), Tulsa Downtown Lions Club, Soc. for Preservation and Encouragement of Barbershop Quartet Singing in Am. Republican. Southern Baptist. Avocation: barbershop quartets. Home: 5803 E 75th Pl Tulsa OK 74136-7255 Home Phone: 918-481-8725. Personal E-mail: RMccull207@aol.com.

MCCULLOUGH, V. BETH, pharmacist, educator; b. Harrison, Ark., May 15, 1953; d. A. G. and Willene L. (McLain) McC.; m. David Mark Pearson, Oct. 25, 1980; children: Colin McCullough-Pearson, Emily McCullough-Pearson, Kaitlyn McCullough-Pearson. BS in Edn. cum laude, S.W. Mo. State U., 1976; BS in Pharmacy, U. Mo., 1981. Registered Pharmacist, Mo. Chief pharmacist Mt. Vernon Park Pharmacy, Springfield, Mo., 1981-89; dir. pharmacy Foster Health Care Group, Springfield, 1989-96; chief pharmacy ops. Balanced Care Corp./Foster Health Care Group, Springfield, 1996-97; cons. pharmacist Managed Healthcare Pharmacy divsn. Omnicare Corp., Springfield, 1997-2001; owner Med. Park Pharmacy, Eureka Springs, Ark., 2001—. Long term care pharmacy cons. Foster Health Care Group, Springfield, 1981-83, Managed Healthcare Pharmacy, Springfield, 1997-2001. Mem. NOW, Springfield, 1982—, assoc. mem. Animal Shelter League of the Ozarks, Nixa, Mo. Mem. Am. Soc. Cons. Pharmacists, Southwest Mo. Humane Soc., Mo. Equine Coun., Mo. Pharmacy Assn., Long Term Care Acad., Biokinetics (instnl. rev. bd. 1999-2001). Avocations: watercolor painting, jewelry making, horse breeding and showing. Office: 146 Passion Play Rd Eureka Springs AR 72632-9495 Home: 146 CR 238 Berryville AR 72616 Office Phone: 479-253-9751. E-mail: medparkpharm@aol.com.

MCCULLY, EMILY ARNOLD, illustrator, writer; b. Galesburg, Ill., 1939; d. Wade E. and Kathryn (Maher) Arnold; m. George E. McCully, 1961 (div. 1975); children: Nathaniel, Tad. BA, Brown U., 1961; MA, Columbia U., 1964; LittD (hon.), Brown U., 2002. Author: How's Your Vacuum Cleaner Working? O'Henry Collection, 1977, A Craving, 1982, (novel) Picnic, 1984 (Christopher award), First Snow, 1985, (novel) Life Drawing, 1986, The Show Must Go On, 1987, School, 1987, You Lucky Duck!, 1988, New Baby, 1988, The Grandma Mix-up, 1988, The Christmas Gift, 1988, Zaza's Big Break, 1989, Grandma's at the Lake, 1990, The Evil Spell, 1990, Speak Up, Blanche!, 1991, Mirette on the Highwire, 1992 (Caldecott medal 1992), Grandma's at Bat, 1993, The Amazing Felix, 1993, My Real Family, 1994, Crossing The New Bridge, 1994, Little Kit, or: The Industrious Flea Circus Girl, 1995, The Pirate Queen, 1995, The Ballot Box Battle, 1996, The Bobbin Girl, 1996, Popcorn at the Palace, 1997, Starring Mirette and Bellini, 1997, an Outlaw Thanksgiving, 1998, Beautiful Warrior, 1998, Mouse Practice, 1999, Monk Camps Out, 2000, The Orphan Singer, 2001, Four Hungry Kittens, 2001, Squirrel and John Muir, 2004; illustrator: Sea Beach Express, 1966, The Seventeenth Street Gang, 1966, Rex, 1967, Luigi of the Streets, 1967, That Mean Man, 1968, Gooney, 1968, Journey From Peppermint Street, 1968 (Nat. Book award 1969), The Mouse and the Elephant, 1969, The Fisherman, 1969, Tales from the Rue Brocca, 1969, Here I Am, 1969, Twin Spell, 1969, Hobo Toad and the Motorcycle Gang, 1970, Slip! Slop! Gobble!, 1970, Friday Night is Papa Night, 1970, Maxie, 1970, Steffie and Me, 1970, The Cat and the Parrot, 1970, Gertrude's Pocket, 1970, Go and Hush the Baby, 1971, Finders Keepers, 1971, Ma n Da La, 1971 (Bklyn. Mus. award 1976, N.Y. Pub. Libr. award 1976), Hurray for Captain Jane!, 1971, Michael Is Brave, 1971, Finding Out With Your Senses, 1971, Henry's Pennies, 1972, Jane's Blanket, 1972, Grandpa's Long Red Underwear, 1972, Girls Can Too!, 1972, The Boyhood of Grace Jones, 1972, Black Is Brown Is Tan, 1973, Isabelle the Itch, 1973, When Violet Died, 1973, That New Boy, 1973, How To Eat Fried Worms, 1973, Jenny's Revenge, 1974, Her Majesty, Grace Jones, 1974, Tree House Town, 1974, I Want Mama, 1974, Amanda, the Panda and the Redhead, 1975, The Bed Book, 1976, My Street's A Morning Cool Street, 1976, Professor Coconut and the Thief, 1977, Martha's Mad Dog, 1977, That's Mine, 1977, Where Wild Willie, 1978, No Help At All, 1978, Partners, 1978, The Twenty-Elephant Restaurant, 1978, What I Did Last Summer, 1978, The Highest Hit, 1978, I and Spraggy, 1978, Edward Troy and the Witch Cat, 1978, My Island Grandma, 1979, Whatever Happened to Beverly Bigler's Birthday?, 1979, Last Look, 1979,

Ookie-Spooky, 1979, The Black Dog Who Went Into the Woods, 1980, How I Found Myself at the Fair, 1980, How We Got Our First Cat, 1980, Oliver and Allison's Week, 1980, Pajama Walking, 1981, The April Fool, 1981, I Dance in My Red Pajamas, 1982, The Halloween Candy Mystery, 1982, Go and Mush the Baby, 1982, Mitzi and the Terrible Tyrannosaurus Rex, 1983, Best Friend Insurance, 1983, Mail-Order Wings, 1984, Gertrude's Pocket, 1984, Fifth Grade Magic, 1984, The Ghastly Glasses, 1985, Fourth of July, 1985, The Explorer of Barkham Street, 1985, Wheels, 1986, Lulu and the Witch Baby, 1986, Richard and the Vratch, 1987, Molly, 1987, Molly Goes Hiking, 1987, Jam Day, 1987, The Boston Coffee Party, 1988, The Take-Along Dog, 1989, Selene Goes Home, 1989, The Magic Mean Machine, 1989, It Always Happens to Leona, 1989, The Grandpa Days, 1989, Dinah's Mad, Bad Wishes, 1989, Stepbrother Sabotage, 1990, Lulu Goes to Witch School, 1990, The Day Chubby Became Charles, 1990, The Christmas Present Mystery, 1990, Sky Guys to White Cat, 1991, Meatball, 1991, Leona and Ike, 1991, The Butterfly Birthday, 1991, Yankee Doodle Drumsticks, 1992, One Very Best Valentine's Day, 1992, Meet the Lincoln Lions Band, 1992, Jingle Bells Jam, 1992, In My Tent, 1992, Anne Flies the Birthday Bike, 1993, Amzat and His Brothers, 1993, Leo the Magnificent, 1996, Old Home Day, 1996, The Divide, 1997, Rabbit Pirates, 1999, Sing a Song of Piglets: A Calender in Verse, 2002, One, Two, ILove You, 2004.

MCCULLY, JOANNA PATRICIA, small business owner; b. NYC, May 17, 1939; d. Joseph McCully Jr. and Emma Maria Ferrucci; children: Rick Bernard, Kevin Bernard. BS, Cornell U., Ithaca, NY, 1990. Lic. real estate broker Fla. Radio host, announcer WLW Radio, Cin., 1964—66; restaurant owner St. Bernard Inn, Breckenridge, Colo., 1967—70, Fat Flounder Tavern, East Hampton, NY, 1970—78; restaurant pub. rels. specialist McCully's Rooftop, Bonita Springs, Fla., 1980—89; owner Joanna McCully Realty, Bonita Springs, 1980—90; internat. advisor U. Ctrl. Fla., Orlando, 1990—97; motivational spkr. McCully Enterprises, Ltd., Lady Lake, Fla., 2001—. Corr. Cornell Alumni Mag., 2006—. Recipient Kindness to Animal award, Huntington Humane Soc., 1953, New Profl. award, Nat. Assn. Internat. Educators, Orlando, 1995, Cert. Recognition, NY State Coll. Human Ecology, Cornell U., 1989, Internat. Orgn., U. Ctrl. Fla., 1997; NY State Regents scholar, 1957. Mem.: Mensa. Avocation: scuba diving. Home and Office: 1607 Hilton Head Blvd Lady Lake FL 32159

MCCULLY, THOMAS RICHARDSON, lawyer; b. Rushville, Ind., Mar. 10, 1941; s. Kenneth Brody and Frances (Richardson) McCully; m. Susan C. McCully, Dec. 5, 1998; children: Julie A., Thomas R. II, Michael G. stepchildren: Keith W. Long, Thomas Long. BA Polit. Sci., Philosophy, Wabash Coll., Crawfordsville, Ind., 1963; JD with distinction, Ind. U., Bloomington, 1966. Bar: Ind. 1966, U.S. Dist. Ct. (So. Dist.) Ind. 1966, U.S. Dist. Ct. (No. Dist.) Ind. 1968, U.S. Ct. Appeals (7th cir.) 1973, U.S. Supreme Ct. 1973. Assoc. Stuart & Branigin, LLP, Lafayette, Ind., 1966—71, ptnr., 1971—. Guest lectr. Purdue U., Lafayette, Ind.; frequent speaker, author Ind. Continuing Legal Edn. Forum, Lohrman Bus. Ctr., Lafayette; speaker Greater Lafayette Small Bus. Devel. Ctr.; bd. dirs. LSB Fin. Corp. and Lafayette Savings Bank, Ind., 1999—. Pres. Highland Sch. PTA; exec. com. Gus Macker, Lafayette, 1997—2001; Elder Ctrl. Presbyn. Ch., Lafayette; bd. dirs. Ctrl. Presbyn. Found., Lafayette Legal Aid Corp., Tippecanoe County, Ind., 1974—96, pres., 1987—89; bd, visitors Ind. U. Sch. Law, Bloomington, Ind., 1994—; bd. dirs. Jr. Achievement of Greater Lafayette, 1994—, Harrison Trails and Sagamore Couns., Boy Scouts Am. (past), Lafayette, Vol. Bur. Tippecanoe County (past). Named one of Best Lawyers in Am., 1987—; recipient Pro Bono Publico award, Ind. Bar Found., 1995. Master: Ind. Bar Found. (fellow); mem.: ABA, Am. Health Lawyers Assn., Ind. State Bar Assn. (mem. spl. com. to revise Ind. Zoning Laws 1982—88, chmn. land use and zoning sect. 1992—94, chmn. health law sect. 2006—), Tippecanoe County Bar Assn., John Purdue Club, Lafayette Country Club (legal counsel 1977—), Ind. U. Varsity Club, Elks Lodge 143, Phi Delta Phi. Office: Stuart & Branigin LLP 300 Main St Ste 900 Lafayette IN 47902 Home Phone: 765-447-7181; Office Phone: 765-423-1561. Office Fax: 765-742-8125. Business E-Mail: trm@stuartlaw.com.

MCCUMBER, CHRIS, communications executive; b. 1968; Sr. v.p., on-air promotion USA Network, sr. v.p., Mktg. and Brand Strategy, 2004—. Launched Characters Welcome campain; mem. NBC Universal mktg. coun. Named one of 40 Executives Under 40, Multichannel News, 2006. Office: USA Network 30 Rockefeller Plz New York NY 10112

MCCUNE, BRENDA L., lawyer; BS, Western State Univ., 1994, JD, 1995. Bar: Calif. 1996. Atty. McCune Family Law, Yorba Linda, Calif. Contbr. articles to profl. jours. Named a Rising Star, So. Calif. Super Lawyers, 2004—06. Mem.: ABA, State Bar Calif., Orange County Bar Assn. (dir. family law sect. 2001—04), Peter M. Elliott Inns of Ct. Office: McCune Family Law Ste 206 4676 Lakeview Ave Yorba Linda CA 92886 Office Phone: 714-695-0502. Office Fax: 714-695-0568. Business E-Mail: brenda@bmccunefamilylaw.com.

MCCUNE, JOHN BRIAN, broadcast engineer; b. Richmond, Va., Aug. 17, 1960; s. Horace Glenn Jr. and Mamie Ray (Potts) McC. Student, J. Sargeant Reynolds Community Coll., Richmond, 1979-80, 85-86, No. Va. Coll., 1984. Lic. 2d class radiotelephone operator. Engr. Sta. WRVA, Richmond, 1975, Sta. WLEE, Richmond, 1979-86, Sta. WCVE-TV, Richmond, 1980-82, Sta. WTVR-TV, Richmond, 1982-83, Richmond Subscription TV, 1982-84, Sta. WXGI, Richmond, 1984-86, Sta. WXEX-TV, Richmond, 1986-87, Sta. WRGF, Richmond, 1986-88; rec. engr. Audio Communications, Richmond, 1986—; with Ray Sports Network Sta. WRLH-TV, Richmond, 1988—; with dept. media svcs. Richmond Pub. Schs., Richmond, 1990—. Mem. Soc. Broadcast Engrs. (cert.). Avocations: amateur radio, rebuilding old broadcast equipment. Home: 1000 Pond View Ln Richmond VA 23231-4643 Office: Richmond Pub Schs Dept Media Svcs 2907 North Ave Richmond VA 23222-3612

MCCUNE, PHILIP SPEAR, lawyer; b. Spokane, Wash., Sept. 14, 1965; s. Calmar A. McCune and Katrina Y. Spear; m. Patricia Ann Ryan; children: Emma Sophia, Jackson Spear. BA magna cum laude, Dartmouth Coll., 1987; JD cum laude, U. Mich., 1991. Bar: Wash. 1991, US Dist. Ct. (we. dist.) Wash. 1991, US Dist. Ct. (ea. dist.) Wash. 1996, US Ct. Appeals (9th cir.) 1991, US Dist. Ct. (no. dist.) Utah 1996, US Supreme Ct. 2004. Law clk. Hon. John C. Coughenour chief judge U.S. Dist. Ct. (we. dist.) Wash., Seattle, 1991—93; with Heller, Ehrman, White and Maculliffe, Seattle, 1993—97; ptnr., founder Summit Law Group, Seattle, 1997—. Author: The Forest Practices Act, Washington Environmental Law and Practice; sr. editor U. Mich. Jour. Law Reform; contbr. articles to profl. jours. Bd. dirs. Friends of Ind. Schs. and Better Edn., Seattle Repertory Theater, Am. Friends St. Michael's U. Sch. Recipient Rising Star and Super Lawyer awards, Wash. Law and Politics Mag. Mem. ABA, Wash. State Bar Assn., King County Bar Assn., Wash. Athletic Club, U. Mich. Law Sch. Barristers. Avocations: hiking, running. Office: Summit Law Group 315 Fifth Ave S Ste 1000 Seattle WA 98104-2682 Office Phone: 206-676-7038. E-mail: philm@summitlaw.com.

MCCUNNEY, ROBERT JOSEPH, physician; b. July 4, 1948; s. Robert H. McCunney; m. Marilyn Stanton, Nov. 7, 1987; children: Robby, Kelsey. BSCE, Drexel U., 1971; MS in Environ. Health, U. Minn., 1972; MD, Jefferson Med. Coll., 1976; MPH in Occupl. Health, Harvard U., 1981. Intern, resident Northwestern U. Med. Ctr., Chgo., 1976-78; occupl. medicine fellow Harvard Sch. Pub. Health, Boston, 1979-81; emergency rm. physician Choate Meml. Hosp., Woburn, Mass., 1979-80, Sancra Maria Hosp., Cambridge, Mass., 1979-80; med. dir. occupl. health svc. Sturdy Meml. Hosp., Attleboro, Mass., 1981-83; med. dir. Goddard Occupl. Health Svcs., Stoughton, Mass., 1982-90; chief occupl. & environ. medicine, dir. occupl. med. residency program Boston U. Med. Ctr., 1983-94; corp. med. dir. Cabot Corp., Boston, 1983—; dir. environ. med. svc. med. dept. MIT, Cambridge, 1994—. Instr. anatomy Thomas Jefferson U., 1973; instr. medicine Brown U., Providence, 1982-85; adj. asst. prof. pub. health Boston U., 1983—; clin. asst. prof. Med. Coll. Wis., Milw., 1989—; lectr. medicine Harvard Med. Sch., Boston; staff physician Mass. Gen. Hosp., Boston. Editor: Handbook of Occupational Medicine, 1988, A Practical Approach to Occupational and Environmental Medicine, 1994, A Manager's Guide to Occupational Health Services, 1995, Occupl. & Environ. Medicine Report, Medical Center Occupational Health and Safety, 1999, Occupational and Environmental Medicine Self Assessment Guide, 1998; co-editor Health & Safety Manual, 1992; contbr. chpts. to books and articles to profl. jours. Fellow Am. Occupl. Medicine Assn., Am. Coll. Preventive Medicine; mem. AMA, APHA, Am. Conf. Govtl. Indsl. Hygienists, Am. Coll. Occupl. & Environ. Medicine (bd. dirs. 1991-94, 95—, chair pubs. com. 1985-88, house dels. 1983-89, govt. affairs com. 1989-93, past pres. New Eng. chpt. 1984-86, dir. residency sect. 1988-93), Tau Beta Pi, Phi Beta Upsilon. Roman Catholic. Avocations: athletics, photography, boating. Office: MIT Dept Biol Engring 77 Massachusetts Ave 16-771 Cambridge MA 02139-4307 Office Phone: 617-258-5650. E-mail: mccunney@mit.edu.

MCCURDY, CHRISTOPHER ROBERT, pharmacist, educator; s. Robert William and Myrna Woodward McCurdy; m. Nancy Ruth Nordling, July 8, 2000; children: Robert Byron, Sean Thomas. BS in Pharmacy, Ohio No. U., Ada, 1994; PhD, U. Ga., Athens, 1998. Prof. U. Miss., University, 2001—. Pharmacist SuperValu Pharms., Mpls., 1998—2001, Publix Supermarkets, Atlanta, 1994—98. Fellow, U. Minn., Mpls., 1998—2001. Mem.: Am. Assn. Pharm. Scientists (chair-elect drug design and discovery 2004—). Office: U Miss Sch Pharmacy 419 Faser Hall University MS 38677 Home Phone: 662-915-5882; Office Phone: 662-915-5882. Office Fax: 662-915-5638. Business E-Mail: cmccurdy@olemiss.edu.

MCCURDY, DAVID KEITH, trade association administrator, former congressman; b. Canadian, Tex., Mar. 30, 1950; s. Thomas L. and Aileen (Geis) McC.; m. Pamela Mary Plumb, Aug. 14, 1971; children: Josh, Cydney, Shannon. BA, U. Okla., 1972, JD, 1975; postgrad., U. Edinburgh, Scotland, 1977-78. Bar: Okla. 1975. Asst. atty. gen. State of Okla., 1975-77; assoc. Luttrell, Pendarvis & Rawlinson, Norman, Okla., 1978-79; pvt. practice Norman, 1979-80; mem. US Congress from 4th Okla. dist., Washington, 1981—95; mem. armed svcs. com., sci., space and tech. com.; chmn., CEO McCurdy Group LLC; pres. Electronic Industries Alliance, Arlington, Va., 1998—2007, Alliance Automobile Manufacturers, Inc., Washington, 2007—. Chmn. Nat. Dem. Leadership Coun. Fellow Internat. Rotary Club; recipient Disting. Svc. award U. Okla., 1991. Mem. Okla. State Bar Assn., Norman C. of C., Omicron Delta Kappa, Rotary. Office: Alliance Automobile Manufacturers Inc 1401 I St NW Ste 900 Washington DC 20005 *

MCCURDY, HARRY WARD, otolaryngologist; b. Branchton, Pa., Aug. 15, 1918; s. Adam Oscar and Sarah Fern (Hindman) McC.; m. Joan Jacqueline Talty, Dec. 10, 1955; children: Bridget Elizabeth, Peter Adam. AB, Allegheny Coll., 1940; MD, U. Pa., 1943. Diplomate Am. Bd. Otolaryngology. Intern Geisinger Meml. Hosp., Danville, Pa., 1944, resident in otolaryngology, 1944-45, 48-49; resident in pathology Hamot Hosp., Erie, Pa., 1945-48; mem. staff Geisinger Med. Center, Danville, 1948-50; commd. 2d lt. U.S. Army, 1945, advanced through grades to col., 1962-74; mil. cons. Surgeon Gen., U.S. Army, 1964-74; ret., 1974; exec. v.p. Am. Acad. Otolaryngology-Head and Neck Surgery, Washington, 1974-84; mem. staff Walter Reed Army Hosp. Resources coun. Gallaudet Coll., 1975-80; nat. adv. coun. Sertoma Found., 1976-84; chmn. FDA Panel on Otolaryngologic Med. Devices, 1974-78, cons., 1978-84 Mem. ACS, AMA, Royal Soc. Medicine (U.K.), Am. Acad. Otolaryngology, Mil. Surgeons Assn., Am. Soc. Assn. Execs., Soc. Med. Consultants to Armed Forces, AAAS, Am. Soc. Facial Plastic Surgery, Soc. Mil. Otolaryngologists, Am. Acad. Facial Plastic and Reconstructive Surgery, Am. Laryngol., Rhinol. and Otol. Soc., Anglo-Am. Med. Soc., Am. Audiology Soc., Royal Soc. Health, Osler Med. Soc., Acad. Medicine, Soc. Univ. Otolaryngologists, Am. Council Otolaryngology, Pan-Am. Soc. Bronchoesophagology., Internat. Fedn. Otolaryngol. Socs. (sec. gen. 1981—), Soc. Mil. Cons. to Armed Forces (sec. 1993—). Clubs: Army Navy, Press, Mil. Attaches of London, Les Chevaliers du Tastevin. Republican. Methodist. Home and Office: 6006 Dellwood Pl Bethesda MD 20817-3812

MCCURDY, LARRY WAYNE, automotive parts company executive; b. Commerce, Tex., July 1, 1935; s. Weldon Lee and Eula Bell (Quinn) McC.; m. Anna Jean Ogle, June 2, 1956; children: Michael, Kimberly, Laurie. BBA, Tex. A&M U., 1957. Jr. acct. Tenneco Inc., Houston, 1958-60; sr. acct. Tenneco Oil Co., Houston, 1960-64; acctg. supr. Tenneco Chems., Houston, 1964-69, from divsn. controller to v.p. fin. Saddle Brook, NJ, 1970-78; sr. v.p. fin. Tenneco Automotive, Deerfield, Ill., 1978-80; pres. Walker Mfg. Co., Racine, Wis., 1980-81; exec. v.p. N.Am. ops. Tenneco Automotive, Deerfield, 1981-82; v.p. fin. Echlin Inc., Branford, Conn., 1983; pres., COO Echlin, Inc., Branford, Conn., 1983-85, pres., 1997—; pres., CEO Moog Automotive Inc., St. Louis, 1985-94; exec. v.p. ops. Cooper Industries, Houston, 1994-97; chmn. bd., pres., CEO Echlin, Inc., Branford, Conn., 1997-98; pres. Dana Automotive Aftermarket Group, 1998-2000; ret., 2000. Bd. dirs. Lear Corp., Mohawk Industries, Inc., Gen. Parts, Inc., Affinia Group Inc. Trustee Somerset County Coll., Somerville, N.J., 1974-78, Millikin U., Decatur, Ill., 1991-97, St. Raphaels's Hosp., New Haven, Conn., 2002—; former mem. bd. dirs. Jr. Achievement, Chgo.; bd. dirs. Sam Houston coun. Boy Scouts Am., 1995-97; mem. adv. coun. Tex. A&M U. Engring. Sch., 1995-97; dir. New Haven Symphony Orch., 2002—. Mem. Fin. Execs. Inst., Nat. Assn. Accts., Motor Equipment Mfrs. Assn. (chmn. bd. dirs. 1989). Personal E-mail: larrywmccurdy@aol.com.

MCCURDY, LAYTON, medical educator; b. Florence, SC, Aug. 20, 1935; m. Gwendolyn A. McCurdy, 1958; children: Robert Jr., David Barclay. BS, U. NC, 1956; MD, Med. U. SC, 1960. Resident in psychiatry NC Meml. Hosp., Chapel Hill, 1961—64; with psychiatry tng. br. NIMH, Bethesda, Md., 1964—66; asst. prof. dept. psychiatry Sch. Medicine Emory U., Atlanta, 1966—68; prof., chmn. dept. psychiatry and behavioral scis. Med. U. SC, 1968—82, v.p. med. affairs, dean, 1990—2001, dean emeritus, disting. prof., 2001—; prof. psychiatry Sch. Medicine U. Pa., Phila., 1982—90; psychiatrist-in-chief Inst. of Pa. Hosp., Phila., 1982—90. Vis. colleague Inst. Psychiatry, U. London, 1974—75; nat. adv. mental health coun. NIMH, 1980—83; apptd. Pa. Adv. Com. for Mental Health and Mental Retardation, 1984—87. Recipient Disting. Alumnus award, Med. U. SC, 1988, George C. Ham. Soc., 1990, Earl B. Higgins Diversity Achievement award, 1999, Humanatati award, La Soc. Francaise, 2002. Fellow: Am. Coll. Psychiatrists (pres. 1993—94, Bowis award 1997); mem.: Am. Bd. Psychiatry and Neurology (pres. 1993), Assn. Academic Psychiatry (pres. 1970—71), SC Commn. on Higher Edn. (chmn. 2005—), Royal Coll. Psychiatrists (UK), Am. Psychiat. Assn. (joint commn. pub. affairs 1981—84, chmn. com. on diagnosis and assessment 1988—94), Cosmos Club. Office: Med Univ SC Inst Psychiatry PO Box 250861 Charleston SC 29425 Home Phone: 843-723-1186; Office Phone: 843-792-2084. Business E-Mail: mccurdy@musc.edu.

MCCURDY, MICHAEL CHARLES, illustrator, author; b. NYC, Feb. 17, 1942; s. Charles Errett and Beatrice (Beatson) McC.; m. Deborah Lamb, Sept. 7, 1968; children: Heather, Mark. BFA, Tufts U., 1964, MFA, 1971. Dir. Penmaen Press, Lincoln, Mass., 1968-85; instr. Concord (Mass.) Acad., 1972-75, Wellesley (Mass.) Coll., 1976. Illustrator: The Man Who Planted Trees, 1985, American Tall Tales, 1991, American Buffalo, 1992, The Way West: Journal of a Pioneer Woman, 1993, Giants in the Land, 1993, The Gettysburg Address, 1995, The Seasons Sewn, 1996; author, illustrator: Hannah's Farm, 1988, Trapped by the Ice, 1997, The Sailor's Alphabet, 1998, An Algonquian Year: The Year According to the Full Moon, 2000; editor, illustrator: Escape From Slavery: The Boyhood of Frederick Douglass in His Own Words, 1994, American Fairy Tales, 1996, War and the Pity of War, 1998, Tarzan, 1999, The Wizard of Oz, 1999, Iron Horses, 1999, The Signers: The 56 Stories Behind the Declaration of Independence, 2002, Walden by H.D. Thoreau, 2004, Tales of Terror, 2004, The Founders: The 39 Stories Behind the U.S. Constitution, 2005. Mem. Great Barrington (Mass.) Housing Authority, 1990-93. Small press grantee Nat. Endowment Arts, 1978, Mass. Arts and Humanities, 1978. Mem. Soc. Printers, St. Botolph Club. Democrat. Episcopalian. Personal E-mail: mccurdy@michaelmccurdy.com.

MC CURDY, PATRICK PIERRE, editor; b. Angers, France, Sept. 14, 1928; s. Joseph Alexander and Constance Yolande (Hillairet de Boisferon) McC.; m. Eiko Yamada, May 30, 1953; children: Alan J., Wendy C., Alec J., Jeffrey R. BS in Chem. Engring., Carnegie Inst. Tech., 1949. Chem. engr. tech. service dept. Humble Oil & Refining Co., Baytown, Tex., 1949-50; chem. engr. Callery Chem. Co., Pa., 1954-56; sr. chem. engr. U.S. Army Engr. R & D Labs., Ft. Belvoir, Va., 1956-60; asst. editor Chem. & Engring. News, Washington, 1960-61, NYC, 1961-62, bur. head Frankfurt, Germany, 1962-64, Tokyo, 1964-67, mng. editor Washington, 1967-69, editor, 1969-73; editor in chief Chemical Week, 1973-80, 84-87, editor-in-chief, assoc. pub., 1987-88; dir. communications Am. Chem. Soc., 1988-91, dir. industry rels., 1991-93, founding editor Today's Chemist at Work, 1989-97; cons. American Chemical Soc., 1993-97; pub. issues mgr. Dow Chem. Co., Midland, Mich., 1980-82, dir. tech. communications, 1982-84. Cons. in field, 1997—; editl. cons. Chem. Heritage mag., 1997—. Served U.S. Coast Guard, Great Lakes, 1945, first lt. C.E. AUS, 1950-54. Recipient Jesse H. Neal award, 1979, finalist 1985; recipient Carnegie Mellon Univ. Alumni Merit award, 1988. Mem.: Societe de Chimie Industrielle (past pres. Am. sect.), Chemists Club, Fgn. Corrs. Club Japan, Am. Chem. Soc., Tokyo Am. Club, Tau Beta Pi, Phi Kappa, Theta Tau, Phi Kappa Phi. Home and Office: 11717 Chauncey Ln Mason Neck VA 22079-4140 Personal E-mail: mccurdypp@aol.com.

MCCURINE, WILLIAM, JR., lawyer; b. Chgo., June 14, 1947; BA, Dartmouth Coll., 1969; MA, Oxford U., Eng., 1971; JD, Harvard U., 1975. Bar: Calif. 1975, U.S. Dist. Ct. (so. dist.) Calif. 1975. Ptnr. Gray, Cary, Ames & Frye, San Diego; magistrate judge US Dist Ct (so. dist.) Calif., San Diego. Bd. dirs. Cristian Conciliation Svc. San Diego, Inc., 1982—; civil arbitrator panel Superior Ct., San Diego. Mem. ABA, Am. Arbitration Assn., State Bar Calif., San Diego County Bar Assn. (sec. 1982-83, v.p. 1980-83). Office: US Dist Ct (so dist) Calif 880 Front St Ste 4290 Courtroom C 1st Fl San Diego CA 92101 Office Phone: 619-557-6624.

MCCURLEY, CARL MICHAEL, lawyer; b. Denton, Tex., July 15, 1946; s. Carl and Geneva McCurley; m. Mary Jo Trice, June 5, 1983; 1 child, Melissa Renee. BA, N. Tex. State U., 1968; JD, So. Meth. U., Dallas, 1972. Bar: Tex. 1972, US Dist. Ct. (no. dist.) Tex. 1972, US Supreme Ct. 1977. Ptnr. McGuire, Levy & McCurley, Irving, Tex., 1972—82, Koons, Fuller, McCurley & Vanden Eykel, Dallas, 1982—92, McCurley, Orsinger, McCurley, Nelson & Downing, Dallas, 1992—. Contbr. articles to profl. jours. Mem.: Tex. Acad. Family Law Specialists (Sam Emison award 2001), Am. Coll. Family Trial Lawyers (Named Law Dragon 500 2006), Internat. Acad. Matrimonial Lawyers, Am. Acad. Matrimonial Lawyers (treas. 1990—93, v.p. 1993—96, pres.-elect 1997, pres. 1998), Family Law Coun. (chmn. 1991—93). Home: 4076 Hanover Ave Dallas TX 75225-7009 Office: McCurley Orsinger McCurley Nelson & Downing 5950 Sherry Ln Ste 800 Dallas TX 75225-6533 Office Phone: 214-273-2400.

MCCURLEY, MARY JOHANNA, lawyer; b. Baton Rouge, Oct. 3, 1953; d. William Edward and Leora Elizabeth (Block) Trice; m. Carl Michael McCurley, June 6, 1983; 1 stepchild, Melissa Reneé McCurley. BA, Centenary Coll., 1975; JD, St. Mary's U., 1979. Bar: Tex. 1979; cert. family law. Assoc. Martin, Withers & Box, Dallas, 1979-82, Raggio & Raggio, Inc., Dallas, 1982-83; ptnr. Bruner, McColl, McColloch & McCurley, Dallas, 1983-87; assoc., ptnr. Selligson & Douglass, Dallas, 1987-90; jr. ptnr. Koons, Fuller, McCurley & VandenEykel, Dallas, 1990—92; ptnr. McCurley, Orsinger, McCurley,. Nelson & Downing, Dallas, 1992—. Contbr. articles to profl. jours. Adv. Women's Service League, Dallas, 1993—. Master: Annette Stewart Am. Inn. Ct. (sec.-treas. 2003—04); mem.: Dallas Bar Assn., Tex. Acad. Family Law Specialist, Tex. State Bar Assn. (sec. 2001, vice-chair 2001, treas. 2001, chair 2003—, family law coun.), Dallas Bar Assn. (chair family law sect. 1985), Am. Acad. Matrimonial Lawyers (treas. Tex. chpt. 1993—95, sec. 1995—96, pres. 1997, pres. Tex. chpt. 1997—98, bd. govs. 2000, nat. sec. 2000—02, nat. v.p. 2002—, nat. bd. dirs.). Methodist. Avocations: golf, travel, jogging, horseback riding. Home: 4076 Hanover Ave Dallas TX 75225-7009 Office: McCurley Orsinger McCurley Nelson & Downing LLP 5950 Sherry Ln Ste 800 Dallas TX 75225-6533 Office Phone: 214-273-2400.

MCCURLEY, ROBERT LEE, JR., lawyer, educator; b. Gadsden, Ala., Sept. 7, 1941; s. Robert Lee and Nellie Ruth McC.; m. Barbara; 1 child, Allison Leah. BS, U. Ala., 1963, JD, 1966. Bar: Ala. 1966, D.C. 1973, U.S. Ct. Mil. Appeals 1966, U.S. Supreme Ct. 1970, U.S. Ct. Appeals (5th cir.) 1972, U.S. Ct. Appeals (11th cir.) 1973, U.S. Ct. Appeals (fed. cir.) 1981. Asst. to dir. Fed. Savs. & Loan Ins. Corp., Washington, 1966-67; partner firm Rains, Rains, McCurley & Wilson, Gadsden, Ala., 1967-75; city judge Southside, Ala., 1970-75; dir. Ala. Law Inst., 1975—; assoc. dir. U. Ala. Center Public Law and Service, 1981-82; asst. dean Sch. Law U. Ala., 1978-81. Panelist White House Conf. on Volunteerism; pres. Gadsden Jaycees, 1972; mem. White House Fifty States Project; adj. prof. Ala. Sch. Law, 1975-2006, Cumberland Sch. Law, 2005-07. Editor: Divorce, Alimony and Child Support Custody, 4th edit., 2005, Land Laws of Alabama, 9th edit. rev., 2007, The Legislative Process, 9th edit., 2007, Alabama Law Office Practice Deskbook, 10th edit., 2007, Federally Mandated State Legislation, 1990, Alabama Legislation, Cases and Statutes, 6th edit., 2007, Alabama Election Handbook, 12th edit., 2006. Pres. Gadsden Boys Club, 1971, Kiwanis Internat. Found., 1998—2000; mem. Nat. Dem. Charter Commn., 1974. Recipient Svc. award, Ala. Bar Commr., 2004, Guin award, Ala. State Bar, 2000, Bar Commnrs. award, 2004, Roger Sayers Disting. Svc. award, U. Ala., 2005; Henry Toll fellow, Coun. State Govt., 1992. Fellow ABA, Ala. Bar Assn., mem. Am. Law Inst. (life), Order of Coif, Scribes, Farrah Law Soc., Commn. Uniform State Laws, Kiwanis (pres. Tuscaloosa club 1976, gov. Ala. dist. 1984, 91-92, v.p. 1998-2000, Internat. Found. pres.), Indian Hills County Club, Univ. Club. Presbyterian. Office Phone: 205-348-7411.

MCCURN, NEAL PETERS, federal judge; b. Syracuse, NY, Apr. 6, 1926; LL.B., Syracuse U., 1952, JD, 1960. Bar: N.Y. 1952. Ptnr. Mackenzie Smith Lewis Mitchell & Hughes, Syracuse, 1957-79; judge U.S. Dist. Ct. (no. dist.) N.Y., 1979-88; chief judge U.S. Dist. Ct. (no. dist.), NY, 1988-93; sr. judge, 1993—. Del. N.Y. State Constl. Conv., 1976; mem. 2d Cir. Jud. Council, 1987-93. Pres. Syracuse Common Coun., 1970-78. Mem. ABA, N.Y. State Bar Assn. (chmn. state constn. com.), Onondaga County Bar Assn. (past pres.), Am. Coll. Trial Lawyers, Am. Judicature Soc. (bd. dirs. 1980-84). Office: US Dist Ct 100 S Clinton St Rm 344 Syracuse NY 13261-6100 Office Phone: 315-234-8590. Business E-Mail: juwest@nynd.uscourts.gov.

MCCURRY, EDDIE JOE, entertainer; b. Gastonia, NC, Apr. 9, 1943; s. Lee and ODell Mosteller McCurry; m. Anna Prince McCurry; 1 child,

Vandi Rene. DD, Universal Life Ch., 2004. Cert. ordination Deep Springs Bapt. Ch., 1974. Broker NC Real Estate, 1979—. Mem.: NC Sheriffs Assn., Masons. Avocations: guitar, mandolin, reading, art, photography.

MCCURRY, MARGARET IRENE, architect, furniture, interior designer, educator; b. Chgo., Sept. 26, 1942; d. Paul D. and Irene B. McC.; m. Stanley Tigerman, Mar. 17, 1979. BA, Vassar Coll., 1964. Registered arch., Ill., Mass., Mich., Tex., Wis., Pa., Ind., Fla.; registered interior designer, Ill. Design coord. Quaker Oats Co., Chgo., 1964-66; sr. interior designer Skidmore, Owings & Merrill, Chgo., 1966-77; pvt. practice architect Margaret I, Chgo., 1977-82; ptnr. Tigerman McCurry Archs., Chgo., 1982—. Vis. studio critic Art Inst. Chgo., 1985-86, 88, 98, lectr., 1988, 98; vis. studio critic U. Ill., Chgo., Miami U., Oxford, Ohio, 1990; juror Internat. furniture awards Progressive Architecture mag., NYC, 1986, advt. awards, 1988; juror design grants Nat. Endowment for Arts, Washington, 1983; NEA Challenge Design Rev., 1992; peer reviewer design excellence program GSA, 1992—; juror, Wis., Minn., Calif., Va., Washington, Pitts., Ky., Ga. Conn. Soc. Archs., Detroit, NYC, Memphis, Austin, LA, Toledo, Jacksonville chpts. AIA, Am. Wood Coun., AIA Students Design Competition, 1993. Author: Margaret McCurry: Constructing 25 Short Stories, 2000; contbr. Chgo. Archtl. Club Jour.; designer, contbr. archtl. exhibit Art Inst. Chgo., 1983-85, 93, 99, 2005, Chgo. Hist. Soc., 1984, Gulbenkian Found., Lisbon Portugal, 1989, Chgo. Athenaeum, 1990, Gwenda Jay Gallery, 1992, Women of Design Traveling Exhbn., 1992-96; archtl. drawings and models in permanent collection Art Inst. Chgo. and Deutsches Architektur Mus., Frankfurt. Chmn. furniture sect. fundraising auction Sta. WTTW-TV, PBS, Chgo., 1975-76; mem. Chgo. Beautiful Com., 1968-70; pres. alumni coun. Grad. Sch. Design, Harvard U., 1997-2000; bd. dirs. Architecture and Design Soc. Art Inst. Chgo., 1988-97, mem. textile adv. bd. textile dept. Loeb fellow Harvard U., 1986-87; recipient Builders Choice Grand award Builders Mag., 1985, Interior Design award Interiors Mag., 1983, Dean of Architecture award Chgo. Design Source and the Mdse. Mart, 1989, Designer of Distinction award ASID, 2002; named a Dean of Design, Archtl. Digest, 2005, AD 100 award, 2007; inducted into Interior Design Hall of Fame, Interior Design Mag., 1990, ASID Design Excellence Residential Ill. Chpt. award, 2005, Hist. Preservation award, 2005, Corp. Office award, 2005. Fellow AIA (mem. coll. fellows, v.p. bd. dirs. Chgo. chpt. 1984-89, chair 1993, nat. design com., lectr. Colo. chpt. 1985, nat. conv. 1988, 97-98, Monterey Design Conf. 1989, Washington Design Ctr. 1989, Nat. Honor award 1984, Nat. Interior Architecture award 1992, 98, Disting. Bldg. award Chgo. chpt. 1984, 86, 91, 94, 99-2000, Disting. Interior Architecture award 1981, 83, 88, 91, 97, product display Neocon award 1985, 88, Gold award best of Neocon 1998, Associated Lic. Archs. Silver Medal Design award 2003), Internat. Interior Design Assn., Chgo. Network, Am. Soc. Interior Designers (v.p. bd. dirs. Chgo. chpt., Nat. Design award 1992, 94, Ill. chpt. Design award 1994, 2005, Design Excellence award in hist. preservation, 2005, in corp. interiors, 2005), Chgo. Archtl. Club, Arts Club Chgo., Harvard Alumni Assn. (dir. 2000-06, v.p. Chgo., 2004-06, pres. 2006-), Harvard Club of Chgo. Episcopalian. Avocations: drawing, writing, travel, golf, gardening. Office: Tigerman McCurry Archs 444 N Wells St Ste 206 Chicago IL 60610-4501 Home Phone: 312-944-5418; Office Phone: 312-644-5880. E-mail: mimccurry@tigerman-mccurry.com.

MCCUSKER, THOMAS J., lawyer, insurance company executive; b. South Bend, Ind., 1943; BA, U. Notre Dame, 1965, JD cum laude, 1969. Bar: NY 1970, Nebr. 1973, US Tax Ct. 1971. Exec. v.p., gen. counsel Mutual of Omaha Ins. Co. Mem.: Nebr. Bar Assn. Office: Mutual of Omaha Ins Co Mutual Of Omaha Plz Omaha NE 68175-1008 *

MCCUTCHAN, GORDON EUGENE, retired lawyer, insurance company executive; b. Buffalo, Sept. 30, 1935; s. George Lawrence and Mary Esther (De Puy) McC.; m. Linda Brown; children: Lindsey, Elizabeth. BA, Cornell U., 1956, MBA, 1958, LLB, 1959. Bar: N.Y. 1959, Ohio 1964. Pvt. practice, Rome, NY, 1959-61; atty., advisor SEC, Washington, 1961-64; ptnr. McCutchan, Druen, Maynard, Rath & Dietrich, 1964-94; mem. office of gen. counsel Nationwide Mut. Ins. Co., Columbus, Ohio, 1964-94, sr. v.p., gen. counsel, 1982-89, exec. v.p., gen. counsel, 1989-94; exec. v.p. Law and Corp. Svcs., Nationwide Ins. Enterprise, 1994-98; ret., 1998. Trustee, bd. govs. Franklin U., 1992-97; trustee Ohio Tuition Trust Authority, 1992-97. Mem. Columbus Bar Assn., Ohio Bar Assn., Am. Corp. Counsel Assn., Assn. Life Inst. Counsel (bd. govs. 1990-94), Fedn. Ins. and Corp. Counsel, Am. Coun. Life Ins. (chair legal sect. 1992-93). Home: 2376 Oxford Rd Columbus OH 43221-4011 E-mail: tunkpa@columbus.rr.com.

MCCUTCHAN, WILLIAM M., banker; b. Evansville, Ind., Apr. 10, 1954; s. Harold O. and Carol A. (Blackman) McC.; m. Donna D. Mushrush, Aug. 11, 1984 (div. July 1990); 1 child, William A.; m. Tatyana Tkachenko, Sept. 15, 1999 (div. Oct. 2006); 1 child Luba McCutchan. BS, Ind. U., 1976; diploma comml. lending, Am. Inst. Banking, 1986; loan rev. cert., Bank Adminstrn. Inst., 1990. Mgmt. trainee Citizens Nat. Bank, Evansville, 1977—79; with Old Nat. Bank, Evansville, 1979—86, loan rev. officer, 1984—86; dir. loan rev., asst. v.p. Old Nat. Bancorp, Evansville, 1986—96; mgr. loan rev., v.p. Fidelity Fed. Bancorp, 1997—99; comml. loan officer CSB State Bank, Cynthiana, Ind., 2000—06; sr. underwriter Am. Gen. Fin., 2006—. Trustee, treas. Willard Libr., Evansville, 1986-99; sec.-treas. McCutchanville (Ind.) Cemetery Assn., 1980—; bd. dirs. So. Ind. Higher Edn., 1995-2002; mem. McCutchanville Cmty. Ch Mem. Am. Mensa Ltd., Evansville Kennel Club. Republican. Methodist.

MCCUTCHEN, TAMMY DEE, lawyer, former federal agency administrator; b. Kewanee, Ill., Oct. 20, 1965; BA, Western Ill. U., 1987; JD, Northwestern U., 1990. Clk. US Ct. Appeals (7th Cir.), 1991—92; assoc. Skadden, Arps, Slate, Meagher and Flom, Chgo., 1992—95, Matkov, Salzman, Madoff anf Gunn, 1995—99; sr. counsel Hershey Foods Corp., 1999—2001; adminstr. wage and hour divsn. US Dept. Labor, Washington, 2001—04; ptnr. Dickstein Shapiro LLP, Washington, 2004—07; shareholder Littler Mendelson, P.C., Washington, 2007—. Mem.: ABA, DC Bar Assn., Ill. Bar Assn., The Federalist Soc. Office: Littler Mendelson PC 1150 17th St NW Ste 900 Washington DC 20036 E-mail: tmccutchen@littler.com. *

MCCUTCHEN, WILLIAM WALTER, JR., retired management educator; b. Hamlet, NC, Aug. 26, 1940; s. William Walter and Edith Wall (Rucker) McC.; m. Irene Katherine Lilly, June 16, 1962; 1 child, William Walter III. BS in Civil Engring., Duke U., 1962; MBA, Harvard U., 1967; PhD, Ind. U., 1988. Sales rep. Eli Lilly and Co., San Francisco, 1967-69, analyst econ. studies Indpls., 1969-70, mgr. econ. studies, 1970-72, mgr. personnel (mktg.), 1972-73; dir. nat. sales Elizabeth Arden, NYC, 1973-76; mng. dir. Lilly Industries Pty. Ltd., Sidney, Australia, 1976-79; dir. corp. communications Eli Lilly & Co., Indpls., 1980-83; assoc. prof. mgmt. Zicklin Sch. Bus., Baruch Coll., CUNY, NYC, 1988—2006, dep. chmn. dept. mgmt., 1995—2006; ret., 2006. Capt. USMC, 1962-65. Mem. Acad. Mgmt., Am. Econ. Assn., Woodstock Club, Univ. Club, Shorehaven Golf Club, Phi Delta Theta, Beta Gamma Sigma. Congregationalist.

MCCUTCHEON, ALLAN LEE, statistics educator; b. Clarinda, Iowa, Mar. 15, 1950; s. Merle Marvin and Margaret Lucille (Larabee) McC.; m. Nancy Ann Cooper, June 13, 1970 (div. May 1975); 1 child, Jennifer; m. Elisabeth Jean Crockett, May 25, 1985. BS, Iowa State U., 1972; MA, U. Chgo., 1977, PhD, 1982. Asst. prof. sociology U. Del., Newark, 1982-88, assoc. prof. sociology, 1988-96, assoc. chair dept. sociology, 1989-95; Donald O. Clifton chair survey rsch. U. Nebr., Lincoln, 1996—, dir. Gallup Rsch. Ctr., 1996—; sr. scientist Gallup Orgn., 1996—. Cons. Disaster Rsch. Ctr., Newark, 1986-88; vis. scientist Max Planck Inst., Freiburg, Germany, 1988-89; dozent U. Cologne (Germany), 1989, 96, 2001, 07; instr. European Consortium for Polit. Rsch. U. Essex (Eng.), 1990—; mem. sci. adv. coun. German Ctr. for Survey Rsch. and Methodology, 1998-2004. Author: Latent Class Analysis, 1987; editor (with J. Hagenaars): (book) Applied Latent Class Analysis, 2002 (newsletter) States and Societies, 1988-95; contbr. articles to profl. jours. Resource cons. Leadership Del. United Way, Wilmington, 1991-92. U. Chgo. rsch. fellow, 1974-77; Deutscher Akademischer Austauschdienst scholar, 1990; Fulbright scholar, The Netherlands, 1995-96. Fellow Am. Statis. Assn.; mem. World Assn. for Pub. Opinion Rsch. (sec.-treas. 2000-2004, gen. sec. 2004—), Coun. for European Studies, Am. Assn. for Pub. Opinion Rsch., Midwest Assn. for Pub. Opinion Rsch. (v.p. 2002-2003, pres. 2003-2004), Am. Sociol. Assn., Sigma Xi. Avocations: German culture, literature. Office: U Nebr Gallup Rsch Ctr 200 N 11th St Lincoln NE 68508-1406 E-mail: AMcCutcheon1@unl.edu.

MCCUTCHEON, JENNIFER LYNNE, horse breeder, lawyer; d. David Wesley and Lynne Reineman McCutcheon. BA in English Lit., Miami U., Oxford, Ohio, 1995, MAT, 1997; JD, No. Ill. U., DeKalb, 2000; LLM, Aberdeen U., Scotland, 2003. Vol. coord. Sexual Assault & Abuse Svcs., DeKalb, 1998—2000; instr. Parkland CC, Champaign, Ill., 2001; asst. state's atty. Coles County State Atty.'s Office, Charleston, Ill., 2001—02; intern Popovich Def. Team, The Hague, Netherlands, 2007; pres. Russell L. Reineman Stable, Inc., Chgo., 2005—. Mem.: Ill. Bar Assn., Ill. Thoroughbred Horsemen's Assn. (bd. dirs. 2006—), Keeneland Club, Thoroughbred Club Am. Office: 3355 W 31st St Chicago IL 60623

MCCUTCHEON, JOHN TINNEY, JR., retired journalist; b. Chgo., Nov. 8, 1917; s. John Tinney and Evelyn (Shaw) McC.; m. Susan Dart, Feb. 1, 1943; children: Anne McCutcheon Lewis, Mary, John Tinney III. BS, Harvard U., 1939. Reporter City News Bur., Chgo., 1939-40, Chgo. Tribune, 1940-51, editor column A Line O' Type or Two, 1951-57, editorial writer, 1957-71, editor editorial page, 1971-82, columnist, 1967-70. Pres. Lake Forest (Ill.) Libr., 1970—72. With USNR, 1941—46. Mem. Soc. Midland Authors, Am. Soc. Newspaper Editors, Nat. Conf. Editorial Writers, Geog. Soc. Chgo. (pres. 1955-57), Chgo. Zool. Soc. (hon. trustee), Chgo. Hist. Soc. (life trustee), Inter Am. Press Assn. (dir., freedom of press com. 1978-87), Wayfarers Club (Chgo.), Tryon (N.C.) Country Club, Sigma Delta Chi. Home: 10 Fox Paw Ln Saluda NC 28773-9527

MCCUTCHEON, STEVEN CLIFTON, civil and environmental engineer, hydrologist; b. Decatur, Ala., Oct. 29, 1952; s. Bernard Clifton and Rosa May (Askenburg) McC.; m. Sherry Lynn Sharp; children: Michael Ian, Alexander Tavis. BS, Auburn U., 1975; MS, Vanderbilt U., 1977, PhD, 1979. Registered profl.engr., La., Miss. Hydrologist U.S. Geol. Survey, Bay St. Louis, Miss., 1977-86; sr. environ. engr. U.S. EPA, Athens, Ga., 1986—. Adj. asst. prof. Tulane U., New Orleans, 1984-85; panel mem. Nat. Rsch. Coun., Washington, 1989-92; adj. prof. forestry, mem. faculty engring., U. Ga., Athens, 1993—; asst. prof. Clemson (S.C.) U., 1990-97; program evaluator Accreditation Bd. Engring. & Tech., 1992—. Author: Water Quality Modeling, vol. 1, 1989, Water Quality, Handbook of Hydrology, 1993; editor and author (with others): Manual for Performing Estuarine Waste Load Allocations, 1990, Hydrodynamics and Transport for Water Quality Modeling, 1999, editor and author: Phytoremediation, 2003; editor Jour. Environ. Engring., 1992—94, mem. editl. bd. Ecol. Engring., 1995—, Internat. Jour. Phytoremediation, 2000—, Hazardous Toxic and Radioactive Waste Mgmt., 1996—97, co-editor Environ. Sci. and Pollution Rsch., 2003—05, adv. editor, 2006—; contbr. chapters to books, articles to profl. jours. Mem. Zoning Commn., St. Tammany Parish, La., 1984-85; vice=chmn. Planning Adv. Bd., St. Tammany Parish, 1985; asst. den leader Cub Scouts Am., Athens, pack 83, 1991-92, pack 96, 1998-99, den leader, 1999-2001. Co-recipient EPA Sci. Achievement award in waste mgmt., Air and Waste Mgmt. Assn., 1995, EPA Sci. Achievement award in Chemistry, Am. Chem. Soc., 1997, Sci. and Tech. Achievement award, EPA, 1999, 2006, Bronze medal, 2001, 2002; recipient medal and plaque, Korea Soc. Water Pollution Rsch. and Control, Seoul, 1986, Engr. of Yr. award in EPA, NSPE, 1992, Engr. of Yr. in Govt. award, Ga. Engr. Week Com., 2004. Mem.: ASCE (br. pres. 1983—84, sect. dir. 1984—85, 1995—2001, sect. v.p. 2001—03, sect. pres.-elect 2003—04, rep. Dist. 14 coun. 2003—04, sect. pres. 2004—05, pres. 2004—05, nat. dir. Dist. 14 2004—06, exec. com. 2006—07, nat. dir. region 5 2006—07, Young Civil Engr. of Yr. award 1984, Richard R. Torrens award 1994, Govt. Civil Engr. of Yr. award 2004, Outstanding Membership Chair 2004), Internat. Soc. Phytotechnologies (charter), Am. Acad. Water Resources Engrs. (elected charter diplomate 2005), Water Environ. Fedn., Internat. Assn. Hydrologic Scis., Internat. Water Assn., Internat. Soc. Environ. Ethics (charter), Am. Geophys. Union, Am. Ecol. Engring. Soc. (chair com. registration and certification 2001—04, v.p., pres.-elect 2004—05, pres. 2005—06, past pres. 2006—07, charter), Phi Theta Kappa, Phi Kappa Phi, Sigma Xi (chpt. sec. 1982—84, membership com. 1984—85). Achievements include research in phytoremediation and ecological engring. to clean up federal facilities and response to Exxon Valdez oil spill. Home: 147 Spalding Ct Athens GA 30605-3716 Office: U Ga Faculty of Engring Driftmier Engring Ctr Athens GA 30602 Home Phone: 706-543-6972; Office Phone: 706-542-1455. Personal E-mail: EnvironHyd@aol.com. Business E-Mail: StevenMc@uga.edu.

MCDADE, HERBERT H., III, investment company executive; m. Martha McDade, 1989. BA, Duke U.; MBA, U. Mich., 1983. Corp. bond trader Lehman Brothers Holdings Inc., 1983—91, head, corp. bond dept., 1991—95, head, high grade credit bus., 1995—98, global head, debt capital markets, 1998—2000, co-global head, fixed income divsn., 2000—02, head, global fixed income divsn., 2002—05, mng. dir., mem. exec. com., global head equities, 2005—. Mem. nat. adv. council Fannie Mae. Mem.: Bond Market Assn. (v. chmn.), Winged Foot Golf Club (bd. govs.). Office: Lehman Brothers Holdings Inc 745 Seventh Ave New York NY 10019 *

MCDADE, JAMES RUSSELL, management consultant; b. Dallas, Jan. 15, 1925; s. Marion W. and Jeannette (Reneau) McD.; m. Elaine Bushey, Sep. 10, 1955. BSEE, So. Meth. U., Dallas, 1947; MBA, Northwestern U., Evanston, Ill., 1950. Asst. to pres. Davidson Corp., Chgo., 1951-52, Mergenthaler Linotype Co., Bklyn., 1952-53, comml. works mgr., 1953-56; chief indsl. engr. Tex. Instruments, Inc., Dallas, 1956-57, product gen. mgr., 1958-60, v.p., 1961-64; chmn. bd. McDade Properties Co., Aspen (Colo.), Denver, Dallas, 1964—. Bd. dirs. Pitkin County Bank, Aspen; chmn. bd. dirs. Harley-Davidson Tex., Westec Security of Aspen, Aspen Security, Inc. Founding mem. Aspen Art Mus., 1980; mem. Ballet Aspen, 1980—; pres. club Aspen Valley Hosp., 1984—. Served to 1st lt. USAF, 1943-46. Mem.: Presidents Assn., Am. Mgmt. Assn., Rep. Senatorial Inner Circle. Avocations: skiing, horseback riding, camping, swimming. Personal E-mail: jrmco@jrmco.com.

MCDADE, ROBERTA CLARK, secondary school educator; b. Balt., Dec. 19, 1951; d. Joseph Thomas and Esther Claire Clark; children: Edward Matthew Day, Rebecca Marie Day. BA in English and Elem. Edn., Salisbury State Coll., Md., 1973; MEd in Secondary Math., U. Del., Newark, Del., 1976. Lic. profl. tchr. Colo. Dept. Edn., 2002. Resident asst. Salisbury State Coll., Md., 1971—73; tchr. Kent County Pub. Schs., Chestertown, Md., 1973—76; home daycare provider Chestertown, Md., 1976—82; instr. math. Chesapeake Coll., Wye Mills, Md., 1982—83; tchr. Anne Arundel County Pub. Schs., Annapolis, Md., 1983—87; substitute tchr. Colo. Springs, 1987—88; instr. Basic Skills Edn. Program, Fort Carson, Colo., 1989; tchr. Colo. Springs Dist. 11, Colo., 1990—. Mem. com. Md. State Dept. Edn., Balt., 1980—83; participant step program NASA, Houston, 1996. Coach baseball Severna Pk. (Md.) Little League, 1986; coach wrestling Severna Pk. (Md.) Parks and Recreation, 1985—86; sec. Boy Scouts Am., Cape St Claire, Md., 1986—87, mem. troop com. Pikes Peak Coun. Colo. Springs, 1989—2006; leader Girl Scouts Am., Arnold, Md., 1986—87, leader wagon wheel coun. Colo. Springs, 1992—97; host parent Am. Field Svc., Colo. Springs, 1991—2000; adv. youth Sr. H.S. Chapel at Peterson AFB, Colo. Springs, 1987—89, Asbury United Meth. Fellowship, Salisbury, Md., 1970—73; tchr. christian edn. St Francis Assisi Ch., 1994—97, coord. christian edn., 1998—2001, mem. discernment com., 2005—06. Home: 1811 Summernight Terr Colorado Springs CO 80909-2725 Office: Sprng Creek Youth Svcs Ctr 3190 E Las Vegas St Colorado Springs CO 80906 Home Phone: 719-550-9114. Personal E-mail: beccyesmom@hotmail.com. Business E-Mail: ackerrc@d11.org.

MCDADE, SANDY D., lawyer, paper company executive; BA, Whitman Coll., 1974; JD cum laude, Seattle U., 1979. Mem. law dept. Weyerhaeuser Co., Federal Way, Wash., 1980—2000, corp. sec., 1993—2000, v.p. strategic planning, 2000—03, sr. v.p. Can., 2003—05, sr. v.p., indsl. wood products and internat. bus., 2005—06. Mem. camping svcs. bd. Seattle Met. YMCA; mem. Wash. State Corp. Act Revision Com. Mem.: Wash. State Bar Assn. (past chmn. corp. law dept. sect.), Am. Soc. Corp. Secs. Office: Weyerhaeuser Co PO Box 9777 Federal Way WA 98063-9777

MCDADE, SEAN, market research company executive; BAA, Temple U., 1990, PhD in Bus. Mgmt., 1996. With Gallup Orgn.; dir. rsch. LRA Worldwide, founder, pres. PeopleMetrics, Inc., 2000—. Named one of 40 Under 40, Phila. Bus. Jour., 2006. Office: PeopleMetrics, Inc Ste 3220 1717 Arch St Philadelphia PA 19103 Office Phone: 215-979-8030. Office Fax: 215-979-8049.

MCDAID, JENNIFER DAVIS, archivist; b. Norfolk, Va., Apr. 18, 1965; m. Christopher Ludden McDaid, Oct. 5, 2001; 1 child, Katharine Ludden. MA, Coll. William and Mary, 1990. Asst. editor Va. Cavalcade Libr. of Va., Richmond, 1996—99, archives rsch. coord., 1999—. Dep. coord. State Hist. Records Adv. Bd., Richmond, 1999—; local records appraisal archivist Libr. Va., 2007—. Contbr. Mem.: So. Assn. Women Historians (Listserv co-editor 1997—). Office: Libr of Virginia 800 E Broad St Richmond VA 23219 Office Phone: 804-692-3648.

MCDANIEL, A. STEPHEN, lawyer; b. Memphis, Nov. 13, 1946; BBA, U. Memphis, 1968, JD, 1973. Bar: Tenn. 1973, Mo. 1975, cert.: Tenn. Commn. Continuing Legal Edn. and Specialization (estate planning specialist). Estate and gift tax atty. US Treasury Dept., 1973—75; positions up to mng. ptnr. Williams, McDaniel, Wolfe & Womack, P.C., Memphis, 1975—. Instr. estate planning and estate & gift tax U. Memphis Sch. Law, 1990—2000. Contbr. articles to profl. jours. Named one of Top 100 Attys., Worth mag., 2006. Fellow: Am. Coll. Trust and Estate Counsel; mem.: Tenn. Bar Assn., Memphis Bar Assn. Office: Williams McDaniel Wolfe & Womack 5521 Murray Ave Memphis TN 38119 Office Phone: 901-767-8200. E-mail: sMcDaniel@wmww.com. *

MCDANIEL, DUSTIN, state attorney general; b. Fayetteville, Ark., Apr. 29, 1972; m. Amanda Miller; 1 child, Emma Grace. BA in Pub. Adminstrn., U. Ark., Fayetteville, 1994; JD, U. Ark. Law Sch., 1998. Patrol officer Jonesboro Police Dept., 1994—96; legal counsel Craighead County Dem. Ctrl. Com.; ptnr. McDaniel & Wells, Jonesboro, Ark.; mem. Ark. Ho. Reps. from dist. 75, Little Rock, 2005—06; atty. gen. State of Ark, Little Rock, 2007—. Named Outstanding State Legislator, Ark. Mcpl. League; named one of 10 Best Legislators, Ark. Dem. Gazette, 2005. Mem.: Craighead County Bar Assn., Ark. Trial Lawyers Assn. (mem., Bd. Governors), Ark. Bar Assn. (chairman, Civil Litig. Sect. 2002—03, chair, Consumer Law Handbook Com., Golden Gavel award, Disting. Svc. award). Democrat. Office: Office of Atty Gen 200 Tower Bldg 323 Center St Little Rock AR 72201-2610 Office Phone: 501-376-1500, 800-482-8982. Office Fax: 501-376-1507. *

MCDANIEL, JAMES EDWIN, lawyer; b. Dexter, Mo., Nov. 22, 1931; s. William H. and Gertie M. (Woods) McD.; m. Mary Jane Crawford, Jan. 22, 1955; children: John William, Barbara Anne. AB, Washington U., St. Louis, 1957, JD, 1959. Bar: Mo. 1959. Assoc. firm Walther, Barnard, Cloyd & Timm, 1959—60, McDonald, Barnard, Wright & Timm, 1960—63, ptnr., 1963—65, Barnard, Timm & McDaniel, St. Louis, 1965—73, Barnard & Baer, St. Louis, 1973—82, Lashly & Baer, St. Louis, 1982—2002, of counsel, 2002—; pros. atty. Glendale, Mo., 1968—. City atty. City of Glendale, Mo., 1996—; bd. dirs. Eden. Theol. Sem.; lectr. Latvian U., Riga, Inst. Fgn. Rels., Banking in Am., 1992-93. Leader legal del. Chinese-Am. Comparative Law Study, China, 1988, Russian-Am. Comparative Law Study, Russia, 1990; trustee, past chmn., past treas. 1st Congl. Ch. St. Louis. With USAF, 1951-55. Fellow Am. Bar Found. (life), St. Louis Bar Found. (life; bd. dirs. 2005-, pres. 2007—); mem. ABA (bd. govs. 1997-2000, ho. of dels. 1976-80, 84-92, 97-2000, state del. 1986-92, chmn. lawyers conf., jud. adminstrn. divsn. 1992-95, 8th cir. rep. standing com. on fed. jud. 1995-98, mem. standing com. on jud. qualification, tenure and compensation 1996-97, adv. com. law and nat. security 1999-), The Mo. Bar (pres. 1981-82, bd. govs. 1974-83), Mo. Assn. Def. Counsel, Bar Assn. Met. St. Louis (pres. 1972), Internat. Assn. Ins. Counsel, Assn. Def. Counsel St. Louis (past pres.), Phi Delta Phi. Home: 767 Elmwood Ave Saint Louis MO 63122-3216 Office: Lashly & Baer 714 Locust St Saint Louis MO 63101-1699 Office Phone: 314-621-2939. Personal E-mail: jemglendale@earthlink.net. Business E-Mail: jemcdaniel@lashlybaer.com.

MCDANIEL, JAMES MARK, JR., health care executive; b. Harrisonburg, Va., Mar. 18, 1953; s. James Mark and Mary (Jones) McD.; m. Lynne Stewart, Mar. 21, 1981; children: Diane Marie, Laura Elizabeth. BA, U. N.C., Greensboro, 1975. Pres. Rock-O-Lawn Mfrs., High Point, N.C., 1976-81; ins. exec. R.P.M. Assocs., Raleigh, N.C., 1981-84; adminstr. White Eye Clinic, Greenville, N.C., 1984-85; pres. S.I.S.I., Greensboro, N.C., 1988—; chief exec. officer Southeastern Eye Ctr., Greensboro, N.C., 1985—. Pres. Salem Optical Co., Winston-Salem, N.C., 1988—. Football coach Lewisville (N.C.) Titans Athletic Assn., 1982-83, 85-87, Pfafftown (N.C.) Packers Football Assn., 1988—; basketball coach Clemmons (N.C.) Basketball Assn., 1981-84; elder Community in Christ Presbyn. Chr., Forest Oaks, N.C., 1976. Republican. Avocation: coaching football and basketball. Office: Southeastern Eye Ctr 3312 Battleground Ave Greensboro NC 27410-2400 also: 146 Sycamore Ridge Dr Advance NC 27006-7476

MCDANIEL, JARREL DAVE, lawyer; b. Clovis, N.Mex., Oct. 17, 1930; s. Raymond Lee and Blanch (Booth) McD.; m. Anne Louise McAllister; children: Jarrel Dave Jr., Julia Anne. AA, Riverside Coll., 1951; BA, U. Tex., 1956, LLB, 1957. Bar: Tex. 1957. Assoc. Vinson & Elkins, Houston, 1957-69, ptnr., 1969-96; of counsel Sheinfeld, Maley & Kay, Houston, 1997-2001; sr. counsel Akin Gump Strauss Hauer & Feld LLP, Houston, 2001—06; of counsel King & Spalding, LLP, Houston, 2007—. Author, lectr. in field. Served with USAF, 1950-54. Mem.: ABA, Am. Bankruptcy Inst., State Bar Tex., Am. Coll. Bankruptcy, Houston Club. Roman Catholic. Home: 1217 Potomac Dr Houston TX 77057-1919 Office: King & Spalding LLP 1100 Louisiana Ste 4000 Houston TX 77002-5213 Office Phone: 713-751-3251. Business E-Mail: jmcdaniel@kslaw.com.

MCDANIEL, JOANAVA B., nurse; b. St. John, Barbados, May 22, 1948; d. Charles and Etheline Griffith; 1 child, Shelley Johnson. AA in Liberal Arts with honors, Delaware County C.C., Media, Pa., 1986; BA in Orgnl. Mgmt. with honors, Ea. U., St. Davids, Pa., 1993. Cert. health mgmt. nurse, Barbados, pub. health nurse, W.I. Sch. Pub. Health, midwife, Tercentenary

Sch. Nursing, Barbados, RN Eng. Staff nurse Ministry of Health, Barbados, 1972—77, pub. health nurse, 1977—83; pvt. duty nurse Lansdale Agy., Newtown Square, Pa., 1984—88; pvt. duty and vis. nurse PRN Health Care Svcs., Inc., Ardmore, Pa., 1986—88, dir. profl. svcs., 1988—91; asst. dir. clin. svcs. Home Nurse, Inc., Wayne, Pa., 1992—2001; clin. support specialist Bayada Nurses, Moorestown, NJ, 2001—. Missionary nurse Project Word Found., Inc., Pa., 1995—, pres. Wayne, Pa., 2000—; bd. dirs. Life Bible Inst., Ardmore, 2002. Avocations: reading, sewing, cooking, gardening, Scrabble. Office: Bayada Nurses 286 Chester Ave Moorestown NJ 08057 Office Phone: 856-778-5300.

MCDANIEL, RAYMOND W., JR., financial information company executive; b. 1958; BS in Polit. Sci., Colgate U.; JD, Emory U., 1983. Bar: NY 1984. Joined Moody's Corp., 1987, sr. analyst asset securitization dept., mng. dir. internat., 1996—2000, sr. v.p. internat., 2000—01, sr. v.p. global ratings and rsch., 2001—03, exec. v.p. global ratings and rsch., 2003—04, bd. dirs., 2003—, COO, 2004—05, pres., 2004—05, chmn., CEO, 2005—; sr. mng. dir. global ratings and rsch. Moody's Investors Svc., 2001, pres., 2001—05. Bd. dirs. John Wiley & Sons, Inc., 2005—, Nat. Coun. Econ. Edn. Mem.: Fixed Income Analysts Soc. Office: Moodys Corp 99 Church St New York NY 10007 Office Phone: 212-553-0300. Office Fax: 212-553-7194. *

MCDANIEL, RODERICK ROGERS, petroleum engineer, consultant; b. High River, Alta., Can., 1926; s. Dorsey Patton and Daisy (Rogers) McD.; m. Trudy Ethier, Apr. 15, 2000; children: Nancy, Leslie. BS, U. Okla., 1947. Petroleum reservoir engr. Creole Petroleum Corp., 1947, Imperial Oil Ltd., 1948-52, chief reservoir engr., 1952-55; founder McDaniel Cons., Calgary, Canada, 1955—; chmn. Can. Airlines Ltd., Calgary, 1974-91, Can. Regional Airlines, Calgary, 1991-92. Hon. dir. Calgary Exhbn. and Stampede, 1979-88, hon. bd. dirs., 1988—; dir. Calgary Stampeder Football Team, 1988. Mem. Assn. Profl. Engrs. Alta (hon. life), Can. C. of C. (bd. dirs. 1973), Calgary C. of C. (past pres.), Calgary Petroleum Club (past pres.), Calgary Highlanders (hon. col. ret.), Calgary Golf and Country Club, Outrigger Club (Honolulu), Mission Hills Country Club. Home: # 2200 255 5 Ave SW Calgary AB Canada T2P 3G6 Office: McDaniel & Assoc 2200 255 5th Ave SW Calgary AB Canada T2P 3G6

MCDANIEL, SARA SHERWOOD (SALLY MCDANIEL), trainer, consultant; b. St. Louis, Apr. 24, 1943; d. Edward Leighton and Dolores Edic (Pitts) Sherwood; m. Allen Polk McDaniel, Dec. 29, 1967; children: James Polk, Fontaine Maury. AA, Mt. Vernon Coll., 1963; BS, Vanderbilt U., 1965. Tchr. Kanawha Valley Schools, Charleston, W.Va., 1965-66, Fulton County Schools, Atlanta, 1966-68, Trinity Sch., 1969-71; tournament dir. Atlanta Classic, 1972-77; dir. alumni affairs Leadership Atlanta, 1988-89; pvt. practice cons., trainer Atlanta, 1988—. Bd. dirs. AID Atlanta, The High Mus. Art, Leadership Coun. Kennedy Ctr. of Vanderbilt U., UNICEF-Atlanta, The Atlanta Women's Found., Leadership Atlanta. Bd. dirs. Girl Scouts U.S., Ga., High Mus. Art, Atlanta Opera, UNICEF Atlanta, Aid Atlanta, Fine Art Collectors; active Com. on Women and Minorities for 1996 Olympics; mem. exec. com. Leadership Atlanta, Jr. League; mem. Friends of Spelman; trustee Mt. Vernon Coll.; bd. chair Atlanta Women's Fund; bd. dirs. Pub. Leadership Edn. Network, Ga. Women of Achievement. Mem. Am. Soc. Trainers and Dirs., Atlanta Women's Network (bd. dirs., pres.), Vanderbilt U. Alumni Assn., Alumni Assn. Peabody Coll., The Atlanta Girls Sch. Presbyterian.

MCDANIEL, SUE POWELL, writer; b. Jefferson City, Mo., Mar. 13, 1946; d. Ernest Gayle and Ruth Angeline (Raithel) Powell; m. Walter Lee Zimmerman, Aug. 14, 1966 (div. 1980); m. Olin Cleve McDaniel, June 23, 1985 (div. 2002). BS in Edn., U. Mo., 1968, MEd in Edn., 1977, EdS, 1980, PhD, 1985. Cert. tchr., Mo. Tchr. Jefferson City Pub. Schs., 1968-80; fiscal assoc. Mo. Coordinating Bd. for Higher Edn., Jefferson City, 1980-90; exec. dir. Mo. Women's Coun., Jefferson City, 1990-99; exec. dir. Skillpath Seminars, 2000—03; pres. Alternatives, Jefferson City, Mo., 1999—; dir. Heisinger Hope Found., 2004. Author: (with C. Dixon) Learning, Changing, Leading: Keep to Success in the 21st Century, 1998, Missouri Women Today, 1993, Status of the Women, 1994, I.M. Heart, 2006. Mem. Zonta Internat. Avocations: reading, music, drawing, flower garden, photography. Home: 1600 Stadium Blvd Jefferson City MO 65109-2418

MCDANIEL, THOMAS R., utilities executive; BS in Civil Engring., UCLA; postgrad., Calif. State U., LA, U. So. Calif. Joined So. Calif. Edison, 1971; CEO, dir. Edison Capital, 1987—2005; CEO, pres. Edison Mission Energy, Irvine, Calif., 2002—05, chmn., 2003—05; exec. v.p., CFO, treas. Edison Internat., Rosemead, Calif., 2005—. Active Huntington Youth Shelter; dir. Sr. Care Action Network. Office: Edison Internat 2244 Walnut Grove Ave Rosemead CA 91770-0800 *

MCDANIELS, AUDREY EVELYN, microbiologist; b. Grants Pass, Oreg., Feb. 11, 1928; d. Charles Pixley and Ruby Clark Best; divorced; 1 child, David Douglas. BS in Microbiology, Oreg. State U., 1950; BS in Edn., U. Wash., 1964; MS in Gen. Scis., Oreg. State U., 1965; PhD in Environ. Sci., U. Mich., 1980. Jr. scientist GE, Hanford, Wash., 1950-53; microbiologist City of Seattle, 1954-57, Wash. State Pub. Health, Seattle, 1957-60; 4th grade tchr. Amity (Oreg.) Elem., 1965-68; biology tchr. Rainier (Oreg.) H.S., 1968-72; microbiologist EPA, Cin., 1980—. Home: 1029 Fashion Ave Cincinnati OH 45238 Office: US EPA 26 W Martin Luther King Dr Cincinnati OH 45268 Office Phone: 513-569-7332. Personal E-mail: audrey6341@aol.com.

MCDANIELS, WILLIAM E., lawyer; b. Needham, Mass., July 1, 1941; BA, Williams Coll., 1963; JD, Georgetown U., 1966. Bar: D.C. 1967, Md. 1983. Grad. fellow criminal law, litigation U. Pa., Phila., 1966-68; pub. defender Phila. Pub. Defender's Office, 1966-68; adj. prof. evidence, criminal law, advanced criminal procedure Georgetown U. Law Ctr., Washington, 1970-87; mem. Williams & Connolly LLP, Washington, 1968—. Instr. Nat. Inst. Trial Advocacy, 1975—. Fellow Am. Coll. Trial Lawyers; mem. ABA, Md. State Bar Assn, D.C. Bar. Office: Williams & Connolly LLP 725 12th St NW Washington DC 20005-5901 Office Phone: 202-434-5055. Business E-Mail: wmcdaniels@wc.com.

MCDANNALD, CLYDE ELLIOTT, JR., management consultation company executive; b. June 29, 1923; s. Clyde E. and Evelyn (Tunison-Morgan) McD.; m. Virginia Washington, Apr. 25, 1953; children: Leslie Ann McDannald Malarchick, Clyde Elliott III, Bruce Robert, Bonnie Washington McDannald Jefferis, Brian Christopher (dec.), Laura Leigh. Market rsch. analyst J. Walter Thompson Co., NYC, 1948-50; asst. dir. market rsch. Nat. Lead Co., NYC, 1950-51; product rsch. supr., account exec. Foote, Cone & Belding, Inc., NYC, 1951-52; product mgr., asst. advt. mgr. Am. Safety Razor Corp., NYC, 1953-54; account exec., account supr. Meldrum & Fewsmith, Inc., Cleve., 1954-56; sr. account exec. Young & Rubicam, NYC, 1956-58; exec. asst. to v.p., advt. mgr. Brown & Williamson Tobacco Corp. subs. Brit.-Am. Tobacco Co., Ltd., Louisville, 1959-63; dir. advt. and mktg. svcs., dir. mktg. Miller Brewing Co., Milw., 1963-65; divsn. gen. mgr., v.p. consumer products, corp. v.p. Revere Copper & Brass Inc., NYC, 1966-71; pres., COO H.H. Pott Distillers Ltd. U.S. subs. H.H. Pott NFGR, NYC, 1972-80; pres., CEO Oxbridge Cons., Inc., NYC, 1981—; ptnr. Hilbert, Peers and Young, Inc., NYC, 1984—. Bd. dirs. West Indies Distillers, Ltd., Distilled Spirits Inst., Washington, McFrank & Williams Inc. and Cooperating Cons. Corp., N.Y.C.; vis. prof. mktg. Fairfield U. Sch. Bus., 1975-77. Apptd. to staff Col. Ky. Govs., 1959-63, 92—; mem. Ky. Hwy. Commn., 1960-63, N.Y. Gov.'s Indsl. Com., 1967-72; bd. govs. N.Y. Mil. Acad., 1970-76, trustee, 1975-92. Capt. Inf. USAAF, 1942-45, ETO. Decorated D.F.C., Air medal with 4 oak leaf clusters; recipient Conspicuous Svc. Cross State of N.Y. with 5 oak leaf clusters, Valor medal UDC, Knickerbocker Greys City of N.Y., War Cross, Sons of Confederate Vets., Medaille de la France Liberee, Croix de Guerre (Belgium, France), Roi Leopold III, Battle of Britain, Knight Mil. Order of Malta, Knight Sovereign Mil. Order Temple Jerusalem. Mem. SAR, SR (bd. mgrs. 1988—), Alumni Fedn. Columbia U., Am. Mgmt. Assn., NAM (mktg. con.), Audit Bur. Circulation, Navy League, St. Andrews Soc. State of N.Y., Am. Revolution Round Table, Am. Legion, VFW, N.Y. Soc. Mil. and Naval Officers World Wars, Sons of Confederate Vets., Soc. Colonial Wars, St. George Soc., Soc. Mayflower Descs., Nat. Huguenot Soc., St. Nicholas Soc. of City of N.Y. Columbia U. Club, Explorers Club, Univ. Club, Sigma Chi (life), Alpha Chi Sigma. Democrat. Presbyterian. Home: Clarendon Gardens 5 Red Fox Run Pinehurst NC 28374-9031 E-mail: cmcdann398@aol.com.

MCDARRAH, FRED WILLIAM, photographer, editor, writer; b. Bklyn., Nov. 5, 1926; s. Howard Arthur and Elizabeth (Swahn) McD.; m. Gloria Schoffel, Nov. 5, 1960; children: Timothy Swann, Patrick James. BA in Journalism, NYU, 1954. Mem. staff Village Voice Newspaper, NYC, 1959—, picture editor, 1971—; book reviewer ASMP Infinity Mag., 1972-73, Photo Dist. News, 1985-88, The Picture Profl., 1990—2002. Exhibited in Soho Photo Gallery, 1973, Whitney Mus., 1974, 76-77, Dallas Mus. Art, 1974, San Francisco Mus. Art, 1975, Wadsworth Atheneum, 1975, Sidney Janis Gallery, 1976, Basel (Switzerland) Art Fair, 1976, Alfred Stieglitz Gallery, 1976, Empire State Mus., Albany, NY, 1978, Lightworks Gallery, Syracuse, NY, 1981, Cape Cod Gallery, Provincetown Mass., 1982, Galleria di Franca Mancini, Pesaro, Italy, 1983, Musée du Quebec, 1987, Anita Shapolsky Gallery, NYC, 1988, Hartnett Gallery U. Rochester, NY, 1989, G. Ray Hawkins Gallery, LA, 1989, Read Gallery Antioch Coll., Ohio, 1989, Mus. Art/Sci./Industry, Bridgeport, Conn., 1989, NYC Gallery Queens Mus., 1989, Ctr. Photography, Woodstock, 1989, Frumkin/Adams Gallery, 1990, Musée d'Art Moderne De La Ville de Paris, 1990, Musée d'Art Contemporain, Montreal, 1990, Pollack-Krasner Mus., East Hampton, NY, 1990, Found. Cartier, Paris, 1990, Marty Carey Pictures Gallery, Woodstock, NY, 1992, Galerie Gilles Ringuet, Belfort, France, 1992, Galerie Contre Jour, Belfort, France, 1992, Galleria La Pescheria, Cesena, Italy, 1994, Whitney Mus. Am. Art, 1995—, Nat. Portrait Gallery, 1996, Candice Perich Gallery, 1996; exhbns. include Jack Kerouac Visions of the Road, Les Rencontres D'Arles, Arles, France, 1991, Jack Kerouac Travelling Writers, Saint-Malo (France) Internat. Festival, 1991, 97, Images of Greenwich Village NY Camera Club, 1992, Walker Art Ctr., Mpls., 1996, M.H. de Young Meml. Mus., San Francisco, 1996, Whitney Mus. Am. Art, 1997-98, New York Stories, Chiostro del Bramante, Rome, 1999, Detroit Inst. Arts, 2000, Great Modern Pictures, NY, 2000, MOCA, Wexner Ctr., Parrish Mus., 2000, Mus. Nat. Modern Art 2001, Gallerie Comunale d'Arte Moderna, Rome, 2001, Mus. City of NY, 2001, Centre Pompidou, Paris, 2001, Albright-Knox Art Gallery, 2002, Mus. Contemporary Art, LA, 2002, Fahey/Klein Gallery, L.A., 2002, Grimaldi Forum, Monaco, 2003, Snap Galleries, Birmingham, Eng., 2004, Castello di Rivoli, Turin, 2004, Triennale di Milano, 2004, Provd Galleries, 2005, Steven Kasher Gallery, NYC, 2007, Shooting Gallery, Hollywood, Calif., 2007; represented in permanent collections: J. Paul Getty Mus., Nat. Portrait Gallery; author: The Beat Scene, 1960, The Artist's World in Pictures, 1961, rev. edit. 1988, Greenwich Village, 1963, NYC, 1964, Sculpture in Environment, 1967, Museums in New York, 1973, French edit., 1979, 5th edit., 1990, Photography Marketplace, 2d edit., 1977, Stock Photo and Assignment Source Book, 1977, 2d edit., 1984, Gay Pride: Photographs from Stonewall to Today, 1994, Frommer's Virginia Guide, 2d edit., 1994, Fodor's Cancun, Cozumel, Yucatan Peninsula, 1996, Kerouac and Friends: A Beat Generation Album, 1984, Japanese edit, 1990, 2nd edit, 2002, Frommer's Atlantic City and Cape May, 4th edit., 1991, 5th edit., 1993, New York Stories, 2001, Anarchy, Protest & Rebellion & the Counter Culture that Changed America, 2003; co-author: The New Bohemia, 1967, 2d edit., 1990, Guide for Ecumenical Discussion, 1970, Greenwich Village Guide, 1992, Frommer's Virginia, 1992, 2d edit. 1994; author: (with Timothy S: LA Pop Art Negli Anni '60 Chiostro del Bram Ante, 1999; author: (with Gloria S. McDarrah) Beat Generation: Glory Days in Greenwich Village, 1998; The Beat Generation: Glory Days in Greenwich Village, editor, 1996; editor: (with Gloria S. McDarrah and Timothy S. McDarrah) The Photography Encyclopedia, 1999; author: (with Gloria S. McDarrah) The Artist's World in Pictures, 2d edit., 1988; Saturday Rev. Executive Desk Diary, 1962-64; photographer: Personality Posters, Fotofolio (post cards) (polit. and social figures); contbr. articles, picture features to various publs. including NY Mag., Vanity Fair. Paratrooper US Army, 1944-47. Recipient numerous photography awards including 1st place spot news photo award. NY Press Assn. 1964, 68, 1st place feature photo award 1967, 1st place picture story award 1969, 2nd place spot news photo award 1967, 70, 3d place spot news photo award 1965, 3d place feature photo award 1965, 3d place picture story award 1970, 1st place Best Pictorial Series Nat. Newspaper Assn., 1966, Page One award Newspaper Guild NY, 1971, 80; Guggenheim fellow in photography, 1972. Mem. N.Y. Press Photographers Assn., Authors Guild, N.Y. Press Club, Am. Soc. Picture Profls. Office: 36 Cooper Sq New York NY 10003-7118 Office Fax: 212-254-5547. Personal E-mail: gloriamcdarrah@earthlink.net.

MCDARRAH, GLORIA SCHOFFEL, editor, writer; b. Bronx, NY, June 22, 1932; d. Louis and Rose Schoffel; m. Fred W. McDarrah, Nov. 5, 1960; children: Timothy, Patrick. BA in French, Pa. State U., 1953; MA in French, NYU, 1966. Editorial asst. Crowell-Collier, NYC, 1957-59; exec. asst. to pub. Time Inc., NYC, 1959-61; libr., tchr. N.Y.C. Pub. Schs. and St. Luke's Sch., 1972-76; exec. asst. to pres. Capital Cities Communications Inc., NYC, 1972-76; analyst N.Y.C. Landmarks Preservation Commn., 1976-79; project editor Grosset & Dunlap Inc., NYC, 1979-80; sr. editor Prentice Hall trade div. Simon & Schuster Inc., NYC, 1980-88; pres. McDarrah Media Assocs., NYC, 1988—. Editor book rev. The Picture Profl., 1989—; book reviewer Pub.'s Weekly, 1994—. Author: Frommer's Guide to Va., 1992, Frommer's Guide to Va. 2d edit., 1994—95, Frommer's Atlantic City and Cape May, 1984, Frommer's Atlantic City and Cape May 4th edit., 1991, Frommer's Atlantic City and Cape May 5th edit., 1993—95, The Artist's World 2d edit., 1988, Photography Encyclopedia, 1999; co-author: Museums in N.Y. 5th edit., 1990, Photography Marketplace, 1975, The Beat Generation: Glory Days in Greenwich Village, 1996, Anarchy, Protest and Rebellion and the Counter-Culture That Changed Am., 2003; co-editor: Exec. Desk Diary Saturday Rev., 1962—64; contbg. editor (quar.): Dollarwise Traveler, Fodor's Cancun, Cozumel, Yucatan Peninsula, Fodor's Ariz.

MCDAVID, DOUGLAS WARREN, executive research consultant; b. San Francisco, Feb. 25, 1947; s. James Etheridge and Elizabeth Rae (Warren) McD.; m. Nancy Kathleen Somers, June 1968 (div. 1982); 1 child, Amy Kemp; m. Carleen Ann Richmond, Feb. 14, 1987; 1 child, Amanda Claire. BA in Sociology, U. Calif., Santa Cruz, 1969; MA in Libr. Sci., San Jose State U., 1972. Libr. Palo Alto (Calif.) City Libr., 1969-81; systems analyst Tymnet (Tymshare), Cupertino, Calif., 1981-84; mgr. systems architecture Tymnet McDonnell Douglas, San Jose, Calif., 1984-86; data modeling cons. Fireman's Fund Ins., Terra Linda, Calif., 1986-87, Bank of Calif., San Francisco, 1988; systems cons. Pacific Bell, San Ramon, Calif., 1989-93; prin. Integrated Info., 1993—; exec. cons. IBM Global Svcs., 1995—, IBM Almaden Rsch Ctr., 2002—. Mem. IBM Acad. Tech., 2000—; spkr. Entity/Relationship Conf. Internat., Burlingame, Calif., 1991, DAMA Internat. Conf., 1994—; sr. cons. in bus. semantic modeling for object oriented applications IBM Corp., 1994—; 1996 spkr. Bus. Rules Conf. OOPSLA, IBM Object Technology Conf., Ind. Labor & Mgmt. Coun.; cons. IBM, 1994-98, mgr. knowledge devel., 1999—; consulting rschr. IBM Almadea Rsch. Ctr., 2002—; spkr. in field. Assoc. editor: Handbook of Object Technology. Mem. IEEE, Assn. for Computing Machinery, Data Adminstrn. Mgmt. Assn. (San Francisco bd. dirs. 1987-91, Sacramento bd. dirs. 1992, spkr. 1991, 92), Data Processing Mgmt. Assn. (spkr. 1992), Am. Assn. Artificial Intelligence (spkr. 1993), Internat. Soc. Sys. Sci. (spkr. 1999), New Media Consortium (visionary bd. mem. 2007—). Avocations: golf, gardening, creative writing, investing, swimming. Home and Office: 8611 Kingslynn Ct Elk Grove CA 95624-3135 Office Phone: 916-549-4600. Business E-Mail: mcdavid@us.ibm.com.

MCDAVID, GEORGE EUGENE (GENE MC DAVID), retired newspaper executive; b. McComb, Miss., June 30, 1930; s. O. C. and Inez S. McDavid; m. Betty Ernestine Tinsley, Sept. 24, 1949; children: Carol, Martha Gene Newman. BBA cum laude, U. Houston, 1965. Owner, pub. Wilk Amite Record, Gloster, Miss., 1949-58; with Houston Chronicle, 1958—, prodn. mgr., 1967-74, v.p. ops., 1974-85, v.p., gen. mgr., 1985-90, pres., 1990-98, ret., 1998. Mem. adv. bd. Am. Press Inst.; past pres., bd. dirs. S.W. Wch. Printing Mgmt. Chmn. Greater Houston chpt. ARC, 1st vice-chmn.; pres.'s counsel Houston Bapt. U; vice-chmn. Sam Houston Boy Scouts Am., United Negro Coll. Fund, Asia Soc. Goodwill Industries, YMCA; chmn. Houston Forum, Houston region Am. Cancer Soc., bd. regents, 1997—; spl. deacon Second Bapt. Ch., Houston.; bd. dirs. Nat. Conf. Christians and Jews; nat. bd. govs. Greater Houston chpt. ARC; bd. dirs. Greater Houston Partnership; bd. dirs., pres. Houston Symphony; bd. dirs., v.p. Books of the World; vice-chmn. devel. bd. U. Houston, chair bd. regents, 2003. Recipient Franklin award, U. Houston, 1961, Disting. Alumnus award, 1990, 1997, Taggart award, Tex. Newspaper, 1992, Man of Yr. award, NCCJ, 1993, named Outstanding Ex-Citizen Gloster, 1973, Hon. Father of Yr., 1996, named to Miss. Jour. Hall of Fame, 2002. Mem.: So. Newspaper Pubs. Assn. (pres.), Am. Newspaper Pubs. Assn. (chmn. tech. com.), Pine Forest Country Club, Houston C. of C. (Houston Citizen's Cmty. Svc. award 1993, named Houston Cultural Leader of Yr. 1998), Tex. Daily Newspaper Assn. (pres.), Crown Colony Country Club, Beta Gamma Sigma, Phi Kappa Phi. Address: 4 Hunters Park Ln Houston TX 77024-5438 Personal E-mail: gene.mcdavid@chron.com.

MCDAVID, JANET LOUISE, lawyer; b. Mpls., Jan. 24, 1950; d. Robert Matthew and Lois May (Bratt) Kurzeka; m. John Gary McDavid, June 9, 1973; 1 child, Matthew Collins McDavid. BA, Northwestern U., 1971; JD, Georgetown U., 1974. Bar D.C. 1975, U.S. Ct. Appeals (fed. cir.) 1975 (D.C. cir. 1976), U.S. Supreme Ct. 1980, U.S. Ct. Appeals (5th cir.) 1983, (9th cir.) 1986. Assoc. Hogan & Harston, Washington, 1974-83, ptnr., 1984—. Gen. counsel ERAmerica, 1977-83; mem. antitrust task force Dept. Defense, 1993-94, 96-97; mem. antitrust coun. U.S. C. of C., 1994—; advisor Bush adminstrn. transition team, 2001. Contbr. articles to profl. jours. Participant Clinton and Bush adminstrn. transition team FTC. Mem. ABA (antitrust sect., vice chmn. civil practice com. 1986-89, sect. 2 com. 1989-90, chmn. franchising com. 1990-91, coun. mem. 1991-94, program officer 1994-97, vice chair 1997-98, chair-elect 1998-99, chair 1999-2000, immediate past chair, governing com. of forum on franchising 1991-97), ACLU, U.S. C. of C. (antitrust coun. 1995—), Washington Coun. Lawyers, D.C. Bar Assn., Fed. Bar Assn., Womens Legal Def. fund. Democrat. Office: Hogan & Hartson 555 13th St NW Washington DC 20004-1109 Office Phone: 202-637-8780. Business E-Mail: jlmcdavid@hhlaw.com.

MCDAVID, SARA JUNE, librarian; b. Atlanta, Dec. 21, 1945; d. William Harvey and June (Threadgill) McRae; m. Michael Wright McDavid, Mar. 20, 1971. BA, Mercer U., 1967; MLS, Emory U., 1969. Head librarian Fernbank Sci. Ctr., Atlanta, 1969-77; dir. rsch. libr. Fed. Res. Bank of Atlanta, 1977-81; mgr. mem. services SOLINET, Atlanta, 1981-82; media specialist Parkview High Sch., Atlanta, 1982-84; ptnr. Interncontinental Travel, Atlanta, 1984-85; librarian Wesleyan Day Sch., Atlanta, 1985-86; mgr. info. svcs. Internat. Assn. Fin. Planning, Atlanta, 1986-90; dir. rsch. Korn Ferry Internat., Atlanta, 1990-95; Atlanta rsch. coord. Lamalie Amrop Internat., Atlanta, 1995-98; dir. practice splty. teams LAI Ward Howell, 1998; prin. McDavid Rsch. Assocs., Atlanta, 1998-99; lead rschr. The Boston Consulting Group, Atlanta, 1999—. Bd. dirs. Southeastern Library Network, Atlanta, 1977-80, vice chmn. bd., 1979-80. Contbr. articles to profl. jours. Pres., mem. exec. com. Atlanta Humane Soc., 1985-86, bd. dirs. aux., 1978-90. Mem. Ga. Libr. Assn. (v.p. 1981-83), Spl. Librs. Assn. (treas. libr. mgmt. divsn. 1998-2000, editor Libr. Mgmt. Quar. 1996-98, 2002). Home: 1535 Knob Hill Dr NE Atlanta GA 30329-3206 Office: Boston Consulting Group Inc 600 Peachtree St NE Ste 3800 Atlanta GA 30308-2218 Office Phone: 404-877-5200. Business E-Mail: mcdavid.sara@bcg.com.

MCDAVID, WILLIAM HENRY, lawyer; b. NYC, May 10, 1946; m. Sylvia Noin, Dec. 21, 1984; children: Andrew, Madeline, William, Flora. AB, Columbia Coll., NYC, 1968; JD, Yale U., 1972. Assoc. Debevoise & Plimpton, NYC, 1972-81; asst. gen. counsel Bankers Trust Co., NYC, 1981-83, assoc. gen. counsel, 1983-84, v.p., 1984-85, v.p., counsel, 1986-88; gen. counsel J.P. Morgan & Co., NYC, 1988—2000, J.P. Morgan Chase & Co., NYC, 2000—03, co-gen. counsel, 2004—. Office: JP Morgan Chase & Co Office Gen Coun 270 Park Ave Fl 8 New York NY 10017-2014 *

MCDAVIS, RODERICK J., academic administrator; b. Dayton, Ohio, Oct. 17, 1948; m. Deborah Moses; children: Ryan, Tony. BS in Social Scis. in Secondary Edn., Ohio U., 1970; MS in Student Pers. Adminstrn., U. Dayton, 1971; PhD in Counselor Edn., U. Toledo, 1974. Asst. prof. edn. grad. divsn. Siena Heights Coll., Adrian, Mich., 1973—74; asst. prof. edn. dept. counselor edn. Coll. Edn. U. Fla., Gainesville, 1974—79, assoc. prof. edn. dept. counselor edn. Coll. Edn., 1979—82, prof. edn. dept. counselor edn. Coll. Edn., 1982—89, acting asst. dean for grad. studies Grad. Sch., 1984—85, assoc. dean Grad. Sch. and Minority Programs Grad. Sch., 1986—89, prof. edn. dept. counselor edn. Coll. Edn., 1994—99, dean Coll. Edn., 1994—99; prof. counselor edn. dept. edn. leadership, counseling and founds. Coll. Edn. U. Ark., Fayetteville, 1989—94, dean Coll. Edn., 1989—94; prof. edn. divsn. ednl. studies Sch. Edn. Va. Commonwealth U., Richmond, 1999—2004, provost, v.p. acad. affairs, 1999—2004; pres. Ohio U., Athens, 2004—. Vis. prof. edn. dept. counselor edn. and human svcs. Grad. Sch. Edn. U. Dayton, 1979—83, 1992. Named Person of Yr. in Edn., The Gainesville Sun, 1995; recipient Disting. Svc. award for cmty. outreach through TV media, Fla. Assn. for Counselor Edn. and Supervision, 1978, Key to the City, City Commn., Gainesville, 1995, Outstanding Alumnus award, Ohio U. Coll. Edn., 1996, Black Achiever's award in edn., Fla. Conf. Black State Legislators, Tallahassee, 1997. Mem.: Nat. Alliance Black Sch. Educators, Am. Coll. Pers. Assn., Phi Kappa Phi, Phi Delta Kappa (Post-secondary Outstanding Educator award North Ctrl. Fla. chpt. 1996). Office: Office of the Pres 108 Cutler Hall Athens OH 45701 Home: 29 Park Pl Athens OH 45701 Office Phone: 740-593-1804. E-mail: mcdavis@ohio.edu. *

MCDEMMOND, MARIE VALENTINE, academic administrator, consultant; b. New Orleans, Feb. 4, 1946; d. George Graham and Marie Valentine (Prudeaux) McD.; m. Louis Saulny, June 15, 1966 (div. 1972); children: Alan Peter, Eric W. Reid; m. Roy Russell Mouton, Sept. 18, 1987. BA, Xavier U., 1968; MEd, U. New Orleans, 1971; postgrad, SUNY, Albany; EdD, U. Mass., 1985. Tchr. Kohn Jr. High Sch., New Orleans, 1968-70; dir. Community Leadership Program, New Rochelle, N.Y., 1970-72, Community Leadership Consortium, Westchester County, N.Y., 1972-73; assoc. Higher Edn. Opportunity Program Office, Albany, N.Y., 1973-74; instr. dept. edn. Ithaca (N.Y.) Coll., 1974; with bus. office, dept. acctg. Bronx (N.Y.) Phychiatric Ctr., 1974-77; assoc. higher edn. N.Y. State Bd. Regents, Albany, 1977-78; dir. fin. Mass. Bd. Regional Community Colls., Boston, 1979-80; assoc. vice chancellor U. Mass., Amherst,

1980-84; v.p. budget & fin. Atlanta U., 1984-85; asst. v.p. for fin. Emory U., Atlanta, 1985-86; pres. McDemmond & Assoc., Boca Raton, Fla., 1986-89; asst. prof. edn. U. New Orleans, 1987-88; asst. v.p. adminstrn. & fin. Fla. Atlantic U., Boca Raton, 1988-89, v.p. adminstrn. & fin., 1990-96; pres. Norfolk (Va.) State U., 1996—. Adj. asst. prof. Coll. New Rochelle, N.Y., 1971-73; adj. prof. edn. U. Mass., Amherst, 1984; hostess Sta. WTCC, Springfield, Mass., 1983-84; lectr. in economic redevel., 1989; adv. bd. mem. Historically Black Coll. and U. Author tng. course. Civil svc. examiner State N.Y., Albany, 1976-78; precinct coord. Democrats for Jackson, Amherst, 1984; advisor Palm Beach Judicial Bldg., West Palm Beach, Fla., 1991; bd. dirs. Lumina Found., United Way, Urban League, Hampton Roads. Named Fla. Woman Who Makes a Difference Nat. Assn. Women Bus. Owners, 1990, Adminstr. of Yr. Va. Assn. Ed. Office Profl.; recipient Pioneer award Outstanding Profl. Women of Hampton Roads. Mem. Bus. and Profl. Women's Club Am. (Woman of Achievement award 1991), New England Minority Women (pres. 1982-84), So. Assn. Coll. and Bus. Officers (exec. com. 1991—), Nat. Assn. Coll. and Univ. Bus. Officers, Coun. Minority Edn. (pres. 1982-84). Roman Catholic. Avocations: gardening, reading. Office: Norfolk State U 700 Park Ave Norfolk VA 23504-8090

MCDERMID, MARGARET E. (LYN MCDERMID), information technology executive, engineer; b. 1948; B in bus., Mary Baldwin Coll.; MBA, U. Richmond. With Stone and Webster Engrng. Corp.; joined Va. Power, 1982, various positions engrng. & construction dept., 1982—86, dir. adminstrv. svcs., 1986—98; v.p. info. tech., CIO Dominion Resources Inc., 1998—2000, sr. v.p. info. tech., CIO, 2000—. Mem. apptd. by Gov. Gilmore CIO Adv. Bd., 2000; bd. dirs. Fed. Res. Bank, Richmond, 2007—. Active with United Way, Big Brothers, Big Sisters; bd. trustees Mary Baldwin Coll.; found. bd. J. Sargeant Reynolds Cmty. Coll.; bd. dirs. Greater Richmond Tech. Coun., Children's Mus. Richmond Bus. Com., CIO Forum; mem. Va. Rsch. and Tech. Adv. Coun. Achievements include first woman to enter the Apprentice Program at Newport News Shipyard where she completed the Patternmaker's program. Office: Dominion Resources Inc 120 Tredegar St Richmond VA 23219 Office Phone: 804-819-2000. *

MCDERMOTT, AGNES CHARLENE SENAPE, philosophy educator; b. Hazelton, Pa., Mar. 11, 1937; d. Charles G. and Conjetta (Ranieri) Senape; children: Robert C., Lisa G., Jamie C. BA, U. Pa., Phila., 1956, PhD, 1964; postgrad., U. Calif., Berkeley, 1960—61, U. Amsterdam, Netherlands, 1965, U. Wis., 1967—69. Instr. math. Drexel Inst. Tech., Phila., 1962-63; asst. prof. philosophy SUNY-Buffalo, 1964-65, Hampton Inst., Va., 1966-67; asst. prof. U. Wis.-Milw., 1967-70; assoc. prof. philosophy U. N.Mex., Albuquerque, 1970-80, prof., dean grad. studies, 1981-86; dean in residence Coun. of Grad. Schs., Washington, 1985-86; provost, v.p. acad. affairs CUNY, 1986-89, prof. philosophy, 1986-91; dean for acad. and student affairs, cons. Albuquerque Acad., 1991-93; ind. cons. Corrales, N.Mex., 1993—. Vis. assoc. prof. U. Wash., Seattle, 1974, U. Calif.-Berkeley, 1973-74, U. Hawaii, Honolulu, 1975; vis. prof. U. Calif.-Berkeley, 1980; vis. prof. Semester at Sea, U. Pitts., fall 1994; bd. dir. Juvenile Diabetes Rsch. Found.; lectr., panelist in field. Author: An Eleventh Century Buddhist Logic of 'Exists', 1969, Boethius' Treatise on the Modes of Signifying, 1980; compiler, editor anthology: Comparative Philosophy: Selected Essays, 1983; rev. editor Phil. East West, 1986—; contbr. articles and stories to profl. and literary jours. Active Albuquerque Care Alliance, 1988—2000; mem. lay rsch. rev. com. Juvenile Diabetes Rsch. Found., N.Mex. AAUW postdoctoral fellow, 1965-66; NEH Younger Humanist fellow, 1971-72; faculty rsch. fellow U. N.Mex., 1978, 79, 80; U. Pa. grad. fellow, 1961-62; S. Fels Found. fellow, 1963-64; U. Pa. tuition scholar; Pa. Hist. Soc. scholar Mem. NY Acad. Scis., Am. Philos. Soc., Am. Philos. Assn. (exec. com. 1977-80), Assn. Asian Studies (exec. com. 1977-80), Am. Oriental Soc., Western Assn. Grad. Schs. (pres. 1986-87), Phi Beta Kappa, Pi Mu Epsilon. Democrat. Avocations: skiing, fly fishing. Personal E-mail: mcdcott@netzero.com.

MCDERMOTT, ALICE, writer; b. Bklyn., June 27, 1953; married; 3 children. BA, SUNY, Oswego, 1975; MA, U. N.H., 1978. Instr. U. Calif., San Diego, Am. U., Washington; lectr. in English U. N.H.; writer-in-residence Lynchburg Coll., Va., Hollins Coll., Va.; prof. The Writing Seminars Johns Hopkins U., Balt. Author: A Bigamist's Daughter, 1982, That Night, 1987 (Pulitzer Prize finalist, Nat. Book Award finalist, L.A. Times Book Prize finalist, PEN Faulkner award finalist), At Weddings and Wakes, 1992 (Pulitizer prize finalist), Charming Billy, 1998 (Nat. Book Award), After This, 2006 (Pulitizer prize finalist); contbr. short stories to numerous profl. publs. Recipient Whiting Writers award. Office: Farrar Straus and Giroux 19 Union Sq W New York NY 10003 Office Phone: 212-838-7777.

MCDERMOTT, ANN ELIZABETH, chemistry professor; b. Enumclan, Wash., Oct. 12, 1960; d. Andrew Oliver and Lila Anne (Diemert) McD. BS, Harvey Mudd Coll., 1981; PhD, U. Calif., Berkeley, 1987. Postdoctoral rschr. MIT Nat. Magnet Lab., Cambridge, Mass., 1988-89, U.C.L. an dC.P., Brussels, 1990-91; asst. prof. Columbia U., NYC, 1991-96, assoc. prof., 1997, prof., 1998—. Contbr. articles to sci. jours. Recipient ACS award in pure chemistry, 1996. Mem.: NAS. Office: Columbia U Chemistry Dept New York NY 10027

MCDERMOTT, DYLAN, actor; b. Waterbury, Conn., Oct. 26, 1961; s. Richard "Mac" and Diane McDermott; m. Shiva Rose Afshar, Nov. 19, 1995; children: Colette, Charlotte Rose. BA in Drama, Fordham U., 1983. Appeared in films: Hamburger Hill, 1987, Twister, 1988, Steel Magnolias, 1989, In The Line Of Fire, 1993, The Cowboy Way, 1994, Miracle on 34th Street, 1994, Destiny Turns On The Radio, 1995, Home For The Holidays, 1995, 'Til There Was You, 1996, Three to Tango, 1999, Texas Rangers, 2001, Party Monster, 2003, Wonderland, 2003, Edison, 2005, The Tenants, 2006, Unbeatable Harold, 2006, The Messengers, 2007; TV films: The Neon Empire, 1989, Into the Badlands, 1991, The Fear Inside, 1992, A House Divided, 2006; TV series: The Practice, 1997-2003, The Grid, 2004, dir. 1997; TV guest appearances Ally MacBeal, 1997, Tales from the Crypt, Will & Grace, 2003; stage The Treatment, 2006. Recipient Golden Globe award, 1999. Address: William Morris Agy 151 El Camino Dr Beverly Hills CA 90212 *

MCDERMOTT, FRANCIS OWEN, retired lawyer; b. Denver, Feb. 25, 1933; s. Paul Harkins and Agnes (Clark) McD.; divorced; children: Diana, Daniel, Christopher, Anthony, Justine; m. Estella Marina Idiaquez, June 6, 1986; stepchildren: Bernard, Michael, Nicole, Marie, Steven. JD, Am. U., 1960. Bar: D.C. 1960, U.S. Dist. Ct. D.C., 1960, U.S. Ct. Appeals (D.C. cir.) 1960, u.S. Tax Ct. 1961, U.S. Supreme Ct. 1964. Trial atty. office regional counsel IRS, Washington, 1961-65; mem. profl. staff com. on fin. U.S. Senate, Washington, 1965-68; tax counsel Assn. Am. R.R.s, Washington, 1968-73; assoc. Hopkins & Sutter, Washington, 1973-76, ptnr., 1976-98, ret., 1999; ret. ptnr. Foley & Lardner, Washington, 2001—02. Gen. counsel Inst. Ill., Washington, 1987-96. Mem. ABA, Fed. Bar Assn., Nat. Def. Transp. Assn. (v.p., gen. counsel 1974—). Roman Catholic. Avocation: tennis. Home: 1 S Montague St Arlington VA 22204-1007 Office Phone: 202-945-6092. E-mail: fmcdermott@foley.com.

MCDERMOTT, JAMES A., congressman, psychiatrist; b. Chgo., Dec. 28, 1936; m. Therese Hansen; 2 children. BS, Wheaton Coll., Ill., 1958; MD, U. Ill. Med. Sch., Chgo., 1963. Intern Buffalo Gen. Hosp., 1963-64; resident adult psychiatry U. Ill. Hosps., Chgo., 1964-66; resident child psychiatry U. Wash. Hosps., Seattle, 1966-68; asst. clin. prof. dept. psychiatry U. Wash., Seattle, 1970-83; mem. Wash. State House Reps. from 43rd Dist., 1971-72, Wash. State Senate, 1975-87; regional med. officer US Fgn. Svc., 1987-88; mem. US Congress from 7th Wash. dist., 1989—, mem. ways and means com., ranking minority mem. human resources subcommittee. Mem. exec. and edn. com. Nat. Conf. State Legislatures, chair ethics com.; co-chmn. Congl. task force internat. HIV/AIDS, Congl. Caucus on India and Indian Ams., Africa Trade and Investment Caucus, Congl. Kidney Caucus. Mem. Wash. State Arts Commn., Wash. Coun. for Prevention Child Abuse and Neglect; Dem. nominee for gov., 1980. Lt. comdr. M.C. USN, 1968—70. Mem. Am. Psychiat. Assn., Wash. State Med. Assn., King County Med. Soc. Democrat. Episcopalian. Office: US House Reps 1035 Longworth House Office Bldg Washington DC 20515 Office Phone: 202-225-3106. *

MCDERMOTT, JOHN E., lawyer; b. Ravenna, Ohio, Oct. 25, 1946; BA, Ohio Wesleyan U., 1968; JD, Harvard U., 1971. Bar: Calif. 1972, US Supreme Ct., US Dist. Cts. (no., ea., ctrl. & so. dists.) Calif., DC, (ea. dist.) Ohio, (ea. dist.) Va., US Cts. of Appeals (9th & DC cirs.). Lectr. U. So. Calif. law Sch., 1974—81; ptnr. Howrey LLP, LA. Dir. Western Ctr. on Law and Poverty, Inc, 1977—81. Editor (Book): Indeterminacy in Education, McCutchan, 1976. Recipient So. California's Super Lawyers, Law & Politics mag., LA mag. Mem. ABA, State Bar Calif. 1972-, LA County, Phi Beta Kappa, mem. Am. Assn. Bus. Trial Lawyers. Office: Howrey LLP 550 S Hope St Ste 1100 Los Angeles CA 90071 Office Phone: 213-892-1815. Office Fax: 213-892-2300. Business E-Mail: mcdermottj@howrey.com.

MC DERMOTT, JOHN FRANCIS, psychiatrist, physician; b. Hartford, Conn., Dec. 12, 1929; s. John Francis and Camilla R. (Cavanaugh) McD.; m. Sarah N. Schemm, Dec. 27, 1958; children: Elizabeth C., John Francis III. AB, Cornell U., 1951; MD, N.Y. Med. Coll., 1955. Diplomate in psychiatry and child psychiatry Am. Bd. Psychiatry and Neurology. Intern Henry Ford Hosp., Detroit, 1955-56; resident in psychiatry U. Mich. Med. Center, 1956-58, resident in child psychiatry, 1960-62; practice medicine, specializing in psychiatry and child and adolescent psychiatry Honolulu, 1969-95; instr., asst. prof., assoc. prof. psychiatry U. Mich. Sch. Medicine, 1962-69; prof., chmn. dept. psychiatry U. Hawaii Sch. Medicine, 1969-95, prof. emeritus, 1995—; scholar-in-residence Rockefeller Found. Study Ctr., Bellagio, Italy, 1985, 92. Chmn. com. cert. in child psychiatry Am. Bd. Psychiatry and Neurology, 1974-78, bd. dirs., 1983-91, chmn. R&D com., 1985-91; sr. vis. scientist dept. exptl. psychology Oxford (Eng.) U., 1993; sr. vis. fellow Inst. Criminology Cambridge U., Eng., 1998, 2000; vis. prof. numerous univs.; cons. in field. Author: Psychiatry for the Pediatrician, 1970, Childhood Psychopathology, 1972, Mental Health Education in New Medical Schools, 1973, Roles and Functions of Child Psychiatrists, 1976, Psychiatric Treatment of the Child, 1977, New Directions in Childhood Psychopathology, vol. I, 1980, vol. II, 1982, Raising Cain (and Abel Too), 1980: People and Cultures of Hawaii, 1980, Culture Mind and Therapy: An Introduction to Cultural Psychiatry, 1982, Japanese edit., 1984, The Complete Book on Sibling Rivalry, 1987, German edit., 1991; editor Jour. Am. Acad. Child and Adolescent Psychiatry, 1987-97; contbr. over 150 articles to profl. jours.; mem. editorial bds. numerous psychiat. jours. Served with USN, 1958-60. Named Disting. Alumnus N.Y. Med. Coll., 1976; life mem. Clare Hall, Cambridge (Eng.) U. Fellow Am. Psychiat. Assn. (disting. life, Agnes Purcell McGavin award 1998), Am. Orthopsychiat. Assn. (life), Am. Acad. Child and Adolescent Psychiatry (life), Am. Coll. Psychiatrists, World Psychiat. Assn. (chmn. child and adolescent psychiatry 1977-89), Benjamin Rush Soc. (sec.-treas. 2000-02, v.p. 2002-04, pres. 2004-06), Cosmos Club, Outrigger Canoe Club.

MCDERMOTT, JOHN H., lawyer; b. Evanston, Ill., June 23, 1931; s. Edward Henry and Goldie Lucile (Boso) McD.; m. Ann Elizabeth Pickard, Feb. 19, 1966; children: Elizabeth A., Mary L., Edward H. BA, Williams Coll., 1953; JD, U. Mich., 1956. Bar: Mich. 1955, Ill. 1956. Assoc. McDermott, Will & Emery, Chgo., 1958-64, ptnr., 1964-99, of counsel, 2000—. Bd. dirs. Patrick Industries Inc. 1st lt. USAF, 1956-58. Mem. ABA, Chgo. Bar Assn. Clubs: Commerical of Chgo., Econ. of Chgo., Legal Chgo. (pres. 1981-82), Law Chgo. (pres. 1986-87). Home: 330 Willow Rd Winnetka IL 60093-4130 Office: McDermott Will & Emery 227 W Monroe St Ste 4400 Chicago IL 60606-5096 Home Phone: 847-446-2022; Office Phone: 312-984-7562. Personal E-mail: mcdermott330@cs.com.

MCDERMOTT, KATHLEEN E., lawyer; b. July 1949; BS in fgn. svc., Georgetown U., JD. Bar: 1975. Assoc. Collier, Shannon, Rill & Scott, Washington, 1975—81, ptnr., 1981—93; exec. v.p., chief legal officer Am. Stores Inc. (now Albertson's Inc.), Salt Lake City, 1993—99; sr. v.p., gen. counsel Nash Finch Inc., Mpls., 2002—06. Mem.: ABA (vice chair corp. counseling com. antitrust sect.). *

MCDERMOTT, KEVIN R., lawyer; b. Youngstown, Ohio, Jan. 26, 1952; s. Robert J. and Marion D. (McKeown) McD.; m. Cindy J. Darling, Dec. 11, 1976; children: Ciara, Kelly. AB, Miami U., Oxford, Ohio, 1974; JD, Ohio State U., 1977. Bar: Ohio 1977, U.S. Dist. Ct. (so. dist.) Ohio 1978, U.S. Dist. Ct. (no. dist.) Ohio 1988, U.S. Dist. Ct. (we. dist.) Mich. 1993, U.S. Supreme Ct. 1990, U.S. Ct. Appeals (3rd cir.) 1996, U.S. Ct. Appeals (6th cir.) 1988. Assoc. ptnr. Murphey Young & Smith, Columbus, Ohio, 1977-88; ptnr. Squire Sanders & Dempsey, Columbus, Ohio, 1988-90, Schottenstein Zox & Dunn, Columbus, Ohio, 1990—. Adv. bd. mem. Capital U. Legal Asst. Program, Columbus, Ohio, 1988—. Bd. pres. Easter Seal Soc. Ctrl. Ohio, Columbus, 1992-94, bd. mem. 1988-92; pres. Upper Arlington Civic Svc. Commn., Columbus, Ohio, 1988-93. Office: Schottenstein Zox & Dunn 250 West St Columbus OH 43215 Office Phone: 614-462-5001. Business E-Mail: kmcdermott@szd.com.

MCDERMOTT, ROBERT J., commissioner; b. Bklyn., Sept. 5, 1944; AB, Georgetown U., 1966; JD cum laude, NYU, 1970, LLM in Taxation, 1974. Bar: NY 1971. Ptnr. Dewey Ballantine, NYC; commr. tax appeals tribunal NY State, 2005—. Mem. ABA, NY State Bar Assn. (exec. com., tax sect. 1980-91), Assn. of Bar of City of NY, Order Coif. NY State Bar Found. (life fellow), NYU Law Alumni Assn. (pres. 1989-91) Office: Divsn Tax Appeals Riverfront Pro Tower 500 Federal St Troy NY 12180 Office Phone: 518-266-3000. Office Fax: 518-272-5178.

MCDERMOTT, SANDRA, national park administrator; d. Joseph McDermott and Julia Ferrari; children: Jennifer Faulkner, Benjamin Faulkner. BA in Psychology, U. Alaska, 1975, BA in History, 1980; MA in History, U. Oreg., 1984. Grad. tchg. fellow U. Oreg., 1982—84; adj. faculty U. Alaska, 1984—97; acting asst. supt. Joshua Tree Nat. Pk., Twenty-Nine Palms, Calif., 2004; hist. preservation program mgr. Nat. Pk. Svc., Anchorage, 1987—92, regional historian, 1992—2004, dep. assoc. regional dir. intermountain region Denver, 2004—. Nat. mgmt. coun. for cultural resource stewardship & partnership Nat. Pk. Svc., Office of the Assoc. Dir., Washington, 2000—; instr., Alaska nat. interest conservation act US Dept. of Interior U., 2003; spkr. Alaska Humanities Forum Speakers Bur., 1996—98. Book reviewer (professional journal) Journal of Public History; contbr. articles to profl. jours. Co-chair Alaska at War Internat. Conf., 1993; pres. Nat. History Day in Alaska, 1989—2004, Alaska Hist. Soc., 1992—98; chair, publs. com. Cook Inlet Hist. Soc., Anchorage, 1997—2000; mem. program com. Western Mus. Assn., Alaska, 1997—98. Recipient President's award, Alaska Hist. Soc., 1989, Fed. Employee of the Yr., Team Leader award, Fed. Employees Assn., 1996, Spl. Svc. Act award, Nat. Pk. Svc., 1997, Nat. Partnership award, Hon. Mention, Nat. Pk. Found., 2001, Cert. of Appreciation, Nat. Coun. for History Edn., 2003, Spl. award for Contributions to Alaska History, Alaska Hist. Soc., 2004, Cert. of Merit in Hist. Preservation, Alaska State Hist. Preservation Office, 2004, Lifetime Achievement award, Nat. History Day in Alaska, 2004, STAR award, NPS-Cultural Resource Adv. Coun., 2004. Mem.: Am. Hist. Assn. (assoc.). Avocation: music. Office: Nat Pk Svc PO Box 25287 Denver CO 80225-0287

MCDERMOTT, THOMAS JOHN, JR., lawyer; b. Santa Monica, Calif., Mar. 23, 1931; s. Thomas J. Sr. and Etha Irene (Cook) McD.; m. Yolanda Amante Jatap; children: Jodi Friedman, Kimberly E., Kish S. BA, UCLA, 1953, JD, 1958. Bar: Calif. 1959. Ptnr. Gray, Binkley and Pfaelzer, LA, 1964-67, Kadison, Pfaelzer, Woodward, Quinn and Rossi, LA, 1967-87, Rogers & Wells, LA, 1987-93, Bryan Cave, LA, 1993-95, Manatt, Phelps & Phillips, LLP, LA, 1995-99, Shanks and Herbert, San Diego, 1999—2003. Served with U.S. Army, 1953-56, Korea, 1999-2003. Fellow Am. Coll. Trial Lawyers; mem. ABA, Assn. Bus. Trial Lawyers (pres. 1980-81, mem. exec. com. 9th cir. jud. conf. 1993—, chair 1997), State Bar Calif. (chair litigation sect. 1993-94), UCLA Law Alumni Assn. (pres. 1961-62), Order of Coif. Office: McDermott & DeLalteur LLP 74-770 Highway 111 Ste 201 Indian Wells CA 92210 Office Phone: 760-346-8200. Business E-Mail: tmcdermott@mcdelaw.com.

MCDEVITT, CHARLES FRANCIS, retired judge, lawyer; b. Pocatello, Idaho, Jan. 5, 1932; s. Bernard A. and Margaret (Hermann) McDevitt; m. Virginia L. Heller, Aug. 14, 1954; children: Eileen A., Kathryn A., Brian A., Sheila A., Terrence A., Neil A., Kendal A. LLB, U. Idaho, 1956. Bar: Idaho 1956. Ptnr. Richards, Haga & Eberle, Boise, 1956-62; gen. counsel, asst. sec. Boise Cascade Corp., 1962—68; mem. Idaho State Legislature, 1963-66; sec., gen. counsel Boise Cascade Corp., 1965-67, v.p. sec., 1967-68; pres. Beck Industries, 1968-70; group v.p. Singer Co., NYC, 1970-72, exec. v.p., 1973-76; pub. defender Ada County, Boise, 1976-78; co-founder Givens, McDevitt, Pursley & Webb, Boise, 1978-89; justice Idaho Supreme Ct., Boise, 1989-97, chief justice, 1993-97; ptnr., founder McDevitt & Miller, LLP, Boise, 1997—. Served on Gov.'s Select Com. on Taxation, Boise, 1988-89; mem. State Select Com. on Campaign Ethics and Campaign Finances, State Select Com. on Legis. Compensation. Chair Idaho Jud. Coun., 1993-97, Cts. Advisors Coun., 1994-98; mem. Multi-State Tax Com. Recipient Legal Merit award, Univ. of Idaho, 2002, Professionalism award, Idaho State Bar, 2005. Home: 4940 Boise River Ln Boise ID 83716-8816 Office: McDevitt Miller 420 W Bannock Boise ID 83702-6034 Office Phone: 208-343-7500. Business E-Mail: chas@McDevitt-Miller.com.

MCDEVITT, HUGH O'NEILL, immunologist, educator; b. Cin., Aug. 26, 1930; MD, Harvard U., 1955. Diplomate: Am. Bd. Internal Medicine. Intern Peter Bent Brigham Hosp., Boston, 1955-56, sr. asst. resident in medicine, 1961-62; asst. resident Bell Hosp., 1956-57; research fellow dept. bacteriology and immunology Harvard U., 1959-61; USPHS spl. fellow Nat. Inst. Med. Research, Mill Hill, London, 1962-64; physician Stanford U. Hosp., Calif., 1966—; assoc. prof. Stanford U. Sch. Medicine, Calif., 1969-72, prof. med. immunology Calif., 1972—, prof. med. microbiology Calif., 1980—2001, Burt and Marian Avery Prof. Immunology Calif., 1988—2001. Cons. physician VA Hosp., Palo Alto, Calif., 1968— Served as capt. M.C., AUS, 1957-59. Recipient Abbott Lab. award in Clin. and Diagnostic Immunology, Am. Soc. Microbiology, 2003. Mem. NAS, AAAS, Am. Fedn. Clin. Rsch., Am. Soc. Clin. Investigation, Am. Assn. Immunologists, Transplantation Soc., Inst. Medicine, Royal Soc. (fgn.). Office: Sherman Fairchild Bldg Stanford U Sch of Medicine 299 Campus Dr MC5124 Stanford CA 94305-5124 Business E-Mail: hughmcd@stanford.edu.

MCDEVITT, JAMES A., prosecutor, lawyer; b. July 1943; Bachelor, U. Wash.; MBA, JD, Gonzaga U. Asst. atty. gen. State of Wash., Office of Atty. Gen., 1975—77; from sr. ptnr. to mng. ptnr. Reed & Geisa, Spokane, Wash., 1977—94; ptnr. Preston, Gates & Ellis, Spokane, Wash., 1994—2002; US atty. (ea. dist.) Wash. US Dept. Justice, 2002—. With USAF, 1965—71, brig. gen. Wash. Air Nat. Guard, ret. Office: US Attys Office PO Box 1494 Spokane WA 99210 *

MCDEVITT, JERRY S., lawyer; BS cum laude, U. Pa., 1973; JD cum laude, Duquesne U. Sch. Law, 1980. Bar: Pa. 1980, US Dist. Ct., Western Dist. Pa. 1980, Pa. Supreme Ct. 1980, US Ct. of Appeals, 3rd Cir. 1985, US Court Appeals, 2nd Cir. 1992, US Supreme Ct. 1994, US Ct. Appeals, 8th Cir. 1994, US Dist. Ct. (ea. dist Wis.) 2003, US. Ct. Appeals 11th Cir. 2004, Numerous pro hac vice admissions in various State and Fed. Cts. Ptnr. Kirkpatrick & Lockhart Nicholson Graham, LLP, Pitts. Exec. recent decisions editor Duquesne Law Review. Officer USMC, 1973—76. Named one of Top 10 Litigators, Nat. Law Jour., 2003. Mem.: Pa. Bar Assn., ABA, Allegheny County Bar Assn. (Pro Bono award for Representation of Death Row Inmate 1990). Office: Kirkpatrick & Lockhart Nicholson Graham LLP Henry W Oliver Bldg 535 Smithfield St Pittsburgh PA 15222-2312 Office Phone: 412-355-8608. Office Fax: 412-355-6501. Business E-Mail: jmcdevitt@klng.com.

MCDEVITT, JOHN, delivery service executive; b. Upper Darby, Pa., Aug. 15, 1958; m. Lori McDevitt; children: Kelly, Tara, Shannon, John. BS in Polit. Sci., Rutgers U., 1980; grad., U. Mich., 1999. Part-time loader UPS, Edison, NJ, 1976—77, part-time supr. Bound Brook, 1977—80, package car driver, 1980—81, supr., 1981—84, mgr. Parsippany, 1984—87, divsn. mgr. Meadowlands, 1987—92, dist. mgr. East Long Island, NY, 1992—94, West Long Island, 1994—96, v.p. corp. compliance Atlanta, 1996—98, mgr. corp. labor rels., 1998—99, v.p. air ops., 1999—2003, sr. v.p. strategic integration, 2003—05, sr. v.p. global transp. services, 2005—. Office: UPS 55 Glenlake Kwy NE Atlanta GA 30328 *

MCDEVITT, LARRY S., lawyer; b. Asheville, NC, June 2, 1942; AB, Univ. NC, 1964, JD, 1968. Bar: NC 1968, US Supreme Ct. 1974. Ptnr. Van Winkle, Buck, Wall, Starnes and Davis, PA, Asheville, NC. Mayor, city councilman, Asheville, NC, 1981—85. Fellow: Am. Coll. Trial Lawyers, Am. Bar Found.; mem.: Am. Judicature Soc., NC Assn. Def. Attys. (bd. dir. 1983—85), NC Bar Assn. (bd. govs. 1983—86, 1988—91, pres. 1989—90), ABA (bd. govs. 2006—). Office: Van Winkle Buck Wall Starnes 11 North Market St PO Box 7376 Asheville NC 28802-7376 Office Phone: 828-258-2991. Office Fax: 828-255-0255. Business E-Mail: lmcdevitt@vwlawfirm.com.

MCDEVITT, SHEILA MARIE, retired lawyer, energy executive, business consultant; b. St. Petersburg, Fla., Jan. 15, 1947; d. Frank Davis and Marie (Barfield) McD. AA, St. Petersburg Jr. Coll., 1966; BA in Govt., Fla. State U., 1968, JD, 1978. Bar: Fla. 1978. Rsch. asst. Fla. Legis. Reference Bur., Tallahassee, 1968-69; adminstr., research assoc. Constitution Revision Commn. Ga. Gen. Assembly, Atlanta, 1969-70; adminstrv. asst., analyst Fla. State Sen., Tallahassee, Tampa, 1970-79; assoc. McClain, Walkley & Stuart, P.A., Tampa, Seminole, Fla., 1979-81; govtl. affairs counsel Tampa Electric Co., 1981-82, corp. counsel, 1982-86; sr. corp. counsel TECO Energy, Inc., Tampa, 1986-89, asst. v.p., 1989-92, v.p., asst. gen. counsel, 1992-99, corp. compliance officer, 1993-99, v.p., gen. counsel Tampa, 1999—2001, sr. v.p., gen. counsel, chief legal officer, 2001—. Mem. Worker's Compensation adv. coun. Fla. Dept. Labor, Tallahassee, 1984-86; trustee St. Leo U., 1999—, vice chair, 2001-2005, chair 2005-; mem. bd. visitors Fla. State U. Coll. Law, 1996—, chmn., 2003-2005; mem. bd. advisors The Centre for Women, 1998—, Met. Ministries, 1996-99; mem. ethics adv. bd. U. Tampa Ctr. for Ethics, 1997-99; mem. jud. nominating commn. 13th Jud. Cir., 2001-2003; mem. Fla. bd. govs. State Univ. sys., 2003, vice chair, 2006-. Mem. Fla. Rep. Exec. Com., Tallahassee, 1974-75, Hillsborough County Rep. Exec. Com., 1974-75, Fed. Jud. Adv. Commn., 1989-93, Fla. Humanities Coun., 2000-2004, WW Women's Leadership, 2004—; bd. dirs. Vol. Ctr. Hillsborough County, Tampa, 1984-85, Hillsborough County Easter Seal Soc., 1994-95, Fla. Aquarium, 1999-2000, Lowry Park Zoo Soc., 1999-2004, chmn., trustee, 1986-94, also legal advisor; mem. transition team for Fla. Gov. Bob Martinez, 1986-87; trustee St. Leo U., 1999, vice chair, 2001-05, chair, 2005-07; trustee Fla. Orch., 2004—. Named Alumni of Yr., Fla. State U.

Coll. Law, 2006; recipient Spl. Contbn. award for pioneering efforts in bus. ethics, U. Tex. Ctr. for Ethics, 2007. Mem ABA, Fla. Bar (vice chmn., then chmn. energy law com. 1984-87, jud. nominating procedures com. 1986-91, jud. adminstrn. selection and tenure com. 1991-93), Hillsborough Bar Found. (trustee 2002-), Hillsborough County Bar Assn. (chmn. law week com. 1990, corp. counsel com. 1986-87, internat. law com. 1994-95, Corp. Counsel of Yr. award 2003), Am. Corp. Counsel Assn. (bd. dirs. Ctrl. Fla. chpt. 1986-87), Hillsborough County Bar Found., Tampa Club, Tiger Bay Club, Tampa Yacht and Country Club. Roman Catholic. Avocations: bicycling, reading. Office: TECO Energy Inc PO Box 111 702 N Franklin St Fl 5 Tampa FL 33602-4440 Business E-Mail: smmcdevitt@tecoenergy.com.

MCDEVITT, THOMAS P., publishing executive; b. Gary, Ind., 1952; 5 children. B. Govt. & Bus., U. Md. With Washington Times, 1994—2005, bus. dir., mktg. dir., spl. asst. to pres., gen. mgr. Mag. divsn., v.p.; sr. v.p. mktg. & comm. Points of Light Found., 2005—07; pres. Washington Times Corp., 2007—. Office: Washington Times 3600 New York Ave NE Washington DC 20002-1947 Office Phone: 202-636-3000. E-mail: tmcdevitt@pointsoflight.org. *

MCDIARMID, BRUCE W., lawyer; b. San Jose, Calif., June 27, 1947; AB, U. Calif., Berkeley, 1968; JD magna cum laude, Harvard U., 1974. Bar: Calif. 1974. Ptnr. Pillsbury Madison & Sutro, San Francisco; (Pillsbury Madison & Sutro merged with Winthrop, Stimson, Putnam, 2001); ptnr., chmn. mktg., distribution & franchising practice group Pillsbury Winthrop LLP, San Francisco, 2001—05; (Pillsbury Winthrop LLP merged with Shaw Pittman LLP, 2005); ptnr., chmn. mktg., distribution & franchising practice group Pillsbury Winthrop Shaw Pittman LLP, San Francisco, 2005—. Mem.: ABA (mem. antitrust section, mem. forum on franchising). Office: Pillsbury Winthrop Shaw Pittman LLP 50 Fremont St San Francisco CA 94105 Office Phone: 415-983-1043. Office Fax: 415-983-1200.

MCDIARMID, LUCY, literature educator, writer; b. Louisville, Mar. 29, 1947; BA, Swathmore Coll., Pa., 1968; MA, Harvard U., 1969, PhD, 1972. Asst. prof. Boston U., 1972-74; from asst. prof. to assoc. prof. Swarthmore Coll., 1974-81; asst. prof. U. Md. Baltimore County, Balt., 1982-84; prof. Villanova (Pa.) U., 1984—. Vis. prof. English Princeton U., 1995; Carole and Gordon Segal vis. chair Irish lit. Northwestern U., 2005; mem. exec. com. Am. Conf. for Irish Studies, 1987-91, v.p., 1995-97, pres., 1997-99, past pres., internat. rep., 1999—2001. Author: Saving Civilization: Yeats, Eliot and Auden Between the Wars, 1984, Auden's Apologies for Poetry, 1990, The Irish Art of Controversy, 2005; co-editor: Selected Writings of Lady Gregory, 1995, High and Low Moderns: Literature and Culture, 1889-1939, 1996; contbr. articles to profl. jours. ACLS grantee, 1976; NEH fellow, 1981-82, Bunting Inst. fellow, 1981-82, Guggenheim fellow, 1993-94, vis. fellow N.Y. Inst. Humanities, 1993-95, fellow Dorothy and Louis B. Cullman Ctr. Scholars and Writers, NY Pub. Libr., 2005-06. Mem. MLA (exec. com. Twentieth Century Lit. divsn.), Internat. Assn. for Study Anglo-Irish Lit. (Am. sec.-treas. 1994-96), Phi Beta Kappa.

MCDIARMID, ROBERT CAMPBELL, lawyer; b. NYC, July 13, 1937; s. Norman Hugh and Dorothy (Shoemaker) McD.; m. Ruth Sussman, 1963 (div. 1996); children: Jennifer, Alexander Samuel; m. Frances Enseki Francis, 1996. BS in Mech. Engring., Swarthmore Coll., 1958; MS in Engring. Physics, Cornell U., 1960; LLB, Harvard U., 1963. Bar: D.C. 1964, Va. 1964, U.S. Supreme Ct. 1967, U.S. Ct. Appeals (4th, 6th and 9th cirs.) 1965, U.S. Ct. Appeals (3d, 5th and 10th cirs.) 1966, U.S. Ct. Appeals (7th, 8th and D.C. cirs.) 1967, U.S. Ct. Appeals (2d cir.) 1970, U.S. Ct. Appeals (1st cir.) 1979, U.S. Ct. Appeals (11th cir.) 1981. Assoc. Weaver & Glassie, Washington, 1963-64; trial atty. civil divsn. appellate sect. Dept. Justice, Washington, 1964-68; asst. to gen. counsel Fed. Power Commn., Washington, 1968-70; assoc. Law Office of George Spiegel, Washington, 1970-73; ptnr. Spiegel & McDiarmid, Washington, 1973—. Mem. alumni coun. Swarthmore Coll., 1986-89. Mem. ABA, Va. State Bar, Bar Assn. D.C., D.C. Bar, Energy Bar Assn. (exec. com. 1982-83, bd. dirs. 1997-2000). Democrat. Mem. Soc. Of Friends. Home: 3625 Fulton St NW Washington DC 20007-1452 Office: Spiegel & McDiarmid 1333 New Hampshire Ave NW Washington DC 20036 Office Phone: 202-879-4040. Business E-Mail: robert.mcdiarmid@spiegelmcd.com.

MCDONAGH, STEVE, chef; life ptnr. Dan Smith; 1 adopted child, Nate. Co-founder, bus. mgr. The Hearty Boys catering co., Chgo.; co-founder The Cafe at Hearty Boys, Lakeview, Ill., 2003—, HB restaurant, The Cafe at Hearty Boys, Lakeview, Ill., 2005—. Co-host Party Line with the Hearty Boys; co-author: Solving the Run of the Mill; featured in Chgo. Mag., guest appearances ABC, NBC, CBS, FOX, CLTV. Achievements include appearing on several radio shows, TV commercials, and the Chgo. stage; co-winning The Next Food Network Star with ptnr. Dan Smith, 2005. Office: The Hearty Boys Caterers 3404 N Halsted Chicago IL 60657 Office Phone: 773-244-9866. Office Fax: 773-244-8088. *

MCDONALD, ALDEN J., JR., bank executive; m. Rhesa Ortique; 3 children. Grad., La. State U. Sch. Banking, Columbia U. Comml. Banking Mgmt. Prog. Positions up to v.p. consumer lending Internat. City Bank, New Orleans, 1966—72; pres., CEO Liberty Bank & Trust, Baton Rouge, 1972—. Bd. mem. FannieMae, Minority Alliance Capital, Ernest N. Morial Convention Ctr., Port Authority New Orleans, Stewart Enterprises, Inc.; mem. adv. bd. Entergy New Orleans; chmn. New Orleans C. of C. Mem. adv. coun. So. U., New Orleans; mem. fin. coun. Archdiocese New Orleans; chmn. Lindy Boggs Med. Ctr.; bd. mem. Tulane U. Sch. Medicine; mem. bd. trustees Loyola U.; bd. mem. United Negro Coll. Fund; mem. 100 Black Men Metro New Orleans; mem. met. area com. Com. for Better New Orleans. Named to Bus. Hall of Fame, Jr. Achievement; recipient Loving Cup, Times-Picayune, 2001, A.G. Gaston Lifetime Achievement award, Black Enterprise, 2005, Whitney Young award, Urban League Greater New Orleans, Civil Rights award, Nat. Dental Assn., Minority Suppliers award, J.C. Penney. Mem.: La. Bankers Assn., Nat. Bankers Assn. (R.R. Wright Presdl. award), Am. Bankers Assn. Office: Liberty Bank & Trust PO Box 74108 Baton Rouge LA 70874-4108 *

MCDONALD, ANGUS WHEELER, farmer; b. Washington, Apr. 21, 1927; s. John Yates and Dorothy Helen (Bosworth) McD.; m. Mary Joan Mooney, May 8, 1952 (div. Sept. 1958); children: Mary Ann Hetzer, Paul Yates. BA, Columbia Union Coll., 1974. Farmer, owner Pleasant View Farm, Charles Town, W.Va., 1953—. Presdl. candidate Democratic Party, 1987-88, 92, 2000. With U.S. Army, 1946-47. Mem. AARP, Jefferson County Farm Bur., W.Va. State Hort. Soc., No. W.Va. Automobile Club, Am. Legion, The Moose. Avocations: photography, travel, attending historical events. Home and Office: Pleasant View Farm 2225 Flowing Springs Rd Charles Town WV 25414-9413 Office Phone: 304-725-7238.

MCDONALD, APRIL D., writer; b. Arlington County, Va., May 29, 1981; d. Butler Cassell William, Jr. and Veronica Denise McDonald. Degree in Journalism, No. Va. Coll., 2003. Cert. A+ NOVA, 2001. CEO ADM Publishing LLC, Nocross, Ga. Author: Sex, Lies & Consequences, 2005. Mentor Big Sister program, Atlanta, 2005—. Independent. Avocations: travel, jet skiing, writing, public speaking. Home Phone: 770-369-6550. Business E-Mail: aprilmcdonaldinc@yahoo.com.

MCDONALD, AUDRA ANN, actress, vocalist; b. Berlin, July 3, 1970; d. Stanley and Kathryn McDonald; m. Peter Donovan, Sept. 10, 2000; 1 child, Zoe Madeline Donovan. BFA in Voice, Juilliard Sch., 1993; attended, Sch. Arts., Calif. Stage appearances include (regional) Man of La Mancha, Evita, The Wiz, A Chorus Line, Grease, Anything Goes, The Real Inspector Hound, Anyone Can Whistle, 2005;(Broadway) The Secret Garden, Man of La Mancha, 1989, Carousel, 1994 (Tony award best featured actress in a musical, 1994, Outer Critics Circle award outstanding actress in a musical, 1994), Master Class, 1995-97 (Tony award best featured actress in a musical, 1996, LA Ovation award best featured actress in a musical, 1996), Ragtime, 1998-99 (Tony award best featured actress in a musical, 1998), Sweeney Todd, 2000, A Raisin in the Sun, 2004 (Tony award best featured actress in a play, 2004, Drama Desk award best featured actress in a play, 2004), See What I Wanna See (formerly titled R Shomon), 2005, 110 in the Shade, 2007 (Drama Desk award outstanding actress in a musical 2007); (TV series) Bill Cosby pilot, 1996, Mister Sterling, 2003; (TV Movies) Having Our Say: The Delaney Sisters' First 100 Years, 1999, Annie, 1999, The Last Debate, 2000, Wit, 2001 (Emmy award nom. best supporting actress, 2001); (films) Seven Servants, 1996, The Object of My Affection, 1998, Cradle Will Rock, 1999, It Runs in the Family, 2003, The Best Thief in the World, 2004; concert performances include S'Wonderful, Some Enchanted Evening, Christa Ludwig and James Levine Recital, Revelation in Courthouse Park, Requiem Canticles; singer: (albums) Leonard Bernstien's New York, 1996, Sings Rodgers & Hart, 1996, George & Ira Gershwin: Standards & Gems, 1998, George Gershwin: 100th Birthday Celebration, 1998, Broadway in Love, 2000, Marie Christine: A New Musical, 2000, Broadway Cares: Home for the Holidays, 2001, Dreamgirls in Concert, 2002, (solo albums) Way Back to Paradise, 1998, How Glory Goes, 2000, Happy Songs, 2002, Build a Bridge, 2006. Recipient Theatre World award, 1994, Drama League award distinguished achievement in musical theatre, 2000. Office: Gersh Agency Inc 41 Madison Ave Fl 33 New York NY 10010-2210 *

MCDONALD, BERNARD ROBERT, retired federal agency administrator; b. Kansas City, Nov. 17, 1940; s. Bernard Luther and Mabel McD.; m. Jean Graves, June 7, 1963 (div. 1996); children: Aaron Michael, Elizabeth Kathleen; m. Joann Huffaker, Aug. 2, 1997. BA in Math., Park Coll., Parkville, Mo., 1962; MA in Math. and Physics, Kans. State U., 1964; PhD in Math., Mich. State U., East Lansing, 1968. Prof. dept. math. U. Okla., Norman, 1968—83, chmn. dept. math., 1981—83; program dir. div. math. scis. NSF, Washington, 1983—86, program dir. spl. projects, 1986—88, dep. dir. div. math. scis., 1988—2004; ret., 2004. Author: R-linear Endomorphism, 1983, Geometric Algebra, 1976, Finite Rings, 1974, Ring Theory III, 1980. Recipient Meritorious Svc. award, NSF, 1995, Disting. Svc. award, 1999. Mem. AAAS, Am. Math. Soc., Math. Assn. Am., Soc. Ind. and Applied Math., Assn. Women Math., Sigma Xi. Home: 5016 35th St N Arlington VA 22207-2816 Personal E-mail: math1940@aol.com.

MCDONALD, BRADLEY G., lawyer; m. Ann Gilbert, Sept. 3, 1964; 1 child, Perry. BA, U. Okla.; JD, Georgetown U., 1961. Bar: D.C. 1961, U.S. Ct. Appeals (D.C., 11th and 4th cirs.), U.S. Supreme Ct. With McDonald & Karl, Washington. Guest lectr. Wash. Coll. of Law, Am. Univ., Washington. Mem. nat. alumni adv. coun. U. Okla; mem. Arlington Com. of 100; bd. dirs gen. counsel, sec. Close Up Found.; trustee Randolph Macon Acad.; bd. dirs. Montessori Sch. of McLean. 1st lt. USMC, 1956-58. Recipient 1st Regent's Alumni award U. Okla. Mem. Sigma Nu (trustee Ednl. Found.). Office Phone: 202-293-3200.

MCDONALD, BRENNA CATHLEEN, psychologist; d. Daniel Ford and Georgia Marie McDonald. BA, Williams Coll., Williamstown, Mass., 1994; MA, Widener U., Chester, Pa., 1998; Psy.D., MBA, Widener U., 2000. Cert. sch. psychologist Pa., 1999, NH, 2005, lic. psychologist NH, 2002, Ind., 2007. Clin. assoc., instr. Dartmouth Med. Sch., Hanover, NH, 2002—04, asst. prof. psychiatry, 2004—07; asst. prof. radiology and neurology Ind. U. Sch. Medicine, 2007—. Recipient Student Loan Repayment award, NIH, 2003—05; Rsch. grantee, Partnership for Pediatric Epilepsy Rsch., 2004—07. Mem.: APA, Orgn. Human Brain Mapping, Am. Neuropsychiat. Assn., Phila. Neuropsychology Soc., Nat. Acad. of Neuropsychology, Internat. Neuropsychol. Soc. Office: Dept Radiology Divsn of Rsch 950 W Walnut St R2 E124 Indianapolis IN 46202 Office Phone: 317-278-8878. Business E-Mail: mcdonalb@iupui.edu.

MCDONALD, BRONCE WILLIAM, community activist, advocate; b. Dayton, Ohio, Mar. 21, 1949; s. Lawrence and Pauline Elizabeth (Macknight) McD. Student, Wright State U., 1968-71, U. Dayton, 1971, Dayton Art Inst., 1967-68. Trainer, cons. Nat. Assn. Youth Orgns. United, Washington, 1971-73; program assoc. Dayton Model Cities, 1973-74; child care worker II Montgomery County Children's Svcs. Bd., Dayton, 1974-78; inventory control Mark Morris Tires, San Francisco, 1979-82; office mgr. Bio-Feedback Internat., San Francisco, 1978-84; speaker, bd. dirs. Dayton Area AIDS Task Force, 1987—, AIDS Found. Dayton, 1988-92; community activist People With AIDS, Dayton, 1987—. Co-chair Dayton HIV Prevention Cmty. Planning Group Montgomery County Combined Health Dist.; com. mem. Direct Svcs. Dayton Area AIDS Task Force, 1987-92, speaker bur., 1987-92, edn. com., 1987-92, AIDS Found. Miami Valley, 1992—, speaker bur., 1992—, edn. com., 1992—, Pub. Policy and Conflict Mgmt., Ohio Statewide HIV Prevention Cmty. Planning Group, Ohio Dept. Health, The Prevention Summit: HIV Prevention Cmty. Planning Co-chairs meeting, Ctr. for Disease Control and Prevention, Nat. Alliance of State & Territorial AIDS Dirs., Nat. Minority AIDS Coun., Atlanta, 1995—; hotline vol. Dayton Lesbian & Gay Ctr., 1988—; mem. minority AIDS coalition Montgomery County Health Dept., Dayton, 1987—, minority health and social issues coalition, 1988—; bd. dirs. The African Am. Forum on AIDS, Dayton, 1990—, nat. AIDS awareness program So. Christian Leadership Conf., Dayton, 1993—; speaker numerous orgns. on AIDS; bd. dirs. Miami Valley AIDS Partnership, mem. membership, outreach, and needs assessment coms., 1995—; CFO, CEO Life Inc., 2003—. Founding mem., treas. Dayton Area People with AIDS Coalition, 1987—92, Men of All Colors Together, Dayton, 1988—90; co-chair Regional Cmty. Prevention Coord. Com., 1996—, AIDS Prevention Coun., Dayton; mem. bd. State of Ohio HIV Prevention Cmty. Planning Group, mem. cmty. info. com., 1996—; mem. membership com., mktg. com. Dayton AIDS Prevention Group; mem. exec. com. Consumer Adv. Coun.; exec. dir. Positive People Organized with Every Resource, 1990—2002, bd. chmn., CEO, 1995—2002; bd. dirs. Ohio AIDS Coalition, 1997, mem. healing com. the leadership tng. program com., 1996—; bd. dirs. Dayton Ryan White Consortium, mem. fin. com., promotion evaluation com., 1994—. Recipient Pres.'s Citation, 1989, Ohio AIDS Svc. award Ohio Dept. Health, 1990, Cert. of Merit Ohio Dept. Health, Columbus, 1994, Plaque of Vol. Outstanding Merit Montgomery County Combined Health Dist., Dayton, 1995, Outstanding Vol. Svc. Plaque Ohio Dept. Health, 1995, Man of Yr. award Met. Cmty. Ch., Cmty. Unity Health and Wholeness Project, Dayton, 1995; named Miami Valley Hero, 1998. Mem. Nat. Assn. Black and White Men Together. Avocations: drawing, painting, writing. Home: 4813 Shiloh View Dr Dayton OH 45415-3218 Home Phone: 937-586-3660; Office Phone: 937-681-5709. E-mail: broncemcdonald@sbcglobal.net.

MCDONALD, CAPERS WALTER, biomedical engineer, manufacturing executive, entrepreneur, educator; b. Georgetown, SC, Nov. 29, 1951; s. WalBern and Cecilia (Lockwood) McD.; m. Marion Elizabeth Kiper, Aug. 23, 1975; 1 child, Adam Capers. BS in Engring. magna cum laude, Duke U., 1974; MS in Mech. Engring., MIT, 1976; MBA, Harvard Bus. Sch., 1983. Dir. mktg. Becton Dickinson Co., Sunnyvale, Calif., 1978-81; cons. Booz, Allen & Hamilton, San Francisco, 1982-84; v.p. Siegen Corp., Mountain View, Calif., 1984, HP Genenchem, South San Francisco, Calif., 1984-87; bio-analytic systems mgr. Hewlett-Packard Corp., Palo Alto, Calif., 1986—87; v.p. Orion Instruments, Inc., Redwood City, Calif., 1987-89, Spectroscopy Imaging Systems Corp., Fremont, Calif., 1989-90, pres., bd. dirs., 1991—92; pres., CEO, bd. dirs. BioReliance Corp., Rockville, Md., 1992—2004; pres., CEO MAGENTA Corp., Rockville, 1993—2000; chmn., dir. MAGENTA Svcs., Ltd., Stirling, Scotland, 1994-2000; dir. BioReliance Holdings GmbH, Heidelberg, Germany, 1996—2004, Q-One Biotech Group Ltd., Glasgow, Scotland, 2003—04; exec. in residence, faculty mem. Johns Hopkins U., 2004—. Bd. dirs. Expion, Inc., Olney, Md.; bd. visitors U. Md. Biotech Inst., 1996-00, Duke U. Sch. Engring., 2001—, chmn. edn. and student affairs com., 2005-; bd. advisors Md. Partnership for Workforce Quality, 1996-98, Washington Bus. Jour., 2003-05; vice chmn. High Tech. Coun. Md., 1998-01; chmn. Tech. Coun. Md., 2001-04; mem. industry adv. bd. Chesapeake Bay Area chpt. ISPE, 1998-2000; mem. mfg. extension partnership nat. adv. bd. US Dept. Commerce, 2007—; lectr. in field. Contbr. chpts. to books; patentee flow microfluorometer; contbr. articles to profl. jours. Asst. scoutmaster Boy Scouts Am., Georgetown, SC, 1965-66; trustee Bethesda Acad. Performing Arts, 1998-01; mem. oversight bd. advanced tech. consortium Montgomery Coll., 1998-01; mem. steering com. Biotech. Industry Orgn., 2003 Ann. Meeting, 2002-03; mem. econ. adv. coun. Montgomery County, 1998-05; mem. founding exec. bd. Greater Washington Regional Partnership, 1998-01; mem. leadership coun. Treatment and Learning Ctrs., 1998-2000; with Capstone Co., Johns Hopkins U., 2003-04; mem. Md. Advanced Tech. Bus. Devel. Commn., 2003; state planning com. for postsecondary edn. Md. Higher Edn. Commn., 2004; chmn. Md. Adv. Tech. del. to Peoples Republic China, 2004; chmn. Eagle Career Day, Greater Washington, 2002-03. Scholar Duke U., 1970-74, MIT scholar, 1974-76; hon. fellow NSF, 1974; recipient Leadership in Tech. award Md. High Tech. Coun., 1996, Employer of Yr. award Md. Pvt. Industry Coun., 1996, Region's Most Admired Bosses award Washington Techway Mag., 2000, Good Scout award Nat. Capital Area Coun., 2000, Nat. Disting. Eagle Scout award Boy Scouts Am., 2001, Export award Scottish Coun. Devel. and Industry, 2001, Stevie award Am. Bus. Awards, 2003, Disting. Alumnus award Pratt Sch. Engring., Duke U., 2005, Excellence in Mentoring and Advising, 2005; named Greater Washington Entrepreneur of Yr. in Life Scis., 2002. Mem. AAAS, ASME, Acad. Mgmt., Biomed. Engring. Soc., NC Acad. Sci., Md. C. of C. (bd. dirs. 1996-00), Soc. Cincinnati, Order Founders and Patriots Am., St. Andrews Soc. of Washington, Harvard U. Alumni Assn., Duke U. Alumni Assn., MIT Alumni Assn., Huguenot Soc. SC, Johns Hopkins Club, Iron Dukes, Congl. Country Club, Sigma Xi, Tau Beta Pi (chpt. pres. 1973-74, nat. fin. devel. com. 2007-), Phi Eta Sigma, Pi Mu Epsilon. Methodist. Avocations: fishing, travel. Office: Johns Hopkins Univ 9601 Med Ctr Dr Rockville MD 20850 Home Phone: 301-299-6504. Business E-Mail: capersmcd@jhu.edu.

MC DONALD, CHARLES J., dermatologist, educator; b. Tampa, Fla., Dec. 6, 1931; s. George B. and Bertha C. (Harbin) McDonald; m. Maureen McDonald; children: Marc S. McDonald, Norman D. McDonald, Eric S. McDonald. BS magna cum laude, A and T Coll., NC, 1951; MS, U. Mich., 1952; MD with highest honors, Howard U., Washington, DC, 1960. Diplomate Am. Bd. Dermatology. Rotating intern Hosp. St. Raphael, New Haven, 1960-61, asst. resident in medicine, 1961-63; asst. resident, dermatology Yale U., 1963-65, spl. USPHS rsch. fellow, chief resident dermatology, 1965-66, instr. medicine, pharmacology, 1966-67, asst. prof. medicine, pharmacology, 1967-68; asst. prof. med. sci. Brown U., Providence, 1968-69, assoc. prof., 1969-74, prof., 1974—, dir. dermatology program, 1970-74, head subsect. dermatology, 1974-82, dir. divsn. dermatology, 1982—96, chair dept. dermatology, 1996—; dir. dermatology Roger Williams Gen. Hosp., 1968-97; physician in chief, dept. dermatology RI Hosp., 1989—. Mem. com., task force, chmn. task force minority affairs Am. Acad. Dermatology, 1975—80; mem. dermatology adv. panel Fed. Drug Adminstrn., 1975—78, cons., 1978—; chmn. com. pub. edn., dir., v.p. RI divsn. Am. Cancer Soc., 1978—80, pres., 1980—83, bd. dir. nat. soc., 1983—, nat. dir. at large, 1990—95, mem. nat. exec. com., 1991—99, nat. officer, 1995—2001, pres. elect, 1997—98, pres., 1998—99; mem. pharm. scis. rev. commn. NIH, 1979—83; mem. residency rev. com. dermatology ACGME, 1992—97, mem. bd. accreditation, 1999—; vice chmn. RRC dermatology, 1996—97; mem. adv. com. Arthritis, Muscular, Skeletal, Skin Disease Inst., NIH, 1993—95; bd. dirs. Lifespan RI. Editor: Post Grad. Med. Jour., 1970—85; mem. editl. bd.: Jour. of Am. Acad. Dermatology, 1981—86; contbr. numerous articles to med. publs. Bd. trustees Citizens Bank of RI, 1975—97, chair cmty. reinvestment com., 1991—97; trustee Howard U., 1993—, chair health affairs com., 1994—98, mem. exec. com., 1994—98; chair adv. bd. Howard U. Cancer Ctr., 2005—; chair bd. advisors Sch. Medicine, 1998—2005; founding mem., bd. dirs. Providence Health Care Found., 1968—76, chmn. mem. adv. com., 1976—87; bd. dirs. Providence Fund for Edn., 1986—90, Providence Pub. Libr., 1977—2000, R.I. Cancer Coun., 1999—2001, Lifespan Hosp. Consortium, RI, 2001—; sec. Providence Pub. Libr., 1991—96; mem. R.I. State Bd. Edn., 1970—72. Maj. USAF, 1952—56. Recipient Disting. Svc. award, Hosp. Assn., RI, 1971, Disting. Alumni award, Howard U. Coll. Medicine, 1983, St. George medal, Nat. Divsn. award, Am. Cancer Soc., 1992, WW Keen award, Brown Med. Alumni, 2002, Candle award, Morehouse Coll., 2005, Disting. Alumni award for medicine and cmty. affairs, Howard U., 2005, Cmty. Svc. and Medicine award, RI Black Heritage Soc., 2005. Mem.: Assn. Profs. Dermatology (bd. dirs. 1991—94), Dermatology Found. (chmn. sci. com. 1972—76), New Eng. Dermatology Soc., Am. Soc. Clin. Oncology, Nat. Med. Assn. (chmn. sect. dermatology 1973—75), Am. Acad. Dermatology (bd. dirs. 1987—91), Am. Fedn. Clin. Rsch., Soc. Investigative Dermatology, Noah Worcester Dermatol. Assn. (bd. dirs. 1983—86), RI Dermatol. Assn., New Eng. Cancer Soc. (Lifetime Achievement award 2007), New Eng. Dermatol. Soc. (v.p. 1983—84, pres. 1984—85), Am. Dermatol. Assn. (bd. dirs. 1995, pres elect 2002, pres. 2003—04), AAAS, Beta Kappa Chi, Alpha Kappa Mu, Alpha Omega Alpha, Sigma Xi. Democrat. Office: RI Hosp Dept Dermatology 593 Eddy St Providence RI 02903-4971 Office Phone: 401-444-7137. Business E-Mail: charles_mcdonald@brown.edu.

MCDONALD, CHRISTIE ANNE, literature and language professor, writer; b. NYC, May 4, 1942; d. John Denis and Dorothy (Eisner) McD.; m. Eugene Augustus Vance, June 11, 1965 (div. June 1986); children: Adam Vance, Jacob Vance; m. Michael David Rosengarten, Dec. 4, 1987. AB, Mt. Holyoke Coll., 1964; PhD, Yale U., 1969; MA (hon.), Harvard Coll., 1994. Acting instr. Yale U., New Haven, 1968-69; asst. prof. French U. Montreal, Que., Canada, 1969-77, assoc. prof. French Que., 1977-83, prof. Que., 1983, 86-93; prof. modern langs. Emory U., Atlanta, 1984-86; prof. romance langs. and. lits. Harvard U., Cambridge, Mass., 1994—, chmn. romance langs. and lits., 2000—06. Author: The Dialogue of Writing, 1985, Dispositions, 1986, The Proustian Fabric, 1991; editor: The Ear of the Other, 1988, The Extravagant Shepherd, 1993, 2d edit., 2007, Transpositions, 1994, Images of Congo, 2005. Decorated chevalier Order Palmes Academiques; recipient Clifford prize Am. Assn. 18th-Century Studies, 1994-95. Mem.: Royal Soc. Can. Office: Harvard U 431 Boylston Hall Cambridge MA 02138

MCDONALD, CRAYDON DEAN, psychologist; b. Denver, Dec. 22, 1946; s. Donald D. and Irene (Dunlavy) McDonald; children: Ian, Brendan, Tavis, Morgynne. BFA, Parsons Sch. Design, NYC, 1970; MDiv cum laude, St. Paul Sch. Theology, Kansas City, Mo., 1979; D of Ministry, Wesley Theol. Sem., Washington, 1982; PhD, Boston U., 1987. Diplomate Am. Bd. Profl. Psychology, lic. psychologist Mass., Wis., Ill., Ariz., approved supr. Am. Assn. Marriage and Family Therapy; ordained to ministry United Meth. Ch., 1982. Psychologist Worcester (Mass.) Pastoral Counseling Ctr., 1982-87; chief psychologist Dr. McDonald & Assocs., Inc., 1982—; assoc. prof., asst. program dir. Loyola U., Chgo., 1987-88; clin. psychologist Lake Geneva, Wis., 1987-93; psychology faculty No. Ariz. U., 1993—2006. Examiner Am. Bd. Profl. Psychology. Author: Personality and Cognitive Theology, 1982, Type A Coronary Prone Behavior and Narcissism, 1987. Fellow: Acad. Family Psychology; mem.:

APA (mem. program com. divsn. 43), Am. Assn. Pastoral Counselors, Human Factors Soc. Democrat. Office: 1100 N San Francisco St Ste C Flagstaff AZ 86001-3260 Office Phone: 928-774-1100. *I have seldom found what a person does to be as significant as the motivation for doing it.*

MCDONALD, DAVID EUGENE, transportation operator; b. Decatur, Ill., July 6, 1956; s. Robert Alexander McDonald and Ida Jane (Varvil) Crowell; m. Lynda Jean Christensen McDonald, Apr. 23, 1983; children: Melanie Ann, Joshua Glen and Jordan David (twins). BS in History, Ill. State U., Normal; student, Parkland C.C., Champaign, Ill. Asst. mgr. Gen. Cinema Corp., Decatur, Champaign, Chgo., 1978-81; mgr. Classic Cinemas, Elmhurst, Ill., 1981-83, World Mgmt. Inc., Downers Grove, Ill., 1983-87; driver UPS, Addison, Ill., 1987—. Active Jr. Achievement, 1971-75, Dupage County Rep., Wheaton, Ill., 1993-2002; treas. Local Luth. Laymans League, 2000—. Named Mr. Exec. Jr. Achievement, Decatur, Ill., 1975; recipient Internat. Literary award Manuscripts Internat., Dayton, Wash., 1988. Republican. Lutheran. Avocations: politics, photography, reading, writing. Home: 841 Prospect Ave Elmhurst IL 60126-4862 Office: UPS 150 S Lombard Rd Addison IL 60101-3020

MCDONALD, DOUGLAS JOEL, orthopedic surgeon, educator; b. Thief River Falls, Minn., Aug. 4, 1956; BS in Biology, St. John's U., Collegeville, Minn., 1978; MD, U. Minn., Mpls., 1982; MS in Orthop. Surgery, Mayo Grad. Sch. Medicine, Rochester, Minn. Cert. Am. Bd. Orthop. Surgery, 1990. Resident orthop. surgery Mayo Grad. Sch. Medicine, 1987, fellow orthop. oncology, 1987; fellow orthop. surgery Istituto Ortopedico Rizzoli Universita Di Bologna, Italy, 1988; prof., vice chmn., residency program dir. dept. orthop. surgery St. Louis U.; prof. orthop. surgery Washington U., St. Louis, chief orthop. oncology. Contbr. articles to med. jours., chapters to books. Named one of Am.'s Top Drs., Castle Connolly Med. Ltd., 2005, 2006. Fellow: Am. Acad. Orthop. Surgeons; mem.: Internat. Soc. Limb Salvage, Internat. Skeletal Soc., Mid-Am. Orthop. Assn., Musculoskeletal Tumor Soc., Am. Orthop. Assn., Acad. Orthop. Soc. Office: Washington U Sch Medicine Dept Orthop Surgery Campus Box 8233 660 S Euclid Ave Saint Louis MO 63110 Office Phone: 314-747-2563. E-mail: mcdonaldd@wustl.edu.

MCDONALD, DOUGLAS ROBERT, non profit agency executive; b. San Francisco, May 27, 1949; s. Robert Angus and Shirley Anne (Beine) McD.; m. Karen Bachanas, June 24, 1978; children: Jennifer, Cameron. AB, Stanford Univ., 1971; MBA, Santa Clara Univ., 1974. Dist. exec. Boy Scouts Am., San Mateo, Calif., 1971-74, exec. Palo Alto, Calif., 1974-76; regional sales-mgr. Baron Data Systems, San Leandro, Calif., 1976-81; field dir., COO Boy Scouts Am., San Mateo, Calif., 1981-86, assoc. reg. dir. Sunnyvale, Calif., 1986-88, scout exec., CEO Stockton, Calif., 1988-92, San Jose, Calif., 1992-99, Sacramento, 1999—2003, scout exec., COO Redlands, Calif., 2003—. Active 1910 Soc. Boy Scouts Am. Recipient Paul Harris fellow Rotary Internat., 1990, St. George award Roman Cath. Diocese of Sacramento, 2000; James E. West fellow Boy Scouts Am., 1993. Mem. Am. Fundraising Profls., Sigma Alpha Epsilon, Alpha Phi Omega, Silicon Valley Planned Giving Coun., Rotary Internat., Scouting Heritage Soc., KC. Republican. Roman Catholic. Avocations: travel, computers, investments. Personal E-mail: drmcdon@aol.com.

MCDONALD, FRANCES D., government official, editor, lawyer; b. Washington, July 6, 1949; BA, U. Va., 1971; JD, Cath. U. Am., 1981. Bar: Va. 1982. Legal publs. specialist Office Fed. Register. Nat. Archives and Records Adminstrn., Washington, 1980-82, atty., 1982-86, dir. legal svcs., 1986-91, dir. presdl. and legis. divsn., 1991-96, mng. editor, 1996—. Mem. Pi Gamma Mu. Office: Office Fed Registr Nat Archives-Recs Adminstrn 800 N Capitol St Rm 700 Washington DC 20408-0001 Office Phone: 202-741-6002. Business E-Mail: frances.mcdonald@nara.gov.

MCDONALD, FRANCIS MICHAEL, judge trial referee, retired state supreme court justice; b. Waterbury, Conn., Jan. 22, 1931; s. M. Francis and Margaret (Kelly) McD.; m. Mary Kelly, Jan. 28, 1956; children: Michael, Mary Ann, John K. AB, Holy Cross Coll., 1953; LLB, Yale U., 1956. Bar: Conn. 1956. Spl. agt. FBI, Washington, 1956-57; asst. U.S. atty. Dist. of Conn., New Haven, 1958-60; asst. prosecutor Cir. Ct., Waterbury, 1961-68; state's atty. Waterbury, 1968-84; judge Superior Ct., Waterbury, 1984-96; assoc. justice Conn. Supreme Ct., Hartford, 1996-99, chief justice, 1999-2001, judge trial referee Conn., 2001—. Avocations: fishing, skiing, fly tying. Home: 257 Christian Rd Middlebury CT 06762-2908 Office: Superior Ct 400 Grand St Waterbury CT 06702-1900

MCDONALD, FRANK G., lawyer, energy executive; BA, JD, Tex. Tech U. Sr. counsel Grace Energy Corp.; sr. v.p., gen. counsel, asst. sec. XTO Energy, 1993—. Shareholder Kliewer and Hood, P.C. Office: XTO Energy Inc 810 Houston St Fort Worth TX 76102-6298 Office Phone: 817-870-2800.

MC DONALD, GAIL FABER, musician, educator; b. Jersey City, Oct. 24, 1917; d. Samuel and Jennie (Weiss) Faber; m. George Walther, Nov. 17, 2000; children from previous marriage: Lora McDonald Ferguson, Charles McDonald, Henry McDonald. Diploma, Mannes Music Sch., NYC, 1938; BA, U. Md., 1962; MusM, Cath. U., 1968; DMus Arts, U. Md., 1977. Legis. asst. Capitol Hill, 1943-46; pvt. tchr. piano and music theory Washington and Md., 1950—. Piano soloist Nat. Gallery Art, 1977; rec. artist Educo Records; lectr., performer Bach Sinfonias and Mendelssohn's Complete Songs Without Words; recorded complete solo piano works of Daniel Gregory Mason. Author: Muzio Clementi and the Gradus Ad Parnassum, 1968. Mem. D.C. Music Tchrs. Assn., Md. Music Tchrs. Assn. (pres. 1977-1981), D.C. Fedn. Music Clubs, Nat. Guild Piano Tchrs. (adjudicator 1972-2005), Friday Morning Music Club (performing mem.). Address: 801 N Monroe St Apt 601 Arlington VA 22201-2372 E-mail: gailmcdonald@comcast.net.

MCDONALD, GREGORY CHRISTOPHER, author; b. Shrewsbury, Mass., Feb. 15, 1937; s. Irving Thomas and Mae (Haggerty) M.; m. Susan Aiken, Jan. 12, 1963 (div. Oct. 1990); children: Christopher Gregory, Douglas Gregory; m. Cheryle Higgins, May 25, 2001. BA, Harvard U., 1958. Bd. dirs. Camaldon Corp. Author: (novels) Running Scared, 1964, Fletch, 1974, Confess, Fletch, 1976, Flynn, 1977, Love Among the Mashed Potatoes, 1978, Fletch's Fortune, 1978, Fletch Forever, 1978, Who Took Toby Rinaldi, 1980, Fletch and the Widow Bradley, 1981, The Buck Passes Flynn, 1981, Fletch's Moxie, 1982, Fletch and the Man Who, 1983, Carioca Fletch, Flynn's In, 1984, Fletch Won, Safekeeping, 1985, Fletch, Too, 1986, (non-fiction) The Education of Gregory Mcdonald, 1985, Fletch Chronicle, Vol. 1, (drama) Bull's Eye, 1986, A World Too Wide, 1987, Exits and Entrances, 1988;: Fletch Chronicle, Vol. 3, 1988, Merely Players, 1988, The Brave, 1991, Son of Fletch, 1993, Fletch Reflected, 1994, Skylar in Yankeeland, 1997, Flynn's World, 2003; editor: Last Laughs, 1986; dir.: Bach Cantata Singers, 1973—80; author: (stage play) CDI pour SDF, 2003. Mem. vis. com. Boston Mus. Fine Arts, 1970-73, 85—; mem. Lincoln Recreation Com., 1977, 78; mem. Winthrop House Sr. Commons Harvard Coll. 1982—. Recipient Humanitarian of Yr. award Tenn. Assn. Fed. Execs., 1989, Citizen of Yr. award Nat. Assn. Social Workers, 1990, Roger William Straus award NCCJ, 1990, Alex Haley award, 1992. Mem. Authors Guild, Dramatists Guild, Mystery Writers Am. (dir. 1977—, pres. 1985-86, Poe award 1975, 77), Crime Writers Eng., Writers Guild Am., Mass. Chiefs Police Assn., Giles Countians United, Mid-Tenn. Harvard-Radcliffe Assn. Clubs: Harvard (Boston); Overseas Press (N.Y.C.); Hillcrest Country (Pulaski, Tenn.). Office: care Arthur Greene Esq 101 Park Ave New York NY 10178-0002

MCDONALD, JAMES FRANCIS, electronics company executive; b. Louisville, Feb. 17, 1940; s. Matthew Joseph and Eileen Frances (Schmidt) McD.; m. Paula S. Smith; children: Jimmie L., Susan J., Ashley K. BSEE, U. Ky., 1962, MSEE, 1964. Mgr. prodn. engring. IBM Corp., Boulder, Colo., 1974-75, mgr. devel. lab., 1975-76, mgr. task force, 1976-77, mgr. bus. planning and product planning office products, 1977, systems mgr. copier products, 1977-78, lab. dir. office parts, 1978-80, gen. mgr. mfg. systems products Boca Raton, Fla., 1980-84; pres., chief operating officer Gould, Inc., Rolling Meadows, Ill., 1984-86, chief operating officer, 1984, chmn., chief exec. officer, 1986-88; pres., chief exec. officer J.H. Whitney & Co., 1989-91, gen. partner, 1991-93; pres. and CEO Scientific-Atlantic, Inc., Norcross, Ga., 1993—. Mem. Robot Inst. Am., (bd. dirs.), United Telecommunications, Inc. (bd. dirs. 1986—). Office: Scientific Atlanta 5030 Sugarloaf Pkwy Lawrenceville GA 30044-2869

MCDONALD, JAMES S., investment company executive; b. Titirangi, New Zealand, 1953; arrived in U.S., 1960; AB, Harvard Coll., 1974; JD, U. Va., 1977. With Choate, Hall & Stewart, 1977—86, Boston Harbor Trust Co., N.A. (now Pell Rudman), 1988—; pres. Boston Harbor Trust N.A. (formerly Pell Rudman Trust Co. N.A.), 1988; COO Pell Rudman Trust Co., N.A., 1993—98, CEO, 1998—2000, Rockefeller & Co., Inc., NYC, 2000—. Bd. dirs. NY Stock Exch., NYC, 2003—06, NYSE Group, Inc., 2006—. Office: Rockefeller & Co Inc 30 Rockefeller Plaza New York NY 10112 also: NYSE Group Inc c/o Corp Sec 11 Wall St New York NY 10005

MCDONALD, JOHN CLIFTON, surgeon; b. Baldwyn, Miss., July 25, 1930; s. Edgar Hone and Ethel (Knight) McD.; m. Martha Dennis, Sept. 9, 1956; children: Melissa Lee, Karen Ann, Martha Knight. BS, Miss. Coll., 1951; MD, Tulane U., 1955. Diplomate Am. Bd. Surgery. Intern Confederate Meml. Med. Ctr., Shreveport, La., 1955-56; asst. resident Meyer Meml. Hosp., Buffalo, 1958-62, resident, 1962-63, from asst. attending surgeon to attending surgeon, 1963-68, assoc. dir. surg. research lab., 1965-68; from asst. attending surgeon to attending surgeon Deaconess Hosp., Buffalo, 1965-69, head sect. transplantation, 1966-68; dir. transplantation Charity Hosp. of La., New Orleans, 1969-77, vis. surgeon, 1969-77; clin. asst. surgeon Touro Infirmary, New Orleans, 1969-77; med. staff So. Bapt. Hosp., New Orleans, 1969-77; assoc. dept. surgery Hotel Dieu Hosp., 1969-77; surgeon in chief La. State U. Med. Ctr., Shreveport, 1977-2000, prof., chmn. dept. surgery, 1977-2000, chancellor, dean, 2000—. Buswell rsch. fellow in immunology SUNY-Buffalo, 1963-65, instr. surger, 1963-65, assoc. prof., 1965-68; asst. prof. surgery SUNY-Buffalo, 1965-68; cons. surgeon various La. Hosps., 1969-77; dir. La. Organ Procurement Program, 1971-77; cons. N.W. La. Emergency Med. Services, 1977—; assoc. prof. surgery Tulane U. Sch. Medicine, 1969-72, prof., 1972-77, assoc. prof. microbiology and immunology, 1969-77, dir. surg. research labs., 1969-77, dir. transplantation labs., 1969-77, dir. Med. Ctr. Histocampatability Testing Lab., 1969-77. Contbr. articles to med. jours. Served to capt. USAF, 1956-58. Recipient Owl Club award for outstanding teaching Tulane U., 1977; grantee Kidney Found., 1966-67, NIH, 1969—, Schlieder Found., 1970-73, Cancer Assn. Greater New Orleans, 1971-72, La. Regional Med. Program, 1971-73. Mem. AMA, ACS, Am. Assn. Clin. Histocompatibility Testing (founding), Am. Assn. Immunologists, Am. Soc. for Artificial Internal Organs, Am. Soc. Transplant Surgeons (founding, pres. 1987), Buffalo Surg. Soc. (sec. 1968, Roswell Pk. medal 2002), So. Surg. Assn. (Arthur H. Shipley award 1972, treas. 1988-91, sec. 1991-3, pres. 1993-94), Surg. Assn. La. (dir. 1977—, pres. 1983), Am. Assn. for Surgery of Trauma, Transplantation Soc., Southeastern Surg. Congress, Am. Surg. Assn., Halsted Soc. (pres. 1991), Soc. U. Surgeons, La. Med. Soc., Shreveport Med. Soc., United Network for Organ Sharing (pres. 1986-88), Am. Assn. Endocrine Surgeons, Am. Hepato-Pancreato-Biliary Assn., Internat. Liver Transplantation Soc., Soc. Critical Car Medicine, Soc. Laparoendoscopic Surgeons. Office: La State U Health Scis Ctr Shreveport Office of Chancellor Shreveport LA 71130 E-mail: jmcdon@isuhsc.edu.

MCDONALD, JOHN F., publishing executive, restauranteur; BA in Polit. Sci., Columbia U. Mgr., owner Merc Bar, Soho, NY, 1993; publishing exec. Desert Living, 1997; opened restaurants including Canteen, Dos Caminos and Lever House; founder, editl. dir., publisher CITY Mag., 1999—. Recipient Nat. Mag. award for Photo Portfolio (CITY Mag.), Am. Soc. Mag. Editors, 2007. Office: CITY Magazine 151 Mercer St New York NY 10012 *

MCDONALD, JOHN FRANCIS PATRICK, electrical engineering educator; b. Narberth, Pa., Jan. 14, 1942; s. Frank Patrick and Lulu Ann (Hegedus) McD.; m. Karen Marie Knapp, May 26, 1979. BSEE, MIT, 1963; MS in Engring., Yale U., 1965, PhD, 1969. Instr. Yale U., New Haven, 1968-69, asst. prof., 1969-74; assoc. prof. Rensselaer Poly. Inst., Troy, NY, 1974-86, prof., 1986—. Founder Rensselaer Ctr. for Integrated Electronics, 1980—. Contbr. more than 285 articles to profl. pubs. Recipient numerous grants, 1974—. Mem. ACM, IEEE (sr., assoc. editor Transactions on VSLI Design 1995—), Optical Soc., Acoustical Soc., Vacuum Soc., Materials Rsch. Soc. Achievements include patents in field. Office: Rensselaer Poly Inst Ctr for Integrated Electronics Troy NY 12181 Office Phone: 518-276-2919. Business E-Mail: mcdonald@unix.cie.rpi.edu.

MCDONALD, JOHN GREGORY, financial investment educator; b. Stockton, Calif., 1937; m. Melody McDonald. BS, Stanford U., 1960, MBA, 1962, PhD, 1967. Mem. faculty Grad. Sch. Bus. Stanford U., Calif., 1968—, now The Stanford Investors prof. fin. Grad. Sch. Bus. Vis. prof. U. Paris, 1972, Columbia Bus. Sch., 1975, Harvard Bus. Sch., 1986; gov., vice-chmn., bd. govs. NASD/NASDAQ Stock Market, 1987—90; mem. adv. bd. InterWest Venture Capital; bd. dirs. Growth Fund of Am., New Perspective Fund, Inc., Plum Creek Timber Co., Scholastic Corp., Euro-Pacific Growth Fund. Contbr. articles to profl. jours. Bd. overseers vis. com. Harvard U. Bus. Sch., Cambridge, Mass., 1994-2000. Fulbright scholar, Paris, 1967—68. Office: Stanford U Grad Sch Bus 518 Memorial Way Stanford CA 94305

MCDONALD, JOHN J., JR., lawyer; b. St. Paul, Dec. 12, 1954; BA, Univ. St. Thomas, 1977; JD, Creighton Univ., 1981. Bar: Minn. 1982, Wis., US Dist. Ct. (Minn., Wis., ND dist.), US Ct. Appeals (1st, 7th, 8th cir.), US Supreme Ct. Ptnr., comml. litigation, mem. mgmt. com. Meagher & Geer PLLP, Mpls. Named a Minn. Super Lawyer, Minn. Law & Politics, 2000—04. Mem.: ABA, Am. Bd. Trial Advocates, Internat. Assn. Def. Counsel, Def. Rsch. Inst., Minn. State Bar Assn., Wis. State Bar Assn. Office: Meagher & Geer PLLP Suite 4200 33 S 6th St Minneapolis MN 55402 Office Phone: 612-347-9120. Office Fax: 612-338-8384. Business E-Mail: jmcdonald@meagher.com.

MCDONALD, JOHN JOSEPH, electronics executive; b. NYC, Apr. 18, 1930; s. John J. and Margaret (Shanley) McD.; m. Tessa de R. Greenfield, Aug. 22, 1956; children: Kathryn, Elizabeth, Andrew. BA, Bklyn. Coll., 1951. With Sperry Rand Corp., Blue Bell, Pa., 1954-75, v.p., 1972-75; mng. dir. Casio Electronics Ltd., London, 1975-78, pres. Casio Europe, 1975-78; pres., CEO Casio, Inc., Dover, NJ, 1978-99, also bd. dirs.; chmn. Casio Can. Ltd., 1988—99; pres., CEO McDonald Assoc., Dover, NJ, 1999—, Electric Fuel Corp. (Instant Power subs.), 2002. Mem. exec. com. Electronic Ind. Found., 1994—. Chmn. Electronics Industries Found., 1997-98; trustee Bklyn. Coll., CUNY, 1997—. Served with US Army, 1952-54. Mem. Electronic Industries Assn. (bd. gov.), Electronic Industries Found. (trustee 1987—), Consumer Electronics Assn.(dir.). Home and Office: PO Box 322 Hope NJ 07844-0322 Office Phone: 908-459-5386. Personal E-mail: johnmac@nac.net.

MC DONALD, JOHN RICHARD, lawyer; b. Connersville, Ind., Aug. 8, 1933; s. Vernon Louis and Thelma (Venham) McD.; m. Mary Alice Boyd, Aug. 17, 1957; children: Anne Elizabeth, John Richard, Colleen Lynn. BA, U. Ariz., 1957, LL.B., 1960. Bar: Ariz. 1960. Since practiced in, Tucson; assoc. Richard N. Roylston, 1961-62; pvt. practice, 1963-65; ptnr. McDonald & Rykken, 1965-68, DeConcini & McDonald (now DeConcini, McDonald, Yetwin, Lacy, and Richardson P.C.), 1968—. Mem. adv. bd. Dependable Nurses, Inc., 1994—. Mem. Ariz. Law Rev. Pres., bd. dirs. emeritus Comstock Children's Hosp. Found.; v.p. Ariz. Sch. Bds. Assn., 1979, pres., 1981; v.p. All Ariz. Sch. Bd., 1981; v.p., bd. dirs. Tucson Assn. for Blind, 1966-86; trustee Catalina Foothills Sch. Dist., 1976-82; bd. dirs. Tucson Unified Sch. Dist. Ednl. Enrichment Found., 1994-2003, Ariz. Acad., 1981-89, Tucson Symphony Soc., 1997-2003, Catalina Foothills Sch. Dist. Found., 1998-2004, Grand Canyon Music Festival, 2003—. Recipient Outstanding Svc. in Sch. Law award, Ariz. Sch. Bds. Assn., 2006. Mem. Ariz. Bar Assn., Ariz. Law Rev. Assn. (pres. 1994), Pima County Bar Assn. (dir. 1978-86, pres. 1984-85), Nat. Coun. Sch. Attys. (dir. 1992-96), Delta Chi. Independent. Presbyterian. Home: 6151 N Camino Almonte Tucson AZ 85718-3729 Office: 2525 E Broadway Blvd Tucson AZ 85716-5398 Home Phone: 520-299-9077; Office Phone: 520-322-5000. Personal E-mail: mjm85718@aol.com. Business E-Mail: jmcdonald@dmyl.com. E-mail: mjm@aol.com.

MC DONALD, JOHN WARLICK, diplomat; b. Coblenz, Germany, Feb. 18, 1922; s. John Warlick and Ethel Mae (Raynor) McD.; m. Barbara Jane Stewart, Oct. 23, 1943 (div.); children: Marilyn Ruth, James Stewart, Kathleen Ethel, Laura Ellen; m. Christel Meyer, Oct. 24, 1970. AB, U. Ill., 1943, JD, 1946; PhD (hon.), Mt. Mercy Coll., 1989, Teikyo Marycrest U., 1991, Salisbury State U., 1993; JD (hon.), St. John's U., 2007. Bar: Ill. 1946, U.S. Supreme Ct. 1951. With legal div. Office Mil Govt., Berlin, 1947; asst. dist. atty. U.S. Mil. Govt. Cts., Frankfort, Germany, 1947-50; with Allied High Commn., Bonn, Germany, 1950-52; U.S. mission to NATO and OEEC, Paris, 1952-54; fgn. affairs officer Dept. State, Washington, 1954-55; exec. sec. to dir. ICA, Washington, 1955-59; U.S. econ. coord. for CENTO affairs Ankara, Turkey, 1959-63; chief econ. and comml. sect. Am. Embassy, Cairo, 1963-66; student Nat. War Coll., Washington, 1966-67; dep. dir. office econ. and social affairs Bur. Internat. Orgn. Affairs, Dept. State, 1967-68, dir., 1968-71; coord. UN Multilateral Devel. Programs, Dept. State, 1971-74, acting dep. asst. sec. econ. and social affairs, 1971, 73; dep. dir. gen. ILO, Geneva, 1974-78; pres. INTELSAT Conf. Privileges and Immunities, 1978; U.S. coord. Tech. Coop. among Developing Countries, 1978; rep. with rank of amb. to UN Conf., 1978—83. Sec. gen. 27th Colombo Plan Ministerial Meeting, 1978; U.S. coord. UN Decade on Drinking Water and Sanitation, 1979; U.S. coord., amb. Third World Conf. on Indsl. Devel., 1979, World Assembly on Aging, 1980-82; chmn. fed. inter-agy. com. Internat. Yr. of Disabled Persons, 1980-81; U.S. rep. Internat. Youth Yr., 1981-83; coord. multilateral affairs Ctr. Study of Fgn. Affairs, 1983-87; profl. lectr. in law George Washington U. Nat. Law Ctr., 1987-88, lectr. in conflict resolution, multilateral diplomacy and art of negotiation; pres. Iowa Peace Inst., Grinnell, 1988-92; prof. polit. sci. Grinnell Coll., 1989-92; Disting. vis. prof. George Mason U., Fairfax, Va., 1992-93; chmn., CEO Inst. for Multi-Track Diplomacy, Washington, 1992—; mem. Fgn. Affairs Res. Corps., 1993—; adj. prof. Union Inst., 1993-94, 97-98; adj. prof. conflict resolution, 1998-01, 05-06. Author: The North-South Dialogue and the UN, 1982, How to Be a Delegate, 1984, 2nd edit., 1994; co-editor: International Negotiation, 1985, Perspectives on Negotiation, 1986, Conflict Resolution: Track Two Diplomacy, 1987, 2nd edit., 1995, U.S. Soviet Summitry, 1987, US Bases Overseas: Negotiations with Spain, Greece and The Philippines, 1990, Multi-Track Diplomacy, 1991, Chinese edit., 2006, Defining A U.S. Negotiating Sytle, 1996; contbr. articles on aging, terrorism, water and conflict resolution; featured in exhibit Va. Hist. Soc., 2006. Bd. dirs. Global Water, 1982-, chair, 1982—, Touchstone Theatre, 1982-88, World Com.-UN Decade of Disabled Persons, 1987—, Countdown 2001, 1987-93, People-to-People Com. on Disability, 1987—2003, Am. Impact Found., 1987-89, chmn. bd., 1988-89; dir. Am. Assn. Internat. Aging, 1983—2003, chmn., 1983—2003; v.p. nat. capital area UN Assn., 1993-98, mem., 1978—. Recipient Superior Honor award, State Dept., 1972, Presdl. Meritorious Svc. award, State Dept., 1984, Peace Builders award Search for Common Ground Internat., 2005, Alumni Achievement award U. Ill. Sch. Liberal Arts and Sci., 2004, Alumni of Yr. award U. Ill., 2006; named Patriot of Yr., Kansas City, 1987; nominee Nobel Peace prize, 1994. Mem. ABA, Am. Fgn. Svc. Assn., U.S. Assn. for Club of Rome (chair 2002-05), People to People Internat. (bd. trustees 2003-), Soc. Profls. in Dispute Resolution, Consortium of Peace Rsch., Edn. and Devel., Va. Hist. Soc., USA Club Rome (Donella Meadows award 2006), Cosmos Club, Delta Kappa Upsilon, Phi Delta Phi. Office: IMTD 1901 Fort Myer Drive Ste 405 Arlington VA 22209 Home Phone: 703-525-9755; Office Phone: 703-528-3863. Business E-Mail: jmcdonald@imtd.org.

MCDONALD, JOSEPH LEE, insurance broker; b. Bremerton, Wash., Aug. 15, 1931; s. Joseph Okane and Ida Elizabeth (Finholm) McDonald; m. Glorietta Maness, Jan. 22, 1954 (dec. 1984); children: Holly Ann Chaffin, Andrew Lee; m. Beverly Mae Falkner, June 22, 1986 (div. Nov. 2005). BS, U. Wash., 1954. Various mgmt. positions AT&T, 1956-62; broker, ptnr. McDonald & McGarry Co., Seattle, 1962-84; ptnr., exec. McDonald Ins. Group, Kirkland, Wash., 1984—. V.p., bd. dirs. Chimayo Inc., Seattle, 1990—94, Santa Fe Food Corp., Seattle, 1991—96. Commr. Water Dist. # 97, Bellevue, 1967—71, Lake Hills Sewer Dist., Bellevue, 1965—71; pres. Wash. State Assn. Sewer Dists., Seattle, 1969; city councilman City of Bellevue, Wash., 1971—75. With US Army, 1954—56. Mem.: Apt. Assn. Seattle and King County, Seattle Master Builders Assn., Ind. Ins. Agts. Assn., Western Assn. Ins. Brokers, Nature Conservancy, Nat. Wildlife Fedn., Roche Harbor Yacht Club, Overlake Golf and Country Club, Coll. Club Seattle, Chi Phi. Avocations: skiing, sailing, tennis. Office: McDonald Ins Group 416 6th St S Kirkland WA 98033-6718 Home: 14220 N Creek Dr Apt 1938 Mill Creek WA 98012-5377 Home Phone: 425-585-0501; Office Phone: 425-827-7400. E-mail: bevnjoe@comcast.net.

MCDONALD, JOSEPH VALENTINE, neurosurgeon; b. NYC, June 7, 1925; m. Carolyn Alice Patricia Petersen, Apr. 30, 1955; 5 children. AB, Coll. Holy Cross, 1946; MD, U. Pitts., 1949. Intern St. Vincent's Hosp., NYC, 1949-50; rsch. fellow neuroanatomy Vanderbilt U., 1950-51; gen. surgery asst. resident Cushing VA Hosp., Boston, 1951-52; neurology extern Lenox Hill Hosp., 1952; asst. resident neurosurgery Johns Hopkins Hosp., 1953-55, resident neurosurgeon, 1955-56; practice medicine specializing in neurol. surgery Rochester, NY, 1956—; emeritus prof. neurosurgery U. Rochester Med. Sch. Mem. Soc. Neurol. Surgeons, A.C.S., Am. Assn. Neurol. Surgeons, Congress Neurosurgeons. Home: 800 Allens Creek Rd Rochester NY 14618-3412

MCDONALD, KRISTEN, lawyer; b. Newport Beach, Calif., Oct. 3, 1973; BA summa cum laude, UCLA, 1995; JD, George Washington Univ., 1999. Bar: Ga. State Ct., Ga. Superior Ct., U.S. Ct. Appeals Eleventh Dist., U.S. Dist. Ct. Middle, No. Dists. Ga. Assoc. atty., health care law Epstein, Becker & Green, P.C., 1999—. Mem.: ABA, Am. Health Lawyers Assn. Office: Epstein Becker and Green PC Ste 2700 Resurgens Plz 945 East Paces Ferry Rd Atlanta GA 30326 Fax: 404-323-9099.

MCDONALD, LINDA L., massage therapist; b. Morgantown, W.Va., Dec. 18, 1946; d. Bonita Viola Wittebort; children from previous marriage: Tatiana Denning, Leo Konchesky, Chad. BSc in Psychology, Davis Elkins Coll., 1985; degree in Therapeutic Massage, Cayce/Reilly Sch. of Masseotherapy, 1999. Cert. massage therapist, colon therapist, hypnotherapist 2005. Lab. asst. Monogahela Gen. Hosp., Morgantown, W.Va., 1965—66; doctor's aide Meml. Gen. Hosp., Elkins, W.Va., 1977—81; direct care provider Immediate Crisis Intervention Ctr., Elkins, 1995—96; massage therapist Cayce/Reilly Sch. of Masseotherapy, Va. Beach, Va., 1999—; pvt. practice Va. Beach, 1999—. Hospice vol. Elkins, W.Va., 1995—; vol. Adult Literacy Coun., Fairbanks, Ala., 1996—, Chrysler Ctr., Va. Beach, 1999—, Options Self-Actualizing Ctr., Shefield, Mass., 2001. Author: Song's On The Wind, 1997, Shadow Walker, 1999. Vol. Adult Literacy Coun., Fairbanks, Alaska, 1996, Hospice, Elkins, W.Va., 1995. Mem.: Internat. Massage Therapist Assn. Avocations: painting, writing, travel, nutrition/alternative medicine, reading. Office: Heritage Holistic Ctr 314 Laskin Rd Virginia Beach VA 23457 Home: 315 33rd St Apt 6 Virginia Beach VA 23451-2945 Personal E-mail: dolphynspirit@yahoo.com.

MCDONALD, MACKEY J., apparel executive; With VF Corp., Greensboro, NC, 1983—, pres., 1993—2006, CEO, 1996—, chmn., 1998—. Bd. dirs. Hershey Foods Corp., 1st Union Corp., Tyco Internat. Ltd. Trustee Davidson Coll. Mem.: Am. Apparel Mfrs. Assn. (bd. dirs.). Mailing: VF Corp PO Box 21488 Greensboro NC 27420-1488 Office: VF Corp 105 Corporate Ctr Blvd Greensboro NC 27408 *

MCDONALD, MALCOLM WILLIS, retired real estate company executive; b. Mpls., Nov. 17, 1936; s. Malcolm Blanchard and Ruth Virginia (Stees) McD.; m. Judy Glynn Ballard, Aug. 22, 1959 (dec. 2003); children: Malcolm Scott, Margaret Alice, Philip Brian; m. Patricia Kathleen Condon, Oct. 8, 2005. BA magna cum laude with high honors and high orations, Yale Coll., 1958; MBA, Harvard U., 1960. V.p. First Nat. Bank of St. Paul, 1960-77; dir., sr. v.p., trustee Space Center, Inc., St. Paul, 1977—2002. Adj. prof. grad. programs in mgmt. U. St. Thomas, St. Paul, 1975—94; mem. adv. bd. Firstar Bank of Minn., St. Paul, 1999—2001; bd. dirs. Scherer Bros. Lumber Co., Mpls.; vice chair adv. com. Minn. State Bd. of Investment, St. Paul, 1982—; mem. adv. bd. Sherbrooke Capital, 2002—, Hill Monastic Manuscript Libr., St. John's U., Collegeville, Minn., 1980—97; bd. dirs. HMN Fin., Inc. Mem. North Oaks Home Owners Assn., 1996; trustee, sec., chmn. audit com., investment com. Amherst H. Wilder Found., St. Paul, 1971—; trustee Bigelow & FR Bigelow Found., St. Paul, 1967-98, Lee and Rose Warner Found., 1990-2002, Manitou Fund, 1990-2002, Adelaide and Harry G. McNeely Found., St. Paul, 1980-98; trustee Minn. State Fair Found., 2002—, chmn., 2006—; trustee Episcopal Diocese Minn., 2004-, v.p., 2004, 05—; trustee Grotto Found., St. Paul, 1980—, 2d v.p., 2005—; trustee Way to Grow, 2006—; pres. Minn. Taxpayers Assn., 1994-96; former bd. dirs. Guthrie Theater, Minn. Orchestral Assn.; chmn. Minn. Landmark, Minn. Kids First, 2004—. Mem. Mpls. Club (bd. govs. 2002-06), North Oaks Golf Club, White Bear Racquet & Swim Club, St. Paul C. of C. (Bravo awards), Colony Found., Phi Beta Kappa, Phi Beta Kappa Assocs., Phi Gamma Delta. Republican. Episcopalian. Avocations: physical fitness, gardening, travel, encouraging 3, 4 and 5 yr. olds to want to read. Home: 21 E Oaks Rd North Oaks MN 55127-2527 Office Phone: 651-484-7714. Personal E-mail: malcolmmcdonald@comcast.net.

MCDONALD, MARIANNE, classicist; b. Chgo., Jan. 2, 1937; d. Eugene Francis and Inez (Riddle) McD.; children: Eugene, James, Bryan, Bridget, Kirstie (dec.), Hiroshi. BA magna cum laude, Bryn Mawr Coll., 1958; MA, U. Chgo., 1960; PhD, U. Calif., Irvine, 1975; doctorate (hon.), Am. Coll. Greece, 1988; diploma (hon.), Am. Archaeol. Assn.; DLitt (hon.), U. Athens, 1994, U. Dublin, 1994, Aristotle U., 1997, U. Thessalonika, 1997, Nat. U. Ireland, 2001. Instr. Greek, Latin, English, mythology, cinema U. Calif., Irvine, 1975-79; founder, rsch. fellow Thesaurus Linguae Graecae Project, 1975-97. Tchg. asst. U. Calif., Irvine, 1972-74; vis. prof. U. Ulster, Ireland, 1997, U. Dublin, 1990—, Univ. Coll. Dublin, 1999, 2002, U. Cork, 1999-; adj. prof. theatre U. Calif., San Diego, 1992-94, prof. theatre and classics, 1994—; bd. dirs. Centrum. Author: (novels) Semilemmatized Concordances to Euripides' Alcestis, 1977, Semilemmatized Concordance to Euripides Cyclops, 1978, Terms for Happiness in Euripides, 1978, Cyclops, Andromache, Medea, 1978, Heraclidae, Hippolytus, 1979, Hecuba, 1984, (play) And Then He Met A Woodcutter, 2005 (San Diego Critics Cir. award for best play, 2005), (critical works) Hercules Furens, 1984, Electra, 1984, Ion, 1985, Trojan Women, 1988, Iphigenia in Taurus, 1988, Euripides in Cinema: The Heart Made Visible, 1983, The Living Art of Greek Tragedy, 2003; translator: The Cost of Kindness and Other Fabulous Tales (Shinichi Hoshi), 1986, Views of Clytemnestra, Ancient and Modern, 1990, Classics and Cinema, 1990, Modern Critical Theory and Classical Literature, 1994, A Challenge to Democracy, 1994, Ancient Sun/Modern Light: Greek Drama on the Modern Stage, 1990, Star Myths: Tales of the Constellations, 1996, Sole Antico Luce Moderna, 1999, Mythology of the Zodiac: Tales of the Constellations, 2000, Antigone by Sophocles, 2000, Mythology of the Zodiac, 2000, Sing Sorrow: Classics, History, Heroines in Opera, 2001; translator: (with Michael Walton) Euripides Andromache, 2001; translator: Euripides' Electra, 2004, Euripides' Hecuba, 2005; editor (with M. McDonald and Michael Walton): Six Greek Tragedies, 2002; editor: (with Michael Walton) Amid Our Troubles: Irish Versions of Greek Tragedy, 2002, Canta la tua Pena, 2002; contbr. chapters to books, articles in field to profl. jours., reviews. Bd. dirs. Am. Coll. of Greece, 1981-90, Scripps Hosp., 1981, Am. Sch. Classical Studies, 1986-; mem. bd. overseers U. Calif., San Diego, 1985-; nat. bd. advisors Am. Biog. Inst., 1982—; pres. Soc. for the Preservation of the Greek Heritage, 1990-, Asian Am. Repertory Theatre, 2003; founder Hajime Mori Chair for Japanese Studies, U. Calif., San Diego, 1985, McDonald Ctr. for Alcohol and Substance Abuse, 1984, Thesaurus Linguarum Hiberniae, 1991-, Hiroshi McDonald Mori Performing Arts Ctr. Recipient Ellen Browning Scripps Humanitarian award, 1975, Disting. Svc. award U. Calif., Irvine, 1982, 2001, Irvine medal, 1987; named one of the Cmty. Leaders Am., 1979-80, Philanthropist of Yr., 1985, Headliner San Diego Press Club, 1985, Philanthropist of Yr. Honorary Nat. Conf. Christians and Jews, 1986, Woman of Yr. AHEPA, 1988, San Diego Woman of Distinction, 1990, Woman of Yr. AXIOS, 1991; recipient Bravissimo gold medal San Diego Opera, 1990, Gold Medal Soc. Internationalization of Greek Lang., 1990, Athens medal, 1991, Piraeus medal, 1991, award Desmoi, 1992, award Hellenic Assn. of Univ. Women, 1992, Acad. of Achievement award AHEPA, 1992, Woman of Delphi award European Cultural Ctr. Delphi, 1992, Civis Universitatis award U. Calif., San Diego, 1993, Hypatia award Hellenic U. Women, 1993, Am.-Ireland Fund Heritage award, 1994, Contbn. to Greek Letters award Aristotle U. Thessaloniki, 1994, Mirabella Mag. Readers Choice One of 1000 Women for the Nineties, 1994, citations from U.S. Congress and Calif. Senate, Alexander the Gt. award Hellenic Cultural Soc., 1995, made hon. citizen of Delphi and gold medal of the Amphiktuonon, Del. Bus. award for Fine Arts San Diego Bus. Jour., 1995, Vol. of Decade Women's Internat. Ctr., 1994, 96, Gold Star award San Diego Arts League, 1997, Golden Aeschylus award Inst. Nat. Drama Antkg. Siracusa, 1998, Women Who Mean Bus., Fine Arts award San Diego Bus. Jour., 1998, Fulbright award, 1999, Ellis Island award, 1999, Spirit of Scripps award 1999; Theatre Excellence award KPBS Patte, 2001, Laud and Laurels, U. Calif. Disting. Alumni award Hellenic Cultural Soc. San Diego, 2003, Sledgehammer Theatre award, 2003, New Path award, 2003, Egeria award Women's Internat. Ctr., 2004, Billie award, 2004, Patté award, 2004. Mem. MLA, AAUP, Am. Philol. Assn. (disting. svc. award 1999), Soc. for the Preservation of the Greek Heritage (pres.), Libr. of Am., Am. Classical League, Philol. Assn. Pacific Coast, Am. Comparative Lit. Assn., Modern and Classical Lang. Assn. So. Calif., Hellenic Soc. (coun. award 2000), Calif. Fgn. Lang. Tchrs. Assn., Internat. Platform Assn., Royal Irish Acad., Greece's Order of the Phoenix (comdr. 1994), KPBS Prodrs. Club, Hellenic Univ. Club (bd. dirs.). Avocations: Karate, harp (medieval), skiing, diving. Home: PO Box 929 Rancho Santa Fe CA 92067-0929 Office: U Calif at San Diego Dept Theatre La Jolla CA 92093 Office Phone: 858-481-0107. E-mail: mmcdonald@ucsd.edu.

MCDONALD, MARK DOUGLAS, electrical engineer; b. Princeton, NJ, Aug. 3, 1958; s. James Douglas and Jacquelyn (Milligan) McD.; m. Patricia Joann Watson, Sept. 12, 1980. BSE, Duke U.; MS, N.C. State U. Product engr. Exide Electronics, Raleigh, NC, 1981—84; rsch. asst. N.C. State U., Raleigh, 1985—86; tech. staff Avantek (Hewlett Packard), Newark, Calif., 1987—90; prin. engr. Nat. Semiconductor, Santa Clara, Calif., 1990—92, engrng. project mgr., 1992—95; design engrng. mgr. Linear Tech. Corp., Milpitas, Calif., 1995—2001; dir. RF/Analog Bermai Inc, Palo Alto, Calif., 2001—02; dir. McDonald Watson and Assocs., Campbell, Calif., 2002—; v.p. hardware devel. Altierre Corp., San Jose, 2003—. Session chmn. Wireless Symposium, Santa Clara, 1993-2002, RF and Microwave Applications Conf., Santa Clara, 1992; mem. com. Symposium on VLSI Circuits Program, 1995-97. Contbr. articles to profl. jours. Precinct capt. various polit. campaigns, Fremont, Calif., 1988. Mem. IEEE (sr.), Cairn Terrier Club of No. Calif. (asst. chair 1995, splty. show chair 1996-97, bd. govs. 1996-99), Cairn Terrier Club Am., Sacramento Valley Cairn Terrier Club (treas. 2004-06), No. Calif. Terrier Assn. (bd. govs. 2002-05). Achievements include U.S. and foreign patents in area of high-speed analog circuits; designed front-end integrated circuits in first wireless digital European cordless telecomm. transceiver (DECT) for voice comm.; design of first selective frequency trip circuit for parallel uninterruptible power supplies. Personal E-mail: markm@altierre.com.

MCDONALD, MARY ANN MELODY, investment management executive; b. Sandwich, Ill., Apr. 30, 1944; d. Theodore Harvey and Sarah Elizabeth (Irving) Larson; m. John G. McDonald, June 19, 1973. MusM, New England Conservatory, 1970; studied with Nadia Boulanger, Paris, 1971; MusD, Stanford U., 1975; MBA, Harvard U., 1986. Credit analyst Wells Fargo Bank, San Francisco, 1976-77, loan officer, 1977-79, asst. v.p., 1979-80; chmn. bd. dirs. Cornwall Corp., Stanford, Calif., 1980-84; dir. client svcs. RCM Capital Mgmt., San Francisco, 1986-92, ptnr., 1988-98, mng. dir., 1998—. Active Ill. Youth Commn., 1963-66. Recipient Rockefeller grantee Oberlin (Ohio) Coll. 1967; winner Miss Boston-Miss Am. Pageant, 1968. Mem. Senatorial Inner Cir. (life), Stanford Alumni Assn., Harvard Alumni Assn., Lincoln Club, Sigma Alpha Iota, Kappa Delta (Telford Cup). Republican. Lutheran. Office: DRCM Capital Mgmt 4 Embarcadero Ctr Ste 3100 San Francisco CA 94111-4106

MC DONALD, MEG, public relations executive; b. Santa Monica, Calif., Oct. 11, 1948; Dir. radio & TV svcs. Fran Hynds Pub. Rels., 1969-75; owner, CEO Mc Donald Media Svcs., 1975—. Recipient Buccaneer award PIRATES, 1980, 82, Prisms award Pub. Rels. Soc. Am., 1981, Pro awards Publicity Clubs. of L.A. Mem. Pub. Rels. Soc. Am. (sec. 1985), Radio ane TV News Assn. of So. Calif. (mem. bd. dirs. 1973-88), Publicity Club of L.A. (pres. 1979-80), L.A. Advt. Women (v.p. 1984-85), Print Interactive Radio and TV Ednl. Soc. (pres. 1998-00), Radio and TV News Assn. Office: Mc Donald Media Svcs 11076 Fruitland Dr Studio City CA 91604-3541 Business E-Mail: mcdmedia@earthlink.net.

MCDONALD, MICHAEL EUGENE, lawyer, educator, clergyman; b. Buffalo, Aug. 13, 1956; s. Ned and Margaret (Hereford) McD.; m. Darlene Carver, July 1, 1989; 1 child, Miranda Danielle. AA, BS, Middle Tenn. State U., 1979; MPA, So. Ill. U., 1984; JD, John Marshall Sch. Law, Chgo., 1987; MDiv, Vanderbilt U., 1989—91. Bar: Ill. 1986, Tenn. 1990; cert. adminstr. elections, Tenn., 1994; cert. civil mediator; ordained to ministry United Meth. Ch., 1996. Legis. intern Office of the Speaker, Ill. Ho. of Reps., Springfield, 1982-83; fellow Exec. Office of the Gov., State of Ill., Springfield, 1983-84; law clk. intern U.S. Dist. Ct. No. Dist. Ill., Chgo., 1984-85; adminstrv. asst. to dir. Ill. Dept. State Police, Chgo., 1984-87; asst. atty. gen. Ill. Atty. Gen.'s Office, Chgo., 1986-87; spl. asst. to mayor Exec. Office of the Mayor, Nashville, 1987-90; assoc. King & Ballow, Nashville, 1991-93; election adminstr. Davidson County Election Commn., Nashville, 1993—. Adj. prof. polit. sci., bus. law and paralegal studies program Middle Tenn. State U., Murfreesboro, 1987—; gen. counsel Gov.'s Alliance for a Drug Free Tenn., Davidson County, 1987—; asst. prof. The Honors Program, Tenn. State U., 1996—; instr. U. Tenn. Ctr. for Govt. Tng., 1995—' instr. Ptnrs. in Policymaking, Tex., Kans., Mo., Tenn., N.J., Ga.; mediator U.S. EEOC, 1998-99. Vol. Buddies of Nashville, 1988—; loaned exec. United Way Mid. Tenn., 1990; mem. Leadership Nashville, 1990-91, Citizens Police Acd., 1997; ordained deacon Bethlehem Ctrs. of Nashville, 2000—; mem. design com. Internat. Convocation of Deacons and Diaconate Mins., Dalals, 2003. Recipient Disting. Young Alumni Achievement award Middle Tenn. State U., 1987, Disting. African Am. Alumni Achievement award; Coun. on Legal Edn. Opportunity fellow, Thurgood Marshall scholar, 1984-87. Mem. ABA (del. ho. of dels.), Nat. Bar Assn., Ill. State Bar, Alpha Phi Alpha, Phi Alpha Delta. Avocations: basketball, running, Karate, sport card collecting, playing guitar. Home: 1603 Benjamin St Nashville TN 37206-2511 Office: Election Commn Met Govt of Nashville Howard Sch Bldg Rm 153 2d Ave S Nashville TN 37210-0650

MCDONALD, MICHAEL SCOTT, lawyer; b. Ft. Stockton, Tex., Feb. 6, 1962; s. Roland R. and Harriett L. McD.; m. Sara; children: Matthew, Michael. BA, U. Tex., El Paso, 1984; JD, U. Tex., Austin, 1987. Bar: Tex. 1987, U.S. Ct. Appeals (5th and 10th cirs.), U.S. Dist. Ct. (all dists.) Tex. With Littler Mendelson, Dallas; mng. shareholder Littler, Mendelson, Dallas. Co-author, editor: (chapter 9) The National Employer, The Texas Employer; contbg. editor: Covenents Not to Compete-A State by State Survey, 1995—, Employee Duty of Loyalty, 1995—, Trade Secrets-A State by State Survey, 1998—; contbr. articles to profl. jours. Mem. ABA (litigation sect., labor and employment law sect.), Tex. Bar Assn. (labor and employment law sect.), Tex. Assn. Bus., Dallas Bar Assn. (employment law sect., chmn. 2000, exec. com. 1994-2001). Office: Littler Mendelson 2001 Ross Ave Ste 2600 Dallas TX 75201-2931

MCDONALD, NATASHA L., school psychologist, educator; d. Richard L. Story and Donna J. Carlton-Vish; m. Tom C. McDonald, Sept. 13, 2003. BA in Psychology, Ea. Ill. U., Charleston, 2001, Specialist Degree in Sch. Psychology, 2004. Cert. brain injury specialist level one SC, 2006. Sch. psychologist II Horry County Schs., Myrtle Beach, SC, 2004—. Adj. instr. Coastal Carolina U., Conway, SC, 2006—. Mem.: NASP (assoc.).

MCDONALD, PATRICK ALLEN, lawyer, educator, arbitrator; b. Detroit, May 11, 1936; s. Lawrence John and Estelle (Maks) Mc D.; m. Margaret Mercier, Aug. 10, 1963; children: Michael Lawrence, Colleen Marie, Patrick Joseph, Timothy, Margaret, Thomas, Maureen. PhB cum laude, U. Detroit, 1958, JD magna cum laude, 1961; LLM (E. Barrett Prettyman Trial scholar, Hugh J. Fegan fellow), Georgetown U., 1962. Bar: D.C. 1961, Mich. 1961, Colo. 1993. Case worker Dept. Pub. Welfare, Detroit, 1958; field examiner NLRB, Detroit, 1961; practiced in Washington, 1961-62; trial cons. NIH, Bethesda, Md., 1962; staff judge adv. USAF, France, 1962-65; ptnr. Monagham, LoPrete, Mc Donald, Yakima & Grenke, Detroit, 1965—. Bd. dirs., past chmn. Delta Dental Plan Mich.; past chmn. Delta Dental Plan Ohio; bd. dirs., chmn. Guest House, Lake Orion, Mich., Rochester, Minn., Detroit Athletic Club, Brighton Hosp.; instr. polit. sci. and law U. Md., 1963-65, U. Detroit Law Sch., adj. prof., 1965-2004; adj. prof. Ave Maria Law Sch., 2003—. Co-author: Law and Tactics in Federal Criminal Cases, 1963; author magnet plans for schs., Detroit, Boston. Mem. Detroit Bd. Edn., 1966-76, pres.; sec., trustee Mt. Elliott Cemetary Assn.; mem. U. Detroit Sports Hall of Fame; mem. adv. bd. Providence Hosp., Southfield, Mich.; exec. bd. U. Detroit Pres.'s Cabinet. Named one of Five Outstanding Young Men of Mich., Outstanding Young Man of Detroit. Mem. ABA, Detroit Bar Assn., State Bar Mich. (commr.), U. Detroit Alumni Assn. (bd. dirs.), Mensa, Blue Key, Alpha Phi Omega (pres. Eta Pi chpt. 1955), Alpha Sigma Nu (v.p. 1960). Home: 13066 Lashbrook Ln E Brighton MI 48114-6002 Office: 40700 Woodward Ave Bloomfield Hills MI 48304-2211 Office Phone: 810-220-3444. Office Fax: 248-642-9460. Personal E-mail: pmcd101@sbcglobal.net. *In the field of law, as an attorney, professor and arbitrator, I have prayed and attempted to be able in argument, accurate in analysis, correct in conclusion, candid with clients, honest with adversaries, and responsible for obligations assigned to me. I have advocated moderation in all things with the exception of my love for Him who created me.*

MCDONALD, PETER D., air transportation executive; m. Diane McDonald; children: Megan, Katie. B, Judson Coll., 1976. Various positions United Airlines Corp., 1969—, v.p., op. svcs., 1999—2001, sr. v.p. airport ops., 2001—02, exec. v.p. ops., 2002—04, exec. v.p., COO, 2004—. *

MCDONALD, PEYTON DEAN, brokerage house executive; b. Kansas City, Kans., Feb. 6, 1936; s. Charles H. and Myra (Miller) McD.; m. Frances B. Beighley, June 14, 1958; children: Peyton D., Todd B. BS, Bucknell U., 1958. Sales rep. Sprout Waldron and Co., Inc., Muncy, Pa., 1958-67; v.p. Blair & Co., Williamsport, Pa., 1967-69; v.p., mgr. Hugh Johnson, Williamsport, 1969-77, E.F. Hutton & Co. Inc., Williamsport, 1977-87; sr. v.p. Smith Barney, Williamsport, 1987—2006; v.p. Merrill Lynch, 2006—. Mem. N.Y. Stock Exchange; pres. Hope Enterprizes. Pres. United Way, Williamsport, 1977-80, Pa. Coll. Found., 1985-86; campaign chmn. Heinz for Senator, Lycoming County, Pa., 1978, 96; bd. dirs., treas. Divine Providence Hosp., chmn.; mem. Susquehanna Health Care Bd. 1st lt. U.S. Army, 1958-59. Mem. Ross Club, Williamsport Country Club, Farmington Country Club, Masons. Republican. Presbyterian. Avocation: golf. Home: 1545 Grampian Blvd Williamsport PA 17701-1917

MCDONALD, R. BRUCE, corporate financial executive; B Commerce, McMaster Univ., Hamilton, Ont. With Lucas Varity plc; v.p., fin. TRW Inc.; corp. controller Johnson Controls Inc., Milw., 2001—02, corp. v.p., corp. controller, 2002—04, corp. v.p., asst. CFO, 2004—05, corp. v.p., CFO, 2005—06, exec. v.p., CFO, 2006—. Office: Johnson Controls Inc 5757 N Green Bay Ave Milwaukee WI 53201 *

MCDONALD, ROBERT ALAN (BOB MCDONALD), consumer products company executive; b. Gary, Ind., June 20, 1953; s. Ray Wellington and Froso (Manolios) McD.; m. Diane Janine Murphy, Dec. 31, 1977; children: Jennifer Elizabeth, Robert Wade. BS in Engring., U.S. Mil. Acad., 1975; MBA, U. Utah, 1978. Asst. Solo brand Procter & Gamble, Cin., 1980-81, asst. mgr. Dawn brand, 1981-82, asst. mgr. Cascade brand, 1982-83, mgr. Cascade brand, 1983-84, mgr. Tide brand, 1984—86, assoc. advt. mgr., 1986—89, mgr. laundry prod. P&G Canada, 1989—91, gen. mgr. P&G Far East, 1991—94, v.p., gen. mgr. P&G Far East, 1994—96, regional v.p. Japan, P&G Asia, 1996—99, v.p. NE Asia, 1999, pres. NE Asia, 1999—2001, pres. global fabric care & home care, 2001—04, vice chmn. global ops., 2004—07, vice chmn., COO, 2007—. Instr. econs. Meth. Coll., Golden Gate U., Campbell U., Fayetteville, N.C., 1979-80; bd. dir. Xerox Corp., GS1. Deacon Knox Presbyn. Ch., Cin., 1982-85, Mt. Washington Presbyn. Ch., Cin., 1986; mem. bd. vis. Fuqua Sch. Bus., Duke Univ.; mem. bd. adv. Northwestern Integrated Mktg. Communications. Advanced through grades to capt. US Army, 1975—80. Fellow Royal Soc. of Arts of London (Silver medal 1975); mem. Phi Kappa Phi, Beta Gamma Sigma, Commonwealth Club. Republican. Avocations: reading, running, painting. Office: Procter & Gamble 1 Procter And Gamble Plz Cincinnati OH 45202-3393 Mailing: Procter & Gamble PO Box 599 Cincinnati OH 45201-0599 *

MCDONALD, SALLY J., lawyer; b. Ind., 1964; d. Homer C. and Esteleen M. McD.; m. Richard M. Levin, Oct. 16, 1993. BS, Ind. U., 1986; JD, Duke U., 1990. Bar: Ill. 1990, Ill. Supreme Ct., US Dist. Ct. (no. dist. Ill.), US Ct. Appeals (7th cir.), Fed. Trial Bar. Assoc. Bell, Boyd & Lloyd, Chgo., 1990-92, Piper Rudnick, Chgo., 1992-98, hiring ptnr., 1998—99; ptnr., labor, employment group, co-nat. hiring ptnr. Piper Rudnick (now DLA Piper), 1999—. Gen. counsel Gtr. Chgo. Food Depository, 1995-99. Contbr. chpt. to book. Bd. mem. Pub. Interest Law Initiative; pres. bd. dir. CARPLS; outside counsel Greater Chgo. Food Depository. Mem. ABA, Chgo. Bar Assn. (bd. mgrs. 1998-2000, chair Young Lawyers sect. 1996-97, Maurice Weigle award 1994), Chgo. Bar Found. (bd. dir., treas.), Women's Bar Assn. Office: DLA Piper Suite 1900 203 N LaSalle St Chicago IL 60601-1293 Office Phone: 312-368-8927. Office Fax: 312-236-7516. Business E-Mail: sally.mcdonald@dlapiper.com.

MCDONALD, THERESA BEATRICE PIERCE (MRS. OLLIE MCDONALD), church official, minister; b. Vicksburg, Miss., Apr. 11, 1929; d. Leonard C. Pierce and Ernestine Morris Templeton Pierce; m. Ollie McDonald, Apr. 23, 1966. Student, Tougaloo Coll., 1946-47, U. Chgo. Indsl. Rels. Ctr., 1963-64; BA in Sociology with deptl. honors, Roosevelt U., 1997; student, Chgo. Theol. Sem., 1997—. Ordained to Gospel Ministry, 1997. Vol. rep. Liberty Bapt. Ch., Am. Legion Aux., VA West Side Hosp., Chgo., 1971-73; nat. instr. ushers dept. Prog. Nat. Bapt. Conv. Inc., Washington, 1973-75, nat. sec. ushers dept., 1975-76, v.p. at large, 1980-82, chmn. pers. com., 1982-84; mem. faculty Congress of Christian Edn., 1978-85; mem. pub. rels. staff Liberty Bapt. Ch., Chgo., 1973-79, trustee, 1987-91; asst. Christian edn. dir. Maryland Ave. Bapt. Ch., Chgo., 1995-99; assoc. min. Md. Ave. Bapt. Ch., Chgo., 1997—; Tchr. Tng. Instr., 1998, 2000; dir. Christian edn. Md. Ave. Bapt. Ch., Chgo., 2000—02. Cons., lectr. in field; Sunday ch. sch. tchr.; bible class instr.; guest speaker TV and radio programs. Participant White House Regional Confs., 1961. Recipient Christian Svc. award Prog. Nat. Bapt. Conv. Inc., 1986, 92, 94, Disting. Svc. award, 1990-94, Dedicated Svc. award, 1998. Mem. VFW (life mem. Hunt aux. 2024), Bethlehem Bapt. Dist. Assn. Chgo. (asst. sec. 1982-84), Ch. Women United in Greater Chgo. (Ecumenical Actions com. 1981-83), Am. Legion (Outstanding Svc. award 1972, 73), Bapt. State Conv. Ill. (life), Order Ea. Star. Address: 9810 S Calumet Ave Chicago IL 60628-1432

MCDONALD, THOMAS ALEXANDER, lawyer; b. Chgo., Aug. 20, 1942; s. Owen Gerard and Lois (Gray) McD.; m. Sharon Diane Hirk, Nov. 25, 1967; children: Cristin, Katie, Courtney, Thomas Jr. AB, Georgetown U., Washington, DC, 1965; JD, Loyola U., Chgo., 1968. Bar: Ill. 1969, US Dist. Ct. (no. dist.) Ill. 1969. Ptnr. Clausen Miller, PC, Chgo., 1969—2001, McDonald & McCabe, LLC, Chgo., 2001—. Mem.: ABA, Chgo. Bar Assn., Ill. Bar Assn. Office: McDonald & McCabe LLC 225 S Wacker Dr Ste 2100 Chicago IL 60606-1299 Office Phone: 312-845-5190. Business E-Mail: tmcdonald@mcdonaldmccabe.com.

MCDONALD, WARREN GEORGE, accountant, mortage company, savings and loan association executive, consultant; b. Oakland, Calif., Feb. 14, 1939; s. George Daniel and Barbara (Sainsot) McD.; m. Roberta Anne Peterson, Apr. 27, 1968; children: Edward Bruce, Deborah Lynn. BA, San Francisco State Coll., 1962. CPA, Calif. Ptnr. Main Lafrentz & Co., CPAs, San Francisco, 1969-74; v.p., treas. Imperial Corp. Am., San Diego, 1975-80; v.p. fin. No. Calif. Savs. & Loan, Palo Alto, 1980-82; sr. v.p. fin. Unified Mortgage Co., Santa Clara, Calif., 1982-85; pres. Saratoga Savs., 1985-89; pvt. practice cons. San Francisco, 1989—2003; ret., 2003. Co-author: Power Above The Law, 1990. Served to capt. USCGR. Mem. AICPA, Calif. Soc. CPAs, Inst. Mgmt. Accts., Res. Officers Assn., Naval Inst., Navy League, Mil. Officers Assn. Am. (nat. bd. dirs. 2004—). Home: 1430 Wendy Way Menlo Park CA 94025-6022 Personal E-mail: mcdcpa@gmail.com.

MCDONALD, WESLEY S., retail executive; b. 1962; B cum laude, Bucknell U., Lewisburg, Pa.; MBA, Wharton Sch., Phila., 1988. Various fin. positions Target Corp., 1988—2000; v.p., CFO Abercrombie & Fitch,

New Albany, Ohio, 2000—03; exec. v.p., CFO Kohl's Corp., Menomonee Falls, Wis., 2003—. Office: Kohls Corp N56 W17000 Ridgewood Dr Menomonee Falls WI 53051-5660 Office Phone: 262-703-7000. *

MCDONALD, WILLIAM HENRY, manufacturing executive; b. Ottawa, Ont., Can., Sept. 8, 1924; s. Joseph and Constance Mary (Gordon) McD.; m. D. Gwen Selkirk, July 8, 1950; 1 child, Barbara Elaine. Grad. high sch. Credit and operating mgr. B.F. Goodrich Co., Winnipeg, Man., Canada, 1945-49; fin. adminstrn. officer Govt. Can., Ottawa, 1949-55; asst. gen. mgr. mortgages Bank of N.S., 1955-66; mng. dir. Boyd Stott & McDonald Ltd., Toronto, Ont., 1966-79; exec. v.p., dir. Morguard Trust Co., 1966-74; chmn. bd. Can. Comml. Bank, Toronto, 1976-81, chmn. exec. com., 1981-84; chmn. bd. Can. Comml. Bank Mortgage Investment Corp., 1983-84; pres., CEO, dir. Boyd Stott and McDonald Techs., Ltd., 1984—2003. Pres. Thornton McDonald Assocs., Inc. Mem. bd. govs. J. Douglas Ferguson Hist. Research Found., 1971—. Served with RCNVR, 1943-45. Mem. Can. Paper Money Soc. (hon. pres.), Internat. Bank Note Soc. (life), Can. Credit Inst., Classical & Medieval Numismatic Soc. (exec. sec.). Conservative. Anglican. E-mail: billmcdo@idirect.com.

MCDONALD, WILLIAM HENRY, lawyer; b. Niangua, Mo., Feb. 27, 1946; s. Milburn and Fannie M. McDonald; m. Janice E. Robinson, July 13, 1968; children: Melissa L., Meghan M. BS in Pub. Adminstrn., Southwest Mo. State U., 1968; JD, U. Mo., 1971. Bar: Mo. 1971, U.S. Dist. Ct. (we. dist.) Mo. 1973, U.S. Supreme Ct. 1978, U.S. Ct. Appeals (8th cir.) 1982. Ptnr., pres. Woolsey, Fisher, Whiteaker & McDonald, PC, 1973-95; pres. William H. McDonald & Assocs., PC, Springfield, Mo., 1995—. Chmn. blue ribbon task force on Delivery of Mental Health Services to Southwest Mo., Mo. Commn. Continuing Legal Edn.; pres. Tan Oaks Homeowners Assn.; mem. fin. com. Child Adv. Council, Rep. Nat. Com., Mo. Rep. Com., Greene County Nat. Com.; active various Southwest Mo. State U. Clubs; bd. dirs. Greene County div. Am. Heart Assn., Ozarks regional Am. Athletic Union Jr. Olympics; pres., bd. dirs. Springfield Little Theatre; v.p. pub. affairs Springfield Area C. of C., bd. dirs., 1995-98. Capt. U.S. Army, 1971-73. Named one of Outstanding Young Men Am., 1978, 81, Outstanding Young Men Springfield, 1980. Fellow ABA (life, antitrust and litigation and torts and ins. sects.); mem. ATLA, Fed. Bar Assn., Mo. Bar Assn. (chmn. spol. com. on mandatory continuing edn., various coms., Pres.'s award 1986), Mo. Assn. Trial Attys. (bd. govs. 1998-2001), Springfield Met. Bar Assn. (bd. dirs., chmn. pub. edn. speakers bur.), Met. Bar Assn. St. Louis, Def. Rsch. Inst., Am. Judicature Soc., Am. Bd. Trial Advs. (state coord.), Nat. Bd. Trial Advs., Am. Coll. Barristers, Million Dollar Forum, 31st Jud. Cir. Bar Com. (chmn.), Supreme Ct. Hist. Soc., U. Mo.-Kansas City Sch. Law Found., Springfield Claims Assn. (pres.), U.S. Cavalry Assn. (life), Am. Legion, 1st Inf. Divsn. Soc., K.T., Beta Omega Tau, Kappa Epsilon. Presbyterian. Home: 4857 E Royal Dr Springfield MO 65809-2425

MCDONALD, WILSON, lawyer; m. Betsy McDonald; 2 children. BBA, JD, Univ. So. Carolina. Former asst. gen. counsel Fleet Mortgage Group; former v.p., So. Carolina state mgr. Old Republic National Title Insurance Co.; former v.p., dep. gen. counsel Resource Bancshares Mortgage Group; former v.p. mktg. and underwriting So. Carolina Investors Title Insurance Co.; exec. v.p., gen. counsel LIME Fin. Co., 2004—. Home: LIME Fin Co Ste 600 5885 SW Meadows Rd Lake Oswego OR 97035

MCDONALD TERLAJE, PATRICIA, counselor; b. Tamuning, Mar. 16, 1962; d. Charles H. and Lucia G. McDonald; m. Paul J. Terlaje, Jan. 11, 2001; children: Pedro C. Lizama, Allen M. McDonald, Trinity E. Terlaje. BA in Secondary Edn. English (hon.), U. Guam, Mangilao, 1985, MA in Counseling, 2001. Tchr. English Guam Pub. Sch. Sys., Hagatna, Guam, 1985—99; counselor Acad. Our Lady Guam, 2000—01, Guam C.C., Mangilao, 2002—. Career resource network counselor U.S. Dept. Edn. Perkins Act, Mangilao, 2002—03. Mem.: Am. Coll. Counseling Assn., Guam Sch. Counselor Assn., Am. Sch. Counselor Assn., Am. Counseling Assn. Home: 557 Chalan Macajna Agana Heights GU 96910 Office: Guam CC PO Box 23069 Barrigada GU 96921 Home Phone: 671-472-8764; Office Phone: 671-735-5564. Office Fax: 671-734-5238; Home Fax: 671-734-5238. Business E-Mail: pterlaje@guamcc.edu.

MCDONALD-WEST, SANDI MACLEAN, director, consultant; b. Lowell, Mass., May 8, 1930; d. Walter Allan and Celina Louise (Lalime) MacLean; m. Thomas D. McDonald, Sept. 8, 1951 (div.); children: Todd F., Brooke Goodfriend, Ned M., Reid A., Heather McDonald McLean. BA, DePauw U., 1951; MA, Fairleigh Dickinson U., 1966; MEd, North Tex. State U., 1980. Cert. in Montessori teaching. Tchr., adminstr. Hudson (Ohio) Montessori Sch., 1966-68, Berea (Ohio) Montessori Sch., 1968-70, Creative Learning Ctr., Dallas, 1970-71; tchr., head of lower sch. The Selwyn Sch., Denton, Tex., 1971-83; tchr., headmaster Cimarron Sch., Enid, Okla., 1983-87; cons. Corpus Christi (Tex.) Montessori Sch., 1987-89, Azlann-Eren Horn Montessori Sch., Denton, 1989-95, Highland Meadow Montessori Acad., Southlake, Tex., 1994-2001, various pub. and pvt. Montessori Schs., 1999—. Ednl. dir., pres. Southwestern Montessori Tchg. Ctr., Inc., Denton, 1974—; adj. prof. North Tex. State U., Denton, 1979-80; cons., lectr. Am. Montessori Soc., N.Y.C., 1970—, Japanese Montessori Soc., 1978—, also pub. and pvt. schs., 1972—; chair commn. for accreditation Montessori Accreditation Coun. Tchr. Edn., 1991-97, chair emerita, 1997—; cons. Public Montessori Programs, 1995-. Developer various Montessori materials; contbr. articles to profl. jours. Mem. AAUW, No. Ohio Montessori Assn. (pres. 1968-70), Assn. Montessori Internat., N.Am. Montessori Tchrs. Assn Avocations: ecology, golf, reading, travel. Home: 2005 Marshall Rd Denton TX 76207-3316 Personal E-mail: swest4smtc@aol.com.

MCDONELL, HORACE GEORGE, JR., instrument company executive; b. NYC, Sept. 23, 1928; s. Horace Gustave and Anabel (Armstrong) McD.; m. Eileen Romar, Sept. 6, 1952; children: Victoria (dec.), Diane, Horace. AB, Adelphi Coll., 1952; postgrad., Harvard U., 1962; DHL, Adelphi Coll., 2002. Engr. Sperry Gyroscope Co., NYC, 1952; with Perkin-Elmer Corp., Norwalk, Conn., 1963—, mgr. instrument group, 1967-77, v.p., 1966-69, sr. v.p., 1969-77, exec. v.p., 1977-80, pres., 1980-85, chmn., 1985-90, ret., 1990. Bd. dirs. Perkin Elmer, Ltd., U.K. UniRoyal, Inc., Perkin Elmer Internat., Inc., Harvey Hubbell, Inc., Ethan Allen Inc.; Mem. adv. task force on export controls U.S. Def. Sci. Bd., 1975—, chmn. instrumentation subcom., 1975— Mem. Bd. Edn., Ridgefield, Conn., 1969; Bd. dirs. Conn. Sci. Fair.; Trustee, bd. dirs. Danbury (Conn.) Hosp.; trustee Adelphi U.; bd. dirs. Danbury Health Svcs. With AUS, 1946-48. Mem. Sci. Apparatus Maker Assn. (dir., chmn. analytical instrument sect.), Am. Inst. Physics, AAAS, Instrument Soc. Am., Am. Electronics Assn. (bd. dirs. 1984-89, chmn. 1987) E-mail: hmcdonell@comcast.net.

MCDONELL, ROBERT TERRY, magazine editor, novelist; b. Norfolk, Va., Aug. 1, 1944; s. Robert Meinard and Irma Sophronia (Nelson) McD.; m. Joan Raffeld Hitzig, June 15, 1981; Robert Nicholas Campbell, Thomas Hunter Campbell. Student, U. Calif., Berkeley, 1962-63, San Jose State U., 1963-64; BA in Art, U. Calif., Irvine, 1967. With AP, NYC, 1970-72; reporter Los Angeles Weekly, 1972-73; asso. editor San Francisco mag., 1974-76, City mag., San Francisco, 1976-77; sr. editor San Francisco mag., 1977, Outside mag., San Francisco, 1978-79; founding editor Rocky Mountain mag., Denver, 1979-80; mng. editor Rolling Stone mag., NYC, 1980-83; asst. mng. editor Newsweek Mag., NYC, 1983-86; founder Smart mag., NYC, 1986-90; editor-in-chief Esquire mag., NYC, 1990-93; editor-in-chief, pub. Sports Afield Mag., NYC, 1994-97; editor Men's Journal, 1997-99; v.p. Wenner Media, 1997—; editor-in-chief US Weekly, NYC, 2000—02; mng. editor Sports Illustrated, NYC, 2002—. Author: California Bloodstock, 1980, paperback edit., 1989; screenwriter: Miami Vice, China Beach. Office: US Weekly 1290 Avenue Of The Americas Fl 2 New York NY 10104-0298

MCDONELL, TERRY, publishing executive, writer, editor; b. Santa Cruz, Calif. m. Joanie McDonell; children: Robert Nicholas, Thomas Hunter. Attended, U. Calif. at Berkeley and Irvine. Worked on film in Tehran, Iran; began career in journalism as freelance photographer; writer, photographer NY Associated Press, 1971; founder, writer, editor Outside, 1977, Rocky Mountain, 1979; mng. editor Rolling Stone, 1981—83; asst. mng. editor Newsweek, 1983—88; founder, pres., editor Smart, 1988—90; editor-in-chief Esquire, 1990—93; editor-in-chief, publishing editor Sports Afield, 1993—97, publishing/editorial dir., 1997; editor Men's Jour., 1997—99, editor-in-chief, 1999—2000, Us Weekly, 2000—02; mng. editor Sports Illus., 2002; editor Sports Illus. Group Time Inc. Author: California Bloodstock, 1980; screenwriter: TV series Miami Vice, China Beach. Avocations: painting, surfing. Office: Sports Illustrated 1271 Avenue of the Americas New York NY 10020 Office Phone: 212-522-1650. Office Fax: 212-522-7117. E-mail: Terry_McDonell@simail.com. *

MCDONNELL, BOB (ROBERT FRANCIS), state attorney general, former state legislator; b. Phila., June 15, 1954; m. Maureen Patricia Gardner; children: Jeanine, Cailin, Rachel, Robert, Sean. BBA in Mgmt., U. Notre Dame, 1976; MBA, Boston U., 1980; MA, JD, Regent U., 1989. Various positions Am. Hosp. Supply Corp., 1981—85; policy intern, Rep. Policy Com. US Ho. Reps, 1988; law clk. Office Commonwealth's Atty., Chesapeake, 1989, asst. Commonwealth atty. Virginia Beach, 1990—91; mem. Va. State Legis., 1992—2006, asst. majority leader, 2002—06, mem. cts. of justice com., mem. edn. com., mem. health welfare & insts. com., mem. Chesapeake and its tributaries com.; ptnr. Huff, Poole & Mahoney, P.C., Virginia Beach, 1992—2006; atty. gen. State of Va., Richmond, 2006—. Served in US Army, 1976—81 USAR, 1981—97. Named Legislator of Yr., Network of Victims of Crime, 1996, Family Found., 1998, 2001, Nat. Legislator of Yr., Nat. Child Support Enforcement Assn., 1998, Legislator of Yr., Va Sheriff's Assn., 2005. Republican. Roman Catholic. Office: Office Atty Gen 900 E Main St Richmond VA 23219 Office Fax: 804-786-2071. *

MCDONNELL, DAVID CROFT, diversified financial services company executive; Nat. mng. ptnr. Grant Thornton Internat. (UK office), 1989—2001; global CEO Grant Thornton Internat., 2001—. Office: Grant Thornton Internat 175 W Jackson Blvd Chicago IL 60604

MCDONNELL, JOSEPH B., lawyer; b. Salina, Kans., Nov. 20, 1935; s. John Francis and Edith (Engle) McD.; m. Betty E. Marlin, Nov. 27, 1965; children: Jean Elizabeth, Jennifer Ann. BS in Govt., St. Louis U., 1958, LLB, 1960. Bar: Ill. 1960, Mo. 1960, U.S. Ct. Appeals (7th cir.) 1973. Law clk. U.S. Dist. Ct., Springfield, Ill., 1960-61; assoc. Pope & Driemeyer, East St. Louis, Ill., 1961-66; ptnr. Dixon & McDonnell, Belleville, Ill., 1966-75, 1975—98, Churchill, Nester & McDonnell, Belleville, 1998—. Mem. character and fitness com. Ill. Supreme Ct., 1978-83. Committeeman St. Clair County Democratic Party, 1974. With USAR, 1953-61. Fellow Ill. Bar Found.; mem. ABA, Ill. Bar Assn., St. Clair County Bar Assn. (pres. 1977-78, del. assembly 1986-92), Acad. Ill. Laureates. Roman Catholic. Home Phone: 618-394-0526; Office Phone: 618-259-7308. Personal E-mail: jbm@greensfelder.com.

MCDONNELL, SANFORD NOYES, air transportation executive; b. Little Rock, Oct. 12, 1922; s. William Archie and Carolyn (Cherry) McD.; m. Priscilla Robb, Sept. 3, 1946; children: Robbin McDonnell MacVittie, William Randall. BA in Econs., Princeton U., 1945; BS in Mech. Engring., U. Colo., 1948; MS in Applied Mechanics, Washington U., St. Louis, 1954. With McDonnell Douglas Corp. (formerly McDonnell Aircraft Corp.), St. Louis, 1948—, v.p., 1959-66, pres. McDonnell Aircraft div., 1966-71, corp. exec. v.p., 1971, corp. pres., from 1971, chief exec. officer, from 1972, chmn., 1980-88, chmn. emeritus, 1988—. Mem. exec. bd. St. Louis and nat. councils Boy Scouts Am.; trustee, elder Presbyn. Ch.; chmn. emeritus Character Edn. Partnership, Washington, 1993-2005, chmn. emeritus, 2005—. Fellow AIAA; mem. Navy League U.S. (life), Tau Beta Pi Office: McDonnell Douglas Corp PO Box 516 Saint Louis MO 63166-0516

MCDONNELL, THOMAS A., information technology executive; b. Kansas City, Mo. BSBA in Acctg., Rockhurst Univ., 1966; MBA, Univ. Pa., 1968. With DST Systems, Inc., 1969—, pres., 1973—84, 1987—, treas., 1973—95, vice chmn., 1984—95, CEO, 1984—. Bd. dir. DST Systems Inc., 1971—, BHA Group Holdings Inc., Blue Valley Ban Corp., Commerce Bancshares Inc., Computer Sci. Corp., Euronet Worldwide Inc., Garmin Ltd., Janus Capital Corp., Ascential Software Inc., Asurion. Trustee Ewing Marion Kauffman Found., 2003—; chmn. Greater Kansas City C. of C., 1994, Civic Coun. Greater Kansas City, 1999—2001; bd. dir. Greater Kansas City Cmty. Found., Midwest Rsch. Inst., Harry S Truman Libr. Inst.; trustee Rockhurst Univ. Office: DST Systems 333 W 11th St Kansas City MO 64105 Office Phone: 816-435-1000. *

MCDONOUGH, BRIDGET ANN, music theatre company director; b. Milw., June 19, 1956; d. James and Lois (Hunzinger) McD.; m. Gregory Paul Opelka, Sept. 20, 1986 (div. Aug. 1993); m. Robert Markey, Feb. 29, 2000. BS, Northwestern U., 1978. Bus. mgr. Organic Theater Co., Chgo., 1979-80; mng. dir., founder Light Opera Works, Evanston, Ill., 1980—. U.S. rep. European Congress Musical Theatre, 1995. Founder, mem. Chgo. Music Alliance, 1984—, pres., 1995-98; mem. Ill. Arts Alliance; bd. dirs., Nat. Alliance for Musical Theatre, 2001-2005, sec., 2001—04; bd. dirs. Evanston Convention Visitors Bur., 1999-2002; mem. alumni adv. bd. Northwestern U. Sch. Speech, 1999-2002; bd. dirs. Around the Coyote Arts Festival, 2002—. Recipient Women on the Move award Evanston YWCA, 1991. Mem. Evanston C. of C. (bd. dirs., 1993-99), North Shore Internat. Network, Rotary (pres. Evanston chpt. 1999-00), Union League Club. Avocation: birdwatching. Office: Light Opera Works 927 Noyes St Evanston IL 60201-6206

MCDONOUGH, JOHN MICHAEL, lawyer; b. Evanston, Ill., Dec. 30, 1944; s. John Justin and Anne Elizabeth (O'Brien) McD.; m. Susan J. Moran, Sept. 19, 1981; children: John E., Catherine Anne. AB, Princeton U., 1966; LLB, Yale U., 1969. Bar: Ill. 1969, Fla. 1991. Assoc. Sidley & Austin, Chgo., 1969-75, ptnr., 1975—. Bd. dirs. Met. Planning Coun., 1978—, pres., 1982-84; bd. dirs. Ctr. Am. Archeology, 1980-85, chmn., 1982-84; bd. dirs. Leadership Greater Chgo., 1984-90, sec.-treas., 1987-90; bd. dis. Brian Rsch. Found., 1985—, pres., 1989-94, chmn. 1999-. With JAGC, USAR, 1969-75. Mem. ABA, Racquet Club, Saddle & Cycle Club, Commonwealth Club, Phi Beta Kappa. Democrat. Episcopalian. Home: 1407 N Dearborn St Chicago IL 60610-1505

MCDONOUGH, KENNETH LEE, pharmaceutical company medical administrator; b. Buffalo, Apr. 7, 1953; s. Sidney Lee and Jeanne Francis (Sheets) McD.; children: Jameson, Laurel, Meghan; m. Connie Kay Staley; stepchildren: Audrey, Kelsie. BS, U. Minn., 1975, MD, 1979, MS, 1986. Diplomate Am. Bd. Quality Assurance and Utilization Rev. Physicians. Resident in occupl. medicine U. Calif., San Francisco, 1984; v.p. Indsl. Health and Hygiene Group, Mpls., 1982-86; pvt. practice occupl. medicine, 1985—92; v.p. Am. Gen. Ins., Dallas, 1986-88, Mut. of Omaha Ins., Omaha, 1988-91, sr. v.p., 1991-95; med. dir. Stuart Disease Mgmt. Svcs. Inc., Wilmington, Del., 1995-98; asst. clin. prof. dept. preventive medicine and pub. health Creighton U. Sch. Medicine, 1994—; med. dir. AstraZeneca Pharms., Wilmington, Del., 1998—; instr. Monmouth (NJ) U., 2004—. Instr. nursing Gustavus Adolphus Coll. Nursing, St. Paul, 1984-86; instr. astronomy Met. State U., St. Paul, 1982-83; prin. rsch. into cost effectiveness of Dr. Dean Ornish's coronary reversal program in collaboration with Harvard Med. Sch., 1992-95. Author and designer of computer software. Instr. Sci. Mus. of Minn., St. Paul, 1982. Recipient Design Excellence award Seako, Inc., 1987, 3M Creativity award Minn. Mining & Mfg., 1971; recipient acad. scholarships. Mem. Am. Coll. Med. Quality, Am. Coll. Occupl. and Environ. Medicine, Nat. Assn. Managed Care Physicians, Gt. Plains Occupl. Medicine Assn. (nominating com. 1990-91), Am. Lung Assn. Nebr. (bd. dirs. 1995—), Disease Mgmt. Assn. Am. (bd. dirs. 2005—), Phi Kappa Phi. Avocations: genealogy, travel, astronomy, medical informatics, ancient history. Home: 9 Devonshire Ct Greenville DE 19807-2572 Office: Astrazeneca Pharmaceuticals 1800 Concord Pike Wilmington DE 19803-2902 Office Phone: 302-886-2001. Business E-Mail: kenneth.mcdonough@astrazeneca.com.

MCDONOUGH, KRISTIN, library director; Positions through chief libr. Baruch Coll. CUNY, 1971—96; Robert & Joyce Menschel dir. NYPL Sci., Ind. & Bus. Libr., NYC, 1996—. Recipient John Jacob Astor award, Continuing Edn. Initiative for Spl. Rsch. Libraries, 2003. Office: Science Industry & Business Library 188 Madison Ave New York NY 10016

MCDONOUGH, RAENELL, musician, educator; b. Amarillo, Tex., Aug. 19, 1946; d. Ray Sam and Doris Winnie (Williams) Roberts; m. Jerome F. McDonough, Dec. 21, 1978 (dec.); 1 child, Brian Christopher. BA in Music Edn., W. Tex. State U., Canyon, 1968, MEd, 1971. Music edn. cert., elem. edn. cert. Music educator Amarillo Ind. Sch. Dist., 1968—73; music educator, piano accompanist, performer W. Tex. State U., Canyon, 1973—89; pianist Amarillo Opera, 1989—; coach, accompanist, instr. music theory and organ Amarillo Coll., 2000—. Mem. textbook com. Amarillo Ind. Sch. Dist., 1970. Mem. W. Tex. State U. Friends Fine Arts Assn., 1980—, Amarillo Little Theatre Guild, 1980—, Friends Aeolian Skinner, Amarillo, 2004—, Amarillo United Citizens Forum, 2006, W. Tex. A&M U. Found., Canyon, Amarillo Youth Choir Orgn., Sta. KACV-TV PBS Orgn., Amarillo; mem., sec. exec. bd., trustee Amarillo Opera, 2006—; organist, music coord. St. Paul Meth. Ch., Amarillo, 1968—. Named Outstanding Young Women Am., 1980; recipient Bill and Louise Dee Vol. award, Amarillo Opera, 1997—98. Mem.: Amarillo Symphony Guild, Tex. CC Tchrs. Assn., Amarillo Art Force (sec. exec. bd. 2006—), Am. Guild Organists (sub-dean 1990—95). Avocations: travel, crafts, reading, theater. Home: 6106 Dartmouth Amarillo TX 79109

MCDONOUGH, RICHARD MICHAEL, philosophy educator; b. Pitts., Jan. 29, 1950; s. Walter and Marilyn (Duman) McD.; m. Mary Lau, July 26, 1991. BA summa cum laude, U. Pitts., 1971; MA, Cornell U., 1974, PhD, 1975. Asst. prof. philosophy Bates Coll., Lewiston, Maine, 1975-82; sr. lectr. Nat. U. Singapore, 1982-91; asst. prof. philosophy U. Tulsa, 1991—; assoc. prof. philosophy, psychology U. Putra Malaysia, Selangor, 1997-98; prof. philosophy Overseas Family School: The College, Republic of Singapore, 1999—; assoc. lectr. PSB Acad., 2005—; lectr. philosophy and psychology lectr. U. Md. Asia divsn., 2007—. Editor Wittgenstein and cognitive sci. spl. issue Idealistic Studies, 1999; tchr. math. dept. U. Md., 2007. Author: The Argument of the Tractatus, 1986, Martin Heidegger's Being and Time, 2006; contbr. articles to profl. jours. Woodrow Wilson fellow, 1971-72, NSF fellow, 1971-74; postdoctoral rsch. grantee NEH, Ind. U., 1980-81. Mem. Australasian Debating Fedn. (hon. life, adjudicator 1991—), Phi Kappa Phi. Achievements include prodn. of original interpretation of Wittgenstein's logical-metaphys. sys., original application Kantian Copernican Revolution to philosophy of lang.; significant interdisciplinary work logic, linguistics, psychology & philosophy. Business E-Mail: rmcdonough@asia.umuc.edu. E-mail: richmary@pacific.net.sg, the_philosopher1950@yahoo.com.

MCDONOUGH, RUSSELL CHARLES, retired state supreme court justice; b. Glendive, Mont., Dec. 7, 1924; s. Roy James and Elsie Marie (Johnson) McD.; m. Dora Jean Bidwell, Mar. 17, 1946; children: Ann Remmich, Michael, Kay Jensen, Kevin, Daniel, Mary Garfield. JD, George Washington U., 1949. Bar: Mont. 1950. Pvt. practice, Glendive, Mont., 1950-83; judge Gen. Jurisdiction State of Montana, Glendive, 1983-87; justice Mont. Supreme Ct., Helena, 1987-93, ret., 1993. City atty. City of Glendive, 1953-57; county atty. Dawson County, Mon., 1957-63; del. Mont. Constl. Conv., Helena, 1972. 1st lt. USAAF, 1943-45, ETO. Decorated DFC. Mem. Mont. Bar Assn. Roman Catholic. Home: 210 Gresham St Glendive MT 59330 Personal E-mail: swedemc@yahoo.com.

MCDONOUGH, THOMAS P., health care company executive; BBA, Northeastern U. COO Jardine Group Svcs. Corp., 1988—93; pres. Harrington Svcs. Corp., 1993—95; sr. v.p. claim svcs. United HealthCare, Inc., 1995—97, exec. v.p. customer svc. group, 1997, CEO Uniprise, 1997—98; exec. v.p., COO Coventry Health Care, Bethesda, Md., 1998—2005, pres., 2005—. Bd. dir. FireLogic Homes. Office: Coventry Health Care 6705 Rockleged Drive Bethesda MD 20817 *

MCDONOUGH, WILLIAM ANDREWS, architect; b. Tokyo, Feb. 20, 1951; s. James Edwin and Sara (Andrews) McDonough; m. Elizabeth Demetriades, May 30, 1981. AB, Dartmouth Coll., 1973; postgraduate studies in Art, Yale U., 1973-76, M.Arch., 1976. Registered architect, NY. Photographer, Kilkenny Design Workshop, Ireland, 1974; architect, builder William A. McDonough, Cork, Ireland, 1974-77; architect Davis, Brody & Assocs., NYC, 1977-81; prin. Mad River Hydro, Warren, Vt., 1981—; prin. McDonough, Rainey Architects, NYC, 1981-85, McDonough Nouri Rainey & Assocs., Inc., NYC, 1985—; founding ptnr., William McDonough & Ptnrs.; dean sch. architecture, U. Va., Charlottesville, 1994-99, founder, McDonough Braungart Design Chemistry, 1995-; cons. Inst. for Indsl. Rsch. and Standards, Dublin, Ireland, 1975-77; dir. North Wind Power Co., Inc., Moretown, Vt., 1982; dir. Am. Residential Architecture Found., NYC, 1983—. Founder Solar Energy Soc. Ireland, Dublin, 1976. Mem AIA. Club: Yale (NYC); Author: (with Michael Braungart) Hannover Principles: Design for Sustainability, 1992, Cradle to Cradle: Remaking the Way We Make Things, 2002; Recipient: Presdl. award for Sustainable Devel., 1996, Design of Yr. award, Bus. Week & Archtl. Record mags., 1997, Presdl. Green Chemistry award, 2003, Nat. Design award, 2004; named one of 50 Who Matter Now CNNMoney.com Bus. 2.0, 2006. Office: William McDonough & Ptnrs 700 E Jefferson St Charlottesville VA 22902 *

MCDONOUGH, WILLIAM J., diversified financial services company executive; b. Chgo., 1934; married. BS, Coll. of Holy Cross, 1956; MA, Georgetown U., 1962. With Dept. of State, 1961-67, 1st Nat. Bank of Chgo., 1967-89, asst. v.p. internat. banking dept., 1967-70, v.p., gen. mgr. Paris, 1970-72, area head, Europe, Mid. East and Africa, 1972-73, sr. v.p., head internat. banking dept., 1973-75, exec. v.p., 1975-86, CFO, 1982-89, chmn. asset and liability mgmt. com., until 1989; vice chmn. 1st Chgo. Corp. and 1st Nat. Bank Chgo., 1986-89; exec. v.p., head markets group Fed. Res. Bank of N.Y., NYC, 1992-93, pres., CEO, 1993—2003; chmn. Pub. Co. Acctg. Oversight Bd., Washington, 2003—05; vice chmn. Merrill Lynch & Co., Inc., NYC, 2006—. Bd. dirs. N.Y. Philharm. Orch.; chmn. investments com. joint staff pension fund UN. Home Phone: 212-838-1188; Office Phone: 212-449-0871. Business E-Mail: william_mcdonough@ml.com.

MCDONOUGH-TREICHLER, JUDITH DIANNE, medical educator, consultant; b. LA, Aug. 15, 1938; d. William Charles and Eleanor (Lewis) Anderson; m. Raymond Milan McDonough, Mar. 2, 1957 (div. Oct. 2, 1974); children: Joyce Churchill, Steven McDonough, Jill Cannon; m. John Rex Treichler, June 2, 1985. BS in Health Edn., Calif. State U., Long

Beach, 1978; MS in Health Care Adminstrn., U. LaVerne, Calif., 1981; PhD in Pub. Health, Loma Linda U., Calif., 1991. Cert. registered nurse, Calif., health edn. specialist nat. Commn. for Health Edn. Credentialing. Dir. health edn. Nat. Med. Enterprises, Lakewood, Calif., 1972-80, Taif, Saudi Arabia, 1980-82, health educator Manila, Philippines, 1983; dir. health promotion and edn. Med. Ptnrs. US Family Care, Montclair, Calif., 1992-97; adj. faculty prof. U. LaVerne, Calif., 1986—, U. Phoenix, Ontario, Calif., 1996—, Crafton Hills Coll., Yucaipa, Calif., 1997—; owner, exec. v.p. JJS Health Edn. Cons., Rancho Cucamonga, Calif., 1996—. Rsch. asst. Loma Linda (Calif.) U., 1995-97; adv. bd. mem. Cerritos (Calif.) Coll., 1975-80, U. LaVerne, Calif., 1996—. Contbr. articles to profl. jours. Contbg. mem. La Liga Flying Samaritans, Rosario Mex., 1978-80, Friendship For Animals, Rancho Cucamong, Calif., 1995—. Recipient Dean's fellowship Loma Linda (Calif.) U., 1988. Mem. APHA, Calif. Scholarship Fedn., Nat. Coun. Against Health Fraud, World Clowns Assn., Clowns of Am. Internat., Calif. State U. Alumni Assn., Alpha Gamma Sigma. Avocation: clowning. Office: U LaVerne Dept Health Svcs Mgmt 1950 3d St La Verne CA 91750 Home: 5152 Breckinridge Ave Banning CA 92220-7153

MCDOUGAL, STUART YEATMAN, comparative literature educator, author; b. LA, Apr. 10, 1942; s. Murray and Marian (Yeatman) McDougal; m. Menakka Weerasinghe, Apr. 29, 1967 (div. 1977); children: Dyanthe Rose, Gavin Rohan; m. Nora Gunneng, Aug. 4, 1979; children: Angus Gunneng, Tobias Yeatman. BA, Haverford Coll., 1964; MA, U. Pa., 1965, PhD, 1970. Lectr. U. Lausanne, Switzerland, 1965-66; asst. prof. Mich. State U., East Lansing, 1970-72; from asst. prof. to prof. English, comparative lit. and film /video U. Mich., Ann Arbor, 1972-85; dir. program in comparative lit. U. Mich., Ann Arbor, 1981-97, asst. to dean spl. projects, 1997-98; Dewitt Wallace prof. English, chair English Dept. Macalester Coll., St. Paul, 1998—2005; vis. scholar Cornell U., 2006—. Vis. prof. film Aegean Inst., Greece, 1994; vis. scholar Senapulli, Brazil, 1996. Author: Ezra Pound and the Troubadour Tradition, 1972 (Bredvold prize 1973), 1973; Made into Movies: From Literature to Film, 1985, Korean edit., 2002; editor: Dante Among the Moderns, 1985; co-editor: Play It Again, Sam: Retakes on Remakes, 1998; editor: Stanley Kubrick's A Clockwork Orange, 2003; contbr. articles to profl. jours. Am. Council of Learned Socs. fellow, 1974-75; U. Mich. Rackham Research grantee, 1975-76; Fulbright Assn. sr. lectr., Italy, 1978; recipient Faculty Recognition award, U. Mich., 1987. Fellow Dirs. Guild Am. (summr workshop, 1993); mem. MLA, Am. Comparative Lit. Assn. (sec.-treas. 1983-89, v.p. 1989-91, pres. 1991-93), Internat. Comparative Lit. Assn., Soc. Cinema Studies. Democrat. Office: Cornell U English Dept Ithaca NY 14850 Business E-Mail: mcdougal@macalester.edu, sym23@cornell.edu.

MCDOUGAL, WILLIAM SCOTT, urology educator; b. Grand Rapids, Mich., 1942; s. William Julian and Verna Wilma (Pasma) McD.; m. Mary Stuart Logan, Sept. 19, 1992; 1 child, Molly Katherine. AB, Dartmouth Coll., 1964; MD, Cornell U., 1968. Intern in surgery U. Hosps., Cleve., 1968-69, resident in surgery, 1969-75, attending urologist, 1977-80; postdoctoral fellow in physiology Yale U., New Haven, 1971-72; postdoctoral fellow in surgery Case-Western Res. U., Cleve., 1972-75; chief, burn study div. Inst. Surg. Rsch. Brooke Army Med. Ctr., Ft. Sam Houston, 1975-77; instr. surgery U. Tex., San Antonio, 1975-77; asst. prof. urology Case Western Res. U., Cleve., 1977-78, assoc. prof., 1978-80, Dartmouth Coll., Hanover, NH, 1980-84, chmn. dept. urology, 1982-84; prof., chmn. dept. urology Vanderbilt U., Nashville, 1984-90; Walter S. Kerr Jr. prof. urology Harvard Med. Sch., 1996—; chief urology Mass. Gen. Hosp., Boston, 1990—. Office: Mass Gen Hosp Dept Urology Fruit St Boston MA 02114

MCDOUGALL, DONALD BLAKE, retired provincial official, librarian; BA, BEd, U. Sask., 1966; BLS, U. Toronto, 1969; MLS, U. Alta., 1983, cert. pub. adminstrn., 1990. Classroom tchr. Regina Bd. Edn., Sask., 1960-63, vice prin., 1963-68; asst. chief libr. Stratford Pub. Libr., Ont., Canada, 1969, chief libr., 1970-72; supr. info. svcs. Edmonton Pub. Libr., Alta., Canada, 1972, head pub. svcs., 1973-74; legislature libr. Legis. Assembly Alta., Edmonton, 1974-87, asst. dep. min., legis. libr., 1987—93; ret., 1993. Editor microfilm: Alberta Scrapbook Hansard, 1906-1964, 1976; editor: A History of the Legislature Library, 1979; author: Princess Louise Caroline Alberta, 1988, Premiers of the Northwest Territories and Alberta, 1876-1991, 1991; co-author, editor: Lieutenant-Governors of the Northwest Territories and Alberta, 1876-1991; (pamphlet) Canadian Parliamentary Libraries, 1989. Govt. Sask. scholar, 1965; recipient Queen's Silver Jubilee medal Govt. Can., 1977; named Hon. Clk.-At-The-Table, Legis. Assembly Alberta, 1987-93. Mem. Alta. Govt. Librs. Coun. (chmn. 1975), Assn. Parliamentary Librs. in Can. (pres. 1980-82), Edmonton Libr. Assn., Hist. Soc. Alta. (v.p. Edmonton chpt. 1987), Libr. Assn. Alta., Can. Libr. Assn., Edmonton Jaguar Drivers Club, Edmonton Jazz Soc., Can. Vintage Motorcycle Assn., Beta Phi Mu. Presbyterian.

MC DOUGALL, DUGALD STEWART, retired lawyer; b. Indpls., May 15, 1916; s. George and Effie (Barclay) McD.; m. Carol Brueggeman, Aug. 1938; children: George, Duncan, Walter, Robert; m. Judith Stephen, Dec. 1967. AB, U. Chgo., 1935, JD, 1937. Bar: Ill. 1937. Since practiced in, Chgo.; sr. ptnr. McDougall, Hersh & Scott, 1961-87. Sec., dir. Aladdin Industries, Inc. Served with USNR, 1942-46. Fellow Am. Coll. Trial Lawyers; mem. ABA, Am. Patent Law Assn., Patent Law Assn. Chgo., Law Club Chgo., Union League (Chgo.). Clubs: Union League (Chgo.); Olympia Fields (Ill.) Country. Office: 25 Pine Forest Ln Haines City FL 33844-9675

MCDOUGALL, HEATHER RENEE, political science professor; d. William D. McDougall, II and Diane D. McDougall; m. Jason Craig Widen, Nov. 26, 2004. BA, Denver U., 1996; MA, U. Calif., Santa Barbara, 1998; PhD, Ind. U., Bloomington, 2005. Asst. prof. Christopher Newport U., Newport News, Va., 2006—; dir. Global Inst. Leadership and Civic Devel., Inc., Bloomington, Ind., 2000—. Mem.: Midwest Polit. Sci. Assn., Am. Polit. Sci. Assn., Phi Beta Kappa. Office: Christopher Newport Univ 1 University Pl Newport News VA 23606 Home Phone: 812-219-1660; Office Phone: 757-594-8400. Business E-Mail: heather.mcdougall@cnu.edu.

MCDOUGALL, IAIN ROSS, nuclear medicine educator; b. Glasgow, Scotland, Dec. 18, 1943; came to U.S., 1976; s. Archibald McDougall and Jean Cairns; m. Elizabeth Wilson, Sept. 6, 1968; children: Shona, Stewart. MB, ChB, U. Glasgow, 1967, PhD, 1973. Diplomate Am. Bd. Nuclear Medicine (chmn. 1985-87), Am. Bd. Internal Medicine (gov. 1984-86). Lectr. in medicine U. Glasgow, 1969-76; fellow Harkness-Stanford Med. Ctr., 1972-74; assoc. prof. radiology and medicine Stanford U., Calif., 1976-84, prof. radiology and medicine, 1985—. Contbr. numerous articles to sci. jours. Fellow Royal Coll. Physicians (Glasgow), Am. Coll. Physicians; mem. Am. Thyroid Assn., Soc. Nuclear Medicine, Western Assn. for Clin. Research. Office: Stanford U Med Ctr Divsn Nuclear Medicine Stanford CA 94305 Office Phone: 650-725-4711. Business E-Mail: rossmcdougall@stanford.edu.

MCDOUGALL, RONALD ALEXANDER, restaurant executive; b. Chgo., Aug. 12, 1942; s. John A. and Doris E. (Sengstock) McD.; m. Dale O. Ryser, Feb. 1, 1964 (div. July 1969); children: Timothy, Jonathan; m. Carolyn Kay Conley, Aug. 9, 1979; 1 child, Matthew. BBA, U. Wis., 1964, MBA, 1965. With Procter & Gamble, Cin., 1967-68, Sara Lee, Deerfield, Ill., 1969-72, The Pillsbury Co., Mpls., 1972-74, S&A Restaurant Corp., Dallas, 1974-82, Burger King, Miami, Fla., 1982-83; pres., CEO,& COO Brinker Internat., Dallas, 1983—. Bd. dirs. Brinker Internat., Excel Comm., Inc. With U.S. Army, 1965-67. Mem. Nat. Restaurant Assn., Am. Mgmt. Assn., Bent Tree Country Club, Aerobics Activity Ctr., Employment Policies Inst. Republican. Presbyterian. Avocations: running, bicycling, golf.

MC DOW, JOHN JETT, biosystems engineering educator; b. Covington, Tenn., Jan. 6, 1925; s. Robert Simpson and Lucy Ann (Cocke) McD.; m. Dorothy Virginia Glass, Dec. 22, 1946 (dec. Dec. 2004); children: Ronald Allan, Jane Virginia. Student, Franklin and Marshall Coll., 1944-45; BS, U. Tenn., 1948; MS, Mich. State U., 1949, PhD, 1957. Registered profl. engr., Tenn., La. Instr. Mich. State U., 1949, Okla. State U., 1949-51, asst. prof. agrl. engring., 1951; assoc. prof. La. Poly. U., 1951-57, prof., 1957-62, head agrl. engring. dept., 1953-62; prof., head dept. biosys. engring. U. Tenn., Knoxville, 1962-73, dean admissions and records, 1973-83, prof. agrl. engring., 1983-92, prof. emeritus, 1992—. Cons., collaborator Agrl. Research Service, US Dept. Agr., 1970-76; leader Rotary Internat. Found. Group Study Exchange Team to Philippines, 1984; mem. scholarship selection com. N.Am. Philips Corp., 1976-88. Contbr. articles to profl. jours. Mem. La. Engring. Coun., 1955-56; bd. dirs. Tenn.-Venezuela-Amazonas Partners, 1977-80; vol. Internat. Centennial Olympic Summer Games, Atlanta, 1996. With USN, 1943—46, comdr. USNR, to 1977. So. Fellowship grantee, 1957. Mem. Am. Soc. Agrl. Engring. (dir. 1973-75), Am. Soc. Engring. Edn. (sec. agrl. engring. div. 1971-72, vice chmn. 1972-73, chmn. 1973-74), Sigma Xi, Tau Beta Pi, Pi Mu Epsilon, Omicron Delta Kappa, Gamma Sigma Delta, Phi Kappa Phi (v.p. 1971-77, nat. pres. elect 1977-80, pres. 1980-83, pres. found. 1974-78). Lodges: Rotary (pres. 1989-90, chmn. dist. scholarship selection com., 1982-87, 88-91). Presbyterian. Home: 2008 Walnut Hills Dr Knoxville TN 37920-2946

MCDOWELL, BARBARA, artist; b. Paducah, Ky., Jan. 6, 1921; d. William Bryan Rouse and Mary Marguerite Thomasson; m. William Wells McDowell, Jan. 6, 1944 (dec. 1976). AA, Delmar Coll., Corpus Christi, 1940; BA with hons., Corpus Christi State U., 1986; MA in Studio Art, Tex. A&M U., Corpus Christi, 2003. Artist Davison Paxon, Atlanta, 1944—45; layout artist Tucker Wayne & Co., Atlanta, 1945—46; fashion illustrator Lichtenstein's, Corpus Christi, 1948—49, 1951—52; artist, art dir. Adcraft Advt. Agy., Corpus Christi, 1952—79; owner, artist, writer B. McDowell Graphic Design, Corpus Christi, 1979—2000. One-woman shows include Corpus Christi Mus. Sci. and History, 1973, Bayfront Plz Auditorium, Corpus Christi, 1976, Art Ctr. of Corpus Christi, 1983, 2003, 2006, Tex. A&M U., Kingsville, 1990, Galeria LaVentana, Corpus Christi, 1992—94, Galvan House, 2001, 2002, 2004, exhibited in group shows at S. Tex. Art League, 1972—2006, S.W. Sculpture Soc., 1972—2006, Tex. Watercolor Soc., San Antonio, 1968, 1978, 1982, 1998, Tex. Fine Arts Assn., Austin, 1975, 1979, 1986, Southwestern Watercolor Soc., Dallas, 1985, Hill Country Arts Found., Igram, Tex., 1990, Art Mus. S. Tex., 1990, 2000, 2006, Tex. A&M U. Alumni Show, Corpus Christi, 1992, Upstairs Gallery, 1992, 1996, Third Biennial Gulf of Mex. Symposium, 1995, Gallery Leszarts - Les Cerquex Sous Passavant, France, 1998, Watercolor Art Soc. Houston, 1998, Estelle Stair Art Gallery, Rockport, Tex., 1999, Rockport Ctr. for Arts, 2000, Wilhelmi-Holland Art Gallery, 2000, Watercolor Soc. of S. Texas, Corpus Christi. Donor Art Ctr. Coll. Design, Pasadena, Calif., 1979—, Corpus Christi Botanical Gardens, 1991—, Driscoll Children's Hosp., Corpus Christi, 1995—, Art Mus. S. Tex., 1995, Tex. A & M U., Corpus Christi, 2000—; mem. Rockport Ctr. for Arts; pres. Art Ctr. of Corpus Christi, 2004—05; mem. Art Mus. of S. Tex., Corpus Christi, 1994—, bd. govs., 2005—; mem., com. chair Mcpl. Arts Commn., Corpus Christi, 1986—92. Recipient Nat. Drawing and Sculpture award, Del Mar Coll., 1986, 1993, 1998, Vol. Cert. of Excellence, Caller Times, 1993, prize, NCECA Regional Juried Ceramics Exhibit, Arlington Mus. Art, Ft. Worth, 1995, Purchase award, Tex. A&M U., Corpus Christi, 2002. Mem.: S.W. Sculpture Soc., Watercolor Soc. S. Tex. (pres. 1977—), S. Tex. Art League (chmn. 1976—). Avocations: gardening, ceramics, painting. Home: 302 Glenmore St Corpus Christi TX 78412

MCDOWELL, CARTER K., lawyer; b. Baton Rouge, Nov. 6, 1958; m. Jeanne Renaudin, Oct. 30, 1981; 3 children. BA, Univ. Tex., Austin, 1980; JD, La. State Univ., 1985; LLM, Boston Univ., 1986. Bar: La. 1985, Mass. 1986, D.C. 1989, Ohio 1991. Atty. Goodwin Proctor LLP, 1986—91, Bank One Corp., 1991—2001, legis. counsel Washington, 1995—2000, mgr. compliance dept., 1997—2001, Washington Representative Washington, 2000; sr. counsel Com. Fin. Svc., U.S. Ho. Rep., Washington, 2001—02, chief counsel, 2003—. Episcopalian. Office: Committee on Financial Services Room 2129 Rayburn House Office Building Washington DC 20515-6050 Office Phone: 202-225-7502.

MCDOWELL, CHARLES EAGER, lawyer, retired military officer; b. Manchester, NH, Sept. 9, 1923; s. Joseph Curry and Mildred (Eager) McD.; m. Carolyn A. Gibbons, June 21, 1947; children— Robin, Patricia. AB, Dartmouth Coll., 1947; JD, U. Va., 1950. Bar: Tex. 1950, Va. 1981, D.C. 1981. With land div. Shell Oil Co., Houston, 1950; commd. lt. (j.g.) USN, 1951, advanced through grades to rear adm., 1976; staff legal officer Comdr. Service Force, U.S. Pacific Fleet; staff judge adv., head internat. law div. Naval War Coll., 1963-66; staff legal officer, comdr. 7th Fleet, 1966-68; sr. Navy mem. ad hoc com., dep. asst. judge adv. gen. Office Judge Adv. Gen. Dept. Def., Washington, 1968-72; staff judge adv. on staff comdr. in chief U.S. Naval Forces, Europe, London, 1972-75; comdg. officer Naval Justice Sch., Newport, RI, 1975-76; dep. judge adv. gen. Navy Dept., Washington, 1976-78, judge adv. gen., 1978-80; pvt. practice Dumfries, Va., 1981-96. Served to 2d lt. AUS, 1943-46. Decorated D.S.M., Bronze Star, Joint Service Commendation medal, Navy Commendation medal with Combat V, Purple Heart, Combat Inf. badge. Mem. FBA, Tex. Bar Assn., Va. Bar Assn., Judge Advs. Assn., Order of Coif, Chi Phi, Square Dancer Club. Methodist. Home: 1106 Croton Dr Alexandria VA 22308-2008

MCDOWELL, DAVID LYNN, mechanical engineering educator; b. Red Oak, Iowa, Dec. 20, 1956; s. Leland Lee and Wilma McDowell; m. Kathryn M. McDowell, May 26, 1979; children: Matthew Todd, Andrew Joel, James Neal. BSME, U. Nebr., Lincoln, 1979; PhDME, U. Ill., Champaign, 1983. Asst. prof. mech. engring. Ga. Inst. Tech., Atlanta, 1983-87, assoc. prof., 1987-92, prof., 1992—, regents prof., 1996—, Carter N. Paden Jr. Disting. chair in metals processing, 1998—. Dir. Mech. Properties Rsch. Lab., 1992—; presenter in field. Mem. editl. bd. Internat. Jour. Plasticity, Fatigue and Fracture of Engring. Material Structure, Internat. Jour. Damage Mechs., Jour. Multiscale Computational Engring., Mechanics Advanced Materials and Structures; contbr. over 300 articles to profl. jours. and confs. Recipient Alfred Noble prize ASCE, 1986, Ralph R. Teetor award Soc. Automotive Engrs., Outstanding Young Faculty award Dow Chem. Soc., 1990, Presdl. Young Investigator award NSF, 1986. Fellow ASME (Henry Hess award 1988, Nadai award 1997, editor Jour. Engring. Material Tech. 1997-2002); mem. ASTM (ann. fatigue lectr., 2002), Am. Soc. Metals Internat., Materials Rsch. Soc., Am. Acad. Mechanics, Am. Soc. for Engring. Edn., Soc. Engring. Sci. (v.p. 2001, pres. 2002), Pi Tau Sigma (Gold medal 1987). Office: Ga Inst Tech GWW Sch Mech Engring Atlanta GA 30332-0405

MCDOWELL, DAVID MICHAEL, psychiatrist, educator, researcher; b. Middletown, Conn., Mar. 16, 1963; s. Arthur Vanall and Jacqueline Larson McDowell. MD, Columbia Coll. Physicians and Surgeons, 1989. Bd. cert. psychiatry Am. Bd. Psychiatry and Neurology, 1993, cert. addiction psychiatry Am. Bd. Psychiatry and Neurology, 1996. Fellow in addiction psychiatry NYU Med. Ctr., NYC, 1993—95; instr. psychiatry Bellevue Hosp./NYU Med. Ctr., NYC, 1995—; asst. prof. clin. psychiatry Columbia U. Coll. Physicians and Surgeons, NYC, 1995—; dir. buprenorphine program Columbia U.; founder, med. dir. STARS the Substance Treatment and Rsch. Svc. Columbia U., NYC, 1997—. Cons. Malinkrodt Pharmaceuticals, St. Louis, 2002—; cons. psychiatrist The Actors Fund. Author: (textbook) Substance Abuse: From Principles to Practice; contbr. chapters to books, articles to profl. jours. Bd. mem. The Three Dollar Bill Theater Co., NYC, 1995—99. Named one of Best Dr.'s in Am.; grantee, NIH/Nat. Inst. on Drug Abuse, 2000—. Fellow: APA (sr. disting.), Am. Psychiat. Assn. (vice chair sci. program com. 2000—, disting.); mem.: Charaka Club. Achievements include Advisor for Creative work including the Golden Globe Award winning film Quills, and other plays and film scripts. Avocations: cooking, singing. Office: 37 West 57th St 6B New York NY 10019 Home: 160 W 86th St # 6 B New York NY 10027 Office Phone: 212-750-7801. Personal E-mail: drdave@bway.net.

MCDOWELL, DONNA SCHULTZ, lawyer, educator; b. Cin., Apr. 23, 1946; d. Robert Joseph and Harriet (Parronchi) Schultz; m. Dennis Lon McDowell, June 20, 1970; children: Dawn Megan, Donnelly Lon. BA in English with honors, Brandeis U., Waltham, Mass., 1968; MEd, Am. U., Washington, DC, 1972; C.A.S. with honors in Reading, Johns Hopkins U., Balt., 1979; JD with honors, U. Md., 1982, postgrad.; MS, Hood Coll., Frederick, Md., 1995. Bar: Md. 1982; cert. tchr. reading K-12, D.C.; advanced profl. cert. in English, law, biology, reading, Md. Instr. Anne Arundel & Prince George's C.C., Severna Park and Largo, Md., 1977-78; coll. adminstr. Bowie State Coll., Md., 1978—79; assoc. Miller & Bortner, Lanham, Md., 1982-83; pvt. practice Lanham, 1983—87, Gaithersburg, Md., 1987—; sci. tchr. DC Pub. Schs., Washington, 1999-2000; chair dept. English Montgomery County Pub. Schs., Md., 2000—, English lit. tchr. Md., 2002—03, lit. lead tchr. Md., 2003—05, instrnl. specialist Md., 2005—06, lit. coach, devel. curriculum literacy and law Md., 2006—. Ednl. cons.; presenter in field. Mem. Solid Waste Adv. Com., Montgomery County, Md.; election judge; presenter in field. Recipient Am. Jurisprudence award U. Md., 1981; Michael Jordan grantee, 2000, D.C. Pub. Schs. grantee. Mem. Phi Kappa Phi. Democrat. Avocations: gardening, reading, bluebirds, movies. Home: 24308 Hipsley Mill Rd Gaithersburg MD 20882-3132 Personal E-mail: donnasmcd@aol.com.

MCDOWELL, ELAINE, retired federal government executive, educator; b. Balt., June 28, 1942; d. McKinley and Lena (Blue) McDowell; children: Nathan H. Jr. Murphy, Michael W. Murphy. BA, Morgan State U., Balt., 1965; MSW, U. Md., 1971, PhD, 1988. Drug abuse adminstr., acting regional dir. State Md. Drug Abuse Adminstrn., Balt., 1971-72; social sci. analyst, pub. health advisor Nat. Inst. Drug Abuse, Rockville, MD, 1972-76, dep. dir., dir. div. community assistance, 1976-82, dep. assoc. dir. for policy devel., 1981-82, dir. div. prevention and communications, 1982-85; exec. asst. to adminstr. Alcohol, Drug Abuse & Mental Health Adminstrn., Rockville, Md., 1985; dep. dir. Nat. Inst. on Drug Abuse, Rockville, MD, 1985-88; dir. Ctr. for Substance Abuse Prevention, 1988-96; acting adminstr. Alcohol, Drug Abuse and Mental Health Adminstrn., Rockville, Md., 1992, Substance Abuse and Mental Health Svcs. Adminstrn., Rockville, Md., 1992-94. Expert cons. in substance abuse, treatment, and mental health fields; prof. Morgan State U., Balt. Chmn. non-alcoholic internat. gen. svc. bd. Alcoholics Anonymous, 2001—05, trustee emeritus, 2005—; active Presbyn. Ch. U.S.A., Balt., 1998—; bd. dirs. Rosalynn Carter Inst. for Human Devel., 1996—2004. Recipient Outstanding Leadership in Improving Health Care in Black Cmty. award Nat. Med. Assn., 1989, Sec.'s commendation HHS, 1989, Disting. Svc. award, 1990, Nat. Coun. on Alcoholism and Drug Dependence Ind., Pres. award for outstanding fed. leadership, 1991, Presdl. Meritorious Exec. Rank award, 1991, Presdl. Meritorious Disting. Rank award, 1993, Clyde Bailey, Sr. Meml. award Nat. African Am. Drug Policy Coalition, 2006. Mem.: NASW, Sr. Execs. Assn. Personal E-mail: JLuvenia@aol.com.

MCDOWELL, ELIZABETH MARY, retired pathology educator; b. Kew Gardens, Surrey, Eng., Mar. 30, 1940; arrived in U.S., 1971; d. Arthur and Peggy (Bryant) McD. B Vet. Medicine, Royal Vet. Coll., London, 1963; BA, Cambridge U., 1968, PhD, 1971. Gen. practice vet. medicine, 1964-66; Nuffield Found. tng. scholar Cambridge (Eng.) U., 1966-71; instr. dept. pathology U. Md., Balt., 1971-73, asst. prof., 1973-76, assoc. prof., 1976-80, prof., 1980-96, ret., 1996. Co-author: Biopsy Pathology of the Bronchi, 1987; editor: Lung Carcinomas, 1987; contbr. over 120 articles to sci. jours., chpts. to books. Rsch. grantee, NIH, 1979—92. Avocations: conservation education, gardening, swimming.

MCDOWELL, EUGENE CHARLES, systems analyst, bioethicist; b. Washington, Jan. 13, 1940; s. Charles Jacob and Voilet Marie (Brown) McDowell; m. Jill Perry Huntley, May 4, 1986 (dec. 1989); m. Hendrika Maria Ram, Mar. 21, 1992. BA, Am. U., Washington, DC, 1962; MA, U. Chgo., 1966, MA, 1976; adv. cert. in Pub. Adminstrn., US Dept. of Agr. Grad. Sch., 1973; grad. cert., Mastery U., 1995. Rsch. asst. ops. rsch. office Johns Hopkins U., Bethesda, Md., 1958-61; rsch. asst. Rsch. Analysis Corp., McLean, Va., 1961-66, ops. rsch. analyst, 1966-71, Nat. Bur. Standards, Gaithersburg, Md., 1971-80, mgmt. analyst, 1980-82; ops. rsch. analyst NOAA, Rockville, Md., 1982-87, computer systems analyst, 1987—2005; mem. bioethics com. and policy subcom. Washington Hosp. Ctr., Washington, 1996—; guest rschr. Nat. Inst. Stds. and Tech., Gaithersburg, Md., 2005—. Mem. US Fed. pub. key infrastructure steering com., 1999-2003, US Fed. Identity Credentialing Com., 2003—, mem. legal/policy working group, 1999—, chmn., 2001—, mem. tech. working group, 2000—, others; convenor Symposium on Legis. for Physician-Assisted Suicide, Bethesda, Md., 1996; mem. bioethics adv. panel Superior Ct. of DC, 1997—; mem. rsch. working group Md. Atty. Gen., 1997-98. Student condr. Nat. Symphony Orch., Washington, 1960. Pres. Hemlock Soc. Nat. Capital Area, Washington, 1991-93, mem. bd. dirs., 1990-97, Nuclear Free Am., Balt., 1991-94, mem. bd. dirs., 1989—, Garrett Park (Md.) Citizens Assn., 1982-84; originator nuclear-free zone movement in US, Garrett Park, Md., 1982; auditor North Bethesda Congress of Citizens Assn., 1982-84; mem. U. Chgo. Profl. Achievement Award Com., Washington, 1977—, chmn. 1982-84. Recipient Spl. Svc. citation Nat. Oceanic and Atmospheric Adminstrn., 1991, US Dept. of Commerce Bronze medal, 1995, Govt. Computer News citation, 1995. Mem. Hemlock Soc. USA (life), AAAS (life), Philos. Soc. Washington (life, bd. dirs. 1996-98), Azalea Soc. Am., Metropolitan Washington Bioethics Network (bd. dirs. 1996—), Standards Engring. Soc. (chmn. bd. govs. 1983-84, sr. 1982). Democrat. Unitarian Universalist. Avocations: gardening, reading. Home: 901 Mill Pond Rd Frederick MD 21701-9312

MCDOWELL, HEATHER L., lawyer; b. Pitts., Apr. 12, 1965; BS with distinction, Pa. State Univ., 1987; JD, George Washington Univ., 1990. Bar: Md. 1990, Va. 1991, DC 1993. Ptnr., adv., mktg., new media communications Venable LLP, Washington, 2000—. Mem. FTC, 1991—94, FCC, 1994—96. Office: Venable LLP 575 Seventh St NW Washington DC 20004 Office Phone: 202-344-4897. Office Fax: 202-344-8300. Business E-Mail: hlmcdowell@venable.com.

MCDOWELL, JENNIFER, sociologist, composer, playwright; b. Albuquerque; d. Willard A. and Margaret Frances (Garrison) McD.; m. Milton Loventhal, July 2, 1973. BA, U. Calif., 1957; MA, San Diego State U., 1958; postgrad., Sorbonne, Paris, 1959; MLS, U. Calif., 1963; PhD, U. Oreg., 1973. Tchr. English Abraham Lincoln H.S., San Jose, Calif., 1960-61; free-lance editor Soviet field, Berkeley, Calif., 1961-63; editor, pub. Merlin Papers, San Jose, 1969-80, Merlin Press, San Jose, 1973—; rsch. cons. sociology San Jose, 1973—; music pub. Lipstick and Toy Balloons Pub. Co., San Jose, 1978—, Abbie & Dolley Records, 2003—; composer Paramount Pictures, 1982-88. Tchr. writing workshops; poetry readings, 1969-73; co-producer radio show lit. and culture Sta. KALX, Berkeley, 1971-72. Author: (with Milton Loventhal) Black Politics: A Study and Annotated Bibliography of the Mississippi Freedom Democratic Party, 1971 (Smithsonian Inst. 1992), Contemporary Women Poets, 1977,

The Women's Basketball Songbook, 2007; co-author: (plays off broadway) Betsy and Phyllis, 1986, Mack the Knife Your Friendly Dentist, 1986, The Estrogen Party To End War, 1986, The Oatmeal Party Comes to Order, 1986, (plays) Betsy Meets the Wacky Iraqi, 1991, Bella and Phyllis, 1994, The She Revues, The Burkas' Can-Can, Cinderella With a PhD, Hello Joyce, 2007; author numerous poems; contbr. articles and short stories to profl. jours, local newspapers; writer: (songs) Money Makes a Woman Free!, 1976, 2004; 3 songs featured in Parade of Am. Music, 1976-77; co-creator mus. comedy Russia's Secret Plot To Take Back Alaska, 1988; (Cassingle) Intern Girl, 1998, Smithsonian, 2002; (CDs) Our Women Are Strong, 2000, 02, The Wearing of the Green Burkas, 2003; (musical revs., CD) She, A Tapestry of Women's Lives, 2004. Recipient 8 awards Am. Song Festival, 1976-79, Service to Poetry award, 1977, Bill Casey Award in Letters (Soviet Studies), 1980, SHE award, Calif. State U.-ERFA Found., 2004, collected by Nobel Inst. for 2003 Nobel Peace Prize laureate Shirin Ebadi; doctoral fellow AAUW, 1971-73; grantee Calif. Arts Coun., 1976-77. Mem. AAUW, Am. Assn. for Advancement of Slavic Studies, Soc. Sci. Study of Religion, Am. Sociol. Assn., Dramatists Guild, Phi Beta Kappa, Sigma Alpha Iota, Beta Phi Mu, Kappa Kappa Gamma. Democrat. Office: care Abbie and Dolley Records PO Box 5602 San Jose CA 95150-5602 Personal E-mail: jeditorphd@earthlink.net.

MCDOWELL, JOHN HENRY, JR., lawyer; b. Las Cruces, N.Mex., June 1, 1957; s. John H. and Jacqueline (O'Sullivan) McD.; 1 child, Michal Jillian. BA in Econs., Stanford U., 1979; JD, U. Va., 1982. Bar: Tex. 1983, US Dist. Ct. (no. dist. Tex.) 1983, US Dist. Ct. (ea. dist. Tex.) 1985, US Dist. Ct. (we. dist. Tex.) 1987, US Dist. Ct. (so. dist. Tex.) 1995. Ptnr. Hughes & Luce, LLP, Dallas. Spkr. in field. Named one of Best Lawyers in Dallas, D Mag., 2005. Fellow: Dallas Bar Found., Tex. Bar Found., Dallas Assn. Young Lawyers Found. (life; chair fellows prog. 2004); mem.: Am. Intellectual Property Law Assn. (antitrust com.), Dallas Assn. Young Lawyers (pres. 1991), Tex. State Bar Assn. (long range planning com. 1990—91), Tex. Young Lawyers Assn. (bd. dir. 1991—93, Award of Achievement 1990), Dallas Bar Assn. (bd. dir. 1990—91), ABA (antitrust com. litig. sect., litig. and antitrust sect. Award of Achievement 1990). Office: Hughes & Luce LLP 1717 Main St Ste 2800 Dallas TX 75201 Office Phone: 214-939-5413. Office Fax: 214-939-5849. E-mail: john.mcdowell@hughesluce.com. *

MCDOWELL, KAREN ANN, lawyer; b. Ruston, La., Oct. 4, 1945; d. Paul and Opal Elizabeth (Davis) Bauer; m. Gary Lee McDowell, Dec. 22, 1979. BA, U. La., Monroe, 1967; JD, U. Mich., 1971; diploma, John Robert Powers Sch., Chgo., 1976, Nat. Inst. Trial Advocacy, 1990. Bar: Ill. 1973, Colo. 1977, US Dist. Ct. (so. dist.) Ill. 1973, US Dist. Ct. Colo. 1977. Reference libr. assoc. Ill. State Libr., Springfield, 1972-73; asst. atty. gen. State of Ill., Springfield, 1973-75; pvt. practice Boulder, Colo., 1978-79, Denver, 1979—. Mem. hate violence task force, Colo. Lawyers Com.; foster mom for young kittens Recycled Critter Rescue. Mem.: DAR, ABA, Colo. Women's Bar Assn. (editor newsletter 1982—84), Denver Bar Assn., Colo. Bar Assn., Am. Assn. Retired Persons, Humane Soc. US, Survivors United Network (legal coord. 1992—93), Ams. of Royal Descent, Toastmasters Internat. (Able Toastmaster Bronze 1992), Colonial Dames, Survivors United Network Profls. (exec. com. 1992), Mensa (local sect. Ann Arbor, Mich. 1968), Nat. Soc. Magna Carta Dames, Colonial Order of Crown, Sovereign Colonial Soc., Alpha Lambda Delta, Sigma Tau Delta, Phi Alpha Theta. Avocations: stamp collecting/philately, chess, needlecrafts, dinosaurs, horatio alger stories. Office: 1525 Josephine St Denver CO 80206-1406 Home Phone: 303-355-0444; Office Phone: 303-830-2627. Business E-Mail: kamcdowell@qwest.net.

MCDOWELL, MALCOLM, actor; b. Leeds, Eng., June 13, 1943; m. Mary Steenburgen, 1980 (div.); 2 children; m. Kelley Kuhr, 1991; children: Beckett Taylor, Finnian Anderson; m. Margot Dullea (div.). Began career with: Royal Shakespeare Co., Stratford, Eng., 1965-66; early TV appearances include: role of Dixon of Dock Green in Z Cars, British TV; other TV appearances: Little Red Riding Hood, Faerie Tale Theatre, Showtime TV, 1983, Gulag, HBO, 1985, Our Friends in the North, 1996, Lexx: The Dark Zone, 1996, The Great War, 1996, Captain Simian and The Space Monkeys, 1996, The Little Riders, 1996, Pearl, 1996-97, Nazis: The Occult Conspiracy, 1998, Beings, 1998; stage appearance: Look Back in Anger, N.Y. Stage, 1980, In Celebration, N.Y.C., 1984, Hunting Cockroaches, L.A. Stage, 1987, Another Time - Stage, 1993; films include: Poor Cow, 1967, If..., 1969, Figures in a Landscape, 1970, The Raging Moon, 1971, A Clockwork Orange, 1971, O Lucky Man, 1973, Royal Flash, 1975, Aces High, 1976, Voyage of the Damned, 1977, Caligula, 1977, The Passage, 1978, Time After Time, 1979, Cat People, 1981, Britannia Hospital, 1984, Blue Thunder, 1983, Get Crazy, 1983, Cross Creek, 1983, Sunset, 1987, Buy and Cell, 1989, Class of 1999, 1989, Assassin of the Tsar, 1990, Bopha!, 1993, Milk Money, 1994, The Caller, Star Trek: Generations, 1997, Tank Girl, 1995, Yesterday's Target, 1996, Where Truth Lies, 1996, Asylum, 1996, Superman, 1996, Mr. Magoo, 1997, Hugo Pool, 1997, 2103 The Deadly Wake, 1997, The Gardener, 1998, Beings, 1998, World of Moss, 1998, Y2K, 1999, Southern Cross, 1999, My Life So Far, 1999, Love Lies Bleeding, 1999, Gangster #1, 2000, Island of the Dead, 2000, Just Visiting, 2001, Dorian, 2001, Between Strangers, 2001, I Spy, 2002, I'll Sleep When I'm Dead, 2003, Tempo, 2003, The Company, 2003, Red Roses and Petrol, 2003, Bobby Jones, Stroke of Genius, 2004, (voice) Pinocchio 3000, 2004, (voice) Dinotopia: Curse of the Ruby Sunstone, 2004, Halloween, 2007; TV guest appearances Tales From the Crypt, 1989, Spider-Man, 1995, Superman, 1996, Ruby, 1999, (voice) South Park, 2000, numerous others.

MCDOWELL, RICHARD WILLIAM, academic administrator; b. McDonald, Pa., Aug. 20, 1936; s. William Murdock and Cora Josephine (Brackman) McD.; m. Ann Brammer, May 27, 1961; children: Susan, Kathleen, Karen. BS, Indiana U. of Pa., 1960, MEd, 1962; MS, Purdue U., 1967, PhD, 1969. Cert. tchr., Pa. Tchr. Penn Hills Sch. Dist., Pa., 1960-67; divsn. chmn. Cmty. Coll. Allegheny County, West Mifflin, Pa., 1969-71; dean, acting pres. C.C. Beaver County, Monaca, Pa., 1971-72; exec. dean C.C. Allegheny County, Monroeville, Pa., 1972-80, v.p. strategic planning Pitts., 1980-81; pres. Schoolcraft Coll., Livonia, Mich., 1981—. Mgmt. cons., Pa. and Ill., 1975-80; chmn., mem. evaluation team Middle States Assn., Phila., 1972-80; trainer workshop leaders Higher Edn. Mgmt. Inst., Washington, 1976-77. With USNC, 1954-56. Recipient Outstanding Tchr. award Spectroscopy Soc., Pitts., 1966, Edn. award Plymouth C. of C., Mich., 1982. Mem. Am. Assn. Cmty. and Jr. Colls., Mich. C.C. Assn. (bd. dirs. exec. com.), W.E. Mich. League C.C. (chmn.), North Central Assn., Assn. C.C. Trustees. Office: Schoolcraft Coll 18600 Haggerty Rd Livonia MI 48152-3932

MCDOWELL, ROBERT M., commissioner; b. 1963; m. Jennifer McDowell; 2 children. AB cum laude, Duke U., 1985; JD, Coll. William and Mary. Bar: Va. 1990, U.S. Dist. Ct. (ea. dist.) Va., U.S. Ct. Appeals DC (1st, 4th, and 5th cir.), U.S. Supreme Ct. Chief legis. aide Va. Ho. of Delegates; with Arter & Hadden, Washington; exec. v.p., gen. coun. Am. Carriers Telecomm. Assn.; sr. v.p., asst. gen. counsel COMPTEL, 1999—2006; commr. FCC, 2006—. Mem. North Am. Numbering Coun.; bd. dirs. North Am. Numbering Plan Billing and Collection, Inc. Mem. gov.'s advisory bd. Safe and Drug-Free Va., Va. Bd. Contractors; chmn. bd. McLean Project for Arts; counsel Bush-Cheney Fla. Recount Team, 2000. Office: FCC 445 12th St SW Washington DC 20554

MCDOWELL, WILBUR BENEDICT, retired chemist consultant; b. Omaha, Feb. 27, 1920; s. Samuel Brownlee and Rose Gwendolen (Benedict) McDowell; m. Jean Erskine Clapp, Aug. 9, 1947 (dec. Aug. 1996); children: Linda Jane, Wendy Sue, Bruce Benedict. BSc, Ohio State U., 1941, MSc, 1942, PhD, 1944. Asst. Ohio State U., Columbus, 1942—43, tchg. fellow, 1943—44; rsch. assoc. The Squibb Inst., New Brunswick, NJ, 1944—52, section head, 1953—58, sr. rsch. assoc., 1958—66; mgr. prof. svc. dept. Squibb Corp., NYC, 1966—69, Princeton, NJ, 1970—85; ret., 1985. Cons., archivist Squibb Corp., 1985—89, Bristol-Myers Squibb Co., Princeton, 1989—99, New Brunswick, NJ, 2000—. Mem., v.p., pres. BOE, East Brunswick, NJ, 1957—65. Fellow: AAAS; mem.: Soc. Nuclear Medicine, Am. Chem. Soc., Sigma Xi. Achievements include 8 patents in field of manufacturing processes for phamaceuticals. Home: 4 Fairview Ave East Brunswick NJ 08816 E-mail: benmcdowell@prodigy.net.

MCDOWELL-CRAIG, VANESSA DENNISE, supervisor, consultant; b. Washington, Dec. 9, 1954; d. John David and Ossie Ola McDowell; m. John Maurice Craig, May 19, 1984. BS, U. DC, 1995; MEd, Trinity U., Washington, 2000; postgrad., Gallaudet U., 2001—. Cert. mgmt. change leadership Gallaudet U., elem. edn. DC, emergins leaders program DC, ednl. rsch. and dissemination program Am. Fedn. Tchrs. Tng. instr. Blue Cross - Blue Shield, Washington, 1980—87; claims supr. Mut. Omaha, Washington, 1987—88, Health Plus, Riverdale, Md., 1988—89; supr., team mgr. Humana Group Health Plan, Washington, 1989—93; elem. tchr. grades 1-6 DC Pub. Sch. Sys., 1993—2001, instrnl. facilitator, supr., 2002—, spl. edn. coord., supr., cons. Cons. TechAgility LLC, Washington, 2004—. Mem.: ASCD (assoc.), Assn. Childhood Edn. Internat. (assoc.), Internat. Reading Assn. (assoc.; corr. sec. DC reading coun. 1999—2002), Delta Sigma Theta (life). Democrat. African Methodist Episcopal. Avocations: travel, reading, bicycling, singing, dance. Home: 7134 Marbury Court District Heights MD 20747 Office: DC Pub Sch Sys Turner Elem Sch 3264 Staton Rd SE Washington DC 20020 Home Phone: 301-736-5912; Office Phone: 202-698-1167. Office Fax: 202-698-1166; Home Fax: 301-736-2365. Personal E-mail: vannettie@aol.com. Business E-Mail: vanessa.craig@k12.dc.us.

MCDUFFIE, KEITH A., literature educator; b. Spokane, Wash., Feb. 12, 1932; s. Clair L. and Helen Marie (Yaeger) McD.; m. Helen E. Ferry, June 5, 1965 (div. July 1995); children: Anne Leslie, Andrew Keith; m. Pamela Philips Bacarisse, Aug. 10, 1995 (dec. Mar. 1996). BA in English, Gonzaga U., Spokane, 1954; MA in Spanish, Middlebury Coll., Vt., 1960, Univ. Complutense, Madrid, Spain, 1960; PhD in Hispanic Lit., U. Pitts., 1969. Prof. U. Mont., 1969-74; Mellon postdoctoral fellow U. Pitts., 1974, prof., chair dept. Hispanic lit., 1975-92, prof. Hispanic lit., 1975-99, ret., 1999. Editor Revista Iberoamericana, Pitts., 1991-96; pres. Univ. Senate, 1995-97. Co-author: Co-Textes: Cesar Vallejo, 1987; co-editor: Texto y Contexto-Actas 19 Congreso del IILI, 1980, En Este Aire de America: Homenaje a Alfredo Roggiano, 1990. With U.S. Army Security Agy., 1954-56. Mellon Predoctoral fellow U. Pitts., 1965, Title VI fellow U.S. Govt., 1966; Spanish Govt. scholar Spanish Govt., 1959-60. Mem. Instituto Internacional de Literatura Iberoamericana (contbg., bd. dirs. 1991-96, exec. dir. 1991-96). Democrat. Home: 220 N Dithridge St Apt 1001 Pittsburgh PA 15213-1425 E-mail: kamcd@pitt.edu.

MC DUFFIE, MALCOLM, oil industry executive; b. San Francisco, Nov. 14, 1915; s. William Chester and Mary (Skaife) McD.; m. Mary Sutherland de Surville, Dec. 8, 1951; children: Cynthia de Surville, Duncan de Surville. AB in Econs, Stanford U., Calif., 1940. With O.C. Field Gasoline Corp., 1940-41, Wilmington Gasoline Corp., 1941-42; with Mohawk Petroleum Corp., 1945-80, pres., dir., 1969-80; dir. Res. Oil & Gas Co., 1973-80, sr. v.p., 1977-80; sp. asst. to pres. Getty Oil Co., Los Angeles, 1980-82. Bd. overseers Huntington Library, Art Gallery and Bot. Gardens, 1972-98; bd. dirs. Calif. Inst. Tech. Assos., 1976-82. Mem. Nat. Petroleum Refiners Assn. (Dir. 1970-80), Ind. Refiners Assn. Calif. (pres. 1967-69, 77-78, dir. 1950-80), Rancheros Visitadores. Clubs: California (Los Angeles); Bohemian (San Francisco); Valley Hunt (Pasadena, Calif.), Annandale Golf (Pasadena, Calif.); Birnam Wood (Santa Barbara, Calif.), Valley (Montecito, Calif.). Republican. Episcopalian. Home and Office: 457 Eastgate Ln Santa Barbara CA 93108-2249

MCEACHEN, RICHARD EDWARD, banker, lawyer; b. Omaha, Sept. 24, 1933; s. Howard D. and Ada Carolyn Helen (Baumann) McE.; m. Judith Ann Gray, June 28, 1969; children: Mark E., Neil H. BS, U. Kans., Lawrence, 1955; JD, U. Mich., 1961. Bar: Mo. 1961, Kans. 1982; cert. trust and fin. advisor Inst. for Cert. Bankers, 1991. Assoc. Hillix, Hall, Hasburgh, Brown & Hoffhaus, Kansas City, Mo., 1961-62; sr. v.p. First Nat. Bank, Kansas City, Mo., 1962-75; exec. v.p. Commerce Bank Kansas City, Mo., 1975-85, Centerre Bank of Kansas City N.A., 1985-87, Security Bank Kansas City, Kans., 1987-88; exec. v.p., trust officer UMB Overland Park Bank, 1988-93; atty. Ferree, Bunn, O'Grady & Rundberg, Chartered, Overland Park, 1994—2005. Gov. Am. Royal Assn., Kansas City, Mo., 1970-2002, amb., 1980-2004, com. mem., 1995-2005; bd. dirs. Harry S. Truman Med. Ctr., Kansas City, 1974-86, mem. fin. com., 1975-86, treas., 1979-84, bd. govs., 1986-2002, mem. bldg. and grounds com., 1993-2002, mem. pension com., 1976-93, 96-2000; trustee Clearinghouse for Midcontinent Founds., 1980-87; bd. dirs. Greater Kansas City Mental Health Found., 1963-69, treas., 1964-69, v.p., 1967-69; adv. bd. urban svcs. YMCA, Kansas City, 1976-83; cubmaster Kanza dist. Boy Scouts Am., 1982-83, dist. vice chmn., 1982-83, troop com., 1983-90, treas., 1986-88; bd. dirs. Scout Booster Club, Inc., 1989-94; mem. planned gift com. William Rockhill Nelson Gallery Art, Children's Mercy Hosp. Planned Gift Coun., 1991—2005; mem. adv. com. Legal Assistance Program Avila Coll., 1978-80, adv. coun. Future Farmers Am., 1972-82; mgr. Oppenstein Bros. Found., 1979-85; trustee Village Presbyn. Ch., 1987-90, chmn., 1989-90, elder, 1994-97; found. com. Am. Royal Charitable Found., 1995—; bd. dirs. Village Presbyn. Ch. Found., 1987-89, 94-97, chmn., 1996-97, mem. adv. bd., 1997-2001; bd. dirs. Estate Planning Coun., 1984-86; mem. Kansas City Fed. Estate Planning Symposium Com., 1992-98; bd. dirs. Shawnee Mission Med. Ctr. Found., 1988—, fin. com., 1989-92, 2002—, mem. planned giving com., 1996-, mem. investment com., 2000—; mem. adv. coun. Shawnee Mission Edn. Found., 2003. Recipient Eagle Scout, Boy Scouts Am., 1948. Mem. Nat. Assn. Securities Dealers Inc. (bd. arbitrators 1994—2004), Am. Arbitration Assn. (panel arbitrators 1994-96), Estate Planning Soc. Kansas City, Mo. Bar Assn., Kans. Bar Assn., Johnson County Bar Assn., Estate Planning Assn. (pres. 1974-75), Kansas City Jr. C. of C. (v.p. 1964-66), Ea. Kans. Estate Planning Coun., 40-Yrs. Ago Column Club (program com. 1999-2000, pres. 2001, trustee 2001-04), Indian Hills Club, Delta Tau Delta Alumni (v.p. Kansas City chpt. 1978-80). Republican. Home: 9100 El Monte St Shawnee Mission KS 66207-2627

MCEACHERN, ALLAN, lawyer; b. Vancouver, BC, Can., May 20, 1926; s. John A. and Blanche L. (Roadhouse) McE.; m. Gloria, July 17, 1953 (dec. Sept. 1997); children: Jean Williams, Joanne Evans; m. Mary Victoria Newbury. BA, U. B.C., Vancouver, 1949, LLB, 1950, LLM (hon.), 1990. Assoc., sr. ptnr., barrister, solicitor Messrs. Russell & DuMoulin, Vancouver, 1950-78; chief justice Supreme Ct. B.C., Vancouver, 1979-88, Ct. Appeals B.C., Vancouver, 1988—2001; assoc. counsel Faskin Martineau, Vancouver, 2001—; chancellor U. B.C., 2002—. Pres. Kats Rugby Club, Vancouver, 1953-64, B.C. Lions Football Club, Vancouver, 1967, 68, 69, We. Football Conf., 1964, Can. Football League, 1967-68, commr. 1967-68. Mem. Can. Bar Assn. (bd. dirs.), Vancouver Bar Assn. (bd. dirs.), Legal Aid Soc. (pres. 1977-78), Law Soc. B.C. (bencher 1971-79). Avocations: sailing, gardening, walking. Office: Faskin Martineau 1075 W George St Vancouver BC V6E 3G2 Canada Home Phone: 604-261-4970; Office Phone: 604-631-4955. Business E-Mail: amceachern@van.fasken.com.

MCEACHERN, BEVERLEY C., priest; b. Topeka, Kans., July 12, 1941; d. Melvin A. and Rosalie Conner; m. P. John McEachern, July 29, 1963; children: John, Conner. BS, Fla. State U., Tallahassee, 1962; MDiv, Va. Theol. Sem., Alexandria, 1979. Ordained Episc. Ch., 1980. Pub. sch. tchr. Dougherty County, Albany, Ga., 1965—66; curate St. Thomas Episcopal Ch., Columbus, Ga., 1979—88; pastoral counselor Pastoral Inst., Columbus, 1988—94; assoc. priest Trinity Ch., Columbus, 1994—99; rector, priest St. Nicholas Ch., Hamilton, Ga., 1999—. Chaplain Bradley Ctr., Columbus, 1991—94, Auburn U., 1998—99. Fellow: Am. Assn. Pastoral Counselors; mem.: Kappa Alpha Theta. Republican. Home: 5130 Fortune Hole Rd Hamilton GA 31811 Office: St Nicholas Ch 69 Mobley Rd Hamilton GA 31811 Office Phone: 706-628-7272. Personal E-mail: revbeverley@aol.com.

MCEACHERN, STEPHEN MATHEW, accountant; b. Nacogooches, Tex., Oct. 18, 1948; s. Maxie Neil and Exa Julia (Stephenson) McE.; m. Rebecca Brookshire, Dec. 29, 1968 (div. Sept. 1973); 1 child, Mathew Clayton; m. Sherry Jane Fears, Sept. 1, 1974; 1 child, Stephene Lee. BBA in Acctg., Tex. A&M U., 1971. CPA, Tex. Staff acct. Ernst & Whinney, Houston, 1971-75; sr. acct. Fitts, Roberts & Co., Houston, 1975—77, ptnr., 1977—97, pres., mng. ptnr., 1997—. Deacon, chmn. personnel and bldg. fin. com. Met. Bapt. Ch., Houston, 1984-86; committeeman Houston Livestock Show and Rodeo., 1983—. Mem. AICPA (auditing standards bd., 1995-98, tech. standards com., 2000-02, chair, 2002-05) Am. Inst. CPA's, Tex. Soc. CPA's (bd. dirs., v.p. Houston chpt. 1985—), Houston CPA Soc. (pres. 2004-05) Lodges: Rotary (sec. 1985—). Republican. Office: Fitts Roberts & Co Inc 3707 Fm 1960 Rd W Houston TX 77068-3526 Home: 16710 Saddle Ridge Pass Cypress TX 77433

MCELDOWNEY, NANCY, diplomat; b. Fla. m. Tim Hayes; 1 child, Jessica. BA, New Coll.; grad., Columbia U., Nat. Def. U. With Office of Sec. Def. Pentagon; Office of Soviet Affairs US Dept. State, Office of European Security Affairs, Front Office, European Bur., Office of Dep. Sec.; dir. European Affairs, Nat. Security Coun. White House; dep. chief of mission, US Embassy in Baku US Dept. State, Azerbaijan, dep. chief US Mission to Turkey Ankara, 2005—, chargé d'affaires in Turkey. Recipient Disting. Writing award, Nat. War Coll., Sinclair Linguistic award, Superior Honor award, US Dept. State. Mailing: 7000 Ankara Pl Washington DC 20521-7000

MC ELHANEY, JOHN HESS, lawyer; b. Milw., Apr. 16, 1934; s. Lewis Keck and Sara Jane (Hess) McE.; m. Jacquelyn Masur, Aug. 4, 1962; children— Scott, Victoria. BBA, So. Meth. U., 1956, JD, 1958. Bar: Tex. bar 1958. Pvt. practice law, Dallas, 1958—; ptnr. Locke, Liddell & Sapp, L.L.C., Dallas, 1976—. Lectr. law So. Meth. U., 1967-76 Contbr. articles to legal jours. Trustee St. Mark's Sch. Tex., 1980-86. Fellow Am. Coll. Trial Lawyers; mem. Am. Bd. Trial Advs., ABA, Tex. Bar Assn., So. Meth. U. Law Alumni Assn. (pres. 1972-73, dir. 1970-73), Town and Gown Club (pres. 1981-82). Presbyterian. Home: 5340 Tanbark Dr Dallas TX 75229-5555 Office: Locke Liddell & Sapp 2200 Ross Ave Ste 2200 Dallas TX 75201-6776 Home Phone: 214-363-7700; Office Phone: 214-740-8000.

MCELHATTEN, BETTY SHREVE, writer, illustrator; b. Union City, Pa., June 4, 1930; d. Earl Milton and Rachel Wilson Shreve; m. Nelson McElhatten, June 4, 1953 (dec. 1994). RN, City Hosp. Sch. Nursing, Meadville, Pa., 1951. Emergency room and surg. scrub nurse Meadville City Hosp., 1951—53; pvt. duty RN U. Pa. Hosp., Phila., 1953—54; gen. duty RN Vets. Hosp., Phila., 1953—54. Scenic designer drama dept. Byram Hills H.S., Armonk, NY, 1970—73; mem. arts forum Village Gallery, San Diego, 1994—. Co-author: The General's Women: MacArthur's' Loves, 2004; co-author, illustrator Stringer and the Blue Bat Mystery, 2003 (finalist San Diego Book award, 2004), illustrator (storyboards) Miss Billy's Story Hour TV show, N.Y.C., 1972, numerous cookbooks, brochures, ads, directories, 1962—74. Neighborhood chair Girl Scouts Am., Mt. Kisco, NY, 1970—71; troop leader Hillside Ch. Pioneer Girls, Armonk, NY, 1971—73; facilitator bereavement support group Rancho Bernardo Presbyn. Ch., San Diego, 1990—93, deacon. Mem.: Am. Pen Women, Press Club North San Diego County. Avocations: art projects, snorkeling, cruising, reading.

MCELHATTON, JERRY, credit card company executive; m. Jane McElhatton. B degree in Indsl. Mgmt., Franklin U.; attended graduate degree program, Western Michigan U. Held exec. mgmt. positions in ops. and tech. Ameritrust, Cleve., Banl One, Columbus, Ohio; pres., CEO First Republic Bank Svcs. Corp., Payment Systems Tech. & Consulting, Inc., Dallas; sr. exec. v.p., global tech. and ops. Mastercard Internat., O'Fallen, Mo., 1994—. Bd. advisors BMC; bd. dir. Mascon. Mem. bd. trustee Nat. Coun. of the Washington U. Olin Sch. Bus., St. Louis U.; bd. dir. St. Louis Sci. Ctr., United Way, St. Louis Variety Club, Rainbow Village. Avocation: model trains. Office: Mastercard Internat 2200 Mastercard Blvd O Fallon MO 63366

MCELHENY, JOSIAH G., sculptor; b. Boston, 1966; BFA, Rhode Island Sch. Design, 1989. Apprentice to master glassblower Jan-Erik Ritzman, 1989—91, Sven-Ake Carlsson, 1989—91, Lino Tagliapietra, 1992—97; artist-in-residence Isabella Stewart Gardner Mus., 1998, U. Nev., Las Vegas, 2000; vis. critic Yale U. Sch. Art, 2001—03. Spkr. in field. One-man shows include Henry Art Gallery, Seattle, Isabella Stewart Gardner Mus., Boston, 1999, Johnson County CC, Overland Park, Kans., 2001, Art Inst. Chgo., Centro Galego de Arte Contemporanea, Spain, 2002, Brent Sikkema, NYC, 2000, 2003, Donald Young Gallery, Chgo., 1995, 1997, 2000, 2004, others, exhibited in group shows at Site Santa Fe, N.Mex., Whitney Biennial, Whitney Mus. Am. Art NYC, 2000, The Saatchi Gallery, London, Nordic Inst. Contemporary Art. Recipient award, Louis Comfort Tiffany Found., 1995, Bagley Wright Fund award, Seattle, 1998, 15th Rakow Commission, Corning Mus. Glass, Corning, NY, 2000; MacArthur Fellow, John D. and Catherine T. MacArthur Found., 2006. Office: c/o Donald Young Gallery 933 W Washington Blvd Chicago IL 60607

MCELHINNEY, BRUCE, finance company executive; BA, Dartmouth Coll. Mktg. & mgmt. positions Procter & Gamble, A.C. Nielsen, Citicorp, Drackett Products; positions through sr. v.p. merchant rels. Visa USA, San Francisco, 1992—2005, exec. v.p. client services, 2005—. Mailing: Visa USA PO Box 194607 San Francisco CA 94119-4607 *

MCELHINNEY, JAMES LANCEL, artist, educator; b. Abington, Pa., Feb. 3, 1952; s. James and Joan Howland (Carpenter) McE.; m. Victoria Maria Dávila, Sept. 12, 1981 (div.), m. M.L. Burnell Shively, May 14, 2003 (div. 2006). Scholarship student, Skowhegan Sch. Painting and Sculp, Maine, 1973; BFA, Temple U., 1974; MFA, Yale U., 1976. Asst. prof. Moore Coll. Art, Phila., 1977-78, Skidmore Coll., Saratoga Springs, NY, 1979-87; instr. Milw. Inst. Art and Design, 1991-93; vis. artist East Carolina U., Greenville, NC, 1994-98; head painting and drawing program visual arts dept. U. Colo., Denver, 1998—2003; vis. assoc. prof. Pratt Inst., NYC, 2004—. Adj. instr. UCLA, 1983, Moore Coll. Art, 1983, Tyler Sch. Art, Phila., 1983—86, U. Arts, 1985—89; artist in residence Harper's Ferry Nat. Hist. Pk., 1999; dir. study abroad program Feltre, Veneto, Italy, 2000—02; lectr. USAF Acad., 2001; faculty Art Students League NY, 2005—, coord. apprentice program, 2007; lectr. in field. Exhibited in group shows at Chrysler Mus., Norfolk, Va., 1999, Allen Sheppard Gallery, NYC, 1999, Ucross Found., 2000, Nicolayseu Mus., 2000, Newarts Gallery, Litchfield, Conn., 2005, Kent Gallery, Conn., 2005, Reinstallation Hamilton Wing, Inst. Western Art, Denver Art Mus., 2006, one-man shows include Peninsula Ctr. for Fine Arts, Newport News, Va., 1993, Danville Mus., Va., 1993, Second St. Gallery, Charlottesville, Va., 1995, F.A.N. Gallery, Phila., 1995, 1998, Greenville Mus. Art, NC, 1996, Lee Hansley Gallery, Raleigh, NC, 1996, 1998, 1999, Asheville Art Mus., NC, 1996, William Havu Gallery, Denver, 2001—02, Mus. of SW, Midland, Tex.,

2003, William Havu Gallery, 2001, Letterkenny Arts Ctr., Donegal, Ireland, 2003, The Painting Ctr., NYC, 2005, Represented in permanent collections Chrysler Mus. Art, Denver Art Mus., Asheville Art Mus.; author: (manual) The Instruction of Civil War Pioneer Troops, 2004; web editor (drawing and edn.) Newington Cropsey Study Ctr., NY; contbr. articles to various profl. mag.; contbr., editor: articles to profl. jours. Vol. Richmond (Va.) Nat. Battlefield Park, 1991—, Frontier Army Living History Corps of Discovery, U.S. Army C.E. Lewis and Clark Bicentennial, Topog. eng. 1st Divsn. Staff, Hdqs. A.N.V (U.S.C.W.). Grantee painting, NEA, 1987—88, Ptnrs. in Arts, Richmond Arts Coun., 1995; rsch. grant, U. Colo., 2000, Faculty Devel. grant, 2003. Mem. Coll. Art Assn., SAR, Civil War Preservation Trust, Frontier Army L.H. Assoc.,Foote Family Assoc. Office: Art Students League of NY 215 W 57th New York NY 10019 Office Phone: 518-929-6295. Personal E-mail: mcelhinney@aol.com.

MCELHINNY, HAROLD JOHN, lawyer; b. San Francisco, Jan. 5, 1947; s. Harold James and Margaret I. (Mahoney) McE.; m. Mary Ellen McElhinny, June 22, 1968; children: Hannah, Jennifer, William. BA in Polit. Sci., U. Santa Clara, 1970; JD, U. Calif., Berkeley, 1975. Bar: Calif. 1976, U.S. Supreme Ct. 1983. Vol. Peace Corps., Tripoli, Libya, 1968-69; juvenile counselor Santa Clara County (Calif.) Juvenile Hall, 1969-72; law clk. U.S. Dist. Ct., Hartford, Conn., 1975-76; ptnr. Morrison & Foerster, San Francisco, 1976—. Mem. ABA, Calif. Bar Assn., State Bar Calif. (rev. dept. 1986-89, chmn. 1988), San Francisco Bar Assn., Am. Intellectual Property Law Assn., Assn. Bus. Trial Lawyers (bd. govs. 1992-97, pres. 1997). Democrat. Roman Catholic. Office: Morrison & Foerster 425 Market St Fl 34 San Francisco CA 94105-2482 Office Phone: 415-268-7265. E-mail: hmcelhinny@mofo.com.

MCELHINNY, WILSON DUNBAR, banker; b. Detroit, July 27, 1929; s. William Dunbar and Elizabeth (Wilson) McE.; m. Barbara Cheney Watkins, June 6, 1952 (dec.); children: David Ashton, Ward Cheney, Edward Wilson, William Dunbar; m. Lisa Lesher, Mar. 27, 1993. BA, Yale U., 1953. With Union and New Haven Trust Co., 1952-63, Reading Trust Co., Pa., 1963-68, pres., 1968-70, Nat. Ctrl. Bank (formerly Reading Trust Co.), Pa., 1970-79, CEO, 1975-79; chmn. bd. dirs., pres., CEO Hamilton Bank (formerly Nat. Ctrl. Bank), Lancaster, Pa., 1979-81, chmn. bd. dirs., CEO, 1981-83, chmn. bd. dirs., 1981-90; pres. CoreStates Fin. Corp., Phila., 1983-86, vice chmn., 1986-90; pres., chmn. Hamilton Bank, Lancaster, 1988-90. Bd. dirs. Reading Eagle Co., 1st Bank Idaho, SIGCO, Portland, Maine. Mem. St. Luke's Wood River Found. Mem. Pa. C. of C. (chmn. 1990-92), Yale Club N.Y., The Valley Club. Home and Office: PO Box 3070 Ketchum ID 83340-3070

MCELLIGOTT, JAMES PATRICK, JR., lawyer; b. Chgo., Jan. 11, 1948; s. James Patrick and Helen Cecelia (Hogan) McE.; children: Michael Sean, Andrew David; m. Trina Reff, Aug. 25, 1985. BA, U. Ill., Urbana, 1970; JD, Harvard U., 1973. Bar: Va. 1974, U.S. Dist. Ct. (ea. and we. dists.) Va. 1974, U.S. Ct. Appeals (4th cir.) 1974, U.S. Supreme Ct. 1979. Research asst. U. Ill., 1970; assoc. McGuire, Woods & Battle, Richmond, 1973-79; ptnr. McGuire Woods, Richmond, 1979—. Mem. exec. com. Va. Home for Boys, Richmond, 1976-92, pres. bd. govs., 1981-83; mem. Leadership Metro Richmond-Met. C. of C., 1984-85; bd. dirs. ARC Greater Richmond Chpt., 1990-96, chmn., 1994-95. Recipient Clara Barton award ARC Richmond Chpt., 1997. Mem. ABA, Va. Bar Assn. (exec. com., chmn. pub. rels. com. 1978-82, producer pub. svc. message 1973, Hot Spot award 1973), Coll. of Labor and Employment Lawyers, Richmond Bar Assn., Fed. Bar Assn. (pres. Richmond chpt. 1986), Nat. Sch. Bds. Assn., Coun. of Sch. Attys., Coll. Labor and Employment Lawyers, Phi Beta Kappa, Phi Kappa Phi, Omicron Delta Epsilon. Home: 203 Cyril Ln Richmond VA 23229-7740 Office: McGuire Woods LLP One James Ctr Richmond VA 23219-3229 E-mail: jmcelligott@mcguirewoods.com.

MC ELRATH, RICHARD ELSWORTH, retired insurance company executive; b. Thompsontown, Pa., Oct. 11, 1932; s. Clayton Ellsworth and Jane Elizabeth (Shoop) McE.; m. Donna Gail Booher, Aug. 18, 1952; children: Leslie Jo, Jennifer Jo, Josie Arlene Elizabeth, Rebekah Clare. BS cum laude, Elizabethtown Coll., Pa., 1955; MBA cum laude, Harvard U., 1961. Research asst. Harvard U., 1961-62; asst. to pres. Callaway Mills Co., LaGrange, Ga., 1963-65; with Irving Trust Co., NYC, 1965-73, v.p., 1969-73; treas. Tchrs. Ins. Annuity Assn. and Coll. Retirement Equities Fund, 1973-81; v.p. Met. Life Ins. Co., 1982-95. Pres., dir. MetLife Funding, Inc., MetLife Credit, Inc., 1984-95. Author articles, case studies. Trustee Elizabethtown Coll.; mem. Society Valley Hosp., Ridgewood, N.J.; mem. Boston Rep. Com., 1961-63, Troup County (Ga.) Rep. Com., 1964-65; bd. dirs. Family Counseling Svc., Ridgewood, 1986-92. Lt. comdr. USNR, 1956-59. Mem. Assn. Gov. Bds. Univs. and Colls. Clubs: Harvard (N.Y.C.). Methodist. Home: 17 Cedar St Glen Rock NJ 07452-1608

MCELROY, EDWARD J., labor union administrator; b. Providence, Mar. 17, 1941; s. Edward J. Sr. and Clara (Angelone) McE.; m. Edwina Barbara Ricci, Apr. 20, 1963; children: Kathleen, Mary, Stephen, Elizabeth. AB, Providence Coll., 1962. Cert. tchr. Tchr. Lockwood Jr. HS, Warwick, RI, 1962—72; pres. Warwick Tchrs. Union, Warwick, RI, 1967—69, RI Fedn. Tchrs., Am. Fedn. Tchrs., Providence, 1971—92, RI AFL-CIO, Providence, 1977—92; v.p. Am. Fedn. Tchrs., AFL-CIO, Providence, 1974—92, sec. treas. Washington, 1992—2004, pres., 2004—. Exec. com. mem. RI Dem. State Com., Providence, 1976-92; sec. exec. com. United Way So. New Eng., Providence, 1978-92; devel. commn. RI State, 1984-85, mem. Workforce 2000, 1987-92. Recipient Quirk Inst. award Providence Coll., 1980. Mem. Aurora Civic Assn., bd. dirs., Voices for Working Families, Amalgamated Bank of Chgo. Democrat. Roman Catholic. Avocations: golf, photography, reading. Office: Am Fedn Tchrs 555 New Jersey Ave NW Washington DC 20001-2029 *

MCELROY, GLORIA FREELS, secondary school educator; b. Harriman, Tenn., Oct. 6, 1955; d. H.M. Freels and Ruby Armes; m. Douglas Dale McElroy, Sept. 7, 1981; 1 child, Merritt Marie. BA, U. Tenn., Knoxville, 1976, BS, 1979, MS, 1992, EdS, 1998. Tchr. Vine Mid. Sch., Knoxville, 1991—96, Fulton HS, Knoxville, 1996—. Mem. Project Grad, Knoxville, 2001—. Named Tenn. History Tchr. of Yr., Gilder Lehrman, 2006—; recipient Promethean Points of Light award, Promethean World, Atlanta, 2006; scholar, Coll. Bd., 2006. Mem.: Tenn. Coun. Social Studies (bd. dirs. 2002—, presenter ann. conf., treas. 2004—), Nat. Coun. Social Studies (del. 1991, presenter ann. conf.). Republican. Baptist. Office: Fulton HS 2509 N Broadway Knoxville TN 37917 Office Phone: 865-594-1240. Office Fax: 865-594-1228. Personal E-mail: gfm10655@yahoo.com.

MC ELROY, JOHN HARLEY, electrical and industrial engineering educator; b. Marion, Ohio, June 27, 1936; s. Francis and Alice Marie McElroy; m. Eleonore Hildegard Schmidt, Mar. 18, 1957. BS in Elec. Engring, U. Tex., Austin, 1966; M.E.E., Cath. U. Am., 1973, PhD, 1978. Instr. guided missles Air Defense Sch. U.S. Army, 1957-63; rsch. asst. Quantum Electronics rsch. Lab U. Texas, Austin, 1963-66; staff Goddard Flight Ctr., Greenbelt, Md., 1966-79, 80-82, chief comms. tech. div., 1978-79, dep. dir. ctr., 1980-82; dir. comms. programs NASA Hdqrs., Washington, 1979-80; asst. adminstr. NOAA, Washington, 1982-85; dir. spl. projects Hughes Aircraft Co., Los Angeles, 1985-86; v.p. tech. Hughes Comms., Inc., 1986-87; dean Coll. Engring., prof. elec. engring. U. Tex., Arlington, 1987-96, vice provost for rsch. and grad. studies, 1996-97, prof. elec. and indsl. engring., 1997-2000, dean emeritus Coll. Engring.; chair space studies bd. Nat. Rsch. Coun., 2000—03. Cons. satellite communications and earth observations. Contbr. articles to profl. jours. Served with AUS, 1954-63. Recipient Apollo Achievement award NASA, 1969, Applications Tech. Satellite award, 1975, Earth Resources Satellite award, 1973, Satellite-Aided Search and Rescue award, 1982, Internat. Coop. in Space Sci. medal AIAA, 1997, Pub. Svc. medal NASA, 2003; named Wernher von Braun Meml. Lectr. Smithsonian Instn., 1985, Disting. Hon. Alumnus U. Tex., Arlington, 1998. Fellow AIAA, IEEE, Washington Acad. Scis.; mem. Nat. Acad. Engring. Home: 6231 Island Palm Ave Las Vegas NV 89118 Personal E-mail: jhmcelroy@worldnet.att.net.

MCELROY, KATHLEEN O., dining editor; b. 1961; BA, Texas A&M, 1981. Editor Austin American-Statesman, Newsday; sr. editor, nat. copy chief The National; copy editor, asst. sports editor, dep. sports ed. NY Times, 1991—2002, assoc. mng. editor for weekends, 2002—04, dining editor, 2004—. Co-recipient Am. Copy Editors Soc. headline contest, 2004. Mem.: Nat. Assn. Black Journalists, Culinary Historians NY (co-editor 2001, assoc. editor 2002). Office: NY Times Dining Sect 229 W 43rd St New York NY 10036 Office Phone: 212-556-1435. Office Fax: 212-556-1481. E-mail: mcelroy@nytimes.com.

MCELROY, LINDA SUE, retired elementary school educator; b. Stephenville, Tex., Sept. 14, 1945; d. E. J. McElroy Sr. and Margaret Walsworth McElroy. BME, Tarleton State U., Stephenville, Tex., 1974, MEd, 1980. Cert. English as Second Lang. 1992, Elem. Edn. 1980. With Evant Ind. Sch. Dist., Tex., 1978—80, tchr. k-2, 1979—80; tchr. 1st and 2nd grade Lingleville Ind. Sch. Dist., Tex., 1981—85; elem. music tchr. Granbury Ind. Sch. Dist., Granbury, Tex., 1985—86; spl. edn. tchr. Mineral Wells Ind. Sch. Dist., Mineral Wells, Tex., 1987—88; tchr. ESL and music Huckabay Ind. Sch. Dist., Stephenville, 1988—2003; mgr. Stephenville Mus., 2003—. Sec./treas. Tex. State Gospel Singing Conv. Mem.: AAUW (pres. 1988), Assn. Tex. Profl. Educators. Methodist. Avocations: singing, reading. Home: 2643 W Washington Stephenville TX 76401 Office: Stephenville Mus 525 E Washington Stephenville TX 76401

MCELROY, MICHAEL ROBERT, lawyer; b. Providence, Feb. 7, 1951; s. Gerald Robert and Jeannette (Belanger) McE.; m. Christine Anne O'Donnell, June 5, 1976; children: Brian Robert, Dianne Elizabeth, Erin Christine. BA with highest distinction, U. RI, 1973; JD cum laude, Boston U., 1976; MS in Taxation cum laude, Bryant U., 1985. Bar: Tenn. 1976, Mass. 1985, U.S. Dist. Ct. (ea. dist.) Tenn. 1977, U.S. Ct. Appeals (5th cir.) 1977, U.S. Supreme Ct. 1979, U.S. Ct. Appeals (6th cir.) 1980, R.I. 1981, U.S. Dist. Ct. R.I. 1981, U.S. Ct. Appeals (1st cir.) 1981, U.S. Dist. Ct. Mass. 2000. Staff atty. TVA, Knoxville, 1976-81; counsel RI Pub. Utilities Commn., Providence, 1982-83; spl. asst. atty. gen. Office Atty. Gen., Providence, 1982-83; ptnr. O'Leary & McElroy, Providence, 1981-85, Schacht & McElroy, Providence, 1987—; sole practice Providence, 1985-87. Pres. Utility Cons., Inc., Providence, 1983; ptnr. McElroy, Lawrence, Edge & Assocs., Providence, 1983-85. Legal counsel for candidate Congl. campaign, Providence, 1982; chief speech writer for candidate gubernatorial campaign, R.I., 1984; chief legal counsel for candidate gubernatorial campaign, R.I., 1988, Gov. Bruce Sundlun's successful gubernatorial campaign, 1990; legal counsel to R.I. Pers. Appeal Bd., 1991—; arbitrator Superior Ct. R.I., 1992—; spl. master/commr., 1993—; mediator Superior Ct., 1999—; spl. legal counsel to R.I. Ethics Commn., 2000-02. Danforth Found. hon. fellow, 1973; Rhodes scholar nominee, 1973; honoree for life-saving CPR, TVA, 1980; nominated for judgeship Jud. Nom. Commn. Superior Ct., 1994; elected fellow RI Bar Found., 2007. Mem.: Am. Assn. for Justice, Million Dollar Advs. Forum, RI Assn. for Justice, RI Bar Assn. (chmn. Superior Ct. Bench/Bar com. 2003—06, mem. Supreme Ct. com. 2002—, fed. ct. com. 1983—, exec. com. ho. of dels. 2006—, mem. superior ct. Bench/Bar coms. 1983—). Roman Catholic. Office: PO Box 6721 Providence RI 02940-6721 Home Phone: 401-273-8283; Office Phone: 401-351-4100. Business E-Mail: mcelroymik@aol.com.

MCELVAIN, DAVID PLOWMAN, retired manufacturing, finance company executive; b. Chgo., Oct. 16, 1937; s. Carl R. and Ruth P. (Plowman) McE.; m. Mary Rosalind Hysong, Dec. 20, 1961; children: Jana, Jodi. BBA, U. Ariz., 1961, MBA, 1962. Cert. mgmt. acct. Consolidation acct., exec. divsn. Dresser Industries, Inc., Dallas, 1962-67, corp. fin. controller, 1973-76, dir. fin. svcs., 1976-78, staff v.p. fin. svc. and risk mgmt., 1978-82, exec. v.p. fin. svcs. group, 1982-83, pres. fin. svcs. group, 1984-86, v.p. fin., CFO, 1987-93; owner McElvain Oil Co., Dallas, 1993—. Controller crane, hoist & tower div., Muskegon, Mich., 1967-73. Mem. Nat. Assn. Accts., Beta Gamma Sigma, Phi Delta Theta. Episcopalian. Home: 14828 Bellbrook Dr Dallas TX 75254-7647 Personal E-mail: mcelvaincl@msn.com.

MCELVEEN, JOSEPH JAMES, JR., journalist, writer, newscaster, educator; b. Sanford, Fla., Feb. 23, 1939; s. Joseph James Sr. and Genevieve (Stoll) McE.; m. Mary Louise Young, Aug. 18, 1979; 1 child, Ryan Leighton. BA, Furman U., 1961; MA, U. S.C., 1968. Editor, pub. West Ashley News, Charleston, SC, 1951-57; reporter, photographer Charleston Post, 1955-57; tchr. English and journalism St. Andrew's Parish High Sch., Charleston, 1961-65; dir. info., prof. journalism Columbia Coll., SC, 1965-68; prof. journalism U. S.C., Columbia, 1968-79; sr. pub. affairs specialist FCC, Washington, 1979-81; dir. pub. affairs adminstrn. Nat. Cable TV Assn., Washington, 1981-87; dir. internal communications Corp. for Pub. Broadcasting, Washington, 1987-92, dir. program adminstrn., 1992-96, sr. program officer, 1996-99; media/comms. cons. Vienna, Va., 1999—; tchr. English, Fairfax County Pub. Schs., Vienna, Va., 2002—. Ombudsman, columnist Alexandria Gazette, Va., 1981—88; pres. McElveen Seminars, Vienna, 2000—. Author: Introduction to Creative Writing, 1963, Modern Communications, 1964; contbr. chpt. to Dictionary of Literary Biography (Mencken), 1986, Words, Words, Words: A Journalist's Memoir, 1997, Effective Writing and Editing, 2000, 1940s: Decade on the Threshold, 2000. Mem. Orgn. of News Ombudsmen, Soc. Profl. Journalists, Mencken Soc. Episcopalian. Avocations: photography, reading, desktop pub. Office: 1807 Hursley Ct Vienna VA 22182-2105 Home Phone: 703-281-4237. Personal E-mail: jjmcelveen@aol.com.

MCELVEEN, JUNIUS CARLISLE, JR., lawyer; b. Rogersville, Tenn., Feb. 17, 1947; s. Junius Carlisle and Martha Kathleen (Harrison) McE.; m. Mary Wallace Pyles, Sept. 22, 1973; children: Kathryn Carlisle, Sarah Elizabeth. BA cum laude, U. Va., 1969, JD, 1972. Bar: Va. 1972, Calif. 1975, U.S. Dist. Ct. (ea. dist.) Va. 1976, D.C. 1978, U.S. Ct. Appeals (4th cir.) 1978, U.S. Ct. Appeals (Fed. cir.) 1986, U.S. Ct. Appeals (11th cir.) 1990. Rsch. assoc. Atlantic Richfield, Washington, 1972; assoc. Pender & Coward, Norfolk, Va., 1976-77; from assoc. to ptnr. Seyfarth, Shaw, Washington, 1977—83; ptnr. Jones Day, Washington, 1983—. Mem. adv. com., reproductive hazards in the workplace Office of Tech. Assessment, Washington, 1984-86; mem. adv. council Ctr. Environ. Health, U. Conn., 1986-95; mem. editorial bd. The Occupational and Environ. Medicine Report, 1986—, Human and Ecol. Risk Assessment, 1998—. Contbr. articles to legal jours. Elder Kirkwood Presbyn. Ch., Springfield, Va., 1984-86. Served as lt. USN, 1972-75. Mem. ABA, Va. State Bar, State Bar Calif., Washington Map Soc. (bd. dirs.), Phi Beta Kappa, Phi Delta Phi (sec. local chpt. 1971-72, Outstanding Grad. award 1972). Home: 2121/2 S Pitt St Alexandria VA 22314 Office: Jones Day 51 Louisana Ave NW Washington DC 20001 Home Phone: 703-299-1719; Office Phone: 202-879-3726. Business E-Mail: jcmcelveen@jonesday.com.

MCELVEEN, WILLIAM LINDSAY, broadcasting executive, lecturer; b. Columbia, SC, Sept. 20, 1950; s. Henry Moody and Dorothy Butler (Sligh) McE.; m. Laurie Wells Boyle, Sept. 8, 1969 (div. 1976); 1 child, Earle Sligh; m. Catharine Elizabeth McCaslin, Aug. 13, 1992; 1 child, Kerry Elizabeth McCaslin. BA in English, U. of South, 1972. Acct. exec. Sta. WNOK-FM, Columbia, SC, 1972-73, mng. dir., 1973-79; v.p., gen. mgr. Stas. WNOK-AM-FM, Columbia, 1979-84; pres. Audubon Broadcasting Co., Columbia, 1984-89, Radio South Carolina, Columbia, 1989—. Exec. dir. Bloomington Broadcasting Corp., 1998-2000; lectr. Internat. Media Fund, Washington, 1993—; v.p. s.e. region Citadel Broadcasting, 2000—. Chmn. bd. dirs. Columbia Urban League, 1983-85; bd. dirs. Crimestoppers of Midlands, 1984-88, S.C. Law Inst., Columbia, 1985-88, Helpline of Midlands, 1986-90, U. S.C. Coll. Journalism Partnership, 1996—, Greater Columbia C. of C., 2002-04, Children's Hosp. SC, 2006—; gen. campaign chair United Negro Coll. Fund, Columbia, 1985-86; mem. exec. com. United Way of Midlands, Columbia, 1987-88. Mem. Nat. Assn. Broadcasters (bd. dirs. 1988-92, 96—2000, v.p. 1997-98, chmn. 1998-2000), S.C. Broadcasters Assn. (exec. com., bd. dirs. 1980-87, pres. 1985-86, Hall of Fame inductee 1996), Columbia Advt. Fedn. (pres. 1980-81), Media Club of Columbia (bd. dirs., pres. 1983-84). Presbyterian. Avocations: golf, tennis, travel. Home: 263 Tombee Ln Columbia SC 29209-0804 Office: Radio SC 1801 Charleston Hwy Cayce SC 29033-2019 Office Phone: 803-796-7600. Business E-Mail: bill.mcelveen@citcomm.com.

MCELVEEN-HUNTER, BONNIE, international relief organization executive; b. SC, Jan. 1945; m. Bynum Merritt Hunter, Sr.; 1 child, Bynum Merritt Hunter Jr. Pres., CEO, owner Pace Comm., Inc.; US amb. to Finland Dept. of State, Helsinki, 2001—03; chair Am. Red Cross, Washington, 2004—. Chmn. Alexis de Tocqueville Soc., United Way Greater Greensboro, NC; bd. mem. United Way Am., chair nat. women's leadership giving campaign; chair Women in Philanthropy Summit, Washington; internat. bd. mem. Habitat for Humanity; bd. mem. Internat. Women Build Habitat for Humanity, Habitat for Humanity First Ladies Build. Named Comdr. Grand Cross Order of Lion, Pres. of Finland; recipient Dr. Carl--Christian Rosenbröijer award. Office: American Red Cross National Headquarters 2025 E St NW Washington DC 20006 Office Phone: 202-737-8300.

MCELVEIN, THOMAS IRVING, JR., lawyer; b. Buffalo, Apr. 19, 1936; s. Thomas I. and Edith Marian (Bowen) McE.; m. Ernesta F. McElvein, June 26, 1965; children: Christopher, Andrew, Kathryn. BA, Antioch Coll., 1959; JD, Yale U., 1962. Bar: N.Y. 1962, U.S. Dist. Ct. (we. dist.) N.Y. 1969. Atty. Village Akron, N.Y., 1963-99, spl. project atty., 2000—. Mem. N.Y. State Bar Assn., Erie County Bar Assn. Home: 295 Nottingham Ter Buffalo NY 14216-3125 Office: 1500 Liberty Bldg Buffalo NY 14202-3612 Office Phone: 716-854-2620 x152. Business E-Mail: tmcelvein@brownkelly.com.

MCELVY, JAMES DOUGLAS, lawyer; BS, U. Ala., JD, 1971; student, St. Bernard Coll. Cert.: mediator, Am. Acad. of Atty. Mediators. Of counsel Azar & Azar LLC, Montomery, Ala. Bd. dir. Univ. Ala. Law Sch. Found.; trustee Ala. Law Found.; former chmn. Tuscaloosa Coalition for Character; former adj. prof. of law Univ. Ala. Sch. of Law; former prof., alternative dispute resolution Oak Brook Coll. of Law and Govt. Policy. Christian Legal Soc.; former deacon First Baptist Ch. of Tuscaloosa; former v.p. bd. dir. YMCA Metro. Mem.: Ala. State Bar Assn. (mem. bd. of bar commrs.-3 terms, exec. coun.-4 terms, v.p. 2002—03, pres.-elect 2003—04, pres. 2004—05), Tuscaloosa County Bar Assn. (sec. treas. 1989, pres.-elect 1990, pres. 1990—91, exec. com.). Office: Azar & Azar LLC Floor 4 2740 Zelda Rd Montgomery AL 36106 Office Phone: 334-265-8551. Office Fax: 334-261-3489. Business E-Mail: dmcelvy@azarlaw.com. *

MCELWAINE, GUY, motion picture company executive; b. Culver City, Calif., June 29, 1936; m. Leigh Taylor-Young (div.). Began career in publicity dept. MGM, 1955; with motion picture div. Rogers and Cowers, 1959-64; formed own pub. relations firm; subsequently with CMA; sr. exec. v.p. Warner Bros., 1975-77, Internat. Creative Mgmt. (formerly CMA), 1977-81; pres., chief exec. officer Rastar Films, 1981-82; pres. Columbia Pictures, Burbank, Calif., 1982—86, chief exec. officer, 1983—86, chmn., 1985-86, Weintraub Entertainment Group, West L.A., 1987-89; vice chmn. Internat. Creative Mgmt., 1989—96; co-founder McElwaine/Hayes Co., 1996; pres. motion picture divsn. Trilogy Entertainment Group, 1998—2001; pres. Morgan Creek Prodns., 2002—. Exec. prodr.: (films) The Dangerous Lives of Altar Boys, 2002, I'll Be There, 2003, Exorcist: The Beginning, 2004, Dominion: Prequel to the Exorcist, 2005, Two for the Money, 2005, Man of the Year, 2006, The Good Shepherd, 2006; (TV films) My Brother's Keeper, 2002. Office: Morgan Creek Prodns 10351 Santa Monica Blvd Ste 200 Los Angeles CA 90025 *

MCELWAINE, JAMES WILLIAM, music educator; b. Galveston, Tex., May 18, 1947; s. James Murrell and Kathryn Rhea McElwaine; m. Molly Ann Murphy, 1967 (div. 1970); life ptnr. Katherine Davenny, 1970 (separated 1973); m. Theresa Weedy, 1989; 1 child, Gabriel. MusB, North Tex. State U., 1969; MusM, Yale U., 1971. Instr. San Francisco (Calif.) Conservatory, 1971—72; prof. music Hampshire Coll., Amherst, Mass., 1972—76, Purchase (NY) Coll. - SUNY, 1978—; instr. Nassau CC, Garden City, NY, 1982—84. V.p., exec. com. mem. U. Faculty Senate, Albany, NY, 2000—; guest lectr. Amherst Coll., Smith Coll., Mt. Holyoke, CUNY, SUNY, Brockport, U. Albany, U. Tenn., Cal Tech., U. Tex., U. Calif., Berkeley, Berklee Sch. Orchestrator Starmites (6 TONY nominations); contbr. chapters to books Scribners Encyclopedia of American Lives; composer (orchestrator, conductor, dir.): American Stage Festival, Criterion Times Square Theater, Vineyard Theater, Truck and Warehouse Theater, Collonades Theater, American Place Theater, Asheville Blues Festival, Internat. Ragtime Festival; musician (programmer): Jim Henson's Muppet Babies; Smithsonian Institute, Bar Harbor Festival, Prairie Home Companion, 1984 Olympics; composer (arranger): The Slow Drag, Der Ring Gott Farblonjet (6 Obie nominations); musical dir. Lenny and the Heartbreakers, orchestrator Goblin Market (Critic's Inner Cir. award, 1983); musician (conductor, co-founder): (chamber music ensemble) Musical Elements; musician: (co-founder) New York Quintet; composer (performer, producer, arranger): Warner Bros., SONY-Columbia, Tropique, Importe-12, Pye, Eurodance, Shanachie, Rhino, Carrerre, Seven Arts, Tommy Boy, Ariola, Melodia, Country Music Heritage; composer: (condr.) Charles Ludlam's Ridiculous Theater. Mem.: ASCAP, Am. Fedn. Mus., United U. Professions. Achievements include design of innovative univ. curriculum (BFA, MFA, BMus, MMus) for popular music composition; development of innovative univ. curriculum (BA) for new media studies; innovative univ. curriculum (BFA) for music production. Office: Conservatory Music Purchase Coll 735 Anderson Hill Rd Purchase NY 10577 Home Phone: 203-622-9617; Office Phone: 914-251-6730. Office Fax: 914-251-6739. Business E-Mail: jim.mcelwaine@purchase.edu.

MCELWEE, ANDREW ALLISON, JR., insurance company executive; b. Dover, NJ, Apr. 10, 1955; s. Andrew Allison and Grace Lloyd (Lloyd) M.; m. Connie Chapman, May 24, 1980; children: Alexandra Chapman, Andrew Allison III. BA magna cum laude, Davidson Coll., NC, 1977; JD, U. Va., Charlottesville, 1980. Bar: NY 1981, NJ 1981, US Dist. Ct. (ea. and so. dists. NY). Assoc. Dewey, Ballantine, Bushby, Palmer & Wood, NYC, 1980-83, Morgan Stanley & Co. Inc., NYC, 1984-85; v.p. fin. Bellemead Devel. Corp., Roseland, NJ, 1985, exec v.p., 1995; sr. v.p. mergers and acquisitions Chubb Corp., 1997, internat. field ops. mgr., 2000—02, exec. v.p., mng. dir. Chubb & Son, COO Chubb Personal Ins., 2002—. Bd. dirs. Lamont Fin. Svcs., Inc., Essex Fells, NJ. Bd. dirs. World Impact, Inc., Newark, 1986; elder First Presbyn. Ch., Caldwell, NJ, 1983-87. Mem. ABA, NJ Bar Assn., NY Bar Assn. Office: Chubb Corp 15 Mountain View Rd Warren NJ 07059 Office Phone: 908-903-2000. Office Fax: 908-903-2027. *

MCELWEE, DENNIS JOHN, lawyer, former pharmaceutical company executive; b. New Orleans, July 30, 1947; s. John Joseph and Audrey (Nunez) McE. BS, Tulane U., New Orleans, 1970; JD, U. Denver, 1992. Clean room and quality control analyst Sci. Enterprises Inc., Broomfield, Colo., 1975-76; analytical chemist in toxicology Poisonlab. Inc., Denver,

1977; analytical chemist, then dir. quality control program Colo. Sch. Mines Rsch. Inst., 1977-79; dir. quality control, then dir. compliance Benedict Nuclear Pharms. Co., Golden, Colo., 1979-84; pres. MC Projections Inc., Morrison, Colo., 1985-86; dir. regulatory affairs Electromedics Inc., Englewood, Colo., 1986-89; pvt. practice Denver, 1992—. Author: Mineral Research Chemicals, Toxic Properties and Proper Handling, 2d edit., 1979; mem. editl. bd. CF Network Mag.; contbr. articles to profl. jours. Bd. dirs. Denver chpt. Cystic Fibrosis Found., 1996, Assn. of Vols. for Children's Hosp., Denver, 1999, hon. lifetime mem., 2004. Recipient Sutton prize in internat. law U. Denver Sch. Law, 1991, Finest award Denver Charities, 1999; named first lifetime hon. bd. mem. of bd. dirs., Assn. Vols. Childrens Hosp. Mem. Colo. Bar Assn., 1st Jud. Dist. Bar Assn. Office: 7475 W 5th Ave 315 Lakewood CO 80226 Office Phone: 303-274-2021.

MCELWREATH, SALLY CHIN, corporate communications executive; b. NYC, Oct. 15, 1940; d. Toon Guey and Jean B. (Wong) Chin; m. Joseph F. Callo, Mar. 17, 1979; 1 child, R.J. McElwreath III. BA, Pace Coll., 1963; MBA, Pace U., 1969. Copywriter O.E. McIntyre, NYC, 1963-65; editl. asst. Sinclair Oil Corp., NYC, 1966-70; account exec. Muller, Jordan & Herrick, NYC, 1970-71; regional mgr. pub. rels. United Airlines, NYC, 1971-79; dir. corp. comm. Trans World Airlines, NYC, 1979-86; v.p. pub. rels. TWA Mktg. Svcs., Inc. The Travel Ch. Divsn., NYC, 1986-88; ptnr. The Comm. Group, NYC, 1988-90; gen. mgr. corp. comm. Ofcl. Airline Guides, 1990-91; v.p. corp. comm. Macmillan, Inc., 1991-93; cons. NYC, 1993-94; sr. v.p. corp. comm. Aquila Inc., 1994—2005. Pub. affairs officer USNR, 1973-2000. Ret. Capt. Named Woman of Yr., YWCA, 1980, Alumnus of Yr., Pace U., 1976. Mem. N.Am. Pub. Rels. Assn. (vice chair 2003-05), Wings Club (N.Y.C.). Avocations: sailing, skiing, harpsichord. Personal E-mail: sallymc79@aol.com.

MCELYA, JAMES S., automotive executive; Student, West Chester U., Pa. Pres. Siebe Automotive Worldwide Invensys, PLC; various exec. mgmt. positions including pres. Automotive and corp. v.p. Handy & Harman; corp. v.p. Cooper Tire & Rubber Co.; pres. Cooper-Std. Automotive; pres., CEO Cooper-Std. Holdings, chmn., CEO, 2006—. Bd. mem. Original Equipment Suppliers Assn., Rubber Mfrs. Assn.; adv. Nat. Alliance for Accessible Golf. Office: Coop-Std Holdings 39550 Orchard Hill Pl Novi MI 48375 Office Phone: 248-596-5900. Office Fax: 248-596-6535. *

MCENROE, JOHN PATRICK, JR., professional tennis player; b. Wiesbaden, Fed. Republic Germany, Feb. 16, 1959; s. John Patrick and Kathy McEnroe; m. Tatum O'Neil, Aug. 1, 1986 (div. 1994); children: Kevin, Sean, Emily; m. Patty Smyth, 1997; children: Anna, Ava 1 stepchild, Ruby. Grad., Trinity Sch., NYC, 1977; student, Stanford U. Winner numerous U.S. jr. singles and doubles titles; winner jr. titles French Mixed Doubles, 1977, French Jr. Singles, 1977; winner Nat. Coll. Athletic Assn. Intercollegiate U.S. Men's Singles title, 1978; professional tennis player, 1978-93; played on victorious U.S. Davis Cup Team, 1978, 79, 81, 82, 92; winner Grand Prix Masters Tournament, NYC, 1979, U.S. Open Men's Singles Championship, 1979, 80, 81, 84, World Championship Tennis Championship, 1979, 83, Wimbledon Singles, 1981, 83, 84, Tournament of Champions, 1981, 83, Wimbledon Doubles, 1992; winner (with Jonas Bjorkman) Doubles Title SAP Open, 2006; tennis sportscaster USA Network, 1993; host The Chair, 2002, McEnroe, 2004. Owner John McEnroe Gallery. Co-author (with James Kaplan): (autobiography) You Cannot Be Serious, 2000; author: Serious, 2003. Inducted, Tennis Hall of Fame, 1999. Mem: Men's Seniors' Tour Circuit, 1994. Achievements include winner 21 Singles Titles, Sr. Champions Tour, 1998-2005.

MCENROE, PATRICK, former professional tennis player, sports commentator; b. Manhasset, NY, July 1, 1966; s. John Patrick Sr. and Katy McEnroe. Grad., Stanford Univ. Doubles winner French Open, 1989; winner ATP tournament, Sydney, Australia, 1995. Mem. US Davis Cup team, 1993, 94, 96, captain, 2001—04; commentator CBS Sports and ESPN, 1998—; bd. dir. US Tennis Assn, 1999—2000; player, partial owner NY Sportimes, World Team Tennis; US Olympics Men's Tennis coach, Athens, Greece, 2004; guest host Pardon the Interruption, ESPN; analyst ESPN First Take. Author: (books) Tennis for Dummies, 1998. Achievements include ranked 12th, US Tennis Assn., 1991; ranked 664th, 1999. Office: Sportime at Harbor Island PO Box 783 Mamaroneck NY 10543

MCENTEE, CHRISTINE W., architecture and former medical association administrator; married; 2 children. BS in Nursing, Georgetown Univ., 1977; MS in Health Adminstrn., George Washington U., 1982; student adv. exec. program, Kellogg Sch. Mgmt., Northwestern Univ. Dir., office constituency rels. Am. Hosp. Assn., 1986—90, v.p., dep. dir., fed. rels., 1990—94, exec. v.p., 1994—98; CEO Am. Coll. Cardiology, Bethesda, Md., 1998—2005; exec. v.p., CEO Am. Inst. Architects, Washington, 2006—. Named an Under 40 Mover and Shaker, Crain's Chgo. Bus., 1994; recipient Annual Achievement in Health Care Mgmt. award, Women Health Execs. Network, 1997. Mem.: Greater Washington Soc. Assn. Execs., European Soc. Cardiology (nurse fellow). Office: Am Inst Architects 1735 New York Ave NW Washington DC 20006 Office Phone: 301-897-5400.

MCENTEE, GERALD W., labor union administrator; b. Phila., Jan. 11, 1935; four children. B in Econs., LaSalle U., 1956; postgrad., Temple U., Harvard U. With Am. Fedn. State County and Mcpl. Employees, 1957—, former leader Dist. Coun. 13 Harrisburg, Pa., union internat. v.p., mem. exec. bd., since 1974, internat. pres. Washington, 1981—; v.p., mem. exec. coun., chair polit. edn. com. AFL-CIO. Office: AFSCME 1625 L St NW Washington DC 20036-5687

MCENTIRE, BETTY, health facility administrator; Exec. dir. Am. SIDS Inst., Marietta, Ga. Lectr. in field. Contbr. to articles in profl. jours. Office: Am SIDS Inst 509 Augusta Dr SE Marietta GA 30067-8205 Office Phone: 770-426-8746. Office Fax: 770-426-1369.

MCENTIRE, REBA NELL, musician, actress; b. McAlester, Okla., Mar. 28, 1955; d. Clark Vincent and Jacqueline (Smith) McE.; m. Charlie Battles June 21, 1976 (div. 1987); m. Narvel Blackstock, June 3, 1989; 1 child, Shelby Steven McEntire Blackstock; 3 stepchildren. Student elem. edn., music, Southeastern State U., Durant, Okla., 1976. Rec. artist Mercury Records, 1978-83, MCA Records, 1984—. Albums include Whoever's in New England (Gold award), 1986, What Am I Gonna Do About You (Gold award), 1987, Greatest Hits (Gold award, Platinum award, U.S., Can.), 1987, Merry Christmas To You, 1987, The Last One To Know (Gold award), 1988, Reba (Gold award 1988), Sweet 16 (Gold award 1989, U.S.), Rumor Has It (Gold award 1991, Platinum award 1992, Double Platinum 1992), Reba Live (Gold award 1990, Gold award 1991, Platinum award 1991), For My Broken Heart, 1991, Forever in Your Eyes, 1992, It's Your Call, 1992, Read My Mind, 1994, Starting Over, 1995, What If It's You, 1996, If You See Him, 1998, Forever Reba, 1998, Star Profile, 1999, So Good Together, 1999, I'll Be, 2001, Room to Breathe, 2003; Reba compilation video (Gold award, Platinum award 1992), Reba Live (video), 1995, What If It's You, 1996, Celebrating 20 Years (video), 1996; author: (with Tom Carter) Reba: My Story, 1994; actress: (stage) South Pacific, 2005, (films) Tremors, 1990, The Little Rascals, 1994, North, 1994, One Night at McCool's, 2000, (voice) Charlotte's Web, 2006, (TV films) The Gambler Returns: The Luck of the Draw, 1991, The Man From Left Field, 1993, Is There Life Out There?, 1994, Forever Love, 1998, Secret of Giving, 1999; (TV series) Disney's Hercules, 1998, A Salute to Dustin Hoffman, 1999, Reba (also prodr.), 2001-06; other TV appearances include Country Gold, 1982, Bob Hope Winterfest Christmas Show, 1987, (video) Wrestlemania VIII, 1992; appeared on TV series Evening Shade, 1993, Frasier, 1994, The Roseanne Show, 1998, One Life to Live; (host) Acad. Country Music awards, 2004. Spokesperson Middle Tenn. United Way, 1988, Nat. and State 4-H Alumni, Bob Hope's Hope for a Drug Free Am.; Nat. spokesperson Am. Lung Assn., 1990-91. Recipient numerous awards in Country music including Disting. Alumni award Southeastern State U., Female vocalist award Country Music Assn., 1984, 85, 86, 87, Grammy award for Best Country Vocal Performance, 1987, 2 Grammy nominations, 1994, Grammy award, Best Country Vocal Collaboration for "Does He Love You" with Linda Davis, 1994, Entertainer of Yr. award Country Radio Awards, 1994, Female Vocalist award, 1994; named Entertainer of Yr., Country Music Assn., 1986, Female Vocalist of Yr. Acad. Country Music, 1984, 85, 86, 87, 92, Top Female Vocalist, 1984, 85, 86, 87, 1991, 94, Am. Music award favorite female country singer, 1988, 90, 91, 92, 93, Am. Music award, 1989, 90, 91, 92, Best Album, 1991, Favorite Female Vocalist, 1994, Favorite Female Vocalist, Peoples Choice Award, 1992, Favorite Female Country Vocalist, 1992, 93, Favorite Female Vocalist, TNN Viewer's Choice Awards, 1993, Favorite Female Country Artist, Billboard, 1994, Favorite Country Album award Am. Music Awards, 1995, Favorite Female Country Vocalist, 1995, Favorite Female Artist-Country, 2004, Favorite Female Vocalist award People's Choice Awards, 1995, Top Female Vocalist of Yr. award Acad. Country Music, 1995, Entertainer of Yr. award Acad. Country Music, 1995, Favorite Female Vocalist award TNN Viewer's Choice Awards, 1995, Star on the Walk of Fame, 1999. Mem. Country Music Assn., Acad. Country Music, Nat. Acad. Rec. Arts and Scis., Grand Ol' Opry, AFTRA, Nashville Songwriters Assn. Inc. Avocations: golf, shopping, being with narvel and shelby, horse racing, raising horses. *

MCEVERS, DUFF STEVEN, lawyer; b. LA, Apr. 21, 1954; s. Milton Stoddard and Virginia Mary (Tongue) McE.; m. Jeannine Marie Matthews, July 14, 1984; children: Tay Colleen, Reily Maureen. BA, U. So. Calif., 1976; JD, Western State U., 1980. Bar: Calif. 1981, U.S. Dist. Ct. (so. dist.) Calif. 1993, U.S. Dist. Ct. (ctrl. dist.) Calif. 1982, U.S. Ct. Appeals (9th cir.) 1988. Assoc. Donald B. Black Inc., Laguna Beach, Calif., 1981-85; pvt. practice Laguna Beach and Newport Beach, 1985-88, Assoc. Law Office of Terry J. Coniglio, Inc., Long Beach, Calif., 1988-89, Newport Beach and Sonoma, Calif., 1992-2000; with Barclay Law Corp., 1989-91; of counsel Walker Law Firm, P.C., Newport Beach, 1998—2000; assoc. Cooksey, Toolen, Gage Duffy & Woog, Costa Mesa, Calif., 2000—02; atty. Law Office of Duff S. McEvers, Laguna Niguel, 2002—. Editor: Law Rev., 1979. Referee Am. Youth Soccer Assn.; bd. dirs. Beatrice F. Kroesche Found. Mem.: Assn. Bus. Trial Lawyers, Calif. Bar Assn., Phi Gamma Delta (bd. chpt. advisors U. Calif., Irvine). Office: 27881 LaPaz Rd Ste G Laguna Niguel CA 92677 Office Phone: 949-637-1631. Personal E-mail: dmcevers@cox.net.

MCEVOY, LORRAINE KATHERINE, oncology nurse; b. S.I., NY, Mar. 24, 1950; d. Edward Donald and Josephine (Boyle) McMahon; children: Kelly Ann, Kevin Michael. RN, St. Vincent's Sch. Nursing, 1970; BSN, Seton Hall U., 1994; MSN, Kean U. N.J., 1997. RN, N.J. Staff nurse St. Joseph's Hosp. and Med. Ctr., Paterson, N.J., 1981-88, nurse mgr. oncology, bone marrow transplant, 1988—, cons., educator devel. bone marrow, stem cell and cord blood transplant programs, 1995-98. Adj. prof. Kean U., 1997-98. Recipient Disting. Alumni award Kean U., 1999; Susan G. Komen Breast Cancer Found. grantee, 1997, 98, 99. Mem. Oncology Nursing Soc., Transcultural Nursing Soc., Tri-State Bone Marrow Transplant Nurses Assn., Breast Cancer Connection, Sigma Theta Tau.

MCEVOY, MICHAEL JOSEPH, economist; b. Cork, Ireland, Feb. 16, 1963; came to U.S., 1991. s. Patrick Joseph and Pauline (Heffernan) McE. BA, Univ. Coll., Cork, Ireland, 1984, M in Econ. Sci., 1987; MBA, U. Penn., 1996. Rsch. economist Irish Export Bd., Dublin, 1986-87; sr. analyst economist Fixpoint Ltd., London, 1987-91; rsch. assoc. Micra, Inc., Washington, 1991-92; chief economist Embassy of France, Washington, 1992-96; dir. The Tower Group, Boston, 1996—2002; CEO Nechtain LLC, Boston, 2002—. Dir. Fixpoint Ltd., 1989-91. Co-author: (quarterly pub.) European Business: Forecasts, Strategies, Tactics, 1989-91. Sponsor and supporter animal and environ. concerns. Mem.: Nat. Economists Club, Nat. Assn. Bus. Economists, U.S. Holocaust Meml. Mus. Roman Catholic. Office Phone: 617-243-9500. Business E-Mail: mmce@nechtain.com.

MCEVOY, PAMELA T., clinical psychologist; b. Mar. 8, 1937; d. Renny T. and Pamela (Sweeny) McE.; m. Percy H. Johnston Jr. (dec.); children: Michael B. Anderson, Jeffery A. Thomas, Candy L. Watts, Kenneth L. Anderson. BA, U La Verne, 1978, MS, 1980; PhD, U.S. Internat. U., 1982. Instr. psychology-sociology Allan Hancock Coll., Santa Maria, 1977-78; mental health asst. Santa Barbara City Alcoholism Dept., 1977-78; gen. mgr. Profl. Suites, San Diego, 1978-81; therapist Chula Vista (Calif.) Comty. Counseling Ctr., San Diego, 1978-85; rsch. asst. U.S. Internat. U., 1979-82; rsch. coord. Mil. Family Rsch. Ctr., San Diego, 1981-82; assoc. dir. Acad. Assoc. Psychotherapists, 1982-86; pvt. practice San Diego, 1982—, PsyCareInc, 1997—. Pres. Borrego Springs Med. Clinic, 1993-95, Family Custody Santa Maria Superior Ct., 1994-95, Santa Barbara County Mental Health Assn., Santa Maria, Calif., 1995-96. Bd. dirs. Women's Internat. Ctr., 1984-86, San Diego County Mental Health Assn., 1978-79, Civic Fedn., 1993-95. State fellow, 1979, 80, 81, 82; Calif. State scholar, 1976-77. Mem.: APA, Calif. State Psychol. Assn., Rotary Internat. Republican.

MCEVOY, SHARLENE ANN, law educator; b. Derby, Conn., July 6, 1950; d. Peter Henry Jr. and Madaline Elizabeth (McCabe) McE. BA magna cum laude, Albertus Magnus Coll., 1972; JD, U. Conn., West Hartford, 1975; MA, Trinity Coll., Hartford, 1980, UCLA, 1982, PhD, 1985. Bar: Conn., 1975. Pvt. practice, Derby, 1984—; asst. prof. bus. law Fairfield (Conn.) U. Sch. Bus., 1986—92; adj. prof. bus. law, polit. sci. Albertus Magnus Coll., New Haven, 1978-80, U. Conn., Stamford, 1984-86; acting chmn. polit. sci. dept. Albertus Magnus Coll., 1980; assoc. prof. law Fairfield U., 1992-98, prof. bus. law, 1998—. Chmn. Women's Resource Ctr., Fairfield U., 1989-91. Staff editor Jour. Legal Studies Edn., 1989-94; reviewer Am. Bus. Law Assn. jour., 1988—, staff editor, 1995—; sr. articles editor N.E. Jour. Legal Studies in Bus., 1995-96; editor-in-chief N.E. Jour. Legal Studies, 2003—. Active Derby Tercentennial Commn., 1973—74; justice of the peace City of Derby, 1975—83; alt. mem. Parks and Recreation Commn., Woodbury, 1995—99; v.p. N.E. Acad. Legal Studies in Bus., 2001—02, 2006—, pres-elect., 2003, 2007—, pres., 2003—04, program chair, 2007—08, 2007—; treas. Woodbury Dem. Town Com., 1995—96, corr. sec., 1996—98; bd. dirs. Valley Transit Dist., Derby, 1975—77. Recipient Best Paper award N.E. Regional Bus. Law Assn., 1990, Best Paper award Tri-State Regional Bus. Law Assn., 1991; Fairfield U. Sch. Bus. rsch. grantee 1989, 91, 92, Fairfield U. rsch. grantee, 1994. Mem. ABA, Conn. Bar Assn., Acad. Legal Studies in Bus., Mensa (coord. SINISTRAL spl. interest group 1977—). Democrat. Roman Catholic. Avocations: sailing, tennis, swimming. Office: 198 Emmett Ave Derby CT 06418-1258 Office Phone: 203-254-4000 ext. 2836. Business E-Mail: samcevoy@mail.fairfield.edu.

MCEWEN, ADAM, artist; b. 1965; BA in English Lit., Oxford U., Christ Church Coll., 1987; attended, Calif. Inst. Arts, 1991. One-man shows include Much Better, 17 Rosebery Avenue, London, 2002, Sleeper, Edinburgh, Scotland, 2002, Alessandra Bonomo Gallery, Rome, 2003, The Wrong Gallery, NY, 2003, The McAllister Inst., NY, 2003, History is a Perpetual Virgin..., Nicole Klagsburg Gallery, NY, 2004, Jack Hanley Gallery, San Francisco, 2006, exhibited in group shows at Grapeshot Bullseye Harvest, Attache Gallery, London, 2001, Free Coke, Greene Naftali Gallery, NY, 2001, Art Transplant, British Consulate in NY, 2001, Yes We're Excerpts, Andrew Kreps Gallery, NY, 2002, Happy Birthday newspaper project, Gavin Brown's Enterprise, NY, 2002, I See A Darkness, Blum & Poe, LA, 2003, Melvins, Anton Kern Gallery, NY, 2003, A Matter of Facts, Nicole Klagsburn Gallery, NY, 2003, I Love Music, Creative Growth Gallery, Calif., 2004, The Chaim Soutine: Tattoo Project, Frieze Art Fair, London, 2004, I'll Be Your Mirror: Hotel Project at Frieze Art Fair, 2004, Situational Prosthetics, New Langton Ctr. for Arts, San Francisco, 2005, Post Notes, ICA, London, 2005, in words and pictures, Murray Guy, NY, 2005, OK/OKAY, Swiss Inst. Contemporary Art, NY, 2005, Take it Furthur, Andrew Mummery Gallery, London, 2005, Bridge Freezes Before Road, Barbara Gladstone Gallery, NY, 2005, Drunk vs. Stoned 2, Gavin Brown Enterprise, 2005, Star Star: toward the center of attention, CAC Contemporary Arts Ctr., Cin., 2005, Superstars, Kunsthalle Wien, Vienna, Austria, 2005; curator A Fete Worse Than Death, 2004, Couldn't Get Ahead, Independent Art Space, London, 2004, Power, Corruption and Lies, Roth Horowitz, NY, 2004, Interstate, Nicole Klagsbrun Gallery, NY, 2005. Mailing: c/o Nicole Klagsbrun 526 West 26th St Room 213 New York NY 10001

MCEWEN, ALEXANDER CAMPBELL, legal association administrator, consultant, cadastral studies educator, former Canadian government official, land use planner; b. Ryde, Isle of Wight, Eng., Aug. 22, 1926; emigrated to Can., 1949; s. Walter Scott and Florence Lilian (Goodall) McE.; m. Patricia Stuart Richards, July 27, 1956 (div. 1988); m. Sherry Lee Wilson, June 13, 1993; children: Ann Florence, Sheila Jean, Laura Susan. LL.B., U. London, 1966, PhD, 1979; LL.M., U. East Africa, 1970. Survey adviser Govt. Can., Jesselton, 1954-56; tech. expert UN, Victoria, Seychelles, 1958-61; sr. surveyor H. Wheeler Assocs., Toronto, Ont., Can., 1961-62; sec. treas. Assn. Ont. Land Surveyors, Toronto, 1963-64; prin. Survey Tng. Centre, Dar es Salaam, Tanzania, 1964-70; survey cons. Ottawa, Ont., Can., 1970-72; dir. lands and surveys Govt. Nfld., St. John's, 1972-76; commr. Internat. Boundary Commn., Ottawa, Ont., 1976-90; survey adviser Govt. Can., Lagos, Nigeria, 1989-90; prof. cadastral studies dept. geomatics engring. U. Calgary, Alta., Canada, 1991—96; survey cons. Can. Exec. Svc. Orgn., La Paz, Bolivia, 2002—03; pvt. practice Calgary, Canada, 2004—. Cons. in field. Author: International Boundaries of East Africa, 1971 In Search of the Highlands, 1988; contbr. articles to profl. jours. Served with Royal Armoured Corp. Mem. Can. Inst. Geomatics (mem. coun. 1977-81, 97-2002, Jim Jones award 1967, 83, 90, 99, 2006, Presdl. citation 1981), Western Can. Bd. Examiners for Land Surveyors (registrar, bd. dirs. 1991-96), Assn. Ont. Land Surveyors (sec.-treas. 1963-64), Assn. Nfld. Land Surveyors (bd. examiners 1975-76). Home: 2129 2d Ave NW Calgary AB Canada T2N OG8 Office Phone: 403-283-9087. Personal E-mail: amcewen@telusplanet.net.

MCEWEN, BOB, former congressman; b. Hillsboro, Ohio, Jan. 12, 1950; m. Liz McEwen, 1976. BBA in Econs., U. Miami, 1972. Mem. Ohio Ho. of Reps, 1974—80; mem. from 6th Ohio Dist. US Ho. of Reps, 1981—93, mem. rules com., mem. vet. affairs com., mem. pub. works and transp. com.; v.p. develop. Boebinger Realty, 1976—80; pres. McEwen Enterprises, 1992, Freedom Quest Internat., 1997; sr. counsel Jefferson Group, 1997; sr. adv. Greenebaum, Doll & McDonald, Cin. & Washington, DC. Elder Hillsboro Ch. of Christ. Mem. Gideons, Jaycees, Farm Bur., C. of C., Grange, Sigma Xi Lodges: Optimist; Rotary. Mailing: 7382 Ridgepoint Dr Cincinnati OH 45230

MCEWEN, BRUCE SHERMAN, neuroscientist, educator; b. Jan. 17, 1938; AB summa cum laude, Oberlin Coll., 1959; PhD in Cell Biology, Rockefeller U., 1964. Postdoctoral fellow Inst. of Neurobiology, Goteborg, Sweden, 1964—65; asst. prof. Dept. Zoology, U. Minn., 1966, Rockefeller U., NYC, 1966—71, assoc. prof., 1971—73, prof., head Harold & Margaret Milliken Hatch Lab. of Neuroendocrinology, 1981—, assoc. dean grad. and post-grad. studies, 1985—91, 1993—94, dean, 1991—93, faculty chair Sci. Outreach Program, 1992—, Alfred E. Mirsky prof., 1999—. Mem. MacArthur Found. Socioeconomic Status and Health Rsch. Network, 1996—. Co-author: The Hostage Brain, 1994; contbr. articles to profl. jours.; mem. editl. bd. Brain Rsch., 1972—, Jour. of Neuroendocrinology, 1989—95, assoc. editor Jour. of Neuroscience, 1989—98. Recipient Jacob Javits Award, MERIT Award. Fellow: AAAS, NY Acad. Scis., Am. Acad. Arts and Scis.; mem.: NAS, Internat. Soc. for Psychoneuroendocrinology, Internat. Soc. for Neurochemistry, Internat. Brain Rsch. Orgn., Endocrine Soc., Am. Soc. for Neurochemistry, Am. Assn. of Biological Chemists, Inst. Medicine, Internat. Soc. of Neuroendocrinology (pres. 1992—95), Soc. for Neuroscience (pres. 1996—97, pres.-elect, pres., past pres. 1996—99), Sigma Xi, Phi Beta Kappa. Office: Rockefeller U Lab Neuroendocrinology 1230 York Ave New York NY 10021-6399 Office Fax: 212-327-8634. E-mail: mcewen@mail.rockefeller.edu.

MCEWEN, DORIS ANN, education educator; b. Oxford, Miss., Aug. 6, 1950; d. Earnest Jr. and Mildred (Blackmon) McEwen; m. Grady Walker Jr., June 19, 1971 (div. Aug. 1990); children: Maleika René, Cheo Da'Mu; m. Jerry E. Harris, Aug. 26, 2006. BS, No. Mich. U., 1971; MS, Mich. State U., 1975, PhD, 1981. Cert. tchr. 7-12, secondary adminstr. 5-12; supt. endorsement, Mich.; tchr., adminstr., Nev.; secondary adminstr., supt., Ind., Wash. Tchr. Flint (Mich.) Sch. Dist., 1972; tchr., sch. adminstr. Lansing (Mich.) Sch. Dist., 1973-86; prof. U. Nev., Reno, 1986-88, 96—; asst. prin. Waverly H.S., Lansing, 1988-91; prin. East Lansing (Mich.) H.S., 1991-94; assoc. prof. Ind. U., South Bend, 1994-96; asst. supt. Edmonds Sch. Dist. 15, Lynnwood, Wash., 1996—; supt. Clover Pk. Sch. Dist., Lakewood, Wash., 2000—. Edn. cons. Nev. State Dept. Edn., Carson City, 1986-88 Contbr. articles to profl. jours. Bd. dirs. Lansing Art Gallery, Neutral Zone, Wash., YWCA Pathways for Women, South Bend (Ind.) Meml. Hosp., Spice of Life, Ind.; past advisor Boy Scouts Am.; cadette leader Mich. Capitol Girl Scouts; mem. nominating bd. YWCA; trustee meml. Hosp.; mem. urban youth adv. bd. YMCA. Mem. ASCD, NAACP, Nat. Assn. Secondary Sch. Prins., Nat. Alliance Black Sch. Educators, Am. Assn. Sch. Adminstrs., Mich. Assn. Secondary Sch. Prins., Ind. Assn. Secondary Sch. Prins., Optimist Club, Clover Pk. Rotary, Phi Delta Kappa, Delta Sigma Theta. Avocations: reading, computers, multimedia. Home: 12775 Gravelly Lake Dr SW Lakewood WA 98499-1459 E-mail: mcewendoris@hotmail.com.

MCEWEN, IRENE RUBLE, physical therapy educator; b. Columbus, Ohio, May 19, 1943; d. John Mitchell and Isabel (Ruble) McE. BS in Phys. Therapy, U. Wash., 1965, MEd in Ednl. Psychology, 1973; PhD in Spl. Edn., Purdue U., 1989. Cert. pediatric clin. specialist Am. Bd. Phys. Therapy Spltys. (pediatric splty. coun.); lic. phys. therapist, Okla., Wash. Phys. therapist St. Vincent Hosp., Portland, Oreg., 1965-69; head phys. therapist Lowell Sch., Seattle, 1970-76; physiotherapist Spastic Centre of New South Wales, Mosman, Australia, 1976-77; head phys. therapist Seattle Sch. Dist., 1977-84; phys. therapist Mesa Pub. Sch., Ariz., 1984, Roosevelt Sch. Dist., Phoenix, 1984-86; rsch. fellow Purdue U., West Lafayette, Ind., 1986-89; tech. specialist Ind. Augmentative and Alternative Communication Tech. Team, West Lafayette, 1988-89; assoc. prof. phys. therapy U. Okla. Health Sci. Ctr., Oklahoma City, 1989-97, prof. phys. therapy, 1997—, Presbyn. Health Found. Presdl. prof., 1998, George Lynn Cross rsch. prof., 2003, Ann Taylor chair in pediats. and devel. disabilities in physical therapy, 2006. Rschr., presenter in field. Contbr. Mem.: Rehab. Engring. and Assistive Tech. Soc. N.Am., Internat. Soc. Augmentative and Alternative Comm., Coun. Exceptional Children, Assn. for Persons with Severe Handicaps, Am. Phys. Therapy Assn. (Margaret L. Moore Outstanding New Acad. Faculty mem. award 1992, Dorothy Briggs Sci. Inquiry award 1993, sect. on pediat. rsch. award 1998, sect. on pediat. Bud DeHaven Svc. award 2001, Catherine Worthingham fellow 2006, Lucy Blair Svc. award 2007), Am. Assn. Mental Retardation, Am. Acad.

Cerebral Palsy and Devel. Medicine, Alpha Eta, Sigma Xi, Phi Kappa Phi. Office: U Okla Dept Rehab Sci PO Box 26901 Oklahoma City OK 73190-1090 Office Phone: 405-271-2131 47125. Business E-Mail: irene-mcewen@ouhsc.edu.

MCEWEN, LAURA, publishing executive; m. James McEwen; 1 child, Sean. BA, Fordham U. Pub. New Woman, Snow Country Mag.; sr. pub. Harpers Bazaar, Family Circle; pub. YM Mag., 2000—03; v.p., pub. dir. Readers Digest Mag., 2003—. Mem., planning com. Mag. Pub. of Am., 2003. Mem.: Fragrance Found., N.Y. Advt. Club, Advt. Women of N.Y., Fashion Group Internat. (bd. dirs.), Cosmetic Exec. Women (bd. dirs.). Office: Readers Digest Mag Box 200 Pleasantville NY 10572-0200 Office Fax: 914-244-7599, 212-850-7275, 914-238-4559. E-mail: laura_mcewen@rd.com.

MCFADDEN, CORI ERIN, psychotherapist, educator; b. Woodbury, NJ, Feb. 25, 1975; d. John Thomas and Linnea Maska McFadden; m. Paul Edward McMahon, June 14, 2003. MA in clin. Counseling Psychology, La Salle U., Phila., 2001; PsyD in Clin. Psychology, La Salle U., 3Phila., 2003. Staff clinician, psychotherapist Cmty. Treatment Solutions, Moorestown, NJ, 2003—05, interim dir., 2005; psychotherapist Friends Hosp., Phila., 2005; psychology prof. - part time La Salle U., Phila., 2002—, adj. faculty psychology. Assessment lab coord.; admissions counselor. Mem. Rebuilding Together of Gloucester County, NJ; alumni coun. chairperson Friends Sch., Mullica Hill, NJ, 2004—06. Recipient Grad. Student of the Yr., La Salle U. Dept. of Grad. Psychology, 2001. Mem.: APA (assoc.), Pa. Psychol. Assn. (assoc.), Assn. for Behavior and Cognitive Therapy (assoc.), Rotary Internat. Wooddbury Breakfast Club, Psi Chi (life). Independent. Avocations: travel, art museums, bicycling. Office: La Salle University 1900 West Olney Ave Philadelphia PA 19141 Home Phone: 856-251-0088; Office Phone: 215-951-1270. Personal E-mail: coridoc@aol.com. E-mail: mcfadden@lasalle.edu.

MCFADDEN, CYNTHIA GRAHAM, news correspondent, journalist; b. Lewiston, Maine, May 27, 1956; d. Warren Graham and Arlene McFadden; m. James Hoge (div.); 1 child; m. Michael Davies, 1998 (div.). BA summa cum laude, Bowdoin Coll., 1978; JD, Columbia U., 1984, LLB. Exec. prodr. Media and Soc. Columbia U., NYC, 1984-90; sr. prodr., anchor Court TV, NYC, 1990-94; legal corr. ABC News, NYC, 1994—96, sr. legal corr., 1996—, corr. PrimeTime Live, 1996—2004, co-anchor PrimeTime, 2004—, co-anchor Nightline, 2005—. Mem. gov. bd. dirs. Bowdoin Coll., Brunswick, Maine, 1989-95. Recipient Woman of Distinction award Crohns and Colitis Found. Am., 1997, George Foster Peabody award, six CINE Golden Eagle awards, Ohio State award, two Silver Gavel awards ABA, 1987-88, Grand award N.Y. Film Festival, Blue Ribbon Am. Film Festival, Dupont Award, 2001-02, Emmy, Fgn. Press Club award Mem.: Phi Beta Kappa. Office: ABC News 147 Columbus Ave New York NY 10023-5999 *

MCFADDEN, DANIEL LITTLE, economist, educator; b. Raleigh, NC, July 29, 1937; s. Robert S. and Alice (Little) McFadden; m. Beverlee Tito Simboli, Dec. 15, 1962; children: Nina, Robert, Raymond. BS in physics, U. Minn., 1957, PhD in econs., 1962; LLD, U. Chgo., 1992; degree (hon.), U. Coll. London, 2003; PhD in Sci. (hon.), No. Carolina St. Univ., 2006. Asst. prof. econs. U. Pitts., 1962-63, U. Calif., Berkeley, 1963—66, assoc. prof. econs, 1966—68, prof., 1968—79, E. Morris Cox Chair, prof. econs. Coll. Letters & Sci., 1991—, dir. Econometrics Lab., 1991—95, 1996—, chmn. dept. of econ., 1995—96; vis. assoc. prof. U. Chgo., 1966—67; Irving Fisher research prof. Yale U., New Haven, 1977—78; prof. econs. MIT, Cambridge, Mass., 1978—91, James R. Killian Chair, 1984—91, dir. Stats. Rsch. Ctr. Cambridge, Mass., 1986—88; Sherman Fairchild Disting. Scholar Calif. Inst. Tech., 1990. Mem. econs. adv. panel NSF, 1969—71, Univs. Nat. Bur., 1974—77; chmn. NSF-NBER Conf. Econs. of Uncertainty, 1970—; bd. dirs. Nat. Bur. Econ. Rsch., 1976—77, 1980—83; mem. book com. Sloan Found., 1977—79; mem. rev. com. Calif. Energy Com. Forecasts, 1979; chmn. awards com. AEA, 1981—84. Editor: Jour. Statis. Physics, 1968—70, Econometric Soc. monographs, 1980—83; mem. bd. editors Am. Econ. Rev., 1971—74, Jour. Math. Econs., 1973—77, Transp. Rsch., 1978—80; assoc. editor: Jour. Econometrics, 1977—78; adv. com. Jour. Applied Econs., 1996—; co-editor: Essays on Economic Behavior Under Uncertainty, 1974, Production Economics, Vols. I and II, 1978, Structural Analysis of Discrete Data with Econometric Applications, 1981, Preferences, Uncertainty, and Optimality, 1990, Handbook of Econometrics Vol. IV, 1994; co-author: Urban Travel Demand: A Behavioral Analysis, 1975, Microeconomic Modeling and Policy Analysis, 1984. Mem. adv. com. Transp. Models Project, Met. Transp. Commn., 1975, City of Berkeley Coordinated Transit Project, 1975—76. Recipient Outstanding Tchr. Award, MIT, 1981, Nobel Prize in Econs., 2000, Nemmers prize in Econs., Northwestern U., 2000, Richard Stone prize in Applied Econs., Jour. Applied Economtrics, 2000—01; Ford Found. Behavioral Sci. Fellow, 1958—62, Earhart Fellow, 1960—61, Mellon Post-Doctoral Fellow, 1962—63, Ford Faculty Rsch. Fellow, 1966—67. Mem.: NAS (mem. com. basic rsch. social scis. 1982—87, mem. com. energy demand modelling 1983—84, mem. commn. behavioral and social scis. and edn. 1989—94, mem. commn. sci. engring., pub. policy 1995—, chair sect. 54 econ. scis. 2003—, chair com. forecasting demand/supply of doctoral scientists and engrs. 1997—2000), Am. Phil. Soc., Transp. Rsch. Bd. (mem. exec. com. 1975—78), Math. Assn. Am., Am. Statis. Assn., Econometrics Soc. (Fisher-Schultz lectr. 1979, mem. exec. com. 1983—86, v.p. 1984, pres. 1985, fellow 1969, Frisch Medal 1986), Am. Econ. Assn. (mem. exec. com. 1985—87, v.p. 1994, pres.-elect 2004, John Bates Clark Medal 1975), Am. Acad. Arts and Scis. Democrat. Avocations: bicycling, tennis, squash, sailing, skiing. Office: U Calif Berkeley Dept Econs 549 Evans Hall # 3880 Berkeley CA 94720-3880 Office Phone: 510-643-8428. Office Fax: 510-642-0638. Business E-Mail: mcfadden@econ.berkeley.edu. *

MCFADDEN, DENNIS, psychologist, educator; b. Oakland, Calif., Oct. 2, 1940; s. Samuel John and Evelyn (Dinnerson) McF.; m. Nancy L. Wilson, Dec. 28, 1960; children: Tracie Ann, Devin James. BA, Sacramento State Coll., 1962; PhD, Ind U., 1967. Asst. prof. U. Tex., Austin, 1967-72, assoc. prof., 1972-77, prof., 1977—, Piper prof., 1987, Ashbel Smith prof., 1998—. Contbr. articles to profl. jours. Recipient Jacob K. Javits Neurosci. Investigator award, NIH, 1984-89, Claude Pepper award of Excellence, 1989-91; NIH grantee. Fellow AAAS, Acoustical Soc. Am., Am. Psychol. Soc.; mem. Assn. for Rsch. in Otolaryngology, Com. Hearing, Bioacoustics and Biomechanics (NAS-NRC com. on hearing, bioacoustics and biomechanics), Soc. Neurosci., Soc. for Behavioral Neuroendocrinology, Internat. Acad. for Sex Rsch., Orgn. for Study of Sex Differences. Avocations: jogging, bicycling, birdwatching, travel. Office: U Tex Dept Psychology 1 University Station Seay Bldg A 8000 Austin TX 78712-0187 Business E-Mail: mcfadden@psy.utexas.edu.

MCFADDEN, FRANK HAMPTON, lawyer, former judge; b. Oxford, Miss., Nov. 20, 1925; s. John Angus and Ruby (Roy) McF.; m. Jane Porter Nabers, Sept. 30, 1960; children— Frank Hampton, Angus Nabers, Jane Porter. BA, U. Miss., 1950; LL.B., Yale U., 1955. Bar: N.Y. 1956, Ala. 1959. Assoc. firm Lord, Day & Lord, NYC, 1955-58, Bradley, Arant, Rose & White, Birmingham, Ala., 1958-63, partner, 1963-69; judge U.S. Dist. Ct. No. Dist. Ala., Birmingham, 1969-73, chief judge, 1973-81; sr. v.p., gen. counsel Blount, Inc., Montgomery, Ala., 1982-91, exec. v.p. adminstrn. and govt. affairs, 1991, exec. v.p. legal affairs, 1991-93, exec. v.p., gen. counsel, 1993-95; mem. Capell & Howard, P.C., Montgomery, 1995—. Chmn. Blount Energy Resource Corp., Montgomery, 1983-88. Mem. jud. panel CPR Inst. for Dispute Resolution, 1985—. Served from ensign to lt. USNR, 1944-49, 51-53. Fellow Am. Coll. Constrn. Lawyers; mem. Am. Corp. Counsel Assn. (bd. dirs. 1984-93, chmn. 1989). Office: Capell & Howard PC 150 S Perry St Montgomery AL 36104-4227 Home Phone: 334-241-3700; Office Phone: 334-241-8041. Business E-Mail: fhm@chlaw.com.

MC FADDEN, GEORGE LINUS, retired army officer; b. Sharon, Pa., Oct. 16, 1927; s. George Linus and Frances Jane (Byrne) McF.; m. Floretta Theresa McFadden, Nov. 20, 1948; children: Kenneth William, Mark Edward (dec.), Mary Kathleen, Robert Bernard, George Linus, William. BE, U. Omaha, Nebr., 1961; MS, George Washington U., Washington, 1967; grad., Advanced Mgmt. Program Harvard U., Cambridge, Mass., 1971. Pvt. U.S. Army, 1946, advanced through grades to maj. gen., 1976; comdg. officer (7th inf. div. arty.), Korea, 1969-70; dep. comdg. gen. U.S. Army Security Agy., Arlington, Va., 1972-74; dep. dir. for field mgmt. and evaluation, dep. chief central security service Fort George G. Meade, Md., 1975-78; dep. dir. ops. Nat. Security Agy., 1978-79; comdg. gen. U.S. Army So. European Task Force, Vicenza, Italy, 1979-82; corp. v.p. CompuDyne Corp., 1986-89; sr. v.p. The Abbott Group, Inc., Annapolis, Md., 1989-90; dir. Washington Studies and Analysis Group McDonnell Douglas Corp., 1985-86; dir. security affairs Dept. Energy, 1990-97, cons., 1999—. Pres., chmn. bd. Met. Washington chpt. Arthritis Found., 1986-95. Decorated D.F.C., D.S.M., Silver Star, Bronze Star, Purple Heart, others. Roman Catholic. Personal E-mail: mcfaddengl@verizon.net.

MCFADDEN, JOHN VOLNEY, retired manufacturing company executive; b. NYC, Oct. 3, 1931; s. Volney and Mary Lucile (McConkie) McF.; m. Marie Linstead, June 27, 1953; children— Deborah, John Scott, David. BS in Commerce and Fin, Bucknell U., 1953; JD, Detroit Coll. Law, 1960. Pres., vice chmn. MTD Products, Inc., Cleve., 1960-92; pres. MTD Products Inc., Cleve., 1980-91, vice chmn., 1990-92; gen. ptnr. Camelot Ptnrs., Cleve.; pres. Parkside Acquisition Ptnrs. Ltd., Cleve., 1997—. Bd. dirs. C.E. White Co., Fusion Inc., Flambeau Corp., Hinkley Lighting, Inc., SGS Tool Co.; past chmn. financing adv. bd. State of Ohio Devel.; past pres. Cleve. World Trade Assn. Trustee Cleve. Eye Bank, former trustee Fairview Health Svcs, Cleve. Clinic. Lt. Supply Corps, USN. Mem. Cleve. Yachting Club. Office: Parkside Acq Ptnrs Ltd 20160 Parkside Dr Cleveland OH 44116-1347

MC FADDEN, JOSEPH MICHAEL, historian, educator; b. Joliet, Ill., Feb. 12, 1932; s. Francis Joseph and Lucille (Adler) McF.; m. Norma Cardwell, Oct. 11, 1958; children: Timothy Joseph, Mary Colleen, Jonathan Andrew. BA, Lewis Coll., 1954; MA, U. Chgo., 1961; PhD, No. Ill. U., 1968. Tchr. history Joliet Cath. High Sch., 1957-60; mem. faculty history dept. Lewis Coll., Lockport, Ill., 1960-70, asso. prof., 1967-70, v.p. acad. affairs, 1968-70; prof. history, dean sch. Nat. and Social Sci., Kearney (Nebr.) State Coll., 1970-74; prof. history, dean Sch. Social and Behavioral Scis., Slippery Rock (Pa.) State Coll., 1974-77; pres. No. State Coll., Aberdeen, SD, 1977-82, U. S.D., Vermillion, 1982-88, U. St. Thomas, Houston, 1988-97, pres. emeritus, prof. history, 1997—2007. Served with USNR, 1954-56. Roman Catholic.

MCFADDEN, LEE VERNON, religious organization administrator; b. Manning, SC, Jan. 5, 1968; s. Daisy Rena and Aaron McFadden; m. Landa LaYota Montgomery, July 22, 2001; children: Ricky Antonio Montgomery-McFadden, Lee Vernon Jr., Aliaya Chanell, Destiny Le'anda. B in Bus. Adminstrn., Trinity U., Sioux Falls, SD, 1999. Founder, CEO Youth Ministry Tng. Corps, Sumter, SC, 1996—. Prodr.(composer,musician,choreographer): Testimony. Musician St. Mark Bapt. Ch., Silver, SC, 2006—06. Recipient Dedication and Leadership to Youths award, 2005. Mem.: Alpha Phi Omega. Office: Youth Ministry Tng Corps 2245 Stadium Rd Sumter SC 29154 Office Phone: 803-481-4882. Personal E-mail: flevmcfadden@yahoo.com.

MCFADDEN, MARY JOSEPHINE, fashion industry executive; b. NYC, Oct. 1, 1938; d. Alexander Bloomfield and Mary Josephine (Cutting) McF.; m. Philip Harari; 1 child, Justine. Student, Sorbonne, Paris, Traphagen Sch. Design, 1957, Columbia, 1959-62; DFA, Internat. Fine Arts Coll., 1984. Pub. rels. dir. Christian Dior, NYC, 1962—64; merchandising editor Vogue South Africa, 1964—65, editor, 1965—69; polit. and travel columnist Rand (South Africa) Daily Mail, 1965—68; founder sculptural workshop Vukutu, Zimbabwe, 1968—70; spl. projects editor Vogue U.S.A., 1973; pres. Mary McFadden, Inc., NYC, 1976—; ptnr. MMcF Collection by Mary McFadden, 1991—. Bd. dirs., advisor Sch. Design and Merchandising Kent State U., Eugene O'Neill Meml. Theatre Ctr.; mem. profl. com. Cooper-Hewitt Mus., Smithsonian Inst., Nat. Mus. of Design; designer Collection by Mary McFadden, 2000, Mary McFadden Collection, 2003, Earth-BOUND, N.Y.C., 2003; lectr. U. Phila., 2004, Dept. Ancient Near Eastern Art, Met. Mus. Art, 2004, Sackler Mus., Japan Soc., 2004, U. Archeology and Anthropology, Pa., 2005, Newark Mus., 2005, Freer Gallery, 2006, RMA, N.Y., 2006, Parrish Mus., 2006, CUNY Grad. Sch., 2006, Phipps Westbury Gardens, 2006, Rubin Mus., Queens Coll., NYC, Preservation Soc., Newport, RI, 2007. Fashion and jewelry designer, 1973—; maj. retrospective of fashion, textiles and jewels at Allentown (Pa.) Art Mus., 2004, Ursyline Coll., 2007; author introduction Mary McFadden High Priestess of High Fashion, 2004; artist (exhbn.) Dixon Mus. and Garden, Memphis, 2005. Advisor Nat. Endowment for Arts; active local Police Athletic League, We Care About N.Y., CFDA-Vogue Breast Cancer Initiative, Beth Israel Hosp., The Chemotherapy Found.; curator emeritus Lannan Found., 1973-85; founding trustee Robert Redford's Sundance Inst., 1978-83; trustee Devi Ahilya Bai Holkal Meml. Charitable Trust, Maheshwar, Indore, India. Recipient Am. Fashion Critics award-Coty award, 1976, 78, 79, Audemars Piguet Fashion award, 1976, Rex award, 1977, award More Coll. Art, 1977, Pa. Gov.'s award, 1977, Roscoe award, 1978, Pres.'s Fellows award RISD, 1979, Neiman-Marcus award of excellence, 1979, Design Excellence award Pratt Inst., 1993, award N.Y. Landmarks Conservancy, 1994, NU Breed Fashion award, 1996, Marymount Coll. Fashion award, 1996, Legends award N.Y., 2001, Lifetime Achievement award South Am. Press Assn., Miami, Fla., 2002, Pratt Legions award, 2002, Spirit of Design award Phila. U., 2004; named to Fashion Hall of Fame, 1979; fellow RISD. Mem. Fashion Group (bd. dirs. 1981-82), Council of Fashion Designers Am. (past pres., I Can award). Office: Mary McFadden Inc 525 E 72nd St New York NY 10021 E-mail: mcfbro@aol.com.

MCFADDEN, NANCY ELIZABETH, utilities executive; b. Wilmington, Del., Oct. 20, 1958; d. William P. and Mary Elizabeth (Adams) McF. BA, San Jose State U., Calif., 1984; JD, U. Va., Charlottesville, 1987. Jud. clk. to Hon. John P. Wiese US Claims Ct., Washington, 1987-88; atty. O'Melveny & Myers, Washington, 1988-91; deputy comm. dir. Office of Pres.-Elect, Washington, 1992-93; asst. atty. gen. US Dept. Justice, Washington, 1993, prin. dep. assoc. atty. gen., 1993-95; gen. counsel Dept. Transp., Washington, 1996—2000; dep. chief of staff V.P. Al Gore, Washington; sr. advisor, dep. chief of staff Gov. Gray Davis Adminstrn., Calif.; with Gov. Arnold Schwarzenegger Adminstrn., Calif.; sr. v.p. pub. affairs PG&E Corp., San Francisco. Nat. dep. polit. dir. Clinton for Pres. Campaign, 1992, nat. surrogate dir. Clinton-Gore for Pres. Campaign, 1992; bd. trustees Calif. Mus. for History, Women and the Arts. Named one of 40 Best Lawyers Under 40, Washingtonian mag. Office: PG&E Corp One Market Spear Tower Ste 2400 San Francisco CA 94105-1126 Office Phone: 415-267-7070. Office Fax: 415-267-7268. *

MCFADDEN, P. MICHAEL, physician, surgeon; b. Hobbs, N.Mex., June 16, 1946; s. Paul Marion and Venita Lenora (Bowen) McF.; m. Jennifer Marie James, Apr. 8, 1990; children: Heather Anne, Jennifer Suzanne, Bryn Ellen, Callan Michael. BS, La. State U., 1968; MD, Tulane U., 1974. Diplomate Am. Bd. Surgery, Am. Bd. Thoracic Surgery. Surg. intern, resident Tulane U. Sch. Medicine, New Orleans, 1974-79, instr. surgery, 1974-79, clin. prof. surgery, 1991—; resident in thoracic surgery Ochsner Clinic, New Orleans, 1979-81, cardiovascular and thoracic surgeon, 1991—2006, surg. dir. lung transplantaion, 1991—2006, dir. thoracic surgery program, 1998—2006; cardiovascular and thoracic surgeon Stanford U. Hosp., Calif., 1981-91; chief cardiovascular surgery Palo Alto Med. Clinic, Calif., 1983-91; prof. cardiothoracic surgery, surg. dir. lung transplantation Keck Sch. Medicine, U. So. Calif., 2006—. Contbr. articles to profl. jours. Bd. dirs. YMCA, Palo Alto area, 1988-91; bd. dirs. U. Tulane Health Svcs., 2006—. Capt USNR, 1984-94. Fellow ACS, Am. Coll. Cardiology, Am. Coll. Chest Physicians; mem. AMA, Alton Ochsner Surg. Soc., Am. Assn. for Thoracic Surgery, Am. Soc. Vascular Surgery, Am. Soc. Transplant Surgeons, Am. Heart Assn. (coun. on cardiovascular surgery), Assn. Mil. Surgeons U.S., Internat. Soc. for Cardiovascular Surgery, Internat. Soc. for Heart and Lung Transplantation, Norman E. Shumway Surg. Soc., Pacific Coast Surg. Assn., So. Surg. Assn., So. Thoracic Surg. Assn., Thoracic Surgery Found., Tulane Surg. Soc., Tulane U. Med. Alumni Assn., Western Thoracic Surg. Assn., Alpha Omega Alpha, Alpha Epsilon Delta, Nu Sigma Nu, Kappa Alpha. Republican. Presbyterian. Office: Dept Cardiothoracic Surgery U So Calif Keck Sch Medicine 1520 San Pablo St Ste 4300 Los Angeles CA 90033 Office Phone: 323-442-5849. Business E-Mail: mmcfadden@surgery.usc.edu.

MCFADDEN, PETER WILLIAM, retired mechanical engineering educator; b. Stamford, Conn., Aug. 2, 1932; s. Kenneth E. and Marie (Gleason) McF.; children: Peter, Kathleen, Mary. BSME, U. Conn., 1954, MS, 1956; PhD, Purdue U., 1959. Registered profl. engr., Ind. Asst. instr. U. Conn., 1954-56, prof. mech. engring., 1971-98, dean Sch. Engring., 1971-85, dir. devel., 1985-88, provost, v.p., 1988, exec. asst. to pres., exec. sec. to bd. trustees, 1989-98; mem. faculty Purdue U., 1956-71; prof. mech. engring., head Purdue U. (Sch. Mech. Engring.), 1965-71; postdoctoral research Swiss Fed. Inst., Zurich, 1960-61. Cons. to industry, 1959-98. Achievements include research in cryogenics, heat transfer, mass transfer.

MCFADDEN, ROBBYN KILBANE, interior designer, public policy specialist, artist, advocate; b. Chgo., Oct. 5, 1951; d. Robert Harrison and Adrienne Fay (Seyring) Kilbane; m. James E. McFadden Jr., Dec. 20, 1975; 1 child, Ryan James. BFA in Art History, U. Ill., Urbana, 1969—74; Diploma in Interior Design, Harper Coll., Chgo., 1976. Designer Crate and Barrel Euromarket Designs, 1978-83; project cons. Volo Interiors, 1983-90; educator, art and design dept. Coll. of Lake County, 1981-83; owner, prin. Design Perspectives, 1983—. Design cons. Law Offices of Patricia Hogan, Monadnock Bldg., Chgo., 1989; project designer retail space Historic Harbor House, Waukegan, Ill., 1988, others. Pub. design commns. include NJ symphony Annual Viennese Ball, NYC, 1991, 1992, 1993, US Equestrian Team Polo Fundraiser, 1992, 1993, 1994, Hunterdon Art Ctr. Archival Print System, 1994, Cleve. Edn. Fund. Historic Dallas Bldg., 1998, Kids First Festival, Lake County, Ill., 1998, numerous others; pvt. commns. include residences in Ill., N.J., Ohio, Calif. & England. Mus. edn./vis. svcs. Art Inst. Chgo., 1985-2007; mem. adv. com. to internat. programs LWV USA, Washington, 1994—; nat. bd. dirs. UNIFEM/UN Devel. Fund for Women, N.Y.C., 1999-2004; fundraiser, pub. policy advocate Ctr. for the Humanities and Environment, Jackson Hole, Wyo., 1992-95; adv. mem., cons. Com. for Pub. Art, Cleve., 1995-97; specialist advisor Lake County Women's Coalition Arts, 2003—; mem. women's bd. Hist. Genesee Theater, Lake County, Ill. Recipient Carrie Chapman Catt award LWV, Cleve., 1998. Mem. LWV (bd. dirs. Ill. chpt., Lake County pres. 2003-05, exec. bd. 2007—), Consultive Delegate UN Conf. on Status of Women, 2005, Am. Soc. Interior Designers (allied), Interior Design Soc. Nat. Home Furnishings Assn., PEO, Lake County Dem. Women (bd. dirs.), Waukegan Main St. Design Com. (bd. mem., 2006), Nat. Historic Register Main St. Program (architectural design com. mem., 2006—) Avocations: painting, golf. Personal E-mail: indezyn@aol.com.

MCFADDEN, ROBERT DENNIS, reporter; b. Milw., Feb. 11, 1937; s. Francis Joseph and Violet (Charleston) McF.; m. Judith Marian Silverman, June 20, 1971; 1 son, Nolan Seth. BS cum laude, U. Wis., 1960. Reporter Wis. Rapids Daily Tribune, 1957-58, Wis. State Jour., Madison, 1958-59, Cin. Enquirer, 1960-61; sr. writer, reporter N.Y. Times, 1961—. Mem. adv. coun. St. John's U. dept journalism, 1996-. Co-author: No Hiding Place, 1981, Outrage: The Story Behind the Tawana Brawley Hoax, 1990. With US Army, 1960—61, with USAR, 1961—68. Recipient Pulitzer Prize for Spot News Reporting (N.Y. Times team), 1994, (individual) 1996; Byline award N.Y. Press Club, 1973, 74, 80, 87, 89, 92, Page One award Newspaper Guild N.Y., 1978, Spot News award Uniformed Firemen's Assn., 1967, Spot News award L.I. Press Club, 1984, 95, Chancellor's award for Disting. Svc. U. Wis., 1987, Man of Yr. award Alumni N.Y., 1997, Excellence in Local Reporting award N.Y. Newpaper Publishers Assn., 1988, Spot News award N.Y. Newspaper Publishers Assn., 1988, Spot News award N.Y. State Associated Press, 1989, 91, Continuing Coverage award, 1995, 99, In Depth Reporting award, 1989, 91, Feature Writing award, 1996, Ochs Prize in Journalism, 1989, Best News/Feature Story award Internat. Assn. Fire Fighters, 1991, Nat. Spot News award Asian-Am. Journalists Assn., 1994, Comprehensive Reporting award, N.Y. Uniformed Fire Officers Assn., 1995. Mem. N.Y. Soc. Silurians (Spot News Story award 1977, 2001, Peter Kihss award 1987, Investigative reporting award 1989, Excellence in Journalism award 1994, President's award, 2006, gov. 1988—). Office: NY Times 229 W 43rd St New York NY 10036-3959

MCFADDEN, ROBERT STETSON, hepatologist; b. Houston, Mar. 29, 1951; s. David Barnett and Phyllis Reed (Gowell) McFadden; m. Lesa McFadden, Apr. 29, 2000; 1 child, Jonathan;children from previous marriage: William Gordon, Elizabeth Stetson. BS in Biology, Baylor U., Waco, Tex., 1973; MD, U. Tex., Galveston, 1977. Diplomate in internal medicine and gastroenterology Am. Bd. Internal Medicine; diplomate Am. Bd. Transplant Hepatology. Intern in internal medicine La. State U. Med. Sch., New Orleans, 1977-78, resident in internal medicine, 1978-81; staff physician clinic Pub. Health Hosp., New Orleans, 1981; fellow gastroenterology U. Ala., Birmingham, 1981-83; fellow hepatology U. Miami, Fla., 1983-84; gastroenterologist Diagnostic Clinic Houston, 1984-87, Oklahoma City Clinic, 1987-92; hepatologist Okla. Transplantation Inst., Oklahoma City, 1993-2000; chief of hepatology Liver Disease Ctr., Good Samaritan Regional Med. Ctr., Phoenix, 2000-01; med. dir. liver transplantation and chronic liver disease program Tex. Transplant Inst., San Antonio, 2001—03; staff hepatologist Baylor Regional Transplant Inst., 2003—05; chief liver medicine Christus Santa Rosa Med. Ctr., 2005—. Cons. gastroenterology Diagnostic Clinic of Houston, 1984-87, Oklahoma City Clinic, 1987-92; cons. liver diseases and liver transplant medicine Okla. Transplant Inst., Oklahoma City, 1993-99; med. dir. San Antonio Hepatic Rsch. Contbr. articles to profl. jours. Mem. ACP, AMA, Am. Assn. for Study of Liver Diseases, Internat. Liver Transplantation Soc., Okla. State Med. Assn. Republican. Baptist. Avocations: victorian antiques, gardening. Address: 519 Bluffestates San Antonio TX 78216 Office: 2829 Babcock San Antonio TX 78229 Office Phone: 210-705-6700. Business E-Mail: robert.mcfadden@christushealth.org.

MCFALL, DONALD BEURY, lawyer; b. Charleston, W.Va., Aug. 2, 1941; s. Henry Tucker and Elizabeth Katharine (Beury) McF.; m. Donna Glenn Binion, May 27, 1972; children: Katharine Atkinson, Mary Crawford. BA, Washington and Lee U., 1964, JD, 1969. Bar: Va. 1969, Tex. 1969, U.S. Supreme Ct. 1979, U.S. Dist. Ct. (we., no., so. and ea. dists.) Tex. 1969. Asst. U.S. atty. U.S. Dept. Justice, Houston, 1970-71; assoc. Butler & Binion, Houston, 1971-77, ptnr., 1977-85, McFall, Sherwood & Sheehy, Houston, 1985-2000; shareholder McFall, Sherwood & Breitbeil, P.C., Houston, 2000—. Trustee Humana Hosp.-Sharpstown, Houston,

1984—85, Southmore Med. Ctr., Houston, 1994—98; bd. dirs. Planned Parenthood Houston and S.E. Tex., 1978—88; trustee Woodberry Forest Sch., Orange, Va., 1984—90, Washington and Lee U., 1997—2006. Lt. US Army, 1964—66. Named Super Lawyer, Tex. Monthly Mag., 2003—, Houston's Top Lawyers, Houston Tex. Mag., 2004—. Fellow: Internat. Soc. Barristers, Am. Coll. Trial Lawyers, Houston Bar Found., Tex. Bar Found.; mem.: Def. Rsch. Inst., Tex. Assn. Def. Counsel, Am. Judicature Soc., Am. Bd. Trial Advocates (nat. bd. dirs. 1996—2000), Fedn. Def. and Corp. Counsel, Tex. State Bar Assn., Va. State Bar Assn., Internat. Assn. Def. Counsel, Garland Walker Inn, Am. Inns of Ct. Office: McFall Sherwood & Breitbeil PC 1250 Four Houston Ctr 1331 Lamar St Houston TX 77010-3027 Office Phone: 713-590-9300. Personal E-mail: dbmcf@aol.com. Business E-Mail: dmcfall@mcfall-law.com.

MCFALL, JOHN, performing company executive; b. Kansas City, Mo. Studies with Tatiana Dokoudovska, Conservatory of Music; student, San Francisco Ballet Sch., 1964-65. Formerly with San Francisco Ballet, prin. dancer, 1969; artistic dir. BalletMet, Columbus, Ohio, 1986-94; artistic dir., CEO Atlanta Ballet Co., 1994—. Choreographer Nat. Ballet Can., Am. Ballet Theatre, Dance Theatre Harlem, San Francisco, Hubbard St. Dance Co., Atlanta Ballet, for other artists, including Mikhail Baryshnikov, Cynthia Gregory. Choreographer Commd. 2 world premieres for 1996 Olympic Arts Festival; recently staged: 10 Atlanta prodns., including The Nutcracker. Ford Found. scholar San Francisco Ballet Sch., 1964, Nat. Endowment for Arts fellow, 1978, 1980, 1985. Office: Atlanta Ballet 1400 W Peachtree St Atlanta GA 30309-2906 E-mail: jmcfall@atlantaballet.com. *

MCFARLAN, FRANKLIN WARREN, business administration educator; b. Boston, Oct. 18, 1937; s. Ronald Lyman and Ethel Warren (White) McF.; m. Margaret Karen Nelson, Dec. 17, 1971; children: Andrew, Clarissa, Elizabeth. AB, Harvard Coll., 1959, MBA, 1961, D.BA, 1965. Asst. prof. Harvard Bus. Sch., Boston, 1964-68, assoc. prof., 1968-73, prof. bus. adminstrn., 1973—, prof. emeritus bus. adminstrn., sr. assoc. dean, dir. rsch. Boston, 1991-95, sr. assoc. dean external rels., 1995-2000, sr. assoc. dean, dir. Asia Pacific, 2000—. Dir. Providian Fin. Corp., San Franciso, Li and Fung Corp., HOng Kong, Computer Sci. Corp., L.A. Author: (with Richard Nolan) Information Systems Administration, 1973; (with Linda Applegate and Robert Austin) Corporate Information Management, 6th edit., 2003, (with Linda Applegate and Robert Austin) Creating Business Advantages in Information Age, 2002, (with Cathleen Benko) Connecting the Dots, 2003; editor: (with Richard Nolan) Information Systems Handbook, 1973, Information Systems Research Challenge, 1984; sr. editor MIS Quar., 1986-88. Bd. dirs., pres. Belmont (Mass.) Day Sch., 1982-86; bd. dirs. Dana Hall Sch., Wellesley, Mass., 1982-94, chmn. bd., 1990-93; trustee Mt. Auburn Hosp., 1991-99, ch mn. bd., 1995-98, trustee care group, 1996—; trustee Winsor Sch., 1994-2000, Milton Acad., 2001--. 1st lt. U.S. Army, 1962-67. Mem.: The Country (Brookline, Mass.). Republican. Episcopalian. Office: Harvard Bus Sch Morgan Hall 131 Harvard Way Boston MA 02163-1317 Office Phone: 617-495-6402. E-mail: fmcfarlan@hbs.edu.

MCFARLAND, ALAN ROBERTS, investment banker; b. Washington, Oct. 4, 1942; s. Alan Roberts and Elizabeth (Mathieu) McF.; m. Ellen Michel, Aug. 6, 1966 (div. 1984); children: Andrew Roberts, Gavin Richards; m. Kathleen Troia, Jan. 12, 1985; children: Fiona Fuller, Lucas Haskell Sawyer, Camilla Collins. BA, Yale U., 1964, LLB, 1967. Law clk. U.S. Ct. Appeals, 3d Cir., Phila., 1967-68; assoc. Drinker Biddle & Reath, Phila., 1968-69; v.p. Donaldson Lufkin & Jenrette, NYC, 1969-73; mng. dir. Lehman Bros., NYC, 1973-78; gen. ptnr. Lazard Freres & Co., NYC, 1978-89, McFarland Dewey & Co., NYC, 1989—. Bd. dirs. Placer Dome Inc., Vancouver, B.C., Can., Foxboro Co. Mass., 1990, Premdor Inc., Willowdale, Ont., Can. Trustee Children's Aid Soc., N.Y.C., 1978—; bd. dirs. World Resources Inst., Washington, 1980-94. Republican. Episcopalian. Office: Mcfarland Dewey Securities Co 420 Lexington Ave Suite 2650 New York NY 10170-2699

MCFARLAND, ANN LOUISE, music educator; b. Danville, Pa., Aug. 3, 1953; d. Robert E. and Jane F. Montague; m. James R. McFarland, June 3, 1972; children: Ailie S. Herr, Kevin S., Jennie E., Grant R. MusB, Susquehanna U., Selinsgrove, Pa., 1975; MusM, Temple U., Phila., 1978; PhD in Music Edn., Temple U., 2006. Cert. music and movement tchr. level III Am. Orff Schulwerk Assn., 1999, movement tchr. High Scope, 2005. Tchr. Hempfield Sch. Dist., Lancaster, Pa., 1991—92, Conestoga Valley Sch. Dist., Lancaster, Pa., 1992—99; asst. prof. music edn. West Chester U., Pa., 1999—. Presenter in field. Contbr. articles to profl. jours. Mem.: Internat. Soc. Music Edn., Soc. Ethnomusicology, Am. Orff Schulwerk Assn., Music Educators Nat. Conf. Office: West Chester Univ Sch Music 817 South High St West Chester PA 19383 Personal E-mail: annmcfarland@juno.com. Business E-Mail: amcfarland@wcupa.edu.

MC FARLAND, H. RICHARD, food products executive; b. Hoopeston, Ill., Aug. 19, 1930; s. Arthur Bryan and Jennie (Wilkey) McF.; m. Sarah Forney, Dec. 30, 1967. BS, U. Ill., 1952. With Campbell Soup Co., Camden, NJ, 1957-67, mgr. purchasing, 1961-67; dir. procurement Keebler Co., Elmhurst, Ill., 1967-69; v.p. purchasing and distbn. Ky. Fried Chicken Corp., Louisville, 1969-74, v.p. food svcs., sales and distbn., 1974-75; pres., dir. Mid-Continent Carton Co., Louisville, 1974-75, Ky. Fried Chicken Mfg. Corp., Nashville, 1974-75; owner, pres., dir. McFarland Foods Corp., Indpls., 1975—. Chmn. processed foods com. World's Poultry Congress, 1974; mem. exec. coun., nat. franchise coun. Ky. Fried Chicken, 1979-85; dir. nat. advt. coun. Ky. Fried Chicken, 1985-91, exec. com., 1988-90, chmn., 1989-90; mem. devel. com. U. Ill., 1989—. Mem. U. Ill. Found., 1992—, bd. dirs., 1993-05, life bd. dirs., 2005—, vice chmn., 2001-05, Ind. U. President's Cir., 2005-; chmn. U. Ill. Nat. Advocates, 1992-2001; life pres. U. Ill. Sr. Class of '52; bd. dirs. Ind. Fedn. Children and Youth, 1983-84; Ind. bd. dirs. Fellowship Christian Athletes, 1997-98, Ind. bd. advisors, 1998—; chmn. campaign Ind. Ky. Fried Chicken March of Dimes, 1978-87; nat. trustee McCormick Theol. Sem., 1993-97, mem. adv. coun., 1998-2002; trustee Hanover Coll., 2004—; life trustee Indpls. Mus. Art, 2005—; bd. dirs. U. Ind. Cancer Ctr. Devel., 2004—, Ind. Ovarian Cancer Orgn., 2003—. 1st lt. USAF, 1952-54, Korea. Recipient Award of Merit U. Ill. Coll. Agr., 1988, Achievement award U. Ill. Alumni Assn., 1996. Mem. Ky. Restaurant Asns. (bd. dirs. 1970-75), Nat. Broiler Coun. (bd. dirs. 1971-74), Ind. Restaurant Assn., Am. Shorthorn Breeders Assn., Great Lakes Ky. Fried Chicken Franchise Assn. (bd. dirs. 1975-91, 1st v.p. 1978-79, pres. 1979-80), Delta Upsilon. Clubs: Main Line Ski (Phila.) (pres. 1964); Hillcrest Country. Presbyterian. Home: 10720 Compass Ct Indianapolis IN 46256-9532 Office Phone: 317-842-4532.

MCFARLAND, JAMES WILLIAM, real estate company executive, consultant; b. Montgomery, Ala., Sept. 7, 1948; s. Ward Wharton and Frances Adelia (Morrow) McFarland; m. Miriam Melinda Webster, Feb. 20, 1971 (div.); children: James William, Mimi Morrow. BS, U. Ala., University, 1971. Dir. real estate Ky., Ind. and Tenn. Winn-Dixie Stores, Inc., Louisville, 1970—72; v.p. Ward McFarland, Inc., Tuscaloosa, Ala., 1972—. Dir. Ward McFarland, Inc., Tuscaloosa, Ala.; charter investor chair of real estate U. Ala. Mem. Coun. Devel. of French in La., 1976—, Friends of Libr., 1975—; commr. Dept. Mental Health, Ala., 1987—89; Rep. nominee US Congress Ala. 7th Dist., 1986; chmn. Ala. Rapid Rail Transit Commn.; vice chmn. La.-Miss.-Ala. Rapid Rail Transit Commn., 1983—84, chmn., 1984; state advisor Congl. Adv. Com., Am. Security Coun.; mem. Rep. State Exec. Com., 1991—; chmn. Tuscaloosa County Reps., 1991—; young churchmen adviser Episcopal Diocese Ala., 1976, conv. del.; sr. warden Christ Episc. Ch., 1984; bd. dir. Tuscaloosa Kidney Found. Named hon. citizen of Mobile and New Orleans, hon. mem. mayor's staff, Mobile, Ala. Mem.: Nat. Small Bus. Assn., Tuscaloosa Bd. Realtors, Nat. Assn. Realtors, USCG Aux. (flotilla comdr. and dist. pub. affairs officer 1997, flotilla staff officer 1994—, dist. staff officer 1997—), U. Ala. Alumni Assn., U. Ala. Commerce Execs. Soc., Ala. Assn. R.R. Passengers (pres. 1982, 1990, 1991), Nat. Assn. R.R. Passengers, Kiwanis (Greater Tuscaloosa chpt.), North River Yacht Club, Delta Sigma Pi. Office: 325 Skyland Blvd E Tuscaloosa AL 35405-4030 Office Phone: 205-759-5161.

MCFARLAND, JAMES WILLIAM, JR., real estate manager; b. Tuscaloosa, Ala., Sept. 8, 1979; s. James William McFarland, Sr. and Miriam Melinda (Webster) McFarland. Diploma, Tuscaloosa Acad., Ala., 1987—98. Cert. notary public Ala., accredited residential mgr. Inst. Real Estate Mgmt., 2006. Internship US Ho. Reps., DC, 2003; founder, mng. mem. Buffex LLC, 2004—; mgr. Skyland Apts. Ward McFarland Inc., 2005—. Author: (biography) Ward Wharton McFarland: Veteran, Attorney, Public Servant, Businessman. Mem. Friends Tuscaloosa Pub. Libr., 2003—07; jr. patron Birmingham Mus. Art, 2004—05; vol. Friends Bryce Hosp., Tuscaloosa; mem. Ala. World Trade Assn., Montgomery; founding mem. US Dept. Homeland Security, 2002; hon. col. appointed by Gov. George C. Wallace State Ala., Montgomery, 1987; dept. campaign mgr. Lisa T. Wallace for Ala. State Treas., 2002; exec. com. mem. Ala. Rep. Party, Birmingham, 2003—04; founding chmn. Tuscaloosa Young Reps., 2003—04; del. Rep. Nat. Conv., NYC, 2004, 2006—; v.p. West Ala. Rep. Assembly, 2007; mem. St. Jude League, Chgo., 1998—2005. Staff officer US Coast Guard Aux. Named Hon. Capitol Hill Historian, US Capitol Hill Hist. Soc., 2003, Hon. Citizen, State of Ohio, Gov. Bob Taft, Hon. Citizen, City of New Orleans, City Coun., Mayor Ernest Morial, Hon. Citizen, Father Flanagan's Boys and Girls Town, Nebr., 2006, 2007; recipient cert. of recognition, Ala. Gov. Bob Riley, Montgomery, 2003. Mem.: Internat. Coun. Shopping Ctr. (student mem.), U. Ala. Ins. Soc. Republican. Roman Catholic. Avocations: travel, writing, photography. Office: Ward McFarland Inc 325 Skyland Blvd E Tuscaloosa AL 35405 Mailing: Buffex LLC 130 Wildwood Pky Ste 108 Birmingham AL 35209

MCFARLAND, KATHLEEN TROIA (KT MCFARLAND), government defense consultant; b. Madison, Wis., July 22, 1951; d. August Joseph and Edith (Fuller) Troia; m. Alan Roberts McFarland, Jr., Jan. 12, 1985; 5 children. BA, George Washington U., 1973; MA, Oxford U., Eng., 1978; postgrad., MIT, 1978-81. Research asst. to Dr. H. A. Kissinger Nat. Security Council, Washington, 1970-73; staff mem. Senate Armed Services Com., Washington, 1981-82; asst. to sec. def. Dept. Def., Washington, 1982-83, dep. asst. sec. def., 1983-84, cons., 1985. Campaign for US Senate NY, 2006—. Student trustee George Washington U., 1971-73 Fellow Ford Found., 1979-81, Arms Control and Disarmament Agy., 1980-81, Inst. for Study World Politics, 1980-81 Mem. Council on Fgn. Relations Republican. Episcopalian. Office: KT McFarland for Senate 954 Lexington Ave Box 135 New York NY 10021

MCFARLAND, KAY ELEANOR, state supreme court chief justice; b. Coffeyville, Kans., July 20, 1935; d. Kenneth W. and Margaret E. (Thrall) McF BA in English & History, Washburn U., Topeka, 1957, JD, 1964. Bar: Kans. 1964. Sole practice, Topeka, 1964-71; probate and juvenile judge Shawnee County, Topeka, 1971-73; dist. judge Topeka, 1973-77; assoc. justice Kans. Supreme Ct., 1977-95, chief justice, 1995—. Mem. Kans. Bar Assn., Women Attys. Assn. Topeka., Topeka Bar Assn Achievements include being the first woman appointed justice and chief justice of Kansas' Supreme Court. Office: Kans Supreme Ct Kans Jud Ctr 301 SW 10th Ave Topeka KS 66612-1507 Fax: (785) 291-3274.

MCFARLAND, MARCIE ALLRED, lawyer; b. Macon, Ga., Jan. 17, 1970; m. Charles McFarland; 1 child. BBA with highest honors, U. Tex., 1992, MBA with highest honors, 1993, JD with high honors, 2000. CPA 1994; bar: Tex. 2000, US Dist. Ct. (so. and we. dists. Tex.). Tax assoc. to tax sr. Ernst & Young, 1993—97; with fin. grp. Continental Airlines, 1997; atty. Baker Botts, Houston, 2000—03; assoc. Rusty Hardin & Assocs., P.C., Houston, 2003—. Named a Rising Star, Tex. Super Lawyers mag., 2006. Mem.: Houston Young Lawyers Assn., Houston Bar Assn. Avocations: movies, walking, music, reading. Office: Rusty Hardin & Assocs PC 1401 McKinney Ste 2250 Houston TX 77010 Office Phone: 713-652-9000. *

MCFARLAND, MICHAEL C., academic administrator; b. Boston, 1948; AB in Physics, Cornell U., 1969; M in Elec. Engring., Carnegie M in Elec. Engring., PhD in Elec. Engring., Carnegie Mellon U.; MDiv, Weston Sch. Theology, ThM in Social Ethics. Ordained to ministry Jesuits, 1984. Cons. AT&T Bell Labs., 1985—86; assoc. prof. computer sci. Boston Coll., 1986—96, dept. chair; prof. computer sci., dean Coll. Arts and Scis. Gonzaga U., Spokane, 1996—2000; pres. Coll. of the Holy Cross, Worcester, Mass., 2000—. Bd. dir. Worcester Mcpl. Rsch. Bur., Worcester Cath. Charities; bd. dirs. U. Scranton. Avocation: running. Office: Coll of the Holy Cross 1 College St Worcester MA 01610-2395 Office Phone: 508-793-2525. *

MC FARLAND, NORMAN FRANCIS, bishop; b. Martinez, Calif., Feb. 21, 1922; Student, St. Patrick's Sem. Ordained to ministry Cath. Ch., 1946, consecrated bishop Cath. Ch., 1970. Auxilliary bishop, San Francisco, 1970—74; apostolic adminstr. Diocese of Reno, 1974—76; bishop Diocese of Reno-Las Vegas, 1976—87, Diocese of Orange, Calif., 1987—98. Office: 200 W La Veta Ave Orange CA 92866-1936

MCFARLAND, PHILIP JAMES, secondary school educator, writer; b. Birmingham, Ala., June 20, 1930; s. Thomas Alfred McFarland and Alice Lucile Sylvester; m. Patricia Katherin Connors, July 23, 1960; children: Philip James Jr., Joseph Thomas. BA, Oberlin Coll., 1951; MA, Cambridge U., 1957. Editor textbooks Houghton Mifflin Co., Boston, 1958—64; tchr. English Concord Acad., Mass., 1965—95. Author: A House Full of Women, 1960, Sojourners, 1979, Seasons of Fear, 1984, Sea Dangers, 1985, A History of Concord Acad. 2 vols., 1986, 2000, The Brave Bostonians, 1998, Hawthorne in Concord, 2004, Loves of Harriet Beecher Stowe, 2007; sr. editor Houghton Mifflin Literature Series, 6 vols., 1972, Focus on Literature, 7 vols., 1978; editor: Composition: Models and Exercises, 5 vols., 2d edit., 1971. Lt. j.g. USN, 1951-55. Fellow Mass. Hist. Soc. Democrat. Avocations: bicycling, trekking. Home: 18 Independence Ave Lexington MA 02421-5939 E-mail: pmcf@rcn.com.

MCFARLAND, RICHARD MACKLIN, retired journalist; b. Blockton, Iowa, Mar. 27, 1922; s. William Harold McFarland and Elsie (Sisson) McFarland Chavannes; m. Jacquelyn Jean Folske, Mar. 22, 1955; children: Bethany Rose, Scott Macklin, Elizabeth Ann McFarland Heyda, Kathryn Belle. BA, U. Iowa, 1944. Newsman UPI, Des Moines, 1944, Chgo., 1945, 46-47, bur. mgr. Bismarck, ND, 1944-45, Herrin, Ill., 1945, Sioux Falls, SD, 1947-49, Milw., 1949-51, legis. reporter Des Moines, 1947, Pierre, SD, 1949, Iowa mgr. Des Moines, 1951-54, NW mgr. Mpls., 1954-55, Wis. mgr. Milw., 1956-57, regional exec. sales, 1958-59, bur. mgr. Chgo., 1960-61, Minn. mgr. Mpls., 1961-69, Mich. editor Detroit, 1969-71, Minn. editor Mpls., 1971-84, bur. mgr.-capitol reporter St. Paul, 1985-89; ret., 1989. Former deacon Advent Luth. Ch., Roseville, Minn.; coun. mem. Redeemer Luth. Ch., Bradenton, Fla., 1996—98, pres. coun., 1998—99, coun. mem., 2001—05. With USN, 1943—44. Avocations: reading, music, fishing, backpacking, golf. Home: 7312 5th Ave NW Bradenton FL 34209-1522 Personal E-mail: rmcf@aol.com.

MCFARLAND, ROBERT BRUCE, physician; b. Ames, Iowa, Sept. 18, 1929; s. Julian Ecwart and Winnie Florence (Goering) McF.; m. Zoë Euphrosyne Bucuvalas, June 1, 1958; children: Laura Ann, Bruce Damon. BA, Kenton Coll., 1950; MD, U. Iowa, 1954. Intern San Francisco Gen. Hosp., 1955; house officer Mass. Gen. Hosp., Boston, 1957-59; asst. resident U. Colo. Med. Ctr., Denver, 1959-61; physician pvt. practice, Boulder, Colo., 1961-76, 78-93; prof. U. Mo., Kansas City, 1976-78. Contbg. editor Jour. Psychohistory, 1996—; contbr. articles to profl. jours. Vestryman St. John's Episcopal Ch., Boulder, 1966-69; jail physician Boulder County, Kansas City, 1972-75, 76-78; co-founder Parenting Place, Boulder, 1984-2001; cons., bd. health No. Cheyenne Tribe, Lame Deer, Mont., 1976-84. Comdr. USNR-R, 1955-78. Avocations: hiking, reading. Home: 2300 Kalmia Ave Boulder CO 80304-1931 E-mail: mcfarland73@msn.com.

MCFARLAND, RONALD G. (RON MCFARLAND), composer, music educator, musician; b. San Bernardino, Calif., Apr. 20, 1928; s. George Millard McFarland and Anna Belle Hagy. Student, Arnold Schoenberg Studio, Brendwood, Calif., 1946—48, Carpenter Music Studio, San Bernardino, 1944—48, Leginska Piano Studio, Hollywood, Calif., 1945—52, Sheinfeld Studio, San Francisco, 1969—71, San Francisco State U., 1961—66. Prin. instr. McFarland Piano Studio, Tiburon, Calif., 1962—; piano tchr., composer-in-residence San Domenico Sch., Fairfax, Calif., 1966—72. Mem. artist adv. com. Old First Concerts, San Francisco, 1994—. Musician: (profl. debut) Leginska Symphony Orch., Wilshire Ebell Theatre, 1948—49, Carnegie Hall, 1983; soloist: Beethoven's Piano Concerto in C Major, Tulare County Symphony Orch., 1963, composer numerous works for piano, voice, violin, orch., opera, ballet. Bd. dirs., founding mem. Composers, Inc., San Francisco, 1984—88. Recipient 1st prize, Composers Today Competition, 1984, Std. award, ASCAP, 1996—2006, Honors, McFarland Musical Retrospective, 1998. Mem.: Music Tchrs. Assn. Calif. (registered tchr. piano and composition, chmn. music competition 1970—72, 1st prize 1975, 1988, 1981, 1982, 1985), Landmark Soc., Belvedere-Tiburon Libr. Soc. Avocations: swimming, gardening, travel, reading, architecture. Home and Studio: 765 Tiburon Blvd Belvedere Tiburon CA 94920

MCFARLAND, SAMUEL P., JR., psychologist; b. Atlanta, Oct. 16, 1957; s. Samuel P. and Gladys Blake (Pepper) McF. BA in Psychology, Mercer U., 1983; MA in Gen. and Exptl. Psychology, Fla. Atlantic U., 1987; MS in Clin. Psychology, Nova U., 1993; PhD in Clin. Psychology, Nova Southeastern U., 1998. Store mgr. Reeds Drugs Inc., Atlanta, 1973—81; mental health technician C.P.C. Parkwood Hosp., Atlanta, 1982—84; mental health asst. C.P.C. Ft. Lauderdale Hosp., Fla., 1985, N.M.E. Fair Oaks Hosp., Delray Beach, 1985-87; peer acad. advisor Fla. Atlantic U., Boca Raton, 1986-87; clin. counselor/supr. Henderson Mental Health Ctr./New Vistas, Ft. Lauderdale, 1987-88; adj. faculty instr. Art Inst. Ft. Lauderdale, 1992-93; case mgr., psychologist Bradley Ctr. of St. Francis, Columbus, Ga., 1993—. Therapist Biofeedback Clinic/Nova Clinic, Davie, Fla., 1992, The Family Ctr./Nova U., 1991-92, Child & Adolescent Anxiety Disorders Clinic/Nova Clinic, Coral Springs, 1988-89. Co-sponsor Al-Ateen Group, Atlanta, 1975-76. Mem. APA (nat. treas. 1988-90, mem. divsns. 12 and 37 1994—), Am. Psychol. Assn. Gread. Students (nat. treas. 1988-90), Am. Psychol. Soc., Columbus Psychol. Assn. Office: Bradley Ctr St Francis 2000 16th Ave Columbus GA 31901 Office Phone: 706-320-3766. E-mail: wolf444@charter.net.

MCFARLAND, THOMAS, English literature educator; b. Birmingham, Ala., Sept. 13, 1926; s. Thomas Alfred McFarland and Lucile Sylvester. AB, Harvard U., 1949; AM, Yale U., 1951, PhD, 1953; postgrad., Eberhard-Karls-Universität, Tübingen, Germany, 1953—54; MA (hon.), Oxford U., Eng., 1986. Instr. in English Oberlin Coll., 1954-56, U. Va., 1956-58; asst. prof. Western Res. U., Cleve., 1958-62, assoc. prof., 1962-64, prof., 1964-67, Grad. Ctr. CUNY, 1967-73, disting. prof. English lit., 1973-78; prof. Princeton (NJ) U., 1978-81, Murray prof. English lit., 1981-89; Murray prof. English lit. emeritus Princeton U., 1989—. Vis. prof. U. Colo., 1968, U. Va., 1972, Yale U., 1975; vis. fellow All Souls Coll., U. Oxford, Eng., 1986-87, Humanities Rsch. Ctr., Australian Nat. U., Canberra, 1992, Lechter Inst. for Lit. Rsch., Bar-Ilan U., Ramat Gan, Israel, 1989, U. Otago, Dunedin, New Zealand, 1992; adv. bd. Bull. Rsch. in Humanities, 1978—, Studies in Romanticism, 1982—, Nineteenth-Century Lit., 1986—, Works of Thomas De Quincey, 1990, Romanticism, 1995—; hon. fellow Ctr. for European Romanticism, Glasgow, 1997—; mem. supervising com. English Inst., 1971-74, chmn. 1974; assoc. trustee The Dove Cottage Trust, The Lake Dist., Eng., 1982—; bd. advisors Milton and the Romantics, 1975—; seminar assoc. Columbia U., 1971—; pres. com. English dept. Harvard U., 1987-88; lectr. in field. Author: Tragic Meanings in Shakespeare, 1966, Coleridge and the Pantheist Tradition, 1969, Shakespeare's Pastoral Comedy, 1972, Romanticism and the Forms of Ruin: Wordsworth, Coleridge and Modalities of Fragmentation, 1981, Originality and Imagination, 1985, Shapes of Culture, 1987, Romantic Cruxes: The English Essayists and the Spirit of the Age, 1987, Festschrift: The Coleridge Connection: Essays for Thomas McFarland, 1990, William Wordsworth: Intensity and Achievement, 1992, Romanticism and the Heritage of Rousseau, 1995, Paradoxes of Freedom: The Romantic Mystique of a Transcendence, 1996, The Masks of Keats: The Endeavor of a Poet, 2000; editor: The Opus Maximum of Samuel Taylor Coleridge, 2002; mem. editl. bd. Comparative Criticism, 1977—, European Romantic Rev., 1989—; contbr. 52 articles to scholarly jours. Fulbright scholar, 1953-54; fellow Guggenheim Found., 1964-65, 74-75, Am. Coun. Learned Socs., 1973-74, Ctr. for Advanced Study in Behavioral Scis., Stanford, Calif., 1981-82, NEH, 1981-82, 86-87. Mem. MLA (exec. com. English 9 1970-73, chmn. 1974), Sydney Soc. for Lit. and Aesthetics (hon. life). Home: 1046 Cornwall C Boca Raton FL 33434

MCFARLAND, WILLIAM JOSEPH (JOE MCFARLAND), academic administrator; b. Sterling, Kans., July 25, 1929; s. Armour James and Sylvia Jane Louise (Hutcheson) McF.; m. Mary Roberta Dill, Dec. 21, 1951; children: William Joseph, Kathryn Ann, Matthew Curtis. BA, Sterling Coll., 1951; MA, U. No. Colo., 1957; EdD, Ind. U., 1966; PhD (hon.), Sterling Coll., 1992, Geneva Coll., 2001. Cert. tchr. and adminstr., pilot. Elem. prin., coach, tchr., supt. schs. Turon Pub. Schs., Kans., 1953-59; assoc. prof. edn., dir. student teaching, head edn. dept. Emporia State U., Kans., 1959-68; assoc. exec. sec. Kans. NEA, Topeka, 1968-71; dir. acad. affairs Kans. Bd. Regents, Topeka, 1971-84; pres. Geneva Coll., Beaver Falls, Pa., 1984-92; cons., scholar in residence Christs Coll., Taipei, Taiwan, 1992—2002; headmaster Am. Acad. Nicosia, Cyprus, 2002—. Chmn. scholarship selection com. Beech Aircraft Co., Wichita, Kans., 1979-84; pres. coun. Nat. Assn. Intercollegiate Athletics, Kansas City, Kans., 1984-92. Contbr. articles to profl. jours. Pres. Topeka Fellowship, Inc., 1977-84; mem. exec. coun., v.p. Boy Scouts Am., Emporia and Topeka, 1963-83; legis. liason person NEA, Topeka, 1968-71; chmn. Kans. Commn. on Aerospace Edn., 1971-83, Gov's. Commn. on Sch. to Work, 1995-2001; trustee Sterling Coll., Kans., 1971-84, Geneva Coll., 1973-84; sec. Pa. Found. Ind. Colls.; bd. dirs. United Way, Beaver County, Pa., 1985-92, ARC of Beaver County, 1985-92, Beaver Valley C. of C., 1985-88; mem. Christian Coll. Coalition, 1984-92. With U.S. Army, 1951-53, Korea. Recipient Lieber Meml. Teaching award Ind. U., Bloomington, 1966; Disting. Service award Sterling Coll., 1983; VIP award Sta. WREN, Topeka, 1971; 50 Yr. Recognition award Kansas State H.S. Activities Assn., 2005. Mem. Assn. Governing Bds. (exec. com.), Pa. Assn. Colls. and Univs., Nat. Assn. Ind. Colls. and Univs., Beaver Valley C. of C., ARC (pres. local chpt.), Knife and Fork Club (bd. dirs. 1979-84, Rotary (life, pres. 1986-87, Paul Harris fellow 1988, chmn. scholarship selection com. Rotary Found.), Phi Delta Kappa (v.p. 1969-73) Republican. Presbyterian. Avocations: flying, football officiating, golf, hunting. Home and Office: 2709 SW Boswell Ave Topeka KS 66611-1604 E-mail: joromcf@sbcglobal.net.

MCFARLANE, BETH LUCETTA TROESTER, retired mayor; b. Osterdock, Iowa, Mar. 9, 1918; d. Francis Charles and Ella Carrie (Moser) Troester; m. George Evert McFarlane, June 20, 1943 (dec. May 1972); children: Douglas, Steven(dec.), Susan, George. EdB, U. No. Iowa, Cedar Falls, 1962, MEd, 1971. Cert. tchr. Tchr. rural and elem. schs., Iowa, 1936-50, 55-56; elem. tchr. Oelwein Cmty. Schs., Iowa, 1956-64, jr. high reading tchr., 1964—71, 1983; city council Oelwein, 1981-82; mayor of Oelwein, 1982-89; ret. Evaluator N. Ctrl. Accreditation Assn. Ednl. Programs; mem. planning team confs. Iowa cities N.E. Iowa, 1985; v.p. N.E. Iowa Regional Coun. Econ. Devel., 1986—89; mem. area econ. devel. com. N.E. Iowa, 1985, mem. legis. interim study com. rural devel., 1987—88; mem. policy com. Iowa League Municipalities, 1987—88. V.p. Fayette County Tourism Coun., 1987—88; mem. Iowa State steering com. road use tax financing, 1988—89; chmn. bd. govs. Oelwein Cmty. Ctr., 1990—94, bd. govs., 2001—; chmn. bldg. and fin. com. Reorganized LDS/Cmty. Christ Ch. Bldg., 1980—2007, dist. ch. fin. com., 1992—2001, dist. ch. revolving loan com., 1982—2000. Named Iowa Reading Tchr. of Yr., Internat. Reading Assn. Iowa, 1978; recipient Outstanding Contbn. to Reading Coun. Acitivities award, Internat. Reading Assn. N.E. Iowa, 1978, State of Iowa's Gov.'s Leadership award, 1988. Mem.: Oelwein Bus. and Profl. Women (Woman of Yr. 1983), MacDowell Music and Arts Orgn. (pres. 1978—80), N.E. Iowa Reading Coun. (pres. 1975—77), Area Univ. Women (pres. 1999—2000), Oelwein Area Ret. Sch. Pers. (pres. 1994—96), Oelwien Area C. of C. (bd. dirs. 1986—89, Humanitarian award 1987), Delta Kappa Gamma (pres. 1980—82). Republican. Mem. Cmty. Of Christ Ch. Avocations: hiking, refinishing antiques, gardening, walking, creative sewing. Home: 512 7th Ave NE Oelwein IA 50662-1326

MCFARLANE, DONOVAN ANTHONY, finance educator, poet, researcher; b. Manchester, Jamaica, Apr. 19, 1978; came to U.S., 1997; s. Merceline Agatha Wright. Cert., deCarteret Coll., Jamaica, 1995, Church Tchrs. Coll., 1997; PhD in Parapsychic Sci., Am. Inst. Theology, 2003; diploma in fitness and nutrition, Harcourt Learning Direct, Scranton, Pa., 1999; diploma in mgmt. restaurant and hotel, Profl. Career Devel. Inst., Atlanta, 2000; diploma in bus. mgmt. with highest honor, Stratford Career Inst., Washington, 2000; diploma in small bus. mgmt., Lifetime Career Sch., Archbald, Pa., 2000; BS in Geog. Sci., Bernadean U., North Hollywood, Calif., 2000; PhD in Metaphysics, Am. Coll. Metaphys. Theology, Golden Valley, Minn., 2000, PhD in Comparative Religion, 2002; cert. in paralegal studies, Blackstone Sch., 2002; BS in Parapsychic Sci., Am. Inst. Holistic Theology, 2003, MS in Parapsychic Sci., 2002; MBA, Frederick Taylor U., 2002; MBA in Mgmt., Barrington U., 2003; BSBA, Nova Southeastern U., Fla., 2003; diploma in writing, Inst. Childrens Lit., 2003; B in Metaphys. sci., U. Metaphysics, Calif., 2003; diploma, U. Metaphysics, 2003; cert. metaphysical practitioner, U. Metaphysics Sem., 2003; MBA, Nova Southeastern U., 2005; D in Metaphys. Psychology, U. Sedona, Ariz., 2007. Bd. cert. holistic health practitioner Am. Assn. Drugless Practitioners, 2005, bd. cert. alternative med. practitioner Am. Alternative Med. Assn., 2005; cert. in secondary edn. Tchr. trainee in Spanish and social studies Comprehensive H.S., Jamaica, 1997; tutor gen. sci. Church Tchrs. Coll., Jamaica; curriculum planner pvt. orgn., Fla., essayist Fla., cons. Lauderdale Lakes, Fla., 1998—; clk. Phillips and Phillips, Ft. Lauderdale, Fla., 1997—98; supr. inventory and warehouse Lord's Supermarket, Oakland, Fla., 1999; with Corp. Edu. Rsch., 2001—; prof. bus. studies U. Ft. Lauderdale, 2005—, City Coll. Ft. Lauderdale, 2005. Adj. instr. bus. studies City Coll., Ft. Lauderdale, Fla., 2005—; founder, chief preceptor, chancellor Donovan Soc., LLC, Ft. Lauderdale, 2006. Author: numerous poems; contbr. scientific papers to profl. jours. Recipient cert. excellence in Spanish, social studies, geography, math., history, cert. diligence in spanish, religious edn., cert. outstanding achievement in social studies, cert. outstanding achievement in Spanish, Internat. Poet of Merit award, 2002, Outstanding Achievement in Poetry Silver award, 2003, Commemorative award, 2003; named hon. alumni Oglata Lakota Coll., S.D., 2000. Mem.: Internat. Libr. Poetry (laureate cert. 2002), Internat. Soc. Poets (Editor's Choice award 1998), Nat. Libr. Poetry (Disting. Membership cert. and plaque 1998), Sigma Beta Delta (Outstanding Scholastic Achievement 2005). Avocations: dance, oratory, martial arts, singing, writing. Personal E-mail: don_anthoni@yahoo.com.

MCFARLANE, SETH, animator, director; b. Kent, Conn., Oct. 26, 1973; s. Ron and Perry McFarlane. Grad., RI Sch. Design. Animator Hanna-Barbera Prodns. (now Cartoon Network Studios); writer Walt Disney Animation, Fox Broadcasting Co. Writer, dir. (TV series) Shnookums and Meat Funny Cartoon Show, 1993, writer, dir., actor The Life of Larry, 1995, Larry & Steve, 1996, writer Dexter's Laboratory, 1996—, Jungle Cubs, 1996—98, Ace Ventura: Pet Detective, 1996, Cow and Chicken, 1997—2001, Johnny Bravo, 1997—, writer, dir. Zoomates, 1998, exec. prodr., writer, creator, actor Family Guy, 1999—, cons. prodr. The Pitts, 2003, exec. prodr., writer, dir., actor American Dad!, 2005—.

MCFARLANE, WALTER ALEXANDER, lawyer, educator; b. Richlands, Va., May 4, 1940; s. James Albert and Frances Mae (Padbury) McF.; m. Judith Louise Copenhaver, Aug. 31, 1962. BA, Emory and Henry Coll., 1962; JD, U. Richmond, 1966. Bar: Ba. 1966, U.S. Supreme Ct. 1970, U.S. Ct. Appeals (4th cir.) 1973, U.S. Ct. Appeals (D.C. cir.) 1977, U.S. Dist. ct. (ea. dist.) Va. 1973. Asst. atty. gen. Office Va. Atty. Gen., Richmond, 1969-73, dep. atty. gen., 1973-90; exec. asst., chief counsel, dir. policy Gov.'s Office Commonwealth of Va., 1990-94, supt. Dept. Correctional Edn., 1994—. Acting dir. Dept. Juvenile Justice, 1997, State Bd. Dept. Criminal Justice Svcs., 1994—; prof. adj. staff U. Richmond, 1978—, A.L.Philpott disting. prof. T.C. Williams Sch. Law, 2003; chmn. transp. law com. Transp. Rsch. Bd., Nat. Rsch. Bd. Nat. Acads. Sci. and Engring., Washington, 1977-85, 88-94, chmn. legal affairs com., 1978-85, chmn. environ., archeol. and hist. com., 1985-90; mem. State Water Commn., 1994-96, mem., Coun. of State Govts. Henry Toll Fell., 1988, Legal Task Force, 1988-2002. Contbr. articles to profl. jours. Exec. com., bd. govs. Emory and Henry Coll., 1985-98; pres. Windsor Forest Civic Assn., Midlothian, Va., 1975-76; bd. dirs. Greater Midlothian Civic League, 1980-86, v.p., 1980; instr. water safety ARC, 1962-87; chmn. bldg. com. Mt. Pisgah United Meth. Ch., 1980-85, pres. men's club, 1980-81; bd. dirs. ctrl. Va. chpt. Epilepsy Assn. Va., 1988-91. Capt. JAGC, USAF, 1966-69. Recipient J.D. Buscher Disting. Atty. award Am. Assn. State Hwy. and Transp. Ofcls., 1983, John C. Vance legal writing award Nat. Acads. Sci. and Engring., 4th ann. outstanding evening lectr. award Student Body, U. Richmond, 1980. Mem. Chesterfield Bar Assn., Richmond Bar Assn. (bd. dir. 1989-93), Richmond Scottish Soc. (bd. dirs. 1980-82), Va. Correctional Assn. (pres.-elect 2004-06, pres. 2007—, Lifetime Achievement award 2004), Am. Correctional Assn. (gen. assembly 2002-06, bd. govs. 2006—), Woodland Pond Civic Assn. (bd. dirs. 2005—), Emory and Henry Coll. Alumni Assn. (chpt. pres. 1971-73, regional v.p. 1974-77, pres. 1981-83), Meadowbrook Country Club (bd. dir. 2001-04). Home: 9001 Widgeon Way Chesterfield VA 23838-5274 Office: 101 N 14th St Richmond VA 23219-3684 Office Phone: 804-225-3314. Business E-mail: wamcfarlane@dce.state.va.us.

MCFARLANE, WILLIS MCKEE, buffalo company executive; b. Cleve., May 27, 1933; BA in Econs. cum laude, Amherst Coll., 1955. Exec. Northwestern Mut. Life Ins., 1955-60; ptnr. life ins. co. Files, Cristal, and McFarlane, 1956—; founder AIRCOA, Cleve., 1968-79, Denver, 1979-90; co-owner Denver Buffalo Mktg. Co., 1990—, Buffalo Bar, Idaho Springs, 1995—. Chmn. bd. dirs. Colo. Symphony Orch.; bd. dirs. Colo. Wildlife Heritage Found. Mem. Cherry Hills Country Club. Office: Denver Buffalo Co 5800 Franklin St Ste 101 Denver CO 80216-1249

MCFARLIN, DIANE HOOTEN, publisher; b. Lake Wales, Fla., July 10, 1954; d. Ruffie Denton Hooten and Anna Loraine (Peeples) Huff; m. Henry Briggs McFarlin, Aug. 28, 1976 (div. 1993). BS, U. Fla., 1976. Reporter Sarasota (Fla.) Jour., 1976-77, asst. news editor, 1977-78, city editor, 1978-82; asst. mng. editor Sarasota (Fla.) Herald Tribune, 1983-84, mng. editor, 1985-87; exec. editor Gainesville (Fla.) Sun, 1987-90; from exec. editor to assoc. publ. Sarasota Herald-Tribune, 1990-99, publ., 1999—. Adv. bd. U. Fla. Coll. Journalism and Comm., 1987—; Pulitzer juror Columbia U., 1995-96, 2001-02. Mem. accrediting coun. Edn. in Journalism and Mass Comms., 1994-96. Recipient Alumna of Distinction award U. Fla., 1999. Mem. Am. Soc. Newspaper Editors (com. chair 1992, 94, 96, 2000, bd. dirs. 1994—, treas., sec., v.p. 2001, pres. 2002), Fla. Soc. Newspaper Editors (sec.-treas. 1993, v.p. 1994, pres. 1995). Office: Sarasota Herald-Tribune PO Box 1719 Sarasota FL 34230-1719 also: 801 S Tamiami Trail Sarasota FL 34236-7824

MCFARLIN, RICHARD FRANCIS, retired industrial chemist, researcher; b. Oklahoma City, Oct. 12, 1929; s. Loy Lester and Julie Mae (Collins) McF.; m. Clare Jane Burroughs, Apr. 4, 1953; children: Robin Sue McFarlin Godwin, Richard Prescott, Rebecca Lynn McFarlin Bray, Roger Whitsitt. BS, Va. Mil. Inst., 1951; MS, Purdue U., 1953, PhD, 1956. Rsch. chemist Monsanto Chem. Co., St. Louis, 1956-60; supr. inorganic rsch. Internat. Minerals and Chems., Mulberry, Fla., 1961; mgr. Agr. Rsch. Ctr. Armour Agrl. Chem. Co., Atlanta, 1962; v.p. rsch., ops., devel. & adminstrn. div. agri-chems. U.S. Steel, Atlanta, 1986; tech. dir. Lester Labs. Inc., Atlanta, 1986-88; exec. dir. Fla. Inst. Phosphate Rsch., Bartow, 1988-96; ret., 1996. Mem. bd. advisors engring. coun. U. South Fla., Lakeland, 1990—, U. Fla., Gainesville, 1991—; mem. bd. advisors Inst. Recyclable Materials La. State U., Baton Rouge, 1990—. Capt. USAR, 1951-61. M. M. Cohn Found. scholar, 1947, L. D. Wall scholar, 1949, O. M. Baldinger scholar, 1950. Presbyterian. Achievements include eight U.S. and foreign patents for selective organic reducing agents, fertilizer processes and selective biocides. Home: 3239 Bridgefield Dr Lakeland FL 33803-7903 E-mail: rmcf203@msn.com.

MCFARLING, USHA LEE, journalist; b. Landstuhl, West Germany, June 28, 1967; m. Michael Dickinson; children: Phoebe, Peter. BA in Biology, Brown U., 1988; MA in Biol. Psych., U. Calif., Berkeley, 1998. With Boston Globe; with Washington bur. Knight Ridder; with San Antonio Light; sci. writer planetary and earth scis. LA Times; freelance journalist. Mem. sci. and soc. journalism awards com. Nat. Assn. Sci. Writers, Inc.; mem. judging com. Wistar Inst., 2004—; spkr. in field. Co-recipient John B. Oakes award for Outstanding Environmental Journalism, Columbia U. Grad. Sch. Journalism, 2006, George Polk award for Environmental Reporting, 2006, Walter Sullivan award for Excellence in Sci. Journalism, Am. Geophys. Union, 2007, Pub. Comm. award, Am. Soc. Microbiol., 2007, Print Media award, Am. Inst. Biol. Scis., 2007, Pulitzer Prize for Explanatory Reporting, 2007; recipient award, Wistar Inst., 2004; fellow Knight Sci. Journalism, MIT, 1992—93. *

MCFARLIN-KOSIEC, BARBARA ANN, secondary school educator, literature and language professor, small business owner; b. Lamesa, Tex., Oct. 4, 1937; d. Roy W. and Laura Corine (Daniel) McFarlin; m. Leonard E. Kosiec; 1 child, James Daniel. BA in Spanish, Tex. Christian U., Ft. Worth, 1960; attended, Instituto Tecnologico and Estudios Superiores Monterrey, Mex., 1961, Instituto Tecnologico and Estudios Superiores Monterrey, 1962, Pan Am. Coll., Edinburgh, Tex., 1962, Ea. Wash. State U., Cheney, 1963, attended, 1972, attended, 1974, attended, 1977, attended, 1989, Ctrl. Washington State U., Ellensburg, 1971, attended, 1973, attended, 1976, attended, 1977, attended, 1987, attended, 1988, U. of Ams., Mex. City, Mex., 1966, U. San Carlos, Guatemala City, Guatemala, 1967; MA in Spanish, Tex. Christian U., Ft. Worth, 1964; PhD in Leadership in Edn., Gonzaga U., Spokane, Wash., 1985. Tchr. 2d grade Mercedes (Tex.) Pub. Schs., 1962; tchr. English Instituto Tecnologico and Estudios Superiores Monterrey, Mexico, 1962; tchr. Spanish, English and social studies Dayton (Wash.) HS, 1963—65; tchr. Spanish, Mexican and Latin Am. history Peninsula CC, Port Angeles, Wash., 1965-68; tchr. grades 4-12 Spanish, English and social studies Burbank (Wash.) Pub. Schs., 1968-73; tchr. Spanish, ESL and multicultural rels. evening staff mem. Columbia Basin CC, Pasco, 1973—80; tchr. 1st, 2d, 3d, 4th, 5th and 6th grades, bilingual and migrant edn. programs Pasco (Wash.) Pub. Schs., 1973-82, 1993—95; tchr. Tex.-Wash. migrant edn. program Pasco HS, 1975—77; sub. tchr. Fernie Pub. Schs., East Kootenay CC, BC, Canada, 1982—85, Fernie Pub. Schs., 1990—92; tchr. grade 3 bilingual edn. Othello Pub. Schs., Wash., 1985—93; pres. McFarlin-Kosiec Enterprises, Fernie, 1986—; tchr. Spanish grades 1-8 St. Joseph Sch., Kennewick, Wash., 1995—96; tchr. Spanish, history and psychology Mt. Baker Secondary Sch. Southeast Kootenay Sch. dist. 5, Cranbrook, Canada, 1997—2004. Instr. English as second lang. Inst. Tech. y de Estudios Superios de Monterrey, Mex., 1962, Spanish Big Bend CC, Moses Lake, Wash., 1986-87, Seattle Pacific U., 1986, Columbia Bain CC, Pasco, Wash., 1973-80, 87-89; edn. editor El Sol newspaper, Pasco; writer Temos, Buenos Aires; cons. in field; freelance writer Fernie Free Press; adj. prof. second lang. and culture Seattle Pacific U., 1980; mem. Tri-Cities Higher Edn. Orgn., 1987-88, Kennewick Schs. Facilities Com., 1990-96; activist State Com., Wash., 1995-96; del. ann. gen. meeting BC Tchrs.' Fedn., 2002; labour affiliation rep. Cranbrook Dist. Tchrs.' Assn., 2001-02, rep. Cranbrook Tchrs. Assn. to BC Fedn. Labour Capilano Coll. Labour studies program, 2002; mem. Growth Mgmt. Act Com., Kennewick, 1990-96; v.p. Elk Valley and South Country Health Care Coalition, 2004-05, pres., 2005-06; com. mem. Can. Day, Fernie; guest spkr. and cons. in field. Performer: Recess; choreographer, dir. Phantom of the Opera Ballet Lutacoga Modern Dance Troup, 1991, Hook, 1992; choreographer: Desert, Art of Noise, Water, Fire, Rejoice, Autumn Leaves, Sunday in the Parkm Military Celebration, Snow, Meet Me in St. Louis, 1993; artistic dir.: Desert Storm Charity Show, Pasco, 1991; exhbns. include The US Bank, Othello, 1992, City Hall, Othello, 1993, Mark Twain Elem. Sch., Pasco, 1993, The Fernie Arts Co-op; writer, prodr. actor (play) Windows on Women, Fernie, BC, 2007; contbr. articles to profl. jours.; contbr. short stories various programs. Bd. dirs. Mid Columbia Regional Ballet Co., Richland, Wash.; precinct com. mem. Cen. Com., Benton County, 1991—; del. Benton County and Washington State Dem. Convs., 1988, 92, 94, 96, 04; active various Rep. convs.; deaconess Disciples of Christ Ch., Richland; mem. Columbia Chorale, Kennewick, Wash.; mem. negotiations com. Othello Sch. Dist., 1990—; artistic dir. benefit show Persian Gulf War Vets, UNICEF, 1991, Lutacaga Modern Dance Troupe, 1991—, founder; mem. Arts Coun., Fernie, BC, 1991, Writers' Guild Fernie, 1991; facility com. Kennewick Schs., Kennewick, Wash., 1989—; media and urban design planning commr. Kennewick, Wash., 1991—; parks and rec. commn. Kennewick, Wash., 1991—; active mem. Wash. Recreation and Park Assn, 1993—; pianist, organist, vocalist, dancer, performer Not For Profit Theater; organist Christ Ch. (Anglican), Fernie, 2004-06; precinct committeewoman Dem. Party, 1988-06; mem. Electoral Coll., Wash., 1996, Washington Assn. Fgn. Lang. Tchrs., 1962-90; commr. Parks and Recreation, Kennewick, 1990-96; vol. costumes Royal Winnipeg Balley Key City Theater, Cranbrook, 2000; scrutineer East Kootenay Electoral Dist., 2001, 05; sec. East Kootenay constituency exec. com. New Dem. Party, 2002-06, alt. del. provincial coun., 2002-03, del., 2003, chair nomination conv., 2005, master of ceremonies fundraiser, 2005; master of ceremonies fundraiser Elk Valley and South Country Health Care Coalition, 2005; coord. dance divsn. Performing Arts Festival 2001-05, presenter awards, 2001-06, sec., 2002-04, mem. bd., 2005; dir. Fernie Arts Coop.; mem. Royal Can. Legion, Fernie, 2004, 05; vol. The Can. Cancer Soc., 2005, 06; mem. Fernie Arts Coun., Columbia Chorale, Kennewick, 1990-93; mem. Allied Arts Gallery, Richland, Wash. Honored Spanish Embassy rsch. Lope de Vega, 1962; recipient Helen Gibbs award most talented Miss Walla Walla, 1965, award Assn. Quality Participation, 1989, 90, 91, 92, award Rainbow Rockers to Lutacaga Dance Troupe, Othello, 1992, Recognition award Mayor of Othello, Recognition award Othello City Libr., Recognition award Columbia Basin CC. Mem. AAUW (scholarship, legis. conf. 1977), NEA, Wash. Edn. Assn. (exec. bd. 1992—), Pasco Edn. Assn. (grievance rep. 1975-77, bldg. rep. 1980), Columbia Edn. Assn. (legis. com. 1968-73), Peninsula CC Edn. Assn. (profl. rights and negotiations com. 1966-68), Can. Fedn. U. Women, Internat. Platform Assn., Assn. Quality and Participation (chmn. edn. com. 1991, mem. awards com., v.p. 1996-97), Dance Educators Assn. Washington, Tri Cities Higher Edn. Orgn. (bd. dirs. 1987), Prevential Intermediate Tchr.'s Assn., Tchrs.' Fedn. and Coll. of Tchrs. (chmn. unemployed tchrs. Fernie dist. 1984-85, activist sub. tchrs.), BC Ret. Tchrs.'s Assn., Writer's Guild. Achievements include research in advanced statistics and research design. Avocations: arranging solo piano music, teaching modem dance. Home and Office: PO Box 1275 Fernie BC Canada V0B 1M0 Office Phone: 250-423-6091. E-mail: bkosiec@telus.net.

MCFARQUHAR, GREG M., meteorologist, educator; BSc, U. Toronto, 2007, MSc, 1989, PhD, 1992. Rschr. Scripps Instn. Oceanography, La Jolla, Calif., 1993—94; project scientist Nat. Ctr. for Atmospheric Rsch., Boulder, Colo., 1994—2001; asst., assoc. prof. U. Ill., Urbana, 2001—. Chief scientist atmospheric radiation measurement program aerial vehicle program Dept. of Energy, Washington, 2006—; chief scientist atmospheric radiation measurement program uninhabited aerospace vehicle program Sandia Nat. Labs., Livermore, Calif., 2003—06. Contbr. articles to profl. jours. Rsch. grant, NSF, Dept. of Energy, NOAA, NASA. Mem.: Am. Geophys. Soc., Am. Meteorol. Soc. (chmn. atmospheric meteorol. soc. com. on cloud physics 2007—). Office: Univ Ill 105 S Gregory St Urbana IL 61822 Office Phone: 217-265-5458.

MCFARREN, LELAND CULLEN, educational association administrator, educator; b. Navarre, Ohio, Nov. 13, 1923; s. Cullen Perry and Clara Caroline (Agler) McFarren; m. Beatrice Virginia German, Dec. 21, 1947; children: Michael Leland, Lynne Caroline Morris. BE, Kent State U., Ohio, 1949, MEd, 1952, postgrad., 1952—55, Case Western Res. U., Cleve., 1960. Cert. supt. East Ctrl. Ohio Tchr.'s Assn., 1970. Bricklayer apprentice Timken Roller Bearing, Canton, Ohio, 1941—43; tchr. Plain Local Schs., Canton, 1949—53, prin., 1953—62, asst. supt., 1963—77, supt., 1978—79. Stark County rep. East. Ctrl. Ohio Tchrs. Assn., 1965—69. Contbr. articles to profl. jours. Pres. Otis German Shopping Ctr. Platoon sgt., tank comdr. US Army, 1943—46. Decorated Silver Star medal US Army, Purple Heart, European Theatre medal with three stars, Good Conduct medal, Am. Theatre medal, Victory medal; named to Hall Distinction, Plain Local Schs., 2001, Ohio Mil. Hall Fame for valor, 2006; recipient Disting. Alumni award, Timken H.S., 2006. Mem.: DAV (life), Order Ky. Cols., Stark County Golf Assn. (past pres., dir.), Stark County Fast Pitch Assn. (Hall of Fame), Stark County Mental Health Soc. (bd. dirs.), East Ctrl. Ohio Tchrs. Assn., Buckeye Assn. Sch. Adminstrs., Stark County Elem. Prins. Assn. (pres. 1953—60, past. pres.), Timken HS Alumni Assn. (life disting. alumni 2006), Plain Local Alumni Assn. (life), Order Purple Heart (life), Ft. Lauderdale Country Club, Dapper Dan Club Akron, Willowbrook Lions Club, Canton Rotary Club, Pro Football Hall Fame Luncheon Club (past pres., dir.), Alliance County Club, North Canton Elks, Phi Delta Kappa. Avocations: golf, reading, sports. Home: 1130 Brushmore Ave NW Canton OH 44720 Home (Winter): 2320 Terra Ceia Blvd #401 Palmetto FL 34221

MCFATE, KENNETH LEVERNE, trade association administrator; b. LeClaire, Iowa, Feb. 5, 1924; s. Samuel Albert and Margaret (Spear) McF.; m. Imogene Grace Kness, Jan. 27, 1951; children: Daniel Elliott (dec.), Kathryn Margaret, Sharon Ann. BS in Agrl. Engring., Iowa State U., 1950; MS in Agrl. Engring., U. Mo., 1959. Registered profl. engr., Mo. Agrl. sales engr. Ill. No. Utility Co., Aledo, 1950-51; extension agrl. engr. Iowa State U., Ames, 1951-53, rsch. agrl. engr., 1953-56; prof. agrl. engr. U. Mo., Columbia, 1956-86, prof. emeritus, 1986; dir. Mo. Farm Electric Coun., Columbia, 1956-75; exec. mgr. Nat. Farm Electric Coun., Columbia, 1975-86; pres. Nat. Food and Energy Coun., Columbia, 1986-91, pres. emeritus, 1991; mgr. Electrotechnology Rsch., 1991-93. Bd. dirs. Internat. Congress Agrl. Engrs., Brussels, 1989—94. Editor, author: (with others) Handbook for Elsevier Science, Electrical Energy in World Agriculture, 1989; mem. editl. bd. Energy in Agriculture for Elsevier Sci., Amsterdam, The Netherlands, 1981-88. With USAAF, 1943—45, 2d lt. USAAF, 1945. Recipient Outstanding Svc. awards Nat. Safety Coun., 1975, MOFEC, 1976, Nat. 4-H Coun., 1982, Nat. Hon. Extension Frat., 1984, Hon. Am. Future Farmers Assn. degree, 1991. Fellow Am. Soc. Agrl. Engrs. (George Kable elec. award 1974, Spl. Svc. award, 2000); mem. Alpha Epsilon, Gamma Sigma Delta. Republican. Presbyterian. Avocations: technical writing, gardening, woodworking.

MCFATE, PATRICIA ANN, foundation executive, science educator; b. Detroit, Mar. 19, 1936; d. John Earle and Mary Louise (Bliss) McF.; m. Sidney Norman Graybeal, Sept. 10, 1988. BA (Alumni scholar), Mich. State U., 1954; MA, Northwestern U., 1956, PhD, 1965; MA (hon.), U. Pa., 1977. Assoc. prof. English, asst. dean liberal arts and scis. U. Ill., Chgo., 1967-74, assoc. prof. English, assoc. vice chancellor acad. affairs, 1974-75; assoc. prof. folklore Faculty Arts and Scis., U. Pa., Phila., 1975-81; prof. tech. and soc. Coll. Engring. and Applied Sci., 1975-81, vice provost, 1975-78; dep. chmn. Nat. Endowment for Humanities, Washington, 1978-81; exec. v.p. Am.-Scandinavian Found., NYC, 1981-82, pres., 1982-88; sr. scientist Sci. Applications Internat. Corp., Mc Lean, Va., 1988—, program dir. Ctr. for Nat. Security Negotiations, 1988—; cons. UN, 1994-95. Vis. assoc. prof. dept. medicine Rush U., Chgo., 1970-85; bd. dirs. First Union Corp.; mem. sr. adv. panel Dept. Def., 1998—. Author: The Writings of James Stephens, 1979, Uncollected Prose of James Stephens, 1983; exec. producer Northern Stars, 1985, Diego Rivera: I Paint What I See, 1989, The Bear in the Skies, 1998; contbr. articles in fields of sci. policy and lit. to various jours. Mem. Arms Control and Non-Proliferation Adv. Bd., Dept. of State, 1995-2001; mem. disting. adv. panel Sandia Nat. Labs.; bd. dirs. Raoul Wallenberg Com. of U.S., Swedish Coun. Am., Santa Fe Cmty. Found., Santa Fe Opera, Lensic Performing Arts Ctr. Decorated officer Order of Leopold II Belgium, comdr. Order Icelandic Falcon, comdr. Royal Order of Polar Star (Sweden), comdr. Order of Lion (Finland), comdr. Royal Norwegian Order Merit, Knight 1st class Royal Order Dannebrog (Denmark); U. Ill. Grad. Coll. faculty fellow, 1968; Swedish Bicentennial Fund grantee, 1981 Fellow N.Y. Acad. Scis.; mem. AAAS (chmn. com. on sci., engring. and pub. policy 1984-87, com. on sci. and internat. security 1976-79, 88-93), Coun. on Fgn. Rels., Acad. Scis. Phila. (founding mem., corr. sec. 1977-79), Theta Alpha Phi, Omega Beta Pi, Delta Delta Delta. E-mail: patricia.a.mcfate@saic.com.

MCFAYDEN, SHANNON W., bank holding company executive; b. Sept. 21, 1960; BA in psychology, Davidson Coll. Head human resources Fla. Bank (merged with Wachovia); with Wachovia Corp., 1982—, dir. human resources client svc., 1998—2001, dir. cmty. affairs, 2001—04, sr. v.p., 2004—, head corp. and cmty. affairs, 2004—. Mem. steering com. Bus. Strengthening Am. Bd. dirs. United Way Capital Campaign Planning, KinderMourn, Cmty. Sch. Arts and Child Care Resources, Charlotte -Mecklenburg Pub. Schs. Found. Named one of 25 Most Powerful Women in Banking, US Banker, 2006. Mem.: Davidson Coll. Alumni Assn. Office: Wachovia Corp 1 Wachovia Ctr Charlotte NC 28288 E-mail: shannon.mcfayden@wachovia.com. *

MCFEATTERS, ANN CAREY, journalist; b. Colorado Springs, Colo., June 27, 1944; d. Norman Cromer and Mildred Harriet Carey; m. Dale B. McFeatters, Sept. 27, 1969; children: Dale C., Matthew C., Kirsten C. BA, Marquette U., 1966. Reporter Evansville (Ind.) Press, 1966-68, Pitts. Press, 1969, Washington Daily News, 1969-70, Scripps Howard News Svc., Washington, 1970-99; Washington bur. chief Pitts. Post-Gazette and Toledo Blade, Washington, 1999—2006; polit. columnist Scripps Howard News Svc., 2006—. Author: Sandra Day O'Connor: Justice In The Balance, 2006. Named to Hall of Fame Soc. Profl. Journalists, 1998; recipient Disting. Svc. award Scripps Howard News Svc., 1999. Mem. Nat. Press Found. (chmn. 1996-98), Washington Press Club (pres. 1980-81), The Gridiron Club. Home Phone: 301-229-4999. Personal E-mail: amcfeatters@hotmail.com.

MCFEE, ARTHUR STORER, physician; b. Portland, Maine, May 1, 1932; s. Arthur Stewart and Helen Knight (Dresser) McF.; m. Iris Goeschel, May 13, 1967. BA cum laude, Harvard U., Cambridge, Mass., 1953, MD, 1957; MS, U. Minn., Mpls., 1966, PhD, 1967. Diplomate: Am. Bd. Surgery. Intern U. Minn. Hosp., 1957-58, resident in surgery, 1958-65; asst. prof. surgery U. Tex. Med. Sch., San Antonio, 1967-70, asso. prof., 1970-74, prof., 1974-2001, ret., 2001, prof. emeritus, 2001—. With Univ. Health Sys., Bexar-County, 1968-2003; spl. cons. on emergency med. care text to AAOS. Contbr. articles to profl. jours. Served with USNR, 1965-67. Fellow ACS; mem. AMA, Am. Assn. History of Medicine, Assn. Acad. Surgery, Tex. Med. Assn., Bexar County Med. Soc., Tex. Surg. Soc., Western Surg. Assn., San Antonio Surg. Soc., Soc. Surgery Alimentary Tract, So. Med. Assn., N.Y. Acad. Scis., Royal Soc. Medicine, So. Surg. Assn., Internat. Surg. Soc., Halsted Soc., J. Bradley Aust Surg. Soc., Am. Surg. Assn. Home: 131 Brittany Dr San Antonio TX 78212-1721 Office: MC 7842 7703 Floyd Curl Dr San Antonio TX 78229-3900 Office Phone: 210-567-2164. Business E-Mail: mcfee@uthscsa.edu. *Most of my life has been spent in training surgeons. It has been an informative experience.*

MCFEE, RICHARD, electrical engineer, physicist; b. Pitts., Jan. 24, 1925; s. William and Beatrice (Allender) McF.; m. Anne Stauffer, June 26, 1947 (div. 1960); m. 2d., Joanellen Lewis, Dec. 31, 1974. BEE, Yale U., 1947; MS in Physics, Syracuse U., 1949; PhDEE, U. Mich., 1955. Rsch. asst. Syracuse U. Med. Sch., 1947-48; instr. Syracuse U. elec. engring. dept., 1948-49; rsch. assoc. U. Mich. Med. Sch., 1949-51; engr. Electro-Mech. Rsch. Inc., Ridgefield, Conn., 1951-52; mem. tech. staff Bell Tel. Labs., Whippany, NJ, 1952-57; prof. elec. engring. Syracuse U., 1957-82; ind. rschr. Union Springs, NY, 1982—86, Hawi, Hawaii, 1986—. Contbr. articles on electronics, electrocardiography, magnetocardiography, superconductivity, circuit theory, thermodynamics, elec. measurements; patentee in field. Sgt. U.S. Army, 1943-46. Sci. Faculty fellowship NSF, Stanford U., 1970. Fellow IEEE; mem. AAAS, Sigma Xi. Home and Office: PO Box 989 Kapaau HI 96755-0989 Office Phone: 808-889-5778.

MCFEELY, WILLIAM DRAKE, publishing company executive; b. Port Chester, NY, July 15, 1954; s. William Shield and Mary (Drake) McF.; m. Karen Gail Eliason, Aug. 12, 1978; children: Matthew Bensen, Eric Daniel, Laura Mae. BA cum laude, Amherst Coll., 1976. Coll. traveler W.W. Norton & Co., Inc., NYC, 1976-80, asst. sales mgr., 1980-82, editor, 1982—, v.p., 1990-94, bd. dirs., 1990—, pres., 1994—, chmn., 2000—. Dir. W.W. Norton & Co., Ltd.; trustee Princeton Univ. Press, chmn., 2004-, Ithaka Harbors, Inc. Mem. Pubs. Lunch Club (pres. 1998-99), Seven Bridges Field Club (pres. 1989). Home: 106 Seven Bridges Rd Chappaqua NY 10514-1121 Office: WW Norton & Co 500 5th Ave Fl 6 New York NY 10110-0054

MC FEELY, WILLIAM SHIELD, historian, writer; b. NYC, Sept. 25, 1930; s. William C. and Marguerite (Shield) Mc F.; m. Mary Drake, Sept. 13, 1952; children: William Drake, Eliza, Jennifer. BA, Amherst Coll., 1952, LHD, 1982; MA, Yale U., 1962, PhD, 1966; LD, Washington Coll., 1986. Asst. prof. history and Am. studies Yale U., 1966-69, assoc. prof., 1969-70; dean faculty Mount Holyoke Coll., 1970-73, prof. history, 1970-80, Rodman prof. history, 1980-82, Andrew W. Mellon prof. humanities, 1982-86; Richard B. Russell prof. Am. history U. Ga., Athens, 1986-94, Abraham Baldwin prof. humanities, 1994-97, prof. emeritus, 1997—; Cardozo vis. prof. history Yale U., 2001—. Tchr. Yale-Harvard-Columbia intensive summer studies program, 1967-69; vis. prof. history Univ. Coll. London, 1978-79, Amherst Coll., 1980-81, U. Mass., 1984-85, John J. McCloy prof., 1988-89; cons. to com. on judiciary U.S. Ho. of Reps., 1974 Author: Yankee Stepfather: Gen. O.O. Howard and the Freedmen, 1968, Grant: A Biography, 1981, Frederick Douglass, 1991, Sapelo's People, 1994, Proximity to Death, 1999, Ulysses S. Grant: An Album, 2004, Portrait: The Life of Thomas Eakins, 2006. Recipient Pulitzer Prize in biography, 1982, Francis Parkman prize, 1982, Lincoln prize, 1992, Avery O. Craven award, 1992; Morse fellow, 1968-69, fellow Am. Coun. Learned Socs., 1974-75, Huntington Library, 1976, 83, Guggenheim fellow, 1982-83, assoc. fellow Charles Warren Ctr., 1991-91, fellow Libr. Co. of Phila., 2002-03, Radcliff Instn. Advanced Study, 2006-, vis. scholar W.E.B. Du Bois Inst., Harvard U., 1992—; NEH grantee, 1986-87 Mem. Am. Hist. Assn., So. Hist. Assn., Soc. of Am. Historians, Orgn. Am. Historians, PEN Ctr., Century Assn., Authors Guild. Home: 35 Mill Hill Rd Wellfleet MA 02667-7441

MC FERON, DEAN EARL, mechanical engineer, educator; b. Portland, Oreg., Dec. 24, 1923; s. Wallace Suitor and Ruth Carolyn (Fessler) McF.; m. Phyllis Grace Ehlers, Nov. 10, 1945; children: David Alan, Phyllis Ann, Douglas Dean, Donald Brooks. Student, Oreg. State Coll., 1942-43; BSME with spl. honors, U. Colo., 1945, MSME, 1948; PhD, U. Ill., 1956. Instr. U. Colo., Boulder, 1946-48; assoc. prof. U. Ill., 1948-58; rsch. assoc. Argonne (Ill.) Nat. Lab., 1957-58; prof. mech. engring., assoc. dean U. Wash., Seattle, 1958-82, prof. emeritus, 1983—. Cons. to industry, 1959-80. Served with USNR, 1942-46, to comdr. Res., 1946-72. Co-recipient Outstanding Tech. Applications Paper award ASHRAE, 1974; Ednl. Achievement award Soc. Mfg. Engrs., 1970; NSF faculty fellow, 1967-68 Mem. ASME, Am. Soc. Engring. Edn., U.S. Naval Inst. (life), Sigma Xi (nat. dir. 1972-80, nat. pres. 1978), Tau Beta Pi, Sigma Tau, Pi Tau Sigma. Home: 4008 NE 40th St Seattle WA 98105-5422 Office: U Wash Dept Mech Engring Seattle WA 98195-0001 *What matters most in life is what you can do for others.*

MCFERREN, MARTHA DEAN, writer, librarian; b. Henderson, Tex., Apr. 25, 1947; d. Manley Edward McFerren and Emma Lou Turner; m. Dennis Scott Wall, May 22, 1977. BS, North Tex. State U., 1969, M of Libr. Svcs., 1971; MFA, Warren Wilson Coll., 1988. Cert. secondary tchr., Tex. Libr. San Jacinto Coll., Pasadena, Tex., 1971-76, Jefferson Parish Librs., Metairie, La., 1976-81, New Orleans Schs., 1984-85; instr. Dillard U., New Orleans, 1991. Poetry instr. Slidell (La.) Pub. Schs., 1989. Author: Delusions of a Popular Mind, 1983, Get Me Out of Here!, 1984, Contours for Ritual, 1988, Women in Cars, 1992 (Marianne Moore prize 1992); assoc. editor New Laurel Rev., 1980-88. Recipient Moore prize Helicon Nine, 1992, Poetry prize Deep South Conf., 1985, creative writing fellowship Yaddo Colony, 1985, writer's fellowship NEA, 1991, Artist fellowship La. Endowment for the Arts, 1983. Mem. New Orleans Poetry Forum (publicity dir. 1976-90), Poetry Soc. of Am. Office Phone: 504-218-4248. Personal E-mail: dwall16@cox.net.

MCGAAN, ANDREW RAYMOND, lawyer; b. Highland Park, Ill., Oct. 15, 1961; s. Dean Bailey and Nancy Eva (Acheson) M. AB with honors, Cornell U., 1983, JD magna cum laude, 1986. Bar: Conn. 1986, Ill. 1991, US Dist. Ct. (dist. Conn.) 1987, US Dist. Ct. (so. & ea. dists. NY) 1988, US Dist. Ct. (no. & ctrl. dists. Ill.), US Ct. Appeals (2nd, 7th, 9th & 11th cirs.). Press sec. Com. to Elect Congressman Stewart B. McKinney, Fairfield, Conn., 1986; law clk. to Judge Warren W. Eginton US Dist. Ct. (dist. Conn.), Bridgeport, 1987-88; assoc. Cummings & Lockwood, Stamford, Conn., 1988—90; ptnr. Kirkland & Ellis, Chgo., 1990—. Elder, chmn. bd. trustees Fourth Presbyn. Ch. Chgo. Mem. ABA, Order of the Coif. Presbyterian. Office: Kirkland & Ellis 200 E Randolph Dr Chicago IL 60601 Office Phone: 312-861-2000. Office Fax: 312-861-2200. Business E-Mail: amcgaan@kirkland.com.

MCGAFFEY, JERE D., retired lawyer; b. Lincoln, Nebr., Oct. 6, 1935; s. Don Larsen and Doris McG.; m. Ruth S. Michelsen, Aug. 19, 1956; children: Beth, Karen. BA, BSc with high distinction, U. Nebr., 1957; LLB magna cum laude, Harvard U., 1961. Bar: Wis. 1961. Mem. firm Foley & Lardner LLP, Milw., 1961—2004, ptnr., 1968—2004. Dir. Wis. Gas Co., 1978-00, Smith Investment Co., Northwestern Mut. Trust Co., 2000-06, Lord Balt. Corp.; mem. take-over adv. com., Gov. Wis., 1988-89, commn on state/local partnerships 21st century 2000-01. Author works in field. Chmn. bd. dirs. Helen Bader Found.; former vice chmn. legis. Milw. Met. Assn. Commerce, 1984—2003; former chmn. Wis. Taxpayers Alliance, sec.-treas., 1994—; bd. dirs. Aurora Health Care, 1986—, chmn., 1986—90; chmn. bd. advisors U. Wis. Nursing Sch., Milw. Mem. ABA (chmn. tax sect. 1990-91, ho. dels. 1995-2000, Sect. Taxation Disting. Svc. award 2005), AICPA, Wis. Bar Assn., Wis. Inst. CPAs, Am. Coll. Tax Counsel (chmn. 1996-98), Am. Coll. Trust and Estate Counsel (chmn. bus. planning com. 1994-97, regent 2000-06), Am. Law Inst., Univ. Club, Milw. Country Club, Harvard Club, Phi Beta Kappa, Beta Gamma Sigma, Delta Sigma Rho. Home: 12852 NW Shoreland Dr Mequon WI 53097-2304 Office: Foley & Lardner 777 E Wisconsin Ave Ste 3600 Milwaukee WI 53202-5302 Home Phone: 262-242-1766. Business E-Mail: jmcgaffey@foleylaw.com.

MCGAGH, WILLIAM GILBERT, financial consultant; b. Boston, May 29, 1929; s. Thomas A. and Mary M. (McDonough) McG.; m. Sarah Ann McQuigg, Sept. 23, 1961; children: Margaret Ellen, Sarah Elizabeth. BSBA, Boston Coll., 1950; MBA, Harvard U., 1952; MS, MIT, 1965. Fin. analyst Ford Motor Co., Dearborn, Mich., 1953-55; mem. staff treas. office DaimlerChrysler, Detroit, 1955-64, compt., treas. Canadian divsn. Windsor, 1965-67, staff exec.-fin. Latin Am. ops. Detroit, 1967-68, asst. treas., 1968-75, treas., 1975-76, v.p., treas., 1976-80; sr. v.p. fin., dir. Northrop Grumman Corp., LA, 1980-88. Mem. adv. bd. Santa Monica-UCLA and Orthopaedic Hosp. Mem. bd. regents Mt. St. Mary's Coll.; bd. dirs. L.A. Orthop. Hosp.; chmn. bd. dirs. John Tracy Clinic. Sloan fellow MIT, 1965. Mem. Fin. Execs. Inst. (pres. Detroit chpt. 1979-80), Harvard Club (N.Y.C. and Boston), Beach Club (Santa Monica, Calif.), L.A. Country Club, Calif. Club (L.A.), Eastward Ho Country Club (Chatham, Mass.). Home: 2189 Century Hill Los Angeles CA 90067 Home Phone: 310-557-0992; Office Phone: 310-248-4395. Personal E-mail: wgm9601@aol.com.

MCGAHEE, WILLIS ANDREW, professional football player; b. Miami, Fl, Oct. 20, 1981; s. Willis McGahee and Jannie Jones. Student, U. Miami, 1999—2003. Running back Buffalo Bills, 2004—07, Balt. Ravens, 2007—. Office: Balt Ravens 1101 Russell St Baltimore MD 21230 *

MCGANN, JEROME JOHN, language educator; b. NYC, July 22, 1937; s. John Joseph and Marie Violet (Lecouffe) McG.; m. Anne Patricia Lanni, July 26, 1938; children: Geoffrey, Christopher, Jennifer. BS, Le Moyne Coll., 1959; MA, Syracuse U., 1962; PhD, Yale U., 1966; LHD (hon.), U. Chgo., 1996. From asst. prof. to prof. U. Chgo., 1966-75; prof. Johns Hopkins U., Balt., 1975-80; Dreyfuss prof. humanities Calif. Inst. Tech., Pasadena, 1980-86; John Stewart Bryan univ. prof. U. Va., Charlottesville, 1987—. Author: Swinburne: An Experiment in Criticism, 1972 (Melville Cane award 1972), The Romantic Ideology, 1983, The Beauty of Inflections, 1985, Social Values and Poetic Acts, 1987, Towards a Literature of Knowledge, 1989, The Textual Condition, 1991, Black Riders: The Visible Language of Modernism, 1993; editor: The New Oxford Book of Romantic Period Verse, 1993, Poetics of Sensibility: A Revolution in Literary Style, 1996, Byron: Complete Poetical Works, 7 vols., 1980-93, Dante Gabriel Rossetti and the Game That Must Be Lost, 2000, The Complete Writings and Pictures of Dante Gabriel Rosetti: A Hypermedia Research Archive, 2000—, Radiant Textuality, Literature after the World Wide Web, 2001, Byron and Romanticism, 2002, D.G. Rossetti. Collected Poetry and Prose, 2003, Swinburne, Selected Poetry and Prose, 2004, The Scholar's Art: Literary Studies in a Managed World, 2006, The Point Is To Change It, Literature in the Continuing Present, 2007; author, editor 25 scholarly books and 4 poetry books. Recipient Mellon Achievement award, 2003, Richard Lyman award, 2002, James Russell Lowell award, 2002; Fulbright fellow, Fels Found. fellow, Eng., 1965-66; Guggenheim fellow, Eng., 1970-71, 74-75; NEH fellow, Eng. and Europe, 1975-76, 87-88, 2003—. Fellow: Am. Acad. Arts and Scis.; mem.: MLA. Address: English Department Bryan Hall U VA Charlottesville VA 22903 Office Phone: 434-924-4064. Business E-Mail: jjm2f@virginia.edu.

MCGANN, LISA B. NAPOLI, language educator; b. West Hartford, Conn., Sept. 07; d. James Napoli; m. Edward Harrison McGann, Jr. BA, Vassar Coll., 1980; MA, Columbia U., 1983, postgrad., 1991-95; MA, Middlebury Coll., 1987. Cert. tchr. French, ESL and Italian, Conn. Cmty. English program coord. Tchrs. Coll. Columbia U., NYC, 1982-83; mgr. English tchg. com. Jr. League N.Y., NYC, 1983-84; asst. dir. ESL Fordham U., NYC, 1988-89; ESL instr. Laguardia C.C., CUNY, Long Island City, NY, 1983—, Columbia U., 1983-96. ESL instr. Yale U., 1988, 89; ESL specialist, tchr. UN, N.Y.C., 1990. Big sister Highland Hts., New Haven, 1976-77; ESL tchr. Boys and Girls Club, Astoria, N.Y., 1992. Recipient awards and scholarships. Mem. Nat. TESOL Soc., Am. Assn. Tchrs. Italian, Italian-Am. Hist. Soc., Nat. Italian Am. Found. (coun.), The Statue of Liberty-Ellis Island Found., Inc. Roman Catholic. Avocations: ballet, reading, travel, real estate, tennis.

MCGARR, FRANK JAMES, retired federal judge, consultant; b. Feb. 25, 1921; married; 6 children. BA cum laude, Loyola U., Chgo., 1942, JD, 1950, degree (hon.), 2002. Bar: Ill. 1950. Assoc. Dallstream Schiff Stern & Hardin, Chgo., 1952—54; asst. U.S. atty., chief criminal divsn. No. dist. of Ill., 1954—55, first asst. U.S. atty., 1955—58; ptnr. McKay Solum & McGarr, Chgo., 1958—68; first asst. atty. gen. State of Ill., 1969—70; judge U.S. Dist. Ct. for No. Ill., 1970—88, chief judge, 1981—86, sr. judge, 1986—88; of counsel Phelan Cahill & Quinlan, Chgo., 1988—96, Foley & Lardner, Chgo., 1996—2001; arbitration and medication pvt. practice, 2001—. Instr. Eng. and pub. speaking Loyola U., 1946—48, administrv. asst. to pres., 1948—52; instr. law Loyola U. Law Sch., 1950—52, instr. criminal law, 1953—57, prof. admiralty and maritime law, 1953—57; instr. legal ethics John Marshal Law Sch., 1985—86. Chmn. law observance com. Chgo. Crime Comm., v.p., bd. dirs.; chmn. Law Enforcement Week Com.; pres. Constl. Rights Found., 1994; chmn. Ill Gov.'s Comm. on Death Penalty, 2000. With USN, 1942—45, Pacific Fleet. Named Man of Yr., Cath. Lawyers Guild Chgo., 1985; recipient Alumni Medal of Excellence, Loyola Law Alumni, 1964, Mother Cabrini award, Columbus-Cuneo-Cabrini Med. Ctr., 1978, Dei Gloriam award, St. Ignatius Coll. Prep, 1984, Disting. Jurist award, Loyola U. Law Sch., Chgo. Fellow: Am. Coll. Trial Lawyers; mem.: Soc. Trial Lawyers, Chgo. Bar Assn., Fed. Bar Assn. (pres. chgo. chpt. 1962—63, mem. exec. com.), 7th Cir. Bar Assn. Office: 4146 Venard Rd Downers Grove IL 60515-1908 Home Phone: 630-960-0985; Office Phone: 630-960-4655.

MCGARR, KEITH, information technology executive; Student, Univ. Tenn.; BBA in Fin., Univ. Memphis; MS in Info. Sys., Telecom., Christian Brothers Univ., MBA. With FedEx, 1983—2000, v.p. info tech. engring; COO Internat. Transmission Corp. (subs. FedEx); joined Reed Elsevier, 2000—; with Lexis-Nexis (subs. Reed Elsevir), 2005—06; chief tech. officer Reed Elsevier, NYC, 2006—. Bd. dir. iPhrase, 2001—. Named one of Top 25 Chief Tech. Officers, InfoWorld mag., 2006. Office: Reed Elsevier 125 Park Ave 23d fl New York NY 10017 *

MCGARRELL, JAMES, artist, educator; b. Indpls., Feb. 22, 1930; s. James and Gretchen (Heermann) McG.; m. Anna (Harris), June 24, 1955; children: Andrew Rider, Flora Raven. BA, Ind. U., 1953; MA, U. Calif. at Los Angeles, 1955. Artist in residence Reed Coll., Portland, Oreg., 1956—59; prof. fine arts, dir. grad. painting Ind. U., Bloomington, Ind., 1959—80; prof. fine arts Washington U., St. Louis, 1981—93, prof. emeritus, 1993—; artist in residence Dartmouth Coll., 1993, Roswell, N. Mex. Found., 1999. Exhibitions include Frumkin, Adams Gallery, N.Y.C., 1961, 1964, 1966, Gallery Claude Bernard, Paris, 1967, Gallery Il Fante de Spade, Rome and Milan, 1967, Frumkin, Adams Gallery, N.Y.C., 1968, Gallery Claude Bernard, Paris, 1970, Gallery Il Fante de Spade, Rome and Milan, 1971, Frumkin, Adams Gallery, N.Y.C., 1971, Gallery Il Fante de Spade, Rome and Milan, 1972, Utah Mus. Art, Salt Lake City, 1972, Frumkin, Adams Gallery, N.Y.C., 1973, Gallery Il Fante de Spade, Rome and Milan, 1974, Gallery Claude Bernard, Paris, 1974, Gallery Il Fante de Spade, Rome and Milan, 1976, Frumkin, Adams Gallery, N.Y.C., 1977, Gallery Il Fante de Spade, Rome and Milan, 1979, Frumkin, Adams Gallery, N.Y.C., 1980, Galeria Gian Ferrari, Milan, 1981, Art Mus. Univ. N.Mex., Albuquerque, 1982, Gallery Gian Ferrari, Milan, 1983, Frumkin, Adams Gallery, N.Y.C., 1984, St. Louis Art Mus., 1985, Frumkin, Adams Gallery, N.Y.C., 1986, More Gallery, Phila., 1987, Frumkin, Adams Gallery, N.Y.C., 1988, 1988, Struve Gallery, Chgo., 1988, Frumkin, Adams Gallery, N.Y.C., 1989, Gallery Simonne Stern, New Orleans, 1989, Frumkin, Adams Gallery, N.Y.C., 1989, More Gallery, Phila., 1989, Frumkin, Adams Gallery, N.Y.C., 1990, Struve Gallery, Chgo., 1990, Printworks Gallery, 1990, Gallery Simonne Stern, New Orleans, 1991, Frumkin, Adams Gallery, N.Y.C., 1991, 1993, More Gallery, Phila., 1994, Gallery Simonne Stern, New Orleans, 1994, Frumkin, Adams Gallery, N.Y.C., 1995, Gallery Simonne Stern, New Orleans, 1995, George Adams Gallery, N.Y.C., 1997, Gallery Simonne Stern, New Orleans, 1998, The Art Gallery Univ. N.H., Durham, 1998, Art Mus. U. Ariz., Tucson, 1998, Printworks Gallery, Chgo., 1999, Gallery Simonne Stern, New Orleans, 2000, George Adams Gallery, N.Y.C., 2000, Sonia Zaks Gallery, Chgo., 2001, 2003, Heriard Cimino Gallery, New Orleans, 2003, Represented in permanent collections Mus. Modern Art, N.Y.C., Met. Mus. Art, Whitney Mus. Am. Art, Pa. Acad., Phila., Santa Barbara Mus. Art, Calif., San Francisco Art Mus., Art Inst., Chgo., Joseph Hirshborn Mus., Washington, St. Louis Art Mus., Hamburg Mus. Art, Germany, Centre Georges Pompidou, Paris, Rose Art Mus., Brandeis U. Bd. gov. Skowhegan Sch. Painting and Sculpture. Recipient Am. Acad. Arts and Letters Lifetime Achievement Award, 1995; Fulbright Fellow, 1955-56; Guggenheim Found. Fellow, 1965; Nat. Endowment for Arts grantee, 1967, 85; Bogliasco Found. Fellow, 2003; Rockerfeller Found. Bellagio Ctr. Fellow Mem. Coll. Art Assn. (bd. dir. 1969-73), Academie des Beaux Arts de L'Institut de France, Nat. Acad. Design. Home: PO Box 39 Newbury VT 05051-0039 Office Phone: 802-866-5447. E-mail: bluedeuce@charter.net.

MCGARRIGLE, THOMAS J., lawyer; b. Phila., Aug. 4, 1953; BS in acctg., Villanova U., 1975, JD, 1978. Bar: Pa. 1978, US Ct. Appeals 3rd Cir., US Dist. Ct. Ea. Dist. Pa., US Dist. Ct. Dist. Ariz., Supreme Ct. Pa. Asst. dist. atty., Phila., 1978—85; assoc. Reed Smith LLP, Phila., 1985—90, ptnr., 1990—, Phila./Wilmington practice group leader litig. group. Mem.: Phila. Assn. Def. Counsel, Phila. Bar Assn. Office: Reed Smith LLP 2500 One Liberty Pl 1650 Market St Philadelphia PA 19103 Office Phone: 215-851-8220. Office Fax: 215-851-1420. Business E-Mail: tmcgarrigle@reedsmith.com.

MCGARRY, DOROTHY, librarian; b. Omaha, May 1, 1929; d. Moore and Ruth (Gorelick) Lasher. AB, UCLA, 1949, MLS, 1971. Catalog libr. UCLA, 1971-76, head cataloging divsn. phys. sci. and tech. libr., 1976-93, emerita, 1993—. Mem. vocabulary task force for revision GeoRef Thesaurus, Am. Geol. Inst. Fellow Spl. Libr. Assn. (chair commn. on cataloging 1983-89, 97-99, 2004-05, rep. CIP adv. group 1983-88, rep. Internat. Fedn. Libr. Assns. and Instns. sect. on classification and indexing 1987-95, 2003—, rep. to sect. on cataloguing 1995-2003, chair physics astronomy-math. divsn. 1982-83, chair sci.-tech. divsn. 1991-92, rep. of the SLA geography and map divsn. Anglo-Am. Cataloging com. for Cartographic Materials, 1988—, internat. rels. com. 1989-97, bd. dirs. 1995-97, SLA del. to the Internat. Fedn. of Libr. Assns. and Instns., 1993-97, treas. So. Calif. chpt. 1991-93, pres. So. Calif. chpt. 1994-95, SLA John Cotton Dana award 1991, chair by-laws com. 2000-2002, Hall of Fame 2000—, rep. ALA com. cataloging description and access, 2005-); mem. AAAS, ALA (resources and tech. svcs. divsn., catalog form and function com. 1986-90), Assn. for Libr. Collections and Tech. Svc. (orgn./by-law com. 1999-2001, com. on cataloging desc. and access 1982-85, chair 1986, policy and rsch. com. 1988-92, subject analysis com. 1993-96, mem.-at-large cataloging and classification sect. 1993-96, chair cataloging and classification sect. 1997-98, Margaret Mann Citation, 2005), Map and Geography Round Table (cataloging and classification com., 1999—; honors award 2003), Am. Math. Soc. (libr. com. 1989-98), Am. Phys. Soc., Am. Soc. for Info. Sci. (LA chpt., chair by-laws com. 1986-89, 99-2001, sec. 1987-88, Outstanding Mem. Yr. award 1990, 94, other coms.), Assn. Coll. Rsch. Librs. (sci.-tech. sect., chair ad hoc com. designing conf. proc. style sheet 1984-87, other coms.), Calif. Acad. and Rsch. Libr., Calif. Libr. Assn., Geosci. Info. Soc., Internat. Fedn. Libr. Assns. and Instns. (sect. on classification and indexing, chair 1989-93, sec. 1993-95, 2003—, sect. cataloging 1995-2003, ISBD rev. group), Math. Assn. Am., N.Am. Serials Interest Group, Online Audiovisual Catalogers, South Calif. Tech. Processes Group. Office: UCLA Sci & Engring Libr 8251 Boelter Hl Los Angeles CA 90095-1598 Business E-Mail: dmcgarry@library.ucla.edu.

MCGARRY, FREDERICK JEROME, civil engineering educator; b. Rutland, Vt., Aug. 22, 1927; s. William John and Ellen (Dunn) McG.; m. Alice M. Reilly, Oct. 7, 1950 (dec. Jan. 1971); children: Martha Ellen, Alice Catherine, Joan Louise, Carol Elizabeth, Susan Elizabeth, Janet Marian. AB, Middlebury Coll., Vt., 1950; S.B., MIT, 1950, S.M., 1953. Faculty MIT, 1950—2002, prof. civil engring., 1965—2002, prof. materials sci. and engring., 1974—2002, head materials divsn., 1964—2002, dir. materials rsch. lab., 1964—2002, assoc. dir. inter-Am. program civil engring., 1961—2002, dir. summer session, 1983—2002; ret., 2002. Contbr. numerous articles to profl. jours. Recipient Best Paper award Soc. Plastics Industry, 1968, 91. Mem. AAAS, ASTM, Soc. Rheology, Soc. Plastics Engrs., Am. Soc. Metals, Sigma Xi. Home: 90 Bakers Hill Rd Weston MA 02493-1774 Office: MIT Rm 35-329 77 Massachusetts Ave Cambridge MA 02139-4301 Mailing: PO Box 446 Weston MA 02493

MCGARRY, MARCIA, retired community service coordinator; b. Washington, Dec. 9, 1941; d. Emil Sylvester and Bernice B. (Bland) Busey. BS, Morgan State U., 1964. Cert. tchr., law enforcement officer, Fla. Payroll clk., jr. acct. U.S. Dept. Labor, Washington, 1964-65; English tchr. Taiwan, 1968-70; tchr. Monroe County Sch. Bd., Key West, Fla., 1971-81; exec. dir. Monroe Assn. Retarded Citizens, Key West, 1977-79; dep. sheriff Monroe County Sheriff's Dept., Key West, 1979-83, 86-90; probation/parole officer Fla. State Dept. Corrections, Key West, 1983-91; law enforcement instr. Fla. Keys C.C., 1983-91; cmty. svc. coord. City of Bradenton, 1991-2000; domestic violence specialist II Broward County Sheriff Dept., 2001—06. Mem. judicial nom. commn. Fla. Gov. Lawton Chiles, 1994—96; former mem. rev. bd. Bradenton Police Dept., mem. cmty. rels. com., 1996—2000; mem. adv. bd. Manatee County Sheriff's Dept., mem. eligibility bd., 1996—2000; mem. Mayor's adv. bd. City of Bradenton, 1999—2000. Active local polit. campaigns; co-founder day schs. for under-privileged children; former mem. Big Bros./Big Sisters Am., mem. com., 1985-86, former bd. dirs., Spouse Abuse, former bd. dirs.; bd. dirs. Adv. Coun. Orange-Ridge Elem., 1991-93; bd. dirs. mayor's com., chmn. task force Drug Free Cmtys., 1991-94, bd. dirs., 1996-2001; bd. dirs. Human Rels. Commn., 1991-93, Drug Free Schs. and Cmty. Adv. Coun., 1991-98, T.O.T.S. (These Our Tots), Inc., 1998-2000; former mem. adv. coun. Byrd Edn. Found., Sweet Adelines Internat., 1992-94, commr. 12th Jud. Nominating Commn., 1992-99, cons., facilitator Cultural Diversity Conflict Resolution Workshops, Manatee County High Schs. and Bradenton Police Dept.; attendance adv. com. Bayshore High, 1993, multicultural com., 1994, former rep. Women's Forum; former dir. choir Luth. Ch.; founding mem. Comprehensive Neighborhood Support Network; charter mem. Women's History Month Mus. Recipient Appreciation cert., Lions Club, 1978, 1979, Career Week award, Harris Elem. Sch., 1981, Glynn Archer Elem. Sch., 1989, Trainers award, Probation/Parole Acad., 1987, Cert. of Acknowledgement for Cmty. Svc., AAUW, 1995, awadrd, Vol. Army for the War on Drugs, 1989. Mem.: Delta Sigma Theta (v.p. 1990—91, corr. sec. 1993—95). Republican. Lutheran. Avocations: reading, travel, musuems. Home Phone: 954-741-7037. Personal E-mail: marciadnc@aol.com.

MCGARRY, RICHARD LAWRENCE, lawyer; b. Flushing, NY, Jan. 12, 1960; s. Richard J. and Loretta (McCarthy) McG.; m. Lynda R. Jones, Dec. 21, 1987; children: Abraham A. Eichelberger, Chelsea Eichelberger St. Clair, David B. Eichelberger. BS, Hampden Sydney Coll., 1982; JD, Washington and Lee U., 1989. Bar: Va. 1989, U.S. Dist. Ct. (we. dist.) Va., U.S. Supreme Ct., 1993. Assoc. Jeffrey H. Krasnow and Assocs., Roanoke, Va., 1989-93; ptnr. Johnson & McGarry, P.C., Charlottesville, Va., 1993-94; pvt. practice Roanoke, 1994—. Bd. dirs. Roanoke Valley SPCA. Mem. Va. Trial Lawyers Assn., Assn. Trial Lawyers Am., Roanoke Bar Assn., Va. Bar Assn. Office: 6405 Merriman Rd Ste 201 Roanoke VA 24018

MCGARVIE, BLYTHE J., management consultant; b. Dec. 3, 1956; BA in Economics, Northwestern U., MBA, 1978. CPA. CPA Arthur Andersen & Co., 1978-85; various positions including dir. worldwide planning Kraft Foods, Inc., 1985-88, group contr., dir. fin. and adminstrn., 1988-91; chief adminstrv. officer Pacific Rim Sara Lee Corp., Chgo., 1991-94; exec. v.p., CFO Hannaford Bros. Co., 1995-99, BIC SA, Clichy, France, 1999—2002; pres. Leadership for Internat. Fin. & Enterprise, Williamsburg, Va., 2003—. Bd. dirs. Accenture, LaFarge North Am., Pepsi Bottling Group, 2002-, The St. Paul Travelers Co., 2003-, Wawa, Inc., Viacom Inc., 2007-. Author: Fit In, Stand Out: Mastering the FISO Factor for Leadership Effectiveness in Business and Life, 2005. Trustee Northwestern U., 1984-87; mem. Lyric Opera Chgo. Guild Bd. Recipient Schaffner award Kellogg Grad. Sch. Mgmt. Office: Leadership for International Fin & Enterprise 3025 River Oaks Rd Williamsburg VA 23185 *

MCGARVIE-MUNN, IAIN LACHLAN, real estate agent, curator, writer; b. NYC, Dec. 24, 1949; Dir. restoration, curator Chateau d'Entrecasteaux, France, 1974—95; freelance curator-cord. Hon. vice consul of Guatemala, Marseille, France, 1982—92; pres. Rt. Historique des Hauts Lieux de Provence, France, 1982—92. Recipient prize, Assn. Vielles Maisons Francaise, 1972, Diplome d'Honneur, Assn. Vielles Maisons Francaises, 1990, Prix des Chefs d'Oeuvre en Peril, French Ministry of Culture, 1977, Obelisque du Conseil de l'Europe, European Coun./La Demeure Historique, 1980, Prix de La Fondation Am., Versailles Found., 1986, Label du Meilleur Accueil dans les Musees, Ministry of Culture, 1988, Qualite Var Accueil, State Dept. Tourism, 1994, Marc de Beauvau Craon, La Demeure Historique/Ministry of Culture, 1994, Grand Prix des Depliants Touristiques, Ministry of Tourism, 1995, Tourism medal. Achievements include founding of the association of historical monuments open to the public in Var County, France; founding of the Festival International de Musique d'Entrecasteaux, France. Office Phone: 512-569-6438. Personal E-mail: mail@iainmunn.com.

MCGAUGHEY, CHARLES GILBERT, retired biochemist; b. San Diego, Sept. 8, 1925; s. Gilbert Arthur and Louisa Ellen (Inskeep) McG. BA, U. Calif., Berkeley, 1950; MA, U. So. Calif., 1952. Diplomate Am. Inst. Oral Biology. Scientist radiol. hazards evaluation U.S. Naval Radiol. Def. Lab., San Francisco, 1952; rsch. biochemist VA Med. Ctr., Long Beach, Calif., 1953-81; prin. investigator studied dental caries, plaque and oral cancer Oral Diseases Rsch. Lab., 1978-81. Contbr. articles to profl. jours. Grantee Nat. Inst. Dental Rsch., 1965. Mem. AAAS. Home: 337 N Winnipeg Pl Long Beach CA 90814-2564

MCGAVIN, JOHN DAVID, lawyer; b. Washington, Apr. 15, 1957; s. Thomas A. and Jane Louise (Haupt) McG.; m. Linda Judith Peele, Oct. 6, 1984. BA with distinction, U. Va., 1979; JD, Coll. William and Mary, 1982. Bar: Va. 1982, U.S. Dist. Ct. (ea. dist.) Va. 1983, U.S. Ct. Appeals (4th cir.) 1983, U.S. Dist. Ct. (we. dist.) Va. 1985, U.S. Supreme Ct., 1995, DC, 2002, US DC Circuit, 2004. Law clk. to presiding justice U.S. Dist. Ct. (ea. dist.) Va., Alexandria, 1982-83; assoc. Lewis, Tydings, Bryan & Trichilo, P.C., Fairfax, Va., 1983-87; ptnr. Trichilo, Bancroft, McGavin, Horvath & Judkins, P.C., Fairfax, 1988—. Recipient Furniss award, Va. Assn. Def. Attys., 2006. Fellow Va. Law Found.; mem. Va. Bar Assn. (cir. rep. young lawyers conf. 1988), Fairfax Bar Assn. (chmn. law and medicine com. 1988), No. Va. Young Lawyers Assn (sec. 1986, pres. 1987), Va. Assn. Def. Attys. (pres. 204-05), River Bend Golf and Country Club. Republican. Methodist. Avocations: tennis, golf. Home: 10004 Park Royal Dr Great Falls VA 22066-1847 Office: 3920 University Dr Fairfax VA 22030-2514 Home Phone: 703-759-6432; Office Phone: 703-385-1000. Business E-Mail: jmcgavin@tbmhjlaw.com.

MCGAVRAN, FREDERICK JAEGER, lawyer; b. Columbus, Ohio, Apr. 24, 1943; s. James Holt and Marion (Jaeger) McG.; m. Elizabeth Dowlig, Jan. 5, 1980; children: Sarah Ann, Marian Katherine. BA, Kenyon Coll., 1965; JD, Harvard U., 1972. Bar: Ohio 1972, U.S. Supreme Ct. 1984, Ky. 1992. With Kyte, Conlan, Wulsin & Vogeler, Cin., 1972-78, Frost & Jacobs, Cin., 1978-2000, Frost, Brown & Todd, LLC, Cin., 2000—. Editor-in-chief Sixth Circuit Federal Practice Manual, 1999. Lt. USN, 1965—69. Mem. Fed. Bar Assn. (pres. Cin. chpt. 1984-85, mem. exec. com. Cin. chpt. 1985—), Ohio State Bar Assn. (chmn. com. on fed. cts. 1982-85), Univ. Club of Cin., The Literary Club (trustee). Home: 3528 Traskwood Cir Cincinnati OH 45208 Office: Frost Brown & Todd LLC 2200 PNC Ctr 201 E Fifth St Cincinnati OH 45202 Home Phone: 513-871-4840; Office Phone: 513-651-6940. Business E-Mail: fmcgavran@fbtlaw.com.

MCGEE, EDWIN C., JR., surgeon; b. SC, 1967; MD, Vanderbilt U. Sch. Medicine, 1993. Cert. surgery, thoracic surgery. Surg. resident Mass. Gen. Hosp.; fellow Cleveland Clinic Found., 2001—04; rsch. fellow NIH Nat. Cancer Inst.; surg. dir. heart transplant program Northwestern Meml. Hosp., Chgo., 2004—. Mem. Northwestern Med. Faculty Found.; asst. prof. Feinberg Sch. Medicine. Named one of 40 Under 40, Crain's Chgo. Bus., 2006. Mem.: Alpha Omega Alpha, Phi Beta Kappa. Avocations: fly fishing, dog training, hunting. Office: Galter 19-1000 675 N St Clair Chicago IL 60611 Office Phone: 312-695-4965. Office Fax: 312-695-1903.

MCGEE, HAROLD JOHNSTON, former academic administrator; b. Portsmouth, Va., Apr. 13, 1937; s. Harold Valentine McGee and Clara Mae (Johnston) Webber; m. Mary Frances Eure, Mar. 22, 1959; children: Harold Johnston, Mary Margaret, Matthew Hayden; m. Linda Gayle Stevens, Apr. 3, 1976; 1 child, Andrew Meade. BS, Old Dominion U., 1959; MEd, U. Va., 1962, EdD, 1968; HumD, James Madison U., 1999. Tchr. Falls Church (Va.) City Schs., 1959-62; asst. dean, then dean of admissions Old Dominion U., Norfolk, Va., 1962-65; field rep., program officer, sr. program officer U.S. Office Edn. Bur. Higher Edn., Charlottesville, 1965-70; provost Tidewater Community Coll., Portsmouth, 1970-71; founding pres. Piedmont Va. Community Coll., Charlottesville, 1971-75; various offices including dean grad. sch., asst. to pres., v.p. student affairs, v.p. adminstrv. affairs, sec. bd. visitors James Madison U., Harrisonburg, Va., 1975-86; pres. Jacksonville (Ala.) State U., 1986-99, pres. emeritus, 1999—. Bd. dirs. Gulf South Conf., chmn., 1990—92, Ala. Coun. Univ. Pres., 1991—92; bd. dirs. Trans America Athletic Conf., chmn., 1998—99. Author: Impact of Federal Support, 1968, The Virginia Project, 1976. Mem. United Way Calhoun County Ala., 1986—92, Leadership Ala.; bd. dir. Ala. 529 Fund Savs. Bd., 2004—, Ala. Prepaid Coll. Tuition Bd., 2004—. Mem.: NCAA (coun. 1991—95), Phi Delta Kappa. Episcopalian.

MCGEE, HENRY ALEXANDER, JR., academic administrator; b. Atlanta, Sept. 12, 1929; s. Henry Alexander and Arrie Mae (Mallory) McG.; m. Betty Rose Herndon, July 29, 1951; children: Henry Alexander, Charles Nelson, Kathy Nan. BChemE, Ga. Inst. Tech., 1951, PhD, 1955; postgrad., U. Wis., 1955-56. Rsch. scientist Army Rocket and Guided Missile Agy. and NASA, Huntsville, Ala., 1956-59; from assoc. prof. to prof. chem. engring. Ga. Inst. Tech., Atlanta, 1959-71; prof. Va. Poly. Inst. and State U., Blacksburg, 1971-94, head dept. chem. engring., 1971-82; assoc. provost for engring. Va. Commonwealth U., Richmond, 1994-95, founding dean engring., 1995-99, founding dean emeritus, prof. chem. engring., 1999—; asst. dean engring. and mfg. techs. J. Sargeant Reynolds C.C., 2006—. Vis. prof. Calif. Inst. Tech., 1984; dir. chem. and transport sys. div. NSF, Washington, 1990-93; cons. in field. Author: Molecular Engineering, 1991; editorial adv. bd.: Chemical Abstracts; contbr. numerous articles to profl. publs. Bd. dirs. Greater Richmond Tech. Coun. Recipient Cmty. Svc. award Richmond Joint Engrs. Coun., 2000, Leadership award Greater Richmond Tech. Coun., 2002; Rsch. grantee NSF, NASA, Air Force Office Sci. Rsch.; named one of five Outstanding Young Men of Yr. Atlanta, 1964, Acad. Disting. Engring. Alumni, Ga. Tech., 1994; Danforth assoc.; named to Hall of Fame, Ga. Tech., 2006. Fellow AIChE (chmn. nat. program com., mem. editl. bd. jour), AAAS (chmn. sect. on engring. 1985-86); mem. Am. Chem. Soc.; mem. Sigma Xi. Republican. Home: 6 River Court Ln Richmond VA 23238-5581 Office: Va Commonwealth U Richmond VA 23284 Office Phone: 804-754-5576. Business E-Mail: hmcgee@vcu.edu.

MCGEE, HUGH E., III, investment company executive; BS summa cum laude, Princeton Univ., 1981; JD with honors, Univ. Tex., 1984. With Lehman Bros. Holdings, NYC, 1993—, mng. dir., mem. exec. com., head investment banking div., 2002—. Office: Lehman Bros Holdings 745 Seventh Ave New York NY 10019 Office Phone: 212-526-2863. Business E-Mail: hmcgee@lehman.com. *

MCGEE, HUMPHREY GLENN, retired architect; b. June 26, 1937; s. James Gladney and Elizabeth Adams (Williams) McG. BArch, Clemson U., 1960. Designer Clark, McCall & Leach, Hartsville-Kingstree, S.C., 1961; designer prodn. A. G. Odell & Assocs., Charlotte, N.C., 1962; chief designer Clark, McCall & Leach, Hartsville-Kingstree, 1963; sr. designer LBC & W, Inc., Columbia, SC, 1965—76, sr. v.p. client svcs. and design, 1976; pres. CEDA, Inc., Columbia, S.C., 1976-86; pres., treas. McGee-Howle & Assocs., Vero Beach, Fla., 1986—2002; pvt. practice Indian River Shores, Fla., 2002—05, Chattanooga, 2002—05; ret., 2005. Pub.: Who's Who in Interior Design, 1993-95; cited in 100 Designer's Favorite Rooms, 1993, 94, 95. With USAR, 1961-67. Mem. AIA, Nat. Soc. Interior Designers (award 1972), Am. Soc. Interior Designers (chmn. S.C. chpt. com. on Found. Interior Design Edn. and Rsch. 1976). Personal E-mail: hglennmcgee@aol.com.

MCGEE, JAMES M., federal agency administrator; Pres. Nat. Alliance Postal and Fed. Employees. Named one of Most Influential Black Americans, Ebony mag., 2006. Office: Nat Alliance Postal Federal Employees 1628 11th St NW Washington DC 20001 Office Phone: 202-939-6325. E-mail: JMcGee@NAPFE.ORG.

MCGEE, JAMES SEARS, historian, educator; b. Houston, July 12, 1942; s. William Sears and Mary Elizabeth (Peterson) McG.; m. Mary Arnall Broach, Aug. 20, 1966; children: Elizabeth, Claude. BA, Rice U., 1964; MA, Yale U., 1966, M in Philosophy, 1968, PhD, 1971. Asst. prof. Ga. So. Coll., Statesboro, 1969-71; asst. prof. history U. Calif., Santa Barbara, 1971-78, assoc. prof., 1978-84, prof., 1984—, chmn. dept., 1990-95. Pres. Pacific Coast Conf. on Brit. Studies, 1998-2000. Author: The Godly Man in Stuart England, 1976; co-author: The West Transformed, 2000; editor: The Miscellaneous Works of John Bunyan, Vol. 3, 1987. Named Disting. Tchr. in Soc. Scis., U. Calif., Santa Barbara, 1989; fellow Abraham Found., 1962-63; Woodrow Wilson fellow, 1964-65; recipient summer stipend NEH, 1975. Fellow Royal Hist. Soc.; mem. Am. Soc. Ch. History, Am. Hist. Assn., N.Am. Conf. on Brit. Studies. Democrat. Episcopalian. Avocation: gardening. Office: U Calif Dept History Santa Barbara CA 93106

MCGEE, JANE MARIE, retired elementary school educator; b. Paducah, Ky., Nov. 3, 1926; d. William Penn and Mary Virginia (Martin) Roberts; m. Hugh Donald McGee, Oct. 11, 1946; children: Catherine Jane McGee Bacon, Nancy Ann McGee McManus. BS in Elem. Edn., Murray State U., 1948; cert. in gifted edn., Nat. Coll. Edn., 1976. Tchr. Hazel Pub. Schs., Ky., 1948—49, Pittsford Pub. Schs., Mich., 1949—50, Leal Elem. Sch., Urbana, Ill., 1950-53, Cleveland Elem. Sch., Skokie, Ill., 1953-57; pvt. tutor, pre-sch. tchr., 1953-61; tchr. Woodland Park Elem. Sch., Deerfield, Ill., 1968-83; ret., 1983. Beauty and skin care cons. Mary Kay Cosmetics, Gunnison, Colo., 1984—2002, Sequim, Wash., 2002—; co-owner Eagles Nest B&B, 1996—2002. Soprano Western State Coll. and Cmty. Chorus, Gunnison, 1986-97, European concert tour, 1990. Mem. AAUW, Top o' the World Garden Club (sec. 1984-2002, winner first place at numerous garden club shows). Baptist. Avocations: flower arranging, crafts, knitting, bird watching, rock collecting.

MC GEE, JOHN FRAMPTON, communications company executive; b. Charleston, SC, Jan. 9, 1923; s. Hall Thomas and Gertrude (Frampton) McG.; m. Ruth Bouknight Smedley, June 19, 1971; children: Beverly C. McGee Kinder, Catharine F. McGee Mebane, Charles V. Smedley. BS in Bus. and Polit. Sci., Davidson Coll., 1943. With Charleston Post-News and Courier, 1946-62; asst. gen. mgr. State-Rcords Newspapers, Columbia, S.C., 1962-64, gen. mgr., pres., co-pub., 1964-69; gen. exec. Knight Newspaper, Inc., Miami, Fla., 1969-70; pres., assoc. pub. Charleston (W.Va.) Daily Mail, 1970-87, pub., 1987-90; gen. ptnr. McGee Enterprises, Charleston, 1987—. Pres. Clay Comms., Inc. parent co Charleston Daily Mail, Raleigh Register, Post-Herald, Beckley, W.V.a, Enquirer-Jour., Monroe, NC, Shelby (NC) Daily Star, Sta. WWAY-TV, NC, others; bd. dirs., exec. com. AP, NYC; bd. dirs. Thomson Newspapers, Inc., NYC and Toronto, United Nat. Bank, Charleston, W.Va.; adv. bd. Sch. Journalism, W.Va. U.; vis. prof. Grad. Sch. Journalism, U. Nairobi, Kenya, 1992, 93, Harare Zimbabwe, 1993-94; vis. lectr. media matters USIS Wind Hook Namibia, 1994; print media counselor, Namibia and Botswana, 1995. Vice chmn. Charleston Area Med. Ctr., U. Charleston; chmn. bd. visitors, trustee Davidson (NC) Coll.; co-chmn. McGee Found.; bd. dirs. Coun. for Cmty. and Economic Devel. W.Va.; gen. exec. bd Presbyn. Ch. U.S.A., 1974-76; active SC Commn. for Higher Edn., 1966-69, Capt. inf. U.S. Army, 1943-45. Decorated Purple Heart with oak leaf cluster, Bronze Star with three oak lead clusters, Combat Inf. badge, Croix de Guerre with palm (France and Belgium); recipient Presdl. Merit citation Knight Found., 1995. Fellow Internat. Press Inst. (bd. dirs. Am. com., mem. UNESCO commn. for free press during South African elections 1994); mem. So. Newspaper Pubs. Assn. (bd. dirs. 1967-69, W.Va. Press Assn. (pres. 1977-78, New Eng. Soc. S.C., Cosmos Club (Charleston), Edgewood Country Club of W.Va. Office: McGee Enterprises Bank One Ctr Ste 312 Charleston WV 25301 E-mail: jfm@citynet.net.

MCGEE, LIAM E., bank executive; Grad., U. San Diego; MBA, Pepperdine U.; JD, Loyola Marymount U. Law Sch. With Wells Fargo and Co., Security Pacific Corp.; mem. staff Bank Am. Corp., 1990, pres. So. Calif., 1998—2000, pres. Calif., 2000—01, pres. global consumer banking, 2001—04, pres. global consumer and small bus. banking, 2004—. Dir. Fed. Res. Bank, San Francisco; mem. risk and capital com. Bank Am. Corpn., mem. mgmt. operating com. Bd. trustees Nat. Urban League; bd. dirs. Arts and Sci. Coun., Charlotte, NC; chmn. bd. trustees U. San Diego; chmn. United Way Greater LA. Office: Bank Am Corp Ctr 100 N Tryon St Fl 58 Charlotte NC 28255-0001 *

MCGEE, LINDA MACE, judge, lawyer; b. Marion, NC, Mar. 20, 1949; d. Cecil Adam and Norma Jean (Hogan) Mace; m. B. Gary McGee, Dec. 19, 1970; children: Scott Adam, Jeffrey Sean. BA, U. N.C., 1971, JD, 1973. Bar: N.C. 1973. Exec. dir. N.C. Acad. Trial Lawyers, Raleigh, 1973-78; assoc. Finger, Watson & di Santi, Boone, NC, 1978-80; ptnr. Finger, Watson, di Santi & McGee, Boone, 1980-89, di Santi, Watson & McGee, Boone, 1989-95; judge N.C. Ct. of Appeals, 1995—. Mem. trustee panel U.S. Bankruptcy Ct., Greensboro, N.C., 1980-82; bd. dirs. Legal Services of N.C., Raleigh, 1980-84; mem. N.C. Bd. Law Examiners, 1986-93. Vice-chairperson Watauga County Coun. on Status of Women, Boone, 1979-82; trustee Caldwell C.C. and Tech. Inst., Hudson, N.C., 1980-89; mem. exec. bd. N.C. Assn. C.C. Trustees, 1983-85; trustee Caldwell C.C., 1981-89; mem. Pub. Edn. Commn., 2000—. Mem. ABA, ATLA, AAUW, LWV, ABA Found., Am. Law Inst., N.C. Assn. Women Attys. (charter, treas. 1980-84, chair jud. divsn. 1997, Gwyneth B. Davis award 1997, Outstanding Judge of Yr. award 1999), N.C. Bar Assn. (bd. govs. 1983-86, co-chair lawyers in schs. com., Pro Bono Svc. award, 1992, jud. divsn. Outstanding Judge of Yr. award 1999), N.C. Acad. Trial Lawyers (bd. govs. 1993-95), N.C. State Bar, Boone C. of C. (bd. dirs. 1982-85), N.C. Bus. and Profl. Womens Clubs (chair polit. action com. 1982-83, Young Career Woman 1980), Boone Bus. and Profl. Women's Club (Woman of Yr. 1980), N.C. Women's Forum. Democrat. Presbyterian. Home: PO Box 508 Corolla NC 27927 Office: PO Box 888 Raleigh NC 27602-0888

MCGEE, MICHAEL JAY, protective services official, educator; b. Ft. Worth, June 9, 1952; s. Cecil Carl McGee and Helen Ruth (Peepies) McGee-Furth; m. Carol Lee Garbarino, Sept. 18, 1982; children: Megan Rose, John Michael, Molly Caitlin. Student, U. Tex., 1970-73, Western Oreg. State U., 1983; AAS in Fire Protection Tech., Colo. Mountain Coll., 1990. Cert. EMT Colo.; lic. fire suppression sys. insp. Colo., vocat. educator Colo., cert. hazardous materials technician Colo., 1992, fire investigator 2002, fire safety hazardous materials instr., evaluator. Driver Massengale Co., Austin, Tex., 1970-73; gen. mgr. Sundae Palace, Austin, 1973-74; staff mem. Young Life, Colorado Springs, Colo., 1970-75; mgr. Broadmoor Mgmt. Co., Vail, Colo., 1974-76; technician Vail Cable Comm., 1976-77; dep. chief, fire marshal Vail Fire Dept., 1977—, fire sci. coord., 1995—2000, emergency med. program coord., 1996—2002; v.p. HAZPRO (Hazardous Materials and Fire Safety Consulting Firm), 1996—2000; pres. Fire Protection Tng. & Consulting, Inc., 1999; v.p. OTB, LLC, 2002—07; joint ptnr. OTB, Colo., 2004—. Dist. rep. Joint Coun. Fire Dist., Colo., 1983—85; co-chmn. Eagle County Hazardous Materials, 1984—85, mem. planning com., 1987—90; mem. accountability com. Eagle County Sch. Dist., 1991—96, mem. budget rev. com., 1991—93, vice chair accountability com., 1992—93, chmn. accountability com., 1992—93, mem. policy rev. com., 1993—96, mem. facilities master planning com., 1996—97; bldg. coord., team coach Odyssey of Mind Eagle Valley Elem. Sch., 1994—95, 1997—98, 1998—99, coach Destination Imagination, 1999—2000; invited dir. workshops Colo. Dept. Edn. Dist. Accountability Conv., Colorado Springs, 1995; pres. Fire Protection Tng. and Cons., Inc.; instr., trainer EMP Am. Inc.; mission coord. Van Christian HS, 2007. Mem. planning com. World Alpine Ski Championships, 1999; mission coord. Vail Christian H.S., 2007; disaster chmn. Eagle County chpt. ARC, 1977—80, chmn., 1980—83; tng. officer Eagle Vol. Fire Dept., 1988—90; program coord. Eagle County Driver's Edn.; mem. citizen's adv. com. Colo. Mountain Coll., 1990—91, bd. dirs., 1990. Named Alumnus of the year, Co. Mountain Coll., 2001. Mem.: KC (trustee 2003—, charter Grand Knight, Eagle Count chpt.), Nat. Inst. Cert. Engring. Tech. Cert., Glendale Fire Safety Inst., Colo. State Fire Chiefs Assn., Colo. State Fire Marshals Assn., Nat. Fire Protection Assn., Internat. Assn. Arson Investigators (Colo. chpt.), Internat. Platform Assn. Office: Vail Fire Dept 42 W Meadow Dr Vail CO 81657-5000 Office Phone: 970-479-2135. Business E-Mail: mmcgee@vailgov.com.

MCGEE, MICHAEL VANHOOK, writer, playwright; b. Ft. Smith, Ark., July 23, 1928; s. Lillard Harold Weatherman and Hila VanHook McGee; m. Evelyn Elizabeth Weber; children: Michael VanHook Jr.(dec.), Patricia Lynn Mc Gee Gunderson, Sarah Valerie McGee Cannon. AB polit. sci., Univ. of the South, 1950; LLB, Southern Law U., 1957; MFA, U. Alaska, Fairbanks, 1982. Clk. and announcer Radio Sta. WMPS, Memphis, 1948; bank clk. Union Planters Bank, Memphis, 1950—51, bank teller, 1953—56; real estate ins. sales Galbreath Co., Memphis, 1956—62; writer, 1979—. Contbr. articles publ. to profl. jour. 2nd lt. USAF, 1951—53, ret. as maj. USAF, 1962—79. Mem.: Fairbanks Arts Assn. (bd. dirs. 1981—94, pres. 1994), Shriners, Masons. Anglican. Avocations: fishing, camping, painting. Home: PO Box 56116 North Pole AK 99705 Office Phone: 907-488-3326.

MCGEE, ROBERT MERRILL, oil industry executive; b. Laramie, Wyo., Dec. 15, 1946; s. Gale William and Loraine (Baker) McG.; m. Mary Louise Lehman, July 26, 1969; children: Kirk Lehman, Scott Baker. BA in Polit. Sci., Allegheny Coll., 1969. Bus. assoc. B.F. Goodrich Co., Akron, Ohio, 1969-70; dir. of info. Nat. Petroleum Coun., Washington, 1970-73; asst. dir. pub. rels. Occidental Internat. Corp., Washington, 1973-74, exec. asst. to pres., 1974-76, v.p., 1976-78, exec. v.p., 1978-82, sr. exec. v.p., 1982-91, pres., 1991—; v.p. Occidental Petroleum Corp., 1994—. Mem. Pres.'s Commn. on White House Fellowships, Washington, 1993—2001, Meridian Internat. Ctr., Washington, 1994—98; mem. bd. advisors Pan Am. Devel. Found., Washington, 1985, pres., 1991—93; bd. govs. Ford's Theatre, Washington, 1991—; bd. govs. Karl Landegger Program in internat. bus. diplomacy Sch. Fgn. Svc., Georgetown U., Washington, 1991—2000; bd. dirs. Decatur House, Washington, 1998, vice chmn. bd., 2000, chmn. bd. dirs., 2001—04. Mem. The Econ. Club of Washington, Met. Club Washington, Nat. Press Club. Office: Occidental Internat Corp Ste 400 1717 Pennsylvania Ave NW Washington DC 20006-4614

MCGEE, WILLIAM HOWARD JOHN, library director; b. Rochester, NY, May 15, 1942; s. William Peter and Cecilia Matilda (Kuhn) McG.; m. Sheila Anne Drumm, Sept. 4, 1965; children: Kathleen Moira, Margaret Frances. BA with honors, U. Toronto, Ont., Can., 1965; MEd, U. Toronto, 1973; MLS, U. Western Ont., London, 1980. Tchr. Mimico (Ont.) High Sch., 1966-67; tchr., libr. Applewood Secondary Sch., Mississauga, Ont., 1967-71; libr. Crestwood Secondary Sch., Peterborough, Ont., 1971-74; libr. cons. Cayman Islands Edn. Dept., Grand Cayman, B.W.I., 1975-79; adminstrv. asst. Lake Erie Regional Libr., London, Ont., 1980-83; chief libr. Ft. Erie (Ont.) Pub. Libr., 1983-86; asst. dir. McAllen (Tex.) Pub. Libr., 1986-89; coord. Hidalgo County Libr. System, McAllen, 1989—2001; libr. br. mgr. Lark Cmty. Ctr. Library, McAllen, 2001—. Cons. Grand Ct. Libr., Grand Cayman, 1974-79; mem. Tex. State Libr. Task Force, Austin, Tex., 1991-93; adv. coun. Libr. Svcs. Tech. Act, Austin, 1993—. Editor InTraLogue jour., 1980-83; assoc. editor Can. Jour. Info. Sci., 1980. Bd. dirs. C-ME-CU Credit Union, 1994-99, chmn., 1999. Mem. ALA, Ont. Libr. Assn., Tex. Libr. Assn. (chmn. dist. 4 1994-95, 96-97, intellectual freedom com. 1995-96, profl. rights, responsiblities, and recruitment, 1996—, centennial celebration com. 2000—), Bibliothecaires Francophones Internat. Roman Catholic. Avocations: gourmet cooking, music, travel, reading. Office: Lark Community Center P R PO Box 220 Mcallen TX 78505-0220 Office Phone: 956-688-3320. Personal E-mail: liam_mcgee@hotmail.com. Business E-Mail: wmcgee@mcallen.net.

MCGEE, WILLIAM TOBIN, internist; b. Port Chester, NY, May 23, 1957; s. James R. and Mary (Delzotto) McG.; m. Sarah McGrath; children: Erin, Kelly, Mary, Kate. BA in Physics, Dartmouth Coll., 1979; MD, N.Y. Med. Coll., 1983; M in Health Adminstrn., Clark U., 1997. Diplomate Am. Bd. Internal Medicine with spl. qualifications in Critical Care. Resident in internal medicine Baystate Med. Ctr., Springfield, Mass., 1983-86, intensivist, acting dir. surg. ICU, 1990-95; fellow in critical care St. Louis U./St. John's Mercy Med. Ctr., St. Louis, 1986-88; intensivist critical care divsn. Baystate Med. Ctr., Springfield, Mass., 1990-98, dir. ICU quality improvement, 1998—. DeWitt Wallace fellow rehab. medicine Rusk Inst. NYU Med. Ctr. Fellow Coll. Chest Physicians (Cecile Lehman Mayer award 1993); mem. AMA, Soc. Critical Care Medicine (presdl. citation 2000, internal medicine specialty award 2000), Am. Soc. Parenteral and Enteral Nutrition. Roman Catholic. Avocations: skiing, biking, hiking, sailing, windsurfing. Office: Baystate Med Ctr 759 Chestnut St Springfield MA 01199-1001

MCGEENEY, JOHN STEPHEN, lawyer; b. Manhasset, NY, Dec. 22, 1934; s. John Joseph and Marion Alice (Morse) McG.; m. Diane Tyler; children: Michael Morse, Luke Stephen. AB, Amherst Coll., 1956; LLB, Harvard U., 1959. Bar: Conn., U.S. Dist. Ct. Conn. 1961, U.S. Supreme Ct. 1965, U.S. Dist Ct. (ea. dist.) Va. 1967, U.S. Ct. Appeals (2d cir.) 1969, U.S. Ct. Appeals (4th cir.) 1971, U.S. Dist. Ct. (so. dist.) N.Y. 1980, U.S. Dist. Ct. Mont. 1987. Assoc. Cummings & Lockwood, Stamford, Conn., 1959-68, ptnr., 1968-89, Paul, Hastings, Janofsky & Walker, Stamford, 1989—, chmn., 1994—, mem. policy com. Bd. dirs. Dorr-Oliver Inc., Milford, 1989—. Fellow Am. Coll. Trial Lawyers; mem. ABA, Fed. Bar Coun., Conn. Bar Assn. (Fed. Practice com.). Office: Paul Hastings Janofsky & Walker 1055 Washington Blvd Stamford CT 06901-2216 Office Phone: 203-961-7402. Office Fax: 203-358-8705. Business E-Mail: stevenmcgeeney@paulhastings.com.

MCGEER, EDITH GRAEF, retired neurological science educator; b. NYC, Nov. 18, 1923; d. Charles and Charlotte Annie (Ruhl) Graef; m. Patrick L. McGeer, Apr. 15, 1954; children: Patrick Charles, Brian Theodore, Victoria Lynn. BA, Swarthmore Coll., 1944; PhD, U. Va., 1946; DSc (hon.), U. Victoria, 1987, U. B.C., 2000; DSc, Shiga U., 2006. Rsch. chemist E.I. DuPont de Nemours & Co., Wilmington, Va., 1946—54; rsch. assoc. divsn. neurol. sci. U. B.C., Vancouver, Canada, 1954-74, assoc. prof., 1974—76, prof., acting head, 1976—83, prof., head, 1983—89, prof. emerita, 1989—. Author: (with others) Molecular Neurobiology of the Mammalian Brain, 1978, 2d edit., 1987; editor: (with others) Kainic Acid as a Tool in Neurobiology, 1978, Glutamine, Glutamate, and GABA, 1983; contbr. articles to profl. jours. Decorated officer Order of B.C., Order of Can.; recipient citation, Am. Chem. Soc., 1958, Rsch. award, Clarke Inst., 1992, Lifetime Achievement award, Sci. Coun. B.C., 1995, Hon. Alumnus award, 1996, cert., Internat. Sci. Inst., 2001, medal of svc., Dr. Cam Coady Found., 2003, Lifetime Achievement award, U. B.C. Med. Faculty, 2006. Fellow Can. Coll. Neuropsychopharmacology, Royal Soc. Can.; mem. Can. Biochem. Soc., Internat. Brain Rsch. Orgn., Internat. Soc. Neurochemistry, Soc. Neurosci., Am. Neurochem. Soc. (councilor 1979-83), North Pacific Soc. Neurology and Psychiatry (hon. fellow), Lychnos Soc., Sigma Xi, Phi Beta Kappa. Office: U BC Divsn Neurol Sci 2255 Wesbrook Mall Vancouver BC Canada V6T 1Z3 Home Phone: 604-224-6403; Office Phone: 604-822-7380. Business E-Mail: mcgeer@interchange.ubc.ca.

MCGEEVER, ELIZABETH M., lawyer; b. Waterbury, Conn., Jan. 27, 1956; BA, U. Conn., 1977; JD, Villanova U., 1981. Bar: Del. 1981, DC 1988. Atty. Divsn. Enforcement SEC, 1986—88; ptnr. Prickett Jones & Elliott, Wilmington, Del. Mem. Del. Judicial Nom. Commn.; chair bd. profl. responsibility Del. Supreme Ct.; rules com. Ct. of Chancery. Mem.: ABA (co-chair com. on class actions and derivative suits 1995—98, diversity implementation com. 2002, minority judicial intern program com. 2002, co-dir. divisions 2003, litig. sect. coun. 2004—, bus. law sect.), Del. State Bar Assn. (corp. law coun. 1990—99, exec. com. 2003—, pres.-elect 2006—07, Women's Leadership award 2003). Office: Prickett Jones & Elliott 1310 King St Wilmington DE 19801 Office Phone: 302-888-6521. Office Fax: 302-888-6554. E-mail: emmcgeever@prickett.com.

MCGEGAN, NICHOLAS, music director; b. Eng. Student, Cambridge U., Oxford U. Music dir. San Francisco's Phila. Baroque Orch., 1985—, Irish Chamber Orch; artistic dir. Göttingen Handel Festival, Germany, 1990, Killaloe Festival; prin. guest condr. Scottish Opera, 1992-98; prin. condr. Drottningholm Ct. Theatre, 1993-95; founder, dir., harpsichordist The Arcadian Acad. Guest condr. San Francisco, St. Louis, Houston, Detroit, Indpls., Minn., Nat. Symphony orchs., City of Birmingham Symphony Orch., Halle Orch., Acad. of St. Martin-in-the-Fields in Breat Britain, Montreal Symphony, Nat. Arts Ctr. Orch., Ottawa, Orchestra de la Suisse Romande, Jerusalem Symphony, NY Philharm., Phila. Orch.; condr. Hanover Band, Freiburg Baroque Orch., Orch. of the Age of Enlightment; artist-in-residence, Milw. Symphony Orch.; condr. over 40 operas in Europe and US; artistic ptnr. St. Paul Chamber Orch. Condr. (Operas) Mostly Mozart Festival, NYC, 2003. Office: The St Paul Chamber Orchestra Third Fl of the Hamm Bldg 408 St Peter St Saint Paul MN 55102-1497 *

MC GEHEE, H. COLEMAN, JR., (HARRY COLEMAN MCGHHE), retired bishop; b. Richmond, Va., July 7, 1923; s. Harry Coleman and Ann Lee (Cheatwood) McG.; m. June Stewart, Feb. 1, 1946; children: Lesley, Alexander, Harry III, Donald, Cary. BS, Va. Poly. Inst., 1947; JD, U. Richmond, 1949; MDiv, Va. Theol. Sem., 1957, DD, 1973. Bar: Va. 1949, U.S. Supreme Ct. 1954; ordained to ministry Episcopal Ch., 1957. Spl. counsel dept. hwys. State of Va., 1949-51, gen. counsel employment svc., 1951, asst. atty. gen., 1951-54; rector Immanuel Ch.-on-the-Hill, Va. Sem., 1960-71; bishop Diocese of Mich., Detroit, 1971-90. Adv. bd. Nicaraguan Network, Ctr. for Peace and Conflict Studies, Wayne State U.; bd. dirs. Mich. Religious Coalition for Abortion Rights, 1976-84; trustee Va. Theol. Sem., 1978-93; pres. Episc. Ch. Pub. Co., 1978-85. Columnist Detroit News, 1979—85, weekly commentator pub. radio sta. WDET-AM, Detroit, 1984—90. Mem. Gov.'s Commn. on Status of Women, 1965-66, Mayor's Civic Com., Alexandria, 1967-68; sponsor Nat. Assn. for ERA, 1977-85; pres. Alexandria Legal Aid Soc., 1969-71; bd. dirs. No. Va. Fairhousing Corp., 1963-67; pres. Mich. Coalition for Human Rights, 1980-89 (Humanitarian award 2001); chmn. Citizens' Com. for Justice in Mich., 1983-84; sponsor Farm Labor Orgn. for Children, 1983-85; bd. dirs. Pub. Benefit Corp., Detroit, 1988-90, Mich. Citizens for Personal Freedom, 1989-92, Poverty and Social Reform Inst., Detroit, 1989—, Bread for the World, 1990-94, Ams. United for Separation of Ch. and State, 1990, ACLU Oakland County, Mich., 1991-94; co-chair Lesbian-Gay Found. Mich., 1991—. 1st lt. C.E., U.S. Army, 1943-46. Named Feminist of Yr., Detroit NOW, 1978, Person of Yr., Econ. Justice Commn. Mich., 1997; recipient Humanitarian award Detroit ACLU, 1984, Phillip Hart medal Mich. Women's Studies Assn., 1984, Sayre award for justice and peace Episc. Peace Fellowship, 1988, Spirit of Detroit award, 1989, Archbishop Romero award Mich. Labor Com., 1990, Brotherhood award AME Ch., Detroit, 1993, Ira Jayne award Detroit br. NAACP, 1993, Martin Luther King, Jr. award United Ch. of Christ, 1995, William Scarlett award Episc. Ch. Pub. Co., 1997, Humanitarian award Mich. Coalition for Human Rights, 2001. Mem.: Detroit Econ. Club (bd. dirs.). Episcopalian. Home: 1496 Ashover Dr Bloomfield Hills MI 48304-1215

MCGEHEE, LARRY THOMAS, retired academic administrator; b. Paris, Tenn., May 18, 1936; s. George Eugene and Margaret Elizabeth (Thomas) McG.; m. Elizabeth Hathhorn Boden, Aug. 26, 1961; children: Elizabeth Hathhorn, Margaret Thomas. BA, Transylvania Coll., 1958; BD, Yale U., 1963, MA, 1964, PhD, 1969. Dir., asst. v.p. for univ. relations U. Ala., 1966-68, exec. asst. to pres., 1968-69, exec. v.p., 1969-71; lectr., assoc. prof. dept. Am. studies, 1969-71, acad. v.p., 1971; chancellor U. Tenn., Martin, 1971-79; spl. asst. to pres. U. Tenn. Sys., Knoxville, 1979-82; v.p. coll., prof. religion Wofford Coll., Spartanburg, SC, 1982—2005; emeritus prof. religion, 2005—. Syndicated columnist Southern Seen, 1982—. Danforth fellow Yale U., 1960-66. Home: 1047 Woodburn Rd Spartanburg SC 29302-2867 Office: Wofford Coll 429 N Church St Spartanburg SC 29303-3663 Office Phone: 864-597-4197. E-mail: mcgeheelt@wofford.edu.

MCGEHEE, ROBERT B., energy executive; Grad., Nuclear Power Sch. and Submarine Sch., U.S. Naval Acad.; law degree, U. Tex. Atty. Wise Carter Child & Caraway, Jackson, Miss.; sr. v.p., gen. counsel Carolina Power & Light Co., 1997—99, exec. v.p., gen. counsel, chief adminstrv. officer, 1999—2000; pres., CEO Progress Energy Svc. Co., LLC, 2000—02; exec. v.p. Carolina Power & Light Co. and Fla. Progress Corp., 2000—, Progress Energy, Inc., Raleigh, NC, 2000—02, pres., COO, 2002—04, chmn., CEO, 2004—. Mem. exec. com., past vice-chmn. Nuclear Energy Inst. Lt. USN. Office: Progress Energy PO Box 1551 411 S Wilmington St Raleigh NC 27601-1748 E-mail: bob.mcgehee@pgnmail.com. *

MCGEORGE, DON W., retail executive; Joined Kroger Co., Cin., 1977, sr. v.p., 1997—2000, former pres., Tex. Divsn., exec. v.p., 2000—03, pres., COO, 2003—. Office: Kroger Co 1014 Vice St Cincinnati OH 45202-1100 *

MCGETTIGAN, CHARLES CARROLL, JR., investment banker; b. San Francisco, Mar. 28, 1945; s. Charles Carroll McGettigan and Molly (Fay) McGettigan Pedley; m. Katharine Havard King, Nov. 1, 1975 (div. 1981); m. Meriwether Lewis Stovall, Aug. 6, 1983; 1 child, Meriwether Lewis Fay. AB in Govt., Georgetown U., Washington, DC, 1966; MBA in Fin., U. Pa., Phila., 1969. Assoc., asst. v.p., v.p. Blyth Eastman Dillon, NYC, 1970-75, 1st v.p., 1975-78, sr. v.p. San Francisco, 1978-80, Dillon, Read & Co., San Francisco, 1980-83; gen. ptnr. Woodman Kirkpatrick & Gilbreath, San Francisco, 1983-84; prin. corp. fin. Hambrecht & Quist, Inc., San Francisco, 1984-88; mng. dir., founder McGettigan, Wick & Co., Inc., San Francisco, 1988—; gen. ptnr., founder Proactive Ptnrs., L.P., San Francisco, 1990—, Proactive Investment Mgrs., L.P., San Francisco, 1991—. Gen. ptnr Fremont Proactive Ptnrs., 1991—2001; bd. dirs. Cuisine Solutions, Inc., Alexandria, Va., Corgi Internat., Ltd., Hong Kong; chmn. Modtech, Inc., Perris, Calif., Onsite Energy Corp., Carlsbad, Calif., Tanknology, Inc., Austin, Tex.; adv. dir. Chesapeake Ventures, Balt., 1984—94. Trustee St. Francis Meml. Hosp., San Francisco, 1980-86; mem. United San Francisco Rep. fin. com., 1983—, steering com., 1986—; adv. bd. dirs. Leavey Sch. Bus. Adminstrn., Santa Clara U., Calif., 1984-90. With USN, 1966. Mem. The Brook, Racquet and Tennis Club (NY), The Pacific Union Club, Bohemian Club (San Francisco), San Francisco Golf Club, Burlingame Country Club (Hillsborough, Calif.), Boston (New Orleans), White's (London). Republican. Roman Catholic. Home: 3375 Clay St San Francisco CA 94118-2006 Office: McGettigan Wick & Co Inc 50 Osgood Pl San Francisco CA 94133-4622 Office Phone: 415-986-4433. Business E-Mail: Chas@McGettigan-Wick.com.

MCGETTRICK, MARK F., energy executive; V.p. customer svc. and mktg. Dominion, sr. v.p. customer svc. and metering, sr. v.p., chief adminstrv. officer, 2002, pres. Dominion Resources Svcs. Inc., 2002—03, pres., CEO generation Va. Power, 2003—06, exec. v.p., 2006—, pres., COO generation Va. Power, 2006—. Bd. dirs. Nuc. Energy Inst. Office: Dominion PO Box 26532 Richmond VA 23261-6532 *

MCGHEE, DIANE BAUMANN, dance instructor, consultant; b. Salem, NJ, 1954; d. Nelson Paul and Alice Elizabeth Baumann; children: Christine, Jonathan, Michael Porcaro. BS, Madison Coll., 1972—76; MS, James Madison U., 1976—78. Phys. edn. and dance instr. Salisbury State Coll., Md., 1978—82; resident choreographer; booking and tour mgr. Mandala Folk Ensemble, Boston, 1984—88; dir. of sch. outreach programs and tchr. MJT Dance Co., Boston, 1988—94; sr. tchr. Boston Renaissance/Edison Project Partnership Sch., 1994—97; dir. SE Ctr. for Dance Edn., Columbia Coll., 1997—2000; assoc. prof. Dept. of Theatre and Dance, Winthrop U., Rock Hill, SC, 2000—02; dir., arts for children interdisciplinary program; assoc. prof. of dance SUNY Coll. at Brockport, Brockport, NY, 2002—. Steering and coordinating committees Arts in Basic Curriculum Project, cons., arts edn. leadership inst.; adv. bd. and cons. Am. Dance Legacy Inst.; edn. cons. NY State Summer Sch. of the Arts Sch. of Dance; dir. Etudes Ednl. Project; exec. bd. Project U.N.I.Q.U.E., arts learning lab; art edn. roundtable Greater Rochester Arts and Cultural Coun. Author: (dance education lesson studies) Roots & Branches: Exploring an Evolving Dance Legacy, (dance unit of study) Civil War to Civil Rights: A Lesson in Humanity, Making Connections: Technology, Education, and Dance, American Indian Dance; A Celebration of Survival and Adaptation, Structuring Time and Space: A Dance Hypothesis. Recipient Presdl. Leadership award in Dance, SC. Dance Assn., 1998, Contbn. to Dance Edn., Fidelity Investments (Am. Ballet Gala, Boston), 1999, Artistic Vision, Comittment to Children, Dedication to Dance Edn., MJT Dance Co., 1994. Mem.: Internat. Assn. for Health, Phys. Edn., Recreation, Sport and Dance, SC Dept. Edn. (co-chair, arts tech. standards com., mem. task force, visual and performing arts curricular standards, arts report card task force, SAT improvement com.), Nat. Dance Edn. Org. (exec. bd. and charter mem.). Office: SUNY Brockport 350 New Campus Dr Brockport NY 14420 Home Phone: 585-889-7385; Office Phone: 585-395-5304. Business E-Mail: dmcghee@brockport.edu.

MCGHEE, JAY D., ecologist, educator; b. San Antonio, Tex., Oct. 22, 1971; s. Janice McGhee; m. Abigail Cartwright, Oct. 15, 2005. B in B in Biology, M in Biology, Tex. State U., San Marcos; PhD, Va. Poly. Inst. & State U., Blacksburg, Va., 2001—06. Grad. rsch. assoc. Va. Poly. Inst. & State U., Blacksburg, 2001—06; vis. asst. prof. U. Mary Washintong, Fredericksburg, Va., 2006—. Deacon Evers Rd. Christian Ch., San Antonio, 1999—2001. Airborne specialist US Army, 1989—92, Fort Bragg. Mem.: Va. Acad. Scis. Achievements include research in wild turkey harvest model. Office: Univ Mary Washington 1301 College Ave Fredericksburg VA 22401 Business E-Mail: jmcghee@umw.edu.

MCGHEE, WILLIAM CLEVELAND, retired military officer, retired transportation engineer; b. Nov. 3, 1920; Served with US Marines, US Army; locomotive engr. Va. Railway, Mullens, W.Va., Norfolk & Western R.R., W.Va. 19 murals, Mullens, W.Va., 1980—95;, author 3 books. Scout master Boy Scouts; mem. Baptist Ch., Mullens, W.Va., 1938—. Home: 1111 Woodland Ave Mullens WV 25882

MCGIBBON, JAMES R., lawyer; b. Buffalo, Apr. 3, 1946; AB cum laude, Princeton U., 1967; JD magna cum laude, Harvard U., 1971. Bar: Mass. 1972, Ga. 1973. Mem. Sutherland, Asbill & Brennan, Atlanta, ptnr. Contbr. Mem. State Bar Ga. (mem. exec. com. 1986-1991, chair antitrust sect. 1989-90, chair health care law sect.) 1992-93, mem. ABA Forum Com. Office: Sutherland Asbill & Brennan 999 Peachtree St NE Atlanta GA 30309-3996 Office Phone: 404-853-8122. Business E-Mail: jim.mcgibbon@sablaw.com.

MCGIBBON, PHYLLIS ISABEL, artist, educator; b. Madison, Wis., Jan. 9, 1961; d. W. Henry and G. Louise McGibbon. BFA, U. Wis., 1983, MFA, 1988. Luther Gregg Sullivan vis. artist Wesleyan U., Middletown, Conn., 1989-91; asst. prof. art Pomona Coll., Claremont, Calif., 1991-94, Wellesley (Mass.) Coll., 1994-97, assoc. prof., 1997—. Artist residency Bemis Ctr. for Contemporary Art, Omaha, 1995, Millay Colony, Austerlitz, N.Y., 1996, Va. Ctr. Creative Arts, Sweet Briar, 1997. Solo art installations include Davison Art Ctr., Middletown, Conn., 1990, Orange County Ctr. for Contemporary Art, Santa Ana, Calif., 1992, Sushi Performance and Visual Art, Inc., San Diego, 1994, Davis Mus. and Cultural Ctr., Wellesley, 1996, John Michael Kohler Arts Ctr., Sheboygan, Wis., 1998. Recipient award Elizabeth Greenshields Found., Montreal, Can., 1991, award Western States Arts Found. NEA, 1992, award Art Matters, Inc., N.Y.C., 1994; fellow Kala Inst., Berkeley, Calif., 1992-93, individual artist fellow Nat. Endowment for Arts 1995. Mem. Coll. Art Assn., Am. Print Alliance. Office: Wellesley Coll Dept of Art Jewett Arts Ctr Wellesley MA 02481

MCGIFFERT, MICHAEL, retired historian; b. Chgo., Oct. 5, 1928; s. Arthur Cushman and Elisabeth (Eliot) McG.; m. Genevieve White Mischel, Aug. 13, 1960 (dec. Mar. 15, 2007); m. Elizabeth Eastman, June 19, 1949 (div. 1960). BA, Harvard Coll., 1949; B.D., Yale U., 1952, PhD, 1958; postgrad., Union Theol. Sem., NYC, 1949-50. Instr. history Colgate U., Hamilton, NY, 1954-55, 56-60, U. Md., College Park, 1955-56; asst. prof. history U. Denver, 1960-64, assoc. prof., 1964-69, prof. history, 1969-74; editor William and Mary Quar., Inst. Early Am. History and Culture, prof. history, Coll. William and Mary, Williamsburg, Va., 1972-97; ret. Author: The Higher learning in Colorado, 1964; editor: The Character of Americans, 1964 (rev. edit.), 1969, Puritanism and the American Experience, 1969, (with Robert A. Skotheim) American Social Thought, 1972, God's Plot: The Paradoxes of Puritan Piety, 1972, God's Plot: Puritan Spirituality in Thomas Shepard's Cambridge, 1994. Faculty rsch. grantee U. Denver, 1970, Coll. William and Mary, 1981-82, 89; rsch. fellow NEH, 1977-78. Mem. Am. Hist. Assn., Orgn. Am. Historians, Confr. of Hist. Jours. (pres.1987-89), Am. Antiquarian Soc., Mass. Hist. Soc. Home: 102 Old Glory Ct Williamsburg VA 23185-4914 Personal E-mail: mcgiff@widomaker.com.

MCGILL, DAN MAYS, insurance business educator; b. Greenback, Tenn., Sept. 27, 1919; s. John Burton and Jane (Mays) McG.; m. Elaine Kem, June 22, 1952; children: Douglas Russell, Melanie Mays BA, Maryville Coll., 1940, LLD (hon.), 1982; MA, Vanderbilt U., 1941; PhD, U. Pa., 1947. Assoc. prof. fin. U. Tenn., Knoxville, 1947-48; Julian Price assoc. prof. ins. U. NC, Chapel Hill, 1948-51; assoc. prof. ins. U. Pa., Phila., 1952-56, Frederick H. Ecker prof. life ins., 1959-90, chmn. ins. chpt., 1965—89. Trustee NW Mut. Life Ins. Co., Milw., 1978-90; bd. dirs. NRG Life Reassurance Corp., Phila., 1984-94, Phila. Reins. Corp., 1990—, Independence Blue Cross, 1990—; exec. dir. S.S. Huebner Found., 1954-75, 78-86, chmn., 1965-94; dir. rsch. Pension Rsch. Coun., 1952-90; chmn., mem. governing bd. Leonard Davis Inst. Health Econs., 1967-90; 1st chmn. adv. commn. Pension Benefit Guaranty Corp., 1975-78, mem. 1978-81. Author: An Analysis of Government Life Insurance, 1949, The Fundamentals of Private Pensions, 8th edit., 2005, Legal Aspects of Life Insurance, 1959, Fulfilling Pension Expectations, 1962, Life Insurance, 1967, Preservation of Pension Benefit Rights, 1972, others; editor: (with others) World Insurance Trends, 1959, others. Trustee Presbyn. Med. Ctr., Phila., 1987—96; chmn. Boettner Inst. Fin. Gerontology, 1993—2002; mem. retirement bd. Mass. Bay Transp. Authority, 1980—96; chmn. bd. pensions Presbyn. Ch. USA, 1977—88; trustee Presbyn. Found. for Phila., 1996—2001. Maj. USAF, 1942—46, Maj. USAF, 1951—52. Recipient Disting. Alumni award Maryville Coll., 1962, Huebner Gold medal award Am. Coll., 1977, Gold medal Internat. Ins. Soc., 1987. Mem.: Am. Risk and Ins. Assn. (pres. 1959, Elizur Wright award 1955, 1981), Merion Cricket Club, Union League. Republican. Presbyterian. Avocations: music, travel, sports. Home: 50 Belmont Ave Bala Cynwyd PA 19004-2437

MCGILL, HENRY COLEMAN, JR., pathologist, educator, researcher; b. Nashville, Oct. 1, 1921; s. Henry Coleman and Thursa (Lowry) McG.; m. Cloace Laurite Ferguson, Sept. 12, 1945; children: Margaret Ann, Laurilynn, Elizabeth Gail. BA, Vanderbilt U., 1943, MD, 1946. Intern Vanderbilt Hosp., Nashville, 1946-47; asst. prof. pathology La. State U. Med. Ctr., New Orleans, 1950-55, assoc. prof., 1955-61, prof., chmn. dept., 1961-66; prof. pathology U. Tex. Health Sci. Ctr., San Antonio, 1966-92, chmn. dept., 1966-72; sci. dir. S.W. Found. for Biomed. Rsch., San Antonio, 1978-92, sr. scientist, 1992-96, sr. scientist emeritus, 1996—. Contbr. articles to med. jours. Capt. M.C., U.S. Army, 1948-50. Mem. Phi Beta Kappa, Sigma Xi, Alpha Omega Alpha. Home: 4102 Fawnridge Dr San Antonio TX 78229-4212 Office: PO Box 760549 San Antonio TX 78245-0549 Business E-Mail: hmcgill@icarus.sfbr.org.

MCGILL, JAY, magazine publisher; With Hearst Magazines, 1979—; pub. Country Living, NYC, 1993—97; v.p. pub. Popular Mechanics, 1997—2003; dir., digital integration Hearst Corp., 2001—03; senior v.p. and pub. SmartMoney, NYC, 2003, now pres., pub. dir. Office: Attn Jay McGill Hearst Mags 224 W 57th St New York NY 10019-3212 also: SmartMoney Mag 1755 Broadway New York NY 10019 Business E-Mail: jmcgill@hearst.com.

MCGILL, JOHN KNOX, lawyer; b. Charlotte, NC, Aug. 25, 1956; s. John Charles and Mabel (Hamilton) Mc. BS in Bus. cum laude, Erskine Coll., 1978; MBA, JD, U. N.C., 1982. Bar: NC 1983; CPA, NC. Ptnr., tax atty. Garland & Alala, P.A., Gastonia, NC, 1982—86, McGill & Hassan, P.A., Charlotte, 1999—; CEO John K. McGill & Co. Inc., Charlotte, NC. Chmn., bd. dirs. Select Cons. Inc., Charlotte; bd. dirs., founder, Advanced Pension Systems, Inc., Charlotte. Tax editor: Dental Economics Mag., 1982—; editor-in-chief newsletter The McGill Advisory; contbg. editor: (textbook) Contemporary Marketing, 4th edit., 1983. Trustee Erskine Coll., 1998-04; treas. 1st Assoc. Reformed Presbyn. Ch., Gastonia, N.C., 1989-94, deacon, 1989-94, elder, 1995-04. Recipient Tax Law scholarship, Touche, Ross & Co., CPA's, 1982. Mem. ABA, N.C. Bar Assn., Am. Inst. CPA's, N.C. Assn. CPA's, Sertoma Club (Disting. Svc award, Kings Mt. N.C., 1983). Republican. Avocations: jogging, basketball, baseball, skiing, card/stamp collecting. Home: 2236 Lake Ridge Dr Belmont NC 28012 Office: Lake View Profl Bldg 8816 Red Oak Blvd Ste 240 Charlotte NC 28217

MCGILL, LEONARD JOHN, lawyer; b. Edinburgh, Oct. 26, 1957; s. Alexander and Mary (Thomson) McG.; m. Nancy Ann Fasulo, Sept. 29, 1981. LLB with honors, U. Edinburgh, 1979; JD magna cum laude, Georgetown U., 1985. Bar: D.C. 1986, Calif. 1988. Assoc. Skadden, Arps, Slate, Meagher & Flom, Washington, 1986-87, Gibson, Dunn & Crutcher, LA, 1987—2002; v.p., dep. gen. counsel Fleetwood Enterprises, Inc., 2002—03, sr. v.p., corp. fin. & chief governance officer, 2003—, gen. counsel, sec., 2005—. Mem. ABA (internat. law and practice sect. 1986—, bus. law sect. 1986—), Masons. Democrat. Presbyterian. Avocations: golf, football. Office: Fleetwood Enterprises Inc 3125 Myers St Riverside CA 92503

MCGILL, MAURICE LEON, corporate financial executive; b. Malden, Mo., Aug. 22, 1936; s. William Howard and Iris (Phillips) McG.; m. Wanda Coral Wirt, Feb. 2, 1957; children— Melany, Melinda, William Shannon

BS, U. Mo., 1958, MA, 1959. C.P.A., Mo., Iowa, Ariz. Mgr. Touche, Ross, Bailey & Smart, Kansas City, Mo., 1959-64; fin. v.p., treas. Iowa Beef Packers, Inc., Dakota City, Nebr., 1964-69; exec. v.p., treas. Spencer Foods, Inc., Iowa, 1969-71, also dir. Iowa; sr. v.p. Diamond Reo Trucks, Inc., Lansing, Mich., 1971-72; fin. v.p. Ariz. Colo. Land & Cattle Co., Phoenix, 1972-75; ptnr. Touche Ross & Co., Phoenix, 1975-81; exec. v.p. fin. and adminstrn., treas., bd. dirs. IBP, Inc., Dakota City, Nebr., 1981-89; pres., bd. dirs. Wirmac Corp., Garland, Tex., 1989—. Bd. dirs. Premium Std. Farms, Kansas City, Mo. Mem.: AICPA. Home: 1406 O Shannon Ln Garland TX 75044-3510 E-mail: mandwmcgill@msn.com.

MCGILL, THOMAS CONLEY, physics educator; b. Port Arthur, Tex., Mar. 20, 1942; s. Thomas Conley and Susie Elizabeth (Collins) McG.; m. Toby Elizabeth Cone, Dec. 27, 1966; children: Angela Elizabeth, Sara Elizabeth. BS in Math., Lamar State Coll., 1963, BEE, 1964; MEE, Calif. Inst. Tech., 1965, PhD, 1969. NATO postdoctoral fellow U. Bristol, Eng., 1969-70; NRC postdoctoral fellow Princeton (N.J.) U., 1970-71; from asst. to assoc. prof. applied physics Calif. Inst. Tech., Pasadena, 1971-77, prof., 1977—. Cons. United Techs. Corp., 1988-95, Advance Projects Agy./Def. Sci. Rsch. Coun., Arlington, Va., 1979—; chief Naval Ops. Exec. Panel, 1995-2000; mem. Semiconductor Tech. Coun., 1995-98; mem. adv. bd. Sematech U., 1992-95. Alfred P. Sloan Found. fellow, 1974. Fellow Am. Physical Soc.; mem. AAAS, IEEE, Am. Vacuum Soc., Sigma Xi. Office: Calif Inst Tech Mail Code 128 # 95 Pasadena CA 91125-0001

MCGILL, WILLIAM JAMES, JR., academic administrator, writer; b. St. Louis, Mar. 25, 1936; s. William James Sr. and Ethel (Williams) McG.; m. Ellen Buck, June 18, 1960; children: Sara Louise, Susan Elizabeth, Alison Marcia. BA, Trinity Coll., 1957; MA, Harvard U., 1958, PhD, 1961, grad. Inst. Ednl. Mgmt., 1989; LHD (hon.), Lebanon Valley Coll., 1998. Instr. history Western Md. Coll., Westminster, 1960-62; asst. prof. history Alma (Mich.) Coll., 1962-68, assoc. prof., 1968-72; dean of coll. Washington & Jefferson Coll., Washington, Pa., 1972-75, prof. history, 1972-84; asst. dir., div. edn. programs NEH, Washington, 1984-86; v.p., dean faculty Lebanon Valley Coll., Annville, Pa., 1986-98, acting pres., 1987-88. Author: Maria Theresa, 1972, The Rock Springs Chronicles, 1999, George Herbert, R.S. Thomas and the Argument with God, 2003; contbr. 72 articles to profl. jours., 61 book revs., 20 short stories, numerous poems; poetry editor Spitball Mag., 1993—, mng. editor, 2000—. Assoc. to rector St. Luke's Episc. Ch., Lebanon, Pa., 1986-98; priest-in-charge St. George's Episc. Ch., Waynesburg, Pa., 1974-83; actor Washington Theater Wing, 1984-86, Gretna Playhouse, Mt. Gretna, Pa., 1987-90; bd. dirs. Lebanon County United Way, 1987-95, Gretna Prodns., Mt. Gretna, 1986-90, 91-92, Concertante, 1999-01; trustee Penn Coll. Art and Design, 1992-06. Mem. Phi Beta Kappa. Avocations: sailing, writing, acting. Home and Office: PO Box 333 Annville PA 17003-0333 E-mail: wjmcgill@earthlink.net.

MCGILLICUDDY, JOAN MARIE, psychotherapist, consultant; b. Chgo., June 23, 1952; d. James Neal and Muriel (Joy) McG. BA, U. Ariz., 1974, MS, 1976; PhD, Walden U., 1996. Cert. nat. counselor. Counselor ACTION, Tucson, 1976; counselor, clin. supr. Behavioral Health Agy. Cen. Ariz., Casa Grande, 1976-81; instr. psychology Cen. Ariz. Coll., Casa Grande, 1978-83; therapist, co-dir. Helping Assocs., Inc., Casa Grande, 1982—, v.p., sec., 1982—; cert. instr. Silva Method Mind Devel., Tucson, 1986—. Active Mayor's Com. for Handicapped, Casa Grande, 1989-90, Human Svcs. Planning, Casa Grande, 1985-95, Pinal Gila Srs. Coun. Found., 2005—. Named Outstanding Am. Lectr. Silva Mind Internat., 1988-99. Mem. ACA. Avocations: jogging, singing. Office: Helping Assocs Inc 1901 N Trekell Rd Casa Grande AZ 85222-1706 Office Phone: 520-836-1029. E-mail: haicg@c212.com.

MC GILLICUDDY, JOHN FRANCIS, retired banker; b. Harrison, NY, Dec. 30, 1930; s. Michael J. and Anna (Munro) McG.; m. Constance Burtis, Sept. 9, 1954; children: Michael Sean, Faith Burtis Benoit, Constance Erin Mc Gillicuddy Mills, Brian Munro, John Walsh. AB, Princeton, 1952; LL.B., Harvard, 1955. With Mfrs. Hanover Trust Co. subs. Mfrs. Hanover Corp., NYC, 1958-91, v.p., 1962-66, sr. v.p., 1966-69, exec. v.p., asst. to chmn., 1969-70, vice chmn., dir., 1970, pres., 1971-79, chmn., chief exec. officer, 1979-91; chmn. bd., chief exec. officer Chem. Banking Corp., NYC, 1992-93, ret., 1994. Bd. dirs. Kelso, Inc. Bd. dirs. life trustee, chmn. emeritus N.Y. Presbyn. Hosp.; trustee emeritus Princeton U.; pres. Boy Scouts Am., Greater N.Y. Couns. Lt. (j.g.) USNR, 1955—58. Mem. Westchester Country Club (Rye, N.Y.), Blind Brook Club (Port Chester, N.Y.), Princeton Club (N.Y.C.), Augusta Nat. Golf Club (Ga.), Pine Valley Golf Club (N.J.), Laurel Valley Golf Club (Ligonier, Pa.), Seminole Golf Club (north Palm Beach, Fla.), Links Club (N.Y.C.). Roman Catholic. Office: JP Morgan Chase Corp 270 Park Ave New York NY 10017-2014

MCGINLEY, PAUL ANTHONY, JR., lawyer; b. Allentown, Pa., Apr. 24, 1948; s. Paul A. Sr. and Mary (McGurl) McG.; children: Paige, Laura, Paul Anthony III, Jonathan. AB, Princeton U., 1970; JD, Georgetown U., 1974. Bar: Pa. 1974, U.S. Dist. Ct. (ea. dist.) Pa. 1974, U.S. Supreme Ct. 1987. Assoc. Gross & Brown, Allentown, 1974-76; asst. pub. defender Lehigh County, Allentown, 1976-77, asst. county solicitor, 1977-78; ptnr. Gross, McGinley & McGinley, Allentown, 1976-83, Gross, McGinley, McGinley & LaBarre, Allentown, 1983-86, Gross, McGinley & LaBarre, Allentown, 1986-87, Gross, McGinley, LaBarre & Eaton, Allentown, 1987—. Mem. legal affairs com. Mag. Pubs. Am., 1994—; chmn. hearing com. disciplinary bd. Supreme Ct. of Pa., 1986-90, 1997-2003; co-chmn. bd. dirs. Rodale Inst., 2005—; asst. sec. Rodale Inc., 1999—, gen. counsel, 2000—; dir., sec. Velodrome Fund, 1995— Bd. dirs. Swain Sch., Allentown, 1984-89, Cedar Crest Coll. Bd. Assocs., Allentown, 1986-88; trustee Allentown YWCA, 1985-88. Mem. ABA, Pa. Bar Assn., Lehigh County Bar Assn. (bd. dirs. 1978-84, pres. 1987), Pa. Trial Lawyers Assn., Allentown-Lehigh County C. of C., Princeton Quadrangle Club (bd. dirs.) Democrat. Roman Catholic. Avocations: skiing, tennis. Office: Gross McGinley LaBarre & Eaton 33 S 7th St Allentown PA 18101-2436 Office Phone: 610-820-5450. Business E-Mail: pmcginley@gmle.com.

MCGINLY, WILLIAM C., healthcare association executive; PhD in Adminstrn., Am. U. Cert. Assn. Exec. (CAE). Pres., CEO Assn. for Healthcare Philanthropy (AHP), head AHP Found. and Hosp. Devel. and Ednl. Fund of Can. Bd. dirs. Ctr. on Philanthropy at Ind. U., Indpls., eTapestry, e-PhilanthropyFoundation; tchr. Am. U., Mt. St. Mary's Coll.; spkr. in field. Fellow: I/D/E/A/; mem.: Am. Soc. of Assn. Execs., Greater Washington Soc. Assn. Execs. Office: Assn for Healthcare Philanthropy Ste 400 313 Park Ave Falls Church VA 22046 Office Phone: 703-532-6243. Office Fax: 703-532-7170. Business E-Mail: bill@ahp.org.

MCGINN, TIMOTHY J., lawyer; b. NYC, Dec. 12, 1950; BA, Fordham U., 1972, JD, 1976. Bar: NY 1977, US Dist. Ct. Ea. Dist. NY, US Dist. Ct. So. Dist. NY, US Ct. Appeals 2nd Cir. Asst. dist. atty., Bronx County, NY, 1976—81; ptnr. Wilson, Elser, Moskowitz, Edelman & Dicker LLP, NYC. Mem.: ABA (medicine & law com.), Assn. of the Bar of the City of NY, NY State Bar Assn. Office: Wilson Elser Moskowitz Edelman & Dicker LLP 23rd Fl 150 E 42nd St New York NY 10017-5639 Office Phone: 212-490-3000 ext. 2779. Office Fax: 212-490-3038. Business E-Mail: mcginnt@wemed.com.

MCGINNIS, ARTHUR JOSEPH, JR., public relations executive; b. Jersey City, Mar. 12, 1952; s. Arthur Joseph and Roselind (Diskon) McG.; m. Kim Elizabeth Midgarden; children: Kirsten Elizabeth, Ashley Alexandra. BS, Siena Coll., 1975. Mgr. trainee Lebhar-Friedman, NYC, 1975-76; regional sales mgr. Simmons-Boardman Pub. Corp., Chgo., 1976-77; pub. Plant Location Mag., Simmons-Boardman, NYC, 1977-89; v.p. mktg. Railway Div., Simmons-Boardman, NYC, 1978-88; exec. v.p., sec. Simmons-Boardman Pub. Co., NYC, 1987-88; pres., pub. Simmons-Boardman Pub. Corp., NYC, 1988—; chmn. bd. Simmons-Boardman Pub. Co., NYC, 1991—; pres. Simmons-Boardman Books, Omaha, 1989—, chmn. bd., 1992—96. Bd. dirs. Am. Bus. Press; chmn. bd. dirs. McGinnis Corp.; adv. bd. United Publ., Inc., 2000—, Davison Pub. Co., LLC, Orlando, 2006—. Home: 35 Cheston Ct Belle Mead NJ 08502-4907 Office: Simmons Boardman Pub Corp 345 Hudson St New York NY 10014-4502 Office Phone: 212-620-7200.

MCGINNIS, BARRY EUGENE, music educator, musician; s. Calvin G. and Martha S. McGinnis; m. Amy McGinnis. BS, Towson State U., Md., 1984—91; MusM - Woodwind Specialist, East Carolina U., Greenville, NC, 1991—93; D of Musical Arts - Saxophone Performance, U. Ga., Athens, 1993—2002. Instr. of music Ga. Coll. & State U., Milledgeville, Ga., 1995—97; instr., music Piedmont Coll., Demorest, Ga., 1997—2000; vis. asst. prof., music Adams State Coll., 2000—01, instr., music, 2001—02; asst. prof., music, dir. woodwinds, dir. jazz combo Newberry Coll., SC, 2002—. Author: (profl. journal articles) Nat. Assn. of Coll. Wind and Percussion Instructors. Mem.: S.C. Band Dirs. Assn., S.C. Music Educators Assn., Music Educators Nat. Conf., College Music Soc., Nat. Assn. of Coll. Wind and Percussion Instructors, Internat. Clarinet Assn., North Am. Saxophone Alliance, Delta Omicron, Pi Kappa Lambda, Kappa Kappa Psi. Office: Newberry College Music Department 2100 College St Newberry SC 29108 Home: 2317 College St Newberry SC 29108 Office Phone: 803-321-5178. Personal E-mail: barry.mcginnis@newberry.edu.

MCGINNIS, JAMES LANDON, lawyer; b. St. Louis, May 10, 1954; s. Robert Delmar (Stepfather) and Rosalind Appel Ritchie; children: Lorna Rose, Rowan Grace. BA in History, Yale U., 1976; JD, U. Calif., Berkeley, 1979. Bar: Pa. 1979, Calif. 1980. Assoc. Morgan, Lewis & Bockius, Phila., 1979—80, Jackson, Tufts, Cole & Black, San Francisco, 1980—84; asst. US atty. Ea. and Ctrl. Districts of Calif., Fresno, LA, 1984—88; ptnr. Morgenstein & Jubelirer, San Francisco, 1988—2002, Sheppard, Mullin, Richter & Hampton, San Francisco, 2002—. Author: (article-Nat. Law Jour.) The Impact of Booker on Sentencing in Criminal Antitrust Cases. Mem.: San Francisco Bar Assn., Calif. Bar Assn., ABA. Avocations: weightlifting, tennis, guitar, motorcycling. Home: 23 Sycamore Ave Mill Valley CA 94941 Office: Sheppard Mullin 17th Fl Four Embarcadero Ctr San Francisco CA 94111 Home Phone: 415-388-8276; Office Phone: 415-774-3294, 415-434-9100. Office Fax: 415-434-3947. Business E-Mail: jmcginnis@sheppardmullin.com.

MCGINNIS, JAMES MICHAEL, physician; b. Columbia, Mo., July 12, 1944; s. Leland Glenn and Lillian Ruth (Mackler) McG.; m. Patricia Anne Gwaltney, Aug. 4, 1978; children— Brian, Katherine AB, U. Calif., Berkeley, 1966; MA, MD, UCLA, 1971; M.P.P., Harvard U., 1977. House officer in internal medicine Boston City Hosp., 1971-72; internat. med. officer HEW, 1972-74; dir. Office for Asia and Western Pacific, 1974-75; state coordinator smallpox eradication program WHO, India, 1974-75; fellow Harvard Center for Community Health and Med. Care, Boston, 1976-77; cons. to sec. HEW, Washington, 1977, dep. asst. sec. for health, dir. office disease prevention, 1977-95, asst. surgeon gen., 1980-95, acting dir. office of rsch. integrity, 1992-93; scholar-in-residence NAS, Washington, 1995-99; sr. cons. Robert Wood Johnson Found., Princeton, 1996—99, sr. v.p., dir. Health Grp., 1999—2004, counselor to pres., 2004—05; sr. scholar, Inst. Medicine NAS, 2005—. Instr. medicine George Washington U. Med. Sch., 1973-75; adj. prof. pub. policy Duke U., 1979-81, 99—; chair, sec. task force on smoking and health; chair exec. com. HHS Environ. Health Policy Com.; mem. U.S. Japan Leadership program; chair World Bank/European Commn. Task Force on Reconstrn. of Health Sector, Bosnia, 1996-97; sr. scholar Assn. of Acad. Health Ctrs., 1997-99. Mem. editl. bd. Jour. Med. Edn., 1975-78, Jour. Preventive Medicine, 1987—, Jour. Health Promotion, 1992-98; editor-in-chief: Healthy People, Healthy People 2000, Surgeon General's Report on Nutrition and Health, Determining Risks to Health, Food Marketing to Children and Youth. Bd. dirs. United Way of Nat. Capital, Nemours Found. With USPHS, 1972—75, with USPHS, 1977—95. Recipient Arthur S. Flemming Pub. Svc. award, 1979, USPHS Disting. Svc. medal, 1989, Surgeon Gen.'s medallion, 1995, Fed. Profile in Leadership award, 1989, Wilbur Cohen award, 1995, award for excellence APHA, 1995, Health Leader of Yr. award, 1996. Fellow Am. Coll. Epidemiology, Am. Coll. Preventive Medicine; mem. Inst. Medicine/NAS. Office: 500 5th St NW Washington DC 20001 Office Phone: 202-334-3963. Business E-Mail: mcginnis@nas.edu.

MCGINNIS, JON DAVID, philosopher, educator; b. San Bernardino, Calif., Sept. 11, 1965; s. Oscar and Judy McGinnis. BA, U. North Tex., Denton, 1989, MA, 1991; PhD, U. Pa., Phila., 2000. Asst. prof. philosphy U. Mo., St. Louis, 2000—06, assoc. prof. philosophy, 2006—. Translator: A Reader of Classical Arabic Philosophy; contbr. articles to profl. jours. Recipient Rsch. Bd. award, U. Mo. Sys., 2004; fellow, NEH, 2004—05, 2005—06, Inst. for Advanced Study, 2005—06; scholar, Fulbright Orgn., 1995—96. Mem.: Mid. East Studies Assn., Am. Oriental Soc., Am. Philos. Assn., Soc. Medieval and Renaissance Philosophy (life; mem. exec. com. 2003—06). Democrat. Roman Catholic. Avocation: cooking. Home Phone: 314-863-0795. Personal E-mail: mcginnis@umsl.edu.

MCGINNIS, PATRICIA GWALTNEY, non-profit organization executive; b. Goldsboro, NC, July 19, 1947; d. Thomas McKim Gwaltney and Patricia Anne (Watkins) Schools; m. James Michael McGinnis, Aug. 4, 1978; children: J. Brian, Katherine B. BA, Mary Washington Coll., 1969; MPA, Harvard U., 1975. Dir. spl. studies U.S. Dept. Commerce, Washington, 1975-76; prof. staff mem. U.S. Senate Budge Com., Washington, 1976-77; dep. assoc. dir. U.S. Office Mgmt. and Budget, Washington, 1977-81; sr. cons. Cresap, McCormick and Paget, Inc., Washington, 1981-82; prin. The FMR Group, Inc., Washington, 1982-94; pres., CEO Coun. for Excellence in Govt., Washington, 1994—. Mem. exec. alumni coun. Kennedy Sch. Govt., Harvard U., Cambridge, Mass., 1992-96; dir. Primark Corp., Waltham, Mass., 1995-2000; mem. assoc. coun. George Washington Sch. Bus. and Pub. Adminstrn., 1996-99; bd. dirs. Brown Shoe Co., St. Louis, Imagitas, Inc., Newton, Mass.; bd. visitors U. Md. Sch. Pub. Affairs; dir. Logistics Mgmt. Inst., McLean, Va. Contbr. articles to profl. jours. Fellow: Nat. Acad. Pub. Adminstrn. Office: Coun for Excellence in Govt 1301 K St NW Ste 450W Washington DC 20005-3397

MCGINNIS, ROBERT EARL, lawyer; b. Caldwell, Ohio, May 1, 1931; s. Earl Peregoy and Mary Ethel (Richner) McG.; m. Jane Ann Lindenmeyer, Sept. 12, 1953; children: Sharon Ann, David E. BA, Ohio Weslayan U., 1952; JD summa cum laude, Ohio State U., 1954. Bar: Ohio 1954, Calif. 1956. Asst. judge advocate USAF, 1954-56; sr. ptnr. Luce, Forward, Hamilton, & Scripps, San Diego, 1956—. Counsel to pub. utilities, pub. agys., savs. and loan instns., ins. cos. and contractors. Trustee Wesley Meth. Ch., San Diego, Fine Arts Soc., First Meth. Ch., La Mesa, Calif.; counsel Kensington Community Ch.; dir. San Diego Opera Assn., corp. sec., v.p. Mem. Order of Coif. Republican. Mem. United Ch. Christ. United Ch.Of Christ. Office: Luce Forward Hamilton & Scripps 600 W Broadway Ste 2600 San Diego CA 92101-3372 Office Phone: 619-699-2441. Business E-Mail: rmcginnis@luce.com.

MCGINNIS, TAMMY MARIE, health services manager; b. Dover, Ohio, Sept. 2, 1958; d. Lindy Luck and Rita Marie Williams; life ptnr. James Gordon Geerts; 1 child, Shaun Michael. Cert. office software profl. Bus. & Industry Inst./OSU & COTC, 1999; nat. cert. med. asst. Nat. Ctr. for Competency Testing, 1997, cert. instr. ARC, 2000; food protection mgr. Nat. Restaurant Assn. Edn. Found., 2003, child devel. assoc. The Coun. for Early Childhood Profl. Recognition, 1995. Health services mgr. Kno Ho Co Ashland Head Start, Coshocton, Ohio, 1990—. Birth-five health & social services com. pres. Kno Ho Co Ashland Head Start, Glenmont, 2000—05; early intervention collaborative pres. Early Intervention Help Me Grow, Coshocton, 2003—05. Named Top Med. Sec., Coshocton County Joint Vocat. Sch., 1997; recipient Ohio Head Start Assn. award of Excellence, Ohio Head Start Assn., 2002—05, Colgate-Palmolive award of Excellence, Nat. Head Start Assn., 2004—05, Samuel Harris award, ADA, 2004—06. Mem.: Kno Ho Co Ashland Head Start Birth to Five Yr. Old Health & Social Services Com. (corr.), Holmes County Dept. of Jobs and Family Services Work Force Devel. Com. (corr.), Holmes County Tng. Ctr. Dental Adv. Bd. (corr.), Help Me Grow (corr.), Ashland Dental Clinic Collaborative (assoc.). Democrat. Roman Catholic. Office: Kno Ho Co Ashland Head Start 120 N 4th St Coshocton OH 43812 Home Phone: 330-377-4567; Office Phone: 330-377-4567. Office Fax: 330-377-4595; Home Fax: 330-377-4595. Personal E-mail: tmcginnis2@adelphia.net.

MCGINNIS, W. PATRICK, diversified company executive; BA in Political Science, Univ. Denver, 1970; MBA, Washington Univ, St. Louis, 1972. With Ralston Purina (now Nestle Purina), St. Louis, 1972—; dir. mktg, cons. prod. Ralston Purina Internat., 1978—80; exec. v.p., dir., grocery products Canadian div. Ralston Purina Co., Ontario, Canada, 1980—83, div. v.p., dir. mktg., grocery products St. Louis, Mo., 1983—84; pres., COO, grocery products group Ralston Purina, St. Louis, 1989—92; pres., CEO, grocery products group Ralston Purina Co., St. Louis, 1992—99, pres., CEO, 1999—2001, Nestle Purina, St. Louis, 2001—; corp. v.p., exec. v.p. Ralston Purina, St. Louis, 1984—89. Bd. dir Brown Shoe Co. Recipient Disting. Alumni Award, Olin Sch Bus., Washington Univ., 1993. Office: Nestle Purina Co Checkerboard Sq Saint Louis MO 63164-0001

MCGINNITY, MAUREEN ANNELL, lawyer; b. Monroe, Wis., Apr. 6, 1956; d. James Arthur and Marie Beatrice (Novak) McG.; m. Richard W. Ziervogel, July 17, 1982; 1 child, Brigitte Kathleen. BS, U. Wis., Milw., 1977; JD, U. Wis., 1982. Bar: Wis. 1982, U.S. Dist. Ct. (ea. and we. dists.) Wis. 1982, U.S. Ct. Appeals (7th cir.) 1989, U.S. Ct. Appeals (1st cir.) 1991, U.S. Tax Ct. 1995, U.S. Supreme Ct. 1991. Assoc. Foley & Lardner LLP, Milw., 1982-91, ptnr., 1991—, chairperson tax valuation & fiduciary litig. practice group. Mem. Wis. Supreme Ct. Planning and Policy Adv. Com., Madison, 1991-94; adv. bd. Domestic Violence Legal Clinic, Milw., 1991—. Treas. Waukesha (Wis.) Food Pantry, 1988-94; trustee Boys & Girls Club Greater Milw., 1991—; bd. dirs. Task Force on Battered Women & Children, Inc., 1994-2006. Recipient Outstanding Svc. award Legal Action Wis., Milw., 1984, 93 Outstanding Fundraising awards Boys & Girls Club Greater Milw., 1987-92, Cert. Recognition, Common Coun. Task Force on Sexual Assault & Domestic Violence, Milw., 1991, Cert. Appreciation, Wis. Equal Justice Task Force, Madison, 1991, Cmty. Svc. award Wis. Law Found., 1995. Mem. ABA, State Bar Wis. (bd. govs. 1992-96, Pro Bono award 1990, chair 1993-94), Assn. for Women Lawyers (various offices, pres. 1992-93), Milw. Young Lawyers Assn. (bd. dirs. 1987-92, pres. 1990-91, Pres.' award 1991), Profl. Dimensions. Office: Foley & Lardner LLP 777 E Wisconsin Ave Ste 3800 Milwaukee WI 53202-5367 Office Phone: 414-297-5510. Office Fax: 414-297-4900. Business E-Mail: mmcginnity@foley.com.

MCGINTY, ALAN J., real estate company executive; BSBA, Myers U., Cleve.; MBA, Cleve. State U.; M in Facility Mgmt., Mich. State U. Mgr. facilities engring. Rockwell Automation, Allen-Bradley, Cleve.; mgr. global real estate Rockwell Automation, 1998—2005, dir. global real estate, 2005—. Pres., v.p., treas. Internat. Facility Mgmt. Assn., Cleve., 1993—98; global learning coun. mem. CORENET, Atlanta. Office: Rockwell Automation 1 Allen-Bradley Dr Cleveland OH 44124-6118 Office Phone: 440-646-3408.

MC GINTY, JOHN MILTON, architect, consultant; b. Houston, Apr. 24, 1935; s. Milton Bowles and Ruth Louise (Dreaper) McG.; m. Juanita Jones, May 4, 1957; children: Christopher Harold, Jacqueline Ruth McGinty Carlson. BS, Rice U., 1957; M.F.A., Princeton U., 1961. With archtl. firm Barnes, Landes & Goodman, Austin, Tex., 1957-58, Ingram & Harris, Beaumont, Tex., 1958-59; prin. McGinty Partnership, Architects, Inc., Houston, 1961-89, City Assos., Inc., 1979-91, Bovay-McGinty, Inc., engrs. & architects, Houston, 1989-91; founder, pres. Am. Constrn. Investigations Inc., Houston, 1991-2000, McGinty Archtl. Consultants, LLP, Houston, 2001—. Instr. archtl. design U. Houston, 1965-67; White House fellow, asst. to Sec. of Interior, 1967-68; vis. prof. architecture Rice U., 1969-70 Named Disting. Alumnus Rice U., 1986. Fellow AIA (mem. U.S. delegation to USSR 1972, pres. Houston chpt. 1973, nat. pres. 1977) Office: McGinty Archtl Cons LLP 602 Sawyer St Ste 740 Houston TX 77007 Home: 3614 Montrose Blvd #607 Houston TX 77006 Office Phone: 713-868-7021. Personal E-mail: jmginty@arch.com.

MCGIRR, DAVID WILLIAM JOHN, pharmaceutical executive; b. Glasgow, Scotland, May 19, 1954; arrived in US, 1991, naturalized, 2004; s. Edward McCombie and Diane Curzon (Woods) McG.; m. Margaret Joslin Richardson, May 9, 1981; children: William David, Katherine Joslin, Lucy Ann, Elizabeth Margaret. BSc (hon.), U. Glasgow, 1976; MBA, U. Pa., 1978. Assoc. S.G. Warburg & Co. Ltd., London, 1978—80, exec. dir., 1981—86; mng. dir. S.G. Warburg & Co. Inc., NYC, 1991—95, CFO, 1992—95; assoc. Warburg Paribas Becker Inc., NYC, 1980—81; exec. dir. S.G. Warburg Securities, London, 1986—87; CEO S.G. Warburg Securities Ltd., Toronto, Ont., Canada, 1987—89; COO, CFO Bunting Warburg Inc., Toronto, 1989—91; pres. GAB Robins North Am. Inc., Parsippany, NJ, 1996—99, CEO, 1997—99; COO hippo, Inc., New Haven, 1999—2002, pres., 2001—02; sr. v.p., CFO Cubist Pharm., Inc., Lexington, Mass., 2002—, treas., 2002—03. Selection com. Thouron Scholarship. Bd. dirs. Friends of Glasgow U., Inc., 2003—. Thouron scholar, 1976-78. Mem. Apawamis Club (Rye, N.Y.). Avocations: collecting cars, golf, classic wooden boats. Office: 65 Hayden Ave Lexington MA 02421 Home Phone: 203-629-5607; Office Phone: 781-860-8526. Business E-Mail: david.mcgirr@cubist.com.

MCGIVERIN, ARTHUR A., former state supreme court chief justice; b. Iowa City, Nov. 10, 1928; s. Joseph J. and Mary B. McG.; m. Mary Joan McGiverin, Apr. 20, 1951; children: Teresa, Thomas, Bruce, Nancy. BSc with high honors, U. Iowa, 1951, JD, 1956. Bar: Iowa 1956. Pvt. practice law, Ottumwa, Iowa, 1956; alt. mcpl. judge, 1960-65; judge Iowa Dist. Ct. 8th Jud. Dist., 1965-78; assoc. justice Iowa Supreme Ct., Des Moines, 1978-87, chief justice, 1987-2000, sr. judge, 2000—. Mem. Iowa Supreme Ct. Commn. on Continuing Legal Edn., 1975. Served to 1st lt. U.S. Army, 1946-48, 51-53. Mem. Iowa State Bar Assn., Am. Law Inst. Roman Catholic. Avocation: golf. Office: Iowa Supreme Court State Capitol Building Des Moines IA 50319-0001

MCGIVNEY, JOHN JOSEPH, lawyer; b. Boston, Oct. 31, 1956; s. William A. and Mary Angela (Wall) McG. AB magna cum laude, Boston Coll., 1978, JD cum laude, 1981. Bar: Mass. 1981, U.S. Dist. Ct. Mass. 1982, U.S. Ct. Appeals (1st cir.) 1983, U.S. Supreme Ct. 1990. Assoc. Burns & Levinson, Boston, 1981-87, ptnr., chief appellate sect., 1988-96; ptnr. Rubin and Rudman, Boston, 1997—. Sec. Lynnfield (Mass.) Dem. Town Com., 1974-75, chmn., 1976-77. Mem. Mass. Acad. Trial Attys., Mass. Def. Lawyers Assn. (bd. dirs.), Algonquin Club of Boston. Home: 47 Doncaster Cir Lynnfield MA 01940-2255

MCGLADE, JOHN E., chemicals executive; b. Bethlehem, Pa., 1954; BS, MBA, Lehigh Univ. Mgmt. positions Air Products & Chemicals Inc., Allentown, Pa., 1976—94, gen. mgr. chem. & process ind. div., 1994—96, v.p. chem. & process ind. div., 1996—98, v.p., gen. mgr., chem. & process ind. & energy systems, 1998—2001, v.p., gen. mgr. performance materials div., 2001—03, v.p. chemicals group, 2003, group v.p. chemicals group, 2003—06, pres., COO, 2006—07, pres., CEO, 2007—. Mem.: Nat. Petroleum Refiners Assn. (mem. petrochemical com.), Soc. Chem. Industry. Office: Air Products & Chemicals 7201 Hamilton Blvd Allentown PA 18195-1501 *

MCGLAMRY, MAX REGINALD, retired lawyer; b. Wilcox County, Ga., Sept. 12, 1928; s. Edgar Lee and Allie Bea (Faircloth) McGlamry; m. Jean Louise Hilyer, Dec. 28, 1950; children: Sharon Kay McGlamry Christopher, Michael Lee. BS, Auburn U., 1948; LLB cum laude, Mercer U., 1952, JD cum laude, 1970. Bar: Ga. 1953, U.S. Dist. Ct. (mid. dist.) Ga. 1954, U.S. Ct. Appeals (5th cir.) 1964, U.S. Supreme Ct. 1972, U.S. Ct. Appeals (11th cir.) 1981, U.S. Ct. Appeals (4th cir.) 1985, U.S. Dist. Ct. (no. dist.) Calif. 1988, U.S. Dist. Ct. (no. dist.) Ga. 1989. Pvt. practice, Columbus, Ga., 1953-64; from ptnr. to officer Swift, Pease, Davidson & Chapman (name changed to Page, Scrantom, Harris, McGlamry, & Chapman, P.C.), Columbus, 1964-85; ptnr. Pope, Kellogg, McGlamry, Kilpatrick & Morrison, Columbus, 1985-90, Pope, McGlamry, Kilpatrick & Morrison, LLP, Columbus, 1990-2000; pres. Max R. McGlamry, P.C., Columbus, 2000—04. Exec. com. Muscogee County Dem. Orgn., Columbus, 1956-60; bd. dirs. Columbus Jr. C. of C. Ens. USN, 1948—49, Ens. USNR, 1949—59. Am. Coll. Trust & Estate Counsel fellow, 1973, Lawyers Found. Ga. fellow, 1983. Mem. ABA, State Bar Ga. (emeritus), Ga. Trial Lawyers Assn., Ga. Sr. Golfers Assn., Valley Sr.'s Golf Assn. (pres. 2003), Urban League of Greater Columbus, Inc., Columbus Lawyers Club (pres. 1964-65), Lions (Columbus chpt. pres. 1967-68), Green Island Country Club, Phi Kappa Phi, Alpha Epsilon Delta, Phi Alpha Delta, Pi Kappa Alpha. Democrat. Methodist. Avocations: golf, fishing. Home: 6941 Wethersfield Rd Columbus GA 31904-3317

MCGLASHAN, THOMAS HAMEL, psychiatrist, educator; b. Rochester, NY, Oct. 20, 1941; m. Patricia L. Gwiazdowski, 1964; children: Lara, Jennifer. BA in Chemistry magna cum laude, Yale U., 1963; MD, U. Pa., 1967. Diplomate in psychiatry Am. Bd. Psychiatry and Neurology. Intern Mary Hitchcock Meml. Hosp., Hanover, NH, 1967-68; resident, chief resident psychiatry Mass. Mental Health Ctr., 1968-71; officer in psychiatry, sr. asst. surgeon USPHS, 1971-73; chief clin. rsch. unit psychiat. assessment sect. NIMH, Adult Psychiatry Br., Bethesda, Md., 1973-75; staff psychiatrist Chestnut Lodge, Rockville, Md., 1975-90, dir. adult studies Rsch. Inst., 1977-81, dir. rsch., 1982-90; prof. dept. psychiatry Yale U. Sch. Medicine, 1990—; exec. dir. Yale Psychiat. Inst., New Haven, 1990-2000. Spl. and invited faculty, supr. Washington Sch. Psychiatry, 1978, 81, 82, 83; instr. Washington Psychoanalytic Inst., 1982-89, Western New Eng. Psychoanalytic Inst., 1992-93; clin. assoc. prof. dept. psychiatry Uniformed Svcs. U. of the Health Scis., 1983-88, clin. prof. dept. psychiatry, 1988-90; rsch. prof. dept. psychiatry U. Md. Sch. Medicine, 1986-90; bd. dirs. Parents Found. for Transitional Living, 1991-97; cons. and grant cons. in field; presenter in field; many others. Author: The Documentation of Clinical Psychotropic Drug Trials, 1973, The Borderline: Current Empirical Research, 1985, Schizophrenia: Treatment, Process and Outcome, 1989. Early Intervention in Psychosis, 2001, A Developmental Model of Borderline Personality Disorder, 2003; editl. cons.: Schizophrenia Bull., 1980-82, 84—, Archives of Gen. Psychiatry, 1982—, Am. Jour. Psychiatry, 1982—, Hosp. and Cmty. Psychiatry, 1984—, Jour. Personality Disorders, 1987—, Schizophrenia Rsch., 1987—, Acta Psychiatrica Scand., 1999—, Jour. Abnormal Psychology, 1988, Psychiatry Rsch., 1988—, others; mem. editl. bd.: Jour. Personality Disorders, 1989—, Schizophrenia Bull., 1989—; contbr. chpts. to books, over 200 articles to profl. jours. Recipient Gary Morris Rsch. award Washington Psychoanalytic Soc., 1980, Presdl. award for rsch. Nat. Assn. Pvt. Psychiat. Hosps., 1988, Silvano Arieti award Am. Acad. Psychoanalysis, 1990, Psychiat. Inst. Am. Found. award for rsch. devel. in hosp. psychiatry, 1990, Alexander Granlick award Am. Psychiat. Found., 1997, Established Investigator award Nat. Alliance Rsch. Schizophrenia & Depression, 1997-98; grantee Fund for Psychoanalytic Rsch. Am. Psychoanalytic Assn., 1978, 79, NIMH, 1996—, Norwegian Rsch. Coun., 1997—. Fellow Am. Psychiat. Assn., Am. Psychopathol. Assn.; mem. Western New Eng. Psychoanalytic Inst. and Soc., Soc. for Psychotherapy Rsch., Assn. for Clin. Psychosocial Rsch., Psychiat. Rsch. Soc., Internat. Soc. Study Personality Disorders, Internat. Early Psychosis Assn. Business E-Mail: thomas.mcglashan@yale.edu.

MCGLATHERY, JAMES MELVILLE, retired foreign language educator; b. New Orleans, Nov. 22, 1936; s. Samuel Lyon and Mary Jackson (Garrott) McG.; m. Nancy Judith Beyer, June 1, 1939; children: Samuel Lyon, Daniel Beyer, Andrew James, Benjamin Kim. AB, Princeton U., 1958; AM, Yale U., 1959, PhD, 1964. Instr. German Phillips Andover (Mass.) Acad., 1959-60; lectr. German Harvard U., 1963-64, instr. German, 1964-65; from asst. prof. to assoc. prof. U. Ill. at Urbana-Champaign, 1965-84, prof. German, 1984-2000, prof. emeritus, 2000—, acting dept. head, spring 1985, dept. head, 1985-95. Instr. Colby Coll. Summer Lang. Sch., 1964, Harvard U. Summer Lang. Sch., 1965-66, 70, U. Ill., Urbana-Champaign, 1972, 74, 76, 78, 80, 82, 87, 90, U. Göttingen, Germany, 1993-94, 2001; lectr., presenter in field. Author: Mysticism and Sexuality: E. T. A. Hoffmann, Part One: Hoffmann and His Sources, 1981, Desire's Sway: The Plays and Stories of Heinrich von Kleist, 1983, Mysticism and Sexuality: E. T. A. Hoffmann, Part Two: Interpretations of the Tales, 1985, Fairy Tale Romance: The Grimms, Basile, Perrault, 1991, Grimms' Fairy Tales: A History of Criticism on a Popular Classic, 1993, E.T.A. Hoffmann, 1997, Wagner's Operas and Desire, 1998; editor: German Source Readings in the Arts and Sciences, 1974, Journal of English and Germanic Philology, 1976, The Brothers Grimm and Folktale, 1988, 91, Music and German Literature: Their Relationship since the Middle Ages, 1992; contbg. author: Reader in German Literature, 1969, Moliére and the Commonwealth of Letters: Patrimony and Posterity, 1975, Fairy Tales as Ways of Knowing: Essays on Märchen in Psychology, Society, and Literature, 1981, Reflection and Action: Essays on the Bildungsroman, 1991, A Companion to the Nibelungenlied, 1998, A Companion to Wagner's Parsifal, 2005; mng. editor: Jour. English and Germanic Philology, 1972-00; contbr. articles and book revs. to profl. jours. Princeton U. scholar, 1954-58; undergrad. rsch. assistantship Princeton U., 1956-58; Woodrow Wilson Nat. fellow Yale U., 1958-59, Jr. Sterling fellow Yale U., 1960-61, Nat. Def. Edn. Act fellow in Russian, Yale U., 1961-63; grad. rsch. bd. grantee U. Ill. Urbana-Champaign, 1975, 79-80, 86, 89, 92. Mem.: N.Am. Heine Soc. Home: 1204 Thomas Dr Champaign IL 61821-1632 Home Phone: 217-352-6902. Business E-Mail: mcglath@uiuc.edu.

MCGLAUCHLIN, TOM, artist; b. Turtle, Wis., Sept. 14, 1934; s. Charles Orion and Frances Lenore McGlauchlin; m. Patricia Ann Smith, Aug. 5, 1961; children: Christopher, Jennifer (dec.), Patrick (dec.). BS in Art, U. Wis., 1959, MS in Art, 1960; studied pottery with James McKinnell, 1962. Instr. dept. art and art edn. U. Wis., Madison, 1960-61; instr. art dept. Cornell Coll., Mt. Vernon, Iowa, 1961-64, asst. prof. art dept., 1964-68, assoc. prof., chmn. art dept., 1968-71; instr. Toledo Mus. Art, 1971-82, prof., dir. glass program, 1982-84. One-man exhbns. include Habatat Gallery, Dearborn, Mich., 1979, Glass Art Gallery, Toronto, 1981, 85, Glass Gallery, Bethesda, Md., 1981, 85, 87, 91, Heller Gallery, N.Y.C., 1983, B.Z. Wagman Gallery, St. Louis, 1983, Running Ridge Gallery, Santa Fe, 1990; selected group exhbns. include Toledo Mus. Art, 1972, 88, Glasmuseum Frauenau, Franenau, Germany, 1977, Habatat Gallery, 1980, 84, The Hand and the Spirit Gallery, Scottsdale, Ariz., 1980, Gallery of Contemporary Crafts, Detroit, 1980, The Naples (Fla.) Art Gallery, 1981, The Craftsman's Gallery, Scarsdale, N.Y., 1981, 84, The Nat. Mus. Modern Art, Kyoto and Tokyo, 1981, Perception Gallery, Houston, 1985, The AirLoft Gallery, Honolulu, 1986, The Corning (N.Y.) Mus. Glass, 1987; selected competitive exhbns. include Everson Mus. Art, Syracuse, N.Y., 1961, 62, Mus. Contemporary Crafts, N.Y.C., 1962, Corning Glass Mus., Met. Mus. Art, N.Y.C., Victoria and Albert Mus., London, Musee Ars Decoratif, Paris; public collections include Toledo Mus. Art, The Smithsonian Collection, Washington, Portland (Oreg.) Art Mus., New Orleans Mus. Art, Mus. Contemporary Crafts, Musee des arts decoratifs de la Ville de Lausanne, Switzerland, Minn. Mus. Art, St. Paul, Kunstmuseum, Dusseldorf, Germany, Corning Glass Mus. Grantee Associated Colls. Midwest, 1966-67; recipient First Jury award Toledo Glass Nat. II, 1968. Mem. Am. Crafts Coun., Internat. Sculpture Soc., Ohio Designer-Craftsmen, Glass Art Soc. Office: The Glass Studio 1940 W Central Ave Toledo OH 43606-3944 Office Phone: 419-461-4097. Business E-Mail: tom@mcglauchlin.com.

MCGLOHON, SUSAN MARIE, educational association administrator; d. Samuel D. Senter and Elizabeth Ann Rutland-Senter; m. Charles Norman McGlohon, June 16, 1979; 1 child, Charles Andrew; 1 child from previous marriage, Bradley Norman. BEd, U. Ga., Athens; MEd, Ednl. Specialist, Clemson U., SC; ednl., reading endorsement, Ga. So. U., Statesboro. Sch. support specialist, facilitator dept. sch. improvement Ga. Dept. Edn. Dept., Atlanta, 2003—. Grantee Ga. award, 2006. Mem.: ASCD, Ga. Assn. Ednl. Leaders. Avocations: home decorating, gardening, reading, hiking.

MCGLONE, MICHAEL ANTHONY, lawyer; b. New Orleans, Jan. 6, 1951; s. James Godfrey and Dorothy (Barta) McG.; m. Suzanne Blanchard, Nov. 27, 1976; children: Kevin, Kathleen, Meghan. BBA cum laude, Loyola U., New Orleans, 1972, JD, 1975. Bar: La. 1975, U.S. Dist. Ct. (ea. dist.) La. 1975, U.S. Ct. Appeals (5th and 11 cirs.) 1975, U.S. Dist. Ct. (we. dist.) La. 1978, U.S. Dist. Ct. (mid. dist.) La. 1979, U.S. Supreme Ct. 1981. Law clk. to Hon. Herbert W. Christenberry U.S. Dist. Ct., New Orleans, 1975-76; ptnr. Kean Miller, 1976—. Fellow Am. Coll. Trial Lawyers; mem. ABA, ALA, FBA (bd. dirs. New Orleans chpt. 1986—, pres. 1995-96), La. Bar Assn., Southeastern Admiralty Law Inst., New Orleans Bar Assn., Maritime Law Assn., St. Thomas More Inn of Ct. (master barrister), Alpha Sigma Nu, Beta Gamma Sigma. Democrat. Roman Catholic. Home: 4708 N Turnbull Dr Metairie LA 70002-1447 Office: Kean Miller 601 Poydras St New Orleans LA 70130-6029 Office Phone: 504-585-3059. Business E-Mail: mike.mcglone@keanmiller.com.

MCGLOTHLEN, JOHN M., librarian; s. Gary and Barbara (Myers) McGlothlen; m. Angela Wells, Aug. 17, 1991; children: Emily, Ethan. BS, Charter Oak State Coll., 1995; MA, U. Iowa, 1998. Assoc. libr. Iowa Wesleyan Coll., Mount Pleasant, Iowa, 1998—2000; electronic svcs. libr. Sioux City Pub. Libr., Sioux City, Iowa, 2000—01; libr. The Gazette, Cedar Rapids, Iowa, 2001—. Editor: (web site) The Bible as Music (http://bibleasmusic.com). Mem.: SLA. Avocation: music. Office Phone: 319-398-8328.

MCGLOTHLIN, MICHAEL GORDON, lawyer; b. Richlands, Va., Oct. 31, 1951; s. Woodrow Wilson and Sally Ann (Cook) McG.; m. Sandra Lee Keen, Oct. 1, 1983; children: Michael Alexander, Robert Aaron. BA, U. Va., 1974; JD, Coll. William and Mary, 1976. Bar: Va. 1977, U.S. Dist. Ct. (we. dist.) Va. 1978. Ptnr. McGlothlin, McGlothlin & McGlothlin, Grundy, Va., 1977-79; commonwealth atty. Buchanan County, Grundy, 1980-83; ptnr. McGlothlin & Wife, Grundy, 1984—; atty.for Buchanan County, 1984-89; bd. dirs. Gt. Southwest Home Commn., vice chmn., 1983—. Mem. adv. bd. Clinch Valley Coll.; sec. Buchanan County Dem. Party. Mem. ABA, Va. State Bar Assn., Buchanan County Bar Assn. (pres. 1984), Kiwanis (sec. Buchanan County Dem. Com.), Phi Alpha Delta, Phi Sigma Kappa. Presbyterian. Home and Office: PO Box 810 Grundy VA 24614-0810

MCGLYNN, ELIZABETH A., health policy analyst; PhD, RAND Grad. Sch., 1988; MPP, U. Mich. Assoc. dir. RAND Health, Santa Monica, Calif.; dir. Ctr. Rsch. on Quality in Health Care, Santa Monica, Calif. Adv. com. Nat. Com. for Quality Assurance (NCQA), Nat. Quality Forum (NQF), Coun. Accountable Physician Practices, Am. Med. Group Assn.; editorial bd. Health Svcs. Rsch., Milbank Meml. Fund Quarterly. Mem.: Inst. Medicine. Achievements include development of QA Tools. Office: RAND Health Communications PO Box 2138 1776 Main St Santa Monica CA 90407-2138

MCGLYNN, JAMES FRANCIS, chemistry educator, chemical engineer; b. Hazleton, Pa., Apr. 28, 1965; s. John Francis and Rosemary McGlynn; m. Beth Ann Shaefbook; children: Jessica, Ryan, Patrick. BSChemE, Pa. State U., State College, 1987; cert. tchr., Hood Coll., Frederick, Md., 1999. Chem. engr. DuPont, Aiken, SC, 1988—89, Westinghouse, Aiken, 1989—94, Sci. Applications Internat. Corp., Gaithersburg, Md., 1999—2002; chem. tchr. Penn Manor Sch. Dist., Millersville, Pa., 2000—. Home: 391 Squire Ln Lititz PA 17543 Personal E-mail: james.mcglynn@pennmanor.net.

MCGLYNN, MARGARET G., pharmaceutical executive; b. Buffalo, Sept. 16, 1959; married; 2 children. BS in Pharmacy, SUNY, Buffalo, 1982, MBA in Mktg., 1983. Profl. rep. Merck & Co., Inc., Whitehouse Sta., NJ, 1983—84, mktg. analyst, 1985—86, promotion mgr., 1986, product mgr., 1987—89, dir. bus. devel., 1987—89, 1989—90, sr. dir. mkt. planning, 1990—91, exec,. dir. nat, consumer mktg. U.S. human health, 1991—93, v.p. bus. mgmt. and devel. U.S. human health, 1993, sr. v.p. managed care U.S. human health, 1994—95, sr. v.p. bus. planning proposals and analysis Merck-Medco Managed Care, 1994, sr. v.p. health and utilization mgmt., Merck-Medco Managed Care L.L.C., Whitehouse Sta, 1995—98, sr. v.p. world wide human health mktg., 1998—2001, exec. v.p. customer mktg. and sales U.S. human health, 2001—02, pres. U.S. human health, 2003—05; pres. Merck Vaccines, 2005—. Bd. dir. Air Products and Chemicals. Corp. exec. bd. Phila. Mus. Art; mem. dean's adv. coun. U. Buffalo Sch. Mgmt. Office: Merck & Co Inc One Merck Dr PO Box 100 Whitehouse Station NJ 08889-0100 *

MCGLYNN, SEAN EDWARD, secondary school educator; b. Syracuse, NY, Mar. 14, 1965; s. Edward and Phyllis Jean McGlynn; m. Sheila McGlynn, Nov. 22, 1997; 1 child, Casey. BS in Biology, Binghamton U., NY, 1987; MS in Environ. and Forest Biology, SUNY, Syracuse NY, 1990; MS in Sci. Edn., Syracuse U., NY, 1990. Cert. tchr. N.Y. State Edn. Dept., 1990. Tchr. sci. East Syracuse-Minoa (N.Y.) Ctrl. Schs., 1990—. Home: 316 Albert Road Syracuse NY 13214 Office: East Syracuse-Minoa Central Schools 6400 Fremont Road East Syracuse NY 13057 Home Phone: 315-445-0802; Office Phone: 315-656-7242. Personal E-mail: smcg24@hotmail.com. Business E-Mail: smcglynn@esmschools.org.

MC GLYNN, SEAN PATRICK, physical chemist, educator; b. Dungloe, Ireland, Mar. 8, 1931; arrived in U.S., 1952, naturalized, 1957; s. Daniel and Catherine (Brennan) Mc Glynn; m. Helen Magdalena Salacz-von Dohnanyi, Apr. 11, 1955 (div.); children: Sean Ernst, Daniel Julian, Brian Charles, Sheila Ann, Alan Patrick; m. Maureen G. Potts, Oct. 23, 1985; children: Shane Joseph, Brennan John, Colin Michael. BS, Nat. U. Ireland, 1951, MS, 1952; PhD, Fla. State U., 1956. Fellow Fla. State U., 1956, U. Wash., 1956-57; mem. faculty La. State U., 1957—, prof. chemistry, 1964—, Boyd prof. chemistry, 1967—, dean Grad. Sch., 1981-82, vice chancellor rsch., 1981-91. Assoc. prof. biophysics Yale U., 1961; Humboldt prof. physics U. Bonn, Germany, 1979—80; cons. to pvt. cos. Author (with others): (book) Molecular Spectroscopy of the Triplet State, 1969, Introduction to Applied Quantum Chemistry, 1971, Photophysics and Photochemistry in the Vacuum Ultraviolet, 1985, The Geometry of Genetics, 1988; editor: Wiley-Interscience Monographs in Chem. Physics; contbr. articles to profl. jours., chapters to books. Recipient award, Baton Rouge Coun. Engring. and Sci. Socs., 1962—63, Sr. Scientist award, Alexander von Humboldt Found., 1979, Disting. Rsch. medal, U. Bologna, Italy, 1979; fellow, Rsch. Corp., 1960—63; Sloan fellow, 1964—68. Mem.: AAAS, Am. Phys. Soc., Am. Chem. Soc. (S.W. Regional award 1967, Fla. sect. award 1970, Coates award 1977). Achievements include research in molecular electronic spectroscopy; electronic structure; energy transfer; molecular genetics; bioenergetics; mathematical biology; optoaccoustics; optogalvanics. Home: 12048 Pecan Grove Ct Baton Rouge LA 70810-4835 Office Phone: 225-578-3392. Business E-Mail: chspm@lsu.edu. E-mail: maureenpotts@cox.net.

MCGOFF, WILLIAM STANLEY, speech educator, consultant; b. Cranston, RI, May 14, 1935; s. Charles Vernon McGoff and Alice Wilson Bradt; m. Jane Gayle Friedkin, Feb. 20, 1973; children: Rebecca Erin Owen, Rachel Ann. BAS in Edn. (hon.), Midwestern U., Wichita Falls, Tex., 1973; MA, Midwestern State U., Wichita Falls, Tex., 1976. Demolition specialist USN, N.Mex., 1952—56; armament electronic specialist USAF, Calif., 1956—73; debate coach instr. Midestern State U., Wichita Falls, 1974—76; tchr. speech debate John Tyler HS, Tex., 1976—94; prin. Plyler Alternative Sch., 1994—2000; English cons. Barrett Kendall Publishing Co., Austin, 2000—02; speech/debate cons. North Tex. Debate Assn., Tyler, 2002—. Pres. Smith County Dem. Club, Tyler, Tex., 2006—. Sgt. USAF, 1956—73. Mem.: Nat. Forensic League (life Spl. Distinction 1976, 1994). Democrat. Roman Catholic. Home: 1309 Hubbard Dr Tyler TX 75703-1522 Home Phone: 903-581-8326. Home Fax: 903-581-8326. Personal E-mail: bmcgoff2000@yahoo.com.

MCGOLDRICK, JOHN LEWIS, lawyer; b. Plainfield, NJ, Mar. 2, 1941; s. John Leslie and Sarah (Walker) McGoldrick; m. Ann Chapman Puffer, Oct. 1, 1966; children: Scott Runyon, Jennifer Winslow. BA cum laude, Harvard U., 1963, LLB, 1966. Bar: N.J. 1966, N.Y. 1985. Assoc. McCarter & English, Newark, 1966-73, ptnr., 1974-95; sr. v.p., gen. counsel Bristol-Myers Squibb Co., NYC, 1995—98, sr. v.p., gen. counsel, pres., Med. Devices Group, 1998—2000, exec. v.p., 1995—2006, gen. counsel, 2001—06; sr. v.p. Internat. AIDS Vaccine Initiative, 2006—. Vice-chmn., bd. dirs. N.J. Transit Corp., Newark, 1979—2005; bd. dirs. Bristol-Myers Squibb Found., Zimmer Holdings, Inc., HealthCare Inst. N.J., Regional Plan Assn., N.J. Network Found. Trustee Essex-Newark Found. Legal Svcs. N.J. Montclair State U.; mem. com. to visit The Coll., mem. com. to visit Sch. Pub. Health Harvard U.; mem. Harvard Malaria Initiative Adv. Coun. Fellow: Am. Acad. Appellate Lawyers, Am. Bar Found., Am. Coll. Trial Lawyers; mem.: ABA, Am. Arbitration Assn., Nat. Panel Arbitrators, Coun. Fgn. Rels., Aspen Inst. World Economy, CPR Inst. Dispute Resolution (mem. exec. com.), Coun. Chief Legal Officers (Conf. Bd. Inc.), Assn. Gen. Counsel, Am. Law Inst., Assn. Fed. Bar N.J. (former pres.), Assn. Bar City of N.Y., N.Y. Bar Assn., N.J. Bar Assn., Legal Svcs. N.J. (bd. dirs.), World Econ. Forum, Coun. U.S. and Italy, Harvard Law Sch. Assn. N.J. (former pres.). Home Phone: 609-924-0172; Office Phone: 212-546-4460.

MCGONAGLE, DUNCAN FRANCIS, mental health nurse, substance abuse counselor; b. Bklyn., May 6, 1939; s. John and Kathleen (Rooney) McGonagle; m. Gloria Maria Carrubba, Dec. 5, 1987. AA, Allan Hancock, 1964; AAS in Nursing, CUNY, 1992. Cert. psychiat. and mental health nurse, addictions RN. Substance abuse counselor Pritikin Longevity Ctr., Santa Monica, Calif., 1978-84; paramedic N.Y.C. Emergency Med. Svc., 1987-92; psychiatric nurse Bellevue Hosp. Ctr., NYC, 1992-99; adminstr. Methadone Maintenance Treatment Program, St. Barnabas Hosp., Bronx, NY, 1999—2001; nurse mgr. Methadone Maintenance Treatment Program, Beth Israel Med. Ctr., NYC, 2001—. Founder Methadone Anonymous, N.Y. Aux. police officer N.Y.C. Police Dept., 1985—. With USN, 1956-60, 1961-62, Vietnam. Recipient Nat. award for Clin. Excellence in Nursing, Nat. Nurses Soc. on Addictions, 1995. Mem. Blue Knights, Knights of Life, Rolls Royce Owners Club, Harley Owners Group. Roman Catholic. Avocations: computers, sailing, motorcycling, antique autos. Home: 73 Verona St Brooklyn NY 11231-1612 Office: Beth Israel Med Ctr 160 Water St New York NY 10038-4922 Office Phone: 212-256-2595. E-mail: duncan73@aol.com.

MCGOUGH, BRIAN EDWARD, investment banker, lawyer; b. NYC, Feb. 18, 1964; s. George V. McGough Sr. and Mary Elizabeth (Keaveny) Covell; m. Tamra Ann Pearce, Aug. 1, 1987; children: Michael Christopher, Christopher Thomas, Matthew Steven. BS, Bradley U., 1986; JD, No. Ill. U., 1990. Bar: Ill. 1991, U.S. Dist. Ct. (no. dist.) Ill. 1990, U.S. Tax Ct. 1993, U.S. Ct. Appeals (7th cir.) 1991, U.S. Supreme Ct. 1993. Assoc. Katten Muchin & Zavis, Chgo., 1990-96; v.p. JP Morgan & Co., Chgo., 1996-98; sr. mng. dir. Bank One Capital Markets, Chgo., 1998—2003; mng. dir. RBC Dain Rauscher, Inc., Chgo., 2003—. Spl. asst. atty. gen. State Ill., Chgo., 1992-96. Bd. dirs. Naperville (Ill.) Cmty. Outreach, 1990—; trustee No. Ill. U., DeKalb, 1993, mem. law sch. adv. bd., 1993. Recipient Disting. Alumnae award No. Ill. U., DeKalb, 1998.

MCGOUGH, DUANE THEODORE, economist, consultant, retired federal official; b. Rice Lake, Wis., Aug. 3, 1932; s. James Patrick and Josephine Margaret (Huerth) McG.; m. Donna Mae Jones, June 13, 1959 Student, Wis. State Coll., Eau Claire, 1950-52, U. Wis., Madison, 1952-54, 56-60, BS in Light Constrn. Industry, 1959, MBA in Urban Land Econs., 1962; postgrad., U. So. Calif. Urban Planning, LA, 1968-69. Housing mgmt. officer Pub. Housing Adminstrn. Atlanta, 1960-62; program planning analyst Pub. Housing Adminstrn. Phila., 1962-67; program analyst HUD, Washington, 1967-68, 69-70, industry economist, 1970-73, supervisory economist, 1973-77, dir. housing and demographic analysis, 1977-97, govt. tech. rep. ann. housing survey, 1977-83; govt. tech. rep. Am. Housing Survey, 1984-97; acting dep. asst. sec. for econ. affairs (chief economist) HUD, Washington, 1977, 82, 84-85, ret., 1997. US rep housing subcom. UN Econ. Commn. for Europe, Geneva, 1976, 79, Madrid, 1982; HUD rep. Interagy. Com. on Population Rsch., 1978-97, Interagy. Forum on Aging-Related Stats., 1986-97; mem. Fed. Task Force on Household Survey Redesign, 1988-97; mem. policy com. Year 2000 Census; coord. PRSC Ctr. U.S./Mex. Sem. Housing Stats., Mexico City, 1997. Editor: President's Report on Housing Goals, 1974—78, Nat. Housing Prodn. Report, 1980, 1982, US Housing Market Conditions Report, 1994—97, FEMA National Emergency Management Program, 1967—97, Housing Consultant, 1997—; musician (tenor): Washington Choral Ensemble, 2002—06. With US Army, 1954—56, saxophonist 7th Army Band US Army, Stuttgart, Germany. Fellow Nat. Inst. Pub. Affairs, 1969; recipient Outstanding Performance award Pub. Housing Adminstrn., Phila., 1966, HUD, 1984, 92, 97, Career Edn. award Nat. Inst. Pub. Affairs, 1968-69, Cert. Spl. Achievement, HUD, 1978, 83, 84, 96, Cert. Superior Svc., HUD, 1988, 95, Cert. Appreciation, Bur. Census, 1990. Mem. Lambda Alpha Internat. (v.p. programs 1987-89, chmn. real estate and fin. com. George Washington chpt. 1990-92, dir.-at-large 1992-93), Lambda Chi Alpha. Avocations: music, gardening, rockhounding, web-surfing. Personal E-mail: duanetm@aol.com.

MCGOUGH, WALTER THOMAS, JR., lawyer; b. Pitts., Nov. 7, 1953; s. Walter Thomas and Jane (Fitzpatrick) McGough; m. Rebecca Gai Frazier, June 24, 1978; children: Emily Ann, Walter Thomas III. BA, Princeton U., 1975; JD, U. Va., 1978. Bar: Pa., 1978, DC, US Dist. Ct. We. Dist. Pa. 1980, US Ct. Appeals 3rd cir., 1983, US Ct. Appeals, 6th cir. 1984, Pa. Supreme Ct., 1978, US Supreme Ct., 1983. Law clk. to Hon. Collins J. Seitz U.S. Ct. Appeals 3rd Cir., Wilmington, Del., 1978-79; law clk. to

Hon. William H. Rehnquist US Supreme Ct., Washington, 1979-80; asst. US atty. We. Dist. Pa., 1980-82; assoc. Reed Smith LLP, Pitts., 1982-86, ptnr., 1987—, head of litigation dept., 1998—2006, mem. exec. com., 1998—. Assoc. counsel, Sen. Select Com. on Secret Mil. Assistance to Iran and the Nicaraguan Opposition, Washington, 1987; mem. lawyers adv. com. US Ct. Appeals 3d cir., 1987-89, chmn., 1989; mem. appellate rules com. US Jud. Conf., 1998-2005. Co-author: Fed. Appellate Procedure, 3rd Cir., 1996; contbr. articles to profl. jours. Trustee Sta. WQED, Pitts., 1996-2002, vice chmn, 1997-99, chmn., 1999-2002; mem. 3d Cir. Task Force on Rule 11, 1987-89. Fellow Am. Coll. Trial Lawyers, Am. Acad. Appellate Lawyers; mem. Allegheny County Bar Assn. (ethics com. 1983-86, bd. govs. 1994-2001, pres. 1999-2000), Allegheny County Acad. Trial Lawyers, Duquesne Club, Ross Mountain Club. Office: Reed Smith LLP 435 6th Ave Pittsburgh PA 15219-1886 Office Phone: 412-288-3088. Office Fax: 412-288-3063. Business E-Mail: wmcgough@reedsmith.com.

MCGOVERN, GEORGE STANLEY, former senator; b. Avon, SD, July 19, 1922; s. Joseph C. and Frances (McLean) McG.; m. Eleanor Stegeberg, Oct. 31, 1943 (dec. Jan. 25, 2007); children: Ann, Susan, Teresa (dec. Dec. 13, 1994), Steven, Mary. BA, Dakota Wesleyan U., 1945; MA, Northwestern U., 1949, PhD, 1953. Prof. history & polit. sci. Dakota Wesleyan U., 1949-53; exec. sec. S.D. Dem. Party, 1953-55; mem. US Congress from 1st Dist. S.D., 1957—61; spl. asst. to Pres., dir. Food for Peace, 1961-62; US Senator from S.D., 1963-81; chmn. select com. on nutrition and human needs; pres. Middle East Policy Coun.; US amb. to Food & Agrl. Agencies UN, Rome, 1998—2001, Global Amb. on World Hunger, 2001—. Chmn. Ams. for Common Sense, Washington, 1981-82; guest lectr. Northwestern U., Evanston, Ill., Duke U., Columbia U., Cornell U., Munich, Berlin, and numerous others in U.S. and Europe, 1981- Author: The Colorado Coal Strike, 1913-14, 1953, War Against Want, 1964, Agricultural Thought in the Twentieth Century, 1967, A Time of War, A Time of Peace, 1968, An American Journey, 1974, Grassroots: The Autobiography of George McGovern, 1977, Terry: My Daughter's Life-and-Death Struggle with Alcoholism, 1996, The Third Freedom: Ending Hunger in Our Time, 2002, The Essential America: Our Founders and the Liberal Tradition, 2004, Social Security and the Golden Age: An Essay on the New American Demographic, 2005; co-author: (with Leonard Guttridge) The Great Coalfield War, 1972, (with Bob Dole, Donald Messer): Ending Hunger Now: A Challenge to Persons of Faith, 2005, (with William R. Polk) Out of Iraq: A Practical Plan for Withdrawal Now, 2006. Democratic nominee for Pres. U.S., 1972; candidate for presdl. nomination of Dem. Party, 1984 Served in US Army Air Corps, 1942—45. Decorated Disting. Flying Cross; recipient Presdl. Medal of Freedom, 2000, Food for Life award World Food Program, 2000 Mem. Am. Hist. Assn.; Clubs: Mason (33 deg., Shriner), Elk, Kiwanian. Methodist. *

MCGOVERN, JAMES P., congressman; b. Worcester, Mass., Nov. 20, 1959; m. Lisa Murray; children: Patrick George, Molly Ginette. BA, Am. U., 1981, MA in Pub. Administration, 1984. Aide U.S. Senator George McGovern (Dem. South Dakota); spokesman, legis. dir., sr. aide U.S. Congressman Joe Moakley (Dem. South Boston); mem. U.S. Congress from 3rd Mass dist., 1997—; elected regional whip, mem. transp. & infrastructure com., house rules com. Mgr. George McGovern for Pres., 1984; delivered McGovern presdl. nomination speech Dem. Nat. Convention, San Francisco, 1984; leader Congressional Investigation on El Salvador, 1989 Candidate for U.S. Congress, 1996; vol. Mt. Carmel House; bd. dirs. Jesuit Internat. Vols. Democrat. Roman Catholic. Office: Ho Reps 430 Cannon Ho Office Bldg Washington DC 20515-2103 Home: 34 Mechanic St Worcester MA 01608-2424 *

MCGOVERN, LORE HARP, communications executive, philanthropist; m. Patrick J. McGovern. Undergrad., Calif. State Univ.; MBA, Pepperdine Univ. Co-founder Vector Graphics Inc., 1976; founder Pacific Tech. Venture Fund, San Francisco, 1981, dir., 1983—85; founder Aplex Corp., 1985—89; CEO Good Morning Teacher! Pub., 1990—99; mem. bd. dir. Internat. Data Group. Chmn. bd. assoc. Whitehead Inst. MIT; mem. bd. advisors Women.com, Blue Pumpkin Software, Skillsvillage.com. Named one of 50 Most Generous Philanthropists, Fortune Mag., 2005; recipient Entrepreneur Yr., 1983. Mem.: Am. Elec. Assn. (former chair.). Office: IDG One Exeter Plz Boston MA 02116 Office Fax: 617-423-0240.

MCGOVERN, MICHAEL, lawyer; b. NYC, Mar. 6, 1947; s. Michael Malachy and Annette (Barbot) McG.; m. Christine Anne Beaudet, Sept. 2, 1972; children: Kathleen, Ellen, Maura. AB, Georgetown U., 1969, JD, 1972; LLM in Taxation, George Washington U., 1987. Bar: D.C. 1973, Md. 1978. From assoc. to ptnr. Wilkes & Artis, Washington, 1973-79; sole practice Washington, 1980, 84-87; ptnr. Lambert, Griffin & McGovern, Washington, 1981-84, Venable, Baetjer, Howard & Civiletti, Washington, 1987-93, Montedonico, Hamilton & Altman, Washington, 1994-98, Hanson & Molloy, Washington, 1998—. Bd. dirs. Hist. Soc. Washington, 1984-93, Montgomery County Hist. Soc., 1997-; co-founder, vice-chair, bd. dirs., mem. Greater Bethesda-Chevy Chase Coalition Inc., 1986—; pres. Westmoreland Citizens Assn. Inc., 1988-90; mem. Leadership Washington, 1987—, Washington Estate Planning Coun. Served to capt. USAFR, 1969—82. Recipient Disting. Svc. award, Fed. Bar Assn., 1978. Mem. Columbia Country Club (Chevy Chase), Met. Club (Washington), Barristers, John Carroll Soc. Republican. Home: 5414 Albemarle St Bethesda MD 20816-1825 Office: Hanson & Molloy 1320 19th St NW Ste 300 Washington DC 20036 Office Phone: 202-833-9300. Business E-Mail: mcgovern@hanson-molloy.com.

MCGOVERN, PATRICK J., communications executive; m. Lore Harp. BA in biophysics, M.I.T., 1959. Founder Internat. Data Corp., Framingham, Mass., 1964, chmn., 1976—; founder IDG Comm. Inc., Framingham, 1987, CEO, 1999. Dir. Info. Inds. Assn., Mag. Publishers Assn., Am. Mgmt. Assn; trustee Mass. Inst. Tech., McGovern Inst. for Brain Rsch., Whitehead Inst. Recipient James Smithsonian Bicentennial Medal, Smithsonian Inst., Entrepreneurial Leadership Award, MIT Enterprise Forum of Cambridge, Inc., The Bus. Pub. of the Year award Delaney Report, The Communicator of the Year award N.Y. Chpt. Bus. Profl. Advertisers Assn., The Entrepreneur of the Year award Ernst & Young, Lifetime Achievement award, Am. Soc. Bus. Publ. Editors, 2004, Top Innovator in Bus. Publishing Award, BtoB Media Bus. mag., 2004, Lifetime Achievement award, Mag. Publishers of Am., 2005; Named one of 25 Entrepreneurs We Love, Inc. mag., 2004, 50 Most Generous Philanthropists, Fortune Mag., 2005, Richest Americans, Forbes, 1999-, World's Richest People, 2001-. Fellow: Am. Acad. of Arts and Sciences. Achievements include providing a $350 mil. endowment to M.I.T. Office: Internat Data Group 1 Exeter Plz Fl 15 Boston MA 02116-2848 *

MCGOWAN, ANGELA KAY, government agency administrator, researcher; b. Decatur, Ga., Sept. 6, 1970; d. John E. McGowan, Jr. and Linda Kay (Hudson) McGowan. BA, Coll. William & Mary, 1992; JD, Vanderbilt U., 1995; MPH, Emory U., 1998. Bar: Ga. 1995. Atty. Troutman Sanders, LLP, Atlanta, 1996—97; legal svcs. officer Divsn. Pub. Health Ga. Dept. Human Resources, Atlanta, 1999—2002; epidemic intelligence svc. officer Ctrs. for Disease Control & Prevention, Atlanta, 2002—04, pub. health law analyst, 2004—06, health scientist, 2006—. Pres. Atlanta chpt. William & Mary Alumni Club, 1999—2000; alumni bd. govs. Rollins Sch. Pub. Health, Emory U., Atlanta, 2004—. Mem.: Ga. Bar Assn., Pub. Health Law Assn., Am. Pub. Health Assn. Office: Centers for Disease Control & Prevention 4770 Buford Hwy K-40 Atlanta GA 30341 Office Phone: 770-488-8210. Personal E-mail: angiemcgowan@cs.com. Business E-Mail: amcgowan@cdc.gov.

MCGOWAN, BERNARD WAYNE (BERNIE), venture capitalist, writer; b. Stonington, Colo., May 22, 1925; s. Neal and Lena Elton (Dean) McGowan; m. Betty B. Neill, Apr. 2, 1944; children: Wava K. Morris, Darwin L., Marla G. Farmer, rancher, Walsh, 1943—50; rancher Cotopaxi, Colo., 1951—61; owner, auto, farm equip. dealer Cotopaxi Garage, Cotopaxi, Colo., 1953—60; ptnr. Paul & McGowan Constrn. Co., Cotopaxi, 1955—62; owner Auto/Aircraft Financing & Leasing, Denver, 1962—66; founder, pres. Aircraft Appraisal Assn., 1967—82; pres., pub. Aircraft Bluebook-Price Digest, Oklahoma City, 1967—86; mgr. v.p. Insured Aircraft Title Svc., Oklahoma City, 1970—74; ptnr. McGowan Investment Co., Oklahoma City, 1986—2001; pres. TIVY Math Games Inc., Oklahoma City, 1991—2000, BBM Devel. Co., Real Estate, Bethany, Okla., 2001—. Past editor, pub.: Jour. Aviation Finance. With USAF, 1944—45. Mem.: Okla. Auctioneers Assn., Nat. Auctioneers Assn., Aircraft Fin. Assn., Internat. Flying Bankers Assn., Aviation Writers Assn. Achievements include several copyrights and patents for two math games. Home and Office: 8205 Brownsville Ln Bethany OK 73008-3038 Personal E-mail: bmcgowan2@cox.net.

MCGOWAN, BRUCE EDWARD, social studies educator, secondary school educator; BA, Hartwick Coll., Oneonta NY, 2000. Tchr. social studies H.S. Unadilla Valley Ctrl. Sch., New Berlin, NY, 2000—.

MCGOWAN, JEFFREY, mathematician, educator; s. Paul and Carla McGowan; m. Kim Sobel, Jan. 2, 1988; children: Benjamin, Simcha. BA, Hampshire Coll., 1985; PhD, CUNY, NY, 1992. Prof. Ctrl. Conn. State U., New Britain, NY, 1992—. Asst. chmn. dept. math. Ctrl. Conn. State U., 1998—. Mem.: Am. Math. Soc. Office: Ctrl Conn State Univ 1615 Stanley St New Britain CT 06050 Office Phone: 860-832-2850.

MCGOWAN, MICHAEL JEREMY, lawyer; b. Evanston, Ill., Aug. 28, 1961; s. Melvin Joseph and Lydia Judith McGowan; m. Karen Jean Palmer; children: Genevieve, Quinn, Grace. BA, U. Notre Dame, 1983; JD, Loyola U., 1988. Bar: Ill. States atty. Lake County, Ill. States Atty. Office, Waukegan, 1988—89; assoc. Querrey & Harrow, Ltd., Waukegan, 1989—95, non-equity ptnr. Chgo., 1995—97, O'Hagan, Smith and Amundsen, LLC, Chgo., 1997—2000, equity ptnr., 2000—06, Smith Amundsen LLC, Chgo., 2006—. Trustee St. Martin de Porres HS, Waukegan, 2003—07; mem. Defense Rsch. Inst., Chgo., 2005—, Ill. Ann. Defense Counsel, Chgo., 1995—, U.S. Law Network, 2002—. Named Ill. Super Lawyer, 2006, 2007. Mem.: U. Notre Dame Law Club (bd. dirs. 2001—05). Republican. Roman Catholic. Avocations: history, football, skiing, travel. Office: Smith Amundsen LLC 150 N Michigan Ave Ste 3300 Chicago IL 60601 Home Phone: 847-735-1745; Office Phone: 312-894-3242. Business E-Mail: mmcgowan@salawus.com.

MCGOWAN, PATRICK FRANCIS, lawyer; b. NYC, July 23, 1940; s. Francis Patrick and Sonia Veronica (Koslow) M.; m. Patricia Neil, June 6, 1964; children: Susan Claire, Kathleen Anne. BA, Rice U., 1962; JD, U. Tex., Austin, 1965. Bar: Tex. 1965, U.S. Ct. Appeals (5th cir.) 1969, U.S. Tax Ct. 1972, U.S. Supreme Ct. 1970, U.S. Ct. Appeals (11th cir.) 1981, U.S. Ct. Appeals (fed. cir.) 1993. Briefing atty. Tex. Supreme Ct., Austin, 1965—66; ptnr. Strasburger & Price, Dallas, 1966—98, Akin, Gump, Strauss, Hauer & Feld, Dallas, 1998—. Pres., chmn. bd. Tex Lex, Inc., 1991-98. Contbr. numerous articles on internet, trademark, copyright and franchise law. Bd. advisors Dallas Ft. Worth Sch. Law. Fellow Coll. State Bar Tex. (faculty Franchising Inst. 1987, Intellectual Property Inst. 1992, S.W. Legal Found. Patent Law Inst. 1992, Practising Law Inst. 1996, Ctr. for Am. and Internat. Law I.P. Inst. 2001-04); mem. ABA (alt. dispute resolution, forum com. on franchising, trademark and unfair competition com., patent, trademark and copyright law sect., chair ADR survey com. 2004—05), Internat. Inst. Conflict Prevention and Resolution Tribunal (arbitrator 2005-06), State Bar Tex. (alt. dispute resolution, intellectual property sect., com. CLE, chair ADR com. 2002-06), Dallas Bar Assn. (dir. intellectual property law sect. 1994—, chmn. basics seminar 1999, sect. vice chmn. 2001, chmn. 2002), Internat. Anti-Counterfeiting Assn., Bd. Inst. Law and Tech., Tex. Law Rev. Editors Assn., Pro Bono Coll., Phi Delta Phi. Office: Akin Gump 1700 Pacific Ave Ste 4100 Dallas TX 75201-4675 Office Phone: 214-969-2800. Business E-Mail: pmcgowan@akingump.com.

MCGOWAN, ROSE, actress; b. Florence, Italy, Sept. 5, 1973; Actor: (films) Encino Man, 1992, The Doom Generation, 1995, Bio-Dome, 1996, Kiss & Tell, 1996, Scream, 1996, Going All The Way, 1997, Nowhere, 1997, Lewis & Clark & George, 1997, Seed, 1997, Phantoms, 1998, Southie, 1998, Devil in the Flesh, 1998, Jawbreaker, 1999, Sleeping Beauties, 1999, Ready to Rumble, 2000, The Last Stop, 2000, Monkeybone, 2001, Strange Hearts, 2001, Vacuums, 2002, The Black Dahlia, 2006, Grindhouse, 2007; (TV films) God Is In the T.V., 1999, The Killing Yard, 2001, Elvis, 2005; (TV series) Charmed, 2001—06, (TV appearances) True Colors, 1990, What About Joan, 2001. *

MCGOWAN, STEPHEN T., corporate financial executive; BS, Northeastern Univ.; MBA, Loyola Univ., Chgo. With Sun Microsystems Inc., Santa Clara, Calif., 1992—; v.p. fin. No. Am. & Australia field ops., 1992—94, worldwide fin. ops., 1994—98, computer sys., 1998—2000; v.p. staff ops. global sales ops., 2000—01, v.p. fin., 2001—02; exec. v.p., CFO corp. resources, 2002—. Office: Sun Microsystems 4150 Network Circle Santa Clara CA 95054

MCGOWAN, SUSAN, gifted and talented educator; b. Alameda, Calif., May 12, 1959; d. Thomas and Gladys Mae (Prutzman) McG.; m. Warren Howard Jones, Oct. 31, 1980 (div.); children: Kelly Hardcastle, Reilly James; m. Barry William McLaughlin, May 22, 2004 AS in Edn., No. Va. Community Coll., 1988; BA in Russian Area Studies, George Mason U., 1991; MEd, Marymount U., 1994; postgrad., Coll. William & Mary, 2003—. Cert. tchr. Va. Data processor Tracor, Inc., Virginia Beach, Va., 1982-83; computer operator Hughes, Bendix, Holmes and Narver, Virginia Beach, 1983-84; data analyst Tracor, Inc., Virginia Beach, 1984; systems analyst Advanced Tech., Inc., Virginia Beach, 1984-85, computer programmer Reston, Va., 1986-87; tech. writer Swiger Group, Reston, 1987; tchr. 3rd grade Loudoun Country Day Sch., Leesburg, Va., 1991-93; tchr. 4th and 5th grade Loudoun County Pub. Schs., 1994—2000, Va. Beach City Pub. Sch., 2001—. Master tchr. Nat. Tech. Tchr. Inst., WNVT, Fairfax, 1998-99; translation cons. Systems Ctr., Inc., Reston, 1990— Recipient Presdl. award, Va. Gov.'s Sch., 2005. Mem. ASCD, World Affairs Coun., Golden Key, Phi Theta Kappa, Alpha Chi. Personal E-mail: smjones59@aol.com. Business E-Mail: smmcgo@wm.edu.

MCGOWAN, THOMAS RANDOLPH, retired religious organization administrator; b. Balt., Apr. 19, 1926; s. Robert and Mary (Miller) McGowan; m. Bernice A. Bernard, May 20, 1967 (dec. Nov. 1981); children: Howard, James, Terry; m. Roedean Olivia Oden, Feb. 9, 1985; children: Karen White, Kevin, Kurt. AA, Oakland Jr. Coll., 1964; postgrad., San Francisco State Coll., 1964-68; BS, U. Md., 1978. Lt. security police Oakland (Calif.) Army Base, 1955-60; chief motor pool San Francisco Procurement Agy., Oakland, 1960-64, contract specialist, 1964-68, Harry Diamond Labs., Washington, 1968-79, br. chief procurement divsn., 1972-79; chief procurement directorate Yuma (Ariz.) Proving Ground, 1979-82; dir. ecumenism Roman Cath. Diocese of Oakland, 1983—, dir. African Am. Cath. Pastoral Ctr., 1991—. Bd. dirs. Columbia (Md.) Found., 1972—74, chmn., 1975—79; convenor Interreligious Coun. Oakland, 1988—; trustee Greater Oakland Interfaith Network, 1989—92; bd. dirs. Thea Bowman Manor, Oakland, 1989—, St. Mary's Ctr.; mem. E. Oakland Renewal Task Force, 1990—; div. Bd. Cons., Graymoor, NY, 1990—. With US Army, 1944—46. Mem.: Rotary, Knights Peter Claver. Democrat. Avocations: tennis, woodworking. Home: 139 Pinto Dr Vallejo CA 94591-8451 E-mail: ThomDean@pacbell.net.

MCGOWEN, LORRAINE S., lawyer; b. Phila., 1960; m. Gailon McGowen; 4 children. BS, Georgetown U., 1983; JD, Columbia U., 1986. Bar: N.Y. 1987, U.S. Dist. Ct., So. Dist. N.Y. 1988, U.S. Dist. Ct., Ea. Dist. N.Y. 1988, D.C. 1994, U.S. Ct. Appeals, Second Cir. 1994. Ptnr. Orrick, Herrington & Sutcliffe LLP, NYC, 1996—, co-chair Bankruptcy and Debt Restructuring Group, 2001—. Mem.: Am. Coll. Investment Counsel, Am. Bankruptcy Inst., DC Bar, Assn. Bar City NY, ABA (bus. law com.). Office: Orrick Herrington & Sutcliffe LLP 666 Fifth Ave New York NY 10103 Office Phone: 212-506-5114. Office Fax: 212-506-5151. Business E-Mail: lmcgowen@orrick.com.

MC GOWIN, WILLIAM EDWARD, artist; b. Hattiesburg, Miss., June 2, 1938; s. William Edward and Emily (Ratliff) Mc G.; m. Claudia DeMonte, May 28, 1977; children: Leah, Jill. BS, U. So. Miss., 1961; MA, U. Ala., 1964. Prof. art SUNY, Old Westbury, 1978—, Coll. Old Westbury; mem. faculty Corcoran Gallery Art, 1966-77, head sculpture dept., 1967-74; lectr. in field. One-man shows include Corcoran Gallery Art, Washington, 1962, 71, 75, Martha Jackson Gallery, NYC, 1968, Am. Cultural Ctr., Paris, 1974, Mus. Modern Art, Paris, 1978, Brooks Jackson Gallery, Iolas, NYC, 1978-80, Fendrick Gallery, Washington, 1977-80, U. Colo., New Orleans Contemporary Art Ctr., 1982, Project Studios 1, L.I., NY, Cranbrook Acad., Bloomfield Hills, Mich., 1983, Art Park, Lewiston, NY, 1984, Gracie Mansion Gallery, NYC, 1985-86, 89, Mus. Fine Arts, Miami, Jones, Troyer Gallery, Washington, 1987, 89, 91, Boca Raton (Fla.) Mus., 1991, Margulis-Taplin Gallery, Miami, 1993, Paris-NY-Bangkok Gallery, Bangkok, Thailand, 1994, Grey Art Gallery, NYU, 1995, Siipakorn U., Bangkok, 1997, Genkan Gallery, Tokyo, 1997, Miss. Mus. Art, 2000, Osuna Art, Bethesda, Md., 2005, Mobile Mus. Art., Ala., 2006, PS1 Mus. Modern Art, L.I., 2006; group shows include Contemporary Mus., Houston, Miss. Mus. Art, Whitney Mus., NYC, Detroit Inst. Art, Guggenheim Mus., Speed Mus., Ky., Cologne (Germany) Art Fair, Zurich Art Fair; represented in permanent collections Phillips Collection, Washington, Indpls. Mus. Art, Addison Mus. Art, Andover, Mass, Corcoran Gallery Art, Nat. Collection Fine Arts, Washington, New Orleans Mus. Art, Whitney Mus. Am. Art, NYC, Guggenheim Mus., NYC, Hirshorn Gallery and Sculpture Garden, Ogden Mus. New Oleans, Cabinet des Estampes Musée d'art Eihistoire, Geneva; permanent commn. U.S. Gen. Svc. Adminstrn., 1979, VA, Indpls., 1985, Percent for Art, NYC, 1992, City of Jubai, Saudi Arabia, 1993, Dallas Rapid Transit Authority, 1994, Queens County N.Y. Supreme Ct., 1996, Art in Pub. Places, Socorro, N.Mex., 1997, Met. Transit Authority State NY, Bayside, 1998, Inst. for Internat. Econs., Washington, 2000, St. Marks Gates, Plan de Grass, France, 2002, U. Iowa, Cedar Falls, 2003, Clarette Group, NYC, 2004, N.Mex. Arts Sculpture, Santa Rosa, 2004-05, Broward County (Fla.) Pub. Art Commn., 2006, Ft. Lauderdale Fire Rescue, 2006, Rockville Town Sq., Md., 2007. Recipient Oscar for painting, 1977, Painting prize 9th Internat. Painting Festival, Cagnes-sur-Mer, France, 1977, Miss. Arts and Letters award for visual arts, 1980, Art Commn. Design award N.Y.C., 1998; Nat. Endowment for Arts grantee, 1967-68, 79-80, pub. outdoor sculpture grantee, 1977, Cassandra Found. grantee. Home and Office: 96 Grand St New York NY 10013-2633 Home Phone: 212-966-4496; Office Phone: 212-966-4496. Personal E-mail: edmcgowin@aol.com.

MCGOWN, JOHN, JR., lawyer; b. Bowling Green, Ky., June 15, 1949; s. John Stanley and Margaret (Deatherage) McG.; m. Mary Grunewald, Apr. 20, 1978; children: Erin Margaret, Brenna Kathryn. BS, U. Ky., Lexington, 1971; JD, U. Colo., Boulder, 1974; LLM in Taxation, U. Denver, 1981. Bar: Colo. 1975, US Tax Ct. 1981, Idaho 1982. Dep. dist. atty. Weld County, Colo., 1974-78; assoc. Montgomery, Little, Young, Campbell, & McGrew, Denver, 1979-80; rschr. appellate divsn. IRS, Denver, 1980-81; mem. staff tax dept. Price Waterhouse, Denver, 1981-82; ptnr. Hawley Troxell Ennis & Hawley, LLP, Boise, Idaho, 1982-99, of counsel, 2000—. Adj. prof. Boise State U., 1983, assoc. prof., 2000-02; guest lecturer U. Idaho Coll. Law, Moscow, 1990, 2003, 04, 05, adj. prof., 06; guest speaker various tax seminars, 1983—. Contbr. over 90 articles to profl. jours. Bd. dirs. Assn. for Retarded Citizens Ada County, Inc., 1987-93, pres. 1991-92, Assoc. Taxpayers Idaho, Inc., 1993-2002, exec. com., 1995-2002; audit review panel United Way Ada County, 1986-91; IRS vol. tax asst. program 1982, 87. Fellow Am. Coll. of Trust and Estate Counsel; mem. ABA (taxation sect.), Idaho State Bar Assn. (founding mem., taxation probate and trust law sect.), Idaho Soc. CPAs (fed. and state taxation com. 1984-89, bus. legis. com. 1989-91, pers. fin. com. 2000—), Boise Bar Assn., Pioneer Club, Toastmasters (pres. 1991), Beta Gamma Sigma, Sigma Chi (pioneer). Home: 282 S Mobley Ln Boise ID 83712-8329 Office: Hawley Troxell Ennis & Hawley LLP 877 Main St Ste 1000 Boise ID 83702-5883

MCGRADY, PHYLLIS, television producer; Exec. prodr. PrimeTime Live, NYC, Turning Point; with ABC, 1977—; v.p. and exec. prodr. spl. programming ABC News, 1998—2000; exec.-in-charge Good Morning Am., 1999—; sr. v.p. primetime, early morning and news program devel. ABC News, 2000—. Office: PrimeTime Live 147 Columbus Ave Fl 3D New York NY 10023-5900

MCGRADY, TRACY, professional basketball player; b. May 24, 1979; Forward Toronto Raptors, 1997—2000, Orlando Magic, 2000—04, Houston Rockets, 2004—. Active NBA's Reading Time-Out prog. Named to Ea. Conf. All-Star Team, NBA, 2000—04, Western Conf. All-Star Team, 2005—07, All-NBA 1st Team, 2002, 2003. Achievements include being the NBA scoring champion, 2003. Office: c/o Houston Rockets 1510 Polk St Houston TX 77002 Office Phone: 407 89M AGIC. *

MCGRAIL, JEANE KATHRYN, artist; b. Mpls., May 1, 1947; d. Robert Vern and Mary Virginia (Kees) McGrail. BS, U. Wis.-River Falls, 1970; MFA, Cranbrook Acad. Art, 1972; postgrad., Sch. of Art Inst. of Chgo., 1985, Ill. Inst. Tech., 1993. Tchr. Inst. Contemporary Art. Group exhbns. include Saginaw Art Mus., Mich., 1972, Met. Mus. Art, Miami, Fla., 1974, Lowe Mus. Art, Coral Gables, Fla., 1974, 76, Miller Galleries, Coconut Grove, Fla., 1978, 80, Cicchinelli Gallery, NYC, 1980-82, Harper Coll., 1984, Contemporary Art Ctr. Arlington, Arlington Heights, Ill., 1984, 85, 86, 94, Evanston Art Ctr., 1985, South Shore Cultural Ctr., Chgo., 1990, N.A.M.E. Gallery, 1990, Artemisia Gallery, Chgo., 1991, 92, 93, 94, North Lakeside Art Ctr., Chgo., 1991, 94, 95, Ceres Gallery, NYC, 1992, Harper Coll., Ill., 1993, Environ. Concerns, Chgo., 1993, North Park Coll., Chgo., 1993, Franklin Square Gallery, Chgo., 1994, 95, 96, Space 900 Gallery, Chgo., 1994-2007, Chuck Levitan Gallery, NYC, 1995, Riverwest Art Ctr., Milw., 1995, Nat. Mus. Women in the Arts, Wash., 1996, Gallery 1040, 1997-, "Red", Chgo., 1998, Oakton Coll. Gallery, Ill., 1999-, Women's Works, Woodstock, Ill., 1999, "Paint It Siver", ARC Gallery, Chgo., 1999, Past/Present, Chgo., 1999, "Blue", Northeastern Ill. U., Chgo., 2000, Then and Now, Chgo., 1999, Norris Cultural Ctr., St. Charles, Ill., 1999, others; represented in permanent collections at Chgo. Mus. Sci. and Industry, U. Chgo., Mus. Photography, Chgo., Miami-Dade Pub. Libr., U. Wis.-River Falls, MacGregor Found., Printmakers Workshop, NYC, Norman R. Eppnik Art Gallery Emporia State U., Kans., 2000, Mini Print Internat. Exhbn., Binghamton, NY, 2000, Yale U. Med. Libr., 2000, Columbia U. Med. Ctr., 2000, 06, Mini Print Internat. of Cadaques, Spain, Macy Gallery, Providence, RI, 2000, Brickton Gallery, Park Ridge, Fla., 2001, Mini Print Internat. of Cadaques, Spain, 2001—, Last of Primaries, Coll. of Lake Co., 2003—, Ukrainian Mus. Contemporary Art, Chgo., 2003, Chautauqua Nat. Exhbn., NY, 2004, Rockford Coll., Ill., 2006, Space 900, Chgo., 2006, Inspiring Change for Global Warming, Chgo., 2007others; solo exhbns.

include Cicchinelli Gallery, 1981, Gallery at the Commons, Chgo., 1982, Truman Coll. Gallery, Chgo., 1991, C.G. Jung Inst., Evanston, Ill., 1992, Carlson Tower Gallery, Chgo., 1994, Olcott Ctr. Gallery, Theosophical Soc. Am., Wheaton, Ill., 2001; pub. "Mosaic", 1992, The Best of Printmaking, 1997; contbr. publ. to profl. jour. Cranbrook Acad. Art scholar, 1971; CAAP grantee Dept. Cultural Affairs City Chgo, 1992; recipient Poster Competition award Vizcaya Mus., 1974; Print award Auction WPBT, 1979, Tchr. Inst. Contemporary Art, Art Inst. Chgo., 2004. Mem. Coll. Art Assn., Chgo. Women's Caucus for Art (bd. dirs. 1992-95, sec.), Chgo. Artists Coalition, Sierra Club (sec. chpt. exec. com. 2005-07). Independent. Studio: 1040 W Huron St LL5 Chicago IL 60622-6591 Office Phone: 312-882-8512. E-mail: whoswho@jeanemcgrail.com.

MCGRATH, CHRISTOPHER THOMAS, lawyer; b. Inwood, NY, Nov. 25, 1958; s. John J. and Dolores Marie McG.; m. Monica Jean DiPalma, Sept. 15, 1984; children: Kristin Marie, Kelli Anne, Katelynn. BS cum laude, St. John's U., Jamaica, NY, 1980; JD, U. Dayton, 1983. Bar: N.Y. 1984, U.S. Dist. Ct. (so. and ea. dists.) N.Y. 1984, U.S. Supreme Ct. 1987; bd. cert. civil trial advocacy Nat. Bd. Trial Advocacy. Assoc. Sullivan & Liapakis, NYC, 1983-89, ptnr., 1989-99, Sullivan, Papain, Block, McGrath & Cannavo P.C., NYC, 1999—. Lectr. N.Y. State Bar Assn., N.Y. State Trial Lawyers Assn., Assn. Trial Lawyers Am. Chmn. humanitarian award Nassau County 4th Precinct Police, 1985—. Mem. ATLA, NY State Trial Lawyers Assn., Nassau County Bar Assn. (bd. dirs., chair med. legal com. 1997-98, chair jud. com. 1999—, mem. exec. com. 2000—, pres.-elect 2004-05, pres. 2005-06), NY State Bar Assn., Kiwanis (disting. past pres. Peninsula chpt. 1988-89). Republican. Home: 1348 Hewlett Ln Hewlett NY 11557-2208 Office: Sullivan Papain Block McGrath Cannavo PC 120 Broadway New York NY 10271-0002 also: 55 Mineola Blvd Mineola NY 11501-4220 Office Phone: 576-742-0707. Business E-Mail: cmcgrath@traillaw1.com.

MCGRATH, DANIEL ANDREW, hydrologist; b. Pitts., Mar. 30, 1960; s. Daniel Francis and Grace Leverne McGrath; m. Betty Marie Boyce, June 9, 1984; children: Margaret Lillian, Caroline Amanda, Josephine Marie. BA in Geography and Geosci., Tex. Tech, Lubbock, 1982, MS in Soil Sci., 1984, postgrad., 2004—. Cert. Project Mgmt. Inst., Pa., 1995, sigma black belt BWXT-Honeywell, Tex., 2002. Rsch. asst. N.Mex Bur. of Mines, Socorro, 1985; hydrogeologist Nev. Test Site, Las Vegas, 1986—87, BWXT Pantex, Amarillo, Tex., 1989—. Adv. bd. mem. Holy Cross Cath. Acad., Amarillo, Tex., 2005—. Mem.: Am. Soc. Engring. Mgmt. (assoc.), KC (assoc.; treas. 2002—06, Star award 2004), Project Mgmt. Inst. (assoc.; program chair environ. mgmt. 1996—98). Home: 117 Rolling Trail Amarillo TX 79108 Office: BWXT Pantex PO Box 30020 Amarillo TX 79120 Home Phone: 806-626-0289; Office Phone: 806-477-5567. Office Fax: 806-477-7951. Personal E-mail: mcgrath5@suddenlink.net. Business E-Mail: dmcgrath@pantex.com.

MCGRATH, DON JOHN, bank executive; b. Springfield, Ill., June 15, 1948; s. Donald John and Wilma P. (Beck) McG.; m. Patriaia Ratti, May 7, 1983. BS in Mktg., U. Ill., 1970; MBA, Boston U., 1973. Investment officer Banque Nationale de Paris, San Francisco, 1975-76, treas. San Francisco and L.A., 1976-78, v.p., treas., 1978-80, Bank of the West, San Francisco, 1980, v.p., CFO, 1980-81, sr. v.p., CFO, 1981-84, sr. exec. v.p., CFO, 1984-87, sr. exec. v.p., COO, 1987-91, pres., COO, 1991-95, pres., CEO, 1996—, chmn., CEO, 2005; pres., COO, dir. BancWest Corp., 1998—2004, pres., CEO, dir., 2005—. Bd. dirs. Commonwealth Club Calif., Nature Conservancy Calif., Dominican Univ. San Rafael, Calif. Mem. Calif. Bankers Assn., Univ. Club, St. Francis Yacht Club (San Francisco), Diablo (Calif.) Country Club. Office: BancWest Corp 180 Montgomery St 25th Fl San Francisco CA 94104 Office Phone: 415-765-4823.

MCGRATH, ELEANOR BURNS, editor, writer; b. Gloucester, Mass., July 28, 1952; d. Edward James and Julia Ann (Holloran) McG.; m. Paul Allen Witteman, May 5, 1984; 1 child, Katharine McGrath Witteman. AB magna cum laude, Mt. Holyoke Coll., 1974. Rschr. Time-Life Books, NYC, 1974-76; reporter, staff writer, edn. editor Time Mag., NYC, 1976-86; sr. editor Women's Sports and Fitness Mag., San Francisco, 1986-87; spl. corr. Time Mag., San Francisco, 1988; sr. editor, articles editor Self Mag., NYC, 1991-98; editor Time Mag./Princeton Rev. Coll. Guide, 2000—02; editor and pub. McWitty Press, 2004—. Journalist-in-residence U. Mich., Ann Arbor, 1984-85. Author: My One and Only: The Special Experience of the Only Child, 1989; editor: One Earth, 1990. Trustee Mt. Holyoke Coll., South Hadley, Mass., 1976-79; pres. Greater N.Y. Athletic Assn., N.Y.C. 1980-84. Time fellow, Duke U., 1981. Mem. N.Y. Rd. Runners Club. Home: 110 Riverside Dr New York NY 10024-3715 Personal E-mail: mcwittypress@aol.com.

MCGRATH, J. PAUL, lawyer; b. Rochester, NY, Sept. 9, 1940; s. Thomas E. and Evelyn R. McG.; m. Eileen Robinson, Aug. 29, 1964; children: John P., Patricia, David R., Robyn. AB, Coll. of the Holy Cross, 1962; LL.B., Harvard U., 1965. Mem. firm Dewey, Ballantine, Bushby, Palmer and Wood, NYC, 1965-73, ptnr., 1973-81, 85-92; asst. atty. gen. civil div. Dept. Justice, Washington, 1981-83, asst. atty. gen. antitrust div., 1983-85; v.p., gen. counsel Allied-Signal Inc., 1992—96; sr. v.p., gen. counsel FMC Corp., Chgo., 1996—2000; sr. v.p., gen. counsel, sec. Am. Standard Cos. Inc., Piscataway, 2000—. Fellow Am. Coll. Trial Lawyers. Clubs: Montclair Golf. Republican. Roman Catholic. *

MCGRATH, JAMES THOMAS, real estate investment company executive; b. NYC, Nov. 10, 1942; s. Thomas James and Mary Ita (Finnegan) McG.; m. Paulette L. Franck, Aug. 16, 1980; 1 child, Tara (dec.). BS in Acctg., Providence Coll., 1964. CPA, N.Y.; lic. gen. contractor, N.C., 2006. Sr. auditor Coopers & Lybrand, NYC, 1968-72, mgmt. cons., 1972-74; group contr. IU Internat. Corp., Phila., 1974-77; v.p. fin. Taylor Engring. Corp. subs. IU Internat., Detroit, 1977-78; controller Pool Co. subs. Enserch Corp., Houston, 1978-85; sr. v.p. fin., treas. Lone Star Gas Co. subs. Enserch Corp., Dallas, 1985-91; pres. McGrath & Assocs., Inc., Dallas, 1991—. Ct. Apptd. Spl. Advocate. Bd. dirs. ARC, Dallas chpt., 1990-93. Lt. USN, 1964-68. Mem. AICPA, Dallas Athletic Club, St. Vincent de Paul Soc. Libertarian. Roman Catholic. Avocations: golf, cooking, skiing, scuba diving, sailing. Home and Office: 2838 Colleen Dr Garland TX 75043-1215 Office Phone: 972-271-5803. Personal E-mail: pjmcgrath2@comcast.net.

MCGRATH, JOSEPH W., computer services company executive; B, Rutgers U. V.p. and svc. dir. Gartner Group, worldwide info. tech. cons. firm; with Xerox Corp., 1989—98, v.p. N.Am. sys. sales, v.p. mktg., integrated sys. ops., v.p. strategy and mktg. Xerox Prodn. Sys. Group, v.p. and gen. mgr. Xerox Prodn. Color Sys.; joined Unisys Corp., 1999, sr. v.p. maj. accounts sales and chief mktg. officer, 1999—2000, exec. v.p. and pres. Global Industries, 2000—02, exec. v.p. and pres. Enterprise Transformation Svcs., 2002—04, pres. and COO, 2004—05, pres. & CEO, 2005—. Office: Unisys Corp Unisys Way Blue Bell PA 19424 *

MCGRATH, JUDY (JUDITH ANN MCGRATH), broadcast executive; b. Scranton, Pa., July 2, 1952; BA in English Lit., Cedar Crest Coll. Copy chief Glamour mag.; sr. writer Mademoiselle; copywriter Nat. Advt., Phila.; copywriter, on-air promotion Warner Amex Satellite Entertainment Corp. (predecessor to MTV), 1981; editl. dir. MTV, sr. v.p., creative dir., 1988—92, exec. v.p., creative dir., 1992—93, co-pres., creative dir., 1993—94, pres., 1994—96, MTV, MTV2, 1996—2000, pres. MTV Group, chmn. Interactive Music, 2000—02; pres. MTV Networks Music Group, 2002—04, chmn., CEO, 2004—. Hon. chair Cable Positive. Trustee emeritus Nat. Campaign to Prevent Teen Pregnancy; bd. dirs. Rock the Vote. Named Humanitarian of Yr., T.J. Martell Found. Leukemia, Cancer and AIDS Rsch., 2003; named one of 100 Most Powerful Women in Entertainment, Hollywood Reporter, 2004, 2005, 2006, Most Powerful Women in Bus., Fortune mag., 2005, 100 Most Powerful Women, Forbes Mag., 2006, 50 Most Powerful Women in Bus., Fortune mag., 2006; recipient Cable Ace Award, 1993, Founders award, Rock the Vote, 2001, Friend of the Children award, Harlem Children's Zone, 2001. Office: MTV 1515 Broadway Fl 28 New York NY 10036-8901

MCGRATH, KATHRYN BRADLEY, lawyer; b. Norfolk, Va., Sept. 2, 1944; d. James Pierce and Kathryn (Hoyle) Bradley; children: Ian M., James D. AB, Mt. Holyoke Coll., 1966; JD, Georgetown U., 1969. Ptnr. Gardner, Carton & Douglas, Washington, 1979-83; dir. div. investment mgmt. SEC, Washington, 1983-90; ptnr. Morgan Lewis, Washington, 1990—2002, Crowell & Moring, LLP, Washington, 2002—05, Mayer, Brown, Rowe & Maw LLP, Washington, 2005—. Named Disting. Exec., Pres. Reagan, 1987. Mem. ABA, Fed. Bar Assn. (exec. council securities law com.). Office: Mayer Brown Rowe & Maw LLP 1909 K St NW Washington DC 20006 Home Phone: 703-836-8155; Office Phone: 202-263-3374. Business E-Mail: kmcgrath@mayerbrownrowe.com.

MCGRATH, KEVIN MICHAEL, military analyst, civilian military employee, researcher; b. Huntington, NY, Aug. 7, 1973; s. John Patrick and Michaele Marie McGrath. BA, James Madison U, Harrisonburg, Va., 1995; M, U of MD, Coll. Pk., MA, 1998; PhD in process, U of MD, Coll. Pk., MD, 1998—. Intern Dept. of State, Wash., DC, 1995; intern Dept. of State, Am. embassy, Nicosia, Cyprus, 1996, FBI, Wash., DC, 1997; tchg. asst. Dept. of Polit. Sci., UMD Coll., Coll. Prk., Md., 1997—98; Fgn. policy analyst Dept. of Def., Wash., DC, 1999—. Author: (article) Madison Journal of Undergraduate Studies, 1995. Recipient Sustained Superior Svc., Dept. Def., 1999, Proficiency in Persian Farsi, Dept. State, 2001, Cert. Meritorious Svc., SFOR/NATO, Bosnia, 2001, NATO Svc. medal, Dept. Def., 2001, Civilian combat support, 2001, 2003, 2004, 2005, 2006, Defense Civilian Expeditionary medal, 2003, 2004, 2005, 2006. Mem.: Kennedy Ctr., World Affairs Coun. Democrat. Catholic. Avocations: softball, reading, theater, basketball, gen. outdoor activities. Home: 28 Delancey Drive Geneva NY 14456 Office: Dept of Defense Washington DC

MCGRATH, LYNN BERNARD, surgeon; b. St. John's Newfoundland, Can., Feb. 14, 1951; came to U.S., 1983; m. Melissa McManus, Sept. 18, 1982; children: Lynn Bernard, Jr., Meaghan Claire, Mark Duggan, Sean Ware. Pre-Med. Diploma, St. Francis Xavier U., Antigonish, NS, Can., 1970; BS, Memorial U., St. John's Newfoundland, Can., 1972, MD, 1974. Lic. MD, Newfoundland, Mass., Ala., N.J., Pa.; Diplomate Am. Bd. Surgery, Am. Bd. Thoracic Surgery. Rotating internship, first yr. surg. resident McGill U., Jewish Gen. Hosp., Montreal, Canada, 1974-75, 75-76; gen. surg. resident, chief surg. resident Peter Bent Brigham Hosp./Harvard Med. Sch., Boston, 1976-80, 80; Arthur Tracy Cabot Fellow in Surgery, instr., surgery Harvard Med. Sch.; chief surgical resident, asst. to the Surgeon-in-Chief VA Hosp., West Roxbury, 1981; appointed to the staff Brigham and Women's Hosp.; cardiothoracic surgery residency, chief resident U. Ala.-Univ. Hosp., Birmingham, 1981-82, 82-83, fellowship in congenital heart surgery, 1983-84, instr. surgery, chief resident, cardiovascular surgery and pediatric cardiovascular surgery; asst. prof. surgery, assoc. prof. surgery U. of Medicine and Dentistry of N.J., New Brunswick, 1985-89, 89—; attending surgeon, dir., pediatric surgery Deborah Heart and Lung Ctr., Brown Mills, NJ, 1985—, chmn. dept. surgery, 1989—, v.p., med. affairs, chair med. staff, 1999—; acting dir. Deborah Rsch. Inst., Brown Mills, 1991-92. Presenter in field. Co-author: Decision Making in Surgery of the Chest, 1989, Indications for Heart Valve Repalcement by Age Group, 1989; contbr. numerous abstracts and articles to profl. publs.; mem. editorial bd. The Annals of Thoracic Surgery, 1989—, The Jour. of Investigative Surgery, 1992—, Circulation, 1994—. Grantee Datascope Corp., 1986, Ethicon Corp., 1987, 90, Deborah Rsch. Inst., 1988, 89, 91, 92, Miles Corp., 1990, Shiley Corp., 1991, 92, Baxter-Edwards Corp., 1991, St. Jude Med. Corp., 1991, Max Bayer Rsch. Found., 1991, 92, Gensia Pharm., Inc., 1992, 93. Fellow Am. Coll. Chest Physicians, Am. Coll. Cardiology, The N.J. Thoracic Soc., Acad. of Medicine of N.J., European Sociedad de Cardiocirujanos, North Am. Soc. of Pacing and Electrophysiology, Am. Coll. Surgeons, Am. Coll. Angiology, Phila. Acad. Surgery; mem. AAAS, The Brigham Surg. Soc., The Kirklin Soc., Internat. Soc. for Heart Transplantation, Assn. for Acad. Surgery, The Donald Ross Soc., The Soc. Thoracic Surgeons, Am. Soc. Artificial Internal Organs, Am. Assn. Thoracic Surgery. Achievements include performing more than 10,000 open-heart surgery procedures; has operated on 1,400 children from 91 countries around the world. Through Children of the World, has performed open-heart surgery on children during medical missions to the former Soviet Republic of Georgia and Lithuania. Office: Deborah Hosp Found PO Box 820 Browns Mills NJ 08015 Home: 839 Matlack Dr Moorestown NJ 08057-1444 *

MCGRATH, MARY HELENA, plastic surgeon, educator; b. NYC, Apr. 12, 1945; d. Vincent J. and Mary M. (Manning) McG.; children: Margaret E. Simon, Richard M. Simon. BA, Coll. New Rochelle, 1966; MD, St. Louis U., 1970; MPH, George Washington U., 1994. Diplomate Am. Bd. Surgery, Am. Bd. Plastic Surgery, lic. physician Calif. Resident in surg. pathology U. Colo. Med. Ctr., Denver, 1970-71, intern in gen. surgery, 1971-72, resident in gen. surgery, 1971-75; resident in plastic and reconstructive surgery Yale U. Sch. Medicine, New Haven, 1976—78, chief resident plastic and reconstructive surgery, 1977-78; fellow in hand surgery U. Conn.-Yale U., New Haven, 1978; instr. in surgery divsn. plastic and reconstructive surgery Yale U. Sch. Medicine, New Haven, 1977-78, asst. prof. plastic surgery, 1978-80; attending in plastic and reconstructive surgery Yale-New Haven Hosp., 1978-80, Columbia-Presbyn. Hosp., NYC, 1980-84, George Washington U. Med. Ctr., Washington, 1984-2000, Children's Nat. Med. Ctr., Washington, 1985-2000, Loyola U. Med. Ctr., 2000—02, Hines VA Hosp., 2001—02, U. Calif., San Francisco, 2003—, San Francisco VA Ctr., 2003—, San Francisco Gen. Hosp., 2003—; asst. prof. plastic surgery Columbia U., NYC, 1980-84; assoc. prof. plastic surgery Sch. Medicine, George Washington U., Washington, 1984-87, prof. plastic surgery, 1987-2000, Loyola U. Med. Ctr., 2000—02, U. Calif., San Francisco, 2003—. Bd. dirs. Am. Bd. Plastic Surgery, 1989-95, historian, 1991-95; examiner certifying exam., 1986—; mem. Residency Rev. Com. Plastic Surgery, 2006—; senator med. faculty senate George Washington U., bd. govs. Med. Faculty Assocs.; presenter, cons. in field. Co-editor: (with M.L. Turner) Dermatology for Plastic Surgeons, 1993; assoc. editor: The Jour. of Hand Surgery, 1984-89, Annals of Plastic Surgery, 1984-87, Plastic and Reconstructive Surgery, 1989-95, Contemporary Surgery, 1999-2006, Archives of Surgery, 2004—; advt. editor Plastic and Reconstructive Surgery, 2003-06; guest reviewer numerous jours.; contbr. chpts. to books and articles to profl. jours Recipient numerous rsch. grants, 1978—. Fellow ACS (D.C. chpt. program ann. meeting chmn., 1992, pres. 1994-95, bd. govs. 1995-98, exec. com. 1996-97, chmn. adv. coun. plastic surgery 1995-98, regent 1997—2006, vice-chair bd. regents 2005-06, 1st v.p. elect 2006-07); mem. AAAS, Am. Surg. Assn., Am. Assn. Hand Surgery, Am. Assn. Plastic Surgeons (trustee 1997-00), Am. Burn Assn., Am. Soc. for Aesthetic Plastic Surgery, Am. Soc. Maxillofacial Surgeons, Am. Soc. Plastic and Reconstructive Surgery (chmn. ethics com. 1985-87, chmn. device/tech. evaluation com. 1993-94, chmn. workforce task force 1997-00, bd. dirs. 1994-96, chmn. endowment bd. dirs. 2000-04, trustee 2004—, chmn. bd. trustees 2006-, ednl. found. bd. dirs. 1985-96, treas. 1989-92, v.p. 1992-93, pres.-elect 1993-94, pres. 1994-95), Am. Soc. Reconstructive Microsurgery (edn. com. 1992-94), Am. Soc. Surgery of Hand (chmn. 1987 ann. residents' and fellows conf. 1986-87, rsch. com. 1988-90), Assn. Acad. Chmn. Plastic Surgery (bd. dirs. 1999—), Assn. Acad. Surgery, Chgo. Soc. Plastic Surgeons (treas. 2001-02), Calif. Soc. Plastic Surgeons, San Francisco Surg. Soc., Chgo. Surg. Soc., Internat. Soc. Reconstructive Surgery, Met. D.C. Soc. Surgery Hand (pres. 1995-97), N.Y. Surg. Soc., Northeastern Soc. Plastic Surgeons (treas. 1993-96, pres. 1997-98), Pacific Coast Surg. Assn., Plastic Surgery Rsch. Coun. (chmn. 1990), Surg. Biology Club III, The Wound Healing Soc Office Phone: 415-353-4389. Business E-Mail: mcgrathm@surgery.ucsf.edu.

MCGRATH, MICHAEL G., management consulting firm executive; BS in Chemical Engring., U. Wis., MBA in Acctg. With Accenture Ltd., 1973—, consulting mng. ptnr. St. Louis, 1987—89, country mng. ptnr. Italy, 1989—92, mng. ptnr. Practice Process & Quality, London, 1992—97, CFO, 1997—2001, 2004—06, treas., mng. ptnr. corp. matters, 2001, capital risk officer, 2001—02, chief risk officer, 2002—04, internat. chmn., 2006—. Office: Accenture Ltd 1345 Ave of the Americas New York NY 10105 also: 22 Victoria St HM12 Hamilton Bermuda *

MCGRATH, MIKE, state attorney general; b. Aug. 22, 1947; BS, U. Mont., 1970; JD, Gonzaga U., 1975. Bar: Wash. 75, Mont. 77, U.S. Ct. Appeals (9th cir.) 80, U.S. Supreme Ct. 80. Reginald Heber Smith cmty. lawyer fellow; atty. Washoe County Legal Svcs., Reno, 1975—76; asst. atty. gen. State of Mont., Helena, 1977—82, atty. gen., 2001—; county atty. Lewis and Clark County, Helena, 1983—2001. Bd. dirs. Mont. Legal Svcs. Assn., 1980—2003, pres., 1984—85, 1995—96; bd. dirs. Mountain chpt. Nat. Com. for Prevention of Child Abuse, 1985—90, Big Bros. Sisters, Helena, 1977—83, Friendship Ctr. Helena, 1989—2003, pres., 1995—97; chmn. Conf. Western Atty. Gens., 2003—04. With USAF, 1970—72. Mem.: Mont. County Attys. Assn. (pres. 1996—97), Nat. Dist. Attys. Assn., Mont. Bar Assn., Rock Mountain Elk Found. Home: 514 Hayes Ave Helena MT 59601-6106 Office: Office of Atty General Justice Bldg 215 N Sanders PO Box 201401 Helena MT 59620-1401 Office Phone: 406-444-2026.

MCGRATH, RICHARD, lawyer; b. Chgo., Aug. 10, 1929; s. John Francis and Helen Leone (Hoyer) M.; m. Luisa Sacco y Artze, Aug. 12, 1956; children: Lisa, Deborah, Holly. BA magna cum laude, Georgetown U., 1951; JD cum laude, Harvard U., 1954. Bar: NY 1955, Conn. 1960, US Supreme Ct. 1965. Assoc. Hughes, Hubbard, Blair and Reed, 1954-57; corp. counsel Raytheon Co., 1957-60; assoc. Cummings & Lockwood, Stamford, Conn., 1960-63, ptnr., 1963—2003; counsel Murtha Cullina, LLP, Stamford, 2004—. Gen. counsel, corp. sec. Internat. Exec. Svc. Corps, 1990—. Mem. editl. bd. Harvard Law Rev., 1952-54; contbr. articles to profl. jours.; panelist law seminars. Past pres. Fairfield County Coun. Boy Scouts Am. Mem.: Conn. Bar Assn. (chmn. corp. law com. 1984—86, fee disputes arbitration com. 1980—84), Woodway Country Club (Darien, Conn.) (bd. govs., sec. 1983—91, chmn. nominating com. 2000), Stamford Rotary Club (past pres.), Gold Key Soc., Eta Sigma Phi, Pi Gamma Mu. Avocations: golf, trap, chess. Office: Murtha Cullina LLP 177 Broad St Stamford CT 06901 Office Phone: 203-653-5412. Business E-Mail: rmcgrath@murthalaw.com.

MCGRATH, THOMAS JOHN, lawyer, writer, film producer; b. NYC, Oct. 8, 1932; children: Maura Lee, J. Connell; m. Diahn W. McGrath, Sept. 28, 1974; 1 child, Courtney C. BA, NYU, 1956, JD, 1960. Bar: NY 1960. Assoc. Milbank, Tweed, Hadley & McCloy, NYC, 1960-69; ptnr. Simpson, Thacher & Bartlett, NYC, 1970-95; ret., 1995. Lectr., writer Practicing Law Inst., 1976—, Am. Law Inst. ABA, 1976-81. Author: Carryover Basis Under Tax Reform Act, 1977; contbg. author: Estate and Gift Tax After ERTA, 1982; producer: (film) Deadly Hero, 1977. Bd. dirs. NY Philharm.; pres. Am. Austrian Found. With US Army, 1953-54, Korea. Fellow Am. Coll. Trust and Estate Coun.; mem. ABA, NY State Bar Assn., Assn. Bar City NY Office: Simpson Thacher & Bartlett 425 Lexington Ave New York NY 10017-3954 Office Phone: 212-355-2232. Personal E-mail: mcgrathtwf@aol.com.

MCGRATH, WILLIAM ARTHUR, arbitrator, mediator, lawyer, real estate broker; b. Hackensack, NJ, Jan. 31, 1941; s. Donald Marble and Elinor (Peck) McGrath; m. Diane Gurley, Apr. 25, 1965 (div. Nov. 1976); children: Philip M., Christian P.; m. Jackie Wynne, Aug. 10, 2002. BS, Calif. U., Long Beach, 1963; JD, U. Pacific, 1972. Bar: Colo. 1972, US Dist. Ct. Colo. 1972. Pvt. practice, Breckenridge, Colo., 1972—82, Aurora, Colo., 1982—84; ptnr. McGrath & Callan, P.C., Breckenridge, 1975—80, McGrath & Lavenhar, Esq., Denver, 1984—85; prin. William A. McGrath & Assocs., Denver, 1985—88; pvt. practice San Diego, 1988—, Sacramento, 1993—. Vocat. instr. Colo. Mountain Coll., 1972—80; instr. Sacramento City Coll., 2004—. Mem.: ABA, Nat. Assn. Realtors, Calif. Assn. Realtors, Colo. Trial Lawyers Assn. Republican. Episcopalian. Home: 1916 Bidwell Way Sacramento CA 95818 Office Phone: 916-447-9852. Personal E-mail: wmcgrathppl@aol.com.

MCGRATH, WILLIAM JOSEPH, lawyer; b. Cleve., July 6, 1943; s. William Peter and Marie Agnes (Wolf) McG.; m. Mary Ann Ostrenga; children: William Peter, Geoffrey Walton, Megan Joy. ABcl, John Carroll U., 1965; MA, Loyola U., 1967; JD, Harvard U., 1970. Bar: Ill. 1970. Assoc. McDermott, Will & Emery, Chgo., 1970-75, ptnr., 1976—, mem. mgmt. com., 1993-98, mem. exec. com., 1994-97. Vice chmn. investment com. Glencoe Capital LLC, 1997-2000, vice chmn., mng. dir., 2000—; bd. dirs. Tomy Am., Inc., Torrance, Calif. Trustee Boys and Girls Club Found., 1983; bd. dirs. Ctr. for Econ. Policy and Analysis, 1989—. Mem. ABA, Evanston Golf Club, Union League (Chgo.), Chgo. Club, Met. Club. Chgo. Democrat. Roman Catholic. Home: 943 Edgemere Ct Evanston IL 60202-1428 Office: Glencoe Capital LLC 222 W Adams St Chicago IL 60606

MCGRATTAN, MARY K., state legislator; b. NYC; married; 6 children. RN, St. Catherine's Hosp. Sch. of Nursing. RN NY, Conn.; cert. notary pub., justice of the peace. Mem. town coun. Town of Ledyard, Conn., 1977-83, mayor, 1983—91; pres. Conn. Conf. of Municipalities, 1990-91; mem. Conn. Ho. of Reps., Hartford, 1993—2002; cons. Ledyard Obesity Prevention Project, 2003; coord. Faith in Action Network, 2003—. Vol. Ledyard Fair, Our Lady of Lourdes Festival; event coord. Crop Walk for Hunger; chair Ledyard HEart Fund Charity Dr.; mem. Ledyard Dem. Town Com. Named Legislator of Yr., Conn. Nurses Assn.; recipient cert. of appreciation, C. of C., Breath of Life award, Am. Lung Assn., award of appreciation, Conn. Assn. Optometrists, Nightingale award for excellence in nursing, 2003; Paul Harris fellow, Rotary. Mem.: Avalonia Land Conservancy, Ledyard Libr. Friends, Ledyard Hist. Soc., Rotary. Avocations: reading, sewing, cooking. Address: 13 Lynn Dr Ledyard CT 06339-1312 Home Phone: 860-464-1204; Office Phone: 860-442-0733. E-mail: mary@community-partnerships.com.

MC GRAW, DARRELL VIVIAN, JR., state attorney general; b. Mullens, W.Va., Nov. 8, 1936; s. Darrell Vivian and Julia (ZeKany) Mc Graw; m. Jorea Marple; children: Elizabeth, Sarah, Darrell, Elliott. AB, W.Va. U., 1961, JD, 1964, MA, 1977. Bar: W.Va. 1964. Gen. atty. Fgn. Claims Settlement Commn., US Dept. State, 1964; counsel to gov. State of W.Va., 1965—68; pvt. practice Charleston, Shepherdstown and Morgantown, 1968—76; judge W.Va. Supreme Ct. Appeals, Charleston, 1977—88, chief justice, 1982—83; atty. gen. State of W.Va., Charleston, 1993—. With US Army, 1954—57. Fellow, W.Va. U., Nat. Ctr. Edn. in Politics/Ford Found. Fellow: Am. Polit. Sci. Assn., Rotary. Democrat. Office: Office of Atty Gen 1900 Kanawha Blvd E Rm E-26 Charleston WV 25305-0009 Office Phone: 304-558-2021.

MCGRAW, DONALD JESSE, biologist, science historian, writer; b. Altadena, Calif., Oct. 27, 1943; s. Jesse E. and Mary L. (Hajostek) McG.; m. Laura Lee Hansen, July 13, 1968; children: Adrienne, Holly, Rachel. BS in Biol. Scis., Calif. State Poly. Coll., 1965; MS, Utah State U., 1967; PhD, Oreg. State U., 1976. Registered microbiologist Am. Acad. Microbiology; CCR fed. registration. Research asst. microbiology Utah State U., 1965-66, teaching asst. food and aquatic microbiology, 1966-67; grad. teaching asst. gen. biology Oreg. State U., 1970-72, instr., 1972-73; tchr. phys. and biol. scis. U.S. Bur. Indian Affairs Boarding Sch., Shonto, Ariz., 1974-75; asst. prof. biology Franklin Coll., Ind., 1975-78; adj. asst. prof. biology Ind. Central U., Indpls., 1977-78; adj. asst. prof. Ind. U.-Purdue U., Columbus, 1978; mem. faculty Yavapai C.C., Prescott, Ariz., 1978-79; assoc. dir. Ute Research Lab., Ft. Duchesne, Utah, 1980-81, dir., 1981-82; asst. prof. biology Coll. St. Thomas, Minn., 1985-87; assoc. provost U. San Diego, 1988—2004, prof., 2001—04; independent fed. contractor, 2005—. Summer ranger/naturalist U.S. Nat. Park Svc., 1970—79, 1983—86; vis. prof. Bard Coll., NYC, 1984. Author: Andrew Ellicott Douglass and the Role of the Giant Sequoia in the Development of Dendrochonology, 2001, Edmund Schulman and the Living Ruins: Bristlecome Pines, Tree Rings and Radiocarbon Dating, 2007; contbr. articles to profl. jours. Commr. San Diego County Columbian Quincentennary Commn., 1990-93, chmn. edn. com., 1990-93; mem. pres.'s adv. com. San Diego Zool. Soc., 1995-97; trustee Quail Bot. Gardens Found., 1995-98. Capt. (0-6) USPHS Res. Recipient Disting. Alumnus award, Calif. State Poly. U., 1991, Monrovia H.S., 1991, Meritorious Pub. Svc. award USN, 2003; Eli Lilly doctoral grantee Oreg. State U., 1973-74; NSF grantee, 1998. Mem. AAAS, Cabrillo Hist. Assn. (bd. dirs. 1989-94, vice chair 1992, chair 1993, 94), History of Sci. Soc., Tree Ring Soc., Alpha Scholastic Honor Soc. of Franklin Coll. (pres. 1976-78), Sigma Xi (sec. San Diego chpt. 1996-97, v.p. 1997-98, pres. 1999-2000, assoc. dir. S.W. region 2000-02, bd. dirs. 2004—, Silver medal of achievement San Diego (Calif.) chpt. 2002), Beta Beta Beta. Office Phone: 619-216-4650. Personal E-mail: granttree@yahoo.com.

MCGRAW, HAROLD W., III, (TERRY MCGRAW), information company executive; b. Summit, NJ, Aug. 30, 1948; s. Harold W. McGraw Jr.; m. Nancy Goodrich, Sept. 22, 1973; children: Harold W. IV, Megan G. BA, Tufts U., 1972; MBA, U. Pa., 1976. Fin. mgmt. staff GTE; asst. v.p. pension investment GTE Mgmt. Corp., McGraw-Hill, Inc., NYC, 1980-83, dir. corp. planning systems, 1983-84, v.p. corp. planning, 1984-85; group v.p., pub. transp. group McGraw-Hill Publs. Co., NYC, 1985-86, group v.p., pub. transp., aerospace and def. group, 1986-87, pres., 1987-88, McGraw-Hill Fin. Svcs. Co., NYC, 1988-89; exec. v.p. McGraw-Hill Cos., NYC, 1989-93, pres., COO, 1993-98, pres., CEO, 1998—, chmn., 1999—. Chmn., Bus. Roundtable, 2006-; bd. dirs. Mag. Publ. Am., Am. Bus. Press. Bd. dirs. Hartley House, N.Y.C., 1983—, Prep for Prep, Black Execs. Exchange Program, Nat. Actors Theatre; co-chmn. Carnegie Hall's Corp. Fund. Mem. Assn. Am. Publ. (bd. dirs.). Office: The McGraw Hill Companies Ste C3A 49th Fl 1221 Ave Americas New York NY 10020-1095 *

MCGRAW, HAROLD WHITTLESEY, JR., publishing executive; b. Bklyn., Jan. 10, 1918; s. Harold Whittlesey and Louise (Higgins) McG.; m. Anne Per-Lee, Nov. 30, 1940; children: Suzanne, Harold Whittlesey III, Thomas Per-Lee, Robert Pearce. AB, Princeton U., 1940. With G.M. Basford (advt. agy.), NYC, 1940-41, Brentano's Bookstores, Inc., 1946; with McGraw-Hill Book Co., Inc., NYC, 1947—, successively promotion mgr., dir. co. advt. and trade sales, 1947-55, dir., v.p. charge trade book, indsl. and bus. book depts., co. advt., 1955-61, sr. v.p., 1961-68, pres., 1968-74, McGraw-Hill, Inc., 1974-81, CEO, 1975-83, chmn., 1976-88; chairman emeritus, 1988—. Bd. dirs. McGraw Hill, Inc., 1954-88. Founder, pres., bd. dirs. Bus. Council Effective Literacy and Bus. Press Ednl. Found. Served as capt. USAAF, 1941-45. Mem.: Wee Burn Club (Darien, Conn.), Blind Brook Club (Purchase, N.Y.). Home: Watch Tower Rd Darien CT 06820 Office: The McGraw-Hill Cos 1221 Avenue Of The Americas New York NY 10020-1095

MCGRAW, JACK WILSON, federal agency administrator; b. Balt., May 19, 1943; s. P.W. and Nina (Gwinn) McG.; m. Nancy F. Foster, Aug. 31, 1974; children— David, Mark BA, Morris Harvey Coll., 1964; B.Div., Tex. Christian U., 1967. Ordained minister Christian Ch. (Disciples of Christ). Dir. temporary housing HUD, Washington, 1979-82; asst. assoc. dir. Fed. Emergency Mgmt. Agy., Washington, 1982, dep. asst. dir., 1982-83; dep. asst. adminstr. EPA Office Solid Waste and Emergency Response, Washington, 1983-88, acting asst. adminstr.; dep. regional adminstr. EPA Regional Office, Denver, 1988—2005, ret., 2005; prin., owner Jack McGraw and Assocs. LLC, Englewood, Colo., 2005—. Nominee William H. Jump award HUD, 1972; recipient Presdl. Meritorious award, Presdl. Disting. Exec. award. Presbyterian. Home: 8074 S Oneida Ct Englewood CO 80112-3128 Office: EPA Regional Office 8074 S Oneida Ct Englewood CO 80112

MCGRAW, PATRICK JOHN, judge; b. Detroit, Feb. 3, 1956; s. John William and Elizabeth Kay (Foley) McG.; m. Susan Elaine Borowiak, Jan. 14, 1978; children: Kelly Elizabeth, Ryan Patrick, Brandon David, Kyle Elaine. BS, Cen. Mich. U., 1979; JD, Cooley Law Sch., 1982. Bar: Mich. 1982. Ptnr. McGraw, Martin & Heyn, P.C., Saginaw, Mich., 1982-99; judge Probate Ct. 10th Jud. Cir., Saginaw, Mich., 1999—. Instr. Ctrl. Mich. U., Mt. Pleasant, Mich., 1986-90. Atty. Sch. Program, Saginaw, 1986—; bd. dirs. Saginaw YMCA, 2006—; bd. trustees Saginaw Twp., 1988-1999; sch. coun. mem. Saginaw Nouvel Cath. Ctrl. H.S., 1988-99; apptd. Mich. Bd. of Counseling, 1994-99, apptd. probate judge by Gov. Engler, 1999; elected probate judge, 2000. Mem. ABA, ATLA, Nat. Coll. Probate and Juvenile Judges, Mich. Bar Assn., Saginaw County Bar Assn., Mich. Probate Judges Assn., Phi Alpha Delta. Avocations: Karate (black belt), hunting, fishing, racquetball, computers. Home: 5220 Overhill Dr Saginaw MI 48603-1727 Office: Saginaw County Govtl Bldg 111 S Michigan Ave Saginaw MI 48602-2019 Office Phone: 989-790-5325. Business E-Mail: pmcgraw@saginawcounty.com.

MCGRAW, PHILLIP CALVIN See DR. PHIL

MCGRAW, SUSAN CATHERINE, interior designer; b. Long Beach, Calif., Apr. 16, 1945; d. Thomas Printis and Mary Ruth (Reese) Gregg; m. Don George McGraw, Nov. 21, 1964; children: DeAnna Coulombe, Katrina Daymude. Dental asst. diploma, Career Tng. Inst., 1964. Cert. interior designer, 1993. Ptnr., buyer The Corner, Garden Grove, Calif., 1971-79; interior designer Kris Noel & Assoc., Huntington Beach, Calif., 1980-85; owner, designer A.I. Designs, Huntington Beach, Calif., 1986-94; ptnr., designer Ross-McGraw Studio, Huntington Beach, Calif., 1994—, owner, designer, 1994—. Pres., ptnr. Red Tee Golf, Huntington Beach, 1998-2001. Bd. dirs. Parent Help USA, Huntington Beach, 1992, Serving People IN Need, 2006-07; sec. Seacliff Home Owners Assn., Huntington Beach, 1992-93; v.p. ways and means Friends of Huntington Youth Guild, Huntington Beach, 1994-96, pres., 1996-98; v.p. ways and means com. Friends of Huntington Youth Shelter, 2003-04. Mem. Am. Soc. Interior Design (profl. mem.). Home Phone: 562-592-1285; Office Phone: 562-592-2521. Business E-Mail: suemcgraw@socal.rr.com.

MCGRAW, TIM, country music singer; b. Delhi, La., May 1, 1967; s. Tug McGraw; m. Faith Hill, Oct. 6, 1996; children: Gracie Katherine, Maggie Elizabeth, Audrey Caroline. Musician: (albums) Tim McGraw, 1993, Not a Moment Too Soon, 1994 (triple-platinum, Album of Yr., Acad. Country Music, 1994), All I Want, 1995, Everywhere, 1997 (Album of Yr., Country Music Assn., 1998), A Place in the Sun, 1999 (Album of Yr., Country Music Assn., 1999), Tim McGraw Greatest Hits, 2000, Set the Circus Down, 2001 (Best Country Album, Am. Music Awards, 2002), Tim McGraw and the Dancehall Doctors, 2002, Live Like You Were Dying, 2004 (Most Inspiring Video of Yr., Country Music Television Music award, 2005, Single Record of Yr., Acad. Country Music Awards, 2005, Am. Music Awards Favorite Country Album, 2005), Tim McGraw Reflected Greatest Hits Vol. 2, 2006 (Favorite Country Album Am. Music Awards, 2006), (single) Welcome to the Club, 1992, It's Your Love, 1997 (Single & Song of Yr., Acad. Country Music, 1998), Grown Men, 2001 (Single of Yr., Radio Music Assn., 2001), Live Like You Were Dying, 2004 (Single & Song of Yr., Country Music Assn., 2004, Song of Yr., Acad. Country Music Awards, 2005), (with Nelly) Over and Over, 2004; vocal collaboration (with Faith Hill) Let's Make Love, 2001 (Grammy award, 2001); actor: (films) Black Cloud, 2004, Friday Night Lights, 2004, Flicka, 2006, (TV appearances) The Jeff Foxworthy Show, 1997. Recipient Favorite New Artist, Am. Music Awards, 1995, Favorite Male Country Artist, 2002, 2001, 2003, 2005, Top Male Vocalist, Acad. Country Music, 1994, 1999, 1998, Vocal Event of Yr., 1997, 1998, Country Music Assn., 1997, Male Vocalist of Yr., 1999, 2000, Entertainer of Yr., 2001, Male Artist of Yr., TNN/Music City News, 1999, Favorite Male Artist, Blockbuster Award, 2001, Country Male Artist, Radio Music Awards, 2003, Favorite Male Musical Performer, People's Choice Awards, 2004, Favorite Male Performer, 2006, Best Country Collaboration With Vocals (with Faith Hill), 2006. Office: care Curb Records 3907 W Alameda Ave Burbank CA 91505-4332 *

MCGREEVEY, JIM (JAMES EDWARD MCGREEVEY), former governor; b. Jersey City, Aug. 6, 1957; s. Jack and Veronica McGreevey; m. Karen J. Schutz, 1991 (div. 1997); 1 child, Morag Veronica; m. Dina Matos, 2000 (separated 2004); 1 child, Jacqueline Matos; life ptnr. Mark O'Donnell. BA, Columbia U., 1978; JD, Georgetown U., 1981; MEd, Harvard U., 1982; LLD (hon.), Rider U., 2002. Mem. NJ State Assembly (19th dist), Middlesex, 1990—91; mayor City of Woodbridge, NJ, 1992—2001; mem. NJ State Senate (19th dist.), 1994—97; gov. State of NJ, Trenton, 2002—04; ptnr. Weiner Lesniak LLP, Parsippany, NJ, 2004—05. Atty., regional mgr. Merck & Co., Rahway, N.J., 1987-91; exec.-in-residence, law & ethics, Kean U., 2007-. Co-author (with David France): The Confession, 2006. Campaign com. vol. State Legis. Campaigns, 1983, 85, 87; campaign vol. Middlesex County Freeholder reelection campaigns, 1983-88; atty., policy counsel Assembly Dem. Majority Office, 1983-84; campaign vol. speaker for Congressman Bernard J. Dwyer, 1984, 86, 88, Senator Frank R. Lautenberg, 1988, 94; former chmn. Ctrl. Jersey chpt. ARC. Mem. Nat. Conf. Christians and Jews (former chmn.), Middlesex County Cult and Heritage Commn. (former chmn.), N.J. League Nursing (former trustee), Diocese of Metuchen Cath. Lawyers Guild (past pres.). Democrat. *

MCGREEVEY, LISA S., investment company executive; BA, So. Methodist U. Spl. asst. to Pres. for polit. & intergovernmental affairs The White House, Washington; sr. legis. mgr. US Dept. Treasury, Washington, 1988—92; with Conf. State Bank Supervisors, 1992—99; exec. v.p. for external affairs, pres. Govt. Affairs Coun. The Fin. Services Roundtable, Washington, 1999—2006; exec. v.p., COO Managed Funds Assn., Washington, 2006—. Named one of The Top 40 Lobbyists, The Hill, 2004, The Most Powerful Women in Washington, US Banker, 2005.

MCGREGOR, DOUGLAS A., real estate company executive; Exec. v.p., dir. devel. & ops. The Rouse Co., Columbia, Md., 1989—. Office: The Rouse Co 10275 Little Patuxent Pkwy Columbia MD 21044-3455

MCGREGOR, DOUGLAS HUGH, pathologist, educator; b. Temple, Tex., Aug. 28, 1939; s. Harleigh Heath and Joyce Ellen (Lambert) McG.; m. Mizuki Kitani, July 6, 1969; children: Michelle Sakuya, David Kenji. BA, Duke U., 1961, MD, 1966; postgrad., U. Edinburgh, Scotland, 1961-62. Diplomate Am. Bd. Pathology. Intern, chief resident in pathology UCLA Med. Ctr., 1966-68; surgeon, lt. comdr. Atomic Bomb Casualty Commn., Hiroshima, Japan, 1968-71; chief resident in pathology Queens Med. Ctr., Honolulu, 1971-73; asst., assoc. prof. pathology U. Kans. Med. Ctr., Kansas City, 1973-82, prof., 1982—. Dir. anat. pathology VA Med. Ctr., Kansas City, Mo., 1975-94, chief pathology and lab. medicine, 1994-2003, dir. surg. pathology, 2003—. Contbr. numerous articles to profl. jours., chpts. to books. Leader YMCA Indian Princess Program, Overland Park, Kans., 1977-79, Indian Guide Program, 1978-80, Cub Scout Am., Overland Park, 1980-82, Boy Scouts Am., Leawood, Kans., 1982—. Lt. comdr. USPHS, 1968-71, Japan. Grantee Merck, Sharp and Dohme, 1980. Fellow Coll. Am. Pathologists, Am. Soc. Clin. Pathologists; mem. Am. Assn. Pathologists, Internat. Acad. Pathologists, Soc. Exptl. Biology and Medicine, N.Y. Acad. Scis., AAAS, Kansas City Soc. Pathologists (sec.-treas. 1982-83, pres. 1983-84), Leawood Country Club. Achievements include research in ultrastructure and pathobiology of neoplasms, radiation carcinogenesis, and morphogenesis of atherosclerosis. Home: 9400 Lee Blvd Shawnee Mission KS 66206-1826 Office: VA Med Ctr 4801 E Linwood Blvd Kansas City MO 64128-2226 Business E-Mail: douglas.mcgregor@med.va.gov.

MCGREGOR, EWAN GORDON, actor; b. Crieff, Perthshire, Scotland, Mar. 31, 1971; s. James and Carol McGregor; m. Eve Mavrakis, July 22, 1995; children: Clara Mathilde, Esther Rose; 1 adopted child. LLD, U. Ulster, 2001. Motion picture actor; stage actor; co-founder (with John Lee Miller, Sean Pertwee, Jude Law, Sadie Frost) Natural Nylon (prodn. co.). Actor: (films) Being Human, 1993, Shallow Grave, 1994, The Pillow Book, 1994, Blue Juice, 1995, Emma, 1996, Trainspotting, 1996 (Brit. Actor of Yr., 1996), Brassed Off, 1996, A Life Less Ordinary, 1997, Velvet Goldmine, 1998, Little Voice, 1998, Nora, 1999, Eye of the Beholder, 1999, Star Wars: Episode I-The Phantom Menace, 1999, Moulin Rouge, 2001 (European Film award for Achievement in World Cinema, 2001, Film Actor Award, The Variety Club Showbusiness Awards, 2002), Black Hawk Down, 2001, Star Wars: Episode II-Attack of the Clones, 2002, Down With Love, 2003, Young Adam, 2003, Big Fish, 2003, Star Wars: Episode III-Revenge of the Sith, 2005, The Island, 2005; voice (films) Robots, 2005, Valiant, 2005; actor: (films) Stay, 2005; others, (TV films) Lipstick on Your Collar, 1993, Doggin' Around, 1994, TV guest appearances include Tales from the Crypt, 1989, ER, 1994, Kavanagh QC, 1994; (plays) Guys and Dolls, 2005; actor: (TV films) Motor Bike: Round the World Trip, 2004; (films) The Tourist. Named No. 36 on the list "100 Top Movie Stars of All Time", Empire mag. (UK), 1997, No. 4 on the list, "British Culture's Top 50 Movers and Shakers", BBC 3, 2004; recipient ALFS award, 1997. Office: care Lindy King Drury House 34-43 Russell St Peters etc London WC2B 5HA England

MCGREGOR, JUDITH ANN, education educator; b. Pitts., Aug. 24, 1954; d. William James and Jeanne Harris McGregor. BS in Elem. Edn., Fla. State U., 1976, MS in Elem. Edn. with honors, 1977, PhD in Elem. Edn. with honors, 1992. Instr. Devel. Rsch. Sch., Fla. State U., Tallahassee, 1976—77; asst. prof. St. Petersburg Jr. Coll., Clearwater, 1978—80; instr. Fla. State U., 1981—82; asst. prof. Calif. State U., Long Beach, 1983—87, instr. Fullerton, 1990—91, asst. prof., supr. field work Dominguez Hills, 1992—. Pres. Jeanne Harris Entertainment, LA, 2006—; cons. in field of children and family TV and film. Author: Occupational Protrayal in Television: A Comparative Study of Children and Family Programs, 1993, (children's TV series) Whispie and Company (educational toys and goods), 1994. Mem.: NOW, NEA, AAUW, AAUP, Fla. State U. Alumni Assn. Avocations: skiing, rollerblading, kayaking, golf. Office: Brentwood Village 149 S Barrington Ave Ste 182 Los Angeles CA 90049 Office Phone: 310-650-0774.

MCGREGOR, RUTH VAN ROEKEL, state supreme court justice; b. Le Mars, Iowa, Apr. 4, 1943; d. Bernard and Marie Frances (Janssen) Van Roekel; m. Robert James McGregor, Aug. 15, 1965. BA summa cum laude, U. Iowa, 1964, MA, 1965; JD summa cum laude, Ariz. State U., 1974; LLM, U. Va., 1998. Bar: Ariz. 1974, U.S. Dist. Ct. Ariz. 1974, U.S. Ct. Appeals (9th cir.), U.S. Supreme Ct. 1982. Assoc. Fennemore, Craig, von Ammon, Udall & Powers, Phoenix, 1974-79, ptnr., 1980-81, 82-89; law clk. to justice Sandra Day O'Connor U.S. Supreme Ct., Washington, 1981-82; judge Ariz. Ct. Appeals, 1989-98, vice chief judge, 1993-95, chief judge, 1995-98; justice Ariz. Supreme Ct., 1998—, vice chief justice, 2002—05, chief justice, 2005—. Mem. disciplinary commn. Ariz. Supreme Ct., 1984-89, City of Mesa jud. adv. bd., 1997. Mem., newsletter editor Charter 100, Phoenix, 1981—; bd. dirs., mem. Ctr. for Law in Pub. Interest, Phoenix, 1977-80. Named Dwight D. Operman award for Top Judge in the Nation, Am. Judicature Soc., 2005. Mem. ABA (chmn. state memberships 1985-89; named fellow), Ariz. Bar Assn. (disciplinary com. 1984-89), Ariz. Judges Assn. (exec. com. 1990-98, sec. 1991-92, v.p. 1992-93, pres. 1993-94), Nat. Assn. Women Judges (chair first time attendees com. 1990-91, 1994 conv. com.; exec. com. 1995—), Ariz. Woman Lawyers Assn., 1975-. Democrat. Lutheran. Office: Ariz Supreme Ct 1501 W Washington St Phoenix AZ 85007-3231 *

MCGREGOR, SCOTT A., electronics company executive; BS, MS, Stanford Univ. Dir., interactive intelligence group Microsoft; sr. mgmt. Digital Equip. Corp., 1985—90; sr. v.p. & gen. mgr. Santa Cruz Ops., 1990—98; pres. & CEO, semiconductor div. Royal Philips Electronics, 2001—04; pres., CEO, dir. Broadcom Co., Irvine, Calif., 2005—. Office: Broadcom Co 16215 Alton Pkwy Irvine CA 92618 *

MCGRORY, MARY KATHLEEN, humanities educator, retired academic administrator; b. NYC, Mar. 22, 1933; d. Patrick Joseph and Mary Kate (Gilvary) McG. BA, Pace U., 1957; MA, U. Notre Dame, 1962; PhD, Columbia U., 1969; DHL, Albertus Magnus Coll., 1984; LLD, Briarwood Coll., 1990; DHL, Trinity Coll., 1991. Prof. English Western Conn. State U., Danbury, 1969-78; dean arts and scis. Ea. Conn. State U., Willimantic, 1978-80, v.p. for acad. affairs, 1981-85; pres. Hartford (Conn.) Coll. for Women, 1985-91; sr. fellow U. Va. Commonwealth Ctr., Charlottesville, 1991-92; exec. dir. Soc. Values in Higher Edn./Georgetown U., Washington, 1992-96; chair dept. rhetoric, lang. and culture U. Hartford, dir. profl. and tech. writing, humanities and writing educator, 2002—04, adj. faculty dept. rhetoric, lang., culture, 1999—. Pres. MKM Assocs., Holland, Mass., 1983—. Author: Yeats, Joyce & Beckett, 1975; editor The American Catholic, 2007—. Bd. dirs. Hartford Hosp., 1985-93; chmn. bd. govs. Greater Hartford Consortium Higher Edn., 1989-90. Fellow Fels Found., 1966-67, NEH, 1975; grantee Ludwig Vogelstein Found., 1973, Moseley Fedn., 2005. Mem. New Eng. Jr. Community and Tech. Coll. Coun. (v.p. 1988-91), Am. Assn. Higher Edn., Med. Acad. of Am., Greater Hartford C. of C. (bd. dirs. 1989-91), Hartford Club (bd. dirs. 1988-91). Avocations: writing, swimming, piano. Address: 44 Forest Dr Holland MA 01521-9702 Office Phone: 860-768-4415.

MCGRUDER, AARON, cartoonist; b. Chgo., May 29, 1974; Diploma, U. Md., 1997. Cartoonist, creator The Boondocks cartoon strip, 1996—. Co-author (with Riginald Hudlin): (novels) Birth of a Nation, 2004. Recipient Chmn.'s award, NAACP Image Awards, 2002. Office: The Boondocks Universal Press Syndicate 4520 Main St Kansas City MO 64111 Office Phone: 800-255-6734.

MCGUAN, KATHLEEN H., lawyer; b. May 9, 1954; BA, Am. U., 1975; MA in hist. musicology, U. Pa., 1978; JD, Cath. U., 1981. Bar: DC. Joined Reed Smith LLP, Washington, 1991, ptnr., 1994—. Office: Reed Smith LLP 1301 K St NW, Ste 1100 - East Tower Washington DC 20005 Office Phone: 202-414-9230. Office Fax: 202-414-9299. Business E-Mail: kmcguan@reedsmith.com.

MCGUCKIN, JOHN HUGH, JR., lawyer; b. Bryn Mawr, Pa., Nov. 8, 1946; AB magna cum laude, Harvard Coll., 1968, JD, 1971. Bar: Mass. 1971, Calif. 1973. Assoc. Orrick, Herrington, Rowley & Sutcliffe, 1972-79; sr. counsel legal divsn. Bank Am., 1979-81; exec. v.p., gen. counsel, corp. sec. UnionBanCal Corp./Union Bank Calif., N.A., San Francisco, 1981—. Adj. instr. Hastings Coll. Law U. Calif., 1980-82; judge pro tem San Francisco Superior Ct. Contbr. articles to profl. jours. Mem. ABA, State Bar Calif. (v.p., treas., bd. govs., chmn. subcom. duties and liabilities trustees probate and trust law sect. 1985-86, legal svcs. trust fund commn. 1989-90, minimum CLE com.), Assn. Corp. Coun. (chmn. 2003-04), Phi Beta Kappa. Office: Union Bank Calif NA 16th Fl 400 California St San Francisco CA 94104-1320

MCGUINN, EDWIN J., chemicals executive; b. 1953; BA in Math. and Econ., Colgate U.; MA in Acctg., N.Y. U. cert. CPA. Mng. dir. Lehman Brothers; mgmt. Mabon Securities, Rodman & Renshaw Capital Group, Inc.; exec. v.p., head ops. InterVest Securities, Inc.; pres., CEP Automated Trading Sys., Inc, eLot, Inc., Milford, Conn., 2000—.

MCGUINN, MARTIN GREGORY, retired bank executive, lawyer; b. Phila., Sept. 9, 1942; s. Martin G. and Rita (Horgan) McG.; m. Ann M. Muldoon, Sept. 17, 1977; children: Patrick J., Christopher M. AB, Villanova U., 1964, JD, 1967. Bar: Pa. 1967, NY 1970. Assoc. Sullivan & Cromwell, NYC, 1970-77; mng. counsel The Singer Co., Stamford, Conn., 1977-80; chmn., CEO Mellon Bank, Pitts., 1998—2006; CEO, chmn. Mellon Fin. Corp, Pitts., 1999—2006. Bd. consultors Villanova Law Sch., 1972—, chmn. 1985-87; bd. dirs. U.S.-Japan Bus. Coun., Inc., Allegheny Conf. on Cmty. Devel., chmn., 2003-05; chmn. Fed. Res. Adv. Bd., 2005. Editor in chief Villanova Law Rev., Vol. 12, 1966-67. Bd. dirs. UPMC Health Sys.; trustee Carnegie Mus. of Pitts.; chmn. Hist. Soc. Western Pa., 1997-2002. Mem. The Fin. Svcs. Roundtable (chmn. 2004-05), Fed. Reserve Adv. Bd. (chmn. 2005), Am. Soc. Corp. Secs. (chmn. 1990-91). Business E-Mail: mcguinn.m@mellon.com.

MCGUINN, MICHAEL EDWARD, III, retired army officer; b. Spartanburg, SC, Feb. 22, 1925; s. Michael Edward Jr. and Margaret Cordelia (Shackleford) McG.; m. Betty Gay Corn, 1948 (div. 1951); m. Phyllis Fryer, Oct. 7, 1952 (dec. July 1997); children: Michael Edward IV, Carol Anne McGuinn Branch. Student, Clemson U., SC, 1941-43, 46, Coll. William and Mary, Williamsburg, Va., 1962-63. Served with US Navy, PTO, 1943-46; commd. 2d lt. US Army, 1949, advanced through grades to col., 1971; asst. mil. attache Am. Embassy, Copenhagen, 1958-61; posted to svc. British Army, Longmoor, Eng., 1964-66; served on US Dept. Army Gen. Staff, Washington, 1966-68; comdr. 10th Transp. Bn. US Army, Vietnam, 1968-69; chief transp. div. US Readiness Command, MacDill AFB, Fla., 1969-72; ret. US Army, 1972; chief govt. svc. various locations, 1972-82; chief of staff Ga. State Def. Force, an Agy. of the State of Ga., Atlanta, 1987-95, 2002—05, comdg. gen., 2005—. Decorated Legion of Merit (2), Army Commendation medal (2), Naval Commendation medal; recipient Georgia Oglethorpe Disting. Sv c. medal, Ga. Meritorious Svc. medal. Mem.: US Army Transp. Mus. Avocations: history, photography, woodworking. Home and Office: 6420 Tanacrest Ct NW Atlanta GA 30328-2837 Personal E-mail: sdftrooper@comcast.net. *Since boyhood when a young cadet, I have lived by one code "Duty, Honor and Country". In good times and bad, it has kept me faithful to principles of personal responsibility, personal integrity, and the importance of service to something greater than oneself. The code has never failed our nation nor has it ever failed me.*

MCGUIRE, AMY CATHERINE, school psychologist; b. Upland, Calif., Aug. 22, 1976; d. Patrick Alfred and Janet Louise McGuire. BA in Psychology, Calif. State U., Fullerton, 1999; MA in Ednl. Psychology, Chapman U., Orange, Calif., 2002. Psychologist WACSEP, Whittier, Calif., 2002—. Liberal. Home Phone: 909-899-9294; Office Phone: 562-945-6431.

MCGUIRE, CHARLES EDWARD, musicology educator; b. Mpls., Nov. 24, 1969; s. Charles Leonard and Rose Marie White McGuire. MusB, BA, Oberlin Coll., Ohio, 1992; PhD, Harvard U., Cambridge, Mass., 1998. Asst. prof. James Madison U., Harrisonburg, Va., 2000—01; assoc. prof. musicology Oberlin Coll. Conservatory Music, 2001—. Author monograph and essays. Mem.: Elgar Soc., Am. Musicological Soc., N.Am. Brit. Music Studies Assn. (v.p. 2003—07). Office: Oberlin Coll Conservatory Music 77 W College St Oberlin OH 44074 Office Phone: 440-775-8252. Business E-Mail: cmcguire@oberlin.edu.

MCGUIRE, EDWARD DAVID, JR., lawyer; b. Waynesboro, Va., Apr. 11, 1948; s. Edward David and Mary Estelle (Angus) McG.; m. Karen Elizabeth Jacobson, Dec. 31, 2005; children: Matthew Edward, Kathryn Ann, Georgia Gail. BS in Commerce, U. Va., 1970; JD, Coll. William and Mary, 1973. Bar: Va. 1973, D.C. 1974, Md. 1990, Pa. 1995, U.S. Dist. Ct. (ea. dist.) Va. 1974, U.S. Dist. Ct. D.C. 1974, U.S. Dist. Ct. Md. 1990, Ct. Appeals (4th cir.) 1974, U.S. Ct. Appeals (D.C. cir.) 1974, U.S. Supreme Ct. 1993. Assoc. Wilkes and Artis, Washington, 1973-78; gen. corp counsel Mark Winkler Mgmt., Alexandria, Va., 1978-80; sr. contracts officer Amtrak, Washington, 1980-81; sr. real estate atty., asst. corp. sec. Peoples Drug Stores, Inc., Alexandria, 1981-88; of counsel Cowles, Rinaldi & Arnold, Ltd., Fairfax, Va., 1989-91; sr. assoc. Radigan, Rosenberg & Holmes, Arlington, Va., 1991; pvt. practice Annandale, Va., 1992-97, 2000—05; sr. assoc. Stein, Sperling, Bennett, DeJong, Driscoll, Greenfeig Metro, Rockville, Md., 1997-99; of counsel Hodes, Ulman, Pessin & Katz, P.A., Annandale, 1999-2000; mng. dir., personal trust adminstr. Riggs Bank, N.A., Washington, 2000—03; mng. dir., gen. counsel MFB Holdings, LLC, 2004—. Co-author: Legacy: Plan, Protect and Preserve Your Estate, 1995, Generations: Planning Your Legacy, 1998. Bd. dirs. Dist. XVI Va. Student Aid Found., 1978-85, George Washington dist. Boy Scouts Am., 1986; active William and Mary Law Sch. Assn., bd. dirs., 1983-96, pres., 1987-88, treas., 1990-91. Capt. JAGC, USANG, 1973-79. Mem. ABA, Va. Bar Assn., DC Bar, Md. State Bar Assn., Pa. Bar, William and Mary Alumni Soc. (bd. dirs. D.C. chpt. treas. 1992-94), U. Va. Club of Washington (schs. com. chmn. 1995—, v.p. outreach 1997-99, pres.-elect 1998-99, bd. dirs. 1996-99), Rotary (treas. Springfield chpt. 1985-86, sec. 1986-87, pres.-elect 1987, chmn. World Affairs Conf. 1985-88, bd. dirs. 1984-88, 96-97, Dist. 7610 youth leadership awards chmn. 1994-97, Outstanding Rotarian award 1985). Greek Orthodox. Avocations: racquetball, coaching youth sports. Home and Office: MFB Holdings LLC 14533 Bluebird Park Rd Windermere FL 34786 Office Phone: 407-456-3304, 202-246-6370. Personal E-mail: edwmcg31@aol.com.

MCGUIRE, JACK (JOHN F. MCGUIRE), international relief organization executive; m. Jane McGuire. BS in Chemistry, Iona Coll., 1968; MBA, Harvard U. With DuPont; mng. dir. UK and Belgium Johnson & Johnson Ortho Diagnostics Inc.; pres., CEO Hemasure Inc., 1997—2001; pres. Waltman PLC N.Am., 2001—04; exec. v.p. biomedical services Am. Red Cross, 2004—, interim pres., CEO, 2005—07. Capt. USMC. Recipient Disting. Svc. award, Am. Assn. Blood Banks, 2000. Avocations: golf, fly fishing. Office: American Red Cross National Headquarters 2025 E St NW Washington DC 20006 Office Phone: 202-303-5646. *

MCGUIRE, JOHN LAWRENCE, pharmaceutical executive; b. Kittanning, Pa., Nov. 3, 1942; s. Lawrence F. and Florence G. (Jones) McG.; m. Pamela Hale, Aug. 2, 1969; children: Megan L., Christa H. BS, Butler U., 1965; MA, Princeton U., 1968, PhD, 1969; postgrad., Columbia Sch. Bus., 1981. Asst. in instrn. Princeton U., 1967-69; pharmacologist Ortho Pharm. Corp., Raritan, NJ, 1969-72, sect. head molecular biology, 1972-75, exec. dir. rsch., 1975-80, v.p. preclin. R&D, 1980-88, bd. dirs., 1988—92; sr. v.p. global rsch. and devel., bd. dirs. R.W. Johnson Pharm. Rsch. Inst., Raritan, 1988-92; corp. v.p. bus. devel., pharm./diagnostics group Johnson & Johnson, New Brunswick, NJ, 1992—2004; pres. Ferring Rsch. Insts., Lausanne, Switzerland, 2004—; exec. com. Ferring Pharm. Corp., Lausanne, 2004—; bd. dirs. Ferring Holding SA, St. Prex, Switzerland, 2005—. Adj. assoc. prof. dept. medicine M.S. Hershey Sch. Medicine Pa. State U., 1978—; adj. prof. dept. animal sci. Rutgers U., 1983-92, ob-gyn. East Va. Med. Sch., 1987—, ob-gyn. and reproductive endocrinology U. Medicine and Dentistry of NJ, 1988—; cons. NASA, 1985-87; cons. Nat. Tech. Transfer Ctr., 1997-2000; bd. dirs. MDAdvantage Ins. Co., Lawrenceville, N.J. Mem. editl. bd. Ullman's Ency. Indsl. Chemistry, 1987—; editor numerous books; contbr. articles to profl. jours.; patentee in field. Trustee Hunterdon Med. Ctr. Found., 1986—, chmn., 2002—; trustee NJ State Hosp. Assn., 2002—, NJ State Theater, New Brunswick, 2002—06, August Found., 1997—, pres., 1997—; trustee Raritan Valley CC, North Branch, NJ, 1986—, vice chmn., 1990—2005, chmn., 2005—; trustee Hunterdon Med. Ctr., Flemington, NJ, 1978—2002, vice chmn., 1984—86, chmn., 1988—98; trustee Hunterdon Health Care Sys., Flemington, NJ, 1986—, chmn., 1989—2002; trustee Atlantic Health Sys., Morristown, NJ, 1991—93, vice chmn., 1992—93; trustee The Pennington Sch., NJ, 1995—, pres., CEO, 1996—; exec. bd. Keystone Area coun. Boy Scouts Am., Harrisburg, Pa., exec. bd. George Washington coun. Trenton, NJ, 1980—86, 1995—99, exec. bd. Ctrl. N.J. coun. Princeton, 1999—, pres., 2000—05, mem. N.E. Region bd., 2004—; bd. dirs. United Way of Hunterdon County, NJ, 1983—97, pres. NJ, 1985—87; bd. dirs. Tri-State United Way, NY, 1987—94, Hunterdon County YMCA, NJ, 1982—87, Mid Jersey Health Corp., 1986—88, chmn., 1986—88; bd. visitors Butler U., Indpls., 2004—. Named NJ Hosp. Trustee of Yr., 2001; recipient Silver Beaver award, Boy Scouts Am., 1984, Disting. Eagle Scout award, 2000, Silver Antelope award, 2006, Johnson medal for rsch. and devel., 1990; Population Coun. fellow, 1969. Mem. Am. Soc. Pharmacology and Exptl. Therapeutics, Soc. Exptl. Biology and Medicine, Am. Physiol. Soc., Endocrine Soc., Am. Coll. Ob-Gyn, Am. Soc. Clin. Pharmacology and Therapetics, Soc. Gynecol. Investigation, Licensing Execs. Soc., Biochemistry Soc. Great Britain, Royal Soc. Medicine (UK), Am. Chem. Soc. Clubs: Princeton (NYC). Home: 10 Club House Dr Whitehouse Station NJ 08889-3378 Personal E-mail: John.McGuire@Ferring.com.

MCGUIRE, JOHN THOMAS, lawyer, educator, writer; b. Bronx, NY, Oct. 12, 1966; s. Thomas John and Irene McGuire. BA History magna cum laude, U. Scranton, 1988, MA History, 1988; JD cum laude, U. Buffalo, 1991; PhD Am. History, Binghamton U., 2001. Bar: N.Y. 1991. Trial atty. U.S. Dept. Justice, Washington, 1991—95; pvt. practice Vestal, NY, 1995—. Bd. dirs. Legal Svcs. Ctrl. N.Y., Legal Aid Soc. Mid. N.Y., 2004-07; adj. prof. SUNY, Oneonta, 2000-05, Tampkins-Cortland C.C., 2005—. Author: Making the Democratic Party a Partner: Eleanor Roosevelt the WJLC and the Women's Division of the New York State Democratic Party, 2001, From The Courts to The State Legislatures: Social Justice Feminism, Labor Legislation and The 1920's, 2004, Two Feminist Visions, Social Justice Feminism and Equal Rights, 1899-1940, 2004, Caught in the Middle: Sue Shelton White and the Conflict Between Social Justice Feminism and Equal Rights in New Deal Politics, 2005, Making the Case for Night Work Legislation in Progressive Era New York State, 1911-1915, 2006; contbr.: Historical Dictionary of the Gilded Age, 2003, Encyclopedia of New York State, 2003, Historical Encyclopedia of the Gilded Age and Progressive Era, 2003, Encyclopedia of World War I, 2005; reviewer American Jewish History, 1998, Labor History, 2004, Jour. Women's History, 2005, Jour. So. History, 2007;, author of poems. V.p. Peace Action NY, 2003-05, sec. 2005-07; pres. Broome County Peace Action, 2004-2006 Recipient Philip S. Klein Article prize Pa. Hist. Assn., 2005; rsch. grantee State Hist. Soc. Iowa, 2004; James A. Finnegan fellow, 1987, Albert M. Greenfield Rsch. fellow, 2003, Archie K. Davis Rsch. fellow, 2004, 06. Mem. N.Y. State Bar Assn., Orgn. Am. Historians, Order of Barristers, Alpha Sigma Nu. Home: 422 Clubhouse Rd Vestal NY 13850-3727 Personal E-mail: johnmcguireus@yahoo.com.

MCGUIRE, JOHN W., SR., advertising executive, marketing professional, writer; b. Chgo., May 12, 1952; s. Eugene H. Sr. and Marjorie (Bolger) McG.; m. Mary Sue Roper, June 17, 1972 (div. 1977); 1 child, John William Jr.; m. Lynn L. Rembos, June 21, 1984 (div. April 1991); children: Kelly Lynn, Ryan Michael. AA, Chgo. City Colls., 1972; BA, Northeastern Ill., Chgo., 1974. Janitor Bd. of Edn., Chgo., 1970-74; sales rep. Motorola Comms., Inc., Schaumburg, Ill., 1974-76, Pattis Group, Chgo., 1976-77; midwest sales mgr. Harcourt Brace Jovanovich Pub. Co., NYC, 1977-79; account sales mgr. Cosmopolitan Mag. Hearst Pub. Co., NYC, 1979-81; midwest acct. mgr. Psychology Today Mag. Ziff-Davis Pub. Co., NYC, 1981-82; midwest regional mgr. Pennwell Pub. Co., Tulsa, Okla., 1982-84; western regional sales mgr. Nursing Mgmt. Mag. SN Pub. Co., West Dundee, Ill., 1984-91; western regional sales mgr., midwest regional sales mgr. U.S. Pharmacist Mag. Jobson Pub. Co., NYC, 1991-98; v.p. SK&A Info. Svcs., Irvine, Calif., 1998-99; assoc. pub. Health Mgmt. Technology Mag. Nelson Pub., Nokomis, Fla., 1999; pres., CEO Blossom Pub. Co., Wasco, Ill., 2000—. Author: (book) One Man's Life: A Poetic Review, 1995; co-author: (with Scott Mennie) The Original Parent and Family Logbook, 2002; singer (cassette tapes), designer (creative posters). With USN, 1970. Mem. VFW, Midwest Healthcare Mktg., Arlington Poetry Project. Republican. Roman Catholic. Avocations: writing, scuba diving, horseback riding, travel, skydiving.

MCGUIRE, KANDACE PETERSON, surgeon; b. Danbury, Conn., Sept. 7, 1976; d. John and Katherine Peterson; m. Phillip McGuire, June 12, 2004. MD, Ea. Va. Med. Sch., Norfolk, 2002. Surg. resident Thomas Jefferson U. Hosp., Phila., 2002—, chief surg. resident, 2007—. Contbr. chapters to books, articles to profl. jours. Recipient Resident Tchg. award, Thomas Jefferson U. Hosp., Dept. Surgery, 2005—06. Mem.: ACS, Assn. Acad. Surgery, Alpha Omega Alpha. Office: Thomas Jefferson Univ 1015 Walnut St Curtis 620 Philadelphia PA 19107 Office Phone: 215-317-4203.

MCGUIRE, KATHERINE ANN, academic administrator, voice educator; d. Dale Brian and Carol Ann Truett, Lila Jean Truett (Stepmother) and Darrell Lindborg (Stepfather); m. Clinton Hoke McGuire, July 19, 2003; 1 child, Ian Thomas. BA in Psychology, U. Tex., San Antonio, 1993, MS in Pharmacology, 1997; MusM, Appalachian State U., Boone, NC, 2004. Sr. R & D technician Greer Labs., Inc., Lenoir, NC, 1997—99; adj. instr. ednl. stats. Appalachian State U., Boone, 1999—2000; asst. dir. instl. rsch. Wash. and Lee U., Lexington, Va., 2002—; instr. applied voice So. Va. U., Buena Vista, 2006—. Recipient Prism Talent scholarship, Appalachian State U., 2001—02; grantee, 2000. Mem.: Am. Musicological Soc., Nat. Assn. Tchrs. of Singing, Phi Theta Kappa, Pi Kappa Lambda. Office: Washington and Lee Univ 204 W Washington St #207 Lexington VA 24450 Home Phone: 540-464-5640; Office Phone: 540-458-8184.

MCGUIRE, KATHLEEN ALISON, conductor; b. Melbourne, Australia, May 22, 1965; d. Frank Leonard McGuire and Jeanette Mary Tilson. MusB, U. Melbourne, 1987; grad. diploma arts in music, Victorian Coll. Arts, U. Melbourne, 1990; grad. diploma in edn., Monash U., Melbourne, 1992; MusM with Distinction, U. Surrey, Guildford, UK, 1995; Dr. in Mus. Arts, U. Colo., 2000. Cert. preparing future faculty U. of Colo. at Boulder, 2000, grad. tchr. cert. U. Colo., Boulder, 2000. Music educator Sacre Coeur Girls' Sch., Melbourne, Victoria, Australia, 1983—86; educator Our Lady of Mercy Coll., 1986; music dir. Mentone Old Time Theatre Soc., Melbourne, Victoria, Australia, 1985—88; educator Killester Coll., Melbourne, Victoria, Australia, 1987; music educator Sacred Heart Regional Girls' Coll., Melbourne, Victoria, Australia, 1988; educator Mentone Girls' Secondary Coll., Melbourne, Victoria, Australia, 1988—89; music tchr. McKinnon Secondary Coll., Melbourne, Victoria, Australia, 1988—90, Mentone Girls' Grammar Sch., Melbourne, Victoria, Australia, 1990—94; dir. of music Sandringham East Primary Sch., Melbourne, Victoria, Australia, 1988—89; condr. Musical Theatre Soc., U. Surrey, Guildford, Sussex, England, 1994—95; asst. condr. Symphony Orch., U. Surrey, Guildford, Sussex, England, 1994—95; condr. Wind Symphony, U. of Surrey, Guildford, Sussex, 1994—95; educator Parkdale Secondary Coll., Melbourne, Victoria, Australia, 1995; music dir. St. Aidan's Episcopal Ch., Boulder, Colo., 1996—2000; asst. condr. U. of Colo. at Boulder Symphony Orch., Boulder, Colo., 1996—2000; assoc. condr. Lakewood Symphony Orch., Denver, 1996—2000; artistic dir./condr. The Rainbow Chorus, Fort Collins, Colo., 1997—2000; asst. condr. Lyric Theatre, U. Colo., Boulder, Colo., 1997—2000; assoc. condr. New Music Ensemble, U. of Colo., Boulder, Colo., 1998—2000; lead grad. tchr. U. of Colo. at Boulder, 1999—2000; assoc. condr. Boulder Youth Symphony, Boulder, Colo., 1999—2000; artistic dir., condr. San Francisco Gay Men's Chorus, 2000—; condr. Opera By the Bay, Marin, Calif., 2001, Cmty. Women's Orch., San Francisco, 2005—; music tchr. Convent of the Sacred Heart H.S., San Francisco, 2004—07; music dir. Melbourne U. Choral Soc., Melbourne, Victoria, Australia, Mordialloc Light Opera Co., Melbourne, Victoria, Australia, Nova Theatre, Melbourne, Victoria, Australia, Whitehorse Mus. Theatre, Melbourne, Victoria, Australia; condr., founder Victorian Women's Orch., Melbourne, Victoria, Australia; condr. Kew Philharm. Orch., Melbourne, Victoria, Australia, Steamboat Springs Cmty. Orch.; music dir. Festival Theatre Co., Melbourne, Victoria, Australia, Renaissance Opera Co., Melbourne, Victoria, Australia, Viola Operatic Soc., Melbourne, Victoria, Australia, Melbourne Opera Co., Melbourne, Victoria, Australia, Melbourne Dancers Co., Melbourne, Victoria, Australia, CLOC Musical Theatre, Melbourne, Victoria, Australia, Gilbert and Sullivan Soc., Melbourne, Victoria, Australia, Melbourne U. Gilbert and Sullivan Soc., Melbourne, Victoria, Australia; asst. condr. St. Aidan's Anglican Ch., Melbourne, Victoria, Australia; music dir. Altona City Theatre, Melbourne, Victoria, Australia, Lyric Opera, Melbourne, Victoria, Australia. Instrumentalist Marie Wilson Band, Melbourne, Victoria, Australia, 1992—94; guest condr. for lighting Guildford Philharm., Guildford, Surrey, England, 1995; guest condr. Rocky Mountain Ctr. Mus. Arts, Boulder, Colo., 1996, Boulder Philharm., Boulder, 1996; condr. & founder Colo. Quilt Chorus, Denver, 1997; guest condr. Golden Gate Opera, San Francisco, 2001, Women's Philharm., San Francisco, 2001—02, Sacramento Ballet & Empyrean Ensemble, Sacramento, 2002, Gay Games & Cultural Festival, Sydney, 2002, Chgo., 06, Goat Hall Prodns., San Francisco, 2002, Cmty. Women's Orch., San Francisco, 2005, Victorian Music Theatre Guild Awards, Melbourne, Victoria, Australia, Royal Women's Hosp. Fundraiser, Melbourne, Fairfield Hosp. Fundraiser, Melbourne, Ann. AIDS Requiem Svcs., Melbourne; asst. condr. Byrd-Cage Singers, Melbourne; cantor Toorak Uniting Ch. Choir, Melbourne; condr. Malvern City Coun. - ann. fundraiser, Melbourne; instrumentalist Frankston City Band, Melbourne, Mordialloc City Band, Melbourne, Moomba Youth Band, Melbourne, Victoria, Australia; asst. condr. Intervarsity Choral Festival, Melbourne; instrumentalist Yamaha Youth Music Festival, Melbourne. Arranger (choral music concert suite) SFGMC Does Queen, (choral music) We Shall Overcome, Turn the World Around by Harry Belafonte, Every Time I Feel the Spirit, Harriet Tubman, Silent Night, Land of the Free, Peace Like a River; editor: (choral music) (by Gareth Valentine) Requiem in Memory of Those Who Have Died of AIDS; contbr. article to profl. jour., CD insert, ednl. pubs., electronic newsletter; prodr.: (comml. compact disc recording) Home for the Holidays (winner, OutMusic award, Outstanding New Choral Recording, 2006), Oh, Happy Day! (finalist OutMusic awards, Outstanding New Recording, choir or chorus, 2005), Closer Than Ever (winner, OutMusic Awards, Outstanding New Recording, choir or chorus, 2005); prodr.: (comml. compact disc recording) Divas' Revenge; prodr.(and arranger): (comml. compact disc recording) SFGMC Does Queen (finalist, Outstanding new choral rec., OutMusic awards, 2002); contbr. comml. compact disc recording (Wash. Area Music award and finalist, Outstanding New Rec., OutMusic awards, 2001); composer: (choral music) Magnificat, On Love, May God Shield You, Don't Ask, Don't Tell; music dir. (comml. compact disc recordings) Beginnings, Five Years for Freedom, St. Aidan's Prayer for Lindisfarne. Mem. Bay Area Cmty. Women, San Francisco; grand marshal San Francisco Pride, 2006; musician City of Refuge United Ch. Christ, San Francisco, 2004—; bd. mem. Gay and Lesbian Assn. Choruses, Washington, 2002—03; ex-officio bd. mem. Golden Gate Performing Arts, Inc., San Francisco, 2000—. Fellow Enrollment Enhancement fellowship, U. of Colo., Coll. of Music, 1996 - 1997; Ambassadorial fellow, Rotary Internat., 1994 - 1995, Writing fellow, Choral Jour., Florence Bradford scholar, U. Melbourne, 1991, Ivy-May Pendlebury scholar, 1985. Mem.: ASCAP, Coll. Music Soc., Am. Choral Dirs. Assn., Gay and Lesbian Assn. Choruses, Inc., Am. Symphony Orch. League, Conductors Guild. Achievements include first appointed woman conductor and artistic director of the world's oldest and largest openly gay men's chorus (founded 1978); was one of the same-sex couples married at San Francisco City Hall, February 23, 2004; conducted the Australian premiere of the rock opera, Metropolis; conducted the U.S. and Australian premieres of the world's first AIDS Requiem (by Gareth Valentine - composed in 1991); conducted the Australian premiere of The Apple Tree by Jerry Bock; arranged for men's chorus and conducted John Rutter's renowned Gloria in honor of the work's 30th anniversary (December, 2004); founder of Australia's first women's orchestra; conducted performances at Carnegie Hall (NY), Kennedy Center (DC), Davies Symphony Hall (San Francisco), Salle Wilfrid Pelletier (Montreal, Canada), Grace Cathedral (San Francisco); conducted the Sacramento Ballet and the Empyrean Ensemble at the inaugural season of the Mondavi Center, Sacramento, CA; conducted a choir of 560 voices at the Sydney Opera House (Australia) for Gay Games VI (November, 2002); opening ceremonies Chgo. Gay Games VII (July 2006); performed with many celebrities, including: Carol Channing, Sir Ian McKellen, Alan Cumming, Joanna Gleason, Sharon Gless, B.D. Wong, Armistead Maupin, Nichelle Nichols, Julie Newmar, Cris Williamson; arranged music that has been performed by premier artists, including: Turtle Creek Chorale, Pot Pourri, Les Ms, Boston Gay Men's Chorus, Men Alive, Metropolitan Community Church Choir of San Francisco; arranged music performed by artists including: San Diego Men's Chorus, Atlanta Gay Men's Chorus, Buffalo Gay Men's Chorus, Seattle Men's Chorus, Houston Gay Men's Chorus, Twin Cities Gay Men's Chorus; arranged music performed by artists including: Lesbian/Gay Chorus San Francisco, Oakland Eastbay Gay Men's Chorus, Phila. Gay Men's Chorus, Rochester Gay Men's Chorus, Vancouver Men's Chorus; conducted a choir of 80 at Rosie O'Donnell's wedding at San Francisco City Hall, February 2004; completed AIDS Life Cycle V 585 mile bicycle ride from San Francisco to Los Angeles June 2006. Avocations: travel, culinary arts, outdoor sports, crossword puzzles. Office: Golden Gate Performing Arts Inc 1800 Market St PMB 1000 San Francisco CA 94102 Office Phone: 415-865-3653.

MCGUIRE, MARK M., lawyer, manufacturing executive; BA with distinction in Psychology, George Washington U.; JD, U. Va. Sch. Law. Ptnr. Powell, Goldstein, Frazer & Murphy, Atlanta; with Internat. Paper Co., 1992—2005, gen. counsel Europe, assoc. gen. counsel, v.p., dep. counsel, 2003—05; v.p., gen. counsel Eaton Corp., Cleve., 2005—. J. Hardy Dillard Fellow, U. Va. Sch. Law. Office: Eaton Corp 1111 Superior Ave Cleveland OH 44114-2584 Office Phone: 216-523-4376. *

MCGUIRE, MICHAEL FRANCIS, plastic surgeon; b. St. Louis, Oct. 4, 1946; s. Arthur Patrick and Virginia Claribel (Gannon) McG. BA, Columbia U., 1968, MD, 1972. Diplomate Am. Bd. Surgery, Am. Bd. Plastic Surgery. Intern UCLA, 1972-73, resident in gen. surgery, 1973-77, resident in plastic surgery, 1978-80; fellow in plastic surgery rsch. Stanford (Calif.) U., 1977-78; traveling fellow in plastic surgery Gt. Britain, 1980; chief plastic surgery L.A. County-Olive View Med. Ctr., Sylmar, Calif., 1980-85; pvt. practice Santa Monica, Calif., 1980—; chief plastic surgery St. John's Health Ctr., 1990—; asst. clin. prof. surgery UCLA, 1980-97, assoc. clin. prof., 1998—. Bd. dirs. Calif. Med. Rev., Inc., sec.-treas., 1997, v.p., 1997-99, chmn. bd. dirs. 1999-2003; chmn. surg. rev. St. Johns Health Ctr., 1996-98, chief plastic surgery, 1992-; pres. Pacific Coast Plastic Surgery Ctr., 1988—. Charter patron LA Music Ctr. Opera, 1983—; sponsoring patron LA County Art Mus., 1986—2005; patron Colleague Helpers in Philanthropic Svc., Bel Air, Calif., 1987, 93, 95; pres. Found. for Surg. Reconstrn., 1996-. Fellow ACS, Royal Soc. Medicine; mem. Am. Soc. Plastic Surgeons (membership chmn. 1997-2000, bd. dirs. 2002-05, sec. 2005-2007, chmn. leadership devel. com. 2004-), Am. Soc. Aesthetic Plastic Surgery (ethics chmn. 1998-99, bd. dirs. 2004—07, pub. edn. chmn. 2004-05, commr. comm., 2005-2007, publications chair, 2007-), Am. Health Quality Assn. (bd. dirs. 1999—2005), LA County Med. Assn. (v.p. 1995-97, sec.-treas. 1997-99), Calif. Med. Assn. (del., exec. com., splty. delegation 1994-99), Calif. Soc. Plastic Surgery (exec. com., auditor 1988-89, program chmn. 1990, exec. coun. 1991-94, treas. 1994-97, v.p. 1997-98, acting pres. 1997, pres.-elect 1998-99, pres. 1999-2000, nominating com. chmn. 2000-01, strategic planning com. chmn. 2001—), Am. Assn. Accreditation of Ambulatory Surgery Facilities (ops. com. 1995-96, bd. dirs. 1996-2006, treas. 1996-98, sec. 1998-2000, v.p. 2000-02, pres. 2002-04), Surgery Facilities Resources (founding pres. 2005-), Alpha Omega Alpha. Avocations: golf, travel, collecting antique glass, opera, art. Office: 1301 20th St Ste 460 Santa Monica CA 90404-2054 Office Phone: 310-315-0121. Business E-Mail: mmcguire@ucla.edu.

MCGUIRE, MICHAEL JOHN, environmental engineer; b. San Antonio, June 29, 1947; s. James Brendan and Opal Mary (Brady) McG.; m. Deborah Marrow, June 19, 1971; children: David, Anna. BS in Civil Engring., U. Pa., 1969; MS in Environ. Engring., Drexel U., 1972, PhD in Environ. Engring., 1977. Diplomate Am. Acad. Environ. Engring.; registered profl. engr., Pa., N.J., Calif., Ariz., Tex. San. engr. Phila. Water Dept., 1969-73; rsch. assoc. Drexel U., Phila., 1976-77; prin. engr. Brown & Caldwell Cons. Engrs., Pasadena, Calif., 1977-79; water quality engr. Met. Water Dist. of So. Calif., LA, 1979-84, water quality mgr., 1984-86, dir. water quality, 1986-90, asst. gen. mgr., 1990-92; pres. McGuire Environ. Cons., Inc., Santa Monica, Calif., 1992—2005; v.p. McGuire Malcolm Pirnie, Inc., Santa Monica, 2005—. Cons. to subcom. on adsorbents, safe drinking water com. Nat. Acad. Scis., 1978-79, NRC, Drinking Water Contaminants (comm. mem.), 1998-99; cons. mem. Techs. Workgroup U.S. EPA, DBP Reg. Neg., 1992-93, 97, 98-2000. Editor: (with I.H. Suffet) Activated Carbon Adsorption of Organics from the Aqueous Phase, 2 vols., 1980, Treatment of Water by Granular Activated Carbon, 1983, (with J.L. McLain and A. Obolensky) Information Collection Rule Data Analysis, 2003; contbr. articles to profl. jours. Recipient Best Paper award, WQTD, 2007. Mem. ASCE, Internat. Water Assn. (specialist group on taste and odor control 1982—, chmn. organizing com. 1991, off-flavor symposium 1987-91), Internat. Ozone Assn. (internat. bd. dirs. 1992-95), Am. Water Works Assn. (hon., Calif.-Nev. sect. chmn. water quality and resources divsn. 1982-83, governing bd. 1984-87, 89-96, exec. com. 1989-96, chmn. 1991-92, nat. edn. divsn. chmn. 1982-83, dir. 1994-96, chair taste and odor com. 1993-98, exec. com. 1994-96, water quality and tech. divsn. trustee 2004—, Acad. Achievement award 1978, Fuller award 1994, Publs. award 2001, George A. Elliot award 2005, Hon. Membership award 2006, WQTD Best Paper award 2007), Am. Chem. Soc., Sigma Xi, Sigma Nu, Sigma Tau.

MCGUIRE, MICHAEL WILLIAM, communications executive; b. Pomona, Calif., Aug. 1, 1960; s. Frederick L. and Anna Belle (Crum) McG.; m. Victoria Jean Von Tobel; children: Gordon, Michael Jr. BA in Polit. Sci., U. San Diego, 1984. Spokesman, dir. Congl. affairs Voice of Am., Washington, 1986-88; owner, chief exec. officer McGuire Rsch. Svcs., Las Vegas, Denver and, San Francisco, Washington, 1988—. Cons. various U.S. and multinat. corps. Cons. various candidates for pub. office, 1988. Mem. Hiwan Golf Club. Office: 3264 Keha Dr Kihei HI 96753

MCGUIRE, RAYMOND J., investment banker; b. Dayton, Ohio; AB cum laude, Harvard Coll., 1979; MBA, Harvard Bus. Sch., 1984; JD, Harvard Law Sch., 1984. With Mergers & Acquisitions Group First Boston Corp., 1984—88; joined Wasserstein Perella & Co., 1988, ptnr., mng. dir., 1991—94; mng. dir. Mergers & Acquisitions Group Merrill Lynch, 1994—2000, Morgan Stanley, NYC, 2000—05; co-head Global Investment Banking Citigroup, 2005—. Pres. bd. trustees Internat. Ctr. Photography; trustee Whitney Mus. Am. Art, mem. investment com.; trustee NY Presbyterian Hosp., Enterprise Found.; chmn. Studio Mus. Harlem, bd. dir.; chmn. De LaSalle Acad., bd. dir., The Enterprise Found., Joseph & Claire Flom Found., Howard Gilman Found.; mem. overseers, dirs. nominating com. Harvard U. Recipient Rotary Fellowship, U. of Nice, France, 1980. Office: Citigroup 388 Greenwich St New York NY 10013

MCGUIRE, ROBIN K., engineering company executive; SB in Civil Engring., MIT, Cambridge; MS in Structural Engring., U. Calif., Berkeley, 1969; PhD in Structural Engring., MIT, Cambridge. Pres., prin. Risk Engring., Inc., Boulder, Colo., 1984—. Author: Seismic Hazard and Risk Analysis, 2004. Mem.: NAE. Office: Risk Engring Inc 4155 Darley Ave Ste A Boulder CO 80305 Office Phone: 303-499-3000. Office Fax: 303-499-4850. *

MCGUIRE, SANDRA LYNN, nursing educator; b. Jan. 28, 1947; d. Donald Armstrong and Mary Lue (Harvey) Johnson; m. Joseph L. McGuire, Mar. 6, 1976; children: Matthew, Kelly, Kerry. BSN, U. Mich., 1969, MPH, 1973, EdD, 1988, MSN, 1997. Staff nurse Univ. Hosp., Ann Arbor, Mich., 1969; pub. health nurse Wayne County Health Dept., Eloise, Mich., 1969—72; instr. Madonna Coll., Livonia, Mich., 1973; pub. health coord. Plymouth Ctr. for Human devel., Northville, Mich., 1974—75; asst. prof. cmty. health nursing U. Mich., Ann Arbor, 1975—83; asst. prof. U. Tenn., Knoxville, 1983—88, assoc. prof., 1990—2007, prof., 2007—, coord. gerontol. nurse practitioners program, 1998—, chair MSN program Coll. Nursing. Dir. Kids Are Tomorrow's Srs. Program, 1988—; resource person Gov.'s Com. Unification of Mental Health Svcs. in Mich.; spkr. profl. assns. and workshops; mem. Coun. Accreditation Nurse Anesthesia Ednl. Programs, 2007—. Author (with S. Clemen-Stone and D. Eigsti)): Comprehensive Community Health Nursing, 1981, Comprehensive Community Health Nursing, 5th edit., 1998, Comprehensive Community Health Nursing, 6th edit., 2002. Bd. dirs. Ctr. Understanding Aging, 1987-93, v.p., 1995; bd. dirs. Mich. chpt. ARC, 1980-83, Knoxville chpt., 1984-85; founder Knoxville Intergenerational Network, 1989; mem. nat. policy coun. AARP, 2006-. Recipient John W. Runyan, Jr. Cmty. Health Nursing award U. Tenn. Memphis, 2002, Outstanding Svc. award U. Tenn. Knoxville Libr. Friends, 2004; USPHS fellow, 1972-73, Robert Woodruff fellow Emory U., 1996-97, Hewlett Innovative Tech. fellow U. Tenn., Knoxville, 1999-00, Profl. Devel. awardee U. Tenn. Knoxville, 1996-97, 99-2000. Mem. ANA, AARP Nat. Policy Coun., Tenn. Nurses Assn., Soc. Gerontological Soc. Am., Assn. Gerontology, Nat. Conf. Gerontol. Nurse Practitioner, Nat. Gerontol. Nursing Assn., Coun. on Accreditation Nurse Anesthesia Programs, Mich. Pub. Health Assn. (chmn. mental health sect. 1976, dir., co-chmn. residential svcs. com. 1976-79, chmn. health svcs. 1979-82), Nat. Assn. Retarded Citizens, Mich. Assn. Retarded Citizens, Nat. Coun. on Aging, Ctr. for Understanding Aging (v.p. 1994-95), Plymouth (chmn. residential svcs. com. 1975-77), Tenn. Assn. Retarded Citizens, So. Nursing Rsch. Soc., Sigma Theta Tau, Pi Lambda Theta, Phi Kappa Phi. Home: 11008 Crosswind Dr Knoxville TN 37934 Office: 1200 Volunteer Blvd Knoxville TN 37996 Office Phone: 865-974-7589. Business E-Mail: smcguire@utk.edu.

MCGUIRE, SARAH LEA, biology professor; married; 1 child. BA, Miss. Coll.; MA, U. So. Miss.; PhD, Baylor Coll. Medicine. Faculty mem. to prof. biology Millsaps Coll., Jackson, Miss., 1995—. Contbr. articles to sci. jours. Recipient US Prof. of Yr. award, Carnegie Found. for Advancement of Tchg. and Coun. for Advancement and Support of Edn., 2006. Mem.: Miss. Acad. Scis. (former pres.). Avocations: rock climbing, trombone, birdwatching. Office: Dept Biology Millsaps Coll 1701 N State St Jackson MS 39210-0001 Office Phone: 601-974-1414. E-mail: mcguisl@millsaps.edu. *

MCGUIRE, TIMOTHY WILLIAM, economics and management educator, dean; b. Englewood, NJ, Nov. 30, 1938; s. Charles James and Marie (McCarthy) McG.; children: Timothy William Jr., Gretchen Elizabeth, Michael Joseph; m. Nancy Paule Melone, 1991. BS in Indsl. Mgmt., Carnegie Inst. Tech., Pitts., 1960; MS in Econs., Carnegie Inst. Tech., 1961; PhD in Econs., Stanford U., Calif., 1968. Staff mem. Coun. Econ. Advisors, 1963—64; rsch. assoc. econs. Grad. Sch. Indsl. Adminstrn. Carnegie Mellon U., Pitts., 1964—66, asst. prof. econs. Grad. Sch. Indsl. Adminstrn., 1966—69, assoc. prof. Grad. Sch. Indsl. Adminstrn., 1969—75, prof. Grad. Sch. Indsl. Adminstrn., 1975—79, prof. mgmt. and econs. Grad. Sch. Indsl. Adminstrn., 1982—, dep. dean Grad. Sch. Indsl. Adminstrn., 1983—90, prof. social scis. and econs. Dept. Social Scis., 1981—82; prof. econs., chmn. dept. U. Iowa, Iowa City, 1979—80; dean, Harry B. Miller prof. bus. Charles H. Lundquist Coll. Bus. U. Oreg., Eugene, 1994—98; COO, sr. exec. v.p. Mgmt. Sci. Assocs., Inc., Pitts., 1998—2005, chmn., sr. exec. v.p., 2005—. Sr. visitor U. Cambridge, England, 1970; bd. dirs. Mgmt. Sci. Assocs., Inc., Pitts.; bd. visitors Joseph M. Katz Grad. Sch. Bus., U. Pitts. Contbr. articles to profl. jours. Bd. trustees Point Park Coll.; chmn. corp. adv. bd. Pitts.(Pa.) Ctr. Sports, Arts and Entertainment Mgmt. Fellow, Ford Found., 1962—63, 1970—71; Woodrow Wilson Nat. Hon. fellow, Carnegie Inst. Tech., 1960—61, Stanford U. fellow, 1961—62. Mem.: Soc. Judgment and Decision Making, Omicron Delta Kappa, Tau Beta Pi. Home: 118 Lakeland Dr Mars PA 16046-2114 Office: Mgmt Sci Assocs Inc 6565 Penn Ave Pittsburgh PA 15206-4490 Office Phone: 412-362-2000. Business E-Mail: tmcguire@msa.com.

MCGUIRE, WALLER F., library director; BA, Earlham Coll.; MLS, U. Ky., 1989. Positions including asst. br. mgr., regional coord. and dir. libr. ops. St. Louis Pub. Libr., 1989—94, dep. dir., 1994—2004, exec. dir., 2004—. Bd. dirs. Mo. Libr. Network Corp., 2006—. Bd. trustees St. Louis Pub. Libr. Found. Office: St Louis Pub Libr 1301 Olive St Saint Louis MO 63103 Office Phone: 314-241-2288. Office Fax: 314-241-3840. Business E-Mail: WMcGuire@slpl.org. *

MCGUIRE, WILLIAM, civil engineer, educator; b. S.I., NY, Dec. 17, 1920; s. Edward Joseph and Phoebe (Sellman) McG.; m. Barbara Weld, Feb. 5, 1944; children: Robert Weld, Thomas Rhodes. BSCE, Bucknell U., 1942; MSCE, Cornell U., 1947. Structural designer Jackson & Moreland (engrs.), Boston, 1947-49; faculty Cornell U., Ithaca, 1949—, prof. civil engring., 1960-90, prof. emeritus of civil engring., 1990—; dir. Cornell U. (Sch. Civil Engring.), 1966-68; vis. prof. civil engring. Asian Inst. Tech., Bangkok, Thailand, 1968-70. Vis. research engr. Nat. Bur. Standards, 1972; Gledden vis. sr. fellow U. Western Australia, 1973; cons. structural engr., 1951—; vis. prof. U. Tokyo, 1979, U. Strathclyde, 1986 Author: Steel Structures, 1967; author: (with R.H. Gallagher and R.D. Ziemian) Matrix Structural Analysis, 1979, 2d edit., 2000. Served to lt. USNR, 1942-45. Recipient Naval Letter of Commendation, award for Outstanding Achievement, Bucknell U., 1987, T.R. Higgins Lectureship award Am. Inst. Steel Constrn., 1992, G. Haaijer awrd Am. Inst. Steel Constrn., 2000, L. Beedle award Structural Stability Rsch. Coun., 2005. Fellow ASCE (pres. Ithaca 1964, Norman medal 1962, 94, Hardesty award 1992, honorary mem. 1994); mem. Internat. Assn. Bridge and Structural Engring., Nat. Acad. Engring., Sigma Xi, Chi Epsilon, Kappa Delta Rho. Congregationalist. Home: 121 Simsbury Dr Ithaca NY 14850-1728 Business E-Mail: wm20@cornell.edu.

MCGUIRE, WILLIAM ALBERT, humanities educator; b. St. Louis, Mar. 18, 1944; s. William Albert and Virginia Marie (Grant) McGuire. BA, St. Louis U., 1966; MA, San Francisco State U., 1976. Instr. De Andreas H.S., St. Louis, 1966—69, Presentation H.S., San Francisco, 1977—91, U. San Francisco, 1992—97, San Francisco State U., 1995, City Coll. of San Francisco, 1975—. Coord. humanities City Coll. of San Francisco, 1998—. Mem. Soc. for the Preservation of San Francisco Archl. Heritage, 1986—. E-5 US Army, 1969—71. Mem.: C.C. Humanities Assn., Calif. Humanities Asn., ACLU, UNICEF, Friends of Urban Forest, Amnesty Internat., Vets. for Peace, Sierra Club. Democrat. Roman Catholic. Avocations: music, gardening, cooking, writing. Office: City Coll of San Francisco 50 Phelan Ave San Francisco CA 94112 Office Phone: 415-452-7257. Business E-Mail: wmcguire@ccsf.edu.

MCGUIRE, WILLIAM B(ENEDICT), lawyer; b. Newark, Feb. 14, 1929; children: Joan Ellen, Ralph R., James C., Keith P., Grant W. BS, Fordham U., 1950; JD, Seton Hall U., 1958; LLM in Taxation, NYU, 1963. Bar: N.J. 1958, U.S. Dist. Ct. N.J. 1958, U.S. Supreme Ct. 1971, U.S. Ct. Appeals (3d cir.) 1980, N.Y. 1982. Chief acct. Hanover Fire Ins. Co., NYC, 1950-58; sr. ptnr. Lum, Blunno & Tompkins, Newark, 1958-83, Tompkins McGuire Wachenfeld & Barry LLP, Newark, 1984—, mng. ptnr. Asst. prosecutor Essex County, N.J., 1964-65; trustee St. Barnabas Corp. and St. Barnabas Med. Ctr.; mem. Essex County Ethics Com., 1974-77; chair bd. visitors Seton Hall U., Sch. Law, 2004—. Fellow Am. Coll. Trial Lawyers, Am. Bar Found. (state chmn. 1990-95), Am. Bd. Trial Advocates, Internat. Acad. Trial Lawyers, Internat. Soc. Barristers; mem. ABA, N.J. State Bar Assn. (trustee 1982-89, sec. 1989-90, treas. 1990-91, 2d v.p. 1991-92, 1st v.p. 1992-93, pres.-elect 1993-94, pres. 1994-95), N.J. State Bar Found. (pres. 1988-89), Essex County Bar Assn. (pres. 1975-76), Internat. Assn. Ins. Counsel, Fedn. Ins. Counsel, Def. Rsch. Inst., Maritime Law Assn., Trial Attys. N.J., Assn. Fed. Bar N.J. (pres. 1985-88), Essex County Country Club (pres. 1983), Newark Club. Roman Catholic. Office: Tompkins McGuire Wachenfeld & Barry LLP 4 Gateway Ctr 100 Mulberry St Newark NJ 07102-4007 Office Phone: 973-622-3000. Office Fax: 973-623-7780. Business E-Mail: wmcguire@tompkinsmcguire.com.

MCGUIRE, WILLIAM DENNIS, healthcare consultant; b. Glen Ridge, NJ, Sept. 24, 1943; s. John William and Kathleen Mary (Sexton) McG.; m. Nancy Katherine Hoyne, Aug. 13, 1966; chldren: Kathleen Anne, Colleen Dempsey. BA, U. Notre Dame, 1965; M.H.A., U. Mich., 1968. Asst. adminstr. U. Wis. Hosps., Madison, 1971-74; adminstr. Children's Med. Ctr., Dayton, Ohio, 1974-79; COO Mercy Cath. Med. Ctr., Phila., 1979-80; CEO Wills Eye Hosp., Phila., 1980-85; pres., CEO Mercy Health Care Sys., Scranton, Pa., 1985-89, Mt. Carmel Health, Columbus, Ohio, 1989-92, Incarnate Word Health Svcs., San Antonio, 1992-95, Cath. Med. Ctrs. of Bklyn. and Queens, NYC, 1996—2000, Kaleida Health, Buffalo, 2002—06; pvt. practice San Antonio, 2000—02, 2006—. Instr. U. Wis., Madison, 1972—73; allied health techs. adv. com. Sinclair CC, 1974—79; mem. Dayton Pub. Schs. Lay Adv. Com. on Vocat. Edn., 1974—79; pres. Dayton Area Young Adminstrs. Group, 1977; asst. clin. prof. Wright State U. Sch. Medicine, Dayton, Ohio, 1978—79; asst. prof. Ohio State U., 1990—92; adj. faculty dept health care Trinity U., 1992—95, Harvard Bus. Sch. Club, 2003—06. Trustee Cath. Social Svcs., 1976—79, pres., 1978—79; trustee Cmty. Blood Ctr., 1977—79; pres. elect Greater Dayton Area Hosp. Assn., 1979; mem. Wilkes Coll. Health Adminstrn. Adv. Com., 1988—89; bd. dirs. Coop. Purchasing Corp., 1974—79, Coll. Misericordia Health Care Task Force, 1988—89, Covenant Health Sys., 1992—2003, chmn. fin. com., 2001—03, Fletcher Allen Health Care, 2002—03; consol. Cath. Risk Retention Group, 1992—95, Cath. Charities, 1996—2000, Primary Care Devel. Corp., 1997—2000, Buffalo Niagara Partnership, 2002—06, D'Youville Coll., 2004—06; bd. govs. League Vol. Hosps., 1996—2000, sec., 1997—2000; bd. govs. Fidelis Care NY, 1996—2000, Queensbrook Ins. Ltd., 1996—2000, vice chmn., 1996—97, chmn., 1997—2000; active Health Policy Forum, United Hosp. Fund, United Way, ARC. Fellow Am. Coll. Healthcare Execs. (life), NY Acad. Medicine; mem. Acad. for Cath. Health Care Leadership, Mercy Leadership Group. (nat. commn. Cath. health care ministry), Maj. Cath. Health Alliance (sec. 1990-95, chmn. 1997-99), Health Care Fin. Mgmt. Assn., Am. Assn. Univ. Profs. Ophthalmology, Am. Soc. Law and Medicine, Am. Hosp. Assn., Am. Assn. Eye and Ear Hosps. (pres.-elect 1984-85), Health Mgmt. Edn. Assn. (pres. 1987-88), Hosp. Assn. NY State (bd. dirs. 1998-2000, 02-05), Greater NY Hosp. Assn. (bd. govs. 1997-2000, 02-06), Tex. Hosp. Assn., We. NY Hosp. Assn. (bd. dirs. 2002-05), Ohio Hosp. Assn., Hosp. Assn. Pa., Cath. Health Assn., Am. Pub. Health Assn., Pa. Pub. Health Assn., Del. Valley Hosp. Council, Pa. Emergency Health Svcs. Coun., Del. County Emergency Health Svcs. Coun., Nat. Union Hosp. and Health Care Employees (plan trustee), Pa. Hosps. Ins. Co. Adv. Coun., 1988-89. C. of C., U. Notre Dame Alumni Assn., U. Mich. Alumni Assn., Pres.'s Soc., U. Wis. Med. Sch. Alumni Assn., Wills Eye Soc., Sorin Soc., Badin Guild, Notre Dame Club (pres. 1971, v.p. 1983-84), Dominion Country Club. Office: 6 Clubhouse Green San Antonio TX 78257 Home: 6 Clubhouse Grn San Antonio TX 78257-1295 Office Phone: 210-698-6543. Personal E-mail: billmcg@together.net.

MCGUIRE, WILLIAM JAMES, psychologist, educator; b. NYC, Feb. 17, 1925; s. James William and Anne M. (Mitchell) McG.; m. Claire Vernick, Dec. 29, 1954; children: James William, Anne Maureen, Steven Thomas. BA, Fordham U., 1949, MA, 1950; PhD, Yale U., 1954; PhD (hon.), Eötvös U., Budapest, Hungary, 1990, U. Bologna, Italy, 2005. Postdoctoral fellow U. Minn., 1954-55; assoc. prof. psychology U. Ill., 1958-61; prof. Columbia U., 1961-67, U. Calif., San Diego, 1967-70; vis. prof. London Sch. Econs., 1970-71; asst. prof. Yale U., New Haven, 1955-58, prof. emeritus, 1970—, chmn. dept. psychology, 1971-73. Mem. adv. panel for sociology and social psychology NSF, 1963-65; mem. review panel for social scis. NIMH, 1968-72, cons., 1974-95. Author: Content and Processes in the Experience of Self, 1988, A Perspectivist Approach to Strategic Planning, 1989, Structure of Attitudes and Attitude Systems, 1989, The Content, Structure, and Operation of Thought Systems, 1991, Explorations in Political Psychology, 1993, Creative Hypothesis-Generating in Psychology, 1997, Constructing Social Psychology: Creative and Critical Processes, 1999, After a Half Century of Election Studies: Whence, Where and Whither, 2001; contbr. to Ency. Brit.; editor Jour. Personality and Social Psychology, 1967-70; cons. editor European Jour. Social Psychology, 1978—, Jour. Applied Social Psychology, 1983—, Jour. Exptl. Social Psychology, 1994—, Comm. Rsch., 1988—, Human Comm. Rsch., 2001—, Jour. Commn., 2002—; Applied Psychology in Hungary, 2002—; contbr. Ency. Psychology. With AUS, 1943-46. Recipient Am. Social Psychology award AAAS, 1964, Gen. Electric Found. awards, 1963, 64, 66, Disting. Scientist award Soc. Exptl. Social Psychology, 1992, Disting. Sci. award Internat. Soc. Political Psychology, 1999; grantee NSF, 1960-79, NIH, 1979-99; Fulbright fellow Louvain (Belgium) U., 1950-51, Ctr. for Advanced Study in Behavioral Scis. fellow, 1965-66, Guggenheim fellow, 1970-71, William James fellow Am. Psychol. Soc., 1989—. Fellow APA (pres. divsn. personality and social psychology 1973-74, Disting. Sci. Contbn. award 1988), Am. Acad. Arts and Scis.; mem. Am. Sociol. Assn., Am. Assn. Pub. Opinion Rsch., Sigma Xi. Home: 225 St Ronan St New Haven CT 06511-2313 Office: Yale U Dept Psychology PO Box 208205 New Haven CT 06520-8205 Office Phone: 203-432-4535. Business E-Mail: william.mcguire@yale.edu.

MCGUIRK, RONALD CHARLES, retired bank executive, economic advisor; b. Balt., Dec. 9, 1938; s. Charles F. and Grace E. (Delcher) McG.; m. Katherine Sauer, Oct. 1, 1960; children: Frank D., Ann E. Student, St. John's Coll., Annapolis, Md., 1956-59. Sr. data processing officer 1st Nat. Bank, Balt., 1966-72, v.p. data processing, 1972-76, v.p. mktg., 1976-80, sr. v.p. mktg., 1980-90, sr. v.p. corp. plan, chief of staff to CEO, 1990-94; sr. v.p., corp. sec. 1st Md. Bancorp, Balt., 1995-99; sr. econ. advisor Anne Arundel County, Md., 1999—2006; ret., 2006. Bd. dirs., v.p., treas. Balto-Washington Med. Ctr., Glen Burnie, Md., 1974—, v.p., 1999—; bd. dirs., treas. Internet, Inc., 1990-95, Glen Burnie Town Ctr. Com., 1995-2006, AACO Conf. and Vis. Bd., 1999-2006, Annapolis Symphony, 1991-92; trustee Mt. Washington Pediat. Hosp., 1997—2004; mem. adv. bd. Hist. Annapolis Found., 1982-85, dir., 1985-90; chmn. Annapolis Boundary Commn., 1983-84; mem. Anne Arundel County Coun., 1974-82, Anne Arundel County Libr. Bd., 1974-84; pres. Anne Arundel County Scholarship for Scholars/Bd. Edn., 1983-85, treas., 1985-88; mem. Anne Arundel County Charter Rev. Commn., 1986, Anne Arundel County Govt. Salary Commn., 1985, 89; chmn. Anne Arundel County Impact Fee Study Task Force, 1987; pres. Anne Arundel County YMCA, 1987-89, bd. dirs., 1982-87, 89-90; mem. Commn. for Ednl. Excellence, 1988-90; vice chmn. Ft. Meade Coordinating Coun., 1989-91; mem. Exec. Com. Md. Bus.-Industry PAC, 1991-99, Anne Arundel County Charter and Orgn. Transition Group, 1991; corp. ptnr. Sch. Bus. and Mgmt. Morgan State U., 1991-92; trustee Md. Hist. Soc., 1995-96; co-chair Anne Arundel County transition fin. com., 1998-99; chair adhoc Fire Dept. Com., 2003-04. Mem. Ctr. Club. Democrat. Roman Catholic. Personal E-mail: rm21061@aol.com.

MCGUIRK, TERRENCE, former broadcasting company executive; b. Bklyn., Apr. 2, 1925; s. William Edward and Loretta Beatrice (Lanigan) McG.; m. Gloria Helen Geoghan, June 17, 1950; children: Terence F., Sara McGuirk Duncan, Susan McGuirk Blank, Elizabeth McGuirk Magee, Melissa McGuirk Bowman, Bryan, Michelle McGuirk O'Connor. BS, Fordham U., 1950. Nat. sales mgr. St. WAGA-TV, Atlanta, 1966-68; mgr. Sta. WAGA-TV, Atlanta, 1970-75; eastern sales mgr. Storer TV Sales, NYC, 1968-70; pres., gen. mgr. Sta. WTEN-TV, Albany, NY, 1976-82; pres. Knight-Ridder Broadcasting, Inc., 1982-85; ret. Assoc. trustee Siena Coll., Loudonville, N.Y., 1979-83; trustee Meml. Hosp. Found., 1980-83; dir. Albany chpt. ARC, 1987-91. Served with U.S. Army, 1943-46. Mem. Mariner Sands Country Club, Babylon Yacht Club (hon.).

MCGUIRL, MARLENE DANA CALLIS, law librarian, educator; b. Hammond, Ind., Mar. 22, 1938; d. Daniel David and Helen Elizabeth (Baludis) Callis; m. James Franklin McGuirl, Apr. 24, 1965. AB, Ind. U., 1959; JD, DePaul U., 1963; MALS, Rosary Coll., 1965; LLM, George Washington U., 1978; postgrad., Harvard U., 1985. Bar: Ill. 1963, Ind. 1964, D.C. 1972. Asst. DePaul Coll. of Law Libr., 1961-62, asst. law libr., 1962-65; ref. law librarian Boston Coll. Sch. Law, 1965-66; libr. dir. D.C. Bar Libr., 1966-70; asst. chief Am.-Brit. Law Divsn. Libr. of Congress, Washington, 1970, chief, 1970-90, environ. cons., 1990—; counsel Cooter & Gell, 1992-93; adminstr. Washington Met. Transit Authority, 1994—2004. Libr. cons. Nat. Clearinghouse on Proverty Law, OEO, Washington, 1967-69, Northwestern U. Nat. Inst. Edn. in Law and Poverty, 1969, D.C. Office of Corp. Counsel, 1969-70; instr. law librarianship Grad. Sch. of U.S. Dept. of Agr., 1968-72; adj. asst. prof., 1973-91; assoc. prof. environ. law George Washington U., 1979—; lectr. justice and peace, Georgetown U., Washington, 2007—; judge Nat. and Internat. Law Moot Ct. Competition, 1976-78, 90—; pres. Hamburger Heaven, Inc., Palm Beach, Fla., 1981-91, L'Image de Marlene Ltd., 1986-92, Clinique de Beauté Inc., 1987-92, Heads & Hands Inc., 1987-92, Horizon Design & Mfg. Co., Inc., 1987—; dir. Stoneridge Farm Inc., Gt. Falls, Va., 1984—; lectr. in field. Contbr. articles to profl. jours. Mem. Georgetown Citizens Assn.; trustee D.C. Law Students in Ct.; del. Ind. Democratic Conv., 1964. Recipient Meritorious Svc. award Libr. on Congress, 1974, letter of commendation Dirs. of Pers., 1976, cert. of appreciation, 1981-84. Mem. ABA (facilities law libr. Congress com. 1976-89), Fed. Bar Assn. (chpt. council 1972-76), Ill. Bar Assn., Women's Bar Assn. (pres. 1972-73, exec. bd. 1973-77, Outstanding Contbn. to Human Rights award 1975), D.C. Bar Assn., Am. Bar Found., Nat. Assn. Women Lawyers, Am. Assn. Law Libraries (exec. bd. 1973-77), Law Librarians Soc. of Washington (pres. 1971-73), Exec. Women in Govt. Home: 3416 P St NW Washington DC 20007-2705 Personal E-mail: marlenemcguirl@aol.com.

MCGUNIGLE, BRIAN EDWARD, lawyer; b. Boston, Nov. 2, 1947; s. Daniel H. and Mona (Tyldesley) McG.; m. Mary Ann Caven, Aug. 9, 1974. BA magna cum laude, Harvard U., 1968; MA 1st Honors, Nat. Univ. of Ireland, 1969; JD cum laude, Harvard U., 1973; LLM with distinction, U. London, 1974. Bar: NY 1975. Assoc. Coudert Bros., NYC, 1974-80, ptnr., 1981—, Dorsey & Whitney LLP, NYC. Fulbright scholar, Ireland, 1968-69; Knox fellow, Eng., 1973-74. Office: Dorsey & Whitney LLP 250 Park Ave New York NY 10177 Office Phone: 212-415-9282. Office Fax: 212-953-7201. Business E-Mail: mcgunigle.brian@dorsey.com.

MCGUNNIGLE, GEORGE FRANCIS, lawyer, judge; b. Rochester, NY, Feb. 22, 1942; s. George Francis and Mary Elizabeth (Curran) McG.; m. Priscilla Ann Lappin, July 13, 1968; children: Cynthia A., Brian P. AB, Boston Coll., 1963; LLB, Georgetown U., 1966; LLM, George Wash. U., 1967. Bar: Conn. 1971, Minn. 1972, U.S. Dist. Ct. D.C. 1967, U.S. Dist. Ct. Conn. 1971, U.S. Dist. Ct. Minn. 1972, U.S. Ct. Appeals (2d cir.) 1971, U.S. Ct. Appeals (8th cir.) 1977, U.S. Supreme Ct. 1986. Asst. U.S. atty. Office of U.S. Atty., Bridgeport, Conn., 1971—72; assoc. Leonard, Street and Deinard, Mpls., 1972—73, ptnr., 1974—2000; judge Fourth Jud. Dist., Mpls., 2000—. Editor: Business Torts Litigation, 1992. Bd. dirs. Cath. Charities, 1997—2003, North Ctrl. chpt. Arthritis Found., Mpls., 1986-92, 94—2003, mem. exec. com., 1988-92, 2001—03. Lt. JAGC, USN, 1967-71. Recipient Nat. Vol. Svc. citation Arthritis Found., 1992. Mem. ABA (litigation sect., chmn. bus. torts litigation com. 1988-91, divsn. dir. 1991-92, 97-98, coun. 1992-95, sect. of dispute resolution coun. 2000-01). Avocation: reading. Office: Fourth Judicial Dist C-1251 Hennepin County Govt Ctr Minneapolis MN 55487-0422 Office Phone: 612-596-8822.

MCGURK, CHRISTOPHER JAMIE, film company executive; b. 1957; BS, Syracuse U., 1978; MBA, U. Chgo. Various positions including CFO Pepsico, 1982—88; sr. v.p. fin. Walt Disney Studios, 1988-90, exec. v.p., CFO, 1990—94, pres. motion pictures group, 1994—96; various positions including pres., CEO Universal Pictures, 1996—99; vice chmn., COO Metro-Goldwyn-Mayer Inc., 1999—2005; sr. adv. new ventures IDT Entertainment, 2006—; CEO Overture Films, 2006—. Bd. dirs. DivX, Inc., 2006—. Exec. prodr.: (films) The Brothers Grimm, 2005. *

MCGURK, EUGENE DAVID, JR., lawyer; b. Phila., Feb. 27, 1951; s. Eugene David and Mary Rose (O'Donnell) McG.; m. Kathleen Mary Murphy, Dec. 28, 1973 (dec. Aug. 1978). BA, LaSalle Coll., 1973; JD summa cum laude, Widener U., 1978. Bar: Pa. 1978, N.J. 1978, U.S. Dist. Ct. (ea. dist.) Pa. 1978, U.S. Dist. Ct. N.J. 1978, U.S. Ct. Appeals (3rd cir.) 1981, U.S. Supreme Ct. 1982. Mgmt. analyst Mng. Dirs. Office, Phila., 1974-76; adminstr. Dept. Commerce, Phila., 1976-78; asst. city solicitor law, sr. trial atty. City of Phila., 1978-81; with Raynes, McCarty, Phila., 1981-87, ptnr., 1987—. Guest lectr. Thomas Jefferson U. Med. Sch., 1083, 1984, Del. Law Sch., 1980, U. Pa. Dental Sch., 1985—90, Med. Coll. Pa., Phila., Drexel U. Med. Sch., 2005; vis. instr. Dept. Comty. and Preventive

Medicine, 1983—91, Am. Soc. Law and Medicine, 1987—; lectr. internat. law studies program (summer) U. Nairobi, Kenya, 1990; adj. faculty Widener U. Sch. Law, 1993—; mem. disciplinary bd. hearing commn. Pa. Supreme Ct., Harrisburg, 1993—98, chmn.disciplinary bd. hearing commn., 1995—97, alt. mem. disciplinary bd. hearing commn., 1999—. Articles editor Del. Jour. Corp. Law, 1977-78. Mem. Camden County Bd. Elections, 1970; bd. of overseers Widener U. Sch. Law, Wilmington, Del., 1985—, chmn. 2003-, bd. trustees, 2001—, sec. 2003-. Recipient award Fed. Bar Assn., 1978, Mayoral award City of Phila., Am. Judisprudence award, 1978. Mem. ABA, Assn. Trial Lawyers Am., Pa. Bar Assn., N.J. Bar Assn., Camden County Bar Assn., Phila. Bar Assn. (bench bar com. 1982, profl. responsibility com. 1982, state civil practice), Widener U. Sch. Law Alumni Assn. (bd. dirs. 1980—, v.p. 1982-85, pres. 1985-92), Phila. Ctr. City Proprietors Assn. (adv. bd.), Phi Kapp Phi, Phi Alpha Delta (scholastic award Read chpt. 1978), Omicron Delta Kappa. Office: Raynes McCarty 1845 Walnut St Ste 2000 Philadelphia PA 19103-4767 also: NJ Mng Atty 116 White Horse Pike Haddon Heights NJ 08035-1928 Office Phone: 215-568-6190. Business E-Mail: edmcgurk@raynesmccarty.com.

MCGURK, MICHAEL R., lawyer; b. Abington, Pa., Feb. 11, 1960; BSChemE, U. Del., 1983; JD, George Washington U., 1988. Bar: Pa. 1988, NJ 1988, DC 1990, Mass. 2002, registered: US Patent & Trademark Office, lic.: US Ct. Appeals (Fed. Cir.) 1990, US Supreme Ct. 1993, US Ct. Appeals (9th Cir.) 2000. Examiner US Patent & Trademark Office, 1985—87; with Finnegan, Henderson, Farabow, Garrett & Dunner LLP, 1987—, ptnr., Chem./ Metall. Practice Group, leader, Interference Sect. Adj. prof. George Mason U., 1998—2000. Mem.: Am. Chem. Soc., Am. Intellectual Property Law Assn. (chmn. pub. info. com. 1996—98), ABA (Litig. Sect., Patent, Trademark & Copyright Law Sect.), Fed. Cir. Bar Assn., Pa. Bar Assn., DC Bar Assn. (Patent, Trademark & Copyright Law Sects.), Boston Patent Law Assn., Boston Bar Assn. Office: Finnegan Henderson Farabow Garrett & Dunner LLP 55 Cambridge Pky Cambridge MA 02142 Office Phone: 617-452-1600. Office Fax: 617-452-1666. Business E-Mail: michael.mcgurk@finnegan.com.

MC GURN, BARRETT, communications executive, writer; b. NYC, Aug. 6, 1914; s. William Barrett and Alice (Schneider) McG.; m. Mary Elizabeth Johnson, May 30, 1942 (dec. Feb. 1960); children: William Barrett III, Elizabeth Hehn, Andrew; m. Janice Ann McLaughlin, June 19, 1962; children: Summers, Martin Barrett, Mark Barrett. AB, Fordham U., 1935, LittD (hon.), 1958. Editor-in-chief Fordham Ram, 1934-35; with N.Y. Herald Tribune, 1935-66, asst. corr. Rome, 1939, bur. chief, 1946-52, 55-62, reporting staff NY, 1935-42, 62-66, bur. chief Paris, 1952—55, acting chief bur. Moscow, 1958; with, assignments in Morocco, Algeria, Tunisia, Hungary (1956 revolution), Egypt, Greece, Yugoslavia, Poland, Cen. Africa, Gaza Strip.; press attache Am. Embassy, Rome, 1966-68, counselor for press affairs Saigon, 1968—69; U.S. consular officer, sec. appointed by Pres., 1969; dir. U.S. Govt. Press Ctr., Vietnam, 1968-69; White House and Pentagon liaison for State Dept. spokesman Washington, 1969-72; World Affairs commentator USIA, 1972-73; dir. pub. info. U.S. Supreme Ct., Washington, 1973-82; dir. communications Cath. Archdiocese of Washington, 1984-87; pres. Carroll Pub. Co. pub. Cath. Standard and El Pregonero, 1987-91; dir. Our Sunday Visitor Pub. Co., 1988-98. Mem. Italian-Am. com. to select Italian fellowship winners for study in U.S., 1950-52; mem. U.S. Nat. Cath. Com. on Comm. Policy, 1970-74, White House Com. on Drug Control Info., 1970-72; interdept. com. on U.S. govt. press info. policy, 1970, interdept. U.S. govt. task force to rescue 100 Ams. kidnapped in Jordan, 1970, one-man U.S. Presdl. mission to Cambodia on media news problems, 1970; archivist John Carroll Soc., Washington, 1990-97. Author: Decade in Europe, 1959, A Reporter Looks at the Vatican, 1962, A Reporter Looks at American Catholicism, 1967, America's Court, The Supreme Court and The People, 1997, The Pilgrim's Guide to Rome, 1999, Yank, Reporting the Greatest Generation, 2004; contbg. author: The Best from Yank, 1945, Yank, the GI Story of the War, 1946, Combat, 1950, Highlights from Yank, 1953, Overseas Press Club Cook Book, 1962, I Can Tell it Now, 1964, U.S. Book of Facts, Statistics and Information, 1966, New Catholic Treasury of Wit and Humor, 1967, How I Got that Story, 1967, Heroes for Our Times, 1968, Newsbreak, 1975, Saints for all Seasons, 1978, Informing the People, 1981, The Courage to Grow Old, 1989, Am. Peoples Encyclopedia Yearbook, Close To Glory: Yank Correspondents Untold Stories of World War II, 1992; contbr. articles to profl. jours. Trustee Corrs. Fund, 1965-68; mem. bd. Anglo-Am. Charity Fund in Italy, 1967-68; v.p. Citizens Assn., Westmoreland Hills, Md., 1984-86. Sgt. AUS, 1942-45. Decorated Purple Heart; grand knight Italian Order of Merit; Vietnam Psychol. Warfare medal 1st class; recipient Polk award for outstanding fgn. reporting L.I. U., 1956; named best press corr. abroad Overseas Press Club, 1957; recipient N.Y.C. Fire Dept. Essay Silver Medal, 1924, N.Y. Times Oratorical Contest Bronze Medal, 1930; Christopher award for one of ten most inspiring books of year, 1959; named Man of Year Cath. Inst. Press, 1962, Fordham U. Alumnus of Year in communications, 1963; co-winner ann. Golden Typewriter award N.Y. Newspaper Reporters Assn., 1965, nominated by N.Y. Herald Tribune for Journalism Pulitzer Prize, 1965; outstanding pub. service award N.Y. chpt. Sigma Delta Chi, 1965; recipient Page One award N.Y. Newspaper Guild, 1966, Silurians award, 1966, award N.Y. Newspaper Reporters Assn., 1966, Citation for pub. service N.Y.C. Citizens Budget Commn., 1966, U.S. Govt. medal for civilian svc. in Vietnam, 1969, pres. commendation for Cambodia mission on news problems, 1970, Meritorious Honor award Dept. State, 1972; Lifetime Achievement award Fordham U. Club, Washington, 1986. Mem. Fgn. Press Assn. Italy (v.p. 1951-52, pres. 1961-62), SHAPE Corrs. Assn. Paris (treas. 1955), Authors Guild, Silurians, Am. Fgn. Svc. Assn., Pax Romana Soc. for Cath. Intellectuals, Overseas Press Club (pres. 1963-65), Nat. Press Club, Diplomats and Consular Officers, Ret., Kenwood Club, Cosmos Club, Fordham U. Club Washington (bd. govs. 1980—99). Roman Catholic. Home: 5229 Duvall Dr Bethesda MD 20816-1875 Office Phone: 301-229-7439. Personal E-mail: jmcgurn@erols.com. *Providing information to our democratic public has been the work of my life both as a foreign correspondent, as a government spokesman, and as a lecturer. The newsman and the person who speaks for government share the same objective of explaining government policy. The spokesman has an added responsibility— to help government policy succeed. The reporter and the spokesman sometimes are at war with one another, but it is a war in behalf of the same beneficiary: the people.*

MCGURN, WILLIAM BARRETT, III, lawyer; b. NYC, Apr. 3, 1943; s. Barrett and Mary Elizabeth (Johnson) McGurn; m. Catherine Roche, June 17, 1972; children: Mary Anne, Edward Johnson. BA, Yale U., 1965; JD, Harvard U., 1972. Bar: DC 1973, Paris 1992. Ptnr. Cleary, Gottlieb, Steen & Hamilton LLP, Washington, Paris, Rome, 1972—. Gov. Am. Hosp. Paris, 1991—; chmn. Dem. Abroad, France, 1987—89; bd. dirs. Spl. Olympics Italy, 2005—. Lt. USNR, 1967—69. Mem.: ABA, Am. C. of C. France (bd. dirs. 1996—, v.p. 1998—2000, pres. 2000—02). Democrat. Home: via del Pié di Marmo 16 00186 Rome Italy Office: Cleary Gottlieb Steen and Hamilton LLP Piazza di Spagna 15 00187 Rome Italy

MCGURN, WILLIAM JOSEPH, speechwriter, editor; b. Oceanside, Calif., Dec. 4, 1958; s. William A. and Mary S. (Gormley) McG.; m. Julie Ann Hoffman, Apr. 24, 1993; 3 adopted children: Grace, Maisie, Lucy BA in Philosophy, U. Notre Dame, 1980; MS in Comm., Boston U., 1981. Asst. mng. editor The American Spectator, Bloomington, Ind., 1981-83; mng. editor This World mag., NYC, 1983-84; editl. features editor The Wall St. Jour. Europe, Brussels, 1984-86; dep. editl. page editor The Asian Wall St. Jour., Hong Kong, 1987-89; bur. chief Nat. Rev., Washington, 1989-92; sr. editor Far Eastern Econ. Rev., Hong Kong, 1992—98; chief editl. writer The Wall St. Jour., 1999—2003; exec., Office of the Chmn. News Corp., 2004—05; asst. to Pres. for speechwriting The White House, Washington, 2005—. Mem. editl. bd. The Wall St. Jour., 1998—2003. Editor: Basic Law, Basic Questions, 1988; author: Perfidious Albion: The Abandonment of Hong Kong, 1997; co-author: Is the Market Moral: A Dialogue on Religion, Economics & Justice, 2004 Named to Outstanding Young Men of Am., 1991. Mem. Fgn. Corr. Assn., Nat. Press Club, Notre Dame Club of Hong Kong (pres. 1993—). Office: The White House 1600 Pennsylvania Ave Washington DC 20500

MCGWIRE, MARK DAVID, retired professional baseball player; b. Pomona, Calif., Oct. 1, 1963; s. John and Kathy McGwire; 1 child, Matthew. Student, U. So. Calif. With Oakland Athletics, Calif., 1984—97, St. Louis Cardinals, 1997—2001. Named Am. League Rookie of Yr., 1987, Male Athlete of Yr., AP, 1998; named to All-Star Team, 1987—92, 1995—2000, MLB All-Century Team, 1999; recipient Gold Glove award, 1990. Achievements include being a member of U.S. Olympic Baseball Team, 1984; mem.of World Series Championship Team, 1989; led Am. League in Home Runs, 1987 (49), 1996 (52); led Nat. League in Home Runs, 1998 (70), 1999 (65); led Nat. League in RBI's (147), 1999.

MCHALE, DAVID R., utilities executive; b. Thompson, Conn. BS, So. Conn. State Univ., 1982; MBA, Univ. New Haven, 1986. Intern Northeast Utilities Sys., Hartford, Conn., 1981—82, rsch. analyst, 1982—86, fin. analyst, 1986—93, mgr. project & short-term fin., 1993—95, asst. treas., 1995—98, v.p., treas., 1998—2004, v.p. strategic bus. plans, 2004—05, sr. v.p., CFO, 2005—. Fellow: Am. Leadership Forum (sr.); mem.: Edison Elec. Inst. Mailing: Northeast Utilities Sys PO Box 270 Hartford CT 06141-0270 *

MCHALE, EDWARD ROBERTSON, retired lawyer; b. Chgo., Jan. 24, 1921; s. Edward F. and Martha (Robertson) McH.; m. Helen Louise Lindgren, Aug. 28, 1953; children: Nancy Ellen McHale Kaufman, Sally Jane McHale Cutler, John Robertson. BSS., Northwestern U., 1942; LL.B., Harvard U., 1948. Bar: Calif. 1949. Asst. U.S. atty. U.S. atty. So. Dist. Calif., 1949—61, chief tax div., 1954—61; assoc. Mitchell, Silberberg & Knupp, Los Angeles, 1961—64, ptnr., 1965—86, mgr. litigation dept, 1978—82; pres. Edward R. McHale, P.C., 1979—86; ret., 1986. Lectr. U. So. Calif. Law Center, 1958-61 Co-author: Handling Federal Tax Litigation, 1961. Served to lt. USNR, 1943-46. Mem. Fed. Bar Assn. (past pres. Los Angeles chpt., past nat. v.p. for 9th Circuit), Assn. Bus. Trial Lawyers (bd. govs. 1981-83), State Bar Calif., Delta Sigma Rho. Clubs: South Hills Country (West Covina); Clan Donnachaidh Soc. Lutheran. Home: 1116 S Serena Dr West Covina CA 91791-3754 E-mail: casu8@earthlink.net.

MCHALE, GEORGE T., mathematics and computer science educator; s. William Vincent McHale and Anne Elizabeth McGee; m. Patricia Boyle, Aug. 11, 1973; children: Sean, Brian, Rebecca. MA, West Chester State Coll., Pa., 1973. Cert. tchr. Pa., 1973. Tchr. Tamaqua Area H.S., Pa., 1974—; instr. Pa. State U., Hazleton Campus, Pa., 1984—. Instr. Lehigh Carbon CC, Schnecksville, Pa., 2005—. Tchr., bd. dirs. New Life Assembly of God Ch., Tamaqua, Pa., 1986—. Recipient Acad. Achievement award, West Chester State Coll., 1972. Mem.: Tamaqua Area Edn. Assn. (assoc.). Avocation: running. Home Phone: 570-668-5434.

MC HALE, JOHN JOSEPH, baseball club executive; b. Detroit, Sept. 21, 1921; s. John Michael and Catherine M. (Kelly) McH.; m. Patricia Anne Cameron, Feb. 15, 1947 (dec.); children: Patricia Cameron II, John Joseph, Jr., Kevin K., Anne F., Brian F., Mary M. AB cum laude, U. Notre Dame, 1947. Profl. baseball player, 1941-42, 45-47; asst. dir. minor league clubs Detroit Tigers Baseball Club, 1948, asst. farm dir., 1948-53, dir. minor league clubs, 1954-55, dir. player personnel, 1956-57, gen. mgr., 1957-58; v.p., gen. mgr. Milw. Braves Baseball Club (became Atlanta Braves Baseball Club 1961), 1957-61, pres., gen. mgr., 1961-67; dep. commr. NYC, 1968—82; pres., gen. mgr. Montreal Expos Baseball Club, 1968-87, dep. chmn., CEO, 1987—; ret. Japan Sports Sys. Dir. Perini Corp. Ret. trustee emeritus Intracoastal Hosp. Corp., West Palm Beach, Fla., 1986—; dir. emeritus Schwartz Investment Trust Ave Maria Fund, 2001; bd. dirs. Nat. Baseball Hall of Fame and Mus.; mem. adv. bd. Hospice of Treasure Coast, Fla.; bd. regents Ave Maria U., 2007; mem. adv. bd. First Bank and Trust, Indiantown, Fla., 2007—. Mem. Nat. Monogram Club (U. Notre Dame), Assn. Ret. Ball Players Am. (pres., dir.), Harbour Ridge Club. Address: Harbour Ridge 2014 NW Royal Fern Ct Palm City FL 34990-8025

MCHALE, JUDITH A. (JUDITH OTTALLORAN), former broadcast executive, lawyer; b. NYC, 1947; m. Michael McHale; 2 children. B in Politics, U. Nottingham, Eng.; JD, Fordham U.Law Sch., 1979. Atty. Battle, Fowler, NYC; gen. counsel MTV networks, Discovery Comm., Inc., 1987, sr. v.p., gen. counsel, exec. v.p., gen. counsel, pres., COO, 1995—2004, pres., CEO, 2004—06. Mem. Md. State Bd. of Edn., 1997—2001; bd. dirs. Polo Ralph Lauren, John Hancock Co., Potomac Electric Power Co., Host Marriott Corp., Cable in the Classroom, Vital Voices Global Partnership, Africa Soc., Africare, Sister-to-Sister Everyone Has a Heart Found.

MCHALE, KEVIN EDWARD, professional sports team executive, retired professional basketball player; b. Hibbing, Minn., Dec. 19, 1957; m. Lynn McHale; children: Kristyn, Michael, Joseph, Alexandra, Thomas. Student, U. Minn., 1976—80. Player Boston Celtics, 1980—93; spl. asst. Minn. Timberwolves, 1993—94, asst. gen. mgr., 1994—95, v.p. basketball ops., 1995—, interim head coach, 2005. Named to NBA All Rookie Team, 1981, NBA All-Defensive Second Team, 1983, 89, 90, NBA All-Defensive First Team, 1986-88, All-NBA First Team, 1987, NBA All-Star Team, 1984, 86-91, Basketball Hall of Fame, 1999, Nat. HS Sports Hall of Fame, 2000; named one of Top 50 Players in first 50 years of NBA, 1995; named Top Player in U. Minn. hist.; recipient NBA Sixth Man award, 1984, 85. Achievements include winning NBA Championships as a member of the Celtics, 1981, 84, 86. Office: Minn Timberwolves 600 1st Ave N Minneapolis MN 55403-1416 Office Phone: 612-673-1600. *

MCHALE, MAUREEN BERNADETTE KENNY, controller; b. Scranton, Pa., July 2, 1955; d. John Theodore and Ann Marie (Slowey) McH. BFA cum laude, Wilkes Coll., 1977; postgrad., Wilkes Coll., Rome, 1977; MBA in Acctg. with honors, U. Notre Dame, 1984; MST with honors, Kings Coll., 1995. Internal auditor Cen. Tax Bur., Forty Fort, Pa., 1977-82; placement coord. U. Notre Dame, South Bend, Ind., 1983-84; sr. acct. Laventhol and Horwath, Wilkes Barre, Pa., 1984-88; contr. Greco Holdings, Inc., Wilkes Barre, 1988-97; dir. fin. Mercy Health Care Ctr., Nanticoke, Pa., 1997—2000; CFO Little Flower Manor/St. Thérèse Residence, Wilkes-Barre, Pa., 2000—. Founder Entrepreneurship Lecture Series, U. Notre Dame, 1984. Leader Girl Scouts US, Forty Fort, 1977-82; chmn. County Children's Fingerprinting Program, Kingston, Pa., 1988; mem. exec. com., bd. dirs. Bishop O'Reilly HS, 1990—; bd. dirs. Northeastern Pa. Choral Soc., 1996-2000, Mercy Ctr.; pres. bd. dirs. St. Michael's Sch., 2005—. U. Notre Dame Scholar, 1984. Mem. Jaycees (bd. dirs. 1987-88), U. Notre Dame Alumni Assn. (bd. dirs., pres. Scranton chpt. 2004—) Democrat. Roman Catholic. Avocations: walking, bicycling, football. Home: 31 Virginia Ter Forty Fort PA 18704-4929 Office: 200 S Meade St Wilkes Barre PA 18702-6221 Office Phone: 570-823-6131. E-mail: mmchale@lfmstr.com.

MCHALE, MICHAEL JOHN, lawyer; b. NYC, Apr. 14, 1960; s. Michael Joseph and Mary Beatrice (Graddy) McH. BA, U. of the South, Sewanee, Tenn., 1982; JD, Samford U., Birmingham, Ala., 1985. Bar: Ala. 1986, U.S. Dist. Ct. (no., mid. and so. dists.) Ala. 1986, U.S. Ct. Appeals (11th cir.) 1986, Fla. (cert. admiralty and maritime law) 1991, U.S. Dist. Ct. (mid. and so. dists.) Fla. 1991, U.S. Dist. Ct. (no. dist.) Fla. 1997, U.S. Supreme Ct. 1991; cert. admiralty and maritime lawyer Fla. Bar Bd. of Legal Specialization, mediator, arbitrator Fla. Supreme Ct. Assoc. Wagner, Nugent, Johnson, Roth, Romano, Eriksen & Kupfer, West Palm Beach, Fla., 1989-92; ptnr. Whalen & McHale, West Palm Beach, Fla., 1992-95, Daves, Whalen, McHale & Considine, West Palm Beach, Fla., 1995-98; sole practitioner Jensen Beach, Fla., 1998—; of counsel Deorchis,Hillenbrand & Wiener, LLP, Miami, Fla., 1998—. Author: Strategic Use of Circumstantial Evidence, 2nd edit., 1991, Evaluating and Settling Personal Injury Claims, 1992, supplement through present, Making Trial Objections, 1993, supplement through present, Expert Witnesses: Direct and Cross Examination, 1993, supplement through present, The Deposition Field Manual, 2004, Maritime Law and Practice, 2d edit., 2004, Use of Evidence in Admiralty Proceedings, 2003; editor, author: Litigating TMJ Cases, 1993 and yearly supplements. Named one of Outstanding Young Men of Am., 1988. Mem. ABA (admiralty com.), ATLA, Am. Acad. Fla. Trial Lawyers, Maritime Law Assn. US (procter), Southeastern Admiralty Law Inst., Fla. Bar (admiralty law com. editl. bd., admiralty and maritime cert. com.), Palm. Beach Bar Assn., Martin County Bar Assn., Sigma Nu Phi. Avocation: vessel building. Office: 1925 NE Ricou Terr Jensen Beach FL 34957 Home: 3000 SE Fairway W Stuart FL 34997 Office Phone: 772-225-2078. Personal E-mail: admar1@earthlink.net.

MCHALE, PAUL F., JR., federal agency administrator, former congressman; b. Bethlehem, Pa., July 26, 1950; m. Katherine McHale; children: Matthew, Mary, Luke. BA in Govt. sigma cum laude, Lehigh U., 1972; JD, Georgetown U. Law Sch., 1977. Atty., Bethlehem, 1977—82; mem. Pa. Ho. of Reps., 1983—92, US Congresses from 15th Pa. dist., 1993—99; former mem. nat. security com., mem. sci. com.; mem. Tallman, Hudders and Sorrentino, Allentown, Pa., 1999—2003; asst. sec. for homeland def. US Dept. Def., Washington, 2003—. Infantry officer USMC, 1972—74, Okinawa, Philippines, maj. USMCR, 1990—92, Persian Gulf. Decorated Navy Commendation medal; recipient Disting. Pub. Svc. medal, US Dept. Def., Frank M. Tejada Leadership award, Marine Corps. Reserve Officers Assn., 1997, Reserve Officers Assn. Minuteman of the Year award, 1998. Mem.: Phi Beta Kappa. Democrat.

MCHALE, VINCENT EDWARD, political science professor; b. Jenkins Twp., Pa., Apr. 17, 1939; m. Ann Barbara Cotner, Nov. 8, 1963; 1 child, Patrick James. A.B., Wilkes Coll., 1964; M.A., Pa. State U., 1966, Ph.D. in Polit. Sci., 1969. Asst. prof. polit. sci. U. Pa., Phila., 1969-75, dir. grad. studies, 1971-73; assoc. prof. Case Western Res. U., Cleve., 1975-84, prof., 1984-03, chmn. dept. polit. sci., 1978-03; vis. lectr. John Carroll U., summer 1980, Beaver Coll., 1975; Marcus A. Hanna prof., 2006—. Author: (with A.P. Frognier and D. Paranzino) Vote, Clivages Socio-politiques et Developpement Regional en Belgique, 1974. Co-editor; contbr.: Evaluating Transnational Programs in Government and Business, 1980; Political Parties of Europe, 1983; edtl. adv. bd. Worldmark Ency. of Nations, 1994—. Contbr. chpts. to books, articles to profl. jours. Project cons. Council Econ Opportunity in Greater Cleve., 1978-81; mem. Morris Abrams Award Com., 1977—. Recipient Outstanding Prof. award Lux chpt. Mortar Bd., 1989, 90; named one of Most Interesting People of 1988, Cleve. Mag.; NSF grantee, 1971-72; HEW grantee, 1976-78; Woodrow Wilson fellow, 1968, Ruth Young Boucke fellow, 1967-68; All-Univ. fellow, 1967-68. Mem. Phi Kappa Phi. Home: 3070 Coleridge Rd Cleveland OH 44118-3556 Office: Case Western Res U Cleveland OH 44106 Office Phone: 216-368-2425. Business E-Mail: vem@case.edu.

MCHARD, JAMES LORIN, corporate financial executive, freelance/self-employed composer, writer; b. Bay City, Mich., June 23, 1942; s. James Alvah and Daisy Evelyn McHard; m. Jerilee Miles, June 6, 1964 (div. May 15, 1985); m. Alice Brallie Dekle, May 24, 1997; children: Maureen Day, Clair James Ian. BS, U. Mich., 1964. Cert. secondary sch. tchr. Mich. Engring. fin. analyst Ford Motor Co., Livonia, Mich., 1964—97; pres. J & A Music Enterprises, Mich. Freelance composer, lectr., writer; lectr. music theory. Composer: Tremors, 1991, Virtuals, 1992; editor: Voice of Reason newsletter, 1980—82; author: The Future of Modern Music, 2001, Julio Estrada, Five Years of ONCE, Pape: Cinema Texas, 2002; contbr. articles to profl. jours.; pub.: program notes for premiere of Estrada's opera ISCM New Music Festival. Mem.: Southern Poverty Law Ctr. (name included on Wall of Tolerance), Electronic Music Found., S.E. Mich. Horn Club (assoc.; sec. 1985—88). Home: 28860 Richland Livonia MI 48150 Office Phone: 734-525-6265. Personal E-mail: release10@sbcglobal.net.

MC HARGUE, CARL JACK, lab administrator; b. Jan. 30, 1926; s. John David and Virginia (Thomas) McH.; m. Edith Trovillion, Aug. 28, 1948; children: Anne Odell McHargue Diegel, Carol Virginia Hornberger, Margaret Katherine McHargue; m. Betty Ford, Sept. 30, 1960. BS in Metall. Engring., U. Ky., 1949, MS, 1951, PhD, 1953. Instr. U. Ky., Lexington, 1949-53; with Oak Ridge Nat. Lab., 1953-90, sect. head, 1960-80, program mgr. for materials scis., 1961-88, sr. rsch. staff, 1980-90; prof. materials sci. and engring. U. Tenn., Knoxville, 1991—, dir. ctr. materials processing, 1991—. Vis. prof. U. Newcastle upon Tyne, Eng., 1987; adj. prof. Vanderfilt U., 1988—; bd. dirs. Accreditation Bd. for Engring. and Tech., 1998—; bd. dirs. The Minerals, Metals and Materials Soc. Contbr. numerous articles in field to profl. jours. With AUS, 1944-46. Recipient Disting. Svc. award The Minerals, Metals and Materials Soc., 2001; named to Engring. Hall of Distinction, U. Ky., 1995. Fellow Metall. Soc. AIME, Am. Soc. for Metals; mem. Materials Rsch. Soc., Sigma Xi, Tau Beta Pi. Republican. Presbyterian. Home: 7201 Sheffield Dr Knoxville TN 37909-2414 Office: U Tenn 514 E Stadium Hill Knoxville TN 37996-0750 Office Phone: 865-974-7680. Business E-Mail: crl@utk.edu.

MCHENRY, BARNABAS, lawyer; b. Harrisburg, Pa., Oct. 30, 1929; s. William Cecil and Louise (Perkins) McH.; m. Marie Bannon Jones, Dec. 13, 1952; children: Thomas J.P., W.H. Davis, John W.H. AB, Princeton U., 1952; LLB, Columbia U., 1957. Bar: N.Y. 1957. Assoc. Lord, Day, & Lord, NYC, 1957-62; gen. counsel The Reader's Digest Assn., Inc., NYC, 1962-85; exec. dir. Wallace Funds, NYC, 1985-86; chmn. N.Y. state orgns., 1986—. Trustee, pres. Boscobel Restoration, Inc., 1964; trustee Am. Conservation Assn., 1977; trustee emeritus Met. Mus. Art, 1980; coun. mem. Villa I Tatti, Harvard Sch. Renaissance Studies, 1982; regent emeritus Smithsonian Instn., 1985; commr. Palisades Interstate Park Commn., 1987; chmn. Hudson River Valley Greenway Coun., 1989; co-chair Hudson River Valley Nat. Heritage Assn., 1996. Home: 164 E 72nd St New York NY 10021-4363 Fax: 212-681-4552.

MCHENRY, HENRY MALCOLM, anthropologist, educator; b. LA, May 19, 1944; s. Dean Eugene and Emma Jane (Snyder) McH.; m. Linda Jean Conway, June 25, 1966; children: Lindsay Jean, Annalisa Jane. BA, U. Calif., Davis, 1966, MA, 1967; PhD, Harvard U., 1972. Asst. prof. anthropology U. Calif., Davis, 1971-76, assoc. prof. anthropology, 1976-81, prof. anthropology, 1981—, chmn. dept. anthropology, 1984-88. Fellow AAAS, Am. Anthrop. Assn., Calif. Acad. Sci.; mem. Am. Assn. Phys. Anthropologists (exec. com. 1981-85), Soc. Study Evolution, Soc. Vertebrate Paleontology, Phi Beta Kappa, Phi Kappa Phi. Democrat. Buddhist. Avocation: winemaker. Home: 330 11th St Davis CA 95616-2010 Office: U of Calif Davis Dept Of Anthropology Davis CA 95616 Office Phone: 530-752-1588. Business E-Mail: hmmchenry@ucdavis.edu.

MCHENRY, KATHRYN, forensic specialist; b. Mariemont, Ohio, Nov. 16, 1981; d. Charles Edmund McHenry, Jr. and Debra Sue McHenry. BA, Berea Coll., Berea, Ky., 2000—03. Biology tchg. asst. Berea Coll., 2000—03; forensic DNA analyst DNA Diagnostics Ctr., Fairfield, Ohio,

2005—. Mem.: Am. Acad. Forensic Scis. (assoc.; trainee affiliate 2006—), Internat. Assn. Identification (assoc.). Home: 8329 Landmark Ct Apt 206 West Chester OH 45069 Office: DNA Diagnostics Ctr One DDC Way Fairfield OH 45014 Home Phone: 513-860-0569. Office Fax: 800-310-9746. Personal E-mail: ktmchnry@yahoo.com. Business E-Mail: km1@dnacenter.com.

MCHENRY, MARTIN CHRISTOPHER, physician, educator; b. Feb. 9, 1932; s. Merl and Marcella (Bricca) McH.; m. Patricia Grace Hughes, Apr. 27, 1957; children: Michael, Christopher, Timothy, Mary Ann, Jeffrey, Paul, Kevin, William, Monica, Martin Christopher. Student, U. Santa Clara, 1950-53; MD, U. Cin., 1957; MS in Medicine, U. Minn., 1966. Diplomate Am. Bd. Internal Medicine. Intern Highland Alameda County (Calif.) Hosp., Oakland, 1957-58; resident, internal medicine fellow Mayo Clinic, Rochester, Minn., 1958-61, spl. appointee in infectious diseases, 1963-64; staff physician Henry Ford Hosp., Detroit, 1964-67, Cleve. Clinic, 1967-72, chmn. dept. infectious diseases, 1972-92, sr. physician infectious diseases, 1992-98. Cons. infectious diseases, 1998—2006; asst. clin. prof. Case Western Res. U., 1970-77, assoc. clin. prof. medicine, 1977-91, clin. prof. medicine, 1991—2006; assoc. vis. physician Cleve. Met. Gen. Hosp., 1970-00; cons. VA Hosp., Cleve., 1973-74. Contbr. more than 100 articles to profl. jours., also chpts. to books. Chmn. manpower com. Swine Influenza Program, Cleve., 1976. With USNR, 1961-63. Named Disting. Tchr. in Medicine, Cleve. Clinic, 1972, 90; recipient 1st ann. Bruce Hubbard Stewart award Cleve. Clinic Found. for Humanities in Medicine, 1985, Nightingale Physician Collaboration award Cleve. Clinic Found. Divsn. Nursing, 1995, Clinician of Yr. award Acad. Medicine of Cleve./No. Ohio Med. Assn., 2002. Fellow ACP, Infectious Diseases Soc. Am. (Clinician award 2000), Am. Coll. Chest Physicians (chmn. com. cardiopulmonary infections 1975-77, 81-83), Royal Soc. Medicine of Gt. Britain; mem. Am. Soc. Clin. Pharmacology and Therapeutics (chmn. sect. infectious diseases and antimicrobial agts. 1970-77, 80-85, dir.). Home: 2779 Belgrave Rd Pepper Pike OH 44124-4601 Office: 9500 Euclid Ave Cleveland OH 44195-0001

MCHENRY, PATRICK TIMOTHY, congressman; b. Mecklenburg, NC, Oct. 22, 1975; Attended, NC State U.; BA in Hist., Belmont Abbey Coll., 1999. Exec. DCI/New Media, Inc., Washington; owner & broker McHenry Real Estate, Gastonia, NC; spl. asst. to Sec. Elaine L. Chao US Dept. Labor, Washington, 2000; mem. NC State Ho. Reps., 2003—05, US Congress from 10th NC dist., 2005—. Mem. fin svcs. com. US Congress, 2005—, mem. budget com., mem. oversight and govt. reform com., vice chmn. fin. for exec. com. Nat. Rep. Congl. Com., dep. Rep. whip. Bd. dirs. United Success by Six Youth Prog. Named a Small Bus. Champion, Small Bus. and Entrepreneurship Coun., Hero of the Taxpayer, Ams. for Tax Reform, Protector of Property Rights, Property Rights Alliance; recipient Spirit of Enterprise award, US C. of C. Mem.: Gaston C. of C., NRA, Gastonia Rotary Club. Republican. Roman Catholic. Office: US House Reps 224 Cannon House Office Bldg Washington DC 20515-3310 Office Phone: 202-225-2576. Office Fax: 202-225-0316. *

MCHENRY, POWELL, lawyer; b. Cin., May 14, 1926; s. L. Lee McHenry and Marguerite L. (Powell) Heinz; m. Venna Mae Guerrea, Aug. 27, 1948; children: Scott, Marshall, Jody Lee, Gale Lynn. AB, U. Cinn., 1949; LLB, Harvard U., 1951, JD, 1969. Bar: Ohio 1951, U.S. Ct. Appeals (6th cir.) 1964, U.S. Supreme Ct. 1966. Assoc. Dinsmore, Shohl, Sawyer & Dinsmore, Cinn., 1951-57; ptnr. Dinsmore, Shohl, Coates & Deupree (and predecessors), Cinn., 1958-75; gen. counsel Federated Dept. Stores, Inc., 1971-75; assoc. gen. counsel Procter & Gamble Co., 1975-76, v.p., gen. counsel, 1976-83, sr. v.p., gen. counsel, 1983-91; counsel Dinsmore & Shohl, Cin., 1991—; bd. dirs. Eagle Picher Industries, Inc., 1991-97. Mem. com. Hamilton County Pub. Defender, Cin., chmn., 1996-2000. With USNR, 1944-46. Recipient award of merit Ohio Legal Center Inst., 1969, Lifetime Achievement in Law award, Cin. Bar Found., 2004. Mem. ABA, Ohio Bar Assn., Cin. Bar Assn. (pres. 1979-80, exec. com. 1975-81), Harvard U. Law Sch. Assn. Cin. (pres. 1960-61), Am. Law Inst., Assn. Gen. Counsel (pres. 1986-88), Harvard Club, Western Hills Country Club (bd. dirs. 1964-70, sec. 1966-69, 87-89, treas. 1969-70, 89-90), Queen City Club, Commonwealth Club (pres. 1996-97). Republican. Methodist. Office: Dimsmore & Shohl 1900 Chemed Ctr 255 E 5th St Cincinnati OH 45202-4700 Office Phone: 513-977-8295.

MCHUGH, CARIL EISENSTEIN DREYFUSS, art dealer, art gallery director, consultant; b. New Haven; d. Irving and Gertrude (Lax) Eisenstein; m. Barney Dreyfuss II (div.); children: Caryn, Barney III (Terry), Andrew, Evan; m. James Marshall McHugh Jr., Dec. 31, 1976. BA, Smith Coll. Libr. archivist, mem. staff art rental Washington Gallery of Modern Art, 1963-67; asst. to curator of prints and drawings Nat. Mus. Am. Art, Washington, 1967-69; dir. Studio Gallery, Washington, 1970-75; dir., ptnr. Parsons-Dreyfuss Gallery, NYC, 1976-80; dir. Frank Marino Gallery, NYC, 1981, Humphrey Fine Art, NYC, 1988-90, Gregory Gallery, NYC, 1995-96; freelance curator, adv. bd. Hugo de Pagano Gallery, 1997—2000; rschr. Barnett Newman Found., NYC, 2001—. Art cons., writer, N.Y.C., 1982—; arranger exhbns. Nat. Mus. Am. Art, Washington, 1968-69, USIA, Washington, 1976, Automation House, N.Y.C., 1983; curator Creative Works Exhbn., Smith Coll., 2005. An Homage to Betty Parsons exhbn., 2000, Portraits by Tom Block/Amnesty Internat. Exhbn., 2002, essays to catalogs, articles to profl. mags. Bd. dirs. Women's Nat. Dem. Club, Washington, 1972-76, Friends of the Corcoran, Washington, 1972-76, Smith Club of Washington, 1974-76; Sophia Smith Assoc. Smith Coll., Northampton, Mass., 1985, 90, 95, 2000, 2005, Women in the Arts, 1995—. Avocations: reading, hiking, swimming, poetry. Home: 241 Central Park W Apt 9C New York NY 10024-4545 Personal E-mail: carilmchugh@msn.com.

MCHUGH, JAMES JOSEPH, lawyer; b. Phila., Sept. 15, 1961; s. James Joseph and Helene Anne (Kiernan) McHugh; m. Colette Marie McHugh, May 20, 1989; children: Albert Taylor, James Joseph III, Cole Michael, Sophia Kiernan. BSME, Drexel U., 1985; JD magna cum laude, Villanova U., Pa., 1992. Bar: Pa. 1992, N.J. 1992, U.S. Dist. Ct. (ea. dist.) Pa., U.S. Dist. Ct. N.J. Ptnr. McHugh Plumbing & Heating, Phila., 1984-89; project mgr. Fluidics Mech Contractors, Phila., 1989-92; assoc. Pepper, Hamilton & Scheetz, Phila., 1992-94; ptnr. The Beasley Firm, LLC, Phila., 1994—. Author, editor case notes. Mem. adv. com. Penn Pub. Svc. Program, Sch. Law, U. Pa. Mem. ATLA, Pa. Bar Assn., Phila. Bar Assn., Order of Coif. Home: 65 Brooks Rd Moorestown NJ 08057-3855 Office: Lopez McHugh LLP 1325 Spruce Street Philadelphia PA 19107 Office Phone: 215-732-3137. Business E-Mail: jjm@mchughfirm.com.

MCHUGH, JAMES LENAHAN, JR., lawyer; b. Pitts., June 28, 1937; s. James Lenahan and Annette (Dalton) McH.; m. Mary-Ann Curto, Feb. 16, 1963 (div. 1988); children: Angela Dalton Sherrill, Hillary Lenahan Clagett; m. Rosa Lamoreaux, Sept. 8, 1991. BA, Duquesne U., 1959; LLB, Villanova U., 1962. Bar: DC 1963. Law clk. U.S. Dist. Ct. (ea. dist.) Pa., Phila., 1962-63; law clk. to Assoc. Justice Tom C. Clark, U.S. Supreme Ct., Washington, 1963-64; assoc. Steptoe & Johnson, Washington, 1967-70, ptnr., 1970-94; gen. counsel APA, Washington, 1994—2001, sr. counsel, 2001—. Mem. bd. consultors Law Sch., Villanova U., 1973—; dir. Higher Achievement Program, Washington, 1984-87; coord. Washington Lawyers' Project, Robert F. Kennedy Meml. Found., Washington, 1972-75. Editor-in-chief Villanova Law Rev., Vol. VII, 1961-62; chmn. editl. adv. bd. Fed. Comm. Law Jour., 1981-84. Bd. dirs. Columbia Hosp. for Women's Found., Washington, 1985-96, Children's Radio Theatre, Washington, 1983-86, Cantate Chamber Singers, 2006-; chmn. exec. giving Archbishop's Appeal, Archdiocese of Washington, 1982-84; mem. bd. visitors Ctr. for Study of Orgns. and Mgmt., U. Md. Univ. Coll., 1987-92; bd. dirs. Human Resources Rsch. Orgn., Inc., 1978—; chmn. bd. dirs., 1991—; mem. adv. bd. Inst. for Conflict Analysis and Resolution, George Mason U., 1990-94. Capt. U.S. Army, 1964-67. Mem. ABA (sect. on health law, tax, intellectual property and legal edn.), D.C. Bar Assn., Am. Soc. Assn. Execs. (chmn. Washington Legal Symposium 2002-04, vice chmn. legal sect. coun. 2003-04, chmn. 2004-05), Choral Arts Soc., Villanova Law Alumni Assn. (pres. Greater Balt./Washington area chpt. 2002—04), Order of Coif, Confrerie des Chevaliers du Tastevin. Home: 4112 Fessenden St NW Washington DC 20016-4227 Office: APA 750 1st St NE Washington DC 20002-4242 Office Phone: 202-336-6089. Business E-Mail: jmchugh@apa.org.

MCHUGH, JOHN MICHAEL, congressman; b. Watertown, NY, Sept. 29, 1948; s. Donald and Jane (O'Neill) McHugh. BA in Polit. Sci., Syracuse U. Utica Coll., 1970; MPA, SUNY Nelson A. Rockefeller Grad. Sch. Pub. Affairs, 1977. Asst. city mgr., Watertown, NY, 1968-73; confidential asst. to city mgr., 1971-76; chief rsch., liaison with local govts. Staff of NY State Senator H. Douglas Barclay, 1976-84; mem. NY State Senate, 1985—93, chmn. joint legis. commn. on dairy industry devel., 1987-92; mem. US Congress from 23rd NY dist., 1993—, mem. oversight and govt. reform com., mem. armed svcs. com., ranking mem. mil. pers. subcommittee, mem. permanent select com. on intelligence. Named Hon. First Citien, City of Watertown, NY, 1976; recipient Individual Achievement award, NY State Dept. Econ. Devel., George (Buck) Gillespie award, Blinded Am. Vets. Found., 1999, President's award, Nat. Newspaper Assn., 2000, Outstanding Legislator award, Assn. US Army, 2003, Friend of Zion award, Jerusalem Fund, 2004, Pub. Svc. award, Direct Mktg. Assn. Nonprofit Fedn., 2004, Bertrand H. Snell award, Clarkson U., 2005. Mem. Legis. on State Legislators (nat. conf. state legislators), Nat. Conf. State Legislators (vice chmn. agrl. and internat. trade com. State-Fed. Assembly), Am. Soc. Young Polit. Leaders. Republican. Roman Catholic. Avocations: boating, skiing, music. Office: 120 Washington St Ste 200 Watertown NY 13601-3370 Office Phone: 202-225-4611, 315-782-3150. Office Fax: 315-782-1291. *

MCHUGH, PAUL R., psychiatrist, neurologist, educator; b. Lawrence, Mass., May 21, 1931; s. Francis Paul and Mary Dorothea (Herlihy) McH.; m. Jean Barlow, Dec. 27, 1959; children: Clare Mary, Patrick Daniel, Denis Timothy. AB, Harvard U., 1952, MD, 1956. Diplomate: Am. Bd. Psychiatry and Neurology. Intern Peter Bent Brigham Hosp., Boston, 1956-57; resident in neurology Mass. Gen. Hosp., 1957-60, fellow in neuropathology, 1958-59; teaching fellow in neurology and neuropathology Harvard, 1957-60; clin. asst. psychiatry Maudsley Hosp., London, Eng., 1960-61; mem. neuropsychiatry div. Walter Reed Army Inst. Research, Washington, 1961-64; asst. prof. psychiatry and neurology Cornell U., NYC, 1964-68, assoc. prof., 1968-71, prof., 1971; dir. electroencephalography N.Y. Hosp., 1964-68; founder, dir. N.Y. Hosp. Bourne Behavioral Rsch. Lab., 1967-68, clin. dir., supr. psychiat. edn., founder, dir. Weschester divsn. dept. psychiatry, 1968-73; prof., chmn. dept. psychiatry U. Oreg. Health Sci. Center, Portland, 1973-75; Henry Phipps prof. psychiatry Johns Hopkins, Balt., 1975—2001, chmn. dept. psychiatry, 1975—2001, prof. dept. mental hygiene, 1976—; psychiatrist-in-chief Johns Hopkins Hosp., 1975—2001; dir. Blades Ctr. for Clin. Practice and Rsch. in Alcoholism Johns Hopkins Med. Inst., 1992—2001; chmn. med. staff Johns Hopkins Hosp., 1983-89, trustee, 1983—89. Author: The Perspectives of Psychiatry, 1983, 1998; (with Phillip R. Slavney) Psychiatric Polarities, 1987, Genes, Brain and Behavior, 1990, The Mind Has Mountains: Reflections on Society and Psychiatry, 2006; contbg. author: Cecil-Loeb Textbook of Medicine; mem. editl. bd. Am. Jour. Physiology, Jour. Nervous and Mental Disease, Comprehensive Psychiatry, Medicine, Psychol. Medicine, 1976—, Am. Scholar; contbr. articles to profl. jours. Mem. Md. Gov.'s Adv. Com., 1977—80, U.S. Conf. Cath. Bishops Nat. Rev. Bd. Office of Child and Youth Protection, 2002—, Pres. Coun. on Bioethics, 2001—. Grantee NIH, 1964-68, 67-70, 70-74, 75-96; recipient William C. Menninger award ACP, 1987, Inst. Medicine, 1992. Fellow: Am. Psychiat. Assn., Royal Coll. Psychiatry; mem.: Am. Coll. Psychiatrists (Disting. Svc. award 2002), Pavlovian Soc., Am. Psychopath. Assn. (Joseph Zubin award 1995, Paul Hoch award 2006), Am. Coll. Neuropsychopharmacology, Harvey Soc., Am. Physiol. Soc., Am. Neurol. Assn., Inst. Medicine-NAS, W Hamilton St. Club, Phi Beta Kappa (vis. scholar 2003—04). Home: 3707 St Paul St Baltimore MD 21218-2403 Office: Johns Hopkins Med Insts Meyer 127 600 N Wolfe St Baltimore MD 21287 Office Phone: 410-502-3150. Business E-Mail: pmchugh1@jhmi.edu.

MCHUGH, THOMAS EDWARD, state supreme court justice; b. Charleston, W.Va., Mar. 26, 1936; s. Paul and Melba McHugh; m. Judith McHugh, Mar. 14, 1959; children: Karen, Cindy, James, John. AB, W.Va. U., 1958, LLB, 1964. Bar: W.Va. 1964. Pvt. practice law, Charleston, 1964-66, 69-74; law clk. to presiding judge Harlan Calhoun W.Va. Supreme Ct. of Appeals, 1966-68; chief judge Cir. Ct. (13th cir.) W.Va., Charleston, 1974-80; justice W.Va. Supreme Ct., Charleston, 1980-97; chief justice W. Va Supreme Ct, Charleston, 1984, 88, 92; mediation practice Allen Guthrie McHugh & Thomas, PLLC, Charleston, 1997—. Served to 1st lt. U.S. Army, 1958-61. Mem. W.Va. Jud. Assn., W.Va. Bar Assn., Order of the Coif. Democrat. Roman Catholic. Office: Allen Guthrie McHugh & Thomas PLLC PO Box 3394 500 Lee St E Charleston WV 25333-3394

MCHUGHEN, ALAN, geneticist, educator; b. Ottawa, Ontario, Can., Apr. 13, 1954; m. Donna Greschner; children: Stephanie, Nicola. PhD, Oxford U., Eng., 1979. Lectr. Yale U., New Haven, 1979—82; prof. U. Sasktoon, Canada, 1982—2001; prof., botany and plant scis. U. Calif., Riverside, 2002—. Author: Pandora's Picnic Basket (Book of Yr., CSWA, 2000); contbr. articles to profl. jours. Pres. Internat. Soc. for Biosafety Rsch., Riverside, 1988—2004. Fellow, Am. Coll. Nutrition, 2002. Achievements include patents in field; development of public sector transgenic crop cultivar. Office: Univ Calif University Ave Riverside CA 92521-0124 Home Phone: 951-683-4766; Office Phone: 951-827-7532. Office Fax: 951-827-5717. Business E-Mail: alanmc@ucr.edu.

MCILQUHAM, DAVID J., consumer products company executive; Grad. with honors, Queens Univ. Mgmt. positions GE Canada; mgmt. positions through gen. mgr. Canadian ops. & v.p. mktg. Samsonite Corp.; v.p. mktg., corp. v.p. sales & mktg. Sealy Inc., Trinity, NC, 1990—2001, pres., COO, 2001—06, chmn., pres., CEO, 2006—. Office: Sealy Inc 1 Office Pkwy at Sealy Dr Trinity NC 27370 *

MCILROY, ALAN F., manufacturing executive; b. 1950; Internat. contr. Wheelabrator Corp., 1983-87; bus. unit contr. Gen. Chem., 1987-90; sr. v.p. Harris Chem.; head Greenock Group; CFO Dayton Superior Corp., Miamisburg, Ohio, 1997—. Office: Dayton Superior Corp Ste 130 7777 Washington Village Dr Dayton OH 45459

MCILROY, M. DOUGLAS, computer scientist, educator; m. Barbara McIlroy. BS, Cornell U., 1958; PhD in Applied Math., MIT, 1959. Prof. MIT, 1957—58; joined Bell Labs., Murray Hill, NJ, 1958, head Computing Techniques Rsch. Dept., 1965—86, disting. mem. tech. staff Computing Scis. Rsch. Ctr.; adj. prof. Dept. Computer Sci. Dartmouth Coll., Hanover, NH, 1997—. Vis. lectr. Oxford U., 1967—68. Contbr. articles to profl. jours. Mem.: NAE. Office: Dartmouth Coll Dept Computer Sci 6211 Sudikoff Hall Hanover NH 03755 Office Phone: 603-464-1077. E-mail: mcilroy@dartmouth.edu.

MCILVAINE, JAMES ROSS, lawyer; b. Youngstown, Ohio, July 22, 1944; s. Earl Eugene and Caroline E. (Clawson) McI.; m. Carol Beth Boyer, June 24, 1967; children: Andrew S., Katherine Erin. BA, Muskingum Coll., 1966; JD cum laude, Ohio State Coll., 1969. Bar: Ohio 1969, U.S. Dist. Ct. (no. dist.) Ohio 1971. Assoc. Oestricher, Seamon, Newman & Knoll, Akron, Ohio, 1969-70; asst. prosecuting atty. Summit County Prosecutor's Office, Akron, Ohio, 1970-71; ptnr. Palecek, McIlvaine, Hoffman & Morse, Co., LPA, Wadsworth, Ohio, 1971—. Mem. citizen's adv. bd. Medina County Correctional Facility Study, 1983; founding trustee Wedsworth City Schs. Performing Arts Found., 1994—; mem. bd. edn. Wadsworth City Sch., 1988—; trustee Wadsworth-Rittmann Hosp., 1999—; bd. dirs. Medina County Law Libr., 1979—83, Wadsworth chpt. ARC, 1981—94. Mem. ATLA (state del. 1985-87, bd. govs. 1987-88), Ohio Acad. Trial lawyers (Editor profl. newsletter 1982-84, chair reginal trial sems. 1980-81, sec. 1981-83, lectr. criminal law sem. 1981, ins. law sem. 1980, 84, 86, negligence law sem. 1984, 86, 88, chair student advocacy divsn. 1976-78, pres. 1984-85, trustee, bd. dirs. 1976-83), Medina County Bar Assn. (pres. 1983, dir., chmn. common pleas ct. rules com., lectr. sms. 1986, 87), Ohio State Bar Assn., Wadsworth Area C. of C. (bd. dirs. 1995-99, v.p. 1997-98, pres. 1998-99, Bus. Leader of Yr. award 2007), Lions. Office: 200 Smokerise Dr Ste 200 Wadsworth OH 44281-9460 Office Phone: 330-334-1536. Business E-Mail: jmcilvaine@pmhmlaw.com.

MCILVAINE, PATRICIA MORROW, physician; b. Pitts., Feb. 4, 1947; d. James Morrow McIlvaine and Virginia Fuller Tucker. BS in Chemistry, Simmons Coll., 1969; MD, U. Utah, 1984. Rsch. technician Mass. Gen. Hosp., Boston, 1969-70, MIT, Cambridge, 1970-75, Utah State U., Logan, 1975-80; resident in internal medicine U. Mass. Hosp., Worcester, 1984-87; pvt. practice, Monson, Mass., 1987-2001; mem. pvt. group practice Walla Walla (Wash.) Clinic, 2002—. Staff physician Wing Meml. Hosp., Palmer, Mass., 1987-2001. Vol., trainer IRBIS Enterprises, Mongolia, 1998-2004. NFS summer scholar, 1968, Helena Rubinstein scholar Simmons Coll., 1968-69. Mem. ACP/Am. Soc. Internal Medicine, Sigma Xi. Avocations: fiber crafts, international travel, hiking, gardening, sailing. Home: 913 Bonnie Brae Walla Walla WA 99362

MCILVAINE, ROBERT MORTON, literature educator; b. Vernon, Tex., Dec. 28, 1943; s. Paul Morton McIlvaine and Nancy Juanita Wickliffe; m. Martha Briegel McIlvaine, July 27, 1966; children: Jessica, Miranda. BA, Davis & Elkins Coll., W.Va., 1966; MA, U. Pa., 1967; PhD, Temple U., 1972. From asst. prof. to prof. Slippery Rock (Pa.) U., 1972—83, prof., 1983—. Contbr. articles to profl. jours. Home: PO Box 144 110 McIlvaine Ln Slippery Rock PA 16057 Office: Slippery Rock University 312D Spotts WCB Slippery Rock PA 16057 Office Phone: 724-738-2351. Business E-Mail: robert.mcilvaine@sru.edu.

MCILVANE, EDWARD JAMES, stained glass artist, educator; b. NYC, July 5, 1947; s. Edward James Sr. and Irene (Logue) McI.; m. Rose F. Aloisi, 1970 (div. 1985); children: Jessica, Blake. BS in Edn. and Art Edn., St. John's U., NYC, 1975; MFA, R.I. Sch. Design, 1978. Stained glass craftsman Claude Gaches Studio, LI, 1969-71, The Lamb Studio, N.J., 1971-72, Greenland Studio, NYC, 1972-75, Helmut-Schardt Studio, Northport, N.Y., 1975-78; freelance artist and designer Providence, 1978—. Guest artist Summrvail Workshop for Art, Vail, Colo., 1980, N.Y. Exptl. Glass Workshop, N.Y.C., 1980; program coord. Pilchuck Sch., Stanwood, Wash., 1979; instr. Haystack Mt. Sch. Crafts, Deer Isle, Maine, 1977. Prin. works include Johnson's Wax Co., Rancine, Wis., Temple Beth-El, Prov, R.I., Providence Coll., Bank of Boston, Joseph W. Martin, Jr. Inst. for Law and Soc. Stonehill Coll., North Easton, Mass., Licht residence, Little Compton, R.I., Vinyl Tech. Sch., Middletown, Conn., Presbyn. World Hdqs., Louisville. R.I. State Coun. on the Arts fellow, 1980, 86, Nat. Endowment for the Arts fellow, 1983. Mem. Glass Art Soc. Avocations: tai chi, angling. Home: 329 Pomfret Rd Brooklyn CT 06234 Office Phone: 860-774-4822. Personal E-mail: macdeverre@charter.net.

MCILWAIN, HARRIS H., physician, researcher; s. Cordelia B. McIlwain; m. Linda Fulghum, June 19, 1970; children: Laura E. McIlwain, Kimberly L. McIlwain, Michael Fulghum McIlwain, Daniel E. McIlwain, Virginia H. McIlwain, Lisa Ann McIlwain. MD, Emory U., Atlanta, 1973. Diplomate Am. Bd. Internal Medicine, Am. Bd. Rheumatology, Am. Bd. Geriat. Internal medicine intern Grady Meml. Hosp., Atlanta, 1973—74; resident in internal medicine Emory U., Atlanta, 1974—76, rheumatology fellow, 1976—78; physician Tampa Med. Group, Fla., 1978—. Med. dir. John Knox Village Retirement Ctr., Tampa, 1995—. Contbr. articles to profl. jours. Bd. dirs. Fla. Osteoporosis Bd., Tampa, 1998—2003. Named one of Top Physicians in the US, Town and Country Mag., 1997, Top 100 Physicians in the US, 1998. Mem.: AMA, ACP, Assoc. Profls. in Coll. Pub. Health, Am. Med. Dirs. Assn. (cert.), Fla. Med. Assn., Hillsborough County Med. Assn., Am. Coll. Rheumatology, Alpha Omega Alpha. Avocation: soccer. Office: Tampa Med Group 4700 Habana Ave Ste 303 Tampa FL 33614 Office Phone: 813-875-9742, 813-879-5485. Personal E-mail: hmcil@aol.com.

MC ILWAIN, WILLIAM FRANKLIN, newspaper editor, writer; b. Lancaster, SC, Dec. 15, 1925; s. William Franklin and Docia (Higgins) McI.; m. Anne Dalton, Nov. 28, 1952 (div. 1973); children: Dalton, Nancy, William Franklin III; m. K. L. Brelsford, June 5, 1978 (div. 1983). BA, Wake Forest Coll., 1949; postgrad., Harvard, 1957-58. Various positions with Wilmington (N.C.) Star, 1943, Charlotte (N.C.) Observer, 1945, Jacksonville (Fla.) Jour., 1945, Winston-Salem (N.C.) Jour.-Sentinel, 1949-52, Richmond (Va.) Times-Dispatch, 1952-54; chief copy editor Newsday, Garden City, N.Y., 1954-57, day news editor, 1957-60, city editor, 1960-64, mng. editor, 1964-66, editor, 1967-70; writer-in-residence Wake Forest U., 1970-71; dorm leader Alcoholic Rehab. Ctr., Butner, N.C., 1971; dep. mng. editor Toronto Star, 1971-73; mng. editor The Record, Hackensack, N.J., 1973-77; editor Boston Herald Am., 1977-79; dep. editor Washington Star, 1979-81, exec. mng. editor, 1981; editor Ark. Gazette, 1981-82; founding editor N.Y. Newsday, 1982-84; exec. editor Sarasota (Fla.) Herald-Tribune, 1984-90; sr. editor N.Y. Times Regional Newspaper Group, 1991-92; chmn. Bill Mc Ilwain, Inc., 1993—. Author: The Glass Rooster, 1960, (with Walter Friedenberg) Legends of Baptist Hollow, 1949; collaborator: (with Newsday staff) Naked Came The Stranger, 1969, A Farewell to Alcohol, 1973, Dancing Naked with the Rolling Stones, 2007; contbr. articles to popular mags. including Reader's Digest, Harper's, Esquire, Atlantic Monthly; editor N.C. Writer's Workshop. Mem. Pres. Johnson's Commn. on Civil Rights; adv. bd. Pulitzer Prize, 1982. With USMC, 1944. Named to N.C. Journalism Hall of Fame. Mem. Am. Soc. Newspaper Editors, Soc. Nieman Fellows. Home and Office: 305 N Channel Dr Wrightsville Beach NC 28480-2723 Personal E-mail: bmcilwain77@gmail.com. *As Fats Waller said, "One never knows, do one?".*

MC INDOE, DARRELL WINFRED, retired nuclear medicine physician; b. Wilkinsburg, Pa., Sept. 28, 1930; s. Clarence Wilbert and Dorothy Josephine (Morrow) McIndoe; m. Carole Jean McClain, Aug. 23, 1952; children: Sherri L. McIndoe, Wendy L. McIndoe, Darrell B. McIndoe, Ronald S. McIndoe, Holly B. McIndoe. BS, Allegheny Coll., 1952; MD, Temple U., 1956, MS, 1960. Commd. 2d lt. M.C. US Air Force, 1956, advanced through grades to col., 1971; intern Brooke Army Med. Ctr., San Antonio, 1956-57; resident in medicine Temple U. Med. Ctr., Phila., 1957-60; chief internal medicine and Hosp. svc. Norton AFB, 1960-64; dir. divsn. nuc. medicine St. Joseph Hosp., Towson, Md., 1992-2000; chief internal medicine and hosp. services 7520 U.S. Air Force Hosp., England, 1964-68; vis. rsch. fellow Royal Post Grad. Med. Sch., London, 1968-69; chief endocrinology svcs., chmn. dept. nuc. medicine USAF Med. Ctr.,

Keesler AFB, Miss., 1969-75; dep. dir. Armed Forces Radiobiology Rsch. Inst., Def. Nuc. Agy., Bethesda, Md., 1975-77, dir., 1977-79; staff physician nuc. medicine br., dept. radiology Nat. Naval Med. Ctr., Bethesda, Md., 1979-82; sr. lectr. mil. medicine Uniformed U. of Health Scis., Bethesda, Md., 1975-80; asst. prof. radiology/nuc. medicine and rsch. program coord. Uniformed U. of Health Sci., 1980-82; assoc. divsn. nuc. medicine St. Joseph Hosp., Towson, Md., 1982-91, dir. divsn. nuc. medicine, 1991—2000; ret, 2000. Med. advisor Nev. ops. office Dept. Energy, Las Vegas; cons. in field. Fellow: Am. Coll. Nuc. Physicians (regent ea. USA), Fellow royal Soc. Medicine; mem.: AMA, Soc. Med. Cons.'s to Armed Forces, Assn. Mil. Surgeons U.S., Health Physics Soc. (dir. Balt., Washington chpt.), Md. Soc. Nuc. Medicine (past pres.), Soc. Nuc. Medicine (ho. of dels.), Uniformed Svcs. Nuc. Medicine Assn. (pres. 1975), Air Force Soc. Physicians (bd. govs. 1973—77), Alexander Graham Bell Soc. Home: 15510 Foxpaw Trail Woodbine MD 21797-8000

MCINERNEY, JAMES EUGENE, JR., trade association executive; b. Springfield, Mass., Aug. 3, 1930; s. James Eugene and Rose Elizabeth (Adikes) McInerney; m. Mary Catherine Hill, July 17, 1963; children: Anne Elizabeth, James Eugene III. BS, U.S. Mil. Acad., 1952; MS in Engring., Princeton U., 1960; postgrad., Royal Air Force Staff Coll., 1964; MS in Internat. Affairs, George Washington U., 1970. Commd. 2d lt. USAF, 1952, advanced through grades to maj. gen., 1976, fighter pilot Republic of Korea, Japan and Germany, comdr. tactical fighter squadron S.E. Asia Thailand, 1967, tactical fighter wing Germany, 1971; sr. US adviser Turkish Air Force, 1973—75; dir. mil. assistance and sales Hdqrs. USAF, 1975-78; comdt. Indsl. Coll. Armed Forces, 1978-79; dir. programs Hdqrs. USAF, 1979-80, asst. dep. chief of staff for programs and evaluation, 1980; dir. legis. liaison McDonnell Douglas Corp., Washington, 1980-83, dir. internat. affairs, 1983-86; from v.p. to exec. v.p. Am. League for Exports and Security Assistance, 1986-92, exec. v.p., 1989-92; v.p. Am. Def. Preparedness Assn., 1992-97, Nat. Def. Indsl. Assn., 1997—. Decorated Air Force Cross, D.S.M. (2), Silver Star (3), D.F.C. (7), Bronze Star, Air medal (18), Meritorious Svc. medal (2), Air Force Commendation medal, Vietnamese Crosses of Gallantry with palm and star, Republic of Korea Cheongsu medal, comdr. Order of the Brit. Empire (CBE). Mem. Air Force Assn. (citation of honor 1968, Medal of Merit, 2002), Brit.-Am. Bus. Assn.-Washington (pres. 1982-94, chmn. 1994-96), Brit.-Am. Bus. Coun. (chmn. 1996-97), Am.-Air Mus. in Britain (exec. dir. 1984—), The Jefferson Islands Club, Capitol Hill Club, Congl. Country Club. Roman Catholic. Home: 1031 Delf Dr Mc Lean VA 22101-2009 Business E-Mail: jmcinerney@ndia.org.

MCINERNEY, JAY, writer; b. Hartford, Conn., Jan. 13, 1955; s. John Barrett and Marilyn Jean (Murphy) McI.; m. Linda Rositer, 1979 (div. 1979); m. Merry Reymond, June 2, 1984 (div. 1991); m. Helen Bransford, Dec. 27, 1991 (div. 2000); m. Anne Hearst, Nov. 21, 2006. BA, Williams Coll., 1976; postgrad., Syracuse U. Reporter Hunterdon County Democrat, Flemington, NJ, 1977; textbook editor Time Life Pubs., Osaka, Japan, 1978-79; fact checker New Yorker, NYC, 1980; reader Random House Pubs., NYC, 1980-81; instr. English Syracuse U., 1983; writer, 1983—. Author: (novels) Bright Lights, Big City, 1984, Ransom, 1985, Story of My Life, 1988, Brightness Falls, 1992, The Last of the Savages, 1997, Model Behavior, 2000, How It Ended, 2001, The Good Life, 2006; (non-fiction) Bacchus and Me: Adventures in the Wine Cellar, 2002, A Hedonist in the Cellar: Adventures in Wine, 2006; screenwriter: (films) Bright Lights, Big City, 1988; (TV movies) Gia, 1998; (TV series) Hotel Room, 1993; contbr. articles to profl. jours. Princeton in Asia fellow, 1977. Mem. Authors Guild, PEN, Writers Guild. Home: 25 E 9th St Penthouse New York NY 10003 Home Phone: 631-537-7668; Office Phone: 212-556-5764. Personal E-mail: bitbright@aol.com.

MCINERNEY, MARK A., county official; b. Flushing, NY, Aug. 28, 1964; s. William F. and Nadine T. McInerney; m. Maria R. Calle, Aug. 2, 2003; children: Fiona M, Liana. AA in Bus. Mgmt., LaGuardia C.C., LI, NY, 1993; degree in Security Mgmt., John Jay Coll., NY, 2002. Lic.: NY (notary pub.) 2007; security guard instr. NY, 1997, fire guard NYC, 2006, fire safety dir. NYC, 1996, registered peace officer NY, 2003, lic. security guard NY, 1995. Police officer Port Authority N.Y., N.J., NYC, 1993—94; mgr. Sunrise Investigations, Valley Stream, NY, 1996—97; prin., owner Highlander Security Acad., NY, 1997—2001; dir. ops. Protection Plus Security Cons., Bklyn., 1999—2001; sr. ct. clk. Unified Ct. Sys., NY, 2001—. Mem.: KC, NY State Ct. Officers Assn., NY State Ct. Clks. Assn., United Security Guard Assn., St. Francis Assisi Holy Name Soc., LaGuardia C.C. Alumni (life), Ancient Order Hibernians. Republican. Roman Catholic. Avocations: baseball, football. Home: 16 - 21 160th St Upper Whitestone NY 11357-3242 Office: Unified Court Sys 25 Beaver St New York NY 10004 Home Phone: 347-368-6563; Office Phone: 718-298-0138. Personal E-mail: mcalle7@nyc.rr.com.

MCINERNEY, THOMAS J., Internet company executive; BA, Yale Univ.; MBA, Harvard Univ. Prin. Morgan Stanley, 1988—99; exec. v.p., CFO Ticketmaster, 1999—2003; CEO retailing sector IAC/Interactive Corp., NYC, 2003—05, exec. v.p., CFO, mem. office of chmn., 2004—. Office: IAC 555 W 18th St New York NY 10011 *

MCINERNY, RALPH MATTHEW, philosopher, educator, writer; b. Mpls., Feb. 24, 1929; s. Austin Clifford and Vivian Gertrude (Rush) McI.; m. Constance Terrill Kunert, Jan. 3, 1953 (dec. May 2001); children: Cathleen, Mary, Anne, David, Elizabeth, Daniel. BA, St. Paul Sem., 1951; MA, U. Minn., 1952; PhD summa cum laude, Laval U., 1954; LittD (hon.), St. Benedict Coll., 1978, U. Steubenville, 1984; DHL (hon.), St. Francis Coll., Joliet, Ill., 1986, St. John Fisher Coll., 1994, St. Anselm's Coll., NH, 1995, Holy Cross Coll., New Orleans, 2001, Assumption Coll., Worcester, Mass., 2007. Instr. Creighton U., 1954-55; prof. U. Notre Dame, Ind., 1955—, Michael P. Grace prof. medieval studies Ind., 1988—, dir. dept. Ind., 1978-85, dir. Jacques Martin Ctr., 1978—2005. Vis. prof. Cornell U., 1988, Cath. U., 1971, Louvain, 1983, 95; founder Internat. Cath. U.; disting. vis. prof. Truman State U., Mo., 1999; Gifford lectr. Glasgow U., Scotland, 1999-2000, Joseph lectr. Pontifical Gregorian Inst., Rome, 2003; vis. lectr. Pontifical U. of Holy Cross, Rome, 2006, Ctr. of Applied Law, Cath. U. Chile, 2006. Author: The Logic of Analogy, 1961, History of Western Philosophy, vol. 1, 1963, vol. 2, 1968, Thomism in an Age of Renewal, 1966, Studies in Analogy, 1967, New Themes in Christian Philosophy, 1967, St. Thomas Aquinas, 1976, Ethica Thomistica, 1982, History of the Ambrosiana, 1983, Being and Predication, 1986, Miracles, 1986, Art and Prudence, 1988, A First Glance at St. Thomas: Handbook for Peeping Thomists, 1989, Boethius and Aquinas, 1989, Aquinas on Human Action, 1991, The Question of Christian Ethics, 1993, Aquinas Against the Averroists, 1993, The God of Philosophers, 1994, Aquinas and Analogy, 1996, Ethica Thomistica, 1997, Student Guide to Philosophy, 1999, Vernunftgemässes Leben, 2000, Characters in Search of Their Authors, 2001, Conversion of Edith Stein, 2001, John of St. Thomas, Summa Theologiae, 2001, Defamation of Pius XII, 2001, Very Rich Hours of Jacques Maritain, 2003, Aquinas, 2003; (novels) Jolly Rogerson, 1967, A Narrow Time, 1969, The Priest, 1973, Gate of Heaven, 1975, Rogerson at Bay, 1976, Her Death of Cold, 1977, The Seventh Station, 1977, Romanesque, 1977, Spinnaker, 1977, Quick as a Dodo, 1978, Bishop as Pawn, 1978, La Cavalcade Romaine, 1979, Lying Three, 1979, Abecedary, 1979, Second Vespers, 1980, Rhyme and Reason, 1981, Thicker than Water, 1981, A Loss of Patients, 1982, The Grass Widow, 1983, Connolly's Life, 1983, Getting Away with Murder, 1984, And Then There Were Nun, 1984, The Noonday Devil, 1985, Sine Qua Nun, 1986, Leave of Absence, 1986, Rest in Pieces, 1985, Cause and Effect, 1987, The Basket Case, 1987, Veil of Ignorance, 1988, Abracadaver, 1989, Body and Soil, 1989, Four on the Floor, 1989, Frigor Mortis, 1989, Savings and Loan, 1990, The Search Committee, 1991, The Nominative Case, 1991, Sister Hood, 1991, Judas Priest, 1991, Easeful Death, 1991, Infra Dig, 1992, Desert Sinner, 1992, Seed of Doubt, 1993, The Basket Case, 1993, Nun Plussed, 1993, Mom and Dead, 1994, The Cardinal Offense, Law and Ardor, 1995, Let's Read Latin, 1995, Aguinas and Analogy, 1996, The Tears of Things, 1995, Half Past Nun, 1997, On This Rockne, 1997, Penguin Classic Aquinas, 1997, The Red Hat, 1998, What Went Wrong With Vatican II, 1998, Lack of the Irish, 1998, Irish Tenure, 1999, Grave Undertakings, 1999, Heirs and Parents, 2000, Shakespearean Variations, 2000, Book of Kills, 2001, Triple Pursuit, 2001, Still Life, 2001, Sub Rosa, 2001, Emerald Aisle, 2001, John of St. Thomas, Summa Theologiae, 2001, Law and Ardor, 2001, As Good as Dead, 2002, Celt and Pepper, 2002, Prodigal Father, 2002, Last Things, 2002, Ablative Case, 2003, Irish Coffee, 2003, Requiem For A Realtor, 2004, Green Thumb, 2004, Blood Ties, 2005, Irish Gilt, 2005, Soul of Wit, 2005, (memoirs) Only I Have Escaped to Tell You, 2006, Prudence of the Flesh, 2006, Perambula Fidei, 2006, The Letter Killeth, 2006, The Widow's Mate, 2007; editor New Scholasticism, 1967-89; editor, pub. Crisis, 1982-96; pub. Catholic Dossier, 1995-2002, Fellowship of Cath. Scholars Quar., 2003—. Exec. dir. Wethersfield Inst., 1989-92; bd. govs. Thomas Aquinas Coll., Santa Paula, Calif., 1993-2001; bd. dirs. Southern Cross Found., 1999—; mem. Pres. Bush's Com. on the Arts and Humanities, 2002—. With USMC, 1946-47. Named to Cath. Edn. Found. Hall of Fame, 2007; recipient Thomas Aquinas medal U. Dallas, 1990, Thomas Aquinas Coll., 1991, St. Thomas Aquinas medal for eminence in philosophy, 1993, Maritain medal Am. Maritain Assn., 1994, P.G. Wodehouse award CRISIS Mag., 1995, Cardinal Journet medal Ave Maria U., Fla., 2007; Fulbright rsch. fellow, Belgium, 1959-60, NEH fellow, 1977-78, NEA fellow, 1983, Catholic Scholars fellow, 1992-95; Fulbright scholar, Argentina, 1986, 87, Outstanding Philosophical scholar Delta Epsilon Sigma, 1990; honoree Ralph McInerny Ctr. Thonistic Studies Thomas Internat. U., 2006. Fellow Pontifical Roman Acad. St. Thomas Aquinas; mem. Am. Philos. Assn., Am. Cath. Philos. Assn. (past pres., St. Thomas Aquinas medal 1993), Cath. Acad. Scis., Am. Metaphys. Soc. (pres. 1992), Am. Maritain Assn. (pres. 2004-06), Internat. Soc. for Study Medieval Philosophy, Medieval Acad., Mystery Writers Am. (Lifetime Achievement award 1993), Authors Guild, Fellowship Cath. Scholars (pres. 1992-95, Cardinal Wright award 1996, Premio Roncevalles de Navarre 2002). Office: U of Notre Dame Jacques Maritain Ctr 714 Hesburgh Notre Dame IN 46556-5677

MCINNES, DONALD GORDON, rail transportation executive; b. Buffalo, Nov. 6, 1940; s. Milton Gordon and Blanche Mae (Clunk) McI.; m. Betsy Campbell, Mar. 18, 1967 (dec. Feb. 1995); children: Campbell Gordon, Cody Milton; m. Carol Anne Haverty, Oct. 12, 1996; stepchildren: Molly Caroline, Lawrence Joseph. BA, Denison U., 1963; MS, Northwestern U., 1965; Cert. in Transp., Yale U., 1965. Budget mgr. operating AT&SF R.R. Co., Chgo., 1969-71, from asst. trainmaster to sr. v.p., COO, 1971—94; COO Burlington No. Santa Fe Corp., 1995—2000. Bd. dirs. Nocona Athletic Goods Co., Global Logistics Acquisition Corp.; founding mem. Intermodal Assn. N.Am., 1st chmn., 1991-93. Trustee, vice chair Vt. Acad., Saxtons River; chmn. bd. Found. for Intermodal Rsch. and Edn., Washington; chair bd. Heritage Mus. and Gardens, Sandwich, Mass.; bd. dirs. Highfield Hall, Falmouth, Mass. Served to 2d lt. USAF, 1965-67; capt. U.S. Army, 1967-69. Decorated Bronze Star. Mem. Ballymeade Country Club (North Falmouth, Mass.), Falmouth Yacht Club. Home: 75 Waterside Ave Falmouth MA 02540-3825

MCINNES, ROBERT A., archivist; b. Parkersburg, W. Va, Jan. 2, 1963; s. Richard Lee and E. Jane (Burtis) McInnes. BA in History, Ohio U., Athens, 1985; MA in History, Wright State U., Dayton, Ohio, 1987; MBA, Baker U., Overland Park, 2001. Acad. Cert. Archivists, 1989. Asst. archivist City of Tampa, Fla., 1987—90; assoc. archivist Va. Hist. Soc., Richmond, 1990—92; processing archivist Kans. State Hist. Soc., Topeka, 1993—2002; archivist/libr./site adminstr. New London County Hist. Soc., Conn., 2002—04; curator of manuscripts U. N.C., Charlotte, 2004—. Author: (web page exhibit) Kansas War Letters, 2001; editor: (booklet) The History of the Amistad Captives, by John W. Barber, 2003, (book) The Amistad Incident as reported in the New London Gazette, 2003; author: The Pemberton Papers, 2006, articles to profl. jours. Mem.: Acad. Cert. Archivists, Soc. N.C. Archivists, Soc. Am. Archivists. Avocations: films, woodworking, hiking, photography. Office Phone: 704-687-2321. Business E-Mail: ramcinne@uncc.edu.

MC INNES, WILLIAM CHARLES, priest, academic administrator; b. Boston, Jan. 20, 1923; s. William Charles and Mary (Byrne) Mc Innes. BS, Boston Coll., 1944, AB, 1950, MA, 1951; STL, Weston Coll., 1958; PhD, NYU, 1955; degree (hon.), U. Bridgeport, Sacred Heart U., Xavier U., Cin., U. Scranton, Loyola U., Chgo., Fairfield U. Joined Soc. of Jesus, 1946; ordained priest Roman Cath. Ch., 1957; prof. mktg. and bus. ethics Sch. Bus. Adminstrn. Boston Coll., 1959-63, assoc. dean Sch. Bus. Adminstrn., 1961-63, dir. honors program, 1963-64, mem. citizens seminar planning com., 1959-63, dir. Nat. Jesuit Honor Soc., 1997—2003; pres. Fairfield (Conn.) U., 1964-73, prof. urban problems, 1969-72; pres. U. San Francisco, 1972-77, Assn. Jesuit Colls. and Univs., 1977-89; campus min. U. Conn., Storrs, 1990-96. Vis. fellow Woodstock Theol. Ctr., 1990—91; adj. prof. bus. ethics Boston (Mass.) Coll., 1996—. Life mem. United Cerebral Palsy Assn. Fairfield County; adv. com. Conn. Dept. Social Svcs., 1993—96; priest Chaplain Alumni Assn.; chaplain Boston Coll. Alumni Assn., 1997—; past chmn. bd. dirs. ABCD (cmty. action agys.); bd. dirs. Nat. Better Bus. Bur.; past pres. Conn. Assn. Cmty. Action Programs; founder Fairfield County Cmty. Forum Conn. Charter Oak Coll.; vice chmn. Nat. Better Bus. Bur. Found.; chmn. Calif. Coun. Humanities. Served to capt. USAF, 1942—46, CBI. Mem.: Alpha Epsilon Delta, Phi Kappa Theta, Delta Sigma Pi, Alpha Sigma Nu, Beta Gamma Sigma. Home: Jesuit Cmty Boston Coll Chestnut Hill MA 02467 Business E-Mail: mcinnewi@bc.edu.

MCINNIS, ROBIN LYNN, voice educator; b. Joplin, Mo., Apr. 28, 1969; d. Ralph Harrison and Nancy Kaye Williston; m. Mark Thomas Muetzel (div.); children: Zachary Thomas Muetzel, Hannah Marie Muetzel; m. Scott Allan McInnis, July 8, 2002. BA, Graceland U., Lamoni, Iowa, 1991. Vocal and instrumental music tchr. K-12 Osborn-R.O. Schs., Osborn, Mo., 1991—95; vocal and instrumental music tchr. 6-12 Lathrop Schs., Lathrop, Mo., 1995—98; vocal and gen. music tchr. K-12 North Platte Schs., Dearborn, Mo., 1998—2007, Ctrl. HS, St. Joseph, 2007—. Singer Cantata Singing Ensemble, Platte County, 2003—. Mem.: Mo. State Tchrs. Assn., Music Educators Nat. Conf., Am. Choral Dirs. Assn. (gen. music v.p. 2001—05). Home: 23515 DD Hwy Dearborn MO 64439

MCINNIS, SCOTT STEVE, lawyer, former congressman; b. Glenwood Springs, Colo., May 9, 1953; s. Kohler McInnis and Carol Kreir; m. Lori McInnis; children: Daxon, Tessa, Andrea. BA, Ft. Lewis Coll., 1975; JD, St. Mary's Law Sch., 1980. Atty. Delaney & Balcomb P.C., Glenwood Springs, Colo., 1981—93; mem. Colo. State Ho. of Reps., 1984-93, chmn. agrl. livestock and natural resources com., 1986-90, majority leader, 1990-92; mem. U.S. Ho. Congresses from 3rd Colo. dist., 1993—2005; mem. rules com. U.S. Ho. Reps., 1998, mem. house ways and means com., 2001—, chmn. resources subcom. on forests and forest health; ptnr. Hogan & Hartson LLP, Denver, 2005—. Recipient Florence Sabin award, 1984, Guardian of Small Bus. award Nat. Fed. Ind. Bus., 1990, Lee Atwater Leadership award, 1991, and various awards from United Vets. Commn.; named Legislator of Decade and Legislator of Yr by Colo. Ski Country and Colo. Wildlife Found. Mem. Elks, Rotary, Phi Delta Phi. Republican. Roman Catholic. Office: Hogan & Hartson LLP 1200 17th St Denver CO 80202 E-mail: smcinnis@hhlaw.com.

MCINTIRE, LARRY VERN, biomedical engineering educator; b. St. Paul, June 28, 1943; s. James Lawrence and Lenore Vineal (Converse) McI.; m. Suzanne G. Eskin, June 27, 1997. BChemE, MS, Cornell U., 1966; MA, Princeton U., 1968, PhD, 1970. Registered profl. engr., Tex. Asst. prof. Rice U., Houston, 1970-74, assoc. prof., 1974-78, prof. chem. engring., 1978—2003, E.D. Butcher prof., 1983—2003, chmn. dept., 1981-91, chmn. Bioscis. and Bioengring. Inst., 1991—2003, chmn. rsch. coun., 1988-91, dir. biomed. engring. lab., 1980—99, chmn. dept. biomed. engring., 1997—2003; Wallace Coulter prof. Ga. Tech., 2003—. Adj. prof. medicine Baylor Coll. Medicine, Houston, 1982—, U. Tex. Med. Sch., Houston, 1982—, M.D. Anderson Cancer Ctr., 2001—; chmn. blood/materials working group NIH, Bethesda, Md., 1982-85; surgery and bioengring. study sect. NIH, 1984-88, 99-2003; com. bioprocessing NRC, 1991-94; chmn. rheology subcom. Internat. Coun. Thrombosis and Hemostasis, 1985-89; engring. directorate adv. coun. NSF, 2002-05; chmn. Coulter dept. biomed. engring. Gal Tech., 2003-. Editor-in-chief: Annals of Biomed. Engring., 2002—; contbr. articles to profl. jours. Recipient Merit award NIH, 1989; NSF fellow Cornell U., Princeton U., 1965-69, NATO-NSF postdoctoral fellow Imperial Coll., London, 1976-77. Fellow AAAS, Am. Inst. Med. Biol. Engring. (sec., treas. 1993-96, pres. 1997-98), AICHE (officer local sect. 1980-81, 86, Food Pharm. and Bioengring. divsn. award 1992, divsn. chair 1998), Biomed. Engring. Soc. (bd. dirs. 1992-97, pres. 1995-96, Disting. lectr. 1992); mem. N.Am. Soc. Biorheology (v.p. 1992-94, pres. 1994-96), N.Y. Acad. Scis., Am. Heart Assn. (coun. on thrombosis, exec. com. 1994-98), Faculty Club Rice U. (bd. dirs., chmn. 1982-84), Sigma Xi (nat. lectr. 1993-96), Nat. Acad. Engring. (editor-in-chief Annals Biomed. Engring., 2002-). Presbyterian. Avocations: tennis, squash, classical music, hiking. Office: Ga Tech Dept Biomed Engring Atlanta GA 30332-0535 Office Phone: 404-894-5057. Office Fax: 404-385-5028.

MCINTIRE, MIKE, journalist; BA in Polit. Sci., Hartwick Coll., NY. Investigations editor, reporter The Hartford Courant, 1990—2003; metro. reporter The New York Times, 2003—. Author: (articles) Dangerous Doctors, 2000, US Response to Storms Becomes Weapon for Democrats in NY Race, 2005. Recipient National Public Service Award, Scripps Howard Foundation, 1992, Nat. Press Found. award, 1997, Pulitzer Prize for Breaking News, 1999. Office: New York Times City Hall Rm 9 New York NY 10007 Office Phone: 212-556-1947.

MCINTOSH, ANITA JANE, retired administrative assistant; b. Huntington, W.Va., Mar. 5, 1937; d. Harold Herbert and Edwinna Work (Barnhart) Boyd; m. Melvin Dwight McIntosh, June 21, 1958; children: Kevin Neal, Menita Lynn. Art and Illustration cert. Famous Artists Schs., Conn., 1965. Sec. Life Ins. Co. of Ga., Atlanta, 1955—59, adminstrv. asst. Charlotte, 1982—99; sec. Santee Sales, High Point, NC, 1968—73; tchrs. aide Burke County Dept. Social Svcs., Morganton, NC, 1974—82; art instr. Myers Pk. United Meth. Ch., Charlotte, NC, 1988, 2002, 2005. Author: (poem) Teacher in the Church Today, 1991, (devotions) Upper Room Devotional Book, 2002, (poetry and watercolors) Musings and Images, 2004. Mem.: Charlotte Mecklenburg Sr. Games (Gold award, Silver award, Bronze award), Watercolor Soc. N.C. United Methodist. Avocations: watercolors, water-skiing, swimming. Home: 2832 Morris Ln Denver NC 28037 Home Fax: 704-483-9270. E-mail: waterwood@charter.net.

MCINTOSH, CAROLYN LEIGH, lawyer; b. Boulder, Colo., Dec. 10, 1955; d. Glen Elvis and Alice Joy McIntosh; m. Roger Alan Bucholz, Oct. 4, 1980 (div. Dec. 1998); m. Leland Kioshi Marable, Dec. 11, 1998. BA cum laude, Middlebury Coll., 1978; JD, U. Colo., 1981. Bar: Colo. 1981, U.S. Dist. Ct. Colo. 1981, Mont. 1988 (specially admitted), U.S. Dist. Ct. Mont. 1989, U.S. Ct. Appeals 2000. Rsch. asst. Rocky Mountain Mineral Law Found., Boulder, 1979—80; assoc. Sisk, Foley, Hultin & Driver, Denver, 1981—83, Hultin, Driver & Spaanstra, Denver, 1983—85; asst. atty. gen. Colo. Dept. of Law, Denver, 1986—88; assoc. Cogswell & Wehrle, Denver, 1988—89, shareholder, 1989—90; spl. asst. atty. gen. State of Mont., 1988—90; sr. assoc. Patton, Boggs & Blow, Denver, 1990—92; ptnr. Patton Boggs, LLP, Denver, 1992—, mng. ptnr. Denver office, 1993—2002. Assoc. adj. prof. Colo. Sch. Mines, 1991—2000; mem., atty. program to provide legal svcs. to indigent, Denver, 1982—86. Mem. procedural rules subcom. Colo. Air Quality Control Commn., 1983-84; mem. Lafayette Planning Commn., 1986-87, 95-99, Lafayette City Coun., 1987-99, mayor pro tem, 1989-91, mayor, 1995-99; mem. bd. Denver Regional Coun. Govts., 1990-99; mem. Regional Air Quality Coun., 1992-99, mem. exec. com., 1996-99; mem. Colo. Water Conservation Bd., 2001-04, Urban Drainage and Flood Control Bd., 1995-99. Mem. ABA (natural resources sect.), Colo. Bar Assn., Denver Bar Assn. (legal fees arbitration com. 1983-84, 86-87), Alliance Profl. Women (bd. dirs. 1986-90), Internat. Inst. Environ. Risk Mgmt. (bd. govs. 1996—). Office: Patton Boggs 1801 California St Ste 4900 Denver CO 80202 Office Phone: 303-894-6127. Business E-Mail: cmcintosh@pattonboggs.com. *Notable cases include: Environ. Def. Fund vs. Colo. Dept. Health, 1986, defending against unsuccessful challenge to the State of Colo.'s prevention of significant deterioration air quality regulations; State of Colo. vs. Idarado Mine Co., 1989, prosecution of superfund clean up claims against Idarado; Denver vs. Adolph Coons Co., et al, superfund cost recovery action.*

MCINTOSH, DAVID M., former congressman; b. June 8, 1958; m. Ruthie McIntosh. Grad., Yale Coll., 1980, U. Chgo., 1983. Bar: Ind., U.S. Supreme Ct. Spl. asst. domestic affairs to Pres. Reagan; spl. asst. to Atty. Gen. Meese; liaison Pres.'s Commn. on Privatization; spl. asst. to V.P. Quayle, dep. legal counsel to; exec. dir. Pres.'s Coun. on Competitiveness; sr. fellow Citizens for a Sound Economy; founder Federalist Soc. for Law & Pub. Policy, now co-chmn.; mem. U.S. Congress from Ind., Washington, 1995-2001; ptnr. Mayer, Brown, Rowe and Maw, 2002—; prof., dept of econ. Ball St. Univ. Sch. of Bus., 2002—. Mem. State Bar of Ind. Republican. Office: Mayer Brown Rowe and Maw 1909 K St NW Washington DC 20006 Home: 3432 N George Mason Dr Arlington VA 22207-1840 E-mail: dmcintosh@mayerbrown.com.

MCINTOSH, DENNIS KEITH, veterinarian, consultant; b. Glen Ridge, NJ, June 12, 1941; s. Sheldon Weeks and Enid Nicholson (Casey) McIntosh; children: Kevin, Jamie. BS in Animal Sci., Tex. A&M U., College Station, 1963, BS in Vet. Sci., 1967, DVM, 1968. Asst. county agrl. agt., Cleburne, Tex., 1963—65; owner, operator Park North Animal Hosp., San Antonio, 1970—75, El Dorado Animal Hosp., San Antonio, 1973—. Founding mem. and vet. liaison Tex. Assn. Animal Technicians (now TARVT), 1976-81; co-chmn.m founding mem. vet. tech. adv. coun. Palo Alto Coll., 1995—, tchr. Animal Health Tech., San Antonio Coll., 1985-95; tchr. ethics for vet. students Tex. A&M U. Coll. Vet. Medicine, 1990-; pres., mgr. Bexar County Emergency Animal Clinic, Inc., 1978-81; cons. vet. practice mgmt., mktg., client rels.; spkr. for vet. meetings, assns.; co-host Ask the Vet, Adopt a Pet, Sta. KENS-TV, 1980-93; vet. mem. Tex. Bd. Health, 1984-89, chmn. disease control com., pers. com.; mem. environ. health, hosps. com. Team capt. Alamo Roundup Club and Pres.' Club of San Antonio C. of C., 1970-75; mem. Guadalupe County Youth Fair Bd., 1978-80. Contbg. author: Mosby's Review Questions and Answers for Veterinary Boards, 1998, Chicken Soup for the Pet Lover's Soul, 1998; contbr. articles to profl. jours. With Vet. Corps, USAF, 1968-70. Recipient Alumnus award Guadalupe County 4-H Club, 1979, Outstanding Svc. award San Antonio Coll., 1986-87, Lynn Anderson Outstanding Svc. award San Antonio chpt. Delta Soc., 1990, Outstanding Bus. Ptnrs. award N.E. Ind. Sch. Dist., 1995-96. Mem. AVMA, Tex. Vet. Med. Assn. (pres., chmn. bd. dirs.), Tex. Acad. Vet. Practice (charter mem., pres.), San Antonio C. of C. (life), Tex. County Agrl. Agts. Assn. (4th v.p. 1964), Am. Legion, Tex.

Old Time Fiddler's Assn., Delta Soc. (first pres.and founding mem. San Antonio chpt. 1989-90), Alpha Zeta. Office: 13039 Nacogdoches Rd San Antonio TX 78217-1960 Office Phone: 210-656-1444.

MCINTOSH, ELAINE VIRGINIA, nutrition educator; b. Webster, SD, Jan. 30, 1924; d. Louis James and Cora Boletta (Bakke) Nelson; m. Thomas Henry McIntosh, Aug. 28, 1955; children: James George, Ronald Thomas, Charles Nelson. BA magna cum laude, Augustana Coll., Sioux Falls, SD, 1945; MA, U. S.D., 1949; PhD, Iowa State U., 1954. Instr., asst. prof. Sioux Falls Coll., 1945-48; instr. Iowa State U., Ames, 1949-53, rsch. assoc., 1955-62; postdoctoral rsch. assoc. U. Ill., Urbana, 1954-55; asst. prof. human biology U. Wis., Green Bay, 1968-72, assoc. prof., 1972-85, prof., 1985-90, emeritus prof., 1990—, writer, cons., 1990—, chmn. human biology dept., 1975-80, asst. to vice chancellor, asst. to chancellor, 1974-76. Author 3 books including American Food Habits in Historical Perspective, 1995, Lewis and Clark: Food, Nutrition, and Health, 2003; contbr. numerous articles on bacterial metabolism, meat biochemistry and nutrition edn. to profl. jours. Fellow USPHS, 1948-49. Avocation: travel. Office: LS 455 Human Biology U Wis Green Bay 2420 Nicolet Dr Green Bay WI 54311-7001

MC INTOSH, JAMES EUGENE, JR., interior designer; b. Dadeville, Ala., Nov. 13, 1938; s. James Eugene and Jessie (Latimer) McI. B.Interior Design, Auburn U., Ala., 1961. Designer contract div. Rich's Dept. Store, Atlanta, 1961-64; assoc. William Trapnell & Assocs., Atlanta, 1964-70; dir. Interior Concepts, Inc., Atlanta, 1970-72; dir. design comml. design div. Rich's Dept. Store, 1972-80; v.p. Comml. Interior Designs, Inc., 1980-82; exec. staff Rollins Inc., 1982—; pres. Gene Mc Intosh & Assocs., 1985—. Fellow Am. Soc. Interior Designers (Presdl. citation 1974); mem. Nat. Trust Hist. Preservation, Ala. Hist. Soc., High Mus. Art, Soc. Archtl. Historians. Home: Gene McIntosh & Assocs 130 Church St Decatur GA 30030 E-mail: cmeneg@earthlink.net.

MCINTOSH, JON CHARLES, illustrator, graphics designer, painter; b. Alliance, Ohio, Aug. 8, 1947; s. John Cowles and Lucile Tipple (Ketcham) McI.; 1 child, Forgan Cowles. Student, Hobart Coll., 1965-67; BFA, R.I. Sch. of Design, 1974. Pres. McIntosh Ink, Inc., Key West, Fla., 1971—; exec. v.p. advt. Chill Internat., Inc., 2004—. Mem. bd. overseers New Eng. Conservatory of Music, Boston, 1989-95; bd. dirs. Sail Martha's Vineyard. Illustrator: (book) The Foolish Dinosaur Fiasco, 1978, The Mysterious Zetabet, 1980, The Doctor's Handbook, 1982, Witch Way to The Country, 1995, Witch Way to the Beach, 1997, The Longest Hair in the World, 1999; author, illustrator: Hooked On Golf, 1986, Fineart: Gingerbread Sq. Gallery, Grannary Gallery, Casa Vieja Gallery, W.H. Patterson Gallery, London. Artwork contbr. Ducks Unltd; art for advt. Bose, Wang, Digital, NASA. Recipient Silver medal V.I. Internat. Film Festival, 1976, Gold medal Soc. of Newspaper Designers, 1985, First place Francis Hatch Advt. Awards, 1987, First place New Eng. Newspaper Awards, 1998, Silver award Soc. Newspaper Designers, 2000. Mem. Soc. of Illustrators (Silver Funny Bone 1991), The Country Club. Republican. Episcopalian. Avocations: musician, ski racing, tennis, fishing, skeet shooting. Office: McIntosh Ink Inc 813 Frances St Key West FL 33040 Office Phone: 305-295-2533.

MCINTOSH, MAXWELL DAVID, lawyer; b. Christiansted, St. Croix, V.I., July 19, 1967; BA in Polit. Econs., Tulane U., 1990; JD, U. Pa., 1993. Bar: V.I. 1994, Pa. 1995. Pvt. practice, Christiansted. Mem.: ABA, Assn. Trial Lawyers Am., Nat. Bar Assn., V.I. Bar. Assn. (chmn. scholarship com. 1996—, mem. bd. govs. 1998—99, pres. elect 2005—06, treas., pres. 2006—07). Office: Atty at Law Ste B 1009 North St Christiansted VI 00820 Office Phone: 340-773-4590. Office Fax: 340-773-4599. Business E-Mail: maxmac@viaccess.net.

MCINTOSH, TERRIE TUCKETT, lawyer; b. Ft. Lewis, Wash., July 20, 1944; d. Robert LeRoy and Elda Tuckett; m. Clifton Dennis McIntosh, Oct. 13, 1969; children: Alison, John. BA, U. Utah, 1967; MA, U. Ill., 1970; JD, Harvard U., 1978. Bar: NY 1979, Utah 1980. Assoc. Hughes, Hubbard & Reed, NYC, 1978-79, Fabian & Clendenin, Salt Lake City, 1979-84, shareholder, 1984-86; staff atty. Questar Corp., Salt Lake City, 1986-88, sr. atty., 1988-92, sr. corp. counsel, 1992—. Instr. philosophy Douglass Coll. Rutgers U., New Brunswick, N.J., 1971-72; mem. adv. com. civil procedure Utah Supreme Ct., Salt Lake City, 1987—; mem. jud. nominating com. 5th Cir. Ct., Salt Lake City, 1986-88. Mem. Utah State Bar (ethics and discipline screening panel 1989-96, vice chair ethics and discipline com. 1996-99, 2006—, co-chair law related edn. com. 1985-86, bar examiner rev. com. 2005—), Women Lawyers of Utah (chair exec. com. 1986-87, Woman Lawyer of Yr. award 2005), Salt Lake Legal Aid Soc. (trustee 1999—), Harvard Alumni Assn. Utah (bd. dirs. 1987—), Phi Beta Kappa, Phi Kappa Phi Office Phone: 801-324-5532.

MCINTURFF, FLOYD M., retired state agency administrator; b. Greenback, Tenn., May 1, 1923; s. Samuel Floyd and Hazel Agnes (Vaden) M.; m. Merle Celeste Sosna, May 27, 1950; children: Judith Margaret, Laura Ellen, Melissa Ann. BS, U. Tenn., Knoxville, 1950. Asst. to the chief engr., missiles Rockwell Internat., Columbus, 1957-73; chief, targeted jobs tax credit program Ohio Bur. Employment Svcs., Columbus, 1974-88; ret., 1988. Commd. officer U.S. Army Signal Corps., 1942-46, 51-52. Mem. Opera Columbus, Columbus Astron. Soc., Am. Atheists, Sons of Revolution, First Families of Tenn. Avocations: music, astronomy, photography, elderhostel. Home: 4985 Beatrice Dr Columbus OH 43227-2114

MCINTYRE, BRIAN P., sports association executive; married; 2 children. Grad., Loyola U., Chgo. Dir. mktg. and media info. Chgo. Bulls, 1978—81; dir. pub. rels. NBA, NYC, 1981—89, v.p. pub. rels., 1989—97, sr. v.p. basketball comm., 1997—. Mem. FIBA (Internat. Basketball Fedn.) News Coun.; mem. media adv. com. USA Basketball. Named to Loyola Acad. Athletic Hall of Fame, 1999. Achievements include creating numerous awards for the NBA, including the Sixth Man, the Defensive Player and the Most Improved Player. Office: NBA Olympic Tower 645 5th Ave Fl 10 New York NY 10022-5986 *

MCINTYRE, BRUCE HERBERT, media consultant, marketing professional; b. Takoma Park, Md., Jan. 24, 1930; s. Orrin Raymond and Leila Hazel (Olmsted) McI.; m. Natalie Ann Wolff, Oct. 10, 1953; children: Douglas A., Elizabeth W., Emily O., Catherine N., Jane A. Student, Gannon Coll., 1954-57, U. Akron, 1958-61. Reporter, city editor Erie (Pa.) Times and News, 1949-57; reporter, city editor, asst. to exec. editor Akron (Ohio) Beacon Jour., 1958-67; with Battle Creek (Mich.) Enquirer & News, 1967-71, asst. mng. editor, 1967-68, mng. editor, 1968-71; exec. v.p., editor Oakland Press, Pontiac, Mich., 1971-77, pub., 1977-95; v.p., pub. div. Capital Cities/ABC Inc., 1987-96; chmn. Great Lakes Media Inc., 1995-96; pre. McIntyre Media LLC, West Bloomfield, Mich., 1997—; co-founder Clarkston Fin. Corp., Mich., 1998—, Huron Valley State Bank, 2005; councilman City of Orchard Lake Village, Mich., 1998—2007, mayor, 2001—04. Lectr. Am. Press Inst., 1968—; journalism juror Pulitzer Prizes, 1972— Served with AUS, 1951-53; lt. col. Res. ret. Mem. Soc. Profl. Journalists, Pine Lake Country Club (Bloomfield, Mich.). Episcopalian. Personal E-mail: bhmcintyre@comcast.net.

MCINTYRE, JAMES G., lawyer; b. 1933; 3 children. BS, Stephen F. Austin State U.; LLB, Miss. Coll. Sch. Law. Bar: 1964. Atty. McIntyre Law Firm, Jackson, Miss., 1964—. Achievements include defense atty. for former Neshoba County Sheriff Lawrence Rainey, who won acquittal in the 1967 federal trial; defense atty. for Edgar Ray Killen, convicted of the 1964 manslaughter of 3 civil rights workers, Andrew Goodman, James Chaney and Michael Schwerner in June 2005. Office: McIntyre Law Firm 828 N State St Jackson MS 39202 Office Phone: 601-355-2481.

MC INTYRE, JAMES R., history professor, researcher; b. Media, Pa., Aug. 1970; s. Robert Henry and Florence Elaine Mc Intyre; m. Catherine Louise Yazum, May 27, 2000; 1 child, Jessica De Voe. MS, U. Ill., Urbana-Champaign, 1999. History instr. Moraine Valley Cmty. Coll., Palos Hills, Ill., 2005—. Office: Moraine Valley Cmty Coll 900 W College Pkwy Palos Hills IL 60465-0937

MCINTYRE, JERILYN SUE, academic administrator; b. June 24, 1942; d. Frank Otto and Maxine (Ward) McIntyre; m. W. David Smith. Student, Stanford U., Italy, 1962; AB in History with distinction, Stanford U., 1964, MA in Journalism, 1965, cert. Summer Radio-TV Inst., 1965, tchrs. cert., 1968; PhD in Comms., U. Washington, 1973; postgrad. Inst. Ednl. Mgmt., Harvard U., 1993. Corr. World News Bureau McGraw-Hill Pub. Co., LA, 1965-67; asst. prof. dept. mass comm. Chico (Calif.) State Coll., 1968-70; asst. prof. Sch. Journalism U. Iowa, Iowa City, 1973-77; assoc. prof., prof. dept. comm. U. Utah, Salt Lake City, 1977-2000, assoc. dean Coll. Humanities, 1984-88, assoc. v.p. acad. affairs, 1988-90, interim pres., 1997, v.p. acad. affairs, 1990-98; pres. Ctrl. Wash. U., Ellensburg, 2000—. Dir. Wall St. Jour. Publs. Workshop, Chico State Coll., 1968; mem. edn. adv. bd. NFL, 1996; mem. exec. com. coun. acad. affairs Nat. Assn. State Univs. and Land Grant Coll., 1995—98, chair, 1997; mem. steering com. Utah Edn. Network, 1995—98. Editl. asst. Chemical Week Mag., 1965-66, World News Bureau, 1966-67; mem. editl. bd. Journalism History; co-author: Symbols & Society; contbr. articles to profl. jours., chpts. to books. Mem. Utah Women's Forum. Named a David P. Gardner fellow, 1984; recipient Yesterday's Girl Scout Today's Successful Woman, Utah Girl Scout Coun., 1996, Salt Lake City chpt. Disting. Woman, AAUW, 1994. Mem.: Assn. Edn. in Journalism and Mass Comm. Office: 400 E University Way Ellensburg WA 98926-7501 E-mail: mcintyrej@cwu.edu.

MCINTYRE, JERRY L., lawyer; b. Atlantic City, July 1, 1941; AB, Columbia U., 1963; JD, Fordham U., 1969. Bar: N.Y. 1969, R.I. 1970. Mem. McIntyre, Tate & Lynch, Providence, 1993—. Com. mem. Family Ct. Bench/Bar Com., 1985—. Pres. town coun., Town of Jamestown, R.I., 1983-89. Fellow Am. Acad. Matrimonial Lawyers; mem. ABA (sect. family law), N.Y. State Bar Assn. (sect. trusts and estates law), R.I. Bar Assn., R.I. Bar Found. Office: McIntyre Tate & Lynch 321 S Main St Providence RI 02903-7108 Office Phone: 401-351-7700. Business E-Mail: jlm@mtllaw.com.

MCINTYRE, JOHN ARMIN, physics professor; b. Seattle, June 2, 1920; s. Harry John and Florence (Armin) McI.; m. Madeleine Forsman, June 15, 1947; 1 son, John Forsman. BS, U. Wash., 1943; MA, Princeton U., 1948, PhD, 1950. Mem. faculty elec. engring. Carnegie Inst. Tech., Pitts., 1943; radio engr. Westinghouse Elec. Co., Balt., 1944; research asso. Stanford, 1950-57; mem. faculty Yale, 1957-63, assoc. prof., 1960-63; prof. physics Tex. A&M U., College Station, 1963-95, emeritus prof., 1995—; asso. dir. Cyclotron Inst., 1965-70. Mem. council Oak Ridge Asso. Univs., 1964-71 Contbr. articles to profl. jours. Fellow Am. Phys. Soc., Am. Sci. Affiliation (exec. council 1968-73); mem. AAAS. Presbyterian. Achievements include research and publs. on scintillation counters for gamma ray spectroscopy; determination of nuclear charge distbns. by electron scattering; study of nuclear structure by neutron transfer reactions; devel. variable energy gamma ray beams, gamma ray cameras. Home: 2316 Bristol St Bryan TX 77802-2405 E-mail: jmcintyre@physics.tamu.edu.

MCINTYRE, JOHN GEORGE WALLACE, real estate developer, management consultant; b. Toronto, Ont., Can., July 26, 1920; s. George Crerar and Gwendolyn Alberta (Wallace) McI.; m. Ruth Elizabeth Wilson, July 26, 1945 (dec.); children: Angus, Heather, Robert, Anne. B of Commerce, U. Toronto, 1941; MBA, Harvard U., 1947. Budget acct. Abitibi Paper Co., Toronto, 1947-51; budget mgr., asst. gen. mgr. Ford of Can., Windsor, Ont., 1951-58, gen. mgr. mfg. ops., 1963-65; asst. mng. dir., mng. dir. Ford of Australia, Melbourne, 1958-63; exec. v.p., pres. Columbia Cellulose Ltd., Vancouver, B.C., Canada, 1965-67; v.p. retail devel. and distbn. Hudson's Bay Co., Toronto, 1967-84; pres. Rupert's Land Tng. Co., Hudson's Bay Co. Devels. Ltd.; trustee Internat. Council of Shopping Ctrs., 1970-84; v.p., gen. mgr. Broadcast Ctr. Devel. Project Can. Broadcasting Corp., 1984-88; cons., 1988—. Chmn. Soldiers' Tower Com., U. Toronto, 1998-2004. Served to capt. Royal Can. Ordnance Corps., 1942-45, ETO. Address: Ste 412 Richview Residence 105 Clement Rd Etobicoke ON Canada M9R 4C2

MCINTYRE, JOHN LAWRENCE, lawyer; b. St. Paul, Apr. 25, 1942; s. John F. and Mary E. (Clancy) McI.; m. Mary E. Seifert, May 6, 1967; children: Matthew, Aimee, Brendan. BA in Philosophy, Coll. St. Thomas, 1963; LLB, U. Minn., 1966. Bar: Minn. 1966, U.S. Ct. Appeals (8th cir.) 1966, U.S. Supreme Ct. 1984. Law clk. to judge U.S. Ct. Appeals (8th cir.), 1966-67; mem. Doherty, Rumble and Butler, St. Paul and Mpls., 1967-93; gen. counsel, v.p., sec. The Toro Co., Mpls., 1993—. Mem. ABA (law and acctg. com. bus. law sect.), Minn. Club, Minn. Bar Assn., Hennepin City Bar Assn., Minn. Corp. Counsel Assn. (dir.), Order of Coif. Roman Catholic. Office: The Toro Co 8111 Lyndale Ave S Minneapolis MN 55420-1196 Office Phone: 952-887-8059. Office Fax: 952-887-8920. Business E-Mail: larry.mcintyre@toro.com.

MCINTYRE, MARVIN H., II, financial consultant; Grad., The Citadel, Charleston, SC. Sr. v.p., broker, sr. mng. dir. High Networth Group Legg Mason Wood Walker, Inc., Washington; founding ptnr., mng. dir. wealth mgmt., portfolio mgr., fin. advisor Smith Barney Capitol Wealth Mgmt. Group, Washington. Former mem. bd. dirs. Legg Mason Wood Walker, Inc. Named one of Top 100 Fin. Advisors, Barron's, 2005—06. Office: Smith Barney Capitol Wealth Mgmt Group 1747 Pennsylvania Ave NW Ste 500 Washington DC 20006 Office Phone: 202-778-1381. Office Fax: 202-778-1283. E-mail: marvin.mcintyre@smithbarney.com. *

MCINTYRE, MICHAEL JOHN, lawyer, educator; b. Attleboro, Mass., Mar. 12, 1942; sd. John W. and Margaret E. (McBrien) McI.; m. May Ping Soo Hoo; children: Devin J., Colin J. AB, Providence Coll., 1964; JD, Harvard U., 1969. Bar: Mass. 1969, D.C. 1970. Vol. Peace Corps, Bhopal, India, 1964-66; assoc. Ivins, Phillips and Barker, Washington, 1969-71; dir. tng. Internat. Tax Program, Harvard U., Cambridge, Mass., 1971-75; prof. law Wayne State U., Detroit, 1975—. Cons. govt. of Egypt, State of N.Y., Navajo Tribe, govts. of Spain, Australia, 1975—; cons. UN Group Experts Internat. Coop. Tax Masters. Author: Readings in Federal Taxation, 1983, International Income Tax Rules of United States, 2d edit., 2001, (with Arnold) International Tax Primer, 1995, 2d edit., 2002; editor-in-chief Tax Notes Internat., 1989-91; contbr. articles to numerous publs. Office: Wayne State Univ Law Sch Detroit MI 48202 Office Phone: 313-577-3944. E-mail: mcintyre@wayne.edu.

MCINTYRE, MIKE (DOUGLAS CARMICHAEL MCINTYRE II), congressman; b. Lumberton, NC, Aug. 6, 1956; s. Douglas Carmichael and Thelma Riley (Hedgpeth) McIntyre; m. Lola Denise Strickland, June 26, 1982; children: Joshua Carmichael, Stephen Christopher. BA, U. NC, 1978, JD, 1981. Bar: NC 1981, US Dist. Ct. (ea. dist.) NC 1984, US Dist. Ct. (mid. dist.) NC 1985, US Ct. Appeals (4th cir.) 1987, US Supreme Ct., 1987. Assoc. Law Office Bruce Huggins, Lumberton, 1981-82, McLean, Stacy, Henry & McLean, Lumberton, 1982-86; ptnr. Price & McIntyre PA, Lumberton, 1987-89; prin. McIntyre Law Firm, PA, Lumberton, 1989-96; mem. US Congress from 7th NC dist., 1997—. Mem. law-focused edn. adv. com. NC Dept. Pub. Instrn., 1986-87; mem. US Ho. Com. on Agr., 1997—, Armed Svcs. Com., 1997—; co-chmn. Coalition Task Force on Edn., 1997-98, Congrl. Task Force on Promotion of Fatherhood, Rural Health Care Coalition, 1999-2002, Dem. Task Force on Children, 1999-2000, Coalition Task Force on Bus. and Tech., Spl. Forces Caucus, 2002—; chmn. U.S. H. Agr. Subcom. on Splty. Crops, Rural Devel. and Fgn. Agr.; mem. Pres.'s Summit on Am.'s Future, 1997. Del. Dem. Nat. Conv., NYC, 1980, NC Dems., Raleigh, 1974—; pres. Robeson County Young Dems., Lumberton, 1982; sec.-treas. 7th Congl. Dist. Young Dems., NC, 1983, chmn., 1984; 2nd vice chmn. 7th Congl. Dist. Dems. So. NC, 1986-89, 1st vice chmn., 1989; mem. state adv. bd. North Carolinians Against Drug and Alcohol Abuse, Raleigh, 1984-85; chmn. Morehead Scholarship Selection Com., Robeson County, 1985-94; deacon, elder, clk. of session Presbyn. Ch.; active Boy Scouts Am., Lumberton, 1983; mem. NC Commn. on Children and Youth, 1987-89, NC Commn. on the Family, 1989-91; mem. Young Life Lumberton com., 1987-89; chmn. Robeson County US Constn. Bicentennial com., 1986-87; mem. lawyers' adv. com. to NC Commn. on Bicentennial of US Constn., 1986-89; bd. dirs. Robeson County Grp. Home, Lumberton, 1984-87, Lumberton Econ. Advancement for Downtown, Inc., 1987-90, pres., 1988-89, 89-90; chmn. legis. affairs com. C. of C., 1991, 92, 93, bd. dirs., 1992-94; mem. NC Mus. Hist. Assocs., 1987-89; mem. regional selection com. Gov.'s Award for Excellence in Tchg. Social Studies, 1991. Morehead Found. scholar, 1974-78; named one of Outstanding Young Men in Am., 1981, 84-85, 88; Outstanding Young Dem. Robeson County Young Dems., 1984-85; one of State's Outstanding Young Dems. Young Dems. NC, 1984-85; recipient Algernon Sydney Sullivan award U. NC, 1978, Outstanding Young North Carolinian award NC Jaycees, 1988, Outstanding Young North Carolinians, Heart Robeson Jaycees, 1988, Nat. Bicentennial Leadership award for Individual Achievement Coun. for Advancement of Citizenship and Ctr. for Civic Edn., Washington, 1987, Gov.'s Outstanding Vol. Svc. award, 1989, Thomas Jefferson award Food Distbrs. Internat., 1998, 2002, Guardian of Small Bus. award, Nat. Fedn. Ind. Bus., 1997-99, Nat. Rural Health Legis. award, 1999, 2003, Outstanding Health Svc. award Cmty. Ptnrs. Health Net, 2000, Spirit of Enterprise award, US C. of C., 1997-98, Super Hero award Nat. Assn. Cmty. Health Ctrs., 2001-05, Internat. Pub. Policy award Internat. Assn. Pers. Employment, 2002, Law Enforcement award, NC Narcotics Officers Assn., 2002, Quality Pub. Svc./Pub. Edn. and Health Care award Am. Fedn. Tchrs., 2001, Charles Dick Medal of Merit Nat. Guard Assn., 2000, Disting. Svc. to Agr. award Robeson County Crop Promotion Assn., 2001, Congrl. Partnership award Nat. Assn. Devel. Orgns., 2002, 2004-05, Nat. Leadership award, 2006, Admiral's Cir. award Nat. Marine Mfrs. Assn., 2004, MVP award Sr. Citizens League, 2004, Disting. Christian Statesman award, 2006; named to Legis. Honor Roll So. Econ. Devel. Coun., 1997, 2001-06, Beach Preservationist of Yr., Oak Island Preservation Soc., 2005. Mem. ABA (exec. com. citizenship edn. com. 1985-87, nat. cmty. law week com. 1982-83), Internat. Platform Assn., NC Bar Assn. (chmn. youth edn. and constn. bicentennial com. 1986-87, youth edn. com., exec. coun. young lawyers divsn. 1986-87), Robeson County Bar Assn. (founder, chmn. citizenship edn. com. 1982-94, law day com.), 16th Jud. Dist. Bar Assn., NC Acad. Trial Lawyers, NC Coll. Advocacy, Christian Legal Soc. (state adv. bd. 1986-90, state pres. 1987), Lumberton C. of C. (bd. dirs. 1992-94), Mil. Officers' Assn. (hon. life), Order of Old Well, Lumberton Rotary Club (bd. dirs. 1995-96), Phi Beta Kappa, Phi Eta Sigma. Democrat. Avocations: tennis, skiing, softball, dance, bible study. Office: US House Reps 2437 Rayburn House Office Bldg Washington DC 20515 Office Phone: 202-225-2731. Office Fax: 202-225-5773. E-mail: congmcintyre@mail.house.gov. *

MCINTYRE, NINA M., counseling administrator; b. Hot Springs, Ark., Dec. 12, 1947; d. Stanley L. and V. Edith Lewis; m. Jerry R. McIntyre, June 1, 1974; 1 child, Laura M. BA in Psychology, Henderson State U., 1971; MS in Sch. Psychology, U. Ctrl. Ark., 1976. Nat. cert. sch. psychologist, sch. psychol. specialist, lic. psychol. examiner Ark. Personal sec. U.S. Army Infantry Staff Surgeon, Fort Benning, Ga., 1968—69; rsch. asst. Ctr. for Early Devel., Little Rock, 1971—74; psychologist II State Youth Svcs., Little Rock, 1976—78; sch. psychol. Sp. LPE Little Rock Schs., Little Rock, 1978—. Mem. Cmty. Mental Health Adv. Bd., Little Rock, 1978—79. Mem.: NEA, Ark. Edn. Assn., Ark. Sch. Psychol. Assn., Nat. Assn. Sch. Psychologists. Episcopalian. Avocations: reading, travel. Home: 3208 Foxcroft Rd Little Rock AR 72227 E-mail: ninamcintyre99@hotmail.com.

MCINTYRE, OSWALD ROSS, physician; b. Chgo., Feb. 13, 1932; children: Margaret Jean, Archibald Ross, Elizabeth Geary. AB cum laude, Dartmouth Coll., Hanover, NH, 1953, postgrad, 1953-55; MD, Harvard U., Cambridge, Mass., 1957. Intern U. Pa. Hosp., 1957-58; resident in medicine Dartmouth Med. Sch. Affiliated Hosps., 1958-60; instr. medicine Dartmouth Coll., 1964-66, asst. prof. medicine, 1966-69, assoc. prof., 1969-75, prof., 1976—, James J. Carroll prof. oncology, 1980-95, dir. Norris Cotton Cancer Center, 1975-92, prof. emeritus, 1995—; attending physician VA Hosp., White River Junction, Vt., 1964. Cons. in hematology and oncology; acting chmn. dept. medicine Dartmouth-Hitchcock Med. Ctr., 1987-89; chmn. Cancer and Leukemia Group B., 1990-95. Mem. Am. Soc. Hematology, Am. Assn. Cancer Rsch., Am. Soc. Clin. Oncology, Assn. Cancer Inst. (pres. 1988-89), New Eng. Cancer Soc. (pres. 1989-90). Home: 34 Lamphire Hill Ln Lyme NH 03768-3109

MCINTYRE, PETER MASTIN, physicist, researcher; b. Clewiston, Fla., Sept. 26, 1947; s. Peter Mastin and Ruby Eugenia (Richaud) McI.; m. Rebecca Biek, June 29, 1968; children: Peter B., Colin H., Jana M., Robert J. AB with honors, U. Chgo., 1967, MS, 1968, PhD, 1973. Asst. prof. Harvard U., Cambridge, Mass., 1975-80; group leader Fermilab, Batavia, Ill., 1978-80; assoc. prof. Tex. A&M U., College Station, 1980-84, prof. physics, 1985—, assoc. dean Coll. of Sci., 1990-92; pres. Accelerator Tech. Corp., Bryan, Tex., 1988—. Dir. Tex. Accelerator Ctr., The Woodlands, 1991—93. Recipient IR-100 award, Indsl. Rch. Mag., 1980; fellow, Sloan Found., 1976—78. Fellow: Am. Phys. Soc. (pres. Tex. sect. 1990—91); mem.: AAAS. Achievements include proton-antiproton colliding beams; E-beam assisted removal of mercury and sub-micron carbon particles from power plant exhausts; electronic pasteurization system for killing bacteria in food and removing organic contaminants in water; tesla superconducting magnets for future hadron colliders; silicon microdevices for DNA sequencing; structured cable using high-temperature superconductors for practical coils; flux-coupled isochronous cyclotron driver for thorium-cycle nuclear fission power; creation of Visual Physics, a new laboratory/problem solving curriculum for first-year college physics; hybrid magnet technology for accelerating dipoles and spectroscopy solenoids to 25 Tesla; superconducting accelerator structures using YBCO high-temperature superconductor; a method by which to steer hurricanes; patents for continuous unitized tunneling system, gigatron high power microwave amplifier, microstrip chamber for medical imaging. Home: 611 Montclair Ave College Station TX 77840-2868 Office: Tex A&M U Dept Physics College Station TX 77843-0001 Office Phone: 979-845-7727. Business E-Mail: p-mcintyre@physics.tamu.edu.

MCINTYRE, ROBERT WHEELER, retired conservation organization executive; b. Chgo., Aug. 26, 1936; s. Henry Langenberg and Winifred (Wheeler) McI.; m. Emily Beardsley Taylor, Oct. 12, 1961 (div. 1985); children: W. Burley, Nancy T., Oliver W., Shanna L., Amanda K.; m. Miriam de Jesus Zarate, June 23, 1990 (div. 1998); m. Myung Sook Son, Jan. 6, 2001, 1 child Suzanne Felton. AB in Sociology, Stanford U., Calif., 1959; MBA, Harvard U., Cambridge, Mass., 1964. Loan analyst Wells Fargo Bank, San Francisco, 1964-65; supr. budget analysis Ford Aerospace, Palo Alto, Calif., 1965-69; controller Allied Life Scis., San Leandro, Calif., 1969-70; ptnr. Diplomat Mfg. Co., Palo Alto, 1970-71; staff cons.

Opportunity Through Ownership, San Francisco, 1971-72; gen. mgr. Quality Metal Finishers, San Francisco, 1972-73; sr. v.p., chief fin. officer The Trust for Pub. Land, San Francisco, 1973—2003, ret., 2003. Adv. bd. Peninsula Open Space Trust, Menlo Park, 1978—, audit com., 2005—; adv. com. Marin Headlands, 1978—81; bd. dirs., treas. Robert C. Wheeler Found., Palo Alto, 1965—95; chair, bd. dirs. Families Adopting Interracially, San Jose, 1971—74; adv. Jr. Achievement, 1966; bd. dirs. Environ. Vols., Palo Alto, 1980—, diversity com., 2003—, chmn. fin. com., CFO, 2004—; bd. dirs. Resource Renewal Inst., Sausalito, 1988—98, Water Heritage Trust, Sausalito, 1988—98, Dorothy Erskine Open Space Fund, San Francisco, 1978—, Sempervirens Fund, Mountain View, 2002—, treas., CFO, chmn. fin. com., 2003—07, exec. com., 2003—07, chmn. audit com., 2007—; bd. dirs., treas. Commonwealth Conservancy, Santa Fe, 2007—. Lt. USN, 1959—62, hon. discharge USN, 1964. Recipient Presdl. Citation award Trust for Pub. Land, 1988, Spl. Svc. award Environ. Vols., 1989, Cert. of Recognition for Outstanding Svc. to Environ. Vols. Calif. State Senate, 2005. Mem. Harvard Club NY, Harvard Club Boston, USS Coral Sea Assn., Stanford U. Hist. Soc. (bd. dirs., fin. com. 2005—, co-chmn. fin. com. 2006—), Palo Alto Tennis Club, Alpine Hills Tennis Club Portola Valley, San Francisco Tennis Club, Stanford Diamond Club, University Buck Diamond Club, Cage Diamond Club. Avocations: hiking, backpacking, tennis, travel. Home: 1061 Fulton St Palo Alto CA 94301-3313

MCINTYRE, SARAH ELIZABETH, soprano; b. Jacksonville, NC, Dec. 26, 1978; d. Luther Byron and Anne Elizabeth McIntyre. MusB, Samford U., Birmingham, Ala., 2001; MusM, Belmont U., Nashville, 2003. Pvt. voice tchr. Metropolis Sch. Performing Arts, Arlington Heights, Ill.; pvt. studio voice tchr. Fine Arts Voice, Chgo. Head voice dept. Metropolis Performing Arts Ctr., Arlington Heights; founder Fine Arts Opera, Chgo., Fine Arts Voice, Chgo. Recipient Hon. Diploma, Minister of Culture, Russia, 2001; grantee Acting grantee, Victory Gardens Theatre, Chgo., 2004. Mem.: Nat. Assn. Tchrs. Singing. Office: Fine Arts Voice 410 S Michigan #469 Chicago IL 60605

MCINTYRE, VIRGIE M., retired elementary school educator; b. Chesnee, SC, Feb. 27, 1923; d. Ed Lawson and Etta Rebecca (Jones) Mahaffey; m. Henry Bryson McIntyre, June 8, 1947; children: Teresa, Dawn. BA in edn., Berea Coll., 1945; M in supr. and adminstrn., Western Carolina U., 1964. Cert. advanced standing (reading) Syracuse U., 1968. Elem. tchr. Polk County Pub. Sch., Columbus, NC, 1945—53, 1957—65, Rutherfordton County, Spindale, NC, 1953—56; suprv. Polk County, 1965—67, reading cons., title 1 dir., 1968—70; reading ctr. prof. Western Carolina U., Cullowhee, NC, 1971—84; ret., 1984. Dir. reading conf. Western Carolina U., Cullowhee, NC, 1971—84, reading cons., 1971—84. Author: Reading Strategies and Enrichment Activities for Grades 4-9, 1979, Split Level Christians, 1993; contbr. articles various profl. jours. Vol. Outreach Min., Columbus, NC, 2000, Green Creek Computer Ctr., Tryon, NC, 2002; vol., dir, pianist Ch. Choir, Columbus, NC, 1984—99. Fellowship grant, Syracuse U., 1969. Mem.: Christian Writer's Group, NC Retired Employee Group. Independent. Avocations: painting, travel, swimming, music, volunteerism. Personal E-mail: tvtmacbd@alltel.com.

MCINTYRE-IVY, JOAN CAROL, data processing executive; b. Port Chester, NY, Mar. 1, 1939; d. John Henry and Molly Elizabeth (Gates) Daugherty; m. Stanley Donald McIntyre, Aug. 24, 1957 (div. Jan. 1986); children: Michael Stanley McIntyre, David John McIntyre, Sharon Lynne McIntyre; m. James Morrow Ivy IV, June 1, 1988. Student, Northwestern U., 1956-57, U. Ill., 1957-58. Assoc. editor Writer's Digest, Cin., 1966-68; instr. creative writing U. Ala., Huntsville, 1974-75; editor Strode Pubs., Huntsville, 1974-75; paralegal Smith, Huckaby & Graves (now Bradley, Arant, Rose & White), Huntsville, 1976-82; exec. v.p. Micro Craft, Inc., Huntsville, 1982-85, pres., 1985-89, ceo, chmn. bd., 1989—; also bd. dirs., co-owner. Author: numerous computer operating manuals for law office software, 1978—; co-author: Alabama and Federal Complaint Forms, 1979; editor: Alabama Law for the Layman, 1975; contbr. numerous articles to profl. jours. and short stories to mags. and lit. mags. Hon. scholar Medill Sch. Journalism Northwestern U., 1956. Mem. Huntsville Literary Soc. (bd. dirs. 1976-77). Republican. Methodist. Office: 123 Fairington Rd NW Huntsville AL 35806-2249 Office Phone: 800-225-3147. Personal E-mail: verdictsos@aol.com.

MCIVER, BARBARA BASORE, language educator; b. Oklahoma City; d. George Milroy and Eleanor (Irvin) Basore; m. William Wood McIver. BA, U. Ark., 1968, MA, 1988, PhD, 1994. Tchr. St. Paul H.S., Ark., 1968—69, Ctrl. H.S., Kansas City, Mo., 1970—71; office mgr. AMC, Inc. Mech. Contractors, Fayetteville, Ark., 1972—85; grad. tchg. asst., lectr. U. Ark., Fayetteville, 1985—94; asst. prof., assoc. prof. Claflin U., Orangeburg, SC, 1994—, interim chair dept. English and fgn. langs., 2006—. Dir. Writing Ctr. Claflin U., Orangeburg, 2000—. Contbr. articles to profl. jours.; editor: Claflin Rev., 2003—. Faculty advisor Friends of Earth, Orangeburg, 1998—. Grantee, NEH, 2000—03. Mem.: S.C. Coun. on Langs., South Ctrl. Modern Lang. Assn., Phi Kappa Phi, Alpha Mu Gamma, Sigma Tau Delta. Office: Claflin Univ 400 Magnolia Orangeburg SC 29115 Office Phone: 803-535-5215. Business E-Mail: bmciver@claflin.edu.

MCIVER, DEBORAH KAY, tax specialist, entrepreneur, small business owner; b. Des Moines, Iowa, May 6, 1948; d. Floyd Malcolm and Nora Marguerite McIver. BS, N.Mex. Inst. Mining and Tech., 1970; MBA, Pepperdine U., 1981; postgrad., U. N.Mex., 1985—87. Chem. control technician McGaw Labs., Glendale, Calif., 1971—72; statistician Northrop Corp., Hawthorne, 1972—73; math. analyst TRW Sys. Group, Redondo Beach, 1973—76; sci. programmer ISS/Sperry Univac, Cupertino, 1976—77; mem. tech. staff TRW Sys. Group, Sunnyvale, 1977—78, ArgoSys., 1978—79; sr. sci. programmer Finnigan-MAT Corp., San Jose, 1979—82; software engr. Ford Aerospace Co., Sunnyvale, 1982—83; v.p. software ops. controller Askeri, Inc., Santa Clara, 1983; owner McIver Enterprises, 1983—86, Deborah K. McIver, MBA, EA, 1990—. Gen. contractor own home, 1994—95. Active Sea Scouts Am., LA, 1975—76; friendly visitor United Way, LA, 1977—79; judge Santa Clara County Sci. and Engring. Sci. Fair, 1980, 1982, 1984; instr., coord. AARP Tax-Aide, 1992—, Colo. state coord., 2004—. Mem.: Soc. Women Engrs. (v.p. San Francisco Bay Area sect. 1980—81, pres. 1981—82, sect. rep. 1982—83), N.Mex. Inst. Mining and Tech. Alumni Assn. (life; pres. No. Calif. chpt. 1980—81). Republican. Disciples Of Christ. Home and Office: PO Box 889 Monument CO 80132-0889 Office Phone: 719-488-3022.

MCJUNKIN, JOHN G., lawyer; b. Kingsport, Tenn., Jan. 5, 1962; s. John L. and Wanda (Goode) McJ.; m. Karen Russell, June 16, 1984. BA summa cum laude, Hamden-Sydney Coll., 1984; JD, U. Cin., 1987. Bar: N.C. 1987, D.C. 1989, Va. 1990, Md. 1993. Assoc. Moore & Van Allen, Raleigh, N.C., 1987-89, Taft, Stettinius & Hollister, Washington, 1989-90, Mays & Valentine, Arlington, Va.; ptnr. Bankruptcy & Bus. Reorganization practice, office mng. ptnr. DLA Piper Rudnick Gray Cary, Reston, Va. Active Vol. Lawyers Program, Raleigh, 1987-89; election advisor Rep. Nat. Com., Raleigh, 1988; law firm coord. United Way, Raleigh, 1988. Mem. ABA, N.C. Bar Assn., Va. Bar Assn., D.C. Bar, Arlington County Bar Assn., Order of Barristers, Phi Beta Kappa, Omicron Delta Kappa. Avocations: skiing, golf, tennis, fishing. Office: DLA Piper Rudnick Gray Cary Suite 400 1775 Wiehle Ave Reston VA 20190-5159 Office Phone: 703-773-4154. Office Fax: 703-773-6279. Business E-Mail: john.mcjunkin@dlapiper.com.

MCKAGAN, DUFF (MICHAEL ANDREW MCKAGAN), bassist; b. Seattle, Feb. 5, 1964; m. Amanda Brixx, May 28, 1988 (div. May 1, 1990); m. Linda Johnson, Sept. 1992 (div. Sept. 1995); m. Susan Holmes, Aug. 28, 1999; children: Grace, Mae Marie. Band mem. Fastbacks, 1980—81, The Fartz, 1981—82, 10 Minute Warning, 1982—84; bassist Guns n' Roses, 1985—97; re-formed 10 Minute Warning, 1998; bassist Velvet Revolver, 2002—. Albums: (with Guns n' Roses) Live Like a Suicide, 1986, Appetite for Destruction, 1987 (Am. Music awards Favorite Heavy Metal/Hard Rock Album, 1990, one of 100 Greatest Albums, VH1, 2001, #1, Spin mag.'s Greatest Metal Albums, 2002, one of 500 Greatest Albums of All Time, Rolling Stone, 2003), Guns n' Roses Lies, 1988, Use Your Illusion I, 1991, Use Your Illusion II, 1991, The Spaghetti Incident?, 1993, (solo album) Believe in Me, 1993, (with Velvet Revolver) Contraband, 2004, Libertad, 2007; songs: (with Guns N' Roses) Welcome to the Jungle, 1987, Sweet Child O' Mine, 1987, (Am. Music Awards Favorite Pop/Rock Single, 1989, MTV Video Music awards Best Heavy Metal Video, 1989), November Rain, 1991, (MTV Video Music awards Best Cinematography, 1992); contbr.: (albums) Brick by Brick, by Iggy Pop, (films) The Dead Pool, 1988, Lean on Me, 1989, Interview with the Vampire, 1994, Grosse Point Blank, 1997, Hulk, 2003, (video games) Grand Theft Auto: San Andreas, 2004; actor: (TV series) Sliders, 1997. Named Best New Artist, MTV Video Music awards, 1988, Favorite Hard Rock Artist, Am. Music awards, 1990, 1992, World's Best Selling Hard Rock Artist of Yr., World Music awards, 1993; named one of 100 Greatest Artists of Hard Rock, VH1, 2000, Sexiest Artists, 2002; recipient Video Vanguard award, MTV Video Music awards, 1992.

MCKAGAN, MICHAEL ANDREW See MCKAGAN, DUFF

MCKANE, DAVID BENNETT, business executive; b. Salem, Mass., July 10, 1945; s. Vernon Wilson and Barbara Inez (Bennett) McK.; m. Wilson Lineburgh Baldwin, Apr. 16, 1977; adopted daughters, Taylor A., Lee and Paige Baldwin. BA, Dartmouth Coll., 1967; MBA, Amos Tuck Sch., 1969. Product mgr. Church & Dwight Co. Inc. (Arm and Hammer Products), NYC, 1969-72; v.p. NTA Inc. NYC, Nanuet, NY, 1972-75; v.p., exec. asst. to chmn. Schick Inc., Westport, Conn., 1975-77, sr. v.p., 1977-79, COO, exec. v.p., 1979-84, treas., 1980-84; chmn., CEO A.I. Friedman, Inc., NYC, 1985-87; chmn. McKane Robbins & Co. Inc., NYC and Westport, 1986-96; mng. gen. ptnr. Riverland and Indian Sun, L.C., Westport, 1996—. Bd. dirs. Oakhurst Dairy, Portland, Maine, Impax Corp., Westport. Bd. trustees Greens Farms (Conn.) Acad., 1991—. Mem. New Eng. Soc. in City N.Y., Mass. Mayflower Soc., Union Club (N.Y.C.), Country Club Fairfield, John's Island Club (Vero Beach, Fla.), RedStick Golf Club (Vero Beach, Fla.), Tucker's Point Club (Bermuda). Episcopalian. Home: 48 Owenoke Park Westport CT 06880-6833

MCKAY, ALEXANDER GORDON, classics educator; b. Toronto, Dec. 24, 1924; s. Alexander Lynn and Marjory Maude Redfern (Nicoll) McKay; m. Helen Jean Zulauf, Dec. 24, 1964; stepchildren: Julie Anne Stephanie Brott, Danae Helen Fraser. BA, U. Toronto, 1946; MA, Yale U., 1947, Princeton U., 1948, PhD, 1950; LLD (hon.), U. Man., 1986, Brock U., 1990, Queen's U., 1991; DLitt (hon.), McMaster U., 1992, U. Waterloo, 1993. Mem. faculty classics Wells Coll., 1949-50, U. Pa., 1950-51, U. Man., 1951-52, 55-57, Mt. Allison U., 1952-53, Waterloo Coll., 1953-55; mem. faculty McMaster U., 1957-90, prof., chmn. dept. classics, 1962-68, 76-79, dean humanities, 1968-73, mem. univ. senate, 1968-73, 85-87, prof. emeritus, 1990—; Disting. vis. prof. classics U. Colo., 1978; prof. in charge Intercollegiate Center for Classical Studies, Rome, 1975; vis. mem. Inst. Advanced Study, Princeton, 1979, 81. Vis. scholar U. Tex., Austin, 1987, Hardt, Vandoevres, Geneva, 88; vis. fellow Trinity Coll., Cambridge, 1988; adj. prof. humanities York U., 1990—96; Disting. vis. lectr. Concordia U., Montreal, 1992—93, prof. emeritus, 2001—; vis. scholar Rockefeller Study and Conf. Ctr., Bellagio (Como), Italy, 1993. Author: Naples and Campania: Texts and Illustrations, 1962, Roman Lyric Poetry: Catullus and Horace, 2d edit., 1974, Vergil's Italy, 1970, Cumae and the Phlegraean Fields, 1972, Naples and Coastal Campania, 1972, Houses, Villas and Palaces in the Roman World, 1975, reprint, 1998, Roman Satire, 1976, Vitruvius, Architect and Engineer, 1978, 2d edit., 1985, Römische Häuser, Villen und Paläste, 1980, Roma Antiqua: Latium and Etruria, 1986; co-author: Selections from Vergil, Aeneid I, IV and VI (Dido and Aeneas), 1988, Festschrift, The Two Worlds of the Poet: New Perspectives on Vergil, 1992, Tragedy, Love, and Change: Roman Poetic Themes and Variations, 1994, Arma Virumque: Heroes at War (Aeneid 10 and 12), 2 vols., 1998, Classics at McMaster (1890-2000), 2000, A Song of War: Readings from Vergil's Aeneid, 2003. Pres., bd. govs. Hamilton Philharm. Orch., 1967-69, Hamilton Chamber Music Soc., 1965-67, Hamilton br. Archtl. Conservancy Ont., 1965-67, Hamilton and Region Arts Coun., 1971-72; bd. dirs. Can. Fedn. Humanities, 1980-82; v.p., dir. Internat. Acad. Union, 1978-90; v.p. U. Bristol Inst. Greece, Rome and Classical Tradition, 1997—; trustee Hamilton Found., 1972-75; bd. govs. Art Gallery Hamilton; bd. govs., dir. Boris Brott Summer Music Festival, 1989-2000 (pres. 2001), Montreal Chamber Music Festival, 1997—; presdl. bd. trustees McMaster U. Art Gallery, 1985-91; pres. Sir Ernest MacMillan String Ensemble, 1988-90, pres. Nat. Acad. Orch., 2001--; mem. adv. bd. Inst. for Classical Tradition, Boston U., 1987-88; v.p., dir. Bach-Elgar Choral Soc., Hamilton, 1992-95. Decorated knight comdr. Order St. John of Jerusalem; officer Order of Can.; recipient Silver Jubilee medal Queen Elizabeth II, 1977, 125th Anniversary medal Can. Confedn., Golden Jubilee medal Queen Elizabeth II, 2002; Woodrow Wilson fellow, 1947-48, Can. Coun. fellow, 1973-74, Killam rsch. fellow, 1979-80, fellow Vanier Coll., York U., 1991—, vis. scholar, 1996—. Fellow Royal Soc. Can. (hon. editor 1970-83, pres. 1984-87, past pres. 1987-89, Centennial medal 1982); mem. Vergilian Soc. (pres. 1972-74, Hon. Pres. for Life 1988—, chmn. Villa Vergiliana mgmt. com. 1993—), Classical Assn. Mid. West and South (pres. 1972-73, award of merit com. 1989-91), Classical Assn. Can. (v.p. 1970-72, 76-78, pres. 1978-80), Ont. Classical Assn. (hon. pres. 1994—), Master Print and Drawing Soc. (Toronto) (v.p. 1998-2001, pres. 2001-05), Yale Club (N.Y.C.), Tamahaac Club (Ancaster), Arts and Letters Club (Toronto), X Club (Toronto), Univ. Club (McMaster). Home: 15 Inglewood Dr Hamilton ON Canada L8P 2T2 E-mail: ag.mckay@sympatico.ca.

MCKAY, BERNARD L., lawyer; b. Maysville, Ky., July 3, 1969; BBA, Morehead State U., 1991; JD, Salmon P. Chase Coll. Law, 1994. Bar: Ohio 1994, Ky. 1995. Ptnr. Frost Brown Todd LLC, Cin. Chmn., Local Rules Com. Hamilton County Probate Ct.; mem. Cin. Estate Planning Coun. Treasurer Salmon P. Chase Coll. Law Bd. Governors, 2003—04, pres. elect, 2004—05, pres., 2005—06; pres., Class of 2004 Leadership Northern Ky., mem., Class of 2005 Steering Com.; mem., Red Mass Com. St. Thomas More Soc.; mem. Friendly Sons of St. Patrick; mem., Bd. Dirs. Women's Crisis Ctr., chmn., Devel. Com.; mem., Bd. Dirs. Caracole, Inc. Named one of Ohio's Rising Stars, Super Lawyers, 2005, 2006, 40 Under 40, Cin. Bus. Courier, 2006; named to Best Lawyers in Am., 2006. Mem.: ABA (mem., Real Property, Probate and Trust Com.), Northern Ky. Bar Assn. (mem., Bus. and Tax Com., mem., Probate Com.), Ky. Bar Assn. (mem., Taxation Com., mem., Probate and Trust Law Com.), Ohio State Bar Assn. (mem., Estate Planning, mem., Trust and Probate Law Com.), Cin. Bar Assn. (mem., Taxation Com., mem., Adv. Estate Planning and Probate Inst. Com.). Office: Frost Brown Todd LLC 2200 PNC Ctr 201 E Fifth St Cincinnati OH 45202-4182 Office Phone: 513-651-6800. Office Fax: 513-651-6981.

MCKAY, DAVID E., mathematics professor; b. Long Beach, Calif., Aug. 4, 1951; s. John James McKay and Belva Jean Leithead. BA, U. Calif., Riverside, 1974; MA, U. Calif., Irvine, 1978. Math. tchr. Orange Coast, Costa Mesa, Calif., Calif. State U., Long Beach, Santiago Canyon Coll., Orange, Calif. Home: 20062 Midland Ln Huntington Beach CA 92646

MCKAY, DIANNE BRENDA, nephrologist; b. Nov. 11, 1954; MD, Chgo. Med. Sch., 1983. Bd. cert. Nephrology, Internal Medicine, United Network for Organ Sharing (UNOS) cert. Transplant Nephrologist. Nephrologist Scripps Clin., La Jolla, Calif.; and Scripps Ctr. Organ and Cell Transplantation, La Jolla, Calif. Mem.: Am. Assn. Immunologists, Am. Soc. Nephrology (Women in Nephrology), Am. Soc. Transplantation (founder, Com.on Women and Transplantation, Wyeth Clin. Sci. Career Devel. award (Asst. Prof. Level) 2007). Office: Scripps Clin Torrey Pines 10666 N Torrey Pines Rd IMM-1 La Jolla CA 92037 Office Phone: 858-784-9716. Office Fax: 858-784-8069. *

MC KAY, EMILY GANTZ, civil rights and nonprofit professional; b. Columbus, Ohio, Mar. 13, 1945; d. Harry S. and Edwina (Bookwalter) Gantz; m. Jack Alexander McKay, July 3, 1965. BA, Stanford U., 1966, MA, 1967. From pub. info. specialist to rsch. assoc. Cmty. Action Pitts., 1967—70; freelance cons., 1969—70; pub. rels. and materials specialist Met. Cleve. JOBS Coun., 1971—72; rsch. and mgmt. cons. BLK Group, Inc., Washington, 1970—73; dir. tech. products Am. Tech. Assistance Corp., McLean, Va., 1973—74; rsch. and mgmt. cons. CONSAD Rsch. Corp., Pitts., 1974—76, v.p., 1976—78; spl. asst. to pres. for planning and eval. Nat. Coun. La Raza, Washington, 1978—82, v.p. rsch., advocacy & legislation, 1981—88, exec. v.p., 1983—88, cons. to pres., 1988—90, v.p. instl. devel., 1991—93, sr. v.p. instl. devel., 1993—94. Pres. Mosaica: Ctr. for Nonprofit Devel. and Pluralism, 1994—; cons. resource devel. New Israel Fund, 1989-91; cons. City of Cleve., Nat. Assn. Cmty. Devel., Nat. Coun. La Raza, 1975-78, Ford Found., 1989, Nat. AIDS Network, 1988-89, Am. Cultural Ctr., Israel, 1990, Nat. Hispana Leadership Inst., 1993; vol. orgnl. cons. SHATIL, Jerusalem and cmty. based groups in Israel, 1987—; guest faculty Union Inst. Grad. Sch., 1975-78; adj. faculty Sch. Internat. Svc. Am. U., Washington, 1995—; mem. faculty Salzburg (Austria) Seminar on Leadership, 2003. Author orgnl. devel. tng. materials and HIV/AIDS tech. assistance materials. Co-chmn. Citizens Adv. Com. to D.C. Bar, 1986-87; mem. Mayor's Commn. Coop. Econ. Devel., 1981-83; non-lawyer bd. govs. D.C. Bar, 1982-85; exec. com., bd. dirs. Indochina Resource Action Ctr., 1982-92; bd. dirs. exec. com. Southeast Asia Resource Action Ctr., 1993-97; co-chmn. Citizens Commn. Adminstrn. Justice, 1982-84; exec. com. Coalition on Human Needs, 1981-88; Washington area steering com. New Israel Fund, 1989-91; co-chmn. adv. com. to Washington dist. office dir. Immigration and Naturalization Svc., 1984-88; chair Refugee Women in Devel., 1987-90, vice-chair, 1990-94; nat. adv. bd. Project Blueprint United Way of Am., 1992-94, diversity com., 1994-96; vice-chair, treas. Fund for Future of Our Children, 1994—; sec. bd. dirs. New Bosnia Fund, 1995-99, U.S. vice-chair, 1997-99; bd. advisors Internat. Ctr. for Residential Edn., 1994-96; bd. dirs. Mary's Ctr. Maternal and Child Care, 1995-2000, treas., 1996-2000; treas., bd. dirs. AVODAH: The Jewish Svc. Corps., 1996-99; bd. dirs. Acad. of Hope, 2001—; bd. dirs. Nat. Hispana Leadership Inst., 1997-2003, treas., 1998-2003, Hispanic Link Journalism Found., Washington, D.C., 2004—; working group Memorandum of Understanding between HHS and Israeli Ministry of Labour and Social Welfare, 1990-94, chair subcom. Youth at Risk, 1992-94; adv. merit sel. panel Superior Ct. D.C., 1987-90; planning task force U.S.-Israel Women to Women, 2000-01. Recipient I. Pat Rios award Guadalupe Ctr., 1988, Milagros Beanfield award Ayuda, 2004; Ford Found. nat. honors fellow, 1966-67. Mem. NAACP, Nat. Coun. La Raza, Phi Beta Kappa. Democrat. Home: 3200 19th St NW Washington DC 20010-1006 Office: 1522 K St NW Ste 1130 Washington DC 20005-1225 Office Phone: 202-887-0620. Business E-Mail: Emily@mosaica.org.

MCKAY, JOANN, retired musician, composer; b. Cin., Feb. 16, 1939; d. Frederic Lawrence Ott and Gladys Leona Phillips; m. John Patrick McKay, Apr. 21, 1961; children: John Philip, Thomas Jeffrey. MusB in Performance, Cin. Coll. Conservatory Music, 1960; postgrad., Union Theol. Sem., NYC, 1960—61; MA in Music, San Francisco State Coll., 1965. Organist St. Martin's Episc. Ch., Pompano Beach, Fla., 1953—56, Faith Meth. Ch., Champaign, Ill., 1998—99; organist, choir dir., recitalist Bethlehem Meth. Ch., Cin., 1958—60, First Congl. Ch., Medford, Mass., 1961—62, St. Peter's Episc. Ch., Oakland, Calif., 1962—65; organist, recitalist First Meth. Ch., Urbana, 1967—74, Wesley Meth. Ch., Urbana, Ill., 1975—89, 2001—04; ret., 2004. Performer Tuesday Morning Musicale, Champaign, 1970—2003. Vol. with prisoners, charitable orgns. Mem.: Am. Guild Organists (registrar 1963—65, sub-dean 1975—76, winner Young Organists competition, San Francisco 1965). Avocation: reading and speaking French. Home: 915 W Charles St Champaign IL 61821

MCKAY, JOHN, former prosecutor, lawyer, law educator; b. Seattle, June 19, 1956; s. John Larkin and Kathleen (Tierney) M. BA, U. Wash., 1978; JD, Creighton U., 1982. Bar: Wash. 1982, US Dist. Ct. (we. dist.) Wash. 1982, US Supreme Ct. 1990, US Ct. Appeals (9th cir.) 1990, DC 1999. Ptnr. Lane Powell Spears Lubersky, Seattle, 1982-92, Cairncross & Hempelmann, Seattle, 1992-97; pres. Legal Svcs. Corp., Washington, 1997—2001; US atty. (we. dist.) Wash. US Dept. Justice, 2001—07; sr. v.p., gen. counsel Getty Images, Inc., Seattle, 2007—. Vis. prof. law Seattle U. Law Sch., 2007—. White House fellow, Washington, 1989-90; named Pro Bono Lawyer of Yr. Wash. State Bar Assn., 1995, Assn. Award of Merit, 2001 Mem. ABA (bd. govs. 1991-94), Wash. State Bar Assn. (pres. young lawyers divsn. 1988-89). Republican. Roman Catholic. Avocations: soccer, golf. Office: Getty Images Inc 601 N 34th St Seattle WA 98103 Office Phone: 206-925-6006. Business E-Mail: jmckay@seattleu.edu, john.mckay@gettyimages.com. *

MCKAY, JOHN DOUGLAS, lawyer; b. Wheeling, W.Va., Feb. 27, 1960; s. Douglas and Margaret Ann McK.; children: John Wallace, Megan Diane, Hannah Nadine, Katherine Lorraine. BA with distinction, U. Va., 1982; JD, U. Maine, 1985. Bar: W.Va. 1985, Maine 1985, U.S. Dist. Ct. (so. dist.) W.Va. 1985, U.S. Dist. Ct. Maine 1985, U.S. Ct. Appeals (1st cir.) 1986, Va. 1988, U.S. Ct. Appeals (4th cir.) 1988, U.S. Dist. Ct. (we. dist.) Va. 1988, Colo. 1997, Fla. 1999, N.Y. 2002, Calif. 2002. Assoc. Petruccelli, Cohen, Erler & Cox, Portland, Maine, 1985-88, Taylor & Zunka, Ltd., Charlottesville, Va., 1988-91; ptnr. McKay & Cattano PLC, Charlottesville, 1991-97; prin. McKay Law Offices, Charlottesville, 1997—2006; ptnr. McKay Lewis PLC, Charlottesville, 2007—, NYC, 1997—. Founder, editor (legal newsletter) Equine Law & Bus. Letter, 1990-95; contbr. articles to profl. jours. Recipient Best Adv. award U. Maine Sch. of Law, 1985. Mem. Va. State Bar (7th dist. disciplinary com. 1994-2000). Office Phone: 802-253-4079.

MCKAY, KENNETH GARDINER, retired physicist, electronics company executive; b. Montreal, Quebec, Canada, Apr. 8, 1917; came to U.S., 1946, naturalized, 1954; s. James Gardiner and Margaret (Nicholas) McK.; m. Irene C. Smith, July 25, 1942; children— Margaret Craig, Kenneth Gardiner B.Sc., McGill U., 1938, M.Sc., 1939; Sc.D, MIT, 1941; D.Eng. (hon.), Stevens Inst. Tech., 1980. Research engr. Nat. Research Council Can., 1941-46; with Bell Telephone Labs., 1946-66, 73-80, dir. solid state device devel., 1957-59, v.p. systems engring., 1959-62, exec. v.p. systems engring., 1962-66, exec. v.p., 1973-80; v.p. engring AT&T, 1966-73; chmn. bd. Bellcomm Inc., 1966-73, Charles Stark Draper Lab., 1982-87; ret., 1987. Advisor Min. of Transp. and Comms., Republic of China, 1982-95. Trustee Stevens Inst. Tech., 1974-87; bd. govs. McGill U., 1972-77, N.Y. Coll. Osteo. Medicine, 1980-89; mem. vis. com. for engring. Stanford U., 1974-87; mem. sci. and acad. adv. com. U. Calif., 1980-88; mem. Sci. and Tech. Adv. Group, Republic of China, 1982-96. Fellow IEEE, Am. Phys. Soc., N.Y. Acad. Scis.; mem. NAS, NAE (councillor 1970-73), Century Assn.

MCKAY, LAURA L., bank executive, consultant; b. Watonga, Okla., Mar. 3, 1947; d. Frank Bradford and Elizabeth Jane (Smith) Drew; m. Cecil O. McKay, Sept. 20, 1969; 1 child, Leslie. BSBA, Oreg. State U., 1969. Cert. cash mgr., Treasury Mgmt. Assn. New br. rsch. U.S. Bank, Portland, Oreg., 1969-80, cash mgmt. officer, 1980-82, asst. v.p., 1982-87, v.p., 1987-94; founder, cons. LLM Cons., Milw., 1994-97; co-founder, mng. ptnr. DMC & Assocs. LLC, Portland, 1997—2001; v.p. treasury mgmt., sales mgr. West Coast Bank, 2000—06, sr. v.p. mgr., treasury mgmt., 2006—. Cert. trainer Achieve Global and Edge Learning. Chmn. Budget Com., North Clackamas Sch. Dist., 1982-84. Mem. Assn. for Fin. Profls., Nat. Assn. Bank Women (chmn. Oreg. group 1979-80), Portland Treasury Mgrs. Assn., Portland C. of C. Republican. Office: Ste 100 5000 Meadows Rd Lake Oswego OR 97034 Home Phone: 503-632-3564; Office Phone: 503-603-8052. E-mail: mckayl@wcb.com.

MCKAY, MARGO MARQUITA, federal agency administrator, lawyer; b. Baltimore, Md., Oct. 9, 1946; d. Gordon and Gary Venetia (Jones) M.; m. James Phillip Allen, Jr., June 10, 1978; children: Marja Allen, Eric Allen, Kaila Allen. BA, Fisk U., Nashville, Tenn., 1968; JD, Georgetown U., DC, 1975. Bar: Penn. 1975, Va. 1982. Trial atty. US Dept. Justice, Washington, 1975-78; atty. Am. Legal Cons., 1979; br. chief Dept. Army US Dept. Def., 1980-81; mng. atty. Legal Serv. No. Va., Alexandria, 1982-83; exec. asst. to vice-chmn., sr. advisor, US Merit Systems Protection Bd., Washington, 1983-91; dep. dir. for ethics US Dept. Housing & Urban Devel., Washington, 1990; adminstrv. judge, temp. panel Office Employee Appeals, DC; dir. compliance, assoc. gen. counsel Fannie Mae; asst. sec. for civil rights USDA, Washington, 2006—. Author (high sch. textbook): Street Law, 1975. Recipient numerous employment awards, 1970—. Mem. ABA, Federal Circuit Bar Assoc. Office: USDA Jamie L Whitten Bldg 14th St & Independence Ave SW Rm 240-W Washington DC 20250

MCKAY, MARIE CONYERS, librarian, writer; b. Brumley, Mo., Aug. 18, 1930; d. Raymond Harold Conyers and Nellie Mae Bunch; m. Julius S. McKay, Oct. 19, 1964; children: Michelle Leighanne O'Beirne, Rosemary Susan O'Hern. AA, S.W. Bapt. Coll., Bolivar, Mo., 1948; BA, Okla. Bapt. U., Shawnee, 1950; MA in Libr. Sci., George Peabody Coll. Tchrs. (now Vanderbilt U.), Nashville, 1951; M in Religious Edn., So. Bapt. Theol. Sem., Louisville, Ky., 1959. Libr. cataloger N.E. Mo. State Coll. (now Harry Truman State U.), Kirksville, 1951—53; libr. S.W. Bapt. Coll. (Now U.), Bolivar, Mo., 1953—57; dep. libr. Hong Kong Bapt. U., Kowloon, 1960—64, curator archive on the history of Christianity in China, 1996—98; libr. cataloger Miss. State U., Starkville, 1987—96. Contbr. articles to profl. jours. Missionary So. Bapt. Fgn. Mission Bd., Richmond, Va., 1959—64. Mem.: ALA. Baptist. Home: 108 Kyle Ct Gardendale AL 35071 Personal E-mail: mmckay@bellsouth.net.

MCKAY, MELINDA, hotel executive; b. Sydney, Australia, 1974; Corp. mktg. devel., rsch. svcs. Jones Lang LaSalle Hotels Asia Pacific; mktg. rsch. Jones Lang LaSalle Hotels, rsch. mgr. Chgo., 1997—99, sr. v.p., 2001—. Named one of 40 Under Forty, Crain's Chgo. Bus., 2005. *

MCKAY, MICHAEL DENNIS, lawyer; b. Omaha, May 12, 1951; s. John Larkin and Kathleen (Tierney) McK.; children: Kevin Tierney, Kathleen Lindsay, John Larkin. BA in Polit. Sci. with distinction, U. Wash., 1973; JD, Creighton U., 1976. Bar: Wash. 1976, U.S. Dist. Ct. (we. dist.) Wash. 1978, U.S. Dist. Ct. (ea. dist.) Wash. 1982, U.S. Ct. Appeals (9th cir.) 1982, U.S. Supreme Ct. 1993. Sr. dep. pros. atty. King County, Seattle, 1976-81; ptnr. McKay & Gaitan, Seattle, 1981-89; U.S. atty. we. dist. Wash. Seattle, 1989-93; ptnr. Lane Powell Spears Lubersky, Seattle, 1993-95, McKay Chadwell PLLC, Seattle, 1995—. Bd. dirs. Mental Health North, Seattle, 1982-85, St. Joseph Sch. Bd., 1984-87, Our Lady of Fatima Sch. Commn., 1994-97, Creighton U., 1988-90; mem. stadium adv. bd. Seattle Kingdome, 1987-89; mem. U.S. Atty. Gen. Adv. Com., 1991-93, vice chmn., 1992; mem. Washington Citizens' Commn. on Salaries for Elected Officials, 1997—; vice chmn., 1999—; vice chmn. Seattle Expert Rev. Panel, 1999; vice chair Washington State George W. Bush Campaign, 2000, 2004. Mem. Creighton U. Alumni Assn. (pres. 1988-90, nat. alumni bd. 1988-92), Wash. Athletic Club, Columbia Tower Club. Republican. Roman Catholic. Avocations: golf, reading. Office: McKay Chadwell PLLC 600 University St Ste 1601 Seattle WA 98101 Business E-Mail: mdm@mckay-chadwell.com.

MCKAY, MICHAEL KEVIN, nurse, priest; b. Chgo., Jan. 10, 1952; s. Gilbert Angus and Winifred Mary (Endebrock) McKay; m. Susan Replogle, Jan. 1, 1985; m. Kathryn Jane Young, July 10, 1976 (div. Apr. 1, 1980); stepchildren: Deborah Aldrich, Kimberly Lacore, William Noble, Rebecca Nicholson. AA, St. Petersburg Coll., Fla., 1974; AS in Nursing, St. Petersburg Coll., Pinellas Park, Fla., 1985; Cert. LPN, St. Petersburg Vocat.-Tech. Inst., 1981. RN Fla., 1985. Pastor, founder Regina Caeli Old-Cath. Ministries, Clearwater, Fla., 2004—; hospice nurse Hernando/Pasco Hospice, New Port Richey, Fla., 2006—; founder, cleric regular Servants of St. Camillus (de Lellis), Clearwater, 2007—. Archbishop Fla. Ref. Cath. Ch. Am., Bremerton, Wash., 2005—. Chaplain AMVETS Post 67 USS Cole, Clearwater, 2003; mem./chaplain Dunedin Vol. Emergency Response Team, Fla., 2006; sr. chaplain, bd. dirs. Emergency Med. Chaplains Assn., Chilhowie, Va., 2006. With USN, 1970—72. Republican. Catholic. Personal E-mail: fr-nevin-mary@earthlink.net.

MCKAY, MICHAEL WENDELL, lawyer; b. Beaufort, SC, Dec. 14, 1949; s. John W. and Alice (Thornhill) M.; m. Leah H. McKay; children: Wendell, Slater, Watson, Harris. BA, La. State U., Baton Rouge, 1971, JD, 1974. Bar: La. 1974, U.S. Dist. Ct. (mid. dist.) La. 1974, U.S. Dist. Ct. (we. dist.) La. 1976, U.S. Dist. Ct. (ea. dist.) La. 1977, U.S. Ct. Appeals (5th cir.) 1977, U.S. Supreme Ct. 1977, U.S. Ct. Appeals (11th cir.) 1981. Assoc./ptnr. Brewer & McKay, Baton Rouge, 1974-80; ptnr. Roy, Kiesel, Patterson & McKay, Baton Rouge, 1980-84; pvt. practice Baton Rouge, 1984-88; dir. Hoffman Sutterfield, Baton Rouge, 1988-97; of counsel Shows, Cali & Burns, Baton Rouge, 1997-99; ptnr. McKay Williamson Lutgring & Cochran, LLC, Baton Rouge, 1999—2004, McKay Lutgring & Cochran, LLC, Baton Rouge, 2004—. Bd. dirs. Baton Rouge Area Found., 1994-97; treas., bd. dirs. Capital Area Legal Svcs. Corp., Baton Rouge, 1978-83. Mem. ABA, La. State Bar Assn. (bd. govs. 1995-98, treas. 1999-2000, pres., 2004-05, Pres.'s award 1997, Pro Bono Publico award 1994), Baton Rouge Bar Assn. (pres., sec., treas. 1989-93), La. Bar Found. (bd. dirs. 1998-2000), La. Assn. Def. Counsel (bd. dirs. 1999-2001), Am. Inns of Ct., La. Trial Lawyers Assn. (bd. govs. 1980-). Democrat. Episcopalian. Avocation: tennis. Office: McKay Lutgring & Cochran 2431 S Acadian Thruway Ste 290 Baton Rouge LA 70808 Business E-Mail: mike@mlclawyers.com. *

MCKAY, MONROE GUNN, federal judge; b. Huntsville, Utah, May 30, 1928; s. James Gunn and Elizabeth (Peterson) McK.; m. Lucile A. Kinnison, Aug. 6, 1954; children: Michele, Valanne, Margaret, James, Melanie, Nathan, Bruce, Lisa, Monroe. BS, Brigham Young U., 1957; JD, U. Chgo., 1960. Bar: Ariz. 1961. Law clk. Ariz. Supreme Ct., 1960-61; assoc. firm Lewis & Roca, Phoenix, 1961-66, ptnr., 1968-74; assoc. prof. Brigham Young U., 1974-76; prof., 1976-77; judge US Ct. Appeals (10th cir.), Denver, 1977-91, chief judge, 1991-94, sr. judge, 1994—. Mem. Phoenix Community Council Juvenile Problems, 1968-74; pres. Ariz. Assn. for Health and Welfare, 1970-72; dir. Peace Corps, Malawi, Africa, 1966-68; bd. dirs., pres. Maricopa county Legal Aid Soc., 1972-74. Served with USMCR, 1946-48. Mem. Ariz. Bar Assn. Mem. Lds Ch. Office: US Ct Appeals 10th Cir Fed Bldg 125 S State St Ste 6012 Salt Lake City UT 84138-1181 *

MCKAY, PATRICIA A., consumer products company executive; CPA. V.p. fin., contr. Dole Food Co., 1993—96; various positions including sr. v.p. fin. AutoNation Inc., 1997—2003; exec. v.p., CFO Restoration Hardware Inc., 2003—05, Office Depot, Delray Beach, Fla., 2005—. Bd. dirs. Office Depot, 2004—05. Office: Office Depot 2200 Old Germantown Rd Delray Beach FL 33445 *

MCKAY, PAUL PATRICK, healthcare educator; b. Pawtucket, RI, Dec. 18, 1964; s. Kenneth John McKay and Ann Virginia Graham; m. Susan Marie Phelps; children: Kristin Nicole, Alannah Kathryn; m. Tambra Mae Sommer. Dir. N.Am. Brain Tumor Coalition, DC, 2001; pres. Brain Tumor Action Network, Zephyrhills, Fla., 2002—. Founder, pres. Brain Tumor Action Network, Zephyrhills, Fla., 2002; tri-state coord. Fathers 4 Justice. E-4 USAF, 1982—86, Ramstein AFB, W.Germany. Recipient Mgr. of Yr. award, San Diego Bus. Jour., 1997. Mem.: Mensa. Independent. Achievements include having an integral role in passing the Benign Brain Tumor Cancer Registries Amendment Act of 2002. Personal E-mail: pmckay@btan.org.

MCKAY, RENEE, artist; b. Montreal, Que., Can. came to U.S., 1946, naturalized, 1954; d. Frederick Garvin and Mildred Gladys (Higgins) Smith; m. Kenneth Gardiner McKay, July 25, 1942; children: Margaret Craig, Kenneth Gardner. BA, McGill U., 1941. Tchr. art Peck Sch., Morristown, NJ, 1955-56. One woman shows include Pen and Brush Club, N.Y.C., 1957, Cosmopolitan Club, N.Y.C., 1958; group shows include Weyhe Gallery, N.Y.C., 1978, Newark Mus., 1955, 59, Montclair (N.J.) Mus., 1955-58, Nat. Assn. Women Artists, Nat. Acad. Galleries, 1954-78, N.Y. World's Fair, 1964-65, Audubon Artists, N.Y.C., 1955-62, 74-79, N.Y. Soc. Women Artists, 1979-80, Provincetown (Mass.) Art Assn. and Mus., 1975-79; traveling shows in France, Belgium, Italy, Scotland, Can., Japan; represented in permanent collections: Slater Meml. Mus., Norwich, Conn., Norfolk (Va.) Mus., Butler Inst. Am. Art, Youngstown, Ohio, Lydia Drake Libr., Pembroke, Mass., Nat. Arts Club, N.Y.C., Provinceton Mus.- Mass., Provincetown, many pvt. collections. Recipient Jane Peterson prize in oils Nat. Assn. Women Artists, 1954, Famous Artists Sch. prize in watercolor, 1959, Grumbacher Artists Watercolor award 1970, Solo award Pen and Brush, 1957, Sadie-Max Tesser award in watercolor Audubon Artists, 1975, Peterson prize in oils, 1980, Michael Engel prize Nat. Soc. Painters in Casein and Acrylic, 1983. Mem. Nat. Assn. Women Artists (2d v.p. 1969-70, adv. bd. 1974-76), Audubon Artists (pres. 1979, dir. oils 1986-88), Artist Equity (dir. 1977-79, v.p. 1979-81), N.Y. Soc. Women Artists, Pen and Brush, Nat. Soc. Painters in Casein and Acrylic M.J. Kaplan prize 1984, Nat. Arts Club, Provincetown Art Assn. and Mus., Key West Art Assn., Cosmopolitan Club.

MCKAY, RICHARD JAMES, professional sports team executive; b. Eugene, Oreg., Mar. 16, 1959; s. John H. and Nancy Jean (Hunter) McK.; m. Terrin Lea Few, May 19, 1984; children: K. Hunter, John Crosby. BA, Princeton U., 1981; JD, Stetson Coll. Law, St. Petersburg, Fla., 1984. Bar: Fla. 1984, U.S. Dist. Ct. (mid. dist.) Fla. 1984. Law clk. to Hon. William Terrell Hodges U.S. Dist. Ct. (middle dist. Fla.), Tampa, 1984-86; ptnr. Hill, Ward & Henderson, Tampa, Fla., 1986-92; gen. mgr. Tampa Bay Bucaneers, 1993—2003; pres., gen. mgr. Atlanta Falcons, 2003—. Adj. prof. Stetson Coll. Law, St. Petersburg, 1989-92; co-chmn. NFL Competition Com., 1994—. Office: Atlanta Falcons 4400 Falcon Pkwy Flowery Branch GA 30542

MCKAY, ROBERT CONNALLY, lawyer; b. Tyler, Tex., Apr. 28, 1950; s. Connally and Glee (McCrary) McK.; m. Bonnie Swain, Mar. 31, 1979; children: Robert Connally, Sarah Catherine, Caroline Swain. BA, Baylor U., 1972, J.D., 1975. Bar: Tex., U.S. Dist. Ct. (so. dist.) Tex.; cert. in Oil, Gas and Mineral Law Tex. Bd. Legal Specializaiton. Asst. counsel com. on pub. works and transp. U.S. Ho. of Reps., Washington, 1975-77; dir. Scott, Robins, McKay, Smith & Rigsby, Victoria, Tex., 1977-85; chmn., chief exec. officer McKay, Smith, Robins, Russell & Rigsby, 1986-87; chmn., chief exec. officer McKay & Russell, P.C., 1987-92, McKay & Crain, P.C., 1992-96, Stephenson & McKay, L.L.P., 1996-2001, Cole, Cole & Easley, P.C., 2001——; pres. Victoria Savs. Assn., 1985; mem. Tex. State Ethics Adv. Commn., 1983-88. Bd. dirs. Victoria Regional Mus. Assn., 1981-84, Victoria Econ. Devel. Corp., 1983-89; mem. Mayor's Image Com., Victoria, 1983-84. Mem. Coll. of State Bar of Tex., Tex. Bar Found., Victoria County Bar Assn. (pres. 1989-90), Rotary. Presbyterian. Home: 303 Leisure Ln Victoria TX 77904-1670 Office: 302 West Forrest Victoria TX 77901 Office Phone: 361-575-0551.

MCKAY-WILKINSON, JULIE ANN, minister, marriage and family therapist; b. Washington, Feb. 26, 1953; d. Charles William and Evelyn Loretta (Starr) McKay; m. Grover Gene Wilkinson, Jan. 13, 1990; 1 child, Angela Starr Gotti. AS, Camden County Coll., 1975; BA, Rowan U., 1978; grad., Unity Sch. Christianity, Lee's Summit, Mo., 1997. Cert. pastoral addictions counselor, and lic. addictions counselor, co-dependency counselor. Probation officer York County Probation, Pa., 1983—86; therapist pvt. practice, York, 1985—90, New Insights, York, 1985—87, Clare Ctr., York, 1987—90; founder, min., therapist Unity Christ Ch., Lubbock, Tex., 1997—2003. Host weekly TV program Spiritual Lifelines. Editor: (monthly newsletter) Spiritual Lifelines, 1997—2003. Chairperson Christmas toy dr. Unity Christ Ch., 1997—2003, founder, Christmas bear dr., 2003—. Mem.: Lubbock Ecimenical Orgn. Democrat. Avocations: gardening, music, movies. Office: Unity Ctr Spiritual Living 7300 Mallard Creek Rd Charlotte NC 28262 Home: 2540 Pickway Dr Charlotte NC 28269 Office Phone: 704-599-1180. Personal E-mail: revjulie3@carolina.rr.com.

MCKEACHNIE, GAYLE F., former lieutenant governor; b. Vernal, Utah, Jan. 26, 1943; s. Colton Orville and Helen (Fletcher) McK.; m. Kathlene Argyle, Dec. 16, 1967; children: Brett, Michelle, Jared, Ashley, Dana Marie, Jonathan, Jacob. BA, Coll. So. Utah, 1967; JD, U. Utah, 1970. Bar: Utah 1970, U.S. Dist. Ct. Utah 1970, U.S. Ct. Appeals (10th cir.) 1970, U.S. Tax Ct. 1985, U.S. Supreme Ct. 1985. Assoc. Senior & Senior, Salt Lake City, 1970-72; adj. prof. UT State U., 1972—2000; prin. Gayle F. McKeachnie & Assocs., Vernal, 1972-78; ptnr. McKeachnie & Allred, Vernal, 1978-81, Nielson & Senior, Vernal, 1981-89, pres., 1988-89, also bd. dirs.; adj. prof. BYU J. Reuben Clark Law School, 1996—2000; lt. gov. State of UT, Salt Lake City, 2003—05. Atty. Daggett County, Manila, Utah, 1974-79; dep. atty. Uintah County, Vernal, 1976-79; appointed to Utah Commn. on Adminstrn. Justice in the Dist. Cts. 1986; chmn. Utah Constl. Review Commn., 1989-01; mem. task force Mgmt. and Regulation of the Practice of Law, Utah Supreme Ct., 1990-92; bd. dirs. Utah Bar Commrs., 1990-94; adv., rural affairs advisor Utah Gov. Mem. Utah Ho. of Reps., Vernal, 1979-88; Utah Bd. State Lands and Forestry, 1992-94. Recipient Disting. Lawyer of Yr. award, Utah Bar Assn., 1997, Disting. Alumnus award, So. Utah U., 1995. Mem. Kiwanis (pres. 1977-78), Utah State U. (chmn., bd. trustees 1994-04), BYU J. Reuben Clark Law Sch. (bd. visitors 1998-00). Office Phone: 435-789-4908. Business E-Mail: gmckeachnie@mckeachnie.com.

MCKEAG, DOUGLAS BRUCE, physician, educator; b. Berwyn, Ill., July 21, 1945; s. Diane (Dolan) McKeag; children: Heather, Kelly, Ian. BS in Zoology, Iowa State U., 1968; MS in Cardiov. Phys., Mich. State U., 1970, MD, 1973. Diplomate Am. Bd. Family Practice. Intern Presbyn. Hosp., Pacific Med. Ctr., San Francisco, 1973-74; resident in family practice Grand Rapids Area Med. Edn. Ctr., Mich., 1974-76; fellow in family practice Mich. State U., East Lansing, 1976-77, fellow in adolescent medicine, 1976-77, team physician dept. intercollegiate athletics, 1977—95, assoc. dir., coordinator sports medicine, 1984—95, adj. assoc prof. sch. health edn., 1986—95; dir. Primary Care Sports Medicine. vice chmn. Dept. Family Medicine and Orthopedic Surgery U. Pitts., 1995—99, Arthur J. Rooney Sr. chair for sports medicine, 1995—99; chmn. Dept. Family Medicine Ind. U. Sch. Medicine, 1999—, OneAmerica prof. preventive health medicine, 1999—, dir. Ctr. Sports Medicine, 1999—. Mem. com. Nat. Bd. Med. Examiners, 1988—; mem. drug testing and drug edn. subcom. NCAA, 1988—; cons. Kuwait U. Faculty of Medicine, Walt Disney Ednl. Svcs., Puerto Rico Olympic Com.; presenter in field. Editor series Primary Care Sports Medicine, 1988—, Basketball (Handbook of Sports Medicine and Science), 2003; assoc. editor: Medicine and Science in Sports and Exercise, 1987; mem. editorial bd. various jours. in field; contbr. articles to profl. publs. Grantee Mich. Heat Assn., 1975-76, NIH, 1980-81, 81-82, 84, 85, Nat. Collegiate Athletic Assn., 1983, 88, Mich. Acad. Family Physicians, 1986; NIH fellow, 1968-70; named one of America's Top Doctors, 2005. Fellow Am. Coll. Sports Medicine (trustee 1987), Am. Acad. Family Physicians; mem. N.Am. Primary Care Rsch. Group, Soc. Tchrs. Family Medicine, Soc. Adolescent Medicine, Am. Medical Soc. for Sports Medicine, Am. Bd. of Family Practice, Am. Coll. Sports Medicine, Ind. Acad. Family Physicians. Office: Ind U Dept Family Medicine 1110 W Michigan St Indianapolis IN 46202 Office Phone: 317-278-0360. Business E-Mail: dmckeng@iupui.edu.

MCKEAGUE, DAVID WILLIAM, judge; b. Pitts., Nov. 5, 1946; s. Herbert William and Phyllis (Forsyth) McKeague; m. Nancy L. Palmer, May 20, 1989; children: Mike, Melissa, Sarah, Laura, Elizabeth, Adam. BBA, U. Mich., 1968, JD, 1971. Bar: Mich. 1971, US Dist. Ct. (we. dist.) Mich. 1972, US Dist. Ct. (ea. dist.) Mich. 1978, US Ct. Appeals (6th cir.) 1988. Assoc. Foster, Swift, Collins & Smith, Lansing, Mich., 1971-76, ptnr., 1976-92, sec.-treas., 1990-92; judge US Dist. Ct., (we. dist.) Mich., Lansing, Mich., 1992—2005, US Ct. Appeals (6th cir.), 2005—. Adm. prof. Mich. State U. Coll. Law, 1998—. Mem. nat. com. U. Mich. Law Sch. Fund, 1980—92, bd. trustees, 2007—; gen. counsel Mich. Rep. Com., 1989—92; mem. adv. coun. Wharton Ctr. Mich. State U., 1996—2002; adv. bd. Corp. Supportive Housing, 2002—. With USAR, 1969—75. Mem.: FBA (bd. dirs. Western Mich. chpt. 1991—), Federalist Soc. Law and Pub. Studies (lawyers divsn. Mich. chpt. 1996—), Am. Inns Ct. (pres. Mich. State U. Coll. Law chpt. 1999—2001), Mich. Bar Assn., Country Club Lansing (bd. govs. 1988—92, 1995—2001). Roman Catholic. Office: US Ct Appeals 315 W Allegan Rm 119 Lansing MI 48933 Office Phone: 517-377-1563. Business E-Mail: ca06-mckeague_chambers@ca6.uscourts.gov. *

MCKEAN, HENRY P., mathematics institute administrator; b. Wenham, Mass., Dec. 14, 1930; AB, Dartmouth Coll., 1952; PhD, Princeton U., 1955; PhD (hon.), U. Paris, 2002. Instr. Princeton U., NJ, 1955-57, MIT, Cambridge, 1958-63, prof., 1964-66, Rockefeller U., NYC, 1966-70; dep. dir., chmn. dept. math., Courant Inst. Math. Scis. NYU, NYC, 1984-88, prof., Courant Inst. Math. Scis., 1970—, dir., Courant Inst. Math. Scis., 1988—92. Vis. prof. Kyoto U., 1957-58, Rockefeller U., 1963-64; George Eastman prof. Balliol Coll., Oxford U., 1979-80. Co-author (with K. Ito) Diffusion Processes and Their Sample Paths, 1965, (with H. Dym) Fourier Series and Integrals, 1972, (with H. Dym) Stationary Gaussian Processes, 1976, (with V. Moll) Elliptic Curves, 1997; author Stochastic Integrals, 1969; Contbr. numerous articles to profl. jours. Recipient Leroy P. Steele prize for Lifetime Achievement, Am. Math. Soc., 2007. Mem. NAS, Am. Acad. Arts and Scis. Office: NYU Courant Inst Math Scis 251 Mercer St New York NY 10012-1110 Office Phone: 212-998-3252. Office Fax: 212-995-4121. Business E-Mail: mckean@cims.nyu.edu. *

MC KEAN, JOHN ROSSEEL OVERTON, university dean; b. Cortland, NY, July 31, 1928; s. Norman Dodge and Janet (Passage) McK.; m. Ruth MacDonald, July 2, 1955; children: Janet, Annalise. BA, Coll. William and Mary, 1951; M.Ed., Cornell U., 1956, Ed.D., 1961. Tchr. Landon Sch. for Boys, Washington, 1952-53; tchr. Central Sch., Homer, NY, 1953-55; asst. prof. history, dean students Allegheny Coll., 1957-67; headmaster Kingswood Sch. for Girls, Cranbrook, Bloomfield Hills, Mich., 1967-68; dean Hobart Coll., 1968-73; v.p. Coll. Kenyon Coll., Gambier, Ohio, 1973-77; dean arts and scis. State U. N.Y. at Canton, 1977-92. Mem. SUNY Coun. Deans Arts and Scis., Nat. Assn. Student Personnnel Adminstrs. (pres. Pa. 1958-59), SUNY Coun. Two-Yr. Bus. Adminstrs., Nat. Assn. Student Personnel Adminstrs. (dir. 1959-61), Am. Assn. Higher Edn., C.C. Gen. Edn. Assn., Middle States Assn. Colls. and Secondary Schs., Direct Descs. Signers Declaration Independence (historian), St. Lawrence County Hist. Soc., Geneva Concerts Assn., (dir. 1969-72), Am. Hist. Assn., Round Table, English-Speaking Union, St. Andrews Soc., Chapel Hill Tennis Club, Rotary, Phi Delta Kappa, Kappa Sigma. Home: 25 Flemington Rd Chapel Hill NC 27517-5638

MCKEAN, KEVIN S., publishing executive, writer; b. Ann Arbor, Mich; BA in English cum laude, Yale U. Police reporter City New Bur. Chgo., 1974; gen. assignment writer, broadcast editor AP, Denver and New Orleans, 1975; nat. sci. writer NY, 1978; staff writer, sr. editor Discover mag., 1981—87; sr. editor, founding new media editor Money mag., 1987—97; asst. mng. editor for business and finance Time Inc. New Media; exec. editor Forbes.com; editl. dir., v.p. PC World mag., 2000—03; editorial dir., CEO InfoWorld Media Group, San Francisco, 2002—05; v.p. editl. dir. Consumers Union (Consumer Reports Publ.). Spkr. in field. Sci. editor (3 hr. WGBH-produced pub. TV spl.) Living Against the Odds, 1991; contbr. chapters to books; appeared (TV programs) NBC'S Today show, CBS This Morning, CNN, CNBC, CNNfn. Named to Power Media 50, B2B Mag., 2005. Office: Consumers Union 101 Truman Ave Yonkers NY 10703-1057 *

MCKEAN, MICHAEL, actor; b. NYC, Oct. 17, 1947; s. Gilbert and Ruth McKean; m. Susan McKean; children: Colin Russell, Fletcher. Student, Carnegie Inst. Tech., NYU. Toured with satirical comedy group The Credibility Gap; TV appearances include The Goodtime Girls, More Than Friends, American Bandstand, The TV Show; regular on ABC-TV series Laverne and Shirley, 1976-83, Grand, 1989, Dream On, 1990, Sessions, 1991, Spinal Tap Anniversary Spl., 1992, Saturday Night Live, 1994, Road Rovers, 1996, Clerks: The Animated Series, 2000, Life's Too Short, 2000, The Lone Gunmen, 2001, Primetime Glick, 2002; actor: (films) 1941, 1979, Used Cars, 1980, Young Doctors in Love, 1982, This is Spinal Tap, 1984, Clue, 1985, D.A.R.Y.L., 1985, Jumpin Jack Flash, 1986, Light of Day, 1987, Planes, Trains, & Automobiles, 1987, Short Circuit II, 1988, Earth Girls Are Easy, 1989, Flashback, 1989, The Big Picture, 1989, Book of Love, 1991, True Identity, 1991, Memoirs of an Invisible Man, 1992, Man Trouble, 1992, Mojo Flats, 1993, Coneheads, 1993, Airheads, 1994, Radioland Murders, 1994, The Brady Bunch Movie, 1995, The Pompatus of Love, 1996, Jack, 1996, Still Breathing, 1997, That Darn Cat, 1997, Nothing to Lose, 1997, Small Soldiers (voice), 1998, Mystery, Alaska, 1999, Teaching Mrs. Tingle, 1999, True Crime, 1999, Best in Show, 2000, Beautiful, 2000, Little Nicky, 2000, My First Mister, 2001, Never Again, 2001, Dr. Doolittle 2, 2001, Teddy Bear's Picnic, 2001, The Guru, 2002, Auto Focus, 2002, 100 Mile Rule, 2002, A Mighty Wind, 2003, Haunted Lighthouse, 2003, Candor City Hospital, 2003; (Broadway) Accomplice, 1989, Hairspray, 2004; (off-broadway) A Second Hand Memory, 2004; (TV movies) More Than Friends, 1978, Classified Love, 1986, Murder in High Places, 1991; (video) Casper: A Spirited Begining, 1997, The Pajama Game, 2006, Love Song, 2006; rec. artist: (with David Lander) Lenny and the Squigglones, This is Spinal Tap; songwriter (with co-writers Christopher Guest and Eugene Levy), A Mighty Wind (Grammy award for Best Song Written For A Motion Picture, Television Or Other Visual Media 2004). Office: care William Morris Agy 151 S El Camino Dr Beverly Hills CA 90212-2704 *

MCKEAN, ROBERT JACKSON, JR., retired lawyer; b. NYC, Dec. 21, 1925; s. Robert Jackson and Isabel (Murphy) McKean; m. Sally H. Ament; children from previous marriage: Katherine, Douglas, Lauren, Andrew. BA, Amherst Coll., 1950; LL.B., Harvard U., 1953. Bar: NY 1954. Assoc. Simpson Thacher & Bartlett, NYC, 1953-62, ptnr., 1962-85. Trustee Amherst Coll., Mass., Folger Shakespeare Libr., Washington. With US Army, 1944—46, ETO. Recipient medal for eminent svc., Amherst Coll., 1968. Mem.: Phi Beta Kappa. Democrat.

MCKEAN, SHERRY LYNN, medical technician; b. Owosso, Mich., Mar. 3, 1953; d. William Ash and Myrtle Viola (Darling) Salander; m. Brian Patrick McKean, May 31, 1997; 1 child, Jennifer Lynn Bentley. A, John Wesley Coll., 1979; degree, Calif. Coll. Health Scis., 2002. Neurodiagnostic supr. Dr. Gary Roat, Flint, Mich., 1978—95; neurodiagnostic tech. Flint Osteo. Hosp., 1993—95, Dr. I. Zachar Dyme, Lansing, 1995—, Meml. Healthcare, Owosso, 1995—. Mem.: Assn. Polysomnographic Technologists. Avocations: hiking, travel, reading, sewing, walking. Office: 826 W King St Owosso MI 48867

MCKEAN, THOMAS WAYNE, retired dentist, retired military officer; b. Adams County, Ind., May 18, 1928; s. Gorman F. and Elmira B. (Staley) McK.; m. Marilyn Kimberlin, Aug. 9, 1952; children: Thomas Wayne, Randall K., Dana K. D.D.S., Ind. U., 1953; grad., Naval Dental Sch., 1963. Diplomate: Am. Bd. Oral Surgery. Commd. ensign Dental Corps USN, 1949, advanced through grades to rear adm., 1980; stationed at Naval Tng. Ctr., Great Lakes, Ill., 1953; dental officer U.S.S. Randall, 1953-56; head dental svc., asst. dental officer U.S. Naval Acad./Naval Hosp., Annapolis, Md., 1956-59; dental officer FASRON III; asst. dental officer U.S. Naval Sta., Bermuda, 1959-63; postgrad. student Naval Dental Sch., Bethesda, Md., 1963-64; resident oral and maxillofacial surgery Naval Hosp., Great Lakes, Ill., 1964-66; dental officer U.S.S. America, 1966-68; chief oral surgery Naval Hosp., Orlando, Fla., 1968-70; dir. oral surgery and gen. practice residency tng. programs Naval Regional Med. Ctr., Great Lakes, 1970-74, chmn. dept. dentistry, 1970-74; cons., lectr. U.S. Army, Fort Sheridan, Ill., 1970-74; dir. oral surgery and gen. practice residency tng. programs Naval Regional Med. Ctr., Oakland, Calif., 1974-78, chmn., dept. dentistry, 1974-78; lectr. oral surgery Letterman Army Med. Ctr., San Francisco, 1974-78; clin. lectr. dept. oral surgery U. of Pacific Sch. Dentistry, San Francisco, 1974-78; comdg. officer Naval Regional Dental Ctr., Pensacola, Fla., 1978-80; lectr. oral surgery Pensacola (Fla.) Jr. Coll., 1978-80; cons., lectr. Dwight D. Eisenhower Army Regional Med. Ctr., Augusta, Ga., 1978-80; insp. gen. dental Bur. Medicine and Surgery, Dept. of Navy, Washington, 1980-81; comdg. officer Naval Regional Dental Ctr., San Diego, 1981-82; insp. gen. Naval Med. Command, Washington, 1983-85; ret., 1985. Contbr. articles to profl. jours. Chmn. bd. trustees UMC, Winter Park, 1992, mem. bd. adminstrs. 1995-98; bd. dirs. Circle of Friends Fla. Hosp. Found., 1989-91, Fla. Hosp. Found., 1991—, chmn. bd., 1995-96; bd. dirs., chmn. Fla. Hosp. Found., 1991—, Ctrl. Fla. Veterans, Inc., 2007-; chmn. Fla. Hosp. Shares (Internat. Med. Missions), 1994—; mem. Fla. Hosp. Cmty. Benefits subcom., 1996—. Decorated Humanitarian Service medal, Legion of Merit with Gold Star, Meritorious Service medal, Nat. Def. Service medal with star, Vietnam Service medal, Republic of Vietnam Campaign medal with device, others; recipient Alumnus of Yr. award Ind. U. Sch.of Dentistry Alumnus Assn., 1988. Fellow Am. Dental Soc. of Anesthesiology, Internat. Coll. Dentists, Am. Coll. Dentists, Internat. Assn. Oral Surgeons; mem. Am. Assn. Oral and Maxillofacial Surgeons, ADA, Western Soc. Oral Surgeons, Assn. Mil. Surgeons U.S. (medal), Fla. Soc. Oral Surgeons, Delta Sigma Delta, Sigma Chi (Significant Sig award 1983). Home: 1309 Temple Grove Ct Winter Park FL 32789-2716 Personal E-mail: tmckean1@cfl.rr.com.

MCKEAND, PATRICK JOSEPH, newspaper publisher, educator; b. Anderson, Ind., June 10, 1941; s. William Dale and Iya Pearl (Shaw) McK. BA, Ind. U., 1963; MA, Ball State U., 1983. Staff writer The St. Petersburg (Fla.) Times, 1963; mng. editor The Anderson (Ind.) Herald, 1968-79; adminstr. analyst Ind. Medicaid Program, Indpls., 1980-81; assoc. prof. Defense Info. Sch., Ft. Ben Harrison, Ind., 1981-89; owner p.m. ink!, Indpls., 1989—. Pub. bd. dirs. Student Pub. at Ind. U., Purdue U. at Indpls., 1992-2003; bd. dirs. Miss Ind. Scholarship Pageant, Indpls., 2005—. Capt. U.S. Army, 1964-68. Recipient Ind.'s Sagamore of the Wabash award, 2003; decorated Bronze Star, Army Commendation medal with 1 oak leaf cluster. Mem. Soc. Profl. Journalists (bd. dirs.), Soc. Newspaper Design, Assn. Educators in Journalism and Mass Comm., Associated Press Mng. Editors Assn., Investigative Reporters and Editors, Ind. Collegiate Press Assn. (bd. dirs., exec. dir.), Coll. Media Advisors (Disting. Newspaper Adviser award 1998), Faculty Club IUPUI (bd. dirs. 2002—). Home: 4450 E 56th St Indianapolis IN 46220-5710 E-mail: pmckeand@iupui.edu.

MCKEE, BETTY DAVIS, English language educator; b. St. Pauls, NC, June 30, 1946; d. John Chesley and Ernestene King Davis; m. Danny Lee McKee, July 13, 1980; children: Brooke Elizabeth Burgess, Ginger Rae Fears, Amanda Lea. AA, Chowan Coll., Murfreesboro, NC, 1966; BA, Campbell Coll., Buies Creek, NC, 1968. Cert. Collegiate Profl. Va., 1970. Tchr. Pinkston St. Sch., Henderson, NC, 1968—70, Western Br. Jr. HS, Chesapeake, Va., 1970—71, 1971—73, 1975—91, chair English dept., 1976—80, 1990—91; tchr. Deep Creek Jr. HS, Chesapeake, 1974—75; tchr., chair, team leader Western Br. Mid. Sch., Chesapeake, 1991—2006, internal coord. So. Assn. Colls. and Schs., 2004—, mem. faculty adv. com. Mem. AAUW, Portsmouth, Va., 2001—05; bd. dirs. Campbell U. Alumni Assn., Buies Creek, 1978—94; yearbook sponsor, 1971—85; pres. Tidewater chpt. Campbell U. Alumni Assn., Chesapeake, 1978—98. Named Tchr. of Yr., We. Br. Jr. H.S., 1987. Mem.: NEA, PTA (life), Chesapeake Edn. Assn. (treas. 2000—04), Va. Edn. Assn., Delta Kappa Gamma Beta Iota (assoc.; rec. sec. 2000—02, pres. 2002—04). Avocations: reading, travel. Home Phone: 757-483-2372.

MCKEE, CATHERINE LYNCH, lawyer, educator; b. Boston, June 7, 1962; d. Robert Emmett and Anne Gayle (Tanner) Lynch; m. Bert K. McKee Jr., Dec. 25, 1990; children: Timothy Kingston, Shannon Lancaster. BA in Biol. Sci., U. Calif. Berkeley, 1984; JD, U. San Diego, 1988. Bar: Calif. 1988, U.S. Dist. Ct. (cen., so. and ea. dists.) Calif. 1989, U.S. Ct. Appeals (9th cir.) 1989. Assoc. Parkinson, Wolf, Lazar & Leo, LA, 1988—89, McCormick & Mitchell, San Diego, 1989—91; prof. Mt. San Antonio Coll., Walnut, Calif., 1994—, mock trial coach, 1994—2000, dir. paralegal program, 1999—2003, 2004—05. Cert. rev. hearing officer, Orange County, 1994-2004; legal counsel Imperial Valley Lumber Co., Valley Lumber and Truss Co., 1998—; coach nat. champion C.C. mock trial team, 2000; mem. acad. senate exec. coun. Mt. San Antonio Coll., 1996-2000, chmn. campus equivalency com., 1999, chair paralegal program adv. com., 1999-2003, 04-05, verifier for cert. of online tchg., 2005—, adv. student club Paralegal Soc., 2006; mem. East San Gabriel Valley regional occupl. program adv. com., 2003—. Contbr. weekly newspaper column, 1993-99; prodr., star videos An Attorney's Guide to Legal Research on the Internet, 1998, 99; co-author: Jeff and Catherine's World's Best List of Legal (and Law-related) Internet Sites. Chair scholarship com. U. Calif. Alumni Assn., Berkeley, 1995—; capt. auction team SCATS Gymnastics, 2000—02; sec. bd. dir. AC Alliance Youth Soccer Club, Calif. Polytech. U., Pomona, 2007—. Named Cmty. Person of Yr., Diamond Bar C. of C., 1995. Mem. NEA, State Bar Calif. (probation monitor 1993—), Ea. Bar Assn. L.A. (trustee 2000—), Calif. Tchrs. Assn., Am. Inns of Ct., Calif. Assn. Lanterman-Petris-Short Hearing Officers. Avocations: weightlifting, photography, reading. Office: Mount San Antonio Coll 1100 N Grand Ave Walnut CA 91789-1341 Office Phone: 909-594-5611 ext. 4907. Business E-Mail: cmckee@mtsac.edu.

MCKEE, CHRISTOPHER FULTON, historian, educator; b. Bklyn., June 14, 1935; s. William Ralph and Frances McKee; m. Ann Adamczyk, 1993; children: Sharon, David. AB, U. St. Thomas, Houston, 1957; AMLS, U. Mich., 1960. Catalogue libr. Washington and Lee U., Lexington, Va., 1958-62; social sci. libr. So. Ill. U., Edwardsville, 1962-66, book selection officer, 1967-69, asst. dir., 1969-72; libr. of coll. Grinnell Coll., Iowa, 1972—2006, Samuel R. and Marie-Louise Rosenthal prof. Sec. of Navy rsch. chair naval history Naval Hist. Ctr., Washington, 1990—91; trustee Bibliog. Ctr. Rsch., Denver, 1984—88; scholar in res., Obermann Ctr. for Advanced Studies U. Iowa, 2006—. Author: (book) Edward Preble, 1972, A Gentlemanly and Honorable Profession: The Creation of the U.S. Naval Officer Corps 1794-1815, 1991, Sober Men and True: Sailor Lives in the Royal Navy 1900-1945, 2002. Mem. vestry Trinity Episcopal Ch., Iowa City. Recipient U.S. Naval History prize, 1985, John Lyman Book award, N.Am. Soc. Oceanic History, 1991, Samuel Eliot Morison Disting. Svc. award, USS Constn. Mus., 1992; fellow NEH-Newberry Libr., 1978—79, Newberry Libr.-Brit. Acad., 1995—96. Mem.: U.S. Naval Inst., Soc. Historians Early Am. Republic, Orgn. Am. Historians, Soc. Mil. History, Navy Records Soc., Can. Nautical Rsch. Soc., Soc. Nautical Rsch. Democrat. Episcopalian. Home: 2382 Willowbrooke Ln Iowa City IA 52246-1834 Office: Obermann Ctr for Advanced Studies Univ Iowa N103 Oakdale Hall Iowa City IA 52242-5000 Home Phone: 319-351-7594; Office Phone: 319-335-4034.

MCKEE, CHRISTOPHER FULTON, physicist, astronomer, educator; b. Washington, Sept. 6, 1942; m. Suzanne P. McKee; 3 children. AB in Physics summa cum laude, Harvard U., 1963; PhD in Physics, U. Calif., Berkeley, 1970. Physicist Lawrence Livermore (Calif.) Labs., 1969-70, cons., 1970—; rsch. fellow in astrophysics Calif. Inst. Tech., Pasadena, 1970-71; asst. prof. astronomy Harvard U., Cambridge, Mass., 1971-74; asst. prof. physics and astronomy U. Calif., Berkeley, 1974-77, assoc. prof., 1977-78, prof., 1978—, Miller Rsch. prof., 1984-85, 99, 2001, chair dept. physics, 2000—04; assoc. dir. Space Scis. Lab., Berkeley, 1978-83, acting dir., 1983-84, dir., 1985-98, Theoretical Astrophysics Ctr., Berkeley, 1985. Co-chair Astronomy and Astrophysics Survey com. NRC, 1998-2001. Fannie and John Hertz Found. fellow, 1963-69, Guggenheim fellow, 1998; Sherman Fairchild Disting. scholar, 1981, NAS, 1992. Fellow AAAS, Am. Phys. Soc. (exec. com. astrophysics divsn. 1986-88); mem. Am. Astron. Soc. (councillor 1981-84), Am. Acad. Arts and Scis., Internat. Astron. Union, Phi Beta Kappa. Office: U Calif Dept Physics Berkeley CA 94720-0001

MCKEE, DAVID CHARLES, neurologist; b. May 19, 1961; m. Marie-Laure Mazquiain, Dec. 29, 1984; children: Tyvand, Camille, Charlotte, Alexanne. BA in Chemistry, Macalaster Coll., 1983; MD, U. Wis., 1987. Diplomate Am. Bd. Psychiatry and Neurology, Am. Bd. Electrodiagnostic Medicine. Resident in neurology Oreg. Health Scis. U., 1987—91; Jeanne Timmins fellow Montreal Neurol. Inst., 1991—92; clin. neurologist Northland Neurology and Myology, Duluth, Minn., 1992—; chief sect. neurology St. Lukes Hosp. and Regional Trauma Ctr., Duluth, 1993—; assoc. prof. neurology Duluth Med. Sch. U. Minn., 1993—; pres. Northland Med. Assocs., 2000—02. Chmn. bd. dirs. Care North Health Sys., 2001—02. Comdr. USNR med. corp., 1998—. Fellow: Am. Assn. Electrodiagnostic Medicine; mem.: European Neurol. Soc., Am. Acad. Neurology, Alpha Omega Alpha, Phi Beta Kappa. Office: 1000 E 1st St Ste 202 Duluth MN 55805-2297 Home: 2215 E Superior St Duluth MN 55812

MCKEE, ELLSWORTH R., food products executive; BA in Bus. and Econs., So. Adventist U., 1954; postgrad., Andrews U., 1987. Shipping/receiving clk. Jack's Cookie Co., Charlotte, NC, 1949-50; various positions McKee Foods, Collegedale, 1951-54, v.p. prodn. and fin., 1954-62, exec. v.p., treas., 1962-71, pres., CEO, 1971-96, also bd. dirs., 1954—, chmn. bd. dirs., 1997—. Bd. dirs. So. Adventist U., Collegedale, Andrews U., Berrien Springs, Mich., 1976—2000. Recipient Pvt. Sector Initiative Commendation, Pres. Ronald Reagan, 1988. Office: McKee Foods PO Box 750 Collegedale TN 37315-0750

MCKEE, FRANCIS JOHN, medical association consultant, lawyer; b. Bklyn., Aug. 31, 1943; s. Francis Joseph and Catherine (Giles) McK.; m. Antoinette Mary Sancis; children: Lisa Ann, Francis Dominic, Michael Christopher, Thomas Joseph. AB, Stonehill Coll., 1965; JD, St. John's U., 1970. Bar: N.Y. 1971. Assoc. Samuel Weinberg, Esquire, Bklyn., 1970-71, Finch & Finch, Esquire, Long Island City, NY, 1971-72; staff atty. Med. Soc. of State of NY, Lake Success, NY, 1972-77; prin. Francis J. McKee Assocs., Clinton, NY, 1984—2001, McKee Assocs., Clinton, NY, 2005—; exec. dir. Suffolk Physicians Rev. Orgn., East Islip, NY, 1977-81, NY State Soc. Surgeons, Inc., Clinton, NY, 1981-2000, NY State Soc. Orthopaedic Surgeons, Inc., Clinton, NY, 1981—2000, Upstate NY chpt. ACS, Inc., Clinton, NY, 1981-2000, NY State Ophthalmol. Soc., 1984-92, NY State Soc. Obstetricians and Gynecologists, 1985-2001, Orthopac of NY, 1986-2000, Nat. Com. for the Preservation Orthopaedic Practice, New Hartford, NY, 1989-2000, L.I. Ophthalmol. Soc., 1994-2000. Coun. Suffolk County Med. Soc., Hauppauge, NY, 1977-81; sec. Thomas J. McKee Assocs., LLC, 2005—, mgr., 2006—. With U.S. Army, 1966-68. Mem.: NY State Bar Assn., Am. Legion, Taberna Country Club, Elks. Republican. Roman Catholic. Home and Office: 908 Taberna Cir New Bern NC 28562 Personal E-mail: frank4mets@earthlink.net.

MCKEE, GEORGE MOFFITT, JR., civil engineer, consultant; b. Valparaiso, Nebr., Mar. 27, 1924; s. George Moffitt and Iva (Santrock) McK.; m. Mary Lee Taylor, Aug. 11, 1945; children: Michael Craig, Thomas Lee, Mary Kathleen, Marsha Coleen, Charlotte Anne. Student, Kans. State Coll. Agr. and Applied Sci., Manhattan, 1942—43, Bowling Green State U., Ohio, 1943; BSE, U. Mich., Ann Arbor, 1947. Registered profl. civil engr., Kans., Okla., land surveyor, Kans. Draftsman Jackson Constrn. Co., Colby, Kans., 1945-46; asst. engr. Thomas County, Colby, 1946; engr. Sherman County, Goodland, Kans., 1947-51; salesman Oehlert Tractor & Equipment Co., Colby, 1951-52; owner, operator George M. McKee, Jr.; cons. engrs. Colby, 1952-72; sr. v.p. engring. Contract Surety Cons., Wichita, Kans., 1974-2000; engring. cons. Wichita, 2000—. Adv. rep. Kans State U., Manhattan, 1957-62; adv. com. N.W. Kans. Area Vocat. Tech. Sch., Goodland, 1967-71; chmn. ofcl. bd. Meth. Ch., 1966-67. With USMCR, 1942-45. Mem. Kans. Soc. Profl. Engrs. (pres. N.W. profl. engrs. chpt. 1962-63, treas. cons. engrs. sect. 1961-63), Kans. County Engr.'s Assn. (dist. v.p. 1950-51), N.W. Kans. Hwy. Ofcls. Assn. (sec. 1948-49), Nat. Soc. Profl. Engrs., Kans. State U. Alumni Assn. (life, pres. Thomas County 1956-57), Am. Legion (Goodland 1st vice comdr. 1948-49), Alumni Assn. U. Mich. (life), Colby C. of C. (v.p. 1963-64), Goodland Jr. C. of C. (pres. 1951-52), Masons (32 degree, Shriner), Order of the Ea. Star. Home: 3636 North Ridge Rd Apt 229 Wichita KS 67205-1219

MCKEE, JUDITH NELSON, elementary school educator, educational consultant; b. Iowa Falls, Iowa, Nov. 8, 1939; d. Herbert and Emma (Czako) Nelson; m. Bernard B. McKee, Oct. 20, 1962; children: Susan Jennifer Ziegler, Blair David. BA, U. No. Iowa, 1961; MA, Roosevelt U., 1967; postgrad., Ill. State U., Nat. Louis U. Cert. tchr. K-9, learning disabilities K-12. Tchr. 2d grade Dist. 25 Pub. Schs., Arlington Heights, Ill., 1961-67; itinerant tchr. learning disabilities NW Suburban Spl. Edn. Dist., Palatine, Ill., 1968-72; tchr. Winnetka Pub. Sch. Nursery, Ill., 1974-75; tchr. spl. edn. North Suburban Spl. Edn. Dist., Glenview, Ill., 1975-76; tchr. gifted Worlds of Wisdom and Wonder, Evanston, Ill., 1985-87; instr. astronomy North Cook County Ednl. Svc. Ctr., Glenview, 1987; mem. faculty Nat. Louis U., Evanston, Ill., 1991—2000, DePaul U., Chgo., 2000—01; tchr. primary grades dist. 39 Wilmette, Ill., 1976—99; faculty U. No. Iowa, Cedar Falls, 2002—. Presenter, state, nat. and internat. confs. Co-author: Integrating Instruction: Literacy and Science, 2005; author (with others): Physical Science Activities for Elementary and Middle School, 1987, Fact, Fiction, and Fantasy, 1995; contbr. articles to profl. jours. Named Ill. Honors Sci. Tchr. NSF, Ill. State. U., 1989-91. Mem. Internat. Reading Assn., Nat. Reading Conf., Nat. Sci. Tchrs. Assn. (ret. adv. bd. 2000-03, chair 2002-03, pre-sch. and elem. tchrs. standing com., 2007), Coun. Elem. Sci. Internat., Ill. Sci. Tchrs. Assn., Phi Delta Kappa. Presbyterian. Home: 315 Fairview Ave Winnetka IL 60093-4210

MCKEE, KATHRYN DIAN GRANT, human resources consultant; b. LA, Sept. 12, 1937; d. Clifford William and Amelia Rosalie (Shacher) G.; m. Paul Eugene McKee, June 17, 1961; children: Scott Alexander, Grant Christopher. BA, U. Calif., Santa Barbara, 1959; grad. Anderson Sch. Mgmt. Exec. Program, UCLA, 1979. Cert. compensation and benefits. Mgr. Mattel, Inc., Hawthorne, Calif., 1963-74; dir. Twentieth Century Fox Film Corp., LA, 1975-80; sr. v.p. 1st Interstate Bank, Ltd., LA, 1980-93; sr. v.p. and human resources dir. Am.'s Std. Chartered Bank, 1993-95; pres. Human Resources Consortia, Santa Barbara, Calif., 1995—. V.p. cons. Right Mgmt. Cons., 1997-98; dir. Accordia benefits of Southern Calif., 1991-96, mem. exec. com. H.R. div. of Am. Bankers Assn., 1991-93; bd. dirs. Bank Certification Inst. Am. Bankers Assn., 1992-94; treas. Pers. Accreditation Inst., 1983-86, pres., 1986. Co-author: Leading People Through Disaster, 2006; contbr. articles to profl. jours. Pres. GEM Theatre Guild, Garden Grove, Calif., 1984-86; bd. dirs. Vis. Nurses Assn., L.A., 1984-88, SHRM, 1986-92, treas., 1989, vice-chmn., 1990, chmn., 1991, pres. SHRM Found., 1994, 95; bd. dirs. Laguna Playhouse, 1996-2000, pres., 1998-99; dir. Old Spanish Days, 2001-, Ensemble Theatre Co., 2002-; mem. U. Calif. Santa Barbara Found., 2001-, vice chmn. stewardship, 2001-. Recipient Sr. Honor Key award U. Calif., Santa Barbara, 1959, William Winter award Am. Compensation Assn., 1986, Excellence award L.A. Pers. Indsl. Rels. Assn., 1990, Profl. Excellence award SHRM, 1994; named Outstanding Sr. Woman, 1959. Mem. Internat. Assn. Pers. Women (various offices, past nat. pres., Mem. of Yr. 1986), U. Calif. Santa Barbara Alumni Assn. (bd. dirs. 1995-2001, pres.-elect 1999, pres. 1999-2000). Office: Human Resources Consortia 3730 Cedar Vis Santa Barbara CA 93110-1578 E-mail: kmckee3730@cox.net.

MCKEE, KEITH EARL, manufacturing technology executive; b. Chgo., Sept. 9, 1928; s. Charles Richard and Maude Alice (Hamlin) McK.; children: Pamela Ann Houser, Paul Earl. BS, Ill. Inst. Tech., 1950, MS, 1956, PhD, 1962. Engr. Swift & Co., Chgo., 1953-54; rsch. engr. Armour Rsch. Found., Chgo., 1954-62; dir. design and product assurance Andrew Corp., Orland Park, Ill., 1962-67; dir. engring. Rsch. Ctr. Ill. Inst. Tech., Chgo., 1967-80, dir. mfg. prodn. ctr., 1977—. Prof. Ill. Inst. Tech., Chgo., 1979—, dir. indsl. programs, 1994—; coord. Nat. Conf. on Fluid Power, Chgo., 1983-88; mem. com. on materials and processing Dept. Def., Washington, 1986-92. Author: Productivity and Technology, 1988; co-author: Managing Technology Dependence Operation, 2004; editor: Automated Inspection and Process Control, 1987; co-editor: Manufacturing High Technology Handbook, 1987; mng. editor: Manufacturing Competitiveness Frontier, 1977-97. Capt. USMC, 1950-54. Recipient oustanding presentation award Am. Soc. of Quality Control, Milw., 1983. Fellow World Acad. Productivity Scis.; mem. ASCE, Am. Def. Preparedness Assn. (pres. Chgo. chpt. 1972-95), Am. Assn. Engring. Soc. (Washington) (coor. com. on productivity 1978-88), Inst. of Indsl. Engrs., Soc. Mfg. Engrs. (Gold medal 1991), Am. Assn. for Artificial Intelligence, Robotic Industry Assn. (bd. dir. 1978-81), Assn. for Mfg. Excellence, Soc. for Computer Simulation. Democrat. Roman Catholic. Home: Ste 504 3115 S Michigan Ave Chicago IL 60616 Office: Illinois Inst Tech Mfg Productivity Ctr 3424 S State St Ste 4001 S Chicago IL 60616 Home Phone: 312-326-3750; Office Phone: 312-567-3650. Business E-Mail: mckee@iit.edu.

MCKEE, LYNN B., human resources specialist; B in Acctg., St. Joseph's U.; MBA, Drexel U. Various positions including dir. employee rels., dir. human resources and exec. devel. Aramark Corp., Phila., 1980—86, mgr. hqtrs. human resources, 1986—89, dir. human resources, 1989, v.p. exec. devel. and compensation, 1998—2001, sr. v.p. human resources, 2001—04, exec. v.p. human resources, 2004—. Mem. human resources roundtable group; mem. conf. bd. advisory coun. human resources mgmt. Office: Aramark Corp Aramark Tower 1101 Market St Philadelphia PA 19107-2988 Office Phone: 215-238-3000. Office Fax: 215-238-3333.

MCKEE, MARCY D'ETTE, voice educator; d. Tony and Penney McKee. MusM in Performance, West Tex. A&M U., Canyon, 2002. Asst. prof. voice Bemidji State U., Minn., 2003—. ND Dist. winner, Met. Opera Nat. Coun., 2003, 2004. Mem.: Nat. Assn. Tchrs. Singing, Mu Phi Epsilon (v.p.), Pi Kappa Lambda (assoc.). Democrat. Office: Bemidji State U 1500 Birchmont Dr NE Bemidji MN 56601 Home Phone: 218-444-7355; Office Phone: 218-755-3930. Business E-Mail: mmckee@bemidjistate.edu.

MCKEE, MARGARET JEAN, federal agency administrator; b. New Haven, June 20, 1929; d. Waldo McCutcheon and Elizabeth McKee. AB, Vassar Coll., 1951. Staff asst. United Rep. Fin. Com., NYC, 1952, N.Y. Rep. State Com., NYC, 1953—55, Crusade for Freedom (name later changed to Radio Free Europe Fund), NYC, 1955—57; researcher Stricker & Henning Rsch. Assocs., Inc., NYC, 1957—59; exec. sec. New Yorkers for Nixon (name later changed to N.Y. State Ind. Citizens for Nixon Lodge), NYC, 1959—60; asst. to Raymond Moley, polit. columnist NYC, 1961; asst. campaign com. Louis J. Lefkowitz for Mayor, NYC, 1961; rsch. programmer, treas. Consensus, Inc., NYC, 1962—67; spl. asst. to U. S. Senator Jacob K. Javits NY, 1967—73; adminstr. asst. NY, 1973—75; dep. adminstr. Am. Revolution Bicentennial Adminstrn., 1976, acting adminstr., 1976—77; chief of staff Perry B. Duryea (minority leader) N.Y. State Assembly, 1978; pub. affairs cons., 1979—80; dir. govt. rels. Gen. Mills Restaurant Group, Inc., 1980—83; exec. dir. Fed. Mediation and Conciliation Svc., 1983—86; mem. Fed. Labor Rels. Authority, 1986—89, chmn., 1989—94; mem. Nat. Partnership Coun., 1993—94; chmn. adv. bd. Workplace Solutions, 1996—98. Mem. U.S. Adv.Commn. on Pub. Diplomacy, 1972—82; dir. scheduling and spkrs.' bur. N.Y. Com. to Re-elect the Pres., 1972; mem. bd. govs. Women's Nat. Rep. Club, NYC, 1963—66; mem. N.Y. State Bingo Control Commn., 1965—72; pres. Bklyn. Heights Slope Young Rep. Club, 1955—56; co-chmn. Bklyn. Citizens for Eisenhower-Nixon, 1956; chmn. 2nd Jud. Dist. Assn. N.Y. State Young Rep. Clubs, Inc., 1957—58, vice chmn., mem. bd. govs., 1958—60, v.p., 1960—62, pres., 1962—64; mem. exec. com. Fedn. Women's Rep. Clubs N.Y. State, Inc., 1960—64; asst. campaign mgr. Kenneth B. Keating for Judge Ct. Appeals, NY, 1965; dir. scheduling Gov. Rockefeller campaign, 1966, Sen. Charles E. Goodell campaign, 1970; dir. planning and strategy Conn. Reagan-Bush campaign, Hartford, 1980; mem annual fund adv. com. Vassar Coll., 1992—96, chmn. 50th Reunion, 2001; trustee Vassar Coll. and Assoc. Alumni, 2005—. Mem.: Conn. Olmsted Heritage Alliance (treas. 2005—), Nat. Assn. Olmsted Parks (trustee 2003—), New Eng. Hist. Geneal. Soc. (mem. adv. coun. 2001—03, trustee 2003—06, mem. adv. coun. 2006—), Nat. Women's Edn. Fund. (former mem. bd.), Exec. Women on Govt. (chmn. 1986), DAR (Lady Fenwick chpt.), Nat. Soc. Colonial Dames, Vassar Club (past dir., Bklyn.), Am. Newspaper Women's Club, Jr. League of Bklyn. (past dir.). Republican. Episcopalian. also: 3001 Veazey Ter NW Apt 1225 Washington DC 20008-5407 Also: 532 S Brooksvale Rd Cheshire CT 06410

MCKEE, RAE ELLEN (RAE ELLEN MCKEE-DOUCETTE), special education educator; b. W. Va. BA in Elem. Edn., Shepherd Coll., Shepherdstown, W. Va., 1979; MA in Clin. Reading, W. Va. Univ., Morgantown, 1983, MA student in Ednl. Supervision. Tchr. remedial reading Slanesville

(W.Va.) Elem. Sch.; cons. Barbara Bush Found. for Family Literacy, Houston. Recipient Nat. Tchr. of Yr. award, 1991. Office: Barbara Bush Found Family Literacy Ste 1400 4400 Post Oak Pkwy Houston TX 77027 *

MCKEE, RICHARD MILES, retired agricultural studies educator; b. Cottonwood Falls, Kans., Oct. 8, 1929; m. Marjorie Fisk, June 22, 1952; children: Dave, Richard, Annell, John. BS in Agriculture, Kans. State Coll. Agriculture and Applied Sci., 1951; MS in Animal Husbandry, Kans. State U., 1963; PhD in Animal Science, U. Ky., 1968. Herdsman Moxley Hall Hereford Ranch, Coun. Grove, Kans., 1951-52, 54-55, Luckhardt Farms, Tarkio, Mo., 1955-58; asst. mgr. L&J Crusoe Ranch, Cheboygan, Mich., 1958-59; asst. instr., cattle herdsman Kans. State U., Manhattan, 1959-65, from asst. prof. to assoc. prof., 1959-65, prof., departmental teaching coord., 1976-99; ret., 2005. Program participant and/or official judge numerous shows, field days including Kans. Jr. Hereford Field Day, Kans. Jr. Shorthorn Field Day, Better Livestock Day, Kans. Jr. Livestock Assn., Am. Jr. Hereford Assn. Field Day, Cheyenne, Wyo., 1973, Kans. Jr. Polled Hereford Field Day, Am. Jr. Shorthorn Assn., Kans. City, Mo., 1965, Am. Internat. Jr. Charolais Assn. Show, Lincoln, Nebr., 1976, Am. Royal 4-H Livestock Judging Contest, Kans. City, 1975, Jr. Livestock Activities various cattle breed assns. nationwide, 1977-81; served on many breed assn. coms.; judge County Fairs; official judge 14 different Nat. Beef Breed Shows U.S. and Can.; conducted 60 livestock judging and showmanship schs. at county level. Contbr. articles to profl. jours. Deacon 1st Presbyn. Ch., Manhattan, 1969-75, Sunday Sch. tchr., Chancel choir, elder; project leader com. mem. 4-H; foster parent Kans. State U. Football Program. Lt. USMC, 1952-54, Korea. Named Hon. State Farmer of Kans.; Hall of Merit Honoree for Edn. by Am. Polled Hereford Assn., 1985; NDEA scholar U. Ky., 1966-67; Miles McKee Student Enrichment Fund established at Kans. State U. Mem. Am. Soc. Animal Sci., Kans. Livestock Assn. (beef cattle improvement com. 1970-78, cow-calf clinic com. 1973, 74, 75, 76, 77, 78), Nat. Assn. Colls. and Tchrs. Agriculture, Block and Bridle Club, Am. Jr. Hereford Assn. (hon.), FarmHouse, Sigma Xi, Phi Kappa Phi, Alpha Zeta, Gamma Sigma Delta, Alpha Tau Alpha (hon.). Home: 901 Juniper Dr Manhattan KS 66502-3148 Office: Dept of Animal Scis & Industry Kansas State U Manhattan KS 66506 Office Phone: 785-532-1237. Personal E-mail: mmckee15@cox.net.

MCKEE, ROGER CURTIS, retired federal judge; b. Waterloo, Iowa, Feb. 11, 1931; s. James A. and Leonace (Burrell) McK.; m. Roberta Jeanne Orvis, Sept. 3, 1954; children: Andrea Jane, Brian Curtis, Paul Robert. BA, State Coll. of Iowa, 1955; MA, U. Ill., 1960; JD, U. San Diego, 1968. Bar: Calif. 1970, US Dist. Ct. (so. dist.) Calif. 1969, US Ct. Appeals (9th cir.) 1971. Telegrapher, agt. Ill. Cen. R.R., 1950-55; tng. asst. No. Ill. Gas Co., Aurora, 1959-60; with indsl. rels. dept. Convair div. Gen. Dynamics Corp., San Diego, 1960-68; contract adminstr. and supr. Datagraphix div. Gen. Dynamics Corp., San Diego, 1968-69, asst. counsel, 1969-70; ptnr. Powell & McKee, San Diego, 1970-75, Millsberg, Dickstein & McKee, San Diego, 1975-83; magistrate judge U.S. Dist. Ct. for So. Dist. Calif., San Diego, 1983-97; presiding magistrate judge, 1993-97. Bd. trustees So. Calif. Presbyn. Homes, LA, 1979-81; moderator Presbytery of San Diego, 1980. Capt. USNR, 1949-85. Mem. Calif. Bar Assn., Fed. Magistrate Judges Assn., Navy League US, Naval Res. Officers Assn., Res. Officers Assn., Dixieland Jazz Soc. (bd. dirs. San Diego chpt. 1984—). Republican. Home Fax: 858-277-0444. Personal E-mail: rcmckee10@sbcglobal.net.

MCKEE, THEODORE A., federal judge; b. Rochester, NY, 1947; BA, SUNY, Cortland, 1969; JD magna cum laude, Syracuse U. Coll. of Law, 1975. Dir. of minority recruitment & admissions SUNY, Binghamton, 1969—72; atty. Wolf, Block, Schorr & Solis-Cohen, Phila., 1975—77; asst. US atty., Eastern Dist. Pa., 1977—80; asst. US atty., Eastern Dist. Gen. Crimes Unit, Narcotics and Firearms Unit, then Polit. Corruption Unit; lectr. Rutgers U. Coll. of Law, 1980—91; dep. city solicitor Law Dept., Phila., 1980—83; gen. counsel Phila. Parking Auth., 1983; judge Ct. of Common Pleas, 1st Jud. Dist. Pa., 1984—94, judge major felony program, 1986, judge orphans' ct. divsn., 1992; judge US Ct. Appeals (3d cir.), Phila., 1994—. Bd. dirs. Diagnostic and Rehab. Ctr. of Phila. Trustee Edna McConnell Clark Found.; mem. adv. bd. City Yr. for Phila. Mem.: ABA, Pa. Bar Assoc., Phila. Bar Assoc., Temple Inn of Ct., Barristers' Assn. Phila., Am. Law Inst., Nat. Bar Assn., Crime Prevention Assn. (bd. dirs.). Office: 20614 US Courthouse 601 Market St Philadelphia PA 19106 *

MCKEE, THOMAS FREDERICK, lawyer; b. Cleve., Oct. 27, 1948; s. Harry Wilbert and Virginia (Light) McK. BA with high distinction, U. Mich., 1970; JD with high distinction, Case Western Rs. U., 1975. Bar: Ohio 1975, U.S. Dist. Ct. (no. dist.) Ohio 1975, U.S. Supreme Ct. 1979. Assoc. firm Calfee, Halter & Griswold, Cleve., 1975-81, ptnr., 1982—, also co-chmn. exec. com.; bd. dirs. Home Décor, Harden Furniture, Stanton Carpet, Data Trail Internat., Case We. Res.U., Musical Arts Assn. Contbg. editor Going Public, 1985. Mem. ABA (com. fed. regulation securities law sect.), Bar Assn. Greater Cleve., Order of Coif., Union Club, Tavern Club, Country Club, 50 Club, Pepper Pike Club. Home: 210 Pheasant Run Dr Chagrin Falls OH 44022-2968 Office: Calfee Halter & Griswold 800 Superior Ave E Ste 1400 Cleveland OH 44114-2601

MCKEE, TIM, chef; b. 1967; married. Prep cook Azur, Mpls.; exec. chef D'Amico Cucina; co-owner, exec. chef La Belle Vie, Stillwater, Minn., 1998—2005, Mpls., 2005—, Solera, Mpls., 2003—. Nominee Best Chef: Midwest, James Beard Found., 2007; named Best New Chef, Food and Wine Mag., 1997, Best Local Chef, City Pages, 1999—2003, 2006, Best Overall Chef, Twin City's Taste mag., 2003. Office: Le Belle Vie 510 Groveland Ave Minneapolis MN 55405 Office Phone: 612-874-6440. *

MCKEE, TIMOTHY CARLTON, taxation educator; b. South Bend, Ind., Mar. 9, 1944; s. Glenn Richard and Laura Louise (Niven) McK.; m. Linda Sykes Mizelle, Oct. 13, 1984; children: Brandon Richard. BS in Bus. Econs., Ind. U., 1970, MBA in Fin., 1973, JD, 1979; LLM in Taxation, DePaul U., 1980. Bar: Ill. 1980, U.S. Dist. Ct. (no. dist.) Ill. 1980; CPA, Va.; cert. govt. fin. mgr. Procedures analyst Assocs. Corp., South Bend, 1969-71; asst. dir. fin. Ind. U., Bloomington, 1971-79; sr. tax mgr. Peat Marwick Mitchell & Co., Chgo., Norfolk, Va., 1979-84; corp. counsel K & K Toys, Norfolk, 1984; assoc. prof. acctg. Old Dominion U., Norfolk, 1985-98, chmn. dept., 1994-95, chmn. acctg., fin. and law dept., 1995, univ. prof. dept. acctg., 1998—. Computer coord. Peat, Marwick, Mitchell & Co., 1982-84; micro computer cons. Old Dominion U., 1985-91. Contbr. articles to profl. jours. Active Friends of Music, Bloomington, 1978, Art Inst., Chgo., 1981; loan exec. United Way, Chgo., 1981; telethon chmn. Va. Orch. Group, Norfolk, 1983. Mem. Assn. Govt. Accts., Am. Acctg. Assn., Am. Assn. Atty. CPAs, Inc., Am. Tax Assn., Fin. Execs. Inst. (pres. 1995-96), Hampton Rds. Tax Forum, Inst. Internal Auditors, Beta Alpha Psi, Beta Gamma Sigma. Home: 412 Rio Dr Chesapeake VA 23322-7144 Office: Old Dominion U Constant Hall Rm 2153 Norfolk VA 23529

MCKEEN, ALEXANDER C., retired engineering executive, foundation administrator; b. Albion, Mich., Oct. 10, 1927; s. John Nisbet and Janet (Callander) McK.; m. Evelyn Mae Feldkamp, Aug. 18, 1951; Jeffrey, Brian, Andrew. BSME, U. Mich., 1950; MBA, Mich. State U., 1968. Registered profl. engr., Mich. From asst. supt. maintenance to supt. final assembly Cadillac Motor Car divsn. GM, Detroit, 1961-69; asst. dir. reliability cadillac motor car divsn. GM, Detroit, 1969-72, exec. engr. product assurance Warren, Mich., 1972-75, from asst. dir. to dir engring. analysis, 1975-87; pres., owner Engring. Analysis Assocs., Inc., Bingham Farms, Mich., 1987-99; cons. Detroit Exec. Svc. Corps, 1999—; pres. McKeen Found., 2002—. Pres. Dells of Bloomfield Home Owners Assn., Bloomfield Hills, Mich., 1987-88; trustee Kirk in Hills, Bloomfield Hills, 1990-93, 2003-06, elder, 1995-97. Mem. Soc. Auto. Engrs., Am. Soc. Quality Control, Econ. Club Detroit, Detroit Athletic Club, Bloomfield (Mich.) Lions Club (pres. 2004-05), Stonycroft Hills Golf Club (treas.), Pelican Nest Golf Club, Beta Gamma Sigma. Avocations: tennis, golf, photography, travel, gardening. Office: Detroit Executive Service Corps 16250 Northland Dr Ste 390 Southfield MI 48075

MC KEEN, CHESTER M., JR., retired manufacturing executive; b. Shelby, Ohio, Mar. 18, 1923; s. Chester Mancil and Nettie Augusta (Fox) McKeen; m. Alma Virginia Pierce, Mar. 1946 (dec. Feb. 1998); children: David Richard(dec.), Karin, Thomas Kevin; m. Sally Ann Werst, Nov. 1999; 1 stepchild, Stephen Harry Werst. BS in Mil. Sci., U. Md., 1962; MBA, Babson Coll., Wellesley, Mass., 1962. Advanced through grades to maj. gen. U.S. Army, 1942-77; dir. logistics Bell Helicopter Internat., Tehran, Iran, 1977-79; v.p. procurement Bell Helicopter Textron, Ft. Worth, 1979-82, v.p. materiel, 1982-89; pres. Logistics Svcs. Internat., Arlington, Tex., 1990—2002; ret., 2002. Decorated D.S.M., Legion of Merit (3), Commendation medal (3); named to U.S. Army Ordnance Hall of Fame. Mem. Nat. Def. Indsl. Assn., Assn. U.S. Army, Ridglea Country Club, Rotary, Masons (33 degree), Shriners, Sojourners, Sigma Pi. Home: 2310 Woodsong Trail Arlington TX 76016-1037 Personal E-mail: cmmckeen@aol.com. *To live for oneself is to pursue emptiness. To live for others is to insure fulfillment.*

MCKEEVER, EDNA, archivist, educator; b. Bklyn. d. Paul Edward McKeever and Edna Moloney. BA, St. Joseph Coll. for Women, Bklyn., 1966; MA in French, Bklyn. Coll., 1970. Permanent cert. tchr. K-12 NY, lic. tchr. NY. Tchr. Holy Cross Sch., Bklyn., 1953—55, St. Brendan Elem. Sch., Bklyn., 1955—59, Our Lady of Good Counsel Sch., Bklyn., 1959—62, St. Francis of Assisi Sch., Bklyn., 1962—66, St. Athanasius Sch., Bklyn., 1966—67, St. Brendan Diocesan HS, Bklyn., 1967—71, St. Angela Hall Acad. HS, Bklyn., 1972—74, Holy Cross HS, Flushing, NY, 1978—83, Sacred Heart Acad. HS, Hempstead, NY, 1983—91; rschr. Maryknoll Cloister, NY, 1971—72; prayer apostolate Bethel Ho. of Prayer, Brentwood, NY, 1974—77; asst. to archivist Congregation of Sisters of St. Joseph, Brentwood, 1991—94, archivist, 1994—. Archives cons. Cenacle Sisters, Ronkonkoma, NY, Good Shepherd Sisters, Jamaica, NY, Daus. of Wisdom; presenter in field. Contbr. articles to profl. jours. Mem.: Soc. Am. Archivists, New Eng. Archivists of Religious Instns., Archivists for Congregations of Women Religious (election com. 1994—96, nat. bd. sec. 1996—98, v.p. 2000—01, pres. 2001—02, past pres., bd. dirs. 2002—03), Mid. Atlantic Regional Archives Conf. Avocations: classical music, piano, reading, swimming, puzzles. Office: Sisters of St Joseph 1725 Brentwood Rd Brentwood NY 11717

MCKEEVER, JOHN EUGENE, lawyer; b. Phila., Oct. 24, 1947; s. John James and Marie Julia (Supper) McKeever; m. Kathleen Marie Wynne, Dec. 9, 1995; children: John Joseph, Jeannine Marie. BA magna cum laude with distinction, U. Pa., 1969, JD magna cum laude, 1972. Bar: Pa. 1972, U.S. Dist. Ct. (ea. dist.) Pa. 1972, U.S. Dist. Ct. (mid. dist.) Pa. 1977, U.S. Ct. Appeals (3d cir.) 1979, U.S. Ct. Appeals (DC cir.) 1981, U.S. Supreme Ct. 1981. Assoc. Schnader, Harrison, Segal & Lewis, Phila., 1972-80, ptnr., 1980-98, DLA Piper US LLP, Phila., 1998—. Trustee Lawyers Com. Civil Rights Under Law, Washington, 2002, dir., 2003—, mem. exec. com., 2005—, regional vice chair, 2007—. Mem. Bus. Leadership organized Cath. Schs., Phila., 1984—87; co-chair Oblates St. Francis De Sales Capital Campaign, 1998—99; capt. spl. gifts com. Cath. Charities Appeal, Phila., 1986—91; bd. dir. Jr. Achievement, Phila., 1986—2006; mem. pres.'s coun. De Sales U., Center Valley, Pa., 1980—; mem. adv. com. De Sales Sch. Theology, Washington, trustee, 1988—91. Mem.: Am. Bar Assn., Phila. Bar Assn., St. Thomas More Soc. (gov. 1979—91, pres. 1981—82), Phi Beta Kappa, Order of Coif, Pi Gamma Mu. Democrat. Roman Catholic. Office: DLA Piper US LLP One Liberty Pl 1650 Market St Ste 4900 Philadelphia PA 19103 Office Phone: 215-656-3310.

MCKEEVER, JOSEPH FRANCIS, III, lawyer; b. Weymouth, Mass., July 21, 1950; s. Joseph Francis Jr. and Virginia Agnes McK.; m. Janice Danielle Kearney, Oct. 17, 1970. BA, George Washington U., 1972, JD, 1978. Bar: D.C. 1978, U.S. Supreme Ct. 1989. Editor Congl. Rsch. Svc. Libr. Congress, Washington, 1974-78; law clk. Honorable Harry Wood U.S. Ct. Claims, Washington, 1978-79, Honorable Wilson Cowen U.S. Ct. Claims, Washington, 1979-80; atty. Sutherland, Asbill & Brennan, Washington, 1980-85; ptnr. Davis & Harman LLP, Washington, 1985—. Author, editor: Annuities Answer Book, 1999; contbr. articles to profl. jours. Mem. ABA (chair sect. on taxation com. on ins. cos. 2000-02); Nat. Assn. for Variable Annuities (chmn., 2002-2003) Avocations: gardening, bicycling. Home: 2812 34th Pl NW Washington DC 20007-1405 Office: Davis & Harman LLP Willard Office Bldg 1455 Pennsylvania Ave NW Washington DC 20004-1008 Office Phone: 202-347-2252.

MCKEEVER, KENT, library director, law librarian; b. Southampton, NY, Sept. 6, 1952; BA, SUNY, Oswego, 1974; MLS, JD, La. State U., 1980. Bar: La. 1980. Ref. libr. Fordham U. Sch. Law Libr., 1981—82; internat., fgn. and comparative law libr. Columbia U. Law Sch. Libr., NYC, 1982—83, assoc. law libr., head collection devel. and tech. svcs., 1983—93, acting law libr., 1994—95, dir. Diamond Law Libr., 1996—. Lectr. Fudan U., Shanghai, 1986, Columbia U. Sch. Libr. Svc., NYC, 1986—91, Columbia Summer Program, Leiden, Netherlands, 1998—2000; cons. Beijing U., Dept. of Treaty and Law, China, MetaMetrics, Inc.; grant application evaluator NEH. Class of 1950 scholar, La. State U., Supr.'s scholar, Tullis-Herget scholar. Office: Diamond Law Libr 435 W 116th St New York NY 10027 Office Phone: 212-854-4228. Office Fax: 212-854-3295. Business E-Mail: mckeever@law.columbia.edu. *

MCKEIGHEN, RONALD EUGENE, physicist; b. Marion, Ill., Oct. 17, 1942; s. George A. and Aileen (Reach) McK.; m. Loretta M. Ward, Sept. 3, 1966; children: Kevin, Christy. BS in Engring. Physics, U. Ill., 1964, MS in Nuclear Engring., 1965, PhD in Physics, 1971. Postdoctoral in cancer rsch. and nuclear medicine Oak Ridge Nat. Lab., 1972-73; sr. prin. rsch. scientist Searle/Siemens Ultrasound, Des Plaines, 1973-79; sr. R&D engr. KB-Aerotech, Lewistown, Pa., 1979-83; staff scientist Advanced Diagnostic Rsch., Tempe, Ariz., 1983-85; prin. staff engr. Motorola Space Elect. Scottsdale, Ariz., 1985-86; mgr. advanced devel. Advanced Tech. Labs., Bothel, Wash., 1986-93; dir. advanced devel. Acoustic Imaging inc., Phoenix, 1993—2001; prin. rsch. engr., SAR signal processing Lockheed-Martin, Litchfield Park, Ariz., 2001—. Contbr. articles to profl. jours., chapters to books. Spl. fellow in nuclear engring. AEC. Mem. IEEE. Mem. Pentecostal Ch. Achievements include development of ultrasonic transducer arrays and sensors; patents for concept of digital beam former for ultrasonic phased array; research in synthetic aperture radar signal processing at Lockheed-Martin. Office: Lockheed-Martin Litchfield Park AZ Home Phone: 623-536-2512; Office Phone: 623-925-7178. E-mail: ronelori@cox.net.

MCKELDIN, WILLIAM EVANS, management consultant; b. Richmond, Va., Aug. 14, 1927; s. Robert A.W. and Mary E. (Burk) McK.; children: William Evans, Roberts Evans; m. Phyllis Shellhase, Jan. 23, 1982. BSBA, Temple U., 1951, postgrad., 1951—53, U. Pitts., 1953—54. Various mgmt. positions Westinghouse Corp., Pitts., 1950-62, Farrel Corp., Rochester, NY, 1963-66, Gen. Signal Corp., Norwalk, Conn., and Watertown, N.Y., 1966-71, Copperweld Steel Co., Warren, Ohio, 1971-75, Tenn. Forging Steel, Knoxville, 1975-77, Val Bradley Assocs., West Chester, Pa., 1977-79; pres., owner McKeldin Assocs., West Chester, 1979-95; founder, co-owner McKeldin Group, Bala Cynwyd, Pa., 1995—. Contbr. articles to profl. jours. Bd. dirs. United Fund, YMCA, ARC, Rochester Inst. Tech., Jefferson C.C., Kent State U. With USAAF, 1945—47. Mem. Inst. Mgmt. Cons., Am. Soc. Safety Engrs., Am. Soc. Personnel Adminstrn., C. of C. (bd. dirs.), Masons, Rotary. Republican. Presbyterian. Office: The McKeldin Group 24 Timber Ln Hilton Head Island SC 29926-1002 Office Phone: 843-837-6565. Personal E-mail: mckeldin@webtv.net.

MCKELL, CYRUS M., retired dean, plant physiologist, consultant; b. Payson, Utah, Mar. 19, 1926; s. Robert D. and Mary C. (Ellsworth) McK.; m. Betty Johnson; children: Meredith Sue, Brian Marcus, John Cyrus. BS, U. Utah, 1949, MS, 1950; PhD, Oreg. State U., 1956; postgrad., U. Calif., Davis, 1957. Instr. botany Oreg. State U., Corvallis, 1955-56; range rsch. plant physiologist U. Calif. USDA-Agrl. Research Service, Davis, 1956—61; prof., dept. chmn. U. Calif., Riverside, 1961—69; prof. dept. head., dir. Utah State U., Logan, 1969-80; v.p. research NPI, Salt Lake City, 1980-88; dean Coll. of Sci. Weber State U., Ogden, Utah, 1988-94; pres., prin. Applied Ecol. Svcs. Inc., Logan, Utah, 1995—. Cons. Ford Found. 1968-72, Rockefeller Found., 1964-70, 89, UN, 1978, 90, NAS, 1980, 89, 91, 92, 93, USAID, 1972, UN Devel. Program, 1989; mem. faculty of sci. adv. bd. UAE Nat. U., 2000-02. Editor: Grass Biology and Utilization, 1971, Useful Wildland Shrubs, 1972, Rehabilitation of Western Wildlife Habitat, 1978, Paradoxes of Western Energy Development, 1984, Resource Inventory and Baseline Study Methods for Developing Countries, 1983, Shrub Biology and Utilization, 1989, Wilderness Issues, Arid Lands of the Western United States, 1992; contbr. over 230 articles to profl. jours. Chmn. Cache County Planning Commn., Logan, 1974-79; mem. Utah Energy Conservation and Devel. Coun., 1976-79, Gov.'s Sci. Adv. Coun., 1988-97, chmn., 1990-91, 96-97; mem. Commn. of the Californias, Riverside, 1965-68; mem. Holladay City Planning Commn., 2003—. Recipient Utah Gov.'s Sci. and Tech. medal, 1990, Gardner Prize in Sci., awarded by Utah Acad. Scis., Arts and Letters, 1999; Fulbright scholar Spain, 1967-68; World Travel grantee Rockefeller Found., 1964. Fellow: AAAS (com. chmn. 1979—89, sci. exchange to China grantee 1984—85, 1989, sci. panel U.S.-Chile 1987); mem.: Am. Soc. Agronomy, Soc. Range Mgmt. (pres. Calif. sect. 1965, pres. Utah sect. 1982). Mem. Lds Ch. Avocations: travel, photography, history. Home: 2248 E 4000 S Holladay UT 84124-1864 Home Phone: 801-278-6469. Business E-Mail: cmmc1@xmission.com.

MCKELLEN, SIR IAN, actor; b. Burnley, England, May 25, 1939; s. Denis Murray and Margery (Sutcliffe) McK.; life partner Sean Mathias. Grad., Cambridge U. Prof. Oxford U., 1990-91. First stage appearance as Roper in A Man for All Seasons, Belgrade Theatre, Coventry, Eng., 1961; numerous other parts include title roles in Henry V, Luther, Ipswich, 1962-63, Aufidius in Coriolanus, Arthur Seaton in Saturday Night and Sunday Morning, title role in Sir Thomas More, Nottingham Playhouse, 1963-64; London debut as Godfrey in A Scent of Flowers, 1964, Claudio in Much Ado About Nothing, Andrew Cobham in Their Very Own and Golden City, 1966; title part in O'Flaherty, V.C. and Bonapart in The Man of Destiny, 1966, (Broadway debut) Leonidik in the Promise, London, 1966-67, Richard II, Edward II, Hamlet, Prospect Theatre Co., 1968-71; Captain Plume in The Recruiting Officer; founder-mem. Actors' Co., Edinburgh Festival, 1972 and touring as Giovanni in Tis Pity She's a Whore, Page-Boy in Ruling the Roost, title role Wood Demon; debut with R.S.C. as Dr. Faustus, Edinburgh Festival, 1974; title role in The Marquis of Keith, Philip the Bastard in King John, 1974-75, Young Vic Colin in Ashes, 1975; Royal Shakespeare Co.: Burglar in Too True to be Good, Romeo, MacBeth, Leontes in the Winter's Tale, Face in the Alchemist, Bernick in Pillars of the Community, Langevin in Days of the Commune, 1976-78, Ivanov in Every Good Boy Deserves Favour, Toby Belch in Twelth Night, Andrei in The Three Sisters, Max in Bent, 1979, Amadeus, N.Y.C., 1980, Iago in Othello, The Other Place, Stratford, 1989; European tour of one-man show Acting Shakespeare, 1983, also L.A., N.Y.C., 1984, one-man show A Knight Out at the Lyceum (devised especially for Gay Games IV U.K. and South Africa tour), 1994, An Enemy of the People, 1997, Peter Pan, 1998, The Seagull, 1998, Present Laughter, 1998, The Tempest, 1999, Dance of Death, N.Y.C, 2001-02, London, 2003, Sydney, 2004; assoc. dir. Nat. Theatre, London, 1984-86; dir. first prodn. The Prime of Miss Jean Brodie, Liverpool Playhouse, 1969, A Private Matter, 1973, The Clandestine Marriage, 1975; plays include: All in Good Time, 1963, The Alchemist, 1977, Amadeus, 1980, Venice Preserved, Wild Honey (recipient, Laurence Oliver Theatre award for Best Actor in a Revival, 1985), Coriolanus, Duchess of Malfi, The Cherry Orchard, King Lear, Richard III (recipient Laurence Olivier Theatre award for Best Actor (Royal Nat. Theatre), 1991, Acting Shakespeare, Napoli Milionaria, Uncle Vanya, An Enemy of The People, Peter Pan, Aladdin, 2004, and several others; films include Alfred the Great, 1968, A Touch of Love/Thank You All Very Much, 1968, The Promise, 1969, The Keep, 1983, Zina, 1985, Plenty, 1986, Scandal, 1988, I'll Do Anything, 1992, The Ballad of Little Jo, 1992, Last Action Hero, 1993, Six Degrees of Separation, 1993,, The Shadow, 1994, Jack and Sarah, 1994, Restoration, 1995, Richard III, 1996 (also exec. prodr., writer), Surviving Friendly Fire, 1997, Bent, 1997, Swept From the Sea, 1997, Apt Pupil, 1998, Gods and Monsters, 1998, X-Men, 2000, Lord of the Rings: The Fellowship of the Ring, 2001 (Outstanding Performance by Male Actor in Supporting Role SAG award 2002, nominee Best Supporing Actor Acad. Award 2002, Best Supporting Actor Saturn award 2002; nominee Best Performance by Actor BAFTA Film award, Empire award, Golden Satellite award, MTV Movie award, and OFCS award 2002), Lord of the Rings: The Two Towers, 2002, X2: X-Men United, 2003, The Lord of the Rings: The Return of the King, 2003, Emile, 2004, The Lord of the Rings: The Third Age (voice), 2004, Eighteen (voice), 2004, The Lord of the Rings: The Battle for Middle-Earth (voice), 2004, Sprung!The Magic Roundabout (voice), 2005, Asylum, 2005, Coronation Street, 2005, Neverwas, 2005, Doogal (voice), 2006, X-Men: The Last Stand, 2006, The Da Vinci Code, 2006, Flushed Away (voice), 2006, Stardust, 2007; TV appearances include: Sunday Out of Season, 1965, The Trial ans Torture of Sir John Rampayne, 1965, David Copperfield, 1966, Hay Fever, 1968, What If It's Just Green Cheese?, 1969, Ross, 1970, The Tragedy of King Richard II, 1970, Edward II, 1970,Keats, 1970, The Last Journey, 1971, Hamlet, 1972, The Recruiting Officer, 1973, Graceless Go I,1973, Hedda Gabler, 1974, Macbeth, 1979, Priest of Love, 1979, Every Good Boy Deserves Favour, 1978, Dying Day, 1980, Loving Walter, 1982, Acting Shakespeare, 1982, The Scarlet Pimpernel, 1982, Walter and June, 1983, Windmills of the Gods, 1988, Othello, 1988, Countdown to War, 1989, Sleepers, 1991 (TV mini series), Tales of the City, 1993 (TV mini series), And the Band Played On, 1993 (Emmy nomination, Supporting Actor, 1993), Cold Comfort Farm, 1994, Rasputin, 1996 (Emmy nomination, Supporting Actor,1996) David Copperfield, 1999, The Simpsons: The Regina Monologues, 2003; (voice) To Die For, 1994, Cirque du Soleil: Journey of Man, 2000. Recipient Clarence Derwent award, 1964, Variety and Plays and Players awards, 1966; Actor of Year, Plays and Players, 1976, Soc. of West End Theatres for Best Actor in Revival award, 1977, for Best Comedy Performance, 1978, for Best Actor in a New Play, 1979, Tony Award for Best Actor, Drama Desk award, Outer Critics Circle award, N.Y. Drama League award, 1981, Performer of the Yr. award Royal TV Soc., 1983, Soc. London Theatre Spl. award, 2006; decorated comdr. Order Brit. Empire, Knight Bachelor. Mem. Brit. Actors' Equity (coun. 1970-71). Office: ICM Oxford House 76 Oxford St London W1D 1BS England *

MCKELLIPS, GORDON WAYNE, JR., lawyer, land developer; b. Phoenix, Feb. 6, 1941; s. Gordon Wayne and Eunice J. (Fife) McK.; m. Joslyn M. Guerin, Aug. 4, 1964; children: Briant W., Eric G. BA, Duke U., 1962; JD, U. Ariz., 1965. Bar: Ariz. 1965, US Ct. Appeals (9th cir.) 1978, US Supreme Ct. 1968. Officer, dir. McKellips Land Corp., Phoenix, 1966—, Gem Land Co., Phoenix, 1982—, Willow Valley Water Co., Inc., Mohave Valley, Ariz., 1966-94, Granite Reef Farms, Inc., Mohave Valley, Ariz., 1966—; assoc. Carson Messinger Elliott Laughlin and Ragan,

Phoenix, 1965-70, ptnr., 1971—. Editorial bd. Ariz. Law Rev., 1965. Com. mem. North Phoenix Young Life, 1989—. Fellow Ariz. Bar Found. Republican. Office: Carson Messinger Elliott Laughlin and Ragan PLLC 3300 N Central Ave Ste 1900 Phoenix AZ 85012-2515 Home Phone: 602-997-1946; Office Phone: 602-264-2261. Business E-Mail: wmckellips@carsonlawfirm.com.

MCKELVEY, ANDREW J., former advertising executive; b. Oct. 13, 1934; m. Dena McKelvey; 1 son, Stuart J. McKelvey. BA, Westminster Coll. Chmn., CEO Monster Worldwide Inc. (formerly TMP Worldwide, Inc.), NYC, 1967—2006, chmn. emeritus, 2006. Co-founder, McKelvey Found.; bd. dirs. Yellow Pages Pubs., Mem. Assn. Director Mktg. (bd. dirs. 1994-96). Business E-Mail: andrew.mckelvey@monsterworldwide.com. *

MCKELVEY, JAMES MORGAN, chemical engineering educator, retired dean; b. St. Louis, Aug. 22, 1925; s. James Grey and Muriel (Morgan) McK.; m. Edith Rothbauer, Dec. 28, 1957; children: James, Robert; m. Judith Hood Forgotson, Sept. 4, 1992. BS, U. Mo.-Rolla, 1945; MS, Washington U., St. Louis, 1947, PhD, 1950. Research engr. E.I. DuPont de Nemours & Co., Inc., 1950-54; asst. prof. chem. engring. Johns Hopkins U., Balt., 1954-57; mem. faculty Washington U., St. Louis, 1957—, dean Sch. Engring. and Applied Sci., 1964-91, prof. chem. engring., 1991-98, sr. prof. chem. engring., 1998—. Recipient Disting. Educator award Soc. Plastics Engrs., 1979 Home: 9861 Copper Hill Rd Saint Louis MO 63124-1063 Office Phone: 314-935-4836. Personal E-mail: jmckelvey@aol.com.

MCKELVY, MICHAEL JOHN, chemist, research scientist; b. Berkeley, Calif., Apr. 19, 1954; s. Andy Milton and Dagmar Marie (Johnson) McK.; m. Margaret Knight Riddall, Aug. 2, 1975; children: Robin, Adam, Evan. BS in Chemistry, U. Calif., Berkeley, 1975; MS in Chemistry, Ariz. State U., 1981, PhD in Chemistry, 1985. Engr. crystal growing lab., ctr. solid state sci. Ariz. State U., Tempe, 1976—82, materials sci. engr. II, 1982—84, rsch. specialist, 1984—90, mgr. materials facility, 1986—94, assoc. rsch. scientist, 1990—99, affiliate assoc. prof. sci. & engring. of materials PhD program, 1993—99, dir. materials facility, 1994—2005, dir. Goldwater materials sci. labs., 1995—2005, acting dir. ctr. solid state sci., 1997, sr. rsch. scientist, 1999—, affiliate prof. sci. and engring. materials grad. program, 1999—2006, mgr. Goldwater materials facilities, 2006—, affiliate prof. Sch. Materials, 2006—. Invited asst. prof. Inst. des Matériaux de Nantes, U. Nantes, France, 1993; dir. Sci. is Fun Program Ariz. State U., Tempe, 1997-; NRC sr. rsch. assoc. Albany (Oreg.) Rsch. Ctr., 2002; proposal reviewer Petroleum Rsch. Fund, Washington, 1992-94, U.S. Dept. Energy, 2000—. Contbr. articles to profl. jours.; manuscript reviewer Chemistry of Materials, 1994-2002, Jour. Physics and Chemistry of Solids, 1995, Jour. Solid State Chemistry, 1996—, Molecular Crystals and Liquid Crystals, 1997-98, Journal of American Chemical Society, 1998-2001, Journal of American Ceramic Society, 2001-02, Environmental Science and Technology, 2003—. Coach Chandler (Ariz.) Youth Baseball, 1988-95, Chandler Am. Little League, 1996-97; com. chmn. cub scouts Boy Scouts Am., Mesa, Ariz., 1992, mem. Boy Scout com., Chandler, 1993-95. Recipient Outstanding Cmty. Impact award, Acad. Cmty. Engagement Svcs., ASU, 2002; rsch. grantee NSF, 1986—, Petroleum Rsch. Fund, 1992-95, Dept. Energy, 1995—; NRC sr. rsch. assoc., 2002. Mem. Am. Chem. Soc., Materials Rsch. Soc., Minerals, Metals and Materials Soc. Democrat. Presbyterian. Achievements include patents for method for detection of chemical components, chemical switch and method for detection of chemical compounds, and chemical switch for detection of chemical components; co-development of atomic-level imaging of lamellar intercalation reaction processes using dynamic high-resolution transmission electron microscopy and scanning tunneling microscopy/spectroscopy; research in new materials synthesis, materials reaction mechanisms, carbon dioxide mineral sequestration, intercalation chemistry, thermal chemistry and analysis, materials sci. edn. Office: Ariz State U LeRoy Eyring Ctr for Solid State Science Tempe AZ 85287-1704 Office Phone: 480-965-4535. Business E-Mail: mckelvy@asu.edu.

MCKENDRICK, JOHN, director; b. London, Eng., Nov. 1, 1949; m. Eva Wirsig, May 10, 1972; 1 child, Michael John. MA in Mass Comm., U. Leicester, Eng., 2005. CCRS Bishops' Conf. of Eng., Wales, and No. Ireland, 1996. Vp Quadric Software, Dallas, 1988—91; co-dir. Centro de Informatica, Soller, Baleares, Spain, 1991—98; tech. coord. HFN Cath. Sch., Irving, Tex., 1998—2004, OLPH Cath. Sch., Dallas, 2004—. Cons. tech. and comm., Dallas, 1998. Author short stories. Affiliate Maryknoll, Dallas, Tex., 1998. Mem.: Internat. Comm. Assn.

MCKENDRICK, RYAN PARKER, music educator, conductor; b. Charlotte, Aug. 10, 1982; s. Robert P and Vicki D McKendrick, Gregg Hardee (Stepfather) and Julie McKendrick (Stepmother). MusB, Furman U., 2005; MusM, Ga. State U., 2007. Dir. music John Calvin Presbyn. Ch., Greenville, SC, 2003—05; choirmaster Rivercliff Luth. Ch., Atlanta, 2006—. Fellow Music Theory, Furman U., 2003—05. Mem.: Am. Choral Dirs. Assn., MENC, Phi Mu Alpha Sinfonia (music dir. 2004—05). Republican. Lutheran. Avocations: reading, travel. Home Phone: 404-274-0580; Office Phone: 770-993-4316.

MCKENDRY, JOHN H., JR., lawyer; b. Grand Rapids, Mich., Mar. 24, 1950; s. John H. and Lois R. (Brandel) McK.; m. Linda A. Schmalzer, Aug. 11, 1973; children: Heather Lynn, Shannon Dawn, Sean William. BA cum laude, Albion Coll., Mich., 1972; JD cum laude, U. Mich., Ann Arbor, 1975. Bar: Mich. 1975. Assoc., then ptnr. Landman, Latimer, Clink & Robb, Muskegon, Mich., 1976-85; ptnr. Warner, Norcross & Judd, Muskegon, 1985—. Dir. debate Mona Shores High Sch., Muskegon, 1979-90; adj. prof. of taxation (employee benefits), Grand Valley State U., 1988—; debate instr. Muskegon C.C., 1999-2001. Pres. local chpt. Am. Cancer Soc., 1979; bd. dirs. West Shore Symphony, 1993-00, v.p. 1995-97, pres., 1997-99; bd. dirs. Cath. Social Svcs., 1998-04; chair profl. divsn. United Way, 1994, 98; chair bd. dirs. Deaf Hard of Hearing Connection, 2003—; bd. dirs. Mona Lake Watershed Coun., 2003-05, Hackley Life Counseling, 2007-; chair Charter Commn. City of Norton Shores, 2003-06. Recipient Disting. Service award Muskegon Jaycees, 1981; named 1 of 5 Outstanding Young Men in Mich., Mich. Jaycees. 1982; named to Hall of Fame, Mich. Speech Coaches, 1986, Diamond Key Coach Nat. Forensic League, 1987. Mem. ABA, Mich. Bar Assn., Muskegon County Bar Assn. (dir. 1992-98, pres. 1996-97), Muskegon C. of C. (bd. dirs. 1982-88), Mich. Interscholastic Forensic Assn. (treas. 1979-86), Optimists (pres. 1992). Republican. Roman Catholic. Home: 1575 Brookwood Dr Muskegon MI 49441-5276 Office Phone: 231-727-2637. Business E-Mail: mckendjh@wnj.com.

MCKENNA, ALVIN JAMES, lawyer; b. New Orleans, Aug. 17, 1943; s. Dixon N. Sr. and Mabel (Duplantier) McK.; m. Carol Jean Windheim, 1963; children: Sara, Alvin James Jr., Martha, Andrea, Erin, Rebecca. AB, Canisius Coll., 1963; JD, Notre Dame U., 1966. Bar: N.Y. 1966, Ohio 1967, U.S. Dist. Ct. (so. dist.) Ohio 1968, U.S. Dist. Ct. (no. dist.) Ohio 1978, U.S. Ct. Appeals (6th cir.) 1969, U.S. Supreme Ct. 1977. Law clk. to judge of U.S. Dist. Ct. (so. dist.), Columbus, Ohio, 1966-68; asst. U.S. atty., 1968-70; ptnr. Porter, Wright, Morris & Arthur, 1970—. Mem. Gahanna (Ohio) City Coun., 1972-80, 82-84; chmn. Gahanna Charter Rev. Commn., 1981, 06; pres. Cmty. Urban Redevel. Corp., Gahanna, 1984-. Named one of Ten Outstanding Young Persons in Columbus, Jaycees, 1974. Mem. ABA, Ohio Bar Assn., Fed. Bar Assn. (pres. Columbus chpt. 1973-74), Columbus Bar Assn. (chair fed. cts. com. 1972-74). Roman Catholic. Home: 202 Academy Ct Columbus OH 43230-2104 Office: Porter Wright Morris & Arthur 41 S High St Ste 2800 Columbus OH 43215-6194 Home Phone: 614-475-1511; Office Phone: 614-227-1945. Business E-Mail: amckenna@porterwright.com.

MCKENNA, ANDREW JAMES, wholesale distribution, printing company, sports association executive; b. Chgo., Sept. 17, 1929; s. Andrew James and Anita (Fruin) McK.; m. Mary Joan Pickett, June 20, 1953; children: Suzanne, Karen, Andrew, William, Joan, Kathleen, Margaret. BS, U. Notre Dame, 1951; JD, DePaul U., 1954. Bar: Ill. Chmn. Schwarz Paper Co. (name now Schwarz), Morton Grove, Ill., 1964—; non-exec. chmn. McDonald's Corp., 2004—. Bd. dir. Skyline Corp., AON Corp., McDonald's Corp., 1991—; Chgo. Bears Football CLub; chmn. Chgo. White Sox, 1975—81, Chgo. Cubs, 1981—84. Trustee, Univ. Notre Dame, chmn. 1992-2000; trustee, past chmn. Mus. Sci. and Industry, Chgo.; bd. dir. Cath. Charities of Chgo., Children's Meml. Med. Ctr. Chgo., Lyric Opera, United Way Metro. Chgo.; founding chmn. Chgo. Metropolis 2020. Mem. Comml. Club Chgo., Econ. Club Chgo., Lyric Opera (bd. dirs.), Execs. Club Chgo., Glenview Golf Club, Old Elm Club, Merit Club, Casino Club, The Island Club. Home: 60 Locust Rd Winnetka IL 60093-3751 Office: Schwarz 8338 Austin Ave Morton Grove IL 60053-3288 Business E-Mail: ajm@schwarz.com.

MCKENNA, ANN K., nutritionist, educator; d. Mary Giannavola and Joseph Peter Kupchak; m. Robert William McKenna, Aug. 10, 1963; children: Rodney William, Scot Robert, Stacy McKenna Brazil, Alison McKenna Rothwell, Cynthia McKenna Holmes. BS in Nutrition and Edn., Marywood Coll., Pa., 1959, MS in Nutrition and Dietetics, 1992. Registered Dietitian Am. Dietetic Assn., 1968, Cert.in Family and Consumer Sci. Am. Assn. of Family and Consumer Sci., 1985, lic. Dietitian, Nutritionist Pa., 2002. Adminstrv. dietitian Flower & Fifth Ave. Hosp., NYC, 1959—62; clin. dietitian Moses Taylor Hosp., Scranton, Pa., 1971—82; cons. dietitian, self employed in long term care facilities and home health orgns. Pa., 1982—; nutrition cons. Scranton Head Start Program, Scranton, 1984—; part-time faculty Marywood U., 1984—; clin. dietitian, educator Moses Taylor Hosp. Diabetes Edn. Program, 1998—2004. Bd. mem. NE Pa. Dietetic Assn., Scranton, Wilkes-Barre, Pa., 1995—; health adv. bd. mem. Scranton Lackawanna Head Start Program, Scranton, 1990—; coordinating cabinet mem. Marywood U. Nutrition and Dietetics Program, 1990—. Recipient Kappa Kappa Nu, Honor Soc. for Nutrition Grads. through Marywood Coll., 1992, Anita Owen award for Dietetic Profls., N.E. Pa. Dietetic Assn., 1998, Outstanding Dietetic Educator, Pa. Dietetic Assn., 1999, Dietetic Educators of Am. Dietetic Assn., 1999, Woman Yr., Head Start Program Scranton Lackawanna Human Devel. Agy., 2000. Mem.: Am. Assn. of Family and Consumer Sci. (assoc.), Am. Dietetic Assn. (assoc.), Pa. Dietetic Assn. (assoc.; bd. mem. 1999—2000), NE Pa. Dietetic Assn. (assoc.; career guidance, job referral chair 1996—2005). Avocations: fitness, gourmet cooking, reading. Home: 1329 Electric St Dunmore PA 18509 Office: Marywood Univ Adams Ave Scranton PA 18509 Home Phone: 570-346-6422; Office Phone: 570-346-6422. Home Fax: 570-346-6422. Personal E-mail: akmrd@aol.com.

MCKENNA, GEORGE LAVERNE, art museum curator; b. Detroit, Dec. 7, 1924; s. John LaVerne and Carolyn Georgia (Schwab) McK.; m. Janice Ballinger, July 22, 1966. Student, U. Oreg., 1943-44, U. Calif., Berkeley, 1948-49, U. Chgo., 1950; AB, Wayne State U., 1948, MA, 1951. Curator prints, drawings and photographs Nelson-Atkins Mus. Art, Kansas City, Mo., 1952-96, cons, 1997—. Cons. Hallmark Cards, Inc., Kansas City, 1974-76. Curator, author exhbn. and coll. catalogues. With U.S. Army, 1943-46. Mem. Am. Assn. Mus., Print Coun. Am. Office: Nelson-Atkins Mus Art 4525 Oak St Kansas City MO 64111-1873

MCKENNA, JEANETTE ANN, archaeologist; b. NYC, Aug. 6, 1953; d. Edward Patrick and Ann Jeanette (O'Brien) McKenna; children: Stephanie Jane, Daniel Glen Edward. AA in Phys. Edn., Mount San Antonio Jr. Coll., 1974; BA in Anthropology, Calif. State U., Fullerton, 1977, MA in Anthropology, 1982; postgrad., Ariz. State U., Tempe, 1981-84, U. Calif., Riverside, 1991-92. Field archaeologist Archaeol. Rsch., Inc., Costa Mesa, Calif., 1976-79; rsch. asst. Calif. State U., 1979; lab. dir. Environ. Rsch. Archaeologists, LA, 1978-79; staff archaeologist Ariz. State U., Tempe, 1979-82; rsch. archaeologist Soil Systems, Inc., Phoenix, 1982-84, Sci. Resource Surveys, Huntington Beach, Calif., 1984-87; co-owner, prin. Hatheway & McKenna, Mission Viejo, Calif., 1987-89; owner, prin. McKenna et al., Whittier, Calif., 1989—; dir. Divsn. Cultural Resource Mgmt. Svcs. EIP Assocs., Chino, Calif., 1996-97. Contbr. numerous articles to profl. jours. and reports. Bd. dirs. Whittier Conservancy, 1987-98, interim treas., 1994, pres., 1994-95, bd. dirs. Residents' Voice, 1998—. Recipient Gov.'s award for Hist. Preservation/Calif., The Whittier Conservancy, 1995, Woman of Achievement award for sci. and rsch. YWCA San Gabriel Valley, 2006. Mem. Soc. Profl. Archaeologists (bd. dirs. 1993-97), Archaeol. Inst. Am., Am. Soc. Conservation Archaeology, Am. Mus. Natural History, Soc. Am. Anthropology, Ariz. Archaeol. Coun., Ariz. Hist. Found., Calif. Hist. Soc., Nat. Arbor Day Found., Nat. Parks and Conservation Assn., Nat. Trust for Historic Preservation, Soc. Calif. Archaeology, Soc. Hist. Archaeology, S.W. Mus. Assn., Wilderness Soc., Whittier Conservancy, Southwestern Anthrop. Assn., Gene Autry Western Heritage Mus. Assn., Nature Conservancy, Smithsonian Assocs., Sierra Club, others. Democrat. Roman Catholic. Avocations: travel, reading, hiking, camping, gardening. Office: McKenna et al 6008 Friends Ave Whittier CA 90601-3724 Office Phone: 562-696-3852. Business E-Mail: jmckena@earthlink.net.

MCKENNA, JULIET JOANN, federal judge; b. Valparaiso, Ind. d. Jon F. and Sherrie McKenna; m. Douglas Townsend Kendall, May 2, 1998. BA summa cum laude, Georgetown U., 1992; JD, Yale Law Sch., 1995. Assoc. Crowell & Moring, 1995—96; atty. Office of Corp. Counsel (now Office of the Atty. Gen.), DC, 1996—98; program dir. Lawyers for Children Am., 1998—2001, nat. exec. dir., 2001—02; magistrate judge Superior Ct. DC, 2002—05, assoc. judge, 2005—. Mem. Family Ct. Implementation Com., Family Ct. Panels Com., Advisory Rules & Standards Com. Superior Ct. DC; mem. steering com. DC Bar Family Law Sect., 2001—04. Recipient Unsung Hero of the Law award, DC Bar Assn., 2001; Arthur Liman Pub. Svc. fellow, Yale Law Sch., 1999. Office: Superior Ct DC JM-640 500 Indiana Ave NW Washington DC 20001 Office Phone: 202-879-0422. *

MCKENNA, MARGARET ANNE, former academic administrator; b. RI, June 3, 1945; d. Joseph John and Mary (Burns) McK.; children: Michael Aaron McKenna Miller, David Christopher McKenna Miller. BA in Sociology, Emmanuel Coll., 1967; postgrad., Boston Coll. Law Sch., 1968; JD, So. Meth. U., 1971; LLD (hon.), U. Upsala, NJ, 1978, Fitchburg State Coll., Mass., 1979, Regis Coll., 1982; LLD (hon.), Emmanuel Coll., 2000, Episcopal Divinity Sch., 2005. Bar: Tex. 1971, D.C. 1973. Atty. Dept. Justice, Washington, 1971-73; exec. dir. Internat. Assn. Ofcl. Human Rights Agys., Washington, 1973-74; mgmt. cons. Dept. Treasury, Washington, 1975-76; dep. council to Pres. White House, Washington, 1976-79; dep. undersec. Dept. Edn., Washington, 1979-81; dir. Mary Ingraham Bunting Inst., Radcliffe Coll., Cambridge, Mass., 1981-85; v.p. program planning Radcliffe Coll., Cambridge, 1982-85; pres. Lesley U., Cambridge, 1985—2007. Bd. dirs. Dominion Resources, Inc., Cisco Learning Inst. Bd. dirs. Am. Assn. Coll. for Tchr. Edn., Coun. for Higher Edn. Accreditation, Datatel Scholars Found.; chmn. higher edn. task force Clinton Transition, 1992-93; chmn. edn. task force Mayor Thomas Menino Transition Com., 1994; mem. Princeton Adv. Bd. ACE Policy Adv. Com., Campus Compact Policy Com., MassNetworks. Recipient Outstanding Contribution award Civil Rights Leadership Conf., 1978; named Woman of Yr. Women's Equity Action League, 1979, Outstanding Woman of Yr. Big Sister Assn., 1986, Pinnacle award for Lifetime Achievement, Lelia J. Robinson award Women's Bar Assn. Mass., 1996, Valeria Addams Knapp award, The Coll. Club, 1995; named Margaret A. McKenna Day, Gov. DePrete, R.I. Mem. Boys Scouts Am., Big Sisters Ass. Boston, Y.W.C.A. Cambridge, Women's Equity Action League, Nat. Women's Polit. Conf., Nat. Assn. Official Human Rights Agencies. Democrat. *

MCKENNA, PETER DENNIS, lawyer; b. Amityville, NY, Aug. 15, 1937; s. John Paul and Margaret (Foley) McK.; children: Michael A., Suzanne E. AB cum laude, Coll. of the Holy Cross, Worchester, Mass., 1959; JD cum laude, N.Y.U., 1968. Bar: N.Y. 1968, U.S. Dist. Ct. (so. dist.) N.Y. 1970, U.S. Supreme Ct. 1973, U.S. Ct. Appeals (4th cir.) 1977, U.S. Ct. Appeals (7th cir.) 1979, U.S. Ct. Appeals (2nd cir.) 1983. Assoc. Wachtell, Lipton, Rosen & Katz, NYC, 1968-71, ptnr., 1972-91, of counsel, 1992—2001. Mem. pres.'s coun. NYU, Weinfeld Ptnr. NYU Law Sch.; regent mem. pres.'s coun. Coll. Holy Cross. Editor-in-chief N.Y.U. Law Review, 1967-68; contbr. articles to profl. jours. Mem. Cmty. Sch. Bd. Dist. 26, Queens, N.Y., 1973-77; adv. bd. St. Aloyisius Sch. for Cen. Harlem Inner-City Children, 1992—, mem. exec. com., 1994-2001; founding dir. Ctrl. Harlem Initiative for Learning and Devel., 1994—; bd. dirs. Mt. St. Michael Acad., 1994-2001, mem. exec. com., 1994-99. Lt. USN 1959-65. MEM. ABA, Am. Arbitration Assn. (comml. and securities panels), Assn. of Bar of City of N.Y., Order of Coif. Democrat. Roman Catholic. Avocations: history, public affairs, travel, swimming, golf. Address: 21205 NE 37th Ave Apt 1607 Aventura FL 33180-4056 E-mail: ppeter68@aol.com.

MCKENNA, ROB, state attorney general, former councilman; b. Ft. Sam Houston, Tex., Oct. 1, 1962; m. Marilyn McKenna; children: Madeleine, Katie, Robert, Connor. BA in Econs. and Internat. Studies, 1985; JD, U. Chgo., 1988. Bar: Wash., 9th Cir. US Ct. Appeals, US Supreme Ct. Atty. Perkins Cole, Bellevue, Wash., 1988—95; councilman King County, Wash., 1996—2004; atty. gen. State of Wash., 2005—. Co-founder, bd. mem. Eastside Human Svcs. Forum; bd. mem. Econ. Devel. Coun. of Seattle & King County; mem. Sound Transit Bd., 1996—2001; chair Eastside Transp. Partnership, 1999—2001, Wash. State Transp. Improvement Bd., 2001—03. Mem. King County Open Space Citizens Oversight Com., 1990—94; founder, bd. dirs. Advance Bellevue, 1991—2001; past pres., bd. mem. Bellevue Schs. Found., 1993—2002; mem. Bellevue Rotary, 1993—; bd. mem. King County Open Space Citizens Oversight Com., 1995—98; co-chair City of Hope Walk for Hope to Cure Breast Cancer, 1998, 1999; co-founder, bd. mem. Evergreen Forest Trust, 2000—; bd. mem. Bellevue CC Found., 2000—; mem. steering com. Citizens for Renton Schs., 2002—03; mem. exec. bd. Chief Seattle Coun. Boy Scouts Am., 2003—; mem. St. Louise Cath. Parish, 1977—; Eagle Scout. Named Elected Ofcl. of Yr., Nat. Assn. Indsl. and Office Properties, 1999; named one of The 25 Smartest People in Wash., Wash. Law & Politics, 2003; recipient Doug Mason Meml. award, Mcpl. League King County, 1991, 40 under 40 award, Puget Sound Bus. Jour., 2000, Advance Bellevue 10th Anniversary Legacy award, 2003. Mem.: King County Bar Assn., Wash. State Bar Assn. Republican. Office: Office Atty Gen 1125 Washington St SE PO Box 40100 Olympia WA 98504-0100 Office Phone: 360-753-6200. Business E-Mail: rob.mckenna@atg.wa.gov.

MCKENNA, TERENCE PATRICK, retired insurance company executive; b. Oldham, Lancashire, Eng., Sept. 3, 1928; came to U.S., 1929, naturalized, 1939; s. Patrick A. and Mary F. McKenna; m. Patricia Buckley, Aug. 22, 1973 (dec. July 1, 2006); m. Suzanne Caffey, Feb. 17, 2007. Student, St. Thomas Coll., Bloomfield, Conn., 1946—48. With John Hancock Mut. Life Ins. Co., 1951-87, gen. agt. Cherry Hill, NJ, 1963-67, field v.p. gen. agy. dept. Atlanta, 1967-69, field v.p. dist. agy. dept. Boston, 1969-73, 2d v.p. mktg. ops. dept., 1973-74, v.p. dept., 1974-76, sr. v.p. dept., 1976-83, sr. v.p. gen. agy. sales dept., 1983-87; ret., 1987. V.p., also bd. dirs. John Hancock Variable Life Ins. Co.; chmn. bd. mgrs. I.V.A.; bd. dirs. John Hancock Distbrs. Inc., John Hancock Property and Casualty Ins. Co. Served with USMC, 1952-54. Mem.: Am. Soc. CLUs, Am. Coll. Life Underwriters, El Niguel Country Club (Laguna Niguel, Calif.), Woods Hole Golf Club (Falmouth, Mass.). Personal E-mail: tpmckenna@cox.net.

MCKENNA, WILLIAM JOHN, retired textile products executive; b. NYC, Oct. 11, 1926; s. William T. and Florence (Valis) McK.; m. Jean T. McNulty, Aug. 27, 1949 (dec. Nov. 1984); children: Kevin, Marybeth, Peter, Dawn; m. Karen Lynne Hilgert, Aug. 6, 1988; children: Katherine Lynne, William John IV. BBA, Iona Coll., 1949; MS (Univ. Store Service scholar), NYU, 1950. V.p. Hat Corp. Am., NYC, 1961-63, v.p. mktg., 1961-63, exec. v.p., 1963-67; pres. Manhattan Shirt Co., NYC, 1967-74; pres., dir. Lee Co., Inc., Shawnee Mission, Kans., 1974-82, Kellwood Co., St. Louis, 1982—, chief exec. officer, 1984—, also bd. dirs., chmn., CEO, 1991-97, chmn., 1991-99, chmn. emeritus, 1999—. Dir. United Mo. Bank of St. Louis. Trustee emeritus St. Louis U., Boys Hope; permanent deacon Archdiocese St. Louis. With USN, 1944-46, PTO. Mem. Sovereign Mil. Order Malta, St. Louis Club, Bellerive Country Club. Roman Catholic. E-mail: william_mckenna@kellwood.com.

MCKENNA, WILLIAM MICHAEL, advertising executive; b. Washington, Apr. 4, 1951; s. William H. and Betty Ann (Cashin) McK.; m. Lynn Stevenson, Dec. 18, 1976; children: James Langdon, Lee Stevenson. BA, Wesleyan U., 1973; MS in Journalism, Boston U., 1978. V.p., creative dir. Ingalls Quinn & Johnson, Boston, 1981-88; sr. v.p., creative dir. Young & Rubicam, NYC, 1988-94; chief creative officer, exec. v.p. AF GL Internat., NYC, 1994-95; mng. dir., chief creative officer Citigate Albert Frank, NYC, 1996-99; mng. dir., COO, Marsteller, NYC, 1999-2000; pres., CEO Marsteller Advt., NYC, 2000—. V.p. comm. Middlebury Coll., Vt., 2005—. Recipient CLIO, Hatch, N.Y. Film Soc. creative advt. awards, 1982-95, Telly award. Office: Burson Marsteller 230 Park Ave S New York NY 10003-1513 Home: 869 James Rd Middlebury VT 05753-9538

MCKENNON, KEITH ROBERT, chemical company executive; b. Condon, Oreg., Dec. 25, 1933; s. Russel M. and Lois E. (Edgerton) McK.; m. Patricia Dragon, Sept. 30, 1961; children: Brian, Marc, Kevin. BS, Oreg. State U., 1955. Rsch. chemist Dow Chem. Co., Pittsburg, Calif., 1955—67, sales mgr. Houston, 1967, from research mgr. to exec. v.p. Midland, Mich., 1968—87, bd. dirs., 1983—92, 2003—06, exec. v.p., 1987-92; pres. Dow USA, 1987-90; chmn., chief exec. officer Dow Corning Corp., 1992-94, also bd. dirs.; chmn. PacifiCorp, Portland, Oreg., 1994-99, CEO, 1998-99. Patentee. Recipient Chemical Industry medal Soc. of Chemical Industry, 1994 Republican. Presbyterian. E-mail: kmck96@aol.com.

MCKENZIE, BRIAN BRUCE, finance educator; b. Kelowna, BC, Canada, Nov. 23, 1948; arrived in U.S., 2003; s. Rex Bruce and Dorothy McKenzie; m. Molly Kathleen Farrend, Mar. 21, 1970. BA, U. BC, Vancouver, Can., 1974; MBA, U. Victoria, Can., 1997, PhD, 2003. Cert. qualification - boatbuilding Province of BC, 1990. Pres. Brian McKenzie Boatbuilding, Inc, Victoria, Canada, 1982—97; lectr. U. Victoria, 1997—2002; asst. prof. U. Calif., East Bay, 2003—. Vis. instr. Worcester (Mass.) Poly. Inst., 1999—2000. Contbr. scientific papers, rsch. to profl. jours. Recipient Entrepreneurship Theory and Practice Best Conceptual Paper award, 2004. Fellow: Students Free Enterprise (Sam Walton fellow 2005—06); mem.: Can. Anthrop. Assn., Small Bus. Inst., N.Am. Case Rsch. Assn., Acad. Mgmt. (chair nontraditional academics com.entrepreneurship divsn., Innovations in Pedagogy award 1999), U.S. Assn. Small Bus. and Entrepreneurship (Model Undergraduate Program award 2000), Oral History Assn. Office: Calif State U 25800 Carlos Bee Blvd Hayward CA 94542 Home Phone: 510-881-4652; Office Phone: 510-885-2858. Personal E-mail: brian@brian-mckenzie.com. Business E-Mail: brian.mckenzie@csueastbay.edu.

MCKENZIE, DENISE, religious organization administrator, academic administrator; b. Lackawanna, NY, Mar. 2, 1950; d. John Patrick and Dolores Marguerite McKenzie. AAS, Trocaire Coll., 1972; BA in Religious Studies, Canisius Coll., 1973, MA in Religious Studies, 1980. Religion tchr. Mt. Mercy Acad., Buffalo, 1973—89; prof. religious studies Trocaire Coll., Buffalo, 1984—89; dir. campus ministry D'Youville Coll., Buffalo, 1989—96, prof. religious studies, 1989—96; diocesan dir. of religious edn. Diocese of Buffalo, 1996—2002, sec. edn., 2002. Vocal cantor Nat. Shrine of Our Lady of Victory; mem. Fidelis health bd. Cath. Health Sys., Buffalo, 2002—; bd. mem. Cantilican Ctr. for Learning, Buffalo, 2002—; mem. bd. Cath. edn. Diocese of Buffalo, 1997—. Recipient Vol. of Yr., Mary Agnes Manor Nursing Home, 1992, Disting. Alumni, Trocaire Coll., 2003, Mt. Mercy Acad., 1998, Adminstr. of Yr., D'Youville Coll., 1992. Mem.: Nat. Conf. Cathechetical Leadership, Nat. Cath. Edn. Assn., Chief Administrators of Cath. Edn. Office: Diocese of Buffalo 795 Main St Buffalo NY 14203 Office Phone: 716-847-5520. Business E-Mail: dmckenzie@buffalodiocese.org.

MCKENZIE, ELIZABETH MCDANIEL, law librarian; b. Lexington, Ky., June 27, 1954; d. William E. and JoAnn E. (Harris) McDaniel; m. James A. McKenzie, May 20, 1978; children: Joseph D., E. Alexa. BA with distinction, Transylvania U., 1975; JD, U. Ky., 1981, MLS with distinction, 1984. Bar: Ky. 1981, U.S. Dist. Ct. (ea. dist.) Ky. 1981. Reginald Heber Smith community lawyer fellow Cen. Ky. Legal Svcs., Lexington, 1981-83; info. specialist Ky. Dept. for Environ. Protection, Frankfort, Ky., 1984-85; readers svcs. librarian St. Louis U. Law Library, 1986-96; dir. Suffolk U. Law Libr., Boston, 1996—. Owner, mgr. Juris Data Legal Rsch. Co., Lexington, 1985-86; bd. dirs. Law Libr. Microforms Consortium, 2005—; steering com. China-US Conf. on Legal Info. and Law Libr., 2007—. Contbr. articles to profl. jours. Recipient Article of Yr. award Law Libr. Jour., 1999; Nat. Merit scholar Transylvania U., 1972-75. Mem. ABA, Ky. Bar Assn., Am. Assn. Law Libraries, Law Libraries New England, New England Law Library Consortium, Assn. Boston Law Libraries. Democrat. Roman Catholic. Office: Suffolk U Law Sch 120 Tremont St Boston MA 02108-4977 Business E-Mail: emckenzi@suffolk.edu.

MCKENZIE, JAMES FRANKLIN, lawyer; b. Mobile, Ala., May 3, 1948; s. Frank L. McKenzie and Mary K. (Crow) McKenzie O'Neal; m. Randy Jo Jones, June 25, 1977; children: Katherine J., J. Alistair. BA magna cum laude, U. W. Fla., 1970; JD with honors, U. Fla., 1973. Bar: Fla. 1973, U.S. Dist. Ct. (no. dist.) Fla. 1973, U.S. Ct. Appeals (5th cir.) 1975, U.S. Ct. Appeals (11th cir.) 1982, U.S. Supreme Ct. 1988. Lectr. bus. law U. Fla., Gainesville, 1972-73; assoc. Levin, Warfield et al, Pensacola, Fla., 1973-76; ptnr. Myrick & McKenzie, PA, Pensacola, Fla., 1976-82, McKenzie & Hall, PA, Pensacola, Fla., 1982—. Contbr. chpts. to books, articles to profl. jours. Pres. N.W. Fla. Easter Seal Soc., Pensacola, 1975; bd. dirs. Five Flags Sertoma Club, 1977; trustee Fla. Lawyers Action Group, Tallahassee, 1996-97; adv. bd. Lupus Soc., N.W. Fla., 1992; deacon, United Ch. Christ. Mem.: 1st Cir. Justice Assn. (pres. 1984, founding mem.), AAJ (bd. govs. 2001—05, pres. club), ABA, Million Dollar Advocates Forum, Civil Justice Found. (founding sponsor), Nat. Bd. Trial Advocacy (cert. civil trial advocacy), Escambia-Santa Rosa Bar Assn., Fla. Bar Assn. (cert. in civil trial law), Fla. Justice Assn. (bd. dirs. 1986—93, exec. com. 1990—91, bd. dirs. 2000—05, coll. diplomates, Silver Eagle award 1989, ABCD award 1991, Silver Eagle award 2002, Crystal Eagle award 2006, named one of Top 100 Fla. Super Lawyers 2006, Crystal Eagle award 2006), Pensacola Country Club, Order of Coif, Phi Delta Phi, Omicron Delta Kappa, Phi Kappa Phi. Democrat. United Ch. Of Christ. Office: McKenzie & Hall PA 905 E Hatton St Pensacola FL 32503-3931 Home: 2800 Blackshear Ave Pensacola FL 32503 Business E-Mail: jmckenzie@mckenzielawfirm.com.

MCKENZIE, JAMES W., JR., lawyer; b. Oct. 3, 1959; AB, Dartmouth Coll., 1982; MBA, JD, U. Pa., 1987. Bar: Pa. 1987. Assoc. Morgan, Lewis & Bockius LLP, Phila., 1987—95, partner, 1995—2000, 2002—; exec. v.p., gen. counsel VerticalNet, Inc., 2002—02. Named one of 12 "Dealmakers of the Yr.", The American Lawyer, 2004. Office: Morgan Lewis & Bockius LLP 1701 Market St Philadelphia PA 19103-2903

MCKENZIE, JOHN F., lawyer; b. Chgo., Sept. 28, 1947; s. John Cummings and Mary Jane (Manny) McK.; m. Lucy A. Roman, Jan. 14, 1978; children: Melissa Ann, Sean Cummings. BA magna cum laude, Williams Coll., 1969; JD cum laude, Harvard U., 1976. Bar: Calif. 1976, U.S. Dist. Ct. (No. Dist.) Calif. 1976, U.S. Ct. Appeals (10th Cir.) 1984, Ct. Internat. Trade. Assoc. Baker & McKenzie LLP, San Francisco, 1976-83, ptnr., 1983—. Spkr. in field. Contbg. author, editor Computers & Software, 4th edit., 1989; contbr. articles on export controls, anti-boycott regulations and software licensing to profl. publs.; articles editor Harvard Law Review, 1975-76. Mem. ABA (internat. law sect.), State Bar of Calif. (internat. sect.), Bar Assn. San Francisco, Santa Clara Valley World Trade Assn., Assn. Freight Forwarders and Customs Brokers (assoc. mem.), Am. Electronics Assn. (lawyers com.), Calif. Coun. on Internat. Trade (mem. legis. coun.), Dist. Export Coun. for Northern Calif., U.S. Dept. Commerce (no. Calif. dist. export coun.); Phi Beta Kappa (Magna Cum Laude) Home: 10 Mann Dr Kentfield CA 94904-1034 Office: Baker & McKenzie LLP 2 Embarcadero Ctr Ste 2400 San Francisco CA 94111-3909 also: Baker & McKenzie 1 Prudential Pla 130 E Randolph St Ste 3700 Chicago IL 60601-6316 Office Phone: 415-576-3033. Business E-Mail: john.f.mckenzie@bakernet.com.

MCKENZIE, KATHLEEN JULIANNA, artist; b. Jan. 20, 1957; Artist, Torrington, Conn., 1987—. Paintings featured in 7th, 9th and 11th Encyclopedia of Living Artist, Internat. Encyclopaedic Dictionary of Modern and Contemporary Art in Casa Editrice Alba. Home: 2493 Poole Rd Greer SC 29651-5046 Office Phone: 864-895-1581.

MCKENZIE, KEVIN PATRICK, performing company executive; b. Burlington, Vt., Apr. 29, 1954; s. Raymond James and Ruth (Davison) McKenzie. Grad. high sch., Washington. Mem. corps de ballet Nat. Ballet of Washington, 1972-74; prin. Joffrey Ballet, NYC, 1974-78, Am. Ballet Theatre, NYC, 1979-91; artistic assoc. Washington Ballet, 1991-92; artistic dir. Am. Ballet Theatre, NYC, 1992—; assoc. artistic dir. New Amsterdam Ballet. Pres. bd. dirs. Am. Ballet Theatre Dancers Fund, Inc., 1982—89; assoc. dir. New Amsterdam Ballet, NYC, 1984—; founding bd. mem. Kaatsbaan Internat. Dance Ctr., 1991—. Performer: (films) Unicorn, 1971; dancer Houston Ballet, 1978, Spoleto Festival, 1980, 1984, Theatre des Champs Elysees, Paris, 1981, Sadler's Wells Theatre, London, 1981, Asami Maki Ballet Co., Tokyo, 1983, Aspen Festival, 1982; prodr., dir. The Party of the Year, 1982; choreographer Groupo Zambaria Ballet, 1984, Liszt Etudes, 1991, Lucy and the Count, 1992, The Nutcracker, 1993; created roles Adrienne Dellos' The Blind Man's Daughter, Seoul, Korea, 1986, Amnon V'Tamar, S.P.E.B.S.Q.S.A., appeared with Martine Van Hamel Swan Lake, Nat. Ballet of Cuba, Havana, 1986, appeared with Merrill Ashley Tchaikowsky Pas de Deux, Bolshoi Theatre, Moscow, 1986; dancer La Bayadere, Carmen, Cinderella, Coppelia, Dim Lustre, Don Quixote, Giselle, The Garden of Villandry, Jardin aux lilas, The Leaves Are Fading, Pillar of Fire, Raymonda, Requiem, Rodeo, Romeo and Juliet, The Sleeping Beauty, Swan Lake, La Sylphide, Paquita, Sylvia Pas de Deux, Theme and Variations. Named Kevin McKenzie Day, City of Burlington, 1985; recipient Silver medal, Varna Internat. Ballet Competition, Bulgaria, 1972, Artistic Achievement medal, Dept. State, U.S. Govt., 1972, Mayor Burlington, Vt., 1984, Performing Arts award, Am. Ireland Fund, 1994. Office: Am Ballet Theatre 890 Broadway New York NY 10003-1211 *

MCKENZIE, LAWRENCE J., composition educator; b. Cumberland, Md., Oct. 9, 1970; s. Lawrence J. McKenzie, Sr. and Judith A. Crumbaugh-Erlewine. BA in Philosophy/Religion, U. Charleston, 1994; MA, Meth. Theol. Sch., Delaware, Ohio, 1998. Cert. candidate for ordination W.Va., 1993. Theol. intern/assoc. pastor St. Andrew United Meth. Ch., St. Albans, W.Va., 1993—96; assoc. pastor/cmty. youth dir. Ostrander United Meth. Ch., Ohio, 1994—96; pastor Hyatt's United Meth. Ch., Ohio, 1997—98; instr. of humanities U. Charleston, W.Va., 1998—2000; instrn. of composition/lit. W.Va. State Coll., Institute, 1998—2000; paralegal The Law Office, Parkersburg, W.Va., 2000—01; prof. of composition W.Va. U., Parkersburg, 2000—. Exec. bd. sec., acquisitions editor Mountain State Press, Charleston, W.Va., 2000—05; faculty senate rep. W.Va. U., Parkersburg, 2002—, mem. humanities spkr. series, 2002—, asst. forensic coach, 2003—, mem. internationalization com., 2007—; mem. W.Va. Assn. of Devel. Educators, Institute, 2002—, W.Va. Consortium for Faculty and Course Devel. in Internat. Studies, Morgantown, 2004—; acquisitions editor W.Va. Writers Assn., Inc., Charleston, 2003—. Pres. Cmty. Acres Homeowners Assn., Inc., Davisville, W.Va., 2003—05; assoc./intern United Meth. Ch., Charleston, W.Va., 1987—89; mem. Order of St. Luke, Delaware, Ohio, 1994—98; interim pres. Cmty. Acres Homeowners Assn., Inc., Davisville, W.Va., 2002—03. Recipient Unsung Hero award, W.Va. U., 2003, Svc. award;, W.Va. Humanities Coun., 2002. Mem.: MLA, ASCD (hon.), W.Va. Assn. Devel. Educators, Nat. Coun. Tchrs. of English. Achievements include development of Erik J. Bitterbaum Pres.'s Award for Innovation in Tchg; Gear Up For Success (GUS) Innovation in Tchg. Avocations: fly fishing, national/international travel, fiction/non-fiction, academic writing. Office: W Va U 300 Campus Dr Parkersburg WV 26104 Home Phone: 304-485-0619; Office Phone: 304-424-8000. Office Fax: 304-424-8315. Business E-Mail: lawrence.mckenzie@mail.wvu.edu.

MC KENZIE, LIONEL WILFRED, economist, educator; b. Montezuma, Ga., Jan. 26, 1919; s. Lionel Wilfred and Lida (Rushin) McK.; m. Blanche Veron, Jan. 2, 1943 (dec. July 1999); children— Lionel Wilfred (dec.), Gwendolyn Veron (dec.), David Rushin. AB, Duke U., 1939; MA, Princeton U., 1946, PhD, 1956; BLitt, Oxford U., Eng., 1949; postgrad., U. Chgo., 1950-51, LLD (hon.), 1991; D of Econs. (hon.), Keio U., Japan, 1998; DPhil (hon.), Kyoto U., Japan, 2004. Asst. economist WPB, 1942; instr. Mass. Inst. Tech., 1946; from asst. prof. to assoc. prof. Duke, 1948-57; prof. econs. U. Rochester, 1957-64, John Munro prof. econs., 1964-67, Wilson prof. econs., 1967-89, Wilson prof. emeritus, 1989—, chmn. dept., 1957-66. Taussig research prof. Harvard U., 1980-81; Mem. math. divsn. NRC, 1960-63, mem. behavioral scis. divsn., 1964-70; mem. math., social scis. bd. Center Advanced Study in Behavioral Scis., Palo Alto, Calif., 1964-70, chmn., 1969-70 Author: Classical General Equilibrium Theory, 2002; assoc. editor Internat. Econs. Rev., 1964-96, Jour. Econ. Theory, 1970-73, Jour. Internat. Econs., 1970-84, Econ. Theory, 1991-95; contbr. articles to profl. jours. Lt. (s.g.) USNR, 1943-45. Recipient Rising Sun award Japan, 1995; Rhodes scholar Oriel Coll. Oxford U., 1939; Guggenheim fellow, 1973-74, fellow Center for Advanced Study in Behavioral Scis., 1973-74. Fellow Econometric Soc. (coun. 1973-78, pres. 1977), Am. Acad. Arts and Scis., Am. Econ. Assn.; mem. NAS, Royal Econ. Soc., Am. Math. Soc., Am. Econ. Assn. (Disting. Fellow 1993), Phi Beta Kappa (chpt. v.p. 1968-70, chpt. pres. 1972-73). Home: 225 Dorchester Rd Rochester NY 14610-1322

MCKENZIE, MARY BETH, artist; b. Cleve. d. William Jennings and Mary Elizabeth (McCray) McK.; m. Tony Mysak, May 8, 1974; children: Zsuzsa McKenzie Mysak, Maria McKenzie Mysak. Student, Mus. Fine Arts, Boston, 1964-65, Cooper Sch. Art, Cleve., 1965-67; diploma, NAD, NYC, 1974. Painting instr. NAD, 1981—, Art Students League, 1995—. Author: A Painterly Approach, 1987; contbr. articles to profl. jours.; one-woman shows include Nat. Arts Club, N.Y.C., 1976, FAR Gallery, 1980, Perin and Sharpe Gallery, New Canaan, Conn., 1981, Frank Caro Gallery, N.Y.C., 1988—89, Joseph Keiffer Gallery, 1991, Union County Coll., 1998, exhibited in group shows at Sindin Gallery, N.Y.C., 1985—86, Ice Collection, 1995—96, Met. Mus. Art, 2001, Represented in permanent collections The Butler Mus. Am. Art, Met. Mus. Art, N.Y.C., Mus. City of N.Y., NAD, Art Students League of N.Y., Nat. Mus. Women in the Arts, Nat. Mus. Am. Art, Smithsonian Instn., Bklyn. Mus. Art, New Britain Mus. Am. Art, N.Y. Hist. Soc., exhibitions include Met. Mus. Art, 2001. Recipient Nat. Scholastic award Mus. Fine Arts, Boston, numerous awards including Thomas B. Clark prize and the Isaac N. Maynard prize Nat. Acad. Design, Greenshields Found. grantee, Stacey Found. grantee. Mem. Nat. Acad. Design, Pastel Soc. Am. (Best In Show, Award of Exceptional Merit, Exhbn. Com. award), Allied Artists Am. (Gold medal, The Jane Peterson award, Grumbacher Cash award, Silver medal), Audubon Artists (Pastel Soc. Am. award). Home: 525 W 45th St New York NY 10036-3414 Personal E-mail: mckenzie525@netscape.net.

MCKENZIE, RALPH NELSON, mathematician, educator; b. Cisco, Tex., Oct. 20, 1941; s. Milton Woodrow and Annie Laurie (Rosenquest) McK.; m. Laura Kathryn Brown, May 19, 1961; children: Deborah, Kathryn Ann. BA, U. Colo., 1963, PhD, 1966. Instr. U. Calif., Berkeley, 1966, asst. prof., 1967—71, assoc. prof., 1971—78, prof., 1978—2004; disting. prof. Vanderbilt U., Nashville, 1994—, prof. emeritus, 1994—. Vis. asst. prof., U. Colo., 1970-71; mem. Inst. for Advanced Study, Princeton, 1971-72; vis. prof. U. Hawaii, 1983, U. Siena, Italy, 1984; vis. researcher, LaTrobe U., Melbourne, 1989; Ulam prof., U. Colo., 1990; chmn. Fulbright Adv. Com. for Math., 1991-94; invited lectr. in field. Co-author: Structure of Finite Algebras, 1987, Commutator Theory for Congruence Modular Varieties, 1984, Algebras, Lattices, Varieties, 1986; mem. editl. bd. Algebra Universalis, 1970-, Internat. Jour. Algebra & Computation, 1990-, Global Jour. Math. and Math. Sciences, 2004-, Internat. Jour. Pure and Applied Math. Sciences, 2004-; contbr. articles to profl. jours. NSF Grad. Fellow, 1963-66, NSF Postdoctoral Fellow, 1971-72, Alfred P. Sloan Found. fellow, 1973-75, Fulbright Sr. Scholar, Australia, 1989; Rsch. grantee NSF, 1980-92, 94-. Avocations: reading, fly-fishing, mountain climbing. Office: Vanderbilt Univ Math Dept 1326 Stevenson Ctr Nashville TN 37240-0001 Office Phone: 615-322-7456. Business E-Mail: rn.mckenzie@vanderbilt.edu, ralph.n.mckenzie@vanderbilt.edu.

MCKENZIE, ROBERT ERNEST, lawyer; b. Cheboygan, Mich., Dec. 7, 1947; s. Alexander Orlando and Edna Jean (Burt) McK.; m. Theresia Wolf, Apr. 26, 1975; 1 child, Robert A. BA in Pers. Adminstrn., Mich. State U., 1970; JD with high honors, Ill. Inst. Tech., 1979. Bar: Ill. 1979, US Dist. Ct. (no. dist.) Ill. 1979, US Tax Ct. 1979, US Ct. Appeals (7th cir.) 1979, US Supreme Ct. 1984; lic. pvt. pilot; enrolled agnet with IRS. Revenue officer IRS, Chgo., 1972-78; ptnr. McKenzie & McKenzie, Chgo., 1979-2000, Arnstein & Lehr LLP, 2000—. Author: Representation Before the Collection Divison of the IRS, 1989, 2007; co-author: Representing the Audited Taxpayer Before the IRS, 1990, 2007, Representation Before the US Tax Court, 2006; contbr. articles to profl. jours. Mem. tax adv. com. Nat. Bankruptcy Rev. Commn., 1997; bd. mem. Ctr. for Econ. Progress, 1999-2005; del. Rep. Nat. Conv., Detroit, 1980. 2nd lt. US Army, 1970, capt. US Army, 1978. Recipient scholarship Mich. State U., 1966-70, State of Mich., 1966-70, Silas Strawn scholarship ITT, 1977, Excellence in Edn. award, NAEA Edn. Found., 2001; fellow Am. Bar. Fellow Am. Bar Found., mem. ABA (chmn. employment tax com. tax sect. 1992-94, co-chmn. bankruptcy task force 1997-98, coun. tax sect. 1998-2001, vice chmn. tax sect. 2003-05, chmn Pro Bono Com., 2007-), Chgo. Bar Assn. (chmn. com. devel. and tax coms. 1996-97), Am. Coll. Tax Counsel (bd. regents 2007-), Union League Chgo. Avocations: travel, flying. Office: Ste 1200 120 S Riverside Plz Chicago IL 60606 Home Phone: 847-981-1441; Office Phone: 312-876-6927. Business E-Mail: remckenzie@arnstein.com.

MCKENZIE, SCOTT ARTHUR, public health service officer, consultant; s. Harry Arthur and Betty Jeane (Palmquist) McKenzie; m. Jacklyn Ethel Shaul, June 7, 1991; 1 child, Jeremiah Joseph. BS in gen. studies, SUNY, 1992; MPA, Webster U., St. Louis, 2000. Cert. health care adminstr. USN, 2001, exec. medicine Dept. Def., 2002; registered environ. health specialist & sanitarian Nat. Environ. Health Assn., 1998. Head preventive medicine dept. Naval Sta., Mayport, Fla., 1996—98; dep. divsn. surgeon, environ. health officer 2d Marine Divsn., Camp Lejeune, NC, 1998—2001; chief prevention svcs. Naval Hosp., Rota, Spain, 2001—04, head preventive medicine dept. Camp Pendleton, Calif., 2004—06; theater pub. health officer Multi-National Corps, Iraq, 2005—06; dir. navy preventive medicine technician sch. USN, San Diego, 2006—. Cons. Navy Environ. Health Ctr., Norfolk, Va., 1996—. Leader Boy Scouts Am., 1980—2007. Lt. comdr. USN, 1980—2007. Decorated Bronze star; recipient Rear Adm. Stevenson award, Navy Environ. Health Ctr., 1998, Navy Environ. Health Officer of Yr. award, USN, 2003, Wood Badge award, Boy Scouts Am., 2007. Mem.: Nat. Environ. Health Assn. (assoc.), Nat. Eagle Scout Assn. (life). Mem. Lds Ch. Avocations: camping, hiking, travel. Home: 1326 Borrego Springs Rd Chula Vista CA 91915-1508 Personal E-mail: samckenzie@hotmail.com.

MCKENZIE, WALTER L., information technology executive, consultant; b. Boston, Mass., Oct. 31, 1960; s. Walter L. McKenzie and Mary D. Golden; m. Carleen R. Fisher; children: Christopher Michael, Mallory Elise. BS in Edn., Ohio State U., 1985; MEd in Instrnl. Tech., George Mason U., 2000. Tchr. Fredericksburg City Schs., Va., 1985—86; tchr./gifted coord. King George County Schs., Va., 1986—95; tchr./trainer Spotsylvania County Schs., Va., 1995—99; sr. tech. tng. specialist Advanced Tech. Sys., McLean, Va., 1999—2000; dept. chair, presenter, course developer Classroom Connect, El Segundo, Calif., 1999—2005; tech. coord. Arlington Pub. Schs., 2000—03; dir. info. sys. Salem Pub. Schs., Salem, Mass., 2003—. Webmaster, surfaquarium.com The One and Only Surfaquarium, Amesbury, Mass., 1995—2005, webmaster, multiple intelligence pages, 1996—2005; cons. Surfaquarium, Amesbury, Mass., 1997—2005; editor Innovative Tchg. Newsletter, Amesbury, Mass., 1998—2005; participant, the arts in every classroom Annenberg Project, Washington, 2001—02; participant, changing edn. through the arts Kennedy Ctr., Washington, 2002—03; editor Va. Soc. Tech. Educators Jour., Blacksburg, Va., 2002—05; dir. Mass. Computer Using Educators, Wellesley, Mass., 2004—05; editor Digital Dozen Newsletter, Amesbury, Mass., 2004—05. Contbr. articles to profl. jours.; author: (book) Multiple Intelligences and Instructional Technology: A Manual for Every Mind, Standards-Based Lessons for tech-Savvy Students: A Multiple Intelligences Approach; prodr.: (online collaborative project) eEditarod Project, Art & Architecture, Build a Better Mousetrap, 2004 National CyberConvention, The Presidents' Project; editor (contributing author): (book) NETS S Curriculum Series: Social Studies Units for Grades 9—12; editor: Va. Soc. Tech. Educators. Judge ThinkQuest, Mass., 1999; sponsor Ann. Top Ten Online Educators Awards, Amesbury, Mass., 2003—05. Grantee Instrnl. Devel. Project, Va. Coun. Fine Arts, 2002. Mem.: ASCD, Internat. Soc. Tech. in Edn., MassCUE (dir., webmaster 2003—05). Achievements include development of surfaquarium digital communities of practice, 2004. Avocations: writing, music, reading, travel. Office: Salem Pub Schs 29 Highland Ave Salem MA 01970 Home Phone: 978-388-0032; Office Phone: 978-825-3608. Personal E-mail: walter@surfaquarium.com. E-mail: waltermckenzie@salem.k12.ma.us.

MCKENZIE-SWARTS, MOLLY, human resources specialist, hotel executive; b. Calif. BA, U. So. Calif. Dir. human resources Berkhemer & Kline Pub. Rels., LA; various human resources positions in employment, facilities, adminstrn., compensation, benefits, and human resource info. systems Hilton Hotels Corp., Beverly Hills, Calif., sr. v.p. human resources, 1999—. Mem. Juniors of Social Svc., Nat. Charity League. Office: Hilton Hotels Corp 9336 Civic Center Dr Beverly Hills CA 90210 Office Phone: 310-278-4321. Office Fax: 310-205-7678.

MCKEON, HOWARD PHILLIP (BUCK MCKEON), congressman, former mayor; b. LA, Sept. 9, 1938; m. Patricia Kunz; 6 children. BS, Brigham Young U., 1985. Mem. city coun. City of Santa Clarita, Calif., 1987-92, mayor, 1987—92; mem. U.S. Congress from 25th Calif. dist., 1993—; mem. armed services com.; chmn. edn. and workforce com., 2006—. Founding dir., chmn. Valencia Nat. Bank, 1987-92; co-owner Howard & Phil's Western Wear, Inc., 1963-. Hon. chmn. Leukemia Soc. Celebrity program, 1990, Red Cross Community Support Campaign, 1992; active Dist. Com. Boy Scouts Am.; chmn., trustee William S. Hart Sch. dist., 1979-87; chmn., dir. Henry Mayo Newhall Meml. Hosp., 1983-88; mem. Calif. Rep. State Ctrl. Com., 1988-92; bd. dirs. Santa Clarita Valley Sml. Bus. Devel. Ctr., 1990-92, Canyon Country C. of C., 1988-92. Named Newsmaker of the Yr. award, Santa Clarita Press Club, 1996; recipient Silver Spur award for Outstanding Community Svc., Coll. of the Canyons Found., 2000, Robert J. Collier award, Nat. Aeronautic Assn., 2001, Advocacy of Ind. Higher Edn. award, Nat. Assn. Ind. Colleges & Universities, 2002. Republican. Mem. Lds Ch. Office: US Ho Reps 2351 Rayburn Ho Office Bldg Washington DC 20515-0525 E-mail: tellbuck@mail.house.gov. *

MCKEOUGH, SUSAN ANNE, elementary school educator; d. Richard Blair McKeough and Barbara Jean Mckeough. BS, St. Francis Coll., Biddeford, Maine, 1976; MA, Sacred Heart U., Bridgeport, Conn., 1982. Cert. tchr. Conn. Supr. tchr. Child Devel. Ctr., Bellefonte, Pa., 1976—78; tchr. St. Gabriel Sch., Stamford, Conn., 1978—85, Greenwich (Conn.) Cath., 1986—88, Saxe Mid. Sch., New Canaan, Conn., 1988—97, 2001—, Grace Episcopal Sch., Ocala, Fla., 1998—2000. Spl. edn. aide, sub- tchr. Saxe Mid. Sch., New Canaan, 1985—86. Recipient Sci. award, State of Fla., 1998. Home: 3 Valley View Rd #17 Norwalk CT 06851 Office: Saxe Mid Sch 468 South Ave New Canaan CT 06840 Home Phone: 203-846-6104; Office Phone: 203-594-4500. Personal E-mail: smckeo2621@aol.com.

MCKEOUGH, WILLIAM DARCY, supply company executive; b. Chatham, Ont., Can., Jan. 31, 1933; s. George Grant and Florence Sewell (Woodward) McK.; m. Margaret Joyce Walker, June 18, 1965; children: Walker Stewart, James Grant. BA, U. Western Ont., 1954; LLD (hon.), Wilfred Laurier U., 1980; DDiv, Huron Univ. Coll., 2003. Chmn. McKeough Supply Inc. Bd. dirs. Can. Gen. Tower Ltd.; former chmn. Ridley Coll. Found., Huron Coll. Found. Former mem. exec. com. Anglican Diocese of Huron; former mem. Gen. Synod, Anglican Ch., Can.; mem. Chatham City Coun., 1960-63; also mem. Planning Bd. and Lower Thames Valley Conservation Authority; former mem. Chatham-Kent adv. bd. Can. Nat. Inst. of the Blind; former bd. dirs. Chatham YMCA, Chatham Little Theatre; former chmn. and pres. bd. govs. pres. Ridley Coll.; former bd. govs. Stratford Shakespearian Festival, Wilfrid Laurier U.; former mem. Can. group Trilateral Commn.; mem. Ont. Legislature, 1963-78, minister without portfolio, 1966, minister mcpl. affairs, 1967; treas. and minister of econs., also chmn. Treasury Bd., 1971-72, minister mcpl. affairs, 1972, treas. and minister of econs. and intergovtl. affairs, 1972, parliamentary asst. to premier Ont., 1973, minister of energy, 1973-75, treas. and minister econs. and intergovtl. affairs, 1975-78; former chmn. Ridley Coll. Found., Huron Coll. Found. Decorated officer of Order of Can. Home and Office: PO Box 940 Chatham ON Canada N7M 5L3 Home Phone: 519-676-5866; Office Phone: 519-352-7110.

MCKEOWN, H. MARY, lawyer, educator; b. West Palm Beach, Fla., Sept. 17, 1952; d. Honore Stephen McKeown and Margaret Berg McKeown Growney; m. Jon Henry Barber, Sept. 18, 1981; children: Sean Patrick, Mary Kathleen. AA, St. Petersburg Jr. Coll., Fla., 1970; BA in Polit. Sci. and Sociology, U. South Fla., 1972; JD cum laude, Samford U., 1976. Bar: Fla. 1976, U.S. Dist. Ct. (mid. dist.) Fla. 1977, U.S. Ct. Appeals (5th and 11th cirs.) 1981, U.S. Supreme Ct. 1992. Asst. state atty. 6th Jud.

Ct., Clearwater, Fla., 1976-90; ptnr. Growney, McKeown & Barber, St. Petersburg, 1976—. Adj. prof. Stetson Coll. of Law, St. Petersburg, 1990—. Chairperson Child Welfare Std. and Tng. Coun., 1995—98; mem. nominee qualifications rev. com. Health and Human Svcs. Bd. Dist. 5, 1992—2000; mem. Study Commn. Child Welfare, 1990—91; leader Girl Scouts U.S., 1991—2001; bd. dirs. Suncoast Girl Scout Coun., 2006—. Recipient Victim Advocacy award Pinellas County Victims Rights Coalition, 1984, Law and Order award Elks, Pinellas County, 1991. Mem.: St. Petersburg Bar Assn., Fla. Bar Assn., Acad. Fla. Trial Lawyers, Phi Alpha Delta. Office: 7763 Starkey Rd Seminole FL 33777

MCKEOWN, JAMES CHARLES, finance educator, consultant; b. Cleve., Nov. 3, 1945; s. Charles Joseph and Dara Ferrol (Prew) McK.; m. Mary Alinda Park, Jan. 2, 1965 (div. May 1980); children— Jeffrey Charles, Pamela Lynn; m. 2d, Nancy Ann Stratton, Jan. 3, 1981 BS in Math. with high honors, Mich. State U., 1966, PhD in Bus. Adminstrn., 1969. Asst. prof. accountancy U. Ill., Urbana-Champaign, 1968-73, assoc. prof., 1973-76, prof., 1976-80, Weldon Powell prof. accountancy, 1980-83, A.C. Littleton prof. accountancy, 1983-89; disting. prof. acctg. Pa. State U., University Park, 1989-92, Ernst & Young prof. acctg., 1992-99, Mary Jean and Frank P. Smeal chaired prof. acctg., 1999—. Cons. research, computers; expert witness. Editor: Inflation and Current Value Accounting, 1979; author computer-delivered acctg. course PLATO for Elementary Accounting, 1978; contbr. numerous articles to acad. jours. Recipient Instructional award U. Ill., Urbana-Champaign, 1970, Weldon Powell award, 1973; Fred Roedgers Research award U. Ill., 1978; Ford Found. fellow, 1967-68 Mem. Am. Acctg. Assn. (Manuscript award 1970, Outstanding Acctg. Educator 2003), Am. Statis. Assn., Decision Scis. Inst. Republican. Office: Pa State U 314 Business Bldg University Park PA 16802 Business E-Mail: jcm@psu.edu.

MCKEOWN, JAMES T., lawyer; b. Columbus, Ohio, Aug. 16, 1958; s. James J. and M. Eileen (O'Neill) McK.; m. Kathleen E. McKeown, Dec. 28, 1981; children: Bridget, Caitlin, Neil, Aislinn. BA in Econs., St. John's U., Collegeville, Minn., 1980; JD, U. Minn., 1984, MA in Pub. Affairs, 1985. Bar: Wis. 1984, U.S. Ct. Appeals (7th cir.) 1985, U.S. Dist. Ct. (ea. dist.) Wis. 1985, U.S. Supreme Ct. Law clk. Hon. Harlington Wood, Jr. U.S. Ct. Appeals for 7th Cir., Springfield, Ill., 1984-85; assoc. Foley & Lardner LLP, Milw., 1985-93, ptnr., 1993—, chmn. antitrust practice group. Adj. asst. prof. Marquette U., 1993-95. Contbr. articles to profl. jours. Civil svc. commr. Village of Shorewood, Wis.; fin. com. chmn. St. Robert Parish, Shorewood, 1993-94. Mem. Milw. Young Lawyers Assn. (Svc. award 1991). Office: Foley & Lardner LLP 777 E Wisconsin Ave Ste 3800 Milwaukee WI 53202-5367 Office Phone: 414-297-5530. Business E-Mail: jmckeown@foley.com.

MCKEOWN, LORRAINE LAREDO, travel company executive, writer; b. NYC, Mar. 20, 1928; d. Frank A. and May (Collins) Laredo; m. William Taylor McKeown, July 9, 1964; children: Beth Ellison, Kate Taylor, Suzanne Harris. Talent agt. Carl Eastman, NYC, 1960-65; cooking/travel columnist Camping Jour./Boating Jour., NYC, 1968-70; travel agt. Beecher Travel, NYC, 1968-70; founding ptnr. Computer Travel Info., NYC, 1984, v.p., pres., 1985-90, CEO, 1990—. Contbr. articles to various publs. Bd. dirs. Chapin-Brearley Exch., N.Y.C., 1980, Howland Cultural Ctr., 2002—, Howland Cultural Ctr., 2002—. Mem. Freelance Assocs., Beacon Conservation Coun. Personal E-mail: mckeown6@verizon.net.

MCKEOWN, MARY MARGARET, federal judge; b. Casper, Wyo., May 11, 1951; d. Robert Mark and Evelyn Margaret (Lipsack) McKeown; m. Peter Francis Cowhey, June 29, 1985; 1 child, Megan Margaret. BA in Internat. Affairs and Spanish, U. Wyo., 1972; JD, Georgetown U., 1975. Bar: Wash. 1975, DC 1982. Assoc. Perkins Coie, Seattle, 1975—79, Washington, 1979—80; spl. asst. US Dept. Interior, Washington, 1980—81, The White House, Washington, 1980—81; ptnr., mem. exec. com. Perkins Coie, Seattle, 1981—98, mng. dir. strategic planning and client rels., 1990—95; judge US Ct. Appeals (9th cir.), San Diego, 1998—. Trustee The Pub. Defender, Seattle, 1982—85; rep. 9th Cir. Judicial Conf., San Francisco, 1985—89; mem. gender bias task force, 1992—93; jud. conf. Com. on Codes of Conduct, 2001—; exec. com. 9th Cir., 2001—; lect. U. Wash. Law Sch., 2000—01; adj. prof. U. San Diego, 2003—; bd. dirs. RAND Inst. for Civil Justice, 2003—. Author: Girl Scout's Guide to New York, 1990; contbr. chpt. to book and articles to profl. jours. Nat. bd. dirs. Girl Scouts US, NYC, 1976—87; mem. exec. com. Corp. Coun. for the Arts, Seattle, 1988—98; bd. gen. counsel Downtown Seattle Assn., 1986—89; mem. exec. com. Wash. Coun. Internat. Trade, 1994—; bd. dirs. YMCA Greater Seattle, 1998—, Family Svcs., Seattle, 1982—84. Named one of 100 Young Women of Promise, Good Housekeeping, 1985, Washington's Winningest Trial Lawyers, Washington Jour., 1992, Top 50 Women Lawyers, Nat. Law Jour., 1998; recipient Rising Stars of the 80's award, Legal Times Washington, 1983; fellow Japan leadership, 1992—93. Fellow: ABA (ho. of dels. 1990—, Jud. Adv. Com. to Standing Com. on Ethics 2000—, chair 2002—, Joint Commn. to Evaluate Code of Jud. Conduct 2003—); mem.: Louis M. Welsh Chpt. Am. Inns of Ct., Am. Judicature Soc. (bd. dirs. 2001—), Assn. Bus. Trial Lawyers (bd. dirs. 2003—), Am. Intellectual Property Law Assoc., Am. Law Institute, Nat. Assn. Iolta Programs (bd. dirs. 1989—91), Wash. Women Lawyers (bd. dirs., pres. 1978—79), Legal Found. Wash. (trustee, pres. 1989—90), Seattle-King County Bar Assn. (trustee, sec. 1984—85, Outstanding Lawyer award 1992), Wash. Bar Assn. (chmn. jud. recommendations 1989—90), Fed. Bar Assn. (trustee western dist. Wash. 1980—90), White House Fellows Found. (bd. dirs. 1998—, pres. 2000—01). Avocations: travel, classical piano, hiking, gourmet cooking, tennis. Office: US Ct Appeals 401 West A St Ste 2000 San Diego CA 92101-7908 E-mail: Judge_McKeown@ca9.uscourts.gov. *

MCKEOWN, WILLIAM P., retired lawyer; m. Elizabeth McKeown; 4 children. B Comm., McGill U., Montreal, Que., 1956; LLB, U. Toronto, 1959. Queen's counsel Ont. 1983. Counsel Dept. Health, Province Ont., Toronto, 1962-63, McMillan Binch, Toronto, 1963-64, Can. GE, Toronto, 1965-74; dep. dir. investigation and rsch. Bur. Competition Policy, Ottawa, Ont., 1974-77; ptnr. Stephens French McKeown, Toronto, 1977-86; judge Supreme Ct. Ont., Toronto, 1986-90; judge gen. divsn. Ont. Ct. Justice, Toronto, 1990—93; judge trial divsn. Fed. Ct. Can., Ottawa, Canada, 1993—2002; chmn. Competition Tribunal, Ottawa, 1993—2002; sr. counsel Fasken, Martineau, DuMoulin, LLP, Toronto, 2002—06; ret., 2006. Mem. Toronto Lawyers' Club. E-mail: mckeown41575@rogers.com.

MC KEOWN, WILLIAM TAYLOR, magazine editor, author; b. Ft. Collins, Colo., July 4, 1921; s. Stuart Ellison and Eunice Harris (Akin) Mc K.; m. Lorraine Laredo; children: Elizabeth Ellison, Katherine, Suzanne. AB, Bowdoin Coll., 1942; student, Columbia U. Grad. Sch., 1948. Editor Fawcett Library Series, 1953-56; founding editor True's Boating Yearbook, 1955-56, Popular Boating mag., 1956, editor-in-chief, 1956-62; CEO The Mc Keown Co., NYC, 1993—; editl. dir. Computer Travel Info., 1994—. Travel editor Davis Publs.; outdoor/boating/travel editor Popular Mechanics, 1971-82; sr. editor Outdoor Life, 1983-93. Author weekly NEA syndicated newspaper column American Afloat, 1959-65; contbr. fiction, non-fiction to nat. mags., 1947—; author: Boating Handbook, 1956, Boating in America, 1960. Pilot USAAF, WW II, ETO. Mem. Am. Power Boat Assn., U.S. Power Squadrons, 357 FIghter Group Assn., N.Y. Yacht Club, Overseas Press Club, Royal Danish Yacht Club (Copenhagen), Turtles Internat. Avocation: international competitor in power and sail racing events. Office: The Mc Keown Co 52 Monell Pl Beacon NY 12508-1424

MCKEOWN-MOAK, MARY PARK, educational consultant; d. John Paton and Sophie Cichon Park; m. Lynn Martin Moak, Oct. 4, 1997; children: David Lynn Moak, Susan Marie Moak; m. James Charles McKeown, Jan. 2, 1965 (div.); children: Jeffrey Charles McKeown, Pamela Lynn McKeown; m. Kenneth Forbis Jordan, Jan. 2, 1982 (div. Sept. 1993). BA, MA, Mich. State U., East Lansing, 1966; PhD, U. Ill., Urbana-Champaign, 1974. Cert. tchr. Mich., 1966, real estate agent Ill., 1977. Bus. mgr. U. Ill. Found., Champaign, 1974—77; sch. fin. specialist, asst. prof. pub. adminstrn. Ill. Bd. Edn., Sangamon State U., Springfield, 1977—80; assoc. dir. fin. and facilities Md. State Bd. Higher Edn., Annapolis, 1980—87; dir. strategic planning Ariz. State U., Tempe, 1987—94; assoc. exec. dir., sr. fin. officer Ariz. Bd. Regents, Phoenix, 1994—98; sr. ptnr. MGT, Inc., Austin, Tex., 1998—. Pres. Fiscal Issues Spl. Interest Group Am. Edn. Rsch. Assn., Washington, 1990—91, pres., chair Futures Planning Spl. Interest Group, 1992—93; pres. Am. Edn. Fin. Assn., Denver, 1996—97. Contbr. articles to profl. jours. Pres. Coll. Bus. Faculty Wives, Champaign, 1971—73; troop leader Girl Scouts, Boy Scouts, Champaign, 1974—78; treas. Champaign-Urbana PTA Coun., 1978—80; pres. Alameda Estates Homeowners Assn., Tempe, Ariz., 1988—95, v.p., 1988—95, sec., 1988—95. Mem.: Impact Austin, Assn. Inst. Rsch., Soc. Coll. U. Planning, Nat. Assn. Coll. U. Bus. Officers, Travis Audubon Soc., Phi Delta Kappa (sec. Ariz. chpt. 1987—91). Avocations: gardening, travel, birdwatching. Home: 8800 Gallant Fox Road Austin TX 78737 Office: MGT Am Inc 502 E 11th Street Ste 300 Austin TX 78701 Office Phone: 512-476-4697. Business E-Mail: mmoak@mgtamer.com.

MCKERNS, CHARLES JOSEPH, lawyer; b. Shenandoah, Pa., July 17, 1935; s. Charles Francis and Bridgett Ann (Barrett) McK.; m. Helen Patricia Nott, Feb. 13, 1960; children: Charles J. Jr., Michael H., Patricia B. BS, Georgetown U., 1957, JD, 1960. Bar: D.C. 1960, U.S. Ct. Appeals (D.C. cir.) 1961, U.S. Supreme Ct. 1971, Va. 1992. Law clk. to assoc. judge U.S. Ct. Appeals (D.C. cir), Washington, 1960—61; assoc. Dow, Lohnes & Albertson, Washington, 1961—65, ptnr., 1965—91, of counsel, 1991—95; ptnr. McKerns and McKerns, Heathsville, Va., 1991-96, of counsel, 1996—98. 1st lt. US Army, 1957—59. Mem. ABA, University Club (Washington), Belle Haven Country Club (Alexandria, Va.), Indian Creek Yacht and Country Club (Kilmarnock, Va.). Republican. Roman Catholic. Avocations: hiking, reading, swimming. Home: Windy Blue PO Box 248 Ophelia VA 22530 Office: McKerns Law Office PO Box 220 Heathsville VA 22473-0220 also: Dow Lohnes & Albertson 1200 New Hampshire Ave NW Washington DC 20036-6802 Office Phone: 804-580-8225. Personal E-mail: cmckerns@yahoo.com.

MC KETTA, JOHN J., JR., chemical engineering professor; b. Wyano, Pa., Oct. 17, 1915; s. John J. and Mary (Gelet) McK.; m. Helen Elisabeth Smith, Oct. 17, 1943; children: Charles William, John J. III, Robert Andrew, Mary Anne. BS, Tri-State Coll., Angola, Ind., 1937; BSE., U. Mich., 1943, MS, 1944, PhD, 1946; D.Eng. (hon.), Tri-State Coll., 1965, Drexel U., 1977; Sc.D., U. Toledo, 1973. Diplomate: registered profl. engr., Tex., Mich. Group leader tech. dept. Wyandotte Chem. Corp., Mich., 1937-40, asst. supt. caustic soda div., 1940-41; teaching fellow U. Mich., 1942-44, instr. chem. engring., 1944-45; faculty U. Tex., Austin, 1946—, successively asst. prof. chem. engring., assoc. prof., then prof. chem. engring., 1951-52, 54—, E.P. Schoch prof. chem. engring., 1970-81, Joe C. Walter chair, 1981-94, prof. emeritus, 1994—. Asst. dir. Tex. petroleum research com., 1951-52, 54-56, chmn. chem. engring. dept., mem. bd. regents, Tri State Univ, 56-, disting. service in truteeship, 2002, 1950-52, 55-63, dean Coll. Engring., 1963-69; exec. vice chancellor acad. affairs U. Tex. System, 1969-70; editorial dir. Petroleum Refiner, 1952-54; pres. Chemoil Cons., Inc., 1957-73; chmn. Tex. AEC, So. Interstate Nuclear Bd., 1963-70; mem. Tex. Radiation Adv. Bd., 1978-84; chmn. Nat. Energy Policy Com., 1970-72, Nat. Air Quality Control Com., 1972-85; mem. adv. bd. Carnegie-Mellon Inst. Research, 1978-84; pres. Reagans's rep. on U.S. Acid Precipitation Task Force, 1982-88; apptd. mem. Nuclear Waste Tech. Rev. Bd., 1992-97. Author: series Advances in Petroleum Chemistry and Refining (10 vols.); Chmn. editorial com.: series Petroleum Refiner; mem. adv. bd.: series Internat. Chem. Engring. mag; exec. editor: series Ency. of Chem. Processing and Design (68 vols.). Recipient Bronze plaque Am. Inst. Chem. Engrs., 1952, Charles Schwab award Am. Steel Inst., 1973, Lamme award as outstanding U.S. educator, 1976, Joe J. King Profl. Engring. Achievement award U. Tex., 1976, Gen. Dynamics Teaching Excellence award, 1979, Triple E award for contbns. to nat. issues on energy, environment and econs. Nat. Environ. Devel. Assn., 1976, Boris Pregal Sci. and Tech. award NAS, 1978, Internat. Chem. Engring. award, Italy, 1984, Pres. Herbert Hoover award for advancing well-being of humanity and developing richer and more enduring civilization Joint Engring. Socs., 1989, Centennial award exceptional contbn. Am. Soc. Engring. Edn., 1993; named Disting. Alumnus U. Mich Coll. Engring., 1953, Tri-State Coll., 1956; fellow Allied Chem. & Dye, 1945-46; named Disting. fellow Carnegie-Mellon U., 1978; Chem. Engring. Dept. at U. Tex. named The John J. McKetta Ctr. for Excellence in Chem. Engring. Edn. in his honor, 1995, Chem. Engring. Dept. at Tri State U. named The Dr. John J. McKetta Chem. Engring. Dept. in his honor, 1998. Mem. Am. Chem. Soc. (chmn. Central Tex. sect. 1950), Am. Inst. Chem. Engrs. (chmn. nat. membership com. 1955, regional exec. com., nat. dir., nat. v.p. 1961, pres. 1962, service to soc. award 1975), Am. Soc. Engring. Edn., Chem. Markets Research Assn., Am. Gas Assn. (adv. bd. chems. from gas 1954), Houston C. of C. (chmn. refining div. 1954, vice chmn. research and statistics com. 1954), Engrs. Joint Council (dir.), Engrs. Joint Countil Profl. Devel. (dir. 1963-85), Nat. Acad. Engring., Sigma Xi, Chi Epsilon, Alpha Psi Omega, Tau Omega, Phi Lambda Upsilon, Phi Kappa Phi, Iota Alpha, Omega Chi Epsilon, Tau Beta Pi, Omicron Delta Kappa. Home: 4100 Jackson Ave Apt 229 Austin TX 78731-6070 Office Phone: 512-471-5227. Business E-Mail: mcketta@mail.utexas.edu.

MCKETTA, JOHN J., III, lawyer; b. Austin, Tex., May 5, 1948; s. John J. and Helen Elisabeth (Smith) McK.; m. Sallie Martin Sharp, Aug. 6, 1977; children: Elisabeth, Mary Elliott, Sarah, John. BA, Harvard U., 1969; JD, U. Tex., Austin, 1977. Bar: Tex. 1977, D.C. 1978, U.S. Ct. Appeals (D.C. cir.) 1978, U.S. Dist. Ct. D.C. 1978, U.S. Dist. Ct. (we. dist.) Tex. 1982, U.S. Ct. Appeals (5th cir.) 1982. Assoc. Covington & Burling, Washington, 1977-82, Graves, Dougherty, Hearon & Moody, Austin, Tex., 1982-84, ptnr., 1984—, pres., 1998—. Fellow: Am. Coll. Trial Lawyers; mem.: Am. Law Inst. (coun. 1998—). Democrat. Episcopalian. Office: PO Box 98 Austin TX 78767-0098 Business E-Mail: mmcketta@gdhm.com.

MCKHANN, GUY MEAD, neurologist, educator; b. Boston, Mar. 20, 1932; s. Charles Fremont and Emily (Priest) McKhann; m. Katherine E. Henderson, Nov. 30, 1957 (div. 1983); children: Ian, James, Emily, Guy, Charles; m. Marilyn S. Albert, Sept. 27, 1997; children: Joshua, Katie. Student, Harvard U., 1948—51; MD, Yale U., 1955; MD (hon.), Hebei Med. Coll., Shijiazhuang, China, 1994. Intern N.Y. Hosp., 1955—56; asst. resident pediat. Johns Hopkins Hosp., Balt., 1956—57; clin. assoc. NIH, Bethesda, Md., 1957—60; resident neurology Mass. Gen. Hosp., Boston, 1960—63; asst. and assoc. prof. pediat. and neurology Stanford (Calif.) U., 1963—69; prof. neurology Johns Hopkins, Balt., 1969—, Kennedy prof. neurology, head neurology dept., 1969—88, dir. Zanvyl Krieger Mind Brain Inst., 1988—2000, 2004—; acting dir. for clin. activities Nat. Inst. Neurol. Diseases and Stroke NIH, 2000—01. Prin. investigator Neurologic and Cognitive Outcomes Following Coronary Artery Bypass Grafting; sci.cons. Dana Found.; sci. adv. Brain in the News. Served with USPHS, 1957—60. Named to Macy Faculty Ward, 1982; recipient Med. Student Teaching Award, Medical Student Teaching Award, Johns Hopkins, 197, 1974, Weinstein-Goldenson Rsch. Award, United Cerebral Palsy, 1978, Undergrad. Teaching Award, Johns Hopkins, 1996; scholar in Acad. Medicine, John and Mary R. Markle, 1964—69, Joseph P. Kennedy Jr., 1963—69. Fellow: AAAS, Royal Coll. Physicians; mem.: Inst. Medicine, Soc. Neurosci., Am. Neurol. Assn. (hon.), Am. Neurochem. Soc., Alpha Omega Alpha. Achievements include research in on normal and abnormal human nervous system. Home: 6526 Montrose Ave Baltimore MD 21212-1023 Office: Zanvyl Krieger Mind/Brain Inst 338 Krieger Hall Johns Hopkins U 3400 N Charles St Baltimore MD 21218-2685 Office Phone: 410-516-8640. E-mail: guy.mckhann@jhu.edu. *

MCKIBBEN, HOWARD D., federal judge; b. Apr. 1, 1940; s. James D. and Bernice McKibben; m. Mary Ann McKibben, July 2, 1966; children: Mark, Susan. BS, Bradley U., 1962; MPA, U. Pitts., 1964; JD, U. Mich., 1967. Assoc. George W. Abbott Law Office, 1967-71; dep. dist. atty. Douglas County, Nev., 1969-71, dist. atty. Nev., 1971-77; dist. ct. judge State of Nev., 1977-84; judge U.S. Dist. Ct. Nev., Reno, 1984—. Mem. Nev. Bar Assn., Am. Inns of Ct. (pres. Nev. chpt. 1986-88). Methodist. Avocations: tennis, golf, racquetball. Home: PO Box 588 Verdi NV 89439-0588 Office: US Dist Ct 400 S Virginia St Ste 804 Reno NV 89501-2197

MCKIBBIN, RALPH DAVID, gastroenterologist, consultant; s. Ralph Eddowes, Jr. and Ida Mae McKibbin; m. Eileen Maria Mulligan, July 10, 1983 (div.); children: Ralph Matthew, James Joseph, William Scott. BA, U. Pa., Phila., 1981; MD, Hahnemann U., Phila., 1986. Diplomate Am. Bd. Internal Medicine, 1987, Am. Bd. Gastroenterology, 1993. Intern in internal medicine Hahnemann U. Hosp., Phila., 1986—87, resident in internal medicine, 1987—89, chief resident in internal medicine, 1989—90, fellow in gastroenterology; gastroenterologist Blair Gastroenterology Assocs., Altoona, Pa., 1992—, Cons. McKibbin Enterprises, LLC, Altoona, 2002—; ptnr. McKibbin Food Svcs., LLC, State College, Pa., 2003—. Contbr. articles to profl. jours. Founder, mng. dir. Colon Cancer Prevention Found., Altoona, 2001—07. Named Resident of the Yr., Hahnemann U. Hosp., 1989; recipient Acad. Honors in Pathology, 1989, Kamarov prize competition, 1992. Fellow: ACP; mem.: AMA, NRA (life), Assn. Clin. Rsch. Profls., Am. Gastroent. Assn., Am. Coll. Physician Execs., Safari Club Internat., Alpha Epsilon Delta. Independent. Buddhist. Avocations: travel, hunting, fishing. Office: Blair Gastroenterology Assocs 810 Valley View Blvd Altoona PA 16602 Home Phone: 814-941-0633; Office Phone: 814-946-5469.

MCKIBBIN, WILLIAM ALEX, artist; b. Phila., May 7, 1940; s. William A. and Jane Harrison (Pippin) McK.; m. Dorothy K. McKibbin, Jan. 26, 1963; children: Erin P., William Alex IV. Student, Barnes Found., Merion, Pa., 1958-59, 60-61; BFA, Temple U., Phila., 1963; MFA, The Claremont Grad. Sch., 1965; postgrad., U. Hartford, Conn., 1967-68. Instr. Mt. Pleasant (Del.) Jr. High Sch., 1965-66, U. Hartford Coll. Basic Studies, 1966-68; instr. evening divsn. Cen. Conn. State Coll., 1967-68; instr. Aegean Sch. Fine Arts, Paros, Greece, summers 1967-68; asst. prof. Western Coll., 1968-74, acting chair, 1968, 69, 70-71; instr. Cin. Art Acad., 1972-74; asst. prof. Miami U., Oxford, Ohio, 1974-77, assoc. prof., 1977-84, full prof., 1984—. Juried various exhbns. throughout U.S. One-man shows at Evansville (Ind.) Mus. Arts and Scis., Main Artist Gallery, 1985, Museum of the Maya Culture, Chetumal, Q.R., Mex., 2002, Casa de la Cultura de Cancun, Mex., 2001, Carrollton Cultural Art Ctr., Ga., 2006, Cultural Arts Coun. Douglasville, Douglas County, Ga., 2006, Springfield Art Mys., Mo., 2007; exhibited in over 200 exhbns. including group shows at East Carolina U., Greenville, N.C., 1981, Second Crossing Gallery, Valley City, N.D., 1981, 93, Okla. Art Ctr., Oklahoma City, 1981-82, U. N.D., Grand Forks, 1982, 85, Art Chgo. Internat. Art Expo, 1982-90, Trenton (N.J.) State Coll., 1983, Fort Hays (Kans.) State U., 1984, 88, Owensboro (Ky.) Mus. Fine Arts, 1984, Middletown (Ohio) Fine Arts Ctr., 1985, Cameron U., 1986, Springfield (Mo.) Art Mus., 1988-90, 94, 2003, La Fond Galleries, Inc., Pitts., 1994, numerous others; represented by Zaks Gallery, Chgo., The Art Exch., Columbus, Boody Fine Arts, Inc., St. Louis, Nancy Mulle Assocs., Cleve., Steinway Gallery, Chapel, N.C., Yvonne Rapp Gallery, Louisville, Orbe Gallery, Cancun, Mex., Gallery Henoch, N.Y.C.; pub. collections include Pomona Coll., Claremont, Calif., Thomas More Coll., Ft. Mitchell, Ky., The Springfield Mus., Ind. U. East, Richmond, Evansville (Ind.) Mus. Art and Sci., Art Ctr., Inc., South Bend, Ind., Cin. Art Mus., Grinnell (Iowa) Coll., Ft. Hays State U., Hays, Kans., Des Moines Art Ctr., Charles H. MacNider Mus., Mason City, Iowa, Ohio State U., Columbus, Clark State U., Springfield, Ohio, U. N.C., Chapel Hill, Ohio State U. Law Sch., So. Alleghenies Mus. of Art, Loretto, Pa., Blanden Meml. Art Mus., Ft. Dodge, Iowa, Ark. Arts Ctr., Little Rock, Taos Art Mus., Taos, N.Mex., Casa de la Cultura de Cancun, Mex., Fitton Ctr. for Creative Arts, Hamilton, Ohio; pvt. collections, 70 corporate collections; reprodns. of work appear in (books) Watercolor Bold and Free, 1980, Figure Drawing, 5th edit., 2000, The Watercolor Solution Book, 1988, Splash I, 1990, The Art of Responsive Drawing, 1992, Splash II, 1993, Watercolor Step-By-Step, 1993, Watercolor School, 1993, Collins' Artist's Manual, 1995, Splash IV, 1995, The Encyclopedia of Watercolour Landscape Techniques, 1996, Painting Shapes and Edges, 1996, North Light Illustrated Book of Watercolor Techniques, Splash VIII, 2004; (mags.) Artist's Mag., The Bull., Jiangsu Pictorial, China, Watercolor Magic, Tropo a la una, Cancun, Mex., Internat. Artist, 2000, Vibrant Watercolours, 2006; work included as cover art on CDs Music for Winds, The Miami Wind Quintet, Vol. 1, 1995, Vol. 2, 1996. Recipient Cert. of Merit Tyler Sch. of Art Temple U., Gen. Alumni Assn., 1991, First State Bank award for watercolor Vechten-Lineberry, Taos Art Mus., 18 cash and purchase awards from various orgns. Studio: PO Box 31 77760 Akumal QR Mexico Office: 435 Tacoma Ave Buffalo NY 14216 Home: 199 Berkley Dr Villa Rica GA 30180-2400

MCKILLIP, PATRICIA CLAIRE, operatic soloist; b. Milw., Apr. 28; d. Lester J. and Ruth J. (Lohneis) McK.; m. Mark Richard McKillip, June 16, 1990. BA in English-Drama, Creative Writing, Lit., Alverno Coll., 1980, MusB in Applied Music, 1981; postgrad., Wis. Conservatory of Music, 1981-82; MS in Fine Arts Edn., U. Wis., Milw., 1996; postgrad., The Juilliard Sch., 1982-84, Am. Acad. Dramatic Arts, 1983-84, Adelphi U., 1984; MA in English-Creative Writing and Lit., U. Wis., Milw., 1997; postgrad., Milw. Inst. Art and Design, 2003—. Soloist Amadeus Opera Co.; instr. vocal music seminars various high schs., NY. Co-founder, co-dir. The Masque Consort, N.Y.C., 1990-91, exec. v.p., 1991; v.p., co-founder Creative Learning Assocs.; instr. Cardinal Stritch Coll., Milw., 1994—. Performer Florentine Opera Co., Music Under the Stars Prodns., Milw. Opera Co., Westchester Lyric Opera Co., Profl. Opera Workshop at Lincoln Ctr., Met. Opera Co., N.Y. Grand Opera Co., Monteverdi Opera Guild Prodns., Republic Opera Co., La Puma Opera Co., others; puppeteer, costumer, designer Puppet Art Troupe; author: (poetry and artwork) Springdrift, 2003; author numerous poems. Exec. v.p. Masque Consort, a multi-media theatrical orgn. Music dept. scholar Alverno U.; named Woman of Yr., Am. Biographical Inst. Bd. Internat. Rsch., 2003. Mem. AFTRA, SAG, Nat. Assn. Music Tchrs., Music Educators Nat. Conf. (treas.), Internat. Platform Assn., Wis. Fedn. Music Clubs, Music Clubs Am., Am. Guild Mus. Artists, Q'ahal-Liturgical Music Soc., Acad. Am. Poets, Milw. Artists Resource Network, Walker's Point Ctr. for Arts, Delta Omicron (v.p., chaplain, warden Gamma Gamma chpt., WMA State and Regional Vocal award 1978, Star of Delta Omicron award 1980, 40 music medals from state and dist. WSMA), Alpha Sigma Tau. Democrat. Roman Catholic. Avocations: dance, creative writing, art. Home: 4860 S 69th St Greenfield WI 53220-4452 Personal E-mail: celticdramaticsoprano@yahoo.com.

MCKIM, PAUL ARTHUR, management consultant, retired gas industry executive; b. Milford, Conn., Feb. 1, 1923; s. Arthur and Helen Agnes McK.; m. Daisy Flora Brown, June 18, 1945; 1 dau., Meredith Ann. Student, Lamar Inst. Tech., 1940-42; BS in Chem. Engring., La. State U.,

1943, MS, 1947, PhD, 1949; grad. Advanced Mgmt. Program, Harvard, 1959; grad. Aspen Inst. Humanistic Studies Exec. Program, 1970. With Ethyl Corp., 1949-62, asst. gen. mgr. research and devel. operations, 1958-62; v.p., gen. mgr. rsch. and devel. Atlantic Refining Co., Phila., 1962-66; v.p. Atlantic Richfield Co., 1966-78; v.p. comml. devel. Arco Chem. Co., 1966-69, v.p. nuclear operations and comml. devel., 1969-73; exec. v.p. Sinclair Koppers Co., 1973; pres. Arco Polymers, Inc., 1974-78; asst. to pres. Tex. Eastern Corp., 1978-80, v.p., 1980-84, sr. v.p., 1985-88. Chmn. US Organizing com. for 12th World Petroleum Congress, Houston, 1987. Past chmn. bd. mgrs. Franklin Inst. Research Labs; past vice chmn. bd. mgrs. Spring Garden Coll., Phila. Coll. Art.; past vice chmn. World Affairs Council of Phila. Served to lt. (j.g.) USNR, 1944-46. Mem. AIChE, Alpha Chi Sigma, Omicron Delta Kappa, Tau Beta Pi, Phi Lambda Upsilon, Phi Kappa Phi, Delta Kappa Epsilon. Home: Sterling Glen of Darien 50 Ledge Rd Apt 252 Darien CT 06820 Personal E-mail: paulmckim@yahoo.com.

MCKIM, RUTH ANN, financial planner; b. Keokuk, Iowa, Nov. 26, 1932; d. Carl Edward and Ruby Irene (Martin) McKim; m. William James Ashbrook, Aug. 15, 1959 (div. 1974); children: Leslie, Diane Hodges. BS, U. Louisville, 1955, MS in Cmty. Devel., 1977. Dir. art therapy Ky. Bapt. Hosp., Louisville, 1955—56; co-dir. art therapy Norton-Children's Hosps. Inc., 1956—57; dir. art therapy NKC Hosps., 1957—59; rschr. Bd. Aldermen, 1976; pub. rels. staff Dept. Consumer Affairs, 1976—78; realtor assoc. Century 21, 1979—86; fin. planner Nat. Life Vt., 1986—. Tutor Ky. Assn. Specific Perceptual-Motor Disability, Louisville, 1970—74. Author: Banking Survey, 1977. Arts festival com., 1975—77; coord. Louisville Food Day, 1978; vol. and art donor PBS, 1985—88; voter registration canvasser, 1976, 1978, 1982; active Rep. Nat. Com., Rep. Presdl. Task Force, Nat. Rep. Senatorial Com., Nat. Rep. Congl. Com. Com.; sec., treas. St. Francis in the Fields Espicopal Ch., Louisville, 1975—76. Recipient Rep. Presdl. Legion of Merit medal, Order of Merit; scholar Allen R. Hite Art Inst., 1952—54; Bd. Realtors scholar, 1979—. Mem.: Inst. Community Devel. Assn., Ky. Artists and Craftsmen, Louisville Craftsmans Guild (life), U. Louisville Alumni Assn. Republican. Episcopalian. Avocation: oil and acrylic painting. Home: No 43 410 Mockingbird Valley Rd Louisville KY 40207-1318

MCKIM, SAMUEL JOHN, III, lawyer; b. Pitts., Dec. 31, 1938; s. Samuel John and Harriet Frieda (Roehl) McK; children: David Hunt, Andrew John; m. Eugenia A. Leverich. AA cum laude, Port Huron Jr. Coll., 1959; BA cum laude, U. Mich., 1961, JD cum laude, 1964. Bar: Mich. 1965, US Dist. Ct. (so. dist.) Mich. 1965, US Ct. Appeals (6th cir.) 1969, US Supreme Ct. 1994. Assoc. Miller, Canfield, Paddock and Stone, PLC, Detroit, Bloomfield Hills, 1964-71, sr. mem., 1971—, head state and local tax sect., 1985—, chmn. tax dept., 1989-94, mng. ptnr., 1979-85, chmn., mng. ptnr., 1984-85. Mem. tax coun. State Bar Mich., 1981-94, chmn. state and local tax com. real property sect., 1982-90; adj. prof. law sch. Wayne State U., 1993-. Assoc. editor Mich. Law Rev. Bd. dirs., past chmn. Goodwill Industries of Greater Detroit, 1970-2000; dir. Goodwill Industries Found., 1982-95; Stevens min., commd. lay assoc. pastor First Presbyn. Ch., Lapeer, Mich. Fellow: Am. Coll. Tax Counsel; mem.: ABA, Barrister's Soc., Detroit Bar Assn., Mich. Bar Assn., Mariner Sands Country Club, Port Huron Golf Club, Order of Coif, Phi Delta Phi. Home (Summer): 8351 Lakeshore Rd Lexington MI 48450 Home (Winter): 6403 SE Brandywine Ct # 124 Stuart FL 34994 Office: Miller Canfield Paddock & Stone 150 W Jefferson Ave Ste 2500 Detroit MI 48226-4416 Office Phone: 313-496-7546. Business E-Mail: mckim@millercanfield.com.

MCKINLEY, ANNE C., lawyer; b. 1974; m. John R. Wickstrom, May 6, 2000. BA, Northwestern U., 1996; grad., U. Ill. Coll. Law. With US SEC, Chgo., 1998—, br. chief enforcement divsn., 2003—. Named one of 40 Under 40, Crain's Chgo. Bus., 2006. Office: US SEC Midwest Regional Office Ste 900 175 W Jackson Blvd Chicago IL 60604 Office Phone: 312-353-7390. E-mail: chicago@sec.gov.

MCKINLEY, CAMERON SHARBEL, elementary school educator; married. BA in Corp. Fin., Mktg. magna cum laude, Univ. Ala. Nat. Bd. Cert. Tech. tchr. Riverchase Elem. Sch., Hoover, Ala. Named Ala. Elem. Tchr. of Yr., 2006, Ala. Tchr. of Yr., 2007. Office: Riverchase Elem Sch 1950 Old Montgomery Hwy Birmingham AL 35244 Office Phone: 205-402-0509. Business E-Mail: camruns@gmail.com. *

MCKINLEY, CRAIG R., career military officer; BSBA, So. Meth. U., 1974; MS in Mgmt. and Econs., Webster Coll., 1979; postgrad., Squadron Officer Sch., 1984, Air Command and State Coll., 1990; postgrad. in Nat. Security Strategy, Nat. War Coll., 1995; postgrad., Nat. Security Mgmt. Course, Syracuse, NY, 1997, Capstone, Ft. Lesley J. McNair, Washington, 1998, Combined Forces Air Component Comdr. Course, Maxwell AFB, Ala., 2002, US-Russia Security Program, Harvard U., 2004. Commd. 2nd lt. USAF, 1974, advanced through grades to lt. gen., 2006, T-38 instr. pilot Craig AFB, Ala., 1975-77, comdr. air force mil. tng. ctr. Lackland AFB, Tex., 1977-78, T-38 instr. pilot Laughlin AFB, Tex., 1978-80, F-106 alert pilot 125th Fighter Interceptor Group Jacksonville, Fla., 1980-82, F-106 instr. pilot, chief of safety 125th Fighter Interceptor Group, 1982-87, F-16 instr. pilot, chief of standardization/evaluation 125th Fighter Interceptor Group, 1987-88, dep. comdr. ops. 125th Fighter Interceptor Group, 1988-91, group comdr. 125th Fighter Interceptor Group, 1991-94, wing comdr. 125th Fighter Interceptor Wing, 1995-96, vice comdr. Southeast Air Def. Sector Tyndall AFB, Fla., 1996, comdr. Southeast Air Def. Sector, 1996-98; dep. dir. Air Nat. Guard, Arlington, Va., 1998—2001; comdr. Air Nat. Guard Readiness Ctr., Andrews AFB, Md., 1998—2001; dep. insp. gen. USAF, Washington, 2001—02, comdr. 1st Air Force, Air Combat Command, comdr. continental US NORAD region Tyndall, Fla., 2002—04; dir., mobilization & reserve affairs directorate US European Command, Stuttgart-Vaihingen, Germany, 2004—05; asst. dep. chief of staff for plans & programs USAF, Washington, 2005—06; dir. Air Nat. Guard, Arlington, Va., 2006—. Decorated Def. Disting. Svc. medal, Disting. Svc. medal with oak leaf cluster, Def. Superior Svc. medal, Legion of Merit, Meritorious Svc. medal with two oak leaf clusters, Air Force Tng. Ribbon, Armed Force Res. medal, Air Force Commendation medal with two oak leaf cluster, Air Force Achievement medal with two oak leaf clusters, Air Force Outstanding Unit award, Combat Readiness medal with four oak leaf clusters, Nat. Def. Svc. medal with bronze star, Global War on Terroris, Svc. medal, Humanitarian Svc. medal, Air Force Longvity Svc. award with silver oak leaf cluster, Armed Forces Reserve meal with silver hourglass; Recipient I.G. Brown trophy, 1993, Disting. Alumni award So. Methodist U., 2003. Office: Air Nat Guard 1411 Jefferson Davis Hwy Arlington VA 22202-3231

MCKINLEY, ELLEN BACON, priest; b. Milw., June 9, 1929; d. Edward Alsted and Lorraine Goodrich (Graham) Bacon; m. Richard Smallbrook McKinley, III, June 16, 1951 (div. Oct. 1977); children: Richard, Ellen Graham, David Todd, Edward Bacon. BA cum laude, Bryn Mawr Coll., 1951; MDiv, Yale U., 1976; STM, Gen. Theol. Sem., NYC, 1979; PhD, Union Theol. Sem., NYC, 1988. Ordained deacon Episcopal Ch., 1980, as priest Episcopal Ch., 1981. Intern St. Francis Ch., Stamford, Conn., 1976-77; pastoral asst. St. Paul's Ch., Riverside, Conn., 1979-80, curate, 1980-81; asst. St. Saviour's Ch., Old Greenwich, Conn., 1982-90; interim asst. Trinity Ch., Princeton, NJ, 1990—91; priest assoc. All Saints Ch., Princeton, NJ, 1992—97, St. Christophers Ch., Chatham, Mass., 1997—. Episc. election com. Diocese of Conn., 1986—87, com. on human sexuality, 1987—90, donations and bequests com., 1987—90; major chpt. mem. Trinity Cathedral, Trenton, NJ, 1992—96; interim rector All Saints Ch., Princeton, NJ, 1993. Sec. Greenwich Com. Drugs, 1970—71; active Episcopal Women's Caucus; bd. dirs. Greenwich YWCA, 1971—72, Chatham Old Village Assn., 1998—2004. Mem.: Colonial Dames Am.

MCKINLEY, JAMES FRANK, JR., retired manufacturing executive; b. Chgo., Feb. 17, 1943; s. James F. Sr. and Annabell I. (Williams) McK.; m. Sharon M., Dec. 7, 1968; children: James P., Scott J., Rebecca L. BS, Monmouth Coll., Ill., 1964; MS, Ill. Inst. Tech., Chgo., 1966; MBA, Stanford U., Calif., 1987. Salesman Joseph T. Ryerson & Son, Chgo., 1961-66, Scot Forge Co., Cicero, Ill., 1966-71, v.p. sales, 1971-76, exec. v.p., 1976-85, pres., COO, 1985-92, pres., CEO, COO, 1992—; pres., bd. dirs. Ringmasters (formerly Ovaco Ajax), Wayne, Mich., 1996—; ptnr. N.Am. Forgemasters, 1997, vice-chmn., 2001, ret., 2002; owner Classic Electric Boats, 2004—. Dir. Fox Waterway Agy., state office, 1997—, chmn. 2000—. Capt. USCG Aux., Fox Lake, Ill., 1985—; dir. Allendale Sch., Lake Villa, Ill., 1983-96; regent Milw. Sch. Engring., 1995; McHenry County mem. Sheriff Merit Commn., 2000. Mem. Am. Soc. Metals, Forging Industry Rsch. Found., Forging Industry Assn. (bd. dirs. 1986—, gov. coun. 1990—, dir. 1998, v.p. 1999, pres. 2000—), Ill. St. Andrews Soc. (bd. govs., v.p. 1996-97), Profl. Capts. Assn., McHenry C. of C. (chmn. 1999). Republican. Avocations: boating, skiing, scuba diving, golf. Office Phone: 715-356-9483. Personal E-mail: jmkinleyjr@msn.com.

MCKINLEY, JIMMIE JOE, small business owner; b. Bertram, Tex., July 23, 1934; s. Joseph Crofford and Velma Anne (Barnett) McK. AA, Kilgore Coll., Tex., 1953; BJ, U. Tex., Austin, 1955; MS, U. Ky., Lexington, 1964. Asst. libr. Bethel Coll., McKenzie, Tenn., 1961—63, reference libr., 1966—70, acting head libr., 1970—71; owner, mgr. Longview Book Co., Tex., 1974—. Former mem., bd. dirs. Longview-Piney Woods chpt. ARC; trustee Bethel Coll., 1977-86. Mem. East Tex. Hist. Assn., Gregg County Hist. Soc., Burnet County Heritage Soc., History Club East Tex., East Tex. Oil Mus. Guild (pres. 1996-97), Kilgore Hist. Preservation Found., U.S. Lighthouse Soc. Presbyn. Office: PO Box 1748 Longview TX 75606-1748

MCKINLEY, JOHN, information technology executive; Grad., U. Pa., 1979. With Ernst & Young LLP, 1982—95, ptnr., 1992; sr. v.p., chief tech. and information officers GE Capital Corp., 1995; sr. v.p., chief tech. officer Merrill Lynch & Co., 1998, exec. v.p., head global technology and svcs.; chief tech. officer, pres. AOL Technologies AOL, Dulles, Va., 2003—04, pres. digital services bus., 2004—, interim chief tech. officer, 2006—. Office: AOL 22000 AOL Way Dulles VA 20166 Office Phone: 703-265-1000. Office Fax: 703-265-1101.

MC KINLEY, JOHN KEY, retired oil company executive; b. Tuscaloosa, Ala., Mar. 24, 1920; s. Virgil Parks and Mary Emma (Key) McK.; m. Helen Grace Heare, July 19, 1946; children: John Key Jr., Mark Charles. BS in Chem. Engring, U. Ala., 1940, MS in Organic Chemistry, 1941, LL.D. (hon.), 1972; grad., Advanced Mgmt. Program, Harvard U., 1962; LL.D. (hon.), Troy State U., 1974. Registered profl. engr., Tex. With Texaco Inc., 1941-86, asst. dir. research Beacon, NY, 1957-59, asst. to v.p., 1959-60, mgr. comml. devel., 1960, gen. mgr. petrochem. dept. NYC, 1960-67, v.p. petrochem. dept., v.p. in charge supply and distbn., 1967-71, sr. v.p. worldwide refining, petrochems., also supply and distbn., 1971, pres., dir., 1971-80, pres., chief operating officer, chmn. exec. com., 1980, chmn. bd., pres., chief exec. officer, 1980-83, chmn. bd., chief exec. officer, 1983-86, ret., 1986. Bd. dirs. emeritus Federated Dept. Stores, Inc. Patentee for chem. processing. Hon. bd. dirs. Met. Opera Assocs.; nat. chmn. Met. Opera Centennial Fund, 1980; bd. dirs. The Ams. Soc.; mem. Bus. Coun. Maj. AUS, 1941-45, ETO. Decorated Bronze Star; recipient George Washington Honor medal Freedoms Found., 1972; Andrew Wellington Cordier fellow Columbia U.; named to Ala. Bus. Hall of Fame, 1982, Ala. Acad. Honor, 1983, State of Ala. Engring. Hall of Fame, 1992. Fellow Am. Inst. Chem. Engrs.; mem. Am. Petroleum Inst. (hon. dir.), Wee Burn Country Club, Brook Club, Augusta Nat. Golf Club, Blind Brook Country Club, North River Yacht, Sigma Xi, Tau Beta Pi, Gamma Sigma Epsilon, Kappa Sigma. Office: 1 Canterbury Grn Stamford CT 06901-2032 Office Phone: 203-967-3000.

MCKINLEY, LORI, education educator; b. Tuscumbia, Mo., July 23, 1957; d. Luchin Lymoin and Lura Maxine McKinley; children: Dana Michelle Petrechko, Jonathan Lukas Petrechko, Daniel Ryan Petrechko. BA in Psychology, U. Mo., Columbia, 1979, MEd in Counseling, 1982, PhD, 2003. Program specialist Dept. Mental Health, Jefferson City, Mo., 1989—90; counselor U. Hosp. and Clinics, Columbia, Mo., 1990—93; adj. prof. Columbia Coll., 1995—96; project devel. specialist U. Mo., Columbia, 1997—2003, rsch. asst. prof., 2003—. Recipient Donald K. Anderson Tchg. award, U. Mo., 1996. Mem.: Rotary, Nat. Alliance for Mentally Ill (assoc.). Office: Univ Mo-Columbia 3 Hospital Dr Rm 135 Columbia MO 65211 Home Phone: 573-529-6857; Office Phone: 573-882-1498. Home Fax: 573-884-1010. Personal E-mail: mckinleyda@health.missouri.edu.

MCKINLEY-HAAS, MARY, artist; b. St. Louis; d. Lee Carrington and Florence (Dowden) McK.; m. Saul Haas; children: Christopher, Matthew. BA, Smith Coll.; student, Art Students League, 1973—74, Nat. Acad. Design, 1965—66, Studio and Forum Stage Design. Head costume design dept. ABC-TV, NYC, 1968-73. One-woman shows include Tarlowe Gallery, Westhampton Beach, NY, 1974, Fontbonne Gallery, St. Louis, 1977, Gallery Yssa, NYC, 1979, Vered Gallery, East Hampton, NY, 1981, Netherlands Bank & Ludlow-Hyland Gallery, NYC, 1981, U. Tex., Austin, 1988, RVS Fine Art, Southampton, NY, 1990, TSS Gallery, NYC, 1992, U. Tex., Austin, 1992, TAI Gallery, NYC, 1999, Ezair Gallery, NYC, 2007; exhibited in group shows at Guild Hall, East Hampton, 1974-76, 78, 81, 85, 96, Parrish Art Mus., Southampton, 1975-76, 78, 81, Water Mill Mus., 1983, 92, Vared Gallery, East Hampton, 1985, Lincoln Ctr., NYC, 1989-90, Queens Coll. Art Ctr., Flushing, NY, 1991, Dorothy Chandler Pavillion, LA, 1993, Stony Brook U. Art Gallery, NY, 1994, Women in Art and Culture, Beijing, 1995, Elite Gallery, Moscow, 1995, Nat. Mus. Women in Arts, Washington, 1996, Soho 20 Gallery, NYC, 1998—, Canajoharie Libr. and Art Ctr., NY, 2000, Weill Cornell Med. Libr., NYC, 2002, Noho-NY Art Walk, 2004-05, 07, Venezuelan Consulate, NYC, 2006-07, others; represented in permanent collections at Nat. Mus. Women in Arts, Washington, Tari Women's Cultural Ctr., Papua, New Guinea, Fontbonne Coll., St. Louis, No. Trust Naples, Fla.; pvt. collections; costume designer for Broadway and network TV shows, Harkness Ballet, Holiday on Ice, others. Mem. United Scenic Artists, Women in the Arts, N.Y. Artists Equity. Office: 284 Lafayette St Loft 5B New York NY 10012-3303 Office Phone: 212-334-8030.

MCKINNELL, HANK (HENRY A. MCKINNELL JR.), pharmaceutical executive; b. Victoria, BC, Can., Feb. 23, 1943; 4 children. BA, U. BC, 1965; MBA, Stanford U., 1967, PhD in Bus., 1969. Joined Pfizer, Inc., Tokyo, 1971; pres. Pfizer Asia, Hong Kong; chief fin. officer, pres. med. technology group Pfizer, Inc., exec. v.p., 1992—99; pres. Pfizer Pharms. Group, prin. oper. divsn., 1997—2001; COO Pfizer, Inc., NYC, 1999—2000, pres., 1999—2001, chmn., CEO, 2001—06, chmn., 2006, bd. dir., 1997—. Mem. Presidential Advisory Council on HIV/AIDS; bd. dirs. ExxonMobil Corp., Moody's Corp., John Wiley & Sons, Inc., Trilateral Commn., Bus. Coun.; chmn. Bus. Roundtable, 2003—06; chmn. emeritus Pharm. Rsch. and Mfrs. of Am.; vice chmn. Com. Econ. Devel.; chmn. Food and Drug Law Inst. Bd. trustee NY Pub. Libr., NYC Police Found., Econ. Club of NY; chmn. Stanford U. Grad. Sch. of Bus. Adv. Coun.; chmn. emeritus, Bus.-Higher Edu. Forum. Fellow, NY Acad. of Medicine. Office: Pfizer Inc Bd Directors 235 E 42d St New York NY 10017-5755 *

MCKINNELL, ROBERT GILMORE, retired zoologist, biology professor, geneticist; b. Springfield, Mo., Aug. 9, 1926; s. William Parks and Mary Catherine (Gilmore) McK.; m. Beverly Walton Kerr, Jan. 24, 1964; children: Nancy Elizabeth, Robert Gilmore, Susan Kerr. B in Naval Sci., U. Notre Dame, 1946; AB, U. Mo., 1948; BS, Drury Coll., 1949, DSc (hon.), 1993; PhD, U. Minn., 1959. Rsch. assoc. Fox Chase Cancer Ctr., Phila., 1958-61; asst. prof. biology Tulane U., New Orleans, 1961-65, assoc. prof., 1965-69, prof., 1969-70; prof. zoology U. Minn., Mpls., 1970—76, prof. genetics and cell biology St. Paul, 1976—99, prof. emeritus, 1999—. Vis. scientist Dow Chem. Co., Freeport, Tex., 1976; guest dept. zoology U. Calif., Berkeley, 1979; Royal Soc. guest rsch. fellow Nuffield dept. pathology John Radcliffe Hosp., Oxford U., 1981-82; NATO vis. scientist Akademisch Ziekenhuis, Ghent, Belgium, 1984; faculty rsch. assoc. Naval Med. Rsch. Inst., Bethesda, Md., 1988; secretariat Third Internat. Conf. Differentiation, 1978; organizer, secretariat 6th Internat. Conf. on Pathology of Reptiles and Amphibians, 2001; mem. amphibian com. Inst. Lab. Animal Resources, NRC, 1970-73, mem. adv. coun., 1974; mem. panel genetic and cellular resources program NIH, 1981-82, spl. study sect., Bethesda, 1990. Author: Cloning: Amphibian Nuclear Transplantation, 1978, Cloning, A Biologist Reports, 1979; sr. editor: Differentiation and Neoplasia, 1980, Cloning: Leben aus der Retorte, 1981, Cloning of Frogs, Mice and Other Animals, 1985, (with others) The Biological Basis of Cancer, 1998, 2d edit., 2006, (with D.L. Carlson) Pathology of Reptiles and Amphibians, 2002, also symposium procs. in field; mem. bd. advisors Marquis Who's Who; contbr. articles to profl. jours. Served to lt. USNR, 1944-47, 51-53. Recipient Outstanding Teaching award Newcomb Coll., Tulane U., 1970; Disting. Alumni award Drury Coll., 1979, Morse Alumni Tchg. award U. Minn., 1992; Rsch. fellow Nat. Cancer Inst., 1956-58, Prince Hitachi award Japanese Found. Cancer Rsch., 1998; Sr. Sci. fellow NATO, 1974. Fellow AAAS, Linnean Soc. (London); mem. Am. Assn. Cancer Rsch. (emeritus), Am. Assn. Cancer Edn. (sr.), Am. Assn. History of Medicine, Indian Soc. Devel. Biology (lifetime emeritus), Internat. Soc. Differentiation (pres. 1994-96), Minn. Acad. Medicine, Gown-in-Town Club, Sigma Xi. Office: 140 Gortner Lab Biochemistry 1479 Gortner Ave Saint Paul MN 55108 Home Phone: 651-646-3690. Business E-Mail: mckin002@umn.edu.

MCKINNEY, ALEXANDER STUART, retired neurologist; b. NYC, Feb. 3, 1933; s. John McDowell and Katherine Elizabeth (Morse) McK.; m. Carolyn Clifton Braman, Aug. 15, 1958 (div. July 1985); children: James, David, Mark; m. Susan Lowe Childress, July 30, 1985; children: Josephine, Mary, Jennifer. AB, Princeton U., 1955; MD, Columbia U., 1959. Diplomate Am. Bd. Neurology. Intern St. Luke's Hosp., NYC, 1959-60; resident N.Y. Neurological Inst., 1960-63; prof. neurology Emory U., Atlanta, 1965-85; pvt. practice Mountain Med. Assocs., Clyde, N.C., 1985-95; chief of staff Haywood County Hosp., Clyde, N.C., 1989-90. Contbr. articles to profl. jours. Served to lt. comdr. USNR, 1963-65. Fellow Am. Acad. Neurology (sr.); mem. N.C. Neurol. Soc. (pres. 1992). Avocations: travel, gardening. Home: 9 Charles Wesley Dr Waynesville NC 28786-3066 Personal E-mail: smsck@charter.net.

MCKINNEY, CYNTHIA ANN, former congresswoman; b. Atlanta, Ga., Mar. 17, 1955; d. Billy and Leola McKinney; 1 child, Coy Grandison. BA in internat. rels., U. So. Calif., 1978; MA, Tufts U. Fletcher Sch. Law & Diplomacy; postgrad., Ga. State U., U. Wis. Former instr. Clark Atlanta U., Atlanta Met. Coll.; mem. Ga. Ho. Reps., 1988-92, US Congress from 4th Ga. dist., 1993—2003, 2005—07, mem. com. on armed svc., com. on budget. Mem. HIV Health Services Planning Coun., Atlanta, 1991—92; Frank H.T. Rhodes vis. prof. Cornell U., Ithaca, NY, 2003—04. Named a Diplomatic fellow, Spellman Coll., 1984; named one of Most Influential Black Americans, Ebony mag., 2006; recipient Edgar Wayburn award, Sierra Club, 1998, Outstanding Contribution award, Nat. Orgn. Sierra Leonians in N Am., 2000. Mem.: Progressive Caucus, Congl. Black Caucus, Agrl. Com., Sierra Club, Nat. Coun. Negro Women, Metro Atlanta, NAACP. Democrat. Roman Catholic. Achievements include the first African American woman elected to Congress from Georgia. Office: N DeKalb Mall Ste D-46 2050 Lawerenceville Hwy Decatur GA 30033 Office Phone: 202-225-1605. Office Fax: 202-226-0691. *

MCKINNEY, DAVID DUANE, museum director, architectural historian; b. Danville, Va., Nov. 14, 1956; s. Lafayette Wadsworth and Katie Jones McKinney. AB in History, Coll. William & Mary, 1979; MA in Archtl. History, U. Va., 1984, PhD in Archtl. History, 1992. Archivist, asst. curator Ash Lawn Coll. William & Mary, Charlottesville, 1981—84; reference staff Alderman Libr. U. Va., Charlottesville, 1984—91; dir. programming Very Spl. Arts, Washington, 1991—95; instrnl. designer, sr. scientist Human Resources Rsch. Orgn., Alexandria, Va., 1995—97; dir. statewide partnerships Va. Mus. Fine Arts, Richmond, 1997—2003; dir. US Dept. of the Interior Mus., Washington, 2003—06; chief cultural resources divsn. Office of Sec., Interior Dept., 2006—. Lectr. archtl. history Goucher Coll., Washington, 1996—97; bd. dirs. Va. Assn. Museums, Richmond, 1998—2005; lectr. art history Va. Commonwealth U., Richmond, 2000—01; mem. steering com. stds. learning devel. Va. State Bd. Edn., 2000—02, mem. governor's adv. bd. on gifted edn., 2001—02. Contbr. dictionary, exhibition catalogue, articles to profl. jours. Fellow Alumni Dissertation fellow, U. Va., 1990—91; scholar, Scottish Rite Order, 1977—79; Governor's scholar, Commonwealth Va., 1981—83, Dewey Lee Curtis scholar, Am. Decorative Arts Trust, 1988, Maverick fellow, Attingham Program, 1988, Resident scholar, Lewis Walpole Libr., Yale U., 1989, Va. Mus. fellow, Va. Mus. Fine Arts, 1989—90, Dumas Malone Meml. Traveling fellow, U. Va., 1989—90, Fiske Kimball Meml. fellow, 1990—91. Mem.: Va. Assn. Museums (dir. art 1998—2005, bd. dirs. 1998—), Am. Assn. Museums. Home: 1239 Vermont Ave NW #409 Washington DC 20005 Office: US Department of the Interior Mail Stop 2266 1849 C Street NW Washington DC 20240 Home Phone: 202-294-2754; Office Phone: 202-208-7017. Office Fax: 202-208-1535. Business E-Mail: david_d_mckinney@nbc.gov.

MC KINNEY, DAVID E(WING), retired information processing products company executive, museum administrator; b. Harriman, Tenn., Nov. 28, 1934; s. David Lloyd and Mattie (Ewing) McK.; children: Mary, John, James, Mark; m. Nancy Coates Hale, Aug. 29, 1991. Student (Founders scholar), Vanderbilt U., 1952-53; BS in Mktg. (Gen. Electric scholar), U. Tenn., 1956. With IBM, 1956—, br. mgr. New Orleans, 1966-68, exec. asst. to chmn. bd. Armonk, N.Y., 1971-73, pres. info. records div. Princeton, N.J., 1975-76, v.p. office products div. Franklin Lakes, N.J., 1976-77, v.p. personnel Armonk, 1979-80; asst. group exec. IBM Gen. Bus. Group, White Plains, NY, 1980; v.p., asst. group exec. IBM Info. Systems Group, Rye, 1982; pres. IBM World Trade, Americas/Far East Corp., 1986, v.p. communications, sr. v.p. corp. ops. staff, mgmt. com., corp. mgmt. bd., 1987—89; pres., dir. gen. IBM Europe, Paris, 1989-91; sr. v.p. IBM Corp., Armonk, NY, 1991—92, ret., 1992. Pres. Met. Mus. of Art, NYC, 1999—2005; bd. dirs. Gen. Re. Corp., Paxar Corp. Mem. adv. bd. T. J. Watson Found., Providence; bd. dirs., corp. mem. Brown U.; bd. dirs. Internat. Exec. Svc. Corps, N.Y. Philharmonic; trustee Am. U., Paris; elder 1st Presbyn. Ch., New Canaan, Conn. Served to lt. US Army, 1957—58. Mem.: Country Club of New Canaan.

MCKINNEY, DONALD JOSEPH, music educator, musician; b. Pitts., May 10, 1977; s. Nina Lee Ziegler and Bernard Scott McKinney. B, Duquesne U., Pitts., 2009; M, Indiana U. Pa., 2004. Asst. dir. bands Kiski Area Sch. Dist., Vandergrift, Pa., 2000—04; grad. asst. Indiana U. Pa., 2002—04; assoc. condr. ensembles Duquesne U., Sch. Music, Pitts., 2004—. Clinician St. Mary's Sch. Dist., Pa., 2003, 05, Mt. Lebanon Sch. Dist., Pa., 2006, Pa. Fedn. Contest Judges, Pitts., 2006; cons. Gloria Dei Artes Found., Orleans, Mass., 2006—; cover condr., coach Butler County

Symphony Orch., Pa., 2006—07; asst. condr. Opera Theater Pitts., Pitts., 2006. Musician: (recording) Teaching Music through Performance Reference Recordings; prodr.: (recording) Wind Music of Duquesne University Composers; contbr. chapters to books. Fellow, Conductors Inst. SC, 2005; scholar, Indiana U. Pa., 2002—04, New Eng. Conservatory of Music, 2004. Mem.: Music Educators Nat. Assn., Pa. Music Educators Assn., Coll. Band Dirs. Nat. Assn. Home: 1218 Berkshire Ave Pittsburgh PA 15226 Office: Duquesne Univ 600 Forbes Ave Pittsburgh PA 15282 Home Phone: 724-448-4149; Office Phone: 412-396-6080. Office Fax: 412-396-5479.

MCKINNEY, DONALD LEE, magazine editor; b. Evanston, Ill., July 12, 1923; s. Guy Doane and Cora Redfield (Brenton) McK.; m. Mary Frances Joyce, Dec. 14, 1958; children— Jennifer Joyce, Douglas Guy. AB, U. N.C., 1948. Salesman textbooks John Wiley & Sons, NYC, 1949-52; freelance writer mostly comic books with some short articles and fiction, 1952-54; asst. mng. editor True mag., NYC, 1955-62; editor articles Saturday Evening Post, 1962-69; spl. features editor N.Y. Daily News, 1969-70; mng. editor McCalls mag., NYC, 1969-86; Gonzales prof. journalism U. S.C., Beaufort, 1986-90, prof. emeritus, 1990—. Author: Magazine Writing That Sells, 1994; reporter, book reviewer. Served with USNR, 1943-46. Democrat. Home: 10520 Shadowlawn Dr Raleigh NC 27614 *I learned early that it is important to speak up if you think you are being treated unfairly; sometimes it's true, and nobody else will complain if you don't. I also learned that in my business, and probably in most others, it is best to always say what you think. Truth is usually more helpful than any assortment of euphemisms, and it also saves a lot of worry over who you have lied to and just what you've said. Truth is not only the best policy— by all odds it's the easiest to keep track of.*

MCKINNEY, E. KIRK, JR., retired insurance company executive; b. Indpls., Mar. 27, 1923; s. E. Kirk and Irene M. (Hurley) McK.; m. Alice Hollenbeck Greene, June 18, 1949; children: Kirk Ashley, Alan Brooks, Nora Claire McKinney Hiatt, Margot Knight. AB, U. Mich., 1948. Asst. treas. Jefferson Nat. Life Ins. Co., Indpls., 1949-52, asst. to pres., asst. treas., 1952-53, treas., asst. to pres., 1953-55, v.p., treas., 1955-59, pres., 1959-90, chmn. bd., 1970-90; vice chmn. bd. Somerset Group Inc., 1986-89; ret., 1990. Corp. rels. com. U. Mich.; former pres., former CEO, bd. govs., treas., bd. dirs., exec. com. Indpls. Mus. Art; past bd. dirs. (hon.) Greater Indpls. Progress Com.; former vice chmn. Indpls.-Marion County Bd. Ethics; former dir. Park Tudor Sch., Cmty. Svc. Coun. Indpls., Hosp. Devel. Corp., Ind. Repertory Theater; past adv. com. Indpls. Retirement Home; former bd. dirs., and pres. Episcopal Cmty. Svcs., Inc.; former vice chmn., life trustee Nature Conservancy; mem. adv. bd. Ind. U., Purdue U.; active Indpls. Symphony Orch.; former bd. dirs. Ind. Pub. Broadcasting Soc.; bd. dirs. Indpls. Civic Theater, 2001—, Athenaeum Found., 2000—. Mem. Life Office Mgmt. Assn. (bd. dirs. 1981-83), Am. Coun. Life Ins. (state v.p. 1973-75, dir., exec. com. 1976-79), Assn. Ind. Life Ins. Cos. (pres. 1969-71), Indpls. C. of C., Sigma Chi. Clubs: Economic of Indpls. (bd. dirs.). Democrat. Home: 250 W 77th St Indianapolis IN 46260-3608 Office: 1330 W 38th St #100 Indianapolis IN 46208-4103 Office Phone: 317-925-2223. Personal E-mail: ekirkjr@sbcglobal.net.

MCKINNEY, GEORGE HARRIS, JR., training systems analyst; b. Birmingham, Ala., Nov. 23, 1943; s. George Harris and Elizabeth Dickey (Fikes) McK.; m. Lynda Jeanne Ponder, June 26, 1965 (div. Aug. 18, 1992; children: Michael Thomas, Carol Elizabeth; m. Tambri Sue Hillis, Aug. 19, 1992. BS in Polit. Sci., U.S. Air Force Acad., 1965; MS in Psychology, Troy State U., 1977. Fighter pilot U.S. Air Force, worldwide, 1965-85, commd. 2d lt., 1965, advanced through grades to lt. col., 1981, ret., 1985; pvt. practice Milton, Fla., 1985—. Decorated D.F.C. (5), Air medal (26), Purple Heart, Meritorious Svc. medal (3). Mem. Order of Daedalians, USAFA Assn. Grads., Air Force, Assn., Am. Def. Preparedness Assn. Avocations: whitetail deer hunting, fishing. Home: 3101 Chippewa Dr Milton FL 32571-9603 Office Phone: 850-452-1001 ext 1730. Personal E-mail: geortamb@bellsouth.net.

MCKINNEY, JAMES DEVAINE, JR., lawyer; b. Muscatine, Iowa, Dec. 13, 1931; s. James D. and Jeffie Lillian (Eblen) McKinney; m. Betty A. Guy, June 10, 1966; children: James D. III, Cynthia Dee, Jennifer Jean. BA, U. Iowa, 1956, LLB, 1958. Bar: Iowa 1958, D.C. 1960, U.S. Ct. Appeals (D.C. cir.) 1961, U.S. Supreme Ct. 1962. Trial atty. FPC, Washington, 1958-60; assoc. Law Offices Charles E. McGee, Washington, 1960-65, Ross, Marsh & Foster, Washington, 1965-68, ptnr., 1968—. Mem. ABA, D.C. Bar Assn., Energy Bar Assn. (exec. com. 1979-82), Met. Club, Washington Golf and Country Club. Home: 6105 Lee Hwy Arlington VA 22205-2110 Office: Ross Marsh & Foster 2001 L St NW Washington DC 20036-4910

MCKINNEY, JOHN ADAMS, JR., lawyer; b. Washington, Mar. 10, 1948; s. John A. and Cleo G. (Turner) McK., m. Carol A. Cowen, Dec. 22, 1970; children: John III, Thomas. BA, Principia Coll., 1970; JD, Coll. William and Mary, 1973. Bar: N.J. 1973. Assoc. Mason, Griffin & Pierson, Princeton, NJ, 1973-77; gen. atty. Nabisco, Inc., East Hanover, NJ, 1977-79; asst. counsel Republic Steel Corp., Cleve., 1979-84; atty. and sr. atty. AT&T, Berkeley Heights, NJ, 1984-90; ptnr. McCarter & English LLP, Newark, 1990—2003; mem. Wolff & Samson PC, West Orange, NJ, 2003—. Adj. prof. Sch. of Law, Seton Hall U., 1997—; charter mem., program chair Justice Pollock Environ. Am. Inn of Ct., 2004—; mem. N.J. Historic Sites Coun., 2005-. Co-author: The RCRA Practice Manual, 2d edit., 2004; co-editor: CERCLA Enforcement, 1996. Mem. N.J. Hist. Sites Coun., 2005—; trustee Hackettstown (N.J.) Free Pub. Libr., 1998—2005, Drumthwacket Found., 2003—. Mem. ABA (vice-chair sect. natural resources energy and environ. law solid and hazardous waste com. 1990-98, chair, teleconf. programs 1994-97), N.J. Bar Assn. (dir. environ. law sect. 1992-96, chair 1996-97). Office: Wolff & Samson PC One Boland Dr West Orange NJ 07052-3698 Home Phone: 908-850-3336; Office Phone: 973-530-2036.

MCKINNEY, JOHN PAUL, performing company executive; b. Birmingham, Ala., Dec. 27, 1956; s. Clifford Littleton and Lisa Michelle (Lankford) McKinney; m. Pamela Elaine Whitaker (div.); 1 child, John Paul II. Cert. in radiological tech., C.C. of the Air Force, 1977; attended, Bethany Bible Coll., 1990; D in biblical studies (hon.), Progressive Life Ch., 1993, D (hon.) in counseling, 1993. Cert. drug and alcohol counseling Alpha & Omega Inc. Pastor, CEO Trinity Cmty. Fellowship, Aptos, Calif., 1987—96; caregiver, adminstr. Trinity Ministries, So. San Francisco, Calif., 1996—2001; min., founder Prepare Ye the Way Ministries, Tuscaloosa, Ala., 2001—04; global relief outreach Solicitor Fund Raiser, Talladega, 2003; writer, dir. Full Moon Inst., Talladega, 2003—04. Pres., founder Trinity Ministries, So. San Francisco, Calif., 1996—2001, Prepare for the Way Ministries, Ala., 2001—04; pres. Full Moon Inst., Talladega, 2003—04. Sgt. USAF, 1976—80. Mem.: Full Moon Insight Soc. Democrat. Baptist. Avocations: chess, reading, golf, hiking. Office: Alpha Omega Inc 110 Coffee St Talladega AL 35160

MCKINNEY, JUDSON THAD, broadcast executive; b. Sacramento, Aug. 21, 1941; s. Judson Bartlet and Mildred Eoline (Taylor) McK. Student, Sacramento State U., 1959-61, Western Bapt. Bible Coll., 1961-62, Am. River Coll., 1962-63. Prodn. dir. Sta. KEBR, Sacramento, 1962-65; prodn. dir. Sta. KEAR, Merced, Calif., 1965-68; sta. mgr. Sta. KAMB, 1968-75, Sta. KEAR, San Francisco, 1975-78, 79-88, WFME, Newark, 1978; western regional mgr. Family Stas. Inc., 1988—. Pres. Abounding Love Ministries, 2000-04; instr.for study of electronic Christian media Grad. Theol. Union. V.p. New Millennium Strings, 2003—04, pres., 2005—; sec., treas. Trinity Lyric Opera, 2005—; chmn. 1st. Bapt. Ch. San Francisco, 1985—91; recording engr. 1st Bapt. Ch. Los Altos, Calif. Mem. Gideons. Republican. Baptist. Office: Family Stations Inc 290 Hegenberger Rd Oakland CA 94621-1436 E-mail: thad@familyradio.org.

MCKINNEY, LARRY J., federal judge; b. South Bend, Ind., July 4, 1944; s. Lawrence E. and Helen (Byers) McK.; m. Carole Jean Marie Lyon, Aug. 19, 1966; children: Joshua E., Andrew G. BA, MacMurray Coll., Jacksonville, Ill., 1966; JD, Ind. U., 1969. Bar: Ind. 1970, U.S. Dist. Ct. (so. dist.) Ind. 1970. Law clk. to atty. gen. State of Ind., Indpls., 1969-70, dep. atty. gen., 1970-71; ptnr. Rodgers and McKinney, Edinburgh, Ind., 1971-75, James F.T. Sargent, Greenwood, Ind., 1975-79; judge Johnson County Cir. Ct., Franklin, Ind., 1979-87, U.S. Dist. Ct. (so. dist.) Ind., Indpls., 1987—, chief judge, 2001—. Presbyterian. Avocations: reading, jogging. Office: US Dist Ct 204 US Courthouse 46 E Ohio St Indianapolis IN 46204-1903

MCKINNEY, MARK A., finance educator; b. Hampton, Va., Nov. 9, 1967; s. Thurman B. McKinney, Sr. and Gladys G. McKinney; m. JoAnn J. Collins, June 15, 2002; children: Mark A. McKinney, Jr., Anusha S. BA, U. Nev., 1996; MPA, Webster U., 1998, MA, 1999; PhD, Madison U., 2002, Capella U., 2005. Cert. nurse aide State Md., 2002. State trooper Nev. Hwy. Patrol, Las Vegas, 1990—94; asst. mgr. Prestige Stations, Inc., Las Vegas, 1995—96; paralegal asst. Jordan Enterprises. Ltd., San Bernardino, Calif., 1996—97; human resrouces sgt. U.S Army, 1997—2001; med. adminstrn. officer USAR, 2002; project asst. Force 3 Corp., Crofton, Md., 2003—04; assoc. dean Aims C.C., Greeley, Colo., 2004—. Content evaluator Am. Coun. Edn., Washington, 2004—; instr. Strayer U., Millersville, Md., 2000—03, Nat. Am. U., Kans. City, Mo., 2003—04; instr. online Park U., Parkville, Mo., 2003—; cons. in field. Author: The Financial Workbook: An everyday guide to financial freedom for the average income individual., Healthcare Diversity: Addressing Professional and Societal Needs. Bd. dirs. Greeley (Colo.) Ctr. Independence, 2004; mem. Greeley (Colo.) Art Commn., 2004. Mem.: Assn. Mil. Surgeons U.S. (peer reviewer 2003—), Am. Health Info. Mgmt. Assn., Health Info. & Mgmt. Sys. Soc., Am. Soc. Pub. Adminstrn., Health Care Compliance Assn., Am. Coll. Healthcare Exec., Mil. Officers Assn. Am., Phi Beta Sigma Frat., Inc. Home Phone: 954-961-5109. Personal E-mail: mark_1914@yahoo.com. E-mail: mark_mckinney@doh.state.fl.us.

MCKINNEY, MEGAN, writer; b. Columbia, Mo., July 11; d. Fred and Margery (Mulkern) McKinney; m. Robert Whitfield, June 6, 1958 (separated 1981); 1 child, Katherine Whitfield. BA, U. Mo., Columbia, 1956. Writer TV Guide, N.Y.C., 1956—58; sr. press rep. CBS TV Network, N.Y.C., 1958—64; v.p. Frank Sullivan Assoc., Chgo., 1979—84; dir. pub. rels. Swedish Covenant Hosp., Chgo., 1985—86; editor Ave. M. Mag., Chgo., 1986—90; freelance columnist, writer, 1990—. Pres. Art Resources in Tchg., Chgo., 1980—82; mem. Womans Bd. Northwestern Meml. Hosp., Chgo., 1979—, pres., 1988—90; mem. gov. bd. English Speaking Union, 1986—2002; chmn. Passavant Cotillion, Chgo., 1983, Ascot Ball, Chgo., 1989; co-chmn. Salute to Mike Wallace Mus. Broadcast Comm., Chgo., 1989, co-chmn. Salute to Betty White, 1990, co-chmn. Salute to A.C. Nielsen Jr., 1991, co-chmn. Salute to Irv Kupcinet, 1994. Mem.: Pi Beta Phi. Episcopal. Home: One East Scott Chicago IL 60610

MCKINNEY, MELISSA A., lawyer; 1 child. BS in Criminal Justice, U. North Tex., 1999; JD, So. Meth. U. Dedman Sch. Law, 2003. Bar: Tex. 2003. Assoc. Barrett, Burke, Wilson, Castle, Daffin & Frappier, L.L.P., Addison, Tex. Named a Rising Star, Tex. Super Lawyers mag., 2006. Mem.: Dallas Young Lawyers Assn., Dallas Bar Assn. Office: Barrett Burke Wilson Castle Daffin & Frappier LLP 15000 Surveyor Blvd Ste 100 Addison TX 75001 Office Phone: 972-386-5040. *

MCKINNEY, ROSS ERWIN, SR., civil engineering educator; b. San Antonio, Aug. 2, 1926; s. Roy Earl and Beatrice (Saylor) McK.; m. Margaret McKinney Curtis, June 21, 1952; children: Ross Erwin, Margaret E., William S., Susanne C. BA, BSCE, So. Meth. U., 1948; SM, MIT, 1949, ScD, 1951. San. scientist S.W. Found. for Research and Edn., San Antonio, 1951-53; asst. prof. MIT, 1953-58, assoc. prof., 1958-60; prof. U. Kans., 1960-63, chmn. dept. civil engring., 1963-66, Parker prof. civil engring., 1966-76, N.T. Veatch prof. environ. engring., 1976-93, prof. emeritus, 1993—. Adj. prof. Tongji U., Shanghai, Peoples Rep. China, 1985; v.p. Rolf Eliassen Assocs., Winchester, Mass., 1954-60; pres. Environ. Pollution Control Services, Lawrence, Kans., 1969-73; adj. prof. environ. engring. Duke U., 1997-2002. Author: Microbiology for Sanitary Engineers, 1962, Environmental Pollution Control Microbology, 2004; editor: Nat. Conf. on Solid Waste Research, 1964, 2d Internat. Symposium for Waste Treatment Lagoons, 1970. Mem. Cambridge (Mass.) Water Bd., 1953-59, Lawrence-Douglas County Health Bd., 1969-76, Kans. Water Quality Adv. Council, 1965-76, Kans. Solid Waste Adv. Council, 1970-76, Kans. Environ. Adv. Bd., 1976-85. With AOM 3c, V6 & V12 USNR, 1943—46, appointed ensign USNR, 1947, with civil engring. corps. USNR, 1949, lt. CEC USNR, 1950—55. Recipient Harrison P. Eddy award, 1962, Rudolph Hering award, Water Pollution Control Fedn., 1964, U.S. Presdl. Commendation, 1971, Environ. Quality award, EPA Region VII, 1979, Chancellors Tchg. award, U. Kans., 1986, Lifetime Achievement award, Enviro.-Water Resources Inst./ASCE, 2001. Mem.: AAAS, NAE, ASCE (hon.), Am. Soc. Microbiologists, Am. Chem. Soc., Water Pollution Control Fedn. (Thomas R. Camp medal 1982), Am. Water Works Assn., Kans. Water Pollution Control Assn. (hon. Gordon M. Fair medal 1991), Tau Beta Pi, Chi Epsilon, Kappa Mu Epsilon, Sigma Tau, Sigma Xi. Democrat. Unitarian Universalist. Achievements include patent for water treatment process. Home: 750 Weaver Dairy Rd # 248 Chapel Hill NC 27514-1493 Office Phone: 919-918-2623. E-mail: remck@mindspring.com.

MCKINNEY, SALLY VITKUS, state official; b. Muncie, Ind., Aug. 6, 1944; d. Robert Brookins and Mary (Mann) Gooden; m. Alan George Vitkus (div. Jan. 1979); m. James Larry McKinney, Feb. 1, 1986. AA, William Woods U., 1964; BS, U. Ariz., 1966; postgrad., U. Nev., Las Vegas, 1966-68. Tchr. Las Vegas Day Sch., 1972—76; salesperson Globe Realty, Las Vegas, 1976—79; owner, pres. Realty West, Las Vegas, 1979—96; chief investigator State of Nev. Real Estate Divsn., 1996—2000; prin., owner McKinney Realty, Las Vegas, 2000—; corp. broker, v.p., dir. bus. and devel. Real Estate Temps, Las Vegas. Rec. sec. Clark County Rep. Cen. Com., Las Vegas, 1982, 1st vice chmn., 1985; vice-chmn. Nev. Rep. com., 1986, chmn., 1987-88; active Assistance League Las Vegas; state chmn. Nev. Rep. Party. Mem. Nat. Assn. Realtors, Nat. Assn. Home Builders, Las Vegas Bd. Realtors, Greater Las Vegas C. of C., Gen. Fedn. Womens Clubs (nominee Outstanding Young Woman Am. 1979, exec. bd. 1980-82), Jr. League Las Vegas (sustaining), Mesquite Club (chmn. pub. affairs com. 1986-87, past pres., secret witness exec. bd. 1994-96, vice chmn.). Presbyterian. Avocations: bridge, fly fishing. Home: 511 Mountain Dell Ave Henderson NV 89012-2509

MCKINNEY, TIMOTHY RICHMOND, music educator; b. Ft. Worth, Mar. 17, 1956; s. James Carroll and Elizabeth Richmond McKinney; m. Cynthia Lynn Cavender, Mar. 18, 1978; children: Erin Elizabeth, Brian Richmond. BS in Viola Performance, William Jewell Coll., 1978; MusM in Music Theory, Southwestern Bapt. Theol. Sem., 1981; PhD in Music Theory, U. North Tex., 1989. Asst. prof. music theory U. Tex., Arlington, 1989—95, assoc. prof. music theory, 1995—2002, assoc. dean Coll. Liberal Arts, 2001—02; assoc. prof. music theory Baylor U., Waco, Tex., 2002—. Fellow Mannes Inst. for Advanced Music Theory, NYC, 2001. Contbr. articles to profl. jours. Children and youth choir leader Broadway Bapt. Ch., Ft. Worth, 1998—2002, ordained deacon, 2001; youth choir vol. asst. Seventh and James Bapt. Ch., Waco, 2003—; violist Ft. Worth Symphony Orch., 1975—76. Named Oustanding Alumnus, Coll. Music, U. North Tex., 2006. Mem.: South Ctrl. Soc. for Music Theory (archivist 1991—99), Am. Musicol. Soc., Soc. for Music Theory, Tex. Soc. for Music Theory (pres. 2003—06), Pi Kappa Lambda (pres. Iota Zeta chpt.), Phi Kappa Phi, Sigma Alpha Iota (hon.; nat. art assoc.). Office: Baylor Univ Sch Music One Bear Pl #97408 Waco TX 76798 Office Phone: 254-710-1417.

MCKINNEY, VIRGINIA ELAINE ZUCCARO, educational administrator; b. San Francisco, Nov. 18, 1924; d. Salvadore John and Elaine Agnes (Shepard) Zuccaro; BA, Calif. State U., LA, 1968; MA, Calif. State U., Northridge, 1969; PhD, Claremont Grad. Sch., 1983; children: Joe, Walter Clifton. Official ct. reporter LA County Superior Cts., 1948-59; tchr. speech-reading, adult edn. LA Bd. Edn., 1966-71; lang., reading specialist Marlton Sch. for the Deaf, LA, 1971-79; founder, pres., dir. communication skills program Ctr. for Communicative Devel., Inc., LA, 1969-; part-time lectr. spl. edn. Calif. State U., LA, 1971-1978; cons. for various univs. and programs for the hearing-impaired; mem. State Ind. Living Coun., 1993-2000, adv. com. for deaf Calif. Dept. Rehab., 1979—1984, Atty.'s Gen. Commn. on Disability, 1987-1990. Recipient Leadership award Nat. Leadership Tng. Program in Area of Deaf, Calif. State U., Northridge, 1974; NEA Project Life grantee, 1970, Gallaudet Coll. Ctr. for Continuing Edn. grantee, 1974. Mem. Calif. Educators for Deaf and Hard of Hearing, Calif. Assn. For Postsecondary Edn. and Disability, Beverly-Hollywood (Calif.) Hearing Soc. (pres. 1967-68). Republican. Presbyterian. Author: The Picture Plus Dictionary, 1997, (CD) Picture Plus Vocabulary, 2000, developer, producer audio-visual media, including 22 films and 4 books, to aid in speechreading and auditory tng., 1963-68; participant research project with Project Life on devel. of communication skills for multiply-handicapped deaf adults, 1970; developer, pub. Toe-Hold Literacy Packet, 1973, Linguistics 36, interactive computer lang. devel. program, 1986. Office: 3460 Wilshire Blvd Ste 200 Los Angeles CA 90010 Office Phone: 213-738-8176. Personal E-mail: ccdcom40@yahoo.com.

MCKINNEY, WILLIAM T., psychiatrist, educator; b. Rome, Ga., Sept. 20, 1937; BA cum laude, Baylor U., 1959; MD, Vanderbilt U., 1963. Diplomate Nat. Bd. Med. Examiners (mem. psychiatry test com. 1982-87, chmn. 1984-87); cert. Am. Bd. Psychiatry and Neurology (sr. examiner 1979-90, bd. dirs. 1991—, mem. rsch. com., co-chair part I test com., chair added qualifications in geriatric psychiatry test com., mem. part II audio visual com., mem. disability accomodations com., rep. to residency rev. com.). Intern in medicine Bowman Gray Sch. Medicine, Wake Forest U., Winston-Salem, NC, 1963-64; resident dept. psychiatry Sch. Medicine, U. N.C., Chapel Hill., 1964-66, Sch. Medicine, Stanford (Calif.) U., 1966-67; clin. assoc. psychosomatic sect. adult psychiatry br., tng. specialist, asst. br. chief NIMH, Bethesda, Md., 1967-69; asst. prof. psychiatry dept. psychiatry Sch. Medicine, U. Wis., Madison, 1969-72, assoc. prof. psychiatry, 1972-74, prof. psychiatry, 1974-93; Asher prof. of psychiatry dept. psychiatry and behavioral scis., dir. Asher Ctr. for Study and Treatment of Depressive Disorders Med. Sch., Northwestern U., Chgo., 1993—. Part-time clin. pvt. practice, Bethesda, 1967-69; NIMH rsch. career investigator Sch. Medicine, U. Wis., Madison, 1970-75, rsch. psychiatrist Primate Lab., 1974-93, affiliate sci. Wis. Regional Primate Rsch. Ctr., 1974-93, affiliate prof. psychology dept. psychology, 1974-93, chmn. dept. psychiatry, 1975-80, dir. Wis. Psychiat. Rsch. Inst. Ctr. Health Scis., 1975-80; sr. staff psychiatrist William S. Middleton Meml. VA Hosp., Madison, Wis., 1974-93; rschr. sub dept. animal behaviour U. Cambridge, Eng., 1974; mem. rsch. rev. com. VA Behavioral Scis., 1976-79; Abbott Sigma XI Club lectr., 1976; Milw. Psychiat. Hosp. lectr., 1977; mem. program adv. com. and workshop chmn. Dahlem Found. Internat. Conf. on Depression, Berlin, 1982; U. Minn. lectr. at Festshrift, 1982; cons. grad. sch. U. Minn., 1982; fellow Ctr. Advanced Study in Behavioral Scis., Stanford, Calif., 1983-84; mem. external adv. bd. Clin. Rsch. Ctr. Dept. Psychiatry U. N.C., Chapel Hill, 1984—, cons., bd. advisors clin. rsch. fellow tng. program dept. psychology, 1988—; William F. Orr lectr. Vanderbilt U., 1985; vis. prof. dept. psychiatry U. Tex. Health Scis. Ctr., Dallas, 1986, U. Utah Sch. Medicine, Salt Lake City, 1987, U. Minn. Sch. Medicine, Mpls., 1988; cons. biol. scis. tng. br. divsn. manpower and tng. programs NIMH, 1975-76, mem. psychiatry spl. tng. com. 1983, plenary lectr., Clearwater, Fla., 1987, co-chairperson Workshop on Non-Human Primate Models of Psychopathology, 1987, mem. biol. psychopathology spl. rev. com., 1992—; mem. sci. core group MacArthur Found. Mental Health Rsch. Network I: The Psychobiology of Depression and Other Affective Disorders, 1988-93; vis. spkr. So. Calif. Psychiat. Soc., L.A., 1988; plenary lectr. Soc. Biol. Psychiatry ann. meeting, Montreal, 1988; vis. prof. Dalhousie U. Sch. Medicine, N.S., 1989, HCA Riveredge Hosp., Chgo., 1989, U. Pa., Phila., 1991, U. N.Mex., Albuquerque, 1992, Northwestern U., Chgo., 1992; invited spkr. Animal Models in Psychopharmacology Symposium, Duphar, Amsterdam, 1990; vis. spkr., cons. CIBA-GEIGY, Basel, Switzerland, 1990; mem. minority instns. rsch. devel. rev. com. Alcohol, Drug Abuse and Mental Health Adminstrn., 1990; guest spkr. Inst. Pa. Hosp., Phila., 1991; reviewer Human Frontier Sci. Program, 1992—; external cons. dept. psychiatry Mental Health Clin. Rsch. Ctr. U. Tex. Southwestern Med. Ctr., Dallas, 1992—; presenter in field. Author: Animal Models of Mental Disorders: A New Comparative Psychiatry, 1988; co-author: Mood Disorders: Towards a New Psychobiology, 1984; mem. editl. bd. Archives of Psychiatry and Neurol. Scis., Contemporary Psychiatry, 1981-82, Ethology and Sociobiology, Experientia, 1982-89, Trends in Neurosciences, 1982-86, Neuropsychopharmacology, 1987-90; manuscript and book reviewer numerous sci. jours.; contbr. articles to profl. jours. USHPS fellow in biostats. Vanderbilt U., 1962; recipient Beauchamp award Vanderbilt U. Med. Sch., 1963, Rsch. Career Devel. award NIMH, 1975, Rsch. Leave award U. Wis., 1983-84, Am. Acad. Pediats. award, 1991. Fellow Am. Psychiat. Assn. (cons. psychiat. edn. consultation svc. 1983—), Am. Coll. Psychiatrists, Am. Coll. Neuropsychopharmacology (mem. constn. and rules com. 1985-87, mem. ethics com. 1987-89, mem. fin. com. 1990-92, panel chair San Juan, P.R. 1992, panel presenter 1992); mem. Am. Soc. Primatologists, Am. Psychosomatic Soc. (mem. program com. 1975-76), Internat. Primatology Soc., Internat. Coll. Neurobiology, Biol. Psychiatry and Psychopharmacology (lectr. Zurich 1985), Internat. Soc. Devel. Psychobiology, Internat. Soc. Ethological and Behavioral Pharmacology (bd. advisors 1983—), Collegium Internat. Neuro-Psychopharmacologicum, Psychiat. Rsch. Soc., Soc. Neuroscience, Wis. Psychiat. Assn. (chmn. program com. 1972, co-chairperson task force on sexual misconduct and membership edn. 1986-88, pres.-elect 1989-91, pres. 1991-93).

MCKINNIS, MICHAEL BAYARD, lawyer; b. St. Louis, May 31, 1945; s. Bayard O. and Doris (Lammert) McK.; m. Patricia Butow, Aug. 24, 1968; children: Scott, Christopher, Elizabeth. BS, Drake U., 1967; JD, U. Mo., 1970. Bar: Mo. 1970, U.S. Dist. Ct. (ea. dist.) Mo. Ptnr. Bryan Cave LLP, St. Louis, gen. counsel, mem. firm operating group. Editor U. Mo. Law Rev., 1969-70. Mem. ABA, Mo. Bar Assn., Order of Coif, Phi Delta Phi. Office: Bryan Cave LLP One Metropolitan Square 211 N Broadway, Ste 3600 Saint Louis MO 63102-2733 Office Phone: 314-259-2000. E-mail: mbmckinnis@bryancavellp.com.

MCKINNISH, RICHMOND D., manufacturing executive; From mem. staff to pres., CEO Carlisle Cos. Inc., Charlotte, NC, 1974—2001, pres., CEO, 2001—07. Bd. dir. Carlisle Cos. Inc. Office: Carlisle Cos Inc 13925 Ballantyne Corp Place Charlotte NC 28277

MCKINNON, ARNOLD BORDEN, retired transportation company executive; b. Goldsboro, NC, Aug. 13, 1927; s. Henry Alexander and Margaret (Borden) McK.; m. Oriana McArthur, July 19, 1950; children: Arnold Borden Jr., Colin McArthur, Henry Alexander. AB, Duke U., 1950, LLB, 1951; grad. Advanced Mgmt. Program, Harvard U., 1972. Bar: D.C.

1951, N.C. 1966. With Norfolk So. Corp. (formerly So. Ry. Sys.), Va., 1951-2000, from v.p. law to chmn., 1971-92, chmn. exec. com., 1992-2000, ret., 2000. Bd. trustees Chrysler Mus. Art; active Mil. Civilian Liaison Group; bd. dirs. Norfolk Forum, Inc. With US Army, 1946—47. Mem.: ABA, Am. Soc. Corp. Execs., D.C. Bar Assn., N.C. Bar Assn., Rotary, Norfolk German Club, Bonita Bay Club, Met. Club, Chevy Chase Club, Norfolk Yacht and Country Club. Presbyterian. Home: 552 Mowbray Arch Norfolk VA 23507-2130 Office: Norfolk So Corp 3 Commercial Pl Norfolk VA 23510-2108

MCKINNON, CAROLYN ANN, retired child care center director; b. Bangor, Maine; d. Joseph Russell and Muriel Ann (Capen) Johnston; m. James Coolidge McKinnon, July 24, 1967; step-children: Michael, Ronald, Shaun, Jeannine; children: William, John. RN, D.C. Gen. Hosp., Washington. RN, N.Y., Colo., Maine. Nurse D.C. Gen. Hosp., Washington, Onondago Gen. Hosp., Syracuse, NY, Colo. Gen. Hosp., Denver, Bangor Mental Health Inst., Maine; dir., adminstr. A Small World Day Care Ctr., Bangor; ad copy writer Interactive Mktg. Group, Bangor; ret., 2006. Spkr. TV and radio programs, 1997. Author: Insanity, Inc., 1996. Mem. PETA, ASCPA, HSUS, NHES, ALDF, IDA, IFAW, PCRM, others. Mem.: Physicians Com. for Responsible Medicine, Internat. Fund for Animal Welfare, In Def. of Animals, Animal Legal Def. Funds, Nat. Humane Edn. Soc., Humane Soc. US, People for Ethical Treatment Animals. Roman Catholic. Avocation: theater and musical organizations. Home: 287 Birch St Bangor ME 04401-4025 Office: A Small World Day Care Ctr 300 Forest Ave Bangor ME 04401-3947 also: Interactive Mktg Group 304 Hancock St Bangor ME 04401-5123

MC KINNON, CLINTON DAN, aerospace transportation executive; b. San Bernardino, Calif., Jan. 27, 1934; s. Clinton Dotson and Lucille V. McK.; m. Janice Bernard; children: Holly Jean, Sherri Lynn, Clinton Scott, Lisa Caroline BA, U. Mo., 1956; doctorate (hon.), Nat. U., 1987. Page U.S. Ho. of Reps., 1950-52; reporter, photographer, advt. salesman Sentinel Newspaper, San Diego, 1960-62; owner, pres. KSON Radio, San Diego, 1962-85, KSON-FM, San Diego, 1964-85; pub. La Jolla (Calif.) Light Jour., 1969-73; owner House of Hits (book and music pub.), San Diego, 1972—; co-owner KIII-TV, Corpus Christi, Tex., 1964—, KBMT-TV, Beaumont, Tex., 1976—, KUSI-TV, San Diego, 1992—; chmn. CAB, Washington, 1981-84; with spl. projects CIA, 1985-86; founder, chmn., pres. North Am. Airlines, Jamaica, NY, 1989—2005. Author: Bullseye--One Reactor (aka Bullseye Iraq), 1986, The Ten Second Message, 1994, Words of Honor, 1995, Rescue Pilot, 2002, Safe Air Travel Companion, 2002. Chmn. exec. com. Greater San Diego Billy Graham Crusade, 1976, commr., Nat. Guard and Reserves Commn., 2005-. Served as aviator USNR, 1956—60. Recipient Advt. Man of Year award San Diego Advt. and Sales Club, 1971; Radio Sta. Mgr. of Year award Billboard Mag., 1973; Internat. Pres.'s award Youth for Christ, 1975; Man of Distinction award Mexican-Am. Found., 1976; George Washington Honor medal Freedoms Found., 1976; Headliner of Yr. (govt.), San Diego Press Club, 1985; named to Country Radio Hall of Fame, 2003. Mem. Country Music Assn. (pres. 1977, Pres. award 1980), C. of C. (dir.), Nat. Assn. Broadcasters (bd. dirs. 1970-74), Calif. Broadcasters Assn. (dir.), Navy League (Media Man of Yr. 1980), Wings Club (bd. govs. 1995-2003, pres. 2002-2003), San Diego Rotary. Achievements include setting Navy helicopter peacetime rescue record of 62 air/sea rescues, 1958; 1st person to close down fed. govt. regulatory agy., CAB, 1984. Office: 1125-101 Pacific Beach Dr San Diego CA 92109

MCKINNON, FLOYD WINGFIELD, textile executive; b. Columbus, Ga., Dec. 1, 1942; s. Malcolm Angus and Sarah C. (Bullock) McK.; m. Barbara Evans Roles, June 18, 1966; children: James Wingfield, Sarah Elizabeth, Robert Kent. AB, Washington and Lee U., 1964. Lic. airplane pilot. Pres. Cotswold Industries, Inc., NYC, 1966—, also bd. dirs.; v.p., corp. sec. Cen. Textiles, Inc., S.C., 1984—, also bd. dirs. S.C. Arbitrator Am. Arbitration Assn., 1983-2001; bd. dirs. Scarsdale Leasing Corp. Pres. Berkley-in-Scarsdale Assn., 1980; admissions rep. Washington and Lee U., 1979-89, 93-99. Mem. Aircraft Owner's and Pilot's Assn., St. Andrews Soc. N.Y., Union League Club N.Y. (bd. govs. 1974-77, 88-91, 97—, sec. 1981-83, chmn. admissions com. 1996, pres. 2005-07), Scarsdale Golf Club (bd. govs. 1983-91, pres. 1990-91) (Hartsdale, N.Y.), Bras Coupe Club (exec. com. 1980—) (Maniwaki, Can.). Republican. Episcopalian. Home: 26 Taunton Rd Scarsdale NY 10583-5610 Office: Cotswold Industries 10 E 40th St Rm 3410 New York NY 10016-0367 Business E-Mail: wink@cotswoldindustries.com. E-mail: wink85wm@optonline.net.

MCKINNON, F(RANCIS) A(RTHUR) RICHARD, utilities executive; b. Delburne, Alta., Can., Mar. 5, 1933; s. John Donald and Ruth Rebecca (Sundberg) McK.; m. Elma Lorraine Lebsack, June 1, 1957; children: Kenneth Richard, Stephen David, Karen Diane. B. Commerce, U. Alta., 1954; postgrad., Stanford Exec. Program, Stanford U., 1982. With Alta. Gas Trunk Line Co. Ltd., Calgary, 1960-75, treas., 1971-75; dir. fin. TransAlta Utilities Corp. (formerly Calgary Power Ltd.), 1975—, treas., 1976-81, v.p. fin., 1981—, Trans Alta Energy Corp., Trans Alta Corp.; pres. ELM FARMS CONS., INC., Calgary, 1996—. Bd. dirs. AEC Power Ltd. Past bd. dirs. Foothills Gen. Hosp., Calgary. Fellow Inst. Chartered Accts. of Alta.; mem. Can. Inst. Chartered Accts., Fin. Execs. Inst. Can. (past chmn., past pres., bd. dirs. Calgary chpt., v.p.), Fin. Execs. Inst. (bd. dirs.). Clubs: Calgary Petroleum, Canyon Meadows Golf and Country. Office: ELM FARM CONS INC 1412 Windsor St NW Calgary AB Canada T2N 3X3

MCKINNON, KARL LUTHER, museum director; b. Asheboro, NC, Mar. 31, 1962; s. George F. and Barbara Ann (Johnson) McKinnon; m. Maribeth Bryan, Dec. 9, 1995. BA Biology, U. N.C., Greensboro, 1984. Zookeeper, docent Natural Sci. Ctr., Greensboro, NC, 1981—83; dir., head naturalist Dan Nichols Park Nature Ctr., Salisbury, NC, 1984—85; exec. dir. Rocky Mount Children's Mus., NC, 1985—95; dep. dir. Nat. Sci. Ctr., Greensboro, NC, 1995—2002; exec. dir. Dakota Sci. Ctr., Grand Forks, ND, 2002—03; exec. dir. Imagination Sect. Sci. Mus., Wilson, NC, 2003—. Chmn. fin. com. NC Grassroots Sci. Mus. Collaborative, 2000—02, bd. dirs., 2003—. Mem.: N.C. Mus. Assn., Summit Rotary Club (Greensboro, N.C.) (pres. elect 2002—, Rotarnet chmn. 1998—2000), All Am. Kiwanis Club (Wilson, N.C.) (bd. dirs., 2000—02, Kwwiet Kiwanian 2004, Pres. award 2004), Wilson Rotary Club (bd. dirs.). Office Phone: 252-291-5113.

MCKINNON, RUSSELL F., professional society administrator; b. Springfield, Mass., Feb. 11, 1944; s. John McKinnon and Margret Louise Bates; m. Deborah Oplinger, July 11, 1987; 1 child, John. AB in History, Coll. Holy Cross, 1966; M in Mgmt., George Washington U., 1988. Pres. The Mackinnon Co., Alexandria, Va., 1972—; exec. Nat. Rural Electric Coop. Assn., Arlington, Va., 1994—; pres. Internat. Theos Found., Alexandria, 1998—. Photographer Parade Mag., 1989. Lt. USNR, 1966-72. Mem. Am. Soc. Assn. Execs. (cert.), Assn. Meeting Planners. Avocations: skiing, golf. Office: Nat Rural Electric Coop Assn 4301 Wilson Blvd Arlington VA 22203-1867 E-mail: md1995@erols.com.

MCKINSTRY, RONALD E., retired lawyer; b. Bakersfield, Calif., Aug. 11, 1926; s. Melville Jack and Lillian Agatha (Saner) McKinstry; m. Shirley Danner, June 19, 1948; children: Michael R., Jill I. McKinstry Epperson, Jeffrey A., Carol A. McKinstry Sundquist. BS, U. Wash., 1950, JD, 1951. Bar: Wash. 1951, US Ct. Claims 1970, US Ct. Appeals (DC cir.) 1981, US Supreme Ct. 1982. Assoc. Evans, McLaren, Lane, Powell & Beeks, Seattle, 1951-55, Bogle, Bogle & Gates, Seattle, 1955-61; ptnr. Bogle & Gates, Seattle, 1962-91, chmn. litigation dept., 1970-91; sr. trial ptnr. Ellis Li & McKinstry, Seattle, 1992—2004; ret., 2004. Apptd. spl. master US Dist. Ct. (we. dist.) Wash., 1976—81, apptd. settlement mediator, 1980—. Editor-in-chief: Washington Civil Procedure Before Trial Deskbook, 1981, Supplement to Deskbook, 1986; contbr. articles to profl. jours. With USN, 1944—46, PTO. Recipient Svc. award, Western Ctr. Law and Religious Freedom, 1990. Fellow: Am. Coll. Trial Lawyers (regent 1978—82); mem.: ABA, CPR Panels Disting. Legal Neutrals, Internat. Assn. Def. Counsel (mem. exec. com. 1974—78), AAA Club Wash. (mem. exec. com. 1983—98). Avocations: golf, travel. Personal E-mail: rsmckinstry@west.net.

MCKINZIE, CARL WAYNE, lawyer; b. Lubbock, Tex., Dec. 3, 1939; s. J. Clyde and Flora (Cates) McK.; m. Rowena Ann Williams; children: Wayne, Clinton, Morgan (dec.). BBA, Tex. Tech U., 1962, MBA, 1963; JD, So. Meth. U., 1966. From assoc. to ptnr. Nossaman, Guthner, Knox & Elliot, LA, 1966-80; prin. Riordan & McKinzie, LA, 1980—2003; ptnr. Bingham McCutchen (merged with Riordan & McKinzie), 2003—. Bd. dirs., exec. com., Saint John's Health Ctr., Santa Monica, Calif., 2001—, vice chair, 2002-2003, chair, 2003-. Contbr. articles to law jours. Trustee Jaquish Found., 2000-04, Raymond Marshall Found., 1993-2003; bd. visitors Sch. Law So. Meth. U., Dallas, 1979-82, 90—, bd. dirs., 1970-73, 84-89, chmn. exec. com., 1996-98; bd. visitors Ariz State U. Coll. Law, 1990-98; bd. dirs. Riordan Found., 1992—, Rx for Reading, 1992—, The Welk Group, 2004—; bd. dirs., exec. com. Libr. Found. LA, 2002—, vice chair, 2003-04; bd. dirs., exec. coun. Pub. Counsel, 1996-99, Calif. Cmty. Found., 1994-98; bd. advisors Coll Law, U. Wyo., 1987-91, 2001—. Recipient disting. alumni award, So. Meth. U., Dallas, 1994. Mem. ABA (chmn. current devel. subcom., com. tax problems 1978-80), Nat. Assn. Real Estate Investment Trusts (bd. govs. 1986-89), Calif. Bar Assn., Los Angeles County Bar Assn., Jonathan Club, City Club on Bunker Hill, L.A. Country Club. Republican. Home: 527 21st Pl Santa Monica CA 90402-3047 Office: Bingham McCutchen 44th Fl 355 S Grand Ave Los Angeles CA 90071-3106 Home Phone: 310-393-3692; Office Phone: 213-229-8484. Business E-Mail: carl.mckinzie@bingham.com.

MCKINZIE, JAMES S., librarian; b. Sweetwater, Tex., Dec. 15, 1951; s. John O. and Laverne McKinzie; m. Anna B. Baker; children: Amy, Jane, Jonathan, William. BA in History, Tex. A&M U., 1975; MA in History, E. Carolina U., Greenville, NC, 1982; MLS, Vanderbilt U., 1988. Social sci. libr. Dickinson Coll., Carlisle, Pa., 1988—2006; libr. dir. Catawa Coll., Salisbury, NC, 2006—. Contbr. articles and book revs. to profl. jours. Presbyterian. Home: 6307 Elk Trail Salisbury NC 28147 Office: Catawa Coll Libr 2300 Innes St Salisbury NC 28147 Office Phone: 704-637-4449. Business E-Mail: smckinzi@catawba.edu.

MCKIRAHAN, RICHARD DUNCAN, classics and philosophy educator; b. Berkeley, Calif., July 27, 1945; s. Richard Duncan and Helen Marion (Hixson) McK.; m. Voula Tsouna, June 3, 1961; 1 child, Helen Hamilton. AB, U. Calif., Berkeley, 1966; BA, U. Oxford, Eng., 1969; MA, Oxford U., Eng., 1979; PhD, Harvard U., 1973. Teaching fellow, tutor Harvard U., Cambridge, Mass., 1971-73; asst. prof. classics and philosophy Pomona Coll., Claremont, Calif., 1973-79, assoc. prof., 1979-87, E.C. Norton prof. classics and philosophy, 1987—, chair dept. classics, 1992—. Author: Socrates and Plato, A Comprehensive Bibliography, 1958-1973, 1978, Plato's Meno, 1986, Principles and Proofs: Aristotle's Theory of Demonstrative Science, 1992, Philosophy Before Socrates, 1994, A Presocratics Reader, 1996, Cicero, De Natura Deorum I, 1997, Simplicius, On Aristotle's Physics, book 8, chpts. 6-10, 2001; contbr. articles on Greek philosophy, math. and scis. Marshall Aid Commemoration Commn. scholar, U. Oxford, 1966-69, Fulbright Sr. scholar, 1999, Overseas Vis. scholar St. John's Coll., Cambridge, 1999; Woodrow Wilson Found. fellow, 1966-67; NEH grantee, 1975, 85, 90, 98, 2004. Mem. Am. Philol. Assn., Soc. Ancient Greek Philosophy, Phi Beta Kappa. Office: Pomona Coll Dept Classics 140 W 6th St Claremont CA 91711-4301 Business E-Mail: rmckirahan@pomona.edu.

MCKISSOCK, DAVID LEE, retired manufacturing company executive; b. Boston, Mar. 27, 1933; s. Allan and Elizabeth (Lee) McK.; m. Diana Parish, Sept. 1, 1956; children: David Lee Jr., Christopher Lee. BA, Middlebury Coll., 1955. Salesman Am. Flange and Mfg. Co., NYC, 1957-62, asst. to v.p. sales Linden, NJ, 1962-64, salesman rip cap closures, 1964-73, v.p. rip cap closures, 1973-89, also bd. dirs. With USNR, 1955-57. Mem. Rumson Country Club, Seabright Lawn Tennis and Cricket Club. Republican. Unitarian Universalist. Avocations: tennis, golf, platform tennis. Home: 20 Hance Rd Fair Haven NJ 07704-3210 Personal E-mail: dlmpaddle@aol.com.

MCKITRICK, JAMES THOMAS, retired retail executive; b. Cin., Sept. 14, 1945; s. Harry J. and L. May (Buck) McK.; m. Margaret J. Haynes, Sept. 6, 1975; children: Angela, Greg, Randal, Paul, Sheri, Richard, Mike. Student, Salem Coll., 1963-64. Dir. mdse. K Mart Corp., Troy, Mich., 1965-84; exec. v.p., gen. mgr. T.G. & Y. Stores, Oklahoma City, 1984-86, exec. v.p. merchandising and mktg., 1986; pres., chief exec. officer Warehouse Club, Skokie, Ill., 1986-87; pres., chief operating officer G.C. Murphy Co. subs. Ames, Rocky Hill, Conn., 1987-89; chmn. Zayre Discount, Rocky Hill, 1988-89; pres. & CEO Builders Emporium, Irvine, Calif., 1989-92, Quality Stores Inc. (formerly Central Tractor Farm & Country), Muskegon, Mich., 1992—2000. Republican. Methodist. Office: Quality Stores Inc PO Box 1002 Muskegon MI 49443-1002

MCKITTRICK, WILLIAM WOOD, lawyer; b. Mt. Carmel, Ill., July 11, 1915; s. Lafe E. and Mary Lynn (Wood) McK.; m. Carolyn Lenne Davis, Dec. 19, 1942; children: Lynn McKittrick Pond, Bruce W. AB, DePauw U., 1936; JD, Northwestern U., 1939. Bar: Ill. Assoc. Pope & Ballard, Chgo., 1939-48, ptnr., 1948-52; atty. Office Gen. Counsel, Panama C.Z., 1942; ptnr. Vedder, Price, Kaufman & Kammholz, Chgo., 1952-95; lectr. on labor law Northwestern U. Sch. Law, Chgo., 1961-62. Case note editor, mem. editorial bd. Ill. Law Rev., 1938-39. Life trustee Orchestral Assn. of Chgo. Symphony Orch., 1980—, Chgo. Symphony Musicians Pension Trust, 1987-98; bd. dirs. Am. Symphony Orch. League, 1986-93, mem. exec. com., 1988-91; trustee Newberry Libr., Chgo., 1984-98, life trustee, 1998—, exec. com., 1989-98; vice chmn. exec. bd. Libr. Coun., Northwestern U., 1984-96; chmn. Friends of Ryerson & Burnham Librs., Art Inst. Chgo., 1988-90, mem. com. on librs., 1982—. Lt. USNR, 1943-45, PTO. Recipient Svc. award Northwestern U., 1968. Mem. ABA, Ill. Bar Assn., Chgo. Bar Assn. (lectr. various programs 1940-70, bd. mgrs. 1961-63), Lawyers Club of Chgo., Univ. Club (Chgo.), Michigan Shores Club, Skokie Country Club, Caxton Club of Chgo. (v.p. 1982-83, pres. 1983-85). Home: 232 Essex Rd Kenilworth IL 60043-1122

MCKNIGHT, CARL PHILLIP, psychologist; b. Bogota, Colombia, Jan. 20, 1969; (parents Am. citizens); s. Elwin D. and Elsa V. McKnight; m. Susan A. Kasparrow, July 18, 1998; children: Christopher children: Angela. BS, Tex. A&M U., 1991; MA, Stephen F. Austin State U., 1995; PsyD, Pepperdine U., 2000. Lic. psychologist Calif. Bd. Psychology. Pediatric psychologist Children's Hosp. Orange (Calif.) County, 2001—06; project behavioral psychologist Med. Ctr. U. Calif., Irvine, 2003—06; clin. psychologist II L.A. County Dept. Mental Health, 2006—. Cons. St. Joseph's Hosp., Orange, 2005—06. Contbr. columns in mags. Mem. childhood obesity steering com. Children and Families Commn. Orange County, Irvine, Calif., 2002—04. Lt. USAR, 1990—98. Pediatric and Clin. Child Psychology fellow, Children's Hosp. L.A. and U. So. Calif. Sch. of Medicine, 1999—2001. Mem.: APA, Soc. Pediatric Psychology. Achievements include development of pilot psychological screening and treatment program for morbidly obese children and adolescents. Office: Los Angeles County DMH 921 E Compton Blvd 1st Fl Compton CA 90221-1683 Office Phone: 310-668-6925. Business E-Mail: cmcknight@lacdmh.org.

MCKNIGHT, FREDERICK L., lawyer; b. Kansas City, Mo., Nov. 28, 1947; s. Harry A. and Donna Ruth (Breining) McK.; m. Linda Jean McKnight, June 20, 1970; children: Justin Teague, Cristin Ruth. AB honors, Princeton U., 1969; JD, U. Calif., Berkeley, 1972. Bar: Calif. 1973, N.Y. 1973. Regional mng. ptnr. Jones Day Reavis & Pogue, LA, 1997; now ptnr.-in-charge LA office Jones Day. Adv. com. Jones, Day, Reavis & Pogue, Cleve. Bd. dirs. Econ. Devel. Corp., L.A., 1992—, St. Vincent Med. Ctr. Found., L.A., 1994—. Fellow Am. Coll. of Trial Lawyers; mem. Assn. Bus. Trial Lawyers. Office: Jones Day 555 S Flower St # 50 Los Angeles CA 90071-2300 Office Phone: 213-243-2777. Office Fax: 213-243-2539. Business E-Mail: fmcknight@jonesday.com.

MCKNIGHT, GREGORY RICHARD, research director; b. Sparta, NC, Feb. 18, 1968; s. James Richard and Carol Norman McKnight; life ptnr. Steven B. McGinnis, 1996. BA, Wake Forest U., Winston-Salem, NC, 1990. Rsch. analyst Wake Forest U. Health Scis., Winston-Salem, 1997—2000, dir. prospect rsch./mgmt., 2000—. Mem.: Carolina's Assn. Profl. Rschrs. for Advancement (dir., treas. 2002—06). Moravian. Avocations: travel, motorcycling, bicycling. Office: Wake Forest U Health Scis Medical Center Blvd Winston Salem NC 27157-1021 Home: 225 Banner Ave Winston Salem NC 27127

MCKNIGHT, JOSEPH WEBB, lawyer, educator, historian; b. San Angelo, Tex., Feb. 17, 1925; s. John Banning and Helen Katherine (Webb) McK.; m. Julia Ann Dyer, July 20, 1957 (dec. Jan. 1972); children: John Banton, Joseph Adair; m. Mildred Katherine Virginia Payne, Aug. 9, 1975 BA, U. Tex., Austin, 1947, Oxford U., Eng., 1949, BCL, 1950, MA, 1954; LLM, Columbia U., NYC, 1959. Bar: Tex. 1951, U.S. Ct. Appeals (5th cir.) 1982. Assoc. Cravath, Swaine & Moore, NYC, 1951-55; asst. prof. So. Meth. U., Dallas, 1955-57, assoc. prof., 1957-63, prof. law, 1963—, acad. dean, 1977-80, Larry and Jane Harlan faculty fellow, 1991—. Vis. prof. various univs. Gen. editor Creditors' Rights in Texas, 1963, History of the Texas Supreme Court, 1998—; author: (with William A. Reppy, Jr.) Texas Matrimonial Property Law, 1983, 10th edit. 2007; contbr. articles to profl. jours. Pres., Tex. Old Missions and Forts Restoration Assn., 1977-79, 99-2001; bd. dirs. San Jacinto Mus. History Assn., 1976-99; exec. coun. Tex. State Hist. Assn., 1988-91, fellow, 2004; bd. trustees Tex. Supreme Ct. His. Soc., 1990-; dir. History of Tex. Supreme Ct. History Project, 1998-. Lt. USNR, 1942-47 Rhodes scholar, 1947-50; James Kent fellow Columbia Law Sch., 1958-59; Academico, Acad. Mexicana de Derecho Internat., 1988, Hall of Legends, State Bar of Texas Fam. Law Sec., 1997. Fellow, Soc. for Advanced Legal Studies (London), 1998; mem. ABA, State Bar Tex., Dallas Bar Assn., Tex. Bar Found. (v.p. 1959), Nat. Legal Aid and Defenders Assn. (bd. dirs. 1963-66), Selden Soc., Am. Soc. Legal History (v.p. 1967-68, bd. dirs. 1967-75), Inst. Texan Cultures (exec. bd. 1990-95), Oxford and Cambridge Club (London), Sigma Chi. Democrat. Episcopalian. Office: So Meth U Law Sch 3315 Daniel Ave Dallas TX 75275-0116 Office Phone: 214-768-2591, 214-768-3851. Business E-Mail: jmcknigh@smu.edu.

MCKNIGHT, PATRICIA GAYLE, musician, artist, writer, educator; b. Rochester, Minn., Aug. 9, 1935; d. William Robert and Maxine Matilda (Hutchings) McK.; m. James Russell Grittner, Nov. 24, 1962; children: Leah Kristin, Rachel Anne. BS in Music, U. Wis., Superior, 1982, MA in Art, 1990, MA in Art History, 1993; postgrad. in Musicology, U. Iowa, Iowa City, 1982—83. Asst. MS editor Am. Acad. Ophthalmology and Otolaryngology, Rochester, Minn., 1958-63. Musician U. Iowa Symphony Orch., U. Iowa Opera Orch., U. Iowa Small Ensembles, U. Wis. Superior Symphony Orch., Rochester Symphony Orch. Exhibited in group shows including Kruk Gallery, Rochester Art Ctr., Rochester Cmty. Coll., Duluth Art Inst. Biennial, 1988, 90, Port Wing Gallery, Tile Show, Wis., 2006; author: Zenith City Arts newspaper. Mem. Hist. Preservation Commn. City of Superior, 1996—. Avocations: playing cello, viola da gamba, piano, art. Home: 2325 Hughitt Ave Superior WI 54880-4920

MCKNIGHT, ROBERT B., JR., sporting goods manufacturing executive; BS, Univ. So. Calif. Co-founder, bd. dir. Quicksilver Inc., Huntington Beach, Calif., 1976—, pres., 1979—91, chmn., CEO, 1991—. Office: Quicksilver Inc 15202 Graham St Huntington Beach CA 92649 *

MCKNIGHT, STEVEN LANIER, molecular biologist; b. El Paso, Tex., Aug. 27, 1949; s. Frank Gillespie and Sara Elise (Stevens) McK.; m. Jacquelynn Ann Zimmer, Sept. 16, 1978; children: Nell, Grace, Frances, John Stevens. BA summa cum laude, U. Tex., 1974; PhD, U.Va., 1977. Fellow U. Va., 1975—76; postdoctoral fellow Carnegie Instn. Washington, Balt., 1977—80, staff assoc., 1980—81, mem. staff, 1984-92; co-founder, dir., dir. rsch. Tularik Inc., San Francisco, 1992—; with U. Tex. Southwestern Med. Ctr., Dallas, 1996—, prof., chmn. biochemistry dept., 2000—, disting. chair Basic Biomed. Rsch. Dallas, Sam. G. Winstead and F. Andrew Bell disting. chair biochemistry. Prof., chmn. dept. biochemistry U. Tex. Southwestern Med. Ctr., 1995—; hon. prof. Johns Hopkins U., scientific rev. bd. Howard Hughes Med. Inst., 1997—; trustee Carnegie Inst., Washington, 2000. Mem. editl. bd. numerous peer-reviewed jours.; contbr. articles to jours. in field. With U.S. Army, 1969-71, Vietnam. Decorated ARCOM medal; recipient Eli Lilly award Am. Soc. Microbiology, 1987, Newcomb-Cleveland award, AAAS, 1989, NAS Molecular Biology award Nat. Acad. Sci., 1991, Pioneer award, NIH, 2004. Fellow Carnegie Inst. Washington (hon.), Am. Soc. Microbiology (hon.); mem. NAS (Monsanto award 1991), Am. Acad. Arts and Scis., Am. Soc. for Biochemistry and Molecular Biology, Am. Chem. Soc., Am. Soc. for Cell Biology, Japanese Biochem. Soc. (hon.), Inst. Medicine. Achievements include research in leading to the discovery of genes that control the body's internal clock and regulate processes such as sleep, wakefulness and hunger. Home: 3717 Euclid Ave Dallas TX 75205-3161 Office: U Tex Southwestern Med Ctr Dept Biochemistry 5323 Harry Hines Blvd Dallas TX 75390-7208 also: Tularik Inc Two Corp Dr South San Francisco CA 94080 Office Phone: 214-648-9152. Business E-Mail: steven.mcknight@utsouthwestern.edu.

MCKNIGHT, THOMAS FREDERICK, artist; b. Lawrence, Kans., Jan. 13, 1941; m. Renate Hödl. BA cum laude, Wesleyan U., Middletown, Conn., 1963; postgrad., Columbia U., 1963-64. One-man shows Basel (Switzerland) Art Fair, 1975-77, Tomic Galerie, Dusseldorf, Germany, 1976, Hartmann Gallery, Munich, 1977, Newport (R.I.) Art Assn., 1981, Kobe (Japan) Mcpl. Art Mus., 1993, R^2 Gallery, N.Y.C., 2002; exhibited in group shows Llubljana, Yugoslavia, 1981, Tokyo, 1989, Davison Art Ctr., Wesleyan U., 1988, 98, numerous others; represented in permanent collections Davison Art Ctr., N.Y. State Mus., Albany, Smithsonian Instn., Washington, Met. Mus. Art, N.Y.C.; represented in Art in Embassies program; commns. include poster and print U.S. Constn. Bicentennial, 1989, prints Am.'s Cup, 1992, paintings and prints Urban Fair, Kobe, Japan, 1991, White House Christmas card, 1994, 95, 96; author: Thomas McKnight: Voyage to Paradise, 1993, Thomas McKnight's Arcadia, 2006. Recipient Disting. Alumni award Wesleyan U., 1998. Office Phone: 860-618-5441. Personal E-mail: info@thomasmcknight.com.

MCKOOL, MIKE, JR., lawyer; b. Dallas, Aug. 18, 1949; BA magna cum laude, U. Notre Dame, 1971; JD with honors, U. Tex. Sch. Law, 1974. Bar: Tex. 1974, US Supreme Ct., US Ct. Appeals (1st, 5th and fed. cirs.), US Dist. Ct. (all dists. Tex.), NY Supreme Ct. Atty. Johnson & Gibbs, Dallas; founder to prin. McKool Smith, P.C., Dallas, 1991—. Adj. prof. law So.

Meth. U., Dallas, 1981—86. Named one of Best Lawyers in Dallas, D Mag., 2001, 2003, 2005, 2006, Tex. Super Lawyers, Tex. Monthly, 2003—06, Best Lawyers in Am., Dallas/Ft/ Worth's Top 15 Bus. Def. Attys., Dallas Bus. Jour., Five Tex. "Go To" Civil Litigation Attys., Tex. Lawyer Newspaper. Mem.: Dallas Bar Assn., ABA. Office: McKool Smith PC 300 Crescent Court Ste 1500 Dallas TX 75201 Office Phone: 214-978-4002. Office Fax: 214-978-4044. E-mail: mmckool@mckoolsmith.com.

MCKOWEN, DOROTHY KEETON, librarian, educator; b. Bonne Terre, Mo., Oct. 5, 1948; d. John Richard and Dorothy (Spoonhour) Keeton; m. Paul Edwin McKowen, Dec. 19, 1970; children: Richard James, Mark David. BS, Pacific Christian Coll., 1970; MLS, U. So. Calif., 1973; MA in English, Purdue U., 1985, PhD, 2003. Libr.-specialist Doheny Libr., U. So. Calif., LA, 1973-74; asst. libr. Pacific Christian Coll., 1974-78; serials cataloger Purdue U. Librs., 1978-88; head children's and young adult svcs. Kokomo-Howard County Pub. Libr., Ind., 1988-89, coord. children's and tech. svcs. Ind., 1989-91; cataloger, network libr. Ind. Coop. Libr. Svcs. Authority, 1991-2001. Mem. adj. faculty Ivy Tech. C.C. of Ind., 2001—; lectr. Purdue U., 2003—. Mem. ALA, MLA, Soc. Early Americanists, Assn. for Libr. Collections and Tech. Svcs. (bd. dirs. 1986-90, 95-96, vice chair, chair-elect coun. of regional groups 1986-88, chair 1988-90, conf. program com. 1986-88, internat. rels. com. 1986-88, micropub. com. 1986-87, subject analysis com., membership com. 1988-90, planning and rsch. com. 1988-90, chair program initiatives com. 1991-93, orgn. and bylaws com. 1991-92, 99-2001), Network OCLC Svc. Mgrs. (MARC Task Force 2000-01), Ind. Coun. Libr. Automation (bibliog. stds. task force), Ind. Libr. Fedn. (chair tech. svcs. divsn. 1984-85), Ohio Valley Group Tech. Svcs. Libr. (chmn. 1985-86). Republican. Home: 7625 Summit Ln Lafayette IN 47905-9729 E-mail: mckowens2@yahoo.com.

MCKOWN, CHARLES HENRY, dean; b. Huntington, W.Va., Dec. 29, 1934; BS, W.Va. U., 1956; MD, Med. Coll. Va., 1960. Intern Med. Coll. Va., 1961; resident in radiology McGuire VA Hosp., 1961—62; fellow NIH, 1964—67; prof. radiology, chmn. dept. radiology Marshall U., Huntington, W.Va., 1975—88, v.p. health scis., dean Sch. Medicine, 1989—. Office: Marshall U Joan C Edwards Sch Medicine Ste 3400 1600 Medical Center Dr Huntington WV 25701-3655

MC KOY, BASIL VINCENT CHARLES, theoretical chemist, educator; b. Trinidad, Wis., Mar. 25, 1938; came to U.S., 1960, naturalized, 1973; s. Allan Cecil and Doris Augusta McK.; m. Anne Ellen Shannon, Mar. 18, 1967; 1 son, Christopher Allan. B.Chem. Eng., N.S. Tech. U., 1960; PhD in Chemistry (Univ. fellow), Yale U., 1964. Instr. chemistry Calif. Inst. Tech., 1964-66, asst. prof. chemistry, 1966-69, asso. prof., 1969-75, prof. theoretical chemistry, 1975—, chmn. of faculty, 1985-87. Cons. Lawrence Livermore Lab., U. Calif., Livermore, 1974—, Inst. Def. Analysis, 1984—; vis. prof. Max Planck Inst., Munich, Ger., 1976—, U. Paris, 1968—, U. Campinas, Brazil, 1976—; lectr. Nobel Symposium, Goteborg, Sweden, 1979. Contbr. articles to Jour. Physics, London, chem. Physics Lettters, Phys. Rev., Jour. Chem. Physics; bd. editors; Chem. Physics Jour., 1977-79, mem. adv. editoral bd., 1992—; co-editor: Electron-Molecule and Photon-Molecule Collisions, 1979, 83, Swarm Studies and Inelastic Electron-Molecule Collisions, 1986; co-author: Electron-Molecule Collisions and Photoionization Processes, 1982. Recipient medal Gov.-Gen. Can., 1960; Alfred P. Sloan Found. fellow, 1969-73; Guggenheim fellow, 1973-74 Fellow Am. Phys. Soc. Home: 3855 Keswick Rd La Canada Flintridge CA 91011-3945 Office: Calif Inst Tech Divsn Chemistry Pasadena CA 91125-0001 Office Phone: 626-395-6545. Business E-Mail: mckoy@caltech.edu.

MCKUSICK, VICTOR ALMON, geneticist, educator, physician; b. Parkman, Maine, Oct. 21, 1921; s. Carroll L. and Ethel M. (Buzzell) Mc K.; m. Anne Bishop, June 11, 1949; children: Carol Anne, Kenneth Andrew, Victor Wayne. Student, Tufts Coll., 1940-43; MD, Johns Hopkins U., 1946; DSc (hon.), N.Y. Med. Coll., 1974; MD (hon.), Liverpool U., 1976; DSc (hon.), U. Maine, 1978, Tufts U., 1978, U. Rochester, 1979, Meml. U., Nfld., 1979; DMCh (hon.), U. Helsinki, 1981; D Med. Sci. (hon.), Med. U. S.C., 1979; MD (hon.), Edinburgh U., 1984; DSc (hon.), Aberdeen U., 1988, Med. Coll. Ohio, 1988, Bates Coll., 1989; PhD (hon.), Tel Aviv U., 1989; MD (hon.), Zurich U., Switzerland, 1990; DSc (hon.), Colby Coll., 1991, U. Chgo., 1991, Mt. Sinai Sch. Medicine, 1992; DSc (hon.), Med. Coll. Wis., 1998, Rockefeller U., 2002. Diplomate Am. Bd. Internal Medicine. Tng. in clin. medicine, lab. rsch. Johns Hopkins U./USPHS, 1946-52; instr. medicine Johns Hopkins Sch. Medicine, 1951-54, asst. prof., 1954-57, assoc. prof., 1957-60, chief divsn. med. genetics, dept. medicine, 1957-73, prof. medicine, 1960-85, prof. epidemiology, biology, 1969-78, William Osler prof. medicine, 1978-85, chmn. dept. medicine, 1973-85; physician-in-chief Johns Hopkins Hosp., 1973-85, Univ. prof. medical genetics, 1985—, chief div. med. genetics, 1957-73, 85-89. Mem. rsch. adv. com. Nat. Found., 1959—78; mem. adv. bd. Howard Hughes Med. Inst., 1967—83; com. mapping and sequencing of human genome Nat. Acad. Sci., 1986—88; pres. Internat. Med. Congress, Ltd., 1972—78; mem. Nat. Adv. Rsch. Resources Coun., 1970—74; mem. bd. sci. advisors Roche Inst. Molecular Biology, 1967—71; trustee Jackson Lab., 1979—; founding mem. Am. Bd. Med. Genetics, 1979—82; pres. 8th Internat. Conf. Human Genetics, Washington, 1991; mem. human genome adv. com. NIH, 1988—92, NIH/DOE work group on ethical, legal and societal implications of human genome project, 1990—95; co-chmn. Centennial of Johns Hopkins Hosp., 1989—90; co-founder, co-dir. ann. short course in med. and exptl. mammalian genetics, Bar Harbor, Maine, 1960—, European Sch. Med. Genetics Sestri Levante and Bertinoro, 1988—; chmn. com. on DNA tech. in forensic sci. NRC/NAS, 1989—92, adv. update com., 1993—96; mem. sci. adv. bd. Celera Genomics, 1998—; founding fellow Am. Coll. Med. Genetics. Author: Heritable Disorders of Connective Tissue, 1956, 60, 66, 72, 93, Cardiovascular Sound in Health and Disease, 1958, Medical Genetics 1958-60, 1961, Human Genetics, 1964, 69, On the X Chromosome of Man, 1964, Mendelian Inheritance in Man, 1966, 68, 71, 75, 78, 83, 86, 88, 90, 92, 94, 98, Medical Genetics Self-Instruction Guide, 1993, (with others) Osler's Textbook Revisited, 1967, Genetics of Hand Malformations, 1978, Medical Genetic Studies of the Amish, 1978, A Model of its Kind, 1989, Osler's Legacy, 1990, A Century of Biomedical Science at Johns Hopkins, 1993; author, editor: Online Mendelian Inheritance in Man, 1985—; editor-in-chief Medicine jour., 1985—; founding co-editor-in-chief Genomics jour. 1987—; editor med. textbook. Named hon. citizen of Genoa, 1997; named to Internat. Pediat. Hall of Fame, 1987; recipient Disting. Achievement award, Modern Medicine, 1965, John Phillips award, ACP, 1972, Silver medal, U. Helsinki, 1974, Gairdner Internat. award, 1977, Premio Internazionale Sanremo per le Ricerche Genetiche, 1983, Col. Saunders award, March of Dimes, 1988, Disting. Alumnus award, Johns Hopkins U., 1983, Alumnus Svc. award, Johns Hopkins Med. Sch., 1989, Passano award, 1989, Disting. Svc. award, Miami Biotech. Winter Symposium, 1991, Frank Bradway Rogers Info. Advancement award, Med. Libr. Assn., 1991, Silver Columbus medal, Comune di Genova, 1992, Maine prize (with twin), 1993, Mendel medal, Villanova U., 1995, Big "M" award, Maine State Soc. Washington, D.C., 1995, Coriell medal, Coriell Inst., Camden, N.J., 1997, Lasker award for lifetime achievement in med. sci., 1997, City of Medicine award, Durham, N.C., 1997, James P. McGovern Compleat Physician award, 2000, Albert Lasker award for Special Achievement in Medicine, Lasker Found., 2000, Nat. medal of sci., 2002, Rsch. Achievement award, Am. Heart Assn., 2002. Fellow AAAS (chair med. scis. sect. 1991), Am. Acad. Orthopedic Surgeons (hon.), Royal Coll. Physicians (London), Hastings Ctr., Am. Coll. Med. Genetics (hon.); mem. Nat. Acad. Sci. (James Murray Luck award 1982), Am. Philos. Soc. (v.p. 1996—, Benjamin Franklin medal for disting. achievement in scis. 1996), Am. Soc. Human Genetics (pres. 1975, Wm. A. Allan award 1977), Assn. Am. Physicians (Kober medal 1990), Am. Soc. Clin. Investigation (v.p. 1967), Human Genome Orgn. (founder pres. 1988-89), Am. Acad. Arts and Sci., Little People of Am. (hon. life), Acad. Nat. Médecine (France; corr.), Phi Beta Kappa, Alpha Omega Alpha, Johns Hopkins Club, West Hamilton St. Club, St. Andrew's Soc. Balt. Presbyterian (elder). Office: Johns Hopkins Hosp Inst Genetic Medicine-Blalock 1007 600 N Wolfe St Baltimore MD 21287-4922 Home: 1055 W Joppa Rd Unit 528 Towson MD 21204-3747

MCKUSICK, VINCENT LEE, retired chief justice, arbitrator, lawyer, mediator; b. Parkman, Maine, Oct. 21, 1921; s. Carroll Lee and Ethel (Buzzell) McK.; m. Nancy Elizabeth Green, June 23, 1951; children: Barbara McKusick Liscord, James Emory, Katherine McKusick Ralston, Anne Elizabeth. AB, Bates Coll., 1943; SB, SM, MIT, 1947; LLB, Harvard U., 1950; LLD, Colby Coll., 1976, Nasson Coll., 1978, Bates Coll., 1979, Bowdoin Coll., 1979, Suffolk U., 1983; LHD, U. So. Maine, 1978, Thomas Coll., 1981. Bar: Maine 1952. Law clk. to Chief Judge Learned Hand, 1950-51; to Justice Felix Frankfurter, 1951-52; partner Pierce, Atwood, Scribner, Allen & McKusick and predecessors, Portland, Maine, 1953-77; chief justice Maine Supreme Jud. Ct., 1977-92; of counsel to Pierce Atwood LLP (formerly Pierce, Atwood, Scribner, Allen, Smith, & Lancaster), 1992—. Mem. adv. com. rules civil procedure Maine Supreme Jud. Ct., 1957-59, chmn., 1966-75, commr. uniform state laws, 1968-76, sec. nat. conf., 1975-77; mem. Conf. Chief Justices, 1977-92, bd. dirs., 1980-82, 91-92, pres.-elect, 1989-90, pres., 1990-91, standing com. past pres., 1992—; dir. Nat. Ctr. for State Ctrs., 1988-89, chmn.-elect, 1989-90, chmn., 1990-91; spl. master U.S. Supreme Ct. Conn. v. N.H., 1992-93, La. v. Miss., 1994-96, Kans. v. Nebr., 1999-2003; spl. master Mass. S.J.C. Liquidation Am. Mutual Liability Ins. Co., 1995-96; leader Am. Judges Del. to China, 1983, USSR, 1988, U.S. State Dept. Rule of Law Del. to Republic of Ga., 1992; mem. permanent com. Oliver Wendell Holmes Devise, 1993-2001. Author: Patent Policy of Educational Institutions, 1947, (with Richard H. Field) Maine Civil Practice, 1959, supplements, 1962, 67, (with Richard H. Field and L. Kinvin Wroth) 2d edit., 1970, supplements, 1972, 74, 77; also articles in legal publs. Trustee emeritus Bates Coll.; mem. adv. com. on pvt. internat. law US State Dept., 1980-85, Fed.-State Jurisdiction com., Jud. Conf. of US, 1987-89. With AUS, 1943-46. Recipient The Maine prize U. Maine Sys., 1993, Benjamin E. Mays award Bates Coll., 1994, Big M award Maine State Soc. Washington, 1995, Paul C. Reardon award Nat. Ctr. for State Ctrs., 1999. Fellow Am. Bar Found. (bd. dirs. 1977-87), Am. Philos. Soc. (coun. 1990-96, 97-02, v.p. 2002-); mem. ABA (chmn. fed. rules com. 1966-71, bd. editors jour. 1971-80, chmn. 1976-77, mem. study group to China 1978, house dels. 1983-87, coun. sr. lawyers divsn. 1997-01), Maine Bar Assn., Cumberland County Bar Assn., Am. Arbitration Assn. (bd. dirs. 1994-2006), Am. Judicature Soc. (dir. 1976-78, 92-98), Am. Law Inst. (coun. 1968—), Maine Jud. Coun. (chmn. 1977-92), Inst. Jud. Adminstrn., Supreme Ct. Hist. Soc. (trustee 1994-2006), Rotary Club (hon., past pres. Portland club), Phi Beta Kappa, Sigma Xi, Tau Beta Pi. Republican. Unitarian Universalist. Home: 1152 Shore Rd Cape Elizabeth ME 04107-2115 Office: 1 Monument Sq Portland ME 04101-1110 Office Phone: 207-791-1100. Personal E-mail: judgemac@maine.rr.com. Business E-Mail: vmckusick@pierceatwood.com.

MCLACHLAN, SARAH, musician, composer; b. Halifax, Nova Scotia, Jan. 28, 1968; m. Ashwin Sood, Feb. 7, 1997; 1 child, India. Founder, performer Lilith Fair. Albums include Touch, 1989, Solace, 1991, Live EP, 1992, Fumbling Towards Ecstasy, 1994, Freedom Sessions, 1995, Rarities, B-Sides, and Other Stuff, 1996, Surfacing, 1997, Mirrorball, 1999, Sarah McLachlan Remixed, 2001, Afterglow, 2003, Wintersong, 2006, Mirrorball: The Complete Concert, 2006; appearances include Gravity, 1991, Island of Circles: A Nettwork C, 1991, No Alternative, 1993, Christmas at Mountain Stage, 1994, Testimonial Dinner: the Songs of Xt, 1995, Memories of the Soul Shack Survivor, 1996, Heroine, 1996, Bloom, 2005; worked with Delerium, Donovan. Recipient Order of Canada, Best Female Pop Vocal Performance award Grammy, 1997, 1999, Best Pop Instrumental Performance award, 1997; nominated for Grammy for Best Female Pop Vocal Performance for "Fallen," 2003. Achievements include founding Lilith Fair, all-female peformance concert tour, 1997-1999. Office: Nettwerk Mgmt 1650 W 2nd Ave Vancouver BC V6J 4R3 Canada

MCLACHLIN, BEVERLEY, Canadian supreme court chief justice; b. Pincher Creek, Alta., Can., Sept. 7, 1943; m. Roderick McLachlin (dec. 1988); 1 child, Angus; m. Frank E. McArdle, 1992. BA, U. Alta., MA in Philosophy, LLB, LLD (hon.), 1991, U. B.C., 1990, U. Toronto, 1995, York U., 1999, Law Soc. Upper Can., 2000, U. Ottawa, 2000, U. Calgary, 2000, Brock U., 2000, Simon Fraser U., 2000, U. Victoria, 2000, U. Alberta, 2000, U. Lethbridge, 2001, Bridgewater State Coll., 2001, Mt. St. Vincent U., 2002, U. PEI, 2002, U. Montreal, 2003, U. Man., 2004, Queen's U., Belfast, 2004, Dalhousie U., 2004, Carleton U., 2004, U. Ft. Kent, Maine, 2005, Ateneo de Manila U., 2006. Bar: Alta. 1969, B.C. 1971. Assoc. Wood, Moir, Hyde and Ross, Edmonton, Alta., Canada, 1969—71, Thomas, Herdy, Mitchell & Co., Fort St. John, B.C., Canada, 1971—72, Bull, Housser and Tupper, Vancouver, 1972—75; from lectr. to prof. U. B.C., 1974—81; appointed to County Ct., Vancouver, 1981; justice Supreme Ct. of B.C., 1981—85, B.C. Ct. of Appeal, Canada, 1985—88; chief justice Supreme Ct. of B.C., Canada, 1988; justice Supreme Ct. Can., Ottawa, Ont., Canada, 1989—2000, chief justice Can., 2000—. Co-author: B.C. Supreme Court Practice, B.C. Court Forms, Canadian Law of Arch. and Engring.; contbr. articles to profl. jours. Office: Supreme Ct Bldg 301 Wellington St Ottawa ON Canada K1A 0J1 Office Phone: 613-992-6940.

MCLAFFERTY, FRED WARREN, chemist, educator; b. Evanston, Ill., May 11, 1923; s. Joel E. and Margaret E. (Keifer) McLafferty; m. Elizabeth E. Curley, Feb. 5, 1948; children: Sara L., Joel P., Martha A., Samuel A., Ann E. BS, U. Nebr., 1943, DSc (hon.), 1983, MS, 1947; PhD, Cornell U., 1950; DSc (hon.), U. Liege, Belgium, 1987, Purdue U., 1995. Fellow U. Iowa, 1949-50; rsch. chemist, divsn. leader Dow Chem. Co., 1950-56; dir. Eastern Rsch. Lab., 1956-64; prof. chemistry Purdue U., 1964-68, Cornell U., 1968-92, Peter J.W. Debye prof. chemistry emeritus, 1992—. Chem. sci. and tech. bd., numerical data adv. bd., bd. Army sci. tech., bd. radioactive waste mgmt. NRC; chem. co-chmn. World Bank's Chinese Univ. Devel. Project. Author: Mass Spectrometry of Organic Ions, 1963, Mass Spectral Correlations, 2d edit., 1981, Interpretation of Mass Spectra, 4th edit., 1993, Tandem Mass Spectrometry, 1983, Advances in Analytical Chemistry and Instrumentation; (with C.N. Reilley), Vols. 4-7, 1967-70, Index and Bibliography of Mass Spectrometry, (with J. Pinzelik), 1967, Atlas of Mass Spectral Data; (with E. Stenhagen and S. Abrahamsson), 1969, Registry of Mass Spectral Data, 1974; (with D.B. Stauffer) Wiley/NBS Registry of Mass Spectral Data, 1989, Important Peak Index of Mass Spectral Data, 1991; editor: Accounts of Chemical Research, 1986-94; co-editor: (with E. Stenhagen and S. Abrahamsson) Archives of Mass Spectral Data, 1969-72. With AUS, 1942-45, ETO. Decorated Purple Heart, Combat Inf. badge, Bronze Star with 4 oak leaf clusters, Presdl. Unit citation; recipient Pitts. Spectroscopy award Spectroscopy Soc. Pitts., 1975, Gold medal U. Naples, 1989, Robert Boyle Gold medal Royal Soc. Chemistry, 1992, Bijvoet medal U. Utrecht, 1997, W.L. Evans award Ohio State U., 1987, Jaroslav Heyrovsky Gold medal Czech Acad. Scis., 1999, Guilio Natta Gold medal Italian Chem. Soc., 2000, Torbern Bergman medal Swedish Chem. Soc., 2001, Lavoisier medal French Chem. Soc., 2004; John Simon Guggenheim fellow, 1972, Overseas fellow Churchill Coll., Cambridge (Eng.) U., 1979. Fellow: AAAS, NAS, Am. Acad. Arts and Scis., N.Y. Acad. Scis.; mem.: Internat. Assn. Protein Structure and Analytical Proteomics (Pehr Edman award 2006), Italian Nat. Acad. Scis. XL (fgn.), Am. Inst. Chemists (Chem. Pioneer award 1996), Am. Soc. Mass. Spectrometry (founder, sec. 1957—58, Disting. Contbn. in Mass Spectrometry award 2003), Assn. Analytical Chemists (Anachem award 1985), Internat. Spectrometry Orgn. (Sir J.J. Thomson gold medal 1985), Am. Chem. Soc. (chmn. analytical chem. divsn. 1969, chmn. Midland sect. 1956, Northeastern sect. 1964, award chem. instrumentation 1971, award analytical chemistry 1981, Nichols medal N.Y. sect. 1984, Oesper award Cin. sect. 1986, award mass spectrometry 1989), Soc. Analytical Chemists (Pitts. Analytical Chemist award 1987, Pioneer Analytical Instrumentation award 1994), Alpha Chi Sigma, Phi Lambda Upsilon, Sigma Xi. Home: 103 Needham Pl Ithaca NY 14850-2120 Office Phone: 607-255-4699. Business E-Mail: fwm5@cornell.edu.

MCLAIN, DENNIS O., lawyer; b. Detroit, Aug. 11, 1945; s. Francis William McLain and Hazel Joyce (Owen) Horton. BA, U. Mich., 1971; JD, Detroit Coll. Law, 1975. Bar: Mich. 1975. Assoc. Collins & McCormick, Ypsilanti, Mich., 1972—77; gen. ptnr. McLain & Winters, Ypsilanti, Mich., 1977—. Mem.: Mich. Trial Lawyers Assn., Ypsilanti C. of C., Ypsilanti Bar Assn., Washtenaw County Bar Assn., Mich. Bar Assn., Fed. Bar Assn. Democrat. Roman Catholic. Office: McLain & Winters 61 N Huron St Ypsilanti MI 48197-2675 Office Phone: 734-481-1120. E-mail: mwatty@voyager.net.

MCLAIN, PAUL KING, systems analyst; b. Bremerton, Wash., June 10, 1946; s. Paul Gaylon and Frances Marilyn McLain; m. Maureen Elizabeth Miner, Aug. 23, 1969 (div. Dec. 16, 1986); children: Paul Joseph, Andrew John; m. Donna Joan Miller, Nov. 19, 1988. BA in Psychology, U. Wash., 1973, BA in History, 1975; cert. in bus. computing, North Seattle CC, 1979; MDiv, Seattle U., 2002. Ordained min. Universal Life Ch. Warehouse clk. Seattle Transfer and Storage, 1969—70; returns supr. Transcontinental Music Co., Seattle, 1970—71; entry mgr. A. L. Tokin Custom Ho. Broker, Seattle, 1973—74; import adminstr. Eckert Overseas Agy., Seattle, 1974—76; warehouse and container terminal clk. Port of Seattle, 1976—79; sys. analyst Boeing Co., Seattle, 1979—2001; point-of-sale clk. Sinnett's Market Pl., Longview, Wash., 2004—05; sys. analyst Longview Fibre Co., Wash., 2005—. Presenter in field; lectr. in field. Actor: (musical) The Fantastics. Del. Dem. State Conv., Tacoma, 2004; mem. Cowlite County Dem. Women's Club; treas. Aspire! for Unitarian Universalist Ministerial Candidates, Boston, 2000—01; pres. Saltwater Unitarian Universalist Ch., Kent, Wash., 1993—94; chpt. pres. Toastmasters Internat., Kent, Wash., 1988—89, area gov., 1989—90. With USN, 1965—69. Decorated Navy Unit Commendation (2) USN, Vietnam Svc. Medal (3), Republic of Vietnam Campaign medal Dept. of Def. Mem.: VFW, Red River Heritage Assn., Am. Bus. Women's Assn., Alexandria Unitarian Universalist Fellowship (pres. 2007—), Mensa. Liberal. Unitarian Universalist. Achievements include reduction of time required for work center loading system; design of webpage timeline. Avocations: digital video, computing, music. Home: PO Box 190 Dry Prong LA 71423-0190 Personal E-mail: uuseeker@earthlink.net.

MCLAIN, WILLIAM ALLEN, lawyer; b. Chgo., Oct. 19, 1942; s. William Rex and Wilma L. (Raschka) McL.; divorced; children: William A., David M., Heather A.; m. Kristine R. Zierk. BS, So. Ill. U., 1966; JD, Loyola U., Chgo., 1971. Bar: Ill. 1971, U.S. Dist. Ct. (no. dist.) Ill. 1971, U.S. Ct. Appeals (7th cir.) 1971, Colo. 1975, U.S. Dist. Ct. Colo. 1975, U.S. Ct. Appeals (10th cir.) 1975. Law clk. U.S. Dist. Ct. (no. dist.) Ill., Chgo., 1971-72; assoc. Sidley & Austin, Chgo., 1972-75; ptnr. Welborn, Dufford, Brown & Tooley, Denver, 1975-86; pres. William A. McLain PC, 1986—; ptnr. McLain & Singer, Denver, 1990—. Mem. Dist. 10 Legis. Vacancy Commn., Denver, 1984-86. Served with U.S. Army, 1966-68. Recipient Leadership and Scholastic Achievement award Loyola U. Alumni Assn., 1971. Mem. Colo. Bar Assn. (lobbyist 1983-85), Denver Bar Assn., Colo. Assn. Commerce and Industry (legis. policy coun. 1983-88), Colo. Mining Assn. (state and local affairs com. 1978-88), Inst. Property Taxation, Roundup Riders of the Rockies Club, Masons, Shriners, Scottish Rite, York Rite. Republican. Home and Office: 3962 S Olive St Denver CO 80237-2038 Office Phone: 303-759-0087. E-mail: wamclain@comcast.net.

MCLANE, CHARLES D., JR., metal products executive; b. Richmond, July 15, 1953; m. Betty McLane; 2 children. B in Acctg., Va. Commonwealth U., Richmond, 1978, M in Acctg., 1984. Various fin. positions including divsn. contr. Reynolds Metals, dir. fin. and adminstrn. Global Can bus. unit, 1990—95, asst. contr., 1995—99, asst. treas., 1999—2000; dir. investor rels. Alcoa, Inc., 2000—02, v.p. Bus. Support Svcs., corp. contr. NYC, 2002, CFO, 2007—. Mem. com. on corp. reporting Fin. Execs. Inst. Office: Alcoa Inc 390 Park Ave New York NY 10022 Office Phone: 212-836-2600. *

MCLANE, FREDERICK BERG, lawyer; b. Long Beach, Calif., July 24, 1941; s. Adrian B. and Arlie K. (Burrell) McL.; m. Lois C. Roberts, Jan. 28, 1967; children: Willard, Anita. BA, Stanford U., 1963; LLB, Yale U., 1966. Bar: Calif. 1967, U.S. Dist. Ct. (cen. dist.) Calif. 1967. Assoc. prof. law U. Miss., Oxford, 1966-68; assoc. O'Melveny & Myers LLP, LA, 1968-74, ptnr., 1975—2005, of counsel, 2005—. Lectr. in field. Pres., bd. dirs. Legal Aid Found., L.A., 1974-83; deacon Congl. Ch., Sherman Oaks, Calif., 1979-83; vice-chair L.A. Music Ctr., Unified Fund, 1992-94; bd. dirs. Calif. Sci. Ctr. Found., 1991-2000. Mem.: ABA (banking com., fed. regulation of securities com.), Calif. Bar Assn. (fin. insts. com., uniform comml. codes), Calif. Club (L.A.), L.A. Country Club (bd. dirs.), The Quarry at La Quinta, Order of Coif. Democrat. Avocations: golf, walking, reading. Office: O'Melveny & Myers LLP 1999 Ave of the Stars Los Angeles CA 90067-6035 Office Phone: 310-246-8554. Business E-Mail: fmclane@omm.com.

MCLANE, ROBERT DRAYTON, JR., food products company executive; b. Cameron, Tex., July 22, 1936; s. Robert Drayton and Gladys (Blaylock) McL.; m. Mary Elizabeth Cockrell, Feb. 2, 1972; children: Robert Drayton III, Denton. BBA, Baylor U., 1958; MS, Mich. State U., 1959. With McLane Co., Inc., Temple, Tex., 1957—, v.p., 1964-74, exec. v.p., sec.-treas., 1974-78, chief exec. officer, pres., 1978—, also bd. dirs. Bd. dirs. First Nat. Bank, Temple, Tex. Pres. United Way Campaign, Temple, 1985—; mem. Tex. State Bd. Mental Health and Mental Retardation, 1985—, exec. bd. Heart O'Tex. Council Boy Scouts Am., 1968—; bd. dirs. Scott and White Meml. Hosp., Temple, 1985—. Recipient Mgmt. Excellence and Achievement award Coll. Bus. Mgmt. U. Ga., 1986; named Entrepreneur of Yr. Arthur Young/Venture, Dallas, 1987; named one of Forbes' Richest Americans, 2006. Mem. Nat. Am. Wholesale Grocers Assn. (chmn. 1986-88), Nat. Assn. Convenience Stores, Grocery Mfrs. Am., Tex. Food Industry Assn. Baptist. Avocation: tennis. Office: McLane Group PO Box 549 Temple TX 76503-0549

MCLANE, WILLIAM DELANO, mechanical engineer; b. Ralls, Tex., Aug. 22, 1936; s. Clyde and Lillian Helen (Earp) McL.; m. Mary Ann Clark, Feb. 17, 1962; children: William Devin, Keri, Kristi, Mandy. BSME, Tex. Tech. U., 1961. Profl. engr. Tex. Engr. Texaco Inc., Tulsa, 1961-63; plant engring. mgr. Owens-Corning Fiberglas Corp., Toledo, 1963-72; pres., CEO Tucker-McLane Tire Corp., Waxahachie, Tex., 1972-89; commr. County of Ellis, Waxahachie, 1989-93; engr. Morrison Knudsen Corp., Dallas, 1993-94, MK-Ferguson, Albuquerque, 1994-95, Parsons Brinckerhoff, Dallas, 1995-96; quality control mgr. Sedalco, Inc., Ft. Worth, 1996-97; engring. mgr. Fortra Fiber-Cement, LLC., Waxahachie, Tex., 1997-2001; constrn. mgr. FWTA commuter rail project Parsons Brinckerhoff Constrn. Svcs., Inc., Dallas, 2001—02, sr. project mgr., Bush Internat. Airport Svcs. Improvement program Houston, 2002—05; constrn. mgr. Dallas County Cmty. Coll. Dist., Irving, Tex., 2005—. Mem. adv. bd. Guaranty Fed. Bank, Waxahachie, 1993—, Citizens Nat. Bank, Waxahachie, 1991-92, City of Waxahachie, 1990-91, Tex. State Tech. Coll., Inc., Waco, 1998—, Navarro Coll., Corsicana, 1998—, Portland Cement Assn.,

Skokie, Ill., 1998—. Sec. bd. Waxahachie Sch. Dist., 1979-88; vice chmn. Ctrl. Tex. Econ. Devel. Dist., Waco, 1989-93; mem. adv. com. Tex. State Tech. Coll., Waco, 1998—. Mem. ASME, ASCE, NSPE, Tex. Soc. Profl. Engrs., So. Bldg. Code Congress Internat., Internat. Soc. Tribologists and Lubrication Engrs., Internat. Conf. Bldg. Officials, Waxahachie C. of C. (pres. 1977). Republican. Presbyterian. Avocations: civic and political volunteer work, golf, fishing, cooking. Home: 1612 Alexander Dr Waxahachie TX 75165-1902 Office: Parsons Brinckerhoff Constrn Svcs 2777 Stemmons Fwy Ste 1333 Dallas TX 75207 Personal E-mail: delmclane@sbcglobal.net.

MCLAREN, BRIAN, pastor, christian activist; b. 1956; m. Grace McLaren; 4 children. BA in Eng., U. of Maryland, Coll. Park, 1978, BA in Eng., 1981; Doctor of Divinity (hon.), Carey Theological Seminary, Vancouver, 2004. Teacher coll. eng., 1978—86; founding pastor Cedar Ridge Comm. Church, 1986—2006. Author: (novels) The Church on the Other Side, 1998, Finding Faith, 1999, A New Kind of Christian, 2001 (Christianity Today's Award of Merit, 2002), More Ready Than You Realize: Evangelism as Dance in the Postmodern Matrix, 2002, A Is for Abductive, 2002; co-author Adventures in Missing the Point, 2003, Church in Emerging Culture: Five Perspectives, 2003; author The Story We Find Ourselves In, 2003, A Generous Orthodoxy, 2004, The Last Word and the Word After That, 2005, The Secret Message of Jesus: Uncovering the Truth that Could Change Everything, 2006, contbr. multiple articles to periodicals, including Leadership, Sojourners, Worship Leader, and Conversations. Named one of 25 Most Influential Evangelicals, Time Magazine, 2005. Mem.: Orientacion Cristiana, Red Letter Christians, Sojourners/Call to Renewal, international steering team for Emergent Village. Christian. Achievements include teaching or lecturing at several seminaries in the U.S. and abroad. His books have been or are being translated into many languages, including Korean, Chinese, French, Swedish, Norwegian, and Spanish. Avocations: fishing, art, ecology, hiking, kayaking, song writing, camping, literature. Office: Emergent Village PO Box 390104 Minneapolis MN 55439 *

MCLAREN, RICHARD WELLINGTON, JR., lawyer; s. Richard Wellington and Edith (Gillett) McL.; m. Ann Lynn Zachrich, 1971; children: Christine, Richard, Charles. BA, Yale U., 1967; JD, Northwestern U., 1973. Bar: Ohio 1973, Ill. 1997, U.S. Dist. Ct. (no. dist.) Ohio 1973, U.S. Dist. Ct. (no. dist.) Ill. 1997, U.S. Ct. Appeals (6th cir.) 1978, U.S. Ct. Appeals (7th cir.) 1997, U.S. Ct. Appeals (fed. cir.) 1997, U.S. Supreme Ct. 1981. Assoc. Squire, Sanders & Dempsey, Cleve., 1973-82, ptnr., 1983-87; prin., counsel Ernst & Whinney, Cleve., 1988-89; assoc. gen. counsel Ernst & Young, Cleve., 1989-93; prin. counsel Centerior Energy Corp., Cleve., 1994-96; prin. Welsh & Katz, Ltd., Chgo., 1997—. 1st lt. U.S. Army, 1967-70. Mem. ABA (litigation, intellectual property and corp. law), FBA, Am. Judicature Soc., Ohio Bar Assn., Ill. Bar Assn. Home: 638 S Monroe St Hinsdale IL 60521-3926 Office: 120 S Riverside Plz Fl 22 Chicago IL 60606-3913 Office Phone: 312-655-1500. Business E-Mail: rwmclaren@welshkatz.com.

MCLARNEY, CHARLES PATRICK, lawyer; b. Hemple, Mo., Mar. 28, 1942; s. Charles Joseph and Owatonna Mary (Sayles) McL.; m. Martina Borkowski, Aug. 28, 1965; children: Ellen, Megan, Michael. BS, St. Benedict's Coll., 1964; JD, U. Mo., 1968. Bar: Mo. 1968, U.S. Dist. Ct. (we. dist.) Mo. 1968, U.S. Ct. Appeals (8th cir.), U.S. Supreme Ct. 1968. Assoc. Shook, Hardy & Bacon LLP, Kansas City, Mo., 1968-72, ptnr., 1972-93, mng. ptnr., 1985-88, 91—, shareholder, pres., 1993-96, mng. ptnr., 1996. Active Friends of Art, Kans. City, 1980—; v.p. Civic Coun. Greater Kansas City. Named Outstanding Lawyer Kans. City Met. Bar Assn., 2004, Legal Leader of Yr. The Daily Record, 2005. Fellow Internat. Soc. Barristers (bd. dirs. 1989-94), Am. Coll. Trial Lawyers; mem. Kansas City Met. Bar, Lawyers Assn. Kansas City (pres. 1987-88), Mo. Bar (bd. govs., bd. dirs. 1991-94), Kansas City Soc. Fellows, Eight Twenty-Two Club, Kansas City Club, Plaza Bus. Breakfast Club (pres. 1983-84), Kansas City Met. Bar Assn. Democrat. Roman Catholic. Avocations: tennis, golf, skiing. Office: Shook, Hardy & Bacon LLP 2555 Grand Blvd Kansas City MO 64108 Office Phone: 816-474-6550. Home Fax: 816-421-5547. Business E-Mail: pmclarney@shb.com.

MCLARNEY, THOMAS JOSEPH, physician; b. Waterbury, Conn., May 22, 1957; s. James Joseph McLarney and Dorothy Rose Calhoun; m. Patricia Lynn Swider; children: Kathryn Helene, James Joseph. BS in Biology, Fairfield U., Conn., 1979; MD, Georgetown U., Washington, 1984. Bd. cert. family medicine and geriatrics Am. Acad. Family Physicians. Intern Naval Hosp. Charleston, SC, 1984—85, resident, 1987—89; staff physician Naval Hosp., Newport, RI, 1989—94; clin. dir. Family Practice Residency, Middletown, Conn., 1994—2002; med. dir. Cmty. Health Ctr., East Hartford, Conn., 2002—. Physician vol. Spl. Olympics, New Haven, 1994—95; vol. We Are The Children, Hartford, 2006. Decorated Meritorious Svc. medal US Navy, Achievement medal; recipient Physician Yr., Naval Hosp., Newport, 1982, D. Schmidt Tchg. award, U. Conn., Dept. Family Practice, 2003, 2005. Mem.: Conn. Acad. Family Practice (K. McShane Execellent Physician medal 1999), St. Paul's Men's Club. Democrat. Roman Catholic. Home: 131 Old Farms Rd South Glastonbury CT 06073 Office: East Hartford Cmty Health Ctr 94 Connecticut Blvd East Hartford CT 06108

MCLARNON, MARY FRANCES, neurologist; b. Montreal, Que., Canada, May 13, 1944; came to U.S., 1969; d. John Francis and Patricia Jessica (Dore) McL.; m. Malcolm Weiner, Dec. 21, 1975; m. Lawrence Zingesser, Oct. 12, 1982; children: Andrea, Eliza. BS, McGill U., 1965, MD, 1969. Intern St. Vincent's Hosp., NYC, 1969-70; fellow seizure unit Boston Children's Hosp., 1970-71; resident in neurology Albert Einstein Coll. Medicine, Bronx, N.Y., 1971-73; resident in radiology N.Y. Hosp.-Cornell Med. Ctr., NYC, 1973-76; pvt. practice. Home: 752 Cove Rd Mamaroneck NY 10543-4324 Office Phone: 917-856-8301. Personal E-mail: mmclmd@hotmail.com.

MCLARTY, THOMAS F., III, (MACK MCLARTY), former White House Chief of Staff; b. Hope, Ark., June 14, 1946; s. Thomas Franklin and Helen (Hesterly) McL.; m. Donna Kay Cochran, June 14, 1969; children: Mark Cochran, Franklin Hesterly BA, U. Arkansas, Fayetteville, 1968. Founder, pres. McLarty Leasing System Inc., Little Rock, 1969-79; pres. McLarty Cos., 1979-83; with Arkla Inc., Shreveport, from 1983, pres., CEO Arkla Gas divsn., 1983; pres., COO Arkla Gas divsn. Arkla, Inc., Shreveport, 1984, chmn., pres., CEO, 1985—93; chief of staff to Pres. The White House, Washington, 1993-94, sr. adv. to Pres., 1994—97, counselor to Pres., spl. envoy for Americas, 1994—97; pres. Kissinger McLarty Assocs., Washington, 1998—; vice chmn. Asbury Automotive Group, 2002—06; sr. adv. The Carlyle Group, 2003—. Chmn. Arkla Energy Mktg. Co., Shreveport, La., Arkla Chem. Corp., Shreveport, AER-Ark. Gas Transit Co., Shreveport; chmn., CEO, Miss. River Transmission Corp., St. Louis, MRT Energy Mktg. Co., St. Louis, Ark. La. Fin. Corp., Shreveport; bd. dirs. Union Pacific Corp., 2006- Mem. Ark. Ho. of Reps., 1970-72; chmn. Ark. Dem. Com., 1974-76; treas. David Pryor Gubernatorial Campaign, 1974, Gov. Bill Clinton campaign, 1978; bd. dirs. Hendrix Coll., Conway, Ark.; bd. visitors U. Ark., Little Rock; former chmn. United Negro Coll. Fund Campaign, fund-raising campaign Ark. Symphony Recipient Humanitarian award, Nat. Conf. Christians & Jews, 1991, Fair Share award, NAACP, 1991, DSM, US Dept. State, Order of the Aztec Eagle. Mem. Greater Little Rock C. of C. (pres. 1983) Office: Kissinger McLarty Assocs 1775 Pennsylvania Ave NW Washington DC 20006-4605 also: The Carlyle Group 1001 Pennsylvania Ave Washington DC 20004 *

MCLAUGHLIN, BARBARA LYN, elementary school educator; b. Watseka, Ill., Jan. 18, 1950; d. LaVerne Melvin and Marian Barbara (Borchers) Reitz; m. Steven Joseph McLaughlin, Oct. 7, 1972; children: Laurie Lyn Peterson, Lisa Kay Kolavennu, Angela Marie Erickson. BS in Edn., Ea. Ill. U., 1971; MA in Edn., Olivet Nazarene U., 1999. Std.Spl. Tchg.K-12 Ill., 1971, Std. Elem. Tchg.K-9 Ill., 1971. Kindergarten tchr. Danville Elem. Schs., Ill., 1971—72; first grade tchr. Clifton Elem., Clifton, Ill., 1972—73; substitute tchr. Ctrl. Unit Sch. Dist. 4, 1973—78; spl. edn. tchr. Chebanse Elem., Chebanse, Ill., 1978—. Chair spl. edn. dept. Ctrl. Unit Sch. Dist. 4, Clifton, Ill., 2000—, mentor spl. edn. dept., Chebanse, Ill., 2004—; mem. sch. improvement team Chebanse Elem., Ill., 1990—2002, 2005—, guest tchr., 2003—; online guest tchr. U. Wash., 2004—05. Contbr. chapters to books. Supporter Spl. Olympics. Recipient Disney Am. Tchr. award Honoree, Walt Disney Co., 2002-2003, Disting. Educator award, Ea. Ill. U., 2004;, First of Am. ednl. grantee, 2004, Ednl. scholar, Target, 1998. Mem.: Assn. Supervision and Curriculum Devel., Coun. for Exceptional Children, Pi Lambda Theta, Kappa Delta Pi (hon.), Delta Kappa Gamma (hon.; sec. 2000—04). Lutheran. Avocations: reading, conservation of natural resources, gardening, sports. Home: 440 East 3200 North Rd Clifton IL 60927 Office: Chebanse Elem 475 School Street Chebanse IL 60922 Home Phone: 815-421-0011; Office Phone: 815-697-2642. Personal E-mail: grove@dlogue.net.

MCLAUGHLIN, CALVIN STURGIS, biochemistry professor; b. St. Joseph, Mo., May 29, 1936; s. Calvin Sturgis and Agnes Jane McLaughlin; m. Chin Helen Moy, Sept. 7, 1960; children: Heather Chin Chu, Christine Leng Oy, Andrew Calvin Moy. BS, King Coll., 1958; postgrad., Yale U., 1958-59; PhD, MIT, 1964. Postdoctoral fellow Institut de Biologie Physico-Chimique, Paris, 1964-66; prof. biochemistry U. Calif., Irvine, 1966—, dir. Cancer Rsch. Inst., 1981-83; vis. prof. Sch. Botany Oxford U., Eng., 1976, 80. Mem. peer rev. panels Am. Cancer Soc., NSF, NIH, VA Contbr. numerous articles to profl. jours.; mem. editl. bds. Jour. Bacteriology, 1975-80, Exptl. Mycology, 1980-86; reviewer profl. jours. Bd. dirs. Am. Cancer Soc., Orange County, 1980-89; mem. Traffic Affairs Com., Newport Beach, Calif., 1972-78. Named Outstanding Tchr. U. Calif.-Irvine, 1978, Gabriel Lester Meml. Lectr. Reed Coll., 1979; fellow Rockefeller Found., 1958-59, Upjohn Found., 1959-60, Nutrition Found., 1960-61, NIH, 1961-64, Am. Cancer Soc., 1964-66 Mem. Genetics Soc. Am., Am. Soc. Biochemistry and Molecular Biology, Am. Soc. Microbiology, Am. Soc. Mycology, Am. Soc. for Cell Biology, Yeast Genetics and Molecular Biology Soc. Am. (co-chair 1986-88), Electrophoresis Soc. Anglican. Office: U Calif Irvine Dept Biol Chemistry Irvine CA 92697-1700 Office Phone: 949-824-5325. Business E-Mail: cal@uci.edu.

MCLAUGHLIN, DAVID, foundation administrator; Grad., M.B.A., Dartmouth Coll.; PhD (hon.), Colby-Sawyer Coll. Pres. Dartmouth College, 1981—87; chmn. Aspen Institute, 1987—88; chmn., CEO Orion Safety Products, 1988—; former chmn. CBS Corp., NYC; mem. bd. of gov. American Red Cross, 1998—, chmn., 2001—. Mem.: Ausbon Sargent Land Preservation Trust, Lake Sunapee Protective Assoc., Friends of the John Hay National Wildlife Refuge, Colby-Sawyer Coll. Bd. of Trustees. Office: Amer Red Cross 6900 Georgia Ave NW Washington DC 20307

MCLAUGHLIN, HARRY ROLL, architect; b. Indpls., Nov. 29, 1922; s. William T. and Ruth E. (Roll) McL.; m. Linda Hamilton, Oct. 23, 1954. Registered Ind., Ohio, Ill., cert. Nat. Coun. Archtl. Registration Bds. Past pres. James Assocs. Inc., Indpls. Restorations include Old State Bank State Meml, Vincennes, Ind., Andrew Wylie House, Bloomington, Ind., Old Opera House State Meml, New Harmony, Ind., Old Morris-Butler House, Indpls. (Merit award 1972), Market St. Restoration and Maria Creek Baptist Ch., Vincennes, Benjamin Harrison House, Old James Ball Residence, Lafayette, Ind (1st Design award 1972), Lockerbie Sq. Master Plan Park Sch., Indpls., Knox County Ct. House, Vincennes, 1972, J.K. Lilly House, Indpls., 1972, Waiting Station and Chapel, Crown Hill Cemetery, Indpls., 1972, Blackford-Condit House Ind. State U., Terre Haute, Indian houses Angel Mounds Archaeol. Site and Interpretative Ctr., Ind.; architect: Glenn A. Black Mus. Archaeology, Ind. U., Bloomington; Restoration Morgan County Ct. House, Indpls. City Market, Hist. Schofield House, Madison, Ind., Ernie Pyle Birthplace, Dana, Ind., Phi Kappa Psi Nat. Hdqrs, Indpls., 1980 (Design award), East Coll. Bldg, DePauw U., Greencastle, Ind., Pres.'s House Restoration, DePauw U., 1992; contbr. articles to profl. jours.; Illustrator: Harmonist Construction. Past chmn. bd., past pres., now chmn. emeritus Historic Landmarks Found., Ind.; bd. dirs., past archtl. adviser, bd. advisers Historic Madison, Inc.; mem. adv. coun. Historic Am. Bldgs. Survey, Nat. Park Svc., 1967-73; past mem. Ind. profl. rev. com. for Nat. Register nominations, 1967-81; past adv. bd. Conner Prarie Mus., Patrick Henry Sullivan Found.; past adviser Indpls. Historic Preservation Commn.; past mem. preservation com. Ind. U.; past mem. Meridian St. Preservation Commn., Indpls., 1971-2001; hon. mem. Ind. Bicentennial Commn.; bd. dirs. Park-Tudor Sch., 1972-85; past nat. bd. dirs. Preservation Action; life bd. dirs. Historic New Harmony; trustee Masonic Heritage Found.; past bd. dirs. Ind. Masonic Home, 1984-91, Inpls. Pub. Libr. Found., treas. 1988, 95—, v.p., 1989, pres. 1990; past trustee Eiteljorg Mus. Western Art, mem. adv. and planning com., 1999; past mem. Hamilton County Tourism Commn., 1989-91. Recipient Gov.'s citation State of Ind., 1967, Sagamore of Wabash award, 1967, 80, 82, Mayor's citation City of Indpls., 1972, Sec. Interior citation U.S. Dept. Interior, 1970, Design and Environ. citation, 1975, Citation of Spl. Merit, Park Tudor Sch., 1993, Disting. Achievement award Ball State U., 2004. Fellow AIA (nat. com. historic bldgs., chmn. 1970); mem. Ind. Soc. Architects (state preservation coord. 1960-85, Biennial award 1972, Design award 1978), Nat. Trust Historic Preservation (past trustee, bd. advisers), Soc. Archtl. Historians (Wilbur D. Peat award Ctrl. Ind. chpt. outstanding contbns. to understanding and appreciation of archtl. heritage 1993, past bd. dirs., Disting. Achievement in Hist. Preservation award 2005), Indpls. Mus. Art. (trustee, chmn. bldgs. com., bd. govs. 1986-95), Zionsville C. of C. (hon. bd. dirs.), U.S. Capitol (hon. trustee), Ind. Hist. Soc. (pres. 1999, trustee 1989-99, bldg. com.), Marion County Hist. Soc. (past v.p., bd. dirs.), Zionsville Hist. Soc. (hon. life), Navy League U.S. (life), Ind. State Mus. Soc. (life), English Speaking Union (past bd. dirs. Indpls.), Hamilton County Hist. Soc. (life), Woodstock Club (bd. dirs. 1982-86, pres. 1985, ex-officio 1986), Literary Club Found. (trustee 1990-2007), Skyline Club (life), Packard Club, Masons (33 deg.). Home and Office: 950 W 116th St Carmel IN 46032-8864

MCLAUGHLIN, JAMES LEE, musician, director; b. Hillsboro, Ohio, Mar. 27, 1946; s. Robert Barker McLaughlin and Virgie Lee Prine-McLaughlin. BFA, Ohio U., Athens, 1968. Cert. music dir. West Ohio Conf. United Meth. Ch., 1973. Organist Hillsboro Ch. Christ, Ohio, 1960—64, First Christian Ch., Athens, 1964—68; tchr. vocal music Zanesville City Schs., Zanesville, 1968—99, dept. chair vocal music, 1991—99; dir. music Faith United Meth. Ch., 1968—86, Ctrl. Trinity United Meth. Ch., 1986—. Founder and dir. Optimists Boys Club Choir, 1981—92; pres. Thursday Music Club, Zanesville, Ohio, 1984—86, 1994—96, 2002—04; dir. music and condr. Zanesville Civic Chorus, 1993—; mem. and asst. condr. Y-City Barbershop Chorus, 2000—; organ recitalist; coach voice, piano, organ; accompanist. Performer: Robert Shaw Chorus. Advisor Virgie Lee McLaughlin Fund Found. Appalachian Ohio, 2002—; bd. dirs. So. Ohio Symphony Orch., New Concord, Ohio, 1974—76, Zanesville Concert Assn., 1979—, pres., 1981—84, booking agt., 2006—; bd. dirs. Katherine B. Geis Scholarship, 1991—. Named an Outstanding Educator, Phi Delta Kappa, 1999; scholar, Stewart-Glapat Company, 1999, Matha Holden Jennings Found., 1982—83. Mem.: Am. Guild Organists, Fellowship of United Meth. Musicians, Ohio Music Edn. Assn. (adjudicator 1993—, dist. 9 pres. 1988—90). Avocations: travel, philanthropy. Home: 413 Moore Ave Zanesville OH 43701-1234 Office: Ctrl Trinity United Meth Ch 62 S Seventh St Zanesville OH 43701 Office Phone: 740-453-1210.

MCLAUGHLIN, JOHN EDWARD, former federal agency administrator; b. McKeesport, PA, June 15, 1942; married; 2 children. BA, Wittenberg U., 1964; MA, Johns Hopkins U., 1966; postgrad., SAIS Ctr., Bologna, Italy, U. Pa. With CIA, 1972—2004, with US Dept. State, Bur. European & Can. Affairs, 1984—85, deputy dir. Office European Analysis, 1985—89, dir. European analysis, 1989, dir. Slavic and Eurasian analysis, 1989—95, acting chmn. Nat. Intelligence Coun., 1995—97, dep. dir. intelligence, 1997—2000, dep. dir., 2000—04, acting dir., 2004; non-resident sr. fellow Brooking Instn., Washington, 2005—; sr. fellow, Philip Merrill Ctr. for Strategic Studies John Hopkins U., Washington, 2005—; adv. on nat. security CNN, 2005—. With US Army, 1966—69.

MCLAUGHLIN, JOHN J., broadcast executive, television producer, journalist, political commentator; s. Augustus Hugh and Eva Philomena (Turcotte) McL.; m. Ann Dore Lauenstein, Aug. 23, 1975 (div. 1992); m. Cristina Vidal, Jun. 22, 1997. AB, Boston Coll., 1951, MA in Philosophy, 1952, BDiv, 1959, MA in English, 1961; PhD, Columbia U., 1967. Ordained priest Roman Catholic Ch., 1960. Mem. Jesuit Order, N.E., NY and Washington; resigned order and active ministry, 1975; tchr., dir. communications Fairfield (Conn.) Univ. and Preparatory Sch., 1960-64; assoc. editor America Mag., NYC, 1967-70; speech writer & dep. spl. asst. to Pres. Richard Nixon and Gerald Ford, Washington, 1971-74; pres. McLaughlin and Co. Pub. Policy Cons., Washington, 1975-79; radio talk-show host Sta. WRC-AM, Washington, 1979-82; pres., chmn. bd. dirs. Oliver Prodns., Inc., Washington, 1983—. Lectr. numerous univs., corps. and orgns. nationwide and abroad, 1963—; host various TV series, Sta. WJAR-TV, Providence, 1962-63, Sta. WNHC-TV, New Haven, 1963, Sta. WTIC-TV, Hartford, 1963, Sta. WOR-TV, N.Y.C., 1964; host, exec. producer Biafra Today report ABC-TV Network, 1969; radio commentator Sta. WSTC, Stamford, Conn., 1964, CBS Network Radio, N.Y.C., 1964, Nat. Pub. Radio All Things Considered, Washington, 1981-85; dir. film insts. Yale U., Holy Cross Coll., Manhattanville Coll.; juror Am. Film Festival, 1969; congressional testimony pub. broadcasting and TV license renewal, Washington, 1967, 69. Author: Love Before Marriage, 1970; editor National Review, Washington, 1981-89, columnist From Washington Straight, 1982-89; TV host and exec. producer The McLaughlin Group NBC and PBS TV stas., 1982—, John McLaughlin's One on One, 1984—, McLaughlin CNBC cable system, 1989-94; TV appearances (host spl. episode) Cheers, 1990, (cameo) Murphy Brown, 1995, Lateline, 1998; Motion picture appearances: Dave, 1993, Mission Impossible, 1996, Independence Day, 1996, Murder at 1600, 1997, Bulworth, 1998. Rep. candidate U.S. Senate, R.I., 1970. Recipient Excellence in Journalism award Cath. Press Assn., 1969, News Media award VFW, 1984; nominee Nat. Acad. Cable Programming ACE award, 1989, 90, 91, 94; The McLaughlin Group named Best Polit. Talk Show, Washingtonian mag., 1987-93, George Mag., 1998. Mem. NATAS (Emmy award 1984), Am. Fedn. TV and Radio Artists, Screen Actors Guild. Office: 1717 Rhode Island Ave NW Ste 640 Washington DC 20036 E-mail: slucian@mclaughlin.com.

MCLAUGHLIN, JOHN SHERMAN, lawyer; b. Pitts., Apr. 1, 1932; s. John H. and Dorothy I. (Schrecongost) McL.; m. Suzanne Shaver, June 5, 1971; children: Dorothy, Sarah, Martha. AB, Harvard U., 1954, LLB, 1957. Bar: Pa. 1958, U.S. Supreme Ct. 1967. Assoc. Reed, Smith, Shaw & McClay, Pitts., 1957-71, ptnr., 1971—2002, of counsel, 2002—. Trustee Harmarville Rehab. Ctr., Inc., 1980-87; pres., trustee Western Pa. Sch. for the Deaf, 1985—; pres. Pa. NG Assn., 1976-78; justice of peace Borough of Edgewood, 1963-73; trustee Winchester Thurston Sch., 1987-2002; life trustee Carnegie Libr. of Pitts., Carnegie Inst., 1994—, Carnegie Mus. Art, 1997—; dir. Pitts. Symphony, 1985-95, adv. 1996-99; emeritus coun. mem. Scotch Irish Soc. USA. Lt. col. Air NG, 1957-79. Mem.: Am. Coll. Trust and Estate Counsel, Allegheny County Bar Assn., Am. Law Inst., Rolling Rock Club (Ligonier, Pa.), Duquesne Club. Office: Reed Smith LLP 435 6th Ave Pittsburgh PA 15219-1886 Home Phone: 412-731-7195. Business E-Mail: jmclaughlin@reedsmith.com.

MCLAUGHLIN, JOSEPH, lawyer; b. Newark, Aug. 1, 1941; s. Joseph Nicholas and Genevieve Veronica (Lardiere) McL.; m. Elisabeth Lippold, July 31, 1965; children: Elisabeth Rogers, Jessica Lierzer, Emilie McLaughlin AB, Columbia U., 1962, LLB, 1965. With Sullivan & Cromwell, NYC, 1968-76; v.p., gen. counsel Goldman, Sachs & Co., 1976-88, cons., 1988-90; ptnr. Sidley Austin LLP, NYC, 1993—. Adj. prof. law NYU Sch. Law, 1988-92; spkr., presenter in field. Author (with C.J. Johnson Jr.): Corporate Finance and the Securities Laws, 4th edit., 2006; contbr. articles to profl. jours. Trustee Greenwich (Conn.) Acad., 1988-2000; treas. Presbyn. Ch. Old Greenwich, 1988-91; bd. dirs. United Way, Greenwich, 1993-97; mem. Rep. Town Com., Greenwich, 1993-96. Jervey fellow Parker Sch. Fgn. Comparative Law, Columbia Law Sch., U. Munich, 1966-68. Mem. ABA (sect. bus. law, fed. regulation securities com., subcom. broker-dealer matters 1985—, subcom. civil litigation and SEC enforcement matters 1989—, chair task force rule 10b-6 1995-97, co-chair task force sellers' due diligence and similar defenses under fed. securities laws 1989-92), Am. Law Inst., Assn. of Bar of City of NY (internat. law com. 1979-84, chair 1981-84, civil rights com. 1984-87, internat. arms control and security affairs com. 1988-90), NY Stock Exch. (legal adv. com. to bd. govs. 1985-88, subcom. corp. governance, subcom. internat. issues 1988—), Securities Industry Assn. (fed. regulations com. 1978-88, chair 1982-84), Nat. Assn. Securities Dealers, Inc. (corp. financing com. 1983-86), Am. Arbitration Assn. (dir. 1986-90). Republican. Congregationalist. Office Phone: 212-839-5312. Business E-Mail: jmclaughlin@sidley.com.

MCLAUGHLIN, JOSEPH MICHAEL, federal judge; b. Bklyn., Mar. 20, 1933; s. Joseph Michael and Mary Catherine (Flanagan) McLaughlin; m. Frances Elizabeth Lynch, Oct. 10, 1959; children: Joseph, Mary Jo, Matthew, Andrew. AB, Fordham Coll., 1954, LL.B., 1959; LL.M., NYU, 1964; LL.D., Mercy Coll., White Plains, NY, 1981; LLD, Fordham U., 1998. Bar: NY 1959. Assoc. Cahill, Gordon, NYC, 1959—61; prof. law Fordham U., NYC, 1961—71, dean Sch. of Law, 1971—81, adj. prof., 1981—90; judge US Dist. Ct. Eastern Dist. NY, Bklyn., 1981—90, US Ct. Appeals (2nd cir.), NYC, 1990—98, sr. judge, 1998—; editor-in-chief Fed. Practice Guide. Adj. prof. St. John's Law Sch., NYC, 1982—97; chmn. NY Law Revision Commn., Albany, 1975—82. Author (with Peterfreund): New York Practice, 1964; author: Evidence, 1979, also articles. Capt. Corps of Engineers US Army, 1955—57, Korea. Mem.: ABA, NY State Bar Assn., Assn. of Bar of City of NY, Lotos Club. Roman Catholic. Office: US Courthouse US Ct Appeals 40 Foley Sq Rm 2402 New York NY 10007-1502 *

MCLAUGHLIN, JOSEPH THOMAS, lawyer; b. Boston, Mar. 30, 1944; s. James Francis and Madeline Louise (Hickman) McL.; m. Christine E. Mullen, Sept. 2, 1967; children: Amy Melissa, Caitlin Christine, Ian Michael. BA magna cum laude, Boston Coll., 1965; JD, Cornell U., 1968. Bar: Mass. 1969, N.Y. State 1968, U.S. Supreme Ct. 1974. Research asst. Brit. Council of Archaeology, Winchester, Eng., 1964, site supr., 1966; legis. asst. Rep. Thomas P. O'Neill, Washington, 1967; research asst. Cornell U., 1967-68; law clk. to chief justice Mass. Superior Ct., 1968-69; assoc. Shearman & Sterling, NYC, 1969-76, ptnr., 1976-97; exec. v.p., legal and regulatory affairs Credit Suisse First Boston, 1997—2001; chmn. Credit Suisse First Boston Found. Trust, 2001—02; ptnr., chmn. Heller Ehrman LLP, NYC, 2002—. Adj. prof. Fordham Law Sch., 1981-88; vis.

prof. Cornell Law Sch., 1995-96. Author: Federal Class Action Digests, 1974, 1976; contbr. articles to profl. jours. Exec. dir. Brooklyn Heights Draft Counseling Svc., 1970-74, Presbyn. Task Force for Justice Counseling Svc., 1973-75; v.p., bd. dirs. Brooklyn Heights Assn., 1973-77; bd. dirs. Willoughby Settlement House, Inc., Ingersoll-Willoughby Cmty. Ctr., Inc., 1970-75, United Neighborhood Houses, 1976-78, Good Shepherd Svcs., Resources for Children with Spl. Needs, Inc., Internat. House, Bklyn. Mus. Art; mem. CRR Inst. for Dispute Resolution. Mem. ABA, Assn. of Bar of City of N.Y. (mem. com. on profl. discord 1986—, chmn. com. to promote diversity in the legal profession), N.Y. State Bar Assn. (chmn. com. on marijuana and drug abuse 1972-75), Am. Law Inst., Am. Arbitration Assn., N.Y. Lawyers for Pub. Interest (chmn. bd. dirs.) ABAC (com. on promoting settlements), Heights Casino Club. Office: Heller Ehrman LLP Times Square Tower 7 Times Square New York NY 10036 Office Phone: 212-847-8789. Office Fax: 212-763-7600. Business E-Mail: joseph.mclaughlin@hellerehrman.com.

MCLAUGHLIN, LEIGHTON BATES, II, retired journalist, reporter, educator; b. Evanston, Ill., Apr. 10, 1930; s. Leighton Bates and Gwendolyn I. (Markle) McL.; m. Beverly Jean Jeske, May 5, 1962; children: Leighton Bates III, Jeffrey, Steven, Patrick. Student, Kenyon Coll., Gambier, Ohio, 1948-50, Northwestern U., 1951; BA in English Lit., UCLA, 1983; MA in Comms., Calif. State U., Fullerton, 1990. Copyboy, reporter, rewriteman City News Bur., Chgo., 1957-58; reporter, rewriteman Chgo. Sun-Times, 1958-62; rewriteman, asst. city editor Ariz. Jour., Phoenix, 1962; reporter Miami (Fla.) Herald, 1962-64; successively rewriteman, night city editor, 1st asst. city editor, telegraph editor Chgo. Sun-Times, 1964-74; dir. Chgo. Daily News/Sun-Times News Service, 1974-79; editorial coord. electronics newspaper div. Field Enterprises, 1975-79; adminstr. reference libr. and communications ctr. Field Newspapers, 1976-79; editor News Am. Syndicate, Irvine, Calif., 1979-85; mng. editor San Gabriel Valley Daily Tribune, 1986; assoc. prof. journalism Riverside (Calif.) C.C., 1987-96, chmn. performing arts and media dept., 1993-96, coll. publs. editor, ret., 1996-99; lectr. in journalism Calif. State U.-Fullerton, 1984-96. Copy editor The Press-Enterprise, Riverside, Calif., 1988-95; lectr., condr. seminars in field. Author articles in field. Served to 1st lt. USMC, 1951-54. Recipient Stick-o-Type award for best feature story Chgo. Newspaper Guild, 1961, Best News story award Ill. AP and UPI, 1967 Mem. Chgo. Journalists Assn., Verban Soc., Psi Upsilon. *Reporting the news is like any other intellectual activity in that it involves research, verification, organization, and clarity of presentation. But news reporting is unique in that all this is done on a dead run, in time for the day's editions.*

MCLAUGHLIN, MARGARET BROWN, adult education educator, writer; b. Miami Beach, Fla., Aug. 24, 1926; d. J. Clifford and Grace Lindsey (DuPre) Brown; m. Francis Edward McLaughlin, Oct. 30, 1982 (dec.). BA cum laude, U. Miami, 1946; MA, Duke U., Durham, NC, 1949; PhD, Tulane U., New Orleans, 1976. Instr., lectr. in English U. Miami, Coral Gables, Fla., 1946-47, 56-61, 73-91, 2000; English tchr. Narimasu Am. Sch., Tokyo, 1963-65; asst. prof. Manchester Coll., North Manchester, Ind., 1965-67; instr. Miami-Dade C.C., 1977, 81; dir. writing workshop for fgn. students U. Miami Sch. Medicine, 1991-92; adj. prof. English, Asian and liberal studies Osher Lifelong Learning Inst., Fla. Internat. U., Miami, Fla., 1997—; instr. humanities Barry U., Miami, 2004. Prodr. Dade County Cable TV series Caribbean Writers and Their Art, 1991; prodr., host cable tv series Haiti Cherie, 1993-94. Contbr. articles to popular Japanese and U.S. mags. and newspapers; contbr. play reviews to Internet pub. Trustee Mus. Sci., Miami, 1977-78. Mem. Am. Lit. Assn. (Henry Adams Soc.), Egyptology and Asian Civilizations Soc. Miami (bd. dirs., pres. 1976-78, 83-85), South Fla. Internat. Press Club (bd. dirs., scholarship chmn. 2002—), South Fla. Writers' Assn. Avocations: writing, travel, editing. Home and Office: 1621 S Bayshore Dr Miami FL 33133-4201 Personal E-mail: margaretj711@comcast.net.

MCLAUGHLIN, MICHAEL JOHN, retired insurance company executive; b. Cambridge, Mass., Feb. 14, 1944; s. Michael John and Evelyn Katherine (Quinn) McL. AB, Boston Coll., 1965; JD, NYU, 1968. Bar: NY, Mass. With NY Life Ins. Co., 1968—, sr. v.p. info. sys. and services dept., 1982-88, sr. v.p., 1988-91, sr. v.p., dep. gen. counsel, 1991-95, sr. v.p., gen. counsel, 1995-2000. Mem. ABA, NY State Bar Assn. Personal E-mail: mmclau2260@aol.com.

MCLAUGHLIN, PATRICK J., lawyer; b. 1947; BA summa cum laude, U. Minn., 1971, JD magna cum laude, 1975. Bar: Minn. 1975. Ptnr., banking, trial practice groups, chair, corp. trust svcs. group Dorsey & Whitney LLP, Mpls. Gen. counsel Minn. Police Relief Assn. Lectr. in field. Office: Dorsey & Whitney LLP Ste 1500 50 S Sixth St Minneapolis MN 55402-1498 Office Phone: 612-340-2975. Office Fax: 612-340-2643. Business E-Mail: mclaughlin.patrick@dorsey.com.

MCLAUGHLIN, PATRICK MICHAEL, lawyer; b. Monahans, Tex., July 23, 1946; s. Patrick John and Ann (Donnelly) M.; m. Christine Manos, Aug. 21, 1970; children— Brian Patrick, Christopher Michael, Conor Andrew B Gen. Studies, Ohio U., 1972; JD, Case We. Res. U., 1976. Bar: Ohio 1976, U.S. Dist. Ct. (no. dist.) Ohio 1978, U.S. Ct. Appeals (6th cir.) 1979, U.S. Supreme Ct. 1980; U.S. Dist. Ct. (so. dist.) Ohio 1989, U.S. Ct. Appeals (5th cir.). Dir. vets. edn. project. Am. Assn. Cmty. and Jr. Colls., Washington, 1972—73; law clk. Common Pleas Ct., Cleve., 1976—77; law clk. to judge 8th Jud. Dist. Ct. of Appeals, Cleve., 1977—78; asst. U.S. atty. No. Dist. Ohio, Cleve., 1978—82, chief civil divsn., 1982—84, U.S. atty. Cleve., 1984—88; ptnr. Janik & McLaughlin, Cleve., 1988—89, Mansour, Gavin, Gerlack & Manos Co., LPA, Cleve., 1989—97; apptd ind. spl. prosecutor Ohio Attys. Gen., 1993—96; mng. ptnr. McLaughlin & McCaffrey, LLP, Cleve., 1997—. Cons. Nat. League of Cities, U.S. Conf. Mayors, 1971-72; co-creator Opportunity Fair for Veterans Concept, 1971 Editor-in-chief Case Western Res. Jour. Internat. Law, 1975-76 Chmn. North Ohio Drug Abuse Task Force, 1986-88; chmn. Law Enforcement Coordinating Commn., North Ohio, 1985-88; chmn. civil issues subcom. Atty. Gen.'s Adv. Com., 1986-88; exec. v.p. Greater Cleve. Vets. Meml., Inc., 1993, pres., 1994—. Decorated Silver Star, Bronze Star, Purple Heart, Army Commendation medal, Vietnamese Cross of Gallantry with Silver and Bronze Stars; named to Ohio Vets. Hall of Fame, 2003, Ohio Mil.Hall of Fame for Valor, 2004. Fellow Am. Coll. Trial Lawyers; mem. ABA, FBA, Ohio Bar Assn., Cleve. Bar Assn., Nat. Assn. Former U.S. Attys., Soc. 1st Divsn., 18th Inf. Regiment Assn., Order of Ahepa, Vietnam Vets. Am., Nat. Vietnam Vets. Network (Disting. Vietnam Vet. award 1985), Nat. Assn. Concerned Vets. (nat. v.p. external affairs 1971-72, exec. dir. 1972-73), Cuyahoga County Vets. (award 1985), Nat. Soc. SAR (law enforcement commendation medal 1989), Judge John Manos Inn of Ct. (pres., master bencher 2005—). Republican. Roman Catholic. Office: McLaughlin & McCaffrey LLP Eaton Ctr 1111 Superior Ave Ste 1350 Cleveland OH 44114-2500 Home Phone: 216-371-0296; Office Phone: 216-623-0900. Business E-Mail: pmm@paladin-law.com.

MCLAUGHLIN, PHILIP VANDOREN, JR., mechanical engineering educator, researcher, consultant; b. Elizabeth, NJ, Nov. 10, 1939; s. Philip VanDoren and Ruth Evans (Landis) McL.; m. Phoebe Ann Feeney, Aug. 19, 1961; children: Philip VanDoren III, Patrick Evans, Christi M. Barton. BSCE, U. Pa., 1961, MS in Engring. Mechanics, 1964, PhD in Engring. Mechanics, 1969. Assoc. engr. Boeing-Vertol, Morton, Pa., 1962-63, engr. II, 1963; rsch. engr. Scott Paper Co., Phila., 1963-65, rsch. project engr., 1965-69, sr. rsch. project engr., 1969; asst. prof. theoretical and applied mechanics U. Ill., Urbana, 1969-73, asst. dean engring., 1971-72; project mgr. Materials Scis. Corp., Blue Bell, Pa., 1973-76; assoc. prof. mech. engring. Villanova (Pa.) U., 1976-81, prof., 1981—2003, prof. emeritus, 2003—. Cons. Naval Air Engring. Ctr., Lakehurst, N.J., 1977-79, U.S. Steel Corp., Trenton, 1980-82, RCA Corp., Moorestown, N.J., 1986, Coal Tech Corp., Merion Station, Pa., Air Products and Chems., Inc., Allentown, Pa., 1988, Aircraft divsn. Naval Air Warfare Ctr., Patuxent River, Md., 1995-96, Christini Technologies, Phila., 1999—, Alpha Sci. Corp., Southeastern, Pa., 2000-01, Materials Rsch. & Design, Inc., Rosemont, Pa., 2002-, DETechs., King of Prussia, Pa., 2002—; vis. prof. dept. engring. U. Cambridge, Eng., 1990-91. Reviewer: for sci. and tech. jours.; contbr. numerous articles to profl. jours. Rsch. grantee NSF, 1970-72, Naval Air Engring. Ctr., 1978-84, Lawrence Livermore Nat. Lab., 1979-81, Naval Air Devel. Ctr., 1985-86, RCA Corp., 1986-87, Materials Scis. Corp., 2003-05; sr. rsch. assoc. NRC, Washington, 1983-84; USN-Am. Soc. for Engring. Edn. sr. faculty fellow, 1995. Mem.: ASME (life; chmn. applied mechanics divsn. Phila. sect. 1981—83, materials divsn. com. on composites 1992—2003), ASCE (life; chmn. engring. mechanics divsn. com. on inelastic behavior 1977—79, assoc. editor Jour. Engring. Mechanics Divsn. 1977—79, aerospace divsn. com. on structures and materials 1986—95), Am. Soc. Composites, Am. Soc. Engring. Edn., Am. Acad. Mechanics, Sigma Xi. Achievements include research and consulting on composite materials and structures, structural analysis and design and inelastic behavior. Office: Villanova U Dept Mech Engring 800 Lancaster Ave Villanova PA 19085-1681 Office Phone: 610-291-2023. Business E-Mail: philip.mclaughlin@villanova.edu.

MCLAUGHLIN, SLADE HAYES, lawyer; b. Phila. JD, Villanova U., Pa., 1982. Mem. The Beasley Firm, LLC, Phila., 1994—. Named one of Best Lawyers in Am., Woodward/White, Inc., 2005—07, Pa. Top 10 Super Lawyer, Law and Politics Mag., 2007. Mem.: ABOTA, Am. Bd. Profl. Liability Attys. (diplomate), Nat. Bd. Trial Advocacy (bd. cert. civil trial atty.), Million Dollar Advocates Forum. Office: The Beasley Firm LLC 1125 Walnut St Philadelphia PA 19107 Office Phone: 215-931-2674. Business E-Mail: shmac@comcast.net.

MCLAUGHLIN, SYLVIA CRANMER, volunteer, environmentalist; b. Denver, Dec. 24, 1916; d. George Ernest and Jean Louise (Chappell) Cranmer; m. Donald Hamilton McLaughlin, Dec. 29, 1948; children: Jean Katherine McLaughlin Shaterian, George Cranmer McLaughlin. AB, Vassar Coll., 1939. Co-founder Save San Francisco Bay Assn., Berkeley-Oakland, Calif., 1961-99, pres., 1993-95. Mem. waterfront adv. com. City of Berkeley, Calif., 1964—68; sec., bd. dirs. Resource Renewal Inst., 1989—, Citizens for East Shore State Pks., 1984—2005, 2005—; founder, bd. dirs. Pub. Trust Group, Oakland, Calif., 1997—; mem. awards com. Berkeley Cmty. Fund, 1998—; mem. adv. bd. Greenbelt Alliance, San Francisco, 1982—; mem. nat. adv. coun. Trust for Pub. Land, San Francisco, 1986—, Ecocity Builders, Berkeley, 1990—; bd. dirs. Ptnrs. for Liveable Cmtys., Washington, 1975—78. Mem. Nat. Aubudon Soc. (bd. dirs. 1970-76), Nat. Recreation and Parks Assn. (bd. dirs. 1974-78), East Bay Conservation Corps (bd. dirs. 1985-97), Student Conservation Assn. (bd. dirs. 1979-84). Avocations: reading, travel, grandchildren, environmental causes. Home: 1450 Hawthorne Ter Berkeley CA 94708-1804

MCLAUGHLIN, T. MARK, lawyer; b. Salem, Mass., Apr. 20, 1953; s. Terrence E. and Mary E. (Donlon) McL.; m. Sandra L. Roman, Oct. 16, 1982; children: Daniel, Kathleen, Eileen. BA in Econs., U. Notre Dame, 1975, JD, 1978. Bar: Ill. 1978, U.S. Dist. Ct. (no. dist.) Ill. 1978, U.S. Dist. Ct. (cen. dist.) Ill. 1992, U.S. Dist. Ct. (ea. dist.) Wis. 1992, U.S. Ct. Appeals (7th cir.) 1982, U.S. Ct. Appeals (11th cir.) 1982, U.S. Ct. Appeals (8th cir.) 1998. Assoc. Mayer Brown Rowe & Maw LLP, Chgo., 1978-84, ptnr., 1985—. Adj. faculty law Loyola U., Chgo., 1983, 86-90. Bd. dirs. no. Ill. affiliate Am. Diabetes Assn., Chgo., 1985-94. Mem. ABA (franchising forum com. antitrust law sect.), Phi Beta Kappa. Office: Mayer Brown Rowe & Maw LLP 71 S Wacker Dr Chicago IL 60606-4637 Home Phone: 708-246-4234. Business E-Mail: mmclaughlin@mayerbrownrowe.com.

MCLAUGHLIN, WILLIAM IRVING, space technical manager, writer; b. Oak Park, Ill., Mar. 6, 1935; s. William Lahey and Eileen (Irving) McL.; m. Karen Bjorneby, Aug. 20, 1960; children: William, Margot, Walter, Eileen. BS with highest honors, U. Calif., Berkeley, 1963, MA, 1966, PhD, 1968. Mem. tech. staff Bellcomm, Inc., 1968-71, Jet Propulsion Lab., Pasadena, Calif., 1971-99. Supr. terrestrial planets mission design group, 1981-83, mission design mgr. for Infrared Astron. Satellite, 1976-83, mgr. flight engring. office for Voyager/Uranus project, 1983-86; mgr. mission profile and sequencing sect., 1986-92; dep. mgr. astrophysics and fundamental physics program office, 1992-96, mgr. mission and syss. architecture sect., 1996-99. Served with USMC, 1957-60. Recipient Apollo Achievement award, 1969, Pioneer 10 Mission Analysis Team Group Achievement award, 1974, Exceptional Svc. medal NASA, 1984, Outstanding Leadership medal NASA, 1986; asteroid 4838 Billmclaughlin named in his honor. Fellow Brit. Interplanetary Soc. (L.J. Carter Meml. lectr. London 2002, Space Achievement Bronze medal 1993); mem. Philosophy Sci. Assn., Internat. Acad. Astros., Phi Beta Kappa, Sigma Xi.

MCLAURIN, HUGH MCFADDIN, III, military officer, museum program director; b. Sumter, SC, Jan. 30, 1936; s. Hugh McFaddin and Louise Mellette (Nettles) McL.; m. Virginia Anne Harvin, Aug. 22, 1958; children: Mary Louise, Virginia Harvin, Hugh IV. BS, Clemson U., 1959; grad. (hon.), Command & Gen. Staff Coll., Ft. Leavenworth, Kans., 1978. Commd. 2d lt. U.S. Army, 1958, advanced through grades to col., 1985; exec. officer 151st Field Arty. Brigade, Sumter, 1975-85; dir. pers. S.C. NG, Columbia, 1986-91, dir. logistics, 1991-95, rank of brig. gen., ret., 1996; owner McLaurin Farms, Wedgefield, SC, 1999—. Cons. S.C. Ednl. TV, Columbia, 1992-93; moderator Nat. Def. Seminar, Washington, 1978. Author: History of South Carolina National Guard and Militia, 1989. Deacon, elder, Presbyn. Ch., Wedgefield, 1961, moderator Presbytery Coun., 2001-04; v.p. Com. for Progress, Sumter, 1963; chmn. bd. dirs. S.C. NG Mus., Columbia, 1982-99; trustee Thornwell Home for Children and Sch. Fellow Coll. Mil. Historians; mem. Field Arty. Soc. S.C. (pres. 1987), SAR (historian), Sumter County Hist. Soc. (dir. 1996-99, pres. 2000), The Sumter Assembly (pres. 1991), Soc. of High Hills of Santee (steward 2002), Hon. Order St. Barbara, Fortnightly Club (pres. 2007). Avocation: American Revolution research. Home: Stirling Plantation 6380 McLaurin Rd Wedgefield SC 29168-9393

MCLAURIN, JOCEE ELIZABETH, elementary school educator; b. Fayetteville, NC, Aug. 11, 1962; d. Colin Marshall and Kathryn Sessoms McLaurin. BA, Meth. U., Fayetteville, 1984; MA, Fayetteville State U., NC, 1990. Cert. mid. childhood generalist Nat. Bd. Profl. Tchg. Stds., 2001. Tchr. Gray's Creek Elem. Sch., Fayetteville. Named Tchr. of Yr., Gray's Creek Elem. Sch., 2004—05. Democrat. Methodist. Avocations: reading, singing. Office: Gray's Creek Elem Sch 2860 Alderman Rd Fayetteville NC 28306 Home: 3443 Beard Rd Fayetteville NC 28312

MCLAWHON, RONALD WILLIAM, pathology educator, biochemist; b. Chgo., Sept. 10, 1957; s. William Columbus and Esther Shirley (Bukowski) McL. AB in Biol. Scis., U. Chgo., 1979, MS in Biochemistry, 1980, PhD in Biochemistry, 1982; MD, Rush Med. Coll., 1986. Diplomate Am. Bd. Pathology. Rsch. assoc. pediat. Joseph P. Kennedy Jr. Mental Retardation Rsch. Ctr., Chgo.; rsch. assoc. pediatrics U. Chgo. Pritzker Sch. Medicine, 1982-83; resident in pathology Rush-Presbyn.-St. Luke's Med. Ctr., Chgo., 1986-87, pathologist, 1987-88; instr. Rush Med. Coll., Chgo., 1986-87, asst. prof., 1987-88; resident in pathology U. Chgo. Med. Ctr., 1988-90; asst. prof. U. Chgo. Pritzker Sch. Medicine, 1990-96, assoc. prof., 1996—2007; dir. clin. chemistry, attending physician U. Chgo. Med. Ctr., 1990—2007; dir. outreach and clin. support svcs. U. Chgo. Hosps. and Health Sys., 1997—98, dir. regional lab. svcs. and med. dir. of hosp. labs., 1998—2007; prof., head divsn. lab. medicine dept. pathology U. Calif. San Diego Sch. Medicine, 2007—; dir. clin. labs., attending physician U. Calif. San Diego Med. Ctr., 2007—. Contbr. articles to Jour. Biol. Chemistry, Molecular Pharmacology, Jour. Neurochemistry, Jour. Membrane Biology, Procs. of NAS, Am. Jour. Clin. Pathology, Clin. Chemistry. US Pub. Health Predoctoral fellow NIH, 1981-82; James B. Herrick scholar Rush Med. Coll., 1986-87; recipient Young Investigator award Acad. Clin. Lab. Physicians and Scientists, 1990. Fellow: Am. Soc. Clin. Pathologists, Coll. Am. Pathologists, Nat. Acad. Clin. Biochemistry; mem.: AAAS, Am. Soc. Cell Biology, Am. Soc. Biochemistry and Molecular Biology, Am. Soc. Investigative Pathology, Am. Assn. Clin. Chemistry (chair Chgo. sect. 2005, Chgo. Chpt. Past Chmn. award 2006), Sigma Xi. Achievements include research in biochemistry of cell membrane receptors and signal transduction in the nervous system, molecular pharmacology of opiates and opioid peptides, regulation of complex carbohydrate and lipid metabolism, clinical laboratory automaton and robotics. Office Phone: 619-543-5816.

MCLEAN, ARTHUR FREDERICK, mechanical engineer; b. Bristol, Eng., Apr. 16, 1929; came to U.S., 1959; naturalized, 1966; s. Frederick Robert and Edith (Hawkings) McL.; m. Oriole R. Robinson, Aug. 30, 1952; children: Mark F., Peter A. Nat. and Higher Nat. degrees in Mech. Engring., Bristol Coll. Tech., 1952. Sr. engr. aircraft control sys. Bristol Aero.-Orenda Engines Can., 1954-59; sr. engr. power sys. rsch. Bendix Corp., Southfield, Mich., 1959-61; supr. turbine sys. sect. Ford Motor Co., Dearborn, Mich., 1961-66, mgr. turbine R & D, 1967-78, mgr. ceramic materials rsch., 1979-86, mgr. materials engring., 1987-88; pvt. practice Oceanside, Calif., 1988—. Patentee in field; contbr. articles to profl. jours. With RAF, 1951-54. Recipient Soichiro Honda medal. Fellow ASME (past chmn. vehicular com., ceramics com.), Am. Ceramic Soc.; mem. Soc. Automotive Engrs. (past turbine com.), Inst. Mech. Engrs. Home: 3764 Southridge Way Oceanside CA 92056-5428 Office Phone: 760-724-3102. Personal E-mail: artmcl@cox.net.

MCLEAN, CRAIG ELLIOTT, retired non-commissioned officer; b. Muskegon, Mich., Dec. 12, 1950; s. Elliott Garber and Margaret Irene (Carlson) McL. BA, Kans. State U., 2007. Enlisted U.S. Army, 1971, advanced through ranks to sgt. first class; served in continental U.S., West Germany and West Berlin; ret., 1992. Contbr. short stories and poetry to profl. publs. Field rep. Law Enforcement Alliance Am., Falls Church, Va., 1998—; mem. Coun. Conservative Citizens, St. Louis, 1999—. Decorated French Commando Badge, French Army, 1981. Mem. DAV, VFW, Golden Key Nat. Honor Soc., U-Boot-Archiv (full friend), Sigma Tau Delta. Avocations: study of world war ii and u-boat history, writing.

MCLEAN, DAVID J., lawyer; m. Tammy Lynne Ross, May 26, 1985; children: Emily, Michael. BA summa cum laude, Washington & Lee U., 1978; grad student, U. Edinburg, Scotland, 1979; JD magna cum laude, Geogetown U. Law Ctr., 1982. Bar: Calif. 1982, DC 1991, N.Y. 2004, (various others). Assoc. Latham & Watkins, LA, 1982—89; ptnr., litigation dept. Latham & Watkins LLP, LA, 1989—2003, ptnr. in charge of tng., 1999—2002, office managing ptnr. Newark, 2004—. Bd. govs. Fed. Bar Assn., Commn. on ADR, Washington, 2000—03; exec. comm. CPR Inst. for Disputre Resolution, NYC, 2003—. Trustee San Martino (Calif.) Schs. Found., 1999—2002. Mem.: ABTL (LA) (bd. of governors, alternative dispute resolution section), CPR Ctr. for Dispute Resolution (standing com. on dispute resolution), Chancery Club (litig. section). Office: Latham & Watkins LLP One Newark Ctr Newark NJ 07101 Office Phone: 973-639-1234. Business E-Mail: david.mclean@lw.com.

MC LEAN, DON, singer, instrumentalist, composer; b. New Rochelle, NY, Oct. 2, 1945; s. Donald and Elizabeth (Bucci) McL.; m. Patrisha Shnier, Mar., 1987. Student, Villanova U., 1964; BBA, Iona Coll., 1968. Pres., owner The Benny Bird Co., Inc., Fairfield, Conn.; recorded for United Artists, Artista Records, EMI Records. Star BBC-TV spls., 1973, 78, numerous concert appearances. Albums include Tapestry, 1972, American Pie, 1972, Don McLean, 1972, Playin' Favourites, 1973, Homeless Brother, 1974, Solo, 1976, Prime Time, 1987, Chain Lightning, 1979, Very Best of, 1980, Believers, 1982, Dominion, 1983, The Best of Don McLean, 1987, Don McLean's Greatest Hits Then & Now, 1987, Love Tracks, 1988, For the Memories, 1989, Don McLean's Greatest Hits Live, 1990, Headroom, 1991, Classics, 1992, The River of Love, 1995, Solo, 1995, Greatest Hits Live, 1997, Don McLean's Christmas Dreams, 1997; singles include American Pie, 1971, Vincent, 1971, Crying, 1980; wrote Perry Como hit And I Love You So, 1973; performances include America's Millenium, Washington, Starry Starry Night (TV special). Mem. bd. Hudson River Sloop Restoration, World Hunger Yr., Advs. for Arts; fund raiser Scenic Hudson, Hudson River Fisherman's Assn. Recipient more than 30 gold and platinum records worldwide, 5 grammy award nominations and others; Israel Cultural award, 1981. Mem. Coffee House Club. Office: Atlantic Records 1290 Avenue Of The Americas New York NY 10104-0184 also: PO Box 307 Camden ME 04843-0307

MC LEAN, DONALD MILLIS, microbiologist, educator, pathologist, pediatrician; b. Melbourne, Australia, July 26, 1926; s. Donald and Nellie (Millis) McL.; married. BSc, U. Melbourne, 1947, MB, 1950, MD, 1954. Fellow Rockefeller Found., NYC and Hamilton, Mont., 1955; vis. instr. bacteriology U. Minn., Mpls., 1957; med. officer Commonwealth Serum Labs., Melbourne, 1957; virologist Research Inst., Hosp. for Sick Children, Toronto, Ont., Canada, 1958-67; assoc. prof. microbiology, assoc. in pediatrics U. Toronto Med. Sch., 1962-67; prof. med. microbiology U. B.C. Med. Sch., Vancouver, Canada, 1967-91, prof. emeritus Pathology, 1991—. Author: Virology in Health Care, 1980, Immunological Investigation of Human Virus Disease, 1982, Same-Day Virus Diagnosis, 1984, Virological Infections, 1988, Medical Microbiology Synopsis, 1991, Acute Viral Infections, 1991; contbr. articles to profl. jours. Fellow Royal Coll. Physicians (Can.), Royal Coll. Pathologists; mem. Am. Epidemiological Soc., Am. Soc. Tropical Medicine, Can. Med. Assn., Am. Soc. Virology, Soc. for Vector Ecology, Soc. for Gen. Microbiology, Infectious Diseases Soc. Am. Home and Office: 2720 Yukon St V5Y 3R1 Vancouver BC Canada Office Phone: 604-263-9076.

MCLEAN, IAN P., utilities executive; m. Kathryn McLean; 4 children. BS with honors in Math., Teesside U., Eng. Mng. dir. London trading operation Engelhard Corp., 1985, sr. v.p. USA Group, 1987, group v.p. indsl. commodities mgmt.; sr. v.p., pres. nat. mktg. divsn. PECO Energy Exelon Corp., 1999, pres. Exelon Power Team, 1999—, exec. v.p., 2002—. Office: Exelon Corp 10 S Dearborn St 37th Fl PO Box 805398 Chicago IL 60680-5398 Office Phone: 800-483-3220. *

MCLEAN, JAMES ALBERT, artist, educator; b. Gibsland, La., Nov. 25, 1928; s. Charles Edward and Lucille (Bowdon) McL.; m. Ocelia Jo Perkins, Nov. 27, 1954; 1 child: Gregory Scott. BA, Southwestern La. Inst., 1950; BD, So. Meth. U., 1953; MFA, Tulane U., 1961. Meth. student dir. Centenary Coll., Shreveport, La., 1957-59; head art dept. LaGrange (Ga.) Coll., 1964-66; assoc. prof. art Ga. State U., Atlanta, 1967-68, prof. art, 1968-95; ret., 1995. Exhibited in numerous group shows including Brooklyn Mus., 1976-77, Positive/Negative Exhbn., 1988, Siggraph Exhbn. 1988, 89, Clemson U. Nat. Print and Drawing Exhbn., 1989, Purdue U. Small Print Exhbn., 1990. Mem. Siggraph. Avocations: animation, puppetry. Home: 1256 Dunwoody Knoll Dr Atlanta GA 30338-3219 E-mail: mcle231@bellsouth.net.

MCLEAN, KATHLEEN, exhibition consultant, museum director; Mus. curatorial specialist Oakland Mus.; dir. exhibts and publications Md. Sci. Ctr.; dir. exhibitions and publications Bklyn. Children's Mus.; dir. Ctr. for Pub. Exhbn. Exploratorium, San Francisco; prin. Ind. Exhibitions. Co-founder ExhibitFiles. Author: Planning for People in Museums, 1992. Named to Centennial Honor Roll, Am. Assn. Museums, 2006. Mem.: Visitors Studies Assn. Mailing: Assn Science Technology Centers 1025 Vermont Ave NW Ste 500 Washington DC 20005-6310 *

MCLEAN, R. BRUCE, lawyer; b. NYC, Nov. 15, 1946; BS with honors, Ind. U., 1968, JD cum laude, 1971. Bar: Ind. 1971, DC 1974. Atty. appellate ct. br. Nat. Labor Rels. Bd., 1971—73; chair, litig. practice Akin, Gump, Strauss, Hauer & Feld L.L.P., Washington, 1982—94, now chmn. Bd. visitors Ind. U. Sch. Law, 1989—, vice chair, 1998—; bd. visitors Georgetown Law Ctr., 2002—. Mem. Fed. City Coun. Mem.: ABA, DC Bar, Fed. Bar Assn., Order of Coif, Phi Alpha Delta. Office: Akin Gump Strauss Hauer & Feld LLP Robert S Strauss Bldg 1333 New Hampshire Ave NW Washington DC 20036-1564 Office Phone: 202-887-4022. Office Fax: 202-887-4288. Business E-Mail: bmclean@akingump.com.

MCLEAN, ROBERT, III, real estate company executive; b. Balt., May 23, 1928; s. Robert Jr. and Mary Somerville (Iglehart) McL.; m. Elizabeth Madison Lewis, May 21, 1960; children: Elizabeth, Alexander, Mary, John. BA, Yale U., 1950; MA, U. Pa., 1965. Mktg. exec. Owens-Ill., Toledo, 1957-65; mktg. cons. Old Phila. Devel. Corp., Phila., 1966-70; 2001vice chmn. Cushman & Wakefield, NYC, 1970—2001; chmn. directorate Cambridge Inst. of Applied Rsch., McLean, Va., 2001—. Mem. real estate investment com. Yale U., New Haven, Conn., 1982-90; mem. bd. Cushman & Wakefield, N.Y.C., 1986-2000. Author: Countdown to Renaissance II, The New Way Corporate America Builds, 1984. Chmn. Nat. Bldg. Mus., Washington, 1992-95; mem. bd. Washington Nat. Cathedral, 1980-88. S/Sgt. USMC, 1953-56. Mem. Rolling Rock Club, Metropolitan Club, Center Club, Gibson Island Club. Republican. Episcopalian. Avocations: tennis, golf, skiing. Home: 631 Stillwater Rd Gibson Island MD 21056 Office: Cambridge Inst 7008 Capital View Dr Mc Lean VA 22101 Office Phone: 703-893-0101. Personal E-mail: rmclean06@aol.com.

MCLEAN, ROBERT ALEXANDER, lawyer; b. Memphis, Oct. 24, 1943; s. Albert A and Harriet Spencer (Pond) McLean; m. Sydney Ross, July 16, 1977; children: Robert Alexander, Ross Andrew. BA with honors, Rhodes Coll., 1965; MA, Princeton U., 1968, PhD, 1974; JD, U. Memphis, 1978. Bar: Tenn 1979, US Dist Ct (we dist) Tenn 1979, US Dist Ct (ea dist) Wis 1985, US Ct Appeals (5th cir) 1986, US Dist Ct (ea and we dists) Ark 1990, US Ct Appeals (8th cir) 1990, US Ct Appeals (10th cir) 1991, US Ct Appeals (6th cir) 1998, US Supreme Ct 1998. Asst. prof. Russian lit. U. Calif., Santa Cruz, 1971-76; staff atty. FCA, Washington, 1979-81; assoc. Wildman, Harrold, Allen, Dixon & McDonnell, Memphis, 1981-88, ptnr., 1988-89; ptnr. McDonnell Boyd, Memphis, 1989-94; mem. McDonnell Dyer, PLC, Memphis, 1994-95; spl. counsel Wolff Ardis, P.C., Memphis, 1995-96, shareholder, 1997; mem. Farris Mathews Branan Bobango & Hellen, PLC, 1997—; asst. city atty. Germantown, Tenn., 1981—. Adj asst prof Russian lang Rhodes Col, Memphis, 1982—86. Translator: (book) Mozart and Salieri, 1973; mem: journal Univ Memphis Law Rev, 1977—78. Mem session Germantown Presbyn. Ch, Tenn., 1988—, chmn fin comm. Tenn., 1989—94, Tenn. Fellow Charlotte Elizabeth Procter, Princeton Univ, 1968, Fulbright, USSR, 1969, Regents, Univ Calif, Santa Cruz, 1975. Mem.: ABA, Memphis Bar Assoc., Tenn Bar Assoc. Republican. Avocations: golf, quail hunting. Home: 8820 Somerset Ln Germantown TN 38138-7375 Office: Farris Matthews et al Ste 2000 One Commerce Sq Memphis TN 38103 Home Phone: 901-755-8453; Office Phone: 901-259-7100. Business E-Mail: ram@farris-law.com. E-mail: envtlatty@aol.com.

MCLEAN, VINCENT RONALD, former manufacturing company financial executive; b. Detroit, June 1, 1931; s. Frederick Ronald and Bernice Mary (Vincent) McL.; m. Joyce Adrienne Koch, July 23, 1960; children—Judith Adrienne, Bruce Ronald BBA, U. Mich., 1954, MBA, 1955. Fin. analyst Ford Motor Co., Detroit, 1954—55, Mobil Oil Corp., NYC, 1958—69; treas. Mobil Chem. Co., NYC, 1966—69; v.p. fin., treas. NL Industries, NYC, 1969—76, exec. v.p. fin. and planning, dir., 1976—82; exec. v.p., CFO, dir. Sperry Corp., NYC, 1982—86; sr. advisor Wertheim Schroder & Co., NYC, 1988—89. Bd. dirs. Legal and Gen. Am., Inc., William Penn Life Ins. Co. NY, Banner Life Ins. Co., Md. Served with U.S. Army, 1955-57 Mem. N.Y. Soc. Security Analysts, Econ. Club N.Y. Home: 702 Shackamaxon Dr Westfield NJ 07090-3408

MCLEAN, WALTER FRANKLIN, government agency administrator, business consultant, legislator, minister; b. Leamington, Ont., Can., Apr. 26, 1936; s. J.L.W. McL.; m. Barbara Muriel Scott, Aug. 19, 1961; children: Scott, Chima, Ian, Duncan BA, Victoria Coll., U. B.C., 1957; M.Div., Knox Coll., U. Toronto, 1960; LLD (hon.), Wilfrid Laurier U., 1995; DD (hon.), Knox Coll., 2002. Ordained to ministry, Presbyterian Ch. Min. Knox Presbyn. Ch., Waterloo, 1971-79; mem. House of Commons, Ottawa, Ont., Canada, 1979—93, Sec. of State of Can., 1984—85, sworn to Privy Coun., 1984, min. of immigration, 1985—86; min. responsible for status of women Govt. of Can., 1984-86. CUSO, Nigeria coord., 1962-67; chaplain U. Nigeria, 1962-67; dep. dir. Internat. Program Can. Centennial, 1967; exec. dir. Man. Assn. for World Devel., 1970; past chmn. World Concerns Commn. Canadian Cun. Chs.; Can. del. Gen. Assemblies UN, 1986-93; apptd. prime minister's spl. rep. Commonwealth and South African affairs, 1989-93; Can. rep. So. Africa Devel. Coordination Conf., 1987-93; del. Commonwealth Fgn. Mins. Against Apartheid, 1987-93, African Devel. Bank, 1990-91, Assn. West European Parliamentarians Against Apartheid, 1988-89; leader fact finding mission to Mozambique, 1987, Can. delegation UN Conf. on Women, Nairobi, 1985; led Parliamentary del. to observe the pre-election process and attended Namibian Indpedence, Mar. 21, 1990; chmn. paliamentary Com. on Devel. and Human Rights; Commonwealth observer South African and Sri Lanka elections 1994; pres. Franklin Cons. Ltd., 1993—; chair McLean and Assocs., 2004—; bd. dirs. TAB Internat. Energy Corp. Alderman City of Waterloo, Ont., 1976-79; co-founder UN based Parliamentarians Global Action; hon. consul of the Rep. of Namibia, 1994—; convenor Millenium Celebration Presbyn. Ch., 1998-00; prin. The Osborne Group, 2000—; bd. dirs. Toronto Sch. Theology, 2005-; adv. bd. Royal Rds. U., Victoria BC, 1995—. Chaplain 404 wing RCAF, 1976-03; mem. Ont. Criminal Injuries Compensation Bd., 2000-03. Recipient Can. U. Svcs. Overseas award, 1990, Can. Bur. Internat. Edn. award, 1994, Disting. Alumni award U. Victoria, 2002; Paul Harris fellow, 1984. Mem. UN Assn. Can. (chair human rights com.), Rotary. Progressive Conservative. Office Phone: 519-578-5932. E-mail: walter@mcleanandassociates.ca.

MCLEAN, WILLIAM RONALD, retired electrical engineer, consultant; b. Bklyn., Mar. 26, 1921; s. Harold W. and Helena Winifred (Farrell) McL.; m. Cecile L. Mills, Aug. 17, 1946 (div.); m. Evelyn Hupfer, Nov. 29, 1968. BA in Math., Bklyn. Coll., 1980, BS in Computational Math., 1981. Chief electrician U.S. Mcht. Marine, 1942-64, elect. designer, engr., 1965-76; sr. elect engr. M. Rosenblatt & Son, Inc., NYC, 1976-86; cons., 1986-98; ret., 1996. Mem. AAAS, IEEE, Soc. Naval Archs. and Marine Engrs., Am. Soc. Naval Engrs. Home: 1270 67th St # 507 Brooklyn NY 11219 Home Phone: 718-331-6342.

MCLEER FREE, LAUREEN DOROTHY, drug development and pharmaceutical professional; b. NYC, Feb. 5, 1955; d. William Myers and Una Lee (Massey) McLeer; m. Martin Kevin Free, Apr. 27, 2007. BS, Columbia U., 1977; MBA, U. London, 1981. RN N.Y., D.C., state reg. nurse, Eng., registered state nurse, Wales. Staff nurse NYU Med. Ctr., NYC, 1977-78; charge nurse Scripps Clinic and Rsch. Found., La Jolla, Calif., 1979-80; clin. rschr. Ayerst Labs., NYC, 1982; sales rep. Pfizer, Inc., NYC, 1983-87, Cahners Pub. Co., NYC, 1988-89; dir. bus. devel. Pro Clinica, NYC, 1990-91; account supr. Salthouse Torre Norton, Inc., Rutherford, N.J., 1992-93; dir. bus. devel. Med. & Tech. Rsch. Assocs., Inc., Wellesley, Mass., 1993-94; sr. project dir. Quiltiles Inc., Arlington, Va., 1994-99; project mgr. product devel. and commercialization Aventis Pharms., Inc., Berwyn, Pa., 1999—2002; clin. trial mgmt. leader AstraZeneca, LP, Wilmington, Del., 2002—, assoc. dir., 2005—. Mem. com. for healthcare issues and legis. United Hosp. Fund, NYC, 1992—94. Chmn. Help Our Neighbors Eat Yr. 'Round, NYC, 1987—89; trustee Murray Hill Com., NYC, 1988—90; bd. dirs. East Midtown Svcs. for Older People, 1987—94; vol. nurse Whitman Walker Clinic, 1995—99; bd. dirs. Cecil Land Trust, 2002—06, v.p., 2006—; bd. dirs. Eastern Shore Land Conservancy, 2003—, treas., exec. bd. dirs., 2005—. Named Md. Wildlife Farmer of Yr., Md. Dept. Natural Resources, 2004. Mem.: Drug Info. Assn., Regulatory Affairs Profl. Soc. Home: PO Box 681 Chesapeake City MD 21915 Office: AstraZeneca LP 1800 Concorde Pike Wilmington DE 19802-4034 Home Phone: 410-885-5255; Office Phone: 302-885-5213. Business E-Mail: laureen.mcleer@astrazeneca.com.

MCLELLON, RICHARD STEVEN, aerospace engineer, consultant; b. Lawton, Okla., May 28, 1952; s. Robert Nelson and Jane (Warriner) McL. BSME, Old Dominion U., 1979. Aerospace engr. Naval Engring. Support Office, Norfolk, Va., 1979-82, U.S. Army Aviation Systems Commd., Ft. Eustis, Va., 1982-86; mission lead dynamicist Astronautics Space Launch Sys., Lockheed Martin Corp., Denver, 1986—2005, stress analyst, loads analyst, Workshare, Tech. Ops., 2005—. Cons. Aircraft Devel., Inc., Littleton, Colo., 1991—.

MCLEMORE, JOAN MEADOWS, librarian, consultant; b. Bivens, Tex., Aug. 24, 1929; d. James Leon Jr. and Dell (Crawford) Meadows; m. Kenneth Lyons McLemore, May 6, 1950 (dec.); 1 child, Ken Malcolm. Student, Miss. State Coll. for Women, 1947-49; BS, U. So. Miss., Hattiesburg, 1976, MLS, 1983. Libr. Franklin County Pub. Libr., Meadville, Miss., 1976-90; libr. dir. Copiah-Lincoln C.C., Natchez, Miss., 1990—2003. Story teller, presenter conf. The Delta Kappa Gamma Soc. Internat., Louisville, 1991, Nashville, 1994; internat. spkr. Delta Kappa Soc., Red Deer, Can., 1994; mem. faculty Elderhostel, Natchez, Miss., 1990—; presenter Southeastern Regional Conf., Delta Kappa Gamma Soc. Internat., Charleston, S.C, 1997; pres. Franklinc. Mus., 1999-2004, Franklin County Mus., Meadville, Miss., 2002—, Inst. Lng. in Retirement, 2003—. Contbr. articles to profl. jours. Libr. trustee Franklin County, Meadville, 1962-76, Lincoln-Lawrence-Franklin Regional Libr., Brookhaven, Miss., 1971-76; trustee Franklyn County Meml. Hosp., 1997-2001, jury com., 1998-2001; deacon Presbyn.Ch., 2003-06; Miss. com. Humanities Spkrs. Roster, 2004—. Mem. Miss. Libr. Assn. (com. chair, exec. dir. libr. week activities 1989), Colonial Dames (gov. George Harlan chpt., 2nd v.p. 2002-05, parliamentarian 2005—), DAR (Homochitlo River chpt. 1979-1999, Natchez chpt. 2000—), Dames of the Ct. of Honor (treas. 2001—, chaplain 1999-2003, treas. 2004—), Mis. Soc. DAMES of the South, Daughters of Soc. of War of 1812 (sec., treas. 2007—), Natchez Garden Club, Natchez Hist. Soc. (trustee 2005—, sec. 2007—), Miss. Hist. Soc., Order of the First Families (chaplain 2002-05, historian 2005-07, dep. gov. gen. 2007—), First Families Twin Territories, Delta Kappa Gamma (pres. 1979-80, 1979-97 Rho chpt.), Progressive Study Club (sec. 2006-), Natchez Women's Book Soc., Friends of Armstrong Libr., Rose Craft Club, Scottish Heritage Soc., Natchez Retiree Partnership. Avocations: genealogy, reading, baking, historial research, story telling. Home: Apt A 310 S Dr M L King Jr St Natchez MS 39120-3533 Personal E-mail: joanmc11@bellsouth.net.

MCLEMORE, LAURA LYONS, archivist, history educator; b. Shreveport, La., July 21, 1950; d. Val Alexander and Bobbie Chennault Lyons; m. Jim Ray McLemore, June 7, 1975; children: Havard Roland, Austen Laurence, Ivy Elizabeth. BA, So. Meth. U., 1971; MA, Tex. A&M U., 1991; PhD, U. of North Tex., 1998. Coll. archivist Austin Coll., Sherman, Tex., 1987—2004; adj. instr. Grayson County Coll., Denison, Tex., 1998—; archivist La. State U., Shreveport. Author: (book) Inventing Texas: Early Historians of the Lone Star State. Mem. Hist. Preservation Adv. Bd., Denison, 2003—04; pres. Red River Hist. Mus., Sherman, 1996—97; mem. Shreveport Symphony Orch., 2005—. Named Outstanding Grad. Student in History, U. of North Tex., 1995—96; recipient Hatton W. Sumners Dissertation fellowship, 1996. Mem.: North La. Hist. Assn., La. Hist. Assn., Tex. State Hist. Assn. (John H. Jenkins Rsch. fellowship 1996), La. Archives and Manuscripts Assn., Acad. of Cert. Archivists (regent for outreach 2004—), Soc. of S.W. Archivists (pres. 1998—99), Soc. of Am. Archivists, Phi Kappa Phi. Episcopalian. Avocations: choral singing, gardening, bridge, reading, tennis. Office: La State U One University Pl Shreveport LA 71115 Office Phone: 318-797-5378. Business E-Mail: Laura.McLemore@lsus.edu.

MCLENDON, BRIAN ANDREW, lab administrator, educator; s. Fredrick Levonne and Peggy Rae McLendon. Student, U. SC, Columbia, 1989—95. Bldg. supr. U. SC, Columbia, 1990—94, alumni fund solicitor, 1994—95; lab technician Eckerd Drug Corp., Columbia, 1996, group leader, 1996, lab supr., 1996—97, lab mgr., 1998, tng. lab. mgr., 1998—. Named Lab Mgr. of Quarter, Eckerd Drug Corp., 2004. Mem.: Soc. Photofinishing Engrs., Photo Mktg. Assn. Internat. (cert. photographic cons. 2001—), Am. Mensa Ltd. Avocations: cabinet making, horology, photography, astronomy. Office: Eckerd Drug Corp 4730 Forest Dr Columbia SC 29206

MCLENDON, LLOYD, professional baseball coach, retired baseball player; Former infielder Cin. Reds, 1987—88, Chgo. Cubs, 1989—90, Toronto Blue Jays, 1990, Pitts. Pirates, 1990—94, former mgr.; bullpen coach Detroit Tigers, 2006, hitting coach, 2006—. Office: Detroit Tigers Comerica Park 2100 Woodward Ave Detroit MI 48201 *

MCLENDON, ROGER EDWIN, neuropathologist, educator; s. Vivian W. and Harold Edwin Mclendon; m. Patti Swain, 1982; children: Patrick Edwin, Erin Elizabeth, Ryan Hodges. MD, Med. Coll. of Ga., 1983. Diplomate Am. Bd. Pathology, 1987. Prof. Duke Sch. of Medicine, Durham, NC, 1992—; asst clin. prof. pathology Mercer U. Sch. of Medicine, Macon, Ga., 1988—2006. Dir. anatomic pathology, chief of neuropathology Duke Sch. of Medicine, Durham, NC, 2006—. Contbg. editor: Russell And Rubinstein's Pathology of Tumors of The Nervous System, 2000; author: Pathology of Tumors of the Central Nervous System. Scoutmaster Boy Scouts Of Am., Durham, NC, 2000—06. Fellow: Coll. of Am. Pathologists (ednl. com. mem. 2003—06); mem.: Am. Assn. Neuropathology (bd. councilors 2006—), Am. Bd. Pathology (neuropathology com. mem. 1997—2006). Avocations: coaching youth baseball, reading. Office Phone: 919-684-6940.

MCLENDON, SUSAN MICHELLE, lawyer; b. NYC, Mar. 5, 1964; d. James McLendon, Sr. BSN, SUNY, 1986; JD, Temple U., 1990. Bar: NJ (adm.) 1991, Wash., DC 1998, NY 2000; RN NY, 1986. Asst. regional counsel Social Security Adminstrn., Office Gen. Counsel, NYC, 1990-98; pvt. practice, 2000—. Cons. in field. Editor-in-chief: Environ. Law Digest, 1989—90. Named Landmark Affirmative Action Baby, 1967, World's Smartest Genius, 1967; scholar, NY State Regents, 1982—86, 1982—86, 1989—90. Avocations: singing, writing, running, tennis, skiing.

MCLENNAN, BARBARA NANCY, tax specialist; b. NYC, Mar. 25, 1940; d. Sol and Gertrude (Rochkind) Miller; m. Kenneth McLennan, Aug. 14, 1962; children: Gordon, Laura. BA magna cum laude, CCNY, 1961; MS, U. Wis., 1962, PhD, 1965; JD, Georgetown U., 1983. Bar: DC 1983, U.S. Ct. Internat. Trade 1988, U.S. Ct. Appeals (DC cir.) 1988, U.S. Supreme Ct. 1988, Va. 1991; cert. accredited valuation analyst Nat. Assn. Cert. Valuation Analysts, 2004. From asst. prof. to assoc. prof. Temple U., Phila., 1965—78; budget analyst Com. Budget, U.S. Ho. of Reps., Washington, 1978—81; legis. asst. fin. and budget Senator Dan Quayle, Washington, 1981—84; internat. tax specialist IRS U.S. Dept. Treasury, Washington, 1984—89; dep. asst. sec. trade, info. and analysis U.S. Dept. Commerce, Washington, 1989—91; prin., atty.-at-law Bitonti and Wilhelm, PC., McLean, Va., 1991—93; staff v.p. govt.-legal affairs consumer electronics group Electronic Industries Assn., Washington, 1993—94, staff v.p. tech. policy, consumer electronics group, 1994—95; v.p. Van Scoyoc Assocs., Washington, 1995—96; cons. on tax related issues in U.S., former Soviet Union, and West Bank and Gaza McLean, Va., 1996—. Adj. prof. Coll. William and Mary, 2005—; sr. polit. scientist SRI-Internat., Arlington, Va., 1971—74; vis. prof. Am. Coll., Paris, 1975—76; cons. UNESCO, Paris, 1977—78. Author: (book) Comparative Political Systems, 1975; contbr. articles to profl. jours. Mem. parents adv. coun. Randolph-Macon Coll., Ashland, Va., 1989—92. Fellow NDEA, 1962—65. Mem.: ABA, Va. Bar Assn., Fed. Bar Assn., DC Bar Assn., Am. Soc. Assn. Execs., Phi Beta Kappa. Home: 1620 Harbor Rd Williamsburg VA 23185 E-mail: barb.mcl@cox.net.

MCLENNAN, HAMISH, advertising executive; Account mgr. George Patterson Bates, internat. client svcs. dir. Hong Kong, 1994, mng. dir. Melbourne, nat. mng. dir., 1999; chmn., CEO Young & Rubicam Brands, Australia, New Zealand, 2002—06; global CEO Y&R Advt., NYC, 2006—. Office: Y&R Advt 285 Madison Ave New York NY 10017 Office Phone: 212-210-3000. *

MCLEOD, CHANSE L., lawyer; b. Dallas, 1965; BBA with honors in Fin., U. Tex., Austin, 1988; JD, Houston U., 1991. Bar: Tex. 1991. Ptnr., Real Estate Andrews Kurth LLP, Houston. Assoc. editor Houston Law Rev., 1989—91. Mem.: Houston Bar Found., Tex. Bar Found., Houston Bar Assn., Houston Young Lawyers Assn., State Bar Tex., Tex. Young Lawyers Assn., ABA, Phi Delta Phi. Office: Andrews Kurth LLP 600 Travis St Ste 4200 Houston TX 77002-3090 Office Fax: 713-238-7257, 713-220-4020. Business E-Mail: cmcleod@andrewskurth.com.

MCLEOD, E. DOUGLAS, real estate developer, lawyer; b. Galveston, Tex., Aug. 6, 1941; s. Vaughan Watkins McLeod and Dorothy (Milroy) Burton; m. Sarah Jackson Helms, Mar. 20, 1965 (div. 1979); children: Chanse, Alexandra, Lindsey; m. Joan Margaret Williams, Dec. 26, 1979; 1 child, Joanie stepchildren: Meg, Libbie. BBA, U. North Tex., 1965; postgrad., So. Meth. U., 1965-66; JD, South Tex. Coll. Law, 1990; LLM, U. Houston, 1993. Bar: Tex., U.S. Dist. Ct. (so. dist.) Tex.; lic. real estate broker. Pres., owner McLeod Properties & co., Galveston, 1967—; tchr. Galveston Ind. Sch. Dist., 1967-69, pres., trustee, 1969—73; banker W. L. Moody & Co., Galveston, 1969-72; developer, broker McLeod Properties/Builders, Galveston, 1972-82; developer Moody Found., Galveston, 1982—. Bd. dirs. Am. Nat. Ins. Co., Galveston, Nat. Western Life Ins. Co., Austin, Anrem Corp., Galveston, Colonel Inc., Galveston, Moody Gardens Inc., Galveston, chmn., 1984—. Mem. editl. bd.: Currents Internat. Trade Law Jour., 1992—. Mayor pro-tem, mem. city coun. City of Galveston, 1973—76; state legislator Tex. Ho. Reps., Austin, 1976—83; bd. visitors South Tex. Coll. Law, 1990—96, bd. dirs., 2000—; mem. adv. bd. U. Houston, 1986—95; bd. dirs. STCL, Ronald McDonald House, 1986—93, Trinity Episcopal Sch., 1990—96, Galveston Econ. Devel. Partnership, 1998—2002; vestryman, sr. warden, chancellor Episc. Ch. With USMC, 1961—67. Mem.: ABA, Am. Judicature Soc., Galveston County Bar Assn., Tex. Bar Assn., Marine Corps League. Avocations: physical fitness advocate, legal history collector. Home: 53 Cedar Lawn Cir Galveston TX 77551-4631 Office: The Moody Found 2302 Post Office St Ste 704 Galveston TX 77550-1994 Office Phone: 409-797-1521. Business E-Mail: dmcleod@moodyf.org.

MCLEOD, HARRY O'NEAL, JR., retired petroleum engineer, consultant; b. Shreveport, La., Feb. 26, 1932; s. Harry O'Neal Sr. and Odelle Nan (Crow) McL.; m. Sandra Lou Mahaffey, Feb. 6, 1959; children: Kathleen Odelle, Bryan O'Neal. Degree in engring., Colo. Sch. Mines, 1953; MS in Petroleum Engring., U. Okla., 1963, PhD in Engring. Sci., 1965. Prodn. engr. Phillips Petroleum Co., 1953—58; rsch. engr. Jersey Prodn. Rsch. Co., Tulsa, 1963—64; sr. rsch. engr. Dowell divsn. Dow Chem. Co., Tulsa, 1965—69; dir. info. svcs. dept. U. Tulsa, 1969—75; from sr. prodn. engr. to sr. staff engr. Conoco, Inc., Houston, 1975—86, engring. profl., 1986—91, sr. engring. profl., 1992—97; pvt. practice cons. Houston, 1998—2003; ret., 2004. 1st lt. U.S. Army, 1954-56. Mem. Soc. Petroleum Engrs. (Prodn. Engring. award 1989, Disting. Mem. award 1995, disting. author, 1983, disting. lectr. 1987-88, 96-97), Sigma Xi. Republican. Methodist. Home: 2006 Southwick St Houston TX 77080-6315 E-mail: homcleod@aol.com.

MCLEOD, WALTON JAMES, lawyer, state legislator; b. Walterboro, SC, June 30, 1937; s. Walton James Jr. and Rhoda Lane (Brown) M.; m. Julie Edwina Hamiter, Feb. 15, 1969; 1 child, Walton James IV. BA, Yale U., 1959; LLB, U. S.C., 1964; postgrad., U. Minn., 1972. Bar: S.C. 1964, U.S. Supreme Ct. 1974. Law clk. to Chief Judge Clement Haynsworth U.S. Ct. Appeals (4th cir.), Richmond, Va., 1964-65; assoc. Pope and Schumpert, Newberry, SC, 1965-67; asst. U.S. Atty. Columbia, SC, 1967-68; gen. counsel S.C. Dept. Health & Environ. Ctrl., Columbia, 1968-94, spl. counsel, 1994-96; dep. S.C. atty. gen. Columbia, 1987-88. Magistrate Newberry County, Little Mountain, S.C., 1973-81; mcpl. judge Town of Little Mountain, 1981-83, mayor, 1983-89, 93-96; mem. S.C. Ho. of Reps., Columbia, 1996—. Author: Legal Perspectives of Environmental Health, 1973; co-author: Environmental Quality Law, 1975, Hospital Franchising Law and Regulation, 1979. Pres. Newberry (S.C.) Jaycees, 1967; bd. dirs. S.C. Housing Fin. & Devel. Authority, Columbia, 1977-96, Newberry County Coun. Aging, 2001—, Newberry Coll. Found., 2005—; chair Ctrl. Midlands Coun. Govts., Columbia, 1981-82, 2001-03; trustee S.C. State Mus., Columbia, 1981-85. Lt. (j.g.) USN, 1959-61, served to Capt. USNR, 1961-92, ret. Recipient Outstanding Jaycee award Newberry Jaycees, 1967, Howell Excellence award Naval Res. Law Program, Washington, 1991, Outstanding Legislator award Gift of Life Trust Fund, 1999, Legislative Appreciation award SC Assn. Conservation Dists., 2006, Outstanding Svc. award SC Am. Legion, 2006; named Outstanding Freshman Rep. of Yr. Carolina Hist. Found. Soc., Inc., 1997. Fellow S.C. Bar Found.; mem. S.C. Magistrates Assn. (pres. 1976-77, Disting. Jud. Svc. award 1975, 77), Judge Advs. Assn. (nat. pres. 1991-92), S.C. Res. Officers Assn. (state pres. 1981-82, Res. Officer of Yr. 1998), S.C. Soc. (pres. 1990-93). Democrat. Luth. Avocations: reading, physical fitness. Home: 308 Pomaria St Little Mountain SC 29075-9003 Office: SC House of Reps PO Box 11867 Columbia SC 29211-1867 Fax: 803-345-0770.

MCLESKEY, CHARLES HAMILTON, anesthesiologist, educator, pharmaceutical executive; b. Phila., Nov. 8, 1946; s. W. Hamilton and Marion A. (Butts) McL.; m. Nanci S. Simmons, June 3, 1972; children: Travis, Heather. BA, Susquehanna U., 1968; MD, Wake Forest U., 1972. Diplomate Am. Bd. Anesthesiology. Intern Maine Med. Ctr., Portland, 1972-73; resident in anesthesiology U. Wash. Sch. Medicine, Seattle, 1973-76, NIH rsch. trainee, 1974-75; clin. teaching assoc. dept. anesthesiology U. Calif., San Francisco, 1976-78; asst. prof. anesthesiology Wake Forest U. Bowman Gray Sch. Medicine, Winston-Salem, NC, 1978-83, assoc. prof., 1983-84, U. Tex. Med. Br., Galveston, 1985-87; assoc. prof. anesthesiology U. Colo. Health Sci. Ctr., Denver, 1987-91, prof., 1991-93, dir. acad. affairs, 1987-93; prof., chmn. dept. anesthesiology Tex. A&M U., 1993-2000; chmn. dept. anesthesiology, med. dir. perioperative svcs. Scott and White Clin. and Meml. Hosp., Temple, Tex., 1993-2000; assoc. med. dir. Scott and White Health Plan, 1995-2000; sr. dir. clin. devel. Abbott Labs., Abbott Park, Ill., 2000—02, global med. dir., global mktg. dir.

anesthesia and sedation, 2002—06; v.p. clin. affairs ZARS, Salt Lake City, 2006—07. Cons., lectr. Janssen Pharmaceutica, Piscataway, N.J., 1980-98, Alza Corp., Palo Alto, Calif., 1986-99; cons. Glaxo-Wellcome Co., Research Triangle Park, N.C., Abbott Labs., Chgo., Hoechst, Marion, Roussel, Kansas City, Kans., Aspect Med., Natick, Mass., Baxter Labs., Chgo., Scott Labs., Lubbock, Tex.; lectr. to over 500 nat. and state med. orgns., 1982—; examiner Am. Bd. Anesthesiology; lectr. Ohmeda, Liberty Corner, N.J. Assoc. editor Anesthesiology Rev., Anesthesiology News, Pharmacy Practia News; editor Geriatric Anesthesiology, 1997; contbr. numerous articles to med. jours. Mem. choir Friendswood (Tex.) Meth. Ch., 1985-87; mem. Friendswood Fine Arts Commn., 1985-87; mem. Temple Chamber Arts Adv. Coun., 1997-99. Lt. comdr. M.C., USN, 1976-78. Woodruff-Fisher scholar, 1964-68. Mem.: Temple C. of C., Evergreen Newcomers, Soc. Acad. Anesthesia Chairs (councilman 1996—99), Soc. for Ambulatory Anesthesia (program chair 1999), Internat. Anesthesia Rsch. Soc., Colo. Soc. Anesthesiologists (past pres.), Soc. for Edn. in Anesthesiology (past v.p., past pres., SEA-Duke Edn. prize), Am. Soc. Anesthesiologists (del. 1983—85, 1988—90), Assn. U Anesthesists, Nat. Spkrs. Assn., Internat. Platform Assn., Mensa, Alpha Omega Alpha. Republican. Presbyterian. Avocations: running, fishing, racquetball, squash. Personal E-mail: charles.mcleskey@comcast.net.

MCLESTER, SCOTT G., lawyer, hospitality executive; Ptnr. Carpenter, Bennett and Morrissey, Newark; v.p. law dept. Merrill Lynch, NYC; sr. counsel Cendant Corp., 2000—01, v.p. legal, 2001—02, group v.p. legal, 2002—04, sr. v.p. legal, 2004—06; exec. v.p., gen. counsel Wyndham Worldwide Corp., Parsippany, NJ, 2006—. Office: Wyndham Worldwide Corp Seven Sylvan Way Parsippany NJ 07054 Office Phone: 973-428-9700. *

MCLEVISH, TIMOTHY R., food products executive; BS in Acctg., U. Minn., 1982; MBA, Harvard U., 1985. CPA. Various mgmt. positions through div. pres. & gen. mgr. Mead Corp., Dayton, Ohio, 1987-99, v.p., CFO, 1999—2002; sr. v.p., CFO Ingersoll-Rand Co. Ltd., 2002—07; exec. v.p., CFO Kraft Foods Inc., Northfield, Ill., 2007—. Office: Kraft Foods Inc 3 Lakes Dr Northfield IL 60093 *

MCLIN, RHINE LANA, mayor, former state legislator; b. Dayton, Ohio, Oct. 3, 1948; d. C. Josef, Jr. and Bernice (Cottman) McL. BA in Sociology, Parsons Coll., 1969; MEd, Xavier U., 1972; postgrad. in law, U. Dayton, 1974-76; AA in Mortuary Sci., Cin. Coll., 1988. Lic. funeral dir. Tchr. Dayton Bd. Edn., 1970-72; divorce counselor Domestic Rels. Ct., Dayton, 1972-73; law clk. Montgomery Common Pleas Ct., Dayton, 1973-74; v.p., dir., embalmer McLin Funeral Homes, Dayton, 1972—; mem. Ohio Ho. of Reps. from 36th & 38th dists., Columbus, 1988-94, Ohio Senate from 5th dist., Columbus, 1994—2002; mem. Ways & Means Com.; controlling bd., ins. commerce comm. ranking mem.; state and local govt. com. Columbus; minority whip Ohio Senate, Columbus, 1994—2001; mayor City of Dayton, 2002—. Instr. Central State U., Wilberforce, Ohio, 1982-97; mem. Ohio Tuition Trust Authority. Mem. Dem. Nat. Com., Children's Def. Fund. Toll fellow; Paul Harris fellow; Flemming fellow; BLLD fellow; named Ohio Legislator of Yr., Ohio Social Workers Assn., 1999. Mem. Nat. Funeral Dirs. Assn., Ohio Funeral Dirs. Assn., Montgomery County Hist. Soc., NAACP (life), Nat. Coun. Negro Women (life), Delta Sigma Theta. Achievements include being first female mayor of Dayton. Office: City Hall 2nd Fl 101 W Third St Dayton OH 45402 Office Phone: 937-333-3653. Business E-Mail: Rhine.McLin@cityofDayton.org.

MCLIN-BRONSON, HATTIE ROGERS, school system administrator; b. Prentiss, Miss., Dec. 8, 1946; d. Javan Wilson Sr. and Alberta (Davis) Rogers; m. Prentiss McLin, June 29, 1968 (dec.); m. Gus Bronson, Sr.; children: Alberta Marie Detter, Prentiss II, Dawn Javan Wilson. BS, Jackson State U., 1968, MA, 1972, EdS, 1981, EdD, 1987; student, Howard U., Ohio State U., U. Southern Miss., Millsaps Coll., Baylor U. Tchr. Hinds County Pub. Schs., Clinton, Miss.; assoc. prof. edn. Paul Quinn Coll., Waco, Tex.; asst. prin. Jackson Public Separate Sch. Dist., Miss., 1992; prin. Johnson Elem. Sch., Jackson. Adj. prof. Jackson State U., Hinds Community Coll., Jackson; leader of ednl. ministry; prin. coach, 2006-. Sec. Jackson City Planning Bd.; bd. dirs. Nurture for Bapt. Chs., Greater Fairview Bapt. Ch.; mem. PTA., Youth Leadership Jackson C. of C., C. of C. Youth Devel. Named Outstanding Elem. Prin., Miss. Educator of the Yr., Adminstr. of Yr., 2006-07; Levi Strauss grantee, 1985, 86. Mem. ASCD, Miss. ASCD, NEA, Miss. Assn. Educators, Nat. Assn. Young Children, Bus. Profl. Women Orgn., Kappan Honors Orgn., Kappa Pi Honor Soc., Zeta Phi Beta. Office: Johnson Elem Sch 3319 Oak Park Dr Jackson MS 39212-4124 Home: 4052 Rainey Rd Jackson MS 39212-5324 Business E-Mail: hmclin@jackson.k12.ms.us.

MCLORIE, GORDON ARTHUR, urologist, educator; b. St. John, New Brunswick, Can., May 2, 1945; arrived in U.S., 2003; m. Blair Hilton, Dec. 20, 1968; children: Scott, David, Graham, Megan. MD, U. Toronto, Can., 1969. Cert. Am. Bd. Urology, 1982. Intern Toronto Gen. Hosp., Canada, 1969; resident in urology and renal transplant U. Toronto, Canada, 1971—76; fellowship dept. urology UCLA, 1976—77; fellowship in pediatric surgery Harvard U., Boston, 1981—82; chief pediatric urology Childrens Hosp. Mich., Detroit, 2002—06; prof. pediatric urology Wayne State U., Detroit, 2002—06; chief pediatric urology Wake Forest U., Winston-Salem, NC, 2006—. Fellow: Royal Coll. Physicians and Surgeons Can., Am. Acad. Pediat.; mem.: Am. Urology Assn., Can. Urology Assn. (pres.). Achievements include research in vesicourethral reflux, and reconstructive surgery of infants and children with congenital anomalies of the genitourinary system; invention of special interest in bladder reconstruction and replacement in children. Avocations: skiing, golf. Office: Wake Forest Sch Medicine Medical Center Blvd Winston Salem NC 27157 Home Phone: 336-725-4947; Office Phone: 336-716-8141. Personal E-mail: gmclorie@wfubnc.edu.

MCLUCAS, WILLIAM ROBERT, lawyer, former federal agency administrator; b. Altoona, Pa., Aug. 12, 1950; s. James Daniel and Ruth Virginia (Sweeney) McL. BA in Polit. Sci. with distinction, Pa. State U., 1972; JD, Temple U., 1975. Bar: Pa. 1975, DC 1998, NY 1999. Atty. Fed. Home Loan Bank Bd., 1975-77; staff atty. through assoc. dir. SEC, Washington, 1977—89, dir., div. of enforcement, 1989—98; ptnr., co-chmn. Securities dept. Wilmer Cutler Pickering Hale & Dorr, Washington. Rsch. editor Temple Law Quar., 1972-75; contbr. articles to profl. jours. Named a Leading Lawyer in securities & corp. governance, Legal Times, 2004; named one of Top 30 Lawyers in Washington, Washingtonian mag., 2004, 100 Most Influential Lawyers in Am., Nat. Law Jour., 1997; recipient Nat. Pub. Svc. award, Nat. Soc. Pub. Adminstrn., 1996, Tom C. Clark Outstanding Lawyer award, Fed. Bar Assn., 1997. Mem. Phi Beta Kappa. Office: Wilmer Cutler Pickering Hale & Dorr 1875 Pa Ave NW Washington DC 20006 Office Phone: 202-663-6622. Office Fax: 202-663-6363. Business E-Mail: william.mclucas@wilmerhale.com.

MC LURE, CHARLES E., JR., economist, consultant; b. Sierra Blanca, Tex., Apr. 14, 1940; s. Charles E. and Dessie (Evans) McL.; m. Patsy Nell Carroll, Sept. 17, 1962. BA, U. Kans., 1962; MA, Princeton U., 1964, PhD, 1966. Asst. prof. econs. Rice U., Houston, 1965-69, assoc. prof., 1969-72, prof., 1972-79, Allyn R. and Gladys M. Cline prof. econs., 1973-79; exec. dir. for research Nat. Bur. Econ. Research, Cambridge, Mass., 1977-78, v.p., 1978-81; sr. fellow Hoover Instn., Stanford U., 1981—; dep. asst. sec. Dept. Treasury, 1983-85. Sr. staff economist Coun. Econ. Advisers, Washington, 1969-70; vis. lectr. U. Wyo., 1972; vis. prof. Stanford U., 1973; cons. U.S. Treasury Dept., Labor Dept., World Bank, UN, OAS, Interam. Devel. Bank, Tax Found., Com. Econ. Devel., IMF, Internat. Tax and Investment Ctr., govts. Can., Colombia, Malaysia, Panama, Jamaica, Bolivia, Indonesia, New Zealand, Brazil, Trinidad and Tobago, Venezuela, Guatemala, Peoples Republic China, Egypt, Malawi, Mex., Bulgaria, Brazil, Russia, Ukraine, Romania, Kazakhstan, South Africa, Vietnam, Chile, Argentina. Author: Fiscal Failure: Lessons of the Sixties, 1972, (with N. Ture) Value Added Tax: Two Views, 1972, (with M. Gillis) La Reforma Tributaria Colombiana de 1974, 1977, Must Corporate Income Be Taxed Twice?, 1979, Economic Perperspectives on State Taxation of Multijurisdictional Corporations, 1986, The Value Added Tax: Key to Deficit Reduction, 1987; co-author: Taxation of Income from Business and Capital in Colombia, 1989; also numerous articles on econs., tax law and public finance. Ford Found. faculty research fellow, 1967-68, Disting. Svc. medal, US Treas. Dept., 1985, Daniel M. Holland medal, Nat. Tax Assn., 2004. Mem. Am. Econ. Assn., Nat. Tax Assn., Beta Theta Pi. Home: 250 Yerba Santa Ave Los Altos CA 94022-1609 Office: Stanford U Hoover Instn Stanford CA 94305-6010 Office Phone: 650-723-2657. Business E-Mail: mclure@hoover.stanford.edu.

MCLURE, HOWARD A., pharmaceutical executive; BBA, Univ. Ga. CPA. Mgmt. positions through sr. v.p., controller Magellan Health Services Inc., 1984—98; sr. v.p. chief acctg. officer Caremark Inc., 1998—2000, exec. v.p., CFO, 2000—05, sr. exec. v.p., COO, 2005—07; exec. v.p., pres. Caremark Pharm. Services CVS Caremark Corp., Woonsocket, RI, 2007—. Mem.: Am. Inst. CPAs. Office: CVS Caremark Corp 1 CVS Dr Woonsocket RI 02895 *

MCLURE, JOHN DOUGLAS, management consultant, former Canadian government official; b. Melita, Man., Can., July 10, 1942; s. Malcolm Alexander and Rachel (Simpson) McL.; m. Nicole Lafrance, Aug. 26, 1967. BSc, U. Man., Winnipeg, 1963; Ammunition Tech. Officer, Royal Mil. Coll. Sci., Shrivenham, Wiltshire, Eng., 1964. Program analyst Treasury Bd. Secretariat, Ottawa, Canada, 1975-79, group chief industry and natural resources divsn., 1979-80, dir. industry and natural resources divsn., 1980-82, asst. sec. econ. devel., 1982-84; asst. dep. min. small bus. and spl. projects Dept. Regional Indsl. Expansion, Ottawa, 1984-85, asst. dep. min. crown investments and spl. projects, 1985-86, asst. dep. min. native econ. devel., 1986-87; asst. dep. min. fin., pers., adminstrn. Dept Industry, Sci. & Tech., Ottawa, 1987—89; asst. dep. min. fin. Dept. Nat. Def., Ottawa, 1989—96, assoc. dep. min., 1996; dep. min. Dept. Western Econ. Diversification, Ottawa, 1996—97; sr. v.p. Hill and Knowlton Can. Ltd., Ottawa, 1997—2000, sr. assoc., 2000—. Chmn. bd. Def. Constrn. Can.; pres., CEO JDM Consulting Inc., 2000—. Maj. Can. Land Forces, 1960-75. Recipient N.Am. Best Practice recognition, Ctr. Creative Leadership, Greensboro, N.C., 1994, Leadership award, Assn. Profl. Exercs., 1995. Mem. Club Link Le Fontainebleau Golf Club, Rideau Club. Avocations: golf, alpine skiing. Office: Hill and Knowlton Can Ltd 55 Metcalfe St Ste 1100 Ottawa ON Canada K1P 6L5 Home: 202-375 Lisgar St Ottawa ON Canada K2P 0E3 Home Phone: 613-612-0070. Business E-Mail: john.mclure@hillandknowlton.ca.

MCLURKIN, THOMAS CORNELIUS, JR., lawyer; b. LA, July 28, 1954; s. Thomas Cornelius and Willie Mae (O'Connor) McL.; m. Charmaine Bobo. BA, U. So. Calif., 1976, MPA, 1980, postgrad., 1998; JD, U. LaVerne, 1982. Bar: Calif. 1984, U.S. Dist. Ct. (ctrl. dist.) Calif. 1984, U.S. Dist. Ct. Hawaii 1984, U.S. Ct. Appeals (9th cir.) 1984, U.S. Dist. Ct. (ea., no. and so. dists.) Calif. 1985, U.S. Tax Ct. 1988, U.S. Ct. Mil. Appeals 1989, U.S. Army Ct. Mil. Rev. 1993, U.S. Supreme Ct., 1995. Law clk. dept. water and power City of L.A., 1979-82; jud. clk. cen. dist. U.S. Dist. Ct., LA, 1982-83; law clk. Office City Atty., LA, 1983-84, dep. city atty., 1984—. Author (with others): Facts in American History, 1968, 2nd edit., 1989. Mem. L.A. World Affairs Coun., 1980—, Smithsonian Assocs.; bd. dirs. L.A. Area coun. Boy Scouts Am., Hillsides Homes for Children; provisional patron Tournament of Roses Assn., Pasadena, 1994—; mem. Verdugo Hills Area coun. Boy Scouts Am., Eagle Scout, 1970. Mem. ABA, ALA, ASPA, Los Angeles County Bar Assn., Assn. Trial Lawyers Am., Langston Law Assn. L.A., U. So. Calif. Gen. Alumni Assn. (bd. govs. exec. bd. 1986-90), U. So. Calif. Black Alumni Assn.-Ebonics (pres. 1988-89), U. So. Calif. Pres.'s Cir., Elks, Am. Legion, Phi Alpha Delta, Kappa Alpha Psi. Republican. United Methodist. Avocations: sailing, tennis, volunteer work, American and world history. Office: LA City Atty Office 200 N Main St Ste 600 CHE Los Angeles CA 90012-4110 Home Phone: 818-244-3530; Office Phone: 213-978-6952. Business E-Mail: thomas.mclurkin-jr@lacity.org.

MCLUSKIE, ED, communications educator; s. Clarence Edward and Francis McLuskie, Irma McLuskie (Stepmother); m. Ariel Thomas Haney, Oct. 4, 2004; m. Mary Elizabeth Trapp, Aug. 11, 1974 (div. Jan. 11, 1986); 1 child, Melissa Davis. BA, Mont. State U., Billings, 1970; PhD, U. Iowa, Iowa City, 1975. Prof. U. Wis., Whitewater, 1974—78, Fla. Atlantic U., Boca Raton, 1978—80, Boise State U., 1981—; Fulbright prof. U. Vienna, 1996—97, guest prof., 2002; Fulbright prof. Tbilisi State U., Georgian Inst. Pub. Affairs, Georgia, 2004—05. Contbr. articles to profl. jours., chapters to books. Bd. dirs. Snake River Alliance, Boise, 1987—88; keynote spkr. Leadership Boise, 2005. Fellow, NEH, 1979, Fulbright Commn., 1996—97, 2004—05; grantee, Can. Embassy, 1983. Mem.: Internat. Comm. Assn. (life). Office: Boise State Univ Dept Communication 1910 Univ Dr Boise ID 83725-1920 Home Phone: 208-345-6937; Office Phone: 208-426-1927. Personal E-mail: emclusk@bigfoot.com. Business E-Mail: emclusk@boisestate.edu.

MCMAHON, ANDREW PAUL, embryologist, educator; BA in Zoology, U. Oxford, Eng.; PhD in Mammalian Devel., Univ. Coll., London. Postdoctoral rschr. Calif. Inst. Tech., 1981; staff scientist Nat. Inst. Med. Rsch.; with Roche Inst. Molecular Biology, NJ, 1988; Frank B. Baird Jr. prof. sci. dept. molecular and cellular biology Harvard U., Cambridge, Mass. Adj. prof. dept. genetics and molecular biology Columbia U., NYC; mem. sci. adv. coun. UTEK Corp., 2004. Contbr. articles to sci. jours. Recipient Senator Jacob Javits award in the Neurosciences, 2004. Fellow: Royal Soc. UK. Office: Harvard U 16 Divinity Ave Rm 1059 Cambridge MA 02138 Office Phone: 617-496-3757. E-mail: mcmahon@mcb.harvard.edu.

MCMAHON, DALTON EDWARD, history professor, social sciences educator, department chairman; b. Rapid City, SD, Nov. 12, 1945; s. Dalton William and Rosemary Lucille McMahon; m. Annie Buendia McMahon, Apr. 28, 1972; children: Annie Christina Norman, Dalton Edward Jr. BS in Edn., U. S.D., 1967, MA, 1975; DA, U. N.D., 1986. Social sci. tchr. Newman Grove (Nebr.) H.S., Dept. Def. Overseas Schs., Subic Bay Naval Station, Philippines, 1969—74, Giessen, Germany, 1974—82; grad. tchg. asst. history U. N.D., Grand Forks, 1982—85, instr. history, 1985—86; asst. prof. history Marymount of Kans., Salina, 1986—89; prof. history/social sci. Mayville (N.D.) State U., 1989—, chair liberal arts divsn., 2003—. Mem. coun. coll. faculties N.D. U. Sys., Bismarck, 1991—98, v.p. coun. coll. faculties, pres. coun. coll. faculties, 1994—95; mem. faculty senate Mayville State U., 1994—95, pres. faculty assn., 1995—97; lectr. in field. Judge DAR Outstanding Am. History Tchr. Contest, ND, 2002—03, Voice of Democracy Contest, Mayville, 1997—99; trustee United Ch. of Christ, Mayville, 1999—2003. Named U. N.D.Outstanding Grad. Historian, Phi Alpha Theta, U. N.D., 1985, Outstanding Tchr., Mayville State U., 1996, I.A. O'Shaughnessy Disting. Prof. of Humanities, Marrymount Coll. Kans., 1988—89; Atlantic-Bridges fellow, 2006. Mem.: Phi Alpha Theta. Home: 605 State Ave Portland ND 58274 Office: Mayville State University 330 3rd St NE Mayville ND 58257 Office Phone: 701-788-4808.

MCMAHON, DONALD AYLWARD, investor, corporate director; b. NYC, Feb. 20, 1931; s. William F. and Anne (Aylward) McM.; m. Nancy Lantz, Apr. 12, 1953; children: Gail, Brian, Lisa, Glenn, Anne, Carol, William, Douglas. MBA, Emory U., 1982. With Dime Savs. Bank, Bklyn., 1952; salesman Monroe Calculating Machine Co., Bklyn., 1952-55; asst. br. mgr. Pitts., 1955-56, br. mgr. Phila., 1956-63, asst. gen. sales mgr. Orange, N.J., 1963-64, Eastern regional gen. sales mgr., 1964-65, v.p. mktg., 1965-66; pres. Monroe Calculator Co. div. Litton Industries, Inc., Orange, 1966-70; v.p. Litton Industries, 1967-70; pres., chief operating officer, dir. Baker Industries, Inc., Parsippany, N.J., 1970-74; pres., chief exec. officer, dir. Royal Crown Cos., Inc., Atlanta, 1975-85. Bd. dirs. Intelligent Systems Corp., Atlanta. Bd. dirs. Boys Clubs Metro Atlanta. Mem. Sovereign Order of Knights of Malta. Home: 1665 Winterthur Close NW Atlanta GA 30328-4688

MCMAHON, ED, television and radio personality; b. Detroit, Mar. 6, 1923; m. Pam Hurn; children: Claudia, Michael (dec.), Linda, Jeffrey, Katherine Mary; 1 stepson, Alexis. Student, Boston Coll.; BA, Cath. U. Am., 1949. Author: For Laughing Out Loud: My Life and Good Times, 1998, Here's Johnny!: My Memories of Johnny Carson, The Tonight Show, and 46 Years of Friendship, 2005; TV announcer: Tonight Show, 1962-92; appeared in films The Incident, 1967, Fun with Dick and Jane, 1975, Butterfly, 1982, Love Affair, 1994, (tv movie) The Kid from Left Filed, 1979, The Great American Traffic Jam, 1980, (mini series) The Golden Moment, 1980, The Star Maker, 1981, Bewitched, 2005; host TV series The Kraft Music Hall, 1968, Whodunnit?, 1979, TV's Bloopers and Practical Jokes, Ed McMahon's Star Search; host TV specials: Thanksgiving Day Parade, (co-host) Jerry Lewis Labor Day Telethon; appeared on TV, The Tom Show, 1997; now host Lifestyles Live, USA Radio Network, Orlando; numerous other TV appearances; appeared on Broadway in The Impossible Years. Active Muscular Dystrophy Assn.; mem. bd. dirs. Horatio Alger Assn. With USMC, PTO; col. res., ret. Office: Lifestyles Live Bldg 22-A, Ste 245 1000 Universal Studios Plaza Orlando FL 32819 Office Phone: 407-224-3162. Office Fax: 407-224-3163.

MCMAHON, EDWARD RICHARD, lawyer; b. Jersey City, June 7, 1949; s. Edward Barnawall and Jean (Sullivan) McM.; m. Ellen Mary Bosek; children: Meghan Jean, Kerry Eileen, Ryan Edward. AB, Colgate U., 1972; JD, Seton Hall U., 1975. Bar: N.J. 1975, U.S. Dist. Ct. N.J. 1975, U.S. Ct. of Appeals (3rd circ.) 1980. Law clk. to judge U.S. Dist. Ct., Newark, 1975-77; assoc. Lum, Biunno & Tompkins, Newark, 1977-83; ptnr. Lum, Danzis, Drasco, & Positan, LLC, Roseland, NJ, 1983—. Mem. Essex County Chancery Ct. Mediation Prog., 1992—, Supreme Ct. of N.J. Dist. Ethics Com., 1994—97, Supreme Ct. of N.J. Dist. Fee Arbitration Com., 2000—; founding mem. and couns. Morris & Essex Inn of Transactional Counsel, 2001—; mem. U.S. Dist. Ct. Arbitration Prog., 2001—, New Jersey Ct. Approved Mediator, 2002—. Mem. Morris County Rep. Com., N.J., 1982-94; mem. Chatham (N.J.) Boro Rep. com., 1982-94, chmn., 1986-94; bd. dirs. Madison area YMCA, 1989-95; bd. trustees Richard J. Hughes Found., 2001-; mem. N.J. State Rep. Com., 1994-. Mem.: ABA (litigation and banking sects.), Colgate U. Alumni Assn. (class rep. 1993—), 200 Club Morris County, Delbarton Sch. Alumni Assn. (class rep. 1984—), Essex County Bar Assn. (Essex County Chancery Ct. Mediation program 1992—, Supreme Ct. of N.J. dist. ethics com. 1994—97, Supreme Ct. of N.J. dist. fee arbitration com. 2000—, founding mem., counselor Morris & Essex Inn of Transactional Counsel 2001—, U.S. Dist. Ct. Arbitration program 2001—, N.J. Ct. approved mediator 2002—), Morris County Bar Assn., Am. Judicature Soc., Assn. Fed. Bar N.J., N.J. Bar Assn., Colgate (No. N.J.), Phi Alpha Delta, Delta Upsilon. Republican. Roman Catholic. Home: 150 Van Houton Ave Chatham NJ 07928-1239 Office: Lum Danzis Drasco & Positan LLC 103 Eisenhower Pky Roseland NJ 07068-1029 also: 325 Broadway New York NY 10007

MCMAHON, FRANK V., insurance company executive; m. Vikki McMahon; 3 children. B in Econs., Villanova U., Pa.; MBA, Duke U., Durham, NC. With Merrill Lynch, 1994—99; positions up to mng. dir. Lehman Bros. Holdings, Inc., 1999—2006; vice chmn., CFO First Am. Corp., Santa Ana, Calif., 2006—. Bd. dirs. First Advantage Corp., 2006—. Office: First Am Corp 1 First American Way Santa Ana CA 92707 Office Phone: 714-250-3000. *

MCMAHON, GERALD LAWRENCE, lawyer; b. Youngstown, Ohio, July 16, 1935; s. Lawrence J. and Lee Z. McM.; m. Donna Ghio, June 17, 1956; children: Maria, Michael, Mark, Matthew, Angela. BS cum laude, U. So. Calif., 1956; JD summa cum laude, U. San Diego, 1964. Bar: Calif. 1965, U.S. Dist. Ct. (so. dist. Calif.), U.S. Ct. Claims 1966, U.S. Ct. Appeals (9th cir.) 1966, U.S. Supreme Ct 1966. Chief of contracts Centaur space vehicle program Gen. Dynamics Astronautics, San Diego, 1960-64; from assoc. to chmn. & head litigation dept. Seltzer Caplan McMahon Vitek, San Diego, 1964—. Adj. prof. Univ. San Diego Sch. Law, 1969—72; lectr. Calif. Western Law Sch. Editor: San Diego Law Rev., 1963-64; frequent speaker & legal edn. panelist. Trustee, Sidney Kimmel Cancer Ctr.; chmn. bd. vis., U. San Diego Law Sch., 1979-80, 1996-98. Aviator with USN, 1956-59. Fellow Am. Coll. Trial Lawyers; mem. ABA, San Diego Bar Assn. (vp., dir. 1974-77), State Bar of Calif. (disciplinary referee pro tem 1977-79), Am. Judicature Soc., Am. Bd. Trial Advocates (pres. San Diego chpt. 1981), Calif. Trial Lawyers Assn., Am. Arbitration Assn., Am. Acad. Matrimonial Lawyers, San Diego Inn of Ct. (panelist 1975, dir. 1979), Phi Alpha Delta, Order of the Coif. Republican. Roman Catholic. Avocations: tennis, skiing, lic. pvt. pilot. Office: Seltzer Caplan McMahon Vitek Symphony Towers 750 B St San Diego CA 92101 Office Phone: 619-685-3114. Office Fax: 619-702-6803. Business E-Mail: mcmahon@scmv.com.

MCMAHON, JAMES CHARLES, lawyer; b. Bklyn., Dec. 4, 1951; s. James Charles and Rosemary Margaret (Gilroy) McM.; m. Nancy M. Neble, Oct. 30, 1984; children: Deirdre Kathleen Wright, Laura Elizabeth, Elizabeth Jane. BA, Boston Coll., 1973; JD, Fordham U., 1977. Bar: NY 1978, Mass. 1996, US Supreme Ct. 1996. Assoc. Winthrop Stimson Putnam & Roberts, NYC, 1977-78, Brodsky, Linett, Altman, Schechter & Reicher, NYC, 1978-82; ptnr. Brodsky, Altman & McMahon, LLP, NYC, 1982—2003, mng. ptnr., 1988—2003, McMahon & Kelly LLP, NYC, 2003—. Exec. sec., counsel NY Movers Tariff Bur., Inc., NYC, 1984-99; gen. counsel Mass. Movers Assn., South Attleboro, 1986—; Movers and Warehousemen's Assn. Greater NY, 1984-98, Met. Moving & Storage Assn., 1979-1998, USA Section of FIDI Inc., 1984—, Commonwealth Transp. Compensation Corp., Andover, Mass., 1992—, Transport Health Plan, Woburn, Mass., 1994-2003, NY State Movers and Warehousemen's Assn., NYC, 1984-2002, Nat. Moving and Storage Assn., Fairfax, Va., 1988-98, Am. Moving & Storage Tech. Found., Alexandria, Va., 1988-2006; adj. prof. bus. law Queens Borough Cmty. Coll., City Univ. NY, 2004-06. Mem. editl. bd. Fordham Urban Law Jour., 1976; author: Warehouseman's Lien & Auctions, 1991. Recipient Disting. Svc. award Mass. Movers Assn., 1992. Mem. NY State Bar Assn. (labor and employment law sect.), Assn. Bar City NY (transp. com. 1997-99), Assn. Comml. Fin. Attys., Transp. Lawyers Assn., Assn. for Transp. Law, Logistics and Policy, NY Athletic Club. Democrat. Roman Catholic. Home: 196 Pinesbridge Rd Ossining NY 10562-1428 Office: McMahon & Kelly LLP 60 E 42d St Ste 1540 New York NY 10165-1544 also: 55 Donimo Dr Concord MA 01742 Office Phone: 212-986-4444. E-mail: jmcmahon@mcmahonlaw.com.

MCMAHON, JAMES E., lawyer, former prosecutor; b. 1951; m. Kathy McMahon; 3 children. BS, Morningside U.; JD, U. S.D., 1977. Asst. atty. gen. State of SD, 1978—81; ptnr. Boyce, Murphy, McDowell & Greenfield, 1981—2002; pvt. practice Sioux Falls, SD, 2002—; US atty. Dist. SD US Dept. Justice, Sioux Falls, SD, 2002—05. Recipient Trial Lawyer of Yr. award, S.D. Trial Lawyers Assn., 2000.

MCMAHON, JAMES PATRICK, ecologist, consultant; b. Chgo., July 10, 1951; s. James Patrick and Helen Margaret (Walter) McM.; children: J. Emrys, Jacqueline Anne. BS in Ecology, U. Ill., 1974; postgrad., Ctrl. Wash. U., Ellensburg, 1975-76, Naropa Inst., Boulder, 1993-94. Owner Seattle Recycling, Inc., 1976-79; program planner City of Seattle, 1979-80; divsn. mgr. Fibres Internat., Bellevue, Wash., 1980-85; owner Environ. Enhancement Group, Lynnwood, Wash., 1985-88; regional mgr. 20:20 Recycle Ctrs., Inc., LA, 1987-88; nat. mktg. dir. May Mfg., Denver, 1990-94; ptnr. Agua Fria Enterprises, Prescott, Ariz., 1992-98; project dir. Nature Conservancy, 1994-98; dir. of Virgin River Programs Grand Canyon Trust, 1999—2002; active Sweetwater, LLC, 2002—. Sr. fellow Independence Inst., Golden, Colo., 1990-93; participant 50 for Colo. leadership program Colo. Assn. Commerce and Industry, 1993; condr. numerous bus. seminars; developer original recycling strategy City of Seattle; expatriot in Saint Martin, French West Indies, 1989. Exec. prodr. (video) Recycling in Washington State, 1985; contbr. many articles on Western pub. lands, natural resources, Philippine Eagle recovery, logging and men's issues to newspapers, mag. and other publs., U.S. and London; frequent radio commentator. Mem. survey and nat. conf. coms. Dept. Ecology, 1985-86; bd. dirs. Nat. Recycling Coalition, 1983-86. Mem. Greater Seattle C. of C., Rocky Mountain Angling Club, Trout Unltd. Avocations: skiing, fly fishing, scuba diving, hiking, camping. Home and Office: 375 Cedar Tree Dr Brookside UT 84782 E-mail: jim@jamespmcmahon.com.

MCMAHON, JOHN ALEXANDER, law educator; b. Monongahela, Pa., July 31, 1921; s. John Hamilton and Jean (Alexander) McMahon; m. Betty Wagner, Sept. 14, 1947 (div. Mar. 1977); children: Alexander Talpey, Sarah Francis, Elizabeth Wagner, Ann Wallace; m. Anne Fountain Willets, May 1, 1977 (dec. June 1996); m. Anne Hall Davis, Apr. 18, 1999. AB magna cum laude, Duke U., 1942; student, Harvard U. Bus. Sch., 1942—43; JD, Law Sch., 1948; LLD, Wake Forest U., 1978; DSc (hon.), Georgetown U. Sch. Medicine, 1985. Bar: N.C. 1950. Prof. pub. law and govt., asst. dir. Inst. Govt. U. N.C., 1948—59; gen. counsel, sec.-treas. N.C. Assn. County Commrs., Chapel Hill, 1959—65; v.p. spl. devel. Hosp. Saving Assn., Chapel Hill, NC, 1965—67; pres. N.C. Blue Cross and Blue Shield, Inc., Chapel Hill, 1968—72, Am. Hosp. Assn., Chgo., 1972—86; chmn. dept. health adminstrn. Duke U., Durham, NC, 1986—92, exec.-in-residence Fuqua Sch. Bus., 1992—. Mem. Chapel Hill bd. N.C. Nat. Bank, 1967—72; bd. govs. Blue Cross Assn., 1969—72; mem. Orange County Welfare Bd., 1956—63; chmn. N.C. Comprehensive Health Planning Coun., 1968—72, Health Planning Coun. of Ctrl. N.C., 1963—69; mem. Pres.'s Com. on Health Edn., 1971—72; mem. com. health svcs. industry and health industry adv. com. Econ. Stblzn. Program, 1971—74; mem. adv. coun. Kate Bitting Reynolds Health Care Trust, 1971—95, Northwestern U., 1973—86; mem. med. adv. com. VA, 1975—85; bd. dirs. The Forest at Duke, Durham, NC, 1994—2002, Exec. Svc. Corps of Greater Triangle, 1986—99, mem. adv. bd., 2000—. Author: North Carolina County Government, 1959, The North Carolina Local Government Commission, 1960; editor: N.C. County Yearbook, 1959—64, Proceedings of the Annual National Forum on Hospital and Health Affairs, 1993—2000. Chmn. bd. trustees Duke U., 1971—83, chmn. emeritus, 1983—; bd. mgrs., mem. exec. com. Internat. Hosp. Fedn., London, 1975—85, pres., 1981—83; mem. Orange County Dem. Exec. Com., also chmn. Kings Mill Precinct, 1964—68; bd. dirs. Rsch. Triangle Found., 1971—83, 1992—, Nat. Ctr. for Health Edn., 1974—86. With USAF, 1942—46, col. Res., ret. Recipient Citation Disting. Svc. by Layman, AMA, 1978, Special award, Ill. Hosp. Assn., 1985, Dallas-Fort Worth Hosp. Coun., 1985, many others. Mem.: Inst. Medicine of NAS (Disting. Svc. award 1979), N.C. State Bar, Duke Alumni Assn. (pres. 1968—70, Silver Medal award 1986), Dunes Golf and Beach Club (Myrtle Beach), Hope Valley Country Club (Durham). Republican. Presbyterian. Home: 181 Montrose Dr Durham NC 27707-3929 Office: Duke U Fuqua Sch Bus Durham NC 27708-0120 Office Phone: 919-660-7760.

MCMAHON, JOHN P., electronics executive; BS, Mercy Coll.; MS in Human Resource Mgmt., Upsala Coll., East Orange, NJ. Leadership position human resources Raytheon Corp., ITT Corp.; sr. v.p. global human resources Terra Lycos, S.A., Fisher Sci.; sr. v.p., chief human resources officer UMass Meml. Health Care Sys.; sr. v.p. corp. human resources Arrow Electronics, Inc., Melville, NY, 2007—. Office: Arrow Electronics Inc 50 Marcus Dr Melville NY 11747-4210 Office Phone: 631-847-2000. *

MCMAHON, JOSEPH EINAR, lawyer, consultant; b. Chgo., Aug. 26, 1940; s. Reynold Bernard and Dorothy Marie (Oftedahl) McM. BA cum laude, Denison U., Granville, Ohio, 1962; JD, U. Mich., 1965. Bar: Mass. 1968, DC 1980. Asst. to Atty. Gen. and Senator Edward Brooke, Boston and Washington, 1965-67; exec. asst. Lt. Gov. Sargent of Mass., Boston, 1967-69; v.p. BedStuy D&S Corp. Restoration, Bklyn., 1969-74; dir. govt. regulations Westinghouse Electric Corp., Washington, 1974-78; v.p. corp. affairs Federated Dept. Stores, Cin., 1978-80; atty., cons. McMahon and Assocs., Washington, 1980—; v.p. pub. policy Covenant House, 2001—06. Exec. dir. (part time), bd. dirs. The Get Ahead Found./USA, 1991-99. Life trustee Denison U.; visitor U. Mich. Law Sch.; 1st v.p. Boston Rep. Com., 1968-69; presdl. appointee Nat. Coun. Econ. Opportunity, 1975-76; exec. dir. Nat. Bus. for Reagan-Bush Com., 1980; dir. emeritus Luther Inst., Washington, Rodale Inst., Emmaus, Pa.; dir. Luth. Lesbian and Gay Min., San Francisco, 1994-2003; mem. outreach bd. Evang. Luth. Ch. in Am., 1995-2001. Mem. Capitol Hill Club, Phi Delta Phi, Pi Sigma Alpha, Omicron Delta Kappa. Lutheran. Office: McMahon & Assocs 1125 Meridian Ave Miami Beach FL 33139 Office Phone: 202-293-6464. Personal E-mail: mcmahon@aol.com.

MCMAHON, JULIAN, actor; b. Sydney, July 27, 1968; s. William and Sonia McMahon; m. Dannii Minogue, Jan. 2, 1994 (div. 1995); m. Brooke Burns, Dec. 22, 1999 (div. 2001); 1 child, Madison. Attended, U. Sydney. Actor: (TV series) The Power, the Passion, 1989, Home and Away, 1989—91, Another World, 1992—94, Profiler, 1996—2000, Charmed, 2000—03, Nip/Tuck, 2003—06; (TV films) Another Day, 2001; guest appearance (TV series) Will & Grace, 1998, Charmed, 2005; actor: (films) Wet and Wild Summer!, 1992, Magenta, 1996, In Quiet Night, 1998, Chasing Sleep, 2000, Fantastic Four, 2005, Prisoner, 2007, Premonition, 2007; actor, exec. prodr.: Meet Market, 2004. Nominee Best Actor in a TV Series (Drama), 62nd Ann. Golden Globe Awards, 2005. *

MCMAHON, LINDA E., sports association executive; b. New Bern, NC, Oct. 4, 1948; d. Henry and Evelyn Edwards; m. Vincent K. McMahon, Aug. 6, 1966; children: Shane, Stephanie. BA French, East Carolina U., 1969. Co-founder, bd. dirs. World Wrestling Entertainment, Inc., Stamford, Conn., 1980—, pres., 1993—2000, CEO, 1997—. Prodr.: (TV series) WWE: Raw is War, 1997—, WWE: Sunday Night Heat, 1998—, WWE: Smackdown!, 1999—; exec. prodr.: WWE Experience, 2004. Office: World Wrestling Entertainment Inc Titan Towers 1241 E Main St Stamford CT 06902

MCMAHON, PAUL FRANCIS, finance company executive; b. Malone, NY, Apr. 28, 1945; s. Philip Francis and Shirley (Roy) M.; m. Sheila Ann Lester, Nov. 30, 1963; children: Michael, Marsha BS, Syracuse U., 1968. CPA, N.Y., Oreg.; cert. mgmt. acct., mgmt. cons. With Ernst & Young, Syracuse, NY, 1968—79, mgr., 1975-79, ptnr. in charge of mgmt. cons. in Europe Brussels, 1979-84, vice-chmn. Cleve., 1984-87; exec. ptnr. Ernst & Young Internat., NYC, 1987-93; chmn. Ernst & Young Ea. Europe, 1990-93; regional dir. Asia/Pacific Ernst & Young Internat., Singapore, 1994-96; contr. Coop. Mktg. Agy., Syracuse, 1973-75; COO Amrop Internat., Brussels, 1997-2001; ptnr. Network Journey, 2002—04. Treas. Chamber Music N.W.; chair lit. and hist. com. Arlington Club; bd. mem. Oreg. Coun. of Humanities; mem. adv. bd. Humaninet; treas. Health Bridges Internat.; mem. adv. bd. Humaninet. Mem.: AICPA, Nat. Acad. Scis., Coun. Consulting Orgns. (past chmn.), Assn. Mgmt. Consulting Firms (bd. dirs.), Inst. Mgmt. Acctg., N.Y. Soc. CPAs, Oreg. Soc. CPAs. Democrat. Roman Catholic. Avocations: sculpture, travel, gardening, biographies. Home: 1030 SW Jefferson St Apg 261 Portland OR 97201 Office Phone: 503-708-4336. Personal E-mail: pfmcmahon@earthlink.net.

MCMAHON, ROBERT M., physician, lawyer; b. Chambersburg, Pa., Sept. 6, 1949; s. Robert James and Bernice G. (Moore) McM.; 1 child, Natalie Ann. BA, U. Calif., San Diego, 1971; JD, U. Calif., San Francisco, 1974; MD, Washington U., St. Louis, 1989. Bar: Mo., Calif., U.S. Supreme Ct.; diplomate Am. Bd. Internal Medicine, Am. Bd. Gastroenterology. Staff counsel State Bar of Calif., LA, 1975-80; sole practice law Beverly Hills, Calif., 1980-85; physician Jewish Hosp., St. Louis, 1989-92, St. Joseph's Hosp., St. Charles, Mo., 1992-93, U. Ark., Little Rock, 1993-95; pvt. practice in gastroenterology Little Rock, 1995-97, St. Louis, 1997—. Judge pro tem Superior Ct., L.A., 1983-85. Dir. South Ctrl. Bar Assn., Compton, Calif., 1983-85. Fellow Am. Coll. Legal Medicine; mem. Am. Soc. Gastrointestinal Endoscopy, St. Louis Met. Med. Soc. (councillor 2000-03). Avocations: computer hobbyist, graphic arts, model aircraft. Office: St Louis GE Cons PC 10012 Kennerly Rd Ste 101 Saint Louis MO 63128

MCMAHON, VINCE (VINCENT KENNEDY MCMAHON), sports entertainment company executive; b. Pinehurst, NC, Aug. 24, 1945; s. Vincent James McMahon; m. Linda Edwards, Aug. 6, 1966; children: Shane, Stephanie. BS in Mktg., Ea. Carolina U., 1964. Announcer World Wrestling Fedn (formerly World Wide Wrestling Fedn.), 1971—82; acquired Capitol Wrestling Corp., 1982; chmn. World Wrestling Entertainment Inc. (formerly World Wrestling Fedn.), Stamford, Conn., 1982—. Office: World Wrestling Entertainment Inc Titan Towers 1241 E Main St Stamford CT 06902-3521 *

MCMANAMAN, KENNETH CHARLES, lawyer; b. Fairfield, Calif., Jan. 25, 1950; s. Charles James and Frances J. (Holys) McM.; m. Carol Ann Wilson, Apr. 15, 1972; children; Evan John, Kinsey Bridget, Klerin Rose. BA cum laude, S.E. Mo. State U., 1972; JD, U. Mo., Kansas City, 1974; grad., Naval Justice Sch., Newport, RI, 1975; MS in Bus. Mgmt. summa cum laude, Troy State U., Montgomery, Ala., 1978; LLM in Advanced Litigation, Nottingham-Trent U., 2004. Bar: Mo. 1975, US Dist. Ct. (we. dist.) Mo. 1975, Fla. 1976, US Dist. Ct. (No. and mid. dists.) Fla. 1976, US Dist. Ct. Mil. Appeals 1977, US Ct. Appeals (5th and 8th cirs.) 1977, US Dist. Ct. (ea. dist.) Mo. 1978, US Supreme Ct. 1978, D.C. 1991; cert. mil. judge spl. 1996, gen. ct. martials 1998; diplomate Am. Bd. Forensic Examiners; cert. Homeland Security, Level III, Am. Coll. Forensic Examiners Internat.; qualified mil. judge gen. ct. martial, Navy-Marine Corps. Prof. bus. law Troy (Ala.) State U., 1976-78; pvt. practice; ptnr. O'Loughlin, O'Loughlin & McManaman, Cape Girardeau, Mo., 1978—2002, Kenneth C. McManaman, Esq., 2002—06, Kenneth C. McManaman, LLC, 2006—; prof. bus. law S.E. Mo. State U., Cape Girardeau, 1978-84, prof. criminal justice, 1998—; prof. leadership Sch. Law William Woods U., 1998—; prof. bus. mgmt. Sch. Law Nat. Inst. Trial Advocacy. Mem. Cape Girardeau County Coun. on Child Abuse, 1980—89; membership dir. S.E. Mo. scouting coun. Boy Scouts Am., 1980—82; mem. Cape Girardeau County Mental Health Assn., 1982—92; sponsor drug edn./prevention program in schs.; sec., pres. Jackson Area Soccer Assn., 1987—93; mem. Jackson R-2 Alt. Sch. Bd., 1999—; mem. dept. acctg. and fin. adv. bd. S.E. Mo. State U., 2001—03; active local and state Dem. Party, del. Dem. Nat. Conv., San Francisco, 1984; chmn. County Dem. Com., 1984—96; mem. 8th Congl. Dist. Dem. Com., 1984—86, 27th State Dem. Senatorial Com., 1980—90; ward committeeman Dem. Party, 1984—96; hon. chmn., bus. adv. coun. Nat. Rep. Congl. Com.; bd. dirs. Area-wide Task Force on Drug and Alcohol Abuse, 1984—87, Cape County chpt. Nat. Kidney Found., 1988—93, S.E. Mo. State Alumni Assn., 2006—. Capt. JAGC USNR, 1994—2003. Recipient Robert Chilton award City of Jackson for Leadership, Integrity and Responsibility, 1995-97, Nat. Leadership award, 2006; named One of Outstanding Young Men Am., 1981, 82, 84, 85, Outstanding Pub. Svc. award Cape Girardeau Police Dept. Fellow Am. Bd. Forensic Examiner; mem. ABA (Mo. del. young lawyers divsn. 1982-83), Mo. Bar Assn. (chmn. trial advocacy task force 1983), Mo. Bar (young lawyers sect. coun. rep. dist. 13 1980-85), Fla. Bar Assn., Kansas City Bar Assn., Assn. Trial Lawyers Am., Fed. Bar Assn., Nat. Coll. Dist. Attys., Cape Girardeau County Bar Assn. (founder, pres. young lawyers sect. 1981-82), Cape County Bar Assn. (sec. 1999, treas. 2000, v.p. 2001, 06, pres. 2007), Naval Res. Assn. (v.p. S.E. Mo/So. Ill. chpt. 1980-85, 2001—), Grand Praetor So. Mo. Province, Order of Constantine, S.E. Mo. State U. Alumni (bd. dirs., mem. coun.), Sigma Chi (numerous awards), Sigma Tau Delta, Pi Delta Epsilon. Roman Catholic. Home: 1162 Trail Ridge Dr Jackson MO 63755-3507 Office: Blattner Bldg Ste One 1028A N Kings Hwy Cape Girardeau MO 63701 Home Phone: 873-845-7829; Office Phone: 573-335-8522. Personal E-mail: kenmcm@sbcglobal.net, kmcmanaman@charter.net.

MCMANIS, JAMES, lawyer; b. Haverhill, Mass., May 28, 1943; s. Charles and Yvonne (Zinn) McM.; m. Sara Wigh, Mar. 30, 1968. BA, Stanford U., Palo Alto, Calif., 1964; JD, U. Calif., Berkeley, 1967. Bar: Calif. 1967, U.S. Dist. Ct. (no. dist.) Calif. 1967, U.S. Ct. Appeals (9th cir.) 1967, U.S. Supreme Ct. 1971. Dep. dist. atty. Santa Clara County Dist. Atty., 1968-71; mem. McManis, Faulkner & Morgan, San Jose, Calif., 1971—. Spl. master tech. equities litig., 1987-98; spl. examiner State Bar Calif., 1995-98; prof. law Lincoln U. Law Sch., San Jose, 1972-82; lectr. Calif. Continuing Edn. of Bar, 1989-90; instr. U. Calif. Law Sch., 1992-96, Stanford U. Sch. Law, 1994-99. Pres. Santa Clara County Bar Assn. Law Found., 1996, dir., 1987—. Fellow Am. Coll. Trial Lawyers, Internat. Acad. Trial Lawyers, Am. Bar Found.; mem. ABA, State Bar Calif., Calif. Trial Lawyers Assn., Santa Clara County Bar Assn., Boalt Hall Alumni Assn. Avocations: history, books, travel, running. Office: McManis Faulkner & Morgan 50 W San Fernando St 10th fl San Jose CA 95113 Office Phone: 408-279-8700. Fax: 408-279-3244. Business E-Mail: jmcmanis@mfmlaw.com.

MCMANN, EDITH BROZAK (EDITH BROZAK), performing and visual artist; b. Totowa, NJ, Mar. 26, 1929; d. Henry and Lena (Ulmer) Brozek; m. Frank Richard McMann, May 26, 1957; children: Robert, Stephen. Dance student, Sch. Am. Ballet, NYC, 1945—58; student art, Westchester Art Workshop; student, Art Student's League, NYC; student art, SUNY, Purchase, NY, 1976—84; B in Profl. Studies in Dance and Visual Arts, SUNY, 1984; MS in Studio Art, Coll. of New Rochelle, 1989. Performing artist Alicia Alonso's Nat. Ballet Cuba tours, Mex., Ctrl. Am., S. Am., 1948-50, Lincoln Kirstein and George Balanchine's N.Y.C. Ballet, 1950—58; visual artist NYC, 1970—; intern Silvermine Coll. Art, 1989. Exhibitions include Depicting Dance in Art, Gutman Gallery, White Plains, 1990, Xavier Gallery, New Rochelle, NY, 1989—94, Mamaroneck Artist Guild Gallery, Larchmont, NY, 1990—, Beaux Arts Exhibits, 1991—94, Manhattanville Coll., Purchase, NY, 1991, Town Ctr. Gallery, Mamaroneck, 1993—, NYC Ballet, 1993—, Westbeth Gallery, NYC, 1994, Hammond Mus., Salem, NY, 1994, Town House Gallery, Stamford, Conn., 2000—, Tower Perrins, Stamford, 2000—02; represented in archives Ohio State U., Columbus, Libr. of Performing Arts, NYC, Lincoln Center, NYC Ballet Archives, Nat. Mus. for Women in Arts, Washington, Harvard Theater Collection, Mass., San Francisco Performing Arts Libr. and Mus., Nat. Resource Ctr. Dance, U. Surrey, Eng.; dancer (ballets) Alicia Alonso's Nat. Ballet Cuba, Mex., Ctrl. Am., South Am., 1948—50, Balachine's NYC Ballet, 1950—58, Apollo, Sleeping Beauty, Pas de Quatre, Ensayo Symphonica, Swan Lake, Symphony C, Con Amore, Nutcracker. Recipient Cert. of Merit U.S. Senator-N. Spano, 1989, U.S. State Assemblyman-R. Brodsky, 1989, Letter of Appreciation U.S. Senator Pat Moynihan, 1989, Letter of Congratulations U.S. Congressman -B. Gilman, 1989, others Mem. Allied Artist of Am., Hudson River Contemporary Artists, Nat. Mus. for Women in Art, Silvermine Guild of Artists, Scarsdale Art Soc., Stamford Art Assn., Mamaroneck Artists Guild (bd. dirs. assoc. rep. 1990-91, receiving com. 1992). Home: 10 Burkewood Rd Hartsdale NY 10530-2933 Personal E-mail: emcmann200@aol.com.

MCMANNON, TIMOTHY J., history professor; AA in Liberal Arts, Coll. So. Idaho, Twin Falls, 1982; BA in History, Pepperdine U., Malibu, Calif., 1985; MA in History, Pepperdine U., 1987; PhD in History, U. Wash., Seattl, 1994. Sr. assoc. Inst. Ednl. Inquiry, Seattle, 1992—2003; history instr. Highline Cmty. Coll., Des Moines, Wash., 2000—. Bd. dirs. Inst. Ednl. Inquiry, Seattle, 2007—. Contbr. chapters to books, articles to profl. jours. Mem.: Orgn. Am. Historians, Am. Hist. Assn., Wash. State Hist. Soc. Office: Highline Cmty Coll PO Box 98000 MS 11-1 Des Moines WA 98198-9800 Business E-Mail: tmcmanno@highline.edu.

MCMANUS, ANTHONY AIDAN, judicial organization executive; b. Dover, NH, Mar. 4, 1939; s. Patrick Henry McManus and Mary Wilhemena Cavanaugh; children: Meghan DiPasquale, Brendan, Moira McKinnon. BS, Georgetown U., Washington, 1960; LLD, Boston Coll., 1963. Bar: NH 1963, Mass. 1963, US Supreme Ct. 1989. Pub. defender Mass. Defenders, Boston, 1964—66; city atty. Dover, 1967—73; pvt. practice, 1973—2001; mem. NH Ho. of Reps., 1973—74, 1975—76, 1978, 1979—81, vice chair ho. jud. com., 1973—76; exec. sec. NH Jud. Conduct Com., Dover, 2001—. Mem. Dover Planning Bd., 1998—; bd. dirs. NH Legal Assistance, Manchester, Dover Day Care Ctr., 1972—75, Stratford Hospice, 1990, NH Symphony, Dover Main St., 2006—. Fellow: NH Bar Found. (hon.; bd. govs.); mem.: NH Bar Assn. (bd. govs.). Home: 39 Glenhill Dr Dover NH 03820 Office: 383 Central Ave Ste 303 Dover NH 03820 Office Phone: 603-749-4464. Office Fax: 603-749-5780.

MCMANUS, DECLAN PATRICK See COSTELLO, ELVIS

MC MANUS, EDWARD JOSEPH, federal judge; b. Keokuk, Iowa, Feb. 9, 1920; s. Edward W. and Kathleen (O'Connor) McM.; m. Sally A. Hassett, June 30, 1948 (dec.); children: David P., Edward W., John N., Thomas J., Dennis Q.; m. Esther Y. Kanealy, Sept. 15, 1987. Student, St. Ambrose Coll., 1936-38; BA, U. Iowa, 1940, JD, 1942. Bar: Iowa 1941. Gen. practice of law, Keokuk, 1946-62; city atty., 1946-55; mem. Iowa Senate, 1955-59; lt. gov. Iowa, 1959-61; chief U.S. judge No. Dist. Iowa, 1962-85, sr. U.S. judge, 1985—. Del Democratic Nat. Conv., 1956, 60. Served as lt. AC USNR, 1942-46. Office: US Dist Ct 329 US Courthouse 101 1st St SE Cedar Rapids IA 52401-1202 Office Phone: 319-286-2350. Business E-Mail: edward_mcmanus@iand.uscourts.gov.

MCMANUS, JAMES WILLIAM, lawyer; b. Kansas City, Mo., Aug. 1, 1945; s. Gerald B. and Mary M. McManus. BA, Rockhurst Coll., 1967; JD, St. Louis U., 1971. Bar: Mo. 1971, U.S. Dist. Ct. (we. dist.) Mo. 1972, U.S. Ct. Appeals (8th cir.) 1974, U.S. Supreme Ct. 1979, U.S. Ct. Appeals (10th cir.) 1984, U.S. Dist. Ct. Kans., 1995. Law clk. to presiding justice U.S. Dist. Ct. (we. dist.) Mo., 1971-73; assoc. Shughart, Thomson & Kilroy, P.C., Kansas City, 1973-76, dir., 1977-94; counsel Dysart, Taylor, Lay, Cotter & McMonigle, P.C., Kansas City, 1994—2002, DeWitt & Zeldin, L.L.C., Kansas City, 2002—04, McManus Law Offices, Kansas City, 2005—. Course lectr. med. jurisprudence U. Health Scis., Coll. Osteo. Medicine, Kansas City, 1994; lectr. in field. Adv. coun. St. Joseph Health Ctr., 1989-2002. Named to Best of the Bar, Appeals and Trials, Kansas City Bus. Jour., 2003, 2005, 2006; recipient Congenial Counselor award, Kansas City Metro Bar Assn., 2003, Exceptional Trial and Appellate atty. award, Mo. Ho. Reps., 2003. Fellow Am. Bar Found.; mem. ABA, AAJ (membership com. 2003-), Mo. Bar Assn., Kansas City Lawyers Assn., Kansas City Met. Bar Assn. (chmn. alternate dispute resolution com. 1996-97, vice chmn. 1994-95, chmn. med. malpractice com. 1989, Congenial Counselor award 2003), Mo. Assn. Trial Attys., Nat. Lawyers Assn., St. Louis Alumni Assn. (pres. 1984-92), St. Louis U. Law Sch. Alumni Assn. Home: 6824 Valley Rd Kansas City MO 64113-1929 Office: McManus Law Offices 1111 Main St Ste 700 Kansas City MO 64105 Office Phone: 816-474-3018. Business E-Mail: jamesmcmanus@justice.com.

MCMANUS, JASON DONALD, retired editor-in-chief; b. Mission, Kans., Mar. 3, 1934; s. John Alan and Stella Frances (Gosney) McM.; m. Patricia Ann Paulson, Oct. 18, 1958 (div. Feb. 1966); 1 child, John Alan; m. Deborah Hall Murphy, Dec. 2, 1973; children: Sophie Eleanor, Mage Caroline. BA, Davidson Coll., 1956, Litt.D. (hon.), 1979; M.P.A., Princeton U., 1958; postgrad., Oxford U., 1958-59; LittD (hon.), Monmouth Coll., 1988, U. N.C., 1991, Loyola U., Balt., 1992. Common Market bur. chief Time Mag., Paris, 1962-64, assoc. editor NYC, 1964-68, sr. editor, 1968-75, asst. mng. editor, 1975-78, exec. editor, 1978-83, mng. editor, 1985-87; corp. editor Time Inc., NYC, 1983-85; editor-in-chief Time Warner Inc., NYC, 1987-95; ret. Author: short stories Introduction, 1960. Mem. presdl. adv. commn. Internat. Edn. Exchange, 1982-83. Rhodes scholar, 1958-59. Mem.: Century Assn. (N.Y.C.).

MCMANUS, JOANNA QUILALA, medical device sales manager, physician assistant; d. Jimmy Ortanez and Filipina Caneda Quilala. BA in Chemistry, Calif. State U., Fullerton, 1994—2000; MS in Physician Asst. Studies, Western U. of Health Scis., Pomona, Calif., 2000—02. Field rschr., phlebotomist RAND, Santa Monica, Calif., 1998—2005; dist. mgr. Cook Med., Inc., 2005—. Physician asst. helper U. So. Calif./L.A. County Med. Ctr., 1997—2000. Allied Health Careers Scholarship, Kaiser Permanente, 2000—01. Mem.: Calif. Acad. Physician Assts. (assoc.), Western U. Alumni Assn. (life). Roman Catholic. Avocations: travel, dance, singing. Personal E-mail: qtkeylala@aol.com.

MCMANUS, PATRICK FRANCIS, editor, educator, writer; b. Sandpoint, Idaho, Aug. 25, 1933; s. Francis Edward McManus and Mabel Delana (Klaus) DeMers; m. Darlene Madge Keough, Feb. 3, 1954; children: Kelly C., Shannon M., Peggy F., Erin B. BA in English, Wash. State U., 1956, MA in English, 1962, postgrad., 1965-67. News reporter Daily Olympian, Olympia, Wash., 1956; editor Wash. State U., Pullman, 1956-59; with Ea. Wash. U., Cheney, 1959—; ret., 1983; news reporter Sta. KREM-TV, 1960-62; assoc. prof. Ea. Wash. U., Cheney, 1971-74, prof., 1974-83, prof. emeritus, 1983—. Author: A Fine and Pleasant Misery, 1978, Kid Camping from Aaaaiii! to Zip, 1979, They Shoot Canoes, Don't They?, 1981, Never Sniff a Gift Fish, 1983, The Grasshopper Trap, 1985, Rubber Legs & White Tail-Hairs, 1987, The Night The Bear Ate Goombaw, 1989, Whatchagot Stew, 1989, Real Ponies Don't Go Oink!, 1991, The Good Samaritan Strikes Again, 1992, How I Got This Way, 1994, Never Cry "Arp!" and Other Great Adventures, 1996, Into the Twilight, Endlessly Grousing, 1997, The Deer on a Bicycle, Excursions Into the Writing of Humor, 2000, The Bear in the Attic, 2002, The Blight Way, 2006, Avalanche, 2007, Kerplunk!, 2007; (stage play) A Fine and Pleasant Misery: The Humor of Patrick F. McManus, 1994, Misery II: McManus In Love, 1995, Pat McManus, Endlessly Grousing, 1997, Pott's Luck, 1999; assoc. editor Field & Stream mag., 1977-81; editor-at-large Outdoor Life, 1981—. Recipient Booksellers award P.N.W. Booksellers, 1983, Trustees medal EWU, 1984, Gov.'s award Wash. State Libr., 1985, Excellence in Craft award OWAA, 1986, Disting. Achievement award WSU, 1994, Founder's Day award EWU, 1994, Circle of Honor award The Outdoor Channel, 2004; named to Idaho's Hall of Fame, 1995, Legendary Communicator, Nat. Fresh Water Fishing Hall Fame, 2004. Mem.: Mystery Writers Am., Outdoor Writers Am. (bd. dirs. 1981—84, Excellence award 1986), Authors Guild. Roman Catholic. Avocations: outdoor sports, woodworking, travel.

MCMANUS, PAUL M., hotel executive; Mgmt. position The St. Regis Hotel, Waldorf-Astoria Hotel; sales and mktg. position Regent Internat. Hotels, Rockresorts, Princess Hotels Internat.; v.p. mktg. Leading Hotels of the World, Ltd., 1992—93, exec. v.p., 1993, pres., CEO, 1998—. Adv. bd. mem. Preston Robert Tisch Ctr. for Hospitality, Tourism and Travel Adminstrn., NYU, Inst. Travel, Hotel and Restaurant Adminstrn., Niagara U.; spkr. in field. Office: Leading Hotels of the World Ltd 99 Park Ave New York NY 10016-1601 Office Phone: 212-515-5600. Office Fax: 212-515-5899. *

MCMANUS, RICHARD PHILIP, lawyer, agricultural products executive; b. Keokuk, Iowa, Oct. 20, 1929; s. Edward William and Kathleen (O'Connor) M.; m. Marjorie Theresa Mullaney, Nov. 5, 1955; children: Michael L., Mark J., Matthew A. BA, St. Ambrose U., Davenport, Iowa, 1949; JD, U. Mich., 1952; MBA, Roosevelt U., Chgo., 1965. Bar: Calif. 1982, Ill. 1958, Iowa 1952. Ptnr. McManus & McManus, Keokuk, 1953-63; div. counsel USN Facility Engring. Command, Great Lakes, Ill., 1963-66; v.p., dir. law Household Fin. Corp., Chgo., 1966-81; exec. v.p., sec. Security Pacific Fin. Svcs., Inc., San Diego, 1981-91, gen. counsel, 1981—91; exec. v.p./sec. Bank Am. Fin. Svcs., San Diego, 1991-92, gen. counsel, 1991—92; pres., chmn. bd. dirs. Mosamac Co., Inc., 1992—2006. Mem. gen. com. Conf. Consumer Fin. Law, Chgo., 1975-92; mem. adv. bd. Hostler Inst. Internat. Affairs, San Diego State U., 2005— Contbr. articles to profl. jours. Bd. dir., treas., atty. Tijuana/San Diego Habitat for Humanity, Inc., 1992-95; trustee Village of Lake Bluff, Ill., 1974-78; bd. dir. Charles Hostler Inst. World Affairs, San Diego State U., 2004-. Recipient San Diego Vol. Lawyer Disting. Svc. award, 1995-2007, Pres. Calif. Bar Pro Bono Svs. award, 1998; named San Diego Pro Bono Atty. of Yr., 2005. Mem. Calif. Bar Assn., San Diego Bar Assn., Calif. Fin. Svcs. Assn. (chmn. law com. 1981-92), Am. Fin. Svcs. Assn. (chmn. law forum 1980-81, Disting. Svc. award 1990), Lions, Elks, KC, Beta Gamma Sigma. Democrat. Roman Catholic. Avocations: golf, flying, sailing, woodworking. E-mail: mcman1000@peoplepc.com.

MCMANUS, SEAN JOSEPH, broadcast executive; b. Feb. 16, 1955; s. James Kenneth and Margaret Dempsey McManus; m. Tracy Lynne Torre, May 23, 1998. BA in English & History, cum laude, Duke U., 1977. Prodn. asst. to assoc. prodr. ABC Sports, NYC, 1977—79; assoc. prodr. to prodr. NBC Sports, NYC, 1979—81, v.p. planning, devel., 1981—87; sr. v.p. US TV sales, programming Trans World Internat. (TV divsn. IMG), NYC, 1987—96; pres. CBS Sports, NYC, 1996—, CBS News, NYC, 2005—. Dir. CBS SportsLine, 1997—.

MCMANUS, WILLIAM PAUL, police chief; married; 3 children. Bachelor's degree, Villanova U.; MS, Johns Hopkins U. Police officer Met. Police Dept., Washington, asst. police chief, 1998—2001; police chief City of Dayton, Ohio, 2001—03, City of Mpls., 2004—06, City of San Antonio, 2006—.

MCMASTER, BELLE MILLER, religious organization administrator; b. Atlanta, May 24, 1932; d. Patrick Dwight and Lila (Bonner) Miller; m. George R. McMaster, June 19, 1953; children: Lisa McMaster Stork, George Neel, Patrick Miller. BA, Agnes Scott Coll., 1953; MA, U. Louisville, 1970, PhD, 1974. Assoc. corp. witness Presbyn. Ch. USA, Atlanta, 1974-77, dir. corp. witness, 1977-81, dir. div. corp. and social mission, 1981-87, dir. social justice and peacemaking unit Louisville, 1987-93; acting dir. program women in theology and ministry Candler Sch. Theology Emory U., 1993-96, dir. advanced studies Candler Sch. Theology, 1995—2003. Vice-moderator chs. commn. internat. affairs World Coun. Chs., 1984-91, mem. justice, peace and creation commn., 1991-99; chair commn. internat. affairs Nat. Coun. Chs., NYC, 1986-89, v.p., 1990-95, exec. bd., 1986-2003, chair ch. world svc. and witness unit com., 1990-2003; chair fin. com. Ch. World Svc. and Witness Unit Com., NC, 1997-99, bd. dirs., 1995-2003. Author: Witnessing to the Kingdom, 1982, book columnist "What I Have Been Reading" in Church and Society Magazine, 1993-2001; contbr. articles to profl. jours. Pres. League of Women Voters, Greenville, S.C., 1963-64; bd. dirs. Interfaith Housing, Atlanta, 1975-81. Danforth fellow, 1969-74. Mem.: MLA, Soc. for Values in Higher Edn., Acad. Am. Religion, Phi Beta Kappa. Presbyterian. Business E-Mail: bmcmast@emory.edu.

MCMASTER, BRIAN JOHN, artistic director; b. May 9, 1943; With internat. artists dept. EMI, 1968-73; contr. opera planning English Nat. Opera, 1973-76; mng. dir. Welsh Nat. Opera, Cardiff, 1976-91; dir. Edinburgh Internat. Festival, Scotland, 1991—2006; artistic dir. Vancouver Opera, BC, Canada, 1983-89. E-mail: brian.mcmaster@hotmail.com.

MCMASTER, GLORIA (GLORIA BUGNI JUHN), mezzo-soprano, educator; b. Montreal, Wis., Oct. 22, 1926; d. Anton George and Rose (Gatto) Bugni; m. Chester L. McMaster (dec. 1972); children— Chester Anthony, Raymond Dale, Brian Monroe, Maureen Anne, Heather Lynn; m. Martin Juhn, July 30, 1977. Student U. Minn.; B.S., Juilliard Sch. Music, N.Y.C.; postgrad. Columbia U., U. Detroit, SUNY-Brockport; Mus.M., Eastman Sch. Music, U. Rochester. Prin., voice instr. McMaster Music Studios, Rochester and Dansville, N.Y., 1987—. Performed in concert, oratorio, opera throughout U.S., including solo appearances with Juilliard Opera Theater, Chautauqua Opera Assn., Rochester Opera Theater; appeared as soloist with Mpls. Symphony, Rochester (N.Y.) Philharm. Buffalo Philharm. Music Theater of Rochester, Eastman Rochester Symphony, Rochester, Hornell (N.Y.) Symphony, Sarasota Opera, 2003—; recitals at Youngstown, Ohio, Ironwood, Mich., Hornell, Alfred U., and Rochester, N.Y.; concerts Nazareth Art Ctr., Nat. Opera Assn., New Orleans, Sarasota, Fla.; dir. Dansville Music Theater; asst. prof. Youngstown State U., State U. Coll., Geneseo, N.Y.; prof. Houghton (N.Y.) Coll; judge scholarship com. Sarasota Opera, Artist Series, Fla. Soloist Republican Nat. Convention, Miami; appeared in title role Nat. Edn. Television prodn. The Medium; appeared in plays by Phil Gelb, Sarasota, 1986-87. Mem. pres.'s leadership council U. Rochester. Mem. AAUW (past pres. Dansville area br.), AAUP (past chpt. exec. bd.), Nat. Opera Assn., Nat. Assn. Tchrs. Singing, Juilliard Alumni Assn., Eastman Alumni Assn., N.Y. Music Tchrs. Assn. Address: 3830 Glen Oaks Manor Dr Sarasota FL 34232 Personal E-mail: gloriajuhn@comcast.net.

MCMASTER, HENRY DARGAN, state attorney general; b. Columbia, SC, May 27, 1947; s. John Gregg and Ida Bacot (Dargan) McM.; m. Peggy Jean McAbee, Mar. 18, 1978 BA, U. SC, 1969, JD, 1973. Bar: SC, US Dist. Ct. SC, US Ct. Claims, US Ct. Appeals (4th cir.), US Supreme Ct. Atty., legis. asst. US Senator Strom Thurmond, Washington, 1973-74; ptnr. Tompkins & McMaster, Columbia, SC, 1974—81, 1985—2003; US atty. Dist. SC, Columbia, 1981-85; atty. gen. State of SC, 2003—. Mem. US Atty. Gen.'s adv. com. of US Attys., Washington, 1981-83; chmn. Com. on Ct. Rules and Legislation, Washington, 1983-85. Contbr. articles to legal publs. Mem. region IV youth adv. bd. EPA, Atlanta, 1972; mem. SC Commn. on Higher Edn., 1991-94; chmn. SC Rep. Party, 1993-2002; bd. dirs. SC Policy Coun., 1991-2003; atty. gen. SC, 2003-. Mem. Richland County Bar Assn. (prog. com. 1978), SC Bar, ABA, Nat. Assn. R.R. Trial Counsel, Def. Rsch. Inst., Centurian Soc., Caroliniana Ball Club, St. Andrew's Soc. (Columbia), Phi Delta Phi, Blue Key, Kappa Alpha (dep. province comdr. 1974-75, province comdr. 1975-91). Republican. Presbyterian. Office: 1731 Senate St Columbia SC 29201 also: Office of Atty Gen Rembert C Dennis Office Bldg PO Box 11549 Columbia SC 29211-1549 Office Phone: 803-734-3970. *

MCMASTER, JULIET SYLVIA, English language educator; b. Kisumu, Kenya, Aug. 2, 1937; emigrated to Can., 1961, naturalized, 1976; d. Sydney Herbert and Sylvia (Hook) Fazan; m. Rowland McMaster, May 10, 1968; children: Rawdon, Lindsey. BA with honors, Oxford U., Eng., 1959; MA, U. Alta., Can., 1963, PhD, 1965. Asst. prof. English U. Alta., Edmonton, Canada, 1965—70, assoc. prof., 1970—76, prof. English, 1976—86, univ. prof., 1986—2000, prof. emeritus, 2000—. Author: Thackeray: The Major Novels, 1971, Jane Austen on Love, 1978, Trollope's Palliser Novels, 1978; author: (with R.D. McMaster) The Novel from Sterne to James, 1981; author: Dickens the Designer, 1987, Jane Austen the Novelist, 1995, Reading the Body in the Eighteenth Century Novel, 2004, Woman Behind the Painter: The Diaries of Rosalie, Mrs. James Clarke-Hook, 2006; co-editor: Jane Austen's Business, 1996, Cambridge Companion to Jane Austen, 1997, The Child Writer From Austen to Woolf, 2005; gen. editor: Juvenilia Press, 1993—2002, illustrator/editor: children's picture book (by Jane Austen) The Beautifull Cassandra, 1993; contbr. articles to profl. jours. Fellow Can. Coun., 1969-70, Guggenheim Found., 1976-77, Killam Found., 1987-89; recipient Molson prize in Humanities for Outstanding Contbn. to Canadian Culture, 1994, Alberta Centennial medal, 2005. Fellow Royal Soc. Can.; mem. Victorian Studies Assn. Western Can. (founding pres. 1972), Assn. Can. Univ. Tchrs. English (pres. 1976-78), MLA, Jane Austen Soc. N.Am. (dir. 1980-91). Office Phone: 708-436-5284. Business E-Mail: juliet.mcmaster@ualberta.ca.

MCMASTERS, JAMES, law librarian, educator; BS, Northwestern U., JD, 1990; MLIS, Dominican U. Litig. assoc. Bell, Boyd & Lloyd, Chgo., 1990—94; lectr. comm. and legal reasoning Northwestern U. Sch. Law, Chgo., staff mem. Pritzker Legal Rsch. Ctr., 2002—, acting dir.; reference libr. Loyola U., Chgo., 2000—02. Office: Pritzker Legal Rsch Ctr Northwestern U Sch Law 357 E Chicago Ave Chicago IL 60611 Office Phone: 312-503-8449. E-mail: j-mcmasters@law.northwestern.edu. *

MCMATH, LULA WRAY, retired elementary school educator, realtor; b. Grenada, Miss., Apr. 27, 1933; d. Alva and Augusta McMath; m. Jesse C. Terry; 1 child, Damita. BS in Edn., Chgo. State U., 1971, MS in Urban Edn., 1972, MS in Corrections, 1974. Lic. realtor Chgo. (Ill.) Bd. Realtors, 1986. Seamstress Hart Schaffner and Marx, Chgo., 1952—65; tchr. Chgo. (Ill.) Bd. Edn., 1965—93; realtor Ronald Waters, Chgo., 1986—. Author: How 8th Grade Students View Discipline, 1973, Places I Have Visited, 1994, My Lovely Garden, 1994. Vol. gardener City of Chgo., 1989; vol. literacy educator Roosevelt U., Chgo., 1993; ballot giver Dem. Party, Chgo., 1988, poll watcher, 1984, judge, 1990, registrar, 1988. Recipient Valuable Svc. award, Faith Temple Ch., 1975, Meritorious award, United Negro Colls., 1991. Mem.: Am. Fedn., Ret. Tchrs. Avocations: gardening, singing, dance, interior decorating. Home: 10621 S Wood St Chicago IL 60643-2717

MCMECHAN, GEORGE, science educator; b. Vancouver, B.C., Canada, Aug. 21, 1947; BASc, U. BC, Vancouver, Can., 1970; MS, U. Toronto, 1971; BS, U. Victoria, Can., 1983. Registered profl. engr., B.C. Prof. geosci. U. Tex. at Dallas, Richardson, 1983—, dir. Ctr. for Lithospheric Studies, 1985—. Rsch. scientist Pacific Geosci. Ctr., Sidney, BC, 1972—82. Contbr. articles to profl. jours. Mem.: Seismol. Soc. Am., Am. Geophys. Union, Soc. Exploration Geophysicists (Virgil Kauffman Gold medal 1997). Avocations: physical fitness, movies. Office: Univ of Tex at Dallas 2601 N Floyd Rd Richardson TX 75080 Office Phone: 972-883-2419. Business E-Mail: mcmec@utdallas.edu.

MCMEEKIN, DOROTHY, botanist, plant pathologist, educator; b. Boston, Feb. 24, 1932; d. Thomas LeRoy and Vera (Crockatt) McM. BA, Wilson Coll., 1953; MA, Wellesley Coll., 1955; PhD, Cornell U., 1959. Asst. prof. Upsala Coll., East Orange, NJ, 1959-64, Bowling Green State U., Ohio, 1964-66; prof. natural sci. Mich. State U., East Lansing, 1966-89, prof. botany, plant pathology, 1989—. Author: Diego Rivera: Science and Creativity, 1985; contbr. articles to profl. jours. Mem. Am. Phytopath. Soc., Mycol. Soc. Am., Soc. Econ. Bot., Mich. Bot. Soc. (former bd. dirs.), Mich. Women's Studies Assn., Sigma Xi, Phi Kappa Phi. Avocations: gardening, sewing, travel, drawing. Home: 1055 Marigold Ave East Lansing MI 48823-5128 Office: Mich State U Dept Botany-Plant Pathology 100 N Kedzie Hall East Lansing MI 48824-1031 E-mail: mcmeekin@msu.edu.

MCMEEKIN, THOMAS OWEN, dermatologist; b. Shelby, Nebr., Apr. 17, 1945; s. Wallace Walton and Evajane (Taber) McM.; m. Dale Goodwin, 1999; children: Michele, Sean. BA with distinction, Stanford U., 1967; MD with honors, U. Rochester, 1971. Intern Beth Israel Hosp., Boston, 1971-72; resident U. Rochester (N.Y.), 1974-76, Mass. Gen. Hosp., Boston, 1976-78; clin. prof. depts. medicine, pediatrics, dermatology U. Rochester Sch. Medicine, 1978—; dermatologist pvt. practice, Rochester, 1978—; clin. asst. prof. SUNY, Buffalo, 1997—. Pres. Geneese Valley Laser Ctr., Rochester, 1990—. Capt. USPHS, 1972—74. Kohn fellow U. Rochester, 1980-81; recipient Doren J. Stephens Alumni award U. Rochester, 1971, Brian Flanagan Teaching Svc. award, 1995, 2003. Fellow Am. Acad. Dermatology (Svc. award 1993), Am. Bd. Internal Medicine, Am. Soc. LAser MEdicine (co-chmn. 1993-94), Am. Soc. Dermatologic Surgery (edn. com. 1983—); mem. N.Y. State Dermatological Soc. (v.p. 1993, treas. 1992), Buffalo Rochester Dermatological Soc. (pres. 1990), Rochester Dermatological Soc. (pres. 1980-89), Alpha Omega Alpha. Avocations: golf, tennis, computers. Office: 300 White Spruce Blvd Rochester NY 14623-1606 Office Phone: 585-424-6770. Personal E-mail: 041745@msn-.com.

MCMEEKING, ROBERT MAXWELL, mechanical engineer, educator; b. Glasgow, Scotland, May 22, 1950; came to U.S., 1972; s. Robert Maxwell and Elizabeth Higginson (Craighead) McM.; m. Norah Anne Madigan, Sept. 4, 1976; children: Gavin Robert, Anne Catherine. BSc with 1st class honors, U. Glasgow, 1972; MS, Brown U., 1974, PhD, 1977. Acting asst. prof. Stanford (Calif.) U., 1976-78; asst. prof. U. Ill., Urbana, 1978-82, assoc. prof., 1982-85; prof. U. Calif., Santa Barbara, 1985—, chmn. mech. and environ. engring., 1992—95, 1999—2003. Cons. in field. Co-editor Intermetallic Matrix Composites, 1990; assoc. editor Jour. Applied Mechanics, 1987-93; editor Jour. Applied Mechanics, 2002—; contbr. articles to profl. jours. Recipient Alexander von Humboldt Rsch. award for Sr. U.S. Scientists, 2004, Alumni medal Brown Engring., 2007, Arthur Newell Talbot Lectr. award U. Ill., 2007; vis. fellow Cambridge U., 1983, 95-96. Fellow ASME, Am. Acad. Mechanics; mem. AAAS, NAE, Inst. Sci. Info. (Highly Cited Rschr. award) Sigma Xi. Office: U Calif Materials Dept Mech Engring Dept Santa Barbara CA 93106 Home Phone: 805-962-8511; Office Phone: 805-893-8434. Business E-Mail: rmcm@engineering.ucsb.edu.

MC MEEL, JOHN PAUL, newspaper syndicate and publishing executive; b. South Bend, Ind., Jan. 26, 1936; s. James E. and Naomi R. (Reilly) McM.; m. Susan S. Sykes, Apr. 16, 1966; children: Maureen, Suzanne, Bridget. BS, U. Notre Dame, 1957. Sales dir. Hall Syndicate, 1960-67; asst. gen. mgr., sales dir. Publishers-Hall Syndicate, 1968-70; co-founder Universal Press Syndicate, Kansas City, Mo., 1970; pres. Andrews McMeel Universal, 1970—. Chmn. bd. Andrews McMeel Pub., 1973—; mem. arts and letters U. Notre Dame. Co-founder Christmas in October, Kansas City, 1984—, James F. Andrews fellowship program, U. Notre Dame, 1981, adv. com. program in journalism; mem. The Civic Coun. Greater Kansas City. Mem. Fed. Assn. USA, Sovereign Mil. Order Malta. Home: Three Sunset Pl 5300 Sunset Dr Kansas City MO 64112-2358 Office: Andrews McMeel Universal 4520 Main St Kansas City MO 64111-1816 Office Phone: 816-932-6602. Business E-Mail: jmcmeel@amuniversal.com.

MCMEEN, ALBERT RALPH, III, writer, technical trainer, multimedia programmer, financial services executive; b. Lewistown, Pa., Oct. 4, 1942; s. Albert Ralph and Margaret McDowell (Parker) McM.; m. A. Mary Kelley, June 6, 1965 (div.); children: Albert Ralph, Christopher Benjamin. BA in Econs., Williams Coll., 1964; MBA in Fin., Columbia U., 1966. Asst. v.p. Chem. Bank, NYC, 1966-75; v.p. Irving Leasing Co., NYC, 1975-80, USI Capital and Leasing, NYC, 1980-83; pres. Tng. Assocs., Inc., 1983—2000; owner guest house Designer's Dock, 2002—. Assoc. adj. prof. NYU, 1979-93; asst. prof. L.I. U., 1986-93; tng. cons. Citibank, 1986-87 Barclay's Bank, 1986-89; lectr. Am. Mgmt. Assn., 1986-93, Am. Bankers Assn., 1992-94, Kocbank, Istanbul, 1993, Fund Democracy and Devel., Moscow, 1995; computer based tng. cons. Depository Trust Co., 1998. Author: Treasurers and Controllers New Equipment Leasing Guide, 1984, Equipment Leasing Guide for Lessees, 1990, Debt Repayment Capacity, 1992, Financial Statement Analysis, 1993, Guide to Consumer Lending Computer-Based Training, 1995, Commercial Credit for Lenders, 1998. Mem. legis. com. Citizens' Union, 1968-75; bd. dirs. Columbia U. Alumni Assn., 1970-75; sec. Gay Fathers Inc. Scholar Columbia Internat. Fellows, 1964; recipient Columbia Bus. Sch. svc. award, 1966. Democrat. Office Phone: 508-487-0385. Personal E-mail: mcmeen@designersdock.com.

MCMEEN, ELMER ELLSWORTH, III, lay minister, musician, retired lawyer; b. Lewistown, Pa., June 3, 1947; s. Elmer Ellsworth II and Frances Josephine McM.; m. Sheila Ann Taenzler, July 31, 1971; children: Jonathan Ellsworth, Daniel Biddle, James Cunningham and Mary Josephine (twins). BA cum laude, Harvard U., 1969; JD cum laude, U. Pa., 1972. Bar: 1973, U.S. Ct. Appeals (2nd cir.) 1973, U.S. Dist. Ct. (so.and ea. dists.) NY 1975. Assoc. Cravath, Swaine & Moore, NYC, 1972-75, LeBoeuf, Lamb, Greene & MacRae, LLP, NYC, 1975-78, ptnr., 1979-99, of counsel, 2000, retired, 2001. Lectr. Editor U. Pa. Law Rev., 1970-72. Author guitar books, Celtic Treasures for String Trio, Hard Times: A Christian Handbook for Getting Through Them, 2007, The Good News is...Freedom, 2007, Do You Have Time For Some Good News!, 2007; musician: (solo instrnl. audio and DVD lessons and performance DVDs) Stefan Grossman's Guitar Workshop and Rounder Records; co-author: The Passion Dialogues, 2006, musician numerous solo guitar recordings; contbr. articles to legal jours. Chmn. N.Y.C. regional com. U. Pa. Law Sch., 1984-86; class sec. Northfield Mt. Hermon Sch. Class of 1965, Mass., 1984-91. Named Musician of Yr., Internat. Biography Ctr., Cambridge, Eng., 2003. Mem.: Rockaway River Country Club. Office: 34 Angelo Dr Sparta NJ 07871 E-mail: mcmeen_el@yahoo.com.

MCMEEN, SHEILA TAENZLER, retired lawyer; b. Morristown, NJ, Aug. 26, 1946; d. William Paul and Mary Cunningham Taenzler; m. E. Ellsworth McMeen, III, July 31, 1971; children: Jonathan, Daniel, James, Mary. AB summa cum laude, Muhlenberg Coll., Allentown, Pa., 1968; JD cum laude, U. Pa., 1971. Bar: N.Y. 1972, U.S. Supreme Ct. 1979. Assoc. Davis Polk & Wardwell, NYC, 1971—80; ret. Editor: U. Pa. Law Rev. Pastoral care vol. staff Andover (N.J.) Rehab Ctr., 2004—; mem. Bd. of Edn., Mountain Lakes, NJ, 1993—2001, Sussex County Child Placement Rev. Bd., Newton, NJ, 2003—. Mem.: Phi Beta Kappa. Avocations: needlework, cryptic puzzles, reading. Home: 34 Angelo Dr Sparta NJ 07871 E-mail: elmcmeen@ptd.net.

MCMENAMIN, JOHN ROBERT, lawyer; b. Evanston, Ill., Sept. 30, 1946; BA, U. Notre Dame, 1968, JD, 1971. Bar: Ill. 1971. Law clk. to presiding judge U.S. Ct. Appeals (7th cir.), 1971-72; ptnr. Mayer, Brown & Platt, Chgo., 1978-89, McDermott, Will & Emery, Chgo., 1989—. Chmn. adv. bd. Holy Trinity High Sch., Chgo., 1986-88; pres. Lawyer's Club Chgo., 2003-04. Mem. ABA, Lawyers Club, U. Club, Econ. Club. Roman Catholic. Office: McDermott Will & Emery 227 W Monroe St Ste 3100 Chicago IL 60606-5096

MCMENAMIN, RICHARD F., lawyer; b. Nov. 23, 1946; BA, St. Joseph's Coll., 1968; MA, Boston U., 1971; JD, Temple U., 1977. Bar: Pa. 1977. Ptnr. Morgan, Lewis & Bockius, Phila. Office: Morgan Lewis & Bockius 1701 Market St Philadelphia PA 19103-2903 Home Phone: 215-640-0848; Office Phone: 215-963-5596. Business E-Mail: rmcmenamin@morganlewis.com.

MCMENNAMIN, MICHAEL J., savings and loan executive, investment banker; b. Berlin, NH, June 27, 1945; s. John Lester and Ruth Ellen (Donaldson) McM.; children: Kelly, Tricia. AB in Econs., Ohio U., 1967; MBA in Banking and Fin., Case Western Res. U., 1972. Exec. v.p. Nat. City Bank, Nat. City Corp., Cleve., 1968-81; vice chmn. Bank One Columbus (Ohio), NA, 1981-85; chief investment officer Banc One Corp., Columbus, 1981-85; ptnr., v.p. Meuse Rinker Chapman Endres & Brooks, Columbus, 1985-88; chmn. Midwest Savs. Bank, Degraff, Ohio, 1986-87; chmn., chief exec. officer Buckeye Fed. Savs. & Loan, Buckeye Fin. Corp., Columbus, 1988-90, Bank One, Columbus, 1990-95; exec. v.p. finance Banc One Corp., Columbus, 1995—. Lectr. Grad. Sch. Banking, U. Wis., Madison, 1975-80; mem. treasury and fed. agy. com. Pub. Securities Assn., 1977-81, 85; mem. exec. com. funds mgmt. div. Am. Bankers Assn., 1977-79. Author articles in field. Mem. The Golf Club (Columbus), The Capital Club (Columbus), The Athletic Club (Columbus), Wedgewood Country Club (Columbus), Pinehurst (N.C.) Nat. Golf Club, Pinehurst Country Club. Republican. Roman Catholic. Avocations: golf, squash, tennis, reading.

MCMENNAMY, ROGER NEAL, automotive executive; b. Amarillo, Tex., Oct. 9, 1942; s. Wilson Foch and Mildred Evelyn (Freudiger) McMennamy; m. Marilyn Kay Gibbons, Jan. 1, 1967; children: Timothy Neal, Traci Nicole. Student, Abilene Christian U., 1961-62; BBA in Mgmt. cum laude, U. Tex., Arlington, 1970; MBA in Fin., U. Tex., Austin, 1971. CPA Tex. Contr., treas. E. N. Wolcott Corp., Houston, 1971-73; mem. corp. staff ELPAC, Inc., Houston, 1973-74; gen. mgr. BS&B Mfg., Houston, 1974-75; gen. mgr. adminstrn. Gulf Interstate Co., Houston, 1975-77; exec. v.p., CFO NWS Supply Group, Houston, 1977-83; v.p., CFO Newpark Resources, Inc., Metairie, La., 1983-86; sr. v.p., CFO Gemcraft, Inc., 1986-88; exec. v.p., CFO Cooper Cmtys., Inc., Bella Vista, Ark., 1988-90, pres., CEO, 1990-97; pres., CEO, gen. mgr. Daryl Hickman Chevrolet, Inc., Siloam Springs, Ark., 1998—2005; pres., CEO Guaranteed Auto Fin., Inc., 2003—, SHAC, Inc., 2003—. With USMC, 1962—66, Vietnam. Avocations: travel, golf, waterfowl hunting. Office: Guaranteed Auto Fin Inc PO Box 730 Tontitown AR 72770 Office Phone: 479-361-4300.

MCMICHAEL, DONALD EARL, lawyer; b. Denver, Aug. 8, 1931; s. Earl L. and Charlotte F. McM.; m. Zeta Hammond, July 6, 1955; children: Lauren A. McMichael Burnett, Thomas D., Susan E. McMichael Markle. AB, Dartmouth Coll., 1953; LLB, U. Colo., 1956. Bar: Colo. 1956, U.S. Dist. Ct. Colo. 1956, U.S. Ct. Appeals (10th cir.) 1956. Assoc. Holme Roberts & Owen, 1956-58; pres. Corp. Ins. Assocs., 1958-70; dir. trust devel. Ctrl. Bank Denver, 1970-72; ptnr. Brenman, Sobol & Baum, Denver, 1972-74, McMichael, Benedict, Multz & Lipton, Denver, 1974—99; of counsel Schmidt & Horen, Denver, 2000—02; pvt. practice, 2002—. Chmn. Denver Ctrl. YMCA, 1971-73. Capt. USAR, 1956—64. Named Layman of Yr. Denver Ctrl. YMCA, 1973, named to Denver Metro YMCA Hall of Fame, 1989. Mem. Colo. Bar Assn., Denver Bar Assn., Denver

Estate Planning Coun. (sec. 1971-73). Republican. Methodist. Office: 6325 W Mansfield Ave Unit 234 Denver CO 80235-3015 Home Phone: 303-987-0543; Office Phone: 303-716-8406. E-mail: dmcmic@aol.com.

MCMILLAN, CAMPBELL WHITE, pediatrician, educator, hematologist; b. Soochow, China, Jan. 10, 1927; arrived in U.S., 1940; s. Henry Hudson and Leila McNeill (Memory) McM.; m. Florence Jean MacKenzie, June 11, 1955; children: Ian Johnson, Sally Hudson, Donna Jean, Andrew Duncan, Bridget White, Wendy McNeill. BS summa cum laude, Wake Forest Coll., 1948; MD, Bowman Gray Sch. Medicine, 1952. Diplomate Am. Bd. Pediatrics, Pediatric Hematology-Oncology. Intern Harvard Med. Service, Boston City Hosp., 1952-53; resident in pediatrics Children's Hosp. Med. Center, Boston, 1953-55; registrar in pediatrics St. Mary's Hosp., London, 1955; pediatrician Nemazee Hosp., Shiraz, Iran, 1956-58; fellow in pediatric hematology Harvard U., 1958-60; instr. pediatrics, 1960-61; gen. practice pediatrics Laurinburg, NC, 1961-63; asst. prof. pediatrics U. N.C., Chapel Hill, 1963-68, asso. prof., 1968-72, prof., 1972-92, chief div. pediatric hematology, 1963-83, prof. emeritus, 1992—. Asso. dir. Clin. Research Center, U. N.C., 1966-78 Assoc. editor: Blood Diseases of Infancy and Childhood, 1978, 84; contbr. articles profl. jours., chpts. in books. Served with USNR, 1945-46. Recipient Lederle Med. Faculty award, 1964, Disting. Alumnus award Bowman Gray Sch. Medicine, 1972, Outstanding Career Achievement award Nat. Hemophilia Found., 1998. Fellow Am. Acad. Pediatrics; mem. Soc. Pediatric Rsch., Am. Pediatric Soc., Phi Beta Kappa, Alpha Omega Alpha. Democrat. Episcopalian. Home: 408 Ridgecrest Dr Chapel Hill NC 27514-2103 *It was my extremely good fortune to live and to work in a time of the most explosive growth medical knowledge had ever undergone.*

MCMILLAN, CHARLES WILLIAM, consulting company executive; b. Ft. Collins, Colo., Feb. 9, 1926; s. Charles and Margaret (Jennings) McM.; m. Jardell Hollier, Feb. 12, 1951; children: Brett W., Kurt C., Scott P. BS, Colo. State U., 1948. Asst. 4-H agt., Denver, 1948; county agrl. agt. LaJara, Colo., 1949-50, Julesburg, 1950-53; faculty Colo. State U., 1954; div. head, agrl. research dept. Swift & Co., Chgo., 1954-59; exec. v.p. Am. Nat. Cattlemen's Assn., 1959-77; v.p. Nat. Cattlemen's Assn., 1977-81; asst. sec. for mktg. and inspection services USDA, Washington, 1981-85; pres. McMillan and Farrell Assocs., Inc., Washington, 1985-94, C.W. McMillan Co., Alexandria, Va., 1994—. Served to lt. (j.g.) USNR, World War II. Mem. Sigma Alpha Epsilon. Home: 4003 Pine Brook Rd Alexandria VA 22310-2144 Office: PO Box 10009 Alexandria VA 22310-0009

MC MILLAN, GEORGE DUNCAN HASTIE, JR., lawyer, former state official; b. Greenville, Ala., Oct. 11, 1943; s. George Duncan Hastie and Jean (Autrey) McM.; m. Ann Louise Dial, Nov. 20, 1971; children: George Duncan Hastie, III, Ann Dial. BA magna cum laude, Auburn U., 1966; LL.B. (Southeastern Regional scholar), U. Va., 1969. Bar: Ala. bar 1969. Research asst. dept. agronomy Auburn U., summers 1963-65; law clk. firm Lange, Simpson, Robinson & Somerville, Birmingham, Ala., summers 1967-68; law clk. to judge U.S. Dist. Ct. No. Dist. Ala., 1969-70; instr. U. Ala. Law Sch., 1969-70; individual practice law Birmingham, 1970-71; ptnr. firm McMillan & Spratling, Birmingham, 1971-86; of counsel Haskell, Slaughter, Young and Lewis, 1986; ptnr. McMillan, Jones and Assocs., 1987-90; pres. McMillan Assocs., 1990—; mem. Ala. Ho. of Reps., 1973, Ala. Senate, 1974-78; lt. gov. Ala., 1979-83. Vice-chmn. Nat. Conf. Lt. Govs., 1980-82; mem. Permanent Study Commn. on Ala.'s Jud. System, 1975-79 Chmn. Ala. Film Commn., 1976-83; mem. Arts Task Force, Nat. Conf. State Legislatures, 1978-80, Multi-State Transp. Adv. Bd., 1974-79; mem. exec. com. So. Growth Policies Bd., 1974-83, vice chmn., 1981-83; bd. dirs. Campfire, Inc., 1975-82, Met. YMCA, Birmingham, Boys and Girls Ranches, Ala., Positive Maturity, 1987—; chmn. bd., pres. Birmingham Cultural and Heritage Found., 1988—; pres., bd. dirs. Birmingham Repertory Theatre, 1989—; exec. prodr. City Stages, 2003—; vice chair Black Belt Cmty. Found. Served to lt. USAR, 1969. Recipient award Ala. Nurses Assn., 1975; named Legislator of Yr. Ala. Forestry Assn., 1978; Hardest Working Senator Capitol Press Corps, 1976; 1 of 4 Outstanding Young Men Ala. Jaycees, 1977; 1 of 10 Most Outstanding State Legislators Assn. Govtl. Employees, 1978; award Birmingham Emancipation Assn., 1977; award Ala. Hist. Commn., 1978; James Tingle award, 1979, Citizen of Yr. award City of Birmingham, 1990. Mem. Birmingham Bar Assn., Ala. Bar Assn., Am. Bar Assn., Birmingham Jaycees, Ala. Jaycees (dir. 1970-72), Birmingham Urban League, United Negro Coll. Fund. Democrat. Mem. Ch. of Christ. Club: Rotary (Birmingham). Office: Mc Millan Assocs Ste 900 1929 3rd Ave N Birmingham AL 35203 Home Phone: 305-871-7462; Office Phone: 205-324-6881. Business E-Mail: george@mcmillan-associates.com.

MCMILLAN, LEE RICHARDS, II, lawyer; b. New Orleans, Aug. 26, 1947; s. John H. and Phoebe (Skillman) McM.; m. Lynne Clark Pottharst, June 27, 1970; children: Leslie Clark, Hillary Anne, Lee Richards III. BS in Commerce, Washington and Lee U., 1969; JD, Tulane U., 1972; LLM in Taxation, NYU, 1976. Bar: La. 1972. Assoc. Jones, Walker, Waechter, Poitevent, Carrere & Denegre, New Orleans, 1976-79, ptnr., 1979—, sect. head, corp. and securities sect., 1987—90, 1994—2002, exec. com., 1990—94, 1996—99, 2001—02, chmn. exec. com., 1991—94, 1996—98, 2001—02. Vice chmn. Mech. Equipment Co., Inc., New Orleans, 1980—86, chmn. bd., 1986—, pres., 1989—99; mem. The Bus. Coun. Greater New Orleans, 1998—, exec. com., 1999—; bd. dirs. The Chamber/New Orleans and the River Region, 1996—98; trustee Alton Ochsner Med. Found., 1995—2003. Trustee New Orleans Mus. Art., 1989-95; bd. dirs. Bur. Govt. Rsch. New Orleans, 1987-93, Louise S. McGehee Sch., New Orleans, 1982-88, co-chmn. capital fund dr., 1984-86, pres. bd. dirs., 1986-88; bd. govs. Isidore Newman Sch., New Orleans, 1991-95. Lt. JACG USNR, 1972-75. Mem. ABA (com. on negotiated acquisitions 1986-94), La. State Bar Assn. (chmn. corp. and bus. law sect. 1985-86, mem. com. on bar admissions 1986-87), Young Pres. Orgn., Washington and Lee U. Alumni Assn. (bd. dirs. 1995-99). Republican. Episcopalian. Avocation: sailing. Office: Jones Walker Waechter Poitevent Carrere & Denegre 201 Saint Charles Ave Ste 5100 New Orleans LA 70170-5101

MCMILLAN, M. SEAN, lawyer; Diploma, U. Munich, 1963; cert., Internat. Sch., Copenhagen, Denmark, 1962; SB, U. So. Calif., 1967; JD, Harvard U., 1970. Bar: Calif. 1971. Spl. projects dir. Mass. Gen. Hosp., Boston, 1967-70; ptnr. Keatinge, Libbott, Bates & Loo, Los Angeles, 1970-74, Loo, Merideth & McMillan, Los Angeles, 1974-85, Bryan Cave LLP, Los Angeles/Santa Monica, 1986—2001, Greenberg Traurig LLP, LA, 2001—. Editor: Harvard Internat. Law Jour., 1968-70. Mem. ABA, Am. Soc. Internat. Law. Office: Greenberg Traurig LLP 2450 Colorado Ave Ste 400E Santa Monica CA 90404 Office Phone: 310-586-7700. Business E-Mail: mcmillan@gtlaw.com.

MCMILLAN, MARY BIGELOW, retired minister, volunteer; b. St. Paul, July 30, 1919; d. Charles Henry and Allison (McKibbin) Bigelow; m. Richard McMillan, June 26, 1943; children: Richard Jr., Charles B., Douglas D., M. Allison, Anne E. BA, Vassar Coll., 1941; MDiv, United Theol. Sem. Twin Cities, 1978, DDiv (hon.), 1989. Ordained to ministry Presbyn. Ch., 1978. Asst. min. House of Hope Presbyn. Ch., St. Paul, 1978-82; interim pres. United Theol. Sem. Twin Cities, New Brighton, Minn., 1982-83, ret., 1987. Contbg. author The Good Steward, 1983. Regional dir. Assn. Jr. Leagues, NYC, 1959—61, pres. St. Paul chpt., 1957—59; vice chair Ramsey County Welfare Bd., St. Paul, 1962—66, St. Paul Health and Welfare Planning Coun., 1964—70, F.R. Bigelow Found., St. Paul, 1988—95, also 1st vice chair; 1st vice chair, trustee Wilder Found., 1973—89; active Presbyn. Homes Found., 1996—; trustee Minn. Ch. Found., Mpls., 1984—99, United Theol. Sem. Twin Cities, 1977—89, also chmn. bd. trustees; bd. dirs. Inst. for Ecumenical and Cultural Rsch., Collegeville, Minn., 1982—2003. Recipient award for cmty. planning United Way, 1965, also for yr. round leadership, 1973, Leadership in Cmty. Svc. award YWCA, 1980, Sisterhood award NCCJ, Mpls., 1989, Outstanding Vol. Fundraiser award Minn., 2005; named Disting Alumna, St. Paul Acad. and Summit Sch., 1988 Mem.: Univ. Club, New Century Club. Avocations: knitting, reading. Home: 2925 Lincoln Dr #713 Roseville MN 55113 Personal E-mail: mbmcmo@comcast.net.

MCMILLAN, MICHAEL REID, retired orthopedic surgeon; b. Conway, SC, Aug. 28, 1941; s. Hoyt and Sara Best (Sherwood) McM.; BS, Citadel, 1963; MD, Duke U., 1967. Diplomate Nat. Bd. Med. Examiners, Am. Bd. Orthopedic Surgery; lic. physician, 1971-2001, SC; Intern in medicine Balt. City Hosps., 1967-68; fellow in medicine Johns Hopkins Hosp., Balt., 1967-68; resident in orthopedic surgery Greenville Hosp. Sys. and Greenville Shriners Hosp., 1971-75; practice medicine specializing in orthopedic surgery, Conway, 1975—2000, ret. 2000; Mem. staff Conway Hosp., 1975—2000, chief orthopedics, 1975-82; bd. dirs. Burroughs and Chapin Co., 1990-96, Burroughs Co., Snow Hill Co., Conway. Trustee Burroughs Found., Conway, 1979—. Served to lt. comdr. MC, USN, 3d marine divn., 1968-71; Vietnam. Mem. AMA, NRA, SC Orthopedic Assn., Horry County Med. Soc., Citadel Alumni Assn., Stelling Soc. Bapt., Forest Landowners Assn., Pres.'s Club Heritage Found., Pres.'s Coun. Brookgreen Gardens, Nat. Trust, SC Hist. Soc., Found. Econ. Edn., Save-the-Redwoods-League, Am. Legion, Civil War Preservation Trust, Third Bn. Third Marines RVN Assn., Horry County Citadel. Republican. Home: 1400 9th Ave Conway SC 29526-4106

MCMILLAN, NATHANIEL (NATE MCMILLAN), professional basketball coach; b. Raleigh, NC, Aug. 3, 1964; m. Michelle McMillan; children: Jamelle, Brittany Michelle. Student, Chowan Coll., Murfreesboro, NC, 1982—84, NC State U., 1984—86. Player Seattle SuperSonics, 1986—98, asst. coach, 1998—2000, interim head coach, 2000—01, head coach, 2001—05, Portland Trail Blazers, 2005—. Named to All-NBA Defensive Second Team, 1994, 1995, Nat. Jr. Coll. Men's Basketball Coaches Assn. Hall of Fame, 2001. Achievements include holding the NBA single-game record for rookie assists. Avocation: football. Office: Portland Trail Blazers Rose Garden One Center Ct Portland OR 97227 *

MCMILLAN, ROBERT RALPH, lawyer; b. NYC, May 21, 1932; s. Harry and Vivian (Beatty) McM.; m. Phoebe Parker Bunn, Nov. 2, 1996; children: Robin, Karen, Kenneth. Student, Adelphi U., 1951-52, 55-56; JD, Bklyn. Law Sch., 1960. Bar: N.Y. 1960. Spl. asst. staff of Richard M. Nixon, NY., Washington, 1960, 64-65; counsel Senator Kenneth B. Keating, Washington, 1960-62; govt. rels. advisor Mobil Oil Co., NYC, 1962-63, 65-68; v.p. Avon Products, NYC, 1973-78, 79-85; sr. v.p. A&S Dept. Stores, NYC, 1978-79; counsel Rivkin, Radler, Bayh, Hart & Kremer, Uniondale, NY, 1986-91; ptnr. McMillan, Rather, Bennett & Farinoci, P.C., Melville, NY, 1991—2003, Fischbein Badillo Wagner Harding, Melville, 2003—05, Bee Ready Fishbein Hatter & Donovan LLP, Melville, 2005—. Chmn. Panama Canal Commn., 1993-94; mem. nat. adv. coun. FannieMae, 1998-2000, co-hosts Face-Off, PBS, NY. News commentator Sta. WLIW-TV, 1993—; columnist, Anton Community Newspapers, Long Island; occasional columnist for Newsday. Trustee Adelphi U., 1984-89; bd. dirs. L.I. (N.Y.) Assn.; chmn. L.I. Housing Parntership, 1988-2002. 1st lt. U.S. Army, 1952-54. Decorated Bronze Star; recipient Excellence in Leadership award, Helen Keller Services for the Blind, Humanitarian award, Alzheimer's Assn. Mem.: AMA (bd. trustees 2002—), Suffolk County Bar Assn., Nassau County Bar Assn. Republican. Avocations: golf, fishing. Home Phone: 516-746-1193; Office Phone: 516-746-5599. E-mail: mcmillanr@aol.com.

MCMILLAN, TERRY L., writer, educator; b. Port Huron, Mich., Oct. 18, 1951; d. Edward McMillan and Madeline Washington Tillman; 1 child, Solomon Welch; m. Jonathan Plummer, 1998 (div. 2005). BA in Journalism, U. Calif., Berkeley, 1979; postgrad., Columbia Univ., NYC, 1979. Instr. U. Wyoming, Laramie, 1987-88; prof. U. Ariz., Tucson, 1988-91. Author: Mama, 1987 (Nat. Book award Before Columbus Found.), Disappearing Acts, 1989, Waiting to Exhale, 1992, How Stella Got Her Groove Back, 1996, A Day Late & A Dollar Short, 2001, The Interruption of Everything, 2005 (NY Times and Publishers Weekly hardcover bestseller list); editor: Breaking Ice: An Anthropology of Contemporary African-American Fiction, 1990; screenwriter (with Ron Bass) (movies) Waiting to Exhale, 1995, How Stella Got Her Groove Back, 1998. Recipient NY Found.for the Arts Fellowship, 1986, Nat.Endowment for the Arts fellowship, 1988, Doubleday/Columbia Univ. Lit. Fellowship, MacDowell Colony fellow, Yaddo Artist Colony fellow (three times).

MCMILLAN, WILLIAM P., lawyer; b. Roanoke Rapids, NC, Mar. 22, 1960; BA with highest distinction, U. Va., 1982; JD with high honors, Duke U., 1985. Bar: Tex. 1985, NC 1994. Ptnr. real estate and creditor's rights Katten Muchin Zavis Rosenman, Charlotte, NC. Mem.: ABA, NC Bar Assn., Mecklenburg County Bar Assn. Office: Katten Muchin Zavis Rosenman 401 S Tryon St, Ste 2600 Charlotte NC 28202 Office Phone: 704-444-2030. Office Fax: 704-344-3065. E-mail: william.mcmillan@kmzr.com.

MCMILLEN, ELIZABETH CASHIN, artist; b. Chgo. d. James Blaine and Hortense (Fears) Cashin; m. John Stephen Jerabek; 1 child, Michael N. Student, Western Coll. for Women, 1961-63; BA, Bard Coll., 1965. Coord. com. and juror Spectra I, sponsor state exhbn. women artists Westbrook Coll., Portland, Maine, 1979; dir. Hancock County Auditorium Art Gallery, Ellsworth, Maine, 1984, 85. Exhibited at Frick Gallery, Belfast, Maine, 1993, 94, Maine Coast Artists Juried Show, Rockport, 1994, Portland Children's Mus., 1995, Lakes Gallery, Sebago, Maine, 1995—, Maine Coast Artists, Rockport, 1998, Portland Mus. Art Biennial, 1998, 2001, American Embassy Santiago Chili, 1998—, Maine Art Gallery, Wiscasset, 2001, Payson Gallery, Portland, 2002, June Fitzpatrick at MECA, Portland, 2004, 05, 07, U. Maine Mus. Art., Bangor, 2005, Ctr. for Maine Contemporary Art, Rockport, 2005, Portland, 2007, Portland Mus. Art Biennial, 2007; one-person shows include Area Gallery, Portland, 1994, Frick Gallery, Belfast, Maine, 1995, Lakes Gallery, Sebago, Maine, 1997, June Fitzpatrick Alternative, Portland, 1999, June Fitzpatrick Gallery, Portland, 2001; two persons show Maine Coast Artists, Rockport, 1996. Dem. chair Town of Lamoine, Maine, 1984-85, 86-87, 88-89; legislation coord. Amnesty Internat., Ellsworth, 1991-97. Democrat. Episcopalian. Avocations: writing, politics, teaching, African-American history.

MCMILLEN, MARIETA LOUISE, art educator; b. Kansas City, Kans., May 2, 1937; d. John Sanford and Dorothy Louise Spurgeon; adopted children: Jon Jason(dec.), Wayne Carey. EdB, Kans. U., 1964, M in Art Edn., 1964; postgrad., Art Inst., Kansas City, Mo., 1973—75. Artist Hallmark Cards, Kansas City, Mo., 1955—58; H.S. art tchr. Unified Sch. Dist. 500, Kansas City, Kans., 1962—65, elem. and secondary sch. art tchr., 1971—95; jr. and sr. H.S. art tchr. Unified Sch. Dist. 458, Basehor, Kans., 1966—71; adj. prof. Davis Coll., Johnson City, NY, 2001—. Infant and toddler tchr. U. Mo. Berkeley Ctr., Kansas City, 1960—99; asst. to phys. therapy Presbyn. Manor, Kansas City, Kans., 1971—72. Author: (novels) Death is Belligerent, 2004, Death is Compulsive, 2005. Adoptive parent Kansas City Kans. Black Adoption Agy., 1973, 1980; foster parent Kansas City Kans. S.S., 1985—95; acdtive fgn. exch. students Am. Field Svc., Kansas City, Kans., 1989—91; art tchr. Home Schoolers, Johnson City, 2004—06; active Bethel Bapt. Ch. Scholar, David Nance S. Found., 1958—62, Maude Ellsworth S. Found., 1961—62. Republican. Avocations: creative writing, camping, fishing, fossil records. Office: Davis College 400 Riverside Dr Johnson City NY 13790

MCMILLEN, ROBERT STEWART, lawyer; b. Yonkers, NY, Feb. 25, 1943; s. David Harry and Blodwyn Elizabeth (Evans) McM; m. Dorothea Anne Murray, July 2, 1966; children: Elissa London (Mrs. Elliott Aten), Tara Evans. BS, U. Rochester, 1964; JD cum laude, Albany Law Sch. Union U., 1969. Bar: N.Y. 1969, U.S. Dist. Ct. (no. dist.) N.Y. 1969. Assoc. Clark, Bartlett & Caffry, Glens Falls, NY, 1969-73; ptnr. Caffry, Pontiff, Stewart, Rhodes & Judge, Glens Falls, 1974-80; prin. Bartlett, Pontiff, Stewart & Rhodes, P.C., Glens Falls, 1981—. Sr. law examiner N.Y. State Bd. Law Examiners, Albany, 1986-2001, bd. mem. 2001—; bd. dirs. Cmty. Title Agy., Inc., Glens Falls, 1984—, pres., 1984-99, v.p., sec., 1999—. Editor-in-chief Albany Law Rev., 1968-69. Bd. dirs., officer Voluntary Action Ctr. of Glens Falls Area, Inc., 1970-97; bd. dirs., treas. Arts and Crafts Ctr. of Warren County, Inc., Glens Falls, 1984-94; mem. Warren County Rep. Com., Queensbury, N.Y., 1979-2001; alt. or del. Rep. Jud. Nomination Com. 4th Jud. Dist. N.Y., 1977—. Recipient Disting. Svc. award Voluntary Action Ctr. of Glens Falls Area, Inc., 1990. Mem. ABA, Nat. Conf. Bar Examiners (mem. multistate performance test com. 2001-04, multistate essay examination com. 2005—), N.Y. State Bar Assn. (mem. com. profl. ethics 1990-99, 2000—), Warren County Bar Assn. (bd. dirs. 1979-82, treas. 2001-07, v.p. 2007—), Adirondack Regional C. of C. (bd. dirs. 1997-2000, vice chmn. 1999-2000, counsel 2000—), Rotary. Avocations: travel, downhill skiing, boating. Home: 147 Assembly Point Rd Lake George NY 12845-5201 Office: 1 Washington St Glens Falls NY 12801-2963 Office Phone: 518-792-2117. Business E-Mail: rsm@bpsrlaw.com.

MCMILLER, ANITA WILLIAMS, leasing company executive; b. Chgo., Dec. 23, 1946; d. Chester Leon and Marion Claudette (Martin) Williams; m. Robert Melvin McMiller, July 29, 1967 (div. 1980). BS in Edn., No. Ill. U., 1968; MBA, Fla. Inst. Tech., 1979; M of Mil. Arts and Sci., U.S. Army Command & Gen. Staff Coll., 1990; postgrad., U.S. Army War Coll., Carlisle, Pa., 1993-94. Social worker Cook County, Chgo., 1968-69; recruiter analyst, dir. pers. State of Ill., Chgo., 1969-75; commd. 1st lt. U.S. Army, 1975, advanced through grades to col., 1996; dep. comdr., ops. officer Bremerhaven (Germany) Terminal, Ft. Eustis, Va. and Okinawa; comdr. 1320th Port Batt, 1991-93; comdr. 1320th Port Battalion U.K. Terminal, Felixstowe, Great Britain, 1991-93; dep. legis. asst. to Chmn. Joint Chiefs of Staff The Pentagon, Washington, 1994-98; pres., CEO Trove Internat., 1999—2002; v.p. ATC Leasing, Kenosha, Wis., 1999—; cons. Trove Internat., Washington, 2002—. Instr. Ctrl. Tex. Coll., Hanau, Germany, 1981-83, Phillips Bus. Coll., Alexandria, Va., 1983-84, City Colls. Chgo., 1987-89. Editor: Rocks, Inc. Pictoral Album, 1996, Alpha Kappa Alpha 75th Commemorative Album, 1997; contbr. articles to profl. jours. Child adv., foster mother Army Cmty. Svc., Hanau, 1980-83; tutor Parent-Tchr. Club Hanau Schs., 1981-83; vol. Vis. Nurses Assn. No. Va., 1983-85; coord., English tutor Adopt-a-Sch. Project, Washington, 1983-85; treas. Bremerhaven Girl Scouts Coun., 1987-89; bd. dirs. Project 2000, Boys and Girls Club of Kenosha. Mem.: NAACP, Internat. Coach Fedn., Links, Inc., Nat. Coun. Negro Women, Army Women's Profl. Assn., Internat. Platform Assn., Am. Hist. Assn., Rocks, Inc., Fedn. Bus. Profl. Women, Am. Mgmt. Assn., Am. Soc. for Quality, Assn. U.S. Army, World Affairs Coun., Nat. Def. Transp. Assn. (bd. dirs., v.p.), Army-Navy Club (Washington), Jr. League Washington, Am. Legion, Alpha Kappa Alpha. Avocations: golf, historical research. Home: 404 129th Infantry Dr Joliet IL 60435-5174

MCMILLIN, DAVID ROBERT, chemistry professor; b. East St. Louis, Ill., Jan. 1, 1948; s. Robert Cecil and Clara Rose McMillin; m. Nicole Wilson, Nov. 3, 1974; children: Robert Stephen, Andrew Wilson. BA, Knox Coll., 1969; PhD, U. Ill., 1973. Postdoctoral fellow Calif. Inst. Tech., Pasadena, 1974; asst. prof. chemistry Purdue U., West Lafayette, Ind., 1975-80, assoc. prof., 1980-85, prof., 1985—. Contbr. articles to profl. jours. Recipient F.D. Martin Teaching award Purdue U., 1975. Mem. Am. Chem. Soc., Inter-Am. Photochem. Soc. (sec. 1986-90, v.p. 1994-96, pres. 1996-98), Phi Beta Kappa, Sigma Xi. Presbyterian. Avocations: sports, reading. Office: Purdue U Dept Chemistry 560 Oval Dr West Lafayette IN 47907-2084 Home Phone: 764-463-4815. E-mail: mcmillin@purdue.edu.

MCMILLIN, STEPHEN S., federal official; b. 1966; m. Dawn McMillin; children: Spencer, Christian. BA, U. Tex. Legis. asst. to Sen. Phil Gramm U.S. Senate, fin. economist, legis. dir.; staff mem. com. on banking, housing and urban affairs US Senate; assoc. dir. gen. govt. programs Office Mgmt. & Budget, Exec. Office of the Pres., 2001—05, dep. dir., 2006—, acting dir., 2007—; dep. asst. to Pres., advisor to chief of staff The White House, 2005—06. Office: Exec Office of Pres Eisenhower Exec Office Bldg 1650 Pennsylvania Ave NW Rm 252 Washington DC 20503 *

MCMILLION, MARGARET KIM, foreign service officer; b. New Brighton, Pa., Nov. 4, 1951; d. Theodore M. and Margaret Jane (Houlette) McM. BA, Eisenhower Coll., 1973; MPIA, U. Pitts., 1975; cert., Nat. War Coll., 1990. Analyst, intern Gulf Oil Corp., Pitts., 1974; polit. and consular officer U.S. Embassy, Kigali, Rwanda, 1975-77, consular officer Taipei, Taiwan, 1977-79; travel svcs. officer Am. Inst. in Taiwan, Taipei, 1979; desk officer Office of West African Affairs U.S. Dept. of State, Washington, 1979-81; with tng. dept. Fgn. Svc. Inst., Washington, 1981—82; polit. officer. U.S. Embassy, Pretoria, South Africa, 1982—85; with Thai lang. tng. dept., Washington, 1985-86; prin. officer U.S. Consulate, Udorn, Thailand, 1986—89; asst. dir. Office of Korean Affairs, Washington, 1990—91; spl. asst. under sec. for polit. affairs U.S. Dept. State, Washington, 1991—92; polit. counselor U.S. Embassy, Bangkok, 1992—95; dep. chief Mission in Vientiane, Laos, 1996—99; dir. Office for Analysis of Africa, Bur. Intelligence and Rsch., 1999—2001; U.S. amb. to Rwanda, 2001—04; dep. comdr. internat. affairs U.S. Army War Coll., 2004—06; ret. State Dept., 2006. Presbyterian. Achievements include speaks French, Afrikaans, Thai and Lao. Avocations: swimming, hiking, music, reading. Office: 191 Surawangse Rd Bangkok 10500 Thailand Office Phone: 66-861-076-260. Personal E-mail: mkmcmillion@aol.com.

MCMILLON, DOUG, retail executive; Degree in Acctg., U. Ark.; MBA in Fin., U. Tulsa. Buyer and merchandise mgr. various cos.; buyer trainee in sporting goods Wal-Mart Stores, Inc., 1984—91, v.p. and gen. merchandise mgr. Sam's Club Internat., sr. v.p. and gen. merchandise mgr., 1999—2002, exec. v.p. merchandising Sam's Club div., 2002—, pres., CEO Sam's Club div. Bentonville, Ark., 2005—. Office: Wal-Mart Stores Inc 702 SW Eighth St Bentonville AR 72716

MCMINDES, ROY JAMES, aggregate company executive; b. Essex, Md., July 12, 1923; s. Roy Preston and Edith S. (Sh) McMindes; m. Prudence Atsinger, June 8, 1946; children: Gail Karen, Joan Susan, James Lee. BS, U. Md., 1948. Pres. Sheridan Corp., Lebanon, Pa., 1951—, Grays Ferry Brick Co., Lebanon, 1971—2001, Waylite Co., Lebanon, 1976-88. Chmn. bd. Peoples Nat. Bank, Lebanon, 1984—92, dir., 1965—92. Bd. dirs. Lebanon YMCA, 1968—86, Good Samaritan Hosp., Lebanon, 1970—93. With A.C. USN, 1943—46, with USNR, 1946—52. Recipient Founders Day award, Lebanon Valley Coll., 1987. Mem.: Lebanon Valley C. of C. (pres. 1973), Lebanon Country Club, Jesters, Shriners. Republican. Presbyterian. Office: 1212 W Maple St Lebanon PA 17046-2701

MCMINN, J. B., retired philosophy educator, composer; b. Pt. Neches, Tex., Nov. 12, 1922; s. Joe Byron and Mary Thelma (Odom) McMinn; m. Dorothy Louise Smith, Aug. 31, 1944 (div. May 15, 1969); children: Jan Branton, Robert Errol. BA in English and religious studies, La. Coll., 1943; ThM in Hellenistic Greek, So. Sem., 1946; postgrad., La. State U., 1948; PhD in Hellenistic Greek, So. Sem., 1951; MA in Classical Greek and Philosophy, Tulane U., 1960, postgrad., 1968, U. Athens, 1970, postdoctoral in Modern Greek, 1979. Asst. prof. English La. Coll., 1948—51; tchg.

asst. in classics Newcomb Coll., 1951—52, Tulane U., 1952—54, asst. prof. classics, 1953—58; from asst. prof. philosophy to assoc. prof. to prof. philosophy U. Ala., 1960—87. Vis. prof. philosophy Miles Coll., 1990; vis. assoc. prof. philosophy and classics Tulane U., 1960, 61; spkr., lectr., presenter in field. Contbr. articles to profl. jours.;, composer piano and vocal pieces; contbr. spirit song for Million Dollar Band of U. Ala. Fight On to Victory, 1987, poetry to anthologies; author: (book of poetry and songs) Une Petite Ménagerie, 1997, (plays) Waiting for Gotdough, 1995, (book) "Mythtaken": Le Mot de L' Énigme, 2002. Rep. commr., New Orleans, 1956—60; mem. So. Soc. Christian Leadership Conf., New Orleans, 1954—60. Cadet officer USNR, 1941—42. Recipient Merit award, U. Ala. Band Assn., 1991, VIP award, Internat. Soc. Poets, 1996, grad. scholarship in classical langs., Tulane U., 1951—54, tchg. assistantship in classical langs., 1951, Fulbright Adj. Lectr. award., 1972, West Germany Lectr. award, 1973, tchg. and rsch. grants in field, Internat. Poet of Merit award, 1996. Mem.: ASCAP, Poetry Soc. Am., Acad. Am. Poets, Nat. Acad. Popular Music-Songwriters Hall of Fame, Internat. Soc. Poets (life), Eta Sigma Phi. Home Phone: 432-366-4534.

MCMORRIS, JERRY, transportation company, sports team executive; Past CEO NW Transport Svc, Denver; chair, pres., CEO Colorado Rockies, Denver, 1993—. Office: 4765 Oakland St Denver CO 80239-2717

MCMORRIS RODGERS, CATHY, congresswoman; b. Salem, Oreg., May 22, 1969; m. Brian Rodgers, Aug. 5, 2006; 1 child, Cole McMorris. BA in Pre-Law, Pensacola Christian Coll., Fla., 1990; MBA, U. Wash., 2002. Mem. Wash. State Ho. Reps. from 7th Dist., 1994—2004, minority leader, 2002—03; mem. US Congress 5th Wash. dist., 2005—, mem. armed svcs. com., nat. resources com., edn. & labor com. Recipient Cornerstone award, Assn. Wash. Bus., 1995—96, Sentinal award, Wash. State Law Enforcement Assn., 1996, Guardian of Small Bus. award, Nat. Fedn. Ind. Bus., 1996, Gold Medal, Ind. Bus. Assn., 1996. Mem.: Wash. Women for Survival of Agr., Wash. Rural Health Assn., Wash. State Farm Bur. (Legislator of the Year 1997), Wash. State Cattlemen's Assn., N.E. Wash. Women in Timber. Republican. Office: 1708 Longworth Ho Office Bldg Washington DC 20515-4705 also: 10 N Post 6th Fl Spokane WA 99201 Office Phone: 202-225-2006. *

MCMORROW, MARY ANN GROHWIN, retired state supreme court justice; b. Chgo., Jan. 16, 1930; m. Emmett J. McMorrow, May 5, 1962; 1 dau., Mary Ann. Attended, Rosary Coll., 1948—50; JD, Loyola U., 1953. Bar: Ill. 1953, U.S. Dist. Ct. (7th dist.) Ill. 1960, U.S. Supreme Ct. 1976. Atty. Riordan & Linklater Law Offices, Chgo., 1954—56; asst. state's atty. Cook County, Chgo., 1956-63; sole practice Chgo., 1963-76; judge Cir. Ct. Cook County, 1976-85, Ill. Appellate Ct., 1985-92; justice Ill. Supreme Ct., 1992—2006, chief justice, 2002—05. Faculty adv. Nat. Jud. Coll., U. Nev., 1984. Contbr. articles to profl. jours. Mem. Chgo. Bar Assn., Ill. State Bar Assn., Women's Bar Assn. of Ill. (pres. 1975-76, bd. dirs. 1970-78), Am. Judicature Soc., Northwestern U. Assocs., Ill. Judges Assn., Nat. Assn. Women Judges, Advocates Soc., Northwest Suburban Bar Assn., West Suburban Bar Assn., Loyola Law Alumni Assn. (bd. govs. 1985—), Ill. Judges Assn. (bd. dirs.), Cath. Lawyers Guild (v.p.), The Law Club of the City of Chgo., Inns of Ct.

MCMULLAN, WILLIAM PATRICK, III, investment banker; b. Newton, Miss., Dec. 29, 1952; s. William Patrick Jr. and Rosemary (Lyons) McM.; m. Rachel Smylie McPherson, Oct. 16, 1982. BA, Vanderbilt U., 1974; MBA, U. Pa., 1976. V.p. Lehman Bros. Kuhn Loeb, NYC, 1976-82; assoc. dir. Prudential-Bache Securities, NYC, 1982-85; mng. dir. Donaldson, Lufkin & Jenrette Securities Corp., NYC, 1985-2000; mng. dir., chmn. global health care Credit Suisse First Boston, NYC, 2000—03; sr. mng. dir., co-head global healthcare Bear, Stearns & Co., NYC, 2003—. Bd. dirs. Scenic Hudson, Gilda's Club Worldwide, Lar Lubovitch Dance Co., Project Reach Youth, Consolidated Corp. Fund, Lincoln Ctr., Good Dog Found. Mem. Met. Club, Mashomack Fish and Game Club, Confrerie des Chevaliers du Tastevin. Home: 607 6th St Brooklyn NY 11215-3701 Office: Bear Stearns & Co 383 Madison Ave New York NY 10179 Office Phone: 212-272-2392. Personal E-mail: pmcmullan@bear.com.

MCMULLEN, CURTIS T., mathematics professor; b. May 21, 1958; BA, Williams Coll., 1980; PhD, Harvard U., 1985. Faculty MIT, Cambridge, Mass., 1985, MSRI, 1986, Inst. Advanced Study, Princeton, NJ, 1986—87, Princeton U., NJ, 1987—90; prof. U. Calif., Berkeley, 1990—97, Harvard U., Cambridge, Mass., 1997—. Author: Logic Minimization Algorithms for VLSI Synthesis, 1984, Complex Dynamics and Renormalization, 1994, Renormalization and 3-Manifolds which Fiber over the Circle, 1996, (course notes) Riemann surfaces, dynamics and geometry, 1998, Hyperbolic manifolds, discrete groups and ergodic theory, 1996, Complex Manifolds, 1996, Complex Analysis, 1993, 1995, Theichmuller Theory, 1993; contbr. articles to profl. jours. Recipient Fields medal, 1998; grantee Guggenheim Fellowship, 2004. Mem.: AAAS, NAS, Am. Acad. Arts & Sci. (elected mem. 1998). Office: Mathematics Dept Harvard U One Oxford St 523 Science Center Cambridge MA 02138-2901 Office Phone: 617-495-0396. Office Fax: 617-485-5132. *

MCMULLEN, SUSAN TAYLOR, librarian; b. Oneida, NY, Mar. 7, 1956; d. Bert L. and Doris A. Taylor; m. John G. McMullen, June 4, 1977; children: Allison, Benjamin. BA, SUNY, Geneseo, 1977, MLS, 1978; MSc, Syracuse U., 2002. Head reference libr. Pawtucket Pub. Libr., RI, 1979—87; sr. reference/electronic info. libr. Seekonk Pub. Libr., Mass., 1987—95; libr. info. resources Roger Williams U., Bristol, RI, 1995—. Presenter in field. Contbr. articles to profl. jours. Mem.: NEA, ALA, Assn. Coll. and Rsch. Librs. Democrat. Episcopalian. Avocations: gardening, reading, weaving. Home: 10 Musket Rd Swansea MA 02777 Office: Roger Williams Univ One Old Ferry Rd Bristol RI 02809 Office Phone: 401-254-3086. Business E-Mail: smcmullen@rwu.edu.

MCMULLEN, W. RODNEY, financial officer; BS in Acctg., U. Ky., 1981, BBA in Fin., 1981, MS in Acctg., 1982. CPA. Fin. analyst The Kroger Co., Cin., 1985-88, asst. treas., 1988-90, v.p. planning and capital mgmt., 1990-93, v.p. fin. svcs. and control, 1993-95, group v.p., chief fin. officer, 1995-97, chief fin. officer, sr. v.p., 1997-2000, exec. v.p. strategy, planning and fin., 2000—03, vice chmn., 2003—. Dir. Cin. Fin. Corp. Office: The Kroger Co 1014 Vine St Cincinnati OH 45202-1100

MCMULLIN, RUTH RONEY, retired publishing executive; b. NYC, Feb. 9, 1942; d. Richard Thomas and Virginia (Goodwin) Roney; m. Thomas Ryan McMullin, Apr. 27, 1968; 1 child, David Patrick. BA, Conn. Coll., 1963; M Pub. and Pvt. Mgmt., Yale U., 1979. Market rschr. Aviation Week Mag., McGraw-Hill Co., NYC, 1962-64; assoc. editor, bus. mgr. Doubleday & Co., NYC, 1964-66; mgr. Natural History Press, 1967-70; v.p., treas. Weston (Conn.) Woods, Inc., 1970-71; staff assoc. GE, Fairfield, Conn., 1979-82; mng. fin. analyst GECC Transp., Stamford, Conn., 1982—84; credit analyst corp. fin. dept. GECC, Stamford, Conn., 1984-85; sr. v.p. GECC Capital Markets Group, Inc., NYC, 1985-87; exec. v.p., COO, CEO, John Wiley & Sons, NYC, 1987—90, pres., CEO; CEO Harvard Bus. Sch. Pub. Corp., Boston, 1991-94; mem. chmn.'s com., acting CEO UNR Industries Inc., Chgo., 1991-92, also bd. dirs.; mgmt. fellow, vis. prof. Sch. Mgmt. Yale U., New Haven, 1994-95; chairperson trustees Eagle-Picher Personal Injury Settlement Trust, 1996—; chairperson Claims Processing Facility, Inc., 1998—. Bd. dirs. Bausch & Lomb, Rochester, N.Y.; vis. prof. Sch. Mgmt., Yale U., New Haven, 1994-95. Mem. dean's adv. bd. Sch. Mgmt. Yale U., 1985—92; bd. dirs. Yale U. Alumni fund, 1986—92, Yale U. Press, 1988—99, Math. Scis. Edn. Bd., 1990—93; bd. dirs., treas. Mighty Eighth Air Force Heritage Mus., 2000—; chmn. Mighty Eighth Found., 2003—; bd. dirs. Savannah Symphony, 1999—2003, The Landings Club, 2002—04. Mem. N.Y. Yacht Club, Yale Club. Avocations: sailing, skiing, golf, tennis. Home: 8 Breckenridge Ln Savannah GA 31411-1701 Office: Eagle Picher Trust P O box 206 652 Main St Cincinnati OH 45202-2542 Personal E-mail: rrmcmullin@aya.yale.edu. Business E-Mail: ruthmcmullin@direcway.com.

MCMURPHY, MICHAEL ALLEN, energy company executive, lawyer; b. Dothan, Ala., Oct. 1, 1947; s. Allen L. and Mary Emily (Jacobs) McM.; m. Maureen Daly, Aug. 8, 1970; children: Matthew, Kevin, Patrick. BS, USAF Acad., 1969; MA, St. Mary's U., San Antonio, 1972; JD, U. Tex., 1975. Bar: Tex. 1975, U.S. Supreme Ct. 1977, U.S. Ct. Mil. Appeals, D.C. 1978, U.S. Ct. Appeals (fed. cir.) 1982. Commd. 2d lt. USAF, 1969, advanced through grades to capt.; instr. Air U., Ala., 1975-79; resigned USAF, 1979; atty., advisor Oak Ridge (Tenn.) ops. U.S. Dept. Energy, 1979-83; gen. counsel COGEMA, Inc., Washington, 1983-87, v.p., 1987-88, pres., CEO, Bethesda, Md., 1988—; pres. Areva T&D, Inc., 2005—. Pres., CEO Va. Fuels, Inc., Lynchburg, 1987-92; co-CEO AREVA Enterprises, Inc., Washington, DC, 2002-03, vice chmn., pres., 2003—; bd. dirs. Soc. Gen. Techs. Nouvelles, S.A., St. Quentin, France, Transnuclear, Inc., Columbia, Md., Canberra Industries, Meriden, Conn., Cogema Resources, Inc, Casper, Wyo., Areva, Inc., Lynchburg, Va. and Richland, Wash.; bd. govs. Duke Cogema Stone & Webster, LLC, Charlotte, N.C., 1998—; pres. Uranium Producers Am., 1991-92 Mem. editorial bd. Air Force Law Rev., 1977-79. Lt. col. USAFR ret., 1992. Decorated chevalier Nat. Order of Merit (France). Avocation: skiing. Home: 9324 Garden Ct Potomac MD 20854 Office: COGEMA Inc 1 Bethesda Ctr 4800 Hampden Ln Ste 1100 Bethesda MD 20814 Business E-Mail: mcmurphy@cogema-inc.com.

MCMURRAY, CLAUDIA ANNE, federal agency administrator, lawyer; d. Raymond D. and Sally Kathryn (Martin) McM.; m. Donald V. Moorehead, June 6, 1987. AB with honors, Smith Coll., 1980; JD, Georgetown U., 1984. Bar: D.C. 1985. Legis. asst. to Rep. Bill Emerson US Ho. Reps, Washington, 1980-81; law clk. Office of Counsel to the Pres. The White House, Washington, 1983-84; atty. Patton, Boggs & Blow LLP, 1984-87, Kirkland & Ellis LLP, 1987-89; legis. counsel to Senator John W. Warner US Senate, 1989-90, minority counsel Com. on Environment and Pub. Works, 1991—95, gen. counsel to Senator Fred Thompson, 1996—98; v.p. Van Scoyoc Associates, Inc., 1998—2000; assoc. dep. adminstr. & chief of staff to dep. adminstr. EPA, 2000—03; dep. asst. sec for environ., Bur. Oceans & Internat. Environ. & Sci. Affairs US Dept. State, Washington, 2003—06, asst. sec. for oceans, internat. environ., & scientific affairs, 2006—. Editor The Tax Lawyer. Office: US Dept State Harry S Truman Bldg 2201 C St NW Rm 7831 Washington DC 20520

MCMURRAY, JAMIE, race car driver; b. Joplin, Mo., June 3, 1976; Race car driver Brewco Motorsports, Central, Ky., Roush Racing. Film appearances: Talladega Nights: The Ballad of Ricky Bobby, 2006. Fundraiser Autism Soc. Am. Named Champion, Lebanon I-44 Speedway, 1997, Nascar Winston Cup Rookie of Yr., 2003. Achievements include won his first NASCAR cup race at Lowe's Motor Speedway in 2002, becoming the first race car driver in Winston/Nextel cup series history to win in his second career start.

MCMURRY, IDANELLE SAM, educational consultant; b. Morganfield, Ky., Dec. 6, 1924; d. Sam Anderson and Aurelia Marie (Robertson) McM. BA, Vanderbilt U., 1945, MA, 1946. Tchr. English Abbot Acad., Andover, Mass., 1946-50, Hockaday Sch., Dallas, 1951-54, San Jacinto High Sch., Houston, 1954-55; dean of girls Kinkaid Sch., Houston, 1955-63; headmistress Harpeth Hall Sch., Nashville, 1963-79, Hockaday Sch., Dallas, 1979-89; ret.; now pvt. sch. cons. The Edn. Group, Dallas. Bd. dirs. Ednl. Records Bur., 1979-85, trustee, 1980-85. Bd. dirs. Tex. council Girl Scouts U.S., 1980-82, Town North YMCA; trustee Winston Sch., 1979-85, Spl. Care Sch., 1979-81, Asheville Sch., Manzano Day Sch. Mem. Nat. Study Sch. Evaluation (bd. dirs. 1979-83), Headmasters Assn., Nat. Assn. Ind. Schs. (bd. dirs. 1974-84, acad. com. 1974-79, sec. 1978-80, chmn. 1980-84), So. Assn. Ind. Schs. (pres. 1974-75), Tenn. Assn. Ind. Schs. (pres. 1967-68), Mid-South Assn. Ind. Schs. (pres. 1972-73), Ind. Schs. Assn. S.W. (v.p. 1967—), Nat. Assn. Prins. Schs. for Girls (sec. 1970-72, pres. 1975-77, coun. 1970-79), Nat. Assn. Secondary Sch. Prins., Country Day Sch. Headmasters Assn. (exe. com. 1984-87, v.p. 1988-89), So. Assn. Colls. and Schs. (adminstrv. coun. 1974-77, ctrl. reviewing com. 1972-77, vice chmn. secondary commn. 1975-76, chmn. 1976-77, bd. dirs. 1976-81), Ladies Hermitage Assn., Vanderilt Aid Soc. (sec. 1971-73, pres. 1994-96), Ind. Edn. Svcs. (trustee 1980-88, chmn. 1986-88), Susan Komen Found. (adv. bd.), Belle Meade Club, Centennial Club, Phi Beta Kappa, Pi Beta Phi. Democrat. Presbyterian. Office: 5 Strawberry Hill Nashville TN 37215-4118

MCMURRY, JAMES FINLEY, JR., endocrinologist, researcher; b. Sentinel, Okla., Aug. 25, 1940; s. James Finley and Anna Jo McMurry; m. Rebecca L. Lomax, May 21, 1987. MD, U. Okla., 1965. Diplomate Am. Bd. Internal Medicine. Chief, med. services USAF Hosp., Dover, Del., 1969—71; endocrinologist Scott and White Clinic, Temple, Tex., 1972—81; assoc prof., internal medicine Tex. A & M U., Temple, 1979—81; asst prof. internal medicine U. Ky., Lexington, 1981—84, Georgetown U., Washington, 1984—87; pvt. practice Rockville, Md., 1984—. Editor: Jefferson, Callender and the SALLY Story, 2000; co-author: Anatomy of a Scandal: Thomas Jefferson and the SALLY Story, 2002. Capt. USAF, 1969—71. Fellow: ACP; mem.: Montgomery County Med. Assn., Md. (com. chmn. 1987—89), Am. Diabetes Assn. (pres. South Tex. chpt. 1980—81, pres. DC chpt. 1986—87, chmn. Ky. affiliate 1983—84), Endocrine Soc. Independent. Avocations: history, photography, gardening. Office: 11119 Rockville Pike Ste 409 Rockville MD 20852-3143 Office Phone: 301-468-1820.

MCMURRY, JOHN EDWARD, chemistry professor; b. NYC, July 27, 1942; s. Edward and Marguerite Ann McMurry; m. Susan Elizabeth Sobuta, Sept. 4, 1964; children: Peter Michael, David Andrew, Paul Matthew. BA, Harvard U., 1964; MA, Columbia U., 1965, PhD, 1967. Prof. chemistry U. Calif., Santa Cruz, 1967-80, Cornell U., Ithaca, NY, 1980—. Author: textbooks; assoc. editor: Accounts of Chem. Rsch., 1975—95. Recipient Humboldt Sr. Sci. award, 1987; Sloan Found. fellow, 1969-71; Career awardee NIH, 1975-80. Fellow AAAS; mem. Am. Chem. Soc. Home: 625 Highland Rd Ithaca NY 14850-1411 Office: Cornell Univ Dept Chemistry Baker Lab Ithaca NY 14853 Office Phone: 607-255-4819. E-mail: jem24@cornell.edu.

MCMURTRY, GARY MICHAEL, geochemist, educator; b. Upland, Calif., Feb. 25, 1950; s. James Samuel and Grace Marietta (Tomlinson) McM.; m. Francine Emy Yagawa, Mar. 3, 1979. BS with honors, U. Calif., Riverside, 1972; MS, U. Hawaii, 1975, PhD, 1979. Research geologist U. Calif., San Diego, 1979-80; asst. geochemist U. Hawaii, Honolulu, 1980-86, assoc. geochemist, 1986-88; sci. dir. Hawaii Undersea research 1980-86, assoc. geochemist, 1986-88; sci. dir. Hawaii Undersea research Lab., Honolulu, 1983-88; grad. faculty mem. U. Hawaii, Honolulu, 1982—, assoc. prof. oceanography, 1988—. Cons. TRW Corp., Redondo Beach, Calif., 1979-80; assoc. dir. Electron Microscopy Lab., Honolulu, 1983-86; panelist Nat. Undersea research program NOAA, Washington, 1985—; guest scientist Los Alamos Nat. Lab., 1991-92; affiliate scientist Jet Propulsion Lab., Caltech, Pasadena, Calif., 1999-2000. Contbr. articles to profl. jours. Recipient Antarctic Service medal NSF, 1979. Mem. AAAS, Am. Geophys. Union, Hawaii Acad. Sci., Marine Tech. Soc., Soc. Econ. Paleontologists and Mineralogists, The Planetary Soc., Sigma Xi. Avocations: tennis, surfing, computing. Office: U Hawaii Sch Ocean & Earth Sci/Tech Dept Oceanography 1000 Pope Rd Honolulu HI 96822-2336 Home Phone: 808-395-1005; Office Phone: 808-956-6858. Business E-Mail: garym@soest.hawaii.edu.

MC MURTRY, JAMES GILMER, III, neurosurgeon; b. Houston, June 11, 1932; s. James Gilmer and Alberta Elizabeth (Matteson) McMurtry. Student, Rice U., Houston, 1950—53; MD cum laude, Baylor U., Houston, 1957. Intern Hosp. U. Pa., Phila., 1957—58; resident gen. surgery Baylor U. Affiliated Hosps., Houston, 1958—59; asst. neurol. surgery Coll. Physicians and Surgeons, Columbia U., NYC, 1959—60; asst. resident neurol. surgery and neurology Neurol. Inst. N.Y., Columbia Presbyn. Med. Ctr., NYC, 1960—62, chief resident neurol. surgery, 1963—65, assoc., 1965—68, asst. prof. clin. neurol. surgery, 1968—73, assoc. prof., 1973—89, prof., 1989—2003, Herbert and Linda Gallen prof. neurol. surgery, 2003—05, Herbert and Linda Gallen prof. neurol. surgery emeritus, 2005—. Asst. attending neurol. surgeon Neurol. Inst. N.Y., NYC, 1964—73, assoc. attending neurol. surgeon, 1973—89, attending neurol. surgeon, 1989—2005; chief neurol. surgery clinic Vanderbilt Clinic, Columbia Presbyn. Med. Ctr., NYC, 1964—68; attending-in-charge neurosurgery Lenox Hill Hosp., NYC, 1970—91; assoc. cons. neurol. surgery Englewood (N.J.) Hosp., 1964—70; asst. cons. neurol. surgery Harlem Hosp., NYC, 1964—75; cons. neurol. surgery Bronx (N.Y.) VA Hosp., 1964—65; mem. NIH Parkinson Rsch. Group, Columbia U., 1965—70; mem. med. adv. bd. N.Y. State Athletic Commn. Author: Medical Examination Review Book-Neurological Surgery, 1970, rev. edit., 1975, Neurological Surgery Case Histories, 1975; contbr. articles to profl. jours. Trustee Glimmerglass Opera, Morris-Jumel, Opera Manhattan. Fellow Allen fellow dept. neurol. surgery, Columbia U., 1964—65; scholar Jesse H. Jones scholar, Baylor U. Coll. Medicine, 1953—57. Fellow: ACS, Linnean Soc. (London); mem.: AMA, AAAS, AAUP, Hoover Inst. (coun. mem.), The Med. Soc. of London, Med. Strollers, Baylor U. Coll. Medicine Alumni Assn., Osler Soc., N.Y. County Med. Soc., Med. Soc. State N.Y., N.Y. Neurosurg. Soc., N.Y. Acad. Sci., N.Y. State Neurosurgery Soc., N.Y. State Soc. Surgeons, Pan Am. Med. Assn., Am. Soc. Stereotaxic Surgeons, European Congress Pediatric Neurosurgery, Am. Assn. Neurol. Surgeons, The Harveian Soc., Norfolk Yacht and Country, The Garrick Club (London), The Union Club, The Atheneum (London), Met. Opera Club (N.Y.C., dir. and v.p. 2002), Alpha Omega Alpha. Home: 1 Cobb Ln Tarrytown NY 10591-3003

MCMURTRY, LARRY JEFF, writer; b. Wichita Falls, Tex., June 3, 1936; s. William Jefferson and Hazel Ruth (McIver) McM.; m. Josephine Ballard, July 15, 1959 (div. 1966); 1 child, James. BA, N. Tex. State Coll., 1958; MA, Rice U., 1960. Instr. Tex. Christian U., Ft. Worth, 1961-62; lectr. in English and creative writing Rice U., Houston, 1963-69; co-owner Booked Up Book Store, Washington, from 1970. Vis. prof. George Mason Coll., 1970, Am. U., 1970-71. Author: (novels) Horseman, Pass By, 1961 (Jesse H. Jones award Texas Inst. of Letters 1962), Leaving Cheyenne, 1963, The Last Picture Show, 1966, Moving On, 1970, All My Friends Are Going to be Strangers, 1972, Terms of Endearment, 1975, Somebody's Darling, 1978, Cadillac Jack, 1982, The Desert Rose, 1983, Lonesome Dove, 1985 (Pulitzer prize for Fiction 1986), Texasville, 1987, Anything for Billy, 1988, Some Can Whistle, 1989, Buffalo Girls, 1990, The Evening Star, 1992, Streets of Laredo, 1993, The Late Child, 1995, Dead Man's Walk, 1995, Comanche Moon, 1997, Duane's Depressed, 1999, Boone's Lick, 2000, Sin Killer: The Berrybender Narratives Book One, 2002, The Wandering Hill: The Berrybender Narratives Book Two, 2003, By Sorrow's River: The Berrybender Narratives Book Three, 2003, Folly and Glory: The Berrybender Narratives Book Four, 2004, Loop Group, 2004, Telegraph Days, 2006, When the Light Goes: A Novel, 2007; Co-author (with Diana Ossana) Zeke and Ned, 1997, Pretty Boy Floyd, 1994; Author (non-fiction) Walker Benjamin at Dairy Queen, 1999, Roads: Driving America's Great Highways, 2000, Paradise, 2000, Sacagawea's Nickname: Essays on the American West, 2001, The Colonel and Little Missie: Buffalo Bill, Annie Oakley, and the Beginnings of Superstardom in America, 2005, Oh What a Slaughter: Massacres in the American West: 1846-1890, 2005; (essays) In a Narrow Grave: Essays on Texas, 1968, It's Always We Rambled: An Essay on Rodeo, 1974, Film Flam: Essays on Hollywood, 1987; screenwriter: (with Peter Bogdanovich) The Last Picture Show, 1971 (Academy award nomination best adapted screenplay 1971), Texasville, 1990, Montana, 1990, Falling From Grace, 1992, (with Cybill Shepard) Memphis, 1992, Brokeback Mountain, 2005 (best screenplay-motion picture Hollywood Fgn. Press Assn., Golden Globe award, 2006, British Acad. Film & TV Arts award for adapted screenplay, 2006, Adapted Screenplay, Acad. Motion Pictures Arts & Sciences, 2006); also articles, essays, book revs. in N.Y. Times, Saturday Rev., Washington Post, Am. Film, others. Wallace Stegner fellow, 1960, Guggenheim fellow, 1964; recipient Barbara McCombs/Lon Tinkle award Texas Inst. of Letters, 1986. Mem. Tex. Inst. Letters (Jesse H. Jones award 1962). Mailing: Author Mail Simon & Schuster 1230 Ave of the Americas New York NY 10020-1586 *

MCMURTRY, R. ROY, federal judge; b. Toronto, Ont., Can., May 31, 1932; s. Roland Roy and Doris Elizabeth (Belcher) McM.; m. Ria Jean Macrae, Apr. 18, 1957; children: Janet, James, Harry, Jeannie, Erin, Michael. BA with honors, U. Toronto, 1954; LLB, Osgoode Hall Law Sch., 1958; LLD (hon.), U. Ottawa, 1983, Leeds U., UK, 1988, York U., 1991, U. Toronto, 1998. Bar: Called to bar 1958, created Queen's counsel 1970. Partner firm Benson, McMurtry, Percival and Brown; mem. Provincial Parliament for Eglinton, 1975-85; atty. gen. for Ont., 1975-85; solicitor gen. for Ont., 1978-82; high commnr. for Can. to Gt. Brit. and No. Ireland, 1985-88; ptnr. Blaney, McMurtry Stapells, Toronto, 1988-91; chmn. Can. Football League, 1989-91; assoc. chief justice Ont. Ct. Justice, Toronto, 1991-94, chief justice, 1994-96; chief justice of Ont. Ont. Ct. of Appeal, Toronto, 1996—. Freeman of City of London, 1986. Mem. United Ch. of Can. Office: Ont Ct of Appeal 130 Queen St W Toronto ON Canada M5H 2N5 Office Phone: 416-327-5803. Personal E-mail: cathy.lanni@ontario.ca.

MCNABB, CORRINE RADTKE, librarian; b. Detroit, Dec. 18, 1956; d. Eugene R. and Dorothy A. (Dorosz) Radtke; children: Brynne Catherine, Kalen Daniel. BA, Aquinas Coll., 1978; MS, Drexel U., 1982, cert. advanced study, 1997. Cert. tchr. Pa. Dept. Edn., 1997, SC Dept. Edn., 2005. Assoc. Nat. Libr. Medicine, Bethesda, Md., 1982-83; dir. libr. svcs. Carbondale (Pa.) Gen. Hosp., 1983-85; libr. dir. Interboro Libr., Peckville, Pa., 1985-86; reference libr. U. Scranton, Pa., 1986-87; libr. Cmty. Med. Ctr., Scranton, 1987-95; elem. libr. Carbondale Area Sch. Dist., 1995-96, Mountain View Sch. Dist., Kingsley, Pa., 1996—; adj. faculty Univ. Scranton, 2002—. Bd. dirs. Carbondale Pub. Libr., 1993—. Mem. ASCD, ALA, Pa. Sch. Librs. Assn. Roman Catholic. Avocations: reading, travel, walking. Home: 214 Stoney Creek Rd Clarks Summit PA 18411 Office: Mountain View Elem Libr RR 1 Box 339A Kingsley PA 18826-9778 Home Phone: 570-586-8000; Office Phone: 570-434-2181. Personal E-mail: santafe13@hotmail.com.

MCNABB, DAVID E., business educator, writer; b. LA, Nov. 29, 1932; s. Jay B. McNabb and Josephine P. Recagno; m. Janet C. Lagerquist, June 12, 1962; children: Meghan, Michael, Sara. BA, Calif. State Coll., Fullerton, 1965; MA, U. Wash., Seattle, 1968; PhD, Oreg. State U., Corvallis, 1980. Prof. Pacific Luth. U., Tacoma, 1979—; vis. prof. UMUC-Europe, Heidelberg, Germany, 1998—99, The Evergreen State Coll., Olympia, Wash., 1999—2000, Stockholm Sch. Econs., Riga, Latvia, 2000—07. Vis. scholar Thunderbird Internat. U., Phoenix, 1990. Author: Research Methods for Public Administration, 2002, Research Methods for Political Science, 2004, Public Utilities: Management Challenges, 2005, Knowledge Management In The Public Sector, 2006. Served with USN, 1952—54. Mem.: ASPA, Acad. Polit. Sci., Acad. Mgmt., Rotary. Home: 605 E Barbary Rd Shelton WA 98584 Business E-Mail: mcnabbde@plu.edu.

MCNABB, DIANNE LEIGH, investment banker, accountant; b. Huntsville, Ala., Sept. 7, 1956; d. Walter David and Mary Josephine (Hawkins) McN.; m. William Roland Lantz, July 1, 1983; 1 child, Sarah Elizabeth. BS in Acctg., U. Ala., Tuscaloosa, 1976. CPA, Ga., Ala. Acct. Lilly Flagg Assocs. & Subsidiaries, Huntsville, 1977-78; mgr. Johnston, Joyce & Wigginton, CPA's, Huntsville, 1978-84; sr. mgr. KPMG Peat Marwick, CPA's, Atlanta, 1984-91; mng. dir. A.G. Edwards & Sons, Inc., Atlanta, 1991—. Mem. ways and means com. Atlanta Jr. League, 1991-98; instr., advisor Jr. Achievement, Atlanta, 1985-88; mem. hospitality com. Dem. Nat. Conv., Atlanta, 1988; vol. Ga. Spl. Olympics, Atlanta, 1989-91. Mem. AICPA, Govt. Fin. Officers Assn. (spl. rev. com. 1991-95), Ga. Soc. CPA (govtl. acctg. and auditing com. 1992), Assn. of Govt. Accts. (bd. dirs. Atlanta chpt. 1990-92), Ala. Soc. CPA (sec.-treas. 1984), Am. Soc. Women Accts. (pres. Huntsville chpt. 1983-84), U. Ala. Alumni Assn. (treas. 1983-84), Zeta Tau Alpha (advisor 1988-93, v.p. 1983, treas. 1987-89, pres. 1984, 89-91, panhellenic del. 1988-91, dist. pres. 1993-95, Cert. of Merit 1992, Zeta Lady award 1991, Alum Chum award 1991). Avocations: tennis, scuba. Home: 2530 Alpine Way Duluth GA 30096-4440 Office: A G Edwards 3399 Peachtree Rd NE Ste 1100 Atlanta GA 30326-1150 Office Phone: 404-995-8930.

MCNABB, DONOVAN, professional football player; b. Chgo., Nov. 25, 1976; s. Samuel and Wilma McNabb; m. Raquel Nurse, 2003. Grad. in Speech Comm., Syracuse U., NY, 1998. Backup guard basketball team Syracuse U., 1995—97; quarterback Phila. Eagles, 1999—. Co-host (with Beasley Reece) The Donovan McNabb Show. Established own scholarship found.; mem. Life as a Rookie panel Rookie Symposium, 2000. Named NFL Player of Yr., CBS Radio, 2000; named to All Madden Team, 2000, Nat. Football Conf. Pro Bowl Team, 2000—04. Office: Phila Eagles One NovaCare Way Philadelphia PA 19145 *

MCNABB, DUNCAN J., career military officer; b. Shaw AFB, SC, Aug. 8, 1952; BS, USAF Acad., 1974; MS in Internat. Rels., U. Southern Calif., LA, 1984. Commd. 2d lt. USAF, 1974, advanced through grades to gen., 2005; instr. navigator 14th Mil. Airlift Wing Squadron, Norton AFB, Calif., 1978-79, instr., pilot, chief pilot, 1980-83; gen.'s aide Air Force Inspection and Safety Ctr., Norton AFB, 1983-84; chief plan integration br. Hdqrs. Mil. Airlift Command, Scott AFB, Ill., 1984-86; aide to the comdr. in chief U.S. Transp. Command and Mil. Airlift Command, Scott AFB, 1986-88; chief pilot to ops. officer 17th Mil. Airlift Squadron, Charleston AFB, S.C., 1988-90; comdr. 41st Mil. Airlift Squadron, Charleston AFB, 1990-92; dep. group comdr. 437th Ops. Group, Charleston AFB, 1992; chief Logistics Readiness Ctr. the Joint Staff, Logistics, the Pentagon, Washington, 1993-95; comdr. 89th Ops. Group, Andrews AFB, Md., 1995-96, 62nd Airlift Wing, McChord AFB, Wash., 1996-97, Tanker Airlife Control Ctr., Hdqrs. Air Mobility Command, Scott AFB, 1997—99; dep. dir. programs, Office of Dep. Chief of Staff for Plans & Programs USAF, Washington, 1999, dir. programs, 1999—2002, dep. chief of staff plan & programs, 2002—04; dir. logistics (J-4) The Joint Staff, Washington, 2004—05; comdr. Air Mobility Command, Scott AFB, Ill., 2005—07; vice chief of staff USAF, Washington, 2007—. Decorated Def. Superior Svc. medal, Def. Meritorious Svc. medal, Meritorious Svc. medal with oak leaf cluster, Joint Svc. Commendation medal, Air Force Commendation medal with oak leaf cluster, Air Force achievement medal, Combat Readiness medal with oak leaf cluster, Nat. Def. Svc. medal, Legion of Merit with oak leaf cluster, Armed Forces Expeditionary medal, Southwest Asia Svc. medal with two bronze stars, Humanitarian Svc. medal, Kuwait Liberation medal (Kingdom of Saudi Arabia), Kuwait Liberation medal (Kingdom of Kuwait); recipent Orville Wright award Order of Daedalians. Office: USAF 1670 Air Force Pentagon Washington DC 20330 *

MCNAIR, EMMA LOUISE, minister; b. Ellisville, Miss., Mar. 11, 1935; d. Will and Chanie Prince Bell; m. Willie Charles McNair Jr., Mar. 16, 1956 (dec. Dec. 1967); children: Ruth, Channie, Willie C. Jr., Victor D., Karen L., Yul L. AA in Edn., Prentiss Inst., Miss., 1974; BA in Social Work, Rust Coll., 1979; MDiv, Memphis Theol. Sem., 1983; cert., East Miss. State Hosp., 1991. Ordained deacon 1981, ordained elder 1993. Pastor Victor/Taylor Charge, Senatobia, Miss., 1981—83, Marion/Walhall Parish, Columbia, Miss., 1983—84, Enterprise (Miss.) Cir., Brookhaven (Miss.) Charge, 1988—89; staff chaplain East Miss. Hosp., Meridian, Meth. Med. Ctr., Jackson, Miss., 1991—2000. Address: 153 Dacetown Rd Ellisville MS 39437

MCNAIR, JOHN WILLIAM, JR., civil engineer; b. Asheville, NC, June 17, 1926; s. John William and Annie (Woody) McN.; m. June Clemens Kratz; childrn: Jeffry, Marsha, Cathy. BS in Forestry, Pa. State U., 1950; BSCE, Va. Poly Inst. State U., 1955; postgrad., U. Va., 1957—2004. Registered profl. engr., VA, NC, MD, WV, PA, NY, KY. Forester U.S. Forest Svc., Flagstaff, Ariz., 1950, U.S. Gypsum Co., Altavista, Va., 1951; mem. engring. faculty U. Va., Charlottesville, 1955—58; prin. John McNair & Assocs., Waynesboro, Va., 1958—; owner Brucheum Group, Waynesboro, 1983—; chmn., CEO Info. Systems Support, Inc., Waynesboro, 1998—2007. With Va. Bd. Architects, Profl. Engrs. and Land Surveyors, 1969-79, v.p., 1977-78, pres., 1978-79. Author numerous engring. and land mgmt. study reports. Mem. Waynesboro City Coun., 1968-72, vice mayor, 1970-72; chmn. Waynesboro Indsl. Devel. Authority, 1984-2000. Capt. AUS, 1944-46, 51-53, France, Okinawa. Recipient Disting. Svc. cert. Va. Soc. Profl. Engrs., 1971. Fellow ASCE; mem. Acad. Environ. Engrs. (diplomate), Rotary, Rappahannock River Yacht Club (founding mem.). Republican. Presbyterian. Office Phone: 540-942-1161. Business E-Mail: jmcnair@brucheum.com.

MCNAIR, MARCIA L., language educator, writer, editor; BA in English, Dartmouth Coll., Hanover, 1980; MA in Writing, NYU, NYC, 1989. Asst. editor Essence Mag., NYC, 1980—83; program coord. NYU, NYC, 1984—87; program coord., adj. lectr. CUNY, NYC, 1987—94; asst. prof. English Nassau CC, Garden City, NY, 1995—. Adj. prof. Molloy Coll., Rockville Center, NY, 2002—; ednl. cons. African Am. Mus., Hempstead, NY, 2005—; workshop facilitator Nassau CC, 2005, lectr., 06. Contbr. essays; creative dir.: Diary of a Mad Black Feminist; author: E-males; editor (arts and entertainment): Lakeview Cmty. News, 2006—. Coord. Nassau Cmty. Co. Nat. African Am. Read In, Garden City, NY, 2002—. Recipient Hon. Mention, New Millenium Writers Creative Non-Fiction Contest, 2002; grantee, LI Coun. Arts, 2006. Mem.: Schomburg Ctr. Rsch. Black Culture, Assn. Black Women Higher Edn., LI Writers Guild, Sigma Delta Chi. Office: Nassau CC English Dept One Education Dr Garden City NY 11530

MCNAIR, RUSSELL ARTHUR, JR., lawyer; b. Detroit, Dec. 2, 1934; s. Russell Arthur and Virla (Standish) McN.; m. Rosemary M. Chesbrough, Apr. 6, 1957; children: Julie McNair Schwerin, Russell Arthur III, Douglas S. AB in Econs. cum laude, Princeton U., 1956; JD with distinction, U. Mich., 1960. Bar: Mich. 1960, Fla. 2001. Assoc. Dickinson, Wright, Moon, Van Dusen & Freeman (now Dickinson Wright PLLC), Detroit, 1960-67, ptnr., 1968-98, chmn., 1994-98, cons. mem., 2007—. Adj. prof. U. Detroit Sch. Law, 1968-72; mem. adv. bd. Fin. Transactions Inst., 1984-94; adj. prof. Wayne State U. Law Sch., 1994-96; spkr. in field. Trustee Children's Home, Detroit, 1975-95, pres. 1986-87, hon. trustee 1995—; mem. community leaders coun. United Way, 1994-98; dir. Mich. Jobs Commn., 1995-98, TED Ctr., Delray Beach, Fla., 2006—. Mem.: Mich. Bar Found., Am. Coll. Real Estate Lawyers, Am. Law Inst., Fla. Bar Assn., Mich. Bar Assn. Republican. Presbyterian. Avocations: golf, tennis, platform tennis. Home: 4383 Gleneagles Dr Boynton Beach FL 33436-4802 Office: PO Box 243351 Boynton Beach FL 33424-3351 Home Phone: 561-740-1037; Office Phone: 313-223-3511. Personal E-mail: mcnairs47@bellsouth.net.

MCNAIR, STEVE LATREAL, professional football player; b. Mount Olive, Miss., Feb. 14, 1973; m. Mechelle McNair; 1 child, Tyler. Student, Mt. Olive H.S.; BA, Alcorn State U., 1994. Quarterback Houston Oilers, 1995—96, Tenn. Oilers, 1997—98, Tenn. Titans, 1999—2006, Baltimore Ravens, 2006—. Named to AFC Pro-Bowl Team, 2003, 2005; recipient NFL MVP award, AP, 2003. Office: Baltimore Ravens 1101 Russell St Baltimore MD 21230

MCNALL, SCOTT GRANT, sociologist, educator, academic administrator; b. New Ulm, Minn., Jan. 16, 1941; s. Everett Herman and Dorothy Grant (Brown) McNall; m. Sally Anne Allen, Oct. 31, 1960; children: Miles Allen, Amy Ellen. BA, Portland State U., 1962; PhD, U. Oreg., 1965. Instr. sociology U. Oreg., Eugene, 1964-65; asst. prof. U. Minn., Mpls., 1965-70; from assoc. prof. to prof. Ariz. State U., Tempe, 1970-76; prof., chmn. dept. sociology U. Kans., Lawrence, 1976-89, prof, chmn. dept. Am. studies, 1989-90; dean Coll. Arts and Scis. U. Toledo, 1990-94; provost Calif. State U., Chico, 1994—2007, interim pres., 2003—05; dir. Inst. Sustained Devel., 2007—. Fulbright lectr., Greece, 1968—69; vis. lectr. Mid-Am. State U. Assn., 1982—83. Author: (book) The Sociological Experience, 1969, 3d edit., 1974, The Greek Peasant, 1974, Social Problems Today, 1975, Career of a Radical Rightist, 1975; author: (with Sally A. McNall) Plains Families: Exploring Sociology Through Social History, 1983, The Road to Rebellion, 1988; editor: The Sociological Perspective, 1968, 4th edit., 1977, Theoretical Perspectives in Sociology, 1979, Current Perspectives in Social Theory, 1980, 6th edit., 1985, Political Economy: A Critique of American Society, 1981; editor: (with others) Studies in Historical Social Change, 1986—, The Road to Rebellion: Class Formation and Kansas Populism, 1865-1900, 1988; editor: (with Rhonda Levine) Bringing Class Back in, 1991; editor: (with Sally A. McNall) Sociology, 1992; editor: Current Perspectives in Social Theory, 1980—87; adv. editor: Sociol. Quar., 1969—72, assoc. editor: Am. Sociologist, 1975—78, Jour. Polit. and Mil. Sociology, 1982—; contbr. articles to profl. jours. East-West Ctr. Vis. fellow, 1978, Fulbright grantee, 1983. Mem.: Pacific Sociol. Soc., Am. Sociol. Assn. (chair Marxist sect. 1989—90), Midwest Sociol. Soc. (pres. 1982—83). Democrat. Congregationalist. Home: 520 Crestwood Dr Paradise CA 95969-3825 Office: Calif State U VPAA Office Chico CA 95929 Office Phone: 530-898-6101. Business E-Mail: smcnall@csuchico.edu.

MCNALLY, ANDREW, IV, publishing executive, director; b. Chgo., Nov. 11, 1939; s. Andrew and Margaret C. (MacMillin) McN.; m. Jeanine Sanchez, July 3, 1966; children: Andrew, Carrie, Ward BA, U. NC, 1963; MBA, U. Chgo., 1969. Bus. mgr. edn. divsn. Rand McNally & Co., Chgo., 1967—70, exec. v.p., sec., 1970—74, pres., 1974—97, CEO, 1978—97, also chmn. bd. dirs., 1993—97; ptnr. McNally Investments, Chgo., 1998—. Bd. dirs. Hubbell Inc., Seneca Inc., Boyt Harness, Qualis. Trustee Newberry Libr.; bd. dirs. Children's Meml. Hosp. With Air Force N.G., 1963-69. Mem. Chgo. Club, Saddle and Cycle Club, Commonwealth Club, Racquet Club, Links (NYC) Office: 333 N Michigan Ave Ste 2200 Chicago IL 60601-4104

MCNALLY, JAMES HENRY, physicist, defense consultant; b. Orange, NJ, Dec. 18, 1936; s. James Osborne and Edith Maude (Jones) McN.; m. Nancy Lee Eudaley, July 4, 1976. B in Engring. Physics, Cornell U., 1959; PhD in Physics, Calif. Inst. Tech., 1966. Staff mem. program mgr. Los Alamos (N.Mex.) Nat. Lab., 1965-74; asst. dir for laser and isotope separation tech. AEC/ERDA, Washington, 1974-75; assoc. div. leader, dep. for inertial fusion, asst. for nat. sec. issues Los Alamos Nat. Lab., 1975-86; dep. asst. dir. Arms Control and Disarmament Agy., Washington, 1986-88; dir. office staff Los Alamos Nat. Lab., 1988-90; pvt. practice, 1990—96; cons. US Dept. of State, 2004—. U.S. del. Geneva Conf. on Disarmament, 1969, 73, 74, Threshold Test Ban Treaty, Moscow, 1974, Nuclear Testing Talks, Geneva, 1986-88. Bd. dirs. Wilson Mesa Met. Water Dist., 1976-88; mem., v.p., pres. Mountain Canine Corps, 1994-98. Recipient Meritorious Honor award Arms Control and Disarmament Agy., 1988, Superior Honor award Dept. of State, 2005. Mem. AAAS, Am. Phys. Soc., Internat. Inst. Strategic Studies. Home: 41 Bowen Rd Kittery ME 03904-1355

MCNALLY, MICHELE, editor, photographer; Sales rep. Sygma Photo News, 1977; picture editor Time Life's Mag. Develop. Group, Fortune Mag., 1986—2004; dir. photography The New York Times, 2004—05, asst. mng. editor, 2005—. Judge Pictures of the Year Contest, White House News Photographers Contest, World Press Photography Contest, Overseas Pres Club Photography Contest, Am. Photography Contest; nominating com. mem. W. Eugene Smith Grant in Humanistic Photography; chair, US divsn. World Press; featured spkr., vis. prof. Duke U., U. N.C., Chapel Hill, Syracuse U., Parsons Sch. Design, NYU, Internat. Ctr. Photography. Editor: Day in the Life series. Office: The New York Times 229 West 43rd St New York NY 10003 Office Phone: 212-556-1234.

MCNALLY, RICHARD JAMES, clinical psychologist, educator; b. Detroit, Apr. 17, 1954; s. George Vincent and Marjorie Frances (Tobin) McN.; m. Margaret Cain, Aug. 16, 1985 (div. 2005). BS in Psychology, Wayne State U., 1976; MA in Clin. Psychology, U. Ill., Chgo., 1980, PhD in Clin. Psychology, 1982. Clin. psychology intern dept. psychiatry Temple U. Med. Sch., Phila., 1982-83, postdoctoral fellow dept. psychiatry, 1983-84; from asst. prof. to assoc. prof. dept. psychology U. Health Scis., Chgo. Med. Sch., North Chicago, Ill., 1984-91; assoc. prof. dept. psychology Harvard U., Cambridge, Mass., 1991-95, prof., 1995—. Assoc. editor Behavior Therapy, 1992-95; author: Panic Disorder: A Critical Analysis, 1994, Remembering Trauma, 2003; contbr. articles to Psychol. Bull., Psychol. Rev. Recipient Disting. Scientist award, Soc. for the Sci. of Clin. Psychology, 2005; rsch. grantee NIMH Fellow Assn. for Psychol. Sci.; mem. APA (mem. DSM-IV task force 1989-94), Assn. for Behavior and Cognitive Therapies. Democrat. Office: Harvard U Dept Psychology 33 Kirkland St Cambridge MA 02138-2044 Business E-Mail: rjm@wjh.harvard.edu.

MCNALLY, TERRENCE, playwright; b. St. Petersburg, Fla., Nov. 3, 1939; s. Hubert Arthur and Dorothy Katharine (Rapp) McNally. BA, Columbia U., 1960. Stage mgr. Actors Studio, NYC, 1961, tutor, 1961-62; film critic The Seventh Art, 1963-65; asst. editor Columbia Coll. Today, NYC, 1965-66. Author: (plays) The Lady of the Camellias, 1963, And Things That Go Bump in the Night, 1964, Apple Pie and Last Gasps, 1966, Sweet Eros, Witness, Tour, Cuba Si!, Noon, 1968, Next, 1969, Where Has Tommy Flowers Gone?, Botticelli, Bringing It All Back Home, 1971, Bad Habits, 1971 (Obie award, 1971), Whiskey, 1973, The Tubs, 1974, The Ritz, 1975 (Obie award best play, 1974), The Golden Age, 1975, Broadway, Broadway, 1979, The Five Forty-Eight, 1974, It's Only a Play, 1982, The Rink, 1984, Frankie and Johnny in the Clair de Lune, 1988, The Lisbon Traviata, 1989, Up in Saratoga, 1990, Kiss of the Spider Woman, 1990 (Tony award best book of a musical, 1993), Andre's Mother, 1990 (Emmy award), Preludes, Fuges & Rifts, Lips Together, Teeth Apart, 1991, (screenplay) Frankie and Johnny, 1991, A Perfect Ganesh, 1993 (Pulitzer prize for drama nomination, 1994), Kiss of the Spiderwoman, 1993, Love! Valour! Compassion!, 1994 (Outer Critics' Circle award best Broadway play, 1995, N.Y. Drama Critics Best Am. play, Tony award for Best Play), Master Class, 1994, Ragtime, 1997 (Tony award Best Book of a Musical Corpus Christi, 1998), The Full Monty, 2000, The Visit, 2001, Frankie and Johnny in the Clair de Lune, 2002, Chita Rivera: The Dancer's Life, 2005, Deuce, 2007, Some Men, 2007. Recipient Dramatists Guild Hull-Warriner award, 1973, 1988, 1990; Guggenheim fellow, 1966—69. Mem.: Am. Acad. Arts and Letters, Dramatists Guild (v.p. 1981—98). Office: care Peter Franklin William Morris Agy 1325 Avenue Of The Americas New York NY 10019-6026 *

MCNALLY, VINCENT JOSEPH, historian, educator; b. Phila., Feb. 6, 1943; s. Joseph Edward and Dorothy Elizabeth (Connor) McNally. PhD, Univ. of Dublin, Trinity College, Dublin, Ireland, 1971—77. Prof. ch. history Sacred Heart Sch. of Theology, Hales Corners, Wis., 1992—; asst. prof. history Simon Fraser U., Burnaby, B.C., Canada, 1987—92. Author: (Book) Education Facsimiles 241-260: Catholic Emancipation, 1793-1829, 1976, A History of the Roman Catholic Diocese of Victoria, B.C., 1990, Reform, Revolution and Reaction: Archbishop John Thomas Troy and the Catholic Church in Ireland, 1787-1817, 1995, The Lord's Distant Vineyard: A History of the Oblates and the Catholic Community in British Columbia, 2000, "Hope for the Future: the Church's Challenges of the New Millennium", 2000, (book) Christianity and Native Cultures: Christian and Native Spiritualities in British Columbia: The Historic Struggle to Respect Diversity and Ambiguity, 2004, (Journal: Historical Studies) Challenging the Status Quo: An Examination of the History of Catholic Education in British Columbia, 1999, (Journal: Western Oblate Studies) "Fighting for a Foundation: Oblate Beginnings in Far Western Canada, 1847-1864, 1996, (Journal: Canadian Church Historical Soci) "Fighting City Hall: The Church Tax Exemption Battle Between the City and Roman Catholic Diocese of Victoria", 1992, (Journal of Church and State) "Church-State Relations and American Influence in British Columbia before Confederation", 1992, (Catholic Historical Review) "Archbishop John Thomas Troy and the Establishment of St. Patrick's, Maynooth, 1791-1795", 1981, (Research Project) Practicing What We Preach: Testing and Publishing a Guide for Implementing a Pastoral Theology of Acceptance and Reconciliation in Northern Ireland", 2001 (Assoc. of Theological Schools in US and Canada: Lilly Research Award, 2001), (Research Project:) "Challenging Prejudice: Creating a Theology of Acceptance and Reconciliation in the Schools of Northern Ireland, 2000 (Pew Charitable Trusts, 2000), (Research Award) Researching, Writing and Publishing of a survey history: Irish Catholics: The Catholic Church in Ireland from the Reformation to the Present, 1999 (Eli Lilly Fellowship, 1999), Developing Healthy Theological Imaginations, 1998 (Lilly Endowment Fellowship for Teaching and Learning in Theology and Religion, 1998), Challenging Ourselves: A Practical Guide for Moving Beyond Prejudice in the Schools of Northern Ireland, 2004. Recipient Rsch. award, NEH, 2004, fellowship U. Chgo., 2005.: American Catholic Historical Society (Peter Guilday Prize 1981). Avocations: drawing, harpsichord, painting, travel. Office: Sacred Heart School of Theology PO Box 429 Hales Corners WI 53130 Office Phone: 414-425-8300 ext. 181. Office Fax: 414-529-6999. Business E-Mail: vmcnally@shst.edu.

MCNAMARA, BRENDA NORMA, retired secondary school educator; b. Blackpool, Lancashire, Eng., Aug. 8, 1945; arrived in U.S., 1946; d. Milford Hampson and Nola (Welsby) Jones; m. Michael James McNamara, July 19, 1969. BA in History, Calif. State U., Long Beach, 1967; postgrad., Calif. State U., various campuses, 1967—. Cert. secondary tchr. and lang. devel. specialist Calif. Tchr. history West HS, Torrance, Calif., 1968—, dept. chair, 1989-99, 2000—04; ret., 2004. Cons. Golden State Exam. in History Calif. State Dept. Edn., 1998; state del. NEA Annual Meeting, 2000, 02, local del., 03, 04; cons. in field. Co-author: (book) World History, 1988. Western Internat. Studies Consortium grantee, 1988. Mem.: NEA (retired 2004), Am. Hist. Assn., Nat. Coun. Social Studies, So. Calif. Coun. Social Studies, Torrance Tchrs. Assn. (bd. dirs. 1992—2004), Calif. Coun. Social Studies, Calif. Tchrs. Assn. (retired 2004). Avocations: travel, theater, mystery reading, gourmet cooking. E-mail: brenmcnamara@cox.net.

MCNAMARA, FRANCIS JOSEPH, JR., retired foundation executive, lawyer; b. Boston, Nov. 30, 1927; s. Francis Joseph and Louise (English) McN.; m. Noreen E. O'Connor, June 18, 1953 (dec. Feb. 1984); children: Francis Joseph III, Moira Patricia (Mrs. Lance F. James), John Allen, Kathleen Louise (Mrs. Robert J. Hugin), Martha Jeanne (Mrs. James R. Bordewick), Mark Jeffrey; m. Lois L. Magner, Jan. 17, 1986. AB, Georgetown U., 1949, LLB, 1951; LLD, Fairfield U., 1983. Bar: Conn. 1952. Assoc. firm Pullman, Comley, Bradley & Reeves, 1953; asst. U.S. Atty., dist. Conn., 1953-57; assoc. firm Cummings & Lockwood, Stamford, Conn., 1957-59, ptnr., 1959-91. Guest lectr. Salzburg (Austria) Seminar, 1981; chmn. grievance com. U.S. Dist. Ct. Conn., 1983-89; mem. panel comml. arbitrators Am. Arbitration Assn., Ctr. Dispute Resolution. Trustee Fairfield (Conn.) U., 1968-80, trustee emeritus, 1980—; trustee Charles E. Culpeper Trust, 1968-2001; chmn. bd. Charles E. Culpeper Found., 1968-99, pres., 1991-99. With USNR, 1946, 51-53. Fellow Am. Bar Found., Am. Coll. Trial Lawyers (state com. 1985-91, state chmn. 1989-90); mem. U.S. Supreme Ct. Hist. Soc. (Conn. state chmn. 1989-91, trustee 1992-2000), Navy League U.S., Knight of Holy Sepulchre, Knight of Malta, Knight of St. Gregory the Great, Wee Burn Country Club (Darien, Conn.), Orchid Island Golf and Beach Club (Vero Beach, Fla.). Republican. Roman Catholic. Home: 110 Island Plantation Terrace Vero Beach FL 32963-5000

MCNAMARA, J. DONALD (JOHN DONALD MCNAMARA), retired lawyer, business executive; b. Bridgeport, Conn., Feb. 28, 1924; s. John T. and Agnes (Keating) McN.; m. Shirley Addison Holdridge, Nov. 5, 1960. BA, Dartmouth Coll., 1945; MA in Govt., Harvard U., 1947, LLB, 1950. Bar: NY 1951, Conn. 1951. Assoc. Hall, Haywood, Patterson & Taylor, NYC, 1951-53, 55-56; asst. U.S. Atty. So. Dist. N.Y., 1953-55; assoc. Wickes, Riddell, Bloomer, Jacobi & McGuire, NYC, 1956-57; assoc., then ptnr. Nottingham & McEniry (and successor), NYC, 1957-59; sec., gen. counsel Interpub. Group of Cos., Inc., NYC, 1960-79, dir., 1965-85, sr. v.p., 1966-73, exec. v.p., 1973-79, pres., 1980-85; ret., 1985. Chmn. U.S. Nat. Tennis Championships, 1965. Served to lt. (j.g.) USNR, 1943-46 Mem. Am. Ceramic Cir., The Silver Soc. (London), River Club, Univ. Club, Met. Opera Club (bd. dirs. 1999-2006, pres. 2004-06), Ekwanok Country Club (bd. govs. Manchester, Vt. 1991-95), Dorset (Vt.) Field Club (bd. govs. 1996-99, pres. 1997-98), West Side Tennis Club (pres. Forest Hills, N.Y. 1964-66, 79-80) Home: 350 E 57th St New York NY 10022-2953 also: River Rd Manchester VT 05254

MCNAMARA, JAMES O., physician, scientist; b. Portage, Wis., Sept. 25, 1942; s. Louis Vincent and Lucille (O'Connell) McN.; m. Ann Marilyn Niebler, Aug. 15, 1964; children: Dennis, Brigid, James, Michael, Brian. AB in Philosophy, Marquette U., 1964; MD, U. Mich., 1968. Diplomate Am. Bd. Psychiatry and Neurology, 1976, Am. Bd. Clin. Neurophysiology, 1977. Neurologist U.S. Army Hosp., Fort Hood, Tex., 1971-73; dir. epilepsy ctr. VA Med. Ctr., Durham, NC, 1976-86, neurologist, 1986—; asst. prof. neurology Duke U. Med. Ctr., Durham, NC, 1975-80, assoc. prof. neurology, 1980-85, asst. prof. pharmacology, 1981-86, dir. Duke Ctr. for Adv. Study of Epilepsy, 1982—, prof. neurology, 1985—, assoc. prof. pharmacology, 1986—, prof. neurobiology, 1990—, Carl R. Deane prof. neuroscience, 1993—, chair neurobiology dept., 2002—. Mem. editl. bd., cons. to numerous jours.; mem. com. ad-hoc grant review; mem. Klingenstein Neuroscience Adv. Com., 1994—, Sandoz Pharmaceutical Duke Adv. Com. Contbr. articles to profl. jours. Maj. U.S. Army, 1971-73. Recipient grant NIH, 1980, 1994, Merit Review grantee Veterans Adminstrn., 1992-95, 95—; Postdoctoral fellow Nat. Multiple Sclerosis Soc.; CIBA-Geigy award for VA Coop. Study on Antiepilectic Drugs Internat. League Against Epilepsy, Epilepsy Rsch. award Am. Soc. Pharmacology & Exptl. Therapeutics, Rsch. Recognition award, Am. Epilepsy Soc., 2 Jacog Javits Neuroscience Investigator awards, NIH. Mem. Am. Epilepsy Soc. (pres. 1993, Rsch. Recognition award 1994) Epilepsy Found. Am. (bd. dirs. 1987-92), N.C. Soc. Neuroscience (pres. 1990-91), Soc. Neuroscience (edn. com. 1993-96), Inst. Medicine. Roman Catholic. Achievements include discovery of an auto-immune cause of Rasmussen's encephalitis. Home: 403 Lakeshore Ln Chapel Hill NC 27514-1730 Office: Duke U Med Ctr Box 3676 401 Bryan Rsch Bldg Durham NC 27710-0001 E-mail: jmc@neuro.duke.edu.

MCNAMARA, JOHN J(OSEPH), advertising executive, writer; b. Yonkers, NY, Mar. 7, 1934; m. Patricia A. Widmann, Sept. 14, 1963; children: Mary, John. BS, Yale U., 1956; MBA, NYU, 1963. Pres. Young & Rubicam Inc., from 1982; later pres. McCann Erickson Worldwide, ret., 1990. Cons. in field. Author: Advertising Agency Management, 1989; columnist: Gulf Stream mags. Pres. Pelham United Way, NY; chmn. Pelham Manor Planning Bd.; trustee Village of Pelham Manor, mayor, 1989—90; pres. Boys and Girls Club, Indian River County, Fla.; pres., bd. dirs. John's Island Property Owners Assn. Mem.: John's Island Club (bd. dirs.), Winged Foot Club, Pelham Country Club (pres.). Office: PO Box 8204 Vero Beach FL 32963-8204

MCNAMARA, JOHN REGIS, psychology educator; b. Binghamton, NY, May 27, 1941; s. Regis Charles and Jane (Bradley) McN.; m. Lucille J. Martel, Dec. 5, 1972; children: Brian, Paul. BA, U. Notre Dame, 1963; MA, Xavier U., 1967; PhD, U. Ga., 1972. Diplomate Am. Bd. Profl. Psychology. Asst. prof. psychology and medicine U. Mo., Kansas City, 1971-72; prof. clin. psychology Ohio U., Athens, 1972—. Cons. U.S. Army, Panama Canal Zone, 1972, U.S. Gen. Acctg. Office, Washington, 1977-81; trainer U.S. AID-Mideast, Athens, 1994. Author: Overcoming Dating Anxiety, 1991; editor: Behavioral Approaches to Medicine, 1979, Critical Issues, Developments and Trends in Professional Psychology, Vol. 1, 1982, Vol. 2, 1984, Vol. 3, 1987. Fellow APA, Sigma Xi. Home: 23 Coventry Ln Athens OH 45701-3718 Office: Ohio U Porter Hall Dept Psychology Athens OH 45701 Home Phone: 740-592-4588; Office Phone: 614-593-1707. Business E-Mail: mcnamara@ohio.edu.

MCNAMARA, JOHN STEPHEN, artist, educator; b. Cambridge, Mass., Feb. 16, 1950; s. John Stephen and Mary (Adams) McN. BFA in Painting, Mass. Coll. Art, Boston, 1971, MFA in Painting, 1977. Tchr. Mus. Fine Arts Sch., Boston, 1983, 90-92; undergrad. and grad. painting tchr. Mass. Coll. Art, Boston, 1988; undergrad. painting tchr. Boston Archtl. Ctr., Boston, 1977; color fundamentals tchr. Mass. Coll. Art, Boston, 1987, undergrad. drawing and painting, 1975-88. Vis. lectr. San Francisco Art Inst., 1992, 93, U. Calif., Berkeley, 1993—. One-man shows include The Exhbn. Space at 112 Greene St., N.Y.C., 1982, Stavaridis Gallery, Boston, 1983-85, 86-89, Bess Cutler Gallery, N.Y.C., 1984, 85, 86, 88, Mass. Coll. Art, 1986, Honolulu Acad. Fine Art, 1987, Nielsen Gallery, 1990, 92, Miller Block Gallery, Boston, 1995, Ebert Gallery, San Francisco, Clark Gallery, Lincoln, Mass., 2002, others; exhibited in group shows at Boston Collects, Mus. Fine Arts, Stavaridis Gallery, 1986, Bess Cutler Gallery, N.Y.C., 1987, Am. Painters and Sculptors, Met. Mus. Art, N.Y.C., 1988, Resonant Abstraciton, Fuller Mus. Art, Brockton, Mass., 1989-90, Tucson Mus. Fine Art, 1996, DeCordova Mus., Lincoln, Mass., 2002, Painting in Boston, 1950-2000. Recipient Outstanding Alumnus award, Mass. Coll. Art, 1986, Faculty Outstanding Mentorship award, Grad. Student Instr., U. Calif., Berkley, 2005; grantee, Mass. Arts and Humanities Grant, 1980, 1983, 1986, 1989, Equitable Life and the Rockefeller Found. Awards in the visual arts, 1982, Equitable Life and the Rockefeller Found., 1983, 1986, 1989, Nat. Endowment Arts, 1981; McDowell Colony fellow, Peterborough, NH, 1985. Home: 1501 Park Ct Novato CA 94945-1472 Office Phone: 510-642-2582. Business E-Mail: namara@berkeley.edu.

MC NAMARA, JOSEPH DONALD, researcher, retired protective services official; b. NYC, Dec. 16, 1934; s. Michael and Eleanor (Shepherd) McN.; divorced; children: Donald, Laura, Karen. BS, John Jay Coll., 1968; fellow, Harvard Law Sch., 1970; DPA (Littauer fellow), Harvard U., 1973. Served to dep. insp. Police Dept., NYC, 1956-73; police chief Kansas City, Mo., 1973-76, San Jose, Calif., 1976-91; rsch. fellow Hoover Instn., Stanford U., 1991—. Adj. instr. Northeastern U., 1972, John Jay Coll., 1973, Rockhurst Coll., 1975-76, San Jose State U., 1980; cons. U.S. Civil Rights Commn., 1978; lectr., appearances on nat. TV; apptd. nat. adv. bd. U.S. Bur. Justice Stats., 1980, U.S. Drug Control Policy Office, 1993; commentator Pub. Broadcasting Radio. Author: (non-fiction) Safe and Sane, 1984, (novel) The First Directive Crown, 1985, Fatal Command, 1987, The Blue Mirage, 1990, Code 211 Blue, 1996; contbr. articles to profl. publs. Bd. dirs. Drug Policy Found., Washington; active NCCJ. Served with U.S. Army, 1958-60. Named one of 200 Young Am. Leaders Time mag., 1975; recipient disting. alumni award John Jay Coll., 1979, Pres.'s award Western Soc. Criminology1979, Morrison Gitchoff award Western Soc. Criminology, 1992, H.B. Spear award Drug Policy Found., 1992; Kansas City police named Best in Country by Nat. Newspaper Enterprises, 1974, San Jose Police Dept. named Nat. Model U.S. Civil Rights Commn., 1980; named Law Enforcement Officer of Yr., Calif. Trial Lawyers Assn., 1991. Mem. Internat. Assn. Chiefs of Police, Calif. Police Chiefs Assn., Calif. Peace Officers Assn., Major Cities Police Chiefs Assn., Police Exec. Research Forum (dir.) Office: Hoover Instn Stanford CA 94305 Office Phone: 650-723-1475. E-mail: mcnamara@hoover.stanford.edu. *In our country, social mobility is possible for people from even the most humble backgrounds. Despite problems, our nation has provided more liberty and dignity for the common individual than any other civilization in history. Continuation of our free society depends upon how successful we are in teaching each new generation an appreciation of our precious freedoms and the patience to achieve progress within our democratic process.*

MCNAMARA, JULIA MARY, academic administrator, foreign language educator; b. NYC, Dec. 13, 1941; d. John P. and Julia (Dowd) McNamara. BA in History and French, Ohio Dominican Coll., 1965; MA in French, Middlebury Coll., 1972; MPhil, Yale U., PhD in French Lang. and Lit., 1980; DHL (hon.), Sacred Heart U., Hamden, Conn., 1984. Mem. faculty St. William Sch., Pitts., 1963-64, Holy Spirit Sch., Columbus, Ohio, 1964-65, Newark (Ohio) Cath. High Sch., 1965-66, Northwest Cath. High Sch., West Hartford, Conn., 1966-69, St. Vincent Ferrer High Sch., NYC, 1969-70, St. Mary's High Sch., New Haven, 1971-74; lectr. french Albertus Magnus Coll., New Haven, 1976-80, dean of students, 1980-82, acting pres., 1982-83, pres., 1983—. Prof. French Albertus Magnus Coll., 1981—; mem. Conn. Health and Edn. Facilities Authority, Hartford, 1983—; chair Conn. Conf. Ind. Colls., Hartford, 1990-92, sec.-treas. 1986—, chmn., 1990-92; lectr. in field; assoc. fellow Yale U., Morse Coll.; bd. dirs. New Haven Savs. Bank. Chairperson United Way Greater New Haven, 1987; bd. dirs. St. Mary's High Sch., New Haven, 1982-91, ARC, New Haven Savs. Bank, 1990—; trustee Yale-New Haven Hosp., 1984—(chair med. com., 1989-91 vice chair bd., 1991-), chair, Yale-New Haven Health Sys.; adv. bd. Bank of Boston-Conn., 1983-87; adv. com. Jr. League Greater New Haven, 1985; trustee Hartford Sem., 1985-91. Fulbright fellow, Paris, 1977-78; Yale U. fellow, 1974-78, Am. Council on Edn. fellow, 1981; recipient Disting. Woman in Leadership award New Haven YWCA, 1984, Veritas award Providence Coll., 1987, Greater New Haven Jr. Achievement Ann. award, 1990. Mem. Fulbright Alumni Assn., New Haven C. of C. (bd. dirs. 1984-90), New England Assn. Schs. and Colls. (appeals bd. 1986-88). Roman Catholic. Office: Albertus Magnus Coll Office of the President 700 Prospect St New Haven CT 06511-1224

MCNAMARA, KEVIN JOHN, museum administrator; b. Abington, Pa., Oct. 6, 1957; s. John Kerwin and Dolores Ann (Auchinleck) McNamara; m. Juliane Cary Roebuck, July 17, 1982 (div. Dec. 2005); children: Hilary Megan, Whitney Morgan. BA, Temple U., 1989; cert., U. Pa., 1994; MA, Temple U., 1995; cert., U. Va., 2000, Stanford U., 2007. Journalist Calkins Newspapers Inc., Doylestown, Pa., 1981-85; congl. aide U.S. Rep. R. Lawrence Coughlin, Washington, 1985-88; asst. dir. Fgn. Policy Rsch. Inst., Phila., 1988-93, rapporteur, 1990-93, adj. scholar, 1994—; dir. devel. Intercollegiate Studies Inst., Wilmington, Del., 1994—98; assoc. v.p. Drexel U., Phila., 1998—2004; v.p. Independence Seaport Mus., Phila., 2004—. Author: The Presidency, 2000; contbg. editor Directors and Boards, 1989-90, Orbis: A Jour. of World Affairs, 1990-93; contbr. articles to profl. jours. Vol. Sam Katz for Gov., 1994, Craig Snyder for Congress, 1992, George Bush for Pres. Com., 1987-88, Snyder for State Ho. Com., 1990; cons. Coughlin for Congress Com., 1986; bd. dirs. Abington Free Lib., 1992-93. Grantee, Tawani Found., 2004; Earhart Found. fellow, 2003—04. Mem. Phila. Com. Fgn. Rels., Assn. of Fundraising Profls. Republican. Avocations: reading, writing, gardening. Office: 211 S Columbus Blvd and Walnut St Philadelphia PA 19106-3199

MCNAMARA, LAWRENCE JOHN, lawyer; b. Evergreen Park, Ill., Aug. 10, 1950; s. William Francis and Florence M.; m. Martha Ann Sanchez, Jan. 7, 1992. BA cum laude, Ill. Coll.; JD, Vanderbilt U. Bar: Tex. 1976, D.C. 1988, U.S. Dist. Ct. (so. dist.) Tex. 1977, U.S. Dist. Ct. (ea. dist.) Tex. 1978, U.S. Dist. Ct. (no. dist.) Tex. 1985, U.S. Dist. Ct. (we. dist.) Tex. 1991, U.S. Ct. Appeals (5th cir.) 1976, U.S. Ct. Appeals (11th cir.) 1981, U.S. Ct. Appeals (7th cir.) 1989, U.S. Ct. Appeals (9th cir.) 1991, U.S. Ct. Appeals (8th cir.) 1994, U.S. Supreme Ct. 1979. Assoc. Baker & Botts, Houston, 1976-85; ptnr. Baker, Smith & Mills, Dallas, 1985-87; ptnr., shareholder Johnson & Gibbs, Dallas, 1987-95; ptnr. Locke Liddell & Sapp (and predecessor firm), Dallas, 1995—. Mem. ABA, Tex. Bd. Legal Specialization (cert.), Phi Beta Kappa. Roman Catholic. Avocations: golf, running. Office: Locke Liddell & Sapp 2200 Ross Ave Ste 2200 Dallas TX 75201-6776

MCNAMARA, MARTIN BURR, lawyer, former gas industry executive; b. Danbury, Conn., Sept. 10, 1947; s. William Joseph and Geraldine Margaret (Young) McN. BA in English, Providence Coll., 1969; JD, Yale U., 1972. Bar: NY 1973, US Dist. Ct. (so. and ea. dists.) NY 1973, US Dist. Ct. (no. dist.) Tex. 1993, US Dist. Ct. (so. dist.) Tex. 1994, US Ct. Appeals (2d cir.) 1973, Tex. 1980, US Ct. Appeals (5th and 11th cirs.) 1981. Assoc. Shea & Gould, NYC, 1972-76; asst. US atty. (so. dist.) NY, NYC, 1976-79; v.p., gen. counsel, sec. Tex. Oil & Gas Corp., Dallas, 1979-91; gen. counsel, sr. v.p. adminstrn. Delhi Gas Pipeline Corp., Dallas, 1979-91; ptnr. litig. and corp. securities Gibson, Dunn & Crutcher LLP, Dallas, 1991—, and ptnr.-in-charge Dallas office. Mem. exec. com. Gibson Dunn & Crutcher, bd. dirs. Transocean Sedco Foret, Inc.; lectr. State Bar Tex., Dallas Bar Assn., U. Tex. Corp. Counsel Inst., Okla. Bar Assn., U. Tex. Mem. exec. com. Yale Law Sch. Assn., 1983-86. Mem. State Bar of Tex. (chmn. 1988-89), Bar Assn. Fifth Fed. Cir., Assn. Bar. City of NY, NY State Bar Assn., Fed. Energy Bar Assn. Clubs: Petroleum. Republican. Roman Catholic. Office: Gibson Dunn & Crutcher LLP Ste 1100 2100 McKinney Ave Dallas TX 75201-6912 Office Phone: 214-698-3127. Office Fax: 214-571-2938. Business E-Mail: mmcnamara@gibsondunn.com.

MCNAMARA, MARY ELLEN, not-for-profit executive; b. Mpls., Dec. 18, 1943; d. Edward Emmanuel and Gladys Theresa (Mattson) Bjorklund; m. Peter Alexander McNamara II (div.); children: Peter Alexander III, Nathaniel Paul. BA, Carleton Coll., 1965; MDiv, Harvard U., 1968. Cert. fin. planner. Program dir. St. Peter's Ch., NYC, 1968-72, program dir., dep. exec., 1977-80; program dir. Ct. Ch. on-the-Green, 1972-74; program developer Westminster Presbyn. Ch., Springfield, Ill., 1974-77; assoc. Gen. Assembly Coun. Presbyn. Ch. (USA), NYC, 1980—86; dir. not-for-profit sector City of NY, 1986—90; pres., exec. dir. Interchurch Ctr., NYC, 1990-99; interim pres. Union Theol. Sem., NYC, 1998—99, exec. v.p., 1999—; mem. exec. com. Assn. Theol. Sch., 2003—. V.p. Pathways for Youth, Bronx, NY, 1987—96; pres. Morningside Area Alliance, NYC, 1991—98; parish assoc. Fifth Ave. Presbyn. Ch., 1998—2002. Moderator Presbyn. NYC, 1995—96, chair com. on ministry, 1992—95, chair implementation task force, 1996—98, chair nominating com., 2005—; chmn. bd. dirs. exec. com. Presbyn. Conf. Ctr., Stony Point, NY, 1996—2002, chmn. nominating com., 2005—; bd. dirs. Blanton/Peale Inst. on Religion and Health, 1994—2001, Wartburg Adult Care Cmty., 1999—, chair elect, 2001—03, chair, 2003—, chmn. pers. com., exec. com., 2001—03. Mem.: Assn. Theol. Seminaries (exec. com. 2004—, bd. dirs. 2005—). Home: 99 Claremont Ave Apt 621 New York NY 10027-5711 Office: Union Theol Sem 3041 Broadway New York NY 10027-5710

MCNAMARA, MICHAEL, electronics executive; BS, Univ. Cinn.; MBA, Santa Clara Univ. Prin. Pittiglio Rabin Todd & McGrath; v.p. mgr. ops. Anthem Electronics; v.p. No. Am. ops. Flextronics Internat., 1994—97, pres. Americas' ops., 1997—2001, COO Singapore, 2002—05, CEO, 2006—. Office: Flextronics Internat 2 Changri S Lane Singapore 486123 Singapore

MCNAMARA, MICHAEL J., law educator; b. Arlington, Mass., Aug. 20, 1970; m. Sylwia Malgorzata Uniwersal, May 5, 2004; 1 child, Drew Asher. BA, Johns Hopkins U., Balt., 1991; JD, MBA, Boston U., Mass., 1994; LLM, Fordham U., NYC, 1996. Bar: NY 1994, Mass. 1994, N. 1995, cert.: NY (notary) 2002, lic.: NY (real estate agt.) 2002; registered Series 4, 7 and 63 NASD, 2002. In-house counsel Fed. Res. Bank of NY, NYC, 1994—96; equity options market maker various, NYC, 1997—2003; adj. prof. Centenary Coll., Parsippany, NJ, 2003—, Capella U., White Plains, NY, 2005—; Am. Contract Bridge League bridge dir., tchr. The Bridge Deck, White Plains. Recipient Best Brief in Country, Kaufman Nat. Moot Ct. Competition, 1994, Winner, Wheel of Fortune, 1994. Master: Am. Contract Bridge League (life; Silver life master, 1st pl. Nat. Non-Life Master Pairs 1995, 2d pl. Flight B Grand Nat. Team 1997); mem.: MENSA (life). Home: 20 Leather Stocking Ln White Plains NY 10603-2836 Home Phone: 914-831-0759. Home Fax: 914-831-0759. Personal E-mail: mcnamaramike@optonline.net.

MCNAMARA, MICHAEL JOHN, lawyer; b. Hutchinson, Minn., July 1, 1948; s. John Oliver and Lucille Violet (Wedell) M.; m. Kathleen Elizabeth Dahl; children: Jennifer, Kelly. BA, U. Utah, 1976; JD, U. Minn., 1980. Bar: Minn. 1981, U.S. Dist. Ct. Minn. 1981, U.S. Ct. Appeals (8th cir.) 1982, U.S. Supreme Ct. 1988, Wis. 1992. Pvt. practice, Mpls., 1981—. Contbr. articles to profl. jours. Sgt. U.S. Army, 1968-71, Vietnam. Nat. Merit scholar. Mem.: Nat. Assn. Criminal Def. Attys., The Federalist Soc., Minn. State Bar Assn., Hennepin County Bar Assn. (spkrs. bur.), Am. Assn. for Justice. Avocations: jogging, biking, hiking. Office: Henderson Howard et al 6200 Shingle Creek Pkwy Ste 385 Minneapolis MN 55430-2176 Home Phone: 952-944-8058; Office Phone: 763-566-8832. Business E-Mail: mjmc@hhpandm.com.

MCNAMARA, MICHAEL LEE PERRY, automation engineer; b. Clarion, Pa., Sept. 1, 1981; s. Patrick Michael and Maxine Renee McNamara; m. Christina Renee Thacher, Aug. 4, 2001. B in Computer Sci., Slippery Rock U., Pa., 2004. Quality assurance analyst, automation engr. McKesson Automation, Cranberry Township, Pa., 2004—. Office: McKesson Automation 500 Cranberry Woods Dr Cranberry Township PA 16066 Home: 6029 Valencia Rd Gibsonia PA 15044 Home Phone: 724-992-1293; Office Phone: 724-741-8080. Personal E-mail: skully@zoominternet.net.

MCNAMARA, MICHAEL T., lawyer; b. Kansas City, Mo., June 26, 1969; AB summa cum laude, Duke U., 1990; JD magna cum laude, Harvard U., 1996. Bar: Md. 1996, DC 1997. Economist US Dept. Commerce, Washington; with Arent Fox Kintner Plotkin & Kahn, Washington; ptnr. Sonnenschein Nath & Rosenthal LLP, Washington, 2002—. Office: Sonnenschein Nath & Rosenthal LLP Ste 600, E Tower 1301 K St NW Washington DC 20015 Office Phone: 202-408-6477. Office Fax: 202-408-6399. Business E-Mail: mmcnamara@sonnenschein.com.

MCNAMARA, PATRICK JAMES, lawyer; b. Bethpage, NY, Mar. 27, 1959; s. James Francis and Kathleen (Marrinan) McN.; m. Kimberly McNamara, Dec. 7, 1991; children: James Patrick, Emma Kathleen, Connor Ryan. BA in History, Rutgers U., New Brunswick, NJ, 1981, MA in Polit. Sci., 1985; JD, Rutgers U., Camden, NJ, 1987. Bar: N.J. 1987, U.S. Dist. Ct. N.J. 1987, Pa. 1987. Legal sec. to Hon. Neil F. Deighan Jr., Appellate Divsn. N.J. Superior Ct., 1987-88; with Giordano, Halleran & Ciesla, Middletown, N.J., 1988-91; ptnr. Carpenter, Bennett and Morrissey, Newark, 1991-94, Scarinci & Hollenbeck, Secaucus, N.J., 1994—. Gen. counsel Nat. Assn. Flavor and Food Ingredient Systems, Inc., 1995—, Chem. Sources Assn., 1998—, Soc. Flavor Chemists, 2001—, Flavor Heritage Soc., 2004—. Assoc. editor Food Exec. mag., 1997, Food Product Design mag., 1999; contbr. author to profl. jours. Mcpl. atty. Township of Aberdeen, 1992-95; spl. counsel Twp. of Aberdeen, 1996-97, Fredon Twp. Zoning Bd. of Adj., 1999-, Borough of S. River, 2001-, Hamilton Twp. Planning Bd., 2005-; lead counsel City of Elizabeth Planning Bd., 1999—; active Matawan-Aberdeen Edn. Found. Rutgers U. Grad. fellow Eagleton Inst. Politics, 1984-85. Mem. N.J. State Bar Assn. (treas. environ. law sect. 2004-05), Environ. Law Inst., N.J. Group Small Chem. Businesses, Rutgers Alumni Assn. Avocations: sports, travel, golf, politics. Office: 1100 Valley Brook Ave PO Box 790 Lyndhurst NJ 07071 Office Phone: 201-896-4100. Office Fax: 201-896-8660. Business E-Mail: pmcnamara@njlegalink.com.

MCNAMARA, RICHARD BEDLE, lawyer; b. Elizabeth, NJ, July 4, 1950; s. Robert Daniel and Doris (Bedle) McN.; m. Linda Battista, June 10, 1973; children: Jennifer Beth, Christopher Brendan, Julie Bridget. AB, Boston Coll., 1972, JD, 1975. Bar: N.H. 1975, U.S. Dist. Ct. N.H. 1975, U.S. Ct. Appeals (1st cir.) 1978, U.S. Supreme Ct. 1979. With Atty. Gen.'s Office, Concord, N.H., 1975-77, asst. atty. gen., 1977-79; assoc. Wiggin & Nourie, Manchester, N.H., 1979-82, ptnr., 1983—. Author: New Hampshire Criminal Practice and Procedure, 1980, Constitutional Limitations on Criminal Procedure, 1982, New Hampshire Personal Injury Practice, 1988. Mem. ABA, N.H. Bar Assn. (chmn. com. on rules of criminal procedure 1985, pres. 2006-07), Manchester Bar Assn. Republican. Roman Catholic. Office: Wiggin & Nourie Ste 305 670 N Commercial St Manchester NH 03105 Office Phone: 603-629-4590. E-mail: rmcnamara@wiggin-nourie.com.

MC NAMARA, ROBERT A., construction company executive; b. 1953; BA in Econs., Brown U., 1975. Contracts mgr. Limbach Co., Woburn, Mass., 1975-78; v.p. sales and mktg. Marshall Contractors Inc., Rumford, RI, 1978-83; exec. v.p. to pres, COO Marshall Contractors Inc. (acquired by Fluor Corp.), Rumford, RI, 1983—96; various positions including sr. group pres. responsible for China Fluor Corp., 1996—2006; pres., CEO LVI Services Inc., 2006—. Office: LVI Services 80 Broad St 3rd fl New York NY 10004

MCNAMARA, ROBERT STRANGE, former world bank president, secretary of defense; b. San Francisco, June 9, 1916; s. Robert James and Clara Nell (Strange) McN.; m. Margaret Craig, Aug. 13, 1940 (dec. Feb. 3, 1981); children: Margaret Elizabeth, Kathleen, Robert Craig; m. Diana Masieri Byfield, Sept. 16, 2004. AB, U. Calif., 1937, LLD (hon.); MBA, Harvard U., 1939, LLD (hon.), U. Mich., Columbia U., George Washington U., Princeton U., Amherst Coll., Williams Coll., U. Ala., Ohio State U., NYU, U. Notre Dame, U. Pa., U. St. Andrews, U. Philippines, Aberdeen U., Oxford U., U. SC. Asst. prof. bus. adminstrn. Harvard U., 1940-43; exec. Ford Motor Co., 1946-61, contr., 1949—53, asst. gen. mgr., Ford divsn., 1953—55, v.p., gen. mgr. Ford divsn., 1955—57, dir., group, v.p. car divsn., 1957-61, pres., 1960-61; sec. U.S. Dept. Def., 1961-68; pres. World Bank, 1968-81; ret., 1981. Mem., trustee pub. and pvt. instns. including Overseas Devel. Coun., Urban Inst., Enterprise Found., Brookings Inst., Royal Dutch Petroleum, 1981-87, Bank of Am., 1981-87, Corning, 1981-90, Washington Post Corp., 1981-89; spl. cons. War Dept., 1942. Author: The Essence of Security: Reflections in Office, 1968, One Hundred Countries-Two Billion People, 1973, The McNamara Years at the World Bank, 1981, Blundering Into Disaster, 1986, Out of the Cold: New Thinking for American Foreign and Defense Policy in the 21st Century, 1989, (with Brian Vandemark) In Retrospect: The Tragedy and Lessons of Vietnam, 1995, Argument Without End: In Search of Answers to the Vietnam Tragedy, 1999, Wilson's Ghost: Reducing the Risk of Conflict, Killing, and Catastrophe in the 21st Century, 2001; Film appearances: The Fog of War: Eleven Lessons from the Life of Robert S. McNamara, 2003; TV appearances: JFK Remembered, 1988, Cold War (mini-series), 1998, Vietnam: A Descent Into Hell, 1999. Served as lt. col. USAAF, 1943-46. Decorated Legion of Merit, D.S.M.; recipient Presdl. Medal of Freedom with distinction, 1968, Disting. Svc. medal, 1968, Christian A. Herter Meml. award, Albert Pick Jr. award U. Chgo., 1979, Albert Einstein Peace prize, 1983, Franklin D. Roosevelt Freedom from Want medal, 1983, Sidney Hillman Foundn. award, 1987, Olive Branch award for Outstanding Book on subject of World Peace, 1987, Onassis Athinai prize, 1988, Am. Assembly Svc. to Democracy award, Dag Hammarskjold Hon. medal, Entrepreneurial Excellence award, Yale Sch. Orgn. & Mgmt. Mem. Phi Beta Kappa. Office: 325 7th St NW Ste 600 Washington DC 20004

MCNAMARA, STEPHEN, newspaper executive; b. Chgo., July 9, 1934; s. Robert Charles McNamara Jr. and Susan (Deuel) Shattuck; m. Hanne Mogensen Petterson, Feb. 21, 1960 (div. Aug. 1970); children: Lise, Natalie, Kevin; m. Kay Copeland, June 10, 1978; children: Christopher, Morgan. AB in Am. History, Princeton U., 1955. Reporter Winston-Salem Jour., NC, 1955—57; sports writer Miami Herald, 1957—59; contbg. European editor Car & Driver, NYC, 1960; asst. news editor, exec. sports editor, Sunday editor San Francisco Examiner, 1961—66; CEO, editor, pub. Pacific Sun, Mill Valley, Calif., 1966—2004; co-pub. The Ark, Tiburon, Calif., 1987—99; pres. Marin Sun Printing Co., Mill Valley, 1967—93; mng. gen. ptnr. Sunlight Investment Co., Mill Valley, 1980—. Vis. lectr. San Francisco State U., 1967; mem. innovation and planning commn. Calif. Dept. Edn., Sacramento, 1980; co-founder, pres. Marin Solar Village Corp., Mill Valley, 1976—, Marin Cmty. Video, Mill Valley, 1973-78. Mem. Soc. Profl. Journalists, Nat. Assn. Alternative Newsweeklies (pres. 1978-81), Calif. Assn. Alternative Newsweeklies (pres. 1990-92), Calif. Soc. Newspaper Editors (pres. 1985-86, bd. dirs. 1983-93), Calif. Newspaper Pubs. Assn. (bd. dirs. 1989-93), San Francisco Press Club (1st place newspaper writing award 1967, 3-2d place awards), Cap and Gown Club (Princeton U.). Democrat. Home: 2 Bradford Way Mill Valley CA 94941-1111 Personal E-mail: smcnamara@aol.com.

MCNAMARA, TED (THOMAS EDMUND MCNAMARA), federal official, former ambassador; b. New Haven, Sept. 16, 1940; s. Joseph Michael and Anne Marie (Meehan) McN.; m. Emma Julia Fonseca, June 11, 1966; children: David Fonseca, Michelle Anne. BA, Manhattan Coll., 1962; MA, Notre Dame U., 1964. Joined fgn. svc. State Dept., 1965; 2nd sec. Am. Embassy, Paris, 1967-69; BENELUX desk officer European bur. US Dept. State, 1969-71; consul Am. Consulate, Lubumbashi, Zaire, 1971-72, Bukavu, Zaire, 1972-73; with Armed Forces Staff Coll., Norfolk, Va., 1973-74; internat. affairs officer Arms Control & Disarmament Agy., 1974-75; chief external divsn., polit. sect. Am. Embassy, Moscow, 1976-78; office dir., polit.-mil. bur. US Dept. State, Washington, 1978-80; dep. chief of mission Am. Embassy, Kinshasa, Democratic Republic of Congo, 1980-83; dept. asst. sec., bur. polit.-mil. affairs US Dept. State, Washington, 1983-86; sr. seminar Fgn. Svc. Inst., Washington, 1986-87; dir. counterterrorism and narcotics Nat. Security Coun., 1987-88; US amb. to

Colombia US Dept. State, Bogota, 1988-91; special asst. to the Pres. for nat. security affairs The White House, Washington, 1991-92; coord. for counter-terrorism US Dept. State, Washington, 1992-93, prin. dep. asst. sec., bur. polit.-mil. affairs, 1993-94, asst. sec., bur. polit.-mil. affairs, 1994—98; pres., CEO Am. Soc. & Coun. Americas, NYC, 1998—2001; sr. adv. for counter-terrorism & homeland security US Dept. State, Washington, 2001—04; program mgr. Program Mgr. Info. Sharing Environ., Washington, 2006—. Adj. prof. Elliott Sch. Internat. Affairs George Washington U. Contbr. articles to profl. jours. Recipient Superior Honor award US Dept. State, 1980, 84, 86. Mem. Am. Fgn. Service Assn., Army-Navy Club.

MCNAMARA, TOM, scientific consulting corporation executive; b. Battle Creek, Mich., May 23, 1944; s. George P. (Stepfather) and Mildred E. Lunt; m. Ellen K. LaRue, Sept. 24, 1977 (div. Dec. 2005); 1 child, George Lunt. Grad. in Chemistry, Boston U., 1966; MBA, Northeastern U., 1970. With corp. planning dept. Reynolds Aluminum, Richmond, Va., 1970—72; sr. cons. Technomic Cons., Chgo., 1972—74; founder, pres. NUVENTURES Cons., Chgo. and San Diego, 1975—97. Spkr. trade convs. and confs. worldwide; frequent guest TV and radio talk shows; on water advisor Am.'s Cup, 1988, 91, 94. Author: Henry Lunt and The Ranger, 1991, Henry Lunt and The Spymaster, 1994; co-author: America's Changing Workforce, 1990; editor: George and The Pitching Machine, 1994; contbr. articles to profl. publs. Mem. various coms. United Fund and Chgo. Assn. Commerce and Industry, 1975—79; spokesman 200th Anniversary U.S. Bill of Rights tour, 1991; Rep. nominee Ill. Gen. Assembly, 1974, 1976. Recipient Presdl. Commendation for heroism, 1974, Commendation award, Chgo. Police Dept., 1974, Pulitzer Prize nomination, 1991. Mem.: Acacia, Sarasota Yacht Club, San Diego Tennis and Racquet Club, Bahia Corinthian Yacht Club. Avocation: scuba diving (cert. diver, NAUI Worldwide, 1980). Personal E-mail: tommcnamara2008@earthlink.net.

MCNAMEE, BRIAN, medical products executive; B in Journalism, St. Bonaventure U., NY; M in Indsl. and Labor Rels., Cornell U., Ithaca, 1987. Various human resources positions GE, 1988—99; sr. v.p. human resources NBC, 1998—99; v.p. human resources Dell Computer Corp., 1999—2001; sr. v.p. human resources Amgen, Inc., Thousand Oaks, Calif., 2001—. Office: Amgen Inc One Amgen Center Dr Thousand Oaks CA 91320-1799 Office Phone: 805-447-1000. Office Fax: 805-447-1010. *

MCNAMEE, SISTER CATHERINE, educator; b. Troy, NY, Nov. 13, 1931; d. Thomas Ignatius McNamee and Kathryn McNamee Marois. BA, Coll. of St. Rose, 1953, DHL (hon.), 1975; MEd, Boston Coll., 1955, MA, 1958; PhD, U. Madrid, 1967. Grad. asst. Boston Coll., 1954-55, asst. registrar Grad. Sch., 1955-57; mem. faculty Coll. St. Rose, Albany, NY, 1960-65, acad. v.p., 1968-75; dir. liberal arts Thomas Edison Coll., Trenton, 1975-76; pres. Trinity Coll., Burlington, Vt., 1976-79, Coll. St. Catherine, St. Paul, 1979-84; dean Dexter Hanley Coll., U. Scranton, Pa., 1984-86; pres. Nat. Cath. Ednl. Assn., Washington, 1986-96; sr. scholar Ctr. for Cath. Studies, U. St. Thomas, St. Paul, 1996-2000; prof. U. Catolica, Talca, Chile, 2000—05; disting. vis. scholar Coll. St. Catherine, St. Paul, 2005—. Cons. Archdiocese St. Paul, 2005—. Trustee assoc. Boston Coll. Spanish Govt. grantee, 1965-67; OAS grantee, 1967-68; Fulbright grantee, 1972-73 Mem. Inter-Am. Confedn. Cath. Edn., Internat. Orgn. Cath. Edn., Nat. Cath. Ednl. Assn., Internat. Fedn. Cath. Univs., Delta Epsilon Sigma. Roman Catholic. Home: 1880 Randolph Ave Saint Paul MN 55105 Office: Archdiocese of St Paul/Mpls 226 Summit Ave Saint Paul MN 55105 Personal E-mail: cmncsj@hotmail.com.

MCNAMEE, LAWRENCE ROSS, JR., manufacturing executive; b. Gary, Ind., June 7, 1931; s. Lawrence Ross and Pearl Agnes (Heyburn) McNamee; m. Mary Ann Youlden, 1956; children: Lawrence R. III, Catherine Ann, John Charles. BA, Claremont McKenna Coll., 1957; MBA, Claremont Grad. U., 1958; postgrad., UCLA. Supr. Gen. Dynamics, Pomona, Calif., 1958-61; mem. staff Arthur D. Little, Inc., LA, 1961-65; dir. Booz Allen & Hamilton, LA, 1965-70; gen. mgr. Hydril Co., LA, 1970-76; pres. Diogenes Group, LA, 1976-91; chmn., CEO Radiant Tech. Corp., Fullerton, Calif., 1991—2005, GreenBridge Tech., Inc., Fullerton, 2006—. With U.S. Army, 1952-54. Mem.: Ops. Rsch. Soc. Am., Turn Around Mgmt. Assn., Semiconductor Equipment and Materials Internat., Malibu Orchid Soc. (pres. 2003), Getty Villa Coun., Calif. Yacht Club. Avocations: sailing, fishing, photography, art collecting. Office: GreenBridge Tech Inc 1 Center Pointe Dr La Palma CA 90623

MCNAMEE, MARK, academic administrator; BS in Chemistry, MIT, 1968; PhD, Stanford U., 1973. Postdoctoral assoc. Columbia U. Coll., 1973—75; asst. prof. U. Calif., Davis, 1975—85, prof., 1985, chair dept. biochemistry and biophysics, 1990—93, dean divsn. biol. scis., 1993—2001; provost, v.p. Va. Tech., Blacksburg, 2001—. Office: Va Tech Univ Provost and VP for Acad Affairs 210 Burruss Hall Blacksburg VA 24061 *

MCNAMEE, PATRICK, health products executive; Chief info. officer, gen. mgr. e-Bus. GE Transp. Systems, 1999—2001; sr. v.p., chief info. officer, chief quality officer NBC, 2001—02; pres. GE OEC Med. Systems, 2002—03; pres., gen. mgr. Physician Systems Misys Healthcare Systems, 2003—05; sr. v.p., chief info. officer Express Scripts, Inc., Md. Heights, Mo., 2005—. Office: Express Scripts Inc 13900 Riverport Dr Maryland Heights MO 63043 Office Phone: 314-770-1666. *

MCNAMEE, STEPHEN M., federal judge; b. 1942; BA, U. Cinn., 1964; MA, U. Ariz., 1967, JD, 1969. US atty. Dist. of Ariz., Phoenix, 1985-90; judge US Dist. Ct. Ariz., Phoenix, 1990—, chief judge, 1999—2006. Office: US Dist Judge Sandra Day O'Connor US Ct 401 W Washington St SPC 60 Phoenix AZ 85003-2158 Office Phone: 602-322-7555.

MCNAUGHTON, KENNETH JOHN, former publisher; b. Melbourne, Australia, July 22, 1940; arrived in U.S., 1970, naturalized, 2005; s. Charles Dudley and Lilian May (Besant) McN.; m. Victoria Ann Yocum, Oct. 28, 1972 (div. Oct. 1982); children: Aurelius John, Candace Ann. B in Chem. Engring., U. Melbourne, 1962; M in Engring. Sci., Monash U., Clayton, Australia, 1964. Dir. comm. network Found. Faith, NYC, 1966-77; asst. editor Chemical Engring., NYC, 1978-81, assoc. editor, 1981-86; editor-in-chief Industrial Chemist, NYC, 1986-89; dir. new publs. divsn. sci. and tech. Warren Gorham & Lamont, NYC, 1989-90; mng. editor Physics Today, NYC, 1991-94; assoc. pub. The Industrial Physicist, College Park, Md., 1995—2004. Pres. McNaughton Comms., N.Y., 1978—. Contbr. over 100 articles to profl. jours.; photo exhibitions, Ellicott City, Md., 2005. Mem. Friends of Benjamin Banneker Hist. Park, Oella, Md., 1996—; founder Campaign to Save the Trees, Roosevelt Island, N.Y., 1991; pres. PTA H.S. for the Humanities, N.Y., 1990-91; pres. bd. dirs. Greystone Condominiums, 2002-2003; mem. Romnet Newsgroup, 1997-99. Recipient Broadcast awards Coun. of Chs., 1976, 78, 79, Golden Mike awards Am. Legion, 1978, 79. Mem. SAG, AFTRA, Port Phillip Pioneers Group, Clan Macnachtan Assn. Worldwide. Avocations: music, dance, films, swimming, walking. Home: 3778 College Ave Ellicott City MD 21043-4662 Personal E-mail: kjmcn@comcast.net.

MCNAUGHTON, WILLIAM JOHN, retired bishop; b. Lawrence, Mass., Dec. 7, 1926; s. William John Sr. and Ruth Irene (Howe) McN. BA, U. of State of N.Y., Ossining, 1948, B of Sacred Theology, 1953; M in Religious Edn., Maryknoll Sem., Ossining, 1953. Ordained Maryknoll priest, 1953; cert. in Korean Lang. Studies, Yale U., 1954. Pastor Pouk Moun Ro Cath. Ch., Chong Ju Diocese, Korea, 1955-57, Nae Duk Dong Cath. Ch., Chong Ju Diocese, Korea, 1957-60; consultor Chong Ju Diocese, 1958-59, vicar gen., 1959-60; consecrated bishop Inchon (Korea) Diocese, 1961—2002, ret., 2002. Roman Catholic. Address: 39 Woodburn Dr Methuen MA 01844-2812

MCNEAL, JANE ERSKINE, music educator, musician; b. Somers Point, NJ, Oct. 29, 1958; d. James Kelley and Jane Emma McNeal. BA Psychology, Stockton State Coll., 1983; music studies, Wheaton Coll., Ill., 1976—78; Kindermusik Cert., Westminster Choir Coll., Princeton, NJ, 1997; Crescendo Music Cert., Acad. Cmty. Music, Ft. Washington, Pa., 2005. Choir dir., NJ, 1991—95; piano instr. NJ, 1975—; vocal instr. Vineland, NJ, 1999—; profl. accompanist NJ, 1976—; ch. and synagogue organist NJ, 1983—; organ and piano recitalist NJ, 1989—. Advocate for mentally ill. Scholar Nat. Merit Corp. Scholarship, Sun Shipbuilding, Chester, Pa., 1976—78; music scholar, Wheaton Coll., 1976. Mem.: Local Musicians Union, Am. Guild Organists, Nat. Guild Piano Tchrs., Psi Chi. Avocations: walking, classical music, jazz, reading. Office: St Bernadette Cath Ch 1421 New Rd Northfield NJ 08225 Home: 2112 Newcombtown Rd Millville NJ 08332 Office Phone: 609-646-5611.

MCNEAL, LYLE GLEN, science educator, rancher, consultant; b. Glendale, Calif., May 16, 1942; s. Darrell Glenn and Elizabeth Bessie McNeal; m. Nancy Coles Wilkie, Aug. 10, 1962; children: Tamara A., Sean E., Joshua M., Travis G., Susannah R., Jenny L., Ian B., Ilene L. BS in Animal Husbandry, Cal Poly Coll., 1964; MS in Animal Breeding, U. Nev., 1966; PhD in Reproductive Physiology, Utah State U., 1978. Shepherd Cal Poly Coll., Pomona, 1962—64; prof. animal sci. Cal Poly State U., San Luis Obispo, Calif., 1969—79; grad. rsch. asst. U. Nev., Reno, 1964—66, extension agt. Minden, 1966—69; rsch. scientist U.S. Sheep Experiment Sta., Dubois, Idaho, 1972—77; founder, exec. dir. Navajo Sheep Project, Logan, Utah, 1977—2002; prof. animal sci. Utah State U., Logan, 1979—. Ranch hand Bar Lazy B Ranch, Ronan, Mont., 1959—61; asst. ranch mgr. Hidden Trails Ranch, Agoura, Calif., 1960—61; Arabian horse showman Kellogg Arabian Horse Ranch, Pomona. Author: Small Ruminant Production Medicine, 2002; contbr. chapters to books. 1st lt. USAF, 1959—61, Norton AFB. Named Tchr. of Yr, U.S.D.A., 1969—94; recipient award, NHL, 1994, Nat. Camptender award, Am. Sheep Industry Assn. Mem.: Am. Livestock Breeds Conservancy (Conservation Breeder of Yr. 1996), Soc. Range Mgmt., Am. Soc. Animal Sci. (mem. tchg. com. 1972—77, Nat. Tchr. of Yr. 1996), Am. Sheep Ctr. (mem. founding bd. 1999—), Navajo-Churro Sheep Assn. (life; hon. 1986—), Dine' be'iina (life; hon. 1991—). Achievements include rescued from extinction the first domestic sheep brought to North America by the Spanish conquistadores; saved and bred back this famous Navajo-Churro sheep for the benefit of Navajo and Hispanic cultures, 1977-2002. Avocations: horseback riding, fly fishing, piloting aircraft, history, reading. Home: 85 Quarter Circle Dr Logan UT 84321 Office: Animal & Vet Dept Utah State U 4815 Old Main Hill Logan UT 84322-4815 E-mail: sheepman@cc.usu.edu.

MCNEAL, MARY KAY, secondary school educator; b. Denver, June 28, 1957; d. Elizabeth Ann and Charles Edwin Willis (Stepfather); m. Johnny Ray McNeal, Feb. 17, 1978; children: Joshua Allen, Sarah Nicole. BA in History and Edn., Augusta State U., Ga., 1986; MA in Tchg. and Learning, Nova Southeastern U., Orlando, Fla., 2002. Nat. bd. cert. tchr. 1999. Tchr. Greenwood Lakes Mid. Sch., Lake Mary, Fla., 1986—90, Rock Lake Mid. Sch., Longwood, Fla., 1991—92, Indian Trails Mid. Sch., Winter Springs, Fla., 1992—. Fundraiser Southeastern Guide Dogs, Inc., Palmetto, Fla., 1990—2006; women's leader Dorcus, Sanford, Fla., 1996—97. With US Army, 1976—79. Named Indian Trails Mid. Sch. Tchr. of Year, 1996, Indian Trails Mid. Sch. Social Studies Tchr. of Year, 2000, Orlando Sentinel Tchr. of Week, 2001. Mem.: NEA (assoc.), Fla. Geog. Alliance (assoc.), Nat. Coun. for the Social Studies (assoc.). Republican. Lutheran. Avocations: reading, gardening. Home: 105 Garden Ct Sanford FL 32771 Office: Indian Trails Middle School 415 Tuskawilla Rd Winter Springs FL 32708 Home Phone: 407-321-2772; Office Phone: 407-320-4348. Personal E-mail: mmcneal728@aol.com. Business E-Mail: mary_mcneal@scps.k12.fl.us.

MCNEAL, PHYLLIS PAULETTE, parole agent; d. Earline Brown. BA in Psychology, Calif. State U., Long Beach, 1982; MSW, Calif. State U., San Bernardino, 2003. Mental health intern Jenesse Domestic Violence Ctr., LA, 2001—01, Los Padrinos Juvenile Hall, Downey, Calif., 2002—03; group supr. Calif. Youth Authority, Norwalk, 1981—84, youth counselor Ontario, 1984—89; parole agt. I parole and cmty. svcs. divsn. Calif. Dept. Corrections, Inglewood, 1989—99, asst. unit supr. LA, 1999—. Sponsor Calif. Youth Authoity, Ontario, 1986—89; small group tng. instr. Calif. Youth Authority, Onartio, 1986—89; founder, CEO Straight Talk Program, Inc., Corona, Calif., 1990—; coll. internship coord. parole and cmty. svcs. divsn. Calif. Dept. Corrections, Ingelwood, 1990—98, defensive tactics instr., LA, 1991—99. Author: Corrections in America an Introduction, 9th edit. (Correctional Champions, 2001); editor: Corrections Today Mag. (Best in the Bus., 1998). Prison min. Abundant Living Family Ch., Rancho Cucamonga, Calif., 2003—05; prison com. mem. Nat. Assn. Equal Justice in Am., Compton, Calif., 2002—05; bd. dirs. Cornerstone Accelerated Learning Acad., LA, 2001—05. Named Parole Agt. of the Yr., Calif. Probation, Parole, and Correctional Assn., 1998, Citizen of the Week, KNX Newsradio CBS, 1998, Hero Of the Week, UPN Channel 13, 1998; recipient Cmty. Stars award, Staples, 1999, award, Freedom Jour., 2000, Trailblazer Award, First AME Ch., 2004, amb. of Progress, Blackwall St., 2005, Local Heroes Neighborhood Excellence award, Bank of Am., 2005. Mem.: Save Our Sons (assoc.; publicity com. mem. 2000—05), Black Women 's Network (assoc.), Delta Sigma Theta (life; dean pledge 1980). Office: Straight Talk Program Inc PO Box 5693 Norco CA 92860 Home Phone: 951-272-5747. Business E-Mail: straighttalkprogram@charter.net.

MCNEAL, RALPH B., social studies educator; BA in Sociology, U. Miami, Coral Gables, 1990; MA in Sociology, U. NC, Chapel Hill, 2002, PhD in Sociology, 1994. Vis. asst. prof. Wake Forest U., Winston Salem, NC, 1994—95; asst. prof. U. Conn., Storrs, Conn., 1995—2000, assoc. prof., 2000—. Dir. grad. studies U. Conn., 1997—2003. Author: Intersections; Readings in Sociology, 2000, 2006, Boundaries: Readings in Deviance, Crime & Criminal Justice, 2002, 2006, Frameworks: Introduction to Sociology; contbr. articles various profl. jours. Coach WAIM Soccer, Mansfield, Conn., 2005, Mansfield Little league, Conn., 2007; vice chair Region #19 Bd. of Edn., Storrs, 1995—2001; mem. Dem. Town Com., Ashford, Conn., 1995—2002; mem., bd. dirs. EASTCONN, Windham, 1995—2001. Nominee Nat. Tchr. of Yr. award, Nat. Soc. Collegiate Scholars, 2005; recipient Teaching Promise award, AAUP - Conn. Chpt., 1999, Citation for Teaching Excellence, State Conn., Tchr. of Yr. award, Nat. Soc. Collegiate Scholars, U. Conn. Chpt., 2005. Office: U Conn 344 Mansfield Rd Sociology U-2068 Storrs Mansfield CT 06268 Home Phone: 860-429-7973; Office Phone: 860-486-4423. Home Fax: 860-486-6356. Business E-Mail: ralph.mcneal@uconn.edu.

MCNEALEY, ERNEST, college president; m. Earnestine Green; children: Ernest II, David. BS, Ala. State U.; MAT, Ind. U.; PhD, Ohio State U. V.p. acad. affairs undergrad. acad. affairs Claflin (S.C.) U.; assoc. provost, dean of undergrad. acad. affairs SUNY, Stony Brook; pres. Stillman Coll., Tuscaloosa, Ala., 1997—. Office: Stillman Coll PO Box 1430 Tuscaloosa AL 35403-1430 E-mail: emcnealey@stillman.edu.

MCNEALY, SCOTT GLENN, information technology executive; b. Columbus, Ind., Nov. 13, 1954; s. Raymond William and Marmaline McNealy; m. Susan Ingemanson, 1994; 4 children. BA, Harvard U., Cambridge, Mass., 1976; MBA, Stanford U., Calif., 1980. With Rockwell Internat. Corp., Troy, Mich., 1976-78, sales engr.; staff engr. FMC Corp., Chgo., 1980-81; dir. ops. Onyx Systems, San Jose, Calif., 1981-82; co-founder Sun Microsystems, Inc., Santa Clara, Calif., 1982, v.p. ops., 1982—84, COO, 1984, pres., 1984—99, 2002—04, CEO, 1984—2006, chmn., 1984—. Bd. dirs. Sun Microsystems, Inc., 1982—. Named one of World's Richest People, Forbes Mag., 400 Richest Ams., Am.'s Most Powerful People. Avocation: hockey. Office: Sun Microsystems Inc 4150 Network Cir Santa Clara CA 95054 Office Phone: 650-960-1300. *

MCNEELY, JAMES LEE, lawyer; b. Shelbyville, Ind., May 4, 1940; s. Carl R. and Elizabeth J. (Orebaugh) McN.; m. Rose M. Wisker, Sept. 5, 1977; children: Angela, Susan, Meg, Matt. AB, Wabash Coll., 1962; JD, Ind. U., 1965. Bar: Ind. 1965, U.S. Dist. Ct. (so. dist.) Ind. 1965, U.S. Ct. Appeals (7th cir.) 1970. Assoc. Pell & Matchett, Shelbyville, 1965-70; ptnr. Matchett & McNeely, Shelbyville, 1970-74; sole practice Shelbyville, 1974-76; sr. ptnr. McNeely & Sanders, Shelbyville, 1976-86, McNeely, Sanders & Stephenson, Shelbyville, 1986-89, McNeely, Sanders, Stephenson & Thopy, Shelbyville, 1989-96, McNeely, Stephenson, Thopy & Harrold, Shelbyville, 1997—. Guest lectr. Franklin Coll., Ind., 1965-72; judge Shelbyville City Ct., 1967-71. Chmn. Shelbyville County Rep. Cen. Com., 1968-88; bd. dirs. Ind. Lung Assn., 1972-75, Crossroads Council Boy Scouts Am., 1982; trustee Wabash Coll., 2004—; bd. dirs., pres. Shelbyville Girls Club. Named Sagamore of the Wabash, Gov. Ed Whitcomb, 1971, Gov. Otis Bowen, 1977, Gov. Robert Orr, 1986, 88, Gov. Evan Bayh, 1996, Gov. Frank O'Bannon, 1999; recipient Lifetime Citizenship award for growth Shelby County C. of C., 2003. Fellow Ind. Bar Found. (patron, sec. 1999-2000, chair elect 2000-01, chmn. 2002-03); mem. ABA, Ind. Bar Assn. (sec. 1985-87, bd. dirs. 1976-78, chair-elect Ho. Dels. 1994-95, chair 1995-96, v.p. 1996-97, pres.-elect 1997-98, pres. 1998-99), Shelby County Bar Assn. (pres. 1975), Ind. Lawyers Commn. (pres., dir.), Fed. Merit Selection Commn. (adv. mem. 1988-92, chmn. 2001—), Shelbyville Jaycees (Distinguished Service award 1969, Good Govt. award 1970), Wabash Coll. Nat. Assn. Wabash Men (dir. 1983-89, sec. 1989-91, v.p. 1991-93, pres. 1993-95, Man of Yr. 1995), Kappa Sigma Alpha Pi chpt. (Hall of Fame 1995). Lodges: Lions, Elks, Eagles. Methodist. Avocations: golf, travel. Home: 1902 E Old Rushville Rd Shelbyville IN 46176-9569

MCNEELY, PATRICIA GANTT, communications educator; b. Winnsboro, SC, Dec. 2, 1939; d. William Adolphus and Alice (Woodson) Gantt; m. Alfred Raymond McNeely, Apr. 8, 1960; children: Allison Patricia, Alan David. BA, Furman U., 1960; MA, U. S.C., 1975. Reporter Greenville (S.C.) News, 1958-60, Columbia (S.C.) Record, 1960-66, 66-72, news editor, 1979-80; reporter The State, Columbia, 1965-66; prof. journalism U. S.C., Columbia, 1972—, Eleanor M. and R. Frank Mundy prof. of journalism, 2000—, dir. print and electronic sequence, 2000—. State mgr. Voter News Svc., N.Y., 1972—; workshop dir. Reader's Digest, Pleasantville, N.Y., 1985—. Author: Fighting Words: A History of the Media of South Carolina, The Palmetto Press: The History of South Carolina's Newspapers and the Press Association. Mem. Assn. for Edn. in Journalism and Mass Comm. (sec. mag. divsn. 1995-96, head newspaper divsn. 1988-89, standing profl. freedom and responsibility com. 1995-98). Office: Univ SC Coll Journalism Mass Comm Blossom At Assembly Sts Columbia SC 29208-0001

MCNEESE, BEVERLY DIANE, language educator; b. Turlock, Calif., Apr. 4, 1952; d. Jesse Audry and Willie Jean Doty; m. Timothy Dean McNeese; children: Noah Michael, Summer Elizabeth. AA, York Coll., Nebr., 1973, BA in English, 1995; MA in Edn., Drury U., Springfield, Mo., 2003. With White County Libr., Searcy, Ark., 1974—75; presch. tchr. East Grand Ch. of Christ, Springfield, Mo., 1976—91; learning disabilities paraprofessional Strafford Pub. Schs., Mo., 1991—92; libr. aide Levitt Libr., York Coll., Nebr., 1992—94; adj. faculty dept. English, York Coll., 1995—2002, asst. prof. English, 2003—. Mem.: Kappa Omicron Nu, Sigma Tau Delta (York Coll. chpt. pres. 1995—96, York Coll. chpt. faculty sponsor 1998—2006). Republican. Mem. Ch. Of Christ. Avocations: refinishing antiques, reading, travel. Home: 5 Arbor Ct York NE 68467 Office: York Coll Dept English 1125 E Eighth St York NE 68467 Office Phone: 402-363-5690. Office Fax: 402-363-5699. E-mail: bdmcneese@york.edu.

MCNEIL, BARBARA JOYCE, radiologist, educator; b. Cambridge, Mass., Feb. 11, 1941; d. Archibald Pius and Katherine (Joyce) McNeil. AB, Emmanuel Coll., 1962; MD, Harvard U., 1966, PhD, 1972. Diplomate Am. Bd. Nuc. Medicine. Intern Mass. Gen. Hosp., Boston, 1966—67, resident in nuclear medicine, 1971—73; radiologist nuclear medicine Brigham and Women's Hosp., 1974—, Dana-Farber Cancer Inst., Boston, 1976—; prof. radiology and clin. epidemiology Harvard Med. Sch. and Brigham & Women's Hosp., Boston, 1983—88, dir. ctr. for cost effective care, 1980—93; chmn. Dept. Health Care Policy Harvard Med. Sch., 1988—, Ridley Watts prof. health care policy, 1990—, acting dean, 2007. Chmn. Blue Cross-Mass. Hosp. Assn. Fund for Coop. Innovation, 1981—87; mem. Prospective Payment Assessment Commn., 1983—91; mem. nat. adv. coun. Agy. for Health Care Policy, Rsch. and Evaluation, 1991—96; mem. med. adv. com. Blue Cross Blue Shield, 1993—; mem. coverage adv. com. Medicare, 2001—. Contbr. articles to profl. jours. Recipient Rsch. Career Develop. award, Nat. Inst. Health, 1976—81. Fellow: AAAS, Am. Coll. Nuc. Physicians (Presdl. award 1995); mem.: Soc. Nuc. Medicine, Am. Coll. Radiology, Inst. Medicine (coun. 1991—97), Am. Acad. Arts and Scis. Office: Harvard Med Sch Dept Health Care Policy 180 Longwood Ave Rm 202-A Boston MA 02115-5821 Office Phone: 617-432-1909. Business E-Mail: mcneil@hcp.med.harvard.edu.

MCNEIL, BARRY, lawyer; b. Lubbock, Tex., June 29, 1944; BA, Tex. Tech U., 1966; JD, U. Tex., 1969. Bar: Tex. 1969, admitted to practice: US Supreme Ct. 1969, US Dist. Ct. (Ea. Dist.) Tex., US Dist. Ct. (So. Dist.) Tex., US Dist. Ct. (No. Dist.) Tex., US Ct. Appeals (5th Cir.). Trial atty. antitrust divsn. Dept. Justice, 1970-75, chief Dallas office antitrust divsn., 1975-79; ptnr. & head Antitrust & Securities Group Haynes and Boone LLP, Dallas. Co-editor: Internal Corp. Investigations (2nd edit.). Fellow: Am. Coll. Trial Lawyers; mem.: ABA (chmn. Litig. Sect. 1996—97). Office: Haynes and Boone LLP 901 Main St Ste 3100 Dallas TX 75202-3789 Office Phone: 214-651-5580. Office Fax: 214-200-0535. Business E-Mail: barry.mcneil@haynesboone.com.

MCNEIL, CHRISTOPHER RYAN, emergency physician, military officer; b. Lincoln, Nebr., Aug. 28, 1975; s. Gale Lee and Carol Joy McNeil; m. Annjanett Marie Kuligowski, Nov. 26, 1997; children: Trevor Ryan, Andrew Sayer. BS, U. Nebr., Lincoln, 1996; MD, U. Nebr. Med. Ctr., Omaha, 2002. Cert. Am. Bdf Emergency Medicine, 2006, ACLS Am. Heart Assn., 2002, advanced trauma life support ACS, 2002. Chemist Novartis Pharmaceuticals, Lincoln, 1996—98; tng. coord., tissue specialist Nebr. Organ Retrieval Sys., Omaha, 2000—02; commd. 2d lt. US Army, 2002, advanced through grades to capt.; asst. prof. emergency medicine residency program Brooke Army Med. Ctr., San Antonio, 2005—, simulation lab. coord., 2005—; squadron surgeon 1-10 Cav., 2nd Brigade, 4th Inf. Divsn., US Army, Baghdad, Iraq, 2006—07. Decorated Bronze Star US Army, Army Commendation Medal U.S. Army; recipient Outstanding Sr. Resident Clinitian Award, SAUSEC Emergency Medicine Residency Program, 2005; U. Founds. scholar, U. Nebr., 1993—97, HPSP scholar, US Army, 1998—2002. Mem.: Am. Coll. Emergency Physicians. Achievements include research in utility of portable ultrasounography in diagnosis and triage of patients in a combat zone. Home: 4015 Albright San Antonio TX 78247 Office: Brooke Army Med Ctr 3851 Roger Brooke Dr Fort Sam Houston TX 78234-4501 Home Phone: 210-403-3258; Office Phone: 210-916-0808.

MCNEIL, DONALD G., JR., journalist; With NY Times, NYC, 1976—, sci. reporter. Co-recipient Madeline Dane Ross award, Overseas Press Club Am., 2007, Grand prize, Robert F. Kennedy Journalism Awards, 2007. Office: NY Times 229 W 43rd St New York NY 10036 *

MCNEIL, EDWARD WARREN, real estate company executive; b. Alhambra, Calif., Jan. 5, 1942; s. Murray Charles and Helen Katherine (Curtis) McN.; m. Jutta Bocking, Apr. 1, 1941; children: Anja Britt, Bradley Stuart. Student, U. Calif., Berkeley, 1960-63. Structures engr. Peter Kiewit Sons Co., various cities, Calif., 1961-63; project engr. Huntington Harbour, Sunset Beach, Calif., 1963-64; project supt. Coordinated Realty, Inc., Anaheim, Calif., 1964-65; field ops. mgr. Lear Siegler, Saigon, Vietnam, 1965-67; project engr. Constructora Emkay, Rio Blanco, Chile, 1968-69; ptnr. The Pyramid Cos., Syracuse, NY, 1969-75, The Pioneer Group, Syracuse, 1975-95, ret., 1995. Past chmn., bd. dirs. Crouse Irving Meml. Hosp. Found., Syracuse, 1986—2005; emeritus bd. dirs. Crouse Iving Meml. Hosp. Found., Syracuse, 2005—; trustee, past vice-chmn. Everson Mus. Art, Syracuse, 1981—94; past chmn., vice-chmn., bd. dirs. Syracuse Stage, 1981—93; chmn. Adirondack chpt. Nature Conservancy, 1994—2001, trustee, 2002—, trustee NY state bd., 1998—; trustee Adirondack Land Trust, 1990—2002, chmn., 1994—2001; trustee Manlius Pebble Hill Sch., 1984—86, 1994—99, emeritus, 1999—; vol. pilot Nature Conservancy, No. Wings. Recipient award for svc. to the arts, Cultural Resource Coun., Syracuse, 1987. Mem. Seaplane Pilots Assn., Slocum Soc., Lake Amphibian Flyers Club, Warbirds of Am., No. Lake Flyers Club. Avocations: sailing, fly fishing, seaplane flying, aviation writing, filmmaking.

MCNEIL, HELEN JO CONNOLLY, nursing educator, public health administrator; b. Olympia, Wash., June 15, 1925; d. James Ambrose and Corinne Marie (Bordeaux) Connolly; m. Robert Phillip McNeil, Aug. 16, 1947; children: Sheryl Ann Andrews, Robert John, Maureen Connolly McNeil, Kevin Charles. BSN, Seattle Coll., 1947; MSN, U. Wash., Seattle, 1961, postgrad., 1974—80. RN Wash., S.C., Tex., Va., cert. pub. health nurse, 1962. Clinic nurse Schutt Clinic, Bremerton, Wash., 1947-49; staff nurse Providence Hosp., Seattle, 1950-60, Overlake Hosp., Bellevue, Wash., 1961-62; pub. health nurse Seattle King County Health Dept. and Vis. Nurse Svc., 1962-64, pub. health nurse supr., 1964-65, assoc. dir. pub. health nursing and vis. nurse svc., 1965-70, health planning and evaluation specialist, 1970-73, adminstr. S.E. dist., 1973-78, adminstr. Ctrl. dist., 1979-81, adminstr. N. dist., 1981-84, dir. nursing rsch., 1984-85; lectr. Sch. Nursing U. Wash., Seattle, 1985-87; mem. faculty S. Puget Sound C.C., Olympia, 1987-88; vis. faculty Sch. Nursing Clemson U., SC, 1988; instr. coll. nursing allied health U. Tex., El Paso, 1988-90; dir. pub. health nursing Commonwealth Va., Richmond, 1990-93; lectr. Sch. Nursing Seattle U., 1995; cons. Seattle, Seaview, 1995—. Mem. panel in nursing edn. Am. Assn. Colls. of Nursing, 1985—87; adj. assoc. prof. Sch. Pub. Health U. N.C., Chapel Hill, 1980—92; adj. asst. prof. U. Wash. Sch. Nursing, 1965—85; rev. com. nursing census USPHS, 1970—72; health care cons., Kuwait, 1976; lectr. Congress on Nutrition, Rio de Janeiro, 1978. Author: Feasting on a Moveable Island, 1980, Reaching Out, 1998; contbr. articles to profl. jours., chpts. to books. Mem. task force Seattle Health Policy, 1981, Seattle 2000 Commn., 1973; lectr. Internat. Congress Social Psychiatry, Athens, 1974; with Project Hope Internat. Approaches in Health Care of Elderly, Milwood, Va., 1983-84; co-project dir. occupl. health con. edn. for cmty. nurses divsn. nursing U. Wash., 1983-86; mem. ARC Disater Team, Seattle, 1995-97, Parent and Home Health Bd., Richmond, Va., 1990-93; vol. Red Cross, 1994-97. With U.S. cadet nursing corps USPHS, 1943-47. Stress Rsch. grantee Heath Resources Adminstrn., 1974, W. K. Kellog Found. grantee U. Tex., El Paso, 1990, grantee U. Wash., 1983-86; recipient Nursing Adminstrn. Recognition award Jour. Nursing Adminstrn., 1993. Fellow: APHA (nursing sect. pres. 1992—93, Ruth B. Freeman Disting. Career award 1998); mem.: Assn. State and Territorial Dirs. Nursing (emeritus), Seattle Mgmt. Assn. (pres. 1976, Disting. Adminstrv. Svc. award City of Seattle 1976), Wash. State Pub. Health Assn. (pres. 1976—77, Adminstrv. Svc. award 1975), Assn. Cmty. Health Nurse Educators (founder, pres. 1985), Seattle U. Alumni (mem. nursing adv. bd. 1993—96, Cmty. Svc. Alumni award 1992), Sigma Theta Tau (internat. rsch. conf. Seoul, South Korea 1984). Avocations: gardening, travel, writing, cooking, paddocks for six hourses. Home and Office: PO Box 173 Seaview WA 98644-0173 Office Phone: 360-642-4958.

MCNEIL, PAUL JOSEPH, JR., financial analyst; b. Winthrop, Mass., Oct. 11, 1941; s. Paul Joseph Sr. and Helen Margaret (Carr) McN. Cert. in ins., U. R.I., 1965; cert. in travel agts., Travel Sch. of Am., 1968; cert., Labor Sch. of Boston, 1976, Labor Studies Inst., 1989. Field investigator R.I. Food Stamp Unit, Providence, 1965-68; cmty. rels. Coordinator Ecology Action for Rhode Island, 1970-71; sec. and rsch. asst. R.I. Worker Assn., 1973-74; enumerator R.I. Polk & Co., Providence, 1970-83; sr. employment security interviewer R.I. Dept. Employment Tng., Providence, 1984-96; sr. employment & tng. interviewer R.I. Dept. Labor & Tng., Providence, 1996—2003, benefits claims specialist, 2003—04; bd. trustees Warwick Pub. Libr., 2003—, vice chair bd. trustees, 2006—. Rec. sec. Local 189 New Eng. chpt., Boston, 1973-76, treas., 1989—; mem. bd. dirs. of R.I. Workers Assn., 1973-74, 75-76, census enumerator U.S. Census Bur., Providence, 1990; mail handler U.S. Post Office, Providence, 1980; claims interviewer R.I. Dept. Employment Security, Providence, 1979-84; rec. sec. R.I. Employment Security Alliance, Providence, 1980-90; v.p. Community Econs. Edn. Ctr., Providence, 1988-91. Exec. com. R.I. State Employees Assn., 1966-68, Community Labor Organizing Com., Providence, 1983-89, Sane Freeze, Washington, 1989-90; shop steward Local 401 SEIU, Providence, 1990-92, 1st v.p., 1992-96; rec. sec. R.I. Sane Freeze, Providence, 1988-94; mem. Nat. Com. Peace Action, 1993—; v.p. Peace Action R.I., 1994-95, pres., 1995—; coord. R.I. Nation Readers Group, 1995—; state committeeman Amvets Dept. R.I., 1965-69, 96—, adj. posts, 1965-68, trustee post 6, 1995-96; v.p. Labor Party R.I., 1994-97, treas., 1997-, pres., 1999, chmn., 1999; exec. bd. R.I. Coalition for Consumer Justice, 1997-2006, v.p., 2006; bd. dirs. Injured Workers R.I., 1996—, Warwick Cmty. Action, 1967-69, R.I. Legal Svcs., 1967-69; founder East Greenwich Dem. Youth Club, 1959; co-chmn. Human Rights Action Coun., Warwick, 1968-70; del. R.I. Dem. State Conv., 1976, 78; mem. R.I. Dem. State Com., 1980-86, bd. dirs., 1985-87; mem. Third Rep. Com., 1976-86, Dem. Study Group R.I., 1986-88, Warwick Democratic City Com., 2000-; organizer United Farm Workers, 1968-71; mem. Fox Point Neighborhood Housing Corp. Dirs., 1980-87, pres., 1981-83, sec., 1983-87; pres. Coalition Consumer Justice, 2000-05. With U.S. Army, 1960-63, ETO. Mem. Internat. Assn. Pers. in Employment Security (R.I. chpt. bd. dirs. 1989-93, sec. 1991-93), Greater R.I. Indsl. Rels. Rsch. Assn., R.I. ACLU (bd. dirs. 1974-80, bd. sec. 1975-77, exec. com. 1979-80), Union of Peace Profls. (exec. bd. 1988-90), Nat. Writers Union, R.I. Cen. Am. Network, Cath. Peace Fellowship, Pax ChristiAncient Order, Order of Hibernians (rec. sec. Providence chpt. 1990-91, 97-98, v.p., 1998-2003, pres. 1991-92, state sec. 1993-96, 99-2005, state pres. 1996-99, state organizer, 2001-03, sec. Providence County 2003—), K. of C., Sierra Club, Newport Mus. Irish History, Am. Irish Hist. Soc., R.I. Hist. Soc., R.I. Labor History Soc., Gaspee Days Com., Americans for Dem. Action, Debs Found., Edward Bellamy Meml. Assn., R.I. Irish Famine Meml. Com., Am. Legion, Indsl. Rels. Rsch. Assn., Assn. Can.-Am., Am. French Geneal. Soc., Irish Nat. Caucus, Am. Irish Polit. Edn. Com., Friendly Sons of St. Patrick (East Greenwich, R.I.), Progressive Democrats of Am. Democrat. Avocation: writing. Home: 155 Hilton Rd Warwick RI 02889-2932

MCNEIL, RAMSEY ENGLISH, religious studies educator; b. Franklin County, Va., Sept. 28, 1937; d. George Wilson and Eva Woody English; m. Carl Nixon McNeil, June 2, 1967; 1 child, Carl Nixon. BS in Edn., Radford Coll., Va., 1958; MS in Edn., Radford U., Va., 1968. Sch. tchr. Franklin County Pub. Sch., Rocky Mount, Va., 1958—59, Danville City Pub. Sch., Danville, Va., 1959—63, Roanoke City Sch., 1963—67, Mongomery County Sch., Christiansburg, Va., 1967—70; tchr. Bible quiz local chs., Va., 1978—89, tchr. adult Sunday sch. Va., 1996—, tchr. Wed. A.M. women's Bible study, 1998—. Den leader Boy Scouts Am., Christiansburg, 1978—80; sch. vol. Mongomery County, Va., 1976—91; v.p. Auxiliary Va. Auctioneers, 2005—06; sec. bd. dirs. Montgomery Mus., Christiansburg, Va., 1995—; foster parent, 1976—86. Mem.: United Daus. Confederacy (pres. 1974—99, 1st dist. chair 1997—99, org. new chpts. com. 1999—2003, v.p. 1999—2006, 1st dist. chair 2003—05, org. new chpts. com. 2005—07), Ea. Star (pianist 1989—96, chaplain 1998—). Republican. Baptist. Avocations: reading, antiques, flowers, travel. Home: 5234 Old Pagelyn Rd Radford VA 24141-6518

MCNEIL, WENDY LAWSON-JOHNSTON, foundation administrator; d. Peter and Dorothy Stevenson Hammond Lawson-Johnston; m. Thomas K. McNeil; 1 child, Lawson Johnston McNeil Wijesooriya. V.p. Solomon R. Guggenheim Found. Bd. trustees Solomon R. Guggenheim Mus. Office: Solomon R Guggenheim Found 1071 Fifth Ave New York NY 10128

MCNEILL, CORBIN ASAHEL, JR., utilities executive; b. Santa Fe, July 6, 1939; s. Corbin Asahel and Madeline (Thielen) McN.; m. Dorice Schiller, June 16, 1962; children: Michele, Corbin IV, Kevin, Alicia, Timothy. BS in Marine Engring., U.S. Naval Acad., 1962; postgrad., Naval Nuclear Power Sch., Mare Island, Md., 1962-63, U. Calif., Berkeley, 1975-76, Syracuse U., 1983-84. Commd. ensign USN, 1962, advanced through grades to comdr., 1981, ret., 1981; sr. v.p. nuclear generation N.Y. Power Authority, White Plains, 1981-85, Pub. Service Electric & Gas Co., Hancocks Bridge, N.J., 1985-88; exec. v.p. nuclear div. PECO Energy Co., 1988-90; pres., COO Phila. Electric Co., 1990-95, pres., CEO, 1995—, also chmn., 1997—. Pres. Adwin Equipment Co., Phila., 1990—. Trustee The Meml. Hosp. of Salem County (N.J.) Inc., 1986; chmn. TeamWalk March of Dimes, Salem, 1986; bd. dirs. Oswego (N.Y.) C. of C., 1982-83. Mem. Am. Nuclear Soc., Nuclear Utility Mgmt. and Resources Com. Avocations: skiing, reading. Office: PECO Energy Co PO Box 8699 2301 Market St Philadelphia PA 19101

MCNEILL, DAN K., career military officer; b. NC, July 23, 1946; m. Maureen McNeill; 1 child, Dan. BS in Agr. and Forestry, NC State U., 1968; grad., US Army War Coll., 1989; attended, Inf. Officer Basic and Advanced Cources, US Army Command and Gen. Staff Coll.; degree (hon.), NC State U., 2003. Advanced through grades to gen. US Army, 2004, commd. 2nd lt., 1968, sr, aide-de-camp to commdg. gen., 1st Inf. Divsn. (mechanized) Fort Riley, Kans., 1971—72, fixed wing avaitor, later asst. ops. officer, later ops. officer, 55th Aviation Co., 52d Aviation Bn., Korea, 1972—73, asst. S-3 (ops.) (air), 2d Bn. (airborne), 505th Inf., 82 Airborne Divsn. Fort Bragg, NC, 1974, commdr., combat support co., 2d Bn. (airborne), 505th Inf., 82 Airborne Divsn., 1974—76, commdr., E Co., 2d Bn. (Airborne), 505th Inf., 82d Airborne Divsn., 1977—78, sec. to gen. staff, US Army So, European Vicenza, Italy, 1984—85, exec. officer, 1st Bn., 509th Inf., later renamed 4th Bn., 325th Inf., 1982—84, commdr.,1st Bn., 325th Inf., 82d Airborne Divsn. Fort Bragg, NC, 1986—88, asst. chief of staff, G-3 (Ops.), 82d Airborne Divsn., Operation Just Cause, Panama and Operation Desert Shield/Storm, Saudi Arabia, 1989—91, commdr., 3d Brigade, 82d Airborne Corps, 1991—93, asst. S-3 (Ops.), later S-3 (Ops.), 3d Brigade, 82d Airborne Divsn., 1976—77, asst. chief of state, G-3 (Ops.), XVIII Airboboure Coprs., 1993—95, asst. divsn. commdr., 2d Inf. Divsn, Korea, 1995—96, chief of staff, XVIII Airborne Corp. Fort Bragg, NC, 1996—97, dep. commdg. gen., I Corps and Fort Lewis Wis., commdg. gen. 82d Airborne Divsn. Fort Bragg, NC, 1998—2000, commdg. gen., combined joint task force-180 Afghanistan, 2000—03, commdg. gen., XVIII Airborne Corps and Fort Bragg, NC, 2000—03; dep. commdg. gen., chief of staff US Army Forces Command, Fort McPherson, Ga., 2003—04, commdg. gen., 2004—07; comdr., Internat. Assistance Security Force NATO, 2007—; comdr. Combined Forces Command, Afghanistan, 2007—. Asst. prof. mil. sci., first reserve officer tng. corps region Ga. Mil. Coll., Milledgeville, Ga., 1978—80; doctrine author, dept. tactics US Army Command and Gen. Staff Coll., Fort Leavenworth, Kans., 1981—82. Decorated Defense Superior Svc. medal, Legion of Merit wirh 2 Oak clusters, Bronze Star medal with 2 oak leaf clusters, Meritorious Svc. medal with 3 Oak Clusters, Army Commendation medal with 2 Oak Leaf Clusters, Army Achievement medal, Expert Infantryman badge, Army Avaitor badge, Master Parachutist badge with Bronze star, Spl. Forces Tab. Office: ISAF-Kabul (AFG) Pub Info Office Feldpost 64298 Damstadt Germany *

MCNEILL, DANIEL RICHARD, writer; b. San Francisco, June 1, 1947; s. Daniel Harry and Maureen Evangeline (Sherriff) McN.; m. Rosalind Deborah Gold, Dec. 20, 1984. AB, U. Calif., Berkeley, 1975; JD, Harvard U., 1982. Author: Fuzzy Logic, 1993 (L.A. Times Book prize in sci. and tech. 1993), The Face, 1998. Mem. Authors Guild. Avocations: photography, bodybuilding. Home and Office: 8110 Redlands St #306 Playa Del Rey CA 90293

MCNEILL, FELITA GALE, nurse, military officer; b. Tampa, Fla., Aug. 4, 1956; d. Claude and Violet Branton; m. Charles McNeill (div. June 1996); children: Malikah Dawkins Daffin, Kahlilah L Dawkins, Rashad Dawkins. BSN, U. So. Fla., 1990; M in edn., 2000; EdS, U. Sarasota, 2002; EdD, Argosy U., 2004. RN Manatee County Health Dept., Bradenton, Fla., 1991—94; sch. nurse Pinellas County Health Dept., St. Petersburg, Fla., 1992—94; LPN instr. Pinellas County Sch. Bd., St. Petersburg, 1994—2001, CNA instr., 1994—2001, tchr. sci., 1994—2001; faculty/rsch. instr. U. So. Fla., Tampa, 2002—; capt./instr. U.S. Army Res., Jacksonville, Fla., 1990—. Major USAR, 1990—, St. Petersburg. Office: Felita Gale McNeill Fine Arts Studio 1600 4th St S Saint Petersburg FL 33712 Home: 3285 40th Way S Apt C Saint Petersburg FL 33711-3993

MCNEILL, G. DAVID, psychologist, educator; b. Santa Rosa, Calif., Dec. 21, 1931; s. Glenn H. and Ethel G. (Little) McN.; m. Nobuko Baba, Dec. 17, 1957; children: Cheryl, Randall L.B. AB, U. Calif., Berkeley, 1953, PhD, 1962. Research fellow Harvard U., 1962-65; asst. prof. psychology U. Mich., 1965-66, assoc. prof., 1966-68; prof. psychology and linguistics U. Chgo., 1969—2001, chmn. dept. psychology, 1991-97, prof. emeritus, 2001—. Vis. fellow Ctr. for Humanities, Wesleyan U., Middletown, Conn., 1970; mem. Inst. Advanced Study, Princeton, 1973-75; fellow Netherlands Inst. for Advanced Studies, 1983-84; visitor Max Planck Inst. for Psycholinguistics, Nijmegen, Netherlands, 1998-99 Author: The Acquisition of Language, 1970, The Conceptual Basis of Language, 1979, Psycholinguistics: A New Approach, 1987, Gengo Shinrigaku, 1991, Hand and Mind: What Gestures Reveal about Thought, 1992, Gesture and Thought, 2005; editor: Language and Gesture, 2000. Recipient Faculty Achievement award, 1991, Ann. Excellence in Pub. award Assn. Am. Pubs., Gordon G. Laing prize U. Chgo. Press, 1995; Guggenheim fellow, 1973-74; grantee NSF, 1983-89, 97—, Spencer Found., 1979-82, 89-92, 95-99, NIDCD, 1992-96, Advanced Rsch. and Devel. Agy., 2003—. Fellow AAAS, Am. Psychol. Soc.; mem. Internat. Soc. Gesture Studies (v.p. 2002-05, hon. pres. 2007—), Cognitive Sci. Soc., Linguistic Soc. Am., Violoncello Soc., Phi Beta Kappa, Sigma Xi Office: U Chgo Dept Psychology 5848 S University Ave Chicago IL 60637-1515 Office Phone: 773-702-8833. Business E-Mail: dmcneill@uchicago.edu.

MCNEILL, JOHN HUGH, pharmaceutical sciences educator; b. Chgo., Dec. 5, 1938; s. John and Agnes Margaret (McLean) McN.; m. Sharon Keneffly, July 27, 1963; children: Sandra, Laurie. BS, U. Alta., Can., 1960, MS, 1962; PhD, U. Mich., 1967. Lectr. pharmacy Dalhousie U., 1962-63, U. Alta., 1963; research assoc. U. Mich., Ann Arbor, 1963-65, teaching fellow, 1965-66; asst. instr. Mich. State U., East Lansing, 1966-67, asst. prof., 1967-71; assoc. prof. U. B.C., 1971-72, assoc. prof., chmn. div. pharmacology and toxicology, 1972-75, dir. rsch. and grad. studies Faculty Pharm. Scis., 1977-78, prof. Faculty Pharm. Scis., 1975—2004, dean Faculty Pharm. Scis., 1985-96, asst. dean, 1978-81, Med. Rsch. Coun. rsch. prof., 1981-82, prof., assoc. dean rsch. and grad. studies, 1982-84, prof. and dean emeritus, 2004—. Contbr. more than 800 tech. articles to profl. jours. Fellow Royal Soc. Can., Internat. Acad. Cardiovasc. Scis., Can. Acad. Health Scis., Am. Coll. Nutrition; mem. Pharm. Soc. Can. (various coms. 1974-88, coun. 1977-83, v.p. 1979, pres. 1980-81), Am. Soc. for Pharm. and Therapeutics (J.J. Abel award com. 1981, Upjohn award com., 1978-80, chmn. mem. com. 1983-86), Western Pharm. Soc. (coun. 1977-81, pres. 1979-80, past pres. 1980-81), N.Y. Acad. Scis., Internat. Soc. for Heart Rsch. (coun. 1986-95), AAAS, B.C. Coll. Pharms. (coun. 1985-96), Internat. Union Pharmacologists (Can. rep. 1982-88), Am. Pharm. Assn. Office: Univ BC Fac Pharm Scis 2146 East Mall Vancouver BC Canada V6T 1Z3 Home Phone: 604-224-5456; Office Phone: 604-822-9373. E-mail: jmcneill@interchange.ubc.ca.

MCNEILL, ROBERT PATRICK, investment advisor; b. Chgo., Mar. 17, 1941; s. Donald Thomas and Katherine (Bennett) McN.; m. Martha Stephan, Sept. 12, 1964; children— Jennifer, Donald, Victoria, Stephan, Elizabeth BA summa cum laude (valedictorian), U. Notre Dame, 1963; M.Letters, Oxford U., 1967. Chartered investment counselor. Assoc. Stein Roe & Farnham, Chgo., 1967-72, gen. ptnr., 1972-77, sr. ptnr., 1977-86, exec. v.p., 1986-89; pres., mng. dir. Stein Roe Internat., Chgo., 1989—. Underwriting mem. Lloyds of London, 1980—; dir. Comml. Chgo. Corp.; vice chmn. bd. Hill Internat. Prodn. Co., Houston, 1982—; dir., adv. bd. Touche Remnant Investment Counselors, London, 1983—; dir. TR Worldwide Strategy Fund, Luxembourg, Konrad Adenauer Fund for European Policy Studies, Fed. Republic Germany. Voting mem., sec Ill. Rhodes Scholarship Selection Com.; voting mem. Ill. rep. Great Lakes Dist. Rhodes Scholarship Selection Com.; bd. dirs. Kennedy Sch. for Retarded Children, Palos Park, Ill., 1972—, Winnetka United Way, Ill., 1984—, Division St. YMCA, Chgo., 1972—; assoc. Rush-Presbyterian-St. Lukes Med. Ctr., Chgo., 1975—; mem. leadership com. Rush Alzheimer's Disease Ctr. Rhodes scholar, 1963 Fellow Fin. Analysts Fedn.; mem. Chgo. Council on Fgn. Relations (bd. dirs., treas. 1975—), Inst. European Studies (bd. govs., vice-chmn. 1981—), Investment Analysts Soc. Chgo. (chgo. com., com. on fgn. affairs, com. on internat. and domestic issues), Assn. for Investment Mgmt. and Rsch., Chgo. Soc. Clubs, Econ. Club of Chgo, Sunset Ridge Country (bd. dirs. Northfield, Ill., 1983—). Avocations: coin collecting/numismatics, bridge, golf, skiing, art. Office Phone: 312-368-7684. Business E-Mail: rmcneill@sric.net.

MCNEILL, SAMUEL GAITHER, farm management extension agent, educator, engineering educator; b. Jefferson, NC, Sept. 5, 1952; s. Peter T. and Anna L. McNeill. BS in Agrl. Engring., U. Ky., Lexington, 1974, MS in Agrl. Engring., 1979; PhD, U. Tenn., Knoxville, 1996. Rsch. engr. U. Ky., Lexington, 1975—78, ext. agrl. engr. Princeton, 1979—97, asst. ext. prof., 1998—2003, assoc. ext. prof., 2004—. Mem. St. Thomas More Cath. Ch., Paducah, Ky., 2000—06, choir mem., 2004—06, parrish coun. mem., 2006—. Grantee Optimization of aeration systems for value-added crop preservation, Nat. Inst. Rsch., 2001—05, Integrating IPM strategies in on-farm stored wheat, US Dept. Agr., 2001—05, Converting soybean oil to hydrogen gas, Ky. Soybean Promotion Bd., 2002—03, Tours of ethanol and biodiesel prodn. facilities in Ky., US Dept. Energy, 2004—05. Mem.: Am. Soc. of Agrl. and Biol. Engineers (mem. grain processing and storage com. 1979—2006, chair textbooks and monographs com. 2000—06, mem. biomass energy com. 1982—2006, Ednl. award for extension 1997, Ednl. award for extension methods 2003), Ky. Asssociation of State Ext. Professionals (bd. dirs. 2004—06, Outstanding Program award 2006), UK Coll. of Agr. Alumni Assn. (life), Chain Reaction Cycling Club, West Ky. Runner's Club. Roman Catholic. Avocations: running, bicycling, swimming, triathlon. Office: U Ky 1205 Hopkinsville St Princeton KY 42445-0469 Office Phone: 270-365-7541. Office Fax: 270-365-2667. Business E-Mail: smcneill@uky.edu.

MCNEILL, THOMAS RAY, lawyer; b. Pitts., June 2, 1952; s. Thomas William McNeill and Mary (Shiveley) Hiss; m. Patsy Lynch, June 25, 1977; children: Elizabeth, Kathleen, Thomas. BSBA, U. Fla., 1974; JD, Emory U., 1977. Bar: Ga. 1977, U.S. Dist. Ct. (no. dist.) Ga. 1977. Assoc. Powell Goldstein LLP, Atlanta, 1977-84, ptnr., 1984—, mgr. corp. dept., 1993-95, bd. ptnrs., 1998—2004, co-leader Bus. Transactions Group, 2003—05, leader, 2005—. Mem. ABA (mem. com. on corp. laws 2007-), Ga. Bar Assn. (exec. com. bus. law sect., 2001—), Emory U. Alumni Assn. (pres. exec. com. 1988-89, Law Sch. coun. 1990-2000, 2003—, chmn. 2005-07), Soc. of Internat. Bus. Fellows, Beta Gamma Sigma. Office: Powell Goldstein LLP 1201 W Peachtree St NW 14th Fl Atlanta GA 30309-3488 Office Phone: 404-572-6681. E-mail: tmcneill@pogolaw.com.

MCNEILL, WILLIAM HARDY, retired historian, writer; b. Vancouver, BC, Can., Oct. 31, 1917; s. John Thomas and Netta (Hardy) McN.; m. Elizabeth Darbishire, Sept. 7, 1946; children: Ruth Netta, Deborah Joan, John Robert, Andrew Duncan. BA, U. Chgo., 1938, MA, 1939; PhD, Cornell U., 1947; 20 hon. degrees. Faculty U. Chgo., 1947-87, prof. history, 1957-87, Robert A. Millikan Disting. Svc. prof., 1969-87, prof. emeritus, 1987—, chmn. dept., 1961-67; pres. Demos Fund, 1968-80; chmn. bd. Demos Found., 1980-86. George Eastman vis. prof. Oxford (Eng.) U., 1980-81 Author: Greek Dilemma, War and Aftermath, 1947, Report on the Greeks, 1948, History Handbook of Western Civilization, 1948, rev. and enlarged 6th edit., 1986, America, Britain and Russia, Their Cooperation and Conflict, 1941-46, 1953, Past and Future, 1954, Greece: American Aid in Action, 1947-56, 1957, Rise of the West: A History of the Human Community, 1963, 9th edit., 1991 (Nat. Book award, Gordon J. Laing prize), Europe's Steppe Frontier, 1500-1800, 1964, A World History, 1967, 4th edit., 1998, The Contemporary World, 1967, 2d edit., 1975, The Ecumene: Story of Humanity, 1973, Venice, the Hinge of Europe, 1081-1797, 1974, The Shape of European History, 1974, Plagues and Peoples, 1976, revised edit., 1998, Metamorphosis of Greece since World War II, 1978, The Human Condition, An Ecological and Historical View, 1980, Pursuit of Power, 1982, The Great Frontier, 1983, Mythistory and other Essays, 1986, A History of the Human Community, 1986, 6th edit., 1998, Polyethnicity and National Unity in World History, 1987, Arnold J. Toynbee: A Life, 1989, Population and Politics Since 1750, 1990, Hutchins' University: A Memoir of the University of Chicago 1929-50, 1991, The Global Tradition: Conquerors, Catastrophies and Community, 1992, Keeping Together in Time: Dance & Drill in Human History, 1995, Colebrook: An Historical Sketch, 1996, De excentriciteit van het wiel en audere wereld-historische essays, 1996, The Disruption of Traditional Forms of Nurture, 1998; (with J.R. McNeill) The Human Web: A Birdseye View of World History, 2003, The Pursuit of Truth: A Historian's Memoir, 2005; editor: Lord Acton, Essays in the Liberal Interpretation of History, 1967, (with others) Readings in World History, Vols. I-X, 1968-73, Human Migration, 1978, Jour. Modern History, 1971-79, Jour. Modern Greek Studies, 1983-85, Berkshire Ency. World History, 2005; mem. editl. bd. Ency. Brit., 1981-98; contbr. articles to profl. jours., chpts. to books. Trustee Athens Coll., 1970-88; vice chmn. Christopher Columbus Quincentenary Jubilee Commn., 1985-93; co-chair curriculum task force Nat. Commn. on Social Studies, 1987-89; mem. Bradley Commn. on the Teaching of History, 1986-89; vice chmn. Nat. Coun. for History Edn., 1990-94, Nat. Coun. for History Standards, 1992-94. Fulbright Rsch. scholar Royal Inst. Internat. Affairs, Eng., 1950-51; Rockefeller grantee, 1951-52, 76; Carnegie grantee, 1957-62, 63-64, Josiah H. Macy grantee, 1973-74; Ford Faculty fellow, 1954-55, Guggenheim fellow, 1971-72, 86-87; recipient Erasmus prize, 1996 Fellow Am. Philos. Soc., Am. Acad.

Arts and Scis., Brit. Acad. Arts and Scis. (corr.), Royal Hist. Soc. (corr.); mem. Am. Hist. Assn. (council, del. Am. Council Learned Socs., pres. 1985) Office: PO Box 45 Colebrook CT 06021-0045

MCNEILLY, KATHY EDEN, librarian, library director; b. St. Louis, Mo., Oct. 24, 1948; d. Edwin Winfield Eden and Florence Sybil (Brown) Eden Day; m. Gregory Scott McNeilly, Jan. 13, 1968; 1 child, Meghan Scott. BS, Fla. State U., Tallahassee, 1966—69; MSc in Libr. Sci., U. Tenn., Knoxville, 1973—74. Libr. asst. Oak Ridge Pub. Libr., Tenn., 1971—76, libr., cataloger, 1976—87, libr., reference, 1987—89, asst. dir., 1989—98, libr. dir., 1998—. Coord. One City, One Book, Oak Ridge, 2005—07. Mem.: DAR (historian Clinch Bend chpt. 2003—06, vice regent 2006, regent 2007—), ALA, Tenn. Libr. Assn., East Tenn. Libr. Assn. (pres. 2002—03), Oak Ridge Breakfast Rotary (literacy chair 2002—03, cmty. svc. chair 2007—), Beta Phi Mu. Office: Oak Ridge Pub Libr 1401 Oak Ridge Turnpike Oak Ridge TN 37830 Office Phone: 865-425-3455.

MC NELLY, FREDERICK WRIGHT, JR., psychologist; b. Bangor, Maine, Apr. 14, 1947; s. Frederick Wright and E. Frances (Cutter) McNelly; 1 adopted child, Roger McNelly foster children: Joseph, Ronald, Michael, Jeffrey, Jeremy. BA magna cum laude, U. Minn., 1969; MA, U. Mich., 1971, PhD, 1973. Registered clin. psychologist Ill., cert. profl. qualification, state and provincial bds. of psychology, early intervention program provider Ill. Rsch. coord. NSF project U. Minn., Morris, 1968-69, lab. instr., 1969, trainee USPHS, 1969-70, 72; teaching fellow psychology U. Mich., Ann Arbor, 1970-72; ednl. examiner Ann Arbor Pub. Schs., 1971; dir. psychol. svcs. Children Devel. Ctr., Rockford, Ill., 1972-82, program dir., 1982-86; cons. psychologist, 1986—. Lectr. Rock Valley Coll., Rockford, 1974—75; part-time pvt. practice psychology, Rockford and Belvidere, Ill., 1980—86, Beloit, Wis., 1985—86; full time, 1986—; mental health cons. Rockford Head Start, 1982—, United Cerebral Palsy, Blackhawk Region, 1986—, Access Svcs., Mendota, Ill., 1992—; mem. health svcs. adv. com. human resources dept. City of Rockford, 1985—; presenter state and regional workshops and confs. Contbr. articles to profl. jours. Active Boy Scouts Am., 1978—83, Big Bros./Big Sisters; chmn. spl. edn. regional adv. com. Bi-County Office Edn., Rockford, 1976—78; mem. Nat. and Ill. Com. Child Abuse, 1975—85; co-chmn. Winnebago County Child Protection Assn., 1980; elder Willow Creek United Presbyn. Ch., Rockford, 1980—83; mem. stronghold renovation session com. Presbytery Blackhawk, Oregon, Ill., 1985. Named U.S. Jaycees Outstanding Young Man of 1977. Mem.: Ill. Assn. Infant Mental Health, No. Ill. Alliance Mentally Ill, Nat. Assn. Mentally Ill, Nat. Assn. Disability Examiners, State Provincial Bds. Psychology, Nat. Register Health Svc. Providers Psychology, Coun. Exception Children, No. Ill. Pvt. Practice Mental Health Assn. (v.p. 1993, pres. 1994—95), No. Ill. Psychol. Assn., Ill. Psychol. Assn. Home: 11591 Beverly Ln Belvidere IL 61008-8708

MCNELLY, JOHN TAYLOR, retired journalist, educator; b. Lancaster, Wis., Oct. 2, 1923; s. Stephen Sumner and Caroline Hurd (Taylor) McN.; m. Pamela Edith Thompson, Dec. 20, 1952; children: Barbara, Duncan. BA, U. Wis., 1946, MA, 1957; PhD, Mich. State U., 1961. Reporter AP, Milw., 1948-52, Reuters, London, 1952-53; news editor U. Wis. News Service, Madison, 1957; instr., then assoc. prof. Mich. State U., East Lansing, 1957-66; assoc. prof., then prof. U. Wis., Madison, 1966-82, Evjue-Bascom prof., 1982-88, prof. emeritus, 1988—. Asst. dir. Inter-Am. Mass Communications Program, San Jose, Costa Rica, 1961-62; vis. prof. Berlin Inst. Mass. Communication in Developing Nations, W.Ger., 1965, Agrarian U., Lima, Peru, 1968-69; communication cons. UNESCO, Latin Am., 1970-75; lectr. USIA, Latin Am., 1968, 74, 80 Co-author: Communication and Social Change in Latin America, 1968; assoc. editor: Journalism Quar., 1975-77; contbr. monographs and articles to communication publs. Served with USAF, 1942-43. Fulbright-Hays Faculty fellow Lima, Peru, 1968-69 Home and Office: 134 Larkin St Madison WI 53705-5116 Business E-Mail: dtmcnelly@facstaff.wisc.edu.

MCNERNEY, JAMES, JR., (W. JAMES MCNERNEY), aerospace transportation executive, former manufacturing executive; b. Providence, Aug. 22, 1949; m. Haity McNerney, 1987; 3 children. BA in American Studies, Yale U., 1971; MBA, Harvard U., 1975. Brand mgr. Proctor & Gamble, 1975—78; sr. mgr. McKinsey & Co., 1978—82; gen. mgr., GE Mobile Communications GE Co., 1982—86; pres. GE Info. Svcs., Rockville, Md., 1988—89; exec. v.p. GE Fin. Services and Capital, Stamford, Conn., 1989—91; pres., CEO GE Elec. Distribution and Control, Plainville, Conn., 1991—92, GE Lighting, Cleveland, Ohio, 1995—97; pres. GE Asia-Pacific, Hong Kong, 1993—95; pres., CEO GE Aircraft Engines, Cin., 1997—2000; chmn., CEO 3M Co, St. Paul, 2001—05; chmn., pres., CEO The Boeing Co., Chgo., 2005—. Bd. dir. The Boeing Co., 2001—, Proter & Gamble Co.; bd. trustee World Bus. Coun. for Sustainable Develop., Bus. Roundtable, Bus. Coun.; mem. spl. programs com. The Boeing Co. Dir. Greater Twin Cities United Way; bd. trustee Northwestern U. Fellow: Am. Acad. Arts & Scis. Office: The Boeing Co 100 N Riverside Plz Chicago IL 60606-1596 *

MCNERNEY, JERRY (GERALD M. MCNERNEY), congressman, engineer; b. Alburquerque, June 18, 1951; m. Mary McNerney; children: Michael, Windy, Gregory. Attended, US Mil. Acad., West Point, NY, 1969—71; BS, U. N.Mex., 1973, MS, 1975, PhD in Math., 1981. Contractor Sandia Nat. Laboratories, Kirkland Air Force Base; sr. engr. Kenetech Inc., 1985—94; cons. manufacture of wind turbines, 1994—98, 2003—04, CEO, 2004—; sr. engr., field mgr. Wind Turbine Co., 1999—2003; CEO Hawt Power Inc., 2003—04; mem. US Congress from 11th Calif. dist., 2007—, mem. vets affairs com., transp. & infrastructure com., sci. & tech. com., select com. on energy independence & global warming. Author: 3 novels. Mem.: Am. Math. Soc., Am. Soc. Mech. Engineers. Democrat. Roman Catholic. Avocations: reading, hunting, running, hiking. Office: 312 Cannon House Office Bldg Washington DC 20515 also: 5776 Stoneridge Mall Rd Ste 175 Pleasanton CA 94588 *

MCNEVIN, CHRISTOPHER J., lawyer; b. Davenport, Iowa, Sept. 6, 1958; BS summa cum laude, U. Miami, 1979; JD, Stanford U., 1983. Bar: Calif. 1983, Calif. Supreme Ct., US Dist. Ct. (all Calif. dist., we. dist. Pa.), US Ct. Appeals (3d, 9th cir.). Ptnr. Pillsbury Winthrop Shaw Pittman, LA. Spl. counsel Orange County Water Dist.; co-leader environ. litig. team Pillsbury Winthrop Shaw Pittman, LA. Contbr. articles to profl. jours. Named a So. Calif. Super Lawyer, LA Mag., 2004, 2005, 2006. Office: Pillsbury Winthrop Shaw Pittman LLP 725 S Figueroa St Ste 2800 Los Angeles CA 90017-5406 Office Phone: 213-488-7507. Office Fax: 213-629-1033. Business E-Mail: chrismcnevin@pillsburylaw.com.

MCNEW, BENNIE BANKS, retired finance educator; b. Greenbrier, Ark., Nov. 12, 1931; s. Roland H. and Stella (Avery) McNew; m. Bonnie Lou Stone, Mar. 31, 1956; children: Bonnie Banks, Mary Kathleen, William Michael. BS, Ark. State Tchrs. Coll., 1953; MBA, U. Ark., 1954; PhD, U. Tex., 1961. Asst. nat. bank examiner, 1954-56; indsl. specialist Indsl. Rsch. and Ext. Ctr. U. Ark., 1956-59; lectr. finance U. Tex., 1959-61; prof. banking U. Miss., University, 1961-65, dean Sch. Bus. Adminstrn., 1965-79; dean Sch. Bus. Mid. Tenn. State U., Murfreesboro, 1980-88; prof. econs. and fin. U. Ctrl. Ark., Conway, 1988-98; ret., 1998. Asst. dir., v.p. Grad. Sch. Banking La. State U., 1966—97. Author (with Charles L. Prather): (book) Fraud Control for Commercial Banks, 1962; co-author: Money and Banking Casebook, 1966, The Bankers Handbook, 1966, A History of Mississippi, 1973. Pres. Faulkner County Singing Conv., Ark., 2002—04. With US Army, 1950—51. Named Disting. Undergraduate Alumnus, Sch. Bus. Adminstrn., U. Ctrl. Ark., 2002. Mem.: Ward Family Singers and Gospel Music. Soc. (pres. 2002—03), Lions (pres. Oxford, Miss. 1964—65, Edward Dalstrom Disting. Svc. award 2002, Melvin Jones fellow 2003). Home: 12 Bainbridge Dr Conway AR 72034-7217

MCNICHOLS, GERALD ROBERT, consulting company executive; b. Cleve., Nov. 21, 1943; s. Charles Wellington and June Beatrice (Kalal) McN.; m. Paula Kay Austin, Dec. 26, 1964; children: G. Robert Jr., Katherine Lynn Loftis, Melissa Sue Cardon. BS with honors, Case-Western Res. U., 1965; MS, U. Pa., 1966; ScD, George Washington U., 1976. Cert. cost estimator/analyst. Sr. ops. analyst Office of Sec., Dept. of Def., Washington, 1970-76; v.p. GenTech, Inc., Bethesda, Md., 1976-77, J. Watson Noah, Inc., Falls Church, Va., 1977-78; pres., chief exec. officer Mgmt. Cons. and Rsch., Inc., McLean, Va., 1978-99; sr. v.p. GRC Internat. (acquired Mgmt. Cons. and Rsch., Inc.), 1999-2000, also bd. dirs.; CEO McNichols & McNichols, Inc., Middleburg, Va., 2000—. Pres. McNichols Family Found., 2000—; chmn. bd. Metier, Ltd.; bd. dirs. Magicsoft Corp.; mem. bd. advisors Arrowhead Corp., The Baldwin Group; vice chmn. com. arts Kennedy Ctr., Wash., 2005—, also bd. dirs. Co-author: Operations Research for Decision Making, 1975; contbg. author: Software Reliability, 1986, Software System Design Methods, 1986, Electronic Systems Effectiveness and Life Cycle Costing, 1983; editor Cost Analysis, 1984; contbr. articles to profl. jours. Pres. Rondelay Civic Assn., Fairfax Sta., Va., 1985-87; bd. dirs. Kennedy Ctr. Cir., 1995-2000. Capt. USAF, 1966-70. Recipient Meritorious Achievement award, Case Western Res U., 1995, Engr. Alumni Achievement award, George Washington U., 1989. Mem. Inst. Cost Analysis (pres. 1985-88), Internat. Soc. Parametric Analysts (bd. dirs. 1982-84, Frieman Lifetime Achievement award 1990), Ops. Rsch. Soc. Am. (chmn. mil. applications sect.), Assn. for Small Rsch., Engring., and Tech. Svcs. Cos. (pres.), Mil. Ops. Rsch. Soc. (sec., treas. 1986-87, v.p. adminstrn. 1987-88, bd. dirs. 1985-88, 92-96), Soc. Cost Estimating and Analysis (bd. dirs. 1990-93, Lifetime Achievement award 2000), Century Club George Mason Univ. (bd. dirs. 1997-2000). Home: 23349 Parsons Rd Middleburg VA 20117-2817 Office: McNichols & McNichols Inc PO Box 2226 Middleburg VA 20118-2226 Business E-Mail: drmcnichols@mcnichols.org.

MCNICOL, DAVID LEON, retired federal official, researcher; b. South Gate, Calif., May 18, 1944; s. Charles D. and Mary W. (Heisel) McN.; m. Lore Anne Long, Mar. 25, 1967; children: Katharine Anne, Elizabeth Mary. BA magna cum laude, Harvard U., 1966; MS, MIT, 1968, PhD, 1973. Asst. prof. econs. U. Pa., Phila., 1971-75; sr. staff economist Pres.'s Coun. of Econ. Advisors, Washington, 1976; vis. assoc. prof. econs. Calif. Inst. Tech., Pasadena, 1976-77; sr. economist Office of the Sec., U.S. Dept. of Treasury, Washington, 1977-79; dir. Office of Econ. Analysis U.S. Dept. Energy, Washington, 1980-81, dep. asst. adminstr. Office of Applied Analysis, 1981-82; dir. Econ. Analysis and Resource Planning Divsn. Office of Sec. of Def., Office of Program Analysis and Evaluation, Washington, 1982-88, dep. asst. sec., dep. dir., 1988—2002, chmn. cost analysis improvement group, 1988—2002; sr. fellow, mem. rsch. staff, dir., cost analysis and rsch. divsn. Inst. for Def. Analyses, Alexandria, Va., 2002—. Author over 20 publs. on commodity markets, regulatory econs., energy issues and econ. aspects of the U.S. def. program. Recipient Spl. Svc. award Dept. Energy, 1981, Presdl. Rank award U.S. Govt., 1988, 93, 96, 2001, Disting./Meritorious Civilian Svc. medal Dept. Def., 1988, 91, 93, 96, 97, 2001, 2002. Home: 6901 Pineway University Park MD 20782-1163 Office: Inst for Defense Analyses 4850 Mark Center Dr Alexandria VA 22311-1882 Office Phone: 703-573-4991. Business E-Mail: dmcnicol@ida.org.

MCNIESH, CELESTE ANGELA, sales executive; b. Vienna, Va., June 28, 1973; d. Barbara Louise Young; m. Michael Lawrence McNiesh, Jan. 17, 2004. BA, James Madison U., Harrisonburg, Va., 1995; MA, Appalachian State U., Boone, NC, 1997. Cert. nationally cert. counselor 1997. Counselor Alamance Burlington Sch. Sys., Graham, NC, 2001—03; coord. sophomore initiative Loyola Coll., Balt., 2003—04; sales mgr. PepsiCo Food Svc., Owings Mills, Md., 2004—; asst. area coord. U. SC, Columbia, SC, 1997—98; asst. dir. residence life Elon U., Elon, NC, 1998—2001. Instr. Dealing with Difficult People, Alamance Burlington Sch. Sys., Graham, NC, 2002—03, Prime for Life Alcohol Prevention Program, Elon U., Elon, NC, 1999—2003; dir. The Thinking CAP, Elon U., 1999—2001; instr. U. 101, U. SC, Columbia, SC, 1997—98, Leadership Devel., Appalachian State U., Boone, NC, 1996—97; crisis team coord. Alamance Burlington Sch. Sys., 2001—03; exec. bd. program chair NC Housing Officers Assn., NC, 1999—2000; conf. chair RA Drive-in Annual Conf., NC, 2000; staff devel. and tng. coord. Elon U., Student Life, 1998—2000. Author: The Space Between, 2003 (10th Nat. Students in Transition Conf. award, 2003). Pres. Five Oaks Homeowners Assn., Owings Mills, Md., 2004—; host com. chair NAMES Project AIDS Meml. Quilt, Elon, NC, 1999—2001. Named Team Player 4th qtr., PepsiCo Food Svc. Mid-Atlantic Zone, 2004; recipient Commitment to Multiculturalism award, Appalachian State U., 1996, Academic Resource Programming award, South Eastern Housing Officers, 1999—2000. Mem.: Nat. Bd. Cert. Counselors. Independent. Roman Catholic. Avocations: travel, reading. Home and Office: PepsiCo Food Svc and Vending 4664 Mews Dr Owings Mills MD 21117 Office Fax: 410-902-7309. Personal E-mail: celeste95@msn.com.

MCNISH, SUSAN KIRK, retired lawyer; b. San Jose, Calif., Nov. 4, 1940; d. Wallace Garland and Dorothy (Kirk) Shaw; m. Thomas A. McNish, May 12, 1989 (dec. Dec. 2001); children: Jenifer, Michael. BA, U. Calif., 1962; JD, U. Santa Clara, Calif., 1981; postgrad., Stanford U., 1979, U. Mich., 1981. Bar: Mich. 1981, U.S. Dist. Ct. (ea. dist.) Mich. 1981. Various positions Stanford (Calif.) U., 1968-79; law clk. U.S. Dist. Ct. (no. dist.) Calif., San Francisco, 1979; atty. Consumers Power Co., Jackson, Mich., 1981-88; v.p., gen. counsel, corp. sec. Mich. Consol. Gas Co., Detroit, 1988-98; ret. Mem. clin. svcs. adv. bd. Detroit Med. Ctr., Wayne State U.; dir. Vista Maria Corp., Dearborn Heights, Mich. Mem. Am. Arbitration Assn. (arbitrator, Mich. adv. panel). Home: 1809 Bay Meadow Ct Raleigh NC 27615-5482 E-mail: susankmcnish@yahoo.com.

MCNITT, WILLARD CHARLES, food products executive; b. Chgo., June 6, 1920; s. Willard C. and Louise (Richardson) McN.; m. Charlotte D. Boyd, Sept. 14, 1946; children: Willard Charles, James D., Peter B. McNitt. BA, Amherst Coll., 1942; A.M., Harvard Grad. Sch. Bus. Adminstrn., 1942; student, Northwestern Grad. Sch. Bus. Adminstrn., U. Chgo. Sch. Bus. Adminstrn., 1947. Asst. market planning and research Foote, Cone & Belding Co., Chgo., 1946-47; asst. sales promotion and advt. Bell & Gosset Co., Morton Grove, Ill., 1947-48; v.p. sales and mktg. Bowes Industries, Inc., Chgo., 1948-54; gen. mgr. sales and mktg. Clayton Mark & Co., Evanston, Ill., 1954-58; pres., dir. Bowey's, Inc., Chgo., 1958-62; pres., dir., mem. exec. com. H.M. Byllesby Co., Chgo., 1962-63; group v.p., dir. Consol. Foods Corp., Chgo., 1963-67; exec. v.p. consumer products group W.R. Grace & Co., NYC, 1967-72; exec. v.p., dir., mem. exec. com. Ward Foods, Inc., Wilmette, Ill., 1972-73, chief operating officer, pres., dir., mem. exec. com., 1973-76; pres., chief exec. officer, dir. Westgate-Calif. Corp., and Sun Harbor Industries, San Diego, 1977-80; pres., chief exec. officer Nalley's Fine Foods, Tacoma, 1980-83; chmn., dir. Joseph Magnin Inc., 1982-85; chmn. Blue Moon Cheese Co., Thorpe, Wis., 1983—; operating ptnr. Wallner & Co., La Jolla, Calif.; vice chmn., pres., CEO, dir., exec. com. Foremost Dairies, Inc., San Francisco, 1983—85. Chmn. Epcom; bd. dirs. ATI, NCIC, Blue Moon Cheese, Del. Lightweight. Troop head local Boy Scouts Am., 1957-67. Lt. (s.g.) USNR, 1942-46. Mem. Execs. Club (Ch, Amherst Club, Harvard Bus. Sch. Club (Chgo., NYC), Indian Hill Country Club (Winnetka), Dairymen's Club (Boulder Junction, Wis.), Chi Psi. Republican. Congregationalist.

MCNULTY, CARRELL STEWART, JR., retired manufacturing executive, architect; b. Newark, Dec. 4, 1924; s. Carrell Stewart and Marjorie (Yaegerlehner) McN.; m. Barbara Brokaw, June 21, 1952; children: Peter Carrell, Susan Abigail. Student, Emory U., 1941-43, U. N.C., 1943-44; BArch, Columbia U., 1950, MS in Urban Planning, 1963. Registered architect, Conn. Assoc. SMS Architects, Stamford, Conn., 1950-58, gen. ptnr., 1958-73; pvt. practice architecture Weston, Conn., 1973-76; pres. CMW Co., Weston, 1975-77, NB Products, Inc., Horsham, Pa., 1976-94, NB Instruments, Inc., Horsham, 1979-93, Environ. Svcs. and Products, Inc., Horsham, 1994-96; ret. Mem. Conn. Soc. Architects, 1963-73, sec., 1964-67, pres., 1969-70. Chair S.W. Regional Planning Agy., Norwalk, Conn., 1967-71; mem. Gov.'s Com. on Environment, New Haven, 1970, chair Gov.'s Task Force on Housing, Norwalk, 1972; bd. dirs., sec. Habitat for Humanity of Greater Bucks, Doylestown, Pa., 1990-97; pres. Ctrl. Bucks Crossroads, 1995-96. Lt. (j.g.) USNR, 1943-46; PTO. Recipient citation Am. Assn. Sch. Adminstrs., 1960, 6th Biennial Design award HUD, 1973; grantee HUD, Housing Rsch., 1970. Fellow AIA (mem. urban design com. 1963-73, chmn. 1971); mem. Bucks County Choral Soc., Sigma Nu. Democrat. Mem. United Ch. of Christ (deacon 1965-71, elder 1989-92). Avocations: computers, watercoloring, choral music. Home: 14179 SE 88th Ct Summerfield FL 34491 Personal E-mail: llerracm@earthlink.net.

MCNULTY, JAMES F., construction company executive; m. Judy McNulty; children: Darby, Anne, Brigid. BS in Engring., US Mil. Acad., 1964; MS in Nuc. Physics, Ohio State U., 1970; MS in Mgmt., MIT, 1985. Rsch. assoc. Lawrence Livermore Nat. Lab., 1972—74; asst. dir. Office Mil. Applications US Dept. Energy, 1978—80; officer nuc. weapon requirements Ops. and Plans Office Dept US Army, 1980—82, sys. mgr. Pershing II Missle Sys., 1982—84, program mgr. ground based laser sys., 1985—88; dir. bus. devel. Parsons Corp., 1988—89, v.p. Washington, 1991—92, sr. v.p., mgr. sys. divsn. Pasadena, 1992—95, pres. infrastructure and tech. group, 1996, pres., CEO, 1996—, chmn., 1998—. Fellow Alfred P. Sloan, MIT. Avocations: hiking, walking, golf, reading. Office: Parsons Corp 100 W Walnut St Pasadena CA 91124-0001 Office Phone: 626-440-2000. Office Fax: 626-440-2630.

MCNULTY, JAMES FRANCIS, engineering executive; b. New Bedford, Mass., July 16, 1929; s. Francis and Mary (Cantwell) McN.; m. Pauline Antoinette Gillotti, Dec. 15, 1962; children: Diana Valencia, Kevin, Irene, James, Theresa. AE in Elec. Engring., Jersey City Tech. Inst.; student, MIT. Supr. Raytheon R&D Lab., Waltham, Mass., 1952-59; elec. engr. Sperry Products, Danbury, Conn., 1959-62; elec. engr. A6A Aircraft Grumman Aircraft, Bethpage, NY, 1963-66; exec. v.p. Adtech Power, Inc., Anaheim, Calif., 1973-80; dir. engring. Datapower, Inc., Santa Ana, Calif., 1980-85; mfg. ops. mgr. Pacific Power Source, Huntington Beach, Calif., 1985-88; v.p., gen. mgr. Powerstar, Inc., Irvine, Calif., 1988-89; dir. engring. and ops. On-Line Power, City of Commerce, Calif., 1989-92; v.p. ops. Tasertron, Corona, Calif., 1992—2001. Cons. On-Line Power, 1993-94, Seimelweis Corp., Bloomington, Calif., 1997, Len Gordon Co., Las Vegas, 1998, Vogt & Resnick Law Corp., Newport Beach, Calif., 1998. Contbr. articles to profl. jours. Sgt. U.S. Army. Mem. VFW. Achievements include patent for ultrasonic testing apparatus and method, patent for control of filament current and voltage, patent for shockley diode pulser, patent for the only non-lethal alternative to the deadly anti-personnel landmine, others. Office: 1731 Medical Ctr Dr Unit #163 Anaheim CA 92801 Office Phone: 714-774-4529. Personal E-mail: jfmcnult@yahoo.com.

MCNULTY, JAMES FRANCIS, JR., lawyer, consultant; s. James Francis, Sr. McNulty and Anna Mae Fiorenza; m. Be Thi Tu, Dec. 19, 1986; 1 child, Thomas Vi. Cert. in Elec. Tech., Santa Ana Coll., 1981, AA, 1982; BA in Sociology, Calif. State U., Fullerton, 1990; JD, Glendale U., 1991; MA in Mgmt., Claremont Grad. U., 2002; AS in Microbiology, Crafton Hills Coll., Calif., 2002. Cert. engring. graphics, Riverside Coll., Calif., 2003; bar: Calif. 1993. Assoc. quality engr. Allen Bradley - West, Fullerton, Calif., 1981—83; plant ops. mgr. Taser Industries, Inc., Monrovia, Calif., 1983—86; CEO E.I.D. Labs, Sierra Madre, Calif., 1986—90; v.p. mktg. and product devel. Tasertron, Newport Beach, Calif., 1990—91; atty. pvt. practice, Calimesa, Calif., 1993—2004; atty., mkt. rsch., product designer Def. Tech. Corp., an Armor Holdings, Inc. Co., 2004—06; atty. Law Enforcement Assoc., Inc., a Sirchie Affiliate, 2004—06; v.p. in ho. counsel Atelier McA'Nulty Designs, Inc., 2006—. Mem.: Mensa, Phi Theta Kappa, Alpha Gamma Sigma, Alpha Kappa Delta, Delta Theta Phi. Republican. Achievements include patents in field. Avocations: bicycling, drafting and designing, scientific and technical illustrating. Home and Office: 5020 Indian River Dr Unit 421 Las Vegas NV 89103 Personal E-mail: macslaw2000@yahoo.co.in.

MCNULTY, JAMES J., former mercantile exchange executive; BA, U. Ill., 1973; MA, U. Coll. Dublin, 1974. Ptnr. O'Connor & Assocs., 1989—93; mng. dir., co-head corp. analysis & structuring team Warburg Dillon Read; pres., CEO Chgo. Mercantile Exch., 2000—03, Chgo. Mercantile Exch. Holdings Inc., 2001—03. Bd. dirs. Chgo. Mercantile Exch., 2002—03, Chgo. Mercantile Exch. Holdings Inc., 2002—03; non-exec. dir. ICAP plc., mem. nominating com., mem. risk com., mem. remunerations com.; bd. dirs. Archipelago Holdings, Inc., 2004—06, NYSE Group, Inc., 2006—. Office: NYSE Group Inc 11 Wall St New York NY 10005 Office Phone: 212-656-3000.

MCNULTY, JOHN KENT, lawyer, educator; b. Buffalo, Oct. 13, 1934; s. Robert William and Margaret Ellen (Duthie) McN.; m. Linda Conner, Aug. 20, 1955 (div. Feb. 1977); children: Martha Jane, Jennifer, John K. Jr.; m. Babette B. Barton, Mar. 23, 1978 (div. May 1988). AB with high honors, Swarthmore Coll., 1956; LLB, Yale U., 1959. Bar: Ohio 1961, U.S. Supreme Ct. 1964. Law clk. Justice Hugo L. Black US Supreme Ct., Washington, 1959—60; vis. prof. Sch. Law U. Tex., 1960; assoc. Jones, Day, Cockley & Reavis, Cleve., 1960—64; prof. law U. Calif., Berkeley, 1964—91, Roger J. Traynor prof. law, 1991—2002, Roger J. Traynor prof. emeritus, 2002—. Of counsel Baker and McKenzie, San Francisco, 1974-75; acad. visitor London Sch. Econs., 1985, Cambridge U., 1994, U. Edinburgh, 1994; vis. fellow Wolfson Coll., Cambridge, 1994, U. Innsbruck, 1996, Trinity Coll., Dublin, 1997; vis. prof. Yale U., U. Tex., U. Leiden, U. Tilburg, U. Tokyo, U. San Diego, Hastings, Vienna Econ. U., Cologne, others; lectr. in field; mem. adv. bd. Tax Mgmt. Author: Federal Income Taxation of Individuals, (with Lathrope) 7th edit., 2004, Federal Estate and Gift Taxation, (with McCouch) 6th edit., 2003, Federal Income Taxation of S Corporations, 1992; (with Westin & Beck) Federal Income Taxation of Business Enterprises, 1995, 2d edit., 1999; mem. bd. overseers Berkeley Jour. Internat. Law. Guggenheim fellow, 1977 Mem. ABA, Am. Law Inst. (life), Internat. Fiscal Assn. (coun. U.S. br.), Order of Coif, Phi Beta Kappa. Home: 1176 Grizzly Peak Blvd Berkeley CA 94708-1741 Office: U Calif Sch Law 463 Boalt Hl Berkeley CA 94720-7200 Home Phone: 510-549-1750; Office Phone: 510-642-1928. Business E-Mail: jmcnulty@law.berkeley.edu.

MCNULTY, KATHLEEN ANNE, social worker, consultant, psychotherapist; b. Hackensack, NJ, Oct. 6, 1958; d. Alfred Edward and Gertrude Natalie (Currie) McN.; m. Henry Stanislaw Kowal, Sept. 16, 1988. BA, Rutgers U., 1980; MSW, Smith Coll., 1984; postgrad., Fielding Grad. Inst., 2001—. Lic. marriage and family therapist; lic. clin. social worker; lic. psychologist. Mental health aide Belleville (N.J.) Mental Health Clinic, 1980-82; clin. social worker Albert Einstein Coll. Medicine, Bronx, N.Y., 1984-86, Family Guidance Bergen, Hackensack, 1986-87, Cliffwood Mental Health Ctr., Englewood, N.J., 1986-87; pvt. practice Rutherford, N.J., 1987-99, Ridgewood, N.J., 1999—. Cons. Meadowlands Weight Control, Rutherford, 1988—, St. Lukes-Roosevelt Hosp. Ctr., N.Y.C., 1988.

Contbr. articles to profl. jours. Mem. Am. Orthopsychiat. Assn., Acad. Cert. Social Workers (cert.), Nat. Assn. Social Workers. Avocations: painting, singing, sports, poetry. Home Phone: 201-768-1644; Office Phone: 201-444-4010. Personal E-mail: kam1058@aol.com, relationsconnect@aol.com.

MCNULTY, MICHAEL ROBERT, congressman; b. Troy, NY, Sept. 16, 1947; s. John J. and Madelon McNulty; m. Nancy Ann Lazzaro; children: Michele, Angela, Nancy, Maria. Grad., St. Joseph's Inst., Barrytown, NY, 1965, Loyola U. Rome Ctr., 1968, Hill Sch. Ins., NYC, 1970; BA in Polit. Sci., Coll. Holy Cross, Worcester, Mass., 1969; LHD honoris causa (hon.), Coll. St. Rose, Albany, NY, 1991; LLD honoris causa (hon.), Siena Coll., Loudonville, NY, 1993, Rensselaer Poly. Inst., Troy, NY, 1995, Excelsior Coll., Albany, NY, 2000. Town supr., Green Island, NY, 1969-77; mayor, 1977-81; mem. NY State Assembly from 106th dist., 1982-88, mem. adminstrv. regulations rev. commn., 1983-88; mem. US Congress from 23rd NY dist., 1989-92, US Congress from 21st NY dist., 1993—, at-large whip, mem. ways and means com., ranking mem. select revenue measures subcommittee. Chmn. United Way campaign, 1982 Mem. staff com. on edn. NY State Constl. Conv., 1967; campaign mgr. John J. McNulty Jr. for Sheriff of Albany County, NY, 1973; participant 1974 polit. campaign mgmt. inst. Kent State U., Ohio Recipient Freedom award, Armenian Nat. Com., 1996. Democrat. Roman Catholic. Office: US House Reps 2210 Rayburn House Office Bldg Washington DC 20515-3221 Office Phone: 202-225-5076. Office Fax: 202-225-5077. *

MCNULTY, PAUL J., lawyer, former federal agency administrator; b. Pitts., Jan. 21, 1958; m. Brenda Millican; 4 children. BA, Grove City Coll., 1980; JD, Capital U., 1983. Counsel US House Com. on Standards of Official Conduct, Washington, 1983—85; dir. congl. affairs Legal Svcs. Corp., Washington, 1985—87; minority counsel House Judiciary Subcom. Crime, 1987—90, chief counsel, 1995—99; dep. dir. Office Policy Devel., dir. Office Policy and Comms. US Dept. Justice, Washington, 1990—93, prin. assoc. dep. atty. gen., 2001, US atty. (ea. dist.) Va. Alexandria, Va., 2001—06, acting dep. atty. gen. Washington, 2005—06, dep. atty. gen., 2006—07; counsel Shaw Pittman LLP, 1993—95; chief counsel, dir. legis. ops. Office of Majority Leader US Ho. Reps., Washington, 1999—2001; ptnr. Baker & McKenzie LLP, Washington, 2007—. Office: Baker & McKenzie LLP 815 Conecticut Ave NW Washington DC 20006 *

MCNULTY, ROBERT HOLMES, non-profit executive; b. Oakland, Calif., June 20, 1940; s. Frederick James and Ruth (Holmes) McN.; m. Penelope Cuff, Dec. 27, 1964; children: Maria, Abigail. BS in Bus. Administrn., U. Calif., Berkeley, 1962, JD, 1965. Bar: Calif. 1965. Property acquisition planner Safeway Stores, Internat., Oakland, 1962; archeol. asst. Colonial Williamsburg, Va., 1968; rsch. asst. Nat. Mus. of History and Tech. The Smithsonian Instn., Washington, 1968-69, asst. to the dir., 1969-70; environ. advisor GSA, Washington, 1970-71; asst. dir. architecture and environ. arts program NEA, Washington, 1971-78; acting dir. grad. program in hist. preservation Sch. Architecture Columbia U., NYC, 1978-79; pres. Ptnrs. for Livable Communities, Washington, 1979—. Cons. Task Force on Land Use and Urban Growth, 1972, Task Force on Neighborhood Economic Development, 1976, German Marshall Fund, Washington, 1978; bd. visitors U. Ind. Sch. Pub. Administrn., 1991—; mem. NY St. Council of the Arts, Architecture & Enviromental Arts Prgm (panelist 1973-74, advisor 1974-75), Taskforce under President Reagan on Private Sector Initiatives, 1981, Urban Land Inst. Cultural Fac. (co-chair adv. comm.) 1984, The Micronesian Inst. (adv. council) 1985—90, Oversight Comm. of L'Axe Majeur de Cergy-Pontoise, Paris, 1988, Internat. Prgm. Adv. Comm. to the Natl. Endowment for the Arts, 1990-92, Internat. Ecotourism Soc., 1992-99, City Innovation Natl. Adv. (bd. mem.) 1993-2005, President's Natl. Preparatory Comm. for the Human Settlements Conference, Istanbul, 1996, Inst. for the Regl. Community (bd. trustees) 1997-98, Am. Assembly on Improving the Economic Hlth. of Am. Distressed Communities, 1997, UNESCO, Bangkok, 2003-; mem. U.S. bd. advisors Griffith U., Brisbane, Australia, 2004; vis. scholar Oxford U., 2007; lect. in field. Author: Neighborhood Conservation: A Handbook of Methods and Techniques, 1976, Economics of Amenity, 1985, Entrepreneurial American City, 1985, Return of the Livable City, 1986, Culture Builds Community: How to put culture to work to enhance your community, 2005, Heritage Tourism Development for Community Value, 2006; editor: (book) Better Cities Book, 1989, (report) State of the American Community, 1994, Livable City Revitalizing Urban Communities, 2000; contbr. articles to profl. journals. Pres. Brookmont and Vicinity Civ. League, 1976-77, bd. mem., 1975-76, 77-78, 91-92; served to capt. U.S. Army, 1966-68. Smithsonian Inst. grantee, 1972, 73, Graham Found. grantee 1978; Loeb fellow Harvard U., 1973-74, Pierson Coll. guest fellow, Yale U., 1985, adj. sr. fellow Hudson Inst., 1989-2000; recipient AIA Gold Medal to the Architecture, Planning & Design Prgm. of NEA, 1979. Mem. Calif. Bar Assn., Nat. Press Club., Royal Soc. for the Arts in the U.S. (fell. 1992-95), Inst. of Current World Affairs, Lambda Alpha Internat. Office: Ptnrs for Livable Community 1429 21st St NW Washington DC 20036-5902 Fax: 202-466-4845. E-mail: bmcnulty@livable.com.

MCNULTY, TERENCE PATRICK, metallurgist, consultant; b. Los Angeles, Nov. 24, 1938; s. John Lambert McNulty and Nelle Mae (Kearney) Knaebel; m. Carol Susan Couch, Oct. 1, 1976; children: Darcy, Dan, Lisa, Peter; children from previous marriage: Tracy, John. BSChemE, Stanford U., 1961; MS in Metall. Engring., Mont. Sch. Mines, 1963; PhD in Metall. Engring., Colo. Sch. Mines, 1967. Registered profl. engr., Colo. Rsch. engr. The Anaconda Co., Anaconda, Mont., 1960-65, sr. rsch. engr. Tucson, 1967-70; concentrator supt. Anaconda Can. Ltd., Bathurst, N.B., 1970-72; supr. process engring. The Anaconda Co., Tucson, 1972-74, dir. metall. rsch. Tucson, Denver, 1974-79; v.p. tech. ops. Kerr-McGee Chem. Corp., Oklahoma City, 1979-83; pres. and chief exec. officer Hazen Rsch. Inc., Golden, Colo., 1983-88; pres. T.P. McNulty and Assocs. Inc., 1989—. Bd. dirs. Hazen Internat. Inc., Golden, Colo., Hazen-Quinn Process Equipment Co., Denver, Hazen Rsch., Inc., Golden, USMX, Denver, Iron Carbide Devel. Corp., Denver. Author 29 tech. papers, 1963-91; patentee in field of mineral processing tech. Trustee, v.p. Colo. Innovation Found., Golden, 1987—; trustee Colo. Sch. Mines, Golden Colo.; bd. dirs. Nat. Mining Mus., Leadville, Colo., 1988-91; chmn. Mines Alumni Ann. Fund., Golden, 1985-88; accreditation visitor Accreditation Bd. for Engring. and Tech., 1977—. Mem. NAE, The Metall. Soc. (Henry Krumb Traveling Lectr. in Metallurgy 1989), Soc. Mining Engrs., Mining and Metall. Soc. Am., Northwest Mining Assn., Colo. Mining Assn., Mining Club of the Southwest (Tucson). Republican. Episcopalian. Avocations: hiking, photography, woodworking. Office: T P McNulty and Assocs Inc 4550 N Territory Place Tucson AZ 85750 Office Phone: 520-529-3355. Office Fax: 520-529-3943. E-mail: Tpmacon1@aol.com.

MCNULTY, TIMOTHY J., editor; b. 1948; BA, Wayne State U.; MA, Georgetown U. Fgn. corr. Chgo. Tribune, nat. news corr., Washington bur. Washington, White House corr., Tempo sect. editor Chgo., nat. editor, fgn. editor, assoc. mng. editor fgn. news, 1991—2006, pub. editor, 2006—. Bd. dirs. World Press Inst., St. Paul. Co-recipient Robert F. Kennedy Journalism award, 1985, Sidney Hillman Found. award, 1985; recipient Beck award, Chgo. Tribune, 1978, 1982, 1989. Mem.: Chgo. Headline Club, Soc. Profl. Journalists. Office: Chgo Tribune 435 N Michigan Ave Chicago IL 60611-4041 Office Phone: 312-222-3348. E-mail: publiceditor@tribune.com, tmcnulty@tribune.com. *

MCNUTT, MARCIA KEMPER, geophysicist; b. Mpls., Minn., Feb. 19, 1952; widowed, 1988; 3 children. BA in Physics, Colo. Coll., 1973; PhD in Earth Sciences, Scripps Inst. Oceanography, 1978; DSc (hon.), Colo. Coll., 1988. Geophysicist US Geol. Survey, 1979-82; asst. prof. geophysics MIT, 1982-86, assoc. prof., 1986-89, prof. geophysics, 1989—95, Griswold prof., 1991, assoc. dir. Sea Grant Coll. Program, 1993—95; pres. & CEO Monterey Bay Aquarium Rsch. Inst., 1997—; prof. geophysics Stanford U., 1998—. Bd. dirs. Monterey Bay Aquarium, 1998—; chmn. Pres. Com. on Ocean Exploration, 2000—; mem. exploration of the seas com. Nat. Rsch. Coun., 2001—. Sr. editl. bd. Science mag., 2000—. Mem. Am. Geophys. Union (pres. tectonophysics sect., 1994, pres., 2000-02, chmn., Macelwane award com., 1996-98, Macelevane award 1988), NAS. Office: MBARI 7700 Sandholt Rd Moss Landing CA 95039-9644

MCNUTT, MONA BELLE, social worker; b. Rogers, Ark., Aug. 31, 1934; d. John Harmon McNuff and Effie Eliza Bell. BS in Edn., U. Ark., Fayetteville, 1955; MA in Social Group Work, Scarritt Coll. for Christian Workers, Nashville, 1961; M in Social Work, U. Tenn., Nashville, 1975. Diplomate Am. Bd. Clin. Social Workers; LCSW Tenn. Social group worker Bethlehem Bd. Missions of Meth. Ch., Spartanburg, SC, 1955—57; cmty. social worker Bethlehem Ctr., Spartanburg, SC, 1961—63, Bethlehem Ctr., Nat. Bd. Missions, Nashville, 1963—70; vocat. rehab. counselor Mid. Ten. Mental Health Inst., State Tenn. Dept. Edn., Nashville, 1970—74; psychiatric social work supr. Mid. Tenn. Mental Health Inst. State Tenn. Dept. Edn., Nashville, 1975—98; dir. social work svc. Mid. Tn. Mental Health Inst., State Tenn. Dept. Edn., Nashville, 1998—2000; ret., 2000—. Deaconess United Meth. Ch., 1961—; chief trustee Glendale United Meth. Ch., Nashville, 2000—06, coord. older adult ministries, 2007—. Mem.: Nat. Alliance Mentally Ill, Nat. Assn Deaconesses and Home Missioners. Democrat. Avocations: travel, crafts, photography, gardening, reading. Home: 5041 Kingsview Ct Nashville TN 37220

MCNUTT, RALPH LEROY, JR., astrophysicist; b. Ft. Worth, Tex., Oct. 29, 1953; s. Ralph Leroy McNutt and Mozelle Mercer; m. Nancy Brenda Auclair, July 5, 1980; children: Stephen Andrew, Christopher James, Matthew David Lee. BS in Physics, Tex. A&M U., College Sta., 1975; PhD in Physics, MIT, Cambridge, Mass., 1980. Prin. profl. staff applied physics lab. Johns Hopkins U., Laurel, Md., 1992—. Recipient Group Achievement award, NASA, 1981, 1986, 1990, 1998, 1998, 2002, 2002. Fellow: Brit. Interplanetary Soc.; mem.: AIAA, Am. Astonomical Soc. and DPS, Internat. Acad. Astronautics (corr.), Am. Geophys. Union. Office: Johns Hopkins Univ Applied Physics Lab 11100 Johns Hopkins Rd MP3-E116 Laurel MD 20723-6099 Home Phone: 410-750-8974; Office Phone: 443-778-5435.

MCNUTT, RICHARD HUNT, manufacturing executive; b. Princeton, NJ, Mar. 11, 1943; s. John and Dorothy Elizabeth (Hunt) McN. Student, Delaware Vly. Coll. Sci./Agr., 1965-68, Temple U., 1978-81; BS in Indsl. Engring., Shelbourn U., 1986. Cert. in vocat. edn.; cert. mfg. engr. Diemaker Custom Tool Co., 1964-67; toolmaker Penn Engring., 1967-69; machine shop mgr., R&D engr. Inertial Motors Corp., 1969-73; machinery design engr. Phila. Rivet Co., Doylestown, Pa., 1973-76; R&D mgr. PHL, Inc., Doylestown, 1976-82; asst. chief engr. PHL Inc./Levr/Air Inc., Prefco Products Inc., 1982-85, chief engr., 1985-86, v.p. ops., 1986-89, dir. engring., 1989—2003; owner Sunrise Solar Heat Co.; cons. Pipersville, Pa.; ptnr. Mediation Assocs., 1990—; R&D engr. fire/smoke divsn. Perfect Air Control, Inc., Pipersville, 2003—04; engring. dir. PHL, Inc., 2004—. Founder: Gateway Tidal River Jour., 2007—. Exec. v.p. Del. Water Study Citizens Group for Sound Resource Mgmt.; councillor Probational Vol. Svcs.; founding bd. dirs. Del-Aware Unltd., Inc., Del-Art Inc., Ctr. for Performing Arts, Bucks County, Pa., Del. River Greenway Partnership, Inc.; mem. Environ. Polit. Action Com.; founder AWARE, Montgomery County, 1985—, STAND, Bucks County, 1986—, Holicong CSA; mem. exec. bd. Earth Day, 1990, Earth Days Alliance, Bucks County Conservation Dist., 1993—, Del. River Greenway, 1994-96, vice chmn., 1995-96, chmn., 1996-98; v.p. Del. River Greenway Partnership Inc., 1998-99, pres., 1999-2004; mem. econ. devel. com. Del. River Wild and Scenic Study Commn., Dept. Interior Nat. Park Svc., 1994-96; founder Solebury Forum, Bucks County, Environ. Party Com.; mem. Plumstead Twp. Parks and Recreation Commn., sec., 1992-97, vice chmn., 1997-98, chmn., 1998—2004; vice chmn. Plumstead Twp. Shade Tree Commn., NJ, 1992—; planning commn. tech. adv. com. Cape May County, 2001—04; founding ptnr. Rising Nation, Native Am. Cultural Heritage Project, 2000-; Indian Coun. mem. Lenape Nation of Pa., 2003—; founder Tidewaters Gateway Partnership, 2004—, pres. 2005—. Served with USMC, 1960-64; designer tidewater trail, NJ Dept. Coastal Zone Mgmt. Office, 2007—. Mem. ASHRAE, NRA (life), VFW, DAV (life), Soc. Mfg. Engrs., Bucks County Assn. Corrections and Rehab., Am. Legion (life), Vietnam Vets. Am. (life), Ctrl. Bucks County C. of C. (environ. and govt. com. 1986—), Internat. Air Movement and Control Assn. (mem. code rev. com., fire-smoke engring. com.), Nat. Fire Protection Assn., Underwriters Lab. (standards com.). Republican. Zen Buddhist. Office: PHL Inc 5556 Stump Rd Pipersville PA 18947-1090 E-mail: phltech@pil.net.

M'CORMACK, FREDANNA ANTOINETTE DUROSIMI, dietician, educator; b. Freetown, Sierra Leone, Apr. 13, 1977; d. Frederick D. Adekumbi and Joanna Aquila May M'Cormack. BS in Health Sci., U. North Fla., Jacksonville, 2000; MS in Food and Nutrition, So. Ill. U., Carbondale, 2003. Cert. dietician Commn. Dietetic Registration, 2003. Nutritionist Human Devel. Corp., St. Louis, 2003—04; intern divsn. for advancement for women UN Secretariat, NYC, 2005; grad. asst. office vice chancellor So. Ill. U., 2005—; dietitian Am. Diabetes Assn., Camp Korelitz, Cin., 2006. Dietetic intern Family Care Health Ctr. and St. Louis Area Agy. for Aging, St. Louis, 2002, Heartland Regional Med. Ctr., Carbondale, 2002; presenter in field. Student Affairs Leadership scholar, U. North Fla., 1997—2000, Undergraduate Student Govt. Women's Leadership scholar, 1999, Women's Caucus Travel scholar, So. Ill. U., 2005, Delbert Oberteuffer scholar, Am. Assn. Health Edn., 2007. Mem.: Am. Sch. Health Assn., Am. Assn. Health Edn., Coll. Adv. Com. (bd. dirs. 2006—07), UN Assn. USA (bd. dirs. 2005—07), Eta Sigma Gamma (treas. 2006—07). Anglican. Avocations: travel, entertaining, fundraising, dance. Office: Southern Ill U Carbondale 1250 Linclon Dr Mail Code 4632 Carbondale IL 62901 Home Phone: 618-203-1023; Office Phone: 618-453-6964. Office Fax: 618-453-1829; Home Fax: 618-453-1829. Personal E-mail: fredannamc@yahoo.com.

MCPARLAND, ROBERT PATRICK, literature educator, writer; b. Mar. 7, 1958; BA, Fordham U.; MA, St. John's U., 1996, Montclair State U., 1997; MPhil, Drew U., 2004, PhD, 2005. Asst. prof. English Felician Coll., Lodi/Rutherford, NJ, 1997—. Author: The Speech of Angels, 2003, In the Nick of Time, 2004, Music and Literary Modernism, 2005, Dickens and Melodrama, 2006. Home: 39 Rosedale Ave Elmwood Park NJ 07407-3033 Office: Dept English 262 S Main St Lodi NJ 07644 Office Phone: 201-559-6105. Business E-Mail: mcparlandr@felician.edu.

MCPARTLAND, JAMES MICHAEL, academic administrator; b. NYC, Sept. 26, 1939; s. James J. and Helen M. (Leddy) McP. BS, Cornell U., 1961, MS, 1963; PhD, Johns Hopkins U., 1968. Rschr. U.S. Office Edn., Washington, 1965-67, U.S. Commn. Civil Rights, Washington, 1967-68; asst. dir. Ctr. Social Orgn. Schs., Johns Hopkins U., Balt., 1968-75, co-dir., 1976-94, dir., 1994—. Co-author: Equality of Educational Opportunity, 1966, Encyclopedia of Educational Research, 1992, Review of Research in Education, 1993; co-editor: Violence in Schools, 1977, Comprehensive Urban School Reform, 2002. Mem. Am. Ednl. Rsch. Assn., Am. Sociol. Assn., Am. Statis. Assn. Democrat. Roman Catholic. Avocation: music. Home: 1102 S Streeper St Baltimore MD 21224-4873 Office: Johns Hopkins U CSOS 3003 N Charles St Ste 200 Baltimore MD 21218-3888 Office Phone: 410-516-8803. E-mail: jmcpartland@csos.jhu.edu.

MCPARTLAND, PATRICIA ANN, adult education educator; b. Passaic, NJ; d. Daniel and Josephine McP. BA, U. Mo., 1971; MCRP, Ohio State U., 1975, MS in Preventive Medicine, 1975; EdD in Higher and Adult Edn., Columbia U., 1988; cert. distance edn., Tex. A&M U., 2000, cert. distance edn. web pub. cert., 2001. Cert. health edn. specialist, distance edn. web pub., grants specialist; workforce devel. profl. Sr. health planner Merrimack Valley HSA, Lawrence, Mass., 1977—79; planning cons., adminstr. Children's Hosp., Boston, 1979—80; exec. dir. Assn. Workforce Alternatives, Rsch. & Devel., Inc., Marion, Mass., 1980—; dir. adult continuing edn. Upper Cape Cod Regional Tech. Sch., Bourne, Mass., 2005—. V.p., cons. New Bedford (Mass.) Cmty. Health Ctr, 1993—94; chmn. edn. and tng. com. Health and Human Svc. Coalition, 1988—89; mem. project expert panel Office of Minority Health, 1997—2003; mem. New Eng. Regional Minority Health Conf. Com., 1997—99; vis. lectr. Bridgewater State Coll.; lectr. in field; project expert panel Office Minority Health's Culturally and Linguistically Appropriate Svcs.; mem. New Eng. Regional Minority Health Conf. Com., 2001—03. Author: Promoting Health in the Workplace, 1991; mem. editl. bd. Jour. Healthcare Edn. and Tng., 1989-93; reviewer Qualitative Health Rsch. Jour.; editor-in-chief, mem. editl. bd. Jour. Workforce Devel.; editor-in-chief Internat. Electronic Jour. Health Edn.; contbr. articles to profl. jours. Vol. spkr. March of Dimes Found., Wareham, Mass., 1992-93; coll.-wide vocat. Cape Cod C.C., Hyannis, Mass., 1989—; planning adv. 2nd Internat. Symposium, Pasco, Wash., 1992; v.p. New Bedford chpt. Am. Cancer Soc., 1985-90. Recipient award Excellence in Continuing Edn. Nat. AHEC Ctr. Dirs. Assn., 1994, 95, 96, 97, Sec.'s awards for Outstanding Progam in Community Health, Nat. Cancer Inst., Washington, 1990. Mem.: APHA, Nat. Assn. Workforce Devel. Profls. (bd. dirs.), Nat. Planning Conf. (mem. com. 1984—87), Southeastern Mass. Health Planning (bd. dirs., sec. 1982—87), Inst. for Disease Prevention (steering com. 1982—). Avocations: writing, acting, dance, theater, travel. Home: PO Box 1116 Marion MA 02738-0020 Office: Assn for Workforce Alternatives R&D Inc PO Box 69 2 Spring St Marion MA 02738-1519 Office Phone: 508-759-7711 ext. 258. Personal E-mail: pcmcpartland@comcast.net. Business E-Mail: pmcpartland@uppercapetech.org.

MCPEAK, MERRILL ANTHONY, retired military officer, investor, company director; b. Santa Rosa, Calif., Jan. 9, 1936; s. Merrill Addison McPeak and Winifred Alice (Stewart) McPeak Bendall; m. Elynor Fay Moskowitz, Nov. 10, 1956; children— Mark Allen, Brian David. AB in Econs., San Diego State Coll., 1957; MS in Internat. Relations, George Washington U., Washington, 1974. Commd. 2d lt. USAF, 1957, advanced through grades to gen., 1988; pilot USAF Thunderbirds, Nellis AFB, Nev., 1966-68; comdr. Misty Forward Air Controllers, Phu Cat, Republic of Vietnam, 1969, 20th Tactical Fighter Wing RAF, Upper Heyford, England, 1980-81, Twelfth Air Force, Bergstrom AFB, Tex., 1987-88; comdr.-in-chief Pacific Air Forces, Hickam AFB, Hawaii, 1988-90; chief of staff USAF, Washington, 1990-94; co. dir., cons., 1994—. Chmn. ECC Internat., 1997-2003, Ethicspoint, 2003-. Decorated DSM, Silver Star, Legion of Merit, DFC. Mem. Air Force Assn., Coun. Fgn. Rels., Daedalians, Sigma Chi. Home: 123 Furnace St Lake Oswego OR 97034 also: 8758 Cliff Swallow Dr Redmond OR 97756 E-mail: mamcpeak@comcast.net.

MCPEEK, BRADLEY, lawyer; b. Cin., Feb. 5, 1973; BA, U. Notre Dame, 1995; JD, U. Cin., 1999. Bar: Ohio 1999, US Dist. Ct. Southern Dist. Ohio 2000. Ptnr. Lindhorst & Dreidame Co., L.P.A., Cin. Named one of Ohio's Rising Stars, Super Lawyers, 2006. Mem.: Ohio State Bar Assn., Cin. Bar Assn. Office: Lindhorst & Dreidame Co LPA 312 Walnut St Ste 2300 Cincinnati OH 45202-4091 Office Phone: 513-421-6630. Office Fax: 513-421-0212.

MCPETERS, SHARON JENISE, artist, writer; b. San Bernardino, Calif., Oct. 17, 1951; d. Cecil L. and Mary I. (Tanner) McPeters; 1 child, Angela M. BA in Journalism and English, U. So. Calif., 1981. Prin. works include My Professors, 1993, Interpretations, 1994, The Thoughts of Socrates, 1995, Self Portrait, 1995, Happiness, 1996, My True Self, 1998, Czechoslovakia 1923, 1999, Liszt, 1999, Portrait of Ten Artists, 2000; author: (autobiography) A Human Mind, 1997, (novels) Domestic Symphonies, 1986, The Broken Heart of the World, 1999, An Illuminated Manuscript, 1994, (short stories) The Library of Heaven, 2000, A Girl Without A Name, 2001, A Sanctified Heart, Selected Poems, 1974-2002, 2003, An Intellect's Goodness, 2004, Professor Scapegoat Speaks, 2006. Avocations: classical music, philosophy.

MCPHEE, GEORGE, professional sports team executive; BA in Bus., Bowling Green State U., 1982; JD, Rutgers U., 1992. Hockey player Guelph Platers, 1978, Bowling Green State U., 1978—82, NY Rangers, 1982, NJ Devils; v.p., dir. hockey ops. Vancouver Canucks, 1992—97, alt. gov., 1992—; gen. mgr., v.p Washington Capitals, 1997—. Recipient Hobey Baker Meml. award, 1982. Office: Washington Capitals Market Sq N 401 9th St NW Ste 750 Washington DC 20004

MC PHEE, HENRY ROEMER, lawyer; b. Ames, Iowa, Jan. 11, 1925; s. Harry Roemer and Mary (Ziegler) McP.; m. Joanne Lambert, May 19, 1956 (div. Dec. 1991); children: Henry Roemer III, Joanne, Larkin, Charles; m. Selby Fleming, Jan. 27, 1999. AB cum laude, Princeton U., 1947; LLB, Harvard U., 1950. Bar: N.J. 1951, Ill. 1961, D.C. 1966. Exec. asst. to gov. State of N.J., Trenton, 1950-52; assoc. R.E. & A.D. Watson, New Brunswick, N.J., 1952-54; asst. to gen. counsel FTC, Washington, 1954; exec. asst. White House, Washington, 1954-57; dep. spl. counsel Pres. U.S., Washington, 1957-58, assoc. spl. counsel, pres., 1958-61; ptnr. Hamel & Park, Washington, 1961-88, mem. mgmt. com., 1975-85, mng. ptnr., 1980-83; ptnr. Hopkins & Sutter, 1988-93, of counsel, 1994—2002, Foley & Lardner, 2002—. Sec. N.J. Commn. on Interstate Cooperation, 1952-54; gen. counsel Rep. Nat. Fin. Com., 1968-73, Rep. Nat. Com., Washington, 1968. Chmn. bldg. com. Potomac (Md.) Presbyn. Ch., 1965-67; v.p. Rep. Club, Princeton, 1952-54; bd. dirs. Eisenhower Inst., 1983-2006, treas., 1991-93, mem. exec. com., 1991-2006. Mem. ABA, D.C. Bar Assn., N.J. Bar Assn., Lincoln's Inn Soc. Harvard Law Sch. Clubs: Tower (Princeton U.); Princeton (Washington) (pres. 1970-72), Metropolitan (Washington), Capitol Hill (Washington). Republican. Presbyterian. Avocation: tennis. Office: Foley & Lardner 3000 K St NW Ste 500 Washington DC 20007

MCPHEE, JOAN, lawyer; b. May 29, 1958; BA, Princeton Univ., 1980; JD magna cum laude, Harvard Univ., 1984. Bar: Mass. 1986, N.Y. 1986, R.I. 1991. Law clk. Judge Abraham D. Sofaer, US Dist. Ct. So. N.Y.; asst. U.S. atty. & dep. chief appeals unit U.S. Dept. Justice, So. Dist. N.Y.; ptnr. litigation dept. Ropes & Gray, Boston, 1990—, chair diversity com. Co-chair Govt. Enforcement Practice Group. Editor (articles): Harvard Law Rev. Mem.: ABA, R.I. Bar Assn., Boston Bar Assn., Phi Beta Kappa. Office: Ropes & Gray 1 International Pl Boston MA 02110-2624 Office Phone: 617-951-7535. Office Fax: 617-951-7050. Business E-Mail: jmcphee@ropesgray.com.

MCPHEE, JOHN ANGUS, writer; b. Princeton, NJ, Mar. 8, 1931; s. Harry Roemer and Mary (Ziegler) McP.; m. Pryde Brown, Mar. 16, 1957; children: Laura, Sarah, Jenny, Martha; m. Yolanda Whitman, Mar. 8, 1972; stepchildren: Cole Harrop, Andrew Harrop, Katherine Harrop, Vanessa Speir. AB, Princeton U., 1953; postgrad., Magdalene Coll., Cambridge U., Eng., 1953-54; LittD (hon.), Bates Coll., 1978, Colby Coll., 1978, Williams Coll., 1979, U. Alaska, 1980, Coll. William and Mary, 1988, Rutgers U., 1988; ScD, Maine Maritime Acad., 1992. TV playwright for Robert Montgomery Presents, NYC, 1955-56; contbg. editor, assoc. editor Time mag., 1957-64; staff writer The New Yorker mag., 1965—; Ferris prof. journalism Princeton U., 1975—. Author: A Sense of Where You Are, 1965, The Headmaster, 1966, Oranges, 1967, The Pine Barrens, 1968, A Roomful of Hovings, 1968, Levels of the Game, 1969, The Crofter and the Laird, 1970, Encounters with the Archdruid, 1971, The Deltoid Pumpkin Seed, 1973, The Curve of Binding Energy, 1974, Pieces of the Frame, 1975, The Survival of the Bark Canoe, 1975, The John McPhee Reader, 1976, Coming into the Country, 1977, Giving Good Weight, 1979, Basin and Range, 1981, In Suspect Terrain, 1983, La Place de la Concorde Suisse, 1984, Table of Contents, 1985, Rising from the Plains, 1986, The Control of Nature, 1989, Looking for a Ship, 1990, Assembling California, 1993, The Ransom of Russian Art, 1994, The Second John McPhee Reader, 1996, Irons in the Fire, 1997, Annals of the Former World, 1998, The Founding Fish, 2002, Uncommon Carriers, 2006. Recipient award in lit., Am. Acad. and Inst. Arts and Letters, 1977, Woodrow Wilson award, Princeton U., 1982, Journalism award, Am. Assn. of Petroleum Geologists, 1982, 1987, John Wesley Powell award, US Geol. Survey, 1988, John Burroughs medal, 1990, Walter Sullivan award, Am. Geophys. Union, 1993, James H. Shea award, Nat. Assn. Geology Tchrs., 1995, award for Outstanding Achievement, Am. Inst. Petroleum Geologists, 1997, award of merit, Field Mus. Natural History, 1998, Pulitzer Prize for Gen. Non-Fiction, Annals of the Former World, 1999, Pres.'s award for disting. tchg., Princeton U., 1999, Pub. Svc. award, Geol. Soc. Am., 2002, Gold medal for Distinction in Natural Art, Acad. Natural Scis. Fellow Geol. Soc. Am.; mem. Am. Acad. Arts and Letters.

MCPHEE, JONATHAN, music director, conductor, composer, interim artistic coordinator; LRAM, Royal Acad. Music; BM, MM, Juilliard Sch. Music dir., prin. condr. Boston Ballet, 1988—; mus. dir. Symphony by the Sea, Boston, 2001—04; prin. condr., artistic advisor Lexington Sinfonietta. Condr.: dance cos. The Joffrey Ballet, The Martha Graham Dance Co., The Dance Theatre of Harlem, Am. Ballet Theatre, N.Y.C. Ballet, The Royal Ballet, Covent Garden, Nat. Ballet of Can., orchs. including Buffalo Philharm., Joffrey Ballet Orch., Rochester Philharm, Opera Orch., BBC Scottish Symphony, Hague Philharm., Boston Pops, Syracuse Symphony, San Diego Symphony, San Francisco Symphony, Orchestre Colonne, The Nat. Philharm. Orch., Danish Radio Symphony Orch; rec. (films) Martha Graham works, Cave of the Heart, Errand Into the Maze, El Penintent, Michael Gandolfi's Caution to the Wind; author: (rev.) version Stravinsky's Rite of Spring; arrangements pub.: by Boosey & Hawkes. Office: Boston Ballet 19 Clarendon St Boston MA 02116-6100 also: P O Box 1425 Marblehead MA 01945

MCPHEE, KATHARINE HOPE, singer; b. Sherman Oaks, Calif., Mar. 25, 1984; d. Peisha Burch and Daniel McPhee. Contestant & second-place winner American Idol, 2006; signed to 19 Recordings Ltd./RCA Records, 2006—. Singer: (singles) Somewhere Over the Rainbow/My Destiny, 2006, (albums) Katharine McPhee, 2007; actor: (plays) Annie Get Your Gun, The Ghost & Mrs. Muir, 2005; (films) Crazy, 2006. Office: 19 Entertainment Ltd 33 Ransomes Dock 35-37 Parkgate Rd London SW11 4NP England Office Phone: 818-788-3056. *

MCPHEE, MARK STEVEN, gastroenterologist, educator; b. Kansas City, Mo., Nov. 8, 1951; s. William Robert and Mary Kay (Paige) McP.; m. Christina Marie Luebke, July 14, 1974; children: Molly Amanda, Ian Andrew. BA magna cum laude, Pomona Coll., Claremont, Calif., 1973; MD summa cum laude, U. Kans., Kansas City, 1976. Diplomate Nat. Bd. Med. Examiners; diplomate in internal medicine and gastroenterology Am. Bd. Internal Medicine. Intern, resident, fellow Harvard U. Med. Sch., Boston, 1976-80; dir. gastrointestinal endoscopy unit Kans. U. Med. Ctr., Kansas City, 1980-85; chief sect. gastroenterology St. Luke's Hosp., Kansas City, Mo., 1988-93, chair dept. medicine, 1992-97, assoc. dir. med. edn., 1995-97, dir. med. edn., 1997—; assoc. dean U. Mo.-Kansas City Med. Sch., 1997—. Asst. prof. medicine U. Kans., KansasCity, 1980-85, assoc. prof., 1985; clin. prof. medicine U. Mo., Kansas City, 1970-97, prof. medicine, 1997—. Author: Annotated Key References in Gastroenterology, 1982; contbr. chpts. to textbook, articles to profl. jours. Bd. dirs. St. Luke's Hosp., Kansas City,Mo., 1993—, Am. Digestive Health Found., Bethesda, Md., 1996—. Fellow ACP, Am. Coll. Gastroenterology; mem. Am. Gastroent. Assn. (mem. governing bd., treas.), St. Lukes Hosp. Physicians Assn. (bd. dirs.), HealthNet Physician Ptnrs. (bd. dirs.), Alpha Omega Alpha. Episcopalian. Avocations: poetry, hiking/camping, golf, tennis, sporting clay target shooting. Office: St Lukes Hosp Dept Med Edn 44th and Wornall Rd Kansas City MO 64111

MCPHEETERS, EDWIN KEITH, architect, educator; b. Stillwater, Okla., Mar. 26, 1924; s. William Henry and Eva Winona (Mitchell) McP.; m. Patricia Ann Foster, Jan. 29, 1950 (div. 1981); children: Marc Foster (dec.), Kevin Mitchell, Michael Hunter; m. Mary Louise Marvin, July 21, 1984. BArch, Okla. State U., 1949; MFA, Princeton U., 1956. Instr. architecture U. Fla., 1949-51; asst. prof. Ala. Poly. Inst., Auburn (Ala.) U., 1951-54; fellow Princeton U., 1955, 81; from asst. prof. to prof. U. Ark., 1956-66; prof. Rensselaer Poly. Inst., 1966-69, dean, 1966-69; prof. Auburn U., 1969-89, dean Sch. Architecture and Fine Arts, 1969-88, dean, prof. emeritus, 1989—. Mem. Ala. Bd. Registration for Archs., 1978-87; profl. adviser South Ctrl. Bell Tel. Co., 1977-79, So. Co., 1979-81, Ala. Power Co., 1979-81, Okla. State U., 1983, Ala. Sch. Fine Arts, 1985-86; cons. Taliesin Archs., 1988-92, adj. prof. Frank Lloyd Wright Sch. of Architecture, 1992-94. Served to 2d lt. USAAC, 1943-45; capt. USAFR 1945-57. Recipient Disting. Arch. award Ala. Archtl. Found., 2001. Fellow AIA (pres. Ala. coun. 1978, Merit award 1976, East Ala. Design awards 1986, 87, 90, 92); mem. Assn. Collegiate Schs. Arch. (bd. dirs. 1970-77, Disting. Prof. 1989), Blue Key, Kappa Sigma, Omicron Delta Kappa, Kappa Kappa Psi, Tau Sigma Delta, Rotary; signature mem. Watercolor Soc. Ala. (pres. 2000—). Episcopalian. Office Phone: 334-887-8779.

MCPHERSON, ALICE RUTH, ophthalmologist, educator; b. Regina, Sask., Can., June 30, 1926; came to U.S., 1938, naturalized, 1958; d. Gordon and Viola (Hoover) McP. BS, U. Wis., 1948, MD, 1951, DSc (hon.), 1997. Diplomate Am. Bd. Ophthalmology. Intern Santa Barbara (Calif.) Cottage Hosp., 1951-52; resident anesthesiology Hartford (Conn.) Hosp., 1952; resident ophthalmology Chgo. Eye, Ear, Nose and Throat Hosp., 1953, U. Wis. Hosps., 1953-55; ophthalmologist Davis and Duehr Eye Clinic, Madison, Wis., 1956-57; clin. instr. U. Wis., 1956-57; fellow retina svc. Mass. Eye and Ear Infirmary, 1957-58; ophthalmologist Scott and White Clinic, Temple, Tex., 1958-60; practice medicine specializing in ophthalmology and retinal diseases Houston, 1960—. Staff Meth., St. Luke's, Tex. Children's Hosps., Harris County Hosp. Dist., Houston; clin. asst. prof. Baylor Coll. Medicine, Houston, 1959-61, asst. prof. ophthalmology, 1961-69, clin. assoc. prof., 1969-75, clin. prof., 1975-98, prof., 1998—; cons. retinal diseases VA Hosp., Houston, 1960—, Ben Taub Hosp., Houston, 1960—; mem. adv. com. for active staff appt. sect. ophthalmology Meth. Hosp., 1986-91, mem equipment com., 1993-95, mem. grievance panel, 1997; vol. clin. faculty appts. and promotions com., 1993; bd. dirs. Highlights of Ophthalmology; v.p. N.Am. Highlights of Ophthalmology Internat. Editor: New and Controversial Aspects of Retinal Detachment, 1968, New and Controversial Aspects of Vitreoretinal Surgery, 1977, Retinopathy of Prematurity: Current Concepts and Controversies, 1986. Amb. Houston Ballet, mem. Houston Ballet Found.; mem. pres.'s coun. Houston Grand Opera; condrs. cir. Houston Symphony, mem. Houston Symphony Soc.; mem. campaign for 80s Baylor Coll. Medicine; mem. Assn. for Cmty. TV, BBB, Physicians' Benevolent Fund, South Tex. Diabetes Assn. Inc., Jr. League Houston; bd. dirs. U. Wis. Found., Madison. Recipient Award of appreciation KT Eye Found., 1978, Woodlands Medal for Outstanding Contbn. to the Econ. Devel. of Cmty., 1988, spl. recognition award Assn. for Rsch. in Vision in Ophthalmology, Crystal award Recognizing Generous Support-Ptnrs. with an Eye for Vision Found. Am. Acad. Ophthalmology, 2000, Benjamin Boyd Humanitarian award Pan Am. Assn. Ophthalmology, 2001, Philip Corboy Meml. award Disting. Svc. Ophthalmology, 2002, Women of Vision Houston Delta Gamma Found., 2002; Alice R. Mc Pherson Lab. for Retina Rsch. dedicated Baylor Ctr. for Biotech., 1988; Alice R. Mc Pherson Day proclaimed in her honor Mayor of City of Houston, Mar. 12, 1988. Fellow: ACS (credentials and Tex. credentials com., com. on applications), Am. Acad. Ophthalmology (2nd v.p. 1979, vice chmn. program devel. found. bd. trustees 1993—, nominating com. subspecialty/specialized sect. of coun. 2001, com. for pub. and profl. rels., bd. dirs. opthalmology ednl. trust fund found., laureate award selection com., mem. coun. representing PAAO, honor award 1956, sr. honor award 1986, guest of honor 1998 meeting, Visionary Soc. Gold Mem.); mem.: AMA, Internat. Coun. Ophthal. Found. (bd. dirs. 2006—), Highlights Ophthal. Internat., Schepens Internat. Soc. (sec. 1986—93, v.p. 1993—95, pres. 1995—97), U. Wis. Ophthal. Alumni Assn. (founding pres. 1990—93, founded Alice R. McPherson lectureship 1994), Assn. Rsch. Surgeons, Pan Am. Assn. Ophthalmology Found., Tex. Ophthal. Assn., So. Med. Soc., Rsch. to Prevent Blindness, Pan Am. Assn. Opthalmology (v.p. 1991—92, pres. elect 1992—95, AJO lectr. 1993, pres. 1995—97, pres. found. 1997, bd. dirs., membership com., Benjamin Boyd Humanitarian award 2001), Macula Soc. (credentialing com. 1992), Internat. Soc. Eye Rsch. (credentials com. 1992), Houston Ophthal. Soc. (pres. 1990—91, credentials com.), Harris County Med. Soc., Am. Bd. Laser Surgery, Am. Soc. Contemporary Ophthalmology (Charles Schepens Hon. award), Internat. Coll. Ocular Surgeons (vice regent 1991), Retina Soc. (v.p. 1976—77, pres. 1978—79, credentials com.), Am. Med. Women's Assn., Internat. Coll. Surgeons (vice regent 1991—), Tex. Med. Assn., Vitreous Soc., Jules Gonin Club. Achievements include research in vision and ophthalmology. Office: Tex Med Ctr 6560 Fannin St Ste 2200 Houston TX 77030-2715 E-mail: alicem@bcm.tmc.edu.

MCPHERSON, BRUCE A., former state official, former state legislator; b. Santa Cruz, Jan. 7, 1944; m. Mary McPherson; children: Tori, Hunter (dec. 2001). Mem. Calif. State Assembly from 27th dist., 1993-96, Calif. State Senate from 15th dist, 1996—2004; vice-chair edn. com. Calif. State Senate from 15th dist., mem. appropriations com., environ. quality com., pub. safety com., revenue and taxation com.; sec. state State of Calif., Sacramento, 2005—07. Mem. joint coms. on arts, headwaters forest and fisheries/aquaculture. Active Santa Cruz City Sch. Dist.; active literacy program Santa Cruz County. Recipeint Friend of Higher Edn. award Calif. State U. Alumni Coun., 1995, Simon Wiesenthal Mus. of Tolerance award, 1998; named Legislator of Yr., U. Calif. Alumni Assn., 1997, Pub. Ofcl. of Yr., Monterey Bay Nat. Marine Sanctuary Coun., 1997, 1998 Friend of C.C., Assn. Calif. C.C. Adminstrs., 1998. Mem. Calif. Coastal Conservancy, Santa Cruz Rotary Club (pres.). Republican. *

MCPHERSON, CRAIG A., cardiologist, educator; s. Lester F. and Gloria K. Mcpherson; m. Anita K. Kerbeshian, 1948; children: Marianne E., Christina R. AB, Columbia U., NYC, 1972; MD, Tufts U., Boston, 1976. Lic. internal medicine Am. Bd. of Internal Medicine, cardiovasc. diseases Am. Bd. of Internal Medicine, cardiac electrophysiology Am. Bd. of Internal Medicine, Am. Bd. of Internal Medicine. Asst. prof. of medicine Yale U., New Haven, Conn., 1984—89, assoc. prof. of medicine, 1989—2006, clin. prof. of medicine, 2006—. Dir. cardiac electrophysiology Bridgeport Hosp., Conn., 1992—, dir. cardiology tng., 1995—. Named Tchr. of the Yr., Bridgeport Hosp., 1995, 2005; recipient Hands and Heart award, Dept. of VA, 1989. Fellow: Am. Coll. of Cardiology; mem.: ACP, Am. Heart Assn., Heart Rhythm Soc., Alpha Omega Alpha. Office: Bridgeport Hosp Yale Univ 267 Grant St Bridgeport CT 06610 Home Phone: 203-887-9925; Office Phone: 203-384-3442. Business E-Mail: pcmcph@bpthosp.org.

MCPHERSON, DONALD PAXTON, III, lawyer; b. Balt., Aug. 9, 1941; s. Donald Paxton Jr. and Janet Lewis Russell McPherson; m. Anna Mary Teaff; children: David Russell, Cynthia Quandt. AB, Princeton U., 1963; LLB, Columbia U., 1966. Bar: Md. 1966, U.S. Dist. Ct. Md. 1967, U.S. Ct. Appeals (4th cir.) 1967. Assoc. Piper & Marbury, Balt., 1966-74, ptnr., 1974-98, head real estate dept., 1980-94, of counsel, 1998—. Mem. ABA, Md. Bar Assn. Democrat. Presbyterian. Avocations: swimming, bicycling, hiking. Office: DLA Piper US LLP 6225 Smith Ave Baltimore MD 21209-3600

MCPHERSON, DONALD SCOTT, labor and employment arbitrator/mediator; b. Sharon, Pa., June 11, 1947; s. Donald McMillan and Lily (Smith) McP.; m. Linda Jo Leighty, Aug. 16, 1969; 1 child, Kimra Leigh. BA, Indiana U. of Pa., 1969, MA, 1971; PhD, U. Pitts., 1977. Dir. residence life Indiana U. of Pa., 1969-77, prof. employment rels., 1977-93, chmn. dept., 1977-87, disting. univ. prof., 1993—2004, prof. emeritus, 2005—. Pres. Assn. Pa. State Coll. and Univ. Faculty, Indiana U. Pa. chpt., 1980. Author: Resolving Grievances, 1983; contbr. articles to profl. jours. Elder Calvary Presbyn. Ch., 1983—; sec. St. Andrew's Soc. of Indiana, 1991-94. Recipient disting. faculty award for svc., Commonwealth of Pa., 1983, Outstanding Alumni award, Indiana U. of Pa., 1983. Mem. Nat. Acad. Arbitrators, Labor and Employment Rels. Rsch. Assn. (exec. dir. Western Pa. chpt. 1982-89), Found. for Ind. U. of Pa. (bd. dir. 1977-82), Ind. Coun. on the Arts, Ind. U. of Pa. Alumni Assn. (pres. 1975-79), Clan MacPherson Assn. (life), Phi Kappa Phi. Democrat. Presbyterian.

MCPHERSON, ELIZABETH WRIGHT, clinical geneticist; b. Battle Creek, Mich., Feb. 27, 1950; d. John Burton and Barbara Cray (Wright) McP.; m. Owen R. Christianson, June 27, 1976; children: Caitlin Ase, Knut Andrew, Olav Iain. BA, Pomona Coll., 1971; MD, U. Wash., 1975; MS, U. Wis., 1975. Diplomate Am. Bd. Pediatrics, Am. Bd. Med. Genetics. Intern and resident U. Wis., Madison, 1975-77, fellow in clin. genetics, 1977-79, clin. geneticist, 1979-81, Children's Hosp. Buffalo, 1981-86, Johns Hopkins U., Balt., 1986-87; pediatrician, geneticist Kaiser Permanent, Washington, 1987-90; pediatric geneticist West Penn Hosp., Pitts., 1990-93; med. geneticist, dysmorphologist Magee-Women's Hosp., Pitts., 1993—. Leader Girl Scouts Am., Reston, Va., 1987-90, Boy Scouts Am., McCandless, Pa., 1990—. Fellow Am. Coll. Med. Genetics, Am. Acad. Pediatrics (mem. exec. com. sect. on genetics). Avocations: medieval re-enactment, camping, skiing, Tae Kwon Do.

MCPHERSON, GAIL, publishing, real estate executive; b. Ft. Worth; d. Garland and Daphne McP. Student, U. Tex.-Austin; BA, MS, CUNY. Advt. sales exec. Harper's Bazaar mag., NYC, 1974—76; sr. v.p., fashion mktg. dir. L'Officiel USA mag., NYC, 1976—80; fashion mgr. Town & Country Mag., NYC, 1980—82; v.p. advt. and mktg. Ultra mag., NYC, Tex., 1982—84; fragrance, jewelry and imported automotive mgr. M. Mag., NYC, 1984—85; sr. real estate sales exec. Fredric M. Reed & Co., Inc., NYC, 1985—88; AT&T security system rep. Home-Watch Inc., Amarillo, Tex., 1989—92; sales rep. Universal Comm., Dallas, 1992—94; acct. exec. Corp. Mktg., Inc., Dallas, 1994—98; sales rep. Pub. Concepts, Dallas, 1998—2006; investor, cons. Dallas, 2006—. NY sponsor Southampton Hosp. Benefit Com.; jr. com. Mannes Sch. Music, NYC, Henry St. Settlement; mem. Dallas Mus. Art League. Mem. Fashion Group NY, Advt. Women NY, Real Estate Bd. NY, U. Tex. Alumni Assn. of NY (v.p.), Corviglia Club (St. Moritz, Switzerland), Doubles, El Morocco Club (jr. com.), Le Club. Republican. Presbyterian. Home: 17850 Sunmeadow Dr #2009 Dallas TX 75252-5382

MC PHERSON, HARRY CUMMINGS, JR., lawyer; b. Tyler, Tex., Aug. 22, 1929; s. Harry Cummings and Nan (Hight) McP.; m. Clayton Read, Aug. 30, 1952 (div.); children: Courtenay, Peter B.; m. Mary Patricia DeGroot, Oct. 17, 1981; 1 child, Sam B. BA, U. South, Sewanee, Tenn., 1949, DCL, 1965; student, Columbia U., NYC, 1949—50; LLB, U. Tex., Austin, 1956. Bar: Tex. 1955, DC 1969. Asst. gen. counsel Democratic policy com. US Senate, 1956-59, asso. counsel, 1959-61, gen. counsel, 1961-63; dep. under sec. internat. affairs Dept. Army, 1963-64; asst. sec. ednl. and cultural affairs Dept. State, 1964-65; spl. asst. and counsel to Pres. Johnson, 1965-66, spl. counsel, 1966-69; sr. ptnr. Verner Liipfert Bernhard McPherson & Hand, Washington, 1969—2002; ptnr., Fed. Affairs & Legis., Govt. Affairs practices DLA Piper, Washington, 2002—. Chmn. task force on domestic policy Dem. Adv. Coun. Elected Ofcls., 1974-76; mem. Pres.'s Commn. on Accident at Three Mile Island, 1979; vice chmn. John F. Kennedy Ctr. for Performing Arts, 1969-76, gen. counsel, 1977-91; bd. dirs. Woodrow Wilson Internat. Ctr. for Scholars, 1969-74; pres. Fed. City Coun., 1983-88; apptd. vice chmn. U.S. Internat. Cultural and Trade Ctr. Commn., 1988-93. Author: A Political Education, 1972, 88, 95. Mem. US Base Closure and Realignment Commn., 1993. 2d lt. USAF, 1950-53. Recipient Disting. Civilian Svc. award Dept. Army, 1964, Arthur S. Flemming award, 1968, Judge Learned Hand Human Rels. award Am. Jewish Com., 1994. Mem. DC Bar Assn., NY Council on Fgn. Relations (dir. 1974-77), Econ. Club. Washington (pres. 1992-99). Democrat. Episcopalian. Home: 10213 Montgomery Ave Kensington MD 20895-3325 Office: DLA Piper 1200 19th St NW Washington DC 20036-2412 Office Phone: 202-861-6464. Office Fax: 202-689-8570. Business E-Mail: harry.mcpherson@dlapiper.com.

MCPHERSON, JAMES ALAN, writer, educator; b. Savannah, Ga., Sept. 16, 1943; s. James and Mable (Smalls) McP.; 1 dau., Rachel Alice. BA, Morris Brown Coll., 1965; LLB, Harvard, 1968; MFA, U. Iowa, 1971. Asst. prof. lit. U. Calif., Santa Cruz, 1969-71, Morgan State U., 1975-76; assoc. prof. English U. Va., Charlottesville, 1976-81; prof. English U. Iowa, 1981—. Mem. lit. panel Nat. Endowment for Arts, 1977-80; lectr., Japan, 1989-90; vis. scholar Yale Law Sch., 1978-79. Author: Hue and Cry, 1969, Railroad, 1976, Elbow Room, 1977 (Pultizer prize 1978), A World Unsuspected, 1987, The Prevailing South, 1988, Confronting Racial Differences, 1990, Lure and Loathing, 1993, Crossings, 1993, Crab Cakes, 1998, Fathering Daughters, 1998, The View From Exile, 2000; editor Double Take Mag., 1995—; contbr. editor Atlantic Monthly, Boston, 1969. Atlantic grantee, 1968; Guggenheim fellow, 1972-73, Ctr. Behavioral Studies fellow, Stanford, Calif., 1997-98, 2002-03; Recipient award in lit. Nat. Inst. Arts and Letters, 1970, MacArthur Found. award, 1981, Excellence in Tchg. award U. Iowa, 1991, Green Eyeshades award Sec. So. Journalists, 1994; stories selected for O'Henry Collection and Best American Short Stories, 1969, 73, Best Am. Short Stories of the 20th Century, Best Am. Essays various Norton Anthologies, 1990, 93, 94, 95, Pushcart prize, 1995, 96, award Cannon Found., 2002. Mem. ACLU, NAACP, P.E.N., Am. Acad. Arts and Scis. (elected mem. 1995), Authors League. Office Phone: 319-335-0416.

MCPHERSON, JAMES E., judge; B in Pub. Adminstrn., San Diego U., 1977, JD, 1981; grad., Naval Justice Sch., 1982; LLM in Mil. Law, Judge Advocate Gen. Sch., 1991. Bar: U.S. Supreme Ct., Calif. Enlisted mil. police USAR; commd. ensign JAGC USNR, 1979, intern Naval Legal Svc. Office San Diego, 1979, asst. force judge advocate comdr. staff U.S. Naval Air Force, U.S. Atlantic Fleet, 1982—83, with Naval Legal Svc. Office Norfolk, 1983—85, judge advocate Naval Air Sta. Cubi Point, Philippines, 1985—88, command judge advocate USS Theodore Roosevelt, 1988—91, sr. def. counsel Naval Legal Svc. Office, 1991—92, sr. trial counsel, 1992—94, asst. legal and legis. matters to chief naval ops., 1995—97, spl. counsel to chief naval ops., 1997—2000, comdr. Trial Svc. Office East Norfolk, 2000—02, dep. JAG naval legal svc. command, 2002—. Decorated Legion of Merit (two awards), Meritorious Svc. Medal (four awards), Army Commendation Medal, Navy Achievement Medal (two awards).

MC PHERSON, JAMES MUNRO, history professor; b. Valley City, ND, Oct. 11, 1936; s. James Munro and Miriam (Osborn) McPherson; m. Patricia Rasche, Dec. 28, 1957; 1 child, Joanna Erika. BA, Gustavus Adolphus Coll., 1958; PhD, Johns Hopkins U., 1963. From mem. faculty to prof. Princeton U., 1962—91, George Henry Davis '86 prof. Am. history, 1991—2004, prof. emeritus, 2004—. Jefferson lectr., 2000. Author: Struggle for Equality, 1964 (Ainsfield-Wolf award race rels., 1965), The Negro's Civil War, 1965, Marching Toward Freedom: The Negro in the Civil War, 1968, Blacks in America: Bibliographical Essays, 1971, The Abolitionist Legacy: From Reconstruction to the NAACP, 1975, Ordeal by Fire: The Civil War and Reconstruction, 1981, 1992, Battle Cry of Freedom: The Civil War Era, 1988 (Pulitzer prize for history, 1989), Abraham Lincoln and the Second American Revolution, 1991, Images of the Civil War, 1992, What They Fought For 1861-1865, 1994, The Atlas of the Civil War, 1994, Drawn With the Sword: Reflections on the American Civil War, 1996, For Cause and Comrades: Why Men Fought in the Civil War, 1997 (Lincoln prize, 1998), Lamson of the Gettysburg: The Civil War Letters of Lt. Roswell H. Lamson, U.S. Navy, 1997 (Theodore and Franklin D. Roosevelt prize in naval history, 1998), Is Blood Thicker than Water? Crisis of Nationalism in the Modern World, 1998, Writing the Civil War: The Quest to Understand, 1998, To the Best of My Ability, 2000, The American Presidents, 2000, Days of Destiny, 2001, Crossroads of Freedom: Antietam, 2002, Hallowed Ground: A Walk at Gettysburg, 2003, Illustrated Battle Cry of Freedom, 2003, This Mighty Scourge: Perspectives on the Civil War, 2007. Recipient Pritzker Mil. Library Lit. award, 2007; fellow, Huntington-Nat. Endowment for Humanities, 1977—78, Behavioral Scis. Ctr., Stanford U., 1982—83, Huntington-Seaver Inst., 1987—88; Danforth fellow, 1958—62, Guggenheim fellow, 1967—68. Mem.: Soc. Am. Historians (pres. 1999—2000), Orgn. Am. Historians, So. Hist. Assn., Am. Hist. Assn. (pres. 2003—04), Am. Philos. Soc., Phi Beta Kappa (Jefferson lectr. 2000). Home: 15 Randall Rd Princeton NJ 08540-3609 Office Phone: 609-258-4173. Business E-Mail: jmcphers@princeton.edu.

MCPHERSON, JOHN EDWIN, JR., zoologist, educator, entomologist, researcher; b. San Diego, June 8, 1941; s. John Edwin McPherson, Sr. and Nadine McPherson; m. Jean Marie LeSarge, Sept. 10, 1966; children: Jay Scott, Anne Marie Arthurs. BS Zoology, San Diego State U., 1963, MS Biology, 1964; PhD Entomology, Mich. State U., 1968. Asst. prof. zoology So. Ill. U., Carbondale, 1968—74, assoc. prof. zoology, 1974—79, prof. zoology, 1979—. Author: The Pentatomoidea (Hemiptera) of Northeastern North America, 1982; author: (with R.M. McPherson) Stink bugs of economic importance in America north of Mexico, 2000; contbr. articles to profl. jours. Named Outstanding Tchr. of Yr., So. Ill. U., Coll. of Sci., 1996—97. Mem.: Entomol. Soc. of Am. (hon.; editor, Am. Entomologist 1993—2001, governing bd. 1994—96, governing bd., officer 2001—03, pres. 2002, Nat. Svc. award 1991, 1993, Disting. Achievement Tchg. award (N. Ctrl. br.) 1993, Nat. Svc. award 1996, C.V. Riley Achievement award (N. Ctrl. br.) 1997, Nat. Svc. award 2001, 2002, Merit award (N. Ctrl. br.) 2006). Office Phone: 618-453-2087. Business E-Mail: mcpherson@zoology.siu.edu.

MCPHERSON, LARRY EUGENE, photographer, educator; b. Newark, Ohio, May 1, 1943; s. Eugene Edward and Ethel Grace (Lehman) McP. BA, Columbia Coll., Chgo., 1976; MA, No. Ill. U., 1978. Instr. Columbia Coll., 1971-76; assoc. prof. photography U. Memphis, 1978—. Instr. Sch. of Art Inst. Chgo., spring 1972; workshop instr. Ohio State U., Columbus, summer 1980, VSW Summer Inst., Rochester, N.Y., summer 1988. One-man shows include Art Inst. Chgo., 1969, 78, 81, Dayton Art Inst., 1992; exhibited in group shows at Mus. Modern Art, N.Y.C., 1978, Corcoran Gallery Art, Washington, 1982, George Eastman House, Rochester, N.Y., 1982, New Orleans Mus. Art, 1992, Milw. Art Mus., 1996, Birmingham Mus. Art, 1996, Art Inst. Chgo., 1997; represented in permanent collections Mus. Modern Art, Art Inst. Chgo., George Eastman House, New Orleans Mus. Art, Mus. Fine Arts, Houston, Memphis Brooks Mus. Art, The Dayton Art Inst., Birmingham Mus. Art, Milw. Mus. Art, Ogden Mus. So. Art; author: "Memphis", Santa Fe, NM: Center for

American Places, 2002, Beirut City Center, 2006, The Cows, 2007. Faculty Devel. grantee U. Memphis, 1983, 92, 99; grantee-fellow Nat. Endowment for Arts, 1975, 79; Guggenheim fellow, 1980. Mem. Soc. Photog. Edn. Home: 7725 Shadow Bend Ln Arlington TN 38002-8051 Office: U Memphis Dept Art Memphis TN 38152-0001 Office Phone: 901-678-2122. Business E-Mail: lmcphrsn@memphis.edu.

MCPHERSON, MICHAEL STEVEN, academic administrator, economist; b. June 6, 1947; married; 2 children. BA Math., U. Chgo., 1967, MA Econs., 1970, PhD Econs., 1974. Instr. econs. dept. U. Ill., Chgo., 1971—74; asst. prof. econs. Williams Coll., 1974—81, assoc. prof. econs., 1981—84, prof. econs., 1984—96, chmn. econs. dept., then dean of faculty, 1986—91; pres. Macalester Coll., St. Paul, 1996—2003, Spencer Found., Chgo., 2003—. Cons. Data Resources, Inc., 1979, Nat. Rsch. Coun. Commn. Human Resources, 1979, Modern Lang. Assn., 1980, Nat. Acad. Edn., 1980, Smith Coll., 1982, The Coll. Bd., 1983, Rand Corp., 1985—86, U.S. Dept. Edn. Ctr. Statis., 1986. Co-author (with M.O. Shapiro): Keeping College Affordable: Government and Educational Opportunity, 1991, The Student Aid Game: Meeting Need and Rewarding Talent in American Higher Education, 1998; co-author: (with D. Hausman) Economic Analysis and Moral Philosophy, 1996; editor: The Demand for the New Faculty in Science and Engineering, 1980, Democratic Development and the Art of Trespassing: Essays in Honor of Albert O. Hirschman, 1986; contbr. articles to profl. jours. Trustee Coll. Bd., 1997—. Fellow Study fellow, Am. Coun. Learned Socs., 1977—78, vis. fellow, Princeton U., 1977—78, sr. fellow, Brookings Inst., 1984—86; grantee, Ford Found., 1981—83, Mellon Found., 1984—86. Office: The Spencer Foundation 625 N Michigan Ave Ste 1600 Chicago IL 60611-3109

MCPHERSON, PETER (M. PETER MCPHERSON), publishing executive, educational association administrator; b. Grand Rapids, Mich., Oct. 27, 1940; s. Donald and Ellura E. (Frost) McP.; m. Joanne McPherson; 4 children. BA in Polit. Sci., Mich. State U., 1963; MBA, Western Mich. U., 1967; JD, Am. U., 1969; LLD (hon.), Mich. State U., 1984; LHD (hon.), Va. State U., Mt. St. Mary's Coll., 1996. Tax law specialist IRS, 1969—75; spl. asst. to Pres. Ford, dep. dir. presdl. pers. The White House, Washington, 1975—77; ptnr. Vorys, Sater, Swymour & Pease, Washington, 1977—80; adminstr. AID, 1981—87; dep. sec. US Dept. Treasury, Washington, 1987—89; group exec. v.p. Bank Am., 1989—93; pres. Mich. State U., East Lansing, 1993—2004, pres. emeritus, 2004—; co-chair, founder Partnership to Cut Hunger and Poverty in Africa, 2005—; pres. Nat. Assn. State Univs. and Land-Grant Colls., 2006—; and chmn. Dow Jones & Co., NYC, 2007. Chmn. bd. Overseas Pvt. Investment Corp., 1981—87; dir. econ. policy Coalition Provisional Authority, Baghdad, Iraq, 2003. Vol. Peace Corps, Peru, 1964—65; gen. counsel Reagan-Bush Transition, 1980—81. Recipient Humanitarian of Yr. award, Am. Lebanese League, 1983, Jewish Nat. Fund Tree of Life award, 1998, UNICEF award for outstanding contributions to child survival, Disting. Svc. award, US Dept. Treasury, 2004, US Presdl. Certificate of Outstanding Achievement, Sec. State's Disting. Leadership award. Mem. DC Bar Assn., Mich. Bar Assn. Republican. Methodist. Office: 499 South Capitol St SW Ste 500B Washington DC 20003 also: NASULGC 1307 New York Ave NW Ste 400 Washington DC 20005-4722 Home Phone: 703-387-0222. E-mail: pmcpherson@nasulgc.org. *

MCPHERSON, SHERRY LYNN, social worker; b. Bklyn., Mar. 8, 1969; d. George Cephano and Mary Sue McPherson. BA, Hofstra U., Hempstead, NY, 1992; MSW, Adelphi U., Garden City, NY, 1996. Cert. sch. social worker. Program coord. Colonial Youth and Family Svcs., Mastic, NY, 1993; sch. social worker Cmty. Counseling Ctr., Franklin Square, NY, 1996—97; cons. Elmont Pre-Kindergarten, NY, 1997, Glen Cove Child Day Care, NY, 1997—98; sch. social worker Patchogue-Medford Schs., NY, 1997—. Bd. dirs., sec. Pronto LI; liaison coord. tobacco free schs. grant NY State, NY, 2007. Sec. sub com. on youth criminal justice Criminal Justice Coordinating Counsel Suffolk County, 2007; mem. site based mgmt., faculty chair Patchogue-Medford High. Grantee, MidEast Suffolk Tchrs. Ctr., 2007. Mem.: NASW, NAACP, Sch. Social Work Assn. Am., Nat. Assn. Black Social Workers (treas. 2002—04), Black/Hispanic Alumni Assn. Hofstra U., Lupus Alliance. Roman Catholic. Avocations: travel, baseball. Office: Patchogue Medford Sch Sys 241 S Ocean Ave Patchogue NY 11772 Personal E-mail: senigma9@aol.com.

MCPHERSON, STEPHEN, broadcast executive; b. Pitts., Oct. 28, 1967; BA in polit. sci., Cornell U., 1986. Fgn. exchange trader Commodities Corp., NYC, 1986—91; dir. devel. Witt-Thomas Prodns., LA, 1991—93; dir. current programming Fox Broadcasting Co., LA, 1993—94; sr. v.p. creative affairs ABC Prodns., Burbank, Calif., 1994—95; v.p. Primetime Series NBC, Burbank, 1995—98; exec. v.p. Buena Vista Prodns. Walt Disney Co., 1998—2000, pres. Touchstone TV, 2000—04, pres. ABC Primetime TV, 2004—. Recipient Diversity award, Director's Guild Am., 2005. Office: ABC Entertainment 500 S Buena Vista St Burbank CA 91521

MCPHERSON, TED R. (EDWARD RUSSELL MCPHERSON), former federal agency administrator; b. Balt., Sept. 18, 1945; s. Donald Paxton and Janet (Russell) McP.; m. Sally Thompson, May 12, 1969; children: Beth, Edward. BA, Williams Coll., 1967; MS, George Washington U., 1971. Mgmt. cons. Klein & Saks Inc., Washington, 1968, Booz Allen & Hamilton, Washington, 1971-73; v.p. corp. planning & investor relations Republic Bank Dallas, 1973-76; sr. v.p. corp. planning and investor relations RepublicBank Corp., Dallas, 1978-83, sr. v.p., CFO, 1983-84, exec. v.p., CFO, 1984-87, First RepublicBank Corp., Dallas, 1987—2001; pres., CEO InterSolve Group, Dallas, 1989—2001; CFO USDA, Washington, 2001—04; under sec. US Dept. Edn., Washington, 2004—05, sr. advisor to sec., 2005—. Mem., Pres. Mngmt. Coun. Trustee Hockaday Sch., Dallas, 1987, Dallas Fiscal Affairs Com., 1983-87. Served to lt. USN, 1968-71.

MCPHERSON, VANZETTA PENN, magistrate judge; b. Montgomery, Ala., May 26, 1947; d. Luther Lincoln and Sadie Lee (Gardner) P.; m. Winston D. Durant, Aug. 17, 1968 (div. Apr. 1979); 1 child, Raegan Winston; m. Thomas McPherson Jr., Nov. 16, 1985. BS in Speech Pathology, Howard U., Washington, 1969; MA in Speech Pathology, Columbia U., 1971, JD, 1974. Bar: N.Y. 1975, Ala. 1976, U.S. Dist. Ct. (so. dist.) N.Y. 1975, U.S. Dist. Ct. (mid. dist.) Ala. 1980, U.S. Ct. Appeals (2d cir.) 1975, U.S. Ct. Appeals (11th cir.) 1981, U.S. Supreme Ct. Assoc. Hughes, Hubbard & Reed, NYC, 1974-75; asst. atty. gen. Ala. Atty. Gen. Office, Montgomery, 1975-78; pvt. practice Montgomery, 1978-92; magistrate judge U.S. Dist. Ct. (mid. dist.) Ala., Montgomery, 1992—. Former co-owner Roots & Wings, A Cultural Bookplace, Montgomery, 1989—2000. Dir. Ala. Shakespeare Festival, Montgomery, 1987—, Montgomery Symphony Orch., 1995-98; chmn. trustees Dexter Ave. King Meml. Bapt. Ch., Montgomery, 1988; chmn. Leadership Montgomery; bd. mem. Lighthouse Counseling Ctr., Montgomery, 1981-84, Montgomery County Pub. Libr., 1989-90; v.p. Lanier H.S. Parent Tchr. Student Assn., Montgomery, 1990-91, Metro-Montgomery YMCA, 2000—, Ala. Arts Coun., 2001-. Recipient cert. Ala. Jud. Coll.; named Woman of Achievement Montgomery Advertiser, 1989, Boss of Yr. Montgomery Assn. Legal Secs., 1992. Mem. ABA (law office design award 1985), FBA (pres. Montgomery chpt.), Nat. Bar Assn., Ala. State Bar Assn. (chmn. family law sect. 1989-90), N.Y. State Bar Assn., Montgomery Inn of Cts. (master bencher 1992—), Ala. Black Lawyers Assn. (pres. 1979-80). Office: US Dist Ct Mid Dist Ala PO Box 1629 One Church St Montgomery AL 36104

MCPHIE, NEIL ANTHONY GORDON, federal official; b. Port of Spain, Trinidad, June 13, 1945; came to the U.S., 1970; s. Sydney Claudius and Rosarita (Francesca) McP.; m. Judith Butler, June 22, 1972 (div. 1979); m. Regina Chow, June 18, 1982; children: Abigail Clarissa, Sydney Frederick. BA in Econs., Howard U., 1973; JD, Georgetown U., 1976. Bar: Iowa 1977, D.C. 1979, Va. 1982, N.Y. 1982. Journalist Trinidad Guardian, Port of Spain, 1963-65; sales rep. Shell Oil Co., Port of Spain, 1965-70; atty. U.S. EEOC, Washington, 1976-82; asst. atty. gen. State of Va, Richmond, 1982—88, sr. asst. atty. gen., 2002—03; exec. dir. Va. Dept. Employment Dispute Resolution, Richmond, 1998—2002; vice chmn. Merit Systems Protection Bd., Washington, 2003—04, acting chmn., 2003—04, chmn., 2004—. Fellow ABA (vice chair constrn., litigation coms.); mem. Va. State Bar Assn. (chair spl. com. 1988-92), Phi Beta Kappa. Avocations: soccer, horticulture, landscaping. Office: 1615 M St NW Rm 680 Washington DC 20419

MCQUADE, EUGENE M., finance and former bank executive; BBA, St. Bonaventure U. CPA. With Peat Marwick Mitchell & Co., until 1980; dep. contr. Mfrs. Hanover Trust Co., 1980-85, sr. v.p., 1982—, contr., 1985—; sr. v.p., contr. Mfrs. Hanover Corp.; joined Fleet Boston Fin. Group, 1992, CFO, 1993, vice-chmn., 1997, pres.,COO, 2002—04; pres. Bank of Am. Corp., 2004; pres., COO Fed. Home Loan Mortgage Corp. (Freddie Mac), 2004—07. Dir. XL Capital Ltd. With USAR. Office: Freddie Mac 8200 Jones Branch Dr MS 400 Mc Lean VA 22102

MC QUADE, LAWRENCE CARROLL, lawyer, investment company executive; b. Yonkers, NY, Aug. 12, 1927; s. Edward A. and Thelma (Keefe) McQuade; m. Morrissey de Rosset Parker, Aug. 3, 1968 (dec. Oct. 1978); 1 child, Andrew Parker McQuade; m. Margaret Osmer, Mar. 15, 1980. BA with distinction, Yale U., 1950; BA, Oxford U., Eng., 1952, MA, 1956; LLB cum laude, Harvard U., 1954; MA (hon.), Colby Coll., 1981. Bar: N.Y. 1955, DC 1968. Assoc. Sullivan & Cromwell, NYC, 1954-60; spl. asst. to asst. sec. internat. security affairs U.S. Dept. Def., Washington, 1961-63; dep. asst. sec. U.S. Dept. Commerce, Washington, 1963-64, asst. to sec., 1965-67, asst. sec., 1967-69; pres. Procon Inc., Des Plaines, Ill., 1969-75, CEO, dir., 1969-75; v.p. Universal Oil Products Co., 1972-75, W.R. Grace & Co., NYC, 1975-78, sr. v.p., 1978-83, exec. v.p., 1983-87, also bd. dirs.; vice chmn. Prudential Mut. Fund Mgmt., NYC, 1988-95; mng. dir. Prudential Securities Inc., 1988-92; chmn. Qualitas Internat., 1994—. Chmn., CEO Universal Money Ctrs., 1987—88; co-chmn. River Capital Internat., 1997—; expert advisor commn. on transnat. corps. UN, 1989—93; bd. dirs. Quixote Corp., Oxford Analytica; chmn. Nucon RF, Inc., 2007—. Author (with others): The Ghana Report, 1959; contbr. articles to profl. jours. Dir. Paul and Daisy Soros Fellowships New Ams., 1998—, Asian Bus. Cooperation Program, 2006—; bd. dirs. Fgn. Bondholders Protective Coun., NYC, 1978—85, Am. Forum, 1985—96, Am. Coun. on Germany, 1985—94, Asian Programs Found., 2006—; trustee Colby Coll., 1981—89, trustee emeritus, 1989—; dir. Czech and Slovak Am. Enterprise Funds, 1994—96, chmn., 1995—96. Rhodes scholar, Oxford U., 1952. Mem.: Pres.'s Cir. NAS, Overseas Devel. Coun. (bd. dirs. 1974—87), Mgmt. and Devel. Inst. (bd. dirs. 1970—99), Atlantic Coun. U.S. (bd. dirs. 1969—99), Nat. Fgn. Trade Coun. (bd. dirs. 1979—87), Chgo. Coun. Fgn. Rels. (bd. dirs. 1969—75), Coun. Fgn. Rels., N.Y., Met. Club (Washington), Century Club, Harvard Club, Phi Beta Kappa. Office Phone: 212-973-9800. Business E-Mail: lmcquade@rivercapital.com.

MCQUAID, KIM, historian, educator, writer; b. Norwalk, Conn., Nov. 2, 1947; s. Francis Walter McQuaid and Margaret Fitzgerald Phelan. BA, Antioch Coll., Yellow Springs, Ohio, 1970; MA, Northwestern U., Evanston, Ill., 1973, PhD, 1975. Asst. prof. dept. history Lake Erie Coll., Painesville, Ohio, 1977—83, assoc. prof., 1983—89, prof., 1989—. Mary Ball Washington vis. prof. U.S. History U. Coll. Dublin, 1985—86; Fulbright lectr. U. Sci. Malaysia, 1995—96. Co-author: (book) Creating the Welfare State, 1980, 1994; author: Big Business and Presidential Power, 1982, A Response to Industrialism: Liberal Businessmen and The Evolving Spectrum of Capitalist Reform 1886-1960, 2d edit., 2003, The Anxious Years: America in the Vietnam-Watergate Era, 1989, Uneasy Partners: Big Business in American Politics, 1945-1990, 1994; contbr. to profl. jours. Woodrow Wilson fellow, 1970. Green Party. Avocations: wilderness hiking, art. Home: Apt 208 686 E Erie St Painesville OH 44077 Office: Lake Erie Coll 391 W Washington St Painesville OH 44077 Office Phone: 440-375-7177. E-mail: mcquaid@lec.edu.

MCQUARRIE, CLAUDE MONROE, III, lawyer; b. Ft. Benning, Ga., Oct. 15, 1950; s. Claude Monroe Jr. and Rosanne (Sprinkle) McQ.; children: Kevin Andrew, Ryan Christopher, Erin Elizabeth. BS, U.S. Mil. Acad., 1972; JD with distinction, St. Mary's U., San Antonio, 1978. Bar: Tex. 1978, U.S. Dist. Ct. (so. dist.) Tex. 1982, U.S. Ct. Mil. Appeals 1979. Commd. 2d lt. U.S. Army, 1972, advanced through grades to capt., 1976, resigned, 1982; assoc. Fulbright & Jaworski, Houston, 1982-89, ptnr., 1989—. Editor Law Rev., 1977-78. Mem. Houston Bar Assn., John M. Harlan Soc., Phi Delta Phi. Avocations: golf, skiing. Office: Fulbright & Jaworski LLP 1301 Mckinney St Ste 5100 Houston TX 77010-3031 Home: 20887 Sweetglen Dr Porter TX 77365 Office Phone: 713-651-5416. E-mail: cmcquarrie@fulbright.com.

MCQUEARY, CHARLES E. (CHUCK MCQUEARY), federal agency administrator; MS in Mech. Engring., U. Tex., PhD in Engring. Mechanics, 1966. Head of dept. Missile OPs. Dept. Bell Labs., AT&T Corp., 1971—73, dir. Undersea Systems Devel. Lab., 1983—87, v.p. Fed. Systems Advanced Technology Divsn., 1987—93; pres., v.p. bus. units AT&T, Lucent Techs., 1994—97; pres. Gen. Dynamics Advanced Tech. Sys., Greensboro, NC, 1997—2002; under sec. for sci. & tech. US Dept. Homeland Security, Washington, 2003—06; dir. operational test & evaluation US Dept. Def., Washington, 2006—. Chair bd. dirs., campaign chair United Way, Greensboro; trustee N.C. Agrl. and Tech. State U.; mem. pres. CEO adv. com. Guilford Tech. C.C.; bd. mem. World Trade Ctr. N.C.; chair Action Greensboro Pub. Edn. Initiative; bd. mem. Guilford County Edn. Network. Named Disting. Engring. Grad., U. Tex., 1997. Office: US Dept Def 1700 Def Pentagon Rm 3A1075 Washington DC 20301

MCQUEEN, JUSTICE ELLIS (L. Q. JONES), actor, television director; b. Beaumont, Tex., Aug. 19, 1927; s. Justice Ellis and Pat (Stephens) McQ.; m. Sue Helen Lewis, Oct. 10, 1950 (dec.); children: Marlin Randolph, Marilyn Helen, Steven Lewis. Student, Lamar Jr. Coll., 1944, Lon Morris Coll., 1949, U. Tex., 1950-51. Actor, writer, dir.: motion picture films including A Boy and His Dog, 1975 (Hugo award, Sci. Fiction Achievement award for dramatic presentation, Golden Boot award, Internat. Star award, Reel Cowboys Silver Spur award, Western Walk of Fame); actor White Line Fever, 1975, Mother, Jugs & Speed, 1976, Winterhawk, 1976, Fast Charlie, The Moonbeam Rider, 1979, Timerider: The Adventures of Lyle Swann, 1982, The Beast Within, 1982, Sacred Ground, 1983, Lone Wolf McQuade, 1983, Bulletproof, 1988, River of Death, 1989, The Legend of Grizzly Adams, 1990, Lightning Jack, 1994, The Friends of Harry, 1995, Casino, 1995, Ben Johnson: Third Cowboy on the Right, 1996, The Edge, 1997, The Patriot, 1998, The Mask of Zorro, 1998, Route 666, 2001, Prairie Home Companion, 2006, numerous others; tv movies include The Sacketts, 1979, Tornado!, 1996, In Cold Blood, 1996, The Jack Bull, 1999, numerous others; appeared in tv series including Gunsmoke, 1955, Alias Smith and Jones, 1971, Cannon, 1971, Cade's County, 1971, Kung Fu, 1972, Matt Helm, 1975, Charlie's Angels, 1976, Columbo: The Conspirators, 1978, The Dukes of Hazzard, 1979, The Fall Guy, 1981, The Yellow Rose, 1983, The A-Team, 1983, Walker, Texas Ranger, 1993, numerous others; producer The Big Thickett, Come In, Children, The Witchmaker; author, prodr.: The Brotherhood of Satan, 1971; dir., prodr. The Devil's Bedroom, 1964, (tv series) The Incredible Hulk, 1978. Served with USNR, 1945-46. Nominee 4 Emmy awards. Mem. Screen Actors Guild, Dirs. Guild Am. Republican. Methodist. Home and Office: 2144 1/2 N Cahuenga Blvd Los Angeles CA 90068-2708 Office Phone: 323-465-4201. *Contribute to a space that no one can or will fill.*

MCQUEEN, REGENIA, writer; b. Summerville, SC, Oct. 29, 1945; d. William and Mary (Stoutamire) McQueen; m. John Ray Sanders Teasley, Oct. 11, 1961; children: John Ray Sanders Teasley, Tonya Teasley, Ieishia Teasley, Nairobi Teasley, Rhodesia Teasley, Donnish Lindsey Teasley, DeJong Lindsey Teasley. A, Cin. Tech. Coll., 1985; cert., Blackstone Sch. of Law, Dallas, 2000; BA, No. Ky. U., 2005. Clk. Western-So. Life Ins., Cin., 1967-72, IRS, Covington, Ky., 1985-87. Author: Regenia McQueen: Born to Search, 2000, Nairobi Teasley: 1-1/2 Hour Defenseless Lamb, 2001, Witnesses to the Impossible Dreams, 2002, Regenia McQueen: Life Stolen, Name, Land, City Government and History Theft in South Carolina, 2003, Regenia McQueen's Documents, Name, Land, Oil, Government and History Theft of William McQueen in South Carolina vol. 1-4, 2004, John Teasley and Nairobi Teasley: Unlawfully Made Guilty until Lawfully Proven Innocent vol. 1 and 2, 2004, Regenia McQueen, One of the Richest Women in the World yet, I Have Not a Dime to Spend, 2006, Regenia McQueen A Queen that Lives in the Ghetto, 2006, My Vision from God Concerning the Virginia Company...Join the Search, 2007. V.p. 13th St. Tenant Assn., 1979—85; Rosa Parks co-chmn.; trustee Owning the Realty, 1983—85. Recipient Achievement award, Ho. of Reps., Ohio, 2000, Wall of Tolerance award, Nat. Campaign Tolerance, 2002. Avocation: researching. Mailing: PO Box 15311 Covington KY 41015 E-mail: r.teasley@insightbb.com.

MC QUEEN, ROBERT CHARLES, retired insurance executive; b. Santiago, Chile, Jan. 23, 1921; s. Charles Alfred and Grace Juanita (Abrecht) McQ.; m. Donna Marie Ikeler, Oct. 6, 1945; children: Scott, Jerry, Monte, Donald. AB, Dartmouth Coll., 1942. Mathematician, Equitable Life Assurance Soc., NYC, 1945-49; group actuary Union Central Life Ins. Co., Cin., 1949-57; with Mut. Benefit Life Ins. Co., Newark, 1957-85, exec. v.p., 1969-71, sr. exec. v.p., chief adminstrv. officer, 1971-85, dir., 1978-85. Bd. dirs. St. Barnabas Corp. (formerly Trimark Corp.). Pres. Millburn Twp. (N.J.) Bd. Edn., 1969-71; chmn. BBB Met. N.Y., 1978-80; chmn. bd. trustees St. Barnabas Hosp., Livingston, N.J., 1983-91, trustee, 1991—. With OSS, 1943-45. Fellow Soc. Actuaries; mem. Am. Acad. Actuaries, Canoe Brook Country Club. Republican. Episcopalian. Home: 11408 Oakmont Ct Fort Myers FL 33908 Personal E-mail: coach1921@yahoo.com.

MCQUEEN, SCOTT ROBERT, broadcast executive; b. Peekskill, NY, June 30, 1946; s. Robert Charles and Donna Marie (Ikeler) McQ.; children: Geoffrey Scott, Mallory Morgan, Brian Daniel; 1 child, by previous marriage, Tasha Lea. BA, Dartmouth Coll., 1968. Founder Sconnix Radio Ent., Inc., Laconia, NH, 1968, Sconnix Radio Ent., Inc. (became Sconnix Group Broadcasting, Inc.), 1971, pres., 1971—; chmn. Bluewater Broadcasting Co., 2003—. Pres. Charisma Ventures, Ltd., 1995—. Chmn. bd. advisors Pine Crest Sch., Boca Raton, Fla., 2000-02, chmn. bd. trustees, 2003—. With N.H. N.G., 1968-69. Mem. Nat. Assn. Broadcasters, Nat. Radio Broadcsters Assn., Lakes Region C. of C. (dir. 1977-81),Royal Palm Yacht and Country Club. Home: 431 E Coconut Palm Rd Boca Raton FL 33432-7915

MCQUEENEY, HENRY MARTIN, SR., publisher; b. NYC, Oct. 29, 1938; s. John Henry and Catherine Mary (Quigg) McQ.; m. Elizabeth Bernino, May 14, 1960; children: Mary E., Henry M. Jr., John P., Matthew S. BBA, St. Johns U., 1961; postgrad., U. Rochester, 1965-67. Advt. sales Curtis Circulation div. Curtis Pub. Co., 1960-62, asst. mgr. NYC, 1962-63, field mgr. Rochester, NY, 1964-67, dept. mgr., account exec. Phila., 1968-74; v.p. sales, exec. v.p. mktg. Manor Books, Inc., NYC, 1974-79; pres. Scott Mag. Dist. Corp., NYC, 1979—93, Kearny Pub., Inc., NYC, 1993-96, Princeton Pub., Inc., NYC, 1996-98; v.p. Irish Connections Mag., NYC, 2000—, Iron Cross, Ltd., NYC, 1998—, Koolhouse Pub. Inc., 2003—, The Irish Examiner USA Newspaper, 2006—. Rep. Western N.Y. Pubs.; cons. Bipad Ednl. Program. Pres. parish bd. Roman Cath. Ch., 1965, editor newspaper, Spencerport, N.Y., 1965, diocesan leader, mem. lay bd., Rochester, 1964-67; certified as tchr. Confraternity Christian Doctrine, Diocese of Rochester, 1964. Served with USAFR, 1956-64. Mem. Am. Legion, Ancient Order of Hiberninas. Home: 12 Blenheim Ln Centerport NY 11721-1704 Office: DMI Worldwide PO Box 603 Centerport NY 11721-0603 Office Phone: 631-261-6273. Fax: 631-261-6532. E-mail: dmi33@aol.com.

MCQUERRY, PATRICIA ANN, painter, retired secondary school educator; b. Long Beach, Calif., Dec. 8, 1934; d. Jack Wendell and Estella Woodruff (Atkinson) M.; m. stepmother Hazel Parnell (dec. 1968); m. stepmother Mary Noble M. (dec. 2006). BA in Art, North Tex. U., 1955; postgrad. in History, U. Ariz., Tucson, 1961-65; postgrad., Stanford U., Calif., 1962-63; diploma in econs., Tex. A&M U., 1974. Tchr. art and social studies Roswell (N.Mex.) Ind. Sch. Dist., 1955-59; grad. asst. history dept. U. Ariz., Tucson, 1959-65; tchr. remedial English, Salpointe Cath. Sch., Tucson, 1961-62; hostess Sequoia-Kings Canyon Nat. Park, 1963; tchr. art Poly. H.S., Ft. Worth, 1966-88; tchr. history Western Hill H.S., Ft. Worth, 1988; tchr. Vision Quest, Elfrida, Ariz., 1991. Counsellor Camp Cruces Episc., Tex., 1968. Author: (plays) New World Playhouse, 1981, Larkenportal, 1993; one-woman show Com. for Artist's Ctr., Ft. Worth, 1990 (citation 1990). Eyewitness U.S.-Mex. Border Patrol; mem. Sky Island Alliance; mem. youth criminal justice subcom. Suffolk County Criminal Justice Coord. Com., 2006—. Recipient various art awards; Fredrich Usher History scholar U. Ariz., 1964. Mem.: Phi Alpha Theta, Alpha Rho Tau.

MCQUIGGAN, JOHN A., theater producer, writer; b. Detroit, Jan. 12, 1935; s. Paul F. and Elizabeth A. McQuiggan; 1 child, Ruth A. BA, Wash. and Lee U., 1956; degree in Theatre Arts, Neighborhood Playhouse Sch. of Theatre, NY, NY, 1959. Founder and prodr. Assn. Producing Artists, NYC, 1959—61; founder, prodr. Milw. (Wis.) Repertory Theatre, 1962—65, Assn. Producing Artists, NYC, 1967—69; exec. prodr. Unity Theatre*Television*Film Co. Inc., Bklyn., 1979—. Mem. drama bd. Yale U., New Haven, 1985—90. Prodr.: (plays) Quartermaine's Terms (8 Obie awards, 1983), Birds of Paradise (2 Drama Desk awards, 1987), The Baby Dance, The Foreigner (Outer Critics' Cir. award and 2 Obies, 1985); prodr.; prodr.: (plays) The Common Pursuit, (Outer Critics' Cir. award, Lucille Lortel award, 1986), Forbidden Broadway; (films) The Common Pursuit, Project Discovery: The First Film School in Cyberspace; author: (screenplay) Time and Madness, In Your Dreams. Grantee, NEA, 1964—65, 1996—97. Office: Unity TheatreTelevision Film Co Inc 150 Joralemon Street Suite 11B Brooklyn NY 11201 Home Phone: 718-855-6133; Office Phone: 718-855-6133. Office Fax: 718-855-2228; Home Fax: 718-855-2228. Personal E-mail: mcq@owf.org.

MCQUILKIN, JOHN ROBERTSON, theology studies educator, writer, academic administrator; b. Columbia, SC, Sept. 7, 1927; s. Robert C. and Marguerite (Lambie) McQ.; m. Muriel Elaine Webendorfer, Aug. 24, 1948 (dec. Sept. 2003); children: Helen Marguerite, Robert Paul (dec.), David John, Virginia Anne, Amy Lambie, Douglas Kent; m. Deborah Jones Sink, Jan 1, 2005. BA, Columbia Internat. U., 1947; M.Div., Fuller Theol. Sem., 1950. Prof. Greek, religious edn. and theology Columbia (S.C.) Internat. U., 1950-52; pres. Internat. U., 1968-90. Headmaster Ben Lippen Sch., Asheville, N.C., 1952-55; missionary The Evang. Alliance Mission, Japan, 1956-68; acting pres. Tokyo Christian U., 1963-65. Author: Measuring the Church Growth Movement, 1974, Understanding and Applying the Bible, 1992, The Great Omission, 1984, An Introduction to Biblical Ethics, 1995,

Life in the Spirit, 1997, A Promise Kept, 1998, Living the Life, 2000; contbr. articles to profl. jours. Mem. Evangel. Missiological Soc. (gen. dir. 1994-97). Personal E-mail: robertsonmcquilkin@earthlink.net.

MCQUILLAN, LAURENCE JOSEPH, communications consultant, educator; b. Bridgeport, Conn., Aug. 4, 1945; s. John Osborne and Mary Catherine McQuillan; m. Geraldine Marie Kenny, Apr. 8, 1972; 1 child, Sean Patrick. BS in Journalism, St. Bonaventure U., 1969; MA in Polit. Sci., SUNY, Albany, 1975. White House corr. UPI, Washington, 1976—80; asst. Washington bur. chief N.Y. Daily News, Washington, 1980—82; Washington corr. San Francisco Examiner, Washington, 1982—84; news editor Scripps Howard News Svc., Washington, 1984—86; dir. of pub. rels. Am. Fedn. of Tchrs., Washington, 1986—87; sr. White House corr. Reuters News Svc., Washington, 1987—99; White House corr. USA Today, Washington, 1999—2004; spokesman, media cons. U.S. Commn. on the Intelligence Capabilities of the U.S., Washington, 2004—05; dir. of comm. Am. Insts. for Rsch., Washington, 2004—. Adj. prof. Sch. of Comm., Am. U., Washington, 2005—06. With US Army, 1969—71, Vietnam. Mem.: White Ho. Corr.'s Assn. (hon.; pres., bd. of dirs. 1993—2004), Gridiron Club of Washington, D.C. (assoc.). Roman Catholic. Office: Am Insts for Rsch 1000 Thomas Jefferson St NW Washington DC 20007 Home Phone: 301-460-3396; Office Phone: 202-403-5119. E-mail: lmcquillan@air.org.

MCQUILLAN, MARK K., school system administrator; married; 3 children. BA, U. Calif., Berkeley; EdD, Harvard U. Asst. supt., Beverly, Mass., 1986—91; supt. Andover, Mass., 1991—94, Lincoln, Mass., 1994—2002; dep. commr., chief operational officer Mass. Dept. Edn., Malden, 2002—04; exec. dir., pres. EDCO Collaborative /Edn. Collaborative for Greater Boston, Waltham, 2004—07; commr. edn. Conn. Dept. Edn., Hartford, 2007—. Office: Conn State Dept Edn 165 Capitol Ave Hartford CT 06106 Office Phone: 860-713-6543. *

MCQUILLEN, JEREMIAH JOSEPH, distribution executive; b. Buffalo, Jan. 7, 1941; s. Joseph Bernard and Marca Rita (Ammerman) McQ.; m. Maureen Elaine Brett; children: Michael, Karen, Kathleen. BS, Canisius Coll., 1962. Nat. sales mgr. Birge Wallcoverings, Buffalo, 1973-74, v.p., gen. mgr., 1976-79; v.p. mktg. Reed Decorative Products, Toronto, 1974-76, exec. v.p. Atlanta, 1979-81, Northeastern Wallcoverings, Boston, 1981-88, pres. 1989-91; pres. comml. wallcoverings Forbo Wallcoverings Inc., 1991-92; exec. v.p. Hytex Industries, Randolph, Mass., 1992-98, pres., CEO, 1998—. Served to 1st lt., U.S. Army, 1962-64. Mem. Wallcovering Distbrs. Assn. (sec., treas. 1987—, v.p. 1988, pres. 1989-90), Wallcovering Info. Bur. (pres. 1980), Wallcovering Mfg. Assn. (v.p. 1980), Di Gamma (life). Republican. Roman Catholic. Avocations: tennis, racquetball. Home: 3 Nauset St Medfield MA 02052-3006 Office Phone: 781-963-4410. Personal E-mail: jjmhytex@aol.com.

MCQUILLEN, MICHAEL PAUL, neurologist, educator; b. NYC, Sept. 9, 1932; s. Paul and Dorothy Marian (Moore) McQ.; m. Louise Devlin; children: Daniel, Thomas, Patrick, Kathleen. BA cum laude, Georgetown U., 1953, MD, 1957; MA, U. Va., 1994. Diplomate Am. Bd. Psychiatry and Neurology (bd. dirs. 1991-95, exec. com. 1995), added qualification in clin. neurophysiology. Rotating intern Royal Victoria Hosp., Montreal, Que., Canada, 1957—58; resident in neurology Georgetown U. Med. Center, 1958—60; fellow in physiology Johns Hopkins U. Med. Sch. and Hosp., 1960—62, instr. medicine, 1962—65; mem. faculty U. Ky. Med. Center, 1965—74, prof. neurology, 1972—74, prof., chmn. neurology, 1987—93; prof. neurology, chmn. dept. Med. Coll. Wis., Milw., 1974—87; clin. faculty mem. dept. neurology U. Va. Health Sci. Ctr., Charlottesville, 1993—94; prof. neurology U. Rochester, NY, 1995—2005; clin. prof. neurology and neurol. scis. Stanford (Calif.) U., 2006—. Vis. sci. Inst. Neurophysiology U. Copenhagen, 1971-72; vis. prof. U. Ky. Med. Ctr., 1978, Royal Coll. Surgeons, Ireland, 1983. Contbr. articles to profl. jours. Mem. Cath. Commn. on Intellectual Affairs. Recipient Neurology medal Georgetown U. Med. Sch., 1957; Clin. Teaching award Med. Coll. Wis., 1976; Disting. Service award N.Y. Med. Coll., 1983; named to Johns Hopkins Soc. Scholars, 1981 Fellow Am. Acad. Neurology; mem. AMA, Royal Acad. Medicine Ireland, Nat. Myasthenia Gravis Found. (chmn. 1981-83), Am. Neurol. Assn., Am. Assn. Electromyography and Electrodiagnosis, Wis. Neurol. Assn. (pres. 81-82), Rochester Acad. Medicine, Alpha Omega Alpha. Office: Stanford Univ 300 Pasteur Dr Rm H3152 Stanford CA 94305 Home: 3611 Louis Rd Palo Alto CA 94303 Office Phone: 650-723-5297. Personal E-mail: michael_mcquillen@comcast.net. Business E-Mail: mmcquillen@stanfordmed.org.

MCQUILLIN, RICHARD ROSS, management consultant; b. Elyria, Ohio, Oct. 15, 1956; s. Wayne Rupp and Frana Rose (Romp) McQuillin; m. Riko Koga; children: Richard K., Sean K. BS, Ohio State U., 1979; MS, U. So. Calif., LA, 1983; MBA, UCLA, 1990. Sr. staff mem. TRW Inc., Redondo Beach, Calif., 1979-88; sr. cons. Deloitte & Touche, LA, 1990-91; cons. mgr. NetBase Computing, El Segundo, Calif., 1993-2000; chief tech. officer When2Click.com, El Segundo, Calif., 2000—04, Casting Networks, Inc., Hollywood, 2004—. Treas., contr. Patio Creek Homeowners Assn., Torrance, Calif., 1986—91, pres., 1991—. TRW Investment Club, Redondo Beach, 1984—87. UCLA fellow, 1989. Mem.: IEEE, Beta Gamma Sigma. Home: 1281 Tennyson St Manhattan Beach CA 90266-6956 Business E-Mail: marquis@mcqcorp.com.

MCQUISTON, ROBERT EARL, lawyer; b. Pitts., Feb. 4, 1936; s. Theodore O. and Bertha L. (Kegley) McQ.; m. Mary Hope Missimer, June 30, 1962; children: Mary Hope, Elizabeth Ann. BA magna cum laude, Yale U., 1958; JD cum laude, Harvard U., 1961. Bar: Pa. 1962. Assoc. Ballard, Spahr, Andrews & Ingersoll, LLP, Phila., Balt., Denver, Washington, Salt Lake City, 1962—69, ptnr., 1969—2001, sr. counsel, 2001—. Mem. nat. adv. group to Commr. IRS, Washington, 1985-87; lectr. in law Temple U., 1968-69, also various tax insts.; bd. dirs. Macromedia Inc., Hackensack, N.J., Gateway Communications, Inc., Binghamton, N.Y. Contbr. articles to profl. jours. Mem. Rep. Fin. Com., Harrisburg, Pa., 1983-86; trustee Am. Soc. Hypertension, 1992-98. Mem. ABA (active numerous coms. sect. taxation 1969—, including coun. mem. 1979-85, vice chmn., sec. 1982-85), Phila. Bar Assn. (bd. govs. 1978-80, mem. coun. 1969-84, sec. treas sect. on taxation 1973-75, vice chmn. 1976-78, chmn. 1978-80), Am. Coll. Tax Counsel (charter, regent 1990-98, vice chmn. 1993-94, chmn. 1994-96), Am. Tax Policy Inst. (trustee 1996-2003, pres. 2001-03), Nat. Conf. Lawyers and CPAs, Exec. Svc. Corps (exec. com. 2005—), Merion Cricket Club, Yale Club N.Y.C. Episcopalian. Home: 1218 Round Hill Rd Bryn Mawr PA 19010-1938 Office: Ballard Spahr Andrews et al 1735 Market St Ste 5100 Philadelphia PA 19103-7599 Office Phone: 215-864-8327.

MCQUOWN, JUDITH HERSHKOWITZ, writer, consultant, financial planner; b. NYC, Apr. 8, 1941; d. Frederick Ephraim and Pearl (Rosenberg) H.; m. Michael L. McQuown, Jan. 13, 1969 (div. 1980); m. Harrison Roth, Dec. 8, 1985 (dec. 1997); m. Harold Allen Lightman, Jan. 2, 2005. AB, Hunter Coll., 1963; postgrad., N.Y. Inst. Fin., NYC, 1965-67. Chief underwriting div. mcpl. securities City of N.Y., 1972-73; CEO Judith H. McQuown & Co., Inc., NYC, 1973—. Author: Tax Shelters That Work for Everyone, 1979, The Fashion Survival Manual, 1981, Playing the Takeover Market, 1982, How to Profit After You Inc. Yourself, 1985, Keep One Suitcase Empty: The Bargain Shopper's Guide to the Finest Factory Outlets in the British Isles, 1987, Keep One Suitcase Empty: The Bargain Shopper's Guide to the Finest Factory Outlets in Europe, 1988, Use Your Own Corporation to Get Rich, 1991, Inc. Yourself: How to Profit by Setting Up Your Own Corporation, 10th edit., 2002, 1,001 Tips for Living Well with Diabetes: Firsthand Advice That Really Works, 2004; contbg. editor: Boardroom Reports, Physician's Fin. News, Physician's Guide to Money Mgmt.; contbr. seminars The Learning Annex, seminars The Discovery Ctr., seminars Boston Ctr. for Adult Edn., seminars First Class, seminars Learning Connection, seminars Knowledge Network. Mem. Am. Soc. Journalists and Authors. Home and Office: One Gracie Ter Apt 9C New York NY 10028

MCRAE, HAMILTON EUGENE, III, lawyer; b. Midland, Tex., Oct. 29, 1937; s. Hamilton Eugene and Adrian (Hagaman) McR.; m. Betty Hawkins, Aug. 27, 1960; children: Elizabeth Ann, Stephanie Adrian, Scott Hawkins BSEE, U. Ariz., 1961; student, USAF Electronics Sch., 1961-62; postgrad., U. Redlands, Calif., 1962-63; JD with honors and distinction, U. Ariz., 1967; LHD (hon.), Sterling Coll., 1992; vis. fellow, Darwin Coll. and Martin Ctr., Cambridge U., Eng., 1996-97. Bar: Ariz. 1967, U.S. Supreme Ct. 1979; cert. real estate specialist, Ariz. Elec. engr. Salt River Project, Phoenix, 1961; assoc. Jennings, Strouss & Salmon, Phoenix, 1967-71, ptnr., 1971-85, chmn. real estate dept., 1980-85, mem. policy com., 1982-85, mem. fin. com., 1981-85, chmn. bus. devel. com., 1982-85; ptnr. and co-founder Stuckey & McRae, Phoenix, 1985—; co-founder, chmn. bd. Republic Cos., Phoenix, 1985—. Magistrate Paradise Valley, Ariz., 1983-85; juvenile referee Superior Ct., 1983-85; pres., dir. Phoenix Realty & Trust Co., 1970—; officer Indsl. Devel. Corp. Maricopa County, 1972-86; instr. and lectr. in real estate; officer, bd. dirs. other corps.; adj. prof. Frank Lloyd Wright Sch. Architecture, Scottsdale, Ariz., 1989—; instr. Ariz. State U. Coll. Architecture and Environ. Design; lead instr. ten-state-bar seminar on Advanced Real Estate Transactions, 1992; evaluation com. for cert. real estate specialist Ariz. Bar, 1994-96; mem. real estate adv. commn. Ariz. Bar, 1996—. Author: Development in Third World Countries, 2002; exec. prodr. film documentary on relief and devel. in Africa, 1990; contbr. articles to profl. jours. Elder Valley Presbyn. Ch., Scottsdale, Ariz., 1973-75, 82-85, 96-98, chair evangelism com. 1973-74, corp. pres., 1974-75, 84-85, trustee, 1973-75, 82-85, chmn. exec. com., 1984, mem. mission com. 1993—, chmn. 1998; trustee Upward Found., Phoenix, 1977-80, trustee, Valley Presbyn. Found., 1982-83, Ariz. Acad., 1971—; trustee, mem. exec. com. Phi Gamma Delta Ednl. Found., Washington, 1974-84; trustee Phi Gamma Delta Internat., 1984-86; bd. dirs. Archon, 1986-87, Hall of Fame Ariz., 1999; founder, trustee, pres. McRae Found., 1980—; bd. dirs. Food for Hungry Inc. (Internat. Relief), 1985-95, exec. com., 1986-95, chmn. bd. dirs., 1987-92; chmn. bd. dirs. Food for Hungry Internat., 1993-95, pres. adv. coun., 1995—, mem. building com., 1999—; trustee, mem. exec. com. Ariz. Mus. Sci. and Tech., 1984—, 1st v.p., 1985-86, pres., 1986-88, chmn. bd. dirs., 1988-90, exec. com. 1984-90, exhibits com. 1990—, strategic planning com., 1999—, svc. recognition 1999; Lambda Alpha Internat. Hon. Land Econs. Soc, 1988-98; sec.-treas. Ariz. State U. Coun. for Design Excellence, 1989-90, bd. dirs. 1988-99, pres. 1990-91, trustee 1999—; mem. Crisis Nursery Office of the Chair, 1988-89, Maricopa C.C. Found., 1988-2002, bd. dirs., 1988-2002, sec. 1990-91, 2d v.p. 1993-94, 1st v.p. and pres. elect 1994-95, pres. 1995-96, mem. Elsner scholarship com., 1999—, web site com., 1999, capital campaign cabinet, 1995-96, 98-99, mem. of chair, 1998-99, mem. nominating com., 1997—, deferred gifts com., 1999—, strategic planning com., 2000—, mem. adv. bd., 2002–; mem. Phoenix Cmty. Alliance, 1988-90, Interchurch Ctr. Corp., 1987-90, Western Art Assocs., bd. dirs., 1989-91, Phoenix Com. on Fgn. Rels., 1988-99, U. Ariz. Pres.'s Club, 1984—, chmn., 1991-92; bd. dirs. Econ. Club of Phoenix, 1987—, sec.-treas., 1991-92, v.p., 1992-93, pres. 1993-94; bd. dirs. Ctrl. Ariz. Shelter Svcs., 1995—, bd. dir., Ariz. Cmty. Found., 1996—, invest. com., 1996—, chair, 2000-, exec. com. 1997—, treas. 1997—, chair nominating com. 1997-98, vice chair bd. dirs., 1999—, chair devel. com., 1999—, advancement com., 1999-2000, chair, 1999—, fin. and adminstrn. com. 1999—; founding mem. Alliance linking poverty and homelessness, 1996-98, bd. dirs., 1996-98, mem. exec. com., 1996-98, co-chair long range planning com., 1997-98; mem. adv. bd. Help Wanted USA, 1990-92; vol. fund raiser YMCA, Salvation Army, others; bd. dirs. Frank Lloyd Wright Found., 1992—, chair fin. com. 1997-98, chmn. bd. dirs., 1998—; mem. Taliesin Coun., 1985—; bd. dirs. Taliesin Arch., 1992-98, Taliesin Conservation Com. (Wis.), 1992—; founding mem. Frank Lloyd Wright Soc., 1993—; mem. fin. com. Kyl for Congress, 1985-92, bd. dir. campaign bd. Kyl for U.S. Senate, 1993-94, 99—; Senator Kyl Council, 1995-98; campaign com. Symington for Gov. '90, 1989-90, mem. gubernatorial adv. bd., 1990-91; mem. Gov.'s Selection Com. for State Revenue Dir., 1993; mem. bond com. City of Phoenix, 1987-88; mem. Ariz. State U. Coun. of 100, 1985-89, investment com., 1985-89; bd. govs. Twelve Who Care Hon Kachina, 1991; mem. adv. coun. Maricopa County Sports Authority, 1989-93; mem. Ariz. Coalition for Tomorrow, 1990-92; founding mem., bd. dirs. Waste Not Inc., 1990-94, pres., 1990-92, chmn., 1992-94, adv. bd. 1996—; bd. dirs. Garden Homes at Teton Pines Home Owners Assn., 1996—, v.p., 2000-04, pres., 2004—; selected as bearer for the Olympic Torch Relay Team, 1996; adv. bd. KAET TV PBS (Channel 8) 1999-2000. 1st lt. USAF, 1961-64. Recipient various mil. awards; 1st place award Ariz. Bar exam, 1967; named to Ariz. Hall of Fame, 1999. Mem. ABA, AIEE, AIME, Ariz. Bar Assn., Maricopa County Bar Assn., U. Ariz. Alumni Assn., Nat. Soc. Fund Raising Execs. (Philanthropy award Ariz. chpt. 1991, 97), Clan McRae Soc. N.Am. Phoenix Exec. Club, Internat. Platform Assn., Am. Friends of the U. Cambridge (Eng.), Jackson Hole Racquet Club, Teton Pines Country Club, Tau Beta Pi. Republican. Address: Republic Cos 11811 N Tatum Blvd Ste 1005 Phoenix AZ 85028-1617 Home Phone: 480-991-0603; Office Phone: 602-494-0202. Personal E-mail: repcos@aol.com, hemcrae3@aol.com.

MCRAE, LESLIE, minister; b. Chaplain, New Zealand, Nov. 22, 1922; s. Alex and Carolyn Lilian McRae; m. Mary Margaret Summers, Sept. 13, 1947; children: Anne, Robert, John. BA, Lycoming Coll., Williamsport, Pa., 1950; MST, Wesley Theol. Sem., Washington, DC, 1953. Minister Ctrl. Pa. Conf., United Meth. Ch., Mechanicsburg, Pa., 1947—85; asst. pastor 1st Meth. Ch., Bradenton, Fla., 1986—90, Parrish United Meth. Ch., Fla., 1991—97. Chaplain USAF, 1956—72, maj. USAF, 1952—72. Decorated Commendation medal USAF. Mem.: Coast Guard Aux., Kiwanis (sec., pres., lt. gov. 1985—2006), Masonic Lodge, Eastern Star. United Methodist. Avocations: golf, music, scuba diving. Home: 222 Old Main St Apt 102 Bradenton FL 34205

MCRAITH, JOHN JEREMIAH, bishop; b. Hutchinson, Minn., Dec. 6, 1934; s. Arthur Luke and Marie (Hanley) McR. BA, Loras Coll., Dubuque, Iowa, 1956. Ordained priest Roman Cath. Ch., 1960. Assoc. pastor St. Mary's Ch., Sleepy Eye, Minn., 1960—64, 1968—71; pastor St. Michael's Ch., Milroy, Minn., 1964—67, St. Leo's Ch., St. Leo, Minn., 1967—68; dir. Nat. Cath. Rural Life, Des Moines, 1971—78; vicar gen. Diocese of New Ulm, Minn., 1978—82; bishop Owensboro, Ky., 1982—. Roman Catholic. Home: 501 W 5th St Owensboro KY 42301-0765 Office: 600 Locust St Owensboro KY 42301-2130 Office Phone: 270-683-1545 ext 339.

MCRANEY, GERALD, actor; b. Collins, Miss., Aug. 19, 1947; m. Beverly Root, 1967, (div. 1971); m. Pat Rae Moran, 1981 (div.); children: Jessica, Angus, Kate; m. Delta Burke, May 28, 1989. Student drama, U. Miss.; studied acting under Jeff Corey, Los Angeles. Repertory experience in New Orleans; 1st TV appearances include Roots II, The Law; co-star TV series Simon & Simon, 1981-88; appeared in films The Never Ending Story, 1984, Jackals, 1986, Murder in the Neighborhood, 1993, Blind Vengeance, 1994, Comanche, 2000, Hansel & Gretel, 2002, Saving Shiloh, 2006; lead role CBS series Major Dad, 1989-93; TV series include Central Park West, 1996, Promised Land, 1996-99, Commando Nanny, 2004, Deadwood, 2005-06, Jericho, 2006-; TV films: Take Me Home: The John Denver Story, 2000, Danger Beneath the Sea, 2001, Untitled Ricky Blitt Project, Tornado Warning, 2002, Untitled Dan Finnerty Project, 2003, Going for Broke, 2003, Ike: Countdown to D-Day, 2004.

MCRANEY, JOAN KATHERINE, artist; b. Magee, Miss., Mar. 21, 1936; d. Harold Bryce and Ruth Katherine (Graves) McRaney; m. William Cummings Hollis, Mar. 14, 1966 (div. June 1970); m. Richard Felder, 1997. At, La. State U., Shreveport, 1954—66, U. Ala., Birmingham, 1965—66; BFA, Inst. Allende, San Miguel de Allende, Mex., 1975; postgrad., U. So. Miss., Hattiesburg, 1990—; studied with sculptor Dan Askew, 1999—2000. Profl. portrait artist and contemporary sculptor, McComb, Hattiesburg, Miss., 1979—. Lectr. Lauren Rogers Mus. Art, Laurel, Miss., 1996. Exhibitions include Inst. Allende Gallery, 1973, Bellas Artes Gallery, San Miguel de Allende, 1974, Gulf South Gallery, McComb, 1982—84, New Orleans World Fair, 1984, Cottonlandia Mus., Greenwood, Miss., 1985—86, Woods Gallery U. So. Miss., 1990, Saenger Gallery, Hattiesburg, 1990, Woods and Locke Gallery U. So. Miss., 1992—96, Lucille Parker Gallery, William Carey Coll., 1993, Lauren Rogers Mus. Art, Laurel, Miss., 1996, 1999, Meridian (Miss.) Mus. Arts, 1997, USM Mus. Art, 1998, Meridian Mus. Art, 1999, Exit Gallery, Hattiesburg Downtown Gallery Walk, 1999—2000, Impressions Gallery, 2000—01, McComb Pub. Libr., 2000, Southwest C.C., 2002, one-woman shows include Gulf South Gallery, McComb, 2003, Meridian Mus. Art, 2004, Impressions Gallery, 2004, Edgewood Gallery, McComb, 2005—06, Good Karma Gallery, 2005—06, Hattiesburg A Gallery, 2006, New Yokel Market, Hattiesburg, 2006—07, Represented in permanent collections Ole Miss Law Sch. Named winner juried competition, Laurel Arts League, 1999; recipient Louie B. Holmes Meml. award, McComb, 1980, 1981, Hon. Mention, Nat. Portrait Seminar, 1981, 1st pl. Pastel award, S. Miss. Art Assn. Cloverleaf Show, 1992, 1st pl. Drawing award, 1992, Dean's Outstanding Creativity award, 1993, 1994, 1st pl. Painting award, Umpteenth Ann. Student Show, Woods Gallery, 1995, Fred A. Walts Endowment, 1995, 1st Pl. Drawing award, 1995, Best of Show award Mixed Media Sculpture, Miss. Collegiate Art Competition, 1997, Best Sculpture award, Dept. Art Annual Student Exhbn., 1998, Honor, Hattiesburg Arts Coun., 1998, winner juried competition, Meridian Mus. Art, 1999. Mem.: Golden Key Soc., Kappa Delta. Avocations: gardening, photography, yoga, meditation, reading. Home and Studio: 308 2nd Ave Hattiesburg MS 39401-3879 Office Phone: 601-818-4131. Personal E-mail: mcraneyart@comcast.net.

MCREE, LISA, television host, producer; b. Ft. Worth; m. Don Granger. BA in Comm., U. Calif., San Diego. Co-anchor news broadcasts WFAA-TV, 1989-91; anchor Lifetime Mag. ABC News; reporter ABC News mag.; anchor World News Now ABC News, NYC, 1992-94; co-anchor news broadcasts KABC-TV Eyewitness News, LA, 1994-97; co-anchor Good Morning America ABC News, NYC, 1997-99; host & corr. California Connected, LA, 2002—. Recipient Alfred I DuPont-Columbia U. award, 2007, Nat. Headliner award for Documentary/Series, 2007. Office: California Connected PO Box 27237 Los Angeles CA 90027-0237 *

MCREYNOLDS, MARY ARMILDA, lawyer; b. Carthage, Mo., Sept. 2, 1946; d. Allen and Virginia Madeliene (Hensley) McR. BA, Mt. Holyoke Coll., South Hadley, Mass., 1968; JD, Georgetown U., Washington, DC, 1971; LLM, Harvard U., Cambridge, Mass., 1973. Bar: DC 1971, US Ct. Appeals (DC cir.) 1971, US Ct. Appeals (2d cir.) 1975, US Ct. Appeals (4th cir.) 1979, US Ct. Appeals (1st, 5th, 6th, 9th 10th cirs.) 1980, US Supreme Ct. 1980, US Ct. Appeals (11th cir.) 1981, US Ct. Appeals (3rd, 7th, 8th cirs.) 1983, US Ct. Appeals (fed. cir.) 1988. Law clk. U.S. Ct. Appeals for D.C. cir., 1971-72; assoc. Wilmer, Cutler & Pickering, Washington, 1973-77; sr. trial atty. civil divsn. fed. program br. U.S. Dept. Justice, 1977-79, mem. appellate staff, 1979-81; ptnr. McReynolds & Mutterperl, Washington, 1981-83, Wilner & Scheiner, Washington, 1983-89, Haley, Bader & Potts, 1989-92; pvt. practice Washington, 1992—. Bd. dirs., gen. counsel Washington Bach Consort, 1977-81, 1985-92, pres. 1981-82, 89-90; pres. bd. dirs., ArtsAm., 1993—; chancellor, sec., mem. synod coun. Anglicon Dist. Va., 2007-. Contbr. articles to profl. jours. Chancellor, sec., vestry mem. All Saints' Ch., Chevy Chase, Md., 2006—; chancellor Anglican Dist. Va., 2006—. Mem. ABA, Kenwood Club, City Tavern Club. Anglican. Home: 2101 Connecticut Ave NW Apt 26 Washington DC 20008-1754 Office: 10th Fl 1050 Connecticut Ave NW Washington DC 20036 Office Phone: 202-429-1770. Business E-Mail: mamcreynoldspc@aol.com.

MCREYNOLDS, NEIL LAWRENCE, management consultant; b. Seattle, July 27, 1934; s. Dorr E. and Margaret (Gillies) McR.; m. Nancy Joyce Drew, June 21, 1957; children: Christopher, Bonnie. BA in Journalism, U. Wash., 1956, postgrad. bus. and fin., 1973-76. Assoc. editor Bellevue (Wash.) Am., 1956-60, editor, 1960-67; press sec. to Gov. Dan Evans State of Wash., Olympia, 1967-73; N.W. regional mgr. for pub. rels. and pub. affairs ITT Corp., Seattle, 1973-80; v.p. corp. rels. Puget Sound Power & Light, Bellevue, 1980-87, sr. v.p., 1987-95; prin. McReynolds Assocs., Seattle, 1995-97; v.p. external affairs Kaiser/Group Health, Seattle, 1997-99; pres. McReynolds Assocs., Inc. (Donworth/McReynolds), Seattle, 1999—; strategic dir. Buerk Dale Victor, Seattle, 2002—. Bd. dirs. HomeStreet Bank, Seattle, Eastern Wash. U., Cheney; chmn. exec. adv. com. Edison Electric Inst., 1984—88; rsch. adv. coun. Electric Power Rsch. Inst., 1989—90; adj. prof. Grad. Sch. Bus. U. Wash., 2002—. Nat. pres. Electric Info. Coun., 1988; chmn. bd. trustees Bellevue CC, 1976—77; chmn. bd. dirs. Leadership Tomorrow, Seattle, 1987, Fred Hutchinson Cancer Rsch. Ctr., 1993—95, Seattle-King County Econ. Devel. Coun., 1994, Eastside Bus. Roundtable, Bellevue, 2003—04; pres. Seattle Ctr. Found., 1979—80, Horizon House, Seattle, 2007—; bd. dirs. Seattle Symphony, 1980—89, Ind. Colls. of Wash., 1984—95, Corp. Coun. for Arts, 1985—94, Mus. History and Industry, 1995—2006, Wash. Nat. Pks. Fund, 1995—2000, Seattle Repertory Theatre, 1996—2002, Wash. Dental Svc. Found., 2002—, United Way of King County, 2002—; state chmn. Nature Conservancy, 1988—90; chmn. King County 2000, 1988—90; mem. Wash. State Commn. on Trial Cts., 1990; chair U. Wash. Bus. and Econ. Devel. Ctr., 1996—98. Named Citizen of Yr., Bellevue, One of Wash. State's Three Outstanding Young Men; recipient Pres. medal Pacific Luth. U. Mem. Pub. Rels. Soc. Am. (accredited; lifetime achievement award, 2003), N.W. Elec. Light and Power Assn. (pres. 1982-83), Greater Seattle C. of C. (officer 1979-81), Soc. Profl. Journalists, Rainier Club (trustee 1995-01, v.p. 1997-98, pres. 1999-2000), Overlake Golf and Country Club (trustee 1993-96), Rotary (pres. Downtown Seattle Club 1991-92). Republican. Episcopalian. Avocations: golf, hiking, skiing, photography, mountain climbing. Home: 14315 SE 45th St Bellevue WA 98006 Office Phone: 206-621-7272. Personal E-mail: nmcreyolds@seanet.com.

MCREYNOLDS, STEPHEN PAUL, lawyer; b. Sacramento, Oct. 16, 1938; s. Leslie N. and Mary C. McR.; m. Chodi D. Greeno, Sept. 29, 1970. AB, U. Calif., Davis, 1969; JD, U. Calif., 1972. Bar: Calif. 1972. Sole practice, Sunnyvale, Calif., 1972—. With USN, 1956—62. Mem.: Mensa Internat. Office: 1111 W El Camino Real # 329 Sunnyvale CA 94087-1056

MCROBERTS, J. WILLIAM, urologist, surgeon, researcher; s. Jerry William McRoberts and Ruth Margaret Parsons; m. Marlie Richards Richards; 1 child, W. Porter; 1 child, Jane Parsons. BA, Princeton U., NJ, 1955; MD, Cornell U., NYC, 1959. Diplomate Nat. Bd. Med. Examiners, Am. Bd. Urology. Surg. intern NY Hosp., Cornell U. Med. Coll., NYC, 1959—60; surg. resident Mayo Clinic, Rochester, Minn., 1960—61, urology resident, 1961—63, chief resident urology, 1963—64; instr. dept. urology U. Wash. Sch. Medicine, Seattle, 1967—69, asst. prof. dept. urology, 1969—72, assoc. prof. dept. urology, 1972; assoc. prof. surgery, chief divsn. urology dept. surgery U. Ky. Sch. Medicine, Lexington, 1972—74, prof. surgery, chief divsn. urology dept. surgery, 1974—97, prof. surgery divsn. urology, 1997—2001, emeritus prof. surgery, 2001—, acting chmn. dept. surgery, 1983, 1984—86. Pediat. fellow Hosp. for Sick

Children, London, 1981—82; sr. vis. fellow U. London and Inst. Urology, 1981—82. Capt. USNR, 1965—95. Mem.: AMA, ACS, AAUP, So. Soc. Urologic Surgeons, Internat. Soc. Urology, Nat. Urologic Forum, Nat. Kidney Found., Soc. Univ. Urologists, Soc. for Pediat. Urology, Ky. State Med. Assn., Assn. Mil. Surgeons US, Assn. Acad. Surgery, Am. Urol. Assn. (southeastern sect.), Am. Fertility Soc., Am. Assn. Genito-Urinary Surgeons, Am. Acad. Pediat., St. Peter's Soc. Home: 137 Kentucky Ave Lexington KY 40502 Home Phone: 859-225-4785; Office Phone: 859-225-4785. Personal E-mail: jwilliammcrobertsmd@msn.com.

MCROBERTS, SHERYL A., art educator; b. Kalamazoo, Mich., Aug. 14, 1950; d. James Burton McRoberts and Janet Alice Ligtvoet McRoberts; m. Thomas Johnson, June 13, 1970; 1 child, Anders Johnson. BA, Augsburg Coll., Mpls., 1973; MFA in Sculpture, Ind. U., Bloomington, 1978. Prof. art Doane Coll., Crete, Nebr., 1980—84, U. Wyo., Laramie, 1984—88, Normandale C.C., Bloomington, Minn., 1989—. Fellow, Fulbright Found., 1995. Office: Normandale CC 9700 France Ave S Minneapolis MN 55431

MCRORIE, WILLIAM EDWARD, retired insurance company executive; b. Rutherfordton, NC, Apr. 8, 1940; s. Cyrus Brown and Rosalie (Thompson) McR.; m. Hope Evangeline Foster, Sept. 9, 1962; children: Mark Edward, Jennifer Lynn. LLB, U. N.C., 1964. CLU; Bar: N.C., Va. State mgr. Sturdivant Life Ins. Co., Lynchburg, Va., 1965-68; sr. v.p., gen. counsel First Colony, Lynchburg, 1969-2000. Sec. Jamestown Life Ins. Co., Lynchburg, 1981-2000. Councilman City of Lynchburg. Mem. Va. Bar Assn., Assn. Life Ins. Counsel, John Lynch Soc. (sec. 1970—). Home: 2600 Link Rd Lynchburg VA 24503-3012 E-mail: wem@ntelos.net.

MC ROSTIE, CLAIR NEIL, economics professor; b. Owatonna, Minn., Dec. 16, 1930; s. Neil Hale and Myrtle Julia (Peterson) McR.; m. Ursula Anne Schwieger, Aug. 29, 1968. BSBA cum laude, Gustavus Adolphus Coll., 1952; MA in Mktg., Mich. State U., 1953; PhD in Fin., U. Wis., 1963; postgrad., U. Minn., 1971-72, Am. Grad. Sch. Internat. Mgmt., 1980-81; cert., Coll. for Fin. Planning, 1990. Cert. fin. planner. Faculty Gustavus Adolphus Coll., St. Peter, Minn., 1958-96; emeritus prof., 1996—; chmn. dept. econs. and bus. Gustavus Adolphus Coll., 1967-83, chmn., mem. various coms., 1971-96; teaching asst. Sch. Commerce, U. Wis., 1960-62. Lectr. European divsn. U. Md., 1966—67; vis. prof. Am. Grad. Sch. Internat. Mgmt., 1980—81; pres. Minn. World Trade Week, Inc., 1987; bd. dirs. Rite Care Childhood Lang. Clinic. Editor: Global Resources: Perspectives and Alternatives, 1978, The Future of the Market Ecomomy, 1979. Congregation pres. First Luth. Ch., St. Peter, Minn., 1972-73, 93, chmn. pastoral call com., 1968-69, chmn. staffing com., 1975, mem. ch. council, 1968-74, 89-93; chmn. social ministry com. Minn. Synod, Luth. Ch. Am., 1975, mem. long range planning com. Southwestern Minn. Synod; chmn. Rep. council arts professions, scis., Minn., 1968-70, co-chmn. state task force on Vietnam, 1968; mem. adv. commn. Minn. Dept. Manpower Services, 1967-71; mem. North Central Regional Manpower Adv. Com.; bd. dirs. Midwest China Resource Study Center; del. White House Conf. Aging, 1971. Served with U.S. Army, 1954-56. Recipient Leavey Found. award Freedoms Found., Valley Forge, Pa.; rsch. fellow Fed. Res. Bank Chgo., 1962-63. Mem. Fin. Execs. Inst., Fin. Planners Assn., Minn. Econs. Assn. (bd. dirs. 1974-75, 79-80), Masons (master, Royal Arch chpt., commandry Zuhrah Shrine Temple, Scottish Rite), Royal Order Scotland, Alpha Kappa Psi, Iota Delta Gamma, Sigma Epsilon. Lutheran. Avocations: bird watching, backpacking, fitness and health. Home: 1208 Pine Pointe Curv Saint Peter MN 56082-1344 Home Phone: 507-934-6920.

MCSHAN, CLYDE GRIFFIN, II, diversified financial services company executive; b. New Orleans, Feb. 8, 1945; s. Clyde G. and Ursula C. (Mumme) McS.; m. Deborah A. Lark, Oct. 16, 1971; children: Madylin, Kristy, Suzanne. BA, Southeastern La. U., 1966. Cert. internal auditor, cert. govt. fin. mgr., cert. office automation profl. Auditor Office of the Inspector Gen., New Orleans, 1965-72; audit br. chief Cen. Voucher Payment Ctr., New Orleans, 1972-73; evaluation staff chief Nat. Fin. Ctr., New Orleans, 1973-74, processing br. chief, 1974, ops. div. chief, 1974-78, acctg. div. chief, 1978-79, ops. div. chief, 1979-80, dep. dir., 1980-81, dir., 1981-93; dep. chief fin. officer, dir. fin. mgmt. U.S. Dept. Commerce, 1993-97; v.p. Affiliated Computer Svcs., Inc., New Orleans, 1997-2001, sr. v.p. affiliated computer svcs., 2001—03; with Lockheed Martin, 2003—04, Savantage Solutions, Inc., 2004—05, Computer Scis. Corp., 2005—06. Contbr. articles to profl. jours. Chmn. CASU Tenant Bd. Dirs., New Orleans, 1989-93, policy com. Fed. Exec. Bd., New Orleans, 1990-93, chmn., 1989-90, 92-93; chmn. unit I United Way of Greater New Orleans, 1989-90, chair mktg. and comm., 1991, vice chmn. cmty. resources divsn. 1991, chair 1992-93, trustee, 1990-94, 98—, chmn. unit VII, 1990, chmn. CFC, 1989, chair cmty.-wide campaign, 2001-02; mem. Tulane U. pub. adv. com. for computer info. sys., 1987—2003; acctg. dept. advt. bd. U. New Orleans, 1991-93; pres. acctg. bd. U. New Orleans, 1992-93, bd. dirs. La. Tech. Coun., vice chair bd., 2004—; bd. dirs. Ctr. for Non-profit Resources, 1997-2002; bd. dirs. YMCA Greater New Orleans, 1990-93, 1997—, chmn. bd., 2002-04; vice chair La. Tech. Coun., 2000—. With U.S. Army, 1965-71. Recipient Leadership award United Way, 1989, Communication and Leadership award Toastmasters, 1991, award New Orleans chpt. Federally Employed Women, 1990, 91, Presdl. Meritorious Rank award, 1988, 95, New Orleans Fed. Exec. Bd. award for outstanding leadership, 1989, Spl. award Office of the Comptroller Gen., 1989, Disting. Exec. Svc. award Sr. Exec. Assn. USDA, 1989, Elmer Staats Disting. Leadership award, 1993, Donald L. Scantlebury Meml. award for Disting. Leadership in Fin. Mgmt., 1995, Robert W. King Meml. award for disting. career accomplishments, 1997, Disting. Achievement award Internat. Inst. Bus. Techs.; named one of Outstanding 1990 Campaign Vols. of Yr., United Way, 1991, Fed. 100 Info. Systems Mgrs., Fed. Computer Wk., 1990, 96, to Info. Tech. Hall of Fame, 1997. Mem. Assn. Govt. Accts. (New Orleans chpt. pres. 1972-73, dir. 1970-71, 73-74, 74-75, 76-77, S.W. region v.p. 1975-76, South Ctrl. region v.p. 1981-82, mem. nat. exec. com. 1983-84, 93-96, chmn. fin. mgmt. enhancement bd. 1988-89, chmn. emerging issues 1990-91, chmn. tech. program com. 1991-93, nat. pres.-elect 1993-94, nat. pres. 1994-95), Inst. Internal Auditors, Sr. Exec. Assn., Fed. Exec. Inst. Alumni Assn. Republican. Roman Catholic. Avocation: gardening. Home: 5500 Toby Ln Kenner LA 70065 Office Phone: 504-722-2100. E-mail: cmcshanii@aol.com, cmcshan@savantage.net.

MCSHANE, BERNARD, purchasing agent; b. Wyandotte, Mich., Sept. 22, 1964; s. Vincent Patrick and Margaret Mary McShane; m. Lanee Marie McGee, Dec. 12, 1992; children: Amber Victoria, Bernard Patrick. A in Comm., CC Air Force, Colorado Springs, 1988; B in Bus. Adminstrn., Lawrence Technol. U., Southfield Mich., 1990; MBA, Ctrl. Mich. U., Southfield, 1996. Purchasing mgr. Siemens E&A, Roebuck, SC, 2000—. Baseball and soccer coach YMCA, Anderson, SC. Sgt. USAF, 1984—92, Crete, Greece. Decorated Commendation medal US Air Force, Achievement medal, 3 Yr. Good Conduct medal. Mem.: Am. Legion (life). Home: 303 Surrey Ln Anderson SC 29621 Office: Siemens Energy and Automation Inc 1320 Old Georgia Rd Roebuck SC 29376-9631 Home Phone: 864-332-0391; Office Phone: 864-595-4775. Office Fax: 864-595-4736; Home Fax: 864-595-4736. Business E-Mail: bernard.mcshane@siemens.com.

MCSHANE, IAN, actor; b. Blackburn, Lancashire, Eng., Sept. 29, 1942; s. Harry McShane; m. Ruth Post (div. 1976); m. Suzan Farmer, 1965 (div. 1968); m. Gwen Humble, 1981; children: Kate, Morgan. Actor: (films) The Pleasure Girls, 1965, Sky West and Crooked, 1966, If It's Tuesday, This Must Be Belgium, 1969, Battle of Britain, 1969, Pussycat, Pussycat, I Love You, 1970, Tam Lin, 1970, Villain, 1971, Freelance, 1971, Sitting Target, 1972, Left Hand of Gemini, 1972, The Last of Sheila, 1973, Ransom, 1975, Journey Into Fear, 1975, The Fifth Musketeer, 1979, Yesterday's Hero, 1979, The Great Riviera Bank Robbery, 1979, Cheaper to Keep Her, 1980, Exposed, 1983, Torchlight, 1984, Ordeal by Innocence, 1984, Too Scared to Scream, 1985, Grand Larceny, 1987, Con Man, 1992, Sexy Beast, 2000, Bollywood Queen, 2002, Agent Cody Banks, 2003, Nemesis Game, 2003, Nine Lives, 2005, Scoop, 2006, We Are Marshall, 2006; (TV series) You Can't Win, 1966, Wuthering Heights, 1967, Bare Essence, 1983, Lovejoy, 1986, Dallas, 1989, Madson, 1996, Deadwood, 2004—06 (Golden Globe award for best actor TV series - drama, 2005); (TV miniseries) Roots, 1977, Jesus of Nazareth, 1977, Life of Shakespeare, 1978, Disraeli, 1979, Marco Polo, 1982, Evergreen, 1985, A.D., 1985, War and Remembrance, 1988, Trust, 2003; (TV films) The Wild and the Willing, 1962, Funny Noises with Their Mouths, 1963, Funeral Games, 1968, Whose Life Is It Anyway?, 1972, The Lives of Jenny Dolan, 1975, Code Name: Diamond Head, 1977, The Pirate, 1978, High Tide, 1980, The Letter, 1982, Grace Kelly, 1983, Braker, 1985, Rocket to the Moon, 1986, The Murders in the Rue Morgue, 1986, The Great Escape II: The Untold Story, 1988, Young Charlie Chaplin, 1989, Dick Francis: Twice Shy, 1989, Dick Francis: In the Frame, 1989, Dick Francis: Blood Sport, 1989, Perry Mason: The Case of the Desperate Deception, 1990, Columbo: Rest in Peace, Mrs. Columbo, 1990, White Goods, 1994, Soul Survivors, 1995, Babylon 5: The River of Souls, 1998, D.R.E.A.M. Team, 1999, Man and Boy, 2002. *

MCSHANE, JOSEPH MICHAEL, academic administrator, priest; b. NYC, June 19, 1949; s. Owen Patrick and Catherine Veronica (Shelley) McS. AB, AM, Boston Coll., 1972; MDiv, STM, Jesuit Sch. Theology, Berkeley, Calif., 1977; PhD, U. Chgo., 1981. Ordained priest Roman Cath. Ch., 1977. English tchr. Canisius H.S., Buffalo, 1972-74; asst. prof. religious studies LeMoyne Coll., Syracuse, NY, 1982-87, assoc. prof. religious studies, 1987-91, prof., 1991-92, chairperson, 1991-92; dean Fordham U., Bronx, NY, 1992-98, prof. theology, 1992-98, pres., 2003—; pres., prof. theology U. Scranton, 1998—2003. Vis. prof. history Loyola House, Berkley, Mich., 1986—87. Author: Sufficiently Radical: Catholicism, Progressivism and the Bishops' Program of 1919, 1986; author chpt. to book; creator video: The Pilgrimage of the People of God: An Introduction to the Study of Church History, 1991; contbr. articles to profl. jours. Bd. dirs. U. Scranton, Pa., Scranton Prep. Sch., Pa., Fordham U., NYC, Fordham Prep. Sch., Bronx, NY, Regis H.S., NYC, Canisius Coll., Buffalo, St. Joseph's Prep. Sch., Phila. Recipient First prize, Cath. Press Assn., 1992. Mem.: Am. Soc. Ch. History, Am. Cath. Hist. Assn., Phi Beta Kappa. Democrat. Roman Catholic. Office: Office of Pres Fordham U Bronx NY 10458 Office Phone: 718-817-3000. Business E-Mail: jmcshane@fordham.edu.

MCSHANE, MICHAEL, manufacturing executive; BBA in Acctg., U. Tex., Austin. CPA. Various fin. mgmt. positions including corp. contr. and regional contr. Far East Ops. Reed Tool Co.; with BJ Svcs. Co., 1987—2002, v.p. fin., CFO, 1990—98, sr. v.p. fin., CFO, bd. dirs., 1998—2002; pres., CEO, bd. dirs. Grant Prideco, Houston, 2002—, chmn., 2003—. Office: Grant Prideco Inc Ste 900 400 N Sam Houston Pky E Houston TX 77060 *

MCSHANE, SYBIL BRIGHAM, library director; Dir. reference & law svcs. Vt. Dept. Librs., Montpelier, info. systems dir., state libr., 1997—. Mem.: ALA, Vt. Libr. Assn., Chief Officers of State Libr. Agencies (legis. com. 2004—06). Office: Vt Dept Libraries Pavillion Office Bldg 109 State St Montpelier VT 05609 Office Phone: 802-828-3265. Office Fax: 802-828-2199. E-mail: sybil.mcshane@dol.state.vt.us. *

MCSHEFFERTY, JOHN, retired research scientist, personal care industry executive, consultant; b. Akron, Ohio, Mar. 14, 1929; s. John and Jean McS.; m. Glenna Gloria Childs, Apr. 18, 1959; children: John III, Amy Childs. BSc, U. Glasgow, 1953, PhD, 1957. Various rsch. positions Sterling Winthrop Rsch. Inst., Rensselaer, NY, 1957-62; dir. pharm. devel. Ortho Pharm. Corp. divsn. Johnson and Johnson, Raritan, NJ, 1962-75; dir. rsch. Janssen R & D, Inc. divsn. Johnson & Johnson, Piscataway, NJ, 1975-77; v.p. R & D family products Internat. Playtex, Paramus, NJ, 1977-79; pres. Gillette Rsch. Inst., Gaithersburg, Md., 1979-97; ret., 1997. Cons. in field. Fellow Royal Pharm. Soc. of Gt. Britain; mem. Indsl. Rsch. Inst. (bd. dirs. 1988-92, emeritt com. 1998—), Am. Acad. Dermatology, Am. Mgmt. Assn. (bd. dirs. 1994-97), Am. Chem. Soc., Am. Pharm. Assn., N.Y. Acad. Scis., Soc. Cosmetic Chemists, Dirs. Indsl. Rsch., Assn. Rsch. Dirs., Rotary, Sigma Xi. Personal E-mail: jmcs2@roadrunner.com.

MCSHERRY, WILLIAM JOHN, JR., lawyer, consultant; b. NYC, Oct. 28, 1947; s. William John Sr. and Mary Elizabeth (Dunphy) McS.; m. Elizabeth Ann Crosby, June 8, 1974; children: Brendan, Sean, Rory. AB cum laude, Fordham U., 1969; JD cum laude, Harvard U., 1973. Bar: N.Y. 1974, U.S. Dist. Ct. (so. dist.) N.Y. 1975, U.S. Ct. Appeals (2d cir.) 1977. Assoc. Spengler, Carlson, Gubar, Brodsky & Frischling, NYC, 1973-78, ptnr., 1979-88, Bryan, Cave, McPheeters & McRoberts, NYC, 1989-91, Battle Fowler LLP, NYC, 1991—. Exec. dir. U.S. Football League, N.Y.C., 1985-86; chmn. litigation dept. Battle Fowler, 1992-96; pres., bd. dirs. Playtex Mktg. Corp.; bd. dirs. Questron Tech., Inc. Author: (with others) Tender Offer Regulation: The Federal SEC's Challenge and New York State's Response. Derivatives Risk and Responsibility, 1996, Attorney Client Privilege in tge Second Circuit, 1998. Mem. Zoning Bd. Appeals, Village of Larchmont, N.Y., 1988-91, dep. mayor, 1992-98, bd. trustees, 1991-98. Served with USAR, 1970-75. Mem. ABA (litigation, antitrust, entertainment and sports, corp. banking and bus. law sects., subcom. litigation 1940 Act; vice-chair com. alt. dispute resolution), Assn. of Bar of City of N.Y. (mem. 1979-82 com. state cts. superior jurisdiction, 1987-90, com. arbitration and alternative dispute resolution, mem. sports law com. 1998—), Fed. Bar Council, Council N.Y. Law Assocs. (bd. dirs., treas. 1975), Phi Beta Kappa. Roman Catholic. Avocations: community involvement, sports, writing. Home: 2 Summit Ave Larchmont NY 10538-2930 Address: 75 E 55th St New York NY 10022-3205

MCSLARROW, KYLE E., telecommunications association executive, former federal agency administrator; b. Va. m. Allison McSlarrow. BA, Cornell U., 1982; JD, U. Va., 1985. Asst. to gen. counsel of U.S. Army office sec. U.S. Army, 1985—89; assoc. Hunton & Williams, Washington; dep. chief of staff, chief counsel to majority leaders Bob Dole and Trent Lott US Senate, 1995—97, chief of staff to Senator Paul Coverdell, 1997—2000; nat. chmn. Quayle 2000 Presdl. Campaign, 1998—2000; v.p. polit. and govt. affairs, lead Washington office Grassroots.com, 2000—01; chief of staff to sec. Spencer Abraham US Dept. Energy, Washington, 2001—02, dep. sec., 2002—05; pres., CEO Nat. Cable & Telecom. Assn., Washington, 2005—. Mem. Arlington County, Va. Planning Commn.; co.-chmn. US-Russia Energy Working Group, 2002—05. Democrat. Office: Nat Cable & Telecom Assn 1724 Massachusetts Ave NW Washington DC 20036

MCSORLEY, RITA ELIZABETH, adult education educator; b. Baraboo, Wis., Feb. 13, 1947; d. Charles Gervase and Bertie Ellen (Baker) Collins; m. William David McSorley III, June 6, 1967; children: William David IV, Kathryn Rita, Stephen Charles, Matthew Thomas. B Liberal Studies, Mary Washington Coll., Fredericksburg, Va., 1988; MEd, U. Va., Charlottesville, 1994. Adult edn. instr. Waipahu (Hawaii) Cmty. Sch. for Adults, 1989-91, literacy coord., 1990-91; dir. religious edn. Marine Meml. Chapel, Quantico, Va., 1992-94; adult edn. instr. Prince William County Schs., Quantico, 1992-93; coord. computer assisted lang. learning project Literacy Coun. No. Va., Falls Church, 1995-96; ednl. cons. Fairfield Lang. Techs., Harrisonburg, Va., 1996-97; adult edn. coord. N.E. Ind. Sch. Sys., San Antonio, 2000—06; ret., 2006; part-time gt. ctr. tng. staff Tex. Ednl. Svc. Ctr. Region XX, 2004—. Lectr. in field. Mem. sch. bd. Quantico Dependent Schs., 1980-82; vol. Boy Scouts Am., Quantico and Pearl City, Hawaii, 1985-97. Mem. TESOL, Commn. on Adult Basic Edn., Daus. Union Vets. Civil War, U. Va. Alumni Assn. Roman Catholic. Avocations: quilting, genealogy, travel.

MCSPADDEN, JODY SODD, lawyer; b. Corsicana, Tex., Feb. 21, 1975; BS, Tex. A&M U., 1998; JD, Baylor U. Law Sch., 2002. Bar: Tex. 2002. Ptnr. Dawson & Sodd, P.C., Corsicana, Tex. Named a Rising Star, Tex. Super Lawyers mag., 2005—07. Office: Dawson & Sodd PC 121 N Main St PO Box 837 Corsicana TX 75151 Office Phone: 903-872-8181. E-mail: jody@dawsonsodd.com.

MCSPADDEN, PETER FORD, retired advertising agency executive; b. Montclair, NJ, Oct. 2, 1930; s. Chester F. and Janet (Chase) McS.; m. Barbara Dodds, June 30, 1956; children— Douglas Dodds, David Ford, Peter Chase. AB, Dartmouth, 1952. Account exec. McCann-Erickson, Inc., NYC, 1956-59; with Dancer-Fitzgerald-Sample, Inc., NYC, from 1959, v.p., account supr., 1965-68, sr. v.p., mgmt. supr., 1968-72, exec. v.p., 1972-74, pres., chief operating officer, from 1974; chmn. bd., chief operating officer Saatchi & Saatchi DFS Inc., NYC, 1986-88, also bd. dirs., ret., 1988. Pres., bd. dirs. DFS/Dorland Worldwide; bd. dirs. Am. Advt. Fedn., Am. Assn. Advt. Agys., TriState U.; mem. Nat. Advt. Rev. Bd.; bd. trustees Bradford Coll; vice chmn. Broadstreet TV Inc, 1989—. Chmn. bd. visitors Rockefeller Ctr., Dartmouth Coll., 1989-97; pres. Greenwich (Conn.) Young Republican Club, 1966-67; bd. dirs. United Way of Tri-State, 1995 Spl. Olympic Games; campaign mgr. Congressman Lowell P. Weicker, 1968, Senator Weicker, 1970, 76, 82, 88; mem. Rep. Town Com., Greenwich, 1965-68; trustee, mem. exec. com. Greenwich Hosp.; trustee Farnsworth Mus., Rockland, Maine. Served to lt. (j.g.) USNR, 1952-55. Mem. Am. Assn. Advt. Agys. (dir.) Clubs: Riverside (Conn.) Yacht, Greenwich Country, Megunticook Golf. Home: 46 Carriglea Dr Riverside CT 06878-2402

MC SWAIN, ANGUS STEWART, JR., retired law educator; b. Bryan, Tex., Nov. 26, 1923; s. Angus Stewart and Lois (Pipkin) McS.; m. Betty Ann McCartney, June 3, 1956 (dec. May 30, 2002); 1 child, Angus Earl. BS in Civil Engring., Tex. A. and M. U., 1947; LLB, Baylor U., 1949; LL.M., U. Mich., 1951. Bar: Tex. 1949. Mem. faculty Baylor U. Law Sch., 1949—, prof. law, 1956—, dean, 1965-84, ret., 1994. Mem. panel arbitrators Fe. Mediation and Conciliation Service. Author: (with Wendorf) Cases and Materials on Texas Trusts and Probate, 1965, Supplementary Cases and Materials on Property, 1965, 78, (with Norvell and Simpkins) Cases and Materials for Texas Land Practice, 1968. Served to 1st lt., C.E. AUS, 1943-46. Mem. ABA, Tex.Bar Assn. (chmn. family law sect. 1967-69, chmn. com. on standards of admission 1972-73, 77-79), Tau Beta Pi, Phi Alpha Delta Home: 4600 Kenny Ln Waco TX 76710-2059

MCSWAIN, BYRDIE ENGLE, laboratory scientist, immunohematologist; b. Ethel, Ark., Oct. 13, 1939; d. James Marvin and Katherine Engle (Martin) McSwain. BS, U. Ark., 1968; BS in Med. Tech., U. Ark. Sch. Medicine, 1969; MS, U. Ctrl. Ark., 1973; Specialist in Blood Banking, U. Ark. Med. Scis., 1976. Cert. in regulatory affairs (RAPS). Supr. blood bank Univ. Ark. Med. Scis., Little Rock, clin. instr.; dir. tech. svcs., dir. product mgmt. ARC Blood Svcs., dir. transplantation svcs., dir. regulatory affairs, South Ctrl. area dir. tech. and regulatory svcs., acting area dir. quality assurance. Contbr. 13 articles to profl. jours. Grad. scholar Am. Soc. Med. Tech.; recipient Omicron Sigma award, Am. Soc. for Med. Tech., Outstanding Svc. award, Disting. Alumni award U. Ark. for Med. Scis. Mem. Ark. Soc. Clin. Lab. Scientists (Med. Technologist of Yr.), Am. Assn. Blood Banks, South Ctrl. Assn. Blood Banks (pres., author, editor), Am. Soc. Clin. Lab. Scientists, Clin. Lab. Mgmt. Assn. (pres. Ark. chpt.), Am. Soc. Clin. Pathologists, Regulatory Affairs Profl. Soc., Am. Soc. Quality Assurance, Phi Beta Kappa.

MCSWAIN, LARRY LEE, religious studies educator; b. Pond Creek, Okla., Nov. 10, 1940; s. Joseph Kelly McSwain and Glorene May Brown Kirk; m. Rebecca Sue Stidham, Aug. 26, 1963; children: Laura Suzanne, Michael Lee. BA, Okla. State U., 1963; BD, Southwestern Bapt. Theol. Sem., 1966; STD, So. Bapt. Theol. Sem., 1970. Ordained to ministry So. Bapt. Conv., 1962. Pastor Morrison (Okla.) Bapt. Ch., 1961-63, Vernon (Ind.) Bapt. Ch., 1967-69; sr. rsch. asst. urban studies ctr. U. Louisville, 1968-70; asst. to prof. ch. and community So. Bapt. Theol. Sem., Louisville, 1970-88, dean sch. theology, 1988-91, provost, 1991-93; pres. Shorter Coll., Rome, Ga., 1993-2000; prof. ethics/leadership McAfee Sch. Theology, Mercer U., Atlanta, 2002—. Bd. dirs. Acts, Nashville, 1988-91. Co-author: Conflict Ministry in Church, 1981, Church Organization Alive, 1987; contbg. author numerous books; contbr. articles, book reviews to religious jours. Pres. Rome and Floyd County United Way. Curriculum grantee Assn. Theol. Schs., 1976-77; named Cons. of Yr. So. Bapt. Conv., 1987, also Recognition award, 1988. Mem. Rotary Internat. (bd. dirs.), Assn. of So. Bapt. Colls. and Schs., Ga. Found. for Ind. Colls. Democrat. Home Phone: 770-754-9443; Office Phone: 678-547-6442. E-mail: mcswain_ll@mercer.edu.

MCSWAIN, NORMAN ELLSWORTH, JR., surgeon, educator; b. Albertville, Ala., Feb. 10, 1937; s.Norman Ellsworth Sr. and Mildred (Johnston) McS.; 1 child, Merry Johnston. BS, U. of the South, 1959; MD, U. Ala., 1963; D Emergency Med. Svcs. (hon.), U. Okoboji, 1979. Diplomate Am. Bd. Surgery; cert. diving medicine, hyperbaric medicine. Resident in surgery Bowman Gray Sch. Medicine, Winston-Salem, N.C., 1963-65, Grady Hosp., Atlanta, 1967-70; instr. in surgery Emory U. Affiliated Hosps., Atlanta, 1969-73; pvt. practice Atlanta, 1970-73; assoc. prof. Kans. U. Sch. Medicine, Kansas City, 1973-77; prof. surgery Tulane U. Sch. Medicine, New Orleans, 1977—. Dept. surgeon New Orleans Police Dept., 1979-, vis. prof. Alexandra Hosp., Edmundson, Alta., Can., 1982, Med. Ctr. Cen. Ga., Macon, 1983, Uniformed Svcs. U. of the Health Scis., Bethesda, Md., 1983, 89, Walter Reed Army Hosp., Washington, 1983, Ea. Va. Med. Sch., Norfolk, 1984, Meml. Med. Ctr., Savannah, Ga., 1985, U. Bufflao, 1987, Uniformed Svcs. U. of the Health Scis., 1987-88, White House, Washington, 1988, Med. Coll. Wis., 1988, U. Tenn. Med. Ctr., Knoxville, 1988, U. Nijmegen Sch. of Medicine, The Netherlands, 1988, Nederlandsche Vereeniging van Artsen-Automobilisten VVAA, Utrecht, The Netherlands, 1988, Hartford (Conn.) Hosp., 1989, Lothian and Borders Fire Brigaade, Edinburgh, Scotland, 1989; mem. staff Charity Hosp. at New Orleans, sr. vis. surgeon Dept. Surgery, Tulane div., 1988—, also chief Trauma Divsn. Co-author: Retroperitoneal Trauma, 1991, Atlas of Emergency Surgical Procedures, 1991; editorial cons. Emergency Care and Transportation of the Sick and Injured, 3d edit., 1981, 4th edit., 1985; contbr. articles to med. jours., chpts. to textbooks; editor The Emergency Med. Technician Jour., 1978-81, Jour. of Prehosp. Care, 1984-86, Emergency Medicine, Trauma Rounds, 1984—c; sci. editor Am. Assn. Automotive Med. Quar., 1976-82; med. editor Current Concepts in Trauma Care, 1977-85, Current Concepts in Wound Care, 1985-87; edit. cons. Emergency Tng., 1980—, Annals of Emergency Medicine, 1981; mem. editorial bd. Comprehensive Therapy, 1977—, Emergency Med. Care, 1981, Emergency Medicine, 1981—, Emergency Med. Svcs., 1982—, Emergency Medicine Reports, 1983-86, Emergency Medicine Quar., 1984—, Advanced Clin. Updates, 1985—, Jour. Prehosp. Medicine, 1988-89, The Inside Edge, 1988—, Trauma Chronicle, 1990—, Prehosp. and Disaster Medicine, 1990—; editorial cons. Mil. Medicine, 1987—; mem. adv. bd. Rescue-EMS News, 1989—. Capt. M.C., USNR, 1965-90. Recipient New Mem. of Yr. award Atlanta Sports Car Club Am., 1971, Sportmanship award Savannah Internat. Raceway Sports Car Club Am., 1971, Excellence award Kans. Emergency Med. Tng. Assn., 1977, Appreciation award Mid-Am. Regional Coun. Emergency Rescue, 1977, helicopter jump and med. evacuation award Offshore Flight Medic Wings,

1987, Med. Commendation award U.S. Power Boat Assn., 1987. Fellow ACS (sr. mem. com. on trauma 1985—, numerous other coms.), Am. Assn. for Surgery of Trauma, Am. Coll. Surgeons/Com. on Trauma (numerous coms.); mem. ACT Found. (med. adv. bd. 1978-84), Am. Heart Assn. bd. dirs. 1974-76, other offices), Am. Motorcycle Assn. (med. dir. 1975—), Am. Surg. Assn., Am. Trauma Soc. (charter mem., bd. dirs. 1978-83), Assn. for Acad. Surgery (exec. coun. 1974-76), Ea. Assn. for the Surgery of Trauma (publs. com. 1990—), Internat. Soc. Aquatic Medicine (exec. com. 1975, dir. continuing med. edn., 1975—), Internat. Soc. Surgeons, Johnson County Med. Soc. (med. dir. emergency med. svcs 1974-77), La. Med. Soc., Nat. Assn. Emergency Med. Technicians (bd. dirs. 1975-85, chmn. publs. com. 1979-85, bd. govs. 1982-85, med. dir. PHTLS com. 1982—, bd. govs. in Reno 1988—, Pres.'s Leadership award 1980, "Deke" Farrington award 1983, Pres.'s award 1984), Nat. Registry Emergency Med. Technicians (chmn. bd. dirs. 1988—), New Orleans Surg. Soc., Orleans Parish Med. Soc., Shock Soc., Sports Car Club Am. (Southeastern Regional dir. 1972-74, dir. med. safety, 1974-76, Val D. Scroggie award 1977), Surg. Assn. La., J.C. Throughman Surg. Soc., U. Assn. Emergency Med. Svcs., Am. Assn. Automotive Medicine (A.J. Mirkin Svc. award 1987), Nu Sigma Nu, Sigma Alpha Epsilon. Achievements include first to introduce Pre-Hospital Trauma Life Support (PHLTS), a nationally recognized protocol for the pre-hospital care of trauma patients; one of several health-care workers who helped save numerous lifes in the days following the Hurricane Katrina disaster, recognized for his heroic work by media outlets such as MSNBC and CNN. Office: Tulane U Sch Medicine Dept Surgery 1430 Tulane Ave New Orleans LA 70112

MCSWEENEY, FRANCES KAYE, psychology professor; b. Rochester, NY, Feb. 6, 1948; d. Edward William and Elsie Winifred (Kingston) McSweeney. BA, Smith Coll., 1969; MA, Harvard U., 1972, PhD, 1974. Lectr. McMaster U., Hamilton, Ont., Canada, 1973—74; asst. prof. Wash. State U., Pullman, 1974—79, assoc. prof., 1979—83, prof. psychology, 1983—2004, Regents prof. psychology, 2004—, chmn. dept. psychology, 1986—94, vice provost for faculty affairs, 2003—. Cons. in field. Contbr. articles to profl. jours. Woodrow Wilson fellow, Sloan fellow, 1968—69, NIMH fellow, 1973. Fellow: APA, Assn. Behavior Analysis (pres. 2005—06), Assn. for Psychol. Sci.; mem.: Psychonomic Soc., Phi Kappa Phi, Sigma Xi, Phi Beta Kappa. Home: 860 SW Alcora Dr Pullman WA 99163-2053 Office: Wash State U Dept Psychology Pullman WA 99164-4820 Home Phone: 509-332-2320; Office Phone: 509-335-2738. Business E-Mail: fkmcs@mail.wsu.edu.

MCSWEENEY, MAURICE J. (MARC MCSWEENEY), lawyer; b. Chgo., July 3, 1938; s. Thomas J. and Margaret F. (Ahern) McS.; m. Sandra A. Panosh, Sept. 30, 1967; children: Erin, Sean. BS, DePaul U., 1960; JD, U. Chgo., 1963. Bar: Wis. 1963. With Foley and Lardner, Milw., 1963—, mem. mgmt. com., 1984—93, chmn. litig. dept., 1993—2002, chief diversity ptnr., 2003—. Bd. dirs. Harambee Elem. Sch., 1989-00, Internat. Clown Hall of Fame, 1995-02. Bd. dirs. Milw. Pub. Schs., 1973-79, Milw. chpt. ARC, 1979-85, Alverno Coll., Milw., 1984—, chmn., 2005-, Health Edn. Ctr. of Wis., 1987-96. Fellow Am. Coll. Trial Lawyers; mem. ABA, Wis. Bar Assn., Milw. Bar Assn., Am. Judicature Soc. (bd. dirs. 1988-93), Milw. Area Tech. Coll. Found., Rotary (bd. dirs. Milw. 1986-88). Avocations: skiing, tennis, Karate. Office: Foley & Lardner LLP 777 E Wisconsin Ave Ste 3800 Milwaukee WI 53202-5367 Office Phone: 414-297-5520. Business E-Mail: mmcsweeney@foley.com.

MCSWEENEY, SEAN THOMAS, director; b. Evergreen Park, Ill., Nov. 29, 1967; s. Dennis and Barbara McSweeney; m. Connie McSweeney, June 30, 2001; children: Kayla, Meghan. MA, Nat. Louis U., Wheeling, Ill., 2000; cert. in Advanced Study, St. Xavier U., Chgo., 2001. Cert. educator Ill., 2002. Tchr. Bremen HS Dist. 228, Midlothian, Ill., 1993—2003; dir. social studies curriculum Cmty. HS Dist. 218, Oak Lawn, Ill., 2003—. Mem.: ASCD. Office: Cmty HS Dist 218 10701 South Kilpatrick Oak Lawn IL 60453 Home Phone: 312-813-6271; Office Phone: 708-424-2000.

MCSWEENEY, WILLIAM LINCOLN, JR., retired publishing executive; b. Nov. 9, 1930; s. William Lincoln and Ruth Patricia (Desmond) McS.; m. Anne Cornelia Bulman, Aug. 18, 1956; children: Anne C., William L., Siobhan White, Arthur J., Sean B. BS, Boston Coll., 1953; MLA, So. Meth. U., 1980; LHD, Rockhurst Coll., 1997. Tchr. English Killingly (Conn.) H.S., 1956-57; with Hallmark Cards, Inc., Kansas City, Mo., 1957-86, area pers. mgr., 1968, sales tng. mgr., 1969-86, dir. corp. tng. and devel., 1970-86; pub. Nat. Cath. Reporter Co., 1986-96. Bd. dirs. Cath. Social Svcs., Kansas City Archdiocese, 1975-88, pres., 1980-84; bd. dirs. United Cmty. Svcs. Kansas City, 1978-84, mem. exec. com., 1978-84; bd. dirs. Kansas City Amigos De Las Americas, 1977-80, pres., 1979; bd. dirs. Johnson County YMCA, 1978-79, Jesuit Vol. Corps, Midwest, 1989-95, Mex. Am. Cultural Ctr., San Antonio, 1990—, Minority Mus., 1994-2000; bd. dirs. Pan Ednl. Inst., 1979-83, pres., 1980-81; mem. Boston Coll. Alumni Admissions Coun., 1976-96; mem. chancellor's adv. bd. Met. Cmty. Colls., 1979-80; mem. Dem. Com., Johnson County, Kans., 1980-86; bd. advisors Sch. Social Welfare U. Kans., 1983-2000, chair, 1983-91, 93-94, Avila Col., 1991-2000; chair Mayor's UN Day Dinner, Kansas City, Mo., 1990, Mayor's Breakfast, 1994—2000; trustee NCCJ, 1991-95, co-chmn., 1995; mem. Cath. Charities Devel. Bd., Diocese of Venice, Fla., 2007—. With U.S. Army, 1953-56. Recipient Kansas City World Citizen of Yr. award, 1995, William V. McKenney award Boston Coll., 2000. Mem. Internat. Rels. Coun. of Kansas City (bd. dirs. 1989-2000), Cath. Press Assn., Assoc. Ch. Press, Internat. Press Inst. (bd. dirs. Am. Com. 1999), UN Assn., Boston Coll. Alumni Assn. (past bd. dirs.), Boston Coll. Club (Kansas City), Knights of Malta. Roman Catholic. Office: 115 E Armour Blvd PO Box 419281 Kansas City MO 64141-6281

MCSWEENY, DOROTHY PIERCE, art association administrator; b. Montgomery, Ala., Apr. 17, 1940; d. George Everill and Mary Dorothy Goodrich Pierce; m. William Francis McSweeny, Jan. 20, 1969; children: Ethan Madden Maverick, Terrell Pierce. BA, Brown U., Providence, 1962. Exec. tng. program U.S. Treasury Dept., Washington, 1962—64; officer Agy. Internat. Devel. U.S. Overseas Mission, Saigon, Vietnam, 1964—65; edn. writer The Boston Globe, 1965—67; presdl. oral historian The White Ho., Washington, 1967—69; Lyndon Johnson oral history project U. Tex., Austin, 1969—70; spl. counsel to spkr. U.S. Ho. Reps., Washington, 1970—72; cons. oral historian, 1972—90; chair D.C. Commn. on the Arts & Humanities, Washington, 1995—. Presdl. trustee John F Kennedy Ctr. Performing Arts, Washington, 1976—81; trustee and v.p. Nat. Symphony Orch., 1981—; founder, trustee and chair Washington Episcopal Sch., Bethesda, Md., 1985—; dir. and vice chair The Washington Ballet, 1986—; founder and vice chair Discovery Creek Children's Mus., 1993—; vice chair Mid Atlantic Arts Found., Balt., 1999—; dir. Nat. Assembly State Art Agencies, Washington, 2002—05; dir. and D.C. chair Nat. Mus. Am. Indian, 2002—06; D.C. cultural del. Senegal, Washington, 2006—, Ghana, 2006—, South Africa, 2006—. Founding dir. Nat. Race for the Cure, 1989—2006; founding mem. and mem. women's com. Nat. Mus. Women in the Arts, Washington, 1986—2006; co-chair Lombardi Cancer Rsch. Ctr. Georgetown U. Hosp., Washington, 1994—96; inaugural disch. com. Nat. Coun. Negro Women, Washington, 1996—2000; adv. coun. Katzen Arts Ctr. Am. U., 2003—06; eucharistic lay minister Episcopal Ch.; bd. dir. Boston U. Sch. Medicine, 1988—2000; founding mem. Lady Bird Johnson Wildflower Rsch. Ctr., Austin, Tex., 1988—2006; founder, chair, then vice chair EnvironMentors Nat. Environ. Edn. and Tng. Found., Washington, 1993—2006. Named Outstanding Fundraising Vol., Nat. Capital Philanthropy, 2002, Washingtonian of the Yr., Washingtonian Mag., 1995; recipient Founders award, Washington Episcopal Sch., 1999, Lifetime Achievement award, DC Youth Orch., 1999, Patron of the Arts award, Cultural Alliance of Greater Washington, 2000, Laura Phillips Angel of the Arts award, Cathedral Choral Arts Soc., 2004, Lifetime Achievement Art award, Mayor, Washington, 2007. Mem.: Fed. City Coun. (trustee 2000—06), D.C. C. of C. (trustee 2000—05), Women's Nat. Dem. Club (life), Order St. John of Jerusalem (comdr. 1987), Internat. Neighbors Club III (pres. then v.p. 1993—2006). Episcopalian-Eucharistic Lay Minister. Avocations: scuba diving, skiing, hiking, reading, tennis. Home: 5021 Millwood Lane NW Washington DC 20016 Office: DC Commn Arts & Humanities 410 Eighth St NW Washington DC 20004 Home Phone: 202-686-1818; Office Phone: 202-724-5613. Office Fax: 202-724-4135.

MCSWEENY, WILLIAM FRANCIS, petroleum company executive, author; b. Haverhill, Mass., Mar. 31, 1929; s. William Francis and Mary Florence (Doyle) McS.; m. Dorothy Pierce, Jan. 20, 1969; children: William Francis III, Cathy Ann, Ethan Madden Maverick, Terrell Pierce. Reporter, columnist, fgn. corr. Hearst Newspapers, 1943—67; dep. chmn., dir. pub. affairs Dem. Nat. Com., 1967—68; spl. asst. to White House Chief Staff, 1968—69; from sr. exec. v.p. to pres. Occidental Internat. Corp., LA, 1969—91; from exec. v.p. to cons. to chmn. Occidental Petroleum Corp., LA, 1984—91; bd. dirs. Chevy Chase FSB, 1985—. Mem. Lloyd's of London; pres.'s envoy to USSR, 1979; mem. Pres.'s Inaugural Com., 1980, 84, 92; Presdl. spl. amb. to Oman, 1980, Bolivia, 1982; Pres.'s com. Korean War Meml., 1987; Pres.'s commr. Exec. Exch., 1976-81; Pres.'s trustee The Kennedy Ctr., 1995—, Pres.'s rep. to Korea, 2000; mem. N.E. White Ho. Fellows Bd.; dir. Collaborative Initiatives MIT; mem. U.S. Com. UNESCO; co-chair NATO 50th Summit; spl. counsel spkr. Ho. of Reps., 1971-72; chmn. Maverick-McSweeny Cattle Co. Author: Go Up for Glory, 1965, Violence Every Sunday, 1966, The Impossible Dream, 1967; contbr. articles to profl. jours Bd. overseers Fletcher Sch. Law and Diplomacy, Tufts U.; bd. advisors Karl F. Landegger Program Internat. Bus. Diplomacy, Sch. Fgn. Svc., Georgetown U.; trustee, pres. Holton Arms; chmn. Washington Episc. Sch.; chmn. Meridian House Internat., life trustee; mem. World Affairs Coun.; bd. dir. The Atlantic Coun., Overseer Exec. Coun. Fgn. Diplomats, Dept. of State, The Brookings Instn. Coun., 1991-98; vice chmn. Sec. State Fine Arts Commn.; chmn. Ford's Theatre, 1988-95, life trustee; bd. dir. Very Spl. Arts, Arena Stage, Corcoran Gallery Art, Africare, Fed. City Coun., Washington Opera, Folger Shakespeare Theater, Cities in Schs. Nat. Learning Ctr., USO, Arms Control Assn., Nat. Assn. So. Poor, Duke Ellington Sch., Washington Ednl. TV, 1989-95; v.p. Ct. Mary Rose, Portsmouth, Eng.; pres. Commn. to Preserve U.S. Cultural Heritage Abroad; co-chmn. State Dept. diplomatic rooms endowment; chmn. Lombardi Cancer Ctr. Coun., Georgetown U. Med. Ctr.; pres. Ams. Internat. Insts. Advanced Studies; vice-chmn. Kennedy Ctr. Cmty. Bd., 1991-92; trustee V.P. Residence Found., Lyndon Baines Johnson Sch. Pub. Affairs, U. Tex.; trustee Washington Coll.; 1995-05; juror The Heinz Found., 1995-2000; chmn. Chevy Chase Cmty. Com., Coun. Ct. Excellence, 1996-99. Maj. inf. U.S. Army, 1950-53 Decorated Combat Inf. badge; recipient Outstanding Young Man award, Boston Jaycees, 1961, US Disting. Svc. award, Jaycees, 1968, US Outstanding Svc. spl. award, 1969, DC Disting. Citizen award, 1981, Paul Hill award, Kennedy Ctr., 1983, DC Cultural award, 1983, Armenian Earthquake Hero medal, 1989, Lincoln medal, 1991, Helen Hayes award, 1991, Washingtonian of Yr. award, 1995, Golden Plate award, Am. Acad. Achievement, 1999, Cultural Alliance award, 2000, Torch of Liberty award, Anti Defamation League, 2001, awards for domestic reports and reporting from Vietnam and Mid. East, including Best U.S. Reporting award, 1964, Angel of Arts award, Cathedral Choral Soc., 2004. Mem. Smithsonian Instn. (nat. adv. com. Kellogg Project), Mus. Native Ams. (dir.), Alfalfa Club, Cosmos Club, 1925 F St. Club (trustee), Internat. Club (trustee) Office Phone: 240-497-7323.

MCSWINEY, CHARLES RONALD, lawyer; b. Nashville, Apr. 23, 1943; s. James W. and Jewell (Bellar) Mc.; m. Jane Detrick McSwiney, Jan. 2, 1970. BA, Kenyon Coll., Gambier, Ohio, 1965; JD, U. Cin., 1968. Assoc. Smith & Schnacke, Dayton, Ohio, 1968-72, ptnr., 1972-89, pres. and mng. ptnr., 1984-89; sr. v.p., gen. counsel The Danis Cos., Dayton, 1989-92, 99-2000; vice chmn. Carillon Capital, Inc., Dayton, 1992-99; dir. devel. Youth Haven, Inc., 2002—. Chmn., CEO Crysteco, Inc., Wilmington, Ohio, 1995-99; pres. interchange exec. Presdl. Commn. on Pers. Interchange, Washington, 1972-73. Chmn., pres. bd. trustees Dayton Ballet Assn., 1985-88; trustee Columbus (Ohio) Symphony Orch., 1981-84; chmn. Dayton Performing Arts Fund, 1989-92, Dayton Devel. Coun., 1987-90, Wright State U. Found., Dayton, 1988-94, Miami Valley Sch., Dayton, 1988-94, Arts Ctr. Found., 1986-2000; mem. bd. advisors Wright State U. Coll. Bus. Adminstrn., 1988-98; bd. vis. U. Cin. Coll. Law, 1987-89; mem. pres.'s coun. Internat. Coll. Recipient Bronze Medal for Performance U.S. EPA, 1973. Mem. Dayton Area C. of C. (trustee 1987-90). Republican. United Ch. Of Christ. Home: 1872 Timarron Way Naples FL 34109 E-mail: ronmcswiney@comcast.net.

MCTAGGART, TIMOTHY ROBERT, state agency administrator, lawyer; b. Phila., May 6, 1960; s. James Francis and Patricia Ann (Berry) McT. AB cum laude, Harvard U., 1982, JD, 1985. Bar: Mass. 1985, D.C. 1987. Atty. gen. counsel's office Bd. Govs. FRS, Washington, 1985-87; assoc. Morrison & Foerster, Washington, 1987-89, Fried, Frank, Harris, Shriver & Jacobson, Washington, 1989-91; counsel U.S. Senate Com., 1991-94, Del. Bank Commr., 1994-98; ptnr. Nixon Peabody LLP and predecessor firm, Washington, 1999—2003, Willkie Farr & Gallagher, 2003—. Mem. ABA, Mass. Bar Assn., D.C. Bar Assn. Avocations: reading, basketball, movies. Home Phone: 301-913-5404; Office Phone: 202-303-1127. E-mail: tmctaggart@willkie.com.

MCTAGUE, JOHN PAUL, materials scientist, educator, chemist, researcher; b. Jersey City, Nov. 28, 1938; s. James Aloysius and Teresa Eugenia (Hanley) McT.; m. Carole Frances Reilly, Dec. 30, 1961 (dec. Jan. 1997); children: Kevin W., Catherine E., Margaret A., Maureen E.; m.Margaret Ann Danna, Oct. 15, 2004. BS in Chemistry with honors, Georgetown U., 1960; PhD in Phys. Chemistry, Brown U., 1965, DSc (hon.), 1997. Mem. tech. staff N.Am. Rockwell Sci. Ctr., Thousand Oaks, Calif., 1964—70; prof. chemistry, mem. Inst. Geophysics and Planetary Physics UCLA, 1970—82; chmn. Nat. Synchrotron Light Source Dept. Brookhaven Nat. Lab., 1983; dep. dir. Office Sci. and Tech. Policy, Exec. Office of Pres., Washington, 1983—86, acting sci. advisor to Pres. Reagan, 1986; v.p. rsch. Ford Motor Co., Dearborn, Mich., 1986—90, v.p. tech. affairs, 1990—99; v.p. lab. mgmt., Office of Pres. U. Calif., Oakland, 2001—03, prof. materials Santa Barbara, 2001—. Adj. prof. chemistry Columbia, U., 1982-83. Mem. Pres.'s Coun. Advisors on Sci. and Tech., 1990-93; mem. adv. bd. Sec. Energy, 1990—; chmn. bd. overseers Fermilab, 1994-99. Alfred P. Sloan Research fellow, 1971-73; NATO sr. fellow, 1973; John Simon Guggenheim Meml. fellow, 1975-76. Fellow AAAS, Am. Phys. Soc. (George E. Pake prize 1998), Calif. Coun. Sci. and Tech.; mem. Am. Chem. Soc. (Calif. sect. award 1975), Nat. Acad. Engring., Sigma Xi. Personal E-mail: jmctague1@aol.com.

MCTEE, CINDY, classical musician, educator; b. 1953; BM, Pacific Luth. U., 1976, studied with David Robbins; MM, Yale U., 1978, studied with Krzysztof Pendereckl, Jacob Druckman, and Bruce MacCombie; PhD, U. Iowa, 1981, studied with Richard Hervig; studied with Penderecki, Marek Stachowski, and Krystyna Moszumanska-Nazar, Higher Sch. Music, Cracow, Poland. Tchr. Pacific Luth. U., Tacoma, 1981-84; asst. to full prof. music composition U. North Tex., Denton, 1984—. Fulbright-Hayes Sr. Lectr. fellow in computer music Acad. Music, Cracow, 1990. Recipient commns. from Dallas Symphony Orch., Nat. Symphony Orch., Big Eight Band Dirs. Assn., Voices of Change, Barlow Endowment for Music Composition, Am. Guild Organists, Coll. Band Dirs. Nat. Assn., Phi Kappa Lambda Bd. Regents, Houston Symphony Commn.; works performed by Dallas Symphony Orch., Am. Symphony Orch., Detroit Symphony Orch., Chgo. Symphony Orch., Indpls. Symphony Orch., Nat. Repertory Orch., St. Louis Symphony, Memphis Symphony, Honolulu Symphony, Pitts. New Music Ensemble, Nat. Symphony Orch., Nippon Housou Kyoukai (NHK) Symphony Orch., Philharm. Orch., London. Recipient BMI award, Guggenheim Fellowship, 2001; grantee Wash. State Arts Commn.; Composers fellow NEA, Goddard Lieberson fellow AAAL; Acad. award in Music, AAAL, 2002; winner Louisville Orch. Composition Competition, 2001. Home: Apt 501 3839 McKinney Ave Dallas TX 75204

MCTEER, ROBERT D., JR., former academic administrator, bank executive; b. Oct. 1942; married; 2 children. BBA in Econ., U. GA, 1963, PhD in Econ., 1971. With Fed. Reserve Bank Richmond, 1968—91; sr. v.p. Baltimore branch Fed. Reserve Bank of Richmond, 1980—91; pres., CEO Fed. Res. Bank Dallas, Tex., 1991—2004; chancellor Texas A&M U. System, College Station, Tex., 2004—06. Adj. prof. U. Richmond, Va. Commonwealth U., Johns Hopkins U.; bd. dirs. Nat. Coun on Econ. Edn.; bd. overseers U. Ga. Terry Coll. Bus. *

MCTIER, CHARLES HARVEY, foundation administrator; b. Columbus, Ga., Jan. 28, 1939; s. Roy and Julia (Harvey) McT.; m. Margaret Lucy Ruyl, Aug. 23, 1962; children: Margaret Marie, Charles Harvey Jr. BBA, Emory U., 1961. Administrv. asst. hosp. Emory U., Atlanta, 1961-63, bus. mgr. dept. psychiat. Sch. Med., 1963-66, assoc. dir. personnel, 1966-69, asst. to pres., bd. trustees, 1969-71; sec. Robert W. Woodruff Found., Joseph B. Whitehead Found., Lettie Pate Evans Found., Inc., Lettie Pate Whitehead Found., Inc., Atlanta, 1971-77, sec., treas., 1977-87, v.p., sec., treas., 1987-88, pres., 1988—. Chmn. Atlanta Founds. Forum, 1985-86; trustee Southeastern Coun. Founds., Atlanta, 1985-92, chmn. membership com., 1986-89, chmn. program com., 1989, chmn. bd. trustees, 1989-90; vice chmn. Coun. on Founds., Washington, 1995-97, program com., 1985-87, nominating com., 1987-88, chmn. audit and fin. com., 1990-95, chmn. mgmt. com., 1996-97; chmn. bd. trustees Found. Ctr. N.Y.C., 1994-2000, fin. and audit com., 1991-2000, exec. com., 1992-93, chmn. nominating com.; former pub. mem. Joint Commn. on Accreditation of Health Care Orgns., 1994-2003; dir. SunTrust Bank of Ga., SunTrust Bank Atlanta, 1995—, Coca-Cola FEMSA. Trustee, North Ga. United Meth. Found., 1985—; trustee, treas. Meth. Found. Ret. Mins., 1980; chmn. new ch. devel. com. North Ga. United Meth. Conf., 1980-85; mem. bd. vis. Emory U., 1985-87. Mem. Assn. Emory Alumni (bd. govs. 1987-91), Pres.'s Cir. of NAS/Inst. of Medicine, Commerce Club (bd. dirs.), Peachtree Golf Club, Piedmont Driving Club. Avocations: golf, travel. Office: Robert W Woodruff Found Inc 50 Hurt Plz SE Ste 1200 Atlanta GA 30303-2951 Office Phone: 404-521-2810. Personal E-mail: pmctier@bellsouth.net.

MCTIERNAN, CHARLES E., JR., lawyer, energy executive; b. Aug. 1944; m. Barbara K. Farrell; children: Michael, Christopher, Stephen. BA, Coll. St. Thomas, Minn.; JD cum laude, Bklyn. Law Sch. Bar: NY 1972, US Dist. Ct. (ea. and so. dists. NY) 1972, US Ct. Appeals (2nd cir.) 1972, US Ct. Appeals (4th cir.) 1990. Law clk. Hon. Charles D. Breitel, NY, 1970—72; assoc. Wickes, Riddell, Blomer, Jacobi & McGuire, 1972—76, Kelley, Drye & Warren, 1976—81; atty. Consol. Edison Inc., NYC, 1981—85, assoc. gen. counsel comml. litig., 1985—2002, gen. counsel, 2003—. Mem. Gen. Counsel Roundtable; mem. litig. adv. com. Edison Electric Inst. Editor (mng.): Bklyn. Law Rev. Office: Consol Edison Inc 4 Irving Pl New York NY 10003 *

MCTIGUE, MAURICE P., director; b. Methven, New Zealand, 1940; Ed., St. Bede's Coll., Christchurch, New Zealand, 1958. Cabinet min., mem. parliament, New Zealand, 1985—97; dir. govt. accountability project Mercatus Ctr., George Mason U., Arlington, Va. Spkr. in field; mem. bd. Performance Mgmt. Adv. Com. Contbr. articles numerous prof. jours. Recipient Queen's Svc. Order, Queen Elizabeth II, 1999; scholar disting. vis. scholar, George Mason U. Office: 3301 N Fairfax Dr Arlington VA 22201-4433 Office Phone: 703-993-4930.

MCTYEIRE, ROBERT ADAMS, sound engineer, music company executive, consultant; b. Birmingham, Ala., July 21, 1949; s. William Walter Jr. and Katherine Elizabeth (Meadow) McT.; m. Pamela Ann Huffstutler, Apr. 18, 1978. BS in Commerce and Bus. Adminstrn., U. Ala., Tuscaloosa, 1972. Ind. sound engr., Tuscaloosa, 1972-73; owner, chief engr. Ram Sound, Tuscaloosa, 1973-89, Mary Esther, Fla., 1989—. Charter mem. nominating com. Ala. Music Hall of Fame, Muscle Shoals; cons. Klipsch and Assocs., Inc., Hope, Ark., 1984-; bd. dirs. Iron Art, Inc., The Krewe of Bowlegs, Navarre Land Enterprises, M4 Properties, Ltd., McTyeire Enterprises, Inc. Sound engr. for numerous entertainers including Tony Bennett, Dave Brubeck, Ray Charles, Ry Cooder, Fats Domino, Roy Orbison, Bob Hope, Tom Jones, B.B. King, Wynton Marsalis, Dolly Parton, Bonnie Raitt, Ray Stevens, Ramsey Lewis, George Jones, B.J. Thomas, and many others. Mem. Tuscaloosa Arts Coun. With U.S. Air N.G., 1969-71. Mem. Muscle Shoals Music Assn. Republican. Avocations: boating, travel, music, motorcycling. Home and Office: Ram Sound 369 W Miracle Strip Pky Mary Esther FL 32569-1833

MCVEIGH-PETTIGREW, SHARON CHRISTINE, communications consultant; b. San Francisco, Feb. 6, 1949; d. Martin Allen and Frances (Roddy) McVeigh; m. John Wallace Pettigrew, Mar. 27, 1971; children: Benjamin Thomas Pettigrew, Margaret Mary Pettigrew. BA with honors, U. Calif.-Berkeley, 1971; diploma of edn., Monash U., Australia, 1975; MBA, Golden Gate U., 1985. Tchr., adminstr. Victorian Edn. Dept., Victoria, Australia, 1972—79; supr. Network Control Ctr. GTE Sprint Comms., Burlingame, Calif., 1979—81, mgr. customer assistance, 1981—84, mgr. state legis. ops., 1984—85, dir. revenue programs, 1986—87; comm. cons. Flores, Pettigrew & Co., San Mateo, Calif., 1987—89; telemktg. Apple Computer Inc., Cupertino, Calif., 1989—94; prin. The Call Ctr. Group, San Mateo, Calif., 1995—. Telecomm. cons. PPG Svcs., 1994—; telecomm. spkr. Dept. Consumer Affairs, Sacramento, 1984. Panelist Wash. Gov.'s Citizens Coun., 1984; founding mem. Maroondah Women's Shelter, Victoria, 1978; organizer nat. conf. Bus. Women and the Polit. Process, New Orleans, 1986; mem. sch. bd. Boronia Tech. Sch., Victoria, 1979. Recipient Tchr. Spl. Responsibilities award, Victoria Edn. Dept., 1979. Mem.: Women's Econ. Action League, Am. Telemktg. Assn. (bd. dirs. 1992), Peninsula Profl. Women's Network, Am. Mgmt. Assn., Women in Telecom. (panel moderator San Francisco 1984). Democrat. Roman Catholic. Office Phone: 650-579-1298.

MCVEY, FRANCIS DANIEL, mechanical engineer, software developer, educator; b. St. Louis, Jan. 19, 1929; s. Martin Patrick and Marguy Josephine (Boeckler) McV.; m. Anna Elizabeth Moss, Nov. 26, 1958 (dec. Dec. 1990); children: Mark Andrew, Mary Denise, Michael Sean. BS in Mech. Engring., Washington U., St. Louis, 1952, MS, 1954. Instt. mech. engring. Washington U., St. Louis, 1954-55; group project engr., missiles engring. divsn. McDonnell Aircraft Co., St. Louis, 1955-58, assoc. scientist rsch. divsn., 1961-64, br. mgr. engring. tech. divsn., 1964-74, prin. staff engr., 1974-83; chief aerodynamicist Cleve. Pneumatic Co., Washington, 1959-61; engring. fellow McDonnell Douglas, 1983-86, sr. fellow, 1986-97, dir. CAD/CAM St. Louis, 1986-97; sr. tech. fellow Boeing Co., St. Louis, 1997—, staff engring. dir., 1997-99; retired, 1999. Lectr. St. Louis U., 1964—70, 2000—, U. Mo.-Rolla extension, 1971; adj. prof. aero. and mech. engring. dept. St. Louis U., 2000—; engring. and automotive cons. Mem. exec. adv. com. on engring. St. Louis U., 1998—2007. With AUS, 1946—48. Recipient Lloyd R. Koenig prize in engring. Washington U., 1952. Fellow: AIAA (assoc.; chmn. St. Louis sect. 1963—66, mem. mgmt. com. 1998—2002); mem.: Am. Rocket Soc. (chmn. St. Louis sect.), Sigma Xi. Roman Catholic. Avocation: reading. Home: 7030 Delmar Blvd University City MO 63130-4301 Personal E-mail: fmcveyd@aol.com.

MCVEY, HENRY HANNA, III, retired lawyer; b. Richmond, Va., Aug. 12, 1935; s. Henry Hanna Jr. and Eva Lawson (Jennings) McVey; m. Reba Jean Robinson, Dec. 12, 1964; children: Margaret Anne McVey Singleton, Lewis Lawson, Ian Douglas. BS, BA magna cum laude, Hampden-Sydney Coll., Va., 1957; LLB, U. Va., Charlottesville, 1960. Bar: Va. 1960, U.S. Dist. Ct. (ea. dist.) Va. 1960, U.S. Ct. Appeals (4th cir.) 1965, U.S. Supreme Ct. 1970. Assoc. Battle, Neal, Harris, Minor & Williams, Richmond, 1960-66; ptnr. McGuireWoods LLP and predecessor firms, Richmond, 1966—99; ret., 1999. Mem. adv. group under Civil Justice Reform Act of 1990 U.S. Dist. Ct. (ea. dist.) Va. Trustee Hampden-Sydney Coll., 1989—94, 1995—2001, vice chair, 2001—03, chair bd. trustees, 2003—; mem. Commn. on Archtl. Rev. City of Richmond, 1985—95; mem. Planning Commn. Gloucester County, 2001—, vice chmn., 2006—; bd. dirs. Richmond Symphony, 1977—86, 1987—99, v.p., 1979—81, exec. v.p., 1981—83, pres., 1983—85, chmn. bd. dirs., 1985—87, pres. Symphony Coun., 1999—2001; bd. dirs. Carpenter Ctr. for Performing Arts, 1982—89, Rosewell Found., 1999—2004, pres., 2001—02, v.p., 2002—03. Recipient Algernon Sydney Sullivan medallion for svc. to coll., Hampden Sydney Coll., 2001, Alumni Citation for loyal Svc., Hampden-Sydney Coll., 2002, Excellence in Civil Litigation award, Va. Assn. Defense Attys., 2006. Fellow: Am. Bar Found., Am. Coll. Trial Lawyers; mem.: Va. Bar Assn., Va. Assn. Def. Attys. (v.p. 1981—83, treas. 1983—84, pres.-elect 1984—85, pres. 1985—86), Ware River Yacht Club (bd. dirs. 2000—05). Presbyterian. Home: PO Box 8 Ware Neck VA 23178 Personal E-mail: hmcvey@cox.net.

MCVEY, SUSAN C., library director; b. Duncan, Okla. MLS, U. Tex., Austin; MPA, U. Okla. Reference libr. Okla. City U., dir.; legis. reference libr. Okla. Dept. Libraries, 1986, dep. dir., 1996—2001, dir., 2001—. Mem.: Chief Officers of State Libr. Agencies (v.p./pres. elect 2006—08, chair Continuing Edn. com. 2004—06), Okla. Libr. Assn. (pres. 1987—88, Disting. Svc. award). Office: Okla Dept Libraries 200 NE 18th St Oklahoma City OK 73105-3298 Office Phone: 405-521-2502. Office Fax: 405-525-7804. E-mail: smcvey@oltn.odl.state.ok.us. *

MC VICKER, CHARLES TAGGART, artist, educator; b. Canonsburg, Pa., Aug. 31, 1930; s. Carl Walter and Mary Ruth (Washabaugh) McV.; m. Lucy Claire Graves, Mar. 20, 1954; children— Lauri, Bonnie, Heather. BA, Principia Coll., Elsah, Ill., 1952; B.F.A., Art Center Coll. Design, Los Angeles, 1957. Staff artist Alexander Chaite Studios, 1957-58; freelance illustrator and painter, 1958—. Asst. prof. Pratt Phoenix Sch. Art, NYC, 1979-84, Coll. of NJ, 1985—2003. One-man shows include Thompson Gallery, N.Y.C., 1967, Capitol Hill Club, Washington, 1988, (retrospective exhibit) Coll. N.J., 2006; represented in permanent collections U.S. Capitol, Am. Hist. Assn., Soc. Illustrators, USAF, Princeton U., DuPont Corp., Zimmerli Art Mus. at Rutgers U., Home Life Ins. Co., Wang Corp. With US Army, 1952—54. Recipient Ralph Fabri award Nat. Audubon Artists Ann. Juried Show, 1986, Ralph Fabri medal Nat. Soc. Painters in Casein and Acrylic, 1991, Michael Engel Meml. award Nat. Audubon Artists, 1992. Mem. Soc. Illustrators (exec. com. 1972-74, pres. 1976-78), Am. Watercolor Soc., Graphic Artists Guild (v.p. nat. exec. com. 1978-79), Audubon Artists, Princeton Artists Alliance (pres. 1989—), Am. Artists Profl. League, Garden State Watercolor Soc. (pres. 2006—). Home: 26 Old Orchard Ln Princeton NJ 08540-1939

MCVISK, WILLIAM KILBURN, lawyer; b. Chgo., Oct. 8, 1953; s. Felix Kilburn and June (DePear) Visk; m. Marlaine Joyce McDonough, June 20, 1975. BA, U. Ill. 1974; JD, Northwestern U., 1977. Bar: Ill. 1977, Ind. 1999, U.S. Dist. Ct. (no. dist.) Ill. 1977, U.S. Ct. Appeals (7th cir.) 1978, U.S. Dist. Ct. (no. and so. dists.) Ind. 1999, U.S. Ct. Appeals (10th cir.) 2001. Assoc. Jerome H. Torshen, Ltd., Chgo., 1977-80, Silets & Martin, Chgo., 1980-81, Peterson & Ross, Chgo., 1981-85, ptnr., 1985-95, Johnson & Bell Ltd., Chgo., 1995—. Contbr. articles to profl. jours. Mem.: Ill. Assn. Def. Trial Lawyers (chmn. ins. coverage com. 1999—2003), Ill. Assn. Hosp. Attys. (bd. dirs. 1997—2003, pres. 2002), Am. Health Lawyers Assn., Def. Rsch. Inst. Office: Johnson & Bell 33 W Monroe St Ste 2700 Chicago IL 60603-5713 Home Phone: 708-771-5421; Office Phone: 312-984-0229. Business E-Mail: mcviskw@jbltd.com.

MCWALTERS, PETER, school system administrator; b. Oct. 8, 1946; m. Alice Bond McWalters; children: Jennifer, Molly, Katherine. BA in History and Philosophy, Boston Coll., 1968; MS in Pub. Adminstrn., SUNY Brockport, 1979, cert. advanced study ednl. adminstrn., 1981. Permanent N.Y. State Teaching Cert social studies 7-12, Sch. Adminstrn., Sch. Dist. Adminstrn. Tchr.-trainer Eng. for speakers other langs. U.S. Peace Corps., Rep. Philippines; tchr. Eng. for speakers other langs. City Sch. Dist., Rochester, N.Y., 1970-71; tchr. social studies Interim Jr. High Sch., Rochester, 1971-78; Magnet Sch. planning specialist City Sch. Dist., Rochester, 1978-81, coord. Mgmt. Inst., 1980-81, supervising dir. planning and budgeting, 1981-85, supt. schs., 1985-91; commr. of edn. State of RI, 1992—. Bd. dirs. Nat. Ctr. Edn. and Economy, mem. new standards project; bd. dirs. Ctr. Ednl. Devel., Rochester; mem. Edn. Commn. of States, Coun. Chief State Schs. Officers (past pres.), Coun. Great Cities Schs., 21st Century Edn. Commn.; co-chair, Nat. Task Force on the Arts in Edn. Bd. dirs. Urban League, Rochester; mem. United Way Task Force, Rochester; gov. bd., exec. com. Rochester New Futures Initiative, Inc.; mem. Goals for Greater Rochester, Inc. Mem. Am. Assn. Sch. Adminstrs., Assn. Supervision and Curriculum Devel., Phi Delta Kappa. Office: Elem and Sec Office Shepard Bldg 255 Westminster St Providence RI 02903-3414 *

MCWATERS, JEFFREY L., healthcare executive; b. Paducah, Ky. m. Cynthia Lamb McWaters; 2 children. B in Acctg., U. Ky., 1978. With Ernst and Young, Nashville, 1978—79, Hosp. Affiliates, 1979—93; founder, pres., CEO Options Mental Health (now Value Options), 1990—94; founder, chmn., CEO AMERIGROUP Corp., Virginia Beach, Va., 1994—2007, chmn., 2007—. Bd. dirs. Am. Assn. Health Plans, Man in the Mirror; mem. adv. bd. Monarch Bank, Envest Entrepreneurial Investments. Chmn. Amerigroup Found., 2000—. Named Entrepreneur of Yr., Ernst and Young, 1999; named to Hall of Fame, Gatton Coll. Bus. and Econs., U. Ky., 2003. Office: Amerigroup Corp 4425 Corporation Ln Virginia Beach VA 23462 *

MCWETHY, JOHN FLEETWOOD, journalist; b. Aurora, Ill., Feb. 28, 1947; s. John Adams and Mary Helen (Bell) McW.; m. Laurie Duncan, June 25, 1971; children: Adam Duncan, James Ian. BA, DePauw U., Greencastle, Ind., 1969, Doctorate (hon.) in Journalism, 2002; MS, Columbia U., NYC, 1970. Def. writer Congl. Quar., Washington, 1970-72; sci. editor U.S. News & World Report, Washington, 1972-77, chief White House corr., 1977-79; chief Pentagon corr. ABC News, Washington, 1979-84; chief corr. ABC News Nat. Security and Sr. State Dept., Washington, 1984—2003; spl. corr. ABC News, 2003—06. Sr. media mentor US Army Command Staff Coll., Ft. Leavenworth, Kans., 2005—; moderator News and Terrorism program Radio TV Dirs. Assn. and Dept. Homeland Security, 2004—. Contbg. author: Power of the Pentagon, 1972. Recipient DuPont award Columbia U. Sch. Journalism, 1984, 2002; 5 Emmy awards, 1984, 91, 92, 99, 2002, Overseas Press Club award for Inside the Other Side, 1987, Peabody award for coverage of Sept. 11, 2001.

MCWETHY, PATRICIA JOAN, educational association administrator; b. Chgo., Feb. 27, 1946; d. Frank E. and Emma (Kuehne) McW.; m. H. Frank Eden; children: Kristin Beth, Justin Nicholas. BA, Northwestern U., 1968; MA, U. Minn., 1970; MBA, George Washington U., 1981. Geog. analyst CIA, McLean, Va., 1970-71; rsch. asst. NSF, Washington, 1972-74, spl. asst. to dir., 1975, assoc. program dir. human geography and regional sci. program, 1976-79; exec. dir. Assn. Am. Geographers, Washington., 1979-84, Nat. Assn. Biology Tchrs., Reston, Va., 1984-95, Nat. Sci. Edn. Leadership Assn., Arlington, Va., 1995-97; edn. dir. Nat. Alliance for Mentally Ill, Arlington, 1998-99. Prin. investigator grant on biotech. equipment ednl. resource partnership NSF, 1989-93, NSF funded internat. symposium on Basic Biol. Concepts: What Should the World's Children Know?, 1992-94; co-prin. investigator NSF grant, 1995-97; mem. chmn.'s adv. com. Nat. Com. Sci. Stds. and Assessment, 1992-95; mem. Commn. for Biology Edn., Internat. Union Biol. Sci., 1988-97; mem. exec. com. Alliance for Environ. Edn., 1987-90, chmn. program com., 1990; condr. seminars in field; lectr. in field. Author monograph and papers in field; editor handbook. NSF grantee, 1989-93, 95-97; NSF fellow, 1968-69; recipient Outstanding Performance award, NSF, 1973. Mem. Phi Beta Kappa.

MCWHINNEY, EDWARD WATSON, Canadian government legislator; b. Sydney, May 19, 1924; s. Matthew and Evelyn Annie (Watson) McW.; m. Emily Ingalore Sabatzky, June 27, 1951. LLB, U. Sydney, 1949; LLM, Yale U., 1951, D Juridical Sci., 1953; diploma, Acad. de Droit Internat., The Hague, 1950; LLD, U. Thessaloniki, Greece, 1998. Bar: called to Australian bar 1949, apptd. Queen's counsel, Can 1967. Crown prosecutor, Sydney, 1949-50; lectr., then asst. prof. Law Sch. and Grad. Sch., Yale U., 1951-55; prof. law, mem. Centre Russian Studies, U. Toronto, Ont., Canada, 1955-66; prof. law, dir. Inst. Air and Space Law, McGill U., Montreal, Que., Canada, 1966-71; prof. law, dir. internat. and comparative legal studies U. Ind., Indpls., 1971-74; disting. prof. Simon Fraser U., Burnaby, BC, 1974—93, prof. emeritus, 1992; mem. Permanent Ct. Arbitration, The Hague, 1985-91; Paul Martin prof. U. Windsor, Canada, 1986; pres., dir. Found. Internat. and Comparative and Fed. Law, 1996—; M.P. Ho. of Commons, Ottawa, Ont., Canada, 1993-2000; co-chmn. joint standing com. Senate and Ho. of Commons, Ottawa, Ont., Canada, 1993-95, parliamentary sec. (fisheries and oceans), 1996-97, parliamentary sec. (fgn. affairs), 1997-2000; fed. govt. rep. nat. unity commn. Govt. of B.C., 1997-98. Vis. prof. Ecole Libre des Hautes Etudes, 1952, Heidelberg and Max-Planck-Inst., 1960-61, 90, NYU, 1954, Faculté Internat. de Droit Comparé, Luxembourg, 1959-60, U. San Antonio, 1963, U. Laval, Que., 1967, U. Paris, 1968, U. Madrid, 1968, U. Aix-Marseille, 1969, U. Nat. Autónoma de México, 1965, Inst. U. Luxembourg, 1972, 74, 76, Acad. Internat. Law, The Hague, 1973, 90, 2002, Aristotelian U., Thessaloniki, Greece, 1974, 78, 85, 96, 2003, U. Nice, 1976-77, Jagellonian U., Cracow, Poland, 1976, U. Paris I (Sorbonne), 1982, 85, Coll. de France, Paris, 1983, Meiji U., Tokyo, 1987, Inst. Internat. Relations, Bejing, 1987, 92, Sch. Internat. Rels., Tehran, 2003; legal cons. UN, 1953-54; cons. Japanese Commn. Constn., mem. prime minister Ont. Adv. Com. Confedn., 1964-71; cons. U.S. Naval War Coll., 1961-68; legal cons. Ministère de la Justice, Que., 1969-70; 74-75; constl. adviser to prime minister of Que., 1974-75; royal commr. Commn. Lang. Rights. Que., 1968-72; cons. U.S. Senate select com. presdl. campaign activities, 1973; spl. commr. inquiry Legislature B.C., 1974-75; chief adv. Fed. Govt.'s Task Force on Nat. Unity, 1978; commr. of enquiry, City of Vancouver, 1979; constl. adv. Fedn. Can. Municipalities, 1978-82; spl. advisor Can. del. UN Gen. Assembly, ann. sessions, 1981-83, 96; constl. adviser Indian Nations (Treaties 6-9), Can., 1980-82; mem. Assoc. de l'Inst. de Droit Internat., 1967, membre titulaire, 1975, pres. 1999-2001; mem. Assoc. de l'Acad. Internat. de Droit Comparé, Paris, 1986, mem. titulaire, 2002-- Author: Judical Review, 4th edit, 1969, Canadian Jurisprudence, 1958, Föderalismus und Bundesverfassungsrecht, 1961, Constitutionalism in Germany, 1962, Comparative Federalism, 2d edit, 1965, Peaceful Coexistence and Soviet-Western International Law, 1964, Law Foreign Policy and the East-West Détente, 1964, Federal Constitution- Making for a Multi-National World, 1966, International Law and World Revolution, 1967, Conflit idéologique et ordre public mondial, 1970, (with M.A. Bradley) The Freedom of the Air, 1968, New Frontiers in Space Law, 1969, The International Law of Communications, 1970, Aerial Piracy and International Law, 1971, (with Pierre Pescatore) Federalism and Supreme Courts and the Integration of Legal Systems, 1973, Parliament and Parliamentary Power Today, 1976, The Executive and Executive Power Today, 1977, (with J-D Gendron and others) La situation de la lanque française au Québec (3 vols.), 1973, The Illegal Diversion of Aircraft and International Law, 1974, Parliamentary Privilege and the Broadcasting of Parliamentary Debates, 1975, The International Law of Detente, 1978, The World Court and the Contemporary International Law-making Process, 1979, Quebec and the Constitution, 1979, Municipal Government in a New Canadian Federal System, 1980, Conflict and Compromise: International Law and World Order in a Revolutionary Age, 1981, Constitution-Making: Principles, Process, Practice, 1981, Canada and the Constitution, 1982, United Nations Law Making, 1984, Supreme Courts and Judicial Law-Making, 1986, Les Nations-Unies et la Formation du Droit, 1986, Aerial Piracy and International Terrorism, 1987, The International Court of Justice and the Western Tradition of International Law, 1987, (with Nagendra Singh) Nuclear Weapons and Contemporary International Law, 1988, Judicial Settlement of International Disputes, 1990, (with G.I. Tunkin and V.S. Vereshchetin) From Coexistence to Cooperation: International Law and Organisation in the Post-Cold War Era, 1991, (with J. Zaslove and W. Wolf) Federalism-in-the-Making, Contemporary Canadian and German Constitutionalism, National and Transnational, 1992, Judge Shigeru Oda and the Progressive Development of International Law, 1992, Judge Manfred Lachs and Judicial Law-Making, 1994, The United Nations and a New World Order for a New Millennium, 2000, (with N. Ando and R. Wolfrum) Liber Amicorum Judge Shigeru Oda, 2002, Self-Determination of Peoples and Plural-Ethnic States. Secession and State Succession and the Alternative, Federal Option, 2003, Chretien and Canadian Federalism, Politics and the Constitution, 1993-2003, 2003, The September 11 Terrorist Attacks and Invasion of Iraq in Contemporary International Law, 2004, The Governor General and the Prime Ministers, 2005, (with Mariko Kawano) Judge Shigeru Oda and the path to judicial wisdom, 2006, Self-Determination of Peoples and Plural- Ethnic States in Contemporary Internat. Law, 2007; bd. editors Australian Quar., 1949-50, Can. Yearbook of Internat. Law, 1963—, Jour. Media Law and Practice, 1980-85, Annuaire International de Justice Constitutionnelle, 1987—; edtl. adv. com. Ency. Brit., 1985—; mem. bd. adv. Chinese Jour. Internat. Law, 2002—; contbr. to Ency. Brit. Served as officer Australian Air Force, 1943-45. Recipient Aristotle medal, Govt. of Greece, 1997, Queen's Golden Jubilee medal, 2002; Carnegie Endowment fellow, 1951, Fulbright fellow, 1950-51, Sterling fellow Yale, 1950-51, Rockefeller fellow, 1960-61, 66-68, Can. Coun. fellow, 1960-61, fellow Am. Soc. Internat. Law, 1962-63, Marco Polo fellow Xi'an Jiaotong U., China, 2007-. Mem. Australian Inst. Polit. Sci. (dir.), Internat. Law Assn. (pres. Toronto br. 1964-66, pres. Montreal br. 1970-71, chmn. exec. com. Canadian br. 1972-75), Canadian Bar Assn. (council Ont. 1956-58), Yale Law Sch. Assn. (pres. Can. 1964-69), Canadian Civil Liberties Assn. (v.p. 1965-67), Am. Soc. Internat. Law (coun. 1965-68, patron 2002—), Am. Fgn. Law Assn., Inst. interamericano de Estudios Juridicos Internacionales (dir. 1965—), Inst. Grand-Ducal de Luxembourg, Internat. Commn. Jurists (mem. coun. Can. br. 1988—), German Soc. for Völkerrecht (hon.), Knights of Mark Twain (U.S., hon.). Home: 1949 Beach Ave Ste 402 Vancouver BC Canada V6G 1Z2

MCWHINNEY, MADELINE H. (MRS. JOHN DENNY DALE), economist, director; b. Denver, Mar. 11, 1922; d. Leroy and Alice (Houston) McW.; m. John D. Dale, June 23, 1961; 1 child, Thomas Denny. BA, Smith Coll., 1943; MBA, NYU, 1947. Economist Fed. Res. Bank, NYC, 1943-73, chief fin. trade statis. divsn., 1955-59, mgr. market stats. dept., 1960-65, asst. v.p., 1965-73; pres. First Women's Bank, NYC, 1974-76, Dale, Elliott & Co., Inc., Red Bank, NJ, 1977-97. Trustee Retirement System Fed. Res. Bank, 1955-58; vis. lectr. NYU Grad. Sch. Bus., 1976-77; mem. NJ Casino Control Commn., 1980-82, Women's Econ. Round Table, 1978-89, chmn. 1987-88; bd. govs. Am. Stock Exch., 1977-81; trustee Monmouth Mus., 1995—, Vis. Nurse Assn. Ctrl. Jersey, 1995-2004, Planned Parenthood Ctrl. Jersey, 1995-2003, Carnegie Corp. NY, 1974-82, Central Savs. Bank NY, 1980-82, Monmouth Conservatory Music, 2002-; trustee Charles F. Kettering Found., 1975-93, chmn. 1987-91; trustee Inst. Internat. Edn., 1975-, Investor Responsibility Rsch. Ctr., Inc., 1974-81; asst. dir. Whitney Mus. Am. Art, 1983-86; dir. Atlantic Energy Co., 1983-93; trustee Mgrs. Funds, 1983-2004; mem. adv. com. profl. ethics NJ Supreme Ct., 1983-98. Recipient Smith Coll. medal, 1971, Alumni Achievement award NYU Grad. Sch. Bus. Adminstrn. Alumni Assn., 1971, NYU Crystal award, 1982. Mem. Am. Fin. Assn. (past dir.), Money Marketeers (v.p. 1960, pres. 1961-62), Alumni Assn. Grad. Sch. Bus. Adminstrn. NYU (dir. 1951-63, pres. 1957-59), Soc. Meml. Ctr., NJ Com. Humanities, Phi Beta Kappa Fellows (v.p. 1979-87). Office: PO Box 458 Red Bank NJ 07701-0458 Home: 192 Heritage Court Little Silver NJ 07739 Personal E-mail: mdale38569@comcast.net.

MCWHIRTER, BRUCE J., retired lawyer; b. Chgo., Sept. 11, 1931; s. Sydney and Martha McWhirter; m. Judith Hallett, Apr. 14, 1960; children: Cameron, Andrew. BS, Northwestern U., 1952; LLB, Harvard U., 1955. Bar: DC 1955, Ill 1955, US Ct Appeals (7th cir) 1963, US Supreme Ct. Assoc. Lord, Bissell & Brook, Chgo., 1958-62; from assoc. to sr. ptnr. Ross & Hardies, Chgo., 1962-95, of counsel, 1996—2003. Editor: Donnelley SEC Handbook, 1972—87; contbr. articles to profl jours. With US Army, 1955—57. Mem.: ABA, Harvard Law Soc Ill., Chgo. Bar Assn., Harvard Club (N.Y.C.), Lawyers Club Chgo., Phi Beta Kappa. Democrat. Home: 111 Sheridan Rd Winnetka IL 60093-4223 Personal E-mail: jbmcw@aol.com.

MCWHIRTER, GLENNA SUZANNE (NICKIE MCWHIRTER), retired columnist; b. Peoria, Ill., June 28, 1929; d. Alfred Leon and Garnet Lorene (Short) Sotier; m. Edward Ford McWhirter (div.); children: Suzanne McWhirter Orlicki, Charles Edward, James Richard. BS in English Lang. and Lit., U. Mich., postgrad., 1960-63. Editl. asst. McGraw-Hill Pub. Co., Detroit, 1951-54; staff writer Detroit Free Press, Inc., Detroit, 1963-70, asst. city editor, 1971-77, columnist, 1977-88, Detroit News Inc., Detroit, 1988-97; advt. copy writer Campbell-Ewald Co., Detroit, 1967-68; ret., 1997. Author: Pea Soup, 1984 Winner 1st Place Commentary award UPI, Mich., 1979; 1st Place Columns AP, Mich., 1978, 81; 1st Place Columns Detroit Press Club Found., Mich., 1978; Disting. Service award State of Mich., 1985 Mem. Women in Comm. (Headliner award 1978), Alpha Gamma Delta. Avocations: flower gardening, interior design. Home: 495 Lake Shore Ln Grosse Pointe Woods MI 48236 Personal E-mail: nickiemcwhirter@earthlink.net.

MCWHORTER, DIANE, writer; b. Tupelo, Miss., Nov. 1, 1952; BA in Comparative Lit., Wellesley Coll. Writer, NYC. Author: Carry Me Home: Birmingham, Alabama,The Climactic Battle of the Civil Rights Revolution, 2001 (Pulitzer prize for gen. nonfiction, 2002, named NY Times Notable Book, winner, Southern Book Critics Circle award, 2001, J. Anthony Lukas Book prize, 2002, English Speaking Union Ambassador award, 2002, Sidney Hillman Found. award, 2002), A Dream of Freedom: The Civil Rights Movement from 1954 to 1968, 2004 (NY Times Notable Children's Book, 2004, USA Today Best Children's History, 2004, on ALA Best New Book for Young Adults list, 2004); contbr. articles to newspapers, chapters to books. Recipient Clarence Cason award, 2003. Personal E-mail: dmcwhorter@earthlink.net.

MCWHORTER, HOBART AMORY, JR., lawyer; b. Birmingham, Ala., Dec. 24, 1931; s. Hobart Amory and Marjorie (Westgate) McW.; remarried Feb. 1, 1997; children: Margaret G., Marjorie W. BA, Yale U., 1953; LLB, U. Va., 1958. Bar: Ala. 1958. Ptnr. Bradley Arant Rose & White, Birmingham, 1958—. 1st lt. U.S. Army, 1953-55. Fellow Am. Coll. Trial Lawyers; mem. Internat. Assn. Ins. Counsel, Nat. Assn. r.R. Counsel. Republican. Presbyterian. Office: Bradley Arant Rose & White One Federal Pl 1819 Fifth Ave N Birmingham AL 35203-2104 Office Phone: 205-521-8241. Business E-Mail: hmcwhorter@bradleyarant.com.

MCWHORTER, KATHLEEN, orthodontist; b. Houston, May 29, 1953; d. Archer and Lucile (Taft) McW. BA summa cum laude, U. Houston, 1986; DDS with honors, Baylor Coll., 1990. Mgr. Am. Internat. Rent-A-Car, Houston, 1974-79; mktg. researcher Concoco Oil Co., Houston, 1979-83; orthodontist Baylor Coll. Dentistry, Dallas, 1990—. Presenter Am. Assn. Dental Rsch., Montreal, Que., Can., 1988, Cin., 1990; rsch. fellow Baylor Coll. Dentistry, Dallas, 1987, 88, 89. Contbr. articles to profl. jours. Mem. ADA, Am. Assn. Orthodontists, Am. Assn. Women Dentists, Am. Assn. Dentistry for Children, Internat. Assn. Dental Rsch., Am. Assn. Dental Rsch., Tex. Dental Assn., Dallas County Dental Soc., The Crescent Club. Avocations: tennis, walking, music, water-skiing. Office: Baylor U Coll Dentistry Dept Orthodontics 3302 Gaston Ave Dallas TX 75246-2027

MCWHORTER, SHARON LOUISE, engineering executive, inventor, consultant; b. Feb. 22, 1951; d. Leroy Byron Harris Jr. and Josiebell (Richards) Harris Aaron; m. Abner McWhorter II, Mar. 15, 1969 (div. Aug. 1974); 1 child, Abner III. BA, Wayne State U., 1988; cert., SBA, Detroit, 1978; cert. in sound engring., Detroit Rec. Inst., Warren, Mich., 1982. Directory asst. Mich. Bell Telephone Co., Detroit, 1969; quality control clk. Chevrolet Gear & Axle, Detroit, 1971-74; circulation clk. Wayne County C.C., Detroit, 1977-85, mem. libr. standing com. and open house com., 1983-84; pres. Galactic Concepts & Designs, Detroit, 1977-88, cons., 1983—. Gen. ptnr., mgr. S.M.J. Corridor Devel., Detroit, 1982—, hist. rschr., 1982; del. Small Bus. Conf., 1981; ad hoc mem. Minority Tech. Coun., 1981-82; elected alt. Mich. del. White House Conf. on Small Bus., Washington, 1985-86; lectr., cons. Author, editor: Creative Dilemma newsletter, 1985—; co-patentee cup holding apparatus. Vol. counselor Barat House/March of Dimes, Detroit, 1977; active Concerned Citizens Cass Corridor, Detroit, 1982-87, Cass Corridor Citizen's Patrol, Detroit, 1983-84, Empowerment Zone Devel. Corp., Detroit, 1996—, bd. dirs., corp. chair, 1997—; pres. Wayne County chpt. MADD, Mich., 1987-88; apptd. citizen rev. com, 1988—; mem. adv. bd. Neighborhood Family Initiative, Southeastern Cmty. Found.; pres. Am. Res. Tng. Sys., Inc., 1990—. Recipient Hist. Landmark award Dept. Interior, 1983, cert. appreciation Tri-County Substance Abuse Awareness Com., 1984. Mem. Inventors Coun. Mich. (bd. dirs. 1985-88), Black Women in Bus. (sec. 1984-85), Greater Detroit C. of C., South Cass Bus. Assn. (v.p. 1987-88, pres. 1988-89), Detroit Econ. Club. Democrat. Methodist. Avocations: photography, filmmaking. Office: SMJ Corridor Devel Co 453 Myrtle St Ste 102 Detroit MI 48201-2311

MCWHORTER, STANLEY BRUCE, retired language educator; b. Osco, Ky., June 17, 1930; s. Stanley Vergil and Myrtie Alice (Stearns) M. BA, Transylvania Univ., Lexington, 1954; MA, U. Ky., 1961, PhD, 1963. Life Cert. Edn. Ky., 1950. Instr. English Southwestern Coll., Winfield, Kans., 1959-60, Morehead State Univ., Ky., 1960-61, Ea. Ky. State Univ., Richmond, 1961-63; asst. prof. English W. Va. Wesleyan Coll., Buckhannon, 1963-67; assoc. prof. English Univ. S. C., Florence, 1967-70; prof. English Xavier Univ., Cincinnati, 1972-75, Univ. Dayton, Ohio, 1975-95; ret., 1995—. Ednl. coord. Natl. Folk Festival Assoc. Am., Wash. D.C., 1963-67. Author: Annotated Bibliography of William Wordsworth's Writings and Ana from 1935-1941, 1961, The Annual Anthology of College Poetry and Literature, 1965, The Idea of Religious Struggle in Four Seventeenth Century English Poets, 1967, The Use of the Folk Ballad in the English Class, 1971, Superstitions of Appalachia, 1975. Dir. civic activities Lions Clubs, Jamestown, Ky., 1953-55. Grantee continued study in chosen field, 1965; recipient Southwestern grant for Tchg. Excellence, 1959-60, Cmty. Leadership award, Lions Club Am., 1961-63, Wesleyan plaque Internat. Rels., 1963-67 Wesleyan grant for study Brit. Am.

Balladry, 1963-67. Life mem. MLA Am. (editl. supervisor, 1963-67, scholarship advanced studies, 1963), Nat. Coun. Tchrs. English, Nat. Edn. Assn. Am., Coll. Assn. English Tchrs., Am. Assn. Univ. Profs. D-Conservative. United Methodist. Avocations: running, swimming, travel. Office: Univ Dayton 300 Coll Park Ave Dayton OH 45469 Home: P O Box 3455 Dayton OH 45401 Personal E-mail: mcwhrca@aol.com.

MCWILLIAMS, C. PAUL, JR., engineering executive; b. Louisville, June 4, 1931; s. Cleo Paul and Audrey Dora (Hale) McW.; m. Barbara Ann Sparks, Feb. 22, 1950 (div. 1962); children: Bruce Kevin, Craig Tinsley; m. Barbara Ann Heintz, Apr. 25, 1980; 1 stepchild, Kimberly Jean Moorhouse Beaumont. B Chem. Engring., U. Louisville, 1954, M Engring., 1972. Lic. profl. engr., N.Y., N.C., Pa. Sr. process devel. engr. Olin Mathieson Chem. Corp., Brandenburg, Ky., 1958-66, Rochester, NY, 1958-66; sr. chem. engr. GTE Sylvania, Seneca Falls, NY, 1966-74, Eastman Kodak Co., Rochester, 1974-81; prin., treas. Flint & Sherburne Assocs., P.C., Rochester, 1981-89; project engr. Roy F. Weston, Inc., Rochester, 1989-92; engring. mgr. ECCO, Inc. (Environ. Cons. Co., Inc.), Buffalo, 1992-94; pres. ECCO Engring., Buffalo, 1993-94; staff engr. Environ. Products & Svcs., Inc., Rochester, NY, 1994-96; pvt. cons. engr. Webster, NY, 1996—. Cons. water tech. Water Tech. Corp., Tonawanda, N.Y., 1973-76; product rsch. panel Chem. Engring. Mag., 1982-83. Author: Waste Disposal Manual, 1976. Life mem. Rep. Presdl. Task Force, Webster, N.Y., 1986—; mem. Rep. Nat. Com., Webster, 1991-92. 1st lt. USAF, 1954-58, ret. lt. col. USAF, 1982. Decorated Meritorious Svc. medal. Mem. NSPE, AIChE, Soc. Am. Mil. Engrs., Res. Officers Assn. (life), Monroe Profl. Engrs. Soc. (environ. com. 1972-75, chmn. 1973-75, bd. dirs. 1982-84, program chmn. 1984), Cons. Engrs. Coun. N.Y. State (program chmn. Rochester chpt. 1986-87, sec. 1987-88, treas. 1989). Episcopalian. Achievements include rsch. in replacing boiler feedwater regulators, related instrumentation and control systems and blowdown; design of dry fabric dust collectors to remove fly ash from coal-fired boilers' flue gas. Home and Office: C Paul McWilliams PE Cons Engr 1132 Woodbridge Ln Webster NY 14580-8709 Home Phone: 585-872-0505; Office Phone: 585-872-0505. Business E-Mail: paulmcw@frontiernet.net.

MCWILLIAMS, DALLAS, technical educator; b. June 20, 1962; AS in Electronics Engring. Tech., Hamilton Tech. Coll., Davenport, Iowa, 1985; BS in Tech. Mgmt., Wayland Baptist U., Anchorage, 2000. Cert. installer low voltage sys., BICSI: A Telecom. Assn.; competent and qualified person full protections rated OSHA. Electronics technician FBI, Anchorage, 1991—2002, instr., 2002—. Precision measurement electronic lab. technician USAF, 1987—91, Elemendorf AFB, Alaska. Decorated Air Force Achievement medal USAF, Elemdorf AFB. Mem.: Mensa. Home: PO Box 843 Fredericksburg VA 22404

MCWILLIAMS, EDWIN JOSEPH, banker; b. Spokane, Washington, Aug. 11, 1919; s. Frank S. and Alice (Conlan) McW.; m. Betty J. Galbreath, Aug. 15, 1944; children: Lawrence, Barbara Anne, Marijoan, Peter. Student, U. Notre Dame, Ind., 1937-38, Marquette U., Milw., 1938-40; BS in Bus. Adminstrn, Gonzaga U., Spokane, Wash., 1943. With Fidelity Mutual Savings Bank, Spokane, 1940-82, exec. v.p., 1955-58, pres., 1958-82, Fidelity Service Corp., 1983-87. Mem. adv. council Wash. State Dept. Commerce and Econ. Devel., 1977-80; U.S. del. Internat. Savs. Bank Inst., 1975, 76, 79; vice chair, dir. NW Edn. Loan Assn Pres. United Crusade Spokane County, 1966; pres., mem. exec. bd. Inland Empire coun., region 11 exec. com. Boy Scouts Am.; pres. Spokane Unltd.; mem. adv. coun. Sch. Bus., Gonzaga U.; bd. dirs., mem. exec. com. Expo '74 World's Fair, 1973-74; mem. bd. regents Ft. Wright Coll., Spokane, 1960-72; bd. dirs. Sacred Heart Med. Ctr., 1961-70, Fairmont Meml. Assn.; chmn. bd. mem. Spokane Housing Assn., 1972-87; chmn. Spokane C. of C., 1973-75; bd. regents Wash. State U., 1979-92. Lt. USNR, 1943—45. Mem. Nat. Assn. Mut. Savs. Banks (chmn. 1976-77), Mut. Savs. Banks Assn. State of Wash. (pres. 1980), Am. Savs. and Loan Inst. (past gov. dist. XI), Spokane C. of C. (pres. 1974-75, chmn., 1975-77), Clubs: Rotary of Spokane, K.C. Roman Catholic. Home: 2408 E Deerwood Ct Spokane WA 99223

MCWILLIAMS, JOHN LAWRENCE, III, lawyer; b. Phila., Dec. 21, 1943; s. John Lawrence Jr. and Elizabeth Dolores (Chevalier) McW.; m. Paula Ann Root, July 19, 1969 (dec.); children: John Lawrence, IV, Robert Root, Anne Elizabeth, David Stanford, Peter Farrell; m. Kathleen Nolan Pradella, Apr./ 3, 1993. BS, St. Joseph's U., 1965; JD, Seton Hall U., 1969. Bar: N.J. 1969, N.Y. 1975, U.S. Supreme Ct. 1975, Fla. 1977. Trial atty., regional office SEC, NYC, 1969-72; assoc. Mudge Rose Guthrie & Alexander, NYC, 1972-77; mem. Freeman, Richardson, Watson & Kelly, P.A., Jacksonville, Fla., 1977-89, chmn., pres., 1984-89; ptnr. Squire, Sanders & Dempsey, Jacksonville, 1989-98, Livermore, Freeman & McWilliams, P.A., Jacksonville, 1998—. Trustee Mcpl. Svc. Dist. Ponte Vedra Beach, 1981-85, chmn. bd. trustees, 1984-85; treas. Ponte Vedra Cmty. Assn., 1980-82; mem. Leadership Jacksonville, 1981, steering com., 1982; dir. Jacksonville Country Day Sch., 1985-87; pres. Jacksonville Beaches Ponte Vedra Unit Am. Cancer Soc., 1988-90; bd. dirs. Sawgrass Property Owners Assn., Inc., 2000-02. Fellow Am. Coll. Bond Counsel; mem. Nat. Assn. Bond Lawyers, The Fla. Bar, Jacksonville C. of C., Jacksonville Cmty. Coun. Inc., Univ. Club, Ponte Vedra Club, Sawgrass Club, River Club. Republican. Roman Catholic. Home: 3040 Timberlake Pt Ponte Vedra Beach FL 32082-3726 Office: Livermore Freeman & McWilliams PA 320 N First St Ste 603 Jacksonville Beach FL 32250 Home Phone: 904-285-2499; Office Phone: 904-399-0500. Personal E-mail: jmcwilliams3@gmail.com. Business E-Mail: jmcwilliams@lfmlaw.net.

MCWILLIAMS, JOHN MICHAEL, lawyer; b. Annapolis, Md., Aug. 17, 1939; s. William J. and Helen (Disharon) McW.; m. Frances Edelen McCabe, May 30, 1970; children: M. Edelen, J. Michael Jr., James McC. BS, Georgetown U., 1964; LL.B., U. Md., 1967; LLD (hon.), U. Balt., 1993. Bar: Md. 1967, U.S. Supreme Ct. 1970, U.S. Ct. Internat. Trade 1991, U.S. Ct. Mil. Appeals 1992; cert. mediator NASD. Law clk. Chief Judge Roszel C. Thomsen, U.S. Dist. Ct. Md., 1967-68; assoc. Piper and Marbury, Balt., 1968-69; asst. atty. gen. Md., 1969-76; gen. counsel Md. Dept. Transp., 1971-76; sr. ptnr. Tydings and Rosenberg, Balt., 1977-97; pres. McWilliams Dispute Resolution, Balt., 1997—. Permanent mem. 4th Jud. Conf.; mem. panel of disting. neutrals CPR Inst. for Dispute Resolution, 1994—2001; mem. Md. Alt. Dispute Resolution Commn., 1994—2002. Asst. editor Law Rev., U. Md., 1967; mem. nat. bd. advisors Ohio State Jour. Dispute Resolution. Chmn. Md. adv. coun. to Nat. Legal Svcs. Corp., 1975-78; mem. Gov.'s Commn. to Revise Annotated Code of Md., 1973-78; transition dir. Md. Gov.-Elect Harry Hughes, 1978-79; mem. Md. Indsl. Devel. Financing Authority, 1980; mem. Greater Balt. Com., 1979-94; mem. exec. com. Econ. Devel. Coun. Greater Balt., 1979-83; vice chmn. bd. Washington/Balt. Regional Assn., 1980-83; mem. Md. Econ. and Cmty. Devel. Adv. Commn., 1983-87; chmn. bd. Md. Econ. Devel. Corp., 1984-89. Served to 1st lt. U.S. Army, 1958-60. Fellow Am. Bar Found. (bd. dirs. 1986-88, 91-93), Internat. Acad. Mediators (pres. 2006—07), Coll. Comml. Arbitrators (pres. 2004-05), Md. Bar Found. (dir. 1980-82); mem. ABA (pres. 1992-93, mem. ho. of dels. 1976—, chmn. 1986-88, chmn. Md. del. 1976-86, bd. editors jour. 1986-88, 91-93) Md. Bar Assn. (pres. 1981-82), Nat. Conf. Bar Pres. (exec. coun. 1982-85), Bar Assn. Balt. City, Am. Law Inst., Am. Judicature Soc. (dir. 1974-81, exec. com. 1975-77), Am. Acad. Judicature Edn. (dir. 1977), Md. Law Rev. (trustee 1980-83), Md. Inst. Continuing Edn. Lawyers (trustee 1980-83), Inst. Internat. Bus. Law and Practice (corr.), Md. Club, Rule Day Club. Democrat. Roman Catholic. Home: 3 Merryman Ct Baltimore MD 21210-2815 Office: 1106 N Charles St Ste 300 Baltimore MD 21201 Office Phone: 410-244-8124.

MCWILLIAMS, KAREN JOAN, writer; b. Alexandria, La., Oct. 12, 1943; d. Steve Peters and Nettie Beatrice Barricklow; step-father: Paul F. McWilliams; m. Charles F. Slezak, June 16, 1973 (div. 1976); m. Julio Espinosa, July 26, 1980 (div. 1988). BA in Elem. Edn., U. No. Colo., 1966; MA in Ednl. Tech./Libr. Sci., San Diego State U., 1976. Tchr. 2d grade Motherlode Union, Diamond Springs, Calif., 1966-67; tchr. 3d grade Redlands (Calif.) Unified Sch. Dist., 1967-69, Dept. of Def. Overseas Schs., various locations, 1969-77; sch. libr. Dept. of Edn., St. Croix, V.I., 1977-83; passage writer Harcourt Brace Edn. Measurement, 1995—97, Pearson Edn. Measurement, 2006—. Author: Pirates, 1989, The Journal of Leroy Jeremiah Jones, 2001, A Fugitive Slave: The Diary of a Slave Girl, Ruby Jo, 2002, The Journal of Darien Dexter Duff Emancipated Slave, 2003 (Royal Palm Young Adult Lit. award, 2003); contbr. articles to Writer's Digest, The Writer, others; children's book reviewer Ind. Pub. mag. Soc. of Children's Book Writers grantee, 1985. Mem. The Authors Guild, Soc. Children's Book Writers and Illustrators (book reviewer). Office Phone: 239-353-0856. Personal E-mail: ksophiedog@aol.com.

MCWILLIAMS, KENNETH L., lawyer; b. Grove City, Pa., Mar. 1, 1953; s. Kenneth C. McWilliams and Edith B. McWilliams; m. Ligia Salcedo, Apr. 9, 1994; children: Jessica Lynn Talley, Kenneth Kyle, Jennifer Lee Grace, Brian James Kenneth. BA, Mt. Union Coll., Alliance, Ohio, 1975; MS, U. So. Calif., LA, 1987; JD cum laude, Georgetown U., Washington, 1998. Bar: Va. 1998, DC 1999. Commd. ens. USN, 1976, advanced through grades to comdr., ret., 1998; assoc. atty. Latham & Watkins, Washington, 1998—2002; sr. atty. Patton Boggs LLP, Washington, 2006—. Decorated Meritorious Svc. medal Sec. of Navy, Navy Achievement mnedal Comdr. Fighter Wing One. Office: Patton Boggs LLP 2550 M St NW Washington DC 20037 Home Phone: 540-882-3157; Office Phone: 202-457-5312.

MCWILLIAMS, MARGARET ANN, home economist, educator, writer; b. Osage, Iowa, May 26, 1929; d. Alvin Randall and Mildred Irene Edgar; children: Roger, Kathleen. BS, Iowa State U., 1951, MS, 1953; PhD, Oreg. State U., 1968. Registered dietitian. Asst. prof. home econs. Calif. State U., LA, 1961-66, assoc. prof., 1966-68, prof., 1968-92, prof. emeritus, 1992—, chmn. dept., 1968-76; pres. Plycon Press, 1978—. Author: Food Fundamentals, 1966, 8th edit., 2006, Nutrition for the Growing Years, 1967, 5th edit., 1993, Experimental Foods Laboratory Manual, 1977, 5th edit., 2000, 6th edit., 2005, Lifelong Nutrition, 2001, (with L. Kotschevar) Understanding Food, 1969, Illustrated Guide to Food Preparation, 1970, 8th edit., 1998, 9th edit., 2005, (with L. Davis) Food for You, 1971, 2d edit., 1976, The Meatless Cookbook, 1973, (with F. Stare) Living Nutrition, 1973, 4th edit., 1984, Nutrition for Good Health, 1974, 2d edit., 1982, (with H. Paine) Modern Food Preservation, 1977, Fundamentals of Meal Management, 1978, 4th edit., 2005, (with H. Heller) The World of Nutrition, 1984, Foods: Experimental Perspectives, 1989, 4th edit. 2000, 5th edit., 2005, Food Around the World: A Cultural Perspective, 2003, 2d edit., 2007. Chmn. bd. Beach Cities Symphony, 1991-94. Recipient Alumni Centennial award Iowa State U., 1971, Profl. Achievement award, 1977; Phi Upsilon Omicron Nat. Founders fellow, 1964; Home Economist in Bus. Nat. Found. fellow, 1967; Outstanding Prof. award Calif. State U., 1976. Mem. Am. Dietetic Assn., Inst. Food Technologists, Phi Kappa Phi, Phi Upsilon Omicron, Omicron Nu, Iota Sigma Pi, Sigma Delta Epsilon, Sigma Alpha Iota. Home: PO Box 220 Redondo Beach CA 90277-0220 Personal E-mail: mmcwredondo@aol.com.

MCWILLIAMS, MICHAEL, writer, publisher; b. Detroit, Aug. 28, 1952; s. Henry and Mary (Toarmina) McW. BA, Wayne State U., 1975; MFA, Columbia U., 1978. Free-lance writer Monthly Detroit mag., 1979-82, Village Voice, Rolling Stone, TV Guide, Advt. Age, N.Y. Daily News, L.A. Herald Examiner, NYC, 1982-87; TV critic, 1988—2001; pub. MaryBooks, 2002—. Author: TV Sirens, 1987, (with others) The Premiere Guide to Movies on Video, 1991. Recipient Assn. of Sunday and Feature Editors award, 1st pl. Arts Criticism, 1992. Mem. Phi Beta Kappa. Avocations: television, movies, theater, music.

MCWILLIAMS, MIKE C., lawyer; b. Dallas, Nov. 10, 1948; s. Earl Dewitt and Mary Louise (Campbell) McWilliams; m. Sally Swatzell, Sept. 1, 1973; children: Michael, Matthew. BBA in Fin., U. Tex., 1969, JD, 1973. Bar: Tex. 1973. Assoc. Elliott, Meer, Vetter, Denton & Bates, Dallas, 1973-78; ptnr. Denton & Generis, Dallas, 1978-80, Moore & Peterson, P.C., Dallas, 1980-89, Winstead, Sechrest & Minick, Dallas, 1989—. Editor: Texas International Law Journal, 1972—73. Mem.: Dallas Bar Assn., Tex. State Bar Assn., Beta Gamma Sigma, Phi Delta Phi. Office: Winstead Sechrest & Minick 5400 Renaissance Tower 1201 Elm St Ste 5400 Dallas TX 75270-2199 Office Phone: 214-745-5631. Business E-Mail: mmcwilliams@winstead.com.

MCWILLIAMS, ROBERT HUGH, federal judge; b. Salina, Kans., Apr. 27, 1916; s. Robert Hugh and Laura (Nicholson) McW.; m. Catherine Ann Cooper, Nov. 4, 1942 (dec.); 1 son, Edward Cooper; m. Joan Harcourt, Mar. 8, 1986. AB, U. Denver, 1938, LL.B., 1941. Bar: Colo. bar 1941. Dep. dist. atty. Denver, Co, 1941—42; special agent US Office of Naval Intelligence, 1942—45; sgt. US Army, Office of Strategic Services, 1945—46; dist. atty. Denver, Co., 1946—49; private practice Denver, Co, 1949—52; judge municipal ct., Denver, 1949—52, dist., city, and county, Denver, 1952—61, supreme ct. of Co., 1967—70; instructor U. of Denver, 1954—60; judge US Ct. Appeals (10th cir.), Denver, 1970—84, sr. judge, 1984—. Served with AUS, World War II. Mem. Phi Beta Kappa, Omicron Delta Kappa, Phi Delta Phi, Kappa Sigma. Republican. Episcopalian. Home: 137 Jersey St Denver CO 80220-5918 Office: Byron White US Courthouse 1823 Stout St Rm 216 Denver CO 80257-1823 *

MCWILTON, CHRIS A., finance company executive; BBA summa cum laude, St. Bonaventure Univ. CPA. Acct. KPMG, 1980—92, ptnr., SEC reviewing ptnr., 1992—2002; corp. controller MasterCard Worldwide, Purchase, NY, 2003, CFO, mem. policy com., 2003—. Office: MasterCard Worldwide 2000 Purchase St Purchase NY 10577 *

MEACHAM, CHARLES HARDING, federal agency administrator; b. Newman, Calif., Sept. 21, 1925; s. Vernon A. and Sara (Paulsen) M.; m. June Lorraine Yunker, June 22, 1946; children— Charles Paulsen, Bruce Herbert. BS, Utah State U., 1950. Biologist Calif. Dept. Fish and Game, 1950-56, Alaska Dept. Fisheries, 1956-59; regional supr. regions II and III Alaska Dept. Fish and Game, 1959-68; dir. internat. fisheries Office Gov. Alaska, 1968-69; commr. U.S. Fish and Wildlife Service, Dept. Interior, 1969-70, dep. asst. sec. for fish and wildlife, pks. and marine resources, commr. Internat. North Pacific Fisheries Commn. and Gt. Lakes Fishery Commn., 1969-70, commr. Internat. Pacific Salmon Fisheries Commn., 1969-70, commr. Great Lakes Fishery Commn., 1969-70, spl. asst. to area dir. Alaska, 1971-74; dir. internat. affairs Office of Gov., Juneau, Alaska, 1975-80; pres. Meacham & Assocs., Anchorage, 1980—. Dep. commr. US North Pacific Fur Seal Commn.; mem. Pacific and North Pacific Fisheries Mgmt. Councils, 1976-81; chmn. nat. park system adv. bd. US Dept. Interior. Bd. dir. Resource Devel. Coun. for Alaska. With USMCR, 1943-46. Mem. Am. Fisheries Soc., Wildlife Soc., Pacific Fisheries Biologists, Internat. Assn. Game, Fish and Conservation Commrs., Ducks Unlimited, Alaska Miners Assn., Am. Legion, USMC Raiders Assn. (pres. 2003—04), Elks. Address: PO Box 428 Sequim WA 98382-0428

MEACHAM, JON E., editor; b. Chattanooga, 1969; m. Keith Meacham; 2 children. BA summa cum laude in English Lit., U. of South, 1991; LHD (hon.), Berkley Div. Sch., 2005. Writer Newsweek mag., NYC, 1995, nat. affairs editor, 1995—98, mng. editor, 1998—2006, editor, 2006—. Contbg. editor The Washington Monthly; writer NY Times Book Review, Washington Post, LA Times Book Review, Washington Post Book World. Editor: Voices in Our Blood: America's Best on the Civil Rights Movement, 2001; author: Franklin and Winston: An Intimate Portrait of an Epic Friendship, 2003 (NY Times bestseller, LA Times Book of the Year, Emery Reves award, Churchill Centre, 2005), American Gospel: God, the Founding Fathers, and the Making of a Nation, 2006 (NY Times bestseller). Mem. Coun. on Fgn. Relations; bd. regents U. of the South; leadership coun. Harvard Divinity Sch.; nat. advisory group Wash. Nat. Cathedral; communicant, serves on Vestry St. Thomas Ch. Fifth Ave.; Vestry Trinity Ch. Wall St. Office: Newsweek 251 W 57th St New York NY 10019-1894 *

MEACHAM, SCOTT, state official; b. Okla. m. Susan Meacham; 4 children. BA in Fin., Univ. Okla., MBA, JD, Univ. Okla. Cert. CFP. Atty.; CEO First Nat. Bank & Trust, Elk City, Okla.; state tres. State of Okla., 2005—. Office: State Treas Rm 217 2300 N Lincoln Blvd Oklahoma City OK 73105 Office Phone: 405-521-3191. Office Fax: 405-521-4994. Business E-Mail: Okla.Treas@treas.state.ok.us. *

MEACHIN, DAVID JAMES PERCY, investment banker; b. Teignmouth, Devon, Eng., Jan. 1, 1941; arrived in U.S., 1969, naturalized, 1990; s. James Alfred and Ena Annie Meachin; m. Barbara Marshall Maxwell, Sept. 25, 1971; children: Jonathan J.M., Philip D.M. BS in Phys. Sci., U. Natal, South Africa, 1960; BSChemE, U. Cape Town, South Africa, 1963; MS in Petroleum Engring., French Petroleum Inst., Paris, 1965; diploma in Indsl. Mgmt., Cambridge U., Eng., 1966; MBA with distinction, Harvard U., 1971. Project engr. Humphreys and Glasgow Ltd., London, 1966-69; 2nd v.p. investment banking Smith Barney and Co. Inc., NYC and Tokyo, 1971-75; v.p., gen. mgr. internat. corp. fin. Salomon Bros., NYC and London, 1975-81; mng. dir. investment banking divsn. Merrill Lynch Capital Markets, NYC, 1981-91; chmn., CEO Cross Border Enterprises L.L.C., 1991—. Bd. dirs. Lyondell Chem. Co.; mem. adv. bd. Gow & Ptnrs., 2003—, Structured Credit Internat. Corp., 2003—, South African C. of C. Am., 2005—; mem. Corp. Dir. Club, Chief Exec. Officers Club. Past chmn. Brit. Am. Ednl. Found.; elder Brick Presbyn. Ch., N.Y.C., 1988—; bd. dirs., vice-chmn. U. Cape Town Fund, N.Y.C., 1985—. Mem.: Kelvin Grove Club (South Africa), Union Club, Harvard Club, United Oxford and Cambridge Club (UK), Misquamicut Club (former bd. govs.). Avocations: sailing, golf, tennis, squash. Home: 351 E 84th St New York NY 10028 Office: Cross Border Enterprises LLC 441 Lexington Ave New York NY 10017-3910 Home Phone: 212-717-5495; Office Phone: 212-682-7400 ext. 230. Business E-Mail: dmeachin@crossborderent.com.

MEAD, ANDREW M., state supreme court justice; Grad., U. Maine; JD, NY Law Sch. With Paine, Lynch & Weatherbee, Bangor, Maine, 1976—81; chief judge Penobscot Tribal Ct., Maine, 1979—90; ptnr. Mitchell & Stearns, Bangor, 1981—90; judge Maine Dist. Ct., 1990—92, Maine Superior Ct., 1992—2007, chief justice, 1999—2001; assoc. justice Maine Supreme Jud. Ct., 2007—. Jud. liaison Maine Rules of Evidence Adv. Com.; chair Task Force on Electronic Ct. Records; adj. faculty mem. U. Maine. Office: Maine Supreme Jud Ct PO Box 368 Portland ME 04112-0368 *

MEAD, CHRISTOPHER, lawyer; b. Richmond, Va., Mar. 20, 1959; BA magna cum laude, Yale Coll., 1981; JD, Yale Law Sch., 1985. Bar: Md. 1985, DC 1988, Va. 1995, admitted to practice: US Ct. Appeals (4th Cir.) 1986, US Ct. Appeals (2nd Cir.) 1986, US Ct. Appeals (7th Cir.) 1986, US Ct. Appeals (11th Cir.) 1986, US Ct. Appeals (DC Cir.) 1986, US Dist. Ct., Dist. Md. 1986, US Dist. Ct. (DC) 1988, US Dist. Ct. (Ea. and Western Dists. Va.) 1995. Law clk. to Hon. Joseph H. Young US Dist. Ct., Dist. Md., 1985—86; assoc. Williams & Connolly, 1986—89; asst. US atty. Dist. Md., 1989—94, spl. asst. US atty., 1994; ptnr. London & Mead, Washington. Named one of 75 Best Lawyers in Washington, Washingtonian Mag., 2002. Mem.: Va. State Bar, Md. State Bar Assn., DC Bar. Office: London & Mead 1225 Nineteenth St NW Ste 320 Washington DC 20036 Office Phone: 202-331-3334. Office Fax: 202-785-4280. Business E-Mail: cmead@londonandmead.com.

MEAD, FRANK WALDRETH, taxonomic entomologist; b. Columbus, Ohio, June 11, 1922; s. Arlington Alfred and Edith May (Harrison) M.; widowed; children: David Harrison, Gregory Scott. BS, Ohio State U., 1947, MS, 1949; PhD, N.C. State U., 1968. Rsch. asst. dept. physiology Ohio State U., Woods Hole, Mass., summer 1941, rsch. asst. dept. entomology Columbus, 1948-50; Japanese beetle scout bur. entomology and plant quar. USDA, Columbus, summer 1948, biol. aid bur. entomology and plant quar., 1950-53; entomologist div. plant industry Fla. Dept. Agr., Gainesville, 1953-58, 60, biologist IV, 1983-95, emeritus, 1995—; rsch. asst. N.C. State U., Raleigh, 1958-60; state survey entomologist Fed.-State Coop. Survey, Gainesville, 1969-80. Courtesy assoc. prof. dept. entomology U. Fla., Gainesville, 1973-95, emeritus, 1995—, Fla. A&M U., Tallahassee, 1977-95, emeritus, 1995—. Co-editor Tri-ology Technical Report; contbr. articles to profl. jours. Bd. dirs., treas. Alachua Audubon Soc., Gainesville, 1968-75, 77-82; bd. dirs. Alachua County Hist. Soc. (hon. lifetime mem. 1998), Gainesville, 1980-82; former mem. steering com. Civitan Regional Blood Bank, Gainesville, 1977-79; vol. photographer P.K. Yonge Devel. Rsch. Sch. U. Fla., Gainesville, 1978—; vol. Project Graduation, U. Fla., 1994-2002; mem. Alachua Conservation Trust, 2003—, Fla. Conservation Trust, 2006—. Nominee Cmty. Svc. award, Gainesville Sun, 2002; named to Registry of Remembrances, Nat. World War II Meml.; recipient award, P.K. Yonge Devel. Rsch. Sch., 2001; fellow, Ohio Acad. Sci., 1966. Mem. VFW, Internat. Order of Merit, Cambridge, Entomol. Soc. Am. (bd. dirs. S.E. br. 1978-79), Ga. Entomol. Soc., Fla. Entomol. Soc. (hon., sec. 1968-82, Cert. of Appreciation 1975, 82, 91, 2004, Cert. of Merit 1986), Fla. Mosquito Control Assn., SAR (Benjamin Franklin chpt. Columbus, Ohio), The Am. Legion (life), Sierra Club, Fla. Track Club, Military Book Club. Avocations: photography, history, birding. Home: 2035 NE 6th Ter Gainesville FL 32609-3758 Office: Fla Dept Agr and Cons Svcs Divsn Plant Industry PO Box 147100 Gainesville FL 32614-7100

MEAD, JAMES MATTHEW, insurance company executive; b. Erie, Pa., June 10, 1945; s. James Leonard and Olga (Richter) M.; m. Rhoda Ginsburg, Sept. 2, 1967 (div. 1971); m. Elaine Margaret Lytle, Mar. 8, 1975. BS, Pa. State U., 1967, MA, 1970. Instr. bus. Pa. State U., Middletown, 1968-71; asst. to ins. commr. Commonwealth of Pa., Harrisburg, 1971-74; asst. to pres. Capital Blue Cross, Harrisburg, 1974-78, sr. v.p., 1978-84, pres., CEO, 1984—2004, vice chmn., 2004—; mng. dir. JM Mead, LLC, 2004—. Bd. dirs. BCS Fin., Chgo., 1987-, Fed. Res. Bank Phila., 1991-95, chmn., 1994-95; bd. dirs. Found. Enhancing Cmtys., Harrisburg, 2002-, Internat. Life Scis. Inst., Washington, 2004-; trustee, vice chmn. Lawyers Fund Client Security, Pa. Supreme Ct., Harrisburg, Pa., 2005-, Lebanon Valley Coll., Annville, Pa., 2003—; venture ptnr. Radius Venture LLC, NYC, 2006—. Contbr. articles on health care to profl. publs. Mem. bd. advisors Pa. State U., 1985-93; chmn. savs. bond campaign for Ctrl. Pa., U.S. Treasury Dept., Harrisburg, 1986-87; bd. dirs. United Way Capital Region, 1994-98, campaign chair, 1994; bd. dirs. Harrisburg Symphony Assn., 2000-, Found. Enhancing Cmty., 2001-, Pa. Lawyers Fund for Client Security, Pa. Supreme Ct. Paul Harris fellow Rotary Internat., 1988, Alumni fellow Pa. State U., 1986. Mem. Capital Region C. of C. (bd. dirs., treas. 1987-90), West Shore Country Club, Blue Ridge Country Club. Home: 1752 Conway Heath Camp Hill PA 17011 Home Phone: 717-763-1490; Office Phone: 717-763-1678. Personal E-mail: jamesmmead@aol.com.

MEAD, JEAN HENRY, freelance/self-employed photojournalist; d. Howard Garrett Hammond and Minnie Carter Henry; m. Willard Dodge

Mead, June 20, 1969; children: Terry Lynne Anderson, Lynda Joyce Kirtland, Lisa Anne Bachman-Johnson, Susan Ilene Myers, William Christopher. BA, U. Nev., Las Vegas, 1995. Staff writer, photographer Hanford Sentinel, Calif., 1968—70, Star News, Chula Vista, Calif., 1971—77, Casper Star-Tribune, Wyo., 1978—80; editor In Wyo. Mag., Casper, 1980—81; freelance photojournalist Casper, 1981—; pub. Misty Mountain Press, Casper, Wyo., 1984—86, Medallion Books, Evansville, Wyo., 2003—. Author: (book) Shirl Lock & Holmes, Escape on the Wind: a Wyoming Novel, Maverick Writers (named number 1 book MidWest Book Rev. List), Westerners: Candid & Historic Interviews, Poet profiles and poetry; author: (photographer) Wyoming in Profile, Casper Country: Wyoming's Heartland. Dir. youth YMCA, Hanford, 1968—70; all-star mgr. Girl's Softball League, Hanford, 1969; scout leader Girl Scouts Am., Hanford, 1962. Recipient Best Writing on Web award, Zino, 2000. Mem.: Wyo. Press Women's Assn. (historian 1974—75), Mystery Writers Am., Wyo. Writers Inc. (pres. 1979—80), We. Writers Am., Inc. (dir. pub. rels. 1980—85, sec. 1980—85, treas. 1980—85). Avocations: travel, computers, interior decorating, sports. Home Phone: 307-235-6456. Personal E-mail: jean henry-mead@aol.com.

MEAD, KENNETH MINOR, lawyer, former federal agency administrator; b. May 14, 1947; m. Elizabeth Guerry; children: Jennifer, Hillary. Baccalaurette Degree, So. Conn. U., 1970; JD, U. S.C., 1975; John F. Kennedy Sch. Sr. Mgrs. in Govt., Harvard U., 1991. Sr. atty. Office Gen. Counsel U.S. Gen. Acctg. Office, Washington, 1975-82, asst. dir. Office Quality Assurance, 1982-86, assoc., asst. dir. transp., dir. transp. & telecom. issues, 1986-96, dep. asst. comptr. gen. for policy, 1996-97; inspector gen. U.S. Dept. Transp., Washington, 1997—2006; spl. counsel Baker Botts LLP, Washington, 2006—. Mem. Pres. Coun. on Integrity and Efficiency, 1997-05, Comptr. Gen.'s U.S. Domestic Accountability Bd., 2001-05. With USN, 1970—72. Recipient GAO Disting. Svc. award, Meritorious Svc. award. Mem. Am. Numismatic Assn., D.C. Bar Assn., Fed. Bar Assn., Assn. Govt. Accountants Office: Baker Botts LLP The Warner 1299 Pennsylvania Ave NW Washington DC 20004 Office Phone: 202-639-7744. Business E-Mail: ken.mead@bakerbotts.com.

MEAD, LAWRENCE MYERS, JR., retired engineering executive; b. Plainfield, NJ, May 11, 1918; s. Lawrence Myers and Eleanor Whitman (Machado) M.; m. Janet Chase, Feb. 21, 1942; children— Lawrence Myers, Kirtland Chase, Jonathan Taylor, Bradford Machado. BSE., Princeton U., 1940, C.E., 1941; postgrad. mgmt., Harvard Bus. Sch., 1964. With Grumman Corp., Bethpage, NY, 1941-93; v.p. tech. ops. Grumman Aerospace Corp., Bethpage, NY, 1972-75, sr. v.p. dept. ops., 1975-81, sr. v.p. tech. ops., 1981-83; sr. mgmt. cons., 1983-93. Patentee in field. Trustee, police commr., dep. mayor Village of Huntington Bay, N.Y., 1975-80; trustee N.Y.C. Hall of Sci. Fellow Poly. U., 1981. Fellow AIAA; mem. NAE, L.I. Forum on Tech. (bd. dirs., past chmn. bd.), Soc. Logistic Engrs., Soc. Advancement Materials and Process Engring., Princeton U. Alumni Assn. Democrat. Achievements include designing A6A Intruder Navy All Weather Bomber, Gulfstream III Exec. Jet Transport. Home: 88 Notch Hill Rd Apt 253 North Branford CT 06471-1851 E-mail: lmmead@aol.com.

MEAD, MATTHEW HANSEN, former prosecutor; b. 1962; Graduate, Trinity U., U. Wyo. Sch. Law. Deputy Co. Atty. Cambell Co. Atty Office, Wyo., 1987—90; Asst. US atty. and Special Asst. US atty. dist. Wyo. US Dept. Justice, 1991—95; ind. practice, 1995—97; ptnr. Mead and Phillips, 1997—2001; US atty. dist. Wyo. US Dept. Justice, 2001—07. *

MEAD, PHILIP BARTLETT, healthcare administrator, educator, retired obstetrician; b. Poughkeepsie, NY, June 23, 1937; s. Ralph Allen and Altina (Gervin) Mead; m. Ann Elaine Smith, June 27, 1964; children: Ralph Allen II, David Smith. BA, Hamilton Coll., 1959; MD, Cornell U., 1963. Diplomate Nat. Bd. Med. Examiners, Am. Bd. Ob-gyn. Intern in medicine Bellevue Hosp., NYC, 1963-64; resident in ob-gyn. N.Y. Hosp./Cornell Med. Ctr., NYC, 1964-69; asst. prof. U. Vt. Coll. Medicine, Burlington, 1971-76, assoc. prof., 1976-81, prof., 1981—2001, prof. emeritus, 2001—; hosp. epidemiologist Med. Ctr. Hosp. of Vt., Burlington, 1984-93; dir. clin. sys. Vt. Acad. Med. Ctr., Burlington, 1993-95; sr. v.p., med. dir. Fletcher Allen Health Care, Burlington, 1995-97; prof., chmn. ob-gyn. U. Vt. Coll. Medicine, 1997—2001, prof. and chmn. emeritus, 2001—; physician leader women's health care svcs. Fletcher Allen Health Care, Burlington, 1997—2001. Lt. comdr. M.C. USN, 1969—71. Fellow: ACOG, Infectious Disease Soc. Am.; mem.: Soc. Hosp. Epidemiologists, Infectious Disease Soc. Ob-Gyn. (pres. 1987—88), Phi Beta Kappa, Alpha Omega Alpha. Home: 203 Pinehurst Dr Shelburne VT 05482-6882 E-mail: PBMeadMD@aol.com.

MEAD, WILLIAM CHARLES, physicist; b. Hazleton, Pa., Dec. 6, 1946; s. Norman Joseph and Ruth Crawford Mead; m. Carol Edna Jerome, May 24, 1969; 1 child, Bennett R. BS, Syracuse U., Syracuse, NY, 1968; MA, Princeton U., Princeton, NJ, 1970, PhD, 1974. Physicist Lawrence Livermore Nat. Lab., 1973—83; physicist, mgr. Los Alamos Nat. Lab., 1983—94; pres., chief scientist Adaptive Network Solutions Rsch. Inc., 1995—. Cons. Lawrence Livermore Nat. Lab., Livermore, Calif., 1995—99, Whistlesoft, Inc., Los Alamos, N.Mex., 1996—98, Ctr. for Adaptive Sys. Applications, Inc., Los Alamos, N.Mex., 1999, Complexica, Inc., Santa Fe, 1999—, Impulse Devices Inc., Grass Valley, Calif., 1999—2003, Los Alamos (N.Mex.) Nat. Lab., 2000—03, Gen. Fusion, Inc., 2003, Environ. Safety Svcs., 2004—. Contbr. articles to profl. jours. Second lt. USAF, 1973—73. Fellow: Am. Phys. Soc. (fellowship 1987); mem.: Internat. Neural Network Soc. Achievements include being head designer for Cairn 50X Intermediate density target, the first laser-driven target to achieve compression of DT to 10 g/cc and a major milestone of the Inertial Confinement Fusion Program; designed and developed C++ engine for Agent-Based Crisis Simulator; development of the Connectionist Hyperprism Classification network to perform task of automated ion mobility spectrum analysis; Adaptive Teaching and Learning Lab. and an Adaptive Tutor for teaching basic arithmetic facts; research in theoretical and computational effort to explore feasibility of Sonic-Cavitation-Driven Fusion; numerical simulations extending knowledge in areas such as the behavior of fluid instabilities in high-gain ICF pellets and the scaling of laser-driven ablation; testing and extending the understanding of ICF physics, providing ideas, simulations and guidance for laser-plasma coupling experiments. Avocations: classical music, photography. Office: Adaptive Network Solutions Research 10 Bonito Pl Los Alamos NM 87544 Office Phone: 505-662-9475. E-mail: wcmead@ansr.com.

MEADE, DALE MICHAEL, experimental physicist; b. Lodi, Wis., Aug. 7, 1939; children: Loretta, Carla Fleming. BS with high honors in Elec. Engring., U. Wis., 1961, MS in Physics, 1962, PhD in Physics, 1965. Asst. prof. physics U. Wis., Madison, 1967-69, assoc. prof., 1969-72, prof., 1972-74; from head FM-1 to head Fire Project Princeton (N.J.) Plasma Physics Lab., 1973—98, head Fire Project, 1998—2004, Fusion Innovation Rsch. and Energy, 2005—. Recipient Disting. Svc. Citation U. Wis. Coll. Engring., Madison, 1990, Disting. Assoc. award U.S. Dept. Energy, Washington, 1994, 2005, Leadership award Fusion Power Assocs., 1999, Disting. Career award Fusion Power Assocs., 2005; Disting. Alumni fellow physics dept. U. Wis., 2002. Fellow AAAS, Am. Phys. Soc. Office: Princeton U Plasma Physics Lab PO Box 451 US Rt 1 N Princeton NJ 08543 E-mail: dmeade@pppl.gov.

MEADER, JOHN DANIEL, judge; b. Ballston Spa, NY, Oct. 22, 1931; s. Jerome Clement and Doris Luella (Conner) M.; m. Joyce Margaret Cowin, Mar. 2, 1963; children: John Daniel Jr., Julia Rae, Keith Alan. BA, Yale U., 1954; JD, Cornell U., 1962. Bar: N.Y. 1963, U.S. Dist. Ct. (no. dist.) N.Y. 1963, U.S. Ct. Appeals (2d cir.) 1966, U.S. Supreme Ct. 1967, U.S. Ct. Mil. Appeals 1973, Ohio 1978, U.S. Dist. Ct. (no. dist.) Ohio 1979, Fla. 1983, U.S. Ct. Appeals (4th cir.) 1992, U.S. Ct. Appeals (fed. cir.) 1993. Sales engr. Albany (N.Y.) Internat. Corp., 1954-59; asst. track coach Cornell U., 1959-62; asst. sec., asst. to pres. Albany Internat. Corp., 1962-65; asst. atty. gen. State of N.Y., Albany, 1965-68; ops. counsel, attesting sec. GE, Schenectady, 1968-77; gen. counsel, asst. sec. Glidden div. SCM Corp., Cleve., 1977-81; chmn. bd., pres. Applied Power Tech. Co., Fernandina Beach, Fla., 1981-84; pres. Applied Energy, Inc., Ballston Spa, 1984-88; judge N.Y. State Workers Compensation Bd., Albany, 1988—. Dir. Saratoga Mut. Fire Ins. Co. Author: Labor Law Manual, 1972, Contract Law Manual, 1974, Patent Law Manual, 1978. Candidate U.S. Ho. of Reps., 29th Dist. N.Y., 1964, N.Y. Supreme Ct., 1975, 87, 93. Col. JAGC, USAR, 1968-1984, dep. staff judge adv. 3d U.S. Army & Ctrl. Command, 1984, brig. gen. JAGC and Fin. Corps, N.Y. Guard, 1984-2002, state staff judge adv. and state comptr. Nat. AAU High Sch. 1000 Yard Indoor Track Champion, 1949, Nat. AAU Prep. Sch. 440 and 880 Yard Indoor Track Champion, 1950, Nat. AAU Outstanding Performer award, Melrose Games Assn., 1950, Heptagonal Track 880-Yard Champion 1954. Mem. ABA, N.Y. State Bar Assn., Fla. Bar, Amelia Island Plantation Club, Cyprus Temple Club, Yale Club Jacksonville (pres.), Masons. Republican. Presbyterian. Home: 271 Round Lake Rd Ballston Lake NY 12019-1714 Office: NY State Workers Compensation Bd 100 Broadway Albany NY 12241-0001 Office Phone: 518-474-6662. Business E-Mail: john.meader@wcb.state.ny.us.

MEADERS, DONALD W., lawyer; b. Dahlonega, Ga., May 3, 1947; AB, Harvard U., 1969, JD, 1973. Bar: Calif. 1973, States Dist. Ct. (ctrl. dist.) Calif. Atty. Kindel & Anderson, LA; ptnr. Manatt Phelps & Phillips LLP. Prog. chmn. 1988 Ann. Meeting Western Pension and Benefits Conf.; mem. steering com. LA chpt. Western Pension and Benefits Conf., 1988-90, sec., 1990-91, pres.-elect, 1991-92, spk. in fields. Contbr. Mem. ABA (mem. employee benefits com., tax sect.), State Bar Calif., LA County Bar Assn. (chmn. employee benefits com., tax sect. 1982-83, mem. exec. com. 1979-82), Calif. Bar Assn., mem. planning com.U. So. Calif. Tax Inst. 2003-2005. Office: Manatt Phelps & Phillips LLP 11355 W Olympic Blvd Los Angeles CA 90064 Office Phone: 310-312-4000, 310-312-4345. Office Fax: 310-312-4224. Business E-Mail: dmeaders@manatt.com.

MEADOR, CHARLES LAWRENCE, management and systems consultant, educator; b. Dallas, Oct. 7, 1946; s. Charles Leon and Dorothy Margaret (Brown), m. Diane E. Collins, May 18, 1985. BSME with honors, U. Tex., 1970; MSME, MS in Mgmt., MIT, 1972. Engring. staff Union Carbide Corp., Houston, 1967-68; instr. Alfred P. Sloan Sch. Mgmt. MIT, Cambridge, 1972-75, asst. dir. Ctr. Info. Systems Rsch., 1976-78, lectr. Sch. Engring., co-dir. Macro-Engring. Rsch. Group, 1978-99. Founder, pres. Decision Support Tech., Inc., 1974-92; co-founder, vice-chmn., dir. Software Productivity Rsch., Inc., 1985-87; pres., dir. The Softbridge Group, 1989-92; founder, CEO, Mgmt. Support Tech. Corp., 1992-99; sr. v.p., chief info. officer CIGNA Property and Casualty, 1995-98; vice-chmn., dir. Condor Tech. Solutions, Inc., 1998-2000; co-founder, chmn., dir. MGI Strategic Solutions, 2001—; commr. Nat. Imagery and Mapping Agy., 2000-01; mem. Def. Sci. Bd. Task Force, 2001. Editor: How Big and Still Beautiful? Macro-Engineering Revisited, 1980, Macro-Engineering: The Rich Potential, 1981, Macro-Engineering and the Future: A Management Perspective, 1982, Macro-Engineering: Global Infrastructure Solutions, 1992, Macro-Engineering: MIT Brunel Lectures on Global Infrastructure, 1997; mem. editorial bd. Computer Comm., 1979-91; contbr. articles to profl. jours. NSF trainee, 1970; MIT Wilfred Lewis fellow, 1971, Draper Lab. fellow, 1974. Mem. Computer Soc. IEEE (vice-chmn. Ea. Hemisphere and Latin Am. Area Com. 1977-83), Am. Soc. for Macro-Engrng. (bd. dirs. 1992-96), Cosmos Club, Sigma Xi, Tau Beta Pi, Pi Tau Sigma. Office: MGI Strategic Solutions 85 Speen St Framingham MA 01701

MEADOR, DANIEL JOHN, law educator; b. Selma, Ala., Dec. 7, 1926; s. Daniel John and Mabel (Kirkpatrick) M.; m. Janet Caroline Heilmann, Nov. 19, 1955; children: Janet Barrie, Anna Kirkpatrick, Daniel John. BS, Auburn U., 1949; JD, U. Ala., 1951; LLM, Harvard U., 1954; LLD (hon.), U. S.C., 1998. Bar: Ala. 1951, Va. 1961. Law clk. to Justice Hugo L. Black U.S. Supreme Ct., 1954-55; assoc. firm Lange, Simpson, Robinson & Somerville, Birmingham, Ala., 1955-57; faculty U. Va. Law Sch., Charlottesville, 1957-66, prof. law, 1961-66; prof., dean U. Ala. Law Sch., 1966-70; James Monroe prof. law U. Va., Charlottesville, 1970-94, prof. emeritus, 1994—; asst. atty. gen. US Dept. Justice, 1977-79; dir. grad. program for judges, 1979-95. Fulbright lectr., U.K., 1965-66; vis. prof. U.S. Mil. Acad., 1984; chmn. Southeastern Conf. Assn. Am. Law Schs., 1964-65; chmn. Cts. Task Force Nat. Adv. Commn. on Criminal Justice, 1971-72; dir. appellate justice project Nat. Ctr. for State Cts., 1972-74; mem. Adv. Coun. on Appellate Justice, 1971-75, Coun. on Role of Cts., 1978-84; bd. dirs. State Justice Inst., 1986-92; exec. dir. commn. on structural alternatives Fed. Ct. Appeals, 1998-99. Author: Preludes to Gideon, 1967, Criminal Appeals-English Practices and American Reforms, 1973, Mr. Justice Black and His Books, 1974, Appellate Courts: Staff and Process in the Crisis of Volume, 1974, (with Carrington and Rosenberg) Justice on Appeal, 1976, Impressions of Law in East Germany, 1986, American Courts, 1991, 2000, Appellate Courts in the United States, 1994, 2nd edit., 2006, His Father's House, 1994, Unforgotten, 1999, (with Baker and Steinman) Appellate Courts: Structures, Functions, Processes, and Personnel, 1994, 2nd edit., 2006; editor: Hardy Cross Dillard: Writings and Speeches, 1995; editor Va. Bar News, 1962-65; contbr. articles to profl. jours. 1st lt. U.S. Army, 1951-53; col. JAGC, USAR ret. Decorated Bronze Star.; IREX fellow German Dem. Republic, 1983 Mem. ABA (chmn. standing com. on fed. jud. improvements 1987-90), Ala. Bar Assn., Va. Bar Assn. (exec. com. 1983-86), Am. Law Inst., Am. Judicature Soc. (bd. dirs. 1975-77, 80-83), Soc. Pub. Tchrs. Law, Am. Soc. Legal History (bd. dirs. 1968-71), Order of Coif, Raven Soc., Phi Delta Phi, Omicron Delta Kappa, Kappa Alpha. Presbyterian. Office: U Va Sch Law 580 Massie Rd Charlottesville VA 22903-1738

MEADOR, JOHN MILWARD, JR., dean, librarian; b. Louisville, Nov. 4, 1946; s. John Milward and Ruth Inez (Miller) M.; m. Judith Ann Hay, Dec. 22, 1969; children: John Milward III, Elise Kathleen. BA, U. Louisville, 1968; MA, U. Tex., 1972, MLS, 1973. Cert. tchr., Ky., Tex. English bibliographer M.D. Anderson Libr., U. Houston, 1973-74, head reference dept. social scis. and humanities, 1974-77, head gen. reference dept., 1977-80; asst. dir. pub. svcs. Marriott Libr., U. Utah, Salt Lake City, 1980-84; dean libr. svcs. S.W. Mo. State U., Springfield, 1984-93; dean librs. U. Miss., Univeristy, 1993—2003; dir. librs. SUNY, Binghamton, 2003—. Bd. dirs. S.W. Mo. Libr. Network, Springfield; cons. Dayco Corp., Springfield, 1984-86; chmn. Mo. Northwestern Online Total Integrated Sys. Users Group, 1988-89. Co-author: The Robinson Jeffers Collection at the University of Houston, 1975; contbr. articles to profl. jours. Sponsor Cmty. Alternative Svc. Program, Springfield and St. Louis, 1985-93; governing bd. Mo. Rsch. and Edn. Network, 1991-93; bd. dirs. Broome Libr. Found., Inc., 2005-07, Broome Leadership Inst. Alumni Assn., 2006—. With U.S. Army, 1969-71, Vietnam. Recipient Nat. Essay award Propeller Club of U.S., 1964; named to Honorable Order of Ky. Colonels, Gov. Ky., 1978; summer scholar English-Speaking Union, Edinburgh, Scotland, 1968; Apple Computer's Higher Edn. Acad. Devel. Donation Program grantee, 1990. Mem. ALA, Am. Assn. for Higher Edn., Assn. Coll. Rsch. Librs., Bibliography Soc. Am., Libr. Adminstrn. and Mgmt. Assn., English-Speaking Union Club, Rotary (chmn. students guests com. Springfield chpt. 1986-89, chmn. scholarships com. 1989-90, bd. dirs. 1990-91, bd. dirs. Oxford chpt. 1995-96), Phi Kappa Phi. Avocations: fishing, book collecting. Office: Binghamton Univ SUNY Bartle Library Binghamton NY 13902-6012 Office Phone: 607-777-2346. Business E-Mail: jmeador@binghamton.edu.

MEADOR, MICHAEL ANTHONY, chemist, researcher; b. Albuquerque, Oct. 2, 1956; s. Charles Thomas and Clara Margaret Meador; m. Mary Ann Babin, Mar. 1, 1958; children: Michael Joseph, Jonathan Charles. BA, Ithaca Coll., NY, 1978; PhD, Mich. State U., East Lansing, 1983. Chemist NASA Lewis Rsch. Ctr., Cleve., 1983—87, dep. chief, polymers br., 1987—88; chief polymers br. NASA Glenn Rsch. Ctr., 1988—. Grad. faculty U. Akron, Ohio, 1998; editl. adv. bd. High Performance Polymers, Nanotech Briefs, Polymer. Contbr. articles to profl. jours. Cantor St. Emilian's Byzantine Cath. Ch., Brunswick, Ohio, 1998, coord. catechism program, 1998—2005. L.L. Quill Grad. fellow, Mich. State U., Dept. Chemistry, 1978—81. Mem.: Am. Chem. Soc. Achievements include 5 US patents in high performance polymers. Office: NASA Glenn Rsch Ctr 21000 Brookpark Rd MS 49-3 Cleveland OH 44135 Office Phone: 216-433-9518. Office Fax: 216-977-7132. E-mail: michael.a.meador@nasa.gov.

MEADOR, RON, newspaper editor, writer; b. Buffalo, Nov. 24, 1952; s. Meril E. and Evelyn (Lyons) M.; divorced; 1 child, Benjamin Brian. BA, Ind. U., 1975. Copy editor The Courier-Journal, Louisville, 1975-78, The New York Times, 1978-80; reporter, state editor, city editor, asst. mng. editor Star Tribune, Mpls., Minn., 1980-96, mem. editl. bd., editl. writer, 1996—. Mem. Investigative Reporters and Editors, Inc., Nat. Conf. Editl. Writers, Soc. Environ. Journalists, Insts. for Journalism and Natural Resources (mem. adv. bd.). Office: Star Tribune 425 Portland Ave Minneapolis MN 55488-0002

MEADOR, ROSS DESHONG, lawyer; b. Mexico City, Aug. 23, 1954; s. Bruce Staffel and Betty Lee M.; m. Michelle Hyunae Chang, Mar. 14, 1997; children: Amy Chang, Leah Chang, Daniel Ross. BA in Comm. and Visual Arts, U. Calif., San Diego, 1980; JD, U. Calif., Berkeley, 1986. Bar: Calif. Co-dir. Overseas Operations Friends of Children of Vietnam, 1974—75; atty. Morrison & Foerster, San Francisco, 1986—89; fgn. legal advisor Kim & Chang, Seoul, 1989—95, Soewito, Suhardiman, Eddymurthy & Kardono, Jakarta, Indonesia, 1996—97; of counsel Morrison & Foerster, 1997—99, Howard, Rice et al, 2000; ptnr. Preston Gates & Ellis, 2001—02, Rogers & Meador, 2003—; internat. legal adv. Vietnam Internat. Law Firm, 2005—. Photographer Escape From Saigon, Gerald Ford Presdl. Mus. Permanent Collection; one man shows include U. Calif. San Diego, 1980; exec. editor Internat. Tax & Bus. Lawyer, 1985-86. Bd. dirs. Theatre Bay Area, San Francisco, 1988—89. Nominee Presdl. Medal of Freedom, 2005. Mem. ABA, Calif. Bar Assn. (exec. com. internat. law sect. 2001-04, sec. 2004-05, adv. emeritus 2006—), Am. C. of C. in Korea (chmn. legal svcs. com. 1993), Korean Am. C. of C. of No. Pacific Coast (v.p. 1998-99, pres. 2000-01), U.S.-Vietnam C. of C. (vice chair 2005), Am. C. of C. Vietnam. Avocations: travel, photography. Home: 1270 Campus Dr Berkeley CA 94708-2045

MEADORS, ALLEN COATS, health facility and academic administrator, educator; b. Van Buren, Ark., May 17, 1947; s. Hal Barron and Allene Coats (Means) Meadors. AA, Saddleback Coll., 1981; BBA, U. Ctrl. Arki., 1969; MBA, U. No. Colo., 1974; MPA, U. Kans., 1975; MA in Psychology, Webster U., 1979, MA in Health Svcs. Mgmt., 1980; PhD in Adminstrn., So. Ill. U., 1981. Assoc. adminstr. Forbes Hosp., Topeka, 1971-73; asst. dir. health svcs. devel. Blue Cross Blue Shield of Kans., Topeka, 1973-76; asst. dir. Kansas City Health Dept., Mo., 1976-77; program dir., asst. prof. So. Ill. U., Carbondale, 1977—82, Webster U., St. Louis, 1979—82; mem. faculty Calif. State U., Long Beach, 1977-81; assoc. prof., dir. divsn. health adminstrn. U. Tex., Galveston, 1982-84; exec. dir. N.W. Ark. Radiation Therapy Inst., Springdale, 1984-87; mem. grad. faculty Sch. Bus. Adminstrn. U. Ark., Fayetteville, 1984-87; prof., chmn. dept. health adminstrn. U. Okla., Oklahoma City, 1987-90, dean Coll. Pub. Health, 1989—90; dean Coll. Health, Social and Pub. Svcs. Ea. Wash. U., Cheney, 1990—94; chancellor U. NC, Penbroke, 1994—99, Pembroke, 1999—. Cons. Surgeon Gen. Office and Air Force Sys.; bd. dirs. Lumbar Guartoner Bank, Southeastern Regional Med. Ctr. Contbr. articles to profl. jours. Command bd. dirs. Blair County Hall of Fame, Blair County Hist. Soc., Martin Luther King Hosp., Health Care Svcs. Adv. Bd.; bd. dirs., exec. com. Altoona Symphony Orch.; bd. dirs. Home Health Agy., NC Retirement Fund, Southwestern Regional Med. Ctr. With Med. Svc. Corps USAF, 1969—73. Fellow: Am. Coll. Healthcare Execs.; mem.: Am. Hosp. Assn., C. of C. (v.p.). Office: U NC at Pembroke Chancellors Office PO Box 1510 Pembroke NC 28372-1510 Home: PO Box 97 Pembroke NC 28372 Office Phone: 910-521-6201. Business E-Mail: acm@uncp.edu.

MEADORS, C. BRIAN, lawyer; b. Lawrence, Kans., Aug. 18, 1969; s. Carey Wayne Meadors and Norma Meadors Senyard; m. Erika Esterbrook, Feb. 12, 2000; children: August Carey, Tabitha Grace. BS in Engring., U. Mich., Ann Arbor, 1991; JD cum laude, Georgetown U., Washington, 1999. Cert. profl. engr., Va., 1998, Ark., 1998; bar: Va. 1999, DC 2000, Ark. 2001, Mo. 2006, Fla. 2007. Atty. Morgan, Lewis & Bockius LLP, Washington, 1999—2002, Pryor, Robertson, Beasley, Smith & Karber PLLc, Fort Smith, Ark., 2002—. Elder First Presbyn. Ch., Fort Smith, 2003—06. Naval nuclear submarine officer USN, 1991—96. Decorated Navy Achievement medal. Mem.: ATLA, Am. Nuc. Soc. Avocations: reading, piano. Home: 10712 Hunters Point Rd Fort Smith AR 72903 Office: Pryor Robertson Beasley Smith & Karber PLLC PO Drawer 848 315 N 7th St Fort Smith AR 72902-0848 Home Phone: 479-285-6809; Office Phone: 479-782-8813. Office Fax: 479-785-0254. Personal E-mail: brianmeadors@gmail.com. Business E-Mail: cbmeadors@prbsklaw.com.

MEADORS, HOWARD CLARENCE, JR., electrical engineer; b. Chgo., July 31, 1938; s. Howard Clarence and Eileen May (Baker) M.; m. Phyllis Anne Rennebaum, July 18, 1964; children: Henry Charles, William Howard, Laura Phyllis, Pamela Susan. SB, MIT, 1960, SM, 1962, Profl. Degree in Elec. Engring., 1964; PhD, Poly. Inst. NY., 1976. Mem. tech. staff Bell Tel. Labs., Inc., Holmdel, NJ, 1966—82; disting. mem. tech. staff AT&T Info. Sys. Labs., Holmdel, 1983—85, supr. product devel., 1985—86; supr. adv. data comm. AT&T Bell Labs., Middletown, NJ, 1986—91; disting. mem. tech. staff AT&T Bus. Comm. Sys., Holmdel, 1991—91, AT&T Network Sys., Holmdel, 1994—96, Lucent Technologies, Holmdel, 1996—2001. Ednl. counselor MIT, 1973-2003, regional vice chmn., 1983-96, ctrl. NJ chmn., 1996-2003. Inventor in field. With Signal Corps, U.S. Army, 1964-66. Mem. IEEE (sr.), Sigma Xi, Eta Kappa Nu. Personal E-mail: hcmeadorsjr@yahoo.com.

MEADOW, CHARLES, information scientist, writer; b. Paterson, NJ, Dec. 16, 1929; s. Abraham and Florence (Troub) M.; m. Harriet Reiss, Sept. 9, 1956 (div.); children: Debra Lynne, Sandra Lee; m. Mary Louise Shinskey, June 24, 1972; children: Alison Maria, Benjamin Niland. BA, U. Rochester, 1951; MS, Rutgers U., 1954. Mathematician David Taylor Model Basin USN, Washington, 1954-55; asst. mathematician RAND Corp., Lexington, Mass., 1955-56; unit mgr. GE Co., Bethesda, Md., 1956-60; sr. sys. analyst IBM Corp., Gaithersburg, Md., 1960-68; chief sys. devel. divsn. US Nat. Bur. Stds., Gaithersburg, Md., 1968-71; tech. asst. Office of Sci. and Tech. Exec. Office of the Pres., Washington, 1970-71; asst. dir. divsn. mgmt. info. and telecom. sys. US AEC, Washington, 1971-74; prof. Drexel U., Phila., 1974-82; project mgr. Dialog Info. Svcs., Inc., Palo Alto, Calif., 1982-84; prof. faculty info. studies U. Toronto, 1984—94, assoc. dean, 1990—94, prof. emeritus, 1994—. Vis. prof. U. Sheffield, 1980-81, U. West Indies, 1990-91, U. Wash., 1993, U. NC, 1995; mem. bd. visitors Coll. Communication and Info., U. Tenn., 2002-05.

Author or co-author 12 books, including (with Bert R. Boyce, Donald H. Kraft and Carol Barry) Text Information Retrieval Systems, 3d edit., 2007; (with Bert R. Boyce and Donald H. Kraft) Measurement in Information Science, 1994, Ink Into Bits: A Web of Converging Media, 1998, Making Connections: Communications Through the Ages, 2002, Messages, Meaning and Symbols, 2006; editor Jour. Am. Soc. for Info. Sci., 1976-84, Can. Jour. Info. Sci., 1986-87. 1st Lt. USMC, 1951-53. Mem. Am. Soc. Info. Sci. and Tech. (disting. lectr. award NJ chpt. 1986, ann. rsch. award 1995, info. sci. book of yr. award 2000), Can. Assn. Info. Sci. (pres. 1994), NY Acad. Sci. (honorable mention children's sci. book awards 1975), Ret. Academics and Librs. U. Toronto (exec. com. 2000-02, coms. dir. 2001-02), Sigma Xi. Avocation: photography. Home: 1047 Richardson St Victoria BC Canada V8V 3CG E-mail: ct.meadow@shaw.ca.

MEADOW, LYNNE (CAROLYN MEADOW), theater producer; b. New Haven, Nov. 12, 1946; d. Frank and Virginia R. Meadow. BA cum laude, Bryn Mawr Coll., 1968; postgrad., Yale U., 1968-70. Dir. Theatre Communications Group, 1978-80. Adj. prof. SUNY, Stony Brook, 1975-76, Yale U., Circle in the Sq., 1977-78, 89-91, NYU, 1977-80; theatre and music/theatre panelist Nat. Endowment for Arts, 1977-88; artistic advisor Fund for New Am. Plays, 1988-90. Artistic dir. Manhattan Theatre Club, N.Y.C., 1972—; guest dir. Nat. Playwrights Conf., Eugene O'Neill Theatre Ctr., 1975-77, Phoenix Theatre, 1976; dir. Ashes for Manhattan Theatre Club and N.Y. Shakespeare Festival, 1977; prodr. off-Broadway shows Ain't Misbehavin', 1978, Crimes of the Heart, 1981, Miss Firecracker Contest, 1984, Frankie and Johnny, 1987, Eastern Standard, 1988, Lisbon Traviata, 1989, Lips Together, Teeth Apart, 1991, Four Dogs and a Bone, 1993, Love! Valour! Compassion!, 1994; dir. Principia Scritoriae, 1986, Woman in Mind, 1988 (Drama Desk award), Eleemosynary, 1989, Absent Friends, 1991; dir. Broadway prodn. A Small Family Business, 1992, The Loman Family Picnic, 1993, Nine Armenians, 1996 (Drama Desk nominee), Captains Courageous: The Musical, 1999, The Tale of the Allergist's Wife, 2000; (dir. Broadway prodn. and nat. tour), Last Dance, 2003, Rose's Dilemma, 2003, Moonlight and Magnolias, 2005; co-prodr. Off-Broadway and Broadway show Mass Appeal, 1981. Recipient Citation of Merit Nat. Coun. Women, 1976, Outer Circle Critics award 1977, Drama Desk award, 1977, Obie award for Ashes, 1977, Margo Jones award for Continued Encouragement New Playwrights, 1981, Critics Circle award Outstanding Revival on or off Broadway for Loot, 1986, Lucille Lortel award for Outstanding Achievement, 1987, Spl. Drama Desk award, 1989, N.Y. Drama Critics Circle award Best Fgn. Play for Aristocrats, 1989, Torch of Hope award, 1989, Manhattan Mag. award, 1994, Lee Reynolds award League Profl. Theatre Women, 1994; named Northwood Inst. Disting. Woman of Yr., 1990, Person of Yr., Nat. Theatre Conf., 1992, SDCF "Mr. Abbott" award, 2003. Office: Manhattan Theatre Club 311 W 43rd St Fl 8 New York NY 10036-6413 Office Phone: 212-399-3000 x 114.

MEADOWS, JOHN FREDERICK, lawyer; b. Manila, Mar. 7, 1926; s. Grover Cleveland and Millie M.; m. Karen Lee Morris, Nov. 17, 1962; children: Ian Joseph, Marie Irene. AA, U. Mich., 1944; BA (Freshman Alumni Scholar, 1943), U. Calif., Berkeley, 1948; LLB, Boalt Hall, 1951. Bar: Calif 1952, U.S. Dist. Ct. (no. dist.) Calif. 1952, U.S. Ct. Appeals. (9th cir.) 1952, U.S. Supreme Ct. 1958. Assoc. Wallace, Garrison, Norton & Ray, San Francisco, 1952-56; atty. advisor Maritime Adminstrn, U.S. Dept. Commerce, Washington, 1956; trial atty., Admiralty and Shipping Sect. U.S. Dept Justice, West Coast Office, San Francisco, 1956-64, atty. in charge, 1964-72; sr. resident ptnr. Acret & Perrochet, San Francisco, 1972-76; sr. ptnr. Meadows, Smith, Lenker, Sterling & Davis, San Francisco, 1976-93, Long Beach, Calif., 1976-93, Seattle, 1976-93; mng. ptnr. west coast Kirlin, Campbell, Meadows & Keating, NYC, 1993; ptnr. Jedeikin, Meadows & Schneider, San Francisco, 1994. Cons. maritime law UN; lectr. in field. Author: Preparing a Ship Collision Case for Trial, 1970, Ship Collision Cases: Technical and Legal Aspects; Investigation and Preparation for Suit, 1997, contbr. articles to legal publs. Lt. M.I. AUS, 1944—46. Mem. ABA, Maritime Law Assn. Republican. Roman Catholic. Home: 205 The Uplands Berkeley CA 94705-2818 Office: 333 Pine St 5th Floor San Francisco CA 94104-3319 Office Phone: 415-477-8826. Office Fax: 415-421-5658. Business E-Mail: jmeadows@jsmslaw.com.

MEADOWS, JUDITH ADAMS, law librarian, educator; b. Spartanburg, SC, June 5, 1945; d. Thomas Taylor and Virginia (Dayton) Adams; m. Bruce R. Meadows; children: Beth Ann Blackwood, Ted Adams Meadows. BA, Am. U., 1967; MLS, U. Md., College Park, 1979. Law libr. Aspen Sys. Corp., Gaithersburg, Md., 1979-81; dir. Fairfax (Va.) Law Libr., 1981-84, State Law Libr., Helena, Mont., 1984—. Vis. prof. U. Wash., Seattle, 1994; adj. prof. U. Great Falls, Mont., 1989-96; presiding ofcl. Gov.'s Conf. on Libr. Info. Svc., Helena, Mont., 1991; cons. Nat. Ctr. for State Cts., 2000—. Author: (book chpts.) From Yellow Pads to Computers, 1991, Law Librarianship, 1994, Encyclopedia of Library and Information Science, 2007; contbr. articles to profl. jours. Bd. dirs. Helena Presents, 1986-92, Holter Mus. Art, 1995-2002, Mont. Supreme Ct. Commn. on Tech., Mont. Equal Justice Task Force, 2001-; bd. dirs. Helena Edn. Found., v.p., 2003, pres. 2005-06; chair Mont. Supreme Ct. Commn. on Self-Represented Litigants, 2004—; mem. Mont. Commn. Continuing Legal Edn., 2006—. Recipient Disting. Svc. award State Bar of Mont., 1991, Pro Bono Pub. award, 2002. Mem. Am. Assn. Law Librs. (treas. 1992-95, v.p. 1996—, pres. 1997-98, past pres. 1998—), N.W. Consortium of Law Librs. (pres.), Mont. Libr. Assn. (sec. 1986-88). Office: State Law Libr Mont PO Box 203004 Helena MT 59620-3004

MEADOWS, VICKERS B., federal agency administrator; Grad., Green Mountain Coll. Procuremen, dir. presdl. gifts The White House, Washington, 1985—87, spl. asst. to the v.p. for adminstrn., 1987—89; dep. dir., dir. exec. svc. US Dept. Transp., Washington, 1989—93; dir. adminstrn. to Gov. Bush State of Tex., 1995—2000; spl. asst. to Pres., dir. White House Mgmt. The White House, Washington, 2001, dir. adminstrn. Bush-Cheney Transition; asst. sec. for adminstrn. office, CIO, chief human capital officer US Dept. Housing & Urban Devel., Washington, 2002—04; chief adminstrv. officer, US Patent & Trademark Office US Dept. Commerce, Washington, 2005—. Republican. Office: US Patent & Trademark Office 2121 Crystal Dr Arlington VA 22202

MEADS, DONALD EDWARD, management services company executive; b. Salem, Mass., Sept. 23, 1920; s. Laurence G. and Gertrude F. Meads; m. Jane Lightner, June 15, 1943; children: Edward G., Robert C., Laurence G., Judith C. Antrim, Suzanne M. O'Neil, Clifford L., Nancy Chapin. AB in Pre-Law, Dartmouth Coll., 1942; MBA in Fin., Harvard U., 1947. V.p., vice chmn. investment com. N.Y. Life Ins Co., NYC, 1947-61; v.p. fin., chmn. investment com. Investors Diversified Svcs. Inc., Mpls., 1961-65; pres., CEO Internat. Basic Economy Corp., NYC, 1965-67, chmn., CEO, 1967-71; exec. v.p., dir., CFO, chmn. investment com. INA Corp., Phila., 1971-74; chmn. bd., CEO CertainTeed Corp., Valley Forge, Pa., 1974-78, dir., 1973-78; chmn. Mateer-Burt Co., Inc., Plymouth Meeting, Pa., 1984-87, Phila. First Group Inc., 1982-90, Carver Assocs., Inc., West Conshohocken, Pa., 1978—. Hon. life trustee Valley Forge Mil. Acad. and Coll., Wayne, Pa.; hon. dir. Marine Corps Scholarship Found., Princeton, N.J. Capt. USMC, 1942-45. Decorated DFC, Air medals (6). Mem. Harvard Club N.Y.C., Union League (Phila.).

MEADS, MINDY, retail executive; b. 1952; m. Larry Meads; 1 child, Griffin. BS, U. Ill., 1974. With Denver Dry Goods, 1974—78; sr. v.p., v.p., merchandising administr., v.p., store mgr., jeans collection buyer R.H. Macy and Company Inc., 1978—89; operating exec. The Limited, 1989—90; v.p., gen. merchandising mgr. Lands' End Inc., 1991—94; sr. v.p merchandising & design Lands' End, Inc., 1994—96, exec. v.p merchandising & design, 1998—2003; sr. v.p., gen. merchandising mgr., merchandising design planning and allocation Gymboree Corp., 1996—98; gen. mgr. apparel Sears Roebuck and Co., 2003—04, exec. v.p., 2003—; pres. Lands' End, Inc., Dodgeville, Wis., 2003—05, CEO, 2004—05; pres. Victoria's Secret Direct, 2005—07; pres., chief merchandising officer Aeropostale, Inc., NYC, 2007—. Office: Aeropostale Inc 112 W 34th St 22nd Fl New York NY 10120 *

MEADS, WALTER FREDERICK, communications executive, consultant, writer; b. Ft. Wayne, Ind., Mar. 11, 1923; s. Frederick C. and Minnie E. (Stephenson) M.; m. Mary E. Smith, Mar. 21, 1975; children by previous marriage: Kenneth W., Catherine L. BS, Kent State U., 1948; MA, Fairfield U. With Norman Malone & Assos., Akron, Ohio, 1946-48, Griswold-Eshleman Co., Cleve., 1949-53, Fuller, Smith & Ross, Cleve., 1953-55; sr. v.p., head of creative svc., mem. mgmt. com., vice chmn. plans and rev. bds. J. Walter Thompson Co., NYC, 1955-72; pres. Meads & Assocs., 1972—. With USAAF, 1943-45. Recipient numerous nat. and local advt. industry awards. Home: 6761 Trail Ridge Dr Lakeland FL 33813-1844 Personal E-mail: chipmeads@tampabay.rr.com. *Creative freedom is probably the core concept at the heart of my life— not only for myself but for others. Life is never static; it either deteriorates or grows. All growth, to me, springs from the creative doers of the world. The rest of humanity goes along for the ride. And creative growth, in any field or endeavor, demands an attitude of freedom to shake off the shackles of habit and find new and better ways of doing things.*

MEAGHER, ANTHONY L., lawyer; b. Balt., Oct. 18, 1963; BA summa cum laude, Tex. Luth. Univ., 1985; JD with honors, Univ. Md., 1988. Bar: Md. 1988. Ptnr., co-chmn. Construction Litigation practice group DLA Piper Rudnick Gray Cary, Balt. Contbr. articles to profl. jours. Mem.: ABA, Md. State Bar Assn., Order of the Coif. Office: DLA Piper Rudnick Gray Cary 6225 Smith Ave Baltimore MD 21209-3600 Office Phone: 410-580-4214. Office Fax: 410-580-3001. Business E-Mail: anthonymeagher@dlapiper.com.

MEAGHER, GEORGE VINCENT, mechanical engineer; b. Halifax, NS, Can., Apr. 23, 1919; s. John Nicholas and Blanche Margaret (Seals) M.; m. Evelyn Margaret Hamm, June 2, 1945; children: Maureen, Lindsey, Lise, Shelagh. BSc, Dalhousie U., Halifax, 1940; B of Engring., McGill U., 1942. Engring. and mgmt. positions in industry, 1942—56; with Dilworth, Secord, Meagher & Assocs. Ltd., Toronto, Canada, 1957—92, chmn., 1985—96; chmn., CEO Champlain Power Products, Ltd., 1970—80; vice chmn. Tata-DSMA, Bombay, 1970—93; pres., CEO DSMA Internat., Inc., 1980—88; dir. State Bank India, Can. Ltd., Toronto, 1984—94; founding dir., past chmn. Can.-India Bus. Coun.; pres. George V. Meagher Inc., Tatacan, Ltd., 1985—. Fellow: Engring. Inst. Can.; mem.: Profl. Engrs. Ont. Home: 500 Avenue Rd Apt 1402 Toronto ON Canada M4V 2J6 Office Phone: 416-929-8286. E-mail: meaghergv@sympatico.ca.

MEAGHER, JAMES PROCTOR, editor; b. Rock Island, Ill., June 2, 1935; s. Edmund Joseph and Pauline Marie (Proctor) M.; m. Marie Therese Lyman, Sept. 12, 1959; children: Kathleen Ann Raffa, Christopher James. BA, U. Notre Dame, 1957. Copy editor Chgo. Tribune Co., 1959-61; staff writer Nat. Observer, Washington, 1961-62, news editor Silver Spring, Md., 1962-65, sr. editor, 1965-76, asst. mng. editor, 1976-77; assoc. editor Barron's Bus. and Fin. Weekly, NYC, 1977-78, news editor, 1978-82, asst. mng. editor, 1982-86, dep. editor, 1986-92, mng. editor, 1992-93, editor, 1993-95; exec. editor Dow Jones Mag. Group, NYC, 1995—2002; ind. editl. cons., 2002—. Served to 1st lt. US Army, 1957—59. Mem. Soc. Profl. Journalists, Sigma Delta Chi. Roman Catholic. Home: 25 Hedges Ave Chatham NJ 07928-2503 Personal E-mail: meagherj@optonline.net.

MEAGHER, JOSEPH PATRICK, law educator, consultant; s. Francis and Alma Meagher; m. Rani Parker, June 4, 1989; 1 child, Asha. JD magna cum laude, Harvard Law Sch., 1989. Bar: NY 1990, Washington 1991. Educator Peace Corps, Kisangani, Zaire, 1982—84; atty. Patton, Boggs, Washington, 1989—91, Shearman & Sterling, 1991—92; sr. assoc. Checchi & Co. Cons., Inc., 1992—94; assoc. dir. IRIS Ctr., U. Md., College Park, 1994—. Adj. prof. law Cath. U., Washington, 1991—93. Co-author, editor: Devolution and Development, 2004; contbr. chapters to books, articles to jours. Fellow, Harvard U, Ford Found., 1987—88; grantee, World Bank Netherlands Trust Fund, 1998—2000; Fulbright scholar, Inst. Internat. Edn., 1989. Mem.: Phi Beta Kappa. Office: IRIS Ctr U Md 2105 Morrill Hall College Park MD 20742 Home Phone: 301-270-3803; Office Phone: 301-405-5468. E-mail: meagher@iris.econ.umd.edu.

MEAKEM, CAROLYN SOLIDAY, investment executive, financial planner, money manager, consultant; b. Columbus, Ohio, Jan. 11, 1936; d. Junius Dean and Mary Elizabeth (Thomas) Soliday; m. Thomas James Meakem, Aug. 26, 1956; children: Thomas James III, Timothy Dean, Traci Lynn. BS, West Liberty Coll., 1959; MEd., U. Md., 1970. cert. fin. planner, cert. trust specialist. Tchr. Westchester Elem. Sch.; Ellicott City, Md., 1956-59, Riverdale (Md.) Elem. Sch., 1959-60, Buckingham Elem. Sch., Willingboro, N.J., 1962-64, Beacon Heights Elem Sch., Riverdale, 1964-68; dir. Christian edn. Forest Lake Presbyn. Ch., Columbia, S.C., 1961-62; supr. student tchrs U. Md., College Park, 1968-69; tchr. Norwood Sch., Bethesda, Md., 1975-77; with Ferris and Co. Inc., Bethesda, 1978-88, v.p., 1984-86, sr. v.p., mem. pres.'s coun., chmn.'s coun., 1986-88, also bd. dirs.; sr. v.p. Legg Mason, Inc., Bethesda, 1988—2005, Smith Barney, Bethesda, 2005—. Guest lectr. George Washington U., 1982-83; trustee, tchr. Wharton Sch. Security Industry Inst., Phila., 1986-95, tchr., speaker Bus. Inst. for Educators, Bethesda, 1987-95. Author: Teachers Activity Guide for Dental Health Education, 1973. Trustee, bd. dirs. Holton-Arms Sch., Bethesda, 1985-94; trustee Nat. Econ. Edn. Found., Security Industry Assn., continuing edn. com., chair ethics edn. sub-com.; founding bd. dirs., treas. Leadership Montgomery, Montgomery County, Md.; hon. bd. dirs. Found. for Boys and Girls Homes Md.; bd. dirs. Child Care Connection; trustee, governing bd. Coun. on Econ. Edn. Md. Mem. LWV (corp. bd. Montgomery County), Nat. Adv. Coun., Security Industry Assn. (regional coord. econ. edn., Best Dist. award 1992), Internat. Assn. Fin. Planners. Presbyterian. Avocations: snow and water skiing, sailing, reading, rose gardening. Home: 10215 Gainsborough Rd Potomac MD 20854-4039 Office: Wachovia Securities 600 Wisconsin Ave Ste 100- Bethesda MD 20814 Office Phone: 301-897-3600. E-mail: carolyn.meakem@wachoviasec.com.

MEAL, DOUGLAS H., lawyer; b. Feb. 12, 1955; BA summa cum laude, Univ. Pa., 1976; JD cum laude, Harvard Univ., 1980; MALD, Fletcher Sch. Law & Diplomacy, Tufts Univ., 1981. Bar: Mass. 1980, N.Y. 1983, US Dist. Ct. (Mass., So., Ea., We. & No. N.Y.), US Ct. Appeals (1st, 2d, 4th, 7th, 11th & D.C. cir.). Law clk. Judge Robert J. Ward, US Dist. Ct. So. N.Y., 1980—82; assoc. Ropes & Gray, Boston, 1985—89, ptnr. litigation dept., 1989—, chmn. hiring com. Editor (Notes & Comments): Harvard Internat. Law Jour. Office: Ropes & Gray 1 International Pl Boston MA 02110-2624 Office Phone: 617-951-7517. Office Fax: 617-951-7050. Business E-Mail: douglas.meal@ropesgray.com.

MEAL, LARIE, chemistry professor, researcher, consultant; b. Cin., June 15, 1939; d. George Lawrence Meal and Dorothy Louise (Heileman) Fitzpatrick. BS in Chemistry, U. Cin., 1961, PhD, 1966. Rsch. chemist U.S. Indsl. Chems., Cin., 1966-67; instr. chemistry U. Cin., 1968-69, asst. prof., 1969-75, assoc. prof., 1975-90, prof., 1990—, rschr., 1980—. Cons. in field. Contbr. articles to profl. jours. Mem. AAAS, N.Y. Acad. Scis., Am. Chem. Soc., NOW, Planned Parenthood, Iota Sigma Pi. Democrat. Avocation: gardening. Home: 2231 Slane Ave Norwood OH 45212-3615 Office: U Cin 2220 Victory Pky Cincinnati OH 45206-2822 Home Phone: 513-631-5249; Office Phone: 513-556-4364. Business E-Mail: meall@uc.edu.

MEALIE, CARL A., emergency physician, educator; b. Astoria, NY, Jan. 26, 1948; s. Patrick and Natalie (Previti) M.; m. Maureen Frances Maybury, Apr. 24, 1993; children: David, Ian, Daniel. BA, NYU, 1969; MD, N.Y. Med. Coll., 1974. CCRN. Chmn. Dept. Emergency Medicine St. Mary's Hosp., Roswell, N.Mex., 1975-83; emergency dept. attending physician Guadalupe Med. Ctr., Carlsbad, N.Mex., 1979-83, L.I. Jewish Med. Ctr., New Hyde Park, N.Y., 1993—, chmn. disaster preparation com., 1991—, asst. chief emergency dept., 1989-95, chief clin. ops., 1995; asst. prof. emergency medicine Albert Einstein Coll. Medicine, NYC, 1995. Mem. ambulance adv. bd. Chavez County Med. Soc., Roswell, 1980-83, ambulance bd., 1981-87. Mem. City Roswell EMS Bd., 1981-93. Fellow Am. Coll. Emergency Physicians (key contact 1987—), N.Y. Acad. Medicine; me,. AMA, Am. Acad. Emergency Medicine, N.Y. State Med. Soc., Soc. Acad. Emergency Medicine. Roman Catholic. Avocations: skiing, sailing, hunting, golf. Home: 33 Heights Rd Northport NY 11768-2629 Office: LI Jewish Med Ctr Lakeville New Hyde Park NY 11040 Personal E-mail: carl_mealie@msn.com.

MEALMAN, GLENN, corporate marketing executive; b. Prescott, Kans., June 10, 1934; s. Edgar R. and Mary E. (Holstein) M.; m. Gloria Gail Proch, June 12, 1955; children: Michael Edward, Cathy Gail. BS in Bus., Kans. State Coll., Emporia, 1957; postgrad., Harvard U., 1970. With Fleming Cos., Topeka, 1957—, sr. v.p. mktg., 1981-82, exec. v.p. mktg., 1982-86, exec. v.p. Mid-Am. region, 1986-93, exec. v.p. nat. accts., 1994-96; mng. ptnr. Bus. Solutions Assocs. Dir. PBI-Gordon Co., Furrs Supermarkets. Pres. bd. Topeka YMCA, 1981; trustee Ottawa U., Kans., 1980. Served with USNR, 1954-56. Mem. Kans. State C. of C. and Industry (bd. dirs. 1991—), Blue Hills Country Club, Gainey Ranch Country Club, Rotary, Sigma Phi Epsilon (Kans. chpt.). Presbyterian. Office: PO Box 7448 Shawnee Mission KS 66207-0448

MEAMBER, LAURIE ANN, marketing educator; b. Sacramento, Calif., Aug. 20, 1966; d. Ernest and Holly Meamber. BA, U. Calif., Davis, 1988; MBA, U. Calif., Riverside, 1991; PhD in Mgmt., U. Calif., Irvine, 1997. Mktg. educator George Mason U., Fairfax, Va. Contbr. chapters to books Ethnoconsumerist Methodology for Cultural and Cross-Cultural Research, Art as Life - Life as Art: The Embeddedness of Art in Life and Life in Art in Postmodernity, Cyberspace as the Next Marketing Frontier (?) - Questions and Issues. Fellow Regent's fellow, U. Calif., Irvine, 1991—95, Grad. Sch. Mgmt., U. Calif., Irvine, 1995—96, U. Calif., 1997; Rsch. grant, Sch. Mgmt., George Mason U., 1999—2001, 2003. Mem.: Aesthetics Acad. Network, Assn. Consumer Rsch. (conf. program com. 2000—00), Am. Mktg. Assn. (collegiate chpt. advisor 1999—2004), Beta Gamma Sigma. Avocation: performing arts. Office: George Mason Univ 4400 University Dr Fairfax VA 22030-4444

MEANS, DAVID HAMMOND, retired advertising executive; b. Lebanon, Pa., Dec. 15, 1928; s. W. Horace and June (Zimmerman) M.; m. Nancy N. Downes, June 21, 1952; children: Elizabeth N., Susan Z., Emily M., David H. BA, Amherst Coll., 1950. With CIA, 1950-53, N.W. Ayer Inc., 1953-89, exec. v.p., 1976-89; ret., also bd. dirs. Mng. dir. Ayer U.S.A. and Ayer Enterprises, Inc. Bd. dirs. Waveny Care Ctr., New Canaan Nature Ctr., Schoolhouse Apts., Get About Inc. 1st lt. USAF, 1953. Mem. Bus. Profl. Advt. Assn., Merion (Pa.) Golf Club, Amherst Club (N.Y.C.), Country Club New Canaan (Conn.), Gridiron Club (New Canaan), Sr. Men's Club (New Canaan, bd. dirs.), Psi Upsilon. Episcopalian. Home: Wahackme Ln New Canaan CT 06840 Personal E-mail: davenan28@aol.com.

MEANS, DWIGHT BARDEEN, JR., financial consultant, educator; b. Pitts., July 21, 1943; s. Dwight B. Sr. and Betty (Feick) M.; div.; children: Melissa Means Morris, Blake Elizabeth. BSEE, Carnegie-Mellon U., Pitts., 1965; MBA, U. Pitts., 1969, PhD, 1984. Various positions Bell Telephone Co. Pa., Pitts., 1965-70; asst. prof., dept. chair CC Allegheny County, Pitts., 1970-78; from asst. to assoc. prof. Saginaw Valley State U., Mich., 1978-86; prof., dept. chair Clarion U. Pa., Pa., 1986-88; asst. prof. U. Memphis, 1988-95; adj. prof. numerous univs., 1996—; cons. Pitts., 1995—. Presenter in field. Reviewer Fin. Practice and Edn., Jour. Econs. and Fin., Jour. Real Estate Rsch., Jour. Applied Bus. Rsch; contbr. articles to profl. jours. Mem. Acad. Fin. Svcs. (program com. 1990-95), Am. Econ. Assn., Midsouth Acad. Econs. and Fin. (dir. 1993-95), Fin. Mgmt. Assn. (program com. 1989), Midwest Fin. Assn. (program com. 1995-96), S.W. Fin. Assn. (program com. 1994-95), So. Fin. Assn. (program com. 1992-95). Avocations: hunting, fishing, camping, reading. Home and Office: 138 Owendale Ave Pittsburgh PA 15227-1951 Office Phone: 412-881-0398. Personal E-mail: meansdb@aol.com.

MEANS, ELIZABETH-ROSE THAYER, financial planner, lawyer, writer; b. NYC, Aug. 29, 1960; d. Cyril Chesnut and Rosaline (Limtiuco y Sy-Sung-Song) M. Student, Sch. of Am. Ballet-Lincoln Ctr, NYC, 1970-75, Harvard Coll., 1980, Tufts U., 1981, Fletcher Sch. Law/Diplomacy, 1983-84; BS, Chatham Coll., 1983; cert. in comparative law, Heidelberg U., 1988; JD, Samford U., 1989; LLM in Internat. Banking Law, Boston U., 1990. Bar: Mass. 1991, Pa. 1991; cert. for piloting, seamanship and small boat handling USCG Aux. Dancer The NYC Ballet Co., 1970—71, Balanchine Cast for PBS The Nutcracker Suite, NYC, 1970—71; docent The Hammond Castle Mus., Gloucester, Mass., 1982-85; asst. mgr. The Gallery, Rockport, Mass., 1977-83; cons. The Galleries, Ltd., Wellesley, Mass., 1988; legal intern U. Ala. Health Svcs. Found., Birmingham, 1988-89; loan officer UN/UNFCU, NYC, 1984-86; overnight counselor Germaine Lawrence Sch., Arlington, Mass, 1989-90; contracts mgr. for Eastern Region Unisys Corp.; Berkeley Heights, NJ, 1990-92; fin. cons. Innovatech, Lexington, Mass., 1992-93, 94-95; contract analyst Guy Carpenter & Co., Inc., NYC, 1994; gen. counsel Mojo Working Prodns., NYC, 1996. Chair Cordell Hull Speakers' Forum, Birmingham, 1988-89; alumnae class sec. Chatham Coll. Class of 1980s, Pitts., 1983-87, 97—. Clk. of vestry The Ch. of the Resurrection, NYC, 1993-95, mem. vestry, 1995-97, acolyte, 1970s, Sunday sch. tchr., 1970s; overnight counselor The Germaine Lawrence Sch., Arlington, Mass., 1989-90; mem. ladies' altar guild The Ch. of Advent, Westbury, NY, 2006—. Recipient Cert. of Appreciation 1990 Alumni award Cumberland Sch. Law, 1990; named to Nat. Dean's List, 1989-90. Mem. DAR (Cape Ann chpt. const. week chair 1993-94, Mass. const. week chair 1995-97, NYC chpt. jr. com. mem. Sons and Daus. Gala Ball 1996), The Federalist Soc. (Cumberland chpt. treas. 1988-89, adv. bd. 1983, sec. 1987-88), Clan Menzies Soc. N.Am., Clan Menzies Soc. Scotland, Thayer Families Assn., Daus. Union Vets. of Civil War 1861-65: Hudson Valley-NY Metro Tent, Mass. Soc. Mayflower Descs., Baronial Order Magna Charta, Dames of Ct. of Honor, Nat. Soc. Magna Charta Dames and Barons, Nat. Soc. Col. Daus. Seventeenth Century (Rensselaerswyck chpt.), Nat. Soc. First Families of Minn., Soc. of the Friends of St. George's and Descs. of Knights of the Garter, Soc. of Desc. of Knights of the Most Noble Order of the Garter, Hugnenot Soc. Am., Order of Wash., NY State Continental Soc. Daus. of Indian Wars 1607-1900, St. Georges Soc. NY, First Families Ohio, Colonial Order the Crown, The Sovereign Colonial Soc. Ams. of Royal Descent, The Plantagenet Soc., Nat. Soc. Descs. of Early Quakers, Nat. Soc. Colonial Daus. of the 17th Century. Libertarian-Republican. Episcopalian. Avocations: lobstering, sailing, fishing, swimming, bicycling.

MEANS, JAMES ANDREW, retired engineer; b. Heavener, Okla., Oct. 11, 1937; s. Edward Andrew and Lorena (Nobles) M.; Therese Louise

Zimmermann, Feb. 21, 1959; children: James A. Jr., William R., Charles E., Vicky M. BSEE, U. Ariz., 1962, MSEE, 1966; PhD, U. Calif., Santa Barbara, 1972; MS in Computer Sci., Chapman U., Orange, Calif., 1988. Engr. Pacific Missile Test Ctr., Pt Mugu, Calif., 1962-72, engr. mgr., 1972-79; tech. dir. Space and Missile Test Orgn., Vandenberg AFB, Calif., 1979-89; sr. tech. advisor SRI Internat., Menlo Park, Calif., 1990—2006. Cons. Agri-Craft, Camarillo, Calif., 1968-70, Astro-Geo-Marine, Ventura, Calif., 1972-74; pres. Internat. Found. for Telemetering, 1989-95. Patentee in field. Recipient Allen R. Matthews award, Internat. Test and Evaluation Assn., 1991, Pioneer award, Internat. Found. Telemetering, 2006. Democrat. Baptist. Avocations: water-skiing, fishing, hunting, old cars. Home: 284 St Andrews Way Lompoc CA 93436-1355 Personal E-mail: jim_means@verizon.net.

MEANS, JOHN BARKLEY, director, language educator; b. Cin., Jan. 2, 1939; s. Walker Wilson and Rosetta Barkley (Miller) Means. BA, U. Ill., 1960, MA, 1963, PhD, 1968. U.S. govt. intelligence rsch. analyst on Brazil CIA, Washington, 1962-64; assoc. prof. Spanish and Portugese Temple U., Phila., 1972-82, prof. Portuguese and critical langs., 1982—2003, prof. emeritus, 2003—, co-chmn. dept. Spanish and Portuguese, 1971-75, dir. dept. critical langs., 1975—2003, dir. Inst. for Langs. and Internat. Studies, 1987—2003, chmn. dept. Germanic and Slavic Langs. and lit., 1992-94, chair univ. core programs, 1995-97. Portugese lang. examiner U.S. Peace Corps, Brazil, 1967—68; cons. on Brazilian-Portuguese and second lang. acquisition and self instrnl. programs for less commonly taught langs., 1968—2003; cons. editor for langs. Norton Pubs., 1979—95; cons. in field. Editor: Essays on Brazilian Literature, 1971; author (with others): Language in Education: Theory and Practice, 1988—; editor: NASILP Manual, 1996; co-dir. CD-ROM Critical Language Series, 1999—; contbr. articles to profl. jours. Trustee Bristol Riverside Theatre, Pa., 1990—2002, 2005—; mng. trustee Means Charitable Trust, 1993—2004. 1st lt. US Army, 1960—62. Fellow, U. Ill., 1966—68; grantee, U.S. Dept. Edn., 1979—83, Japan Found., 1980, 1982, 1989—91, ARCO Chem. Found., 1991, 1993; NDEA fellow, 1962, 1964. Mem.: AAUP, MLA, Joint Nat. Com. for Langs. (bd. dirs.), Nat. Assn. State Univs. and Lang Grant Colls. (commn. on internat. affairs), Nat. Coun. Orgns. Less Commonly Taught Langs. (exec. sec.-treas. 1990—2001), Am. Coun. on Tchg. Fgn. Lang., Nat. Assn. Self-Instrnl. Lang. Programs (exec. dir. 1977—98, editor jour. 1978—94, exec. dir. emeritus 1999—), Nat. Coun. on Langs. and Internat. Studies (bd. dirs.), Sigma Delta Pi, Phi Lambda Beta, Pi Kappa Phi. Home: PO Box 829 Washington Crossing PA 18977-0829 Office: Temple U Dept Critical Langs Anderson Hall 1114 W Berks St Philadelphia PA 19122-6090 Business E-Mail: means@temple.edu.

MEANS, MARIANNE, columnist; b. Sioux City, Iowa, June 13, 1934; d. Ernest Maynard and Else Marie Johanne (Andersen) Hansen; m. Warren Weaver, Jr. (dec.); m. James J. Kilpatrick. BA, U. Nebr., 1956; JD, George Washington U., 1977. Copy editor Lincoln (Nebr.) Jour., 1955-57; woman's editor No. Va. Sun, Arlington, 1957-59; Washington bur. corr. Hearst Newspapers, 1959-61, White House corr., 1961-65; polit. columnist Hearst Newspapers and King Features Syndicate, 1965—, N.Y. Times News Svc., 1994—; commentator Spectrum CBS radio, Mut. Broadcasting Network, Voice of Am., U.S.I.A. World Network, Post Newsweek Stas., Nat. Pub. Radio. Author: The Woman in the White House, 1963. Recipient Front Page award N.Y. Newspaper Women, 1962; Tex. Headliners award, 1976, Hall of Fame-Sigma Delta Chi, 1988. Mem.: Internat. Women's Media Found. (bd. dirs.), Nat. Press Found. (chmn.), White House Corrs. Assn., Nat. Press Club, Cosmos Club, Gridiron Club (pres.), Sigma Delta Chi (Hall of Fame), Phi Beta Kappa, Delta Delta Delta. Office Phone: 202-263-6415.

MEANS, MICHAEL DAVID, hospital administrator; b. Lakeland, Fla., Jan. 19, 1950; married. B, U. Fla., 1971, MHA, 1974. Adminstrv. resident Manatee Meml. Hosp., Bradenton, Fla., 1974, adminstrv. asst., 1974-78; asst. dir. Orlando (Fla.) Regional Med. Ctr., 1978-80, assoc. exec. dir., 1980-81, exec. v.p., chief oper. officer, 1981-88; pres., chief exec. officer Holmes Regional Healthcare System, Melbourne, Fla., 1988—, Health First, Melbourne, Fla. Mem. Fla. Hosp. Assn. Office: Health First 6450 US Highway 1 Rockledge FL 32955-5747

MEANS, ROBERT TAYLOR, JR., hematologist, educator, researcher; b. Midland, Tex., July 14, 1957; s. Robert Taylor and Anna Therese (Cassidy) M.; m. Stacey W. McKenzie, May 23, 1992; children: Anna, Robert III, Patrick. BA in Biochemistry, Rice U., Houston, 1979; MD, Vanderbilt U., Nashville, 1983. Diplomate Am. Bd. Internal Medicine; cert. in hematology. Resident Baylor Coll. Medicine, Houston, 1983-86; fellow in hematology Vanderbilt U., Nashville, 1986-88, instr. medicine, 1988-90, asst. prof. medicine, 1990-92; assoc. investigator VA Med. Ctr., Nashville, 1988-91, asst. chief hematology/oncology Cin., 1992-98; assoc. prof. med. U. Cin., 1992-98; prof. med., head hematology, assoc. divsn. chief Med. U. S.C., 1998-2000, dir. divsn. hematology-oncology, 2000—04; chief hematology/oncology VA Med. Ctr., Charleston, SC, 1998—2004, prof. internal medicine, 2004—, chief med. svc. Lexington, Ky., 2004—06; prof. internal medicine U. Ky., 2004—, assoc. chair for rsch., internal medicine, 2004—, interim assoc. dean, 2004—06. Interim dir. Markey Cancer Ctr., 2006—. Editor (assoc.) Jour. Investigative Medicine; mem. editl. bd. Internat. Jour. Hematology, Am. Jour. Med. Sci., Winthrobe's Clinical Hemotology, 12th edit.; contbr. chpts. to books, articles to profl. jours. Recipient Career Devel. award Dept. Veterans Affairs., 1988, Henry Christian award Am. Fedn. Clin. Rsch., 1991, Chief Resident's Faculty of Yr. award, U. Ky., 2006. Fellow Am. Coll. Physicians; mem. Am. Soc. Hematology, Internat. Soc. Exptl. Hematology, Am. Fed. Med. Rsch. (v.p. mtgs., programs, 1998-2002), Southern Soc. Clin. Investigation (councillor, 2005-), Phi Beta Kappa. Achievements include being first to report response of anemia of chronic disease to erythropoietin; first description of erythropoietin receptor in polycythemia. Home: 2204 Abbeywood Rd Lexington KY 40515 Office: U Ky Markey Cancer Ctr Rm CC455 800 Rose St Lexington KY 40536 Home Phone: 859-971-8184; Office Phone: 859-323-6556. Business E-Mail: robert.means@uky.edu.

MEANS, TERRY ROBERT, federal judge; b. Roswell, N.Mex., July 3, 1948; s. Lewis Prude and Doris Emaree (Hightower) M.; m. JoAnn Huffman Harris, June 2, 1973; children: Robert, MaryAnn, Emily. BA, So. Meth. U., 1971, JD, 1974. Bar: Tex. 1974, U.S. Dist. Ct. (no. dist.) Tex. 1976, U.S. Ct. Appeals (5th cir.) 1978, U.S. Dist. Ct. (we. dist., ea. dist.) Tex. 1991. Ptnr. Means & Means, Corsicana, Tex., 1974-88; Presdl. elector, 1980; justice 10th Ct. Appeals, Waco, Tex., 1989-90; judge U.S. Dist. Ct. (no. dist.) Tex., Ft. Worth, 1991—. Chmn. Navarro County Rep. Party, Corsicana, 1976-88; pres. YMCA, Corsicana, 1984, Ft. Worth Youth Soccer Assn., 1996-97. Recipient Disting. Alumni award for jud. svc. So. Meth. U., 2006. Mem. State Bar Tex., Tarrant County Bar Assn. (Silver Gavel award 2006). Baptist. Avocations: coaching soccer, racquetball. Office: 201 US Courthouse 501 W 10th St Fort Worth TX 76102-3637

MEANS, THOMAS CORNELL, lawyer; b. Charleston, SC, Oct. 3, 1947; s. Thomas Lucas and Dean (Cornell) M.; m. Judith Faye Perlmutter, Sept. 10, 1977; children: Benjamin, Samuel. AB, Dartmouth Coll., 1969; postgrad., Princeton Theol. Sem., 1970-71; M of Pub. Adminstrn., U. Colo., 1975; JD, George Washington U., 1978. Bar: D.C. 1978, U.S. dist. ct. (D.C. dist.), U.S. Ct. Appeals (4th and D.C. cirs.) 1979, U.S. Ct. Appeals (10th cir.) 1983, U.S. Ct. Appeals (6th and 11th cirs.) 1989, U.S. Ct. Appeals (9th cir.) 1992, U.S. Ct. Appeals (8th cir.) 1993, U.S. Ct. Appeals (5th cir.) 1996. Social worker Vinyard Childcare, Ann Arbor, Mich., 1969-70; rsch. analyst, registered lobbyist Colo. Counties, Inc., Denver, 1972-75; assoc. Jones, Day, Reavis and Pogue, Washington, 1978-79; assoc. then ptnr. Crowell & Moring LLP, Washington, 1979—. Mem. state adv. coun. on pub. Pers. Mgmt., Colo. State Govt., Denver, 1974-75; lectr. mining law; chmn. coal com. Energy and Mineral Law Found., 1988-89, chmn. spl. insts., ass. sec., 1989-91, sec., 1991-92, v.p., 1992-93, pres., 1993-94, exec. com., 1989-96, trustee, 1989—, mem. bd. editors, 1994—; bd. advisors Nat. Law Ctr., 1993-94, adv. bd. W. Va. Law Review on Nat. Coal Issues, 2004—. Contbr. articles to profl. jours. Named Best Lawyers in Am., 2006—07; recipient Pres.' award, Energy and Mineral Law Found., 2002, Daniel Levy award, Nat. Immigration Project, 2004, John L. McClaugherty award, Energy & Mineral Law Found., 2005. Mem. George Washington Law Alumni Assn. (bd. dirs. 1986-96, exec. com. 1987-96, treas. 1987-88, sec. 1988-90, pres. 1992-94), Order of Coif, Cosmos Club (Washington), Phi Beta Kappa. Home: 6411 Dahlonega Rd Bethesda MD 20816-2101 Office: Crowell & Moring LLP 1001 Pennsylvania Ave NW Fl 10 Washington DC 20004-2595 Home Phone: 301-229-1702; Office Phone: 202-624-2735.

MEANY, PHILIP AUGUSTUS, retired library director; b. Oakland, Calif., Oct. 20, 1938; s. John Philip and Mary Gertrude (Deasy) M. BA, St. Mary's Coll., Moraga, Calif., 1960; M Librarianship, U. Wash., 1963. Asst. libr. Centralia (Wash.) Coll., 1963-68, media svcs. and tech. processes libr., 1969-88, libr. dir., 1988—2002; ret., 2002. Mem. Wash. State Bicycling Adv. Com., Olympia, 1990-99; pres. Destination Centralia Mktg. Assn., 1999-2001. Recipient Platinum Pedal, N.W. Bicycle Fedn., 1997. Mem. Coll. Librs. and Media Specialists Wash. State (pres. 1987-88), N.W. Mgmt. Ednl. Tech. Assn. Avocation: bicycling.

MEARA, ANNE, actress, playwright, writer; b. Bklyn., Sept. 20; d. Edward Joseph and Mary (Dempsey) M.; m. Gerald Stiller, Sept. 14, 1954; children: Amy, Benjamin. Student, Herbert Berghoff Studio, 1953-54. Apprentice in summer stock, Southold, L.I. and Woodstock, N.Y., 1950-53; off-Broadway appearances include A Month in the Country, 1954, Maedchen in Uniform, 1955 (Show Bus. off-Broadway award), Ulysses in Nightown, 1958, The House of Blue Leaves, 1970, Bosoms and Neglect, 1986, After-Play, 1996; Shakespeare Co., Two Gentlemen of Verona, Ctrl. Park, N.Y.C., 1957, Romeo and Juliet, 1988; Broadway plays: Spookhouse, 1982, Eastern Standard, 1989, Anna Christie, 1993 (Tony nomination Best Supporting Actress); film appearances include The Out-of-Towners, 1968, Lovers and Other Strangers, 1969, The Boys From Brazil, 1978, Fame, 1979, Nasty Habits (with husband Jerry Stiller), 1976, An Open Window, 1990, Mia, 1990, Awakenings, 1991, Reality Bites, 1994, Daytrippers, 1997, The Fish in the Bathtub, 1998, Southie, 1999, The Independent, 2001, Like Mike, 2002, comedy act, 1963—; appearances Happy Medium and Medium Rare, Chgo., 1960-61, Village Gate, Phase Two and Blue Angel, N.Y.C., 1963, The Establishment, London, 1963, QE II, 1990; syndicated TV series Take Five with Stiller and Meara, 1977-78; numerous appearances on TV game and talk shows, also spls. and variety shows; rec. numerous commls. for TV and radio (co-recipient Voice of Imagery award Advt. Bur. N.Y.); star TV series Kate McShane, 1975, Archie Bunker's Place, 1979, Alf, 1986-88; other TV appearances The Sunset Gang, 1990, Avenue Z Afternoon, 1991, Murphy Brown, 1994, Homicide, 1996 (Emmy nomination), Will and Grace, 2002, Sex in the City, 2002-04, The King of Queens, 2003-05, Good Morning Miami, 2003; (TV movie) Jitters, 1997, All My Children, 1994-99, (TV movie) What Makes a Family, 2001; writer, actress TV movie The Other Woman, 1983 (co-recipient Writer's Guild Outstanding Achievement award 1983), Alf, To Make Up to Break Up, The Stiller and Meara pilot; author, actor (play) After-Play, 1996; author (play) Down the Garden Paths, 2000; video host (with Jerry Stiller) So You Want to Be an Actor? Recipient Outer Critic's Cir. Playwriting award for After-Play, 1995, 4th ann. Alan King award in Jewish Humor, 2003, Productive Aging award Jewish Coun. Aging, 2004, Thalia award (w/ Jerry Stiller) Humbert Coll. Toronto; received joint star with husband on the Hollywood Walk of Fame, 2007.

MEARS, CAROLYN LUNSFORD, education educator; b. Hampton, Va., Sept. 17, 1947; d. John Blackwell and Myrtle Louise (Marshall) Lunsford; m. Connally E. Mears, Feb. 27, 1971; children: Brian Connally, Austin Douglas. B, Ea. Ky. U., Richmond, 1969; M, U. Ky., Lexington, 1971; D, U. Denver, 2005. Curriculum assessment Denver Pub. Schs., 1985—95; program coord. goals Sheridan Pub. Schs., Colo., 1995—97; progra, coord. grants, tchr. edn. program U. Denver, 2000—, faculty coll. engring., 2005—. Contbr. articles to profl. jours. Guest spkr. Colo. Victims Assn., 2005—06; vol., counselor Boy Scouts Am., Colo., 1994—2001. Mem.: Am. Oral History Assn., Am. Edn. Rsch. Assn., Internat. Oral History Assn., Phi Delta Kappa. Office: U Denver Coll Edn 2135 E Wesley Ave Denver CO 80208

MEARS, CASEY, race car driver; b. Bakersfield, Calif., Mar. 12, 1978; s. Roger Mears. Profl. race car driver NASCAR, 2002—. Achievements include winner Jim Russell USAC Triple Crown Championship, 2005; finished second Daytona 500, 2006. Office: c/o NASCAR 1801 Internat Speedway Blvd Daytona Beach FL 32115

MEARS, MICHELLE MORGAN, archivist; b. Austin; BA in Art History, U. Tex., Austin, 1977, M in Libr. and Info. Sci., 1991; MA in History, Baylor U., Waco, 2001. Archives intern Tex. Sch. for the Deaf, Austin, 1990; archivist Scott White Meml. Hosp., Temple, Tex., 1991—99; libr., records adminstr. Tex. Hist. Commn., Austin, 1999—2004; sr. libr., archivist U. Tex., MD Anderson Cancer Ctr., Houston, 2004—06; archivist U. N. Tex., Denton, 2006—. Chmn. Bell County Hist. Commn., 1997—99; mem. Denton County Hist. Com., 2006—. Mem.: Tex. Oral History Assn. (pres. 1997), Soc. SW Archivists, Soc. Am. Archivists. Office: U N Tex U Archives Willis Libr PO Box 305190 Denton TX 76203 Business E-Mail: mmears@library.unt.edu.

MEARS, PATRICK EDWARD, lawyer; b. Oct. 3, 1951; s. Edward Patrick and Estelle Veronica (Mislik) M.; m. Geraldine O'Connor, July 18, 1981. BA, U. Mich., 1973, JD, 1976. Bar: N.Y. 1977, Ill. 1996, U.S. Dist Ct. (so. and ea. dists) N.Y. 1977, Mich. 1980, U.S. Dist. Ct. (we. and ea. dists.) Mich. 1980, U.S. Ct. Appeals (6th cir.) 1983, Ill. 1996, U.S. Dist. Ct. (no. dist.) Ill. 1998. Assoc. Milbank, Tweed, Hadley & McCloy, NYC, 1976-79; ptnr. Warner, Norcross & Judd, Grand Rapids, Mich., 1980-91; sr. mem. Dykema Gossett PLLC, Grand Rapids, 1991—2002; equity mem. Dickinson Wright, PLLC, Grand Rapids, 2002—04; equity ptnr. Barnes & Thornburg LLP, 2004—. Adj. prof. Grand Valley State U., Allendale, Mich., 1981-84; dir. Children's Law Ctr., 1994, Grand Rapids Ballet, 1994-99, East Grand Rapids Pub. Sch. Found., 1994-98. Author: Michigan Collection Law, 1981, 2d edit., 1983, Basic Bankruptcy Law, 1986, Bankruptcy Law and Practice in Michigan, 1987, 1995, Revised Article 9 of the UCC in Michigan, 2001; co-author: Strategies for Secured Creditors in workouts and Foreclosures, 2004; contbg. author Collier Bankruptcy Practice Guide; contbr. articles to profl. jours.; editor: Jour. of the Hist. Soc. of the U.S. Dist. Ct. for the Western Dist. of Mich., 2003—. Chmn. legis. com. East Grand Rapids PTA, Mich., 1992—94; bd. dir. Grand Rapids Sister Cities Internat., 2004—06, sec., 2004—06. Fellow: Mich. State Bar Found. (sec. coun. real property sect. 1993—97, chair Uniform Comml. Code com. bus. law sect. 2000—), Am. Coll. Bankruptcy; mem.: ABA (chmn. workouts, bankruptcy and foreclosures 2002—04, vice chair real estate financing group 2004—06, chair real estate financing group 2006—), Fed. Bar Assn. (chmn. bankruptcy sect. We. Mich. chpt. 1992—94, newsletter editor 1998—2002, pres. 2001—02), Am. Law Inst., Am. Bankruptcy Inst., Mich. State Bar Assn., East Hills Athletic Club. Office: Barnes & Thornburg LLP 300 Ottawa Ave NW Ste 500 Grand Rapids MI 49503 Office Phone: 616-742-3936. Business E-Mail: pmears@btlaw.com.

MEARS, WALTER ROBERT, retired journalist; b. Lynn, Mass., Jan. 11, 1935; s. Edward Lewis and Edythe Emily (Campbell) M.; m. Sally Danton, Dec. 28, 1956 (dec. Dec. 1962); children: Pamela (dec.), Walter Robert Jr. (dec.); m. Joyce Marie Lund, Aug. 4, 1963 (div. 1983); children: Stephanie Joy, Susan Marie; m. Carroll Ann Rambo, Mar. 1, 1986 (div. 1995); m. Frances R. Richarson, July 5, 1997. BA, Middlebury Coll., 1956, LittD (hon.), 1977. Newsman AP, Boston, 1956, corr. Montpelier, Vt., 1956-60, state house corr. Boston, 1960-61, newsman Washington, 1961-69, chief polit. writer, 1969-72, asst. chief Washington bur., 1973-74, spl. corr., 1975, chief, 1977-83, v.p., 1978-2001, exec. editor, 1984-88, v.p., columnist, 1989-2001. Author: (with John Chancellor) The News Business, 1983, The New News Business, 1995, Deadlines Past, 2003. Trustee Middlebury Coll., 1980-84. Recipient ann. award AP Mng. Editors Assn., 1973; Pulitzer prize for Nat. Reporting, 1977. Mem.: Govs. Club, Burning Tree Club, Gridiron Club, Delta Kappa Epsilon, Phi Beta Kappa.

MEATH, JAMES V., lawyer; b. Norfolk, Va., May 26, 1948; BA, Old Dominion U., 1971; MUA, Va. Polytechnic Inst. and State U., 1974; JD, U. Richmond, 1979. Bar: Va. 1979, D.C. 1985. Atty. Williams Mullen, Richmond, Va., vice chmn. bd. dirs., regional head Richmond, Charlottesville, chmn. labor and employment sect. Adj. prof. labor law U. Richmond, mem. bd. assocs., 1998—, mem. dean's adv. coun., 1997—. Co-editor: Virginia Employment Law Letter, 1990—2002; contbr. articles to profl. jours. Bd. dirs. Richmond Soc. Prevention of Cruelty to Animals. Named Number One Employment Defendant Atty in Va., Chambers USA; named one of Legal Elite, Va. Bus. Mag.; fellow, Coll. Labor and Employment Lawyers. Mem.: ABA (mem. developing labor law com., mem. alternate dispute com.), Am. Arbitration Assn. (large complex case panel arbitrator 1985—, comml. panel arbitrator, employment panel arbitrator), D.C. Bar Assn., Va. Bar Assn. (chmn. labor rels. and employment sect. 1995—97, mem. exec. com. 2002—, chmn., bd. govs. 2003, pres.-elect 2004, pres. 2005—). Office: Williams Mullen Two James Ctr 1021 E Cary St Richmond VA 23219 also: Williams Mullen PO Box 1320 Richmond VA 23218-1320 Home Phone: 804-783-6507; Office Phone: 804-783-6507. E-mail: jmeath@williamsmullen.com. *

MEAUX, ALAN DOUGLAS, retired computer technician, artist; b. Joliet, Ill., Sept. 10, 1951; s. Berry Lee and Luella Ann (Ferguson) M.; m. Letta Sue Nygaard, Sept. 15, 1984; children: Ashley Nicole, Lacey Marie. Student, Joliet Jr. Coll., 1969-71, Bradley U., 1971-72, U.S. Dept. Agr. Grad. Sch., 1972, Skagit Valley Coll., 1983-85. Cert. specialist water distbn. Wash. state, 2002, Wash. state, 2003. Photographer J.J.C. Blazer, Joliet Herald News, Joliet, 1969-71; auto mechanic Pohanka Olds and Fiat, Hillcrest Heights, Md., 1972-74, Hoffman Olds and Rolls Royce, Hartford, Conn., 1974-75; carpenter Klappenbach Constrn. Co., Moscow, Idaho, 1975-79; property mgr. Olympic Builders, Oak Harbor, Wash., 1979-86; maintenance technician Troubleshooters Inc., Oak Harbor, 1986-87; facilities technician Island County Govt., Coupeville, Wash., 1987—. Chmn. safety com. Island County Govt., 1997, 98, 99, 2000, 03; bronze sculptor Ronin Art Prodns., Oak Harbor, 1979—; appraiser class A Mid-Am. Appraisers Assn., Springfield, Mo., 1986—; bd. dirs. North West Token Kai, U. Wash., Seattle, 1989—, lectr., 1985; contbr. Nanka Token Kai, L.A., 1985-. Author: Japanese Samurai Weapons, 1989; prin. works exhibited at Mini Guild Children's Orthopedic Show, Ballard, Wash., 1986, Worldfest/Ethnic Heritage Coun., Seattle, 1988, 89, 90, Stanwood (Wash.) Invitational Art Show, 1988. Asst. coach Whidbey Islanders Soccer League, 1997-99; safety com. chmn. Island County Govt., 1998-2003. Mem. NRA (life), Law Enforcement Alliance Am. (life), Japanese Sword Soc. U.S. (life), N.W. Token Kai (charter, bd. dirs. 1989-91), Western Mus. Conf., Wash. Mus. Assn., Ethnic Heritage Coun., Nanka Token Kai, Japan Soc., Wash. Arms Collectors Assn., North Whidbey Sportmen's Assn. (chmn. range com., trustee), Leisure Acres Water Assn. (pres. 1998-2000), Internat. Defensive Pistol Assn., Ctrl. Whidbey Sportmen's Club, Whidbey Islanders Futbol Club (asst. coach for girls under 12, 1997-99). Avocations: hunting, fishing, woodworking, reading, collecting Japanese antiques. Office: Ronin Art Prodns 1287 E Hideaway Ln Oak Harbor WA 98277

MEBANE, JULIE S., lawyer; b. San Antonio, Mar. 13, 1957; d. John Cummins and Mildred (Hill) Mebane; m. Kenneth Jerome Stipanov, Jan. 21, 1984; children: Thomas Kenneth Stipanov, Kristen Hill Stipanov. BA in Polit. Sci., UCLA, 1978, JD, 1981. Bar: Calif. 1981, U.S. Dist. Ct. (so. dist.) Calif. 1981. Assoc. Gray, Cary, Ames & Frye, San Diego, 1981-85, Sheppard, Mullin, Richter & Hampton, San Diego, 1986-90; ptnr. Scalone, Stipanov, Yaffa & Mebane, San Diego, 1990-94, Stipanov & Mebane, San Diego, 1994—2004, Duane Morris LLP, San Diego, 2005—. Panelist Calif. Continuing Edn. Bar, 2000—01, Lorman Edn. Svcs., 2006—07. Bd. dirs. Episcopal Diocese San Diego, 1992—95, Francis Parker Sch., 2003—. Mem.: San Diego Lawyers Club, San Diego County Bar Assn., ABA, Nat. Assn. Women Bus. Owners (bd. dirs. San Diego chpt. 1996—97), UCLA Alumni Assn. (gen. counsel, bd. dirs. 1992—96), Phi Beta Kappa, Kappa Alpha Theta. Avocations: sports, travel. Office: Duane Morris LLP 101 W Broadway Ste 900 San Diego CA 92101-3544 Office Phone: 619-744-2211. Business E-Mail: jmebane@duanemorris.com.

MEBANE, WILLIAM BLACK, controller, financial consultant; b. Vernon, Tex., Dec. 15, 1927; s. David Mitchell and Ida Virginia (Black) M.; m. Joan Hebbard Dumper, Nov. 24, 1956; children— David Alexander, Virginia Ann. BBA, Tex. A&M U., 1952; MBA, Harvard U., 1954. Mem. treas.'s office staff Gen. Motors Corp., NYC, 1954-70; sec.-treas. Alfred P. Sloan Found., NYC, 1971-78; dir. fin. and adminstrn. Am. Diabetes Assn., NYC, 1979-80, dir. planning, 1981; v.p., comptroller NCCJ, Inc., NYC, 1981-86, v.p. for fiscal affairs, 1987-88; fin. cons. Internat. House, NYC, 1989-90; ind. fin. cons., 1990-91; contr. Better Bus. Bur., NYC, 1991-99. Vol. Essex Council Boy Scouts Am., 1967—. Served with USAAF, 1946-49. Recipient Silver Beaver award Boy Scouts Am., 1982 Mem.: Harvard Bus. Sch. (N.Y.C.); Short Hills (N.J.). Republican. Episcopalian. Home: 36 Haddonfield Rd Short Hills NJ 07078-3402

MEBANE, WILLIAM DEBERNIERE, newspaper publisher; b. Durham, NC, Jan. 14, 1949; s. John Gilmer and Harriet deBerniere (Elmore) M.; m. Catharine Frampton McGee, May 30, 1970; children— William deBerniere, Harriet Bacot, Jane Bacot, Catharine Frampton, John McGee, Beverly Canby BA, U. N.C., 1971, cert. in exec. program, 1981. V.p. Greenville News-Piedmont, S.C., 1976-82, bus. mgr. S.C., 1976-78, gen. mgr. S.C., 1978-81, co-pub. S.C., 1981-84, pres. S.C., 1982—, pub. S.C., 1984-92, 97-99; v.p. Multimedia Newspaper Co., Greenville, 1984-92, pres., 1989-95; v.p. Multimedia Inc., 1989-95; sr. group pres., newspaper divsn. Gannett Co. Inc., Gannett newspaper operating com., 1995-99; pres. Crescent Pub. LLC, 1999—. Commr. SC Mental Retardation Commn., 1983-89, vice chmn., 1988; past pres. Greenville Symphony Assn.; campaign chmn. United Way Greenville County, 1984, v.p. resource devel., 1985, v.p. mktg. and comms., 1986, 1st v.p., 1987, pres., 1988; treas. Goodwill Industries Upper SC, 1980-81; past pres. Greenville Assn. Retarded Children; mem. First Amendment Congress Bd., 1987-88, NC Soc. Cin., Corp. Coalition Infant Mortality, 1988; bd. dirs. Greenville Hosp. System, 1993-99, chmn. 1999; communicant Christ Episcopal Ch., vestry, 2003-05. Mem. AP (com. 1985—, nominating com. 1991—, chmn. 1992-95), Am. Newspaper Pubs. Assn. (com. 1982—), So. Newspaper Pubs. Assn. (treas. 1990, chmn. com. 1983-84, pres. 1992, chmn. 1993, found. treas. 1996-99), Urban League of Upstate (chair 2006), So. Govs. Assn., SC Press Assn. (treas. 1984-85, v.p. dailies 1986, pres. 1987), Young Pres.'s Orgn., Huguenot Soc., Anglican Compass Rose Soc., Telecom. Commn. Anglican Commmunion, Greenville C. of C. (bd. dirs., v.p. 1981-82, bd. dirs. 1987-88), Poinsett Club, Delta Kappa Epsilon. Avocation: outdoor activities. Home: 119 Crescent Ave Greenville SC 29605-2812 Office: Crescent Pub LLC 109 Laurens Rd Ste 4-C Greenville SC 29607-1860 Office Phone: 864-250-4446. Business E-Mail: bmebane@crescentsc.com.

MECCIA, FRANCIS (FRANK) ANTHONY, physician assistant; s. Aniello J. and Marie Celeste Meccia. AA, Kendall Coll., 1976; BS, Columbus Univ., 1998; MS, Trinity So. U., 2000; cert. physician asst., Cook County Hosp., 1989. Cert. advance cardiac life support. Enlisted U.S. Army, 1976, advanced through ranks to staff sgt., 1985, sr. med. aidmen Spangdahlem, Germany, 1976-80, sr. med. advisor Hdqrs. 2d Inf. White House Washington, 1980-83, med. recruiter Ft. Sheridan, Ill., 1983-87, ret., 1987; physician asst. Montefiore Med. Ctr., Bronx, NY, 1989-91; cardio-vasc. physician asst. Murphy Otto and Assocs., Evanston, Ill., 1991-98; sr. physician asst. for cardiovasc. svcs. Resurrection Hosp., Chgo., 1998—; staff physician asst. Our Lady of the Resurrection Med. Ctr., Chgo., 2001—; staff physician asst. for cardiovasc. surgery St. Francis Hosp., Evanston, Ill., 2001—. Preceptor U. Health Scis., Chgo. Med. Sch., North Chgo., 1993-94, Cook County Hosp. Physician Asst. Program, Chgo., preceptor 1993—; bd. trustees Alexian Bros. Bonaventure Ho., Chgo., 2005—. Decorated Meritorious Svc. medal USAR, Washington, 1992, Army Commendation medal with oak leaf cluster, 1997; recipient The David award Allied Health Pers., Chgo., 1993. Mem. Am. Assn. Physician Assts. (cert., editor/treas. AAPA caucus GLPA 2003—), Am. Assn. Physician Assts. Surgery, Am. Heart Assn. (cert. advance trauma life support), Assn. Physician Assts. Cardiovasc. Surgery, Ill. Acad. Physician Assts. Avocations: scuba diving, sky diving, skiing. Home: 6219 W Cornelia Ave Chicago IL 60634-4120 Office: Resurrection Hosp 7435 W Talcott Ave Ste 1 Chicago IL 60631-3746 Office Phone: 773-792-7942. E-mail: frank1906@aol.com.

MECCIA, NEIL ROCCO, health facility administrator, physician; b. Evanston, Ill., July 3, 1954; s. Aniello Joseph and Marie Celeste (Fischerelli) Meccia. BA, Northwestern U., 1976; MA, No. Ill. U., 1978; MPA, U. So. Calif., 1980, PhD, 1988; D of Naprapathy, Nat. Coll. Naprapathic Medicine, 2001; D of Naturopathy, Naprapathic Acad. Sci. and Rsch., Chgo., 2004. Diplomate Am. Coll. Healthcare Execs., bd. credentialied Am. Acad. Med. Adminstrs. Advanced through ranks to lt. col. USAF, 1988—; patient squadron comdr. USAF Med. Ctr., Wright Patterson AFB, Ohio, 1988—90, dep. dir. patient adminstrn., 1988—90, assoc. adminstr. hosp. svcs., 1990—91; command tng. mgr. med. scis. HQ AFMC, Wright Patterson AFB, 1991—95; assoc. to dir. managed care integration Dept. of Def. Health Svc. Region 5, Wright Patterson AFB, 1995—97; assoc. to dep. comdr. 74th Med. Support Squadron, Wright Patterson AFB, 1997—98, assoc. to comdr., 1998—2005; chief resident Noble Family Ctr. for Health, Chgo., 2002—05; assoc. to chief med. edn. and assoc. dean Air Force Inst. Tech., Wright Patterson AFB, 2005—. Cons. adminstr. Great Lakes Podiatric Group, Valparaiso, Ind., 1995—, Family Stress and Pain Clinic, Chgo., 2002—. Contbr. articles to profl. jours. Coord. USMCR Toys for Tots, Chgo., 1997—2004; sci. fair judge Our Lady Immaculate Acad., Oak Park, Ill., 2002—05; charter sponsor Air Force Meml., Washington, 2005—06. Decorated Nat. Def. medal USAF, Air Force Achievement medal, Air Force Commendation medal, Mil. Outstanding Volunteerism Svc. medal USAF; recipient David award for Sci., Italo-Am. Nat. Union, 1990. Fellow: Am. Coll. Healthcare Execs., Am. Acad. Med. Adminstrs. (sec.-treas. 1993—95); mem.: Nutrition for Optimal Health Assn., Assn. Mil. Surgeons US, Chgo. Health Execs. Forum, Healthcare Execs. SW Ohio (charter mem. 1990—91), Mil. Officers Assn. Am. (treas. 2003, cert. of appreciation 2004), Air Force Assn., Am. Legion, Alpha Theta Xi, Phi Theta Kappa, Pi Alpha Alpha, Pi Sigma Alpha, Tau Epsilon Phi. Republican. Roman Catholic. Avocations: aviation, plastic model aircrafts, movies. Home: 6219 W Cornelia Ave Chicago IL 60634-4120 Office: Air Force Inst Tech/ENEM Rm 120 2275 D St Wright Patterson Afb OH 45433-7221 Home Phone: 773-545-1658. Office Fax: 847-982-9855. Personal E-mail: majormeccia@hotmail.com.

MECH, TERRENCE FRANCIS, library director; b. Birdorup Park, Wiltshire, Eng., Feb. 24, 1953; s. Emil Paul and Madelyn Mech. BS, U. Wis., Stevens Point, 1975; MS, Ill. State U., 1978; MLS, Clarion U., 1979; EdD, Pa. State U., 1994. Pub. svcs. libr. Tusculum Coll., Greensville, Tenn., 1979-80; libr. dir. Coll. of the Ozarks, Clarksville, Ark., 1980-82, King's Coll., Wilkes-Barre, Pa., 1982—, dir. libr., 1982—, v.p. for info. and instrnl. techs., 1994—2001. Bd. dirs. Northeastern Pa. Bibliographic Ctr., 1982—; mem., officer Coun. Pa. Libr. Networks, 1984-89, chair, 1987-89. Contbr. chpts. to books and articles to profl. jours. Mem. ALA, Pa. Libr. Assn. (bd. dirs. 1986-87, various coms. 1985—). Office: Kings Coll 133 N River St Wilkes Barre PA 18711-0801

MECHAM, GLENN JEFFERSON, lawyer, mayor; b. Logan, Utah, Dec. 11, 1935; s. Everett H. and Lillie (Dunford) M.; m. Mae Parson, June 5, 1957; children: Jeff B., Scott R., Marcia, Suzanne. BS, Utah State U., 1957; JD, U. Utah, 1961; grad., Air Command and Staff Coll., 1984, Air War Coll., 1984. Bar: Utah 1961, Supreme Ct. U.S., U.S. Ct. Appeals (10th cir.), U.S. Dist. Ct. Utah, U.S. Ct. Claims. Gen. practice law, 1961-65; atty. Duchesne County, Utah, 1962, City of Duchesne, 1962; city judge Roy City, Utah, 1963-66; judge City of Ogden, Utah, 1966-69, mayor, 1992-2000. Lectr. law and govt. Stevens-Henager Coll., Ogden, 1963-75; asst. U.S. atty., 1969-72; ptnr. Mecham & Richards, Ogden, Utah, 1972-82; pres. Penn Mountain Mining Co., South Pacific Internat. Bank, Ltd.; mem. Bur. Justice Stats. Adv. Bd., U.S. Dept. Justice, U.S. Conf. Mayors; chmn. Marina Capital Inc. Chmn. Ogden City Housing Authority; chmn. bd. trustees Utah State U., Space Dynamics Lab; mem. adv. coun. Fed. Home Loan Bank; pres. Utah League Cities and Towns, 1981—82; vice chmn. Wasatch Front Reg. Coun. Col. USAF, 1957; No. Utah liaison U.S. Sen. Robert F. Bennett. Recipient Disting. Svcs. award, Utah State U., Weber State U. Mem ABA, Weber County Bar Assn. (pres. 1966-68), Utah Bar Assn., Am. Judicature Soc., Weber County Bar Legal Svcs. (chmn. bd. trustees 1966-69), Utah Assn. Mcpl. Judges (sec.), Ogden-Weber C. of C. (Order of the Big Hat), Sigma Chi, Phi Alpha Delta. Home: 1715 Darling St Ogden UT 84403-0556 Office Phone: 801-725-6666.

MECHAM, STEVEN RAY, school system administrator; b. Salt Lake City, Oct. 10, 1938; s. Milton Claudius and Marjorie (White) M.; m. Donna Jean Johnson, Jan. 22, 1943; children: Brian Paul, Allan LeRoy. AS, Weber State Coll., 1958; BS, U. Utah, 1963; MA, Tchrs. Coll., Columbia U., 1965; postgrad., McGill U.; PhD, U. Calif., Santa Barbara, 1981. Prin. Montreal Oral Sch., 1966-70; state dir. hearing impaired Conn. Dept. Edn., 1970-71; dir. guidance Lexington Sch. for Deaf, NYC, 1971-72; supt. Exton Elem., Ana Frank Jr. and sr. H.S., Mexico City, 1972-77; coord. spl. edn. Weber Sch. Dist., Ogden, Utah, 1977-78; prin. Roosevelt Elem. Sch., Ogden, 1978-82; asst. supt. Weber County Schs., Ogden, 1982-87; assoc. supt. Utah Schs., 1990-93; supt. Weber Sch. Dist., 1993-98, dir. Odyssey Sch., 1998—2003. Instr. U. Utah, 1965-66, St. Joseph Coll., Hartford, Conn., 1970-71; pres. Finnish Mission-LDS Russia and Baltic States, 1987-90; adj. prof. McGill U.; instr. Tchrs. Coll., Columbia U., 1968-70; acting chmn. dept. edn. U. Americas, Mexico City, 1976-77; cons. Far West Labs., San Francisco. Contbr. articles to profl. jours. Bd. dirs. Instituto Mexicano Norte Americano de Relaciones Culturales, Mexico City, 1975-76; bishop, stake pres. Ch. Jesus Christ of Latter-day Saints, pres. Finnish Mission; bd. dirs. Am. Cancer Soc. Weber County. Mem. Am. Orgn. Educators Hearing Impaired (pres.), Can. Hearing Soc. (dir.), Utah Assn. Elem. Sch. Prins., Nat. Assn. Elem. Sch. Prins., Internat. Reading Assn., Am. Assn. Sch. Adminstrs., Utah Supt. Assoc., Alexander Graham Bell Assn., PTA, Rotary.

MECHANIC, DAVID, social sciences educator; b. NYC, Feb. 21, 1936; s. Louis and Tillie (Penn) Mechanic; m. Kathleen Mars Wiltshire; children: Robert Edmund, Michael Alexander. BA, CCNY, 1956; MA, Stanford U., 1957, PhD, 1959. Faculty U. Wis., Madison, 1960—79, prof. sociology, 1965—73, John Bascom prof., 1973—79; dir. U. Wis. (Center for Med. Sociology and Health Services Research), 1971—79, chmn. dept. sociology, 1968—70; prof. social work and sociology Rutgers U., New Brunswick, NJ, 1979—, acting dean faculty arts and scis., 1980—81, Univ. prof., dean faculty arts and scis., 1981—84, Univ. prof. and Rene Dubos prof. behavioral scis., 1984—, dir. Inst. for Health, Health Care Policy and Aging Research, 1985—. Panelist on health svcs. rsch. Pres.'s Sci. Adv. Com., 1971—72; coord. panel Pres.'s Commn. Mental Health, 1977—78; mem. Nat. Adv. Coun. Aging, NIH, 1982—86; treatment com. on reduction of cancer mortality Nat. Cancer Inst., 1984; expert adv. panel on mental health WHO, 1984—89; vice-chmn. com. pain, disability and chronic illness behavior Inst. Medicine-NAS, 1985—86, panel on prevention of disability, 1989—90, panel on new data for an aging world, 1999—2000, com. on capitalizing on social sci. and behavioral rsch. to improve the pubs. health, 1999; health adv. bd. GAO, 1987—95; nat. com. on vital and health stats. HHS, 1988—92; commn. on med. edn. Robert Wood Johnson Found., 1990—92, nat. adv. com. scholars in health policy rsch. program, 1993—, nat. dir. investigators awards in health policy rsch. program, 2000—, tech. adv. com. scholars in health policy rsch. program, 2001—02, nat. adv. com. health and soc. scholar's program, 2003—; mem. Com. on Prevention of Mental Disorder, 1992—94; panel on tech., ins. and health care sys. Office of Tech. U.S. Congress, 1992—95; commn. on behavioral and social scis. and edn. NRC, 1992—95; adv. com. Picker/Commonwealth Scholars Program, 1992—99; panel on rethinking disability policy Nat. Acad. Social Ins., 1993—96; vis. scholar Kings Fund Inst., London, 1994—95; professionalism adv. com. Am. Bd. Internal Med. Found., 2002—05; bd. dirs. Acad. Health. Author: Students Under Stress, 1962, 1978, Medical Sociology, 1968, 1978, Mental Health and Social Policy, 1969, 2007, Public Expectations and Health Care, 1972, Politics, Medicine and Social Science, 1974; author: (with Charles E. Lewis and Rashi Fein) A Right to Health, 1976; author: Growth of Bureaucratic Medicine, 1976, Future Problems in Health Care, 1979, From Advocacy to Allocation: The Evolving American Health Care System, 1986, Painful Choices: Research and Essays on Health Care, 1989, Inescapable Decisions: The Imperatives of Health Reform, 1994, The Truth About Health Care: Why Reform is Not Working in America, 2006; author, editor: Symptoms, Illness Behavior and Help-Seeking, 1982; editor: Handbook of Health, Health Care and the Health Professions, 1983, Improving Mental Health Services: What the Social Sciences Can Tell Us, 1987, General Hospital Impatient Psychiatry, 1997, Managed Behavioral Health Care: Current Realities and Future Potential, 1998; co-editor (with Robert Hauser, Archibald Haller and Tess Hauser): Social Structure and Personality, 1982; co-editor: (with Linda Aiken) Applications of Social Science to Clinical Medicine and Social Policy, 1986; co-editor: Paying for Services: Promises and Pitfalls of Capitation, 1989; co-editor: (with Marian Osterweis and Arthur Kleinman) Pain and Disability: Clinical Behavior and Public Policy Perspectives, 1987; co-editor: (with Carl Taube and Ann Hohmann) The Future of Mental Health Services Research, 1989; co-editor: (with Lynn Rogut, David Colby, and James Knickman) Policy Challenges in Modern Health Care, 2005. Recipient Ward medal, CCNY, 1956, Carl Taube award, APHA, 1990, Remc Lapouse award, 2003, Disting. Investigator award, Assn. for Health Svcs. Rsch., 1991, Disting. Contbn. award mental health sect., Soc. for Study of Social Problems, 1991, Emily Mumford medal, Columbia U., 1991, Investigator award in health policy rsch., Robert Wood Johnson Found., 1995—99, Health Svcs. Rsch. prize, Assn. of U. Programs in Health Adminstrn. and the Baxter Allegiance Found., 1997, Senator Frank R. Lautenberg Ann. award, Sch. Pub. Health, U. Medicine and Dentistry NJ, 2003, Benjamin Rush award, Am. Psychiat. Assn., 2004, First Matilda Riley award and lectr., NIH, 2006; fellow Ford Behavioral Sci. fellow, 1956—57, NIMH rsch. fellow, 1965—66, Ctr. for Advanced Study in Behavioral Scis., 1974—75, Guggenheim fellow, 1977—78, Disting. fellow, Assn. Health Svcs. Rsch., 1996. Fellow: AAAS (chmn. sect. social, econ. and polit. scis. 1985), Assn. Health Svcs. Rsch. (disting. 1996); mem.: NAS, Nat. Acad. Sciences, Hogg Found. Mental Health (nat. adv. coun. 1987), Nat. Acad. Social Ins. (founding), Am. Acad. Arts and Scis., Inst. Medicine-NAS (governing coun. 1972—74), Sociol. Rsch. Assn. (pres. 1991—92), Am. Sociol. Assn. (chmn. med. sociol. sect. 1969—70, governing coun. 1977—78, chmn. publs. com. 1989—91, chmn. mental health sect. 1992—93, Disting. Med. Sociologist award 1983, Lifetime Achievement award mental health sect. 1994, Disting. Career award 2001, Disting. Career award for Practice of Sociology 2004), Phi Beta Kappa. Office: Rutgers U Inst Health Policy Aging Rsch 30 College Ave New Brunswick NJ 08901-1283 Home: 5 Overbrook Dr Princeton NJ 08540-3924 Office Phone: 732-932-8415. Business E-Mail: mechanic@rci.rutgers.edu.

MECHANIC, JONATHAN L., lawyer; b. Paterson, NJ, Oct. 1, 1952; s. Mayer and Bernadine J. Mechanic; m. Wendy Sue Levine, Nov. 7, 1987. BA magna cum laude, Brandeis U., 1974; JD, NYU, 1977. Bar: NY 1978, US Dist. Ct. (so. and ea. dists.) NY 1978. Gen. counsel HRO Internat. Ltd., 1983-87; ptnr. Fried, Frank, Harris, Shriver & Jacobson LLP, NYC, 1987—. Bd. dirs. NYU Real Estate Inst., Chgo. Title Ins. Co., Wall St. Rising, YMCA, Eldridge St. Synagogue, Modell Found. Named a Dealmaker of Yr., Am. Law mag., 2007, recipient Am. Jurisprudence award. Mem. ABA, Assn. Bar City of NY, Real Estate Bd. NY (exec. com., bd. govs.), Real Estate Roundtable, Order of Coif. Office: Fried Frank Harris Shriver & Jacobson 1 New York Plz Fl 22 New York NY 10004-1980 Office Phone: 212-859-8222. Office Fax: 212-859-4000. E-mail: mechajo@friedfrank.com. *

MECHE, GIL (GILBERT ALLEN MECHE), professional baseball player; b. Lafayette, La., Sept. 8, 1978; children: Landon, Ella. Draft pick Seattle Mariners, 1996, pitcher, 1999—2006, Kans. City Royals, 2006—. Mem. US Jr. Olympic Team, 1995. Named The Sporting News Comeback Player of Yr., 2003; named to Am. League All-Star Team, 2007. Mailing: Kans City Royals One Royal Way Kansas City MO 64129 *

MECHEM, CHARLES STANLEY, JR., retired broadcast executive; b. Nelsonville, Ohio, Sept. 12, 1930; s. Charles Stanley and Helen (Hall) Mechem; m. Marilyn Brown, Aug. 31, 1952; children: Melissa, Daniel, Allison. AB, Miami U., Oxford, Ohio, 1952; LLB, Yale U., New Haven, Conn., 1955. Bar: Ohio 1955. Practice in Cin., 1955—67; ptnr. Taft, Stettinius & Hollister, 1965—67; chmn. bd. Taft Broadcasting Co., Cin., 1967—90; commr. LPGA, Daytona Beach, Fla., 1990—95, commr. emeritus, 1995—; chmn. U.S. Shoe, 1993—95; chmn. Cin. Bell, Inc., 1996—98, Convergys Corp., 1998—2000; cons. Arnold Palmer Enterprises, Cin., 1996—. Bd. dirs. Messer Constrn., Inc. Capt. JAGC US Army, 1956—59. Mem.: Cin. C. of C. (pres. 1977), Comml. Club. Office: Taft Stettinius & Hollister LLP 425 Walnut St Ste 1800 Cincinnati OH 45202-4122

MECIMORE, CHARLES DOUGLAS, retired accounting educator; b. Belmont, NC, Aug. 20, 1934; s. John Edgar and Hattie (Bolick) M.; m. Barbara Jean Chiddie, June 7, 1959; children: Laura Jean, Charles D. Jr., John Amos. BS, Pfeiffer Coll., 1958; MS, U. N.C., 1962; PhD, U. Ala., 1966. CPA, N.C.; CMA. Asst. prof. U. Ala., Tuscaloosa, 1966-67; assoc. prof. U. Ga., Athens, 1967-71; prof. U. Cin., 1971-79; prof. acctg. Sch. Bus. and Econs., U. N.C., Greensboro, 1980-98; ret., 1998. Head dept. U. N.C. Sch. Bus. and Econs., 1980-89, 96-98. With USAF, 1951—55. Univ. scholar, 1963-66; Haskins and Sells fellow, 1962-64; Beyer bronze medal, 1974. Mem. AICPAs, N.C. Assn. CPAs (Outstanding Educator 1985), Inst. Mgmt. Acctg. Home: 430 Marshall View Ct Winston Salem NC 27101-5285 Personal E-mail: MecimoreC@bellsouth.net.

MECKE, WILLIAM MOYN, public information officer; b. Detroit, May 7, 1957; s. Theodore Hart McCalla Jr. and Mary Eleanor (Flaherty) M.; m. Katherine E. Bauer. BA, Georgetown U., 1979; MA, Am. U., 1982; postgrad., Oxford U., 1982, U. N.C., 1982-85. Asst. dir. Found. Study Presdl. and Congrl. Terms, Washington, 1979-82; acct. exec. Hill and Knowlton, Inc., Chgo., 1985-86; tchr. The Bolles Sch., Jacksonville, Fla., 1986-88, St. Andrew's Sch., Savannah, 1988-91, Joseph Walker Sch., Marietta, Ga., 1991-92; polit. cons. various Democratic candidates, 1992-95; tech. writer Total Sys. Svcs. Inc., Columbus, Ga., 1995; dir. mktg. Habitat for Humanity Internat., Americus, Ga., 1995-2000, media svcs. mgr., 2000-2001; comm. dir. Ga. Regional Transp. Authority, 2001—. Co-author, editor: Presidential and Congressional Term Limitation: The Issue That Stays Alive, 1981. Asst. dir. Found. Study Presd. and Congl. Terms, Washington, 1979-82; mem. Regional Leadership Forum. Mem. Pub. Rels. Soc. Am., Atlanta Press Club. Office: Ga Regional Transp Authority Ste 900 245 Peachtree Ctr Ave NE Atlanta GA 30303 Office Phone: 404-463-3011. Business E-Mail: wmecke@grta.org.

MECKEL, PETER TIMOTHY, arts administrator, educator; b. Yankton, SD, Nov. 28, 1941; s. Myron Eugene and Cynthia Ann (Turnblom) Meckel; m. Louise Gloria Mudge, Sept. 8, 1962; children: Christina Louise, Christopher Mark; m. Adrienne Dawn Maravich, Dec. 30, 1972; children: Moya Ann, Jon-Peter. Student, Rockford Coll., Occidental Coll. Founder, gen. dir. Hidden Valley Music Seminars, Carmel Valley, Calif., 1963—; dir. Hidden Valley Opera Ensemble, Masters Festival of Chamber Music, Master Class Series. Cons. in field. Mem. Music Educators Nat. Conf. Congregationalist. Office: Hidden Valley Opera Ensemble PO Box 116 Carmel Valley CA 93924-0116 Office Phone: 831-659-3115. E-mail: hvms@aol.com.

MECKLENBURG, GARY ALAN, hospital executive; m. Lynn Kraemer; children: John, Sarah. BA, Northwestern U., 1968; MBA, U. Chgo., 1970. Adminstrv. resident Presbyn.-St. Luke's Hosp., Chgo., 1969-70, adminstrv. asst., 1970-71, asst. supt., 1971-76, assoc. supt., 1976-77, U. Wis. Hosps., Madison, 1977-80; adminstr. Stanford U. Hosp. Clinics, Calif.; pres., CEO St. Joseph's Hosp., Milw., 1980-85; pres., dir. Franciscan Health Care Inc., Milw., 1985; pres., CEO Northwestern Meml. Hosp., Chgo., 1985—2001, Northwestern Meml. HealthCare, Chgo., 2001—. Preceptor, guest lectr., mem. adv. bd. Kellogg Sch. Mgmt., chgo., 1986—; pres., chief exec. officer, dir. Northwestern Healthcare Network, 1990-92. Recipient Todd Scout award Boy Scouts Am., 1998, Chgo. Bus. Hall of Fame award Jr. Achievement, 2000, GSB Disting. Pub. Svc./Pub. Sector Alumnus award U. Chgo., 2000. Mem. Am. Hosp. Assn. (sect. met. hosps., governing coun. 1984-92, chmn. 1991, 2001, trustee 1996-2002, exec. com. 1997-2002, chmn., 2001, mem. regional policy bd., #5 1984, 87-89, 91-93, 95-99, chmn. 1996-99, 2001, mem. ho. dels. 1984, 87-89, 91—, mem. com. on med. edn. 1976-80), Ill. Hosp. Assn. (bd. dirs. 1988-95, chmn. 1994, mem. adv. panel coun. tchg. hosps. 1997—), U. Chgo. Hosp. Adminstrn. Alumni Assn. (pres. 1985-86), Econ. Club Chgo., Comml. Club Chgo.

MECKSTROTH, WILMA JEAN, piano and organ educator, accompanist; b. Dayton, Ohio, July 5, 1928; d. Edgar B. and Olive M. Andrew; m. Robert C. Meckstroth, Oct. 7, 1950; children: David, John, Carol. MusB, Northwestern U., Evanston, Ill., 1950. Nat. cert. tchr. music Music Tchrs. Nat. Assn. Organist The Luth. Ch. of Our Savior, Dayton, 1957—2003; pvt. piano tchr. Dayton, 1957—; accompanist The Music Appreciation Choral Club, 1957—; chmn. Dayton Organ Acad., 1980—; adjudicator Nat. Guild Piano Tchrs., Am. Coll. Musicians, Austin, 1980—2006. Mem.: Am. Guild Organists (dean 1981—83), Ohio Music Tchrs. Assn. (chmn. west dist. 1994—96, Piano Tchr. of Yr. 1999), Dayton Music Club (pres. 1987—89), Dayton Piano Tchrs. Study Club (pres. 1978—79), Mu Phi Epsilon (pres. 1958—60, 2000—02, Dayton chpt. alumni). Lutheran. Avocations: cooking, tennis. Home: 2142 E Rahn Rd Kettering OH 45440

MECONI, HONEY, musicologist, writer; d. Patrick and Mary Evelyn Meconi; m. Michel Jean-Marie Godts, Mar. 5, 1988; 1 child, Yannick Corentin Godts. BA, Pa. State U., 1974; AM, Harvard U., 1980, PhD, 1986. From asst. to full prof. Rice U., Houston, 1987—2004, dir. Medieval studies, 1998—2004; prof. music U. Rochester, NY, 2004—; prof. musicology Eastman Sch. Music, Rochester, 2004—. Mem. Harvard Grad. Soc. Coun., Cambridge, Mass., 1990—96; mem. adv. bd. Houston Early Music, 2000—02; bd. dir. The Hildegard Project; conf. dir. Constructing Hildegard: Reception and Identity 1098-1998, 1998; music cons. U.S. Cath. Conf., Washington, 1998—99; bd. dirs. Pegasus Early Music. Author: Pierre de la Rue, 2003; editor: Early Musical Borrowing, 2004, (music edit.) Fortuna Desperata, 2001; contbr. articles to profl. jours. Recipient Arts and Architecture Alumna award, Pa. State U., 2006; fellow, Fulbright, Belgium, 1982—84, Villa I Tatti, Florence, Italy, 1986—87, Andrew W. Mellon, U. Pa., 1990—91, Ctr. for the Study of Cultures/Rice U., 2002—03. Mem.: Coll. Music Soc., Internat. Musicol. Soc., Am. Musicol. Soc. (pres. S.W. chpt. 1999—2001, bd. dirs. 2005—06, Noah Greenberg award 2006). Avocation: quilting. Office: Univ Rochester 207 Todd Union Rochester NY 14627-0052 Office Phone: 585-275-9399.

MEDAK, SUSAN LEE, performing company executive; b. Chgo., Dec. 30, 1953; d. Herman and Vivian Hannah (Fried); m. Gregory Scott Murphy, Aug. 1, 1982. BA cum laude, Lawrence U., 1976. Tour asst. The Guthrie Theater, Mpls., 1974; regional svcs. dir. Milw. Repertory Theatre, 1976-80, dir. audience devel., 1980-83; mng. dir. The People's Light and Theatre Co., Malvern, Pa., 1983-84, Northlight Theatre, Evanston, Ill., 1984—, Berkeley Repertory Theatre, 1990—. Sec. League of Resident Theatres, 1988; treas. League of Chgo. Theatres, Chgo., 1987-89. Adv. bd. Evanston Jr. League, 1988—, Cameron Kravit Found. of Evanston Hosp., 1989—. Office: Berkeley Repertory Theatre 2025 Addison St Berkeley CA 94704

MEDAL, CAROLE ANN, library director; b. Chgo., Sept. 17, 1949; d. Edward Charles and Helen Ward Medal. MusB, Millikin U., 1972; MusM, U. Ill., 1975; MLS, Ind. U., 1979; cert. bus. adminstrn., U. Ill., Chgo., 1998. Asst. dir. children's svcs. Elk Grove Village (Ill.) Pub. Libr., 1976-77; tech. supr. Schaumburg (Ill.) Twp. Dist. Libr., 1979; reference libr. Barrington (Ill.) Area Libr. Dist., 1979-80; dir. adult svcs. & circulation Rolling Meadows (Ill.) Libr., 1980-84, exec. dir., 1984-99; chief visual & performing arts divsn. Chgo. Pub. Libr., 1999—2004; dir. Gail Borden Pub. Libr. Dist., Elgin, Ill., 2004—. Mem. exec. bd. Night Owl Reference Svc., Inc., Arlington Heights, Ill., 1995-99; mem. adv. coun. North Suburban Libr. Sys., Wheeling, Ill., 1993-97; pres. Libr. Adminstrs. Conf. No. Ill., 1997-98. Mem. Rolling Meadows 2000, 1996. Mem. ALA (Marshall Cavendish award, 2006), Pub. Libr. Assn. (bus. coun. 1994-98), Libr. Adminstrn. and Mgmt. Assn., Ill. Libr. Assn., Rolling Meadows C. of C., Rotary Club (Rotarian of Yr. 1992, Paul Harris fellow 1995, pres. Rolling Meadows club 1994-95). Avocations: music, travel, photography. Office: Gail Borden Pub Libr Dist 270 N Grove Ave Elgin IL 60120 Office Phone: 847-742-2411. Office Fax: 847-742-0485.

MEDALIE, RICHARD JAMES, lawyer; b. Duluth, Minn., July 21, 1929; s. William Louis and Mona (Kolad) M.; m. Susan Diane Abrams, June 5, 1960; children: Samuel David, Daniel Alexander. BA summa cum laude, U. Minn., 1952; cert., U. London, 1953; A.M., Harvard U., 1955, JD cum laude, 1958. Bar: DC 1958, NY 1963. Law clk. to Hon. George T. Washington U.S. Ct. Appeals, Washington, 1958-59; asst. solicitor gen. U.S., 1960-62; assoc. Kaye, Scholer, Fierman, Hays & Handler, NYC, 1962-65; dep. dir. Ford Found. Inst. Criminal Law and Procedure, Georgetown U. Law Ctr., 1965-68; ptnr. Friedman & Medalie and predecessors, Washington, 1968-98; pres. Pegasus Internat., Washington, 1970—; exec. dir. The Appleseed Found., Washington, 1993-94, chmn. bd., 1993—2002, chmn. emeritus, 2003—, pres., 1995-98; of counsel Brock Ptnrs. LLC, NYC, 1995—; pvt. practice Washington, 1998—2006, Hull, Mass., 2006—. Adj. prof. adminstrv. and criminal law Georgetown U. Law Center, 1967—70; mem. D.C. Law Revision Commn., 1975—87; chmn. Criminal Law Task Force, exec. com., 1978—82; mem. panel comml.

arbitrators Nat. Arbitration Forum, 2004—; vice chmn. Harvard Law Sch. Fund, 1981—84, chmn. nat. maj. gifts, 1984—86, dep. chmn., 1986—87, chmn., 1987—89; v.p., bd. dirs. Trial Lawyers for Pub. Justice, Washington, 1998—2006. Author: From Escobedo to Miranda: The Anatomy of a Supreme Court Decision, 1966; co-author: Federal Consumer Safety Legislation, 1970; co-author, editor: Commercial Arbitration for the 1990s, 1991; co-author, co-editor American Students Organize: Founding the National Student Association after World War II, 2006; co-editor: Crime: A Community Responds, 1967; staff: Harvard Law Rev., 1956-58; case editor, 1957-58; contbr. articles to legal jours. Bd. dir. alumni assn. Experiment in Internat. Living, Brattleboro, Vt., 1961-64, pres., 1962-63. Fulbright scholar, 1952-53; Ford fellow, 1954-55. Fellow Am. Bar Found., Harvard Law Sch. Assn. D.C. (pres. 1976-77, nat. v.p. 1977-78), Harvard Alumni Assn. (law sch. dir. 1991-95); mem. ABA (program chair 1984, 90, chair legis. subcom. 1986-89, ADR/arbitration com., rep. on adv. com. nat. conf. Emerging ADR Issues in State and Fed. Cts. 1991, vice-chmn. 1991-94, arbitration com. litigation sect., co-chair nat. conf. Critical Issues in Arbitration 1993), Am. Arbitration Assn. (panel comml. arbitrators 1964—), D.C. Unified Bar, Assn. Bar City of N.Y., Am. Law Inst. (life, consultative group, model penal code sentencing), Cosmos Club, Harvard Club of Washington, Phi Beta Kappa, Phi Alpha Theta. Office: 46 P St Hull MA 02045 Home Phone: 781-925-0138; Office Phone: 202-659-0880. Personal E-mail: rmedalie@att.net.

MEDALIE, SUSAN DIANE, lawyer, management consultant; b. Boston, Oct. 7, 1941; d. Samuel and Matilda (Bortman) Abrams; m. Richard James Medalie, June 5, 1960; children: Samuel David, Daniel Alexander. BA, Sarah Lawrence Coll., 1960; MA, George Washington U., 1962, cert. pubs. spec., 1977; JD, Am. U., 1986. Bar: Pa. 1987, DC 1987. Pres. Medalie Cons., Washington, 1980—; dep. dir. U.S. Holocaust Meml. Coun., Washington, 1980—82; assoc. pub. Campaigns & Elections, Washington, 1983—84; legis. analyst Subcom./House Energy and Commerce, Washington, 1985; ea. regional dir. Josephson Found. for Adv. Ethics, LA, 1986—88; asst. dean for external affairs George Washington U. Nat. Law Ctr., Washington, 1988—90; exec. dir. Internat. Soc. Global Health Policy, Washington and Paris, 1990—93; pvt. practice Washington, 1993—2000, 2005—07, Hull, Mass., 2007—; exec. dir. Women's Campaign Fund, Washington, 2000—04. Corp. liaison First Hosp. Corp., Norfolk, Va., 1986—88. Editor, pub.: Getting There mag., 1977—80, sr. editor: Am. U. Law Rev., 1984—86; assoc. prodr., cons. (TV series) Prof. Arthur Miller's "Headlines on Trial", 1987—91. Exec. bd., DC Bar rep. Coalition Against Drugs and Violence, 1997—2000; nat. dep. fin. dir. Edward M. Kennedy for Pres. Com., Washington, 1979—80; del. DC Ward 3 Dem. Ctrl. Com., 1996—2000; bd. dirs., exec. com. Women's Campaign Fund, 1999—2000. Mem.: ABA, DC Unified Bar. Home and Office: 46 P St Hull MA 02045 Office Phone: 781-925-0138. Personal E-mail: susanmedalie@att.net.

MEDAROV, BORIS I., pulmonologist, researcher, critical care physician; b. Stara Zagora, Bulgaria, Aug. 7, 1971; m. Aniko Holler. MD, Semmelweis U., Budapest, Hungary, 1997. Cert. paramedic Hungarian Nat. Emergency Svc., 1997, lic. physician Conn., 2004, diplomate Am. Bd. Internal Medicine, Am. Bd. Pulmonary Medicine, Am. Bd. Critical Care Medicine. Resident in internal medicine SUNY, Bklyn., 1999—2002; fellow in pulmonary and critical care medicine L.I. Jewish Med. Ctr., L.I. Campus of Albert Einstein Coll. of Medicine, New Hyde Park, NY, 2002—05. Named Dr. of Yr., Kings County Hosp. Ctr., 2002. Mem.: Am. Thoracic Soc., Am. Coll. Chest Physicians. Achievements include research in circadian variation of lung functions. Office: LI Jewish Med Ctr 270-05 76th Ave New Hyde Park NY 11040 Office Phone: 860-496-6666. Personal E-mail: medaroff@yahoo.com. Business E-Mail: bmedarov@lij.edu.

MEDAVOY, MIKE, film company executive, producer; b. Shanghai, Jan. 21, 1941; arrived in U.S., 1957, naturalized, 1962; s. Michael and Dora Medavoy; m. Irena Medavoy; children: Nicholas, Brian. BA, UCLA, 1963. With Casting dept. Universal Studios, 1963; agt. Bill Robinson Assos., LA, 1963—64; v.p. motion picture dept. GAC/CMA Co., 1965—71, IFA Co., 1971—74; sr. v.p. United Artists Corp., 1974—78; one of founders, exec. v.p. Orion Pictures Co., Burbank, Calif., 1978—82; exec. v.p. Orion Pictures Corp. (formerly Orion Pictures Co.), Century City, Calif., 1982—90; chmn. Tri-Star Pictures, Inc., Culver City, Calif., 1990—, Phoenix Picture Corp., 1995—. Jury chmn. Tokyo Film Festival 1994; hon. co-chair St. Petersburg (Russia) Film Festival, 1992; adv. bd. Shanghai Film Conf.; co-chmn. Am. Cinematheque, 1997-2004, chmn. emeritus, 2004—. Author: You're Only as Good as Your Next One, 2002. Co-founder Sundance Film Inst.; bd. govs. Sundance Inst., 1980-86; bd. dirs. Calif. Mus. Sci. and Industry, 1984-87, U. Tel-Aviv., UCLA Found.; commr. L.A. Bd. Parks and Recreation, 2001; exec. adv. bd. Calif. Anti-Terrorism Info. Ctr., 2002; bd. advs. Harvard's Kennedy Sch. Gov., co-chair UCLA Burkle Ctr. Internat. Rels., mem. coun. fgn. rels., 2004. Named to Hollywood Walk of Fame, 2005; recipient Acad. award (mem. of team that green lit), One Flew Over the Cuckoo's Nest, Rocky, Annie Hall, Amadeus, Platoon, Dances with Wolves, Silence of the Lambs, Motion Picture Pioneer award, 1992, Career Achievement award, UCLA Alumni, 1997, Prodrs. award, Cannes Film Festival, 1998, Neil H. Jacoby award, 1999, Fred Zinneman award, Anti-Defamation League, 2001, Film Theater and Prodrs. Guild Am. Vision award, UCLA, 2005, Prodr. of Yr. award, Hollywood Film Festival, 2006, 2007. Mem. Acad. Motion Picture Arts and Scis. (gov. 1977-81, Hollywood Walk of Fame Star 2005) Business E-Mail: mmedavoy@phoenixpictures.com.

MEDBURY, SCOT DANIEL, botanical garden executive; b. Columbus, Ga., Jan. 28, 1959; s. Paul Randall Medbury and Janet Elaine Stewart; m. Brian K. Lym, Oct. 13, 2003. BA in Internat. Studies, U. Wash., Seattle, 1987, MS in Forest Resources, 1990; studied, U. Calif., Berkeley, 1992—97. Nursery mgr. Nat. Tropical Bot. Garden, Kauai, Hawaii, 1982—83; gardener Crown Estate Commn., Windsor, England, 1985, Pukekura Park, New Plymouth, New Zealand, 1986; edn. assoc. Ctr. for Urban Horticulture, Seattle, 1986—90; curator Honolulu Bot. Gardens, 1990—92; dir. San Francisco Bot. Garden and Conservatory of Flowers, 1999—2005; pres., CEO Bklyn. Botanic Garden, 2005—. Hort. cons. Plant Collections Planning and Mgmt., Berkeley, Calif., 1992—99; bd. dirs. Am. Assn. Botanical Gardens & Arboreta, 2001—04. Author: San Francisco Botanical Garden - A World of Plants, 2005; contbr. articles to profl. jours. Named to Centennial Honor Roll, Am. Assn. Museums, 2006. Mem.: Internat. Dendrology Soc. (coun. mem. 2001—), Garden Club Am. Office: Brooklyn Botanic Garden 1000 Washington Ave Brooklyn NY 11225 Office Phone: 718-623-7269. Business E-Mail: presidentsoffice@bbg.org.

MEDDING, WALTER SHERMAN, retired environmental engineer; b. St. Louis, Mar. 4, 1922; s. Walter Lyman and Elizabeth Steele (Sherman) M.; m. Mary Agnes Patty Johnson, Apr. 22, 1944; children: Jean, Walter, Mauri. BSCE, Va. Poly. Inst., 1947, MS in Sanitary Engring., 1970. Registered profl. engr., Va., N.C., Kans. Various positions U.S. Army, 1942-64; student officer advanced course The Engr. Sch., Ft. Belvoir, Va., 1952—54, head fixed bridges sect., 1954—55; asst. engr. Asmara Eritrea, chief design br. Mediterranean Divsn., Gulf Dist., Tehran, Iran, 1955-57; asst. divsn. engr. 9th Infantry Divsn., Ft. Carson, Colo., 1957-59; resident engr. USACAG, chief constrn. ops. U.S. Army Engring. Command Europe, Frankfurt, Germany, 1959-72; chief contract adminstrn. U.S. Army Engring. Divsn. Europe, Frankfurt, Germany, 1972-75; chief environ. engring. Office, Chief of Engrs., U.S. Army, Washington, 1975-86; sr. engr. Romem Aqua Sys. Co., Woodbridge, Va., 1986-97. Cons. U.S. army Ctr. for Pub. Works, Ft. Belvoir, Va., 1997-98; music tchr. Co-author: (textbook) Non-standard Military Fixed Bridges, 1954, (with E. Farago) Which Musical Instrument Shall I Play?, 1985; editor, pub. Letter to Lyman, 1978; contbr. articles to profl. jours. Mem. ASCE, Am. Waterworks Assn., Water Environ. Fedn., Conf. of Fed. Environ. Engrs. Republican. Episcopalian. Achievements include development of mil. bridge classification procedures for load carrying and rapid field design. Home: 204 Brooke Dr Fredericksburg VA 22408-2004 Personal E-mail: wsmedding@aol.com.

MEDEARIS, MARK A., lawyer; BS in Civil Engring. with honors, U. Colo., 1975; MS in Structural Engring., Stanford U., 1976; JD, Stanford Law Sch., 1979. Bar: Calif., Colo. Co-founder Venture Law Group (merged with Heller, Ehrman, White, & McAuliffe LLP), 1993—2003; atty., shareholder Heller, Ehrman, White, & McAuliffe LLP, Silicon Valley, Calif., 2003—. Co-author: Counseling the Boar on Pre-Bid Defensive Planning, 1991. Office: Heller Ehrman 275 Middlefield Rd Menlo Park CA 94025-3592 Office Phone: 650-233-8307. Office Fax: 650-324-0638. E-mail: markm@vlg.com.

MEDEARIS, MILLER, lawyer; b. Liberty, Mo., Jan. 19, 1921; s. Thomas Whittier and Mara (Miller) Medearis; children: Christy Crochet, Kellee Reed. LLB, Cumberland U., 1948; JD, Stamford U., 1969. Bar: Okla. 1948, Calif. 1957. Claims adjustor Transit Casualty Co., LA, 1950-56, atty., trial counsel, 1956-58; ptnr. Hagenbaugh, Murphy & Medearis, LA, 1958-69, Medearis and Grimm, LA, 1969—2004; adminstrv. law judge Calif. Employee Ins. Appeals Bd., Sherman Oaks, 2004—. Sec., bd. dirs. Med. Quality Assurance, Sacramento, 1979—84, v.p., 1984—86; commr. LA Bd. Transp., 1986—92; bd. mem. Calif. Unemployment Ins. Appeals Bd., 2000—04; mem. Dem. Bus. Coun., LA, 1980; adminstrv. law judge Calif. Unemployment Ins. Appeals Bd., 2004—; bd. dirs. Pico Rivera Cmty. Hosp., 1975—85. With USN, 1945—46. Mem.: ABA, Okla. Bar Assn., Calif. Trial Lawyers Assn., State Bar Calif., Lawyers Club LA. Democrat. Baptist. Avocations: boating, water-skiing, downhill skiing. Home: 2175 Ridge Dr Los Angeles CA 90049-1153 Office: 15303 Venture Blvd Ste 1260 Sherman Oaks CA 91403 Home Phone: 310-471-8900; Office Phone: 818-461-3468.

MEDEIROS, JENNIFER LYNN, school psychologist, consultant; b. New Bedford, Mass., Feb. 5, 1974; d. Antone and Joan Elaine Medeiros. BA in Psychology, Bridgewater State Coll., 1995; MEd, U. Mass., Boston, 2004. Tchr. I.H. Schwartz Children's Rehab. Ctr., New Bedford, Mass., 1995—97; children's intensive support services mgr. TILL, Inc., Dedham, Mass., 1997—2001; therapeutic mentor Family Intervention Network, Wakefield, Mass., 1999—2002; cons. Charles River Assn. for Retarded Citizens, Needham, Mass., 2001—; rsch. asst. Ctr. for Social Devel. and Edn., Boston, 2001—04; sch. psychologist Boston Pub. Schools, 2004—. Student rep. Ctr. for Exceptional Children Divsn. of Rsch., Arlington, Va., 2003—04. Mem.: Coun. for Exceptional Children (student rep.divsn. of rsch. 2003—04), Mass. Assn. of Sch. Psychologists, Nat. Assn. Sch. Psychologists. Home: 90A Dexter Ave Watertown MA 02472 Office: Boston Pub Sch 443 Warren St Dorchester MA 02121 Home Phone: 617-775-8748; Office Phone: 617-635-9676. Personal E-mail: jen_medeiros@yahoo.com.

MEDEIROS, L. JEFFREY, hematologist, educator; b. New Bedford, Mass., Sept. 25, 1954; s. Leonard L. and Albertina G. Medeiros; m. Carrie A. Rafferty, Jan. 4, 2003; children: Christina Grace, Caroline Grace. MD, U. Mass., Worcester, 1980. Prof. M.D. Anderson Cancer Ctr., Houston, 1998—, chmn. dept. hematopathology, 1998. Office: MD Anderson Cancer Ctr Box 72 1515 Holcombe Blvd Houston TX 77030 Home Phone: 713-662-0933; Office Phone: 713-794-5446. Office Fax: 713-745-0736. Business E-Mail: ljmedeiros@mdanderson.org.

MEDEIROS, MATTHEW FRANCIS, lawyer; b. Little Compton, RI, Apr. 30, 1945; s. Manuel S. and Marie F. (Goulart) M.; m. Sarah Judith Medjuck, July 26, 1970. AB, Brown U., 1967; JD, NYU, 1970. Bar: R.I. 1970, Mass. 1985, U.S. Dist. Ct. R.I. 1971, D.C. 1971, U.S. Dist. Ct. D.C. 1971, U.S. Ct. Appeals (1st cir.) 1972, U.S. Ct. Appeals (D.C. cir.) 1972, U.S. Supreme Ct. 1974. Summer assoc. Lewis & Roca, Phoenix, 1969; law clk. to chief judge U.S. Dist. Ct. R.I., 1970-71; assoc. Covington & Burling, Washington, 1971-76; on leave with Neighborhood Legal Svcs. Program, Washington, 1973; ptnr. Edwards & Angell, Providence, 1977-87, Flanders & Medeiros Inc., Providence, 1987-2000, Little, Bulman, Medeiros & Whitney, P.C., 2000—. Chmn. planning com. 1st Cir. Jud. Conf., 1980-81; mem. jud. screening coms. U.S. Bankruptcy Judge and U.S. Magistrate, 1981-82; mem. adv. com. for U.S. Ct. Appeals (1st cir.), 1983-88; adj. prof. fed. trial practice So. New Eng. Sch. Law, 1986-88; editor: NYU Law Rev., 1969-70; bd. dirs. Associated Alumni Brown U., 1969-71; bd. dirs. R.I. br. ACLU, 1977-79. Mem. ABA, Am. Bd. Trial Advocates, Fed. Bar Assn. (pres. R.I. chpt. 1978-80), R.I. Bar Assn. Office: Little Medeiros Kinder Bulman & Whitney 72 Pine St Providence RI 02903 Office Phone: 401-272-8080. Business E-Mail: mfm@lmkbw.com.

MEDEL, REBECCA ROSALIE, artist; b. Denver, Mar. 26, 1947; d. Natividad and Josefa (Apodaca) Medel. BFA, Ariz. State U., Tempe, 1970; MFA, UCLA, 1982. Asst. prof. fibers dept. head Tenn. Technol. U., Smithville, 1983-88; lectr. Dept. of Design, UCLA, 1989-91; studio artist, 1991—; prof. Tyler Sch. Art Temple U., 1995—. Lectr. N.C. State U., Raleigh, San Diego State U., SUNY, Purchase, 1992, Penland Sch. Asheville, NC, Textile Study Group, NYC, Calif. Coll. of Arts & Crafts, Oakland, Calif., San Jose State U., Am. Ctr., Kyoto, Japan, City Ctr., Sapporo, Japan, 1986; vis. artist U. ND, 1985. One-woman shows include Thirteen Moons Gallery, Santa Fe, 2003, 05, Brown Grotta Gallery, Wilton, Conn., 1996, Neuberger Mus. of Art, Purchase, NY, 1992-93, Bellas Artes Gallery, NYC, 1991, N.D. Mus. Art, Grand Forks, 1985, Maya Behn Galerie, Zurich, 1984, UCLA, 1982, Thirteen Moons Gallery, Santa Fe, 2003, 05; group shows include Bellas Artes Gallery, Santa Fe, N.Mex., 1992, NC State U. Gallery, 1992, Portland Art Mus., 1995, Madison Art Ctr., Wis., 1995, Santa Monica Art Gallery, 1995, Maya Behn Gallerie, 1991, Mus. Van Bommel-Van Dam, Venlo, Netherlands, 1990, Palo Alto Cultural Ctr., 1990, Barbican Ctr. Concourse Gallery, London, 1998, Montclair State U. Gallery, NJ, 1998, Art Inst. Chgo., 1999, Yokohama Mus. Art, Japan, 1999, Biennial 2000, Del. Art Mus., Wilmington, LA Mus. Art, 2000, Soc. Contemporary Crafts, Pitts., 2001, Westport Arts Ctr., Conn., 2003, many others. Recipient bronze medal Triennial of Tapestry, 1985; visual artist fellow Nat. Endowment for Arts, 1986, 88, fellow for emerging visual artists So. Arts Fedn. NEA, 1985; Pew fellow in the arts, 1999, 2003, fellow Pa. Coun. on Arts, 2001, 03, 07; scholar to Arcosanti, Nat. Endowment for Arts, 1986, 88. Home: 2920 Meyer Ave Glenside PA 19038-1920 Office Phone: 215-782-2728. Business E-Mail: rmedel@temple.edu.

MEDEPALLI, KAMESH, engineer, researcher, educator; b. Kakinada, Andhra Pradesh, India, Nov. 17, 1975; s. Srirama Rao and Kalyani Alivelu Manga Medepalli; m. Yeshoda Devi Yedevelly; 1 child, Sruthi Kalyanasai. PhD, Stanford U., Calif., 2006. Tech. staff Bell Labs, Holmdel, NJ, 1998—2003; rsch. scientist Telcordia Technologies, Piscataway, NJ, 2003—06; sr. staff engr. Beceem Comm., Santa Clara, Calif., 2006—. Presenter in field. Contbr. articles to profl. jours., chapters to books. Sec. Dept. Electronics & Comm., Visakhapatnam, Andhra Pradesh, India, 1993—94. Analog Devices scholar, Analog Devices, 1996. Mem.: IEEE. Hindu. Achievements include patents for efficient automatic repeat request method using variable length sequence numbers; patents pending for enhancement of framing protocol frame format to support quality of svc; multiplexing IP datagrams inside an MPLS frame; peak-picking enhanced airlink QoS (PEAQ) scheduler for CDMA2000's 1X-EVDO airlink; a channel state dependent method to enforce minimum and maximum throughputs for QoS differentiation in wireless networks; a techniue for reliable point to multipoint wireless comm; load equalizing smart antennas for wireless local area networks; channel partitioning for wireless local area networks; collaborative comm. for wireless local area networks. Avocations: running, music, philosophy. Office: Beceem Comm 3960 Freedom Cir Santa Clara CA Home Phone: 408-387-5060; Office Phone: 408-387-5060. Business E-Mail: kmedepalli@gmail.com.

MEDEROS, CAROLINA LUISA, public policy consultant; b. Rochester, Minn., July 1, 1947; d. Luis O. and Carolina (del Valle) Mederos. BA, Vanderbilt U., 1969; MA, U. Chgo., 1971. Adminstrv. asst. Lt. Gov. Ill., Chgo., 1972; sr. rsch. assoc. U. Chgo., 1972; project mgr., cons. Urban Dynamics, Inner City Fund and Cmty. Programs Inc., Chgo., 1972-73; legis. asst. to Senate pres. Ill. State Senate, Chgo. and Springfield, 1973-76; program analyst Dept. Transp., Washington, 1976-79, chief, trans. assistance programs div., 1979-81, dir. programs and evaluation, 1981-88, chairwoman, sec.'s safety rev. task force, 1985-88, deputy asst. sec. for safety, policy and internat. affairs, 1988-89; cons. Patton Boggs LLP, Washington, 1990—. Recipient award for Meritorious Achievement, Sec. Transp. 1980, Superior Achievement award U.S. Dept. Transp., 1981, Sec.'s Gold Medal award for Outstanding Achievement, 1986, Presdl. Rank award, 1987. Home: 2723 O St NW Washington DC 20007-3128 Office: Patton Boggs LLP 2550 M St NW Washington DC 20037-1350 Home Phone: 202-337-4107; Office Phone: 202-457-5653. Business E-Mail: cmederos@pattonboggs.com.

MEDFORD, JAMES A., lawyer; b. Norfolk, Va., May 25, 1945; AB, U. N.C., 1967; student, Johannes Gutenberg Universitaet, Mainz, Germany; JD cum laude, Harvard U., 1971. Bar: NC 1971, US Ct. of Appeals (4th cir.) 1972, US Ct. of Appeals (fed. cir.) 1987, US Dist. Cts.(ea., mid. & we. dists.) NC. Law clk. to Hon. J. Braxton Craven Jr. U.S. Ct. Appeals (4th cir.), 1971-72; atty. Smith Helms Mulliss & Moore, Greensboro, NC; ptnr. Smith Moore LLP, Greensboro, NC. Contbr. articles to profl. jours. Mem. sci. adv. bd. U. NC, Greensboro; mem. NC World Trade Ctr. Morehead scholar, Fulbright scholar, NC Super Lawyer 2006, Bus. NC's Legal Elite 2004-06, Best Lawyers Am. 2001-07. Mem. Am. Law Inst., Phi Beta Kappa, Phi Eta Sigma, Internat. Bar Assn., Am. Health Lawyers Assn., NC Bar Assn. (Sect. Internat. Law, coun. 1994-1997, 1998-2001, 2005-2008), ABA (White Collar Crime com. sect. criminal justice), Wong Sun soc. Office: Smith Moore LLP 300 N Greene St Ste 1400 Greensboro NC 27401 Office Phone: 336-378-5265. Office Fax: 336-378-5400. Business E-Mail: jim.medford@smithmoorelaw.com.

MEDH, JHEEM D., medical educator, biochemist, researcher; BS in Chemistry and Biochemistry, U. Bombay, India, 1982; MS in Biochemistry, U. Bombay, 1984; PhD in Biochemistry, U. Tex. Med. Br., Galveston, 1990. Jr. rsch. fellow, dept. physiology L.T.M. Med. Coll., Bombay, 1984-86; rsch. asst., dept. human biol. chemistry and genetics U. Tex. Med. Br., 1986-90; postgrad. rsch. biochemist, dept. medicine U. Calif., San Diego, 1991-93; asst. rsch. scientist, adj. asst. prof., dept. medicine U. Iowa Coll. Medicine, Iowa City, 1993—. Presenter in field of role of LDL receptor-related protein, receptor-associated protein and lipoprotein lipase on the regulation of lipoprotein metabolism. Juvenile Diabetes Internat. Found. fellow 1992-93; recipient nat. grand-in-aid award Am. Heart Assn., 1995-98; recipient Gip Hudson award Nat. Student Rsch. Forum, 1989, Stephen C. Silverthorne award Grad. Sch. Biomed. Scis., U. Tex. Med. Br. Mem. Am. Heart Assn. (coun. for basic science), Am. Soc. Cell Biology, Juvenile Diabetes Found. Internat. Office: U Iowa Coll Med 200 CMAB Iowa City IA 52242

MEDICI, ROCHELLE, psychologist, brain researcher; b. Morris, Minn., Dec. 31, 1933; d. Albert and Johanna (Ulvestad) Johnson; m. Michael A. Medici, July 4, 1970 (div. 1995); 1 child, Bianca Cristina. BA magna cum laude, U. Minn., 1954, PhD, 1962. Lic. psychologist, Calif. USPHS postdoctoral fellow U. Minn., Mpls., 1965-67; asst. biologist Calif. Inst. Tech., Pasadena, 1967-68; assoc. prof. anatomy Brain Rsch. Inst., UCLA, 1968-79; pvt. practice neuropsychology, San Marino, Calif., 1980—. Cons. AEC, Washington, 1976, WHO, Washington, 1976, Neuroscis. Rsch. Program, Boston, 1977. Rschr. numerous publs.; contbr. articles to profl. jours (Nature, Brain Research, et al) Mem. APA, AAAS, Explorers Club, Phi Beta Kappa. Democrat. Avocations: music, art, travel, politics, literature. Home: 2220 El Molino Pl San Marino CA 91108-2317

MEDICUS, HEINRICH ADOLF, physicist, researcher; b. Zurich, Switzerland, Dec. 24, 1918; came to U.S., 1950; naturalized, 1995; s. Friedrich Georg and Clara Anna (Frey) M.; m. Hildegard Julie Schmelz, June 15, 1961. Diploma, Swiss Fed. Inst. Tech., Zurich, 1943, DSc, 1949. Rsch. assoc. Swiss Fed. Inst. Tech., Zurich, 1943-50; visitor Lawrence Berkeley (Calif.) Lab., 1950-51, MIT, Cambridge, Mass., 1951-52, instr., vis. asst. prof., 1952-55; from assoc. prof. to prof. exptl. nuc. physics and history of modern physics Rensselaer Poly. Inst., Troy, NY, 1955-87, prof. emeritus, 1987—. Vis. scientist Atomic Energy Research Establishment Harwell, Eng., 1967-68, Swiss Inst. Nuclear Research, Villigen, 1974-75. Co-author: Fields and Particles, 1973; contbr. articles to profl. jours. Bd. mem. Albany Symphony Orch., NY, 2006—. With Swiss Army, 1937—50. Fellow Swiss Found., 1950-52 Mem. Am. Phys. Soc., Swiss Phys. Soc., Swiss Am. Hist. Soc., Hudson-Mohawk Swiss Soc. (pres. 1974-06), Delta Tau Delta (pres. house corp. Upsilon chpt. 1984-91, faculty adv. 1991-95), Swiss Alpine Club. Presbyterian. Avocation: wine education. Home: 1 The Knoll East Acres Troy NY 12180 Office: Rensselaer Poly Inst Dept Physics Troy NY 12180 Business E-Mail: medich@rpi.edu.

MEDICUS, HILDEGARD JULIE, retired dentist, orthodontist, educator; b. Frankfurt, Germany, July 25, 1928; came to U.S., 1961, naturalized, 1995; d. Gustav and Elizabeth Berta (Neunhoeffer) Schmelz; m. Heinrich Adolf Medicus, June 15, 1961. DMD, U. Marburg, W. Germany, 1953; orthodontics diploma, U. Düsseldorf, W. Germany, 1957. lic. dentist, N.Y. Postdoctoral fellow dental sch. U. Zürich, Switzerland, 1957; postdoctoral fellow U. Liège, Belgium, 1958, Forsyth Dental Ctr., Boston, 1959, orthodontic rsch. affiliate, 1963—74; sch. dentist Pub. Sch. Sys., Zürich, 1975—76; dental hygiene instr. Hudson Valley C.C., Troy, NY, 1976—77; pvt. practice Troy, NY, 1977—89; ret., 1989. Active Hudson Mohawk Swiss Soc. Mem. AAUW, ADA, European Orthodontic Soc., German Orthodontic Soc. Achievements include study of functional orthodontic appliances and growth and development. Home: 1 The Knoll Troy NY 12180-7284

MEDIN, A. LOUIS, computer company executive; b. Balt., Oct. 2, 1925; s. Nathan and Bessie (Zell) Medin; m. Julia A. Levin, Dec. 24, 1950; children: Douglas, David, Thomas, Linda. BSChemE, Johns Hopkins U., Balt., 1948; PhDChemE, Ohio State U., Columbus, 1951. Registered profl. engr., Md. Chem. engr. AEC, Wilmington, Del., 1951-53; rsch. engr. Ford Motor Co., Dearborn, Mich., 1953-55; chief chem. nuclear reactor tech. ALCO Products, Schenectady, 1955-58; head nuclear rsch. engr. U.S. Steel, Monroeville, Pa., 1958-63; project mgr. missile design AVCO Corp., Wilmington, Mass., 1963-65; mgr. sci. applications IBM, Manassas, Va., 1965-72, mgr. advanced applications, 1975-87; exec. dir. Inst. for Simulation and Tng., Orlando, Fla., 1987-2000. Chmn. sci. and engring. tech. divsn. Nat. Def. Indsl. Assn.; dir. environment and life scis. Dept. Def., 1972—74; lectr. in field. Contbr. articles to profl. and tech. jours. Mem. Monroeville Parks and Recreation Commn., 1960; chmn. Monroeville Mental Health Assn., 1961; mem. Monroeville Zoning and Planning Commn., 1961; chmn. sci. and engring. tech. divsn. Nat. Def. Indsl. Assn., 1999—; dep. precinct chmn. Montgomery County Rep. Com., 1982. With USN, 1944—46, PTO. Recipient award, Am. Chem. Soc., 1957. Fellow: Am. Inst. Chemists; mem.: Am. Metall. Soc., Am. Def. Preparedness Assn. (chmn. sci. and engring. tech. divsn. 1981—, ednl. advisor Def. Jour., Am. Def. award 1984, Gold medal 1990), Am. Inst. Chem. Engrs., Nat. Security Indsl. Assn., Ohio State U. Alumni Assn., Johns Hopkins U. Alumni Assn.

Home: 11401 Ridge Mist Ter Potomac MD 20854-7002 Office Phone: 301-762-1290. Personal E-mail: lmedin@comcast.net.

MEDIN, ALICE LOUISE, librarian; b. Eau Claire, Wis., July 17, 1935; d. Ongle Ever and Esther Moholt; m. Myron James Medin, May 14, 1955; children: John, Kāren, Anne. BA in Edn., Ea. Wash. U., 1957; MA in Libr. Sci., U. Wis., Madison, 1977. Libr. asst. U. Wis. Fond du Lac Ctr., 1979; reference libr. Plaza br. Kansas City (Mo.) Pub. Libr., 1984-86, describer old and rare books main libr., 1985; dir. Rogers (Ark.) Pub. Libr., 1987—2000. Mem. N.W. Ark. C.C. Found. Bd., Rogers, 1987—95. Bd. dirs. Bella Vista Pub. Libr., 2002—03. Recipient Intellectual Freedom Fighter award, ALA/Freedom to Read Found., 1999. Mem. AAUW (pres. Fond du Lac br. 1973-75), Ark. Libr. Assn. (mem. intellectual freedom com. 1993-2000), N.W. Ark. Libr. Assn. (v.p. 1988-89), Round Table Lectr. Club (v.p. 1979). Lutheran. Avocations: reading, knitting, theater. Home: 1 Audley Cir Bella Vista AR 72714-5645

MEDIN, DOUGLAS, psychology professor; Chmn. Psychology Dept. Northwestern U., Ill., prof. Ill., dir. program in culture, language and cognition Ill., co-dir. program in cognitive studies of environ. Ill. Recipient Disting. Sci. Contribution award, APA, 2005. Fellow: Am. Psychol. Soc. (bd. dirs. 2005—); mem.: NAS. Office: Psychology Dept Northwestern Univ 222 Swift Hall Evanston IL 60208 Office Phone: 847-467-1660. Office Fax: 847-491-7859. E-mail: medin@northwestern.edu.

MEDIN, JULIA ADELE, mathematics professor, researcher; b. Dayton, Ohio, Jan. 16, 1929; d. Caroline (Feinberg) Levitt; m. A. Louis Medin, Dec. 24, 1950; children: Douglas, David, Thomas, Linda. BS in Maths. Edn., Ohio State U., Columbus, 1951; MA in Higher Edn., George Washington U., Washington, 1977; PhD in Counseling and Math. Edn., Am. U., Washington, 1985. Cert. tchr. Fla., Md. Rsch. engr. Sun Oil Co., Marcus Hook, Pa., 1951-53; tchr. maths. Montgomery County Pub. Schs., Rockville, Md., 1973-88; asst. prof. maths. U. Ctrl. Fla., Orlando, 1988-90, sr. ednl. technologist Inst. for Simulation and Tng., 1990-99; sr. assoc. Mgmt. and Ednl. Tech. Assocs., 1999—. Adv. steering com. U.S. Dept. Edn. Title II, Washington, 1985-89; sr. math. educator, rschr. Inst. for Simulation and Tng., Orlando, 1988-90; judge, co-chair GII Nat. Awards; co-acad. advisor I/ITSEC Conf.; condr. nationwide rsch. project on effective use of technology in the classroom; spkr. in field Author: Loc. of Cont. and Test Anxiety of Mar. Math. Studies, 1985, Single Sex Public Schools, Who Needs Them and Why, 2005; co-author: Single Sex Public Schools, 2005; contbg. author: Math for 14 & 17 Yr. Olds, 1987; editor: Simulation and Computer-Based Technology for Education; contbr. articles to profl. jours. Dem. committeewoman Town of Monroeville, Pa., 1962; religious sch. dir. Beth Tikva Religious Sch., Rockville, 1971; cons. Monroeville Mental Health, 1960 Mem. Nat. Coun. Tchrs. Math., Math. Assn. Am. (task force on minorities in math.), Women in Math. in Edn., Nat. Coalition for Tech. in Edn. and Tng., Phi Delta Kappa, Kappa Delta Pi. Home and Office: 11401 Ridge Mist Ter Potomac MD 20854-7002 Personal E-mail: jmedin@comcast.net.

MEDIN, MYRON JAMES, JR., city manager; b. Ladysmith, Wis., July 8, 1931; s. Myron James and Mildred Clara (Johnson) M.; m. Alice Louise Moholt, May 14, 1955; children: John, Karen, Anne. BA, St. Olaf Coll., 1954; MPA, U. Mich., 1959. Adminstrv. asst. to city mgr. City of Fond du Lac, Wis., 1959-64, city mgr. Wis., 1967-83, City of New Ulm, Minn., 1964-67; city adminstr. City of Kansas City, Kans., 1983-85; pres., gen. mgr. Bella Vista Village Property Owners Assn., Ark., 1986-92. Mem. com. human devel. Nat. League of Cities, Washington, 1974-80, com. on govtl. relations, 1971-73; chmn. City Plan Commn., Fond du Lac, Wis., 1967-83 Bd. dirs. United Way, Kansas City, Kans., 1984-85, YMCA, 1984-85, Kansas City C.C. Found., 1984-85; mem. Gov.'s Regionalism Task Force Adv. Com., Madison, Wis., 1968-70; trustee Phillips Pro-Celebrity Golf Tennis Charity Classic, 1991-92; mem. transition task force Bella Vista Incorporation, 2005-06; vol. historic house mus. and gardens. Lt. USAF, 1955-57. Recipient Community Service award Fond du Lac Assn. of Commerce, 1978 Mem. Internat. City Mgmt. Assn., Wis. City Mgmt. Assn. (pres. 1975-76), Wis. League of Municipalities (bd. dirs. 1978-80), Wis. Alliance of Cities (v.p. 1972-73), Am. Soc. Pub. Adminstrn. (bd. dirs. 1984-85, Pub. Adminstr. of Yr. award 1985), Bella Vista-Bentonville C. of C. (bd. dirs. 1987-91), Nat. Trust for Hist. Preservation, Benton County Hist. Soc. Lutheran. Avocations: swimming, reading, tennis, gardening, genealogy. Home: 1 Audley Cir Bella Vista AR 72714-5645

MEDINA, DAVID, state supreme court justice; b. Galveston Island, Tex., 1958; BS, Southwest Tex. State U., 1980; JD, S. Tex. Coll. of Law, 1989. Joined Cooper Industries Inc., Houston, 1987—89, litigation counsel, 1989; judge 157th State Dist. Ct., Tex., 1990—99; assoc. gen. counsel Cooper Industries Inc., Houston, 2000—04; gen. counsel Gov. Rick Perry, Tex., 2004—05; justice Tex. Supreme Ct., 2005—. Former adjunct prof. S. Tex. Coll. of Law. Former bd. mem. Habitat for Humanity, Houston Metro; bd. mem. Spring Klein Baseball Assn. Mem.: ABA, Mexican Am. Bar Assn., Assn. for Advancement of Mexican Am., Houston Bar Assn. Office: Tex Supreme Ct PO Box 12248 Austin TX 78711 Office Phone: 512-463-1316. Office Fax: 512-463-1365.

MEDINA, JANE S., music educator; d. Harry R. and Anna M. Peirce; m. Pablo Medina, June 14, 1980; children: Anna M., Joel L. BA in Music Edn., Azusa Pacific U., Calif., 1975; EdM, Calif. State U., Fullerton, 1999. Tchr. Orange Unified Sch. Dist., Calif., 1977—. Adj. prof. Calif. State U., Fullerton, 1999—2004, adv. bd. Author: (book) My Name Is Jorge on Both Sides of the River, 1999 (Noteable Book, 1999), The Dream on Bianca's Wall, 2004 (America's award, 2005), Tomas Rivera, 2004. Edwin Carr Fellow, Calif. State U., 1999. Mem.: NEA, Nat. Coun. Tchrs. English, Internat. Reading Assn. (reviewer 1999—). Avocations: writing, music, walking, photography. Personal E-mail: medinajane@sbcglobal.net.

MEDINA, JESSE JAMES, protective services official, educator; b. Roma, Tex., May 18, 1956; s. Benigno and Celia Gonzalez M.; m. Dina Pena, May 25, 1979; children: Gerardo J., Rebecca A. AAS, Laredo CC, Tex., 1977; BS, St. John's U., Springfield, Mo., 2000. Dep. sheriff Starr County, Rio Grande City, Tex., 1975-78; police officer City of Pharr, Tex., 1978-79, detective sgt. Tex., 1984-99, lt. Tex., 1984-90, capt. Tex., 1990-92, asst. chief police Tex., 1992-96, chief police Tex., 1996—. Sgt.-at-arms Rio Grande Valley Chief Assn., 1998. Editor State Mag. Chmn., 1983. V.p. Self Sufficiency Counsel, 1999; sec. treas. team plan com. Traffic Problem, 2000; mem. Internat. Bridge Traffic Adv. Coun., 2002--. Recipient Leadership award, Mexican Govt., 1999. Fellow Tex. Atty. Gens. Office (Excellence award 1989). Republican. Menonite. Avocations: hunting, fishing, camping. Home: 810 Tarrant Cir Pharr TX 78577-3942 Office: Pharr Police Department 1900 N Cage Blvd Pharr TX 78577-1802 E-mail: jmedina@pharrpd.net.

MEDINA, KATE (KATHRYN BACH MEDINA), publishing executive, editor; b. Plainfield, NJ; d. F. Earl and Elizabeth E. Bach; 1 child. BA, Smith Coll., Northampton, Mass.; MA, NYU. With Doubleday Pub. Co., Inc., NYC, 1965-85; assoc. pub., exec. editl. dir., sr. v.p. Random House Inc., NYC, 1985—, assoc. pub. Random House Publishing Group, 2007—. Assoc. fellow Jonathan Edwards Coll., Yale U., New Haven, 1982—; fellow Bunting Inst., 1994—95; cons., 1995—96, Coun. Fgn. Rels. Editor: books by James Atlas, Peter Benchley, Elizabeth Berg, Amy Bloom, Bill Bradley, Tom Brokaw, Anita Brookner, Ethan Canin, Michael Chabon, Robert Coles, Agnes deMille, E.L. Doctorow, Jane Fonda, Max Frankel, Charles Frazier, Henry Louis Gates, Jr., Carol Gilligan, Mary Gordon, David Halberstam, Kathryn Harrison, John Irving, Tracy Kidder, Wynton Marsalis, Bobbie Ann Mason, Jon Meacham, James A. Michener, Sandra Day O'Connor, Jane Pauley, Anna Quindlen, Nancy Reagan, James Reston, William Safire, Maggie Scarf, Gloria Steinem, Christopher Tilghman, Alice Walker, Daniel Yergin. Office: Random House Inc 1745 Broadway New York NY 10019

MEDINA, KRISTA LISDAHL, neuropsychologist, educator; d. Alan James and Carol Jean Lisdahl; m. Mario Medina, Sept. 16, 2000. BA summa cum laude, U. Minn., Mpls., 1998; MA, U. Cin., 2002, PhD, 2005. Clin. neuropsychology intern U. Ariz., Tucson, 2004—05; asst. prof. U. Cin., 2007—. Vol. Chrysalis, A Ctr. for Women, Mpls., 1996—98; vol. therapist Talbert Ho., Women's Jail, Cin., 2001—02; vol. neuropsychologist San Diego Vets. Adminstrn., 2005—. Recipient Golden Key, Nat. Honors Soc., 1994—98, Early Career Investigator Travel award, Nat. Inst. on Drug Abuse, 2005, Rsch. Tng. Inst. Travel award, 2006, Nelson Butters award, Nat. Acad. Neuropsychology, 2006, Jr. Investigator award, Nat. Inst. on Alcohol Abuse and Alcoholism, 2006, Coll. Problems Drug Dependency, 2007; fellow, U. Calif., San Diego, 2005—07; Postdoctoral Fellowship, Nat. Inst. on Drug Abuse, 2005—07. Mem.: APA (assoc.), Internat. Neuropsychological Soc. (assoc.). Democrat. Avocations: mountain biking, travel, bicycling, photography. Office: U Cin Dept Psychology 424 Dyer Hall Cincinnati OH 45221

MEDINA, RUBENS, law librarian; b. Paraguay; arrived in US, 1964; Degree in Law, Nat. U. Asunción; MS in Legal Institutions, U. Wis., Madison, 1966, PhD in Law and Sociology, 1970. Lawyer, Paraguay; prof. Nat. U. Paraguay; chief Hispanic law divsn. Libr. of Congress, Washington, 1971—94, law libr., 1994—, mem. libr. mgmt. team, dir. Global Legal Info. Network. Tchr. Nat. U. Asunción, Paraguay, U. Catolica de Valparaiso, Chile, U. Wis. Law Sch., NYU Law Sch.; lectr. in field. Bd. dirs. Burton Found. Recipient Federal 100 Award, 2007; fellow Land Tenure Ctr., U. Wis., Orgn. Am. States. Office: Law Libr Congress 101 Independence Ave, SE Washington DC 20540 *

MEDINA MILGROM, GENIE, pharmaceutical company executive; b. Havana, Cuba, Feb. 7, 1955; came to U.S., 1960; d. George O. and Isabel Medina; m. Sergio Salvador Hernandez, Sept. 8, 1974 (div. Aug. 1990); m. Michael Milgrom, July 12, 1992; children: Sergio, Nicole. Dir. Farma Internat., Miami, Fla., 1973—. Mem., advisor Dist. Export Coun., Miami, Fla., 1998-2001. Fin. v.p. Young Israel of Kendall, Miami. Recipient Pres.'s E award for export excellence U.S. Sec. of Commerce, 1984, 98; named Hispanic Bus. Woman of Yr., Region VI U.S. Hispanic C. of C., 1998, # 7 in nation of fastest-growing Hispanic exporters Hispanic Bus. Mag., 1992—. Republican. Jewish. Avocations: miniature arts dioramas, parchment crafts, paper art. Office: Farma Internat 9501 Old S Dixie Hwy Miami FL 33156 Fax: (305) 670-4417. E-mail: geniemlgrom@hotmail.com.

MEDISH, MARK, federal government official; b. Washington, Dec. 10, 1962; BS, Georgetown U., 1984; MS, Harvard U., 1987, JD, 1990. Bar: DC 1990. Atty. in pvt. practice, Wash., 1990—92, Covington & Burling, Wash., 1992—94; adminstr. UN Devel. Programs, NYC, 1994-95, AID, Washington, 1995-97; dep. asst. sec. for Eurasia and Middle East, Dept. of the Treasury, Washington, 1997—2000; spl. asst. (to pres.)and sr. dir. US Nat. Security Coun. (for russian, ukrainian and eurasian Affairs); ptnr. Akin Gump Strauss Hauer & Feld, LLP, Wash., DC. Adj faculty Harvard U, Georgetown U, John Hopkins U; fin. and strategic adv. Govts. Balkans region (including fed. rep. of Yugoslavia). Contbr. articles to profl. jour. Recipient Luce award, 1990, Shintaro-ABC award, 1996; Mellon grantee, 1984, Fulbright grantee, 1985. Mem. Coun. on Fgn. Rels., vis. fellow Japan Inst. of Internat. Affairs, Tokyo, 1990-1991. Office: Akin Gump Strauss Hauer Feld LLP 1333 New Hampshire Ave NW Washington DC 20036 Office Phone: 202-939-2323. Office Fax: 202-887-4288. Business E-Mail: mmedish@akingump.com.

MEDLAND, MAURICE BLUE, writer; b. Centerville, Iowa, Sept. 29, 1936; s. William C. and Avis N. (Blue) M.; m. Karen A. McFarland, Aug. 7, 1965; children: Melissa A., Steven W. BS, Truman State U., 1961; MBA, Pepperdine U., 1977. Mgmt. sys. analyst Rockwell Internat. Corp., Downey, Calif., 1961-70; dir. Fluor Corp., Irvine, Calif., 1970-85; v.p. PacifiCare Health Sys., Cypress, Calif., 1985-87; novelist Calif., 1987—; instr. U. Calif., Irvine, 1998—. Advisor Calif. State U. Fullerton Writers Program, 1998—. Author: Point of Honor, 1997, China Star, 2007. With USN, 1954-57. Recipient Apollo Achievement award, NASA, 1969. Mem. The Authors Guild, Internat. Thriller Writers. Home: 19842 Villager Cir Yorba Linda CA 92886-4454 E-mail: mauricemedland@yahoo.com.

MEDLAND, WILLIAM JAMES, university chancellor; b. Logansport, Ind., Jan. 1, 1944; s. Thomas Gallagher and Mary Elizabeth (Hassett) M.; m. Donna Lee Bahnaman, Mar. 12, 1977; children: Bridget Marie, Mark David, Jeanne Nicole. BA, U. Notre Dame, Ind., 1966; student, St. Louis U., 1972-74; MA in History, Ball State U., Muncie, Ind., 1967, MA in Edn., 1979, PhD in History, 1980; postgrad., Inst. for Mgmt. Lifelong Edn., Harvard U., 1985, Ctr. Internat. Cooperation and Security Studies, U. Wis., 1988, Ctr. Internat. Studies, MIT, 1989, Freie Universitat, Berlin, 1991; DHL (hon.), Vitelbo U., 2005. Instr. history and philosophy Donnelly coll., Kansas City, Kans., 1967-70; curricular advisor Ball State U., Muncie, Ind., 1970-71, teaching fellow, 1977-80; asst. dean St. Louis U., 1971-75; employee supr. Wilson, Inc., Logansport, 1975-76; ops. mgr. Watson-Jenkins, Inc., Indpls., 1976-77; dean of coll., asst. prof. history Springfield Coll., Ill., 1980-81; acad. dean, assoc. prof. history and edn. Marymount Coll., Salina, Kans., 1981-86; exec. v.p., provost, prof. history St. Mary's U., Winona, Minn., 1986-91; pres., prof. history Viterbo U., LaCrosse, Wis., 1991—2006, also bd. dirs., CEO, 1991—2006, univ. chancellor, 2006—. Edn. cons. Am. Inst. Banking, Springfield, 1980-81; advisor Adv. Com. to Sch. Bd., Salina, 1984, Salina Diocesan Bd. Edn., 1981-83; evaluator North Ctrl. Assn., Chgo., 1987-2000. Author: Cuban Missile Crisis of 1962-Needless or Necessary?, 1988, reprint, 1990, A Guide to Writing College Research Papers, 1989, The Catholic School: A Bibliographical Resource Guide, 1990; editor: Ind. Acad. Social Scis. jour., 1979, Perspectives: A Liberal Arts Exchange (faculty jour.), 1988. Coll. solicitor United Way, St. Louis, 1973; coord. Coll./Cmty. Artist Series, Salina, 1981—84; mem. Franciscan-Skemp Healthcare Cmty. Bd., 2002—; adv. Hmong Cultural Ctr., 2005—; bd. dirs. Immaculate Heart of Mary Sem., Winona, 1987—91, La Crosse Med. Health Sci. Consortium, 1993—2004, Wis. Found. for Ind. Colls., 1994—98, Assn. Franciscan Colls. and Univs., 1999—2004; chair La Crosse Diocesan Edn. Commn., 1994—2001; bd. dirs. Mathy Ctr., 2003—, Cath. Charities, LaCrosse, Wis., 2006—. Named Iverson-Freking Ecumenical award, 2003, LaCrosse Tribune Person of the Yr., 2003; named to Hall of Fame, Boys and Girls Club, 2007, Boys and Girls Club Wall of Fame, 2007; recipient Nat. Man and Youth award, Boys and Girls Clubs, 2004, Collaboration Achievement award, Ladco, 2004, Svc. award, LaCross C. of C., 2004, Disting. Svc. award, Pope John XXIII, 2006; Ctr. Internat. Studies fellow, MIT/Harvard U., 1989. Mem.: Wis. Assn. Ind. Colls. and Univs. (bd. dirs. 1991—2006), Am. Assn. Ind. Coll. Pres., Coun. Coll. Pres.; Am. Assn. Higher Edn., La Crosse C. of C. (bd. dirs. 2000—04, exec. com. 2001—04, Cmty. Svc. award 2004), Rotary, KC, Phi Delta Kappa, Phi Alpha Theta (rsch. award Ball State U. 1979). Roman Catholic. Avocations: reading, research. Home: 119 Calla Ct Onalaska WI 54650-8317 Office: Viterbo Univ Office of Chancellor 900 Viterbo Dr La Crosse WI 54601-4777 Office Phone: 608-796-3000. Business E-Mail: wjmedland@viterbo.edu.

MEDLIN, HOMER LEWIS, engineering executive; b. Midland, Tex., Sept. 3, 1920; s. Lewis Jerome and Mary Lydia (Ward) M.; m. Dorothy Adeline Jordan, May 3, 1947; children: Debra Sue, Dianne Cecile, Gary Lewis. Student, Howard Payne Coll., Brownwood, Tex., 1939-40; BSEE, Tex. Tech U., 1943; Cert. in Comms. Engring., Washington U., St. Louis, 1963. Registered profl. engr., Tex. Various engring. positions S.W. Bell Telephone, Dallas, 1946-54, 55-61; sr. egnr. #5 X-B switching ewuipment Western Electric Co., Chgo., 1954; equipment engring. gen. staff S.W. Bell Telephone, St. Louis, 1961-63, with North Tex. engring. of equipment divsn. Dallas, 1963-68; engr. of equipment AT&T, NYC, 1968-69; engr. of equipment North Tex. S.W. Bell Telephone, Dallas, 1969-73, engring. mgr. equipment and bldgs., 1973-79, divsn. mgr. network engring., 1979-85. Joint editor: The Engineering Manager Concept, 1969. Chmn. bd. Mt. Auburn Christian Ch., Dallas, 1953; chmn. bd. Lakeview Christian Ch., Dallas, 1973, 94, chmn. trustees, 1995, 96. Cpl. Signal Corps, U.S. Army, 1943-45; ensign USN, 1945-46. Mem. NSPE, IEEE (life), Tex. Soc. Profl. Engrs., Dallas Electric Club (pres. 1964), Tex. Soc. Telephone Engrs., Telephone Pioneers Am. (pres. Dallas 1989-90), Tau Beta Pi. Republican. Mem. Christian Ch. (Disciples Of Christ). Home: Apt 602 5455 La Sierra Dr Dallas TX 75231-4147

MEDLIN, JOHN GRIMES, JR., banker, director; b. Benson, NC, Nov. 23, 1933; s. John Grimes and Mabel (Stephenson) M. BS in Bus. Adminstrn., U. N.C., 1956; grad., The Exec. Program, U. Va., 1965. With Wachovia Bank & Trust Co., Winston-Salem, NC, 1959—98, pres., 1974; pres., CEO Wachovia Bank and Wachovia Corp., Winston-Salem, NC, 1977-93; chmn. bd. Wachovia Corp., Winston-Salem, NC, 1987-98, chmn. emeritus, 1998—. Trustee Nat. Humanities Ctr., Wake Forest U., The Duke Endowment, The Rsch. Triangle Found., Kenan Inst. for Ethics; mem. State Jud. Coun. N.C., 2000—; active numerous civic and svc. orgns. With USNR, 1956-59. Mem. Phi Delta Theta. Office: Wachovia Corp 100 N Main St Winston Salem NC 27101 Office Phone: 336-732-5000.

MEDLOCK, DONALD LARSON, lawyer; b. Port Chester, NY, Mar. 8, 1927; s. Harold and Emma Adelaide (MacLennan) Medlock; m. Katharine Smedes Nicholson, May 21, 1955; children: Katharine Baird, Margaret MacLennan, William Nicholson. BA with honors, Yale U., 1947, LLB, 1950. Bar: N.Y. 1950, U.S. Dist. Ct. (so. dist.) N.Y. 1951, U.S. Ct. Appeals (2d cir.) 1951, U.S. Dist. Ct. (ea. dist.) N.Y. 1952, U.S. Tax Ct. 1952, U.S. Ct. Custom and Patent Appeals. Assoc. Winthrop, Stimson, Putnam & Roberts, NYC, 1950-56, ptnr., 1957-94, sr. counsel, 1995—. Bd. dirs. Bancard Sys. N.Y. Inc. Editor: Yale Law Jour., 1948—50; former dir. Fin. Times Publs., Economist Newspaper Group. Bd. dirs. Yale Alumni Fund, 1955—, chmn., 1984—86, mem. exec. com., 1980—88; bd. dirs. Port Washington Estates Assn., 1958—61; sec., bd. dirs. Port Washington Cmty. Chest, 1959—61; bd. mgrs., mem. exec. com. William Sloane Ho. YMCA Greater N.Y., 1979—84; chmn. Yale Law Sch. Fund, 1974—76; mem. exec. com. Assn. Families U. Denver, 1982—84; mem. ann. fund patents com. Taft Sch., 1979—81; chmn. univ. coun. com. Law Sch. Yale U., 1979—86; mem. devel. bd. Yale U., 1984—88, mem. exec. com., 1984—86, Yale Law Sch., 1975—79, hon., 1979—. Recipient citation, Yale Law Sch., 1977, Yale Alumni Fund Chmn.'s award, 1979, 1987, Yale medal, 1994. Mem.: Assn. Bar City of N.Y. (mem. com. profl. ethics 1958—61), Fed. Power Bar Assn., India House, Corbey Ct. Yale Law Sch., Assn. Yale Alumni (rep.-at-large 1979—82, mem. com. undergraduate admissions 1979—82, mem. com. Yale medal 1981, bd. dirs. 1984—86), Mory's Assn., Yale Club N.Y.C., Manhasset Bay Yacht Club, Tuscarora Club (Margaretville, N.Y.) (bd. dirs. 1963—95, sec. 1970—86, v.p. 1984—86), Country Club Landfall, Scroll and Key Soc., Phi Beta Kappa, Phi Delta Phi. Avocations: trout fishing, tennis, reading, crossword puzzles, golf. Home: Landfall 800 Oyster Landing Wilmington NC 28405-5292

MEDNICK, ROBERT, accountant; b. Chgo., Apr. 1, 1940; s. Harry and Nettie (Brenner) Mednick; m. Susan Lee Levinson, Oct. 28, 1962; children: Michael Jon, Julie Eden, Adam Charles. BSBA, Roosevelt U., Chgo., 1962. CPA Ill. Staff asst. Arthur Andersen, Chgo., 1962-63, sr. acct., 1963-66, mgr., 1966-71, ptnr., 1971-98, mng. dir. SEC policies, 1973-76, mng. dir. auditing procedures, 1976-79. Vice chmn. com. on profl. stds. Andersen Worldwide, 1979-82, chmn. com., 1982-98, mng. ptnr. profl. and regulatory matters, 1993-98; mem. faculty Northwestern U. Kellogg Grad. Sch. Mgmt., 1999; mem. panel disting. neutrals in banking, acctg. and fin. svcs. Internat. Inst. for Conflict Prevention and Resolution, 2003—. Contbr. articles to profl. jours. Bd. dirs. Roosevelt U., Chgo., 1977—, vice chmn., 1986-94, sr. vice chmn., 1994—, life trustee, 1999—; bd. dirs. Auditorium Theatre Coun., 1990-96, Lake Shore Drive Synagogue, 1992—; co-chmn. adv. coun. Chgo. Action for Soviet Jewry, Highland Park, Ill., 1983-87; bd. dirs., mem. exec. com. Am. Judicature Soc., 1990-95, vice chmn., 1993-95; bd. overseers Rand Corp. Inst. Civil Justice, 1994-98; bd. dirs. Nat. Bur. of Econ. Rsch., 1998—, treas., 1999—; acccountability adv. coun. to the Comptr. Gen. of the U.S., 2000—. Sgt. USAFR, 1965-69. Recipient Silver medal Ill. CPA Soc., 1962; named One of Ten Outstanding Young Men in Chgo., Chgo. Jr. C. of C., 1973-74; recipient Rolf A. Weil Disting. Service award, Roosevelt U., Chgo., 1983; Max Block award N.Y. State C.P.A. Soc., 1984; Ann. Literary award Jour. Accountancy, 1986, 88; Andrew D. Bradin award for distinctive contbns. to discipline of accountancy Case Western Res. U., Cleve., 1996; Disting. Alumni award Roosevelt U. Walter E. Heller Coll. Bus. Adminstrn., 1997; Disting. Vis. scholar Hebrew U., Jerusalem, 1999, 2000, Coll. Mgmt., Rishon Litzion, 2003, 05, 06, 07, hon. fellow, 2005. Mem. AICPA (bd. dirs. 1986-87, 92-94, 95-98, vice chmn. 1995-96, chmn. 1996-97, numerous coms., Elijah Watt Sells award 1962, Gold Medal for Disting. Svc. 1998), Ill. CPA Soc. (acctg. prins. com. 1973, legal liability com. 1986-89, mgmt. of acctg. practice com. 1991-94, regulation and legis. com. 1998—), Internat. Fedn. Accts. (chmn. compliance adv. panel 2003—). Jewish. Avocations: collecting art, travel. Home Phone: 312-642-4326; Office Phone: 312-642-0571. E-mail: bobmednick@aol.com.

MEDNICK, SHELDON IRA, pharmacist; b. Balt., Apr. 8, 1955; s. Sol Abraham and Doris Asbell Mednick. BSc in Pharmacy, Phila. Coll. Pharmacy, 1979. Registered pharmacist Pa., NJ, Md. Pharmacy intern Cooper U. Hosp., Camden, NJ, 1979—80; staff pharmacist Trenton Psychiat. Hosp., NJ, 1981—86, Phila. Geriatric Ctr., 1986—95, Neighborcare Pharmacy, King of Prussia, Pa., 1997—2001, Girard Med. Ctr., Phila., 2001—. Mem.: Masons (sr. deacon Burlington lodge 1984—85). Jewish. Avocations: reading, music, travel. Home: 2801 Wingate Ct Edgewater Park NJ 08010

MEDOFF, MARK HOWARD, playwright, scriptwriter; b. Mt. Carmel, Ill., Mar. 18, 1940; s. Lawrence Ray and Thelma Irene (Butt) M.; m. Stephanie Thorne, June 24, 1972; children: Debra, Rachel, Jessica. BA, U. Miami, 1962; MA, Stanford U., 1966; DHL, Gallaudet Coll., 1981. Instr. English and drama N.Mex. State U., 1966-79, dramatist-in-residence, 1974—, head dept. drama, 1978-87, prof. drama, 1979-93, artistic dir., 1982-87, Am. S.W. Theatre Co., 1984-87. Artistic dir. Creative Media Inst. N.Mex. State U., 2006. Author: (plays) When You Comin' Back, Red Ryder?, 1974, The Wager, 1975, The Kramer, 1975, The Halloween Bandit, 1978, The Conversion of Aaron Weiss, 1978, Firekeeper, 1978, The Last Chance Saloon, 1979, Children of a Lesser God, 1980 (Soc. West Theatres best play award 1982), The Majestic Kid, 1981, The Hands of Its Enemy, 1984, Kringle's Window, 1985, The Heart Outright, 1986, Road to a Revolution, 2001, Prymate, 2004, The Same Live Over, 2004, (novel) Dreams of Long Lasting: (films) When You Comin' Back, Red Ryder?, 1979, Off Beat, 1986, Apology, 1986, Children of a Lesser God, 1986, Good Guys Wear Black, 1978, Clara's Heart, 1988, The Majestic Kid, 1988, City of Joy, 1992, Homage, 1995, Santa Fe, 1997, Who Fly On Angel's Wings, 2000, Children On Their Birthdays, 2002, 100 MPG, 2006; works appear in Best Plays, 1973-74, 75-75, 79-80, Best Short Plays, 1975, The Homage that Follows, 1987; plays Stumps, 1989, Stefanie Hero, 1990, Showdown On Rio Road, 1995, Gila, 1995, A Christmas Carousel, 1996,

Crunch Time, 1996, Gunfighters, A Gulf War Chronicle, 1997, A Christmas Carousel, 1998, Tommy J and Sally, 2000, Prymate, 2004; dir. (film) Children on Their Birthdays. Guggenheim fellow, 1974-75; recipient Obie award, Drama Desk award, Outer Critics Circle award, Media award Pres.'s Com. Employment Handicapped, Tony award, Kennedy Ctr. medal Excellence in Edn. and Artistic Achievement, 2006; Oscar award nominee for Best Screenplay for Children of A Lesser God, 1987; Reynolds Eminent scholar Fla. State U., 2003-06, Artistic Dir. Creative Media Isnt N.Mex. State U., 2006-. Mem. SAG, Coll. Fellows Am. Theater, Dramatists Guild, Writers Guild Am., Actors Equity Assn., PEN, Coll. Fellows of the Am. Theatre.

MEDVECKY, PATRICIA, retired elementary school educator; b. NYC, Feb. 2, 1936; d. Patrick and Katherine Conneally; m. Thomas E. Medvecky, Aug. 25, 1967; 1 child, Thomas E. II. BA, Hunter Coll., 1961, MS in Edn., 1965. Cert. notary pub. Conn. Tchr. elem. sch. Bd. Edn., NYC, 1961—67, Ridgefield, Conn., 1967—73, ret., 1973; real property abstractor Law Office of T.E. Medvecky, Bethel, Conn., 1973—96. Mem.: Hunter Coll. Alumni Assn., Sheffield Art League. Republican. Roman Catholic. Avocations: history, watercolor painting and etching. Home: PO Box 23 99 Washinee Heights Rd Taconic CT 06079 Personal E-mail: oldpatsy@yahoo.com.

MEDVECKY, ROBERT STEPHEN, lawyer; b. Bridgeport, Conn., Feb. 12, 1931; s. Stephen and Elizabeth (Petro) M.; m. Ellen R. Munt, Nov. 11, 1966; children— Allison L., Beth A., Craig R. AB, Dartmouth, 1952; JD, Harvard, 1955. Bar: Ill. bar 1955, Conn. bar 1958, D.C. bar 1972, Fla. bar 1989. Asso. firm Lord, Bissell & Brook, Chgo., 1955-57; gen. atty. So. New Eng. Telephone Co., New Haven, 1957-71; v.p., gen. counsel, sec. Amtrak, Washington, 1971-75; partner firm Lord, Bissell & Brook, Washington, 1975-78, Reid & Priest, NYC, 1978-87. Clubs: Harvard (N.Y.C.), Fiddlesticks Country (Ft. Meyers, Fla.), Saphire Valley Country (Cashlers, N.C.). Office: 15491 Kilbirnie Dr Fort Myers FL 33912-2424 Home (Summer): 457 Round Hill Rd Sapphire NC 28774 Personal E-mail: bmedvecky@yahoo.com.

MEDVECKY, THOMAS EDWARD, lawyer; b. Bridgeport, Conn., Apr. 22, 1937; s. Stephen and Elizabeth P. Medvecky; m. Patricia Conneally, Aug. 25, 1967; 1 son, Thomas Edward, II. A.B., Bowdoin Coll., 1959; LL.B., St. John's U., 1962. Bar: Conn. 1962. Assoc., Louis Katz, Danbury, Conn., 1963-68; sole practice, Bethel, Conn., 1968—; asst. town counsel Town of Bethel, 1963-67; assoc. dir. State Nat. Bank Conn. Mem. budget com. Danbury (Conn.) Community Chest, 1966-68. Served with USAR, 1962-68. Recipient Am. Jurisprudence award 1962. Mem. ABA, Conn. Bar Assn., Danbury Bar Assn. Democrat. Lutheran. Office: 99 Greenwood Ave PO Box 272 Bethel CT 06801-0272 E-mail: oldlawyer@yahoo.com.

MEDVED, ROBERT ALLEN, lawyer; b. Cleve., July 22, 1945; s. Joseph Jack and Mary (Blasko) Medved. BBA, Kent State U., 1968; JD cum laude, Seattle U., 1975. Bar: Wash. 1976, US Ct. Appeals (9th cir.) 1976, US Dist. Ct. (we. dist.) Wash. 1976, US Dist. Ct. (ea. dist.) Wash. 1979, US Supreme Ct. 1981, US Ct. Appeals (DC cir.) 1989. Fin. analyst Ford Motor Co., Sandusky, Ohio, 1972; rsch. asst. Seattle U., 1973—75; law clk Judge U.S. Ct. Appeals (9th cir.), 1974; asst. to labor arbitrator Tacoma, 1975; law clk. to Judge U. S. Dist. Ct. (ctrl. dist.) Calif., 1976; assoc. Graham & Dunn, Seattle, 1976—81, ptnr., 1981—82, Drake and Whiteley, Bellevue, Wash., 1982—86, Foster, Pepper & Shefelman, Seattle, 1986—97; pvt. practice Mercer Island, 1997—. Spl. dist. counsel 8th Congl. Dist., Wash., 1983—86. Editor-in-chief: Seattle U. Law Rev. Bd. dirs. Bellevue CC found., 1986—98. Lt. USN, 1968—71. Seattle U. scholar, 1974. Mem.: Wash. State Bar Assn., Fed. Bar Assn. (chair intellectual property com.). Roman Catholic. Office: 7238 SE 32nd St Mercer Island WA 98040-2641 Office Phone: 206-232-5800. Business E-Mail: bob@ramedved.com.

MEDVINSKY, NATHALIA, library director; b. Kiev, Ukraine, Aug. 1, 1961; arrived in U.S., 2003; d. Vladimir Kroutoy and Ioanna Tabachnikov; m. Boris Dregalo (div.); m. Felix Medvinsky, Jan. 24, 2003. BLS, Kiev Inst. Culture, 1982; MLS, Sch. Libr. Info. and Archives, Jerusalem, Israel, 2001. Chief librarian Conservatory and HS of Jerusalem Acad. Music and Dance, 1992—2002; libr. dir. Fla. Nat. Coll., Hialeah, 2004—. Mem.: ALA, Fla. Libr. Assn. Home: 20336 NE 10th Court Rd N Miami FL 33179-2522 Office: Fla Nat Coll 4425 W 20th Ave Hialeah FL 33012

MEDWEDEFF, FRED M., retired dentist; b. Flint, Mich., Nov. 20, 1926; s. Marshall Herbert and Elsie Ella (Miller) M.; m. Joan Lenore Kampmeier, June 17, 1950 (div. 1973); children: Carol Medwedeff Grosvenor, Linda Medwedeff Mello, John Davis; m. Carolyn Adams Payne Gothard, Dec. 30, 1977; 1 child, Carol Lynn Gothard. BS, U. Mich., 1949; DDS, Emory U., 1954. Diplomate Am. Bd. Oral and Maxillo-Facial Radiology. Gen. practice dentistry, Nashville, 1955—2007; instr., then asst. prof. Vanderbilt U. Sch. Medicine, Nashville, 1955-83; staff mem. Vanderbilt U. Hosp., 1955-83; asst. prof. Meharry Med. Coll., 1970; ret., 2007. Founder, pres. Precision X-Ray Co., Nashville, 1964-74; cons. The Masel Co.; lectr. tour on x-rays to dentists, Japan, 1973; graphic designer U. Tex., 2007-. Contbr. articles to profl. jour.; patentee in field. Served with USAAF, 1945. Mem. ADA (named Father of Rectangular Collimation 2004), Tenn. Dental Assn., Nashville Dental Soc., Am. Acad. Oral and Maxillo Facial Radiology, Mid. Tenn. Acad. Implant Dentistry (founding), Pierre Fauchard Acad. (life), Psi Omega. Achievements include working on the only system of rectangular collimation of X-ray beam to fit film and meet all general guidelines. Home: 9646 New Hwy 96 W Franklin TN 37064-4782 Office: Ste 303 21st Plaza Bldg 121 21st Ave N Nashville TN 37203-5213 Office Phone: 615-327-4246. Personal E-mail: monotype9646@aol.com.

MEE, MAUREEN ADELE See DOZE, MAUREEN

MEECE, ROGER A., ambassador; b. Indpls., Oct. 1949; BS, Mich. State U., 1971. Former dep. chief of mission Am. Embassy, Brazzaville, Republic of the Congo; consul gen. Halifax, Nova Scotia, Canada; dep. chief of mission Am. Embassy, Kinshasa, Democratic Republic of Congo, 1995—98; dir., Ctrl. African affairs US Dept. State, Washington, 1998—2000, U.S. amb. to Malawi Lilongwe, 2000—03; charge d' affaires Am. Embassy, Abuja, Nigeria, 2003—04; US amb. to Dem. Republic of Congo US Dept. State, Kinsasha, 2004—. Vol. Peace Corps, Sierra Leone, 1971, assoc. dir., Niger, Cameroon, dep. dir., Republic of the Congo, dir., Gabon. Office: DOS Amb 2220 Kinshasa Pl Washington DC 20521-2220 *

MEEGODA, JAY NAMUNU, engineering educator, professional engineer; b. Colombo, Sri Lanka, May 16, 1956; arrived in US, 1981, naturalized; s. Don G. and Dona S. (Abeywickrama) M.; m. Lily B. Wang, Oct. 19, 1986; children: Eleanor D., Olivia S. MS, U. Calif., Davis, 1983, PhD, 1985. Asst. prof. to assoc. prof. to prof. NJ Inst. Tech., Newark, 1985—. Vis. lectr. U. P.R., Mayaguez, 1985, cons. Earthtechnology Corp., Long Beach, Calif., 1985, UN Devel. Program, 1994, 06, World Bank, 1995 Contbr. articles to profl. jours., chapters to books; editor 3 books. Disting. scholar, U. Calif., 1983, Earle C. Anthony fellow, 1984, rsch. grantee, NSF, 1987, 1997, 2004. Mem.: ASCE (com., Educator of Yr. NJ sect. 2005), ASTM (com.). Achievements include patents for method to incorporate petroleum contaminated soils into asphalt concrete; research in micromechanics of construction materials, centrifugal modeling, ultrasound and underground infrastructure. Office: NJ Inst of Tech 323 Martin Luther King Jr Blvd Newark NJ 07102-1824 Office Phone: 973-596-2464. Business E-Mail: meegoda@njit.edu.

MEEHAN, JEAN MARIE ROSS, human resources, occupational health and safety management consultant; b. Chgo., Mar. 16, 1954; d. A. Ronald Gonzalez and Barbara Marx Shipley; m. John J. Meehan, 1993; 1 child, Jenna A.; 1 child from previous marriage, Justin L. Ross. Diploma in Nursing, St. Mary of Nazareth Hosp., Chgo., 1974; BS in Health Arts with high honors, U. St. Francis, 1988; MPA with honors, Roosevelt U., 2000. Cert. occupl. health nurse specialist, cert. pharmacy technician (CPhT); ordained minister Universal Life Ch., 2003; cert. senior professional in human resources. Staff nurse St. Mary of Nazareth Hosp., Chgo., 1973—75; head nurse ambulatory care Edgebrook Med. Diagnostic Ctr., Chgo., 1975—76; occupl. health nurse Williams Electronics, Inc., Chgo., 1976—84; adminstr. safety and benefits Reliable Power Products, Franklin Park, Ill., 1984—90; dir. corp. human resources MacLean-Fogg Co., Mundelein, Ill., 1990—2005, Navitus Health Solutions LLC, Madison, Wis., 2005—. Pres. Auriel Mgmt. Group, LLC, Island Lake, Ill., 1992—, Claim Masters, LLC, 1998—99; adv. bd. dir. Gt. Lakes Health Care Alliance, 1996—97; spkr. in workshops. Poetry included in Visions of Beauty, 1999 (Editor's Choice award 1999), Tides of Memory, 2000, America at the Millennium—The Best Poems and Poets of the 20th Century, 2000. Guest spkr. local schs. and environ. groups, also I.E.P.A. and U.S. E.P.A. workshops; mem. Ill. Pollution Prevention Adv. Coun., Springfield, Ill., 1993-98; mem. Lake County Employer Coun. Bus./Govt. Partnership, 1996-99; faculty Am. Occupl. Health Conf., 2003-04. Recipient Leadership Civic citation United Way Charities of Lake County, 1993, 94. Mem. Am. Assn. Occupl. Health Nurses, Soc. for Human Resources Mgmt., Lake County Violence Intervention and Prevention, Lake County Employer Coun. Avocations: writing, interior design, reading, arts patronage. Office: Auriel Mgmt Group LLC PO Box 86 Wauconda IL 60084 Home Phone: 847-526-4418; Office Phone: 608-827-7567. Business E-Mail: hrpro@email.com.

MEEHAN, MARTIN THOMAS (MARTY MEEHAN), academic administrator, former congressman, lawyer; b. Lowell, Mass., Dec. 30, 1956; s. Martin T. and Alice (Britton) Meehan; m. Ellen T. Murphy; children: Robert Francis, Daniel Martin. BA in Polit. Sci., Edn. cum laude, U. Mass., Lowell, 1978; MPA, Suffolk U., 1981, JD, 1986; student, Harvard U., 1987-88. Adminstrv. asst. to mayor City of Lowell, Mass., 1978-79; press asst. to Rep. James M. Shannon US Congress, Mass., 1979-81; del. Dem. Nat. Conv., 1980, 84, 88; head rsch. analyst Joint Com. on Elec. Laws Mass. State Senate, 1981-84; dir. pub. affairs Commonwealth of Mass., 1985-86, dep. sec. state securities & corporations, 1986-90; 1st asst. dist. atty. Middlesex County, Mass., 1991-92; mem. U.S. Congress from 5th Mass. dist., 1993—2007, mem. armed services. com., judiciary com.; chancellor U. Mass., Lowell, 2007—. Adj. instr. U. Mass., Lowell, 1984-85, U. Harvard, 1987-88 Named Student of Yr. Lowell Exchange Club, 1975. Mem. ABA, Mass. Bar Assn., U. Lowell Alumni Assn., The Newspaper Guild, Internat. Fedn. Journalists. Democrat. Roman Catholic. Office: U Mass Lowell Office of Chancellor One University Ave / Cumnock Hall 2nd Fl Lowell MA 01854 E-mail: Martin_Meehan@uml.edu. *

MEEHAN, MICHAEL JOSEPH, lawyer; b. St. Louis, Aug. 28, 1942; s. Joseph Michael and Frances (Taylor) M.; m. Sharon Kay McHenry (div. 1988); m. Patricia Ann Shive, July 8, 1989 (dec. 1999); m. Shelley Fujiko Lee, 2002. BS in Engring., U.S. Coast Guard Acad., 1964; JD with high distinction, U. Ariz., 1971. Bar: Ariz. 1971, U.S. Ct. Appeals (6th, 8th, 9th and 10th cirs.), U.S. Supreme Ct. 1975. Law clk. Assoc. Justice William H. Rehnquist, U.S. Supreme Ct., 1972; assoc. Molloy, Jones & Donahue, P.C., Tucson, 1971-75, shareholder, 1975-93; chmn. exec. com., head trial dept., 1986-93; founder Meehan & Assocs., Tucson, 1993-2001; ptnr. Quarles & Brady/Striech Long, Tucson, 2001—03; pvt. practice Tucson, 2003—; of counsel Munger Chadwick P.L.C., Tucson, 2006—. Mem. fed. appellate rules adv. com. Jud. Conf. U.S., 1994-99; steering com. mem. Nat. Conf. Appellate Justice; mem. adv. bd. William H. Reinquist Ctr. Constl. Structures Govt., 2006—. Author chpt. on appellate advocacy: State Bar of Arizona Appellate Practice Handbook. Fellow Am. Acad. Appellate Lawyers (past pres.); mem. Am. Law Inst., Ariz. Bar Assn. (past chair appellate practice sect. 1999-00), Nat. Conf. Appellate Justice (mem. steering com. 2005). Lutheran. Avocation: golf. Office: Munger Chadwick PLC 333 North Wilmot Rd Ste 300 Tucson AZ 85711 Office Phone: 520-721-1900. Business E-Mail: mmeehan@mungerchadwick.com.

MEEHAN, PATRICK LEO, prosecutor; b. 1955; BA, Bowdoin Coll., 1978; JD, Temple U., 1986. Assoc. Dilworth, Paxon, Kalish and Kauffman; sr. counsel, exec. dir. US Senator Arlen Specter; dist. atty. Delaware County, Pa., 1986—2001; US atty. (ea. dist.) Pa. US Dept. Justice, 2001—. Mem. corp. fraud task force panel Atty. Gen., 2002—, mem. adv. com., mem. exec. working group. Office: US Attys Office 615 Chestnut St Philadelphia PA 19106 *

MEEHAN, ROBERT HENRY, human resources, business educator, electronics executive; b. Hackensack, NJ, June 19, 1946; s. Horace Miles and Pauline Jeannette (Pente) M.; m. Ruth Ann Auletta, Sept. 28, 1969; children: Robert Michael, Brian John. BA, Montclair State U., 1968; MA magna cum laude, Fairleigh Dickinson U., 1972; D in Profl. Studies, Pace U., 1997. Cert. secondary sch. tchr. of social studies, N.J., compensation and benefits profl. Job analyst Citicorp, NYC, 1969-70, sr. job analyst, 1970-72, ofcl. asst., 1972, project specialist human resources practices/policy rev., 1973, project specialist attitude surveys, 1973-75, human resources officer nat. banking group, 1975-76; asst. dir. human resources N.Y. Power Authority, White Plains, 1976-84, dir. compensation, 1984-93, dir. compensation and human resources info. sys., 1993-94, dir. compensation and benefits strategy and devel., 1994-95, dir. compensation and benefits, 1995-98; dir. compensation Philips Electronics N.Am., 1998-2000; mng. dir. R.H. Meehan Assocs., Human Capital Cons., Maywood, NJ, 2000—01; dir. compensation, benefits and HRIS, ASML, Tempe, Ariz., 2001—; CEO Chaparral Capital, LLC, Scottsdale, Ariz., 2005—. Instr. World at Work, Scottsdale, Ariz., 1986—, course coord., 1992-94, mem. cert. and currency com., 1988-89, direct compensation com. 1990-91, chmn. 1992-93, bd. dirs. 1993; adj. assoc. prof. Lubin Grad. Sch. Bus., Pace U., 1995-2001; mem. N.Y. Power Pool Salary com., 1990-98, chair, 1998; spkr. at profl. confs. Sr. author: Managing a Direct Pay Program, Cert. Course 4A, 1991, Determining Compensation Costs: An Approach to Estimating and Analyzing Expense, 1991; editor books; mem. exec. adv. panel Acad. Mgmt. Exec., 1993—; contbr. articles to profl. jours. Scoutmaster, Boy Scouts Am., Ridgefield Park, N.J., 1968; also scouting coord., Maywood, N.J., 1982-83; vestryman, sr. warden St. Martin's Episcopal Ch., Maywood, 1977-84. Mem. Soc. Human Resource Mgmt. (mem. compensation and benefits com. 1998-01), Metro Phoenix Human Resource Assocs., 2002—, Human Resources Assn. NY (compensation com. 1998-01), Acad. Mgmt. (exec. adv. panel jour. The Exec.), NY Compensation Assn., Order DeMolay (master councilor 1963, 65, scribe, adv. bd. 1965-68, Meritorious Svcs. award 1965), Psi Chi, Delta Mu Delta, Beta Gamma Sigma. Episcopalian. Avocations: golf, sailing, furniture making. Office: ASML 8555 S River Pkwy Tempe AZ 85284 Office Phone: 480-383-4043. Business E-Mail: rhmeehan@cox.net.

MEEHAN, SANDRA GOTHAM, corporate financial executive, consultant, writer; b. Tokyo, June 9, 1948; d. Fred C. and Evelyn (Dirr) Gotham; m. James P. Jenkins, June 15, 1970 (div.); m. Dayton T. Carr, Dec. 27, 1986 (div. 1989), m. Michael J. Meehan, II, Jan. 16, 1992. Student, Stanford-in-France, Tours, 1968-69; BA, Stanford U., Calif., 1970, MA, 1971. Acct. exec. Young & Rubicam Inc., NYC, 1972-78, acct. supr., 1978-80; pres. Gotham Prodns., NYC, 1980-82; v.p., mgmt. supr. Ogilvy & Mather, NYC, 1982-85; v.p. Steuben Glass, NYC, 1985-88; sr. v.p. Siegel & Gale, NYC, 1988-92; prin., mng. ptnr. Gotham Meeham Ptnrs., NYC, 1992—. Sr. v.p., dir. corp. comm. Bionutrics, Inc., 1997-98; cons. Congl. coms., FDA, FTC for exec. program Am. Assn. Advt. Agys., Washington, 1978-80; cons. Ctr. Arctic Studies Sorbonne, Paris, in US and Can., 1980-82; seminar dir. NY chpt. Women in Bus., NYC, 1983-84. Author, editor: TV documentary Inuit! The Universal Cry of the Eskimo People, 1981. Trustee, bd. dirs. Rensselaerville Inst., NY; exec. com., bd. dirs. Checkerboard Film Found.; NYC Mayor's rep. to bd. dirs. Bot. Gardens; bd. dirs. Paris Rev. Mag., The Accompanied Literary Soc., NYC, Agora Found. Home: 220 E 73rd St New York NY 10021-4319 Office: Gotham Meehan Ptnrs 220 E 73rd St Ste 5G New York NY 10021-4319 Home Phone: 212-734-1249; Office Phone: 212-628-6810. Office Fax: 212-628-6747. Personal E-mail: gmp7777@aol.com.

MEEHAN, TAMIYE MARCIA, library director; b. Chgo., Oct. 14, 1942; d. Thomas and Virginia Fujibayashi; m. Rudolph J. Trejo, Jr., Sept. 1, 1962 (div. 1980); m. James E. Meehan, Jr., Oct. 4, 1981; children: Terrence, Theodore, Timothy, Rosalind. MALS, Rosary Coll., Fremont, Calif., 1974; MBA, De Paul U., Chgo., 1980. Librarian Chgo. Pub. Libr., 1974-75, br. libr. head, 1975-77, dist. chief, 1977-96, staff devel., 1996-97; dir. Indian Trails Pub. Libr. Dist., Wheeling, Ill., 1997—. Mem. ALA (chmn. ethnic multicultural and info. roundtable 1998-99, chmn. APALA 2001-2002), Ill. Libr. Assn. (bd. dirs. 1999-2002, treas. 2000-02, pres. 2006-07), Wheeling Rotary Club (pres. 2004-05). Office: Indian Trails Pub Libr Dist 355 S Schoenbeck Rd Wheeling IL 60090-4467 Office Phone: 847-459-4100. Business E-Mail: TMeehan@indiantrailslibrary.org.

MEEHAN, WILLIAM A., air transportation executive; Pres., COO Continental Micronesia, Inc. Continental Airlines, Inc., Guam, 1998—2002, v.p. Cleve. hub, 2002—03, v.p. Houston hub, 2003—04, sr. v.p. airports svcs. Houston, 2004—. Office: Continental Airlines Inc PO Box 4607 Houston TX 77210 Office Phone: 713-324-5000. Office Fax: 713-324-2637. *

MEEK, BARBARA SUSAN, elementary school educator; b. Monaca, Pa., Feb. 8, 1951; d. Michael Frederick and Sarah Ellen (Hall) Fronko; m. Joseph William Meek Jr., Nov. 25, 1977. BS in Edn., Ohio U., Athens, 1973; MA in Edn., Marietta Coll., Ohio, 1999. Cert. elem. tchr., Ohio. 3d grade tchr. Warren Local Schs., Vincent, Ohio. Martha Holden Jennings scholar, 1976-77. Mem. NEA, Ohio coun. Tchrs. Math., Ohio Coun. Internat. Reading Assn., Ohio Edn. Assn., Warren Local Edn. Assn. Home: 5371 Veto Road Vincent OH 45784-5118

MEEK, DAVID JASON, recreational facility executive, real estate developer; b. Cin., Aug. 25, 1976; s. Donald George Meek and Karen Leigh Steeves. BS, Ohio State U., Columbus, 2000. Asst. golf course supt. The Golf Club at Stonelick Hills, Batavia, Ohio, 2001—05, golf course supt., 2005—. Master gardener vol. Master Gardener Program, Cin., 2004—07. Mem.: GCSAA (assoc.), Kappa Sigma (life). Home: 3537 Rawson Pl Cincinnati OH 45209 Office: The Golf Club at Stonelick Hills 3155 Sherilyn Ln Batavia OH 45103 Home Phone: 513-509-5387; Office Phone: 513-735-4654. Personal E-mail: dmeek24@msn.com.

MEEK, FORREST BURNS, retired trading company executive; b. Tustin, Mich., June 11, 1928; s. Robert B. and Electa I. (Gallup) Meek; m. Jean R. Grimes, June 26, 1953; children: Sally, Thomas, Nancy, Charles. AA, Spring Arbor Coll., 1950; AB, Mich. State U., 1953; postgrad., U. Ga., 1965; MA, Ctrl. Mich. U., 1967. Exec. sec., chmn. bd. Edgewood Press, Clare, 1971—; gen. mgr. Blue Water Imports, 1985; dir. Ctr. for Chinese-Am. Scholarly Exchs., Inc., 1989—97; gen. mgr. Blue-Water Internat. Trading Co., Inc., ret., 1998. Vis. prof. Wuhan U., China, 1986—87; dist. office mgr. Fed. Decennial Census, 1990; instr. phys. geology and astronomy Mid Mich. C.C., 2002, instr. astronomy, 2001—03; mem., chmn. Red team East Ctrl. Mich. Planning and Devel. Regional Commn.; bd. sec. ITC Shanghai Maglev, Inc., 2003. Author: Michigan Timber Battleground, 1976, Michigan Heartland, 1979, One Year in China, 1988, Michigan Logging Railroad Era, 1850-1963, 1989, Railways and Tramways, 1990, Lumbering in Eastern Canada, 1991, Pearl Harbor Remembered, 1991, Heroes of The Twentieth Century, 2000. Coord. Clare County Bicentennial Com., 1975-76; Rep. fin. chmn., Clare County, 1966-71, asst. treas. 10th dist. Mich, 1967-69; trustee local sch. bd., 1992-96; chmn. local county jury bd., 1991-98; mem. bd. commrs. Clare County Dist. 4 Commn., 1998-2006. Mem. Am. Entrepreneur Assn., Mich. Sci. Tchrs. Assn., Mich. Hist. Soc., Heartland Mich. Geneal. Soc., White Pine Hist. Soc. (exec. sec.), Steam Locomotive History Soc. Republican. Avocations: astronomy, silviculture. Personal E-mail: forrestmeek@hotmail.com.

MEEK, KENDRICK B., congressman; b. Miami, Sept. 6, 1966; m. Leslie Meek; 2 children. BS, Fla. A&M U., 1989. Devel. rep. Wackenhut Corp.; mem. Fla. Ho. of Reps., Tallahassee, 1994-98; mem. for dist. 36 Fla. State Senate, Tallahassee, 1998—2002; mem. US Congress from 17th Fla. dist., 2003—; mem. armed svcs. com., homeland security com. Vice chair Com. on Criminal Justice Appropriations Fiscal Responsibility Coun., 1996-97; mem. Com. on Crime and Punishment Justice Coun., 1996-97. Mem. Fla. Young Dems., 1985—, Gtr. Miami Svc. Corp Bd., All Peoples Dem. Club, South Fla. Food Recovery Bd., North Shore Med. Ctr. Bd., IMPACT Miami, Met. Dade County Urban Revitalization Task Force; capt. Fla. Hwy Patrol, 1989-94; founder, mem. Men Against Drugs, Defending Against Drugs and Social Disorder (MAD DADS); founder Positive African-Am. Role Models Lillie C. Evans Elem. Sch., 1990; mem. adv. bd. Dems. 2000 Elected Officials; bd. dirs. Metro-Dade Cmty. Action Agy. Flemming fellow Ctr. for Policy Alternatives, 1996-97; recipient Outstanding Svc. award MADD, 1990, Positive African-Am. Role Models award Lillie C. Evans Elem. Sch., 1991, #1 award Scott-Carver Pack, 1991, award Dade Ptnrs. for Safe Neighborhoods, 1995, Legis. award MADD, 1995, Cmty. Svc. award Fla. Meml. Coll., 1995, award IMPACT Miami, 1996, Stellar Cmty. Svc. award South Fla. Assn. Black Journalists, 1996, Legis. Achievement honor Fla. Divsn. Emergency Mgmt., 1996; named St. Joseph Delaney Hurricane Hero Metro Dade County Commn., 1995, one of 50 Leaders of Tomorrow Ebony Mag., 1995, one of Most Influential Black Americans, 2006, Up and Comers finalist Price Waterhouse, 1996 Quality Floridian Fla. League of Cities, 1996. Mem. NAACP (life, chmn. Miami-Dade br. Oper. Voter Registration 1995-96, v.p., Adams-Powell Civil Rights award 1996, Gwen Sawyer Cherry Meml. award Fla. Conf. NAACP brs. 1997), North Ctrl. Dade Cmty. Assn. (chmn. pub. safety com.), Fla. Agr. and Mech. U. Alumni Assn., Disabled Police Officers Assn. (adv. bd.), Omega Psi Phi. Democrat. Office: US Ho Reps 1039 Longworth Ho Office Bldg Washington DC 20515-0917 Office Phone: 202-225-4506. Office Fax: 202-226-0777. *

MEEK, VIOLET IMHOF, retired dean; b. Geneva, Ill., June 12, 1939; d. John and Violet (Krepel) Imhof; m. Devon W. Meek, Aug. 21, 1965 (dec. 1988); children: Brian, Karen; m. Don M. Dell, Jan. 4, 1992. BA summa cum laude, St. Olaf Coll., 1960; MS, U. Ill., 1962, PhD in Chemistry, 1964. Instr. chemistry Mount Holyoke Coll., South Hadley, Mass., 1964-65; asst. prof. to prof. Ohio Wesleyan U., Delaware, Ohio, 1965-84, dean for ednl. svcs., 1980-84; dir. annual programs Coun. Ind. Colls., Washington, 1984-86; assoc. dir. sponsored programs devel. Rsch. Found. Ohio State U., Columbus, 1986-91, dean, dir. Lima, 1992—2003; ret., 2003. Vis. dean U. Calif., Berkeley, 1982, Stanford U., Palo Alto, Calif., 1982, reviewer GTE Sci. and Tech. Program, Princeton, N.J., 1986-92, Goldwater Nat. Fellowships, Princeton, 1990-98. Co-author: Experimental General Chemistry, 1984; contbr. articles to profl. jours. Bd. dirs. Luth. Campus Ministries, Columbus, 1988-91, Luth. Social Svcs., 1988-91, Americom Bank, Lima, 1992-98, Art Space, Lima, 1993—, Allen Lima Leadership, 1993—, Am. House, 1992—, Lima Vets. Meml. Civic Ctr. Found., 1992—; chmn. synodical coms. Evang. Luth. Ch. Am., Columbus, 1982; bd.

trustees Trinity Luth. Sem., Columbus, 1996—; chmn. Allen County C. of C., 1995—, chair bd. dirs., 1999; bd. dirs. Lima Syphomy Orch., 1993—, pres. bd. dirs., 1997— Recipient Woodrow Wilson Fellowship, 1960. Mem.: Am. Assn. Higher Edn., Nat. Coun. Rsch. Adminstrs. (named Outstanding New Profl. midwest region 1990), Phi Beta Kappa. Avocations: music, skiing, woodworking, civil war history, travel. Home: 209 W Beechwold Blvd Columbus OH 43214-2012 Office: Ohio State Lima 8521 Libra Rd Dublin OH 43016-9022

MEEKER, GUY BENTLEY, banker; b. Calcutta, India, Nov. 4, 1945; (parents Am. citizens); s. Lincoln Voght and Fortune Helen (Bentley) M.; m. Lavenia Yale Nelson, Apr. 27, 1967 (div. 1979); children: G. Bentley Jr., Melissa Anne; m. Marcia Lee Zink, Nov. 4, 1984 (div. 1993). BSBA, Georgetown U., 1967; MBA, George Washington U., 1970. Cons. OAS, Washington, 1971-73; v.p. The Deltec Banking Corp., Nassau, Bahamas & NYC, 1973-78, Comml. Credit Internat. Banking Corp., Balt., 1978-82; sr. v.p., gen. mgr. Union Planters Internat. Bank, NYC, 1982-84; exec. v.p., gen. mgr. Worthen Bank Internat., NYC, 1984-86; exec. v.p. and chief exec. officer N.Am. Bank Cen. Asia, NYC, 1984-95; supervisory dir. BCA Bank Europe N.V., Amsterdam, The Netherlands, 1993-95; pres. G.B. Meeker & Co., NYC, 1996—99; writer, mgmt. fin. cons. Miami, 1999—. Author articles and management programs in field. Mem. Bankers Assn. Fgn. Trade (internat. adv. coun. 1992-95, vice chmn. IAC 1994-95), Inst. Internat. Bankers (legis. and regulatory com. 1992-94, bd. trustees 1994-95), Asia Soc. (corp. coun. 1987-95), River Club, Dutch Treat Club, Coffee House Club. Roman Catholic.

MEEKER, MARY G., brokerage house executive; b. Portland, Ind., Sept. 1959; BA in Psychology, DePauw U., 1981; MBA in Fin., Cornell U., 1986. Stockbroker Merrill Lynch, Chgo., 1982; tech. rsch. analyst Salomon Bros., 1989, Cowen & Co., 1990—91; mng. dir. Internet, new media and PC software equity rsch. Morgan Stanley, Dean Witter, Discover & Co. (now Morgan Stanley), NYC, 1991—. Named Queen of the Net, Barron's. Avocations: golf, fishing, skiing. Office: Morgan Stanley 1585 Broadway New York NY 10036-8200 Fax: 212-761-0472. E-mail: mmeeker@ms.com.

MEEKERS, DOMINIQUE ARMAND, public health professor, demographer; b. Diepenbeek, Belgium, June 23, 1962; arrived in US, 1987; BA magna cum laude, Free U. Brussels, 1985; MA, U. Pa., 1988, PhD, 1990. Rschr. Free U. Brussels, 1985-87; rsch. assoc. NAS, Washington, 1990-91; asst. prof., rsch. assoc. Pa. State U., University Park, 1992-96; assoc. Johns Hopkins U., Balt., 1996-2001; rsch. dir. Population Svcs. Internat., Washington, 1996—2001; prof. dept. internat. health and devel. Tulane U., New Orleans, 2001—, chair, 2005—. Cons. John Snow, Arlington, Va., 1992—93, Demographic and Health Surveys, Macro Internat., Calverton, Md., 1993—97, Population Svcs. Internat., 2001—, Hewlett Found., 2003—; invited mem. Com. Reproductive Health, 2000—03, Internat. Union Sci. Study Population. Contbr. articles to profl. publs. Rsch. grantee Spencer Found., 1995, U. Md., 1996, UNICEF, Bucharest, Romania, 1997, UNAIDS, 1997, Deloitte Touche Tohmatsu, 2002, UNICEF, 2002, USAID/Health Comm. Partnership, 2002-2007. Mem. APHA, Population Assn. Am. Office: Tulane U Dept Internat Health and Devel 1440 Canal St Ste 2200 New Orleans LA 70112 Home: 5633 Durham Dr New Orleans LA 70131 Office Phone: 504-988-3655. E-mail: dmeekers@tulane.edu.

MEEKINS, DEBORAH, bank executive; b. 1953; 2 children. Pres., CEO Sonoma Nat. Bank, Santa Rosa, Calif., 1991—. Bd. mem. Western Ind. Bankers, Cmty. Bankers. Bd. mem. Santa Rose Jr. Coll. Found., Santa Rosa Meml. Hosp. Found., United Way, Santa Rosa Chamber of Commerce. Named one of 25 Women to Watch, US Banker, 2006. Achievements include first woman Sonoma County Bank Pres. Office: Sonoma National Bank 801 Fourth St Santa Rosa CA 95404 *

MEEKISON, MARYFRAN, writer; b. Napoleon, Ohio, Apr. 9, 1919; d. Frank J. and Elizabeth (Keyes) Shaff; m. David Meekison, June 17, 1939; children: Maureen Meekison Houppert, David Francis, Beth Ann. Student, St. Mary's Coll., Notre Dame, Ind., 1936-39. Hist. writer, photographer, Napoleon, 1963—, St. Augustine Ch., 1983—; citizen com. Napoleon Area HS Award, 2005—. Author: (photographer) Canal Days to Modern Ways Revisited, 1984, History of St. Augustine's 1882-1982, History of St. Augustine Ch., 1983, centennial edit.; (brochure) Canal Days to Modern Ways, 1963; mem. editl. adv. bd. Courier mag., 1989-91; contbr. articles to mags. Steering com. Napoleon Susquicentennial, 1984; trustee Napoleon Pub. Lib., 1976-01. Recipient Spl. citation Courier Alumnae mag., others, Pres.'s medal, St. Mary's Coll., Notre Dame, Ind., 1991; named Citizen of Yr., Napoleain Area C. of C., 1990; named to St. Mary's Coll. Athletic Hall of Fame Notre Dame, 2001. Mem. Alumnae Assn. St. Mary's Coll. (bd. dirs. 1985-91), Literary Club. Democrat. Roman Catholic. Avocations: tennis, sailing. Home: PO Box 253 Napoleon OH 43545-0253

MEEKS, GREGORY WELDON, congressman; b. NYC, Sept. 25, 1953; s. James Weldon and Mary (McNeal) Meeks; m. Simone-Marie Meeks; children: Ebony Renee, Aja J., Nia-Aiyana. BA in Hist., Adelphi U., Garden City, NY, 1975; JD, Howard U. Sch. Law, Washington, 1978. Asst. dist. atty. Queens Dist. Atty.'s Office, 1978-81; asst. spl. narcotics prosecutor Office of Spl. Narcotics Prosecutor, NYC, 1981-83; asst. counsel State Investigations Commn., 1983-84; hearing officer NY Family Ct., 1984-85; judge NY State Workers' Compensation Bd., 1985-87, supervising judge, 1987-93; mem. NY State Assembly, 1993-98, US Congress from 6th NY dist., 1998—, mem. fin. svcs. com., mem. internat. rels. com., mem. New Dems. Caucus. Bd. dirs. Rockaway Peninsula Civic Assn., 1983-1991, Peninsula Gen. Hosp., 1989-; chmn. bd. Joseph P. Addabbo Family Health Care Ctr., 1990-92. Recipient NAACP Polit. Leadership award, 1989, Outstanding Vol. Mentor award, NY Mentoring, 1990, Cmty. Leader award Boy Scouts Am., 1992, William Garvin Pub. Svc. award, 2004, Congl. Leadership award, Nat. Urban League, 2006; named one of Most Influential Black Americans, Ebony mag., 2006. Mem. Macon B. Allen Black Bar Assn. (v.p.), Queens County Bar Assn., Far Rockaway NAACP (Polit. Leadership award 1989). Democrat. Baptist. Office: 153-01 Jamaica Ave 2nd Fl Jamaica NY 11432 Office Phone: 202-225-3461, 718-725-6000. Office Fax: 718-725-9868. *

MEEKS, JACQUELYNN, city health department administrator; MPH, Tulane U.; DPH, Harvard U. Corp. dir. quality assurance Mutual of Omaha; dir. quality improvement Group Health Plan, Inc.; rsch. assoc. Washington U. Sch. Medicine; dir. dept. health St. Louis County, 2001—04; health dir. Maricopa County, Ariz., 2005—. Office: Maricopa County Dept Health 4041 N Central Ste 1400 Phoenix AZ 85012 Office Phone: 602-506-6902. Office Fax: 602-506-0272. Business E-Mail: jacquelynnmeeks@mail.maricopa.gov.

MEEKS, PATRICIA LOWE, literature and language educator, consultant; b. Enid, Okla., Oct. 21, 1928; d. Henry Preston and Veda Gay (Combs) Lowe; m. James Donald Meeks, Feb. 28, 1953 (div. Aug. 1975); children: Mary Gay, Ann Lowe, James Robert David. BA, Phillips U., 1951; MA in English, U. Colo., 1973. Cert. tchr., Colo., Okla. Tchr. English Garber HS, Okla., 1952-53; tchr. English and journalism Hillcrest HS, Dallas, 1955-57; tchg. asst. U. Colo., Boulder, 1965-66; tchr. English Cherry Creek HS, Englewood, Colo., 1966-91; supr. grades K-12 reading and lang. arts Oklahoma City Pub. Schs., 1991-98; English cons., 1998—. Adj. prof. English, Oklahoma City CC, 2002-06, CC Denver, 2006-; cons. Coll. Bd. Rocky Mt. Region, Denver, 1973-91; advanced placement reader, table leader Coll. Bd. and Ednl. Testing Svc., Princeton, N.J., 1970-90, SAT reader, 1989-94, table leader, 1994-98, reader, 1999-04. Grantee Fulbright Found., 1980-81; grantee NEH, 1986; English-Speaking Union, 1987; IDEA fellow. Mem. ACLU, English-Speaking Union (pres. Oklahoma City chpt. 1998-2006), Nature Conservancy, Audubon Soc., US Humane Soc., Defenders of Wildlife, Nat. Resources Defense Coun., Denver Art Mus. Episcopalian. Avocations: art history, bird watching, jazz, reading. Home: 8155 Fairmount Dr 711 Denver CO 80230 Personal E-mail: plmeeks@comcast.net.

MEEKS, WILLIAM HERMAN, III, lawyer; b. Ft. Lauderdale, Fla., Dec. 30, 1939; s. Walter Herman Jr. and Elise Walker (McGuire) M.; m. Patricia Ann Rayburn, July 30, 1965; 1 son, William Herman IV; m. 2d, Miriam Andrea Bedsole, Dec. 28, 1971; 1 child, Julie Marie. AB, Princeton U., 1961; LLB, U. Fla., 1964; LLM in Tax, NYU, 1965. Bar: Fla 1964, US Dist. Ct. (so. dist.) Fla. 1965, US Tax Ct. 1966, US Ct. Appeals (11th cir.) 1981, US Supreme Ct. 1985. Ptnr. McCune, Hiaasen, Crum, Ferris & Gardner, Ft. Lauderdale, 1964-89, Fleming, O'Bryan & Fleming, Ft. Lauderdale, 1990-95, Dobbins, Meeks, Raleigh & Dover, Ft. Lauderdale, 1995—. Dir. Attys. Title Svcs., Inc., 1978-79, Attys. Title Svcs. of Broward County, Inc., 1971—, chmn., 1976-77; mem. Attys. Real Estate Coun. Broward County. Mem. ABA, Fla. Bar Assn., Broward County Bar Assn., Attys. Title Ins. Fund, Ft. Lauderdale Hist. Soc., Ft. Lauderdale Mus., Kiwanis, Lauderdale Yacht Club, Tower Club (Ft. Lauderdale), Phi Delta Phi. Democrat. Presbyterian. Office: Dobbins Meeks Raleigh & Dover 3081 E Commercial Blvd Ste 204 Fort Lauderdale FL 33308 Home Phone: 954-567-9151; Office Phone: 954-491-1100. E-mail: whmeeks@ndmrd.com.

MEENAN, ALAN JOHN, clergyman, theology studies educator; b. Belfast, No. Ireland, Feb. 7, 1946; arrived in US, 1970, naturalized; s. John and Elizabeth (Holland) M.; m. Vicky Lee Woodall, May 6, 1974; children: Kelly Elizabeth, Katie Michelle, Kimberly Brooke. BA, Queen's U., Belfast, 1970; MDiv, Asbury Theol. Sem., Wilmore, Ky., 1972, ThM, 1975; PhD, Edinburgh U., 1981. Ordained to ministry Presbyn. Ch., U.S.A., 1973. Pastor Wilmore Presbyn. Ch., 1972-74; asst. pastor St. Giles' Cathedral, Edinburgh, Scotland, 1974-77; sr. pastor 3d Presbyn. Ch., Richmond, Va., 1977—84, First Presbyn. Ch., Amarillo, Tex., 1989-97, Hollywood Presbyn. Ch., Calif., 1997—2005; head staff Canoga Park Presbyn. Ch., Calif., 1984-89; founder, pres. The Word Is Out, LA. Vis. lectr. Nairobi Grad. Sch. Theology, Kenya, 1983, 89; adj. prof. W. Africa Theol. Sem., Lagos, Nigeria, 2004-. Contbr. revs. to religious publs., including Asbury Bible Commentary. Tchr. Chogoria High Sch., Meru, Keyna, 1965-66. Yale U. rsch. fellow, 1976—77. Mem. Tyndale Fellowship for Bibl. Rsch., Theta Phi. Presbyterian. Avocations: travel, photography, reading, swimming, squash racquets. Office: 11271 Ventura Blvd Ste 509 Studio City CA 91604 Office Phone: 323-969-9090.

MEENGS, WILLIAM LLOYD, cardiologist; b. Zeeland, Mich., Dec. 23, 1942; s. Lloyd Stanley and Gertrude (Wyngarden) M.; m. Helen Delores Van Dyke, June 10, 1964; children: Michelle Rene, William Lloyd, Lisa Ann. AB, Hope Coll., 1964; MD, U. Mich., 1968. Diplomate Am. Bd. Cardiology, Am. Bd. Interventional Cardiology, Am. Bd. Nuc. Cardiology. Intern in internal medicine U. Hosp., Ann Arbor, Mich., 1968-69, resident in internal medicine, 1971-73, fellow in cardiology, 1973-75; practice medicine specializing in cardiology, interventional cardiology and nuc. cardiology Petoskey, Mich., 1975—. Cardiologist Burns Clinic Med. Center, Petoskey, 1975-99, chmn. dept. cardiology and cardiac surgery, 1978-89; med. dir. No. Mich. Heart Center, 1989-95; pres. Petoskey Cardiology, P.C., 1999—; chief sect. cardiology No. Mich. Hosps., 2000—; cardiologist Little Traverse Hosp., Petoskey, 1975—, dir. coronary care unit, 1986-89; dir. cardiac catheterization lab. No. Mich. Hosps., Petoskey, 1985-87, 92—, adult spl. care units, 1986-89; vice chmn. bd. dirs. Burns Clinic Med. Ctr., 1989-92. Contbr. med. articles to profl. jours. Trustee Mich. Heart Assn., 1979-83. Served as surgeon USPHS, 1969-71. Named one of Best Drs. in Am. 2001-02, Best Drs. Inc., 2002, Best Drs. in Am. 2003-04, 2004, Best Drs. in Am. 2005-06. Fellow: Soc. Cardiovasc. Angiography and Interventions, Am. Coll. Cardiology; mem.: Am. Heart Assn. (fellow Coun. on Clin. Cardiology), Alpha Omega Alpha. Home: 1224 Autumn Ln Petoskey MI 49770-9019 Office: Petoskey Cardiology 560 W Mitchell St Ste 400 Petoskey MI 49770-2274 Office Phone: 231-487-2490.

MEER, JON DOUGLAS, lawyer; b. Amherst, NY, Dec. 8, 1963; s. Ronald Lewis and Sharon (Fisher) M. BS with honors, Cornell U., 1986; JD, Boston U., 1989. Bar: Calif. 1989, US Dist Ct. (no. & ctrl. dist Calif., Nev., ea. dist Mich.), US Ct. Appeals (6th, 9th cir.). Assoc. Paul, Hastings, Janofsky & Walker, LA; atty. Akin, Gump, Strauss, Hauer & Feld LLP, LA; ptnr., chmn. LA sect. Labor & Employment practice DLA Piper Rudnick Gray Cary, LA, 2002—. Lectr. Lawyer in Classroom prog., Constitutional Rights Found. Named a So. Calif. Super Lawyer, LA Mag., 2004. Mem. ABA, LA County Bar Assn., Beverly Hills Bar Assn., Phi Kappa Phi, Phi Eta Sigma. Office: DLA Piper Rudnick Gray Cary 4th Fl 1999 Ave of the Stars Los Angeles CA 90067-6022 Office Phone: 310-595-3004. Office Fax: 310-595-3304. Business E-Mail: jon.meer@dlapiper.com.

MEEROPOL, RACHEL, lawyer; b. 1976; BA, Wesleyan U., 1997; JD, NYU, 2002. Staff atty., fellow Ctr. Constitutional Rights, 2002—. Author, co-editor: Jailhouse Lawyers Handbook; editor: America's Disappeared: Secret Imprisonment, Detainees, and the "War on Terror". Named one of Top 40 Lawyers Under 40, Nat. Law Jour., 2005, Litigation's Rising Stars, The Am. Lawyer, 2007. Mem.: Nat. Lawyers Guild NYC Chpt. (v.p.). Office: Nat Lawyers Guild 143 Madison Ave 4th Fl New York NY 10016 also: Ctr Constitutional Rights 666 Broadway New York NY 10012 Office Phone: 212-679-6018, 212-614-6420. Office Fax: 212-679-6178. *

MEEROW, ALAN WILLIAM, geneticist, horticulturist, botanist; s. Jack and Lillian Meerow; m. Linda Lee Fisher, May 29, 1982; children: Sara Anne, Andrew Todd, Erica Lynn. BS, U. Calif., Davis, 1978; MS, U. Fla., Gainesville, 1983, PhD, 1986. Prof. U. Fla., Ft. Lauderdale, Fla., 1987—99; rsch. plant geneticist Agrl. Rsch. Svc. USDA, Miami, Fla., 1999—. Rsch. assoc. Fairchild Tropical Bot. Garden, Miami, Fla., 1989—; chmn., bulb specialists group Species Survival Commn. World Conservation Union, Geneva, 1993—2005. Author: Betrock's Guide to Florida Landscape Plants, 1989, Betrock's Guide to Landscape Palms, 1992, Ornamental Palm Horticulture, 2000, Betrock's Cold Hardy Palms, 2005, Betrock's Landscape Palms, 2006; contbr. over 12 chapters to books, over 100 articles to profl. jours. Named Hort. Writer of the Yr., Fla. Nursery and Growers Assn., 1990, Hort. Educator of the Yr., 1991; recipient Presdl. Recognition cert., U. Fla., 1985, Best Ph.D Dissertation of Yr. award, 1986, Superior Accomplishment award, 1996; fellow, World Wildlife Fund/Garden Club Am., 1984, Fla. Fedn. of Garden Clubs, 1985; grantee, NSF, 1984—86, 1996—98, 2002—05, Am. Floral Endowment, 1990—94, Hort. Rsch. Inst., 1992, U. Fla., USDA Coop. Ext. Svc., 1993—99, Floyd L. Wray Found., 1993—96, Growing Technologies, 1993, EZ Soil Co., 1993, Plumeria Soc. Am., 2003, Am. Iris Soc., 2004—06; scholarship, Garden Writers Assn. Am., 1984, H. Harold Hume fellowship, 1985. Mem.: Internat. Soc. Hort. Sci., Internat. Assn. Plant Taxonomy, Am. Soc. Plant Taxonomists (assoc. editor Systematic Botany 2003—, Peter Raven Sci. Outreach award 2005), Am. Soc. Hort. Sci. (assoc. editor Hort Sci. 2001—04), Bot. Soc. Am., Internat. Palm Soc., Internat. Bulb Soc. (life; pres. 2001—06, editor Herbertia 1999—, William Herbert medal 1998). Achievements include research in phylogenetic systematics of Amaryllidaceae and other plant taxa; genetics of coconut varieties; molecular markers in tropical ornamental plants; new tropical plant cultivar development; tropical botany and horticulture; patents in field.

MEERSCHAERT, JOSEPH RICHARD, retired physician; b. Detroit, Mar. 4, 1941; s. Hector Achiel and Marie Terese (Campbell) M.; m. Jeanette Marie Ancerewicz, Sept. 14, 1963; children: Eric, Amy, Adam. BA, Wayne State U., 1965, MD, 1967. Diplomate Am. Bd. Phys. Medicine and Rehab., Am. Bd. Pain Medicine. Intern Harper Hosp., Detroit, 1967-68; resident in phys. medicine and rehab. Wayne State U. Rehab. Inst., Detroit, 1968-71; chief divsn. phys. medicine Naval Hosp., Chelsea, Mass., 1971-73; attending physician William Beaumont Hosp., Royal Oak, Mich., 1973—2006, med. dir. rehab. unit, 1979-87; pvt. practice medicine specializing in phys. medicine and rehab. Royal Oak, 1973—2006; pvt. practice specializing in pain medicine, 1990—2006; ret., 2006. Mem. med. adv. bd. Nat. Wheelchair Athletic Assn., 1973—, U.S. team physician VII World Wheelchair Games, Stoke Mandeville, Eng.; clin. instr. Wayne State U., 1973-83, clin. asst. prof. phys. medicine and rehab., 1983—; mem. Mich. Dept. Licensing and Regulation State Bd. Phys. Therapy, 1978-81. Contbr. articles to profl. jours. With M.C. USN, 1971-73. Recipient John Hussey award Mich. Wheelchair Athletic Assn., 1981. Fellow Am. Coll. Pain Medicine; mem. Am. Acad. Phys. Medicine and Rehab. (reviewer, presenter) Am. Congress Rehab. Medicine, Mich. Phys. Medicine and Rehab. Soc., Am. Geriatrics Soc., Am. Assn. Electromyography and Electrodiagnosis, Mich. Rheumatism Soc., Mich. Acad. Phys. Medicine and REhab. (pres. 1986-87, chmn. program com. 1977-78, trustee 1980—, pres. bd. dirs. 1994-97), Oakland County Med. Soc. (bd. dirs. 1991, 97), Alpha Omega Alpha. Roman Catholic.

MEESE, ED (EDWIN MEESE III), law and public policy educator, former United States attorney general; b. Oakland, Calif., Dec. 2, 1931; s. Edwin and Leone M. Meese; m. Ursula Herrick, 1958; children: Michael James, Dana Lynne. BA, Yale U., 1953; JD, U. Calif., Berkeley, 1958; LLD, Del. Law Sch., Widener U., U. San Diego, Valparaiso U., Calif. Luth. Coll. Dep. dist. atty. Alameda County, Calif., 1959-67; legal affairs sec. to Gov. Ronald Reagan, State of California, Sacramento, 1967-69; exec. asst., chief of staff to Gov. Ronald Reagan, State of Calif., Sacramento, 1969-75; v.p. Rohr Industries, Chula Vista, Calif., 1975-76; pvt. law practice, 1976-80; prof. law U. San Diego, 1977—81, dir. Ctr. for Criminal Justice Policy; counselor to Pres. The White House, Washington, 1981-85; atty. gen. US Dept. Justice, Washington, 1985-88; disting. fellow, Ronald Reagan Chair in Pub. Policy Heritage Found., Washington. Mem. NSC, 1981—85, Iraq Study Group, 2006; disting. vis. fellow Hoover Instn. Stanford U.; disting. sr. fellow Inst. for US Studies U. London; bd. regents Nat. Coll. of Dist. Atty.; bd. dirs. Capital Rsch. Ctr., Landmark Legal Found.; co-chmn. bd. governors The Reagan Ranch Program. Author: With Reagan: The Inside Story, 1992. V.p. Lutheran Ch., El Cajon, Calif. Served with US Army. Office: Heritage Found 214 Massachusetts Ave NE Washington DC 20002-4958 Office Phone: 202-546-4400. *

MEESTER, HOLLY, elementary school educator, music educator, sales executive; b. Grafton, ND, Sept. 1, 1966; d. Gordon and (Alice) Jane Thompson; m. Brent Meester, Sept. 27, 1991; children: Emily, Daniel. BS in Music Edn., N.D. State U., 1989; MA in Music Edn., U. St. Thomas, 2003. Lic. profl. educator N.D., 1989. Asst. dir. Red River Boy Choir, Fargo, ND, 1988—90; tchr. elem. music Fargo Pub. Schs., 1989—; founder, music dir. Lake Agassiz Girls Choir, Fargo, 1990—97. Ind. cons. Mary Kay Cosmetics, Fargo, 1993—; mentor Fargo Pub. Schs., 1999—2002, dir. elem. hand chimes performing group, 1991—, dir. elem. choir, 1989—; adj. prof. Minn. State U., Moorhead, 2004—. Bldg. liaison Fargo Edn. Assn.; bd. mem. Lake Agassiz Girls Choir, Fargo, 1990—98; steering com. mem. North Ctrl. Accreditation - Lewis & Clark Elem., 1992—2005. Mem.: N.D. Music Educators Assn. (state pres. collegiate chpt. 1988—89, Outstanding Collegiate Music Educator 1989), Music Educators Nat. Conf., Orgn. Am. Kodaly Educators, No. Plains Kodaly Chpt. (pres., v.p., past pres., member-at-large 1997—2005), Kappa Delta (life; corr. sec. 1986—87), Sigma Alpha Iota (life). Achievements include Performance at National Organization of American Kodaly Educators while Director of Lake Agassiz Girls Choir. Avocations: reading, piano, scrapbooks, choir. Office: Fargo Pub Schs 1040 29th St N Fargo ND 58102 Home Phone: 701-235-8098; Office Phone: 701-446-4854.

MEEZAN, ELIAS, pharmacologist, educator; b. NYC, Mar. 5, 1942; s. Maurice and Rachel (Epstein) M.; m. Elisabeth Gascard, May 14, 1967; children: David, Nathan, Joshua. BS in Chemistry, CCNY, 1962; PhD in Biochemistry, Duke U., 1966. Asst. prof. physiology and pharmacology Duke U., Durham, NC, 1969-70; asst. prof. pharmacology U. Ariz., Tucson, 1970-75, assoc. prof., 1975-79; prof., chmn. dept. pharmacology U. Ala., Birmingham, 1979-89, prof., dir. Metabolic Diseases Rsch. Lab., 1989-93, prof. dept. pharmacology & toxicology, 1993—. Mem. sci. adv. bd. Aegis Therapeutics, 2004—. Assoc. editor: Life Sci., 1973-79. Helen Hay Whitney postdoctoral fellow, 1966-69; recipient NIH Rsch. Career Devel. award, 1977-79. Mem. Am. Soc. Pharmacology and Exptl. Therapeutics, Am. Soc. Biol. Chemistry, AAUP, AAAS, N.Y. Acad. Sci., Assn. Med. Sch. Pharmacology. Democrat. Jewish. Achievements include isolation of retinal and brain microvasculature; development of method for isolating ultrastructurally and chemically intact basement membranes; co-inventor of method for enhancing nasal absorption of drugs. Home: 1202 Cheval Ln Birmingham AL 35216-2037 Office: U Ala Dept Pharmacology Birmingham AL 35294-0001 Office Phone: 205-934-4577. Business E-Mail: Elias.Meezan@ccc.uab.edu.

MEEZAN, WILLIAM ALAN, social work educator, consultant; b. NYC, Mar. 10, 1947; s. Joseph and Beatrice (Rauch) Meezan. BA in Psychology, U. Vt., 1967; MSW, Fla. State U., 1969; cert. in advanced social welfare, Columbia U., NYC, 1973; DSW, Columbia U., 1978. Social worker The Children's Village, Dobbs Ferry, NY, 1969—70; rsch. asst. child welfare rsch. program Sch. of Social Work Columbia U., NYC, 1970-72, part-time rsch. asst. child welfare rsch. program, 1972-73; rsch. assoc. Ctr. for N.Y.C. Affairs New Sch. for Social Rsch., NYC, 1973-75; study dir. Child Welfare League of Am., NYC, 1975-77; cons. Children's Bur., Adminstrn. for Children, Youth and Families, Office Human Devel. Svcs. HEW, Washington, 1978; asst. prof. Jane Addams Coll. of Social Work U. Ill., Chgo., 1978-81, assoc. prof. Jane Addams Coll. of Social Work, 1981-86, chair PhD program, prof. Jane Addams Coll. of Social Work, 1986-88; John Milner prof. child welfare Sch. Social Wk., U. So. Calif., LA, 1988—99, chair PhD program, 1989—94; Marion Elizabeth Blue prof. children and families U. Mich. Sch. Social Work, 1999—2005; dean Coll. Social Work Ohio State U., Columbus, 2005—. Part-time instr. Ctr. of Social Work and Social Rsch., Fairleigh Dickinson U., Teneck, N.J., 1974-75, Adelphi U. Grad. Sch. of Social Work, Garden City, N.Y., 1978; adj. asst. prof. NYU Sch. of Social Work, N.Y.C., 1975-78; spl. asst. to exec. dir. Jewish Children's Bur., Chgo., 1986-88, steering com., sec. Group for Advancement Doctoral Edn., 1990-94; sec. Soc. For Social Work and Rsch., 2002-05; bd. dirs., v.p. Inst. Advancement Social Work Rsch., 2003—. Author: Adoption Without Angencies: A Study of Independent Adoptions, 1978, Care and Commitment: Foster Parent Adoption Decisions, 1985, Evaluating Family Based Services, 1995, Family Preservation and Family Functioning, 1997, (monographs) The Impact of Welfare on Family Stability, 1975, Foster Care Needs and Alternatives to Placement: A Projection for 1975-85, 1975, Adoptions Services in the States, 1980, Evaluation of the Wayne County Foster Care Pilot Project, 2003; editor: Child Welfare: Current Dilemas-Future Decisions, 1983, Rationing Child Protection, 1995, Research Methods with Gay, Lesbian, Bisexual and Transgender Populations, 2003, The Rewards, Frustrations, Trials and Tribulations of Doing Social Work Research "On the Ground", 2 vols., 2005-2006; mem. editl. bd. Social Work Rsch., Child Welfare, Children and Youth Svcs. Rev., Jour. Pub. Child Welfare, Reflections: Narratives Profl. Helping, others; contbr. chpts. to books, articles to jours. HEW fellow, 1967-68, NIMH fellow, 1972-73, AAAS Congl. Sci. fellow,

1984-85; HEW scholar, 1975-77, U.S. Dept. Health and Human Svcs. scholar, 1980-83, 2000-04; Stuart Found. scholar, 1989-95, Fulbright scholar, 1994-95, State of Calif., 1996-99, Kellogg Found., 2000-04, State of Mich., 2000-02, Aspen Inst., 2000-03, Skillman Found., 2003-04, Mich. Nonprofit Rsch. Program, 2003-05. Mem. NASW, Am. Orthopsychiat. Assn., Acad. Cert. Social Workers, Coun. on Social Work Edn., Soc. Social Work and Rsch. Office: Ohio State U Stillman Hall 1947 College Rd Columbus OH 43210 Home: 2796 Powell Ave Bexley OH 43209 Home Phone: 614-237-9159; Office Phone: 614-292-5300. E-mail: meezan.1@osu.edu.

MEFFERT, JEFFREY JOHN, dermatologist; s. Roland Mathew and Marcella Czarnecki Meffert; m. Paula Marie Lyons, May 18, 1980; children: Austin Lyons, Ian Lyons. BA in Biology, Rice U., Houston, 1977; MD, U. Tex. Health Sci. Ctr., San Antonio, 1981. Diplomate Am. Bd. Family Practice, 1984, Am. Bd. Dermatology, 1995. Commd. officer USAF, 1978, advanced to col., family physician, dir. emergency svcs. Langley AFB, Va., 1984—86, chief flight medicine, squadron med. element Elmendorf AFB, Alaska, 1986—89, chief clinic svcs, Brooks AFB, Tex., 1989—92; dermatologist, assoc. program dir. USAF, US Army, Brooke Army Med. Ctr., Brooks AFB, 1995—2000; program dir., dermatology USAF, US Army, Lackland AFB, Tex., 2000—05; ret. USAF, 2006; assoc. clin. faculty dermatology U. Tex. Health Sci. Ctr., San Antonio, 2006—; pvt. practice dermatology San Antonio, 2006—. Co-author to profl. jours. albums. Decorated Legion Merit USAF; named Outstanding Program Dir., San Antonio Uniformed Svcs. Health Edn. Consortium, 2004. Mem.: Med. Dermatology Soc., San Antonio Dermatologic Soc. (pres. 2000—03), Am. Acad. Dermatology (chmn. bioterrorism and natural disaster task force 2005—), Assn. Mil. Dermatologists (life; pres. 2000—01). Independent. Buddhist. Home: 105 Cas Hills Dr San Antonio TX 78213 Office: Dermatology Center at Texas MedClinic 1007 NE Loop 410 Suite 110 San Antonio TX 78209 Home Phone: 210-348-8485; Office Phone: 210-826-3258. Office Fax: 210-826-5520. Personal E-mail: jmeff@aol.com. Business E-Mail: dermronin@yahoo.com.

MEFFERT, ROLAND MATTHEW, periodontist, educator; b. Cross Plains, Wis., June 30, 1932; s. John Michael and Lorraine Catherine (Garfoot) Meffert; m. Marcella Ann Czarnecki, June 12, 1954; children: Jeffrey, Lisa, Sarah, Gregory, Douglas. DDS, Marquette U., 1955; cert. in periodontics, U. Tex., Houston, 1961; cert. in periodontics, Wilford Hall USAF Med. Ctr., 1962. Commd. 1st lt. USAF, 1954, advanced through grades to col., 1970, ret., 1974; prof. dept. periodontics U. Tex. Health Sci. Ctr., San Antonio, 1974—84, 1992—2003, cons. continuing dental edn., 2003—; assoc. prof. dept. prosthodontics U. Tex. Med. Ctr., San Antonio, 2003—; prof., chmn. dept. periodontics La. State U. Sch. Dentistry, New Orleans, 1984—92. Editor emeritus Implant Dentistry; editor emeritus: Practical Periodontics and Aesthetic Dentistry; contbr. chapters to books, articles to profl. jours. Recipient Spl. Citation award, Am. Acad. Periodontology, 1993, 1997, Meffert-Mutlu Implant Inst. named in honor, Ankara, Turkey, 1997. Master: Am. Acad. Implant Prosthodontics; fellow: Internat. Colll. Dentists, Am. Coll. Dentists; mem.: Am. Soc. Osseointegration (diplomate, pres. 1992, Oral Implantologist of Yr. 1988), Internat. Congress Oral Implantology (diplomate, pres. 1990, Internat. Edn. award 1992, 1994), Am. Bd. Periodontology (diplomate, dir., chmn. 1990—96). Business E-Mail: meffert@uthscsa.edu.

MEGALLI, MAGUID RAMZI, health facility administrator; b. Cairo, Jan. 26, 1942; arrived in U.S., 1969; s. Ramzi and Lydia Megalli; m. Viviane Wassef, Jan. 28, 1968; children: Michael, Mark. MD, MBA, Cairo U., 1965. Lic. Am. Bd. of Urology. Resident in urology Columbia U., NYC, 1970—74; chief of urology St. Joseph Med. Ctr., Yonkers, NY, 1982—88; chief med. officer Cath. Health Care Sys. Resources, 1999—2002; pres. Benifice Advantage, the Self-Insuring Co. for Archdiocese of N.Y., 2002—; exec. v.p., chief med. officer Our Lady of Mercy Med. Ctr., Bronx, NY, 2003—. Founder, chmn. Servitas IPA, NYC, 1994—99. Contbr. articles to profl. publs. (Valantine Fellowship award, 1974). Lt. col. USAR, 1972—84. Fellow: ACS (life). Home: 35 Island Dr Rye NY 10580 Office: Our Lady of Mercy Med Ctr 600 E 233d St Bronx NY 10466 Office Phone: 718-920-9590. Home Fax: 914-967-3613. Business E-Mail: mmegalli@chcsnet.org.

MEGGERS, BETTY JANE, anthropologist, researcher; b. Washington, Dec. 5, 1921; d. William Frederick and Edith (Raddant) M.; m. Clifford Evans, Sept. 13, 1946. AB, U. Pa., 1943; MA, U. Mich., 1944; PhD, Columbia U., 1952; D (hon.), U. de Guayaquil, Ecuador, 1987, U. Fed. Rio de Janeiro, Brazil, 1994, U. Nat. La Plata, Argentina, 1997, U. Católica de Goiás, Brazil, 1999; D (hon.), U. Fed. do Parana, Brazil, 2006. Instr. anthropology Am. U., Washington, 1950-51; rsch. assoc. Smithsonian Instn., 1954—, expert, 1981—; founder, pres. Taraxacum Inc., 1977—. Hon. prof. U. de Azuay, Ecuador, 1991. Author: Environmental Limitation on the Development of Culture, 1954, Ecuador, 1966, Amazonia, 1971, 2d edit., 1996, Prehistoric America, 1972, Evolucion y Difusion Cultural, 1998, Ecologia y Biogeografia de la Amazonia, 1999, (with Clifford Evans) Archeological Investigations at the Mouth of the Amazon, 1957, Archeological Investigations in British Guiana, 1960, (with Clifford Evans and Emilio Estrada) Early Formative Period of Coastal Ecuador, 1965, (with Clifford Evans) Archeological Investigations on the Rio Napo, Eastern Ecuador, 1968; editor: Prehistoria Sudamericana, 1992. Recipient award for sci. achievement Washington Acad. Sci., 1956; gold medal 37th Internat. Congress of Americanists, 1966; Order Al Merito Govt. Ecuador, 1966; Order Bernardo O'Higgins Govt. Chile, 1985; Sec.'s Gold medal for exceptional service Smithsonian Instn., 1986; Order Andres Bello Govt. Venezuela, 1988; Order Al Mérito por Servicios Distinguidos Govt. Peru, 1989, Order Al Mérito Científico, Casa de la Cultura Ecuatoriana, 2006. Fellow: AAAS, Assn. Tropical Biology (hon.; councilor 1976—78, pres.-elect 1982, pres. 1983); mem.: Ecol. Soc. Am., New Eng. Antiquities Rsch. Assn., Academia Nacional Historia Ecuador (corr.), Am. Anthrop. Assn. (exec. sec. 1959—61), Museo Antropológico de la Cultura Andina (hon.), Soc. Am. Archaeology (exec. bd. 1962—64), Am. Ethnol. Soc., Anthrop. Soc. Wash. (treas. 1955—60, v.p. 1965—66, pres. 1966—68), Phi Beta Kappa, Sigma Xi. Home: 1227 30th St NW Washington DC 20007-3410 Office: Smithsonian Instn Washington DC 20560-0001

MEGGINSON, ELIZABETH R., legislative staff member, director, lawyer; b. Clarksdale, Miss., Oct. 27, 1947; d. Mitford Ray and Cleo Ruth (Faggard) M.; m. Mark W. Menezes; children: Paige Jennings, Marisa Menezes. BM, La. State U., 1969, MM, 1970, JD, 1977. Pvt. practice, 1977-78; counsel natural resources com. La. Ho. Reps., 1978-81, legis. svc. coord. comml. regulation divsn., 1981-84; asst. atty. gen. environ. enforcement divsn. La. Dept. Justice, 1984-88; asst. sec. for office legal affairs and enforcement La. Dept. Environ. Quality, 1988-89; adminstrv. asst. to Rep. W.J. Billy Tauzin, Washington, 1989-90; staff dir. counsel Subcommittee on Coast Guard and Navigation Com. on Merchant Marine and Fisheries, U.S. Ho. Rep., Washington, 1990—95; counsel to chair Com. on Resources, U.S. Ho. Rep., Washington, 1995—96, chief counsel, 1997—2000, Com. on Transp. & Infrastructure, U.S. Ho. Rep., Washington, 2001—. Mem. Phi Kappa Phi. Office: Committee on Transportation & Infrastructure Room 2165 Rayburn House Office Building Washington DC 20515-6256 *

MEGGS, WILLIAM JOEL, toxicologist, allergist, emergency physician, educator; b. Newberry, SC, May 30, 1942; s. Wallace Nat and Elizabeth (Pruitt) M.; m. Susan Nancy Spring, June 11, 1966 (div. June 1998); m. Susan Krause Martin, Apr. 21, 2001; children: Jason Nathaniel, Benjamin Maffey, Thomas Clute. BS, Clemson U., 1964; PhD, Syracuse U., 1969; MD, U. Miami, 1979. Diplomate Am. Bd. Internal Medicine, Am. Bd. Allergy and Immunology, Am. Bd. Emergency Medicine, Am. Bd. Med. Toxicology. Resident in internal medicine Rochester (N.Y.) Gen. Hosp., 1979-82; staff fellow in allergy and clin. immunology Nat. Inst. Allergy and Infectious Diseases, Bethesda, Md., 1982-85; asst. dir. med. edn. emergency dept. Washington Hosp. Ctr., 1985-88; from asst. prof. allergy, immunology to sr. vice chmn. Sch. Medicine E. Carolina U., Greenville, NC, 1988—2004, sr. vice chmn. Sch. Medicine, 2004—; chmn., dir. emergency dept. Lenoir Meml. Hosp., Kinston, NC, 1990-91. Mem. Emergency Svcs. Com. Lenoir Meml. Hosp., Kinston, 1988-92; mem workshop on immune testing, Agy. for Toxic Substances and Diseases Registry, 1992, workshop on equity in environ. health, U.S. EPA, 1992, workshop on multiple chem. sensitivity syndrome, NRC, 1991; mem. rsch. adv. com. on Gulf War illnesses Dept. VA, 2002-; fellow med. toxicology NYU, 1992-96. Co-author: The Inflammation Cure, 2003; co-editor: Health and Safety in Agriculture, 1997; contbr. numerous articles and abstracts to profl. jours. Vol. physician Indigent Clinic E. Carolina U., Pitt County Med. Soc., 1988—, Pitt County Shelter, 1989—; advanced cardiac life support instr. E. Carolina U. Sch. of Medicine, 1988-2000, advanced trauma life support instr., 1991-2002; mem. Pitt County Traffic Injury Prevention Program, 1989-92; bd. dirs. Rachael Carson Coun., 1988—; mem. adv. bd. Pamplico Tar River Found., 1990—. Named Woodrow Wilson Hon. fellow, 1964, NSF post-doctoral fellow, 1969; granter N.C. United Way, 1988-89, Greer Labs., 1989-90, Am. Lung Assn. N.C., 1992-93. Fellow Am. Coll. Emergency Physicians, Am. Coll. Med. Toxicology; mem. AMA, Am. Acad. Allergy and Immunology, Am. Acad. Clin. Toxicology, Pitt County Med. Soc., N.C. State Med. Soc., Soc. for Acad. Emergency Medicine, N.C. Thoracic Soc. (physicians' sect.). Achievements include creator of the biological homing theory of the origins of life. Office: E Carolina U Sch Medicine Dept Emergency Medicine Brody Bldg 4-W54 600 Moye Blvd Greenville NC 27858-4300 Office Phone: 252-744-2954. Business E-Mail: meggsw@ecu.edu.

MEGHREBLIAN, ROBERT VARTAN, manufacturing executive, physicist; b. Cairo, Sept. 6, 1922; arrived in U.S., 1923, naturalized, 1929; s. Vahan V. and Mary (Kurkjian) M.; m. Mary J. Walton, 1955 (div. 1977); Children: David V., Susan M.; m. Margaret M. Gordon, 1987. B in Engring. (Gotshall-Powell scholar), Rensselaer Poly. Inst., 1943; MS (Guggenheim fellow), Calif. Inst. Tech., 1950, PhD magna cum laude (Guggenheim fellow), 1953. Lectr. Oak Ridge Nat. Lab., 1952-55, assoc. project mgr., 1955-58; chief sect, Physics Jet Propulsion Lab., Calif. Inst. Tech., 1958-60, mgr. space scis. divsn., 1960-68, dep. asst. lab. dir., 1968-71, assoc. prof. applied mechanics, 1960-61; v.p. rsch. and engring. Cabot Corp., Boston, 1971-79, v.p., 1971-87; pres. Distrigas Corp., 1979-85; gen. mgr. Cabot Crystals Bus. Unit, 1985-86, dir. corp. planning and devel., 1986-87. Author: Reactor Analysis, 1960. Vice chair Montecito Planning Commn., Calif., 2003, chair, 2004—06. Lt. (j.g.) USN, 1941—46, PTO, ATO. Fellow: AIAA (assoc.), Am. Nuc. Soc.; mem.: Montecito Assn. (bd. dir. 1992—98, chair archtl. rev. com. 1993—95, v.p. 1994, pres. 1995, 1996, elected hon. dir. 2007, Montecito Citizen of Yr. 2002), Art Found. Santa Barbara (v.p.), Santa Barbara Club, Tennis Club Santa Barbara, Sigma Xi. Home: 440 Woodley Rd Montecito CA 93108-2006

MEGIDDO, NIMROD, mathematician, computer scientist; BSc in Math. and Physics, Hebrew U., Jerusalem, 1968, MSc in Math., 1969, PhD in Math., 1972. Prof. ops. rsch. Tel Aviv U., 1972—98; rsch. staff mem. Almaden Rsch. Ctr., San Jose, Calif., 1984—. Contbr. articles to profl. jours. Achievements include 32 patents in field.

MEGILL, ALLAN, historian; b. Regina, Sask., Apr. 20, 1947; arrived in US, 1980; s. Ralph Peter and Jean Tudhope (Dickson) M.; div.; children: Jason Robert, Jessica Susan, Jonathan David; m. Rita Felski; 1 child, Maria Megill Felski. BA, U. Sask., 1969; MA, U. Toronto, 1970; PhD, Columbia U., NYC, 1975. From instr. to prof. history U. Iowa, Iowa City, 1974—90; prof. history U. Va., Charlottesville, 1990—. Rsch. fellow in history of ideas Australian Nat. U., Canberra, 1977—79, temp. lectr. modern European studies, 1979; vis. prof. Sch. Advanced Studies in Social Scis., Paris, 1997. Author: Prophets of Extremity, 1985, Karl Marx: The Burden of Reason, 2002, Historical Knowledge, Historical Error: A Contemporary Guide to Practice, 2007; editor: Rethinking Objectivity, 1994; co-editor: The Rhetoric of the Human Sciences, 1987; cons. editor Jour. of History of Ideas, 1986—89, mem. editl. bd., 1990—, v.p., 2004—05, pres., 2005—; mem. editl. bd.: U. Press of Va., 1991—94, Rethinking History, 1996—; contbr. articles to profl. jours. Chmn. Page-Barbour and Richard Lectures com. U. Va., 1994-96. Mem.: Internat. Commn. for the History and Theory of Historiography, Internat. Soc. for Intellectual History, Am. Hist. Assn. Office: Univ Va Corcoran Dept History PO Box 400180 Charlottesville VA 22904 Office Phone: 434-924-6414. Business E-Mail: megill@virginia.edu.

MEGNA, STEVE ALLAN, retired secondary school educator; Secondary tchr. Vernon (NJ) H.S., ret., 2006. Recipient Tech. Excellence award Internat. Tech. Edn. Assn. and Tech. Edn. Assn. N.J., 1992, Tech. Program of Yr. award Tech. Edn. Assn. N.J., 1989; named Innovative Tech. Educator, Martinson Family Found., 2002.

MEHAFFEY, JOHN ALLEN, marketing executive, publishing executive; b. Brainerd, Minn. m. Mary Jean Mehaffey; children: Mark, Scott, Chris. Student, Minn. Sch. Bus. With Mehaffey Internat., Naples, Fla., 1954—. Bd. govs. Verified Audit Circulations. Ga. Nat. Newspaper Assn., Newspaper Assn. Am., Nat. Press Club (Washington), Ill. Press Assn., Assn. Free Cmty. Papers, Ind. Free Papers Assn., Fla. Free Papers Assn., Am. Mktg. Assn., Inland Press Assn., Fla. Press Assn., Soc. Profl. Journalists, Chgo. Headline Club, Internat. Platform Assn., Am. Telemktg. Assn., Naples Area C. of C., Suburban Newspaper Assn., Ctrl. States Circulating Mgrs. Assn., Inland Press Assn., Southeastern Advt. Pubs. Assn., Brainerd Lakes Area C. of C., St. Joseph's Med. Ctr. Found. (charter), Nat. Alliance for Mentally Ill., Greater Chgo. and Alll. Alliance for Mentally Ill, Motion Picture and TV Assn., Marine Habitat Found. (founding), Naples Aquarium (founding), Founding One Thousand, Naples Philharm. Ctr. for Performing Arts, Naples Conservancy, Northland Arboretum, Paul Bunyan Nature Learning Ctr. (life), Nat. Rails-to-Trails Conservancy, Internat. Press Club (Chgo.), Naples Press Club, Elks, Moose, Sigma Delta Chi. Avocation: boating. Home and Office: Mehaffey Internat PO Box 2956 Naples FL 34106-2956

MEHALCHIN, JOHN JOSEPH, entrepreneur, finance company executive; b. Hazleton, Pa., Aug. 8, 1937; s. Charles and Susan (Korba) Mehalchin; 1 child from previous marriage, Martin. BS with honors (1st in class), Temple U., 1964; MBA, U. Calif., Berkeley, 1965; postgrad., U. Chgo., 1964; LHD (hon.), U. Colo., 2002. Supr. costs Winchester-Western, New Haven, 1965-67; mgmt. cons. Booz-Allen & Hamilton, NYC, 1967-68; mgr. planning TWA, NYC, 1968-69; officer Smith Barney, NYC, Paris, 1970-74; CFO Storage Tech., Louisville, 1974-79; sr. v.p. Heizer Corp., 1979; pres., founder Highline Fin. Svcs., Inc. and fgn. subs., Boulder, Colo., 1979—, London, Paris, Frankfurt, Germany. Strategic planning com. Coll. and Grad. Sch. Bus., U. Colo., Denver; bd. advisors U. Colo. Ctr. Entrepreneurship, U. Colo. Bus. Sch., Wolf Ventures. With US Army, 1958—61. Recipient Mack Easton award for Excellence, 1998, Univ. medal, U. Colo., 2002; fellow, U. Calif., Berkeley, 1964, 1965; scholar, U. Chgo., 1964. Mem.: Equipment Leasing Assn., Fin. Execs. Inst., Omicron Delta Epsilon, Beta Gamma Sigma. Home and Office: Highline Fin Svcs Inc 2930 Center Green Ct Ste 200 Boulder CO 80301-5419 Office Phone: 303-443-7267.

MEHALIK, MATTHEW M., industrial engineer, educator; b. Pitts., Pa., Jan. 11, 1970; s. Gilbert G. and Sandra L. Mehalik; m. Deborah L. McGaughey, Apr. 28, 2006. BS in Aerospace Engring. with distinction, U. Va., Charlottesville, 1992, MS in Sys. Engring., 1997; PhD, U. Va., Charlottesville, 2001. Postdoctoral assoc. Sci., Tech., and Soc. U. of Va., Charlottesville, 2001—02; fellow in pub. affairs Coro Ctr. for Civic Leadership, Pitts., 2002—03; postdoctoral rsch. assoc. Learning R&D Ctr. U. of Pitts., Pitts., 2003—05, vis. asst. prof. indsl. engring., 2005—. Cons. Sustainable Pitts., Pitts., 2004—. Author, researcher: Ethical and Environmental Challenges to Engineering, ISO 14001 Concepts and Cases; contbr. articles to profl. jours. (Lous T. Rader award in sys. engring., 2001). Mem. adv. bd. Nat. Found. for Tchg. Entrepreneurship, Pitts., 2003—04; mem. planning com. Nat. Aviary, Pitts., 2006. Recipient Product Realization for Global Opportunities grant, Nat. Collegiate Inventors and Innnovators Alliance, 2005—07, Earth Systems Engring. and Mgmt. Course Devel. grant, AT&T, 2001—03, Bringing Design into Urban High Schools to Teach Sci. grant, NSF, 2005—07, Inventing for a Better Global Environment: A Comparative Analysis of Two Networks grant, 1998—99. Mem.: Assn. for Practical and Profl. Ethics (assoc.), Soc. for the Social Studies of Sci. (assoc.), Am. Soc. for Engring. Edn. (assoc.), Am. Ednl. Rsch. Assn. (assoc.), Inst. for Indsl. Engrs. (assoc.). Office: U Pitts Indsl Engring 1048 Benedum Hall Pittsburgh PA 15261 Office Phone: 412-624-7245. Office Fax: 412-624-7439. Business E-Mail: mmehalik@pitt.edu.

MEHAN, GEORGE TRACEY, III, former federal agency administrator; b. June 1949; Grad., St. Louis U. Dir. Mo. Dept. Natural Resources, 1989—91; assoc. deputy adminstr. EPA, 1992—93; dir. Office of Great Lakes, Mich. Dept. Environ. Quality; asst. adminstr. water EPA, Washington, 2001—04.

MEHIEL, DENNIS, investment company executive; Co-founder Four M Corp., Balt., 1966, Valhalla, NY, 1970; former owner Box USA, Sweetheart Cup Co.; now chmn., prin. shareholder Four M Capital Inc.

MEHL, ALBERT L., pediatrician, poet, composer; s. Clinton Mehl and Alberta Wells; m. Annie Kempe, Aug. 4, 1979; children: Sarah Kempe-Mehl, James Kempe-Mehl. BA, Colo. Coll., Colorado Springs, 1976; MD, U. Colo. Health Scis. Ctr., Denver, 1980. Diplomate Am. Bd. Pediat. Pediatrician Kaiser Permanente, Lafayette, Colo., 1987—. Editl. cons. various publs., Various US states, 1988—; asst. clin. prof. U. Colo. Health Scis. Ctr., Denver, 2001—; chmn. peer rev. com. Exempla Good Samaritan Med. Ctr., Lafayette, Colo., 2005—. Singer, songwriter: albums Asphalt Cowboy, writer, performer: albums Cowboy Pottery; contbr. articles to profl. jours. Mem. expert working group effective interventions infants and young children with hearing loss U.S. HHS; gubernatorial appointee Colo. Children's Trust Fund Child Abuse Prevention, Denver, 1992—97, vice chmn., 1995—96; chmn. infant hearing adv. com. Colo. State Dept. Health and Environment, Denver, 1997—. Recipient Peak Performance award, Colo. Acad. Audiology, 1998, Communities Helping Young Children award, Frances Owens, First Lady of Colo., 2005; Boettcher Found. scholar, 1973—77. Fellow: Am. Acad. Pediat. (chmn. nat. task force infant hearing 2005—, appointee U.S. joint com. infant hearing 2005—). Avocations: fly fishing, skiing, golf. Office: Kaiser Permanente Med Offices 280 Exempla Cir Lafayette CO 80026

MEHLENBACHER, DOHN HARLOW, civil engineer, consultant; b. Huntington Park, Calif., Nov. 18, 1931; s. Virgil Claude and Helga (Sigfridson) M.; m. Nancy Moss; children: Dohn Scott, Kimberly Ruth, Mark James, Matthew Lincoln. BSCE, U. Ill., 1953; MS in City and Regional Planning, Ill. Inst. Tech., Chgo., 1961; MBA, U. Chgo., 1972. Registered profl. engr., Ill.; lic. structural engr., Ill. Structural engr., draftsman Swift & Co., Chgo., 1953-54, 56-57, DeLeuw-Cather Co., Chgo., 1957-59; project engr. Quaker Oats Co., Chgo., 1959-61, mgr. constrn., 1964-70, mgr. real property, 1970-71, mgr. engring. and maintenance LA, 1961-64; chief facilities engr. Bell & Howell Co., Chgo., 1972-73; v.p. design Globe Engring. Co., Chgo., 1973-76; project mgr. I.C. Harbour Constrn. Co., Oak Brook, Ill., 1976-78; dir. estimating George A. Fuller Co., Oak Brook, 1978; pres. Food-Tech. Co., Willowbrook, Ill., 1979-80; dir. phys. resources Ill. Inst. Tech., Chgo., 1980-92; cons. Exec. Svc. Corp., Chgo., 1994—; cons. structural engr. Mem. AAA Nat. Roster of Neutrals. With USAF, 1954-56. Fellow ASCE. Home and Office: 436 Leitch Ave La Grange IL 60525-6126 Office Phone: 708-354-7131. Personal E-mail: dohnh@comcast.net.

MEHLER, GORDON, lawyer, former federal prosecutor; b. Denver, Feb. 27, 1955; s. Irving Martin and Bernice (Steinberg) M.; m. Ariel Zwang; children: Grace, Rachel. BS, U. Colo., 1976; JD, NYU, 1982. Bar: NY 1983, US Dist. Ct. (ea. and so. dists.) NY 1983, US Ct. Appeals (10th cir.) 1984, US Ct. Appeals (2d cir.) 1986, US Supreme Ct. 2000. Assoc. Skadden, Arps, Slate, Meagher & Flom, NYC, 1982-83; law clk. to presiding judge US Ct. Appeals (10th cir.), Denver, 1983-84; fed. prosecutor US Atty.'s Office (ea. dist.), NYC, 1984—99, chief spl. prosecutions (pub. integrity), 1996-98; dep. asst. atty. gen. US Dept. Justice, Washington, 1999-2000; pvt. practice Law Offices of Gordon Mehler, PLLC, NYC, 2000—. Adj. assoc. prof. legal law Fordham U. Law Sch., NYC, 1988-92; US Dept. Justice resident legal advisor to Romania, Bucharest, 1992. Co-author: (with Gleeson and James) Federal Criminal Practice, 8th edit., 2007; co-editor: New York Criminal Practice, 2d edit., 2005; contbr. articles in field to profl. jours. and newspapers. Bd. dirs. Health Jam, 2004—, Jacob Riis Settlement House, 2007—. Mem. ABA, Fed. Bar Coun., NY State Bar Assn., NYC Bar Assn., NY Coun. Def. Lawyers. Office: 747 Third Ave 32nd Floor New York NY 10017-2803 Office Phone: 212-661-2414. Business E-Mail: gmehler@mehlerlaw.com.

MEHLER, PHILIP S., internist; m. Leah Mehler. BA in Biology, U. Colo., Denver, 1979, MD, 1983. Internship and residency U. Colo. Health Sci. Ctr., 1983—87; staff attending physician Denver Health Med. Ctr., Denver, 1987—, chief internal medicine, 1994—2004; assoc. med. dir. Denver Health Denver, 2003—. V.p. Colo. Prevention Ctr., Denver, 1995—; Prof. of Medicine and Glassman endowed chair Internal medicine U. Colo. Sch. Medicine, Denver, 2000—. Contbr. articles to profl. jours. Recipient Ciba-Geigy Tchg. award, U. Colo. Sch. Medicine, 1986, Outstanding Faculty award, 1991, Outstanding Tchr. Yr., Denver Health Med. Ctr., 1996, Safety award, NAPH, 1997, Academic Excellence award, Denver Health, 2005. Fellow: Am. Coll. Physicans; mem.: Phi Beta Kappa, Alpha Omega Alpha. Office: Denver Health Med Ctr 777 Bannock St MC0278 Denver CO 80204 Office Phone: 303-436-3234.

MEHLINGER, HOWARD DEAN, education educator; b. Hillsboro, Kans., Aug. 22, 1931; s. Alex and Alice Hilda (Skibbe) Mehlinger; m. Carolee Ann Case, Dec. 28, 1952; children: Bradley Case, Barbara Ann, Susan Kay. BA, McPherson Coll., Kans., 1953; MS in Edn, U. Kans., 1959, PhD, 1964. Co-dir. social studies project Pitts. pub. schs., 1963-64; asst. dir. fgn. relations project North Central Assn. Schs. and Colls., Chgo., 1964-65; mem. faculty Ind. U., Bloomington, 1965-97, prof. history and edn., 1974-97, dean Sch. Edn., 1981-90, dir. Ctr. for Excellence in Edn., 1990-99. Social studies adviser Houghton Mifflin Pub. Co.; cons. U.S. Office Edn. Co-author: American Political Behavior, 2d edit., 1977, Count Witte and the Tsarist Government in the 1905 Revolution, 1972, Toward Effective Instruction in the Social Studies, 1974, School Reform in the Information Age, 1995, Technology and Teacher Education: A Guide for Educators and Policymakers, 2002; editl. bd. Education and Society, history tchr.; editor: UNESCO Handbook on the Teaching of Social Studies, 1981; co-editor: Yearbook on the Social Studies, 1981. STAG grantee Dept. State, 1975 Mem. NEA, Nat. Council Social Studies, Phi Beta Kappa, Phi Alpha Theta, Pi Sigma Alpha, Phi Delta Kappa. Home: 3271 N Ramble Rd E Bloomington IN 47408-1094 Business E-Mail: mehlinge@indiana.edu.

MEHLMAN, BRUCE P., trade association and formal federal agency administrator; s. Arthur and Judy Mehlman; married; 3 children. Grad., Princeton U., U. Va. Gen. counsel Nat. Rep. Congl. Com., 1996—99; gen. counsel, policy dir. House Rep. Conf.; telecom. policy counsel Cisco Sys., 1999—2001; asst. sec. for tech. policy US Dept. Commerce, Washington, 2001—04; exec. dir. Computer Systems Policy Project, Washington, 2004—. Republican. Office: Computer Systems Policy Project Ste 1100 1341 G St NW Washington DC 20005

MEHLMAN, EDWIN STEPHEN, endodontist; b. Hartford, Conn., Nov. 30, 1935; s. Sol Abraham and Rose (Slitt) M.; m. Lesley Judith Lunin, June 13, 1959; children: Jeffrey Cole, Brian Scott, Erik Van. BA, Wesleyan U., 1957; DDS, U. Pa., 1961; cert. endodontics, Boston U., 1965. Diplomate Am. Bd. Endodontists. Instr. oral medicine Sch. Dental Medicine Harvard U., Boston, 1965—67; clin. instr. endodontics Sch. Dental Medicine Tufts U., Boston, 1968—70; lectr. endodontics Sch. Dental Medicine, Harvard U., Boston, 1970—72, asst. clin. prof. endodontics, 1972—; staff assoc. Forsyth Dental Ctr., Boston, 1965—; asst. prof. endodontics Boston U. Sch. Dental Medicine, 1995—; pvt. practice Providence, 1965—. Vis. lectr. dental hygiene U. R.I., Kingston, 1965-71, Community Coll. R.I., Lincoln, 1990—; cons. com. on accreditation of Dentists and Dental Aux. Edn. Programs, 1974-78. Contbr. articles to profl. jours. Pres. Temple Habonim, Barrington, R.I., 1968-70, Bur. Jewish Edn. of R.I., 1980-84; area v.p. Jewish Fedn. R.I., 1975-78; mem. R.I. Legis. Commn. to Study Malpractice Crisis, 1985-86; chmn. R.I. Dental Polit. Action Com., 1987-90. Capt. USAF, 1961-63. Recipient Etherington award Six N.E. Dental Assns. for Outstanding Contbns. to Dentistry, Disting. Fellow Internat. Coll. Dentists, 2004, Dist. Alumni award for svc. to dentistry Boston U. Goldman Sch. Dentistry, 2005 Fellow Am. Coll. Dentists (Vol. Yr. 2004), Internat. Coll. Dentists (dep. regent 1994-98), Pierre Fauchard Acad. (Merit award, Leadership award 2006, Rida Kershaw award for outstanding contbn. to cmty. 2006); mem. ADA (coun. on govt. affairs and fed. dental svcs. 1988-92, vice-chmn. 1991-92, 1st v.p. 1994-95, 1st dist. trustee 1999-2003), Am. Assn. Endodontists (dir. 1988-91), R.I. Dental Assn. (pres. 1986-87), N.E. Dental Assns. (Outstanding N.E. Dentist 1995, Disting. Practitioner 2000). Jewish. Avocations: reading, civic activities. Home: 3 Hanley Farm Rd Warren RI 02885-4376 also: 130 Waterman St Providence RI 02906-2010

MEHLMAN, KEN(NETH) (BRIAN), lawyer, former political organization administrator; b. Balt., Aug. 21, 1966; s. Arthur and Judy Mehlman. BA, Franklin & Marshall, 1988; JD, Harvard U., 1991. Bar: DC, Md. Assoc. Akin Gump Strauss Hauer & Feld LLP, 1991—94; legis. dir. to Rep. Lamar Smith US Congress, 1994—96, chief of staff to Rep. Kay Granger, 1996—99; mid-west regional polit. dir. Rep. Primaries, 1999; nat. field dir. Bush-Cheney campaign, 2000; dep. asst. to Pres. & dir. pub. affairs The White House, 2001—03; chmn. Bush-Cheney campaign, 2004, Rep. Nat. Com., 2005—07; ptnr. Akin Gump Strauss Hauer & Feld LLP, Washington, 2007—. Campaign worker William Weld's campaign for gov. of Mass., 1990, Pres. George H. W. Bush re-election campaign, 1992, Ohio Senator Mike DeWine's campaign, 1994, Senator Bob Dole's campaign, 1996; mem. bd. trustees Franklin & Marshall Coll., 2003—. Named Campaign Mgr. of the Yr., Am. Assn. Polit. Consultants, 2005. Mem.: Phi Kappa Tau. Republican. Jewish. Office: Akin Gump Strauss Hauer & Feld LLP Robert S Strauss Bldg 1333 New Hampshire Ave NW Washington DC 20036 *

MEHLMAN, MARK FRANKLIN, lawyer; b. LA, Dec. 18, 1947; s. Jack and Elaine Pearl (Lopater) M.; m. Barbara Ann Novak, Aug. 20, 1972; children: David, Jennifer, Ilyse. BA, U. Ill., 1969; LLB, U. Mich., 1973. Bar: Ill. 1973; U.S. Dist. Ct. (no. dist.) Ill. 1973. Assoc. Sonnenschein, Nath & Rosenthal LLP, Chgo., 1973—80, mem. policy and planning com., 1989—2006. Trustee Groveland Health Svcs., Highland Park (Ill.) Hosp., 1991-97; trustee, treas., exec. com. Spertus Inst. Jewish Studies, Chgo., 1992-97, vice chmn. bd. trustees, 1996—; vice-chmn. regional bd. Anti-Defamation League, 1987-89, hon. life mem. nat. commn., 1993—. Fellow Am. Bar Found.; mem. ABA (chmn. mortgages and other debt financing subcom. 1991-95, supervisory coun. 1997-2000, sec. RPPT sect. 2004-05), Am. Coll. Real Estate Lawyers (exec. com. bd. govs. 2000—, sec. 2003-04, treas. 2004-05, v.p. 2005-06, pres.-elect 2006—, chmn. MDP com. 2000—, chmn. mem. selection com. 2000-01), Anglo-Am. Real Property Inst., Legal Club of Chgo., Lake Shore Country Club, Standard Club, Exec. Club of Chgo. Office: Sonnenschein Nath & Rosenthal LLP Ste 7800 233 S Wacker Dr Chicago IL 60606-6491 Office Phone: 312-876-8023. Business E-Mail: mmehlman@sonnenschein.com.

MEHLMAN, MAXWELL JONATHAN, law educator; b. Washington, Nov. 4, 1948; s. Jacob and Betty (Hoffman) M.; m. Cheryl A. Stone, Sept. 15, 1979; children: Aurora, Gabriel. BA, Reed Coll., 1970, Oxford U., England, 1972; JD, Yale U., 1975. Bar: D.C. 1976, Ohio 1988. Assoc. Arnold & Porter, Washington, 1975-84; asst. prof. Case Western Res. U., Cleve., 1984-87, dir. Law-Medicine Ctr., 1986—, assoc. prof., 1987-90, prof. law, 1990-96, Arthur E. Petersilge prof., 1996—, prof. biomed. ethics, 1998—. Spl. counsel N.Y. State Bar, N.Y.C., 1988-94, Nat. Kidney Found., 1991; cons. Am. Assn. Ret. Persons, Washington, 1992. Editor: High Tech Home Care, 1991, (with T. Murray) Encyclopedia of Ethical, Legal and Policy Issues in Biotechnology; author: (with J. Botkin) Access to the Genome: The Challenge to Equality, 1998, (with Andrews and Rothstein) Genetics: Ethics, Law and Policy, 2002, 06, Wondergenes: Genetic Enhancement and the Future of Society, 2003; contbr. articles to profl. jours. Active steering com. AIDS Commn. Greater Cleve., 1986-90. Rhodes scholar, 1970; Rsch. grantee NIH, 1992-94, 97—. Mem. Am. Assn. Law Schs. (chmn. sect. on law, medicine and health care 1990), Phi Beta Kappa. Avocations: skiing, music, kayaking. Office: Case Western Reserve U Sch Law-Law Medicine Ctr Gund Hall 11075 E Blvd Cleveland OH 44106 Office Phone: 216-368-3983. Business E-Mail: mjm10@case.edu.

MEHLMAN, MYRON A., medical educator, toxicologist; m. Constance Mehlman, Sept. 4, 1960 (dec. June 1997); children: Mara Appel, Hope Hurowitz, Alison Fox; m. Karyl Norcross, Apr. 14, 1999. BS, CCNY, 1957; PhD, MIT, 1964. Prof. biochemistry Rutgers U., Newark, 1965-69; prof. biochemistry Coll. of Medicine U. Nebr., Omaha, 1967-71; chief biochem. toxicology FDA, Washington, 1972-73; spl. asst. toxicology dept. HEW, Washington, 1973-75; interagy. liaison officer NIH, Bethesda, Md., 1975-77; dir. toxicology Mobil Oil, Princeton, NJ, 1977-89; prof. U. Medicine and Dentistry of N.J., Piscataway, 1990—, Mt. Sinai Sch. Medicine, NY, 1980, U. Tex. Med. Br., Galveston, 2003—. Editor Jour. Environ. Pathology and Toxicology, 1977-81, Jour. Toxicology and Indsl. Health, 1975-78, Jour. Clean Tech. and Environ. Sci., 1989—; contbr. over 300 articles to profl. jours.; edited over 60 books. 1st lt. U.S. Army, 1958-60. Fellow Acad. Toxol. Soc., Am. Coll. Toxicology, Collequim Ramazzin (founding dir., mem. bd. dirs., Ramazzin award 2002). Achievements include research in toxicology, environmental health, and nutritional and biomedical science. Office: 7 Bouvant Dr Princeton NJ 08540-1208 Home Phone: 409-744-4137.

MEHLTRETTER, KATHLEEN M., former prosecutor; b. 1954; BS, Univ. of Dayton; JD, State Univ. of NY at Buffalo. Bar: New York 1979. U.S. atty. (we. dist.) NY U.S. Dept. Justice, Buffalo, 2005—06.

MEHO, LOKMAN I., library and information scientist, educator; arrived in US, 1996; s. Ibrahim Y. Meho and Layla S. Hussein. BA in Polit. Sci., Am. U. Beirut, 1991, MA in Polit. Sci., 1996; MS in Libr. Sci., N.C. Ctrl. U., Durham, 1996; PhD in Info. and Libr. Sci., U. N.C., Chapel Hill, 2001. Libr. asst. Am. U. Beirut, 1986—95; freelance bibliographer Lebanon and U.S., 1991—; lectr. Sch. Libr. and Info. Scis. N.C. Ctrl. U., Durham, 1997—98; tchg. fellow Sch. Info. and Libr. Sci. U. N.C., Chapel Hill, 1999—2001; asst. prof. SUNY, Albany, 2001—04, Ind. U., Bloomington, 2004—. Author: Libraries and Information in the Arab World, 1999, Kurdish Culture and Society, 2001, Kurdish Question in U.S. Foreign Policy, 2004, Censorship in the Arab World, 2006. Sec. Lebanese Kurdish Charity Assn., Beirut, 1992—95; youth mem. Lebanese Red Cross, Beirut, 1989—95. Mem.: Assn. Libr. and Info. Sci. Edn., Assn. Coll. and Rsch. Librs., ALA, Am. Soc. Info. Sci. and Tech. Avocations: soccer, reading, painting. Office: Ind Univ 1320 E 10th St LI 011 Bloomington IN 47405 Home Phone: 812-320-0437; Office Phone: 812-856-2323. Office Fax: 812-855-6166. Business E-Mail: meho@indiana.edu.

MEHRA, PUSHKAR, director, educator; s. Mahendra Kumar and Sheila Mehra; m. Deepika Bhargava, Feb. 17, 2002. DDS, King Georges Med. Coll., India, 1992; DMD, Boston U., 1995; fellowship in Maxillofacial Reconstructive Surgery, Baylor U. Med. Ctr., 2000; postgrad., Tufts U., 1999, Boston U., 1999. Resident Lucknow U., India, 1992—93; clin. dir. Dept of Oral and Maxillofacial Surgery, Boston, 2000—02; asst. prof. Boston U., Boston, 2000—; dir., dept of oral and maxillofacial surgery Boston Med. Ctr., Boston, 2002—. Contbr. articles various profl. jours., chapters to books. Named one of Am.'s Best Dentists Maxillofacial Surgery; recipient Straumann award, Outstanding Rsch., Am. Assn. of Oral and Maxillofacial Surgeons, 2000. Fellow: Am. Coll. of Oral and Maxillofacial Surgeons, Am. Bd. of Oral and Maxillofacial Surgery (life); mem.: ADA (assoc.), Am. Soc. of TMJ surgeons, Mass. Dental Soc. (assoc.), Am. Assn. of Oral and Maxillofacial Surgeons. Achievements include clin. rsrch. in facial reconstructive surgery. Office: Boston U Medl Ctr 100 E Newton St Ste G-407 Boston MA 02118 Office Phone: 617-638-4350. Personal E-mail: pushkar.mehra@bmc.org. E-mail: pmehra@bu.edu.

MEHRA, RAMAN KUMAR, aerospace and defense technology executive, automotion and control engineering researcher; b. Lahore, Punjab, India, Feb. 10, 1943; came to U.S., 1964; s. Madan Mohan and Vidya Vati (Khanna) M.; m. Anjoo Talwar; children: Archana, Mandira, Kunal. BEE, Punjab Engring. Coll., 1964; MS in Engring., Harvard U., 1965, PhD, 1968. Assoc. prof. Harvard U., Cambridge, Mass., 1972-76; pres., chief exec. officer Sci. Systems, Co., Inc., Woburn, Mass., 1976—. Author: System Identification, 1976; also tech. papers on model algorithmic control (Best Paper award Internat. Fedn. Automatic Control, 1983). Recipient Eckman award Am. Automatic Control Coun., St. Louis, 1971. Fellow IEEE. Avocations: hiking, golf, tennis. Home: 5 Angier Rd Lexington MA 02420-1608 Office: Sci Systems Co Inc 500 W Cummings Park Woburn MA 01801-6503 Office Phone: 781-933-5355. Personal E-mail: rkmehra@rcn.com. Business E-Mail: rkm@ssci.com.

MEHRBERG, RANDALL ERIC, lawyer, utilities executive; b. Bklyn., Dec. 29, 1955; s. Julius and June (Shapiro) M.; m. Michele Schara, Oct. 20, 1984; children: Dillon, Sam, Eric. BS magna cum laude in Econs., U. Pa., 1977; JD, U. Mich., 1980. Bar: Ill. 1980, US Dist. Ct. (no. dist. Ill.) 1980, US Ct. Appeals (7th cir.) 1981, US Supreme Ct. 1987. With Jenner & Block, Chgo., 1980—93, equity ptnr., 1997—2000; gen. counsel, lakefront dir. Chgo. Pk. Dist., 1993—97; sr. v.p., gen. counsel Exelon Corp., Chgo., 2000—02, exec. v.p., gen. counsel, 2002—, chief adminstrv. officer, chief legal officer. Asst. sec. Chgo. Pacific Corp., 1984—85; bd. mem. Nuc. Electric Ins. Ltd. V.p. bd. dirs. Gus Giordano Jazzdance Chgo. Recipient Hope for the People award, HOPE Fair Housing, Ill., 1982, commendation for work for the poor, Cath. Charities, 1986, award for def. of civil liberties, ACLU, 1987, Mex. Am. Legal Def. and Edn. Fund Legal Svcs. award, 2001. Mem. ABA, Chgo. Bar Assn. (exec. com. young lawyers sect. 1988-89, David C. Hilliard award), Chgo. Counsel Lawyers, Law Club Chgo. Avocations: tennis, skiing, hockey. Office: Exelon Corp 10 S Dearborn St 37th Fl PO Box 805398 Chicago IL 60680-5398 Office Phone: 800-483-3220. *

MEHRETU, JULIE, artist; b. Addis Ababa, Ethiopia, 1970; Attended, U. Cheik Anta Diop, Dakar, Senegal, 1990—91; BA, Kalamazoo Coll., 1992; MFA with honors, RI Sch. Design, 1997. Greater New York, P.S.1 Contemporary Arts Ctr., NY, 2000, exhibited in group shows, Ctr. Curatorial Studies, Bard College, Annandale-on-Hudson, 2000, Free Style, Studio Mus. Harlem, 2001, The Americans, Barbican Gallery, London, 2001, Busan Biennale, Korea, 2002, 8th Baltic Triennial Vilnius, Lithuania, 2002, Drawing Now: Eight Propositions, Mus. Modern Art, 2002, Painting at the Edge of the World, Walker Art Ctr., 2003, one-woman shows include, Sol Kofler Gallery, Providence, RI, 1995, Ancestral Reflections, Archive Gallery, NY, 1995, Bombastic Righteous Passively Become Apparent Absurdities, Sol Kofler Gallery, Providence, RI, 1996, Recent Work, Barbara Davis Gallery, Houston, 1998, Module, Project Row Houses, Houston, 1999, The Project, NYC, 2001, Art Pace, San Antonio, Tex., 2001, White Cube, London, 2002, Julie Mehretu: Drawing into Painting, Walker Art Ctr. (travelling), 2003, REDCAT, LA, Calif., 2004, Albright-Knox Art Gallery, Buffalo, NY, 2004, Matrix, U. Calif. Berkeley Art Mus., 2004, earlier 1 gebauer, Berlin, Germany, 2004, Drawing, The Project, NYC, 2005, Current, St. Louis Art Mus., 2005, exhibited in group shows at Carnegie Internat., Carnegie Mus. Art, Pitts., Pa., 2004, Sao Paulo Biennial, San Paulo, Brazil, 2004, Whitney Biennal, The Whitney Mus. Am. Art, NYC, 2004, Back to Paint, C&M Arts, NYC, 2004, Firewall, Ausstellungshalle Zeitgenössische Kunst, Munster, Germany, 2004. Recipient Cry of My Birth, Visiting Artist Residency Project, Sch. Art Inst. Chgo., 1999, Excellence Award, RI Sch. Design, 1996, Penny McCall Award, 2001; Core Fellowship, Artist in Residence, Glassell Sch. Art, Mus. Fine Arts, Houston, 1997—99, MacArthur Fellow, John D. and Catherine T. MacArthur Found., 2005. Address: 37 W 57th St 3rd Fl New York NY 10019

MEHRINGER, CHARLES MARK, medical educator; b. Dickinson, ND, Nov. 21, 1945; m. Ruth Herrman; 1 child, Sydney. BS in Biology, Lamar U., 1966; MD, U. Tex., 1970. Diplomate Am. Bd. Radiology, Am. Bd. Neuroradiology. Intern UCLA Hosp., 1970-71; resident in diagnostic radiology Harbor-UCLA Med. Ctr., Torrance, Calif., 1971-74, fellow in neuroradiology, 1976-77; asst. prof. dept. radiology UCLA Sch. Medicine, 1977-80, dir. spl. procedures, 1980-94, assoc. prof. dept. radiology, 1986-96, prof. dept. radiology, 1996—, acting chmn. radiology, 1996—. Vice-chmn. dept. radiological scis. UCLA Sch. Medicine, Torrance, 1992—, acting chmn. dept. radiology, 1992—, chief diagnostic radiology, 1983-92; chief radiological svcs., cons. U.S. Air Force for Japan and Korea, 1974-76; cons. U. Calif./Irvine (Calif.) Med. Ctr., 1988—, St. Marys Med. Ctr., Long Beach, Calif., 1986—, Long Beach VA Hosp., 1979—, L.A. County Dept. Chief Med. Examiner-Coroner, 1977—; bd. dirs. Rsch. and Ednl. Inst.; presenter in field. Co-author: (with others) Neurological Surgery of the Ear and Skull Base, 1982, Vascular Surgery, 1984, 2d edit., 1994, Youman's Neurological Surgery, 1990, Common Problems in Infertility and Impotence, 1990, Intraluminal Imaging of Vascular and Tubular Organs: Diagnostic and Therapeutic Applications, 1993, Neuroradiology, A Study Guide, 1995; contbr. articles to profl. jours. Bd. dirs., exec. com. Med. Found. Harbor-UCLA Med. Ctr., 1992—. Recipient numerous grants for rsch., 1977—. Mem. Am. Coll. Radiology, Am. Soc. Neuroradiology (sr. mem.), Western Neuroradiologic Soc., L.A. Radiologic Soc. Office: Harbor UCLA Med Ctr Box 27 1000 W Carson St Torrance CA 90502-2004

MEHRINGER, RICHARD PATRICK, design educator, artist; s. Joseph A. and Iva D. Mehringer. BFA, Ft. Hays State U., 1981, MA, 1986, cert. in tchg., 1986. Art, lang. arts instr. Fowler Secondary Sch., Colo., 1986—88; art, fine arts chair St. Pauls H.S., NC, 1988—93; art instr., fine arts chair Roosevelt Mid. Sch., Coffeyville, Kans., 1993—99; design instr. Larned H.S., 2000—. Mem., exec. com. Fine Arts League S.E. Colo., LaJunta, 1986—88; mem. Cape Fear Studios Inc., Fayetteville, NC, 1989—93; founding mem. Santa Fe Trail Creative Arts Guild, Larned, 2004—. Artist, photographer (exhibitions) The Dancer, artist, prodr. (one-man shows) Frozen Motion, artist Down Many Roads, Through Many Eons, artist, curator (group shows) Santa Fe Trail Artist and Crafter Guild Invitational; two-person shows, Santa Fe Trail Artist and Crafter Guild Invitational. Named Kans. Secondary Art Educator of Yr., Kans. Art Edn. Assn., 2001-2002, Western Region Secondary Art Educator of Yr., Nat. Art Edn. Assn., 2002-2003, Dist. Tchr. of Yr., Kans. Dept. Edn., 2004-2005; Grad. Assistanship scholar, Ft. Hays State U. Art Dept., 1986. Mem.: Kans. Exemplary Educator's Network (assoc.; team leader 2004—), Santa Fe Creative Arts Guild (assoc.; founding mem. 2004—, pres. 2004), Creative Art Soc. (pres. 1979—81), Phi Delta Kappa (assoc.). Achievements include design of visual arts curriculum. Home Phone: 620-285-2977. Personal E-mail: arknat@yahoo.com.

MEHROTRA, BHOOMI, hematologist, oncologist; MD, U. Delhi, India, 1985. Diplomate in internal medicine, hematology, and med. oncology Am. Bd. Internal Medicine, 1990. Atttending physician LI Jewish Med. Ctr., New Hyde Park, NY, 1994—. Office: Long Island Jewish Med Ctr 270-05 74th Ave New Hyde Park NY 11040 Office Phone: 718-470-8934.

MEHTA, ARIZ RUYINTAN, physiatrist, researcher; b. Summit, NJ, Sept. 19, 1977; s. Ruyintan Erach and Monica R. Mehta; m. Dorothy Diane Prusaczyk, May 24, 2003. AB, Cornell U., Ithaca, NY, 1999; MD, NY Med. Coll., Valhalla, 2003. Chief resident Kessler Inst. Rehab. U. Medicine and Dentistry NJ, Newark, 2006—; pvt. practice Jersey City, 2007—, NYC. Fellow, Sinai Hosp. of Balt., Orthop. Spine Specialists, 2008. Mem.: AMA (assoc.), Am. Acad. Phys. Medicine and Rehab. (mem. performance measures devel. 2006—), Am. Assn. Cardiovasc. and Pulmonary Rehab. (assoc.), Internat. Soc. Phys. Rehab. Medicine (assoc.), Am. Assn. Neuromuscular and Electrodiagnostic Medicine (assoc.), Assn. Acad. Physiatrists (assoc.). Zoroastrian. Achievements include research in rehabilitation, Musculoskeletal Pain, Pain Medicine, Spinal Cord Injury, Cardiac Rehabilitaton, Electrodiagnosis, Spasticity, Botulinum Toxin Injections, Medical Education, Sports Medicine. Home Phone: 914-420-8037.

MEHTA, EILEEN ROSE, lawyer; b. Colver, Pa., Apr. 1, 1953; d. Richard Glenn and Helen (Wahna) Ball; m. Abdul Rashid Mehta, Aug. 31, 1973. Student, Miami U., 1971-73; BA with distinction, Fla. Internat. U., 1974; JD cum laude, U. Miami, 1977. Bar: Fla. 1977, U.S. Dist. Ct. (so. dist.) Fla. 1977, U.S. Ct. Appeals (11th cir.) 1981. Law clk. to presiding judge U.S. Dist. Ct. (so. dist.) Fla., Miami, 1977-79; asst. atty. County of Dade, Miami, 1979-89; shareholder Fine Jacobson Schwartz Nash Block & England, Miami, Fla., 1989-94; ptnr. Eckert Seamans Cherin & Mellott, Miami, 1994-98, Bilzin Sumberg Baena Price & Axelrod, Miami, 1998—. Lectr. in field; v.p., bd. dirs. Shalimar Homes Inc., Anderson, S.C. Miami U. scholar, 1971-73. Mem. Fla. Bar Assn., Dade County Bar Assn. Office: Bilzin Sumberg Baena Price & Axelrod 2500 Wachovia Fin Ctr Miami FL 33131 Office Phone: 305-350-2380. Business E-Mail: emehta@bilzin.com.

MEHTA, JATIN VINODRAI, biomedical engineer; b. Bombay, Maharastra, June 7, 1966; s. Vinodrai Purushottamdas and Ramaben Vinodrai Mehta; m. Parul Manharlal Timbadia, Apr. 16, 1994; 1 child, Sarth. BE, TKIET, Kolhapur, India, 1987; PhD, Indian Inst. Tech., 1993; MBA, U. Mass., 2005. Trainee engr. Godrej and Boyce, Bombay, 1987-88; chief biomed. engr. Jaslok Hosp., Bombay, 1993-96; dep. chief biomed. engr. Bahrain (India) Internat. Group WLL, 1996; asst. prof. dept. biomed. engring. DJ Sanghui Coll. Engring., U. Mumbai (India), 1997-98; lead software developer Software Internat. Inc., NJ, 1998-99; sr. cons. Mgmt. Info. Consulting, Va., 1999—2002; sr. application developer Lifeline Systems, Inc., Mass., 2002—05. Dir. tech. Jesica Securities Ltd., Bombay, 1995—96, Insight Meditronics, Bombay, 1995—; CEO MetaSense Inc., 1999. Editor Modern Medicine Internat., 1995-96; contbr. articles to profl. jours. With Indian Army, 1977-81. Ministry Human Resource Devel. fellow; Coun. for Sci. and Indsl. Rsch. fellow. Mem. Nat. Soc. Fluid Mechanics and Fluid Powers, Inst. Elec. and Telecomm. Engrs., Inst. for Pub. Health Engrs., Indian Soc. Tech. Edn., Indian Assn. Biomed. Scientists, Nat. Biomed. Engrs. Soc., Toastmasters Internat. Avocations: basketball, cricket, acting, mime. Office Phone: 856-873-9950. Personal E-mail: mehtajatin@hotmail.com. Business E-Mail: jmehta@metasenseusa.com.

MEHTA, JATINDER S., mathematics professor; s. Jagjit S. and Rajinder K. Mehta; m. Kathleen F. Gender, Mar. 26, 1982. M of Stats., U. Wis., Madison, 1966, PhD, 1968. Asst. prof. math. Temple U., Phila., 1968—72, assoc. prof. math., 1972—78, prof. math., 1978—. Contbr. articles to profl. jours. Avocation: travel. Home: 1011 Dixon Rd Elkins Park PA 19027 Office: Temple U 11822 N Broad St Philadelphia PA 19122 Home Phone: 215-635-3173; Office Phone: 215-204-7283. Personal E-mail: mehta1007@comcast.net. E-mail: mehta@temple.edu.

MEHTA, JAWAHAR LAL, cardiologist; b. India, Aug. 10, 1946; arrived in US, 1970; s. Mohan L. and Ishwar D. (Valecha) M.; m. Paulette Smedresman, Oct. 20, 1977; children: Asha, Jason. MD, GN Med. Coll. U. Amritsar, 1968; PhD, Uppsala U., Sweden. Diplomate Am. Bd. Internal Medicine, Am. Bd. Cardiovascular Diseases. Intern N.Y. Med. Coll., Valhalla, NY, 1970, resident in pediat., 1971; resident in internal medicine Mt. Sinai-Beth Israel Hosp., NYC, 1971-73; fellow in cardiology SUNY, NY, 1973-75; from asst. prof. to prof. medicine & physiology U. Fla. Coll. Medicine, Gainesville, 1976-2000; dir. cardiovasc. medicine, Stebbins chair in cardiology U. Ark. for Med. Sci., Little Rock, 2000—. Rsch. fellow, instr. in medicine U. Minn., Mpls., 1975—76; staff physician VA Med. Ctr., Gainesville, 1976—2000, clin. investigator, 1980—85; dir. cardiology svcs. Ctrl. Ark. Vets. Healthcare Sys., 2000—. Fellow: ACP, Am. Heart Assn., Am. Coll. Cardiology; mem.: Assn. Univ. Cardiologists, Assn. Am. Physicians, Am. Soc. Clin. Investigation. Office: U Ark for Med Scis Slot 532 Little Rock AR 72205-7199 Business E-Mail: mehtajl@uams.edu.

MEHTA, KIRAN H., lawyer; AB magna cum laude, Cornell U., 1978; JD cum laude, Harvard U., 1981. Bar: NC 1983. Law clk. Chief Judge Frank A. Kaufman, US Dist. Ct. (Md. Dist.), 1982—82; ptnr. litigation dept. Kennedy Covington, Charlotte, NC. Contbr. articles to profl. jours., chapters to books. Dean, solid & hazardous waste Charlotte C. of C. Environ. Sch., 1991—94, chmn. hazardous waste/superfund com., 1992—94; dir. Cmty. Sch. Arts, 1997—; mem. supt. council Charlotte-Mecklenburg Sch. Sys., 1999. Mem.: ABA, NC Bar Assn., Mecklenburg County Bar Assn., Phi Beta Kappa. Office: Kennedy Covington Hearst Tower 47th Fl 214 N Tryon St Charlotte NC 28202 Office Phone: 704-331-7437. Office Fax: 704-353-3137. Business E-Mail: kmehta@kennedycovington.com.

MEHTA, KISHOR CHANDULAL, civil engineering educator; b. Ahmedabad, Gujarat, India, Feb. 19, 1936; came to the U.S., 1954; s. Chandulal Harilal and Vimala Chhaganlal (Shah) Mehta; m. Mary Ann Gaffney, Dec. 27, 1960; children: David, Jatin, Anna, Raajan. BS in Civil Engring., U. Mich., 1957, MS in Civil Engring., 1958; PhD in Structural Engring., U. Tex., 1965. Design engr. Merritt-Chapman & Scott Corp.,

NYC, 1958-61, Page, Ariz., 1958—61; rsch.-tchg. asst. U. Tex., Austin, 1961-64; from asst. to P.W. Horn prof. civil engring. Tex. Tech. U., Lubbock, 1964—, former dir. Wind Engring. Rsch. Ctr., 1988—2003. Prin. MMY Wind Engrs., Lubbock, 1970—; chmn. Nat. Rsch. Coun.-Com. NaturalDisasters, Washington, 1983-87; pres. Am. Assn. for Wind Engring., Baton Rouge, La., 1985-89. Author/editor Minimum Design Loads for Building, 1995 (Nat. Hurricane Conf. Svc. awards, 1997, 2000). Pres. Christ The King Sch. Bd., Lubbock, 1973-75. Recipient Svc. award Am. Assn. for Wind Engring., L.A., 1989. Mem. ASCE (hon. mem., local chpt. pres. 1971-72, chmn. wind load com. 1978-95), NSPE (local chpt. pres. 1975-76), NAE, Am. Meteorol. Soc., Internat. Assn. for Wind Engring. (pres. 1999—2003). Achievements include establishment of one of a kind wind engineering research field laboratory under the sponsorship of the National Science Foundation to investigate wind effects on buildings, a multidisciplinary program to conduct research in mitigation of windstorm effects; chaired the development of the national standards in 1982, 1988 and 1995 for wind loads on buildings; direction of TTV/TTU/NIST Cooperative Agreement for Windstorm Mitigation. Home: 3808 55th St Lubbock TX 79413-4620 Office: Tex Tech Univ PO Box 41023 Lubbock TX 79409-1023 E-mail: kishor.mehta@ttu.edu.

MEHTA, LINN CARY, literature educator; b. Chgo., Aug. 8, 1955; d. William Lucius and Katherine L.F. (Cooper) Cary; m. Ved Mehta, Dec. 17, 1983; children: Alexandra Sage, Natasha Cary. BA in English and French, Yale U., 1977; MA in English, Oxford U., 1979; MPhil in Comparative Lit., Columbia U., 1989, PhD in Comparative Lit., 2004. Asst. to pres. Ford Found., NYC, 1980—82, asst. program officer, 1982—85; preceptor Columbia U., NYC, 1990—91; instr. Yale U., New Haven, 1993; instr., adj. asst. prof. English dept. Vassar Coll., Poughkeepsie, NY, 1994—97; lectr. English dept. Barnard Coll., NYC, 2000—. Chair bd. Am. Friends St. Hilda's Coll., Boston, 1995-02; sec. bd. alumnae Wrexham Found., New Haven, 1988-94; lit. advisor English adaptation of play "Allende" for Theater for a New City, 2006. Bd. pres. Ctr. for Traditional Music and Dance, NYC, 1989-94, v.p., 2000—; pres. Lexington 79th Corp., NYC, 1993-97; bd. dirs. Norman Rockwell Mus., Stockbridge, Mass., 1991-96, NY Soc. Libr., 2002—, Goddard Riverside C0mty. Ctr., 2007—; adv. bd. Appalshop, Whitesburg, Ky., 1990-92. Mem. MLA, Am. Comparative Lit. Assn., Thursday Evening Club (pres. 1998-2001) Avocations: music, running, languages. Home: 139 E 79th St New York NY 10021-0324 Office: English Dept Barnard Coll Columbia U 3009 Broadway New York NY 10027 Business E-Mail: lmehta@barnard.edu.

MEHTA, MAUSMI, oceanographer; b. Spring, Tex., Aug. 19, 1978; d. Pravin and Lata Mehta; m. Paul Deeds, Mar. 18, 2006. BS in Biology, MIT, Cambridge, Mass., 1999; PhD, U. Wash., Seattle, 2006. Rsch. asst. U. Wash., Seattle, 1999—2006. Achievements include discovery of hyperthermophilic nitrogen fixer. Home Phone: 206-595-0900. Personal E-mail: mausmi.mehta@gmail.com.

MEHTA, MINESH P., oncologist, educator; s. Praful P. and Sudha P. Mehta; children: Tej, Sanjli. MD, U. Zambia, Lusaka, 1981. Prof. dept. human oncology U. Wis., Madison, 1997—. Chmn. RTOG Brain Tumor Com., Phila., 2000—06. Contbr. articles to profl. jours. Examiner ABR, Tucson, 2004—06. Grantee, NIH, 2001—06. Mem.: ASTRO (ednl. com. mem. 2000—04). Achievements include first to Tomotherapy. Office: U Wis Dept Human Oncology 600 Highland Ave Madison WI 53792 Home Phone: 608-837-6714; Office Phone: 608-263-1668. Office Fax: 608-263-5009; Home Fax: 608-263-5009. Business E-Mail: mehta@humonc.wisc.edu.

MEHTA, NARINDER KUMAR, marketing executive; b. Lahore, Punjab, India, Feb. 18, 1938; came to U.S., 1959; s. Raj Rani Mehta and Puran Chand; m. Narayanaswamy Sampath; children: Kiren, Ravi. B of Commerce, U. Delhi, India, 1958; MA, U. Minn., 1961. Program dir. All India Mgmt. Assn., New Delhi, 1963—67; with Am. Express Co., Chgo., 1968—82, dir. nat. sales NYC, 1975—80, v.p. sales, 1980—82; sr. v.p. Shearson Lehman/Am. Express, Boston, 1982—85; sr. v.p. mktg. & sales Capital Credit Corp., Fairfield, NJ, 1985—94; sr. v.p. internat. mktg. Outsourcing Solutions, Inc., 1994—97; pres. Mehta Cons. Group, Dover, Mass., 1997—. Sr. v.p. Temporary Investment Funds, 1982-85, Trust for Short Term Fed. Securities, 1982-85, Mcpl. Fund for Calif. Investors, 1983-85; conducted seminars for profl. assns., colls. and univs. Contbr. articles to profl. jours. Nat. v.p. Muscular Dystrophy Assn., NYC, 1984-86; student body pres. U. Delhi, India, 1958-59. Recipient 1st prize inter-coll. debate, 1958. Mem. Am. Mgmt. Assn., Tau Kappa Epsilon. Avocations: running, swimming, travel, reading. Office: Mehta Cons Group PO Box 547 4 Bryant Ln Dover MA 02030-0547 Home Phone: 508-878-9627. Personal E-mail: nkmehta@aol.com.

MEHTA, PARINDA APURVA, pediatrician, medical educator, hematologist, oncologist; d. J. V. and B. Amlani; m. Apurva C. Mehta, Nov. 26, 1996; children: Parth, Shlok. MBBS, Seth Gordhandas Sunderdas Med. Coll., Mumbai, India, 1993; MD, Upstate Med. U., Syracuse, NY, 2002. Intern King Edward Meml. Hosp., Mumbai, India, 1993—94; resident Lokmanya Tilak Mcpl. Med. Coll., 1994—96; pediatrician pvt. practice, 1996—97; resident Upstate Med. U., SUNY, 1999—2002; fellow Cin. Children's Hosp. Med. Ctr., 2002—05, asst. prof. pediat., blood and marrow transplantation, 2005—. Reviewer: jours. British Jour. Hematology, 2005, Pharmacogenomics Jour., 2005, Clin. Cancer Rsch., 2005, Leukemia, 2006; contbr. articles to profl. jours. Named Tchr. of Yr., Dept. Pediat., UMU, SUNY, 2000—01, 2001—02; Rsch. grant, Cancer-Free Kids Pediatric Rsch. Alliance, 2004—05, Translational Rsch. Initiative, Cin. Children's Hosp. Med. Ctr., 2005—06, Astellas, Inc., 2007—. Mem.: Am. Soc. Pediatric Hematology Oncology, Am. Soc. Blood and Marrow Transplantation, Am. Soc. Clin. Oncology (Young investigator award 2006—07, Rsch. grant 2006—), Am. Soc. Hematology (mem. clin. rsch. training inst. 2005—06). Office: Cincinnati Children's Hospital Medical C MLC 7015 3333 Burnet Avenue Cincinnati OH 45229 Office Phone: 513-636-4913. Office Fax: 513-636-3549. E-mail: parinda.mehta@cchmc.org.

MEHTA, RAKESH KUMAR, physician, educator; b. Gidderbaha, Punjab, India, Aug. 18, 1952; came to U.S., 1985; s. Parkash Chander and Sheela (Thukral) M.; m. Anita Gupta; children: Sonika Deepali Mehta, Shivam Parkash Mehta. MB BS with gold and silver medal, Med. Coll., Amritsar, Punjab, 1975; MD, Postgrad. Inst. Med. Edn., Chandigarh, 1978. Diplomate Am. Bd. Internal Medicine. Intern Victoria Jubilee, Amritsar, 1975; resident in medicine Hosp. Postgrad. Inst., Chandigarh, India, 1976-78, sr. resident in medicine, 1978-79, All India Inst. of Med. Scis., New Delhi, 1979-81, U. Alta., Edmonton, Can., 1981-83; clin. fellow in oncology Cross Cancer Inst., Edmonton, 1984-85, N.Y. Med. Coll., NYC, 1985-86; cons. med. oncologist Vets. Affairs, Castle Point, NY, 1986-97; clin. asst. prof. medicine N.Y. Med. Coll., Valhalla, 1990—. Chief oncology program VA Hudson Valley, 1986—, program mgr. splty. care svcs., 2003-. Contbr. articles to professional jours. Fellow ACP, Royal Coll. Physicians and Surgeons of Can., Am. Coll. Internat. Physicians; mem. Am. Soc. of Clin. Oncologists, Hudson Valley Assn. Physicians from India (pres.-elect). Avocations: travel, jogging, photography. Office: Vets Affairs VA Med Ctr Castle Point NY 12511

MEHTA, RAVI RAVINDER SINGH, commodities trader, consultant; b. Rawalpindi, Punjab, Pakistan, May 20, 1945; s. Harbans Singh and Swinder Kaur (Duggal) M.; m. Davinder Kaur Kohli, Nov. 7, 1977; 1 child, Gurpreet. BSc, Delhi U., 1967, MSc, 1970; MLitt, Punjabi U., Patiala, India, 1976; PhD, Panjab U., Chandigarh, India, 1991. Cert. trade specialist. Rsch. scholar Panjabi U., Patiala, 1971-74; officer operational banking Punjaband Sind Bank, Bombay, 1977-80, officer trainer Chandigarh, 1980-96, mgr. internat. banking tng., 1996-2000. Author: Sociology of Banking, 1976, Autobiography of a Cheque, 1982, Fundamentals of Banking, 1984, Signature Verification, 1990, Journey Through British Banking, 1991, Banking on Lombard Street, 1993, Bank Training in the U.K., 1994, Pictorial Biography of a Bank Training Centre in Switzerland, 1994, Early Banking in England, 1994, Export L/C Management: A Handbook for the Exporter, 2003, World's Most Influential LC Specialist-Kim Christensen, 2006; Editor: LCViews in USA; assoc. editor The Exporter Mag., 1997—; contbg. editor LCMonitor, Ont.; contbr. articles to mags.; contbr. articles to profl. and trade jours. Recipient several awards. Mem. Indian Inst. Bankers (life), Internat. Trade and Banking Inst. (bd. dirs.). Sikh. Avocations: travel, gardening, stamp collecting/philately. Personal E-mail: aea16@hotmail.com.

MEHTA, SHAILESH J., banker; b. Bombay, Maharashtra, India, Apr. 22, 1949; came to U.S., 1971; s. Jayantilal B. and Manjula J. Mehta; m. Kalpa S. Doshi, Dec. 19, 1973; children: Sameet, Sheetal BS in Mech. Engring., Indian Inst. Tech., 1971; MS in Ops. Research, Case Western Res. U., 1973, PhD in Ops. Research and Computer Sci., 1975. Sr. ops. analyst Cleve. Trust Co., 1973-75, ops. officer, 1975-76, asst. v.p. card ops., 1976-77, v.p. corp. ops. adminstrn., 1979, v.p. advanced systems planning, 1977-78, v.p. info. systems, 1979-82; exec. v.p. banking services AmeriTrust, Cleve., 1974-86; exec. v.p., COO First Deposit Corp., San Francisco, 1986-88, pres., CEO, 1988—; chmn. bd. First Deposit Nat. Bank, Tilton, NH, 1986—; pres., chief exec. officer, chmn. bd. First Deposit Savs. Bank, Redding, Calif., 1986-90; CEO, chmn. bd. First Deposit Nat. Credit Card Bank, Concord, NH, 1990-93; exec. v.p. Providian Corp., San Francisco, 1993-94, pres., COO, 1994-97, chmn., CEO, 1998—. Pres., dir. A.T. Venture Capital Group, Cleve., 1982-86; pres. Granite Hill Capital Ventures LLC. Mem. community adv. coun. U. Calif., Berkeley, 1991—. Mem. Am. Bankers Assn. (telecommunications group 1984—), Ohio Venture Assn., Calif. Commn. for Econ. Devel's. Adv. Coun. on Asia.

MEHTA, SONNY (AJAY SINGH MEHTA), publishing executive; b. India, 1943; Student, Cambridge U. Worked in paperback pub., England; formerly with Pan and Picador Pubs., England; pub., pres. Alfred A. Knopf divsn. of Random House, NYC, 1987, pres., editor-in-chief; former pres., editor-in-chief Knopf Pub. Group, NYC, chmn., editor-in-chief, 2005—. Office: Knopf Pub 1745 Broadway #B1 New York NY 10019-4305

MEHURON, WILLIAM OTTO, retired federal official; b. Hammond, Ind., Nov. 20, 1937; s. Arthur and Margaret Irene M.; m. Charlotte Anne Nyheim, Aug. 26, 1982; children: Kimberly Anne, Kristine Lynn, Susan, Geoffrey. BSEE, Purdue U., 1959; MSEE, U. Pa., 1962, PhD, 1966. Tech. dir. naval intelligence Dept. Navy, Washington, 1974-81; dir. rsch. and engring. Nat. Security Agy., Ft. Meade, Md., 1981-85; v.p., gen. mgr. data systems div. Ampex Corp. subs. Allied-Signal Co., Redwood City, Calif., 1985-86; sr. v.p. product ops. Daisy Systems Corp., Mountain View, Calif., 1986-88; v.p., gen. mgr. Networks and Info. Security div. Security div. Unisys Def. Systems, McLean, Va., 1988-91; pres. Mehuron Assocs. Inc., 1991-95; dir. sys. acquisition office NOAA, USG, Washington, 1995-99; dir. Info. Tech. Lab., Nat. Inst. Stds. and Tech., Gaithersburg, Md., 1999—2002; pres. Mehuron Assocs., Inc., 2002—. Avocations: amateur radio, golf, cooking. Home: 803 S Clay St Hinsdale IL 60521-4541 Personal E-mail: wmehuron@comcast.net.

MEI, ANHUA, mechanical engineer, researcher; b. Chongqing, China, Oct. 5, 1955; arrived in US, 2002; s. Dedong Mei and Jiyu Liu; m. Jinghui Wang, May 28, 1984; 1 child, Da. BS, Chongqing U., 1982; MS, Wuhan Tech. U. Surveying and Mapping, China, 1995; D Engring., Lamar U., Beaumont, Tex., 2006. Asst. prof., lectr. Wuhan Tech. U. Surveying and Mapping, 1982—93, assoc. prof., 1993—98; prof. Wuhan U., 1998—2002; prin. lectr. Harare Poly. U., Zimbabwe, 1999—2002; sr. mech. engr. Perry Equipment Corp., Mineral Wells, Tex., 2006—. Presenter in field. Contbr. articles to profl. jours. Mem.: ASME, Am. Soc. Optical Engrs. Avocations: swimming, ping pong/table tennis. Home: 1676 Holland Lake Dr # 1206 Weatherford TX 76086 Office: Perry Equipment Corp 118 Washington Ave Mineral Wells TX 76086 Personal E-mail: anhuamei2002@yahoo.com.

MEI, CHIANG CHUNG, civil engineer, educator; b. Wuhan, China, Apr. 4, 1935; m. Caroline J. Schmitt, 1965; 1 child. BS, Nat. Taiwan U., 1955; MS, Stanford U., 1958; PhD, Calif. Inst. Tech., 1963. Rsch. fellow engring. sci. Calif. Inst. Tech., 1963-65; mem. tech. staff Nat. Engring. Sci. Co., Calif., 1965; from asst. prof. to prof. MIT, Cambridge, 1965-93, Edmund K. Turner prof. civil engring., 1993—2001, acting head dept., 2001—02, Donald and Martha Harleman prof. civil engring., 2001—. Hon. prof. U. Hong Kong, 1992—; instr. mechanics Chinese Acad. Sci., Beijing, 1994. Recipient J.T. Hsieh award, 1984, Rosenstiel award, 1988, Moffatt & Nichol award, 1992. Fellow Acad. Sinica; mem. ASCE, Nat. Acad. Engring., Am. Phys. Soc., Am. Geophys. Union, Soc. Indsl. and Applied Math. Office: Dept Civil Environ & Engr MIT Cambridge MA 02139 E-mail: ccmei@mit.edu.

MEI, TOM Y. K., lawyer; b. Kuantan, Malaysia, July 24, 1940; came to U.S., 1958. s. Hung Po and Hannah (Chung) M.; m. Margene Suzuki Mei, Sept. 1964; children: Rodney, Todd. BA in econ., Calif. State U. at L.A., 1963; JD, Western State U. Coll. Law, 1975. Bar: Calif. 1976. Claim rep. CNA Ins., LA, 1964-66, claim supr. San Diego, 1966-76; assoc. attorney Murchison & Cumming, Santa Ana, 1976-88, ptnr., 1988—. Pres. San Diego Claims Mgr. Council, 1973. Mem. Am. Bd. Trial Advocates (bd. dirs.), Defense Rsch. Inst., Orange County Bar Assoc. Avocations: skiing, travel. Office: Murchison & Cumming 200 W Santa Ana Blvd Ste 801 Santa Ana CA 92701-4134 Office Phone: 518-605-6476.

MEIDAV, JOSHUA SINCLAIR ETHAN, ecologist, researcher; b. June 24, 1965; BA, U. Calif., Santa Cruz, 1989; MS, U. Calif., Davis, 2000. Rschr. U. Calif., Tahoe Rsch. Group, Davis, 1997—2000; ecol. surveyor US Forest Svc., Albany, Calif., 2003—05; rschr. U. Calif., Tahoe Environ. Rsch. Ctr., Davis, 2002—. Scholar, Nat. Scholars Honor Soc., Bartlett, Ill., 2006. Mem.: Soc. Ecol. Restoration, Ecol. Soc. Am. Home: 811 Adams St Albany CA 94706

MEIER, BARRY, reporter; b. May 10, 1949; m. Ellen Joan Pollock; 1 child. BA, Syracuse U. Reporter Wall Street Jour.; spl. reporter NY Newsday; reporter NY Times, 1989—, consumer news reporter. Frequent guest Nat. Pub. Radio. Contbr. chapters to books. Recipient George Polk award for bus. reporting, 2006. Office: NY Times 229 West 43rd St New York NY 10036 Office Phone: 212-556-1917. Office Fax: 212-556-1448. E-mail: meier@nytimes.com.

MEIER, BEVERLY JOYCE LOEFFLER, science educator, educational consultant; b. Balt., Md., June 28, 1941; d. John Thonas and Frances Lillian Loeffler; m. Thomas Meier, June 8, 1963; children: Thomas Jr., John H. BS, U. Colo., Boulder, Colo., 1963; MA, U. Colo., 1969. Sci. tchr. Cherry Creek Sch. Dist., Denever, Colo., 1963—65; potter Boulder Potter's Guild, Boulder, Colo., 1970—77; part owner Sturtz Copeland Florist, Boulder, Colo., 1970—75; sci. tchr. Boulder Valley Sch. Dist., Boulder, Colo., 1977—. Cons. sci. edn. Nat. Oceanic Atmosphere Adminstrn., Boulder, Colo., 1993—, Nat. Renewal Energy Lab, Golden, Colo., 1989—90; cons. Am. Indian Sci. Engr. Soc., Boulder, Colo., 1994. Contbr. articles to profl. jour. Adv. bd. Colo. Sci. and Engring. Fair, Ft. Collin., 1990—; dir. sci. fair Boulder Valley Sch. Dist., 1982—. Grantee Boulder Valley Impact grant, 2000, Toyota Tapestry-NSTA, 1998, Boulder Valley Impact on Edn. grant, 2006. Mem.: NSTA, Phi Delta Kappa. Avocations: anthropology, archaeology. Office: Broomfield Heights Mid Sch 1555 Daphne St Boulder CO 80305

MEIER, GEORGE KARL, III, minister, lawyer; b. Glen Ridge, NJ, Jan. 13, 1944; s. George Karl and Mary Claire (Myers) M.; children: G.K., Leslie; m. Therese DesCamp, Oct. 10, 1992. BS, Washington and Lee U., 1966; JD, Dickinson Sch. Law, 1969; MDiv, Pacific Sch. of Religion, 1992. Bar: N.J. 1969, Oreg. 1970, U.S. Dist. Ct. N.J. 1969, U.S. Dist. Ct. Oreg. 1970, U.S. Ct. Appeals (9th cir.) 1971, U.S. Ct. Appeals (fed. cir.) 1987, U.S. Supreme Ct. 1973. Law clk. N.J Superior Court Appellate Div., 1969-70; assoc. Stoel, Rives, Boley, Jones & Grey, Portland, Oreg., 1970-75, ptnr., 1976-89; spl. dep. atty. gen. State of Idaho, 1988-89; spl. asst. to pres. Pacific Sch. Religion, Berkeley, Calif., 1992; pastor Pioneer Congl. Ch., Sacramento, Calif., 1992-1998, Cmty. Ch. Monterey Peninsula, Carmel, Calif., 1998—. Co-founder Ctrl. City Concern, 1978, SW Youth Svc. Ctr., Portland; chmn. ctrl. adv. bd. Dept. Human Resources; pres. consistory Hillside Cmty. Ch., Portland, 1984-85; acad. com. Pacific Sch. Religion, 1989-91; interim dir. youth programs Epwirth Meth. Ch., 1992; bd. dirs. No. Calif. Nev. Conf. the United Ch. Christ, 1993-97; v.p., 1995-96, pres., 1996-97, Francis House, 1992-98; chmn. 1995-96, Cathedral Pioneer Ch. Homes, Inc., 1992-98; Samaritan Counseling Ctr., 1997-98;co-founder, bd. dirs. InterFaith Pastoral Counseling Ctr. Monterey County, 1999-2005; panel vol. United Way Fund Distbn., 1999-2000; Leadership Monterey Peninsula Class of 2000; bd. dirs. Legal Svcs. for Srs., 2004—. Recipient Outstanding Svc. award Cen. City Concern 1976-89. Mem. Oreg. State Bar Assn; mem. Carmel Valley Rotary Club, 1999—. Mem. United Ch. of Christ. Office Phone: 831-624-8595.

MEIER, JOSEPH M., lawyer; b. Balt., June 5, 1959; 3 children. BA, U. Oreg., Eugene, 1981; JD, Willamette Coll. Law, Salem, Oreg., 1984. Bar: Oreg. 1984, Idaho 1985. Atty. Cosho, Humphrey, Greener, Welsh, PA, Boise, Idaho, 1985—2005, Cosho Humphrey, LLP, Boise, 2005—. Lawyer rep. 9th Cir. Ct. Appeals, San Francisco, 2002—. Fellow: Am. Bankruptcy Coll.; mem.: Idaho State Bar (dir. comml. and bankruptcy law sect. 1995—2001, governing bd. 1995—2001, Professionalism award 2003). Office: Cosho Humphrey LLP 800 Park Blvd Ste 790 Boise ID 83712 Office Phone: 208-344-7811. E-mail: jmeier@cosholaw.com.

MEIER, KENNETH JOHN, political scientist; b. Aberdeen, SD, Mar. 3, 1950; s. John and Elizabeth (Malsam) M.; m. Diane Jones Meier, Dec. 31, 1972. BA, U. S.D., 1972; PhD, Syracuse U., 1975. Prof. polit. sci. Rice U., Houston, 1975-78, U. Okla., 1978-85, U. Wis., Madison, 1985-89, Milw., 1989-97; Charles Puryear prof. liberal arts Tex. A&M U., College Station, 1998—2005, Sara Lindsey prof. govt., 2001—04, Charles Gregory chair in liberal arts, 2006—. Fellow com. for hispanic pub. policy issues Inter Univ. Program Social Sci. Rsch. Coun., 1991-92; dir. Ctr. for Presdl. Studies, Policy and Governance, 2001-02. Author: Race, Class and Education, 1989, The Politics of Hispanic Education, 1991, Politics and the Bureaucracy, 1993, The Politics of Sin, 1994, The Case Against School Choice, 1995, Regulation and Consumer Protection, 1995, Applied Statistics for Public Administration, 1997, What Works: A New Approach to Program and Policy Analysis, 2000, The Politics of Fertility Control, 2001, Politics, Policy and Organizations, 2003; editor Am. Jour. Polit. Sci., 1994-98; assoc. editor Jour. Pub. Adminstrn. Rsch. and Theory. Recipient Clarence A. Kulp award, 1990, Gustavus Myers award, 1991, 93, Herbert Kaufman award, 1992, 2002, Herbert A. Simon award, 1999, award Acad. Mgmt., 2000, disting. rsch. award, Nat. Assn. Schs. Pub. Affairs and Adminstrn./ASPA, 2003; Big XII Faculty fellow, 2003. Fellow: Nat. Acad. Pub. Adminstrn. (Charles Levine award 2005, William Mosher award 2005), Advanced Inst. Mgmt. (Joseph Wholey award 2004); mem.: APHA, MW Polit. Sci. Assn. (pres.-elect 2004—05, pres. 2005—06), Nat. Pub. Mgmt. Rsch. Assn. (pres. 2003—05), SW Polit. Sci. Assn. (pres.-elect 1998—99, pres. 1999—2000), Am. Polit. Sci. Assn. (Latino Mentor award 2005, John Gaus award 2006). Office: Tex A&M U Dept Polit Sci TAMUS 4384 College Station TX 77843-0001 Office Phone: 979-845-4232. Business E-Mail: kmeier@polisci.tamu.edu.

MEIER, LISA M., lawyer; b. Springfield, Vt., Aug. 22, 1977; BA in Hist. and Russian Lang. and Lit., Smith Coll., 1999; JD, William Mitchell Coll. Law, 2002. Bar: Minn. 2002. Children's prog. intern Minn. Advocates for Human Rights, Mpls., 2000; devel. asst. Office of Instl. Advancement William Mitchell Coll. Law, St. Paul, 2000; law clk. Honsa & Michales, P.A., Mpls., 2001—02, atty., 2002—. Named a Rising Star, Minn. Super Lawyers mag., 2006. Mem.: Dakota County Bar Assn., ABA, Minn. State Bar Assn. (mem. family law sect.), Ramsey County Bar Assn. (mem. family law sect.), Hennepin County Bar Assn. (mem. family law sect., sec. family law exec. com.). Avocations: reading, hiking, walking. Office: Anne M Honsa 5500 Wayzata Blvd Ste 1075 Minneapolis MN 55416 Office Phone: 763-797-9855. *

MEIER, MARK FREDERICK, research scientist, educator, artist, small business owner; b. Iowa City, Dec. 19, 1925; s. Norman C. and Clea (Grimes) M.; m. Barbara McKinley, Sept. 16, 1955; children: Lauren G., Mark S., Gretchen A. BSEE, U. Iowa, 1949, MS in Geology, 1951; PhD in Geology and Applied Mechanics, Calif. Inst. Tech., 1957. Instr. Occidental Coll., LA, 1952-55; chief glaciology project office U.S. Geol. Survey, Tacoma, 1956-85; dir. Inst. Arctic and Alpine Rsch. U. Colo., Boulder, 1985-94; owner MeierArt, 2005—. Vis. prof. Dartmouth Coll., Hanover, N.H., 1964; rsch. prof. U. Wash., Seattle, 1964-86; prof. geol. scis. U. Colo., 1985-96, prof. emeritus, 1997—; pres. Internat. Comn. on Snow and Ice, 1967-71; pres. Internat. Assn. Hydrol. Scis., 1979-83; Mendenhall lectr. U.S. Geol. Survey, 1982, Walter Orr Roberts Disting. lectr. Aspen Global Change Inst., 1992. Contbr. articles to profl. jours. With USN, 1945—46. Named Meier Valley (Antarctica) in his honor; recipient 3 medals, Acad. Scis., Moscow, 1970—85, Disting. Svc. award (Gold medal), U.S. Dept. Interior, 1968, Internat. Hydrology prize, Internat. Assn. Hydrol. Scis./World Meteor. Orgn./UNESCO, 1999, Goldthwait Polar medal, Ohio State U., 2002. Fellow: AAAS (John Wesley Powell Meml. lectr. 1994), Am. Geophys. Union (com. chmn., Robert E. Horton medal 1996); mem.: Arctic Inst. N.Am. (gov. 1987—93), Internat. Glaciol. Soc. (v.p., coun., Seligman Crystal 1985), Geol. Soc. Am. (com. mem.). Office: U Colo Inst Arctic Alpine Rsch 1560 30th St Boulder CO 80309-0450 Business E-Mail: mark.meier@colorado.edu.

MEIER, RAYMOND A., former state legislator, lawyer; b. Rome, Oct. 23, 1952; s. Alfred and Irene Meier; m. Kimberly Davis; children: Monica, Erik. BA in Polit. Sci., Syracuse U., JD. Mem. 47th Dist. N.Y. Senate, Albany, 1997—, chair vets. and mil. affairs com., mem. codes, crime victims, crime and corrections com., mem. energy, telecom., higher edn. coms., mem. housing, constrn., and cmty. devel. coms., mem. jud., racing, gaming and wagering coms., mem. social svcs. and transp. coms.; assoc. Law Office of Paul A. Worlock, 1977-83; ptnr. McMahon and Grow, Rome, 1985-91; of counsel Siegel, Hester, Stephens, Kahler, and Manion, Utica; ptnr. Bond, Schoeneck & King, Syracuse, NY, 2007—. Mem. Oneida County Legis., 1986-91, asst. majority leader, chmn. econ. devel., cts. and law enforcement coms.; mem. Gov. Pataki's Transition Team, Gov.'s Task Force on Welfare Reform and Medicaid. Mem. N.Y. State Assn. Counties (bd. dirs., 1st v.p.). Office: Bond Schoeneck & King One Lincoln Ctr Syracuse NY 13202-1355 Office Phone: 315-218-8108. Office Fax: 315-218-8100. Business E-Mail: rmeier@bsk.com.

MEIER, RICHARD ALAN, architect; b. Newark, Oct. 12, 1934; s. Jerome and Carolyn (Kaltenbacher) M.; m. Katherine Gormley, Jan. 21, 1978 (div.); children: Joseph Max, Ana Moss. BArch, Cornell U., Ithaca,

NY, 1957; PhD (hon.), U. Naples, Italy, 1991, Parsons Sch. Design, 1998, Wheaton Coll., 1998, Pratt Sch. Fine Arts, 1999, U. Bucharest, 2001, NC State U., 2004, Mercy Coll., 2004. Registered profl. arch., NY, NJ, Conn., Mich., Va., Fla., Ind., Ga., Calif., Ill., Iowa, Tex., Oreg. Arch. Frank Grad & Sons, NJ, 1957, Davis, Brody & Wisniewski, NYC, 1959, Skidmore, Owings & Merrill, 1959—60, Marcel Breuer & Assocs., 1960—63; prin. arch. Richard Meier & Assocs., NYC, 1963—80; arch., prin. Richard Meier & Ptnrs., 1980—. Resident arch. Am. Acad. Rome, 1973-74; vis. critic Pratt Inst., 1960-62, 65, Princeton, 1963, Syracuse U., 1964; William Henry Bishop vis. prof. architecture Yale U., 1975, 77, vis. critic, 1967, 72, 73, 77; vis. prof. Harvard U., 1977, UCLA, 1988, Eliot Noyes vis. critic in architecture, 1980-81; Harvey S. Perloff vis. prof. architecture UCLA, 1987, 88, 90, 2000; adj. prof. architecture Cooper Union, NYC, 1963-73; mem. adv. coun. Cornell U. Coll. Art, Architecture and Planning; mem. Jerusalem Com. Exhbns., XV Triennale, Milan, 1973, Mus. Modern Art, NYC, 1975, 81, Princeton U., Biennale, Venice, Italy, 1976, Cooper-Hewitt Mus., NYC, 1976-77, Leo Castelli Gallery, NYC, 1977, 94, Rosa Esman Gallery, NYC, 1978, 80, NJ State Mus., 1978, Modernism Gallery, San Francisco, Wadsworth Atheneum, Hartford, Conn., High Mus. Art, Atlanta Harvard U., Max Protech Gallery, 1980, Syracuse U., Whitney Mus. Art, NYC, 1982, Knoll Internat., Tokyo, Japan, 1988, October Gallery, London, 1990, Royal Palace, Naples, Italy, 1991, Palazzo delle Esposizione, Rome, 1993, Aichi Prefectural Mus. Art, Nagoya, Japan, 1996; adj. prof. Cooper Union, 1963-66, 66-69, 69-73. Prin. works include Westbeth Artists Housing, NYC, Bronx Devel. Ctr., NY, Smith House, Darien, Conn., Douglas House, Harbor Springs, Mich., Shamberg House, Mt. Kisco, NY, Hoffman and Saltzman Houses, East Hampton, NY; houses in Old Westbury, NY, Pound Ridge, NY, Palm Beach, Fla., Pitts.; Twin Parks NE Housing, NYC, Atheneum, New Harmony, Ind., NY, Hartford Sem., Conn., Mus. für Kunsthandwerk, Frankfurt, Germany, Des Moines Art Ctr., High Mus. Art, Atlanta, Bridgeport Ctr., NY, Daimler-Benz Office and Lab. Complex, Ulm, Germany, Weishaupt Forum, Schwendi, Germany, City Hall and Cen. Libr., The Hague, The Netherlands, Corp. Hdqs., Royal Dutch Paper Mills, Hilversum, The Netherlands, Cornell U. Alumni and Admissions Ctr., Ithaca, NY, Canal Hdqs., Paris, Espace Pitot, Montpellier, France, Maybury Office Pk., Edinburgh, Hypolux Bank Bldg., Luxembourg, Mus. Contemporary Art, Barcelona, Spain, Arp Mus., Rolandswerth, Germany, Swiss Volksbank, Basel Office Bldg., Singapore, The Getty Ctr., LA, SwissAir Hdqs., Melville, NY, Fed. Courthouse, Islip, NY, Phoenix, Mus. TV & Radio, LA, Gagosian Gallery, LA, Rachofsky House, Dallas, Ch. of Yr. 2000, 173 & 176 Perry St., NYC, 2002 (Royal Inst. Brit. Archs. award 2006), Frieder Burda Collection Mus., Baden-Badem, Germany, 2004 (Royal Inst. Brit. Archs. award 2006), Rome, Ara Pacis, Rome, 2006, 165 Charles St., NYC, 2006, others; author: Richard Meier Architect, vol. 1, 1964-68, vol. 2, 1985-91, vol. 3, 1992-99, vol. 4, 2000-04, On Architecture, 1982, Richard Meier Collages, 1990, The Getty Ctr. Design Process, J. Paul Getty Trust, 1991, Richard Meier Sculpture, 1994; contbr. articles to profl. jours. Decorated officer de l'Ordre des Arts et des Lettres (France), 1984; recipient Arnold Brunner Meml. prize AAAL, 1972, Albert S. Bard Civic award City Club NY, 1973, 1st honor award for excellence in architecture and urban design, 1977, R.S. Reynolds Meml. award, 1977, Archtl. Record award of excellence for design, 1964, 68, 69, 70, 77, Am. Inst. Steel Constrn. award, 1978, 79, design award 1st prize Kunsthandwerk Competition, Frankfurt am Main, Fed. Republic Germany, 1980, Pritzker Prize for Architecture, 1984, Praemium Imperiale, Japan, 1997, Am. Inst. Architects, LA Chpt. Gold Medal, 1998, El Gobierno del Distrito Federal "Huesped Distinguido de la Ciudad de Mexico," 2000, AIA 25-Yr. award for Smith House, 2000, NY Mag. award for Arch., 2003, Frate Sole Internat. award for Sacred Architecture, 2004, Dedalo Minosse Internat. Prize for Commissioning a Bldg. - Quinquennial Hon. award, Associazione Liberi Architetti, 2004, Pratt Legend award, 2004, Sidney L. Strauss award, NY Soc. Archs., 2004. Fellow AIA (medal of honor NY chpt. 1980, nat. design com. 1972-74, 30 AIA nat. awards 1968-2006, 50 chpt. awards NY 1965-2006, Chgo. Arch. award, 1995, 5 Progressive Architecture awards 1979, 89, 90, 91, 95, Gold medal 1997), Am. Acad. Arts & Sci., 1995; mem. NAD (academician), Internat. Inst. Archs., Royal Inst. Brit. Archs. (Royal Gold medal 1989), Belgian Royal Acad. Art (Lifetime Achievement award Guild Hall 1991, commdr. de l'Ordre des Arts et Lettres, France, 1992). Office: Richard Meier & Ptnrs 475 10th Ave Fl 6 New York NY 10018-1120 Office Phone: 212-967-6060. Office Fax: 212-967-3207. E-mail: mail@richardmeier.com.

MEIER, STEVEN W., orthopedist, surgeon, consultant; b. Elmhurst, Ill., Jan. 11, 1967; s. William P. and Donna L. Meier. MD, Loyola Med. Sch., Chgo., 1993. Diplomate Am. Bd. Orthop. Surgery, 2003. Orthop. surgeon Ctr. Advanced Sports Medicine, Summit, NJ, 2001—06, Adult and Pediatric Orthop. Specialists, Orange and Mission Viejo, Calif., 2006—. Contbr. articles to profl. jours. Mem.: Am. Acad. Orthop. Surgeons (assoc.). Office: Apos 1310 West Stewart Drive #508 Orange CA 92868-3856 Home Phone: 1-201-220-0312; Office Phone: 1.714.633.2111. Office Fax: 1.714.633.5615. Personal E-mail: oblio54@aol.com.

MEIER, THOMAS KEITH, academic administrator, language educator; b. Houston, Apr. 12, 1940; s. Herbert H. and Madeleine (Keith) Meier; m. Milla Hillard Meier, June 30, 1962; children: John Hillard, Keith Reilly. BA, U. Tex., 1962; AM, Columbia U., 1963, PhD, 1969; MBA, Harvard U., 1967. Fin. mgr., employee rels. mgr. Exxon Co., U.S.A. and Exxon Rsch. Engrng. Co., Houston, Florham Park, NJ, 1969-79; pres. Castleton State Coll., Vt., 1979-87; pres., Simeon Benjamin prof. English lit. Elmira Coll., NY, 1987—. Regent Lee Coll., Baytown, Tex., 1972—73; pres. Vt. Higher Edn. Coun., 1981—82; mem. Johnson Found. (Troutbeck) Leadership Seminar, 1991—; mem. adv. coun. Pres.'s Found. Support Higher Edn.; bd. dirs. Chemung Canal Trust Co., Coll. Consortium Finger Lakes, NY, Ind. Coll., Fund NY, Coun. Ind. Colls. and Univs., Christopher Isnerwood Found. Author: Defoe and the Defense of Commerce, 1987; contbr. articles to profl. jours. Bd. dirs. Union County Urban League, Elizabeth, NJ, 1973—76, Rutland Region C. of C., 1982—86, Arnot Art Mus., 1987—99, So. Tier Econ. Growth, 1987—, N.E.-Midwest Congl. Leadership Coun., 1988—, Chemung County United Way, 1990—93, chmn., 1992—93; mem. exec. coun. Five Rivers Coun. Boy Scouts Am., 1998—, mem. exec. bd. N.E. region, 2004—; corp. bd. dirs. Rutland Hosp., 1980—87; bd. dirs. Ind. Coll. Fund, 1995—97. Lt. US Army, 1963—65. Recipient Outstanding Periodical Essay award, Tex. Books Rev., 1979, medal of merit, Elmira Coll. Alumni Assn., 1991, medallion, Presidential Univ. InterAm. de Panama, 2002, Silver Beaver award, Boy Scouts Am., 2006; Weaver fellow, 1968. Mem.: Harvard Club Boston, Harvard Club NYC, Univ. Club NYC, Clmira City Club, Pico Ski Club (Vt.), Elmira Country Club, Phi Beta Kappa, Lambda Iota Tau, Sigma Beta Delta, Alpha Sigma Lambda, Theta Xi, Omicron Delta Kappa, Phi Alpha Theta, Phi Eta Sigma. Episcopalian. Home: The President's Home 855 College Ave Elmira NY 14901-2001 Office: Elmira Coll Office of Pres Elmira NY 14901

MEIERAN, EUGENE STUART, materials scientist; b. Cleve., Dec. 23, 1937; s. Elias and Rae (Linetsky) M.; m. Rosalind Berson, Mar. 25, 1962; children: Sharon Elizabeth, Andrew Marc. BS in Metallurgy, MIT, 1961, ScD in Material Sci., 1963; Doctorate (hon.), Purdue U., 2004. Mem. tech. staff Fairchild R&D, Palo Alto, Calif., 1963-73; engrng. mgr. Intel Corp., Santa Clara, Calif., 1973-77, sr. mgr. quality assurance, 1977-84, Intel fellow, 1984—, mgr. applications lab., 1989—, Intel sr. fellow, 2003. Dir. rsch. LFM program MIT, 1993—; vis. lectr. Technion, Haifa, Israel, 1970-71, H.H. Wills Physics Lab., Bristol, Eng., 1970-71; mem. adv. bd. Lawrence Berkeley Lab., 1984— Contbr. articles to profl. jours. AEC fellow, 1960; recipient Internat. Reliability awards, 1970, 79, 85, Carnegie medal, 2004; named Disting. Engrng. Alumnus Purdue U., 1988, Purdue Band Alumni, 2000, GIA Wall of Fame, 2004. Mem. AIME (chmn. electronic material symposium 1973—), NAE, Electron Microscope Soc. U.S.A., Tau Beta Pi, Phi Lambda Upsilon. Democrat. Jewish. Home: 5421 E Camello Rd Phoenix AZ 85018-1910 Office: Intel Corp 5000 W Chandler Blvd Chandler AZ 85226-3699 Business E-Mail: gene.s.meieran@intel.com.

MEIERHENRY, JUDITH KNITTEL, state supreme court justice; b. Burke, SD, Jan. 20, 1944; m. Mark Vernon Meierhenry, May 14, 1961; children: Todd, Mary. BA in English, U. S.D., 1966, MA, 1968, JD, 1977. Bar: S.D. 1977. H.S. tchr. English Plattsmouth (Nebr.) Pub. Schs., 1966-67; instr. U. SD, 1968-70, Hiram Scott Coll., Scottbluff, Nebr., 1970; tchr. Todd County Pub. Schs., Mission, SD, 1971-74; ptnr. Meierhenry, DeVaney, Krueger & Meierhenry, Vermillion, SD, 1977-79; cabinet sec. SD Dept. Labor, Pierre, 1980-84; sr. mgr., asst. gen. counsel Citibank SD, 1985-88; cabinet sec. edn. and cultural affairs State SD, 1983-84, cir. ct. judge, 1988—2002; justice SD Supreme Ct., 2002—. Mem.: Nat. Assn. Women Judges, SD Bar Assn. Office: SD Supreme Ct 500 E Capital Ave Pierre SD 57501 *

MEIGHER, S. CHRISTOPHER, III, communications and media executive, publisher; b. NYC, Sept. 23, 1946; s. Stephen Christopher and Denise (Connor) Todd; m. Grace Tebbutt, Aug. 8, 1970; children: Elizabeth, Amanda Powers. BA, Dartmouth Coll., 1968; grad. program mgmt. devel., Harvard U., 1974. Dir. circulation Fortune mag., NYC, 1972-74, Sports Illustrated mag., NYC, 1974-76, Time mag., NYC, 1976-79; v.p. circulation Time, Inc., NYC, 1981-83; pres. Time Distbn. Svc., NYC, 1979-81; pub. People mag., NYC, 1983-85, exec. v.p., group pub., 1985-90; pres. Time Inc. Mags. NY, NYC, 1990—92; gen. ptnr., CEO, chmn. Meigher Comm., L.P., NYC, 1993—; CEO Questmedia LLC, 2000—. Bd. dirs. Individual Investor Group, 1998—; bd. vis. Rockefeller Ctr. at Dartmouth Coll., 1997—; delegate U.S. State Dept. USA-USSR, 1988; mem. Bilateral Info. Talks, Moscow. Pub. Saveur mag., Garden Design mag., Quest mag., Smarth Health mag., Friends mag., 1992-2000. Trustee Boys Club NYC, 1979—, Internat. House, 1985—92, Am. Ballet Theatre, 1993—, South St. Seaport, 1987—97, St. Paul's Sch., 1997—2002; mem. dream team Meml. Sloan Kettering, 1990—; mem. comm. com. St. James Episcopal Ch., 1989—95. Recipient Disting. Service award Brandeis U., 1983 Mem.: Mag. Publs. Assn. (bd. dirs. 1988—92, 1997—2002), Am. Pubs. Assn. (bd. dirs. 1988—92), Everglades Club (Palm Beach), Saratoga Reading Room, Clove Valley Rod and Gun Club, Lake George Club (trustee 1995—2002), NY Yacht Club (trustee 1987—92), Racquet & Tennis Club (NY), Brook Club, Bath & Tennis Club (Palm Beach), River Club. Office Phone: 646-840-3402. E-mail: scmiii@aol.com.

MEIGS, JOHN FORSYTH, lawyer; b. Boston, Dec. 4, 1941; s. Charles H. Meigs and Florence S. Truitt; m. Carolyn J. Adams, Aug. 11, 2002; children: Amory, Perry, John. BA, Yale U., 1964; LLB, U. Pa., 1969. Bar: Pa. 1969, US Supreme Ct. 1977. Assoc. Saul, Ewing, Remick & Saul (now Saul Ewing, LLP), Phila., 1969-76, ptnr., 1976—. Co-chair estates and trusts Saul Ewing, LLP, 1997—2003, chair personal wealth svcs., 2000—. Contbr. articles to profl. jours. Trustee Independence Seaport Mus., 1978—, Woodmere Art Mus., 1987—. Named one of Top 100 Attys., Worth mag., 2005—06. Mem.: ABA, Phila. Bar Assn., Pa. Bar Assn. Episcopalian. Office: Saul Ewing LLP Centre Sq W 1500 Market St 38th Fl Philadelphia PA 19102-2186 Office Phone: 215-972-7812. Office Fax: 215-972-1870. E-mail: jmeigs@saul.com.

MEIGS, MONTGOMERY CUNNINGHAM, JR., retired military officer, educator; b. Annapolis, Md., Jan. 11, 1945; s. Montgomery Cunningham and Elizabeth Shoemaker (Griggs) M.; m. Mary Ann Mellenbruch, July 6, 1968; children: William Bradford, Matthew Montgomery. BS, U.S. Mil. Acad., West Point, NY, 1967; MA in History, U. Wis., 1977, PhD in History, 1982. Commd. 2d lt. U.S. Army, 1967, advanced through grades to gen.; internat. affairs fellow Coun. Fgn. Rels., NYC, 1981-82; exec. officer 2d Armored Cavalry Regiment, Nurnberg, Germany, 1982-84; commdr. 1st Squadron, 1st Cavalry, 1st AD, Schwabach, Germany, 1984-86; rsch. fellow Nat. Def. U., Washington, 1986-87; chief strategic applications br. J-5 Joint Staff, Washington, 1987-90; comdr. 2d Bde 1st Armored Divsn., Desert Storm, Erlangen, Germany, 1990-91; chief of staff V U.S. Corps, Frankfurt, Germany, 1993-94; dep. chief of staff Ops. HQ USAREUR & 7th Army, Heidelberg, Germany, 1994; comdg. gen. 3d Infantry Divsn., 1995-96, 1st infantry Divsn., Wurzburg, Germany, 1996-97, COMEAGLE, Bosnia-Herzegovina, 1996-97, Combined Arms Ctr., Ft. Leavenworth, Kans., 1997-98; commdg. gen. U.S. Army, COMSFOR, Bosnia-Herzegovina, 1998-99; comdg. gen. U.S. Army Europe and 7th Army, 1998—2002. Tom Slick vis. prof. LBJ Sch., U. Tex., Austin, 2003—04; Louis A. Bantle chair Maxwell Sch. Syracuse U., 2004—; dir. OSD's Joint IED Defeat Org., 2005—. Author: Slide Rules and Submarines, 1990; contbr. articles to profl. jours. Decorated Legion of Merit with oak leaf cluster, Bronze Star medal with V device and 2 oak leaf clusters, Purple Heart, officer French Legion of Honor, German Nat. Svc. Order with star, Bavarian Svc. Order, Army Disting. Svc. medal with oak leaf cluster. Avocations: history, hunting. Home: 70 Marvelle Rd Fayetteville NY 13066 Office Phone: 703-601-3837. Business E-Mail: montgomery.meigs@jieddo.dod.mil.

MEIGS, WALTER RALPH, lawyer, dry dock and shipbuilding company executive; M, Maritime Mgmt.; BA, Birmingham So. Coll., 1970; JD, U. Ala., 1973, postgrad., 1982, Auburn U., 1974. Bar: Ala. 1973, U.S. Dist. Ct. (no. dist.) Ala. 1974, U.S. Dist. Ct. (so. dist.) Ala. 1989, U.S. Ct. Appeals (11th cir.) 1990, US Ct. Appeals (5th cir.) 1992, US Ct. Appeals (9th cir.) 1994, US Supreme Ct. 1992. Law clk. Jud. br. State of Ala., 1973—74; assoc. firm Hubbard, Waldrop and Jenkins, Tuscaloosa, Ala., 1974—75; ho. counsel Ala. Dry Dock and Shipbldg. Co., Mobile, 1975—85; corp. sec., counsel Addsco Industries Inc., 1985—92; gen. counsel Atlantic Marine Ala., 1992—. Past trustee D.R. Dunlap Jr. Meml. Trust, Kate Middleton Charitable Trust; past vice-chmn. Excess, Surplus Lines and Reins. Com.; troop com. chmn. Boy Scouts Am.; past chmn. Mobile Pre-sch. for Sensory Impaired; bd. dirs. Mobile chpt. ARC, past chmn.; past mem. adv. bd. Tex. A&M U., Galveston. Mem.: ABA, Ala. State Bar Assn., Mobile Bar Assn., Maritime Law Assn., Ala. Hist. Soc., Leadership Mobile, Mobile C. of C., U.S. Navy League (Mobile chpt.), Propeller Club U.S., Mobile Touchdown Club, Kiwanis. Home: 155 Provident Ln Mobile AL 36608-1417 Office: Atlantic Marine Ala PO Box 190 Mobile AL 36601-0190 Office Phone: 251-690-7100. Business E-Mail: walterm@atlanticmarine.com.

MEIJER, HANK, retail company executive; b. 1952; BA, U. Michigan, 1973. Asst. advt. dir. Meijer, Grand Rapids, Mich., mktg. dir., vice chmn. bd. dirs., co-chmn. bd. dirs., 1990—, CEO, 2002—05, co-CEO, 2005—. Office: 2929 Walker Ave NW Grand Rapids MI 49544 *

MEIJER, PAUL HERMAN ERNST, physicist, educator; b. The Hague, Netherlands, Nov. 14, 1921; came to U.S., 1953, naturalized, 1959; s. Herman Willem and Elisabet (Kossmann) M.; m. Marianne Schwarz, Feb. 17, 1949; children: Onko Frans (dec.), Miriam, Daniel, Mark, Corinne. PhD, U. Leiden, Netherlands, 1951. Research assoc. U. Leiden, 1952-53, Duke U., 1954-55; vis. lectr. Case Inst. Tech., 1953-54; asst. prof. U. Del., 1955-56; asso. prof. Cath. U., Washington, 1956-60, prof. physics, 1960-92, prof. emeritus, 1992—, chmn. dept., 1980-83. Vis. prof. U. Paris, 1964-65, 72, 78, U. Nancy, 1984, 88; part-time appointment Nat. Inst.Stds. and Tech.; short time appointments at Naval Ordnance Lab., Livermore Radiation Lab., Naval Research Lab., Night Vision Lab., Ft. Belvoir. Author:(with P. Papon, J. Leblond) The Physics of Phase Transitions, 2006, (with E. Bauer) Group Theory, 2004; editor: Group Theory and Solid State Physics, 1964. Fulbright grantee, 1953-55, 77-78; Guggenheim grantee, 1964-65; Fulbright sr. fellow, 1978 Fellow Am. Phys. Socs.; mem. European Phys. Soc., Phys. Soc. Netherlands, Fedn. Am. Scientists, Fulbright Alumni Assn., Sigma Xi. Research, publs. statis. mechanics solids and liquids, group theory and other fields. Home: 1438 Geranium St NW Washington DC 20012-1518 Office: Cath U Am Dept Physics Hannan Hall Washington DC 20064 Office Phone: 202-319-5324. Business E-Mail: meijer@cua.edu.

MEIKLE, PHILIP G., engineer, retired government agency executive; b. Glendale, W.Va., Dec. 5, 1937; s. Philip and Caroline Elizabeth (Stephens) M.; m. Linda Kay Price, July 14, 1961 (div. Aug. 1976); children: Philip Kevin, Melissa Kay BS in Mining Engring., W.Va. U., 1961, MS in Mining Engrng., 1965; M.Engrng. Adminstrn., George Washington U., 1980. Registered profl. engr. Mining engr. Duquesne Light Co., Pitts., 1961-63; research engr. W.Va. U., Morgantown, 1963-66; materials engr. Mobay Chem. Co., New Martinsville, W.Va., 1966-68; asst. dir. Nat. Ash Assn., Washington, 1968-72; staff mining engr. U.S. Bur. Mines, Washington, 1972-82, divsn. chief, 1982-95; ret., 1995. Mem. U.S. Nat. Com. for Tunneling Tech., Nat. Acad. Scis., Washington, 1985-90, chmn., 1988-89; adj. prof. George Washington U., 1985—; pres. Clan Lamont Soc. N.Am., 1998-2002. Contbr. articles to profl. jours., chpts. to books Recipient Superior Svc. award Dept. Interior, 1980, Meritorious Svc. award, 1986, Disting. Svc. award, 1991, Presdl. Rank award, 1991. Mem. Nat. Assn. Ret. Fed. Employees (life), Sr. Execs. Assn. (life), Coun. Former Fed. Execs. (bd. dirs., 2004-06), Sigma Xi, Tau Beta Pi, Sigma Gamma Epsilon, Masons, Shriners. Republican. Baptist. Home: 6819 Brian Michael Ct Springfield VA 22153-1004

MEIKLEJOHN, ALVIN J., JR., state legislator, lawyer, accountant; b. Omaha, June 18, 1923; m. Lorraine J. Meiklejohn; children: Pamela Ann, Shelley Lou, Bruce Ian, Scott Alvin. BS, U. Denver, JD, 1951; LLD (hon.), U. No. Colo., 2000. Mem. Colo. state Senate from 19th Dist., 1976-96, chmn. com. edn.; mem. Edn. Commn. of States, 1981-96; chmn. Colo. Commn. on Ach. in Edn., 1995, mem., 1993-96, Jefferson Sch. Dist. No. R-1 Bd. Edn., 1971-77, pres., 1973-77; commr. Commn. on Uniform State Laws, 1988-96. Dir. Red Rocks C.C. Found., Wings Over the Rockies Air and Space Mus. Capt. US Army, 1940—46, maj. USAF, 1947—51. Mem. Arvada C. of C., Masons, Shriners, Transp. Lawyers Assn. (pres. 1972-73). Republican. Home: 7540 Kline Dr Arvada CO 80005-3732 Office: Jones & Keller PC 1625 Broadway Ste 1600 Denver CO 80202-4727 Office Phone: 303-573-1600. E-mail: ajmeiklejohn@joneskeller.com.

MEIKLEJOHN, DONALD STUART, lawyer; b. Chgo., Oct. 27, 1950; s. Donald and Elizabeth (Moore) M.; m. Rebecca Schneider, Aug. 9, 1975; children: David Alexander, Sarah. AB, Harvard U., 1971, JD, 1975. Bar: N.Y. 1976, U.S. Dist. Ct. (so. and ea. dists.) N.Y. 1976, U.S. Ct. Appeals (2d cir.) 1981, U.S. Ct. Appeals (5th cir.) 1982, U.S. Supreme Ct. 1986, U.S. Ct. Appeals (1st and 8th cirs.) 1990, U.S. Ct. Appeals (3d cir.) 1996, U.S. Ct. Appeals (9th cir.) 1997, U.S. Ct. Appeals (D.C. and 11th cirs.) 1998. Assoc. Sullivan & Cromwell, NYC, 1975-83, ptnr., 1983—, sr. councel. Bd. dirs. Union Settlement, N.Y.C., Lawyer's Com. Civil Rights Under Law, Legal Aid Soc. Mem. ABA, N.Y. State Bar Assn., Assn. of Bar of City of N.Y. Office: Sullivan & Cromwell 125 Broad St New York NY 10004-2489 Office Phone: 212-558-4000. Office Fax: 212-558-3588. Business E-Mail: meiklejohns@sullcrom.com.

MEIKSIN, ZVI H., electrical engineering educator; b. 1926; BSEE, Israel Inst. Tech., Haifa, 1950, Dipl. Ing., 1951; MSEE, Carnegie Mellon U., 1953; PhDEE, U. Pitts., 1959. Registered profl. engr., Pa. Design engr. McGraw Edison, Cannonsburg, Pa., 1953-54; sr. project engr. Westinghouse Electric Corp., Pitts., 1956-59; prof. dept. elec. engring. U. Pitts., 1959-91, prof. emeritus, 1991—; pres. Transtek, Inc., Pitts., 1995—2004; mng. ptnr. Analog Digital Mfg. Co., 2006—. Cons. entr. 33 orgns. in U.S., Europe, 1959-95; expert witness in field, 1991-95; cons. Transtek, Inc., 2004—. Author: Thin & Thick Films, 1976, Active Filter Design, 1990; co-author: Electronic Design, 1980, 84, Microprocessor Based Design, 1986; jour. referee profl. publs., 1970—; contbr. articles to profl. jours.; inventor, holder 8 patents in field. Fellow IEEE (award coms.); mem. Eta Kappa Nu, Sigma Xi. E-mail: meiksin@pitt.edu.

MEILAN, CELIA, food products executive; b. Bklyn., Jan. 21, 1920; d. Ventura Lorenzo and Susana (Prego) Meilan. Student, CCNY, 1943—46. Codes and ciphers translator security divsn. U.S. Censorship Office, NYC, 1942—46; sec., treas. Albumina Supply Co., NYC, 1946—55; co-founder, co-owner, sec., treas., fin. officer Internat. Proteins Corp. (now Animal-Feeds Internat. Corp.), Clark, NJ, 1955—86, exec. v.p., 1986—92, pres., 1992—94, chair emeritus, bd. dirs., 1994—, v.p., co-owner, 1998—. Bd. dirs. Pesquera Taboquilla, Panama City, Panama, Inversiones Pesqueras S.A., British Virgin Islands; v.p., bd. dirs. Atlantic Shipers of Tex. Inc., Port Arthur, 1989; bd. dirs. Atlantic Shippers Inc., Morehead City, NC, Empacadora Nacional S.A., Panama City; v.p., dir. AnimalFeeds, Internat., Santiago, Chile. Named One of Top 50 Women Bus. Owners, Working Woman Mag./Nat. Found. Women Bus. Owners, 1994, 1995. Mem.: Nat. Found. Women Bus. Owners, Spanish Benevolent Soc. (bd. dirs. 1955—62). Avocation: Avocations: travel, hand crafts, backgammon, puzzles. Office Fax: 732-827-0188.

MEILINK, JACQUELINE RAE, music educator; b. St. Louis, Mo., Mar. 4, 1956; d. Raymond John and Dorothy Virginia Meiners; m. Michael Steven Meilink, May 19, 1979; children: Steven M., Kristin R. BMusEd, U. Mo., Kansas City, 1978, MMusEd, 1999. Pvt. piano tchr., 1971—94; tchr. music North Kansas City Sch. Dist., Kansas City, Mo., 1978—85; choir dir. Northminster Presbyn. Ch., 1983—85; dir. children's choir Northgate Bapt. Ch., 1987—94, ch. pianister, 1988—2002; music tchr. North Kansas City Sch. Dist., 1994—. Sponsor Jr. Achievement, Kansas City, 2005—06; cultural art chmn. Oakwood Manor Parent Tchr. Student Assn., Kansas City, Mo.; reflections chmn. Antioch Mid. Sch. Parent Tchr. Student Assn., Gladstone, 1997, Maple Park Mid. Sch. Parent Tchr. Student Assn., Kansas City, 1998. Mem.: Am. Choral Dirs., Music Educators Nat. Conf., Mu Phi Epsilon (pres. Alpha Kappa chpt. 1977, Outstanding Jr. 1977). Republican. Baptist. Avocations: bicycling, exercise, reading, piano. Office: Northgate Mid Sch NE 48th St Kansas City MO 64118

MEILMAN, EDWARD, physician; b. Boston, Apr. 6, 1915; s. Harry and Jennie (Sholofsky) M.; m. Rhoeda Berman, Mar. 6, 1946. AB, Harvard U., 1936, MD, 1940. Intern Mt. Sinai Hosp., NYC, 1940-42; resident Beth Israel Hosp., Boston, 1946-48, assoc. in med. and med. research, 1948-53; chmn. dept. medicine L.I. Jewish-Hillside Med. Center, New Hyde Park, NY, 1953-82, chmn. emeritus dept. medicine, 1982—. Prof. medicine SUNY, Stony Brook, 1971— Contbr. articles to profl. jours. Served with USAAF, 1942-46. Fellow N.Y. Acad. Medicine, N.Y. Acad. Scis.; mem. Am. Heart Assn. (fellow council clin. cardiology, council arteriosclerosis), Am. Fedn. Clin. Research, Harvey Soc., Am. Rheumatism Assn., Phi Beta Kappa, Alpha Omega Alpha. Clubs: Harvard (N.Y.C.); Harvard (L.I.). Democrat. Jewish. Office Phone: 516-487-4203. E-mail: emeilman@optonline.net.

MEILMAN, ROY K., lawyer; b. NYC, June 7, 1946; BA, Franklin & Marshall Coll., 1968; JD, Harvard U., 1973. Bar: Pa. 1973, N.Y. 1977. Mem. Mudge Rose Guthrie Alexander & Ferdon, NYC; ptnr. Chadbourne & Parke LLP, Seyfarth Shaw LLP, NYC, 2007—. Mem. ABA, NY State Bar Assn., Phi Beta Kappa. Office: Seyfarth Shaw LLP 1270 Ave of Americas Ste 2500 New York NY 10020-1801 Office Phone: 212-218-4650. Office Fax: 212-218-5526. Business E-Mail: rmeilman@seyfarth.com.

MEILTON, SANDRA L., lawyer; b. 1946; BA, Bethany Coll., 1968; attended, U. Pitts.; JD, Dickinson Sch. Law, 1980. Bar: Pa. 1980. Assoc. Hepford, Swartz and Morgan, 1980—87, ptnr., 1987—98; shareholder Tucker Arensberg, P.C., 1998—2006; ptnr. Daley, Zucker, Meilton, Miner & Gingrich, Harrisburg, Pa., 2006—. Bd. dirs. Mechanicsburg Children's Home. Named one of Best Lawyers in Am., 2005. Mem.: ABA, Dauphin County Bar Assn., Am. Acad. Matrimonial Lawyers. Office: Daley Zucker Meilton Miner & Gingrich 1029 Scenery Dr Harrisburg PA 17109 Home Phone: 717-697-8810; Office Phone: 717-657-4795. Business E-Mail: smeilton@dzmmglaw.com.

MEIMA, RALPH CHESTER, JR., retired diplomat, real estate company executive; b. Chgo., Mar. 29, 1927; s. Ralph Chester and Grace Georgine (Larson) Meima; m. Elizabeth B. Frazier, 1994; children from previous marriage: Ralph Chester III, Stephen H. BA, U. Ams., Mexico City, 1952; MBA, Am. U., 1964. With Carborundum Co., Perth Amboy, 1952-53, Johns-Manville Corp., NYC, 1953-58, Security Storage Co., Washington, 1958-61, Dept. of Commerce, 1961-68; joined U.S. Fgn. Svc., 1968; consul gen. Marseille, France, 1977-80; on loan export devel. cons. State of Md., 1980-82; pres. Atlantic Eastern Corp., 1982-87, Phoenix Internat. Mktg. Corp., 1987-89; pres., chief exec. officer FTI Inc., Annapolis, Md., 1989-95; pres. DERCO, Inc., Balt., 1995—2002. In govt. rels. iJET Travel Risk Mgmt., Inc. With USN, 1945—46. Office: Champion Realty 541-B Baltimore Annapolis Blvd Severna Park MD 21146-3934 Office Phone: 443-994-6342. Personal E-mail: r.meima@att.net.

MEINCKE, CARL RUSSELL, music educator, director; b. Green Bay, Wis., June 23, 1952; s. Arnold Carl and Rose Maria Meincke; m. Judith Kay Ellingson, Sept. 1, 1984; children: Anthony James, Alexander Carl, James Arnold, Dominic Phillip. MusB in Edn., U. Wis., Eau Claire, 1975; MEd, U. Minn., Mpls., 1982. Lic. instrumental music tchr. Wis., 1975. Band dir. Hudson Jr. HS, Wis., 1975—94, Hudson Mid. Sch., 1994—. Adjudicator Wis. Sch. Music Assn., 1979—. Cub scout den leader Boy Scouts Am., Hudson, 1994—2004, asst. cub master, 1996—2003, asst. scout master, 2000—, merit badge counselor Eagle Bluff dist., 1998—, chmn. Order of Arrow elections; pres. Mt. Zion Luth. Ch., Hudson, 1986—88, dir. summer music, 1984—. Named Vigil mem., Order of the Arrow; recipient Excellence in Tchg. award, Hudson Edn. Found., 2005, Silver Beaver award, Northern Star Boy Scout Coun. Mem.: NEA, Wis. Youth Band Dirs. Assn., St. Croix Valley Music Educators Assn. (sec. 2000—), Wis. Edn. Assn., West Ctrl. Edn. Association-Hudson Unit (treas. 1992—), Wis. Music Educators Assn. (v.p. 2002—05), Music Educators Nat. Conf., Internat. Assn. Jazz Edcuators, Nat. Band Assn. (assoc.), Phi Mu Alpha Sinfonia. Avocation: tennis. Office: Hudson Mid Sch 1300 Carmichael Rd Hudson WI 54016 Home Phone: 715-386-8744; Office Phone: 715-7377-3820. Office Fax: 715-377-3821. Business E-Mail: meinckcr@hudson.k12.wi.us.

MEINDL, JAMES DONALD, electrical engineering educator, academic administrator; b. Pitts., Apr. 20, 1933; s. Louis M. and Elizabeth F. (Steinhauser) Meindl; m. Frederica Ziegler, May 21, 1961; children: Peter James, Candace Ann. BS, Carnegie Mellon U., 1955, MS, 1956, PhD, 1958. Engr. Autonetics Co., Downey, Calif., 1957, Westinghouse Co., Pitts., 1958-59; head sect. microelectronics US Army Electronics Command, Ft. Monmouth, NJ, 1959-62, chief br. semiconductors and microelectronics, 1962-65, dir. divsn. integrated electronics, 1965-67; assoc. prof. elec. engring. Stanford U., 1967-70, prof., 1970-84, John M. Fluke prof. elec. engring., 1984-86, assoc. dean rsch., 1984-86, dir. integrated circuits lab., 1969-84; co-founder Telesensory Systems Inc., 1971-84; dir. Electronics Labs. Stanford U., 1972-86, dir. Ctr. Integrated Systems, 1981-86; v.p. acad. affairs, provost Rensselaer Poly. Inst., Troy, NY, 1986-88, prof. sci. and engring., 1986-93, sr. v.p. acad. affairs, provost, 1988-93; Joseph M. Pettit Chair prof. microelectronics Ga. Inst. Tech., Atlanta, 1993—, dir. Microelectronics Rsch. Ctr., 1997—. Cons. to govt., industry. Author: Micropower Circuits, 1969; editor: Brief Lessons in High Technology, 1989; patentee integrated cir. field; contbr. numerous articles to profl. publs. Served to 1st lt. AUS, 1959-61. Recipient Arthur S. Flemming Commn. award Washington Jr. C. of C., 1967; J.J. Ebers award IEEE Electron Devices Soc., 1980, Univ. Rsch. award Semiconductor Industries Assn., 1999. Fellow IEEE (Solid State Circuits Coun. editor jour. 1966-71, Internat. Outstanding Paper ann. awards 1970, 75-78, Beatrice K. Winner award Internat. conf. 1988, solid State Circuits medal 1989, Edn. medal 1990, Third Millenium medal 2000, Medal of Honor 2006), AAAS, Am. Acad. Arts and Scis.; mem. AAUP, NAE, Am. Soc. Engr. Edn. (Benjamin Garver Lamme medal 1991), Electrochemical Soc., Biomedical Engring. Soc. (co-editor Annals of Biomedical Engring. 1976-80), Sigma Xi, Tau Beta Pi, Eta Kappa Nu, Phi Kappa Phi. Office: Ga Inst Tech Microelectronics Rsch Ctr 791 Atlantic Dr Atlanta GA 30332-0001 E-mail: james.meindl@mirc.gatech.edu. *

MEINDL, ROBERT JAMES, language educator, poet; b. Wausau, Wis., Sept. 17, 1936; s. George Martin and Adeline Emilie (Goetsch) M.; m. Victoria Lynn Chavez; children: Karin Rose, George Andrew, Damian Kurt, Erika Wittmer, Christopher Smith, Gabrielle Remelia. BS, U. Wis., 1958; MA, U. Conn., 1960; PhD, Tulane U., 1965; postgrad., U. Calif., Berkeley, 1967—68, Goethe Inst., Liblar, Germany, 1970, U. Cologne, Germany, 1970. Teaching asst. U. Conn., Storrs, 1958—60; teaching fellow Tulane U., 1960—62; lectr. U. Wis., Green Bay, 1963—65; asst. prof. to full prof. English Calif. State U., Sacramento, 1965—2002, prof. emeritus English, 2002—. Translator: Studies in John Gower, 1981; book rev. editor Studia Mystica Jour., 1984-89; contbr. numerous articles to profl. jours. With USNR, 1953-61, 79-96. Fellow, NEH, 1982. Mem. MLA (life), Medieval Acad. Am. (life), John Gower Soc. Office: Calif State U 6000 J St Sacramento CA 95819-2605 Office Phone: 916-278-7704. Business E-Mail: rmeindl@csus.edu.

MEINEL, ADEN BAKER, optics scientist; b. Pasadena, Calif., Nov. 25, 1922; s. John G. and Gertrude (Baker) M.; m. Marjorie Steele Pettit, Sept. 5, 1944; children: Carolyn, Walter, Barbara, Elaine, Edward, Mary, David. AB, U. Calif., Berkeley, 1947, PhD, 1949; DSc (hon.), U. Ariz., 1990. Assoc. prof. Yerkes Obs., U. Chgo., Williams Bay, Wis., 1950-58; dir. Kitt Peak Nat. Obs., Tucson, 1958-61; prof. U. Ariz., Tucson, 1961-85; dir. Steward Obs., Tucson, 1962-66, Optical Scis. Ctr., Tucson, 1966-73; Disting. scientist Jet Propulsion Lab., Pasadena, 1985-92; ret., 1993. Regent Calif. Luth. Coll., 1961-71; cons. USAF Spl. Projects Office, 1965-80. Co-author: Applied Solar Energy, 1976, Sunsets, Twilights and Evening Skies, 1983. Recipient Warner prize Am. Astron. Soc., 1954, Van Blesbroeck award Astron. Soc. Pacific, 1990, NASA Exceptional Scientific Achievement medal, 1993; Meinel bldg. U. Ariz., dedicated 1993 Fellow Am. Acad Arts and Scis., Optical Soc. Am. (pres. 1972-73, Adolph Lomb medal 1952, Ives medal 1980), Internat. Optical Engring. Soc. (Goddard award 1984, Kingslake medal, 1993, 2000, Gold medal 1997). Home: 2548 Eclipsing Stars Dr Henderson NV 89044 Personal E-mail: ammeinel@cox.net.

MEINER, SUE ELLEN THOMPSON, adult nurse practitioner, consultant, gerontologist; b. Ironton, Mo., Oct. 24, 1943; d. Louis Raymond and Verna Mae Thompson; m. Robert Edward Meiner, Mar. 5, 1971; children: Diane Romeril, Suzanne. AAS, Meramec C.C., 1970; BSN, St. Louis U., 1978, MSN, 1983; EdD, So. Ill. U., Edwardsville, 1991. RN, Nev.; cert. gerontol. nurse practitioner; cert. clin. specialist in gerontol. nursing. Staff RN St. Joseph's Hosp., St. Charles, Mo., 1976-78; nursing supr. Bethesda Gen. Hosp., St. Louis, 1975-76, 71-74; adult med. dir. Family Care Ctr.-Carondelet, St. Louis, 1978-79; program dir., lectr. Webster Coll./Bethesda Hosp., Webster Groves, Mo., 1979-82; diabetes clin. specialist Washington U. Sch. Medicine, St. Louis, 1982; asst. prof. St. Louis C.C., 1983-88; vis. nurse assoc. St. Louis, 1970—71; chmn. dept. nursing, asst. prof. Barnes Hosp. Sch. Nursing, 1988-89; instr. U. Mo., St. Louis, 1989; assoc. prof. St. Charles County C.C., St. Peters, Mo., 1990-92, Deaconess Coll. of Nursing, 1991-93; patient care mgr. Deaconess Hosp., St. Louis, 1993-94; assoc. prof. Jewish Hosp. Coll. of Nursing and Allied Health, 1994-99; gerontol. nurse, rschr. Wash. U. Sch. Med., St. Louis, 1996-2000; asst. prof. nursing U. Nev. Coll. Health Scis., Las Vegas, 2000—05; pvt. practice Nev., 2005—. Nat. dir. edn. Nat. Assn. Practical Nurse Edn. and Svc., Inc., St. Louis, 1984-86; mem. task force St. Louis Met. Hosp. Assn., 1987-88; mem. adv. com. Bd. Edn. Sch. Nursing, St. Louis, 1986-90; grant coord. Kellogg Found. Gerontology and Nursing, 1991-92; project dir. NIH, NIA Grant Washington U. Sch. Medicine, St. Louis, 1996-00; mem. editorial bd. Geriatric Nursing Journ., 1999-02; legal nurse cons. Author and editor profl. books; contbr. articles to profl. jours. Chmn. bd. dirs. Creve Coeur Fire Protection Dist. Mo., 1984-89; vice chmn. Bd. Cen. St. Louis County Emergency Dispatch Svc., 1985-87; asst. leader Girl Scouts U.S., St. Louis, 1975; treas. Older Women's League, St. Louis, 1992-93. Recipient Woman of Worth award Gateway chpt. Older Women's League, 1993. Mem.: ANA, Am. Soc. of Aging, Nat. League for Nursing, Am. Nurses Found., Am. Coll. Nurse Practitioners, Am. Acad. Nurse Practitioners, Job's Daus. (guardian 1979—80), Order Ea. Star (chaplain 1970), Creve Coeur C. of C., Sigma Theta Tau (fin. chmn. 1984, archivist 1985—87, Zeta Kappa chpt. v.p. 2001—03), Kappa Delta Pi, Sigma Phi Omega (Iota chpt. pres. 1990—91). Avocations: travel, reading. Home and Office: 3722 Violet Rose Ct Las Vegas NV 89147-7400 Personal E-mail: agingwell@earthlink.net. *Personal philosophy: From my earliest memories, I have established goals that were obtainable only through very hard work and perseverance. I always sought support and assistance from significant others as each goal was reached before setting another one. My life has been enriched by family and very dear friends. An important belief and practice has been to return the benefits of my education to my community and to be an advocate for those persons needing assistance. I hold a special place for support of all older adults.*

MEINERT, EDWARD, computer scientist, management consultant; MS, U. Oxford, Eng., 2001. Sr. project mgr. Diligenti Healthcare, NYC, 2000—02; chief software engr. MedAbiliti Software, Inc., NYC, 2002—04; mng. dir. Meinert Schivers & Co., Cambridge, Mass., 2004—06; rsch. asst. Harvard Med. Sch., Boston, 2006—. Author: (novel) In between Boston and a New York Chronicle, 2005. Mem.: IEEE, AAAS, ABA (assoc.), NAACP, Am. Soc. Bioethics and Humanities, Am. Med. Informatics Assn., Brit. Computer Soc. Achievements include patents pending for substance abuse management system and method. Office: 700 Huron Ave Ste 12J Cambridge MA 02138 Home Phone: 617-943-4326; Office Phone: 617-326-3841. Office Fax: 617-812-2583. Business E-Mail: emeinert@meinertschivers.com.

MEINERT, JOHN RAYMOND, apparel executive, investment banker; b. White Cloud, Mich., Aug. 11, 1927; m. Joyce Macdonell, Nov. 5, 1955; children: Elizabeth Tinsman, Pamela Martin. Student, U. Mich., 1944-45; BS, Northwestern U., 1949. CPA Ill., 1952. With Hart Schaffner & Marx/Hartmarx Corp., Chgo., 1950-90, exec. v.p., 1975-80, vice chmn., 1981-85, sr. vice chmn., 1985-86, chmn., 1987-90, chmn. emeritus, 1990—, also bd. dirs.; prin. investment banking J.H. Chapman Group, LLC, Rosemont, Ill., 1990—, chmn., 1995—. Bd. dirs. County Seat Stores, Inc., N.Y.C., 1998-99, The John Evans Club, BBB, Chgo. C.of C.; trustee Amalgamated Ins. Fund, 1980-90, Rotary Internat. Retirement Fund, 2000-02; dir. Evanston Hosp., 1988-94, Clothing Mfrs. Assn., pres., 1982-87, chmn. 1987-90; instr. acctg. Northwestern U., 1949; faculty Lake Forest Grad. Sch. Mgmt., 1994-95; arbitrator Am. Arbitration Assn., 1993—. Chmn. bus. adv. coun. U. Ill., 1989-90; mem. Fin. Acctg. Stds. Adv. Coun., 1989-92, Chgo. Coun. Fgn. Rels., Sisters City Com.; mem. adv. coun. Northwestern U. Kellogg Grad. Sch. Recipient Alumni Merit award Northwestern U. Kellogg Grad. Sch., 1989; named Humanitarian of Yr., Five Hosp. Found., 1995. Mem. AICPA (v.p. 1985-86, bd. dirs. 1975-78, coun. 1971-93, trustee benevolent fund 1992-95, gold medal 1987), Ill. CPA Soc. (pub. svc. award 1996, pres. 1982-83, bd. dirs. 1966-68, 81-84, hon. award), Chicagoland C. of C. (bd. dirs.), Rotary (pres. Chgo. 1989-90, trustee found. 1991-95, asst. dist. gov. 1997-2000), Univ. Club, Execs. Club, Rolling Green Country Club. Presbyterian (elder). Home: 634 N Ironwood Dr Arlington Heights IL 60004-5818 Office: J H Chapman Group LLC 9700 W Higgins Rd Rosemont IL 60018-4796 Office Phone: 773-693-4800. Business E-Mail: jmeinert@jhchapman.com.

MEINHOLD, CHARLES BOYD, health physicist; b. Boston, Nov. 1, 1934; s. Russell and Jane (Boyd) M.; m. Anne Elizabeth DuVally, Oct. 20, 1956; children: Anne Frances, Patricia Marie, Michael John, Peter Russell, Catherine Louise. BS in Physics, Providence Coll., 1956; postgrad., U. Rochester, 1956-57. Cert. Am. Bd Health Physics 1967. Staff scientist health physics div. Brookhaven Nat. Lab., Upton, NY, 1957-72, head, sr. health physicist safety and environ. div., 1972-88, sr.scientist, div. head, 1988-91, sr. scientist radiol. sci. divsn. Dept. Advanced Tech., 1991-2001; guest scientist Dept. of Non-Proliferation and Nat. Security, 2001—. Mem. Internat. Commn. on Radiol. Protection, 1978-01, vice chmn., 1992-01, emeritus mem., 2002—; mem. Nat. Coun. on Radiol. Protection and Measurement, 1977-01, pres., 1991-02, pres. emeritus, 2002—; Lauren S. Taylor lectr. Pres. South Haven Bd. Edn., Brookhaven, N.Y., 1965-87. Named Hon. Prof., China Inst. Atomic Energy, 1995, China Inst. Radiation Protection, 1997. Fellow Health Physics Soc. (pres. 1980-81); mem. Internat. Radiation Protection Assn. (v.p. 1988-92, pres. 1992-96), Hon. mem. Conf. Radiation Control Program Dirs. Democrat. Roman Catholic. Avocations: woodworking, sailing. Home: 41 Old South Country Rd Brookhaven NY 11719-9526 Office: Brookhaven Nat Lab Bldg 197D Upton NY 11973-5000 Personal E-mail: cbmeinhold@optonline.net.

MEINIG, DONALD WILLIAM, geography educator; b. Palouse, Wash., Nov. 1, 1924; s William August and Annie (Malsed) M.; m. Lee McAuliffe, June 29, 1946; children: Laurel, Kristin, Lee. BS, Georgetown U., 1948; MA, U. Wash., 1950, PhD, 1953; DHL (hon.), Syracuse U., 1994. From asst. prof. to assoc. prof. U. Utah, Salt Lake City, 1950-59; assoc. prof. geography Syracuse U., NY, 1959-73, Maxwell prof. geography NY, 1973-89, Maxwell rsch. prof., 1990—2005. Lectr. St. Andrews U., Scotland, 1973, Charles Homer Haskins lectr. ACLS, 1992; vis. prof. Hebrew U., Jerusalem, 1974; adv. editor Wadsworth Pub. Co., 1957-61, Harper & Row, N.Y.C., 1965-83; chief editl. cons. Nat. Geog. Soc., Washington, 1982-88; councilor Am. Geog. Soc., 1993-96. Author: On the Margins of the Good Earth, 1962, The Great Columbia Plain, 1968, Imperial Texas, 1969, Southwest, 1971, The Shaping of America, Vol. 1: Atlantic America 1492-1800, 1986, Vol. 2: Continental America 1800-1867, 1993, Vol. 3: Transcontinental America 1850-1915, 1998, Vol. 4: Global America 1915-2000, 2004; editor: The Interpretation of Ordinary Landscapes, 1979. Mem. N.Y. Council for Humanities, 1979-86. Served to 2d lt. U.S. Army, 1943-46. Recipient Emil and Kathleen Sick award in Western History, 1968, award of Merit Seattle Hist. Soc., 1968, award of Merit Am. Assn. State and Local History, 1969, Summerfield G. Roberts award Sons Republic of Tex., 1969, Faculty Enrichment award Can Embassy, 1980, Master Tchr. award Nat. Coun. for Geog. Edn., 1986, Charles P. Daly medal Am. Geog. Soc., 1986; Fulbright rsch. scholar U. Adelaide, 1958; Guggenheim fellow, 1966-67, NEH fellow, 1987-88. Fellow Brit. Acad. (corr.); mem. Assn. Am. Geographers (councilor 1965-67, Meritorious Contbn. award 1965, Presdl. Achievement award 2005, John Brinkerhoff Jackson award 2005), Am. Antiquarian Soc. Office: Syracuse U Dept Geography Syracuse NY 13244-0001

MEINWALD, JERROLD, retired chemistry professor; b. Bklyn., Jan. 16, 1927; s. Herman and Sophie (Baskind) M.; m. Yvonne Chu, June 25, 1955 (div. 1979); children: Constance Chu, Pamela Joan; m. Charlotte Greenspan, Sept. 7, 1980; 1 child, Julia Eve. PhB, U. Chgo., 1947, BS, 1948; MA, Harvard, 1950, PhD (hon.), 1952; PhD, U. Göteborg, 1989. Mem. faculty Cornell U., 1952-72, 73—, Goldwin Smith prof. chemistry, 1980—2005, grad. sch. prof., 2006—, mem. sci. directing group Cornell Inst. Rsch. Chem. Ecology, 1992—, emeritus prof., 2006—; rsch. dir. Internat. Centre Insect Physiology and Ecology, Nairobi, 1970-77; A. Mellon Term prof., 1992-95; prof. chemistry U. Calif. at San Diego, 1972-73. Chem. cons. Schering-Plough Rsch. Inst., 1957-99, Procter & Gamble Pharms., 1958-95, Cambridge Neurosci. Rsch., 1988-92, Du Pont, 2006; mem. sci. adv. bd. ENTOMED Inc., 2002-05; vis. prof. Rockefeller U., 1970, Harvard Med. Sch., 1997; Camille and Henry Dreyfus Disting. scholar Mt. Holyoke Coll., 1981, Bryn Mawr Coll., 1983, Dartmouth Coll., 1996; Kolthoff lectr. U. Minn., 1985; Beckman lectr. Calif. Inst. Tech., 1986; Swiss "Troisième Cycle" Lectr., 1986; Russell Marker lectr. Pa. State U., 1987; mem. vis. com. chemistry Brookhaven Nat. Lab., 1969-72, chmn., 1972; mem. med. A chemistry study sect. NIH, 1963-67, chmn., 1965-67; mem. adv. bd. Petroleum Rsch. Found., 1971-73; mem. adv. coun. chemistry dept. Princeton U., 1978-83; mem. adv. bd. Rsch. Corp., 1978-83; mem. adv. bd. chemistry div. NSF, 1979-83; organizing chmn. Sino-Am. Symposium on Chemistry of Natural Products, Shanghai, 1980; mem. adv. bd. A.P. Sloan Found., 1985-91; Frontiers of Rsch. lectr. Coun. Chem. Rsch., 1987; mem. sci. adv. bd. Agridyne Corp., 1989-93; adv. com. chem. ecology Max-Planck Soc., 1994-96, Nat. Inst. Sericulture and Entomol. Scis., Tsukuba, Japan, 1997-01; adv. bd. Xerces Soc., 1995—; adv. com. Biosphere 2, 1999-03; Carlton Coll. Convocation, 1993; Mary Aldridge lectr. Am. U., 1993; K. Pfister lectr. MIT, 1992, Hilldale lectr. U. Wis., 1991, Nat. Undergrad. Rsch. Symposium, Plenary lectr., Mpls., 1992; UNOCAL lectr. Calif. State U., Long Beach, 1992; Max T. Rogers lectr. Mich. State U., 1994; Jean Day lectr. Rutgers U., 1994, Disting. Grad. Sch. lectr. U. Md., 1994. Merck lectr. Lafayette Coll.; plenary lectr. 3d Pan Am. Chem. Congress; Inaugural Paul G. Gassman lectr. Canisius Coll., 1996, Disting. Sci. Lectr. Bard Coll., 1996, hon. visiting sci., Taiwan, 1997, Gassman lectr. U. Minn., 1999, Ptnrs. in Sci. lectr., Rsch Corp., 2000, Iscol award lectr., Cornell U., 2000, Chemistry as a life sci. X Symposium, 2000, IUPAC plenary lectr., Brazil, 2000, W.S. Johnson Symposium, Stanford, 2000, Berzelius Days plenary lectr., Stockholm, 2001, ICSN Symposium on Chemistry of Nat. Products, Gif-sur-Yvette, 2003, Nat. ACS Organic Symposium lectr., 2001, 05, others; mem. internat. sci. com. Programa Brasileiro de Ecologia Molecular/Amazonia, 1997-03; Grandpierre lectr. Columbia U., 1998; sci. adv. bd. Inst. Chemistry and Biochemistry, Czechoslovak Acad. Sci., 1999-05; Gilbert Stork lectr. Columbia U., 2005; mem. Princeton Area Organic Symposium, 2005. Mem. bd. editors Jour. Organic Chemistry, 1962-66, Organic Reactions, 1968-78, Organic Synthesis, 1968-72, Jour. Chem. Ecology, 1974—, Insect Sci., 1979-90, Current Organic Chemistry, 1999—, Chemistry & Biodiversity, 2004—, Procs. Nat. Acad. Sci., 2006—; contbr. articles to profl. jours. Recipient Tyler Environ. Achievement prize U. So. Calif., 1990, Gustavus J. Esselen award for Chemistry in the Pub. Interest, 1991, Heyrovsky medal Acad. Scis. of the Czech Rep., 1996, Pioneer's award Am. Inst. Chemists, 1997; Sloan fellow, 1958-62, Guggenheim fellow, 1960-61,76-77, spl. postdoctoral fellow NIH, 1967-68, fellow Japan Soc. Promotion of Sci., 1983, Ctr. for Advanced Study in Behavioral Sci., 1990-91; Fogarty internat. scholar NIH, 1983-85; Bert L. and Natalie K. Vallee Found., Inc. fellow, 1997. Mem. NAS (exch. scholar 1987), AAAS, Am. Acad. Arts and Scis. (sec. 2005-), Am. Philos. Soc., Am. Chem. Soc. (chmn. organic divsn. 1969, E Guenther award 1985, Disting. Scientist award Kalamazoo sect. 1985, A.C. Cope Scholar award 1989, Roger Adams award in Organic Chemistry 2005, Grand Prize of La Maison de la Chimie, Paris, 2006, R.C. Fuson lectr., U. Nev., 2006, R. Sandin lectr., U. Alberta, 2006, R. Hirschmann lectr., U. Wis., 2006, Novartis lectr., MIT, 2006, John D. Roberts lectr., Caltech, 2007), Internat. Soc. Chem. Ecology (pres. 1988, Silver medal 1991), Phi Beta Kappa, Sigma Xi (nat. lectr. 1965, 75, 92-94). Home Phone: 607-257-0035; Office Phone: 607-255-3301. Business E-Mail: circe@cornell.edu.

MEINZER, BEVERLY ANNE, chemist, educator; d. David Lathrop and Anna Lee (Floyd) Edmiaston; m. Alan Lester Meinzer, Dec. 30, 1989; 1 child, Natalie. BS, Lyon Coll., Batesville, Ark., 1986; MS, U. Ark., Fayetteville, 1989. Chemist IV Tenn. Dept. Health, Jackson, 1990—95; lab. mgr., instr. Lyon Coll., Batesville, 1995—2003; chemistry educator U. Ark. CC, Batesville, 2003—. Sci. fair judge various secondary schs. Pianist Faith-Hopewell Cumberland Presbyn. Ch., Batesville, 1996—. Presbyterian. Avocations: piano, sewing. Office: Univ Ark Cmty Coll PO Box 3350 Batesville AR 72503 Business E-Mail: bmeinzer@uacch.edu.

MEIRELLES, FERNANDO, film director; b. São Paulo City, Brazil, Nov. 9, 1955; Student in Architecture, Univ. São Paulo. Co-founder Olhar Electronico studio. Dir.: (films) Olhar Electronico, 1986, the Nutty Boy 2, 1998, Golden Gate, 2002, The Constant Gardener, 2005 (ALMA award, Nat. Coun. La Raza for outstanding dir. for motion picture, 2006, Golden Globe nominee for best dir., 2005); co-dir.: City of God, 2002 (Acad. award nomination for direction, 2004); dir., writer: (TV episodes) Brava Gente, 2000, Cidade dos Homens, 2002, 2005; prod: Contra Todos, 2003. Mailing: c/o John Lesher Endeavor Agy 10th fl 9601 Wilshire Blvd Beverly Hills CA 90212

MEIROWITZ, RANDY EMIL, research scientist, consultant; b. Queens, NY, Feb. 1, 1953; B, Boston U., 1978, PhD, 1983. Chartered chemist Royal Soc. of Chemistry, Eng. (fellow), 1997, chartered scientist Royal Soc. of Chemistry, Eng., 2004. Dir. rsch. devel. & engring. Waters Corp., Milford, Mass., 1994—97; chief tech. officer Nextec Applications Inc, Vista, Calif., 1997—2003; pres. RND Tech. Solutions Inc, San Diego, 2003—. Contbr. articles to profl. jours. E-4 US Army, 1971—74, Germany. Recipient Connect award, U. Calif. San Diego Connect, 1998; grantee, US Dept. Def., 1998; Rsch. fellow, Boston U., 1982. Mem.: Am. Inst. Chemistry, Assn. Consulting Chemists and Chem. Engrs., Am. Chem. Soc., Am. Assn. Textile Chemists and Colorists. Achievements include patents for water-wettable chromatographic media for solid phase extraction; nonwoven webs containing shaped fibers; nonwoven fabric having durable wettability; absorbent structure for masking and distributing a liquid; nonwoven web containing shaped fibers; method of making polyolefin articles; polyester articles; method of providing a polyester article with a hydrophilic surface; enhanced soil removal from paper machine forming fabrics; water-wettable chromatographic media for solid phase extraction; absorbent structure comprising superabsorbent, staple fiber, and binder fiber; interlabial sanitary pad. Office: RND Tech Solutions Inc 18285 High Mesa Ct San Diego CA 92127 Office Phone: 619-675-9385. Office Fax: 619-675-9386. Business E-Mail: randy@rndtechnicalsolutions.com.

MEIS, PAUL JEAN, retired obstetrics and gynecology educator; b. Sioux City, Iowa, Oct. 29, 1934; s. Lee Francis and Dorothy (Trexlar) M.; m. Marcia Rose Donsker, June 28, 1958; children: Steven James, Douglas John. BS, U. Iowa, 1956, MD, 1959. Diplomate Am. Bd. Ob-Gyn., Am. Bd. Maternal-Fetal Medicine. Intern Martin Army Hosp., Ft. Benning, Ga., 1959-60; resident ob/gyn. SUNY Upstate Med. Ctr., Syracuse, 1962-65; pvt. practice, La Crosse, Wis., 1965-75; fellow Harbor Gen. Hosp., Torrance, Calif., 1975-77; asst. prof. dept. ob-gyn. Bowman Gray Sch. Medicine Wake Forest U., Winston-Salem, NC, 1977-80, assoc. prof., 1980-85; prof. Bowman Gray Sch. Medicine Wake Forest U. Sch. Medicine, 1985—2006; prof. emeritus, 2006—. Capt. M.C., U.S. Army, 1959-62. Office: Wake Forest U Sch Medicine Dept Ob-Gyn Medical Center Blvd Winston Salem NC 27157-0001 E-mail: pmeis@wfubmc.edu.

MEISBURG, RONALD EDWARD, federal agency administrator, lawyer; b. Bowling Green, Ky., July 28, 1947; s. Edward Austin and Jean Lavelle (Knadler) M.; m. Elizabeth Ann Ruark, July 27, 1969 (div. Dec. 1975); m. Roseann Karene Finigan, July 14, 1984 (dec. 1997); m. Mary Helen Ratchford, June 9, 1999. BA, Carson-Newman Coll., 1969; JD, U. Louisville, 1974. Bar: Ky., D.C., U.S. Ct. Appeals (2nd, 3rd, 4th, 5th, 6th, 7th, D.C., and 9th cirs.). Atty. U.S. Dept. Labor, Washington, 1974-80; assoc. Smith, Heenan and Althen, Washington, 1980-85, ptnr., 1985-97, Heenan Althen & Roles, Washington, 1997—2002; atty., shareholder Ogletree, Deakins, Nash, Smoak & Stewart LLP, Washington, 2002—03; mem. NLRB, Washington, 2004, spl. asst. to assoc. gen. counsel for enforcement, 2005—06, exec. asst. to dep. gen. counsel, 2005—06, gen. counsel, 2006—. Pres., Energy & Mineral Law Found., 1994-95; mem., exec. com. Ea. Mineral Law Found., W.Va. U., Morgantown, 1990—, asst. v.p., 1991-93, v.p., 1993-94, pres., 1994-95; mem., US Coun. Internat. Bus., 1993-98, Employment Lawyers Advisory Coun., 1996-98, Nat. Assn. Mfrs., 1996-98. Contbr. articles to profl. jours. and proceedings; editl. adv. bd. Jour. Natural Resources and Environ. Law, 1987—. Recipient Disting. Achievement award U.S. Sec. of Labor, Washington, 1978. Mem. ABA, Ky. Bar Assn., DC Bar. Roman Catholic. Office: NLRB Office Gen Counsel 1099 14th St NW Rm 10100 Washington DC 20570

MEISEL, ALAN, law educator; b. Newark, Dec. 24, 1946; s. Stanley and Beatrice (Katz) M.; m. Linda Serody, Mar. 6, 1982; 2 children. BA, Yale U., 1968, JD, 1972. Bar: Conn. 1972, Pa. 1973, U.S. Dist. Ct. Conn. 1972, U.S. Dist. Ct. (we. dist.) Pa. 1973, U.S. Ct. Appeals (3d cir.) 1985. Prof. psychiatry U. Pitts., 1973—, prof. law, 1976—, Dickie, McCamey Chilcote prof. bioethics/law and psychiatry, 1995—, dir. Ctr. for Bioethics and Health Law, 1987—. Asst. dir. for legal studies Pres.'s Commn. for Study of Ethical Problems in Medicine and Biomed. and Behavioral Rsch., Washington, 1982; mem. ethics working group Presdl. Task Force on Healthcare Reform, 1993; mem. adv. coun. NHLBI, 1998—2004. Author: The Right to Die, 1989, 2d edit., 1995, 3d edit. 2004; co-author: Informed Consent: A Study of Decision Making in Psychiatry, 1984, Informed Consent: Legal Theory and Clinical Practice, 1987; contbr. articles to legal and med. jours. Grantee NIMH, grantee Pres.'s Commn. for Study of Ethical Problems in Medicine and Biomed. and Behavioral Rsch., 1981-82, Founds. Fund for Rsch. in Psychiatry grantee, 1979-82, Legal Svcs. Corp. grantee, 1985-87; fellow Hastings Ctr.; award for The Right to Die Am. Assn. Publs., 1989; Pellegrino medal Contbns. Am. Health Care Ethics Law in Selfless Spirit of Edmund D. Pellegrino, Samford U., 2005. Mem.: Am. Soc. Bioethics and Humanities, Am. Soc. Law, Medicine and Ethics, Am. Health Lawyers Assn. Office: U Pitts Sch Law 3900 Forbes Ave Pittsburgh PA 15260 Business E-Mail: meisel@pitt.edu.

MEISEL, DAN, chemist; b. Tel Aviv, July 4, 1943; s. Arie and Mariasha Miriam (Ribak) M.; m. Osnat Meisel, Dec. 30, 1965; children: Einat, Omer. BSc, Hebrew U., 1967, MSc, 1969, PhD, 1974. Prof. chemistry U. Notre Dame, Ind., 1998—, dir. Radiation Lab. Ind., 1998—2004. Adv. bd.: Jour. Phys. Chem., 1993—2002; editor: Photochem. Energy Conversion, 1989, Semiconductors Nanoclusters, 1997. Mem. AAAS, Am. Chem. Soc., Am. Phys. Soc. Office: U Notre Dame Radiation Lab Notre Dame IN 46556 Office Phone: 574-631-5457. Business E-Mail: dani@nd.edu.

MEISEL, GEORGE VINCENT, lawyer; b. St. Louis, Sept. 24, 1933; s. Leo Otto and Margaret (Duggan) M.; m. Joy C. Cassin, May 18, 1963 BS summa cum laude, St. Louis U., 1956, JD cum laude, 1958. Bar: Mo. 1958. Assoc. Grand Peper & Martin, St. Louis, 1961-64, ptnr., 1965; jr. ptnr. Bryan Cave McPheeters & McRoberts, St. Louis, 1966-69; ptnr. Bryan Cave, LLP, St. Louis, 1970-2000, of counsel, 2000—. Served to 1st lt. USAF, 1958-61 Mem. ABA, Bar Assn. Met. St. Louis, Mo. Bar Assn. Clubs: Saint Louis, Mo. Athletic (St. Louis). Roman Catholic. Home: 2029 S Warson Rd Saint Louis MO 63124-1151 Office Phone: 314-259-2268. Business E-Mail: gvmeisel@bryancavellp.com.

MEISEL, JOHN, political scientist; b. Vienna, Oct. 23, 1923; s. Fryda and Ann M. BA, U. Toronto, 1948, MA, 1950; PhD in Polit. Sci., London Sch. Econs., 1959; LLD, Brock U., 1983, U. Guelph, 1985, Carleton U., 1990, U. Toronto, 1993, Queen's U., 1996, U. Regina, 1999, U. Calgary, 2000; DU (hon.), U. Ottawa, 1983; D of Social Scis. (hon.), Laval U., 1988; LittD (hon.), U. Waterloo, 1998. Head dept. polit. studies Queen's U., Kingston, Ont., Canada, 1963-67, Hardy prof. polit. sci., 1963-80, Sir Edward Peacock prof. polit. sci., 1983-93, prof. emeritus. Former chmn. Can. Radio-TV and Telecomms. Commn.; moderator symposia on finding common grounds for polit. issues confronting Yugoslavia, UN, Vienna, 1995. Author: The Canadian General Election of 1957, 1962, Papers on the 1962 Election, 1964, Ethnic Relations in Canadian Voluntary Associations, 1972, Working Papers on Canadian Politics, 1975; editor: Internat. Polit. Sci. Rev., 1979-95, (with Jean Laponce) Debating the Constitution/Débat sur la constitution, 1994. Decorated companion Order of Can.; recipient Killam award Can Coun., 1968-73. Fellow Royal Soc. Can. (pres. 1992-95); mem. Univ. Club (Toronto). Home (Summer): Colimaison Tichborne ON Canada K0H 2V0 Office: Queen's U Kingston ON Canada K7L 3N6 Home (Winter): 70A Johnson St Kingston ON Canada K7L1X7 Business E-Mail: meiselj@post.queensu.ca.

MEISEL, MARTIN, retired English and comparative literature educator; b. NYC, Mar. 22, 1931; s. Joseph and Sally (Rössler) Mörsel; m. Martha Sarah Winkley, Dec. 22, 1957; children: Maude Frances, Andrew Avram, Joseph Stoddard AB, Queens Coll., 1952; MA, Princeton U., 1957, PhD, 1960; postgrad., U. Rome, 1959. Instr. English Rutgers U., New Brunswick, N.J., 1957-58; instr., asst. prof., assoc. prof. Dartmouth Coll., Hanover, N.H., 1959-65; prof. English U. Wis., Madison, 1965-68; prof. English and comparative lit. Columbia U., NYC, 1968—, Brander Matthews prof. dramatic lit., 1987—, chmn. dept., 1980-83, 99-01, acting v.p. arts and scis., 1986-87, v.p. arts and scis., 1989-93, prof. emeritus, 2004—. Trustee Columbia U. Press, 1990-94. Author: Shaw and the 19th Century Theater, 1963, Realizations: Narrative, Pictorial, and Theatrical Arts in 19th Century England (George Freedley Meml. award Theater Libr. Assn. 1984, Barnard Hewitt award Am. Theatre Assn. 1984), 1983, How Plays Work: Reading and Performance, 2007; mem. editl. bd. Jour. Victorian Studies, PMLA, Jour. Contemporary Lit., Bull. Rsch. in the Humanities, 19th Century Contexts. Served with U.S. Army, 1954-56 Fellow Guggenheim Found., 1963-64, 1987-88, Am. Council of Learned Socs., 1970-71, Inst. for Advanced Studies in the Humanities, Edinburgh, 1977, Huntington Library and Art Gallery, 1978, 80, 83, Nat. Humanities Ctr., 1983-84, Wilson Ctr., Smithsonian Instn., 1987-88. Mem. MLA, Am. Soc. Theatre Rsch., North Am. Victorian Studies Assn., Assn. of Historians of 19 Century Art, Century Assn., Internat. Shaw Soc. Home: 18 Bacon Hill Rd Pleasantville NY 10570-3502 Personal E-mail: mm28@columbia.edu.

MEISEL, MICHAEL J., lawyer; s. William J. and Patricia A. Meisel; m. Brenda J. Meisel; children: Erin, Nicholas. BA summa cum laude, Siena Coll., 1982; JD, Union U., 1985; MS in Nat. Resource Strategy, Nat. Def. U., 2002. Bar: N.Y. 1985. Judge adv. U.S. Army, Fort Riley, Kans., 1986—89; chief civilian pers. law team U.S. Army Legal Svcs. Agy., Arlington, Va., 1990—93, chief civilian pers. litig., litig. divsn., 1993—2001, dep. chief litig. divsn., 2002—03, dir. civil law and litig., 2003—. Lectr. Judge Adv. Gen.'s Sch. U. Va., Charlottesville, Va., 1993—2001. Capt. US Army, 1985—90. Decorated Army Commendation medal U.S. Army, Army Achievement medal; recipient Commander's award for Civilian Svc., 1990, Superior Civilian Svc. award, 2001. Mem.: Am. Legion, KC. Avocations: travel, reading. Office: US Army Legal Svcs Agy 901 North Stuart St Ste 716 Arlington VA 22203-1837

MEISELES, DANIEL, sports association executive; m. Stephanie Meiseles. Grad., St. John's U. Assoc. prodr. NBC, 1988, NBA, NYC, 1990, sr. v.p. prodn. and programming, 2006—. Office: NBA Olympic Tower 645 5th Ave Fl 10 New York NY 10022-5986 *

MEISELS, GERHARD GEORGE, academic administrator, chemist, educator; b. Vienna, May 11, 1931; came to U.S., 1951, naturalized, 1961; s. Leo and Adele Josefa Maria (Seehofer) M.; m. Sylvia Claire Knopsnider, June 28, 1958; 1 dau., Laura Germaine. Student, U. Vienna, 1949-51, 52-53; MS, U. Notre Dame, Ind., 1952, PhD, 1956. Postdoctoral rsch. assoc. U. Notre Dame, 1955-56; chemist Gulf Oil Corp., Pitts., 1956-59; part-time instr. Carnegie Inst. Tech., Pitts., 1956-58; chemist nuclear divsn. Union Carbide Corp., Tuxedo, NY, 1959-63, asst. group leader, 1964-65; assoc. prof. U. Houston, 1965-70, prof., 1970-75, dept. chmn., 1973-75; prof., chmn. dept. chemistry U. Nebr., Lincoln, 1975-81, dean Coll. Arts and Scis., 1981-88; provost, COO U. South Fla., Tampa, 1988-94; dir. Coalition Sci. Literacy, 1994—, Suncoast Area Ctr. for Ednl. Enhancement (SACEE), 1996-99. Cons. Union Carbide Corp., Gearhart-Owen Industries. Editor (spl. issue) Jour. Radiation Physics and Chemistry, 1980; contbr. writings in field to profl. publs. Sec., pres. Ramsey (N.J.) Jr. C. of C., 1959-64; active rsch. bd. All Children's Hosp.; chmn. Fla. Coalition for Improving Math. and Sci. Edn., 1998—, interim exec. dir. Fulbright fellow, Smith-Mundt fellow, 1951-52; sr. fellow Sci. Rsch. Coun., Eng., 1976. Mem. Am. Chem. Soc. (com. chmn.), Am. Soc. for Mass Spectrometry (charter, com. chmn., v.p. 1984-86, pres. 1986-88, bd. dirs. 1988-90), Fla. Acad. Scis., AAAS, Am. Phys. Soc., Coun. Sci. Soc. Pres. (exec. bd. 1989-92, chmn. elect 1990, chmn. 1991, chmn. com. on sci. priorities), Nat. Alliance State Sci. and Math. Coalitions (bd. dirs. 1999—, v.p., 2007—), Coun. for Chem. Rsch. (bd. dirs. 1982-85), Conformation Judges Assn. Fla. (pres. 1996—), Fla. Higher Edn. Consortium Math. and Sci. (ctrl. steering com. 1995—, chmn. 1998-2000), Houston Kennel Club (bd. dirs. 1968-70), Cornhusker Kennel Club (pres., bd. dirs., del. to Am. Kennel Club 1976-88), St. Petersburg Dog Fanciers Assn. (sec. 1996-98, 2000-04, del. to Am. Kennel Club 1998—), Lakeland-Winter Haven K.C. (pres. 2006—), Sigma Xi. Home: PO Box 1347 Thonotosassa FL 33592-1347 Office: U South Fla 4202 E Fowler Ave/CHE 205 Tampa FL 33620 Office Phone: 813-974-7183. Business E-Mail: meisels@csl.usf.edu.

MEISELS, JUDITH A., pianist, music educator; b. Budapest, Hungary, July 23, 1938; came to U.S., 1957; d. Stephan and Margaret Benjamin; m. Irving M. Meisels, May 30, 1964; children: Jason D. Meisels, Adrienne C. Meisels. Diploma in piano performance, Buda Acad. Music and Budapest Conservatory of Music, Budapest, Hungary, 1950-54; student, Franz Liszt Acad. Music, Budapest, 1954-56; Matura diploma in Humanities and Natural Scis., Veres Palne Women's Gymnazium & Coll., Budapest, 1956; student, Bklyn. Coll., NYC, 1958-61; Piano pedagogy cert., New Sch. Music Studies, Princeton, NJ, 1977; postgrad., Westminster Choir Coll., Princeton, 1984—90. Cert. profl. tchr. music, N.J. Music Tchrs. Assn., nat. cert. profl. tchr. music Music Tchrs. Nat. Assn. Tchr. piano, theory and harmony, chamber music, music history and appreciation. Mem. exec. bd. rsch., planning and selecting internat. artists series, Spectrum Com., Monmouth County Arts Coun., 1980-85; cultural com., exec. bd. internat. concert and lecture series Monmouth County "Y", 1971-93; spkr., lectr. in field; panelist, conductor master classes Piano Tchrs.' Groups, NJ and N.Y.C., 1976-2006; adjudicator high level prestigious piano auditions and competitions. Piano performances: classical solo and ensemble Radio Budapest, Hungary, Ministerium of Fgn. Affairs, 1948-49, Franz Liszt Acad., Budapest, 1948-56, solo performances Hungary, Austria, U.S.A., 1954-56, 73-80. Grantee Franz Liszt Acad., 1956-57. Mem. Music Tchrs. Nat. Assn., N.J. Music Tchrs. Assn., Leschetizky Assn. N.Y., Piano Tchrs. Cong. N.Y., Nat. Guild Piano Tchrs., Shore Music Educators Assn.(exec. bd., publicity chair 1976-80, recording sec. 1987-93), Cecilian Music Club of Freehold, N.J. Avocations: power walking, swimming, reading, music, arts. Office Phone: 732-531-5042. Personal E-mail: jimeisels@aol.com.

MEISINGER, LOUIS M., lawyer; b. NYC, Dec. 12, 1942; BA, UCLA, 1964, JD, 1967. Bar: Calif. 1968. Atty. Hill Wynne Troop & Meisinger, LA; exec. v.p., gen. coun. Walt Disney Co., Burbank, Calif., 1997—2003; sr. advisor Sheppard, Mullin, Richter & Hampton, LLP, Los Angeles, Calif., 2003—. Editor: UCLA Law Rev., 1965-67. Recipient Entertainment Lawyer of the Yr., Beverly Hills Bar Assoc./ Calif., 1999. Mem. State Bar Calif., L.A. County Bar Assn., Century City Bar Assn., Order of Coif, Phi Beta Kappa, Sigma Delta Pi, Phi Delta Phi. Office: Sheppard Mullin Richter & Hampton 333 S Hope St Los Angeles CA 90071

MEISINGER, SUSAN, human resources specialist; BA, Mary Washington Coll.; JD, George Washington U. Cert. sr. profl. Human Resources Certification Inst. Spl. legal counsel Associated Builders and Contractors, Washington; dep. under sec. employment standards adminstrn. U.S. Dept. Labor, Washington; v.p. govt. and pub. affairs Soc. Human Resource Mgmt., Alexandria, Va., 1987—97, sr. v.p., 1997—99, exec. v.p., COO, 1999—2002, pres., CEO, 2002—. Mem.: DC Bar Assn. Office: Soc Human Resource Mgmt 1800 Duke St Alexandria VA 22314

MEISLIN, HARVEY WARREN, emergency healthcare physician, professional society administrator; b. Rochester, NY, June 19, 1946; s. Milton M. and Celia (Weiner) M.; m. Loretta Marie Bielski, Apr. 30, 1977; children: Justin, Jonathan, Megan. BS in Chemistry, Purdue U., 1968; MD, Ind. U., 1972. Diplomate Am. Bd. Emergency Medicine (chmn.), Am. Bd. Med. Spltys. (del. 1990, fin. com. 1992, exec. com. 1994); cert. cardiac life support, ACLS instr., advanced trauma life support instr. Intern U. Chgo. Hosps. and Clinics, 1973-75, resident, 1975-77, dir. div. emergency medicine, 1975-77; asst. prof. internal and emergency medicine UCLA Emergency Med. Ctr., 1977-80, resident dir. emergency medicine, 1977-80, assoc. dir., 1977-80; assoc. prof. dept. surgery emergency medicine Coll. Medicine, U. Ariz., Tucson, 1980-83, assoc. prof., 1983-85; assoc. head, dept. surgery U. Ariz., Tucson, 1995—; prof. Coll. Medicine, U. Ariz., Tucson, 1985—; chief emergency medicine U. Ariz., Tucson, 1980—; chief sect. emergency medicine dept. surgery Ariz. Health Scis. Ctr., Tuscon, 1980—, dir. emergency svcs. Univ. Med. Ctr., 1980—, dir. Ariz. Emergency Med. Rsch. Ctr., 1990—; med. dir. MEDTRAN-Aeromed. Ambulance Corp., 1985-88. Mem. emergency med. svc. com. Mid-South Health Planning Orgn., Chgo., 1974; coord. Mid-South Disaster Plan, Chgo., 1974; mem. com. revision of Disaster Plan Billings Hosp., 1974-76; mem. faculty Am. Hosp. Assn. Inst. Disaster Preparedness, 1975; vis. prof. dept. emergency medicine Denver Gen. Hosp., 1977; bd. trustees Emergency Med. Found., 1978-81; mem. med. adv. com. L.A. City Fire Dept., 1979-80; chmn.-elect Tuscon Met. EMS Coun., 1983-84, chmn., 1984-85; chmn. Tuscon Pre-Hosp. Care Coun., 1981; mem. trauma steering com. So. Ariz. Regional Trauma Ctr., 1986-88; mem. ETHICON emergency physicians adv. panel Johnson & Johnson Co., 1987-92; presenter and lectr. in field. Editor: Purdue Rivet, 1971-72, abstract sect. Annals Emergency Medicine, 1982-90, EMS sect., 1989-90; guest editor: Topics in Emergency Medicine, 1979; sci. editor: Drug Therapy, 1984—; mem. editorial bd.: Annals Emergency Medicine, 1977-90, Emergency Dept. News, 1979-87, Emergency Dept. and Ambulatory Care News, 1987-90, Digest of Emergency Medicine Care, 1981-87; contbr. articles and revs. to profl. jours. Mem. select med. adv. com. City of Tucson, 1981, med. dir. emergency med. svcs., 1982-83, 84-85; bd. dirs. so. Ariz. divsn. Am. Heart Assn., 1985-90; mem. emergency cardiac care com. so. divsn. Ariz. Heart Assn., 1986-88; mem. med. dirs. commn., dept. health svcs. State of Ariz., 1992—, also mem. Mex. border commn., 1991—; mem. med. direction commn. State of Ariz. (appointed by gov.), 1993—. Recipient Pres. gavel and plaque Am. Bd. Emergency Medicine. Fellow Am. Coll. Emergency Physicians (State of Ill. chpt.): mem. sci. adv. com. 1975, mem. sci. edn. com. 1975-76, mem. grad./undergrad. edn. com. 1976-79, mem. ethics com. 1976-77, mem. surgery/trauma task force bd. cert. exam. 1976-77, bd. dirs. 1976-77, chmn. edn. com. 1976-77; State of Calif. chpt.: mem. hosp. and contract com. 1978-79, mem. EMS and legis. com. 1978-79, mem. spl. task force on emergency dept. distbn. 1979-80, mem. membership com. 1979-80, mem. legis. com. 1979-80, mem. sci. assembly planning com. 1980-81, bd. dirs. 1979-81, mem. rsch. com. 1981; State of Ariz. chpt.: bd. dirs. 1982-92, 92—, chmn. pub. rels. com. 1982-83, v.p. and sec. 1983-84, counselor 1984-87, mem. credentials com. 1986-91, chmn. 1987-90, mem. test com. 1986-87, mem. ad hoc com. for combined tng. 1987-88, chmn. task force on emergency medicine 1987-89, mem. exec. com. 1988—, mem. fin. com. 1988—, sec./treas. 1989-90, mem. EMS com. 1990—, pres.-elect 1990-91, pres. 1991-92, chair stds. com., mem. faculty Nat. Sci. Assembly 1974-76, Cert. Appreciation award 1990); mem. APHA, Am. Coll. Physician Execs., Am. Trauma Soc., Am. Bd. Med. Specialties (mem. fin. com. 1992, mem. exec. com. 1995—, pres., 2004), Ariz. Med. Assn., Pima County Med. Soc. (bd. dirs. 1991—), Phi Rho Sigma. Avocations: racquetball, golf, skiing, automobiles. Office: U Ariz Med Ctr Sect Emergency Med 1501 N Campbell Ave Tucson AZ 85724-0001

MEISNER, JAY, plastic surgeon; s. George and Pauline Meisner; 4 children. BA, Columbia U., NYC, 1978, MA, 1979; MD, Mt. Sinai Sch. Medicine, NYC, 1983. Diplomate Am. Bd. Plastic Surgery, 1992, Am. Bd. Surgery, 1989, Nat. Bd. Med. Examiners. Pvt. practice plastic surgeon, NYC, 1991—; chief plastic surgery James J. Peters VA Med. Ctr., Bronx, NY, 1991—. Asst. clin. prof., plastic surgery Mt. Sinai Sch. Medicine, NYC, 1991—; attending plastic surgeon Beth Israel Med. Ctr., NYC, 1991—, Mt. Sinai Hosp., NYC, 1994—; lectr. in field. With (documentaries) Catherine's Story - The Learning Channel; contbr. articles to profl. jours. Exec. com. Octoberwoman Found. for Breast Cancer Rsch., Park Ridge, NJ, 2003—06; trustee Temple Beth Haverim, Mahwah, NJ, 1998—2000. Recipient Merck award for Clin. Excellence, Mt. Sinai Sch. Medicine, 1983, Tchr. of Yr. award, Mt. Sinai Plastic Surgery Tng. Program, 2000, 2006. Master: Upsilon Pi Epsilon (Delta chpt. v.p. 1979); fellow: ACS; mem.: NY Regional Soc. Plastic Surgeons, Am. Soc. Plastic Surgeons, Med. Soc. State NY. Achievements include research in cardiac surgery; plastic surgery. Avocations: computers, basketball. Office: 605 Park Ave New York NY 10021-7016 Home Phone: 201-818-1008; Office Phone: 212-794-1500.

MEISNER, MARY JO, foundation administrator, former newspaper editor; b. Chgo., Dec. 24, 1951; d. Robert Joseph and Mary Elizabeth (Casey) M.; 1 child, Thomas Joseph Gradel. BS in Journalism, U. Ill., 1974, MS in Journalism, 1976. Copy editor Wilmington (Del.) News Jour., 1975-76, labor and bus. reporter, 1976-79; labor and gen. assignment reporter Phila. Daily News, 1979, city editor, 1979-83, met. editor, 1983-85; PM city editor San Jose (Calif.) Mercury News, 1985-86, met. editor, 1986-87; city editor The Washington Post, 1987-90; mng. editor The Ft. Worth Star-Telegram, 1991-93; editor and v.p. The Milw. Jour., 1993-95; editor, sr. v.p The Milw. Jour. Sentinel, 1995-97; editor, vice chmn. Cmty. Newspaper Co., Needham, Mass., 1997—2001; v.p., comm., external affairs Boston Found., 2001—. Mem. AP Mng. Editors (bd. dirs. 1992-95), Am. Soc. Newspaper Editors, Internat. Press Inst. (bd. dirs 1994-2000, Pulitzer prize juror 1994, 96). Mass. Newspaper Pubs. Assn. (bd. dirs.); bd. dir., WorldBoston. Office: Boston Foundation 10th Fl 75 Arlington St Boston MA 02116 Business E-Mail: mjm@tbf.org.

MEISSNER, EDWIN BENJAMIN, JR., retired real estate broker; b. St. Louis, Dec. 27, 1918; s. Edwin B. and Edna (Rice) Meissner; m. Nina Renard, Dec. 17, 1946; children: Edwin Benjamin III, Wallace, Robert; 1 child, Donald. BS, U. Pa., Phila., 1940. Joined St. Louis Car Co., 1934, asst. to pres., v.p., exec. v.p., 1950-56, pres., gen. mgr., 1956-61; pres. St. Louis Car div. Gen. Steel Industries, Inc., 1961-67; sr. v.p., dir. Gen. Steel Industries, Inc., 1968-74; v.p. Bakewell Corp., 1974-85; real estate broker, v.p. Hilliker Corp., St. Louis, 1985-96. Mem. pres.' coun. St. Louis U.; bd. dirs. Washington U. Med. Ctr. Redevel. Corp., Barnard Free Skin and Cancer Hosp.; past bd. dirs. James S. McDonnell USO; overseer St. Louis Symphony Soc.; hon. dir. Humane Soc. Mo.; v.p. Gateway Ctr. Met. St. Louis; past chmn. Ladue Police and Fire Commn., Mo.; mem. Jefferson Nat. Expansion Meml. Commn.; mil. affairs com. Regional Commerce; dir. Ctrl. Inst. for Deaf. Mem. Am. Ordnance Assn. (life), Internat. Assn. Chiefs of Police (assoc.), Mo. Assn. Chiefs of Police, Mo. Athletics Club, Westwood Country Club, Bridlespur Hunt Club, St. Louis Club, Beta Gamma Sigma. Office: Barton Bldg Ste 302 200 S Bemiston Saint Louis MO 63105-1915 Office Phone: 314-863-2440.

MEISSNER, KATHERINE GONG, municipal official; b. Stockton, Calif., 1955; BA, U. Phoenix, Stockton, Calif., 1999. Mem. comty. planning dept. staff City of Stockton, Calif., 1982-85, exec. asst. city clk., 1985-96, city clk., 1996—. Office: City Stockton Office City Clk 425 N El Dorado St Stockton CA 95202-1997 Office Phone: 209-937-8458. Business E-Mail: city.clerk@ci.stockton.ca.us.

MEISSNER, MICHAEL G., lawyer; b. Panama City, Fla., 1954; BA cum laude, U. Notre Dame, 1976; JD cum laude, Harvard U., 1979. Bar: Ohio 1979, US Ct. of Fed. Claims, US Tax Ct. Mem. Squire, Sanders & Dempsey, Cleve., ptnr. Contbr. articles to profl. jours. Trustee and vice-chair Cleve. Coun. on World Affairs; trustee Tax Club Cleve. Mem. ABA (mem. sect. taxation), Tax Practitioners Cleve., Ohio State Bar Assn., Cleve. Bar Assn. (former chmn. gen. tax com.), former gen. chair Cleve. Tax Inst. Bd. editors: Harvard Law Review, 1979. Office: Squire Sanders & Dempsey 4900 Key Tower 127 Public Sq Ste 4900 Cleveland OH 44114-1304 Office Phone: 216-479-8593. Office Fax: 216-479-8780. E-mail: mmeissner@ssd.com.

MEISSNER, WALT, dean; BA, Texas A & M; MFA in theatre mgmt. & directing, Boston U. Assoc. dean-adminstr. affairs Boston U. Coll. Fine Arts, 1993—2001, acting dean, 2001—02, dean ad interim, 2002—. Office: Boston U Coll Fine Arts 855 Commonwealth Ave Room 230 Boston MA 02215 Office Fax: 617-353-3350. E-mail: cfadean@bu.edu.

MEISTER, BERNARD JOHN, retired chemical engineer; b. Maynard, Mass., Feb. 27, 1941; s. Benjamin C. and Gertrude M. Meister; m. Janet M. White, Dec. 31, 1971; children: Mark, Martin, Kay Ellen. BSChemE, Worcester Poly. Inst., 1962; PhD in Chem. Engring., Cornell U., 1966. From engring. rschr. to rsch. scientist Dow Chem. Co., Midland, Mich., 1966—92, rsch. scientist, 1992—2005, ret., 2005. Contbr. articles to profl. jours. Mem.: AIChE, Soc. Rheology, Soc. Plastic Engrs., Am. Chem. Soc., Sigma Xi. Methodist. Home: 2925 Chippewa Ln Midland MI 48640-4181 E-mail: bjjm1@aol.com. *Free the mind of things you can't change, and let it focus on things you can accomplish.*

MEISTER, JULIA B., lawyer; b. Ft. Thomas, Ky., Nov. 16, 1969; BA, Xavier U., 1991; JD, Notre Dame Law Sch., 1995. Bar: Ohio 1995, Ct. of Appeals Sixth Cir., US Dist. Ct. Southern Dist. Ohio, US Dist. Ct. Southern Dist. Ind. Ptnr. Taft, Stettinius & Hollister LLP, Cin. Mem. Bd. for Cin. Area Sr. Services. Named a Rising Star, YWCA Acad. Career Women of Achievement; named one of Ohio's Rising Stars, Super Lawyers, 2006; named to Best Lawyers in Am. Mem.: Cin. Bar Assn. (vice chair, Admissions Com., mem., Unauthorized Practice of Law Com.). Office: Taft Stettinius & Hollister LLP 425 Walnut St Ste 1800 Cincinnati OH 45202-3957 Office Phone: 513-357-9330.

MEISTER, MARK JAY, museum director, professional society administrator; b. Balt., June 26, 1953; s. Michael Aaron and Yetta (Haransky) M.; m. Carla Steiger, Aug. 7, 1977; children: Rachel, Kaitlin. AB, Washington

U., St. Louis, 1974; MA, U. Minn., 1976; cert. mus. mgmt., U. Calif., Berkeley, 1983. Asst. lectr. St. Louis Art Mus., 1974; asst. coord. young people's program Mpls. Inst. Arts, 1975—76, coord. mobile program, 1976, coord. tchrs. resource svcs., 1976—77; dir. Mus. Art and History, Port Huron, Mich., 1978—79, Midwest Mus. Am. Art, Elkhart, Ind., 1979—81; exec. dir. Children's Mus., St. Paul, 1981—86; dir. Mus. Art, Sci. and Industry, Bridgeport, Conn., 1986—89; exec. dir. Archaeol. Inst. of Am., Boston, 1989—99; exec. dir. Archl. Inst. Am. Inst. Archeologique d'Amerique, Boston and Toronto, 1994—99; exec. dir. Dayton Soc. Natural History, 2000—06, pres., CEO, 2006—. Adj. lectr. museology Kenyon Coll., Gambier, Ohio, 1977; adj. lectr. art history Ind. U., South Bend, 1980—81; regional reviewer Inst. Mus. Svcs., Washington, 1985—86, Washington, 1989; treas., vice chmn. Minn. Assn. Mus., St. Paul, 1983—86; ex-officio trustee U.S. com. Internat. Coun. on Monuments and Sites, 1995—99. Bd. dirs. Seaway Arts Coun., St. Clair County, Mich., 1978-79; bd. dirs. Dayton Sister Cities Com., 2000-05, chair, 2003-05; bd. dirs. Dayton Peace Accords Project, 2000-05, vice chair, 2003; bd. dirs. Glen Helen Ecology Inst., 2003—2007, Dayton Coun. on World Affairs, 2005-, pres.-elect 2006-; Greater Dayton Pub. TV, 2006-07, cmty. advisor bd, 2007-; mem. Mayor's Arts Adv. Com., Elkhart, 1981; mem. exec. com., Conf. Adminstrv. Officers, Am. Coun. Learned Socs., 1994-97; pres. Asian Arts Ctr., Dayton, 2002-05; bd. trustees, Dayton: A Peace Process, 2004-, co-chair, 2007-; Prevent Blindness Ohio, Dayton chpt. leadership coun., 2004—, chmn., 2006-. NEH museology fellow, Mpls. Inst. Arts, 1976-77, Kress fellow U. Minn. 1977-78, Bush leadership summer fellow, Bush Found., St. Paul, 1983; named One of Outstanding Young Men Am., 1981. Mem.: Archaeological Conservancy, Assn. Children's Mus., Ohio Mus. Assn., Assn. Sci. and Tech. Ctrs., Assn. Zoos and Aquariums, Assn. Sci. Mus. Dirs., Archaeological Inst. Am., Am. Assn. Mus. Office: Dayton Soc Natural History 2600 Deweese Pkwy Dayton OH 45414-5499 Business E-Mail: mmeister@boonshoftmuseum.org.

MEISTER, PAUL M., medical products executive; BA, Univ. Mich., 1974; MBA, Northwestern Univ., 1976. Mng. dir. Henley, 1986—92; sr. v.p. Abex, Inc., 1992—95; sr. v.p., CFO Fisher Sci. Internat., Hampton, NH, 1995—98, exec. v.p., CFO, 1998—2001, vice chmn., 1998—2006; chmn. Thermo Fisher Scientific, Waltham, Mass., 2006—. Bd. dir. M & F Worldwide Corp., Minerals Tech., Inc., Nat. Waterworks, Inc., LKQ Corp. Office: Thermo Fisher Scientific 81 Wyman St Waltham MA 02454 *

MEITNER, PAMELA, lawyer, educator; b. Phila., Aug. 23, 1950; d. Alfred Victor Meitner and Claire Jane (Carroll) Harmer; m. William Bruce Larson, Sept. 13, 1980; 1 child, William Bruce, Jr. BS in chem. engring., Drexel U., 1973; JD, Del. Law Sch., 1977. Bar: Del. 1977, U.S. Dist. Ct. Del. 1977, U.S. Patent and Trademark Office 1977. Engr. DuPont Co., Deepwater, N.J., 1973-77, lawyer Wilmington, Del., 1977. Prof. Del. Law Sch., Wilmington, 1985-89. Commr. State Emergency Response Com., Dover, Del., 1986-90, 97—. Mem. Del. Bar Assn. Clubs: DuPont Country (Wilmington) (bd. govs. 1984-85). Home: 211 Welwyn Rd Wilmington DE 19803-2951 Office: DuPont Co Legal Dept 1007 S Market St Wilmington DE 19801-5227 Home Phone: 302-654-2097; Office Phone: 302-774-8720. Business E-Mail: pamela.meitner@usa.dupont.com.

MEJIA, BARBARA OVIEDO, retired chemistry professor; b. San Francisco, Apr. 14, 1946; d. Louis Jerome and Alice May (Beall) O. AA, Sierra Coll., 1967; BS, U. Calif., Davis, 1969, PhD, 1973. Cert. community coll. tchr., Calif. Lectr. U. Calif., Davis, summer 1977, Calif. State U., Chico, 1973-76, asst. prof., 1976-80, assoc. prof., 1980-85, prof., 1985—2001, emeritus, 2001—. Contbr. articles to profl. jours. Judge Calif. Cen. Valley Sci.-Engring. Fair, Chico, 1977, 89, 81, 81, 88, bd. dirs., 1978-79; judge Butte County Sci. Fair, Chico, 1985-90. Mem. AAAS, Am. Chem. Soc., Congress of Faculty Assns., Cal Aggie Alumni Assn., Assn. Calif. State Univ. Profs., Sigma Xi. Home: 6 Laguna Ct Chico CA 95928-7431 Office: Calif State U Dept Chemistry Chico CA 95929-0001 Business E-Mail: Bmejia@csuchico.edu.

MEJIA, JOSE A., telecommunications industry executive; b. Venezuela; married; 2 children. BS in Indsl. and Ops. Engring., U. Mich.; MBA in Fin. and Ops. Rsch., Duke U. With IBM, Ford Motor Co.; v.p. supplier mgmt. Bay Networks, Inc., Calif., 1996—98; v.p. external mfg. strategy Nortel Networks (formerly Bay Networks), 1999; joined Lucent Techs., Murray Hill, NJ, 1999, chief procurement officer, 1999—2000, v.p. and chief supply chain officer, 2000—01, pres. supply chain networks, 2001—. Named Engr. of Yr., Hispanic Engr. Nat. Achievement Awards Corp., 2003; named one of Top 25 Execs. That Made A Difference, Electronic Buyer News, 1997, 50 Most Important Hispanics in Tech. & Bus., Hispanic Engr. & Info. Tech. mag., 2005. Office: Lucent Techs 600 Mountain Ave New Providence NJ 07974

MEKEEL, ROBERT K., lawyer; b. Ossining, NY, Mar. 21, 1950; s. Ira III and Carmen E. (Munson) M.; m. Martha J. Keller, Sept. 29, 1979; 1 child, Meryl Fox. BA, Wesleyan U., Middletown, Conn., 1972; JD, U. Puget Sound, 1978. Bar: NH 1978, NY 1979, US Dist. Ct. (so. dist.) NY 1980, US Ct. Appeals (2d cir.) 1981, US Dist. Ct. NH 1983, US Ct. Appeals (1st cir.) 1983. Asst. dist. atty. Westchester County NY Dist. Atty., White Plains, NY, 1979-82; assoc. Craig Wenners & McDowell, Manchester, NH, 1983-84; clk. ct. Coos County Superior Ct., Lancaster, NH, 1985; ptnr. McKible & Mekeel, P.A., Concord, NH, 1986-89, Cullity Kelley & McDowell, Manchester, NH, 1989-93, McDowell & Mekeel P.A., Manchester, 1994-96; prin. Robert K. Mekeel, P.A., Concord, 1996—. Mem. mentor program Franklin Pierce Law Sch., Concord, 1992; lectr. Nat. Bus. Inst., Eau Claire, Wis., 1993-95; mem. Million Dollar Advocates forum; mediator NH Superior Cts.; pvt. mediator, arbitrator disputes involving personal injury claims, pvt. mediation svcs. Coach Hopkinton Lacrosse Club, NH, 2002—03. Fellow NH Bar Found., NH Bar Assn. (com. on cooperation with cts., lectr. evidence seminar 1994), Coös County Bar Assn. Democrat. Avocations: running, biking, swimming, drawing, wood working. Office: Old Coos County Courthouse 148 Main St 3d Fl Lancaster NH 03584-3059 Home: 91 Mt Prospect Rd Lancaster NH 03584-3305 Office Phone: 603-788-4455. Business E-Mail: mekeelaw@usa.net.

MEKKAWI, MOHAMED, library director; BA, U. Paris; diploma in Econ. and Social Devel. Planning, Inst. Planning and Devel.; MA in Polit. Sci., Am. U. Beirut; MLS, U. Pitts.; MA cum laude, Georgetown U. Joined Howard U. Librs., Washington, 1972, dir., 1994—. Bd. mem. Chesapeake Info. and Rsch. Libr. Alliance (CIRLA). Contbr. articles to profl. jours. Office: Howard U Librs 500 Howard Place, NW Washington DC 20059 Office Fax: 202-806-7234. E-mail: mmekkawi@howard.edu. *

MEKLER, L. ARLEN, lawyer, chemist; b. NYC, May 4, 1943; s. Lev A. and Ethel (Fox) M.; children from previous marriage: Jeffrey Arlen, Rebecca Ann, Ann-Marie Laura, Victoria Arlene, Lamar Adam, Lars Arlen; m. Molly L. Malone, Feb. 3, 1995. BS in Chemistry, Reed Coll.-San Jose State U., 1953; MS in Organic Chemistry, Iowa State U., 1955; PhD, Ohio State U., 1958; JD, Temple U., 1972. Bar: Del. 1972, Pa. 1972, U.S. Supreme Ct. 1976. Sr. rsch. chemist E.I. du Pont de Nemours & Co., Wilmington, Del., 1958-69; ptnr. Mekler and Maurer, Wilmington, 1972—. Chief appellate div. Office Pub. Defender, State of Del., 1973-77; pres. Del. Law Ctr., Wilmington, 1973—; instr. constl. law Wilmington Coll., 1976-80; dir. Bar Rev. Del., 1972—; mem. 3d Circuit Ct. Appeal Jud. Nominating Commn., 1977-81, 3d Circuit Ct. Appeals Jud. Conf. Contbr. monographs to legal publs. Pres. Mental Health Aux. for Gov. Bacon Health Ctr., 1964-66; mem. Citizens Conf. for Modernization of State Legislatures, 1964-68; state chmn., Reform Commn. for Modernization Polit. Party Rules, 1965-68; pres. Del. Citizens for Fair Housing, 1965-69; state commr. Nat. Conf. on Uniform State Laws, 1972—; pres. Democratic Forum Del., 1966-70; mem. Del. Dem. Platform Com., 1966, 68, 72, 76; research dir. Del. Citizens for Humphrey-Muskie, 1968, Citizens for Biden, 1972, 78, 84, Citizens for McDowell, 1986—, Biden for Pres., 1986, 2005; del. Dem. Nat. Conv., 1980; mem. social action com. Unitarian Ch., Wilmington, 1962-68. Recipient Keyman award, 1964, 65; State Govtl. Affairs award, 1964, 65 Mem. ABA, Del. Bar Assn. (com. on rules of criminal procedure 1973-74, supreme ct. com. on revision of criminal law 1973—, supreme ct. com. on rules of evidence 1976—, com. on revised rules of evidence 1976—, com. on revised rules of Del. Supreme Ct. 1974—, family law com. 1979—, continuing legal edn. com. 1981—), Pa. Bar Assn., Am. Chem. Soc., N.Y. Acad. Scis., Chem. Soc. (London), AAAS, Catalyst Club Phila., Wilmington Organic Chemists Club, ACLU (bd. dirs.), Sigma Xi, Phi Alpha Delta Home: Brandywine Hills 714 W Matson Run Pky Wilmington DE 19802-1912 Office: Del Law Ctr Inc 1216 N King St Ste 100 Wilmington DE 19801-3237 Home Phone: 302-762-4008; Office Phone: 302-498-5297. Business E-Mail: drlaw@comcast.net.

MEKONNEN, ADEME, meteorologist; s. Mekonnen Aberra and Tiru-ihil Bizuneh; 1 child, Nathnael Ademe. BSc, Addis Ababa U., Ethiopia, 1986; MSc, U. Reading, Eng., 1998; PhD, U. Albany, NY, 2007. Cert. Indian Meteorol. Dept., 1990, Israel Meteorol. Dept., 1991. Asst. meteorologist Ethiopian Meteorol. Svcs., Addis Ababa, 1986—91, meteorologist, forecaster, 1992—96, lectr., 1994—2000, sr. meteorologist, 1997—2000; rsch. asst. U. Albany, 2001—. Co-author: Handbook on Methods for Climate Change Impacts Assessment and Adaptation Strategies; editor: Ethiopian Communication to the UN (cert. Appreciation for Valuable Contbn. in Climate Change Rsch., 2001). Mem. Ethiopian Red Cross, Addis Ababa, 1990—94. Mem.: Am. Geophys. Union, Ethiopian Meterol. Soc., Ethiopian Phys. Soc., Am. Meteorol. Soc., Ethiopian Econ. Soc. (assoc.). Office: U Albany Atmospheric Sci 1400 Washington Ave Albany NY 12222 Office Phone: 518-442-4569. Personal E-mail: ademe_mekonnen@yahoo.com.

MELAMED, ARTHUR DOUGLAS, lawyer; b. Mpls., Dec. 3, 1945; s. Arthur Charles and Helen Beatrix (Rosenberg) M.: m. Carol Drescher Weisman, May 26, 1983; children: Kathryn Henrie, Elizabeth Allyn. BA, Yale U., 1967; JD, Harvard U., 1970. Bar: D.C. 1970, U.S. Ct. Internat. Trade 1985, U.S. Ct. Appeals (9th cir.) 1971, U.S. Ct. Appeals (2d cir.) 1975, U.S. Ct. Appeals (D.C. cir.) 1978, U.S. Ct. Appeals (8th cir.) 1981, U.S. Ct. Appeals (fed. cir.) 1985, U.S. Ct. Appeals (4th cir.) 1989, U.S. Ct. Appeals (10th cir.) 1993, U.S. Supreme Ct. 1981. Law clk. U.S. Ct. Appeals for 9th Circuit, 1970-71; assoc. Wilmer, Cutler, Pickering, Hale & Dorr, Washington, 1971-77, ptnr., 1978-96, 2001—, co-chmn. Antitrust & Competition dept.; prin. dep. asst. atty. gen. U.S. Dept. Justice, 1996-2000, acting asst. atty. gen. antitrust divsn., 2000-2001. Vis. prof. Georgetown U. Law Ctr., 1992-93, adj. prof., 1993-94. Editor, Harvard Law Rev.; contbr. articles to profl. jours. Mem. coun. Yale U., 2006—; trustee Nat. Child Rsch. Ctr., 1990-93, Sidwell Friends Sch., 2000— Mem. ABA, Am. Law Inst., Yale Club (N.Y.C.), Kenwood Country Club. Office: Wilmer Cutler Pickering Hale & Dorr 1875 Pennsylvania Ave NW Washington DC 20006 Office Phone: 202-663-6090. Office Fax: 202-663-6363. Business E-Mail: doug.melamed@wilmerhale.com.

MELAMED, LEO, global consulting firm executive; b. Bialystok, Poland, Mar. 20, 1932; arrived in U.S., 1941, naturalized, 1950; s. Isaac M. and Fayga (Barakin) M.; m. Betty Sattler, Dec. 26, 1953; children: Idelle Sharon, Jordan Norman, David Jeffrey. Student, U. Ill., 1950-52, LittD (hon.), 1999; JD, John Marshall Law Sch., Chgo., 1955. Bar: Ill. 1955. Sr. ptnr. Melamed, Kravitz & Verson, Chgo., 1956-66; chmn., CEO Dellsher Investment Co., 1965—93, Sakura Dellsher, Inc., Chgo., 1993—2000, Melamed & Assoc., Inc., Chgo., 1993—2002; co-chmn. Stevenson, Melamed and Assocs., Chgo., 2002—, Hua Mei Capital Co., 2005—, Stevenson, Melamed and Assocs., 2002—. Mem. Chgo. Merc. Exch., 1953—. mem. bd. govs., 1967—91, chmn. emeritus, 1991—, chmn. bd., 1969—71, 1975—77, chmn. exec. com., 1985—91, also spl. counsel, apptd. sr. policy advisor, 1997—; chmn. bd. Internat. Monetary Market, 1972—75, spl. counsel, 1976—91; mem. Chgo. Bd. Trade, 1969—; mem. corp. adv. bd. U. Ill., Chgo., 1991—; mayor Chgo. Coun. Manpower and Econ. Advisors, 1972; adv. coun. mem. Grad. Sch. Bus. U. Chgo., 1980—, Leo Melamed endowed chair future markets, 1991; hon. prof. Renmin U., Beijing, 2003; hon. dean Derivatives Sch. Peking U., China, 2007. Author: (sci. fiction novel) The Tenth Planet, 1987, Leo Melamed on the Markets, 1993, Escape to the Futures, 1996; editor: The Merits of Flexible Exchange Rates, 1988. Mem. bd. trustees John Marshall Law Sch., 1991—; coun. mem. US Holocaust Meml. Mus., 1992—, dir. Named Man Yr., Israel Bonds, 1975; recipient Human Rights medallion, Am. Jewish Com., 1991, Lifetime Achievement award, Anti-Defamation League, 2001; Betty and Leo Melamed Rsch. scholar biomed. rsch., Weizmann Inst. Sci., 1998, Leo Melamed fellow in internat. bus. and trade law, John Marshall Law Sch., 2000. Fellow: Internat. Assn. Fin. Engrs. (sr.); mem.: ABA, Chgo. Bar Assn., Ill. Bar Assn., Am. Judicature Soc., Nat. Futures Assn. (chmn. 1982—89, spl. advisor 1989—), Am. Contract Bridge League (life master), Standard Club, Union League Club, Econs. Club Chgo. Avocations: writing, jogging, bridge. Office: Melamed & Assocs Inc 10 S Wacker Dr Ste 3275 Chicago IL 60606-7442 Office Phone: 312-930-3310. Business E-Mail: lmelamed@melamedassoc.com. E-mail: lm@sdinet.com.

MELANCON, CHARLES, congressman; b. Napoleonville, La., Oct. 3, 1947; s. Joe and Brownie Melancon; m. Alida (Peachy) Clark; children: Charles, Claire. BS, Univ. Southwestern La. Owner Melancon Ins. Agy.; mem. La. Ho. Rep., 1987—93; pres. Am. Sugar Cane League, 1993—2004; mem. US Congress from 3rd La. dist., 2005—. Mem. La. State Dem. Ctrl. Com., 1987—93. Chmn. LSU Agr. Devel. Council; vice chmn. La. Econ. Council. Recipient Outstanding Legislator award, La. Municipal Assn., Disting. Svc. award, La. Restaurant Assn., 1990. Mem.: Ducks Unlimited, UL Lafayette Alumni Assn. Democrat. Roman Catholic. Office: US Ho Reps 404 Cannon Ho Office Bldg Washington DC 20515-1803 Office Phone: 202-225-4031. Office Fax: 202-225-3944. *

MELANÇON, RENÉE M., lawyer; b. Lakenheath, Eng., May 23, 1971; BS cum laude, U. Fla., 1992; MS, U. Ariz., 1997, JD magna cum laude, 1997. Bar: Tex. 2002. Jud. law clk. to Hon. Robert E. Jones US Dist. Ct. (dist. Oreg.), 1998—99; jud. law clk. to Hon. Martha Craug Daughtrey US Ct. Appeals (6th cir.), 2000—01; assoc. appellate sect. Baron & Budd, P.C., Dallas. Contbr. articles to profl. publs. Named a Rising Star, Tex. Super Lawyers mag., 2006. Mem.: Dallas Bar Assn., Dallas Trial Lawyers Assn., Tex. Trial Lawyers Assn., Trial Lawyers for Pub. Justice, Am. Trial Lawyers Assn., ABA, Phi Beta Kappa. Office: Baron & Budd PC 3102 Oak Lawn Ave Ste 1100 Dallas TX 75219 Office Phone: 214-521-3605. *

MELANI, KENNETH R., insurance company executive; MD, Bowman Gray Sch. of Med., NC, 1979. Pres., CEO West Penn Cares Inc.; pres. Keystone Health Plan West; with Highmark Inc., Pittsburgh, 1989—, exec. v.p. strategic bus. devel. and health services, pres., CEO, 2003—. Mem.: Am. Coll. of Physician Executives, Am. Soc. of Internal Med., Penn. Soc. of Internal Med., Am. Med. Assn., Penn. Med. Soc., Allegheny County Med. Soc. Office: Highmark Inc 120 5th Ave Pittsburgh PA 15222-3099 Office Phone: 412-544-7000.

MELANSON, DOROTHY, political organization administrator; b. Boston, Sept. 21, 1953; AS, Westbrook Coll., Maine, 1980. Com. woman Maine Dem. Nat., Maine, 1996; chairwoman Dem. Com., Cumberland County, Maine, 1996—2002; com. woman Maine Dem. Nat., Maine, 2000; Presdl. Elector Maine, 2000; com. woman Maine Dem. Nat., 2001—03; chairwoman Maine Dem. Party, 2003—; registered nurse Maine Med. Ctr., Maine. A longtime dem. party activist.

MELBINGER, MICHAEL S., lawyer; b. Chgo., Sept. 5, 1958; s. Donald G. and Joyce A. (Haynes) M.; m. Karen Mary Melbinger, June 16, 1984; children: Peter Donald, Charlotte Anna, Lucy Grace. BA, U. Notre Dame, 1980; JD, U. Ill., 1983. Bar: Ill., 1983. Assoc. McDermott, Will & Emery, Chgo., 1983-88, ptnr., 1989-93; ptnr., head employee benefits dept. Schiff, Hardin & Waite, Chgo., 1993—97; ptnr., chmn. employee benefits and exec. compensation Winston & Strawn LLP, Chgo., 1997—. William M. Trumbull adj. prof. law Northwestern U.; author, speaker Coll. for Fin. Planning, Denver, 1990—. Mem. editorial bd. Practical Tax Strategies, Taxation for Lawyers, N.Y.C., 1989—, Employee Benefits Counselor, 1993—, Pension Management, 1995—; author Executive Compensation, 2004, author: Employee Benefit Trust Compliance Manual; contbr. articles to profl. jours. Pro bono Adoptive Families Am., Adoption Advocates. Mem. ABA, Nat. Assn. Stock Plan Profls. Home: 2699 Independence Ave Glenview IL 60025-7730 Office: Winston & Strawn LLP 35 W Wacker Dr Chicago IL 60601-9703 Office Phone: 312-558-7588. Office Fax: 312-558-5700. E-mail: mmelbinger@winston.com.

MELBOURNE, ROBERT ERNEST, civil engineer; b. Oceanside, Calif., July 17, 1929; s. Thomas Powell and Helen Millicent (Plausse) M.; m. Jeanne Edith Kuhn, Apr. 8, 1961; children: Ann Teresa Farley, Maria Helen Hayes, Steven Thomas, Louise Clare Vance. BSCE, U. So. Calif., 1951, PhD in History, 1996; MSCE, Stanford U., 1955; MA in History, U. San Diego, 1990. Registered civil engr., Calif. Engr. Morrison-Knudsen Co., Boise, Noxon, Mont., 1955-57, J.E. Haddock Ltd., Pasadena, Calif., 1957-58; pres. R.E. Melbourne Co. Inc., San Luis Rey, Calif., 1958-66; engr. constrn. and design, chief engr. San Diego County Water Authority, San Diego, 1966-90; mil. historian in pvt. practice, 1990—. Mem. adv. bd. Colorado River Bd., L.A., 1967-83. Commr. Oceanside Historic Preservation, 1997—. Lt. USN, 1951-54, PTO. Fellow ASCE; mem. U.S. Naval Inst., Soc. Mil. History, Navy League of U.S., Marine Corps Heritage Found. Republican. Roman Catholic. Home: PO Box 9 San Luis Rey CA 92068-0009

MELBY, DONNA D., lawyer; b. 1950; BA, U. Calif., Santa Barbara, 1972; attended, Loyola U. Sch. Law, 1977—78, Calif. Western Sch. Law, 1975—77, JD, 1978. Bar: Calif. 1979. Ptnr. Sonnenschein Nath & Rosenthal LLP, LA, 2002—05, Paul, Hastings, Janofsky & Walker, LA. Mem. Calif. Judicial Selection Adv. Coun., 2004. Named one of The Most Influential & Talented Women Trial Lawyers in Calif., LA Daily Jour. & San Francisco Recorder, 2002—06, 16 leading litigators in the US, Minority Corp. Counsel Assn., 2004, The 100 Most Influential Attorneys in State of Calif., LA Daily Jour. & San Francisco Recorder, 2004, The 50 Most Influential Women Lawyers in Am., Nat. Law Jour., 2007; named to Top 5% So. Calif. Super Lawyers, LA Mag., 2003—06; recipient Rothchild Pro Bono Award, Sonnenschein Nath & Rosenthall LLP, 2004. Fellow: Internat. Soc. Barristers, Am. Coll. Trial Lawyers; mem.: Fed. Bar Assn., Women Lawyers of LA, Calif. Women Lawyers, Assn. Bus. Trial Lawyers, Assn. So. Calif. Def. Counsel, Def. Rsch. Inst. (labor & employment com.), Fedn. Def. and Corp. Counsel, Internat. Assn. Def. Counsel (faculty mem. trial sch.), Am. Bd. Trial Advocates (faculty mem. trial sch. 1993—, mem. bd. dirs. 1994—, mem. found. bd. trustees 2001—, v.p. 2003, pres.-elect 2004, pres. 2005, pres. LA chpt. 2004, Guardian of Constitution award), Chancery Club. Office: Paul Hastings Janofsky & Walker 515 S Flower St 25th Fl Los Angeles CA 90071 Office Phone: 213-683-6098. Office Fax: 213-996-3098. *

MELBY, EDWARD CARLOS, JR., veterinarian; b. Burlington, Vt., Aug. 10, 1929; s. Edward C. and Dorothy H. (Folsom) M.; m. Jean Day File, Aug. 15, 1953; children: Scott E., Susan J., Jeffrey T., Richard A. Student, U. Pa., 1948—50; DVM, Cornell U., 1954. Diplomate Am. Coll. Lab. Animal Medicine. Practice vet. medicine, Middlebury, Vt., 1954-62; instr. lab. animal medicine Johns Hopkins U. Sch. Medicine, Balt., 1962-64, asst. prof., 1964-66, assoc. prof., 1966-71, prof., dir. div. comparative medicine, 1971-74; prof. medicine, dean Coll. Vet. Medicine, Cornell U., Ithaca, NY, 1974-84; v.p. R & D SmithKline Beecham Animal Health, 1985-90, v.p. sci. and tech. assessment, 1990-91; ind. cons., 1992—. Cons. VA, NRC, NIH. Author: Handbook of Laboratory Animal Science, Vols. I, II, III, 1974-76. Served with USMC, 1946-48. Mem. Am., N.Y. State, Md., Pa. Vet. Med. Assns., Am. Assn. Lab. Animal Sci., Am. Coll. Lab. Animal Medicine, AAAS, Phi Zeta. Home: PO Box 248 Charlotte VT 05445-0248 Office: 736 Lime Kiln Rd Charlotte VT 05445-9141 Home Phone: 802-985-3368; Office Phone: 802-985-3368. Personal E-mail: ecmelby@verizon.net.

MELBY, JOHN B., composer, educator; b. Whitehall, Wis., Oct. 3, 1941; s. John B. Sr. and Margaret (Edmundson) M.; m. Carol A. Wurtz, July 7, 1961 (div. 1977); 1 child, John; m. Jane H. Thompson, June 15, 1978; children: Kirsten, Charles. MusB, Curtis Inst., 1966; MA, U. Pa., 1967; MFA, Princeton U., 1971, PhD, 1972. Assoc. prof. West Chester (Pa.) U., 1971-73; prof. music U. Ill., Urbana, 1973-97, prof. emeritus, 1997—. Assoc. U. Ill. Ctr. for Advanced Studies, 1989-90. Composer numerous mus. works for live performers, computer-synthesized tape, vocal, chamber, choral and orchestral works including 2 symph., works pub. by Associated Music Pubs., Merion Music, Inc.; recs. on Composers Recs., Inc., New World Records, Advance Records, Centaur Records, Zuma Records. Recipient 1st prize 7th Internat. Electroacoustic Music Awards, Bourges, France, 1979, Am. Acad./Inst. Arts and Letters award, 1984; Guggenheim fellow, 1983. Mem.: ACLU, Am. Composers Alliance (bd. govs.), Am. Music Ctr., Broadcast Music Inc., Herpetologists' League, Am. Atheists, Green Party. Avocations: railroading, cooking, herpetology. Home: 5 Walter St Salem MA 01970-2518 E-mail: jbmelby@johnmelby.com.

MELBY, THOMAS EDWIN, clinical virologist, medical writer; s. James Melby and Cheryl Mackrell. BS, Ea. Mich. U., Ypsilanti, 1994; MS, Duke U., Durham, NC, 1998. Rsch. assoc. Glaxo Wellcome, NC, 1999—2001; sr. scientist, clin. virology Trimeris, Inc., Morrisville, NC, 2001—. Rsch. Fellowship, NSF, 1995—98, James B. Duke Fellowship, Duke U., 1995—98. D-Liberal. Achievements include research in HIV coreceptor use and pathogenesis. Avocation: gardening. Office: Trimeris Inc 3500 Paramount Pkwy Morrisville NC 27560 Home Phone: 919-323-6292; Office Phone: 919-408-5049. Business E-Mail: tmelby@trimeris.com.

MELCHER, ELIZABETH, musician; b. Phoenixville, Pa., Oct. 1, 1965; d. William Diehl Lober and Caroline Merroth Melcher; 1 child, Amy Elizabeth Winger. MusB, The Curtis Inst. Music, 1987; MusM, The Juilliard Sch., 1990; DMA, Eastman Sch. Music, 1994. Fellow in ch. music Christ and St. Stephen's Episc. Ch., NYC, 1988—89; asst. organist Brick Presbyn. Ch., NYC, 1989—90; organist/choirmaster Ch. of Ascension, Rochester, NY, 1991—94; min. music Ascension Luth. Ch., Balt., 1994—97; dir. music The Luth. Ch. St. Andrew, Silver Spring, 1997—2001; min. music The Ch. Good Shepherd, Burke, Va., 2001—03; organist/choirmaster Grace and Holy Trinity Episc. Ch., Richmond, Va., 2003—. Asst. organist John Wanamaker Grand Ct. Organ, Phila., 1985—87; pvt. tchr. organ and piano, 1999—. Organist: CD recording Pageant, 2001. Recipient 2d prize, Naples (Fla.) Internat. Organ Festival Competition, 1993, Arthur Poister Nat. Organ Competition, 1995, 1988. Mem.: Am. Guild Organists (recitalist, adjudicator various competitions, 1st prize Nat. Young Artists Competition, Region III 1991, Finalist Nat. Young Artists Competition 1996, 1992). Avocations: tennis, swimming, reading, concerts, travel. Office: Grace and Holy Trinity Episc Church 8

North Laurel St Richmond VA 23220-4797 Home Phone: 804-282-4159; Office Phone: 804-359-5628 ext. 20. Office Fax: 804-353-2348. Business E-Mail: emelcher@ghtc.org.

MELCHER, JOE A., audiologist, educator; b. Slaton, Tex., Dec. 19, 1943; s. Louie A. and Iris A. Melcher; life ptnr. Glenn L. Jones. BA, Tex. Tech U., Lubbock, 1965; MA, Tex. Tech. U., Lubbock, 1966; PhD, La. State U., Baton Rouge, 1973. Cert. clin. competency in audiology Am. Speech Lang. Hearing Assn., 1981. Prof. Xavier U. of La., New Orleans, 1970—, chmn. dept. comm. Mem. Human Rights Campaign, Gay, Lesbian, Straight Educators Network; bd. dirs. Parents, Family and Friends of Lesbians and Gays, New Orleans. Recipient Scholar-Mentor award, Nat. Black Assn. for Speech Lang. Hearing, 2005, Cmty. Spirit award for edn., Met. Cmty. Ch., 2003; Freeman fellow, Salzburg Seminar, 2002, Minority Biomedical Rsch. Support grantee, NIH, 1983—91, Edn. Enhancement grantee, La. Bd. of Regents, 1994, 1995, 2005. Fellow: Am. Acad. Audiology, Am. Speech Lang. Hearing Assn. (mem. bd. multicultural issues 2001—03, Dr. Jeanette Laguaite award for contbns. to higher edn. 2003); mem.: Lesbian, Gay Audiologist and Speech Pathologists (co-chair 1995—97), Nat. Acad. Pre-Profl. Programs in Comm. Scis. and Disorders (pres. 1988—89), La. Speech Lang. Hearing Assn. (pres. 1985, Honors of Assn. 1988). Office: Xavier Univ of Louisiana # 1 Drexel Dr New Orleans LA 70125 Home Phone: 504-944-6013; Office Phone: 504-520-5099. Business E-Mail: jmelcher@xula.edu.

MELCHIOR, IB JORGEN, scriptwriter, author, film director; b. Copenhagen, Sept. 17, 1917; arrived in U.S., 1938; s. Lauritz Lebrecht Hommel and Inger Thora (Nathansen) M.; m. Harriet Hathaway Kale, Mar. 15, 1942 (div. 1960); 1 child, Leif; m. Cleo Baldon, Jan. 18, 1964; stepchild, Dirk Arin. Degree, Stenhus Kostskole, Denmark, 1936; Cand.Phil, U. Copenhagen, 1937. Actor, stage mgr., co-dir. English Players, Paris, 1937—39; stage mgr. Radio City Music Hall, Ctr. Theater, NYC, 1941—42; actor, writer NYC, 1946—49; assoc. dir. CBS-TV, NYC, 1949—50; dir. Perry Como Show, NYC, 1951—54; assoc. prodr. G-L Enterprises, NYC, 1952—53; screenwriter, dir., novelist, 1957—. Author: (novels) Order of Battle, 1973, Sleeper Agent, 1975, The Haigerloch Project, 1977, The Watchdogs of Abaddon, 1979, The Marcus Device, 1980, The Tombstone Cipher, 1983, Eva, 1984, V-3, 1985, Code Name: Grand Guignol, 1987, (biography) Quest, 1990, Order of Battle: Hitler's Werewolves, 1991, (autobiography) Case by Case, 1993; author: (with Cleo Baldon) Steps & Stairways, 1989, Reflections on the Pool, 1997, Lauritz Melchior: The Golden Years of Bayreuth, 2003; screenwriter Live Fast, Die Young, 1957, The Angry Red Planet, 1959, Reptilicus, 1962, Journey to the 7th Planet, 1962, Ambush Bay, 1965, Robinson Crusoe on Mars, 1964, The Time Travelers, 1964, others; dir. Angry Red Planet, The Time Travelers; translator, narrator (tapes) Hans Christian Andersen Fairy Tales, 1986; creator Space Family Robinson (spl. advisor Lost in Space, 1997-98); subject of biography: (by Robert Skotak) Ib Melchior: Man of Imagination, 2000. Adv. bd. Mayor's Narcotics Info. Clinic, LA, 1972-73; adv. coun. Danish Immigrant Mus., Elk Horn, Iowa, 1985—. With U.S. Army Mil. Intelligence, 1942-46. Decorated Bronze Star, Knight Commander Cross, Militant Order of St. Brigitte of Sweden, 1965; recipient King Christian X Erindringsmedalje, 1948, Medal of Merit Old Guard, 1965, Golden Scroll award Best Writing Acad. Sci. Fiction, 1976, Hamlet award Best Legitimate Play Shakespeare Soc. Am., 1982; named Scandinavian of Yr. Am. Scandanavian Found. L.A., 1995, Mem. Writers Guild Am. West, Dirs. Guild Am., Acad. Sci. Fiction (hon.), Manuscript Soc., Authors Guild Inc., Royal Danish Guard Assn., Danish Luncheon Club (L.A.), Adventures Club (L.A.). Home and Office: 8228 Marmont Ln Hollywood CA 90069-1624 Personal E-mail: ijmelchior@aol.com.

MELCONIAN, LINDA JEAN, state senator, lawyer, educator; b. Springfield, Mass. d. George and Virginia Elaine (Noble) Melconian. BA, Mt. Holyoke Coll.; MA, George Washington U.; JD, George Mason U. Asst. counsel to Spkr. Thomas P. O'Neill, Jr. U.S. Ho. of Reps., Washington; pros. atty. Hampden County Dist. Atty., Springfield, Mass.; state senator Mass. Gen. Ct., Boston, 1983—2004, majority leader emeritus Mass. State Senate. Instr. Mt. Holyoke Coll., Am. Internat. Coll.; vis. asst. prof. Suffolk U., Boston. Ex Officio trustee Ella T. Grasso Found., Conn.; active Dem. State Com., Mass. Home: 465 Dwight Rd Springfield MA 01108 Office Phone: 413-374-3671. Business E-Mail: lindamelconian@comcast.net, lindamelconi@suffolk.edu. E-mail: lmelconi@suffolk.edu.

MELCZEK, DALE J., bishop; b. Nov. 9, 1938; AB, St. Mary Coll., Orchard Lake, Mich.; MDiv, St. John Sem., Plymouth, Mich.; MA in Edn., U. Detroit; postgrad., U. Notre Dame. Ordained priest Roman Cath. Ch., 1964, apptd. aux. bishop Roman Cath. Ch., 1982. Assoc. pastor St. Sylvester Ch., Warren, Mich., 1964—70, co-pastor, 1970—72; pastor St. Christine Ch., Detroit, 1972—75; vicar West Detroit Vicariate, 1973—75; asst. vicar for parishes Archdiocese of Detroit, 1975—77, sec. to archbishop and vicar gen., 1977—82, archdiocesan consultor, 1972—83, aux. bishop, titular bishop of Trau, 1982—92; regional bishop Detroit N.W. Region, 1983—92; apostolic adminstr. Diocese of Gary, 1992—95, coadjutor Bishop of Gary, 1995—96, bishop of Gary, 1996—. Roman Catholic. Office Phone: 219-769-9292.

MELDER, KEITH E., retired curator; b. May 1932; Asst. curator Nat. Mus. Am. Hist., Smithsonian Inst., Washington, 1962—63, assoc. cur., 1964—85, cur. polit. hist., 1986—94, cur. emeritus, 1995—. Author: City of Magnificent Intentions: A History of Washington, District of Columbia, 1983, Hail to the Candidate: Presidential Campaigns from Banners to Broadcasts, 1992. Mem. Capitol Hill Cmty. Coun., Washington, 1961—68. Named to Centennial Honor Roll, Am. Assn. Museums, 2006.

MELDMAN, ROBERT EDWARD, lawyer; b. Milw., Aug. 5, 1937; s. Louis Leo and Lillian (Gollusch) M.; m. Sandra Jane Setlick, July 24, 1960; children: Saree Beth, Richard Samuel. BS, U. Wis., 1959; LL.B., Marquette U., Milw., 1962; LL.M. in Taxation, NYU, 1963. Bar: Wis. 1962, Fla. 1987, Colo. 1990, U.S. Ct. Fed. Claims, U.S. Tax Ct. 1963, U.S. Supreme Ct. 1970. Practice tax law, Milw., 1963—; pres. Meldman, Case & Weine, Ltd., Milw., 1975-85; dir. tax div. Mulcahy & Wherry, SC, Milw., 1985-90; shareholder Reinhart, Boerner, Van Deuren, S.C., 1991—2006, of counsel, 2006—. Adj. prof. taxation U. Wis., Milw., 1970—2000, mem. tax adv. coun., 1978—2000, dir. Low Income Taxpayer Clinic, 2005—; adj. prof. Marquette U. Sch. Law, Milw., 2001—02, The U. of Queensland T.C. Beirne Sch. Law, 2002; vice chmn. Internat. Revenue Svc. Taxpayer Adv. Panel, 2003—04; sec. Profl. Inst. Tax Study, Inc., 1978—; bd. dirs. Wis. Bar Found., 1988—94; exec. in residence Deloitte & Touche Ctr. for Multistate Taxation, U. Wis., Milw., 1996—2000. Co-author: Federal Taxation Practice and Procedure, 1983, 1986, 1988, 1992, 1998, 2004, 2007, Practical Tactics for Dealing with the IRS, 1994, A Practical Guide to U.S. Taxation of International Transactions, 1996, 1997, 2004, Federal Taxation Practice and Procedure Study Guide/Quizzes, 1998; editor: Jour. Property Taxation, 1996—2002; mem. editl. bd.: Tax Litigation Alert, 1995—2000; contbr. articles to legal jours. Recipient Adj. Taxation Faculty award UWM Tax Assn., 1987; named Outstanding Tax Profl. 1992 Corp. Reports Wis. Mag. and UWM Tax Assn. Fellow Am. Coll. Tax Coun.; mem. ABA, Fed. Bar Assn. (pres. Milw. chpt. 1966-67), Milw. Bar Assn. (chmn. tax sect. 1970-71), Wis. Bar Assn. (bd. dirs. tax sect. 1964-78, chmn. 1973-74), Internat. Bar Assn., The Law Assn. for Asia and the Pacific (chair tax sect. 2000—, dep. chair bus. law sect.), Friends of Gold Meir Libr. (bd. dirs.), Marquette U. Law Alumni Assn. (bd. dirs. 1972-77), Milw. Athletic Club, Wis. Club (bd. dirs. 2003—), B'nai B'rith (trustee, Ralph Harris Meml. award Century Lodge 1969-70), Phi Delta Phi, Tau Epsilon Rho (chancellor Milw. chpt. 1969-71, supreme nat. chancellor 1975-76, v.p. Wis. chpt., tech. 1992-2000). Jewish (trustee congregation 1972-77). Office: 1000 N Water St Ste 2100 Milwaukee WI 53202-3197 Office Phone: 414-298-8181. Business E-Mail: rmeldman@reinhartlaw.com.

MELE, ALFRED R., philosophy educator; b. Detroit, May 22, 1951; s. Alfred Emil and Rosemary (Pardo) M.; children: Al, Nick, Angela. BA, Wayne State U., 1973; PhD, U. Mich., 1979. Asst. prof. philosophy Davidson (N.C.) Coll., 1979-85, assoc. prof., 1985-91, prof., 1991-95, Vail prof., 1995-2000; William H. and Lucyle T. Werkmeister prof. Fla. State U., Tallahassee, 2000—. Author: Irrationality, 1987, Springs of Action, 1992, Autonomous Agents, 1995, Self-Deception Unmasked, 2001, Motivation and Agency, 2003, Free Will and Luck, 2006; contbr. articles to profl. jours. Fellow NEH, 1985-86, 92-93, 99-2000, 2007—, Nat. Humanities Ctr., Rsch. Triangle Park, NC, 1992-93, Australian Nat. U., 1999. Mem. Am. Philos. Assn., So. Assn. Philosophy and Psychology, Internat. Soc. for Rsch. on Emotion. Avocation: racquetball. Office: Dept Philosophy Fla State Univ Tallahassee FL 32306-1500

MELEN, ALEX, entrepreneur, Internet company executive; b. 1984; s. Arkady and Alla Melen. Grad., Babson Coll., Wellesley, Mass., 2006. Pres., founder T35 Hosting, Fair Lawn, NJ, 1999—. Named one of Best Entrepreneurs Under 25, BusinessWeek mag., 2006; recipient Student Bus. Initiative award, Babson Coll. Alumni Assn., 2006. Office: T35 Hosting 42-09 Naugle Dr Fair Lawn NJ 07410 E-mail: president@t35.net. *

MELENDEZ, BRIAN, lawyer; b. Silver Creek, NY, Sept. 26, 1964; s. Gilbert Raymond and Dolores Maried (Valone) M. AB in Govt., Harvard U., 1986, MA in Theological Studies, 1991, JD cum laude, 1991. Bar: Minn., US Ct. Appeals (Fed. Cir.), US Dist. Ct. (Dist. Minn.). Adminstrv. sec. Harvard-Radcliffe Undergrad. Coun., Cambridge, Mass., 1983-84, 85-88; mgr. Copyrite Copy Ctrs., Winter Park, Fla., 1984; rsch. asst. Harvard U., Office of the Sec., Cambridge, 1985, Prog. on Info. Resources Policy, Cambridge, 1986-87; summer assoc. Avrell, Fons, Radey & Hinkle, Tallahassee, 1988, Greenberg, Travrig, Hoffman, Lipoff et al, Miami, Fla., 1989; ptnr. Faegre & Benson LLP, Minneapolis. Counselor Fla. Am. Legion Boys State, Tallahassee, 1982-89; v.p. Ctrl. Minn. Legal Services, 2003-05; bd. trustees Lawyers' Com. Civil Rights Under Law; bd. dirs. Vol. Lawyers Network, Ltd., Fair Vote Minn., 2002-05; mem. adv. com. on gen. rules of practice Supreme Ct. Minn., 2000-04, Minn. Citizens Commn. for Preservation of an Impartial Judiciary; chmn. Dem.-Farmer-Labor Party Minn., Minneapolis Dem.-Farmer-Labor Party, 1999-2005; pres. Harvard Divinity Sch. Alumni Assn., 2001-03. Fellow, Am. Bar Found.; mem. ABA (law student div., chmn. young lawyers divsn. 2000-01, mem. House of Delegates 1997-2004, presdl. appointments com. 2003-04, coun. mem. bus. law sect. 2001-03), Nat. Sr. Classical League (nat. pres. 1985-86), Am. Inst. of Parliamentarians, Hennepin County Bar Assn. (pres. 2001-02), Minn. Bar Assn. (chmn. ct. rules and adminstrn. com., 1998-2001; pres.-elect 2006, pres. 2007), Nat. Assn. Parliamentarian; mem. Minn. Distance Running Assn. Office: Faegre & Benson LLP 2200 Wells Fargo Ctr 90 S 7th St Minneapolis MN 55402-3901 Office Phone: 612-766-7309. Office Fax: 612-766-1600. E-mail: bmelendez@faegre.com.

MELENDEZ, SONIA IVETTE, counselor; b. Rio Piedras, PR, Dec. 12, 1952; d. Ramon Melendez and Bienvenida Miray. Faith educator, ISTEPA, Rio Piedros, 1983; Psychology Social Work, Career Stratford Inst., Washington, 2001; child psychology, Career Stratford Inst., 2002, Sex and Drug Counselor, 2003. Tchr. Colegio San Antonio, Rio Piedros, 1983—85, Colegio Catolice Notre Dame, Cigues, PR, 1985—89; spiritual counselor Casa Cristo Redentor, Aguas Buenas, PR, 1990—2001; cons., trainer Family Devel. Dept. Families P.R., San Juan, 1995—2006; pres. San Agustin Coqui Inc., Aguas Buenas, 1991—. Chaplain CAP, Bayamon, PR, 2000—06. Mem.: ACA, Assn. Puertarriqueni de Psicologia Individual, Am. Type Assn. Roman Catholic. Avocations: music, sports, gardening, tai chi.

MELENDY, DAVID RUSSELL, newscaster, reporter; b. Corpus Christi, Tex., Oct. 19, 1948; s. Harold Orville and Marguerite Doris (Waller) Melendy; m. Lorna Sandra Katz, Mar. 19, 1972; children: Seth Howard, Andrew Scott. Student, George Washington U., 1966-70; BA magna cum laude, U. Hartford, 1972. News dir. Sta. WINY, Putnam, Conn., 1971-77; news anchor, reporter Sta. WPOP, Hartford, Conn., 1977-80; news dir. Sta. WNVR, Waterbury, Conn., 1980-81; news anchor, reporter St. WDRC, Hartford, Conn., 1980—81; news anchor Sta. WCBS-FM, NYC, 1981; prodr., assignment editor, anchor, reporter AP Broadcast, Washington, 1981—. Instr. journalism Briarwood Coll., Southington, Conn., 1977—81, mem. broadcast adv. com., 1978—81. Prodr., writer, reporter: Star Wars: Strategic Defense Initiative, 1985, Flashback, 1986—2005. Publicity chmn. Woodstock Players Cmty. Theater, Conn., 1972—77, Quinebaug Valley C.C. Found., Danielson, Conn., 1973—75, fundraising chmn., 1976; neighborhood coord. Am. Heart Assn., Washington, 1994, 1999, 2001, 2006, 2007; troop com. mem. Boy Scouts Am., 1998—99, 2005—, pack com. chmn., 2000—01, asst. scoutmaster, 2001—05, advancement chmn., 2003—, vice chmn. mktg. Horizon dist/nat. Capital Area coun., 2005—06. Recipient Edward R. Murrow award, Radio and TV News Dirs. Assn., 2002. Mem.: Nat. Press Club, Com. Concerned Journalists, News Media Guild/TNG-CWA (v.p.), Radio and TV News Dirs. Assn., Ho. and Senate Radio-TV Corr. Assn., Elks. Avocations: personal computers, photography, hiking, swimming. Office: AP 1825 K St NW Ste 800 Washington DC 20006-1202

MELENHORST, JAN JOSEPH, immunologist; b. Geldrop, Netherlands, Mar. 6, 1965; s. Jan Marius Melenhorst and Hendrika Josepha Melenhorst-Alsters; m. Ling Zhao, Mar. 30, 1966; children: Anne Xinyi, Matthew Xinwei. PhD, Leiden U., Netherlands, 1997. Postdoctoral fellow Leiden U. Med. Ctr., Netherlands, 1997—98, NIH, Nat. Heart, Lung & Blood Inst., Bethesda, Md., 1998—2002, staff scientist, 2002—. Fogarty Vis. fellowship, NIH, 1998-2002. Mem.: Am. Soc. of Hematology, Am. Assn. of Immunologists. Achievements include the development of a cell culture system for the efficient induction of CD4 and CD8 T cell responses against viral and leukemia antigens for adoptive immunotherapy; Demonstrated that the clonal CD8 population in large granular lymphocyte leukemia consist of memory and effector T cells; Demonstrated that some patients with myelodysplastic syndrome have large expansions of clonal CD8 T cells; isolated and characterized autoreactive Tcells from a patient with aplastic anemia. Office: NIH NHLBI Bldg 10-CRC 10 Center Dr Bethesda MD 20892-1202 Home Phone: 301-519-2001; Office Phone: 301-435-2622. Office Fax: 301-480-2664. Business E-Mail: melenhoj@nhlbi.nih.gov.

MELESSE, ASSEFA MEKONNEN, engineering educator, researcher; s. Mekonnen and Aselef (Belay) Melesse; m. Zomanesh Aysheshim Abate, Mar. 25, 1970; children: Yonatan Assefa, Henok Assefa. BSc, Alemaya U., Ethiopia, 1986; M of Eng. Sci., Nat. U. Ireland, Dublin, 1991; M of Engring., U. Fla., Gainesville, 2000; PhD, U. Fla., 2002. Cert. profl. engr., Fla., ND. From grad. asst. II to asst. prof. II Alemaya U., Ethiopia, 1987—98; asst. prof. U. ND, Grand Forks, 2002—04, Fla. Internat. U., Miami, 2004—. Grad. sch. coord. Alemaya U., 1996, dir. ctr. continuing edn., 1995—97. Fellow, Irish Govt., 1989—91. Mem.: Am. Geophys. Union, Am. Soc. Agrl. Engrs., Alpha Epsilon (life). Office: Dept Environmental Studies ECS 339 Fla Internat Univ 11200 SW 8th St Miami FL 33199 Business E-Mail: melessea@fiu.edu.

MELGREN, ERIC FRANKLIN, prosecutor, lawyer; b. Minneola, Kans., Dec. 16, 1956; s. Carl James and Louise C. (Loechnor) M.; m. Denise Melgren, June 16, 1979; children: David W., Susan C., Peter J., Abigail J. B, Wichita State U., 1979; JD, Washburn U., Topeka, 1985. Bar: Kans. 1985, US Dist. Ct. Kans. 1985, US Ct. Appeals (10th cir.) 1987, US Tax Ct. 1988, US Supreme Ct. 1995. Law clk. US Dist. Ct. Kans., Wichita, 1985-87; assoc. Foulston, Siefkin, Powers & Eberhardt, Wichita, 1987-92; ptnr. Foulston & Siefkin, Wichita, 1992—2002; US atty. dist. Kans. US Dept. Justice, 2002—. Trustee Leadership Wichita, 1994—. Mem. Christian Legal Soc. (state dir. 1989-94), Wichita State Alumni Assn. (exec. com. 1993—), West Wichita Rotary Club. Republican. Office: US Attys Office 1200 Epic Ctr 301 N Main Wichita KS 67202 Office Phone: 316-269-6481. *

MELI, SALVATORE ANDREW, lawyer; b. NYC, Sept. 18, 1947; s. Andrew and Marie (Ruggiero) M.; m. Barbara Ann Chiesa, Aug. 16, 1970. BA, St. John's U., Jamaica, NY, 1969, JD, 1975. Bar: NY 1976, Fla. 1976, US Dist. Ct. (ea. and so. dist.) NY 1976, US Supreme Ct. 2004. Sole practice, Flushing, NY, 1976-78, 1997—, Lake Worth, Fla., 1997—2005; ptnr. Muratori & Meli, Flushing and Lake Worth, Fla., 1978-97. Lectr. Lawyers in the Classroom program, NYC, 1977-81; mem. adv. bd. Title Ins. Co., Queens, NY, 1985—. Recipient Regents Scholarship, NY State Bd. Regents, 1965. Mem. ABA, NY State Bar Assn., Fla. Bar Assn., Queens County Bar Assn. Office Phone: 718-886-4660. Business E-Mail: lawyer1@nyc.rr.com.

MELICHER, RONALD WILLIAM, finance educator; b. St. Louis, July 4, 1941; s. William and Lorraine Norma (Mohart) M.; m. Sharon Ann Schlarmann, Aug. 19, 1967; children: Michelle Joy, Thor William, Sean Richard. BSBA, Washington U., St. Louis, 1963, MBA, 1965, DBA, 1968. Asst. prof. fin. U. Colo., Boulder, 1969-71, assoc. prof., 1971-76, prof. fin., 1976—, chmn. fin. divsn., 1978-86, 90, chmn. fin. and econ. divsn., 1993-2000, MBA/MS programs dir., 1990-93, chmn. fin. divsn., 2003—. Assoc. dir. space law bus. and policy ctr. U. Colo., 1986-87; rsch. cons. FPC, Washington, 1975-76, GAO, Washington, 1981, RCG/Hagler, Bailly, Inc., 1985—, Ariz. Corp. Commn., 1986-87, Conn. Dept. Pub. Utility Control, 1989, US SEC, 1992-95; cons. tech. edn. IBM Corp., 1985-91; dir. ann. Exch. Program for Gas Industry, 1975-94; instr. ann. program Nat. Assn. Regulatory Utility Commrs., Mich. State U., 1981-94. Co-author: Real Estate Finance, 1978, 3d edit., 1989, Financial Management, 5th edit., 1982, Finance: Introduction to Markets, Institutions and Management, 1980, 1984, 1988, 1992, Finance: Introduction to Institutions, Investments and Management, 9th edit., 1997, 12th edit., 2006, Entrepreneurial Finance, 2003, 2d edit., 2006; assoc. editor Fin. Mgmt. Jour., 1975—80, The Fin. Rev., 1988—91. Recipient News Ctr. 4 TV Tchg. award, 1987, MBA/MS Assn. Tchg. award, 1988, Boulder Faculty Assembly Tchg. award, 1988, Grad. Bus. Students Tchg. award, 1995, 98; grantee NSF, 1974, NASA, 1986, 87; scholar W.H. Baughn Disting., 1989-2000, U. Colo. Pres.'s Tchg., 1989—. Mem. Fin. Mgmt. Assn. (mem. com. 1974-76, regional dir. 1975-77, v.p. ann. mtg. 1985, v.p. program 1987, pres. 1991-92, exec. com. 1991-93, bd. trustees 1992-99, chmn. 25th Anniversary com. 1994-95, mem. search com. for editor of Fin. Mgmt. Jour., 1995-96, chmn. search com. editor of Fin. Practice and Edn. Jour. 1996, mem. search com. for sec./treas. 1999, 2001), Am. Fin. Assn. Western Fin. Assn. (bd. dirs. 1974-76), Fin. Execs. Inst. (acad. mem. 1975—), Ea. Fin. Assn., Southwestern Fin. Assn., Midwest Fin. Assn. (bd. dirs. 1978-80), Alpha Kappa Psi, Beta Gamma Sigma. Office: U Colo Coll Bus PO Box 419 Boulder CO 80303 Office Phone: 303-492-3182. Business E-Mail: ronald.melicher@colorado.edu.

MELICK, CLIFFORD FRANCIS, sociologist, researcher; b. Albany, NY, Sept. 6, 1947; s. Francis Joseph Melick, Marion Dorothy Campbell; m. Evelyn Louise Mazo, Feb. 24, 2004. BA, Siena Coll., Loudonville, NY, 1971; MA, SUNY, Albany, 1973, PhD, 1979. Rsch. scientist N.Y. State Divsn. for Youth, Albany, 1980—83, dir. revenue and reporting svcs., 1983—86, chief program analysis and rsch., 1986—90; dir. rsch. Greater Balt. Med. Ctr., 1990—2002, dir. clin. info. and rsch., 2002—04; program evaluator Balt. City Pub. Sch. Sys., 2005—. Mem. editol adv. bd. Rsch. in Healthcare Fin. Mgmt., Balt., 2000—; prin. advisor NEMA Rsch., Inc., NYC, 1997—; mem. Greater Balt. Med. Ctr. Instnl. Rev. Bd., Balt., 1990—; bd. dirs. Analytica, Ltd., Albany, NY; adj. Johns Hopkins Sch. Pub. Health, 2005—. Contbr. book Chronic Wound Care, 2nd edit., 1997, Chronic Wound Care, 3d edit., 2001, Current Surgical Therapy, 4th edit., 1992, Current Surgical Therapy, 5th edit., 1995, articles to profl. jours. Mem.: APHA, Soc. of Clin. Rsh. Assoc., Am. Urogynecologic Soc., Acad. Health, Soc. for the Art and Sci. Wound Mgmt., Internat. Soc. for Rschs. in Healthcare Fin. Mgmt., Free State Corvette Club. Avocation: sports cars. Home: 8207 Spring Bottom Way Baltimore MD 21208 Office: Balt City Pub Sch Sys Rsch Evaluation Assessment Account 200 E North Ave Baltimore MD 21202 Office Phone: 410-396-8956. Personal E-mail: cmelick@comcast.net. Business E-Mail: cmelick@bcps.k12.md.us.

MELILLO, JERRY M., ecologist; BA, Wesleyan Univ., Middletown, Conn., 1965, MAT, 1968; MFS, Yale Univ., 1972, PhD, 1977. Biology instr. Kakamega Secondary Sch., Kenya, 1966—67, Weston (Conn.) H.S., 1968—73, Foote Sch., 1972—73; tchg. asst. Yale Univ., 1973—75, assoc. rsch., Hubbard Brook Ecosystem Study, 1975—76; dir., ecosystems studies NSF, Washington, 1986—88; assoc. dir., environ., Office of Sci., Tech. Policy Office of Pres., Washington, 1996—97; asst. scientist, Ecosystems Ctr. Marine Biol. Lab, Woods Hole, 1976—82, assoc. scientist, 1982—87, sr. scientist, 1987—, acting dir., 1988—89, co-dir., 1989—. Trustee H. John Heinz III Ctr. Sci., Econ, Environ. Recipient Disting. Alumni award, Wesleyan Univ. Fellow: Am. Acad. Arts & Scis.; mem.: Nat. Assn. Advancement Sci., Am. Geophysical Union, Ecological Soc. Am. (pres.-elect), Cosmos Club. Office: Ecosystems Ctr Marine Biological Lab 7 MBL St Woods Hole MA 02543 Business E-Mail: jmelillo@mbl.edu. *

MELILLO, JOSEPH VINCENT, theater producer; b. New Haven, Nov. 15, 1946; s. Vincent and Viola (Fucci) M. BA, Sacred Heart U., 1968; MFA, Cath. U. Am., 1972. Adminstr. City Ctr. Music and Drama, NYC, 1972-75; mktg. dir. The Walnut St. Theatre, Phila., 1975-76; dir. FEDAPT, NYC, 1976-80; gen. mgr. New World Festival of Arts, Miami, Fla., 1982; dir. Next Wave Festival, NYC, 1983-89; artistic dir. N.Y. Internat. Festival, NYC, 1990-91, exec. prodr., 1999—; producing dir. Bklyn. Acad. Music, 1991—, exec. prodr., 1999—. Trustee EnGarde Arts, N.Y.C., 1991-96; v.p., bd. dirs. Assn. Performing Arts Presenters, Washington, 1991-93; cons.-specialist Opera Am. Washington, 1991-93; cons. The Japan Found. "Performing Arts Japan", The Bush Found., St. Paul, Arts Internat., N.Y.C.; adj. prof. Theater Dept. Bklyn. Coll.; co-chair Internat. Presenters Forum; mem. cultural challenge panel N.Y.C. Dept. Cultural Affairs; bd. advisors Etantdonnes, 2000-02; curator Internat. Soc. Performing Arts, 2005. Editor: Market the Arts, 1980. Mem. adv. bd. materials for arts Africa Exch. 651 program com. NJ Performing Arts Ctr., Newark, 1999—; mem. New Haven Festival of the Arts and Ideas; advisor Rolex Mentor and Protege Program, 2002—03; program adv. panel Pew Fellowships in the Arts, 2003, chmn. multidisciplinary panel, 2003, 2007; moderator The Berkshire Conf.; curator panels Internat. Soc. Performing Arts Found., 2005; adv. bd. Rolex Mentor and Protege Program, 2005—. Decorated Order Brit. Empire, chevalier and officer Order of Arts and Letters; recipient Documents of Dance award, Dance Library of Israel, 2003, Svc. to Artistic Cmty. award Bang on a Can. Mem.: Century Assn. Democrat. Avocations: reading, travel. Office Phone: 718-636-4107. Business E-Mail: programming@bam.org.

MELIN, ROBERT ARTHUR, lawyer; b. Milw., Sept. 13, 1940; s. Arthur John and Frances Magdalena (Lanser) M.; m. Mary Magdalen Melin, July 8, 1967; children: Arthur Walden, Robert Dismas, Nicholas O'Brien, Madalyn Mary. BA summa cum laude, Marquette U., Milw., 1962, JD, 1967. Bar: Wis. 1966, US Dist. Ct. (ea. dist.) Wis. 1966, US Ct. Appeals (7th cir.) 1966, US Ct. Mil. Appeals 1967, US Supreme Ct. 1975. Law clk. U.S. Dist. Ct. (ea. dist.), Wis., 1966; instr. bus. law U. Ga., Hinesville, 1968; lectr. bus. law U. Md., Asmara, 1970; lectr. law Haile Salassie I. U. Law Faculty, Addis Ababa, Ethiopia, 1971-72; with Walther & Halling, Milw., 1973-74, Schroeder, Gedlen, Riester & Moerke, Milw., 1974-82; ptnr. Schroeder, Gedlen, Riester & Melin, Milw., 1982-84, Schroeder, Riester, Melin & Smith, Milw., 1984—. Author: Evidence in Ethiopia, 1972; contbg. author Ann. Survey African Law, 1974; contbr. numerous articles to legal jours. Rep. Class of 2000, West Point Parent Assn. Wis., 1996—, exec. bd., 1997—; lectr. charitable solicitations and contracts Philanthropy Monthly 9th Ann. Policy Conf., NYC, 1985; chmn. Milw. Young Dems., 1963-64. Capt. JAGC, AUS, 1967-70. Mem.: ABA, Wis. Acad. Trial Lawyers, Wis. Bar Assn., Milw. Bar Assn., Friends Ethiopia, Am. Legion, Delta Theta Phi, Phi Alpha Theta, Pi Gamma Mu. Roman Catholic. Home: 8108 N Whitney Rd Milwaukee WI 53217-2752 Office: 135 W Wells St Milwaukee WI 53203-1807 Home Phone: 414-351-2416; Office Phone: 414-351-0539.

MELIN, STACY M., literature and language educator; b. Dallas, Oct. 27, 1977; d. Billy Joe Sr. and Suzanne Denise Melin. BA in Lit. cum laude, U. North Tex., Denton, 2003. Cert. tchr. English and lang. arts grades 4-12 State of Tex., 2004. Tchr. lit. grades 7-8 St. Pius X Cath. Sch., Dallas, 2004—. Speech team coach St. Pius X Cath. Sch., Dallas, 2004—. Recipient Work of Heart award, Cath. Diocese of Dallas, 2006. Office: St Pius X Catholic Sch 3030 Gus Thomasson Rd Dallas TX 75228 Home Phone: 214-336-1318; Office Phone: 972-279-2339.

MELINSON, GREGG R., lawyer; b. Phila., 1954; s. James and Monica Melinson. BA, LaSalle Univ., 1986; JD, Duke Univ., 1989. Bar: Pa. 1989, NJ 1990. Law clerk, Hon. Edward R. Becker US Dist. Ct. Appeals (3d cir.), 1989—90; assoc. Drinker Biddle & Reath LLP, Phila., 1990—94, rejoined, 1997—, now ptnr., chair, govt. affairs practice group; dep. gen. counsel Gov. Tom Ridge, 1994—97. Co-chair Pa. Lawyers for Bush/Cheney. Frequent writer, lectr. in field. Vice chair Am. Heart Assn. Southeastern Pa. affiliate. Mem.: Pa. Economy League (chmn. 2003—). Republican. Office: Drinker Biddle & Reath LLP One Logan Sq 18th & Cherry Sts Philadelphia PA 19103-6996 Office Phone: 215-988-2648. Office Fax: 215-988-2757. Business E-Mail: gregg.melinson@dbr.com.

MELISSINOS, ADRIAN CONSTANTIN, physicist, researcher; b. Thessaloniki, Greece, July 28, 1929; came to U.S., 1955, naturalized, 1970; s. Constantin John and Olympia (Abbott) M.; m. Mary Joyce Mitchell, June 7, 1960; children: Constantin John, Andrew William. Student, Royal Naval Acad., Greece, 1945-48; MS, Mass. Inst. Tech., 1956, PhD, 1958. Naval cadet Greek Navy, 1945-48, commd. ensign, 1948, advanced through grades to lt., 1951; ret., 1954; teaching and research asst. Mass. Inst. Tech., 1955-58; instr. U. Rochester, NY, 1958-60, asst. prof. physics, 1960-63, assoc. prof., 1963-67, prof., 1967—, chmn. dept. physics and astronomy, 1974-77. Vis. scientist CERN European Center for Nuclear Research, 1968-69, 77-78, 89-90; cons. Brookhaven Nat. Lab., 1970-72, 75-79; vis. prof. U. Athens, 1996; vis. scientist Deutsches Electronen Synchrotron, 1997; cons. Stanford Linear Accelerator Ctr., 1995-98. Author: Experiments in Modern Physics, 1966, (with J. Napolitano) 2d edit., 2003, (with F. Lobkowicz) Physics for Scientists and Engineers, 1975; (with A. Das) Quantum Mechanics, 1985, Principles of Modern Technology, 1990. Decorated Swedish Order of Sword. Fellow Am. Phys. Soc.; mem. Greek Nat. Acad. (corr.) Achievements include experimentation with elementary particles at most major high energy accelerators in the U.S. and Europe, experimentation with high power lasers, searches for dark matter, search for high frequency gravitational waves. Home: 177 Whitewood Ln Rochester NY 14618-3223 Office: U Rochester Dept Physics Rochester NY 14627 Home Phone: 585-473-1197; Office Phone: 585-275-2707. Business E-Mail: meliss@pas.rochester.edu.

MELLANBY, SCOTT EDGAR, retired professional hockey player; b. Montreal, June 11, 1966; Right wing Phila. Flyers, 1986—91, Edmonton Oilers, 1991—93, Fla. Panthers, 1993—2001, St. Louis Blues, 2001—04, Atlanta Thrashers, 2004—, capt., 2005—07. *

MELLBERG, JAMES RICHARD, retired dental research chemist; b. Manitowoc, Wis., June 3, 1932; s. Millard Filmore Mellberg and Marion Eleanor (Elmer) Zimmerman; m. Gail Maureen Loehning, Sept. 26, 1956; children: Eric, Diane, Laura. BS, Wis. State U., Oshkosh, 1955; MS, Loyola U., Chgo., 1960. Head dental rsch. dept. Kendall Co., Barrington, Ill., 1958-75; assoc. dir. dental rsch. Colgate-Palmolive Co., Piscataway, NJ, 1975-94; ret. Cons. Naval Dental Rsch. Inst., Great Lakes, Ill., 1972-94. Author: Fluoride in Preventive Dentistry, 1983; patentee in field; contbr. over 100 articles in field to sci. publs. Recipient 20 sci. exhibit awards ADA, 1964-87. Mem. Internat. Assn. Dental Rsch. (Disting. Scientist award). Avocations: bicycling, woodworking. Home: 675 Ridge Top Rd Tryon NC 28782 Personal E-mail: mellberg1@alltel.net.

MELLBERG, LEONARD EVERT, physicist; b. Springfield, Mass., Dec. 18, 1935; s. Evert and Dorothy (Baker) M.; m. Pamela Narbeth. BS in Physics, U. Mass., Amherst, 1961; MS in Physics, Trinity Coll., Hartford, Conn., 1968. Rsch. physicist Navy Underwater Sound Lab., New London, Conn., 1961—68, SACLANT Undersea Rsch. Ctr., LaSpezia, Italy, 1968—72, Office of Naval Rsch., London, 1968—72, Naval Underwater Sys. Ctr., Newport, RI, 1972—91; sr. scientist Marine Acoustics Inc., Newport, 1991—94; chief scientist Sci. Applications Internat. Corp., San Diego, 1994—2000, Ocean Physics Assocs., South Dartmouth, Mass., 2000—. Govt. and profl. tech. adv. bds. and coms. Contbr. over 70 articles to profl. jours. Pres. Verdandi Swedish Cultural Found., Providence, 1992-97; bd. dirs. Verdandi Chorus Am. Union Swedish Singers, Providence, 1992—. Recipient Naval Underwater Sys. Ctr. Excellence in Sci. award, 1977, 84, Civilian Navy Meritorious Svc. medal Dept. of Navy, 1991. Fellow Acoustical Soc. Am.; mem. IEEE (sr.), AIAA (Svc. award 1977), Am. Geophys. Union, Oceanic Soc. of IEEE. Achievements include research in ocean physics, ocean acoustic propagation, anti-submarine warfare acoustics, Arctic sea-ice ridges and lighter than air vehicles. Home and Office: 109 Wilson St South Dartmouth MA 02748-3021 Home Phone: 508-994-9599. E-mail: lpmellberg@ieee.org.

MELLEMA, DONALD EUGENE, retired radio news reporter and anchor; b. Chgo., Mar. 30, 1937; s. Raymond Cornelius and Dorothy Sofia (Miller) M.; m. Freda Dieterlen Mellema, Sept. 23, 1961; children: Darryl Emerson, Duane Edward. BA in Speech, Beloit Coll., Wis., 1959. News dir. WGEZ Radio, Beloit, 1959; evening host, newsman WOSH Radio, Oshkosh, Wis., 1959-63; morning host, newsman WANE Radio, Ft. Wayne, Ind., 1963-65; news dir. WATI Radio, Indpls., 1965-67; news writer WGN Radio, Chgo., 1967-69; news reporter, anchor WBBM Radio, Chgo., 1969-96; ret., 1996. Mem. publs. adv. bd., pres's adv. coun., cons. Beloit Coll., 1996-00, also profl.-in-residence; Lewis and Clark lectr. Taft HS, 2002—; part time faculty Coll. Lake County, Grayslake, Ill., 2002-. Spkr., motivator Chgo. Pub. Sch. Youth Motivation Program, 1993-96; advisor, cons. media rels. to various police and civic orgns.; commr., unit leader Boy Scouts Am., 1971-81; ch. deacon Park Ridge (Ill.) Presbyn. Ch., 1980-83. Recipient regional award Radio TV News Dirs. Assn., 1994, Newsfinder award AP, 1995, career recognition award Chgo. Police Dept., 1997, Mark Twain award Ill. AP, 1997; named to Taft H.S. Hall of Fame, 1995. Mem. Ill. News Broadcasters Assn. (Silver Dome 1st Place award 1994), Soc. Profl. Journalists (Peter Lisagor award 1991, 96, Lewis and Clark lectr. 2002—), Am. Legion. Republican. Avocations: woodworking, reading, photography, birding, travel. Personal E-mail: donmellema@netscape.net.

MELLE MEL, See GLOVER, MELVIN

MELLEN, FRANCIS JOSEPH, JR., lawyer; b. Williamsport, Pa., Dec. 19, 1945; s. Francis Joseph and Mary Emma (Oberst) M.; m. Mary Wilder Davison, Aug. 2, 1975 (div. 1987); m. Beverly Joan Glascock, Sept. 2, 2000; children: Elizabeth, Catherine, Robert, Christine. BA, U. Ky., 1967, MA, 1971; JD, Harvard U., 1973. Bar: NY 1974, Ky. 1975, US Dist. Ct. (so. dist.) NY 1974, US Dist. Ct. (ea. dist.) Ky. 1977, US Dist. Ct. (we. dist.) Ky. 1978, US Ct. Appeals (2d cir.) 1975, US Ct. Appeals (6th cir.) 1982, US Supreme Ct. 2005. Assoc. atty. Rogers & Wells, NYC, 1973-75, Wyatt, Grafton & Sloss, Louisville, 1975-80; ptnr. Wyatt, Tarrant & Combs, Louisville, 1980—. Co-author: Kentucky Mineral Law, 1986, Kentucky Forms and Transactions, 1991; contbr. articles to profl. jours. Spl. study com. Uniform Comml. Code, Ky. Legis. Rsch. Commn., Frankfort, 1984-91; bd. dirs. Leadership Louisville Found., 1995-02, counsel, 1996-98, 2000-02; bd. dirs. Stage One: The Louisville Children's Theatre, 1995-01, v.p., 1997-98, pres., 1998-00; bd. dirs. Louisville-Jefferson County A.W.A.R.E. Coalition, 1994-98; bd. trustees Cherokee Gardens, 2005—. Lt. (j.g.) USNR, 1967-69. Mem. ABA, Am. Arbitration Assn. (panel), Nat. Arbitration Forum (panel), Ky. Bar Assn. (ho. of dels. 1986-92, ethics com. 2004—, arbitration panel 2005—), Louisville Bar Assn. (chmn. com. profl. responsibility 1992-94), Jefferson Club, Filson Club, Am. Mensa, Hon. Order Ky. Cols. Republican. Home: 2944 Lexington Rd Louisville KY 40206-2934 Office: Wyatt Tarrant & Combs LLP 2800 PNC Plz Louisville KY 40202 Home Phone: 502-893-9254; Office Phone: 502-562-7290. E-mail: fmellen@wyattfirm.com.

MELLENCAMP, JOHN (JOHN COUGAR), singer, lyricist; b. Seymour, Ind., Oct. 7, 1951; m. Vicky C. (div.); children: Michelle, Teddy Joe, Justice; m. Elaine Irwin, Sept. 5, 1992; children: Hud, Spec Wildhorse. A. in Broadcasting, Vincennes U., Ind., 1973; Doctorate (hon.), Ind. U., 2000. Albums include Chestnut Street Incident, 1977, Biography, 1978, Johnny Cougar, 1979, Nothing Matters and What If It Did, 1980, Night Dancin, 1980, American Fool, 1982, Uh-huh, 1983, Scarecrow, 1985, The Lonesome Jubilee, 1988, Big Daddy, 1989, Whenever We Wanted, 1991, Human Wheels, 1993, Dance Naked, 1994, Mr. Happy Go Lucky, 1996, The Best That I Could Do...1997, John Mellencamp, 1998, Rough Harvest, 1999, Cuttin' Heads, 2001, Trouble No More, 2003, Words & Music: John Mellencamp's Greatest Hits, 2004, Freedom's Road, 2007; performed one song for Folkways: A Vision Shared (A Tribute to Woody Guthrie and Leadbelly), 1988; film actor, dir., soundtrack performer: Falling From Grace, 1992, Seeing in the Dark, 2000; actor (films) Madison (voice only), 2001, After Image, 2001, Lone Star State of Mind, 2002; TV appearance Bob Dylan: The 30th Anniversary Concert Celebration, 1993, Farm Aid '96, 1996. Co-founder, bd. dirs. Farm Aid, 1985—. Recipient Century award for Creative Achievement, Billboard, 2001, Woody Guthrie award, 2003. Office: John Mellencamp PO Box 6777 Bloomington IN 47407-6777 also: c/o Randy Hoffman Hoffman Entertainment Inc 362 5th Ave Ste 804 New York NY 10001 *

MELLER, JAROSLAW, biotechnologist, information scientist, educator; m. Halina Meller; children: Artur, Adam. PhD, Nicholas Copernicus U., Torun, Poland, 1996; D, Polish Acad. Sci., Warsaw, 2004. Assoc. Hebrew U., Jerusalem, 1996—97; fellow Kyoto U., 1997—98; rsch. assoc. Cornell U., Ithaca, NY, 1999—2001; asst. prof. Children's Hosp. Rsch. Found., Cinn. Contbr. articles to profl. jours. Mem.: Internat. Soc. Computational Biology, AAAS. Achievements include discovery of using computational approaches, proposed links between several classes of proteins, including tumor suppressor pVHL and RNA Pol II and a gene regulating the size of the tomato fruit and RAS oncogene. Office: Children's Hosp Rsch Found 3333 Burnet Ave Cincinnati OH 45229 Office Phone: 513-636-0270.

MELLERT, LUCIE ANNE, writer, photographer; b. Charleston, W.Va., June 6, 1932; d. Wilbur Conant and Grace Martin (Taylor) Frame; m. William Jennings Mellert, March 15, 1957; 1 child, James Floyd Kelly III. Student, Mason Coll. of Music Fine Arts, Charleston, 1937-49, W.Va. U., Morgantown, 1950-51. Pub. rels. exec., asst. treas., office mgr. J. H. Milam, Inc., Dunbar, W.Va., 1959-71; pub. rels. exec., office mgr. Hallcraft, Inc., Dunbar, 1972-74; office mgr. Kanawha Stone Co. Inc., Nitro, W.Va., 1975-78. Vol. photographer Charleston Gazette, 1997—. Beautification commr. City of Dunbar, 1969-72; activity coord., program dir. Dunbar Bicentennial Com., 1971; founder, coordinator Dunbar City wide Beautification and Improvement Com., 1969-72; coord. Kanawha County Elem. Students Anti-Litter Program, Planting the Seed, 1996-03; pres. United Meth. Women of St. Marks; active U. Charleston Builders, W.Va. Humanities Coun., Friends of W. Va. Culture and History, Friends of Clay Ctr.; judge various cmty. events, 1995-04; commr. Kanawha County Pks. and Recreation Commn., 2000—; vol. photographer Charleston Gazette On the Town, 1997-. Named Disting. Mountaineer, W.Va. Gov. Joe Manchin III, 2005; recipient West Virginian award, Gov. Cecil Underwood, 2000, Gov. Bob Wise, 2001, West Va. Vol. Spirit award, W. Va. Women's Commn., 2003, commendation for vol. svc., W.Va. Gov. Bob Wise, 2004. Mem. Nat. Mus. Women in the Arts, Nat. Fedn. Press Women, Pioneer Women's (past pres.), Libr. of Congress Assn., Kanawha Valley and Nat. Trust Hist. and Preservation Soc., East End Assn., Women of Moose, Woman's Club Charleston, W.Va. Soc.Assn. Execs., Mental Health Assn., Mid Atlantic Arts Found. Methodist. Avocations: church activities, music, travel, art, photography. Home: 1604 Virginia St E Charleston WV 25311-2114

MELLETTE, JULIAN RAMSEY, JR., dermatologist, dermatologic surgeon; b. Florence, SC, June 27, 1939; s. Julian Ramsey and Mary (Brown) Mellette; m. Elizabeth Odom, May 22, 1945; children: Elizabeth Erhelens, Julian Ramsey III, Bradford. AB, Wofford Coll., 1961; MD, Med. U. S.C., 1969. Spl. agt. in charge Atlanta field office Mil. Intelligence, 1962—64; chief aerospace medicine Lyster Army Hosp., Fort Rucker, Ariz., 1971—73; chief dermatology Fitzsimmons Army Med. Ctr., Aurora, Colo., 1982—90; prof. dermatology U. Colo. Health Sci. Ctr., 1990—2003, Mohs fellowship dir., 1995—2003. Brig. gen. Joint Svc. Detachment, State of SC, 2003. Contbr. chapters to books, articles to profl. jours. Col. US Army, 1961—90. Mem.: Colo. Dermatology Surg. Soc. (pres. 1989—), Internat. Soc. Dermatology Surgeons (bd. dirs. 1999—2001), Am. Coll. Mohs Surgery and Cutaneous Oncology (bd. dirs. 1993—96). Avocations: skiing, golf, scuba diving, flying. Office Phone: 720-848-0510. E-mail: ramsey.mellette@uchsc.edu.

MELLEY, STEVEN MICHAEL, lawyer; b. Rhinebeck, NY, Jan. 3, 1950; s. James Christopher and Virginia (Madonna) M.; children: Aliza, Steven Jonathan, Olivia, Bennett; m. Phoebe Kirwood. BA in Russian Studies with honors, Colgate U., 1972; JD, Tulane U., 1975. Bar: N.Y. 1976, U.S. Dist. Ct. 1976, U.S. Supreme Ct. 1980. Law clk. to hon. Matthew Braniff Criminal Dist. Judge, Orleans Parish, New Orleans; assoc. Woody N. Klose Law Offices, Red Hook, N.Y., 1975-78; ptnr. Klose & Melley, Rhinebeck, 1978-83; pvt. practice Rhinebeck, 1983—. Atty. Village of Tivoli, N.Y., 1977-78. Contbg. editor: New York Motor Vehicle Accidents, 1999; assoc. editor Tulane Forum, 1974-75. Named to, NY Superlawyers, 2007. Mem. ABA, AAJ (sustaining), NY State Bar Assn. (past com. mem. on specialization), Dutchess County Bar Assn. (sustaining), NY State Trial Lawyers Assn., Christian Trail Lawyers Assn., Million Dollar Advocates Forum, Phi Alpha Delta, Kappa Delta Rho. Office: 24 Closs Dr Rhinebeck NY 12572 Home Phone: 845-876-3210; Office Phone: 845-876-4057. Business E-Mail: melleyinjurylaw@aol.com.

MELLI, MARYGOLD SHIRE, law educator; b. Rhinelander, Wis., Feb. 8, 1926; d. Osborne and May (Bonnie) Shire; m. Joseph Alexander Melli, Apr. 8, 1950; children: Joseph, Sarah Bonnie, Sylvia Anne, James Alexander. BA, U. Wis., 1947, LLB, 1950. Bar: Wis. 1950. Dir. children's code revision Wis. Legis. Coun., Madison, 1950-53; exec. dir. Wis. Jud. Coun., Madison, 1955-59; asst. prof. law U. Wis., Madison, 1959-66, assoc. prof., 1966-67, prof., 1967-84, Voss-Bascom prof., 1985-93, emerita, 1993—. Assoc. dean U. Wis., 1970-72, rsch. affiliate Inst. for Rsch. on Poverty, 1980—; mem. spl. rev. bd. Dept. Health and Social Svcs., State of Wis., Madison, 1973—2002. Author: (pamphlet) The Legal Status of Women in Wisconsin, 1977, (book) Wisconsin Juvenile Court Practice, 1978, rev. edit., 1983, (with others) Child Support & Alimony, 1988, The Case for Transracial Adoption, 1994; co-editor: Child Support: The Next Frontier, 1999; contbr. articles to profl. jours. Bd. dirs. Am. Humane Assn., 1985-95, Frank Lloyd Wright - Wis., 2004; chair A Fund for Women, Madison, Wis., 2002, 2003. Named one of five Outstanding Young Women in Wis., Jaycees, 1961, Woman of Distinction, YWCA, Madison, Wis., 2007; grantee NSF, 1983; recipient Belle Case LaFollette award for outstanding svc. to the profession, 1994, Outstanding Contbn. to Advancement of Women in Higher Edn. award, 1991, Lifelong Contbn. to Advancement of Women in the Legal Prof. award, 1994, Sr. Svc. award Rotary, Madison, Wis., 2002. Fellow Am. Acad. Matrimonial Lawyers (exec. editor jour. 1985-90); mem. Am. Law Inst. (cons. project on law of family dissolution), Internat. Soc. Family Law (v.p. 1994-2000, 2002-05), Wis. State Bar Assn. (reporter family law sect., 1976-2005), Nat. Conf. Bar Examiners (chmn. bd. mgrs. 1989, editl. adv. com.). Democrat. Roman Catholic. Avocations: walking, swimming, collecting art. Home: 2904 Waunona Way Madison WI 53713-2238 Office: U Wis Law Sch Madison WI 53706 Home Phone: 608-222-2003; Office Phone: 608-262-1610. Business E-Mail: msmelli@wisc.edu.

MELLINGER, KEITH E., mathematician, educator; b. Lancaster, Pa., Mar. 18, 1973; m. Sara Mellinger, 1998; 1 child, Gabriel. BS, Millersville U., Pa., 1995; MS, U. Del., Newark, 1997, PhD, 2001. Rsch. asst. prof. U. Ill., Chgo., 2001—03; asst. prof. math. U. Mary Wash., Fredericksburg, Va., 2003—. Cons. in field. Musician: (albums) New Day Dawning by the Fall Line Bluegrass Band, Bookends - an acoustic duo; contbr. articles to mags., to profl. jours. Grantee, Nat. Security Agy., 2005—07. Mem.: Am. Math. Soc., Math. Assn. Am. (fellow). Office: Univ Mary Washington 1301 Coll Ave Fredericksburg VA 22401 Home Phone: 540-368-3128; Office Phone: 540-654-1333. Business E-Mail: kmelling@umw.edu.

MELLINKOFF, SHERMAN MUSSOFF, medical educator; b. McKeesport, Pa., Mar. 23, 1920; s. Albert and Helen Mussoff Mellinkoff; m. June Bernice O'Connell, Nov. 18, 1944; children: Sherrill, Albert. BA, Stanford U., 1941, MD, 1944; LHD (hon.), Wake Forest U., 1984, Hebrew Union Coll., LA, 1988. Diplomate Am. Bd. Internal Medicine, Am. Bd. Gastroenterology, Am. Bd. Nutrition. Intern asst. resident Stanford U. Hosp., San Francisco, 1944—45; asst. resident Johns Hopkins Hosp., Balt., 1947—49, chief resident, 1950—51, instr. in medicine, 1951—53; fellow in gastroenterology Hosp. of U. Pa., Phila., 1949—50; from asst. prof. to prof. medicine UCLA Sch. of Medicine, LA, 1962—86; dean UCLA Sch. Medicine, LA, 1962—86, emeritus prof. of medicine, 1990—; disting. physician of VA Wadsworth VA Medical Ctr., LA, 1990-93. Mem. sci. adv. panel Rsch. to Prevent Blindness, Inc., NYC, 1975—93; mem. program devel. com. Nat. Med. Fellowships, Inc., NYC, 1984—. Editl. bd.: The Pharos, 1986; contbr. articles to profl. jours. Apptd. by Gov. of Calif. to McCone Com., 1965. Capt. US Army, 1945—57. Recipient Abraham Flexner award, Assn. Am. Med. Colls., 1981, J.E. Wallace Sterling Disting. Alumnus award, Stanford U. Sch. of Medicine, 1987. Master: ACP; fellow: Royal Coll. of Physicians; mem.: The Johns Hopkins Soc. of Scholars, Am. Acad. of Arts and Scis., Inst. of Medicine of NAS, Assn. Am. Physicians, Am. Gastroenterol. Assn. Assn. Avocations: reading, hiking. Office: UCLA Dept Medicine 44 138 Chs Los Angeles CA 90095-0001

MELLINS, CLAUDE ANN, psychologist; BA in Psychology, Brown U., 1982; MS in Clin. Psychology, U. So. Calif., LA, 1987; PhD in Clin. Psychology, U. So. Calif., 1990. Assoc. prof. clin. psychology HIV Ctr.; co-dir. and dir. rsch. Spl. Needs Clinic Children & Families Columbia Presbyn., NYC, 1992—; assoc. prof. clin. psychology dept. psychiatry and sociomed. scis. N.Y. State Psychiat. Inst. and Columbia U., NYC, 1994—. Neurodevel. supr. Women and Children's Care Ctr., Presbyn. Hosp.; mem. sci. adv. group Pediat. HIV AIDS Cohorts Study; co-founder spl. needs clinic NY Psychiat. Hosp., co-dir. Contbr. chpts. to books and articles to profl. jours. Aaron Diamond Found. fellow. Mem. APA (pediat. psychology subdivsn.).

MELLINS, HARRY ZACHARY, radiologist, educator; b. NYC, May 23, 1921; s. David J. and Ray (Hoffman) M.; m. Judith Alice Weiss, Dec. 26, 1950; children— Elizabeth, William, Thomas. AB, Columbia Coll., 1941; MD, L.I. Coll. Medicine, 1944; MS in Radiology, U. Minn., 1951; AM (hon.), Harvard U., 1970. Intern Jewish Hosp., Bklyn., 1944-45, asst. resident in radiology, 1945-46; resident in radiology U. Minn., Mpls., 1948-50, instr. radiology, 1950-52, asst. prof., 1952-53; clin. asst. prof. radiology Wayne State U., Detroit, 1953-56; dir. radiology Sinai Hosp., Detroit, 1953-56; prof., chmn. dept. radiology SUNY, Coll. Medicine, NYC, 1956-69; chief radiology Kings County Hosp. Center, Bklyn., 1956-69; radiologist-in-chief State Univ. Hosp., Bklyn., 1966-69; prof. radiology Harvard Med. Sch., Boston, 1969—87, prof. radiology emeritus, 1991—; dir. diagnostic radiology Peter Bent Brigham Hosp., 1969-79, Brigham and Women's Hosp., 1980-87, dir. edn. and tng., dept. radiology, 1987-94; co-dir. edn. and tng. dept. radiology, 1994-97; chief of radiology Harvard U. Health Svc., 1988-97; radiologist Brigham and Women's Hosp., 1998-99. Nat. cons. in radiology to surgeon gen. U.S. Air Force, 1968-79; mem. radiation study sect. NIH, 1967-71; mem. subcom. for written exam. in diagnostic radiology Am. Bd. Radiology, 1970-75; mem. radiology tng. com. research tng. grants br. Nat. Inst. Gen. Med. Scis.; mem. diagnostic research adv. group div. cancer biology and diagnosis Nat. Cancer Inst., 1975-79; guest examiner Am. Bd. Radiology. Served to capt. M.C. USAAF, 1946-48. Mem. Bklyn. Radiol. Soc. (pres. 1965-66), N.Y. Roentgen Soc. (pres 1966-67), Assn. Univ. Radiologists (pres. 1969-70, Gold medal 1986), Soc. Uroradiology (pres. 1975-76, Gold medal 2000), Am. Roentgen Ray Soc. (pres. 1977-79, Gold medal 1989), Radiol. Soc. N.Am., New Eng. Roentgen Ray Soc. (pres. 1986-87), Soc. Gastrointestinal Radiology, Alpha Omega Alpha (alumnus).

MELLINS, ROBERT B., pediatrician, educator; b. NYC, Mar. 6, 1928; s. David J. and Ray H. (Hoffman) M.; m. Sue Mendelsohn, Apr. 19, 1959; children: Claude Ann, David Rustin. AB, Columbia U., 1948; MD, Johns Hopkins U., 1952. Intern Johns Hopkins Hosp., 1952—53; mem. epidemic intelligence svc, founder poison control program Ctr. Disease Control, Chgo., 1953—55; resident in pediat. N.Y. Hosp., 1955—56, Presbyn. Hosp., NYC, 1956—57, dir. pediat. ICU, 1970—75; assoc. prof. pediat. Columbia U., NYC, 1970—75, prof. pediat., 1975—, dir. Cystic Fibrosis Ctr., 1976—91, dir. pediat. pulmonary divsn., 1972—97. Christmas Seal prof. Can. Lung Assn., 1979-80; 1st Deans Disting. lectr. in clin. scis. Columbia U. Coll. P&S, 1982; mem. Am. Bd. Pediat., founding mem. sub-bd. on pediat. pulmonology; bd. dirs. A.P. Gold Found. to promote humanism in medicine. Mem. editl. bd. Am. Rev. Respiratory Diseases, 1974-81, assoc. editor, 1984-90; contbr. articles to profl. jours. V.p. Am. Lung Assn., 1987—89; chmn. steering com. multi-ctr. study heart and lung complications of HIV infection in children NIH, 1989—2003; bd. dir. Am. Lung Assn., 1981—83, LA Jonas Found., 1970—78, 1990—, Symphony of UN, 1990—; bd. dirs. Am. Lung Assn. City of N.Y., 2001—05. Recipient Career Devel. award NIH, 1966-71, Career Scientist award Health Rsch. Coun. NYC Health Rsch. Coun., 1975, Stevens Triennial Rsch. award

Columbia U., 1980, Health Edn. Rsch. award Nat. Asthma Edn. Program, 1992, Will Ross medal Am. Lung Assn., 1996, 2001, Life & Breath award Am. Lung Assn. NY, Outstanding Alumnus award Babies Hosp., Columbus, 2006. Mem.: Am. Acad. Allergy and Immunology, Soc. Critical Care Medicine, Am. Thoracic Soc. (bd. dir. 1975, 1981—84, nat. pres. 1982—83, v.p., Disting. Achievement award 1996), Am. Acad. Pediat. (Med. Edn. Lay Edn. award 1995, Kendig award 2003), Am. Soc. Pharmacology and Exptl. Therapeutics, Am. Physiol. Soc., Soc. Pediat. Rsch., Am. Pediat. Soc., Fleischner Soc. (pres. 1995—), Gold Humanism Honor Soc., Alpha Omega Alpha. Office: Childrens Hosp NY-Presbyn 3959 Broadway CHC 746 New York NY 10032 Home: 22 W 66th St Apt 5 New York NY 10023-6207 Home Phone: 212-362-3461; Office Phone: 212-305-8430. Business E-Mail: rbm3@columbia.edu.

MELLITS, MARC ANDREW, composer; b. Balt., Mar. 29, 1966; s. Edwin David and Janet Gloria Mellits; m. Cristina Miruna Buciu, Apr. 25, 1999; children: Nina Ileana children: Mara Rose. MusB, Eastman Sch. Music, 1988; MusM, Yale U., 1991; MusD, Cornell U., 1996. Bd. dirs. Music Journeys, Inc., Fayetteville, NY. Composer: Piano Concerto, 1984, Intervals, 1985, Piano Quartet, 1985, Duo for Alto Flute & Cello, 1986, String Quartet, 1986, 10 Pieces for Piano Solo, 1987, Road Trip, 1987, Whales Save Us, 1988, Insect Heads, 1988, Dark Age Machinery, 1988, Hooley Fooley, 1989, Music for 22 Strings, 1989, Fanfare, 1990, Bucket, 1991, Aggravated Assault, 1991, O, 1991, 11 Pieces for Flute and Piano, 1992, Trio, 1993, Aro, 1993, Polysorbate 60, 1994, Merge Left, 1994, Piccolo Concerto, 1995, Spam, 1995, Blue, 1996, 11 Miniatures for Baroque Ensemble, 1996, Large Man Looms, 1996, Five Chanukah Etudes for the Frascas, 1996, Fruit Loops, 1997, Spank Me, 1997, Jaana, 1997, Fruity Pebbles, 1997, Spin, 1998, Edible Vinyl, 1998, Parking Violation, 1999, 8 Etudes for 2 Guitars, 1999, Phase, Inc., 1999, Zoot Suit Riot, 1999, 5 Machines, 2000, Two Pieces for Flute & Guitar, 2000, Canonada, 2001, Machine V, 2001, Machine III, 2001, Dreadlocked, 2001, Troica, 2001, Opening, 2001, Machine IV, 2001, Lefty's Elegy, 2001, The Misadventures of Soup, 2001, Paranoid Cheese, 2001, Broken Glass, 2001, Zrenden Rodendan, Marija!, 2001, Groove Canon, 2002, M/W, 2002, Haiku, 2003, Season's Songs, 2003, Disciples of Gouda, 2003, Platter of Discontent, 2004, Agu, 2004, String Quartet No. 2, 2004, Tight Sweater, 2005, Gonzalo Speaks, 2005, Brick, 2005, 5 Quiet Machines, 2006, Farfalle Cotte, 2006. Recipient Bernard Rogers Best Composer prize, Eastman Sch. Music, 1987, John Day Jackson prize, Yale U., 1990, award, Found. for Contemporary Performance Arts, 2005; fellow, Cornell U., 1991—95, Tanglewood, 1997; George Eastman scholarship, Eastman Sch. Music, 1984—88. Mem.: Soc. New Music (v.p. 2005—), Common Sense Composers Collective, ASCAP (Young Composers award 1994, 1996).

MELLMAN, LEONARD, real estate developer, consultant; b. Mar. 23, 1924; s. Morris and Luba (Levin) Mellman. BA, Temple U., 1949. Prin., owner L. Mellman Co., Phila., 1949-84, Mellman Investments, Phila., 1960—; ptnr. Mellman, Blume Co., Phila., 1979—, Cunniff, Mellman Co., Phila., 1982—. Gen. ptnr. Diamond Acres, Phila., 1981—86, Van Pelt Ct. Ltd., pres., 1985—91, MLC Bd. Settlement Music Sch., Phila., 1985—91, sec. ctrl. bd., 1985—91, v.p. ctrl. bd., 1997—; bd. visitors Temple U. Coll. Liberal Arts, 2004—. Bd. dirs. Art Growth 2000, 1998—; pres. arts and sci. alumni bd. Temple U., Phila., 1976—78, bd. visitors Coll. Liberal Arts, 2004—. With US Army, 1943—46. Named Settlement 100 honoree, 2007. Mem.: Phila. Bd. Realtors, Credit Mchts. Assn. (pres. 1970—72, Man of the Yr. award 1970), Opera Vols. Internat. (treas. 1999—2003), Union League Phila. (chair, trustee Scholarship Found.), Phila. Vols. Internat., Phila. Opera Guild (bd. dirs. 1995—, pres. 1997—99, chmn. bd. dirs. 1999—2003, hon. chmn. 2003—), Singing City Choir (bd. dirs., pres. 1988—90), Temple U. Gen. Alumni Assn. (pres. 1992—94, Disting. Alumni award 1985). Democrat. Jewish. Home and Office: 220 W Rittenhouse Sq Apt 22C Philadelphia PA 19103 Personal E-mail: mellmanl@aol.com.

MELLO, CRAIG C., molecular medicine educator, researcher; b. 1960; BS in Biochemistry, Brown U., 1982; PhD in Biology, Harvard U., 1990. Postdoctoral rsch. fellow Fred Hutchinson Cancer Rsch. Ctr.; investigator Howard Hughest Med. Inst., 2000—; with U. Mass. Med. Sch., Worcester, Mass., 1994—, Blais U. chair in molecular medicine, 2003—, prof. in the program in molecular medicine. Contbr. articles to profl. journals. Co-recipient Nobel Prize in Physiology or Medicine, Nobel Found., 2006; recipient Lewis S. Rosenstiel award for Disting. Work in Basic Med. Sci., Massry prize, Wiley Prize in Biomedical Sciences, 2003, Gairdner award, Gairdner Found., 2005, Dr. Paul Janssen award for Biomedical Rsch., Johnson & Johnson, 2006, Paul Ehrlich and Ludwig Darmstaedter prize, 2006; Pew scholar, U. Calif., San Francisco, 1995. Mem.: NAS (award in molecular biology 2003). Office: Univ Mass Med Sch Biotech Two Ste 219 373 Plantation St Worcester MA 01605 also: Howard Hughes Inst Medicine 4000 Jones Bridge Rd Chevy Chase MD 20815-6789 Office Phone: 508-856-1602, 301-215-8500. Office Fax: 508-856-2950. Business E-Mail: craig.mello@umassmed.edu.

MELLO, DAWN, retail executive; b. Lynn, Mass. Student, Modern Sch. Fashion and Design, Boston. Model; asst. to fashion dir. B. Altman & Co., NYC, fashion dir., 1971—75; from corp. buying officer to v.p. and gen. merchandise mgr. May Dept. Stores Co.; v.p., fashion dir. to exec. v.p., dir. fashion merchandising Bergdorf Goodman, NYC, 1975—84, pres., 1984—89, 1994—99; creative dir. Gucci, 1989—94; cons. Dawn Mello and Assocs., NYC, 1999—. Recipient Eleanor Lambert award, Coun. Fashion Designer's Am., 2001. Office: Dawn Mello Assocs Inc 12 W 57th St # 802 New York NY 10019 *

MELLO, KERRY L., pharmacist; b. Nov. 22, 1976; PharmD, U. RI, Kingston, 2000. Registered pharmacist RI, Mass. Staff pharmacist Pharmacare Specialty Pharmacy, Providence, 2001—05; clin. pharmacist Butler Hosp., Providence, 2005—. Clin. asst. dir. pharmacy Butler Hosp., 2007—. Mem.: Coll. Psychiatric and Neurologic Pharmacists, Am. Coll. Clin. Pharmacy. Office: 345 Blackstone Blvd Providence RI 02906

MELLOAN, GEORGE RICHARD, editor; b. Greenwood, Ind., Nov. 10, 1927; s. James and Sara Ollie (Merideth) M.; m. Joan Minner, July 1, 1951; children: James, Melissa, Maryanne. BS, Butler U., 1950. Reporter Logansport (Ind.) Press, 1950, Muncie (Ind.) Press, 1951, Wall Street Jour., Chgo. and Detroit, 1952-59, bur. mgr. Cleve. and Atlanta, 1959-61, page one writer NYC, 1961-66, fgn. correspondent London, 1966-70, editl. writer NYC, 1970—2006, dep. editor, internat., 1973—, op-ed columnist, 1987—2006; ret., 2006. Co-author: The Carter Economy, 1978. Sgt. U.S. Army, 1946-47. Recipient Gerald Loeb award G&R Loeb Found., 1981, Daily Gleaner awards Inter-Am. Press Assn., 1983, 87. Mem. Coun. on Fgn. Rels., Dutch Treat Club, Echo Lake Country Club. Avocations: travel, golf, hiking, photography. Office: Wall Street Jour 200 Liberty St New York NY 10281-1003

MELLON, MATTHEW J., urologist; b. Royal Oak, Mich., Apr. 16, 1978; s. Andrew J. and Suzanne K. Mellon; m. Michelle Anne Crone, Nov. 10. BS, U. Mich., Ann Arbor, 2000; MD, Vanderbilt U., Nashville, 2004. Resident in urology Clarian Health, Ind. U. Sch. Medicine, Indpls., 2004—. Contbr. articles to profl. jours. Recipient award in humanities, Xerox. Mem.: AMA, ACS, Am. Urol. Assn., Golden Key, Phi Psi, Phi Kappa Phi, Gamma Sigma Alpha.

MELLON, SEWARD PROSSER, brokerage house executive; b. Chgo., July 28, 1942; s. Richard King and Constance Mary (Prosser) Mellon Burrell; m. Karen Leigh Boyd, Sept. 10, 1966 (div. 1974); children—Catharine Leigh, Constance Elizabeth; m. Sandra Springer Stout, 1975. Grad., Choate Sch., 1960; BA, Susquehanna U., 1965, DH, 1993. With Mellon Nat. Corp., Pitts., 1965-69; with T. Mellon & Sons, Pitts., 1969-71; pres. Richard K. Mellon & Sons, Ligonier, 1971—. Bd. dirs. Mellon Bank N.A., Mellon Fin. Corp. Trustee Richard King Mellon Family Found.; trustee, pres. Richard King Mellon Found.; chmn. real estate com., chmn. bd. mem. fin. and exec. com. Valley Sch. Ligonier. Mem. Western Pa. Conservancy (life), LoyalHanna Assn. (pres.), Vintage Club (Palm Springs, Calif.), Duquesne Club (Pitts.), Laurel Valley Golf Club (Ligonier), Rolling Rock Club, Rolling Rock Hunt, Phi Mu Delta. Republican. Home: Huntland Downs Box K Ligonier PA 15658 Office: PO Box Rkm Ligonier PA 15658-0780 Home Phone: 724-238-9517; Office Phone: 724-238-6671.

MELLON, TAMARA, apparel executive; b. Bershire, Eng., July 7, 1967; d. Tom Yeardye and Ann; m. Matthew Mellon II, 2000 (div. 2005); 1 child, Araminta. Shop asst. Browns; with Phyllis Walters Pub. Rels., Mirabella; accessories editor Brit. Vogue, 1990—96; founder, pres. Jimmy Choo, 1996—. Office: Jimmy Choo Ltd Ixworth House 37 Ixworth Pl London SW3 3QH England *

MELLOR, CHIP (WILLIAM H. MELLOR), lawyer; Grad., Ohio State U., 1973; JD, U. Denver, 1977. Public interest lawyer Mountain States Legal Found., 1979—83; pres. Pacific Research Institute for Public Policy, 1986—91; pres., gen. counsel, founder Inst. for Justice, 1991—. Office: Institute For Justice 901 N Glebe Rd Ste 900 Arlington VA 22203-1854 E-mail: wmellor@ij.org.

MELLOR, ELI, diversified financial services company executive, writer; b. Bozeman, Mont., Jan. 31, 1945; Student, Sioux Falls Coll., SD, 1963—64, U So. Calif., LA, 1966—69. Cardiovasc. surg. technician LAC, U. So. Calif., LA, 1964—69; founder, CEO Life Sci. Systems, Inc, Burbank, Calif., 1970—75, Better Homes, Upland, Calif., 1978—82; lic. prin, stock broker Bache, Halsey, Stuart, Encino, Calif., 1975—78; exec. recruiter SearchWest, LA, 1983—87; founder, trustee The Time Is Now Inst., Claremont, Calif., 1979—. Author: The Time Is Now, The Time is Still Now, The Time Was or Is Still Now; contbr. articles to profl. publs. Activist The Time Is Now Inst., Claremont, Calif., 1979—2007. Named to Presidents Club, SearchWest, 1983—86. Mem.: Nat. Acad. Polit. Sci. (corr.), LA World Affairs Coun. (corr.). Constitutional. Achievements include patents for Sinbad; Needle-aid; Dia-Kleen; Home Dializer; Shunt-Sim. Office: Time is Now Institute 1500 E Tropicana Ste 100 Las Vegas NV 89119 Home Phone: 702-376-5963; Office Phone: 702-376-5963. Office Fax: 702-952-9977. Business E-Mail: spearshakers@bresnan.net.

MELLOR, JAMES ROBB, retired electronics executive; b. Detroit, May 3, 1930; s. Clifford and Gladys (Robb) Mellor; m. Suzanne Stykos, June 8, 1953; children: James Robb, Diane Elyse, Deborah Lynn. BS in Elec. Engring. and Math., U. Mich., 1952, MS, 1953. Tech. staff Hughes Aircraft Co., Fullerton, Calif., 1955—58; pres. data systems divsn. Litton Industries, Van Nuys, Calif., 1958; exec. v.p. Litton Industries, Inc., Beverly Hills, Calif.; pres., COO AM Internat., Inc., LA, 1981; exec. v.p., dir. Gen. Dynamics Corp., Falls Church, Va., 1981—90, pres., 1990—, COO, 1990—93, CEO, 1993—97, chmn., 1994—97, USEC, Inc., 1998—, interim pres., CEO, 2004—05; dir. AmerisourceBergen, 2001—06, chmn. bd., 2004—06. Bd. dirs. Bergen Brunswig Corp., Kerr, Computer Scis. Corp., Pinkerton, U.S. Surg. Inc. Contbr. articles to profl. jours. Mem. nat. advisory com. U. Mich.; mem. US-Egypt Pres. Coun. 1st lt. Signal Corps US Army, 1953—55. Recipient Officer of the Order of the Crown, his Majesty King Baudouin of Belgium, 1987. Mem.: IEEE, Computer and Bus. Equipment Mfrs. Assn. (past chmn.), Armed Forces Comm. and Electronics Assn. (bd. dirs.), Am. Mgmt. Assn., Burning Tree Club, Congl. Country Club, Eldorado Club, L.A. Country Club, Calif. Club, Phi Beta Kappa, Eta Kappa Nu, Tau Beta Pi, Sigma Xi. Achievements include patents for storage tubes and display systems. Office: USEC 6903 Rockledge Dr Bethesda MD 20817 Office Phone: 301-564-3200.

MELLOR, JOHN WILLIAMS, economist, consultant; b. Paris, Dec. 28, 1928; came to U.S., 1929; s. Desmond W. and Katherine (Beardsley) M.; m. Arlene Patton, June 15, 1950 (div. Sept. 1972); children: Michael, Brian, Mark (dec.); m. Uma Lele, Feb. 17, 1973 (div. Apr. 1992); m. Zarmina Said, Oct. 16, 1997. BS, Cornell U., 1950, MS, 1951, PhD, 1954; Diploma, Oxford U., 1952. Prof. Cornell U., Ithaca, NY, 1953—75; chief economist USAID, Washington, 1975—77; dir. Internat. Food Policy Rsch. Inst., Washington, 1977—91; pres. John W. Mellor Assocs., Inc., Washington, 1991—98; v.p. Abt Assocs., Inc., Washington, 1998—2006; pres. John Mellor Associates, Inc., Washington, 2006—. Mem. bd. on agrl. NAS, 1989-92; mem. Agrl. Credit Commn., Res. Bank India, 1986-88. Author: Economics of Agricultural Development, 1966 (Am. Agrl. Econs. Assn. award 1978), Accelerating Food Production Growth in Sub-Saharan Africa, 1987, Agricultural Price Policy for Developing Countries, 1988 (hon. mention Am. Agrl. Econs. Assn. 1989), Agriculture on the Road to Industrialization, 1992. Mem. Internat. Commn. on Food and Peace, 1988—. Recipient Wihuri Internat. prize Wihuri Found., Helsinki, 1985, Presdl. End Hunger award The White House, 1987, Outstanding Alumni award Cornell U., 1987. Fellow AAAS, Am. Acad. Arts and Scis., Am. Agrl. Econs. Assn. (Best Pub. Rsch. award 1967). Avocations: sailing, skiing. Office: John Mellor Assocs Inc Ste PH18 801 Pennsylvania Ave NW Washington DC 20004-2668 Office Phone: 202-347-8802. Business E-Mail: jmellor@jmassocinc.com.

MELLOR, KATHY, English as a second language educator; b. Providence; BS in Elem. Edn., RI Coll., 1970, MEd, 1977; MA in Teaching, with ESL and Cross Cultural studies, Brown U., 1989. Substitute tchr. Cranston, RI Sch. Dept., 1970—74; ESL tchr. Internat. Inst. RI, 1980—85; continuing edn. tchr., english dept. RI Coll., 1985—86; cons. for ESL North Kingstown Sch. Dept., RI, 1985; ESL tchr. Hamilton Elem. Sch., North Kingstown, RI, Davisville Mid. Sch., North Kingstown, RI, 1985—. Nat. and internat. spokesperson for education, 2004—. Named Nat. Tchr. of Yr., Coun. Chief State Sch. Officers, 2004. Achievements include redesigning her school's ESL program, which provides each student with one to three periods per day in classes for English learners. The amount of instruction given depends on their skill level; providing help to students and their families by forming a local parents group called the "Ladybugs" for speakers of other languages. This improved their ability to help their children; has instructed students from virtually every part of the globe (Laos, Korea, Bolivia, Brazil, Puerto Rico, the Philippines and the Dominican Republic); hosts an International Picnic where her students and their families gather to celebrate their achievements during the school year. Office: Davisville Mid Sch 200 School St North Kingstown RI 02852 Office Phone: 401-541-6300. *

MELLOR, ROBERT E., building materials company executive, lawyer; b. 1943; BA, Westminster Coll., 1965; JD, So. Meth. U., 1968. Atty. legal dept. Union Oil Co. of Calif., 1968-73; atty. U.S. Leasing Internat. Inc., 1973-75; v.p. dir. Alexander & Bolton Inc., 1975-76; with Di Giorgio Corp., San Francisco, 1976-79, v.p., 1979-80, v.p., gen. counsel, 1980-81, v.p., sec., gen. counsel, 1981-87, sr. v.p., gen. counsel, sec., 1987, chief adminstrv. officer, exec. v.p., gen. counsel, sec.; counsel Gibson, Dunn & Crutcher, San Francisco, 1990—97; pres., CEO Building Materials Holding Co., San Francisco, 1997—2002, chmn., pres., CEO, 2002—. Bd. dir. Coeur d'Alene Mines Corp., The Ryland Group, Inc., Monroe Muffler Brake, Inc. Office: c/o BMHC 4 Embarcadero Center San Francisco CA 94111 *

MELLOR, RONALD JOHN, history professor; b. Bklyn., Sept. 30, 1940; s. Ronald Green and Eleanor Teresa (Walsh) M.; m. Anne Tidaback Kostelanetz, June 7, 1969; 1 child, Ronald Blake. AB, Fordham Coll., 1962; cert., U. Louvain, Belgium, 1961; AM, Princeton U., 1964, PhD in Classics, 1968. Asst. prof. Classics Stanford (Calif.) U., 1965-75; assoc. prof. history UCLA, 1976-82, prof. history, 1982—. Vice-chmn. history UCLA, 1985-86, 1991-92, 1998-99, chmn. history, 1992-97; visitor Princeton Inst. Advanced Studies, 1997-98. Author: Thea Rhome, 1975, Tacitus, 1993, Tacitus and the Classical Tradition, 1995, The Roman Historians, 1999, The Ancient Roman World, 2004, The World in Ancient Times: Primary Sources and Reference Volume, 2005; editor: From Augustus to Nero: The First Dynasty of Imperial Rome, 1990, The Historians of Ancient Rome, 2d edit., 2004, Text and Tradition: Studies in Greek History and Historiography in Honor of Mortimer Chambers, 1999, Augustus and the Creation of the Roman Empire, 2005. Fellow NEH, 1969, Am. Coun. Learned Socs., 1972, Humanities Rsch. Ctr. Australian Nat. U., Canberra, Australia, 1990; hon. fellow U. Coll. London, Eng., 1969, 72, 83-85. Mem. Am. Hist. Assn., Am. Philol. Assn., Assn. Ancient Historians, Soc. for the Promotion of Roman Studies. Democrat. Avocations: opera, travel, theater, tennis. Home: 2620 Mandeville Canyon Rd Los Angeles CA 90049-1004 Office: UCLA Dept History 405 Hilgard Ave Los Angeles CA 90095-1473 E-mail: mellor@history.ucla.edu.

MELLORS, ROBERT CHARLES, physician, scientist, educator; b. Dayton, Ohio, 1916; s. Bert S. and Clementine (Steinmetz) Mellors; m. Jane K. Winternitz, Mar. 25, 1944; children: Alice J., Robert C., William K., John W. PhD, Western Res. U., 1940; MD, Johns Hopkins, 1944. Diplomate Am. Bd. Pathology. Intern Nat. Naval Med. Ctr., Bethesda, Md., 1944-45; rsch. fellow medicine Meml. Ctr. Cancer and Allied Diseases, NYC, 1946-50, rsch. fellow pathology, 1950-53, asst. attending pathologist, 1953-57, assoc. attending pathologist, 1957-58. Sr. fellow Am. Cancer Soc., 1947-50; sr. clin. rsch. fellow Damon Runyon Meml. Fund, 1950-53; asst. attending pathologist Meml. Hosp., N.Y.C., 1953-57, assoc. attending pathologist, 1957-58; asst. attending pathologist Ewing Hosp., N.Y.C., 1953-57, assoc. attending pathologist, 1957-58; instr. biochemistry Western Res. U., 1940-42; rsch. assoc. Poliomyelitis Rsch. Ctr. and Dept. Epidemiology Johns Hopkins U. Sch. Hygiene, 1942-44; asst. prof. biology Meml. Ctr. Cancer and Allied Diseases, N.Y.C., 1952-53; asst. prof. pathology Sloan Kettering div. Cornell U., 1953-57, assoc. prof., 1957-58; prof. pathology Cornell U. Med. Coll., 1961-90, prof. emeritus, 1990—; adj. prof. pathology N.Y. Med. Coll., 1997—; assoc. attending pathologist N.Y. Hosp., 1961-72, attending pathologist, 1972-86; pathologist-in-chief, dir. labs., 1958-84, emeritus, 1984-85, hon. staff, 1986—; assoc. dir. rsch. Hosp. for Spl. Surgery, N.Y.C., 1958-69, dir. rsch., 1969-84, emeritus, 1984-85, scientist emeritus, 1986—; mem. rsch. adv. com. NIH, 1962-66; adv. com. Nat. Inst. Environ. Health Sci., 1966-69; com. nomenclature and classification of disease Coll. Am. Pathologists, 1960-64. Author: Analytical Cytology, 1955, 2d edit., 1959, Analytical Pathology, 1957, also 5 med. sch. tchg. documents online. Mem. Conservation Bd., Town of North Castle, Westchester, NY. Served as lt. (j.g.), M.C. USNR, 1944-46. Recipient Kappa Delta award Am. Acad. of Orthopedic Surgeons, 1962 Fellow Royal Coll. Pathologists, Molecular Medicine Soc., Am. Soc. Clin. Pathology; mem. Internat. Soc. for Optical Engring., Am. Assn. Pathologists, Am. Assn. Immunologists, Am. Soc. Biochemistry and Molecular Biology, Am. Coll. Rheumatology, Am. Orthopedic Assn. (hon.), Phi Beta Kappa. Home: 3 Hardscrabble Cir Armonk NY 10504-2222 Personal E-mail: rmellors@optonline.net.

MELLO-THOMS, CLAUDIA, medical educator, researcher; d. Jose Souto de Mello and Maria Gilvanete Barros de Mello; m. Renny Thoms, Oct. 19, 1996. BSc, U. Fed. de Pernambuco, Recife, 1988; MSEE, U. Fed. do Rio de Janeiro, 1991; PhD, Rutgers U., New Brunswick, 2001, U. Medicine and Dentistry of NJ. Rsch. asst. U. Pa., Phila., 1997—2001; rsch. asst. prof. U. Pitts., 2001—. Cons. Network of Advisors, NYC, 2005—. Author: (short stories) Lavraluz, 1983; contbr. articles to profl. jours. Recipient Best Clin. Sci. Paper award, Assn. U. Radiologists, 2003; grantee NIH/Nat. Cancer Inst., 2004—. Mem.: Med. Image Perception Soc. Buddhist. Achievements include research in determining that radiologists do not make decisions to report or dismiss perceived findings based only on the finding itself, but in comparing the finding with the background; demonstrating that the way a radiologist samples the background offers a good indication about whether they will read the case correctly. Avocations: reading, gardening, cats, hiking, movies. Office: U Pitts 3362 Fifth Ave Pittsburgh PA 15213 Office Phone: 412-641-2570. Business E-Mail: cmellothoms@magee.edu.

MELLOTT, JOHN C., publishing executive; Grad., Case Western Reserve U., 1979. CPA. Controller Atlanta Journal-Constitution, 1987—91, v.p. & gen. mgr., 1992—2000, pub., 2004—; treas. Cox Enterprises, 1991—92, v.p. bus. devel. & planning, 2000—02; pres. Dent Wizard Internat., 2002—04. Office: Atlanta Journal-Constitution 72 Marietta St NW Atlanta GA 30303 Mailing: Atlanta Journal-Constitution PO Box 4689 Atlanta GA 30302 Office Phone: 404-526-5892. Business E-Mail: jmellott@ajc.com. *

MELLOY, MICHAEL J., federal judge; b. Dubuque, IA, 1948; m. Jane Anne Melloy; children: Jennifer, Katherine, Bridget. BA, Loras Coll., 1970; JD, U. Iowa, 1974. With O'Conner & Thomas P.C. (formerly O'Conner, Thomas, Wright, Hammer, Bertsch & Norby, Dubuque, Iowa, 1974-86; judge US Bankruptcy Ct. (no. dist.) Iowa, 1986-92, US Dist. Ct. (no. dist.) Iowa, Cedar Rapids, 1992—2002; chief judge, 1992—99; judge US Ct. Appeals (8th cir.), 2002—. With US Army, 1970-72, USAR, 1972-76. Mem. ABA, Comml. Law League Am., Nat. Conf. Bankruptcy Judges, Eighth Cir. Judicial Coun. (bankruptcy judge rep., bankruptcy com.), Iowa State Bar Assn. (coun. mem. bankruptcy and comml. law sect.), Ill. State Bar Assn., Dubuque County Bar Assn., Linn County Bar Assn., Mason L. Ladd Inn of Ct., Rotary. Address: 625 1st St SE #200 Cedar Rapids IA 52401-2032 *

MELLUM, GALE ROBERT, lawyer; b. Duluth, Minn., July 5, 1942; s. Lester Andrew and Doris Esther (Smith) M.; m. Julie Murdoch Swanstrom, July 23, 1966; children: Eric Scott, Wendy Jane. BA summa cum laude, U. Minn., 1964, JD magna cum laude, 1968. Bar: Minn. 1968. Assoc. Faegre & Benson, Mpls., 1968-75, ptnr., 1976—, mem. mgmt. com., 1986-98. Mem. planning com. Garret Corp. and Securities Law Inst., Northwestern U. Law Sch., 1984—; bd. dirs., mem. adv. bd. Quali Tech Inc., Chaska, Minn., 1985-98; corp. sec. Excelsior-Henderson Motorcycle Mfg. Co., Belle Plaine, Minn., 1997-2000. Hockey chmn. LARC Bd., Mpls., 1980—85. Mem. ABA (fed. securities regulation com.), Minn. Bar Assn., Hennepin County Bar Assn. Republican. United Ch. Of Christ. Avocations: tennis, golf, snow and water skiing, handball, boating. Home: 3833 Thomas Ave S Minneapolis MN 55410 Office: Faegre & Benson 2200 Wells Fargo Ctr 90 S 7th St Ste 2200 Minneapolis MN 55402-3901 Home Phone: 612-926-1093; Office Phone: 612-766-7317. E-mail: gmellum@faegre.com.

MELMAN, RICHARD, restauranteur; m. Martha Melman; 3 children. Owner, chef R.J. Grunts, Chgo., 1971; pres. Lettuce Entertain You Enterprises Inc., Chgo. Recipient Outstanding Svc. award, James Beard Found., 2007. Office: Lettuce Entertain You Enterprises Inc 5419 N Sheridan Rd Chicago IL 60640-1900 *

MELMER, RICK, school system administrator; m. Valerie Melmer; children: Tara, Megan, Sean. BA in Elementary Edn. and Psychology, Dakota Wesleyan U.; MA in Elementary Edn., SD State U.; EdD in Ednl. Adminstrn., U. Wyo. Supt. schools Sioux Ctr. Cmty. Sch. Dist., Iowa,

1991—95, Watertown Sch. Dist., 1995—2003; sec. edn. SD Dept. Edn., Pierre, 2003—. Instructed grad. courses U. Sioux Falls, Morningside Coll., Iowa Area Edn. Agy., SD State Univ. Avocations: watching baseball, running, reading. Office: SD Dept Edn 700 Governors Dr Pierre SD 57501 Office Phone: 605-773-5669. Office Fax: 605-773-6139. Business E-Mail: rick.melmer@state.sd.us. *

MELNICHENKO, YURI B., physicist; b. Kiev, Ukraine, Dec. 4, 1953; s. Boris and Inna Melnichenko; m. Galina Kalchenko, July 23, 1977; children: Oleg, Yuri Jr. B in Physics, Kiev State U., 1974, MS in Physics, 1976, PhD in Physics, 1984; DSc, Inst. Macromolecular Chemistry, Ukrainian Acad. Sci., 1992. Rsch. assoc. Kiev State U., 1976—84; sr. rsch. assoc. Inst. Macromolecular Chemistry, Kiev, 1984—93; vis. rschr. Max Plank Inst. for Polymer Rsch., Mainz, Germany, 1993—95; sr. rsch. assoc. Ctr. Neutron Scattering Oak Ridge Nat. Lab., Tenn., 1995—. Author more than 110 papers in peer reviewed phys. jours. Fellow, Humboldt Found., 1992, Am. Physics Soc., 2005. Home: 632 Lark Meadow Dr Knoxville TN 37934 Office: Oak Ridge Nat Lab 1 Bethel Valley Rd Oak Ridge TN 37831-6393 Home Phone: 865-250-8329; Office Phone: 865-576-7746.

MELNICK, JANE FISHER, writer, educator, photographer; b. Boston, Sept. 26, 1939; d. Richard T. and Mary (Holcombe) Fisher; m. Burton A. Melnick, Dec. 1962 (div. 1969); 1 child, Benjamin A.; life ptnr. Eileen Willenborg, 1978—. BA cum laude, Radcliffe Coll., 1962; MA, NYU, 1985, PhD in Am. Studies, 1991. News writer, photographer, freelance editor, 1962—75; editor, writer, photographer In These Times, Chgo., 1976-78; grapnics editor, writer Seven Days, NYC, 1978-81; instr. writing, journalism, Am. lit. and history NYU, 1981-86; instr. writing, Am. lit. Loyola U., Chgo., 1988-91; asst. prof. Elmhurst (Ill.) Coll., 1991-96; writer, coll. prep. tutor Chgo., 1997—2004. Recipient Phi Beta Kappa award for best creative work by an undergrad. Radcliffe Coll., 1959; Mademoiselle mag. fiction contest award, 1962, NEA grantee, 1973, dean's dissertation fellow NYU, 1987. Mem. MLA, Mid-Am. Am. Studies Assn. (exec. bd.) Avocations: home renovation, travel. Home: 5000 N Marine Dr Apt 15A Chicago IL 60640-3226

MELNICK, MICHAEL, geneticist, educator; b. NYC, Sept. 24, 1944; s. Lester and Evelyn (Rosenberg) M.; m. Anita Goldberger, June 19, 1966; children: Cliff, Lynn. BA in Biology, NYU, 1966, DDS, 1970; PhD in Genetics, Ind. U., 1978. Instr. oral medicine Ind. U., Indpls., 1973-74, fellow in med. genetics, 1974-77, asst. prof. med. genetics, 1977-78; rsch. assoc. prof. U. So. Calif., LA, 1978-85, assoc. prof., 1985-89, prof. genetics, 1989—. Cons. in human genetics NIH, Bethesda, Md., 1977-88, grant reviewer, 1978—; manuscript referee Am. Jour. Human Genetics, Chgo., 1980—, Am. Jour. Med. Genetics, Helena, Mont., 1980—; MRC vis. prof. McGill U., Montreal, que., 1990. Author, editor 5 books on human genetics; editor-in-chief Jour. Craniofacial Genetics, 1980-2000; contbr. more than 100 articles to profl. jours. Mem. nat. bd. Com. of Concerned Scientists, N.Y.C., 1983—; vice chmn. Youth Towns of Israel, L.A., 1986—. Capt. M.C. U.S. Army, 1970-73. Recipient Ind. U. Disting. Alumnus award, 1984; Warwick James fellow U. London/Guy's Hosp., 1992. Fellow AAAS; mem. Soc. Craniofacial Genetics (pres. 1978-79), Soc. for Developmental Biology, Am. Soc. Human Genetics, Sigma Xi. Achievements include research in delineated major gene causation of cleft lip and palate; delineated insulin-like growth factor, type 2, receptor control of fetal lung, salvary gland and palate development; delineated molecular pathogenesis of viral-induced birth defects; application of probability neural networks to multi-gene analysis; molecular pathology of embryonic CMV infection. Avocations: art, philosophy, chess. Office: Univ So California Den 4266 Mc 0641 Los Angeles CA 90089-0641 Business E-Mail: mmelnick@usc.edu.

MELNICK, PETER RODGERS, composer; m. Laini Melnick; children: Daniel, Reine. Ed., Harvard Coll., Berklee Coll. Music, Guildhall Sch. Music and Drama; studied jazz with Jaki Byard. Composer: (films) Vampire Knights, 1987, Homesick, 1988, LA Story, 1991, Convicts, 1991, In the Name of the Father, 1992, Only You, 1992, Arctic Blue, 1993, No One Could Protect Her, 1996, The Only Thrill, 1997, Time to Say Goodbye?, 1997, Call Waiting, 2004, Farce of the Penguins, 2007, (TV films) Get Smart, Again!, 1989, The KGB the Computer and Me, 1990, Testing Dirty, 1990, Bad Attitudes, 1991, Running Mates, 1992, 12:01, 1993, Indictment: The McMartin Trial, 1995, Lily Dale, 1996, Grand Avenue, 1996, Two Mothers for Zachary, 1996, For Hope, 1996, Jitters, 1997, Every 9 Seconds, 1997, Mermaid, 2000, Becoming Dick, 2000, Taking Back Our Town, 2001, (TV series) Magic, 1991, (documentaries) Mystery of the Master Builder, The Dinosaurs!, Washington National Cathedral, Edgar Allan Poe: Tales of Mystery and Imagination, 1995, The Original GI Bill, American Masters Portrait: Robert Rauschenberg, Tak for Alt: Survival of a Human Spirit, 1999, (plays) The Curse of Kulyenchikov, Primates, Chinese Cabaret, Sextet, Patter for the Floating Lady, The Last Smoker in America, Adrift in Macao, 2006. Mailing: c/o Jack Tantleff The William Morris Agy 1325 Avenue of the Americas New York NY 10019 *

MELNYK, EUGENE N., professional sports team executive, retired pharmaceutical executive; Founder, pres., CEO Trimel, 1983—91; chmn. bd. dirs. BCI, 1991—94; exec. chmn. Biovail Corp., Mississauga, Ont., Canada, 1994—2007, CEO, 2001—04; owner, gov. & chmn. Ottawa Senators Hockey Club, 2003—. Office: Ottawa Senators 1000 Palladium Dr Kanata ON K2V 1A5 Canada *

MELO, WELTON, professional soccer player; b. Rio de Janeiro, Apr. 17, 1975; Forward Brazilian Club Am., 1995, New Eng. Revolution, 1996, L.A. Galaxy, 1997—98, Miami Fusion, 1999—2001, Pittsburgh Riverhounds, 2001—02, Fredrikstad FK, Norway, 2003, Seattle Sounders, 2004—. Named Maj. League Soccer All-Star, 1996. Mailing: Seattle Sounders PO Box 80966 Seattle WA 98108

MELODY, MICHAEL EDWARD, publishing company executive; b. Streator, Ill., Dec. 22, 1943; s. Giles Lambert and Rose Mary (Moreschi) M.; m. Carol Ann Weir, June 8, 1968 (div.); 1 dau., Alison Anne; m. Bonnie Kaye Binkert, Mar. 26, 1983. BA, Ala. Coll., 1966. Exec. editor, asst. v.p. Prentice-Hall, Inc., Englewood Cliff, NJ, 1974-79; v.p., editor-in-chief coll. divsn. Macmillan Pub. Co., NYC, 1979-80, sr. v.p., pres. coll. divsn., 1980-87, pres. sch. divsn., 1987—88; v.p. higher edn. group Simon & Schuster, NYC, 1988-90; sr. v.p. Houghton Mifflin Co., Boston, 1990-91, exec. v.p., 1991-95; prin. Michael E. Melody Cons., Boston, 1995-96; v.p., gen. mgr. info. prodn. Inso Corp., Boston, 1996-99; pres, CEO, bd. dirs. Sage Pubs., Inc., Thousand Oaks, Calif., 1999—2005. Chmn. bd. dirs. Appleton & Lange, N.Y.C., 1989-90; bd. dirs. Sage Publs., Ltd., London. Bd. overseers Huntington Theatre Co., Boston, 1993-96; bd. advisors Boston U. Sch. for the Arts, 1997-2000; bd. dirs. Judge Baker Ctr. for Children, Harvard U. Med. Sch., 1997-99, mem. exec. com.; pres. adv. coun. Calif. Luth. U., 2001-05; trustee New West Symphony, 2003-05, So. N.H. U., 2003—06; treas., bd. dirs. Santa Fe Symphony Orch., 2006—. Mem. Assn. Am. Pubs. (vice chmn. coll. divsn. 1981-83, chmn. coll. divsn. 1983-86, exec. com. sch. divsn. 1987-88, exec. com. higher edn. divsn. 1990—), Nat. Assn. Coll. Stores (trustee 1986-87, 94-95). E-mail: michael.melody@gmail.com.

MELONE, JOSEPH JAMES, retired insurance company executive; b. Pittston, Pa., July 27, 1931; s. Dominick William and Beatrice Marie (Pignone) Melone; m. Marie Jane DeGeorge, Jan. 23, 1960; children: Lisa, Carol. BS, U. Pa., 1953, MBA, 1954, PhD in Econs., 1961. CPCU; ChFC. Assoc. prof. ins. U. Pa., 1959-66, mem. pension rsch. coun., 1961-66; rsch. dir. Am. Coll. Life Underwriters, 1966-68; v.p. Prudential Ins. Co., Boston, 1969-76, sr. v.p. Newark, 1976-81, exec. v.p., 1981-84, pres., 1984-90, Equitable Life Assurance Soc. U.S., 1990-94, COO, bd. dirs.; pres. Equitable Cos., Inc., 1992-96, COO, bd. dirs., pres. NYC, 1996-98, CEO; chmn. Equitable Life Assurance Soc. U.S., NYC, 1994-98. Chmn., CEO Equitable Variable Life Ins. Co.; bd. dirs. Foster Wheeler Corp., BISYS, Inc.; chmn. bd. dirs. Horace-Mann Educators Corp.; chmn. emeritus Equitable Cos. Author: Collectively Bargained Multi-Employer Pension Plans, 1961; co-author: Risk and Insurance, 1963, Pension Planning, 1966. Trustee Newark Mus.; bd. dirs. Greater N.Y. couns. Boy Scouts Am.; chmn. ins. divsn. Caridnal's Commn. Laity N.Y. Archdioceses; bd. overseers Wharton Sch. U. Pa. Mem.: Baltusrol Golf Club, Lost Tree Golf Club, Morris County Country Club, Alpha Tau Omega. Home: Gen Delivery New Vernon NJ 07976-9999 Office: Equitable Cos Inc 1290 Ave of Americas New York NY 10104 Home Phone: 973-377-6640; Office Phone: 212-314-2060. Personal E-mail: joere@mac.com. Business E-Mail: joseph.melone@axa-financial.com.

MELORO, PEGGY ARM-BOSLEY, retired rehabilitation nurse, small business owner; BSN, West Tex. State U., Canyon, 1978. RN. Nursing supr. Palo Duro Hosp. Care Unit, Canyon, 1980—92, Palo Duro Hosp. Outpatient Chem. Dependency Program, Canyon, 1990—92, interim program dir., 1990—92; owner Peggy's Custom Covers, Amarillo, Tex., 2006—. Avocations: sewing, tatting, crocheting, equestrianship, stock investment. Office: Peggy's Custom Covers 6201 Estacado Ln Amarillo TX 79109 Office Phone: 806-223-5755.

MELOY, JUDITH MARIE, humanities educator; b. Pitts., Oct. 22, 1951; d. John C. and Miriam Meloy. BA, Denison U., 1973; MST, U. Dayton, 1982; PhD, Ind. U., 1986. Admissions counselor Denison U., Granville, Ohio, 1973—74; tchr. Centerville (Ohio) City Schs., 1978—83; program evaluation Conn. State Dept. Edn., Hartford, 1987—89; prof. Vt. State Colls., Castleton, 1989—. Dept. chair, 1994—95; chair tchg. and scholarship com., 2001—03; faculty fellow, 1996—97. Author: (book) Writing the Qualitative Dissertation: Understanding by Doing, 1994, Writing the Qualitative Dissertation: Understanding by Doing, 2d edit., 2002. Comty. Svc., Castleton, 1998—; mem. Hayes Found. Bd., 1992—. Recipient Outstanding Faculty award, Castleton State Coll. Alumni Assn., 2005. Mem.: Am. Ednl. Rsch. Assn. (chmn. qualitative rsch. spl. interest group 2004—06). Office: Castleton State Coll Castleton VT 05735 Business E-Mail: judy.meloy@castleton.edu.

MELOY, SYBIL PISKUR, retired lawyer; b. Chgo., Dec. 1, 1939; d. Michael M. and Laura (Stevenson) Piskur; children: William S., Bradley M. BS with honors, U. Ill., 1961; JD, Chgo. Kent Coll. Law, 1965. Bar: Ill. 1965, Fla. 1985, D.C. 1995, U.S. Dist. Ct. (no. dist.) Ill. 1965, U.S. Supreme Ct. 1972, U.S. Ct. Appeals (fed. cir.) 1983, U.S. Dist. Ct. (so. dist.) Fla. 1985, D.C. 1995. Patent chemist, patent atty., sr. atty., internat. counsel G.D. Searle & Co., Skokie, Ill., 1961-72; regional counsel Abbott Labs., North Chicago, Ill., 1972-78; pvt. practice Arlington Heights, Ill., 1978-79; asst. gen. counsel Alberto Culver Co., Melrose Park, Ill., 1979-83; corp. counsel Key Pharms., Inc., Miami, Fla., 1983-86; assoc. Ruden, Barnett, McCloskey, Smith, Schuster and Russell, Pa., 1987-89, ptnr. Pa., 1990-91, Foley & Lardner, Miami, Washington, 1991—2001. Adj. prof. Univ. of Miami Sch. of Law, 1986-92. Contbr. article on fertility control and abortion laws, book rev. on arbitration to law revs. Recipient Abbott Presdl. award, 1977; Bur. Nat. Affairs prize, 1965; Law Rev. prize for best article. Mem. ABA, Chgo. Bar Assn. (chmn.-elect and vice chmn. internat. and fgn. law com.), Am. Patent Law Assn., Am. Chem. Soc., Licencing Execs. Soc., Phi Beta Kappa, Phi Kappa Phi. Patentee oral contraceptive, 1965. Office: 1676 32d St NW Washington DC 20007-2960 Office Phone: 202-338-5744.

MELROSE, IAN PAUL ELLIS, music educator, director, secondary school educator; MusB in Edn., U. Wis., Madison, 2002; MusM in Tuba Performance, U. Ga., Athens, 2004. Cert. instr. K-12 instrumental music Wis., 2002. Dir. H.S. band Beloit Turner H.S., Wis., 2004—. Musician: Bulldog Brass Quintet. Mem.: Music Educators Nat. Conf.

MELROSE, KENDRICK BASCOM, manufacturing executive; b. Orlando, Fla., July 31, 1940; s. Henry Bascom and Dorothy (Lumley) M.; children: Robert, Velia, Kendra. BS cum laude, Princeton U., 1962; M.Sc., MIT, 1965; MBA, U. Chgo., 1967. Mktg. mgr. Pillsbury Co., Mpls., 1967-69; dir. corp. planning Bayfield Techs., Inc., Mpls., 1969-70; dir. mktg., consumer products Toro Co. (mfrs. outdoor power equipment), Mpls., 1970—73, pres., Game Time Litchfield, Mich., 1973—76, v.p., outdoor power equipment Mpls., 1976—80, exec. v.p. outdoor power equipment div., 1980-81, pres., 1981-88, chief exec. officer, 1983—2005, chmn., 1987—2005, exec. chmn., 2005. Congregationalist. Office: Toro Co 8111 Lyndale Ave S Minneapolis MN 55420-1196

MELROY, PAMELA ANN, astronaut; b. Palo Alto, Calif., Sept. 17, 1961; d. David and Helen M.; married BS in Physics and Astronomy, Wellesley Coll., 1983; MSc in Earth and Planetary Scis., MIT, 1984. Commd. 2nd lt. USAF, 1983, advanced through grades to lt. col.; co-pilot KC-10, aircraft comdr., instr. pilot Barksdale AFB, Bossier City, La.; test pilot C-17 Combined Test Force; shuttle pilot NASA, Houston, pilot STS-92 (Discovery), 2000, pilot STS-112 (Atlantis), 2002, shuttle comdr. STS-120 to Internat. Space Station, 2006, selected as astrounaut, 1994, astronaut, 1995—. Bd. trustee Wellesley Coll. Decorated Air Force Meritorious Svc. medal with oak leaf cluster, Air medal with oak leaf cluster, Aerial Achievement medal with oak leaf cluster, Expeditionary medal with oak leaf cluster. Mem. Soc. Exptl. Test Pilots, Order of Daedalians, 99s. Achievements include being the second female astronaut to command a US orbiter. Avocations: theater, tap and jazz dancing, reading, cooking, flying. Office: Astronaut Office/CB NASA Lyndon B Johnson Space Ctr Houston TX 77058

MELSHEIMER, MEL P(OWELL), venture capitalist; b. LA, July 9, 1939; s. Oscar Merrill M.; m. Sara Sturdevant, Sept. 1, 1962; children: Heidi, Erich, Douglas. AB, Occidental Coll., 1961; MBA, U. So. Calif., 1965. With United Calif. Bank, Los Angeles, 1962-66; sr. fin. analyst Ford Motor Co., Newport Beach, Calif., 1966-67; v.p., chief fin. officer Pepsi Cola Co. Pepsico, Inc., Purchase, NY, 1968-75; exec. v.p., chief operating officer AZL Resources, Inc., 1975-84; chmn. bd., CEO PHX Pacific, Inc., 1984-89; pres., CEO MPM Capital Corp., 1987-89; exec. v.p. Finevest Foods, Inc., Greenwich, Conn., 1989-92; pres., CEO Land-O-Sun Dairies Inc., 1991-92, Atlanta Dairies, Inc., 1991-92; exec. v.p., sec., COO Dairy Holdings, Inc., Johnson City, Tenn., 1992-94; exec. v.p., COO, CFO Sonex Internat. Corp., Brewster, NY, 1994; pres., CEO M.P. Melsheimer & Co., Ridgefield, Conn., 1994-97; pres. NFX, 1995-96; pres., COO, CFO Harris & Harris Group, Inc., NYC, 1997—2004; pres. Linkhorn Capital Advisors, Inc., 2005—; chmn. bd. Patriot Capital Funding Inc., 2006—. Served with U.S. Army, 1961-62. Home: 1418 N Woodhouse Rd Virginia Beach VA 23454 E-mail: melmelsheimer@msn.com.

MELSHEIMER, THOMAS M., lawyer; BA magna cum laude, U. Notre Dame, 1983; JD magna cum laude, U. Tex., 1986. Bar: Tex. 1986. Law clk. to Hon. Homer Thornberry US Ct. Appeals (5th cir.), 1986—87; asst. US atty. No. Dist. Tex., 1990—93; mng. prin. Fish & Richardson, P.C., Dallas. Former prof. U. Tex. Sch. Law, Austin, So. Meth. U. Sch. Law, Dallas. Contbr. articles to profl. jours. Named one of Best Lawyers in Dallas, D Mag., 2005. Mem.: Am. Bd. Trial Advs., Dallas Bar Assn., ABA. Office: Fish & Richardson PC 1717 Main St Ste 5000 Dallas TX 75201-4612 Office Phone: 214-292-4001. Office Fax: 214-747-2091. E-mail: melsheimer@fr.com. *

MELTON, ARTHUR RICHARD, public health administrator; b. Ysleta, Tex., Apr. 28, 1943; s. Francis Charles and Jean (Graham) M.; m. Frances Bay, Aug. 19, 1965; children: David Bay, Amy Elizabeth. BS, U. Utah, 1969; MPH, U. N.C., 1974, D in Pub. Health, 1976. Dir. labs. S.D. Dept. Health, Pierre, 1976-87; microbiologist Utah Dept. Health, Salt Lake City, 1970-73, dir. divsn. lab. svcs., 1987-92, dep. dir., 1992—. Mem.: Assn. State and Territorial Health Ofcls. (pres. elect 1999—2000, pres. 2000—01), SD Pub. Health Assn. (pres. 1980—81, past. pres. 2001—06), Am. Pub. Health Assn. (governing coun. 1980—83). Mem. Lds Ch. Home: 6835 Heather Way West Jordan UT 84084-2304 Office: PO Box 141000 Salt Lake City UT 84114-1000 Office Phone: 801-538-6111. Personal E-mail: dickmelton@yahoo.com. Business E-Mail: dmelton@utah.gov.

MELTON, BARRY, lawyer, musician; b. NYC, June 14, 1947; s. James Gerald and Terry Melton; m. Barbara Joy Langer; children: Kingsley, Kyle. Bar: Calif. 1982, U.S. Dist. Ct. (no. dist.) Calif. 1982, U.S. Dist. Ct. (cen. dist.) Calif. 1983, U.S. Ct. Appeals (9th cir.) 1983, U.S. Dist. Ct. (ea. dist.) Calif. 1985, U.S. Supreme Ct. 1988. Pvt. practice, San Francisco, 1982-94; pub. defender Yolo County, Calif., 2000—. Musician, pub. Seafood Music, San Francisco, 1965—; pro-tem judge San Francisco Mcpl. Ct., 1987—94. Musician, composer various mus. recs., 1965—. Mem. State Bar Calif. (cert. criminal law specialist 1993—, vol. legal svc. awards 1983-87), Calif. Attys. Criminal Justice, Calif. Pub. Defenders Assn. (pres., 2006), Yolo County Bar Assn. (pres. 2004). Office: Yolo County Pub Defender 814 North St Woodland CA 95695-3538 Office Phone: 530-666-8165. E-mail: thefish@counterculture.net.

MELTON, BRIAN CHRISTOPHER, history professor, writer; b. Columbus, Ga., Jan. 29, 1976; s. Clinton Dale and Maragret Ray Melton; m. Kami Rene Harris, May 13, 2000; 1 child, Annora Hope. BS in Philosophy and Religion, Toccoa Falls Coll., Ga., 1998; MA in US History, PhD in US History, Tex. Christian U., Ft. Worth, 2003. Grading asst. Tex. Christian U., Ft. Worth, 1999—2001, tchg. asst., 2001—03; asst. prof. history Liberty U., Lynchburg, Va., 2003—. Adj. instr. Tarrant County Coll., Ft. Worth, 2001—03. Author: Sherman's Forgotten General: Henry W. Slocum; contbr. articles to profl. jours. and mags. Facilitator writers and artists support group Inklings III, Lynchburg, Va., 2004. Recipient Outstanding Svc. award, Tex. Christian U. Dept. History, 2002. Mem.: Popular Culture Assn., So. Hist. Assn., Liberty U. Kumdo Club (asst. instr. 2005, faculty adviser 2005). Independent. Avocations: writing, martial arts, hiking, home improvement, reading. Office: History Dept Liberty Univ 1971 Univ Blvd Lynchburg VA 24502 Home Phone: 434-946-2352; Office Phone: 434-592-4028. Business E-Mail: bmelton@liberty.edu.

MELTON, CAROL A., communications executive; b. St. Augustine, Fla., 1954; m. Joseph M. Hassett; children: Matthew, Meredith Hassett. BA with honors, Wake Forest U., 1976; MA in Journalism and Comm., U. Fla., 1977; JD with honors, Am. U., 1981. Assoc. in comm. grp. Hogan and Hartson, Washington, 1981-82; asst. gen. counsel Nat. Cable TV Assn., 1983-86; legal adv. to Chmn. Mark Fowler FCC, Washington, 1986-87; Washington counsel Warner Comm., 1987-91; v.p. law and pub. policy Time Warner Inc., Washington, 1992-97; exec. v.p. govt. rels., exec. officer Viacom, Inc., Washington, 1997—2005; exec. v.p. global pub. policy, exec. officer Time Warner Inc., 2005—. Trustee The Media Inst., Washington, 1997—2005, Washington Performing Arts Soc., 1997—99, The Potomac Sch., McLean, Va., 1999—2000, Meridian Internat. Ctr., 2001—03; mem. Fed. City Coun., 1997—, Coun. on Fgn. Rels., 2006—. Office: Time Warner Inc 800 Connecticut Ave NW Washington DC 20006

MELTON, DAVID REUBEN, lawyer; b. Milw., Apr. 4, 1952; s. Howard and Evelyn M.; m. Nancy Hillary Segal, May 22, 1981; children: Michelle, Hannah. BA, U. Wis., 1974; JD, U. Chgo., 1977. Bar: Ill. 1977, U.S. Dist. Ct. (no. dist.) Ill. 1977, U.S. Ct. Appeals (7th cir.) 1981, U.S. Supreme Ct. 1982, U.S. Fed. Cir. Ct. Appeals, 1991. Assoc. Karon, Morrison & Savikas, Ltd., Chgo., 1977-83; ptnr. Karon, Morrison & Savikas, Ltd., Chgo., 1983-87, Karon, Savikas & Horn, Ltd., Chgo., 1987-88, Keck, Mahin & Cate, Chgo., 1988-96; counsel Mayer, Brown & Platt, Chgo., 1996-99, ptnr., 2000—07; sr. counsel Foley & Lardner, LLP, Chgo., 2007—. Office: Foley & Lardner LLP 321 N Clark St Ste 2800 Chicago IL 60610 Office Phone: 312-832-4599. Business E-Mail: dmetton@foley.com.

MELTON, DOUGLAS A., molecular and cell biology educator; b. 1954; BS in Biology with honors, U. Illinois, Champaign-Urbana, 1971—75; BA in History, Phil. of Sci., Cambridge U., Eng., 1975—77, PhD in Molecular Biology, 1980. Asst. prof, dept. bio chem. and molecular biology Harvard U., 1981—84, assoc. prof., 1984—87, J.L. Loeb assoc. prof. nat. sci., 1987, prof. dept. molecular and cellular biology Cambridge, Mass., 1988—; biologist (med.) Mass. Gen. Hosp., Boston; assoc. mem. Children's Hosp., Boston, 1994—; investigator Howard Hughes Med. Inst., 1994—; Thomas Dudley Cabot prof. Natural Sci. Harvard U., Cambridge, Mass., 1999—; sci. dir. Harvard Stem Cell Inst. Recipient Richard Lounsbery award NAS, 1995; named Policy Leader of Yr. within the Scientific Am. 50, Scientific Am., 2004; Named one of The World's Most Influential People, TIME Mag., 2007, 50 Who Matter Now, Bus. 2.0, 2007. Mem.: Inst. Medicine. Office: Harvard Univ Dept Molecular & Cellular Bio 7 Divinity Ave Cambridge MA 02138 *

MELTON, EMMA ALEXANDER, educational consultant, retired elementary school educator; b. Louisville, Ky., Aug. 26, 1933; d. Jesse Wilson and Reella Odessa Alexander; m. Brady Melton Jr., Apr. 17, 1960; children: Brady Aldred, Tia Meychelle. BA in English and Speech, Ctrl. State Coll., 1954; MA in Elem. Edn., Ohio State U., 1962; cert. in reading, John Carroll U. English tchr. Xenia (Ohio) City Sch., 1955—57; elem. tchr. Cleve. Pub. Sch., 1957—63, reading cons., 1969—90; social skills cons. Soc. Prevention of Violence, Cleve., 1990—92; diversity trainer of educators Anti-Defamation League, Cleve., 1992—97; worksh. Workshop facilitator Inst. Cultural Affairs Internat., various locations, 1970—2000; spkr. at nat. and internat. conf. and workshops, 1984—. Contbg. author: Sister to Sister, 1999. Adv. bd. Nuc. Age Resource Ctr., Cleve., 1994—2004; deacon First Bapt. Ch., Cleve., 1980—; advocacy bd. Interreligious Ptnrs. in Action, Cleve., 2000—; mem. adv. bd. Cleve. Ecumenical Inst. for Religious Studies, 2006—. Recipient Ecumenical award, Interchurch Coun., Cleve., 1998; grantee, Cleve. Edn. Fund, 1987; Martha Holden Jennings scholar, Jennings Found., 1981. Mem.: Delta Sigma Theta. Democrat. Baptist. Avocations: reading, travel, singing.

MELTON, GARY BENTLEY, psychologist, educator; b. Salisbury, NC, June 4, 1952; s. Harold Sumner Jr. and Marion Adair (Reeves) M.; m. Robin Jo Kimbrough, Aug. 7, 1999; children by previous marriage: Jennifer Lynn, Stephany Beth. BA, U. Va., 1973; MA, Boston U., 1975, PhD, 1978. Asst. prof. psychology Morehead (Ky.) State U., 1978-79, U. Va., Charlottesville, 1979-81; from asst. prof. to full prof. psychology and law U. Nebr., Lincoln, 1981-87, Carl A. Happold prof. psychology and law, 1987-94; prof. neuropsychiatry & behavioral science U. S.C., Columbia, 1994-99, adj. prof. law, pediat. and psychology, 1994-99, dir. Inst. Families in Soc., 1994-99; prof. psychology Clemson U., 1999—. Dir. Inst. Family and Neighborhood Life, Clemson U., 1999—. Author: Child Advocacy: Psychological Issues and Interventions, 1993; co-author: Community Mental Health Centers and the Courts: An Evaluation of Community-Based Forensic Services, 1985, Psychological Evaluations for the Courts: A Handbook for Mental Health Professionals and Lawyers, 1987, 3d edit., 2007, Pediatric and Adolescent AIDS: Research Findings from the Social Sciences, 1992, Ethical and Legal Issues in AIDS Research, 1995, No Place to Go: Civil Commitment of Minors, 1998; editor numerous books. Mem. U.S. Adv. Bd. on Child Abuse and Neglect, 1989-93, vice-chair, 1991-93. Recipient Frederick Howell Lewis award Psi Chi, 1993, Lynn

Stuart Weiss award Am. Psychol. Found., 2000. Fellow: APA (chmn. various coms., cert. recognition for psychology in pub. interest 1981, Disting. Contbn. to Psychology in Pub. Interest award 1985, Nicholas Hobbs award 1992, Harold Hildreth award 1992, Disting. Contbn. to Pub. Svc. award 1999, Disting. Contbn. to Internat. Advancement of Psychology award 2005); mem.: Am. Profl. Soc. on Abuse of Children (Career Achievement in Rsch. award 2005), Prevent Child Abuse Am. (Donna Stone award 1992), Am. Orthopsychiat. Assn. (pres. 2004—05), Am. Psychology-Law Soc. (pres. 1990—91). Unitarian Universalist. Office: Clemson U Inst Family and Neighborhood Life 158 Poole Agrl Ctr Clemson SC 29634-0132 Home Phone: 864-716-9989; Office Phone: 864-656-6271. Business E-Mail: gmelton@clemson.edu.

MELTON, HAROLD D., state supreme court justice; b. Washington; BA, Auburn U.; JD, U. Ga., 1991. Former atty. Ga. Dept. of Law, former section leader, consumer interests div.; former exec. counsel Gov. Perdue; justice Ga. Supreme Ct., 2005—. Former volunteer leader Young Life Ministries. Dir. teen ministry Southwest Christian Fellowship Church; bd. mem. Atlanta Youth Academies. Office: Ga Supreme Ct Ste 300 244 Washington St SW Atlanta GA 30334 Office Phone: 404-656-3470. Office Fax: 404-656-2253. *

MELTON, HOWELL WEBSTER, SR., federal judge; b. Atlanta, Dec. 15, 1923; s. Holmes and Alma (Combee) M.; m. Margaret Catherine Wolfe, Mar. 4, 1950; children— Howell Webster, Carol Anne. JD, U. Fla., 1948. Bar: Fla. 1948. With Upchurch, Melton & Upchurch, St. Augustine, 1948-61; judge 7th Jud. Circuit of Fla., St. Augustine, 1961-77, U.S. Dist. Ct. (mid. dist.) Fla., Jacksonville, 1977-91, sr. judge, 1991—. Past chmn. Fla. Conf. Cir. Judges, 1974; past chmn. coun. bar pres.'s Fla. Bar. Trustee Flagler Coll., St. Augustine. Served with U.S. Army, 1943-46. Recipient Disting. Service award St. Augustine Jaycees, 1953 Mem. ABA, St. Johns County Bar Assn., Jacksonville Bar Assn., Fed. Bar Assn., Fla. Blue Key, Officers Club, Masons, Phi Delta Theta, Phi Delta Phi. Methodist. Office: US Dist Ct 300 N Hogan St Ste 11-300 Jacksonville FL 32202 Office Phone: 904-549-1940.

MELTON, HOWELL WEBSTER, JR., lawyer; b. St. Augustine, Fla., Oct. 26, 1951; BA with high honors, U. Fla., 1973; JD, U. Fla. Coll. Law, 1975. Bar: Fla. 1976, DC 2006, Fla. State Cts., US Dist. Ct. (Middle Dist. Fla.), US Cir. Ct. of Appeals (11th Cir.), US Supreme Ct. With Holland & Knight LLP, NYC, 1975—, mng. ptnr. Tampa, Orlando, Chgo. and NYC offices, 2003—. Bd. dir. Enterprise Fla., Inc., chmn. fin. and compensation com., exec. com.; chmn. Metro Orlando Econ. Develop. Commn., 2000—01; past chmn. Ctrl. Fla. Tech. Partnership. Trustee emeritus U. Fla. Coll. Law; officer, mem. exec. com. bd. trustees Orlando Mus. Art, 1991—97; bd. governors Greater Orlando Region, Nat. Conf. for Community and Justice, 1990—; bd. dir. Ctrl. Fla. Fair, Inc., 1993—; trustee Greater Orlando C. of C.; mem. Orlando Leadership Class, 1990; founder, bd. dir. and sec. Leadership Orlando Alumni Assn.; mem. Orlando Mus. of Art Acquisition Trust, Savant; pres. Fla. Blue Key. Fellow: Fla. Bar Found., Am. Bar Found.; mem.: Internat. Bar Assn., DC Bar Assn., Fla. Justice Assn. (commercial litig. sect.), Am. Assn. for Justice, Am. Arbitration Assn. (panel arbitrators), Am. Judicature Soc., Fed. Bar Assn., Orange County Bar Assn., Fla. Bar Assn. (litig. sect.), ABA (litig. sect.), Phi Delta Theta (pres. 1976), Omega Delta Kappa, Phi Delta Phi, Phi Eta Sigma. Office: Holland & Knight LLP 195 Broadway New York NY 10007-3189 Office Phone: 212-513-3544, 212-513-3200. Office Fax: 212-513-2339. Business E-Mail: howell.melton@hklaw.com.

MELTON, KATHY A., medical transcription educator; b. Corpus Christi, Tex., Mar. 30, 1952; d. Thomas Rodman Smith and Dorothy Frances Hays; m. Lynn E. White (div.); children: Robert Jason White, Jerrald Martin White; m. Claude E. Melton, Jan. 21, 2005. Student, East Ctrl. State Coll., Ada, Okla., 1970—72, U. Tex., Austin, 1976—77, Houston Lighthouse for Blind, 1977—78. Med. transcriptionist Meth. Hosp., Houston, 1978—80, Cardiovascular Assoc., Athens, Tex., 1997—2002; owner, med. transcriptionist Accutrans, Houston, 1981—85; legal sec. Law Office of David Hamilton, Paris, Tex., 1986—91; receptionist Criss Cole Rehab. Ctr., Austin, 1991—94; relay agt. Relay Tex., Austin, 1994—97; owner, instr. med. transcription Kaysclass.com, Kemp, Tex., 2003—. Spkr. in field. Pres. Lake Area Coun. Blind, Athens, 1999—2003; vol. Ark. Enterprises for Blind, 1982—83; mem. team Walk to Emmaus, 1998—. Mem.: Am. Assn. Med. Transcription, Lions Club (sec. 1987—90, bd. dirs. 1998—2002). Avocation: keyboard for church and praise team. Home and Office: 10753 Buddy Parker Rd Kemp TX 75143 Office Phone: 903-498-3659. Business E-Mail: kathy@kaysclass.com.

MELTON, STEPHEN REID, lawyer; b. Savannah, Ga., Dec. 10, 1949; s. Wallace Reid and Doris Cleone (Bragg) M. BA magna cum laude, Armstrong Coll., Savannah, 1973; JD, U. Ga., Athens, 1976. Bar: Ga. 1976, DC 1979, Tex. 1992, US Supreme Ct. 1980, US Dist. Ct. DC 1980, US Ct. Appeals (DC cir.) 1980, US Ct. Appeals (7th cir.) 1980, US Ct. Appeals (10th cir.) 1981, US Ct. Appeals (5th and 11th cirs.) 1985, US Ct. Appeals (4th cir.) 1986, US Ct. Appeals (6th cir.) 1991. Atty., adviser ICC, Washington, 1976-78; staff lawyer FERC, Washington, 1978-81, dep. gen. counsel, 1981-83, acting gen. counsel, 1983-84; assoc. Beveridge & Diamond, Washington, 1984-85; sr. atty. Tex. Oil & Gas Corp., Dallas, 1985-87; asst. gen. counsel United Gas Pipe Line Co., Houston, 1987-89, asst. v.p., asst. gen. counsel, spl. asst. for regulatory affairs, 1989-90, assoc. gen. counsel, 1990-92; of counsel Akin, Gump, Strauss, Hauer & Feld, 1992—97; v.p. gen. counsel and sec. Columbia Gulf Transmission, 1997—2000; asst. sec. Columbia Gas Transmission Corp., 2000—01; assoc. gen. counsel NiSource Corp. Svcs. Co., 2000—02, dep. gen. counsel, 2002—04, dep. gen. counsel FERC compliance officer, 2004—05, v.p., dep. gen. counsel FERC compliance officer, 2005—. Contbr. articles to profl. jours. Recipient Outstanding Handicapped Employee award, US Dept. Energy, 1983, Disting. Svc. award, US Fed. Energy Regulatory Commn., 1984. Mem. ABA (adminstrv. law sect., utility law sect., bus. law sect.), Energy Bar Assn., Houston Bar Assn., DC Bar Assn., Assn. Corp. Counsel, Am. Gas Assn. (exec. legal com.). Office: NiSource Corp Svcs Co 5151 San Felipe Ste 2500 Houston TX 77056 Home Phone: 713-932-1358. Office Fax: 713-267-4755. Business E-Mail: smelton@nisource.com.

MELTON, WAYNE CHARLES, real estate executive; b. Oak Ridge, Tenn., Aug. 30, 1954; s. Charles Estel and Una Faye (Hull) M.; m. Maria Tobar-Conde; 1 child, Ingrid Tatiana. AB in European Intellectual History, U. Ga., 1975; MS in Real Estate, Shepperton U., 2001, PhD in Real Estate, 2003. Mgr. Household Internat., Athens, Ga., 1975—76; asst. mgr. Athens and Hickory, NC, Doraville, Ga., 1976—77; pres., CEO Impact Realty-Melton & Assocs. Inc., Athens, 1987—. Cons. Ga. Furniture, Charlotte Realty, NC, 1987—. Trustee Mu, Inc., Page, Ga. Ho. of Reps., 1968; chmn. Madison County Reps., 1973-74; mem. Congl. Bus. Coun., 2002. Recipient Ronald Reagan award, Rep. Congl. Com., 2004. Mem. Pheonix Club, Pres. Club, Zeta Beta Tau. Office: Impact Realty Melton & Assoc Inc 855 Sunset Dr Ste 11 Athens GA 30606-7718 Business E-Mail: impactrealty@hotmail.com.

MELTON, WILLIAM EVERETT, retired music educator; b. Roanoke, Va., June 28, 1940; s. William Everett and Cordelia Mae Melton; m. Carol Ann Drawdy, Aug. 17, 1963; children: John Morris, Marissa Kaye. BS in Music Edn., Carson-Newman Coll., 1962; MS in Music Edn., U. Tenn., 1970, EdD, 1984. Choral music tchr. Carter H.S., Knoxville, Tenn., 1968—93; instr. Carson-Newman Coll., Jefferson City, Tenn., 1993—2006; ret., 2006. Dir. music ministries Fountain City United Meth. Ch., Knoxville, 1993—2003; min. of music Smithwood Bapt. Ch., Knoxville, 2005—06. Composer, arranger: choral and handbell works. Asst. dir., music dir. Knoxville Nativity Pageant, 1987—95, mem. adv. bd., 1996—2006; vol. Jubilee Project, Sneedville, Tenn., 2004—06; choral clinician, adjudicator East Tenn. Choral Festivals. Recipient Disting. Alumnus award, Carson-Newman Coll., 2001. Mem.: NEA, Tenn. Ret. Tchrs. Assn., Am. Choral Dirs. Assn. (life). Avocations: travel, gardening.

MELTZER, ALLAN H., economist, educator; b. Boston, Feb. 6, 1928; s. George B. and Minerva I. (Simons) M.; m. Marilyn Ginsburg, Aug. 27, 1950; children: Bruce Michael, Eric Charles, Beth Denise. AB, Duke U., 1948; MA, UCLA, 1955, PhD, 1958. Lectr. econs. U. Pa., Phila., 1956-57; faculty Carnegie Mellon U. Grad. Sch. Indsl. Adminstrn., Pitts., 1957-64, prof. econs., 1964—, Maurice Falk prof. econs. and social sci., 1970-80, John M. Olin univ. prof. polit. economy and pub. policy, 1980-91, Univ. prof. polit. economy and pub. policy, 1991-97, Allan H. Meltzer Univ. prof. polit. economy, 1997—. Vis. prof. U. Chgo., 1964-65, Fundacao Getulio Vargas, Rio de Janeiro, 1976-79, City U., London, 1979-2001; vis. fellow Hoover Instn., 1977-78; vis. scholar Am. Enterprise Inst., Washington, 1989—; co-chmn. Shadow Open Market Com., 1974-89, chmn., 1989-2000; cons. US Treasury, joint econ. com. US Congress, 1960; com. on banking and currency US Ho. of Reps., 1963-64; mem. Pres.'s Econ. Policy Adv. Bd., 1988-90; acting mem. Coun. Econ. Advisors, 1988-89; panel econ. advisors Congl. Budget Office, 1995—; cons., bd. gov. FRS, FDIC; dir. Cooper Tire & Rubber Co., 1983-98, chmn. audit and compensation com., 1996-98; hon. advisor Inst. Monetary and Econ. Studies Bank of Japan, 1987-2003; bd. dir. Sarah Scaife Found., Commonwealth Found.; dir. Stillhalter Vision AG, Zurich, 1994-2002, Advanced Materials Group, 1994-2001; chmn. Internat. Fin. Instn. adv. com. to US Congress, 1999-2000; advisor Federal Reserve Bank NY, 2005-. Author: Monetary Economics, 1989, Keynes's Monetary Theory: A Different Interpretation, 1988; (with Karl Brunner) Money and the Economy: Issues in Monetary Analysis, 1993; (with Alex Cukierman and Scott Richard) Political Economy, 1991, Report of the International Financial Institution Advisory Commission, 2000, A History of the Federal Reserve, vol. 1, 2003 (Book award Econ. History Assn. 2004-05); editor: (with Karl Brunner) Carnegie-Rochester Conf. Series, 1976-89; (with Charles Plosser), 1989-97; contbr. articles to profl. jours. Recipient Outstanding Achievement award UCLA, 1983, Money Marketeers, 1997, Educator of Yr. award Pittsburg Hist. Ctr., 2003, Irving Kristol award Am. Enterprise Inst., 2003, David Horowitz prize Israel Bankers Assn., 2004; Social Sci. Rsch. Coun. fellow, 1955-56, Ford Found. fellow, 1962-63; named Man of Yr. in Fin., Pitts., 1995-96. Fellow: Nat. Assn. Bus. Economists (Adam Smith award 2003); mem.: Am. Fin. Assn., Western Econ. Assn. (pres. 1985—86), Internat. Atlantic Econ. Assn. (pres. 1999—2000), Am. Econ. Assn. (v.p. 1990, Disting. fellow 2002), Phila. Soc. (v.p. 1981—83), Cosmos Club. Achievements include research in macroeconomics. Avocations: political economy, monetary history. Office: Carnegie Mellon U Dept Econs Pittsburgh PA 15213 Office Phone: 412-268-2282. Business E-Mail: am05@andrew.cmu.edu.

MELTZER, ARTHUR ADAM, researcher; s. Mayer and Selma Meltzer; m. Adela Valadez-Plascencia. BA, SUNY, Buffalo, 1979; diploma in Human Biology, U. Oxford, 1980; MA, U. Mich., Ann Arbor, 1982; MPH, U. Tex., Houston, 1986, PhD, 1991. Rsch. analyst Ctrs. for Medicare and Medicaid Svcs., Balt., 2000—. Contbr. articles to profl. jours. Mem.: Soc. Epidemiol. Rsch. Achievements include research in population-based health. Avocations: yoga, aerobics. Office: Ctrs Medicare and Medicaid Svcs 7500 Security Blvd Baltimore MD 21224

MELTZER, BRAD, writer; married. Grad., U. Michigan, Columbia Law Sch. Co-creator (TV series) Jack & Bobby, 2004—05; author: The Tenth Justice, 1998, Dead Even, 1999, The First Counsel, 2001, The Millionaires, 2002, Zero Game, 2004, The Book of Fate, 2006, (comic books) Justice League of America, Green Arrow, 2003, Identity Crisis, 2005, (short stories) The Best Seat in the House, Final Farewell, An American Lawyer in London, The Craziest Kid in the World. Address: PO Box 801632 Aventura FL 33180

MELTZER, DANIEL J., law educator; b. Chgo., Dec. 17, 1951; AB in Econs., Harvard U., 1972, JD, 1975. Bar: Ill. 1975, DC 1978, Mass. 1983. Law clk. to Hon. Carl McGowan, 1975-76; law clk. to Hon. Potter Stewart, 1976-77; spl. asst. to sec. Joseph Califano, Jr. Dept. Health, Edn. and Welfare, 1977-78; assoc. Williams & Connolly, 1979-81; asst. prof. law Harvard Law Sch., Cambridge, Mass., 1982-87, prof., 1987—, Story prof. law, 1998—, assoc. dean, 1989-93, vice dean physical planning, 2003—. Co-editor: The Judicial Code and the Rules of Procedure in the Fed. Courts, pub. annually, 1988—2000; co-author: Hart & Wechsler's The Federal Courts and the Federal System, 1973, 1988, 1996, 2003. Fellow: Am. Acad. Arts & Sciences. Office: Harvard Law Sch 1536 Massachusetts Ave Cambridge MA 02138 Office Phone: 617-495-4659. Office Fax: 617-496-4865. Business E-Mail: meltzer@law.harvard.edu.

MELTZER, DONALD RICHARD, retired treasurer; b. Boston, Sept. 1, 1932; s. Leo N. and Betty (Flesher) M.; m. Mary Douglas Seelye, Dec. 7, 1963; children: Kimberly, Christopher. AB, Dartmouth Coll., 1954, MBA, 1955. Mgr. Peat, Marwick, Mitchell & Co., Boston, 1955-67; asst. controller United Fruit Corp., Boston, 1968-69, controller, 1969-70, v.p., controller, 1970-73; v.p., chief acctg. officer United Brands Co., NYC, 1973-74, v.p. fin. and adminstrn., 1974-76; v.p. fin., treas. Instron Corp., Canton, Mass., 1976-88; v.p. fin. and adminstrn., treas., chief fin. officer Dialogue, Inc., Braintree, Mass., 1988-90. Corp. fin. cons., Sudbury, Mass., 1988-96. Overseer Children's Hosp. Med. Ctr., Boston, 1980-94; fin. com. Town of Sudbury, Mass., 1967; chmn. bd. trustees First Parish Ch., Sudbury, 1970-71, treas., 1991-93; pres. Mass. Parents Assn. for Deaf and Hard of Hearing, Boston, 1976-77, bd. dirs., 1973-86. Mem. AICPA, Mass. Soc. CPAs, Fin. Execs. Inst., Am. Assn. Indsl. Mgmt. (bd. dirs. 1980-85), Walk 'N Mass Volkssport Club (co-pres. 1993-95). Avocations: postal history, stamp collecting/philately. Home: 341 Old Lancaster Rd Sudbury MA 01776-2035

MELTZER, JAY H., lawyer, consultant; b. Bklyn., Mar. 30, 1944; s. Solomon G. and Ethel L. (Kraft) M.; m. Joan Pike, Aug. 12, 2006; children from previous marriage: Wendy, Elizabeth, Jonathan. AB, Dartmouth Coll., 1964; JD, Harvard U., 1967. Bar: N.Y. 1968, Mass. 1978, U.S. Dist. Ct. Mass. 1979. Law clk. to U.S. dist. judge, 1967-68; assoc. firm Shearman & Sterling, NYC, 1968-72; with Damon Corp., Needham Heights, Mass., 1972-84, gen. counsel, sec., 1973-84, v.p., 1979-84; v.p., corp. counsel The TJX Cos., Inc., Framingham, Mass., 1984-87, v.p., gen. counsel, sec., 1987-89, sr. v.p., gen. counsel, sec., 1989—2005; mng. dir. Kwatcher Legal Consulting, Boston, 2006—. Dir. coun. Better Bus. Bur., 1990-93. Mem. ABA, Am. Soc. Corp. Secs., Am. Corp. Counsel Assn. (bd. dirs. N.E. chpt. 1991-2000), Retailers Assn. Mass. (bd. dirs., exec. com., sec. 1991-2005), New Eng. Corp. Counsel Assn. (bd. dirs. 1979-2003), Legal Mktg. Assn. Home Phone: 781-259-4360; Office Phone: 617-478-0550. E-mail: jaymeltzer@comcast.net.

MELTZER, MILTON, author; b. Worcester, Mass., May 8, 1915; s. Benjamin and Mary (Richter) M.; m. Hilda Balinky, June 22, 1941; children: Jane, Amy. Student, Columbia, 1932-36. Adj. prof. history U. Mass., Amherst, 1977-80. Author: Mark Twain Himself, 1960; author: (with Walter Harding) A Thoreau Profile, 1962; author: Langston Hughes: A Biography, 1968, Bread and Roses, 1967, Never to Forget: The Jews of the Holocaust, 1976, Dorothea Lange: A Photographer's Life, 1978; editor (with Langston Hughes, C. Eric Lincoln, Jon Michael Spencer): A Pictorial History of African-Americans, 1994; co-editor: Lydia Maria Child: Selected Letters, 1817-1880, 1982, The Black Americans, 1984, Mark Twain: A Writer's Life, 1985, George WAshington and the Birth of Our Nation, 1986, The American Revolutionaries, 1987, Benjamin Franklin: The New American, 1988, Rescue: The Story of How Gentiles Saved Jews in the Holocaust, 1988, Starting From Home: A Writer's Beginnings, 1988, Voices From the Civil War, 1989, Columbus and the World Around Him, 1990, The Bill of Rights: How We Got It and What It Means, 1990, Thomas Jefferson: Revolutionary Aristocrat, 1991, The Amazing Potato, 1992, Slavery: A World History, 1993, Lincoln: In His Own Words, 1993, Andrew Jackson and His America, 1993, Gold, 1993, Cheap Raw Material: How Our Youngest Workers Are Exploited and Abused, 1994, Theodore Roosevelt, 1994, Weapons and Warfare, 1996, Tom Paine, 1996, The Many Lives of Andrew Carnegie, 1997, Ten Queens: Portraits of Women of Power, 1998, Food, 1998, Carl Sandburg, 1999, Witches and Witch Hunts, 1999, Driven from the Land, 2000, They Came in Chains, 2000, Ten Kings, 2001, Ain't Gonna Study War No More, 2002, The Day the Sky Fell, 2002, Great Inventions: The Cotton Gin, 2003, Great Inventions: The Printing Press, 2003, Herman Melville, 2003, Edgar Allan Poe, 2003, Hour of Freedom: American History in Poetry, 2003, Hear That Train Whistle Blow! How the Railroad Changed the World, 2004, Milton Meltzer: Writing Matters, 2005, Emily Dickinson, 2006, Henry David Thoreau, 2007, others. Served with USAAF, 1942-46. Recipient Laura Ingalls Wilder award, Am. Libr. Assn., 2001, Regina medal, Cath. Libr. Assn., 2000. Mem. Orgn. Am. Historians, Authors Guild, P.E.N. Address: 263 West End Ave New York NY 10023-2612

MELTZER, ROBERT CRAIG, lawyer, educator; b. Chgo., July 31, 1958; s. Franklin Richard and Zelma (Cohen) M. BA, U. Colo., 1980; cert., Inst. de Internat., Strasbourg, France, 1984; JD, No. Ill. U., DeKalb, 1985; postgrad., U. Salzburg, Austria, 1985. Bar: Ill. 1985, U.S. Dist. Ct. (no. dist.) Ill. 1985, U.S. Ct. Appeals (7th cir.) 1988, U.S. Supreme Ct. 1989. Law clk. Hurwitz & Abramson, Washington, 1980, Mayer, Brown & Platt, Chgo., 1983; lawyer UN WHO, Geneva, Switzerland, 1985; assoc. Robert C. Meltzer & Assocs., Chgo., 1986-91, Katz, Randall & Weinberg, Chgo., 1991-93, Arnstein & Lehr, Chgo., 1993-98, Grotefeld & Denenberg, Chgo., 1998-99; pres. Visanow.com, Inc., Chgo., 1999—. Adj. prof. internat. law Ill. Inst. Tech/Chgo.-Kent Coll. Law, 1994-98; creator online immigration processing. Contbr. articles to profl. jours.; editor The Globe, Springfield, Ill., 1984-99. Pro bono lawyer Fed. Bar Assn., Chgo., 1985-98. Recipient Medal of Appreciation, Ministry of Justice, Beijing, 1996. Mem. Ill. State Bar Assn. (internat. and immigration law sect. 1985-2000, chair internat. law sect. 1990-91, Editor's award 1989, 94, 99), Am. Immigration Law Assn. Avocations: history, bread baking, golf, arts, music. Office: Visanow com Inc 350 N La Salle St 1400 Chicago IL 60610 E-mail: meltzer@visanow.com.

MELTZER, ROGER, lawyer; b. NYC, Jan. 31, 1951; s. Irwin Samuel and Beula (Jacobs) Meltzer; m. Robin Hirtz, July 20, 1975; children: Justin, Martin, Elizabeth. BA cum laude, Harvard U., 1973; postgrad., Tulane U., 1974-75; JD cum laude, NYU, 1977. Bar: NY 1978, DC 1979. Assoc. Cahill, Gordon & Reindel LLP, NYC, 1977-84, ptnr., 1984—2007, mem. exec. com., 2000—07, chmn. hiring com.; global chmn. corp. & fin. DLA Piper, 2007—. Bd. dir. Hain Celestial Group Inc., 2000—. Mem.: ABA, Order of Coif. Office: DLA Piper 1251 Ave Americas New York NY 10020 E-mail: roger.meltzer@dlapiper.com.

MELTZER, STEVEN LEE, lawyer; b. Rochester, NY, Sept. 6, 1946; s. Seymour Norman and Ruth (Pekarsky) M.; m. Harriet Vivian Lewis, Aug. 29, 1971; children: Debra, Scott, Jeremy. AB cum laude, Brown U., 1968; MBA with high distinction, Harvard U., 1973, JD, 1973. Bar: Md. 1973, D.C. 1974, Va. 1997. From assoc. to mng. bd. Shaw, Pittman, Potts & Trowbridge, Washington, 1973—2005; ptnr., Corp. & Securities, Health Care, Emerging Growth & Tech. practices, mng. bd. Pillsbury Winthrop Shaw Pittman, McLean, Va., 2005—06. Exec. editor Technology Law Notes, 1986-92. Trustee New Eng. Inst. Tech. 1974-, bd. chmn. 1989-; bd, vis. Coll. Life Sci., U. Md., 2004—; sec., exec. com., legal counsel Tech. Coun. Md.; founder, legal counsel Md. Angels Coun. Mem. ABA, Internat. Bar Assn., Info. Tech. Assn. Am., Nat. Assn. Corp. Dir., Mid-Atlantic Venture Assn., No. Va. Tech. Council, Biotechnology Industry Org., D.C. Bar Assn., Md. State Bar Assn., Harvard Bus. Sch. Club. Avocations: golf, tennis. Office: Pillsbury Winthrop Shaw Pittman 1650 Tysons Blvd Ste 1400 Mc Lean VA 22102-4859 Office Phone: 703-770-7950. Office Fax: 703-770-7901. Business E-Mail: steven.meltzer@pillsburylaw.com.

MELVILL, MICHAEL W., aircraft company executive, experimental test pilot; b. 1941; arrived in US, 1970; m. Sally Melvill; 1 child. FAA coml. cert., cert. ASEL, AMEL, instrument airplane, Rotorcraft-helicopter and Glider. V.p., gen. mgr., test pilot Scaled Co., Inc., Mojave, Calif., 1985—. Recipient Ivan C. Kincheloe trophy for work on devel. high altitude flight testing of model 281 Proteus, 1999. Mem.: Experimental Aircraft Assn., Aircraft Owners' and Pilots' Assn., Soc. Experimental Test Pilots (assoc. fellow). Achievements include participated in flight testing for Beech Starship prototype (NGBA), Fairchild's Next Generation Trainer for US Air Force (NGT), ARES, Pond Racer; built and flight tested Model 27 Variviggen; built, tested and flew around world in 1997 with Dick Rutan Model 61 Long-EZ; first flight of Model 72 GRIZZLY prototype, Model 77 SOLITAIRE prototype, Model 81 CATBIRD prototype, Model 120 PREDATOR prototype, Model 144 UAV prototype, Model 202 BOOMERANG, Model 226 RAPTOR; first flight of Model 281 PROTEUS, Model 316 SPACESHIPONE; first flight firing of GAU-12/U25mm cannon in Model 151 ARES jet fighter; only person to have flown Voyager Aircraft besides Dick Rutan and Jeana Yeager; holds 4 World and Nat. speed and altitude records in Catbird and Proteus Aircraft; first private manned mission to space, first civilian to fly a spaceship out of the atmosphere, first private pilot to earn astronaut wings, June 21, 2004; Guinness Book of World Records dubbed rocket launch "first ever privately funded manned spaceflight"; manned SpaceShipOne flight on Sept. 29, 2004, which will mark the first of two successful flight that are needed to win the Ansari X Prize. Office: Scaled Composites Inc 1624 Flight Line Mojave CA 93501 Office Phone: 661-824-4541. Office Fax: 661-824-4174.

MELVIN, BILLY ALFRED, clergyman; b. Macon, Ga., Nov. 25, 1929; s. Daniel Henry and Leola Dale (Seidell) Melvin; m. Marcia Darlene Eby, Oct. 26, 1952; children: Deborah Ruth, Daniel Henry II. Student, Free Will Baptist Bible Coll., Nashville, 1947—49; BA, Taylor U., Upland, Ind., 1951, LLD (hon.), 1984; postgrad., Asbury Theol. Sem., Wilmore, Ky., 1951—53; BD, Union Theol. Sem., Richmond, Va., 1956; DD, Azusa Coll., Calif., 1968, Huntington Coll., 1995. Ordained to ministry Free Will Baptist Ch., 1951; pastor First Free Will Baptist Ch., Newport, Tenn., 1951—53, Richmond, Va., 1953—57, Bethany Ch., Norfolk, 1957—59. Exec. sec. Nat. Assn. Free Will Baptists, 1959—67; exec. dir. Nat. assn. Evangelicals, 1967—95. Baptist. E-mail: bam1929@verizon.net.

MELVIN, CAROLE RAMEY, educational consultant; d. Roy Earl and Marjorie Smithson Ramey; m. James Preston Melvin, June 4, 1966; children: LindaJean Melvin Eastland, Robert Wesley. Med, Regent U., 1997. Mid. sch. math tchr. Va. Beach City Pub. Sch., Va., 1965—72, jr. high math tchr., 1989—94, academic, testing coord., 1994—98, libr., computer, testing coord., 1998—2000, sch. improvement specialist, 2000—; adj. prof. Regent U., Va. Beach, 1997—99. Sch. rep. Va. Beach Edn. Assn., 1997—98; facilitator Sch. Planning Coun., Va. Beach, 1999—; mem. Prins. Adv. Com., Va. Beach. Youth leader Va. Beach Christian Ch., 1989—92. Recipient Disting. Student award, Regent U. Mem.: NEA (assoc.), ASCD (assoc.), Va. Edn. Assn. (assoc.), Va. Beach Edn. Assn. (assoc. Outstanding Math Tchr. award 1993, Math. Tchr. award). Office: Ctr Effective Learning 233 N Witchduck Rd Virginia Beach VA 23462-6507 Business E-Mail: crmelvin@vbschools.com.

MELVIN, CHARLES EDWARD, JR., lawyer; b. Greensboro, NC, July 13, 1929; s. Charles Edward and Mary Ruth (Plunkett) M.; m. Jacklyn McDaniel, Mar. 1, 1958; 1 child, Dana W. BS, U. N.C., 1951, JD with honors, 1956. Bar: N.C. 1956. Of counsel Smith Moore LLP, Greensboro, 1958—. Capt. U.S. Army, 1952-54. Mem. N.C. Bar Assn. (chmn. real property sect. 1981), Am. Coll. Real Estate Lawyers, Greensboro C. of C. (pres. 1978). Office: Smith Moore LLP PO Box 21927 Greensboro NC 27420-1927 Office Phone: 336-378-5204. Business E-Mail: charlie.melvin@smithmoorelaw.com.

MELVIN, PETER JOSEPH, astrophysicist, educator; b. Seattle, Mar. 12, 1944; s. William Leopold and Virginia (Stevens) M.; m. Bernice Stenman, June 6, 1967 (div. July 1974); m. Alice Sue Pfiester, May 25, 1975 (dec. 1994); children: Robert Dennis, Chloe Anne. BA, Western Wash. State Coll., 1965; MS, U. Ill., 1966, PhD, 1970. NASA trainee U. Ill., Urbana, 1966-68, instr. phys. sci., 1970-72, asst. prof., 1972-77; sr. engr. Martin-Marietta Aerospace Co., Denver, 1977-80, staff engr., 1980-83; sr. specialist engr. engring. tech. applications divsn. Boeing Computer Svcs., Seattle, 1983-86; astrophysicist U.S. Naval Rsch. Lab., Washington, 1986-99, ret., 1999; dir. of rsch. B-Gravity, Inc., Waldorf, Md., 1999—. Vis. faculty applied math. divsn. Nat. Bur. Stds. Boulder (Colo.) Labs., 1977. Contbr. articles to sci. jours.; patentee in field. Mem. AIAA, Am. Math. Soc., Soc. Indsl. and Applied Math., Am. Geophys. Uion, Am. Astronautical Soc. Personal E-mail: pjmelvin@comcast.net.

MELVIN, RUSSELL JOHNSTON (JAY MELVIN), magazine publishing consultant; b. New Castle, Pa., Nov. 16, 1925; s. Russell Conwell and Anna Katharine (Johnston) M.; m. Helen Margaret Connery, Aug. 6, 1949; children: Thomas Kirk, Meredith. BA, U. Pa., Phila., 1949. Reporter Phila. Inquirer, 1949; copywriter, then asst. to circulation mgr. Time mag., 1949-53; with Newsweek mag., 1953-86, dir. Pacific edits., 1960-64, mng. dir. internat. edits., 1964-68, mng. editor internat. editorial service, 1969-86; cons. internat. affairs and profl. edn. Mag. Pubs. Am. (formerly Mag. Pubs. Assn.), NYC, 1986—2003. V.p. Newsweek, Inc., 1965-85; founding editor The Journal, Tokyo, 1963; founding dir. Newsweek Feature Service, 1968; mem. UN Communications Adv. Coun. With USNR, 1942—46. Mem. Internat. Advt. Assn. (chmn., CEO 1980-85, exec. dir. Chgos. Corp. 1985-86, bd. dirs. 1988-91, mem. world coun. 1990—), Internat. Fedn. Periodical Press (vice chmn. 1990-94, mgmt. bd.), The Century Assn. Home: 4214 Kendal Way Sleepy Hollow NY 10591

MELZACK, RONALD, psychology professor; b. Montreal, Que., Can., July 19, 1929; s. Joseph and Annie (Mandel) M.; m. Lucy Birch, Aug. 7, 1960; children: Lauren, Joel. BSc, McGill U., Montreal, 1950, MSc, 1951, PhD, 1954; DLitt (hon.), U. Waterloo, 1992; DLaws (hon.), Dalhousie U., 2004. Lectr. Univ. Coll., London, 1957-58; assoc. prof. MIT, 1959-63; lectr. psychology McGill U., 1953-54, prof., 1963—, E.P. Taylor prof., 1986. Author: The Day Tuk Became a Hunter, and Other Eskimo Stories, 1967, Raven, Creator of the World, 1970, The Puzzle of Pain, 1973, Why the Man in the Moon is Happy, and Other Eskimo Creation Stories, 1977; author: (with P.D. Wall) The Challenge of Pain, 1982, 2d edit., 1996; author: Pain Measurement and Assessment, 1983; author: (with P.D. Wall) Textbook of Pain, 1984, 4th edit., 1999; author: (with D.C. Turk) Handbook of Pain Assessment, 1999, 2d edit., 2001; author: (with P.D. Wall) Handbook of Pain Management, 2003. Decorated Officer, Order of Can., 1995, Order of Quebec, 2000; recipient Molson prize Can. Coun., 1985, Gaston Labat award Am. Soc. Regional Anesthesia, 1989, J.J. Bonica award VI World Congress on Pain, 1990, Prix du Que. Marie-Victorin, 1994; recipient Disting. Contbn. award Can. Pain Soc., 1995, Rsch. Recognition award Canadian Anesthesiology Soc., 1997, Janet Travell award Am. Acad. Pain Mgmt., 1997, Killam prize, 2001. Fellow APA, AAAS, Royal Soc. Can., Can. Psychol. Assn. (Disting. Contbns. to Psychol. Sci. award 1986, hon. pres. 1988-89, gold medal award 2002); mem. Internat. Assn. Study of Pain (hon., past pres.). Home: 6111 Du Boisé Apt 5C Montreal PQ Canada H3S 2V8 Home Phone: 514-342-3283; Office Phone: 514-398-6084. Business E-Mail: rmelzack@mcgill.ca.

MELZER, JOHN T.S., translator, editor; b. Sept. 9, 1938; s. John Henry and Dorothy (Garrett) M. AB, Auburn U., 1961; MA, U. Va., 1964; PhD, Tulane U., 1978; diploma (hon.), U. Villareal, Lima, Peru, 1990. Prof. Georgetown (Ky.) Coll., 1964, Columbus (Ga.) State U., 1964-67, U. West Ala., 1977; dir. hist. rsch. St. Augustine (Fla.) Restoration Commm., 1968; drilling fluids cons., 1979—; scholar-in-residence, prof. English, Translex Inst., Miraflores, Lima, 1985-92; editor-in-chief Oakbowery Books, Auburn, Ala., 1994—. Investigator ad honorem Nat. Inst. Culture, Peru, 1989—. Author: Field Spanish, 1985, Bastion of Commerce in the City of Kings, 1991, Oilfield Spanish, 1997; translator: A Dictionary for the Petroleum Industry; contbr. articles to jours., mags. Mem.: SAR, Alpha Phi Omega, Delta Tau Delta, Tau Kappa Alpha. Avocations: hiking, horseback riding, rock collecting, archaeology. Address: 74 Curtis St Camp Hill AL 36850-3362 Personal E-mail: johntmelzer@yahoo.com.

MEMIK, GOKHAN, engineering educator; b. Istanbul, Turkey, Feb. 25, 1975; s. Mehmet and Fatma Humeyra Memik; m. Fatma Seda Ogrenci; 1 child, Eda Defne. PhD, U. Calif., LA, 2003. Rsch. asst. UCLA, LA, 2001—03; asst. prof. Northwestern U., Evanston, Ill., 2003—. Cons. Global Supercomputing Inc., NYC, 2005—. Recipient Career award, Dept. Energy, 2005; Searle fellow, Northwestern U., 2004. Achievements include patents for temperature-aware caches and user-aware architectures. Home Phone: 847-910-5588; Office Phone: 847-467-1168.

MEMISHIAN, JACK, electronics engineer; Fellow Analog Devices, Inc., Cambridge, Mass., 1980, sr. analog circuitry designer. Founding dir. Am. Hot Rod Found., Greenwich, Conn., 2002—. Achievements include development of microchips that can sense motion, currently used in Nintendo Wii remotes; patents for offset trimming for a micromachined sensing device, 1997; reset switch for a micromachined device, 1998; feedback circuit for micromachined accelerometer, 2003; feedback circuit for micromachined accelerometer, 2004; multiple axis acceleration sensor, 2006. Office: Analog Devices 1 Technology Way PO Box 9106 Norwood MA 02062-9106 Office Phone: 781-329-4700. E-mail: john.memishian@analog.com. *

MEMMOTT, SCOTT A., lawyer; b. Hartford, Conn., July 15, 1965; BS with high honors, USCG Acad., 1987; JD, U. Va., 1996. Bar: Va. 1996, DC. Spl. asst. US atty., Norfolk, Va.; trial atty. civil divsn. US. Dept. Justice, Washington; with Shaw Pittman LLP, Washington; ptnr. Sonnenschein Nath & Rosenthal LLP, Washington, 2004—. Vice-chmn. Nat. Health Care Practice Group, 2007—. Editor-in-chief: Va. Jour. Internat. Law. Founder Sept. 11th Pro Bono Legal Relief Project; mem. standing com. pro bono legal svcs. D.C. Cir. Jud. Conf.; gen. counsel Pentagon Meml. Fund, Inc. Served to lt. comdr. USCG. Mem.: ABA (mem. health law sect. & litig. sect.), Healthcare Compliance Assn., Va. Bar Assn., DC Bar Assn. (mem. health law sect., white collar crime com.), Am. Health Lawyers Assn. Office: Sonnenschein Nath & Rosenthal LLP Ste 600 E Tower 1301 K St NW Washington DC 20005 Office Phone: 202-408-9169. Office Fax: 202-408-6399. Business E-Mail: smemmott@sonnenschein.com.

MEMORY, JASPER DURHAM, academic administrator, physics professor; b. Raleigh, NC, Dec. 10, 1936; s. Jasper Livingston and Margaret Moore (Durham) M.; m. Carolyn Hofler, June 4, 1961; children—Margaret Carolyn, Jasper William BS summa cum laude, Wake Forest U., 1956; PhD, U. N.C., 1960. Successively asst. prof., assoc. prof. physics U. S.C., Columbia, 1960-64; assoc. prof. N.C. State U., Raleigh, 1964-67, assoc. dean, physics and math. scis., 1973-82, prof. physics, 1967—98, vice-provost, grad. dean, 1982—86, dir. corp. and govtl. affairs, 1998-99; v.p. for research U. N.C. System, 1986—98, prof. emeritus, 1998—. Bd. govs. Research Triangle Inst., Research Triangle Park, N.C., 1983-84, Triangle Area rsch. dir., 1981-98; cons. NASA Langley, Hampton, Va., 1970-74, Ohio Bd. Regents, 1993-95, Ark. Bd. Regents, 1987, Mass. Bd. Regents, 1998; N.C. State U. rep. Oak Ridge Associated Univs., 1982-85, Grad. Record Exam. Bd., 1985-90, chair, 1989, Policy Coun., Test of English as a Fgn. Lang., 1987-88, chair, 1988. Author: Quantum Theory of Magnetic Resonance Parameters, 1968; (with others) NMR of Aromatic Compounds, 1982, High Resolution NMR in the Solid State: Fundamentals of CP/MAS, 1994. Recipient Outstanding Tchr. award N.C. State U., 1967, Disting. Alumni Service award Wake Forest U., 1981 Fellow Am. Phys. Soc.; mem. Am. Assn. Physics Tchrs., Phi Beta Kappa, Sigma Xi. Democrat. Presbyterian. Home: 4815 Rembert Dr Raleigh NC 27612-6237 Home Phone: 919-781-8558. E-mail: jmemory@nc.rr.com.

MEN, HONGSHENG, biologist, researcher; b. Tongbai, Henan, China, May 18, 1962; s. Jianfeng Men and Shuzhen Li; m. Shunling Tan, May 2, 1989; 1 child, Li. BS, Henan Normal U., Xinxiang, China, 1982—86; MS, Chinese Acad. Scis., Kunming, Yunnan, China, 1986—89; PhD, U. Wis., Madison, 1996—2002. Asst. rschr. Kunming Inst. Zoology, Chinese Acad. Scis., 1986—91, asst. prof., 1992—96; vis. scientist Animal Biotechnology Cambridge Ltd, England, 1991—92; grad. rsch. asst., dept. animal scis. U. Wis., Madison, 1996—2002; rsch. scientist, dept. vet. pathobiology U. Mo., Columbia, 2003—. Rschr. Kunming Inst. Zoology, Chinese Acad. Scis., 1986—96. Contbr. papers to profl. jours. and pubs. Mem.: Soc. Cryobiology, Soc. for Study of Reproduction, Internat. Embryo Transfer Soc. Freedom. Achievements include research in demonstration of cryoinjury to bovine oocytes at DNA level; demonstration of the degeneration mechanism of cryopreserved bovine oocytes to be apotitic in nature during culture; improvement in the cryosurvival of porcine embryos produced in vitro through chemical delipation; improved monospermic penetration of porcine oocytes emplying a modified in vitro fertilization system. Home: 1814 E Broadway 2S Columbia MO 65201 Office: Dept Vet Pathobiology Univ Mo 1600 E Rollins St Columbia MO 65211 Home Phone: 573-256-4396; Office Phone: 573-882-1514. Office Fax: 573-884-7521. Business E-Mail: menho@missouri.edu.

MENA, DANIEL, lawyer, arbitrator; s. Oswaldo and Martha Mena; m. Maite Pilar Portuondo, Nov. 21, 1997; children: Eric, Sofia. Cert. in Spanish History, U. Salamanca, 1991; BA, Fla. Internat. U., 1992; JD, U. Pa., 1995. Bar: U.S. Dist. Ct. (so. dist.) Fla. 1996, U.S. Dist. Ct. (mid. dist.) Fla. 1997, U.S. Dist. Ct. (no. dist.) Fla. 1998, U.S. Ct. Appeals (11th cir.) 1995, U.S. Supreme Ct. 1999. Assoc. atty. Baker & McKenzie, Miami, Fla., 1993—94; intern civil litig. U.S. Atty.'s Office, Phila., 1994—95; assoc. atty. Gunster, Yoakley & Stewart, Miami, 1995—98; ptnr. Holland & Knight LLP, Miami, 1998—. Mem. civil procedure rules com. Fla. Bar, Tallahassee, 2004—. Contbr. articles to profl. jours. Mem. legal bd. Amigos Together For Kids, Miami, Fla., 2003. Named Selected Up & Comer, South Fla. Legal Guide, 2002; named one of State's Legal Leaders, Fla. Trend's Fla. Legal Elite, 2006. Mem.: ABA (com. internat. law), Dade County Bar Assn. (com. internat. litig.), Chamber South. Independent. Roman Catholic. Avocations: travel, scuba diving, fishing, boating. Office: Holland & Knight LLP 701 Brickell Ave Suite 3000 Miami FL 33131 Home Phone: 305-270-1559; Office Phone: 305-789-7528. Office Fax: 305-789-7775. Business E-Mail: daniel.mena@hklaw.com.

MENA, MICHELE M., counselor, educator; b. Paterson, NJ, Nov. 24, 1953; d. Miguel Mena and Catalina Alvarez. BA in Psychology, Montclair State U., 1975, MA in Counseling, 1978; MA in Health Edn., NYU, 1985; PhD in Clin. Christian Counseling, Fla. Christian U., 2004. Vocat. rehab. counselor Addiction Rsch. Treatment Corp., NYC, 1984—88; instr. Boricua Coll., NYC, 1988—90; dir. counseling and human svcs. Iron Bd. Edn. Cultural Ctr., Newark, 1992—94; N.G.O. (philanthrope) UN Earth Summit, 1994—; counselor, educator Bridges of Am., Fla., 2003—. Author: (poetry) Internat. Libr. of Poetry. Guest Presdl. Inaugural-Reagan/Bush, 1984, Nat. Rep. Conv., New Orleans, 1988; mem. Rep. Com. Task Force, Montclair Rep. Com., 1981—91. Recipient grad. assistantship, Dept. Adult Edn., Montclair State U., 1977—78. Mem.: Nat. Assn. Forensic Counselors, Ctrl. Fla. Mental Health Assn., Am. Assn. Christian Counselors, Ctrl. Fla. Soc. for Hist. Preservation, Sanford Hist. Soc., Am. Nat. World War II Mus., The Nature Conservancy, Williamsburg Colonial Found., World Wildlife Fund, The Audubon Soc., Nat. Geographic Soc., Nat. Wildlife Found., Nat. Trust for Hist. Preservation, Montclair State U. Alumni Assn., White House Historical Soc., Eagle Forum, Montclair Hist. Soc., Orange County Regional History Ctr., Women's Club Upper Montclair, Nat. Garden Club. Republican. Protestant. Avocations: gardening, antiques, poetry, archaeology. Home: 2009 S Magnolia Ave Sanford FL 32771 Office: 500 Smith Holly Ave Sanford FL 32771

MENACHEM, ANDREW, financial advisor; m. Shari Menachem; children: Jackson, Cooper. B, George Washington U.; MBA, Nova Southeastern U. Gained cert. investment mgmt. analyst designation Wharton Sch. Bus., U. Pa., obtained alternative investment designation Investment Mgmt. Cons. Assn. Comprehensive training program, NYC, 1995; wealth advisor Morgan Stanley; specialization in asset allocation design, portfolio analysis; experience in creating fin. plans, focusing on risk mgmt. and tax efficiency. Adj. prof. U. Miami; columnist Miami Herald Sunday Money sect.

MENACHERY, ELIZABETH P., physician; Lic. physician Md. Physician Collaborative Inpatient Med. Svc., Balt., 2001—, assoc. dir. hospitalist group, 2001—. Vol. physician Ch., 1998—2007. Mem.: Soc. Hosp. Medicine. Achievements include development of hospitalist elective for medical students and residents.

MENAKER, DANIEL, former publishing executve; b. NYC, 1941; s. Robert Owen and Mary Grace Menaker; m. Katherine Bouton; 2 children. BA in English, Swarthmore Coll., 1963; MA in English Lit., Johns Hopkins U., 1965. H.S. tchr.; joined as a fact checker The New Yorker, 1969, copy editor, sr. editor; v.p., sr. literary editor Random House, Inc., NYC, 1994—2001; exec. editor Harper Collins, NYC, 2001—03; sr. v.p., editor-in-chief Random House Imprint Random House, Inc., NYC, 2003—04, exec. editor-in-chief, 2004—07. Author: (novels) The Treatment, 1998, (collection of short stories) Friends and Relations, 1976, The Old Left and other stories, 1987.

MENAKER, FRANK H., JR., lawyer; b. Harrisburg, Pa., Aug. 23, 1940; s. Frank H. and Romaine (Sadler) M.; m. Sharon Ann Lynch, Feb. 21, 1981; children: Denise L., Jamie E.; children by previous marriage: David C., Michelle R. BA, Wilkes Coll., 1962; JD, Am. U., 1965. Bar: D.C. 1966, Md. 1975, U.S. Supreme Ct. 1975. Formerly staff counsel Office Gen. Counsel, GAO, Washington; asst. divsn. counsel for aerospace ops. Martin Marietta Corp. Aerospace Divsn., 1970—73, asst. gen. counsel, 1973—77, gen. counsel, 1977—81, Martin Marietta Corp., 1981-95, corp. v.p., 1982—95; v.p., gen. counsel Lockheed Martin Corp., 1995-96, sr. v.p., gen. counsel, 1996—2005; ptnr. DLA Piper Rudnick Gray Cary LLP, Washington, 2006—. Spl. counsel U.S. Commn. on Govt. Procurement, 1971. Mem. ABA (mem. sect. pub. contract law, former chair), Md. Bar Assn., Wash. Met. Corp. Counsel Assn. (bd. dirs. 1988-95). Office: DLA Piper Rudnick Gray Cary 1200 Nineteenth St NW Washington DC 20036 Office Phone: 202-861-6302. Business E-Mail: frank.menaker@dlapiper.com.

MENAKER, MICHAEL, biology professor; b. Vienna, May 19, 1934; came to U.S., 1934; s. William and Esther (Astin) M.; m. Shirley Ann Lasch, June 4, 1955; children: Ellen Margaret, Nicholas. BA in Biology, Swarthmore Coll., 1955; PhD in Biology, Princeton U., 1960. Asst. instr. Princeton (N.J.) U., 1955-57; postdoctoral fellow Harvard U., Cambridge, Mass., 1960-62; asst. prof. zoology U. Tex.-Austin, 1962-68, assoc. prof., 1968-72, prof., 1972-79; prof. biology U. Oreg., Eugene, 1979-86, dir. interdisciplinary program for neuroscis., 1979-81, dir. Inst. Neurosci., 1981-85; Commonwealth prof. biology U. Va., Charlottesville, 1987—, chmn. dept., 1987-93; dir. Howard Hughes Undergrad. Rsch. Program in Biol. Sci., Charlottesville, 1989-94; core investigator Sci. and Tech. Ctr. in Biol. Timing U. Va., Charlottesville, 1991—. Benjamin Meaker vis. prof. U. Bristol, Eng., 1986. Assoc. editor Behavioral Neurosci., Jour. Biol. Rhythms; contbr. articles to profl. jours. Recipient Lifetime Achievement award Am. Soc. for Photobiology, 2002, Life Achievement in Sci. award Va.'s Outstanding Scientists and Industrialists, 2003, Peter C. Farrell prize Sleep Medicine, 2007; NSF fellow, 1958-59, 60-62; NIH fellow, 1960-62; Guggenheim Found. fellow, 1971-72. Fellow AAAS, Am. Acad. Arts and Scis., Japan Soc. Promotion of Scis. (sr.); mem. Soc. Neuroscis., Am. Physiol. Soc., Soc. Rsch. Biol. Rhythms. Avocations: literature, music, sailing. Office: U Va Dept Biology Gilmer Hall PO Box 400328 Charlottesville VA 22904-4328 Office Phone: 434-982-5767. Business E-Mail: mm7e@virginia.edu.

MENAKER, RONALD HERBERT, retired bank executive; b. NYC, Dec. 17, 1944; s. Harold L. Menaker and Gladys (Bleiberg) Ross; m. Kathleen Sager Thomas, Sept. 11, 1966; children: Meredith E., Kyri D. Student, Queen's Coll., 1965—66. Mng. dir. J.P. Morgan & Co., Inc., NYC, 1966—2000; ret., 2000. Bd. dirs. Reckson Assocs. Realty Corp., 2002—. Past trustee NYU Med. Ctr. and Health Sys., NYC, 1991, The Am. Kennel Club Mus. of the Dog, St. Louis, 1989—; bd. dirs., chmn. Am. Kennel Club, NYC, 2002; trustee, vice chmn., past chmn. NYU Downtown Hosp., 1991—; bd. overseers U. Pa. Vet. Sch., 2000—. Mem.: Westminster Kennel Club. Avocations: sporting art, judging dogs. Office Phone: 212-696-8359. Business E-Mail: rhm@akc.org.

MENAND, LOUIS, literature educator, writer; m. Emily Menand; 2 children. BA, Pomano Coll., 1973, MA, 1975; PhD in English, Columbia U., 1980. Disting. prof. English Grad. Ctr. CUNY; prof. English Princeton U., Columbia U., U. Va. Sch. Law; Anne T. and Robert M. Bass Prof. of English and Am. Lit. and Language Harvard U., Cambridge, 2003—. Contbg. editor NY Rev. of Books, 1994—; staff writer The New Yorker. Author: Discovering Modernism: T.S. Eliot and His Context, 1986, Metaphysical Club: A Story of Ideas in America, 2001 (Pulitzer Prize for History, 2002, Francis Parkman Prize, 2002, Heartland Prize for Non-Fiction), American Studies, 2002; editor: Pragmatism: A Reader, 1996, The Future of Academic Freedom, 1997, The Best American Essays, 2004; co-editor: The Cambridge History of Literary Criticism, Vol. 7: Modernism and the New Criticism, 2000. Office: Harvard U Barker Ctr Rm 161 12 Quincy St Cambridge MA 02138 Office Phone: 617-495-8780. Office Fax: 617-497-8737. E-mail: menand@fas.harvard.edu.

MENARCHIK, DOUGLAS (EDWARD DOUGLAS MENARCHIK), federal agency administrator; b. 1945; MA, PhD in Internat. Rels., George Wash. U. With air staff, Middle East/African policy divsn. US Dept. Def.; mil. adv. to v.p. The White House; asst. for terrorism policy US Dept. Def.; dir., def. leadership mgmt. prog. Nat. Def. U., 1997—2000; dir. George Bush Presidl. Libr. & Mus., 2000—04; asst. adminstr. for policy & program coordination US Agy. Internat. Devel., 2004—07, asst. adminstr. for Europe & Eurasia, 2007—. Former prof. polit. sci. U.S. Air Force Acad.; former instr. AF Special Ops. Sch.; former prof., dem. def. mgmt. George C. Marshall European Ctr. for Strategic Studies and Def. Econ., Garmisch, Germany. Officer, colonel USAF, 1968—94, vice comdr. 1776 Air Base Wing USAF, Andrews AFB, Md., asst. dir., ops. 443rd Mil. Airlift Wing, Altus AFB, Okla. Office: US Agy Internat Devel 1300 Pennsylvania Ave NW Washington DC 20523 *

MENARCHIK, EDWARD DOUGLAS See **MENARCHIK, DOUGLAS**

MENARD, JOHN R., JR., home improvement retail executive; b. Eau Claire, Wisc., 1940; s. John Menard Sr. and Rosemary; 6 children. BA/BS, U. of Wis. Madison, 1963. Founder, pres., CEO Menard Inc., Eau Claire, Wis., 1972—; owner, pres. Menard Racing, 1979—. Bd. dirs. Polaris Industries. Named one of Forbes' Richest Americans, 1999—, World's Richest People, Forbes Mag., 2001. Avocation: auto racing. Office: Menard Inc 4777 Menard Dr Eau Claire WI 54703-9625 *

MENARD, MICHAEL JOSEPH, museum director; b. Saginaw, Mich., Sept. 25, 1948; s. Louis Raymond and Dorothy Cicelia (Rable) M.; m. Nora Webb, Apr. 3, 1971; children: James T., Karla A. BA, Mich. State U., 1974, MA, 1976. Archivist State of Mich., Lansing, 1975-76; curator archives Mus. We. Colo., Grand Junction, 1977-80; dir. mus. Ft. Caspar Mus., Casper, Wyo., 1981-87; hist. sites adminstr. London Town Publik House and Garden, Edgewater, Md., 1987-92; mus. dir. Koshare Indian Mus., La Junta, Colo., 1992—95; curator archives Mus. Western. Colo., 1997—. Sgt. USAF, 1968-72, Vietnam. Mem. Am. Assn. Mus. (cons. mus. assessment 1986—), Am. Assn. State and Local History, Mid-Atlantic Assn. Mus., Mountain Plains Mus. Assn. (state rep.), Colo.-Wyo. Assn. Mus. (vice chmn. bd. dirs. 1984-87), C. of C. for Annapolis and anne Arundel County. Avocations: carpentry, stained glass. Office: 509 33 Rd Clifton CO 81520-9777

MENASHE, ALBERT ALAN, lawyer; b. Portland, Oreg., Apr. 24, 1950; s. Solomon A. and Faye F. (Hasson) Menashe; m. Laura L. Richenstein, July 23, 1972 (div. Oct. 1979); 1 child, Shawn Nathan; m. Sandra J. Laniado, June 28, 1980 (div. Jan. 1994); m. Julie D. Howe, Oct. 25, 2003. BS in Polit. Sci., U. Oreg., 1971; JD, Willamette U., 1976. Bar: Oreg. 1977, U.S. Dist. Ct. Oreg. 1977, U.S. Ct. Appeals (9th cir.) 1977, U.S. Supreme Ct. 1980. Assoc. Bullivant, Wright et al, Portland, 1976—79; ptnr. Samuels, Samuels et al, Portland, 1979—80; mng. shareholder Gevurtz, Menashe, Larson & Howe, P.C., Portland, 1982—. Frequent spkr. on family law, 1979—; former pro tem judge County of Clackamas, Oreg. Editor-in-chief: Willamutte Law Jour. 1st lt. US Army, 1971—73. Mem.: ABA, Multnomah County Bar Assn. (pres. 1997—98), Oreg. State Bar Assn. (chair family law sect. 1981—82, bd. govs. 2004—, pres.-elect 2006, pres. 2007), Am. Acad. Matrimonial Lawyers (pres. Oreg. chpt. 1996—97), Phi Beta Kappa, Phi Kappa Phi. Office: Gevurtz Menashe Larson & Howe PC 111 SW 5th Ave Ste 900 Portland OR 97204 Business E-Mail: amenashe@gevurtzmenashe.com.

MENCER, JETTA, lawyer; b. Coshocton, Ohio, Apr. 7, 1959; d. William J. and Virginia M. (Fry) M. BS, Ohio State U., 1980, JD, 1983. Bar: Ohio, U.S. Dist. Ct. (so. dist.) Ohio. Assoc. Berry, Owens & Manning, Coshocton, 1983-86; asst. pros. atty. Coshocton County, 1983-86, Licking County, Newark, Ohio, 1986-88, asst. atty. gen., 1988-95; pvt. practice Coshocton, 1995-96; prosecuting atty. Coshocton County (Ohio) Prosecutor's Office, 1997-2001; atty. Lee Smith & Assocs., Columbus, Ohio, 2001—03; pvt. practice Columbus, 2003—. Treas. Coshocton County Dem. Cen. & Exec. Coms., 1984-86; chmn., 1986-88; sec., bd. dirs. Heart Ohio Girl Scout Council, Inc., Zanesville, Ohio, 1985-87; fin. chmn., bd. dirs. YMCA, Coshocton, 1985-87. Mem. Ohio State Bar Assn., Coshocton County Bar Assn., Lions Club. Democrat. Methodist. Office: One S Park Pl Newark OH 43055 Office Phone: 740-345-5171. Personal E-mail: jmencer@columbus.rr.com.

MENCER, SUE (CONSTANCE SUZANNE MENCER), former federal agency administrator; b. Nov. 15, 1947; m. John Mencer; children: Jessie, Alex. BA in Spanish, Ohio St. U., 1968; Grad., JFK Sch. Govt., Harvard U., 2003. Tchr. Spanish, 1968—78; spl. agt. FBI, 1978—85, supervisory spl. agt., 1985—90, supr., 1990—98; pvt. cons. Anti-Terrorism Tng., Denver; exec. dir. dept. pub. safety State of Colo., Denver, 2000—03; exec. dir. Office of State & Local Govt. Coordination & Preparedness US Dept. Homeland Security, Washington, 2003—05; sr. policy advisor govt. rels. group Brownstein Hyatt & Farber, PC, Denver, 2005—. Mem.: Commn. on Jud. Discipline, Soc. Former Spl. Agents. Office: Brownstein Hyatt & Farber PC 410 17th St 22nd Fl Denver CO 80202 E-mail: smencer@bhf-law.com.

MENCH, JOHN WILLIAM, retail executive, electrical engineer; b. NYC, Feb. 27, 1943; s. John William and Edna (Ilgen) M.; m. Rose Irene Miller, Aug. 12, 1962 (dec. Jan. 1997); 1 child, William Ilgen; m. Ann Ward Frentress, Mar. 7, 1998. BSEE, U. S.C., 1969; MBA, Ohio U., 1983; PhD, Calif. Coast U., 1994. Registered profl. engr., Ohio, Ga.; cert. in heating, ventilating and air conditioning; accredited profl. Leadership in Energy and Environ. Design, 2006. Elec. engr. Uniroyal, Shelbyville, Tenn., 1969-74; facility engr. Kroger, Nashville, 1974-77, asst. mgr. facility engring. Atlanta, 1977-79, Kroger mktg. area mgr. facility engring. Columbus, Ohio, 1979-85; divsn. mgr. facility engring., v.p. Safeway Stores, Inc., Oakland, Calif., 1985-86; v.p. constrn., engring. Big V Supermarkets, Inc., Florida, NY, 1986-95; pres. Mench & Assocs. Inc., 1994-98. Assoc. prof. Pa. Coll. Tech., 1996-99; lectr. So. Poly. State U., 1999—; prof. Am. Contr. Exch., 1999-2003. Author: (tech. manuals) Comments on Commercial Refrigeration, 1998, Comments on Commercial Air Conditioning, 1998, Plan Review, 1995, others, (textbook) Finance for Construction Management 5th edit., 2007. Trustee Meth. Ch., 1987—93; bd. dirs. Goshen Day Care Ctr., 1988—95, Elec. Distbn. Systems, 1993—94; past v.p. Tri State V.W. Assn.; exec. adv. bd. Ohio U. Coll. Bus. Adminstrn., 1992—97, life mem.; v.p. Prime Time Group, 2003—05, pres., 2006. Named Ga. Engr. of Yr. in Edn., Ga. Profl. Engring. Soc., 2007; recipient Outstanding Faculty award, So. Poly. State U., 2007, Engr. of Yr., 2007. Mem. ASHRAE, IEEE (sr.), Assn. Energy Engrs. (sr.). Republican. Methodist. Business E-Mail: jmench@spsu.edu.

MENCHER, BRUCE STEPHAN, judge; b. Washington, May 21, 1935; s. Emanuel and Bertha Miriam (Robbin) M.; m. Janet Patricia Whitfield, Nov. 24, 1974; children by previous marriage: Sean Robbin, Marc Nadzo. BA, George Washington U., 1957, JD with honors, 1960. Bar: DC 1960, US Supreme Ct. 1964. Gen. atty. Office Gen. Counsel, Dept. Agr., 1960—61; asst. corp. counsel for D.C., 1961—67; atty.-adviser Office Gen. Counsel, Bur. for Africa, AID, 1967—69; ptnr. Wilkes & Artis, Washington, 1969—75; assoc. judge Superior Ct. D.C., 1975—91, sr. judge, 1991—, presiding judge Family divsn., 1988—90. Professorial lectr. law George Washington U. Nat. Law Ctr., 1982-83; lectr. criminal justice Nat. Cathedral Sch./St. Albans Sch., 1985; faculty advisor Nat. Jud. Coll., 1995. Asst. rsch. editor George Washington Law Rev., 1959-60; contbr. articles to law revs. Mem. gen. alumni gov. bd. George Washington U., 1972-80; bd. dirs. Nat. Child Support Enforcement Assn., 1994-97, The Washington Savoyards Ltd., 1991-96, Trinity Chamber Orch., 2001-. Recipient Alumni Svc. award, 1975, Judge of Yr. award Assn. Plaintiffs Trial Attys., 1983, Samuel Green award for disting. svc. to Washington legal comty. and Phi Delta Phi, 1985, Disting. Alumni Achievement award George Washington U., 1987, also various appreciation and recognition awards local bar assns., DC and fed. govts. for work in area of family law and child support enforcement. Mem. ABA, Bar Assn. D.C., D.C. Bar, George Washington Law Assn. (exec. com. 1972-77), The Barristers (exec. com. 1981), George Washington Am. Inn of Ct. (pres. 1999—2000, Phi Delta Phi (pres. Barrister Inn 1974-75) Office: Superior Ct DC 500 Indiana Ave NW Rm 5520 Washington DC 20001-2131 Office Phone: 202-879-1358. Business E-Mail: mencherbs@dcsc.gov. *While it may sound old-fashioned, I attribute my appointment to the bench, in large part, to hard work, dedication, a love of the law and respect for my fellow man. One should maintain his sense of balance, always try to understand the other person's position and, at all costs, maintain a sense of humor throughout.*

MENCHER, MELVIN, journalist, educator; b. Bklyn., Jan. 25, 1927; s. Peter and Theresa (Sherman) M.; m. Helen Chamberlain, Aug. 27, 1947; children: Thomas, Marianne, Nicholas. Student, U. N.Mex., 1943-44; BA, U. Colo., 1947; postgrad. (Nieman fellow), Harvard, 1952-53. Reporter UP, 1947-50; state polit. corr. Albuquerque Jour., 1951-54; reporter Fresno (Calif.) Bee, 1954-58; asst. prof. journalism U. Kans., Lawrence, 1958-62; asst. prof. Columbia U., NYC, 1962-65, assoc. prof., 1965-75, prof., 1975-90, assoc. dir. summer program for journalism edn. of minorities, 1971, prof. emeritus, 1990—. Contbg. author: Evaluating the Press, 1973; author: News Reporting and Writing, 1977, Basic Media Writing, 1983; editor: The FNMA Guide to Buying, Financing and Selling Your Home, 1973; contbr. articles to profl. jours. Mem. Soc. Profl. Journalists, Nat. Council Coll. Pubs. Advisers, Kappa Tau Alpha. Home: 450 Riverside Dr New York NY 10027-6801 E-mail: mm55@columbia.edu.

MENCHER, STUART ALAN, sales and marketing executive; b. NYC, Apr. 25, 1939; s. Meyer H. and Mildred B. Mencher; m. Judith Leslie Schneider; children: Jane Lizabeth, Tracy Ellen. B in Mgmt. Engring., Rensselaer Poly. Inst., 1960; MBA, NYU, 1965. Sales rep. Sperry Rand Univac, Albany, NY, 1960-62; various sales and mktg. mgmt. positions IBM Corp., White Plains, NY, 1965-78, br. mgr. data processing div. Harrison, NY, 1978-81; dir. market ops. planning, bus. mktg. dept. AT&T, Basking Ridge, NJ, 1981-83; dir. market mgmt., sales and mktg. div. AT&T Info. Systems, Morristown, NJ, 1983, dir. data systems mktg., 1983-84, v.p. mktg., large bus. systems div., 1985-87; sr. v.p. sales and mktg. MCI Communications Corp., Washington, 1987-90; sr. v.p., gen. mgr. U.S. distbn. div. Motorola/Codex Corp., Mansfield, Mass., 1990-91; sr. v.p., gen. mgr. Teleport Communications, NYC, 1992-93, sr. v.p. nat. sales and mktg., 1994-98; v.p. strategic planning AT&T Bus. Svcs., Bridgewater, NJ, 1998-99; mng. ptnr. The Mencher Group LLC, East Hampton, NY, 1999—. Bd. dirs. Broadview Networks, N.Y.C., 2000-05. Pres. Westfield Men's Coll. Scholarship Club, NJ, 1977; coach Westfield Young Soccer Assn., 1976—81; mem. budget rev. com. United Fund, Westfield, NJ, 1983—85; mem. adv. bd. N.Y.C. Tech. Coll., 1993; mem. Mayor's Telecomms. Mutual Aid and Restoration Com., NYC, 1992—93; v.p., bd. dirs. Ctr. Children and Families/Safe Space, NYC, 1999—; chmn. mktg. adv. com. YMCA Greater N.Y., NYC, 1999—2004. Lt. USCGR, 1962—65. Avocations: golf, travel, theater, arts. Office: PO Box 5134 East Hampton NY 11937-6165

MENCHETTI, DAVID BARRY, lawyer; b. Chgo., Dec. 13, 1959; s. Leo and Diane M.; m. Lorraine C. Dorff, June 2, 1984; children, Cecilia, Quinn. BA, Stanford U., 1981; JD, Loyola U., Chgo., 1984. Bar: Ill. 1984. Staff atty. Ill. State Senate, Sprinfield, 1984-86; ptnr. Cullen, Haskins, Nicholson & Menchetti P.C., Chgo., 1986—. Author: (notebook) Penalties in Workers' Compensation Illinois Trial Lawyers WC Notebook, 1990—. Mem. Ill. State Bar Assn. (chair workers compensation com. 1996-97), Chgo. Bar Assn. (chair workers' compensation com., 1993-94), Workers Compensation Lawyers Assn. (pres. Chgo. 1999, bd. dirs. 1997—), Workplace Injury Litigation Group. Democrat. Roman Catholic. Office: Cullen Haskins Nicholson & Menchetti 35 E Wacker Dr Ste 1760 Chicago IL 60601-2271 Office Phone: 312-332-2545.

MENCHIK, PAUL LEONARD, economist, educator; b. NYC, Sept. 16, 1947; s. Irving and Elinor (Swedlow) M.; m. Bettie Ann Landauer, May 28, 1972; children: Daniel Aron, Jeremy Matthew. BA, SUNY, Binghamton, 1969; AM, U. Pa., 1971, PhD, 1976. Lectr. Rutgers Coll., New Brunswick, NJ, 1974-76; rsch. assoc. Inst. for Rsch. on Poverty, U. Wis., Madison, 1976-79; prof. dept. econs. Mich. State U., East Lansing, Mich., 1979—, chairperson dept. econs., 1992-96, dir. grad. studies, 2005—; sr. economist, econ. policy Office Mgmt. & Budget, Washington, 1990-91. Acad. visitor Stanford (Calif.) U., 1980, London Sch. Econ., 1987-88; vis. assoc. prof. U. Pa., Phila., 1982-83; vis. scholar Congrl. Budget Office, 1997-98; cons., advisor in field. Mem. editl. bd. Jour. Income Distbn., Amsterdam, 1992—; contbr. articles to profl. jour.; Hon. Rsch. Fellow, Univ. Coll., London, 2003. Grantee NSF, Social Security Adminstrn., U.S. Dept. Health and Human Svcs.; recipient Best Article of Yr. award Econ. Inquiry, 1987. Mem. Am. Econ. Assn., Nat. Tax Assn., Nat. Bur. Econ. Rsch. Conf. on Income & Wealth. Avocations: bowling, racquetball, golf, travel, camping. Office: Mich State U 101 Marshall Hall E Circle Dr East Lansing MI 48824 Home Phone: 517-349-5261; Office Phone: 517-355-4553. Business E-Mail: menchik@msu.edu.

MENCHIN, ROBERT STANLEY, marketing executive; b. Kingston, NY, Oct. 31, 1923; s. Abraham H. and Gertrude (Gorline) M.; m. Marylin Barsky, Dec. 26, 1949; children: Jonathan, Scott. BA, NYU, 1948. Acct. exec. DKG Advt., NYC, 1949-51; dir. spl. porjects Am. Visuals Corp., NYC, 1952-59; dir. advt. and pub. rels Arthur Wiesenberger & Co., NYC, 1959-65; pres. Wall Street Mktg. Commn., Inc., NYC, 1967-77; dir. mktg. comm. Chgo. Bd. Trade, 1977-83, v.p. comm. and member rels., 1983-87; pres. Wall Street Mktg., Chgo., 1987—. Author: The Last Caprice, 1964, Where There's a Will, 1977, The Mature Market: A Strategic Marketing Guide to America's Fastest-Growing Population Segment, 1989, New Work Opportunities for Older Americans, 1993, 101 Classic Jewish Jokes: Jewish Humor from Groucho Marx to Jerry Seinfeld, 1997. With AUS, 1942-45. Mem. Am. Mktg. Assn., Pub. Rels. Soc. Am., Fin. Planners Assn. Home: The Breakers 5333 Sheridan Rd Apt 21N Chicago IL 60640 E-mail: robertmenchin@sbcglobal.net.

MENDE, HOWARD SHIGEHARU, mechanical engineer; b. Hilo, Hawaii, Nov. 19, 1947; s. Tsutomu and Harue (Kubomitsu) M. BS in Mech. Engring., U. Hawaii, 1969; MS in Mech. Engring., U. So. Calif., 1975. Registered profl. engr., Calif. Mem. tech. staff I Rockwell Internat., Anaheim, Calif., 1970-71, LA, 1971-73, mem. tech. staff II, 1973-77, mem. tech. staff IV, 1984-86; devel. engr. AiRsch. Mfg. Co., Torrance, Calif., 1977-83; mech. engr. Def. Contracts Mgmt. East, Santa Ana, Calif., 1987-94, electronics engr., 1994—. Lectr. Pacific States U., LA, 1974-75. Mem. ASME. Democrat. Buddhist. Home: 1946 W 180th Pl Torrance CA 90504-4417 Office: Def Contract Mgmt Agy 18901 S Wilmington Ave Bldg DH 2 Carson CA 90746-2856 Personal E-mail: hmende@socal.rr.com. Business E-Mail: howard.mende@dcma.mil.

MENDE, ROBERT GRAHAM, retired engineering association executive; b. Newark, Dec. 4, 1926; s. Herman Ernest and Etta (Hillenbrand) M.; m. Joan B. Tamlyn, Apr. 12, 1958; children: Lisa Anne, Robert Graham Jr. Student, Mass. Inst. Tech., 1944-45; degree, N.Y. State Maritime Acad., 1947; BS, Webb Inst. Naval Architecture, 1951. Project engr. Foster Wheeler Corp., NYC, 1953-56; dist. mgr., naval architect Bird-Johnson Co., NYC, 1956-62; sr. naval architect J.J. Henry Co., Inc., NYC, 1962-69; exec. dir. Soc. Naval Architects and Marine Engrs., 1969-91. Mem. marine engring. coun. Underwriters Labs., Inc., 1969-91; ad hoc vis. com. Engrs. Coun. for Profl. Devel., 1970-72. Bd. dirs. Friends of World Maritime U., 1987-91; trustee Webb Inst. Naval Architecture, 1987-91. Lt. USNR, 1951-53. Fellow Royal Inst. Naval Architects, Soc. Naval Architect and Marine Engrs. (hon. life v.p., chmn. N.Y. sect. 1968-69, Vice Admiral E.S. Jerry Land medal 1991, Robert G. Mende Bldg. hdqrs. bldg. named in his honor); mem. ASME, Am. Soc. Naval Engrs., Am. Soc. Assn. Execs., Coun. Engring. and Sci. Soc. Execs. (bd. dirs. 1988-91), Maritime Coll. Assn., N.E. Coast Inst. Engrs. and Shipbuilders, Webb Alumni Assn. (pres. 1970-72). Personal E-mail: robertgmende@aol.com. *Hard work, perseverance, humility and a dash of deprivation almost always insure success. It also doesn't hurt to be in the right place at the right time.*

MENDEL, JERRY MARC, electrical engineering educator; b. NYC, May 14, 1938; s. Alfred and Eleanor (Deutch) M.; m. Letty Susan Grossman, June 26, 1960; children: Jonathan, Aileen. BMechE cum laude, Poly. U., 1959, MEE, 1960, PhD in Elec. Engring., 1963. Registered profl. engr., Calif. Instr. elec. engring. Poly. Inst. Bklyn., 1960—63; engring. scientist and sect. chief McDonnell-Douglas Astronautics Co., Huntington Beach, Calif., 1963-74; prof. dept. elec. engring. systems U. So. Calif., LA, 1974—, chmn. dept., 1984-91, dir. Signal and Image Processing Inst., 1991-94, assoc. dir. edn. Integrated Media Sys. Ctr., 1996—2004. Pres., founder MENTECH, Culver City, Calif., 1983—; pres. United Signals and Systems, Inc., 1989-2001. Author: Discrete Techniques of Parameter Estimation: The Equation Error Formulation, 1973, Optimal Seismic Deconvolution: An Estimation Based Approach, 1983 (Phi Kappa Phi award 1984), Lessons in Digital Estimation Theory, 1987, Maximum-Likelihood Deconvolution, 1990, Lessons in Estimation Theory for Signal Processing, Communications and Control, 1995; editor: Prelude to Neural Networks: Adaptive and Learning Systems, 1994, Uncertain Rule-Based Fuzzy Logic Systems: Introduction and New Directions, 2001; co-editor: Adaptive Learning and Pattern Recognition Systems, 1970. Fellow IEEE (Centennial medal 1984, Third Millennium medal 2000); mem. IEEE Control Systems Soc. (Disting.; pres. 1986), IEEE Neural Networks Soc. (AdCom 2004—). Office: U So Calif Dept Elec Enging Sys Eeb 400 Los Angeles CA 90089-2564 Home Phone: 310-837-1993; Office Phone: 213-740-4445. Business E-Mail: mendel@sipi.usc.edu.

MENDELL, JOSHUA T., molecular biologist, geneticist, educator; b. Columbus, Ohio, Nov. 22, 1973; s. Jerry R. and Joyce N. Mendell; m. Kathryn A. O'Donnell, June 18, 2005. BA, Cornell U., Ithaca, NY, 1996; MD, Johns Hopkins U., Balt., PhD, 2003. Asst. prof. Johns Hopkins U., 2004—. Contbr. articles to profl. jours. Recipient Michael A. Shanoff Rsch. award, Johns Hopkins U. Sch. Medicine, 2003, Postdoctoral Basic Sci. award, Am. Soc. Human Genetics, 2003; fellow, Howard Hughes Med. Inst., 1995, Johns Hopkins U., 2003—04; scholar, NSF, 1990; Rita Allen scholar, Rita Allen Found., 2006, Basil O'Connor scholar, Mar. Dimes, 2004—06. Mem.: RNA Soc., Phi Beta Kappa. Achievements include patents for novel therapeutic targets for cancer; novel method to identify mutated genes in human diseases; research in novel mechanisms through which oncogenes promote tumorigenesis. Office: Johns Hopkins University 733 N Broadway BRB 471 Baltimore MD 21205 Office Phone: 410-502-0428.

MENDELS, JOSEPH, psychiatrist, educator; b. Cape Town, South Africa, Oct. 29, 1937; came to U.S., 1964; s. Max and Lily (Turecki) M.; m. Ora Kark, Jan. 22, 1960; children: Gilla Avril, Charles Alan, David Ralph. MB, BChir, U. Cape Town, 1960; MD, U. Witwatersrand, Johannesburg, South Africa, 1965. Asst. prof., assoc. prof. psychiatry and pharmacology U. Pa., Phila., 1967-73; prof. U. Pa. and VA Hosp., Phila., 1973-80; med. dir. Fairmount Inst., Phila., 1980-81; hon. prof. psychiatry and human behavior Thomas Jefferson Med. Ctr., 1985—; med. dir. Med. Inst., Phila., 1981-95, Therapeutics PC, Phila., 1981-98. Cons., lectr. in field. Author, editor: Concepts of Depression, 1971, Biological Psychiatry, 1973, Psychobiology of Affective Disorders, 1981; contbr. over 200 articles to med. jours. V.p., mem. bd. govs. Am. Jewish Com.; nat. bd. dirs. Project Interchange. Fellow Internat. Coll. Neuropsychopharmacology, Am. Coll. Neuropsychopharmacology. Personal E-mail: jos737@comcast.net.

MENDELSOHN, DANIEL, writer, humanities professor; b. Long Island, NY, 1960; BA summa cum laude in Jour., U. Va., 1982; PhD Mellon Fell. in Humanities, Princeton U., 1994. Weekly book critic NY Mag., 2000—02; freelance jour., 2002—; lectr., dept. Classics Princeton U., 1994—2002; Charles Ranlett Flint Professor of Humanities Bard Coll., 2002—. Contbr. articles NY Times, New Yorker, NY Review of Books, Esquire Mag., The Nation, The Paris Review (Nat. Book Critics Circle award for Reviewing, 2001); author: (memoirs) The Elusive Embrace: Desire and the Riddle of Identity, 1999 (NY Times Notable Book Yr., 1999), The Lost: A Search for Six of Six Million, 2006 (Nat. Books Critics Circle award for Autobiography, 2006); contbr. chapters to books incl. Best Am. Travel Writing, Republicans Can Be Cured!, Best Am. Humor Writing. Recipient George Jean Nathan Prize for Drama Criticism; grantee Guggenheim Fell., 2005. Office: c/o Paradigm Agency 360 N Crescent Dr Beverly Hills CA 90210 Office Fax: 310-288-2000. *

MENDELSOHN, JOHN, oncologist, hematologist, educator, health facility executive; b. Cin., Aug. 31, 1936; s. Joe and Sarah (Feibel) M.; m. Anne Charles, June 23, 1962; children: John Andrew, Jeffrey Charles, Eric Robert. BA in BioChemical Sciences, Harvard U., 1958, MD, 1963. Diplomate Am. Bd. Internal Medicine, Am. Bd. Hematology, Am. Bd. Med. Oncology. Intern, resident Peter Bent Brigham Hosp., Boston, 1963-65, 67-68; fellow in hematology Washington U. Sch. Medicine, St. Louis, 1968-70; asst. prof. to prof. medicine U. Calif., San Diego, 1970-85, Am. Cancer Soc. prof. clin. oncology La Jolla, 1982-85, dir. Cancer Ctr., 1977-85; prof. medicine, vice-chmn. Cornell U. Med. Coll., NYC, 1985-96; Winthrop Rockefeller chmn. dept. medical oncology, co-head, molecular pharmacology and therapeutics program Meml. Sloan Kettering Cancer Ctr., NYC, 1985-96; pres., prof. medicine U. Tex. M.D. Anderson Cancer Ctr., Houston, 1996—; vice chmn. BioHouston, 2001—. Bd. sci. counselors Nat. Cancer Inst., 1986—90, 1996—2001; cons., mem. sci. adv. bd. Progenics Pharms.; founder, 1st dir. U. Calif. San Diego Cancer Ctr.; mem. Nat. Dialogue on Cancer, 1999, Team on Cancer Rsch., 2001, U. Calif. San Diego External Adv. Com., 2000, Gov.'s Biotech. Panel, Ctr. for Houston's Future; mem. external adv. bd. John Hopkins Oncology Ctr., 1993—; faculty U. Tex. Graduate Sch. Biomedical Sciences. Editor-in-chief: (textbook) The Molecular Basis of Cancer; mem. editl. bd. Growth Factors, Jour. Biol. Response Modifiers, Expert Rev. Anticancer Therapy; editor-in-chief Clin. Cancer Rsch.; founding editor Clin. Cancer Rsch.; contbr. articles to profl. jours. Mem. Gov.'s Cancer Coun., Calif., 1981—85; bd. dirs. Am. Cancer Soc., San Diego, 1981—85, Houston Grand Opera, BioHouston, Ctr. for Houston's Future, Houston Forum; bd. dirs., mem. healthcare task force Greater Houston Partnership, 1997; bd. dirs., mem. exec. com. Houston Tech. Ctr., 1998—, nat. cancer policy bd., 1999—; mem. bd. overseers Harvard Med. Sch.; trustee Houston Grand Opera. Named Headliner of Yr. in Medicine, San Diego, 1985; recipient Bourgine award for excellence in cancer rch., Svc. d'Oncologie Med. Pitie-Saltpetriere, 1997, Jill Rose award for oustanding breast cancer rsch., Breast Cancer Rsch. Found., 1999, Gold medal of Paris, 1997, Cancer Rsch. award, Bristol-Myers Squibb, 1997, Joseph H. Burchenal Clin. Rsch. award, Am. Assn. for Cancer Rsch., 1999, Simon Shubitz prize, Univ. Chgo., 2002, David A. Karnofsky award, Am. Soc. of Clin. Oncology, 2002, Freedom to Discover Achievement award in Cancer, Bristol-Myers Squibb, 2004; Fulbright scholar, U. Glasgow, Scotland, 1958—59. Mem.: ACP, AAAS (electorate nominating com. sect. on med. scis. 2001), Am. Clin. and Climatol. Assn., Harvard Overseers' Com., Royal Netherlands Acad. Arts and Scis., Inst. Medicine U.S. NAS, Century Assn., Am. Soc. Hematology, Am. Assn. Cancer Rsch. (4th Joseph H. Burchenal award 1999), Am. Soc. Clin. Oncology (lectr., David A. Karnofsky award 2002), Am. Soc. Clin. Investigation, Assn. Am. Physicians, Phi Beta Kappa. Achievements include rsch. in establishing inhibition of tumor growth by antibodies against growth factor receptors. Office: U Tex MD Anderson Cancer Ctr 1515 Holcombe Blvd # 91 Houston TX 77030-4009 E-mail: jmendelsohn@mdanderson.org.

MENDELSOHN, LOUIS BENJAMIN, financial analyst; b. Providence, Mar. 26, 1948; s. Alvin Harold and Frances (Leitner) M.; m. Illyce Deborah Greenspan, Aug. 29, 1976; children: Lane Jeffrey, Ean Graham, Forrest Lee. BS, Carnegie Mellon U., 1969; MSW, SUNY, Buffalo, 1973; MBA with hons., Boston U., 1977. Rsch. asst. Mass. Gen. Hosp., Boston, 1969-71; regional health planner Comprehensive Health Planning Coun., Buffalo, 1973-74; adminstv. resident New Eng. Hosp., Boston, 1976; mgmt. specialist Humana Hosp. Bennett, Ft. Lauderdale, Fla., 1977-78; asst. exec. dir. Humana Women's Hosp., Tampa, Fla., 1978-80; pres., CEO Market Techs. Corp., Wesley Chapel, Fla., 1979—, CEO, 2004—, Predictive Techs. Group LLC, Wesley Chapel, 2004—. Author: Trend Forecasting with Techinal Analysis: Unleashing the Hidden Power of Intermarket Analysis to Beat the Market, 2000, Forex Trading Using Intermarket Analysis, 2006; contbg. rschr.: The Encyclopedia of Technical Market Indicators, 1988; contbg. author: High Performance Futures Trading, 1990, Virtual Trading, 1995, Artificial Intelligence in the Capital Markets, 1995, Trade Your Way to Financial Freedom, 1999, Trading Chicago Style, 1999; contbg. writer Tech. Analysis of Stocks and Commodities Mag.; editor newsletter Neural-Financial News, 1991; developer investment software ProfitTaker, 1979—, VantagePoint, 1988—. USPHS fellow, 1975-77. Mem. Market Technicians Assn., Colleague Internat. Fedn. of Tech. Analysts, Beta Gamma Sigma. Achievements include pioneering strategy back-testing and optimization in technical analysis software for personal computers, 1983; introduction of first commercial strategy testing trading software in financial industry for personal computers and first intermarket analysis software in financial industry for personal computers. Office: Mkt Techs LLC 5807 Old Pasco Rd Wesley Chapel FL 33544-5108 Office Phone: 813-973-0496. E-mail: ww@tradertech.com.

MENDELSOHN, MARTIN, lawyer; b. Bklyn., Sept. 6, 1942; s. Hyman and Gertrude M.; m. Syma Barbara Rossman, Aug. 15, 1964; children: Alice S., James D. BA, Bklyn. Coll., 1963; LLB, George Washington U., DC, 1966. Bar: DC 1967, Ill., 1973, NY, 2003, US Ct. Appeals (DC cir.) 1967, US Supreme Ct. 1970, US Ct. Appeals (3d cir.) 1971, US Ct. Appeals (7th cir.) 1973, Ill. 1973, US Ct. Appeals (9th cir.) 1987, US Tax Ct. 1988, US Ct. Appeals (2d cir.) 1988, US Ct. of Appeals (5th cir.) 2000, US Ct. Appeals (4th cir.) 2002, US Ct. Appeals (8th cir.) 2004. With Gen. Counsel's Office, HEW, Washington, 1966—67; legal svcs. Washington, 1967—70, Pa., 1971—72, Ill., 1973—75; counsel Legal Svcs. Corp., Washington, 1976; adminstrv. asst. US Congress, Washington, 1977; chief spl. litigation US Dept. Justice, Washington, 1977—79, dep. dir. office spl. investigations, 1979—80; counsel House Judiciary Com., 1980; pvt. practice Washington, 1980—88; ptnr. Dilworth, Paxon, Kalish & Kauffman, 1989—91, Verner, Liipfert, Bernhard, McPherson & Hand, 1991—2002, Schnader, Harrison, Segal and Lewis, Washington, 2002—. Author: (with Aaron Freiwald) The Last Nazi, 1994. Decorated officer Order of Merit (Poland), medal of honor Czech Republic; named Advocate for Justice, Olender Found., 2007; recipient Grand Decoration of High Honor, Austria, 2002, Disting. Achievement in Law award, Bklyn. Coll. Alumni Assn., 2007. Mem.: ABA, DC Bar Assn., Cosmos Club. Jewish. Home: 5705 Mckinley St Bethesda MD 20817-3638 Office: 2001 Pennsylvania Ave NW Ste 300 Washington DC 20006 Office Phone: 202-419-4220. Business E-Mail: martinmendelsohn@comcast.net.

MENDELSON, ALAN CHARLES, lawyer; b. San Francisco, Mar. 27, 1948; s. Samuel Mendelson and Rita Rosalie (Spindel) Brown; children: Jonathan Daniel, David Gary; m. Agnès Marie Barbariol. BA with great distinction, U. Calif., Berkeley, 1969; JD cum laude, Harvard U., 1973. Bar: Calif. 1973. Assoc. Cooley Godward LLP, San Francisco, 1973-80, ptnr. Palo Alto, 1980-2000, mng. ptnr. Palo Alto office, 1990-95, 96-97; sec. acting gen. counsel Amgen Inc., Thousand Oaks, Calif., 1990-91; acting gen. counsel Cadence Design Sys., Inc., San Jose, Calif., 1995-96; sr. ptnr. Latham & Watkins LLP, Menlo Park, Calif., 2000—. Bd. dirs. QLT Inc.; co-chair venture & tech. group Latham & Watkins; mem. bd. advisors Santa Clara Computer and High Tech. Law Jour.; mem. emerging cos. sect.

governing body Biotech. Industry Orgn., 2004—. Bd. dirs. Bay Bio, Calif. Alumni Assn., 2005—; chmn. Piedmont (Calif.) Civil Svc. Commn., 1978-80; fundraiser Harvard Law Sch. Fund, U. Calif. Berkeley Health Scis. Initiative, Lucille Packard Children's Hosp.; pres., mem. exec. com., bd. dirs. No. Calif. chpt. Nat. Kidney Found., 1986-98; mem. Overseers' Com. to visit Harvard Law Sch., 2005—. With USAR, 1969-75. Recipient Disting. Svc. award Nat. Kidney Found., 1992; named U. Calif. Berkeley Alumni scholar, 1966, Scaife Found. scholar, 1966, One of 100 Most Influential Attys. in U.S. Nat. Law Jour., 1994, 97, 2000, 06. Mem. Bohemian Club, Phi Beta Kappa. Jewish. Home: 76 De Bell Dr Atherton CA 94027-2253 Office: Latham & Watkins LLP 140 Scott Dr Menlo Park CA 94025 Home Phone: 650-853-1343; Office Phone: 650-463-4693. Business E-Mail: alan.mendelson@lw.com.

MENDELSON, EDWARD JAMES, English literature educator; b. NYC, Mar. 15, 1946; s. Ralph and Grace Bernice (Stein) M.; m. Cheryl Neel Noble, 1990; 1 child, James. BA, U. Rochester, 1966; PhD, Johns Hopkins U., 1969. Instr. English Yale U., New Haven, 1969-70, asst. prof., 1970-76, assoc. prof., 1976-79; vis. assoc. prof. Columbia U., NYC, 1979-80, assoc. prof. English, 1981-83, prof., 1983—2006, Lionel Trilling prof., 2006—; vis. assoc. prof. English Harvard U., Cambridge, Mass., 1977-78; lit. executor Estate of W.H. Auden. Author: Early Auden, 1981; editor: Homer to Brecht, 1977, Pynchon: A Collection of Critical Essays, 1978, The English Auden, 1978, Later Auden, 2000, The Things That Matter, 2006; editor: Complete Works of W.H. Auden, 1988—; contbg. editor PC Mag. Fellow Am. Council Learned Socs., 1974-75, NEH, 1980-81, Guggenheim Found., 1986-87 Mem. Acad. Lit. Studies, Societe Européene de Culture Office: Columbia U Dept English 602 Philosophy Hall New York NY 10027

MENDELSON, ELLIOTT, mathematician, educator; b. NYC, May 24, 1931; s. Joseph and Helen (Bienstock) M.; m. Arlene Zimmerman, Jan. 25, 1959; children: Julia, Hilary, Peter. AB, Columbia U., 1952; MA, Cornell U., 1954, PhD, 1955. Instr. U. Chgo., 1955-56; jr. fellow Soc. Fellows, Harvard U., 1956-58; Ritt instr. Columbia U., 1958-61; mem. faculty Queens Coll., CUNY, 1961—, prof. math., 1965—. Dir., instr. NSF math. program for high sch. students, 1964-71; researcher axiomatic set theory and math. logic, especially ind. various important propositions of axiomatic set theory, axiom of choice, axiom of restriction; participant NSF Time 2000 Project for future secondary sch. math. tchrs., 1998—. Author: Introduction to Mathematical Logic, 1997, Boolean Algebra and Switching Circuits, 1970, Number Systems, 1973, Beginning Calculus, 1997, 3000 Solved Problems in Calculus, 1988, Differential and Integral Calculus, 1997, Quick Calculus, 1999, Introducing Game Theory and Its Applications, 2004; contbr. articles to profl. jours. Mem. Am. Math. Soc., Math. Assn. Am., Assn. for Symbolic Logic, Phi Beta Kappa. Home: 10 Pinewood Rd Roslyn NY 11576-2420 Office: Queens Coll Dept Math Flushing NY 11367 Office Phone: 516-621-0313. Personal E-mail: emenqc@msn.com.

MENDELSON, JOEL STUART, allergist, immunologist; b. Bklyn., Nov. 2, 1956; BS, Bklyn. Coll., 1978; MD, U. Ctrl. East Dominican Rep., 1982. Diplomate Am. Bd. Allergy/Immunology, Am. Bd. Pediatrics, Am. Bd. Pediatric Infectious Diseases. Pres. pedicatrics St. Lukes Roosevelt Med. Ctr./Columbia U., NYC, 1982-85; fellow allergy, immunology and infectious disease U. Med. and Dentistry N.J., Newark, 1985-87; asst. dir. dept. allergy and immunology Childrens Hosp. N.J., Newark, 1987-88; dir. dept. allergy and immunology Beth Israel Med. Ctr., Newark, 1992—. Cons. in field. Contbr. articles to profl. jours. Fellow Am. Acad. Allergy and Immunology, Am. Coll. Allergy and Immunology, Am. Acad. Pediatrics; mem. Infectious Disease Soc. N.J. Home: 17 Dartmouth Rd Cranford NJ 07016-1651 Personal E-mail: jmendelsonmd@msn.com.

MENDELSON, LEE M., film company executive, producer, director, writer; b. San Francisco, Mar. 24, 1933; s. Palmer C. and Jeanette D. (Wise) M.; children: Glenn, Linda, Jason, Sean. BA, Stanford U., 1954. With Sta. KPIX-TV, 1961-63; chmn. bd., pres. Lee Mendelson Film Prodns. Inc., Los Angeles and Burlingame, Calif., 1963—. Guest instr. in communications Stanford U. Exec. producer, co-writer (miniseries) This Is America, Charlie Brown; producer: Charlie Brown, Cathy, Betty Boop, (TV spls.) John Steinbeck's Travels with Charley, American and Americans, The Fantastic Funnies, You Asked for It, Here Comes Garfield, (animated films) A Boy Named Charlie Brown, Snoopy Come Home, Race for Your Life Charlie Brown, Peanuts, Bon Voyage Charlie Brown (And Don't Come Back), Garfield and Friends, Mother Goose and Grim. Served to 1st lt. USAF, 1954-57. Recipient 7 Emmy awards, 3 Peabody awards. Mem. Writers Guild Am., Dirs. Guild Am. Office: Lee Mendelson Film Prodn Inc 330 Primrose Rd Ste 215 Burlingame CA 94010-4028

MENDELSON, RICHARD DONALD, former communications company executive; b. NYC, Dec. 2, 1933; s. George and Martha (Goodman) M.; m. Marilyn Miller, July 28, 1956; children: Sandra, Kenneth. BS, Wharton Sch. U. Pa., 1955; JD, NYU, 1959. Bar: N.Y., 1960; CPA, N.Y. Asst. atty. gen. N.Y. State Dept. Law, NYC, 1959-70; v.p., treas. Petry TV, NYC, 1971-75; v.p., dir. corp. devel. Katz Communications, Inc., NYC, 1975-77, sr. v.p. ops., 1977-79, sr. v.p., chief fin. officer, 1979-81, exec. v.p., chief operating officer, 1981-82, pres., chief oper. officer, 1982-89; free-lance writer, 1989—. Mem. Employee Stock Ownership Assn. Am. (pres. 1987-88, bd. dirs.), Ballen Isles Country Club (Palm Beach Gardens, Fla.l bd. dirs. 2000-06, pres. 2006). Home and Office: 71 Saint George Pl Palm Beach Gardens FL 33418-4024 Personal E-mail: themeri@aol.com.

MENDELSON, ROBERT ALLEN, polymer scientist, rheologist; b. Cleve., 1930; s. Julius and Theodora Anne M.; m. Lura Lauzon, 1971 (dec. 1999); children: John A. Blackstone, Marie L. Taylor. BS in Indsl. Chemistry, Case Inst. Tech., 1952, PhD in Phys. Chemistry, 1956. From sr. rsch. chemist to sci. fellow rsch. dept. Monsanto Co., Texas City, Tex., 1956-71, sci. fellow Springfield, Mass., 1972-89, sr. sci. fellow, 1989-91; rheology focus area leader Baytown (Tex.) Polymers Ctr. Exxon Chem., 1991-94, rheology prin. investigator, 1995-99; ret., 1999. Mem. com. for pub. policy Am. Inst. Physics, 1985-89; collaborator Univ. Rsch. Programs, Cornell U., 1989-91. Mem. editl. bd. Journal of Rheology, 1986-99; contbr. chpts. to books and articles to profl. jours.; patentee in field. Mem. AAAS, Soc. Rheology (pres. 1989-91, v.p. 1987-89, sec. 1974-78), Am. Chem. Soc. (Arthur Doolittle award div. organic coatings and plastics 1982). Home: 5001 Woodway Dr Unit 1803 Houston TX 77056-1701

MENDELSON, SOL, physical science educator, consultant; b. Checonovska, Poland, Oct. 10, 1926; came to U.S., 1927; s. David C. and Frieda (Cohen) M. BME, CCNY, 1955; MS, Columbia U., 1957, PhD, 1961. Prof. engring. CCNY, 1955-58; sr. scientist Sprague Electric Co., North Adams, Mass., 1962-64, Airborne Instruments Lab., Melville, NY, 1964-65; phys. metallurgist Bendix Rsch. Lab., Southfield, Mich., 1966-67; cons., rschr., writer, NYC and Troy, Mich., 1968-72; adj. prof. phys. sci. CUNY, 1972-87. Contbr. numerous articles to sci. jours. Mem. Am. Phys. Soc., Fedn. Am. Scientists, Sigma Xi, Tau Beta Pi, Pi Tau Sigma. Achievements include research on theory and mechanisms of Martensitic transformations; research on degeneracy in phase transitions and its universal nature which shows that revolutions in science are still possible. *We have to keep reminding each other that data proclaims theory, but theory does not proclaim anything if it is not physical and addresses crucial data. Ambiguous data or unrealistic models have brought prominence to some theories, but those who succeed are based on crucial data and physical models. Such theories give insight into related problems, and to theories of many things and everything.*

MENDENHALL, HARRY BARTON, lawyer; b. Oct. 31, 1946; BA, Colo. Coll., 1968; JD, U. Colo., 1971. Bar: Colo. 1971. Ptnr. Mendenhall & Malouff, R.L.L.P., Rocky Ford, Colo., 1971—. Mem. nominating com. Colo. Supreme Ct., Denver, 1986-91; pres. Colo. Lawyer Trust Account Found., Denver, 1995-97. Mem. Colo. Bar Assn. (pres. 1999-2000). Office: Mendenhall & Malouff 805 Chestnut Ave Rocky Ford CO 81067-1224 Office Phone: 719-254-7606. E-mail: bmendenhall@centurytel.net.

MENDENHALL, ROBERT W., information technology executive; b. Pasadena, Calif., Nov. 18, 1954; s. Winton L. and Margaret E. (Kerr) Mendenhall; m. Kathleen A. White, 1978; children: Jamie, Robert, Christina, Virginia, Kathleen, Lori, Emily. BS in Univ. Studies, Brigham Young U., Provo, Utah, 1977, PhD in Instrnl. Psychology and Tech., 2003. Gen. mgr. Wicat Inst., Orem, Utah, 1977-80; pres., dir. Wicat Systems Inc., Orem, Utah, 1980—92; exec. v.p., dir. Jostens Learning Corp., San Diego, 1992—94; gen. mgr. IBM K-12 Edn., Atlanta, 1994—96, exec. cons., 1997—98; pres. Western Govs. U., Salt Lake City, 1999—. Mem. bd. bus. and econ. devel. State of Utah, 1997—2001; mem. Commn. Tech. and Adult Learning, 1999—2000; adv. bd. Partnership for 21st Century Skills, 2003—04; mem. Sec. of Edn.'s Commn. on Future of Edn., 2005—06. Missionary and bishop LDS Ch.; bd. dir. Oquirrh Inst., 2002—07; bd. dir. and chair Gina Bachauer Internat. Piano Found., 1980—2000. Office: Western Gov U Ste 700 4001 South 700 East Salt Lake City UT 84107 Home Phone: 801-209-4400; Office Phone: 801-274-3280. Business E-Mail: rwm@wgu.edu.

MENDES, EVA, actress; b. Houston, Mar. 5, 1974; Spokesperson Revlon Cosmetics. Actor: (films) A Night at the Roxbury, 1998, My Brother the Pig, 1999, Urban Legends: Final Cut, 2000, Exit Wounds, 2001, Training Day, 2001, All About the Benjamins, 2002, 2 Fast 2 Furious, 2003, Once Upon a Time in Mexico, 2003, Out of Time, 2003, Stuck on You, 2003, Hitch, 2005, The Wendell Baker Story, 2005, Trust the Man, 2005, 3 & 3, 2005, Ghost Rider, 2007; (TV films) The Disciples, 2000; TV appearances include: ER, 1998; Mortal Kombat: Conquest, 1998; VIP, 1999. Office: Creative Artist Agency 9830 Wilshire Blvd Beverly Hills CA 90212-1825 *

MENDES, SAM (SAMUEL ALEXANDER MENDES), film director, theater director; b. Reading, Eng., Aug. 1, 1965; s. James Peter and Valerie Helene Mendes; m. Kate Winslet, May 24, 2003; 1 child. Student, U. Cambridge, Eng. Dir.: (films) American Beauty, 1999 (Outstanding Directorial Achievement in Feature Film Dirs. Guild Am. 1999, Golden Globe for best dir. 1999, Best Dir. award Dallas-Ft. Worth Film Critics Assn. 1999, Best Dir. award Online Film Critics Soc. 1999, Best Dir. award Broadcast Film Critics Assn. 1999, Best Dir. award L.A. Film Critics Assn. 1999, Oscar for best dir. 2000, Dir. of the Yr. London Film Critics Cir. 2000, Hamburg Shakespeare prize 2000), Road to Perdition, 2002, Jarhead, 2005; artistic dir. The Rise and Fall of Little Voice (RNT, Aldwych, Olivier and Evening Standard awards), 1992, Cabaret (Tony award), 1998, The Blue Room, 1998; dir.: (plays) London Assurance, 1989, Cherry Orchard, 1989, Kean, 1990, Plough & the Stars, 1991, Troillis & Cressida, 1991, The Alchemist, 1991, The Sea, 1991, Richard III, 1992, The Tempest, 1993, The Birthday Party, 1994, Othello, 1997, Assasins, Translations, Glengarry Glen Ross, Glass Managerie, Company, Habelis Corpus, Front Page, To the Green Fields Beyond, The Real Thing (Tony award for Best Revival of Play 2000), Take Me Out (Tony award for Best Revival of Play 2003). Office: Scamp Film & Theatre 26-28 Neal St London WC 2H 9QQ England E-mail: mleigh@scampltd.com.

MENDEZ, CELESTINO GALO, mathematics professor, dean; b. Havana, Cuba, Oct. 16, 1944; came to the U.S., 1962; naturalized, 1970. s. Celestino Andres and Georgina (Fernandez) M.; m. Mary Ann Koplau, Aug. 21, 1971; children: Mark Michael, Matthew Maximilian. BA, Benedictine Coll., 1965; MA, U. Colo., 1968, PhD, 1974, MBA, 1979. Asst. prof. maths. scis. Met. State Coll., Denver, 1971-77, assoc. prof., 1977-82, prof., 1982—2002, chmn. dept. math. scis., 1980—83, asst to the v.p. for acad. affairs/provost, 1989—91; vis. assoc. prof. math. U. Mich., Ann Arbor, 2002—03; asst. dir. math program, lectr. dept. applied math. U. Colo., Boulder, 2003—05; dean Coll. Arts and Scis. N.Mex. Highlands U., Las Vegas, N.Mex., 2005—, 2005—, prof. math., 2005. Assoc. editor Denver Met. Jour. Math. and Computer Sci., 1993—2001; contbr. articles to profl. jours. including Am. Math. Monthly, Procs. Am. Math. Soc., Jour. Personalized Instrn., Denver Met. Jour. Math. and Computer Sci. and newspapers. Mem. advt. rev. bd. Met. Denver, 1973-79; parish outreach rep. S.E. deanery, Denver Cath. Cmty. Svcs., 1976-78; mem. social ministries com. St. Thomas More Cath. Ch., Denver, 1976-78, vice-chmn., 1977-78, mem. parish coun., 1977-78; del. Adams County Rep. Conv., 1972, 74, 94, Colo. 4th Congl. Dist. Conv., 1974, Colo. Rep. Conv., 1982, 88, 90, 92, 96, 98, 2000, 02, 04, Douglas County Rep. Conv., 1980, 82, 84, 88, 90, 92, 94, 96, 98, 2000, 02, 04; alt. del. Colo. Rep. Conv., 1974, 76, 84, 2000, 5th Congl. dist. conv., 1976, mem. rules com., 1978, 80, precinct committeeman Douglas County Rep. Com., 1976-78, 89-92, mem. ctrl. com., 1976-78, 89-92; dist. 29 Rep. party candidate Colo. State Senate, 1990; mem. Colo. Rep. Leadership Program, 1989-90, bd. dirs., 1990-98; Douglas County chmn. Rep. Nat. Hispanic Assembly, 1989—95; bd. dirs. Rocky Mountain Better Bus. Bur., 1975-79, Rowley Downs Homeowners Assn., 1976-78; trustee Hispanic U. Am., 1975-78; councilman Town of Parker, Colo., 1981-84, chmn. budget and fin. com., 1981-84; chmn. joint budget com. Town of Parker-Parker Water and Sanitation Dist. Bds., 1982-84; commr. Douglas County Planning Commn., 1993-97; dir. Mile High Young Scholars Program, 1995-98. Recipient Excellence in Tchg. award U. Colo. Grad. Sch., 1965-67; grantee Benedictine Coll., 1964-65, Math. Assn. Am. SUMMA grantee Carnegie Found. N.Y., 1994; program dir., grantee NSF, 1995-98; nominated candidate for first v.p Math. Assn. Am., 1999, for 2d v.p., 2001. Mem. Math. Assn. Am. (referee rsch. notes sect. Am. Math. Monthly 1981-82, gov. Rocky Mountain sect. 1993-96, investment com. 1996-02, devel. com. 1995-01, task force on reps. 1994-96, sci. policy com. 2000-06, bd. govs. 1993-96, 2002-05, membership com. 2005-), Am. Math. Soc., Nat. Coun. Tchrs. Math., Colo. Coun. Tchrs. Math. (bd. dirs. 1994-96), Colo. Internat. Edn. Assn., Assoc. Faculties of State Insts. Higher Edn. in Colo. (v.p. 1971-73). Republican. Roman Catholic. Home: 1855 8th St Las Vegas NM 87701 Office: Coll Arts and Scis NMex Highlands Univ PO Box 9000 Las Vegas NM 87701

MENDEZ, DAVID, information systems and operations research educator; b. Santo Domingo, Dominican Republic, Jan. 27, 1958; s. David Mendez and Dulce Maria Emilien; m. Hildegarde Selig, Mar. 30, 1959; 1 child, Jose David. BS in Civil Engring., Universidad Nacional Pedro Henriquez Urena, 1980; MS in Ops. Rsch./Sys. Sci., Mich. State U., 1987, MS in Applied Stats., 1989, PhD in Mgmt. Sci., 1995. Rsch. assoc. U. Mich. Sch. Pub. Health, Ann Arbor, 1993—95, asst. prof., 1997—2005, assoc. prof., 2005—. Vis. asst. prof. Mich. State U., Eli Broad Coll. Bus., East Lansing, 1996—97. Recipient Excellence in Tchg. award, U. Mich. Sch. Pub. Health, 2000; Paul A. Cornely fellow, 1995—97. Mem.: Prodn. and Ops. Mgmt. Soc., Inst. Ops. Rsch. and Mgmt. Scis., Decision Scis. Inst. (mem. pubs. com. 2003—04). Achievements include research in patterns of adult smoking initiation and cessation. Developed forecasting model to predict future levels of smoking in the US in response to current policy actions; development of Rich Media Instructional Technology Modules in Public Health to be used in face to face or distance learning programs. - Received recognition by the ComputerWorld Honors Program. Office: U Mich 109 Observatory Ann Arbor MI 48109 Home Phone: 734-669-6264; Office Phone: 734-647-0218. Business E-Mail: dmendez@umich.edu.

MENDEZ, MICHELLE ANNETTE, lawyer; b. Clarksburg, W.Va., Nov. 15, 1961; d. Robert Argimiro and Eulaene Kathleen (Prince) M.; m. Luis Ramon Atiles, July 30, 1988. BA, U. Charleston, W.Va., 1983; JD, George Washington U., Washington, 1987. Bar: Tex. 1987, U.S. Dist. Ct. (no. dist.) Tex. 1987, U.S. Dist. Ct. (so. dist.) Tex. 1990, U.S. Dist. Ct. (we. dist.) Tex. 1991, U.S. Dist. Ct. (ea. dist.) Tex. 1992. Assoc. Hutcheson & Grundy, Dallas, 1987, Larson & King; shareholder Greenberg Traurig, Dallas, 2003; with Jenkens & Gilchrist, Dallas; counsel Hunton & Williams LLP, Dallas, 2007—. Vol. Tex. Accts. and Lawyers for Arts, 1989-91; dir., officer The Vivid Theatre Ensemble; v.p., bd. dirs. Sammons Ctr. Arts. Mem. ABA (mem. internat. bankruptcy and insolvency com.), Dallas Bar Assn., Tex. Bar Assn., Tex. Assn. Young Lawyers, Dallas Assn. of Young Lawyers (chair internat. conf. liaison com. 1989-93), Turnaround Mgmt. Assn. Democrat. Methodist. Avocations: Dallas Coun. on World Affairs, Dallas Women's Found. Office: Hunton & Williams LLP Energy Plz 30th Fl 1601 Bryan St Dallas TX 75201-3402

MENDIS, PATRICK, diplomat, writer, educator; b. Polonnaruwa, Sri Lanka, Apr. 7, 1960; arrived in US, 1978, naturalized; m. Cheryl Lynn Pattison, Oct. 8, 1988; children: Gamini, Samantha. BS in Bus. Adminstrn. with hon., U. Sri Lanka, Colombo, 1983; MA in Internat. Devel., Fgn. Affairs, Hubert H. Humphrey Inst. Pub. Affairs, Mpls., 1986; PhD in Geography/Applied Econs., U. Minn., St. Paul, 1989. Grad. Harvard Exec. Leadership Program John F. Jennedy Sch. Govt., Cambridge, Mass., 1996. Vis. scholar in applied econs. U. Minn., 1990—97, lectr. in internat. rels., 1990—97; grad. prof. econs. and govt. U. Md. U. Coll./U.S. Dept. Def., Heidelburg, Germany, 1997—99, U. Md. U. Coll./US Dept. Def., Tokyo, 1999—2000; fgn. affairs officer for sci. and tech. US State Dept., Washington, 2000—01, advisor to US Delegation to UN Commn. on Sustainable Devel., 2001, spl. asst. to Asst. Secy. State and Ednl. and Cult., 2001, Secretariat Dir., 2001—02, vice chair, Sec. of State's Open Forum, 2001—02; cons., economist Ctr. Global Security Rsch., Lawrence Livermore Nat. Lab., US Dept. Energy, 2002—03. Del. UN, and youth ambassador Govt. Sri Lanka, NYC, 1985; cons. World Bank, Washington, 1988-89; advisor US State Dept., Washington, 1991; US Senate Fgn. Relations Com., Washington; chmn. UN Youth Leadership Summit, N.Y.C., 1995; sr. policy fellow Inst. Agr. and Trade Policy, Mpls., 1996-97; vis. faculty Yale U. Ctr. for Internat. and Area Studies, 1996, 97 summers; military prof., U. Md., NATO and Pacific Commands of US Dept. Defense, 1997-2000; spl. Asst. to former NATO Ambassador Harlan Cleveland, UN Univ. Leadership Acad., Amman, Jordan, 1997, Asian Tour of the World Acad. Art and Science, 1995; Governing bd. mem., USDA Graduate Schoo, US Dept. Agr., 2003-, editl. bd. mem. Energy & Environ., 2004 -, dir., editl. bd. mem. The Public Mgr., 2006-.vis. prof. econs. and public policy, U. Pitts. Semester at Sea Program, 2004; adj. prof of diplomacy, Sch. Graduate Studies, Norwich U., 2004-, of internat. relations, Troy U., 2005-. Author: (book) Glocalization: The Human Side of Globalization as If the Washington Consuensus Mattered, 2007; Freedom on the March: An American Voyage to Explore Globalization, 2005; Human Environment and Spatial Relations in Agricultrual Production, 1992; Sri Lanka in Pictures, 1990; Contributing Editor, Asian American Press, 1990-94; advisor (Jour.) Internat. Policy Review, 1991—97; Editor, Global Issues and Economic Perspectives (US State Dept.). Pres. Soc. for Internat. Devel., Minn., 1993-95; v.p. 1995-97; sec. UN Assn., Minn., 1995-96, v.p. 1996-97; founding chair Asian-Pacific Endowment for Cmty. Devel. at St. Paul Found., 1993-95, v.p., 1995-97; bd. dirs. Ctr. for Victims of Torture, Minn., 1997-98, U. Minn. Alumni Assn. Nat. Governing Coun. 1994-97; trustee Humphrey Inst. Alumni Bd. 1993-97; endowed two ann. scholarships in Mgmt. Studies and Leadership U. Sri Jayawardenepura, Sri Lanka, 1993-, Harlan Cleveland Leadership award, U. Moratuwa, 2002-, six Tsunami scholarships, peace prize, Sarvodaya, Sri Lanka, 2006-; named Uhuru Freedom fellow Internat. Republican Inst.; sr. advisor Cultural Heritage Ctr. 2006-; adv. Sen. George Allen senatorial campaign, 2006. Sgt. Army Cadets Corp. Sri Lanka, 1974—76, sgt. Police Cadets Corp. Sri Lanka, 1976—78. Decorated Best Cmdr. Army Cadets Corps Sri Lanka, 1976; recipient UN medal, 1985, Hubert Humphrey Alumni award for outstanding leadership, 1986, MN Gov.'s Asian-Pacific Heritage award, 1994, Aspen Inst. Global Leadership fellowship, 1995, Salzburg Seminar scholarship, 1995, Kennedy Sch, Leadership scholarship Harvard U., 1996, Sasakawa award Sasakawa Found., 1996, Harold Stassen award for UN Affairs, 1997, UN Univ. scholarship Internat. Leadership, Jordan, 1997, Coolidge fellowship Columbia U., 1997, 21st. Century Trust fellow, Oxford U., 2000, Sci. and Diplomacy fellow AAAS, 2000, Socrates Soc. fellow Aspen Inst., 2001, Meritorious Honor award, U.S. State Dept., 2001, Presidential fellow, Salzburg Seminar, 2003, Benjamin Franklin Award, US State Dept., 2003. Fellow World Acad. Arts and Sci.; mem. Am. Com. on Fgn. Rels., U. Minn. Alumni Assn. (bd. dirs. Wash. chpt.), Soc. Internat. Devel. (life), Internat. Inst. for Strategic Studies. Roman Catholic. Avocations: running, hiking. Personal E-mail: patrickmendis@post.harvard.edu.

MENDIUS, PATRICIA DODD WINTER, retired editor, educator, writer; b. Davenport, Iowa, July 9, 1924; d. Otho Edward and Helen Rose (Dodd) Winter; m. John Richard Mendius, June 19, 1947; children: Richard, Catherine M. Graber, Louise, Karen M. Chooljian. BA cum laude, UCLA, 1946; MA cum laude, U. N.Mex., 1966. Cert. secondary edn. tchr., Calif., N.Mex. English tchg. asst. UCLA, 1946—47; English tchr. Marlborough Sch. for Girls, LA, 1947—50, Aztec (N.Mex.) HS, 1953—55, Farmington (N.Mex.) HS, 1955—63; chair English dept. Los Alamos (N.Mex.) HS, 1963—86; sr. technical writer, editor Los Alamos Nat. Lab., 1987—2005. Adj. prof. English, U. N.Mex., Los Alamos, 1970-72, Albuquerque, 1982-85; English cons. S.W. Regional Coll. Bd., Austin, Tex., 1975—; writer, editor, cons. advanced placement English test devel. com. Nat. Coll. Bd., 1982-86, reader, 1982-86, project equality cons., 1985-88; book selection cons. Scholastic mag., 1980-82. Author: Preparing for the Advanced Placement English Exams, 1975; editor Los Alamos Arts Coun. bull., 1986-91. Chair Los Alamos Art Pub. Places Bd., 1987-92; chair adv. bd. trustees U. N.Mex., Los Alamos, 1987-93; pres. Los Alamos Concert Assn., 1972-73, 95-98, 2000-04, pres., 2003-04; chair Los Alamos Mesa Pub. Libr. Bd., 1990-94, chair endowment com., 1995-99. Named Living Treasure of Los Alamos, 2005. Mem. Soc. Tech. Communicators, AAUW (pres. 1961-63, state bd. dirs. 1959-63, Los Alamos coordinating coun. 1992-93, pres. 1993-94, 2002-04, sec. 2001-04), DAR, Order Ea. Star, Mortar Bd., Phi Beta Kappa (pres. Los Alamos chpt. 1969-72, 99, v.p. 1996-99, pres. 2000-01, dir. 2002—), Phi Kappa Phi, Delta Kappa Gamma, Gamma Phi Beta. Avocations: swimming, reading, hiking, astronomy, singing. Home: 124 Rover Blvd Los Alamos NM 87544-3634 Office: Los Alamos Nat Lab Diamond Dr Los Alamos NM 87544 E-mail: pmendius@cybermesa.com.

MENDLER, JOEL A., lawyer; b. New Orleans, Apr. 11, 1944; BA, Tulane U., 1965, JD, 1968. Bar: La. 1968, Ala. 2006. Atty. Baldwin & Haspel, LLC, New Orleans; of counsel Sirote & Permutt, Birmingham, Ala., 2006—. Author: Foreign Base Company Services Income; bd. editors: Tulane Law Rev., 1966-68. Named one of Top 100 Attys., Worth mag., 2005. Fellow Am. Coll. Trust and Estate Counsel; mem. ABA, La. State Bar Assn. (bd. cert. tax atty.), New Orleans Bar Assn., Order of the Coif, Phi Sigma Alpha. Office: Sirote & Permutt 2311 Highland Ave S Birmingham AL 35205 Home: 3540 Wynwood Dr Birmingham AL 35210-3026 Office Phone: 205-930-5243. Office Fax: 205-212-3892. E-mail: jmendler@sirote.com. *

MENDLIN, RONALD C., employment specialist, writer; b. San Francisco, Jan. 8, 1936; s. Joseph and Freda Mendlin; m. Lorraine F. Mendlin, Feb. 15, 1964; children: Andrew Scott, Susan Debra. Student, U. San Francisco, San Francisco State U.; degree, San Francisco City Coll., 1958. Vocat edn. tchg. credential Calif. With City and County of San Francisco,

1962-92; employment specialist No. Calif. Svc. League, San Francisco, 1993—; part-time employment specialist San Mateo, Calif. Job developer San Mateo Employment and Tng. Ctr., Advanced Career Tech., Peninsula Placement Agy.; placement counselor Scofield Employment Agy., San Francisco; lectr. in field. Author (with Marc Polonsky): Putting the Bars Behind You, 5 vols., 2000; author: The Double You, Being Job-Ready, Job Search Tools, Networking and Interviewing for Jobs, Keeping Your Job. With N.G. USAR, 1954—63. Recipient numerous accolades, Mayor's Office. Mem.: Fiesta Gardens Home Owners Assn. (v.p.), No. Calif. Svc. League (mock interviewer 1993—). Achievements include work with California Department of Corrections, California State University's Sacramento Foundation in job placement for ex-felons. Office: No Calif Svc League 28 Boardman Pl San Francisco CA 94103 Office Phone: 415-863-2323.

MENDOLA, JOSEPH ROBERT, philosophy professor, department chairman; b. Rochester, NY, May 2, 1957; s. Joseph R. and Shirley Cook Mendola; m. Therese A. McCarty (div.); 1 child, Lily Yang Griffin. BA, Haverford Coll., Pa., 1979; MA, U. Mich., Ann Arbor, 1981, PhD, 1983. Mellon postdoctoral fellow U. Rochester, 1983—84; vis. asst. prof. NC State U., Raleigh, 1984—85; asst. prof. U. Okla., Norman, 1985—86, U. Nebr., Lincoln, 1986—92, assoc. prof., 1992—98, prof., 1998—, chmn. philosophy dept., 1997—. Author: Human Thought, 1997, Goodness and Justice, 2006. Mem.: Am. Philos. Assn. (program chmn. 2001), Phi Beta Kappa. Office: U Nebr Dept Philosophy 1010 Oldfather Hall Lincoln NE 68588

MENDOZA, GEORGE, poet, author; b. NYC, June 2, 1934; s. George and Elizabeth Mendoza; m. Ruth Sekora, 1967; children: Ashley, Ryan. BA, State Maritime Coll., 1953; postgrad., Columbia U., 1954-56. Author over 100 books for children and adults published worldwide; many included in Boston U.'s George Mendoza Collection, established 1984; children's books on display at the Centre Nat. d'Art et de Culture Georges Pompidou. Works include: And Amedeo Asked, How Does One Become a Man?, (illustrated by Ati Forberg), 1959, The Puma and the Pearl, 1962, The Hawk Is Humming: A Novel, 1964, A Piece of String, Astor-Honor, 1965, Gwot! Horribly Funny Hairticklers (illustrated by Steven Kellog), 1967, The Crack in the Wall and Other Terribly Weird Tales (illustrated by Mercer Mayer), 1968, Flowers and Grasses and Weeds (illustrated by Joseph Low), 1968, The Practical Man (illustrated by Imero Gobbato), 1968, Hunting Sketches (illustrated by Ronald Stein), 1968, A Beastly Alphabet (illustrated by J. Low), 1969, The Digger Wasp (illustrated by Jean Zallinger), 1969, Herman's Hat (illustrated by Frank Bozzo), 1969, The Starfish Trilogy (illustrated by Ati Forberg), 1969, (compiler) The World From My Window: Poems and Drawings (children's writings), 1969, Are You My Friend? (illustrated by F. Bozzo), 1970, The Marcel Marceau Alphabet Book, 1970, The Thumbtown Toad (illustrated by Monika Beisner), 1970, The Inspector, 1970, The Good Luck Spider & other bad luck stories, 1970, The Fearsome Brat (illustrated by F. Bozzo), 1971, Fish in the Sky (illutrated by Milton Glaser), 1971, Moonfish and owl scratchings, 1971, Moonstring, 1971, The Hunter, the Tick and the Gumberoo, 1971, The Marcel Marceau Counting Book, 1971, The Scarecrow Clock (illustrated by Eric Carle), 1971, Big Frog, Little Pond, 1971, The Scribbler, 1971, The Christmas Tree Alphabet Book, 1971, Shadowplay, 1974, Lord, Suffer me to Catch a Fish, 1974, Fishing the Morning Lonely, 1974, (with Carol Burnett) What I Want to Be When I Grow Up, 1975, (with Zero Mostel) The Sesame Street Book of Opposites, 1975, Norman Rockwell's Americana ABC (illustrated by N. Rockwell), 1975, Doug Henning's Magic Book, 1975, Lost Pony, 1976, Norman Rockwell's Boys and Girls at Play, 1976, Secret Places of a Trout Fisherman, 1977, Norman Rockwell's Diary for a Young Girl (illustrated by N. Rockwell), 1978, Magic Tricks, 1978, Mon livre de magic (French edit. of My Book of Magic), Norman Rockwell's Scrapbook for a Young Boy (illustrated by N. Rockwell), 1979, (with Andres Segovia) Segovia, My Book of the Guitar, 1979, Need a House? Call Ms. Mouse! (illustrated by Doris Susan Smith), 1981, Alphabet Sheep (illustrated by K. Reidy), 1982, The Sheepish Book of Opposites, 1982, Silly Sheep and other sheepish rhymes, 1982, Norman Rockwell's Four Seasons, 1982, Norman Rockwell's Happy Holidays, 1983, Henri Mouse (illustrated by Joelle Boucher), 1985, Henri La Souris, 1987, Norman Rockwell's Patriotic Times, 1986, (with Ivan Lendl) Hitting Hot, 1986, (with Sam Snead) Slammin' Sam, 1986, Norman Rockwell's Love and Remembrance, 1986, Top Tennis, 1987, L'Album des Noeuds, 1988, Norman Rockwell's Old Fashioned American Cookbook, 1988, Hairticklers (illustrated by Gahan Wilson), 1989, The Hunter I Might Have Been, reprint 1989, Were You a Wild Duck, Where Would You Go? (illustrated by Jane Osborn-Smith), 1990, Traffic Jam (illustrated by David Stoltz), 1990; also author screenplays for Petals from a Poem Flower, You Show Me Yours and I'll Show You Mine and scripts for Sesame Street; numerous others; over 15 books of poetry including The Hunter I Might Have Been (Lewis Carroll Shelf award 1968), The Mist Men, Goodbye, River, Goodbye; also dozens of articles in The N.Y. Times, Herald Tribune, Stern, Vogue, Harper's Bazaar, Ms., Esquire, Town & Country, Sports Afield, Men's Journal, Philadelphia Inquirer; special travel corr. Toronto Globe & Mail, 1991-94. Cited by Pres. Reagan for Norman Rockwell's Patriotic Times. Avocation: fishing. *I believe we are living in a world where people no longer see each other as individuals. We have become invisible. It is necessary to save our souls. Go out to a field and pick up a fallen leaf. Look at the veins that river the leaf. Follow them until nothing else matters except for the leaf in your hand. Then you will become visible. You will see others and others will see you.*

MENDOZA, JULIE C., lawyer; BA summa cum laude, Tufts U., 1977; JD, U. Chgo., 1981. Bar: DC 1981, US Ct. Internat. Trade, US Ct. Appeals, Fed. Cir. Ptnr., co-chair Internat. Trade Group Kaye Scholer LLP, Washington, DC. Office: Kaye Scholer LLP McPherson Bldg 901 Fifteenth St, NW, Ste 1100 Washington DC 20005 Office Phone: 202-682-3640. E-mail: jmendoza@kayescholer.com.

MENDOZA, KAREN LYNN, special education educator; b. Artesia, New Mex., Feb. 5, 1970; d. Fred Torrez and Esperanza-Mariscal Alvarez; m. Ramon Mendoza; children: Eris, Jadyn. BSc, Eastern New Mex. U., 1993. Cert. tchr. Tex. Tchr., San Antonio, 1993—97; tchr. Arnett Elem. Sch. Lubbock (Tex.) Ind. Sch. Dist., 1997—. Avocations: scrapbooks, photography, reading. Personal E-mail: kamendoza@cox.net.

MENDOZA, MARTHA, reporter; b. LA, 1969; BA, U. Calif. Santa Cruz, 1988. Reporter Madera Tribune, Bay City News Svc., Santa Cruz County Sentinel; nat. investigative reporter Associated Press, San Jose, Calif., 1995—. Co-author: The Bridge at No Gun RI: A Hidden Nightmare from the Korean War, 2001. Recipient Pulitzer prize, 2000, Alumni Achievment award, U. Calif. Santa Cruz, 2002; John S. Knight fellow, Stanford U., 2001. Office: Associated Press 675 N 1st St San Jose CA 95112

MENDOZA, ROBERTO G., JR., banker; b. Cuba, 1945; BA, Yale U., 1967; MBA, Harvard U., 1974. Corp. fin. mgmt. positions with J.P. Morgan & Co., NYC, 1967—90, vice chmn., 1990—2000; mng. dir. Goldman Sachs, NYC, 2000—01; founder & chmn. Integrated Finance Ltd., NYC, 2001—. Bd. dir. Prudential plc, Western Union. Office: Integrated Finance Ltd Ste 2750 630 Fifth Ave New York NY 10111

MENDOZA, RON, chef; Grad., Calif. Sch. Culinary Arts. Hot line Nick and Stef's Steakhouse, LA; tng. pastry chef Patina Restaurant; pastry chef Restaurant Jaan, Sona; exec. pastry chef Ortolan, LA, 2006—. Named one of LA's Rising Stars, StarChefs.com, 2006. Office: Ortolan 8338 W Third St Los Angeles CA 90048 Office Phone: 323-653-3300. *

MENDOZA, RUBEN G., anthropologist, educator, archaeologist; b. Frenchcamp, Calif., June 18, 1956; s. Jose and Josephine Mendoza; m. Linda Marie James, June 2, 1990; children: Natalie Dawn Marie, Maya Nicole. BA, Calif. State U., Bakersfield, 1978; MA, U. Ariz., Tucson, 1980, PhD, 1992. Registered profl. archaeologist 2000. Rsch. asst. SW Mission Rsch. Ctr., Tucson, 1978—79; instr. Bakersfield Coll., Calif., 1982—86; curatorial asst. Photographic Collections, Ariz. State Mus., Tucson, 1988—90; asst. prof. U. Colo., Denver, 1991—95; assoc. prof. Calif. State U., Monterey Bay, Seaside, 1995—2001, prof., 2001—. Instr. Pima Coll., Tucson, 1979—91; prin. investigator Mission San Jaun Bautista, Calif., 1995—, project mgr. mission conservation program, Calif., 2005—; planning faculty Calif. State U. Monterey Bay, Seaside, 1995—97, dir. Inst. Archaeology, 1995—; lit. pl. mentor Scholastic, Inc., NYC, 1996—; contract archaeologist Ruben G. Mendoza, Archaeol. Cons., Salinas, Calif., 2000—; multimedia prodr./content specialist Prentice Hall, Inc., NYC, 2002—03; prin. investigator wireless tech. in archaeology demonstration project, Seaside, 2003—05, Mission San Carlos Borromeo del Rio Carmelo, Calif., 2002—03, Mission San Juan Bautista, Calif., 2005—, project mgr. SJB Mission Conservation program, Calif., 2005—. Photographer, featured archaeologist: 3d grade science text, video, CD-ROM Time Detectives, 1996, 3d grade science text Science, 2001, editl. cons.: children's book Mission Santa Cruz, Mission San Carlos Borromeo del Rio Carmelo, Mission San Juan Bautista, 2000; contbr. chapters to books; photographer (exhibitions) Loveland Gallery, Colo., Mexican Consulate, Denver, Colo., 1994—95, Mex. Heritage Plaza, 2000; contbr. articles to profl. jours. Curatorial rep., old mission San Juan Bautista Calif. Mission Curators and Dirs. Conf., Santa Barbara, 1997; founding faculty mem. CSU Monterey Bay; prin. investigator Royal Presidio Chapel, Monterey, Mission Nuestra Señora de la Soledad; mem. grants rev. com. Calif. Missions Found., San Francisco, 2000—06, bd. dirs. Riverside. Recipient wireless tech. in tchg. and learning award, Congl. Appropriation, 2002—03; fellow, Ford Found., 1990—91, scholar, Nat. Hispanic Scholarship Fund, 1981, 1982, 1987. Mem.: Register Profl. Archaeologists, Am. Anthrop. Assn. (pres. Assn. Latina and Latino Anthropologists 1997—2000, sect. assembly 1998—2000). Achievements include principal investigator Crescent Rockshelter Archaeological Site, Colorado; principal investigator Old Mission San Juan Bautista, California; principal investigator Mission San Carlos Borromeo del Rio Carmelo, California; discovery of California and Southwest mission feast day, equinox and solstice alignments. Avocations: photography, golf, writing, videography, gardening. Office: California State Univ Monterey Bay 100 Campus Center Seaside CA 93955-8001 Office Phone: 831-582-3760. Business E-Mail: ruben_mendoza@csumb.edu.

MENDOZA, STANLEY ATRAN, pediatric nephrologist, educator; b. Pitts., May 7, 1940; s. Joseph William and Marian Ruth (Atran) M.; m. Carole Ann Klein, June 23, 1963; children: Daniel, Joseph. Student, Harvard U., 1957—59; BA, Johns Hopkins U., 1961, MD, 1964. Diplomate Am. Bd. Pediat. Intern Johns Hopkins Hosp., Balt., 1964-65; jr. asst. resident dept. medicine Children's Hosp. Med. Ctr., Boston, 1965-66; asst. attending physician, dir. renal rsch. labs. Children's Meml. Hosp., Chgo., 1969-71; asst. prof. pediat. U. Calif. Sch. Medicine, San Diego, 1971—73, assoc. prof., 1973—79, prof. pediat. dept. pediat. divsn. pediatric nephrology, 1979—, vice chmn. dept. pediat., 1986—87, chmn. dept. pediat., 1992—2000. Contbr. article in field to profl. publ. Served With USPHS, 1966-69. Fogarty Sr. Internat. fellow, 1978-79; Alan J. Wurtzburger rsch. scholar, 1964; recipient Johns Hopkins Med. Soc. award, 1964, hon. mention Borden Undergrad. rsch. award in medicine, 1964; Eleanor Roosevelt internat. fellow Internat. Union Against Cancer, 1984-85. Mem. Am. Fedn. Clin. Rsch., Am. Pediatric Soc., Am. Physiol. Soc., Am. Soc. Nephrology, Am. Soc. Pediatric Nephrology, Internat. Soc. Nephrology. Office: U Calif San Diego Dept Pediat 9500 Gilman Dr # 0696 La Jolla CA 92093-5004 Home Phone: 858-459-0979. E-mail: samendoza@ucsd.edu.

MENEAR, CRAIG, retail executive; b. Flint, Mich. m. Dawn Menear; children: Courtney, Danielle. BA in Bus., Mich. State U., 1979. With IKEA Wholesale, Inc., Builders Emporium, Grace Home Ctrs., Montgomery Ward; divsn. mdse. mgr. Home Depot, Inc., Atlanta, merchandising v.p. S.W. divsn., merchandising v.p. hardware, sr. v.p. merchandising hardlines, 2003—06, sr. v.p. merchandising. Office: Home Depot Inc 2455 Paces Ferry Rd NW Atlanta GA 30339-4024 *

MENEELEY, EDWARD STERLING, artist; b. Wilkes-Barre, Pa., Dec. 18, 1927; s. Edward Sterling and Louina Halter M. Student, Murray Art Sch., Wilkes-Barre, 1947-50, Sch. Visual Arts, NYC, 1952-53, Founder Portable Gallery Press, 1957-67; vis. lectr. Belleville Coll., St. Louis, Art Students League, N.Y.C.; lectr. Lehigh Valley Sch. System, 1987, Rogers College, Istanbul, Turkey, 1991, Lafayette Coll., 1998; pres. ESM Documentations, N.Y.C.; fine arts cons. Arts Initiatives, Inc., N.Y.C.; mem. Penna Artists, 2005. One-man exhbs. include, Donovan Gallery, Phila., 1952, Parma Gallery, N.Y.C., 1962, Teuscher Gallery, N.Y.C., 1966, 68, Inst. Contemporary Arts, London, 1971, Victoria and Albert Mus., London, 1972, U. Sussex, Eng., 1972, Whitechapel Art Gallery, London, 1973, Demos Gallery, Athens, Greece, 1976, Frank Marino Gallery, N.Y.C., 1978, 79, 80, 81, 82, Sordoni Gallery, Wilkes (Pa.) Coll., 1981, Ericson Gallery, N.Y.C., 1980, Portfolio Gallery, Atlanta, 1983, Angela Flowers Gallery, London, 1985, J.T. Gallery, Jim Thorpe, Pa, 1987, 55 Mercer St., N.Y.C., 1987, Anita Shapolsky Gallery, N.Y.C., 1988, Bucknell U. Gallery Art, Lewisburg, 1988, Recent Painting & Sculptute, Coll. Misericordia, Dallas, Pa., 1989, Mixed Media, Craft Alliance Gallery, St. Louis, 1990, Provincetown (Mass.) Art Mus., 1993, De Arte Magick Gallery, Easton, Pa., 1997, New Works, N.Y.C., 1998, 181 Hudson St. N.Y.C., 1998, 70th St. Gallery Collages, 2001, Soho Creative, N.Y.C., 2002, 03, 04, MCI Gallery, 2003, 2004, Anita Shapulsky Art Found., 2005. Served with USNR, 1945-47, 50-52. Nat. Endowment Arts grantee; Pollock-Krasner Found. grantee, 1986, 90, 2002. Mem. Artist Club N.Y.C., Inst. Contemporary Arts London, Josiah White Soc., Weissport, Pa. Office: Anita Shapcsky Found 20 West Broadway Jim Thorpe PA 18229 Personal E-mail: edm7688@yahoo.com.

MENEES, KATHERINE DETERMAN, parochial school educator; b. Keyser, W.Va., Mar. 22, 1941; d. Alphonsus William and Bernadette Cosgrove Determan; m. Timothy Ryan Menees, Aug. 24, 1968; children: Timothy Marion, Rebecca Menees Ciccio. BS, Frostburg State U., Md., 1963. Tchr. Surrattsville Jr. HS, Clinton, Md., 1963—69; substitute tchr. Incirlik Am. Sch., Turkey, 1970—71, Bainbridge Island HS, Wash., 1973—74; tchr. St. Valentine Sch., Bethel Park, Pa., 1985—. Forensics team moderator, coach Southwestern Pa. Forensics League, Pitts., 1995—; advisor St. Valentine Sch. Newspaper, 1996—. Tchr., student advisor St. Mary of Mercy at Meny Red Door Program, Pitts., 1987, 1988, 1999, 2005, Food Bank, McKeesport, Pa., 1990; bd. dirs. Children's Ctr. for Theater Arts, Mt. Lebanon, Pa., 1981—90. MAC grantee, McDonalds, Bethel Park, 2004. Mem.: Nat. Cath. Ednl. Assn., Western Pa. Coun. Tchrs. of English, Nat. Coun. Tchrs. of English. Roman Catholic. Avocations: piano, sewing, gardening, reading. Home: 5001 Highland Ave Bethel Park PA 15102 Office: St Valentine Sch 2709 Mesta St Bethel Park PA 15102 Office Phone: 412-835-3780. E-mail: detcat322@aol.com.

MENEFEE, FREDERICK LEWIS, advertising executive; b. Arkansas City, Kans., Oct. 22, 1932; s. Arthur LeRoy and Vera Mae (Rather) M.; m. Margot Leuze, Sept. 16, 1955; children: Gregory S., Christina Menefee-Anderson. AA, Arkansas City Jr. Coll., 1952; BA, U. Wichita, 1958. Sports editor, bus. mgr. Ark. Light and Tiger Tales, 1949-52; sports reporter Arkansas City Daily Traveler, 1949—52; advt. mgr. Derby Star, Haysville Herald and Sedgwick County News, 1956-57; v.p., account exec. Associated Advt. Agy., 1958-64; with McCormick-Armstrong Adv. Agy. (now Menefee and Ptnrs., Inc.), Wichita, 1964—, agy. mgr., 1964—, account. supr., 1965—, gen. mgr., 1972—, pres., CEO, 1979—, chmn. bd., 1986—2003. Vol. Wichita River Festival, 1974-98; pub. rels. chmn. Wichita Centennial Nat. Art Show and Exhibit, 1969-70. With AUS, 1953-55. Named Henry J. Lawrence Photo award, 1956, Wichita Beacon Advt. award, 1957, KANS Radio award, 1958, Advt. Man of Yr., Advt. Club of Wichita, 1964, Advt. Man of Yr., 9th Dist. Am. Advt. Fedn. Colo., Nebr., Iowa, Mo., Kans., 1965, Adm. Windwagon Smith III Wichita Festivals Inc., 1976. Mem. Am. Advt. Fedn. (nat. bd. dirs. 1969-70, dist. gov. 1968-69, chmn. nat. coun. govs. 1969-70, 1st lt. gov. awards chmn. 1967, 68), Wichita Wagonmasters (founding mem. 1973, capt. 1974-75, dir., charter, founder, commodore 1999), Wichita Advt. Club (bd. dirs. 1958-68), v.p. awards 1961-62, v.p. membership 1962, v.p. programs 1963, pres. 1964-65), PAWS Inc. (founder, 1st pres. 1978-86), Alpha Delta Sigma (pres. 1957-58, Outstanding Svc. award 1958), Quill & Scroll, 1949-50. Home: 2235 Red Bud Ln Wichita KS 67204-5346

MENEFEE, JOHN WILLIAM, III, cinematographer, film producer; b. Washington, Dec. 19, 1944; s. John William Menefee Jr. and Mary Claudia (Tudor) Upchurch. Student, U. Va., 1964-66, Columbia Sch. for Motion Pictures and TV, L.A., 1992. Tour guide Universal Studios, Universal City, Calif., 1970-75, studio transp. driver, 1976; camera asst., trainee Dino d'Laurentis Orgn., Beverly Hills, Calif., 1976, Panavision (formerly Gen. Camera), NYC, 1978; camera person Paramount Pictures, LA, 1980, 20th Century Fox Film Corp., LA, 1987, 96, Sony Pictures Corp., Culver City, Calif., 1992, 97, Paramount Pictures, LA, 2000. Mem. film and TV action com. Bring Hollywood Home, L.A., 1999—; contbr., supporter World Wildlife Fund, Washington, Lambda Legal Def. Fund, N.Y.C., Cato Inst., Washington. Mem. Internat. Cinematographers Guild (cert.), Jamestown Soc. Episcopalian. Avocations: genealogy, vedic astrology, tennis, acting. Home: 1020 San Rafael Ln Pasadena CA 91105-1531

MENEFEE, LINNEA-NORMA, antique dealer; b. Mpls., Mar. 5, 1924; d. Arthur Wesley and Elsie Ida Buck. Student, U. Minn., Mpls., U. Minn., Duluth, McPhail Sch. Music, Mpls. Chmn. State Vet. Home, Buffalo. Founder Albert Lea (Minn.) Art Ctr., 1959; county chairwoman Goldwater for Pres., Albert Lea. Recipient Conscientious award, 2001. Mem. AAUW, Am. Med. Assn. Alliance, Nat. Fedn. Rep. Women, Nat. Women of the Arts, Nat. Am. Legion Aux., Nat. VFW Aux., Nat. Assn. Family and Cmty. Edn., Order of Ea. Star, Gillette Blue Blades, Kiwanis Internat. (Concientious Kiwanian 2002), Zeta Phi Eta, Omega Upsilon, Zeta Beta Chi. Episcopalian. Avocations: writing, reading, painting, sculpting, travel.

MENEFEE, SAMUEL PYEATT, lawyer, academic; b. Denver, June 8, 1950; s. George Hardiman and Martha Elizabeth (Pyeatt) M.; m. Mary W., April 21, 2000; 1 child: Mary Elizabeth. BA in Anthropology and Scholar of Ho. summa cum laude, Yale U., 1972; diploma in Social Anthropology, Oxford U., Eng., 1973, BLitt, 1975; JD, Harvard U., 1981; LLM in Oceans, U. Va., 1982, SJD, 1993; MPhil in Internat. Rels., U. Cambridge, Eng., 1995. Bar: Ga. 1981, U.S. Ct. Appeals (11th cir.) 1982, Va. 1983, La. 1983, U.S. Ct. Mil. Appeals 1983, U.S. Ct. Internat. Trade 1983, U.S. Ct. Claims 1983, U.S. Ct. Appeals (10th cir.) 1983, U.S. Ct. Appeals (fed., 1st, 3d, 4th, 5th, 6th, 7th, 8th and 9th cirs.) 1984, D.C. 1985, Nebr. 1985, Fla. 1985, U.S. Supreme Ct. 1985, U.S. Ct. Appeals (D.C. cir.) 1986, Maine 1986, Pa. 1986. Assoc. Phelps, Dunbar, Marks, Claverie & Sims, New Orleans, 1983-85; of counsel Barham & Churchill PC, New Orleans, 1985-88; sr. assoc. Ctr. for Nat. Security Law U. Va. Sch. Law, 1985—, fellow Ctr. for Oceans Law and Policy, 1982-83, sr. fellow, 1985-89, Maury fellow, 1989—, adv. bd., 1997—. Vis. lectr. U. Cape Town, 1987; vis. asst. prof. U. Mo., Kansas City, 1990; law clk. Hon. Pasco M. Bowman US Ct. Appeals (8th cir.), 1994-95; vis. prof. Regent U., 1996-97, scholar-at-large, 1997—2003, prof., 1998—2003; adv. Am. Maritime Forum/Mariners' Mus., 1997-99; lectr. various nat. and internat. orgns.; mem. ICC Consultative Task Force on Comml. Crime, 1996—. Author: Wives for Sale: An Ethnographic Study of British Popular Divorce, 1981, Contemporary Piracy and International Law, 1995, Trends in Maritime Violence, 1996; co-editor: Materials on Ocean Law, 1982; nat. editor: Assn. Rsch. on Peasant Diaries, 1996-; mem. editl. bd. Internat. Jour. Marine and Costal Law, 1997-2003; contbr. numerous articles to profl. jours. Recipient Katharine Briggs prize Folklore Soc., 1992; Bates traveling fellow Yale U., 1971, Rhodes scholar, 1972; Cosmos fellow Sch. Scottish Studies U. Edinburgh, 1991-92, IMB fellow, ICC Internat. Maritime Bur., 1991—, Piracy Reporting Ctr. fellow, Kuala Lampur, 1993—, Huntington fellow The Mariners Mus., 1997. Fellow Royal Anthrop. Inst., Am. Anthrop. Assn., Royal Asiatic Soc., Royal Soc. Antiquaries Ireland, Soc. Antiquaries Scotland, Royal Geog. Soc., Soc. Antiquaries; mem. ABA (vice-chmn. marine resources com. 1987-90, chmn. law of sea com. subcom. naval warfare, maritime terrorism and piracy 1989—, mem. law of sea com. steering com. 1996—99, mem. working group on terrorism), Southeastern Admiralty Law Inst. (com. mem.), Maritime Law Assn. (proctor, com. mem., chmn. subcom. law of sea 1988-91, vice chmn. com. internat. law of sea 1991—99, chmn. com. internat. law of sea 1999-2003, chair working group piracy 1992—2003, UNESCO study group 1998—), Marine Tech. Soc. (co-chmn./chmn. marine security com. 1991—2004), Selden Soc., Am. Soc. Internat. Law, Internat. Law Assn. (com. mem., rapporteur Am. br. com. EEZ 1988-90, rapporteur Am. br. com. Maritime Neutrality 1992, observer UN conv. on law of sea meeting of states parties 1996, chmn./co-chmn. Am. br. com. on law of sea 1996—2001, rapporteur joint internat. working group on uniformity of law of piracy 1998—2001), Com. Maritime Internat., Am. Soc. Indsl. Security (com. mem.), US Naval Inst., USN League, Folklore Soc., Royal Celtic Soc., Internat. Studies Assn., Royal Scottish Geog. Soc., Royal African Soc., Egypt Exploration Soc., Arctic Inst. N.Am., Internat. Studies Assn., Am. Hist. Soc., Soc. for History of Discoveries, Soc. Nautical Rsch., Internat. Assn. Rsch. on Peasant Diaries, Christian Aid Mission, Nat. Eagle Scout Assn., Raven Soc., Jefferson Soc., Fence Club, Mory's Assn., Elizabethan Club, Yale Polit. Union, Leander Club, Cambridge Union, United Oxford and Cambridge Univ. Club, Yale Club NYC, Paul Morphy Chess Club, Pendennis Club, Round Table Club New Orleans, Phi Beta Kappa, Omicron Delta Kappa. Republican. Avocations: anthropology, archaeology, crew, hiking. Office: PO Box 5291 Charlottesville VA 22905-2591 also: U Va Ctr Nat Sec Law 580 Massie Rd Charlottesville VA 22903-1738 Office Phone: 434-924-7441. Business E-Mail: colp@virginia.edu.

MENELL, PETER SETH, law educator; b. Jersey City, Dec. 2, 1958; s. Allan and Carole M.; m. Claire Marie Sylvia. SB in Econs., MIT, 1980; MA in Econs., Stanford U., Calif., 1982; PhD in Econs, 1986; JD, Harvard U., 1986. Law clk. to presiding judge US Ct. Appeals (2d cir.), Hartford, Conn., 1986-87; assoc. prof. law Georgetown U. Law Ctr., Washington, 1987-90; prof. sch. law U. Calif., Berkeley, 1990—, dir. Ctr. Law and Tech., 1995—. Vis. prof. Harvard Law Sch., 1990, Stanford Law Sch., 1992-93. Co-author (with Richard Stewart): Environmental Law and Policy, 1994; co-author: (with J. Dwyer) Property Law and Policy, 1998; co-author: (with R. Merges & M. Lemley) Intellectual Property in the New Technological Age, 2006; co-author: (with M. Lemley, R. Merges and P. Samuelson) Software and Internet Law, 2006; author: Environmental Law, 2002; contbr. articles to profl. jour. Stanford U. fellow, 1980, Olin fellow Harvard U., 1985, Olin Found. fellow, 1989. Mem. Am. Econs. Assn., Calif. Bar Assn. Jewish. Office: University of California School of Law Boalt Hall, Rm 355 Berkeley CA 94720-7200 Office Phone: 510-642-5489. Business E-Mail: pmenell@law.berkeley.edu.

MENENDEZ, ROBERT (BOB MENENDEZ), senator, former congressman; b. NYC, Jan. 1, 1954; s. Mario and Evangelina (Lopez) M.; m. Jane Jacobsen, June 5, 1976 (div. 2005); children: Alicia, Robert. BA in Polit. Sci. and Urban Studies, St. Peter's Coll., 1976; JD, Rutgers U., 1979. Bar:

NJ 1980. Atty. Diaz and Menendez, Union City, NJ, 1980-92; mayor City of Union City, 1986—92; mem. NJ Gen. Assembly, 1987—91; majority whip NJ State Senate, 1991—92; mem. US Congress from 13th N.J. dist., 1993—2006; Dem. whip at large; US Senator from NJ, 2006—; mem. banking, housing & urban affairs, budget, energy & nat. resources, fgn. rels. com. Co-chair Hillary Rodham Clinton Presdl. Campaign, 2007—. CFO Union City Bd. Edn., 1978-82, trustee, 1974-78; mem. Alliance Civic Assn., 1982-92, pres. 1981; mem. Gov.'s Hispanic Adv. Com., Trenton, N.J., 1984—; mem. Gov.'s Ethnic Adv. Com., Washignton, 1985. Recipient Cmty. Svc. award Gran Logia del Norte, 1981, Outstanding Svc. award Hispanic Law Enforcement, 1981, Outstanding Cmty. Svc. Revista Actualidades, 1982, US Conf. Mayors award, 1987, 1988, 1991, Disting. Citizen award U. Medicine and Dentistry N.J., 1994, Man of Yr. award Kiwanis, 1994, Justice of Cyprus award, Cyprus Federation Am., 1995, Am. Hellenic Inst. Public Svc. Achievement award, 1997, Lifetime Achievement award Hispanic Bus. Roundtable, 2000, Excellence in Edn. award, Ana G. Mendez U. System, 2003, Capital award Nat. Coun. of La Raza, 2003, Paraskevaides award, 16th Annual Cyprus Conf., 2005; named Man of the Year, Armenian Nat. Com. NJ, 2007. Mem. ABA, Fed. Bar Assn. NJ Bar Assn., Hispanic Bar Assn., Hudson County Bar Assn., NJ Employment & Training Commn., NJ Mayors Coalition, NJ Hispanic Leadership Opportunities Program (chmn.), Hispanic Elected and Apptd Ofcls. Orgn. (chmn.); Hoboken Elks Club, North Hudson Lawyers Club (chmn.) Democrat. Roman Catholic. Avocations: chess, racquetball. Office: US Senate 317 Hart Senate Office Bldg Washington DC 20510 also: District Office Ste 1100 One Gateway Ctr Newark NJ 07102 Office Phone: 202-224-4744, 973-645-3030. Office Fax: 202-228-2197, 973-645-0502. *

MENENDEZ CAMBO, PATRICIA, lawyer; b. NYC, June 7, 1966; BBA, U. Miami, 1986; JD, U. Pa., 1989. Bar: Fla. 1991, DC 1993. With Greenberg Traurig, PA, Miami, 1994—2000; chief U.S. legal counsel Telefónica S.A., 2000—02; shareholder, chair internat. practice group Greenberg Traurig, PA, Miami, 2002—. Bd. dirs. Coun. of Americas. Contbr. articles to profl. jours. Trustee Nat. Alliance for Autism Rsch. Named one of Top Up and Comers in So. Fla., So. Fla. Legal Guide, 2004, Top 40 Lawyers Under 40, Nat. Law Jour., 2005, 100 Most Influential Lawyers, 2006, The 50 Most Influential Women Lawyers in Am., 2007. Office: Greenberg Traurig 1221 Brickell Ave Miami FL 33131 Office Phone: 305-579-0766. Office Fax: 305-579-0717. Business E-Mail: pmc@gtlaw.com. *

MENEZES, NELSON, surgeon; b. July 6, 1957; MBBS, U. Bombay, India, 1980, MS, 1984. Diplomate Am. Bd. Surgery, 1997, Am. Bd. Vascular Surgery, 1999. Chief vascular surgeon Bklyn. Hosp. Ctr., 1998—. Mem.: Soc.Vascular Surgery, NY Soc. Vascular Surgery. Home: 121 Dekalb Ave Brooklyn NY 11201-5425

MENG, ANNE L., pediatric nurse practitioner; b. Rochester, NY, Apr. 25, 1948; d. William Charles and Ann Louise Meng. BSN, Salve Regina Coll., Newport, 1970; MSN, U. Pitts., Pa., 1976. Cert. pediat. nurse practitioner U. Tex., 1996, AE-C Associated Asthma Educators. Staff nurse RI Hosp., Providence, 1970—74; instr. U. Rochester, NY, 1976—80; clin. nurse specialist U. Tex. Med. Branch, Galveston, 1981—94, asst. prof., sch. nursing, 1994—2004, special projects coord., 2004—. Author (producer): (DVD) Radical Randy Presents the Camp Rad Children's Asthma Classes, 2006; contbr. articles various profl. jours. Recipient Archor award, Sigma Theta Tau Internat., 1998, Pres. Cabinet award, U. Tex. Med. Branch, 2006. Mem.: Asthma Coalition Tex. (founding mem.). Achievements include invention of 3-D asthma teaching doll "Radical Randy"; development of the Camp RAD children's asthma curriculum. Avocations: tennis, quilting, writing. Business E-Mail: ameng@utmb.edu.

MENG, GUNTER RICHARD, surgeon; b. Brühl, Germany, Mar. 31, 1927; US, 1948; s. Richard and Elise Meng; m. Hilde Maria Farrenkopf, Aug. 14, 1954; children: Karin, Peter. BA, Cornell U., 1951, MD, 1955. Internship, surg. residency Syracuse U., NY, 1955—60; gen. surgeon USAF, 1960—82, chief surgery, chief prof. staff; vice comdr. USAF Wright Patterson Med. Ctr. Surgery cons. for surgeon gen. USAF, Wash., DC, 1978—82; assoc. clin. prof. surgery Wright-State U. Med. Coll., Dayton, Ohio, 1978—84. Contbr. articles to profl. jours. Recipient Legion of Merit, USAF, 1982. Fellow: ACS; mem.: Assn. Mil. Surgeons. Republican. Home: 12211 Lackwood Ct Fort Myers FL 33908

MENG, LINDA, lawyer; BA, Towson State U., Md., 1976; JD, U. Md. Law Sch., 1979. Bar: Oreg. 1979. Law clerk Oreg. Ct. Appeals, 1979—80; assoc., ptnr. Hart, Neil & Weigler Attys., 1983—90; with Legal Dept., Portland, Oreg., 1990—, now city atty. Office: Portland City Atty Rm 430 1221 SW 4th Ave Portland OR 97204 Fax: 503-823-3089.

MENG, LING-JIAN, engineering educator; b. China, Aug. 24, 1970; BA, U. Sci. and Tech. China, 1995; PhD, U. Southampton, Eng., 2001. Rsch. fellow U. Mich., Ann Arbor, 2002—03, rsch. asst. prof., 2003—06; asst. prof U. Ill, Urbana, 2006—. Mem.: IEEE, IEEE Nuc. and Plasma Scis. Soc. Office: U Ill 214 Nuc Engring Labs 213 S Goodwin Ave Urbana IL 61801

MENG, M. KATHRYN, lawyer; JD, Fordham U. Former dist. ct. bur. chief criminal divsn. Legal Aid Soc. Nassau County; ptnr. Cianciulli Meng & Panos P.C., Garden City, NY, 1992—. Dean Nassau Acad. Law; adj. prof. Nassau C.C., 1992—. Columnist Nassau Lawyer. Bd. dirs. Sara's Ctr.; mem. outreach adv. com. St. Brigid's Ch., Westbury, eucharistic ministr. Mem.: ABA (del.), 2d Jud. Dept. Com. on Character and Fitness Adminstrn. Attys. to the Bar, Nassau Legal Aid Soc. (former pres., former bd. dirs.), Criminal Cts. Bar Assn. (former pres., bd. dirs.), N.Y. State Bar Assn. (del.), Nassau County Bar Assn. (pres. 2000—01, mem. civil rights com., mem. lawyers assistance com., former mem. judiciary com.). Office: Cianciulli Meng & Panos PC 99 Quentin Roosevelt Blvd Ste 201 Garden City NY 11530 Office Phone: 516-683-0901. Business E-Mail: kmeng@cmlawgroup.net.

MENG, RU-LING, research scientist; children: Meng Huang, He Huang. BA, Ctrl. So. U. of Tech. Mining and Metallurgy Coll., Hunan, China, 1958. Instr. Ctr. So. U. of Tech. (Mining and Metallurgy Coll.), Hunan, China, 1958—59; rsch. asst. Acad. of Sci., Inst. of Mining and Metallurgy, Beijing, 1959—73; rsch. assoc. Chinese Acad. of Sci., Inst. of Physics, Beijing, 1973—79, U. of Houston, Dept. of Physics, 1979—81; vis. scholar U. of Konstanz, Dept. of Physics, Germany, 1981; rsch. assoc. Acad. of Sci., Inst. of Physics, Beijing, 1982—84, U. of Houston, Dept. of Physics, 1984—; sr. rsch. scientist Tex. Ctr. for Superconductivity at the U. of Houston, Dept. of Physics, 1987—. Sr. cons. Chan-Sha Rsch. Inst. of Mining and Metallurgy, China, 1992. Named one of the most worlds most cited authors, Inst. for Sci. Info. Current Contents, 2000; recipient ranked 25th out of the 1000 most cited physicists, Inst. for Sci. Info., 1981—97, Hon. professorship, Zhong-Shan U. (Sun Yat-Sen U.), 1992, Ctr. So. U. of Tech., 1992, Beijing Polytechnic U., 1998. Mem.: Chinese Assn. of Professionals in Sci. and Tech. (founder/1st pres.), Materials Rsch. Soc., Phi Beta Delta Internat. Assn. Achievements include discovery of high temperature superconducting Y-Ba-Cu-O system; first to succeed in fabricating texturing Y-Ba-Cu-O bar, obtained first record trapped field of 8T at 4.2k by 20 mmx6 mm YBCO discs, first to grow C60 (or carbon 60) single crystal with no defect; development of and the patent for processing techniques for highest transition superconducting temperature Hg-Ba-Ca-Cu-O and co-developed the first Hg-1212 film; first to succeed in fabricating Hg-1223 tape; first to succeed in fabricating Bi-sr-ca-cu-o on a low cost ni metal substrate. Office: Texas Ctr for Superconductivity U of Houston High Pressure Low Temperature Lab Houston TX 77204 E-mail: rmeng@uh.edu.

MENG, SHENG, physicist, researcher; b. Huaibei, Anhui, China, Dec. 25, 1981; s. Ling-Yuan Meng and Yu-Fang Li; m. Jun Ren, July 6, 2006. BS, U. Sci. & Tech. China, Hefei, 1996—2000; PhD in Physics, Chalmers U. Tech., Gothenburg, Sweden, 2002—04; PhD, Chinese Acad. Sci., Beijing, 2004. Post-doctoral fellow Harvard U., Cambridge, Mass., 2005—. Contbr. articles to profl. jours. Mem.: Materials Rsch. Soc., Am. Phys. Soc. Achievements include design of new hydrogen storage material; carbon nanotube machinary for ultrafast DNA sequencing; discovery of melanin molecular structure; carbon nanotube and nucleobase interaction; novel water structure and behavoir on solid surfaces. Home: 196 Hampshire St Cambridge MA 02139 Office: Harvard Univ Physics Dept 17 Oxford St Cambridge MA 02138 Office Fax: 617-495-2545. Personal E-mail: meng.sm@gmail.com. Business E-Mail: shmeng@deas.harvard.edu.

MENG, TERESA H., electrical engineer, educator; b. Taiwan; BSEE, Nat. Taiwan U., 1983; MS in Elec. Engring. and Computer Sci., U. Calif., Berkeley, 1984, PhD in Elec. Engring. and Computer Sci., 1988. Mem. faculty elec. engring. dept. Stanford U., Calif., 1988—, Reid Weaver Dennis prof. elec. engring. Calif., 2003—; founder, bd. dirs. Atheros Comm., Inc., Calif., 1998—, pres., CEO, 1998—99. Contbr. articles to sci. jours., chapters to books; author: Synchronization Design of Digital Systems, 1990; co-editor: VLSI Signal Processing IX, 1996. Bd. trustees Computer Hist. Mus. Named Innovator of Yr., MIT Sloan Sch. eBusiness Awards, 2002; named one of Top 10 Entrepreneurs, Red Herring, 2001; recipient Eli Jury award, U. Calif. Berkeley, 1988, Best Paper award, IEEE Signal Processing Soc., 1989, Presdl. Young Investigator award, NSF, 1989, Young Investigator award, Office of Naval Rsch., 1989, IBM Faculty Devel. award, 1989, Disting. Lectr. award, IEEE Signal Processing Soc., 20/20 Vision award, Chief Info. Officer Mag., 2002, Demo@15 World-Class Innovator award, 2005. Fellow: IEEE; mem.: NAE. Achievements include patents in field. Office: Dept Elec Engring 209 CIS Bldg 420 Via Palou Mall Stanford CA 94305-4070 Office Phone: 650-725-3636. Office Fax: 650-725-3383. E-mail: meng@ee.stanford.edu. *

MENG, YU-JU GLORIA, research scientist; d. Chen-Fu and Chou Ya Chu; 1 child, John Chu. PhD, Columbia U., NYC, 1980; BS in Chemistry, Nat. Tsing Hua U., Taiwan, 1974. Staff scientist Bayer, Berkeley, Calif., 1984—92; sr. scientist (tech.) Genentech Inc., South San Francisco, Calif., 1992—. Grantee, NIH. Mem.: Am. Chem. Soc., Am. Soc. Biochem. and Molecular Biology. Office Phone: 650-225-8289.

MENGDEN, JOSEPH MICHAEL, retired investment banker; b. Houston, Sept. 28, 1924; s. Hippolyt Frederick and Amalia (Dittlinger) M.; m. Suzanne Miner, Sept. 30, 1950 (dec. July 1990); children: Anne Elise Mengden Giliberto, Amanda Mary, Michael Joseph, Charles Louis, Melissa Mary Mengden Bunker, Mary Miner Mengden Fitch; m. Dorothy Duggan, July 27, 1991 (dec. Apr. 2006); m. Carolyn Lounsberry, June 22, 2007. Ph.B., U. Notre Dame, 1949. V.p. Nat. Bank of Detroit, 1950-67; exec. v.p. First of Mich. Capital Corp., Detroit, 1967-90, sr. cons., 1990-95. Served to 1st lt. USAAF, World War II. Decorated Air medal with 2 oak leaf clusters. Home: 17111 E Jefferson #11 Grosse Pointe MI 48230-1941 Personal E-mail: men@comcast.net.

MENGEL, CHARLES EDMUND, internist, educator; b. Balt., Nov. 29, 1931; s. Charles LeRoy and Anna (Apgar) M.; m. Paula Padgett, June 5, 1978; children: Cheryl Lynn, Charles Edmund, Gregory John, Scott Alan, Carol Ann, Michael Daniel. AB in Chemistry, Lafayette Coll., 1953; MD, Johns Hopkins U., 1957. Intern Johns Hopkins Hosp., 1957-58; resident Duke Hosp., 1958-59, 61-62; clin. assoc. NIH, 1959-61; mem. faculty Duke U. Med. Sch., 1961-65; Doan prof., dir. hematology and oncology Ohio State U., 1965-69; prof. medicine U. Mo., Columbia, 1969-82, chmn. dept., 1969-81; pvt. practive gen. medicine Moberly, Mo., 1982-88; prof. medicine Kans. U. Med. Ctr., Kansas City, 1988-98; CEO MEC Enterprises, 1999—. Author textbook; contbr. articles to med. publs. With USPHS, 1959-61. Markle scholar acad. medicine, 1963 Mem. ACP, Am. Fedn. Clin. Rsch., Am. Soc. Hematology, Am. Soc. Clin. Investigation

MENGEL, CHRISTOPHER EMILE, lawyer, educator; b. Holyoke, Mass., Sept. 11, 1952; s. Emile Oscar and Rose Ann (O'Donnell) M.; m. Ellen Christine Creager, Dec. 6, 1991; children: Meredith Anne, Celia Claire; step-children: Cara Elizabeth Creager, Kristen Michele Creager. Student, U. Notre Dame, 1970-71; BA, Holy Cross Coll., 1974; JD, Detroit Coll. Law, 1979. Bar: Mich. 1979, U.S. Dist. Ct. (ea. dist.) Mich. 1989, U.S. Ct. Appeals (6th cir.) 1990. Tchr. Holyoke Pub. Schs., 1974-76; assoc. Fried & Sniokaitis P.C., Detroit, 1980-82; prof. Detroit Coll. Law, 1982-85; pvt. practice Detroit, 1982-91; mng. ptnr. Berkley, Mengel & Vining, PC, 1992—2005, Berkley, Mengel PLC, 2005—. Mem. coun. St. Ambrose Parish, Grosse Pointe Park, Mich., 1985-88, pres. 1986-87; bd. dirs., vice chair Empowerment Zone Coalition Detroit, 2006—. Matthew J. Ryan scholar, 1970; recipient Disting. Brief award Thomas M. Cooley Law Rev., 1996. Mem. ABA, Mich. Bar Assn., Detroit Bar Assn. Democrat. Roman Catholic. Avocations: baseball, sailing, photography. Home: 1281 N Oxford Rd Grosse Pointe MI 48236-1857 Office: Berkley Mengel PLC 225 S Troy St Ste 250 Royal Oak MI 48067 Office Phone: 248-586-0200. Business E-Mail: cmengel@berkleymengel.com.

MENGELING, WILLIAM LLOYD, retired veterinarian, virologist; b. Elgin, Ill., Apr. 1, 1933; s. William Paul and Blanche Joyce (Wormwood) M.; m. Barbara Ann Kethcart, Aug. 23, 1958; children: Michelle, Michael. BS, Kans. State U., 1958, DVM, 1960; MS, Iowa State U., 1966, PhD, 1969. Diplomate M. Coll. Vet. Microbiologists (chmn. 1977-78, bd. dirs. 1975-77). Vet. clinician St. Francis Animal Hosp., Albuquerque, 1960-61; vet. med. officer Nat. Animal Disease Ctr., Ames, Iowa, 1961-69, rsch. leader, 1969—2001, U.S. Sr. Exec. Svc., 1991—; ret., 2001. Cons. numerous state, fed., pvt. U.S. and fgn. agys.; collaborative prof., mem. grad. faculty Iowa State U. Co-editor: Diseases of Swine, 5th, 6th, 7th, 8th editions; contbr. articles to jours., chpts. to books. With U.S. Army, 1953-55. Recipient cert. appreciation USDA, 1978, George Fleming award Brit. Vet. Jour., 1978, Disting. Svc. award USDA, 1984, Gov.'s medal sci. State of Iowa, 1985, Vet. Med. Rsch. award Am. Feed Industry Assn., 1989, Leadership Merit awards USDA, 1989, 90, 91, 93, Alumnus award Kans. State U. Coll. Vet. Medicine and Vet. Med. Alumni Assn., 1999, William P. Switzer award Iowa State U. Coll. Met. Medicine, 2000, Howard Dunne Meml. award, Am. Assn. Swine Vets., 2001; elected to Agrl. Rsch. Svc. Hall of Fame, 2001. Mem. AVMA (Vet. Med. Rsch. award 1989), U.S. Animal Health Assn., Conf. Rsch. Workers in Animal Disease (pres. 1987-88, coun. 1981-86, dedicatee 2005 ann. meeting), Polish Soc. Vet. Sci. (hon.), Kiwanis (pres. 1975-76). Methodist. Avocations: wilderness survival, canoeing, camping, fishing. Home: 4220 Phoenix St Ames IA 50014-3922 Office Phone: 515-292-7060. Personal E-mail: bbmengeling@aol.com.

MENGES, MARTHA, special education educator; d. John and Mary Blake Duff; children: John A., Katherine. BS in Home Econs., William Woods Coll., Fulton, Mo., 1969; postgrad., Harris Tchrs. Coll., St. Louis, 1970—71, Ea. Ill. U., 1987—88. Cert. elem. edn. Ill., cross categorical spl. edn. Ill. State Bd. of Edn., 1988. Elem. tchr. Granite City Sch. Dist., Ill., 1970—72; substitute tchr. Iroquois County schs., Watseka, Ill., 1982—87; cross categorical spl. edn. tchr. Ford-Iroquois Spl. Edn. Assn., Iroquois County, Ill., 1988—96; spl. edn. tchr. students with behavior disorders Kankakee Dist. #111, Ill., 1996—98; cross categorical spl. edn. tchr. Iroquois Spl. Edn. Assn., Donovan and Watseka, Ill., 1998—. Ednl. diagnostician Nexus Ednl. Ctr., Onarga, Ill., 1995—96; spelling contest coord. King Mid. Sch., Kankakee, 1997—97; instrnl. mentor Iroquois Spl. Edn. Assn., Donovan, 1999—2003; sch. improvement plan com., Donovan, 2000—02; ACT accommodations coord. Watseka Comty. H.S., 2003—04. Iroquois County bd. vol. Am. Cancer Soc., Watseka, 2000—03, Reach to Recovery vol., 2000—03; chairperson wills and memorials com. Watseka United Meth. Ch., 2001—03; steering com. Iroquois Valley Youth for Christ, Watseka, 1995—97. Mem.: NEA, Ill. Coun. for Exeptional Children, Ill. Edn. Assn., Nature Concernvancy, Ill. Corn Growers Assn., Gen. Soc. Mayflower Descendants, Iroquois County Hist. Soc. Avocations: family genealogy, Iroquois county history, prairie plants of Illinois. Home Phone: 815-432-6151.

MENGES, SUSAN DEBRA FAVREAU, management consultant, retired protective services official; b. Cleve., Dec. 15, 1955; d. Donald Francis and Helen Patricia (Rafferty) F.; m. William J. Menges, Nov. 17, 2001. Cert., N.Y. State Police Acad., 1974; student, Cornell U., 1984, SUNY, 1986. Comm. specialist N.Y. State Police, Loudonville, 1974—87, comm. specialist divsn. hdqrs., 1987—98; mgmt. cons., sec.-treas., dir. Don Favreau Assocs., Inc., Clifton Park, NY, 1983—86, v.p., 1986—; comm. specialist divsn. hdqrs. N.Y. State Police, Albany, 1987—98, sys. support specialist divsn. hdqrs., 1998—2005, ret., 2005. Adj. faculty Internat. Assn. Chiefs Police; NYSPIN coord. FBI/Nat. Crime Info. Ctr. cert. program, 1986—; ind. sr. beauty cons. Mary Kay Cosmetics, 2003 Author: Teamwork in the Telecommunication Center, 1986, One More Time: How to be a Mature and Successful Telcommunications Manager, 1987, Law Enforcement Terminal Security, 1991; also NYSPIN cert. manuals. Vol. Suncoast Seabird Sanctuary, Indian Shores, Fla., 2005—06; deacon Ch. of the Isles, Indian Rocks Beach, Fla., 2006—. Recipient Dirs. Commendation N.Y. State Police Acad., 1977, Commendation N.Y. State Police, 1978, Supt.'s Commendation, 1986, Y2K Commendation Gov. George Pataki, 2000 Mem. NAFE, N.Y. State Civil Svc. Assn., Emergency Communicators Profl. Assn. (adv. bd.), Colonie Police Benevolent Assn. (hon.), Am. Soc. Law Enforcement Trainers, Assoc. Pub. Safety Comm. Officers (planning commn. Atlantic chpt. 1991, registration chair ann. N.E. conf. 1991), N.Y. State Troopers Police Benevolent Assn. (hon.), Nat. Bus. Women Am., Internat. Assn. Chiefs Police, Am. Horse Shows Assn., Am. Soc. Law Enforcement Trainers, Capital Dist. Hunter/Jumper Coun Republican. Roman Catholic. Avocations: horseback riding, target shooting, reading, sewing. Office: Hdqrs NY State Police State Office Bldg Campus Bldg # 22 Albany NY 12226 Home: 19701 Gulf Blvd Apt 307 Indian Shores FL 33785-2385 E-mail: susan9g6@aol.com.

MENGLER, THOMAS M., dean; b. May 18, 1953; BA in Philosophy magna cum laude, Carleton Coll., 1975; MA in Philosophy, U. Tex., 1977, JD, 1981. Bar: Ill., Tex., D.C., U.S. Ct. Appeals (5th, 7th and 10th cirs.), U.S. Dist. Ct. (we. dist.) Tex. Law clk. to Hon. James K. Logan U.S. Ct. Appeals for 10thCir., Olathe, Kans., 1980-81; assoc. atty. Arnold & Porter, Washington, 1982-83; asst. atty. gen. Office of Atty. Gen. of Tex., Austin, 1983-85; asst. prof. law U. Ill. Coll. Law, Champaign, 1985-89, assoc. prof., 1989-91, prof. law, 1991—2002, assoc. dean for acad. affairs, 1992-93, dean, 1993—2002; dean, prof. law U. St. Thomas Sch. Law, Mpls., 2002—. Contbr. numerous articles to profl. jours. Mem. ABA, Ill. State Bar Assn., Order of Coif, Phi Beta Kappa. Office: U St Thomas Sch Law Mail TMH 440 1000 LaSalle Ave Minneapolis MN 55403-2005

MENICHESCHI, EDWARD JOHN, publishing executive; b. June 20, 1959; Graduate, Fasion Inst. of Tech. Edited the retail trade publ. GQ mag, 1982—86, merchandising editor, 1986—90; v.p. mktg. Bidermann Industries, 1990—92; exec. editor Vogue, 1992—94, assoc. publ., 1994—99; pres. IAM.COM, 1999—2001, WWD Media Worldwide, 2001—06; exec. v.p. Fairchild Publications Inc., 2005—06; v.p., publ. Vanity Fair, 2006—. Named to Digital Coast's Top 100 Internet Exec.; recipient Outstanding Alumni award, Fashion Inst. Tech., 1988. Office: Vanity Fair 4 Time Square 22nd Fl New York NY 10036

MENINGALL, EVELYN L., retired educational media specialist; b. Dothan, Ala., July 22, 1935; d. Earl and Luella Koonce; m. A. Richard Meningall, Jan. 17, 1958; children: Dawn, Tracy, Richard. BS in Edn., Wayne State U., 1975; MLS, Rutgers U., 1979. Cert. ednl. media specialist Dept. Edn. State N.J., elem. sch. dept. Dept. Edn. State N.J., profl. librs. cert. Dept. Edn. State N.J. Tchr. Detroit Bd. Edn., 1975—76; libr. East Brunswick (N.J.) Pub. Libr., 1978—80; ednl. media specialist Piscataway (N.J.) Bd. Edn., 1980—98; ret., 1998. Author: A Way of Life: An Anthology of Poems, 2004, Reflections: A Collection of Poems, 2005. Active New Detroit, Inc., Delta Sigma Theta Sorority Ctrl. Jersey; vol. tutor/reader pub. schs.; vol. to holisitic score English tests Plainfield (N.J.) H.S.; recording sec. Scholarship Fund of St. Paul AME Ch. Mem.: ALA (life), Ednl. Media Assn., Nat. Edn. Assn. (life), NJ Edn. Assn. (life), Nat. Sorority Phi Delta Kappa, Inc. (life; basileus 1987—89, exec. advisor 1989—91), Delta Sigma Theta (life). Methodist. Avocations: poetry, reading, fishing. Home: 23 Vauxhall Rd East Brunswick NJ 08816-1719

MENINO, THOMAS M., mayor; b. Boston, Dec. 27, 1942; m. Angela Faletra; children: Susan, Thomas Michael, Jr. Grad., Chamberlayne Junior Coll., 1963; degree in Community Planning, U. Mass., 1988; cert. in State and Local Govt. Program, Harvard U. Mem. City Coun., Boston, 1985—, pres., 1993; acting mayor City of Boston, 1993, mayor, 1993—. Sr. rsch. asst. Joint Com. Urban Affairs, 1978-83; pres. U.S. Conf. Mayors, 2002-03. Contbr. articles to historic preservation jours. Regional chmn. Nat. Trust Historic Preservation; bd. dirs. Nat. League Cities, 1985—, mem. various coms. Office: Office of Mayor 1 City Hall Plz Fl 5 Boston MA 02201-1001 *

MENITOFF, PAUL ALAN, psychiatrist; b. Boston, May 4, 1946; s. Ralph and Ethel (Bickoff) M.; m. Susan Mathilde Hirsch, June 8, 1980. BA cum laude, Harvard U., 1969; MD, Cornell U., 1973. Diplomate Am. Bd. Psychiatry and Neurology, Subspecialty Psychosomatic Medicine. Intern in surgery Univ. Hosp., Boston, 1973-74; psychiat. resident Payne Whitney Clinic N.Y. Hosp./Cornell Med. Ctr., NYC, 1974-77; forensic psychiat. fellow U. So. Calif./L.A. County Med. Ctr., 1977-78; forensic psychiat. fellow Med. Sch. U. Md., Balt., 1978-79; staff psychiatrist Clifton T. Perkins Hosp., Jessup, Md., 1978-80; mem. med. staff St. John's Hosp., Lowell, Mass., 1980-93; Saints Meml. Med. Ctr., 1993—; chief divsn. psychiatry, 1996—; mem. med. staff St. Joseph's Hosp., Lowell, 1980-93; pvt. practice Chelmsford, Mass., 1980—; mem. med. staff Lowell Gen. Hosp., 1980—, chief dept. psychiatry, 1991-93, New Eng. Rehab. Hosp., Lowell, 1993—. Clin. inst. psychiatry U. So. Calif. Med. Sch., L.A., 1977-78; clin. asst. prof. psychiatry U. Md. Med. Sch., Balt., 1979-80; clin. asst. prof. psychiatry Tufts U. Sch. Medicine, 2006—. Mem. Am. Psychiat. Assn., Mass. Psychiat. Assn., Acad. Psychosomatic Medicine, Am. Acad. Psychiatry and the Law, Mass. Med. Soc. Democrat. Avocations: movies, theater. Office: Greater Lowell Psychiat Assocs 9 Acton Rd Ste 25 Chelmsford MA 01824-3496 Office Phone: 978-256-6579.

MENIUS, ESPIE FLYNN, JR., electrical engineer; b. New Bern, NC, Mar. 5, 1923; s. Espie Flynn and Sudie Grey (Lyerly) M.; adopted children: James Benfield, Ruben Hughes, James Sechler, Steve Walden. BEE, N.C. State U., 1947; MBA, U. S.C., 1973. Registered profl. engr., N.C., S.C., Tenn., Ga., Fla. With Carolina Power & Light Co., 1947-63, asst. to dist. mgr. Raleigh, Henderson, NC, 1947-50, Sumter, SC, 1947-50, elec. engr. Asheville, Southern Pines and Dunn, NC, 1950-52, dist. engr. Hartsville, SC, 1952-63; sr. elec. engr. Sonoco Products Co., 1963-74, engring. group leader, 1974-89, sr. profl. engr., 1989-91; profl. cons. and elec. engr.,

1991—. Instr. Florence-Darlington Tech. Ednl. Ctr. Author: Adoption of Older Children; contbr. articles to profl. jours. Active Hartsville Vol. Fire Dept., 1958-94; Fire dept. and Law Enforcement Chaplain 1985—; Eagle Scout Boy Scouts Am., 1938, scout troop leader New Bern, 1940-41, Raleigh, 1941-47, Henderson, 1948-49, Sumter, 1949-50, Asheville, N.C., 1950, Southern Pines, N.C., 1951-52, Hartsville, 1952-64; bd. mgrs. Nazareth Children's Home, Rockwell, N.C., 1980—; chmn. bd. examiners City of Hartsville, 1980-90; advocate Thornwell Children's Home, Clinton, S.C., 1990—; bd. dir. Darlington (S.C.) County Youth Home, 1992—; active Hartsville Leadership Coun., 1993—; deacon, elder, trustee, tchr. men's Bible class First Presbyn. Ch., Hartsville. Served with US Army, 1943-46. Recipient Citizenship award S.C. State Firemen's Assn., 1993; named Hartsville Citizen of Yr., Rotary, 1960; named to S.C. Fire Fighters Hall of Fame, 1995. Mem. IEEE, AAAS, VFW, Nat. Assn. Engrs., Am. Legion, Knight of St. Patrick, Scabbard and Blade, Eta Kappa Nu, Pine Burr, Phi Eta Sigma, Theta Tau, Beta Gamma Sigma. Presbyn. Home and Office: 423 W Richardson Cir Hartsville SC 29550-5437 Office Phone: 843-332-8502.

MENKE, ALLEN CARL, retired manufacturing executive; b. Huntingburg, Ind., Feb. 16, 1922; s. William Ernest and Clara (Moenkhaus) M.; m. Virginia Lee MacDonald, Apr. 14, 1944; children: Janet, William, Sarah. BS in Mech. Engring, Purdue U., 1943, MS, 1948. Instr. Purdue U., 1946-48; with Trane Co., 1948-68, v.p. sales, 1963-64, exec. v.p. sales, mfg. and engring., 1964-68; v.p. Borg-Warner Corp., Chgo., 1969-76; chmn., pres., CEO Artesian Industries, Northbrook, Ill., 1976-88; ret. Bd. dirs. Trane Co., SPS Techs., Hoover Co., Consolidated Papers Corp., York Corp., Am. Air Filter. Pres. Met. Housing Devel. Corp.; founder, pres. Winnetka Interch. Coun.; bd. dirs., past chmn. Presbyn. Home; past chmn. dean's adv. coun. Krannert Sch. Mgmt. Purdue U.; bd. dirs. McCormick Sem., U. Chgo.; trustee Kenilworth Union Ch. Served to 1st lt. AUS, 1944-46. Named Disting. Alumnus, Purdue U., 1965, Outstanding Engr. Grad., 1991, mem. Purdue Hall of Fame, Ind. Basketball Hall of Fame, 1999. Mem. Sigma Chi (Significant Order Constantine awards). Presbyterian (elder). Lodge: Mason. Home: 2 Arbor Ln #208 Evanston IL 60201

MENKE, SEAN E., air transportation executive; m. Arminda Menke; 3 children. B in Econs. and Aviation Mgmt., Ohio State U.; MBA, U. Denver. Dir. planning Western Pacific Airlines, Inc.; sr. planner domestic schedule planning United Air Lines, Inc.; dir. mktg. and planning Frontier Airlines, Inc., 1999—2000, v.p. mktg. and planning, 2000—03, sr. v.p. mktg., 2003—04, sr. v.p., chief operating officer, 2004—05, pres., CEO, 2007—; exec. v.p., chief comml. officer Air Can., 2005—07, exec. v.p. comml. strategy, 2007. Bd. mem. Frontier Airlines, Inc. Recipient Disting. Alumni award, Ohio State U., 2006. Office: Frontier Airlines Inc 7001 Tower Rd Denver CO 80249 Office Phone: 720-374-4200, 800-265-5505. Office Fax: 720-374-4375. *

MENKEL-MEADOW, CARRIE JOAN, law educator; b. NYC, Dec. 24, 1949; d. Gary G. and Margot (Sinn) Menkel; m. Robert Gary Meadow, Aug. 22, 1971. AB magna cum laude, Columbia U., 1971; JD cum laude, U. Pa., 1974; LLD (hon.), Quinnipiac Coll. Law, 1995. Bar: Pa. 1974, U.S. Ct. Appeals (3d cir.) 1975, Calif. 1979, D.C., 1997. Dir. legal writing U. Pa. Law Sch., Phila., 1974-75, clin. supt., lectr., 1976-79; staff atty. Cmty. Legal Svcs., Phila., 1975-77; prof. UCLA, 1979—, prof. law, 1979-99, Georgetown Law Ctr., Washington, 1996—, A.B. Chettle Jr. chair prof. dispute resolution civil procedure, 2005—; holder Phyllis Beck chair Temple U. Law Sch., Phila., 1999. Cons. ABA, Chgo., 1979—84; panel mem. NAS, Washington, 1986—87, NSF, Washington, 1987—90; vis. prof. law Stanford Law Sch., 1990, Harvard Law Sch., 2001, U. Fribourg, Switzerland, 2003; dir. UCLA Ctr. for Conflict Resolution, 1994—99, Georgetown-Hewlett Program on Conflict Resolution and Problem Solving, 2001—. Author: Mediation: Theory, Practice and Policy, 2000, Dispute Processing: Theory, Practice and Policy, 2003, What's Fair: Ethics for Negotiators, 2004, Dispute Resolution: Beyond the Adversarial Model, 2004, Negotiation: Processes for Problem Solving, 2005, Mediation: Practice, Policy and Ethics, 2005; editor-in-chief Jour. Legal Edn., 2003—; editor-in-chief: Internat. Jour. Law in Context, 2004—; contbr. articles to profl. jours. Chairperson Ctr. for Study of Women, UCLA; chair CPR Commn. on Ethics and ADR; bd. dirs. Western Ctr. on Law and Poverty, LA, 1980—86; bd. advisors Saltmann Ctr. Conflict Resolution, UNLV; internat. adv. com. Monash U., Australia. Recipient William Rutter Found. for Tchg. award UCLA, 1992, 1st prize for Acad. Scholarship on Alternative Dispute Resolution Ctr. for Pub. Resources, 1983, 91, 98, Frank Flegal award for tchg., Georgetown U., 2006; Fulbright scholar, Chile, 2007. Mem.: Acad. Civil Trial Mediators, Am. Law Inst., Am. Bar Found. (exec. com. 1994—2004, bd. dir., sec.), Law and Soc. Assn. (trustee), Ctr. for Law and Human Values (bd. dir.), Assn. Am. Law Schs. (accreditation com. 1987—90, editor-in-chief Jour. of Legal Edn. 2004—, alt. dispute resolution sect., law and social sci. sect., women in law sect.), Soc. Am. Law Tchrs. (trustee), Phi Beta Kappa. Democrat. Office: Georgetown Law Ctr 600 New Jersey Ave NW Washington DC 20001-2075 Office Phone: 202-662-9379. Business E-Mail: meadow@law.georgetown.edu.

MENKEN, ALAN, composer; b. New Rochelle, NY, July 22, 1949; Student, NYU. Composer, lyricist, performer Lehman Engel Mus. Theatre Workshop at BMI; ptnr. with Howard Ashman. Works include: (theatre) Off-Broadway debut God Bless You, Mr. Rosewater, (with Howard Ashman) Little Shop of Horrors, 1982, Kicks, The Apprenticeship of Duddy Kravitz, Diamonds, Personals, Let Freedom Sing, Weird Romance, Beauty and the Beast, 1994, A Christmas Carol, 1995, Sister Act, 2006; (films) The Line, 1980, Little Shop of Horrors, 1986 (Acad. award nominee for best original score 1986), The Little Mermaid, 1988 (Acad. award for best original score 1989, Acad. award for best original song 1989), Beauty and the Beast, 1990 (Acad. award for best original score 1991, Acad. award for best original song 1991), Newsies, 1992, Aladdin, 1992, (Acad. award for best original score 1993, Acad. award best original song 1993, 3 Grammy awards 1994), Life With Mikey, 1993, The Return of Jafar, 1994, The Hunchback of Notre Dame, 1996, Hercules, 1997, King David, 1997, Home on the Range, 2004, Noel, 2004, The Shaggy Dog, 2006; (with Stephen Schwartz) Pocahontas, 1995 (Golden Globe award 1996, Acad. award for best original score 1996, Acad. award for best original song 1996); TV films Act II, 1987, Lincoln, 1992, A Christmas Carol, 2004. *

MENKEN, JANE AVA, demographer, educator; b. Phila., Nov. 29, 1939; d. Isaac Nathan and Rose Ida (Sarvetnick) Golubitsky; m. Matthew Menken, 1960 (div. 1985); children: Kenneth Lloyd, Kathryn Lee; m. Richard Jessor, Nov. 13, 1992. AB, U. Pa., 1960; MS, Harvard U., 1962; PhD, Princeton U., NJ, 1975. Asst. in biostats. Harvard U. Sch. Pub. Health, Boston, 1962-64; math. statistician NIMH, Bethesda, Md., 1964-66; rsch. assoc. dept. biostats. Columbia U., NYC, 1966-69; mem. rsch. staff Office of Population Rsch. Princeton U., 1969-71, 75-87, asst. dir., 1978-86, assoc. dir., 1986-87, prof. sociology, 1980-82, prof. sociology and pub. affairs, 1982-87; prof. sociology and demography U. Pa., Phila., 1987-97, UPS Found. prof. social scis., 1987-97, dir. Population Studies Ctr., 1989-95; prof. sociology U. Colo., Boulder, 1997—, faculty assoc. Population Program, Inst. Behavioral Sci., 1997—; dir. Population Aging Ctr., 2000—, Inst. Behavioral Sci., 2001—, disting. prof., 2002—. Mem. social scis. and population study sect., NIH, Bethesda, 1978-82, chmn., 1980-82, dirs. adv. com., 1995-2000, Nat. Adv. Child Health and Human Devel. Coun., 1988-91, adv. com. Fogarty Internat. Ctr., 2000-02, population adv. com. Rockefeller Found., NYC, 1981-93, com. on population and demography, NAS, Washington, 1978-83, com. on population, 1983-85, 1996-2002, chair 1998-2002, com. nat. stats., 1983-89, com. on AIDS rsch., 1987-93, chair 1990-93; co-chair panel data and rsch. priorities for arresting AIDS in sub-Saharan Africa, 1994-96, Com. on Behavioral and Social Scis. and Edn., 1991-97, chair, steering com., workshop on aging in Africa, 2003-06, chair, sci. adv. com., INDEPTH newtwork, 2002-; cons. Internat. Centre for Diarrhoeal Disease Rsch., Bangladesh, Dhaka, 1984—. Author: (with Mindel C. Sheps) Mathematical Models of Conception and Birth, 1973, (with Ann Blanc and Cynthia Lloyd) Training and Support of Developing Country Population Scientists, 2002; editor: (with Henri Leridon) Natural Fertility, 1979, (with Frank Furstenberg, Jr. and Richard Lincoln) Teenage Sexuality, Pregnancy and Childbearing, 1981, World Population and U.S. Policy: The Choices Ahead, 1986, (with Barney Cohen) Aging in Sub-Saharan Africa: Recommendations for Furthering Research, 2006; contbr. articles to profl. jours. Bd. dirs. Alan Guttmacher Inst., NYC, 1981-90, 93-2000, African Population and Health Rsch. Ctr., Nairobi, Kenya, 2000—. Nat. Merit scholar, 1957; John Simon Guggenheim Found. fellow, 1992-93, Ctr. for Advanced Study in Behavioral Scis. fellow, 1995-96. Fellow AAAS, Am. Statis. Assn.; mem. NAS, Inst. of Medicine, Am. Acad. Arts and Scis., Population Assn. Am. (pres. 1985, Mindel Sheps award 1982), Am. Pub. Health Assn. (Mortimer Spiegelman award 1975), Am. Sociol. Assn., Soc. for Study of Social Biology, Internat. Union for Sci. Study of Population (coun. 1989-97), Sociol. Rsch. Assn. (exec. com. 1991-96, pres. 1996). Office: U Colo IBS#1 483 UCB Boulder CO 80309-0483 Office Phone: 303-492-8148. Business E-Mail: menken@colorado.edu.

MENKES, JOHN HANS, pediatric neurologist; b. Vienna, Dec. 20, 1928; came to U.S., 1940; s. Karl and Valerie (Tupler) M.; m. Miriam Trief, Apr. 14, 1957 (div. Feb. 1978); m. Joan Simon Feld, Sept. 28, 1980 (dec. Nov. 2000); children: Simon, Tamara, Rafael C.; m. Myrna Fox (July 1, 2004). AB, U. So. Calif., 1947, MS, 1951; MD, Johns Hopkins U., 1952. Diplomate Am. Bd. Pediat., Am. Bd. Psychiatry and Neurology. Intern, jr. asst. resident Children's Med. Ctr., Boston, 1952-54; asst. resident pediat. Bellevue Hosp., NYC, 1956-57; resident neurology, trainee pediatric neurology Columbia-Presbyn. Med. Ctr., Neurol. Inst. N.Y., NYC, 1957-60; asst. prof. pediat. Johns Hopkins U., Balt., 1960-63, assoc. prof., 1963-66, asst. prof. neurology, 1964-66, chief pediatric neurology divsn., 1964-66; prof. pediat. and neurology UCLA, 1966-74, chief pediatric neurology divsn., 1966-70, prof. psychiatry, 1970-74; chief Neurology-Neurochem. Lab. Brentwood (Calif.) VA Hosp., 1970-74; clin. prof. psychiatry, neurology and pediat. UCLA, 1974-77, clin. prof. pediat. and neurology, 1977-84, prof. pediat. and neurology, 1985-89, prof. emeritus pediat. and neurology, 1989—. Dir. pediatric neurology Cedars-Sinai Med. Ctr., 1997-99, dir. emeritus pediat. neurology, 1999—; mem. metabolism study sect. NIH, 1968-70, project com., 1969-70; mem. adv. com. Nat. Inst. Child Health and Human Devel., 1985-87; mem. Dept. Health Svcs., Calif., 1980-87; mem. vaccine safety commn. Nat. Inst. Medicine, 1995—; mem. Coun. Child Neurology Soc., Dysautonomia Found., med. adv. bd. Nat. Orgn. Rare Diseases, Nat. Wilson's Disease Found.; trustee Dystonia Med. Rsch. Found., Vancouver, Can., 1985—. Author: Textbook of Child Neurology, 6th edit., 2000; (play) The Last Inquisitor, 1985 (Drama-Logue Critics award 1985), The Salvation of Miguel Toruna, 1987; (screen play) Miguel, Open Ward, 1989, The Countess of Sligo, 1992, The White Darkness, 1996, Lady Macbeth Gets a Divorce, 2001, Native Born, 2003; (novels) The Secret Diary of Alice in Wonderland, 1998, The Angry Puppet Syndrome, 1999, After the Tempest, 2003, The Waiting Game, 2000, A View of Fuji, 2000; contbr. numerous articles to profl. jours. Served with USAF, 1954-56. Mem. Am. Acad. Neurology, Am. Acad. Pediatrics, Am. Chem. Soc., Soc. for Pediatric Rsch., Sociedad Peruana de Neuro-Psiquiatria (hon.), Am. Neurochem. Soc., Am. Neurol. Assn., Am. Pediatric Soc., Child Neurology Soc. (Hower award 1980), Dramatist Guild, PEN. Jewish. Home: 10375 Wilshire Blvd Apt 11H Los Angeles CA 90024-4749 Office: 345 N Maple Dr Ste 376 Beverly Hills CA 90210 Office Phone: 310-246-6582. Personal E-mail: jhansmenk@aol.com. Business E-Mail: jmenkes@ucla.edu.

MENN, JULIUS JOEL, retired research scientist, consultant; b. Danzig, Free City (now Poland), Feb. 20, 1929; came to the U.S., 1950, naturalized, 1959; s. David Gregory and Regina (Ajzenstadt) M.; m. Alma R. Zito, Aug. 31, 1952 (div. 1981); children: Leslie, David (dec.), Diana (dec.); m. Dianne R. Sagner, Apr. 17, 1992. BS, U. Calif., Berkeley, 1953, MS, 1954, PhD, 1958. Dir. biochem. and insecticide rsch. Stauffer Chem. Co., Mountain View, Calif., 1957-79; dir. agrichem. rsch. Zoecon Corp., Palo Alto, Calif., 1979-85; nat. program leader crop protection Agrl. Rsch. Svc., USDA, Beltsville, Md., 1985-88; assoc. dep. area dir. Beltsville Agrl. Rsch. Ctr., 1988-94; sr. agrl. policy adviser USDA/FAS, 1999—2006. Internat. cons. crop protection and agr. biotechnology, 1994-; chmn. Gordon Rsch. Conf., 1989; adj. prof. environ. toxicology San Jose State U., Calif., 1979-84; adj. prof. entomology U. Md., College Park, 1986-95; vis. prof. Pa. State U., 1999-2002; mem. U.S./USSR Team on Environ. Pollution, 1974-85; tech. expert UNIDO, UNDCP, 1995—, The World Bank, 1998.; tech. cons. Inst. Post Harvest Tech., MARD, Hanoi, Vietnam, 2003-. Editor: Insect Juvenile Hormones, 1972, Insect Neuropeptides, 1991, Biopesticides: Use & Delivery, 1999; contbr. articles to profl. jours. Recipient Bussart Meml. award Ea. Br. Entomol. Soc. Am., 1990, Ciba-Geigy Recognition award Ea. Br. Entomol. Soc. Am., 1991, 92. Mem. Am. Chem. Soc. (fellow pesticide chem. divsn. 1973, chmn. 1976, councilor 1981-89, adv. bd. books dept. 1991-94, Agrochem. Divsn. Internat. award for rsch. in pesticide chem. 1979), Internat. Soc. Study Xenobiotics (councilor 1983-86). Achievements include research in pesticide metabolism, selective insect control agents including juvenile hormones and neuropeptides; patentee in field. Office Phone: 443-745-4091. Personal E-mail: menn03@comcast.net.

MENNA, GILBERT G., lawyer; AB magna cum laude, Syracuse U., 1978; JD, Georgetown U., 1982, ML in Taxation, 1983. Bar: Calif. 1982, Mass. 1988. Ptnr., bus. law dept. Goodwin Procter LLP, Boston, mem. mgmt. com. Bd. dir. NYU Real Estate Inst.'s REIT Ctr.; bd. assoc. NAREIT. Frequent lectr., writer in field. Mem.: Phi Beta Kappa. Office: Goodwin & Procter Exchange Pl 53 State St Boston MA 02109-2881 Office Phone: 617-570-1433. Office Fax: 617-523-1231. Business E-Mail: gmenna@goodwinprocter.com.

MENNA, SÁRI, artist, educator; b. San Fracisco, Sept. 29, 1932; m. Ferdinand Carl Menna, Mar. 10, 1949; children: Mark, Diane Menna Clarke. BFA cum laude, Hunter Coll. of CUNY, NYC, 1968, MFA, 1974; post grad., N.Y. U., NYC, 1987—93. Lic. tchr. N.Y. Bd. Edn., 1971. Substitute tchr. Massapequa Pub. Schs., LI, NY, 1968—69; tchr. art N.Y.C. Bd. Edn., 1971—95; ret., 1995. Vol. art tchr. Pres.' Econ. Opportunity Ctr., LI, 1967—68; organizer juried art shows Amity Art League, 1964—67; tchr. cultural workshop Amityville Workshop, LI, 1968. Exhibitions include Salute to Women, Washington, Nairobi, 1991, Women's Art, NYC, 1992, Paintings and Paperworks, CUNY, 1992, Small Works, Kirkland, Wash., 1993, Garden of Delights, Bklyn., 1994, Family Values, NYC, 1994, Hallelujah, 1994, Visions of Reality, Madison, NJ, 1995, A Woman's Pl., NYC, 1995, Points of View, 1995, ADA: Women and Info. Tech., Chgo., 1995—96, The World's Women On Line, Beijing, Tempe, Ariz., online, 1995—96, Fine Arts Mus., LI, NY, 1996, Openings, NYC, 1996, Diversity, 1997, Small Statement Show, Bklyn., 1997, Painterly Forms, NYC, 1997, BWAC 4th Ann. Pier Show, NJ, 1998, Flat Iron Gallery, Peekskill, NY, 1999, Broome St. Gallery, Soho, NYC, 2000, WIA Part II, Canojohri, NY, 2000, Broome St. Gallery, NYC, 2004, Williamsburg Art and Hist. Ctr., Bklyn., 2004, Taller Boriqua Galleries, Julia de Burgos Cultural Ctr., NYC, 2005, Medeung Gallery, Korea, 2005, exhibited in group shows at Pier Show, NYC, 2006, WIA, Venezuelan Ctr., NY, 2007, Represented in permanent collections Nat. Mus. Women in Arts, Washington, Women's Interart Collections, NYC, calendar and cover art, Women Artists, 1983, in pvt. collections, online exhibitions, mini-park, NYC, 1974. Pres. Creative Women's Collective, NYC, 1982—85; mem. Women's Caucus Art (N.Y.C. chpt.), 1982—91; mem. Queens Coun. on Art, 2001—06. Mem.: Creative Women's Collective, Women in the Arts Found, Inc., Women's Studio Ctr., Artists Equity.

MENNIN, GERALD STANLEY, ophthalmologist; b. NYC, Mar. 20, 1932; children: Danielle, Douglas. BA, NYU, 1954; MD, SUNY, NYC. Intern Beth Israel Hosp., NYC, 1958-59; resident Bronx Mcpl. Hosp. Ctr./Einstein Coll. Medicine, 1050-62; pvt. practice Yonkers; chief ophthalmology Yonkers Gen. Hosp., 1986—. Attending ophthalmologist Montefiore Hosp., Bronx, 1962—, Bronx Mcpl. Hosp., 1962—, St. John's Hosp., Yonkers, 1981—, Yonkers Gen. Hosp., 1962—, Manhattan Eye and Ear Hosp., N.Y.C., 1990—. Fellow ACS, Am. Acad. Ophthalmologists, Nat. Arts Club. Avocation: art. Office: 45 Ludlow St Yonkers NY 10705-1947

MENNINGA, CLARENCE, retired geologist; b. Otley, Iowa, Apr. 6, 1928; s. Gysbert and Ethel (Van Engelenhoven) Menninga; m. Irene June Van Prooyen, Oct. 7, 1949; children: Richard Lee children: Douglas Wayne, John Alan, Carol Sue Sunday, Craig Warren, Dianne Joy Shapiro, David Glenn. BA, Calvin Coll., Grand Rapids, 1949; MA in Tchg., Western Mich. U., Kalamazoo, 1959; PhD, Purdue U., West Lafayette, Ind., 1965. Analytical chemist Maytag Co., Newton, Iowa, 1950—56; tchr. Grand Rapids Christian HS, 1956—61; radiochemist Lawrence Radiation Lab., Livermore, Calif., 1966—67; prof. geology Calvin Coll., Grand Rapids, Mich., 1967—90, prof. geology emeritus, 1990—. Author: Science Held Hostage, 1988. Fellow, NSF, 1962—65. Mem.: Nat. Assn. Geology Tchrs., Mich. Basin Geol. Soc., Am. Schools for Oriental Rsch., Am. Sci. Affiliation. Home: 2155 Radcliff Ave SE Grand Rapids MI 49546 Office: Calvin Coll North Hall 1740 Knollcrest Cir SE Grand Rapids MI 49546-4403 Home Phone: 616-956-9046; Office Phone: 616-526-7093. Office Fax: 616-526-6501. Business E-Mail: menn@calvin.edu.

MENNINGER, WILLIAM WALTER, psychiatrist; b. Topeka, Oct. 23, 1931; s. William Claire and Catharine Louisa (Wright) Menninger; m. Constance Arnold Libbey, June 15, 1953; children: Frederick Prince, John Alexander, Eliza Wright, Marian Stuart, William Libbey, David Henry. AB, Stanford U., 1953; MD, Cornell U., 1957; LittD (hon.), Middlebury Coll., 1982; DSc (hon.), Washburn U., 1982; LHD (hon.), Ottawa U., 1986; LLD (hon.), Heidelberg Coll., 1993, Dominican U., 2007. Diplomate Am. Bd. Psychiatry and Neurology, Am. Bd. Forensic Psychiatry. Intern Harvard Med. Svc., Boston City Hosp., 1957-58; resident in psychiatry Menninger Sch. Psychiatry, 1958-61; chief med. officer, psychiatrist Fed. Reformatory, El Reno, Okla., 1961-63; assoc. psychiatrist Peace Corps, 1963-64; staff psychiatrist Menninger Found., Topeka, 1965—2001, coordinator for devel., 1967-69, dir. law and psychiatry, 1981-85, dir. dept. edn., dean Karl Menninger Sch. Psychiatry and Mental Health Scis., 1984-90, exec. v.p., chief staff, 1984-93, CEO, 1993—2001, pres., 1993—96, 1999—2001, chmn. bd. trustees, 2001—; clin. supr. Topeka State Hosp., 1969-70, sect. dir., 1970-72, asst. supt., clin., dir. residency tng., 1972-81; pres. Menninger Clinic, Topeka, 1991-96; staff Stormont-Vail Hosp., Topeka, 1984-94, assoc., 1994—2002. Adj. prof. Washburn U.; mem. Fed. Prision Facilities Planning Coun., 1970—73; mem. adv. bd. Nat. Inst. Corrections, 1975—88, chmn., 1980—84; cons. U.S. Bur. Prisons; mem. adv. bd. US Bank, Topeka, 1999—. Syndicated columnist: In-Sights, 1975—83; author: (book) Happiness Without Sex and Other Things Too Good to Miss, 1976, Caution: Living May Be Hazardous, 1978, Behavioral Science and the Secret Service, 1981, Chronic Mental Patient II, 1987; editor: Psychiatry Digest, 1971—74, Bull. of Menninger Clinic, 2001—; contbr. articles to profl. jours., chpts. to books. Mem. health and safety com. Boy Scouts Am., 1970—, chmn., 1980—85, mem. nat. exec. bd., 1980—90, mem. nat. adv. coun., 1990—; bd. dirs. Nat. Com. Prevention Child Abuse, 1975—83; mem. nat. adv. health coun. HEW, 1967—71; mem. Nat. Commn. Causes and Prevention Violence, 1968—69; rsch. adv. com. U.S. Secret Svc., 1990—2005; pres. Jayhawk coun. Boy Scouts Am., 1998—2001; mem. Kans. Gov.'s Adv. Commn. Mental Health, Mental Retardation and Cmty. Mental Health Svcs., 1983—90, Kans. Gov.'s Penal Planning Coun., 1970; chmn. Kans. Gov.'s Criminal Justice Coun., 1970; mem. Kans. Gov.'s Commn. on Crime Reduction and Prevention/Koch Commn., 1994—98; ruling elder 1st Presbyn. Ch., Topeka, 1992—95; trustee Kenworthy-Swift Found., 1980—; bd. dirs. Police Found., Washington, 1996—, Koch Crime Inst., 1998—2000; trustee Midwest Rsch. Inst., Kansas City, Mo., 1996—. With USPHS, 1959—64. Fellow: ACP, Am. Coll. Psychiatrists, Am. Psychiat. Assn. (chmn. com. chronically mentally ill 1984—86, chmn. Guttmacher award bd. 1990—96); mem.: AMA, Am. Acad. Psychiatry and Law, Am. Psychoanalytic Assn. (chmn. com. psychoanalysis, cmty. and soc. 1984—93), Inst. Medicine NAS, Group Advancement Psychiatry (chmn. com. mental health svcs. 1974—77, 1991—2002), Stanford Assocs. Office: PO Box 4406 Topeka KS 66604-0406 Office Phone: 785-235-3400. Business E-Mail: wmenninger@menninger.edu.

MENNIS, EDMUND ADDI, investment management consultant; b. Allentown, Pa., Aug. 12, 1919; s. William Henry and Grace (Addi) M.; m. Selma Adinoff, Sept. 25, 1945; children: Ardith Grace, Daniel Liam. BA, CCNY, 1941; MA, Columbia U., 1946; PhD, NYU, 1961. Security analyst Eastman, Dillon & Co., NYC, 1945-46; sr. rsch. asst. Am. Inst. Econ. Rsch., Great Barrington, Mass., 1946-50; security analyst Wellington Mgmt. Co., Phila., 1950-61, dir. rsch., 1958-61, v.p., mem. investment com., 1958-66, economist, 1953-66; sr. v.p., chmn. trust investment com. Republic Nat. Bank, Dallas, 1966-72; sr. v.p., chmn. investment policy com. Security Pacific Nat. Bank, LA, 1973-81; pres., dir. Bunker Hill Income Securities, Inc., 1973-81; chmn. bd. Security Pacific Investment Mgrs., Inc., 1977-81; ind. cons. to investment mgmt. orgns., 1982—. Tech. cons. Bus. Coun., Washington, 1962-66, 72-77, 79-81; econ. adviser sec. commerce, 1967-68; mem. investment adv. panel Pension Benefit Guaranty Corp., 1981-83. Author: How the Economy Works, 1991, 2d edit., 1999, Chinese edit., 2000; assoc. editor Fin. Analysts Jour., 1960-88; editor: C.F.A. Digest, 1971-86, Bus. Econs., 1985-99, editor emeritus, 2000—; editor: Banker's Econ. & Investment Alert, 1993—; author or editor books, chpts., numerous articles in field of econs. and investments. Trustee Fin. Analysts Rsch. Found., 1981-86. 1st lt. USAAF, 1942-45; capt. USAF, 1951-53. Fellow Nat. Assn. Bus. Economists (coun. 1967-69, David L. Williams Lifetime Achievement award 1996); mem. Fin. Analysts Fedn. (dir. 1970-72, Graham and Dodd award 1972, Molodovsky award 1972), Am. Econ. Assn., Am. Fin. Assn., LA Soc. Fin. Analysts, Conf. Bus. Econ. (vice chmn. 1977, chmn. 1978), Inst. CFAs (pres. 1970-72, trustee 1968-74, C. Stewart Sheppard award 1978). Home: 721 Paseo Del Mar Palos Verdes Estates CA 90274-1222 Office: PO Box 1146 Palos Verdes Estates CA 90274-7946 Home Phone: 310-378-8026. Personal E-mail: eamennis@cox.net.

MENO, JOHN PETER, chorepiscopus; b. Carlinville, Ill., Aug. 22, 1942; s. John Victor and Margaret Mary (Cena) M.; m. Rolanda A. Abyad, Sept. 14, 1968; 1 child, Peter James. MA, Am. U. Beirut, 1969; STM, Union Theol. Sem., 1972. Ordained priest Syrian Orthodox Ch. of Antioch, 1972, elevated to chorepiscopus, 1983. Gen. sec. Archdiocese of Syrian Orthodox Ch. in the U.S. and Can., Lodi, NJ, 1972—95; cathedral dean St. Mark's Syrian Orthodox Cathedral, Teaneck, NJ, 1975—; gen. sec. Archdiocese of the Syrian Orthodox Ch. for the Ea. U.S., Teaneck, 1996—. Co-sec. Standing Conf. of Oriental Orthodox Chs. in Am., N.Y.C., 1973—; co-chmn. U.S. Roman Cath.-Oriental Orthodox Cons., 1989—. Editor: Hymns of the Syrian Orthodox Church of Antioch, 1976; contbr. The Oriental Orthodox Chs. in the U.S., 1986, Dictionary of Christianity in America, 1990, Oriental Orthodox-Roman Catholic Interchurch Marriages and Other Pastoral Relationships, 1995, Nelson's New Christian Dictionary, 2001, The Encyclopedia of Christianity, 2003. Recipient Golden

Cross of the Archdiocese of the Syrian Orthodox Ch. in U.S., and Can., 1992. Syrian Orthodox. Home: 263 Elm Ave Teaneck NJ 07666-2323 Office: St Mark's Syrian Orthodox Cathedral 260 Elm Ave Teaneck NJ 07666-2318 Personal E-mail: vrjmeno@aol.com.

MENO, LIONEL R., academic administrator; Commr. edn. Tex. Edn Agy., Austin; dist. supt. Board of Coop. Education Services, Angola, NY, 1995—99; dean Coll. Edn. San Diego State U., 1999—. Office: 5500 Cempanile Dr San Diego CA 92182

MENON, JAI M., information technology manager; arrived in U.S., 1977; s. Sreedharan Menon and Radha Sreedharan; m. Sathi Eradi, Aug. 20, 1985; children: Anjali, Vijay V. BS in Tech in Elec. Engring., Indian Inst. Tech., Madras, India, 1977; MS in Computer Sci., Ohio State U., Columbus, Ohio, 1978, PhD in Computer Sci., 1981. From rsch. staff mem. to chief tech. officer IBM, San Jose, Calif., 1982—2003, chief tech. officer, 2003—, dir. storage arch. and strategy, 2003—05, v.p. arch. and strategy, software and storage, 2005—07, v.p. tech. strategy, 2007—. Session chair CompCon, San Francisco, 1983, 95; mem. program com. conf. Very Large Data Base, 1984, rev. panelist, 1992—96; mem. program com. Internat. Symposium Computer Arch., 1995—95; mem. of steering com. FAST, File and Storage Sys. Tech., 2003—; vice chair IBM Acad. of Tech., San Jose, 2007—; presenter in field. Author: Relational Database Machine Architecture; co-author: Advanced Database Machine Architcture, Disk Array and parallel I/O - Theory and Practice; contbr. over 47 articles to profl. jours. (Best Paper award HICSS-25, 1992); mem. editl. bd.: Jour. Distributed and Parallel Databases, 1993—94; editor, 1994. Chmn. campaign IBM United Way, San Jose, Calif., 2001. Named Master Inventor, IBM, 1995; recipient Acad. Tech. award, 1994, Corp. award, 2000, Disting. Alumnus award, Ohio State U., 2004, Indian Inst. Tech., Madras, 2006; fellow, IBM, 2001; scholar, Govt. India, 1977. Fellow: IEEE (Wallace McDowell award 2002, Reynold B. Johnson award 2006). Achievements include patents in field. Business E-Mail: menonjm@almaden.ibm.com.

MENOYO, ERIC FELIX, lawyer; b. NYC, May 9, 1944; s. Enrique and Frances (Villela) M.; m. Deirdre Caitlin Ryan, Aug. 12, 1967; children: Eric Edward, Sarah Micela Holch. AB in English, Georgetown U., 1966, JD, 1969; LLM in Taxation, NYU, 1975. Bar: NY 1969, Mass. 1976, US Dist. Ct. (ea. dist.) Mass. 1976, US Ct. Appeals (1st cir.) 1976. Assoc. Barrett Smith Schapiro & Simon, NYC, 1969-76, Palmer & Dodge, Boston, 1976-77, ptnr., 1978—2005, Edwards Angell Palmer & Dodge LLP, Boston, 2005—. Lectr. law Northeastern U., 1986-87, Mass. Continuing Legal Edn., Boston, 1978—; trustee Cora du Bois Charitable Trust, 1995-. Trustee Nashoba-Brooks Sch. Concord Inc., Mass., 1984-90, 1st Parish Sudbury, 1979-82, Sudbury Valley Trustees, Inc., 1991—, pres., 1994-96. Fellow Am. Coll. Trust and Estate Counsel; mem. ABA, Boston Bar Assn., Am. Law Inst., Larchmont Yacht Club. Unitarian Universalist. Avocations: sailing, hiking. Home: 388 Willis Rd Sudbury MA 01776-1332 Office: Edwards Angell Palmer & Dodge LLP 111 Huntington Ave Boston MA 02199-7613 Home Phone: 978-443-5009; Office Phone: 617-239-0128. Business E-Mail: emenoyo@eapdlaw.com.

MENSCHEL, ROBERT BENJAMIN, investment banker; b. NYC, July 2, 1929; s. Benjamin and Helen (Goldsmith); m. Joyce Virginia Frank, Dec. 5, 1968; children: David F., Lauren E. BS, Syracuse U., 1951, LLD (hon.), 1991; postgrad., NYU, 1951—53. Mem. N.Y. Stock Exchange, NYC, 1950—51; specialist HW Goldsmith and Co., NYC, 1951—54; with Goldman, Sachs & Co., NYC, 1954—66, gen. ptnr. instl. sales, 1966—78, ltd. ptnr., 1979—2000, sr. dir., 2000—. Author: Markets Mobs & Mayhem, 2002. Trustee Nat. Gallery Art; com. on the arts and the humanities Pres. Clinton; former mem. bd. trustees, investment com. Human Rights Watch; chmn., trustee, exec. and fin. com., mem. investment com., co-chmn. photography com. Mus. Modern Art; trustee Inst. Advanced Study, Princeton, Chess in the Schs., NYC; trustee, exec. com. Syracuse U.; former trustee, mem. exec. com. Montefiore Hosp.; former trustee Guild Hall, East Hampton, NY, past chmn. bd.; pres. bd. trustees, mem. exec. com. Dalton Sch., NYC; past bd. advs. Grad. Sch. Inst. Internat. Bus. Pace U.; exec. bd. NY chpt. Am. Jewish Com., NY; bd. dirs., mem. fin. and exec. com. N.Y. Pub. Libr., NYC; bd. dirs. Parks Coun.; mng. dir. Horace W. Goldsmith Found., Vital Projects Fund; bd. dirs. associated YM-YWHA; v.p. bd. trustees, mem. fin. and exec. com. Temple Emanu-El; trustee N.Y. Presbyn. Hosp. Recipient Recipient George Arents medal, Syracuse U., 1984. Mem.: Coun. Fgn. Rels., City Athletic Club, India Ho. Office: Goldman Sachs & Co 85 Broad St New York NY 10004-2456 Home: 980 5th Ave New York NY 10075 also: Further Lane Amagansett NY 11930 Office Phone: 212-902-6913. Business E-Mail: robert.menschel@gs.com.

MENSCHER, BARNET GARY, steel company executive; b. Laurelton, NY, Sept. 5, 1940; s. Samuel and Louise (Zaimont) M.; m. Diane Elaine Gachman, June 12, 1966; children: Melissa Denise, Corey Lane, Scott Jay. Student, Centenary Coll., 1958-59; BBA, U. Tex., 1963. Vice pres. mktg. Ella Gant Mfg., Shreveport, La., 1964-66; warehouse mgr., dir. material control Gachman Steel Co., Fort Worth, 1966-68, gen. mgr. Houston, 1968-70; v.p. sales Gachman Metal Co., Houston, 1971-76; pres. Menko Steel Service, Inc., Houston, 1979—; CEO NEXTLEVEL, Houston, 1998—. Investment cons. D & L Enterprises, 1966—. Mem. solicitation com. United Fund, 1969-76; mem. Nat. Alliance of Businessmen Jobs Program, 1969—. Served with AUS, 1963-65. Mem. Tex. Assn. Steel Importers, Purchasing Agts. Assn. Houston, Credit Assn. Houston, Am. Mgmt. Assn., Assn. Steel Distbrs., Nat. Assn. Elevator Contractors, Phi Sigma Delta, Alpha Phi Omega. Home: Apt 1002 3388 Sage Rd Houston TX 77056

MENSE, ALLAN TATE, research and development engineering executive; b. Kansas City, Mo., Nov. 29, 1945; s. Martin Conrad Mense and Nancy (Tate) Johnson; children from previous marriage: Melanie Georgia, Eileen Mense Hartzell. BS, U. Ariz., 1968, MS, 1970; PhD, U. Wis., 1977; MS in Indsl. Engring., Ariz. State U., 1999. Registered profl. indsl. engr., ASQ cert. reliability engring. Scientist Oak Ridge (Tenn.) Nat. Lab, 1976-79; sr. staff sci. and tech. comm. U.S. Ho. Reps., Washington, 1979-81; sr. scientist McDonnell Douglas Astro. Co., St. Louis, 1981-85; from dep. chief scientist to chief scientist Dept. Def. Strategic Def. Initiative Orgn., Washington, 1985-88; v.p. rsch. Fla. Inst. Tech., Melbourne, 1988-92; pres. Advanced Tech. Mgmt., Inc., Tempe, Ariz., 1992-97; lead sys. engr. Motorola Space Sys. Tech. Group, Chandler, Ariz., 1998—2001; chief engr., sr. engring. fellow Raytheon Missile Sys., 2002—. Vis. scholar Sloan Sch., MIT, 1995-96; mem. U.S. Army Sci. Bd., 2005—. Contbr. over 60 articles to profl. jours. Ariz. State U. scholar, 1996-97. Mem. AIAA (sr. mem.), IEEE (chmn. energy com. 1985—, sr. mem.), Nat. Def. Industries Assn., Am. Phys. Soc., Am. Nuclear Soc., Inst. Indsl. Engrs., Fla. Com. Nat. Space Club (charter), Sigma Xi, Theta Tau, Pi Mu Alpha. Episcopalian. Office: 1151 E Hermans Rd B840/MS8 Tucson AZ 85706 Home: 116 E Camino Limon Verde Sahuarita AZ 85629 Office Phone: 520-794-4720. Business E-Mail: allan_t_mense@raytheon.com.

MENSES, JAN, artist, draftsman; b. Rotterdam, Netherlands, Apr. 28, 1933; emigrated to Can., 1960, naturalized, 1965; s. Jan and Elisabeth Wilhelmina (Schwarz) M.; m. Rachel Régine Kadoch, Dec. 7, 1958; children: Salomon, Hnina Sarah, Nechamah Elisabeth Halo. Student, Acad. Fine Arts, Rotterdam, Officers Acad. Royal Dutch Air Force, 1953-55. Cert. Royal Can. Academician, Academician of Nations, Academician of Europe, Academician of Italy. Lectr. in fine arts Concordia U., Montreal, 1973-76, others. One-man shows include Montreal Mus. Fine Arts, 1961, 65, 76, Isaacs Gallery, Toronto, Ont., Can., 1964, Delta Gallery, Rotterdam, 1965, Galerie Godard Lefort, Montreal, 1966, Gallery Moos, Toronto, 1967, Rotterdam Art Found., 1974, Galerie Mira Godard, Toronto, 1977, Montreal, 1978, Seasons Galleries, The Hague, 1980, U. B.C. Fine Arts Gallery, Vancouver, 1981, Galerie Don Stewart, Montreal, 1981, Mead Art Mus., Amherst, Mass., 1983, Agnes Etherington Art Mus., 1984, Blom and Dorn Gallery, N.Y.C., 1985, 86-93, Marywood Coll. Mus., Scranton, Pa., 1985, Saraya-Wolfson Ctr., Safed, Israel, 1987, Mayanot Gallery, Jerusalem, 1987-88, Esperanza Gallery, Montreal, 1988, 89, Gallery Hamaayan Haradum, Safed, Israel, 1989—, Blom and Dorn Gallery, Hartford, Conn., 1995, Nora Gallery, Jerusalem, 1995, 96, 97, Artist's Colony, Safed, Israel; over 300 group shows include Montreal World Exhbn., 1967, Salon Internat. Art, Basel, Switzerland, 1972, 74, Can. Nat. Exhbn., 1972, Centennial Exhbn., Royal Can. Acad., Toronto, 1980, Que. Biennale I, II, III, Montreal, 1977, 79, 81, Foire Internat. D'Art Contemporain Paris and Internat. Fair Koln Germany, 1986, Migdal Ha-Emek, Israel, 1988, Group of 8 Israel, Toronto, 1990, Royal Can. Acad. Show, Toronto, 1991, Bezalel Acad., Jerusalem, 2004; represented in permanent exhbn. Gallery Hamaayan Haradum, Safed, Profl. Artists' Assn., Artists Colony, Safed, Menses Mus. Contemporary Art, Safed, Israel; represented in permanent collections Pushkin Mus., Moscow, former Soviet Union, U. Coll. Cape Breton Art Gallery, Sydney, NS, Can. Museo Ciani di Villa Caccia, Lugano, Switzerland, The Art Gallery of Hamilton, Ont.,Can., David Giles Carter Collection, New Haven, Gallery of N.S.-Halifax, Can, Jewish Pub. Libr. Collection, Montreal, Cadillac Fairview Collection, Toronto, Mus. Modern Art, NYC, Phila. Mus. Art, Solomon R. Guggenheim Mus., NYC, Yivo Inst., NYC, Bklyn. Mus., Art Inst. Chgo., Cleve. Mus. Art, Detroit Inst. Arts, Yale U., U. Montreal, Queens U., Kingston, Mead Art Mus., Amherst Coll., Jonathan Edwards Coll., New Haven, Victoria and Albert Mus., London, Vatican Mus., Rome, Quebec Art Bank, Concordia U., Montreal, Haifa Mus. Modern Art, Hebrew U., Jerusalem, Govt. of Que., Yad Vashem Holocaust Meml., Jerusalem, Mus. Boymans-van Beuningen, Rotterdam, Stedelijk Mus., Amsterdam, Rijksmuseum, Amsterdam, Nat. Gallery Can., Ottawa, Gallery Stratford, Montreal Mus. Fine Arts, Musée d'Art Contemporain, Montreal, Que. Provincial Mus., Que. Art Bank, Art Bank of the Can. Coun., Ottawa, Ariz. State Mus., Tucson, Hebrew U., Jerusalem, City of Safed-Israel, Holocaust Mus., Majdeanek, Poland, Holocaust Meml. Ctr., Toronto, Lavalin Mus. Coll, Montreal, Oshawa Mus., Ont., Dept. External Affairs Govt. Can., Ottawa, Can. Jewish Congress Mus., Montreal, Israel Mus., Jerusalem, Holocaust Mus., Majdanek, Poland, McGill U., Montreal, Olympia and York Collection, Toronto, CBC Collection, Montreal, Kingston (Ont.) U. Mus. Collection, NY Pub. Libr., Worcester (Mass.) Art Mus., Currier Gallery Art, Manchester, NH, Gallery of U. NH, Durham, Mus. Art. RI Sch. Design, Providence, Olympia & York Collection, Toronto, Collection Rishon Le'Zion, Jerusalem, Rose Art Mus., Brandeis U., Waltham, Mass., C.I.L. Collection Montreal, Tel Aviv U., McGill U. Coll., Montreal, Can. Jewish Congress Mus., Montreal, Young Israel of Montreal (Coll.), Can., Confedn. Art Ctr., Charlottetown-Prince Edward Island, Can., Thomas More Inst., Montreal, Menses Mus. Contemporary Art, Safed, Israel, Pushkin Mus., Moscow, The Bronfman Collection Can. Art Montreal Mus. Fine Arts, CEMP Collection Montreal, Mt. Allison U., Sackville, NS, Ont. Heritage Found., Toronto, Denbo Collection, L.A., Oziel Collection, Israel, Edelstein Collection, Montreal, many others; paintings include Klippoth Series, 1963-78, Kaddish Series, 1964-80, Hechaloth Series, 1973—, Tikkun Series, 1978—, Doomed Children Series, Kings Series, Victor's Series, Metamorphasis Series, ShevirotHakelim Series, Diabolica Series, Lepers Series, Angels Series, Hiroshima Cycle; mural for Montreal Holocaust Meml. Ctr. Mem. pres.'s coun. U. N.H. Served with Royal Dutch Air Force Res., 1953-55. Recipient 5 1st prizes Nat. Art Exhbn., Quebec, Que., 1960-65; Grand prize Concours Artistiques de la Province de Que., 1965; prize X and XI Winnipeg (Man., Can.) Shows, 1966, 68; prize IX Internat. Exhbn. Drawings and Prints, Lugano, 1966; prize Ofcl. Centennial Art Competition, Toronto; 1st prize Hadassah, 1969, 71, 82; Recipient Imago award U. Montreal, 1971; award Reeves of Can., 1969; Tigert award Ont. Soc. Arts, 1970; Loomis and Toles award, 1972; J. I. Segal award J. I. Segal Fund Jewish Culture, 1975; Gold medal Accademia Italia Delle Arte, Italy, 1980; Gold medal Internat. Parliament U.S.A., 1982; Gran Premio delle Nazioni, Italy, 1983, European Banner of Arts with Gold medal, 1984, Oscar d' Italia, 1985, 1st prize III Que. Biennale, 1981, OSA award of merit, Toronto, 1981, 82; World Culture prize Italy, 1984; Golden Flame of World Parliament (U.S.A.) award, 1986; Ish Shalom award Jerusalem, 1993; numerous others; Can. Council sr. arts fellow, 1969-70, 71-72, 81-82; grantee, 1966-67, 67-68; travel grantee, 1968, 73 Mem. Royal Can. Acad. Arts, Acad. Italia Arte e del Lavoro, Acad. Nazioni, Maestro Accademico-Accademia Bedriacense (Italy), Jewish Am. Acad. Arts and Scis., Israeli Art Assn. (Telaviv), Israel Assn. Profl. Artists Safed, Acad. Europa, Academician Italy, Israel Assn. Visual Art (Jerusalem). Jewish. Address: PO Box 43150 HAR NOF Jerusalem 91400 Israel Personal E-mail: jan@janmenses.com. *My works have dealt with death, the eclipse of faith, exile, the Galut. They are shaped by my childhood experiences, real and imagined, in Nazi-occupied Europe; influenced by and rooted in my principles and standards of conduct as an Orthodox Jew in the post-holocaust/pre-Messianic era. They are an attempt to translate these experiences into visual contemporary terms (imagery conflicts and reconciliations of conflicts) in order to ascend from the personal/specific to the universal/general. They are a lament, an elegy, a denial and confirmation, an expression of the attitude of the soul in its debasement and dignity towards its Creator; a striving towards serenity in anticipation of the Redemption: a form of prayer.*

MENTER, M(ARTIN) ALAN, dermatologist; b. Doncaster, Eng., Oct. 30, 1941; came to U.S., 1975; s. Harry Menter and Esme (Green) Behr; m. Pamela Mary Williams, Dec. 4, 1966; children: Keith, Colin, Kerith. MB, BChir, U. Witwatersrand, 1966; MMed in Dermatology, U. Pretoria, 1971. Diplomate Am. Bd. Dermatology. Intern Johannesburg Gen. Hosp., South Africa, 1967, sr. intern, 1968; resident in dermatology U. Pretoria and Pretoria Gen. Hosp., 1968-71; sr. resident in dermatology Guy's Hosp., London, 1972; sr. resident, tutor in dermatology St. John's Hosp. for Disease of Skin, London, 1972-73; cons. dermatologist Pretoria Gen. Hosp., 1973-75; dermatologist Baylor U. Med. Ctr., Dallas, 1975—, chmn. divsn. dermatology, 1992—; dir. Baylor Psoriasis Rsch. Ctr., 2007—; med. dir. Nat. Psoriasis Found. Tissue Bank, Dallas, 1993—99; clin. prof. dermatology U. Tex. Southwestern Med. Sch., 1996—. Fellow dept. dermatology U. Tex. Southwestern Med. Sch., Dallas, 1977-79, assoc. clin. prof. dermatology, 1977-95; med. dir. Psoriasis Ctr., Baylor U. Med. Ctr., Dallas, 1979—; clin. assoc. prof. dept. periodontics Baylor Coll. Dentistry, Dallas, 1985—; presenter in field. Mem. editl. bd. Jour. Am. Acad. Dermatology, 1993—2003; contbr. numerous articles to profl. jours., chpts. to books. Tex. state chmn. Dermatology Found.; rsch. chmn. Nat. Psoriasis Found., med. adv. bd. exec. com.; coach Rugby football team U. Pretoria, 1974; represented S. Africa Nat. Rugby football team, 1968; coach, commr. Boys Under 12 Classic League Soccer, Dallas, 1978-82; active various local civic organizations and coms. Recipient Clin. Rsch. award Imperial Chem. Industries, 1972-73. Mem. AMA, Acad. Dermatology (mem. com. on psoriasis 1988-93, chmn. 1990-93, mem. com. on stds. care for psoriasis 1988-92, 2007, chmn. 1989-92, 2007, dir. Psoriasis Symposium 1990-93, bd. dirs. 1995-97), Am. Acad. Dermatol. Surgery, Brit. Assn. Dermatology, Dallas County Med. Soc. (mem. med. student rels. com. 1989-94), Dallas Dermatol. Soc. (sec.-treas. 1979, pres. 1980, rep. to adv. coun. Am. Acad. Dermatology 1987-89), Dermatol. Therapy Assn. (pres. 1985), Tex. Dermatol. Soc. (program coord. 1987-93, pres. 1995-96), Tex. Med. Assn. (mem. subcom. on joint sponsorship 1992-95), Internat. Psoriasis Coun. (pres. 2005—). Home: 5230 Royal Ln Dallas TX 75229-5525 Office: Baylor Rsch Inst Baylor Medical Pavilion 3900 Junius St #125 Dallas TX 75246-1613 Home Phone: 214-696-5689. Personal E-mail: alanmenter@gmail.com.

MENTHENA, ANURADHA, research scientist; arrived in US, 2000; d. Bangar Raju and Ammaji Mantena. Student, St. Ann's Coll., Hyderabad, India, 1988—89; MBBS, U. Health Sci., Hyderabad, 1996. House officer Shanti Nursing Home, Hyderabad, 1997—2000; rsch. assoc. Live Rsch. Ctr. Albert Einstein Coll. Medicine, Bronx, NY, 2001—05; rsch. assoc. dept. devel. and molecular biology Albert Einstein Coll. Medicine, Bronx, 2005—. Contbr. articles to profl. jours. Mem.: Am. Soc. Cell Biology. Avocations: opera, music, travel, cooking, reading. Office: Albert Einstein Coll Medicine Dept Devel and Molecular Biology 1300 Morris Park Ave Ullmann 405 Bronx NY 10461

MENTZ, HENRY A., III, plastic surgeon; b. New Orleans, Apr. 9, 1958; s. Henry A. Jr. and Ann (Lamantia) M.; m. Paula Comiskey, May 20, 1989; children: Henry A. IV, James August. BS, La. State U., 1980, MD, 1984. Diplomate Am. Bd. Facial Plastic and Reconstructive Surgery, Am. Bd. Otolaryngology, Am. Bd. Plastic Surgery. Intern otolaryngology Tulane U., New Orleans, 1984-89; resident plastic surgery St. Joseph's Hosp., Houston, 1989-91; founder, ptnr. Aesthetic Ctr. for Plastic Surgeons, Houston, 1991—. Clin. assoc. prof. Baylor U., Houston, 1992—, St. Joseph U., Houston, 1992—; chief surgery Sharpstown Gen. Hosp., Houston, 1994—, chief plastic surgery, 1994—; pres., Houston Soc. of Plastic Surgeons, 2000-01. Fellow ACS, Internat. Coll. Surgeons, Am. Acad. Otolaryngology; mem. Am. Soc. Plastic and Reconstructive Surgeons, Am. Soc. Plastic Surgeons, Am. Soc. Aesthetic Plastic Surgeons, Internat. Soc Aesthetic Plastic Surgeons, Am. Acad. Otolaryngology Head and Neck Surg, AMA, Tex. Medical Assn., Houston Soc. Plastic Surgeons, Harris County Medical Soc. Republican. Episcopalian. Office: Aesthetic Ctr for Plastic Surgery Ste 300 Kimberly Profl Bldg 12727 Kimberley Houston TX 77024

MENTZ, LAWRENCE, lawyer; b. NYC, Nov. 5, 1946; s. Joseph Walter and Audrey Cecilia (Armstrong) M.; m. Barbara Antonello, Nov. 10, 1973; children: Kathleen Elizabeth, Lawrence Goodwin. BS in Physics, Rensselaer Poly. Inst., 1968; JD, U. Notre Dame, 1973. Bar: N.Y. 1973, DC 1974. Assoc. Condon & Forsyth, NYC, 1973-80, ptnr., 1981-89, Biedermann, Hoenig, Massamillo & Ruff, NYC, 1990—2005, Kaplan, von Ohlen & Massamillo, LLC, NYC, 2005—; counsellor at law. Spkr. Worldwide Airlines Customer Rels. Assn. Conf., Singapore, 1983, 2d Cir. Spkrs. Bur., Com. on BiCentennial of U.S. Constn., 1987; arbitrator U.S. Dist. Ct. (ea. dist.) Bklyn., 1986—. With USNR, 1969-70. Mem. ABA, N.Y. State Bar Assn. (exec. com. sect. on comml. and fed. litigation, fed. judiciary com., 1993, com, Supreme Cts.), Assn. of Bar of City of N.Y. (com. on aeronautics law, task force on N.Y. Constl. Conv., com. on state legis.), Wings Club. Roman Catholic. Avocations: swimming, running, stamp collecting/philately. Office Phone: 212-455-9248. E-mail: lwmentz@kvolaw.com.

MENTZER, ROSLYN, academic administrator; b. NYC, Oct. 26, 1935; d. Morris and Etta B. (Greenberg) Moskowitz; m. Alan D. Mentzer, June 21, 1953; children: Michelle, Stuart. BA, Queens Coll., 1965; MA, UCLA, 1968. Instr. L.A. Community Coll. Dist., 1968-69; v.p. United Coll. of Bus., LA, 1969—. Pres. CAPPS, Calif., 1984-87. Mem. LWV (v.p. Beverly Hills, Calif. chpt. 1969), Phi Beta Kappa. Avocations: tennis, bridge, writing. Home: 61 Cascade Ky Bellevue WA 98006-1023 Office: United Coll of Bus 445 S Figueroa St Bldg 2400 Los Angeles CA 90071-1602

MENUTIS, RUTH ANN, small business owner; b. Lafayette, La., Aug. 7, 1939; d. Minus and Annie (Duhon) Pellerin; ed. S.W. La. Inst., Patricia Stevens Sch. Modeling; m. Jimmie Menutis, Feb. 15, 1960; children: Jamie, Marika, Dimitri. Comml. announcer, traffic mgr. KLFY-TV, 1957-58; hostess Trans Tex./Tex. Internat. Airlines, also model Dallas Apparel Mart, 1958-68; owner, mgr. Playgril Shop of Am. and Ruth Ann Fashion, New Orleans, 1960-80; owner Natural Energy Unltd., Inc. (doing bus. as Grove), 1980-2004; owner Menutis Investments, New Orleans/Lafayette, La.; pres. Branded Works Inc.; acting pres. French Market Corp.; real estate developer; clothing designer Miss Jane of Miami & More by Ruth Ann. Bd. dirs. Better Bus. Bur., Contemporary Arts Ctr.; chmn. La. del. to White House Small Bus. Conf., 1980; vice chmn. midwest U.S.A. Small Bus. Nat. Unity Council; chmn. New Orleans Mayor's, French Quar. Task Force. Mem. Vieux Carre Action Assn. (v.p.), Bourbon Mchts. Assn. (pres.), Daus. of Penelope. Greek Orthodox. Office: 110 Travis St # 100 Lafayette LA 70503-2453 Home: 108 Royal St Ste 400 New Orleans LA 70130 Business E-Mail: rmenutis@brandedworksinc.com.

MENY, ROBERT GEORGE, former medical research administrator, physician; b. Hackensack, NJ, Jan. 7, 1945; m. Janet McHugh, Apr. 28, 1990; children: Danielle, Ellen, Gus. BS, Tulane U., 1966; MD, Columbia U., 1971. Intern and resident in pediat. N.Y. Hosp., NYC, 1971—73; fellow in neonatology U. Md. Hosp., Balt., 1975—77; mem. staff neonatal ctr. Rutgers Med. Sch., New Brunswick, NJ, 1977—80; dir. Hurley Neonatal Ctr., Flint, Mich., 1980—83; dir. Sudden Infant Death Syndrome Inst. U. Md., Balt., 1983—99; pvt. practice Towson, Md., 1999—. Capt. USAF. Mem.: Am. Assn. Sudden Infant Death Prevention Physicians (pres.-elect 1995, chmn. bd. 1998). Office: O'Dea Bldg #409 7505 Osler Dr Towson MD 21204

MENZ, ROBERT L., psychotherapist, minister; b. Cape Girardeau, Mo., June 29, 1949; s. Robert A. and Vivian Marie Menz; m. Ruth A. Hageman, Jan. 7, 1994; children: Gwendolyn J. Menz Ogle, Shawn E. BS in Edn. and Sci., SE Mo. U., Cape Girardeau, 1975; MDiv, Midwestern Bapt. Sem., Kansas City, Mo., 1979; DMin in Counseling, So. Bapt. Sem., Louisville, 1987. Ordained Am. Bapt. Ch., 1974. Resident chaplain Bapt. Meml. Hosp., Kansas City, 1980—81; chaplain Meml. Med. Ctr., Springfield, Ill., 1981—87; dir. pastoral care Bapt. Home DC, Washington, 1987—91; employee counselor Emerson Climate Techs., Sidney, Ohio, 1991—. Adj. asst. prof. So. Ill. U., Springfield, 1982—87; adj. faculty Edison State Coll., Piqua, Ohio, 1993—. Author: A Memoir of a Pastoral Counseling, 1997, A Pastoral Counselor's Model of Wellness in the Workplace, 2003; editor: Social Change: Vision 2020. Counsel mem., past pres. Shelby County Cmty. Svcs., Sidney, 1991—; counsel mem. Wilson Home Health Hospice, Sidney, 1998—; bd. dirs., past chmn. Shelby County Counseling Ctr., Sidney, 2002—. With US Army, 1970—71, Vietnam. Decorated Commendation medal US Army. Fellow: Am. Assn. Pastoral Counselors; mem.: Employee Assistance Profl. Assn. (bd. cert.), Am. Psychotherapy Assn. (diplomate 2002—), Nat. Employee Assistance. Avocations: flying, running, mountain climbing, hiking, writing. Home: 1290 Dritwood Trail Sidney OH 45365 Office: Emerson Climate Techs 1650 W Campbell Rd Sidney OH 45365

MENZA, CLAUDIA MARCELLA, literary agent; b. NYC, June 11, 1947; d. John Gaetano and Antonina (di Lorenzo) M.; m. James R. Forker, May 29, 1971 (div. 1980); m. Charles Anthony Frye, Dec. 16, 1989 (dec. Oct. 1994). BA, Oberlin Coll., 1969. Asst. editor Evergreen Rev., NYC, 1969-73; gen. editor, prodn. mgr. Grove Press, Inc., NYC, 1973-83; sr. editor Art Dir. News, NYC, 1983-85; ptnr. Menza-Barron Agy., NYC, 1983—. Cons. Riverrun Press, N.Y.C., 1983-96; guest lectr. Tex. A&M U., Prairie View, Tex., 1986, NYU, N.Y.C., 1986-87; cons., panelist Nat. Civil Rights Mus. Conf. The Power of the Word, Memphis, 1995; panelist NYU, 1998, The New Sch., N.Y.C., 2000, The Lost State Writers Conf., Greeneville, Tenn., 2000, Harlem Book Fair, 2001; panelist African Am. Lit. Conf., Raleigh, NC, 2003. Author: Cage of Wild Cries, 1990, The Lunatics Ball, 1994, (play), 2006; contbg. author: The Dream Book: An Anthology of Writing by Italian-American Women, 1985 (Am. Book award, 1985); actor: Damned Pub. Riverside Studios, 1999. Working mem. Congress of Racial Equality, Hempstead, N.Y., 1961, Student Nonviolent Coord. Com., Oberlin, Ohio, 1965, Students for Dem. Soc., Oberlin, 1965,

The West Village Com., N.Y.C., 1980. Mem. PEN (trustee, chair prison writing com.), Internat. Platform Assn., Acad. Am. Poets, Italian-Am. Writers Assn., Assn. Authors Reps. Avocations: reading, music, theater. Office: Menza-Barron Agy 1170 Broadway Ste 807 New York NY 10001-7507 Business E-Mail: claudia@menzabarron.com.

MENZA, MATTHEW A., psychiatrist; b. Sept. 11, 1950; BA, U. Va., 1973; MD, Temple U., 1980; postgrad., Harvard U., 1985. Intern NYU Med. Sch. Bellvue Hosp., NYC, 1980—81, resident, 1981—84; chief divsn. clin. psychopharmacology Robert Wood Johnson Med. Sch., Piscataway, NJ, 1996—, vice chmn. dept. psychiatry, 2003—. Contbr. over 65 articles to profl. jours. Bd. govs. Univ. Med. Group, New Brunswick, N.J., 1999—. Office: Robert Wood Johnson Med Sch Dept Psychiatry 675 Hoes Ln Piscataway NJ 08854-5627 Home Phone: 732-868-0840. Business E-Mail: menza@umdnj.edu.

MENZEL, FEROL SCHRICKER, academic administrator; b. Cin., Mar. 12, 1946; d. Raymond and Esther (Meikle) Schricker; m. Bruce Willard Menzel, Aug. 9, 1969; children: Erich Leith, Evan Douglas. BS in Occupational Therapy, Ohio State U., 1968; MS in Child Devel., Iowa State U., 1975, PhD in Child Devel., 1979. Occupational therapist Spl. Children's Ctr., Ithaca, NY, 1969—70; work evaluator then dir. occupational therapy Woodward State Hosp.-Sch., Iowa, 1970—72, dir. Devel. Ctr., 1972—73; tchg. and rsch. asst. dept. child devel. Iowa State U., Ames, 1973—75; occupational therapist Iowa Area XI Edn. Agy., 1977—79; asst. prof. to prof. psych. Grand View Coll., Des Moines, 1980, prof., 1988, chair dept. psych., 1982—83, head social svcs. divsn., 1983, assoc. dean freshmen, 1986—88, dir. lifelong edn., 1989—90, dir. planning and instl. rsch., 1990; v.p. academic affairs, dean of faculty Wartburg Coll., Waverly, Iowa, 1999—. Lectr. dept. psych. Drake U., 1979; instr. in service tng. for tchrs. of severely and profoundly handicapped Drake U., 1978-79, U. Ga., 1978; instr. occupational therapy U. Iowa, 1981; cons. occupational therapy Iowa State Dept. Pub. Instrn., 1979-80, Mainstream Living, Inc., Ames, Iowa, 1975-76, Ames Pub. Schs., 1975-76; cons.-evaluator North Ctrl. Assn. Colls. and Schs., 1986, mem. accreditation rev. com., 1990, chair, Higher Learning Commn. Contbr. articles to profl. jours. Mem. Sawyer Sch. PTA, Ames, Crawford Sch. PTA, Ames, Supts. Adv. Com., Ames; bd. dirs. Coop. Presch., Ames, Ames Soccer Club; bd. deacons, chair Christian edn. com., tchr. Collegiate Presbyn. Ch., Ames. Mem. APA, Am. Assn. Higher Edn., Soc. Rsch. in Child Devel., Phi Kappa Phi, Phi Eta Sigma (chpt. advisor 1990). Office: Deans Office Wartburg Coll 100 Wartburg Blvd Waverly IA 50677-2215 E-mail: ferol.menzel@wartburg.edu. *

MENZEL, MARYBELLE PROCTOR, volunteer; b. Milledgeville, Ga., Feb. 5, 1940; d. Ennis Hall Proctor and Sara (Evans) McCarthy; m. Robert John Menzel, Sept. 1, 1961; children: Blake, John, Craig. BA cum laude, Wesleyan Coll., Macon, Ga., 1962; MA with highest distinction, U. Ctrl. Fla., Orlando, 1986. Cert. highest level tchr. Fla. Tchr. Spaulding Jr. HS, Griffin, Ga., 1962, East Syracuse (NY) Minoa HS, 1964—65, Coral Gables (Fla.) HS, 1965—66; dir. Gerber Child Care Ctr., Indialantic, Fla., 1981, Brevard CC Coop Presch., Melbourne, Fla., 1982—85; adj. instr. English and Humanities Brevard CC, Cocoa, Fla., 1985. Host, guide, amb. Denver Art Mus., 2006—. Named Million Dollar Woman, Wesleyan Coll., 2005. Mem.: AAUW (Nat. award Fundraising AAUW Ednl. Found. 2001, Garden of Victories award 1993), Colo. AAUW (dir. ednl. found. 2000—01, pres. elect 2001—02, pres. 2002—04, past pres. 2004—05, pub. policy com. 2004—, women's legis. breakfast com. 2005—, state exec. bd., mem. women's lobby), Wesleyan Coll. Million Dollar Women, Nat. Mus. Women in the Arts (friend), Nat. Mus. Women's History (charter), Nat. Trust for Historic Preservation, Phi Kappa Phi. Democrat. Methodist.

MENZER, JOHN BRUCE, retail executive; b. Chgo., Mar. 27, 1951; s. John and Lorraine (Glugla) M. m. Kathleen A. Leahy, Oct. 23, 1976; 1 child, Christine. BBA in Pub. Acctg., Loyola U., 1972, MBA in Fin., 1980. CPA, Ill. Supr. acctg. systems Am. Internat., Mount Prospect, Ill., 1973-75; supr. audit Pannell, Kerr, Forster & Co., Chgo., 1975-77; sr. v.p. Bally Mfg. Corp., 1977-85, Ben Franklin Retail Stores, Carol Stream, Ill., 1985—88, exec. v.p., 1988—91, COO, CFO, 1991—93, pres., 1993—95; exec. v.p., CFO Wal-Mart Stores, Inc., 1995—99; pres., CEO Wal-Mart Internat., 1999—2005; vice chmn. U.S. Wal-Mart Stores, Inc., 2005—. Bd. dirs. Wal-Mart de Mex., Seiyu Ltd., Japan, Emerson Electric, U.S.-China Bus. Coun., Guangdong Province Gov.'s Econ. Advisors in China. Bd. dirs. Jr. Achievement, Chgo., 1973-75. Mem. Fin. Execs. Inst., Ill. State Soc. CPAs, Nat. Retail Mchts. Assn., Am. Inst. CPAs, Internat. Franchise Assn. (chmn. fin. and tax com., conf. coordinator). Avocations: golf, tennis. Office: Wal-Mart Stores Inc 702 Southwest Eighth St Bentonville AR 72716 *

MENZER, ROBERT EVERETT, retired toxicologist, educator; b. Washington, Dec. 21, 1938; s. Russell Ernest and Ora Taylor (Oates) M.; m. Sara Lee Gribbon, Dec. 29, 1962; children: R. Eric, Paul D., Joan Coleraine. BS in Chemistry, U. Pa., 1960; MS, U. Md., 1962; PhD, U. Wis., 1964. Instr. U. Wis., Madison, 1964; mem. faculty U. Md., 1964-89, asst. prof. entomology, 1964-69, assoc. prof., 1969-73, prof., 1973-89, assoc. dean grad. studies and research, 1974-77, acting dean, 1977-80, chmn. grad. program marine-estuarine-environ. scis., 1978-89, dir. Water Resources Research Ctr., 1981-89; dir. environ. rsch. lab. EPA, Gulf Breeze, Fla., 1989-95, sr. sci. advisor Nat. Ctr. for Environ. Rsch. Washington, 1995—2001; ret., 2001. Prof. emeritus U. Md., 1990—; chmn. hazardous substances data bank rev. panel Nat. Library Medicine, 1973-97; cons. in field, 2001-. Contbr. articles to profl. jours. Recipient U. Md. Alumni award, 1974 Fellow Washington Acad. Scis.; mem. AAAS, Am. Chem. Soc., Soc. Toxicology, Estuarine Rsch. Fedn., Sigma Xi, Phi Kappa Phi. Clubs: Cosmos (Washington). Republican. Episcopalian. Home: 90 Highpoint Dr Gulf Breeze FL 32561-4014 Personal E-mail: remenzer@att.net.

MENZIES, HENRY HARDINGE, architect; b. Hickory, NC, Apr. 20, 1928; s. Henry Hardinge and Hallie (Lloyd) M. AB in Lit., U. N.C., 1948; postgrad., U. So. Calif., 1948-49; BArch, N.C. State U., 1958. Founder, ptnr. The Architects Group, Boston, 1962-63; individual practice architecture Boston, 1964-78; ptnr. Menzies and LeMieux, NYC, 1978-82; pvt. practice architecture New Rochelle, N.Y., 1983—. Lectr. in field. Works include coll. and seminary, Natick, Mass., 1964, Heights Sch., Washington, 1965, St. Marie's Ch., Lowell, Mass., 1966, Central Cath. H.S., Lawrence, Mass., 1971, Walker Sch., Needham, Mass., 1972, Baird Residence, Sherborn, Mass., 1972, Layton Cultural Ctr., Brookfield, Wis., 1974, Shellbourne Conf. Ctr., Valparaiso, Ind., 1974, Wespine Study Ctr., Pembroke, Mass, 1982, alterations to residences in Greenwich, Conn., 1984, Garwood Bldg. at Arnold Hall, 1986, Midtown Ctr., Chgo., 1986, Student Ctr., Houston, 1986, Windmoor Ctr., South Bend, Ind., 1986, alterations to student residences in Milw. and Providence, 1989-91, renovation of interior St. Aloysius Ch., New Canaan, Conn., 1993-96, chapel at Warwick House, Pitts., 1993, chapel at Westfield Residence, L.A., 1994, chapel at Allview Ctr., Columbia, Md., 1994, chapel at St. John Fisher Residence, Stamford, Conn., 1994, master plan, crypt chapel St. Mary of the Angels Ch., Chgo., 1996—, Shrine at Conf. Ctr., Schulenberg, Tex., chapel Lincoln Green student residence, Urbana, Ill., 1997—, new facade of St. Aloysius Ch., New Canaan, 1997—, Willows Acad., Chgo., 1997—, Cath. Info. Ctr. Washington, 1999-2000, St. Michael's Ch., Gastonia, N.C., 2000—, Cathedral St. Augustine, Bridgeport, Conn., 2003, Paducah, Ky., 2003, H.S. Charlotte, 2003, St. Ann's Ch., Bridgeport, 2006, Heights Sch. Chapel, 2006, others; contbr. articles to profl. jours. Served to 1st lt. USNR, 1951-55. Mem. AIA (N.Y. chpt. 1978-84, Westchester/Mid-Hudson chpt. 1985—). Roman Catholic. Office: 99 Overlook Cir New Rochelle NY 10804-4501 Office Phone: 914-637-9597. E-mail: hmenzies@gmail.com.

MENZIES, IAN STUART, newspaper editor; b. Glasgow, Scotland, Mar. 11, 1920; came to U.S., 1944, naturalized, 1948; s. John S. and Gertrude (Mephius) M.; m. Barbara Edith Newton, June 16, 1945; children: Marla Ann, Gillian Jean, Alexa Stuart, Deborah Newton. Student, Royal Tech. Coll., 1937-39; LHD, Salem State Coll., Mass., 1978. Reporter Boston Globe, 1948-57, sci. editor, 1957-63, fin. editor, 1963-65, mng. editor, 1965-70, assoc. editor, 1970-85; sr. fellow John McCormack Inst. Pub. Affairs, U. Mass., Boston, 1985—95, sr. fellow emeritus, 1995—. Vis. assoc. Joint Ctr. for Urban Studies, Mass. Inst. Tech.-Harvard, 1970-71. Mem. Hingham Sch. Com., Mass., 1962-68. Served to lt. Royal Naval Vol. Res., 1939-46. Decorated D.S.C.; recipient Pub. Service award Nat. Edn. Writers, 1961, Pub. Service award AAAS, 1963, Heywood Broun award, 1961, Sevellon Brown award, 1959, Rudolph Elie award, 1959, A.P. Big City award, 1958, U.P.I. award, 1959; Neiman fellow Harvard U., Cambridge, Mass., 1961-62. Mem. Harvard Club, Hingham Yacht Club, Brit. Officers Club New Eng. Home and Office: Apt 527 303 Linden Ponds Way Hingham MA 02043-4705

MEOLA, TONY, professional soccer player, actor; b. Belleville, NJ, Feb. 21, 1969; s. Vincent and Maria Meola; m. Colleen Meola; 1 child, Jonathan. Student, U. Va., 1986—89. Goalkeeper U.S. Nat. Team, 1988—94, 1999—2002, U.S. World Cup Team, 1990, 1994, 2002, Brighton Football Club, England, 1990, Fort Lauderdale Strikers, 1991, Long Island Roughriders, 1994—95, NY-NJ MetroStars, 1996—98, 2005—, Kansas City (Mo.) Wizards, 1998—2004. Actor: (plays) Tony N' Tina's Wedding, 1995. Named Hermann Trophy winner, MVP, U.S. Cup, 1993; named to MLS All Star Team, 1996—98, 2000, 2002; recipient Mo. Athletic Club Player of Yr., 1989. Achievements include drafted ctr. fielder N.Y. Yankees; tried out as placekicker for N.Y. Jets, 1994; mem. N.J. State H.S. Soccer Champions, 1986; NCAA Division I Co-Champions, 1989. Office: NY NJ MetroStars 3d Fl 1 Harmon Plz Secaucus NJ 07094

MÉRAS, PHYLLIS LESLIE, journalist; b. Bklyn., May 10, 1931; d. Edmond Albert and Leslie Trousdale (Ross) M.; BA, Wellesley Coll., Mass., 1955; MS in Journalism, Columbia U., NYC, 1954; Swiss Govt. Exchange fellow, Inst. Higher Internat. Studies, Geneva, 1957; m. Thomas H. Cocroft, Nov. 3, 1968. Reporter, copy editor Providence Jour., 1954-57, 59-61; feature writer Ladies Home Jour. mag., 1957-58; editor Weekly Tribune, Geneva, Switzerland, 1961-62; copyeditor, travel sect. NY Times, 1962-68; mng. editor Vineyard Gazette, Edgartown, Mass., 1970-74, contbg. editor, 1974—; assoc. editor Rhode Islander, Providence, 1970-76; travel editor Providence Jour., 1976-95; editor Wellesley Alumnae mag., 1979-96; assoc. in journalism U. RI, 1974-75; adj. instr. Columbia U. Sch. Journalism, 1975-76. Author: First Spring: A Martha's Vineyard Journal, 1972, A Yankee Way With Wood, 1975, Miniatures: How to Make Them, Use Them, Sell Them, 1976, Vacation Crafts, 1978, The Mermaids of Chenonceaux and 828 Other Tales: An Anecdotal Guide to Europe, 1982, Exploring Rhode Island, 1984, Castles, Keeps and Leprechauns: Tales, Myths and Legends of Historic Sites in Great Britain and Ireland, 1988, Eastern Europe: A Traveler's Companion, 1991; co-author: Christmas Angels, 1979, Carry-out Cuisine, 1982, New Carry Out Cuisine, 1986, Rhode Island Explorer's Guide, 2004, Country Editor: Henry Beetle Hough and the Vineyard Gazette, 2006, The Historic Shops and Restaurants of Boston, 2007. Pulitzer fellow in critical writing, 1967. Mem. Soc. Am. Travel Writers. Home: Music St PO Box 215 West Tisbury MA 02575-0215 Office Phone: 508-693-1439. E-mail: pmcocroft@aol.com.

MERBLER, CANDACE ANNE, librarian; b. Bklyn., July 14, 1956; d. Patricia Anne M. Daly and Charles Fuoco; m. Richard Albert Merbler, Feb. 14, 1987 (div. Mar. 5, 2003). BA, U. Albany, 1979, MLS, 1999. Ref. support assoc. U. Albany, 1979—. Pres. United Univ. Profls., Albany, 2001—. Mem. Town of Greenfield UDAG Com., Greenfield Center, NY, 1996—; mem. statewide exec. bd. United Univ. Professions, 2005—; chmn. adv. com. on campus security U. Albany, 2004—. Recipient Excellence award, United U. Professions, N.Y., 1991, Initiatives for Women award, U. Albany, 2002; fellow RASS Dewey fellow, N.Y. Libr. Assn., 1999; scholar Alice-Hastings Murphy scholar, U. Albany Libraries, 1991, Inst. Info. Lit. scholar, Assn. Coll. & Rsch. Libraries, 2002. Mem.: ALA (assoc.), SUNY Librs. Assn. (assoc.), Hudson-Mohawk Libr. Assn. (assoc.), Ea. N.Y. Assn. of Coll. & Rsch. Librs. (assoc.), N.Y. Libr. Assn. (assoc.). Avocations: gardening, crafts, crocheting. Home: 788 Coy Rd Greenfield Center NY 12833 Office: U Albany 1400 Washington Ave Albany NY 12222 Office Phone: 518-442-3564. E-mail: cmerbler@uamail.albany.edu.

MERCADO, DAVID, lawyer; b. Houston, Oct. 28, 1958; AB, Columbia Univ., 1981; JD, Yale Univ., 1984. Bar: NY 1985. Assoc. Cravath Swaine & Moore LLP, NYC, 1984—92, ptnr., corp., 1992—. Mem.: ABA, NY State Bar Assn. Office: Cravath Swaine & Moore LLP Worldwide Plz 825 Eighth Ave New York NY 10019-7475 Office Phone: 212-474-1756. Office Fax: 212-474-3700. Business E-Mail: dmercado@cravath.com.

MERCANDO, ANTHONY DOMINIC, cardiologist; b. Yonkers, NY, Oct. 6, 1954; s. Dominic and Ida Mercando; m. Lee-Ann Davis, May 3, 1980; children: Michelle, Christina, Andrew, Anne Marie. BSEE, Manhattan Coll., Bronx, 1976; MD, Harvard U., 1980. Lic. physician, N.Y. Med. intern Montefiore Med. Ctr., Bronx, 1980-81, med. resident, 1981-83, cardiology fellow, 1984-86, attending arrhythmia svc., 1986-88; ptnr. Westchester Cardiology Assocs., Tuckahoe, N.Y., 1988—. Founder, pres. Amadeus Multimedia Technologies, Ltd., Irvington, N.Y., 1995—; assoc. dir. ACLS Montefiore Hosp., 1991—. Contbr. articles to profl. jours., chpts. to books; computer editor Jour. Pacing and Clin. Electrophysiology, 1993—. Bd. dirs. Home Nursing Assn. Westchester, Tuckahoe, 1994—; tech. com. Irvington Sch. Bd., 1995—. R. Rosen fellow in pacing and electrophysiology N. Am. Soc. Pacing and Electrophysiology, 1986, Sable Meml. Heart fellow United Order Odd Fellows, 1985. Fellow Am. Coll. Cardiology; mem. N.Am. Soc. Pacing and Electrophysiology. Roman Catholic. Avocations: biking, skiing. Office: Westchester Cardiology 688 White Plains Rd # 201 Scarsdale NY 10583-5059

MERCER, EDWIN WAYNE, lawyer; b. Kingsport, Tenn., July 19, 1940; s. Ernest LaFayette and Geneva (Frye) M. MBA, Tex. Tech U., 1963; JD, S. Tex. Coll. Law, 1971. Bar: Tex. 1971, U.S. Dist. Ct. (no. dist.) Tex 1975, U.S. Supreme Ct. 1976, U.S. Ct. Appeals (5th Cir.) 1979. Pvt. practice, Houston, 1971-73; gen. counsel, corp. sec. Alcon Labs., Inc., Ft. Worth, 1973-81; ptnr. Gandy Michener Swindle Whitaker Pratt & Mercer, Ft. Worth, 1981-84; v.p., gen. counsel, corp. sec. Pengo Industries, Inc., Ft. Worth, 1984-90, also bd. dirs.; pvt. law practice, 1990—. Bd. dirs. Soc. for Prevention Blindness, 1979—. Mem. ABA, State Bar Tex., Coll. State Bar Tex., South Tex. Coll. Law Alumni Assn., Tex. Tech U. Ex-Assn., Ft. Worth Club, Delta Theta Phi, Phi Delta Theta. Methodist. Office Phone: 817-731-1959.

MERCER, ERICA SCHALOW, urologist, educator; b. Fla. m. Gregory Mercer. BS in Engring., Tulane U., New Orleans, 1992; MD, U. Fla., Gainesville, 1996. Pediatric urologist Nemours Children's Clinic, Jacksonville, Fla., 2004—; asst. prof. surgery Mayo Clinic, 2004—. Nat. Merit scholar. Office: Nemours Children's Clinic 807 Children's Way Jacksonville FL 32207 Office Phone: 904-390-3748.

MERCER, JAMES LEE, management consultant; b. Sayre, Okla., Nov. 7, 1936; s. Fred Elmo and Ora Lee (Davidson) M.; m. Karolyn Lois Prince, Nov. 16, 1962; children: Tara Lee, James Lee. BS, U. Nev., Reno, 1964, MBA, 1966; postgrad. exec. devel. program, Cornell U., Ithaca, NY, 1979. Cert. in mcpl. adminstrn. U. NC, 1971, lifetime Jr. coll. tchng. credential Calif., cert. mgmt. cons. Methods and results supr. Pacific Tel. & Tel., Sacramento, 1965-66; prodn. control supr. Gen. Dynamics, Pomona, Calif., 1966-67; nuclear submarine project mgr. Litton Industries, Pascagoula, Miss., 1967-70; asst. city mgr. City of Raleigh, NC, 1970-73; nat. program dir. Pub. Tech., Inc., Washington, 1973-76; gen. mgr. Battelle So. Ops., Atlanta, 1976-79; v.p. Korn/Ferry Internat., Atlanta, 1979-81; pres. James Mercer & Assocs. Inc.; mgmt. cons. Atlanta, 1981-86; chief Indsl. Ext. Divsn. Ga. Inst. of Tech., Atlanta, 1981-83, dir. Ga. Productivity Ctr.; dir. govtl. cons. svc. Coopers & Lybrand, 1983-84; regional v.p. Wolfe & Assocs., Inc., 1984-86; pres., CEO, chmn. Mercer, Slavin & Nevins, Inc., 1986-90, The Mercer Group, Inc., 1990—. Ad hoc prof. NC State U., 1972-73; bd. dirs. Taratec Corp., Columbus, Contract Svcs. Assn., Wash., DC., 1990—; lectr., spkr. in field. Author: Public Management Systems, 1978, Public Technology, 1981, Managing Urban Government Services, 1981, Strategic Planning for Public Managers, 1990, Public Management in Lean Years, 1992; contbr. numerous articles to profl. jours. Chmn. Raleigh Mayor's Civic Ctr. Authority Study Commn., 1971; founding bd. dirs. Mordecai Sq. Hist. Soc., Nat. Civic League; founding mem. Calif. Poly. State U., adv. coun. Coll. Bus. Adminstrn., San Luis Obispo, 1980-95, bd. mem. emeritus, 1995—; founding mem., bd. trustees emeritus U. Nev. Found., Reno, 1985-91, trustee emeritus, 1991—; founding mem. U. SC M Pub. Adminstrn. adv. bd., 1987-97. Mem.: NC League of Municipalities (George C. Franklin award 1971), Instit. Mgmt. Cons. (Atlanta Chpt. (v.p. membership 1991—97, bd. dirs. 1991—97), Contract Svcs. Assn. Am. (bd. dirs. Wash. (D.C.) chpt. 1990—), Ga. Indsl. Devel. Assn., Tech. Transfer Soc. (dir. 1978—87, treas. 1985—86), Internat. Pers. Mgmt. Assn., Govtl. Fin. Officers Assn., Inst. Indsl. Engrs. (chpt. pres. 1969—70, past pres.'s award 1970), Am. Soc. Pub. Adminstrn., Internat. City-County Mgmt. Assn., Raleigh Forward Leadership Orgn., U. Nev. Alumni Assn. (exec. com. 1969—79, Oustanding Alumnus), Shriners, Rotary, Atlanta C. of C., Masons, Beta Gamma Sigma. Home: 28 Sierra del Sol Santa Fe NM 87508-2136 Office: 551 W Cordova Rd Ste 726 Santa Fe NM 87505-1825 Office Phone: 505-466-9500. Personal E-mail: mercer@mindspring.com.

MERCER, JOHN LEE, secondary school educator, department chairman; b. Lakewood, Ohio, Sept. 9, 1959; s. Jerry and Molly Hubbard Mercer; m. Ruth Benedict; children: Jacob, Samuel. BA, Bethany Coll., Bethany, W.Va., 1977—81; MA in History, Kent State U., Ohio, 1995—2001. Cert. Comprehensive social studies tchr. 7-12 State Ohio, 2003. Ops. specialist US Ho. Reps., DC, 1978—82; dir. customer support LSW, Inc., Landover, Md., 1982—87; sales rep. Dialcom, Cleve., 1987—89; tchr., dept. chair Olmsted Falls HS, Ohio, 1989—. Actor: (plays) Black River Theatre Company; dir.: (various school plays & musicals). Vestryman Christ Ch., Oberlin, 1991—2006; strategic planning cabinet mem. Olmsted Falls Schs., Ohio, 1992—2004; north ctrl. process steering com. Olmsted Falls HS, Ohio, 1995—2003; pres., bd. mem. MAD Factory, Oberlin, Ohio, 1998—2001; treas. Ohio HS Speech League, 2003—05, chair, 2005—06. Recipient Tchr. of Yr. award, Olmsted Falls HS, 1995, Excellence in Tchg. award, Coll. Wooster, 2000, Outstanding Educator award, Ohio PTA, 2001, Diamond Coach award, Nat. Forensic League, 2002, Ohio Coaches Hall of Fame, Ohio H.Speech League, 2006. Mem.: Nat. Forensic League, Nat. Coun. Social Studies. Episc. Office: Olmsted Falls HS 26939 Bagley Rd Olmsted Falls OH 44138 Home Phone: 440-774-4019.

MERCER, JOHN T.W., lawyer; b. Mpls., 1949; AB, Univ. Mich., 1973, JD, 1977. Bar: Ga. 1977. Assoc. Troutman Sanders LLP, Atlanta, 1978—84, ptnr., corp. and securities, 1985—, and practice group leader, project develop. and fin. Named Ga. Super Lawyer in Securities and Corp. Fin., Atlanta Mag., 2007; named one of Am. Leading Lawyers for Energy and Natural Resources, Chambers USA, 2005, 2006. Mem.: ABA, State Bar Ga. Office: Troutman Sanders LLP 600 Peachtree St NE Ste 5200 Atlanta GA 30308-2216 Office Phone: 404-885-3182. Office Fax: 404-962-6632. Business E-Mail: john.mercer@troutmansanders.com.

MERCER, WILLIAM W., prosecutor; b. Jan. 7, 1964; BA in Polit. Sci., U. Mont., 1986; MPA, Harvard U., 1988; JD, George Mason U., 1993. Counselor to asst. atty. gen., sr. policy analyst Office of Policy Devel. US Dept. Justice, 1989—94, prin. assoc. dep. atty. gen. Washington, 2005—06, acting assoc. atty. gen., 2006—07, asst. US atty. Dist. Mont. Billings, Mont., 1994—2001, US atty., 2001—. Mem. president's adv. coun. U. Mont.; mem. bd. visitors U. Mont. Sch. Law; mem. atty. gen.'s adv. com. Office: US Attys Office PO Box 1478 Billings MT 59103 E-mail: askdoj@usdoj.gov. *

MERCHANT, P. GLENN, JR., military officer, physician; b. Quonset Point, RI, Jan. 6, 1953; s. Paul Glenn and Mary Jean Merchant; m. Debra Colleene Brown, Nov. 25, 1951; children: Nicholas Ryan, Kaitlin Elizabeth, Joshua Daniel. BS in Biology, The Citadel, 1980—83; MD, Med. U. of SC., 1983—87; BA in Polit. Sci., The Citadel, 1971—75; Masters in Pub. Health and Tropical Medicine, Tulane U. Sch. of Pub. Health & Tropical Medicine, 1991—92. Diplomate Am. Bd. of Preventive Medicine, 1994. Marine aviator VMA-542, Cherry Point, NC, 1975—80; commd. 2d lt. USMC, 1975, advanced through grades to capt., 1980; intern in family medicine Naval Hosp., Charleston, SC, 1987—88; flight surgeon 2d MAW, 1988—91; resident in aerospace medicine Naval Aerospace Med. Inst., Charleston, SC, 1992—94; sr. med. officer USS John C. Stennis (CVN 74), Norfolk, 1994—97; prof. Uniformed Svcs. U., Bethesda, 1997—2005; mem. Med. Exam. Review Bd. Dept. of Def., USAF Acad., Colo., 2005—07, dir. Med. Exam Review Bd., 2007—. Chair Am. Bd. Preventive Medicine, Chgo., 2003—07. Recipient Delta Omega Scholastic Honor Soc., Tulane U. Sch. of Pub. Health, 1992, Phi Kappa Phi Honor Soc., The Citadel, 1983. Fellow: Am. Coll. of Preventive Medicine, Aerospace Med. Assn. (v.p. 2001—03); mem.: Am. Bd. Preventive Medicine (chair). Methodist. Office: Dept of Def Med Exam Review Bd 8034 Edgerton Dr Ste 132 U S A F Academy CO 80840-2200 Personal E-mail: glenn.merchant@dodmerb.tma.osd.mil, pgmerchant@mac.com.

MERCHANT, ROLAND SAMUEL, SR., health facility administrator, educator; b. NYC, Apr. 18, 1929; s. Samuel and Eleta (McLymont) M.; m. Audrey Bartley, June 6, 1970; children: Orelia Eleta, Roland Samuel, Huey Bartley. BA, NYU, 1957, MA, 1960; MS, Columbia U., 1963, MSHA, 1974. Asst. statistician NYC Dept. Health, 1957-60, statistician, 1960-63, NY Tb and Health Assn., NYC, 1963-65; biostatistician, adminstrv. coord. Inst. Surg. Studies, Montefiore Hosp., Bronx, NY, 1965-72; resident in adminstrn. Roosevelt Hosp., NYC, 1973-74; dir. health and hosp. mgmt. Dept. Health, City of NY, 1974-76; from asst. adminstr. to adminstr. West Adams Cmty. Hosp., LA, 1976; spl. asst. to assoc. v.p. for med. affairs Stanford U. Hosp., Calif., 1977-82, dir. office mgmt. and strategic planning Calif., 1982-85, dir. mgmt. planning Calif., 1986-90; v.p. strategic planning Cedars-Sinai Med. Ctr., LA, 1990-94; cons. Roland Merchant & Assocs., LA, 1994—. Clin. assoc. prof. dept. family, cmty. and preventive medicine Stanford U., 1986—88; dept. health rsch. and policy Stanford U. Med. Sch., 1988—90. Author: Passion-Sustained Commitment to Excellence: Family-Oriented Parenting and Training, 2004. With US Army, 1951—53. Fellow, USPHS. Fellow: APHA, Am. Coll. Healthcare Execs.; mem.: NY Acad. Scis. Home: 27335 Park Vista Rd Agoura Hills CA 91301-3639 Office Phone: 818-879-8732.

MERCHANT, SUZY, women's college basketball coach; b. Dearborn, Mich., July 26, 1969; married; 1 child, Tyler. BA, Ctrl. Mich. U., 1991; MA in Edn., Saginaw Valley St. Asst. coach Oakland U., 1992—95; head coach Saginaw Valley State U., 1995—98, Ea. Mich. U., 1998—2007, interim assoc. athletics dir., sr. women's adminstr., 2005—06; head coach Mich.

State U., 2007—. Named Coach of Yr., Basketball Coaches Assn. Mich., 2004. Office: Mich State U Womens Basketball Berkowitz Complex Ste 110 East Lansing MI 48824 Office Phone: 517-353-8613. E-mail: msuwbbhoops@ath.msu.edu. *

MERCHENTHALER, ISTVAN JOZSEF, neuroscientist, morphologist; b. Baja, Hungary, Apr. 29, 1949; came to U.S., 1988; s. Istvan and Maria (Gomori) M.; m. Agnes Katalin Major, Nov. 6, 1969; children: Istvan, Boglarka, Nora. MD, U. Med. Sch., Pecs, Hungary, 1974; PhD, Hungarian Acad. Sci., Budapest, 1986; DsC, Hungarian Acad. Sci., 1992; Dr. Habil, Albert Szent-Gyorgyi Med. Sch., Szeged, Hungary, 1997. Asst. prof. dept. anatomy Univ. Med. Sch., Pecs, Hungary, 1974-86, assoc. prof., 1986-92; vis. asst. prof. dept. anatomy U. N.C., Chapel Hill, 1981-83; vis. asst. prof. Hebert Rsch. Ctr. Tulane U., New Orleans, 1984; vis. scientist, head, functional morphology sect. NIEHS/NIH, Research Triangle Park, NC, 1988—94; dir. functional morphology Women's Health Rsch. Inst. Wyeth Rsch., Collegeville, Pa., 1994—2004; prof. dept. epidemiology, preventive medicine U. Md. Sch. Medicine, Balt., 2004—. Adj. prof. dept. anatomy and neurosci.,U. N.C., 1991-94, U. Md. Sch. Medicine, Balt., 2004-05; adj. prof. dept. pathology Ohio State U., Columbia. Contbr. more than 170 articles on the distribution and function of hypothalamic hormones and estrogen receptors to profl. jours. and books. Recipient Lenhossek award Hungarian Assn. of Anatomists, 1984, Outstanding Young Scientist award Hungarian Acad. Scis., 1986. Achievements include mapping neuropeptides and estrogen receptors in the brain; elucidation of physiological significance of co-localization of neuropeptides; contribution to better understand estrogen action in brain in health and disease (stroke/ischemia). Office: Prof Dept Epidemiology Univ Md 10 S Pine St MSTF bldg 9-00F Baltimore MD 21201 Office Phone: 410-706-1350. Business E-Mail: imerchen@epi.umaryland.edu.

MERCIER, EILEEN ANN, pension fund chairman; b. Toronto, Ont., Can., July 7, 1947; d. Thomas Sidley and Frances Katherine (Boone) Falconer; m. Ernest Cochrane Mercier, Feb. 8, 1980 (dec.); children: Jenny, Sheelagh, Peter, Michael, Stuart. BA with honors, Waterloo Luth. U., 1968; MA, U. Alta., Can., 1969; fellow, Instn. Can. Bankers, 1975; MBA, York U., 1977. Mgr. corp. fin. Toronto-Dominion Bank, 1972-78, portfolio mgr. TD capital; dir., U.S. comm. ops. Canwest Capital Corp., Toronto, 1978-81; mgr. fin. strategy & planning Gulf Can. Ltd., Toronto, 1981-86, mgr. corp. fin.; v.p. The Pagurian Corp., Toronto, 1986-87; v.p., treas. Abitibi-Price, Inc., Toronto, 1987-88, v.p. corp. devel., 1989-90, sr. v.p., CFO, 1990-95. Bd. dirs. TeeKay Corp., The CGI Group Inc., ING Bank Can., ING Can., Inc.; chmn. Ont. Tchrs. Pension Plan. Past chmn., mem. bd. govs. Wilfrid Laurier U., Waterloo, Ont., York U. Recipient Outstanding Bus. Leader award Wilfrid Laurier U., 1991, Award for Outstanding Contbn. Schulich Sch. of Bus. York U., 1997. Office: 199 Cranbrooke Ave Toronto ON Canada M5M 1M6

MERCKER, MARY ALICE, aviation school administrator; b. Kansas City, Mo., June 29, 1932; d. Kenneth Foster Rhees and Catherine Mary Henel; m. Reid Martin, Nov. 23, 1950 (div. Nov. 1969); children: Reid J., Kenneth C., Mark T., Mary M., Theodore H., Sylvia R., Ben X., Teresa I. Student, Phoenix Coll., 1949-50; AA, Pima Coll., 1990-93; student, U. Ariz., 1994. Fed. aviation adminstr.; comml. pilot; cert. flight instr. Instr. Ariz. Sch. Aviation, Tucson, 1979, Tucson Cmdr., 1980, AVRA Flt. Ctr., Marana, Ariz., 1976-78; pres., founder Alpha Air, Inc., Tucson, 1980—; sec., treas. Manasco Inc., Tucson, 1987—. Aviation cons., Tucson, 1987—; adj. profl aviation Pima C.C., Tucson, 1988-94, curriculum cons., 1988-93. Author: Northumberland Dreaming, 1998, numerous poems. Recipient 2nd Place Sparrowgrass Poetry Forum, 1996, 1st Place Sparrowgrass Chapbook award, 2001. Mem. Ariz. Pilots Assn., Aircraft Owners and Pilots Assn., 99's (life). Home: 6220 W Belmont Rd Tucson AZ 85743-9212 Office: Alpha Air Inc HC 2 Box 282 Tucson AZ 85735-9709 Home Phone: 520-744-1696. Personal E-mail: alphair@msn.com.

MERCURI, JOAN B., museum administrator; b. NYC; BA, Va. Commonwealth U., 1984. Mgmt. positions various corps., Ill., 1986-96; exec. dir. Frank Lloyd Wright Home and Studio Found., Oak Park, Ill., 1996—; pres., CEO Frank Lloyd Wright Preservation Trust, Oak Park, 2000—. Dir. Oak Park Area Conv. and Vis. Bur. Mem. Am. Assn. Museums, Nat. Trust for Hist. Preservation, Employment Mgmt. Assn., Soc. Human Resource Mgmt., Frank Lloyd Wright Bldg. Conservancy, Assn. Fundraising Profls., Board Source. Office Phone: 708-848-1976. Business E-Mail: mercuri@wrightplus.org.

MERCURIO, RENARD MICHAEL, real estate company executive; b. NYC, June 22, 1947; s. Pasquale J. and Ann F. Mercurio; m. Abbie Gonzalez, June 29, 1968; children— Kristin, Allison. BA, Queens Coll., NYC, 1968; MBA, U. Rochester, 1969. CPA, N.Y.; lic. real estate broker, Calif. Sr. accountant Peat, Marwick & Mitchell, NYC, 1969-73; mgr. Gulf & Western Industries, Inc., NYC, 1973-78; v.p., treas. Famous Players Ltd., Toronto, Ont., Canada, 1978-81; exec. v.p. Famous Players Realty Ltd., Toronto, 1981-84; pres. Design Twenty-Seven Ltd., Toronto, 1984—; v.p. Renric Holdings, Ltd., 1987—; CFO Schickedanz Real Estate, Palm Beach Gardens, Fla., 1999—2003. Mem. AICPA, NY State Soc. CPAs. Personal E-mail: amercu6@aol.com.

MERDEK, ANDREW AUSTIN, publishing and media executive, lawyer; b. Portland, Maine, Oct. 11, 1950; s. Philip and Eleanor (Weiss) M.; m. Jeanne Mullen, July 22, 1983; children: David, Jonathan. AB magna cum laude, Middlebury Coll., 1972; JD, U. Va., 1978. Bar: D.C. 1978, U.S. Dist. Ct. D.C. 1979, U.S. Ct. Appeals (D.C. cir.) 1979, U.S. Supreme Ct. 1982. Reporter, editor Portland Press Herald, 1973-75; assoc. Dow, Lohnes & Albertson, Washington, 1978-86, ptnr., 1986-87; v.p., gen. mgr. Atlanta Constitution and Journal, 1987-92; v.p. legal affairs Cox Enterprises, Inc., Atlanta, 1993—, gen. counsel, 1993—, corp. sec., 1993—. Mem. Newspaper Assn. of Am. (chmn. legal affairs com.), Order of Coif, Phi Beta Kappa. Office: Cox Enterprises Inc 6205 Peachtree Dunwoody Rd Atlanta GA 30328 E-mail: andy.merdek@cox.com. *

MERDINGER, CHARLES JOHN, civil engineer, educator, military officer, academic administrator; b. Chgo., Apr. 20, 1918; s. Walter F. and Catherine (Phelan) M.; m. Mary McKelleget, Oct. 21, 1944; children: Anne, Joan, Susan, Jane. Student, Marquette U., 1935-37; BS, U.S. Naval Acad., 1941; BCE, Rensselaer Poly. Inst., 1945, MCE, 1946; DPhil (Rhodes scholar), Brasenose Coll., Oxford U., Eng., 1949; LHD (hon.), Sierra Nev. Coll., 1987; DLitt (hon.), U. Nev., Reno, 1994. Registered profl. engr., Wis. Commd. ensign USN, 1941, advanced through grades to capt. Civil Engr. Corps, 1959; served aboard USS Nevada, USS Alabama Atlantic and Pacific, 1941-44; design, constrn. pub. works Panama, 1946—47, Washington, Bremerion, Adak, Miramar, 1949—56; comdg. officer, dir. U.S. Naval Civil Engring. Lab., Port Hueneme, Calif., 1956-59; pub. works officer U.S. Fleet activities, Yokosuka, Japan, 1959-62; head English, history and govt. dept. U.S. Naval Acad., Annapolis, Md., 1962-65; asst. comdr. ops. & maintenance Naval Facilities Engring. Command, Navy Dept., 1965-67; pub. works officer Seabees (NSA), DaNang, Vietnam, 1967-68; comdg. officer Western div. Naval Facilities Engring. Command, San Bruno, Calif., 1968-70; pres. Washington Coll., Chestertown, Md., 1970-73; v.p. Aspen Inst. Humanistic Studies, Colo., 1973-74; dep. dir. Scripps Instn. Oceanography, La Jolla, Calif., 1974-80; dir. Avco, 1978—. Author: Civil Engineering Through the Ages, 1963; contbr.: articles to Ency. Britannica; others. Mem. Md., Calif., Oreg. and Nev. Selection Coms. for Rhodes Scholars, sec. Nev. Com., 1982-89; exec. vol. Boy Scouts Am.; sec., mem. exec. com. Md. Ind. Coll. and Univ. Assn., 1971-72; mem. So. Regional Edn. Bd, 1971-73, Nat. Com. History and Heritage of Am. Civil Engring., 1965-72; Alumni trustee U.S. Naval Acad., 1971-74; mem. coun. Rensselaer Poly. Inst., 1972—; trustee Found. for Ocean Rsch., 1976-80, Desert Rsch. Inst. Found., Nev., 1983-92, U. Nev. Reno Found., 1986-93; chmn. bd. trustees Sierra Nev. Coll., 1980-87, chmn. bd. emeritus, 1987; commr. N.W. Assn. Commn. on Colls., 1988-93. Pfc Wis. Nat. Guard, 1935—37. Decorated Legion of Merit with combat V; named All-Am. in lacrosse, 1945, Papal Knight Grand Cross Equestrian Order of Holy Sepulchre of Jerusalem, 1992; inducted into Rensselaer Athletic Hall of Fame, 1983; recipient Disting. Eagle Scout award, 1984. Fellow ASCE (Nat. History and Heritage award 1972), Explorers Club, Soc. Am. Mil. Engrs. (Toulmin medal 1952, 57, 61); mem. NSPE, Soc. History Tech., Am. Soc. Engring. Edn., Brasenose Soc., Pearl Harbor Survivors Assn., Nat. Eagle Scout Assn. (regent), Phalanx, Sigma Xi, Tau Beta Pi, Chi Epsilon. Clubs: Vincent's, Oxford. Roman Catholic. Home: 726 Tyner Way PO Box 7249 Incline Village NV 89452-7249

MEREDITH, DALE DEAN, civil engineering educator; b. Centralia, Ill., Mar. 24, 1940; s. Leslie Edward Meredith and Beulah Marie (McClelland) Nattier; m. Linda Jean Hutson, July 3, 1965; children: Sarah Elizabeth, Laura Jane. AA, Centralia Twp. Jr. Coll., 1961; BS, U. Ill., 1963, MS, 1964, PhD, 1968. Registered profl. engr., N.Y., Ill. Asst. prof. U. Ill., Urbana, 1968-73; assoc. prof. civil engring. SUNY, Buffalo, 1973-79, prof., 1979-2000, chmn. dept. civil engring., 1987-96, prof. emeritus, 2000—. Co-author: Design and Planning Engineering Systems, 1973, 2d edit., 1985; also over 50 articles. Vice pres. Baptist Conv. N.Y., Syracuse, 1982-84, 94-95, chmn. exec. bd., 1987. Grantee U.S. Office Water Research and Tech., 1966-73, 75-78, U.S. Dept. Interior, 1968-79, U.S. Dept. Commerce, 1976-79, various pvt. cos., 1979—, N.Y. State Agys., 1980-2000. Fellow ASCE (chmn. exec. com. Water Resources Planning and Mgmt. div., 1988, editor jour. Water Resources Planning and Mgmt. 1982-84); mem. Am. Geophys. Union, Am. Soc. Engring. Edn., Am. Water Resources Assn. (editor Water Resources Bull. 1990-91). Office: SUNY Dept Civil Engring Buffalo NY 14260-4300 E-mail: ciedale@eng.buffalo.edu.

MEREDITH, LISA ANN MARIE, social studies educator, consultant; b. Reading, Pa., May 2, 1969; d. Robert Lee and Carol Ann Meredith; life ptnr. Thomas J. Unrath. BA, Alvernia Coll., Reading, Pa., 1990—91. Cert. elem. sch. tchr. Commonwealth of Pa., 1991, mid. sch. tchr. Commonwealth of Pa., 2005. Tchr. Reading Sch. Dist., Pa., 1991—2003, Sch. Dist. Phila., 2001—; edn. coord. Nat. Constn. Ctr., Phila., 2003—04. Asst. coord. Ctr. for Civic Edn., Phila., 2003—04; cons. Pa. Gov.'s Inst. for Social Studies Educators, Harrisburg, 2004—. Mem. Champions for Caring, Phila., 2003—04; activist, rep. Reading Edn. Assn., Pa., 1998—2000; activist Phila. (Pa.) Citizens Children and Youth, 2002—03, Phila. Fedn. Tchrs., 2004—05. Grantee, Eisenhower Grants, 1995—96, Tchg. Am. History, 2002—03. Mem.: ASCD, Nat. Coun. Social Studies Tchrs. (assoc.), Phila. Fedn. Tchrs. (assoc.). Liberal. Lutheran. Avocations: history, travel, golf, reading. Office: Sch Dist Phila 238 E Wyoming Ave Philadelphia PA 19120 Office Phone: 215-456-3012. Business E-Mail: lameredith@phila.k12.pa.us.

MEREDITH, THOMAS J., communications, investment company executive; b. 1950; m. Lynn Maureen Mullen; 4 children. BA in Polit. Sci., St. Francis Coll., Loretto, Pa., 1972; JD, Duquesne U. Law, 1975; LLM in Taxation, Georgetown U., 1977; PhD (hon.), St. Francis, Duquesne U. Bus. Sch. Bar: Calif., DC, Pa. Dir. tax rsch. and planning Castle & Cooke, Inc.; sr. tax cons. Arthur Young & Co.; co-founder, gen. mgr. Amdahl Capital Corp., 1979—89; v.p., treas. Sun Microsystems, Inc., 1989—92; sr. v.p., CFO Dell Computer Corp., Round Rock, Tex., 1992—2000, sr. v.p., bus. devel & strategy, 2000—01; mng. dir. Dell Ventures, 2000—01; co-founder, gen. ptnr. Meritage Capital, L.P., 1998—; CEO MFI Capital; acting CFO Motorola, Inc., Schaumburg, Ill., 2007—. Bd. dir. Freemarkets, Inc., Divine, Inc., VoxPath Networks, Tipping Point, 2001—, Motive, Inc., 2003—, Motorola, Inc., 2005—; adj. prof., McCombs Sch. Business Univ. Texas; adv. bd. Wharton Sch., U. Pa., U. Tex., adj. prof., McCombs Sch. Bus. Chair, pres. Meredith Private Found., 1998—; founding investor & chair Austin Idea Network. Mem.: Fin. Execs. Inst. Office: Motorola Inc 1303 E Algonquin Rd Schaumburg IL 60196

MEREDITH, WENDI SUE, music educator; d. Dennis Wayne and L Imogene Meredith. BS in Elem. Edn., Bapt. Bible Coll., 1992, BA in Ch. Music, 1997; MusM, SW Mo. State U., 2001. Level 1 Orff Schulwerk Certification Am. Orff Schulwerk Assn., 1999, Improving Strategies in Tchg.AQA GCSE Music Specification Keynote Ednl., 2004, Form Tutors: Role, Skills and Responsibilities Lighthouse Profl. Devel., 2004. English, music tchr. Quint City Bapt. Sch., Davenport, Iowa, 1992—95; prof. voice Bapt. Bible Coll., Springfield, Mo., 1997—2004; tchr. music Egerton Rothesay Sch., Berkhamsted, Hertfordshire, England, 2004—06, peripatatic singing tchr., 2005—, head music, 2006—, coord. musical events, 2006—. Traveling recruiter Bapt. Bible Coll., Springfield, Mo., 1990—92, 1995—2001, coord. traveling recruitment teams, 1999—2001, co-writer, co-producer of drama, 1998—99; soprano Cmty. Choir SW Mo. State U., Springfield, 1998—2003; coord. program for woman's conf. Cherry St. Bapt. Ch., Springfield, 2000—04, dir. woman's conf., 2003—04; children's and musical dir. Bible Bapt. Ch., Wendover, Buckinghamshire, England, 2003—, worship leader, 2004—, vocal instr., Resonant Praise, 2007; mem. chorus Springfield Regional Opera/Messiah Project, 2003—03; soprano Cmty. Choir Bapt. Bible Coll., Springfield, 2003—04; spkr. in field. Composer: (song) For Such a Time as This. Choir dir. Voices of St. Francis concert Egerton Rothesay Sch., 2006; singing team leader for youth camp and youth events Bapt. Bible Fellowship Internat., Springfield, Mo., 1995—2002; children's choir tchr. Cherry St. Bapt. Ch., Springfield, Mo., 1995—2004; christian sch. tchr. Quint City Bapt. Ch., Davenport, Iowa, 1992—95; music coord. youth event, Berkhamsted, 2006—07; music coord., leader LIFE Camp, Tonbridge, Kent, England, 2006—07. Civilian day camp worker US Army, 1990—93, Rock Island Illinois. Mem.: Nat. Trust, Nat. Union Tchrs., Gospel Music Assn., Am. Orff Schulwerk Assn. Home Phone: 01296395737.

MERENDINO, K. ALVIN, surgeon, educator; b. Clarksburg, W.Va., Dec. 3, 1914; s. Biagio and Cira (Bivona) M.; m. Shirley Emma Jane Hill, July 6, 1943; children: Cira Anne Watts, Nancy Jane Napuunoa, Susan Hill Mitchell, Nina, Maria King Merendino-Stillwell. BA summa cum laude, Ohio U., 1936, LLD (hon.), 1967; MD, Yale U., New Haven, Conn., 1940; PhD, U. Minn., 1946. Diplomate Am. Bd. Surgery, Am. Bd. Thoracic Surgery. Intern Cin. Gen. Hosp., 1940-41; resident U. Minn. Hosp., Mpls., 1941-45; rsch. asst. Dr. Owen H. Wangensteen, 1942-43; trainee Nat. Cancer Inst., 1943-45; dir. program in postgrad. med. edn. in surgery Ancker Hosp., St. Paul, 1946-48; instr. dept. surgery U. Minn., Mpls., 1944-45, asst. prof. dept. surgery, 1945-48; assoc. prof. dept. surgery U. Wash., Seattle, 1949-55, dir. exptl. surgery labs., dept. surgery, 1950-72, prof. dept. surgery, 1955-81, prof. emeritus, 1981—, prof. and adminstrv. officer dept. surgery, 1957-64, prof., chmn., 1964-72; chmn. dept. surgery King Faisal Specialist and Rsch. Ctgr., Riyadh, Saudi Arabia, 1976, dir. med. affairs, 1976-79, dir. Cancer Therapy Inst., spl. cons. to Coun., supr. for exec. mgmt., assoc. dir. med. affairs, 1981-82; dir. ops. King Faisal Med. City, Riyadh, 1981-85. Mem. adv. com. for med. rsch., Boeing Airplane Co., 1959-67, chmn., 1962l cons. Children's Orthopedic Hosp., Seattle, 1972-82; mem. adv. com. on heart disease and surgery for crippled children's svc., Wash. State Dept. Health and Div. Vocational Rehab., 1961; mem. surgery study sect. NIH, 1958-62, subcom. on prosthetic valves for cardiac surgery, chm. 1st Nat. Conf., 1960, mem. adv. com. 2d Nat. Conf. on Prosthetic Heart Valves, 1969, Surgery A study sect. chmn., 1970-72, Nat. Heart and Lung Inst. Tng. Com., 1965-69; cons. VA, Seattle, 1949-59, 65-81; mem. adv. com. on hosps. and clinics, USPHS, 1963-66; mem. surgery test com. Nat. Bd. Med. Examiners, 1963-67; mem. surgery resident rev. com., Conf. Com. on Grad. Edn. in Surgery, 1963-73, vice-chmn., 1972-73; chmn. 2d Saudi Arabian Med. Conf., Riyadh, 1978; mem. com. on postgrad. med. edn., Kingdom of Saudi Arabia Ministry of Health, 1978-79; vis. prof. established open heart surgery program Malaysia U. Hosp., Kuala Lumpur, 1971, edn. and tng. jr. faculty (surg. residents) faculty medicine U. Saigon and Mil. M.C. (army surgeons) Binh Dan Hosp. Saigon, Vietnam. Editor in chief: Prosthetic Valves for Cardiac Surgery, 1961; assoc. editor: Prosthetic Heart Valves, 1969; mem. editorial bd. Am. Jour. Surgery, 1958-83, Jour. Surg. Rsch., 1961-69, Pacific Medicine and Surgery, 1964-68, King Faisal Hosp. Medicine Jour. (renamed Annals of Saudi Medicine), 1981-85; contbr. articles to profl. jours., chpts. to books; producer movies on surgery. Recipient cert. of merit Ohio U. Alumni Assn., 1957, Outstanding W.Va. Italian-Am. award W.Va. Italian Heritage Festival Inc., Clarksburg, W.Va., 1984, Spirit of Freedom award A. James Mancin, Sec. State W.Va., 1984, Disting. W. Virginian award Gov. John D. Rockefeller IV., State of W.Va., 1984, John Baird Thomas Meml. award Ohio U.; named Surgery Alumnus of Yr., U. Minn., 1981, Disting. Citizen Wash. State, Lt. Gov. John Cherberg, 1981, K. Alvin Merendino Day Seattle, Mayor Charles Royer, 1981; NIH grantee, 1951-76; Verdi scholar Yale U. Fellow ACS (numerous coms., bds.), Soc. of Univ. Surgeons (councilman at large 3 yrs.), Internat. Soc. Surgery; mem. Am. Surg. Assn. (adv. mem. com. 1959-64, v.p. 1972-73), Am. Assn. for Thoracic Surgery, Halsted Soc., Henry N. Harkins Surg. Soc., N. Pacific Coast Surg. Assn., Seattle Surg. Soc. (honored special tribute annual meeting 1997), So. Surg. Soc. (Arthur H. Shipley award 1972), Am. Bd. Surgery 1958-64 (vice chmn. 1962-63, chmn. 1963-64, emeritus 1964—); University Club, Seattle Golf Club, Phi Beta Kappa, Sigma Xi, Beta Theta Pi (sec., pres.), Phi Beta Pi (hon.). Republican. Episcopalian. Avocations: golf, fly fishing, bird hunting, gardening. Home: The Highlands Shoreline WA 98177 Personal E-mail: k.merendinomd@comcast.net.

MEREY, JOHN HOWARD, ophthalmologist; s. ERnest Ernd and Ernestine Ily Merey; m. Daisy Breuer, Dec. 26, 1967; children: Deanne, Andrew. BA, Union Coll., Schenectady, NY, 1961; MD, Columbia U., NYC, 1965. Diplomate Am. Bd. Ophthalmology. Resident NYU Med. Ctr., NY, 1966—70; pvt. practice West Palm Beach, Fla., 1971—. Recipient Gala Honor, Israel Cancer Assn., 2003. Fellow: ACS, Am. Acad. Ophthalmology. Office: 5405 Okeechobee Blvd # 302B West Palm Beach FL 33417 Office Phone: 561-686-8202.

MERGENTHALER, FRANK, corporate financial executive; BS, Providence Coll. CPA. Acctg. positions Price Waterhouse, 1983—96; asst., treas., corp. contr. to sr. v.p. fin. Seagram, 1996—2001; sr. v.p., dep. CFO Vivendi Universal, 2001—02; exec. v.p., CFO Columbia House Co., 2002—05, Interpublic Group of Companies, NYC, 2005—. Mem.: AICPA, Fin. Executives Inst., NY State Soc CPAs. Office: Interpublic Group 1114 Ave of the Americas New York NY 10036 *

MERGES, ROBERT PATRICK, law educator, writer; BS, Carnegie-Mellon U., 1981; JD, Yale Law Sch., 1985; LLM, JSD, Columbia Law Sch., 1988. Assoc. prof. Boston U. Sch. Law, 1988—92, prof., 1992—95; prof. law Boalt Hall Sch. Law, U. Calif., Berkeley, 1995—97, co-dir. Berkeley Ctr. Law and Tech., 1997—, Wilson Sonsini Goodrich & Rosati Prof. Intellectual Property Law, 1997—. Vis. prof. U. Calif., Davis Sch. Law, 2002—03; spl. cons. U.S. Dept. Justice; mem. U.S. Dept. Justice Task Force on Intellectual Property. Co-author: Patent Law and Policy: Cases and Materials, Legal Protection for Computer Technology, Intellectual Property in the New Technological Age, 2003, Foundations of Intellectual Property, 2004; contbr. articles to law jours. Grantee Alfred P. Sloan Foundation Grant, 1989—90, Office of Tech. Assessment Contract Rsch. Award, 1993, Sloan Foundation, 1994—, Dept. of Energy grant, 1998. Office: U Calif Sch Law Boalt Hall Berkeley CA 94720 E-mail: rmerges@law.berkeley.edu.

MERGLER, H. KENT, investment counselor; b. Cin., July 1, 1940; s. Wilton Henry and Mildred Amelia (Pulliam) M.; m. Judith Anne Metzger, Aug. 17, 1963; children: Stephen Kent, Timothy Alan, Kristin Lee. BBA with honors, U. Cin., 1963, MBA, 1964. CFA, C.I.C. Portfolio mgr. Scudder, Stevens & Clark, Cin., 1964-68, exec. v.p. Chgo., 1970-73; v.p. Gibralter Rsch. & Mgmt., Ft. Lauderdale, Fla., 1968-70; ptnr. Stein Roe & Farnham, Ft. Lauderdale, 1973-84; ptnr., pres., dir., prin., mem. exec. com. Stein Roe & Farnham, Inc., Chgo., 1984-91; pres. Stein Roe Investment Trust, 1988—91; mng. ptnr., chief investment officer Loomis, Sayles & Co., L.P., Palm Beach Gardens, Fla., 1992-2000; pres. Northstar Capital Mgmt., Inc., 2002—04, chmn., 2005—. Arbitrator Nat. Assn. Security Dealers, Inc., 1976-82. Chmn. adminstrv. bd. Christ United Meth. Ch., Ft. Lauderdale, 1981—83; mem. fin. com. Kenilworth Union Ch., 1989—92; elder, chmn. fin. com. First Presbyn. Ch., Stuart, 2001—04, 2006—; chmn. Presbytery of Tropical Fla.-Coral Gables Trust Fund, 2006—; chmn. investment com. Cmty. Found. Broward, 1992—2001, bd. dirs., chmn. investment com., 1994—2001; mem. Martin County Econ. Coun., 1992—2000; bd. dirs. Pine Crest Prep. Sch., 1982—84, bd. advisors, 1984—87; corp. adv. bd. U. Cin. Coll. Bus. Adminstrn., 1991—94; bd. dirs. Hibiscus House Children's Found., 1993—99, 2001—, chmn. investment, endowment com., 1994—99, 2001—. Mem. Fin. Analysts Soc. So. Fla. (bd. dirs. 1974-78, pres. 1975), Bond Club Ft. Lauderdale (bd. dirs. 1978-82), Cullasaja Club (Highlands, N.C.), Mariner Sands Golf Club, Beta Gamma Sigma, Beta Theta Pi. Republican. Presbyterian. Home: 6306 SE Oakmont Pl Stuart FL 34997 Office: 3801 PGA Blvd Ste 904 Palm Beach Gardens FL 33410 Office Phone: 561-775-5880.

MERGLER, NANCY L., academic administrator; BA in Psychology, Syracuse U., 1972, MA in Developmental Psychology, 1975, PhD in Developmental Psychology, 1977. Tchg. asst. dept. psychology Syracuse U., 1973—75; asst. prof. dept. psychology Washington Coll., 1976—79, asst. prof., 1979—83, assoc. prof. dept. psychology, 1984—94; prof. dept. psychology U. Okla., 1995—, interim sr. v.p., provost Norman, Okla., 1995—96, sr. v.p., provost, 1996—. Dir., honor program U. Okla., 1987—96. Contbr. articles to profl. jours. Syracuse U. Fellow, 1975—76. Mem.: APA, Md. Consortium for Gerontology in Higher Edn., Okla. Psychol. Assn., Southwestern Psychol. Assn., Ea. Psychol. Assn., Gerontol. Soc., Big 12 Provosts, Phi Kappa Phi. Office: Provosts Office 104 Evans Hall Univ Okla Norman OK 73019-0390 Office Phone: 405-325-3221. Office Fax: 405-325-7470. Business E-Mail: nmergler@ou.edu. *

MERIAM, THOMAS C., lawyer; b. Oceanside, NY, Aug. 3, 1951; BA, Coll. Holy Cross, 1973; JD cum laude, Fordham U., 1976. Bar: NY 1977. Ptnr. Chadbourne & Parke LLP, NYC, 1988—, chmn., Bank Fin. Practice Group. Contbr. articles to profl. jour. Mem.: ABA, NY State Bar Assn. Office: Chadbourne & Parke LLP 30 Rockefeller Plz Fl 31 New York NY 10112-0129 Office Phone: 212-408-5355. Office Fax: 212-541-5369. Business E-Mail: tmeriam@chadbourne.com.

MERIDEN, TERRY, physician; b. Damascus, Syria, Oct. 12, 1946; arrived in U.S., 1975; s. Izzat and Omayma (Aidi) Meriden; m. Lena Kahal, Nov. 17, 1975; children: Zina, Lana. BS, Sch. Sci., Damascus, 1968; MD, Sch. Medicine, Damascus, 1972, doctorate cum laude, 1973. Diplomate Am. Bd. Internal Medicine. Resident in infectious diseases Rush Green Hosp., Romford, Eng., 1973; house officer in internal medicine and cardiology Ashford Group Univ. Hosps., England, 1973-74; sr. house officer in internal medicine and neurology Grimsby Group Univ. Hosps., England, 1974; registrar in internal medicine and rheumatology St. Annes Hosp., London, 1974-75; jr. resident in internal medicine Shadyside Hosp., Pitts., 1975-76, sr. resident in internal medicine, 1976-77; fellow in endocrinology and metabolism Shadyside Hosp. and Grad. Inst., Pitts.,

1976-77; clin. asst. prof. U. Ill., Peoria, 1979; pres. Am. Diabetes Assn., Peoria, 1982-84; dir. Proctor Diabetes Unit, Peoria, 1984—, 1984—. Adviser Gov. of Ill. on diabetes. Mem. editl. bd. Diabetes Forecast mag., Clin. Diabetes, 1990; contbr. articles to profl. jours. Fellow: ACP, Am. Coll. Endocrinology; mem.: ADA (chmn. profl. edn. and rsch. 1980—, mem. editl. bd., mem. Spanish lit. bd., nat. bd. dirs. 1986—, vice chmn. nat. com. on diabetes edn. and affiliate svcs. 1986—, Outstanding Svc. award 1984, Outstanding Diabetes Educator award 1986), AMA (Recognition award 1985), Am. Coll. Endocrinology, Am. Assn. Clin. Endocrinology (founding), Am. Cancer Soc. (Life Line award 1983), Obesity Found. (Century award 1984, Recognition award 1985). Home: 115 E Coventry Ln Peoria IL 61614-2103 Office: 900 Main St Ste 300 Peoria IL 61602-1049 Home Phone: 309-673-1616; Office Phone: 309-673-1717. Business E-Mail: tmeriden@aol.com.

MERIDETH, SUSAN CAROL, business administration educator; b. St. Louis, May 25, 1956; d. George Getzel Brody and Jacquie Jean Lammers; m. John Wolf Merideth, July 28, 1979; children: Laura, Michelle. AAS, St. Louis C.C., 1977; BS, Fontbonne U., 1979; Master of Bus. Adminstrn., Maryville U., 1994; PhD, Capella U., 2007. Presch. tchr. various instns., San Diego, 1979—82, Greater San Diego Health Plan, San Diego, 1985—87; supr. Cmty. Care Network, San Diego, 1987—90; mgr. St. John's Mercy Med. Ctr., St. Louis, 1990—95; contracts mgr. Nashua Eye Assocs., Nashua, 1996—98; practice mgr. Found. Med. Ptnrs., Nashua, 1998—99; assoc. prof. bus. adminstrn. Hesser Coll., Manchester, NH, 2000—. Adj. prof. NHCTC, 2006—. Mem.: AAUP, Nat. Bus. Edn. Assn., Alpha Chi. Office: Hesser Coll 3 Sundial Ave Manchester NH 03103

MERIDOR, SALLAI, ambassador; BA, Hebrew U. Policy advisor to min. fgn. affairs State of Israel, 1988—90, advisor to min. def., 1990—92; head settlement divsn. World Zionist Orgn., 1992—97, treas., 1998—99, chmn., 1999—2005; treas. Jewish Agy. for Israel, 1998—99, chmn., 1999—2005; amb. to U.S., 2006—. Office: Israeli Embassy 3514 International Dr NW Washington DC 20008 Office Phone: 202-364-5590. Office Fax: 202-364-5607.

MERIDY, HOWARD WILLIAM, rabbi, anesthesiologist; b. Hartford, Conn., July 11, 1940; s. Saul I. and Ethel O. Meridy; m. Sandra Perler Meridy; children: Pamela, Laura Meridy Heidman. BA cum laude, U. Vt., Burlington, 1962, MD cum laude, 1966; MS in Mgmt., Rensselaer Poly., Hartford, 1993; MS in Jewish Studies, Spertus Coll., Chgo., 2007. Diplomate Am. Bd. Anesthesiology; ordained Rabbi 2003. Attending anesthesiologist Hartford Hosp., 1973—83, Charlotte Hungerford Hosp., Torrington, Conn., 1983—90, dir. med. affairs, 1990—95; v.p. med. affairs St. Johns Regional Med. Ctr., Joplin, Mo., 1995—97, Bethesda Meml. Hosp., Boynton Beach, Fla., 1997—99; chaplain Vitas Innovative Hospice, Ft. Lauderdale, Fla., 2002—. Maj. US Army, 1971—73, Ft. Lee, Va. Mem.: Alpha Omega Alpha, Sigma Xi, Phi Bata Kappa. Office: Rabbi Howard Meridy PO Box 740757 Boynton Beach FL 33474-0757 Office Phone: 561-704-5334.

MERINI, RAFIKA, humanities educator, writer, language educator; b. Morocco; arrived in U.S., 1972; d. Mohamed M. and Fatima Merini. BA in English cum laude, U. Utah, 1978, MA in Romance Langs. and Lits., 1981; postgrad., U. Wash., 1980-82; cert. in translation, SUNY, Binghamton, 1988, PhD in Comparative Lit., 1992. Tchg. asst. U. Utah, Salt Lake City, 1978-80, U. Wash., Seattle, 1980-82; adminstrv. asst., tchr. French, interpreter Internat. Lang. Sch., Seattle, 1982—83; lectr. Pacific Luth. U., Tacoma, 1983; instr. French and Spanish Ft. Steilacoom C.C. (now Pierce C.C.), 1983—85; tchg. asst. dept. romance langs. SUNY, Binghamton, 1985-87, tchg. asst. women's studies dept., 1988, tchg. asst. comparative lit. dept., 1986-88; vis. instr. humanities and French Union Coll., Schenectady, NY, 1988—89; vis. instr. dept. fgn. langs. and lits. Skidmore Coll., Saratoga Springs, NY, 1989-90; asst. prof. dept. modern and classical langs. State U. Coll., Buffalo, 1990—96, assoc. prof. dept. modern and classical langs., 1996—. Coord. Buffalo State Coll. women's studies interdisciplinary unit State U. Coll., Buffalo, 1993-99, adviser French Club, 1990-93; sponsor, founder, dir. Trois-Pistoles French Immersion Program, U. Western Ont.-Buffalo State Coll.1994, 95; presenter, spkr., conf. organizer in field. Author: Two Major Francophone Women Writers, Assia Djébar and Leïla Sebbar: A Thematic Study of Their Works, 1999, 2d printing, paperback edit., 2001; mem. editl. bd. Jour. Middle Eastern and North African Intellectual and Cultural Studies; contbr. articles to profl. jours Grantee Nat. Defense Student award U. Utah, 1974; also numerous other grants and awards. Mem. MLA, Pi Delta Phi. Achievements include being interviewed on Radio-Canada. Office: State Univ Coll-Buffalo Modern & Classical Langs 1300 Elmwood Ave Buffalo NY 14222-1095 Home: PO Box 1063 Buffalo NY 14213-1063

MERIWETHER, HEATH J., newspaper consultant, retired publisher, educator; b. Columbia, Mo., Jan. 20, 1944; s. Nelson Heath and Mary Agnes (Immele) Meriwether; m. Patricia Hughes, May 4, 1979; children: Graham, Elizabeth. BA in History, BJ, U. Mo., 1966; MAT, Harvard U., 1967; Advanced Exec. Program, Northwestern U. Journalism fellow Stanford U.; reporter Miami (Fla.) Herald, 1970—72, editor Broward and Palm Beach burs., 1972—77, exec. city editor, 1977—79, asst. mgr. editor news, 1979—80, mng. editor, 1981—83, exec. editor, 1983—87, Detroit Free Press, 1987—95, pub., 1996—2004; newspaper cons., 2004—. Adj. prof. grad. sch. journalism City U. NY, 2006—. Chair Rails to Trails Conservancy, 2005—07. Lt. USNR, 1967—70. Office Phone: 646-758-7824. Personal E-mail: hjm4491@yahoo.com.

MERK, FREDERICK BANNISTER, biomedical educator, researcher; b. Cambridge, Mass., Feb. 21, 1936; s. Frederick and Lois Alberta (Bannister) M.; m. Linda Jean Poole, Oct. 22, 1966 (dec. Dec. 1994); children: John F., R. Daniel; m. Laura Ann Bradford, July 11, 1998; 1 stepchild, Letty A. Bradford. AB, Harvard Coll., 1958; PhD, Boston U., 1971. Asst. prof. pathology Boston U. Sch. Medicine, 1972-73; assoc. prof. dept. pathology Tufts U. Sch. Medicine, Boston, 1973—2002, assoc. prof. dept. anatomy, 1973—2002, emeritus prof. pathology and anatomy, 2002—, part time tchr. anatomy, 2002—, dir. electron microscopy facility, 1975-85. Cons. electron microscopy Mass. Gen. Hosp., Boston, 1964-85; cons. toxicol. testing Transgenic Scis., Worcester, Mass., 1988-91, U.S. Army, 1998-2001. Contbr. more than 60 articles to profl. jours. Trustee Broadway United Meth. Ch., Lynn, Mass., chmn. 1994-2000; lay rep. Grace United Meth. Ch. to ann. New Eng. Conf., 2000—; trustee Frederick and Paula Anna Markus Found., Audubon Soc., Moultonboro, NH, 2005—. Recipient Disting. Career in Tchr. award, 2002; grantee, NIH, 1994—98. Mem. Am. Soc. Cell Biology, Fedn. Am. Soc. Exptl. Biology, Am. Assn. Anatomists, Microscopy Soc. Am., Boston Cancer Rsch. Assn., Sigma Xi. Achievements include research on biology of cells in target organs responding to hormones with emphasis on benign prostatic hypertrophy (enlargement) and prostate cancer. Avocations: gardening, photography, swimming, scuba diving. Home: 28 Warwick Rd Melrose MA 02176 Office: Tufts Univ Sch Medicine Dept Anatomy 136 Harrison Ave Boston MA 02111-1800 Personal E-mail: fmerk@hotmail.com.

MERK, P. EVELYN, retired librarian; b. Macon, Ga., Dec. 8, 1943; d. Charlie B. and Gladys (Perry) M. BA, Mercer U., 1966; MEd, U. Ga., 1973; MLS, Emory U., 1987. Tchr. East Laurens HS, Dublin, Ga., 1966-68, Westside Sch., McDonough, Ga., 1968-70, Brantley County HS, Nahunta, Ga., 1970-72; sch. media specialist Mary Persons Sch., Forsyth, Ga., 1973-75; tech. services libr. Houston County Pub. Libr., Warner Robins, Ga., 1975-76, reference libr., 1976-77, libr., 1977—96, asst. dir., 1996—2002, libr. cons., trainer, 2002—06; ret., 2007. Bd. dirs. Warner Robins Day Care Ctr. Inc., chmn. 1984-85, 91. Mem. ALA, AAUW, Southeastern Library Assn., Ga. Library Assn., Warner Robins Pioneers. Avocations: reading, candle making, travel. Home: 293 Peachtree Cir Warner Robins GA 31088-4448 Personal E-mail: evelynmerk@aol.com.

MERKEL, PATRICIA MAE, retired school system administrator; b. Spokane, Wash., June 18, 1935; d. Hugo Oscar and Mary Jane (Blackwelder) Koenig; m. Gordon Henry, Nov. 10, 1956 (div. 1973); children: Katherine Marie Merkel Fisk, Karol Ann Merkel Korte, John Henry. BA cum laude, Ea. Washington U., 1989. Cert. ednl. office employee. Acctg. clk. Pacific N.W. Bell, Spokane, 1954-56; book-keeper Edwall (Wash.) Sch. Dist., 1969-75, Reardan (Wash.)-Edwall Sch. Dist., 1975-78, bus. mgr., 1978-82; asst. to supr. fin. Dayton (Wash.) Sch. Dist., 1982-99. Mem. Town of Reardan Planning Commn., 1977-82, sec., 1978-82; treas. Citizens for Edn. Com., Dayton, 1983-91, Columbia County Courthouse Restoration Project, Dayton, 1988-99; fin. adv. com. Dayton Gen. Hosp., 1986-90, Dayton City Coun., 1986-87; vocat. bus. adv. com. Dayton HS, 1990-96. Recipient Mary Shields Wilson Medallion award; George F. Hixson fellow, 2005. Mem. AAUW, Wash. Assn. Ednl. Office Profls. (treas. 1984-86, pres.-elect 1986-87, pres. 1987-88, Ednl. Office Profl. of Yr. award 1990), Nat. Assn. Ednl. Office Profls. (Ednl. Office Profl. of Yr. award 1990), Assn. Assn. Sch. Bus. Ofcls. (chmn. com. 1978-81), S.C. Assn. Ednl. Office Profls. (pres. 1991-92), Blue Mountain Assn. Ednl. Office Profls., Assn. Sch. Bus. Ofcls. Internat. (com. 1984-86, scholar 1987), Order of Eagles, Kiwanis (sec. 1991-99, pres.-elect Tri Cities 2002-03, pres. 2003-04, Kiwaniain of Yr. 1993, 99, George F. Hixson award 2006). Democrat. Methodist. Avocations: reading, quilting, needle work, doll and bear making. Home: 3324 W 19th Ave Trlr 102 Kennewick WA 99338-2292 Personal E-mail: patmmerkel@aol.com.

MERKEL-MORAN, CHRISTA ILSE, investor, linguist, educator; b. Leipzig, Saxony, Germany, Jan. 5, 1946; arrived in US, 1968; d. Erich Harry and Ilse Dora (Waehnert) Merkel; m. William Joseph Moran, May 5, 1967 (dec. Mar. 4, 1979); children: Leslie Paige, Linda Christa. BA, U. Tuebingen, 1968; postgrad., U. Alaska, 1968—69. German linguistics. Clk. Anchorage Westward Hotel, 1969—71; sales mgr. Windsor Park Hotel, Washington, 1971—75; linguist, instr. Def. Lang. Inst., Dept. Def., Washington, 1975—79; investor in real estate, sports cars Atlanta, 1979—. Real estate agt., Northside Realty Co., Atlanta, 1992—. Author: Die Millie Miglia, 1969; Der Nuerburgring, 1975; German Culture, 1977. Chairperson for a United Germany Com., Washington, Atlanta, Leipzig chpt.; fundraiser UNICEF. Named Sportswriter of Yr., ADAC of Germany, 1977. Democrat. Home: PO Box 34165 Pensacola FL 32507-4165 Office: Buckhead Brokers 5395 Roswell Rd NE Atlanta GA 30342-1976 Office Phone: 850-492-0025. Personal E-mail: forsy564@bellsouth.net, christamoran@bellsouth.net.

MERKEN, LEO, lawyer; b. Paris, Feb. 14, 1964; arrived in US, 1982; m. Euginia Chen, Nov. 9, 1990; children: Madeleine Chen, Daniel Chen. BA, Occidental Coll., 1985; BS, Calif. Inst. Tech., 1987; MS, U. Calif., Berkeley, 1988; JD, Columbia U., 1995. Bar: U.S. Patent and Trademark Office 1997. Mem. tech. staff, cognizant engr. Jet Propulsion Lab. NASA, Pasadena, Calif., 1989—92; assoc., ptnr. Pennie & Edmonds LLP, NYC, 1995—2003; ptnr. Jones Day, NYC, 2004—. Harlan Fiske Stone scholar, Columbia U. Law Sch., 1995. Mem.: ABA, N.Y. Intellectual Property Law Assn., Am. Intellectual Property Law Assn., Caltech Alumni Assn. (life), Jones Day N.Y. Ice Hockey Club. Achievements include contributions to the launch and flight operations on the Galileo spacecraft mission. Avocations: travel, ice hockey, soccer. Office: Jones Day 3 Park Plz Irvine CA 92614 Office Phone: 949-851-3939. Business E-Mail: leo.merken@jonesday.com.

MERKER, STEVEN JOSEPH, lawyer; b. Cleve., Feb. 21, 1947; s. Steven Joseph and Laverne (Zamenik) Merker; m. Janet L. Whyatt; children: Steven, Rena, Ashley, Matthew. BS, Case Inst. Tech., 1968; MS, U. Fla., 1973; JD, George Washington U., 1976. Bar: Ohio 1976, U.S. Dist. Ct. (no. dist.) Ohio 1976, U.S. Dist. Ct. Colo. 1979, U.S. Ct. Appeals (10th cir.) 1979, U.S. Supreme Ct. 1989, U.S. Patent & Trademark Office. Assoc. Jones, Day, Reavis & Pogue, Cleve., 1976-78, Davis, Graham & Stubbs, Denver, 1978-82, ptnr., 1983-96, chmn. labor and employment group, 1989-96; chmn. litig., labor and employment groups Merrick, Calvin & Merker, LLP, 1996-97; ptnr. Dorsey & Whitney LLP, Denver, 1997—, mng. ptnr. Denver office, 2000—. Mem. Tenth Cir. Adv. Com., 1997—2000. Bd. dirs. Very Spl. Arts, Colo., 1994—, Am. Liver Found., 2002—; legal counsel Coloradans for Lamm-Dick campaign, Denver, 1982, Nancy Dick for U.S. Senate Com., Denver, 1984, Cantrell for Dist. Atty., Jefferson County, Colo., 1984. Capt. USAF, 1969—72. Mem.: ABA, Denver Bar Assn., Colo. Bar Assn. Office: Dorsey & Whitney LLP 370 17th St Ste 4700 Denver CO 80202-5644 Office Phone: 303-628-1514. Business E-Mail: merker.steve@dorsey.com.

MERKERSON, S. EPATHA, actress; b. Saginaw, Mich., Nov. 28, 1952; m. Toussaint L. Jones, Mar. 1994 (div. Feb. 14, 2006). BFA, Wayne State U. Broadway and Off-Broadway productions include The Piano Lesson, I'm Not Stupid (Obie award 1992), The Old Settler, Birdie Blue, 2005 (OBIE award Village Voice 2006); appeared in films including Terminator II, Jacob's Ladder, Navy Seals, Loose Cannons, Random Hearts, 1999, The Rising Place, 2001, Radio, 2003, Jersey Girl, 2004, Black Snake Moan, 2006; television guest appearances include The Cosby Show, Equal Justice, Elysian Fields, Moe's World; television series roles include Pee Wee's Playhouse, Mann & Machine, Here & Now, Law & Order (Outstanding Supporting Actress in a Drama Series, NAACP Image award, 2006), A Place for Annie, 1994, A Mother's Prayer, 1995, Breaking Through, 1996, An Unexpected Life, 1998, Exiled, 1998, Lackawanna Blues, 2005 (Emmy award for outstanding lead actress in a miniseries or a movie, 2005, best performance by an actress in a mini-series or motion picture made for television, Hollywood Fgn. Press Assn. (Golden Globe award), 2006, outstanding performance by an female actor in a TV movie or miniseries, Screen Actors Guild award, 2006, Outstanding Actress in a TV Movie, Mini-Series, or Dramatic Spl., NAACP Image awards, 2006). Nominated for Tony award, 1990, Drama Desk award, 1990, Helen Hayes award, 1990, L.A. Theater Critics award, 1990. Office: Law & Order c/o Universal Television 100 Universal City Plz Universal City CA 91608-1002 *

MERKIN, ALBERT CHARLES, pediatrician, allergist; b. Chgo., Sept. 4, 1924; s. Harry A. and Goldie (Lamasky) M.; m. Eunice Aprill, Aug. 22, 1948; children: Audrey, Ellen, Joseph. Student, U. Ill., 1942-44; MD, U. Ill., Chgo., 1949. Diplomate Am. Bd. Allergy and Immunology, Am. Bd. Pediat. Intern, resident Cook County Hosp., Chgo.; resident Children's Meml. Hosp., Chgo.; with Valley Pediatric and Allergy Clinic, Las Vegas, Nev. Capt. USAF, 1950-53. Fellow Am. Acad. Pediatrics (state chmn. Nev. 1961-64, sect. allergy and immunology), Am. Coll. Allergy; mem. Am. Acad. Allergy, Allergy Subsplty. Group of Acad. Pediatrics (cert. pediatric allergist). Avocations: reading, travel. Office: Valley Pediat & Allergy Clinic 222 S Rainbow Blvd Ste 119 Las Vegas NV 89145-5343

MERKIN, ARI, advertising executive; b. 1970; 4 children. Copywriter Land Rover, Mobil Oil, Mt. Sinai Hosp., Crispin, Porter & Bogusky, Miaimi, 1998—2003; exec. creative dir. Fallon New York, 2003—05; co-founder, creative dir. Toy, Inc., NYC, 2005—. Named one of the Top Ten "Creatives to Watch", AdAge, Creativity, 2003, 2004, 2005, 40 under 40, Advt. Age, 2007. Office: Toy Inc 132 W 21st St 8th Fl New York NY 10011 Office Phone: 212-488-1555. *

MERKIN, WILLIAM LESLIE, retired lawyer; b. NYC, Apr. 30, 1929; s. Jules Leo Merkin and Rae (Levine) Lesser; children: Monica Jo, Lance Jeffrey, Tiffany Dawn. BA, U. Tex., Austin, 1950; JD, St. Mary's U., San Antonio, 1953. Bar: Tex. 1953, U.S. Ct. Mil. Appeals 1954, U.S. Dist. Ct. (we. dist.) Tex. 1957, U.S. Ct. Appeals (5th cir.) 1969, U.S. Supreme Ct. 1970. Pvt. practice, El Paso, Tex., 1956-71; sr. ptnr. Merkin & Gibson, El Paso, Tex., 1972-78, Merkin, Hines & Pasqualone, El Paso, Tex., 1978-90; ret. Lectr. U. Tex.-El Paso, 1978—; cons. in field. Served to capt. JAGC, U.S. Army, 1953-56. Mem. Tex. State Bar Assn., Soc. Profls. in Dispute Resolution, Am. Trial Lawyers Assn., Tex. Trial Lawyers Assn., Common Cause, Internat. Wine and Food Soc. (pres. 1979-80), Am. Arbitration Assn. (part-time arbitrator), Nat. Assn. Securities Dealers (part-time arbitrator), Del Norte Club (El Paso), B'nai B'rith (pres. 1961-62), Phi Delta Phi. Home and Office: 1442 Seacoast Dr Imperial Beach CA 91932-3183 Office Phone: 619-423-1718.

MERLE, H. ETIENNE, broker, director, restaurateur; b. NYC, July 8, 1944; s. Pierre and Josephine Merle. BS, Cornell U., 1969. Mgr. food and beverage DiviDivi Beach Hotel, Aruba, 1969-70; restaurant mgr., chmn. food dept. Tng. Resources for Youth, NYC, 1971; gen. mgr. L'Auberge du Cochon Rouge, Ithaca, NY, 1971-92; v.p. Pascale Wine Bar and Restaurant, Syracuse, NY, 1982-94; splty. foods broker, pres. Shineola & Assocs., Ithaca, 1992—. Ops. cons. Merle & Roy Assocs., N.Y.C., 1975—; chef, operator Atelier Etienne Corp., Valentine Café, Ithaca, N.Y., 1999-2003. Mem. Cornell Hotel Soc., Chefs de Cuisine Assn. Am., Soc. Culinaire Philanthropique, L'Union Francaise (pres. 1975, 76, 86, 91—). Home: 1146 Danby Rd Ithaca NY 14850-9406 Office: PO Box 6769 Ithaca NY 14851-6769 Office Phone: 607-227-2269.

MERLIN, LISA RUTH, neurologist, researcher; d. Walter and Isabel Merlin; m. Bruce Kiel, June 27, 2000; 1 child, Allison Elizabeth Kiel. BA, CUNY Bklyn. Coll., 1983; MD, SUNY Downstate Med. Ctr., Bklyn., 1986. Diplomate Nat. Bd. Med. Examiners, 1987; cert. in neurology Am. Bd. Psychiatry and Neurology, 1991. Intern in internal medicine Brookdale Hosp. Med. Ctr., Bklyn., 1986—87; resident in neurology SUNY Downstate, Bklyn., 1987—90, clin. asst. prof. neurology, 1990—93, asst. prof. neurology and pharmacology, 1993—98, assoc. prof. neurology, physiology and pharmacology, 1998—2004, prof. neurology, physiology and pharmacology, 2004—. Dir. neurology outpatient svcs. Kings County Hosp., Bklyn., 1992—95; dir. adult neurology residency tng. program SUNY Downstate Kings County, 1995—2002; study sect. mem. NIH, Washington, 2001—03; dir. clin. neurosciences pathway med. student programs SUNY Downstate Coll. Medicine, Bklyn., 2004—. Contbr. scientific papers to profl. jours. Recipient Chancellor's Excellence in Tchg. award, SUNY, 2004; grantee Clin. Rsch. Assoc. award, SUNY Downstate, 1992—94, PhRMA Found., 1996—98, Epilepsy Found. Am., 1996—97, Mentored Clin. Scientist Devel. award, NIH, 1996—2002, Ind. Rsch. Grant, 2001—07, Novartis Pharmaceuticals, 2005—06. Fellow: Am. Acad. Neurology (Dreifuss-Penry Epilepsy award 2002); mem.: Am. Neurol. Assn., Soc. Neuroscience, Assn. U. Professors of Neurology, Am. Epilepsy Soc., Alpha Omega Alpha. Achievements include discovery of role of group I metabotropic glutamate receptors in epileptogenesis. Office: SUNY Downstate Med Ctr 450 Clarkson Ave Box 29 Brooklyn NY 11203 Office Fax: 718-270-2241.

MERLIN, ROBERTO DANIEL, physicist, educator; b. Buenos Aires, Aug. 12, 1950; came to U.S., 1978; MSc, U. Buenos Aires, 1973; PhD, U. Stuttgart, Federal Republic of Germany, 1978. Rsch. asst. Comision de Energia Atomica, Buenos Aires, 1974-75, Max Planck Inst., Stuttgart, 1975-78; rsch. assoc. U. Ill., Urbana, 1978-80; asst. prof. physics U. Mich., Ann Arbor, 1980-85, assoc. prof. physics, 1985-89, prof. physics, 1989—, assoc. chair for rsch. and facilities, dept. physics, 1993-96, dir., Optical Physics Interdisciplinary Lab., joint appt., dept. elec. engring and computer sci., 2000—. Cons. Battelle Labs., Columbus, Ohio, 1985-86, AT&T Bell Labs., Holmdel, N.J., 1981; vis. prof., Max-Planck-Institut FkF, Stuttgart, Germany, 1987, Hong Kong U. Sci. and Tech., 1996, Iberdrola chair U. Automona, Madrid, 1997; Lannin Lectr., dept. physicis, Pa. State U., 2002. Mem. editl. bd. Springer Series in Solid State Sciences, Solid State Comm. Fellow, Von Humboldt Found., Fed. Republic of Germany, 1987, Guggenheim Meml. Found., 2007. Fellow Am. Phys. Soc. (chair Forum on Internat. Physics 1996-97, mem. com. Internat. Freedom Scientists, 2002-04, Frank Isakson prize, 2006), Optical Soc. Am.(gen. chair, Quantum electronics and laser sci. conf., 2006), von Humboldt Found.; mem. AAAS, Argentina Physics Assn. Achievements include patents for Quasiperiodic Layered Structures, Data Storage Using Pulsed Optical Domain Reversal. Office: U Mich Dept Physics 450 Church St Ann Arbor MI 48109-1040 Office Phone: 734-763-9759. Office Fax: 734-764-5153. Business E-Mail: merlin@umich.edu.

MERLISS, HARRY, orthopedist, surgeon; b. Russia, July 19, 1921; arrived in US, 1924; s. Eugene and Nettie Merliss; m. Barbara K. Merliss, Jan. 5, 1974; 1 child, Eugenia; m. Evelyn Merliss (div.); children: Andrew, Lois, Teri, Barbara, David. MD, George Washington U., DC, 1943. Diplomate Am. Bd. Orthop. Surgery. Attending orthopaedic surgeon Hackensack U. Med. Ctr., NJ, 1950—65, 1975—98, dir. dept. orthopaedic surgery, 1965—75; ret., 1998. Capt. US Army, 1944—46. Fellow: ACS, Am. Acad. Orthop. Surgeons; mem.: NJ Orthop. Soc. (past pres.). Home: 916 Amaryllis Ave Oradell NJ 07649

MERLO, LARRY J., retail executive; Sr. v.p. stores CVS Pharmacy, Inc., Woonsocket, RI, 1994—98, exec. v.p. stores, 1998—2000, CVS Corp., Woonsocket, 2000—07; exec. v.p., pres. CVS Pharmacy Retail CVS Caremark Corp., Woonsocket, RI, 2007—. Office: CVS Caremark Corp Corp Hdqrs 1 CVS Dr Woonsocket RI 02895 *

MERMANN, ALAN CAMERON, retired pediatric educator, chaplain; b. Bklyn., June 23, 1923; s. William Joseph and Ada Fischer (McCree) M.; m. Constance Barnes, Sept. 4, 1948 (div. Mar. 1988); children: Edith, Constance, Sarah, Elizabeth; m. Cecily Allen Reynolds, Apr. 15, 1989. BA, Lehigh U., 1943; MD, Johns Hopkins U., 1947; MDiv, Yale U., 1979, MST, 1988, MA, 1999. Diplomate Am. Bd. Pediatrics; med. license, Conn.; ordained to Christian ministry, United Ch. of Christ, 1979. Intern pediatrics Bellevue Hosp., NYC, 1947-48, Johns Hopkins Hosp., Balt., 1948-49; sr. resident pediatrician N.Y. Hosp., NYC, 1949-50; resident pediatrician Meml. Hosp., NYC, 1950-51; rsch. fellow Sloane-Kettering Inst., NYC, 1953-54; pvt. practice pediatrics Guilford, Conn., 1954-82; clin. instr. pediatrics Yale Sch. Medicine, 1954-59, asst. clin. prof. pediatrics, 1959-71, assoc. clin. prof. pediatrics, 1971-79, clin. prof. pediatrics, 1979—2000. Trustee New Eng. Coll., Henniker, N.H., 1969-91; fellow Branford Coll., Yale U., 1979-00; mem. instnl. rev. bd. Union Carbide Corp., Danbury, Conn., 1991—98; lectr. pastoral theology Yale Divinity Sch., 1979-82; asst. pastor First Congregational Ch., Guilford, 1979-82; assoc. pastor Ch. of Christ Congl., United Ch. of Christ, Norfolk, Conn., 1995—2003; chaplain Yale Sch. Medicine, 1982-00, human investigation com., 1983-91, med. ctr. bioethics com., chair pediatrics ethics com., sch. medicine admissions com., com. on well-being of students. Author: Some Chose to Stay: Faith and Ethics in a Time of Plague, 1997, To Do No Harm: Learning to Care for The Seriously Ill, 1999; contbr. articles to profl. jours. Lt. USNR, 1951-53. Fellow Am. Acad. Pediatrics. Democrat. Avocations: dixieland, jazz, dance, gardening. Home: 185 Ashpohtag Rd Norfolk CT 06058

MERMELSTEIN, HOPE LEAH, educational consultant; d. Lothar David Mermelstein and Terry Denman. BA, U. Mass., Amherst, 1992, MA, 1994. Tchr. Pub. Sch. II, NYC, 1994—98; staff developer Dist. 15, Region 8, Bklyn., 1998—99; literacy cons. Columbia U., NYC, 1999—2003;

freelance ednl. cons. Hoboken, NJ, 2005—. Author: Reading, Writing Connections in the K-2 Classroom, 2005, Don't Forget to Share, 2007; co-author (with Lucy Calkins): Launching The Writing Workshop, 2003. Mem.: NY State Assn. Edn. Young Children (mem. adv. bd. 2006—), Internat. Reading Assn., Nat. Coun. Tchrs. English. Avocations: running, yoga, reading.

MERMELSTEIN, JULES JOSHUA, lawyer, educator, commissioner; b. Phila., Apr. 25, 1955; s. Harry and Ellen Jane (Greenberg) M.; m. Ruth Susan Applebaum, Aug. 18, 1974; children: Hannah Leona, Benjamin Isaac. BA, Temple U., Phila., 1977; JD, Am. U., Washington, DC, 1979; MEd, Beaver Coll., Glenside, Pa., 1994. Bar: Pa. 1980, US Dist. Ct. (ea. dist.) Pa. 1980, US Ct. Appeals (3d cir.) 1982, US Supreme Ct. 1983. Ptnr. Mermelstein & Light, Norristown and Hatboro, Pa., 1980-83; v.p., gen. counsel Am. Ins. Cons., Feasterville, Pa., 1983; staff atty. Hyatt Legal Svcs., Phila., 1983-84, mng. atty., 1984-85; pvt. practice Phila./Montgomery County, 1985-93; tchr., social studies coach. The Bridge, 1997-99; atty. Levin & Assocs., Wyncote, Pa., 1998—2001, mng. atty., 2002—03; title agt. Forward Abstract, LLC, Glenside, Pa., 2002—05; social studies tchr. Sch. Dist. Phila., 2005—07, Upper Dublin Sch. Dist., 2007—. Prof. law St. Matthew Sch. Law, Phila., 1985—87; adj. prof. criminal justice Glassboro State U., NJ, 1988; faculty polit. sci. dept. Temple U., 1989; ednl. cons. Interim Ho., 1998—2000. Editor: The Montco Democrat, 1990-92. Vol. atty. ACLU, Phila., 1980-93; chmn. Tikkun Olam (Repair the World) Com., 1989-92, 98-2000; area rep. Montgomery County Dem. Exec. Com., 1982-85, 88-94; treas., 1994-98, candidate coord., 1982, nominee for dist. atty., 1983, committeeman, 1973-77, 82-85, 88-92, campaign mgr. Talbot for state legis., 1988; Upper Dublin chmn. Dukakis-Bentsen, 1988, chair Upper Dublin Dem. Com., 1990-91, commr. Upper Dublin Twp., 1992—, v.p., 2006—; Dem. candidate Pa. State Legis., 2000; bd. dirs. Reconstructionist Congregation Or Hadash, Ft. Washington, Pa., 1988-92, 96-2000, 2001-2003, confirmation tchr., 1994—. Jewish. Home: 18 Northview Dr Glenside PA 19038-1318 Personal E-mail: Jules.Mermelstein@gmail.com.

MERON, THEODOR, judge, educator, researcher; b. Kalisz, Poland, Apr. 28, 1930; came to U.S., 1978, naturalized, 1984; s. Yhiel and Bluma (Lipschitz) Znamirowski; m. Monique Jonquet, Mar. 13, 1981; children: Daniel, Amos. M.J., Hebrew U., 1954; LL.M., Harvard U., 1955, S.JD, 1957; diploma in Pub. Internat. Law, Cambridge U., Eng., 1957. Bar: Israel 1971, N.Y. 1984. Legal advisor to Fgn. Ministry of Israel, 1967-71; Israeli ambassador to Can., 1971-75; permanent rep. U.N., Geneva, 1977; prof. law NYU Law Sch., NYC, 1977—94, Charles L. Denison prof., 1994—2005, Charles L. Denison prof. emeritus, jud. fellow, 2006—. Carnegie lectr. Hague Acad. Internat. Law, 1980; Sir Hersch Lauterpacht Meml. lectr.; vis. fellow All Souls Coll., Oxford U., England, Max-Planck Inst., Heidelberg, Germany; vis. prof. Grad. Inst. Internat. Studies, Geneva, prof. law, 1991—95; pub. mem. U.S. Del. Conf. on Human Dimension Conf. on Security and Coop. in Europe, Copenhagen, 1998; mem. U.S. del. Rome Diplomatic Conf. on the Establishment of an Internat. Criminal Ct.; vis. prof. law Harvard U., Berkeley Law Sch.; counselor on internat. law U.S. Dept. State, 2000—01; judge appeals chamber Internat. Criminal Tribunal for former Yugoslavia, 2001—, Internat. Criminal Tribunal for Rwanda, 2001—, pres., 2003—05. Author: Investment Insurance in International Law, 1976, The United Nations Secretariat, 1977, Human Rights Law-Making in the United Nations, 1986, Human Rights in Internal Strife: Their International Protection, 1987, Human Rights and Humanitarian Norms as Customary Law, 1989, Henry's Wars and Shakespeare's Laws, 1993, Bloody Constraint: War and Chivalry in Shakespeare, 1998, International Law in the Age of Human Rights, 2004, The Humanization of International Law, 2006; editor: Human Rights in International Law, 1984; editor in chief: Am. Jour. Internat. Law, 1983-88; contbr. articles to profl. jours. Rockefeller Found. fellow, 1975-76; Humanitarian Trust student Cambridge U., 1956-57;recipient Rule of Law award, Internat. Bar Assn., 2005. Mem. Am. Soc. Internat. Law (Cert. Merit 1987, Hudon medal 2006); Inst. Internat. Law, Internat. Law Assn., Coun. on Fgn. Rels., Inst. Internat. Humanitarian Law, French Inst. Internat. Law. Office: NYU Law Sch 40 Washington Sq S New York NY 10012-1099 also: Churchillplein 2501 EW The Hague Netherlands Business E-Mail: meront@un.org.

MEROPOL, NEAL J., oncologist, researcher; AB, Princeton U., 1981; MD, Vanderbilt U., 1985. Cert. Am. Bd. Internal Medicine, Internal Medicine, Med. Oncology. Intern, resident in internal medicine Case Western Res. U., Cleve., 1985—88; fellow in med. oncology and hematology U. Pa., Phila., 1988—92; asst. prof. medicine Roswell Park Cancer Inst., 1992—98; dir. Gastrointestinal Cancer Program Fox Chase Cancer Ctr., Phila., 1998—, dir., Gastrointestinal Tumor Risk Assessment Program. Prof. medicine Temple U. Sch. Medicine, 2006—. Contbr. articles to profl. publications. Mem.: Am. Assn. for Cancer Rsch., Am. Soc. Clin. Oncology. Office: Fox Chase Cancer Ctr 333 Cottman Ave Philadelphia PA 19111-2497 Office Phone: 215-728-2570. *

MEROW, JAMES F., federal judge; AB, George Washington U., 1953, JD, 1956. Bar: Va., 1956, DC, 1958. Trial atty., br. dir., civil divsn. US Dept. Justice, Washington, 1959-78; trial judge US Ct. Claims, Washington, 1978-82; judge US Ct. Fed. Claims, Washington, 1982—. With JAGC, US Army, 1956-59. Mem. ABA, Fed. Bar Assn., Va. State Bar, DC Bar. Office: US Ct Fed Claims 717 Madison Pl NW Washington DC 20005

MEROW, JOHN, lawyer; b. Little Valley, NY, Dec. 20, 1929; s. Luin George and Mildred Elizabeth Merow; m. Mary Alyce Smith, June 19, 1957; 1 child, Alison. Student, UCLA, 1947—48; BS in Engring., U. Mich., 1952; JD, Harvard U., 1958. Bar: N.Y. 1958, U.S. Supreme Ct. 1971. Assoc. Sullivan & Cromwell, NYC, 1958-64, ptnr., 1965-96, vice chmn., 1986-87, chmn., sr. ptnr., 1987-94, sr. counsel, 1997—. Bd. dirs. Seligman Group Investment Cos., Aleris Internat. Inc.; trustee, vice chmn. N.Y. Presbyn. Healthcare Sys., Inc.; trustee N.Y. Presbyn. Hosp.; trustee, sec. Friends of the Archbishop of Canterbury's Anglican Communion Fund. Chmn. bd. dirs. Am.-Australian Assn., 1986—99; bd. dirs. Mcpl. Art Soc. N.Y.; mem. exec. com., sec. U.S. Coun. Internat. Bus.; bd. dirs., sec. Met. Opera Club, 1986—94; trustee Anglican Investment Agy. Trust. Lt. USN, 1952—55. Named hon. officer Order of Australia. Mem. Am. Law Inst. (advisor corp. governance project 1978-92), Coun. on Fgn. Rels., Soc. Mayflower Desc., Links Club, Pilgrims, Piping Rock Club, Down Town Assn., Union Club, Griffis Faculty Club, River Club. Home: 435 E 52d St New York NY 10022 also: 51 Fruitledge Rd Glen Head NY 11545-3316 Office: Sullivan & Cromwell LLP 125 Broad St New York NY 10004-2498 Office Phone: 212-558-3616. E-mail: merowj@sullcrom.com.

MERRELL, JAMES LEE, writer, minister; b. Indpls., Oct. 24, 1930; s. Mark W. and Pauline F. (Tucker) M.; m. Barbara Jean Burch, Dec. 23, 1951; children: Deborah Lea Merrell Griffin, Cynthia Lynn Archer, Stuart Allen. AB, Ind. U., 1952; MDiv, Christian Theol. Sem., 1956; LittD, Culver-Stockton Coll., 1972. Ordained to ministry Christian Ch., 1955; asso. editor World Call, Indpls., 1956-66, editor, 1971-73; pastor Crestview Christian Ch., Indpls., 1966-71; editor The Disciple, St. Louis, 1974-89; sr. v.p. Christian Bd. Publ., 1976-89; sr. minister Affton Christian Ch., St. Louis, 1989-94; interim chaplain Culver-Stockton Coll., Canton, Mo., 1995; interim sr. pastor Friedens United Ch. of Christ, Warrenton, Mo., 1995-98, St. Johns United Ch. of Christ, Mehlville, Mo., 1998—2002, Hamilton Christian Ch., Creve Coeur, 2002—03, Redeemer Evang. Ch., St. Louis, 2003—05, Trinity United Ch. Christ, 2005—. Bd. dirs. Horizons mag., 1995-98. Author: They Live Their Faith, 1965, The Power of One, 1976, Discover the Word in Print, 1979, Finding Faith in the Headlines, 1985, We Claim Our Heritage, 1992, Seeing Life: Finding God, 2006. Chmn. bd. Kennedy Meml. Christian Home, Martinsville, Ind., 1971-73; trustee Christian Theol. Sem., 1978-81. Recipient Faith and Freedom award Religious Heritage of Am., 1983; lifetime achievement award Mo. State Sen., 2000. Mem. Associated Ch. Press (award 1973, 79, 80, 81, 82, dir. 1974-75, 78-81, 1st v.p. 1983-85), Christian Theol. Sem. Alumni Assn. (pres. 1966-68), Religious Pub. Rels. Coun. (awards 1979, 80, 84, 87, 90, pres. St. Louis chpt. 1985-86), Sigma Delta Chi (award 1952), Theta Phi. Home: 248 Greycliff Bluff Dr Saint Louis MO 63129-5081 E-mail: JLeeMer@aol.com. *As a religious communicator and as a pastor, I have always believed in applying the same standards in the sacred realm as in the secular. I have tried to pursue the truth, to keep my constituency informed, to celebrate the noble in life, to fight against those who would lie, distort and hide God's truth in the name of some supposed good.*

MERRELL, RONALD CLIFTON, surgeon, educator; b. Birmingham, Ala., June 18, 1946; s. Greene Lawrence and Florence (Jones) M.; m. Marsha Karen Cox, Dec. 24, 1966; children: Alexandria, Alison, R. Clifton. BS in Chemistry, U. Ala., 1967, MD, 1970. Diplomate Am. Bd. Surgery. Resident and fellow in surgery Wash. U., St. Louis, 1970-77; asst. prof. surgery Stanford U., Calif., 1979-84; assoc. prof. surgery U. Tex. Med. Sch., Houston, 1984-88, prof. surgery, 1988—93, M.D. Anderson Cancer Ctr., Houston, 1988—93; assoc. dean clin. affairs U. Tex. Med. Sch., Houston, 1988-92, vice dean, 1992-93; Lampman prof. surgery, chmn. dept. surgery Yale U., 1993—99; Stuart McGuire prof. surgery, chmn. dept. surgery Va. Commonwealth U., Richmond, 1999—2003, prof. surgery, 2003—; dir. Med. Informatics Tech. Applications Consortium, 1997—. Editor-in-chief Telemedicine and e-Health. Contbr. chapters to books, articles to profl. jours. Maj. US Army, 1977—79. Recipient Basil O'Connor award March of Dimes, 1979, Rsch. Career Devel. award NIH, 1979-84, Henry J. Kaiser award Stanford U., 1982, 83, John P. McGovern Outstanding Tchr. award U. Tex. Med. Sch., 1988, Dean's Teaching Excellence award, 1983-89, Pub. Svc. medal NASA, 1998, 2005, 06, Disting. medal as Friend of Democritus, U. Thrace, Greece, 1998; grantee NASA, Dept. Def., Internat. Coop. medal, Russian Space Agy., 2005. Fellow: ACS, Soc. Univ. Surgeons; mem.: Am. Surg. Assn., Am. Assn. Endocrine Surgery, Alpha Omega Alpha. Democrat. Episcopalian. Achievements include research in telemedicine and in the transplantation of islets of Langerhans. Office: Va Commonwealth U PO Box 980480 1101 E Marshall St Richmond VA 23298-0519 Office Phone: 804-827-1020, 804-827-1031. Business E-Mail: rmerrell@mcvh-vcu.edu.

MERRETT, CHRISTOPHER DOUGLAS, geographer, educator; b. Sault Ste. Marie, Canada, Mar. 2, 1961; s. Stanley James and Edna Mary Merrett; m. Mary Catherine Kiritsy, July 1, 1989; children: Grace, Alastair. PhD, U. Iowa, Iowa City, 1994. Prof. Ill. Inst. Rural Affairs, Macomb, 1995—, dir., 1995—. Author: Free Trade: Neither Free nor About Trade. Home: 640 Lincoln Dr Macomb IL 61455 Office: We Ill Univ 1 Univ Cir Macomb IL 61455 Office Phone: 309-298-2281. Office Fax: 309-298-2142. Business E-Mail: cd-merrett@wiu.edu.

MERRIAM, DANIEL F(RANCIS), geologist; b. Omaha, Feb. 9, 1927; s. Faye Mills and Amanda Frances (Wood) M. m. Annie Laura Young, Feb. 12, 1946; children: Beth Ann, John Francis, Anita Pauline, James Daniel, Judith Diane. BS in Geology, U. Kans., 1949, MS, 1953, PhD, 1961; MSc in Geology, Leicester U., England, 1969; DSc, Leicester U., 1975. Geologist Union Oil Co. Calif., 1949-51, 52; asst. instr. U. Kans., 1951-53, instr., 1954, rsch. assoc., 1963-71; geologist Kans. Geol. Survey, 1953-58, head divsn. basic geology, 1958-63, chief geol. rsch., 1963-71; Jessie Page Heroy prof. geology dept. geology Syracuse U., 1971-81, chmn. dept. geology, 1971-80; Endowment Assn. Disting. prof. natural scis. dept. geology Wichita State U., 1981-93, chmn. dept. geology, 1981-87; sr. rsch. scientist Kans. Geol. Survey, U. Kans., 1993-97, emeritus, 1997—. Vis. rsch. scientist Stanford U., 1963; dir. Internat. Field Inst. to Japan, Am. Geol. Inst., 1967; vis. prof. geology Wichita State U., 1968-70; vis. geol. scientist Am. Geol. Inst., 1969; cons. nat. gas survey Fed. Power Commn., 1972-75, 78, chmn. supply tech. adv. com., 1975-77; ad hoc panel earth resources survey NAS/NRC, 1972-73, chmn. U.S. Nat. Com. for Internat. Geol. Correlation program, 1976-79, ex-officio, 1979-80, 81-83, U.S. Nat. Com. on History of Geology, 1989-95; Esso Disting. lectr. U. Sydney, Australia, 1979; mem. U.S. Nat. Commn. for UNESCO, U.S. Dept. State, 1979-85; vis. prof. Centre d'Informatique Geologique, Ecole des Mines de Paris, Fontainebleau, 1980; vis. sr. scientist Kans. Geol. Survey, 1990-91; vis. scientist GeoForschungsZentrum, Potsdam, Germany, 1992; adj. prof. Emporia State U., Kans., 1993—; geol. dept. historian, U. Kans., 2004-. Author: The Geologic History of Kansas: Kansas Geological Survey, 1963, (with J.W. Harbaugh) Computer Applications in Stratigraphic Analysis, 1968, Computer Fundamentals for Geologists: COMPUTe, 1975, Bibliography of Computer Applications in the Earth Sciences, 1988; founder, editor-in-chief Jour. Math. Geology, 1968-76, 94-97, Computers & Geosciences, 1975-95; founder, editor Kansas Geological Survey, Computer Contributions, 1966-71, Syracuse University Geological Contributions, 1973-81; editor (series) Computer Applications in the Earth Sciences, 1969—, Computers and Geology, 1976-90, Computer Methods in the Geosciences, 1982—, (books and vols.) Mathematical Models of Sedimentary Processes, 1972, The Impact of Quantification on Geology, 1974, Random Processes in Geology, 1976, Geomathematics: Past, Present, and Prospects, 1978, Down-to-Earth Statistics: Solutions Looking for Geological Problems, 1981, Current Trends in Geomathematics, 1988, (colloquium) Geostatistics, 1970; translation editor Statistics for Geoscientists, 1987; co-editor Pacific Geology, 1971-83; editl. cons. Geosystems, 1971-83; mem. editl. rev. bd. Colo. Sch. Mines Quarterly, 1974-90; mem. editl. adv. bd. Geophysical Computer Programs, 1975-76, Applied Geochemistry, 1985-93; mem. editl. bd. History of Earth Science Soc., 1982-2000; reviewer for nat. and internat. jours.; contbr. notes, articles to numerous jours. Bd. dirs. Kans Geol. Found., 1989-92; mem. SEPM Found., 2002-. Fullbright-Hayes Sr. Rsch. fellow, UK, 1964-65; recipient Disting. Alumni hon., U. Jans., 1995. Fellow AAAS (sr., electorate nomination com. 1977-80, chairperson sect. E 1983-84, Sci. software adv. panel 1986-91, SWARM 64th local arrangement com. chmn. 1988), Geol. Soc. Am. (sr. fellow, com. on publs. 1973-76, chmn. com. geology dept. 1975-78, history of geology divsn. nominating com. 2006), Geol. Soc. London (William Smith medal 1992), Sigma Xi (sec. Kansas chpt. 1994-96, pres. 1997-98); mem. Am. Assn. Petroleum Geologists (hon., chmn. 1954, 57, ednl. exhibits com., rsch. com., 1964-67, assoc. editor bulletin 1969-75, Geobyte 1985-92, computer applications in geology com. 1971-81, 86-89, NY Dist. rep. 1974-76, Kans. Dist. rep. 1956-57, 1985-91, chmn. 1989-91, Kans. rep. Midcontinent sect. 1988-92, Disting. Svc. award 1987, Cert. of Merit 1987, 93), Soc. Econ. Paleontologists and Mineralogists (hon., chmn. organizer rsch. group in computer tech. 1970-75, 82-82, 89-90, publs. com. 1980-83, chmn. publs. 1981-82, chmn. Pa. Stratigraphy working group Midcontinent sect. 1986-96, ad. hoc. com. databases 1985-88, chmn databases 1986-88, organizer computer applications com. 1988-97, chmn. computer applications 1988-92, procedures com. 1989-2001, chmn. 1993-94, spl. advisor headquarters and bus. com. 1988-91, chmn. 1991-98), SEPM Found., Nat. Assn. Geology Tchrs. (v.p. Kans.-Okla. sect. 1986, pres. 1987-89, sec. 1994-2003), Geosci. Info. Soc. (program com 1980-81), Internat. Union Geol. Scis., Internat. Geol. Correlations Program (U.S. del. 1969, sci. com. 1975-79, 76-77, chmn. ad hoc com. publs. 1980, adv. bd. publs. 1980-89, chmn. 1980-84), Internat. Geol. Congress (alternate U.S. del. VII ordinary sessions coun. 1984, U.S. del. VIII ordinary sessions coun. 1989), Internat. Assn. Math. Geology (first hon. life mem., mem. coun. 1968—, sec.-gen. 1972-76, pres. 1976-80, interim archivist 1989-92, archivist 1992—, William Christian Krumbein medal 1981, pubs. com. 1997—, organizing com. 8th ann. meeting 2001), Leicester Geol. Soc. (hon. life 1965), Sylvester-Bradley Geol. Soc. (hon. v.p. 1978-79; Hornicka Pribram, Czechoslovakia, Horricka Pribram gold medal 1970), Classification Soc. (chmn. mem. com., bd. dirs. 1968-71), NY State Geol. Assn. (exec. sec. 1972-77, pres. 1977-78, bd. dirs. 1987-83), Kans. Geol. Soc. (hon., bd. dirs. 1989-92, dir. many confs., presdl. citation 1989, chmn future plans com. 1989), Kans. Acad. Sci. (life, mem. coun. at large 1983-86, v.p. 1987, pres.-elect 1988, pres. 1989, chmn. com. for 2001, 1989-92, assoc. editor Transactions 1990-92, editor, 1992-2003, strategic planning com. 2000-02, gen. chmn. 119th Ann. Meeting 1987, 131st Ann. Meeting 2001; cert. appreciation 2003), History of Earth Sci. Soc. (Earth Science History editl. bd. 1982-2000), Sigma Gamma Epsilon (pres. Alpha chpt. 1952-53, nat. coun. 1983-95, nat. pres. 1990-95, nat. editor The Compass, 1983-92, hon.), Phi Kappa Phi (life), Sigma Xi (Kans. chpt. sec. 1994-96, pres. 1997-98). Office: U Kans Dept Geology Kansas Geol Survey Lawrence KS 66047 Business E-Mail: dmerriam@kgs.ku.edu.

MERRIAM, DWIGHT HAINES, lawyer, land use planner; b. Norwood, Mass., Apr. 20, 1946; s. Austin Luther and Lillian Diana (Olsen) M.; m. Cynthia Ann Hayes, May 21, 1966 (div. June 1992); children: Sarah Ann Leilani, Jonathan Hayes; m. Susan Manning Standish, May 6, 1995; children: Alexander Harlan, Lucy Caroline. BA cum laude, U. Mass., 1968; M in Regional Planning, U. N.C., 1974; JD, Yale U., 1978. Bar: Conn. 1978, Mass. 1980, U.S. Dist. Ct. Conn. 1981, U.S. Dist. Ct. Hawaii 1984, U.S. Dist. Ct. Colo. 2006, U.S. Supreme Ct. 1990, U.S. Ct. Appeals (4th cir.) 1993. Land use planner Charles E. Downe, Newton, Mass., 1968; assoc. Byrne, Buck & Steiner, Farmington, Conn., 1978, Robinson, Robinson & Cole, Hartford, Conn., 1979-83; ptnr. Robinson & Cole LLP, Hartford, 1984—. Adj. prof. law Western New Eng. Coll., 1978-86, U. Conn., 1982, 84-87, Vt. Law Sch., 1994—; instr. planning U. Bridgeport, 1981-83, U. Conn., 1986-92; mem. faculty Nat. Coll. Dist. Attys., 1983-87, Nat. Jud. Coll., 1994; mem. faculty Am. Law Inst.-ABA Land Use Inst., 1988—; instr. city and regional planning Memphis State U., 1989, 94; spkr. in field. Author: The Complete Guide to Zoning, 2005; co-author: The Takings Issue, 1999; co-editor: Inclusionary Zoning Moves Downtown, 1985, Eminent Domain Use and Abuse: Kelo in Context, 2006; contbr. more than 200 articles and book revs. to profl. jours. Bd. dirs. Conn. chpt. Appleseed Found., 1997-2000, Am. Boat Builders and Repairers Assn., 1995-1999, Growth Mgmt. Inst., Washington, 1992—, Housing Edn. Resource Ctr., 1984-88, Housing Coalition for Capitol Region, Inc., 1984-86; bd. dirs. Conn. Fund for Environment, 1981-85, legal adv. com., 1985-88, legal adv. bd., 1978-81; mem. Environment 2000 environ. plan adv. bd. Conn. Dept. Environ. Protection, 1987-91; assoc. Environ. Law Inst., 1987—; mem. housing task force Conn. Dept. on Aging, 1981; mem. Gov.'s Housing Task Force, Conn., 1980-81. With USN, 1968—75, Vietnam, capt. USNR, 1975-99. USNR, 1975—99. Fellow: Royal Inst. Chartered Land Surveyors, Am. Inst. Cert. Planners (pres. 1988—90); mem.: ABA (comm. dir. state and local govt. sect. 2006—), Am. Coll. Real Estate Lawyers, Assn. State Floodplain Mgrs., Internat. Mcpl. Law Assn. (chmn. sect. on zoning, planning and land devel. 1988—89, chmn. Conn. 1999—2003), Am. Planning Assn. (chmn. legis. com. Conn. chpt. 1978—80, exec. com. planning and law divsn. 1978—88, chmn. planning and law divsn. 1984—86, editl. adv. bd. 1984—92, bd. dirs. 1988—90), Conn. Bar Assn. (exec. com. zoning and planning sect. 1985—87, 1991—). Democrat. Unitarian Universalist. Avocations: sailing, skiing. Home: 80 Latimer Ln Weatogue CT 06089 Office: Robinson & Cole LLP 280 Trumbull St Hartford CT 06103-3597 Home Phone: 860-651-7077; Office Phone: 860-275-8228. Business E-Mail: dmerriam@rc.com.

MERRIAM, ROBERT W., engineering executive, educator; b. Providence, July 18, 1923; s. Paul Adams and Marian Lewis M.; m. Nancy Ann Allen, Dec. 21, 1954; children: Susan Allen Jones, Paul Adams, II. BS in Engring. Sci. and Applied Physics, Harvard Coll., 1949; MS in Engring. Sci. and Applied Physics, Harvard Engring. Sch., 1950. Reg. profl. engr., R.I. Instr. elec. engring. Swarthmore (Pa.) Coll., 1950-52; engr. Metals & Controls Corp., Attleboro, Mass., 1953-55; pres. Merriam Instruments, East Greenwich, R.I., 1955-99. Assoc. prof. U. R.I., Kingston, 1969-79. Editor: History of Wireless Communication in the U.S., 1989; patentee in field; contbr. articles to popular publications. Pres., dir. N.E. Wireless and Steam Mus., East Greenwich, 1964—; chmn. Planning Bd., East Greenwich, 1970s; hon. trustee Heritage Trust of R.I. With U.S. Army Signal Corp., 1942-46, ETO. Recipient Antoinette Downing award State of R.I., 1998; named Engr. of Yr., Nat. Assn. Power Engrs., 1998, award Soc. Indsl. Archeology Gen. Tools, 2001, Preserve R.I. Merit award, 2005. Fellow Radio Club Am. (Batcher award 1979); mem. IEEE (life), Am. Radio Relay League (life), Nat. Marine Electronic Assn. (hon., dir. 1957), Nat. Assn. Power Engrs. (hon.), Vet. Wireless Assn. (Marconi Gold medal 1995), 20:00 Club (Meritorious Amateur Seamanship award 1955), Rhode Soc. Profl. Engrs. (Engr. of Yr. 1999), Hope Club, Harvard Club (Boston).

MERRICK, FRED HAROLD, retired marine engineer; s. Fred C. Merrick and Irene Louise Carpenter; m. Cheryl Ann Cain, Apr. 2, 1977. BS, UCLA, 1963; MDiv, Ch. Div. Sch. Pacific, Berkeley, Calif., 1973—76; Cert. Advanced Profl. Study, Pacific Sch. Religion, Berkeley, 1976—78; Cert. Supervision & Mgmt., San Francisco City Coll., 1994—95. Engr. Nat. Aeronautics & Space Adminstrn., Edwards, Calif., 1962; commd. officer USN, 1963—72, 1st commanding officer deep submergence rescue vehicle 2, 1969—72; sr. marine engr. Planning Rsch. Corp., Marine Sys., San Francisco, 1977—79; project mgr., sr. marine engr. Morris Guralnick Assocs., San Francisco, 1979—90; supervising engr. Earl & Wright Cons. Engrs., San Francisco, 1990—91; asst. program mgr. John J. McMullen Assocs., Inc., San Francisco, 1993—2000; computer sys. mgr. Cammisa & Wipf Cons. Engrs., San Francisco, 2000—05, ret., 2005. Expert witness in marine engring., San Francisco, 1980—. Singer public performances, solos, duets & quartets. Assoc. pastor Christ Ch. Luth., San Francisco, 1981—85; sec. Luth. Campus Ministry, San Francisco, 1982—95; pastor Bayview Luth. Ch., San Francisco, 1986—98; chaplain Vets. Adminstrn. Med. Ctr., San Francisco, 2000—05; publicity dir. Calif. Geneal. Soc., San Francisco, 1985—90; pres., program dir. Landberg Ctr. Health & Ministry, San Francisco, 1985—2006. Lt. USN, 1963—72. Mem.: VFW (life). Reform. Luth. Avocations: singing, genealogy, travel. Home: 1623 12th Ave San Francisco CA 94122 Home Phone: 415-564-2875. Personal E-mail: fmerrick@pacbell.net.

MERRICK, GEORGE BOESCH, aerospace transportation executive; b. Burlington, Iowa, Mar. 9, 1928; s. Dale McKeen and Marjorie May (Boesch) M.; m. Eleanor Gamble Moore, Sept. 1, 1951; children: Charles, Ellen, Elizabeth. BS, U. Minn., 1949. With N.Am. Aviation (name changed to Rockwell Internat.), 1949; dir. Apollo Command and Service Module, Space div., 1966-72; v.p., program mgr. Apollo Program, 1972-74, v.p., program mgr. Space Shuttle Orbiter Program, 1974-76; pres. space div. Rockwell Internat., Downey, Calif., 1976-78, pres. space systems group, 1978-80, corp. v.p., 1980-91, ret., 1991. Recipient Pub. Svc. award, NASA. Fellow Am. Astron. Soc., AIAA.

MERRIFIELD, DONALD PAUL, ministries coordinator; b. Los Angeles, Nov. 14, 1928; s. Arthur S. and Elizabeth (Baker) M. BS in Physics, Calif. Inst. Tech., 1950; MS, U. Notre Dame, 1951; A.M., Ph.L. in Philosophy, St. Louis U., 1957; PhD, MIT, 1962; S.T.M., U. Santa Clara, Calif., 1966; S.T.D. (hon.), U. So. Calif., 1969; D.H.L. (hon.), U. Judaism, 1984, Hebrew Union Coll.-Jewish Inst. Religion, 1986. Joined Soc. of Jesus, 1951; ordained priest Roman Cath. Ch., 1965; instr. physics Loyola U., Los Angeles, 1961-62; lectr. Engring. Sch., Santa Clara, 1965; cons. theoretical chemistry Jet Propulsion Lab., Calif. Inst. Tech., 1962-69; asst. prof. physics U. San Francisco, 1967-69; pres. Loyola Marymount U., Los Angeles, 1969-84, chancellor, 1984—2002; regent, sr. rsch. fellow Charminade U., Honolulu, 2002—; mem. religious ministry Catholic Diocese of Hawaii, 2002—. Contbr. chapters to books. Mem. Sigma Xi. Office: 2727 Pamoa Rd Honolulu HI 96822-1838 Home Phone: 808-988-3464. Personal E-mail: dmerrifield@calprov.org. Business E-Mail:

dmerrifi@chaminade.edu. *In today's world, we all stand in need of that pragmatic hope which allows us to see the possibilities for building a more just society and meeting the challenges before us. Without such hope we are paralyzed before our difficulties. With a less realistic hope, too idealistic, we are continually overwhelmed by failures. But with an openness to possibilities, we can move ahead with determination.*

MERRIFIELD, DUDLEY BRUCE, finance educator, federal official; b. Chgo., June 13, 1921; s. Fred and Anna (Marshall) M.; m. Paula Sorensen, June 8, 1949; children: Bruce, Robert, Marshall. AB in Chemistry, Princeton U., 1942; MS in Chemistry, U. Chgo., 1948, PhD in Chemistry, 1950. Disting. vis. prof. Georgetown U. Bus. Sch., Washington. Sr. rsch. chemist Monsanto, St. Louis, 1950-56; mgr. polymer rsch. Tex.-U.S. Chem. Co., Parsippany, NJ, 1956-63; dir. R & D Petrolite Corp., St. Louis, 1963-68; v.p. tech. and ventures Occidental Petroleum Co., Houston, 1968-77; v.p. tech. and venture mgmt. Continental Group, Stamford, Conn., 1977-82; asst. sec. for productivity, tech. and innovation Dept. Commerce, Washington, 1982-89; undersec. econ. affairs, 1986-87; Walter Bladstrom prof., emeritus Wharton Bus. Sch., U Pa., Phila., 1989-94; pres., CEO Pinnacle Rsch. Inst. Devel. Co., 1991—. Adv. bd. Binat R & D Found., U.S., Israel, France, India, 1979—; disting. vis. prof. mgmt., Georgetown U., Washington. Contbr. articles to profl. jours.; patentee in field. Exec. coun. Episcopal Ch., 1973-79; chmn. Princeton Alumni Coun., 1968-72. With USMC, 1943-46. Fellow AAAS, Inst. for Chemists; mem. Am. Chem. Soc., Indsl. Rsch. Inst. (dir., pres.-elect 1977-82 M. Holland award), Am. Mgmt. Assn. Hall of Fame (trustee, chmn. rsch. coun.), Dirs. Rsch., Sigma Xi Republican. Episcopalian. Office: Pridco Mgmt Corp Ste 604 1316 New Hampshire NW Washington DC 20036 Office Phone: 202-887-0877. Personal E-mail: pridco@verizon.net.

MERRIFIELD, JEFFREY S., commissioner; b. Antrim, NH, 1963; m. Diana M. Merrifield; 3 children. BA magna cum laude, Tufts U., 1985; JD, Georgetown U.Law Ctr., 1992. Bar: NH, DC. Legis. asst. to Senator Gordon Humphrey US Senate, Washington, 1987—90, legis. asst. to Senator Robert Smith, 1990—92; assoc. McKenna & Cuneo LLP, Washington, 1992—95; majority coun. & staff dir. Senate Subcommittee on Superfund, Waste Control and Risk Assessment, Washington, 1995—98; commr. US Nuclear Regulatory Commn., Rockville, 1998—. Mem.: DC Bar Assn., NH State Bar Assn. Achievements include drafting legislation dealing with solid and hazardous waste disposal and cleanup regulation. Office: US Nuclear Regulatory Commn One White Flint N 11555 Rockville Pike Rockville MD 20852-2738 Office Phone: 301-415-1855.

MERRILL, ABEL JAY, retired lawyer; b. Balt., Mar. 25, 1938; s. Yale and Evelyn (Cordish) M.; m. Susan Stein, June 15, 1963; children: Adam L., Julie F. BA, Colgate U., 1959; LLB, U. Md., 1964. Bar: Md. 1964. Law clk. U.S. Ct. Appeals, Balt., 1964-65; assoc. Gordon, Feinblatt & Rothman, Balt., 1965-70; atty. pvt. practice, Annapolis, Md., 1970-78, 83—; prin. Blumenthal, May, Downs & Merrill, Annapolis, 1979-83; mem. firm Merrill & Cruttenden, P.A.; ret., 2006. Mem. inquiry com. Atty. Grievance Commn. Md., 1975-85, character com. Ct. of Appeals, 1987-88; mem. pension oversight bd. Anne Arundel County, Md., 2000-03. Co-author: (software) Lawgic Maryland Wills and Trusts, 2004—. Fellow Am. Coll. Probate Counsel; mem. ABA, Md. Bar Assn., Anne Arundel County Bar Assn. E-mail: abelj@merillaw.com.

MERRILL, ALLAN P., construction executive; BS, Univ. Pa. Mng. dir., co-head glob. resources group Dillon Read & Co., & UBS, 1987—2000; pres. Homebuilder.com div. Move Inc., 2000—01; exec. v.p. corp. develop. & strategy Move Inc., 2001—07; exec. v.p., CFO Beazer Homes USA Inc., Atlanta, 2007—. Bd. mem. Homebuilding Cmty. Found.; mem. policy adv. bd. Joint Ctr. Housing Studies Harvard Univ. Office: Beazer Homes USA Ste 1200 1000 Abernathy Rd Atlanta GA 30328 *

MERRILL, ARTHUR LEWIS, retired theologian; b. Tura, Assam, India, Sept. 14, 1930; s. Alfred Francis and Ida (Walker) M.; m. Barbara Jean Mayer, Aug. 18, 1951 (dec. June 1978); children: Margaret Jean, Katherine Merrill Nelson, Robert L.; m. Margaret Z. Morris, Sept. 11, 1985. BA, Coll. of Wooster, 1951; BD with distinction, Berkeley Bapt. Div. Sch., 1954; PhD, U. Chgo., 1962. Ordained to ministry United Ch. of Christ, 1954. Asst. prof. Bapt. Missionary Tng. Sch., Chgo., 1957-58; assoc. prof. Mission House Theol. Sem., Plymouth, Wis., 1958-62, United Theol. Sem. Twin Cities, New Brighton, Minn., 1962-67, prof., 1967-95, prof. emeritus, 1995—. Author: United Theological Seminary of the Twin Cities: An Ecumenical Venture, 1993; co-author: Biblical Witness and the World, 1967; co-editor: Scripture in History and Theology, 1977; contbr. articles to profl. publs. ATS-Lilly postdoctoral fellow, 1966-67. Mem. Soc. Bibl. Lit., Am. Schs. Oriental Rsch., Israel Exploration Soc., Minn. Theol. Libr. Assn. (pres. 1994-95). Home: 36177 Wabana Rd Grand Rapids MN 55744-6446 Personal E-mail: artgaro@northlc.com.

MERRILL, CHARLES EUGENE, lawyer; b. San Antonio, Aug. 26, 1952; s. Charles Perry and Florence Elizabeth Merrill; m. Carol Ann Rutter, Apr. 28, 1984; children: Elizabeth C., Charles C. AB, Stanford U., 1974; JD, U. Calif., Berkeley, 1977. Bar: Mo. 1977, Calif. 1983, Ill. 1993. Mem. Husch & Eppenberger, LLC, St. Louis, 1977—. Mem. ABA, Bar Assn. of Met. St. Louis. Office: Husch & Eppenberger LLC 190 Carondelet Plz Ste 600 Saint Louis MO 63105-3441 Business E-Mail: charlie.merrill@husch.com.

MERRILL, CHRISTOPHER LYALL, writer; b. Northampton, Mass., Feb. 24, 1957; s. Charles Francis Merrill and Suzanne Sigmund France; m. Lisa Ellen Gowdy, June 4, 1983; children: Hannah Frances, Abigail Rose. BA, Middlebury Coll., 1979; MA, U. Wash., 1982. Dir. Santa Fe Writers Conf., 1987-90, Santa Fe Literary Ctr., 1988-92; William H. Jenks chair Contemporary Letters Coll. of the Holy Cross, Worcester, Mass., 1995-2000; dir. internat. writing program U. Iowa, Iowa City, 2000—. Author: The Old Bridge: The Third Balkan War and The Age of the Refugee, 1995, Watch Fire, 1994, The Grass of Another Country: A Journey Through The World of Soccer, 1993, From the Faraway Nearby: Georgia O'Keefe As Icon, 1992, Only the Nails Remain: Scenes from the Balkan Wars, 1999, Brilliant Water, 2001, Things of the Hidden God, 2005; poetry editor Orion Mag., 1993-2003; contbg. editor Paris Rev., 1991-95; gen. editor-poetry series Gibbs Smith Pub., Layton, Utah, 1987-2001. Recipient Ingram Merrill Found. award, 1991, Pushcart Prize in Poetry, 1990, Arts and Letters chevalier French Govt., 2006. Mem. Acad. Am. Poets (Peter Lavan Younger Poets award 1993, Bosnian Stecak award 2001, Kostas Kyriazis Internat. Lit. award 2005). Episcopalian. Avocations: gardening, hiking, reading. Office: U Iowa Internat Writing Program Shambaugh House Iowa City IA 52242-2020 Office Phone: 319-335-2609. Business E-Mail: christopher-merrill@uiowa.edu.

MERRILL, DANIEL A., program manager; b. NJ; Data ctr. shift supr. Volt Info. Scis., 1984—85; image analyst DBA Sys., 1985—87; data ctr. supr. sys. divsn. TRW, 1987—89; info. tech. ops. mgr. advanced client/server devel. group Wollongong/Attachmate, 1989—99; mgr. internat. CPE cert. global product engring. UUNET Tech., 1999—2001; tech. project mgr. IP VPN product devel., comm. svcs. engring. Worldcom, Inc., 2001—02; info. tech. mgr. RDR, Inc., 2003—04; program mgr. Metters Industries, Inc., 2004—06, ManTech IS&T, 2006—. With USN, 1980—84. Mem.: Armed Forces Comm. and Engring. Assn., Internet Engring. Task Force, Am. Mgmt. Assn., Wash. Network Group, US Tennis Assn., Appalachian Mountain Club, Am. Legion. Home: 2015 Chapel Ct Frederick MD 21702-2624 Home Phone: 301-663-1787; Office Phone: 703-961-9799 ext. 221. Personal E-mail: dan.merrill@earthlink.net.

MERRILL, DONNA, special education educator; b. Raymond, Nebr., Oct. 30, 1933; d. Donald Frank and Edith Marie (Brightenburg) Spellman; m. Robert Henry Merrill, May 29, 1952; children: Nancy, Catherine, Robert, Barbara. BA, Park Coll., Parkville, Mo., 1955; MA, U. Mo., Kansas City, 1975, PhD, 1983. Editor publs. Park Coll., Parkville, Mo., 1953-57; tchr. Smithville Sch. Dist., Mo., 1965-85, Shawnee Mission Sch. Dist., Mo., 1985—2001, St. Agnes Sch., Mission, Kans., 2000—07. Adj. faculty U. Mo., Kansas City, 1985-1995; co-dir. Signet Summer Camp, Kansas City, 1985-88. Mem. Gifted Assn. Mo., Kans. Gifted-Talented Assn., Alpha Delta, Phi Kappa Phi, Pi Lambda Theta, Phi Delta Kappa. Avocation: travel. Home: 19626 SE Dykes Rd Holt MO 64048-8782 Home Phone: 816-320-2408. Personal E-mail: dmerrill915141@embarqmail.com.

MERRILL, EDWARD WILSON, chemical engineering professor; b. New Bedford, Mass., Aug. 31, 1923; s. Edward Clifton and Gertrude (Wilson) M.; m. Genevieve de Bidart, Aug. 19, 1948; children: Anne de Bidart, Francis de Bidart. AB, Harvard U., 1945; DSc, MIT, 1947. Research engr. Dewey & Almy div. W.R. Grace & Co., 1947-50; mem. faculty MIT, 1950-98, prof. chem. engring., 1964-98, Carbon P. Dubbs prof., 1973-96, emeritus, 1998—. Cons. in field. Contbr. articles to profl. jours. Pres. bd. trustees Buckingham Sch., Cambridge, 1969-74; trustee Browne and Nichols Sch., Cambridge, 1972-74, hon. trustee, 1974—. Fellow Am. Inst. for Med. and Biol. Engring., Am. Acad. Arts and Scis.; mem. AIChE (Alpha Chi Sigma award 1984, Charles M.A. Stine award 1993, Founders award 2000), Am. Chem. Soc., Soc. for Biomaterials (Clemson U. Award 1990, Founders award 2003). Achievements include patents for chemical and rheological instruments; research in polymers, rheology, medical engineering. Home: 90 Somerset St Belmont MA 02478-2010 Office Phone: 617-253-4593. Office Fax: 617-489-2165. Business E-Mail: emerrill@mit.edu.

MERRILL, FRANK HARRISON, data processing executive, consultant; b. Pitts., June 20, 1953; s. Edgar Frank and Harriet Margaret (Gallagher) M.; m. Rita Alice Mae Murray, May 27, 1977; 1 child, Laura Margaret. BSMetE, Colo. Sch. Mines., 1971-76; M of Computer Info. Systems, U. Denver, 1988. Cert. sys. profl., computer programmer; cert. PICK profl.; cert. computer profl.; A+ cert., MCSE. Metall. engr. Inspiration Copper Co., Miami, Ariz., 1979-80, Cominco Am., Inc., Bixby, Mo., 1980-81; programmer, analyst M.L. Foss, Inc., Denver, 1981-83, Titsch & Assocs., Denver, 1983; data processing mgr. PBI/BAXA, Inc., Denver, 1983-86; owner, sys. cons. Dynamic Solutions, Denver, 1986—2004; dir. software devel. Drycreek Assocs. Corp., 2004—; sr. devel. programmer Trust Co. Am., 2006—. Cons. in field, Denver, 1985—; instr. continuing edn. User's Group, Denver, 1985—2001; instr. computer info. sys. U. Denver, 1990-97; mem. grad. computer info. sys. faculty Colo. campus, U. Phoenix, 1991-94; bd. dirs. Inst. for Cert. of Computer Profls. 1993-96, Drycreek Assocs. Corp., 2004-. Leader Boy Scouts Am., Denver and Globe, Ariz., 1973-86, Denver, 1996—; mem. Marriage Encounter Interfaith Bd., Denver, 1985-89, chair, 1988-89; mem. coun. Rocky Mountain Aldersgate Marriage Encounter, 1986-94, exec. couple, 1990-94; mem. Volksmarch Steering Com. Lakewood on Parade, 1990-95; mem. St. Andrew's Soc. Colo.; nominating com. Free Meth. Ch., 1989-92, ch. bd. property and fin., 1992-94. 2d lt. U.S. Army, 1977-79. Recipient God and Svc. award Free Meth. Ch., 1984, Silver Beaver award Boy Scouts Am., 2007; named to PICK Industry Accreditation Coun., 1990. Mem. IEEE, SAR, Assn. Sys. Mgmt. (profl. pres. Mile-Hi chpt. 1992-93, mem. internat. cert. adv. com. 1993-95, chmn. 1994-95, mem. divsn. 17 coun. 1994-96, vice chmn. 1995-96, Distinguished Service award 1996), Colo. Pick Users' Group (edn. chmn. 1984—2001), Info. Sys. Security Assn., Scottish-Am. Mil. Soc. (charter, post contr. Post 100 Colo. 1991-95), Cheyenne High Plains Wanderers Club, A.C. Gilbert Heritage Soc. (Rocky Mtn. Regnl. pres. 1994-2000, mem. nat. exec. bd. 1995—2002), Nat. Soc. Magna Charta Dames & Barons. Republican. Mem. Free Methodist Ch. Avocations: model railroading, model rocketry, hiking, camping, mountain climbing.

MERRILL, GEORGE VANDERNETH, lawyer, investment executive; b. NYC, July 2, 1947; s. James Edward and Claire (Leness) M.; m. Janice Anne Humes, May 11, 1985; children: Claire Georgina, Anne Stewart. Student, Phillips Exeter Acad., 1960—64; AB magna cum laude, Harvard U., 1968, JD, 1972; MBA, Columbia U., 1973. Bar: NY 1973, U.S. Dist. Ct. (so. and ea. dists.) NY 1974, U.S. Ct. Appeals (2d cir.) 1974. Assoc. Cleary, Gottlieb, Steen & Hamilton, NYC, 1974-77, Hawkins, Delafield & Wood, NYC, 1977-79; v.p. Irving Trust Co., NYC, 1980-82, Listowel, Inc., NYC, 1982-84, bd. dirs., exec. v.p., 1984-93; v.p. instl. portfolio mgmt. Shawmut Investment Advisors, 1993-95; also co-mgr. Shawmut Growth & Income Equity Mut. Fund; v.p. instl. portfolio mgmt. Fleet Investment Advisors, 1995-96, also co-mgr. Galaxy Growth & Income Equity Mut. Fund.; v.p. trust and instl. portfolio mgmt., mem. Fla. equity com. No. Trust Corp., Chgo., 1996-2000; v.p., sr. personal investment officer, sector head Bank of NY Mellon, NYC, 2000—, mem. investment policy com., 2004—. Pres. Northfield Charitable Corp., NYC, 1986-93; v.p., sec. Brougham Prodn. Co., NYC, 1986-89, sr. v.p., sec., 1990-93; v.p., sec. Marinetics Inc., NYC, 1988-90, sr. v.p., sec., 1991-93; v.p. Sci. Design and Engring. Co., Inc., NYC, 1987-88, exec. v.p., 1989-93 Bd. dirs. Pres. Arell Found., NYC, 1985—93. Recipient Detur award, Harvard U., 1968; John Harvard scholar. Mem. ABA, Am. Mgmt. Assn., Nat. Cum Laude Soc., The Brook, Union Club (NYC), Down Town Assn., Racquet and Tennis Club, Somerset Club (Boston), Signet Soc. (Cambridge), Pilgrims of US. Home: 2 Pierce Rd Riverside CT 06878 Office: The Bank of NY Mellon 5th Fl 1290 Ave of the Americas New York NY 10104

MERRILL, HARVIE MARTIN, manufacturing executive, director; b. Detroit, Apr. 26, 1921; s. Harvie and Helen (Nelson) M.; m. Mardelle Merrill; children— Susan, Linda. BS in Chem. Engring, Purdue U., 1942. Devel. engr. Sinclair Refining Co., 1946-47; research and gen. mgr. 3M Co., St. Paul, 1947-65; v.p. fabricated products Plastics div. Stauffer Chem. Co., NYC, 1965-69; with Hexcel Corp., San Francisco, 1969-86, pres., chief exec. officer, 1969-86, chmn. bd., 1976-88. With USAF, 1942-46. Mem.: Interlachen Country Club. Home: 664 Osceola Ave Winter Park FL 32789

MERRILL, JEAN FAIRBANKS, writer; b. Rochester, NY, Jan. 27, 1923; d. Earl Dwight and Elsie (Fairbanks) M. BA, Allegheny Coll., 1944; MA, Wellesley Coll., 1945. Feature editor Scholastic Mags., 1947-50; editor Lit. Cavalcade, 1956-57; publs. div. Bank St. Coll. Edn., 1964-65. Children's books include Henry, the Hand-Painted Mouse, 1951, The Woover, 1952, Boxes, 1953, The Tree House of Jimmy Domino, 1955, The Travels of Marco, 1956, A Song for Gar, 1957, The Very Nice Things, 1959, Blue's Broken Heart, 1960, Shan's Lucky Knife (Jr. Lit. Guild selection), Emily Emerson's Moon, 1960 (Jr. Lit. Guild selection), The Superlative Horse (Jr. Lit. Guild selection), 1961 (Lewis Carroll Shelf award 1963), Tell About the Cowbarn, Daddy, 1963, The Pushcart War (Lewis Carroll Shelf award), 1964 (Boys Club Am. Jr. Book award), High, Wide & Handsome, 1964 (Jr. Lit. Guild selection), The Elephant Who Liked to Smash Small Cars, 1967, Red Riding, 1968, The Black Sheep, 1969, Here I Come-Ready or Not!, 1970, Mary, Come Running, 1970, How Many Kids are Hiding on My Block?, 1970, Please, Don't Eat My Cabin, 1971, The Toothpaste Millionaire (Dorothy Canfield Fisher Meml. award 1975-76), 1972 (Sequoyah award 1977), The Second Greatest Clown in the World, 1972, The Jackpot, 1972, The Bumper Sticker Book, 1973, Maria's House, 1974, The Girl Who Loved Caterpillars, 1992; poetry books edited include A Few Flies and I, 1969; libretto for chamber opera Mary Come Running, 1983. Fulbright fellow, India, 1952—53. Mem. Authors League, Vt. Arts. Coun., Vt. Inst. Natural Sci., Vt. Nat. Resources Coun., Fulbright Assn., Acad. Am. Poets, Women's Internat. League Peace and Justice, Sierra Club, Audobon Soc., Women's Internat. League Peace and Justice, Phi Beta Kappa. Home Phone: 802-728-9549; Office Phone: 802-728-9549. *My interest in writing children's books may have derived from the impact certain books had on me as a child, and a wish to recreate the quality of that experience. As to my general motivation as a writer, I would say that it is to celebrate those aspects of the human experience that affirm the creative and life-reverencing instinct in man. I always hope that my stories may be essentially liberating, opening the reader to emotional, as well as intellectual experience, and that they may be entertaining, encouraging the capacity for joy by evoking the free play of a reader's curiosity, humor and inventiveness.*

MERRILL, JOHN, chef; b. Long Island, NY; Diploma, Culinary Inst. of Am., 1988. Externship JP Morgan Hotel, Hartford, Conn.; line cook Reach Resort, Key West, sous chef, exec. sous chef; mng. chef Boston Harbor Hotel, Marblehead, Mass.; co-founder gourmet catering co., Weston, Mass.; exec. sous chef Aura, Seaport Hotel, Boston, 1998, chef, 1999—. Guest chef (cooking events) Ready, Set, Cook, Food Network, Boston Wine Expo, The Anthony Spinazzola Gala Festival of Wine & Food, Edible, Share Our Strength's Operation Frontline. Named one of Boston's Rising Stars, StarChefs.com, 2006. Office: Aura The Seaport Hotel 1 Seaport Ln Boston MA 02110 Office Phone: 617-385-4000. *

MERRILL, STEPHEN, lawyer, consultant, retired governor; BA magna cum laude, U. NH, 1969; JD, Georgetown U., 1972. Former personal counsel to Sec. Air Force, Pentagon; atty. gen. State of NH, Concord, 1985—89, gov., 1993—97; of counsel Choate, Hall and Stewart, Boston, 1997—99; pres. Bingham Consulting Group, Boston, 1999—; ptnr. Bingham McCutchen LLP, Boston, 1999, of counsel. Mem. NH task force on Child Abuse and Neglect, former pres., legal counsel. Served to capt. USAF. Recipient AG Profl. award; Georgetown Law Fellow, Ford Found. Scholar, Univ. NH. Fellow: ABA (life); mem.: Pa. Bar Assn., DC Bar Assn., NH Bar Assn., Nat. Attys. Gen. Emeritus (co-chmn.), Nat. Gov.'s Assn. Emeritus, Ea. Assn. Attys. Gen. (chmn.), Phi Beta Kappa (Ford Found. scholar). Office: Bingham McCutchen 150 Federal St Boston MA 02110-1726 Office Phone: 617-951-8828. Office Fax: 617-951-8736. Business E-Mail: stephen.merrill@bingham.com.

MERRILL, STEVEN WILLIAM, research and development company executive; b. Oakland, Calif., Aug. 6, 1944; s. David Howard and Etha Nadine (Wright) Merrill. BA in Chemistry, Calif. State U., Hayward, 2004. Lic. pyrotechnic Calif. Apprentice Borgman Sales Co., San Leandro, Calif., 1960—64; assembler Calif. Fireworks Display, Rialto, Calif., 1970; pyrotechnician Hand Chem. Industries, Milton, Ont., Canada, 1972—74; dir. R&D Pyrospectaculars, Rialto, 1988—92; pyrotechnic cons., 1993—; owner, dir. Merrill Prodns. Ordnance, Crestline. Experimenter in field; chief chemist Baron Blakesly Solvents, Newark, 1987—88; court expert San Francisco Superior Ct., 1971, Victorville Superior Ct., Calif. Counselor Xanthos, Inc., Alameda, Calif., 1970. Mem.: AAAS, Am. Bd. Forensic Examiners, Am. Stats. Assn., Am. Chem. Soc., Internat. Platform Assn. Avocations: woodcarving, sculpting, photography, electronics, auto restoration. Home and Office: Merrill Prodns Ordnance PO Box 676 Crestline CA 92325-0676 Home Phone: 909-338-2913; Office Phone: 909-338-2913. Personal E-mail: birdscare@aol.com.

MERRILL, SUSAN L., financial regulatory service executive, lawyer; b. 1957; Grad. cum laude, U. Md., 1979; JD summa cum laude, Bklyn. Law Sch., 1986. Law clk. to Hon. Francis L. Van Dusen US Ct. Appeals (3rd cir.), 1986—87; assoc. Davis Polk & Wardwell, 1987—2004, ptnr., 1994—2004; exec. v.p. enforcement NYSE Group, Inc. (formerly NY Stock Exch.), 2004—07, Fin. Industry Regulatory Authority, Inc., Washington, 2007—. Office: Financial Industry Regulatory Authority Inc 1735 K St NW Washington DC 20006 Office Phone: 212-656-3000. *

MERRILL, WENDY JANE, financial services company executive; b. Waterbury, Conn., Dec. 4, 1961; d. David Kenneth and Jane Joy (Nevius) Merrill; m. Aidan T. Harrison (div. Nov. 1998); children: Christopher Harrison, Charlotte Harrison, Ryan Harrison; m. Michael G. Kelly, Oct. 2, 1999 (dissolved Nov. 2004). BA in Journalism, George Washington U., 1981; MBA in mgmt., Cornell U., 1992. Intern edn. HEW, Washington, 1978, writer, 1979; rsch. asst. dept. health svcs. adminstrn. George Washington U., Washington, 1979—81; sec. Nat. Assn. Beverage Importers, Washington, 1981; account exec. Staff Design, Washington, 1982; adminstrv. aide Internat. Food Policy Rsch. Inst., Washington, 1983—86; program assoc. Acad. for Ednl. Devel., Washington, 1986—87; pvt. practice cons. Washington, 1987—88; adminstrv. mgr. food and nutrition policy program Cornell U., Ithaca, NY, 1988—92; cons. mgmt. of med. practices Med. Bus. Mgmt., Ithaca, 1994—95; realtor Century 21 Alpha, 1995—97; compensation mgr. Santa Clara U., Calif., 1996—98; sr. compensation analyst Stanford U., Calif., 1998—99; human resources cons. Siemens Info. and Comm. Networks, 2000; compensation and benefits mgr. Kana Comms., 2000—01; U.S. compensation mgr. KLA-Tencor, 2001—02; pres. Total Solutions Ins. Agy., Inc., Calif., 2003—, Total Solutions Comml. Ventures, Inc., 2003—, Global Funding Unltd. LLC, 2007—. Cons., editor George Washington U., 1986; cons., rapporteur Internat. Food Policy Restaurant Inst., Washington and Copenhagen, Denmark, 1987; cons., adminstr. Hansell & Post, Washington, 1987-88, Cornell U., Washington and Ithaca, 1988; pvt. practice cons., 2001—. Sponsor Worldvision, Tanzania, 1988-91. George Washington U. scholar, 1979-81. Mem. Zonta Club (charter pres. Silicon Valley chpt. 2006—), Sigma Delta Xi (scholar 1980). Democrat. Avocations: piano, hiking, swimming. Home: 9000 Las Vegas Blvd S #1102 Las Vegas NV 89123 Business E-Mail: wendy@totalsolutionscv.com.

MERRILL, WILLIAM DEAN, retired architect, medical facility planning consultant; b. Portland, Oreg., June 1, 1915; s. Charles O. and Grace (Ruhl) M.; m. Bernice E. Wickham, Apr. 19, 1943 (dec. Sept. 1996); 1 child, Sue Ann Merrill Boardman; m. Irene Moe, July 30, 2001. Student in Fine Arts and Forestry, Oreg. State U., Corvallis, 1936-38; student in Architecture, U. Oreg., Eugene, 1939-42. Registered architect, Oreg., Calif., NCARB Prin. W.D. Merrill, Architect, Portland, 1956-64; architect, ptnr. Bissell & Merrill, Architects, Stockton, Calif., 1964-68; architect, Kaiser Engrs., Kaiser Found. Hosps. design and constrn., 1968-81; pvt. practice hosp. design and constrn., residential design and constrn., Bay Area, 1981-91; hosp. and sch. constrn. insp. Office of State Health Planning and Devel., State of Calif., 1984-93; ret. 1996. Served as lt. (j.g.) USNR, 1942-44, PTO. Mem. AIA (emeritus). Republican. Home: 25411 E Cedar Glen Loop Welches OR 97067

MERRILL, WILLIAM H., JR., lawyer, corporate financial executive; b. Indpls., Apr. 11, 1942; s. William H. and Jane (Robinson) M.; m. Winifred Jane Baur, July 25, 1964; children: Michele Jane, Betsy Diane. BS, Butler U., 1965; JD, Ind. U., 1967. Bar: Ind. 1967. Trust officer Mchts. Nat. Bank, Indpls., 1965—69; gen. counsel Everett I. Brown Co., Indpls., 1969—85; v.p., gen. counsel Landeco, Inc., Indpls., 1970—85; pres. Bash Seed Co., Indpls., 1975—97; gen. ptnr. Meta Ptnrs., 1984—90. Pres. Meta Investment Co., 1988-90, Meta Mgmt. Co., 1988-90, Northwest Devel. Corp., 1975—, Scotts Garden Ctr., Inc., 1977-97; bd. dirs. Custom Molded Products, Inc. Mem. Carmel (Ind.) City Plan Commn., 1975-85, pres. 1982-85. Mem. ABA, Ind. Bar Assn., Indpls. Bar Assn., Crooked Stick Golf Club. Office: 3205 W 71st St Indianapolis IN 46268-2244 Office Phone: 317-291-1441. Personal E-mail: merrillwhmjr@aol.com.

MERRIMAN, KEVIN THOMAS, lawyer; b. Rochester, NY, Sept. 17, 1966; s. William Emmett and Anne Flaherty Merriman; m. Joy Alexandria Mautner, May 23, 1992; children: Samuel, Alexander. BS, Cornell U., 1989; JD, SUNY, Buffalo, 1992. Bar: N.Y. 1993. Assoc. Allen, Lippes & Shonn, Buffalo, 1993-98; ptnr. Hurwitz & Fine, P.C., Buffalo, 1998—2004, Goldberg Segalla LLP, Buffalo, 2004—. Mem. NY Bar Assn. (Young Lawyers award, Torts, Insurance and Compensation Law Sect., 2002), Def. Rsch. Inst., Erie County Bar Assn., Am. Inns of Ct. Democrat. Home: 590 South St E East Aurora NY 14052-2951 Office: Goldberg Segalla LLP 665 Main St Ste 400 Buffalo NY 14203 Office Phone: 716-566-5411. Business E-Mail: kmerriman@goldbergsegalla.com.

MERRIN, SEYMOUR, computer company executive; b. Bklyn., Aug. 13, 1931; s. Joseph and Esther Bella (Manelis) M.; m. Elaine Cohen, Sept. 4, 1960 (dec. May 1962); m. Elizabeth Jenifer Slack, Oct. 12, 1963 (dec. Mar. 1995); children: Charles Seymour, Mariamne Jenifer Weights; m. Helene Claire Singer, Sept. 1, 2001 BS, Tufts Coll., 1952; MS, U. Ariz., 1954; PhD, Pa. State U., 1962. Geologist Magma Copper Co., Superior, Ariz., 1954, U.S. Geol. Survey, 1956-58; chemist IBM, Poughkeepsie, NY, 1962-64; mgr. package devel., mgr. reliability and failure analysis Sperry Semiconductor divsn. Sperry Rand, Norwalk, Conn., 1965-68; cons. materials tech. Fairfield, Conn., 1967-69; v.p., dir. Innotech Corp., Norwalk, 1969-74; divsn. mgr. Emdex divsn. Exxon Enterprises, Milford, Conn., 1974-78; chmn., dir. Computerworks, Westport, Conn., 1978-85; v.p., dir. personal computing svc. Gartner Group, Inc., Stamford, Conn., 1984-87; pres. Merrin Resources, Southport, Conn., 1987-89, Merrin Info. Svcs., Inc., Santa Fe, 1987—. Bd. dirs. Micrografx Corp., Allen, Tex.; adv. panel Apple Computer Co., Cupertino, Calif., 1982-83; adv. bd. Compaq Computer Corp., Houston, 1984-85, Computer and Software News, NYC, 1984-89; program adv. bd. Comdex, Boston, 1985—; lectr. in field. Contbr. numerous articles to profl. publs.; patentee in field. Bd. dirs. Futures for Children, Albuquerque, 2004—, Santa Fe Internat. Folk Market, Couse Found., Taos, N.Mex. With US Army, 1954—56. Fellow Geol. Soc. Am., Am. Inst. Chemists; Computing Tech. Industry Assn. (founder, pres. 1981-83, bd. dirs. 1981-84). Home and Office: 840 Camino de las Trampas Santa Fe NM 87501 Personal E-mail: smerrin@aol.com.

MERRING, ROBERT ALAN, lawyer, arbitrator, mediator; b. Middletown, NY, Oct. 5, 1951; s. Merton Joseph and Mabel Ruth M.; m. Lynn S. Connor, Mar. 16, 1996. Student, Ohio Wesleyan U., 1969—70; AB with distinction and departmental honors, Stanford U., 1973; JD with honors in Internat. and Fgn. Law, Columbia U., 1977; cert. Pepperdine Sch. Law, Inst. for Dispute Resolution, 1996. Bar: Calif. 1977, U.S. Dist. Ct. (cen. dist.) Calif. 1978, U.S. Dist. Ct. (so. and ea. dists.) Calif. 1980, U.S. Ct. Appeals (9th cir.) 1980, U.S. Dist. Ct. (no. dist.) Calif. 1983, U.S. Supreme Ct. 1987, Colo. 1989. Assoc. Pacht, Ross, Warne, Bernhard & Sears, Inc., LA, 1977-79, Donovan Leisure Newton & Irvine, LA, 1979-81, Cutler and Cutler, LA, 1983-88, Friedemann & Hart, Irvine, 1988-89; pvt. practice Orange County, Calif., 1989—. Civil arbitrator, temporary judge, judge pro tem Orange County Superior Ct., 1993—, arbitrator NASD, 2006; mediator U.S. Bankruptcy Ct. (ctrl. dist.) Calif., 1996—; mediator Orange County Superior Ct., 1998-2002; clin. prof. Loyola U. Law Sch., LA, 1981-82. Editor Columbia Jour. Transnat. Law, 1976-77. Columbia U. Internat. fellow, 1975—76. Mem.: ABA, Orange County Patent Law Assn., Am. Arbitration Assn. (panel comml. arbitrators 1993—, panel mediators 2002—), State Bar Calif. (del. 1998—2003), Assn. Conflict Resolution, Assn. Bus. Trial Lawyers, Orange County Bar Assn. (chair intellectual property and tech. law sect. 2000—01). Office Phone: 714-444-9922. Business E-Mail: rmerring@merringlaw.com.

MERRION, ARTHUR BENJAMIN, mathematics professor, tree farmer; b. Williamstown, NJ, Oct. 25, 1938; s. Anthony Robert and Eva May Merrion; m. Martha Jane Banse, Dec. 26, 1965 (div. May 1977); children: Benjamin Thomas, Elizabeth Jane. Attended, Rutgers U., 1957, Drexel Inst. Tech., 1961; fellowship, Appalachian State U., 1965; AB in Math., Pfeiffer Coll. (now Univ.), 1965; MS in Numerical Sci., Johns Hopkins U., 1976. Navigations scientist Oceanographic Office, Suitland, Md., 1966—72, Def. Mapping Agy. Hydrographic Ctr., 1972—78; fellow ops. rsch. analysis Sec. Army Pentagon, Washington, 1978-80; ops. rsch. analyst Asst. Sec. Army, Washington, 1980-86; tree farmer Huntingtown, Md., 1986-98. Instr. math. and stats. Embry-Riddle Aeronautical U., 1993-94; math. instr. Charles County C.C., 1990-91; tutor Literary Coun., navigation scientist Silas Bent Naval Oceanographic Vessel, 1966. Author: A Short Story By Edgar Allen Pooh. With U.S. Army, 1957-58. Mem. Md. Soc. SAR, Nat. Soc SAR, Internat. Soc. Poets (Poet of Merit award). Achievements include research in applying math. chaos theory to weather modification; invention of upside-down pear-shaped earth reversal maneuver for correcting earth perturbations. Avocations: chess, violin, Judo, wrestling. Home: PO Box 685 Jefferson NC 28640-0685 *The Bible says many different things to many different people. To Thomas Alva Edison it was a "Chemist's Handbook". To me it is the source of all man's creativity, directly from the greatest Creator of all. It is a source of inspiration, a solace for periods of depression, and a prescription when I'm in error.*

MERRISS, PHILIP RAMSAY, JR., banker; b. NYC, June 7, 1948; s. Philip Ramsay and Elisabeth (Paine) M.; m. Janet Henry Hylan, Oct. 27, 1973. AB in Econs. magna cum laude, Lafayette Coll., 1970; MBA with high distinction, Dartmouth Coll., 1972. Assoc. corp. fin. dept. A.G. Becker and Co. Inc., NYC, 1972-73; fin. analyst corp. banking dept. Chase Manhattan Bank, 1973, asst. treas. N.Y.C. dist., 1974-75, 2d v.p. mining and metals div., 1976-78, 2d v.p. petroleum div., 1979-86, client exec., v.p. pub. utilities component, 1987-89, credit supv. officer, div. exec., v.p. U.S. pvt. banking, 1989-94; credit exec. J.P. Morgan Pvt. Bank, NYC, 1994-97, mng. dir. and credit exec., 1997—. Capt. US Army, 1978. Tuck scholar Dartmouth Coll., 1972. Mem. Am. Econ. Assn., Aircraft Owners and Pilots Assn., Weston Gun Club, Yale Club, Fairfield County Hunt Club, Phi Beta Kappa. Republican. Episcopalian. Home: 11 Katydid Ln Weston CT 06883-1808 Office: JP Morgan Chase & Co 345 Park Ave New York NY 10154-1002

MERRITT, BRUCE GORDON, lawyer; b. Iowa City, Oct. 4, 1946; s. William Olney and Gretchen Louise (Kuever) M.; m. Valerie Sue Jorgensen, Dec. 28, 1969; children: Benjamin Carlyle, Alicia Marie. AB magna cum laude, Occidental Coll., 1968; JD magna cum laude, Harvard U., 1972. Bar: Calif. 1973, NY 1996. Assoc. Markbys, London, 1972—73, Nossaman, Krueger & Marsh, LA, 1973—79, ptnr., 1979—81; asst. US Atty., LA, 1981—85; ptnr. Debevoise & Plimpton, LA, 1989—95, NYC, 1996—2001. Adj. prof. law Loyola Law Sch., LA, 2003—. Vestryman St. Mark's Episcopal Ch., Glendale, Calif., 2006—; bd. dir. Inner Law Ctr., LA, 1991—96. Fellow Am. Coll. Trial Lawyers; mem. Calif. State Bar Assn. (exec. com. litig. sect. 1992-95), Phi Beta Kappa, Harvard Club (N.Y.C.). Episcopalian. Office Phone: 818-521-1812. Personal E-mail: brucegmerritt@sbcglobal.net.

MERRITT, CAROLYN, government agency administrator; Diploma, Radford U. Mngr. of solid and hazardous waste and environmental health and safety Champion Intl. Corp., 1988—94; sr. project mngr. RMT/Jones and Neuse, Inc., Houston, 1994; sr. v.p. for Environment, Health and Safety IMC Global Inc., Northbrook, Ill.; chmn, CEO U.S. Chemical Safety and Hazard Investigation Board, 2002—. Office: 2175 K Street NW Ste 400 Washington DC 20037 Office Phone: 202-261-7600.

MERRITT, GILBERT STROUD, federal judge; b. Nashville, Tenn., Jan. 17, 1936; s. Gilbert Stroud and Angie Fields (Cantrell) M.; m. Louise Clark Fort, July 10, 1964 (dec.); children: Stroud, Louise Clark, Eli. BA, Yale U., 1957; LLB, Vanderbilt U., 1960; LLM, Harvard U., 1962. Bar: Tenn. 1960. Asst. dean Vanderbilt U. Law Sch., 1960-61, lectr., 1963-69, 71-75, assoc. prof. law, 1969-70; assoc. Boult Hunt Cummings & Conners, Nashville, 1962-63; asst. metro. atty. City of Nashville, 1963-66; US Dist. atty. for (mid. dist.) Tenn., 1966-69; ptnr. Gullett, Steele, Sanford, Robinson & Merritt, Nashville, 1970-77; judge US Ct. Appeals (6th cir.), Nashville, 1977-2001, chief judge, 1989—96, sr. judge., 2001—. Exec. sec. Tenn. Code Commn., 1977. Mng. editor: Vanderbilt Law Rev, 1959-60; contbr. articles to law jours. Del. Tenn. Constl. Conv., 1965; chmn. bd. trustees Vanderbilt Inst. Pub. Policy Studies. Mem. ABA, Fed. Bar Assn., Tenn. Bar Assn., Nashville Bar Assn., Vanderbilt Law Alumni Assn. (pres. 1979-80), Am. Law Inst., Order of Coif. Episcopalian. Office: US Ct Appeals Customs House 701 Broadway Ste 303 Nashville TN 37203-3967 *

MERRITT, HOWARD SUTERMEISTER, retired art educator; b. Ithaca, NY, June 12, 1915; s. Ernest and Bertha (Sutermeister) M.; m. Florence Sederquest Hill, June 27, 1941; children— Jessica, Stephen, Jonathan, James. BA, Oberlin Coll., Ohio, 1936; M.F.A., Princeton U., NJ, 1942, PhD, 1958. Mem. faculty U. Rochester, N.Y., 1946-80, prof. emeritus, 1980—. Cons. 19th Century Am. Painting, 1960— Contbr. exhbn. catalogues and articles to various publs. Served with AUS, 1942-45. Decorated Bronze Star; Nat. Endowment for Humanities summer grantee, 1966-68 Mem. Coll. Art Assn. Home: 85 Bellevue Dr Rochester NY 14620-2703

MERRITT, JAMES EDWARD, lawyer; b. Hickory, NC, June 10, 1938; s. Eddy Schmidt and Dorothy (Hunt) M.; m. Joan L. Hiscock, June 14, 1960 (div. 1983); children: James Edward Jr., Catherine Hunt; m. Kristine McFadden, May 4, 1983. AB, Duke U., 1959; LLB, Harvard U., 1962. Bar: D.C. 1962, Calif. 1968; cert. tax specialist, Calif. Assoc. Pogue & Neal, Washington, 1962-64; trial atty. regional counsel IRS, San Francisco, 1964-68; assoc. Morrison & Foerster, LLP, San Francisco and Washington, 1968-72, ptnr., 1972—98, sr. counsel, 1998—. Lectr. Golden Gate U., San Francisco, 1970-74; cons. chief counsel IRS, Washington, 1983; mem. adv. bd. Tax Mgmt. Inc., N.Y.C., 1987—. Contbr. articles to profl. jours. Mem. Am. Coll. Tax Counsel (regent, chair 1997-2000), ABA (coun., dir., sect. taxation 1990-93, mem. commn. on legal problems of elderly 1993-96), Bar Assn. D.C., Bar Assn. San Francisco (Outstanding Tax Lawyer 1983), J. Edgar Murdock Inn of Ct. Avocations: travel, gardening, sports. Office: Morrison & Foerster LLP 30 Winster Fax Williamsburg VA 23185-5542 Office Phone: 757-258-3819. Personal E-mail: jimmerritt@aol.com.

MERRITT, JEAN, consulting firm executive, psychotherapist; b. NYC, Oct. 29, 1952; d. Harry and Ruth (Happel) Packman; m. Richard L. Kashinsky, Aug. 2, 1976 (div.); m. Richard L. Merritt, May 5, 1985 (div. June 2002); children: Courtney Morgan, Melissa Morgan Grad. high sch., Bayside, NY. From contr. to v.p., sec., treas. Kaswol Corp., Richmond Hill, NY, 1973—85; corp. exec. Federated Cons. Svc., Inc., Bayside, NY, CFO Jupiter, Fla., 1985—2002, psychotherapist, 2004—, dir. mktg., 2005—. Coach Queens Spl. Olympics, 1985. Mem. Nat. Trust for Hist. Preservation, Nat. Fedn. Wildlife, Ctr. for Environ. Edn., Defenders of Wildlife, Nat. Resource Def. Coun., Humane Soc. of U.S., Sierra Club, Amnesty Internat. Avocations: flying, art collecting, painting, interior design, gourmet cooking. Home: 4856 Katherine Ave Sherman Oaks CA 91423 Office Phone: 917-319-0184. E-mail: jeanie22m@aol.com.

MERRITT, NANCY-JO, lawyer; b. Phoenix, Sept. 24, 1942; d. Robert Nelson Meeker and Violet Adele Gibson; children: Sidney Kathryn, Kurt, Douglas. BA, Ariz. State U., 1964, MA, 1974, JD, 1978. Bar: Ariz. 1978, U.S. Dist. Ct. Ariz. 1978, U.S. Ct. Appeals (9th cir.) 1984. Shareholder Fennemore Craig, P.C., Phoenix. Author: Understanding Immigration Law, 1993; sr. editor: Immigration and National Law Handbook, 1993—; contbr. articles to profl. jours. Chair bd. dirs. TERROS, 1995-97. Fellow Ariz. Bar Found.; mem. ABA, Am. Immigration Lawyers Assn. (chairperson Ariz. chpt. 1985-87, several coms., Pro Bono award), Ariz. Bar Assn. (immigration sect.), Nucleus Club. Democrat. Avocations: modern literature, south american literature, hiking, gardening. Office Phone: 602-916-5411, 702-692-8003. Business E-Mail: njmerritt@fclaw.com.

MERRITT, PAUL, neuroscientist, educator; BS, Colo. State U., Ft. Collins, 1987—96, MS, 1997—99, PhD, 1997—2002. Lic. cognitive neuroscience Colo. State U., 2002. Post doctoral asst. George Wash. U., DC, 2002—04; asst. prof. Tex. A&M U., Corpus Christi, 2002—. Grantee Rsch. Enhancement grant, Tex. Excellence Fund, 2004—05, Tex. Rsch. Devel. Fund, 2005—06. Mem.: Assn. Psychol. Sci., Psychonomic Soc. (assoc.). Office: Texas A&M Univ 6300 Ocean Dr Unit 5827 Corpus Christi TX 78412-5827 Home Phone: 361-739-5914. Office Fax: 361-825-6098. Business E-Mail: paul.merritt@tamucc.edu.

MERRITT, PHYLLIS JUNE, music educator, director; b. Elizabethton, Tenn., Mar. 28, 1939; d. Earl H. and Willie Greene Merritt. BS in Music Edn., East Tenn. State U., 1960; MusM in Edn., Fla. State U., 1972. Tchr. music Kingsley Elem. Sch., Kingsport, Tenn., 1960—61, Weis Elem. Sch., Pensacola, Fla., 1961—62; dir. choral music Brownsville Jr. H.S., Pensacola, Fla., 1962—65, Escambia H.S., Pensacola, 1965—76, Meigs Jr. H.S., Shalimar, Fla., 1976—80, Niceville H.S., Fla., 1980—90; dir. music Trinity United Meth. Ch., Fort Walton Beach, Fla., 1991—98, ret., 1998; founder Phyllis Merritt Singers, Pensacola, 2003—, artistic music dir., 2003—. Singer, conductor Inst. European Studies Concert Tour, 1970, Internat. Assn. Cultural European Concert Tour, 1973, Young Americans Nat. Choral Festival, 1985, Big Apple Choral Festival, 1986. Named Tchr. of Yr., Escambia County, Fla., 1971, Okaloosa County, Fla., 1986; recipient Disting. Alumni in Arts award, East Tenn. State U., 1990. Mem.: Fla. Vocal Assn. (pres. 1988—95, chmn. dist. 1988—95), Am. Choral Dirs. Assn. (sr. pres. 1975—77, pres. divsn. 1979—81, bd. dirs., dir. various convs., musician various concerts, Wayne Hugoboom Disting. Svc. award 1989, So. Divsn. Excellence in Choral Art award 2000). Avocation: travel. Home: 431 Gregory Ave Valparaiso FL 32580

MERRITT, SUSAN MARY, computer science educator, dean; b. New London, Conn., July 28, 1946; d. Nelson Alfred and Mary (Cory) M. BA summa cum laude, Cath. U. Am., 1968; MS, NYU, 1969, PhD, 1982; Cert., Inst. for Edn. Mgmt., Harvard U., 1985. Joined Sisters of Divine Compassion, 1975; permanent cert. tchr., N.Y. Systems programmer Digital Equipment Corp., Maynard, Mass., 1969-70; tchr. Good Counsel Acad. High Sch., White Plains, N.Y., 1970-75; adj. instr. computer sci. Pace U., 1972-78, asst. prof. White Plains, 1978-82, assoc. prof., 1982-85, prof., 1985—, chmn. dept., 1981-83, dean Sch. Computer Sci., 1983—. Spkr. in field, mem. gen. coun. Sisters Divine Compassion, 1988-92. Contbr. articles to profl. jours. Recipient Carol S. Russett Award for Disting. Svcs., ACE Nat. Women's Leadership Network, Recipient Cert. of Appreciation, IEEE, 1990, endowment, Ivan G. Seidenberg Sh. Computer Sci. and Info. Sys., 2005. Mem. Assn. for Computing Machinery (edn. bd. 1988—), Phi Beta Kappa, Sigma Xi. Roman Catholic.

MERRITT, THOMAS BUTLER, lawyer; b. Toledo, Apr. 3, 1939; s. George Robert and Bernice (Gerwin) M.; m. Mary Jane Bothfeld, July 23, 1966; children— Thomas Butler, Haidee Soule, Theodore Bothfeld AB magna cum laude, Harvard U., 1961, LLB cum laude, 1966. Bar: Mass. 1966, NH 1994, Vt. 2006, Maine 2007, US Ct. Appeals (1st cir.) 1999, US Supreme Ct. 1974. With N.Y. State Dept. Civil Svc., Albany, 1961—63; intern Office of Legal Advisr U.S. Dept. State, Washington, 1965; law clk. to assoc. justice Arthur E. Whittemore Supreme Jud. Ct. Mass., Boston, 1966-67; assoc. Nutter, McClennen & Fish, Boston, 1967-69, Palmer & Dodge, Boston, 1969-73; asst. counsel to Gov. Mass., 1973; reporter of decisions Supreme Jud. Ct. Mass., Boston, 1974-94; pvt. practice NH, 1994—. Contbr. articles to profl. jours. Mem. Conservation Commn. Town of Sherborn, Mass., 1969-74, chmn., 1972-74; planning bd. Town of Hollis, NH, 1995-98; mem. NH Bd. Natural Scientists, 2005—. 1st lt. US Army, 1962-63, capt. USAR, 1963-69. Mem.: Vt. Bar Assn., Assn. Reporters Jud. Decisions (pres. 1983—84), Am. Soc. Internat. Law, NH Bar Assn. (sec. sec. mil. law), Mass. Bar Assn., Am. Law Inst. (life), Harvard Faculty Club (Cambridge), Harvard Club Boston, Union Club. Episcopalian. Office: PO Box 324 Littleton NH 03561-0324 Home Phone: 603-444-5354.

MERRITT, THOMAS M., lawyer; b. 1964; BS in Bus. Adminstrn., SUNY, Albany; JD, Hofstra U. Bar: NY 1990. Atty. Suffolk County Atty. Office, NY; asst. chief counsel NASD; dir., asst. gen. counsel Knight Trading Group, 2000—04, interim gen. counsel, 2004—05, chief legal officer & co-head office of gen. counsel, 2005—. Office: Knight Trading Group 545 Washington Blvd Fl 1 Jersey City NJ 07310-1607

MERRITT, WILLIAM ALFRED, JR., retired lawyer, real estate company executive; b. NYC, Aug. 7, 1936; s. William Alfred and Florence Anne (O'Connor) M.; m. Christine Marie Cartnick, Sept. 27, 1969; children— William Tyler, Brian Edward, Elizabeth Cody BA in Econs., Holy Cross Coll., Worcester, Mass., 1958; LLB, Harvard U., 1964. Bar: N.Y. 1965. Assoc. Olwine, Connelly, Chase, O'Donnell & Weyher, NYC, 1964-68; v.p. ops. and controls Bunge Corp., NYC, 1968-81; exec. v.p. TIE/Communications Inc., Seymour, Conn., 1981-90; pres. Wiltel Communications Systems Inc, Rolling Meadows, Ill., 1991-92; ptnr. Seaboard Equities Inc., Stamford, Conn., 1992—; gen. counsel Carolina Barnes Capital Inc., Stamford, 1992—99; ptnr. KM Group, Stamford, Conn., 1992—. Served to capt. USNR, 1958-80. Mem. Wee Burn Club, Harvard Club (N.Y.). Avocations: skiing, boating, golf. Home: 83 Brookside Rd Darien CT 06820-3505 Office: Ste 602 One Dock St Stamford CT 06902 Personal E-mail: w59merr@aol.com.

MERRIWEATHER, FREDA E., education educator; d. Oscar and Eura Merriweather; m. William M. Norvell, III, Apr. 30, 1961 (div.); children: Stacy LePrix Norvell, Tracy Norvell Dukes. BS, So. Ill. U., 1964; MS, U. Wis., Milwaukee, 1971; EdD, U. Louisville, 1992. Cert. tchr. So. Ill. U., 1964, Principal U. Wis., 1972, Superintendent State of Ky., 1991. Tchr. Siefert Elem. Sch., Milw., 1964—73; prin. Md. Ave. Sch., Milw., 1974—76, James Whit Comb Riley, Milw., 1977—80, Price Elem. Sch. - JCPS, Louisville, 1984—87; vice-prin. William McKinley Intermediate Sch., Milw., 1976—80; edn. cons. Ingham Internat. Sch. Dist., Holt, Mich., 1982—84; dir. Jefferson County Pub. Sch., Louisville, 1987—91, exec. dir., 1991—93, asst. supt., 1993—2002, 1993—2002; practitioner in residence U. Louisville, Louisville, 2002—. Mem. Gov.'s Literacy Task Force, Frankfort, Ky.; alumni bd. U. Louisville, 1993—95; alumni Supt. Prepared-McKenzie Group, Washington, 1995. Mem. Jr. Achieve., Louisville, Urban League, Louisville. Recipient Adminstrv. Leadership award, Collaborative for Tchg. and Learning, 2001, award, Sarah Scott Leadership, 1978, Valedictorian, H.S. Class, Alumni Fellow, Coll. of Edn., U. Louisville, 1999, Bingham Fellows, 1993, Grad. Sch. Dean's Citation, 1991, Ky. Edn. Leadership Inst., 1990, Outstanding Prin., Nat. Schools of Excellence, 1987; grantee, Leadership Louisville, 1992, Bd. of Alderman, 1992; Doctoral Program scholarship, Scottish Rites Found. Mem.: NAACP, Greater Louisville Alliance of Black Sch. Educators, Nat. Alliance of Black Sch. Educators, Urban League (dir.), Louisville Chpt. of Moles (parliamentation), Delta Sigma Theta Sorority. Avocations: dancing, card games, reading. Office Phone: 502-852-0635. Personal E-mail: femerr01@aol.com.

MERSEL, MARJORIE KATHRYN PEDERSEN, lawyer; b. Manila, Utah, June 17, 1923; d. Leo Henry and Kathryn Anna (Reed) Pedersen; m. Jules Mersel, Apr. 12, 1950; 1 child, Jonathan. AB, U. Calif., 1948; LLB, U. San Francisco, 1948. Bar: D.C. 1952, Calif. 1955. Pvt. practice, Beverly Hills, Calif., 1961—71, LA, 1997—; staff counsel Dept. Real Estate State of Calif., LA, 1971—97. Pub. counsel, 2000—02. Active L.A.-Guangzhou Sister City. Mem.: ABA, Current Affairs Forum, World Affairs Coun., So. Calif. Women Lawyers Assn. (treas. 1962—63), Trial Lawyers Assn., L.A. County Bar Assn., Beverly Hills Bar Assn., Beverly Hills C. of C., L.A.-Guanghou Sister City Assn., Sierra Club, L.A. Athletic Club. Home and Office: 13007 Hartsook St Sherman Oaks CA 91423-1616

MERSEREAU, HIRAM STIPE, wood products company consultant; b. Portland, Oreg., Aug. 4, 1917; s. E.W. and Ruth (Stipe) M.; m. Margaret Daggett, Dec. 25, 1937; children: Hiram Stipe, John Bradford, Timothy Daggett. Student, George Washington U., 1936-37, Harvard U., 1959. With Weyerhauser Timber Co., Klamath Falls, Oreg., 1937-38, Alexander-Yawkey Lumber Co., Prineville, Oreg., 1938-52; gen. mgr. lumber div. Crossett Co., Ark., 1954-62; corp. sr. v.p., gen. mgr. So. div. Ga.-Pacific Corp., 1963-82, cons., 1982—. Past dir. Citizens & So. Nat. Bank, Augusta, Appalachian Hardwood Mfrs. Inc., Merry Cos., Inc., Augusta. Past bd. dirs. Young Life, Ga. Conservancy, Jr. Achievement Augusta; bd. dirs. Augusta br. Boys Clubs Am., Augusta Cancer Fund; trustee Paine Coll., Augusta. Mem. Nat. Forest Products Assn. (exec. com., dir.) Republican. Presbyterian (elder). Home: 6 Turnberry Ln Sea Pines Plantation Hilton Head Island SC 29928

MERSEREAU, SUSAN, information systems company, data processing executive; b. Portland, Oreg., Sept. 5, 1946; d. Roland William Mersereau and Barbara Munro; m. Robert Stier, June 19, 1968; 1 child, Arran Elizabeth; m. Philip White, Nov. 17, 1989; children: Richard, Brandon. BA in History, Scripps, 1968; MAT in Edn. History, U. Chgo., 1971; MA in Whole Systems Design, Antioch, 1990. Tchr. South Shore High Sch., Chgo., 1969-70; adminstrv. asst. U. Ill., Chgo., 1970; rsch. analyst U. Wash., Seattle, 1971-72; dir. planning rsch. and evaluation Seattle Sch. Dist., 1972-80; program mgr. Weyerhauser Co., Tacoma, 1980-81, mgr. advanced tech., 1981-83, dir. telecom., 1983-88; gen. mgr., v.p. Weyerhauser Info. Systems, Tacoma, 1988-92, v.p. total quality region adminstrv. svcs. and aviation, 1992—98; v.p. organizational effectiveness Weyerhauser Co., Federal Way, Wash., 1998—2003, sr. v.p. info. tech, chief info. officer, 2003—. Bd. dirs. King County Jr. Achievemen, King County United Way. Avocations: skiing, art, hiking, tennis, fishing. Office: Weyerhaeuser Co 33663 Weyerhaeuser Way S PO Box 9777 Federal Way WA 98063-9777 Office Phone: 253-924-2345.

MERSINI - HOUGHTON, LAURA, physicist, educator; d. Nexhat and Stela Mersini; m. Jeffrey Houghton, Feb. 2, 2003. MSc in Physics, U. Md., 1997; PhD, U. Wis., Milw., 2000. Cert. theoretical physics U. Wis., Milw. Physics Dept., 2000. Rsch. fellow Scuola Normale Superiore, Pisa, Italy, 2000—02; postdoctoral fellow Syracuse U., Physics Dept., NY, 2002—03; vis. prof. Perimeter Inst. Theoretical Physics, Waterloo, Ontario, Canada, 2003—04; asst. prof. physics U. NC, Chapel Hill, 2004—. Contbr. articles to profl. jours. Fellow, Fulbright Found., 1994. Achievements include research in addressing fundamental problems of cosmology and modern physics by means of a new field and direction, string cosmology. Connecting and testing models and the new field to astrophysical observables. Office: U NC Dept Physics and Astronomy Phillips Hall UNC-Chapel Hill Chapel Hill NC 27599 Home Phone: 919-967-9302; Office Phone: 919-962-4277. Office Fax: 919-962-0480. Business E-Mail: mersini@physics.unc.edu.

MERSKY, ROY MARTIN, legal association administrator, educator; b. NYC, Sept. 1, 1925; s. Irving and Rose (Mendelson) Mirsky; m. Rosemary Bunnage; children: Deborah, Lisa, Ruth. BS, U. Wis., 1948, JD, 1952, MALS, 1953. Bar: Wis. 1952, U.S. Supreme Ct. 1970, Tex. 1972, U.S. Ct. Appeals (5th cir.) 1981, N.Y. 1983. Cataloger U.S. govt. documents U. Wis.

Law Libr., 1951—52; reference asst. Madison Free Libr., Wis., 1952; pvt. practice law Wis., 1952—54; readers adv., reference and catalog libr., mcpl. reference libr. at City Hall, Milw. Pub. Libr., 1953—54; chief readers and reference svc. Yale Law Libr., 1954—59; dir. Wash. State Law Libr., 1959—63; exec. sec. Jud. Coun. Commn. Wash. Court Report, State of Wash., 1959—63; prof. law, law libr. U. Colo., Boulder, 1963—65; prof. law, dir. rsch. U. Tex., Austin, 1965—, dir. Tarlton Law Libr., Jamail Ctr. Legal Rsch., 1965—, William Stamps Farish Centennial prof. law, 1996—2001, Harry M. Reasoner Regents chair in law, 2001—, prof. Grad. Sch. Libr. and Info. Sci., 1976—. Vis. prof. law, dir. law libr. N.Y. Law Sch., N.Y.C., 1982-84; M.D. Anderson Found. vis. prof. law Queen Mary and Westfield Coll., U. London, 1994; interim dir. Jewish Nat. and Univ. Libr., Hebrew U., 1972-73; vis. fellow Australian Nat. U. Fac. of Law, Canberra, 1999; cons. to legal pubs. and law schs.; panelist various confs.; lectr. in field. Author: A Treasure in Jerusalem, 1974, (with J. Myron Jacobstein) Fundamentals of Legal Research, 7th edit., 1998, 8th, edit., 2002, (with Dunn) Legal Research Illustrated, An Abridgement of Fundamentals of Legal Research, 8th edit., 2002, (with Albert P. Blaustein) The First One Hundred Justices: Statistical Studies on the Supreme Court of the United States, 1978, (with W. Bader) The First One Hundred Eight Justices, 2004, (with Gary R. Hartman, Suzanne F. Young, Jill Duffy and Jake Lisbert) A Documentary History of the Legal Aspects of Abortion in the United States, 1990, 96, 2001 (with Jacobstein Hartman and Bonnie Koneski-White) Reports on Successful and Unsuccessful Nominations, 1992, 95, 96, (with Gary Hartman and Cindy L. Tate) Landmark Supreme Court Cases, 2004 (with Richard Leiter) The Spirit of Lain Librarianship, 2d edit., 2005; contbr. articles to profl. jours., chpts. to books; editor numerous books in field. Bd. dirs. Ctrl. Tex. chpt. ACLU, pres., 1968; bd. dirs. Human Rights Documentation Exch., 1997-2001; mem. bd. advisors Anti-Defamation League, Austin, 1974-78, Tex. Book Festival, 2001-2004; bd. dirs. Hillel Found., 1980-83; bd. dirs. Tex. Com. for Humanities, 1978-80, chair, 1980-82, conf. facilitator, 1982. With U.S. Army, 1944-46, ETO. Decorated Bronze Star. Fellow Am. Bar Found. (life), Tex. Bar Found.; mem. ABA (various coms.), AAUP (chmn. nominating com. 1979-80), Am. Law Inst., Assn. Am. Law Schs. (various coms.), Internat. Assn. Lawyers and Jurists (bd. govs. Am. sect. 1980-95), Nat. Bar Assn., Am. Assn. Law Librs. (chair various coms.), Am. Soc. Info. Sci. (pres. Tex./Okla. chpt. 1992-94), Scribes (bd. dirs. 1974-94, book awards com. 1978-96, pres. 1991-93, chair Scribes Law Review Competition award com. 1993—), Soc. Am. Law Tchrs. (bd. govs. 1979-88, nominations com. 1984), ALA (rsch. librs. group 1987, libr. edn. divsn.), Am. Soc. Indexers, Internat. Assn. Law Librs. (U.S. adv. coun.), Internat. Fedn. Libr. Assns., Nat. Librs. Assn. (pres. 1980-81), Spl. Libr. Assn., State Bar Tex. (mem. edit. bd. jour.), State Bar Wis. (bd. mem. nonresident lawyers divsn. 1992-98, 2003-), Nat. Assn. Coll. and Univ. Attys., Tex. Assn. Coll. Tchrs., Tex. Humanities Alliance (bd. dirs. 1986-88), Tex. Supreme Ct. Hist. Soc. (bd. trustees 1988-94, exec. bd. 2002—, treas. 2005—), Order of Coif (mem. triennial book award com.). Home: 6412 Cascada Dr Austin TX 78750-8157 Office: U Tex Sch Law Tarlton Law Libr 727 E Dean Keeton St Austin TX 78705-3224 Office Phone: 512-471-7735. E-mail: rmersky@law.utexas.edu.

MERSZEI, GEOFFREY E., corporate financial executive; BA, Albion Coll. With Dow Chem. Co., Midland, Mich., 1977—2001, treas. Germany Frankfurt, 1983—85, treas. Ea. Europe, 1985—86, fgn. exch. mgr. Midland, Mich., 1986—88, dir. fin. Asia Pacific Hong Kong, 1988—91, dir. fin. Europe Horgen, Switzerland, 1991—96, v.p., treas. Midland, Mich., 1996—2001; exec. v.p., CFO Alcan, Inc., 2001—05, Dow Chem. Co., Midland, Mich., 2005—, bd. dirs., mem. Office of the Chief Exec., 2005—. Bd. dir. Dow Corning Corpn.; mem. Conf. Bd. Com. Coun. Fin. Execs.; mem. corp. exec. bd. working coun. for CFOs. Office: Dow Chem Co 2030 Dow Ctr Midland MI 48674 *

MERTE, HERMAN, JR., mechanical engineering educator; b. Detroit, Apr. 3, 1929; s. Herman and Anna Marie (Mitterer) M.; m. Bernice Marie Brant, Sept. 17, 1952; children: Kenneth Edward, James Dennis, Lawrence Carleton, Richard Brant, Robert Paul. BS in Marine Engring, U. Mich., Ann Arbor, 1950, BS in Mech. Engring, 1951, MS, 1956, PhD, 1960. Faculty U. Mich., 1959—67, prof. mech. engring. Ann Arbor, 1967—2000, prof. emeritus, 2000—. Vis. prof. Tech. U. Munich, Germany, 1974-75 Served to lt. (j.g.) USNR, 1952-55. NSF sr. postdoctoral fellow, 1967-68 Mem. ASME, AIAA, Am. Soc. Engring. Edn., Am. Assn. U. Profs., Sigma Xi. Home: 3480 Cottontail Ln Ann Arbor MI 48103-1706 Office: U Mich Heat Transfer Lab 2026 G G Brown Lab Ann Arbor MI 48109-2125 Home Phone: 734-662-6253; Office Phone: 734-764-5240. Business E-Mail: merte@umich.edu.

MERTEN, ALAN GILBERT, academic administrator; b. Milw., Dec. 27, 1941; s. Gilbert Ervin and Ruth Anna (Ristow) M.; m. Sally Louise Otto; children: Eric, Melissa. BS, U. Wis., 1963; MS, Stanford U., 1964; PhD, U. Wis., 1970. Asst. prof. U. Mich., Ann Arbor, 1970-74, assoc. prof., 1974-81, prof., 1981-86, assoc. dean, 1983-86; dean U. Fla., Gainesville, 1986-89; dean Johnson Grad. Sch. of Mgmt. Cornell U., Ithaca, N.Y., 1989-96; pres. George Mason U., Fairfax, Va., 1996—. Bd. dirs. Comshare, Inc., Ann Arbor, Citigroup Mut. Funds, Digital Net, Brainbench; mem. Fla. Gov.'s Select Com. on Workforce 2000, 1988-89. Author: Internal Control in U.S. Corporations, 1980, Senior Management Control of Computer-Based Information Systems, 1983. Mem. Airport Authority, Gainesville, Fla., 1986-89. Served to capt. USAF, 1963-67. Lutheran. Home: 11020 Popes Head Rd Fairfax VA 22030-4608 Office: George Mason U Office of Pres Fairfax VA 22030-4444 Office Phone: 703-993-8704. E-mail: amerten@gmu.edu. *

MERTENS, JOAN R., museum curator, art historian; b. NYC, Oct. 10, 1946; d. Otto R. and Helen H. M. BA, Radcliffe Coll., 1967; PhD, Harvard U., 1972. Curatorial asst. Met. Mus. Art, NYC, 1972-73, asst. curator, 1973-76, assoc. curator, 1976-81, curator Greek and Roman dept., 1981—, curator, adminstr., 1983-90, mem. editorial bd. Mus. Jour., 1976—. Lectr. NYU, Inst. Fine Arts, 1992—. Author: Attic White-Ground*Its Development, 1977, Greek Bronzes in the Metropolitan Museum of Art, 1985; author: (with others) Ancient Art from Cyprus: The Cesnola Collection in the Metropolitan Museum of Art, 2000, The Cesnola Collection: Terracottas, 2004, The Art of the Classical World in the Metropolitan Museum of Art, 2007. Mem. Archaeol. Inst. Am., German Archael. Inst. (corr. mem.) Home: 124 E 84th St New York NY 10028-0915 Office: Met Mus Art Fifth Ave at 82nd St New York NY 10028

MERTENS, THOMAS ROBERT, biology professor; b. Fort Wayne, Ind., May 22, 1930; s. Herbert F. and Hulda (Burg) M.; m. Beatrice Janet Abair, Apr. 1, 1953; children: Julia Ann, David Gerhard BS, Ball State U., 1952; MS, Purdue U., 1954, PhD, 1956. Research assoc. dept. genetics U. Wis.-Madison, 1956-57; asst. prof. biology Ball State U., Muncie, Ind., 1957-62, assoc. prof., 1962-66, prof., 1966-93, dir. doctoral programs in biology, 1974-93, George and Frances Ball disting. prof. biology edn., 1988-93, prof. emeritus, 1993—. Author: (with A. M. Winchester) Human Genetics, 1983 (with R.L. Hammersmith) Genetics Laboratory Investigations, 13th edit., 2006 (co-recipient William Holmes McGuffey Longevity award Text and Acad. Authors Assn. 1998); contbr. numerous articles to profl. jours. Co-recipient Gustav Ohaus award for innovative coll. sci. tchg. NSTA, 1986, recipient Disting. Svc. to Sci. Edn. citation, 1987; fellow NSF, 1963-64, Ind. Acad. Scis., 1969. Fellow AAAS; mem. Nat. Assn. Biology Tchrs. (pres. 1985, hon. mem. 1988), Am. Genetic Assn., Genetics Soc. Am. Episcopalian. Home: 4501 N Wheeling 9B-4 Muncie IN 47304-1277 Office: Ball State U Dept Biology Muncie IN 47306-0001 Personal E-mail: t.mertens@att.net.

MERTINS, DETLEF, architect, educator; BArch, U. Toronto, 1980; PhD in Architecture, Princeton U., 1996. Instr. U. Toronto, 1991—2003, Can. Rsch. chair in architecture, 2001—03; prof., chair dept. architecture U. Pa. Sch. Design, 2003—. Vis. prof. Columbia U., Harvard U., Princeton U., Rice U. Author: The Presence of Mies, 1994, The Victory of Building a Style, 2000, others. Recipient Konrad Adenauer Rsch. prize, Alexander von Humboldt Found. and Royal Can. Soc., 2003; vis. scholar fellow, Can. Ctr. for Architecture, 1998. Office: Univ Pa 207 Meyerson Hall Philadelphia PA 19104-6311

MERTINS, JAMES WALTER, entomologist; b. Milw., Feb. 18, 1943; s. Walter Edwin and Harriet Ellen (Sockett) M.; m. Marilee Eloise Joeckel, Dec. 8, 1979. BS in Zoology, U. Wis., Milw., 1965; MS in Entomology, U. Wis., 1967, PhD in Entomology, 1971. Project assoc. dept. entomology U. Wis., Madison, 1971-75, rsch. assoc. dept. entomology, 1975-77; asst. prof. dept. entomology Iowa State U., Ames, 1977-84; entomol. cons. Ames, 1984-89; entomologist Nat. Vet. Svcs. Labs. USDA Animal and Plant Health Inspection Svc., Ames, 1989—. Co-author: (textbook) Biological Insect Pest Suppression, 1977, Russian edit., 1980, Chinese edit., 1988; contbr. articles to profl. jours. NSF Grad. fellow, 1970. Mem. Entomol. Soc. Am. (Insect Photography award 1984, 86, 2003), Entomol. Soc. Can., Mich. Entomol. Soc., Wis. Entomol. Soc. (pres., sec., treas., bd. dirs.), Cyclone Corvettes, Inc. (co-founder, pres. 1978, 79, sec., treas., bd. dirs., Mem. of Yr. 1982), Am. Mensa. Avocations: insect photography, Corvette automobile activities, gardening, movies, insect collecting. Office: USDA Animal and Plant Health Inspection Svc PO Box 844 Ames IA 50010-0844 Business E-Mail: James.W.Mertins@aphis.usda.gov.

MERTON, ROBERT C., economist, educator; b. NYC, July 31, 1944; s. Robert K. and Suzanne (Carhart) M., 3 c. BS in Engring. Math., Columbia U., 1966; MS in Applied Math., Calif. Inst. Tech., 1967; PhD in Econs., MIT, 1970; MA (hon.), Harvard U., 1989; LLD (hon.), U. Chgo., 1991; Prof. honoris causa degree, HEC Sch. Mgmt., Paris, 1995; D Econ. Sci. (hon.), U. Lausanne, Switzerland, 1996; Dr honoris causa, U. Paris Dauphine, 1997, Universidad Nacional Mayor de San Marcos, Lima, Peru, 2004; D of Mgmt. Sci. (hon.), Nat. Sun Yat-sen U., Kaoshiung, Taiwan, 1998; DS (hon.), Athens U. Econs. and Bus., 2003; DPhil (hon.), U. Nacional Federico Villarreal, Lima, Peru, 2004. Instr. econs. MIT, Cambridge, 1969-70; asst. prof. fin. Alfred P. Sloan Sch. Mgmt., 1970-73, assoc. prof., 1973-74, prof., 1974-80, J.C. Penney prof. mgmt., 1980-88; vis. prof. fin. Harvard U., Boston, 1987-88, George Fisher Baker prof. bus. adminstrn., 1988-98, John and Natty McArthur University prof., 1998—. Rsch. assoc. Nat. Bur. Econ. Rsch., 1979—; mem. internat. bd. sci. advisors Tinbergen Inst.; co-founder Long-Term Capital Mgmt., L.P., Greenwich, Conn., 1993—99; mem. governing bd. AlphaSimplex Group, 2001—; acad. adv. bd. Real Option Group, 1999—; bd. dirs. Vical Inc., MF Risk, Inc., Dimensional Funds, Cmty. First Fin. Group, Peninsula Banking Group; co-founder, chief sci. officer, mem. bd. dirs. Integrated Fin. Ltd., 2002—; mem. competitive markets adv. coun. Chgo. Merc. Exch., 2004—. Author: Continuous-Time Finance, 1990, rev. edit., 1992; co-author: Casebook in Financial Engineering: Applied Studies of Financial Innovation, 1995, The Global Financial System: A Functional Perspective, 1995, Finance, 2000, Transparency, Risk Management and International Financial Fragility, 2003; editor: The Collected Scientific Papers of Paul A. Samuelson, vol. III, 1972; mem. editl. bd. Internat. Econ. Rev., 1972-77, Jour. Fin., 1973-77, Jour. Money, Credit and Banking, 1974-79, Jour. Fin. Econs., 1974-83, Jour. Banking and Fin., 1977-79, 92-2003, Fin. India, 1988—, Geneva Papers on Risk and Ins., 1989-96, Jour. Fixed Income, 1991—, Fin. Rev., 1992-97, Jour. Fin. Edn., 1995—, European Fin. Rev. (now Rev. Fin.), 1997-2004; mem. adv. bd. The New Palgrave Dictionary of Money and Finance, Math. Fin., Rev. Derivatives Rsch., Nihon Finance Gakkai, The Brookings-Wharton Papers on Financial Policy, Internat. Jour. Theoretical and Applied Finance, Jour. Investment Mgmt., North Holland Series of Handbooks in Finance, Jour. Banking and Fin., 2003—, Annals of Fin., 2004—, Jour. Fin. Lit., 2004—; mem. adv. coun. Fin. Analyst Jour., 2003—; contbr. articles to profl. jours. Mem. hon. bd. Internat. Raoul Wallenberg Found., 2003—, Angelo Roncalli Internat. Com., 2003—. Recipient Leo Melamed prize U. Chgo. Sch. Bus., 1983, Roger Murray prize Inst. for Quantitative Rsch. in Fin., 1985, 86, Disting. Scholar award Ea. Fin. Assn., 1989, Internat. INA-Nat. Acad. Lincei prize Nat. Acad. Lincei, Rome, 1993, FORCE award for fin. innovation Fuqua Sch. Bus., Duke U., 1993, Fin. Engr. of Yr. award Internat. Assn. Fin. Engrs., 1993, Alfred Nobel Meml. Prize in Econ. Scis., 1997, Heroes Among Us award Boston Celtics, 1997, Michael Pupin medal Columbia U., 1998, Disting. Alumni award Calif. Inst. of Tech., 1999, MFD Lifetime Achievement award Boston U., 1999, Lifetime Achievement award Risk Mag., 2003, Nicholas Molodovsky award Assn. Investment Mgmt. Rsch., 2003, Graham and Dodd award Fin. Analysts Jour., 2003; inducted Derivatives Hall of Fame, 1998, named Risk Hall of Fame, Risk Mag., 2002. Fellow Internat. Assn. Fin. Engrs. (sr.), Econometric Soc., Am. Acad. Arts and Scis., Inst. Quantitative Rsch., Fin. Mgmt. Assn., Am. Fin. Assn. (dir. 1982-84, pres. 1986, fellow 2000—); mem. NAS, Bachelier Fin. Soc., Soc. for Fin. Studies (v.p. 1993), Hon. Order Ky. Cols., Tau Beta Pi, Sigma Xi. Office: Harvard U Grad Sch Bus Adminstrn Baker Libr 353 Soldiers Field Rd Boston MA 02163 Home Phone: 617-374-9511. Business E-Mail: rmerton@hbs.edu.

MERTZ, AARON F., physicist; b. 1984; s. H. Edward and Shirley A. M. BS in Physics and Am. Culture Studies, Washington Univ., St. Louis, 2006; PhD student in Physics, Yale Univ., 2006—07; MPhil. student in History of Sci., Oxford Univ., 2007—. Rhodes Scholar. Mem.: Sigma Xi Scientific Rsch. Honor Soc., Phi Beta Kappa. Achievements include doing physics rsch. Neutron Sci. Ctr., Los Alamos (NM) Nat. Lab.; Gamma-Ray Astronomy Group, Max-Planck-Institut für Extraterrestrische Physik, Garching, Germany; Divsn. Microfluidics, Lucent Tech. Bell Labs, Murray Hill, NJ. *

MERTZ, ANNE MORRIS, writer, researcher, journalist, educator; b. Indpls., Sept. 29, 1913; d. Theodore Hatfield and Lisette Susanna (Krauss) Morris; m. Walter Day Mertz, June 29, 1937; children: Suzanne Day Mertz Smalloy, Elizabeth Morris Mertz O'Brien, Walter Day Jr., Theodore Morris. BA cum laude, Randolph-Macon Woman's Coll., Va., 1935. Cert. Tchr. Pa., 1935. Tchr. ch. sch. Germantown Unitarian Ch., Phila., 1935—50; tchr. Yeadon (Pa.) Sch. Dist., 1935—40; religious edn. dir. Unitarian Ch., Wilmington, Del., 1950—60; mus. guide Hagley Mus., Wilmington, 1964-76; travel writer, lectr., 1965—. Author: (booklets) History of Delaware Colonial Dames Headquarters, 1990, 2001, History of Delaware Mayflower Society, 1993, (books) Morris Migration: A Saga of Forbears and Descendants, 1996, 2000, 2001, Windows into Pilgrim Life and Seven Mayflower Ancestors, 1998, Memoirs of Washington in the Eighteen Sixties Including the Witnessing of Lincoln's Assassination, 2001; author: (with others) Reaching the Summit, 1999, America at the Millennium, 2000; contbr., rschr. (articles) many jours., newspapers, mags., Libr. of Congress Archives, Phila. Inquirer, Wayne Suburban, Ardmore Suburban, Greenville Cmty. News, Wilmington News Jour., Sarasota Herald Tribune, Brandenton Herald, Venice Gondolier, Mayflower Quar., Baby Talk Mag., Del. Geneal. Jour., Hockessin Cmty. News, Bank Notes, Dartmouth Coll. and Randolph-Macon Woman's Coll. Mag. Vol. mus. guide Winterthur Mus., Wilmington, 1956—60; active pres.'s adv. bd. Wilmington Trust of Fla., Stuart, 1990—93; bd. dirs. Wilmington Music Sch., 1952—73, Family Svcs. Del.; spkr., dir., hon. bd. dirs. United Fund Planning Com., Wilmington, 1957—65; hon. bd. dirs. Children and Families First, 1995—; hon. bd. mem. Family and Children's Svcs.; profl. womens' adv. bd. mem. Am. Biog. Inst., Inc.; pres. Travelers Aid Soc., Wilmington, 1954—56, Randolph-Macon Woman's Coll. Alumnae of No. Del., 1949—51, 1965—68; nat. v.p. Randolph-Macon Woman's Coll. Alumnae Assn., Lynchburg, Va., 1961—64. Mem.: AAUW (nat. and local life mem., Wilmington Br. chair trustees, 1st v.p. 1970—75, Scholarship-Grant named for her 1940—), Nat. League Am. PEN Women (active Sarasota and Fla.), Del. Colonial Dames (spkr., rschr., oral history interviewer), Del. Hist. Soc., Mayflower Soc. (life; Del. state pres. 1990—93, bd. dirs., gold medal), Del. Geneal. Soc. Avocations: world travel, flowers, gardening, genealogy, embroidery. Home (Winter): 1526 Pelican Point Dr # 145 Sarasota FL 34231-6792 Home (Summer): 606 Coksbury Village 26 Loveville Rd Hockessin DE 19707-1519 Mailing: 606 Cokesbury Village 726 Loville Rd Hockessin DE 19707-1519 E-mail: mertz.wd@.com.

MERTZ, FRANCIS JAMES, university president; b. Newark, Sept. 24, 1937; s. Frank E. and Marian E. (Brady) M.; m. Gail Williams, Apr. 11, 1964; children: Lynn, Christopher, Suzanne, David, Amy, Jonathan. BA, St. Peter's Coll., 1958; JD, NYU, 1961; LLD (hon.), Felician Coll., 1984, Stevens Inst. Tech., Hoboken, NJ, 1988, Fairleigh Dickinson U., 1999, Kunghnam Univ., 1999, Coll. St. Elizabeth, 2002. Bar: N.J. 1967. Exec. v.p. St. Peter's Coll., Jersey City, 1972-78; v.p., CFO N.Y. Med. Coll., Valhalla, 1978-79; dir. adminstrn. Sage Gray Todd and Sims, NYC, 1979-81; pres. Ind. Coll. Fund N.J., Summit, 1981-90, Assn. Ind. Colls. and Univs. N.J., Summit, 1982-90, Fairleigh Dickinson U., Teaneck, NJ, 1990-99, pres. emeritus. Bd. dirs., chmn. St. Joseph's Home for the Blind, 1998—; mem. bd. regents Seton Hall U., 2002-04; chair N.J. Commn. on Higher Edn., 2004-06, N.J. Higher Edn. Student Assistance Authority, 2004-06, N.J. Ednl. Facilities Authority, 2004-06. Home: 54 Woodcrest Dr Morristown NJ 07960-4541 Home Phone: 973-984-6455; Office Phone: 973-267-1506. Business E-Mail: mertz@fdu.edu.

MERTZ, PAUL ERIC, retired history professor, writer; b. Bartlesville, Okla., Feb. 27, 1943; s. Floyd E. and Mary O. Mertz; m. Lyndall Ruth Kauffman, Jan. 28, 1966; children: Mary Kathryn Mertz Carney, Paul Eric Jr. BA, Phillips U., Enid, Okla., 1965; MA, U. Okla., Norman, 1967, PhD, 1971. Instr. history U. Wis., Stevens Point, 1969—72, asst. prof., 1972—77, assoc. prof., 1977—82, prof. history, 1982—2006; prof. emeritus, 2006—. Chair dept. history U. Wis., Steven Point, 1992—98. Author: New Deal Policy and Southern Rural Poverty, 1978. Chair Dem. Party, Portage County, Wis., 1999; elder Frame Meml. Presbyn. Ch., 1972—. Woodrow Wilson Nat. fellow, 1965—66. Mem.: Wis. State Hist. Soc., So. Hist. Assn., Orgn. Am. Historians. Democrat. Presbyterian. Avocation: leading bicycle tours in Europe. Office: Dept History U Wis Stevens Point WI 54481

MERWIN, GREGORY ALAN, insurance agent, retired special education educator; b. Mt. Pleasant, Mich., Oct. 16, 1946; s. Alexander D. and Carey Mae Merwin; m. Carole Jeanne Ripatte, Aug. 26, 1967; children: Kari Jeanne Pulver, Shelley Ann Dividock. BE, Ctrl. Mich. U., Mt. Pleasant, 1964—68, MA in Spl. Edn., 1974—79. Cert. property & casualty insurance Mich., 2002. Spl. edn. tchr. Mt. Pleasant Pub. Schs., 1972—2002; ins. agt. Kingsley Ins. Grp., Alma, Mich., 2002—. Varsity cross country coach Mt. Pleasant HS, 1977—87, girls varsity track & field coach, 1990—98; work study coord. Mt. Pleasant Pub. Sch., 1999—2001; pre-vocational tchr. Mt. Pleasant Area Tech. Ctr., 2001—02. Recipient Secondary Tchr. of Yr. award, Mt. Pleasant Bd. Edn., 1988, Girls Track Coach of Yr. award, White Pine Conf., 1989—92, Regional Track Coach of Yr. award, Mich. Interscholastic Track Coaches Assn., 1992. Meth. Avocations: nordic ski racing, guitar, photography. Home: 1040 Granada Dr Weidman MI 48893 Office: Kingsley Ins Grp 116 W Superior Ste 1 Alma MI 48801 Home Phone: 989-644-5968.

MERWINE, DAVID KARL, neurophysiologist, educator; b. Harrisburg, Pa. BS, Juniata Coll., Huntingdon, Pa., 1985; PhD in Vision Sci., U. Ala., Birmingham, 1997. Postdoctoral fellow Wake Forest U., Winston-Salem, NC, 1994—95; rsch. assoc. Smith-Kettlewell Eye Rsch. Inst., San Francisco, 1996—2001; rsch. asst. prof. U. So. Calif., LA, 2001—. Cons. Neuropsychology Found., Sun Valley, Calif., 2006—07. Contbr. chapters to books, articles to profl. jours. Bd. mem. Village United, Long Beach, Calif., 2004—06. Recipient Travel award, Fedn. Am. Socs. Exptl. Biology, 2000; grantee ARVO Travel grant, Retina Rsch. Found., 1993. Mem.: AAAS, Soc. Neuroscience, Assn. Rsch. Vision and Ophthalmology. Avocations: martial arts, singing. Office: Univ So Calif 1042 Downey Way DRB 140 Los Angeles CA 90089 Office Phone: 213-821-2072.

MERZ, JAMES LOGAN, electrical and materials engineering educator, researcher; b. Jersey City, Apr. 14, 1936; s. Albert Joseph and Anne Elizabeth (Farrell) M.; m. Rose-Marie Weibel, June 30, 1962; children: Kathleen, James, Michael, Kimarie. BS in Physics, U. Notre Dame, 1959; postgrad., U. Göttingen, Fed. Republic Germany, 1959-60; MA, Harvard U., 1961, PhD in Applied Physics, 1967; PhD (hon.), Linköping U., Sweden, 1993. Mem. tech. staff Bell Labs., Murray Hill, NJ, 1966-78; prof. elec. engring. U. Calif., Santa Barbara, 1978-94, prof. materials, 1986-94, chmn. dept. elec. and computer engring., 1982-84, assoc. dean for rsch. devel. Coll. Engring., 1984-86, acting assoc. vice chancellor, 1988, dir. semiconductor rsch. corp. core program on GaAs digital ICs, 1984-89, dir. Compound Semiconductor Rsch. Labs., 1986-92, dir. NSF Ctr. for Quantized Electronic Structures, 1989-94; Freimann prof. elec. engring. U. Notre Dame (Ind.), 1994—, v.p. for grad. studies and rsch., dean Grad. Sch., 1996-2001, interim dean engring., 2006—. Mem. exec. com. Calif. Microelectronics Innovation and Computer Rsch. Opportunities Program, 1986-92; mem. NRC com. on Japan, NAS/NAE, 1988-90; mem. internat. adv. com. Internat. Symposium on Physics of Semiconductors and Applications, Seoul, Republic of Korea, 1990, Conf. on Superlattices and Microstructures, Xi'an, China, 1992; participant, mem. coms. other profl. confs. and meetings. Contbr. over 400 articles to profl. jours.; patentee in field. Fulbright fellow, Danforth Found. fellow, Woodrow Wilson Found. fellow; Alexander von Humboldt rsch. awardee, 2002. Fellow IEEE, Am. Phys. Soc.; mem. IEEE Lasers and Electro-Optics Soc. (program com. annual mtg. 1980), IEEE Electron Device Soc. (sec. 1994, 95), Am. Vacuum Soc. (exec. com. electronic materials and processing divsn. 1988-89), Materials Rsch. Soc. (editl. bd. jour. 1984-87), Soc. for Values in Higher Edn., Inst. Electronics, Info. and Comm. Engrs. (overseas adv. com.), Sigma Xi, Eta Kappa Nu. Achievements include research in field of optoelectronic materials and devices: semiconductors and ionic materials; optical and electrical properties of implanted ions, rapid annealing; semiconductor lasers, detectors, solar cells, other optoelectronic devices; low-dimensional quantum structures, nanostructures. Home: 1530 Marigold Way South Bend IN 46617-1016 Office: U Notre Dame Dept Elec Engring 203B Cushing Hall Notre Dame IN 46556-5637 Business E-Mail: jmerz@nd.edu.

MERZBACHER, EUGEN, retired physics professor; b. Berlin, Apr. 9, 1921; came to U.S., 1947, naturalized, 1953; s. Siegfried and Lilli (Wilmersdoerffer) M.; m. Ann Townsend Reid, July 11, 1952; children: Celia, Charles, Matthew, Mary (dec.). Licentiate, U. Istanbul, 1943; AM, Harvard U., 1948, PhD, 1950; DSc (hon.), U. N.C., Chapel Hill, 1993. HS tchr., Ankara, Turkey, 1943—47; mem. Inst. Advanced Study, Princeton, NJ, 1950—51; vis. asst. prof. Duke U., Durham, NC, 1951—52; from mem. faculty to Kenan prof. physics U. N.C., Chapel Hill, 1952—91, Kenan prof. emeritus, 1991—; ret., 1991. Vis. prof. U. Wash., 1967-68, U. Edinburgh, Scotland, 1986; Arnold Bernhard vis. prof. physics Williams Coll., 1993; chair Internat. Conf. on Physics of Electronic and Atomic Collisions, 1987-89; sr. advisor APS, 1998-99. Author: Quantum Mechanics, 3d edit., 1998; also articles. NSF Sci. Faculty fellow U. Copenhagen, Denmark, 1959-60; recipient Thomas Jefferson award U. N.C., 1972; Humboldt sr. scientist award U. Frankfurt, Germany, 1976-77. Fellow AAAS, Am. Phys. Soc. (pres. 1990); mem. Am. Assn. Physics Tchrs.

(Oersted medal 1992), Sigma Xi. Achievements include research on applications of quantum mechanics to study atoms and nuclei. Home: 750 Weaver Dairy Rd #119 Chapel Hill NC 27514-1439 Personal E-mail: merzie@mindspring.com. Business E-Mail: merzbach@physics.unc.edu.

MESA, REINALDO HUMBERTO, information scientist, educator; b. NY, June 2, 1966; s. Alexander and Acacia Mesa; m. Yvonne Janice Orr, June 7, 1997; 1 child, Nicholas Chillian Dysart. BSc in Electronics Engring. Tech., ITT Tech. Inst., Sacramento Calif., 1991; student in Workforce Edn. and Devel., U. So. Ill., Fairfield Calif., 2001. Cert. Computer Tng. Industry Assn., journeyman Internat. Soc. Cert. Electronics Technicians. Instr. ITT Tech. Inst., Greenfield, Wis., 1993—95, Rancho Cordova, Calif., 1995—. Adv. ITT br. Alpha Beta Kappa, Rancho Cordova, 1995—. Mem.: IEEE (assoc.; student adv. 1996—). Roman Catholic. Avocations: reading, music, scuba diving. Office: ITT Technical Inst 10863 Gold Ctr Dr Rancho Cordova CA 95670-6034 Office Phone: 916-851-3900. Office Fax: 916-851-9225. Personal E-mail: r_mesa@comcast.net. Business E-Mail: rmesa@itt-tech.edu.

MESAK, HANI IBRAHIM, marketing educator; b. Cairo, Feb. 21, 1944; s. Ibrahim M. Wassif and Mary K. Ghobrial; m. Eugenie Milad Habib, Aug. 23, 1977; 1 child, Irene Ann. BSc, Cairo U., 1965, Grad. Diploma, 1969; PhD, U. Pa., Phila., 1974. Engr. Orgn. Small Scale Industries, Cairo; mgmt. rsch. analyst Wharton Sch. U. Pa., Philad., 1970—73; project leader Data Analysis Ctr., NJ, 1974—75; assoc. prof. U. La., Monroe, 1987—89; prof. La. Tech U., Ruston, 1989—. Asst. prof. Kuwait U., 1975—87. Contbr. articles to profl. jours. (Irwin McGraw-Hill Disting. Paper award SW Fedn. Adminstrv. Disciplines, 1999, Best Theoretical/Empirical Paper award Decision Scis. Inst., 2002, Disting. Paper award Decision Scis. Inst., 2006). Mem.: Decision Sciences Inst. (assoc. editor Decision Scis. jour. 1999—2005, named to Hall of Fame). Democrat. Eastern Orthodox. Avocations: travel, ping pong/table tennis. Home: 904 Monterey Dr Ruston LA 71270 Office: La Tech U PO Box 10318 Ruston LA 71272 Office Phone: 318-257-3506. Business E-Mail: mesak@cab.latech.edu.

MESCHI, JENNIFER MARGARET, technology educator; b. Smithtown, NY, Aug. 2, 1973; m. Richard Meschi. AA in Early Childhood Edn., Suffolk County CC, Selden, NY, 1997; BA in Elem. Edn., St. Joseph's Coll., Patchogue, NY, 1999; MA in Liberal Studies, Stony Brook U., NY, 2003. Tchr. Frank J. Carasiti Elem. Sch., Rocky Point, NY, 2000—02, tech. integration specialist, 2002—. Finalist Tech. & Learning Leader of Yr., Tech. and Learning Mag., 2005; grantee, MESTRACT, 2004, 2007, Best Buy, 2006, 2007, Power to Learn, Cablevision, 2006. Achievements include design of web site for educators. Office: Frank J Carasiti Elem Sch 90 Rocky Point-Yaphank Rd Rocky Point NY 11778 Office Phone: 631-744-1600 3189. Business E-Mail: jmeschi@rockypoint.k12.ny.us.

MESCHKOW, JORDAN M., lawyer; b. Bklyn., Mar. 25, 1957; s. Gerald Meschkow and Florence Y. (Katz) Silverman; m. Susan G. Scher, Aug. 10, 1980; children: Sasha Hayley, Alisha Sadie. BS in Biology, SUNY, Stony Brook, 1979; JD, Chgo. Kent Coll. Law, 1982. Bar: Ariz. 1982, Fla. 1983; registered U.S. Patent Trademark Office 1983. Assoc. James F. Duffy, Patent Atty., Phoenix, Ariz., 1982; ptnr. Duffy & Meschkow, Phoenix, 1983-84; sole practice Phoenix, 1984-92; sr. ptnr. Meschkow & Gresham, P.L.C., Phoenix, 1992—. Frequent talk radio guest spkr. seminars patent, trademark, copyright law. Contbr. article series to profl. jours.; patentee in field. Exec. bd. City Phoenix Fire Pub. Awareness League, 1996—. Mem. Am. Intellectual Property Law Assn., State Bar Ariz. (intellectual property sect. 1982—), State Bar Fla. Avocations: gardening, motorcycling, bicycling, skating, swimming. Office: 5727 N 7th St Ste 409 Phoenix AZ 85014-5818 Home Phone: 480-951-4191; Office Phone: 602-274-6996. Business E-Mail: MG@patentmg.com.

MESCHUTT, DAVID RANDOLPH, historian; b. NYC, May 29, 1955; s. Philip Frederick and Mary Evelyn (Mahanes) M.; m. Sarah Caroline Bevan, July 14, 1990. BA in Journalism, Washington and Lee U., 1977; MA in History Mus. Studies, SUNY, Cooperstown, 1988; postgrad., Attingham Summer Sch., Gt. Britain, 1988-98, postgrad., 2004, Royal Collection Studies Programme, 2000; PhD in Art History, U. Del., 2005. Rschr. Thomas Jefferson Meml. Found., Charlottesville, Va., 1977-78, Frick Art Reference Libr., NYC, 1980-86; curator art West Point (N.Y.) Mus./U.S. Mil. Acad., 1988-98; consulting curator N.Y. State Office of Pks., Recreation and Hist. Preservation, Waterford, NY, 1999—. Guest curator N.Y. State Hist. Assn., Cooperstown, 1986-87, Brandywine River Mus., Chadds Ford, Pa., 1992, Va. Hist. Soc., Richmond, 1999; cons. Curatorial Office, U.S. Dept. Treasury, Washington, 1988, Albany (N.Y.) Inst. History and Art, 1988. Author: A Bold Experiment: John Henri Isaac Browere's Life Masks of Prominent Americans, 1988; co-author: The Portraits and History Paintings of Alonzo Chappel, 1992; assoc. editor Am. Nat. Biography, Oxford U. Press, 1994-99, contbr., 1994—; contbr. articles to profl. jours. Bd. dirs. Friends of Stony Point Battlefield, NJ. Nourse Found. fellow, 1986-87, Nat. Endowment for Arts fellow, 1987, Soc. Colonial Wars fellow, 1988, Andrew W. Mellon fellow Va. Hist. Soc., 1992, Anne S.K. Brown fellow Brown U., 1993, Mayers fellow Huntington Libr. and Art Gallery, 1997. Mem.: Walpole Soc., N.Y. State Hist. Assn., Va. Hist. Soc., Ralph Vaughan Williams Soc., Herbert Howells Soc., Historians Brit. Art, Assn. Historians Am. Art. Methodist. Avocation: music. Office: care Mus of the Shenandoah Valley 901 Amherst St Winchester VA 22601-3802

MESECAR, DOUG, federal agency administrator; BA, Hope Coll. Elem. sch. tchr., Colo.; staff mem. Com. on Edn. and Workforce, US Ho. of Reps.; chief of staff Office of Elem. and Secondary Edn. US Dept. Edn., Washington, dep. chief staff policy, 2004, acting asst. sec., Office Planning Evaluation & Policy Devel., 2006—. Office: US Dept Edn OPEPD 1990 K St NW Washington DC 20006-1103 *

MESELSON, MATTHEW STANLEY, biochemist, educator; b. Denver, May 24, 1930; s. Hymen Avram and Ann (Swedlow) M.; m. Jeanne Guillemin, 1986; children: Zoe, Amy Valor. Ph.B., U. Chgo., 1951, D.Sc. (hon.), 1975; PhD, Calif. Inst. Tech., 1957; Sc.D. (hon.), Oakland Coll., 1964, Columbia, 1971, Yale U., 1987, Princeton U., 1988. Asst. prof. chemistry Calif. Inst. Tech., 1958—59, sr. rsch. fellow chem. biology, 1959—60; assoc. prof. molecular biology Harvard U., 1964—76, Thomas Dudley Cabot prof. natural scis., 1976—. Cons. U.S. Arms Control and Disarmament Agency, 1963; adj. scientist Josephine Bay Paul Ctr. Comparative Molecular Biology and Evolution Marine Biol. Lab., Woods Hole, Mass., 2000—. Recipient Eli Lilly award microbiology and immunology, 1964, Alumni medal U. Chgo., 1971; Lehman award 1975, Presidential award 1983, N.Y. Acad. Scis., 1975; Alumni Disting. Svc. award Calif. Inst. Tech., 1975; Leo Szilard award Am. Phys. Soc., 1978; MacArthur fellow, 1984-89, Lasker award for Special Achievement in Medical Sci., Albert and Mary Lasker Found., 2004. Fellow AAAS (Sci. Freedom and Responsibility award, 1990); mem. NAS (Molecular Biology prize 1963), Inst. Medicine, Am. Acad. Arts and Scis., Fedn. Am. Scientists (chmn. 1986-88, Pub. Svc. award 1972), Coun. Fgn. Rels., Accademia Santa Chiara, Am. Philos. Soc., Royal Society (London), Académie des Sciences (Paris), Genetics Soc. Am. (Thomas Hunt Morgan medal 1995). Office: Harvard U Fairchild Biochem Bldg 7 Divinity Ave Cambridge MA 02138-2019

MESEREAU, THOMAS ARTHUR, JR., lawyer; b. West Point, NY, 1951; m. Heidi Gold (div.). BA cum laude, Harvard U., 1973; MSc, London Sch. Econ., 1975; JD, U. Calif., 1979. Bar: Calif. 1979. Assoc. Hunton & Williams, Washington, 1979—81; dep. dist. atty. Orange County, Calif., 1981—82; exec. Getty Synthetic Fuels Inc., 1982—85; ptnr. Collins, Mesereau, Reddock & Yu, LLP, LA, 1985—. Vol. legal clinic First African Meth. Episcopal Ch. Named Criminal Def. Lawyer Yr., Century City Bar Assn.; named one of The 10 Most Fascinating People of 2005, Barbara Walters Special; recipient Pro Bono award, State Bar Calif., Commendation, LA Bd. Supr., Sarah Allen Trailblazer award, Cert. Appreciation, LA County Supr., Compton award, Calif. Sch. Bd., Humanitarian award, Nat. Assn. Blacks in Criminal Justice. Mem.: Italian Am. Lawyers Assn. (former mem. bd. gov.), Calif. Atty. Criminal Justice. Achievements include leading def. atty. in Michael Jackson child molestation trial, 2005. Office: Mesereau Nuyu LLP 10390 Santa Monica Blvd Ste 220 Los Angeles CA 90025 Office Phone: 213-384-0982. Office Fax: 213-380-4820. Business E-Mail: mesereau@mesereauyu.com. *

MESERLIAN, DONALD C., mechanical engineer, consultant; b. Nov. 4, 1927; BS in Mech. Engring., Stevens Inst. Tech., Hoboken, NJ, 1949, MS in Mech. Engring., 1953. Pres. Tech. Products Co., North Caldwell, NJ, 1973—. Chmn. Voices Safety Internat. Health, Safety and Environ. Stds. Writing Orgns., 2000—. Contbr. numerous articles to profl. publs. Recipient Bronze medal, ASTM, 1998, Autism Awareness Proclamation, Essex County, 2006. Mem.: Nat. Soc. Profl. Engrs. Address: 264 Park Ave North Caldwell NJ 07006-4242 E-mail: dmeserlian@voiceofsafety.com.

MESERVE, RICHARD ANDREW, lawyer, administrator; b. Medford, Mass., Nov. 20, 1944; s. Robert William and Gladys Meserve; m. Martha Anne Richards, Sept. 20, 1966; children: Amy, Lauren. BA, Tufts U., 1966; JD, Harvard U., 1975; PhD in Applied Physics, Stanford U., 1976. Bar: Mass. 1975, DC 1980, U.S. Supreme Ct. 1982. Law clk. Mass. Supreme Jud. Ct., Boston, 1975-76; law clk. to presiding justice U.S. Supreme Ct., Washington, 1976-77; legal counsel Pres. Sci. Adviser, Washington, 1977-81; ptnr. Covington & Burling, Washington, 1981-99, sr. of counsel, 2004—; bd. dirs. Carnegie Instn. Washington, 1992—2003, pres., 2003—; chmn. U.S. Nuc. Regulatory Commn., Washington, 1999—2003. Chmn. com. assess safety and tech. issues Dept. Energy reactors NAS, 1987—88, chmn. com. fuel economy automobiles and light trucks, 1991—92, chmn. com. declassification info. Dept. Energy's environ. programs, 1994—95; chmn. nuc. and radiation studies bd. NAS-NAE, 2004—; co-chmn. AAAS-ABA Nat. Conf. Lawyers and Scientists, 1988—94; mem. bd. overseers arts and scis. Tufts U., 1994—2002; mem. adv. bd. Sec. Energy, 1996—99; bd. dirs. Univs. Rsch. Assn., Inc., 2004—, PG&E Corp., 2006—; chmn. internat. nuc. safety group IAEA, 2003—; mem. Nat. Commn. on Energy Policy, 2006—; bd. overseers Harvard U., 2007—. Recipient Gold medal, Sec. of Energy, 1999. Fellow: AAAS (bd. dirs. 2000—06), Am. Acad. Arts and Scis. (coun. and exec. com. 2005—), Am. Phys. Soc.; mem.: NAE, Am. Philos. Soc., Sigma Xi, Phi Beta Kappa. Democrat. Home: 708 Berry St Falls Church VA 22042-2402 Home Phone: 703-533-0775; Office Phone: 202-387-6404. Business E-Mail: rmeserve@ciw.edu.

MESERVE, WILLIAM GEORGE, lawyer; b. Medford, Mass., June 14, 1940; s. Robert William and Gladys Evangeline (Swenson) M.; m. Susan Mary Rycroft, Oct. 21, 1967; children: Daniel Scott, Susan Elizabeth, Jonathan Robert. BA, Tufts U., Medford, Mass., 1962; LLB, Harvard U., Cambridge, Mass., 1965; MSc, London Sch. Econs., 1966. Bar: Mass. 1966, US Dist. Ct. Mass. 1970, US Ct. Appeals (1st cir.) 1973. Legal asst. to commr. FTC, Washington, 1966-67; staff counsel com. commerce US Senate, Washington, 1967-69; assoc. Ropes & Gray, Boston, 1970-76, ptnr., 1976—2002, sr. counsel, 2002—06, of counsel, 2007—. Geology field asst. McMurdo Sound, Antarctica, 1959-60, Inglefield Land, Greenland, summer 1965. Trustee Tufts U., Medford, 1979—97, AFS Intercultural Programs Inc., NYC, 1979—92, 1993—96, 2006—, Boston Fulbright Com., Inc., 1999—, New Eng. Med. Ctr., Inc., Boston, 1988—97, Lifespan of Mass., Inc., 1997—2002; bd. visitors Fletcher Sch. Law and Diplomacy Tufts U., Medford, 1971—; bd. dirs. United South End Settlements, Boston, 1979—, Earthwatch Inst., Maynard, 1996—, AFS-USA, NYC, 1999—2006, Conservation Edn. and Rsch. Trust, Oxford, England, 2004—07; bd. govs. New Eng. Med. Ctr. Hosps., Boston, 1982—94, 1995—97, 2004—. Fellow Am. Coll. Trial Lawyers; mem. ABA, Boston Bar Assn., Phi Beta Kappa. Clubs: Appalachian Mountain (Boston) (rec. sec. 1977-78). Democrat. Office: Ropes & Gray 1 International Pl Fl 41 Boston MA 02110-2624 Business E-Mail: william.meserve@ropesgray.com.

MESHACK, GENEVA TUCKER, retired elementary school educator; b. Marion, Ala., Aug. 31, 1939; d. Lovelace and Louise (Kynard) Tucker; m. Hugh von Meshack, Aug., 1962 (div. 1978). BS, MS, Prairie View A&M. Tchr. Temple ISD, Temple, Tex., 1965—2004; ret., 2004. Mem. PTO, Temple; music dept. Mt. Zion Bapt. Ch., Temple, Tex., gen. v.p., 2nd v.p. mission. Mem. NEA, Tex. State Tchr. Assn., Nat. Sci. Assn., Ebony Culture Soc., Prairie View A&M U. Alumni, Zeta Phi Beta. Democrat. Home: 1016 E Adams Ave Temple TX 76501-4621

MESHBESHER, RONALD I., lawyer; b. Mpls., May 18, 1933; s. Nathan J. and Esther J. (Balman) M.; m. Sandra F. Siegel, June 17, 1956 (div. 1978); children: Betsy F., Wendy S., Stacy J.; m. Kimberly L. Garnaas, May 23, 1988; 1 child, Jolie M. BS in Law, U. Minn., 1955, JD, 1957. Bar: Minn. 1957, U.S. Supreme Ct. 1966. Prosecuting atty. Hennepin County, Mpls., 1958-61; pres. Meshbesher and Spence Ltd., Mpls., 1961—. Lectr. numerous legal and profl. orgns.; mem. adv. com. on rules of criminal procedure Minn. Supreme Ct., 1971-91; cons. on recodification of criminal procedure code Czech Republic Ministry of Justice, 1994. Author: Trial Handbook for Minnesota Lawyers, 1992; mem. bd. editors Criminal Law Advocacy Reporter; mem. adv. bd. Bur. Nat. Affairs Criminal Practice Manual; contbr. numerous articles to profl. jours. Mem.: ABA, ATLA (bd. govs. 1968—71),Calif. Attys. for Criminal Justice, Trial Lawyers for Pub. Justice, Minn. Assn. Criminal Def. Lawyers (pres. 1991—92, Disting. Svc. award 2001), Minn. Trial Lawyers Assn.(pres 1973—74, (Lifetime Achievement award 2001), Nat. Assn. Criminal Def. Lawyers (pres. 1984—85), Am. Acad. Forensic Scis., Am. Bd. Criminal Lawyers (v.p. 1983, bd.gov.) Am. Bd. Trial Advs., Am. Coll. Trial Lawyers (Lifetime Achievement sward, Minn. chpt., 2006), Internat. Acad. Trial Lawyers, Minn. Bar Assn. Avocations: bicycling, photography, travel, flying, theater. Office: Meshbesher & Spence 1616 Park Ave Minneapolis MN 55404-1695 Home Phone: 952-449-8700; Office Phone: 612-339-9121. E-mail: rmeshbesher@meshbesher.com.

MESHEL, HARRY, former state senator, political party official; b. Youngstown, Ohio, June 13, 1924; s. Angelo and Rubena (Markakis) Michelakis; children: Barry, Melanie. BSBA, Youngstown Coll., 1949; MS, Columbia U., 1950; LLD (hon.), Ohio U., Youngstown State U., Ohio Coll. Podiatric Medicine; LHD (hon.), Youngstown State U. Exec. asst. to mayor City of Youngstown, Ohio, 1964-68, urban renewal dir. Ohio, 1969; mem. 33d district Ohio Senate, Columbus, 1971-93, Dem. minority leader, 1981-82, 85-90, pres. and majority leader, 1983-84, com. mem. econ. develop., sci. & tech., state & local govt., ways & means, commerce & labor, controlling bd., state employment compensation bd., fin. chmn., 1974-81, rules chmn., 1983-84, com. mem. rules, reference & oversight, 1985-90; state chair Ohio Dem. Party, 1993-95. Real estate broker; adj. prof. polit. sci. Ohio U.; faculty mem. (limited svc.) Youngstown State U.; div. mgr. investment firm; Ohio Senate special com. mem. Task Force on Drug Strategies, Ohio Acad. Sci. Centennial Celebration Commn., Motor Vehicle Inspection & Maintenance Program, Legis. Oversight Com., Ohio Boxing Commn., Correctional Inst. Inspection Com., Ohio Small Bus. & Entrepreneurship Coun., Gov.'s Adv. Coun. Travel & Tourism, Legis. Svc. Commn., Capital Sq. Rev. & Adv. Bd., others. Past pres., past lt. gov. Am. Hellenic Ednl. Prog. Assn. (AHEPA); precinct committeeman Mahoning County Dem. Party, ward captain, mem. exec. com.; campaign mgr. local candidates, county campaign mgr. presdl. candidates; del. Dem. Mid-Term Conv., 1981; founder Great Lakes/N.E. Legis. Coalition; chmn., founder Nat. Dem. State Legis. Leaders Assn.; dir. State Legis. Leaders Found.; state/fed. assembly, mem. communications com. Nat. Conf. State Legis., legis. mgmt. com., govt. opers. com.; chair fiscal affairs com. Midwest Conf. Coun. State Govts., task force on econs. & fiscal affairs; del., exec. com. Dem. Nat. Com.; mem. Dem. Leadership Coun., State Dem. Exec. Com.; exec. com. Assn. State Dem. Chairs; bd. trustees Nat. Hall of Fame for Persons with Disabilities; mem. St. Nicholas Greek Orthodox Ch.; mem. Mill Creek Metro Park Bd. Commrs. With USN, 1943-46. Decorated two Bronze Battle Stars; recipient Dist. Svc. award Office of Pres., Top Legislator award Ohio Union Patrolmen Assn., Dist. Citizen award Med. Coll. Ohio, City of Hope Leadership award, 1993, Legis. Leadership award Ohio Coalition for Edn. of Handicapped Children, Phillips Medal of Pub. Svc., Ohio U., John E. Fogarty award Gov.'s Com. of Employment of Handicapped, Gov.'s award, 1992, U. Cin. Award for Excellence, Lamp of Learning award Ohio Edn. Assn., Black Cultural Soc. award East Liverpool, Mahoning Valley Man of Yr. award, Mahoning Valley Econ. Devel. Corp., Office Holder of Yr. award Truman-Johnson Dem. Women, Best Interest of Children award Fathers of Equal Rights, Founders Day award Circle of Friends Found., Helping Hand award Easter Seal Soc., Honorary Riverboat Captain award Mahoning County Dem. Party, Community Svc. and Special Svcs. awards Eastern Orthodox Men's Soc., Periclean award AHEPA, Academy of Achievement award Nat. AHEPA Ednl. Found., Nat. Svc. Dem. award AHEPA, 1994, Disting. Citizen award Youngstown State U. Alumni Assn., numerous appreciation and recognition awards; recipient Outstanding Legislator awards Ohio Acad. Trial Lawyers, Ohio Assn. Pub. Sch. Employees, Ohio Rehab. Assn., League Ohio Sportsmen; recipient Dist. Svc. awards Youngstown State U., Ohio Edn. Assn., Ohio Union Patrolmen Assn., Ohio Disabled Vets., AFL-CIO Ohio Barbers Union, AFL-CIO Nat. Assn. of Theatre Owners of Ohio; named Guardian of the Menorah, Youngstown B'nai B'rith, Outstanding Dem., Fairfield Dem. Club, 1993; named to Ohio Vets. Hall of Fame. Mem. (life) NAACP, ACLU, AMVETS (Legislator of Yr. 1993), VFW, Am. Legion, Cath. War Vets (Dist. Legislator award), Vet. Boxers Assn. Mercer County, Pa., Trumbull County Boxers' Legends of Leather (Man of Yr. award Hall of Fame), William Holmes McGuffey Hist. Soc., Buckeye Elks Lodge (hon.); mem. Kiwanis Internat., Urban League, Alliance C. of C., Southern Community Jaycees (hon.), Soc. for Preservation of Greek Heritage, Greek Am. Progressive Assn., Pan Cretan Assn., Arms Hist. Mus. Soc., Eagles, Moose, The Stambaugh Pillars.

MESHER, JOHN R., lawyer; b. Pitts., Nov. 8, 1952; m. Maureen Mesher; children: Dan, Jeffrey, Rachel, Laura. BA, Ind. U. Pa., 1974; JD, Duquesne U., 1977. Bar: Pa. 1977. With Eckert Seamans Cherin & Mellott, Pitts., 1977—80, Alco Standard Corp., Phila., 1980—88; divsn. counsel Certain Teed Corp., 1988—97; v.p., gen. counsel, sec. Saint-Gobain Corp., Valley Forge, 1997—. Mem.: Am. Corp. Counsel Assn. Office: St Gobain Corp 750 E Swedesford Rd PO Box 860 Valley Forge PA 19482 Office Phone: 610-341-7108. Office Fax: 610-341-7087.

MESHII, MASAHIRO, materials science educator; b. Amagasaki, Japan, Oct. 6, 1931; arrived in US, 1956; s. Masataro and Kazuyo M.; m. Eiko Kumagai, May 21, 1959; children: Alisa, Erica. BS, Osaka U., Japan, 1954, MS, 1956; PhD, Northwestern U., 1959. Lectr., rsch. assoc. dept. materials sci. and engring. Northwestern U., Evanston, Ill., 1959-60, asst. prof., assoc. prof., then prof., 1960-88, chmn. dept. materials sci. and engring., 1978-82, John Evans prof., 1988—2003, John Evans prof. emeritus, 2003—. Vis. scientist Nat. Rsch. Inst. Metals, Tokyo, 1970-71; NSF faculty rsch. participant Argonne (Ill.) Nat. Lab., 1975; guest prof. Osaka U., 1985; Acta/Scripta Metallurgica lectr., 1993-95. Co-editor: Lattice Defects in Quenched Metals, 1965, Martensitic Transformation, 1978, Science of Advanced Materials, 1990; editor: Fatigue and Microstructures, 1979, Mechanical Properties of BCC Metals, 1982; contbr. over 245 articles to tech. publs. and internat. jours. Recipient Founders award Midwest Soc. Electron Microscopists, 1987; named Best Tchr. of Yr., Engring. Students of Northwestern U., 1978; Fulbright grantee, 1956; Japan fellow, 1957. Fellow ASM (Henry Marion Howe medal 1968, Best Acad. Paper award 1994), Japan Soc. Promotion of Sci.; mem. AIME (Meritorious award for Best Paper Iron and Steel Soc. 1993), Metall. Soc., Japan Inst. Metals (hon., Achievement award 1972), Toastmasters Internat. (Disting. Toast Master, 1987, 2007). Office: 22879 NE 127th Way Redmond WA 98053-5657 Office Phone: 425-836-2334. Personal E-mail: mmeshii@hotmail.com.

MESHKE, GEORGE LEWIS, retired drama and humanities educator; b. Yakima, Wash., Oct. 7, 1930; s. George Joseph and Marye Elizabeth (Lopas) Meshke. BA, U. Wash., 1953, MA, 1959, PhD in Drama, 1972. Cert. tchr., Wash. Tchr. English and drama Zillah High Sch., Wash., 1955-58, high sch., Bellevue, Wash., 1958-60, Federal Way, Wash., 1960-70; dir., actor Old Brewery Theatre, Helena, Mont., 1962-66; prof. drama Yakima Valley CC, Yakima, 1970-2000, part-time instr., 2001—05, emeritus, 2005—. Casting dir., dir. summer seminar Laughing Horse Summer Theatre, Ellensburg, Wash., 1989-96, Children's Lit. Inst., 2000; adj. prof. grad. studies Ctrl. Wash. U., Tchr. Exch., London, 1995, People-to People Exch., China, 2000, Mongolia, Manchuria, 2001; lectr. Inquiring Mind series Wash. State Humanities, 1989-91; regional dir. Am. Coll. Theatre Festival, Washington, 1980-86; arts dialogue J.F. Kennedy Ctr., Washington, 1987—; casting dir., actor Hollywood Ind. Prodns.; adv. coun. Kennedy Ctr. Author, producer Towers of Tomorrow, 1985, The Halls of Yesterday-Yakima Hist. drama; appeared in Yakima, Washington, 1998. Regional bd. dirs. Common Cause, Yakima, 1971-73; active Nat. Hist. Soc., Nat. Wilderness Soc., Roosevelt Meml. Found., Wash. State Commn. Humanities, Drama League, People to People Tours, Clinton Libr. With U.S. Army, 1953-55, Austria. Recipient Gold medal Kennedy Ctr., 1985, Wash. State Humanities medal, 1983, NISAD medal, 1989, Wash. State Drama award, 1999. Mem. ACLU, VFW, Wash. Edn. Assn., N.W. Drama Assn., Am. Legion, Am. Edn. Theatre Assn., Am. Fedn. Tchrs., Kennedy Libr., Amnesty Internat. Carter Libr., Libr. Congress (assoc.), Smithsonian Instn., Phi Delta Kappa Democrat. Avocations: travel, mountain climbing, skiing, reading. Home: 5 N 42nd Ave Yakima WA 98908-3214

MESHKI, HAMED, lawyer; b. Tehran, Iran, Dec. 28, 1978; s. Cyrus Meshki and Aida S. McNamara. BA, UCLA, 2000; postgrad., Georgetown U., Washington, 2000—01; JD with hons., U. Chgo., 2003. Bar: Calif. 2003. Assoc. Skadden, Arps, Slate, Meagher & Flom LLP, LA, 2003—05, Kirkland & Ellis LLP, LA, 2005—. Presenter in field; founder, chmn. com. Chgo. Transfer Com., 2002—03; mem. Chgo. Investment Law Group, 2002—03; course instr. Law Sch. Admissions Test, 1999—2000; asst. mgr., sales rep. Bernini, Inc., 1997—2000. Contbr. articles to mags. Pro bono atty. Pub. Counsel, LA, 2003; vol. Habitat for Humanity, LA, 2005; pro bono atty. Small Wonders Found., LA, 2004—05, Hope Renews, Inc., LA, 2004—05, Alliance Children's Rights, LA, 2006. John M. Olin scholar in law and econ., U. Chgo. Law Sch., 2001—02. Mem.: Calif. Young Lawyers Assn., LA County Bar Assn., Calif. State Bar Assn., Order of Coif. Avocations: literature, wine, travel. Office: Kirkland & Ellis LLP 777 S Figueroa St Los Angeles CA 90017

MESHLOVITZ, MARY E., educational consultant, special education educator; b. Buffalo, Apr. 6, 1967; d. John and Kathleen C. Kroll; m. Kenneth Peter Meshlovitz, Mar. 15, 1997; 1 child, Kenneth John. BS in Elem. and Spl. Edn., SUC Geneseo, 1989; MS in Reading Edn., SUNY, Buffalo, 1999. Cert. reading, elem. edn., spl. edn. Spl. edn. tchr. Monroe Boces II, Spencerport, NY, 1989—90, Gateway-Longview Sch., Williamsville, 1990—98; spl. edn. resource tchr. Buffalo Pub. Sch., 1998—99, reading tchr., 1999—2003, reading first coach, 2003—07, staff developer K-6, 2007—. Mem.: Coun. for Exemption Children, Internat. Reading Assn. Democrat. Roman Catholic. Avocations: reading, travel, cross stitch. Home: 302 Hartford Rd Buffalo NY 14226 Office: #70 Buffum St Buffalo NY 14207 Personal E-mail: new1211997@netzero.net.

MESHOWSKI, FRANK ROBERT, business consultant; b. Milw., Sept. 10, 1930; s. Frank Louis and Constance (Mockus) M.; m. Olga Skirka, Jan. 26, 1952; children: David, Laurie, Elaine. B. in Marine Engring., N.Y. State Maritime Acad., 1951; BSME, Newark Coll. Engring., 1954. Project mgr. Curtiss Wright, Woodridge, N.J., 1952-59; v.p. sales/mktg. Gulton Industries, Metuchen, N.J., 1959-68; sr. v.p. Nytronics, Inc., Alpha, N.J., 1968-72; v.p. mktg. Gulf & Western Industries, NYC, 1972-79; pres., chief exec. officer Unicord div. Gulf & Western Industries, Westbury, N.Y., 1979-87; exec. v.p., chief operating officer, dir. OPT Industries, Phillipsburg, N.J., 1987-89. Bus. cons. strategic planning, mktg. and distbn., 1989—. Home and Office: 17 Turnberry Dr Monroe Township NJ 08831 Office Phone: 732-656-3168.

MESHULAM, DEBORAH R., lawyer; b. Lancaster, Pa., Nov. 25, 1956; BA magna cum laude, Univ. Va., 1978; JD, Columbia Univ., 1981. Bar: NY 1982, DC 1988, US Dist. Ct. (so. & ea. NY, Md., DC dist.), US Ct. Appeals (2d, 11th, DC cir.), US Supreme Ct. Asst. chief litigation counsel SEC, Washington, 1990—97; ptnr, head of Litigation group DLA Piper Rudnick Gray Cary, Washington. Co-author: Plain English Guidebook to SEC Recordkeeping & Retention, 2003; contbr. articles to profl. jours. Harlan Fiske Stone scholar. Office: DLA Piper Rudnick Gray Cary 1200 19th St NW Washington DC 20036-2412 Office Phone: 202-861-6470. Office Fax: 202-223-2085. Business E-Mail: deborah.meshulam@dlapiper.com.

MESKELL, KRISTIN MARIE, psychologist; b. Sacramento, Jan. 11, 1973; d. Howard Glen and Marylin Teresa Auble; m. Tim Meskell. BA in Psychology & Sociology, Calif. Luth. U., Thousand Oaks, Calif., 1994; MA in Counseling, Loyola Marymount U., LA, 2004; MA in Ednl. Psychology, Loyola Marymount U., 2006. Spl. events mgr. Loyola Marymount U., 2001—05; sch. psychologist San Diego Unified Sch. Dist., 2005—. Staff senator Loyola Marymount U., 2004—05; mem. psychology governance team San Diego Unified Sch. Dist., 2006. Mem.: Calif. Assn. Sch. Psychologists, Nat. Assn. Sch. Psychologists. Democrat. Luth. Office: San Diego Unified Sch Dist 4100 Normal St San Diego CA 92103

MESKILL, THOMAS J., federal judge; b. New Britain, Conn., Jan. 30, 1928; s. Thomas J.M. Meskill; m. Mary T. Grady; children: Maureen Meskill Heneghan, John Peter, Eileen Meskill Gallupe, Thomas. BS, Trinity Coll., Hartford, Conn., 1950, LL.D., 1972; JD, U. Conn., 1956; postgrad., Sch. Law, NYU; LL.D., U. Bridgeport, 1971, U. New Haven, 1974. Bar: Conn. 1956, DC 1957, US Ct. Appeals (2d cir.) 1975, US Supreme Ct. 1971. Former mem. firm Meskill, Dorsey, Sledzik and Walsh, New Britain; mem. 90th-91st Congresses 6th Conn. Dist.; gov. Conn., 1971-75; judge US Ct. Appeals (2d cir.), New Britain, Conn., 1975—, chief judge, 1992-93, sr. judge, 1993—. Pres. New Britain Council Social Agys.; Asst. corp. council City of New Britain, 1960-62, mayor, 1962-64, corp. counsel, 1965-67; mem. Constl. Conv., Hartford, 1965. Served to 1st lt. USAF, 1950-53. Recipient Disting. Svc. award Jr. C. of C., 1964, Jud. Achievement award ATLA, 1983, Learned Hand medal for Excellence in Fed. Juridprudence, Fed. Bar Coun., 1994. Mem. Conn. Bar Assn. (Henry J. Naruk Jud. award 1994), Hartford County Bar Assn., New Britain Bar Assn., KC. Republican. Office: US Ct Appeals Old Post Office Plz Ste 204 114 W Main St New Britain CT 06051-4223 Office Phone: 860-224-2617. *

MESNIAEFF, GREGORY, economist, securities analyst; b. NYC, Jan. 13, 1958; s. Peter G. and Maria A. (Voropajeff) M.; m. Elizabeth Burke, June 18, 1989. BBA Baruch Sch. Bus., CUNY, NYC, 1986; MA in Econs., Trinity Coll., Hartford, 1989. Market rschr. Blair TV, NYC, 1989-90; industry analyst telecomms. Northern Bus. Info./McGraw Hill, NYC, 1990-94; assoc. v.p. equity rsch. Wheat First Butcher & Singer, Richmond, Va., 1994-96; sr. v.p. equity rsch. Robinson-Humphrey Co., Atlanta, 1996—2002; mng. dir. Bantam Capital, LLC, NYC, 2002—. Fellow Trinity Coll. Bd. Fellows, Hartford, 1994-96. Recipient All-Star Analyst Telecom. Equipment Wall St. Jour., 1998. Mem. NY Soc. Security Analysts (investment strategy com.), NY Yacht Club, Russian Nobility Assn. Am. (bd. dir.), Order of St. John, New England Soc. NY. Republican. Russian Orthodox. Avocations: skiing, sailing, bicycling, historic preservation. Home: PO Box 1021 Sharon CT 06069

MESNIKOFF, ALVIN MURRAY, psychiatrist, educator; b. Asbury Park, NJ, Dec. 25, 1925; s. Nathan and Rachel (Feinberg) M.; m. Wendy Savin, June 15, 1952; children: Nathaniel, Rachel, Joel, Ann. AB, Rutgers U., 1948; postgrad., Yale U., 1948-49, Stanford U., 1949-50; MD, U. Chgo., 1954; cert. Psychoanalytic medicine, Columbia U., 1962. Diplomate: Am. Bd. Psychiatry and Neurology. Pvt. practice, 1958—; collaborating psychoanalyst Columbia U. Psychoanalytic Ctr. for Tng. and Rsch., NYC, 1962—; dir. Washington Heights Cmty., N.Y. State Psychiat. Inst., NYC, 1965—68; assoc. clin. prof. psychiatry Columbia U. Coll. Physicians and Surgeons, 1958—68; prof. psychiatry SUNY, Bklyn., 1968—81; dir. South Beach Psychiat. Ctr., SI, NY, 1968—75; regional dir. N.Y. State Dept. Mental Health, NYC, 1975—78, dep. commr. rsch., 1978—81; Marion E. Kenworthy prof. Psychiatry Columbia U. Sch. Social Work, 1981—89; lectr. Union Theol. Sem., NYC, 1989—90. Cons. St. Vincent's Hosp., S.I., 1970-76; attending psychiatrist S.I. Hosp., 1972-76; sr. attending psychiatrist St. Luke's/Roosevelt Hosp. Ctr., N.Y., 1987—; cons. Ford Found., N.Y.C., 1980-81 Contbr. chpts. to books, articles to profl. jours. Bd. dirs. Reality House, 1967-74; mem. task force med. sch. enrollment and physician manpower N.Y. State Bd. Regents, 1973-75; mem. task force on gen. and splty. hosp. care N.Y. State Health Planning Commn., 1973-74. Served with U.S. Army, 1943-45. Grantee Ford Found., 1982 Fellow Am. Psychiat. Assn. (life); mem. Am. Psychoanalytic Assn., Assn. Psychoanalytic Medicine, Am. Friends Tel Aviv U. (chmn. 1974-75), Phi Beta Kappa. Jewish. Office: 200 W 90th St 1F New York NY 10024 Home Phone: 914-478-3950; Office Phone: 212-663-5701.

MESROBIAN, ARPENA SACHAKLIAN, publishing executive, consultant, editor; b. Boston; d. Aaron H. and Eliza Sachaklian; m. William J. Mesrobian, June 22, 1940 (dec.); children: William S.(dec.), Marian Elizabeth (Mrs. Bruce MacCurdy). Student, Armenian Coll. of Beirut, Lebanon, 1937-38; AA, Univ. Coll., Syracuse U., NY, 1959, BA magna cum laude, 1971; MSsc, Syracuse U., 1993. Editor Syracuse U. Press, 1955-58, exec. editor, 1958-61, asst. dir., 1961-65, acting dir., 1965-66, editor, 1968-85, assoc. dir., 1968-75, dir., 1975-85, 87-88, dir. emeritus, 1985. Dir. workshop on univ. press. pub. U. Malaysia, Kuala Lumpur, 1985; cons. Empire State Coll. Book rev. editor: Armenian Rev., 1967-75; author: Like One Family: The Armenians of Syracuse, 2000; mem. publs. bd. Courier, 1970-94; mem. adv. bd. Armenian Rev., 1981-83; contbr. to Ency. of NY State, 2005; contbr. numerous articles, revs. to profl. jours. Pres. Syracuse chpt. Armenian Relief Soc., 1972-74; sponsor Armenian Assembly, Washington, 1975; mem. mktg. task force Office of Spl. Edn., Dept. Edn., 1979-84, Adminstrn. of Developmental Disabilities, HHS; mem. publs. panel Nat. Endowment for Humanities, Washington; bd. dirs. Syracuse Girls Club, 1982-87; pres. trustees St. John the Bapt. Armenian Apostolic Ch. and Cmty. Ctr., 1991-95. Named Post-Standard Woman of Achievement, 1980; recipient Chancellor's award for disting. service Syracuse U., 1985; Nat. award U.S. sect. World Edn. Fellowship, 1986; N.Y. State Humanities scholar. Mem. Women in Communications, Soc. Armenian Studies (adminstrv. council 1976-78, 85-87, sec. 1978, 85-87), Syracuse U. Library Assocs. (v.p. 1983-88), Am. Univ. Press Services (dir. 1976-77), Armenian Lit. Soc., Armenian Community Center, Assn. Am. Univ. Presses (v.p. 1976-77), UN Assn. (bd. dirs. 1983-88, v.p. 1985), Phi Kappa Phi, Alpha Sigma Lambda. Mem. Armenian Apostolic Ch. (past trustee). Club: Zonta of Syracuse (pres. 1979-80, 1st v.p. 1985-86, dist. historian Dist. 2 Zonta Internat. 1993-96).

MESSA, CHARLES ANGELO, III, plastic surgeon; b. Phila., Feb. 8, 1963; s. Charles Angelo Jr. and Roberta Elizabeth (Price) M.; m. Linda Mary Schultz, Aug. 13, 1988; children: Charles Angelo IV, William Joseph. BA magna cum laude, LaSalle U., 1985; MD, Pa. State U., 1989. Diplomate Am. Bd. Surgery. Intern U. Mass. Sch. Medicine, 1989-90; resident in surgery U. Mass. Sch. Medicine Ctr., Worcester, 1990-94; resident in plastic and reconstructive surgery U. Pa. Med. Ctr., Phila., 1994-96; surgeon Cosmetic Surgery Ctr., Weston, Fla. Presenter in field. Contbr. articles to profl. jours. Fellow ACS (assoc.), Am. Soc. Laser Med. and Surg.; mem. AMA, Pa. Med. Soc., Fla. Med. Assn., Mass. Med. Soc. Republican. Roman Catholic. Office: Weston Cosmetic Surgery Ctr Ste 1 & 2 17180 Arvida Pkwy Weston FL 33326 E-mail: drmessa@westoncosmeticsurgery.com.

MESSEMER, GLENN MATTHEW, lawyer; b. Hartford, Conn., Jan. 7, 1947; s. Joseph M. and Mary S. Messemer. BSBA, Georgetown U., 1968; JD, U. Conn., 1971. Bar: Conn. 1972. Staff atty. Kaman Corp., Bloomfield, Conn., 1972-74; asst. sec., 1974-79; asst. v.p., 1979-81; v.p., gen. counsel, 1981—. Prof. bus. law Sch. Bus. Adminstrn., U. Hartford (Conn., 1974-80; legal counsel Am. Helicopter Soc.; arbitrator Am. Arbitration Assn., 1978-82. Bd. dirs., trustee, regent U. hartford, 1993—. Served with M.I., U.S. Army, 1969-75. Mem. ABA, Conn. Bar Assn. (founding; exec. com., sec.), Hartford County Bar Assn. Clubs: Hartford Golf, Hartford, Masons. Office: Kaman Corp 1332 Blue Hills Ave Bloomfield CT 06002

MESSENGER, BARBARA BEALL, artist; d. John Murray and Anne Bryant (Dorsey) Beall; m. Donald White Messenger, Aug. 16, 1960; children: Colleen Beall Messenger-Baldwin, Melanie Dorsey Messenger Davis. BS, Western Md. Coll., 1960; postgrad., Md. Inst. Art, 1978, Howard C.C., Columbia, Md., 1979—80. Art educator, dept. chair Md. Pub. Sch. Sys., New Carrollton, 1960—66; art dir. Bellassai Gallery, Ellicott City, Md., 1980—84; proprietor Art and Frame Shop Ellicott Mills Gallery, Ellicott City, 1984—2000. Set, costume and program designer Calverton Players, Beltsville, Md., 1970—73; art critic, writer Laurel (Md.) Newsleader, 1974—80; substitute tchr. Howard County Sch. Sys., Ellicott City, 1984, Ellicott City, 85; publicity chmn. Laurel Art Guild. Exhibited in group shows at Laurel Art Guild, 1979, Bellassai Gallery, 1980—84, Villa Julia, Stevenson, Md., 1983, exhibited in group shows, Camden, Maine, 1988, exhibitions include Ellicott Mills Gallery, Md., Represented in permanent collections, Honduras, Turkey, Italy, German, U.S.A., and many islands. Active PTA, Howard County; membership chmn., v.p. Howard County Rep. Women; events coord. Howard County Rep. Party. Recipient Best of Balt. Art Gallery, Balt. Mag., 1980. Mem.: Am. Craft Coun., Howard County Arts Coun., Md. State Arts Coun. (bd. mem. 2003—), Nat. Mus. Women in the Arts (charter). Avocations: painting, crafts, reading, writing, photography. Home and Office: 616 Traveller Ct Lothian MD 20711 Office Phone: 410-741-0959. E-mail: bobbiemessenger@aol.com.

MESSENGER, GEORGE CLEMENT, engineering executive, consultant; b. Bellows Falls, Vt., July 20, 1930; s. Clement George and Ethel Mildred (Farrar) M.; m. Priscilla Betty Norris, June 19, 1954; children: Michael Todd, Steven Barry, Bonnie Lynn. BS in Physics, Worcester Poly U., 1951; MSEE, U. Pa., 1957; PhD in Engring., Calif. Coast U., 1986. Rsch. scientist Philco Corp., Phila., 1951-59; engring. mgr. Hughes Semicondr., Newport Beach, Calif., 1959-61; divsn. mgr. Transitron Corp., Wakefield, Mass., 1961-63; staff scientist Northrop Corp., Hawthorne, Calif., 1963-68; cons. engr. Las Vegas, Nev., 1968—. Lectr. UCLA, 1969-75; v.p., dir. Am. Inst. Fin., Grafton, Mass., 1970-78; gen. ptnr. Dargon Fund, Anaheim, Calif., 1983—; v.p., tech. dir. Messenger and Assoc., 1987—, registered investment adviser, 1989—. Co-author: The Effects of Radiation on Electronic Systems, 1986, Single Event Phenomena, 1997; contbg. author: Fundamentals of Nuclear Hardening, 1972, Nonvolatile Semiconductor Memory Technology, 1998; contbr. articles to profl. jours.; patentee microwave diode, hardened semicondrs. Recipient Naval Rsch. Lab. Alan Berman award, 1982, Best Paper award HEART Conf., 1983, Spl. Merit award, 1983, Pete Haas award, 1992, Goddard award for outstanding profl. achievement Worcester Poly. Inst., 1996, Archimedes award for contbns. to semicondr., solid state and nuc. physics rsch., 2006. Fellow IEEE (Merit award 1986); mem. Rsch. Soc. Am., Am. Phys. Soc. Congregationalist. Home and Office: 3111 Bel Air Dr Apt 7F Las Vegas NV 89109-1510 Personal E-mail: gpmessenger@cox.net.

MESSENKOPF, EUGENE JOHN, real estate developer, hotel executive; b. NYC, Jan. 26, 1928; s. John Philip and Helen Bessie (Holden) M.; m. Martha Ann Crane, Jan. 29, 1955; children: Diane, Nancy, Eugene John, Susan. BBA, Iona Coll., 1950; MBA, NYU, 1956. CPA, N.Y. Sec.-treas. KLM Process Co., NYC, 1952-54; acct. Am. Tobacco Co., NYC, 1954-56; staff acct. Peat, Marwick & Mitchell, NYC, 1956-60; exec. v.p. Donaldson, Lufkin & Jenrette, Inc., NYC, 1960-84, pres., chief exec. officer real estate div., 1977-84; pres., chief exec. officer Meridian Investing and Devel. Corp., 1977-84; pvt. practice cons., 1984—. Mem. adv. bd. NYU Real Estate Inst., 1981-85; mem. exec. coun. small scale devel. Urban Land Inst., 1983-90; chmn. Wall St. Tax Com., N.Y.C., 1965-68; bd. dirs. SIA Acctg. Div., N.Y.C., 1965-79. Trustee, chmn. fin. com. Mt. Vernon Hosp., 1982-87. Served as sgt. AUS, 1950-52, Korea. Recipient Brother Loftus award Iona Coll., 1976. Mem. AICPA, N.Y. State Soc. CPAs, Fin. Execs. Inst. Republican. Roman Catholic. Achievements include walking 2000 mile Appalachian Trail, 1987.

MESSER, ALLEN PERSON, mechanical engineer, construction executive; b. Chicopee, Mass., July 1, 1961; s. Elroy Allen and Roberta Gail Messer; m. Donna Sue Riddle, Nov. 23, 1991. AA, U. Fla., Gainesville, 1980—83, BS in Engring., 1980—83; MBA, Embry-Riddle Aero. U., Daytona Beach, Fla., 1983—85. Cert. profl. engr., Bd. Profl. Engrs., Fla., 2001; leed v2 accredited profl. US Green Bldg. Coun., 2006. Analytical engr. Pratt & Whitney Govt. Aerospace Sys., W.Palm Beach, Fla., 1983—85; material engr. Martin Marietta Denver Aerospace, Denver, 1985—87; bus. devel. mgr. Harris Govt. Aerospace Sys., Melbourne, Fla., 1987—89; sales rep. EDS/McDonnell Douglas, Orlando, Fla., 1989—93; mgr. bus. devel. Briggs Assocs., Inc., Orlando, 1993—94; dir. bus. devel. Coastal Mech. Svcs., Inc., Melbourne, 1994—98; v.p., bus. unit leader Control Solutions, LTD, LLC, Orlando, 1998—2000; lead estimator Centex Constrn., Plantation, Fla., 2000—07; dir. preconstruction Skanska, Dania Beach, 2007—. Adj. prof. Fla. Atlantic U., Ft. Lauderdale, 2003—. Sec. Lake Harney Homeowner's Assn., Geneva, Fla., 1992—99. Mem.: Am. Soc. Profl. Estimators, Am. Soc. Heating, Refrigeration & Air-Conditioning Engrs. (v.p. 2003—05, chmn. rsch. promotion 1997—98, Cert. Appreciation award 1998), Golden Key. Avocations: travel, swimming. Home: 4811 SW 201 Ter Southwest Ranches FL 33332 Office: Skanska 1815 Griffin Rd Ste 204 Dania Beach FL 33004 Home Phone: 954-252-9811.

MESSER, DONALD EDWARD, theology educator, administrator; b. Kimball, SD, Mar. 5, 1941; s. George Marcus and Grace E. (Foltz) M.; m. Bonnie Jeanne Nagel, Aug. 30, 1964; children: Christine Marie, Kent Donald. BA cum laude, Dakota Wesleyan U., 1963, LHD (hon.), 1977; MDiv magna cum laude, Boston U., 1966, PhD, 1969. Asst. to commr. Mass. Commn. Against Discrimination, Boston, 1968-69; asst. prof. Augustana Coll., Sioux Falls, SD, 1969-71; assoc. pastor 1st United Meth. Ch., Sioux Falls, 1969-71; pres. Dakota Wesleyan U., Mitchell, SD, 1971-81, Iliff Sch. Theology, Denver, 1981-2000, pres. emeritus and prof. practical theology, 2000—; exec. dir. Ctr. for the Ch. and Global AIDS, 2007—. Author: Christian Ethics and Political Action, 1984, Contemporary Images of Christian Ministry, 1989, Send Me? The Intineracy in Crisis, 1991, The Conspiracy of Goodness, 1992, Caught in the Crossfire: Helping Christians Debate Homosexuality, 1994, Calling Church and Seminary Into the 21st Century, 1995, Unity, Liberty, and Charity: Building Bridges Under Icy Waters, 1996, How Shall We Die? Helping Christians Debate Assisted Suicide, 1997, The Befuddled Stork: Helping Persons of Faith Debate Beginning of life Issues, 2000, Breaking the Conspiracy of Silence: Christian Churches and the Global AIDS Crisis, 2004; co-author: (with George McGovern, Bob Dole) Ending Hunger Now, 2005; co-editor: Connected Spirits: Friends and Spiritual Journeys, 2007; contbr. articles to Face to Face, The Christian Century, The Christian Ministry. Active Edn. Commn. of U.S., 1973-79; co-chmn. Citizens Commn. Corrections, 1975-76; vice chmn. SD Commn. on Humanities, 1979-81. Dempster fellow, 1967-68; Rockefeller fellow, 1968-69. Mem. Soc. Christian Ethics, Am. Acad. Religion, Assn. United Meth. Theol. Schs. (v.p. 1986-91, pres. 1991-92). Democrat.

MESSERLE, JUDITH ROSE, retired medical librarian, public relations executive; b. Litchfield, Ill., Jan. 16, 1943; d. Richard Douglas and Nelrose B. Wilcox; m. Darrell Wayne Messerle, Apr. 26, 1968; children: Kurt Norman, Katherine Lynn. BA in Zoology, So. Ill. U., 1966; MLS, U. Ill., 1967. Cert. med. libr. Libr. St. Joseph's Sch. Nursing, Alton, Ill., 1967-71, dir. med. info. ctr., 1971-76, dir. info. svcs., 1976-79; dir. ednl. resources and cmty. rels. St. Joseph's Hosp., 1979-84; dir. Med. Ctr. Libr. St. Louis U., 1985-88; libr. Francis A. Countway Libr. Harvard Med. Sch. and Boston Med. Libr., 1989—2004; ret. Instr. Lewis and Clark Coll., 1975, Med. Libr. Assn.; cons. in field. Bd. dirs. Family Svcs. and Vis. Nurses Assn., Alton, 1976-79. Fellow AAAS, Med. Libr. Assn. (search com. for exec. dir. 1979, dir. 1981-84, pres. 1986-87, legis. task force 1986-90, task force for knowledge and skills 1988-92, nominating com. 1996); mem. OCLC (spl. libr. adv. com. 1994-98), AMA (com. on allied health edn. and accreditation 1991-94), Assn. Acad. Health Sci. Libr. Dirs. (editl. bd. for ann. stats. 1989-94, Region 8 adv. bd. 1992-93, joint legis. task force 1992-96, pres. 1993, charting the future task force 2001-03, scholarly communication task force 2003-05), Am. Med. Informatics Assn. (planning com. 1990, publs. com. 1994-96, ann. mtg. com. 1996-98), Ill. State Libr. Adv. Com., Midwest Health Sci. Libr. Network (divsn. health sci. coun.), St. Louis Med. Librs., Hosp. Pub. Rels. Soc. St. Louis, Nat. Libr. Medicine (biomed. libr. rev. com. 1988-92).

MESSERSCHMIDT, WILLIAM HARCLERODE, retired noncommissioned officer, musician; b. Lebanon, Pa., Apr. 30, 1947; s. Harry Edgar and Sylva (Harclerode) M.; m. Janice Andersen, Dec. 28, 1971; children: William F., Ann K., Dorothy R., Edward D. MusB with distinction, Eastman Sch. Music, 1969; postgrad., Cath. U. Am., 1983, Va. Theol. Sem., 1992-96. Enlisted man U.S. Army, 1969, advanced through grades to sgt. maj., 1994; percussionist U.S. Army Field Band, Ft. George G. Meade, Md., 1969-74, U.S. Army Band (Pershing's Own), Ft. Myer, Va., 1974-85, asst. sect. leader, 1985-89, leader percussion sect., 1989-94, leader percussion group, 1994—2002; ret., 2002. Pvt. tchr. percussion, Springfield and Woodbridge, Va., 1975—; adj. instr. percussion No. Va. C.C., Woodbridge, 1983—; percussionist Prince William Symphony Orch., Lake Ridge, Va., 1989-93, The Fifes and Drums of Prince William, III, Woodbridge, 2003—, Lynchburg Symphony Orch., Va., 2003-; timpanist, percussionist orchs. with Nt. Christian Choir, Gaithersburg, Md., 1990—, Old Bridge Chamber Orch., Burke, Va., 1999-. Choir dir. Grace Ref. Presbyn. Ch., Woodbridge, 1985-93, Salvation Army Leadership Coun. Mem. Nat. Audubon Soc., Soc. German Am. Studies, Am. Soc. Prevention Cruelty to Animals, Am. Fedn. Musicians, Vir Firth Edn. Team, Am. Legion, Smithsonian Assocs., SAR, Kappa Delta Pi. Avocations: reading, philosophy, tennis, languages. Home: 5400 Staples Ln Woodbridge VA 22193-3562 Office Phone: 703-590-9834. Personal E-mail: messperc@aol.com.

MESSIAH-JILES, SONCERIA, publishing executive; BA in Polit. Sci., U. Houston; MBA, Tex. So. U. Talk show host KHOU-TV, KRIV-TV; adv. acct. exec. KMJQ-FM; news reporter KYOK-AM; pub. Houston Defender; pres. Nat. Newspaper Pub. Assn. Office: Nat Newspaper Pub Assn 3200 13th St NW Washington DC 20010 Office Phone: 202-588-8764.

MESSICK, ANDREW, sports association executive; BA in Econs. and Psych., U. Calif., Davis; MBA, Yale Sch. Mgmt. With McKinsey & Co., Chgo. and Amsterdam; various bus. devel., mktg. and gen. mgmt. positions Sara Lee Corp.; sr. v.p. internat. NBA. Office: NBA Olympic Tower 645 5th Ave Fl 10 New York NY 10022-5986 *

MESSICK, FREDERIC MORTON, librarian; b. South Bend, Ind., Apr. 20, 1935; s. Francis Morton Messick and Mary Elizabeth Muessel; m. Carol Louise Reitzel, May 15, 1993; m. Claire Laverne Bowen, Dec. 18, 1965 (div. July 15, 1990); children: Elizabeth Ann Webber, David Morton. AB, Ind. U., 1959, AMT, 1963; MLS, U.Mich., 1965. Social sci. tchr. Elkhart Pub. Schools, Ind., 1963—64; ref. libr. Am. U., Washington, 1965—67; libr., bibliographer Ctrl. Mich. U., Mount Pleasant, Mich., 1967—97, ret., 1997, prof. emeritus, 1997—. Author: (reference book) Primary Sources in European Diplomacy, 1914-1945: A Bibliography of Published Memoirs and Diaries. Bd. dirs. Mt. Pleasant Area Internat. Rels. Com., Mich., 1994—2001. Mem.: Am. Hist. Assn. Unitarian. Avocations: sailing, swimming. Home: 1333 Crestwood Dr Mount Pleasant MI 48858 Home Phone: 989-772-0304. Personal E-mail: f.messick@cmich.edu.

MESSIER, MARK DOUGLAS, retired professional hockey player; b. Edmonton, Alta., Can., Jan. 18, 1961; Center Indpls. Racers, 1978, Cin. Stingers, 1979, Edmonton Oilers, Canada, 1979—91, NY Rangers, 1991—97, NY, 2000—05, Vancouver Canucks, Vancouver, 1997—2000; hockey analyst NHL on Versus. Player NHL All-Star Game, 1982—84, 1986, 1988—92, 1994, 1996—98, 2000, 04. Named NHL Player of Yr., 1989, 1990, 1991—92; named to Sporting News All-Star Team, 1981—82, 1982—83, 1989—90, 1991—92; recipient Conn Smythe Trophy, 1984, Lester B. Pearson award, 1989—90, 1991—92, Hart Trophy, 1990, 1992. Achievements include being a member of Stanley Cup Champion Edmonton Oilers, 1984, 1985, 1987, 1988, 1990, NY Rangers, 1994; having his number, 11, retired by NY Rangers, 2006, Edmonton Oilers, 2007.

MESSIER, PIERRE, lawyer, manufacturing executive; b. Montreal, Que., Can., Mar. 3, 1945; s. Lionel and Anita (Caron) M.; m. Ginette Piche, July 11, 1970; 1 child, Mathieu. BA, Coll. St. Viateur, Outremont, Que., 1964; Lic. in Law, U. Montreal, 1968; diploma in adminstrv. scis., Ecole Hautes Etudes Commerciales, Montreal, 1973. Bar: Que. 1969. Assoc. Lemay & Messier, Montreal, 1969-75; v.p., sec. gen. counsel Can. Cement Lafarge, Ltd., Montreal, 1975-84; v.p., sec. Lafarge Corp., 1983-84; v.p. bus. devel., legal affairs Norsk Hydro Can. Inc., Montreal, 1989-98; lawyer Leduc LeBlanc, Montreal, 1998-2000; pvt. practice, cons., 2000—02, 2003—; sr. legal counsel Bombardier, Inc., Montreal, 2002—03. V.p. Que. Bar Svc. Corp., 1995-2006. Pres. Centre Pedagogique Lucien-Guilbault Inc., 1999—; v.p. Coll. Jean de Brebeuf, 1991-97; pres. Greenfield Park Bd. Revision, 1973-74; bd. dirs. Societe Progres Rive Sud, Longueuil, Que., 1974-75, Que. Bar Profl. Liability Ins. Fund, 2006—. Mem. Can. Bar Assn. (pres. young lawyers sect. 1976, nat. exec. 1977-78), Montreal Jr. Bar (treas. 1972), Que. Mfrs. and Exporters Alliance (bd. dirs. 1996-98),

St. Denis Club (Montreal), Que. Secs. and Gen. Counsel Assn. (sec. 1998). Office Phone: 514-344-7081. Business E-Mail: pierre.messier@defense.bombardier.com.

MESSIMER, DONALD MCKEE, JR., language educator; b. Danville, Pa., Apr. 29, 1948; s. Donald McKee and Molly Inkrote Messimer. BS, Bloomsburg U., Pa., 1970, MEd, 1973; post grad., Pa. State U., Univ. Park, 1974—76. Cert. permanent tchr. English 7-12 Pa., 1973. Tchr. English Mifflinburg Area Sch. Dist., Pa., 1970—, dept. chair. Named Tchr. of Yr., Pa. Dept. VFW, 2005—06. Mem.: Pa. State Edn. Assn., Nat. Edn. Assn., Travelers Protective Assn. Democrat. United Ch. Christ. Avocations: music, book collecting, antiques, travel. Office: Mifflinburg HS 75 Market St Mifflinburg PA 17844-1328 Home: 220 Washington Ave Sunbury PA 17801 Office Phone: 570-966-8230.

MESSIN, MARLENE ANN, plastics company executive; b. St. Paul, Oct. 6, 1935; d. Edgar Leander and Luella Johanna (Rahn) Johnson; m. Eugene Carlson (div. 1972); children: Rick, Debora, Ronald, Lori; m. Willard Smith (dec. 1975); m. Frank Messin, Sept. 24, 1982; 5 stepchildren. Bookkeeper Jeans Implement Co., Forest Lake, Minn., 1952-53, 1953—57, Great Plains Supply, St. Paul, 1960-62, Plastic Products Co., Inc., Lindstrom, Minn., 1962-75, pres., 1975—; co-owner, treas. Gustaf's Fine Gifts, Lindstrom, 1985—. Bookkeeper Trinity Luth. Ch., Lindstrom, 1976-81. Recipient award, Diversity 2000/Woman-Owned Bus. in Minn. Mem. Soc. Plastic Engrs., Swedish Inst., Soc. Plastic Industry, Minn. State Hist. Soc., Chgo. County Hist. Soc. Home: 28968 Olinda Trl Lindstrom MN 55045-9429 Office: 30355 Akerson St Lindstrom MN 55045-9456

MESSINA, CHARLES, artist; b. Wilmington, Del., Jan. 6, 1950; s. Joseph and Mae C. Messina; m. Patricia Simmons (div.); 1 child, Charlene. Oil painter, wood carver, sculptor. Represented in permanent collections Rattenni Children Edn. Fund, Wilmington, Am. Diabetes Assn., Leukemia and Lymphoma, Del. Recipient Salute for Participation, Soc. da Vinci, 2004, cert. appreciation, City of Wilmington, 2004. Mem.: Order Sons Italy Am., St. Anthony's Club. Avocations: art, crafts. Home: 1902 W 6th St Wilmington DE 19805

MESSING, DEBRA, actress; b. Bklyn., Aug. 15, 1968; m. Daniel Zelman, Sept. 3, 2000; 1 child, Roman Walker. Grad., Brandeis U.; M in Drama, NYU. Actor: (films) Walk in the Clouds, 1995, McHale's Navy, 1997, Prey, 1997, Celebrity, 1998, Mothman Prophecies, 2002, Hollywood Ending, 2002, Along Came Polly, 2004, (voice) Garfield, 2004, The Wedding Date, 2005, (voice) Open Season, 2006, Purple Violets, 2007, Lucky You, 2007; (TV series) Ned and Stacey, 1995, Prey, 1998, Will & Grace, 1998—2006 (Emmy award best actress in a comedy, 2003); TV appearances include: NYPD Blue, 1994, 1995; Partners, 1995; Seinfeld, 1996, 1997; (voice) King of the Hill, 2002. Office: c/o Gersh Agy 232 N Canon Dr Beverly Hills CA 90210 *

MESSINGER, DONALD HATHAWAY, lawyer; b. Lyons, NY, July 1, 1943; s. Donald H. and Thelma (Hubbard) M.; m. Sara L. Stock, June 3, 1967; children: Michael David, Robert Stephen, Daniel Mark. BA, Colgate U., 1965; JD, Duke U., 1968. Bar: Ohio 1968. Assoc. Thompson Hine LLP, Cleve., 1968-76, ptnr., 1976—, vice chair corp. practice group, 1989-92, ptnr.-in-charge Cleve. office, 1991-96, mem. exec. com., 1996-2000. Sec., bd. dirs. Am. Steel and Wire Corp., 1986-93; sec., bd.dirs. Lee Wilson Engineering C., Inc., 1989-94; bd. dirs. Cedar Fair Mgmt. Co., 1993-2002. Trustee Cmty. Info.-Vol. Action Ctr., 1981-88, pres. 1981-84; trustee Free Med. Clinic Greater Cleve., 1970—, sec., 1970-82, v.p. 1982-86, 96-2002, pres. 2002-04; trustee Cleve. Hearing and Speech Ctr., 1980—, v.p. 1984-86, 92-93, pres., 1986-88, 98-2000; dir. Colgate U. Alumni Corp., 1979-83; trustee U. for Young Ams., 1982-95, sec.,1982- 1982-86, pres., 1986-88, chmn. 1991-95; mem. exec. bd. Boy Scouts Am., 1983-88; Leadership Cleve., 1984—; trustee, sec. Bus. Vols. Unltd., 1992—; sec. Buckeye Area Devel. Corp., 1970-90; mem. adv. bd. Greater Cleve. New Stadium; dir., Cleve. Pops Orch., 2006-. Recipient Cmty. Svc. award Fedn. for Community Planning, 1981-82, Daniel D. Dauby award Cleve. Hearing & Speech Ctr. 2007.; named one of Outstanding Young Citizens of Greater Cleve., 1971-75, BTI Client Svc. All Star 2006. Mem. ABA, Ohio Bar Assn., Cleve. Bar Assn. (trustee 1975-79, chmn. securities law inst. 1983), Nat. Assn. Bond Lawyers Home: 21550 Shelburne Rd Shaker Heights OH 44122 Office: 3900 Key Ctr 127 Public Sq Cleveland OH 44114 Office Phone: 216-566-5571. Business E-Mail: don.messinger@thompsonhine.com.

MESSITTE, PETER JO, judge; b. Washington, July 17, 1941; s. Jesse B. and Edith (Wechsler) M.; m. Susan P. Messitte, Sept. 5, 1965: children: Zachariah, Abigail. BA cum laude, Amherst Coll., Mass., 1963; JD, U. Chgo., 1966. Bar: Md. 1969, DC 1969, US Ct. Appeals (4th cir.) 1977, US Supreme Ct. 1973, US Ct. Appeals (DC cir.) 1982, US Ct. Appeals (5th cir.) 1983. Assoc. Zuckert, Scoutt & Rasenberger, Washington, 1968-71; solo practice Chevy Chase, Md., 1971-75; mem. Messitte & Rosenberg, P.A., Chevy Chase, 1975-81; prin. Peter J. Messitte, P.A., Chevy Chase, 1981-85; assoc. judge Cir. Ct. for Montgomery County Rockville, Md., 1985-93; judge U.S. Dist. Ct. Md., Greenbelt, 1993—. Mem. Internat. Jud. Rels. Com. Jud. Conf. US, 1997-2003. Bd. dirs. Cmty. Psychiat. Clinic, Montgomery County, Md., 1974-85, v.p. 1980-85; Peace Corps vol., Sao Paulo, Brazil, 1966-68; Md. del. Dem. Nat. Conv., NYC, 1980. Recipient tchg. citations Fed. Deposit Ins. Corp. Bank Exam. Sch., 1975, 79, Am. Inst. Banking, 1978, Elizabeth Scull award for Outstanding Svc. to Montgomery County, Md., 1993, Spl. citation Divorce Roundtable Montgomery County, 1993, Gran Cruz da Ordem São José Operário-Brazilian Labor Tribunal, Mato Grosso, 2001, Medalha de Mérito Académico, Academia Paulista de Magistrados, 2002, Contbr. Mental Health Cmty. Psychiat. Clinic, 1986, Leadership in Law award, Md. Daily Record, 2002, Diploma Honor and Merit, Assn. São Paulo Magistrates, 2007; named an honorary citizen Ribeirão Preto, Brazil, 2007, Uberlândia, Brazil, 2007. Fellow: Md. Bar Found. (H. Vernon Eney award for contbn. to adminstrn. of justice 2001); mem.: ABA, Jud. Inst. Md. (bd. dirs. 1989—93), Charles Fahy Inn of Ct. (master 1987—88), Fed. Judges Assn. (4th jud. cir.), Am. Law Inst., Instituto Paulista de Advogados (hon.), Montgomery County Bar Assn. (Century of Svc. award 1999), Md. Bar Assn., DC Bar Assn., Fed. Bar Assn., Montgomery County Inn of Ct. (pres. 1988—90). Jewish. Office: US Courthouse 6500 Cherrywood Ln Greenbelt MD 20770-1249 Office Phone: 301-344-0632.

MESSMAN, JACK L., network management software company executive; b. Clarksburg, W.Va., Mar. 13, 1940; s. Marvin C. and Betty L. (Jones) M.; m. Maggie Saran, Apr. 18, 1997; children: Valerie Lynne, Kyle Andrew. B in Chem. Engring., U. Del., 1962; MBA with Distinction, Harvard U., 1968. Ptnr. Butcher & Singer, Phila., 1971-73; pres. Norcross, Inc., West Chester, Pa., 1973-80; v.p. corp. devel. UGI Corp., Valley Forge, Pa., 1980-81; exec. v.p. Safeguard Scientifics, Inc., King of Prussia, Pa., 1981-83; pres., CEO Novell Data Sys., Inc., Orem, Utah, 1982—83; exec. v.p., CFO, also bd. dir. Warner Amex Cable Comm. Inc., NYC, 1983-86; mng. dir. Mason Best Co., 1986—88; chmn., CEO Somerset House Corp., Houston, 1986-88; CEO, chmn. bd. dirs. US Pollution Control Inc. (subsidiary of Union Pacific Corp.), Oklahoma City, 1988-91; pres. Union Pacific Resources, Inc., 1991—96, CEO, 1991—99, chmn. Ft. Worth, 1996—99; pres., CEO Cambridge Tech. Ptnrs. (merged with Novell, Inc.), Waltham, Mass., 1999—2001; CEO Novell, Inc., Waltham, Mass., 2001—06, chmn., 2001—06. Bd. dirs. Wawa, Inc. (Pa.), Novell Inc., 1985-, Safeguard Scientifics, Inc., 1994-,Cambridge Technology Ptnrs., 1992-, Tandy Corp., U.S. Data., RadioShack Corp., Timminco, Ltd. Served to 1st lt. U.S. Army, 1963-65. Mem. River Crest Country Club (Ft. Worth), Mira Vista Club (Ft. Worth). Republican. Episcopalian. Office: Novell Inc 404 Wyman St Ste 500 Waltham MA 02451

MESSMER, DONALD JOSEPH, business management educator, marketing consultant; b. St. Louis, July 30, 1936; s. Edgar Louis and Lucille Louise (Straub) Messmer; m. Charlotte Jean Fox; 1 child, Angeline Charlotte. BSBA with honors, Washington U., St. Louis, 1969, PhD, 1974. Asst. mgr. M.A. Bell Co., St. Louis, 1956-61; dist. sales exec. U. S. Gypsum Co., St. Louis, 1962-65; br. sales exec. Victor Comptometer Corp., St. Louis, 1965-68; asst. prof. Coll. William and Mary, Williamsburg, Va., 1973-76, assoc. prof., 1976-81, prof., 1981—2006, J.S. Mack prof., 1982—2006; pres. The Wessex Group, Ltd., Williamsburg, 1979—. Bd. dirs. Williamsburg Winery, Ltd., 2005—07, chmn. bd. dirs., 2005—; co-founder Coll. William and Mary Exec. Ptnrs. Editor (assoc ed): Decision Scis Jour, 1985—88; contbr. articles to profl jours. Bd. dirs., treas. Cmty. Action Agy., Williamsburg, 1984—91, United Way Greater Williamsburg, 1985—91, pres., 1989; founder Cmty. Svcs. Coalition, pres., chmn.; owner Hist. Triangle Cmty. Svcs. Bldg. Recipient Pres.'s cmty. svc. award, Coll. William and Mary, 1999. Mem.: Southeastern Decision Scis Inst (pres 1985—86), Am Mkt Asn (Dissertation Award 1974), Decision Scis Inst (mkt coord 1985—86), Rotary (bd. dirs. 1990—92, program chair 2003, bd. dirs. 2003—, pres. 2004, pres.-elect 2003—04), Beta Gamma Sigma, Alpha Mu Alpha. Republican. Avocations: fishing, golf. Home Phone: 757-229-0764; Office Phone: 757-253-5606. Business E-Mail: don.messmer@wessexgroup.com.

MESSMER, HAROLD MAXIMILIAN, JR., (MAX MESSMER), financial services executive; b. Jackson, Miss., Feb. 20, 1946; s. Harold Maximilian and Margaret (Dee) M.; m. Marcia Elizabeth Nesmith, Apr. 5, 1973; children: Michael Christopher, Matthew Gordon. AB summa cum laude, Loyola U., 1967; JD cum laude, NYU, 1970. Ptnr. corp. law and securities O'Melveny & Myers, Los Angeles, 1970-81; sr. v.p., gen. counsel Pacific Holding Corp., Los Angeles, 1981-82, pres., chief operating officer, 1982-85; pres., dir., chief operating officer Cannon Mills Co. (subs.), Kannapolis, N.C., 1982-85; chmn., dir. Castle & Cook Inc., San Francisco, 1985; chmn., pres., chief exec. officer Robert Half Internat. Inc., Menlo Park, 1985—2004, chmn., CEO, 2004—. Adj. prof. Claremont Grad. Sch. Bus.(exec. mgmt. program), 1979-82; bd. dirs. Health Care Property Investors, Los Angeles, BF Enterprises Inc., N.C. Nat. Bank, Charlotte. Trustee Davidson (N.C.) Coll., 1984—; appointee Pres. Reagan's Adv. Com. on Trade Negotiations, 1985-87. Served with USAR, 1971-75. Mem. ABA, Los Angeles County Bar Assn., Calif. Bar Assn. Served with USAR, 1971-75. Office: Robert Half Internat Inc 2884 Sand Hill Rd Ste 200 Menlo Park CA 94025-7059 *

MESSNER, HOWARD MYRON, former professional association executive; b. Newark, June 10, 1937; s. Elias and Freda (Trachtenberg) M.; m. Aletha Bragg, 1960 (div. 1980); children: Jennifer, Linda, David; m. Melba June Meador, June 22, 1986. BA, Antioch Coll., 1960; MA, U. Mass., 1962. Mgmt. analyst, Office Gov. State of Mass., Boston, 1960-61; staff asst. to adminstr. NASA, Washington, 1962-65; mgmt. analyst Bur. Budget, Washington, 1965-71; dir. adminstrn. EPA, Washington, 1971-75, asst. adminstr. for adminstrn., 1983-87; asst. dir. Congl. Budget Office, Washington, 1975-77, Office Mgmt. & Budget, Exec. Office of the Pres., Washington, 1977-83; contr. US Dept. Energy, Washington, 1983; exec. v.p. Am. Cons. Engr. Coun., 1987—99, 2006—07; pres., CEO Nat. Acad. Pub. Adminstrn., Washington, 2004—07. Bd. dirs. Kelly, Anderson Inc. Recipient William A. Jump Meml. award, 1971, Presdl. Disting. Exec. award, 1986, Outstanding Pub. Service award Nat. Capital chpt. Am. Soc. Pub. Adminstrn., 1986, Chancellor's medal U. Mass., 1978. Mem. Nat. Acad. Pub. Adminstrn. (trustee), Cosmos Club. Democrat. Jewish. Personal E-mail: messnermeador@msn.com.

MESSNER, JAMES W., advertising executive; b. 1939; Attended, 1959-61. With Sta. WCSM, Celina, Ohio, 1961-63, Sta. WTOD, Toledo, 1961-63, Detroit Advt. Agy., 1965-68, Norman, Navan, Moore & Bard, 1968-77; chmn., CEO J.W. Messner Inc., Grand Rapids, Mich., 1977—. Office: JW Messner Inc 161 Ottawa Ave NW Ste 403 Grand Rapids MI 49503-2760

MESSNER, LEONARD VINCENT, optometrist, educator; b. Johnstown, Pa., May 17, 1957; s. Leonard Francis and Julia (Pirich) M.; m. Stephanie Ann Saylor, July 25, 1981; 1 child, Jordan Anastasia. BS, U. Pitts., 1979; OD, Pa. Coll. Optometry, Phila., 1984. Diplomate Neuro-ophthalmic Disorders. Resident in optometry, advanced tng. vitreoretinal and neuro-ophthalmic disorders Eye Inst. Pa. Coll. Optometry, 1985; assoc. prof. optometry Ill. Coll. Optometry, Chgo., 1985—. Mem. ocular disease-trauma com., mem. clin. exam. coun. Nat. Bd. Examiners in Optometry, Bethesda, Md., 1994—; chief of staff Ill. Eye Inst., 1996-97, v.p. patient care svcs., 1998—. Contbr. articles to profl. jours., referee. Fellow Am. Acad. Optometry (neuro-ophthalmic disorders diplomate com.); mem. Am. Optometric Assn., Ill. Optometric Assn., Prentice Soc. Avocations: running, golf, baseball. Office: 3241 S Michigan Ave Chicago IL 60616-3849

MESSNER, ROBERT THOMAS, lawyer, bank executive; b. McKeesport, Pa., Mar. 27, 1938; s. Thomas M. and Cecilia Mary (McElhinny) M.; m. Anne Margaret Lux, Dec. 3, 1966; children: Megan Anne, Michael Thomas. AB, Dartmouth Coll., 1960; LL.B., U. Pa., 1963. Bar: Pa. 1965. With firm Rose, Schmidt & Dixon, Pitts., 1965-68; with G.C. Murphy Co., McKeesport, 1968-86, corp. sec., 1974—, gen. counsel, 1975-86, v.p., 1976-86; v.p., gen. counsel, corp. sec. Dollar Bank, Pitts., 1986—2006. Dir. G.C. Murphy Found. Author: Reflections from Braddock's Field, 2005. Mem. Point State Park planning com. City of Pitts.; Rep. candidate Pa. Legis., 1966; mem. Mayor's Com. on Fort Duquesne, Pitts.; bd. dirs. McKeesport YMCA, Downtown Pitts. YMCA, Braddock's Field Hist. Soc., 1994—, Mon-Yough Heritage Found., 2003—; mem. adv. bd. Pa. Human Rels. Commn., 1968—69. 1st lt. US Army, 1963—65. Decorated Commendation medal. Mem. ABA, Pa. Bar Assn. (chmn. corp. law dept. com.), Allegheny County Bar Assn. (coun. on corp., banking and bus. law), Am. Soc. Corp. Secs. (pres. Pitts. regional group, dir.), Am. Mgmt. Assn., Pa. Assn. Savs. Instns. (chmn. legal com. 1989—), Am. Corp. Counsel Assn., Braddock's Battlefield Assn. (bd. dirs. 2004—), Theta Delta Chi. Clubs: Dartmouth Western Pa., Rivers. Home: 1061 Blackridge Rd Pittsburgh PA 15235-2719 Office: Dollar Bank Three Gateway Ctr Pittsburgh PA 15222 Personal E-mail: r.messner@comcast.net.

MESSNER, THOMAS G., advertising executive, copywriter; b. NYC, Jan. 26, 1944; s. Malcolm V. Messner and Virginia M. Burkard; m. Terry Carol Bonaccolta, Nov. 28, 1971; 1 child, Zachary. Letter carrier U.S. Post Office, NYC, 1965-67; copywriter Occidental Life Calif., LA, 1967-68; mail boy D'Arcy Advt., NYC, 1968; copywriter BBDO, NYC, 1968-69, Doyle Dane Bernbach, NYC, 1969-72; creative dir. Ally and Gargano, NYC, 1972-86; founder, ptnr. Messner Vetere Berger Carey Schmetterer, NYC, 1986-92; ptnr. Messner Vetere Berger McNamee Schmetterer Euro RSCG, NYC, 1992—; founder Grand Old Website Co., 1999. Former prof. Sch. Visual Arts, N.Y.C.; copywriter MCI; bd. dirs., US. bd., internat. bd. Eurol RSCG; founder, pres. The Grand Old Website Co., Rep. Advt. Inc. Copywriter Ronald Reagan 1984 Presdl. campaign Repub. Nat. Com., NY, 1984; copywriter George Bush 1988 presdl. campaign, 1988, Bob Franks Senatorial Campaign, 2000, Andrew O'Rourke for Gov., NY, 1986. Named CLIO Hall of Fame. Mem. Mortons Group, E-Media Investment Group, Fenway Club. Roman Catholic. Office: Messner Vetere Berger McNamee Schmetterer Euro RSCG 350 Hudson St Fl 7 New York NY 10014-4509 E-mail: tom.messner@mvbms.com.

MESTAYER, MARY FRANCES, science educator; b. Raceland, La., Sept. 2, 1952; d. Thomas Francis and Del Monte Mary Arabie Mestayer. BA in Edn., U. Southwestern La., Lafayette, 1974; student, Lea Castle Riding Sch., Worcester, Eng., 1977, Moyfield Riding Sch., 1978; cert, in advanced Bible Study, Layman's Sch. Training Christian Cmty. Ch., Pietersburg, South Africa, 1997—99. Cert. Rhema Bible Training Ctr., Johannesburg, South Africa, 1992; tchr. type B State of La., 1977, tchr. South African Tchr.'s Coun., 1986, South African Coun. Educators, 2000, highly qualified sci. and elem. edn. State of La. Tchr. Raceland (La.) Lower Elem. Sch., 1974—86; sci. tchr. Sunward Park H.S., South Africa, 1986—90; staff Rhema Missions Ctr. Rhema Ministries South Africa, Lanseria, 1991—92; sci. tchr. Southside Elem., Bastrop, La., 1993; sci. tchr., coord. and facilitator Pepps Polokwane Prep. Sch. and Coll., Pietersburg, South Africa, 1994—2001; sci. tchr. Larose- Cut Off Mid. Sch., Cut Off, La., 2001—. Sci. fair coord. Pepps Polokwane Prep. Sch. and Coll., Pietersburg, South Africa, 1994—2000; sci. facilitator Sci. Math. Found., 1996, Power Matric, South Africa, 1996, Africa Growth Network, 1996; sch. dir. after care Pepps Polokwane Prep. Sch. and Coll., 1999; sci. fair coord. Larose- Cut Off Mid. Sch., Cut Off, La., 2002—07; sci. fair team mem. Lafourche Parish Schs., Thibodaux, La., 2002—07; fellow Ag in the Classroom, La., 2002—; mem. Nat. Energy Ednl. Devel. Project, 2004—, Jason Project, 2006—07, Immersion, 2007—. Recipient Mestayer Sci. Trophy, Pepps Polokwane Prep. Sch. and Coll., 2000. Mem.: La. Fedn. Tchrs. Republican. Avocations: missions, horseback riding, gardening, reading, travel. Office: Larose Cut Off Mid Sch 13356 W Main St Cut Off LA 70345-2500 Office Phone: 985-693-3273. Business E-Mail: mmestayer@lafourche.k12.la.us.

MESTEL, MARK DAVID, lawyer; b. May 15, 1951; s. Oscar L. and Katherine (Waldner) M.; m. Linda Antonik, Jan. 6, 1984; children: Brenton V., Spenser Andrew. BA, Northwestern U., 1973; JD, U. Mich., 1976. Bar: Mich. 1976, D.C. 1977, Wash. 1978, U.S. Dist. Ct. (we. dist.) Wash. 1979, U.S. Ct. Appeals (9th cir.) 1984, U.S. Dist. Ct. (ea. dist.) Wash. 1986, U.S. Supreme Ct. 1991; cert. criminal trial specialist Nat. Bd. Trial Advocacy, 1982, 86, 91. Atty. EPA, Washington, 1976-77; pvt. practice Washington, 1977-78, Everett, Wash., 1981-84; staff atty. Snohomish County Pub. Defender, Everett, 1978-80, dir., atty., 1980-81; ptnr. Mestel & Muenster, Everett, 1984-94; pvt. practice, 1994—. Mem. Nat. Assn. Criminal Def. Lawyers, Wash. Assn. Criminal Def. Lawyers. Office: Mark D Mestel Inc PS 3221 Oakes Ave Everett WA 98201-4407 Office Phone: 425-339-2383. Personal E-mail: mdmestel@verizon.net.

MESTRE, OSCAR LUIS, financial consultant; b. Havana, Cuba, Nov. 26, 1959; came to U.S., 1960; s. Oscar Luis and Ana Victoria (Arango) M.; m. Margaret M. Bozak, May 17, 1986; children: Melissa Anne, Victoria Elizabeth, Jessica Margaret. BS and BA, U. Del., 1982; cert. CLU, Am. Coll., Bryn Mawr, Pa., 1988, cert. ChFC, 1988. Account exec. Keystone Fin. Group, Bryn Mawr, 1982-87, New Eng. Fin. Group, Radnor, Pa., 1987—91; ptnr. in charge of mktg. internat. ins., liason for Latin Am., internat. banking and securities AG Transnat., Ltd., Radnor and Huntington, N.Y., 1991—. Founding mem. Tech. Resource Alliance, 1998. Chmn. U. Del. golf fundraising com., Newark, 1986-92; bd. dirs. Haverford (Pa.) Sch. Alumni Assn., 1988-98, chmn. annual giving campaign, 1993-94, planned giving coun. 1998—; mem. profl. adv. coun. Cedars Med. Ctr., Miami, Fla., 1990-93; vol. St. Monica's Ch., Berwyn, Pa., Am. Heart Assn., Pa. chpt.; U.S. amateur golf contestant, 1999, British amateur golf contestant, 2000, U.S. Mid-amateur golf contestant, 2000. Named to U. Del. Athletic Hall of Fame, 2001; recipient Hon. Mention All Am. award, NCAA Div. I Golf, 1980—81, Top Club award, Penn Mut. Life Ins. Co., Phila., 1982, Ins. Prodn. Recognition award, Clerical Med. Internat., 1992. Mem. Am. Soc. CLUs and ChFCs (cert.), Tech. Resource Alliance (founding), Leaders Assn. New Eng. Fin., Overbrook Golf Club (bd. dirs. 1999—03, 2006—). Avocations: golf, travel, theater, music. Office: Creative Fin Group Ste 200 16 Campus Blvd Newtown Square PA 19073 Office Phone: 610-355-7885. Business E-Mail: omestre@cfg.nef.com.

MESTRES, RICARDO A., III, film company executive; b. NYC, Jan. 23, 1958; s. Ricardo Angelo Jr. and Ann M.; m. Tracy Stewart (div.); children: Alexander Carson, Carrie Ann (dec.). AB, Harvard U., 1980; postgrad., U. So. Calif., 2007—. Creative exec. Paramount Pictures, LA, 1981-82, exec. dir. prodn., 1982-84, v.p. prodn., 1984-85, Walt Disney Pictures, Burbank, Calif., 1985-86, sr. v.p. prodn., 1986-88; pres. prodn. Touchstone Pictures, Burbank, Calif., 1988-89; pres. Hollywood Pictures, Burbank, Calif., 1989-94; co-founder Great Oaks Entertainment, Burbank, Calif., 1995-97; prin. Ricardo Mestres Prodns., Disney Studios, Burbank, Calif., 1997. Prodr: Jack, 101 Dalmations, Flubber, Home Alone 3, The Visitors, The Hunted. Mem. Acad. Motion Picture Arts and Scis. Personal E-mail: mestres@usc.edu. Business E-Mail: ricardo@rmp.com.

MESTRES, RICARDO ANGELO, JR., lawyer; b. NYC, Aug. 12, 1933; s. Ricardo Angelo and Anita (Gwynne) M.; m. Ann Farnsworth, June 18, 1955; children: Laura, Ricardo III, Lynn, Anthony. AB, Princeton U., NJ, 1955; LLB, Harvard U., Cambridge, Mass., 1961. Bar: NY 1962, US Supreme Ct. 1970. Assoc. Sullivan & Cromwell, NYC, 1961-67, ptnr., 1968-2000, chmn., sr. ptnr., 1995-2000, sr. counsel, 2001—. Trustee Unitarian Ch. All Souls, NYC, 1973-79, 84-87; trustee Phillips Exeter Acad., 1989-99, pres. bd. trustees, 1993-99. Served to lt. USN, 1955-58. Mem.: ABA, Coun. Fgn. Rels., Am. Law Inst., Assn. Bar City N.Y. (corp. law, securities regulation law and state legis. coms.), N.Y. State Bar Assn., Mill Reef Club (Antigua), Links Club, Phi Beta Kappa. Office: Sullivan & Cromwell LLP 125 Broad St Fl 32 New York NY 10004-2498 Office Phone: 212-558-3716.

MESZNIK, JOEL R., investment banker; b. Oct. 3, 1945; m. Lynne Gladstein, Mar. 25, 1979; children: Daniel, Jared, Kara. BS, CCNY, 1967; MBA, Columbia U., 1970. Engr. Ebasco Svcs., NYC, 1967-70; banker Citibank, NYC, 1970-71, Newhouse Capital, NYC, 1971-72, Matthews & Wright, NYC, 1972-76; mng. dir. Drexel Burnham Lambert, NYC, 1976-89; pres. Mesco Ltd., 1990—. Bd. dirs. Pharma/wHealth, Greenfield Online, Muni Funding Co. Am. Office: 470 Main St Ste 315 Ridgefield CT 06877-4516

METCALF, DONALD, biomedical researcher; BSc, U Sydney, Sydney, Australia; MB, BS, U Sydney; MD, U. Sydney. Carden fellow, cancer rsch. Walter & Eliza Hall Inst. Med. Rsch., Victoria, Australia, 1954—, head, cancer rsch. unit, asst. dir., 1965—96; emeritus prof. Walter & Eliza Hall Inst. Med. Rsch., Royal Melbourne Hosp., 1996—; rsch. prof., cancer biology U. Melbourne, Australia, 1986—96. Vis. prof., Australia, England, Canada, France, Netherlands, New Zealand, Switzerland, United States. Contbr. articles to profl. jours. Recipient Armand Hammer prize, 1988, Sloan prize, GM Cancer Rsch. Found., Albert Lasker Clin. Rsch. award, 1993, Louisa Gross Horwitz prize, Columbia U., 1993, Internat. award, Gairdner Found., 1994, Warren Alpert Found. prize, Harvard Med. Sch., 1996, Ernst Neumann award, Internat. Soc. for Exptl. Hematology, 1995, Amgen Australia prize, 1996, Chiron Internat. award, Nat. Acad. Medicine, Italy, 1999, Victoria prize, Australia, 2000, Prime Min.'s prize, 2001, Pres. medal, Australia and New Zealand Soc. for Cell and Devel. Biology, 2002, Centenary medal, Australia, 2003, Mentorship award, Days of Molecular Medicine Found., 2004. Mem.: NAS (fgn. assoc. mem., Jessie Stevenson Kovalenko medal 1994), Assn. Am. Physicians (hon. fgn. mem.), Royal Soc. (Wellcome prize 1986, Royal medal 1995), Polish Soc. Hematology (hon.), Companion Order of Australia, Alpha Omega Alpha (hon.). Achievements include research in clinical use of molecules called colony-simulating factors (CSFs), which control the growth and development of blood cells. Office: Walter and Eliza Hall Inst Med Rsch 1G Royal Parade Parkville VIC 3050 Australia Home Phone: 61-3-9836-1343; Office Phone: 61-3-9345-2555. Business E-Mail: metcalf@wehi.edu.au.

METCALF, JAMES S., manufacturing executive; b. 1959; married; 3 children. BS, Ohio St. Univ., 1980; MBA, Pepperdine Univ., Calif., 1983. Former sr. v.p., L&W Supply Distribution Subs., USG Corp.; with USG Corp., 1981—, dir., retail strategy, 2004, exec. v.p., pres. building sys. divsn., 2005—06, pres., COO, 2006—. Office: USG 125 S Franklin St Chicago IL 60606-4678 Office Fax: 312-606-4093. *

METCALF, KAREN, retired foundation executive; b. Reading, Mass., Dec. 12, 1936; d. Albion Edmund and Natalie Viola (Ives) M. AB, Vassar Coll., 1958; MBA, Harvard U., 1968. CFA. Sec. Radio Liberty Com., NYC, 1958-60; rsch. asst. Air Inc., Cambridge, Mass., 1960-64; sys. analyst Keydata Corp., Watertown, Mass., 1964-66; customer edn. cons. Interactive Data Corp., NYC, 1968; portfolio mgr. Scudder, Stevens & Clark, NYC, 1969-81; v.p. fin. and adminstrn. N.Y. Cmty. Trust, NYC, 1981—2002. Episcopalian. Avocations: travel, opera.

METCALF, LAURIE (LAUREN OPHELIA METCALFE), actress; b. Edwardsville, Ill., June 15, 1955; m. Jeff Perry (div.); 1 child, Zoe; m. Matt Roth; 2 children Will Theron, Mae BA in Theatre, Ill. State U., 1976. Founding ensemble mem. Steppenwolf Theatre, Chgo. Off-Broadway appearances: Balm in Gilead (debut, Theatre World award), 1984; stage appearances: Who's Afraid of Virginia Woolf?, 1982, Coyote Ugly, 1985, Bodies Rest, and Motion, 1986, Educating Rita, 1987 (Joseph Jefferson award best performance by principal actress in a play), Little Egypt, 1987, Killers, 1988, My Thing of Love, 1995, All My Sons, 2006 (LA Ovation award lead actress in a play 2006); films: Desperately Seeking Susan, 1985, Making Mr. Right, 1987, Stars and Bars, 1988, The Appointments of Dennis Jennings, 1988, Candy Mountain, 1988, Miles from Home, 1988, Uncle Buck, 1989, Internal Affairs, 1989, Pacific Heights, 1990, Frankie and Johnny, 1991, JFK, 1991, Mistress, 1992, A Dangerous Woman, 1993, Blink, 1994, The Secret Life of Houses, 1994, Leaving Las Vegas, 1995, Dear God, 1996, (voice) Toy Story, 1995, Hellcab, 1997, U-Turn, 1997, Scream 2, 1997, Bulworth, 1998, (voice) Toy Story 2, 1999, Treasure Planet, 2002, Steel City, 2006, Beer League, 2006, (voice) Meet the Robinsons, 2007; TV films: Execution of Raymond Graham, 1985, Always Outnumbered, 1998, The Long Island Incident, 1998, Ballon Farm, 1999, Two Families, 2002, Phil at the Gate, 2003; TV series: Saturday Night Live, 1981, Roseanne, 1988-97 (Emmy award, Outstanding Supporting Actress in a Comedy Series, 1993, 94), The Norm Show, 1999, (voice) God, The Devil and Bob, 2000; TV appearances: The Equalizer, 1986, The Dharma & Greg, 1997, King of the Hill, 1997, 3rd Rock from the Sun, 1998, The Norm Show, 2001, Malcolm in the Middle, 2004, Frasier, 2004, Without a Trace, 2005, Monk, 2006, Grey's Anatomy, 2006, Desperate Housewives, 2006. Address: care ICM 8942 Wilshire Blvd Beverly Hills CA 90211-1934 *

METCALF, ROBERT CLARENCE, architect, educator; b. Nashville, Ohio, Nov. 7, 1923; s. George and Helen May (Drake) M.; m. Bettie Jane Sponseller, Sept. 15, 1943. Student, Johns Hopkins U., 1943; B.Arch., U. Mich., 1950. Draftsman G.B. Brigham, Jr., Architect, Ann Arbor, Mich., 1948-52; pvt. practice architecture Ann Arbor, 1953—; lectr. architecture U. Mich., Ann Arbor, 1955-58, asst. prof., 1958-63, asso. prof., 1963-68, prof., 1968-91, chmn. dept., 1968-74; dean U. Mich. (Coll. Architecture and Urban Planning), 1974-86; Emil Lorch prof. emeritus U. Mich., 1991—, dean emeritus, 1991—; pvt. practice, 1991—. Sec. Mich. Bd. Registration for Architects, 1975-79, chmn., 1980-82 Designer more than 140 bldgs., Ann Arbor, 1953—. Served with U.S. Army, 1943-46, ETO. Decorated Silver Star; recipient Sol King award for excellent teaching in architecture U. Mich., 1974; named Emil Lorch Professor of Architecture, 1989. Fellow AIA (Pres.'s award 1999); mem. AIA Mich., Assn. Collegiate Schs. Architecture, Phi Kappa Phi, Tau Sigma Delta. Home: 1052 Arlington Blvd Ann Arbor MI 48104-2816 Office: U Mich 2150 Art Architecture Bldg Ann Arbor MI 48109 also: Metcalf Architect 2211 Medford Rd Ann Arbor MI 48104-5004

METCALF, ROBERT JOHN ELMER, industrial consultant; b. Glen Ellyn, Ill., June 27, 1919; s. Elmer Simpson and Vida Marie Metcalf; B.S.M.E., U. Pitts., 1947; m. Rosemarie Rusch, Sept. 11, 1947; children: Kathleen, Karen, Patti, Pamela. Asst. staff supr. Westinghouse Electric Co., Buffalo, 1949-52, assoc. engr., 1952-54; assoc. Gemar Assocs., Inc., Greenwich, Conn., 1954-66. v.p., 1966-83; cons., 1983-92. Served with U.S. Army, 1943-46. Mem. Inst. Mgmt. Cons. (founding). Roman Catholic. Home and Office: 444 Paula Dr N #331 Dunedin FL 34698-1820

METCALF, VIRGIL ALONZO, economics professor; b. Branch, Ark., Jan. 4, 1936; s. Wallace Lance and Luella J. (Yancey) M.; m. Janice Ann Maples, July 2, 1958; children: Deborah Ann, Robert Alan. BS in Gen. Agr., U. Ark., 1958, MS in Agrl. Econs., 1960; Diploma in Econs., U. Copenhagen, 1960; PhD in Agrl. Econs., U. Mo., 1964. Asst. prof. U. Mo., Columbia, 1964-65, asst. to chancellor, 1964-69, assoc. prof., 1965-69, prof., exec. asst. to the chancellor, 1969-71; prof. econs., v.p. adminstrn. Ariz. State U., Tempe, 1971-81, prof. Sch. Agribus. and Natural Resources, 1981-88, prof. internat. bus. Coll. of Bus., 1988—99, prof. emeritus, 2000—. Asst. to the chancellor U. Mo., 1964-69, coord. internat. programs and studies, 1965-69, mem. budget com., 1965-71, chmn., co-chmn. several task forces; cons. Ford Found., Bogota, Colombia, 1966-67; mem. negotiating team U.S. Agy. for Internat. Devel., Mauritania, 1982, cons., Cameroon, 1983, agrl. rsch. specialist, India, 1984, agribus. cons., Guatemala, 1987, 88, asst. dir. Reform Coops. Credit Project, El Salvador, 1987-90; co-dir. USIA univ. linkage grant Cath. U., Bolivia, 1984-89; cons. World Vision Internat., Mozambique, 1989. Contbr. numerous articles to profl. jours. Mem. City of Tempe U. Hayden Butte Project Area Com., 1979; bd. commrs. Columbia Redevel. Authority; mem. workable project com. City of Columbia Housing Authority. Econs. officer USAR, 1963, econ. analyst, 1964-66. Fulbright grantee U. Copenhagen, 1959-60, U. Kiril Metodij, Yugoslavia, 1973. Mem. Am. Assn. Agrl. Economists, Soc. for Internat. Devel., Samaritans (chmn. 1976, bd. dirs. 1976, mem. task force of health svc. bd. trustees 1974, health svc. 1974-78, chmn. program subcom. 1975), Kiwanis, Blue Key, Gamma Sigma Delta, Alpha Zeta, Alpha Tau Alpha. Democrat. Home: 1357 W Crystal Springs Dr Gilbert AZ 85233-6606

METCALF, WAYNE C., III, retired insurance company executive; m. Shirley Imada Metcalf. BA in Polit. Sci., U. Hawaii, 1975; JD, 1978; student, Tufts U., 1992-93. Atty. pvt. practice, 1979—; spl. cons. UN, 1994; ins. commr. Dept. Commerce and Consumer Affairs State Hawaii, 1994—97, 2002—. Staff Senate Jud. Com., 1973-75; staff dir. Senate Pres.'s Office, 1975-78; vice-chmn. House Com. on Jud., 1984-86; chmn. House Com. on Jud., 1986-92; mem. house coms. Comsuner Protection and Commerce, 1984-92, Land Use and Hawaiian Affairs Plannong, 1984-86, Labor and Pub. Employment Transp., 1985-88, Housing, Health Humand Svcs, 1988-90, Housing, Health, 1990-92. Recipient Disting. Alumni award U. hawaii, 1988, Disting. Legislator award, Nat. Dem. State LEgis. Leaders Assn., 1988; named one of Hawaii's five best legislators by polit. columnist Dan Boylan, 1990, 92.

METCALF, WILLIAM EDWARDS, museum curator, educator; b. East Grand Rapids, Mich., Dec. 16, 1947; s. George Ellington and Ruthanne (Schnitzler) M.; m. Margaret Mary Finn, May 21, 1972 (annulled 1984); 1 son, Daniel F.; m. Jane Salinger, Oct. 26, 1991; 1 child, Lydia Qiao Salinger. BA, U. Mich., 1969, MA, 1970, PhD in Classical Studies (Horace H. Rackham prize fellow), 1973. Asst. curator Roman and Byzantine coins Am. Numismatic Soc., NYC, 1973-75, assoc. curator, 1975-78, curator, dep. chief curator, 1978-79, chief curator, 1979-2000, hon. curator, 2000—; prof. classics Yale U., 2002—, curator coins and medals Art Gallery, 2002—. Adj. prof. art history and archaeology Columbia U., 1978—97, adj. prof. classics, 1998; adj. prof. history, 1993; adj. prof. classics NYU, 1996, 2000-01, Princeton U., 1999, Bryn Mawr U., 2000; vis. prof. classics NYU, 2001-02. Author: The Cistophori of Hadrian, 1980, The Silver Coinage of Cappadocia, Vespasian-Commodus, 1996; editor: Studies in Early Byzantine Gold Coinage, 1988, America's Gold Coinage, 1990, Mnemata: Papers in Memory of Nancy M. Waggoner, 1991; adv. com. Lexicon Iconographicum Mythologiae Classicae, 1979—; adv. bd. Am. Jour. Archaeology, 1980-97; editor book revs. Am. Jour. Numismatics, 1989-2000; mem. editl. bd. Revue Suisse de Numismatique, 2002—contbr. articles on Roman and Byzantine coinage to profl. jours. NEA fellow for mus. profls., 1978; mem. Inst. for Advanced Study, 1988-89 Fellow Am. Numismatic Soc. (life); mem. Royal Numismatic Soc., Am. Philol. Assn. (subcom. on classical bibliography 1979-89), Archaeol. Inst. Am. (exec. com. NY 1976-80, chmn. numismatics com. 2000--), Columbia U. Seminar on Classical Civilization, Internat. Numismatic Commn. (1st v.p. 1997-2003), Soc. Antiquaries London. E-mail: william.metcalf@yale.edu.

METCALFE, ELIZABETH BROKAW, art educator; b. St. Louis, Feb. 14, 1941; d. Augustus Van Liew and Elizabeth Cabell Gray Brokaw; m. James Walter Metcalfe, June 7, 1969; children: James Kenneth Brokaw, Elizabeth Cabell. BA, Washington U., St. Louis, 1962, MA, 1965. Instr. Pierce Coll., Athens, Greece, 1966; instr. art history Maryville U., St. Louis, 1968—72, 1981—. Lectr. and book reviewer. Mem. St. Louis Art Mus., 1970—, Chgo. Art Inst., 1970—. Mem.: Archeol. Inst. Am., Nat. Soc. Colonial Dames Am. Republican. Episcopalian. Avocations: reading, walking, running, travel, hiking. Home: 65 Berry Rd Pk Saint Louis MO 63122 Office: Maryville Univ 13550 Conway Rd Saint Louis MO 63141 Personal E-mail: stlouis65@juno.com.

METCALFE, LAUREN OPHELIA See METCALF, LAURIE

METCALFE, ROBERT DAVIS, III, lawyer; b. Bridgeport, Conn., July 2, 1956; s. Robert Davis Jr. and Barbara Ann (Peaslee) M. BA summa cum laude, U. Conn., 1978, JD, 1981; MA, Trinity Coll., 1982, Am. Mil. U., 1997. Bar: Conn. 1981, U.S. Supreme Ct. 1986, D.C. 1990, Md. 1991. Judge adv. USN, Norfolk, Va., 1982-85; spl. asst. U.S. atty. U.S. Dept. Justice, Norfolk, 1985, trial atty. Washington, 1985—. Instr. ARC, Hartford, Conn., 1976-80; legis. asst. Conn. Gen. Assembly, Hartford, 1977. Served to lt. USN, 1982-85. Mem. Fed. Bar Assn., Conn. Bar Assn., Judge Adv. Assn., Mensa, Phi Beta Kappa. Republican. Roman Catholic. Avocations: martial arts, reading, sailing, trap and skeet shooting, stamp collecting/philately.

METCALFE, ROBERT M., venture capitalist, former science engineer, publishing executive, writer; b. Bklyn., Apr. 7, 1946; BS in Electrical Engring. and Computer Sci., B in Mgmt., MIT, 1969; MS in Applied Math., Harvard U., 1970, PhD in Computer Sci., 1973; doctorate (hon.). With computer sci. lab. Xerox Palo Alto Rsch. Ctr., 1973-79; founder 3Com Corp., Santa Clara, Calif., 1979-90; v.p. tech. Internat. Data Group, Boston, 1990—92; CEO, pub. Info World Pub. Co., San Mateo, Calif., 1992—95, columnist, exec. corr., 1995—2000; venture capitalist, gen. ptnr. Polaris Venture Partners, Waltham, Mass., 2001—. Vis. fellow U. Cambridge, 1991—92; bd. dir. Avistar, EarthLink, Ember, IDC, IDG, Jeknscitt, MediaLabEurope, MIT, Nanosys, Narad, MIT Tech. Review Mag., Mintera Corp.; chmn. Paratek; bd. dir. SiCortex; founder (conferences) Pop!Tech, 1997, dir. conferences; produced conferences for Agenda, Vortex. Author: (books) Packet Communication, Internet Collapses and Other InfoWorld Punditry, Beyond Calculation: The Next Fifty Years of Computing. Bd. trustees MIT; bd. dir. St. Mark's Sch. Recipient Grace Murray Hepper award, Assn. for Computing Machinery, 1980, Alexander Graham Bell medal, IEEE 1988, Pub. Understanding of Sci. award, 1995, Medal of Honor IEEE 1996, Nat. Medal Tech., 2005; Marconi Internat. Fellowship 2003; inducted into Bay Shore HS Hall of Fame, 2003, Nat. Inventors Hall of Fame, 2007. Mem. Am. Acad. Arts and Sciences, NAE, Internat. Engring. Consortium Achievements include helping build the early Internet; invention of Ethernet for which he holds four patents. Office: Polaris Venture Partners Ste 3350 1000 Winter St Waltham MA 02451

METCALFE, WALTER LEE, JR., lawyer; b. St. Louis, Dec. 19, 1938; s. Walter Lee and Carol Metcalfe; m. Cynthia Williamson, Aug. 26, 1965; children: Carol, Edward. AB, Washington U., St. Louis, 1960; JD, U. Va., 1964. Bar: Mo. 1964. Ptnr. Armstrong, Teasdale, Kramer & Vaughan, St. Louis, 1964—81; sr. ptnr. Bryan Cave LLP, St. Louis, 1982—, former chmn.; chmn. Fed. Res. Bd., St. Louis. Bd. dirs. BJC Health Care, St. Louis. Bd. dirs. Washington U., St. Louis, Danforth Found., Pulitzer Found. Arts, St. Louis Children's Hosp. Named one of 100 Most Influential Lawyers, Nat. Law Jour., 2006. Mem.: ABA, St. Louis Bar Assn., Mo. Bar Assn., Noonday Club, Bogey Club. Episcopalian. Home: 26 Upper Ladue Rd Saint Louis MO 63124-1675 Office: Bryan Cave 211 N Broadway 1 Metropolitan Sq Ste 3600 Saint Louis MO 63102-2750 Office Phone: 314-259-2000.

METOYER, PAMELA PARADIS, scientific editor, writer; b. Hutchinson, Minn., Sept. 1, 1955; d. Paul Edward, Sr. and Mary LaVerne (Hebert) Paradis; m. Jeffrey Johns Powell, June 17, 1977 (div. July 1982); m. Christopher Allen Tice, Aug. 25, 1997 (div. Sept. 2004),; m. Grady Wilson Metoyer, June 3, 2006. BA, Coll. of St. Scholastica, 1977. Statis./sec. U. Tex. M.D. Anderson Cancer Ctr., Houston, 1978-87; data coord. Baylor Coll. Medicine, Houston, 1987-88, editl. asst., 1988-90, sr. editor, 1992-2000, rsch. assoc., 2000—; dept. editor U. Tex. Med. Sch., Houston, 1990-91; editor, Houston medicine HCA Ctr. for Health Excell., Houston, 1991-92; exec. asst. U. Tex. Sch. Nursing, Houston, 1991-92. Mem. scope and mandate task force, Coun. of Sci. Editors, Chgo., 1996. Editor-in-chief: Am. Med. Writers Assn. Jour., 1992-95 (Apex awards 1995, 96, 97, Matrix award 1996, 2000, 2001, others). Recipient Presdl. Alumni award, Coll. of St. Scholastica, 2003. Mem. Am. Med. Writers Assn. (chpt. sec. 1989-90, chpt. treas. 1990-92, chpt. pres.-elect 1992-93, chpt. pres. 1993-94, chpt. past pres. 1994-95, chpt. dir.-at-large 2001-03, 07-, chair McGovern Award com. 2003-07, Assn. Pres. award 1993, Chpt. Svc. award 1994,, Assn. Leadership award 1995), Coun. Sci. Editors, Bd. Editors in Life Scis. (diplomate 2002). Home Phone: 713-839-7652; Office Phone: 713-798-1087. Business E-Mail: pptice@bcm.edu.

METTEE-MCCUTCHON, ILA, municipal official, retired military officer; b. Mobile, Ala., May 1, 1945; d. John Martin and Anna Ruth (Cleveland) Mettee; m. John Robert McCutchon, Oct. 13, 1974; 1 child, Erin Tempest. BS, Auburn U., Ala., 1967, MS, 1969; grad., various army schs. Rsch. psychologist VA Hosp., Tuskegee, Ala., 1967-69; clin. psychologist U. Ala. Med. Ctr., Birmingham, 1969-71; commd. 1st lt. U.S. Army, 1971, advanced through grades to col., 1992. Officer in charge Alcohol and Drug Abuse Rehab. Ctr., Presidio, San Francisco, 1971-73; strategic intelligence officer 8th Psychol. Bn., 1973-75; tactical intelligence officer, ops. officer, co. comdr. 525th MI Brigade (Airborne), Ft. Bragg, N.C., 1976-79; project officer Command, Control, Comms. and Intelligence Directorate, Combined Arms Combat Devel. Activity, Ft. Leavenworth, Kans., 1979-82; student Command and Gen. Staff Coll., 1982-83; ops. officer Army Spl. Security Group, Washington, 1983-86; Def. Lang. Inst. Presidio of Monterey, 1986-87; chief U.S. So. command Joint Intelligence Ctr., Republic of Panama, 1987-89; comdr. 741st M.I. Bn., Ft. Meade, Md., 1989-91; U.S. Army War Coll., 1991-92; strategic intelligence officer Internat. Mil. Staff NATO, Brussels, 1992-94; comdr. Presidio of Monterey and Ft. Ord, Calif., 1994-96, chief base realignment and closure/environ. mgmt., 1996-97, ret. with honors, 1997. Elected to Marina City Coun., 1998, Rep. ctrl. com. Monterey County, 2000, Mayor City of Marina, 2002—, reelected, 2004; apptd. housing cmty. and econ. devel. policy com. League Calif. Cities', 1999—; chair bd. dirs. Ftord Reuse Auth., 2004 Decorated Army Commendation medal (3), Meritorious Svc. medal (4), Def. Meritorious Svc. medal, Army Achievement award (2), Legion of Merit (2), Def. Superior Svc. medal; named Woman of Yr. Marina, 2001, Philanthropist of Yr., 2001. Mem. NAFE, Nat. Assn. Univ. Women, Nat. Women's Polit. Caucus, VFW, Assn. U.S. Army, Alumni Assn. U.S. Army War Coll., WAC Found., Women in NATO, Am. Legion (post 694), Ft. Ord Alumni Assn. (adv. bd.), Girl Scouts of Monterey Bay (bd. dirs.), Cmty. Human Svcs. (bd. dirs.), Rotary Internat. (local chpt.), Monterey Rep. Women, Marina C. of C., Marina Bus. Assn., Marina Larger Libr. Com. Home: 3181 DeForest Rd Marina CA 93933 Office: City Hall City of Marina 211 Hillcrest Ave Marina CA 93933-3534 Office Phone: 831-884-1278.

METTERS, THOMAS WADDELL, sportswriter; b. Columbus, Ohio, Apr. 17, 1939; s. Thomas Hammond and Charlotte Ann (Waddell) M. BS in Journalism, Ohio U., Athens, 1965. Sports editor The Traveller, Ft. Lee, Va., 1960—62; sports writer The Athens Messenger, Ohio, 1965—. Asst. to officials Legion Baseball, Athens, 1962—. Contbr.: Ohio Interscholastic Athletic Media Guide, 1985. Bd. dirs. Athens H.S. Booster Club, 1975—07, Athens H.S. Athletic Hall of Fame, 2000; ofcl. scorekeeper Am. Legion World Series, Millington, Tenn., 1989. With US Army, 1959-62. Named to Ohio H.S. Basketball Coaches Assn. Hall of Fame, 1993; recipient Contributor award Ohio H.S. Track & Field Coaches Assn., 1995, Ohio H.S. Athletic Assn. Media Svc. award, 1998. Mem. Soc. Profl. Journalists (Recognition plaque 1973), Ohio Associated Press Sports Writers Assn. (pres. 1984), Green & White Club (sec. 1983-2004, historian 2004—, Jonesy Sams award 1987), Ohio Prep Sports Writers Assn. (Hall of Fame 1990), Ky. Colonels, Am. Legion. Republican. Avocation: bowling. Home: 71 Sunnyside Dr Athens OH 45701-1921 Office: The Athens Messenger 9300 Johnson Rd Athens OH 45701 Office Phone: 740-592-6612 x 221.

METTINGER, KARL LENNART, pharmaceutical executive; b. Helsingborg, Sweden, Nov. 1, 1943; came to the U.S., 1989; s. Nils Allan and Anna Katarina (Hallberg) M.; m. Chesne Maree Ryman, 1979; m. Miki Ilaw, 1998. MD, U. Lund, 1973; PhD, Karolinska Inst., 1982. Intern Stockholm Hosps., 1973-74; resident Karolinska Hosp., Stockholm, 1974-77, clin. neurologist, 1977-85; med. dir. Kabi Hematology, Stockholm, 1985-87; dep. gen. mgr. Kabi Cardiovascular, Stockholm, 1987-89; med. dir. Ivax/Baker Norton Pharms., Miami, Fla., 1989-93, sr. clin. rsch. dir., 1993-98, exec. dir., clin. rschr., 1998-2000; sr. v.p. chief med. officer SuperGen, San Ramon, 2000—05; chief med. officer Oncolytics Biotech, Calgary/Berkeley, 2005—. Assoc. prof. Karolinska Inst., Stockholm, 1983-91; cons. neurologist Odenplan Med. Ctr., Stockholm, 1984-89. Author: Cerebral Thromboembolism, 1982, Refaat--Myths and Billions in Biotech, 1987; editor: Coronary Thrombolysis: Current Answers to Critical Questions, 1988, Controversies in Coronary Thrombolysis, 1989. Bd. dirs. Bass Mus. Arts, 1999-2001, Oakland East Bay Symphony, 2002—, UNA USA, East Bay, 2006—; v.p. Friends of Music, U. Miami, 2000-2001. Lt. Swedish Army, 1979 Recipient Silver award Spanish Health Ministry, 1989, Classical Langs. award King Gustav V Found., 1963. Mem. Swedish Stroke Soc. (bd. dirs. 1979-89, pres. 1984-86), Swedish Med. Soc., Swedish Christian Med. Soc. (bd. dirs. 1972-88, pres. 1983-88), Am. Heart Assn., Internat. Assn. Christian Physicians (exec. com. 1975-86). Home and Office: 1367 La Loma Ave Berkeley CA 94708

METZ, ADAM S., real estate company executive; BA, Cornell U.; MMgmt, Northwestern U. Corp. lending officer 1st Nat. Bank Chgo., 1983-87; v.p. Capital Markets Group, JMB Realty, 1987-93; treas., CFO, exec. v.p, dir. acquisitions Urban Shopping Ctrs., Inc., 1993-2000, pres., 2000—01; co-founding ptnr. Polaris Capital LLC, Northbrook, Ill., 2003—. Trustee Amli Residential Properties, 2003—, Ctr. for Urban Land Econs. Rsch., U. Wis., 1997—. Mem. Internat. Coun. Shopping Ctrs. Office: Polaris Capital LLC 1033 Skokie Blvd Ste 660 Northbrook IL 60062 Home Phone: 847-835-4171; Office Phone: 847-480-9180. E-mail: metza@comcast.net.

METZ, BRIAN K., cardiologist; b. Aug. 8, 1966; MD, SUNY-Downstate Med. Sch., 1991. Cert. Internal Medicine, Cardiovascular Disease. Resident, internal medicine Scripps Clinic, La Jolla, Calif.; fellow Cleve. Clinic, Ohio; dir., noninvasive cardiology Meml. Hosp.; cardiologist Parkside Cardiology. Recipient Top Cardiology Doctor, El Paso County, Colo. Springs Bus. Jour., 2004. Fellow: Am. Coll. Cardiology; mem.: Am. Soc. Echocardiography, Colo. Med. Soc., El Paso County Med. Soc., Cleve. Clinic Heart Soc., Soc. Cardiovascular Computed Tomography (founding mem.), ACP. Avocations: tennis, mountain biking. Office: Parkside Cardiology 215 Parkside Dr Colorado Springs CO 80910 Office Phone: 719-471-1775. *

METZ, CATHERINE TAYLOR, performing arts educator; b. Charlotte, NC, Feb. 5, 1952; d. Hier0 Louis and Norma Roberts Taylor; m. James Milton Metz, Nov. 7, 1987. B of Creative Arts, U. N.C., Charlotte, 1975; MFA, U. N.C., Chapel Hill, 1978, Licentiate of Dramatic Arts, 1979. Cert. tchr. N.C. Substitute tchr. Charlotte-Mecklenburg Schs., NC, 1985—2000; tchr. theatre N.E. Jr. HS, Charlotte, 1986—87, South Mecklenburg HS, Charlotte, 1998—99, East Mecklenburg HS, Charlotte, 2000—. Actress Playmakers Rep., Chapel Hill, NC, 1976—79, Actor's Theatre, Charlotte, 1988—90, Children's Theatre, Charlotte, 1988—90. Recipient Joseph Felman scholarship, U. N.C., 1978. Republican. Episcopalian. Avocations: swimming, acting, writing. Home: 10322 Silver Mine Rd Fort Mill SC 29707 Office: East Mecklenburg HS 6800 Monroe Rd Charlotte NC 28212 Office Phone: 980-343-6430. E-mail: catherine.metz@cms.k12.nc.

METZ, CHARLES EDGAR, radiology educator; b. Bayshore, NY, Sept. 11, 1942; s. Clinton Edgar and Grace Muriel (Schienke) M.; m. Maryanne Theresa Bahr, July, 1967 (div. 1988); children: Rebecca, Molly. BA, Bowdoin Coll., 1964; MS, U. Pa., 1966, PhD, 1969. Instr. radiology U. Chgo., 1969-71, asst. prof., 1971-75, assoc. prof., 1976-80, dir. grad. programs in med. physics, 1979-85, prof., 1980—, prof. structural biology, 1984-86, prof. med. physics, 2003—. Mem. diagnostic rsch. adv. group Nat. Cancer Inst., 1980-81; mem. sci. com. Nat. Coun. on Radiation Protection and Measurements, 1982-85, 2001-, Internat. Commn. on Radiation Units and Measurements, 1988-96, chmn. sci. com., 1992-99; cons. and lectr. in field. Assoc. editor: Radiology Jour., 1986—91, Med. Physics Jour., 1992—95, mem. editl. bd.: Med. Decision Making Jour., 1980—84; contbr. over 250 articles to sci. jours. and chpts. to books. Recipient L.H. Gray medal, Internat. Commn. on Radiation Units and Measurements, 2005. Fellow Am. Assn. Physicists in Medicine; mem. Radiol. Soc. N.Am., Am. Assn. Physicists in Medicine, Soc. Med. Decision Making, Assn. Univ. Radiologists, Phi Beta Kappa, Sigma Xi. Achievements include development of software for ROC analysis used in more than 10,000 labs worldwide. Office: U Chgo Dept Radiology MC2026 5841 S Maryland Ave Chicago IL 60637-1463 E-mail: c-metz@uchicago.edu.

METZ, CRAIG HUSEMAN, lawyer; b. Columbia, SC, Aug. 26, 1955; s. Leonard Huseman and Annette (Worthington) M.; m. Karen Angela McCleary, Aug. 11, 1984; 1 child, Preston Worthington. BA, U. Tenn., 1977; JD, U. Memphis, 1986; cert., U.S. Ho. of Reps. Leadership Parliamentary Law Sch., 1987. Bar: S.C., D.C., U.S. Ct. Fed. Claims, U.S. Supreme Ct., U.S. Ct. Appeals (4th cir.). Canvass coord., liaison Campaign to Re-elect Congressman Floyd Spence, 1978; del., chmn. Shelby County Del. to 1983 Tenn. Young Rep. Fedn. Conv.; vice chmn. Shelby County Young Reps., 1983-84, chmn., 1984-85; Shelby County adminstr., asst. to Tenn. state exec. dir. Reagan-Bush Campaign, 1984; field rep. Campaign to Re-elect Congressman Floyd Spence, 1986; spl. asst. to Congressman Floyd Spence, 1986-88; counsel com. on labor and human resources U.S. Senate, 1988-90; commr.'s counsel U.S. Occupl. Safety and Health Rev. Commn., Washington, 1990-91; spl. asst. to asst. sec. for legis. and congl. affairs, dep. asst. sec. for congl. liaison US Dept. Edn., 1991—93; asst. dir. Divsn. Congl. Affairs AMA, Washington, 1993; chief of staff Congressman Floyd Spence, Washington, 1993—2001; adminstr. Office of the Second Congl. Dist. of S.C., U.S. Ho. of Reps., Washington, 2001; govt. rels. mgr. EMC Corp., Arlington, Va., 2001—07; atty. Venable LLP, Washington, 2007—. Judge nat. writing competition U.S. Constn. Bicentennial, SC, 1987—88; mem. U.S. adv. bd. Churchill Archives Ctr., Churchill Coll., U. Cambridge; mem. bd. trustees Dwight D. Eisenhower Soc.; mem. adv. bd. Salvation Army, Alexandria, Va., leadership council; adv. bd. South Carolina Political Collections; mem. Ch. of the Ascension and Saint Agnes, Washington, Friends of the Ch. of the Resurrection, NYC, Guild of All Souls. Recipient award of merit Rep. Party of Shelby County, 1985, Outstanding Leadership award Shelby County Young Reps., 1985, Meritorious Svc. medal Mil. Dept. S.C., Legis. award Res. Officers Assn. U.S., Order of the Palmetto, Palmetto Patriot award, Pres.'s award of N.G. Assn. S.C.; Hon. Washington fellow U. S.C. Washington Fellows Program. Mem.: SAR, Soc. Colonial Wars, Rep. Nat. Lawyers Assn. (state chmn. S.C. chpt. 1987—90), St. David's Soc., NY, Charleston, SC, Supreme Ct. Hist. Soc., St. George's Soc. Balt., Order St. John (serving brother), U. Tenn. Nat. Alumni Assn., Ky. Col., Am. Clan Lockhart Soc., Newcomen Soc. U.S., English Spkg. Union, The Churchill Ctr., Geman Soc. Md., Propeller Club Washington, Nat. Mus. U.S. Army (founding sponsor), Royal Oak Found., Friend of Scouting, Savannah River Valley Geneal. Soc., The Oyster Bay Hist. Soc., Hist. Soc. of Washington County, Va., Randolph County Geneal. Soc., Fairfax Geneal. Soc., Nat. Trust for Hist. Preservation (assoc. Capital region), Sons of Am. Colonists, St. Andrew's Soc. Washington, Royal Soc. St. George, Freedoms Found. Valley Forge, Va. Hist. Soc., Assn. for Preservation Va. Antiquities, Land Trust of Va., Preservation Alliance of Va., Va. Geneal. Soc., U. South Caroliniana Soc., Palmetto Trust for Historic Preservation, Palmetto Conservation Found., Lowcountry Heritage Soc., Orangeburg County Hist. Soc., Mil. Soc. War of 1812, Vet Corps Arty., Gen. Soc. War of 1812, Mil. Order Loyal Legion of U.S., Mil. Order Stars and Bars, Sons and Daus. Colonial and Antebellum Bench and Bar 1565-1861, Soc. King Charles the Martyr, Clan Lockhart, Nat. Cathedral Assn., Soc. of Friends of St George's and Descs. of Knights of the Garter, Friends of Stratford Hall, Touchdown Club, NY Caledonian Club, Phi Alpha Delta (v.p. McKeller chpt., Outstanding Svc. award 1983), Sigma Alpha Epsilon. Republican. Episcopalian. Home: 8505 Westown Way Vienna VA 22182-2513 Office: 575 7th St NW Washington DC 20004

METZ, EMMANUEL MICHAEL, investment company executive, lawyer; b. Pitts., Sept. 19, 1928; s. Solomon and Gertrude (Krieger) M.; m. Janine Spaner, Apr. 3, 1964. BA, Dartmouth Coll., 1949; LLB, Harvard U., 1952; LLM, NYU, 1958. Bar: N.Y. 1952. Atty. ABC, NYC, 1956-58; security analyst Standard & Poor's, NYC, 1958-68; mng. dir. CIBC Oppenheimer Corp., NYC, 1968—. Author: Street Fighting at Wall and Broad, 1982. Lt. USN, 1952-56. Home: 150 E 56th St New York NY 10022-3631 Office: 200 Park Ave New York NY 10166 Home Phone: 212-371-0547; Office Phone: 212-667-5430. Business E-Mail: michael.metz@opco.com.

METZ, FERDINAND, chef, educator, academic administrator; b. Munich; BS, U. Pitts., 1973, MBA, 1975; apprenticeship, Sch. for Hotel and Restaurant Adminstrn., Cooking Trade Coll., Munich, Germany. Cert. master chef, Am. Culinary, Fedn., 1982. European apprentice in cooking and baking, 1956—62; commis tounant Hotel Deutscher Kaiser, Munich; saucier, garde manger, decorateur, sous chef Preakness Hills Country Club, Wayne, NJ; poissonier, garde manger, entremetier Le Pavillon, NYC, 1961—64; banquet chef Plaza Hotel, NYC, 1964—65; with Heinz, U.S.A., Pitts., 1965—80, sr. mgr., new product develop., mgr., new product develop., chief, product develop., exptl. chef; pres. Culinary Inst. Am., Hyde Park, NY, 1980—2001, pres. emeritus Beacon, NY, 2001—. Team mem., capt., team mgr., chmn. US Culinary Olympic Team, 1968-1988 (30 gold medals in internat. competition); mgr. Am. Team (Culinary World Cup, Luxemburg, 1986); head, cons., Ferdinand Metz Culinary Innovations, LLC and Master Chefs' Assocs.; lectr. German Hotel and Restaurant Industry; owner Café Cappuccino, Pitts., Gourmet Cooking Sch. for Food Enthusiasts, Pitts.; Internat. Culinary judge representing U.S.A., 1980-. Author: The Culinary Olympics Cookbook, 1976, 1980, 1984, 1988. Trustee St. Francis Hosp., Poughkeepsie, 1981-90. Co-recipient World Championship, hot foods divsn. Internat. Kockkunst Ausstellung, Internat. Culinary Competition, Germany, 1988; recipient Who is Who in Cooking, 1985, Lifetime Achievement award, James Beard Found. 1999, Medal of French Republic, 1967, Gold Plate award Internat. Foodservice Mfrs. Assn., 1983, Hotel Olympia Gold Medal of the British Chef's Soc., Centennial medal, Soc. Culinaire Philanthropique, Grand prize for Culinary Arts, German Govt., Leadership award, Restaurant Bus. Mag., 1985, Team Grand prize, Culinary World Cup Competition, Luxembourg, 1986, Courvoisier "Order of Napoleon", 1986, Caterina de Medici Edu. award, 1987, Corning Higher Edu. award, Commn. Independent Coll. & U., 1990, Silver Spoon award, Food Arts Magazine, 1995, Lifetime Achievement award, Tastemaster, 1992 & 1999, Ty award, NY Restaurant Assn., 1999, Coll. Diplomates, Nat. Restaurant Assn., Diploma and Medal Hon., Maires Cuisiniers de France, 2001, Hon. Gold medal, Masters Chefs of Frame, 2003; inducted into the Am. Acad. of Chefs Hall of Fame, 2003; named Maitre D'Honneur, La Chaine des Rotisseurs, 1997, Man Yr., Innovator Yr. award, MUFSO, 1998, Top 25 Movers and Shakers, Self Magazine, 1998, Escoffier Soc., 2002. Mem. Am. Culinary Fedn. (pres. 1979-83, chmn., mem. honor soc. 1971-, nat. chmn., culinary and master chef cert. com., 1976-85, named Nat. Chef Yr., 1968, Nat. Culinarian Yr., 1985, Educator Yr., 1998), Internat. Foodsvc. Mfrs. Assn., World Assn. of Cooks Societies (hon. mem., v.p. 1981-85, pres. 2004-), Am. Acad. Chefs, tres. Nat. Restaurant Assn. Edu. Found., 2003-, Societe Culinaire Philanthropique, Vatel Club, Les Amis D'Escoffier Soc., James Beard Found., La Chaine des Rotisseurs; hon. mem. Canadian Chefs de Cuisine, German Chefs' Assn., Am. Dietetic Assn., Internat. Chefs' Assn.; trustee Coun. of Independent Colls. & U. NY, 1983-92, Centre Internat. de Glion, Switzerland, 1987-97, Culinary Inst. Am. 1975-80 (Outstanding Chef Yr., 1975), Nat. Restaurant Assn. Edu. Inst., 1994-. Office: Culinary Inst Am 5 Slocum Rd Beacon NY 12508 Office Phone: 845-838-5448. Office Fax: 845-838-5449. Business E-Mail: F_Metz@msn.com. *

METZ, LARRY EDWARD, lawyer; b. Phila., Mar. 20, 1955; s. Harry Franz and Joan (Nye) Metz; m. Mariko Tomisato, Mar. 26, 1980; children: Marla Jo, Christina Jill. BA, U. Fla., 1976; JD with high honors, Fla. State U., 1983. Bar: Fla. 1983, U.S. Dist. Ct. (so., mid. and no. dists.) Fla. 1984, U.S. Ct. Appeals (11th cir.) 1984, U.S. Supreme Ct. 1987. Assoc. Fleming, O'Bryan & Fleming, Ft. Lauderdale, Fla., 1983-86; atty. Westinghouse Electric Corp., Coral Springs, Fla., 1986-88; pvt. practice Ft. Lauderdale, 1988-91, Coral Springs, 1991-93; assoc. Herzfeld & Rubin, Miami, Fla., 1993-96, ptnr. Ft. Lauderdale, 1996-99; assoc. Unger, Swartwood, Latham & Indest PA, Orlando, Fla., 1999—2000; ptnr. The Unger Law Group PL, Orlando, 2000—06; pvt. practice Eustis, Fla., 2007—. Mem. Sch. Bd., Lake County, Fla., 2004—, vice chmn., 2005—06, chmn., 2006—; mem. Lake County Zoning Bd., 2005—; Rep. nominee U.S. Ho. Reps. 19th dist. Fla., 1992; area leader, sign co-chmn., spkr. George Bush for Pres. Broward County (Fla.) Victory Com., 1988; pres. Broward County Regional Rep. Club, 1991, 1995; mem. exec. com. Broward County Reps., 1988—91, 1993—96, Lake County Reps., 1999—; Rep. candidate Fla. Ho. Reps., 2004; mem. Cmty. Ch. Howey-in-the-Hills, Fla., 1999—2003, chmn. stewardship and fin. com. Fla., 2000—02; mem. Fla. Guardian Ad Litem Program, 1991—97. Capt. USMC, 1976—82. Recipient Outstanding Mem. of the Yr. award, Broward Lawyers Care, 1989, 1990, Disting. Svc. Award, Marine Corps League, N Lake Detachment, Fl., 2002. Mem.: ABA, Order of Coif, Lake County Bar Assn., Marine Corps League (judge adv. North Lake detachment, Fla. 2000—03, trustee 2003—06). Office: 531 N Bay St Eustis FL 32726 Home Phone: 352-324-9752; Office Phone: 352-483-5655. Business E-Mail: larry@metzlawyer.com.

METZ, MARY SEAWELL, retired foundation administrator, retired academic administrator; b. Rockhill, SC, May 7, 1937; d. Columbus Jackson and Mary (Dunlap) Seawell; m. F. Eugene Metz, Dec. 21, 1957; 1 dau., Mary Eugena. BA summa cum laude in French and English, Furman U., 1958; postgrad., Institut Phonetique, Paris, 1962-63, Sorbonne, 1962-63; PhD magna cum laude in French, La. State U., 1966; HHD (hon.), Furman U., 1984; LLD (hon.), Chapman Coll., 1985; DLT (hon.), Converse Coll., 1988. Instr. French La. State U., 1965-66, asst. prof., 1966-67, 1968-72, assoc. prof., 1972-76, dir. elem. and intermediate French programs, 1966-74, spl. asst. to chancellor, 1974-75, asst. to chancellor, 1975-76; prof. French Hood Coll., Frederick, Md., 1976-81, provost, dean acad. affairs, 1976-81; pres. Mills Coll., Oakland, Calif., 1981-90; dean of extension U. Calif., Berkeley, 1991-98; pres. S.H. Cowell Found., San Fransisco, 1999—. Vis. asst. prof. U. Calif.-Berkeley, 1967-68; mem. commn. on leadership devel. Am. Coun. on Edn., 1981-90, adv. coun. Stanford Rsch. Inst., 1985-90, adv. coun. Grad. Sch. Bus., Stanford U.; bd. dirs. PG&E, AT&T, Inc., Union Bank, Longs Drug Stores. Author: Reflets du monde francais, 1971, 78, Cahier d'exercices: Reflets du monde francais, 1972, 78, (with Helstrom) Le Francais a decouvrir, 1972, 78, Le Francais a vivre, 1972, 78, Cahier d'exercices: Le Francais a vivre, 1972, 78; standardized tests; mem. editorial bd. Liberal Edn., 1982—. Trustee Am. Conservatory Theater. NDEA fellow, 1960-62, 1963-64; Fulbright fellow, 1962-63; Am. Council Edn. fellow, 1974-75 Mem. Western Coll. Assn. (v.p. 1982-84, pres. 1984-86), Assn. Ind. Calif. Colls. and Univs. (exec. com. 1982-90), Nat. Assn. Ind. Colls. and Univs. (govt. rels. adv. coun. 1982-85), So. Conf. Lang. Teaching (chmn. 1976-77), World Affairs Coun. No. Calif. (bd. dirs. 1984-93), Bus.-Higher Edn. Forum, Women's Forum West, Women's Coll. Coalition (exec. com. 1984-88), Phi Kappa Phi, Phi Beta Kappa. Address: PO Box 686 Stinson Beach CA 94970-0686 also: 9 Regulus Ct Alameda CA 94501-1015

METZ, ROBERT C., media company executive; b. Feb. 13, 1953; married; 2 children. Grad., U. Mich. With PRIMEDIA Inc. (formally PRIMEDIA Guides, HPC Publs.), 1975—, various positions including publisher, COF, COO, pres., chmn. bd., v.p., 2000—; pres., CEO Consumer Guides. Bd. dirs. Guia Qual. Bd. dirs. Big Brothers program; coach various children's sports teams. Office: PRIMEDIA Consumer Guides Consumer Source Inc 3585 Engineering Dr Norcross GA 30092 Office Phone: 678-421-3000. *

METZ, ROBERT ROY, publishing executive, media consultant; b. Richmond Hill, NY, Mar. 23, 1929; s. Robert Roy, Sr. and Mary (Kissel) M.; m. Susan Lee Blair, 1984; children: Robert Sumner, Christopher Roy. BA, Wesleyan U., Middletown Conn., 1950. Copyboy N.Y. Times, 1951, asst. fgn. news desk, 1952; rewriteman cable desk I.N.S., 1953, overnight cable editor, 1954-56, asst. feature editor, 1956-58; asst. news editor Newspaper Enterprise Assn., 1958, news editor, 1959-63, mng. editor, 1963-66, exec. editor, 1966-68, v.p., 1967-71, editorial dir., 1968-71, pres., editor, dir., 1972-94; dir. Berkeley-Small Inc., 1974-77; chmn. Berkley-Small Inc., 1976-77; v.p., dir. United Feature Syndicate, 1976-77, pres., editor, 1978; pres., editor, dir. United Media, 1978-93, chmn., 1993-94; media cons., 1994—. Pres. Peter Pan Children's Fund, 1997—2005. Mem.: Union League (N.Y.C.). Lutheran. Home: 193 Swamp Rd East Hampton NY 11937

METZ, ROXIE ANNE, art educator; b. New Rochelle, NY, July 2, 1955; d. Calvin Leon and Dorothy Mary (Belton) Metz. BFA, Coll. New Rochelle, 1978, MA in Art/Psychology, 1984. Asst. residence supr. Westchester Assn. for Retarded Citizens, White Plains, NY, 1978-79; art tchr. New Rochelle City Sch. Dist., 1979—. Vol. New Rochelle Hosp. Med. Ctr., 1977—; active New Rochelle Community Action Agy., 1973-74; art tchr. Hawthorne Cedar Knolls Union Free Sch. Dist., NY. Mem. NY State United Tchrs., Am. Fedn. Tchrs. Democrat. Christian. Address: 80 Guion Pl Apt 8T New Rochelle NY 10801-3837 Office Phone: 914-576-4300. Personal E-mail: preciousmetz@optonline.net.

METZ, STEVEN WILLIAM, small business owner; b. Inglewood, Calif., Nov. 30, 1946; s. Glenn Ludwig and Kathleen Martha (Peterson) M.; m. Michelle Marie McArthur, Aug. 11, 1989; 1 child, Glenn Christian. Student, Fullerton Coll., Calif. Supt. Oahu Interiors, Honolulu, 1969-71, Hackel Bros., Miami, Fla., 1971-73; exec. v.p. Tru-Cut Inc., Brea, Calif., 1974-82; gen. mgr. The Louvre', Grass Valley, Calif., 1983-85; mfg. engring. mgr. Rexnord Aerospace, Torrance, Calif., 1986-87; pres., founder Metz/Calcoa Inc., Torrance, Calif., 1987—. Mfg. rep. consul Orange County Spring, Anaheim, 1987—, TALSCO, 1994—, Precision Resources, 1994—, GEMTECH, 1994—; mfg. rep. consul Alard Machine Products, Gardena, Calif., 1988—, v.p. spl. projects, 1997—. Charter mem. Rep. Presdl. Task Force, 1991—; mem. L.A. Coun. on World Affairs, 1991-92. With U.S. Army, 1966-68. Recipient Appreciation awards DAV, 1968, Soc. Mfg. Engrs., 1991. Fellow Soc. Carbide Engrs.; mem. Soc. Carbide and Tool Engrs. (chpt. pres. 1980-82, Appreciation award 1981), Rep. Presdl. Legion of Merit. Avocations: golf, swimming, riding, boating.

METZ, T(HEODORE) JOHN, librarian, educator; b. Erie, Pa., Nov. 5, 1932; s. Theodore John and Dorothy Pearl (Schutte) M.; m. Dorothy Page Neff, June 11, 1955; 1 child, Margaret Elizabeth MusB, Heidelberg Coll., 1954; MA in Music, Miami U., Oxford, Ohio, 1955; MLS, U. Mich., 1959. Libr. II U. Wis., Madison, 1959-61; asst. libr. Lawrence U., Appleton, Wis., 1961-67; dir. librs. U. Wis.-Green Bay, 1967-75; exec. dir. Midwest Region Library Network, Evanston, Ill., 1975-79; coll. libr., assoc. prof. Carleton Coll., Northfield, Minn., 1979-97, coll. libr. emeritus, 1998—. Speaker, participant, coord. numerous confs. and insts., 1969—; chmn. several state libr. groups, 1971-76; mem. several nat. libr. adv. coms., 1974-80; bldg. cons. Carleton Coll., others, 1978—; mem. Citizen Amb. Rsch. Librs. del. to Ea. Europe, 1992. Author: MIDLNET Symposium Report, 1976 Chmn. Green Bay Symphony, 1971-76; mem. various bds. coms., relating to mus. activities; performer Green Bay and other orchs., 1955— Library Service scholar U. Mich., 1957; Library Service fellow U. Mich., 1958 Mem. ALA, Assn. Coll. Rsch. Librs., Internat. Fedn. Libr. Assns. Avocations: music, hunting, fishing, gardening. E-mail: tmetz@carleton.edu.

METZ, THOMAS FREDERIC, career military officer; b. Elkin, NC, Sept. 21, 1948; m. Pamela Redmond; children: Elizabeth, Cade, Patrick. BS, U.S. Mil. Acad., 1971; M in Mech. Engring., N.C. State U., 1980; grad., Command and Gen. Staff Coll., Army War Coll. Registered profl. engr., Va. Enlisted U.S. Army, 1966, commd. 2nd lt. inf., 1971, advanced through grades to lt. gen., 2002, various positions, 1972-76, aide-de-camp for Comdr., Readiness Region VI Ft. Knox, Ky., 1976, comdr. C Co., 4th Bn., 54th Inf., 194th Armor Brigade, 1977-78; asst. prof. mech. engring. dept. U.S. Mil. Acad., West Point, N.Y., 1981-84; S-3/XO 3d Bn., 7th Inf., S-3 197th Separate Inf. Brigade Ft. Benning, Ga.; divsn. chief Inf. Sch. Combat Devel. Directorate, 1984-87; comdr. 4th Bn., 15th Inf., 194th Armor Brigade Ft. Knox, 1987-89; G-3, 2d Inf. Divsn. Republic of Korea, 1990-92; comdr. 2d Brigade, 1st Inf. Divsn., 1992-94; chief of staff Ft. Riley, 1994-95; dir. exptl. force coordination cell, 4th Inf. Divsn. U.S. Army, Fort Hood, 1995-97; asst. divsn. comdr. for support 4th Inf. Divsn., 1997-98; dep. dir. Joint Warfighting Capability Assessment, J8 The Joint Staff, Washington, 1998-2000, vice dir., force structure, resources, & assessment, J-8, 2000—01; comdr., 24th Infantry Divsn. (Mechanized) U.S. Army, Fort Riley, Kans., 2001—03; chief of staff US Centl. Command, Operation Enduring Freedom, 2002—03; comdr., III US Corps U.S. Army, Fort Hood, Tex., 2003—; comdr. Multi-Nat. Corps. Iraq, 2004—05. Decorated Legion of Merit with two oak leaf clusters, Meritorious Svc. medal with three oak leaf clusters, Army Commendation medal with two oak leaf clusters, Good Conduct medal. Office: 6791 Patton Dr Fort Hood TX 76544-1343 E-mail: metztf@js.pentagon.mil.

METZ, WERNER ADAM, physicist; BA in Physics, U. of Chgo., 1975; MS in Physics, Ga. Tech, 1977, PhD in Physics, 1982. Sr. mgmt. and tech. positions Polaroid Corp., Intel Corp., Tex. Instruments. Author: (28 technical papers) J. Applied Physics, Applied Phys. Letters, Electron Device Letters, IEEE Trans on Consum Electronics. Recipient Excellence award in Low power CMOS process, NCR Corp., 1985, Excellence award in std. cell arch., Intel Corp., 1986, Intel award for Arch. of dual mode CMOS based camera, 1996, Intel award for devel. of next generation conf. camera, 1999. Mem.: AAAS, Internat. Soc. for Optical Engring/Soc. for Imaging Sci. and Tech., IEEE, Am. Phys. Soc., Sigma Pi Sigma. Achievements include patents for 18 patents in medicine, Physics, microelectronics, digital imaging products and sci; first to digital still cameras, CMOS image sensors, digital processing algorithms; development of dual mode video/still camera, scanners, digital printers; invention of MXP5x00 image processor architect. Business E-Mail: werner.metz@ieee.org.

METZER, PATRICIA ANN, lawyer; b. Phila., Mar. 10, 1941; d. Freeman Weeks and Evelyn (Heap) M.; m. Karl Hormann, June 30, 1980. BA with distinction, U. Pa., 1963, LLB cum laude, 1966. Bar: Mass. 1966, D.C. 1972, U.S. Tax Ct. 1988. Assoc., then ptnr. Mintz, Levin, Cohn, Glovsky and Popeo, Boston, 1966—75; assoc. tax legis. counsel U.S. Treasury Dept., Washington, 1975-78; shareholder, dir. Goulston & Storrs, P.C., Boston, 1978-98; stockholder Hutchins, Wheeler & Dittmar, P.C., Boston, 1998—2002; of counsel Vacovec, Mayotte & Singer LLP, Newton, Mass., 2003—. Lectr. program continuing legal edn. Boston Coll. Law Sch., Chestnut Hill, Mass., spring, 1974; lectr. grad. tax program Boston U. Law Sch., 2001—03; adv. com. NYU Inst. Fed. Taxation, NYC, 1981—87; practitioner liaison com. Mass. Dept. Revenue, 1985—90; spkr. in field. Author: Federal Income Taxation of Individuals, 1984; authors' panel Jour. Passthrough Entities, 2003—; mem. editl. bd. Am. Jour. Tax Policy, 1995-98; mem. adv. bd. Corp. Tax and Bus. Planning Rev., 1996—; contbr. articles to profl. jours., chpts. to books. Bd. mgrs. Barrington Ct. Condominium, Cambridge, Mass., 1985-86; bd. dirs. Univ. Rd. Parking Assn., Cambridge, 1988—; trustee Social Law Libr., Boston, 1989-93. Mem. ABA (tax sect., vice-chair publs. 2000-02, mem. coun. 1996-99, chair subcom. allocations and distbns. partnership com. 1978-82, vice-chair legis. 1991-93, chair 1993-95, com. govt. submissions, vice liaison 1993-94, liaison 1994-95, North Atlantic region, co-liaison 1995-96, N.E. region, regional liaison meetings com.), FBA (coun. on taxation, chmn. corp. taxation com. 1977-81, chair com. partnership taxation 1981-87), Mass. Bar Assn. (coun. taxation law sect. 2001—, chair coun. taxation law sect. 2006-07), Boston Bar Assn. (coun. 1987-89, chair tax sect. 1989-91, steering com. solo and small firm sect. 2005—), Am. Coll. Tax Counsel (bd. regents 1999-2004), Boston Estate Planning Coun. (exec. com. 1975, 79-82). Avocation: vocal performances (as soloist and with choral groups). Office: Vacovec Mayotte & Singer LLP Two Newton Pl Ste 340 255 Washington St Newton MA 02458-1634 Office Phone: 617-964-0500. Business E-Mail: pmetzer@vacovec.com.

METZER, WALTER STEVEN, neurologist, educator; b. Hot Springs, Ark., Dec. 15, 1949; s. Walter Mathew and Mildred Jean Metzer; m. Teddi Marie O'Kelley, Jan. 24, 1976. BS in Applied Psychology, Ga. Inst. Tech., 1972; MD, U. Ark., Little Rock, 1976. Diplomate Am. Bd. Psychiatry and Neurology. Intern U. Ark. Coll. Medicine, Little Rock, 1976-77; resident in neurology U. Ark. Coll. for Med. Scis., Little Rock, 1980-82, asst. prof. neurology, 1983-89; assoc. prof. neurology U. Ark. Coll. Medicine, 1989—; asst. med. dir. East Little Rock Community Clinic, 1977-79; staff neurologist McClellan Meml. VA Hosp., Little Rock, 1986-89, 96—, chief, neurology svc., 1989-92; pvt. practice North Little Rock, Ark., 1992—97. Author book chpts. rsch. study reports, pharm. submissions, articles, abstracts and letters. Recipient Svc. award East Little Rock Cmty. Clinic, 1979, Honored Faculty award U. Ark. Coll. Medicine, 1985-86, 92, 2007; named to Outstanding Young Men of Am., 1985; Richard P. Moll scholar Ga. Tech., 1972. Fellow Am. Acad. Neurology; mem. Movement Disorder Soc., Am. Assn. Electrodiagnostic Medicine, Am. Clin. Neurophys. Soc., Ga. Inst. Tech. Alumni Assn., Ark. Caduceus Club, Sigma Xi. Avocations: guitar, wood working. Office: Univ Ark 4301 W Markham Little Rock AR 72205 Office Phone: 501-257-6053. Business E-Mail: wmetzer@uams.edu.

METZGER, ERNEST HUGH, aerospace engineer, research scientist; b. Nurnberg, Germany, Oct. 22, 1923; came to U.S., 1939, naturalized, 1943; s. Paul Arthur and Charlotte Babette (Kann) M.; m. Sarah Temple Grinnell, Nov. 19, 1956; children: Lisa Metzger Dunning, Charlotte Bennett (dec.), George Grinnell. BS, CCNY, 1949; MS, Harvard U., 1950. Automatic control engr. Bell Aerospace Co. div. Textron, Buffalo, 1950-54, tech. dir. inertial nav. systems, 1954-60, chief engr., inertial instruments, 1960-70, chief engr., gravity gradiometer systems, 1970-83, dir. gravity sensor systems, 1983-86, exec. dir. engring., 1986-89, cons., 1989-95, Bell Geospace Inc., Buffalo, 1995—. Mem. panel future navigation systems Nat. Acad. Sci., com. on geodesy NRC, 1988-89, accelerator criteria com. NASA, tech. com. navigation guidance and control, AIAA, 1989—; vis. lectr. dept. aernautics and astronautics Stanford U., 1990 Contbr. articles to profl. jours.; patentee in field Served with AUS, 1943-46 Recipient Aerospace Pioneer award Niagara Frontier sect. AIAA, 1977; named to Niagara Frontier Aviation Hall of Fame, 1992. Mem. IEEE, Inst. Navigation (Thurlow award for outstanding contbn. to sci. navigation 1983), AAAS, Air Force Assn., N.Y. Acad. Scis., Explorers Club, Sigma Xi, Tau Beta Pi, Eta Kappa Nu Clubs: Harvard, Buffalo Ski. Home: 663 Downing Ln Williamsville NY 14221 E-mail: semetz@adelphia.net.

METZGER, HENRY, federal research institution administrator; b. Mainz, Germany, Mar. 23, 1932; came to U.S., 1938; naturalized, 1945; s. Paul Alfred and Anne (Daniel) M.; m. Deborah Stashower, June 16, 1957; children: Eran D., Renée V., Carl E. MD, Columbia U., 1957. Chief chem. immunology sect. Nat. Inst. Arthritis & Musculoskeletal & Skin Disease/NIH, Bethesda, Md., 1973—2002; br. chief USPHS, Bethesda, 1983-94, sci. dir., 1987-98, med. officer grade VI, 1975-98; scientist Sr. Biomed. Rsch. Svc., 1999—2002, scientist emeritus, 2002—. Carl Prausnitz Meml. lectr., 1982; Ecker Meml. lectr. Case Western Res. U., Cleve., 1984; Harvey Soc. lectr., 1984; Eli Nadel Meml. lectr. St. Louis U., 1987; Rodney Porter Meml. lectr., 1993; Burroughs-Wellcome lectr., 1994; R.E. Dyer lectr., 1995; mem. health rsch. coun. BMFT, German Govt., 1994-97. Editor: Fc Receptors & the Action of Antibodies, 1990; assoc. editor Ann. Rev. Immunology, 1982-96; contbr. numerous articles to profl. jours.; mem. editl. bd. numerous sci. jours. Recipient Meritorious Svc. award USPHS, 1978, Disting. Svc. award, 1985, 97, Joseph Mather Smith prize Columbia U., 1984. Fellow AAAS, Am. Acad. Allergy and Immunology; mem. NAS, Am. Assn. Immunologists (pres. 1991-92), Am. Soc. Biol. Chem. Molecular Biology, Am. Soc. Cell Biology, Internat. Union Immunol. Soc. (pres. 1992-95), Found. for Advanced Edn. in the Scis. (pres.

1990-92, 2005-), Alpha Omega Alpha. Home: 3410 Taylor St Chevy Chase MD 20815-4024 Office: NIH Rm 9n228 10 Center Dr 9000 Rockville Pike Bethesda MD 20892-1820 E-mail: metzgerh@exchange.nih.gov.

METZGER, JAMES W., career military officer; s. Mr. and Mrs. George Metzger; m. Mary Jane Bachmann; children: Jennifer, Amy. Grad. with distinction, U.S. Naval Acad., 1971; MEE, Mich. State U.; student, Nuc. Power Sch., Bainbridge, Md. Commd. ensign USN, advanced through grades to vice adm., 2000; elec. officer, main propulsion asst. USS George Bancroft; engring. officer USS Indpls., 1977-81; mem. nuc. propulsion examining bd. U.S. Pacific Fleet; exec. officer USS Tautog, Pearl Harbor, Hawaii, 1983-86; comdr. USS Mpls.-St. Paul, 1987-90; dir. Submarine Prospective Comdg. Oficer Sch., 1991; exec. asst. to comdr. in chief U.S. Atlantic Fleet, Norfolk, Va., 1991-93; comdr. Submarine Devel. Squadron 12, 1993; exec. asst. Vice Chief of Naval Ops.; exec. asst., naval aide Sec. of Navy; dep. dir. for strategy and policy USN, Washington, 1997-98, commr. of submarine group 8, 1998—2000, comdr. Seventh Fleet Yokosuka, Japan, 2000—02; asst. to Chmn. of the Joint Chiefs of Staff US Dept. Def., Washington, 2002—04. Decorated Legion of Merit with five gold stars.

METZGER, JANET, librarian; MA in Libr. Sci., Kent State U. Worked in both pub. and sch. libr. settings, 1976—2004; libr., Ramsayer Rsch. Libr. William McKinley Presdl. Libr. & Mus., Canton, Ohio, 2004—. Children's & young adult libr. Louisville Pub. Libr., Ohio, local history libr., Ohio; sch. libr. Our Lady of Peace Sch., Canton, Ohio. Singer church choirs and Canton's City of Flags Chorus and Sweet Adelines. Mem.: Plain Township Hist. Soc., Ohio Genealogical Soc. (Stark County Chpt.). Avocations: reading, piano and organ, singing. Office: William McKinely Presdl Libr & Mus 800 McKinley Monument Dr NW Canton OH 44708 Office Phone: 330-445-7043. Office Fax: 330-455-1137. *

METZGER, JEFFREY PAUL, lawyer; b. Oct. 13, 1950; s. John E. and Ellen J. M; m. Stephanie Ann Stahr, Dec. 27, 1977. BA magna cum laude, Amherst Coll., 1973; JD, Georgetown U., 1976. Bar: D.C. 1977. Legis. asst. U.S. Senator Joseph Biden, Jr., Del., 1973; assoc. Collier, Shannon, Rill and Scott, Washington, 1976-79, Cole and Groner PC, Washington, 1979-82; trial atty. comml. litigation br. civil divsn. U.S. Dept. Justice, Washington, 1982-85; mem. prof. staff Pres.'s Blue Ribbon Commn. on Def. Mgmt., Washington, 1985-86; asst. gen. counsel Unisys Corp., 1986—88, v.p., assoc. gen. counsel, 1989—. Mem. ABA. Office Phone: 703-439-5609. Personal E-mail: Jeffrey.Metzger@unisys.com.

METZGER, JOHN MACKAY, lawyer; b. Princeton, NJ, Mar. 8, 1948; s. Bruce Manning and Isobel Elizabeth (Mackay) M.; m. Sandra Kay Wellington, May 8, 1999. BA cum laude, Harvard U., 1970; JD, NYU, 1973; postgrad., London Sch. Econs., 1973-74. Bar: Pa. 1976, NJ 1976, US Dist. Ct. NJ 1976, US Tax Ct. 1977, DC 1978, US Ct. Appeals (fed. cir.) 1982, US Supreme Ct. 2006. Tax adminstr. N.J. Div. Taxation, Trenton, 1976-86, 88—; atty. McCarthy & Schatzman PA, Princeton, 1986-88. Mem. N.J. Econ. Devel. Coun., 1987-90. Author: A Visit to Colonial Trenton, 2002; contbr. articles to profl. jours. Trustee Friends of N.J. State Libr., 2000—, pres., 2000-03; sec., trustee Witherspoon Inst., 2003—. Mem. ABA, Am. Soc. Internat. Law, Harvard Club of N.Y.C., Supreme Ct. Historical Soc. Republican. Home: 52 Coriander Dr Princeton NJ 08540-9434 Office: 50 Barrack St Trenton NJ 08695-0269 Business E-Mail: John.Metzger@treas.state.nj.us.

METZGER, PAUL LOUIS, theologian, director; b. Elgin, Ill., Mar. 9, 1964; s. William Frank and Audrey Louise Metzger; m. Mariko Tomoda, Aug. 11, 1990; children: Christopher Takasumi William, Julianne Misaki. BA, Northwestern Coll., Roseville, Minn., 1987; MDiv. and MA, Trinity Evang. Div. Sch., Deerfield, Ill., 1992; PhD, King's Coll. London, U. London, 1999. Prof. Christian theology and theology of culture Multnomah Bibl. Sem., Portland, Oreg., 1999—. Founder and dir. of the Inst. for the theology of culture: new wine, new wineskins Multnomah Bibl. Sem., Portland, 2000—. Editor: (journal) Cultural Encounters: A Jou. for the Theology of Culture; author: (book) The Word of Christ and the World of Culture, 2003; editor: Trinitarian Soundings in Systematic Theology, 2005; contbr. articles to profl. jours. and newspapers. Mem.: Ctr. Theol. Inquiry. Protestant Christian. Office Phone: 503-251-6741.

METZGER, ROBERT STREICHER, lawyer; b. St. Louis, Sept. 27, 1950; s. Robert Stanley and Jean Harriet (Streicher) M.; children: Michael, Kristen, Marisa. BA, Middlebury Coll., 1974; JD, Georgetown U., 1977. Bar: Calif. 1978, D.C. 1978. Legis. aide US Rep. Robert F. Drinan, Washington, 1972-73; legis. asst. US Rep. Michael J. Harrington, Washington, 1973-75; rsch. fellow Ctr. for Internat. Affairs Harvard U. Grad. Sch. Arts and Sci., Cambridge, Mass., 1977, Harvard U., Cambridge, Mass., 1978; assoc. Latham & Watkins, LA, 1978-84, ptnr., 1984-90, Kirkland & Ellis, LA, 1990-93, Troop, Meisinger, Steuber & Pasich and predecessor, LA, 1993-97, Gibson, Dunn & Crutcher LLP, LA, 1997—2007; ptnr. corp. and securities Pillsbury Winthrop Shaw Pittman LLP, LA, 2007—. Chmn. Aerospace and Govt. Practice Group, 1997—2006, Telecom. Practice Group, 2000-06; cons. Congl. Rsch. Svc., Washington, 1977-78. Contbr. articles to profl. jours. Trustee Sierra Canyon HS Found.; mem. dean's alumni leadership coun. Kennedy Sch. Govt. Harvard U., 2005—. Mem. ABA (litig. pub. contracts sect.), Fed. Comm. Bar Assn., Internat. Inst. for Strategic Studies, Pacific Coun. on Internat. Policy, Jonathan Club. Office: Pillsbury Winthrop Shaw Pittman LLP 725 S Figueroa St Ste 2806 Los Angeles CA 90017-5406 Office Phone: 213-488-7437, 310-729-9392. Business E-Mail: robert.metzger@pillsburylaw.com.

METZGER, SCOTT, information technology executive; BS Computer Sci., Calif. State Poly. Inst., San Luis Obispo. Sr. sys. cons., corp. rsch. devel. group Baxter; devel. mgr. MCI, Apple, IBM; chief info. officer TrueCredit Co., Chester, Pa. Named one of Top 25 Chief Tech. Officers, InfoWorld mag., 2006. Office: TrueCredit Co 2 Baldwin Pl PO Box 2000 Crum Lynne PA 19022 *

METZGER, SIDNEY, retired communications engineer; b. NY, Feb. 1, 1917; m. Miriam Lipstein; children: David, Sally, Philip. BSEE, N.Y. Univ., 1937; MEE, Polytech. Inst. Bklyn., 1950. Engr. U.S. Signal Corps. Lab., NJ, 1939—45; head radio relay divsn. Fed. Telecommunications Labs. Internat. Tel. & Tel. Corp., 1945—54; mgr. communications engring. Astro Elect. Prod. Divsn. RCA, 1954—63; mgr. engring. divsn. Communications Satellite Corp., 1963-67, asst. v.p. and chief engr., 1968-72, asst. v.p. and chief scientist, 1972-80, v.p. and chief scientist, 1980-82; cons. engr., 1982—93; ret., 1993. Recipient Aerospace award Aerospace & Elec. Systems Soc., 1975, Internat. Communication award IEEE, 1976, Koji Kobayashi Computers & Communication award, 1985, Aerospace Communication award Am. Inst. Aeronaut. & Astronaut., 1984. Fellow IEEE, AIAA; mem. Nat. Acad. Engring, Sigma Xi. Address: 700 John Ringling Blvd Apt N-206 Sarasota FL 34236-1500 Personal E-mail: mimsid7@comcast.net.

METZGER, VERNON ARTHUR, management educator, consultant; b. Baldwin Park, Calif., Aug. 13, 1918; s. Vernon and Nellie C. (Ross) Metzger; m. Beth Alrene Metzger, Feb. 19, 1955; children: Susan, Linda, David. BS, U. Calif., Berkeley, 1947, MBA, 1948. Estimating engr. C.F. Braun & Co., 1949; prof. mgmt. Calif. State U., Long Beach, 1949—89, prof. emeritus, 1989—, founder Sch. of Bus. Mgmt. cons. Mem. Fire Commn., Fountain Valley, Calif., 1959—60; mem. mgmt. task force to promote modern mgmt. in Yugoslavia, U.S. State Dept., 1977; mem. State of Calif. Fair Polit. Practices Commn., Orange County Transit Com.; pres. Orange County Dem. League, 1967—68. With USNR, 1942—45. Recipient Outstanding Citizen award, Orange County. Fellow: Soc. Advancement Mgmt. (life; dir.); mem.: Orange County Indsl. Rels. Rsch. Assn. (v.p.), Acad. Mgmt., Tau Kappa Upsilon, Alpha Kappa Psi, Beta gamma Sigma. Home: 1938 Balearic Dr Costa Mesa CA 92626-3513 Office Phone: 714-557-6415.

METZGER, WYATT K., physicist; s. Phillip and Patricia (O' Rorke) Metzger; m. Mercedes Metzger; children: Andre, Sean. BA in Physics, Bowdoin Coll., Brunswick, Maine, 1992; MS in Physics, U. Colo., Boulder, 1997, PhD in Physics, 2001. Rsch. scientist Battery Automated Tech., Salt Lake City, 1993—95, Boundless Corp., Boulder, Colo., 1996—97, U. Colo., Boulder, 1997—2001, Nat. Renewable Energy Lab., Golden, 2001—. Author: more than 40 rsch. articles in field. Recipient Dir.'s award, Nat. Renewable Energy Lab., 2003. Mem.: IEEE, Am. Chem. Soc., Am. Phys. Soc., Materials Rsch. Soc. Achievements include pioneering contributions in the fields of alternative energy, photovoltaics, and semiconductor devices. Office: Nat Renewable Energy Lab 1617 Cole Blvd Golden CO 80401

METZINGER, TIMOTHY EDWARD, lawyer; b. LA, Aug. 21, 1961; s. Robert Cole and Mary Jean (Cusick) M.; m. Cynthia Lee Stanworth, Nov. 16, 1991. BA, UCLA, 1986; JD, U. San Francisco, 1989. Bar: Calif. 1989, U.S. Dist. Ct. (ctrl., so., ea. and no. dists.) Calif. 1989, U.S. Ct. Appeals (9th cir.) 1989, U.S. Supreme Ct. 1994. Assoc. Bronson, Bronson & McKinnon, LA, 1989-93; ptnr. Price, Postel & Parma, Santa Barbara, Calif., 1999—2006. Santa Barbara County del. State Bar Conf. of Dels., 2001—. Editor-in-chief Santa Barbara Lawyer, 1999-2000. Mem. Santa Barbara Mus. Natural History (bd. advisors), Santa Barbara Barristers Club (pres.), Santa Barbara County Bar Assn (pres., 2004.), Surgical Eye Expeditions Internat. (dir., 2006), Am. Inns. Ct. (master), Santa Barbara Club. Avocations: diving, moutaineering, sailing. Office: Price Postel & Parma 200 E Carrillo St Ste 400 Santa Barbara CA 93101-2190

METZLER, JAMES ROBERT, musician; b. Worcester, Mass., June 20, 1947; adopted s. Robert Adolph Metzler and Olga Slonin; m. Diane Pearl Fought, Aug. 27, 1988; children: Yurii Wynn Fought, Jeffrey David. MusB, Westminster Choir Coll., 1969; MusM, Hartt Coll. Music, U. Hartford, 1972; diploma, Cambridge Soc. Musicians; diploma (hon.), Nat. Coll. Music & Arts; diploma in Choir Tng., Am. Guild Organists, 1977; D in Organ and Musicology, U. Mich., Ann Arbor, 1987. Organist and choirmaster St. James' Episcopal Ch., New London, Conn., 1969—71, First Presbyn. Ch., Hartford, Conn., 1971—72, Trinity Episcopal Ch., Toledo, 1972—96; adj. prof. organ U. Toledo, 1984—89; organist and dir. music Trinity Episcopal Cathedral, Little Rock, 1996—2006, Pk. Congl. Ch., Grand Rapids, 2006—. Recipient S. Lewis Elmer (First Prize on Guild Exams), Am. Guild of Organists, 1977. Mem.: Assn. Anglican Musicians, Am. Guild Organists, Am. Guild of English Handbell Ringers. Episcopalian. Achievements include organ recital at Notre-Dame Cathedral, Westminster Abbey, St. Paul's Cathedral, Norwich Cathedral, King's College Chapel, Westminster Cathedral, and Washington National Cathedral; director of the Canterbury Singers USA for more than 80 choral services at major British cathedrals and Westminster Abbey. Office: Pk Congl Ch 10 E Park Pl NE Grand Rapids MI 49503 Office Phone: 616-459-3203. Office Fax: 616-459-0918. Business E-Mail: jmetzler@parkchurchgr.org.

METZLER, RUTH HORTON, genealogical educator; b. Eden, NY, Aug. 4, 1927; d. John Morris and Bernice Louise (Horton); m. Henry George Metzler, Sept. 4, 1948; children: Kathleen, Ronald, Janice, Margaret. Attended, Wheaton Coll., 1945-48; BA (hon.), Wilmington Coll., 1956; MLS, State Univ. of N.Y., Geneseo, 1962. Cert. tchr., libr. media specialist, N.Y. Cataloging typist Peoria Pub. Libr., Ill., 1949-52; cataloging asst. Wilmington Coll. Libr., Ohio, 1953-56; sch. libr. K-12 Nunda Ctrl. Sch., NY, 1956-65; head libr. media ctr. Irondequoit H.S., Rochester, NY, 1965-84; pres. Rochester Geneal. Soc., NY, 1989-93; instr., lectr. Rochester Mus. and Sci. Ctr., NY, 1990—. Author of several family histories. Organizing instr. Genealogy workshops, Rochester Mus. and Sci. Ctr; contbg. lectr. Nat. Geneal. Conf., Rochester, 1990; others. Mem. N.Y. Libr. Assn.;N.Y. State Tchr. Retirement Sys.; New Eng. Hist. and Geneal. Soc.; Kodak Geneal. Soc., N.Y.; State Coun. of Geneal.; Genealogy Round Table of Monroe County (del. 1996—); Rochester Geneal. Soc.; Geneal. Educators (organizing mem. 1996). Republican. Baptist. Avocations: genealogy, writing.

METZNER, CHARLES MILLER, federal judge; b. NYC, Mar. 13, 1912; s. Emanuel and Gertrude (Miller) M.; m. Jeanne Gottlieb, Oct. 6, 1966. AB, Columbia U., 1931, LL.B., 1933. Bar: N.Y. 1933. Pvt. practice, 1934; mem. Jud. Council State N.Y., 1935-41; law clk. to N.Y. supreme ct. justice, 1942-52; exec. asst. to U.S. atty. Gen. Herbert Brownell, Jr., 1953-54; mem. firm Chapman, Walsh & O'Connell, 1954-59; judge U.S. Dist Ct. (so. dist.) N.Y., 1959—77; sr. judge, 1977—. Mem. Law Revision Commn. N.Y. State, 1959; chmn. com. adminstrn. magistrates system U.S. Jud. Conf., 1970-81; chmn. Columbia Coll. Coun., 1965-66. Pres. N.Y. Young Republican Club, 1941; Trustee Columbia U., 1972-84, trustee emeritus, 1984—; bd. dirs. N.Y.C. Ctr. Music and Drama, 1969-74. Recipient Lawyer Div. of Joint Def. Appeal award, 1961, Columbia U. Alumni medal, 1966, Founders award Nat. Coun. U.S. Magistrates, 1989. Mem. ABA, Am. Law Inst., Fed. Bar Coun. (cert. Disting. Jud. Svc. 1989).

METZNER, DAVID MARK, plastic and reconstructive surgeon; b. Cleve., Jan. 16, 1939; children: Damon Hires, Rowan Aliya von Zanthier. AB, U. Mich., 1960; MD, Case Western Res. U., 1964. Diplomate Am. Bd. Otolaryngology, Am. Bd. Plastic Surgery, Nat. Bd. Med. Examiners; lic. MD, Ohio, Calif., Mass., La. Internship Mt. Sinai Hosp., Cleve., 1964-65, residency in gen. surgery, 1965-66; residency in otolaryngology Harvard Med. Sch., Boston, 1966-69; chief of otolaryngology The Cambridge (Mass.) Hosp., 1971-74; residency in plastic and reconstructive surgery La. State U., New Orleans, 1975-76; active staff Lakeside Hosp., Metairie, La., 1977—, Highland Pk. Hosp., Covington, La., 1977—, Prytania Surgery Ctr., New Orleans, 1986—; pvt. plastic surgery New Orleans & Covington, 1977—; plastic surgeon The Ctr. for CosMedic Rejuvenation and Wellness. Active, courtest staff So. Bapt. Hosp., New Orleans, 1977—; courtesy staff St. Tammany Parish Hosp., Covington, 1977—; clin. instr. Harvard Med. Sch., 1971-75; vis. prof. Nassau County, N.Y. Med. Ctr., 1988, Med. Coll. Wis., 1992; vis. lectr. U. Calif. San Diego, 1991; clin. asst. prof. La. State U., 1994-; lectr. in field. Recipient AMA Physician's Recognition award, 1981, 84, 87, 90, Appreciation award North Am. Med./Dental Assn.; named one of Top Plastic Surgeons, New Orleans Mag. Mem. Am. Soc. Plastic and Reconstructive Surgeons, Inc., The Am. Soc. for Aesthetic Plastic Surgery (Walter Scott Brown award, 1989), Southeastern Soc. Plastic and Reconstructive Surgeons, Inc., Am. Acad. Facial Plastic and Reconstructive Surgery, Inc., Am. Acad. Otolaryngology-Head and Neck Surgery, Inc., La. Soc. Plastic and Reconstructive Surgeons (pres.), The Double Boarded Soc. (pres.), Southeastern Soc. Plastic and Reconstructive Surgeons, La. Soc. Plastic and Reconstructive Surgeons, La. State Med. Soc., Orleans Parish Med. Soc., Harvard Club La. (pres.). Avocations: art, sculpting, jewelry. Office: Lakeside Hosp Med Staff Office Bldg 4720 I-10 Service Rd Ste 407 Metairie LA 70001 also: 106 Park Pl Ste 115 Covington LA 70433 *

MEULEMANS, WILLIAM CHARLES, political science professor; b. Glenwood City, Wis., Dec. 31, 1935; s. Philip Dominic and Frances Barbara Meulemans; m. Janet Beth Banion, Oct. 15, 1983; children: Julie, Jamie. BS in Polit. Sci., U. Wis., River Falls, 1960; MA in Polit. Sci., U. Idaho, Moscow, 1963, PhD in Polit. Sci., 1970. Prof. polit. sci. So. Oreg. U., Ashland, 1964—92, Queen's U. Belfast, Northern Ireland, 1991—2002, Portland State U., Oreg., 2002—. Polit. cons. Dem. Party, Oreg., 1968—82, 3M Co., Oreg., 1978—82; polit. organizer SW Indian Health Project, Oreg., 1979—80. Author: Making Political Choices, 1989, Wy Irish Eyes Are Crying: Portestants and Catholics in the North, 2007. Mem. Marion County Dem. Ctrl. Com., 1990—; bd. dirs. No. Ireland Children Holiday Scheme, Belfast, Northern Ireland, 1995—97, KSYS Pub. TV, Medford, Oreg., 1988—92. With US Army, 1953—56. Fellow, Danforth Found., 1970—72; grantee, Oreg. State Sys. Edn., 1990—92; scholar, Fulbright Found., 1989; Nat. Def. fellow, U. Idaho, 1962—64. Avocation: jazz. Home: 13017 Maple Leaf Ct NE Aurora OR 97002

MEUSER, FREDRICK WILLIAM, retired church administrator, historian; b. Payne, Ohio, Sept. 14, 1923; s. Henry William and Alvina Maria (Bouyack) Meuser; m. Jeanne Bond Griffiths, July 29, 1951; children: Jill Martha, Douglas Griffiths. AB, Capital U., 1945, BD, 1948, DD (hon.), 1989; STM, Yale U., 1949, MA, 1953, PhD, 1956; DD (hon.), Tex. Luth. Coll., 1980, Capital U., 1989; LHD (hon.), Augustana Coll., 1985. Ordained to ministry Am. Lutheran Ch., 1948; asst. pastor 1st Luth. Ch., Galveston, Tex., 1948, Christ Luth. Ch., North Miami, Fla., 1949—51; campus minister Yale U., 1951—53; prof. ch. history Luth. Theol. Sem., Columbus, Ohio, 1953—78, dean grad. studies, 1963—69, pres., 1971—78; exec. sec. div. theol. studies Luth. Council in U.S.A., 1969—71; pres. Trinity Luth. Sem., Columbus, 1978—88; del. World Council Chs., 1968, Luth. World Fedn., 1970; v.p. Am. Luth. Ch., 1974—80; mem. Commn. for a New Luth. Ch., 1982—86; asst. pastor St. Paul Luth. Ch., Westerville, Ohio, 1995—97. Author: The Formation of the American Lutheran Church, 1958, Luther the Preacher, 1983; author: (with others) Church in Fellowship, 1963, Lutherans in North America, 1975; translator: (with others) What Did Luther Understand by Religion, 1977, The Reconstruction of Morality, 1979; editor and author: (with others) Interpreting Luther's Legacy, 1967. Recipient Disting. Churchman's award Tex. Luth. Coll., 1972, Joseph Sittler award Trinity Luth. Sem., 1990; named Outstanding Alumnus Capital U., 1977; Am. Assn. Theol. Schs. fellow, 1961-62 Home: 2055 S Floral Ave Lot 240 Bartow FL 33830-7157 Personal E-mail: fredmeuser@aol.com.

MEVERS, FRANK CLEMENT, state agency administrator, archivist; b. New Orleans, Oct. 10, 1942; s. Lloyd F. and Mary Ashley (Collins) M.; m. Kathryn Ann Hayes, Dec. 23, 1967; children: John F., Lauren K. BA in History, La. State U., 1965; PhD in Am. History, U. NC, 1972; MA, La. State U., 1967. Editor Papers of James Madison, Charlottesville, Va., 1972-74, Papers of Josiah Bartlett, Concord, NH, 1974-77, Papers of William Plumer, Concord, 1977-79; state archivist State of NH, Concord, 1979—. Editor, author: New Hampshire: State That Made US a Nation, 1989. Mem. Pub. Libr. Bd. Trustees, Concord, 1979-99. With US Army, 1967-69, Korea. Episcopalian. Avocation: stamp collecting/philately. Home: 29 Bradley St Concord NH 03301-6432 Office: NH State Archives 71 S Fruit St Concord NH 03301-2410 Office Phone: 603-271-2236. Personal E-mail: eatright@comcast.net. Business E-Mail: fmevers@sos.state.nh.us.

MEW, CALVIN MARSHALL, advertising executive; b. Oakland, Calif., Oct. 27, 1947; s. Thomas Bing and May (Jan) m. Mary Farnham Crawford, Oct. 20, 2001. BA, Yale U., 1969; MDiv, Union Theol Sem., 1973; postgrad., Columbia U., 1973-79, Harvard U., 1984. Tutor Union Theol. Sem., 1973-77; adj. lectr. Hunter Coll., 1977-79; market analyst Kenyon & Eckhart Advt., Inc., NYC, 1979-82, v.p. market plans, 1982-83, rev. v.p. strategic plan, 1983-85, v.p. strategic mktg. svcs., 1985-88, sr.v.p. strategic and forward planning, 1988-90; sr. v.p., mng. dir. Bozell, Inc., 1990-93, exec. v.p., mng. dir., 1993—. Gen. mgr. Bozell Austria, 1994; exec. v.p., regional dir. L.Am. Bozell Worldwide, Inc., 1996; dir. Capitauro Investments, Ltd., 2002; adv. bd. Columbia U. Librs., 2006—. Contbr. articles to profl. jours. Bd. dirs. Union Theol. Sem., 1984—, vice chmn., 1992—; mem. advisory bd. Columbia U. Libr., 2006-. Recipient Cogswell award Yale U., 1969; Columbia U. fellow, Rockefeller Bros. Fund fellow. Mem. Am. Acad. Religion, Soc. Bibl. Lit., Harvard Bus. Sch. Club (mem. adv. bd. N.Y. chpt. 2004). Presbyterian. Home: 895 W End Ave New York NY 10025-3500 Office: Bozell Jacobs Kenyon Eckhart 13801 Fnb Pkwy Omaha NE 68154-5230 Business E-Mail: calvinmew@post.harvard.edu.

MEW, THOMAS JOSEPH, III, (TOMMY MEW), artist, educator; b. Miami, Fla., Aug. 15, 1942; s. Thomas Joseph and Maude Edith (Perry) M.; m. Mary Ann Kelley, June 17, 1966; 1 son, Thomas Joseph IV. BS, Fla. State U., 1962, MA, 1964; PhD, NYU, 1966. Grad. instr. Fla. State U., 1963; asst. prof. art Troy State U., 1966-68, Jacksonville U., 1968-70; prof., chmn. dept. art Berry Coll., 1970—, Dana prof. art. Juror art shows: vis. artist; lectr. in field, cons. art; dir. Fluxus West/Southeast; dir. Moon Gallery. Exhibited in one-man shows Parkway Gallery, Miami, 1962-63, 319 Gallery, N.Y.C., 1968, Meridian (Miss.) Mus., 1976, C.D.O. Gallery, Parma, Italy, 1978, Calif. State U., Sacramento, 1979, Miss. Mus. Art, Jackson, 1979, Art Inst. for Permian Basin, ITex, Arte Studio, Bergamo, Italy, Queen Street Gallery, Belfast, No. Ireland; group shows include High Mus., Atlanta, 1971, 72, 74, New Reform Gallery, Aalst, Belgium, 1975, U. Guelph, Ont., Can., 1975, Neuberger Mus., Purchase, N.Y., 1978, Arte Fiera, Bologna, Italy, 1979; represented in permanent collections, Kansas City Art Inst., Mildura Art Centre, Australia, Wichita Art Mus., Jacksonville (Fla.) Art Mus., Macon Mus. Art, AT&T, Harn Mus., U. Iowa; host: Cable TV show Art: The Mew View, 1978—; Filmmaker, 1966-69; contbr. articles to profl. jours. Bd. dirs. Rome Arts Coun., 1984—, Interface. Recipient Gellhorn award N.Y. U., 1966; Cowperthwaite grantee, 1972; Lilly Found. grantee, 1975; Gulf Life grantee, 1977. Mem. Southeastern Coll. Art Conf., Coll. Art Assn. Am., Am. Fedn. Arts, Nat. Art Edn. Assn., Am. Assn. Art Dealers, Omicron Delta Kappa, Phi Kappa Phi. Home: 28 Virginia Cir Rome GA 30161 Office: Berry Coll Art Dept PO Box 580 Mount Berry GA 30149 Home Phone: 706-292-9234; Office Phone: 706-236-2219. Business E-Mail: tmew@berry.edu. *I've always moved in the direction of my dreams...always tried to make the great dream a reality.*

MEWANI, RAJSHREE R.(AMCHAND), researcher; b. Bombay, Apr. 3, 1969; d. Naraindas and Neena Kotwani; life ptnr. Ramchand Mewani, Dec. 13, 1999. BS, U. Bombay, 1989, diploma in med. lab. tech., 1990, MA, 1994, PhD, 1999. Jr. rsch. fellow Seth G.S. Med. Coll. and K.E.M. Hosp., Bombay, 1990-94, sr. rsch. fellow, 1994-99; parasitologist Inst. of Medicine, Kathmandu, Nepal, 1999-2000; rsch. fellow Georgetown U. Med. Ctr., Washington, 2000—. Contbr. articles to profl. jours. Achievements include patents in field. Office Fax: 202-687-2221. Personal E-mail: dr_rajshreek@yahoo.com. Business E-Mail: rrm6@georgetown.edu.

MEYBURG, ARNIM HANS, transportation engineer, educator, consultant; b. Bremerhaven, W. Ger., Aug. 25, 1939; came to U.S., 1965; s. Friedel and Auguste (Kleeberg) M.; m. Ruth Meyburg; 1 child, Jennifer Susan. Student, U. Hamburg, 1960-62, Free U. Berlin, 1962-65; MS (Fulbright travel grantee), Northwestern U., 1968, PhD, 1971. Research assoc. Transp. Center, Northwestern U., 1968-69; asst. prof. transp. engring. Cornell U., 1969-75, assoc. prof., 1975-78, prof., 1978—, acting chmn. dept., 1977-78, chmn. dept., 1980-85, dir. Sch. Civil and Environ. Engring., 1988-98, chmn. bd. Univ. Transp. Rsch. Ctr., 1992-95; dir. Transp. Infrastructure Rsch. Consortium, 1995—. Vis. mem. faculties U. Calif., Irvine, Tech. U. Munich, Germany, (Fulbright lectr.) U. Sao Paulo, Brazil, 1984, Tech. U. Brunswick, W. Ger., 1985-86; Humboldt Found. research fellow, 1978-79; prin. investigator projects Dept. Transp., NSF, Nat. Coop. Hwy. Research Program, N.Y. State Dept. Transp., U.S. Dept. Transp. Author: (with others) Urban Transportation Modeling and Planning, 1975, Transportation Systems Evaluation, 1976, Survey Sampling and Multivariate Analysis for Social Scientists and Engineers, 1979, Survey Methods for

Transport Planning, 1995; co-editor: (with others) Behavioral Travel-Demand Models, 1976, New Horizons in Travel-Behavior Research, 1981, Selected Readings in Transport Survey Methodology, 1992; contbr. articles to profl. jours., chpts. to books. NSF Research Initiation grantee, 1973; recipient Humboldt U.S. Sr. Scientist award, 1984, Fulbright sr. lectr. award, 1984. Mem. ASCE, AAUP, Transp. Rsch. Bd., Transp. Rsch. Forum, Sigma Xi, Chi Epsilon. Office: Cornell U 220 Hollister Hall Ithaca NY 14853-3501 Office Phone: 607-255-7519. E-mail: ahm2@cornell.edu.

MEYER, ALBERT JAMES, educational researcher; b. Cleve., Sept. 24, 1929; s. Jacob Conrad and Esther Agnes (Steiner) M.; m. Mary Ellen Yoder, Aug. 21, 1954; children: Richard, Anne, Kathryn, Barbara, Elaine. BA, Goshen Coll., 1950; MA, Princeton U., 1952, PhD, 1954. Asst. in teaching and rsch. Princeton (N.J.) U., 1950-53; fellow U. Basel, Switzerland, 1953-54, rsch. assoc., 1956-57; dir. for France, rep. European peace sect. Mennonite Ctrl. Com., 1954-57; asst. prof. physics Goshen (Ind.) Coll., 1958-61, prof., rsch. prof., 1967-89, adj. rsch. prof., 1989—; acad. dean, prof. Bethel Coll., North Newton, Kans., 1961-66, Menno Simons lectr., 1993; exec. sec., pres. Mennonite Bd. Edn., Elkhart, Ind., 1967-95; vis. fellow Princeton (N.J.) U., 1995-96. Exec. for secretariat Puidoux Theol. Confs., 1955-57; former mem. staff Mennonite Student Svcs. Com.; former coord. com. on liberal arts edn. North Ctrl. Assn. Colls. and Secondary Schs.; vis. rsch. scientist U. Paris, 1974-75; vis. rschr. New Coll. Berkeley, 1986-87; presenter in field; former cons. Conrad Grebel Coll., U. Waterloo, Ont., Can.; mem. peace and social concerns com. Mennonite Ch., 1959-71; former mem. Continuation Com. of Hist. Peace Chs.; mem. interch. rels. staff Mennonite Ch. U.S.A., 1997—; mem secretariat Nat. Assn. Ind. Colls. and Univs. Contbr. articles to profl. jours. Princeton U. exch. fellow and Charles Foster Kent fellow Nat. Coun. for Religion in Higher Edn., 1953-54. Mem.: Soc. for Values in Higher Edn., Nat. Assn. Ind. Colls. and Univs. (secretariat), Am. Assn. Physics Tchrs., Denominational Execs. for Ch.-Related Higher Edn. (chmn. 1984—86). Avocations: tennis, hiking. Home: 708 Emerson St Goshen IN 46526-3904

MEYER, ALICE VIRGINIA, state official; b. NYC, Mar. 15, 1921; d. Martin G. and Marguerite Helene (Houzē) Kliemand; m. Theodore Harry Meyer, June 28, 1947; children: Robert Charles, John Edward. BA, Barnard Coll., 1941; MA, Columbia U., 1942; D of Humanitarian Svcs. (hon.), Briarwood Coll., 2006. Tchr. pub. schs., Elmont, N.Y., 1942-43; tchr. Fairlawn (N.J.) High Sch., 1943-47; office mgr., sales rep. NYC, 1948-55; substitute tchr. Pub. Schs., Easton, Conn., 1965-72; state rep., asst. minority leader Conn. State Legislature, Hartford, 1976-93. Mem. Ct. Bd. of Govs. Higher Edn., 1993-05, vice-chair, chair. bd. govs. higher edn.; bd. dirs. 3030 Fairfield Health Ctr., 1994-06. Mem. Edn. Commn. of the States, 1985—87; life trustee Discovery Mus., 1980—; trustee United Way Regional Youth Substance Abuse Project, Bridgeport, 1983—93; mem. strategic planning com. Town of Easton, 1993—96; vice chmn. ct. adv. coun. on intergovtl. rels., 1988—; mem. Conn. Commn. on Quality Edn., 1992—93; supporter Conn. Small Towns, 1988; mem. Conn. Humanities Coun., 1974—76, Conn. Film Commn., 1985—88; co-chair Com. on State Plan of Conservation and Devel., 1985—87; mem. Lt. Gov.'s Commn. on Mandate Reduction, 1995; sec. Easton Free Sch. Scholarship Fund, 1980—; pres. Barnard Class of 1941, 1996—; justice of the peace, 2001—; ct. adv. coun. career and vocat. edn., 1980—88; mem. Easton Rep. Town Com., 1965—, vice chmn., 1970—78; bd. dirs. 3030 Park, 1993—2006; Fairfield County Lit. Coalition Bridgeport, 1988—94. Named Legislator of Yr. Conn. Libr. Assn., 1985; Guardian Small Bus. grantee Nat. Fedn. Ind. Bus., 1987; honoree Fairfield YWCA Salute to Women, 1988, Conn. Assn. Small Towns, 1990; named grant to AAUW Fellowship Fund, Bridgeport Br., 1970, Conn. State AAUW, 1974; recipient Conn. Friends of Libr. Hon. award, 1984, Disting. Svc. award Conn. State Coun. on Voc/Tech. Edn., 1986, Sacred Heart U. Ctr. for Policy Issues award, 1988, citation Conn. Bd. for Acad. Affairs, 1992, citation Charter Oak Coll., 1993, Spl. Day Recognition, Town of Weston, 1993, Cert. of Recognition, Town of Westport, 1993, Citation for Fostering Open Access to Higher Edn., AAUW, 1994, Disting. Rep. award Easton Rep. Town Com., 2000, Pub. Svc. award Conn. Sec. of State, 2003, others; named in her honor Alice U. Meyer Day, Conn., 2005; scholarship named in her honor, 2006. Mem.: LWV, AAUW (local pres. 1976, bd. dirs. 1982), Nat. Order Women Legislators (regional dir. 1987—91, past pres. Conn. chpt.), Conn. Assn. Sch. Adminstrs. (hon.), Bus. and Profl. Women. Congregationalist. Avocations: swimming, sailing, bridge. Home: 18 Lantern Hill Rd Easton CT 06612-2218

MEYER, ANDREAS S., architect, consultant; s. Peter Meyer and Luise Schutzmeister-Meyer; m. Renee LeVerrier, 1999; 1 child, Luis pedro. BS in Elec. Engring., U. Ill., Champaign, 1981; MS, U. Mass., Amherst, 1984—86. Chief tech. officer Zaiq Tech., Woburn, Mass., 1996—2002; verification arch. Cadence Design Sys., Inc, Chelmsford, Mass., 2002—04; chief tech. officer Assertive Design, Inc., Boston, 2004—. Verification cons. Ind. Cons., Newburyport, Mass., 1994—. Author: (technical book) Principles of Functional Verification, 2004, Newness, 2004. Parent-child mediator Cmty. Diversion Project, Greenland, NH, 2000—06. Achievements include patents pending for automated assertion technology. Home Phone: 603-674-3631; Office Phone: 603-674-3631. Office Fax: 760-683-2250. Personal E-mail: andreas.meyer@ameyer.org.

MEYER, ANDREW C., JR., lawyer; b. NYC, June 28, 1949; s. Andrew and Myra Meyer; m. Kathleen A. Sullivan, May 7, 1982; children— Joshua Andrew, Daniel Gregory, Jessica Kathleen. BS, C.W. Post Coll., 1971; JD, Suffolk U., 1974, hon. LLD. Bar: Mass. 1974, US Dist. Ct. Mass. 1974, US Ct. Appeals (1st cir.) 1974. Ptnr. Lubin & Meyer, P.C., Boston, 1974—. Contbr. articles to law jours. Mem. nat. adv. bd., Nat. Ctr. for Patients' Rights. Named one of Boston's Top Lawyers, Boston Mag., Top Ten Lawyers, Mass. Lawyers Weekly. Mem. Mass. Bar Assn. (mem. action subcom. Patients' Rights, chmn. trial practice com. 1983-84, award 1984, seminar speaker, 21st Century Club award 1984, Continuing Legal Edn. Faculty award 1984), Mass. Acad. Trial Attys. (mem. bd. gov.), Boston Bar Assn. Office: Lubin & Meyer PC 100 City Hall Plz Ste 4 Boston MA 02108 Office Fax: 617-720-1229. Business E-Mail: acmj@lubinandmeyer.com.

MEYER, AUGUST CHRISTOPHER, JR., broadcast executive, lawyer; b. Champaign, Ill., Aug. 14, 1937; s. August C. and Clara (Rocke) M.; m. Karen Haugh Hassett, Dec. 28, 1960; children: August Christopher F., Elisabeth Hassett. BA cum laude, Harvard U., Cambridge, Mass., 1959, LLB, 1962. Bar: Ill. 1962. Founding ptr. Meyer-Capel, Champaign, Ill., 1962-77, of counsel, 1977—2003; owner, dir., officer Midwest TV, Inc., Sta. KFMB-TV-AM-FM, San Diego, Sta. WCIA-TV, Champaign, Ill., Sta. WMBD-TV-AM, WMXP, Peoria, Ill., 1968—, pres., 1976—. Bd. dirs. BankIll., Main St. Trust Inc.; spl. asst. atty. gen. State of Ill., 1968-76. Chmn. bd. trustees Carle Found. Hosp., Urbana, Ill. Mem. Ill. Bar Assn., Champaign County Bar Assn. Clubs: Champaign Country. Office: Midwest TV Inc PO Box 197 100 W University Ave # 401 Champaign IL 61824-0197 also: Sta KFMB PO Box 85888 7677 Engineer Rd San Diego CA 92111-1515

MEYER, B. FRED, small business executive, builder, home and product designer; b. LI, NY, Jan. 6, 1918; s. Barthold Fred and Edna May (Clark) M.; m. Mary E. Carman, July 18, 1951; children: Patricia Meyer Sauer, Susan Meyer Sachs. Student, Pratt Inst., 1935-39, Johns Hopkins U., 1946-48, Wayne State U., 1954-55. Registered builder, Fla. Project engr. Lear, Inc., Grand Rapids, Mich., 1948-51; engring. exec. GM Corp., Warren, Mich., 1951-75; pres. BFM Assocs., Inc. (name Fred Meyer, Inc. 1990), Sarasota, Fla., 1975—. Capt. USAAF, 1942-46, ETO. Achievements include 23 patents including pendulum type seat belt retractor, automotive power window switches, automotive power window activator. Avocations: golf, computers, travel. Home and Office: 4753 Antler Trail Sarasota FL 34238 Home Phone: 941-586-4131; Office Phone: 941-925-1707. Personal E-mail: bfredm@hotmail.com.

MEYER, BARRY MICHAEL, motion picture executive; b. NYC, Nov. 28, 1943; s. Perry and Lillian Helen (Katz) M.; m. Barbara Patricia, June 12, 1966; children: Matthew, Elizabeth. BA, U. Rochester, 1964; JD, Case Western Res. U., 1967. Bar: NY, Ohio. Legal counsel ABC, NYC, 1968-70, dir. bus. affairs LA, 1970-71, Warner Bros. TV, LA, 1971—72, v.p. bus. affairs, 1972—78, exec. v.p., 1978—84, Warner Bros. Entertainment, Inc., LA, 1984—94, exec. v.p., COO, 1994—99, chmn., CEO, 1999—. Mem. bd. councilors USC Sch. Cinema-TV; bd. dirs. Motion Picture Assn. Am., Mus. Radio and TV, Am. Film Inst. Contbr. articles to profl. jours. Bd. dirs. Human Rights Watch, San Fernando Valley Child Guidance Clinic, Calif.; bd. trustees U. Rochester. Named one of 50 Most Powerful People in Hollywood, Premiere mag., 2004—06. Mem. Hollywood Radio and TV Soc., Nat. Acad. TV Arts and Scis. (former gov.), Am. Mgmt. Assn., Acad. Motion Pictures Arts & Scis. Office: Warner Bros Entertainment Inc 4000 Warner Blvd Burbank CA 91522-0002 Office Phone: 818-954-1464.

MEYER, BRECKIN, actor; b. Mpls., May 7, 1974; m. Dorothy Kaplan, Oct. 14, 2001; 1 child, Caitlin Willow. Actor: (films) Freddy's Dead: The Final Nightmare, 1991, Payback, 1995, Clueless, 1995, The Craft, 1996, Escape from L.A., 1996, Prefontaine, 1997, Touch, 1997, Dancer, Texas Pop. 81, 1998, 54, 1998, Go, 1999, The Insider, 1999, Tail Lights Fade, 1999, Road Trip, 2000, Rat Race, 2001, Kate & Leopold, 2001, (voice) Pinocchio, 2002, Garfield: The Movie, 2004, Blast, 2004, Herbie: Fully Loaded, 2005, Rebound, 2005, Garfield: A Tale of Two Kitties, 2006; (TV films) Camp Cucamonga, 1990, Betrayed: A Story of Three Women, 1995, Rock Times, 2000; (TV series) Child's Play, 1982, Potato Head Kids, 1985, The Jackie Thomas Show, 1992, The Home Court, 1995, (voice) King of the Hill, 2000—, The Near Future, 2000, Inside Schwartz, 2001, Married to the Kellys, 2003, Robert Chicken, 2005—06. Office: c/o the Gersh Agy PO Box 5617 Beverly Hills CA 90210

MEYER, BRUCE D., lawyer; b. Aug. 31, 1945; BA, U. Ill., 1967, JD with high honors, 1970. Bar: Calif. 1971. Assoc. Gibson Dunn & Crutcher, LA, 1970—73, ptnr., 1979—81, Riyadh, Saudi Arabia, 1981—83, ptnr. corp. transactions and securities LA, 1983—; v.p., asst. gen. counsel Whittaker Corp., LA, 1973—79. Mem. exec. com. Gibson Dunn & Crutcher. Mem.: ABA (chmn. Middle East law com., internat. law section 1984—85), LA County Bar Assn., Order of Coif. Office: Gibson Dunn & Crutcher LLP 333 Grand Ave Los Angeles CA 90071-3197 Office Phone: 213-229-7979. Office Fax: 213-229-6979. Business E-Mail: bmeyer@gibsondunn.com.

MEYER, BRUD RICHARD, retired pharmaceutical executive; b. Waukegan, Ill., Feb. 22, 1926; s. Charles Lewis and Mamie Olive (Broom) M.; m. Betty Louise Stine (dec. 1970); children: Linda (Mrs. Gary Stillabower), Louise (Mrs. Donald Knochel), Janet (Mrs. Gerald Cockrell), Jeff, Karen, Blake, Amy; m. Barbara Ann Hamilton, Nov. 26, 1970. BS, Purdue U., 1949. With Eli Lilly & Co., Indpls., 1949-87, indsl. engr., 1949-56, supr. indsl. engr., 1956-59, sr. personnel rep., 1960-64, personnel mgr. Lafayette, Ind., 1964-67, asst. dir., 1967-69, dir. adminstrn., 1969-79, dir. personnel and public relations, 1980-87, ret., 1987. Bd. dirs. Lafayette Home Hosp., 1977—, Hanna Cmty. Ctr., 1983—, Tippecanoe Hist. Corp., 1985—; bd. dirs. United Way Tippecanoe County, 1970-76, pres., 1974; bd. dirs. Legal Aid Soc. Tippecanoe County, 1973—, Jr. Achievement, pres., 1979; bd. dirs. Lilly Credit Union, 1969-75, pres., 1973-74; mem. Citizen's Com. on Alcoholism, 1966-72; bd. dirs. Greater Lafayette Cmty. Ctrs., 1975-79, pres., 1977-78; bd. dirs. Tippecanoe County Child Care, 1990—, pres., 1998-99; mng. dir. Battle Tippecanoe Outdoor Drama Bd. With USAAF, 1943-45. Mem. Pi Tau Sigma, Lambda Chi Alpha, C. of C. Greater Lafayette (bd. dirs., v.p. 1969-73), Battleground Hist. Soc. Methodist. Home: 4217 Trees Hill Dr Lafayette IN 47909-3451 Office: Eli Lilly & Co PO Box 7685 Lafayette IN 47903-7685

MEYER, CAROL FRANCES, retired pediatrician, allergist; b. Berea, Ky., June 2, 1936; d. Harvey Kessler and Jessie Irene (Hamm) Meyer; m. Daniel Baker Cox, June 5, 1955 (div. Apr. 1962). AA, U. Fla., 1955; BA, Duke U., 1957; MD, Med. Coll. Ga., 1967. Diplomate Am. Bd. Pediatrics, Am. Bd. Allergy and Immunology. Intern in pediat. Med. Coll. Ga., Augusta, 1967-68; resident in pediat. Gorgas Hosp., Canal Zone, 1968-69; fellow in pediat. respiratory disease Med. Coll. Ga., 1969-71, instr. pediat., 1971-72; med. officer pediat. Canal Zone Govt., 1972-79, Dept. of Army, Panama, 1979-82, med. officer allergy, 1982-89, physician in charge allergy clinic, 1984-89; asst. prof. pediat. and medicine Med. Coll. Ga., Augusta, 1990-2000, med. dir. Telemedicine Ctr., 2000-01; ret. Mem. Bd. Canal Zone Merit Sys. Examiners, 1976—79. Contbr. articles to profl. jours. Founding mem., violoncello Curundu Chamber Ensemble, 1979—89; mem. First Bapt. Ch. Orch., 1992—2000. Recipient Exceptional Performance award, US Army, 1985, 1986, 1989, Merck award, Med. Coll. Ga., 1967; J. Hillis Miller scholar, U. Fla., 1954. Mem.: Am. Lung Assn. (Ga. East Ctrl. br. exec. bd. 1990—98), Ga. Ornithol. Soc., Panama Canal Soc. Fla., Am. Acad. Pediat., Am. Acad. Allergy, Asthma and Immunology, Am. Coll. Allergy, Asthma and Immunology, Allergy and Immunology Soc. Ga., Am. Coll. Rheumatology, Altrusa Internat. (co-chair, chair internat. comm. 2003—05, chair Altrusa House fund raiser 2005, chair silent auction 2006, 2006, trustee Altrusa House 2004—), Am. Assn. Ret. Persons, Hawks Nest Village Assn. (1st v.p. 2000—01), Audubon Soc., Nat. Assn. Ret. Fed. Employees, Nature Conservancy, Royal Soc. for Preservation Birds, Willow Run Homeowner's Assn. (pres. 1994—99), Alpha Omega Alpha.

MEYER, CATHERINE DIEFFENBACH, lawyer; b. Seattle, Mar. 27, 1951; d. Patrick Andrew and Hope Dieffenbach; m. Michael E. Meyer, Nov. 21, 1982; children. AB, Bryn Mawr Coll., 1973; JD, Northwestern U., 1979. Bar: Calif. 1979, U.S. Dist. Ct. (cen. dist.) Calif., 1979, U.S. Ct. Appeals (9th cir.) 1982, U.S. Dist. Ct. (ea., no. and so. dists.) Calif. 1987. Assoc. Lillick, McHose & Charles, LA, 1979-85, ptnr., 1985-88, Lillick & McHose, LA, 1988-90, Pillsbury Madison & Sutro, LA, 1990—2001, Pillsbury Winthrop LLP, LA, 2001—05; past co-chmn. Privacy & Data Protection practice, co-chmn. LA Bus. dept. Pillsbury Winthrop Shaw Pittman LLP, LA, 2005—, counsel, 2005—. Bd. dirs. House Ear Inst. Mem.: ABA (past co-chmn. Extraterritorial Application of Law subcommittee), LA County Bar Assn. Office: Pillsbury Winthrop Shaw Pittman Suite 2800 725 S Figueroa St Los Angeles CA 90017 Office Phone: 213-488-7362. Office Fax: 213-629-1033. Business E-Mail: catherine.meyer@pillsburylaw.com.

MEYER, CHRISTOPHER HAWKINS, lawyer; b. Springfield, Mo., Sept. 29, 1952; s. Richard DeWitt and Nancy (Hawkins) M.; m. Karen Anne Adams, Aug. 8, 1987; 1 child, C. Andrew Meyer. BA in Econs. magna cum laude, U. Mich., 1977, JD cum laude, 1981. Bar: D.C. 1981, U.S. Ct. Appeals (D.C. cir.) 1982, U.S. Ct. Appeals (9th cir.) 1983, Colo. 1985, U.S. Ct. Appeals (10th cir.) 1985, Idaho, U.S. Ct. Appeals (8th cir.). Counsel water resources program Nat. Wildlife Fedn., Washington, 1981-84; assoc. prof. U. Colo. Law Sch., Colo., 1984-91; ptnr. Givens Pursley, Boise, 1991—. Counsel Rocky Mountain Natural Resources Clinic, Boulder, Colo., 1984—91. Contbr. articles to profl. publs. Mem. steering com. Idaho Environ. Forum. Named one of Best Lawyers in Am., Chambers USA. Mem. Phi Beta Kappa. Home: 3443 S Millspur Way Boise ID 83716-8648 Office: Givens Pursley LLP 601 W Bannock St Boise ID 83702-7720 Home Phone: 208-336-2485; Office Phone: 208-388-1236. Business E-Mail: chrismeyer@givenspursley.com.

MEYER, SIR CHRISTOPHER J.R., former ambassador; b. Beaconsfield, Eng., Feb. 22, 1944; m. Catherine Laylle; 2 sons, 2 stepsons. Student, Lancing Coll., Eng., Peterhouse, Cambridge, Eng., Paul Nitze Sch., Bologna, Italy; MA in History, Cambridge U., 1965. Joined Diplomatic Svc., London, 1966-68, with Moscow, 1968-70, Madrid, 1970-73; head Soviet sect. East European and Soviet dept. Fgn. and Commonwealth Office, London, 1973-76; speech-writer to fgn. sec. policy planning staff Diplomatic Svc., London, 1976-78; mem. UK rep. to European Comtys., Brussels, 1978-82; polit. counselor British Embassy, Moscow, 1982-84; fgn. office spokesman, press sec. to fgn. sec. Fgn. and Commonwealth Office, London, 1984-88, min. Washington, 1989-92; min., dep. head mission British Embassy, 1992—93, govt. spokesman, press sec. to prime min. London, 1994—96, Brit. amb. to Fed. Rep. Germany, 1997; UK amb. to U.S. Washington, 1997—2003; chmn. U.K. Press Complaints Commn., 2003—. Vis. fellow Harvard U. Ctr. for Internat. Affairs, 1988-89; hon. fellow Peterhouse, Cambridge U., 2001—; chmn. Ambo Consultancy Ltd.; non-exec. dir. GKN plc. Named Knight Comdr. of the Order of St. Michael and St. George, 1998. Avocations: tennis, watching soccer, listening to jazz music. Office: Press Complaints Commn 20/23 Holborn London EC1N 2JD England Office Phone: 44 207 438 1242. Office Fax: 011 44 207 831 0070.

MEYER, CHRISTOPHER RICHARD, lawyer; b. Springfield, Ohio, June 18, 1952; s. Eugene Francis and Marilyn Crawford (Hopping) M.; m. Sharman Elizabeth, Sept. 8, 1973; children: Elizabeth Ann, Emily McClure, Timothy Joseph. BA summa cum laude, Ohio State U., 1974, JD, 1977. Bar: Ohio, US Dist. Ct. (so. and no. dists.) Ohio, US Ct. Appeals (6th cir.), US Supreme Ct. Ptnr. Reese, Pyle, Drake & Meyer, Newark, Ohio, 1977—. Legal counsel Licking Meml. Hosp., Newark Ohio, 1983—, State Farm Ins. Co., Bloomington, Ill., 1977—, spl. coun. Ctrl. Ohio Tech. Coll. Mem. Ohio State Bar Assn. (negligence com., litigation sect.), Ohio Assn. Civil Trial Attys., Soc. Ohio Hosp. Attys., Phi Beta Kappa. Home: 976 Briarhill Dr Newark OH 43055-2249 Office: Reese Pyle Drake & Meyer 36 N 2d St PO Box 919 Newark OH 43058-0919 E-mail: cmeyer@rpdm.com.

MEYER, DANIEL KRAMER, real estate executive; b. Denver, July 15, 1957; s. Milton Edward and Mary (Kramer) M. Student, Met. State Coll., Denver, 1977-78, U. Colo., 1978-80. Ptnr., developer RM & M II (Ltd. Partnership), Englewood, Colo., 1981-87; pres. Centennial Mortgage and Investment, Ltd., Englewood, Colo., 1984-87; prin. Capriole Properties, Greenwood Village, Colo., 1983—. Mng. dir. Heritage Capital Group, 2005—06; prin. Courbette Capital, LLC, 2006—. Alumni mem. bd. trustees Kent Denver Country Day Sch., 1981-83; sec. dist. 37 ctrl. and vacancy com. Colo. Ho. of Reps., 1991-92. Recipient Pamela Davis Beardsley devel. award Kent Denver Sch., 1995. Mem.: Chartered Realty Investor Soc., Greenwood Athletic Club. Republican. Avocations: mountain climbing, rollerblading. Personal E-mail: danielkmeyer@msn.com.

MEYER, DEBORA LYNN, music educator; d. Ronald James and Lorraine Gott; m. Marcus Joseph Meyer, Dec. 20, 1986. BA in K-12 vocal music edn. and vocal performance, Carthage Coll., Kenosha, Wis., 1976; MME in Music Edn., Holy Names Coll., Oakland, Calif., 1990. Cert. Kodaly Orgn. of Am. Kodaly Educators. Pvt. music instr. voice, piano, organ, and guitar, Kenosha and Milwaukee Counties, Wis., 1969—87; profl. vocalist Kenosha, Racine, Milw., Waukesha and Winnebago counties, Wis., 1970—; vocal music specialist K-8, dir. of music St. George Sch. and Ch., Kenosha, Wis., 1976—82; vocal music specialist K-8 St. Stephen Sch., Milw., 1982—87; vocal music specialist K-6, choral dir. Banting Sch. Sch. Dist. Waukesha, Wis., 1987—; clinician music listening, singing sci., children's choral pedagogy Orgn. of Am. Kodaly Educators, Wis. Choral Dirs., Wis. Sci. Tchrs., 1990—. Music mentor acad. decathlon - music mentor Waukesha West H.S., 2001—. Bldg. chairperson campaign United Way of Waukesha County, 2001—05. Recipient Kohl Tchr. Fellowship award, Sen. Herb Kohl, 1998. Mem.: NEA (assoc.), Am. Orff-Schulwerk Assn. (assoc.), Midwest Kodaly Music Educators Assn. (assoc.), Orgn. Am. Kodaly Educators (assoc.; regional rep. mid-west 1 1993—95), Wis. Choral Dirs. Assn. (assoc.; state chair Singing in Wis. and Children's Conv. Choir 1991—94, state chair Conv. Children's Honor Choir 1991—94, rep. Southeastern dist. 1992—94), Am. Choral Dirs. Assn. (assoc.), Nat. Assn. Tchrs. of Singing (assoc.), Wis. Music Educators Assn. (assoc.), Edn. Assn. of Waukesha (assoc.; bldg. union rep. 2000—, NEA del. to nat. assembly in New Orleans 2003), Music Educators Nat. Conf. (assoc.), Sigma Alpha Iota (assoc.). Office: Banting Elem Sch 2019 Butler Dr Waukesha WI 53186-2634 Home Phone: 262-652-8939; Office Phone: 262-970-1250. Personal E-mail: musicmeyer@wi.rr.com. E-mail: dmeyer@waukesha.k12.wi.us.

MEYER, DEBORAH WAHL, automotive executive; b. Detroit, 1962; married; 1 child. BA in Econs., Wellesley Coll., 1986; MBA, U. Pa.; MS in Internat. Studies, Joseph H. Lauder Inst. Mgmt. Internat. Studies, 2005. With Chase Manhattan Bank, NY, Ford Motor Co.; product mgr. W.L. Gore and Assocs.; group mgr. brand strategy and comm. Mazda N.Am. Ops.; corp. mktg. mgr. Toyota Motor Sales, USA, 2001—05, v.p. mktg. Lexus Divsn., 2005—07; v.p., chief mktg. officer Chrysler LLC, Auburn Hills, Mich., 2007—. Mem. hall of achievement com. Am. Advt. Fedn.; bd. dirs. Assn. Nat. Advertisers. Trustee Long Beach Mus. Art, 2005—. Named one of 100 Leading Women in N.Am. Automotive Industry, Automotive News, 2005; named to Hall of Advt. Achievement, Am. Advt. Fedn. Office: Chrysler LLC 1000 Chrysler Dr Auburn Hills MI 48326 *

MEYER, DENNIS IRWIN, lawyer; b. Dayton, Ohio, Oct. 20, 1935; s. Luther Edward and Mary (McGee) M.; m. Rita Murray, June 23, 1962; children: Matthew, Michael, Rita Catherine, Peter, Denise, Abigail. BS, U. Dayton, 1957; LLB, Georgetown U., 1960, LLM, 1962. Bar: Ohio 1960, D.C. 1962. Atty.-advisor U.S. Tax Ct., Washington, 1960—62; sr. counsel Baker & McKenzie, Washington, 1965—. Bd. dirs. United Fin. Banking Cos., Vienna, Va. Mem. ABA, Internat. Fiscal Assn., Met. Club, Belle Haven Country Club, Avenel Golf Club, Robert Trent Jones Golf Club. Roman Catholic. Office: Baker & McKenzie 815 Connecticut Ave NW Washington DC 20006-4004 Home Phone: 703-768-3482; Office Phone: 202-452-7008. Business E-Mail: dennis.i.meyer@bakernet.com.

MEYER, DONALD ROBERT, state agency administrator, lawyer; b. Phoenix, June 4, 1942; s. Donald and Eleanor M.; m. Virginia Whitesel, Sept. 3, 1966; 2 children. BA, U. Calif., Berkeley, 1964, JD, 1967; postgrad., Harvard U., 1968. Bar: Calif. 1972, U.S. Peace Corps. Lectr. Seoul Nat. Univ., Korea, 1969-70; assoc. Graham & James, San Francisco, 1971-76; asst. sec. Calif. First Bank (name now Union Bank), San Francisco, 1973-76, v.p., 1976-78, gen. counsel, 1976-96, sr. v.p., 1978-96; corp. sec., exec. v.p. gen. counsel UnionBanCal Corp., 1996—98; commr. Fin. Institutions, Calif., 2000—. Contbr.: Intro to the Law & Legal System of Korea, 1983. Mem. Habitat for Humanity Internat., Sierra Club; co-chmn. San Francisco/Seoul Sister City Com., 1980-90; trustee Asian Art Found. of San Francisco, 1985-92, 97—; commr. Asian Art Mus., San Francisco, 1985-91. Recipient Key to Seoul, Korea, 1984. Mem. ABA, San Francisco Bar Assn., Am. Bankers Assn. (v.p. Calif. State 1982-83), Calif. Bankers Assn. (chmn. legal affairs com. 1982-84, svc. award 1989), Korean-Am. C. of C. (dir. San Francisco sec., bd. dirs. 1974-93, pres. 1996-98, chmn. 1998-2002), Soc. Calif. Pioneers, Bohemian Club. Republican. Episcopalian. Personal E-mail: dmeyerberk@cs.com. Business E-Mail: dmeyer@dgi.ca.gov.

MEYER, EDMOND GERALD, energy scientist, retired chemistry professor, academic administrator, entrepreneur; b. Albuquerque, Nov. 2, 1919; s. Leopold and Beatrice (Ilfeld) M.; m. Betty F. Knobloch, July 4, 1941; children: Lee Gordon, Terry Gene, David Gary. BS in Chemistry,

Carnegie Mellon U., 1940, MS, 1942; PhD, U. N.Mex., 1950. Chemist Harbison Walker Refractories Co., 1940-41; instr. Carnegie Mellon U., 1941-42; asst. phys. chemist Bur. Mines, 1942-44; chemist research div. N.Mex. Inst. Mining and Tech., 1946-48; head dept. sci. U. Albuquerque, 1950-52; head dept. chemistry N.Mex. Highlands U., 1952-59; dir. Inst. Sci. Rsch., dean Grad. Sch. U. Wyo., 1957—63, dean Coll. Arts and Sci., 1963-75, v.p. rsch., 1974-80, prof. energy and natural resources, 1981-89, prof. and dean emeritus, 1989—. Exec. cons. Diamond Shamrock Corp., 1980; sci. adviser Gov. of Wyo., 1964-90; pres. Coal Tech. Corp., 1981—; cons. Los Alamos Nat. Lab., NFS, HHS, GAO, TVA, Wyo. Bancorp; contractor investigator Rsch. Corp., Dept. Interior, AEC, NIH, NSF, Dept. Energy, Dept. Edn.; Fulbright exch. prof. U. Concepcion, Chile, 1959. Co-author: Chemistry-Survey of Principles, 1963, Legal Rights of Chemists and Engineers, 1977, Industrial Research & Development Management, 1982; contbr. articles to profl. jours.; patentee in field. Mem. Laramie Regional Airport Bd., 1989-93, treas., 1994-97, chair; active Laramie City Coun., 1997-2001, vice mayor, 1998-2001. Lt. comdr. USNR, 1944-46, ret. Recipient Disting. Svc. award Jaycees; rsch. fellow U. N.Mex., 1948-50. Fellow: AAAS, Am. Inst. Chemists (hon.; pres. 1992—93, chmn. 1994—95); mem.: AIChE (sr.), Coun. Coll. Arts and Scis. (pres. 1971, sec.-treas. 1972—75, dir. Washington office 1973), Biophys. Soc., Am. Chem. Soc. (councilor 1962—90, chmn. Wyo. sect. 1997, 2002, nat. vol. svc. award 2006), Assn. Western Univs. (chmn. 1972—74), Laramie C. of C. (pres. 1984), Sigma Xi. Home: 1058 Colina Dr Laramie WY 82072-5015 Office: U Wyo Coll Arts Scis Laramie WY 82073-0966 Office Phone: 307-766-5445. Business E-Mail: egmeyer@uwyo.edu.

MEYER, EDWARD HENRY, retired advertising executive; b. NYC, Jan. 8, 1927; s. I.H. and Mildred (Driesen) M.; m. Sandra Raabin, Apr. 26, 1957; children: Margaret Ann, Anthony Edward. BA with honors in Econ., Cornell U., 1949. With Bloomingdale's div. Federated Dept Stores, 1949-51, Biow Co., 1951-56, Grey Global Group, NYC, 1956—2006, exec. v.p., 1963-68, pres., 1968—2006, chmn., CEO, 1970—2006. Bd. dirs. Ethan Allan Interiors Inc., Harman Internat. Industries, Inc., Jim Pattison Group, Inc. Trustee Solomon R. Guggenheim Mus., NYU Med. Ctr.; bd. mem. Am. Mus. Natural History, Film Soc. of Lincoln Ctr. With USCGR, 1945—47. Mem. Econ. Club (NYC), Univ. Club (NYC), Harmonie Club (NYC), Century Country Club, Atlantic Golf Club.

MEYER, FRANCES MARGARET ANTHONY, educational consultant; b. Stella, Va., Nov. 15, 1947; d. Arthur Abner Jr. and Emmie Adeline (Murray) Anthony; m. Stephen Leroy Meyer, Aug. 2, 1975. BS, Longwood Coll., 1970; MS, Va. Commonwealth U., 1982, PhD, 1996. Cert. tchr. Va. Tchr, health, phys. edn., and dance Fredericksburg City Pub. Schs., Va., 1970—89; coord. AIDS edn. Va. Dept. Edn., Richmond, 1989—90, specialist health edn., 1990—94, specialist comprehensive sch. health program, 1994—2003; ednl. cons. Fredericksburg, Va., 2003—. Mem. rev. bd. Nat. Commn. for Health Edn. and Credentialing, Inc., conf. and profl. devel. rev., 1996-00; mentor Nat. Pub. Health Leadership Inst., 2001. Author, editor: Dance Education, What is it? Why is it important?, 2002; author (with others): Elementary Physical Education: Growing through Movement-A Curriculum Guide, 1982; contbr. articles to profl. jours. Dir. Va. Children's Dance Festival, 1981—96, 1997—99; vol. ARC, Fredericksburg, 1976—84, 1997—2001, Va. affiliate AHA, 1982—93, 1999—2001; mem. ctrl. steering com. Health, Mental Health and Safety in Schs. Nat. Guidelines Project, Am. Acad. Pediat., 2000—02; Va. Affiliate Am. Cancer Soc. Richmond, Va.; mem. Public Health Edn.Coun., Comprehensive Sch. Health Edn. Team, Va. Alliance Adolescents and Sch. Health, 1990—2004; health com. Va. Healthy Pathways Coalition, 2004—; mem. Am. Heart Assn., 2004—; mentor Pub. Health Leadership Inst., 2001; bd. dirs. Va. HIV/AIDS Network ARC, 1997—2001. Recipient gov.'s medal for substance abuse and prevention edn. State of Va., 1997, Alumni Cmty. Svc. award Va. Commonwealth U., 1998, Youth Edn. award for Leadership in the healthy devel. of children Am. Cancer Soc., 2002, Disting. Leadership in Phys. Edn. award Nat. Assn. Sport and Phys. Edn., 2004, Profls. Who Make A Difference award Coll. Edn. and Human Svcs., Longwood U., 2006; Nat. Pub. Health Leadership Inst. fellow, 2000, fellow mentor, 2001; Va. Coordinated Sch. Health Leadership fellow, 2006. Fellow: N.Am. Soc. Health, Phys. Edn., Recreation, Sport and Dance (hon.); mem.: AAPHERD (chmn. divsn. 1970—, chmn. so. dist. applied strategic planning com. 2002—04, pres. so. dist. 2005—06, past v.p., nominating com., strategic planning com., social justice com., bd. govs. 2007—, pres.'s recognition award 1997, svc. award 1997, nat. honor award 1999, svc. award 2007), ASCD, AAUW, NEA, Dance Edn. Orgn. (charter), Va. Assn. for Health, Phys. Edn., Recreation and Dance (various coms. 1970—, health edn. editor Va. Jour. 1994—2003, past pres., Tchr. of Yr. 1983, Va. Honor award 1988, Va. Pioneer award 2003), Va. Alliance for Arts Edn. (adv. bd. 1980—83, 1989—90, 1994—96), Am. Coll. Health Assn. (curriculum and tng. rev. panel 1992—94), Soc. State Dirs. Health, Phys. Edn. and Recreation (legis. affairs com. 1994—98, applied strategic planning com. 1994—2001, pres.-elect 1997, pres. 1998, past pres. 1999, think tank chair 2000—02, Healthis acad. rev. com. 2001—03, applied policy & legis. com. 2002—, Presdl. award 1996, Presdl. Recognition award 1997, 2000, Simon A. McNeely Honor award 2000, Julian B. Smith award 2004), Va. Health Promotion and Edn. Coun. (bd. dirs. 1990—96), Internat. Coun. for Health, Phys. Edn., Recreation, Sport and Dance (internat. commns. for health edn. and commn. for dance and dance edn., jour. articles rev. com.), Va. Mid. Sch. Assn., Va. Edn. Assn., Nat. Mid. Sch. Assn., Nat. Dance Assn. (pres. 2001—03, rep. to AAHPERD bd. govs. 2007—, bd. dirs., presdl. citation 1998, svc. award 1998, 2000, pres.'s merit award 2001, presdl. citation 2007), Nat. Network for Youth Svcs. (adv. bd. 1994—98, rev. panel), Longwood Coll. Alumni Coun. (bd. dirs. 1987—90), Delta Kappa Gamma (pres. Beta Eta chpt. 1988—90). Baptist. Avocations: travel, dance, swimming, reading, theatrical performances.

MEYER, FRED JOSEF, finance company executive; b. Zurich, Switzerland, Jan. 1, 1931; came to U.S., 1959; s. Josef and Claire (Lehmann) M.; m. Beverly Ruth Carter, Apr. 9, 1961 (div. Feb. 1975); children: Fred Jay, Marcus Clinton, Michael Josef; m. Marie-Noelle Vigneron, Oct. 30, 1975. MS, Fed. Inst. Tech., Zurich, 1956; MBA, Harvard U., 1961; LLD (hon.), Sacred Heart U., 1981. V.p. planning & adminstrn. Sandoz, Inc., Hanover, NJ, 1971-73, exec. v.p., chief fin. officer, 1973-78; pres., CEO Sandoz U.S., Inc., Greenwich, Conn., 1978-81; mng. dir., CEO Wander Ltd., Berne, Switzerland, 1981-82; sr. v.p., chief fin. officer CBS, Inc., NYC, 1982-88; chief fin. officer Omnicom Group, Inc., NYC, 1988-98, vice chmn., 1998-99, spl. advisor exec. office, 2000—03. Bd. dirs. Novartis Corp., N.Y.C., Ptnrs. Group USA Inc., NYC Mem. Fin. Execs. Inst., Econ. Club, Harvard Club (N.Y.C.), Greenwich Country Club. Republican. Congregationalist. Office: Omnicom Group Inc 437 Madison Ave New York NY 10022-7001 E-mail: fjmeyer@aol.com.

MEYER, G. CHRISTOPHER, lawyer; b. Fremont, Nebr., Mar. 27, 1948; s. Gerald William and Mildred Ruth (Clauson) M.; children: Kate, Stacy, Jon, Robert. Student, Grinnell Coll., Iowa, 1966—69; BA, U. Kans., 1970; JD, U. Pa. Law Sch., 1973. Bar: Ohio 1973, US Dist. Ct. (no. dist.) Ohio 1975, US Ct. Appeals (6th cir.) 1982. Assoc. Squire, Sanders & Dempsey, L.L.P., Cleve., 1973-82, ptnr., 1982—. Bd. mem. Cleve. Rape Crisis Ctr., past chmn. Named one of Best Lawyers in Am., Ohio Super Lawyers. Mem. ABA, Greater Cleve. Bar Assn., Am. Coll. Bankruptcy. Office: Squire Sanders & Dempsey LLP 4900 Key Tower 127 Public Sq Cleveland OH 44114-1304 Home: 5455 N Marginal Rd Cleveland OH 44114-3951 Office Phone: 216-479-8692. Business E-Mail: cmeyer@ssd.com.

MEYER, GABRIEL R., writer; b. LA, May 29, 1947; adopted s. George Thomas Meyer. Attended, New Eng. Conservatory Music, Boston, 1966—68. Mid. east corr. Nat. Cath. Register, Studio City, Calif., 1986—90, Balkan affairs corr., 1990—94; assoc. editor Twin Cir. Pub., Studio City, 1994—96; sr. writer, contbg. editor Cir. Media, New Haven, 1996—99; exec. dir. Bishop Gassis Sudan Relief Fund, DC, 1999—2003, Windhover Forum, Inc., LA, 2003—05. Author: (books) The Gospel of Joseph, In the Shade of the Terebinth, War and Faith in Sudan. Recipient award for best human interest feature, Cath. Press Assn., 1989, Poetry award, Calif. Writer's Club, 1991, Book of Yr. award, Foreword Mag., 2005; grantee Rsch. grant for writing, Dan Murphy Found., 2006. Mem.: Keats, Shelley, Byron Meml. Assn. (corr.), Ruskin Art Club (hon.; pres. 1998—2007). Personal E-mail: grmncr@aol.com.

MEYER, GEORGE HERBERT, lawyer; b. Detroit, Feb. 19, 1928; s. Herbert M. and Agnes F. (Eaton) Meyer; m. Carol AnnA Jones, 1958 (div. 1981); children: Karen Ann, George Herbert Jr.; m. Katherine Palmer White, Nov. 12, 1988. BA, U. Mich., 1949; JD, Harvard U., 1952; cert., Oxford U., Eng., 1955; LLM in Taxation and Labor Law, Wayne U., 1962. Bar: DC 1952, Mich. 1953. Assoc. firm Fischer, Franklin & Ford, Detroit, 1956-63, mem. firm, 1963-74; established firm George H. Meyer, 1974-78; sr. mem. firm Meyer and Kirk, 1978-85; sr. mem. Meyer, Kirk, Snyder & Safford PLLC, Bloomfield Hills and Detroit, Mich., 1985-99; mng. mem. Meyer, Kirk, Snyder & Lynch PLLC, Bloomfield Hills and Detroit, Mich., 2000—. Curator Step Lively exhibit Mus. Am. Folk Art, NYC, 1992; lectr. Am. Folk Art. Author: Equalization in Michigan and Its Effect on Local Assessments, 1963, Folk Artists Biographical Index, 1986, American Folk Art Canees: Personal Sculpture, 1992. Chmn. Birmingham Bd. Housing Appeals, Mich., 1964—68; vice chmn. Birmingham Bd. Zoning Appeals, 1968—69; mem. Birmingham Planning Bd., 1968—70; trustee Bloomfield Village, Mich., 1976—80, pres., 1979—80; trustee Am. Mus. Folk Art, NYC, 1987—2004; mem. exec. bd. Detroit area coun. Boy Scouts Am., 1976—, counsel, 1986—95; trustee Detroit Sci. Ctr., 1985—99, Assocs. Am. Wing, Detroit Inst. Arts, 2005—. 1st lt. JAG USAF, 1952—55, maj. USAFR. Recipient Silver Beaver award, Detroit area coun. Boy Scouts Am., 1989. Mem.: ABA, Cranbrook Writers Guild (pres. 2002—04), State Bar Mich., Oakland County Bar Assn., Detroit Bar Assn., Am. Folk Art Soc. (pres. 2000—04), Detroit Sci. Mus. Soc. (pres. 1961—74, chmn. 1974—76), Harvard Law Sch. Assn. Mich. (dir. 1959—78, pres. 1970—78), Detroit Athletic Club, Harvard Club NYC, Prismatic Club (pres. 2002—03), Scarab Club, Birmingham Athletic Club, Rotary, Masons, Phi Beta Kappa, Pi Sigma Alpha, Alpha Phi Omega. Republican. Unitarian. Office: Meyer Kirk Snyder & Lynch PLLC 100 W Long Lake Rd Ste 100 Bloomfield Hills MI 48304-2773 Office Phone: 248-647-5111. Business E-Mail: gmeyer@meyerkirk.com.

MEYER, HELEN M., state supreme court justice; BSW, U. Minn.; JD, William Mitchell Coll. Law. Ptnr. Pritzker & Meyer, 1987—96, Meyer and Assocs., 1996—2002; assoc. justice Minn. Supreme Ct., St. Paul, 2002—. Office: Minn Jud Ctr 25 Rev Dr Martin Luther King Jr Blv Saint Paul MN 55155

MEYER, HENRY LEWIS, III, bank executive; b. Cleve., Dec. 25, 1949; s. Henry Lewis and Anne (Taylor) M.; m. Jane Kreamer, July 15, 1978; children: Patrick Harrison, Andrew Taylor, Christopher Bicknell. BA, Colgate U., 1972; MBA, Harvard U., Boston, 1978. Asst. v.p. Soc. Nat. Bank, Cleve., 1972-76, v.p., 1978-81, sr. v.p., 1981-83; exec. v.p. Soc. Bank, Dayton, Ohio, 1983-85, pres., chief operating officer, 1985-87; sr. exec. v.p. Soc. Nat. Bank, Cleve., 1987-89, vice chmn. bd., 1989-90, pres., COO, 1990-93, pres., CEO, 1993-94, chmn. bd., CEO, 1994-95; exec. v.p. Soc. Corp., 1987-91, vice chmn. bd., 1991-94; exec. v.p. KeyCorp, 1994-95, sr. exec. v.p., COO, 1995-96, vice chmn. bd., COO, 1996-97, pres., COO, 1997—2001, chmn., CEO, 2001. Bd. dirs. Continental Airlines, Inc., Fed. Res. Bank Cleve. Trustee Cleve. Mus. Nat. History, Ideastream (WVIZ/PBS and WCPN); with Law Enforcement Found., Northeast Ohio Coun. Higher Edn., United Way Greater Cleve., Univ. Sch.; bd. dirs. U. Hosps. Health Sys., Inc. Mem.: Club at Key Ctr., Chagrin Valley Hunt Club, Pepper Pike Club, The Union Club, Kirtland Country Club. Republican. Episcopalian. *

MEYER, HERMANN BELTON PERRIN, retired neonatologist, health facility administrator, bioethicist; b. Stockton, Calif., Apr. 5, 1935; s. Hermann Perrin and Margaret Anna (Kammerer) Meyer; m. Marion Annette Pinkerton, July 2, 1961; children: Paul Belton, Christopher Charles. AA, Sacramento Jr. Coll., Calif., 1955; BA, U. Calif., Berkeley, 1957; MD, U. Calif., San Francisco, 1960; MS, Ariz. State U., Tempe, 1999, PhD, 2006. Diplomate Am. Bd. Pediat., 1969, perinatal medicine Am. Bd. Pediat., 1975. Rotating internship Highland-Alameda County Hosp., Oakland, Calif., 1960—61; sr. pediat. intern U. Calif. Med. Ctr., San Francisco, 1963—64, pediat. residency, 1964—65; fellowship, NIH Newborn Respiratory Physiology Ctr. for Premature Infants, Stanford U., Palo Alto, Calif., 1965—67; med. dir. newborn transport and intensive care Ariz. State Health Dept., Phoenix, 1967—91; med. dir. nurseries Good Samaritan and Phoenix Children's Hosps., Phoenix, 1967—86, 1990—91; med. dir. Ariz. Health Care Cost Containment Sys., Phoenix, 1992—97, ret., 1997. Mem. cmty. bd. St. Joseph's Hosp. and Med. Ctr., Phoenix, 2002—; trustee Ariz. Perinatal Trust, Phoenix, 1980—; sec., adv. com. Cath. Social Svcs., Phoenix, 2003—06; chmn. bioethics com. Good Samaritan Hosp., 1983—89, Phoenix Children's Hosp.; cons. in field. Contbr. articles to profl. jours. Chmn. premature adv. com. Ariz. Health Dept., 1970—73; chmn. bioethics workgroup Kino Inst. Cath. Diocese, Phoenix, 1980—83. Lt. med. corps. USN, 1961—63, med. officer USN, 1961—62, USS Lenawee, asst. med. officer, med. dept. US Naval Air Reserve Training Sta., 1962—63, Los Alamitos, Calif. Recipient various Lifetime Achievement awards, Dr. William Beaumont Outstanding Contbn. by Physician Under 50 award, AMA, 1978. Mem.: SAR (Ariz. and nat. soc. 2006—), Ariz. Med. Assn. (bd. dirs. 1967—, chmn. govt. svcs. 1983—90, chmn. bioethics 1990—96, A.H. Robins Physician Cmty. Svc. award 1978), Maricopa Med. Soc., Knights Malta (mem. Malta ctr. bd. 1991—98, named Knight Magistral Grace 1991). Democrat. Roman Catholic. Avocations: painting, ceramics, collecting beetles, philosophy, reading. Home: 901 West Monte Vista Rd Phoenix AZ 85007 Personal E-mail: belhpmar@earthlink.net.

MEYER, HORST, physics professor; b. Berlin, Mar. 1, 1926; arrived in US, 1957; BS, U. Geneva, 1949; PhD in physics, U. Zurich, 1953. Fellow Swiss Assn. Rsch. Physics and Math. Studies, Oxford, Eng., 1953-55; Nuffield fellow Clarendon Lab. U. Oxford, 1955-57; lectr., rsch. assoc. dept. engring. and applied physics Harvard U., Cambridge, Mass., 1957-59; from asst. prof. to prof. Duke U., Durham, NC, 1959-84, Fritz London prof. physics, 1984—2004, Fritz London prof. physics emeritus, 2004—. Vis. prof. Technische Hochschule, Federal Republic of Germany, 1965, Tokyo U., 1980, 81, 83; traveling fellow Japanese Soc. for Promotion Sci., 1971, vis. scientist, 1979; guest scientist Inst. Laue-Langevin, France, 1974, 75; Yamada Found. fellow, Japan, 1986; guest scientist USSR Acad. Sci., 1988; guest prof. Toyota Inst. Tech., Nagoya, Japan, Oct. 1998; chmn. Gordon Conf. on Solid H2, 1990; western chmn. conf. quantum crystals, Almaty, Kazakhstan, 1995. Editor Jour. Low Temperature Physics, 1992—, mem. editorial bd., 1988-92; contbr. articles to profl. jours. Alfred P. Sloan fellow, 1961-65. Fellow Am. Phys. Soc. (Jesse Beams prize, 1982, Fritz London prize 1993). Achievements include exptl. rsch. on the properties of liquid and solid helium, critical phenomena in fluids, solid hydrogen and deuterium, magnetic insulators, phase transitions, convection in supercritical helium. Office: Duke U Dept Physics PO Box 90305 Durham NC 27708-0305 Office Phone: 919-660-2520. Business E-Mail: hm@phy.duke.edu.

MEYER, IRWIN STEPHAN, lawyer, accountant; b. Monticello, NY, Nov. 14, 1941; s. Ralph and Janice (Cohen) M.; children: Kimberly B., Joshua A. BS, Rider Coll., 1963; JD, Cornell U., 1966. CPA NJ; bar: NY 1966. Tax mgr. Lybrand Ross Bros. & Montgomery, NYC, 1966—71; mem. Ehrenkranz, Ehrenkranz & Schultz, NYC, 1971—74; prin. Irwin S. Meyer, 1974—77, 1982—97; mem. Levine, Honig, Eisenberg & Meyer, 1977—78, Eisenberg, Honig & Meyer, 1978—81, Eisenberg, Honig, Meyer & Fogler, 1981—82, Janow & Meyer, LLC., 1997—2004; prin. Irwin S. Meyer, LLC, Pearl River, NY, 2004—. With US Army, 1966—71. Mem.: ABA, NY Bar Assn., Am. Assn. Atty.-CPA, NY Assn. Atty.-CPAs, NJ Soc. CPAs. Office: 1 Blue Hill Plz Ste 1006 Pearl River NY 10965-3100 Business E-Mail: irwin@nytaxplanner.com.

MEYER, JACK ALLEN, historian, consultant; b. Sugar Camp, Wis., Nov. 13, 1934; s. John Charles Meyer and Loretta Bertha Basch; m. Martha Elise Robinson, Dec. 18, 1970. BA summa cum laude, U. Md., 1973; MA, U. SC, 1979, PhD, 1984. Enlisted USAF, 1953, advanced through grades to chief master sgt., 1975, ret., 1976; lectr. U. SC, Columbia, 1983—85, vis. asst. prof., 1985—87, sr. lectr., 1987—93; self-employed Tower Armory, Winnsboro, SC, 1993—; commd. SC State Guard, 1993, col., 2001—. Cons. SC State Mus., Columbia, 1979—; presenter in field. Author: South Carolina in the Mexican War, 1996, (monograph) William Glaze & the Palmetto Armory, 1982, 1994; editor: Annotated Bibliography-Napoleonic Era, 1987; contbr. articles to profl. jours. Chmn. Fairfield County Airport Commn., 1976—79, mem., 2006—; bd. mem. Columbia Choral Soc., 1988—90, treas., 1991—92; chmn. Fairfield County Hist. Commn., 1987—89, mem., 1990—94; spl. advisor Laotian Airborne Assn.; trustee Greenbrier United Meth. Ch., 1980—87, 1998—2000, 2002—07, chmn., 2005—06. Decorated Bronze Star, Meritorious Svc. medal, Air Force Commendation medal,; recipient Disting. Faculty award, ROTC, 1992, President's Vol. Svc. award, 2007. Fellow: Internat. Napoleonic Soc.; mem.: SAR, VFW, Royal Soc. St. George, Sumter Guards, SC Soc. SAR (pres. 2001—06), State Guard Assn. US, Internat. Chivalric Inst., Am. Inst. for Conservation and Preservation of Historic and Artistic Works, Orders and Medals Rsch. Soc., Orders and Medals Soc. Am. (Lit. medal 1991), Am. Numismatic Assn., Arms and Armour Soc., SC Arms Collectors Assn., Univ. South Caroliniana Soc., SC State Mus. Found. (founding mem., treas. 1981—83, dir. 1983—88), Fairfield County Hist. Soc. (dir. 1978, pres. 1979—80, dir. 1984—87), Co. Mil. Historians, SC Hist. Soc., Soc. for Army Hist. Rsch., US Parachute Assn., Am. Legion, Soc. for Mil. History, Alpha Sigma Lambda, Phi Kappa Phi, Phi Alpha Theta. Methodist. Avocations: private pilot, skydiving, collecting antiques. Home: Aeolia 1029 Greenbrier/Mossydale Rd Winnsboro SC 29180 Personal E-mail: drjameyer@juno.com.

MEYER, JACK EDWARD, radiologist, educator; b. Davenport, Iowa, Oct. 21, 1939; s. Russell and Ellen Meyer; m. Mary Jean Meyer, Jan. 9, 1966; children: Heather, Hilary. BA, Grinnell Coll., Iowa, 1961; MD, Cornell U., 1965; MS (hon.), Harvard U., 1991. Diplomate Am. Bd. Radiology; lic. physician, Mass., Calif., Mich. Intern San Francisco Gen. Hosp., 1965-66; resident in radiology U. Mich., Ann Arbor, 1968-69, Mass. Gen. Hosp., Boston, 1969-71, asst. radiation medicine, 1971-72, head oncologic diagnostic radiology, 1979-85; chief diagnostic radiology Pondville Hosp., Walpole, Mass., 1972-78, chief radiology, chief staff, 1978-79; prof., chmn. dept. radiology U. Louisville, Ky., 1985-87; acting dir. diagnostic radiology Brigham and Women's Hosp., Boston, 1987-88, dir. diagnostic radiology, 1989-99; dir. breast imaging Dana-Farber Cancer Inst., Boston, 2001—. Asst. prof. radiology Boston U., 1972-74, assoc. clin. prof., 1974-79; asst. prof. U. Mass., Boston, 1976-77, assoc. prof. radiology, 1977-79; asst. prof. radiology Harvard Med. Sch., Boston, 1979-82, assoc. prof. radiology, 1982-85, 87-91, prof. radiology, 1991—; dir. diagnostic oncoradiology Dana-Farber Cancer Inst., Boston, 1991-99; dir. breast imaging, Brigham and Womens Hosp, Boston, 1999—2002. Author: (with others) Interventional Radiology, 1981, Cancer: A Manual for Practitioners, 6th edit., 1982, Lymphatic Imaging, 2d edit., 1985; cons. to editorial bd. jours.; contbr. numerous articles and abstracts to profl. jours. Examiner Am. Bd. Radiology, 1992—. Capt. USAF, 1966-68. Fellow: Soc. Breast Imaging, Am. Coll. Radiology; mem.: Radiol. Soc. N. Am., Mass. Radiol. Soc., Mass. Med. Soc. Office: Brigham and Womens Hosp Dept Diagnostic Radiology 75 Francis St Boston MA 02115-6106 Business E-Mail: jmeyer@partners.org.

MEYER, JAMES SAMPSON, art historian, educator; s. Irving and Charlotte Meyer; life ptnr. Patrick Paul Garlinger. BA, Yale U., New Haven, 1984; MA, NYU, NYC, 1986; PhD, Johns Hopkins U., Balt., 1995. Asst. prof. art history Emory U., Atlanta, 1994—2002, assoc. prof., 2002—06, Winship Disting. assoc. prof., 2006—. Vis. assoc. prof. Northwestern U., Evanston, Ill., 2004; Robert Sterling Clark vis. prof. Williams Coll., Williamstown, Mass., 2006. Author, editor: Minimalism, 2000; author: Minimalism: Art and Costumes, 2001. Mem. Eldredge Prize com. Smithsonian Am. Art Mus., Washington, 2005—06; mem. exhbn. adv. com. Guggenheim Mus., NYC, 2006—. Rsch. grantee, Getty Rsch. Inst., 1999, Rsch. fellow, Obermann Ctr. Art, 2000—01, Clark fellow, Clark Rsch. Inst., 2007. Mem.: Coll. Art Assn. (mem. Mather Prize com. 2004—06). Office: Emory U Art History Dept Atlanta GA 30322

MEYER, JANIS M., lawyer; b. NYC, Apr. 29, 1947; BA, SUNY, Stony Brook, 1969; MA, Ohio State Univ., 1971; JD with distinction, Hofstra Univ., 1981. Bar: N.Y. 1982, US Dist. Ct. (ea. & so. dist. N.Y., no. dist. Ill.), US Ct. Appeals (2d, 7th, 9th cir.). Law clerk, Judge George C. Pratt, US Dist. Ct. ea. N.Y. & US Ct. Appeals, 2d cir.; ptnr. litigation & diversity affairs Dewey Ballantine LLP, NYC, 1995—. Contbr. chapters to books. Bd. trustees Hofstra Univ., 1993—, vice chmn., 1996—99, 2002—. Mem.: ABA (vice chmn. Internat. Litigation com. 1993—94), Assn. Bar City of N.Y. Office: Dewey Ballantine LLP 1301 Ave of the Americas New York NY 10019-6092 Office Phone: 212-259-6030. Office Fax: 212-259-6333. Business E-Mail: jmeyer@dbllp.com.

MEYER, JAROLD ALAN, oil company research executive; b. Phoenix, July 28, 1938; s. Lester M. and Anita (Walker) M.; m. Diane Louise Wheeler; children: Ronald Alan, Sharon Lynne. BSChemE, Calif. Inst. Tech., 1960, MS, 1961. Mgr. process devel. Chevron Rsch., Richmond, Calif., 1978-82; tech. mgr. Chevron U.S.A., El Segundo, Calif., 1982-84; v.p. process rsch. Chevron Rsch., Richmond, 1984-86, pres., 1986—; sr. v.p. Chevron Rsch. and Tech., Richmond, 1990-93; ret., 1993; prin. J.A. Meyer Assocs., Martinez, Calif., 1993—. Bd. dirs. Solvent Refined Coal Internat., Inc., San Francisco; mem. adv. bd. Surface Sci. and Catalysis Program Ctr. for Advanced Materials, Lawrence Berkeley Lab., 1988-91; mem. adv. coun. Lawrence Hall Sci., 1989-94; indsl. advisor Accreditation bd. for Engring. and Tech. Inventor petroleum catalysts; contbr. articles to profl. jours. Bd. visitors U. Calif., Davis, 1986-93, trustee found., 1989—. Mem. Nat. Acad. Engring., Am. Chem. Soc., Nat. Petroleum Refining Assn., Indsl. Rsch. Inst., Conf. Bd. Internat. Rsch. Mgmt. Coun., Accreditation Bd. for Engring. and Tech. Indsl. Advisor, Sigma Xi, Tau Beta Pi. Avocations: electronics design and construction, photography. Home and Office: 849 Corte Briones Martinez CA 94553-5950

MEYER, JOHN FREDERICK, engineering educator; b. Grand Rapids, Mich., July 26, 1934; s. Frederick Albert and Harriet (Stibbs) M.; m. Nancy Shaw Briggs, July 4, 1959; children: John, Patricia, James. BS, U. Mich., 1957; MS, Stanford U., 1958; PhD, U. Mich., 1967. Data systems engr. Douglas Aircraft Corp., Santa Monica, Calif., 1957; research engr. Caltech, Jet Propulsion Lab., Pasadena, Calif., 1958-67; asst. prof. U. Mich., Ann Arbor, 1968-71, assoc. prof., 1971-76, prof. elec. engring. and computer sci., 1976—2002, dir. Computing Research Lab., 1984-89, prof. emeritus elec. engring. and computer sci., 2002—. Cons. Calif. Inst. Tech. Jet

Propulsion Lab., 1979—91, Indsl. Tech. Inst., Ann Arbor, 1985-92, CIMSA, Paris, 1992, Bendix Advanced Tech. Ctr., Columbia, Md., 1977-85, Thomson CSF, Paris, 1975, Italtel, Milan, 1990—99, Applied Scis. Corp., Reading, Mass., 1993, U. Ill., 2002-05. Precinct chmn. 3d ward Democratic Party, Ann Arbor, 1971-74. Recipient Disting. Service Award U. Mich., 1964, Silver Core award IFIP, 1995, Golden Core award 1996; IBM fellow, 1957 Fellow IEEE; mem. AAAS, IEEE Computer Soc. (Cert. of Appreciation 1981, 95, Meritorious Svc. award 1985). Achievements include patents for time division multiplexer; admission control of mixed variable bitrate sources in broadband networks. Home: 1946 Ridge Ave Ann Arbor MI 48104-6306 Office: U Mich 3636 CSE Bldg Ann Arbor MI 48109-2121 Business E-Mail: jfm@umich.edu.

MEYER, JOHN ROBERT, economist, educator; b. Pasco, Wash., Dec. 6, 1927; s. Philip Conrad and Cora (Kempter) M.; m. Lee Stowell, Dec. 17, 1949 (dec.); children: Leslie Karen, Ann Elizabeth, Robert Conrad. Student, Pacific U., 1945-46; BA, U. Wash., 1950; PhD (David A. Wells prize), Harvard U., 1955. Jr. fellow Harvard U., 1953-55, asst. prof., 1955-58, assoc. prof., 1958-59, prof. econs., 1959-68, 1907 Found., prof. transp. and logistics, 1973-83; prof. Yale U., 1968-73; Harpel prof. capital formation and econ. growth Harvard U., 1983-96, prof. emeritus, 1997—. Vice chmn. Union Pacific Corp., 1982-83, dir., 1978-99; trustee Pacific U. Author (with Edwin Kuh): The Investment Decision-An Empirical Inquiry, 1957; author: (with others) Competition in the Transportation Industry, 1959, The Urban Transportation Problem, 1965, Techniques of Transport Planning, 1970, Economics of Competition in the Telecommunications Industry, 1980, Autos, Transit and Cities, 1981, Deregulation and the Future of Intercity Passenger Travel, 1987, Going Private: The International Experience with 'Transport Privatization, 1993, Moving to Market: Restructuring Transport in the Former Soviet Union, 1996, Chile: Political Economy of Urban Development, 2002, other books; contbr. articles. Mem. Presdl. Task Forces on Transp., 1964, 80, Presdl. Commn. on Population Growth and Am. Future, 1970-72; pres. Nat. Bur. Econ. Research, 1967-77. Served with USNR, 1946-48. Recipient Roy W. Crum award, transp. rsch. bd. Nat. Acad. Scis. and Nat. Acad. Engring., 2002; Guggenheim fellow, 1958. Fellow: Econometric Soc., Am. Acad. Arts and Scis.; mem.: Econ. History Assn., Coun. Fgn. Rels., Am. Econ. Assn. (mem. exec. com. 1971—73). Home: 572 Kinzie Island Ct Sanibel FL 33957-5021 Office: Harvard U Jt Ctr Housing Studies 1033 Massachussetts Ave 5th Fl Cambridge MA 02138-5801 Personal E-mail: jrobtmeyer@aol.com.

MEYER, JON KEITH, psychiatrist, psychoanalyst, educator; b. Springfield, Ill., May 6, 1938; m. Eleanor Fumie Yamashita, June 6, 1964; children: David Christopher, Laura Tamiko. AB summa cum laude, Dartmouth Coll., 1960; MD, Johns Hopkins U., 1964; grad., Washington Psychoanalytic Inst, 1980. Intern internal medicine Johns Hopkins Hosp., Balt., 1964-65, resident in psychiatry, 1965-67, 69, St. Elizabeth's Hosp., Washington, 1968; spl. asst. to dir. NIMH, Bethesda, Md., 1969-71; asst. prof. psychiatry Johns Hopkins Med. Sch., Balt., 1971-76, assoc. prof., 1976-83; prof. psychiatry Med. Coll. Wis., Milw., 1983—2003, prof. psychoanalysis, 1996—2003, prof. family medicine, 1990—2003, prof. psychiatry and psychoanalysis emeritus, 2003—; tng. and supervising analyst Chgo. Inst. for Psychoanalysis, 1987—2002; vice chmn. Dept. of Psychiatry, 1993—2003; chief psychiatry Froedtert Meml. Luth. Hosp., Milw., 1994-97; tng. and supervising analyst Wis. Psychoanaltic Inst., Milw., 2001—, Washington Psychoanalytic Inst., 2004—; tchg. analyst Balt.-Washington Psychoanalytic Inst., 2004—; clin. prof. pschiatry Georgetown U. Sch. Medicine, 2006—. Med. dir. Wis., Psychoanalytic Found., Milw., 1987-91, sec. bd. dir., 1988-91; part time assoc. prof. psychiatry Johns Hopkins Med. Sch., 2003-. Author books; editl. bd. Jour. Am. Psychoanalytic Assn., 1991-94; nat. editor: The American Psychoanalyst, 1997-2001; mem. steering com. Psychodynamic Diagnostic Manual; contbr. chpts. to books, numerous articles to profl. jours. Comdr. USPHS, 1967—71. Recipient Dennison Rsch. prize, Johns Hopkins Med. Sch., 1964; Sr. fellow, Dartmouth Coll., 1959—60, Daniel Webster Nat. scholar, 1956—60, Rufus Choate scholar, 1960, Erik Erikson scholar, Austen Riggs Ctr., Stockbridge, Mass., 1991—92, Ctr. Advanced Psychoanalytic Studies, Princeton, NJ, 1998—. Fellow: Am. Coll. Psychoanalysts, Am. Psychiat. Assn.; mem.: Washington Ctr. Psychoanalysis (bd. dirs. 2007—), Wash. Psychoanalytic Soc., Balt.-Wash. Psychoanalytic Soc., William Alanson White Psychoanalytic Soc. (hon.), Can. Psychoanalytic Soc. (hon.), Wis. Psychoanalytic Soc. (pres. 1989—91), Assn. Child Psychoanalysis (candidate councilor 2001—03), Am. Psychoanalytic Assn. (exec. councilor 1993—97, chmn. com. on exec. coun. structure and function 1995—98, sec. 1997—2001, chmn. com. on cmty. clinics 1997—2002, exec. com. 1997—2002, adminstrv. bd. Jour. Am. Psychoanalytic Assn. 1997—2002, com. on insts. 1998—2002, com. on bylaws 2001—02, pres.-elect 2002—04, adminstrv. bd. Jour. Am. Psychoanalytic Assn. 2002—06, exec. com. 2002—06, pres. 2004—06, chmn. exec. com. 2004—06, presiding officer exec. coun. 2004—06, chmn. steering com. 2004—06, exec. councilor 2006—, exploratory subcom. nominating com. 2006—, chair task force on access to care 2007—, Edith Sabshin Tchg. award 1999), Internat. Psychoanalytical Assn. (com. on constn. and by-laws 1997—2001, com. on procedural codes 1997—2001, task force on structure and mission 1997—2001, ho. dels. 1998—2001, chair ho. of dels. 1999—2000). Avocations: photography, hiking, kayaking. Office: 2210 Dalewood Rd Lutherville Timonium MD 21093

MEYER, JOSEPH B., state official; b. Casper, Wyo., 1941; m. Mary Orr; children: Vincent, Warren. Student, Colo. Sch. Mines; BA, U. Wyo., 1964, JD, 1967; postgrad., Northwestern U., 1968. Dep. county atty. Fremont County, Wyo., 1967-69; assoc. Smith and Meyer, 1968-71; asst. dir. legis. svc. office State of Wyo., Cheyenne, 1971-87, atty. gen., 1987-95, sec. state, 1999—2006, state treas., 2007—; spl. asst. to pres. govt. rels. U. Wyo., Laramie, 1995-98. Condr. numerous govt. studies on state codes including Wyo. probate, criminal, state adminstrn., banking, domestic rels.; negotiator with Office of Surface Mining for Wyo. state preemption; instr. Wyo. Coll. Law, fall, 1986; lectr. Rocky Mountain Mineral Law Found., 1977; chmn. Conf. Western Atty. Gen., 1992—93; mem. exec. com. Nat. Assn. Attys. Gen.; mem. Bush-Cheney Transition Team, 2000—01. Chmn. Cheyenne Bd. of Health, 1999—; bd. dirs. Longs Peak coun. Boy Scouts Am.; dir., chmn. Frontier CDC. Mem. Rotary. Republican. Congregationalist. Avocations: golf, tennis, gardening, wood carving, rock hunting. Home Phone: 307-634-8117; Office Phone: 307-777-5333. Office Fax: 307-777-6217. Business E-Mail: jmeyer3@state.wy.us. *

MEYER, JOYCE, television minister, author; b. St. Louis, Missouri, June 4, 1943; m. Dave Meyer; 4 children. PhD in theology, Life Christian U., Tampa, Florida; PhD in Divinity (hon.), Oral Roberts U., Tulsa, Oklahoma; PhD in sacred theology (hon.), Grand Canyon U., Phoenix, Arizona. Mem. Life Christian Church, assoc. pastor, 1980—86; founder Joyce Meyer Ministries, 1986—; television minister Enjoying Everyday Life, 1993—. Author: (novels) Battlefield of the Mind: Winning the Battle in Your Mind, 1993, Me and My Big Mouth: Your Answer is Right Under Your Nose, 2002, How to Hear from God: Learn to Know His Voice and Make Right Decisions, 2003, The Secret Power of Speaking God's Word, 2004, In Pursuit of Peace: 21 Ways to Conquer Anxiety, Fear, and Discontentment, 2004, Straight Talk: Overcoming Emotional Battles with the Power of God's Word, 2005, Approval Addiction: Overcoming Your Need to Please Everyone, 2005, Look Great Feel Great: Joyce shares twelve practical keys that will help you look and feel great, 2006. Founder St. Louis Dream Center, St. Louis. Named one of 25 Most Influential Evangelicals, Time Magazine, 2005. Christian. Office: Joyce Meyer Ministries PO Box 655 Fenton MO 63026 Office Phone: 800-727-9673. E-mail: mediacontact@joycemeyer.org. *

MEYER, JULIE CATHLEEN, marketing executive, director; b. San Francisco, Nov. 16, 1978; d. John William and Catherine Elain Ball. Cert. Armed Forces Sch. Music, Little Creek, Va., 1997. Musician Washington/Idaho Symphony, Pullman, 2002—04; mechanic US Armty N.G., Santa Rosa, Calif., 2002—. Program dir. Ata Martial Arts, Petaluma, Calif., 2006—, tournament chair, 2006—. Chair St. Jude Fundraiser, 2007. Cpl. musical corp USMC, 1996—2000, Japan. Mem.: VFW, Am. Legion, Mensa. Avocations: history, archaeology, geology, music. Office: Ata martial Arts 363 S McDowell Blvd Petaluma CA 94954

MEYER, KARL ERNEST, journalist; b. Madison, Wis., May 22, 1928; s. Ernest Louis and Dorothy (Narefsky) M.; m. Sarah Nielsen Peck, Aug. 12, 1959 (div. 1972); children: Ernest, Heather, Jonathan; m. Shareen Blair Brysac, Jan. 6, 1989. BA, U. Wis., 1951; MPA, Princeton U., NJ, 1953, PhD, 1956. Reporter N.Y. Times, NYC, 1952, mem. editl. bd., 1979-98; editl. writer Washington Post, 1956-65, chief London Bur., 1965-70, N.Y.C. corr., 1970-71; Washington corr. New Statesman, 1961-65; sr. editor, TV critic Saturday Rev., NYC, 1975-79; corr. in residence Fletcher Sch. Law and Diplomacy, Tufts U., 1979; editor World Policy Jour., NYC, 2000—. Vis. journalist fellow Duke U., Durham, NC, 1988; vis. prof. Yale U., New Haven, 1983, New Haven, 90; McGraw prof. in writing Princeton U., 1993—94; vis. prof. Bard Coll., NY, 2002. Author: The New America, 1961, (with Tad Szulc) The Cuban Invasion, 1962, Fulbright of Arkansas, 1963, The Pleasures of Archaeology, 1971, The Plundered Past, 1973, Teotihuacán, 1975, The Art Museum: Power, Money, Ethics, 1979, Pundits, Poets and Wits: An Omnibus of American Newspaper Columns, 1990, (with Shareen Brysac) Tournament of Shadows: The Great Game and Race for Empire in Central Asia, 1999, The Dust of Empire, 2003. Recipient citation for excellence Overseas Press Club, 1961, Bronze medal for editl. writing Sigma Delta; George Foster Peabody Broadcasting award 1983, Disting. Achievement award Sch. Journalism, U. Wis., 1985; Davenport Coll. of Yale U. fellow; Wisenschaftskolleg Inst. Adv. Studies (Berlin) fellow, 1994-95, Reuter fellow Oxford (Eng.) U., 1996-97. Mem. PEN Club Internat., Coun. on Fgn. Rels., NYU Soc. Fellows, Century Assn., Authors League Am Home: 50 W 96th St New York NY 10025-6526 Office: World Policy Jour 66 5 Th Ave Ste 900 New York NY 10011 Office Phone: 212-229-5808 4258. Personal E-mail: karlmeyer@optonline.net. Business E-Mail: meyerk@newschool.edu.

MEYER, KARL WILLIAM, retired university president; b. Ft. Wayne, Ind., May 8, 1925; s. K.W. and L. (Hofacker) M.; m. Margery R. Hamman, Apr. 15, 1950; children— Mary, William, Frederick, Ann, Jean. AB, Valpariaso U., 1948; M.F.S., U. Md., 1949; PhD, U. Wis., 1953; postgrad., U. Basel, Switzerland, 1948-49; postdoctoral fellow, U. Mich., 1958-59. Faculty Valparaiso U., 1952-53, Augustana Coll., 1953-55, Wis. State U., 1955-58; dean instrn., dir. grad. studies Wayne State Coll., 1959-63; asst. dir. bd. regents Wis. State Colls., Madison, 1963-64; pres. U. Wis.-Superior, 1964-87. Author: Karl Liebknecht: Man Without a Country, 1957; Contbr. articles to profl. jours. Served with USAAF, 1943-46, ETO. Home: W7861 Homestead Ct Holmen WI 54636-9440 E-mail: meyk25@aol.com.

MEYER, KATHERINE ANNE, lawyer; BA, Manhattanville Coll., 1973; JD, Columbus Sch. Law, Cath. U. Am., 1976. Bar: DC, Md. With Swankin & Turner, 1976—77, Ctr. for Auto Safety, 1977—79, Pub. Citizen Litigation Group, 1979—89, Harmon, Curran, Gallagher & Spielberg, 1989—93; ptnr. Meyer Glitzenstein & Crystal, Washington, 1993—. Chmn. litigation com. Defenders of Wildlife; adj. prof. law Georgetown U. Law Ctr. (Civil Litigation and Pub. Interest Advocacy), 1986—92; bd. dir. Defenders of Wildlife, Ctr. for Auto Safety, Wildlife Advocacy Project; with DC Cir. Advisory Com. Procedures, 1995—2001; bd. dirs. Ctr. Biol. Diversity. Named one of Best 75 Lawyers in Washington, Washingtonian Mag., 2002. Office: Mayer Glitzenstein & Crystal 1601 Connecticut Ave NW Ste 700 Washington DC 20009-1056 Office Phone: 202-588-5206. Office Fax: 202-588-5049.

MEYER, KELLY LEE, music educator; s. Willard Lee and Donna Jean Meyer; m. April Dawn Meyer, June 19, 1993; children: Kai Lenake children: Talon Lee, Cody Justice, Sage Washtay. AA in Audio Rec. Tech., Nebr. CC, Norfolk, 1991; BS in Music Edn., Wayne State Coll., Nebr., 1998; MusM in Edn., U. SD, Vermillion, 2003. Dir. bands Ponca HS, Nebr., 1998—2003, Coffeyville CC, Kans., 2003—04; asst. prof. music Silver Lake Coll., Manitowoc, Wis., 2004—. Pvt. tchr. music, Manitowoc, Wis., 1998—. Author: Buckets, Bells, and Whistles, 1999, Cadences for the Progressive Drumline, 2001, Rudimental Percussion Ensembles, 2003; composer, arranger over 20 songs; composer: numerous songs. Mem.: MENC (mediator 2004—06), Wis. Music Educators Ass., Nat. Band Dir.'s Assn., Percussive Arts Soc. (assoc.). Office: Silver Lake Coll 2406 S Alverno Rd Manitowoc WI 54220 Home Phone: 920-775-4495; Office Phone: 920-686-6185.

MEYER, LAWRENCE GEORGE, lawyer; b. East Grand Rapids, Mich., Oct. 2, 1940; s. George and Evangeline (Boerma) M.; children from previous marriage: David Lawrence, Jenifer Lynne; m. Linda Elizabeth Buck, May 31, 1980; children: Elizabeth Tilden, Travis Henley. BA with honors, Mich. State U., 1961; JD with distinction, U. Mich., 1964. Bar: Wis., 1965, Ill. 1965, US Supreme Ct. 1968, DC 1972. Assoc. Whyte, Hirschboeck, Minahan, Hardin & Harland, Milw., 1964-66; atty. antitrust div. U.S. Dept. Justice, Washington, 1966-68; legal counsel U.S. Senator Robert P. Griffin, Mich., 1968-70; dir. policy planning FTC, 1970-72; ptnr. Patton, Boggs & Blow, Washington, 1972-85, Arent, Fox, Kintner, Plotkin & Kahn, Washington, 1985-96, Gadsby & Hannah, 1996-2001; pvt. practice Washington, 2001—. Contbr. articles to profl. jours.; asst. editor. U. Mich. Law Rev., 1960-61. Bd. dirs. Hockey Hall of Fame, Toronto, 1993-99, Woodrow Wilson House, 1997—. Recipient Disting. Svc. award FTC, 1972. Mem.: ABA, Ill. Bar Assn., Wis. Bar Assn., DC Bar Assn., Congl. Country Club. Home: 9602 Beman Woods Way Potomac MD 20854-1610 Office Phone: 202-262-1964. Business E-Mail: larry@lawlgm.com.

MEYER, LINDSAY BEARDSWORTH, lawyer; b. Bridgeport, Conn., Apr. 11, 1961; Student, Universite de Rouen, France, 1982; BS cum laude, Univ. Conn., 1983; JD, George Washington Univ., 1987. Bar: Va. 1987, DC 1988; lic. US Customs Svc. Broker. Assoc. Venable, Baetjer, Howard & Civiletti LLP (now Venable LLP), Washington; ptnr., adv., mktg., new media, homeland security practice areas Venable LLP, Washington, and head, internat. trade practice group. Mem. Md.-Washington Dist. Export Coun. Mem.: ABA (chair, internat. trade and customs com.), DC Bar Assn., Va. Bar Assn., Am. Assn. Exporters and Importers, Beta Gamma Sigma. Office: Venable LLP 575 Seventh St NW Washington DC 20004 Office Phone: 202-344-4829. Office Fax: 202-344-8300. Business E-Mail: lbmeyer@venable.com.

MEYER, LYNN NIX, lawyer; b. Vinita, Okla., Aug. 10, 1948; d. William Armour and Joan Ross Nix; children: Veronica, Victoria, David. BA, Baldwin Wallace Coll., 1978; JD, Case Western Res. U., 1981. Bar: Ky. 1982, Colo. 1984. Paralegal Texaco Devel., Austin, Tex., 1976-77; legal asst. Alcan Aluminum, Cleve., 1977-79; assoc. Wyatt, Tarrant & Combs, Lexington, Ky., 1982-83; ptnr. Meyer, Meyer & Assocs., P.C., Denver, 1984-85; gen. counsel Carbon Fuels Corp., 1985-95; in pvt. practice Denver, 1996-97; asst. gen. counsel products Gambro, Inc. (now Gambro BCT), Lakewood, Colo., 1997—. Mem. ABA, Colo. Bar Assn., Ky. Bar Assn., Arapahoe County Bar Assn. Home: 10487 E Ida Ave Englewood CO 80111-3746 Office: Gambro BCT 10810 W Collins Ave Lakewood CO 80215-4439 E-mail: lynn.meyer@gambrobct.com.

MEYER, MARA ELLICE, special education educator, consultant, academic administrator; b. Chgo., Oct. 28, 1952; d. David and Harriett (Lazar) Einhorn; m. Leonard X. Meyer, July 20, 1986; children: Hayley Rebecca, David Joseph. BS in Speech and Hearing Sci., U. Ill., 1974, MS in Speech and Lang. Pathology, 1975, postgrad., 1990—95, Nat. Louis U., Chgo., 2003—. Cert. speech and lang. pathologist, spl. edn. tchr., reading tchr. Speech and lang. pathologist Macon-Piatt Spl. Edn. Dist., Decatur, Ill., 1975-76, Cmty. Consolidated Sch. Dist. # 59, Arlington Heights, Ill., reading specialist, learning disabilities coord., 1976—87; speech and lang. pathologist Adlai Stevenson HS, Lincolnshire, Ill., 2006—07, Lincolnshire-Prairie View Sch. Dist., 2007—. Adj. prof. Nat. Louis U., 1985—87, 2003—; test cons. Psychol. Corp., San Antonio, 1987—89, ednl. cons., 1987—89, Am. Guidance Svc., Circle Pines, Minn., 1989—94; project dir. Riverside Pub. Co., Chgo., 1993—94; pvt. practice ednl. cons., Deerfield, Ill., 1994—; cons. Spl. Edn. Dist., Lake County, 1995—, Lake Zurich Pub. Schs., 1996—98, Waukegan Pub. Schs., Ill., 1997; asst. prin., inclusion coord. Mundelein Sch. Dist., Ill., 1999—2001; spl. edn. adminstr. Wilmette Schs., 2001—03; spl. cons. Avoca Sch. Dist. 37, Wilmette, Ill., 2003—; prin. ednl. cons. Ill. State Bd. Edn., 2004—06. Mem. adv. coun. to Headstart, Dept. Human Svs., Chgo., 1990-99; pres. Park West Condo Assn., Lake County, 1983-88; area coord. Dem. Party, Lake County, Ill., 1978—. Mem. NEA, ASCD, Nat. Assn. Elem. Prins., Nat. Family Partnership Network, Am. Speech-Lang. and Hearing Assn., Ill. Speech-Lang. and Hearing Assn., Ill. Prins. Assn., Internat. Reading Assn., Coun. on Exceptional Children. Avocations: swimming official, leisure reading, technical reading. Home: 1540 Central Ave Deerfield IL 60015-3963 Office Phone: 847-431-0767. Personal E-mail: maraemeyer@comcast.net.

MEYER, MARGARET ELEANOR, retired microbiologist; b. Westwood, Calif., Feb. 8, 1923; d. Herman Henry and Eleanor (Dobson) M. BS, U. Calif., Berkeley, 1945; PhD, U. Calif., Davis, 1961. Pub. health analyst USPHS, Bethesda, Md., 1945-46; swine Brucellosis control agt. Dept. Agr., Davis, 1946-47; bacteriologist U. Calif., Davis, 1947-61; research microbiologist U. Calif. (Sch. Vet. Medicine), 1961-77, prof. vet. pub. health and microbiologist exptl. sta., 1977—; rsch. microbiologist U. Calif. Med. Sch., LA, 1961-77; supr. Brucella identifications lab. WHO, U. Calif., Davis, 1964—87, prof. vet. pub. health, 1973—87, dir. program in preventive vet. medicine, 1987; ret., 1987. Cons. subcom. on Brucella Internat. Com. Bacterial Taxonomy, 1962—, mem., 1966—; mem. 5th Pan Am. Congress Veterinary Medicine, Venezuela, 1966; mem. Internat. Congress Microbiology, Moscow, 1966, Mexico City, 1970, Munich, Ger., 1978, mem., officer, Eng., 1986; mem. Internat. Conf. Culture Collections, Tokyo, 1968; mem. adv. com. to Bergey's Manual Determative Bacteriology, 1967; cons. in resident Pan Am. Health Orgn., Zoonoses Lab., Buenos Aires, 1968; mem. brucellosis tech. adv. com. U.S. Animal Health Assn., 1977; FAO cons. on brucellosis control in dairy animals, Tripoli, Libya, 1981, mem. 3d internat. brucellosis symposium, Algiers, 1983; cons. Alaska Dept. Fish and Game, 1976, FAO, Libya, 1981, Bering Straits Reindeer Herders Assn., Nome, Alaska, 1981; invited speaker Internat. Symposium on Advances in Brucellosis Rsch., Tex. A&M U., 1989, Internat. Bison Conf.; resident cons. on brucellosis control in sheep and goats Am. Near East Refugee Aid, East Jerusalem, 1989; cons. on brucellosis in Yellowstone Nat. Pk., Nat. Pk. Svc., 1991—; invited mem. nat. symposium on brucellosis in the Greater Yellowstone Area, Jackson Hole, Wyo., 1994; cons. on brucellosis control in livestock for Armenia, 1994—. Contbr. articles to profl. jours. Bd. dirs. Carmichael Park and Recreation Dist., Calif., 1975; mem. Sacramento County Grand Jury, 1999-2000. Recipient Research Career Devel. award USPHS-NIH, 1963 Fellow Am. Pub. Health Assn., Am. Acad. Microbiology; mem. Soc. Am. Microbiologists, N.Am. Conf. Animal Disease Research Workers, Am. Coll. Vet. Microbiologists (hon. affiliate), US Animal Health Assn. (chmn. brucellosis tech. advisory com. 1978-79), Internat. Assn. Microbiol. Socs. (mem. 1st intersect. congress 1974), AAUW, No. Calif. Women's Golf Assn., U. Calif. Alumni Assn., Sigma Xi. Clubs: U. Calif. Faculty (Davis); El Dorado Royal Country (Shingle Springs, Calif.); Reno Women's Golf. Home: 5611 Fair Oaks Blvd Carmichael CA 95608-5503 Office: U Calif Sch Vet Medicine Dept Epidemiology & Preventive Medicine Davis CA 95616

MEYER, MARGARET VAUGHAN, librarian, educator; b. Phila., Mar. 13, 1919; d. Clifford and Fannie (Lehman) Vaughan; m. Donald Robert Meyer, Sept. 3, 1949 (dec. Mar. 2002); children: Karen, Frederick E., Julie Meyer; m. Arnoldo Ramos, 1985; 3 children; m. Shelly Brogden, 2000. BEd, UCLA, 1942; MLS, U. So. Calif., 1967. Elem. tchr. Indio Sch. Dist., Indio, Calif., 1942-43, Lawndale Sch. Dist., Lawndale, Calif., 1943-44, L.A. Unified Schs., 1946-53; program libr. City of Pasadena Libr., Pasadena, Calif., 1965-85. Co-author (Spanish-English): Centeno Collection-Annotated, 1977; author (biog. and notes, 2 CDs): Clifford Vaughan classical music. Organizer, chmn. libr. com. PTA, LA, 1961—64, hon. life mem., 1964; vol. Com. Solidarity People of El Salvadore, LA, 1985—97; mem. Citizens Com. Save Elysian Park, LA, 1987—97, L.A. County Mus. Art, 1986—2003, Friends of Pasadena Pub. Libr., 1986—98, Food Bank, Washington, 2004—. Mem.: ALA (del. 1967—80), L.A. Pub. Libr., Libr. Found. (charter mem.), Calif. Libr. Assn., Am. Fedn. Tchrs. (exec. bd. L.A. chpt.), Denishawn Repertory Dancers (hon. bd. dirs.), Sierra Club. Avocations: music, reading, swimming, gardening, games. Home: 1525 Upshur-NW Washington DC 20011

MEYER, MARTIN JAY, lawyer; b. Wilkes-Barre, Pa., Aug. 1, 1932; s. Max and Rose (Wruble) M.; m. Joan Rosenthal, Aug. 24, 1954; children: Leah, Gary. BA, Wilkes Coll., 1954; postgrad., U. Miami, 1956—57; LLB, Temple U., 1959. Bar: Pa. 1960, U.S. Dist. Ct. (mid. dist.) Pa. 1961, U.S. Ct. Appeals (3d cir.) 1966, U.S. Supreme Ct. 1978. Assoc. Mack, Kasper & Meyer, Wilkes-Barre, 1961-66; ptnr. Mack & Meyer, Wilkes-Barre, 1966—80; sr. ptnr. Meyer & Swatkoski, Kingston, Pa., 1980—. Chmn. disciplinary hearing com. Pa. Supreme Ct.; apptd. spl. trial master State Ct., 1995; apptd. cert. mediator U.S. Dist. Ct. (mid. dist.) Pa., 2000. Legal columnist to local newspapers, creator (TV program) Call The Lawyer, (weekly columns) You Be the Lawyer, You Be the Jury. Chmn. Muscular Dystrophy Assn., 1960; co-chmn. March of Dimes, 1962; trustee Temple Israel Wilkes-Barre; bd. dirs. Jewish Home Scranton, Family Svc. Assn.; arbitrator U.S. Arbitration and Mediation of N.E., Inc., Million Dollar Advocates Forum. With U.S. Army, 1955-56. Fellow Pa. Bar Found.; mem. DAV, ATLA, Am. Arbitration Assn. (arbitrator), Assn. for Conflict Resolution, Am. Bd. Trial Advocates, Pa. Soc., Pa. Bar Assn. (former co-chmn., adoption com. family law sect., alt. dispute resolution com.), Nat. Conf. Bar Pres.'s, Pa. Trial Lawyers Assn. (lectr.), Luzerne County Bar Assn. (pres. 1984-85, chmn. Ct. Rules Com. 1994-2000), N.E. Pa. Trial Lawyers Assn., Elks (trustee), Masons (32 degree), B'nai Brith (pres. 1967), Tau Epsilon Rho. Office: 405 3rd Ave Kingston PA 18704-5802 Home Phone: 570-288-0081; Office Phone: 570-288-8482. Office Fax: 570-288-1003. Business E-Mail: mmeyer@meyerswatlaw.com.

MEYER, MAX EARL, lawyer; b. Hampton, Va., Oct. 31, 1918; s. Earl Luther and Winifred Katherine (Spacht) M.; m. Betty Maxwell Dodds, Sept. 22, 1945; children: Scott Maxwell, Ann Culliford. AB, U. Nebr., 1940, JD, 1942. Bar: Nebr. 1942, Ill. 1946. Assoc. firm Lord, Bissell & Brook, Chgo., 1945-53, ptnr., 1953-85; chmn. Chgo. Fed. Tax Forum, 1965, U. Chgo. Ann. Fed. Tax Conf., 1972; mem. Adv. Group to Commr. of IRS, 1967. Lectr. in field. Bd. dirs. Music Acad. of the West, chmn., 1993—94. Mem.: ABA (coun. tax sect. 1969—72), Am. Coll. Tax Counsel, Chgo. Bar Assn. (chmn. taxation com. 1959—61), Nebr. Bar Assn., Ill. Bar Assn. (coun. tax sect. 1973—76), Birnam Wood Golf Club, Valley Club of Montecito, Law Club (Chgo.), Legal Club, Masons. Republican. Presbyterian.

MEYER, MICHAEL EDWIN, lawyer; b. Chgo., Oct. 23, 1942; s. Leon S. and Janet (Gorden) M.; m. Catherine Dieffenbach, Nov. 21, 1982; children: Linda, Mollie, Patrick, Kellie. BS, U. Wis., 1964; JD, U. Chgo., 1967. Bar: Calif. 1968, U.S. Supreme Ct. 1973. Assoc. Lillick & McHose, LA, 1967-73, ptnr., 1974-90, mng. ptnr., 1986-87; ptnr. Pillsbury Madison Sutro, 1990—, mem. mgmt. com., 1990-92; mng. ptnr. Pillsbury Winthrop, LA, 1999—2003, Piper Rudnick LLP (now DLA Piper Rudnick Gray Cary), 2004—. Judge pro tem Beverly Hills Mcpl. Ct., Calif., 1976-79, Los Angeles Mcpl. Ct., 1980-86; lectr. in field. Bd. dirs. Bldg. Owners and Mgrs. Assn. Greater L.A., L.A. coun. Boy Scouts Am., L.A. Sports and Entertainment Commn., L.A. Econ. Devel. Corp.; pub. counsel United Way Greater L.A., Los Angeles County Bar Found., trustee, 1997—, Reviving Baseball in Inner Cities; mem. L.A. County Sheriff Youth Found., Jackie Robinson Found. Recipient Good Scout award L.A. Coun. Boy Scouts Am., 1992, Man of Yr. award United Way, 1996, Real Estate Profl. of Yr. award NACORE, 2002, Reviving Baseball in Inner-Cities CB award Major League Baseball, 2005, Spirit L.A. award L.A. Hdqs. Assn., 2005, Outstanding Cmty. Svc. award Weingart Ctr., 2006; named to Top Ten So. Calif. Super Lawyers LA Mag., 2006, Top Five Calif. Real Estate Lawyers Chambers USA, 2005. Mem. ABA, Am. Arbitration Assn. (arbitrator), Calif. Bar Assn., Los Angeles County Bar Assn. (trustee 1997—), L.A. Bar Assn., Am. Coll. of Real Estate Lawyers, U. Chgo. Alumni Assn. So. Calif. (pres. 1980-82), Calif. Club, U. L.A. Club (dir. 1979-85, pres. 1984-85), L.A. Country Club. Jewish. Office: DLA Piper Rudnick Gray Cary Ste 2300 550 S Hope St Los Angeles CA 90071 Home Phone: 310-546-5500, 213-505-2113; Office Phone: 213-330-7777. Office Fax: 213-330-7577. Business E-Mail: michael.meyer@dlapiper.com.

MEYER, MILTON EDWARD, JR., retired lawyer, artist; b. St. Louis, Nov. 26, 1922; s. Milton Edward and Jessie Marie (Hurley) M.; m. Mary C. Kramer, Nov. 5, 1949 (dec. Dec. 1999); children: Milton E. III, Melanie M. Meyer Francis, Daniel K., Gregory N.; m. Mildred R. Emrick, Nov. 18, 2003. BS in Bus. Adminstrn, Washington U., 1943; LL.B., St. Louis, U., 1950; LL.M., N.Y. U., 1953. Bar: Mo. 1950, Colo. 1956. Trust adminstr. Mississippi Valley Trust Co., St. Louis, 1946-50; asso. firm Burnett, Stern & Liberman, St. Louis, 1953-56; founding partner firm Hindry & Meyer, Denver, 1956-79, chmn. bd., 1970-79; spl. counsel Schmidt, Elrod & Wills, and predecessors, 1979-83, pres., 1980-82; sec. C.A. Norgren Co., Littleton, Colo., 1960-78, dir., 1971-78; ret., 1978. Contbr. articles to profl. jours. Chmn. Denver Rotary's Artists of Am. Exhbn., 1990—92; bd. dirs. Nat. Club Assn., 1971—91, pres., 1976—78; bd. dirs. Denver Cmty. Concert Assn., 1960—64, Sewall Rehab. Ctr., Denver, 1965—68, Carl A. Norgren Found., 1960—70; Denver Leadership Found., 1983—93, Found. Colo. Women's Coll., 1982—86, chmn., bd. dirs., 1984—86; bd. dirs. Conf. Pvt. Orgns., 1982—89, chmn., bd. dirs., 1984—88. Officer, U.S. Airborne Infantry US Army, 1943—46, World War II, officer, U.S. Airborne Infantry US Army, 1950—52, Korean War. Recipient Wisdom Soc. award of honor. Mem.: ABA, Colo. Bar Assn., Denver Bar Assn., Greater Denver Tax Counsels Assn. (founder, chmn. 1957), Denver Estate Planning Coun. (founder, pres. 1958), Am. Coll. Probate Counsel, Knickerbocker Artists, Pastel Soc. Am., Pastel Soc. West Coast (disting. pastellist award), Internat. Assn. Pastel Socs (founder, dir. 1994—2003), Salmagundi Club, Pinehurst Country Clu (pres. 1979—80, dir. 1960—97), Hundred Club Denver, Denver Execs. Club, Cherry Hills Country Club, Rotary (bd. dirs. 1991—93), Phi Eta Sigma, Beta Gamma Sigma, Omicron Delta Kappa, Beta Theta Pi. Republican. Roman Catholic. Home: 7123 W Belmont Dr Littleton CO 80123 E-mail: miltonmeyer@comcast.net.

MEYER, PAUL, information technology executive; Studied Politics, Philosophy and Econs., Oxford U.; grad., Pomona Coll.; JD, Yale U. Rschr. & speechwriter for Pres. Clinton The White House, 1993—95; CEO Endeavor Initiative; with Internat. Rescue Com.; sr. fellow Markle Found.; founder, chmn. IPKO, Kosovo, 1999; co-founder, pres. & CEO Voxiva, Washington, DC, 2001—. Named one of the world's 100 Top Young Innovators, MIT Tech. Review, 100 Global Leaders for Tomorrow, World Econ. Forum; recipient Tech. in Service of Humanity Award, MIT Tech. Review. Fellow: Foreign Policy Assn. Office: Voxiva 1725 K St NW Ste 900 Washington DC 20006-1415

MEYER, PEARL, compensation executive consultant; b. NYC; d. Allen Charles and Rose Weissman; m. Ira A. Meyer. BA cum laude, NYU, postgrad. Statis. specialist, exec. comp. div. Gen. Foods Corp., White Plains, NY; exec. v.p. and cons. Handy Assocs., Inc., NYC; founder, chair Pearl Meyer & Ptnrs., NYC, 1989—. Lectr. exec. compensation confs. and seminars. Contbr. articles to profl. jours. Recipient Woman of Achievement award, Women Bus. Owners NY, Legal Momentum Aiming High award, 2003. Mem.: Pers. Accreditation Inst., Women's Econ. Roundtable, Soc. Human Resources Mgmt. (cert. accredited pers. diplomate), WorldatWork, Am. Mgmt. Assn., Women's Forum, Sky Club, Sedgewood Club, Phi Beta Kappa, Beta Gamma Sigma, Pi Mu Epsilon. Office: Pearl Meyer & Ptnrs 445 Park Ave New York NY 10022-2606

MEYER, PHILIP EDWARD, journalism educator; b. Deshler, Nebr., Oct. 27, 1930; s. Elmer Edward and Hilda Grace (Morrison) M.; m. Sue Quail, Aug. 5, 1956; children: Caroline, Katherine, Melissa, Sarah. BS, Kans. State U., 1952; MA, U. N.C., 1963. Asst. state editor Topeka (Kans.) Daily Capital, 1954-56; reporter Miami (Fla.) Herald, 1958-62; Washington corr. Akron Beacon Jour., 1962-66; nat. corr. Knight-Ridder, Inc., Washington, 1967-78, dir. news research Miami, 1978-81; William Rand Kenan Jr. prof. journalism U. N.C., Chapel Hill, 1981-93; Knight prof., 1993—. Author: Precision Journalism, 1973 (Sigma Delta Chi Disting. Service award 1974), The Newspaper Survival Book, 1985, Ethical Journalism, 1987, The New Precision Journalism, 1991, The Vanishing Newspaper, 2004; co-author: To Keep the Republic, 1975; co-editor: Evaluating Public Journalism, 1998. Project dir. Russell Sage Found., N.Y.C., 1969-70. Served with USNR, 1952-54. Recipient Disting. Contbns. to Journalism award Nat. Press Found., 1994, Disting. Contbns. to Media and Media Studies award Freedom Forum Media Studies Ctr., 1995, award of merit Newspaper Assn. Am. Rsch. Fedn., 1996; Nieman fellow Harvard U., 1966-67, fellow Freedom Forum Ctr. for Media Studies, 1985. Fellow Soc. Prof. Journalists, mem. Am. Assn. for Pub. Opinion Rsch. (pres. 1989-90, award exceptionally disting. achievement 2000), World Assn. for Pub. Opinion Rsch. (pres. 1994-95), Assn. for Edn. in Journalism and Mass Comm. (mem. USA Today bd. contbrs. 1998—), Nat. Press Club (Washington). Democrat. Episcopalian. Avocation: photography. Office: UNC Sch Journalism & Mass Comm Carroll Hall Cb3365 Chapel Hill NC 27599-3365 Office Phone: 919-962-4085. Business E-Mail: philip_meyer@unc.edu.

MEYER, PHILIP GILBERT, lawyer; b. Louisville, June 26, 1945; s. Henry Gilbert and Adele (Gutermuth) M.; m. Jackie Darlene Watson, Jan. 30, 1971 (div. Apr. 1976); m. Sylvia Saunders, Oct. 9, 1976. BBA, U. Mich., Ann Arbor, 1967; JD, U. Tex., Austin, 1970. Bar: Tex. 1970, Mich. 1971, U.S. Tax Ct. 1972, U.S. Dist. Ct. (ea. dist.) Mich. 1971, U.S. Ct. Appeals (6th cir.), 1972, U.S. Dist. Ct. (no. dist.) Ohio 1976, U.S. Dist. Ct. (we. dist.) Mich. 1993, U.S. Dist. Ct. (no. dist.) Ill. 1998. Law clk. Wayne County Cir. Ct., Detroit, 1970-72; atty. Leonard C. Jaques, Detroit, 1972; assoc. Christy & Robbins, Dearborn, Mich., 1972-73; ptnr. Foster, Meadows & Ballard, Detroit, 1973-79; of counsel Christy, Rogers & Gantz, Dearborn, 1979-81, Rogers & Gantz, Dearborn, 1981-86; prin. Philip G. Meyer and Assocs., Farmington Hills, 1986—. Adj. prof. U. Detroit Sch. Law, 1979. Mem. ABA (com. vice chmn. rules and procedure 1982-88), Maritime Law Assn. U.S., Mich. Bar Assn. (vice chmn. admiralty sect. 1978), Tex. Bar Assn., Detroit Bar Assn. (vice chmn. admiralty com. 1991-93, chmn. admiralty sect. 1993-95), Propeller-Port of Detroit Club (pres. 1984-85). Republican. Home: 5905 Independence Ln West Bloomfield MI 48322-1854 Office: Ste 113 30300 Northwestern Hwy Farmington Hills MI 48334-3212 Home Phone: 248-626-4677; Office Phone: 248-737-0700. Business E-Mail: pgm@meylaw.com.

MEYER, PIOTR JAN, electronics engineer; b. Szczecin, Poland, May 31, 1969; arrived in US, 2000; s. Zygmunt and Maria Meyer. MS in Electronics Engring., Tech. U. Szczecin, 1992. Devel. engr., mechatronic sys. Philips Applied Technologies, Eindhoven, Netherlands, 1994—2000, sr. specialist mechatronic sys. Lynnfield, Mass., 2000—. Guest lectr. series MIT, Cambridge, Mass., 2006. Contbr. scientific papers. Mem.: IEEE (chmn. chpt. 2006—), Netherlands-Am. Bus. Group New Eng., Math. Assn. Am., German Scholars Boston (bd. dirs. 2003—06). Achievements include patents for fast and accurate motion of industrial robots; research in mathematical modelling, analysis, simulation and optimization of industrial robot motion for nanometer-level accuracy; development of mathematical modelling, analysis, simulation and optimization of commercial LED-based light sources. Avocations: history, philosophy, fine arts, classical music, mountain climbing. Home and Office: Philips Applied Technologies 20 Lakeview Avenue Lynnfield MA 01940-1920 Home Phone: 781-334-0052; Office Phone: 617-852-2403. Business E-Mail: p.j.meyer@philips.com.

MEYER, PRISCILLA ANN, literature and language professor; b. Aug. 26, 1942; d. Herbert Edward and Marjorie Rose (Wolff) M.; m. William L. Trousdale, Sept. 15, 1974; 1 dau., Rachel V. BA, U. Calif., Berkeley, 1964; MA, Princeton U., 1966; PhD, 1971. Lectr. in Russian lang. and lit. Wesleyan U., Middletown, Conn., 1968-71, asst. prof., 1971-75, assoc. prof., 1975-88, prof., 1988—. Vis. asst. prof. Yale U., 1973, adv. coun. dept. Slavic lang. and lit. Princeton U., 1998-2002. Author: Find What the Sailor Has Hidden: Vladimir Nabokov's Pale Fire, 1988; editor: Life in Windy Weather (by Andrei Bitov), 1986; co-editor: Dostoevsky and Gogol, 1979, Essays on Gogol: Logos and the Russian Word, 1992, Nabokov's World, 2001, Yuz! Essays on the Occasion of the 75th Birthday of Yuz Aleshkovsky, 2005; translator stories; mem. editl. bd. Slavic and East European Jour., 1999—; contbr. articles to profl. jours. Scholar Internat. Rsch. and Exch. Bd., 1973; grantee Ford Found., 1964-68, 70; hon. vis. fellow Sch. Slavonic and East European Studies London U., 1997, 2001. Mem. Am. Coun. Tchrs. Russian (dir. 1983-86), Am. Assn. Tchrs. Slavic and East European Studies, Internat. Vladimir Nabokov Soc. (v.p. 1983-85, 2002-04, pres. 1985-87, 2004-06), Tolstoi Soc., Dostoevsky Soc., Conn. Acad. Arts and Scis. Office: Russian Dept Wesleyan U Middletown CT 06459-0001 Office Phone: 860-685-3127. E-mail: pmeyer@wesleyan.edu.

MEYER, PUCCI, editor; b. NYC, Sept. 1, 1944; d. Charles Albert and Lollo (Offer) M.; m. Michael V. McGill, Oct. 28, 2001. BA, U. Wis., 1966. Asst. editor Look mag., NYC, 1970-71, editorial asst. Paris, 1967-69; reporter Newsday, Garden City, L.I., NY, 1971-73; style editor N.Y. Daily News Sunday Mag., NYC, 1974-76, assoc. editor, 1977-82, editor, 1983-86; sr. editor Prodigy, White Plains, NY, 1987; spl. projects editor N.Y. Post, NYC, 1988-89, style editor, 1990-92, food editor, 1992-93, assoc. features editor, 1993—94, travel editor, 1994—2004. Contbr. articles to various nat. mags. Recipient Pulitzer prize as mem. Newsday investigative team that wrote articles and book The Heroin Trail, 1973.

MEYER, RICHARD CHARLES, microbiologist, educator; b. Cleve., May 2, 1930; s. Frederick Albert and Tekla Charlotte (Schrade) M.; m. Carolyn Yvonne Patton, Apr. 6, 1963; children: Frederick Gustav, Carl Anselm. B.Sc., Baldwin-Wallace Coll., 1952; M.Sc., Ohio State U., 1957, PhD, 1961. Teaching and research asst. Ohio State U., 1956-61, research assoc., 1961-62; microbiologist Nat. Cancer Inst., NIH, Bethesda, Md., 1962-64; asst. prof. vet. pathology and hygiene and microbiology U. Ill., Urbana-Champaign, 1965-68, assoc. prof., 1968-73, prof., 1973-89, prof. emeritus, 1989—. Served with C.E. U.S. Army, 1952-54. Mem. Am. Acad. Microbiology, AAAS, Am. Inst. Biol. Sci., Am. Soc. Microbiology, Sigma Xi, Gamma Sigma Delta, Phi Zeta. Republican. Lutheran. Home: 1504 S Buckthorn Ln Mahomet IL 61853-3632 Office: Dept Vet Pathobiology U Ill at Urbana-Champaign Urbana IL 61801

MEYER, RICHARD W., university librarian; b. St. Louis, Jan. 22, 1943; s. Norman K. Meyer and Melba R. Reisel; m. Clare A. Siesennop, Apr. 12, 1944; children: Sharyn C. Moore, Karyn A. BS in Chemistry, U. Mo., 1967; BA in Libr. Sci., U. Mo., Columbia, 1967; MS in Libr. Sci., U. Ill., Champaign, 1970; MA in Econs., Clemson U., SC, 1986. Asst. libr. E.I. duPont de Nemours, Aiken, SC, 1967—69; dir. libr. tech services Ind. State U., Terre Haute, Ind., 1976—79; asst. dir. libr. U. Tex. at Dallas, Richardson, 1970—76; assoc. dir. libraries Clemson U., 1979—91; dir. libr. Trinity U., San Antonio, 1991—2000; dean, dir. libraries Ga. Inst. Tech., Atlanta, 2000—. Cons. Harris Corp., Melbourne, Fla., 1985—86, Chemists Club, NYC, 1991—92, Mackenzie U., Sao Paulo, Brazil, 1998—99. Contbr. articles to profl. jours. Field svc. rev. team mem. United Way of San Antonio, 1998—2000. Recipient G.K. Saur Best Article award, Coll. and Rsch. Libraries, 1999; grantee, Andrew W. Mellon Found., 1995—2000; Blackwell scholarship, Coll. and Rsch. Libraries, 2002. Mem.: So. Assn. Colls. and Schs. (mem. reaffirmation rev. teams 1999—2002), ALA. Conservative. Office: Georgia Institute of Technology 704 Cherry St Atlanta GA 30332-0900 Office Phone: 404-894-8914. Business E-Mail: richard.meyer@library.gatech.edu.

MEYER, ROBERT ALLEN, finance educator; b. Wisconsin Rapids, Wis., May 31, 1943; s. Charles Harold and Viola Bertha (Stoeckmann) M.; 1 child, Timothy Charles. BA, Valparaiso U., Ind., 1966; MA, Mich. State U., 1967, PhD, 1972, postgrad., 1981. Asst. prof. Muskingum Area Tech. Coll., Zanesville, Ohio, 1972-74; adj. prof. U. Fla., Gainesville, 1974-80; dean acad. affairs Santa Fe Community Coll., Gainesville, 1974-80; asst. prof. Purdue U., W. Lafayette, Ind., 1982-84, Ga. State U., Atlanta, 1985-89; assoc. prof., program coord. U. N. Tex., Denton, 1989-91; Fulbright profl. scholar, Bangkok, 1991-92; coord. travel, tourism, hotel, restaurant mgmt. program U. Hawaii Manoa Campus, Honolulu, 1992-97; dir. distance edn., dir. travel, hotel and restaurant mgmt. SPC, St. Petersburg, Fla., 1997—; 21573325. Investor, asst. mgr. LaSiene Restaurant, Ann Arbor, Mich., 1970-72; investor, cons. Cafe Brittany St. Thomas, U.S. V.I., 1974-80, owner, operator, Houston, 1980; pres. RTM Cons., Honolulu, Hawaii, 1989—; educator World Tourism Orgn., 1993—; mem. vis. ind. coun. C. of C., 1993—; club mgr. Assn. Am., 1994—; dir. edn. Am. Assoc. Real Estate License Law Officials. Contbr. articles to profl. jours. Founding mem. Fla. Distance Learning Consortium, 1998—; bd. dirs., founder Fla. Virtual Campus, 1998—, dir. hospitality program, 1998—. Recipient White House Commendation for Partnerships with Industry and Higher Edn.,1984, George Washington Medal of Honor for innovations in higher edn., Freedoms Found., 1985, 86, Achievement award in hospitality edn. Coun. of Hotel, Restaurant & Instl. Edn., 1987. Mem. Assn. Real Estate Lic. Law Ofcls. (distance edn. coun. bd. mem. 1999—), Tarrant County Hotel and Motel Assn., Dallas Hotel Assn., Am. Soc. Tng. and Devel., Travel Ind. Assn. Tex., Hotel Sales & Mktg. Assn. (bd. dirs. 1985-89), Coun. of Hotel, Restaurant and Instl. Edn. (grad. com. 1989-90). Office: St Petersburg Coll PO Box 13489 Saint Petersburg FL 33733-3489 Home: 13108 Angler St Spring Hill FL 34609-5907 Office Phone: 727-394-6165. E-mail: rmeyer1@tampabay.rr.com.

MEYER, ROGER JESS CHRISTIAN, pediatrics educator; b. Olympia, Wash., May 14, 1928; s. Paul Eugene and Martha Bell Rogers Meyer; m. Joyce Langley, Mar. 14, 1959; children: Paul, John, William, Douglas, Nancy, Liz. BS in Chemistry, U. Wash., Seattle, 1951; MD, Washington U., St. Louis, 1955; MPH, Harvard U., 1959. Cert. pediatric bds. eligible rehab., preventive medicine, family practice. Instr. pediat. Harvard Med. Sch., Boston, 1959-62; asst. prof. U. Vt. Coll. Medicine, Burlington, 1962-65; assoc. prof. U. Va. Sch. Medicine, Charlottesville, 1965-68, Northwestern U., Chgo., 1968-76; asst. dean U. Ill. Sch. Pub. Health, Chgo., 1974-76; prof. pediat. and pub. health Sch. Medicine U. Wash., Seattle, 1976—; with U.S. Army Res. Med. Corps, 1982; advanced through grades to col. U.S. Army, 1986. Chair, bd. dir. community pediatrics sect. Am. Acad. Pediatrics, Evanston, Ill, 1973-74; pres. Child and Family Health Found., 1976—; bd. dir. Nat. Com. Prevention Child Abuse, Chgo., 1974-76. Author 155 books and articles. Bd. dir. N.W. orgn. ARC, Unitarian Universalist Ch., Rotary Internat.; chief pub. health Pacific Rim, U.S. Army Med. Corps 364 Civil Affairs, 1986-93; staff Madigan Army Med. Ctr.; faculty Def. Dept. JMRTC. Decorated Army Achievement medal (2) for disting. svc. 1988-89; recipient NIMH Social Sci. in Medicine award Harvard U., 1961, Children's Hosp. Ann. award, Boston, 1959; Shaller scholar U. Wash., 1950-51, NIMH Health scholar U. Rochester, 1957-58; Oxford fellow, 1992. Mem. APHA, Am. Acad. Pediat. (sect. on child devel., ethics, pediat. mil.), Marine Sci. Soc. Pacific N.W. (N.W. global epidemiology com., pres.), N.W. Pediat. Soc., Res. Officers Assn., Harvard U. Alumni Assn., Washington U. Alumni Assn., Mil. Officers Am. Assn. (historian Rutsap chpt.). Office Phone: 360-479-5534. Personal E-mail: rjcmeyer@aol.com.

MEYER, RON, film company executive; b. 1944; m. Kelly Chapman; children, Jennifer, Sarah, Carson, Eli. With Paul Kohner Agency, 1964-1970; agent William Morris Agency, Beverly Hills, CA, 1970-1975; co-founder, pres. Creative Artists Agency, Inc., Beverly Hills, CA, 1975-95; pres., COO Universal Studios Inc., Universal City, 1995—. Served with USMC. Named one of 50 Most Powerful People in Hollywood, Premiere mag., 2004—06; recipient Milestone award, Producers Guild Am., 2007. Office: Universal Studios Inc 100 Universal City Plz Universal City CA 91608 Office Phone: 818-777-1000.

MEYER, RONALD G., forensic specialist; b. Chicopee, Mass., Oct. 28, 1966; s. Nora J. Meyer; m. Regina Meyer, Nov. 9, 1999; children: Kaitlyn Daniel, Kristine Nora. AS, Holyoke C.C., Mass., 1990; BS, SUNY, Albany, 1997; MS in Forensic Sci., George Wash. U., Washington, 2002. Lic. in forensic medicine Armed Forces Med. Examiner, Rockville, Md., 2002. Spl. agt. US Army Criminal Investigation Command, Fort Hood, Fort Sam Houston, Tex., 1994—99, supervisory spl. agt. Fort Bragg, NC, 1999—2001, asst. ops. officer, investigations and forensic sci. officer Bamberg, Germany, 2002—06, Iraq, 2004, spl. agt. in charge Bagram, Afghanistan, 2005—06; chief advanced investigations and specialized tng. br. US Army Mil. Police Sch., Fort Leonard Wood, Mo., 2006—. Decorated Army Achievement medal US Army, Bronze Star, Meritorious Svc. medal, Army Commendation medal, Armed Forces Expeditionary medal, Global War on Terrorism Svc. medal, Iraq Campaign medal, Afghanistan Campaign medal. Mem.: Mil. Police Regtl. Assn., Am. Acad. Forensic Sci. (assoc.). Office: US Army Military Police School Thurman Hall MANSCEN Loop Ste 2912 Fort Leonard Wood MO 65473 Home Phone: 573-855-3375; Office Phone: 573-563-7816. Business E-Mail: ronald.meyer@us.army.mil.

MEYER, RUSSELL WILLIAM, JR., air transportation executive; b. Davenport, Iowa, July 19, 1932; s. Russell William and Ellen Marie (Matthews) M.; m. Helen Scott Vaughn, Aug. 20, 1960; children: Russell William, III, Elizabeth Ellen, Jeffrey Vaughn, Christopher Matthews, Carolyn Louise. BA, Yale U., 1954; LLB, Harvard U., 1961. Bar: Ohio 1961. Mem. firm Arter & Hadden, Cleve., 1961-66; pres., chief exec. officer Grumman Am. Aviation Corp., Cleve., 1966-74; exec. v.p. Cessna Aircraft Co., Wichita, Kans., 1974-75, chmn. bd., CEO, 1975-2000, 2002—03, chmn., 2004, chmn. emeritus, 2005. Bd. dirs. Fourth Fin., 1975-1995, Westar Energy, 1978-2000, Gen. Dynamics, 1986-1992, Nations Bank, 1995-2001, Pub. Broadcasting Svc., Welfare to Work Partnership; presdl. appointee Aviation Safety Commn., 1987—; mem. Pres. Airline Commn., 1993, FAA Mgmt. Adv. Counsel, 2004—; dir. Pub. Broadcasting Sys. Chmn. bd. trustees 1st Bapt. Ch., Cleve., 1972-74; bd. dirs. United Way, Wichita and Sedgwick County; trustee Wesley Hosp. Endowment Assn., Wake Forest Univ.; bd. govs. United Way Am., 1993—. With USAF, 1955-58. Recipient Collier trophy Nat. Aeronautic Assn., 1986, George S. Dively award Harvard U., 1992, Wright Bros. Meml. trophy, 1995, Disting. Svc. Citation U. Kans., 2000; named Kansan of Yr., 1998. Mem. ABA, Ohio Bar Assn., Kans. Bar Assn., Cleve. Bar Assn., Gen. Aviation Mfrs. Assn. (chmn. bd. dirs. 1973-74, 81-82, 93-94), Wichita C. of C. (chmn. 1988—, bd. dirs.), Wichita Club, Wichita Country Club, Pine Valley Club, Cypress Point Club, Double Eagle Country Club, Flint Hills Nat. Club, Latrobe Country Club, Eldorado Country Club, The Tradition Golf Club. Home: 600 N Tara Ct Wichita KS 67206-1830 Office: Cessna Aircraft PO Box 7704 1 Cessna Blvd Wichita KS 67215-1424 Office Phone: 316-517-8000.

MEYER, SCOTT, communications executive; AB, Brown U.; MBA, Harvard U. Cons. Boston Cons. Group; with Merrill Lynch & Co.; v.p., gen. mgr. bus. to bus. consumer divsn. Multex.com; with NY Times Co., 2000—; v.p. NY Times Digital, 2000—03; gen. mgr. NY Times on the Web, 2000—03; v.p. New Eng. Media Group (NEMG), Boston Globe, 2003—05; pres., CEO About, Inc., 2005—. Bd. dirs., former pres. Harvard Bus. Sch. Club, NY; bd. dirs. Online Publishers Assn.; big brother Mass. Bay Big Brothers program; bd. visitors Boston Ctr. Arts. Office: About Inc 249 W 17th St New York NY 10011

MEYER, TOBIAS, auction house executive; Student, Vienna U. Entry-level position contemporary art dept. Christie's, London, 1989—92; head contemporary art Sotheby's, London, 1992, dir. contemporary art worldwide NYC, 1997—. Auctioneer Orange Marilyn (Andy Warhol), 1988, Michael Jackson and Bubbles (Jeff Koons), 2001. Office: Sotheby's 1334 York Ave New York NY 10021 Office Phone: 212-606-7254. Office Fax: 212-606-7011.

MEYER, URBAN, college football coach; b. Ashtabula, Ohio, July 10, 1964; m. Shelly Mather, 1986; children: Nicole, Gigi, Nate. Grad., U. Cin., 1986. Tight ends coach Ohio State U., 1986, receivers coach, 1987; linebackers coach Ill. State U., 1988, quarterbacks/wide receivers coach, 1989; wide receivers coach Colo. State U., 1990—95, U. Notre Dame, 1996—2000; head coach Bowling Green U., 2001—02, U. Utah, 2003—04, U. Fla., Gainesville, 2005—. Named Mid. Am. Conf. Coach of Yr., 2001, Nat. Coach of Yr., The Sporting News, 2003, Mountain West Conf. Coach of Yr., 2003, 2004, Nat. Coach of Yr., Home Depot, 2004, Eddie Robinson Coach of Yr., Football Writers Assn. Am., 2004; recipient Nat. Coach of Yr., Pro Football Weekly, 2004, George Munger award for Collegiate Coach of Yr., Maxwell Club, 2004, Woody Hayes Trophy award, Columbus Touchdown Club, 2004, Victor award, 2004. Achievements include coaching U. Fla. to the 2006 BCS Nat. Championship. Office: U Fla Gators Ben Hill Griffin Stadium Univ Ave & North South Dr Gainesville FL 32611 *

MEYER-BAHLBURG, HEINO F.L., psychology professor; b. Hamburg, Germany, Feb. 26, 1940; came to U.S., 1969; s. Wilhelm and Marie Luise Meyer-B. Vordiplom in Psychology, U. Hamburg, 1963, Diplom Psychology, 1966; D in Natural Scis., U. Düsseldorf, Germany, 1970. Sci. asst. U. Düsseldorf, 1970; rsch. asst., then rsch. assoc. prof. psychiatry and pediat. SUNY Med. Sch., Buffalo, 1970-77; rsch. scientist N.Y. State Psychiat. Inst., NYC, 1977—; from assoc. clin. prof. med. psychology to prof. clin. psychology in psychiatry Columbia U. Coll. Physicians and Surgeons, 1978—; pediat. behavioral endocrinologist Presbyn. Hosp., NYC, 1978-90, prof. psychologist in psychiat. svc., 1990—. Contbr. numerous articles to profl. publs. Recipient Disting. Sci. Achievement award Soc. for Sci. Study of Sex, 1993; grantee NIMH, NICHD. Mem. AAAS, APA, Soc. Pediat.

Psychology, Internat. Acad. Sex Rsch., German Sexual Rsch. Soc., Soc. Sci. Study Sex, Soc. Rsch. Child Devel., Soc. Sexual Therapy and Rsch., Lawson Wilkins Pediat. Endocrine Soc., Harry Benjamin Internat. Gender Dysphoria Assn. Office: Columbia U Dept Psychiatry 1051 Riverside Dr Unit 15 New York NY 10032-2695 Office Phone: 212-543-5299. Business E-Mail: meyerb@childpsych.columbia.edu.

MEYERHARDT, JEFFREY ABRAHAM, internist, oncologist; b. Englewood, NJ, Oct. 26, 1969; MD, Yale U. Sch. Med., 1997. Resident, internal medicine Beth Israel Deaconess Med. Ctr., Boston, 1997; fellow, med. oncology Dana-Farber Cancer Ctr. Inst., Boston, hosp. appointment, Gastrointestinal Cancer Ctr., dept. med. oncology, 2002—; asst. prof. medicine Harvard Med. Sch., Boston, 2004—. Contbr. articles to profl. jours. Office: Dana-Farber Cancer Inst Mailstop DL 1220 44 Binney St Boston MA 02115 Office Phone: 617-632-6855. Office Fax: 617-632-5370. *

MEYERHOFER, DAVID D., physicist, educator; b. Mar. 6, 1959; AB, Cornell U., Ithaca, NY, 1981; PhD, Princeton U., NJ, 1987. Exptl. divsn. dir. and prof. Lab. for Laser Energetics U. Rochester, NY, 2000—. Fellow: Am. Phys. Soc. Office: Lab Laser Energetics 250 East River Rd Rochester NY 14559 Office Phone: 585-275-0255. Business E-Mail: ddm@lle.rochester.edu.

MEYERHOFF, ERICH, librarian, director; b. Braunschweig, Germany, Nov. 24, 1919; came to US, 1935; s. Karl and Irma Meyerhoff; m. Inge Zuber; children: Tina, C. Michael BS, CCNY, 1943; MS, NY Sch. Social Work, 1949; MSLS, Columbia U., 1951, cert. advanced librarianship, 1974. Social worker various orgns., to 1951; reference librarian Columbia U. Med. Library, NYC, 1951-57; librarian, asst. prof. Downstate Med. Ctr., SUNY, Bklyn., 1957-61; dir. Med. Library Ctr. NY, 1961-67; librarian Health Scis. Library, SUNY-Buffalo, 1967-70, Cornell U. Med. Coll., NYC, 1970-86, asst. dean, 1977-86; chief library svc. VA Med. Ctr., NYC, 1986-88; archives librarian NYU Med. Ctr., 1980-91; asst. curator Ehrman Med. Libr.-Archives, NYU Sch. Medicine, 1991—. Adj. instr. biomed. comms. Columbia U., 1976-81; cons. U. Mich., Ann Arbor, 1968, NY Met. Reference Rsch. Libr. Agy., 1968-69, Coll. Physicians Phila., 1969-70. Fellow AAAS, Med. Library Assn. (cert., bd. dirs. 1972-76, chmn. various coms. 1968-72, 78-81, Inst. for Sci. Info. award 1981-82, Janet Doe lectr. 1977, Marcia C. Noyes award 1997), NY Acad. Medicine; mem. AAUP, Spl. Libraries Assn., Archons Colophon, Am. Assn. History Medicine, Am. Printing History Assn., Met. NY Archivists Roundtable. Avocation: travel. Home: 90 La Salle St New York NY 10027-4719 Office: NYU Med Ctr Archives 550 1st Ave New York NY 10016-6402 Office Phone: 212-263-8280. Business E-Mail: meyere01@library.med.nyu.edu.

MEYERHOFF, JACK FULTON, corporate financial executive; b. Joliet, Ill, May 15, 1926; s. Charles F. and Helen (Ferguson) M.; m. Mary Margaret Williams, Jan. 2, 1949; children— Keith F., Greg H., Deborah S., Todd C. Postgrad., Ohio Wesleyan U., 1944-45; BS, Miami U., Ohio, 1947. CPA, Ohio, Ill.; cert. Advanced Mgmt. Program, Harvard U., 1968. Mgr. Arthur Andersen & Co., Chgo., Cin., Cleve., 1947-59; treas. MacGregor Sports, Cin., 1959-63; v.p., corp. controller Brunswick Corp., Chgo., 1963-77, CFO, 1972-77, v.p. corp. affairs, 1977-80, v.p. human resources, 1980-81; chmn., CEO MarJac Assocs., Nokomis, Fla., 1981—; pres., dir. Charles Oxford Corp., Nokomis, 1984—. Bd. dirs. Sherwood Med. Industries, Inc., Old Orchard Bank & Trust Co., Tech: Time Inc., Nokomis; organizer, vice chmn. bd. trustees Caldwell Trust Co. and Trust Cos. Am., Venice, Fla., 1993—. Treas., bd. dirs. Cove Sch.; bd. dirs., pres. Skokie Valley Cmty. Hosp., No. Ill. Indsl. Assn.; v.p., bd. dirs. Jr. Achievement; bd. dirs. Chgo. Responsibility Growth, Gulf Area Med. Properties; chmn. bd. Bon Secours-Venice Hosp., HMA Regional Med. Ctr., Venice Hosp. Found.; bd. dirs. J. Clifford MacDonald Handicapped Ctr. of Tampa, Sarasota Com. of 100; bd. dirs., treas. Triangle Econ. Devel. Coun.; bd. dirs., Manatee C.C. Found., Boys and Girls Club of Venice, Pillar Cmty., Venice, Fla.; mem. adv. coun. Miami U., Georgetown U., U. So. Fla. With USNR, 1944-46. Mem. AICPA, Ohio Soc. CPAs, Ill. Soc. CPAs, Fin. Exec. Inst., Nat. Assn. Acct., Harvard Bus. Sch. Alumni Assn., Miami U. Exec. Alumni Coun. (bd. dirs., treas.), Venice Area C. of C. (bd. dirs., treas.), Sigma Alpha Epsilon, Delta Sigma Pi, Beta Alpha Psi, Beta Gamma Sigma, Venice Yacht Club, Mid Am. Club, Econ. Club, Misty Creek Country Club, Masons, Rotary. Methodist. Home: 3730 Cadbury Cir 819 Venice FL 34293 Personal E-mail: meyerhoffjm@comcast.net.

MEYERINK, VICTORIA PAIGE, film producer, actress; b. Santa Barbara, Calif., Dec. 27, 1960; d. William Joseph Meyerink and Jeanne Baird; m. Lawrence David Foldes, Apr. 24, 1983. Student, U. So. Calif., 1978-80. Actress, 1962—; v.p. Star Cinema Prodn. Group, Inc., 1981-85; pres. Star Entertainment Group, Inc., LA, 1985—. Mem. faculty Internat. Film & TV Workshops, 1991—; lectr. colls. & film festivals. Prodr. (motion pictures) The Great Skycopter Rescue, 1982, Young Warriors, 1984, Night Force, 1987, Prima Donnas, 1996, Finding Home, 2004; actress (TV series) The Danny Kaye Show, Green Acres, My Three Sons, Family Affair, The FBI, Adam 12, (motion pictures) Speedway, Night of The Grizzly, Seconds, Brainstorm, The Littlest Hobo, (TV spl.) It Isn't Easy Being a Teenage Millionairess, numerous commls. Recipient Mayoral Proclamation for Outstanding Achievement award City of LA, Recognition Cert. for 25 Yrs. Outstanding Contbns. to the Entertainment Industry City of LA, Outstanding Achievement award Acad. Family Films & TV, Former Child Star Lifetime Achievement award, 2006. Mem. Acad. Motion Picture Arts & Scis. (exec. com. Student Acad. Awards 1996—), L.A. Film Tchrs. Assn. Avocations: languages, travel, music, scuba diving, gourmet cooking.

MEYEROWITZ, ELLIOT MARTIN, biologist, educator; b. Washington, May 22, 1951; s. Irving and Freda (Goldberg) Meyerowitz; m. Joan Agnes Kobori, June 17, 1984; 2 children. AB, Columbia U., 1973; MPhil, Yale U., 1975, PhD, 1977; D (hon.), École Normale Supérieure, Lyon, France, 2007. Rsch. fellow Stanford U., Calif., 1977-79; asst. prof. biology Calif. Inst. Tech., Pasadena, 1980-85, assoc. prof., 1985-89, prof., 1989—, George W. Beadle prof. biology, 2002—, chair, divsn. biology, 2000—. Mem. editl. bd. Trends in Genetics, Current Biology, Cell Devel., Genome Biology, Philos. Transactions Royal Soc. B, 2006; mem. editl. bd.: Current Opinion in Plant Biology, Jour. of Biology; contbr. articles to profl. jours. Recipient LVMH Sci. pour l'Art Sci. prize, 1996, Internat. prize for biology, Japan, 1997, Mendel medal, UK, 1997, Wilbur Cross medal, Yale U., 2001, Ross Harrison prize, Internat. Soc. Devel. Biologist, 2005, Balzan prize, 2006; Jane Coffin Childs Meml. Fund fellow, 1977—79, Sloan Found. fellow, 1980—82. Fellow: AAAS; mem.: NAS (councilor 2006—, Lounsbery award 1999), Royal Soc., Soc. Devel. Biology (pres. 2005—06), Academie des Scis. (fgn. mem. France), Internat. Soc. for Plant Molecular Biology (pres. 1995—97), Genetics Soc. Am. (pres. 1999, medal 1996), Bot. Soc. Am. (Pelton award 1994, Centennial award 2006), Am. Soc. Plant Biologists (Gibbs medal 1995), Am. Acad. Arts and Scis., Am. Philos. Soc. Office: Calif Inst Tech Divsn Biology 156 29 Pasadena CA 91125-0001 Home Phone: 626-844-4555; Office Phone: 626-395-6889. Business E-Mail: meyerow@caltech.edu.

MEYERROSE, DALE WILLIAM, federal official, retired military officer; BS in Econs., USAF Acad., 1975; Grad, Squadron Officer Sch., Maxwell AFB, 1977; MBA, U. Utah, 1978; Grad., Nat. War Coll., Ft. Lesley J. McNair, 1992, Sr. Info. Warfare Applications Course, Maxwell AFB, 2000, Program for Nat. & Internat. Security, JFK Sch. Govt., Harvard U., 2001, Joint Flag Officer Warfighting Course, Maxwell AFB, 2003, USN Exec. Bus. Course, U. Calif-Berkeley, 2005. Commd. 2d lt. USAF, 1975, advanced through grades to major gen., 2002, ret., 2005; maintenance officer 4th Combat Comms. Group, Altus AFB, Okla., 1976-77; aide-de-camp, asst. exec. officer to the comdr. European Comms. Divsn., Kapuan Air Sta., West Germany, 1977-79; aide-de-camp to the comdr. Air Force Comms. Command, Scott AFB, Ill., 1979-80; chief of maintenance 1974th Comms. Group, Scott AFB, 1980-82; mem., air staff tng. program officer Sec. of the Air Pers. Coun., The Pentagon, Washington, 1982-83; various assignments Hdqrs. USAF, The Pentagon, Washington, 1983-85, chief future concepts, dep. chief of staff, 1990-91; comdr. 2048th Comms. Squadron, Carswell AFB, 1985-87; comms. support officer Nat. Mil. Command Ctr. the Joint Staff, The Pentagon, Washington, 1987-90; comdr. 3rd Combat Comms. Group, Tinker AFB, Okla., 1992-94; dir. comms. Operation Southern Watch, Riyadh, Saudi Arabia, 1993; dir. comms. and info. Hdqrs. USAF in Europe, Ramstein AB, Germany, 1994-96, Hdqrs. Air Combat Command, Langley AFB, Va., 1996—2000; dir. command control systems & chief info officer N. Am. Aerospace Def. Command & US Space Command, Peterson AFB, Colo., 2000—02; dir. comm. & info. & chief info. officer Hdqs. Space Command, Peterson AFB, Colo., 2002—05; dir. architecture & integration & chief info. officer Hdqs. US No. Command, Peterson AFB, Colo., 2002—05; assoc. dir. & chief info. officer Office Nat. Intelligence, Washington, 2006—. Decorated Disting. Svc. medal, Def. Superior Svc. medal, Legion of Merit with oak leaf cluster, Def. Meritorious Svc. medal woth oak leaf cluster, Meritorious Svc. medal with silver oak leaf cluster, Air Force Commendation medal, Joint Svc. Commendation medal, Air Force Achievement medal, Combar Readiness medal, Nat. Def. Svc. medal with two bronze stars, Southwest Asia Svc. medal with bronze star, Kuwait Liberation medal; Recipient Outstanding Young AFCEAN awars, Armed Forces Comm. & Electronics Assn., 1987, Medal of Merit, 1992; Named Internat. AFCEAN of the Yr., 1999, "Top 100" Info. Tech. Profl., Fed. Computer Weekly, 2005 Office: Office Nat Intelligence NEOB 725 17th St Washington DC 20500

MEYERS, ABBEY S., foundation administrator; b. Bklyn., Apr. 11, 1944; m. Jerrold B. Meyers, Oct. 23, 1966; children: David, Adam, Laura. AAS, N.Y.C. Community Coll., 1962; LHD (hon.), Alfred U., 1994. Comml. artist various advt. agys., NYC, 1962-65; dir. patient svcs. Tourette Syndrome Assn., Bayside, NY, 1980-85; exec. dir., founder Nat. Org. for Rare Disorders, Danbury, Conn., 1985—, pres. U.S. commr. Nat. Commn. on Orphan Diseases, Washington, 1986-89; subcom. human gene therapy NIH, Bethesda, Md., 1989-92, recombinant DNA adv. com., 1992-96; mem. Health Care Payor Adv. Commn. on Conn. Commn. on Hosps. and Health Care, 1992-94; mem. FDA Biol. Response Modifiers Com., 1995-99; DHHS Nat. Human Rsch. Protection Adv. Com., 2000-2002; Partnership for Human Rsch. Protection Pub. Adv. Coun., 2005—. Author: (with others) Orphan Drugs and Orphan Diseases: Clinical Reality and Public Policy, 1983, (with others) Cooperative Approaches to Research and Development of Orphan Drugs, 1985, (with others) Tourette Syndrome: Clinical Understanding and Treatment, 1988, (with others) Physicians Guide to Rare Diseases, 1992. Bd. dirs. Nat. Orphan Drug and Device Found., N.Y.C., 1982-85; leader Coalition to Pass Orphan Drug Act of 1983, 1979-82. Recipient Pub. Health Svc. award HHS, 1985, Commr.'s Spl. citation FDA, 1988. Mem. Nat. Health Coun. (bd. dirs. 1989-94), Alliance of Genetic Support Groups (bd. dirs. 1987-89), European Orgn. for Rare Disorders (hon. pres. 1997—). Avocations: reading, horseback riding. Office: Nat Orgn for Rare Disorders PO Box 1968 Danbury CT 06813-1968 E-mail: orphan@rarediseases.org.

MEYERS, ALAN HOGE, lawyer; b. Brookfield, Mo., Nov. 2, 1949; s. Francis E. and Dorothy K. (Hoge) Meyers; m. Nancy Blaker Mitchell, July 31, 1976; children: Meredith Blaker, Courtney Alyson, Mitchell Cutler. BA with honors, U. Tex., 1973, JD, 1976. Bar: Tex. 1977, U.S. Tax Ct. 1978. Assoc. J.C. Blazier, Austin, 1976—78; from assoc. to ptnr. Cotton, Bledsoe, Tighe & Dawson, Midland, Tex., 1978—96; ptnr. Morgan, Leeton & Meyers, P.C., Midland, 1996—2004; pvt. practice Midland, 2004—. Participant Leadership Midland, 1981—82; elder 1st Presbyn. Ch., Midland; trustee Cmty. Bible Study, Colorado Springs, Colo. Served to 1st lt. U.S. Army N.G., 1971—78. Mem.: Midland County Bar Assn. (pres. 2004—05), Tex. State Bar Assn. Home: 1704 Normandy Ln Midland TX 79705-1701 Office: Law Offices of Alan H Meyers PC 505 N Big Spring Ste 104 Midland TX 79701 Home Phone: 432-683-5665; Office Phone: 432-682-5800. Personal E-mail: meyersll@sbcglobal.net, ahmeyers@sbcglobal.net.

MEYERS, ALBERT IRVING, chemistry professor; b. NYC, Nov. 22, 1932; s. Hyman and Sylvia (Greenberg) M.; m. Joan Shepard, Aug. 10, 1957; children: Harold, Jill, Lisa BS, NYU, 1954, PhD, 1957. Rsch. chemist Cities Svc. Oil Co., Cranbury, NJ, 1957-58; asst., assoc. prof., prof. La. State U., New Orleans, 1958-70; postdoctoral fellow NIH, Harvard U., Cambridge, Mass., 1965—66; Boyd prof. La. State U., New Orleans, 1969; prof. Wayne State U., Detroit, 1970-72, Colo. State U., Fort Collins, 1972—2003, disting. prof., 1986—2003, John K. Stille prof. chemistry, 1993—2003, prof. emeritus chemistry, 2003—. Spl. postdoctoral fellow Harvard U., Cambridge, 1965-66; cons. G.D. Searle Co., Skokie, Ill., 1972-84, Mid-West Rsch. Inst., Kansas City, Mo., 1974-77, NIH, Bethesda, Md., 1977-79, 85-89, Bristol-Myers Squibb Co., 1983-95, Roche Colo., 1989—, GlaxoSmithKline Co., 1994-2001; mem. sci. adv. bd. La Jolla, Calif., Avanir Bioscis., La Jolla. Assoc. editor Jour. Am. Chem. Soc., 1979-85; mem. editl. adv. bd. Jour. Organic Chemistry, 1990-95, Tetrahedron, 1990-2003, Jour. Chem. Soc. Perkin, 1993, Jour. Chem. Soc. Chem. Commn., 1996, Heterocycles, 1974—; contbr. over 500 articles to profl. jours. Recipient Alexander von Humboldt award Fed. Republic of Germany, 1984, Disting. Alumni award NYU, 1990, award in synthetic chemistry Am. Chem. Soc., 1985, A.C. Cope Scholar award, 1987, Yamada prize, Japan, 1996, award Internat. Soc. Heterocyclic Chemistry, 1997; named Man of Yr., New Orleans Jaycees, 1968, Boyd Prof. La. State U., 1969; recipient pioneer award Am. Insts. Chemists, 1998. Fellow AAAS, Nat. Acad. Sci.; mem. Royal Soc. Chemistry (silver medalist 1982), Phila. Organic Chemistry Soc. (Allan Day award 1987). Home: 1500 Hepplewhite Ct Fort Collins CO 80526-3822 Office: Colo State Univ Dept Chemistry Fort Collins CO 80523-0001 Home Phone: 970-223-9055; Office Phone: 970-491-7060. E-mail: aimeyers@colostate.edu.

MEYERS, AMY, museum director; m. Jack Meyers; 1 child, Rachel. BA, U. Chgo.; PhD in Am. Studies, Yale U. Rschr. Dumbarton Oaks; rschr. Ctr. for Advanced Study in Visual Arts, Nat. Gallery; curator Am. Art, Henry E. Huntington Libr., Art Collections and Bot. Gardens, San Marino, Calif.; dir. Yale Ctr. for Brit. Art; prof. art Yale U. Adj. faculty Calif. Inst. Tech.; vice chair, Huntington rep. Assn. Rsch. Insts. in History of Art, 1995—2000. Editor (with Margaret Pritchard): Empire's Nature: Mark Catesby's New World Vision; editor: (with Alan Trachtenberg) Classic Essays on Photography. Office: Yale Ctr for Brit Art PO Box 208280 1080 Chapel St New Haven CT 06520-8280

MEYERS, ARLEN, physician; b. Philadelphia, Pa. MD, Jefferson Med. Coll., 1972; MBA, U. Colo., 1984. Prof. U. Colo. Sch. of Medicine, Denver, 1976—2006. Office: U Colo 4200 E 9th Ave B-205 Denver CO 80262 Office Phone: 303-315-8642. Business E-Mail: arlen.meyers@uchsc.edu.

MEYERS, CAROLYN WINSTEAD, academic administrator, mechanical engineer, educator; b. Hampton, Va., May 11, 1946; d. John Selner and Eva Carroll (Tonsler) Winstead; divorced; m. James E. Cofield, Jr.; children: Timothy C. III, Leslie C., Lisa A.; m. James E. Cofield, Jr. BSME, Howard U., 1968; MSME, Ga. Inst. Tech., 1979, PhD in Metallurgy, 1984. Steam generator analyst Machinery Apparatus Operation div. Machinery Apparatus Ops. div. GE, Schenectady, 1968; systems analyst Info. Svcs. div. Info. Svcs. div. GE, Bethesda, Md., 1969; instr. Atlanta U. Ctr. Corp., 1972-77; instr. mech. engring. Ga. Inst. Tech., Atlanta, 1979-84, asst. prof., 1984-90, assoc. prof., 1990-96; dir. SUCCEED Coalition Ctr. for Profl. Success, 1992-93; assoc. dean rsch. Coll. Engring. Ga. Inst. Tech., Atlanta, 1993-96; dean Coll. Engring. NC A&T State U., Greensboro, 1996, prof. mech. engring., 1996—2006, vice chancellor acad. affairs, 2000—06, provost, 2001—06; pres. Norfolk State U., Va., 2006—. Summer faculty fellow USAF Materials Lab., Wright-Patterson AFB, Ohio, 1988; program officer NSF, 1996-99. Contbr. articles to profl. jours. Chmn. waste volume reduction subcom. Atlanta Mayor's Commn. on Solid Waste Disposal, 1989-92; trustee Westminster Schs., Atlanta, 1989-93; program dir. divsn. undergrad edn. NSF, 1997-99, divsn. human resources devel., Arlington, V., 1999—; bd. dirs. Piedmont Triad Coun. Internat. Visitors, N.C. Sch. Sci. and Math, 2000-, Moses Cone Health Sys., 2003-, United Way Greater Greensboro, 2002-03, Rsch. Triangle Inst., MentorNet; chair, bd. dirs. Nat. Inst. Aerospace, 2003—. Recipient Faculty award for women NSF, 1991, Disting. Alumni award Atlanta-Howard U. Alumni Assn., 1992; named Black Engr. of Yr. in Higher Edn. U.S. Black Engr. Mag. and Coun. Engring Deans, 1990; Pres. Young Investigator grantee NSF, 1988; inducted to Acad. of Disting. Engring. Alumni Ga. Tech. U., 1996; honored alumna in edn. on Charter Day Howard U., 1997. Fellow ASME (Engr. of Yr. 1990); mem. AIME, SAE (Ralph Teetor Ednl. award 1986), Am. Soc. Engr. Edn. (v.p. pub. affairs 2001-2003), Foundry Ednl. Found. (key prof. 1985-95), Soc. Women Engrs. (state pres. Atlanta sect. 1987-90), Am. Foundrymen's Soc. (sponsor student sect. 1987-95, aluminum divsn. sci. merit award 1994), Soc. Black Engrs. (Golden Torch award 2002, Emerald honors Women in Sci and Tech. 2003), Links (pres. Atlanta chpt. 1987-89), Jack and Jill Am., The Girl Friends, Golden Key, Sigma Xi, Tau Beta Pi, Phi Kappa Phi, Alpha Kappa Alpha, Beta Gamma Sigma. Roman Catholic. Office: Office of Pres Norfolk State U 700 Park Ave Norfolk VA 23504 E-mail: president@nsu.edu.

MEYERS, CHRISTINE LAINE, marketing and media executive, consultant; b. Detroit, Mar. 7, 1946; d. Ernest Robert and Eva Elizabeth (Laine) M.; 1 child, Kathryn Laine; m. Oliver S. Moore III, May 12, 1990. BA, U. Mich., 1968. Editor indsl. rels. diesel divsn. Gen. Motors Corp., Detroit, 1968; nat. advt. mgr. J.L. Hudson Co., Detroit, 1969-76, mgr. internal sales promotion, 1972-73, dir. pub., 1973-76; nat. advt. mgr. Pontiac Motor divsn., Mich., 1976-78; pres., owner Laine Meyers Mktg. Cos., Inc., Troy, Mich., 1978—; founder, owner CORP! Mag., 1998—. Dir. Internat. Inst. Met. Detroit, Inc. Contbr. articles to profl. publs. Bus. adv. coun. Ctrl. Mich. U., 1977-79; pub. adv. com. on jud. candidates Oakland County Bar Assn.; adv. bd. Birmingham Cmty. Hosp., Bank of Am., 1999-2001; bd. dirs. YMCA, Mich., 1992-98, Haven, 1997—, Automation Alley, Oakland County, 1999—. Named Mich. Ad Woman of Yr., 1976, one of Top 10 Working Women, Glamour mag., 1978, one of 100 Best and Brightest Advt. Age, 1987, one of Mich.'s top 25 female bus. owners Nat. Assn. Women Bus. Owners, One of Top 10 Women Owned Bus., Mich., 1994; recipient Vanguard award Women in Comm., 1986, Lifetime Achievement award Northwood U., 2002. Mem. Internat. Assn. Bus. Communicators, Adcraft Club, Women's Advt. Club (1st v.p. 1975), Women's Econ. Club (pres. 1976-77), Internat. Women's Forum Mich. (founding pres. 1986-97), Internat. Inst. Detroit (bd. dirs. 1986-89), Detroit C. of C., Troy C. of C., Mortar Bd., Quill and Scroll, Pub. Rels. Com. Women for United Found., Founders Soc. Detroit Inst. Arts, Fashion Group, Pub. Rels. Soc. Am., First Soc. Detroit (exec. com. 1970-71), Kappa Tau Alpha. Office Phone: 248-458-2677 ext.301. Business E-Mail: cmyers@corpmagazine.com.

MEYERS, CHRISTOPHER, humanities educator, consultant; s. Diana Meyers and Ehrhard Bahr (Stepfather); m. Donna Elsdon, Apr. 6, 1997; 1 child, Natasha Leigh Meyers-Cherry stepchildren: Renee Elsdon, Jonathon Elsdon. BA, U. Calif., Santa Cruz, 1980; cert. in clin. ethics, U. Tenn., 1984, D, 1986. Prof. philosophy Calif. State U., Bakersfield, 1986—, exec. dir. Kegley Inst. Ethics, 1987—; clin. ethicist Kern Med. Ctr., Bakersfield, 1997—. Ethics cons., instr. Mercy Healthcare, Bakersfield, 1991—, San Joaquin Cmty. Hosp., Bakersfield, 1995—. Author: (book) A Practical Guide to Clinical Ethics Consulting: Ethics, Power & Expertise, 2007; contbr. articles to profl. jours. Ethics cons., instr. Multiple Bus. and Philanthropic Groups, Bakersfield, 1987—2006. Mem.: Am. Soc. Bioethics and Humanities, Assn. Practical and Profl. Ethics, Am. Philos. Assn. Avocations: fly fishing, hiking, bicycling. Office: Calif State U Bakersfield 9001 Stockdale Hwy Bakersfield CA 93311 Home Phone: 661-588-3449; Office Phone: 661-654-3149. Business E-Mail: cmeyers@csub.edu.

MEYERS, DALE (MRS. MARIO COOPER), artist; b. Chgo. d. Walter Herman and Gertude Wetterer; m. Mario Cooper, Oct. 11, 1964; children: Dale, Steven R. Student, Glendale Coll., Corcoran Gallery Sch. Art, Washington, 1962-63, Art Student's League, NYC, 1964-78. Instr. Art Students League, 1979—; ofcl. artist NASA, USCG.; lectr. Parson's Sch. Design, Nat. Acad. Sch. Author The Sketchbook, 1983; contbr.: Watercolor Bold and Free, Am. Artist mag, Diversion mag.; solo exhbns. include, West Wing Gallery, Ringwood (N.J.) State Park, 1970, Manor Club, Pelham Manor, N.Y., 1970, Apollo Art Gallery, Oklahoma City, 1972, Quadrangle Gallery, Dallas, 1972, Galveston Ctr. for Arts, 1974, Fla. Gulf Coast Art Ctr., 1977, 86, Okura Hotel, Tokyo, Japan, 1977, Owensboro Mus. Art, 1983, Salmagundi Club, 1986, 88, Stehle-Reed Gallery, Midland, Tex., 1987, others; artist-in-residence, Galveston Arts Ctr., 1974, Owensboro Mus. Art, 1983, Asilomar, Calif., 1983, 84; group exhbns. include Two Hundred Years of Watercolor Painting in Am, Met. Mus. Art, 1966, Eyewitness to Space, Nat. Gallery Art, Washington, 1969, Smithsonian Instn., 1961-63, Corcoran Gallery, 1963, Museo de la Acuarela, Mexico City, 1968, 89, London (Ont., Can.) Mus. Art, 1971-72, Art Gallery Hamilton, Ont., Can., 1971-72, Ont. Inst. Edn., 1971-72, Butler Inst. Art, 1962—, Frye Mus., 1962—; represented in permanent collections, Calif. Palace of Legion of Honor, San Francisco, Nat. Acad. N.Y.C., Avon Fine Arts Collection, NASA, EPA, Museo de la Acuarela, Schumacher Gallery, Columbus, Ohio, Slater Mus., Conn., Portland (Maine) Mus., U. Utah Fine Arts Collection, Frye Mus., Seattle, Owensboro Mus. Art, Coll. Misericordia, Dallas, Pa, Canton Art Inst., Ohio, Arnot Mus., Elmira, N.Y.; internat. watercolor exhbn. Can., U.S., Gt. Britain, 1991-94, Chung Cheng Gallery, Taipei, 1994. Recipient Henry W. Ranger award Nat. Acad. Design, 1968, Samuel F.B. Morse medal, 1973, Anna Hyatt Huntington Bronze medal, 1971, Knickerbocker Artists Gold medal, 1981, 88, Allied Artists Am. award, 1969, Gold medal honor Nat. Arts Club, 1972, Anna Hyatt Huntington Gold medal, 1974, Adolf and Cara Obrig award Nat. Acad., 1974, 81, Walter Biggs award, 1976, Allied Arts Gold medal, 1978, Audubon ARtists Silver medal, 1984. Fellow Royal Soc. Arts (Grumbocher Gold medals 1988, 90); mem. Am. Watercolor Soc. (pres. 1993-03, pres. emeritus 2003-, editor jours. 1962-79, Bronze medal honor award 1968, awards 1970, 72, 78, 79, 81, 82, 83, 85, 87, 89, 93, 98, High Winds medal 2001, 05, Dolphin medal 2000), Nat. Acad. (academician), Allied Artists Am. (pres. 1975-78), Art Students League N.Y., La. Watercolor Soc. (hon.), Ky. Watercolor Soc., Ohio Watercolor Soc. (hon.), Watercolor Soc. Mex., Fla. Watercolor Soc. (hon.), Audubon Artists, Salimagundi Club (medal of honor 1994). Office: Art Students League 215 W 57th St New York NY 10019

MEYERS, DAVID GEORGE, internist, cardiologist, educator; b. Muscatine, Iowa, Oct. 5, 1950; BS, Loras Coll., 1972; MD, U. Iowa, 1976; MPH, Med. Coll. Wis., 1998. Cert. in cardiology Am. Bd. Internal Medicine, Am. Bd. Preventive Medicine, Am. Bd. Clin. Lipidology. Intern Creighton U., 1976-77, resident medicine, 1977-79; fellow cardiology Med. Coll. Va., 1979-81; from asst. prof. internal medicine to assoc. prof. Neb. U. Med. Ctr., Omaha, 1981-93; mem. faculty U. Kans. Med. Ctr., Kansas City, 1994, prof. internal medicine and preventive medicine, 1994—, dir. of preventive Cardiology, 1994—. Recipient Chancellor's

Outstanding Classroom Tchg. award, U. Kans., 1997. Fellow ACP, Am. Coll. Cardiology, Am. Coll. Chest Physicians, Am. Heart Assn., Am. Coll. Preventive Medicine, Nat. Lipid Assn.; mem. Am. Coll. Epidemiology, Am. Soc. Preventive Cardiology, Soc. Civil War Surgeons, Internat. Wine and Food Soc., Am. Inst. for Wine and Food. Office: U Kans Med Ctr 3901 Rainbow Blvd Kansas City KS 66160-0001 Office Phone: 913-588-6015. Business E-Mail: dmeyers@kumc.edu. *

MEYERS, ERIC MARK, religion educator; b. Norwich, Conn., June 5, 1940; s. Karl D. and Shirlee M. (Meyer) M.; m. Carol Lyons, June 25, 1964; children: Julie Kaete, Dina Elisa. AB, Dartmouth Coll., 1962; MA, Brandeis U., 1964; PhD, Harvard U., 1969. Lerner prof. religion, archeol., bibl. study, ancient hist. Duke U., Durham, NC, 1969—, dir. grad. program in religion, 1979—86, 2001—06; dir. Annenberg Inst., Phila., 1991-92. Pres. Am. Schs. Oriental Rsch., Boston, 1990—96, 2006—07; commentator on biblical archaeology; dir. 8 digs Israel, Italy, 1970—2000; co-dir. NEH seminar Duke U., 2004; dir. Jewish St. Program, 1972—90, 2002—. Author: 10 books; co-author: The Cambridge Companiion to the Bible, 1997; editor (in chief): The Oxford Encyclopedia of Archaeology in the Near East, 5 vols., 1997; contbr. articles more than 400 to profl. jours.; frequent guest (TV series) A&E channel, Discovery channel; frequent guest: History Channel. Jewish. Avocations: singing (baritone), golf, the arts, travel. Home: 3202 Waterbury Dr Durham NC 27707-2416 Office: Duke U 118 Gray Bldg PO Box 90964 Bldg Durham NC 27708-0964 Office Phone: 919-660-3517. Business E-Mail: emc@duke.edu.

MEYERS, JAN, retired congresswoman; b. Lincoln, Nebr., July 20, 1928; m. Louis Meyers; children: Valerie, Philip AA in Fine Arts cum laude, William Woods Coll., 1948; BA in Communications (hon.), U. Nebr.-Lincoln, 1951; LittD, William Woods Coll., 1986; LLD (hon.), Baker U., 1993. Mem. Overland Park (Kans.) City Coun., 1967-72; pres. Overland (Kans.) Park City Council; mem. Kans. Senate, 1972-84, chmn. pub. health and welfare com., local govt. com.; mem. 99th-103rd Congresses from 3rd Kans. Dist., 1985-97, mem. com. internat. rels., chmn. sml. bus. com., mem. com. on econ. and ednl. opportunities. Chmn. pub. health and welfare com., chmn. local govt. com., vice chmn. transp. com., vice chmn. utilities com. Kans. Senate. 3rd Dist. co-chmn. Bob Dole for U.S. Senate, 1968; chmn. Johnson County Bob Bennett For Gov., 1974; mem. Johnson County Cmty. Coll. Found.; bd. dirs. Johnson County Mental Health Assn.; mem. fundraising com. Johnson County Am. Cancer Soc.; mem. com. for Ctr. for Aging, Kans. U. Med. Ctr.; bd. dirs. Johnson County Libr. Assn. Recipient Outstanding Elected Ofcl. of Yr. award Assn. Cmty. Mental Health Ctrs. Kans., Woman of Achievement Matrix award Women in Communications, Disting. Service award Bus. and Profl. Women Kansas City, William Woods Alumna award of distinction, Cmty. Svc. award Jr. League Kansas City, 1st Disting. Legislator award Kans. Assn. C.C.s, Outstanding Svc. award Kans. Library Assn., United Community Services, Kans. Pub. Health Assn., award Gov.'s Conf. Child Abuse and Neglect, Outstanding Legislator award Kans. Action for Children, Friend award Nat. Assn. County Park and Recreation Ofcls., 1987, Disting. Alumna award, 1991, Spirit of Enterprise award U.S. C. of C., Guardian of Small Bus. award Nat. Fedn. Ind. Bus. Mem. LWV (past pres. Shawnee Mission) Methodist.

MEYERS, JERRY IVAN, lawyer; b. McKeesport, Pa., Mar. 26, 1946; s. Eugene J. and Gladys Claire (Rubenstein) M.; m. Judith Drake Aughenbaugh, June, 26, 1971; 1 child, Lindsey Drake. BA in Philosophy and Rhetoric, U. Pitts., 1972; JD cum laude, U. Miami, 1975. Bar: Pa. 1975, US Dist. Ct. (we. dist.) Pa. 1975. Assoc. Berger & Kapetan, Pitts., 1975-78; ptnr. Meyers, Rosen, Louik & Perry P.C., Pitts., 1978—2004, Meyers, Kenrick & Giuffre, LLC, 2004—06, Meyers, Kennrick, Giuffre & Evans LLC, 2006—. Named to Best Lawyers in Am., Pa. Super Lawyers. Mem. Assn. Trial Lawyers Am., Pa. Trial Lawyers Assn. (past pres. western Pa. chpt., bd. govs. legis. policy com., med.-legis. com.), Acad. Trial Lawyers Allegheny County. Office: Meyers Kerrick Giuffre & EvansLLC Ste 5745 US Steel Tower 600 Grant St Pittsburgh PA 15219 Office Phone: 412-281-4100. E-mail: meyers@meyersmedmal.com.

MEYERS, JOHN ALLEN, magazine publisher; b. Winnetka, Ill., Feb. 21, 1929; s. Fred W. and Ruth B. (Burras) M.; m. Jane Bowers, Sept. 18, 1954; children: Jennifer, Katherine, John. BA, Mich. State U., 1951, Litt.D. (hon.), 1978; postgrad., Columbia U., 1965. Mgr. Cleve. Time mag., 1960-63, mgr. Chgo., 1963-65, mgr. NYC, 1965-68, worldwide advt. sales dir., 1968-72; v.p. Time, Inc., publisher Sports Illustrated mag., 1972-78; pub. Time mag., 1978-85; chmn. Time Inc. Mag. Co., 1985-88; chmn. emeritus Time Inc., 1988—. Appointed presdl. bd. adv. on Pvt. Sector Initiatives; chmn. J.A.M. Enterprises. Editor-in-chief Constitution mag. Bd. dirs., pres., Found. for the U.S. Constn., 1986-2004; Served with USMC, 1951-53. Decorated Purple Heart.

MEYERS, KAREN DIANE, lawyer, educator; b. Cin., July 8, 1950; d. Willard Paul and Camille Jeannette (Schutte) M.; m. William J. Jones, Mar. 27, 1978. BA summa cum laude, Thomas More Coll., 1971; MBA, MEd, Xavier U., 1978; JD, U. Ky., Covington, 1978. Bar: Ohio 1978, Ky. 1978; CLU; CPCU; cert. structured settlement cons. Clk. to mgr. Baldwin Co., Cin., 1970-78; adj. prof. bus. Thomas More Coll., Crestview Hill, Ky., 1978—, CSSC-U. Notre Dame, 1994, CSSC, 1994; asst. sec., asst. v.p., sr. counsel The Ohio Life Ins. Co., Hamilton, 1978-91; prin. KD Meyers & Assocs., 1991; v.p. Benefit Designs, Inc., 1991-96, Little, Meyers & Assocs., Ltd., Cin., 1996—; adj. prof. Miami U., 1998—. Adj. lectr. U. Notre Dame, South Bend, Ind., 2005—. Bd. dirs. ARC, Hamilton, 1978-83, vol., 1978—; bd. dirs. YWCA, Hamilton, 1985-91. Gardner Found. fellow, 1968-71; recipient Ind. Progress award Bus. & Profl. Women, 1990. Fellow Life Mgmt. Inst. Atlanta; mem. ABA, Soc. Chartered Property Casualty Underwriters (instr. 1987—), Cin. Bar Assn., Butler County Bar Assn., Ohio Bar Assn., Ky. Bar Assn. Roman Catholic. Avocations: aerobics, jogging, crafts. Home: 7903 Hickory Hill Ln Cincinnati OH 45241-1363

MEYERS, KENNETH RAYMOND, telecommunications industry executive; b. Chgo., Jan. 16, 1954; s. Raymond F. and Rita L. (Dunlevy) M.; m. Chere L. Lazzare, Mar. 10, 1984; children: Kristin, Kathryn. BBA, Loyola U., Chgo., 1977; M in Mgmt., Northwestern U., 1994. CPA. Various fin. positions including divsn. contr. and audit mgr. The Marmon Group, Chgo., 1977-84; contr. to treas. to v.p. fin. Imi-Tech Corp., Elk Grove, Ill., 1984-87; various sr. mgmt. fin. positions US Cellular Corp., Chgo., 1987—99, exec. v.p., CFO, 1999—2007, Tel. and Data Systems, 2007—. Bd. dirs. US Cellular Corp., Tel. and Data Systems. Mem. alumni adv. bd. Northwestern U. J.L. Kellogg Sch. Mgmt. Mem. AICPA, Fin. Exec. Inst., Cellular Tel. Industry Assn. (fin. com.). Roman Catholic. Avocations: boating, golf. Office: Tel and Data Systems 30 N LaSalle St Ste 4000 Chicago IL 60602 Office Phone: 312-630-1900. Office Fax: 312-630-1908. *

MEYERS, LAWRENCE EDWARD, state judge; m. Barbara Meyers; children: Kelli Kelli, Clay. BA in History and Chemistry, So. Meth. U., 1970; JD, U. Kans., 1973; postgrad., U. Tex., Arlington, Tex. Wesleyan U. Asst. dist. atty. Montgomery County, Kans., 1973—75; pvt. practice Ft. Worth, 1975—88; assoc. justice U.S. Ct. Appeals (2nd cir.), Ft. Worth, 1988—92; judge Ct. Criminal Appeals, Ft. Worth, 1992—. Instr. Tex. Christian U., Ft. Worth. Mem. parish coun. St. Mary's of Assumption, Ft. Worth. Mem.: Tarrant County Bar Assn., State Bar Kans., State Bar Tex. Republican. Office: Court of Criminal Appeals Supreme Ct Bldg 201 W 14th St Austin TX 78701-1614 also: PO Box 12308 Austin TX 78711-2308

MEYERS, LINDA DEE, non-profit administrator, researcher; b. Chgo., Dec. 31, 1945; m. L. Richard Meyers; 2 children. BA in Phys. Edn. & Health with honors, Goshen Coll., 1968; MS in Nutrition, Colo. State U., 1974; PhD in Human Nutrition, Cornell U., 1978. Tchr. Swaneng Hill Secondary Sch., 1968-71; staff Bioteko Rural Coop., Serowe, Botswana, 1972; rsch. asst. dept. food sci. and nutrition Colo. State U., 1973-74; scientist Nat. Ctr. Health Statistics HHS, Washington, 1976-78, sr. nutrition advisor, 1986—, dep. dir. and team leader nutrn., environ. hlth. & sci. coord., 1996—2001; dep. dir. food and nutrition Inst. of Med. of Nat. Acads., Washington, 2001—03, exec. dir., food and nutrition bd., 2003—. Contbr. articles to profl. jours. Mem. APHA, IFT, Am. Soc. Nutrition, Omicron Nu, Phi Kappa Phi. Office: Inst of Med 500 Fifth St NW Washington DC 20001

MEYERS, MARLENE O., retired hospital administrator; m. Eugene Meyers; children: Lori, Lisa, Dean. BSN, U. Sask., 1962; postgrad., U. Oslo, Norway, 1973; MSc, U. Calgary, Alta., Can., 1976; continuing edn., Harvard U., 1980, Banff Sch. Mgmt., 1985, U. Western Ont., Can., 1993; EMT-B, Scottsdale C.C., 2000. RN, Ariz. Various nursing positions, Alta. and B.C., Can., 1962-69; instr., chair Mount Royal Coll. Allied Health, Calgary, 1969-82; asst. exec. dir. Rockyview Hosp., Calgary, 1982-85; v.p. patient svcs. Calgary Gen. Hosp., 1985-91, pres., CEO, 1991-95, Meyers and Assocs. Health Care Mgmt. Cons., Calgary, 1995—98; clin. nurse Scottsdale Behavioral Health Ctr., 1999—2006. Surveyor Can. Coun. on Health Facilities Accreditation, 1986-97; mem. adv. com. for South Caucasus Health info. project, Can. Adv. Com. Named Calgary Woman of Yr. in field of Health, 1982; recipient Heritage of Svc. award, 1992. Mem. Alta. Assn. RNs (hon.), Can. Coll. Health Svcs. Orgn., Can. Exec. Svcs. Orgn., Can. Soc. for Internat. Health (bd. dirs. 1997-2001, South Caucasus adv. com. 2001—), Rotary Internat. also: 10464 E Cannon Dr Scottsdale AZ 85258-4929

MEYERS, MARY ANN, foundation administrator, consultant, writer; b. Sodus, NY, Sept. 30, 1937; d. Harold Galpin and Clarice Mildred (Daniel) Dye; m. John Matthew Meyers, Aug. 22, 1959; children: Andrew Christopher, Anne Kathryn. BA magna cum laude, Syracuse U., 1959; MA, U. Pa., 1965, PhD, 1976. Editorial asst. Ladies' Home Jour., Phila., 1959-62; editor, asst. dir. news bur. U. Pa., Phila., 1962-65, asst. to pres., 1973-75, univ. sec., lectr. Am. civilization, 1980-90; contbg. writer The Pennsylvania Gazette, Phila., 1965—97; dir. coll. rels., editor Haverford Horizons, lectr. in religion Haverford (Pa.) Coll., 1977-80; pres. The Annenberg Found., St. Davids, Pa., 1990-92; v.p. for external affairs Moore Coll. Art and Design, Phila., 1995-97; sr. fellow The John Templeton Found., Radnor, Pa., 1997—. Vis. com. dept. biology U. Pa., 1996—2002; mem. bd. advisors The Peter Gruber Found., St. Thomas, U.S. V.I., 2001—. Author: A New World Jerusalem, 1983, Art, Education and African American Culture: Albert Barnes and the Science of Philanthropy, 2004, 06; contbg. author: Death in America, 1975, Gladly Learn, Gladly Teach, 1978, Coping with Serious Illness, 1980, Religion in American Life, 1987; contbr. articles to profl. jours. Judge recognition program Coun. for Advancement and Support Edn., Washington, 1977—78, chair creative editing and writing workshop, 1978; mem. Picker Found. Program on Human Qualities in Medicine, NYC and Phila., 1980—83; del. Phila.-Leningrad Sister Cities Project, 1986; trustee U. Pa. Press, 1985—2003; vice chmn. U. Pa. 250th Anniversary Commn., 1987—90; mem. steering com. of bd. trustees U. Pa., Annenberg Sch. for Comm., 1990—92; mem. adv. bd. U. Pa., Annenberg Ctr. for the Performing Arts, 1990—98; mem. bd. overseers U. Pa., Sch. Arts and Scis., 1990—97; mem. steering com. of bd. trustees Annenberg Ctr. for Comm., U. So. Calif., LA, 1990—92, The Annenberg Washington Program in Comm. Policy Studies of Northwestern U., Washington, 1990—92; dir., sec. Am. Acad. Polit. and Social Sci., 1992—, World Affairs Coun. Phila., 1990—95; dir. Diagnostic and Rehab. Ctr., Phila., 1993—2002. Recipient Excellence award Women in Communications, Inc., 1973-74, award for pub. affairs reporting Newsweek/Coun. for Advancement and Support Edn., 1977, Silver medal Coun. for Advancement and Support Edn., 1986. Mem. Am. Acad. Polit. and Social Sci. (sec. and dir. 1992-), Cosmopolitan Club, Sunday Breakfast Club, Phi Beta Kappa (mem. steering com. Delaware Valley chpt. 1995-97). Roman Catholic. Home: 217 Gypsy Ln Wynnewood PA 19096-1112

MEYERS, MORTON ALLEN, radiologist, educator; b. Troy, NY, Oct. 1, 1933; s. David and Jeanne Sarah (Dunn) M.; m. Beatrice Applebaum, June 1, 1963; children— Richard, Amy. MD, SUNY, Upstate Med. Coll., 1959. Diplomate Am. Bd. Radiology, 1965. Intern Bellevue Hosp., NYC, 1959-60; resident in radiology Columbia-Presbyn. Med. Ctr., NYC, 1960-63; fellow Am. Cancer Soc., 1961-63; prof. dept. radiology Cornell U. Med. Ctr., NYC, 1973-78; radiologist in chief Stony Brook U. Hosp., 1978—91; prof., chmn. dept. radiology SUNY Sch. Medicine, Stony Brook, 1978-91, prof. dept. radiology, 1991-98, disting. univ. prof., 1998—. Cons. Northport VA Hosp.; vis. investigator St. Mark's Hosp., London, 1976; spkr. in field. Author: Diseases of the Adrenal Glands: Radiologic Diagnosis, 1963, Dynamic Radiology of the Abdomen: Normal and Pathologic Anatomy, 1976, 5th edit., 2000, tranl. in Spanish, 1980, Japanese, 1985, 1991, Italian, 1992, Portuguese, 1999, Iatrogenic Gastrointestinal Complications, 1981; series editor: Computed Tomography of the Gastrointestinal Tract: Including the Peritoneal Cavity and Mesentery, 1986, Neoplasms of the Digestive Tract: Imaging, Staging, and Management, 1998, Happy Accidents: Serendipity in Modern Medical Breakthroughs, 2007, founding editor-in-chief: Abdominal Imaging, 1976—, mem. editl. bd.: Iatrogenics; mem. editl. bd. Surg. and Radiol. Anatomy; contbr. chapters to books, articles to profl. jours. Served to capt. M.C. U.S. Army, 1963-65. Recipient Gold medal, U. Leeds, 1980, Radiol. Soc. Republic of China, 1986, Asian-Oceanian Congress Radiology, 1987, European Congress of Radiology, 1995, Indian Radiol. and Imaging Assn., 1999. Fellow: European Soc. Gastrointestinal and Abdominal Radiology, Am. Coll. Gastroenterology, Am. Coll. Radiology; mem.: European Soc. Urogenital Radiology, NY Acad. Gastroenterology, NY Roentgen Ray Soc., Assn. Univ. Radiologists, Israel Radiol. Soc. (hon.), Italian Radiol. Soc. (hon. Medal of honor 1983), Royal Belgian Soc. Gastroenterology (hon.), Spanish Radiol. Soc. (hon.), European Assn. Radiology (hon.), Soc. Gastrointestinal Radiologists (Cannon medal 1993, Hartman medal 1995), Soc. Uroradiology, Am. Gastroenterol. Assn., Am. Roentgen Ray Soc. (Gold medal 1975, 1980), Radiol. Soc. N.Am. (ann. orator 1986), Alpha Omega Alpha. Home: 14 Wainscott Ln East Setauket NY 11733-3816 Office: SUNY Health Scis Ctr Sch Medicine Dept Radiology Stony Brook NY 11794-8460 Office Phone: 631-751-3685.

MEYERS, NANCY JANE, screenwriter, producer, director; b. Phila., Dec. 8, 1949; d. Irving H. and Patricia (Lemisch) M; m. Charles Shyer. BA, Am. U., Washington, 1971. Writer, prodr.: (films) Private Benjamin (Acad. award nominee, Writers Guild award 1980), Baby Boom, 1987, Father of the Bride, 1991, A Place to be Loved (assoc. prodr.), 1991, I Love Trouble, 1994, Father of the Bride Part II, 1995, Ted Hawkins: Amazing Grace (co-prodr.), 1996, The Affair of the Necklace, 2001, writer: (films) Irreconcilable Differences, 1984, Protocol, 1985, Once Upon A Crime..., 1992; writer, prodr., dir.: (films) Something's Gotta Give, 2003, The Holiday, 2006; prodr., dir.: (films) What Women Want, 2000; writer, dir.: (films) The Parent Trap, 1998. Mem. ASCAP, Acad. Motion Picture Arts and Scis., Writers Guild Am. West. Office: Creative Artists Agy 9830 Wilshire Blvd Beverly Hills CA 90212-1825 *

MEYERS, NICHOLAUS, music educator; s. Walden Augustus and Cheryl Renee Meyers. MusB, Augusta State U., 1997—2002; MusM, U. of Tenn., 2002—04. Grad. libr. asst. U. Tenn., 2003—04; instr. of music Augusta State U., 2004—. Percussion instr. Lakeside H.S., Evans, Ga., 2001—; percussionist Augusta Opera, Augusta, Ga., 2002—; timpanist Augusta Choral Soc., Augusta, Ga., 2004—; percussionist Oakridge Symphony, Oakridge, Tenn., 2004. Composer: (composition) A Glimpse Ahead, Reflections, Three Shorts, Altered Stages, Contrasting Opinions, Two Holy Songs, Two Songs of Love, Concerto for Marimba, The Picture in My Mind, The New Found Feeling. Maxwell Meml. Music scholarship, Augusta State U., 1998—2002, Mauldin Music scholarship, 1999—2002. Mem.: ASCAP, Percussive Arts Soc., Soc. of Composers, Coll. Music Soc. Achievements include research in Guide to Timpani Concertos. Home: 495 Creekwalk Cir Martinez GA 30907 Home Phone: 706-868-5807. Personal E-mail: nmeyers@aug.edu.

MEYERS, PAMELA SUE, lawyer; b. Lakewood, NJ, June 13, 1951; d. Morris Leon and Isabel (Leibowitz) M.; m. Gerald Stephen Greenberg, Aug. 24, 1975; children: David Stuart Greenberg, Allison Brooke Greenberg. AB with distinction, Cornell U., 1973; JD cum laude, Harvard U., 1976. Bar: NY 1977, Ohio 1990. Assoc. Stroock & Stroock & Lavan, NYC, 1976-80; staff v.p., asst. gen. counsel Am. Premier Underwriters, Inc., Cin., 1980-96; legal counsel Citizens Fed. Bank, Dayton, Ohio, 1997-98; gen. counsel, sec. Mosler Inc., Hamilton, Ohio, 1998—2001. Bd. dirs. Hamilton County Alcohol and Drug Addiction Svc. Bd., 1996-2000, Adath Israel Congregation, 1999-2005; dir. Gorman Heritage Farm Found., 2006—; trustee Carpenters Creek Civic Assn., 2004-06; mem. Village Evendale Recreation Commn., 2006—. Mem. Cin. Bar Assn., Harvard Club of Cin. (pres. 1998-99, bd. dirs. 1993-2000), Phi Beta Kappa. Jewish. Avocations: piano, reading, tennis. Home: 3633 Carpenters Creek Dr Cincinnati OH 45241-3824 Personal E-mail: psmeyers@fuse.net.

MEYERS, PHILIP ALAN, geochemistry educator, researcher; b. Hackensack, NJ, Mar. 3, 1941; s. Harold Grove and Gertrude Myra (Smith) M.; m. Judith Arlene Brown, May 15, 1965; children: Shelley, Suzanne, Christopher. BS, Carnegie-Mellon U., 1964; PhD, U. R.I., 1972. Rsch. chemist Inmont Corp., Clifton, N.J., 1967-68; prof. U. Mich., Ann Arbor, 1972—. Cons. Marathon Oil Co., BP Oil Co., Chevron Oil Co., Cities Svc. Oil. Co., 1980; dir. Ct. Lakes and Marine Waters Ctr., U. Mich., 1982-83; vis. prof. Eidgenossische Technische Hochschule, Zurich, Switzerland, 2003. Contbr. articles to profl. jours. Lt. (j.g.) USNR, 1964-67. NOAA summer fellow, 1981, vis. fellow Hanse-Wissenschaftskolleg, 2000; recipient Disting. Svc. award U. Mich. Class of 1938, Engring., 1976, vis. scientist award Ind. U., 1979-80. Fellow AAAS, Geol. Soc. Am., Am. Geophys Union, Geochem. Soc.; mem. Am. Assn. Limnology and Oceanography, European Assn. Organic Geochemists, Huron Valley Tennis Club. Avocations: tennis, travel, photography, running. Office: U Mich 3514 C C Little Bldg Ann Arbor MI 48109-1005 Business E-Mail; pameyers@umich.edu.

MEYERS, REBECKA LOUISE, pediatric general surgeon; b. Salt Lake City, May 11, 1958; MD, Oreg. Health Sciences U. Sch. Medicine, 1985. Cert. Gen. Surgery, Pediatric Gen. Surgery. Intern, gen. surgery U. Calif. Med. Ctr., San Francisco, 1985—88, fellow, cardiovascular diseases, 1988—90, resident, gen. surgery, 1990—92; fellow St. Christopher's Hosp. for Children in Pediatric Surgery, Phila., 1992—94; pediatric surgeon Primary Children's Med. Ctr., Salt Lake City, 1994—; chief, divsn. pediatric surgery Univ. Utah Hosp. (now called U. Utah Health Sciences Ctr.), Salt Lake City, 2001—; asst. prof. U. Utah, Salt Lake City, 1994—99, assoc. prof., 1999. Mem.: Utah Med. Assn., Pacific Assn. of Pediatric Surgeons, Internat. Pediatric Endosurgery Group, Assn. Women Surgeons, Am. Pediatric Surgical Assn., Am. Coll. Surgeons, Am. Acad. Pediatrics. Office: Primary Childrens Med Ctr 100 N Medical Dr Ste 2600 Salt Lake City UT 84113 also: U Utah Health Services Ctr 50 N Medical Dr Salt Lake City UT 84132 Office Phone: 801-588-3350.

MEYERS, WAYNE MARVIN, microbiologist, physician; b. Huntingdon County, Pa., Aug. 28, 1924; s. John William and Carrie Venca (Weaver) Meyers; m. Esther Louise Kleinschmidt, Aug. 26, 1953; children: Amy, George, Daniel, Sara. BS in Chemistry, Juniata Coll., Huntingdon, Pa., 1947, DSc (hon.), 1986; diploma, Moody Bible Inst., Chgo., 1950; MS in Med. Microbiology, U. Wis., 1953, PhD in Med. Microbiology, 1955; MD, Baylor Coll. Medicine, 1959. Instr. Baylor Coll. Medicine, 1955-59; intern Conemaugh Valley Meml. Hosp., Johnstown, Pa., 1959-60; staff physician Berrien Gen. Hosp., Berrien Center, Mich., 1960-61; missionary physician Am. Leprosy Missions, Congo/Zaire, Burundi, 1961-73; prof. pathology Sch. Medicine U. Hawaii, Honolulu, 1973-75; chief microbiology divsn. Armed Forces Inst. Pathology, Washington, 1975-89, chief mycobacteriology, 1989—2005, registrar leprosy registry, 1975—2005, asst. to registrar leprosy registry, 2005—, vis. scientist, 2005—; mem. leprosy panel US-Japan Coop. Med. Sci. Program, 1976-83; mem. sci. adv. bd. Leonard Wood Meml., 1981-85, sci. cons. dir., 1985-87, sci. dir., 1987-90, cons., 1990—2004; rsch. affiliate Tulane U., 1981—. Bd. dirs. Gorgas Meml. Inst. Tropical and Preventive Medicine, Inc., Leonard Wood Meml. Bd. dirs. Jour. Leprosy, 1978—93; contbr. chapters to books, articles to profl. jours. Adv. bd. Damien-Dutton Soc. Leprosy Aid, Inc., 1983—96, corp. bd. dirs., 1996—; adv. bd. Am. Leprosy Missions, Inc., 1979—88, chmn. bd. dirs., 1985—88, program cons. to bd. dirs., 1988—2003, mem. bd. references, 1988—; mem. Hansen's Disease rsch. adv. com. Gillis W. Long Hansen's Disease Ctr., Carville, La., 1985—92, chmn., 1985—92; mem. Buruli Ulcer task force WHO, 1998—2004. With US Army, 1944—46. Allergy Found. Am. fellow, 1957, 1958, WHO Rsch. grantee, 1978—87. Mem.: Internat. Soc. Travel Medicine, Binford-Dammin Soc. Infectious Disease Pathologists (sec.-treas. 1988—91, pres. 1995—96), Am. Soc. Microbiology, Am. Soc. Tropical Medicine and Hygiene, Internat. Soc. Tropical Dermatology, Internat. Acad. Pathology, Internat. Leprosy Assn. (councillor 1978—88, pres. 1988—93), Sigma Xi. Achievements include research in human and experimental leprosy, and other mycobacterial diseases. Office: Armed Forces Inst Pathology Washington DC 20306-6000 Office Phone: 202-782-1873. Personal E-mail: wmekmeyers@comcast.net.

MEYERSON, ADAM, foundation administrator; b. Phila., Aug. 2, 1953; s. Martin and Margy Ellin (Lazarus) M.; m. Nina Hope Shea, Sept. 13, 1986; children: Thomas Abraham, William Ulysses, Henry Elijah. BA, Summa Cum Laude, Yale U., 1974; student, Harvard U., 1977-79. Mng. editor The Am. Spectator, Bloomington, Ind., 1974-77; editorial writer Wall St. Jour., NYC, 1979-83; editor Policy Rev. The Heritage Found., Washington, 1983-98, v.p. ednl. affairs, 1993—2001; pres. Philanthropy Roundtable, Washington, 2001—. Co-editor: The Wall Street Journal on Management, 1985. Home: 3714 Ingomar St NW Washington DC 20015-1820 Office: Philanthropy Roundtable 1150 17th St NW # 503 Washington DC 20036 Office Phone: 202-822-8333. E-mail: ameyerson@philanthropyroundtable.org.

MEYERSON, CHRISTOPHER CORTLANDT, lawyer; b. Princeton, NJ, July 7, 1962; s. Dean and Beatrice Meyerson; m. Megumi Kawaguchi; children: Kenneth, David. BA in Govt. magna cum laude, Harvard U., 1985, cert. in L.Am. studies, 1985, MA in History, 1985; MPhil in Polit. Sci., Columbia U., 1993; LLM, Kyoto U., Japan, 1994; JD, Columbia U., 2001. Bar: D.C. 2001. Intern Bur. Inter-Am. Affairs, Office Policy Planning/Coord. U.S. State Dept., Washington, summer 1982; rsch. asst. Harvard U., 1982-83; intern, rschr. macro econ. rsch. dept. Banco Itau, São Paulo, 1983-84; human rights intern Coalition for Homeless, NYC, summer 1988; legal intern gen. counsel Mus. Modern Art, NYC, summer 1989; law clk. Office of Chief Counsel for Internat. Commerce U.S. Commerce Dept., Washington, summer 1991; editl. asst. Kyoto Comparative Law Ctr., summer 1994, 95; vis. scholar Associated Kyoto Program, 1996. Summer assoc. Venable, Baetjer, Howard & Civiletti, Washington, 1998; law clk. Office of Chief Counsel for Import Adminstrn., U.S.

Commerce Dept., Washington, 1999-2000. Author various publs. on internat. trade. Recipient scholarship, Japanese Govt., 1991—97. Mem. ABA. Episcopalian. Home: 7306 Summit Ave Chevy Chase MD 20815-4030

MEYERSON, HAROLD, journalist; b. LA, 1950; Grad, Columbia Univ. Exec editor L.A. Weekly mag, 1989—2001, polit editor & columnist, 2001—; editor at large The American Prospect. Contbr. columns in newspapers, articles in polit jours. Office: The American Prospect Suite 717 2000 L St NW Washington DC 20036

MEYERSON, IVAN D., lawyer, former corporate financial executive; AB, U. Calif., Berkeley, 1966; JD, Stanford U., 1969. Bar: Calif. 1970. Assoc. Herzstein & Maier, San Francisco, 1970-75, ptnr., 1976-78; atty. SEC, 1975-76; assoc. gen. counsel McKesson Corp., San Francisco, 1984-87, v.p., gen. counsel, 1987-98; exec. v.p., gen. counsel McKesson - HBOC Inc., San Francisco, 1998—2006. *

MEYERSON, LEE A., lawyer; b. NYC, May 11, 1956; AB magna cum laude, Duke U., 1977; JD, NYU, 1981. With Simpson, Thacher & Bartlett, LLP, NYC, 1981—, ptnr., 1989—. Editor: NYU Law Review, 1981. Mem.: Assn. Bar City of NY. Office: Simpson Thacheer & Bartlett LLP 425 Lexington Ave New York NY 10017-3954 Office Phone: 212-455-3675. Office Fax: 212-455-2502. E-mail: lmeyerson@stblaw.com.

MEYERSON, MORTON HERBERT, investor, real estate company executive; b. Ft. Worth, June 3, 1938; s. Maurice Brudus and Bernice Estell (Gressman) M.; m. Marlene Nathan, Apr. 26, 1964; children: David Nathan (dec.), Marti Ann, Leslie. BA in Philosophy and Econs., U. Tex., 1960. Computer software trainee Bell Helicopter; v.p. Electronic Data Systems Corp., Dallas, 1966-71, pres., 1979-86, vice chmn., 1986; pres. E.D.S. Fed. Corp. subs. Electronic Data Systems Corp., Dallas, 1975-79; pres., bd. dirs. duPont Glore Forgan Inc., NYC, 1971-75; pres. Nat. Heritage Ins. Co. (subs. E.D.S.), NYC, 1976-86; now chmn., CEO 2M Companies Inc.; also chmn. Morton H. Meyerson Family Tzedakah Fund; and chmn. E2M Partners real estate fund. Bd. govs. Dallas Symphony Orchestra, chmn. concert hall com., 1980-86, bd. dir. Nat. Park Found. Served with US Army, 1961-63, USAR, 1963-69. Fellow Am. Acad. Arts & Scis. Jewish. Office: 2M Cos 3401 Armstrong Ave Dallas TX 75205-3949 Office Phone: 214-443-1900. Office Fax: 214-443-1980. *

MEYERSON, SEYMOUR, retired chemist; b. Chgo., Dec. 4, 1916; s. Joseph and Rena (Margulies) M.; m. Lotte Strauss, May 22, 1943; children: Sheella, Elana. SB, U. Chgo., 1938, postgrad., 1938-39, 47-48, George Williams Coll., 1939-40; DSc (hon.), Valparaiso U., 1995. Inspector powder & explosives Kankakee Ordnance Works, Joliet, Ill., 1942; chemist Deavitt Labs., Chgo., 1941-42; from chemist to rsch. cons. Standard Oil Co. (Ind.) Rsch. Dept. (now BP Corp. N.Am. Inc.), Whiting, Ind. and Naperville, Ill., 1946—84. Mem. indsl. adv. coun. chemistry dept. U. Okla., Norman, 1967-69; Frontiers in Chemistry lectr. Wayne State U., 1965; invited spkr. James L. Waters Symposium, Pitts. Conf., Chgo., 1995. Charter mem. editl. adv. bd. Organic Mass Spectrometry, 1968-87, Mass Spectromony Revs., 1980-87; author, co-author 190 sci. publs. 2d. lt. AUS, 1943—46, ETO. Mem. Am. Chem. Soc. (Frank H. Field and Joe L. Franklin award for outstanding achievement in mass spectrometry 1993), Am. Soc. for Mass Spectrometry., Phi Beta Kappa. Secular Humanist. Achievements include research in chemistry of gas-phase organic ions; patents in field. Home: 43 Vermont Ct Unit A1 Asheville NC 28806-3058 Personal E-mail: meyerson43@hotmail.com.

MEYLER, WILLIAM ANTHONY, financial analyst; b. Newark, Oct. 29, 1944; s. Raymond Francis and Margaret (Loveless) Meyler; m. Dana Irene Brennan, May 3, 1975; children: Daniel, Diana. BS, St. Joseph's Coll., 1966; MBA, Fairleigh Dickinson U., 1974. CPA N.J. Sr. acct. Ernst & Young, Trenton, NJ, 1970; dir. acctg. Baker Industries, Inc., Parsippany, NJ, 1971—72; mgr. corp. acctg. Witco Chem. Corp., NYC, 1973—75, asst. to contr., 1976—79, asst. contr. world-wide ops., 1977—82, asst. contr. mgmt. info. sys., 1982—84; ptnr. Letters, Meyler & Co. CPA, 1984—91; pvt. practice Middletown, NJ, 1991—. Cons., exec. v.p. Investment Techs., Inc., Edison, NJ, 1985—91, bd. dirs.; exec. v.p., CFO Gateways to Space, Inc., 1994—96, bd. dirs.; adj. prof. Monmouth Coll., 1983—85. Fellow: N.J. Soc. CPA; mem.: AICPA, Am. Acctg. Assn., Middletown C. of C., Rotary. Home: 30 Southview Ter S Middletown NJ 07748-2415 Office: One Arin Park 1715 Highway 35 Middletown NJ 07748-1867 Office Phone: 732-671-2244. Business E-Mail: bill@meylercpa.com.

MEYROWITZ, CAROL M., retail executive; b. 1954; With TJX Cos., Inc., Framingham, Mass., 1983; exec. v.p. merchandising Chadwick's of Boston (divsn. previously held by TJX), 1996—99; sr. v.p. merchandising Marmaxx group TJX Cos., Inc., 1999—2000, exec. v.p. merchandising Marmaxx group Framingham, Mass., 2000—01, exec. v.p., pres. Marmaxx group, 2001—04, sr. exec. v.p., 2004—05, adv. cons., 2005, pres., 2005—, CEO, 2007—. Bd. dirs. Yankee Candle, 2004—, TJX Cos., Inc., 2007—. Named one of 50 Most Powerful Women in Bus., Fortune mag., 2006. Office: TJX Companies 770 Cochituate Rd Framingham MA 01701 *

MEYSTEL, MICHAEL A., Internet company executive; b. Moscow, Feb. 12, 1973; arrived in U.S., 1978; s. Alexander M. and Marina M. (Selitsky) M.; m. Robin L. Weiss, May 25, 1997 (div.); 1 child, Jacob. Student, Drexel U., 1989—94; BBA in Computer Sci. magna cum laude, Ursinus Coll. Sys. and network adminstr. Drexel U., Phila., 1991—94; sr. sys. analyst Bell Atlantic, Malvern, Pa., 1994—95; pres., CEO Cognisphere, Inc., West Chester, Pa., 1995—; sr. sys. analyst Decision One Corp., Malvern, 1995—96; cons., application developer Shared Med. Sys., Malvern, 1996—97, Conectiv Energy, Newark, Del., 1997—98, Anderson BDG, Inc., Allentown, Pa., 1998; project mgr. The Vanguard Group, Valley Forge, Pa., 1998—; dir. info. tech. MRDS, Inc., 1999—2003, COO, 2003—05. Sys. cons. ADREM, Inc., Bala, Pa., 1991-94; rsch. asst. Siemens Corp. Rsch., Princeton, N.J., 1992; pres., CEO ICSC Corp., West Chester, 1995-2000. Chmn. Citizens for Youth Devel. Through Sports, 2005—06. Achievements include inventor/patentee apparatus for text structuring. Office: Cognisphere Inc PO Box 2591 West Chester PA 19380

MEZA, LUIS ALBERTO, internist, researcher; s. Luis Alberto and Susana Cartes Meza; m. Teresa I. Ibarra, Sept. 3, 1966; children: Luis A. Jr., Monica Meza Hernandez, Leticia Ann Canizaro, Lisa Cristina Harrell. MD, U. Nat. Asuncion, Paraguay, 1966. Diplomate Am. Bd. Internal Medicine, Am. Bd. Oncology, Am. Bd. Hematology. Intern Mercy Hosp., Des Moines, 1970—71; resident in internal medicine La. State U., New Orleans, 1971—74; fellow Ochsner Found. Hosp., New Orleans, 1974—76; assoc. prof. medicine La. State U., Lafayette, 1976—; physician SW Oncology, Lafayette, 1979—. Chief med. staff Southpark Hosp., Youngsville, La., 2005—06. Capt. Paraguay Nat. Army, 1964—69. Fellow: ACP, Internat. Soc. Hematology; mem.: Am. Soc. Hematology, So. Assn. for Oncology, La. State Med. Soc., So. Med. Assn., Am. Soc. of Clin. Oncology, Lafayette Parish Med. Soc. Roman Catholic. Achievements include research in growth factor support in treating side effects related to chemotherapy. Avocations: travel, golf, photography. Office: Southwest Oncology 443 Heymann Blvd Ste A Lafayette LA 70503 Home Phone: 337-988-6440; Office Phone: 337-234-4535. Office Fax: 337-235-4272. Personal E-mail: lamezamd@aol.com.

MEZACAPA, EDNA S., music educator, elementary school educator; b. Flint, Mich., Jan. 23, 1948; d. Jack E. and Vlasta A. Tremayne; m. Nicklas A. Mezacapa, July 25, 1970; children: Amy Anne, Sara Marie. MusB, Heidelberg Coll., Tiffin, Ohio, 1970. Gen. music tchr. Bellevue (Ohio) City Schs., 1969—73; youth choir dir. Findlay Episc. Ch., Findlay, Ohio, 1975—78; subs. tchr. Rochester (N.Y.) Schs., 1979—81; youth choir dir. Ch. of the Epiphany, Rochester, 1979—81; music tchr., K-8 St. Mary's Cath. Sch., Kalamazoo, 1981—82, St. Ludmila Cath. Sch., Cedar Rapids, Iowa, 1984—86; tchr. Christian edn. Calvary Episc. Ch., Rochester, Minn., 1986—87; subs. music tchr., 1-6 Rochester City Schs., Rochester, Minn., 1988—90, music tchr., 1-6, 1990—. Dir. Calvary Episc. Youth Choir, 1995—96, Suzuki Orch., 2001—03. Dir. youth choir Calvary Episcopal Ch., 1996—97; dir. Suzuki Orch., 2001—03.

MEZEY, ROBERT, poet; b. Phila., Feb. 28, 1935; s. Ralph and Clara M.; m. Olivia Simpson (div.); children: Naomi, Judah, Eve. Student, Kenyon Coll., 1951-53; BA, U. Iowa, 1959; postgrad., Stanford U., 1960-61. Lectr. Western Res. U., Cleve., 1963-64, Franklin & Marshall Coll., Lancaster, Pa., 1965-66; asst. prof. Fresno (Calif.) State U., 1967-68, U. Utah, Salt Lake City, 1973-76; prof., poet-in-residence Pomona Coll., Claremont, Calif., 1976-99; ret., 1999. Author: (poems) The Lovemaker, 1960 (Lamont award), White Blossoms, 1965, The Door Standing Open, 1970, Selected Translations, 1981, Evening Wind, 1987 (Bassine citation, PEN prize 1989), Collected Poems 1952-1999, 2000 (Poets prize 2002); editor Naked Poetry, 1968, Poems from the Hebrew, 1973, Collected Poems of Henri Coulette, 1990, Selected Poems of Thomas Hardy, 1998, The Poetry of E.A. Robinson, 1999, Poems of the American West, 2002, A Word Like Fire: Selected Poems of Dick Barnes, 2005; translator: Tungsten (César Vallejo), 1988. With US Army, 1953—55. Fellow Ingram Merrill, 1973, 89, Guggenheim Found., 1977, Stanford U., 1960, NEA, 1987; recipient Poetry prize Am. Acad. Arts and Letters, 1982. Avocations: tennis, chess. Home: 960 E Bonita Ave # 28 Pomona CA 91767 Personal E-mail: mezteadancer@aol.com.

MEZGER, JEFFREY T., construction executive; b. Chgo., 1955; BA in Econs., DePauw U., Greencastle, Ind., 1977. Pres. ctrl. Calif. divsn. US Home, Calif., 1983—93; pres. Antelope Valley divsn. KB Home Corp., LA, 1993—95, pres. KB Home Ariz., sr. v.p., regional mgr. SW divsn., 1995—99, exec. v.p., COO, 1999—2006, pres., CEO, 2006—. Mem. exec. bd. USC Lusk Ctr. for Real Estate; mem. policy adv. bd. Harvard Joint Ctr. for Housing Studies. Mem.: Nat. Assn. Home Builders (mem. high prodn. builders coun.). Office: KB Home Corp 10990 Wilshire Blvd 7th Fl Los Angeles CA 90024 *

MEZO, RICHARD EUGENE, literature and language professor, writer; b. Carterville, Ill., Aug. 17, 1938; s. William Leonard Mezo and Madeline Helen Wilkerson; m. Sun Hee Choe Mezo; children: Harmony Suzanne, Julia Ann. AA, San Diego City Coll., 1969; MA, Calif. State U., 1972; PhD, U. ND, 1978. Cert. Teacher 6-12 Western Wash. U., 1988. English instr. Several Overseas U. (Saudi Arabia, Taiwan, Korea), 1979—85, Pierce Coll., Tacoma, 1985—86, Olympic Coll., Bremerton, Wash., 1986—87; asst. prof. Meyille State U., ND, 1988—89; assoc. prof. U. Guam, 1989—99; lectr. U. Md., Asian Divsn., 1992—2001; tchr. Dept. Def. Edn. Activity, Arlington, Va., 2001—. Reader ETS Coll. Bd., Daytona, Fla., 1997—; chmn., divsn. English and applied linguistics U. Guam, 1990—92. Author: (reference book) Am. Nat. Bio., 1999, World Edn. E.ncy, 2001. Mem.: MLA (field bibliographer 2002—), Assn. Lit. Scholars and Critics, Acad. Am. Poets. Democrat. Protestant. Avocation: reading. Home: 9718 Big Bethel Rd Fredericksburg VA 22407 Personal E-mail: remezo@yahoo.com.

MEZROW, CRAIG, plastic surgeon; b. Dec. 5, 1964; BS, MS, Emory U., Atlanta, Ga.; MD, Mt. Sinai Sch. Medicine, NYC, 1996. Cert. Am. Bd. Plastic Surgery. Tng., plastic and reconstructive surgery Med. Coll. Wis.; tng., cosmetic surgery Manhattan Eye Ear and Throat Hosp., NYC; staff mem. Bryn Mawr Hosp., Pa., Laukennu Hosp., Wynnewood, Pa., Paoli Hosp., Pa.; private practice Bala Cynwyd, Pa. Lectr. in field. Contbr. articles to profl. jours. Fellow: ACS; mem.: Am. Soc. Plastic Surgeons. Office: 15 N Presidential Blvd Ste 200 Bala Cynwyd PA 19004 Office Phone: 610-664-5500. Office Fax: 610-664-7548. *

MEZZULLO, LOUIS ALBERT, lawyer; b. Balt., Sept. 20, 1944; m. Judith Scales, Jan. 2, 1970. BA, U. Md., 1967, MA, 1976; JD, T.C. Williams Law Sch., 1976. Bar: Va. 1976, Calif. 2006. Sales rep. Humble Oil (name now Exxon), Richmond, Va., 1970-72; acctg. Marcoin, Inc., Richmond, 1972-73; pvt. practice bookkeeping, tax preparation, Richmond, 1973-76; assoc. McGuire, Woods, Battle and Boothe, Richmond, 1976-79; dir. Mezzullo & McCandlish, Richmond, 1979-2000; mem. Mezzullo & Guare, PLC, Richmond, 2000—03, McGuire Woods, 2004—06, Luce, Forward, Hamilton & Scripps, Carlsbad, Calif., 2006—. Contbr. articles to profl. jours. Former pres. Southampton Citizens Assn., Richmond, 1986; former bd. dirs. Richmond Symphony; bd. dirs. Va. Mus. Fine Arts Found., San Diego Opera. Served with USAR, 1969—75. Mem.: ABA (tax sect., vice chair publs.), Am. Coll. Employee Benefits Counsel, Trust Adminstrs. Coun., Estate Planning Coun. Richmond, Va. Law Found., Am. Bar Found., Va. Bar Assn., Am. Coll. Employee Benefit Counsel, Va. State Bar (tax sect.), Am. Coll. Tax. Counsel (chair), Am. Coll. Trust and Estate Counsel, Internat. Acad. Estate and Trust Law, Willow Oaks Country Club. Home: 7326 Grebe Dr Carlsbad CA 92011 Office Phone: 858-381-8014. Business E-Mail: lmezzullo@luce.com.

MFUME, KWEISI, civil rights association executive, former congressman; b. Balt., Oct. 24, 1948; divorced; children: Donald, Kevin, Keith, Ronald, Michael, Christopher. BS, Morgan State U., 1976; MA, Johns Hopkins U., 1984. Mem. Balt. City Council, 1979-87, 100th-104th Congresses from 7th Md. dist., 1987-96, chmn. congl. black caucus, ranking minority mem., mem. banking and fin. svcs. subcom. on gen. oversight and investigations; mem. small bus. com., mem. joint econ. com.; pres. NAACP, Balt., 1996—2005. Former adj. prof. polit. sci. Morgan State U., Balt. Author (with Ronald Stodghill II): (autobiography) No Free Rule: From the Mean Street to the Mainstream, 1997. Recipient Drum Major for Justice award, SCLC, 1997. Baptist. Home: PO Box 1557 Baltimore MD 21203-1557

MI, CHUNTING CHRIS, engineering educator; s. Zhanyou Mi and Shumei Liu; m. Yuhong Fu, Nov. 15, 1990; children: Juliana, Jonathan. BSc, N.W. Poly. U., Xi'an, China, 1985, MSc, 1988; PhD, U. Toronto, 2000. Assoc. prof. Northwestern Poly. U., Xi'an, 1992—94, Xi'an Petroleum Inst., 1994—96; elec. engr. GE, Peterborough, Ontario, 2000—01; asst. prof. elec. engring. U. Mich., Dearborn, 2001—07, assoc. prof., 2007—. Contbr. articles to profl. jours. Recipient Nat. Innovation award, China State Coun., 1990, Govt. Spl. Allowance award, 1995, Dist. Tchg. award, U. Mich., Dearborn, 2005. Mem.: IEEE (sect. vice chiar 2005—06, Outstanding Engr. award Region 4 sect. 2007, Outstanding Profl. award SE Mich. sect. 2007). Office: Univf Mich Dearborn 4901 Evergreen Rd Dearborn MI 48128-1491 Office Phone: 313-583-6434.

MIALON, HUGO, economics professor; b. Apr. 25, 1977; s. Yves and Elly Mialon; m. Sue Mialon. BA in Econ., McGill U., Montreal, 1999; MS in Econ., U. Tex., Austin, 2001, PhD in Econ., 2004. Asst. prof. Emory U., Atlanta, 2004—. Contbr. articles to profl. jours. Recipient Tchg. Consultation Pairs award, Emory U., 2005; Tchg. Rsch. grant, 2005. Mem.: Can. Econ. Assn., Am. Econ. Assn., Golden Key Nat. Honors Soc. Achievements include research in the economic theory of the Second Amendment's right to bear arms; the economic theory of the Fifth Amendment's right to silence; the economic theory of the Fourth Amendment's search and seizure law; the economic theory of private and public enforcement of the antitrust laws; the economic theory of sexual and domestic violence. Home: 732 Ladson Ct Decatur GA 30033 Office: Emory U Econs Dept 1602 Fishburne Dr Atlanta GA 30322-2240 Home Phone: 404-408-8333; Office Phone: 404-727-0355. Office Fax: 404-727-4639. E-mail: hmialon@emory.edu.

MIAN, LAL SHAH, entomologist, educator; b. Pakistan, Mar. 4, 1945; s. Mohammad Shah M.; m. Judith Anne Conatser, Dec. 26, 1983; children: David Shah and Adam Shah. BSc in Agr. with honors, U. Peshawar, 1967, MSc in Agr. with honors, 1972; MS in Agr., Am. U., Beirut, Lebanon, 1974; PhD in Entomology, U. Calif., Riverside, 1982. Registered environ. health specialist. Tech. asst. forest entomology Forest Rsch. Inst., Peshawar, 1967-68; instr. entomology U. Peshawar, 1969-72, lectr. entomology, 1974-77; vector ecologist San Bernardino (Calif.) County Vector Control Program Pub. Health Dept., 1986-99; adj. lectr. dept. health sci. and human ecology Calif. State U., San Bernardino, 1993, 95, 98, asst. prof., 1999—2003, coord. environ. health sci. program, 2001—, assoc. prof., 2003—06, prof., 2006—. Mem. Africanized Honey Bee task force, steering com., San Bernardino County, 1993—2000; coord. environ. health sci. program Calif. State U., San Bernardino, 2001; mem. faculty coun. Water Resources Inst., 2002; mem. West Nile Task Force, San Bernardino County, 2004—05, Advanced Tech., Environ. Sci. Coun., Coachella Valley, 2005, Emerging/Re-Emergin Disease Com., San Bernardino County, 2006—. Author (with others): Distribution, Transport and Fate of the Insecticides Malathion and Parathion in the Environ., 1981, Interagency Guidelines for the Surveillance and Control of Selected Vector-borne Pathogens in California, 1995, Inland Empire Environ. Quality Paradigm, 2000; reviewer Environ. Entomology; editor (assoc.): Bull. Soc. Vector Ecology, 1991—92; mem. editl. bd. Wing Beats, 1992—94; contbr. more than 80 articles to profl. jours., numerous interviews to newsmedia. Mem. Chancellor's Search Com. for Dean Coll. Natural and Agrl. Scis. U. Calif., 1981, Grad. Student Coun. U. Calif., 1981, Student Mini-Grant Adv. Com. U. Calif. Coop. Ext., 1981-82. Postdoctoral fellow in mosquito rsch. U. Calif., 1982-86; asst. in mosquito rsch. U. Calif., 1981-82; Cmty. Univ. Partnership fellow Calif. State U., 2000-01, summer rsch. faculty fellow, 2000, mini-grant award fellow, 2000-02. Mem.: AAAS, Big Bear Valley (coordinated resource mgmt. plan group 1993—94, univ. diversity com. 2000—04), Soc. Vector Ecology (Southwestern Reg. Dir. 2007—, S.W. regional dir. 2007—), Entomol. Assn. So. Calif., Nat. Environ. Health Assn., Calif. Environ. Health Assn., Mosquito and Vector Control Assn. Calif. (disease control subcom. vector control com. 1990—93, pubs. com. 1990—94, tng. and cert. 1991—2001, chem. control com. 1993—97, Africanized honey bee ad hoc com. 1993—99, pub. edn. 2002—, editor procs. and papers 2004—, paper editor 2004), NY Acad. Sci., Entomol. Soc. Am., Am. Mosquito Control Assn. (recert. and tng. com. 1992—94, recert. com. 1994—95, pub. rels. and edn. com. 1998—2002, Jour. editor 2007—), Am. Registry Profl. Entomologists, Sigma Xi. Democrat. Office: Calif State Univ Dept Health Sci/Human Ecol San Bernardino CA 92407-2397 E-mail: lmian@csusb.edu.

MIANO, LOUIS STEPHEN, arts advisor; b. NYC, July 28, 1934; s. Louis Clyde and Zefira (Palombo) M. BA, Dartmouth Coll., 1955; MA, Columbia U., 1958. Writer Look Mag., NYC, 1960-61; editor Show Mag., NYC and L.A., 1961-63; assoc. producer ABC-TV, NYC and L.A., 1963-66; vice-chmn., dir. creative services AC&R Advt., NYC, 1966-90. Sec. EEE Theatrical Ventures, N.Y.C., 1974—; bd. trustees Met. Opera Guild; cons. in field. Co-producer plays: Design for Living, Corpse, The Seagull, Legends, Inner Voices, 1974-86 Trustee Marymount Manhattan Coll., N.Y.C., 1980-2002; cons. Home Box Office, 1991-92; bd. dirs. Nat. Bd. of Rev. of Motion Pictures, 1995—, Gotham Chamber Opera, 2000—, Met. Opera Guild, 2005—, Circle-in-the Square, sec.; gen. dirs. coun. N.Y.C. Opera, 1998—; bd. dirs. Metro. Opera Guild, 2005— Mem. Century Assn. Home and Office: 430 E 57th St New York NY 10022-3061 Office Phone: 212-753-2860.

MIAO, WUJIAN, chemistry professor; b. Rudong, Jiangsu, China, Dec. 26, 1962; s. Siyou Miao and Bafeng Yang; m. Zhilan Ge, Nov. 25, 1986; children: Jingfan, Kevin Liu. BS, Nantong U., Nantong, China, 1979—82; MSc Courses Diploma, Jinan U., Guangzhou, China, 1985—86; MSc, Zhongshan U., Guangzhou, China, 1988—91; PhD, Monash U., Melbourne, Australia, 1996—99. U. tchr. qualification credential Edn. Commn., Jiangsu Province, China, 1996. Chemistry technician, dir. chemistry dept. labs, lectr., vice-head, dept. chemistry Nantong U., 1982—95; vis. scholar Monash U., Melbourne, Australia, 1995—96; rsch. scientist Commonwealth Sci. and Industrian Orgn., Melbourne, 2000; post-doctoral fellow U. Tex., Austin, 2001—04; asst. prof. U. So. Miss., Hattiesburg, 2004—. Adv. Overseas Exch. Assn. of Nantong City, Jingsu, China, 1998—2002; sec. gen. Chinese Student Club, Monash U., 1996—98. Named Top Young Tchr. in Gen. Univs. and Colls., Edn. Commn, Jiangsu Province, China, 1994; recipient Top Postgrad. award, Zhongshan U., 1991, Dean's Rsch. Initiative Program award, U. So. Miss., 2004; Guanghua Edn. scholar, Zhongshan U., 1990, Yao Wannian scholar, 1990, Study Abroad scholar, State Edn. Commn., China, 1995, Grad. scholar, Monash U., 1996—99, Study Abroad scholar, State Edn. Commn., China, 1997, Internat. Planning Visit grantee, NSF, 2006. Fellow: China's Tchrs. Coll. Assn. Analytical Chemistry, Universities & Colleges Laboratorial Mgmt. Soc., Jiangsu Province; mem.: Miss. Acad. Scis., Soc. Electroanalytical Chemistry, Electrochem. Soc., Am. Chem. Soc. Achievements include patents for methods and compositions for the detection of biological molecules using a two particle complex. Office: Univ So Miss 118 College Dr Box 5043 Hattiesburg MS 39406 Home Phone: 601-579-8990; Office Phone: 601-266-4716. Office Fax: 601-266-6075. Business E-Mail: wujian.miao@usm.edu.

MIAOULIS, IOANNIS NIKOLAOS, mechanical engineer, educator; b. Athens, Greece, July 24, 1961; came to U.S., 1980; s. Nikolaos Ioannis and Titika Photini (Kokkinopoulou) M.; m. Beth Karen, Sept. 23, 1984; children: Marina, Katrina. BSME, Tufts U., 1983, MA in Econs., 1986, PhD, 1987; SMME, MIT, 1984. Asst. prof. mech. engring. Tufts U., Medford, Mass., 1987-93, assoc. prof., 1993-97, prof., 1997—, assoc. dean engring., 1993-94; dean Tufts U. Sch. Engring., Medford, Mass., 1994—2002; interim dean Tufts U. Sch. Arts and Scis., Medford, Mass., 2001, assoc. provost, 2001—02. Pres., dir. Mus. Sci., Boston, 2003—; cons. in field. Contbr. over 100 articles to profl. jours. Elected mem. Mass. Tech./Engring. Edn. Adv. Bd., 1999—, chair 2000—; elected mem. Mass. Math. & Sci. Edn. Bd., 1995-99, Tufts Alumni Coun., Medford, 1994-2002; elected coun. mem. Pompositticut Sch., Stow, Mass., 1993-98; trustee Tufts U. Recipient Presdl. Young Investigator award NSF, 1991, Inventor's Assn. award, New. Eng., 1990, William P. Desmond award Citizen's Edn. Resource Ctr., Mass., 1996, Cmty. & Leadership award Toastmasters Internat., Mass., 1995, Jaycees Outstanding Young Leader award, 1999, Outstanding Svc. Alumni award Tuffi Univ., 2003, Sophia award Hellenic Inst., 2004. Mem. ASME, AAAS, Am. Soc. Engring. Edn., ASTK, Materials Rsch. Soc. Achievements include 2 U.S. patents; research in area of heat transfer in materials processing, microscale heat transfer, comparative biomechanics. Office: Mus Sci 1 Science Park Boston MA 02114

MIAZGA, RONALD C., language educator; b. Chgo., Oct. 10, 1940; s. Edward J. and Mary D. Miazga; m. Marcia A. Barney, May 3, 1992; children: Colleen, Michael, Lauri, Jamie. BA, MA, Ill. State U., Normal, 1965. English instr. Winston Churchill CC, Pontiac, Ill., 1966—68, Glen Oaks CC, Centreville, Mich., 1968—86, Kalamazoo Valley C.C., 1986—. Contbr. articles to profl. publs. Mem.: AAUP. Avocations: writing, travel, fishing, woodworking. Home: 6720 Hayward Dr Vicksburg MI 49097 Office: Kalamazoo Valley CC 6767 W O Ave Kalamazoo MI 49003 Business E-Mail: rmiazga@kucc.edu.

MICA, JOHN L., congressman; b. Binghamton, NY, Jan. 27, 1943; s. John and Adeline Resciniti M.; m. Patricia Szymanek, 1972; children: D'anne, Clark. AA, Miami-Dade C.C., 1965; BA, U. Fla., 1967. Pres. MK Devel. Inc., 1975—92; mem. Fla. Ho. of Reps., 1977—81, mem. appropriations com., mem. ethics com., mem. elections com., mem. cmty. affairs com.; chief of staff US Senate, Washington, 1981—85; mng. gen. ptnr MD Cellular Comm., 1986—92; mem. US Congress from 7th Fla. Dist., Washington, 1993—. Mem. transp. and infrastructure com., govt. reform and oversight com., chmn. subcom. on aviation, 1993—. Author: Factor affecting local government reorganization efforts in Florida, Urban and Environmental Issues. Formerly with Beth Johnson Mental Health Bd., PTA Bd., Zora Neale Hurston Meml. Com. Recipient Outstanding Svc. award Fla. Conservative Union, Outstanding Svc. award Fla. Cancer Soc., Outstanding Svc. award Sertoma, Outstanding Young Men of Am. award; named one of five outstanding Young Men in Fla. Mem.: Fla. Jaycees Statewide (Good Govt. award 1973), Winter Park Jaycees (Good Govt. award 1972), Tiger Bay Club, Kiwanis. Republican. Episcopalian. Office: US HoReps 2313 Rayburn Ho Office Bldg Washington DC 20515-0907 Office Phone: 202-225-4035. *

MICALE, FRANK JUDE, lawyer; b. Pitts., Jan. 10, 1949; s. Frank Jacob and Catherine Anna (Wagner) M.; m. Jane Sincler Czak. BA, Duquesne U., 1971, JD, 1977. Bar: Pa. 1977, U.S. Dist. Ct. (we. dist.) Pa. 1977, U.S. Ct. Appeals (3rd cir.) 1978. U.S. Supreme Ct. 1986; cert. Nat. Bd. Trial Advocacy. Law clk. to judge U.S. Ct. Appeals (3rd cir.), 1977-78, U.S. Dist. Ct. (we. dist.) Pa., 1978-79; assoc. Egler & Reinstadtler, Pitts., 1979-80; dep. atty. gen., sr. dep. atty. gen. in charge torts litigation sect. western region Office of Atty. Gen. Commonwealth of Pa., 1980-92; pvt. practice, 1992—. Mem. ABA, Am. Arbitration Assn., Pa. Bar Assn., Allegheny County Bar Assn., Acad. Trial Lawyers Allegheny County. Home: 5521 Claybourne St Pittsburgh PA 15232-1634 Office: 1042 Summitt St Mc Keesport PA 15132 Personal E-mail: frankmac@msn.com.

MICALI, SILVIO, information scientist, educator; b. Palermo, Italy; Student in Math., U. Rome; PhD in Computer Sci., U. Calif., Berkeley, 1982. Prof. dept. elec. engring. and computer sci. MIT, Cambridge, 1983—, mem. cryptography and info. security grp. Computer Sci. and Artificial Intelligence Lab. Chief scientist, bd. dirs. CoreStreet; co-founder Peppercoin. Contbr. articles to sci. jours.; co-editor: Advances in Computing Rsch. Recipient Gödel prize in Theoretical Computer Sci., Assn. Computing Machinery, 1993, RSA Conf. award, Math., 2004, Rising Star award, Info. Security Exec. New Eng., 2006. Fellow: Am. Acad. Arts & Scis.; mem.: NAS, NAE. Office: MIT Computer Sci and Artificial Intelligence Lab Stata Ctr Bldg 32 32 Vassar St Cambridge MA 02139 Office Phone: 617-253-5949. E-mail: silvio@csail.mit.edu. *

MICCICHE, DANIEL JOHN, lawyer; BA, SUNY, Stony Brook, 1978; JD, U. Chgo., 1981. Profl. corp. ptnr. Akin Gump Strauss Hauer and Feld LLP, Dallas, 1988—. Mem. comptroller's tax adv. group Tex. Comptroller Pub. Accounts. Mem. sch. fin. task force Greater Dallas Chamber; bd. dirs. Tex. C-BAR (Cmty. Bldg. through Atty. Resources), Am. Found. Blind S.W. Region. Mem. ABA, State Bar Tex.(chair state taxation com., 2002-04, chair corp. taxation com., 1998-99), Dallas Bar Assn. (chair tax section, 2001), State Bar N.Y. Office: Akin Gump Strauss Hauer & Feld LLP 1700 Pacific Ave Ste 4100 Dallas TX 75201-4675

MICELI, MARC DOMINICK, lawyer; BA, BM, MM, U. Ill., Urbana-Champaign, 1995; JD, Case Western Res. U., Cleve., 1998; LLM in Taxation, Boston U., 2001. Bar: NJ 1999, Mass. 1999. Assoc. Carella, Byrne, Bain, Gilfillan et al, Roseland, NJ, 2001—. Talent Merit scholar, U. Ill., Urbana-Champaign. Mem.: ABA, Mass. Bar Assn., Essex County Bar Assn., NJ Bar Assn., Insol Internat., Am. Bankruptcy Inst., Pi Sigma Alpha. Office: Carella Byrne Bain Gilfillan Et Al 5 Becker Farm Rd Roseland NJ 07068 Home Phone: 201-944-8604; Office Phone: 973-994-1700. Business E-Mail: mmiceli@carellabyrne.com.

MICHA, DAVID ALLAN, chemistry and physics professor; came to U.S., 1966, naturalized, 1974; s. Simon David and Catalina (Cohen) M.; m. Rebecca Stefan, 1991; children: Michael F., Anna K. MS, U. Cuyo, Bariloche, Argentina, 1962; DSc, U. Uppsala, Sweden, 1966. Rsch. assoc. Theoretical Chemistry Inst. U. Wis., Madison, 1966-67; asst. rsch. physicist Inst. Pure and Applied Sci. U. Calif., La Jolla, 1967-69; assoc. prof. chemistry and physics U. Fla., Gainesville, 1969-74, prof., 1974—, dir. Ctr. Chem. Physics, 1982-91, head phys. chem. divsn., 1999—2004. Vis. prof. U. Gothenburg, Sweden, 1970, Harvard U., 1972, 90, 98, 2000, 01, Max-Planck Inst., Göttingen, Germany, 1976, 96, Imperial Coll., London, 1977, U. Calif., Santa Barbara, 1982, U. Colo. and Weizmann Inst., Israel, 1983, U. Buenos Aires, 1988, 95, Supercomputer Inst., Fla. State U., 1991, Ecole Normale Superieure, Paris 2004, 05; mem. adv. panel div. advanced sci. computing NSF, 1990-92, Max-Planck Inst. Astrophysik, Munich, Germany, 1996, 97. Mem. editl. bd. Internat. Jour. Quantum Chemistry, 1979-88, Few-Body Systems, 1985—; editor Finite Systems and Multiparticle Dynamics, 1990-2005, symposium procs., 3 workshop books; contbr. several book chpts., numerous articles to sci. jours. Recipient U.S. Sr. Scientist award A. Von Humboldt Found., 1976, Sr. Faculty Rsch. award Sigma Xi, 1985; Alfred P. Sloan Found. fellow, 1971-74; Nat. Bur. Standards JILA fellow, 1983. Fellow Am. Phys. Soc. (vice chmn. topical group on few body sys. and multi-particle dynamics 1986-88, chmn. 1988-89); mem. Am. Chem. Soc. Office: U Fla 2318 New Physics Bldg Gainesville FL 32611-8435

MICHAEL, ALFRED FREDERICK, JR., physician, medical educator; b. Phila. s. Alfred Frederick and Emma Maude (Peters) M.; m. Jeanne Jones; children: Mary, Susan, Carol. MD, Temple U., 1953. Diplomate Am. Bd. Pediatrics (founding mem. sub-bd. pediatric nephrology, pres. 1977-79). Pediat. diagnostic lab. immunology and pediatric nephrology intern Phila. Gen. Hosp., 1953-54; resident St. Christopher's Hosp., 1954, Children's Hosp. and U. Cin. Coll. Medicine, 1957-60; postdoctoral fellow dept. pediatrics and biochemistry Med. Sch., U. Minn., Mpls., 1960-63, assoc. prof., 1965-68, prof. pediatrics, lab. medicine and pathology, 1968-88, co-dir. pediatric nephrology, 1968—86, Regents' prof., 1986—, head dept. pediatrics, 1986-97, dean, 1996—2002. Established investigator Am. Heart Assn., 1963-68. Past mem. editl. bd. Internat. Yr. Book of Nephrology, Am. Jour. Nephrology, Kidney Internat., Clin. Nephrology, Am. Jour. Pathology; contbr. articles to profl. jours. Physician founder Vikings Children's Fund, Univ. Pediat. Found.; bd. dirs. St. Mary's Health Clinics. Served with USAF, 1955—57. Recipient Alumni Achievement award Temple U. Sch. Medicine, 1988, John Peters award, 1992, Diehl award, 2003; NIH fellow, 1960-63, Guggenheim fellow, 1966-67, NIH Merit awardee, 1992-2002, Bolles Rogers award, Shotwell award. Fellow AAAS; mem. AMA, Am. Soc. Clin. Investigation, Assn. Am. Physicians, Am. Pediat. Soc., Soc. for Pediat. Rsch., Am. Assn. Investigative Pathology, Am. Soc. Cell Biology, Am. Soc. Nephrology (coun., pres.-elect 1992—, pres. 1993, John Peters award), Internat. Soc. Nephrology, Soc. for Exptl. Biology and Medicine, Minn. Med. Assn. Home: 1986 Lower Saint Dennis Rd Saint Paul MN 55116-2820 Office Phone: 612-625-2715. Business E-Mail: micha003@umn.edu.

MICHAEL, DOUGLAS CHARLES, law educator; b. Omaha, Dec. 8, 1957; s. B.B. and Arleen M. (Heinz) M.; m. Susan Lindsey, Jan. 11, 1986; children: Stuart Douglas, Amanda Lindsey. AB, Stanford U., 1979; MBA, U. Calif., Berkeley, 1982, JD, 1983. Bar: Calif. 1984, D.C. 1988. Staff atty. SEC, Washington, 1983-85, commr.'s counsel, 1985-87; assoc. Arnold and Porter, Washington, 1987-89; asst. prof. U. Ky. Coll. Law, Lexington, 1989-93, assoc. prof., 1993-97, prof., 1997—. Vis. prof. law U. Fla., 2000. Contbr. articles to legal jours.; author: Legal Accounting: Principles and Applications, 1997. Mem. ABA, Order of Coif. Office: U Ky Coll Law Lexington KY 40506-0048 Home: 1224 Sebring Ln Lexington KY 40513 Office Phone: 859-257-1485. Business E-Mail: michaeld@uky.edu.

MICHAEL, ERNEST ARTHUR, mathematics professor; b. Zurich, Switzerland, Aug. 26, 1925; came to U.S., 1939; s. Jakob and Erna (Sondheimer) M.; m. Colette Verger Davis, 1956 (div. 1966); children: Alan, David, Gerard; m. Erika Goodman Joseph, Dec. 4, 1966; children: Hillary, Joshua. BA, Cornell U., 1947; MA, Harvard U., 1948; PhD, U. Chgo., 1951. Mem. faculty dept. math. U. Wash., Seattle, 1953—, asst. prof., 1953-56, assoc. prof., 1956-60, prof., 1960-93, prof. emeritus, 1993—. Mem. Inst. for Advanced Study, Princeton, 1951-52, 56-57, 60-61, 68, Math. Research Inst., E.T.H., Zürich, 1973-74; vis. prof. U. Stuttgart, Ger., 1978-79, U. Munich, Fed. Republic Germany, 1987, 88, 92-93. Editor: Procs. Am. Math. Soc., 1968-71, Topology and Its Applications, 1972-94, Set-Valued Analysis, 1993—; contbr. articles to profl. jours. With USNR, 1944—46. Grantee, AEC, Office Nav. Rsch., NSF, Guggenheim Found., Humboldt Found. Mem. Am. Math. Soc., Math. Assn. Am., ACLU, Amnesty Internat. Jewish. Home: 22200 Chinook Rd Woodway WA 98020-7200 Office: U Washington Dept Math Box 354350 Seattle WA 98195-4350 Personal E-mail: ernie@eemichael.net.

MICHAEL, GEORGE T., real estate manager, developer; s. Lorriane Cooper; m. Terrelyn Michael, Sept. 9, 1989. AA, Bronx C.C., 1978; diploma, NYU Grad. Sch. of Bus., 1980. Mgr., owner various real estate properties, NYC, 1980—. Author: (sch. newspaper) The Communicator, 1975. V.p. Adults & Youth for a Better Baisley Inc., Jamaica, 1984. Avocations: book collecting, stamp collecting/philately, track. Office Phone: 718-468-4481. Office Fax: 718-468-1512. E-mail: gtmdred@aol.com.

MICHAEL, HAROLD KAYE (BUD MICHAEL), sales, marketing and operations executive; b. Tracy, Calif., Dec. 3, 1955; s. Harold Kaye Sr. and Marjorie (Goodwin) M.; m. Barbara Ann Samuels, Sept. 5, 1981; children: Sean Solomon, Stephen Goodwin. BA in Econs., Stanford U., 1978; Grad. Bus., U. Santa Clara, 1981. Mktg. engr. Intel Corp., Santa Clara, Calif., 1978-82, sales engr. El Segundo, Calif., 1982-84; sales exec. Tandem Computers, Culver City, Calif., 1984-85, br. sales mgr., 1985, dist. sales mgr., 1985-86, regional sales mgr., 1986-88; v.p. sales ops. Atalla (a Tandem Co.), San Jose, Calif., 1988-90; dir. field mktg. Sequent Computer Systems, Denver, 1990-92; COO R-Squared Distbg., Denver, 1992-93; pres. Solutions Mktg., Denver, 1993-94; v.p., gen. mgr. RSA, Inc., Denver, 1994-96; v.p. sales & mktg. Client Systems, LLC, Denver, 1996-98; ind. bus. cons., 1998-99; v.p. sales & bus. devel. Decisionism, Boulder, Colo., 1999—2001; exec. v.p. products, chief mktg. officer KANA Software, 2001—03; CEO Biz360, Inc., San Mateo, Calif., 2003—05, Avaiiigent, Inc., San Jose, 2005—. Polit. intern US Congress, Washington, 1975. Mem. Am. Mgmt. Assn., Stanford Alumni Assn. (life), Kiwanis Club (v.p. 1986-87, pres. 1987-88). Republican. Avocations: running, golf, sailing. Home: 1290 Colonial Oaks Dr Los Altos CA 94024-6144 Office Phone: 408-570-3510. Business E-Mail: bmichael@availigent.com.

MICHAEL, JERROLD MARK, public health service officer, educator, retired dean; b. Richmond, Va., Aug. 3, 1927; s. Joseph Leon and Esther Leah M.; m. Lynn Y. Simon, Mar. 17, 1951; children: Scott J., Nelson L BCE, George Washington U., 1949; MSE, Johns Hopkins U., 1950; MPH, U. Calif., Berkeley, 1957; DrPH (hon.), Mahidol U., 1983; ScD (hon.), Tulane U., 1984. Commd. ensign USPHS, 1950, advanced through grades to rear adm., asst. surgeon gen., 1966; ret., 1970; dean Sch. Pub. Health, U. Hawaii, Honolulu, 1971-92, prof. pub. health, 1971-95; emeritus prof. pub. health U. Hawaii, Honolulu, 1995—; adj. prof. global health George Washington U., 1997—. Bd. dirs. Nat. Health Coun., 1967-78, Nat. Ctr. for Health Edn., 1977-90; mem. nat. adv. coun. on health professions edn., 1978-81; chmn. bd. dirs. Kuakini Med. Ctr., Honolulu; sec., treas. Asia-Pacific Acad. Consortium Pub. Health; vis. prof. U. Adelaide, 1993, George Washington, 1994; hon. prof. Beijing Med. U., 1994; adj. prof. internat. pub. health Goerge Washington U., 1997- Contbr. articles to profl. jours.; assoc. editor Jour. Environ. Health, 1958-80, Asia-Pacific Jour. of Pub. Health, 1986-95 Pres. Commd. Officers Found., 2000—. Served with USNR, 1944-47 Decorated Meritorious Svc. medal, comdr. Royal Order of Elephant (Thailand); recipient Walter Mangold award, 1961, J.S. Billings award for mil. medicine, 1964, Gold medal Hebrew U., Jerusalem, 1982, San Karcil Gold medal, Malaysia, 1989, Disting. Svc. award Pacific Island Health Officers Assn., 1992, USPHS awards, Commd. Officers Assn. Brutsche award, 1999, Founders award Asia-Pacific Acad. Consortium Pub. Health, 2003, U.S. Surgeon Gen.'s medallion, 2005, others Fellow Am. Public Health Assn.; mem. Am. Acad. Health Adminstrn., Am. Soc. Cert. Sanitarians, Nat. Environ. Health Assn., Am. Acad. Environ. Engrs. Clubs: Masons

MICHAEL, M. BLANE, federal judge; b. Charleston, SC, Feb. 17, 1943; AB, W.Va. U., 1965; JD, NYU, 1968. Bar: NY 1968, US Dist. Ct. (so. and ea. dists.) NY 1968, W.Va. 1973, US Ct. Appeals (4th cir.) 1974, US Dist. Ct. (so. dist.) W.Va. 1981. Counsel to Gov. W.Va. John D. Rockefeller IV, 1977—80; atty. Jackson & Kelly, Charleston, W.Va., 1981—93; fed. judge US Ct. Appeals (4th cir.), Charleston, W.Va., 1993—. Mem.: ABA, Kanawha County Bar Assn., W.Va. Bar Assn., Phi Beta Kappa. Office: US Circuit Judge Robert C Byrd US Courthouse 300 Virginia St E Rm 7404 Charleston WV 25301-2504 *

MICHAEL, MARK DIXWELL, lawyer; b. Palo Alto, Calif., Feb. 27, 1951; s. J.L. and Elizabeth (Ketcham) M.; m. Eileen Susan Landauer; children: Sarah Kristen Michael, Emily Christine Landauer. BA, Stanford U., 1972; JD, UCLA, 1977. Bar: Hawaii 1977, Calif. 1979. Assoc. Carlsmith, Carlsmith, Wichman & Case, Honolulu, 1977-78, Char, Hamilton, Taylor & Thom, Honolulu, 1979-81, Law Offices of Jerry E. Berg, San Francisco, 1981-84; sr. v.p., gen. counsel, sec. 3Com Corp., Santa Clara, Calif., 1984—2003. Dir. Nollenberger Capital Ptnrs., Inc., Natus Med., Inc. Mem. ABA, Am. Soc. Corp. Secs., Silicon Valley Assn. Gen. Counsel, Calif. State Bar Assn., Hawaii State Bar Assn. E-mail: mark_michael@myway.com.

MICHAEL, NOREEN, academic administrator; PhD in Ednl. Psychology, U. Ill. Commr. of edn. Virgin Islands Dept. Edn., Charlotte, Amalie, Virgin Islands, 2002—07; chief of staff, Office of President U VI, St. Thomas, 2007—. Office: 2 John Brewer's Bay St Thomas VI 00802-9990 Office Phone: 340-774-0100, 340-693-1003. Office Fax: 340-779-7153. Business E-Mail: nmichael@uvi.edu. *

MICHAELIDES, CONSTANTINE EVANGELOS, architect, educator; b. Athens, Greece, Jan. 26, 1930; came to U.S., 1955, naturalized, 1964; s. Evangelos George and Kalliopi Constantine (Kefallonitis) M.; m. Maria S. Canellakis, Sept. 3, 1955; children: Evangelos Constantine, Dimitri Canellakis. Diploma in Architecture, Nat. Tech. U., Athens, 1952; M.Arch., Harvard U., 1957. Practice architecture, Athens, 1954-55, St. Louis, 1963—; asso. architect Carl Koch, Jose Luis Sert, Hideo Sasaki, Cambridge, Mass., 1957-59, Doxiadis Assos., Athens and Washington, 1959-60, Hellmuth, Obata & Kassabaum, St. Louis, 1962; instr. Grad. Sch. Design Harvard U., 1957-59, Athens Inst. Tech., 1959-60; asst. prof. architecture Washington U., St. Louis, 1960-64, assoc. prof., 1964-69, prof., 1969-94, assoc. dean Sch. Architecture, 1969-73; dean Washington U., Sch. Architecture, 1973-93, dean emeritus, 1993—; Ruth and Norman Moore vis. prof. Washington U., St. Louis, 1995. Vis. prof. (Sch. Architecture), Ahmedabad, India, 1970; counselor Landmarks Assn. St. Louis., 1975-79 Author: Hydra: A Greek Island Town: Its Growth and Form, 1967, The Aegean Crucible: Tracing Vernacular Architecture in Post-Byzantine Centuries, 2003; contbr. articles to profl. jours. Mem. Mcpl. Commn. on Arts, Letters, University City, Mo., 1975-81. With Greek Army Res., 1952-54. Fellow AIA (Rsch. award 1963-64, Presdl. Citation 1992); mem. Tech. Chamber of Greece, Soc. Archtl. Historians, Modern Greek Studies Assn., Hellenic Soc. St. Louis (pres. 1991, 95, 96). Home and Office: 735 Radcliffe Ave Saint Louis MO 63130-3139 Business E-Mail: info@delospress.com.

MICHAELIDES, DOROS NIKITA, internist, medical educator; b. Nicosia, Cyprus, Jan. 7, 1936; came to U.S., 1969; s. Nikita P. and Elpinike (Taliadorou) M.; m. Eutychia J. Loizides, Feb. 27, 1965; children: Nike-Elsie, Joanna-Doris. MD magna cum laude (Royal Greek Govt., Scholar) U. Athens, 1962; DTM and H (Greek State Scholarship, Found. Scholar) U. Liverpool, Eng., 1967; MSc in Clin. Biochemistry (Greek State, Scholarship Found. Scholar), U. Newcastle-upon-Tyne (Eng.), 1969. Diplomate Am. Bd. Family Practice, Am. Bd. Allergy and Immunology; qualified Am. Bd. Internal Medicine; cert. in infectious diseases and immunochemistry, Eng. Clk., intern U. Uppsala, Sweden, 1962; resident Nicosia Gen. Hosp., 1963—66; fellow U. Liverpool Hosps., 1967; fellow internal and clin. medicine Royal Infirmary U. Edinburgh, 1967—68; rsch. fellow Royal Victoria Infirmary U. Newcastle-upon-Tyne, 1968—69; resident internal medicine Hamot Med. Ctr., Erie, Pa.; resident internal medicine Bapt. Meml. Hosp., Memphis, 1969—72; fellow in chest diseases We. Okla. Chest Disease Hosp., 1970—71; chief clin. immunology/respiratory care ctr. Erie, Pa.; chief respiratory care ctr. VA Med. Ctr., Erie, 1972—84, acting chief dept. medicine, 1980—81; asst. clin. prof. medicine Hahnemann U. Sch. Medicine, Phila., 1977—, Gannon U., Erie, 1977—. Mem. staff internal medicine Hamot Med. Ctr., immunology and chest diseases Metro Health Ctr., Erie; preceptor medicine St. Vincent's Health Ctr.; affiliate staff Cleveland Clinic Found.; vol. physician Greek Nat. Guard, Cyprus, 1964. Author: The Occurrence of Proteolytic Inhibitors in Heart and Skeletal Muscle, 1969; Blood Gases, Acid-Base and Electrolytes Disturbances, 1980; Immediate Hypersensitivity: The Immunochemistry and Therapeutics of Reversible Airway Obstruction, 1980; The Equivalent Potency of Corticosteroid Preparations used in Reversible Airway Obstruction, 1981; contbr. articles to med. jours. Recipient citation for outstanding svcs. to vets. DAV, 1975, citation Adminstr. U.S. Vets. Affairs, 1978. Fellow ACP (life), Am. Assn. Cert. Allergists, Am. Coll. Allergy and Immunology (com. autoimmune diseases), Am. Assn. Clin. Immunology and Allergy (pulmonary com.), Am. Coll. Chest Physicians (life; critical care com.), Royal Soc. Medicine, Am. Coll. Angiology, N.Y. Acad. Scis., Am. Coll. Clin. Pharmacology, Am. Assn. Cert. Allergists. Greek Orthodox. Home: 4107 State St Erie PA 16508-3129 Office: Doros N Michaelides Md 4107 State St Erie PA 16508-3129 Personal E-mail: dorosmichaelides@yahoo.com. Business E-Mail: dnm777@pol.net.

MICHAELIS, KAREN LAUREE, law educator; b. Milw., Mar. 30, 1950; d. Donald Lee and Ethel Catherine (Stevens) Michaelis; m. Larry Severtson, Aug. 2, 1980 (div. Aug. 1982); 1 child, Quinn Alexandra Michaelis. BA, U. Wis., Madison, 1972, BS, 1974, MS, 1985, PhD, 1988, JD, 1989; MA, Calif. State U., LA, 1979. Bar: Wis. 1990, U.S. Dist. Ct. (we. dist.) Wis. 1990. Asst. prof. law Hofstra U., Hempstead, N.Y., 1990-93; assoc. prof. Ill. State U., Normal, 1993-95, Wash. State U., Pullman, 1995—2002; pvt. practice Madison, Wis., 2003—06, Kenosha, Wis., 2006—. Author: Reporting Child Abuse: A Guide to Mandatory Requirements for School Personnel, 1993, Theories of Liability for Teacher Sexual Misconduct, 1996, Postmodern Perspectives and Shifting Legal Paradigms: Searching for a Critical Theory of Juvenile Justice, 1998, Student As Enemy: A Legal Construct of the Other, 1999; editor: Ill. Sch. Law Quar., 1993—95; mem. editl. bd. Jour. Sch. Leadership, 1991—99, People & Education: The Human Side of Edn., 1991—96, Planning and Changing, 1993—95; author: From Indifference to Injustice: The Politics of School Violence, 2004. Mem.: ABA, Edn. Law Assn. (bd. dirs. 1998—2000, co-chair publs. com. 1998—), Nat. Orgn. Legal Problems Edn. (mem. publs. com. 1993—2001, mem. program com. 1995, exec. bd.), Nat. Coun. Profs. Ednl. Adminstrn. (mem. Morphet Fund com. 1993—2000, mem. program com., mem. editl. bd. 1994—95), State Bar Wis. Office: 5707 Sixth Ave Kenosha WI 53140 Office Phone: 262-997-0026. Business E-Mail: karen@michaelislaw.com.

MICHAELIS, MICHAEL, management and technical consultant; b. Berlin, June 8, 1919; s. George and Martha (Bluth) M.; m. Diana Ordway Tead, Sept. 11, 1954; children: Ordway Peter, David Tead; m. Cintra McIlwain Williams, Mar. 19, 1966 (div. Nov. 1975); m. Caroline Crutcher Bishop, Mar. 17, 1984. BSc in Engring., U. London, 1941. Rsch. asst., group leader Rsch. Labs. Gen. Electric Co., Ltd., U.K., 1935-45, staff physicist and cons., 1945-49; dir. physics divsn. Radiochem. Centre, U.K. Atomic Energy Authority, 1949-51; cons. Arthur D. Little, Inc., Cambridge, Mass., 1951-52, staff cons., 1952-61, sr. asso., 1957-61, head nuclear mgmt. cons. services, 1956-61, internat. bus. devel. services, 1959-61, policy adviser to several large corps, 1954-61, mgr. Washington ops., 1963-72, sr. cons., 1972-81; pres., CEO Partners In Enterprise, Inc., 1981—2000. Cons. to Pres.'s Spl. Asst. Sci. and Tech., The White House, 1961-63; exec. sec. The White House Panel on Civilian Tech., 1961-63; exec. dir. rsch. mgmt. adv. panel, com. on sci. and tech. U.S. Ho. of Reps., 1963-67; dep. coord. then Pres.-elect Carter's Task Force on Sci. and Tech. Policy, 1976; mem. tech. adv. bd. to U.S. Sec. Commerce, 1978-81; mem. citizens adv. coun. Congl. Caucus for Sci. and Tech., 1983-86; mem. nat. com. Am. Goals and Resources, Nat. Planning Assn., 1964-67, mem. adv. com. sci., tech. and economy, 1966-68; vice chmn. com. internat. affairs Atomic Indsl. Forum, 1958-60; assoc. with Anglo-Am. Radar Rsch. Project, World War II. Editor, project dir.: Federal Funding of Civilian Research and Development, 1976; Contbr. articles to profl. jours. Fellow AAAS (chmn. engring. sect. 1980-82, exec. dir. sr. scientists and engrs. program 1989-90); mem. IEEE (sr.), Sci. Film Assn. (founder 1943, sec. 1943-48, v.p. 1948-51), Am. Nuclear Soc., Boston Com. Fgn. Rels., Royal Inst. Physics and Phys. Soc., Soc. Internat. Devel., Royal Instn. Elec. Engrs., Assn. Hosp. Physicists, Nat. Planning Assn., World Future Soc. (dir.), U.S. C. of C. (chmn. com. on govt.-industry rels. in sci. and tech. 1963-64), Interdisciplinary Comm. Assocs. Inc. (dir. 1969-79), Am. Econ. Assn., Am. Soc. Cybernetics, Am. Soc. for Pub. Adminstrn., Atlantic Coun. U.S., Cosmos Club (Washington, sec. 1994-97, v.p. 1997-98, pres. 1998-99), Harvard Faculty Club. Home and Office: 6812 Meadow Ln Chevy Chase MD 20815-5018 Home Phone: 301-657-8847; Office Phone: 301-986-1950. Personal E-mail: zmichael@verizon.net. *The Constitution of the U.S. diffuses power so as to better secure liberty. But it also intends that practice will integrate the dispersed powers into a workable government. It confers upon its branches autonomy but also reciprocity, separateness but also interdependence. It is incumbent on each of us to help make this system work, and to make it responsive to the human needs of our country and the world.*

MICHAELIS, PAUL CHARLES, engineering physicist executive; b. Bronx, June 18, 1935; s. Paul Fredrick and Rose (Landsbury) M.; m. Geraldine A. DeCuollo, June 29, 1958; 1 son, Paul Charles. BS in Elec. Engring, Newark Coll. Engring., 1964, MS in Physics, 1967. With AT&T Bell Labs., Murray Hill and Whippany, NJ, 1953-96; assoc. mem. tech. staff Bell Telephone Labs., 1963-67, mem. tech. staff, 1967-82, tech. mgr., 1982-96, ret., 1996; founder P.C. Michaelis Tech. Cons. Inc., Watchung, NJ, 1996—. Lectr. USSR Acad. Scis., 1972 Contbr. articles to profl. jours.; patentee in optics, magnetics, mechanics and electronics. Mem. IEEE (life; Morris N. Liebmann award 1975), AAAS, Am. Phys. Soc., U.S. Naval Inst., Am. Soc. Naval Engrs., Lions (past pres. Watchung club, Melvin

Jones fellow), Raritan Yacht Club (sec.). Home: 103 High Tor Dr Watchung NJ 07069-5424 also: 151 Amherst Dr Bayville NJ 08721 Office: P C Michaelis Tech Cons Inc 103 High Tor Dr Watchung NJ 07069-5424 E-mail: pmichaelis@optonline.net.

MICHAELS, AL (ALAN RICHARD MICHAELS), sportscaster; b. Bklyn., Nov. 12, 1944; s. Jay Leonard and Lila Ruth (Ross) Michaels; m. Linda Anne Stamaton, Aug. 27, 1966; children: Steven, Jennifer. BA, Ariz. State U., 1966. TV/radio play-by-play announcer Cin. Reds, 1971—73, San Francisco Giants, 1974—76; sports commentator ABC TV Network, NYC, 1976—2006, lead announcer, Monday Night Football, 1986—2006, lead announcer, NBA, 2003—06, NBC Sunday Night Football, 2006—. Recipient Nat. Sportscaster of Yr. award, Nat. Sportscasters and Sportswriters Assn., 1980, 1983, 1986, Emmy award, 1987, Emmy award, Outstanding Sports Personality - Play-by-Play, 2007. Avocations: reading, tennis. Office: c/o NBC Sports 30 Rockefeller Plaza New York NY 10112 *

MICHAELS, ANDREW DAVID, medical educator, cardiologist; MD, U. Calif., San Francisco, 1994, M in Advanced Studies, 1994. Diplomate Calif., 1994. Asst. prof. medicine U. Calif., 2000—06; assoc. prof. medicine U. Utah, Salt Lake City, 2006—. Dir. cardiac catheterization lab. and interventional cardiology U. Utah, 2006—.

MICHAELS, GARY DAVID, lawyer; b. Pitts., Apr. 27, 1955; s. Edgar Wolfe and Norma Flora (Barker) M.; m. Joan Marie Kelly, June 9, 1984; children: Jeffrey Thomas, Abbey Rose. BA, U. Pa., 1977; JD, George Washington U., 1980. Bar: D.C. 1980, U.S. Dist. Ct. D.C. 1981, U.S. Ct. Appeals (D.C. cir.) 1981, U.S. Ct. Appeals (4th cir.) 1985, U.S. Supreme Ct. 1985, U.S. Ct. Appeals (1st cir.) 1987. Assoc. Troy, Malin & Pottinger, Washington, 1981-82, Ballard, Spahr, Andrews & Ingersoll, Washington, 1982-84, Krivit & Krivit P.C., Washington, 1984-98, Fed. Comm. Commn., Washington, 1998—, dep. chief FCC Auctions and Spectrum Access Divsn., 2004—. Bd. dirs. Hinkel-Hofmann Supply Co. Inc., Pitts., 1976—. Mem. The George Washington Law Rev., 1978-80. Vol. legal staff Gary Hart Presdl. Campaign, Washington, 1983, field coord. N.H. and Pa., 1984; bd. dirs. Van Ness South Tenants Assn., Inc., 1986-88, v.p., 1987, pres., 1988, of counsel, 1989-90. Mem. ABA, D.C. Bar Assn. Democrat. Jewish. Home: 11922 Coldstream Dr Potomac MD 20854-3602 Office: Fed Comm Commn 445 12th St SW Washington DC 20554-0001 Office Phone: 202-418-0660. Business E-Mail: gary.michaels@fcc.gov.

MICHAELS, GLEN, artist, sculptor; b. Spokane, Wash., July 21, 1927; s. Paul Frederick and Ethel May Violet (Craddock) Michaels; m. Jacqueline Hosking, Nov. 26, 1960; children: Suzanne Michaels Barbero, John Ross, Paul Robert. Student, Yale U., New Haven, 1950—52; BA, Ea. Wash. Coll. Edn., Cheney, 1957; MFA, Cranbrook Acad. Art, Bloomfield Hills, Mich., 1958. Cert. tchr. 1957. Dir., tchr. Young Peoples Art Ctr. Cranbrook Acad. Art, Bloomfield Hills, 1958—65; asst. prof. sculpture Wayne State U., Detroit, 1966—68, U. Windsor, Ont., Canada, 1970—71. Com. mem. Image and Arts Coun. Troy, Mich., 2006—. El Al Israel Airlines, Rockefeller Ctr., NYC, 1964, Internat. Monetary Fund, Washington, 1965, Soc. Automotive Engrs., Phila., 1983, Clark U., Wooster, Mass., 1991, Baldwin Pub. Libr., Birmingham, Mich., 1991—92, Imaging Ctr., Beaumont Hosp., Royal Oak, Mich., 1997, Alexander Walt Comprehensive Breast Care Ctr., 1998, Barbara Ann Karmanos Cancer Inst., Detroit, 1999, exhibitions include Smithsonian Instn., Washington, 1969—70, travel exhbn., Cranbrook Acad. Art, Bloomfield, 1969—70, Mus. Contemporary Crafts, NYC, 1969—70, US Dept. State, Washington, 1973—80, traveling exhbn., Am. Crafts Coun., 1970, fused glass pool floor, Henry Ford Meml. Libr., Dearborn, Mich., 2004, Represented in permanent collections People Mover, Beaubien Sta., Detroit, Fused GlassPool Fl., Mich. State Libr., Lansing, Assemblage, Providence Hosp., Shiffman Libr. Wayne State U., Detroit, exhibitions include, Lande Bldg, Wayne State U., Represented in permanent collections Waterfall Mosaic, Ford/Weisburg Cancer Ctr., Franklin, Mich., various Oil Portraits, Wayne State U. Selection com. mem. Mich. State Capitol Bldg., 1968. Sgt. US Army, 1945—46. Recipient Internat. Craftsman award, Stuttgart, Germany, 1966, award, Mich. Found. for the Arts, 1983, Artist of Yr. award, Mich. Art Train, 2006; grantee, Ford Motor Co., 1976, Kresge Found., 1986, 1987; Louis Comfort Tiffany grantee, 1973. Mem.: AIA (hon.). Avocations: music, piano. Home: 4800 Beach Rd Troy MI 48098

MICHAELS, JACK D., manufacturing executive; BSME, U. Cin. Various postions Internat. Harvester Co., sr. v.p., gen. mgr. Paris, mng. dir. Germany, worldwide pres. agrl. and constrn. equipment ops., J. I. Case Co.; pres.-internat. Hussmann Corp., pres., CEO; pres. Hon Industries, Inc., Muscatine, Iowa, 1991—96, CEO, 1991—96, chmn., 1996—2004; chmn., pres., CEO Snap-on Inc., Kenosha, Wis., 2004—07, chmn., CEO, 2007—. *

MICHAELS, JENNIFER TONKS, foreign language educator; b. Sedgley, England, May 19, 1945; d. Frank Gordon and Dorothy (Compston) Tonks; m. Eric Michaels, 1973; children: Joseph, David, Ellen. MA, U. Edinburgh, 1967, McGill U., 1971, PhD, 1974. Teaching asst. German dept. Wesleyan U., 1967-68; instr. German dept. Bucknell (Pa.) U., 1968-69; teaching asst. German dept. McGill U., Canada, 1969-72; prodn. asst. Pub. TV News and Polit. program, Schenectady, NY, 1974-75; from asst. prof. to assoc. prof. Grinnell (Iowa) Coll., 1975-87, prof., 1987—. Vis. cons. German dept. Hamilton Coll., 1981; cons. Modern Lang. dept. Colby Coll.; panelist NEH, 1985; spkr. in field. Author: D.H. Lawrence, The Polarity of North and South, 1976, Anarchy and Eros: Otto Gross' Impact on German Expressionist Writers, 1983, Franz Jung: Expressionist, Dadaist, Revolutionary and Outsider, 1989, Franz Werfel and the Critics, 1994; contbr. numerous articles, revs. to profl. jours. Mem. MLA, Rocky Mt. MLA (v.p. 2005), Am. Assn. Tchrs. of German, Soc. Exile Studies, German Studies Assn. (sec. treas. 1991-92, v.p. 1992-94, pres. 1995-96, numerous coms.). Democrat. Avocations: music, travel, reading. Office: Grinnell Coll German Dept PO Box 805 Grinnell IA 50112-0805 Business E-Mail: michaels@grinnell.edu.

MICHAELS, JOHN PATRICK, JR., investment banker, media broker; b. Orlando, Fla., May 28, 1944; s. John Patrick and Mary Elizabeth (Slemons) M.; 1 child, Kimberly Lynn. Grad., Jamaica Coll., Kingston, 1961; BA magna cum laude, Tulane U., 1966; MA in Comm. (ABC fellow), U. Pa., 1968; MA (hon.), St. Leo Coll., 1981. With Times Mirror Co., 1968-72; v.p. mktg. and devel. TM Comms. Co., 1968-72; v.p. Cable Funding, NYC, 1973; founder, chmn. Comm. Equity Assoc., 1973—; chmn. Atlantic Am. Ptnrs., 2000—. Dir. Enterprise Fla. Tulane scholar, 1962-66; Tulane fellow, 1963-66. Fellow Inst. Dir. (London), Royal Overseas Club (UK), RNC Regents (co-chmn.); mem. Master of Fox Hounds, Nat. Cable TV Assn., Cable TV Pioneers, Broadcast Pioneers, Phi Beta Kappa, Phi Eta Sigma, Sigma Chi (Significant SIG). Home: 5117 S Nichol St Tampa FL 33611-4132 Office: 101 E Kennedy Blvd Ste 3300 Tampa FL 33602-5151 Office Phone: 813-226-8844. Business E-Mail: rmichaels@ceaworldwide.com.

MICHAELS, LORNE, television producer; b. Toronto, Ont., Can., Nov. 17, 1944; m. Rosie Schuster, 1973 (div. 1980); m. Susan Forristal, 1984 (div. 1987); m. Alice Barry, 1991; 3 children. Grad., U. Toronto, 1966; doctorate (hon.), Ryerson U. Former prodr. CBC, Toronto; writer Rowan and Martin's Laugh-In, NBC, also other TV series, LA, 1968-75; chmn. bd., founder Broadway Video, NYC; chmn. SNL Studios, 1997—. Writer, prodr. (TV series) The Hart & Lorne Terrific Hour, 1970, writer, exec. prodr. Saturday Night Live, 1975—80, 1985—; prodr.: (TV series) The New Show, 1984; exec. prodr.: Sunday Night, 1988, The Kids in the Hall, 1989—94, Late Night with Conan O'Brien, 1993—, The Vacant Lot, 1994; writer, prodr. (TV special) Lily Tomlin, 1975, The Paul Simon Special, 1977, Steve Martin's Best Show Ever, 1981, The Best of John Belushi, 1985; prodr.: (TV special) Saturday Night Live - Robbin Williams, 1986, The Best of Gilda Radner, 1989, Saturday Night Live: The Best of Eddie Murphy, 1998, Saturday Night Live: The Best of Steve Martin, 1999, Saturday Night Live: The Best of Dana Carvey, 1999, Saturday Night Live: The Best of Chris Rock, 1999, Saturday Night Live: The Best of Will Ferrell, 2002; writer, exec. prodr. (TV special) The Best of Dan Aykroyd, 1986; exec. prodr.: (TV special) Saturday Night Live: The Best of Chris Farley, 1998, Saturday Night Live: The Best of Phil Hartman, 1998, Saturday Night Live: The Best of Mike Myers, 1998, Saturday Night Live: The Best of Adam Sandler, 1999, Late Night with Conan O'Brian: 10 Anniversary Special, 2003, Night of Too Many Stars, 2003, Saturday Night Live: The Best of Cheri Oteri, 2004; co-exec. prodr. (TV special) Rolling Stone Presents Twenty Years of Rock & Roll, 1987; prodr.: (TV films) Things We Did Last Summer, 1977; exec. prodr.: The Rutles: All You Need Is Cash, 1978, Mr. Mike's Mondo Video, 1979, Simon and Garfunkel: The Concert in Central Park, 1982, The Rutles 2: Can't Buy Me Lunch, 2002, America's Most Terrible Things, 2002; (TV series) The Colin Quinn Show, 2002, The Tracy Morgan Show, 2003—04, Sons & Daughters, 2006—; writer, prodr. (TV films) Gilda Live, 1980, (films) Three Amigos, 1986; prodr.: (films) Coneheads, 1983, Nothing Lasts Forever, 1984, Wayne's World, 1992, Coneheads, 1993, Wayne's World II, 1993, Tommy Boy, 1995, Stuart Saves His Family, 1995, Black Sheep, 1996, Kids in the Hall: Brain Candy, 1996, A Night at the Roxbury, 1998, Superstar, 1999, The Ladies Man, 2000, Enigma, 2001, Mean Girls, 2004. Recipient Writers Guild Am. award, 2001, Herb Sargent award for Comedy Excellence, Writers Guild Am., East, 2007, 9 Emmy awards NATAS; named Broadcaster of Yr. Internat. Radio and TV Soc., 1992; recipient George Foster Peabody award for Saturday Night Live, 1990, Order of Canada, 2002, Mark Twain Prize, John F. Kennedy Ctr. for Performing Arts, 2004; named to TV Acad. Hall of Fame, 1999; received star on Hollywood Walk of fame. Office: Broadway Video 1619 Broadway Fl 9 New York NY 10019-7463 *

MICHAELS, MARION CECELIA, newswriter, editor, news syndicate executive; b. Black River Falls, Wis. d. Leonard N. and Estelle O. (Payne) Doud; m. Charles Webb (div.); children: Charles, David, Robert; m. Mark J. Michaels (div.); 1 child, Merry A. BS in Bus. Edn., U. Wis., 1978, MS in Spl. Edn., 1981. Mgr., instr. bus. program Blackwell Job Corps Ctr., 1987-89; mgr. Michaels Secretarial Svc., Black River Falls, Wis., 1979-83; columnist, editor Michaels News, Black River Falls, 1983—, pres., 1989—. Hon. appt. rsch. bd. advisors Am. Biog. Inst., 1996-2001. Author: The Little Cowboy: Pursuing Dana's Dream, 1998, September's Song, 2003—, Dana's Dream, 2004, Loving Lisa, 2005; columnist Single Parenting, 1983—94, Parenting Plus, 1990—2004, editor, contbr. (column) Surviving Single, 1990—95, To Read or Not (Fiction), 1985—, To Read or Not (Non-Fiction), 1985—2004, Report From Planet Earth, 1985—, Travel Tidbits, 1991—95, Surviving Sane, 1995—98. Chmn. Brockway Cmty. Orgn., 1969-71; chair, counselor Brockway Youth Group, 1970-72; chmn. labor com. Dem. Platform Com., Wis., 1975-76; candidate State Assembly, 1978, 82; co-founder Franklin Delano Roosevelt Meml., 1997; mem. LWV. Named to Internat. Poetry Hall of Fame, 1997. Mem.: Assn. Rsch. and Enlightenment, Physicians for Social Responsibility, Union Concerned Scientists, Internat. Soc. Poets (founding laureate mem. 2006, Internat. Poet of Merit award 1999, Outstanding achievement in poetry award 2005, 2006), Humane Soc. of US, Nat. Com. to Protect Soc. Security and Medicare, Peale Ctr. for Positive Living, Friends of the Earth, Nat. Trust for Pub. Edn., Smithsonian (assoc.), Pub. Citizen, Am. United, Nat. Parks, Clean Wis., So. Poverty Law Ctr., Natural Resources Def. Coun., Co-op Am., Amnesty Internat., Inst. for Noetic Sci., League of Conservation Voters, Wilson Ctr., Common Cause, Internat. Fund for Animals, Women's History Mus. (charter mem.), Phi Delta Kappa, Pi Omega Pi. Avocations: singing, dance, walking, swimming.

MICHAELS, MIA, choreographer, dancer; b. Fla. Choreographer for Celine Dion, Ricky Martin, Glorio Estefan, Cirque du Soleil, Anna Vissi, Angelica, Prince, Jimmy Ray, and many others; founder Miami Movement Dance Co., 1989; founder, artistic dir. & choreographer R.A.W. (Reality At Work), NYC; judge, choreographer So You Think You Can Dance?, 2005—. Choreographer (theater) Celine Dion: A New Day, 2003, Fort Chaffee, Arkansas Repertory Theater, WestSide Story, If These Shoes Could Talk, Angelinos Eyes, Coconut Grove Playhouse, Miami, Hello, Dolly, Papermill Playhouse, NJ, 2006, Cirque Du Soleil: Delirium, (TV series) So You Think You Can Dance?, 2005—; contbr. Movment mag., 2006—. Office: c/o Julie McDonald McDonald/Selznick Assocs Inc 1611A N El Centro Ave Hollywood CA 90028 also: c/o Mark D Sendroff Sendroff & Baruch LLP 1500 Broadway Ste 2001 New York NY 10036 Office Phone: 323-957-6680. Office Fax: 323-957-5694, 323-957-6688. *

MICHAELS, RICHARD EDWARD, lawyer; b. Chgo., June 10, 1952; s. Benjamin and Lillian (Borawski) Mikolajczewski; m. Karen Lynn Belau Michaels, May 17, 1980; children: Jonathan R., Timothy R., Matthew R. BS in Commerce summa cum laude, DePaul U., 1973; JD, Northwestern U., 1977. Bar: Ill. 1977, U.S. Dist. Ct. (no. dist.) Ill. 1977, U.S. Ct. Appeals (7th cir.) 1977; CPA, Ill. Acct. Touche Ross & Co., Chgo., 1973-74; assoc. Schuyler, Roche & Zwirner and predecessor firm Hubachek & Kelly Ltd., Chgo., 1977-83; ptnr. Schuyler, Roche & Zwirner, Chgo., 1983—, pres., 1994—. Mem. adv. bd. Thrivent Fin., 2002—. Mem. Northwestern U. Law Rev., 1976-77. Mem. adv. bd. Greater Chgo. agy. Luth. Brotherhood, 1999—2002; chmn. Hawkswimming Maine South H.S., 2001—02; vice chmn. congregation St. Andrew's Luth. Ch., Park Ridge, Ill., 1990—92, chmn. congregation, 1992—94. Mem. ABA, Internat. Bar Assn., Ill. Bar Assn., Chgo. Bar Assn., DePaul U. Alumni Assn., DePaul U. Boosters, Chgo. Athletic Assn., Northwestern Club, C.A.A. Club, Beta Gamma Sigma, Pi Gamma Mu, Beta Alpha Psi. Lutheran. Avocations: photography, golf. Home: 808 Elm St Park Ridge IL 60068-3312 Office: Schuyler Roche & Zwirner 130 E Randolph St Ste 3800 Chicago IL 60601-6342 Office Phone: 312-565-8438. Business E-Mail: rmichaels@srzlaw.com.

MICHAELS, ROBERT A., real estate development company executive; BSBA, JD, U. S.D. With Gen. Growth, 1972—, gen. counsel, exec. v.p., dir. corp. leasing; pres., CEO Gen. Growth Mgmt., Inc.; pres., COO Gen. Growth Properties, Inc. Bd. dirs. Gen. Growth Properties, Inc., Gen. Growth Mgmt., Inc.; bd. dirs. Ctr. for Urban Land Econs. Rsch., Sch. of Bus. U. Wis.-Madison.; spkr. in field. Editor Law Rev., U. S.D.; contbr. articles to profl. jours. Mem. ABA, S.D. Bar Assn., Iowa Bar Assn., Minn. Bar Assn., Internat. Coun. of Shopping Ctrs. (exec. com., bd. trustees, govt. affairs chmn. states Iowa, Nebr., S.D., state dir. Minn., S.D., N.D.). Office: 110 N Wacker Dr Chicago IL 60606-1511

MICHAELS, TODD JORDAN, lawyer; b. Miami, Fla., June 4, 1977; s. Lawrence Ronald and Karen Gilbert Michaels. BA in History, U. of Mich., Ann Arbor, 1999; JD, U. of Miami, Coral Gables, Fla., 2002. Bar: Fla. 2002. Misdemeanor/juvenile atty. Miami-Dade Pub. Defender's Office, Miami, 2002—03, felony atty., 2003—06, felony tng. supr. atty., 2006—. Mem. Eyewitness Identification Reform Panel, Miami, 2006—. Mentor 5000 Role Models, Miami, 2004—06. Mem.: Fla. Assn. Criminal Def. Lawyers (bd. dirs. 2004—06). Democrat. Jewish/Agnostic. Office: Law Office of Bennett H Brummer 1320 NW 14 St Miami FL 33125 Office Phone: 305-670-0077. Office Fax: 305-545-1932. Personal E-mail: toddmichaels33@hotmail.com. Business E-Mail: tmichaels@miltonhirschpllc.com.

MICHAELS, WALTER BENN, English professor, writer; b. 1948; BA, U. Calif., Santa Barnara, 1970, PhD, 1975. Asst. prof. English Johns Hopkins U., 1974—77, prof. English and humanities, 1988—2001; asst. prof. English U. Calif., Berkeley, 1980—86, prof., 1987—88; prof., head Dept. English U. Ill., Chgo., 2001—. Sunderland fellow U. Mich. Law Sch., 1987; Joseph Warren Beach lectr. U. Minn., 1987; Whitney J. Oates fellow humanities Princeton U., 1989; Leventritt lectr. arts Harvard U. Mus., 1994; disting. prof. Am. lit. Tel Aviv U., 1996, Vardi lectr., 99; prof. Sch. Criticism and Theory Cornell U., 1997; Ian Watt lectr. History and Theory of Novel Stanford U., 2001. Editor: The American Renaissance Reconsidered, 1984; author: The Gold Standard and the Logic of Naturalism: American Literature at the Turn of the Century, 1987, Our America: Nativism, Modernism and Pluralism, 1995, The Shape of the Signifier: 1967 to the End of History, 2004, The Trouble With Diversity, 2006; contbr. Promises of American Life: 1880-1920, 2005, editl. bd. mem. Nineteenth Century Studies, 1995—, Cambridge U. Press Am. Lit., 1999—; contbr. articles to profl. jours. Office: U Chgo Dept English 601 S Morgan St Chicago IL 60607-7120 Office Phone: 312-413-2200. E-mail: wbm@uic.edu.

MICHAELS, WILLARD A. (BILL MICHAELS), retired broadcasting executive; b. Omaha, May 13, 1917; s. Gus M. and Bessie (Kerstine) M.; m. Helen Louise Mintel, Nov. 20, 1938 (dec. Sept. 2000); children: Marcella, Lawrence Richard, Betty Michaels Westbrook BA, Trinity U., 1940. Asst. sports editor San Antonio Express, 1937-40; sports announcer, sales mgr., gen. mgr. KABC, San Antonio, 1940-53; gen. mgr. KGBS-TV, 1954; v.p. WJBK-TV, Detroit, 1955-61; dir. Storer Broadcasting Co., Miami Beach, Fla., 1960-85, TV v.p., 1961-66, exec. v.p., 1966-67, pres., 1967-74, chmn., 1974-82, ret., 1982. Chmn. New Boston Garden Corp. (Boston Bruins), 1972-75; dir., mem. exec. com. Northeast Airlines, 1965-72, pres., 1970-72; dir. Delta Airlines, 1972-90, adv. dir., 1990—. Trustee Storer Found. Home: 154 Manchester Way Shavano Pk San Antonio TX 78249

MICHAELSEN, O.V. See OFTENESS, OVE

MICHAELSON, ARTHUR M., lawyer; b. NYC, May 16, 1927; s. Samuel H. and Augusta L. M.; m. Arline L. Kahn, June 30, 1957; children: Barbara L., Sarah E., David N. AB, Columbia U., 1947; LLB, Yale U., 1950. Bar: N.Y. 1950, U.S. Supreme Ct 1964. Partner Wachtel & Michaelson, NYC, 1957-66; v.p. McCrory Corp., NYC, 1966-68, Glen Alden Corp., NYC, 1968-73; partner Miller, Singer, Michaelson & Raives, NYC, 1973-84; counsel Hofheimer Gartlir & Gross, 1984—. Author: (with J. Blattmachr) Income Taxation of Estates and Trusts, 1980, 85, 89, 95, 96, 98. Bd. dirs., mem. exec. com. Amnesty Internat. of U.S.A., Inc., 1972-81, vice chmn., 1975-76. Served with USN, 1945-46. Fellow Am. Bar Found.; mem. ABA, Assn. Bar City N.Y. Office: 530 5th Ave New York NY 10036-5101

MICHAELSON, JON, lawyer; b. Jersey City, Apr. 2, 1948; BA, Pomona Coll., 1969; MA, Univ. Tex., Austin, 1973; JD, Boalt Sch. Law, Univ. Calif., Berkeley, 1978. Bar: Calif. 1978, US Dist. Ct. (Calif. districts), US Ct. Appeals (9th & Fed. cir.), US Supreme Ct. Ptnr., Global Intellectual Property practice Coudert Bros. LLP, San Francisco. Editor (mng.): Indsl. Rels. Law Jour., 1976—77; editor: (articles), 1977—78. Mem.: ABA, Internat. Trademark Assn., State Bar Calif., Santa Clara County Bar Assn. Office: Coudert Brothers Llp 555 S Flower St Los Angeles CA 90071-2300 Office Phone: 415-267-6200. Office Fax: 415-977-6110. Business E-Mail: michaelsonj@coudert.com.

MICHAELSON, MARTIN, lawyer; b. Boston, Apr. 12, 1943; s. Eliot D. and Charlotte (Selib) M.; m. Anne Taylor, Aug. 30, 1987; children: Andrew M., Daniel M.; stepchildren: Rachel T., Hannah T. BA, U. Chgo., 1965; JD, Boston Coll., 1968. Bar: N.Y. 1968, D.C. 1973, U.S. Supreme Ct. 1973, Mass. 1983, U.S. Dist. Ct. N.Y. 1969, D.C. 1973, U.S. Ct. Appeals (1st, 2d, 3d, 4th, 6th and 9th cirs.). Atty. Cravath, Swaine & Moore, NYC, 1968-71; legis. asst. Congressman Robert F. Drinan, Washington, 1971-73; atty. Hogan & Hartson, Washington, 1973-76, ptnr., 1976-83, 89—. Dep. gen. counsel Harvard U., Cambridge, Mass., 1983-88, univ. counsel, 1989, lectr. Harvard Grad. Sch. of Education, 1999. Consulting editor Trusteeship mag. Fellow: Nat. Assn. Coll. and Univ. Attys. Office: Hogan & Hartson Columbia Square 555 13th St NW Ste 800E Washington DC 20004-1161 Office Phone: 202-637-5748. Business E-Mail: mmichaelson@hhlaw.com.

MICHAELSON, PETER LEE, lawyer; b. NYC, Aug. 29, 1952; BS in Elec. Engring. and Econs., Carnegie-Mellon U., 1974, MSEE, 1975; JD, Duquesne U., 1979; LLM in Trade Regulation, NYU, 1985; postgrad., Harvard U., 1993, 96, 97, postgrad., 96, 97, 99. Bar: Pa. 1979, NJ 1980, (US Patent and Trademark Office) 1980, (US Dist. Ct. NJ) 1980, (US Ct. Claims) 1980, (US Ct. Mil. Appeals) 1980, (US Tax Ct.) 1980, (US Ct. Appeals (3rd cir.)) 1981, (US Ct. Appeals (fed. cir.)) 1983, NY 1986, (US Supreme Ct.) 1986, Alaska 2000, cert.: Ctr. Effective Dispute Resolution (mediator), lic.: Chartered Inst. Arbitrators, Eng. (arbitrator). Electronics project engr. Control Systems Research, Inc., Pitts., 1975-76; electronics devel. engr. Aluminum Co. Am., Alcoa Tech. Ctr., Prodn. Equip. Lab., Pitts., 1976-77, Rockwell Internat. Corp., Pitts., 1977-79; corp. patent atty., mem. patent and legal staff Bell Telephone Labs., Holmdel, NJ, 1979-82; atty. Pennie & Edmonds, NYC, 1982-84; prin. Michaelson & Assocs., Counsellors at Law, Red Bank, NJ, 1984—. Mem. disting. panel neutrals tech. ICANN domain names and Y2K panels CPR Inst. Dispute Resolution, NYC; accredited mediator Ctr. Effective Dispute Resolution, London; approved mediator/arbitrator in intellectual property and ICANN domain name and keyword disputes World Intellectual Property Orgn., Geneva; arbitrator ICANN domain name disputes, mem. adv. com. IP panel, bd. dir., mem. transfer dispute resolution policy panel Nat. Arbitration Forum, Mpls.; arbitrator, mediator US Dist. Ct. (ea. dist.) NY; arbitrator London Ct. Internat. Arbitration, N.Am. Coun., Internat. C. of C., Paris, Internat. Ct. Arbitration, US Coun. Internat. Bus., NYC, Nat. Assn. Securities Dealers, NYC, NY Stock Exch., NYC; mediator NJ Superior Ct.; master Justice Marie Garibaldi Am. Inn of Ct. for Alternative Dispute Resolution; mem. Ctr. Dispute Resolution, London, mem. CPR arbitration com., mem. patent commn., mem. e-discovery com.; chartered arbitrator Chartered Inst. Arbitrators, London; arbitrator comml. and tech. panels Am. Arbitration Assn.; presenter in field US and abroad. Contbr. articles to profl. jours. Mem. Sch. Budget Adv. Com., Rumson, NJ, 1981—85, Zoning Bd. Adjustment, Rumson, 1988—93. Fellow: Australian Ctr. Internat. Comml. Arbitration (arbitrator), Chartered Inst. Arbitrators; mem.: AIPPI, Internat. Bar Assn., Am. Arbitration Assn. (nat. patent adv. coun., arbitrator, commercial and tech. panels), Assn. Fed. Bar N.J., Fed. Bar Assn., N.J. Intellectual Property Law Assn., Am. Intellectual Property Law Assn. Home: 15 Holly Tree Ln Rumson NJ 07760-1950 Office: Michaelson & Assocs 1161 Broad St Ste 118 Shrewsbury NJ 07702 Office Phone: 732-542-7800. Office Fax: 732-542-7858. Business E-Mail: pete@mandw.com.

MICHAILOFF, IAN ROBERT, real estate broker, land use planner; b. Santa Clara, Calif., Sept. 13, 1973; s. Michael Gregory and Victoria Jean Michailoff; m. Robyn Michelle Clark, Mar. 10, 2001; children: Raiden Anthony, Jennika Simone. Diploma in bus. mgmt. info. sys. and acctg., Calif. State U., Sacramento, 1998; Microsoft Cert. Sys. Engr., HEALD, Calif., 1999. Cert. Real Estate Broker Calif., 2004. Broker, founder HouseLynk Realty & Loan, Stockton, Calif., 2003—, RentLynk Property Mgmt., Stockton, Calif., 2003—. Land developer DYB, LLC, Stockton, Calif., 2004—. Sgt. US Army, 1991—95. Decorated Airborne Jump Wings U.S. Army, Ranger Tab, Can. Jump Wings, Jordanian Jump Wings. Mem.: Santa Clara Assn. Realtors (licentiate), Lodi Assn. Realtors (licentiate),

Calif. Assn. Realtors (licentiate), Nat. Assn. Realtors (licentiate), Stockton C. of C. (assoc.), Stockton Golf & Country Club (licentiate), Gracie Jiu Jitsu (assoc.), Sigma Phi Epsilon Frat. (assoc.; social chmn. 1997—98). Conservative. Roman Catholic. Avocations: golf, Ju Jitsu, kickboxing, renovating properties. Office: HouseLynk Realty & Loan 1904 Country Club Blvd Stockton CA 95204 Home Phone: 209-598-2612; Office Phone: 209-462-8300. Business E-Mail: robm@houselynk.com.

MICHALAK, JANET CAROL, childhood education educator, coordinator; b. Buffalo, Mar. 22, 1949; d. Theodore and Thelma Ruth (Roesch) Vukovic; m. Gerald Paul Michalak, June 19, 1971; children: Nathan, Justin. BS in Edn., SUNY Coll. at Buffalo, Buffalo, 1970; MS in Edn., SUNY, Buffalo, 1971, EdD, 1981. Cert. tchr. nursery, kindergarten, grades 1-6, reading tchr., English tchr. grades 7-12, N.Y. Reading tchr. Tonawanda (N.Y.) Sch. System, 1971-80; instr. Niagara County C.C., Sanborn, N.Y., 1980-82, asst. prof., 1982-85, assoc. prof., 1985-91, prof., 1991—2004, prof. emeritus, 2004, coord., prof. childhood edn. Adj. lectr. SUNY, Buffalo, 1990—91. Recipient Pres.'s award for Excellence in Teaching, Niagara County C.C., 1990, Nat. Inst. for Staff & Orgnl. Devel. Excellence award, 1991, SUNY Chancellor's award for Excellence in Teaching, 1991. Mem. Coll. Reading Assn., Internat. Reading Assn., N.Y. Coll. Learning Skills Assn., Niagara Frontier Reading Coun. (bd. dirs. 1986-88, 97—). Republican. Avocation: reading. Office: Niagara County CC 3111 Saunders Settlement Rd Sanborn NY 14132-9487 Home: 90 Lord Byron Ln Williamsville NY 14221-1997

MICHALAK, JO-ANN, library director; Grad., Syracuse U., U. Ill., Columbia U. Libr. U. Ill., Ind. U., Columbia U., U. Pitts.; now dir. Tisch Libr. Tufts. U., Medford, Mass. Pres. Boston Libr. Consortium, 2006—; mem. adv. bd. for univ. librs. Carnegie Mellon U., 2006—; bd. dirs. NELINET. Mem.: Soc. For Scholarly Pub. Office: Tisch Libr Tufts U 35 Professors Row Medford MA 02155 Office Phone: 617-627-3345. Office Fax: 617-627-3002. E-mail: jo-ann.michalak@tufts.edu. *

MICHALAK, SARAH C., university librarian; BA in English, Univ. Calif. Riverside, 1969; MLS, UCLA, 1970. Previous head Bio-Agrl. Dept. Univ. Calif. Riverside; previous libr. Univ. Wash., Seattle; dir. J. Willard Marriot Libr. Univ. UT, Salt Lake City, 1995—2004; univ. libr. and assoc. provost for univ. libraries U. NC, Chapel Hill, 2004—. Mem.: Scholarly Pub. and Academic Resources Coalition (steering com.), Libr. Adminstrn. and Mgmt. Assn., Assn. Rsch. Libr. Office: Univ NC Walter Clinton Jackson Library PO Box 26170 Greensboro NC 27402 Office Phone: 919-962-1301. E-mail: smichala@email.unc.edu. *

MICHALEK, ROMUALD, environmental engineer, engineering company executive; b. Myslowice, Silestia, Poland, Apr. 28, 1932; arrived in US, 1961; s. Emanuel and Anna Michalek; m. Maria Baruszynski, Nov. 22, 1964; 1 child, Eva Baran. BSChemE, Politechnic Inst. Silesia, Gliwice, Poland, 1954; MSChemE, NYU, NYC, 1972; MBA, Fairleigh Dickensen U., East Rutherford, NJ, 1982. Cert. profl. engr., NJ, 1976. Mgr. prodn. Chem. Works, Oswiecim, Poland, 1954—61; rsch. engr. Halcon Internat., Little Ferry, NJ, 1962—66; project engr. Engelhard Corp., Newark, 1966—71, mgr. environ. engring., 1980, gen. mgr. svcs., 1981—89, corp. bus. devel. mgr. Metro Park, NJ, 1981—89; v.p., sr. v.p. tech. programs World Environment Ctr., NYC, 1989—99. Adj. prof. Newark Coll., 1977—80. Co-author: Handbook of Pollution Control Management, 1978. Player Polish Nat. Soccer Team, 1953—57. Roman Catholic. Achievements include patents for removal of tritmyed species from gas streams. Avocations: golf, tennis, astronomy, art, music. Home: 70 Primrose Ln Paramus NJ 07652

MICHALIK, JOHN JAMES, legal association administrator; b. Bemidji, Minn., Aug. 1, 1945; m. Diane Marie Olson, Dec. 21, 1968; children: Matthew John, Nicole, Shane. BA, U. Minn., 1967, JD, 1970. Legal editor Lawyers Coop. Pub. Co., Rochester, NY, 1970—75; dir. continuing legal edn. Wash. State Bar Assn., Seattle, 1975—81, exec. dir., 1981—91; asst. dean devel. and cmty. rels. Sch. Law U. Wash., 1991—95; dir., CEO Assn. Legal Adminstrs., Lincolnshire, Ill., 1995—. Fellow: Coll. Law Practice Mgmt.; mem.: Nat. Trust Hist. Preservation, Am. Mgmt. Assn., Am. Soc. Assn. Execs. Lutheran. Office: Assn Legal Adminstrs 75 Tri-State Internat Ctr # 222 Lincolnshire IL 60069-4435 Home Phone: 847-821-9533; Office Phone: 847-267-1360. Business E-Mail: jmichalik@alanet.org.

MICHALSKI, PAUL PETER, lawyer; b. Amsterdam, NY, Aug. 11, 1961; s. Steven Robert (stepfather) and Marilyn Lee (Januszewski) Cevera; m. Elizabeth L. Butterworth, 1994; children: James, Anne. AB, Harvard U., 1983, JD, 1986. Bar: Mass. 1986, N.Y. 1987. Assoc. Cravath, Swaine & Moore LLP, NYC, 1986-94, ptnr., corp., 1994—. Adv. bd. Capital Markets Law Jour. Chmn. Benjamin Franklin Ho. Found., James Beard Found. fellow. Mem. ABA, Internat. Bar Assn., N.Y. State Bar Assn., City of N.Y. Bar Assn., The Blue Hill Troupe Ltd., Mosimann's Club, Harvard Club, New Canaan Soc., Roton Point Assn., Royal Soc. for Encouragement of Arts (Mfg. and Commerce fellow), NY Law Inst. (exec. com.). Republican. Office: Cravath, Swaine & Moore LLP Worldwide Plz 825 Eighth Ave New York NY 10019-7475 Office Phone: 212-474-1868. Office Fax: 212-474-3700.

MICHALSON, GORDON E., JR., academic administrator; BA magna cum laude, Yale U., 1970; RelM in Philosophy of Religion/Theology, Claremont Sch. Theology, 1972; PhD in Philosophy of Religion, Princeton U., 1976. Tchg. asst. Princeton U., 1974—75; from instr. to asst. prof. Dept. Religion Davidson Coll., 1975—79; from asst. prof. to prof. Oberlin Coll., 1977—92, dept. chair, 1989—92; dean, warden New Coll., U. So. Fla., 1992—97, prof. humanities, 1992—; acting pres. New Coll. of Fla., Sarasota, 2001, pres., 2001—. Bd. trustees Leroy Collins Inst. Pub. Policy, 2004. Author: Kant and the Problem of God, 1999; contbr. articles to profl. jours. Mem.: Am. Theol. Soc. Office: New Coll of Fla 5800 Bay Shore Rd Sarasota FL 34243-2109 Office Phone: 941-487-4100. *

MICHAUD, GEORGES JOSEPH, physics professor; b. Quebec, Can., Apr. 30, 1940; s. Marie-Louis and Isabelle (St. Laurent) M.; m. Denise Lemieux, June 25, 1966. BA, U. Laval, Que., 1961, BSc, 1965; PhD, Calif. Tech. Inst., Pasadena, 1970. Prof. U. Montreal, Canada, 1969—2005, prof. emeritus, 2005—; dir. Ctr. Rsch. en Calcul Appliqué, 1992-96, assoc. dean of grad. studies, 1997-2000. Recipient Steacie prize NRC, 1980, Medaille Janssen, Acad. Scis., Paris, 1982, Prix Vincent, ACFAS, 1979; Killam fellow Conseil des Arts, 1987-89. Mem.: Royal Soc. Can., Internat. Astron. Union, Can. Astron. Soc. (Beals award 2006), Am. Astron. Soc. Office Phone: 514-343-6672. Business E-Mail: michaudg@astro.umontreal.ca.

MICHAUD, MICHAEL HERMAN, congressman; b. Millinocket, Maine, Jan. 18, 1955; s. James Leroy and Jean (Morrow) M. Grad., Schenck H.S., 1973; student, U. Maine, 1979. Papermaker Gt. No. Paper Co., 1973-80, mem. staff finishing dept., 1981—; mem. dist. 134 Maine Ho. Reps., Augusta, 1980—94, mem. regional conf. task force on environment, chmn. energy and natural resources com., spkr. pro tem, chmn. appropriations and fin. affairs com., mem. legis. svc. com.; mem. Dist. 3 Maine Senate, Augusta, 1994—2002, pres. pro tem.; mem. US Congress from 2nd Maine dist., 2003—. Mem. com. Eastmill Fed. Credit Union, 1979—; area coord. Merril for Gov. campaign, 1978; v.p. Maine Young Dems., 1978-80, del. state conv., 1980, 82, 84, del. nat. conv., 1979. Mem. Nat. Conf. State Legislators, Katahdin Friend of Retarded Children Assn., East Br. Snow Rovers, KC. Democrat. Office: US Ho Reps 437 Cannon Ho Office Bldg Washington DC 20515-1902 also: Great Northern Paper Co Bowater Main St East Millinocket ME 04430 Home: 3 Birch St East Millinocket ME 04430-1001 *

MICHAUDON, ANDRÉ FRANCISQUE, physicist; b. Cavaillon, Vaucluse, France, May 14, 1929; s. Maurice Louis and Jeanne Francoise (Chatal) Michaudon; children: Claire Hello, Helene Caron. Engring. degree, Ecole Supérieure Ingenieurs Arts et Métiers, Paris, 1951, Ecole Supérieure Électricite, 1953; DS, Sorbonne, 1964. Rsch. engr. Le Materiel Teléphonique, Boulogne, France, 1954-56; group leader Commissariat à Energie Atomique, Cen Saclay, France, 1956-64, 65-72, div. head Bruyeres le Chalel, France, 1972-79, dept. dept. head Limeil, France, 1979-83; theorist MIT, Cambridge, 1964-65; French co-dir. Inst. Laue Langevin, Grenoble, France, 1983-89; prof. Inst. Nat. des Scis. et Techniques Nuclèaires, Saclay, Orsay, France, 1969-84; sr. sci. adv. Los Alamos (N.Mex.) Nat. Lab., 1989. Mem. exec. coun. European Sci. Found., Strasbourg, France, 1987—90; mem. adv. coun. Census Bur. for Nuc. Measurements, European Union, Geel, Belgium, 1990—95; cons. Orgn. for Econ. Cooperation and Devel., Paris, 1989—92. Contbr. articles to profl. jours.; author (author, editor): (book) Nuclear Fission, 1981; editor (co-gen. editor): Neutron Sources, 1983, Neutron Radiative Capture, 1984, Probability & Statistics, 1991. Lt. French Navy, 1953-54. Named knight, Order of Merit, Paris, 1984; recipient written congratulations, Minister of the Navy, France, 1954, award, Acad. des Scis., Paris, 1980. Fellow: Am. Nuclear Soc., Am. Phys. Soc.; mem.: N.Y. Acad. Scis., Francaise de Physique, Cosmos Club. Avocations: music, tennis, skiing, golf, hiking. Home: 333 Otero St Unit 6 Santa Fe NM 87501-6212 Office: Los Alamos Nat Lab Lansce Ns Ms H 855 Los Alamos NM 87545-0001 Home Phone: 505-820-0944; Office Phone: 505-665-2883. Personal E-mail: amichaudon@aol.com. Business E-Mail: michaudon@lanl.gov.

MICHEL, ANTHONY NIKOLAUS, electrical engineering educator, researcher; b. Rekasch, Romania, Nov. 17, 1935; came to U.S., 1952; s. Anton Michel and Katharina (Metz) Malsam; m. Leone Lucille Flasch, Aug. 17, 1957; children: Mary Leone, Katherine Jean, John Peter, Anthony Joseph, Patrick Thomas. BSE.E., Marquette U., 1958, MS in Math., 1964, PhD in Elec. Engring., 1968; D.Sc. in Math., Tech. U. Graz, Austria, 1973. Registered profl. engr., Wis. Engr. in tng. U.S. Army C.E., Milw., 1958-59; project engr. AC Electronics div. Gen. Motors Corp., Milw., 1959-62, sr. research engr., 1962-65; asst. prof. elec. engring. Iowa State U., Ames, 1968-69, assoc. prof., 1969-74, prof., 1974-84; prof. elec. engring. U. Notre Dame, Ind., 1984-87, chmn. dept. elec. and computer engring. Ind., 1984-88, Frank M. Freimann prof. engring. Ind., 1988—2002, dean coll. engring. Ind., 1988—98, dean emeritus, 1998—, prof. emeritus, 2002—. Cons. Houghton Mifflin Co., 1975, Acad. Press, 1983; cons. editor William C. Brown Co. Pubs., Dubuque, Iowa, 1982-83; vis. prof. Tech. U. Vienna, 1992, Ruhr U., Bochum, Germany, 1999, Johannes Kepler U., Linz, Austria, 2004. Author: (with others) Qualitative Analysis of Large Scale Dynamical Systems, 1977, Mathematical Foundations in Engineering and Science, 1981, Ordinary Differential Equations, 1982, Applied Linear Algebra and Functional Analysis, 1993, (with Derong Liu) Dynamical Systems with Saturation Nonlinearities, 1993, (with Kaining Wang) Qualitative Theory of Dynamical Systems, 1994, (with Kaining Wang) Qualitative Theory of Dynamical Systems, 2d edit., revised and expanded, 2001, (with Panos J. Antsaklis) Linear Systems, 1997, (with Derong Liu) Qualitative Analysis and Synthesis of Recurrent Neural Networks, 2002; contbr. articles to profl. jours., chpts. to books. Grantee NSF, 1972—, Dept. Def., 1968-72; fellow Fulbright Found., 1992; recipient Alexander von Humboldt Rsch. award U.S. Sr. Scientists, 1998, Disting. Alumnus award Coll. Engring. Marquette U., 2005 Fellow IEEE (mng. editor Trans. on Cirs. and Sys. 1981-83, Best Trans. Paper award 1978, 83, 93, Centennial medal 1984, Millenium medal 2000); mem. IEEE Cirs. and Sys. Soc. (pres.s 1989, Myril B. Reed Outstanding Paper award 1993, Tech. Achievement award 1995, Golden Jubilee medal 1999), IEEE Control Sys. Soc. (Disting. Mem. award 1998), Russian Acad. Engring. (hon.), Sigma Xi, Eta Kappa Nu, Pi Mu Epsilon, Phi Kappa Phi. Home: 17001 Stonegate Ct Granger IN 46530-6948 Office: U Notre Dame Dept Elec Engring Coll Engring Notre Dame IN 46556 Office Phone: 574-631-4395. Business E-Mail: amichel@nd.edu, anthony.n.michel1@nd.edu.

MICHEL, DONALD CHARLES, editor; b. Ventura, Calif., Nov. 17, 1935; s. Charles J. and Esther Caroline (Heilert) M.; m. Loretta Perron, May 4, 1963; children: Edwin, Robert, Christopher. BA, UCLA, 1958, MS, 1959. Editor San Fernando (Calif.) Sun, 1958-60; successively reporter, weekend editor, mng. editor Valley Times Today, North Hollywood, Calif., 1960-63; feature editor Houston Chronicle, 1963-68; asst. mng. editor features Chgo. Daily News, 1968-77; exec. v.p., editor Chgo. Tribune-N.Y. News Syndicate, 1977-84; v.p. adminstrn. and editl. devel. L.A. Times Syndicate, 1984-93, dir. book devel., 1993-97; cons. L.A. Times Syndicate, 1998-99; ret. Photo exhbn., Sedona, 2001; founder DLM Images, 2003. Home: 3000 Adornos Way Burbank CA 91504-1609 Personal E-mail: donmichel@charter.net.

MICHEL, GREGG L., cruise line executive; m. Adriana Michel; 1 child. BA, Kent State U.; MBA, U. So. Calif. Sr. v.p. fin. and adminstrn. Crystal Cruises, 1988, pres., COO, 2001—, bd. dirs., chmn. sales and mktg. com. Spkr. in field. Office: Crystal Cruises Ste 1400 2049 Century Park E Los Angeles CA 90067 Office Phone: 866-446-6625. *

MICHEL, H. JOHN, JR., lawyer; b. Lewistown, Pa., 1947; AB, Wesleyan, 1970; MA, Univ. Chgo., 1977; JD, Univ. Pa., 1985. Bar: Pa. 1985. Joined Drinker Biddle & Reath LLP, Phila., 1985, ptnr., chair, bus., fin. dept. Office: Drinker Biddle & Reath LLP One Logan Sq 18th & Cherry Sts Philadelphia PA 19103-6996 Office Phone: 215-988-2515. Office Fax: 215-988-2757. Business E-Mail: john.michel@dbr.com.

MICHEL, HARTMUT, biochemist; b. Ludwigsburg, Germany, July 18, 1948; s. Karl and Frieda Michel; m. Ilona S. Leger, 1979 (div.); children: Andrea, Robert Joachim. Doctorate, U. Wurzburg, 1969—74. With Max Planck Inst. Biochemistry, Martinsried, Germany, 1979-87. Co-recipient Nobel prize for chemistry, 1988; recipient Biophysics Prize, Am. Phys. Soc., Otto Klung Prize, Leibniz Prize, Otto-Bayer Prize. Avocation: gardening. Office: Max Planck Inst Biophysics Max-von-Laue-Str 3 60438 Frankfurt Germany E-mail: hartmut.michel@mpibp-frankfurt.mpg.de.

MICHEL, HOWARD E., electrical engineer, director; s. Howard A. and Christine I. Michel; m. Linnea R. Arold, Oct. 2, 1976; children: Kristin L., Megan R. BSEE, NJ Inst. Tech., Newark, 1975; MS, U. So. Calif., Limestone, Maine, 1981, U. Mass., Amherst, 1988; PhD, Wright State U., Dayton, Ohio, 1999. Commd. lt. USAF, 1976, advanced through grades to maj., 1988, ret., 1994; asst. prof. U. Mass., Dartmouth, 1999—2005, assoc. prof., 2005—, assoc. dir. rsch. ctr. rehab. engring., 2005—. Author: (book) Computer Systems Performance Evaluation and Prediction., 2003; contbr. articles to profl. jours. Decorated Def. Meritorious Svc. medal USAF, Meritorious Svc. Achievement medal, Commendation medal; grantee, NSF, 2002—06, NOAA, 2001—02, U. Mass. Mem.: IEEE (chmn. sect. 2003, chmn. area 2004). Achievements include patents for seismic-acoustic detection, tracking, and identification of stealth aircraft. Home: 45 Christine Dr Dartmouth MA 02747 Office: Univ Massachusetts Dartmouth 285 Old Westport Rd Dartmouth MA 02747 Home Phone: 508-636-5790. Office Fax: 508-999-8489. Business E-Mail: hmichel@umassd.edu.

MICHEL, MARY ANN KEDZUF, retired nursing educator; b. Evergreen Park, Ill., June 1, 1939; d. John Roman and Mary Kedzuf; m. Jean Paul Michel, 1974. Diploma in nursing, Little Company of Mary Hosp., Evergreen Park, 1960; BSN, Loyola U., Chgo., 1964; MS, No. Ill. U., 1968, EdD, 1971. Staff nurse Little Co. of Mary Hosp., 1960-64; instr. Little Co. of Mary Hosp. Sch. Nursing, 1964-67, No. Ill. U., DeKalb, 1968-69, asst. prof., 1969-71; chmn. dept. nursing U. Nev., Las Vegas, 1971-73, prof. nursing, 1975—, dean Coll. Health Scis., 1973-90, prof. emeritus coll. health scis., 2006—; pres. PERC, Inc.; mgmt. cons., 1993—95. Mgmt. cons. Nev. Donor Network, 1993; mem. So. Nev. Health Manpower Task Force, 1975; mem. manpower com. Plan Devel. Commn., Clark County Health Sys. Agy., 1977-79, mem. governing body, 1981-86; mem. Nev. Health Coordinating Coun., Western Inst. Nursing, 1971-85; mem. coordinating com. assembly instnl. adminstrs. dept. allied health edn. and accreditation AMA, 1985-88; mem. bd. advisors So. Nev. Vocat. Tech. Ctr., 1976-80; sec.-treas. Nev. Donor Network, 1988-89, chmn. bd., 1988-90. Contbr. articles to profl. jours. Trustee Desert Spring Hosp., Las Vegas, 1976-85; bd. dirs. Nathan Adelson Hospice, 1982-88, Bridge Counseling Assocs., 1982, Everywoman's Ctr., 1984-86; chair Nev. Commn. on Nursing Edn., 1972-73, Nursing Articulation Com., 1972-73, Yr. of Nurse Com., 1978; moderator Invitational Conf. Continuing Edn., Am. Soc. Allied Health Professions, 1978; mgmt. cons. Nev. Donor Network, 1994-95, Donor Organ Recovery Svc., Transplant Recipient Internat. Orgn., SW Eye Bank, SW Tissue Bank. Named Outstanding Alumnus, Loyola U., 1983; NIMH fellow, 1967-68. Fellow Am. Soc. Allied Health Professions, 1991, (chair nat. resolutions com. 1981-84, treas. 1988-90, sec's. award com. 1982-83, 92-93, nat. by-laws com. 1985, conv. chair 1987); mem. AAUP, Am. Nurses Assn., Nev. Nurses Assn. (dir. 1975-77, treas. 1977-79, conv. chair 1978), So. Nev. Area Health Edn. Coun., Western Health Deans (co-organizer 1985, chair, 1988-90), Nat. League Nursing, Nev. Heart Assn., So. Nev. Mem. Hosps. (nursing recruitment com. 1981-83, mem. nursing practice com. 1983-85), Las Vegas C. of C. (named Woman of Yr. Edn.) 1988, Slovak Catholic Sokols, Phi Kappa Phi (chpt. sec. 1981-83, pres.-elect 1983, pres. 1984, v.p. Western region 1989-95, editl. bd. jour. Nat. Forum 1989-93), Alpha Beta Gamma (hon.), Sigma Theta Tau, Zeta Kappa. Office: U Nev Las Vegas 4505 S Maryland Pky Las Vegas NV 89154-9900 Personal E-mail: m.a.michel@worldnet.att.net.

MICHEL, NICOLAS, international organization official; b. Nov. 7, 1949; married with children. PhD in Law, U. Fribourg, Switzerland; MA in Internat. Rels., Georgetown U., Washington, DC. Lic.: (attorney at law). Sec.-gen. Dept. of Edn. and Culture of the canton, Fribourg, Switzerland, 1980—85; acted as the head of the Swiss del. for the presentation of nat. reports before internat. com.; dir., Internat. Law Directorate Swiss Fed. Dept. of Foreign Affairs, 1998—2003, legal advisor, 1998—2004; under-sec.-gen. Legal Affairs and UN Legal Counsel, 2004—. Chmn., consultation and preparatory mtg. on a third protocol to the Geneva Convs. (Emblems), 2000; chmn. Com. of the Legal Advisors on Pub. Internat. Law of the Coun. of Europe, 2003—04; prof., Internat. Law and European Law U. Fribourg, Switzerland, 1987—2004, vice dean of the law faculty, 2003—04; bd. dir. European Law Faculties Assn., 2003—04. Author of numerous books and articles on Internat. and European law. Office: UN Hdqs First Avenue at 46th St New York NY 10017 Office Phone: 212-963-5339. Office Fax: 212-963-6430. *

MICHEL, PAUL REDMOND, federal judge; b. Phila., Feb. 3, 1941; s. Lincoln M. and Dorothy (Kelley) Michel; m. Brooke England, 2004; children: Sarah Elizabeth, Margaret Kelley. BA, Williams Coll., 1963; JD, U. Va., 1966. Bar: Pa. 1967, US Supreme Ct. 1970. Asst. dist. atty. Dist. Atty.'s Office, Phila., 1967—71, dep. dist. atty. investigations, 1972—74; asst. spl. prosecutor Watergate investigation US Dept. Justice, Washington, 1974—75, dep. chief pub. integrity sect., Criminal div. and prosecutor "Koreagate" investigation, 1976—78, assoc. dep. atty. gen., 1978—81; asst. counsel intelligence com. US Senate, 1975—76, counsel and adminstrv. asst. to Sen. Arlen Specter, 1981—88; judge US Ct. Appeals (Fed. cir.), Washington, 1988—2004, chief judge, 2004—. Instr. appellate practice and procedure George Washington U. Nat. Law Ctr., 1991—2002. 2d lt. USAR, 1966—72. Office: US Ct Appeals Fed Cir 717 Madison Pl NW Washington DC 20439 Office Phone: 202-633-6297. E-mail: michelp@cafc.uscourts.gov. *

MICHEL, SANDRA K., lawyer, food products executive; b. Miami, Fla., July 29, 1957; d. Vernon C. and Dorothy A. (Neisman) M. BBA, U. Miami, 1977, JD, 1980. Bar: Fla. Assoc. Greenburg, Tranrig, Miami, 1980-82, Weil, Gotshal & Manges, NYC, 1982-84, Walker, Ellis, Gragg & Deaktor, Miami, 1984; ptnr. Gustafson, Stephens, Ferris, Forman & Hall, PA, Fort Lauderdale, Fla.; sr. counsel legal services group W.R. Grace & Co., 1991—99; deputy gen. counsel, asst. sec. Sunterra Corp., 1999—2000, gen. counsel, sec., 2000—01; sr. v.p., gen. counsel La Quinta Corp., Dallas, 2002; exec. v.p., gen. counsel Krispy Kreme Doughnut Corp., 2007—. Commr. zoning bd. and bd. of adjustment, City of Hialeah, Fla., 1978-82. Republican. Office: Krispy Kreme Doughnut Corp PO Box 83 Winston Salem NC 27102 *

MICHEL, VERLYN LYLE, mayor, consultant; b. Nampa, Idaho, Sept. 25, 1938; s. Wolford and Ruth Alleta (Kimes) Michel; m. Betty Vernette, Nov. 1, 1974; children: Verlyn Lyle II, Eric Ryan. Student, Foothill Coll., Los Altos Hills, Calif., 1969—70, De Anza Coll., Cupertino, Calif., 1969—70, Lassen County Coll., Susanville, Calif., 1971. Com. mem. USAF/State of Idaho, Mountain Home AFB, 1963—67; cons. State Senator Hansen, Mountain Home AFB, 1964—66, Amb. Perez from Peru, Hemet, Calif., 1990; mayor Town of Quartzsite, Ariz., 2000—; com. leader Ariz. Western Coll., Yuma, 2004. Past pres. Western Ariz. Coun. Govts.; mem. exec. com. Western Ariz. Econ. Devel. Dist., Ariz. League Cities and Towns, Pandemia Flu H5N1; mem. com. APS Focused Future; mem. adv. com. Ariz. Western Coll. Staff sgt. USAF, 1963—67. Recipient cert. appreciation, DAV, Good Conduct medal, US Army, Nat. Def. Svc. medal, Armed Forces Res. medal, Presdl. Unit citation, Outstanding Unit award, USAF, Good Conduct medal, Longevity Svc. award ribbon, Tng. Ribbon, Cold War medal. Mem.: Toastmasters, Disabled Vets. Assn., Quartzsite Vets. Assn., Quartzsite Basin Model RR (pres. 2004). Republican. Baptist. Avocations: amateur radio, model railroads, woodworking. Home: PO Box 1353 Quartzsite AZ 85346 Office: Town of Quartzsite PO Box 2812 Quartzsite AZ 85346 Office Phone: 928-927-4333. Fax: 928-927-4400. Business E-Mail: mayormike@ci.quartzsite.az.us.

MICHELI, FRANK JAMES, lawyer; b. Zanesville, Ohio, Mar. 23, 1930; s. John and Theresa (Carlini) Micheli; m. Doris Joan Clum, Jan. 9, 1954; children: Michael John, James Carl, Lisa Ann, Matthew Charles. Student, John Carroll U., Cleve., 1947-48, Xavier U., Cin., 1949-50; LL.D., Ohio No. U., Ada., 1953. Bar: Ohio 1953. Pvt. practice, Zanesville; ptnr. Leasure & Micheli, 1953-65, Kincaid, Micheli, Geyer & Ormond, 1965-75, Kincaid, Cultice, Micheli & Geyer (and predecessor), 1982-92, Micheli, Baldwin, Bopeley & Northrup, 1992—. Instr. bus. law Meredith Bus. Coll., Zanesville, 1956; lectr. med. malpractice, hosp. and nurse liability. Dir. pub. svc. City of Zanesville, 1954. Mem.: ABA, Am. Bd. Trial Advs. (bd. dirs. Ohio chpt. 1991—95, pres. 1997), Am. Arbitration Assn. (mem. nat. panel), Am. Judicature Soc., Ohio Bar Assn., Ohio Def. Assn., Def. Rsch. Inst., Internat. Assn. Ins. Counsel, Elk. Home: 160 E Willow Dr Zanesville OH 43701-1249 Office: PO Box 788 3808 James Ct Ste 2 Zanesville OH 43702-0788 Office Phone: 740-454-2545. E-mail: micheli@cyberzane.net.

MICHELINI, SYLVIA HAMILTON, auditor; b. Decatur, Ala., May 16, 1946; d. George Borum and Dorothy Rose (Swatzell) Hamilton; m. H. Stewart Michelini, June 4, 1964; children: Stewart Anthony, Cynthia

Leigh. BSBA summa cum laude, U. Ala., Huntsville, 1987. CPA, Ala.; cert. govt. fin. mgr., fraud examiner. Acct. Ray McCay, CPA, Huntsville, 1987-88; auditor Def. Contract Audit Agy., Huntsville, 1989-92; auditor-office of inspector general George C. Marshall Space Flight, Center, Ala., 1992-97; contr. Hamilton Hotels, Inc., 1997-2001; ret. Exec. bd. Decatur City PTA, 1976-78; pres., v.p. Elem. Sch. PTA, Decatur, 1977-79; leader Girl Scouts U.S. and Cub Scouts, Decatur, 1972-77; active local ARC, 1973-77. Mem.: AAUW (chpt. treas. 1988—90), AICPA, Inst. Mgmt. Accts. (v.p. comm., dir. program book 1991—94, Dixie coun. dir. newsletters 1992—93, dir. ednl. programs 1992—93, 1993—94, nat. com. ethics 1990—97, nat. fin. com. 1997—98, nat. bd. dirs. 1994—97), Inst. Internal Auditors (dir. awards and recognition 1996—97, sec. 1999—2001, 2003—04), Ala. Soc. CPAs (profl. ethics com. 1993—94, govtl. acctg. and auditing com. 1994—95), Assn. Govt. Accts. (sec. 1992—93, chmn. pub. rels. 1993—94), Am. Soc. Women Accts. (chpt. treas. 1989—90, dir. chpt. devel. 1989—90), Nat. Notary Assn., Nat. Assn. Accts. (dir. cmty. svc. 1987—88, v.p. adminstrn. and fin. 1988—89, pres. 1989—90, nat. com. on ethics 1990—91), Phi Kappa Phi. Baptist. Avocations: reading, walking, sewing, research, music. Home and Office: 2801 Sylvia Dr SE Decatur AL 35603-5643 E-mail: nimi@hiway.net.

MICHELIS, MICHAEL FRANK, nephrologist; b. Bklyn., Dec. 11, 1938; s. Michael and Gisella (Gammer) M.; m. Mary Ann Wolak, July 28, 1973; children: Elizabeth Ann, Katherine Clare. BA, Columbia U., 1959; MD, George Washington U., 1963. Intern, resident Lenox Hill Hosp., NYC, 1963-65; resident Hosp. Med. Coll. Pa., Phila., 1965-67; fellow in renal disease, dept. medicine U. Pitts. Sch. Medicine, 1969-70, asst. prof. medicine, 1971-75; chief renal diagnostic unit VA Hosp., Pitts., 1971-75; asst. prof. clin. medicine NYU Med. Sch., 1975-93; assoc. prof. clin. medicine N.Y. Med. Coll., 1980-87, prof., 1987-92; assoc. prof. clin. medicine Cornell U. Med. Coll., 1992-93; prof. clin. medicine NYU Med. Coll., 1993—; dir. nephrology sect. Lenox Hill Hosp., NYC, 1975—. Spl. lectr. Georgetown U. Med. Sch., 1973-85; lectr. Western Pa. Continuing Edn. for Physicians, 1972-75, vis. prof., 1976; mem. merit rev. bd. VA, 1973-76; cons. clin. fellowship rev. com. NIH, 1981-85; mem. exec. com. End Stage Renal Disease Network, N.Y.C., 1981-85; mem. med. adv. bd. Nat. Kidney Found. of N.Y./N.J., 1987-2001; vice-chair med. adv. bd., trustee Kidney and Urology Found. Am., 2001—, v.p., 2005—. Mem. editl. bd. Clin. Nephrology, 1979-89, Geriat. Nephrology, 1986, Jour. Geriatric Nephrology and Urology, 1989—, Am. editor, 1989-98; contbr. articles to profl. jours. Served to maj. M.C., AUS, 1967-69. Decorated Army Commendation medal; Health, Rsch. and Svcs. Found. grantee, 1970, 72, 74. Mem. AMA (invited lectr. 1973-75), ACP, Am. Fedn. Clin. Rsch., Am. Soc. Nephrology, Internat. Soc. Nephrology, Internat. Soc. for Geriatric Nephrology and Urology (pres. 1999-2003), Ctrl. Soc. Clin. Rsch. Greek Orthodox. Home: 16 Woodland Park Dr Tenafly NJ 07670-3027 Office: Lenox Hill Hosp 100 E 77th St New York NY 10021-1850 Home Phone: 201-871-3769; Office Phone: 212-988-3506. E-mail: mfmich@ix.netcom.com.

MICHEL-KERJAN, ERWANN O., finance educator; b. Paris; PhD, Polytechique, Paris, 2002. Mng. dir. Ctr. for Catastrophic Risk Mgmt., Wharton Sch., Phila., 2002—. Author, editor: Seeds of Disaster. Roots of Response. How Can Private Action Reduce Public Vulnerability, 2006. Mem.: World Econ. Forum's Young Global Leader. Office: The Wharton School 3730 Walnut St Philadelphia PA 19104 Home Phone: 215-735-7395; Office Phone: 215-573-0515. Business E-Mail: erwannmk@wharton.upenn.edu.

MICHELLE, CADIEUX M., writer; d. Ronald Cadieux and Judith Dettman, William Dettman (Stepfather). BA, U. Minn., Mpls., 1992; MBA, San Jose State U., Calif., 2000. Lectr. Silesian U., Karvina, Czech Republic, 1995—96; editor Am. page Globe News, Rome, 1996—97; rsch. dir. San Jose Bus. Jour., 1998—99; tech. writer, trainer Creative Comm., San Francisco, 1998—; sr. tech. trainer Lockheed, San Jose, 2001—02. Spkr. in field. Editor: Jour. English Specific Purpose. Field election dep., San Francisco. Scholar, Black Rock City, 2004. Mem.: ASTD (assoc.). Achievements include patents pending in field. Avocations: search and rescue, diving, films. Personal E-mail: creativecommunications@yahoo.com.

MICHELMAN, DOUGLAS, finance company executive; BA, Duke Univ. Sr. ptnr., regional pres. Fleishman-Hillard; exec. v.p. corp. rels. Visa USA, San Francisco, 2003—. Mailing: Visa USA PO Box 194607 San Francisco CA 94119-4607 *

MICHELMAN, KATE, advocate; married; 3 daughters. Dir. Planned Parenthood, Harrisburg, Pa., 1980-85; pres. Nat. Abortion and Reproductive Rights Action League, Washington, 1985—2004. Spkr. in field. Named one of 100 Most Powerful Elites in the Nation's Capitol Washingtonian Mag., named a fellow of John F. Kennedy Sch. Govt.'s Inst. of Politics Harvard U., 1994. Office: Nat Abortion Rights Action League 1156 15th St NW Ste 700 Washington DC 20005-1744

MICHELS, DALE E., physician; b. Wayne, Nebr., Mar. 24, 1948; s. R.B. and Florence A. (Peterson) M.; m. Roylene C. Gustafson, Jan. 25, 1969; children: Gretchen, Sheila, Joel. BA in Medicine, U. Nebr., Omaha, 1969, MD, 1973. Diplomate Am. Bd. Family Practice with added qualifications in geriatrics. Practicing family physician Lincoln (Nebr.) Family Med. Group, 1974—. Med. cons. Comm. Blood Bank of LCMS, Lincoln, 1992-2007; med. dir. Nebr. Found. for Med. Care, 2001—; pres. EMS, Inc., 2002—; v.p. Wellmark Health Plan of Nebr., Lincoln, 1996-2000; vice-chair bd. trustees Back to the Bible, Lincoln, 1986-2004 chair bd. trustees, 2004—; sec.-treas. Family Care, PC, Lincoln, 1986-97. Pres. Lancaster County Med. Soc., Lincoln, 1991-92, Nebr. Acad. of Family Physicians, Omaha, 1987, Nebr. Heart Assn., 1983, Lincoln Christian Sch. Bd., Lincoln, 1990-97. Recipient J.J. Hanigan award Lincoln Lancaster Comm. Health Dept., 1994, Pub. Health Leadership awrd, 2000; named Family Physician of Yr., Nebr. Acad. Family Physicians, 1999. Mem. Am. Med. Dirs. Assn. (pres. N.E.), Nebr. Med. Dirs. Assn. (pres.), Lancaster County Med. Soc., Nebr. Acad. Family Physicians (Family Physician of Yr. 1999), Christian Med. Dental Soc., Am. Acad. Family Physicians, Nebr. Med. Assn. (pres. 1999-2000). Republican. Avocations: flying, photography, gardening. Office: Lincoln Family Med Group PC 7441 O St Ste 400 Lincoln NE 68510-2466 Home Phone: 402-488-8760; Office Phone: 402-488-7400. E-mail: dale.michels@gmail.com.

MICHELS, DIRK, lawyer; b. Wupperful, Germany, Mar. 10, 1962; s. Wolfgang and Ingrid Michels; m. Claudia I. Olson, Aug. 2, 1995. BWL Vordiplom, U. Hamburg, Germany, 1986, JD Erstes Staatsexamen, 1988; LLM, U. San Diego, 1996. Bar: Hamburg 1992, Calif. 1996. Law clk. Hamburg Ct. Appeals, 1989-92; assoc. Huth Dietrich Hahn, Hamburg, 1992-95, Hillyer & Irwin, San Diego, 1996-2000; assoc. to ptnr. Kirkpatrick & Lockhart Preston Gates Ellis LLP, San Francisco, 2000—. Contbr. articles tp profl. jours. Mem. ABA (internat. sect.), Council of Bars & Law Soc. of European Cmty., German-Am. Bus. Assn. (bd. dir.), Internat. Angel Investor Inst. (bd. adv.), German-Am. Lawyers Assn., German-Am. Cultural Soc., Am. Coun. on Germany. Office: K&L Gates 630 Hansen Way Palo Alto CA 94304 Office Phone: 650-798-6709. Business E-Mail: dirk.michels@klgates.com.

MICHELS, ROBERT, psychiatrist, educator; b. Chgo., Jan. 21, 1936; s. Samuel and Ann (Cooper) M.; m. Verena Sterba, Dec. 23, 1962; children—Katherine, James. BA, U. Chgo., 1953; MD, Northwestern U., 1958. Intern Mt. Sinai Hosp., NYC, 1958-59; resident in psychiatry Columbia Presbyn.-N.Y. State Psychiat. Inst., NYC, 1959-62; mem. faculty Coll. Physicians and Surgeons, Columbia U., NYC, 1964-74, assoc. prof., 1971-74; psychiatrist student health service Columbia U., 1966-74; supervising and tng. analyst Columbia U. Center for Psychoanalytic Tng. and Research, 1972—; attending psychiatrist Vanderbilt Clinic, Presbyn. Hosp., NYC, 1964-74; Barklie McKee Henry prof. psychiatry Cornell U. Med. Coll., NYC, 1974-93, chmn. dept. psychiatry, 1974-91, Stephen and Suzanne Weiss dean, 1991-96; provost for med. affairs Cornell U., 1991-96, Walsh McDermott U. prof. of medicine, 1996—, univ. prof. psychiatry, 1996—; psychiatrist-in-chief N.Y. Hosp., 1974-91, attending psychiatist, 1991—. Attending psychiatrist St. Luke's Hosp. Ctr., N.Y.C., 1966—. Co-author: The Psychiatric Interview in Clinical Practice, 1971, 2d edit., 2006; contbr. articles to profl. jours. Served with USPHS, 1962-64. Mem. Am. Psychiat. Assn., Am. Coll. Psychiatrists, N.Y. Psychiat. Soc., Royal Medico-Psychol. Assn., Psychiat. Rsch. Soc., Assn. Rsch. in Nervous and Mental Diseases, Assn. Acad. Psychiatry, Am. Psychoanalytic Assn., Internat. Psychoanalytic Assn., Ctr. Advanced Psychoanalytic Studies, N.Y. Acad. Scis., Alpha Omega Alpha. Office: Cornell U Med Coll 418 E 71st St New York NY 10021-4894 Office Phone: 212-746-6001. E-mail: rmichels@med.cornell.edu.

MICHELSEN, CHRISTOPHER BRUCE HERMANN, surgeon; b. Boston, Aug. 18, 1940; s. Jost Joseph and Ingeborg Elizabeth (Dilthey) M.; children: Heidi Elizabeth, Matthew Christopher, Joshua Jost. BA, Bowdoin Coll., 1961; MD, Columbia U., 1969. Diplomate Am. Bd. Orthop. Surgery, Am. Bd. Forensic Medicine. Intern Columbia Presbyn. Med. Ctr., NYC, 1969—70, resident, 1970—71; orthop. resident N.Y. Orthop. Hosp., NYC, 1971—73, jr. Anne C. Kane fellow, 1973—74, sr. Anne C. Kane fellow and hip fellow, 1974—75, traveling fellow, 1975—76; intenrat. A-O fellow, postgrad. fellow in biomechanics Case Western Res. U., NYC, 1975—76, instr. biomed. engring., 1975—76; prof. clin. orthop. surgery, orthop. surgeon Columbia Coll. Physicians and Surgeons, 1976, vice chmn. dept. orthop. surgery, 2002—; chief orthop. svc. Allen Pavillion, Columbia Presbyn. Med. Ctr., 1993—, chief orthop. spine surgery svc., 1998—. Col. USAR, ret. Fellow ACS, Am. Assn. for Surgery of Trauma, Am. Orthop. Assn., N.Am. Spine Soc., Am. Acad. Orthop. Surgeons, Internat. Coll. Surgeons, N.Y. Acad. Medicine; mem. AMA, Am. Coll. Physicians Execs., Orthop. Rsch. Soc., Am. Soc. Bone and Mineral Rsch., Royal Soc. Medicine (affiliate). Office: 5141 Broadway New York NY 10034-1159 Home: 10 Rossa Ln Ossining NY 10562-2568

MICHELSEN, CLEO, retired education educator, writer; b. Jan. 22, 1909; d. Hamilton Michelsen and Elizabeth Havens; m. Auriel Bessemer (div.). BA in English, George Washington U., Washington, 1943, MA in Theater Arts, 1952. Tchr. D.C. Pub. Schs., Washington, 1931—45; Eng. instr. U. Calif., Berkeley, 1945—47; asst. prof., supr. of student tchg. D.C. Tchr.'s Coll., 1958—65. Instr., creative dramatics George Washington U., 1953—54; dir., children's playhouse Radio Sta. WCFM, Washington, 1948—49. Co-author: (textbook series) Enjoying English, 1961—. Membership chair World Assn. for World Fedn., Amsterdam, Netherlands, 1982—84; pres., so. Calif. region World Federalist Assn., LA, 1980—86, pres., Va. chpt., 1987—2000. Mem.: World Federalist Assn. (adv. bd. 2000—, pres. 1995), Earth Action (internat. bd. mem. 2003—), Dem. World Federalists (brain trust 2003—). Democrat. Unitarian. Avocations: writing, reading, walking, theater. Home: 3440 S Jefferson St Falls Church VA 22041 E-mail: 1world@cox.net.

MICHELSON, GERTRUDE GERALDINE, retired retail executive; b. Jamestown, NY, June 3, 1925; d. Thomas and Celia Rosen; m. Horace Michelson, Mar. 28, 1947 (dec. Apr. 2002); children: Martha Ann (dec.), Barbara Jane. BA, Pa. State U., 1945; LLB, Columbia U., 1947; LLD with honors, Adelphi U., 1981; DHL with honors, New Rochelle Coll., 1983; LLD with honors, Marymount Manhattan Coll., 1988; PhD in Policy Analysis, Rand Grad. Sch., 2002. Mgmt. trainee Macy's NY, 1947-48, various mgmt. positions, v.p. employee personnel, 1963-70, sr. v.p. labor consumer rels., 1970—72; sr. v.p. pers. labor consumer rels. Macy & Co., Inc., 1972-79, sr. v.p. external affairs, 1979-80, R.H. Macy & Co., Inc., 1980-92, sr. advisor, 1992-94; ret., 1995. Chmn. Helena Rubinstein Found.; chmn. emeritus bd. trustees Columbia U.; life trustee Spelman Coll.; past pres. bd. overseers Tchrs. Ins. Annuity Assn. Am. Coll. Retirement Equities Fund. Recipient Disting. Svc. medal Pa. State U., 1969. Mem. NYC Ptnrship. (vice chmn.), Women's Forum, Econ. Club NY Home: 70 E 10th St New York NY 10003-5102 Office: Federated Dept Stores Inc 151 W 34th St New York NY 10001-2101

MICHELSON, LILLIAN, librarian, researcher; b. NYC, June 21, 1928; d. Louis and Dora (Keller) Farber; m. Harold Michelson, Dec. 14, 1947; children: Alan Bruce, Eric Neil, Dennis Paul. Vol. Goldwyn Libr., Hollywood, Calif., 1961-69; owner Former Goldwyn Rsch. Libr., Hollywood, 1969—; ind. location scout, 1973—. Mem. Motion Picture Libr. Found., 2002—, Friends L.A. Pub. Libr. Mem.: Acad. Motion Picture Arts and Scis. Office: c/o Dreamworks SKG Rsch Libr 1000 Flower St Glendale CA 91201-3007 Home Phone: 323-654-7177; Office Phone: 818-695-6445. E-mail: lmichelson@dreamworks.com.

MICHELSON, LOUIS ELI, lawyer; b. LA, Nov. 24, 1956; s. Irving and Sonia Michelson; m. Judy Michelson; children: Shoshana Helen, Miriam Regina, Aaron Noam, Renina Aliza. BA, U. Chgo., 1977; MA, DePaul U., Chgo., 1982; JD, UCLA, 1988. CPA 1984; bar: Calif. 1988, US Dist. Ct. (ctrl. dist.) Calif. 1988. Sr. acct. PriceWaterhouse, LA, 1982—85; atty. Loch & Loeb, LA, 1988—93, Sanders, Barnet, Goldman, Simons & Musk, LA, 1993—97; tax ptnr. Grohstein Horwath & Co. LLP, LA, 1997—2000; pvt. practice, 2000—07. Apptd. permanent receiver US Dist. Ct., Fed. Trade Commn., 1997—99; apptd. non-profit dir. Superior Ct., Calif. Atty. Gen., 2003. Editor: LA Lawyer Mag., 1993—95. V.p. Young Israel of Century City, LA, 2005—07. Recipient Chancellor's Marshall award, UCLA, Sch. Law, 1988, Am. Juris Prudence award, 1987, 1988. Mem.: State Bar Calif. (co-chair non-profit orgn. com. bus. law sect. 2000—06), LA County Bar Assn. (chair elect taxation sect. 2006—07). Office: 15233 Venture Blvd Penthouse Ste 1 Sherman Oaks CA 91403 Office Phone: 818-784-1700.

MICHELSTETTER, STANLEY HUBERT, lawyer; b. Milw., July 8, 1946; s. Donald Lee and Gloria (Menke) M.; m. Joyce Bladow, Apr. 29, 1972 (div. Jan. 2006); children: Chad S., Chris E. BA in Math., U. Wis., 1968, JD, 1972. Bar: Wis. 1972, U.S. Dist. Ct. (we. dist.) Wis. 1972. Staff atty. Wis. Employment Rels. Commn., Milw., 1972-80; pvt. practice, Milw., 1980—; adminstrv. law judge, equal rights div. adminstrn. Wis. Dept Industry, Labor and Human Rels., Milw., 1992-93. Chmn. North Shore Rep. Club, Milw., 1984-86; bd. dirs. Jewish Family Svcs., 2002-06; with Wis. EMployment Rel. Commn., 2005—. Served to 2d lt. Wis. N.G., 1968-74. Mem. Wis. Bar Assn. (chmn. 1993), Milw. Bar Assn., Nat. Acad. Arbitrators, Indsl. Rels. Rsch. Assn. (bd. dirs. 1987—), Nat. Assn. R.R. Rels. Republican. Jewish. also: PMB 37 5185 Broadway Gary IN 46409-2708 Home: 3032 Providence St Sun Prairie WI 53590 Home Phone: 608-825-1414; Office Phone: 608-266-1180. Business E-Mail: stan@stanm.com.

MICHENER, CHARLES DUNCAN, entomologist, researcher, educator; b. Pasadena, Calif., Sept. 22, 1918; s. Harold and Josephine (Rigden) Michener; m. Mary Hastings, Jan. 1, 1941; children: David, Daniel, Barbara, Walter. BS, U. Calif., Berkeley, 1939, PhD, 1941. Tech. asst. U. Calif., Berkeley, 1939-42; asst. curator Am. Mus. Natural History, NYC, 1942-46, assoc. curator, 1946-48, rsch. assoc., 1949—; assoc. prof. U. Kans., 1948-49, prof., 1949-89, prof. emeritus, 1989—, chmn. dept. entomology, 1949-61, 72-75, Watkins Disting. prof. entomology, 1959-89, acting chmn. dept. systematics, ecology, 1968-69, Watkins Disting. prof. systematics and ecology, 1969-89; dir. Snow Entomol. Museum, 1974-83, state entomologist, 1949-61. Vis. rsch. prof. U. Paraná, Curitiba, Brazil, 1955—56. Author: The Social Behavior of the Bees, 1974, The Bees of the World, 2000, 2d edit., 2007; author: (with Mary H. Michener) American Social Insects, 1951; author: (with S. F. Sakagami) (book) Nest Architecture of the Sweat Bees, 1962; author: (with M. D. Breed and H. E. Evans) The Biology of Social Insects, 1982; author: (with D. Fletcher) Kin Recognition in Animals, 1987; author: (with R. McGinley and B. Danforth) The Bee Genera of North and Central America, 1994; contbr. articles to profl. jours.; Am. editor: Insectes Sociaux, 1954—55, 1962—90; editor: (jour.) Evolution, 1962—64; assoc. editor: Ann. Rev. Ecology and Systematics, 1970—90. Served to capt. San Corps AUS, 1943—46. Recipient Disting. Rsch. medal, Internat. Soc. Hymenopterists, 2002; fellow Guggenheim, U. Paraná, 1955—56, Africa, 1966—67, Fulbright, U. Queensland, 1958—59; scholar Rsch., U. Costa Rica, 1963. Fellow: AAAS, Royal Entomol. Soc. London, Am. Acad. Arts and Sci., Am. Entomol. Soc., Entomol. Soc. Am. (C. V. Riley award 1999); mem.: NAS, Kans. Entomol. Soc. (pres. 1950), Linnean Soc. London (corr.), Russian Entomol. Soc. (hon.), Soc. Systematic Zoologists (hon.; pres. 1969), Netherlands Entomological Soc. (hon.), Brazilian Acad. Sci. (corr.), Internat. Union Study Social Insects (pres. 1977—82), Am. Soc. Naturalists (pres. 1978), Soc. Study Evolution (pres. 1967). Home: 1706 W 2nd St Lawrence KS 66044-1016 Office Phone: 785-864-4610. Business E-Mail: michener@ku.edu.

MICHENER, JAMES LLOYD, medical educator; b. Dec. 19, 1952; m. Gwendolyn Curtis Murphy; children: Rebecca Liane, Joshua Kieran. BA, Oberlin Coll., Ohio, 1974; MD, Harvard Med. Sch., 1978. Diplomate Am. Bd. Family Practice. Resident in family medicine Duke U. Med. Ctr., Durham, NC, 1978-81, Kellogg fellow, 1981-82, prof. dept. cmty. and family medicine, 1994—, chmn. dept. cmty. and family medicine, 1994—; dir. Duke Ctr. Cmty. Rsch., 2006. V.p. Durham Health Care, Inc., 1985-86; project reviewer Ctrs. Disease Control and Prevention, 2002-; vis. prof. work group pub. health and med. edn. Ctrs. Disease Control, Atlanta, 2005. Co-author: Nutrition in Practice, 1990, 2d edit., 1992; contbr. numerous articles to med. pubs. including Academic Medicine, The Jour. of Family Practice, Medical Care, others; mem. editl. bd. Rx Nutrition, 1989-91; presenter in field. Bd. dirs. N.C. Med. Soc. Found., 1995—2004; STFM rep. resource com. on nutrition edn. Am. Acad. Family Practice Found., 1987-91. Grantee The Fullerton Found., Inc., The Josiah Macy, Jr. Found., U.S. Dept. Health and Human Svcs., Kate B. Reynolds Charitable Trust, N.C. Health and Wellness Trust. Mem. AMA, NIH (Fogarty/Ellison fellowship selection com. 2005-06), Assn. Am. Med. Colls. (exec. com. 2001-06, exec. coun. 2001—), Assn. Tchrs. Preventive Medicine (chmn. coun. acad. units 2002—), Am. Acad. Family Physicians Found., N.C. Acad. Family Physicians, Assn. Dept. Family Medicine (bd. dir. 1997—, sec. 1998—2005), Coun. Acad. Socs. (adminstrn. bd. 2000—, chair 2005-06), World Orgn. Nat. Colls., Acads. and Academic Assn. Gen. Practitioners and Family Physicians, Am. Austrian Founds. Internat. Health Forum (mem. steering com.). Home: 4011 Duck Pond Trail Chapel Hill NC 27514-9758 Office: Duke U Med Ctr PO Box 2914 Durham NC 27710-0001 Business E-Mail: miche001@mc.duke.edu.

MICHENFELDER, ALBERT A., lawyer; b. St. Louis, July 21, 1926; s. Albert A. and Ruth Josephine (Donahue) M.; m. Lois Barbara Sullivan, Sept. 03, 1949 (div. May 2, 1967); children: Michael J., Ann C. Michenfelder Yancey, Elizabeth D. Michenfelder Brown; m. Ramona Jo Dysart, July 12, 1968 (dec. Jan. 2, 1998); 1 child, Julie D. Michenfelder Wolfe. B of Naval Sci., Marquette U., 1946; LLB, St. Louis U., 1950. Bar: Mo. 1950, U.S. Dist. Ct. (ea. dist.) Mo. 1950, U.S. Supreme Ct. 1975. Assoc. Flynn & Challis, St. Louis, 1950-54; pvt. practice St. Louis, 1954-55; of counsel Husch & Eppenberger LLC, St. Louis. Mem. 21st Cir. Jud. Commn., St. Louis, 1981-87. Contbr. articles to profl. jours. City atty. City of Webster Groves, Mo., 1966-79; mem. John Marshall Club, St. Louis. Lt. (j.g.) USNR, 1944-47. Mem. Mo. Bar Assn., Bar. Assn. Met. St. Louis, St. Louis County Bar Assn. (pres. 1966), Westborough Country Club. Republican. Avocations: golf, tennis. Office: Husch & Eppenberger LLC 190 Carondelet Plz Ste 600 Saint Louis MO 63105-3441 Home Phone: 314-991-2846; Office Phone: 314-480-1730. Business E-Mail: al.michenfelder@husch.com.

MICHIE, SARA H., pathologist, educator; b. Tulsa, Okla., Jan. 3, 1955; BS in Biology, Stephen F. Austin U., 1977; MD, U. Tex., Houston, 1981. Diplomate Am. Bd. Pathology. Resident anatomic pathology Stanford (Calif.) U. Med. Ctr., 1981—83, postdoctoral fellow immunology dept. pathology, 1983—84, 1986—87, postdoctoral fellow diagnostic immunopathology, 1984—85; resident dept. pathology U. Iowa, Iowa City, 1985—86, postdoctoral fellow, 1986; assoc. investigator lab. svc. VA Hosp., Palo Alto, Calif., 1988—89, staff physician, 1989—, assoc. investigator, 1990—91; clin. instr. pathology dept. Stanford U., 1989—92, asst. prof. pathology, 1992—. Contbr. articles to profl. jours. Recipient Rsch. award, Am. Diabetes Assn., 1996. Mem.: Bay Area Flow Cytometry Group, Soc. Investigative Pathology, Am. Soc. Investigative Pathology, Alpha Omega Alpha, Sigma Xi. Office: VA Hosp Palo Alto 3801 Miranda Ave Stop 154F Palo Alto CA 94304-1207

MICHIELSEN, STEPHEN, chemistry professor; b. NY; BS in Chemistry, SUNY, Stony Brook, 1972; PhD, U. Chgo., 1979. Rsch. assoc. DuPont, Wilmington, Del., 1980—95; assoc. prof. Ga. Inst. Tech., Atlanta, 1995—2003, NC State U., Raleigh, 2004—. Mem.: Am. Phys. Soc., Am. Chem. Soc., Fiber Soc. (treas. 2007). Achievements include patents pending for antiviral surface coatings. Office: North Carolina State Univ 2401 Rsch Dr Raleigh NC 27695-8301 Office Phone: 919-515-1414.

MICHL, MICHAEL W., finance company executive; PhD in Law, Univ. Vienna. Mgmt. positions IBM; global head HR & admin. Avon Products Inc., 1993—98; exec. v.p. ctrl. resources MasterCard Worldwide, Purchase, NY, 1998—2004, chief adminstrv. officer, 2004—. Trustee Manhattanville Coll. Office: MasterCard Worldwide 2000 Purchase St Purchase NY 10577 *

MICHLER, ROBERT E., heart surgeon; b. July 8, 1956; m. Sally Radcliffe Sandercock, May 28, 1983; children: Alexandra Keats, Sarah Radcliffe, Elizabeth Tamsin. BA magna cum laude, Harvard U., 1978; MD, Dartmouth U., 1981. Diplomate Am. Bd. Surgery, Am. Bd. Thoracic Surgery, Am. Bd. Surgery-Critical Care. Intern Columbia-Presbyn. Med. Ctr., NYC, 1981-82, resident gen. surgery, 1982-86, chief resident gen. surgery, 1986-87, resident cardiothoracic surgery, 1987-88, chief resident cardiothoracic surgery, 1988-89; chief resident pediat. cardiothoracic surgery Boston Children's Hosp., Harvard Med. Sch., 1989-90, attending surgeon, 1990-97, dir. cardiac transplant svc., 1993-97; assoc. prof. surgery Columbia U., 1990-97, dir. cardiac transplantation rsch. lab., 1991-97, John G. and Jeanne R. McCoy chair; Karl P. Klassen prof. surgery, chief thoracic surgery Ohio State U., Columbus, 1997—2005; dir. cardiothoracic transplantation and rsch. Ohio State U. Med. Ctr., Columbus, 1997—2005, co-dir. heart and lung inst., 1997—2005; chmn. dept. cardiothoracic surgery Albert Einstein Coll. Medicine, NYC, 2005—; dir. Montefiore-Einstein Heart Ctr. Montefiore Med. Ctr., 2005—. Rsch. fellow cardiopulmonary transplantation Columbia U., Coll. Physicians and Surgeons, N.Y.C., 1984-85; founder, chmn. Heart Care Internat., 1994—; presenter and lectr. in field. Contbr. chpts. to books and articles to profl. jours. Exec. coun. mem. Second Congl. Ch., Greenwich, Conn., 1994—. Recipient Claire Lucille Pace Humanitarian award, 1996, Order of Christopher Columbus; named Person of Week, ABC World News Tonight, 1995; Leopold Schepp scholar Dartmouth Med. Sch., Hanover, N.H., 1981.

Fellow ACS, Am. Coll. Cardiology, Am. Coll. Chest Physicians; mem. AMA, Am. Bd. Surgery, Am. Bd. Thoracic Surgery, Soc. Thoracic Surgeons, Internat. Soc. for Heart and Lung Transplantation, Soc. Pediat. Cardiac Surgery, Soc. Critical Care Medicine, Am. Soc. for Artificial Internal Organs, N.Y. Soc. for Thoracic Surgery, N.Y. Transplantation Soc., Riverside Yacht Club (Greenwich, Conn.), N.Y. Yacht Club. Avocations: sailing, sculling, squash, tennis. Home: 36 Leeward Ln Riverside CT 06878-2409 Office: Dept Cardiothoracic Surgery Montefiore Med Ctr 3400 Bainbridge Ave MAP Bldg 5B Bronx NY 10467 Office Phone: 718-920-2100. E-mail: rmichler@montefiore.org.

MICHLIK, JOHN F., engineer; s. Robert F. and Diane M. Michlik. B of Engring., Stevens Inst. Tech., Hoboken, NJ, 2003. EIT NJ., 2003. Project engr. Syska Hennessy Group, NYC, 2004—. Mem.: ASHRAE (assoc.).

MICHNEY, TODD MICHAEL, history professor; b. Cleve., Ohio, Oct. 1, 1971; s. Michael A. and Patricia A. Michney; m. Laura M. D'Alessandro, July 20, 1996. BA, Case We. Res. U., 1993; MA, U. Minn., 1997, PhD, 2004. Lectr. U. Minn., Mpls., 1999—2000; adj. prof. Cleve. State U., 2005—06; vis. asst. prof. Tulane U., 2006—. Contbr. articles to profl. jours.; actor: Barebones Prodns., 1998, In the Heart of the Beast Mask and Puppet Theater, 2005. Organizer, canvasser Green Party Ohio, Cleve., 2000. Mem.: Orgn. Am. Historians, Am. Hist. Assn., Phi Beta Kappa. Avocations: birdwatching, tai chi. Office: Tulane Univ 125A Hebert Hall Annex New Orleans LA 70118 Office Phone: 504-862-8607. Business E-Mail: tmichney@tulane.edu.

MICHNICH, MARIE E., health policy analyst, consultant, educator; M Health Svs. Adminstrn., UCLA, DrPH Health Svs. Rsch. Asst. prof. health svs. U. Washington; sr. exec. v.p. Health Policy, Am. Coll. Cardiology Clin. Practice and Sci. Svs. Divsn.; dir. Health Policy Programs and Fellowships Nat. Acad. Scis. Inst. Medicine, 2002—. Cons, spkr. in field; legis. asst. health policy Medicare, Medicaid, maternal and child health; legis. asst. U.S. Senate Majority Leader Robert Dole; mem. several nat. health policy groups. Robert Wood Johnson Health Policy fellow. Mem.: Am. Pharm. Assn. Found. (1st pub. mem. bd. dirs. 2002—), Robert Wood Johnson Health Policy Fellows Program (mem. adv. bd., dir.), Health Care Quality Alliance (former chmn.). Office: Office Health Policy Programs Fellowship 500 5th St NW Washington DC 20001

MICHOD, SUSAN ALEXANDER, artist, painter; b. Toledo, Ohio, Jan. 3, 1945; d. Harold Milne and Caroline (Simonds) Alexander; m. Charles Louis Michod Jr., Aug. 16, 1969; children: Alexander Charles, Richard Simonds, Michael Wise. Student, Smith Coll., 1963-66; BS, Univ. Mich., 1967; MFA, Pratt Inst., 1969. Exhibiting mem. Artemisia Gallery, Chgo., 1973-78; exhibitor Jan Cicero Gallery, Chgo., 1978-88, Andre Zarre Gallery, NYC, 1978-80, Susan Caldwell Gallery, NYC, 1980-83, Gwenda Jay Gallery, Chgo., 1988-89, State of Ill. Gallery, Chgo., 1991, Jan Cicero Gallery, Chgo., 1991, Andre Zarse Gallery, NYC, 2003, Biennale Internat. Dell' Arte Contemporanea, Florence, Italy, 2003, That 70's Show- The Age of Pluralism in Chgo., Munster, Ind., 2004, Hinsdale (Ill.) Ctr. Arts, 2004, Whitney Mus. Am. Art, NYC, 2006. Faculty Chgo. Acad. Fine Arts, Chgo., 1969-74; mentor Columbia Coll., Chgo., 1980-90; collaborator and set designer Fluid Measure Organic Theatre, Chgo., 1989, Kast & Co., Links Hall., Chgo., 1992. Author: Some Thoughts on Pattern Painting, 1977; contbr. articles to books. Visual arts panel Ill. Arts Coun., 1977-79. Recipient Artist's grant Ill. Arts Coun., 1984, Collaboration grant Paper Press Gallery, 1987. Mem. Artimisia Gallery (pres. 1973—, founding mem.). Home: 2242 N Dayton St Chicago IL 60614-3612 Office: 1523 N Kingsbury St Chicago IL 60622-2533 E-mail: cmichod@cs.com.

MICHOPOULOS, ARISTOTLE V., humanities educator, researcher; b. Kotylion, Arcadia, Peloponnesos, Greece, Apr. 22, 1944; s. Vassilios A. Michopoulos and Anastasia D. Papazafeiropoulos; m. Despina Dimitropoulos (div. Jan. 30, 1996). BA, U. Athens, 1967; MA, CUNY, 1976; PhD, Fla. State U., Tallahassee, 1980. Translator Greek Orthodox Archdiocese of N.Am. and S. Am., NYC, 1970—71; translator and adminstr. Hellenic Indsl. Devel. Corp., NYC, 1972—74; h.s. tchr. Bd. of Edn. of NYC, 1975—76; adj. instr. Fla. State U., Tallahassee, 1977—78, asst. project dir. and curriculum writer, 1978—80; asst. prof. U. Fla., Gainesville, 1980—87; prof., dir. Greek studies Hellenic Coll., Brookline, Mass., 1987—2007. Dean Hellenic Coll., Brookline, Mass., 1995—2002, Greek studies dept. dir., 1987—; translator, cons. Various Organizations, Many, 1980—. Rep. to U.S. Dept. Edn., Greek Orthodox Archdiocese, N.Y.C., 1992—98; del., com. mem. Coun. on Hellenes Abroad, Chgo., 1995—2002; nat. coord. Paideia project, Greece, 1999—2007. Recipient Socratic award, U. Fla., 1999; fellow, US Dept. HEW, 1976—79; Fulbright awardee, 1977. Mem.: Kotylion Syllogos (cons. 1980—2005, Merit Award 2000), Am. Hellenic Edn. Assn. (AHEPA), Modern Greek Studies Assn. Avocations: tennis, swimming, backgammon, travel. Office: Hellenic Coll 50 Goddard Ave Brookline MA 02445 Office Phone: 617-850-1271.

MICIC, MIODRAG, chemist, researcher; b. Belgrade, Serbia-Monteneg, Sept. 19, 1973; s. Zivorad and Nadezda Micic. B in Mech. and Navel Arch. Engring., Poly. Acad., Belgrade, 1991; BS in Physics and Fundamentals of Engring., U. Belgrade, Serbia, 1996, MS in Phys. Chem., 1998, DS in Phys. Chem., 2001; PhD in Chemistry, MS in Chemistry, U. Miami, Coral Gables, 2002; M in Tech. Mgmt., Wash. State U., Pullman, 2003. Pres., CEO Mimitech D.O.O., Belgrade, Serbia and Montenegro, 1991—98; rsch. assoc. U. Belgrade, Faculty Phys. Chemistry, 1996—98; tchg. and rsch. asst. U. Miami, Chemistry Dept., Coral Gables, 1998—2002; sr. applications scientist Veeco Instruments, Inc., Santa Barbara, Calif., 2003—04; v.p., r & d MP Biomedicals LLC, Irvine, Calif., 2004—. Grants reviewer Inst. for Publich Health and Water Rsch., Napperville, Ill., 2005—, Ministry Sci. and Environ. Protection, Belgrade, 2004—, Vojvodina Region, Provincial Secretariat Sci. and Tech. Devel., Novi Sad, 2004—; symposia chmn. 40th Regional Meeting Western Region Am. Chem. Soc., Annaheim, Calif., 2006—. Fellow, Battelle Meml. Inst., Pacific NW Nat. Lab., Richland, 2002—03. Mem.: Am. Chem. Soc., Exptl. Aircraft Assn., Aircraft Owners and Pilots Assn., Masons (Master Mason 2001, plural membership 2004, 2002), Scottish Rite (32nd degree), Sigma Xi, Alpha Epsilon Lambda (hon.). Achievements include development of FastPrep-24, semi-automated DNA, RNA and proteins extraction system; discovery of methods for AFM imaging of microorganisms; novel photoscwitchable biocompatable hydrogels; research in single molecular electron transfer; first to theorize apertureless NSOM; development of aurora-3/SPEC near field scanning optical microscopy system; discovery of elucidation of the lignin model compunds supramolecular strucutres; research in AFM, FLIM, ESEM and SERS spectroscopy and imaging, langmuir and langmuir blodgett film studies of supramolecular systems; biomaterials; nanoparticles; first to apertureless FLIM development; gold quantum dots conjugates; visualisation of lignin model compound supramolecular structures; novel bioanalytical instruments. Office: MP Biomedicals LLC 15 Morgan Irvine CA 92618 Home Phone: 949-981-1068; Office Phone: 949-833-2500 264. Office Fax: 959-859-5095; Home Fax: 949-387-0841. Personal E-mail: drmicic@aol.com. E-mail: mmicic@mpbio.com.

MICKEL, EMANUEL JOHN, foreign language educator; b. Lemont, Ill., Oct. 11, 1937; s. Emanuel John and Mildred (Newton) M.; m. Kathleen Russell, May 31, 1959; children: Jennifer, Chiara, Heather. BA, La. State U., 1959; MA, U. N.C., 1961, PhD, 1965. Asst. prof. U. Nebr., Lincoln, 1965-67, assoc. prof., 1967-68, Ind. U., Bloomington, 1968-73, prof., 1973—, dir. Medieval Studies Inst., 1976-91, chmn. French and Italian, 1984-95. Cons. NEH; French advisor Soc. Rencesvals, 1995-98; adv. bd. mem. Nineteenth Century French Studies, 1995-, vis. scholar Pembroke Coll., U. Cambridge, 2006. Author: Marie de France, 1974, Eugene Fromentin, 1982, Ganelon Treason and the Chanson de Roland, 1989, Jules Vernes Complete Twenty Thousand Leagues Under the Sea, 1992, Enfances Godefroi and Retour de Cornumarant, 1999. Capt. U.S. Army, 1963-65. Grantee NEH, Washington, 1978-84; Lilly Open fellow Lilly Found., Indpls., 1981-82; Chevalier dans l'Ordre des Palmes Academiques, 1997. Avocations: music, theater, sports, travel, ancient literature. Office: French & Italian Dept Indiana Univ 642 Ballantine Hall Bloomington IN 47401-5020 Office Phone: 812-855-8253. Business E-Mail: mickel@indiana.edu.

MICKELSON, PHIL (PHILIP ALFRED MICKELSON JR.), professional golfer; b. San Diego, June 16, 1970; s. Philip and Mary Mickelson; m. Amy McBride, Nov. 19, 1996; children: Amanda Brynn, Sophia Isabel, Evan. BS in Psych., Ariz. State U., 1992. Profl. golfer PGA, 1992—. Co-author (with Donald T. Phillips): One Magical Sunday (But Winning Isn't Everything), 2005. Founder The Phil and Amy Mickelson Charitable Fund. Recipient Fred Haskins award, 1990, 91, 92, Jack Nicklaus award, 1990, 91, 92; won NCAA Championships, 1989, 90, 92; 1st team All-Am. with Sun Devils; Espy Award for Best Male Golfer, Best Championship Performance, ESPN, 2004. Achievements include 1st left-hander to win US Amateur, 1990; 1st player in PGA history to win same tournament as amateur and profl. (No. Telecom Open); winning The Masters Tournament, 2004, 06; PGA Championship, 2005; Presidents Cup, 1994, 96, 98, 2000, 03; Ryder Cup, 1995, 97, 99, 2001, 04; 32 career PGA Tour Victories; runner-up US open, 2006; shot a career-low 60 in the second round of the 2005 FBR Open; tying record for course in Pebble Beach Pro-Am victory, 2007. Avocation: flying. Office: c/o PGA Box 109601 100 Avenue Of Champions Palm Beach Gardens FL 33418 *

MICKENBERG, DAVID, museum director, art director, historian; b. Bklyn., Apr. 24, 1954; s. Morton and Florence Geri (Merenstein) M.; m. Judith Hope, Apr. 25, 1980; children: Danielle, Julia, Mia. BA with honors, Colgate U., 1976; M in Art History, U. Wis., Milw., 1979. Asst. to dir. Bklyn. Mus., 1975-76; asst. curator Picker Art Gallery, Hamilton, N.Y., 1974-76; program coordinator, asst. dir. adult edn. Indpls. Mus. of Art, 1979-81; exec. dir. Okla. Mus. Art, Oklahoma City, 1981-86; dir. Mary & Leigh Block Gallery Northwestern U., Evanston, Ill., 1986—2001; Ruth Gordon Shapiro dir. Davis Mus. and Cultural Ctr., Wellesley Coll., Mass., 2001—. Editor: (exhbn. catalogue) Maurice Prendergast Large Boston Public Garden Sketchbook, 1981; editor, author: (exhbn. catalogue) Songs of Glory: Medieval Art from 900 to 1500, 1985. Trustee Chamber Orch. of Oklahoma City, 1984-86, Oklahoma City Pub. Sch. Found., 1984-86, Infant Crisis Services, Oklahoma City, 1985-86; advisor mktg. and pub. rels. Okla. Symphony Orch., Oklahoma City, 1984-86, masters of mus. studies program, U. Okla., Norman, 1985; bd. govs. Ill. Art Alliance, 1988-90. Ind. U. fellow, 1979-80, scholar, 1980-81 Mem. Coll. Art Assn., Am. Assn. Museums, Internat. Ctr. of Medieval Art Office: Davis Mus and Cultural Ctr Wellesley Coll 106 Central St Wellesley MA 02481-8203

MICKEY, PAUL F(OGLE), JR., lawyer; b. Washington, Sept. 25, 1949; s. Paul Fogle and Margaret Snowden (Stanley) M.; m. Carol Lynne Forsyth, Mar. 19, 1977; children: Alison Langlands, Suzanne Snowden, Scott Forsyth. AB summa cum laude, Princeton U., 1971; JD, U. Va., 1974. Bar: D.C. 1974, US Ct. Appeals (DC, 7th, 10th cir.), U.S. Supreme Ct. 1981. Law clk. to George E. MacKinnon, U.S. Ct. Appeals, D.C. Circuit, 1974-75; with office of legal adv. U.S. Dept. State, Washington, 1975-77; assoc. Covington & Burling, Washington, 1977-79; v.p., gen. counsel Nat. R.R. Passenger Corp. (Amtrak), Washington, 1979-83, exec. v.p. law and pub. affairs, 1983-85; ptnr. Shaw, Pittman, Potts & Trowbridge, Washington, 1985—2005, mng. ptnr., chmn., 1995—2003; ptnr. Employment & Labor, Litigation practices Pillsbury Winthrop Shaw Pittman, Washington, 2005—. Articles editor, Va. Law Rev.; contbr. articles to legal revs. Mem., bd. govs. Nat. Cathedral Sch.; mem. corp. bd. dirs. Children's Hosp., Nat. Med. Ctr.; bd. dirs. St. Francis Ctr. Mem. ABA, D.C. Bar Assn. (chmn. Individual Employee Rights & Responsibilities subcom.), Am. Arbitration Assn. (arbitrator), Met. Club, Chevy Chase Club. Episcopalian. Office: Pillsbury Winthrop Shaw Pittman 2300 N St NW Washington DC 20037-1128 Office Phone: 202-663-8233. Office Fax: 202-663-8007. Business E-Mail: paul.mickey@pillsburylaw.com.

MICKLE, MARLIN HOMER, electrical engineer, educator; b. Windber, Pa., July 5, 1936; s. Howard T. and Ruth Elma (Corle) Mickle. BS, U. Pitts., 1961, MS, 1963, PhD, 1967. Jr. engr. IBM, 1962; engr. Westinghouse Co., 1964; mem. faculty U. Pitts., 1962—, assoc. prof. elec. engring., 1968-75, prof., 1975—, dir. computer engring. program, 1982-84, Nickolas A. DeCecco prof., 2001—. Program dir. sys. theory & applications NSF, 1974—75; pres. Mickle Computer Techs., Inc., Pitts., 1979—85; v.p., bd. dirs. Power Resources, Inc., Pitts., 1980—84; dir. Univ. R & D Assocs., Inc., 1985—2004; exec. dir. Swanson Ctr. Product Innovation, 2004—06; dir. Radio Frequency Identification Ctr. Excellence, 2005—; cons. in field. Author (with T. W. Sze): Optimization in Systems Engineering, 1972; mem. editl. bd. Jour. Interdisciplinary Modeling and Stimulation, 1978—80; editor-in-chief: Internat. Jour. Paralle and Distributed Systems and Networks, 1997—2002; editor: Internat. Jour. Radio Frequency Tech. Applications, 2004—; contbr. articles to profl. jours. Bd. dirs. Asbury Heights, Pitts., 1982—, Wesley Hills Mt. Lebanon, Pitts., 1985—86; chmn. bd. dirs. Emory Sr. Housing, Pitts., 2000—; dist. lay leader Pitts. dist. United Meth. Ch., 1971—73; elder Shadyside Presbyn. Ch., 2004—. Radar tech. Airborne USAF, 1954—58. Recipient sys. rsch. and cybernetics award, Internat. Inst. Advanced Studies in Sys. Rsch. and Cybernetics, 1988, excellence in corp. innovation award, Carnegie Sci. Ctr., 2005, Pitt Innovator award, 2005, 2006. Fellow: IEEE (life); mem.: Cathedral Learning Soc. Republican. Home: 4601 5th Ave Apt 723 Pittsburgh PA 15213-3657 Office: U Pitts Dept Elec and Computer Engring Pittsburgh PA 15261-0001 Office Phone: 412-600-3606. Business E-Mail: mickle@pitt.edu.

MICKO, ALEXANDER S., corporate financial executive, educator, treasurer; b. Munich, May 8, 1947; came to U.S., 1952, naturalized, 1957; s. Zygmunt and Maria (Huber) M.; m. Sharon E. Judge, June 7, 1969; 1 child, Brian A. BS, LaSalle U., 1969. CPA, NJ, Pa. Audit mgr. Price Waterhouse Coopers, Phila., 1970—77; asst. chief fin. investigations div. of Casino Gaming Enforcement, State of NJ, Trenton, NJ, 1977—79; v.p. fin. TeleScis., Inc., Mt. Laurel, NJ, 1979—87, Nat. Environ. Testing, Inc., Thorofare, NJ, 1988—92; controller AAA Mid-Altantic, Inc., Phila., 1992—2006; pres. Alexander & Assocs., CPA, LLC, 2006—. Cons. United Computer Svcs., Berlin, 1982; lectr. in field. Bd. dirs. Forest Hills Civic Assn., Williamstown, NJ, 1976. With USMC, 1969-75. Recipient Michael A. DeAngelis Outstanding Profl. Achievement award, LaSalle U., Phila., 1985. Mem. AICPA, NJ Soc. CPAs, Pa. Inst. CPAs, Fin. Execs. Inst., Nat. Assn. Accts. Roman Catholic. Avocations: skiing, golf. Home: 5 Huntington Cir Medford NJ 08055-3315 Personal E-mail: amicko@aol.com.

MICOZZI, MARC STEPHEN, medical educator, writer; b. Norfolk, Va., Oct. 27, 1953; s. Edio Dominic and Huguette (Picon) M.; m. Carole Ann O'Leary, Oct. 8, 1982; 1 child, Alicia Madeleine. Cadet, USAF Acad., 1971-72; BA, Pomona Coll., 1974; MD, U. Pa., 1979, PhD, 1986. Diplomate Am. Bd. Pathology. Rsch. fellow City of Hope Nat. Med. Ctr., Duarte, Calif., 1973; chem. engr. Gould Corp., El Monte, Calif., 1974; Luce Found. scholar Mindanao, The Philippines, 1976-77; clin. applications chemist McDonnell-Douglas Corp., Pasadena, Calif., 1978; postdoctoral fellow Allied Inst. Environ. Health, Princeton, N.J., 1979; resident in pathology Pa. Hosp., Phila., 1980-83; med. examiner Dade County Med. Examiner's Office, Miami, Fla., 1983-84; sr. investigator Nat. Cancer Inst., Bethesda, Md., 1984-86; dir. Nat. Mus. Health and Medicine, Washington, 1986-95; exec. dir. Coll. Physicians' of Phila., 1995—2002; exec. dir. Integrative Medicine Thomas Jefferson U. Hosp., Phila., 2002—05. Adj. prof. Uniformed Svcs. U. Health Scis., Bethesda, 1986-95, U. Pa. Sch. Medicine, 1996—; vis. faculty Georgetown U. Sch. Medicine, Washington, 1986—, Johns Hopkins U. Sch. Medicine, Balt., 1988—; adj. prof. dept. phys. medicine U. Pa., 1996—. Editor: Nutrition and Cancer, 1989; assoc. editor Health Care, Jour. Human Orgn., 1983-89; contbr. chpts. to books and numerous articles to profl. jours. Del. White House Conf. on Youth, Estes Park, Colo., 1971, UN Conf. on Human Environ., Stockholm, 1972, NATO Advanced Study Inst., Brussels, 1982; mem. Calif. Gov.'s Adv. Com., 1972-74. Fellow Human Biology coun., Soc. for Applied Anthropology, Am. Anthrop. Assn.; Am. Acad. Forensic Scis., Am. Pub. Health Assn., N.Y. Acad. Scis. Roman Catholic. Office Phone: 301-654-4706.

MICUNIS, GORDON JULES, set designer; b. Lynn, Mass., June 16, 1933; s. Morris and Ida Gordon Micunis; life ptnr. Jay Kobrin, Nov. 30, 1959. BA, Tufts U., Medford, Mass., 1954. Theatrical designer United Scenic Artists, NYC, 1960—90; prin., owner Gordon Micunis Designs Inc., Stratford, Conn., 1976—. Cons. Colliseum Authority, Stamford, Conn. With US Army, 1954—56. Democrat. Avocation: graphic arts. Home: 916 Old Santa Fe Trail Santa Fe NM 87505 Home Phone: 505-231-5856.

MICZEK, KLAUS ALEXANDER, psychology professor; came to U.S., 1967; s. Erich and Irene (Wirthl) M.; m. Christiane Baerwaldt, Aug. 8, 1970; 1 child, Nikolai A. Tchrs. cert., Paedagogische Hochschule, Berlin, 1966; PhD, U. Chgo., 1972. Asst. prof. Carnegie-Mellon U., Pitts., 1972-74, assoc. prof., 1974-79, Tufts U., Medford, Mass., 1979-83, prof., 1983-93, Moses Hunt prof. psychiatry, psychology, pharmacology and neuroscience, 1993—. Cons. Solvay-Pharma v.b., Weesp, The Netherlands, 1984-99, NIH, Rockville, Md., 1984—, Forest Labs., N.Y.C., 2003-; Boehringer Ingelheim, Germany, 2003-; Boerhaave prof. U. Leiden, The Netherlands, 1987; mem. panel on violence, NAS, 1989-92. Editor: Ethopharmacology, 1983, Ethopharmacological Aggression Research, 1984; field editor, coord. editor Behavioral Pharmacology, Jour. Psychopharmacology; contbr. articles on psychopharmacology, 1973—. Rsch. grantee Nat. Inst. Drug Abuse, 1973—, Nat. Inst. Alcoholism and Alcohol Abuse, 1981—; recipient Solvay-Duphar award APA, 1993, Bundesverdienstkreuz Cross of Merit, Fed. Republic of Germany, 1996, Gold medal Charles U., Prague, 2004; named disting. scholar Tufts U., 2006. Fellow AAAS, APA (program chmn. 1981, pres. div. psychopharmacology 1990-91, master lectr. 1999), Behavioral Pharmacol. Soc. (pres. 1992-94), Internat. Soc. for Rsch. on Aggression (councilor 1987); mem. Soc. Neurosci., N.Y. Acad. Scis., Internat. Primatol. Soc. Office: Tufts U Dept Psychology 530 Boston Ave Medford MA 02155-5532 Business E-Mail: klaus.miczek@tufts.edu.

MIDDAUGH, ROBERT BURTON, artist; b. Chgo., May 12, 1935; s. John Burton and Mae Knight (Crooks) M. Student, U. Chgo., 1960-64; BFA, Art Inst. Chgo., 1964. Curator art collection 1st Nat. Bank Chgo., 1971-83. Designed, executed ednl. display, Prehistoric Project at Oriental Inst. of U. Chgo., 1968; one-man shows include, Kovler Gallery, Chgo., 1965, 67, 69, Martin Schweig Gallery, St. Louis, 1970, 72, 79, 83, U. Wis., 1976, 81, 82, Fairweather Hardin Gallery, Chgo., 1977, 80, 83, 85, Rockford Art Mus., 1987, Zaks Gallery, Chgo., 1992, 93, 97, Printworks Gallery, Chgo., 2006; group shows, including, Art Inst. Chgo., 1964, 66, 78, 79, Evanston (Ill.) Art Ctr., 1966, Joslyn Art Mus., Omaha, 1968, U. Notre Dame, 1969, Va. Mus. Fine Arts, Richmond, 1966; represented in permanent collections, Art Inst. Chgo., Boston Mus. Fine Arts, Fine Art Mus. of South, Mobile, Ala., Los Angeles County Mus., Phoenix Art Mus., Worcester (Mass.) Art Mus., Ill. State Mus., Springfield. Served with U.S. Army, 1958-60. Archivist, Chgo. Park Dist., 1998-2005. Mem. Arts Club Chgo.

MIDDELKAMP, JOHN NEAL, pediatrician, educator; b. Kansas City, Mo., Sept. 29, 1925; s. George H. and Clara M. (Ordelheide) M.; m. Roberta Gill, Oct. 3, 1949 (div. 1970); children— Sharon Ann, Steven Neal, Susan Jean, Scott Alan; m. Lois Harper, Mar. 1, 1974 BS, U. Mo., 1946; MD, Washington U., St. Louis, 1948. Diplomate Am. Bd. Pediatrics. Intern D.C. Gen. Hosp., Washington, 1948-49; resident St. Louis Children's Hosp., 1949-50, 52-53; instr. pediatrics Washington U., 1953-57, asst. prof. pediatrics, 1957-64, assoc. prof., 1964-70, prof., 1970-98, prof. emeritus, 1998—; dir. ambulatory pediatrics St. Louis Children's Hosp., 1974-91. Author: Camp Health Manual, 1984; contbr. articles, chpts. to profl. publs. Served to comdr. M.C., USNR, 1943-66. NIH postdoctoral fellow, 1961-62 Mem. Am. Acad. Pediatrics, Am. Soc. Microbiology, Infectious Diseases Soc. Am., Am. Pediatric Soc., Ambulatory Pediatric Assn., Sigma Xi, Alpha Omega Alpha Home: 8845 Paragon Cir Saint Louis MO 63123-1114 Office: Office Asst Dean for Grad Med Edn Washington Univ Sch Medicine 660 S Euclid Box 8033 Saint Louis MO 63110 Office Phone: 314-747-4479.

MIDDENDORF, J. WILLIAM, II, investment banker; b. Balt., Sept. 22, 1924; m. Isabelle Paine, Mar. 7, 1953; children: Frances, Amy, John W. IV, Ralph Henry. B in Naval Sci., Holy Cross Coll., 1945; AB, Harvard U., 1947; MBA, NYU, 1954; LLD (hon.), Troy State U.; LittD (hon.), Sch. of Ozarks, Am. Christian Coll.; D. Social Scis. (hon.), Netherlands-Am. Inst. Commd. ensign USN, 1945, advanced through grades to lt. (j.g.), ret., 1946; with credit dept. Chase Manhattan Bank, 1947-52; ptnr. Wood Struthers and Co., 1958-61; sr. ptnr. Middendorf, Colgate and Co., 1962-69; ambassador to The Netherlands, 1969-73; sec. USN, 1974-77; pres., CEO Fin. Gen. Bankshares, Inc., 1977-81; ambassador to Orgn. Am. States, 1981-85, European Communities, 1985-87; chmn. Middendorf & Assocs., Inc., 1989—. Chmn. presdl. task force Project Econ. and Social Justice, 1986-90; mem. U.S. Del. to supervise elections in Suriname, 1988; treas. Internat. Rep. Inst. Composer 8 symphonies, 100 marches, (opera) King Richard, nat. independence march for Belize, other compositions for Latin Am. countries; guest condr. Boston Pops, St. Louis Symphony, Ind. U., others; contbr. articles to profl. jours. Mem. U.S. Olympic com., 1979-89, U.S. Olympic Selection com. for field hockey; judge field hockey Olympics, Rome, 1960; former mem. vis. com. dept. Am. paintings Met. Mus. Art, N.Y.C., vis. com. dept. Am. Art, Mus. Fine Arts, Boston; hon. v.p. Naval Hist. Found.; treas. Goldwater for Pres. com., 1962-64, Presdl. Transition com. 1968, Rep. Nat. Com., 1964-69; alt. del. for Gov. Reagan, 1980; del. State of Conn., 1964, 68, State of Va., 1996; co-chmn. Virginians for Reagan, 1980, fin. com. Va. GOP, 1980-81; coord. internat. econ. and naval adv. com. Reagan for Pres. campaign, 1980; chmn. Congl. Boosters com., 1978-81; chmn. CIA Transition Team, 1980-81; chmn. fin. com. Pres. Reagan's 1981 Inaugural com.; trustee Naval War Coll. Found., Heritage Found., Washington; past trustee Hoover Instn. for War Revolution and Peace, Corcoran Gallery, N.Y. Hist. Soc., Balt. Mus. Art, Greenwich Hist. Soc., Boston Symphony, Middlesex Sch., Concord, Mass., Nat. Symphony Orch., Mass. Gen. Hosp., Boys Club N.Y.; bd. electors Ins. Hall of Fame; bd. dirs. Georgetown U., John Philip Sousa Meml. Found., Newport Art Mus. and Mariners' Mus., Norfolk, Va.; chmn. bd. dirs. council statesmen Ludwig von Mises Inst.; chmn. Com. for Monetary Rsch. and Edn. Inc., Netherlands-Am. Amity Trust, Def. Forum Found., Navy League Awards com., 1977—; former mem. com. Dept. State Fine Arts Com.; founding chmn. U.S. Navy Meml. Found.; past chmn. Netherlands-Am. Inst., Wolf Trap Farm Park, John Carter Brown Library Assocs., Providence, Asian Composers Expo., European Council of Boy Scouts. Decorated Grand Master Order of Orange Nassau (Netherlands), Order of Arab (Republic Egypt), Grand Master of Order of Naval Merit (Republic Brazil); recipient Superior Honor award Dept. State, 1974, Disting. Pub. Svc. award Dept. Def., 1975, 76, Navy Disting. Pub. Svc. award, 1976, Naval Disting. Svc. medal Republic Brazil, 1976, Ludwig von Mises Free Market award, 1985, Inter-Am. Music Coun. award, 1985, Edwin Franko Goldman award Am.

Bandmasters Assn., 1987, Assn. Harvard Clubs Am. award, Disting. Svc. medal Purdue Univ. Bands, Netherlands Soc. Phila. Gold medal, Good Citizenship medal Nat. Soc. SAR, Medal of Honor, Midwest Nat. Band Assn., Invest in Am. Am. Eagle award, 1988, Eugene J. Keogh Disting. Pub. Svc. award NYU, 1989, Nat. Commendation award Pres.' Coun. Phys. Fitness and Sports, 1989, Leadership award Am. Friends of Turkey, 1989, Adm. Arleigh Burke Leadership award, 1998, Arleigh Burke award 1998, Gold medal Holland Soc., Spl. Recognition award Surface Navy Assn., 2007; named Alumnus of Yr. NYU, 1978; Nat. Masters Sculling champion, 1979. Mem. Am. Antiquarian Soc., Harvard Alumni Assn. (permanent class com. 1947), Soc. Cin. (hon.), ASCAP, Walpole Soc., Co. Mil. Historians, Mil. Order Loyal Legion, SAR, Soc. of SAR, Field Hockey Assn. Am. (past pres., player/mgr. nat. team 1963), U.S. Naval Inst., Navy League. Clubs: Angler's, Downtown Assn., Union (N.Y.C.); Army-Navy, Capitol Hill, Met., Potomac Boat (Washington); Sakonnet Golf (Little Compton, R.I.); Somerset (Boston). Mailing: PO Box 1037 Little Compton RI 02837

MIDDENDORF, JOHN HARLAN, English literature educator; b. NYC, Mar. 31, 1922; s. George Arlington and Margaret (Hofmann) M.; m. Beverly Bruner, July 14, 1943 (dec. 1983); children: Cathie Jean Middendorf Hamilton, Peggy Ruth Middendorf Brindisi; m. Maureen L. MacGrogan, Jan. 31, 1986. AB, Dartmouth Coll., 1943; AM, Columbia U., 1947, PhD, 1953. Lectr. English CCNY, 1946, Hunter Coll., 1946-49; faculty Columbia, 1947—, prof. English, 1965-89, prof. emeritus, 1990—, dir. grad. studies, 1971-74, vice-chmn., 1976-80. Chmn. English test com. Coll. Entrance Exam. Bd., 1967—69. Contbr. articles, revs. to profl. jours.; Editor: English Writers of the Eighteenth Century, 1971; asst. editor: Johnsonian News Letter, 1950-58; co-editor, 1958-78, editor, 1978-90; assoc. editor: Yale edit. Works Samuel Johnson, 1962-66; gen. editor, 1966—. Lt. (j.g.) Japanese translator USNR, 1943—45. Faculty fellow Fund Advancement Edn., 1951-52; grantee Coun. Rsch. Humanities, 1958-59, Am. Philos. Soc., 1962, Am. Coun. Learned Socs., 1962, NEH, 1976-88. Mem. Johnsonians (sec.-treas. 1958-68, chmn. 1969, 79), Univ. Seminar on 18th Century European Culture (chmn. 1973-75, 85-87), Oxford Bibliog. Soc., Grolier Club, English Inst. (mem. supervisory com. 1963-66), Modern Lang. Assn., Soc. Sr. Scholars, Am. Soc. 18th Century Studies, Phi Beta Kappa. Home: 404 Riverside Dr New York NY 10025-1861 Office: Columbia U Dept English New York NY 10027

MIDDLEBROOK, DIANE WOOD, English language educator, writer; b. Pocatello, Idaho, Apr. 16, 1939; d. Thomas Isaac and Helen Loretta (Downey) Wood; m. Jonathan Middlebrook, June 15, 1963 (annulled 1976); 1 child, Leah Wood; m. Carl Djerassi, June 21, 1985. BA, U. Wash., 1961; MA, Yale U., 1962, PhD, 1968; LittD (hon.), Kenyon Coll., 1999, U. Mass., Dartmouth, 2005. Asst. prof. Stanford (Calif.) U., 1966—73, assoc. prof., 1978—83, prof., 1983—2001, prof. emerita, 2002—, dir. Ctr. for Rsch. on Women, 1977—79. Vis. prof. Univ. Coll., London, 2007—. Author: Walt Whitman and Wallace Stevens, 1974, Worlds into Words: Understanding Modern Poems, 1980, Anne Sexton, A Biography, 1991, Suits Me: The Double Life of Billy Tipton, 1998, Her Husband: Hughes and Plath, a Marriage, 2003; editor: Coming to Light: American Women Poets in the Twentieth Century, 1985; author: (poetry) Gin Considered as a Demon, 1983. Founding trustee Djerassi Resident Artists Program, Woodside, Calif., 1980—83, chair, 1994; trustee San Francisco Art Inst, 1993. Finalist Nat. Book award, 1991; recipient Yale Prize for Poetry; fellow Ind. Study, NEH, 1982—83, Bunting Inst., Radcliffe Coll., 1982—83, Guggenheim Found., 1988—89, Rockefeller Study Ctr., 1990. Fellow: Royal Soc. Lit.; mem.: MLA, Authors Guild, Christs Coll. Cambridge (hon.), The Athenaeum Club, Biographers Club. Avocations: collecting art, theater. Home: 1101 Green St Apt 1501 San Francisco CA 94109-2012 Office: Agent Georges Borchardt 136 E 57th St New York NY 10022 Office Phone: 415-474-1866. E-mail: dwm@stanford.edu.

MIDDLEBROOKS, DELORIS JEANETTE, retired nursing educator; b. Cedar Rapids, Iowa, Apr. 9, 1931; d. Harland R. and Rosa V. (Anderson) Hickey; m. Johnnie L. Middlebrooks, Apr. 25, 1962 (dec.); children: James, Kathleen. Diploma, Evang. Hosp. Sch. Nursing, 1956; BSN, State U. Iowa, 1958; MS in Nursing, U. Calif., San Francisco, 1960; EdD, U. Nev., Las Vegas, 1985. Instr., coord. Nev. State Hosp. Sch. Practical Nursing, Sparks, 1963-66; staff nurse St. Mary's Hosp., Reno, 1968; instr., coord. Reno VA Sch. Practical Nursing, 1968-72; instr,. coord. health occupations Wooster High Sch., 1972-73; nursing faculty Truckee Meadows C.C., 1973-94, ret., 1994; intermittent staff nurse VA Hosp., 1984-86; instr., review course Stanley Kaplan Ednl. Ctr., 1987-89; clin. nursing faculty Western Nev. C.C., Carson City, 1987, Northern Nev. C.C., Elko, 1979-93; guest assoc. prof. nursing Lewis-Clark State Coll., Lewiston, Idaho, 1989. Cons. Irish Bd. Nursing, Dublin, Ireland, 1985. Nominated Nev. Voc. Tchr. of Yr., 1975, 79, 88, 89; Recipient March of Dimes Community Leadership award, 1990. Mem.: ANA, Am. Assn. for the History of Nursing, Nev. Nurses Assn., Phi Kappa Phi, Sigma Theta Tau. Home: 1385 Ebbetts Dr Reno NV 89503-1918

MIDDLEBROOKS, EDDIE JOE, environmental engineer; b. Crawford County, Ga., Oct. 16, 1932; s. Robert Harold and Jewell LaVerne (Dixon) M.; m. Charlotte Linda Hardy, Dec. 6, 1958; 1 child, Linda Tracey. BCE, U. Fla., 1956, MS, 1960; PhD, Miss. State U., 1966. Registered profl. engr., Ariz., Miss., Utah, Wash., Colo.; registered land surveyor, Fla. Asst. san. engr. USPHS, Cin., 1956-58; field engr. T.T. Jones Constrn. Co., Atlanta, 1958-59; grad. teaching asst. U. Fla., 1959-60; research asst. U. Ariz., 1960-61; asst. prof., then assoc. prof. Miss. State U., 1962-67; research engr., asst. dir. San. Engring. Research Lab., U. Calif.-Berkeley, 1968-70; prof. Utah State U., Logan, 1970-82, dean Coll. Engring., 1974-82; Newman chair natural resources engring. Clemson U., 1982-83; provost, v.p. acad. affairs Tenn. Tech. U., 1983-88, U. Tulsa, 1988-90, prof. chem. engring., 1988-92, Trustees prof. chem. engring., 1990-92, acting pres., 1990; prof. civil engring. U. Nevada, Reno, 1992-97. Mem. nat. drinking water adv. council EPA, 1981-83; cons. EPA, UN Indsl. Devel. Orgn., Calif. Water Resources Control Bd., City and County of San Francisco, State of Colo., South Fla. Water Mgmt. Dist. (Everglades), also numerous indsl. and engring. firms. Author: Modeling the Eutrophication Process, 1974, Statistical Calculations-How to Solve Statistical Problems, 1976, Biostimulation and Nutrient Assessment, 1976, Water Supply Engineering Design, 1977, Lagoon Information Source Book, 1978, Industrial Pollution Control, Vol. 1: Agro-Industries, 1979, Wastewater Collection and Treatment: Principles and Practices, 1979, Water Reuse, 1982, Wastewater Stabiliation Lagoon Design, Performance and Upgrading, 1982, Reverse Osmosis Treatment of Drinking Water, 1986, Pollution Control in the Petrochemicals Industry, 1987, Natural Systems for Waste Management and Treatment, 1988, 2d edit., 1995, Japanese transl., Natural Wastewater Treatment Systems, 2006; contbr. tech. articles to profl. jours. Fellow ASCE; mem. Water Environment Fedn. (dir. 1979-81, 91-92), Eddy medal 1969), Assn. Environ. Engring. Profs. (pres. 1974), Utah Water Pollution Control Assn. (pres. 1976), Internat. Assn. on Water Quality, Am. Soc. Engring. Edn., Am. Acad. Environ. Engrs. (diplomate, trustee 1992-95, v.p. 1995, pres. 1997-98), Sigma Xi, Omicron Delta Kappa, Phi Kappa Phi (Disting. mem.), Tau Beta Pi, Sigma Tau. Home and Office: 2128 Imperial Ln Superior CO 80027 Office Phone: 303-664-5292. Personal E-mail: Joemiddle@aol.com.

MIDDLEDITCH, LEIGH BENJAMIN, JR., lawyer, educator; b. Detroit, Sept. 30, 1929; s. Leigh Benjamin and Hope Tiffin (Noble) M.; m. Betty Lou Givens, June 27, 1953; children: Leigh III, Katherine Middleditch McDonald, Andrew B. BA, U. Va., 1951, LLB, 1957. Bar: Va. 1957. Assoc. James H. Michael, Jr., Charlottesville, Va., 1957-59; ptnr. Battle, Neal, Harris, Minor & Williams, Charlottesville, 1959-68; legal adviser U. Va., Charlottesville, 1968-72; ptnr. McGuire, Woods, Battle & Boothe (now McGuire Woods LLP), Charlottesville, 1972-99, of counsel, 2000—; v.p. McGuire Woods Cons. LLC, Charlottesville, 2001—. Lectr. Grad. Bus. Sch., U. Va., Charlottesville, 1958-94, lectr. Law Sch., 1970-90. Co-author: Virginia Civil Procedure, 1978, 2d edition, 1992; contbr. articles to profl. jours. Chmn. U. Va. Health Svcs. Found., 1988-97; bd. mgrs. U. Va. Alumni, 1994-2001, pres., 2000-01; bd. dirs., chmn. Va. Health Care Found., 1997-98; trustee Claude Moore Found., 1991—; bd. visitors U. Va., 1990-94; trustee Thomas Jefferson Meml. Found., Monticello, 1994-2002; chair U. Va. Miller Found. for Study of Presidency, 2000—. Fellow Am. Bar Found., Va. Bar Found.; mem. ABA (bd. govs. 1999-2002), Va. State Bar (coun., chmn. bd. govs. various sects.), Charlottesville-Albemarle Bar Assn. (pres. 1979-80), U. Va. Law Sch. Alumni Assn. (pres. 1979-81), U.S. C. of C. (bd. dirs. 1998—2004), Va. C. of C. (pres. 1988-90), Omicron Delta Kappa. Episcopalian. Office: McGuire Woods LLP PO Box 1288 Charlottesville VA 22902-1288 Office Phone: 434-977-2543. E-mail: lmiddleditch@mcguirewoods.com.

MIDDLEKAUFF, ROBERT LAWRENCE, historian, educator, academic administrator; b. Yakima, Wash., July 5, 1929; s. Harold and Katherine Ruth (Horne) M.; m. Beverly Jo Martin, July 11, 1952; children: Samuel John, Holly Ruth. BA, U. Wash., 1952; PhD, Yale U., 1961. Instr. history Yale U., New Haven, 1959-62; asst. prof. history U. Calif., Berkeley, 1962-66, assoc. prof., 1966-70, prof., 1970-80, Margaret Byrne prof. history, 1980-83, prof. history, 1988-92, emeritus prof., 2000—, Preston Hotchkis prof., 1992—; dir. Huntington Libr., Art Gallery and Bot. Gardens, San Marino, Calif., 1983-88; Harmsworth prof. history Oxford (Eng.) U., 1996-97. Mem. coun. Inst. Early Am. History and Culture, Williamsburg, Va., 1974-76, 85-88, chair exec. bd., 1992-96. Author: Ancients and Axioms, 1963, The Mathers, 1971, The Glorious Cause: The American Revolution, 1763-1789, 1982, 2nd edit., rev., 2005, Benjamin Franklin and His Enemies, 1996. Served to 1st lt. USMC, 1952-54, Korea. Recipient Bancroft prize, 1972, Commonwealth Club Gold medal, 1983; fellow Am. Coun. Learned Socs., 1965, NEH, 1973, Huntington Libr., 1977. Fellow Am. Acad. Arts and Scis.; mem. Am. Hist. Assn., Orgn. Am. Historians, Am. Philos. Soc., Soc. Am. Historians, Am. Antiquarian Soc., Assocs. Early Am. History and Culture (chmn. exec. com.), Colonial Soc. Mass. (corr.), Mass. Hist. Soc. Home: 5868 Ocean View Dr Oakland CA 94618-1535 Office: Univ Calif Dept History Berkeley CA 94720-2550 Office Phone: 510-642-1971.

MIDDLEMAN, RAOUL FINK, artist; b. Balt., Apr. 3, 1935; s. Paul B. and Elizabeth (Fink) M.; m. Pat Bird (div.); m. Ruth Katherine Channing, Dec. 2, 1971; children: Raphael Bachrach, Benjamin Jacob, Nathaniel John. BA, Johns Hopkins U., 1955; postgrad., Penn. Acad. Fine Arts, 1957—61, Bklyn. Mus., 1961. Faculty Md. Inst. Coll. of Art, Balt., 1961-85. Vis. critic Vt. Studio Sch. Summer Program,1 985; resident dir. Summer Landscape Painting Program, Md. Inst. Coll. of Art, 1981-83; vis. artist Artists for Environment Found., Walpack Ctr., 1977-81; artist-in-residence Hoffberger Sch. of Painting, 1973-74; lectr. for Figurative Alliance, Studio Sch., N.Y.C., Nat. Gallery in Edinborough, Yale Norfolk, 1980, Md. Inst. Coll. of Art, 1985. One-man shows include Swanston Fine Arts, 1988, Allan Stone Gallery, 1985, 1981,1975, 1972, 1969, 1968, Grimaldis Gallery, 1984, 1981, 1979, 1978, 1999, 2003, William Capro Gallery, 1983, The Water Gap Art Gallery, 1982, The Md. Inst., Coll. of Art, 1974, Krasner Gallery, 1966, Ice Gallery, NYC, 1996, 1997, 1998, Univ. Md., 1999, Troika Gallery, Easton, Md., 1999, MB Modern Gallery, NYC, 2000, Rodger LaPelle Galleries, Phila., 2001, Bavarian Paintings, Murnau, Germany, 2001, Md. Art Place, Balt., 2002; exhibited in groups shows at Nat. Acad. Design, 1990, Md. Inst., 1989-90, Gaumann Cicchino Gallery, 1989, Ingber Gallery, 1989, Bendann Gallery, 1989, Swanston Fine Arts, 1988, Haus der Kunst, 1986, Kornbluth Gallery, 1985, Steven Scott Gallery, and others; respresented in permanent collections at ABC Network, Balt. Mus. Art, Corcoran Gallery, Frye Mus. Art, Johns Hopkins Hosp. NAD, Met. Mus. Art, NY Public Libr., Syracuse Univ., Towson Univ., Univ. Md. Recipient Robert and Rochelle Phillipp prize Nat. Acad. Design, 1990. Mem. Nat. Acad. Design (pres. 1998-2001). Avocation: violin. E-mail: rmiddleman@earthlink.net.

MIDDLETON, CHARLES RONALD, history educator; b. Hays, Kans., Sept. 16, 1944; s. Charles Buster and Dorothy Bryant (Parsons) M.; m. Sandra Leigh Paulson, Dec. 19, 1964 (dec. 1986); children: Charles Christopher, Kevin Andrew, Kathryn Gillian; life ptnr: John S. Geary. AB with honors, Fla. State U., 1965; MA, Duke U., 1967, PhD, 1969. Asst. prof. U. Colo., Boulder, 1969-77, assoc. prof., 1977-85, asst. dean, 1979-80, prof. history, 1985-96, assoc. dean Coll. Arts and Scis., 1980-88, dean Coll. Arts and Scis., 1988-96; prof. history, provost, v.p. acad. affairs Bowling Green (Ohio) State U., 1996—. Contbr. articles to profl. jours. Bd. dirs. Found. for World Health, Denver and Boulder, 1985-87, Boulder County AIDS Project (hon.), 1990-97, The Consenting Adults Theatre Co., Washington, 1992—, OhioLink, 1997—. Recipient Faculty Teaching Excellence award U. Colo., Boulder, 1978; research grantee Am. Philos. Soc., 1977, U. Colo., 1972. Fellow Royal Hist. Soc.; mem. N.Am. Conf. on Brit. Studies, Western Conf. on Brit. Studies (pres.-elect 1985-86, pres. 1986-87), Western Humanities Conf. (bd. dirs. 1990-95), Am. Hist. Assn. (mem. com. gay and lesbian history), Am. Com. for Irish Studies, So. Conf. on Brit. Studies, Rotary, Coun. of Colls. and Arts and Scis. (bd. dirs. 1993-96), Golden Key, Phi Beta Kappa, Phi Eta Sigma, Phi Kappa Phi. Avocations: fishing, cooking, travel, bicycling. Office: Bowling Green State U 230 Mcfall Ctr Bowling Green OH 43403-0001

MIDDLETON, CHRISTOPHER, Germanic languages and literature educator; b. Truro, Cornwall, Eng., June 10, 1926; arrived in US, 1966; s. Hubert Stanley and Dorothy May (Miller) M. BA, U. Oxford, Eng., 1951, DPhil, 1954. Lectr. King's Coll., London, 1955-65; prof. Germanic langs. and lit. U. Tex., Austin, 1966-98. Author: Selected Writings, 1989, Andalusian Poems, 1993, The Balcony Tree, 1992, Intimate Chronicles, 1996, Twenty Tropes for Doctor Dark, 2000, The Word Pavilion and Selected Poems, 2001, Of the Mortal Fire, 2003, Jackdaw Jiving: Essays on Poetry and Translation, 1998, In the Mirror of the Eighth King, 1999, Faint Harps and Silver Voices-Selected Translations, 2000, Crypto-Topographia: Stories of Secret Places, 2002, Palavers and A Nocturnal Journal, 2004, The Anti-Basilisk, 2005, The Tenor on Horseback, 2007. Recipient trans. prize Schlegel-Tieck/Govt. Fed. Republic Germany, 1985, Anglo-Swiss Cultural Rels. prize Max Geilinger Stiftung, Zurich, Switzerland, 1987; Guggenheim Found. poetry fellow, 1974-75, NEH poetry fellow, 1980. Mem. Akademie der Künste Berlin. Office: U Tex Dept Of Germanic Langs Austin TX 78712

MIDDLETON, DAVID, physicist, educator; b. NYC, Apr. 19, 1920; s. Charles Davies and Lucile (Davidson) Middleton; m. Nadea Butler, May 26, 1945 (div. 1971); m. Joan Bartlett Reed, 1971; children: Susan Terry, Leslie Butler, David Scudder Blakeslee, George Davidson Powell, Christopher Hope, Andrew Bartlett, Henry H. Reed. Grad., Deerfield Acad., 1938; AB summa cum laude, Harvard U., 1942, AM, 1945, PhD in Physics, 1947. Tchg. fellow electronics Harvard U., Cambridge, Mass., 1942, spl. rsch. assoc. radio rsch. lab., 1942—45, NSF predoctoral fellow physics, 1945—47, rsch. fellow electronics, 1947—49, asst. prof. applied physics, 1949—54; cons. physicist Cambridge, 1954—2004, Concord, Mass., 1957—71, NYC, 2005—; adj. prof. elec. engring. Columbia U., 1960—61; adj. prof. applied physics and comm. theory Rensselaer Poly. Inst., Hartford Grad. Ctr., 1961—70; adj. prof. communication theory U. R.I., 1966—; adj. prof. math. scis. Rice U., 1979—89. US del. Internat. Radio Union, Lima, Peru, 1975; lectr. NATO Advanced Study Inst., Grenoble, France, 1964, Copenhagen, 80, Luneburg, Germany, 84; invited lectr. Russia Acad. Sci. Acoustic Inst., 1973, 76, 79, 84; mem. Naval Rsch. Adv. Com., 1970—77; mem., cons. Inst. Def. Analyses; mem. sci. adv. bd. Supercomputing Rsch. Ctr., 1987—91; cons. physicist, 1946—, Johns Hopkins U., SRI Internat., Rand Corp., USAF, Cambridge Rsch. Ctr., Comm. Satellite Corp., Lincoln Lab., NASA, Raytheon, Sylvania, Sperry-Rand, Office Naval Rsch., Applied Rsch. Labs., U. Tex., GE, Honeywell Transp. Sys. Ctr. Dept. Transp., Dept. Commerce Office Telecom., NOAA, Office Telecom. Policy Exec. Office Pres., Nat. Telecom. and Info. Adminstrn., Sci. Applications Inc., Naval Undersea Warfare Ctr., Lawrence Livermore Nat. Labs., Planning Rsch. Corp., Applied Physics Labs. U. Wash., 1992—, Kildare Corp., 1995—, Karmanos Cancer Inst., 1997—2001, Air Force Rsch. Lab, Hanscomb Air Force Base, 2006—, Gen. Dynamics Info. Tech. Inst., 2006—, others. Author: Introduction to Statistical Communication Theory, 1960, 3d edit., 1996, Russian edit. Soviet Radio Moscow, 2 vols., 1961, 1962, Topics in Communication Theory, 1965, 1987, Russian edit., 1966; sci. editor: English edit. Statistical Methods in Sonar (V. V. Ol'shevskii), 1978; mem. editl. bd. Info. and Control, Advanced Serials in Electronics and Cybernetics, 1972—82; contbr. articles to tech. jours. Co-recipient Prize Paper award, Nat. Electronics Conf., 1956; recipient Prize paper award (with W.H. Huggins), 1956, First prize, 3d Internat. Symposium on Electromagnetic Compatibility Rotterdam, Holland, 1979, 2 Prize paper awards, US Dept. Commerce, 1978, Wisdom award of Honor, 1970, 1st prize, 3d Internat. Symposium Electromagnetic Compatibility, 1979, Prize Paper award, US Dept. Commerce, 1978. Fellow: NAE, AAAS, IEEE (life, Prize paper award 1977, 1979), Electromagnetics Acad. MIT, N.Y. Acad. Scis., Acoustical Soc. Am., Am. Phys. Soc.; mem.: Am. Math. Soc., Author's Guild Am., Dutch Treat (N.Y.C.), Explorers Club, Cosmos Club (Washington), Harvard Club (N.Y.C.), Sigma Xi, Phi Beta Kappa. Achievements include research in radar, telecommunications, underwater acoustics, oceanography, seismology, systems analysis, electromagnetic compatibility; a founder of Statistical Communication Theory. Home and Office: 127 E 91st St New York NY 10128-1601 Office: David And Joan B Middleton 127 E 91st St New York NY 10128-1601 Office Phone: 212-831-8565.

MIDDLETON, HERMAN DAVID, SR., retired theater educator; b. Sanford, Fla., Mar. 24, 1925; s. Arthur Herman and Ruby Elmerry (Hart) Middleton; m. Amelia Mary Eggart, Dec. 1, 1945; children: Herman David, Kathleen Hart. BS, Columbia U., 1948, MA, 1949; PhD, U. Fla., 1964; postgrad., N.Y. U., 1950, Northwestern U., 1951. Instr., dir. drama and speech Maryville (Tenn.) Coll., 1949-50; instr., designer, tech. dir. theatre U. Del., 1951-55; asst. prof., head dept. drama U. N.C., Greensboro, 1956-59, assoc. prof., head dept. drama and speech, 1959-65, prof., head dept., 1965-74, prof., 1974-79, Excellence Fund prof. dept. communication and theatre, 1979-90, prof. emeritus, 1990. Stage mgr. Unto thee Hills Cherokee Hist. Assn., 1953—56; designer Chucky Jack Gt. Smokey Mountains Hist. Soc., Gatlinburg, Tenn., 1956, designer, dir., 57; comm. cons. NC Nat. Bank, 1968, Jefferson Std. Life Ins. Co., Greensboro, NC, 1969, Gilbarco, Inc., Greensboro, 1969—70, Greensboro, 1973. Drama critic, columnist: Sunday Star, 1952, theater editor: Players Mag., 1959—61, theater columnist: Sunday edits. Greensboro Daily News, 1959—62; contbr. articles to profl. jours. Mem. NC Arts Coun. Commn., 1964—66, Guilford County Bi-Centennial Celebration Commn., 1969—70; pres. Shanks Village Players, Orangeburg, NYC, 1947—48, Univ. Drama Group, Newark, Del., 1954—55; bd. dirs. Broadway Theatre League Greensboro, 1958—60, Greensboro Cmty. Arts Coun., 1964—67, 1969—72, Greensboro Cmty. Theatre, 1983—86, Carolina Theatre commn., 1990—93; organizer-cons. Market Players, W. Market St. United Meth. Ch., 1979—82. With USN, 1943—46. Recipient O. Henry award, Greensboro C. of C., 1966, Gold medallion, Amoco Oil Co., 1973, Suzanne M. Davis award, Southeastern Theatre Conf., 1975, Marian A. smith Disting. Career award, NC Theatre Conf., 1990. Mem.: Assn. Theater Higher Edn., NC Theater Conf. (co-organizer 1971, bd. dirs. 1984—92, pres. 1987—88), NC Drama and Speech Assn. (pres. 1966—67), Carolina Dramatic Assn. (bd. dirs. 1958—59), Southeastern Theatre Conf. (bd. dirs. 1963—68, 1987—92, pres. 1965, pres. pro tem 1966), Nat. Collegiate Players, Speech Communication Assn. Am., Assn. Theatre Higher Edn. (founding mem. 1986—87), Am. Coll. Theatre Festival (regional festival dir. 1973, 1980, regional dir., mem. nat. com. 1978—80), Am. Theatre Assn. (chmn. bd. nominations 1971—72), Am. Nat. Theatre and Acad. (organizer, exec. v.p. Piedmont chpt. 1957—60), Alpha Psi Omega, Theta Alpha Phi, Phi Kappa Phi, Phi Delta Kappa. Democrat. Methodist. Home: 203 Village Ln Unit A Greensboro NC 27409-2517 Personal E-mail: hmiddleton@triad.rr.com.

MIDDLETON, J. HOWARD, JR., lawyer; b. Camden, NJ, Mar. 1, 1939; s. J. Howard and Helen Marie (Casper) M.; m. Betty Jo Bittinger, Aug. 22, 1965; children: J. Howard III, Lucia Katherine. BA, Haverford Coll., 1962; MDiv., Union Theol. Sem., 1965; JD, Georgetown U., 1972. Bar: Va. 1972, U.S. Dist. Ct. (ea. dist.) Va. 1973, U.S. Ct. Appeals (D.C. cir.) 1974, U.S. Supreme Ct. 1976, U.S. Ct. Claims 1978; ordained minister. Manpower analyst U.S. Dept. Labor, Washington, 1971-72; asst. atty. City of Alexandria, Va., 1972-76, dep. atty. Va., 1976-78; sole practice Alexandria, Va., 1978-81; ptnr. Thomas & Fiske P.C., Alexandria, Va., 1981—87, Hazel & Thomas PC, 1987—99, Reed Smith LLP, 1999—. Chmn. Alexandria mcpl. liaison com. Northern Va. Builders, 1986; active Va. legis. com. Washington Bd. Trade, Alexandria, 1986; v.p. sr. svs. Alexandria. Bd. dirs. Circle Terr. Hosp., Alexandria, 1986. Mem. NAIOP, Va. Assn. Comml. Real Estate, Lambda Alpha, Areal Estate Econs. Hon. Soc. Democrat. Office: Reed Smith LLP PO Box 12001 Falls Church VA 22042-0681 Office Phone: 703-641-4225.

MIDDLETON, J. RICHARD, religious studies educator; b. Kingston, Jamaica, Jan. 14, 1955; s. Jack Reginald and Phyllis Merle Middleton; m. Marcia Ann Berry, Aug. 27, 1977; children: Andrew Derek, Kevin Timothy. BTh, Jamaica Theol. Sem., Kingston; MA, U. Guelph, Ont., Canada; PhD, Vrije Universiteit, Amsterdam, Netherlands. Inter-varsity campus min. U. Guelph, 1981—83; assoc. Protestant chaplain U. Rochester, 1986—88; christian ref. chaplain Brock U., St. Catharines, Ontario, Canada, 1988—90; adj. prof. of philosophy Redeemer U. Coll., Ancaster, Ontario, Canada, 1989—91; adj. prof., worldview studies Inst. Christian Studies, Toronto, 1990—95; asst. prof. O.T. interpretation Colgate Rochester Div. Sch., NY, 1996—2001; assoc. prof. Bibl. studies Roberts Wesleyan Coll., Rochester, 2002—. Mem. adv. bd. Brazos Press, Grand Rapids, Mich. Author: The Liberating Image: The Imago Dei in Genesis 1; co-author: Truth Is Stranger Than It Used to Be: Biblical Faith in a Postmodern Age, The Transforming Vision: Shaping a Christian World View; contbr. articles to profl. publs. Recipient Faculty award for Profl. Devel., Roberts Wesleyan Coll., 2004; Grad. scholar, Provincal Govt., Ont., Can., 1983—84, Doctoral fellow, Social Scies. and Humanities Rsch. Coun. Can., 1992—94. Mem.: Am. Acad. Religion, Can. Evang. Theol. Assn., Can. Theol. Soc., Can. Soc. Bibl. Studies, Soc. Bibl. Lit. Office: Roberts Wesleyan Coll 2301 Westside Dr Rochester NY 14624 Office Phone: 585-594-6971. Business E-Mail: middleton_richard@roberts.edu.

MIDDLETON, JACK BAER, lawyer; b. Phila., Jan. 13, 1929; s. Harry C. and Mildred Cornell (Baer) M.; m. Ann (Dodge), Aug. 22, 1953; children: Susan D., Jack B. Jr., Peter C. BA, Lafayette Coll., 1950; JD (hon.), Boston U., 1956. Bar: NH 1956, US Dist. Ct. Vt. 1988, US Ct. Appeals (1st cir.) 1957, US Supreme Ct. 1972. Assoc. McLane, Graf, Raulerson, and Middleton, Manchester, NH, 1956—62; ptnr., dir. McLane, Graf, Raulerson, and Middleton, Manchester, NH, 1962—. Spl. justice Merrimack, NH Dist. Ct., 1964-87; commr. Uniform State Laws, 1971-74. Author: (with others) Summary of New Hampshire Law, l964, Compendium of New Hampshire Law, l969, Trial of a Wrongful Death Action in New Hampshire, l977; editor Boston U. Law Rev., l954-56; contbr. articles to profl. jours. Active Mt. Washington Commn., 1969—, Bedford, NH Sch. Bd.,

1960-66; adv. bd. Merrimack Valley Coll.; trustee, sec. Mt. Washington Obs., 1957—; chmn. bd. trustees White Mountain Sch., 1976-79; campaign chmn. United Way Greater Manchester, 1987, bd. dirs., 1986-92, chmn., 1990-91; bd. dirs. NH Pub. Radio, 1988-91; bd. gov. NH Pub. TV, 1994-2003, chmn., 1997-99; trustee New Eng. Law Inst., 1977-80, Franklin Pierce Law Ctr., 2003—. Sgt. USMCR, 1950-52. Fellow Am. Coll. Trial Lawyers (chmn. NH sect. 1988-90), Am. Bar Found. (life); mem. ABA (ho. dels. 1984-2005, bd. gov. 1996-2002, sec. elect 1998-99, sec. 1999-2002), New Eng. Bar Assn. (bd. dir. 1977-88, pres. 1982-83), NH Bar Assn. (pres. 1979-80), NH Bar Found. (bd. dir. 1979-92, chair 1983-90), Nat. Ctr. State Ct. (dir. 1999-2005), Nat. Conf. Bar Found. (trustee 1985-92, pres. 1989-90), Nat. Conf. Bar Pres. (exec. coun. 1987-95, pres. 1993-94), NH Bus. and Industry Assn. (bd. dir. 1988-2005, sec. 1990-2005), Manchester C. of C. (bd. dir. 1967-89, chmn. 1984-85), New Eng. Coun. (bd. dirs. 1991-2004), New Eng. Legal Found. (bd. dirs. 2001-04). Office: McLane Graf Raulerson and Middleton 900 Elm St Ste 1001 Manchester NH 03101-2029 Home Phone: 603-539-6305; Office Phone: 603-628-1446.

MIDDLETON, JAMES ARTHUR, oil and gas company executive; b. Tulsa, Mar. 15, 1936; s. James Arthur and Inez (Matthews) M.; m. Victoria Middleton; children: Robert Arthur, James Daniel, Angela Lynn; stepson: Andrew Davis Fitzhugh. BA, Rice U., 1958, BS in Mech. Engring., 1959. With Atlantic Richfield Co., 1959-96; design engr. Dallas, 1962-67; tech. planner, 1967-69; mgr. shale devel. Grand Junction, Colo., 1969-72; mgr. engring. dept. Los Angeles, 1972-74; mgr. Prudhoe Bay project Pasadena, Calif., 1974-80; v.p., mgr. corp. planning Los Angeles, 1980-81; pres. ARCO Coal Co., Denver, 1981-82; sr. v.p. ARCO Oil and Gas Co., Dallas, 1982-85, pres., 1985-90, sr. v.p. parent co., 1981-87, exec. v.p. parent co., 1987-94, also bd. dirs.; chmn., CEO Crown Energy Corp., Salt Lake City, 1996-2000; pres. Jam Energy Co., 2000—. Bd. dirs. Tex. Utilities Co., Dallas., ARCO Chem. Co., Berry Petroleum Co. Corp. rep. Circle Ten coun. Boy Scouts Am.; bd. dirs. L.A. coun. Boy Scouts Am., United Way Met. Dallas, Dallas Coun. on World Affairs, Jr. Achievement So. Calif. 2d lt. C.E., AUS, 1959-60 Reicpient ASME Petroleum div. Oil Drop award. Mem. Soc. Petroleum Engrs. of AIME, Tex. Mid-Continent Oil and Gas Assn., Am. Petroleum Inst., Rocky Mountain Oil and Gas Assn., We. States Petroleum Assn. (chmn. bd. dirs.), Nat. Gas Suppliers Assn. (chmn.), L.A. C. of C. (bd. dirs.), L.A. Music Ctr. Founders, Ctr. for Strategic and Internat. Studies (CSIS)-Dallas Round Table, Am. Enterprise Forum Chief Execs. Round Table, Dallas Petroelum Club, Tower, Northwood, Calif. Club, Bel-Air Country Club, L.A. Country Club, Preston Trail Golf Club.

MIDDLETON, JAMES BOLAND, retired lawyer; b. Columbus, Ga., Aug. 19, 1934; s. Riley Kimbrough and Annie Ruth (Boland) M.; 1 child, Cynthia. BA in Psychology, Ga. State U., Atlanta, 1964; JD, Woodrow Wilson Coll. Law, 1972. Bar: Ga. 1972, US Patent Office. Draftsman, paralegal and office mgr. to patent atty., Atlanta, 1955-68; draftsman, paralegal and office mgr. Jones & Thomas, Atlanta, 1968-72, assoc., 1972-76; pvt. practice intellectual property Decatur, Ga., 1976-98; ret., 1998. Mem. editl. bd. Atlanta Lawyer, 1973-82, assoc. editor, 1978-81, editor-in-chief, 1981-82. Dir. arts coun. Unitarian-Universalist Congregation Atlanta, 1989-91; bd. dirs. Unitarian-Universalist Endowment Fund, 1993-96, vice chair, 1994-95, sec., 1995-96; bd. dirs., sec. Decatur Arts Alliance, 1990-94; bd. dirs. Life Enrichment Svcs., Inc., 2002-05, Atlanta Freethought Soc., 2005-07. With US Army, 1957-59. Mem. ABA, Am. Intellectual Property Law Assn., Am. Arbitration Assn. (comml. panel 1983-94), DeKalb Bar Assn., State Bar Ga. (editl. bd. jour. 1985-92, patent trademark and copyright sect. 1972-2000, chmn. 1982-83, pub. rels. com. 1982-88), Fed. Cir. Bar Assn., Atlanta Freethought Soc. (bd. dirs. 2005-07). Personal E-mail: jimbmid@yahoo.com.

MIDDLETON, JOHN EDISON, management consultant; b. Sunnyside, Wash., May 1, 1947; s. John Willbey Middleton and Marion (Brignic) Hoage; children: William Arthur, Rachel Ranee. BBA, UCLA, 1968; MBA, NYU, 1989, PhD, 1987; PhD (hon.), Oxford U., Eng., 1988. Dir. Ramic Prodn., NYC, 1973—75; v.p. Nelson Berry, 1975—79, CEO, 1984—87; exec. v.p. Investment Internat., 1980—84, Am. Video, 1987—89; pres. JBL Assoc., 1989—92; CEO LBJ Assoc. Ltd., 1992—. Exec. dir. National Coalition for Civil Rights. Col. U.S. Army, 1968-72 (Green Beret). Named Big Brother of Yr. Big Bros. N.Y., 1979. Mem. Assn. Pub. Pay Phones (pres. 1991—), Masons, Scottish Rite, Shriners, Am. Purple Heart. Republican. Jewish. Avocations: scuba diving, sky diving. Office: 50 Court St Ste 501 Brooklyn NY 11201-4859 Office Phone: 718-624-7666. Personal E-mail: nccr004@aol.com.

MIDDLETON, MARC STEPHEN, corporate insurance risk manager; b. Louisville, Dec. 7, 1950; s. Joseph Scott and Virginia Marie (Schuler) M.; m. Carmen Teresa Fauscette, Feb. 22, 1969; 1 child, Marc Christopher. AA, Dalton Jr. Coll., 1970; BBA, U. Ga., 1972. Sr. risk analyst Deere and Co., Moline, Ill., 1973-78, mgr. corp. claims, 1978-79, mgr. corp. ins. dept., 1980-86; v.p. risk mgmt. svcs. John Deere Ins. Group, Moline, Ill., 1987-91; dir. risk mgmt. Deere and Co., Moline, Ill., 1992—. V.p. bd. dirs. Tahoe Ins. Co., Reno, 1981-83, Sierra Gen. Life Ins. Co., Reno, 1981-83, Continental Guaranty, Ltd., Hamilton, Bermuda, 1981-83; v.p. John Deere Ins. Co., Rock River Ins. Co., Tahoe Ins. Co., 1990-91, John Deere Life Ins. Co., Sierra Gen. Life Ins. Co., 1991; mem. M200 Risk Mgmt. Forum; mem. FM Global Risk Mgmt. Exec. Coun. Mem. Citizen's Adv. Council to East Moline (Ill.) Sch. Bd., 1978-80; coach YMCA Youth Basketball, Moline, 1978. Mem. Risk and Ins. Mgmt. Soc., Risk Mgmt. Council of Mfrs. Alliance (formerly Machinery and Allied Products Inst.), Captive Ins. Cos. Assn., ESIS (Delphi panel 1985—), Internat. Platform Assn. Roman Catholic. Avocations: tennis, hunting, fishing, woodworking. Home: PO Box 369 6 Eagle Pointe Pass Rapids City IL 61278 Office: Deere & Co 1 John Deere Pl Moline IL 61265-8098 Home Phone: 309-496-3333; Office Phone: 309-765-5865. Business E-Mail: middletonmarcs@johndeere.com.

MIDDLETON, NORMAN GRAHAM, social worker, psychotherapist; b. Jacksonville, Fla., Jan. 21, 1935; s. Norman Graham and Betty (Quina) M.; m. Judy Stephens, Aug. 1, 1968; stepchildren: Monty Stokes, Toni Stokes. BA, U. Miami, Fla., 1960; MSW, Fla. State U., 1962. Casework counselor Family Svc., Miami, 1962-64; psychiat. social worker assoc. firm Drs. Warson, Steele, Wiener, Sarasota, Fla., 1964-66; psychotherapist Sarasota, 1966—. Instr. Manatee Jr. Coll., Bradenton, Fla., 1973-76. Author: The Caverns of My Mind, 1985, Imaginative Healing, 1993, Spirited Imagination, 2002. Pres. Coun. on Epilepsy, Sarasota, 1969-70. Served with USAF, 1954-58. Fellow Fla. Soc. Clin. Social Work (pres. 1978-80); mem. Am. Group Psychotherapy Assn., Am. Assn. Sex Educators and Counselors (cert. sex educator). Democrat. Episcopalian. Home: 16626 Winburn Dr Sarasota FL 34240-9221 Office: 1257 S Tamiami Trail Sarasota FL 34239-2219 Home Phone: 941-322-1897; Office Phone: 941-366-3334. Personal E-mail: imageside@aol.com.

MIDDLETON-DOWNING, LAURA, psychiatric social worker, artist, small business owner; b. Edinburg, Ind., Apr. 20, 1935; d. John Thomas Jr. and Rowene Elizabeth (Baker) Middleton; m. George Charles Downing, 1974 (div. 1986). BA in English Lit., U. Colo., 1966, MFA, 1969, BA in Psychology, 1988; MSW, U. Denver, 1992; Doctor of Clin. Hypnotherapy, Am. Inst. Hypnotherapy, 1995. Cert. clin. hypnotherapist, Calif., Colo.; cert. past life therapist, Colo., In ternat. Bd. for Regression Therapy-Level II cert. Profl. artist, Silver Plume and Boulder, Colo., 1965—; profl. photographer Silver Plume, Boulder, 1975—; art tchr. U. Colo., Boulder and Longmont, 1971-73; mem. survey crew Bur. of Land Mgmt., Empire, Colo., 1984-85; cons. social work and psychotherapy Boulder, 1992—; psychiat. and med. social worker Good Samaritan Health Agy., Boulder, 1993-97; pvt. practice clin. hypnotherapy Boulder, 1995—; pvt. practice past-life therapist, 1995—. Pres. Phoenix LG, Inc., 1998-2004 Author, photographer Frontiers, vol. IV, no. 1, 1979; works exhibited in 18 one-woman shows, 1969—; numerous group exhbns. including one in Colo. History Mus., Denver, 1997-98. Trustee Town of Silver Plume, Colo., 1975-84; co-founder, pres. Alma Holm Rogers Nat. Orgn. Women, Clear Creek County, 1975-82; mem. Ctrl. Mountain Coun., Clear Creek County, 1980; chairperson Mary Ellen Barnes Cmty. Ctr. Project, Silver Plume, Colo., 1983; vol. Rape Crisis Team, Boulder, 1989-90, Child & Family Advocacy Program, Boulder, 1992-97; adv. bd. mem. Good Samaritan Agy., Boulder, 1993-97; caring minister vol. First Congl. Ch., Boulder, 1995-98; founding mem. Front Range Women in the Visual Arts, Boulder, Colo., 1974. Recipient Juried Exhbn. Merit award Colo. Women in the Arts, 1979; Women's Incentive scholar U. Colo., Boulder, 1989; Grad. Sch. Social Work scholar U. Denver, 1991; Colo. Grad. grantee U. Denver, 1992. Mem. AAUW, NASW, DAR, Colo. Advs. for Responsible Mental Health Svcs., Eye Movement Desensitization Reprocessing Network, Internat. Assn. for Regression Rsch. and Therapies, Inc. (Ecocycle, Colo. block leader), Natural Resources Def. Coun., The Nature Conservancy, World Wildlife Fedn., Bus. Women's Leadership Group, Sierra Club, Defender of Wildlife, Psi Chi. Avocations: skipping, photography, travel, volunteerism, bicycling. Office: PO Box 2312 Boulder CO 80306-2312

MIDELFORT, HANS CHRISTIAN ERIK, history professor; b. Eau Claire, Wis., Apr. 17, 1942; s. Peter Albert and Gerd (Gjems) M.; m. Corelyn Forsyth Senn, June 16, 1965 (div. Dec. 1981); children: Katarina, Kristian; m. Cassandra Clemons Hughes, May 25, 1985 (div. April 1996); 1 child, Lucy; m. Anne L. McKeithen, June 22, 1996. BA, Yale U., 1964, MPhil, 1967, PhD, 1970. Instr. Stanford U., Calif., 1968-70; asst. prof. U. Va., Charlottesville, 1970-72, assoc. prof., 1972-87, prof., 1987—, Charles Julian Bishko prof. history, 1996—. Vis. prof. Harvard U., Cambridge, Mass., 1985, U. Stuttgart, Germany, 1988, U. Bern, Switzerland, 1988, Wolfson Coll., Oxford U., 2002, Yale U., 2003; prin. Brown Coll., U. Va., 1996-2001; Dwight Terry lectr. Yale U., 2003; vis. fellow All Souls Coll., Oxford U., 2005. Author: Witch Hunting in Southwestern Germany, 1972 (Gustave Arlt prize 1972), Mad Princes of Renaissance Germany, 1994 (Roland H. Bainton prize 16th Century Studies Conf. 1995), A History of Madness in 16th Century Germany, 1999 (Ralph Waldo Emerson prize, Phi Beta Kappa, 1999, Roland H. Bainton prize 16th Century Studies Conf. 2000), Exorcism and Enlightenment, 2005; editor: Johann Weyer, On Witchcraft, 1998; co-editor: Europe, 1450-1789. Encyclopedia of the Early Modern World, 2003; translator: Imperial Cities and the Reformation (Bernd Moeller), 1972, Revolution of 1525 (Peter Bickle), 1981, Shaman of Oberstdorf (Wolfgang Behringer), 1998. Mem. Soc. Reformation Rsch. (pres. 1992-93). Office: U Va Dept History Charlottesville VA 22903 Business E-Mail: hem7e@virginia.edu.

MIDKIFF, DINAH LEE, retired elementary and middle school educator; b. Ashland, Ky., Dec. 23, 1954; d. Marie Ramey Midkiff. AA, Ashland Cmty. Coll, 1974; BA, Morehead State U., 1976, MA, 1978, cert. in adminstrn. and supervision, 1980. Tchr. Boyd County Bd. Edn., Ashland, 1976—85, Boone County Bd. Edn., Hebron, Ky., 1989—90, Franklin County Bd. Edn., Frankfort, Ky., 1990—2003, Jessamine County Bd. Edn., Nicholasville, Ky., 2003—04; ret., 2004—. Cons. Ky. Dept. Edn., Frankfort, Ky., 1986—89. Co-author: Jazz Up Reading: A Conference Overview, Informal Selection Process for Grade One Placement. Named Ky. Col., 2001; recipient Drug Abuse Resistance Edn. award, 2002. Mem.: NOW, AAUW, Am. Assn. Ret. Persons, Ky. Ret. Tchr. Assn. Democrat. Avocations: travel, reading, gardening. Home: 1338 Shun Pike Nicholasville KY 40356

MIDKIFF, ROBERT RICHARDS, trust company, finance company executive, consultant; b. Honolulu, Sept. 24, 1920; s. Frank Elbert and Ruth (Richards) M.; m. Evanita Sumner, July 24, 1948; children: Mary Lloyd, Robin Starr, Shelley Sumner, Robert Richards Jr., David Wilson. BA, Yale U., 1942; grad. Advanced Mgmt. Program, Harvard U., 1962; LHD, U. Hawaii, 2002. Asst. sec. Hawaiian Trust Co., 1951—56, asst. v.p., 1956—57, v.p., 1957—65; dir. Am. Factors, Ltd., 1954—65; v.p. Amfac, Inc., 1965—68; exec. v.p., dir. Am. Security Bank, Honolulu, 1968—69, pres., dir., 1969—71; pres., CEO, dir. Am. Trust Co. Hawaii, Honolulu, 1971—93; chmn. bd. dirs. Bishop Trust Co. Ltd., Honolulu, 1984—93; pres., CEO Am. Fin. Svcs. of Hawaii, 1984—93. Co-chmn. Gov.'s Archtl. Adv. Com. on State Capitol, 1960-65; co-chmn. Gov.'s Adv. Com. on Fine Arts for State Capitol, 1965-69; past chmn., bd. dirs. Hawaii Visitors Bur.; past pres., bd. dirs. Downtown Improvement Assn., Lahaina Restoration Found., Hawaii Cmty. Found.; bd. dirs., pres. Atherton Family Found.; past chmn. Profit Sharing Rsch. Found.; chmn., bd. dirs. Hawaii Theatre Ctr.; past chmn. bd. dirs. Good Beginnings Alliance; chmn. bd. dirs. Honolulu Cultural and Arts Dist. Mem. Coun. on Founds. (past bd dirs.), Profit Sharing Coun. Am. (past bd. dirs.), Small Bus. Coun. Am. (past bd. dirs.), ESOP Assn. Am. (past bd. dirs.), Pacific Club, Waialae Golf Club, Phi Beta Kappa. Episcopalian. Office: 4477 Kahala Ave Honolulu HI 96816-4924 Office Phone: 808-734-8132. Office Fax: 808-737-9007. Personal E-mail: rrmhi@aol.com.

MIDLARSKY, ELIZABETH RUTH, psychologist, educator, researcher; b. NYC; d. Abraham Allan and Frances Lucille (Wiener) Steckel; m. Manus Issachar Midlarsky, June 25, 1961; children: Susan Rachel, Miriam Joyce, Michael George. BA, CUNY, 1961; MA, Northwestern U., 1966, PhD, 1968. Lic. psychologist, N.J., Mich., Colo. Asst. prof. U. Denver, 1968-73; dir. rsch. and evaluation Malcolm X Mental Health Ctr. (now Park East), Denver, 1973-75; assoc. prof., dir. psychol. tng. program Met. State Coll., Denver, 1975-77; assoc. prof. psychology U. Detroit, 1982—90, prof. psychology, 1983-90, chair dept. psychology, 1978-81, dir. Ctr. Study Devel. and Aging, 1977-83; prof. clin. psychology Tchrs. Coll. Columbia U., NYC, 1990—, dir. Ctr. for Lifespan and Aging Studies, 1992—, founding coord. MA program, 1998—, co-chair dept. counseling and clin. psychology, 2006—; rsch. scholar Phila. Geriatric Ctr., 1997—2000. Mem. initial rev. group NIMH, Bethesda, Md., 1976-82; mem. ad hoc rev. groups NHLBI, Bethesda, 1985-95; mem. study sect. NIH, Bethesda, 1986-91; mem. nat. reviewers reserve, 1991-94. Author: Altruism in Late Life, 1994; co-editor Humboldt Jour. Social Rels., 1985-86, Violence in Schools, 2005; editor Acad. Psychol. Bull., 1982-86, mem. editl bd. Jour. Traumatic Stress, 2000—; contbr. chpts. to books and articles to profl. jours. Mem. exec. coun. Mich. Psychol. Assn. Grantee Nat. Inst. Aging, 1982-85, 87-90, AARP, 1982-83, 88-89, 92-95; postdoctoral rsch. fellow AAUW, 1974-75. Fellow APA (divsn. 12, 20, publs. com. 1990-92, election com. 2005—, student award com. 1990), Assn. Psychol. Soc., Am. Orthopsychiat. Assn., Gerontol. Soc. Am. (exec. com. on program com. 1983-84); mem. Soc. Psychol. Study Social Issues, Internat. Assn. Genocide Scholars. Jewish. Avocations: writing, poetry, needlepoint, piano, reading. Home: 3 Falcon Rd East Brunswick NJ 08816-2716 Office: Columbia U Tchrs Coll Dept Couns & Clin Psych PO Box 148 New York NY 10027-0148 Office Phone: 212-678-3124. Business E-Mail: em142@columbia.edu.

MIDLER, LAURENCE H. (LARRY), lawyer; BA with hon., U. Va., 1987; JD, NYU, 1990. Bar: NY State 1990. Former assoc. atty. Latham & Watkins Law Offices, NYC; former v.p., gen. counsel Serviscope Corp.; former head facilities corp. svcs. dept., gen. counsel Micro Warehouse, Inc.; exec. v.p., gen. counsel CB Richard Ellis Group, 2006—. Office: CB Richard Ellis Ste 2700 355 S Grand Ave Los Angeles CA 90071

MIEARS-CUTSINGER, MARY ELLEN, artist, art gallery owner; b. Ratliff, Okla., Jan. 23, 1931; d. Elmer Cecil and Ruth Collins Miears; m. Leroy Gene Meyers (dec.); children: Kathryn, Melissa, Mary Teresa, Marsha, Donna; m. Charles Wesley Cutsinger, Oct. 10, 1979. Student, Mt. San Antonio Coll., Walnut, Calif., 1975—76. Freelance comml. and portrait artist, 1949—76; staff artist Pomona (Calif.) Progress Bull., 1976—77; studio artist Miears Fine Art, Ridgecrest, Calif., 1979—; art tchr. Studio Eight, Ridgecrest, 1989—96; studio artist Miears Fine Art and Studio Eight Gallery, Ridgecrest, 1979—. Mem. gallery com. Maturango Mus., Ridgecrest, 1990. Recipient Top 100 Paintings award, Premier Arts for the Parks Nat., 1987, Wingspread Guide to N.Mex. award, Ann. Nat. Exhbn., 2000, 2d pl. award, Sierra Pastel Soc. Internat., 2004. Mem.: Allied Artists, Pastel Soc. West Coast (signature mem.), Catharine Lorillard Wolfe Art club (signature mem.). Home: 1125 W Benson Ridgecrest CA 93555 Office: 995 N Norma St Ste # Ridgecrest CA 93555 Office Phone: 760-446-7977. E-mail: mary@kuanyin-images.com.

MIEKKA, JEANETTE ANN, retired science educator; b. Kenmore, NY, Aug. 25, 1931; d. Harry Whittier and Beulah Laura Lambe; m. Richard George Miekka, June 22, 1958; children: James Richard, Frederick Noah, Cynthia Marie Bordas-Miekka. BSc, Boston U., 1949—53, MEd, 1954—57. Teacher of All Sciences Mass., 1954. Tchr. of chemistry, physics, biology, gen. sci. Meridith H.S., Meridity, NH, 1953—54; sci. tchr. and dept. chmn. Hicksville Jr. H.S., 1954—56; biology and physiology tchr. Newton H.S., Mass., 1956—60; instr. of comparative physiology Allied Health Jr. Coll., Holliston, Mass., 1978—79; ret., 1979. Sophomore class advisor Meridith H.S., NH, 1953—54; supr. of student teachers Newton H.S., Mass., 1957—60, advisor, future teachers of am., 1956—60. Contbr. articles to profl. jours. Pres. Am. Field Svc., Natick, Mass., 1964—65; dir. F.I.S.H., Natick, Mass., 1964—65; chmn., publicity Sudbury Women's Club, Mass., 1971—74; mem. Sun Coast Opera Guild; cons. St. Francis Sch., Loiseau, Haiti, 2002—05; assoc. St. Margaret's Convent, Boston; lay eucharistic min. St. Matthews Ch., St. Petersburg, Fla., 2004—05. Mem.: Internat. Women's Writing Guild (assoc.). Episcopal. Avocations: travel, bridge, book club, cooking, writing. Home Phone: 727-866-8682.

MIELE, ANGELO, engineering educator, researcher, consultant, author; b. Formia, Italy, Aug. 21, 1922; arrived in U.S., 1952, naturalized, 1985; s. Salvatore and Elena (Marino) Miele. DCivil Engring., U. Rome, Italy, 1944, DAero. Engring., 1946; DSc (hon.), Inst. Tech., Technion, Israel, 1992. Asst. prof. Poly. Inst. Bklyn., 1952- 55; prof. Purdue U., 1955-59; dir. astrodynamics Boeing Sci. Rsch. Labs., 1959-64; prof. aerospace scis., math. scis. Rice U., Houston, 1964-88, Foyt Family prof. engring., 1988-93, Foyt prof. emeritus engring., aerospace scis., math. scis., 1993—, rsch. prof., 2001—. Cons. Douglas Aircraft Co., 1956—58, U.S. Aviation Underwriters, 1987, Boeing Comml. Airplane Co., 1989, European Space Tech. Engring. Ctr., 2002; cons. Allison divsn. GM Corp., 1956—58; Breakwell Meml. lectureship Internat. Astron. Fedn., 1994; Gaspare Santangelo Meml. lectureship Italian Assn. of Aeronautics and Astronautics, 2001. Author: Flight Mechanics, 1962; editor: Theory of Optimum Aerodynamic Shapes, 1965, Applied Mathematics in Aerospace Science and Engineering, 1994, Advanced Design Problems in Aerospace Engineering, 2003; editor-in chief Jour. Optimization Theory and Applications, 1966—, assoc. editor Jour. Astronautical Scis., 1964—93, Applied Math. and Computation, 1975—, series editor Math. Concepts and Methods in Sci. and Engring., 1975—, Optimal Control Applications and Methods, 1979—, mem. editl. bd. RAIRO-Ops. Rsch., 1990—, mem. adv. bd. AIAA Edn. Series, 1991—98; contbr. articles to profl. jours. Pres. Italy in Am. Assn., 1966—68. Decorated knight comdr. Order Merit Italy; recipient Levy medal, Franklin Inst. of Phila., 1974, Brouwer award, AAS, 1980, Schuck award, Am. Automatic Control Coun., 1988, Latina prize, 2002, Flight Mechanics award, AIAA, 1982, Pendray Aerospace Lit. award, 1982. Fellow: Am. Astronautical Soc., AIAA (hon. Pendray Aerospace Lit. award 1982, Mechs. and Control of Flight award 1982), Franklin Inst.; mem.: Tex. Acad. Engring., Scis. and Medicine, Nat. Acad. Engring. of Argentina (corr.), Internat. Acad. Astronautics, Acad. Scis. Turin (corr.), Russian Acad. Scis. (fgn.), NAE. Achievements include research in aerospace engring., windshear problems, hypervelocity flight, interplanetary flight, math. programming, optimal control theory and computing methods. Home: 3106 Kettering Dr Houston TX 77027-5504 Office: Rice Univ MS-322 Aero-Astronautics Group 6100 Main St Houston TX 77005-1827 Office Phone: 713-348-4907. Business E-Mail: miele@rice.edu.

MIELE, JOEL ARTHUR, SR., civil engineer; b. Jersey City, May 28, 1934; s. Jene Gerald Sr., and Eleanor Natalie (Bergida) M.; m. Faith Roseann Trombetta, July 21, 1952 (div. 1954); m. 2d Josephine Ann Cottone, Feb. 14, 1959; children: Joel Arthur, Jr., Vita Marie, Janet Ann. BCE, Poly. Inst. Bklyn., 1955. Lic. profl. engr. NY, NJ, Fla.; profl. planner NJ; chartered engr., U.K. Civil engr. Yudell & Miele, Queens, NY, 1955-57; chief engr. Jene G. Miele Assocs., 1960—68; prin. and CEO Miele Assocs., 1968—94; commr. N.Y.C. Planning Commn., 1990—94; commr. dept. bldgs. City of N.Y., 1994—96; commr. Dept. Environ. Protection, 1996—2002, N.Y.C. Bd. Stds. and Appeals, 2002—05; pvt. practice cons. engr., 2005—. Mem. NY State Bd. for Engring. and Land Surveying, 1997—, chmn. 2005-. Patentee masonry wall constrn. Mem. Cmty. Bd. 10, Queens, 1971-90, chmn., 1978-90; mem. bd. visitors Creedmoor State Hosp., 1978—, pres., 1979—; trustee Queens Borough Pub. Libr., 1979—, pres., 1995-96; bd. dirs. Peninsula Hosp. Ctr., 1984—, chair, 1990—; bd. mem. Peninsula Gen. Nursing Home, 1985—, chair, 1990—; bd. dirs. Queens County Overall Econ. Devel. Corp., 1989-94, pres., 1991-94; trustee, treas. Queens Pub. Comm. Corp., 1983—; exec. v.p. Queens County and mem. Nat. Coun. Boy Scouts Am., 1991—; bd. mem. Am. Parkinson Disease Assn., 1985—, mem. exec. com., 1987—, v.p., 1996—; pres. Internat. Parkinsons Fond, Netherlands, 1997—; dir. Queens Libr. Found., 1997—; dir. Assn. Met Water Agys., 1997-02, Assn. Met. Sewerage Agys., 1997-02; mem. Nat. Coun. Examiners Engring. & Surveying, 1997—; founder, co-pres., Internat. Parkinsons Fond GmbH, Germany, 2006-. Lt. (j.g.) USN, 1957-60; capt. USNR, 1960-88, ret., 1988; RADM LH NY Naval Militia, 1998. Named Italian-Am. of Yr. Ferrini Welfare League, Queens, 1980, Hon. Mem. of Queens Chpt. AIA, 1994, Hon. Profl. Affiliated Mem. NY Soc. Archs., 1994; recipient Outstanding Cmty. Leader award Boy Scouts Am., 1987, Pride of Queens award, 1990, Pub. Servant Extraordinaire award United Cerebral Palsy of Queens, 1994, Good Scout award Greater NY Coun. Boy Scouts Am., 1994, Nat. Silver Beaver Court of Honor award, Boy Scouts of America, 1997, United Hosp. Funds Disting. Trustee award for Extraordinary Svc., 1997, NYSSPE Outstanding PE Mgr. of Yr. award, 1997, Disting. Alumni award, Poly. U., 1998, Humanitarian of Yr. award Guide Dog Found., 2000, Spl. Recognition for Pub. Svc. award NY Bldg. Congress, 2002, Golden Eagle award Boy Scouts Am., 2002. Fellow ASCE (life), NSPE (trustee polit. action com. 1990-96); mem. N.Y. State Soc. Profl. Engrs. (v.p. 1984-86, pres. 1988-89, nat. dir. 1987-90, Engr. of Yr. 1983), Soc. Am. Mil. Engrs., N.Y. State Assn. of Professions (founding). Democrat. Congregationalist. Home Phone: 718-848-8013; Office Phone: 718-848-8013. Personal E-mail: jmiele2@nyc.rr.com.

MIELE, LUCIO, physician, medical researcher, pharmacologist; b. Naples, Italy, Mar. 13, 1957; s. Armando and Agata Liana (Vassallo-Paleologo) Miele; m. Carolyn Margaret Duncan, Oct. 16, 2005; stepchildren: Charles Joseph Duncan, Margaret Ann Duncan, Caroline Elizabeth Duncan. MD, U. Naples, Italy, 1981—81, PhD, 1987. Vis. fellow NIH, Bethesda, Md., 1986—89, vis. assoc., 1989—93; tenure-track prin. investigator Ctr. for Biologics Evaluation and Rsch., FDA, Bethesda, 1994—96, acting chief lab. cell biology, 1996—98; asst. prof. pathology Loyola U. Med. Ctr., Maywood, Ill., 1998—2001; assoc. prof. pharmacology U. Ill., Chgo., 2001—05; prof. pathology, pharmacology and exptl. therapeutics Loyola U. Med. Ctr., Maywood, Ill., 2005—. Vis. prof. Temple U., Phila.,

2005—06; dir. breast cancer pre-clinical rsch. program Cardinal Bernardin Cancer Ctr., Loyola U. Chgo., Maywood, Ill., 2005—; organizer EMBO Conf. on Notch Signaling, 2005; spkr., cons. in field. Editor: Jour. Expt. Clin. Oncology, 2004—06; mem. editl. bd.: Jour. Cell Biochem., 2003—06, Women's Oncology Reviews, 2002—06; contbr. articles to profl. jours. Drug discovery and molecular pharmacology study sect. Nat. Cancer Inst./NIH, Bethesda, 2002—06; breast cancer rsch. study sections Dept. of Def., Washington, 2002—06; dept. pub. health penny severns women's oncology rsch. awards study sect. State of Ill., Springfield. Recipient Outstanding Young Scientist award, Italian Acad. Medicine and Surgery, 1983, FDA award, 1997, Excellence in Women's Oncology Rsch. award, Ill. Dept. Pub. Health, 2000—01; grantee, NCI, 1999—2004, Ill. Dept. Pub. Health, 1999—2002, 2006—, Nat. Inst. Child Health and Human Devel., 2002—06; Idea grant, DOD, 2004—, Program Project grant, NCI/NIH, 2006—. Mem.: Am. Assn. for Cancer Rsch. Democrat-Npl. Roman Catholic. Achievements include development of recombinant human CC10/Uteroglobin; research in role of notch signaling in various cancers, notch inhibition has anti-neoplastic activity in vivo. Avocations: horsemanship, scuba diving, photography, poetry, philosophy. Office: Loyola Univ Med Ctr 2160 S First Ave Maywood IL 60153 Home Phone: 630-406-0126; Office Phone: 708-327-3298. Office Fax: 708-327-2245. Business E-Mail: lmiele@lumc.edu.

MIELKE, CLARENCE HAROLD, JR., hematologist; b. Spokane, Wash., June 18, 1936; s. Clarence Harold and Marie Katherine (Gillespie) M.; m. Marcia Rae, July 5, 1964; children: Elisa, John, Kristina. BS, Wash. State U., 1959; MD, U. Louisville, 1963. Intern San Francisco Gen. Hosp., 1963-64; resident in medicine Portland VA Hosp., 1964-65, San Francisco Gen. Hosp., 1965-67; fellow in hematology U. So. Calif., 1967-68; tchg. fellow, asst. physician, instr. Tufts-New Eng. Med. Ctr. Hosps., Boston, 1968-71; sr. scientist Med. Rsch. Inst., San Francisco, 1971-90; chief hematology Presbyn. Hosp., San Francisco, 1971-82; asst. prof. clin. medicine U. Calif. Sch. Medicine, San Francisco, 1971-80, assoc. clin. prof., 1979-90, bd. dirs. Inst. Cancer Rsch., 1992—. Trustee, bd. dirs. Med. Rsch. Inst. San Francisco, Sacred Heart Hosp. Found., 1997-2000, Rockwood Clinic Found., 1994—; dir. emeritus Inst. Cancer Rsch.; trustee emeritus, bd. dirs. Med. Rsch. Inst., 1988—; dir. Health Rsch. and Edn. Ctr., Wash. State U., 1989-2005, prof. pharmacology, 1989—, prof. vet. medicine, 1989—, assoc. dean rsch., 1992-2004; dir. Spokane (Wash.) Heart Study, 1994-2006. Editor emeritus Jour. Clin. Aphesis, 1981; contbr. chpts. to books, articles to med. jours. Named Nat. Disting. Eagle Scout, 1998; NIH grantee, 1973-88. Fellow ACP, Am. Heart Assn.; mem. AAAS, AMA, Am. Heart Assn., Internat. Acad. Clin. and Applied Thrombosis and Hemostasis, Internat. Soc. Hematology, Am. Coll. Angiology; mem. Am. Soc. Internal. Medicine, Internat. Soc. Thrombosis and Hemostasis, N.Y. Acad. Scis., Spokane Med. Soc., Internat. Soc. Angiology. Office: PO Box 1495 Spokane WA 99210-1495 Office Phone: 509-358-7630. Business E-Mail: mielkeh@wsu.edu.

MIELKE, JAMES EDWARD, geochemist; b. Toledo, Oct. 6, 1940; s. Herbert Edward and Naomi Hilletje (Raabe) M.; m. Laurie Beth Retter, Dec. 19, 1966; children: Erin Christine, Emily Jane. BS, MIT, 1962; MS, U. Ariz., 1965; PhD, George Washington U., 1974. Mine geologist potash exploration N.S. Rsch. Found., 1962; geologist S.W. field party Universal Engrng. Corp., Boston, 1963-64; geochemist C-14 dating lab. Smithsonian Instn., Washington, 1964-73; specialist in marine and earth scis. Congl. Rsch. Svc./Libr. of Congress, Washington, 1973-2000, retired, 2000. Liaison to Nat. Materials Adv. Bd., Nat. Rsch. Coun., Washington, 1981-86. Author more than 170 publs. including articles in profl. jours., com. prints, Congl. Rsch. Svc. reports; co-author: Strategic and Critical Materials, 1985, Review of Research in Modern Problems in Geochemistry, 1979. Pres. Home Buyers, Inc., Washington, 1976-83. Smithsonian Instn. Rsch. grantee, 1966-69. Mem. AAAS, Am. Geophys. Union. Republican. Lutheran. Avocation: folk dancing. Home: 2803 Washington Ave Chevy Chase MD 20815-3009

MIELKE, PAUL WILLIAM, JR., statistician, consultant; b. St. Paul, Feb. 18, 1931; s. Paul William and Elsa (Yungbauer) M.; m. Roberta Roehl Robison, June 25, 1960; children: William, Emily Spear, Lynn Basila. BA, U. Minn., 1953, PhD, 1963; MA, U. Ariz., 1958. Tchg. asst. U. Ariz., Tucson, 1957—58, U. Minn., Mpls., 1958—60, statis. cons., 1960—62, lectr., 1962—63; from asst. to assoc. prof. dept. stats. Colo. State U., Fort Collins, 1963—72, prof. dept. stats., 1972—. Co-author: Permutation Methods: a Distance Function Approach; contbr. articles Am. Jour. Pub. Health, Jour. of Statis. Planning and Inference, Ednl. and Psychol. Measurement, Biometrika, Earth-Sci. Revs., Weather and Forecasting, Jour. Behavioral and Ednl. Stats. Capt. USAF, 1953-57. Fellow Am. Statis. Assn.; mem. Am. Meteorol. Soc. (Banner I. Miller award 1973, 94), Biometric Soc. Achievements include rsch. in common statistical methods (t test and analysis of variance) based on counter intuitive geometric foundations and provided alternative statistical methods which are based on appropriate foundations. Home: 736 Cherokee Dr Fort Collins CO 80525-1517 Office: Colo State U Dept Stats Fort Collins CO 80523-1877 Office Phone: 970-491-6465. Business E-Mail: paul.mielke@colostate.edu.

MIERS, HARRIET ELLAN, lawyer, former federal official; b. Dallas, Aug. 10, 1945; BS in Mathematics, So. Meth. U., 1967, JD, 1970. Bar: Tex. 1970. Law clk. to Hon. Joe E. Estes US Dist. Ct. (no. dist.) Tex., 1970—72; assoc. Locke Purnell Rain Harrell (formerly Locke, Purnell, Boren, Laney & Neely PC), Dallas, 1972—78, ptnr, 1978—99, pres., 1996—99; mng. ptnr. Locke Liddell & Sapp LLP, Dallas, 1999—2001; asst. to Pres. & staff sec The White House, Washington, 2001—03, asst. to Pres. & dep. chief of staff for policy, 2003—05, gen. counsel to Pres., 2005—07; nominee for assoc. justice US Supreme Ct., 2005, withdrew nomination, 2005; ptnr. Locke Liddell & Sapp LLP, Dallas, 2007—. Chairwoman, Tex. Lottery Commn., 1995-2000; mem. bd. dirs. Capstead Mortgage Corp., Coamerica Bank, Tex. Comments editor Southwestern Law Jour., 1969-70. Mem.-at-large Dallas City Coun., 1989-91; trustee Southwestern Legal Found. Named 1 of Top 50 Most Influential Lawyers Nat. Law Jour., 1998; named Outstanding Young Lawyer of Dallas, Dallas Assn. of Young Lawyers, 1978, Woman of the Year, Today's Dallas Woman, 1997; Woman of Excellence award, Woman's Enterprise Mag., Louise B. Raggio award, Dallas Women Lawyers Assn., Jurisprudence award, Anti-Defamation League, 1996, Hon. Merrill Hartman award, Legal Svcs. of No. Tex., Sarah T. Hughes award, Women in Law Section State Bat of Tex., Am. Jewish Comm. Human Relations award, DBA's Justinian award for Community Svc. Fellow Am. Bar Found., Tex. Bar Found. (life); mem. ABA (jour. bd. editors, ho. dels., chair credentials and admissions com., election law com., bus. and cmty. activities), Dallas Bar Found., Dallas Bar Assn. (chmn. bd. dirs. 1981, pres., 1985-90), State Bar Tex. (pres. 1992-93, dir. 1986-89), Attys. Liability Assurance Soc. (bd. dirs.). Office: Locke Liddell & Sapp LLP 2200 Ross Ave Ste 2200 Dallas TX 75201-6776 *

MIERSWA, DAVID P., lawyer, real estate investor; b. Oshkosh, Wis. s. Joseph and Patricia Mierswa; m. Karen M. Rheingans, Sept. 11, 1999. BBA in Mktg., Human Resources Mgmt., U. Wis., Oshkosh, 1992; MBA, Keller Grad. Sch. Mgmt., Chgo., 1997; JD, Thomas Cooley Law Sch., Lansing, Mich., 1999. Pvt. practice, Skokie, Ill., 1999—. Mem.: Chgo. Bar Assn. (spkr.). Office: 5200 Golf Rd Skokie IL 60077

MIERZWA, JOSEPH WILLIAM, lawyer, consultant; b. Chgo., Nov. 21, 1951; s. Joseph Valentine and Betty Ann (Ray) M.; m. Rolana Conley, May 18, 1974. BA, U. Kans., 1981, JD, 1985. Bar: Kans. 1985, U.S. Dist. Ct. Kans. 1985. Pvt. practice, Prairie Village, Kans., 1985-86; gen. counsel Hyatt Legal Svcs., Kansas City, Mo., 1986-87; corp. counsel NLS Corp., Inc., Lakewood, Colo., 1988; owner, mgr. Joseph W. Mierzwa Cons., Lakewood, 1988-92; pres. Prose Assocs., Inc., Highlands Ranch, Colo., 1991—. Cons. Nat. Legal Shield, Lakewood, 1988-92, Reader's Digest Assn., Pleasantville, N.Y., 1988-02, Hyatt Legal Svcs., Cleve., 1988-94, USLaw.com, 2000-02, ComPsych, 2001—, BestEver.com, 2003—, others; editor OverDrive Sys., Inc., Cleve., 1990-95. Author: The 21st Century Family Legal Guide, 1994. Mem.: ABA. Avocations: cooking, travel, creative writing. Office: 9889 Spring Hill Dr Highlands Ranch CO 80129-4349 E-mail: paibooks@aol.com.

MIES, JOHN CHARLES, Internet company executive; b. Peoria, Ill., Aug. 24, 1946; s. Ernest Gregory and Clara Emma (Reese) M. BS, Ea. Ill. U., 1968. Tchr. Centennial High Sch., Champaign, Ill., 1969-74; ptnr. The Leather Shop, Champaign, 1974-78, The Waterbed Shop, Champaign, 1978-82; pres., CEO Mies Corp., Champaign, 1982—. Mem. adv. bd. Bedroom mag., 1991-93; v.p./gen. mgr. AdvanceNet, 1996; pres. Online Svcs.; gen. mgr. Cambert Ltd., 1997, COO, 1999; ptnr. Ravecomm, LLC. Editor-in-chief The Sleep Connection newsletter; columnist Bedroom Industry Newsletter. Faculty rector Flotation Healthcare Found., chmn. bd., 1996. Mem. Nat. Waterbed Retailers Assn. (exec. com. 1987-92, sec.-treas. 1988-89, pres. 1991, chmn. long-range planning com., co-chmn. liaison com., joint pub. rels. com., named to Waterbed Hall of Fame 1992), Ctrl. State Mktg. Group (pres. 1986-89, 93, sec.-treas. 1990-92, sec. 1994-98, editor New Bedding Vision newsletter), Urbana C. of C. (chmn. leadership planning com.), Monticello C. of C. (bd. dirs. 1998-2003, treas. 2001-02), Champaign C. of C., Waterbed Advt. Coun. (com. mem., bd. dirs. 1990-91), Waterbed Coun. (com. mem., bd. dirs. 1990-91), Waterbed Coun. (bd. dirs. 1994, sec. 1994, dir. pubs. 1995, pres. 1996). Avocations: computers, motorcycle. Office: Mies Corp 201 W Springfield Ave Champaign IL 61820-4834

MIFFLIN, JEFFREY ALLEN, archivist, consultant, historian, researcher; b. St. Louis, 1949; s. Lewis Allen and Helen Louise Mifflin; m. Wendy Sue Kalish, 1988. AB cum laude, Harvard U., Cambridge, Mass., 1980; JD, Northeastern U., Boston, 1983; MA in History, U. Mass., Boston, 1992; MS in Libr. and Info. Sci., Simmons Libr. Sch., Boston, 1998. Asst. archivist McLean Hosp., Belmont, Mass., 1986—90, Harvard Collection Hist. Scientific Instruments, 1990—92; archives and manuscript specialist Mass. Inst. Tech., 1992—; archivist and curator Mass. Gen. Hosp., 1998—. Cons. Pioneer Group, Boston, 1998—2002, Mary B. Wakefield Charitable Trust, Milton, Mass., 2007—. Contbr. articles to profl. jour., chapters to books. Recipient Infinite Mile award, Mass. Inst. Tech., 2001. Mem.: Archivists and Libr. in the History Health Scis., Am. Assn. for the History Medicine, Soc. Am. Archivists. Achievements include research in relationship of historical objects to the documentary record. Home: 18 Douglas Rd Medford MA 02155 Office: Mass Gen Hosp RSL 110 55 Fruit St Boston MA 02114 Office Phone: 617-726-3180.

MIFTAHOF, ROUSTEM NARIMANOVICH, science educator, researcher; b. Kazan, Russia, Apr. 5, 1957; s. Nariman A. and Sofie K. Miftahof; m. Grace S. Sawan, May 20, 1997; 1 child, Jasmine Sofie. MD (hon.), Kazan Med. Inst., Russia, 1980; MS in Applied Math., Kazan State U., Russia, 1981, PhD in Math. and Physics, 1983; DS in Technical Scis., Moscow, 1989. Prof. Korea Advanced Inst. Sci. and Tech., Daejeon, Republic of Korea, 2006. Prin. scientist Acad. Scis., Kazan, 1984—87. Author: Biomechanics of the Small Intestine. Recipient Bronze medal, Acad. Scis., USSR, 1984. Achievements include design of software to simulate the neurogastrobiology of the gastrointestinal tract. Personal E-mail: aincompany@hotmail.com.

MIGALA, LUCYNA J., journalist, broadcast executive, artistic director; b. Krakow, Poland, May 22, 1944; came to U.S., 1947, naturalized, 1955; d. Joseph and Estelle (Suwala) M.; m. Frank A. Cizon, Oct. 9, 1998. Student, Loyola U., Chgo., 1962-63, Chgo. Conservatory of Music, 1963-70; BS in Journalism, Northwestern U., 1966. Radio announcer, prodr. Sta. WOPA, Oak Park, Ill., 1963—66; writer, reporter, prodr. NBC News, Chgo., 1966—69, 1969—71; prodr. NBC local news, Washington, 1969; prodr., coord. NBC network news, Cleve., 1971—78, field prodr. Chgo., 1978—79; v.p. Migala Comm. Corp., 1979—. Program and news dir., on-air personality Sta. WCEV, Cicero, Ill, 1979—; lectr. City Colls., Chgo., 1981, Morton Coll., 1988. Columnist Free Press, Chgo., 1984-87. Founder, artistic dir., gen. mgr. Lira Ensemble (formerly The Lira Singers), Chgo., 1965—, Artist-in-residence, Loyola U., Chgo.; mem., chmn. various cultural coms. Polish Am. Congress, 1970-80; bd. dir. Nationalities Svcs. Ctr., Cleve., 1973-78; bd. dir., v.p. Cicero-Berwyn Fine Arts Coun., Cicero, Ill., 1980-87; v.p. Chgo. chpt. Kosciuszko Found., 1983-86; bd. dir. Polish Women's Alliance Am., 1983-87, Ill. Humanities Coun., 1983-89, mem. exec. com., 1986-87; founder, gen. chmn. Midwest Chopin Piano Competition (later Chgo. Chopin Competition), 1984-86; founding mem. ethnic and folk arts panel Ill. Arts Coun., 1984-87, 92-94; mem. City Arts I and II panels Chgo. Office Fine Arts, 1986-89, 94; bd. dir. Ill. Arts Alliance, 1989-92, Polish-Am. Leadership Initiative, Chgo., 2001—; mem. Polonia Census 2000 Com.; bd. dir.trustee Lincoln Acad. Ill., 2005—; mem. bd. Berwyn Cicero Coun. on Aging, 2007-. Fellow Washington Journalism Ctr., 1969; decorated Cavalier's Cross of Merit Govt. Poland; recipient AP Broadcasters award, 1973, Emmy award NATAS, 1974, Cultural Achievement award Am. Coun. Polish Culture, 1990, award of merit Advocates Soc. Polish Am. Attys., 1991, Human Rels. Media award City of Chgo., 1992, Outstanding Achievement award Minister Fgn. Affairs Rep. of Poland, 1994, Civic Achievement award Polish Am. Hist. Assn., 2000, Nat. Creative Arts award Polish Am. Hist. Soc., 2003, Beautiful Spirit award Keep Chgo. Beautiful, Inc., 2005. Mem. Soc. Profl. Journalists. Office: Sta WCEV 5356 W Belmont Ave Chicago IL 60641-4103 also: The Lira Ensemble 6525 N Sheridan Rd # Sky905 Chicago IL 60626-5344 Business E-Mail: lmigala@liraensemble.com.

MIGDALE, LAWRENCE D., photographer; b. Transvaal, South Africa; arrived in US, 1978; s. Nathan and Jean Migdale; m. Terry Lowenthal, Sept. 17, 1978; children: Daniel, Ari. BA in Photo Journalism, Ctrl. London Poly., 1975. Self employed photographer Pix, Orinda, Calif., 1978—, ptner, 2007—. Stock photo libr. owner Pix, Orinda, 1990—. Photographer, author (28 photography books). Mem.: Am. Soc. Picture Profls. Avocation: scuba diving. Office: PIX PO Box 568 Orinda CA 94563

MIGDOL, MARVIN JACOB, public relations and marketing executive, consultant; b. Rochester, NY, Jan. 11, 1937; s. Frank and Dorothy (Krieger) M.; m. Frances Scheiner, June 13, 1959 (div. June 1970); children: Helene Ellen, Steven Gary, Larry Jay; m. Grace Miron, Dec. 26 1970 (div. Aug. 1986); children: Michael Alan, Susan Renee, Honi Faith; m. Roni Habel, June 30, 1991 (div. Dec. 1992); m. Fay Herschberg, Dec. 27, 2003. BA in Sociology, U. Buffalo, 1959; postgrad., U. Miami, 1959-60; MS in Communications, Boston U., 1961. Dir. pub. rels. United Fund, Reading, Pa., 1961-63, Rensselaer Poly. Inst., Troy, NY, 1963-64, Touro Infirmary, New Orleans, 1964, Hamot Hosp., Erie, Pa., 1964-65, United Jewish Fedn., Buffalo, 1965-68; pres. Marvin J. Migdol Inc., Dallas, 1968—. Instr. Boston U., 1962—, Pa. State U., 1962—, U. Tex., 1962—, Collin County C.C., Plano, 1990-91. Author: Public Relations Handbook, 1963, Comics as a Public Relations Tool in Communications, 1971, The Migdol Manual, 1972, Success in the 1990's, 1987, Greater Virility: Overcoming Impotence, 1993; contbr. numerous articles to profl. jours. Reporter Rep. Nat. Conv., Dallas, 1964; asst. dist. commr. Boy Scouts Am., Dallas, 1980-85; exec. bd. dirs. EPCOT Resorts, Lake Buena Vista, Fla., 1992—; v.p. Am. Jewish Congress, S.W. Region, 2001-05; v.p. Am. Friends of Magen David Adoin, 2004-07; commencement U. Phoenix, Dallas, 2005. Recipient Pub. Rels. award Coun. Jewish Welfare Funds & Fedn., N.Y.C., 1967, Nat. Bus. League, West Palm Beach, Fla., 1968, Merit award Big Brothers & Sisters, Dallas, Tex., 1987, Major League Volleyball award San Jose, Calif., 1987.; named Entrepreneur of the Yr. Venture Mag., Dallas, Tex., 1987 Mem. U.S. Profl. Mktg. Assn. (pres. 1990—), Am. Assn. Indsl. Editors (bd. dirs. 1967-70), Am. Coll. Pub. Rels. Assn. (bd. dirs. 1964-66), Inst. for Info. and Comm. (bd. dirs. 1971—), Dallas Belles (dir. mktg. and pub. rels. 1987—), Jewish Nat. Fund (area dir.), Dallas Bridge Assn. (chmn. publicity), Dallas C. of C. (mem. econ. and internat. coun.), U. Buffalo Alumni Assn. We. Pa. and Tex., 1964-65, Temple Shalom (vice chmn. bldg. fund 1971-72, mem. Brotherhood bd. 1985-86), Jewish Cmty. Ctr., Am. Contract Bridge League (chmn. pub. rels. 1983—, award Memphis chpt. 1983-87), Alpha Epsilon Pi (gov., 1970-79), Phi Delta Phi, (v.p. 1959-60, treas. 1960—). Jewish. Avocations: writer, lecturer, baseball and softball umpire, Boy Scout leader. Home: 18715 Gibbons Dr Dallas TX 75287 Office Phone: 972-233-9942. Personal E-mail: fmmigdol@tx.rr.com.

MIGHELL, KENNETH JOHN, lawyer; b. Schenectady, NY, Mar. 17, 1931; s. Richard Henry and Ruth Aline (Simon) M.; m. Julia Anne Carstarphen, Aug. 24, 1961; children: Thomas Lowry, Elizabeth Anne. BBA, U. Tex., 1952, JD, 1957. Bar: Tex. 1957. Assoc. Scurry, Scurry, Pace & Wood, Dallas, 1957-61; asst. U.S. Atty. Justice Dept., Dallas, 1961-77; 1st asst. No. Dist. Tex., 1972-77; U.S. Atty. No. Dist., Tex., 1977-81; ptnr. Cowles & Thompson, Dallas, 1981-96, of counsel, 1996—. Chmn. bd. mgmt. Downtown Dallas YMCA, 1974-76; pres. Dallas Area Am. Lung Assn., 1985-87; bd. dirs. YMCA Met. Dallas, 1987—; chmn. adv. bd. Southwestern Law Enforcement Inst., 1994-98; mem. SW Legal Found., CLE adv. com. 1999-2003. With USN, 1952-54; capt. USNR, 1954-78. Mem.: FBA, Nat. Assn. Former U.S. Attys. (pres. 1995), State Bar Tex. (bd. dirs. 1994—95), Dallas Bar Found. (trustee 1994—2001, vice chmn. 1999—2000, chmn. 2001—02), Dallas Bar Assn. (bd. dirs. 1984—89, chmn. 1989, v.p. 1990—91, pres. 1993). Democrat. Methodist. Office: Cowles & Thompson 901 Main St Ste 4000 Dallas TX 75202-3793 E-mail: kmighell@cowlesthompson.com.

MIGIELICZ, GERALYN, photojournalist; b. St. Louis, Feb. 15, 1958; d. Edward J. and Mary Ann (McCarthy) M. BJ, U. Mo., 1979. Photographer Emporia (Kans.) Gazette, 1979-80; chief photographer St. Joseph (Mo.) News-Press & Gazette, 1980-83; photo editor, photographer Seattle Times, 1984; picture editor Rocky Mountain News, Denver, 1985-86; graphics editor San Jose (Calif.) Mercury News, 1986-92, dir. photography, 1992—. Mem. faculty Poynter Inst., U. Mo. Workshop, Latin Am. Photojournalism Conf., Stan Kalish Picture Editing Workshop. Knight fellow Stanford U., 2005; recipient Individual Editing awards Soc. Newspaper Designers, 1988-04, Editing awards, 91-01; named for Overall Excellence in Editing, Picture of Yr. Contest, U. Mo., 1993. Office: San Jose Mercury News 750 Ridder Park Dr San Jose CA 95131-2432

MIGIRO, ASHA-ROSE, international organization official; b. Songea, Tanzania, July 9, 1956; m. Cleophas Migiro; 2 children. LLM, U. Dar es Salaam, Tanzania, 1984; LLD, U. Konstanz, Germany, 1992. Mem. faculty of law to sr. lectr. U. Dar es Salaam, head dept. constl. and adminstrv. law, 1992—94, head dept. civil and criminal law, 1994—97; min. cmty. devel., gender and children United Republic of Tanzania, min. fgn. affairs and internat. cooperation, 2006—07; dep. sec.-gen. UN, NYC, 2007—. Mem. Tanzania Law Reform Commn., 1997, UN Com. on Elimination of Discrimination against Women, 2000; pres. UN Security Coun.; chair So. African Devel. Cmty. Ministerial Com. Organ on Politics, Def. and Security Cooperation; chair Coun. of Mins.' meetings Internat. Conf. of Gt. Lakes Region. Contbr. articles to profl. jours. Office: UN First Ave at 46th St New York NY 10017

MIGLIARO, MARCO WILLIAM, electrical engineer; b. NYC, Mar. 29, 1948; s. Marco Salvatore and Anna (Dalton) M.; children: Kristen Marie, Meredith Anne, Marie Angela, Marco Thomas; m. Jasoda Badlu, Nov. 19, 1988. BEE, Pratt Inst., 1969; postgrad., N.J. Inst. Tech., 1970-72. Registered profl. engr., N.Y., N.J., Pa., Mass., Fla. Engr. Am. Electric Power, NYC, 1969-78; staff engr. Gibbs & Hill, Inc., NYC, 1978-81; sr. cons. engr. Ebasco Svcs., Inc., NYC, 1981-88; tech. mgr. ABB Impell Corp., Melville, NY, 1988-90; sr. staff specialist for nuc. engrng. Fla. Power & Light, Juno Beach, 1990-96, chief elec./I&C engr., 1996—2003; pres. ESA Cons. Engrs., PA, Jupiter, Fla., 2003—; pres., CEO IEEE Industry Stds. and Tech. Orgn., 2003—. Developer seminar on stationary batteries, 1987. Contbg. author: Handbook of Power Calculations, 1984, 99, Standard Handbook for Electrical Engineers, 1999, 2006; also articles. Recipient Meritorious Svc. award Am. Nat. Standards Inst., 1994. Fellow IEEE (pres. 2001—, stds. assn. bd. govs. 1998—, bd. dirs. 1990-92, 2001, fin. com. 1990-92, dir. stds. 1990-91, mem. exec. com. 1992, v.p. stds. activities, 1992, 2001, Stds. medal 1986, Stds. Bd. Disting. Svc. award 1993, Charles Proteus Steinmetz award 1996, Third Millennium medal 2000); mem. IEEE Power Engrng. Soc. (Disting. Svc. award 1988, 92), Industry Standards and Tech. Orgn. (bd. dirs. 2000—, chmn. 2000-03). Avocations: fishing, travel, music. Home: PO Box 9253 Jupiter FL 33468-9253 Office: ESA Cons Engrs PA PO Box 9251 Jupiter FL 33468-9251 Home Phone: 561-624-4743; Office Phone: 561-691-1946. Business E-Mail: marco@esaconsulting.com.

MIGLIAZZO, ARLIN C., history professor; b. South Gate, Calif., Sept. 20, 1951; BA, Biola U., La Mirada, Calif., 1974; MA, No. Ariz. U., Flagstaff, 1975; PhD, Washington State U., Pullman, 1982. Asst. prof. history and polit. sci. Judson Bapt. Coll., The Dalles, Oreg.; asst. to full prof. history Whitworth U., 1983—. Editor: (book) Lands of True and Certain Bounty, 2002, Teaching As An Art of Faith, 2002; author: To Make This Land Our Own, 2007. Scholar, Fulbright Found., 1990; Rsch. Fellowship, Weyerhaeuser Ctr. for Faith and Learning, 1999. Mem.: Conf. in Faith and History, Ea. Wash. State Hist. Soc., SC Hist. Soc., So. Hist. Assn., Spokane City-County Hist. Landmarks Commn., Phi Alpha Theta. Office: Whitworth U Dept History 300 W Hawthorne Rd Spokane WA 99251 Home Phone: 509-467-6198; Office Phone: 509-777-4367.

MIGLIORE, MARCUS CHARLES, lawyer; b. Rochester, NY, Apr. 12, 1961; s. Charles T. and Virginia (DeCesare) M. BA, U. Rochester, 1983; JD, George Washington U., 1986. Bar: N.Y. 1987, D.C. 1987. Law clk. to chief judge D.C. Ct. Appeals, Washington, 1986-87; assoc. Dickstein, Shapiro & Morin, Washington, 1987-92; atty. to mng. atty., legal dept. Air Line Pilots Assn., AFL-CIO, Washington, 1993—. Mem. ABA, N.Y. State Bar Assn., D.C. Bar Assn., Order of Coif, Phi Beta Kappa. Office: ALPA 1625 Massachusetts Ave NW Washington DC 20036-2212 Business E-Mail: marcus.migliore@alpa.org.

MIGNONE, MARIO B., language educator; came to U.S., 1960; m. Lois Mignone, June 29, 1968; children: Pamela Anne, Cristina Maria, Elizabeth Maria. BA, CCNY, 1967; MA, Rutgers U., 1969, PhD, 1972. Disting. prof. Italian lang. SUNY, Stony Brook, 1970—, dir. undergrad. studies, 1976-83, dir. grad. studies, 1983-87; founder, exec. dir. Ctr. for Italian Studies, chmn. French and Italian dept., Stony Brook, 1988—98. Author: The Theater of Eduardo De Filippo, 1974, Abnormality and Anguish in the Narrative of Dino Buzzati, 1981, Eduardo De Filippo, 1984, Pirandello in America, 1988, Columbus: Meeting of Cultures, 1993, Italy Today: A Country in Transition, 1995, Italy Today: At the Crossroads of the New Millennium, 1998; assoc. mng. editor Forum Italicum, 1986-94, editor, 1994—; contbr. articles to profl. jours. Mem. coll. coun. SUNY, Old Westbury. Mem. Am. Assn. Tchrs. Italian (pres. 1982-84), Assn. Italian Am. Educators (pres. 1997—), Am. Italian Hist. Assn. (nat. exec. com.). Office: SUNY Dept European Langs Lits Stony Brook NY 11794-3359 Office Phone: 631-632-7444. Business E-Mail: mmignone@notes.cc.sunysb.edu.

MIGNOT, EMMANUEL, medical researcher; Student, Ecole Normale Supérieure, Paris; MD, René Descartes Sch. Medicine, Paris V Univ., 1984; PhD, Paris VI Univ., 1984. Cert. Sleep Disorders Am. Bd. Sleep Medicine. Resident Necker Enfants Malades Hosp., Paris, 1985, intern, 1984; dir. Stanford Ctr. for Narcolepsy Stanford U. Sch. Med., 1993—, acting asst. prof. psychiatry & behavioral sciences, 1993—2001, prof. psychiatry & behavioral sciences, 2001—, assoc. prof. medicine; founder Hypnion Inc., 2000—; investigator Howard Hughes Med. Inst., 2002—. Editorial bd. Sleep, Sleep Medicine, Sleep Rsch. Online; bd. dirs. Nat. Sleep Found., chair Narcolepsy Coun.; Nat. Ctr. for Sleep Disorders adv. panel NIH. Recipient Health Rsch. award, Nat. Sleep Found., Rsch. award, NIH, Profl. Svc. award, Narcolepsy Network, Drs. C. & F. Demuth 11th award for Young Ingestigators in the Neurosciences, WC Dement Academic Achievement award, McKnight Achievement award, W. Alden Spencer award, Jacobaeus Prize. Mem.: Inst. Medicine. Achievements include discovery of cause of narcolepsy. Office: Stanford Hosp Sleep Disorders Clinic #3301 MC 5730 401 Quarry Rd Stanford CA 94305

MIGOYA, CARLOS, bank executive; b. Cuba; Grad., Fla. Internat. U., 1976. With Southeast Bank, 1974—91; pres. Consolidated Bank, 1991; with First Union Nat. Bank; pres. Miami-Dade County region Wachovia Corp., CEO Atlantic region, 2006—. Bd. dirs. Take Stock in Children, Miami-Dade County Cultural Affairs Coun., chmn., 2006; bd. dirs. Miami Bus. Forum. Office: Wachovia Corp 1 Wachovia Ctr Charlotte NC 28288-0013

MIGRO, ASHA-ROSE, international organization official; b. Songea, Ruvuma Region, Tanzania, July 9, 1956; LLB, LLM, U. Dar-es-Salaam; PhD, U. Konstanz. Sr. lectr. faculty of law U. Dar-es-Salaam; min. cmty. devel., gender & children Govt. of Tanzania, 2000—06, min. fgn. affairs & internat. cooperation, 2006—07; dep. sec.-gen. UN, NYC, 2007—. Office: UN UN Plz 46th St at First Ave New York NY 10017

MIGUE, JEAN LUC, economics professor; b. Montreal, Que., Can., Apr. 13, 1933; s. Joseph Alfred and Marie Laurence (Venne) M.; m. Renee Caron, Sept. 13, 1958; children: Paule, Pascal, Nicolas. BA in Econs, U. Montreal, 1953, MA, 1956; PhD in Econs, Am. U., 1968. Researcher Bank of Can., 1957-58; prof. Laval U., 1962-70; prof. econs. Nat. Sch. Public Adminstrn., Quebec, 1970-99. Mem. staff Econ. Coun. Can., 1973-74 Author: The Price of Health, 1974, Le Prix du Transport, 1978, Nationalistic Policies of Canada, 1979, L'Economiste et La chose Publique, 1979, The Public Monopoly of Education, 1989, Federalism and Free Trade, 1993, Etatisme et Declin du quebec, 1999, Le Monopole de La Santé, 2001, Statism and Health in France, 2005, On N'a Pas Les Gouvernements Qu'on Merite, 2006. Fellow Massey Found., 1956, sr. fellow, The Fraser Inst. Fellow Royal Soc. Can.; mem, Mont Pelerin Soc. Roman Catholic. Office Phone: 418-651-1968. E-mail: jlmigue@videotron.ca.

MIHAILA, GEORGE ANDREI, computer scientist, researcher; b. Bucharest, Romania, June 18, 1967; arrived in U.S., 2000; s. Gheorghe and Violeta Marcela Mihaila; m. Haritina Gratiela Dobrescu, Nov. 28, 2000; children: Maria, Irina Violeta. BS, U. Bucharest, 1990; MS, U. Toronto, 1996, PhD, 2000. Jr. rschr. Informatics Rsch. Inst., Bucharest, 1990—91; asst. prof. U. Bucharest, 1990—93; software engr. Omnis Group Inc., Bucharest, 1991—92, Ciel Romania, Bucharest, Romania, 1992—93, Ahearn & Soper Inc., Toronto, Canada, 1993—94; rsch. staff mem. T. J. Watson Rsch. Ctr. IBM, Hawthorne, NY, 2000—. Adj. asst. prof. Columbia U., NYC, 2002—. Author: Publishing, Locating, and Querying Networked Information Sources (award Romanian Acad., 2002). Mem.: Assn. Computing Machinery. Home: 1724 Central St Yorktown Heights NY 10598 Office: IBM TJ Watson Research Center 19 Skyline Drive Hawthorne NY 10532 Office Phone: 914-784-7803. Personal E-mail: george.mihaila@gmail.com. Business E-Mail: mihaila@us.ibm.com.

MIHAL, SANDRA POWELL, research scientist; b. Balt., Dec. 15, 1941; d. Sanford William and Mary Louise (Barry) Powell; m. James George Anderson, June 15, 1963; children: Robin Marie, James Brian, Melissa Lee, Derek Clair; m. Charles Turner Barber, Apr. 18, 1978; stepchildren: Gretchen Jayco, Katrina Hope; m. Ladislaw Paul Mihal, May 25, 1991; stepchildren: Alexander Paul, Suzie May, Natasha Elizabeth, Rudy Darius. BA, Mt. St. Agnes Coll., 1963; MA, N.Mex. State U., 1970, Purdue U., 1975; EdD, Vanderbilt U., 1990. Cert. tchr., Md. Tchr. Ridgely-Dulaney Jr. H.S., Towson, Md., 1964; grad. asst. N.Mex. State U., Las Cruces, 1967—69; acad. advisor, instr. polit. sci. Purdue U., West Lafayette, Ind., 1974—78; prof., acad. sys. analyst U. So. Ind., Evansville, 1978—82; assoc. prof., chair dept. computer info. sys. Henderson (Ky.) C.C., 1982—88; prof. computer tech., divsn. chair Anne Arundel C.C., Arnold, Md., 1988—91; sys. analyst immigration and naturalization svc. Dept. of Justice, Washington, 1991—92, sr. rsch. sys. analyst immigration and naturalization svc. Glynco, Ga., 1995—; dep. program mgr. distributed learning Fed. Law Enforcement Training Ctr., Homeland Security, Glynco, Ga., 2002—. Bd. dirs. Ind. Polit. Sci. Assn., Muncie, 1984-88, Internat. Studies Assn.-Midwest, Chgo., 86-88; pres. Ky. Acad. Computer Users' Group, Lexington, 1985-86; telecom. adv. bd. C.C. Sys., Annapolis, Md., 1990-91; computer sys. network analyst CLARC Svcs., Pt. Charlotte, Fla., 92-95; adj. prof. history and polit. sci. Edison C.C., Punta Gorda, Fla., 1993-95; spkr. in fied Author: Learning By Doing BASIC, 1983, Computers Learning By Doing, 1984; contbr. articles to profl. jours Block coord. several neighborhood assns.; computer adv. bd. Henderson County Sch., 1982-88; chmn. Newburgh (Ind.) Youth Orgn., 78-86; judge Sci. Fair, Annapolis, 1988-90; nomination bd. Ky. Higher Edn. Assn., 1989-91; mem. Charlotte Chorale, Port Charlotte, 1992-94, Peace River Power Squadron, Port Charlotte, 1994-96. Coast Guard Aux., 1995-97. Fellow, Sloan Found., 1973—75, U. Ky., 1984, Ky. Col., 2003; scholar, Md. State Tchr. Bd. Edn., 1960—63. Mem, Soc. Applied Learning Tech., Assn. Computing Machinery (v.p. 85—), Am. Legion, Pi Gamma Mu. Democrat. Mem. Ch. Of Christ. Avocations: sailing, singing, swimming, cooking, music. Home: 112 Oak Ridge Rd Brunswick GA 31523-9741 Office Phone: 912-267-2591. Business E-Mail: sandy.mihal@dhs.gov.

MIHALAS, DIMITRI MANUEL, astrophysicist, educator; b. LA, Mar. 20, 1939; s. Emmanuel Demetrious and Jean (Christo) M.; children: Michael Demetrious, Alexandra Genevieve. BA with highest honors, UCLA, 1959; MS, Calif. Inst. Tech., 1960, PhD, 1963. Asst. prof. astrophys. scis. Princeton U., 1964-67; asst. prof. physics U. Colo., 1967-68; asso. prof. astronomy and astrophysics U. Chgo., 1968-70, prof., 1970-71; adj. prof. astrogeophysics, also physics and astrophysics U. Colo., 1972-80; sr. scientist High Altitude Obs., Nat. Center Atmospheric Research, Boulder, Colo., 1971-79, 82-85; G.C. McVittie prof. astronomy U. Ill., 1985-98; astronomer Sacramento Peak Obs., Sunspot, N.Mex., 1979-82; mem. staff Los Alamos (N.Mex.) Nat. Lab., 1998—2004, fellow, 2004—. Cons. Los Alamos Nat. Lab, 1981-98; vis. prof. dept. astrophysics Oxford (Eng.) U., 1977-78; sr. vis. fellow dept. physics and astronomy Univ. Coll., London, 1978; mem. astronomy adv. panel NSF, 1972-75 Author: Galactic Astronomy, 1969, 2d edit, 1981, Stellar Atmospheres, 1970, 2d edit., 1978, Theorie des Atmospheres Stellaires, 1971, Foundations of Radiation Hydrodynamics, 1984; assoc. editor Astrophys. Jour, 1970-79, Jour. Computational Physics, 1981-87, Jour. Quantitative Spectroscopy, 1984-94; mem. editorial bd. Solar Physics, 1981-89. NSF fellow, 1959-62; Van Maanen fellow, 1962-63; Eugene Higgins vis. fellow, 1963-64; Alfred P. Sloan Found. Research fellow, 1969-71; Alexander von Humboldt Stiftung sr. U.S. scientist awardee, 1984. Mem. U.S. Nat. Acad. Sci., Internat. Astron. Union (pres. commn. 36 1976-79), Am. Astron. Soc. (pub. bd. 1995-99, mem. coun. 2000—03, Helen B. Warner prize 1974), Astron. Soc. Pacific (dir. 1975-77) Home: PO Box 806 Los Alamos NM 87544-0806 Office: Los Alamos Nat Lab X-3 MS-F644 Los Alamos NM 87545-0001 Office Phone: 505-665-4529. Business E-Mail: dmihalas@lanl.gov.

MIHALCEA, RADA FLAVIA, language educator; d. Valentina Maria Alfreda and Dumitru Mihalcea. PhD, So. Meth. U., Dallas, 2001. Asst. prof. U. North Tex., Denton, 2002—. Dir. Lang. and Info. Technologies, Denton, 2002—. Contbr. articles to profl. jours. Recipient Best Paper award, Fla. Artificial Intelligence Rsch. Soc., 1999—2000, Internat. Conf. on Intelligent Text Processing, 2007. Mem.: Assn. for Computational Linguistics. Achievements include research in lexical semantics, languages with scarce resources, graph models for natural lang. processing. Office: Univ North Tex PO Box 311366 Denton TX 76203 Office Phone: 940-369-7630.

MIHALY, EUGENE BRAMER, management consultant; b. The Hague, The Netherlands, Nov. 11, 1934; arrived in US, 1940; s. Eddy and Cecile (Bramer) Kahn; stepson of Eugene Mihaly; m. Stacey Beth Pulner, Apr. 21, 1996; children: Lisa Klee, Jessica; stepchildren: Stephanie Pulner, Andrew Pulner. AB magna cum laude, Harvard U., 1956; PhD, London Sch. Econs. and Polit. Sci., 1964. Aviation/space editor Hartford (Conn.) Courant, 1960-61; internat. economist AID, Washington, 1964-65; dep. dir. Peace Corps, Tanzania, 1966, dir., 1967-68, dep. dir. East Asia/Pacific bur. Washington, 1969, dir. office program devel., evaluation and rsch., 1969-70; assoc. dir. Inst. Internat. Studies, U. Calif., Berkeley, 1970-72; pres. Mihaly Internat. Corp., 1972—; chmn. bd. Mihaly Internat. Can., Ltd., 1992—; sr. lectr. Haas Sch. Bus. U. Calif., Berkeley, 1991-95. Adj. prof. Amos Tuck Sch. Dartmouth Coll., 1997-2002; chmn. adv. bd. Northwood Fund Mgmt. Inc. Author: Foreign Aid and Politics in Nepal: A Case Study, 1965; contbr. articles to profl. jours., chpts. to books. Chmn. emeritus Calif.-S.E. Asia Bus. Coun.; chmn. Global R.I.; dir. Common Cause R.I.; trustee CC of R.I. Found.; chmn. R.I. Pub. Radio. Mem. Coun. on Fgn. Rels. (chmn.), Appalachian Mountain Club (Narragansett chpt.). Home: 4 Half Mile Rd Barrington RI 02806 Office Phone: 401-247-1418.

MIHAN, RICHARD, retired dermatologist; b. Dec. 20, 1925; s. Arnold and Virginia Catherine (O'Reilly) M. MD, St. Louis U., 1949. Diplomate Am. Bd. Dermatology. Intern L.A. County Gen. Hosp., 1949-51, resident in dermatology, 1954-57; pvt. practice in dermatology LA, 1957-95; prof. emeritus U. So. Calif., 1989—. Lt. Comdr. USNR, 1951-53. Fellow ACP; mem. AMA, Pacific Dermatol. Assn. (exec. bd. 1971-74), Am. Acad. Dermatol., Calif. Med. Assn. (chmn. dermatol. sect. 1973-74), L.A. Met. Dermatology Soc. (pres. 1975-76), L.A. Acad. Medicine (pres. 1988-89), Order of St. John of Jerusalem, of Rhodes, and of Malta, Order of St. Lazarus (comdr.), Calif. Club. Roman Cath. Home: 3278 Wilshire Blvd Apt 503 Los Angeles CA 90010-1431

MIHICH, ENRICO, medical researcher; b. Fiume, Italy, Jan. 4, 1928; came to U.S., 1957; s. Milan and Rosina (Lenaz) M.; m. Renata Marisa Mustacchi; 1 child, Sylvia MD, Milan, Italy, 1951, docent, 1962; MD (honoris causa), U. Marseille, 1986. Research asst. Inst. Pharmacology U. Milan, Italy, 1951, asst. prof., 1954-56; vis. research fellow Sloan Kettering Inst. Cancer Research, NYC, 1952-54; head pharmacology lab. Valeas Pharm. Industry, Milan, 1954-56; sr. cancer research scientist dept. exptl. therapeutics Roswell Park Cancer Inst., Buffalo, 1957-59, assoc. cancer research scientist, 1959-66, prin. scientist, 1966-71, dir. pharm. and therapeutics and Grace Cancer Drug Ctr., 1971-2001, v.p. for sponsored programs, 1987-97; prof. pharmacology SUNY-Buffalo, 1960—, research asst., 1960-66, research assoc., 1966-68, research prof. pharmacology, 1968-69; chmn. dept. molecular pharmacology and therapeutics SUNY-Buffalo Roswell Park Divsn., 1969—2006; assoc. prof. biochem. pharmacology Sch. of Pharmacy, 1963-68, adj. prof. biochem. pharmacology, 1968-99, exec. dir. for sponsored programs, disting. mem. dept. pharmacology and therapeutics, 2001—. Cons., lectr. in field; participant numerous symposia; sci. advisor govt. agys., pvt. industry; mem. Nat. Cancer Adv. Bd., 1984-90; mem. coun. Internat. Union Against Cancer, 1998-2002; mem. bd. scientific advisors NCI, 1997-2004. Author more than 265 books, articles, chpts. in books; editor-in-chief for N.Am., China and Japan, Cancer Immunology and Immunotherapy; mem. editorial bd. Advances in Cancer Chemotherapy, Internat. Jour. Immunopharmacology, Cancer and Metastasis Revs., others; adv. editor Oncology Rsch., Selective Cancer Therapeutics jours. Recipient numerous grants for med. rsch.; Fulbright travel fellow, 1952-53, Sloan Found. fellow, 1953-54; recipient Lifetimw Sci. award Inst. Advanced Studies in Immunology and Aging, 1994; named Myron Karon Meml. lectr., 1981. Office: Grace Cancer Drug Ctr Roswell Park Cancer Inst Elm And Carlton St Buffalo NY 14263-0001 Home Phone: 716-832-5757; Office Phone: 716-845-8226. E-mail: enrico.mihich@roswellpark.org.

MIHM, JOHN CLIFFORD, chemical engineer; b. Austin, Tex., July 28, 1942; s. Clifford Henry and Adeline (Cleary) M.; m. Janet Eleanor Skales, May 29, 1964; 1 child, Mary Lynn AA, Frank Phillips Coll., 1962; BSChemE, Tex. Tech. U., 1964. Registered profl. engr., Tex., Okla. With Phillips Petroleum Co., 1964—2003, v.p. corp. engring. Bartlesville, Okla., 1987-92, v.p. R & D, 1992-93, sr. v.p. corp. tech., 1993-99, sr. v.p. tech. and project devel., 1999—2002; engr. mgr. E & P Phillips Petroleum Co., Stavanger, Norway, 1977-82; chmn. bd. Far East Energy Corp., 2005—07, vice chair. nitrogen natural gas, 2006—. Mem. adv. bd. Tex. Tech U., Lubbock, 1985—, pres. deans coun., 1996-98. Bd. dirs. Boy Scouts Am., Bartlesville, 1986—, area III pres., 1998-2002, So. region bd. dirs., 1998—. Named Disting. Engr., Tex. Tech. U., 1984; named to Okla. State U. Coll. of Engring. Arch. and Tech. Hall of Fame, 1999. Fellow ASME (ind. adv. bd. 1989-2002, found. bd. dirs. 2000—); mem. NSPE (mem. adv. bd. 1994-2002), AIChE (ECC divsn., bd. dirs. 1989-93, chmn. 1992-93), Okla. Soc. Profl. Engrs. (Outstanding Engr. in Mgmt. award 1991), Soc. Petroleum Engrs. (bd. dir., 2004-, Disting. Mem. 2000), Okla. Engring. Found. (bd. dirs., pres. 1993-97), Nat. Acad. Constrn. Republican. Roman Catholic. Home: 5413 Braemar Dr Frisco TX 75034 Home Phone: 214-705-7207; Office Phone: 972-658-8583. E-mail: jcmihmr66@aol.com.

MIHM, MARTIN CHARLES, JR., pathologist, educator; s. Martin Charles and Cecilia Matilda (Hepp) M. AB, Duquesne U., 1955; MD, U. Pitts., 1961; MA (hon.), Harvard U., Cambridge, Mass., 1990. Diplomate Am. Bd. Dermatology, Am. Bd. Pathology. Intern Mt. Sinai Hosp., NYC, 1961-62, resident in medicine, 1963-64; resident in dermatology Mass. Gen. Hosp., Boston, 1964-67, resident in Pathology, 1968-72, chief dermatopathology, 1973-94; asst. prof. pathology Harvard U. Med. Sch., Boston, 1972-75, assoc. prof., 1975-79, chief dermatopathology, 1982-93; prof. pathology Mass. Gen. Hosp.-Harvard U., Boston, 1980-93; prof., chief dermatopathology, dermatology Albany (N.Y.) Med. Coll., 1993—. Pathologist Malignant Melanoma Coop. Group, 1972—77; chmn. pathology com. Intergroup Melanoma Study, 1983—88; chief sr. adminstr. Wellman Labs., Mass. Gen. Hosp., 1985—93; cons. WHO, 1985—; adj. prof. pathology Vanderbilt U., 1989—; chmn. pathology standing com., 1991—; clin. prof. pathology Harvard Med. Sch., 1996—; sr. dermatopathologist and pathologist Mass. Gen. Hosp., 1996—; adj. prof. Thomas Jefferson Med. Sch., 2000—; prof. otolaryngology U. of Ark. Sch. of Med. Scis., 2002—. Author: Primer of Dermatopathology, 1984, 2d edit., 1992, Problematic Pigmented Lesions, 1990; co-author: Melanoma and Nevi, 1997, The Melanocytic Proliterations, 2001; editor: Lymphoproliferative Disorders of the Skin, 1986, Pathbiology and Recognition Malignant Melanoma, 1988, Dermatologia Practica, 2005; contbr. articles to med. jours.; overseer Boston Symphonic Orch., 2001—. Bd. overseers Boston (Mass.) Symphony Orch., 2001—. Served to comdr. USPHS, 1967-69. Recipient Gold Humanism award, Harvard Med. Sch., 2004. Fellow: ACP, Am. Soc. Dermatopathology, Am. Acad. Dermatology; mem.: AMA (Harvard Med. Sch. rep. to med. sch. sect. 1991), Annenberg Cir. of Dermatologic Found., Italian Assn. Ambulatory Dermatologists (hon.), Soc. of Dermatology, Mexico (hon.), Italian Soc. of Anatomic Pathology (hon.), Austrian Dermatology Soc. (hon.), Harvard Dermatology House Officer's Assn. (pres. 1982), Fort Orange Club, Albany, Harvard Club (Boston, N.Y.C.), Pi Gamma Mu, Alpha Omega Alpha. Independent. Roman Catholic. Home: 27 Chilton St Brookline MA 02446 Office: Mass Gen Hosp Warren Bldg 827 55 Fruit St Boston MA 02114 Office Phone: 617-724-1350. Business E-Mail: mmihm@partners.org.

MIHM, MICHAEL MARTIN, federal judge; b. Amboy, Ill., May 18, 1943; s. Martin Clarence and Frances Johannah (Morrissey) M.; m. Judith Ann Zosky, May 6, 1967; children— Molly Elizabeth, Sarah Ann, Jacob Michael, Jennifer Leah BA, Loras Coll., 1964; JD, St. Louis U., 1967. Asst. prosecuting atty. St. Louis County, Clayton, Mo., 1967-68; asst. state's atty. Peoria County, Peoria, Ill., 1968-69; asst. city atty. City of Peoria, Ill., 1969-72; state's atty. Peoria County, Peoria, Ill., 1972-80; sole practice Peoria, Ill., 1980-82; U.S. dist. judge U.S. Govt., Peoria, Ill., 1982—; chief U.S. dist. judge U.S. Dist. Ct. (ctrl. dist.) Ill., 1991—98. Chmn. com. internat. jud. rels. U.S. Jud. Conf., 1994—96, mem. exec. com., 1995—97, mem. com. jud. br., 1987—93, mem. com. internat. jud. rels., 1998—2002; mem. Supreme Ct. Fellows Commn., 2000—; adj. prof. law John Marshall Law Sch., 1990—. Past mem. adv. bd. Big Brothers-Big Sisters, Crisis Nursery, Peoria; past bd. dirs. Salvation Army, Peoria, W.D. Boyce council Boy Scouts Am., State of Ill. Treatment Alternatives to Street Crime, Gov.'s Criminal Justice Info. Council; past vice-chmn. Ill. Dangerous Drugs Adv. Council; trustee Proctor Health Care Found., 1991-2002. Recipient Good Govt. award Peoria Jaycees, 1978, Vincent C. Immel Alumni Merit award St. Louis U. Sch. Law, 1997, Disting. Alumnus in Pub. Svc. award Loras Coll., 2000, U.S. AID award for Outstanding Vol. Svc. in Russia, 2004. Mem. Peoria County Bar Assn. Roman Catholic. Office: US Dist Ct 204 Federal Bldg 100 NE Monroe St Peoria IL 61602-1003 Office Phone: 309-671-7113. Business E-Mail: michael_mihm@ilcd.uscourts.gov.

MIKA, JOSEPH JOHN, library director, educator; b. McKees Rocks, Pa., Mar. 1, 1948; s. George Joseph and Sophia Ann (Stec) Mika; m. Marianne Hartzell; 3 children. BA in English, U. Pitts., 1969, MLS, 1971, PhD in Libr. Sci., 1980. Asst. libr., instr. Ohio State U., Mansfield, 1971-73; asst. libr., asst. prof. Johnson State Coll., Vt., 1973-75; grad. asst., tchg. fellow Sch. Libr. and Info. Sci., U. Pitts., 1975-77; asst. dean, assoc. prof. libr. svc. U. So. Miss., Hattiesburg, 1977-86; dir. libr. and info. sci. program Wayne State U., 1986—95, 2002—, prof., 1986—. Co-owner Hartzell-Mika Consulting; cons. to librs. Editor: Jour. Edn. Libr. and Info. Sci., 1995—2005. Retired col. USAR. Decorated DSM. Mem.: ALA (councilor 1983—86, chmn. constn. and bylaws com. 1985—86, councilor 1998—2001), Mich. Ctr. for Book (chair 1994—2001), Soc. Miss. Archivists (treas., exec. bd. 1981—83), Assn. Coll. and Rsch. Librs. (chmn., chmn. budget com. 1982—83), Leadership Acad., Mich. Libr. Assn., Miss. Libr. Assn. (pres.-elect 1985, chair libr. edn. com. 1989), Assn. Libr. and Info. Sci. and Edn. (chmn. nominating com. 1982, chmn. membership com. 1982—83, exec. bd. 1986), Kiwanis (Hattiesburg), Phi Delta Kappa, Beta Phi Mu (pres-elect. 1987—89, pres. 1989—91). Home: 222 Abbott Woods Dr East Lansing MI 48823-1995 Office: Wayne State U Libr and Info Sci Program 106 Kresge Library Detroit MI 48202 Office Phone: 313-577-6196. Business E-Mail: aa2500@wayne.edu.

MIKAELIAN, TSOLINE, aerospace engineer; b. Beirut, Feb. 15, 1980; d. Hratch Kaspar Mikaelian and Alice Karapet Koucherian. BS in Space and Comm. Scis., York U., Toronto, Ont., Can., 2002; MS in Aeronautics and Astronautics, MIT, Cambridge, Mass., 2005. Tchg. asst., rschr. Atomic Physics Lab., York U., 2000—02; rschr. Spectral Applied Rsch., Inc., Concord, Ont., 2002, MIT Computer Sci. and Artificial Intelligence Lab., Cambridge, 2003—. Rsch. cons. Toyota Tech. Ctr., Inc., Cambridge, 2004—06. Contbr. articles to profl. jours. Gen. advisor Armenian Generic Benevolent Union, Young Profls. Group, Boston, 2005. Recipient Herschel prize dept. physics and astronomy, York U., 2000, Ruth Hill Meml. award, 2001, Gold medal of the Faculty of Pure and Applied Sci., 2002, Normal Bethune Coll. Master's prize for academic excellence, 2002, Academic medal, Gov. Gen. of Can., 2002; scholar, Calouste Gulbenkian Found., Portugal, 1999, 2000, 2001; Presdl. fellow, MIT, 2003, Amelia Earhart fellow, Zonta Internat. Found., 2004—05. Mem.: Can. Assn. Physicists, Am. Assn. Artificial Intelligence, MIT Enterprise Forum. Armenian Orthodox. Avocations: painting, photography, travel. Home: 70 Pacific St Apt 402A Cambridge MA 02139 Office: MIT 32 Vassar St Cambridge MA 02139 Personal E-mail: tsoline@alum.mit.edu.

MIKALSON, JON DENNIS, classics educator; b. Milw., Aug. 1, 1943; s. John Martin and Evelyn Kathryn (Heuser) M.; m. Mary Helen Villemonte, Aug. 28, 1966; children: Melissa, Jacquelyn. BA, U. Wis., 1965; postgrad., Am. Sch. Classical Studies, Athens, Greece, 1968-69; PhD, Harvard U., 1970. Asst. prof. classics U. Va., Charlottesville, 1970-75, assoc. prof., 1975-84, prof., 1984—, William R. Kenan Jr. prof. classics, 1999—, chmn. dept. classics, 1978-90. Dir. Echols Scholar Program, 1997-2000; vis. scholar Corpus Christi Coll., Cambridge, Eng., 1977-78; mem. Inst. for Advanced Study, Princeton, N.J., 1984-85; Whitehead prof. Am. Sch. Classical Studies, 1995-96. Author: The Sacred and Civil Calendar of the Athenian Year, 1975, Athenian Popular Religion, 1983, Honor Thy Gods: Popular Religion in Greek Tragedy, 1991, Religion in Hellenistic Athens, 1998, Herodotus and Religion in the Persian Wars, 2003, Ancient Greek Religion, 2004; contbr. articles to profl. and scholarly jours. James Rignall Wheeler fellow Am. Sch. Classical Studies, 1968-69, NEH fellow, 1977-78, Herodotus fellow Inst. for Advanced Study, 1984-85. Mem. Am. Philol. Assn., Am. Sch. Classical Studies, Archeol. Inst. of Am., Classical Assn. of Middle West and South (pres. so. sect. 1989-90), Classical Assn. of Va., Phi Beta Kappa, Phi Eta Sigma, Phi Kappa Phi, Omicron Delta Kappa. Clubs: Lions. Home: PO Box 664 Crozet VA 22932-0664 Office: U Va Dept Classics PO Box 400788 B002 Cocke Hall Charlottesville VA 22904-4788 Home Phone: 434-823-2163; Office Phone: 434-823-2163, 434-924-3008. Business E-Mail: jdm9x@virginia.edu.

MIKAN, G. MIKE, healthcare services company executive; Mgmt. positions, corp. devel. group UnitedHealth Group, Minnetonka, Minn., CFO specialized care svcs., 2001—04, sr. v.p. fin., 2006, exec. v.p., CFO, 2006—; pres. UnitedHealth Networks, Minnetonka, Minn., 2004—06. Bd. dirs. Make-a-Wish Found. Minn., 2004—. Office: UnitedHealth Group PO Box 1459 Minneapolis MN 55440-1459 *

MIKATA, YOZO, mechanical engineer, application developer; b. Nichinan, Miyazaki, Japan, Jan. 29, 1956; arrived in U.S., 1981; s. Chotaro and Fumiko (Kato) Mikata. BSCE, U. Tokyo, 1979, MSCE, 1981; PhD in Mech. Engring., U. Del., Newark, 1984. Postdoctoral fellow Northwestern U., Evanston, Ill., 1984-87; postgrad. rsch. engr. U. Calif., San Diego, 1987-89; rsch. assoc. U. Ill., Urbana-Champaign, 1989-90; asst. prof. Old Dominion U., Norfolk, Va., 1990-96; sr. rsch. scientist ICAM, NASA Langley Rsch. Ctr., Hampton, Va., 1996-99; software engr. Bell Atlantic Network Svcs., Silver Spring, Md., 1999-2000; structural mechanics engr. Lockheed Martin Co., Schenectady, N.Y., 2000—. Contbr. articles to profl. jours. Rsch. grantee, Engring. Found., 1992, NASA Langley Rsch. Ctr., 1993, 1994. Mem.: ASME, Am. Acad. Mechanics, Soc. Indsl. and Applied Math. Achievements include research in on micromechanics of coated fiber composite materials providing analytical solutions, and thereby contributed to the understanding of local mechanical behavior of coatings; on wave propagation, fracture mechanics, dynamic phase transformation. Avocations: swimming, dance, jazz, astronomy, number theory. Office: Lockheed Martin Co PO Box 1072 Schenectady NY 12301

MIKELL, FRANK LEONARD, cardiologist; b. Augusta, Ga., Apr. 26, 1947; s. Frank Leonard and Mary (Herndon) M.; three children. BA, Emory U., 1969; B in Med. Scis., Dartmouth Med. Sch., 1972; MD, Emory U. Med. Sch., 1974. Asst. prof. medicine U. Minn., Mpls., 1979-82; interventional cardiologist Prairie Cardiovasc. Cons., Springfield, Ill., 1982—. Clin. assoc. prof. medicine So. Ill. U. Med. Sch., Springfield, 1987—. Fellow Am. Coll. Cardiology, Am. Coll. Chest Physicians, Am. Coll. Physicians, Soc. Cardiac Angiography & Intervention, Coun. Clin. Cardiology Am. Heart Assn. Avocations: golf, hunting. Office: Prairie Cardiovasc Cons PO Box 19420 Springfield IL 62794-9420

MIKELS, RICHARD ELIOT, lawyer; b. Cambridge, Mass., July 14, 1947; s. Albert Louis and Charlotte Betty (Shapiro) M.; m. Deborah Gwen Katz, Aug. 29, 1970; children: Allison Brooke, Robert Jarrett. BS in Bus. Adminstrn., Boston U., 1969, JD cum laude, 1972. Bar: Mass. 1972, US Dist. Ct. Mass. 1974, US Ct. Appeals (1st Cir.) 1978. Legal examiner ICC, Washington, 1972-74; ptnr. Riemer & Braunstein, Boston, 1974-80; ptnr., chmn. Comml. Law Sect. Peabody & Brown, Boston, 1980-88; mem., chmn. Comml. Law Sect. Mintz, Levin, Cohn, Ferris, Glovsky and Popeo, PC, Boston, 1988—, ptnr. Contbr. articles to profl. jour.; editor: Boston U. Law Rev., 1971—72. Tng. adv. com. Jewish Vocat. Svc., Boston, 1991, 1995, 1996, bd. dir., 1995—99, vice chair microenterprise adv. com., 1997; vice chair lawyers com. Combined Jewish Philanthropies, 1994, 1995; mem. bd. visitors Boston U. Fellow Am. Coll. Bankruptcy (1st cir. regent 2005-06); mem. ABA, Am. Bankruptcy Inst. (bd. dirs. 2000-06), Assn. Comml. Fin. Attys., Comml. Law League Am., Mass. Bar Assn., Boston Bar Assn., Boston U. Law Alumni Assn. (mem. exec. com., pres. exec. com. 2000-01). Office: Mintz Levin Cohn Ferris Glovsky & Popeo PC 1 Financial Ctr Fl 39 Boston MA 02111-2657 Office Phone: 617-348-1691. Office Fax: 617-542-2241. Business E-Mail: rmikels@mintz.com.

MIKESELL, MARVIN WRAY, geography educator; b. Kansas City, Mo., June 16, 1929; s. Loy George and Clara (Wade) M.; m. Reine-Marie de France, Apr. 1, 1957. BA, UCLA, 1952, MA, 1953; PhD, U. Calif.-Berkeley, 1959. Instr. to prof. geography U. Chgo., 1958—, chmn. dept. geography, 1969-74, 83-86. Del. U.S. Nat. Commn. for UNESCO Author: Northern Morocco, 1961; editor: Readings in Cultural Geography, 1962, Geographers Abroad, 1973, Perspectives on Environment, 1974. Fellow Am. Geog. Soc. (hon.); mem. Assn. Am. Geographers (pres. 1975-76, Disting. Career award 1995). Clubs: Quadrangle. Home: 1155 E 56th St Chicago IL 60637-1530 Office: Com Geog Studies 5828 S University Ave Chicago IL 60637-1583 Office Phone: 773-702-8313. Business E-Mail: mmikesel@uchicago.edu.

MIKESELL, RICHARD LYON, lawyer, financial counselor; b. Corning, NY, Jan. 29, 1941; s. Walter Ray and Clara Ellen (Lyon) M.; m. Anna May Creese, Mar. 16, 1973; 1 child, Joel. BSChemE, U. Calif., Berkeley, 1962; LLB, Duke U., 1965; BA in Liberal Studies, UCLA, 1977. Bar: U.S. Supreme Ct. 1971, Ohio 1965, Calif. 1967, U.S. Ct. Appeals (9th cir.) 1982, U.S. Ct. Appeals (2d cir.) 1993, U.S. Patent Office 1967. Patent atty. Procter & Gamble, Cin., 1965-66, Rocketdyne divsn. N.Am. Aviation, LA, 1966-69; pvt. practice law LA, 1969-81; prin. Law Offices of R.L. Mikesell, LA, 1981—. Fin. counselor L.A. Police Dept., 1986—; arbitrator Am. Arbitration Assn., L.A., 1980—. Pres. San Fernando Valley Fair Housing Coun., L.A., 1969-72, Valley Women's Ctr., L.A., 1990; line res. officer L.A. Police Dept., 1969-72. Named Res. Officer of Yr. L.A. Police Dept., 1990, 98; recipient 1st Place award Nat. SPAM Recipe Contest, 1998. Avocation: target rifle shooting. Office: Law Offices of R L Mikesell 14827 Ventury Blvd Ste 216 Sherman Oaks CA 91403 Home Phone: 818-995-4010; Office Phone: 818-376-0376. Personal E-mail: richlyon6713@sbcglobal.net.

MIKHAILOV, STEPAN FEDOROVICH, physicist, researcher; b. Norilsk, Krasnoyarsk region, Russia, Nov. 29, 1960; arrived in US, 2000; s. Feodor K. and Valentina M. Mikhailov; m. Natalia A. Makhanova, June 8, 2000; 1 child, Andrei M. Makhanov. MS, Novosibirsk State Tech. U., Russia, 1982. Rsch. scientist Budker Inst. Nuc. Physics, Novosibirsk, 1982—2000; sr. rsch. scientist FEL Lab. Duke U., Durham, NC, 2000—. Office: Duke U DFEL Lab PO Box 90319 LaSalle St Extension Durham NC 27708-0319 Home: Apt K 103 Misty Woods Cir Chapel Hill NC 27514 Office Phone: 919-660-2647. Office Fax: 919-660-2671. Business E-Mail: smikhail@fel.duke.edu.

MIKHELSON, SERGEI, mathematician, educator; b. Saint Petersburg, Russia, May 17, 1970; s. Stanislav and Eleonora (Guretskaya) Mikhelson. BA, Russian State Pedagogical U., St. Petersburg, Russia, 1993; MA, Russian State Pedagogical U., 1993, Columbia U., NYC, 1994. Math. and logic tchr. Gymnasia 56, St. Petersburg, Russia, 1991—97; program dir., dept. head Ctr. of Alternative Edn., St. Petersburg, 1994—98; vice-prin. Gymnasia 56, St. Petersburg, 1995; math. adj. instr. NYU, NYC, 1999—2005, Borough of Manhattan C.C., NYC, 1998—2001; math. tchr. Bklyn Friends Sch., 2002—. Internat. debate trainer Internat. Debate Edn. Assn., NYC, 1998—2002. Co-author (publication) Mathematics Education in Russia. Mem.: Nat. Coun. of Tchrs. of Math. Home Phone: 718-259-8444. Business E-Mail: ssm21@columbia.edu.

MIKIEWICZ, ANNA DANIELLA, marketing and international business export manager; b. Chgo., Dec. 22, 1960; d. Zdislaw and Lucy (Magnusweska) M. BS in Mktg., Elmhurst Coll., 1982; postgrad., Triton Coll. Asst. to midwestern regional mgr. Melster Pub. Co., Chgo., 1983; sales rep. First Impressions, Elk Grove, Ill., 1984; asst. to Midwestern dist. mgr. Airco Ind. Gases, Broadview, Carol Stream, Ill., 1985; customer svc. & ops. mgr. Yamazen USA, Inc., Schaumburg, Ill., 1985-88; nat. sales & mktg. coord. Kitamura Machinery U.S.A. Inc., 1988-95; mktg. mgr. Beth Lee Boutique, 1995-97; internat. bus. export control sales coord. MHI Machine Tool USA, Inc. subs. Mistubishi Heavy Industries, 1997-99; internat. bus. asst. to exec. v.p. sales America Excel, Inc., Elk Grove Village, Ill., 1999—; internat. bus. Brazil Market JST Sales Am., Inc., Waukegan, Ill., 2000—04; internat. export bus. mgr. global worldwide market Anixter, Inc., 2005—. Named Chgo. Polish Queen Polish Am. Culture Club, 1983-84. Mem.: NAFE. Republican. Roman Catholic.

MIKITKA, GERALD PETER, brokerage house executive, consultant; s. Michael and Helen Mikitka; m. Nancy Mikitka, 1977; children: Richard, Jeffrey, Jennifer. BSBA in Fin., Roosevelt U., 1966, postgrad., 1967. Diplomate: registered investment advisor. Sr. investment exec. Shearson Hammill & Co., Chgo., 1967-73; chmn., pres. Capital Directions, Inc., Chgo., 1973—. Pres. CDI Fin. Advisors, Chgo., 1974—, CDI Properties, Chgo., 1974—, CDI Communications, Inc., Chgo., 1978—, A.B. Properties Inc., Chgo., 1986—, Am. Eagle Realty Inc., Chgo., 1988—, Grand Caribbean Properties Inc., Chgo., 1988, Cain Estates Inc., Chgo., 1988—, Caribbean Sea Properties Inc., Chgo., 1989—. Served with U.S. Army, 1967-69. Mem. Nat. Assn. Securities Dealers, Securities Investment Protection Assn., Broadcast Fin. Mgmt. Assn., Nat. Radio Broadcast Assn., Internat. Assn. Fin. Planning. Lodges: Rotary.

MIKOLAJCZYK, MARK S., publishing executive; b. 1961; Grad., Rochester U., 1982. Prodn. coord. to night ops. mgr. USA Today, 1982—84; spl. projects mgr. Cin. Enquirer, 1984—87; prodn. dir. Times Herald, Port Huron, Mich., 1987—89; v.p. prodn. Cin. Enquirer, 1989—96; dir. prodn. Gannett Co. Newspaper Div., 1996, v.p. prodn., 1997—2003, sr. v.p. ops., 2003—05; pres., CEO Detroit Newspaper Partnership, Mich., 2005—06; pres., publisher Fla. Today, Melbourne, 2006—. Named Corp. Staffer of Yr., Gannett Co., Inc., 2002. Office: Florida Today PO Box 419000 Melbourne FL 32941-9000 Office Phone: 321-242-3500.

MIKSIS, CHRISTINA BARBARA, psychologist; b. Elmhurst, Ill., Jan. 17, 1971; d. Albert Charles Miksis and Regina Vyga Suhr. BS, U. Iowa, 1993; MA, Ill. Sch. Profl. Psychology, 1997, D in Psychology, 2001. Lic. clin. psychologist Ill. Bd. Regulations, 2002. Asst. clin. dir. The MENTA Group, Inc./Fox Tech, North Aurora, Ill., 2002—03; clin. dir. The MENTA Group, Inc/Fox Tech, 2003—04; outpatient coord., clin. tng. coord. Alexian Ctr. Mental Health, Arlington Heights, 2004—. Mem.: APA. Home Phone: 773-227-0734. E-mail: christina.miksis@abnwmhc.net.

MIKULSKI, BARBARA ANN, senator; b. Balt., July 20, 1936; d. William and Christine (Kutz) M. BA in Sociology, Mt. St. Agnes Coll., 1958; MSW, U. Md., 1965; LLD (hon.), Goucher Coll., 1973, Hood Coll., 1978, Bowie State U., 1989, Morgan State U., 1990, U. Mass., 1991; DHL (hon.), Pratt Inst., 1974. Tchr. Vista Tng. Ctr. Mount St. Mary's Sem., Balt.; social worker Balt. Dept. Social Services, 1961-63, 66-70; mem. Balt. City Council, 1971-76, 95th-99th Congresses from 3d Md. Dist., 1977-87; US Senator from Md., 1987—; sec. Dem. Conf. 104th-106th Congress. Adj. prof. Loyola Coll., 1972-76; mem. U.S. Senate labor and human resources com., 1987—, ranking mem. subcom. on aging, 1993—; mem. appropriations com., 1987, ranking mem. subcom. on vets., housing, and ind. agys., 1987—. Bd. visitors U.S. Naval Acad.; bd. adv. Space Awareness Alliance. Recipient Nat. Citizen of Yr. award Buffalo Am.-Polit. Eagle, 1973, Woman of Yr. Bus. & Profl. Women's Club Assn., 1973, Outstanding Alumnus U. Md. Sch. Social Work, 1973, Govt. Social Responsibility award, 1991, Disting. Svc. award Ctrl. and East European Coalition, 1996, Louis D. Brandeis award Baltimore, Md. Zionist Dist., 1996, Public Svc. award Am. Inst. Aeronautics and Astronautics, 1998, Order of Merit Commanders Cross with Star Govt. Poland, 2001, Good Housekeeping/Wyeth award women's health, 2002, Connie Mack Lifetime Avhievement award Susan G. Komen Breast Cancer Found., 2003, Elmer P. Martin Public Svc. award Great Blacks in Wax Mus., 2003, Public Svc. award Emergency Nurses Assn., 2004, Nat. Leadership award Big Brothers and Big Sisters of Ctrl. Md., 2005. Mem. LWV. Democrat. Roman Catholic. Office: US Senate 503 Hart Sen Office Bldg Washington DC 20510-0001 also: Brown's Wharf Ste 400 1629 Thames St Baltimore MD 21231 Office Phone: 202-224-4654, 410-962-4510. Office Fax: 202-224-8858, 410-962-4760. *

MIKUMO, AKIKO, lawyer; BA, U. Calif., Berkeley, 1978; JD, NYU, 1982. Assoc. Weil, Gotshal & Manges LLP, NYC, 1982—90, ptnr., 1990—, head U.S. practice London, 1998—2002. Mem.: ABA (mem. com. on corp. law 1993—), Assn. of the Bar of the City of N.Y. (com. Asian affairs). Office: Weil Gotshal & Manges LLP 767 Fifth Ave New York NY 10153 Office Phone: 212-310-8000.

MIKUS, ELEANORE ANN, artist; b. Detroit, July 25, 1927; d. Joseph and Bertha (Englot) M.; m. Richard Burns, July 6, 1949 (div. 1963); children: Richard, Hillary, Gabrielle. Student, Mich. State U., 1946-49, U. Mex., summer 1948; B.F.A., U. Denver, 1957, MA, 1967; postgrad., Art Students League, 1958, NYU, 1959-60. Asst. prof. Cornell U., Ithaca, NY, 1979-80, assoc. prof., 1980-92, prof. art, 1992-94, prof. emerita, 1994—. Asst. prof. art Monmouth Coll., West Long Branch, N.J., 1966-70, prof. Cornell, Rome, 1989; vis. lectr. painting Cooper Union, N.Y.C., 1970-72, Central Sch. Art and Design, London, 1973-77, Kensington Inst., London, 1974-77, Harrow (Eng.) Coll. Tech. and Art, 1975-76. One-woman shows include Pace Gallery, NYC, 1963-65, O.K. Harris Gallery, NYC, 1971-74, Baskett Gallery, Cin., 1982, 84-85, Claudia Carr Gallery, 1998—, Mitchell Algus Gallery, NYC, 1998, 2003-04, The Drawing Ctr., NYC, 2006-07; represented in permanent collections including Met. Mus. Art, NYC, Mus. Modern Art, NYC, Whitney Mus., NYC, LA County Mus., Cin. Mus., Birmingham Mus. Art, Ala., Norton Simon Mus., Pasadena, Bklyn. Mus., Honolulu Acad. Arts, Indpls. Mus. Art, Nat. Gallery Art, Washington, Victoria and Albert Mus., London, Libr. of Congress, Washington, Tucson Mus. of Art, Blanton Mus. U. Tex., U. Ariz. Mus. Art, Tucson, Univ. Ariz., Tucson, De Cordova Mus., Lincoln, Mass.; subject of book Eleanore Mikus, Shadows of the Real (by Robert Hobbs and Judith Bernstock), 1991. Fellow, Guggenheim, 1966—67, Tamarind, 1968, McDowell, 1969, Yaddo drawing and painting, 2004. Home: PO Box 4775 Ithaca NY 14852-4775 Office: Cornell U Dept Art Tjaden Hall Ithaca NY 14853 also: 270 Luce Rd Groton NY 13073-9747 Office Phone: 607-533-7766. Personal E-mail: mikusart44@hotmail.com.

MIKVA, ABNER JOSEPH, lawyer, retired judge; b. Milw., Jan. 21, 1926; s. Henry Abraham and Ida (Fishman) M.; m. Zoe Wise, Sept. 19, 1948; children: Mary, Laurie, Rachel. JD cum laude, U. Chgo., 1951; DL (hon.), U. Ill., 1980, Am. U., 1991, Northwestern U., 1991, Tulane U., 1993, Ill. Inst. Tech., 1997, Santa Clara U., 2000, Wm. Mitchell Coll. Law, 2001; DHL (hon.), Hebrew U., 1989, U. Wis., 1995, De Paul U. Law Sch., 2002, So. Ill. U., 2006. Bar: Ill. 1951, D.C. 1978. Law clk. to Hon. Sherman Minton U.S. Supreme Ct., 1951; ptnr. Devoe, Shadur, Mikva & Plotkin, Chgo., 1952-68, D'Ancona, Pflaum, Wyatt & Riskind, 1973-74; lectr. Northwestern U. Law Sch., Chgo., 1973-75, U. Pa. Law Sch., 1983-85, Georgetown Law Sch., 1986-88, Duke U. Law Sch., Durham, NC, 1990-91, U. Chgo. Law Sch., 1992-93; mem. Ill. Gen. Assembly from 23d Dist., 1956-66, 91st-92d Congresses from 2d Dist. Ill., 94th-96th Congresses from 10th Dist. Ill., mem. ways and means com., judiciary com.; chmn. Dem. Study Group, 1979; judge U.S. Ct. Appeals (D.C. cir.), 1979-94; chief judge U.S. Ct. Appeals (D.C. cir), 1991-94; counsel to the Pres. The White House, Washington, 1994-96; arbitrator JAMS, Inc., 1997—. Vis. prof., Walter Schaefer chair in pub. policy U. Chgo., 1996-98; vis. prof. U. Ill. Coll. Law, 1998-2000, U. Chgo., 2000—. Author: The American Congress: The First Branch, 1983, The Legislative Process, 1995, An Introduction to Statutory Interpretation, 1997. With USAAF, WWII. Sr. fellow Inst. Govt. & Pub. Affairs U. Ill., 1998-2000; recipient Page One award Chgo. Newspaper Guild, 1964, Best Legislator award Ind. Voters Ill., 1956-66, Alumni medal U. Chgo., 1996, Paul Douglas Ethics in Govt. award, 1998, Thurgood Marshall award, ABA, 2005; named one of Ten Outstanding Young Men in Chgo., Jr. Assn. Commerce and Industry, 1961. Fellow Am. Acad. Arts and Scis.; mem. ABA, Chgo. Bar Assn. (bd. mgrs. 1962-64), D.C. Bar Assn., Am. Law Inst., U.S. Assn. Former Mems. Congress, Order of Coif, Phi Beta Kappa. Home: Ph 6 5020 S Lake Shore Dr Chicago IL 60615-3253 Home Phone: 773-241-5048; Office Phone: 773-834-5852. Business E-Mail: amikva@law.uchicago.edu.

MILAM, CATHY P., dermatologist; b. June 24, 1960; Degree, U. Fla., Gainesville, 1980; MD, U. South Fla., Tampa, 1984. Pvt. practice dermatology, Sarasota, Fla., 1989—. Fellow: Am. Acad. Dermatology; mem.: Fla. Med. Assn. Office: 1750 Osprey Ave Sarasota FL 34239

MILAM, JOHN DANIEL, pathologist, educator; b. Kilgore, Tex., May 22, 1933; s. Ott G. and Effie (White) Milam; m. Carol Jones, Aug. 1, 1959; children: Kay, Beth, John Daniel, Julie. BS, La. State U., 1955, MS, 1957, MD, 1960. Attending pathologist St. Luke's Episcopal Hosp., Houston, 1967—89, chief of staff, 1981—83; emeritus Tex. Children's Hosp., Houston, 2000—; adj. prof. lab. medicine M.D. Anderson Cancer Ctr., U. Tex., Houston, 1990—2001; prof. pathology and lab. medicine U. Tex. Med. Sch., Houston, 1989—2001, prof. emeritus, 2001—; active med. staff Hermann Hosp., Houston, 1988—, med. dir. lab. svcs., 1990—95; chief pathology Lyndon B. Johnson Gen. Hosp., Houston, 1995—2001. Trustee Am. Bd. Pathology, 1985—96, pres., 1995, life trustee, 1996—; cons. in field. Contbr. articles and abstracts to profl. jours., chapters to books. Bd. dirs. Greater Houston area chpt. ARC, 1978—. Recipient Disting. Physician award, Hermann Hosp., 1996. Mem.: Houston Soc. Clin. Pathologists (pres. 1975, Harlan J. Spjut award 2003), Am. Soc. Clin. Pathologists (Commn. on Continuing Edn. Disting. Svc. award 1993, Israel Davidsohn Disting. Svc. award 2001), Tex. Soc. Pathologists (pres. 1978, George T. Caldwell award 1981), Am. Assn. Blood Banks (pres. 1984, Disting. Svc. award 1988). Republican. Baptist. Home: 11927 Arbordale Ln Houston TX 77024-5001 Office: U Tex Houston Med Sch Rm 2-022 Dept Pathology 6431 Fannin St Houston TX 77030-1501 Office Phone: 713-500-5336. Business E-Mail: john.d.milam@uth.tmc.edu.

MILAM, LYNNE MORGAN, special education educator; b. Harlan, Ky., Oct. 19, 1943; d. James T. and Dorothy O. Morgan; m. Jon Milam, June 20, 1970; 1 child, Morgan M. Cressman. BA with distinction in Edn., U. Ky., Lexington, 1967; MA in Spl. Edn., West Ga. Coll., Carrollton, 1990. Cert. tchr. speech grades 7-12 Ky., 1967, Ga., 1989, tchr. learning disabilities grades K-12 Ga., 1991. Tchr. English/speech Loyall Jr. H.S., Ky., 1966—73; tchr. speech/drama James A. Cawood H.S., Harlan, 1969—73; tchr. learning disabilities The Bedford Sch., Fairburn, Ga., 1985—. Named one of Outstanding Young Women in Am, 1967, 1970; recipient Outstanding Young Ky. Speech Tchr., Ky. Assn. Comm. Arts, Lexington, 1969, Outstanding Harlan County Educator, Harlan County Jaycees, 1970. Mem.: Orton Dyslexia Assn., Ga. Coun. Tchrs. of English, Phi Kappa Phi. Republican. Christian. Avocations: reading, writing, singing. Office: The Bedford Sch 5665 Milam Rd Fairburn GA 30213 Business E-Mail: lmilam@thebedfordschool.org.

MILAM, WILLIAM BRYANT, former ambassador, senior policy scholar; b. Bisbee, Ariz., July 24, 1936; s. Burl Vivian and Alice Vera (Pierce) M.; step-children: Erika, Fred. AB, Stanford U., 1959; MA, U. Mich., 1970; postgrad., Am. U., 1973. Polit. officer Dept. State, Washington, 1967-69; fin. economist Dept. State and Am. Embassy, Washington and London, 1970-75; energy economist Dept. State, Washington, 1975-77, dep. office dir., 1977-80, office dir., 1980-83; dep. chief of mission Am. Embassy, Yaounde, Cameroon, 1983-85; dep. asst. sec. Dept. State, Washington, 1985-90; U.S. amb. to Bangladesh, 1990-93; spl. negotiator oceans environ. sci. Dept. State, Washington, 1993-95; chief of mission Am. Embassy, Monrovia, Liberia, 1995-98, U.S. amb. to Pakistan, Islamabad, 1998-2001; with Woodrow Wilson Internat. Ctr. for Scholars, 2002—. Calif. State scholar, 1956-59; recipient James Clement Dunn award Dept. of State, 1981, Superior Honor award, 1983, Pres.'s Meritorious Svc. award U.S. Govt., 1990, Pres. Outstanding Svc. award, 1991. Avocations: reading, golf, writing. Office: One Woodrow Wilson Plz 1300 Pennsylvania Ave NW Washington DC 20004 Business E-Mail: william.milam@wilsoncenter.org.

MILANA-PANOPOULOS, MARIA, artist, inventor, model; b. Oceanside, NY, Nov. 13, 1965; d. Thomas F. and Angelina M. Milana; m. S. Michael Panopoulos, May 1988; children, Thomas, Nicholas Student, Kingsborough CC, Manhattan Beach, NY, 1983—84, Nassau CC, Garden City, NY, 1984—85. Cert. herbologist Herbal Healer Acad. Freelance model, NY, 1981—, Fla.; owner Artistic Creations, 2006—, Custom Faux You!, 2006—, Mia Milana Collections, 2006—. Mem. adv. bd. Trinity Oaks Homeowners Assn., New Port Richey, Fla., 1992-93. Mem. Tarpon Springs Art Assn. (bd. dirs. 1998—), Herbal Healer Acad. Republican. Roman Catholic. Achievements include patent for knee brace. Mailing: PO Box 1234 Elfers FL 34680 Business E-Mail: cre8tive@tampabay.rr.com.

MILANDER, HENRY MARTIN, educational consultant; b. Northampton, Pa., Apr. 17, 1939; s. Martin Edward and Margaret Catherine (Makovetz) M.; children: Martin Henry, Beth Ann. BS summa cum laude, Lock Haven U., Pa., 1961; MA, Bowling Green State U., Ohio, 1962; EdS (Future Faculty fellow 1964), U. No. Iowa, 1965; EdD, Ill. State U., Normal, 1967. Instr. Wartburg Coll., Waverly, Iowa, 1962-64; asst. prof. Ill. State U., 1966-67; dean instrn. Belleville (Ill.) Area Coll., 1967-69; v.p. acad. affairs Lorain County Community Coll., Elyria, Ohio, 1969-72; pres. Olympic Coll., Bremerton, Wash., 1972-87, Northeastern Jr. Coll., Sterling, Colo., 1988-95; ednl. cons., 1995—. Pres. Bremers, Inc., 1986-87. Contbr. articles to profl. jours. Pres. Kitsap County Comprehensive Health Planning Council, 1975-76; pres. Logan County Colo. United Way, 1992-93. Recipient Faculty Growth award Wartburg Coll., 1963, Cmty. Svc. award, 1975, Chief Thunderbird award, 1985. Mem. Am. Assn. C.C., Am. Assn. Sch. Adminstrs., N.W. Assn. Cmty. and Jr. Colls., Wash. Assn. C.C. (pres. 1984-85), Wash. C.C. Computing Consortium (chmn. bd. dirs. 1985-87), Puget Sound Naval Bases Assn. (pres. 1982-86), Wash. Assn. C.C. Pres. (pres. 1984-85), Bremerton Area C. of C. (pres. 1977-78), Colo. Assn. C.C. Pres. (pres. 1993-94), Rotary (pres. Sterling Club 1992-93), Kappa Delta Pi, Phi Delta Kappa. Lutheran. Home: 709 E Pointes Dr West Shelton WA 98584-6305

MILANICH, JERALD THOMAS, archaeologist, writer, curator; b. Painesville, Ohio, Oct. 13, 1945; s. John Joseph and Jean Marie (Bales) M.; m. Maxine L. Margolis, Dec. 20, 1970; 1 child, Nara Bales. BA, U. Fla., 1967, MA, 1968, PhD, 1971. Fellow Smithsonian Inst., Washington, 1971-72; asst. prof. anthropology U. Fla., Gainesville, 1972-75; asst. curator Fla. Mus. Natural History, 1975-77, assoc. curator, 1977-81, chmn. dept. anthropology, 1981-83, 91-94, curator, 1981—. Author: (with Samuel Proctor) Tacachale -- Essays on the Indians of Florida and Southeastern Georgia During the Historic Period, 1978; (with Charles Fairbanks) Florida Archaeology, 1980; McKeithen Weeden Island, 1984; Early Prehistoric Southeast, 1985; (with Susan Milbrath) First Encounters, Spanish Explorations in the Caribbean and the United States, 1492-1570, 1989; The Hernando de Soto Expedition, 1990; Earliest Hispanic-Native America Interactions in the Greater American Southwest, 1991; (with Charles Hudson) Hernando de Soto and the Indians of Florida, 1993, Archaeology of Precolumbian Florida, 1994, Florida Indians and the Invasion of Europe, 1995, The Timucua, 1996, Archaeology of Northern Florida, 1997, Florida Indians From Ancient Times to the Present, 1998, Laboring in the Fields of the Lord: Spanish Missions and Southeastern Indians, 1999, 2006, Famous Florida Sites: Mount Royal and Crystal River, 1999, (with Theodore Morris) Florida's Lost Tribes: Through the Eyes of an Artist, 2004, Frolicking Bears Wet Vultures and Other Oddities: A New York City Journalist in Nineteenth Century Florida, 2005; mem. editl. bd.: Archaeology Mag., 1992-2002, contbg. editor, 2002—. Trustee Archeol. Inst. Am., 2004—. Recipient Ripley P. Bullen award, 1980, Rembert Patrick Book award, 1994-95, James Mooney Book award, 1995, medal Fla. Acad. Sci., 2004, Lifetime Achievement award Fla. Archeol. Coun., 2005; grantee NSF, 1970-71, 73-75, 77-82, 2003, Wentworth Found., 1976-77, 81-84, 91, NEH, 1985, 87-89, Fla. Divsn. Hist. Resources, 1981, 83-89, 91, 96-97, 00-02, 03-04. Mem. Soc. Am. Archaeology (exec. bd. 1990-93), Soc. Profl. Archeologists (cert., pres. 1981-82), So. Anthrop. Soc., S.E. Archeol. Conf. (pres. 1986-88). Office: Fla Mus Natural History Gainesville FL 32611-7800

MILANO, ADAM, film company executive; b. July 17, 1978; Student, U. So. Calif. Intern Columbia Pictures, Culver City, Calif., dir. devel. Achievements include invention of acting as studio executive on such films as Gridiron Gang, The Grudge 2 and Monster House, as well as the upcoming releases Vantage Point and 30 Days of Night. Office: Columbia Pictures 10202 W Washington Blvd Culver City CA 90232 *

MILASKI, JOHN JOSEPH, management consultant; b. Johnson City, NY, Sept. 16, 1959; s. John Walter and Nellie Joan (Panaro) Milaski; m. Ann Mildred Caldwell, Jan. 22, 1994; children: Ian Alexander, Isaac Nicholas, Natalie Ann. AAS, Broome C.C., 1979; BSEE, Rochester Inst.

Tech., 1984; MBA, Syracuse U., 1991. Registered engr., N.Y.; cert. bus. transformation cons. Design engr. IBM, Endicott, NY, 1979-84, systems engr., 1984-85, mktg. cons., 1985-91, cons. Cons. & Sys. Integration Svcs. upstate N.Y., 1992-94, cons. Worldwide Document Mgmt. Solutions Group, 1995-96, con. Worldwide Cons. Svcs., 1996-99; prin. IBM WW BT Cons. Svcs., 2000—. Ga. state advisor to Nat. Rep. Senatorial Com., 1997. Inventor. Vol. IBM Olympic Force Team 1996 Summer Olympics; trust mgr. Nat. Trust for Hist. Preservation; charter mem., life mem. Statue of Liberty-Ellis Island Found., Inc.; charter mem. Nat. WWII Meml.; founding mem. Nat. Wall of Tolerance; charter mem. Nat. D-Day Mus.; active IBM Corp. Tech. Leadership Coun.; life mem. Republican Nat. Com.; mem. presdl. victory team Rep. Nat. Com. Recipient Utilities Industry Mktg. Excellence award IBM Systems Engrng. Symposium, 1989, 91. Mem. IEEE (sr.), ASME (sr.), Am. Mgmt. Assn., Am. Prodn. and Inventory Control Soc. (sr.), Internat. Platform Assn., Computer and Automated Sys. Assn., NY State Sheriff's Assn., Ga. State Sheriff's Assn., Ga. State Troopers Assn., U.S. Holocaust Meml. Mus. (charter), IBM 100 Percent Club, U.S. C. of C., Internat. Directory of Disting. Leadership, Nat. Mus. of the Am. Indian (charter), Nat. WWII Meml. Soc. (charter), Am. Battle Monuments Commn. (charter), Libr. Congress (charter), Nat. Trust for Historic Preservation, Centennial Olympic Pk. Atlanta (constructing donor). Republican. Roman Catholic. Avocations: skiing, travel, boating. Home: 2315 Sagramore Pl Cape Coral FL 33914-2571

MILAZZO, DAVID ANTHONY, mathematics educator; b. Buffalo, Aug. 29, 1982; s. Sam and MaryEllen Milazzo. BS in Math., Buffalo State Coll., 2003, MS in Math. Edn., 2006. Cert. secondary math. edn. N.Y. State. Tchr. Lake Shore HS, Angola, NY, 2005—06, Orchard Pk., 2006—07. With SUNY Niagra County CC, 2004—, D'Youville Coll., NY, 2006—. Recipient Legacy scholarship, Buffalo State Alumni Assn., 2003, Buffalo State Coll. Honors Program scholarship, Buffalo State Honors Program, 2000—03; scholar Balanced Man award and scholarship, Sigma Phi Epsilon, 2000. Mem.: Nat. Coun. Tchrs. of Math., Am. Math. Assn., Math. Assn. of Am., Omicron Delta Kappa (treas. 2002—03), Kappa Delta Pi. Home: 59 Gary Ln Buffalo NY 14227 Home Phone: 716-656-9862. Personal E-mail: milada89@mail.buffalostate.edu.

MILBERG, JOACHIM, retired automotive executive; b. 1943; Doctorate in prodn. engring., Tech. U. Berlin, 1971. Head automatic lathe divsn. Werkzeugmaschinenfabrik Gildemeister AG, 1978; prof. machine tools and ops. rsch. Munich Tech. U., 1981; mem. bd. mgmt. in charge of prodn. BMW, 1993, ret. chmn. bd. mgmt., 1999—2002, dir.; ret. CEO BMW A.G., 1999—2002. Mem. audit review com. Deere and Co., mem. corp. governance com.; dir. Allianza A.G., Festo A.G., MAN A.G. Achievements include raced in the 24hrs of LeMans and won with the BMW LMR.

MILBOURNE, WALTER ROBERTSON, lawyer; b. Phila., Aug. 27, 1933; s. Charles Gordon and Florie Henderson (Robertson) M.; m. Georgena Sue Dyer, June 19, 1965; children: Gregory Broughton, Karen Elizabeth, Walter Robertson, Margaret Henderson AB, Princeton U., 1955; LL.B., Harvard U., 1958. Bar: Pa. 1959. Assoc. firm Pepper, Hamilton & Sheetz, Phila., 1959-65, Obermayer, Rebmann, Maxwell & Hippel, Phila., 1965-67, ptnr., 1968-84, Saul, Ewing, Remick & Saul, 1984-2000, of counsel, 2001—. Bd. dir. Phila. Reins. Corp.; co-chmn. Nat. Conf. Lawyers and Collection Agys., 1979-90; chmn. bus. litigation com. Def. Rsch. Inst., 1986-89, mem. law instsn. com., 1989-95; mem. panel of disting. neutrals CPA Inst. Dispute Resolution, 2000- Chmn. mental health budget sect. Phila. United Fund, 1967—70; pres. Found. Internat. Assn. Def. Counsel, 1997—2001. Fellow: Am. Coll. Trial Lawyers (mem. internat. com. 1992—96); mem.: ABA, Phila. Bar Assn., Pa. Bar Assn., Phila. Lawn Tennis Assn. (pres. 1969—70), Merion Cricket Club. Republican. Home: 689 Fernfield Cir Wayne PA 19087-2002 Office: Saul Ewing LLP 3800 Centre Sq W Philadelphia PA 19102 Office Phone: 215-972-1975. Personal E-mail: Waltermilb@aol.com.

MILBRATH, ROBERT HENRY, retired petroleum industry executive; b. Apr. 17, 1912; s. Paul and Mabel (Volkman) M.; m. Margaret Ripperger, Jan. 19, 1940; children: Robert S., Constance, Susan. BS, U.S. Naval Acad., 1934. With Standard Oil Co. N.J., 1934-74; v.p., gen. mgr. Esso Sociedad Anonima Petrolera Argentina, 1938-42, 45-50; area contact East Coast South Am., mktg. coordination, 1950-52; dir. Internat. Petroleum Co., 1954—, v.p., 1956; v.p., dir. Esso Export Corp. N.Y., 1957-59, exec. v.p., dir., 1959-61; pres., dir. chmn. exec. com. Esso Internat., Inc. (formerly Esso Export Corp.), 1961-66; exec. v.p. Esso Europe, 1966-68; logistics coordinator Standard Oil Co. (N.J.) (now Exxon Corp.), 1968-69, dir., v.p., 1969-70, dir., sr. v.p., 1970-73, ret., 1974. Cons. Boys Clubs Am., 1978-84. Served to lt. comdr. USNR; asst. naval attache 1942, Buenos Aires; chief Latin Am. sect. Army-Navy Petroleum Bd. 1943-45, Washington. Mem. U.S. Naval Acad. Alumni Assn. Clubs: U. (N.Y.C.). Republican. Home: Apt 3221 5200 SW 25th Blvd Gainesville FL 32608 Personal E-mail: rmil@gator.net.

MILBRETT, TIFFENY CARLEEN, professional soccer player; b. Portland, Oreg., Oct. 23, 1972; Degree in comms. mgmt., U. Portland. Mem. U.S. Women's Nat. Soccer Team; profl. soccer player N.Y. Power, 2001—03. Mem. championship team, Montricoux, France, 1993. Named World Cup Champion, 1999; recipient Gold medal, Centennial Olympic Games, 1996, 3d place medal, 1995, Silver medal, World Univ. Games, 1993, Sydney Olympic Games, 2000. Office: c/o US Soccer Fedn 1801 S Prairie Ave # 1811 Chicago IL 60616-1319

MILBURN, RICHARD HENRY, physics professor; b. Newark, June 3, 1928; s. Richard Percy and Lucy Elizabeth (Karr) M.; m. Nancy Jeannette Stafford, Aug. 25, 1951; children— Sarah Stafford, Anne Douglas. AB, Harvard U., 1948, A.M., 1951, PhD, 1954. Instr. Harvard U., Cambridge, Mass., 1954, 56-57, asst. prof., 1957—61; assoc. prof. physics Tufts U., Medford, Mass., 1961-65, prof., 1965-98, John Wade prof., 1990-98, rsch. prof., 1998—2003, prof. emeritus, 2003. Fulbright lectr., India, 1984 Trustee Cambridge Friends Sch., 1989-95. With U.S. Army, 1954-56. Sheldon travelling fellow, 1948-49; NSF fellow, 1952-53; Guggenheim fellow, 1960 Fellow Am. Phys. Soc. (past chmn. New Eng. sect.); mem. Am. Assn. Physics Tchrs., AAAS. Achievements include research on high energy and elementary particles physics. Home: 1 Plymouth Rd Winchester MA 01890-3620 Personal E-mail: rmilburn@tufts.edu.

MILCH, DAVID, screenwriter, producer; b. Buffalo, Mar. 23, 1945; s. Elmer and Molly (Pies) M.; m. Rita Stern, Oct. 30, 1982; children: Elizabeth, Benjamin, Olivia. BA in English summa cum laude, Yale U., 1966; MFA with distinction, Iowa U., 1970. Co-founder Redboard Productions, 2001—. Vis. lectr. Yale U., New Haven, 1971-82. Writer: TV series Hill Street Blues, 1982—84 (Emmy award for Best Writing in a Drama series, Writer Guild award, Humanitas prize, 1982), Bay City Blues, 1983, Murder One, 1995, Total Security, 1997; prodr.: (TV series) Hill Street Blues, 1984—85; exec. prodr.: (TV series) Hill Street Blues, 1985, 1986—87, Beverly Hills Buntz, 1987—88, Brooklyn South, 1997; writer, exec. prodr.: TV series The Big Apple, 2001, NYPB Blue, 1993—2005 (Emmy award for Best Writing in a Drama series, 1997, 1998, Humanitas prize, Edgar award for Screenwriting), Capital News, 1990, Deadwood, 2004—06, John from Cincinnati, 2007—; actor: (TV appearances) L.A. Law, 1987—94; editor: (textbook) History of American Literature, 1974. Recipient Tinker prize for Highest Achievement in English, Yale U. Mem. Writers Guild Am. (Writers Guild award 1983, 84), Phi Beta Kappa (Tinker prize). Office: c/o HBO 1 Time Warner Ctr New York NY 10019 *

MILCH, THOMAS H., lawyer; b. Dec. 27, 1950; BA summa cum laude, Yale Univ., 1973, JD, 1976. Bar: Ind. 1976, D.C. 1977. Ptnr., Environ. Practice Group Arnold & Porter, Washington, chmn., 2006—. Adj. prof. Georgetown Univ. Law Sch., 1989—97. Dir. Migrant Legal Action Project, 1991—93, Environ. Law Inst., 1993—99; bd. dir. RESOLVE, Inc., 1993—, Wildlife Trust Internat. Mem.: ABA (vice chmn., Com. on Environ. Litigation 1994—, chmn. Spec. Com. on Environ. Litigation Techniques 1992—94, mem. Standing Com. on Environ. Law 1996—98), Lawyers Com. on Human Rights (past co-chmn., D.C. Adv. Council). Office: Arnold & Porter 555 Twelfth St NW Washington DC 20004-1206 Office Phone: 202-942-5030. Office Fax: 202-942-5999. Business E-Mail: thomas.milch@aporter.com.

MILCHAN, ARNON, film producer; b. Britis Palestine (now Israel), Dec. 6, 1944; 4 children. Student, London Sch. of Economics, U. Geneva Interpreters Sch. Founder, co-owner New Regency Productions, 1991—. Prodr. (plays) Tomb, It's So Nice To Be Civilized, Amadeus (Paris prodn.), (TV) MASADA, 1981, (TV series) The Client, 1995, (films) Black Joy, 1977, The Medusa Touch, 1978, Dizengoff 99, 1979, The King of Comedy, 1983, Once Upon a Time in America (also actor), 1984, Brazil, 1985, Stripper, 1986, Legend, 1986, Man on Fire, 1987, The Adventures of Baron Munchausen, 1989, Who's Harry Crumb, 1989, The War of the Roses, 1989, Big Man on Campus, 1990, Pretty Woman, 1990, Q&A, 1990, Guilty by Suspicion, 1991, JFK, 1991, Switch, 1991, The Mambo Kings, 1992, Memoirs of an Invisible Man, 1992, The Power of One, 1992, Under Siege, 1992, Sommersby, 1993, Falling Down, 1993, Made in America, 1993, Free Willy, 1993 (exec. prodr.), The Nutcracker, 1993, That Night, 1993, Heaven and Earth, 1993, The New Age, 1993, Striking Distance, 1993, Six Degrees of Separation, 1993, Second Best, 1994, Boys on the Side, 1994, Natural Born Killers, 1994, The Client, 1994, Cobb, 1994, Bogus, 1995, Under Siege 2: Dark Territory, 1995, Free Willy 2: The Adventure Home, 1995, Empire Records, 1995, Copycat, 1995, Heat, 1995, The Sunchaser, 1996, Carpool, 1996, Bogus, 1996, A Time to Kill, 1996, The Mirror Has Two Faces, 1996, Tin Cup, 1996, L.A. Confidential, 1997, Murder at 1600, 1997, Free Willy 3: The Rescue, 1997, The Devil's Advocate, 1997, Breaking Up, 1997, The Man Who Knew Too Little, 1997, Dangerous Beauty, 1998, City of Angels, 1998, The Negotiator, 1998, A Midsummer Night's Dream, 1999, Simply Irresistable, 1999, Goodbye Lover, 1999, Fight Club (exec. prodr.), 1999, Entrapment, 1999, The Hunt for the Unicorn Killer, 1999, Big Momma's House, 2000, Tigerland, 2000, Joe Somebody (exec. prodr.), 2001, Don't Say A Word, 2001, Black Knight, 2001, Freddy Got Fingered (exec. prodr.), 2001, Joy Ride (exec. prodr.), 2001, High Crimes, 2002, Life or Something Like It, 2002, Unfaithful (exec. prodr.), 2002, Daredevil, 2003, Runaway Jury, 2003, Down with Love (exec. prodr.), 2003, The Girl Next Door (exec. prodr.), 2004, Man on Fire, 2004, First Daughter (exec. prodr.), 2004, Elektra, 2005, Mr. and Mrs. Smith, 2005, Bee Season (exec. prodr.), 2005, Stay, 2005, Date Movie, 2006, The Sentinel, 2006, Just My Luck, 2006, My Super Ex-Girlfriend, 2006, The Fountain, 2006; (TV); exec. prodr.: Squach, 2000, Noriega: God's Favorite, 2000 (TV), Up at the Villa, 2000 Named one of World's Richest People, Forbes mag., 2004—. Office: New Regency Enterprises 10201 W Pico Blvd Bldg 12 Los Angeles CA 90064-2606 *

MILDENHALL, JONATHAN, beverage company executive; b. 1967; Student, Manchester Poly.; grad. in Advanced Mgmt. Prog., Harvard Bus. Sch., 2005. Grad. trainee McCann-Erickson, 1990—93; with Bartle Bogle Hegarty, 1993—96; account dir. Smirnoff worldwide Lowe Howard-Spink, 1996—97, bd. dirs., 1997; head account mgmt. HHCL & Ptnrs., 2000—02; joint mng. dir. TBWA\LONDON, 2002—03, mng. dir., 2003—05; strategy dir. Mother Coca-Cola Co., London, 2005—06, v.p. global mktg. strategy and creative comm. Atlanta, 2007—. Co-chair ethnic diversity com. IPA, coun. steering mem. Fellow: British Am. Project. Office: Coca-Cola Co PO Box 1734 Atlanta GA 30301 *

MILDER, JAY, artist; b. Omaha, May 12, 1934; s. Leo and Jeanette M.; children: Rachael, Rifka, Joshua, Isobella. Student, U. Nebr., Omaha, 1953-54, Sorbonne, Paris, 1954-56, Art Inst. of Chgo., 1956-57, Hans Hofmann Sch., Provincetown, Mass., 1958-62. Dfsdfsdfsd. Tchr. art Dayton Art Inst., 1963-65, N.Y. Inst. Tech., N.Y.C., 1965, Pratt Inst., Bklyn., 1966, Brandeis Inst., Santa Susana, Calif., 1967-68, Md. Art Inst., Balt., 1969, Chrysler Mus. Sch., Norfolk, Va., 1970, CUNY, 1971-89, Vt. Studio Sch., Johnson, 1989. Numerous one man shows at various mus. and galleries including City Gallery, NYC, 1958, Sun Gallery, Provincetown, Mass., 1958, Allan Stone Gallery, NYC, 1960, 61, 62, Fulton Gallery, NYC, 1960, Zabriskle Gallery, NYC, 1960, Museo Bellas Artes, San Juan, 1961, Dayton Art Inst., 1963, Ohio Wesleyan U., Del., 1964, Antioch Coll., Ohio, 1965, Gallery Fore, LA, 1965, Bienville Gallery, New Orleans, 1968-72, 73, 74, 77, Rosen Gallery, Laguna Beach, 1968, Temple Israel, Long Beach, 1969, The Chrysler Mus., Norfolk, Va., 1972, Mint Mus. Art, Charlotte, NC, 1973, Ryder Gallery, LA, 1973, Thompson Gallery, Aspen, Colo., 1974, Lerner-Heller Gallery, NYC, 1975, Gallery One, 1976, Art Latitude Gallery, NYC, 1978, Mint Mus. Art, Charlotte, NC, 1978, Ingber Gallery, NYC, 1979, Ad Summun Arts Gallery, NYC, 1980, Ronald Hunning Gallery, NYC, 1981, Oscarsson Hood Gallery, NYC, 1982, Shahin Requicha Gallery, Rochester, NYC, 1984, Sid Deutsch Gallery, NYC, 1986, Richard Green Gallery, NYC, 1986, Gallery Four, Charlotte, Va., 1986, Harcourts Contemporary, San Francisco, 1987, Richard Green Gallery, NYC, 1987-89, Gallery Jupiter, Little Silver, NJ, 1987-89, Anton Gallery, Washington, 1987-89, Yares Gallery, Scottsdale, 1987-89, Eleonore Austerer Fine Art, San Mateo, Calif., 1988, Girgis & Klym Gallery, Fitzroy, Australia, 1988, Yares Gallery, Scottsdale, Ariz., 1989, Schick Art Gallery, Skidmore Coll., Saratoga Springs, NYC, 1991-92, Va. Beach Ctr. Arts, 1991-92, Elizabeth Harris Gallery, NYC, 1994, Alitash Kebede Gallery, LA, 1994, Horace Richter Gallery, Tel Aviv, 1996, Hugo Pagano Gallery, NYC, 1997, Nat. Mus. Fine Arts, Rio de Janeiro, 1999, Andre Zarre Gallery, NYC, 2001, Mus. Modern Art, Salvador, Bahia, Brazil, 2003; numerous group shows including City Gallery, NYC, 1958, 10th St. Gallery, NYC, 1958, Phoenix Gallery, 1958, 77, Sun Gallery, Provincetown, 1959, Ellison Gallery, Ft. Worth, 1959, Stuttman Gallery, NYC, 1960, Zabriskie Gallery, 1960, Dayton Art Inst., Ohio, 1961, Mus. Modern Art, NYC, 1962, 67, Yale U. Art Gallery, New Haven, 1962, Nat. Graphics Show, 1963, Yale U. Art Gallery, New Haven, 1964, Martha Jackson Gallery, NYC, 1965, Am. Fedn. Art U. Mich. Mus. Art, Ann Arbor, 1965, Mus. Modern Art, Mex. City, Mex., 1968, Karen Horney Clinic, NYC, 1969, Sonraed Gallery, NYC, 1970-71, New Sch. Social Rsch., NYC, 1970-71, Mus. NY, 1970-71, North Shore Cmty. Art Ctr., Gt. Neck, NY, 197-71, Dayton Art Inst., 1970-71, Living Arts Ctr. Gallery, 1970-71, Joseloff Gallery, U. Hartford, Conn., 1970-71, East Ctrl. State Coll., Ada, Okla., 1970-71, Gardiner Art Gallery, Okla. State U., Stillwater, 1970-71, Contemporary Arts Found., Okla. City, 1970-71, Bienville Gallery, New Orleans, 1970-71, 74, The Chrysler Mus., Norfolk, Va., 1970-71, Westbeth Artists Gallery, NYC, 1971, City Coll., NYC, 1973, Santa Barbara Mus., Calif., 1974, Mass. U., 1974, San Francisco Art Inst., 1974, Ankrum Gallery, LA, 1974, Aida Hernandez Gallery, NYC, 1974, Pace Coll., NYC, 1974, The Chrysler Mus., Norfolk, 1974, Humanist Ctr., NYC, 1974, La. State U. Gallery, Baton Rouge, 1975, Landmark Gallery, NYC, 1977, Aaron Berman Gallery, NYC, 1977, Skidmore Coll., Saratoga Springs, NYC, 1977, Noyes, Van Cline and Davenport Gallery, NYC, 1977, 10th St. Mexican Mus., Guadalajara, Mex., 1978, Bienville Gallery, New Orleans, 1978, Landmark Gallery, NYC, 1978, Myers Arts Gallery, SUNY, Plattsburgh, 1978, U. Art Gallery, SUNY, Albany, 1978, Union Coll., Cranford, NJ, 1978, St. John's Coll., Annapolis, Md., 1979-80, Castellani Gallery, Niagara Falls, NY, 1979-80, Dowd Art Gallery, SUNY, Cortland, NY, 1979-80, Root Art Ctr., Hamilton Coll., Clinton, NY, 1979-80, Brainerd Art Gallery, SUNY, Potsdam, 1979-80, Del. Art Mus., Wilmington, 1979-80, Bruce Mus., Greenwich, Conn., 1979-80, Tyler Art Gallery, SUNY, Oswego, 1979-80, Firehouse Gallery, Nassau CC, Garden City, NY, 1979-80, Warehouse Gallery, Orlando, Fla., 1984, Provincetown Assn. and Mus., Mass., 1985, Equitable Life AssuranceSoc. and Mendik Co., NYC, 1985, Kenkeleba Gallery, NYC, 1986, Shanghai, China and City U. NY, 1986, Newton Art Ctr., Newtonville, Mass., 1986, Anita Shapolsky Gallery, NYC, 1987, 55 Mercer St. Gallery, 1987, Galerie Helen Grubair, Miami, Fla., 1988, Arthur Robbins Studio, NYC, 1988, Manattan Borough Pres. Gallery, NYC, 1988, Newport Art Mus., RI, 1988, Unipas Gallery, NYC, 1988, RFM Studio, NYC, 1988, Limelight, NYC, 1988, Galerie Helene Grubair, Miami, Fla., 1988, Barbara Ingber Gallery, NYC, 1989, Horace Richter Gallery, Jaffa, Israel, 1990, Anita Shapolsky Gallery, NYC, 1990, Alitash Kebede Fine Art, LA, 1991, Anderson Gallery, Va. Commonwealth U., Richmond, Va., 1991, Greenville Mus., SC, 1993, Kathleen Ross Gallery, Soho, NYC, 1995, Elizabeth Harris Gallery, NYC, 1998, Hugo Pagano Gallery, NYC, 1999, Reina Sofia Mus., Madrid, 2000, many others; represented in permanent collections including New Orleans Mus. Art, Grey Mus., NYU, Mus. Tucson, Pinacoteca Mus., Sao Paulo, RI Sch. Design Mus., Providence, Va. Beach Art Mus., Wichita Art Mus., Kans., Anderson Gallery, Va. Commonwealth U., Richmond, AT&T Corp., NYC, Bayonne Jewish CC, NJ, Brandeis Inst., LA, Best Products, Richmond, Beth El Synagogue, Long Beach, The Chrysler Mus., Dayton Art Inst., Ein Hod Mus., Jerusalem, Flossie Martin Gallery, Radford U., Va., Herbert F. Johnson Mus., Cornell U., Ithaca, Lakeland Cultural Arts Ctr., Littleton, NC, Maler Mus. Art, Randolph-Macon Women's Coll., Lynchburg, Va., Mint Mus. Art, Charlotte, NC, Muscarelle Mus. Art, Williamsburg, Va., Mus. Art, San Juan, Mus. Solidarity, Titograd, Yugoslavia, Neuberger Mus., Purchase, Newark Mus., New Mus., NY, Oakleigh Collection, Boston, Palm Springs Desert Mus., Provincetown Mus., Simon and Shuster Co., NYC, Sinai Temple, LA, Skidmore Coll., Saratoga Springs, Skirball Mus., Hebrew Union Coll., LA, State U. NY, Binghamton, Tel Aviv Mus., Weatherspoon Art Gallery, Greensboro, NC, Yale U., New Haven; contbr. various catalogues and publs. Home and Office: 108 Wooster St New York NY 10012-5207

MILDREN, JACK, bank executive, retired state official; b. Kingsville, Tex., Oct. 10, 1949; s. Larry J. and Mary Glynne (Lamont) M.; m. Janis Susan Butler, Jan. 14, 1972; children: Leigh, Lauren, Drew. BBA, U. Okla., 1972. Cert. petroleum landman. Mem. Balt. Colts Football Team, 1972-73, New England Patriots Football Team, 1974; v.p. Saxon Oil Co., 1972-79; co-founder, pres. Regency Exploration Inc., 1977-88; ind. oil oper., 1988-90; lt. gov. State of Okla., Oklahoma City, 1990-95; pres., CEO Pre-Paid Legal Svcs. Inc., Ada, Okla., 1995; owner LJM Fin., 1997—; vice chmn. Arvest Banks, 2003—. Bd. dirs. Children's Med. Rsch. Found., Arts Coun. Oklahoma City, Nat. Football League Players Found. and Hall of Fame, State Ctr. Com., Jim Thorpe Club; mem. Leadership Okla., Leadership Oklahoma City; mem. Com. to Devel. Biotech. Industry in Okla. Named All-Am. Football Player, 1971, Acad. All-Am., 1971, Nat. Football Found. Hall Fame, 1971, Most Valuable Player Sugar Bowl, 1972, Best QB in U. Oklahoma history, numerous other athletic awards; inducted into Okla. Sports Hall of Fame, 1998, GTE Acad. Hall of Fame, 1998. Mem. Beta Gamma Sigma, Phi Delta Theta (past pres., bd. dirs.) Meth. Home: 1701 Guilford Ln Oklahoma City OK 73120-1013 Office: PO Box 55500 Oklahoma City OK 73155 Office Phone: 405-419-3721. Business E-Mail: jmildren@arvest.com.

MILDVAN, DONNA, infectious diseases physician; b. Phila., June 20, 1942; d. Carl David and Gertrude M.; m. Rolf Dirk Hamann; 1 child, Gabriella Kay. AB magna cum laude, Bryn Mawr Coll., 1963; MD, Johns Hopkins U., 1967. Diplomate Am. Bd. Internal Medicine and Infectious Diseases. Intern, resident Mt. Sinai Hosp., NYC, 1967-70, fellow, infectious diseases, 1970-72; asst., assoc. prof. clin. medicine Mt. Sinai Sch. Medicine, NYC, 1972-87; prof. clinical medicine Dept. Medicine, Mt. Sinai Sch. Medicine, NYC, 1987-88, prof. medicine, 1988-94; physician-in-charge infectious diseases Beth Israel Med. Ctr., NYC, 1972-79, chief, div. infectious diseases, 1980—; prof. medicine Albert Einstein Coll. of Medicine, NYC, 1994—. Mem. AIDS charter rev. com., NIH/Nat. Inst. Allergy and Infectious Diseases, Bethesda, 1987—; cons. FDA, Rockville, 1987—, Ctrs. for Disease Control, Atlanta, 1985-86; among first to describe AIDS, "Pre-AIDS", AIDS Dementia, 1982, among first to study AZT, 1986; Keynote speaker, II Internat. Conf. on AIDS, Paris, 1986 and other achievements in field; Sophie Jones Meml. lectr. in infectious diseases U. Mich. Hosps., 1984. Contbr. numerous articles to profl. jours; co-editor two books, many book chpts. and abstracts on infectious diseases and AIDS; editor: Atlas of AIDS, edits. 1-3. Grantee N.Y. State AIDS Inst., 1986-87; Henry Strong Denison scholar Johns Hopkins U. Sch. Medicine, 1967; recipient Woman of Achievement award AAUW, 1987, Hero in Medicine award Internat. Assn. Physicians in AIDS Care, 2000; contract for antiviral therapy in AIDS, Nat. Cancer Inst./Nat. Inst. Allergy and Infectious Diseases, 1985-86, subcontract Nat. Inst. Allergy and Infectious Diseases, ACTU, 1987-99, prin. investigator, 2000—. Fellow Infectious Diseases Soc. Am.; mem. Am. Soc. Microbiology, AAAS, Harvey Soc., Internat. AIDS Soc. Democrat. Jewish. Avocation: old movies. Office: Beth Israel Med Ctr 1st Ave New York NY 10003-7903

MILEDI, RICARDO, neurobiologist; b. Mexico City, Mex., Sept. 15, 1927; m. Ana Mela Garces, Dec. 17, 1955; 1 child, Rico. BSc, Instituto Cientifico y Literario, Chihuahua, Mex., 1945; MD, U. Nacional Autonoma de Mex., 1955. Researcher Instituto Nacional de Cardiologia, Mexico, 1954-56; fellow John Curtin Sch. Med. Res., Canberra, Australia, 1956-58; mem. faculty U. Coll., London, 1959-85, Foulerton research prof. of Royal Soc., 1975-85, head dept. biophysics, 1978-85; disting. prof. dept. neurobiology and behavior U. Calif., Irvine, 1984—. Recipient Principe de Asturias prize, Spain, 1999. Fellow Royal Soc. London (Royal medal 1999), Am. Acad. Arts and Scis.; mem. AAAS, NAS, 3d World Acad. Scis., (titular) European Acad. Arts, Scis., Humanities, N.Y. Acad. Scis., Hungarian Acad. Scis. (hon.), Mex. Acad. Scis., Mex. Acad. Medicine. Home: 9 Gibbs Ct Irvine CA 92612-4032 Office: U Calif Dept Neurobiology Behavior 2205 Bio Sci Ii Irvine CA 92697-4550 Office Phone: 949-824-4730. Business E-Mail: rmiledi@uci.edu.

MILES, ANTHONY R., lawyer; b. Denver, Sept. 12, 1971; BA with dist., Yale Univ., 1993; JD cum laude, Univ. Mich., 1999. Bar: Wash. 1999, U.S. Ct. Appeals Sixth Circuit 2001, U.S. Supreme Ct. 2002. Assoc. healthcare atty. Preston Gates & Ellis LLP, Seattle. Contbr. articles to numerous profl. jours. Named Wash. Rising Star, SuperLawyer Mag., 2006. Mem.: ABA, Wash. State Soc. Health Care Attys., Am. Health Lawyers Assn. Office: Preston Gates & Ellis LLP Ste 2900 925 Fourth Ave Seattle WA 98104-1158

MILES, DAVID LOREN, museum director; b. Charlevoix, Mich., Feb. 14, 1940; s. Robert Clarence and Esther Miles. BA, MA, U. Mich., 1963. Asst. cashier U. Mich., Ann Arbor, 1966—68, dir. statistical svcs., 1968—70; night mgr. Lodge Motel, Charlevoix, 1972—2000; co-dir. Charlevoix Hist. Soc. Harsha House Mus., 2000—. Writer, prodr., rschr. (town heritage book) Bob Miles' Charlevoix II, 2002. Mem. C. of C. Home: 109 Pk Ave Charlevoix MI 49720 Office: Charlevoix Hist Soc PO Box 525 Charlevoix MI 49720 Office Phone: 231-547-0373. Business E-Mail: chxhistory@sbcglobal.net.

MILES, DAVID MICHAEL, lawyer; b. Jackson, Mich., Aug. 5, 1954; s. Richard George and Joann Marie (Stefanoff) M.; m. Noelle Suzanne McHugh, Sept. 6, 1986; children: Amy Elizabeth, Margaret Noelle, Lane McHugh. Student, U. Mich., 1972-74; BA cum laude, Clark U., 1976; JD magna cum laude, George Washington U., 1979. Bar: D.C. 1979, U.S. Ct. Appeals (4th cir.) 1980, U.S. Dist. Ct. Md. 1980, U.S. Dist. Ct. D.C. 1983, U.S. Supreme Ct. 1983, U.S. Ct. Appeals (D.C. cir.) 1981, U.S Ct. Appeals

(9th cir.) 1984, U.S. Ct. Appeals (2d cir.) 1986. Law clk. to Chief Judge Edward Northrop, U.S Dist. Ct. Md., 1979-80; law clk. to Cir. Judge George MacKinnon U.S. Ct. Appeals, Washington, 1980-81; assoc. Fried, Frank, Harris, Shriver & Jacoboson, Washington, 1981-86, ptnr., 1986-92, Sidley Austin LLP, Washington, 1992—. Co-author: The Law of Financial Services, 1988; contbr. articles to profl. jours. Home: 5229 Westpath Way Bethesda MD 20816 Office: Sidley Austin LLP 1501 K St NW Washington DC 20005 Home Phone: 301-229-9240; Office Phone: 202-736-8556. Personal E-mail: DavidM9876@aol.com. Business E-Mail: dmiles@sidley.com.

MILES, DON CLIFFORD, architect; b. Ft. Knox, Ky., Sept. 17, 1942; s. Don and Kathrine Eva (Gray) M.; m. Pamela Wait, Aug. 6, 1972; children: Katherine Wait, Lesley Gray, Nicole Conel. BArch with honors, U. Wash., 1966; MArch, M of City Planning in Urban Design, Harvard U., 1971. Registered architect, Wash. Assoc. ptnr. Zimmer, Gunsul, Frasca Partnership, Seattle. Cons., lectr. numerous orgns., cities, corps. Prin. projects include Pedestrian Corridor, Major Pub. Open Spaces, CBD Transit Ctr., Bellevue, Wash., Banfield Light Rail Project, Portland, Boise (Idaho) Downtown Major Pub. Open Space, Street Improvements and Transit Malls, Honolulu Rapid Transit Project, Revitalization of State St., Chgo., Midway Corridor Project, Mpls., High Capacity Transit Project, Seattle, Ctrl. Orange County Aerial Fixed Guideway, Mission Valley West Extension Light Rail Project, San Diego, Master Plan for Capitol of State of Wash., Seattle Union Sta. Redevel. Plan, Weyerhauser Corp. Campus, Quadrant Corp. site, Lake Union, Seattle, Whitman Coll. Bd. dirs., founder Project for Pub. Spaces, 1975—; bd. dirs. Seattle Children's Mus., 1978-82; trustee Queen Ann Community Coun., 1978-80. Fellow AIA, Inst. Urban Design. Avocations: skiing, jogging. Home: 611 W Comstock St Seattle WA 98119-3422 Office: Zimmer Gunsul Frasca 925 4th Ave 2400 Seattle WA 98104-1146

MILES, DONALD F., lawyer; b. Marysville, Calif., Apr. 11, 1949; AB with honors, Stanford U., 1971; JD, U. Calif., San Francisco, 1974. Bar: Calif. 1974, U.S. Dist. Ct. (no. dist.) Calif. 1974, U.S. Dist. Ct. (ea. dist.) Calif. 1977, U.S. Dist. Ct. (so. dist.) Calif. 1986, U.S. Supreme Ct. 1987, U.S. Dist. Ct. (ctrl. dist.) Calif. 1991. Law clk. to Hon. William P. Clark Jr. Supreme Ct. Calif., 1974-75; mem. Howard, Rice, Nemerovski, Canady, Falk & Rabkin, P.C., San Francisco. Spl. master U.S. Dist. Ct. (no. dist.) Calif.; instr., adj. faculty mem. Hastings Coll. Law U. Calif.; faculty mem., bd. dirs. Hastings Nat. Coll. Advocacy; mem. adv. com. Calif. Legis. Joint Com. Tort Liability. Author: (with others) Civil Procedure During Trial, vol. II, 1984, 95, California Liability Insurance Practice, 1991, Continuing Education of the Bar Action Guide, 1991; author, narrator: (videotape) Laying a Foundation to Introduce Evidence, 1989; contbr. articles to profl. jours. Bd. chmn. The Glenwood Sch. Found. Mem. ABA (sect. torts and ins. practice), State Bar Calif., Assn. Def. Counsel No. Calif., Bar Assn. of San Francisco, Internat. Assn. Def. Counsel, Def. Rsch. Inst., Thurston Soc., Order of Coif.

MILES, FRANK CHARLES, retired newspaper executive; b. Detroit, Jan. 1, 1926; s. Nelson and Ethel Jane (Mennill) M.; m. Catharine Estelle Coleman, Sept. 4, 1948 (dec. Aug. 2000); children: Barbara Ann, Diana Estelle; m. Joan Ashkin, Feb. 1, 2003. Student, Westervelt Bus. Coll., 1947-48. With Thomson Newspapers Ltd., Cambridge, Ont., Canada, 1950-52, 54-55; bus. mgr. Sarnia (Ont.) Obs., 1952-54; gen. mgr. Pembroke (Ont.) Obs., 1956-58, Moose Jaw (Sask.) Times-Herald, Canada, 1958-62; pub. Austin (Minn.) Daily Herald, 1962-66; sr. v.p., gen. mgr. Thomson Newspapers Inc., Des Plaines, Ill., 1966-89, exec. v.p. acquisitions, 1990-91, ret., 1991, also bd. dirs. Vol. assignments Internat. Media Fund, Baltics, Albania, 1992-93; Knight fellowship Moscow, 1994, Ctrl. for Ind. Journalism, Bucharest, Romania, 1995, Kocise Slovakia, 1996, Internat. Rsch. & Exch. Corp., Zagreb, Croatia, Belarus, 1997, Brest, Minsk, Belarus, 1997-98. Mem. Assn. Integration of Whole Person, Sigma Delta Chi. Republican. Mem. United Ch. of Christ.

MILES, JACK (JOHN RUSSIANO), journalist, educator; b. Chgo., July 30, 1942; s. John Alvin and Mary Jean (Murphy) Miles; m. Jacqueline Russiano, Aug. 23, 1980; 1 child, Kathleen. LittB, Xavier U., Cin., 1964; PhB, Pontifical Gregorian U., Rome, 1966; student, Hebrew U., Jerusalem, 1966—67; PhD, Harvard U., 1971. Asst. prof. Loyola U., Chgo., 1970—74; asst. dir. Scholars Press, Missoula, Mont., 1974—75; postdoctoral fellow U. Chgo., 1975—76; editor Doubleday & Co., NYC, 1976—78; exec. editor U. Calif. Press, Berkeley, 1978—85; book editor L.A. Times, 1985—91, mem. editl. bd., 1991—95; dir. Humanities Ctr. Claremont (Calif.) Grad. U., 1995—97; Mellon vis. prof. Calif. Inst. Tech., 1997—98; sr. advisor to pres. J. Paul Getty Trust, LA, 1999—. Contbg. editor: Atlantic Monthly, 1995—; author: Retroversion and Text Criticism, 1984, God: A Biography, 1995, Christ: A Crisis in the Life of God, 2001; contbr. learned and popular articles to various periodicals; book reviewer. Recipient Pulitzer Prize for biography, 1996; Guggenheim fellow, 1990—91, 2002—, MacArthur fellow, 2003—. Mem.: PEN, Amnesty Internat., Am. Acad. Religion, Nat. Book Critics Cir. (pres. 1990—92). Episcopalian. Office: J Paul Getty Trust 1200 Getty Center Dr Ste 1100 Los Angeles CA 90049-1688

MILES, JESSE MC LANE, retired accounting company executive; b. De Funiak Springs, Fla., June 17, 1932; s. Percy Webb and Dora (Pippin) M.; m. Catherine Rita Eugenio, July 18, 1959; children: Jesse Jr., Catherine, Teresa, John, Thomas, Robert BSBA, U. Fla., 1954. CPA NY. Mem. staff, mgr., prin. Arthur Young & Co., NYC, 1954-63, ptnr., 1963-89; dep. chmn.-internat., 1985-89; chmn. Arthur Young Internat., 1985-89; ptnr. Ernst & Young, 1989-92; co-chmn. Ernst & Young Internat., 1989-92; ret., 1992. Mem. AICPA, N.Y. Inst. CPAs, Boca Pointe Country Club. Home: 7077 Via Mediterrania Boca Raton FL 33433

MILES, JOANNA, actress, playwright, director; b. Nice, France, Mar. 6, 1940; came to U.S., 1941, naturalized, 1941; d. Johannes Schiefer and Jeanne Miles; m. William Burns, May 23, 1970 (div. 1977); m. Michael Brandman, Apr. 29, 1978; 1 child, Miles. Grad. H.S., Putney, Vt., 1958. Mem. Actors Studio, Playwrites and Dirs. Workshop, NYC, 1966; co-founder, mem. LA Classic Theatre, 1986. Founder, artistic dir. Playwrights Group/LAWW, 1991-98. Starred in: (motion pictures) The Way We Live Now, 1969, Bug, 1975, The Ultimate Warrior, 1975, Golden Girl, 1978, Cross Creek, 1983, As Is, 1986, Blackout, 1988, Rosencrants and Guildenstern are Dead, 1991, The Rhinghart Theory, 1994, Judge Dredd, 1994, Alone, 1996, Sex & Breakfast, 2006; numerous television films including In What America, 1965, My Mothers House, 1963, Glass Managerie, 1974, Born Innocent, 1974, Aloha Means Goodbye, 1974, The Trial of Chaplain Jensen, 1975, Harvest Home, 1977, Fire in the Sky, 1978, Sophisticated Gents, 1979, Promise of Love, 1982, Sound of Murder, 1983, All My Sons, 1987, The Right to Die, 1987, The Habitation of Dragons, 1991, Heart of Justice, 1991, Water Engine, 1991, Cooperstown, 1992, Legionnaires, 1992, Life Lessons, 1992, Willing to Kill, 1992, The American Clock, 1993, Dark Reflections, 1993, Outcry, 1994, Everything to Gain, 1995, Small Vices, 1998, Crossfire Trail, 1999, Thin Aire, 1999, Monty Walsh, 2002, Jane Doe: Shaken & Stirred, 2006; episodes in numerous TV series including: Barney Miller, Dallas, St. Elsewhere, The Hulk, Trapper John, Kaz, Cagney and Lacey, Studio 5B, 1989, Star Trek: The Next Generation, 1990, 91, Life Stories, 1991, HBO Life Stories, 1993, Total Security, 1997, Nothing Sacred, 1998, Chicago Hope, 1998-99, ER, 2000, 01, Family Law, 2000, Judging Amy, 2003; stage plays include Once in a Life Time, 1963, Cave Dwellers, 1964, Drums in the Night, 1968, Dracula, 1968, Home Free, 1964, One Night Stands of a Noisy Passenger, 1972, Dylan, 1973, Dancing for the Kaiser, 1976, Debutante Ball, 1985, Kramer, 1977, One Flew Over the Cuckoo's Nest, 1989, Growing Gracefully, 1990, Cut Flowers, 1994; performed in radio shows Sta. KCRW Once in a Lifetime, 1987, Babbit, 1987, Sta. KPFK, Grapes of Wrath, 1989, The White Plague, Sta. KCRW, 1991, Chekhov Short Stories, Sta. KCRW, 1992; playwright, v.p. Brandman Productions; author: (plays) Ethanasia, A Woman in Reconstruction, Hostages, Feathers, On the Shelf, (films) An Offereing of Oranges, Breaking the Rules. Pres. Children Giving to Children. Recipient 2 Emmy awards, 1974, Women in Radio and TV award, 1974, Actors Studio Achievement award, 1980, Dramalogue award, 1996, Vision award 2003; nominated Golden Globe, 1974. Mem. Acad. Motion Picture Arts and Scis. Office: Brandman Prodns 2062 Vine St Apt 5 Hollywood CA 90068-3928 Office Phone: 323-463-3224. Personal E-mail: jmilesb@aol.com.

MILES, JOHN BILL, retired accountant, tax specialist; b. Knox County, Ky., Sept. 18, 1931; s. John Ishmael and Allie Arizona (Engle) M.; m. Mary Patricia Wilson, May 25, 1963; children: Melanie, Jennifer, Dennis. BS in Commerce, Salmon P. Chase Coll., 1962; BS in Acctg., U. Cin., 1972; MBA, Lincoln Grad. Sch. Mgmt., Des Moines, 2001. CPA; accredited tax advisor; enrolled agt. Cost acct. Avco Corp., Cin., 1956—58; chief auditor Pepsi-Cola Bottling Co., Cin., 1958—64; property acct. Monsanto Co., Addyston, Ohio, 1964—66; sec.-treas. Shur-Good Biscuit Co., Inc., Cin., 1966—79; acct. Fabritec Internat. Corp., Cold Spring, Ky., 1980—98; ind. practice acctg. Cheviot, Ohio, 1999—. Lt. Col. ret. Ohio Mil. Res. Mem.: NRA, AICPA, Nat. Assn. Legal Assts., Ohio Assn. Ind. Accts., Nat. Soc. Accts., Ohio Soc. CPAs, State Guard Assn. U.S., Am. Legion, Assn. U.S. Army, Honorable Order Ky. Cols., Fur Takers of Am., Ohio Mil. Res. Assn., Accts. for Pub. Interest, Cheviot Rep. Club. Home: 3816 Roswell Ave Cincinnati OH 45211-3329

MILES, JOHN JEFFRIES, lawyer; b. Roanoke, Va., Mar. 29, 1946; s. Hugh Smith Jr. and Helen Mary (Jeffries) M.; m. Carolyn Ward, Aug. 30, 1969. BS, Va. Tech., 1968, MA, 1971; JD, Washington & Lee U., 1973. Bar: Va. 1973, U.S. Tax Ct. 1973, U.S. Claims Ct. 1973, U.S. Dist. (we. dist.) Va. 1974, U.S. Ct. Appeals (4th cir.) 1974, U.S. Supreme Ct. 1980, D.C. 1982, U.S. Ct. Appeals (D.C. cir.) 1982, U.S. Ct. Appeals (3d cir.) 1983, U.S. Ct. Appeals (fed. cir.) 1990, U.S. Ct. Appeals (8th cir.) 1997. Assoc. Martin Hopkins & Lemon, Roanoke, 1973-75; asst. atty. gen. Office of Atty. Gen., Richmond, Va., 1976-78; trial atty. antitrust divsn. U.S. Dept. Justice, Washington, 1979-92; ptnr. O'Connor & Hannan, Washington, 1982-84, Powers Pyles Sutter & Miles, Washington, 1984-87, Baker & Hostetler, Washington, 1987-88; sr. atty. Jones Day Reavis & Pogue, Washington, 1988-92; ptnr. Ober Kaler, Washington, 1993—. Author: Antitrust Guide for Health Care Coalitions, 1983, Health Care and Antitrust Law, 1992, Antitrust Bull., 1984, Antitrust Law Jour., 1979, 1998. Episcopalian. Home: 6254 Kingfisher Ln Alexandria VA 22312-3913 Office: Ober Kaler 1401 H St NW Fl 5 Washington DC 20005-2175 Office Phone: 202-326-5008.

MILES, LAVEDA ANN, advertising executive; b. Greenville, SC, Nov. 21, 1945; d. Grady Lewis and Edna Sylvia (Mahaffey) Bruce; m. Charles Thomas Miles, Nov. 10, 1974; 1 child, Joshua Bruce. A in Bus. Adminstrn., North Greenville Jr. Coll. Traffic mgr. WFBV-TV, Greenville, 1968-74; pub. svc. dir., traffic mgr. WTCG-TV, Atlanta, 1974-75; traffic mgr. Henderson Advt. Co., Greenville, 1975-77, broadcast coord., 1977-79, dir. broadcast bus., 1979-82, v.p., dir. broadcast bus., 1982-89, bus. mgr. creative dept., 1989-91, dir. creative svcs., 1991-93, sr. v.p., 1994-96, v.p., dir. creative svcs., 2000—06; creative svcs. mgr. The Bounce Agy., 2006—; owner Altamont Mktg., 1996-99. Mem. Leadership S.C., 1994-95; bd. dirs. Boys Home of the South, 2003—. Named one of 100 Best and Brightest Women, Ad Age and Advt. Women of N.Y., 1988. Mem. Advt. Fedn. Greenville (sec. 1979-81), Greenville Ad Club (sec. 1999-2000, pres. 2000—02, Silver medal award 2003). Republican. Baptist. Office Phone: 864-271-8340. E-mail: laveda.miles@thebounceagency.com.

MILES, LELAND WEBER, retired academic administrator; b. Balt., Jan. 18, 1924; s. Leland Weber and Marie (Fitzpatrick) M.; m. Mary Virginia Geyer, July 9, 1947; children: Christine Marie, Gregory Lynn. AB cum laude, Juniata Coll., 1946; MA, U. N.C., 1947, PhD, 1949; postgrad., Duke U., 1949; DLitt (hon.), Juniata Coll., 1969; LHD (hon.), Rosary Hill Coll., 1970; LLD (hon.), Far East U., 1979; DHC (hon.), U. Guadalajara, Mex., 1984; Order of Merit, Alfred U., 1986. Assoc. prof. English Hanover Coll., 1949-50, prof., chmn. English dept., 1950-60; assoc. prof., asst. to head English dept. U. Cin., 1960-63, prof., 1963-64, founder humanities reading program for engrs., 1961; dean Coll. Arts and Scis., U. Bridgeport, Conn., 1964-67; pres. U. Bridgeport, 1974-87; founder U. Bridgeport Sch. Law, 1977; pres. emeritus U. Bridgeport, 1987—; pres. Alfred U., 1967-74. Bd. dirs. United Illuminating, 1978-94, chmn. audit com., 1992-94, Grolier, 1984-88, Wright Managed Investment Funds, 1988-04, Internat. Peace Acad., 1982-90; Danforth scholar Union Theol. Sem., 1956; Lilly fellow Sch. Letters Ind. U., 1959; Am. Council Learned Socs. fellow Harvard, 1963-64; Sr. Fulbright Research scholar Kings Coll. U. London, 1964, vis. scholar, 1972; seminar leader, deans and presidents insts. Am. Council on Edn., 1973-79; chmn. bd. Acad. Collective Bargaining Info. Service, Washington, 1977-79; producer, moderator Casing the Classics CBS Sta. WHAS-TV, Louisville, 1958-61; moderator Aspen (Colo.) Inst. for Humanistic Studies, 1969-70; lectr. Keedick Lecture Bur., N.Y.C., 1956-83; vis. prof. New Coll., Sarasota, Fla., 1989. Author: John Colet and the Platonic Tradition, 1961; editor: St. Thomas More's Dialogue of Comfort Against Tribulation, 1965, Where Do You Stand On Linquistics?, 1964, revised, 1968; sr. editor: (with Stephen Graubard and later Stephen B. Baxter) Studies in British History and Culture, 1965-79, Provoking Thought: What Colleges Should Do For Students, 2001; contbg. editor Nat. Forum, 1983-91; contbr. articles to learned jours., chpts. in books. Trustee Western NY Nuc. Rsch. Ctr., 1967-73; chmn. bd. Coll. Ctr. Finger Lakes, 1968-71; vice-chmn. bd. Empire State Found., 1969-71, chmn., 1971-73; mem. New Eng. Bd. Higher Edn., 1985-87, Ambs. Roundtable World Affairs Forum, 1986-92, Fuld Found./Nat. League Nursing Adv. Coun. on Accreditation, 1986-88; chmn. Ettinger scholarship com. Ednl. Found. Am., 1987-93; bd. dirs. Conn. Grand Opera, 1978-89, Bridgeport Bus. Coun., 1982-88; bd. dirs. Save the Children, 1988-95, chmn. adv. coun., 1990-95; adviser Asolo Theater-Fla. State U. Conservatory Actors Tng., 2004-. 1st lt. USAAF, 1944-45; capt. USAFR. Decorated DFC with oak leaf cluster, Crown Decoration of Honor 3rd Order Iran, 1978; chevalier l'Ordre des Palmes Académique (France), 1984; recipient Rosa and Samuel Sachs prize Cin. Inst. Fine Arts, 1961, Cultural medal Republic of China, 1983, Disting. Svc. award Greater Bridgeport Bar Assn., 1986, Outstanding Civilian Svc. medal Dept. Army, 1988; Miles scholars Alfred U., 1995—. Fellow Royal Soc. Arts, Manufactures and Commerce (life); mem. Renaissance Soc. Am., English Speaking Union (bd. dirs. Greenwich, Conn. chpt. 1998-04), UN Assn. (bd. dirs. Sarasota Manatee chpt., coord. young profl. for internat. coop. 2005-), Internat. Assn. Univ. Pres. (pres. 1981-84, pres. emeritus 1984—, chief UN mission 1988-97, World Peace award 1987, chmn. UN commn. on arms control edn. 1991-96, mem. coun. sr. advisers 1992—), Knights of Malta (order of the Orthodox Knights Hospitaller of St. John of Jerusalem, Russian Orthodox br.), Mil. Officers Assn. Sarasota, West Coast Symphony Assn., Sarasota Opera Guild, Univ. Club (NYC), Sarasota Univ. Club, Phi Delta Kappa. Episcopalian. Home (Summer): 87 Field Point Dr Fairfield CT 06824-6329 Home (Winter): 2110 Ben Franklin Dr Sarasota FL 34236 Office Phone: 941-525-3095. Personal E-mail: lelandwmiles@yahoo.com.

MILES, LES, college football coach; b. Nov. 10, 1953; m. Kathy Miles; children: Kathryn, Leslie, Benjamin, Gracie. BS in Econ., Mich. Univ., 1976. Asst. NFL coach. Dallas Cowboys, 1998—2000; grad. asst. Univ. Mich., 1980—81, asst. coach., 1987—94, Univ. Colo., 1982—86, Okla. State, 1995—97, head football coach, 2001—04, LSU, 2005—. Office: Tiger Stadium Staadium Rd Baton Rouge LA 70803 E-mail: football@lsu.edu.

MILES, MARY ELLEN, retired human resources specialist; d. Monroe and Leona (Simmons) Jackson; m. Monte Sanford, Sept. 21, 1956 (div.); children: Dean Sanford, Marisa Sanford(dec.), Mark Sanford. Degree in secretarial sci., Orlando Jr. Coll., Fla., 1962. Cert. OSHA inspector, EEO investigator. Exec. sec. Dept of Def./AAFES, Montgomery, Ala., 1974, employee devel. specialist Wright Patterson AFB, Ohio, 1974—77, tech. publs. writer/editor Munich, 1977—79, pers. asst Ft. Rucker, Ala., 1979—82, pers. asst, employee devel. specialist Langley AFB, Va., 1982—85, human resources mgr. Ft. Eustis, Va., 1985—87, Ft. Knox, Ky., 1987—91, Ft. Carson, Colo., 1990—93, Ft. Hood, Tex., 1993—95, Hickam AFB, Hawaii, 1995—98, sr. human resources policy specialist/policy devel. Dallas, 1998—2002. HR subject matter expert, cons., Decatur, Ala., 2002. Author: (cookbook) From the Heart. Newsletter writer, editor Newport News Literacy Coun., Va., 1985—86, Clean Cmty. Commn., Newport News, 1985—86; mem. Mayor's Coun. Handicapped Employment, Newport News, 1985—87; vol. Duncanville Pub. Libr., Tex., 2002, Carnegie Visual Arts Ctr., Decatur, 2003; mem. Ala. Citizens for Constn. Reform, Huntsville, 2003—06, Acad. for Lifetime Learning, U. Ala., Huntsville, 2003—05, Leadership Coun., So. Poverty Law Ctr., Montgomery, Ala., 2003, Morgan County Diversity Coun., 2004, Princess Theater, Decatur, 2006; vol. Decatur City Schs., 2004—06, Cmty. Free Clinic, Decatur, 2005, Habitat for Humanity, Decatur, 2006, Morgan County Pub. Libr., Decatur, 2006; docent Carnegie Visual Arts Ctr., 2003. Recipient Commander's Coin, Cold War Recognition Cert. for Fed. Govt. Svc. Mem.: Am. Bus. Women's Assn. Republican. Avocations: reading, writing, art, antiques, collectibles, cooking. Home Phone: 256-584-9893.

MILES, MICHAEL A., JR., retail executive; BA, Yale U., New Haven, 1983; MBA, Harvard U., 1987. Sr. v.p. concept devel. & franchise Pizza Hut Yum! Brands, Inc., 1996—99, COO Pizza Hut, 2000—03; COO Staples, Inc., Framingham, Mass., 2003—, pres., 2006—. Bd. dir. Western Union. Office: Staples Inc 500 Staples Dr Framingham MA 01702 *

MILES, MICHAEL ARNOLD, consumer products executive; b. Chgo., June 22, 1939; s. Arnold and Alice (Morrissey) Miles; m. Pamela L. Miles; children: Michael Arnold Jr., Christopher. BS, Northwestern U., 1961. Various mgmt. positions to v.p., account supr. Leo Burnett Co., Inc., 1961—71; with Heublein, Inc., 1971—82; sr. v.p. mktg. Ky. Fried Chicken, 1971—72; v.p. gen. mgr. grocery products Heublein, Inc., 1972—75, group v.p. internat. ops., 1976—77, v.p. group exec. Internat. group, chmn. food svc. and franchise group Ky. Fried Chicken, 1977—81, sr. v.p. foods Louisville, 1981—82; pres., COO Kraft Gen. Foods, Glenview, Ill., 1982—89; CEO, vice chmn. Philip Morris Cos., Inc., 1989—91, dep. chmn., 1991, CEO, 1991—94; special ltd. ptnr. Forstmann Little & Co., 1995—. Bd. dirs. Sears Holding Corp., Time Warner, 1995—, AMR Corp., Citadel Broadcasting Corp., Dell Inc. Bd. dirs. Jr. Achievement Chgo., Coun. Fgn. Rels., Nat. Multiple Sclerosis Soc., Lyric Opera Chgo.; mem. adv. coun. J.L. Kellogg Grad. Sch. Mgmt. Northwestern U., Evanston, Ill.

MILES, RAYMOND EDWARD, retired dean, organizational behavior and industrial relations educator; b. Cleburne, Tex., Nov. 2, 1932; s. Willard Francis and Wilma Nell (Owen) M.; m. Lucile Dustin, Dec. 27, 1952; children: Laura, Grant, Kenneth. BA with highest honors, U. North Tex., 1954, MBA, 1958; PhD, Stanford U., 1963. Clk. Santa Fe R.R., Gainesville, Tex., 1950-55; instr. mgmt. Sch. Bus. U. North Tex., Denton, 1958-60; asst. prof. organizational behavior and indsl. relations Sch. Bus. Adminstrn. U. Calif.-Berkeley, 1963-68, assoc. prof., 1968-71, prof., 1971—, assoc. dean Haas Sch. of Bus., 1978-81, dean, 1983-90; dir. Inst. Indsl. Relations, 1982-83; cons. various pvt., pub. orgns. Author: Theories of Management, 1975; (with Charles C. Snow) Organization Strategy, Structure and Process, 1978, Fit, Failure, and the Hall of Fame, 1994; co-author: Organizational Behavior: Research and Issues, 1976, (with Grant Miller and Charles C. Snow) Collaborative Entrepeneurship, 2005; co-editor, contbg. author: Organization by Design: Theory and Practice, 1981. Served to 1st. lt. USAF, 1955-58. Mem.: Acad. Mgmt. Democrat. Unitarian Universalist. Home: 8640 Don Carol Dr El Cerrito CA 94530-2733 Office: U Calif Walter A Haas Sch Bus Berkeley CA 94720-0001 Business E-Mail: miles@haas.berkeley.edu.

MILES, RICHARD BRYANT, mechanical and aerospace engineering educator; b. Washington, July 10, 1943; s. Thomas Kirk and Elizabeth (Bryant) M.; m. Susan McCoy, May 14, 1983; children: Thomas, Julia. BSEE, Stanford U., 1966, MSEE, 1967, PhD in Elec. Engring., 1972. Rsch. assoc. elec. engring. dept. Stanford (Calif.) U., summer 1972; asst. prof. mech. and aerospace engring. dept. Princeton (N.J.) U., 1972-78, assoc. prof., 1978-82, prof., 1982—, chmn. engring. physics program, 1980-96, acting chmn. dept. mech. and aero. engring., 2002. Lectr. Northwestern Poly. U., Xian, China, 1987; rsch. scientist CNRS; vis. prof. U. Marseilles, France, 1995; bd. dirs. Precision Optics Corp., Gardner, Mass. Contbr. articles to profl. pubs., chpt. to book and conf. procs.; patentee in field. Bd. dirs. Fannie and John Hertz Found., Livermore, Calif., 1989—; trustee Pacific U., Forest Grove, Oreg. Fannie and John Hertz Found. fellow, 1969-72. Fellow AIAA (Aerodynamic Measurement Tech. TC award 2000) Optical Soc. Am.; mem. IEEE (sr.), Am. Phys. Soc. Office: Princeton U Mech & Aerospace Engring D-414 Eng Quad Olden St Princeton NJ 08544-0001 Office Phone: 609-258-5131. Business E-Mail: miles@princeton.edu.

MILES, THOMAS CASWELL, aerospace engineer; b. Atlanta, Mar. 21, 1952; s. Franklin Caswell and Eugenia Frances (Newsom) M.; m. Linda Susan Duggleby, Aug. 10, 1980. BMET, So. Poly. State U., 1977; postgrad., Troy State U., 1978-80. Assoc. engr. aircraft design Lockheed Martin Aero. Co., Marietta, Ga., 1980-82, engr., aircraft design, 1982-85, sr. engr., aircraft design, 1985-89, group engr., 1989-90, specialist engr., 1990-98, sr. specialist engr., 1998-2001, staff engr., 2001—. Mem. SAE-A-6 Mil. Aircraft & Helicopter Panel, 1987-91, SAE-A-10 Aircraft Oxygen Equipment Com., 1996—. Mem. AIAA, (assoc. fellow), ASME, ASTM, Nat. Mgmt. Assn. (bd. dirs. 1996-2000), Soc. Automotive Engrs. (SAE co. rep., SAE Atlanta sect. vice chmn. aircraft), Oxygen Standardization Coord. Group, Assn. Fraternity Advisors (affiliate), Wick's Lake Homeowners Assn. (pres. 1995, v.p. 1996, 97), Tau Kappa Epsilon (Providence advisor 1999-2002, dist. pres. 1987-88, dist. v.p. 1984-99, chpt. advisor 1980-87, key leader 1985, 90, So. Order of Honor 1989, Edn. Found. medal of excellence 2002). Avocations: sailing, screen printing, bicycling. Home: 1926 Wicks Ridge Ln Marietta GA 30062-6777 Personal E-mail: tekezeke@aol.com.

MILES, WENDELL A., federal judge; b. Holland, Mich., Apr. 17, 1916; s. Fred T. and Dena Del (Alverson) M.; m. Mariette Bruckert, June 8, 1946; children: Lorraine Miles, Michelle Miles Kopinski, Thomas Paul. AB, Hope Coll., 1938, LLD (hon.), 1980; MA, U. Wyo., 1939; JD, U. Mich., 1942; LLD (hon.), Detroit Coll. Law, 1979. Bar: Mich. Ptnr. Miles & Miles, Holland, 1948-53, Miles, Mika, Meyers, Beckett & Jones, Grand Rapids, Mich., 1961-70; pros. atty. County of Ottawa, Mich., 1949-53; U.S. dist. atty. Western Dist. Mich., Grand Rapids, 1953-60, U.S. dist. judge, 1974—, chief judge, 1979-86, sr. judge, 1986—. Cir. judge 20th Jud. Cir. Ct. Mich., 1970-74; instr. Hope Coll., 1948-53, Am. Inst. Banking, 1953-60; adj. prof. Am. constl. history Hope Coll., Holland, Mich., 1979—; mem. Mich. Higher Edn. Commn.; apptd. Fgn. Intelligence Surveillance Ct., Washington, 1989—. Pres. Holland Bd. Edn., 1952-63. Served to capt. U.S. Army, 1942-47. Recipient Liberty Bell award, 1986.

Fellow Am. Bar Found.; mem. ABA, Mich. Bar Assn., Fed. Bar Assn., Ottawa County Bar Assn., Grand Rapids Bar (Inns of Ct. 1995—), Am. Judicature Soc., Torch Club, Rotary Club, Masons. Office: US Dist Ct 236 Fed Bldg 110 Michigan St NW Ste 452 Grand Rapids MI 49503-2363 Home (Winter): 16380 Kelly Cove Dr #305 Fort Myers FL 33908 Home Phone: 616-942-8538; Office Phone: 616-456-2314. Business E-Mail: miles@miwd.uscourts.gov.

MILETICH, IVO, library and information scientist, bibliographer, educator, linguist, literature research specialist; b. Pucisca, Yugoslavia, Apr. 18, 1936; came to U.S., 1966, naturalized, 1972; s. Josip and Mandina (Bagich) M.; m. Mira Pilja, Mar. 11, 1967; children: George Edward, Marina Julie. AB, Acad. Edn., Split, Yugoslavia, 1960; AM in History, U. Skopje, Macedonia, Yugoslavia, 1966; cert. advanced study, English Inst., Chgo., 1969; MA in Libr. Sci., Rosary Coll., River Forest, Ill., 1971. Cert. libr., Va. Tchr. various schs., Yugoslavia, 1959-65; asst. bibliographer Slavic langs. and lit. Joseph Regenstein and Sam Harper Librs., U. Chgo., 1967-71; tchr. Croatian lang. co-edn. YMCA Community Coll., Chgo., 1969-71, 74—; bibliographer Old Dominion U., Norfolk, Va., 1971-74; assoc. prof. libr. sci., bibliographer Chgo. State U., 1974—. Translator, interpreter English, Latin, Croatian, Serbian, Macedonian, Bulgarian, Old Ch. Slavic, Slovene, 1969—; interpreter Berlitz Trans. Ctr. Sch. Langs.; lectr. South Slavonic langs., lit., history and culture, Balkan states culture, heritage and folk lit., transl. techniques; lectr. in field. Contbr. various confs., seminars, workshops, jours., transl. of articles, studies, work on dictionary, Berlitz Transl. Svc. transl. and interpretion. Recipient cert. of appreciation YMCA C.C., Chgo., 1976, cert. Beta Phi Mu, U. Pitts., 1972, Am. Translators Assn., 1980, Assn. Coll. and Rsch. Librs., 1986. Mem. ALA, Am. Fedn. Tchrs., Assn. Coll. and Rsch. Librs., Chgo. Acad. Libr. Coun. Libr. of Congress (assoc.), Soc. Scholarly Publishing, Beta Phi Mu. Home: 618 Exchange Ave Calumet City IL 60409-3903 Office: Chgo State U Rm Lib 203 95th St at King Dr Chicago IL 60628

MILETICH, JOSEPH P., medical products executive; MD, PhD in Molecular Biology, Washington U., St. Louis. Dir. labs. Barnes-Jewish Hosp., St. Louis; prof. internal medicine and pathology, chief divsn. lab. medicine Washington U. Sch. Medicine, St. Louis; sr. v.p. worldwide preclinical devel. Merck Rsch. Labs.; sr. v.p. R & D Amgen, Inc. Contbr. articles to med. jours. Office: Amgen Inc One Amgen Center Dr Thousand Oaks CA 91320-1799 Office Phone: 805-447-1000. Office Fax: 805-447-1010. *

MILEWSKI, BARBARA ANNE, pediatrics nurse, neonatal/perinatal nurse practitioner, critical care nurse; b. Chgo., Sept. 11, 1934; d. Anthony and LaVerne (Sepp) Witt; m. Leonard A. Milewski, Feb. 23, 1952; children: Pamela, Robert, Diane, Timothy. ADN, Harper Coll., Palatine, Ill., 1982; BS, Northern Ill. U., 1992; postgrad., North Park Coll. RN Ill., cert. CPR instr. Staff nurse N.W. Cmty. Hosp., Arlington Heights, Ill., Resurrection Hosp., Chgo.; nurse neonatal ICU Children's Meml. Hosp., Chgo.; day care cons. Cook County Dept. Pub. Health; owner, CEO Child Care Health Cons. CPR instr. Stewart Oxygen Svcs., Chgo., Harper Coll., Children's Meml. Hosp.; instr., organizer parenting and well baby classes and clinics; health coord. CEDA Head Start; mem. adv. bd. Cook County Child Care Resource and Referral; dir. Albany Park Head Start. Vol. Children's Meml. Hosp., Boy Scouts Am. Mem.: Am. Mortar Bd., Sigma Theta Tau. Personal E-mail: barbmilewski@aol.com.

MILEY, GEORGE H., nuclear and electrical engineering educator, plasma engineer, energy conversion scientist; b. Shreveport, La., Aug. 6, 1933; s. George Hunter and Norma Angeline (Dowling) M.; m. Elizabeth Burroughs, Nov. 22, 1958; children: Susan Miley Hibbs, Hunter Robert. BS in Chem. Engring., Carnegie-Mellon U., 1955; MS, U. Mich., 1956, PhD in Chem.-Nuclear Engring., 1959. Nuclear engr. Knolls Atomic Power Lab., Gen. Electric Co., Schenectady, 1959-61; mem. faculty U. Ill., Urbana, 1961—, prof., 1967—, chmn. nuclear engring. program, 1975-86, dir. Fusion Studies Lab., 1976—, fellow Ctr. for Advanced Study, 1985-86; dir. rsch. Rockford Tech. Assocs. Inc., 1990-94; pres., dir. rsch. NPL Assocs. Inc., 1994—; chief scientist Lattice Energy, LLC, 2001—03. Vis. prof. U. Colo., 1967, Cornell U., 1969-70, U. New South Wales, 1986, Imperial Coll. of London, 1987; mem. Ill. Radiation Protection Bd., 1988—; mem. Air Force Studies Bd., 1990-94; chmn. tech. adv. com. Ill. Low Level Radioactive Waste Site, 1990-96; chmn. com. on indsl. uses of radiation Ill. Dept. Nuclear Safety, 1989-2000. Author: Direct Conversion of Nuclear Radiation Energy, 1971, Fusion Energy Conversion, 1976; editor Jour. Fusion Tech., 1980-2001; U.S. assoc. editor Laser and Particle Beams, 1982-86, mng. editor, 1987-91, editor-in-chief, 1991-2002; U.S. editor Jour. Plasma Physics, 1995-2003. Served with C.E. AUS, 1960. Recipient Western Electric Tchg.-Rsch. award, 1977, Halliburton Engring. Edn. Leadership award, 1990, Edward Teller medal, 1995, Scientist of Yr. award Inst. New Energy, 1996, Cert. Recognition award NASA, 2003; NATO sr. sci. fellow, 1975-76, Guggenheim fellow, 1985-86, Japanese Soc. Promotion of Sci. fellow, 1994, CMNS Preparata medal, 2006, Integrity in Rsch. award, 2006. Fellow IEEE (Fusion Engring. and Sci. award, 2004), Am. Nuclear Soc. (dir. 1980-83, Disting. Svc. award 1980, Outstanding Achievement award Fusion Energy divsn. 1992, Radiation Sci. and Tech. award 2004), Am. Phys. Soc., AIAA (assoc.); mem. Am. Soc. Engring. Edn. (chmn. energy conversion com. 1967-70, pres. U. Ill. chpt. 1973-74, chmn. nuclear divsn. 1975-76, Outstanding Tchr. award 1973), Sigma Xi, Tau Beta Pi. Presbyterian. Achievements include research in fusion, energy conversion, reactor kinetics, and fuel cells. Avocations: tennis, hiking. Office: U Ill 214 Nuc Engring Lab 103 S Goodwin Ave Urbana IL 61801-2901 Home Phone: 217-356-5402; Office Phone: 217-333-3772. E-mail: georgehm@aol.com. *My professional goal has been to insure that future generations have a plentiful supply of economical, readily available energy such as offered by fusion. Not only should this insure a continued improvement in the standard of living for persons in all nations, but it should help maintain peace which is threatened by the struggle to obtain and control limited natural sources of energy.*

MILEY, JENNA YVONNE, education educator, consultant; b. S. Charleston, W.Va., Nov. 23, 1951; d. Edgar M. and Retha M. (Barnes) Gillespie; m. Stanley Leon Miley, Apr. 19, 1985; 1 child, James E. Caruthers. AS, Mohegan C.C., Norwich, Conn., 1990; BS, So. Ill. U., 1993; MA, Webster U., St. Louis, 1994; postgrad., Capella U., 2006—. Instr. Owensboro C.C., Ky., 1995—96; summer intern GRADD, Owensboro, Ky., 1996; instr. Jefferson C.C., Louisville, 1997, Carolina C.C., Sanford, NC, 1998—99, Al Ain Women's Coll., United Arab Emirates, 1999—2002; asst. prof. Bainbridge (Ga.) Coll., 2002—. Dir. mini-grant Svc. Learning. Author: (newsletter) College Success. Mem. steering com. Leadership Decatur County, 2004—05. Decorated Outstanding Unit Ribbon USAF; Gov.'s Tchg. fellow, 2005—06. Mem.: AAUW (pres. Bainbridge chpt. 2005—06), AAUP, Lions. Republican. Pentecostal. Avocation: travel, reading. Office: Bainbridge Coll 2500 E Shotwell St Bainbridge GA 39819 Home Phone: 229-246-7162; Office Phone: 229-248-2567. Personal E-mail: jmiley@bainbridge.edu.

MILFORD, FREDERICK JOHN, retired research and development company executive; b. Cleve., July 1, 1926; s. Frederick Charles and Florence M.; m. Jean Irene Olson, Sept. 8, 1951; 1 child, Cheryl Lynn. BS in Physics, Case Inst. Tech., 1949; PhD in Physics, M.I.T., 1952. Instr. Case Inst. Tech., Cleve., 1952-56, asst. prof., 1956-59; div. cons. Battelle Columbus Labs., 1959-62, div. chief, 1962-64, sr. fellow, 1964-66, dir. research in phys. scis., 1966-73, scientist, 1973, dept. mgr., 1973-76, assoc. dir., 1976-85, chief scientist, 1985-87, v.p. spl. programs, 1987-89, ret., 1989. Vis. prof. physics U. Wash., 1969 Author: (with J.R. Reitz) Foundations of Electromagnetic Theory, 1960, 4th edit., 1993. Emeritus mem. adv. bd. Central Ohio Salvation Army. Served with USNR, 1945-46. George Eastman fellow, 1951-52; Focke scholar, 1948-49 Fellow Am. Phys. Soc.; mem. Masons, Kit Kat Club, Ctrl. Ohio Lions Eye Bank (oper. bd. 1993—). Home: 1411 London Dr Columbus OH 43221-1543

MILFORD, MURRAY HUDSON, retired soil science educator; b. Honey Grove, Tex., Sept. 29, 1934; s. Murray Lane and Vivian Ione (Hudson) M.; m. Marsha Ann Rasmussen, July 21, 1961; children: Rebecca Ione, Murray Daniel. BS in Agronomy, Tex. A&M, 1955, MS in Agronomy, 1959; PhD in Soil Science, U. Wis., 1962. Cert. profl. soil scientist. Rsch. assoc. Cornell U., Ithaca, NY, 1962-63, asst. prof., 1963-68, assoc. prof., 1968, Tex. A&M U., College Station, 1968-74, prof., 1974-2001; ret., 2001. Author: (lab. manual) Soils and Soil Science-Lab. Exercises, 1970. 1st lt. USAR, 1955-57. Recipient so. region award for excellence in coll. and univ. tchg. in food and agrl. scis. Nat. Assn. State Univs. and Land Grant Colls., Higher Edn. Program, USDA, 1995. Fellow AAAS, Am. Soc. Agronomy (pres. Tex. chpt. 1982-83, Resident Edn. award 1978), Soil Sci. Soc. Am. (Edn. award 1988); mem. Soil and Water Conservation Soc. (pres. Tex. coun. of chpts. 1987). Democrat. Presbyterian. Home: 3606 Tanglewood Dr Bryan TX 77802-3320

MILGRAM, ANNE M., state attorney general; b. Dec. 1, 1970; BA in English & Polit. Sci., Rutgers Coll., 1992; MPhil in Social & Polit. Theory, U. Cambridge, Eng., 1993; JD, NYU, 1996. Law clk. to Hon. Anne E. Thompson US Dist. Ct. NJ, Trenton, 1996—97; asst. dist. atty. NYC, 1997—2001; prosecutor criminal sect. US Dept. Justice, 2001, lead fed. prosecutor; counsel to Gov. Jon Corzine State of NJ, Trenton, 2005, acting atty. gen., 2006, first asst. atty. gen., 2006—07, atty. gen., 2007—. Recipient Spl. Commendation for Outstanding Svc., US Dept. Justice, 2004, Director's award, 2006. Office: Office Atty Gen Richard J Hughes Justice Complex 25 Market St 8th Fl West Wing Trenton NJ 08625-0080 *

MILGRAM, JEROME H., marine and ocean engineer, educator; b. Phila., Sept. 23, 1938; s. Samuel J. and Fannie M. BSEE, MIT, 1961, BS in Naval Architecture and Marine Engring., 1961, MS, 1962, PhD in Hydrodynamics, 1965. Registered profl. engr., Mass. With Scripps Inst. Oceanography, San Diego, summer 1961; project engr. Block Assocs., Cambridge, Mass., 1961-67; asst. prof. MIT, Cambridge, 1967-70, assoc. prof., 1970-77, prof. ocean engring., 1977-89, William I. Koch prof. marine tech., 1989—, prof. mech. engring., 2005—. Rsch. assoc. in biophysics Harvard U. Med. Sch., 1974-76; vis. prof. in naval architecture and marine engring. U. Mich., 1988-89; design dir. Am. 3 Found., 1991-95; guest investigator Woods Hole Oceanog. Instn., 1996—; vis. prof. Johns Hopkins U., 1996-97; investigator and expert witness for marine casualties. Contbr. articles to profl. jours.; patentee in field. Recipient Am. Bur. Shipping award, 1961, Alan Berman Outstanding Rsch. Publ. award U.S. Naval Rsch. Lab., 1990, AT&T Design Innovation award, 1992. Fellow Soc. Naval Archs. and Marine Engrs. (life); mem. NAE (life), Nat. Rsch. Coun. (marine bd. 1998-2001). Home: 20 Blossom Hill Rd Winchester MA 01890-3455 Office: MIT 77 Massachusetts Ave Rm 5-318 Cambridge MA 02139-4307 Business E-Mail: jmilgram@mit.edu.

MILGRIM, DARROW A., insurance company executive; b. Chgo., Apr. 30, 1945; BA, Calif. State U., San Bernardino, 1968; postgrad., U. So. Calif., 1972. Accredited ins. advisor, cert. ins. counselor; sch. adminstr. Tchr. Rialto Unified Sch. Dist., Calif., 1969-70, Las Virgenes Unified Sch. Dist., Westlake Village, Calif., 1970-78; instr. Calif. State U., Northridge, 1980-84; pres. Darrow Milgrim Ins. Svcs., Inc.; ins. broker, dir. Speare Ins. Brokers, Blade Ins. Svcs., Sherman Oaks, Calif., 1984—2004; sr. v.p. Acordia Calif., Inc., a Wells Fargo Ins. Svcs., Sherman Oaks, 2004—. Cons. Ronald McDonald House Charities, SC, LA, 1986—95, ACA Legis. Task Force and Nat. Pub. Policy com.; bd. dirs. Calamigos Star C Ranch Summer Camp, Malibu, Calif., Calamigos Environ. Edn. Ctr., Malibu. Editor: Legislation and Regulations for Organized Camps, 1987. Pres. Calif. Camping Adv. Coun., Long Beach, 1985—87, 1999—2000; bd. dirs. Calif. Collaboration Youth, Sacramento, 1985—, Camp Ronald McDonald Good Times, 1989—95; commr. dept. pks. and recreation City of Agoura Hills, Calif., 1987—93. Mem.: Market Ins. Co. Agents Coun., Agts. and Brokers State Legis. Coun., Ins. Brokers and Agts. L.A. Coun., Am. Camping Assn. (bd. dirs. So. Calif. sect., mem. nat. pub. policy com. Martinsville, Ind. 1980—98, nat. bd. dirs. 1990—95, legis. liaison, regional honor 1986), United Educators Nat. Broker Adv. Coun. Office: Acordia Calif Inc 15303 Ventura Blvd 7th Fl Sherman Oaks CA 91403 Office Phone: 818-464-9308. Business E-Mail: darrow_milgrim@wellsfargois.com.

MILGRIM, ROGER MICHAEL, lawyer; b. NYC, Mar. 22, 1937; s. Israel and Iola (Lash) Milgrim; 1 child, Justin. BA, U. Pa., 1958; LLB, NYU, 1961, LLM, 1962. Bar: NY, US Supreme Ct. Assoc. Baker & McKenzie, Paris, 1963-65, Nixon Mudge et al, NYC, 1965-68; mem. Milgrim Thomajan & Lee P.C., NYC, 1968-92; ptnr., chmn. intellectual property group Paul, Hastings, Janofsky & Walker LLP, NYC, 1992—2005, chmn. litig. dept., 1999—2000. Adj. prof. sch. law NYU, NYC, 1974—95. Author: Milgrim on Trade Secrets, 1967, supplement, 2007, Milgrim on Licensing, 1990, supplement, 2007. Trustee Coll. Wooster, 1994-97, Bklyn. Hosp., 1982-91; bd. dirs. Fulbright Assn., 1998—2004, chmn. Fulbright Prize com., 1999-2001; bd. dirs. Technip, 1998—; mem. bd. advs. UniStates LLC, 2000-06. Mem. Knickerbocker Club. Republican. Home: 431 Paxinosa Rd E Easton PA 18040-1337 Home Phone: 610-438-4418; Office Phone: 212-318-6010. Business E-Mail: rogermilgrim@paulhastings.com.

MILGROM, FELIX, immunologist, educator; b. Rohatyn, Poland, Oct. 12, 1919; came to U.S., 1958; naturalized, 1963; s. Henryk and Ernestina (Cyryl) M.; m. Halina Miszel, Oct. 15, 1941; children: Henry, Martin Louis. Student, U. Lwow, Poland, 1937-41, U. Lublin, 1945; MD, U. Wroclaw, Poland, 1947; MD (hon.), U. Vienna, Austria, 1976, U. Lund, Sweden, 1979, U. Heidelberg, Fed. Republic Germany, 1979, U. Bergen, Norway, 1980; DSc (hon.), U. Med. Dent., NJ, 1991. Rsch. assoc., prof. dept. microbiology Sch. Medicine U. Wroclaw, 1946-54, chmn. dept., 1954; prof., head dept. microbiology Sch. Medicine, Silesian U., Zabrze, Poland, 1954-57; rsch. assoc. Svc. de Chime Microbienne, Pasteur Inst., Paris, 1957; rsch. assoc. prof. dept. bacteriology and immunology U. Buffalo Sch. Medicine, 1958-62; assoc. prof., then prof. and disting. prof. microbiology Sch. Medicine, SUNY, Buffalo, 1962—, chmn. dept., 1967-85. Author: Studies on the Structure of Antibodies, 1950; co-editor: International Convocations on Immunology, 1969, 75, 79, 85, Principles of Immunology, 1973, 2d edit., 1979, Principles of Immunological Diagnosis in Medicine, 1981, Medical Microbiology, 1982; editor in chief Internat. Archives of Allergy and Applied Immunology, 1965-91; contbg. editor Vox Sanguinis, 1965-76, Transfusion, 1966-73, Cellular Immunology, 1970-83, Transplantation, 1975-78; contbr. numerous articles to profl. jours. Recipient Alfred Jurzykowski Found. prize, 1986, Paul Ehrlich and Ludwig Darmstaedter prize, 1987. Mem. Am. Assn. Immunologists, Transplantation Soc. (v.p. 1976-78), Am. Acad. Microbiology, Coll. Internat. Allergologicum (v.p. 1970-78, pres. 1978-82, hon. mem. 1990—), Polish Acad. Arts and Scis., Sigma Xi. Achievements include research in the serology of syphilis, Tb, rheumatoid arthritis, organ and tissue specificity including blood groups, transplantation and autoimmunity. Home: 474 Getzville Rd Buffalo NY 14226-2555 Office Phone: 716-829-3816. Business E-Mail: milgrom@buffalo.edu.

MILGROM, PAUL ROBERT, economics educator; b. Detroit, Apr. 20, 1948; s. Abraham Isaac and Anne (Finkelstein) M.; m. Jan Thurston, Dec. 10, 1977; children: Joshua, Elana. AB in Math. with high honors, U. Mich., 1970; MS in Stats., Stanford U., 1978, PhD in Bus., 1979; MA (hon.), Yale U., 1983. Actuarial trainee Met. Life Ins. Co., 1970-71; conulting actuary Nelson and Warren, Inc., 1972-75; asst. prof. dept. managerial econs. and decision scis. Kellogg Grad. Sch. Mgmt. Northwestern U., 1979-81, assoc. prof., 1981-82, prof., 1982-83; prof. econs. and mgmt. Yale U., 1983-85, Williams Bros. prof. mgmt. studies, prof. econs., 1985-87; prof. econs. Stanford U., 1987—, Shirley R. and Leonard W. Ely, Jr. prof. humanities and scis., 1993—. Vis. rsch. assoc. econs. Stanford U., 1981; vis. prof. Yale U., 1982-83; Ford vis. prof. econs. U. Calif. Berkeley, 1986-87; IBM rsch. chair Northwestern U., 1981; Williams Bros. chair mgmt. studies Yale U., 1985; Olin disting. lectr. Princeton U., 1988; dir. Stanford Inst. for Theoretical Econs., 1989-1991; past cons. So. New Eng. Telephone Co., Rand Corp., Arctic Slope Regional Corp., Ga. Pacific, Exxon, Pacific Telesis, Bell Atlantic, Govt. of Mex., others; lectr. in field. Author: (with John Roberts) Economics, Organization and Management, 1992, (with John Roberts), Instructor's Manual for Economics, Organization and Management, 1992; assoc. editor Jour. Econ. Theory, 1983-87, Rand Jour. Econs., 1985-89, Econometrica, 1987-90, Jour. Fin. Intermediation, 1989-92, Games and Econ. Behavior, 1990-92; co-editor Am. Econ. Review, 1990-93; contbr. over 50 articles to profl. jours. Recipient Leonard J. Savage Meml. Thesis award, 1980, Rsch. grant NSF, 1980, 82, 85, 88-91, 89, 91, Rsch. award Actuarial Edn. and Rsch. Fund, 1983, John Simon Guggenheim fellowship, 1986, Best Paper of Yr. award, 1987, Rsch. grant Ctr. Econ. Policy, 1988, 90. Fellow Am. Acad. Arts and Scis., Econometric Soc. (plenary lectr. 5th World Congress 1985), Morse Coll., Inst. Advanced Studies Hebrew U. Jerusalem, Ctr. Advanced Study in Behavioral Scis., Soc. Actuaries (Triennial Paper prize 1976); mem. Am. Econ. Assn., NAS. Office: Stanford Univ Dept Econs Stanford CA 94305 E-mail: milgrom@stanford.edu.

MILHOLLAND, TERENCE V., finance company executive; b. Balt., Md. BS, Univ. Md.; MS, George Washington Univ. Mgmt. positions Boeing Co., 1978—99, CIO, 1997—99; sr. v.p., CIO, chief tech. officer EDS, 1999—2005; exec. v.p., chief tech. officer Visa Internat., Foster City, Calif., 2005—. Mailing: Visa Internat PO Box 8999 San Francisco CA 94128-8999 Office: Visa Internat 900 Metro Ctr Blvd Foster City CA 94404 *

MILHORAT, THOMAS HERRICK, neurosurgeon; b. NYC, Apr. 5, 1936; s. Ade Thomas and Edith Caulkins (Herrick) M.; m. Edith Mostile, 1961; children: John Thomas, Robert Herrick. BA, Cornell U., 1957, MD, 1961. Intern, asst. resident in gen. surgery N.Y. Hosp.-Cornell Med. Ctr., 1961—63, asst. resident, chief resident in neurosurgery, 1965—68, asst. neurosurgeon NIH, 1968—71; clin. assoc., dept. surg. neurology Nat. Inst. Neurol. Diseases and Blindness, Bethesda, 1963—65; assoc. prof. neurol. surgery, assoc. prof. child health and devel. George Washington U. Sch. Medicine, Washington, 1971—74, prof. neurol. surgery, prof. child health and devel., 1974—81; chmn. dept. neurosurgery Children's Hosp. Nat. Med. Ctr., Washington, 1971—81; prof. neurol. surgery, dept. chmn. SUNY Health Sci. Ctr., Bklyn., 1982—2001; chmn. dept. neurosurgery North Shore/L.I. Jewish Health System, 2002—; founder, dir. Chiari Inst. North Shore Univ. Hosp., 2002—; dir. Harvey Cushing Insts. Neurosci., Northshore-LI Jewish Health System, 2006—; prof. neurol. surgery NYU Sch. Medicine, 2002—. Neurosurgeon-in-chief Kings County Hosp. Ctr., 1982—2001; regional chmn. neurol. surgery L.I. Coll. Hosp., 1986—2001; program dir. Neurosurgery Rsch. Tng. Program, 1982—2001; mem. Nat. Coun. Scientists NIH, 1969—82; dir. Harvey Cushing Inst. Neurosci. North Shore L.I. Jewish Health Sys., NY, 2006—. Author: Hydrocephalus and Cerebrospinal Fluid, 1972, Pediatric Neurosurgery, 1978, Cerebrospinal Fluid and the Brain Edemas, 1987; (with M.K. Hammock) Cranial Computed Tomography in Infancy and Childhood, 1981; mem. editl. bd. Neurosurgery, 1997—, Neurosug Focus: Syringomyelia, 2000—; contbr. more than 325 articles to profl. jours. Lt. comdr. USPHS, 1963—65. Recipient 1st prize in pathology, Cornell U. Med. Sch. Dept. Ob-Gyn., 1960, Charles L. Horn prize Cornell Med. Sch., 1961, Best Paper award ann. combined meeting N.Y. Acad. Medicine/N.Y. Neurosurg. Soc., 1965, Pudenz award for Excellence in CSF Physiology, 1994, E. Jefferson Browder award for excellence in Neurosurgery, 1996, Arthur A. Kaplan award for excellence in neurosurgery, 1999. Mem. AAAS, Internat. Soc. Pediat. Neurosurgery, Am. Assn. Neurol. Surgery, Am. Syringomyelia Alliance Project (chmn. med. adv. bd. 1996—, bd. dirs. 1996—), Am. Acad. Pediat. (surg. sect.), Soc. Pediat. Rsch., N.Y. Acad. Medicine, N.Y. Soc. Neurosurgery (pres. 1988-90), Bklyn. Neurologic Soc. (pres. 1988-95), Soc. Neurosci., Internat. Soc. Neurosci., Soc. Neurol. Surgeons, Sigma Xi. Avocations: golf, billiards, gardening. Office: North Shore Univ Hosp Dept Neurosurgery Manhasset NY 11030 Office Phone: 516-562-3020. Business E-Mail: milhorat@nshs.edu.

MILIC-EMILI, JOSEPH, physiologist, educator; b. Sezana, Slovenia, May 27, 1931; arrived in Can., 1963; s. Joseph Milic-Emili and Giovanna Milic-Emili Perhavec; m. Ann Harding, Nov. 2, 1957; children: Claire, Anne-Marie, Alice, Andrew. MD, U. Milan, 1955; Dr. honoris causa, U. Louvain, Belgium, 1987, Kunming Med. Coll., China, 1987, U. Montpellier, France, 1994, U. Ferrara, Italy, 1996, U. Athens, Greece, 1998, U. Ljubljana, Slovenia. Asst. prof. physiology and exptl. medicine McGill U., Montreal, Que., Canada, 1963-65, assoc. prof., 1965-69, prof., 1970-97, prof. emeritus, 1998—, dir. Meakins-Christie Labs., 1979-94. Vis. prof. Lab. de Physiologie Faculte de Medecine Saint-Antoine, Paris, Svc. de Pneumologie Hosp. Beaujon, Paris, 1978-79, 94-95, chmn. dept. physiology, 1973-78; vis. cons. medicine Royal Postgrad. Med. Sch., London, 1969-70; vis. cons. Aeronautics Imperial Coll. Tech., London, 1969-70; asst. prof. physiology U. Liege, Belgium, 1958-60; asst. prof. U. Milan, 1956-58. Mem. editl. bd. Jour. Applied Physiology, 1970-76, Rev. Française des Maladies Respiratories, 1979-96, Rivista de Biologia, 1979-86, Am. Rev. Respiratory Disease, 1982-89, Reanimation, Soins Intensifs, Medicine d'Urgence, 1984-95. Mem. applied physiology and bioengring. study sect. NIH, 1975-78. Decorated Order of Can.; recipient Gold medal C. Forlanini U. Pavia, Italy, 1982, Am. Coll. Chest Physicians medal, 1984, 98, Harry Wunderly medal Thoracic Soc. Australia, 1988, medal Italian Sch. Mil. Medicine, 1990, medal Med. Sch. Brest, 1997, medal Med. Sch. Ferrara, 1997, medal Med. Sch. Bologna, 2006, Trudeau medal Am. Thoracic Soc., 2006; author of one of 100-most cited articles in clin. rsch. of 1960s; named one of 1,000 most-cited contemporary scientists, 1965-78, 1998 Presdl. award European Respiratory Soc., 1998 Disting. Lectr. in Physiology Am. Coll. Chest Physicians. Fellow Royal Soc. Can., Slovenian Acad. Sci. (fgn. corr.), Soc. Med. Clin. Bononiensis Sci.; mem. Am. Physiol. Soc., Can. Physiol. Soc., Can. Thoracic Soc., Med. Rsch. Coun. (mem. grants com. 1980), Soc. Pneumologie Belge (hon.), Brazilian Physiol. Soc. (hon.), Hellenic Thoracic Soc. (hon.), Polish Pneumological Soc. (hon.), Chilean Resp. Soc. (hon.). Home: 4394 Circle Rd Montreal PQ Canada H3W 1Y5 Office: McGill U Meakins-Christie Labs 3626 St Urbain St Montreal PQ Canada H2X 2P2 Office Phone: 514-398-3864 ext. 80144. Business E-Mail: joseph.milic-emili@mcgill.ca.

MILIOTIS, DEMITRIOS, physics professor; b. Korinth, Greece, Jan. 1, 1930; s. Menelaos and Angellika Miliotis; m. Louly Grifsa, June 10, 1960; 1 child, Menelaos. Diploma in Physics, Nat. U., Athens, Greece, 1957, PhD in Physics, 1964. Rsch. asst. Nat. Found. Rsch., Athens, 1958-65, rsch. assoc., 1969-71; rsch. asst. physics dept. U. Ill., Urbana, 1965-66, rsch. assoc., 1966-68; asst. prof. physics dept. U. Athens, 1971-72; assoc. prof. U. Ioannina, Greece, 1972-75, prof., chmn. applied physics, 1975-77, head physics and math. depts., 1978-80, prof. dept. physics, 1981-85, prof. emeritus, 1985—. Invited prof. U. Crete, Heraklion, Greece, 1977-78; vis. prof. physics dept. U. Ill., 1980-81. Author books on circuit analysis and semiconductor physics; contbr. articles to profl. jours. Lt. Greek Army, 1954-56. Home: 27A Kifissias Ave 11523 Athens Greece

MILKE, LINDA JEAN, elementary school educator; b. Muskegon, Mich., Sept. 30; d. John Carl and Helen Maxine Milke. BA, Western Mich. U., Kalamazoo, 1973; MEd in Curriculum and Instrn., Ariz. State U., Tempe, 2002. With Smitty's of Ariz., 1973—90; tchr. Tempe Elem. Dist., 1992—98; tchr. in sch. intervention Gililland Mid. Sch., Tempe, 1998—2003, tchr. 6th grade social studies, 2003—. Co-chair pride com. Gililland Mid. Sch., 2000—06, co-chair leadership team, 2003—04, mem. site coun., 2004—, mem. ASIP acad. coun., 2006—. Mem. Project Upward Bound Western Mich. U., 1967—69. Mem.: NEA (assoc.), Nat. Assn. Bilingual Educators (assoc.), Phi Kappa Phi. Avocations: antiques, home decorating, reading. Home: 7026 E Kiva Ave Mesa AZ 85209 Office: Gililland Middle Sch 1025 S Beck Ave Tempe AZ 85281 Office Phone: 480-966-7114 5895. Personal E-mail: lindamilke@msn.com. Business E-Mail: lindamilke@tempeschools.org.

MILKEN, MICHAEL R., think-tank executive, philanthropist; b. Calif., July 4, 1946; m. Lori Milken, Aug. 11, 1968; 3 children. Grad. summa cum laude, U. Calif., Berkeley; MBA, U. Pa. Securities trader Drexel Burnham Lambert, until 1990; chmn. The Milken Inst., 1991—; founder Prostate Cancer Found. (formerly CaPCure), 1993—; chair Knowledge Universe, 1996—; chmn. FasterCures/Ctr. for Accelerating Med. Solutions, 2003—. Author: Taste for Living Series cookbooks. Chair Assn. Cure of Cancer of the Prostate; co-founder Milken Family Found., 1982. Named one of 400 Richest Ams., Forbes mag., 2006. Office: Milken Inst 1250 Fourth St Ste 200 Santa Monica CA 90401 *

MILKMAN, ROGER DAWSON, genetics educator, molecular biologist, researcher; b. NYC, Oct. 15, 1930; s. Louis Arthur and Margaret (Weinstein) M.; m. Marianne Friedenthal, Oct. 18, 1958; children: Ruth Margaret Milkman Atkinson, Louise Friedenthal, Janet Dawson Milkman Lussenhop, Paul David. AB, Harvard U., 1951, A.M., 1954, PhD, 1956. Student, asst., instr., investigator Marine Biol. Lab., Woods Hole, Mass., 1952-72, 88-96; instr., asst. prof. U. Mich., Ann Arbor, 1957-60; assoc. prof., prof. Syracuse U., NY, 1960-68; prof. biol. scis. U. Iowa, Iowa City, 1968-2001, prof. emeritus, 2001—, chmn. univ. genetics PhD program, 1992-93. Vis. prof. biology Grinnell (Iowa) Coll., 1990; mem. genetics study sect. NIH, 1986-87; NSF panelist, 1996-99; adj. scientist Marine Biol. Lab., Woods Hole, 2002—, Josephine Bay Paul Ctr. Translator: (from German) Developmental Physiology, 2d edit., 1971; editor: Perspectives on Evolution, 1982, Experimental Population Genetics, 1983, Evolution jour., 1984-86; mem. editl. bd. Jour. Bacteriology, 1998-2000; contbr. articles to profl. jours. Sec. Soc. Gen. Physiologists, 1963-65, Am. Soc. Naturalists, 1980-82; alumni rep. Phillips Acad., Andover, Mass., 1980-94. NSF grantee, 1959—; USPHS grantee, 1984-87. Fellow AAAS; mem. Am. Soc. for Microbiology, Genetics Soc. Am., Corp. Marine Biol. Lab., Soc. for Gen. Microbiology (U.K.), Soc. study Evolution. Jewish. Avocation: mountain hiking. Home and Office: 12 Fells Rd Falmouth MA 02540-1626 Home Phone: 508-548-6248; Office Phone: 508-289-7390. Business E-Mail: rmilkman@mbl.edu, roger-milkman@uiowa.edu, rogmilkman@adelphia.net.

MILL, THEODORE, chemist, researcher; b. Apr. 17, 1931; BS, Wayne State U., 1953; PhD, U. Wash., 1956. Fellow Hickrill Rsch. Found., Katonah, NY, 1956-57; chemist DuPont Expt. Sta., DuPont Co., Wilmington, Del., 1957-60, Stanford Rsch. Inst., Menlo Park, Calif., 1960-64, dir. phys. organic chemistry dept., 1964-85, sr. scientist, 1985—. Fellow Stanford Rsch. Inst., 1996; cons. in field. Contbr. articles to profl. jours. Patentee in field. Grantee NSF, 1975-80, NIH, 1976-82, EPA, 1976-99, Dept. Energy, 2002-04. Mem. ACS (chmn. local sect. 1976), AAAS, Am. Geophys. Union, Sierra Club, Audubon Soc. Office: SRI 333 Ravenswood Ave PS 239 Menlo Park CA 94025-3493 Home Phone: 650-328-1069; Office Phone: 650-859-3605. Personal E-mail: ted.mill@srl.com.

MILLANE, LYNN, retired municipal official; b. Buffalo, Oct. 14, 1928; d. Robert P. and Justine A. Schermerhorn; m. J. Vaughan Millane Jr., Aug. 16, 1952; children: Maureen, Michele, John, Mark, Kathleen. EdB, U. Buffalo, 1949, EdM in Health Edn., 1951. Coun. mem. Amherst Town Bd., NY, 1982—96, dep. town supr., 1990-96, supr., 1996. Founder, liaison 1st adult day svcs. adv. bd. Town of Amherst, 1988, liaison to ad hoc cable TV com., 1992—96, liaison to Amherst C. of C., 1993—96, 1st records mgmt. adv. bd., liaison ethics bd., 1994—96; legis. liaison SUNY Family Violence Clin. Sch. Law, Buffalo, 1997—98; pres. E.J. Meyer Hosp. Jr. Bd., 1962—64; commr. (apptd. by Gov. George Pataki) NY State Ethics Commn., 1999—2004, 2004—; adv. bd. NY State Office Aging, 1996—2005, chair adv. bd., 1997—2005; spkr. in field. Pres. Aux. to Erie County Bar Assn., 1966-68, Womens Com. Buffalo Philharm. Orch., 1976-78, v.p. adminstrn., 1975-76, v.p. pub. affairs, 1974-75, chair. adv. bd., 1979-82; v.p. Buffalo Philharm. Orch. Soc., Inc., 1976-78, coun. mem., trustee, 1979-87, bd. overseers, 1987-92; dir. 8th jud. dist. NY State Assn. Large Towns, 1989-91; bd. dirs. oper. bd. Millard Fillmore Suburban Hosp., 1992-98; 1st v.p. Fams for 17, 1980-82, Friends of Baird Hall SUNY, Buffalo, 1980-82; exec. bd. Womens Exec. Coun. Erie County Rep. Com., 1969-71, Longview Protestant Home for Children, 1979-85, 2d v.p., 1982-85; bd. dirs. Amherst br. ARC, 1982-91, by-laws com., 1981, 84, chair sr. concerns com., 1982-91, liaison code of ethics com., 1987-89; nat. music com. Womens Assn. for Symphony Orchs. in Am. and Can., 1977-79; coun. mem. Am. Symphony Orch. League; sec. Amherst Sr. Citizens Adv. Bd., 1980-81, liaison from Amherst Town Bd., 1982-96; liaison to the Alternate Fuel and Clean Cities Com., 1994-96; dir.-at-large cmty. adv. coun. SUNY, Buffalo, 1981-91; co-assoc. chair maj. gift divsn. capital campaign Daemen Coll., 1983-84, trustee, 1998-; chair mem. com. Daemen Coll Trustees, 2003—; co-chair Women United Against Drugs Campaign, 1970-72; founding mem. Lunch and Issues, Amherst, 1981—; edn. com., bd. dirs. Network in Aging of Western NY, Inc., 1982-89, housing com., 1987-89; bd. dirs. Amherst Elderly Transp. Corp., 1982-99; committeeman dist. Town of Amherst Rep. Com.; treas. Town and Country Rep. Club, 1980-81; nominating com. Fedn. Rep. Womens Clubs Erie County, 1980; del. NY State Govs. Conf. on Aging, 1995, White House Conf. on Aging, 1995, named mem. aging svcs.; mem. Erie County Indsl. Devel. Agy. Erie County Regional Devel. Corp., 1996-97; mem. adv. bd. Amherst Symphony Orch., 2003-; vol. life project Greater Buffalo chpt. ARC, 2002-05, mem. svc. to older adults com., 2002-05. Named Homemaker of Yr., Family Circle mag., 1969, Woman of Substance, 20th Century Rep. Women, 1983, Woman of Yr., Buffalo Philharm. Orch. Soc., Inc., 1982, Outstanding Woman in Cmty. Svc., SUNY, Buffalo, 1985; recipient Good Neighbor award, Courier Express, 1978, Merit award, Buffalo Philharm. Orch., 1978, Edn. Rep. Womens Clubs Erie County award, 1982, Disting. Svc. award, Town of Amherst Sr. Ctr., 1985, Amherst Adult Day Care and Vis. Nurses Assn., 1994, Susan B. Anthony award, Interclub Coun. Western NY, 1991, Cmty. Svc. award, Amherst Rep. Com., 1991, D.A.R.E. award, Town of Amherst Police Dept., 1994, Amherst South Rotary Club, 1997, Outstanding Cmty. Svc. award, Amherst Sr. Citizen Found., 1997, Lynn Millane Cmty. Svc. award named in her honor, Rep. honoree, award for svc., Town of Amherst Youth Bd., 1996, award for care and assistance to sr. citizens of N.Y. State, Batavia Nursing Home, 2000, Woman of Distinction award, NY State Senate, 2003; hon. Paul Harris fellow. Mem. Amherst C. of C. (VIP dinner com. 1984), LWV, SUNY Buffalo Alumni Assn. (life, presdl. advisor 1977-79), Amherst Symphony Orch. Assn. (bd. dirs. 1981-87, roster chair. 1982-84, nominating chair 1985-86, vice-chair 50th ann. com. 1994-96, trustee 2003-), Niagara Connect, Amherst Rep. Womens Club (bd. dirs. 1963-65, 99), Zonta (pres. Amherst chpt. 1986-88, Zontian of Yr. 1992), Pi Lambda Theta (hon.).

MILLAR, GORDON HALSTEAD, mechanical engineer, agricultural products executive; b. Newark, Nov. 28, 1923; s. George Halstead and Dill E. (McMullen) M.; m. Virginia M. Jedryczka, Aug. 24, 1957; children: George B., Kathryn M., Juliet S., John G., James H. B.M.E., U. Detroit, 1949, D.Sc. (hon.), 1977; PhD, U. Wis., 1952; L.H.D., West Coast U., 1984; D.Sc. (hon.), Western Mich. U., 1986. Registered profl. engr., Fla., Ill., Iowa, Mich., Minn., Ohio. Supr. new powerplants Ford Motor Co., 1952-57; engring. mgr. Meriam Instrument Co., Cleve., 1957-59; dir. new products McCulloch Corp., Los Angeles, 1959-63; with Deere & Co., 1963-84, v.p. engring. Moline, Ill., 1972-84; exec. assoc. Southwest Research Inst., 1987. Mem. Fed. Adv. Com. Indsl. Innovation, 1979; chmn. West Ctrl. Ill. Ednl. Telecom. Corp.; pres. Accreditation Bd. for Engring. and Tech., 1983-85; pres., fellow Accreditation Bd. for Engring. and Tech. Editor: The Sheerline, Antique and Classic Boat Soc. (Sunnyland chpt.), 1995-; contbr. articles to profl. jours.; patentee in field. Chmn. Quad Cities chpt. United Way, 1976-77; bd. dirs.; adv. council Bradley U. Coll. Engring. and Tech.; mem. exec. com. Illowa council Boy Scouts Am., 1977-79. Served with U.S. Army, World War II. Decorated Purple Heart; recipient Alumnus of Year award U. Detroit, 1976, Comdrs. medal for pub. svc. Dept. Army, 1989 Fellow ASME (hon. life mem.), Soc. Automotive Engrs. (pres. 1984, bd. dirs. 1984-86, mem. nat. nominating com.); mem. NAE, NSPE, Engrs. Joint Coun., Indsl. Rsch. Inst., Engring. Soc. Detroit, Am. Soc. Agrl. Engrs., Ill. Soc. Profl. Engrs., Moline C. of C., Aviation Coun. Home: 1840 Wiley Post Trl Port Orange FL 32128-6756 Office Phone: 386-788-0213.

MILLAR, JAMES ROBERT, economist, educator, university official; b. San Antonio, Tex., July 7, 1936; s. James G. and Virginia M. (Harrison) M.; m. Gera Ascher, July 4, 1965; children: Leo Schaeg (dec.), Mira Gail. BA, U. Tex., 1958; PhD in Econs., Cornell U., 1965. Asst. prof. dept. econs. U. Ill., Urbana, 1965-70, assoc. prof., 1970-72, prof., 1973-89, assoc. vice chancellor for acad. affairs, 1984-89, dir. internat. programs and studies, 1984-89; prof. econs. and internat. affairs George Washington U., Washington, 1989—2004, prof. emeritus, 2004—, dir. Inst. for European, Russian and Eurasian Studies, 1989-01, assoc. dean Elliott Sch. Internat. Affairs, 1989-95, acting dean, 1994. Mem. acad. coun. Kennan Inst. Advanced Russian Studies, 1975-84; young faculty exchangee Moscow State U., 1966; cons. to congressmen and various U.S. govt. depts., 1972—; dir. Soviet Interview Project, 1981-88; sec., bd. dirs. Midwest Univs. Consortium for Internat. Activities, 1984-88, chmn. bd., 1988-89; bd. dirs., chair fin. com. Internat. Rsch. and Exchs. Bd., 2002-06. Author: The ABCs of Soviet Socialism, 1981 (non-fiction award Soc. Midland Authors, 1981), The Soviet Economic Experiment, 1990; editor, contbr. The Soviet Rural Community, 1971; editor: Slavic Rev., Am. Quar. Soviet and East European Studies, 1975-80, Problems of Post-Communism, 1996-2003; editor, contbr. Politics, Work and Daily Life, A Survey of Former Soviet Citizens, 1987; editor, contbr. Cracks in the Monolith: Party Power in the Brezhnev Era, 1992, The Social Legacy of Communism, 1994; editor-in-chief: Encyclopedia of Russian History, 4 vols., 2004; contbr. articles on studies on Soviet/Russian economy and econ. history to scholarly jours. Served with Q.M.C. U.S. Army, 1960. Ford Found. fgn. area fellow, 1961-64; sr. scholar rsch. travel grantee to USSR, 1972; Internat. Rsch. and Exchs. Bd./USSR Acad. Scis. travel exchangee, 1979; fellow Woodrow Wilson Internat. Ctr. for Scholars, 1988-89, Guggenheim fellow, 1995-96; Internat. Rsch. and Exchs. Bd. advanced rsch. grantee, 1996. Mem. AAAS, Internat. Com. Ctrl. and East European Studies (bd. dirs., v.p. 2001—), Econ. History Assn., Am. Assn. Advancement Slavic Studies (del. Am. Coun. Learned Soc. 1992-98, bd. dirs. 1995-2001, v.p. 1998-99, pres. 1999-2000, chair coun. mem. insts. 1995-99, treas. 2004—, Disting. Contbn. Slavic Studies award, 2006), Am. Coun. Learned Soc. (treas., bd. dirs. 1996-2002, sec. 1994-96, mem. exec. com. del., chair 1992-95, mem. joint com. with Social Sci. Rsch. Coun. 1990-95), Nat. Coun. for Ea. Europe and Eurasia (bd. dirs. 2004—), N.Y. Acad. Sci., Phi Beta Kappa (pres. Alpha chpt. 1998-01). Home: 2801 New Mexico Ave NW Apt 1215 Washington DC 20007-3942 Office: George Washington U Inst Eur Russ Eurasian Studies 1957 E St NW Ste 412 N Washington DC 20052-0001 Home Phone: 202-337-1428; Office Phone: 202-994-1645. Business E-Mail: millar@gwu.edu.

MILLAR, JOCELYN G., entomologist, educator; PhD in Organic Chemistry, Simon Fraser U., Burnaby, B.C. Canada, 1983. From asst. to prof. dept. entomology U. Calif., Riverside, 1988—. Assoc. editor: Jour. Chem. Ecology, 2003—; contbr. articles to profl. jours., chapters to books. Fellow: AAAS; mem.: Internat. Soc. Chem. Ecology (pres. 2005—), Entomol. Soc. Am. (Syngenta Recognition award Crop Protection 2001, Recognition award 2001, IPM award 2005, C.W. Woodworth award 2006, IPM award 2006), Am. Chem. Soc. Office: U Calif Dept Entomology Riverside CA 92521 Office Fax: 1 951 827 3086.

MILLAR, JOHN DONALD, physician, environmental services administrator, essayist, consultant, musician; b. Newport News, Va., Feb. 27, 1934; s. John and Dorothea Virginia (Smith) M.; m. Joan M. Phillips, Aug. 17, 1957; children: John Stuart, Alison Gordon, Virginia Taylor. BS, U. Richmond, 1956; MD, Med. Coll. Va., 1959; D.T.P.H., London Sch. Hygiene and Tropical Medicine, 1966; D of Pub. Svc. (hon.), Greenville Coll., Ill., 1994. Cert. specialist in Gen. Preventive Medicine 1969. Intern U. Utah Affiliated Hosps., Salt Lake City, 1959-60, asst. resident in medicine, 1960-61; chief Epidemic Intelligence Svc., Ctr. for Disease Control, USPHS, HEW, Atlanta, 1961-63, dep. chief surveillance sect. epidemiology br., 1962-63, chief smallpox unit, 1963-65, dir. smallpox eradication program, 1966-70, dir. Bur. State Svcs., 1970-78, asst. dir. Ctr. for Disease Control for Pub. Health Practice, 1979-80; dir. Nat. Ctr. Environ. Health, Atlanta, 1980-81, Nat. Inst. for Occupation Safety and Health, Atlanta, 1981-93, chmn. exec. com. Nat. Toxicology Program, 1989-93; pres. Don Millar & Assocs., Inc., Atlanta, 1993—. Adj. prof. occupl. and environ. health Sch. Pub. Health Emory U., Atlanta, 1988-98; cons. on smallpox, smallpox eradication, immunization programs and occupl. and environ. health WHO; mem. WHO expert adv. panel on occupl. health; bd. dirs. Farm Safety 4 Just Kids, 1993-98; tech. adv. bd. Ctr. Protect Workers' Rights, 1993; disting. fellow, vice chmn. Pub. Health Policy Adv. Bd., Inc., Washington, 1998-2007; mem. string bass sect. DeKalb Symphony Orch., 1982-06, Gainesville (Ga.) Symphony Orch., 2000-04, N.E. Ga. Mountain Chamber Orch., 2001-05, Truett-Macconnell Coll. Wind Symphony, 2002—, Toccoa Falls Coll. Orch., 2005—, Toccoa Symphony Orch., 2005—. Mem. editl. bd. Am. Jour. Indsl. Medicine, 1985-05, Am. Jour. Occupl. Psychology, 1993-00, Am. Jour. Preventive Medicine, 1993-00; contbr. articles to profl. jours. Recipient Surgeon Gen's. Commendation medal, 1965, Okeke prize London Sch. Hygiene and Tropical Medicine, 1966, Presdl. award for mgmt. improvement, 1972, W.C. Gorgas medal Assn. Mil. Surgeons U.S., 1987, Lucas lectr. Faculty Occupational Medicine Royal Coll. Physicians, London, 1987, Outstanding Med. Alumnus award Med. Coll. Va., 1988; also recipient Equal Employment Opportunity award, 1975, Medal of Excellence, 1977, Joseph W. Mountin lectr. award, 1986, Alexander D. Langmuir MD Meml. lectr. award, 2001, all from Ctrs. for Disease Control, Disting. Svc. medal USPHS, 1983, 88, Exemplary Svc. medal Surgeon Gen. U.S., 1988, Giants in Occupational Medicine lectr. U. Utah, 1989, William S. Knudsen award Am. Coll. Occupational Medicine, 1991, presdl. citation APA, 1991, William Steiger Meml. award Am. Conf. Govtl. Indsl. Hygienists, 1993, Health Watch award for outstanding contbns. toward improving health of minority populations, 1992, Award of Merit Minerva Edn. Inst., 1993, Alumni Disting. Svc. award U. Richmond, 1993, Jeff Lee Mem. Lectr. Am. Indusl. Hygiene Assoc. San Diego, Calif., 2002; named to Order Bifurcated Needle, World Health Orgn., 1978, Faculty Occupational Medicine, Royal Coll. Physicians, London, 1990; elected Safety and Health Hall of Fame Internat., Nat. Safety Coun., 1997. Mem. Am. Indsl. Hygiene Assn. (hon.), Am. Coll. Occupl. and Environ. Medicine, Am. Epidemiol. Soc., Collegium Ramazzini, Am. Assn. Pub. Health Physicians., Assn. Mil. Surgeons U.S., Pub. Health Svc. Commissioned Officers Assn., Alpha Omega Alpha.

MILLAR, MICHAEL WILLIAM, musician; b. NYC, June 22, 1953; s. W. Llewellyn and Janet Josephine (Dean) M.; m. Lisa Rochelle Branch, July 30, 1983 (dec. Aug. 1987); m. Dava Grace Smart, June 25, 1989; children: Emily Ellyn, Matthew Ian. MusB in Performance, U. Colo., Boulder, 1976; MA in Music Performance, Calif. State U., LA, 1980; D in Musical Arts, Claremont Grad. U., 1999; studied with George Roberts, Jeffrey Reynolds, Roy Main, Peter F. Drucker, Jean Lipman-Blumen, Nancy van Deusen. Trombonist Harry James Orch., 1980-85; exec. dir. Santa Clarita Symphony, 2005—. Mem. faculty U. Colo., Denver, 1987, Calif. State Poly. U., Pomona, 2004-, Internat. Trombone Festival, 2001; dir. Entrepreneurship Ctr. for Music, U. Colo., Boulder, 2002-03; has appeared with various brass ensembles, big bands, symphony orchs. and other mus. groups; performed in TV and radio jingles for Budweiser, Toyota, IBM, Texaco, Am. Express, Honda, Delta Airlines, Qantas, Sunny Delight, Disney World, AT&T, numerous others. Appeared in films Patch Adams, Hot to Trot, Sing, For the Boys, The Doors, on TV in Hull High, Jerry Lewis MDA Telethon Orch., 1995-2005; performed with L.A. Philharm., Steve Allen, Ray Anthony, Tex. Beneke Orch., Tony Bennett, George Burns, Ray Charles Orch., Rosemary Clooney, Ray Conniff, Merv Griffin, Jerry Lewis, Shari Lewis, Mills Bros., Liza Minnelli, Helen O'Connell, Patti Page, Debbie Reynolds, Kenny Rogers, Artie Shaw, The Smothers Brothers, numerous others; recs. with Southwest Chamber Music, Ray Anthony, Poco, Les Hooper, Joey DeFrancesco, Bruce Lofgren Jazz Orch., others. Co-recipient Grammy award, with S.W. Chamber Music, 2004. Mem. NARAS, Rec. Musicians Assn., Am. Fedn. Musicians, Ams. for the Arts. Home: 25430 Via Impreso Valencia CA 91355-2709 Home Phone: 661-253-2999; Office Phone: 818-901-6843. E-mail: millar@music.org.

MILLAR, RICHARD WILLIAM, JR., lawyer; b. LA, May 11, 1938; LLB, U. San Francisco, 1966. Bar: Calif. 1967, U.S. Dist. Ct. (cen. dist.) Calif. 1967, U.S. Dist. Ct. (no. dist.) Calif. 1969, U.S. Dist. Ct. (so. dist.) Calif. 1973, U.S. Supreme Ct. Assoc. Iverson & Hogoboom, Los Angeles, 1967-72; ptnr. Eilers, Stewart, Pangman & Millar, Newport Beach, Calif., 1973-75, Millar & Heckman, Newport Beach, 1975-77, Millar, Hodges & Bemis, Newport Beach, 1979—. Trustee Western State U. Coll. Law, 2004—. Fellow: Am. Bar Found. (life); mem.: ABA (litigation sect. trial practice com., ho. of dels. 1990—), Orange County Bar Assn. (chmn. bus. litig. sect. 1981, chmn. judiciary com. 1988—90, sec. 1999, treas., dir. charitable fund 2000, pres.-elect 2001, pres. 2002, treas., dir. charitable fund 2003), Calif. Bar Assn. (lectr. CLE), Pacific Club, Bohemian Club (San Francisco). Home: 71 Hillsdale Newport Beach CA 92660 Office: Millar Hodges & Bemis One Newport Pl Ste # 900 Newport Beach CA 92660 Office Phone: 714-752-7722. Personal E-mail: millar@mhblaw.net.

MILLARD, CHARLES WARREN, III, museum director, writer; b. Elizabeth, NJ, Dec. 20, 1932; s. Charles Warren and Constance Emily (Keppler) M. AB magna cum laude, Princeton U., 1954; MA, Harvard U., 1963, PhD, 1971. Asst. to dir. Fogg Art Mus. Harvard U., Cambridge, Mass., 1963-64; asst. to dir. Dumbarton Oaks, Washington, 1965-66; dir. Washington Gallery Modern Art, 1966-67; teaching fellow Harvard U., 1968-69; curator 19th Century European art L.A. County Mus. Art, 1971-74; chief curator Hirshhorn Mus. and Sculpture Garden Smithsonian Instn., Washington, 1974-86; adj. prof. Johns Hopkins U., Balt., 1983-86; dir. Ackland Art Mus. U. N.C., Chapel Hill, 1986-93, adj. prof., 1986-93; chmn. vis. com. to fine arts dept. Boston U., 1977-80. Chmn. nat. adv. bd. Ackland Art Mus., 2000-04. Author: The Sculpture of Edgar Degas, 1977, La Vie d'Auguste Preault, Auguste Preault Sculpteur Romantique, 1809-1879, 1997; art editor Hudson Rev., 1972-87; contbr. articles to profl. jours. With USN, 1956-59.

MILLARD, DONALD REX, financial executive; b. Atlanta, Ga., June 24, 1947; s. Rex and Martha Nell (Gilstrap_ M.; m. Fay Simmons, Mar. 15, 1968; children: Lisa, Bradley. BBA, U. Ga., 1968. CPA Ga. Audit mgr. Peat, Marwick, Main & Co., Atlanta, 1968-78; v.p. fin. Chick-fil-A Inc., Atlanta, 1978-82; pres. Dental One Inc., Atlanta, 1982-87; v.p. fin, CFO HEalthdyne Inc., Marietta, Ga., 1987—. Pub. chmn., Fin. Execs. Inst., Atlanta, 1987—. Mem. AICPA, Ga. Assn. CPA, Assn. Corp. Growth, Fin. Execs. Inst. (publicity chmn. 1987—). Avocations: racquetball, skiing.

MILLARD, JAMES KEMPER, marketing executive; b. Lexington, Ky., Oct. 28, 1948; s. Lyman Clifford and Cora (Carrick) M.; m. Madelyn (Hooper), Nov. 26, 1983; children: Lyman Clifford III, Sean Duffy, James Kemper Jr., Caroline Carrick. BA, Transylvania Univ., Lexington, Ky., 1971. Writer AP, Lexington, Ky., 1970—71; asst. news. dir. Sta. WLEX-TV, FM, Lexington, Ky., 1971—76; prod. Ky. Dept. Pub. Info., Frankfort, 1973; dir. Univ. rels. Transylvania Univ., Lexington, Ky., 1973—79; acct. supr. Abbott Advt., Inc., Lexington, Ky., 1979—85; mktg. dir. Steak N' Shake, Inc., Indpls., 1985; field mktg. mgr. Blue Bell, Pa., 1985—86; field mktg. dir. Nutri Sys. Inc., Blue Bell, Pa., 1986—88, v.p. comm., 1988—90, sr. v.p. mktg., 1990—91; pres. Mktg. Comm. Overview, Inc., Exton, Pa., 1991—93, Waterwild Mktg., Lexington, Ky., 1993—94; dir. promotion and devel. Sta. WKYT-TV, Lexington, Ky., 1994—99; exec. cons. E Corp., Lexington, Ky., 1999—2000; pres. ConnectedCampus.com., 1999—2000; sr. v.p. devel. strategy Equity Technologies and Resources, Inc., Lexington, Ky., 2000—02; pres. ETCR Mergers and Acquisitions, Inc., Lexington, Ky., 2001—06; pres., CEO Equity Technologies and Resources, Inc., Lexington, Ky., 2002—06, Verified Prescription Safeguards, Inc., Lexington, Ky., 2002—06; ptnr. Waterwild Farm, LLC, Lexington, Ky., 2003—; pres., CEO Found Affordable Housing, Inc., 2006—. Mem. acad. adv. com. Ea. Ky. U., Richmond, 1983-87; treas. Bluegrass Integrated Pest Mgmt., Lexington, 1983-85; case study spkr. Radio Advertisers Bur., 1989-90. Author: C and O Streamliners, 1994. Mem. Comdr. in Chief Leadership Cir., 1990—; pres. Swan Kitchen Car Co., 1990—; mem. Hon. Order Ky. Colonels, 1976—; cons. Jr. Achievement; mem. campaign cabinet United Way Bluegrass, 1995, mem. dream team, 1998—99; mem. devel. coun. Midway Coll., 1995—99; mem. Nat. Coalition Homeless Vets, 2006—, Employee Support Guard and Res., 2006—, Lexingtin FEMA Emergency Food and Shelter Bd., 2007—; deacon Ctrl. Christian Ch., Lexington, Ky., 1984—86; bd. dir. Chesapeake and Ohio Hist. Soc., Clifton Forge, Va., 1983—98; v.p. Chesapeake and Ohio Hist. Soc., Clifton Forge, Va., 1994—97; bd. dir. Found. for Affordable Housing, 1995—, Friends of McConnell Springs, 1998—; chmn. Friends of Mc Connell Springs, 2001—; bd. dir. Bluegrass Trust for Hist. Preservation, 1998—2003, v.p., 1999, pres., 2000—02; trustee Lexington History Mus., Ky., 2000—; mem. bd. Lexington, Fayette Rural Land Mgmt., Ky., 2001—; mem. Am. Assn. Pvt. R.R. Car Owners, 1990—, R.R. Passenger Car Alliance, 1990—. Recipient Great Menu Award Nat. Restaurant Assn., 1982; Key Man Award Jerrico Inc., 1981; Silver and Bronze ADDY Awards Lexington Advt. Club, 1982; Gold Award Fla. Restaurant Assn., 1984; Innovative Idea Award Ky. Broadcasters Assn., 1995. Mem. Rotary Internat., Delta Sigma Phi (pres. U. Ky. corp. bd. 1994-97), Navy League, Ky. Saddle Bred Heritage. Democrat. Address: 2580 Waterwild Ln Lexington KY 40511 Personal E-mail: jmillard@usa.com. Business E-Mail: jmillar KY@foudhousing.org.

MILLARD, NEAL STEVEN, lawyer, educator; b. Dallas, June 6, 1947; s. Bernard and Adele (Marks) Millard; m. Janet Keast, Mar. 12, 1994; 1 child, Kendall Layne. BA cum laude, UCLA, 1969; JD, U. Chgo., 1972. Bar: Calif. 1972, U.S. Dist. Ct. (ctrl. dist.) Calif. 1973, U.S. Tax Ct. 1973, U.S. Ct. Appeals (9th cir.) 1987, N.Y. 1990. Assoc. Willis, Butler & Schiefly, LA, 1972-75; ptnr. Morrison & Foerster, LA, 1975-84, Jones,

Day, Reavis & Pogue, LA, 1984-93, White & Case, LA, 1993—. Instr. Calif. State Coll., San Bernardino, 1975—76; lectr. Practising Law Inst., NYC, 1983—90, Calif. Edn. Bar, 1987—90; adj. prof. U. So. Calif. Law Ctr., LA, 1994—. Mem. citizens adv. com. L.A. Olympics, 1982—84; trustee Altadena (Calif.) Libr. Dist., 1985—86; bd. dirs. Woodcraft Rangers, LA, 1982—90, pres., 1986—88; bd. dirs. Los Angeles County Bar Found., 1990—2000, pres., 1997—98; mem. Energy Commn. county and cities of L.A., 1995—99; mem. jud. procedures commn. Los Angeles County, 1999—, chair, 2000—02; mem. Pub. Safety Commn. LaCanada-Flintridge, 2006—; bd. dirs. Inner City Law Ctr., 1996—99; bd. dirs., sec. LaCanada-Flintridge Ednl. Found., 2002—06; bd. dirs. Alliance Coll.-Ready Pub. Schs., 2004—. Mem.: ABA, Am. Law Inst., Pub. Counsel (bd. dirs. 1984—87, 1990—93), Los Angeles County Bar Assn. (trustee 1985—87), N.Y. State Bar Assn., Calif. Bar Assn., U. So. Calif. Inst. Corp. Counsel (mem. adv. bd. 1998—2006), U. Chgo. Law Alumni Assn. (pres. 1998—2001), Flintridge Riding Club, Calif. Club, Chancery Club, Beach Club, Phi Beta Kappa, Phi Delta Phi, Pi Gamma Mu. Office: White & Case 633 W 5th St Ste 1900 Los Angeles CA 90071-2087 Home Phone: 818-952-3700; Office Phone: 213-620-7773. Business E-Mail: nmillard@whitecase.com.

MILLARD, RICHARD STEVEN, lawyer; b. Pasadena, Calif., Feb. 6, 1952; s. Kenneth A. and Kathryn Mary (Paden) M.; m. Jessica Ann Edwards, May 15, 1977; children: Victoria, Elizabeth, Andrew. AB, Stanford U., 1974; JD magna cum laude, U. Mich., 1977. Bar: Calif. 1977, Ill. 1985. Assoc. Heller, Ehrman, White & McAuliff, San Francisco, 1977-81. Mayer, Brown & Platt, Chgo., 1982-83, ptnr., 1984-99, Weil, Gotshal & Manges, Redwood Shores, Calif., 1999—. Mem. ABA, Order of Coif. Office: Weil Gotshal & Manges 201 Redwood Shores Pkwy Redwood City CA 94065 Office Phone: 650-802-3015. Business E-Mail: richard.millard@weil.com.

MILLARD, ROBERT B., investment company executive; b. 1950; m. Bethany Millard; 4 children. BS, MIT, 1973; MBA, Harvard U., 1976. Joined Kuhn Loeb & Co., 1976; mng. dir. Lehman Brothers Inc., 1983—. Bd. dirs. Weatherford Internat., Inc., 1989—, GulfMark Offshore, Inc., 1996—, L-3 Comm. Corp., 1997—, non-exec. chmn., 2006—; chair vis. physics com. MIT, vis. linguistics & philosophy com., vis. architecture com. Bd. trustees, oper. & adminstrn. com. Assoc. Universities Inc.; bd. trustees, exec. com. Population Coun., 1993—, MIT Corp., 2003—; bd. trustees, exec. com., treas. New Sch. Univ.; bd. govs. Parsons Sch. Design; bd. dirs. Remarque Inst., NYU. Mem.: Coun. Fgn. Rels., The Brook, Edgarton Golf Club, NY Yacht Club. Office: Lehman Brothers 9th Fl 399 Park Ave New York NY 10022 Office Phone: 212-526-9370. Office Fax: 212-526-3597.

MILLARD, WENDA HARRIS, multi-media company executive; b. Alexandria, Va., July 9, 1954; d. Roger and Joan Marie (Kelliher) Harris; m. William John Millard, Oct. 8, 1983. BA in English, Trinity Coll., 1976; MBA, Harvard U., 1983. Sales promotion mgr. Am. Home mag., 1976-77, Ladies' Home Jour., 1977-79; sales devel. mgr. NY mag., 1979-81; gen. mgr. Working Woman Ventures, 1983-85; exec. v.p., group pub. Adweek, Mediaweek and Brandweek mags., NYC, 1985-89; gen. mgr., ptnr. The Peer Group, Westport, Conn., 1989; sr. v.p., pub. Family Circle mag.; pres., group pub. SRDS; founding mem., exec. v.p. DoubleClick, 1996—2000; chief internet officer Ziff Davis Media; pres. Ziff Davis Internet, 2000—01; chief sales officer Yahoo! Inc., 2001—07; pres. media Martha Stewart Living Omnimedia, NYC, 2007—. Exec. prodr. Working Woman radio report, Nat. Commn. on Working Women, 1984; bd. dirs. True North Comms., Martha Stewart Living Omnimedia, 2004—. Editor: Fashion Capital News, 1980; contbr. articles to profl. jours. Bd. trustees Trinity Coll., Hartford, Conn., 1980—. Named Digital Media Master, Advertising Age, 1999; named one of 100 Young Women of Promise, Good Housekeeping mag., 1985; recipient Women at Work Broadcast Award, IABC Award for Innovation, Univ. Settlement House, Gary McQuaid Award for Excellence in Bus. Leadership. Mem.: Advt. Club NY (Andy award 1988, 1999), Women's Equity Action League, Women in Comms., Advt. Women NY, Harvard Club. Republican. Office: Martha Stewart Living Omnimedia Inc 11 W 42nd St New York NY 10036 *

MILLBERG, JOHN C., lawyer; b. New London, Conn., Jan. 4, 1956; s. Melvin Roy and Dorothy (Van Zandt) M.; m. Lori Bruce, Oct. 18, 1981; children: Kathryn Faye, Rebecca Ann, Melvin Roy III. BA, Bowling Green State U., 1977; JD, Wake Forest U., 1980. Bar: Tex. 1980, N.C. 1986, S.C. 2000, U.S. Dist. Ct. (so. dist.) Tex. 1981, U.S. Ct. Appeals (5th and 11th cirs.) 1981, U.S. Dist. Ct. (ea., mid. and we. dists.) N.C. 1986, U.S. Ct. Appeals (4th cir.) 1986, U.S. Dist. Ct. S.C. 2002. Assoc. Crain Caton James & Womble, Houston, 1981—85; assoc., dir. Maupin, Taylor, Ellis & Adams, Raleigh, NC, 1985—94; mng. ptnr. Millberg, Gordon & Stewart, PLLC, Raleigh, NC, 1994—. Mem. bar candidate com. N.C. Bd. Law Examiners, 1988-90. Scholar Wake Forest U. Sch. Law, 1977-80. Mem. N.C. Assn. Def. Attys. (exec. com., v.p. southeastern region), Nat. Assn. R.R. Trial Counsel. Office: Millberg Gordon & Stewart PLLC S 104 1101 Haynes St Raleigh NC 27604-1455

MILLEA, THOMAS FRANCIS, photographer; b. Bridgeport, Conn., Sept. 30, 1944; s. Thomas Francis and Mildred Claire Millea. BA in History, Western Conn. State U., Danbury, 1966. Artist in residence Yosemite Valley Nat. Pk., 1988—99. Photographer (permanent collections), The Getty Mus., The Smithsonian, San Francisco Moma, Boston Mus. Fine Arts, in over 40 museums worldwide. Named Alumnus of Yr., Western Conn. State U., 2006; Rutenburg grant, 1984. Achievements include re-introduction and refinement of platinum printing for photography. Avocations: travel, philosophy. Business E-Mail: tmillea@aol.com.

MILLEN, MATT, professional sports team executive; b. Hokendauqua, Pa., Mar. 12, 1958; m. Patricia Millen; children: Marianne, Michalyn, Marcus; 1 child, Matthew Jr. Student Pa. State U. Linebacker Oakland/L.A. Raiders, 1980—88, San Francisco 49ers, 1989—90, Washington Redskins, 1991; game analyst CBS, Fox TV; pres., CEO Detroit Lioins, 2001—. Named to NFL Pro Bowl Team, 1988. Office: Detroit Lions Inc 222 Republic Dr Allen Park MI 48101-3650

MILLER, ALAN, computer company executive, management consultant; b. Bklyn., Apr. 20, 1954; s. Michael and Lillian Charlotte (Garment) M.; m. Zelda Sara Bochlin, Nov. 16, 1974; children: Michael Glenn, Dara Jennifer. BS in Computer Sci. magna cum laude, SUNY, 1975; MBA in Mgmt. with honors, Adelphi U., 1982. Tech. svcs. mgr. Guardian Life Ins. Co., NYC, 1977-81; project mgr. Mfrs. Hanover Trust Co., NYC, 1981-83; asst. v.p. Bankers Trust Co., NYC, 1983-86; v.p., MIS dir. Bank Am. Trust Co. of N.Y., NYC, 1986-87; assoc. John Diebold and Assocs., NYC, 1987-89; mgr. banking practice AGS Info. Svcs., NYC, 1989-90; v.p. mktg. and bus. devel., product mgr. global trade fin. BIS Banking Systems, NYC, 1990-93; sr. cons. Computer Scis. Corp., 1994-95; solution exec. global fin. industries IBM Software Group, Somers, NY, 1995—98; client exec. Goldman Sachs Group IBM Corp., NYC, 1998—2001; client exec. N.Y. Life, 2002—05; client unit exec. Wall St. Exchs. and Clearing, 2006—. Chmn. Sch. Dist. Adv. Com., Plainview, N.Y., 1981-83; exec. producer Oklahoma prodn. Patio Players, Plainview, 1990-91; bd. dirs. men's club Plainview Jewish Ctr., 1986-95. Mem. Delta Mu Delta. Jewish. Avocations: softball, theater, games shows, volleyball. Home: 21 Beaumont Dr Plainview NY 11803-2507 Office: IBM 33 Maiden Ln New York NY 10038-4598 Home Phone: 516-935-5965; Office Phone: 212-493-2454. Business E-Mail: alan.miller@us.ibm.com.

MILLER, ALAN B., hospital management executive; b. NYC, Aug. 17, 1937; s. Daniel and Mary (Blumenthal) M.; m. Jill K. Stein, Oct. 5, 1968; children: Marc Daniel, Marni Elizabeth, Abby Danielle. BA, Coll. William and Mary, 1958; MBA, U. Pa., 1960. V.p. Young & Rubicam, Inc., NYC, 1964-69; sr. v.p. Am. Medicorp., Inc., LA, 1970, pres., chief exec. officer Phila., 1973-77, chmn. bd., 1977, Hosp. Underwriting Group, 1977-78; founder, chmn., pres., CEO Universal Health Services, King of Prussia, Pa., 1978—; chmn., founder UHT-Real Estate Trust, King of Prussia, Pa., 1986—. Formerly health care adviser Fed. Mediation and Conciliation Svc.; chmn., pres. Universal Health Svcs. Real Estate Investment Trust, N.Y. Stock Exch., 1986—; bd. dirs. CDI Corp., N.Y. Stock Exch., Broadlane, Penn Mut. Life Ins.; mem. exec. bd. Wharton Sch., U. Pa., 1996-2004, mem. bd. overseers, 2005-. Chmn. Opera Co. of Phila.; dir. Regional Performing Arts Ctr. Capt. 77th Inf. Divsn. US Army. Recipient Ellis Island Medal of Honor, 1998, William and Mary medallion, George Washington U. Pres.'s medal. Mem.: Phila. C. of C. (bd. dirs.). Home: 57 Crosby Brown Rd Gladwyne PA 19035-1512 Office: Universal Health Svcs Inc PO Box 61558 367 S Gulph Rd King Of Prussia PA 19406 Office Phone: 610-768-3300.

MILLER, ALAN J., retired financial company executive; b. Bklyn., July 11, 1936; s. Louis and Claire (Maltz) M.; m. Susan Ruth Morris, Oct. 29, 1961; children— Laurie Ann, Adam Louis. BA, Cornell U., 1957. Chartered fin. analyst. Pres. Analysis-in-Depth Inc., NYC, 1965-67; mng. editor Value Line Investment Survey, NYC, 1967-68; rsch. dir. Emanuel Deetjen & Co., NYC, 1968-69; exec. v.p., dir. Intersci. Capital Mgmt. Corp., NYC, 1969-71; pres., dir. ICM Equity Fund Inc., NYC, 1970-71, ICM Fin. Fund Inc., NYC, 1970-71; v.p., assoc. rsch. dir. Bache & Co., Inc., NYC, 1972, G.H. Walker & Co., Inc., NYC, 1972-73; 1st v.p., assoc. rsch. dir. Blyth Eastman Dillon & Co. Inc., NYC, 1974-76; dir. rsch. E.F. Hutton & Co., Inc., NYC, 1976-81, sr. v.p., 1976-80, exec. v.p., 1981-88; dir. Hutton Investment Mgmt., 1976-88; mng. dir. SLH Asset Mgmt. Shearson Lehman Hutton, Inc, NYC, 1988-90; sr. v.p Martin E. Segal Co., NYC, 1990-92. Adj. assoc. prof. Columbia U. Grad. Sch. Bus., 1978-79; mem. faculty NY Inst. Fin., 1977-98; adj. prof. Adelphi U. Coll., 1993-98; rare book dealer, 1998-2006. Author: Socially Responsible Investing: How to Invest with Your Conscience, 1991, Standard and Poor's 401(k) Planning Guide, 1995. Home Phone: 212-300-4488. Personal E-mail: amiller202@aol.com.

MILLER, ALAN M., writer, educator, television host; b. NYC, July 24, 1934; s. Philip and Sylvia (Lubash) M.; children: Neil, Peter, Stephanie Cook, Douglas; m. Sharon A. Tanenbaum, Aug. 29, 1996; step-children: Holly Harouche, Becky Theodoratos. AB, Syracuse U., 1955, LLB, 1958, JD, 1968. Asst. counsel 3 joint legis. coms. NY State Legislature, 1968-70; counsel to minority Nassau County Bd. Suprs., 1974-75; prin. atty. editor Thomson/West, Eagan, Minn., 1985—2004. Faculty film and screenwriting Mpls. Coll., 1999—, Hofstra U., 1990-97, Discovery Ctr., 1990-94, NY Inst. Tech., Old Westbury, 1987-89; humanities faculty, Inver Hills CC, 2004—; bd. mem. Inver Hills Found., 2005—. Columnist South Shore Record, Woodmere, NY, Another Viewpoint, 1985-99 (awards NY Press Assn. 1988, 89, 94, Best column award 1992), Single-Minded, 1991-92, NY Bowler, 1991-93 (Bowling Mag. awards 1990-93, Best column award 1992), Nostalgia Mag., 1990-91; writer-editor USCAdvantage, 1995-99 (Immy awards 1996, 97); editor: Beyond the Bar, Thomson West Group, 2000-02, 05; contbr. articles to publs., including NY Times, Newsday, Newsday Mag., Mpls. Star-Tribune, Humanistic Judaism. Assembly dist. leader NY State Dem. Com., 1965-76; Commr. Village of Woodsburgh, NY, 1980, telecom. com. City of Eagan, Minn., 1999-2005, chmn., 2002, vice-chmn., 2003; citizens adv. com. Minn. Twins, 2000-02; vice-chmn. Minn. Assn. Cable TV Adminstrs., 2002-03; host and prodr. cable TV Access to Democracy, 2001—, TwinsTalk, 2003-; guest host Air Am. Radio, Minn., 2005—; presenter, Holocaust and Genocide Seminar, Met. State U., 2006. Recipient multiple awards for coverage of Persian Gulf War from Israel, 1991, Citizens Impact award Burnsville/Eagan Telecomm., 2003-04, Millenium Club award, 2004, Century Club award, 2005. Mem. Screenwriters Workshop, Ind. Film Pub., Assn. Holocaust Orgns. Jewish. Home: 4316 Aries Ct Eagan MN 55123 Office: 1501 Hennepin Ave T-3068 Minneapolis MN 55403 Personal E-mail: alanmillermn@comcast.net.

MILLER, ALBERT JAY, retired library director; b. Beaver Falls, Pa., Dec. 7, 1927; s. Joseph Jefferson and Alberta Fae (Shaffer) Miller. BS, Geneva Coll., 1952; MLS, Rutgers U., 1958; postgrad., U. Chgo., 1960-61, U. Pitts., 1963-68, U. Mich., 1969. Libr. West Allegheny Jr. H.S., Imperial, Pa., 1959-60, Butler (Pa.) Area Sr. H.S., 1962-67, Pa. State U., New Kensington, 1969-89, tchr.-libr. continuing edn. dept., 1970-89, ret. libr. and info. svcs. dir. emeritus, 1989, prof. emeritus. Author: A Selective Bibliography of Existentialism in Education and Related Topics, 1969, Confrontation, Conflict and Dissent, 1972, Death: A Bibliographical Guide, 1977; book and media rev. editor: Learning Today, 1978—; mem. editl. bd. Learning Today, 1979—. Tchr., judge Nat. Baton Twirling Assn., 1998; instr. water safety ARC, New Kensington, 1969—, Citizens Gen. Hosp., 1971—72; active Boy Scouts Am., 1970—; bd. dirs. Westmoreland County, Butler County mental health issues; mem. Allegheny-Kiski Human Rels. Coun., 1976—77; bd. dirs. Allegheny-Kiski Sr. Citizens Ctr., 1976—77, fund raising chmn., 1989—90, 2d v.p., 1997—98, pres., 1998—; mem., pub. rels. dir. Twirling Unlimited, Akron, Ohio; baton twirler Kensington Firemens Band; entrepreneur Al's Terrific Twirling Tricks-Catch It; book reader People's Libr., New Kensington; Sunday sch. tchr. Manchester Reformed Presbyn. Ch., 1970—, elder, clk. session, 1984—, Sabbath sch. supt., 1990; elder emeritus Eastvale Reformed Presbyn. Ch., mem. Christian edn. com., tchr. adult Sabbath sch., 2003; bd. corporators Geneva Coll., Beaver Falls, Pa., 1987—. Named Twirling champion, N.Y. State Hall of Fame, 1999. Mem.: ALA, NEA (life), U.S. Twirling Assn., Pa. Libr. Assn., Pa. Edn. Assn. (life). Democrat. Home: 160 Crosswynds Dr Beaver Falls PA 15010-1182 Office Phone: 724-891-2369. Personal E-mail: millercrosswynds@comcast.net.

MILLER, ALLAN JOHN, retired lawyer, oil industry executive; b. Beachwood, Ohio, Oct. 17, 1921; s. Carl Frederick and Rhoda (Warren) M.; m. Marjorie Hewitt Pirtle, Aug. 10, 1946; children: James W., Patricia Anne Costas. BBA, Fenn Coll., 1946; LLB, Western Res. U., 1948; D (hon.), Dyke Coll., Cleve., 1986. Bar: Ohio 1948. With Standard Oil Co., Ohio, 1948-77, treas., 1967-77; mem. firm Kiefer, Knecht, Rees, Meyer & Miller, Cleve., 1977-81. Dir. United Screw & Bolt Corp., 1977—97. Pres. South Euclid-Lyndhurst Recreation Com., Ohio, 1953-56; division chair unit plan divsn., United Way Cleve., 1966-69; Chmn. bd. dirs. Luth. Med. Ctr., Cleve., 1967-82; pres. Luth. Med. Ctr. Med. Staff Found., 1979-85; bd. dirs. Christian Residencies Found., 1972-77, St. Luke's Hosp. Assn., 1973-84; chmn. bd. trustees Dyke Coll., Cleve., 1971-86; vol. tax aide AARP, 2005-. Sgt. Corp. Engrs. US Army, 1943—46, Asiatic Pacific. Named Man of Yr., Cleve. State U. Alumni, 1982, Lutheran Med. Ctr., Cleve., 1984. Mem. Capri Isles Golf Club (Venice, Fla.). Presbyterian. Avocations: golf, bridge, music. Home: Apt 531 900 Tamiami Trl S Venice FL 34285-3627

MILLER, ALLAN MARQUESS, hematologist; b. Indpls., Aug. 1, 1943; s. Myron George and Edythe Louise Marquess Miller; m. Diane Marie Gehrke, Aug. 12, 1967; children: Emily Marie Danler, Eric Allan, Elisabeth Diane. BS in Pharmacy, Purdue U., W. Lafayette, Ind., 1965; MD, Ind. U., Indpls., 1971. Diplomate Am. Bd. Internal Medicine, 1974, subspecialty in hematology Am. Bd. Internal Medicine, 1976, subspecialty in oncology Am. Bd. Internal Medicine, 1981. Intern Ind. U. Hosps., 1971—72, resident, 1972—73; fellow hematology & med. oncology Harvard U., Cambridge, Mass., 1973—76; asst. prof. La. State U. Sch. Medicine, Shreveport, 1978—81; physician Daniel Den Hoed Kliniek, Rotterdam, Netherlands, 1981—82, Allan M. Miller, MD, Inc., Bloomington, Ind., 1982—2001, Internal Medicine Assocs., Bloomington, 2001—04, Colo. Hematology-Oncology, Denver, 2004—. Clin. asst., assoc. prof. medicine Ind. U. Sch. Medicine, 1982—2004. Lt. comdr. USN, 1976—78, Bethesda, Md. Mem.: Internat. Soc. Exptl. Hematology, Am. Soc. Clin. Oncology, Am. Soc. Hematology. Protestant. Avocation: travel. Office: Colo Hematology-Oncology 10103 Ridge Gate Pky #106 Lone Tree CO 80124 Office Fax: 720-344-0686. Personal E-mail: allanmmill@msn.com.

MILLER, ALLEN TERRY, JR., lawyer; b. Alexandria, Va., Sept. 19, 1954; s. Allen Terry and Eleanor Jane (Thompson) M.; m. Maureen Ann Callaghan, June 22, 1985; children: Brendan Allen, Patrick Joseph, Brigit Eleanor. BA, U. Va., 1977; JD, Seattle U., 1982. Bar: Wash. 1982, U.S. Dist. Ct. (we. dist.) Wash. 1982, U.S. Ct. Appeals (9th cir.) 1985, U.S. Dist. Ct. (ea. dist.) Wash. 1986, U.S. Dist. Ct. (no. dist.) N.Y. 1990, U.S. Dist. Ct. (we. dist.) Mich. 1990, U.S. Supreme Ct. 1990, U.S. Ct. Appeals (2d and 6th cirs.) 1991. Legis. asst. Congressman Paul N. McCloskey Jr., Washington, 1978-79; asst. atty. gen. State of Washington, Olympia, Wash., 1982-92; prin. Connolly, Tacon & Meserve, 1992—2004; chief dep. prosecuting atty. Thurston County Crthse., 2004—06; atty. pvt. practice, Olympia, 2006—. Adj. prof. environ. law Seattle U., 1991—2001. Commr. Olympia Planning Commn., 1987-92, vice-chair, 1991, chair, 1992; sec. North Capitol Campus Heritage Pk. Devel. Assn., 1989-90, pres., 1991—; pres. Olympia Chorale and Light Opera Co., 1984-85; active St. Michael's Sch. Bd., 1993-96, chair, 1994-96; bd. dirs. South Sound YMCA, 1996—, Olympia Symphony, 1999-2001, Olympia Sch. Dist. Found., 1998-2002; pres. bd. dirs. United Way Thurston County, 1998-2003, pres. 2000-02, campaign chair, 2002-05; pres. Olympia Yashiro Sister City Assn., 2001-02. Recipient Merit award Am. Planning Assn., 1989, 92, Citizen of Yr. award Thurston County, 1998. Mem. ABA, Wash. Bar Assn. (mem. environ. law sect. 1984—, ct. rules com. 1985-89, jud. recommendation com. 1991-94, legis. com. 1994-97, ct. improvement com. 1997-2000, character and fitness com. 2002-06, vice chmn. 2004-06), Thurston County Bar Assn., Leadership Thurston County, Olympic-Thurston C. of C. (trustee 1996-00, pres. 1998), Rotary (Olympia, bd. dirs. 2002—, pres. 2006-). Roman Catholic. Avocations: mountain climbing, kayaking, tennis, piano. Home: PO Box 6059 Olympia WA 98507-6059 Office: 1801 W Bay Dr SW Ste 205 Olympia WA 98502 Office Phone: 360-754-9156. Business E-Mail: allen@atmlawoffice.com.

MILLER, ALWIN VERMAR, educational association administrator, consultant; b. Dardanelle, Ark., Oct. 12, 1922; s. William Marshall and Ollie Vernice (Green) M.; m. Patricia Jane Knox, Dec. 31, 1945; children: Carol, Alwin, William, Nitiya, Thomas. AA, Ark. Poly. Inst., 1939; BS, UCLA, 1947, BA with honors, 1947, MEd, 1948, EdD, 1956; cert., Internat. Inst. Ednl. Planning, (UNESCO), 1967—68. Instr. Chico (Calif.) State Coll., 1948-49; assoc. prof. So. Oreg. Coll., Ashland, 1949-57; edn. advisor AID, Washington, 1957-75; pvt. practice Upper Marlboro, Md., 1975—. Cons. in field. Lt. col. USAF, 1942-46. Mem. ASTD, Soc. Internat. Devel., Internat. Soc. Ednl. Planning, Res. Officers Assn. (v.p. DC dept. 1986-87, treas. 1991-97, pres.-elect 1997-98, pres. 1998-99, Reilly Meml. Scholarship com. 1999-2002, retirement com. 2002—), Am. Legion (post comdr. 1995-96, 99-2000, 2007-, dept. vice comdr. 1996-97, dept. comdr. 1997-98, vice chmn. nat. security 1999-2004), Mil. Order World Wars (chpt. pres. 1999-2002, nat. security com. 2002—, nat. legis. com. 2002—, sr. vice comdr. Dept. of Md., 2003-04, comdr. dept. Md. 2004—06), Nat. Sojourners (v.p. 2006-07, pres. 2007—), Mil. Order of Temple of Jerusalem, Forty and Eight (grand conducteur 2000-01), Lions, Masons (trustee Mt. Hermon lodge no. 179, 2005-06, treas. 2005—), Shriners, K.T., Phi Delta Kappa. Democrat. Office: 8107 Bird Ln Greenbelt MD 20770-2104 Office Phone: 301-441-8201. Personal E-mail: avmiller46@verizon.net.

MILLER, ANDRE, professional basketball player; b. Mar. 19, 1976; BS in Soc., Univ. Utah, 1998. Basketball player Cleveland Cavaliers, 1999—2002, LA Clippers, 2002—03, Denver Nuggets, 2003—. Named to NBA All-Rookie Team, 1999—2000. Office: Denver Nuggets 1000 Chopper Cir Denver CO 80204

MILLER, ANDREW PICKENS, lawyer; b. Fairfax, Va., Dec. 21, 1932; s. Francis Pickens and Helen (Hill) M.; m. Penelope Farthing, Nov. 18, 1990; children: Julia Lane, Andrew Pickens, Elise Givhan, Winfield Scott, Lucia Holcombe. AB magna cum laude, Princeton U., 1954; postgrad., New Coll., Oxford U., Eng., 1954-55; LLB, U. Va., 1960. Bar: Va. 1960, U.S. Supreme Ct. 1967, D.C. 1979. Asso. Penn, Stuart & Stuart, 1960-62; ptnr. Penn, Stuart & Miller, Abingdon, Va., 1963-69; atty. gen. State of Va., 1970-77; ptnr. Mays, Valentine, Davenport & Moore, Richmond, Va., 1977-78, Dickstein, Shapiro, Morin & Oshinsky, LLP, Washington, 1979—2002, Powell Goldstein LLP, Washington, 2002—. Pres., Young Democratic Clubs Va., 1966-67; chmn. Washington County Dem. Com., 1967-69; Dem. nominee for U.S. Senate from Va., 1978; bd. dirs. Barter Found., 1962-69, Nat. Maritime Heritage Found., 2005—; trustee King Coll., 1966-74; mem. adv. bd. Ams. for Effective Law Enforcement, 1973-77, Ctr. for Oceans Law and Policy, 1975-79; vice-chmn. Va. Bd. Corrections, 1983-86. Served to 1st lt. AUS, 1955-57. Fellow Am. Bar Found., ABA (ho. dels. 1971-76, action commn. to reduce ct. costs and delay 1979-84, commn. on pub. understanding about the law 1992-95); mem. So. Conf. Attys. Gen. (vice chmn. 1972-73, chmn. 1973-74), Nat. Assn. Attys. Gen. (exec. com. 1973-74, chmn. antitrust com. 1971-76, Wyman Meml. award 1976), Va. Bar Assn. (chmn. young lawyers sect. 1967-68, exec. com. 1985-88), Am. Judicature Soc. (bd. dirs. 1973-76, exec. com. 1974-76), Soc. of Cin. (Va. standing com. 1986-89, 93-96, asst. sec., 1992-95, sec. gen. 1995-98), Nat. Maritime Heritage Found. (bd. dirs. 2006—), The John Marshall Found. (pres. 1987-89), Phi Beta Kappa, Omicron Delta Kappa. Presbyterian. Home: 1503 35th St NW Washington DC 20007-2729 Office: Powell Goldstein LLP 3rd Fl 901 New York Ave NW Washington DC 20001-4413 Home Phone: 202-337-1726; Office Phone: 202-624-7386. Business E-Mail: amiller@pogolaw.com.

MILLER, ANITA DIANE, psychologist; b. Lewistown, Pa., Oct. 31, 1968; d. Fred A. and Sarah A. Miller; life ptnr. James McMartin Long; 1 child, Hannah Nicole Keener. BA, Bucknell U.; PhD, Vanderbilt U., 1998. Lic. clin. psychologist NY, 2002. Rsch. cons. James Long Co., Caroga Lake, NY, 2002—05; asst. prof. Skidmore Coll., Saratoga Springs, 2005—. Contbr. articles to profl. jours. Mem. Resident's Com. Protect Adirondacks, Blue Mountain Lake, NY, 2004—05, Adirondack Nature Conservancy, Keene Valley, 2004—05. Recipient Still prize, Bucknell U., 1989, Nat. Rsch. Svc. award, NIMH, 1994—97, 1999—2002, Rsch. award, 1999, Young Investigator award, Nat. Alliance for Rsch. on Schizophrenia and Depression, 2000—03; fellow, Pew Sci. Found., 1989, U. Pitts., 1998—2002; scholar, U. Wis., 1999. Mem.: APA (assoc.), Am. Psychol. Soc., NY Psychol. Assn. (assoc.), Soc. Rsch. Child Devel. (assoc.), Soc. Neurosci. (assoc.), Soc. Rsch. Psychopathology (assoc.), Internat. Neuropsychological Soc. (assoc.), Soc. Psychophysiological Rsch. (assoc.), Sigma Xi, Phi Beta Kappa, Psi Chi, Alpha Lambda Delta, Phi Eta Sigma. Achievements include research in Psychophysiology Device Development, with James Long. Home: PO Box 685 Caroga Lake NY 12032-0685 Office: Skidmore Coll 815 North Broadway Saratoga Springs NY 12866-1632 Home Phone: 518-835-8111. Personal E-mail: anita_miller_phd@yahoo.com.

MILLER, ANN G., lawyer; b. San Francisco, Nov. 1, 1944; BA, U. San Diego, 1966; JD, U. San Francisco, 1970. Bar: Calif. 1971. Law clk. U.S. Dist. Ct. (no. dist.) Calif., 1970-71; ptnr. Lillick & Charles, San Francisco, Nixon Peabody LLP, San Francisco, 2001—. Mem. Ninth Cir. Judicial Nominating Com. Mem.: ABA, Computer Law Assn., Bar Assn. San

Francisco, Maritime Law Assn. (chair Passenger Vessel and Cruise Com.). Office: Nixon Peabody LLP Two Embarcadero Ctr San Francisco CA 94111-3996 Office Phone: 415-984-8236. Office Fax: 415-984-8300. E-mail: amiller@nixonpeabody.com.

MILLER, ANNETTE K. See MATEMA, ZSUN-NEE

MILLER, ANTHONY BERNARD, physician, researcher; b. Woodford, Eng., Apr. 17, 1931; married, 1952; 5 children. BA, U. Cambridge, 1952, MB, BChir, 1955; MA, 2004, MD, 2006. House officer Oldchurch Hosp., Romford, Eng., 1955-57; med. registrar Luton and Dunstable Hosp., Eng., 1959-62; mem. sci. staff Med. Research Council Tb and Chest Disease Unit, London, 1962-71; assoc. prof. preventive medicine and biostats. U. Toronto, 1972-76, prof., 1976-96, chmn. dept., 1992-96, dir. grad. program in epidemiology, 1986-91; dir. epidemiology unit Nat. Cancer Inst. Can., Toronto, 1971-86; dir. Nat. Breast Screening Study, 1980—, WHO Collaborating Ctr. on Evaluation of Screening for Cancer, 1991-2000; prof. emeritus pub. health scis., 1997—; head divsn. of clin. Epidemology German Cancer Rsch. Ctr., Heidelberg, 1999—2003. Nat. Health scientist, 1988-93; mem. working cadre Bladder Cancer Project, U.S., 1973-75; mem. epidemiology com. Breast Cancer Task Force, U.S., 1973-77, chmn., 1975-77; mem. Fed. Task Force Cervical Cytol. Screening, Can., 1974-76, 80-81, Union Internat. Contre le Cancer com., controlled therapeutic trials, 1978-82, Multidisciplinary project breast cancer, 1978-82, chmn. project on screening, 1982-93; mem. sci. council Internat. Agy. Research Cancer, Lyon, 1981-85, chmn., 1985; mem. com. on diet, nutrition and cancer NRC of U.S., 1980-83, mem. oversight com. radioepidemiologic tables, 1983-84, com. on diet and health, 1986-89, com. on dietary guidelines implementation, 1988-91, chmn. com. on environmental epidemiology, 1990-94; chmn. Ont. Task Force on Primary Prevention of Cancer, 1994-95; mem. Coun. Can. Strategy Cancer Control, 2000-06; mem. adv. coun. Can. Partnership Against Cancer, 2007—. Served with RAF, 1957-59. Mem. Can. Oncology Soc. (sec.-treas. 1975-79, pres. 1980-81), Soc. Epidemiology Research, Internat. Epidemiology Assn., Am. Soc. Preventive Oncology (pres. 1983-85), Am. Coll. Epidemiology (bd. dirs. 1987-89). Personal E-mail: ab.miller@sympatico.ca.

MILLER, ARJAY, retired university dean; b. Shelby, Nebr., Mar. 4, 1916; s. Rawley John and Mary Gertrude (Schade) M.; m. Frances Marion Fearing, Aug. 18, 1940; children: Kenneth Fearing, Ann Elizabeth (Mrs. James Olstad). BS with highest honors, UCLA, 1937; postgrad., U. Calif., Berkeley, 1938-40; LLD (hon.), Washington U., St. Louis, 1964; LLD, Whitman Coll., Walla Walla, Wash., 1965, U. Nebr., 1965, Ripon Coll., Wis., 1980. Teaching asst. U. Calif. at Berkeley, 1938-40; research technician Calif. State Planning Bd., 1941; economist Fed. Res. Bank San Francisco, 1941-43; asst. treas. Ford Motor Co., 1946-53, controller, 1953-57, v.p., controller, 1957-61, v.p. finance, 1961-62, v.p. of staff group, 1962-63, pres., 1963-68, vice chmn., 1968-69; dean Grad. Sch. Bus., Stanford U., 1969-79, emeritus, 1979—. Former chmn. Automobile Mfrs. Assn., Econ. Devel. Corp. Greater Detroit; councillor The Conf. Bd.; past chmn., life trustee Urban Inst.; mem. Public Adv. Commn. on US Trade Policy, 1968-69, Pres.'s Nat. Commn. on Productivity, 1970-74. Trustee Internat. Exec. Svc. Coirps.; hon. trustee The Brookings Instn.; dir. emeritus S.R.I. Internat.; former chmn. Pub. Policy Inst. Calif.; former pres. Detroit Press Club Found.; former chmn. Bay Area Coun. Capt. USAAF, 1943—46. Recipient Alumnus of Year Achievement award UCLA, 1964, Disting. Nebraskan award, 1968, Nat. Industry Leader award B'nai B'rith, 1968; named to Automotive Hall of Fame, 2006. Fellow Am. Acad. Arts and Scis. Clubs: Pacific Union, Bohemian. Presbyterian.

MILLER, ARNOLD, electronics executive; b. NYC, May 8, 1928; s. Sam and Mina (Krutalow) M.; m. Beverly Shayne, Feb. 5, 1950; children: Debra Lynn, Marla Jo, Linda Sue BS in Chemistry, UCLA, 1948, PhD in Phys. Chemistry, 1951; DHL (hon.), So. Calif. Coll. Optometry, 2007. Registered profl. engr., Calif. Rsch. phys. chemist Wrigley Rsch. Co., Chgo., 1951; supr. phys. chemistry Armour Rsch. Found., Chgo., 1951-54, mgr. chemistry and metals, 1954-56; chief materials sci. dept. Borg-Warner Rsch. Ctr., Des Plaines, Ill., 1956-59; dir. rsch. Rockwell Corp., Anaheim, Calif., 1959-66, dir. microelec. ops., 1967-68; group exec. materials ops. Whittaker Corp., LA, 1968-70; pres. Theta Sensors, Orange, Calif., 1970-72; mgr. xeroradiography Xerox Corp., Pasadena, Calif., 1972-75, corp. dir. rsch. and adv. devel. Stamford, Conn., 1975-78, El Segundo, Calif., 1978-81, v.p. electronics div., 1981-84, pres. electronics div., 1984-87, corp. officer Stamford, 1984-87; pres. Tech. Strategy Group, Fullerton, Calif., 1987—; prodr. Remembrance Films, 2004—. Bd. dirs. Spectro Diode Labs, San Jose, Calif., Semicondr. Rsch. Corp., Colorep Inc., Carlsbad, Calif.; bd. dirs., chair audit com. Merisel Computer Products, El Segundo, Calif., lead dir., 1989—; mem. vis. com. on materials sci. U. So. Calif., L.A., 1966-68; mem. State of Calif. Micro Bd., 1984-2000. Editorial adv. bd. Advances in Solid State Chemistry; co-editor Electronics Industry Development; contbr. numerous articles to profl. jours. and monographs; patentee in field. Mem. civilian adv. group Dept. Commerce, 1959-60; mem. 5th decade com., also adv. com. on engring. and mgmt. program UCLA, 1984-; mem. com. on scholarly commn. with People's Republic of China, Tech. Transfer Task Force, Nat. Acad. Sci., Washington, 1985; bd. dirs. Orange County Pacific Symphony, Fullerton, Calif., 1982-; mem. univ.'s adv. bd. Calif. State U.-Fullerton, 1986-2006, chair, 1991-2006; v.p., bd. dirs. Heritage Pointe Home for the Aging, 1987-97; chmn. Indsl. Assocs. sch. engring. and computer sci. Calif. State U., 1987-97, trustee continuing learning ctr., 1993-; mem. Overseas Devel. Coun., 1988-; mem. Nat. Com. U.S.-China Rels., 1990-; trustee So. Calif. Coll. of Optometry, 1996-, sec.-treas. 1997-2003; bd. mem. Cmty. Found., 1995-, v.p., 1997-. Recipient Sci. Merit award Navy Bur. Ordnance/Armour Rsch. Found., 1952, IR-100 award, 1964, 69, U. medal Inst. Gerontology Calif. State U., Fullerton, 2002; named Hon. Alumnus Calif. State U., Fullerton, 1996, Hon. Dr. Humane Letters So. Calif. Coll. Optometry, 2007. Fellow AAAS; mem. IEEE, AIME, Am. Chem. Soc., So. Calif. Coalition Edn. Mfg. Engring. (bd. dirs. 1994-98), Elec. Industry Assn. (past chmn. microelectronics), Phi Beta Kappa, Sigma Xi, Phi Lamda Upsilon Home: 505 Westchester Pl Fullerton CA 92835-2706 Office: Tech Strategy Group PO Box 5769 Fullerton CA 92838-0769 Office Phone: 714-447-8887. Business E-Mail: amiller@fullerton.edu.

MILLER, ARTHUR HAROLD, lawyer; b. Plainfield, NJ, Sept. 21, 1935; s. Leon Daniel and Bertha Zelda (Madoff) M.; m. Lynn Fieldman, Aug. 24, 1958; children: Jennifer, Jonathan. BA, Princeton U., 1957; JD, Columbia U., 1960. Bar: N.Y. 1961, U.S. Supreme Ct. 1965, N.J. 1969. Assoc. Wachtel & Michaelson, NYC, 1961-65, Netter, Lewy, Dowd, NYC, 1965-67, Dannenberg Hazen & Lake, NYC, 1967-69; ptnr. Clarick, Clarick & Miller, New Brunswick, NJ, 1971-78, Miller, Miller & Tucker PA, New Brunswick, NJ, 1979—. Chmn. Middlesex County Legal Svcs. Corp., New Brunswick, 1975-83; vis. lectr. Princeton U., 2004, 2006. Active Sch. Bd. Highland Park, N.J., 1981-84. Mem. N.J. Bar Assn. (trustee 2006—, chmn. availibility legal svcs. com. 1983-85, lawyer referral com. 1986-88), Middlesex County Bar Assn. (pres. 1993-94, lawyer achievement award 1996), Middlesex County Bar Found. (pres. 1997-98, chmn. capital campaign 2003-04), Middlesex County C. of C. (trustee and legal counsel 1990-93). Democrat. Jewish. Office: Miller Miller & Tucker 96 Paterson St New Brunswick NJ 08901-2109 Home Phone: 732-985-0943; Office Phone: 732-828-2234. Business E-Mail: amiller@millerandmiller.com.

MILLER, ARTHUR HAWKS, JR., librarian, archivist; b. Kalamazoo, Mich., Mar. 15, 1943; s. Arthur Hawks and Eleanor (Johnson) M.; m. Janet Carol Schroeder, June 11, 1967; children: Janelle Miller Moravek, Andrew Hawks. Student, U. Caen, Calvados, France, 1963-64; AB, Kalamazoo Coll., 1965; AM in English, U. Chgo., 1966, AM in Librarianship, 1968; PhD, Northwestern U., 1973. Reference libr. Newberry Libr., Chgo., 1966-69, asst. libr. pub. svcs., 1969-72; coll. libr. Lake Forest (Ill.) Coll., 1972-94, archivist and libr. for spl. collections, 1994—. Co-author: 30 Miles North: A History of Lake Forest College, Its Town, and Its City of Chicago, 2000, Lake Forest Estates, People, and Culture, 2000, Classic Country Estates Lake Forest, 2003, One Hundred Rare and Notable Books, 2004, co-editor, Lake Forest College: A Guide to the Campus, 2007. Pres. Lake Forest/Lake Bluff Hist. Soc., 1982-85, bd. dirs., 2003—06; pres. Ill. Ctr. for Book Bd., 1992-93; pres. Ragdale Found., 1992-96; dir. Lake Forest Found. for Hist. Preservation, 1997—, v.p., 2000-02, 2006-07, pres., 2007—; dir Ctr. For Railroad Photography and Art, 1999—, sec., 2005—. Mem. Caxton Club. Presbyterian. Home: 169 Wildwood Rd Lake Forest IL 60045-2462 Office: Lake Forest Coll Donnelley and Lee Libr/LIT 555 N Sheridan Rd Lake Forest IL 60045-2399 Office Phone: 847-735-5064. E-mail: amiller@lakeforest.edu.

MILLER, ARTHUR MADDEN, lawyer, investment banker, brokerage house executive; b. Greenville, SC, Apr. 10, 1953; s. Charles Frederick and Kathryn Irene (Madden) M.; m. Roberta Beck Connolly, Apr. 17, 1993; children: Isabella McIntyre Madden, Roberta Beck Connolly. AB in History, Princeton U., 1973; MA in History, U. NC, 1976; JD with distinction, Duke U., 1978; LLM in Taxation, NYU, 1982. Bar: N.Y. 1979, U.S. Dist. Ct. (so. dist.) N.Y. 1979. Assoc. Mudge Rose Guthrie Alexander & Ferdon, NYC, 1978—85; v.p. pub. fin. Goldman, Sachs & Co., NYC, 1985—. Trustee Convent of the Sacred Heart, NY, 2003—, St. Andrew's Sch., Del., 2003—; adv. bd. Mary Baldwin Coll., Staunton, Va., 1982—86; trustee Princeton U. Rowing Assn., NJ, 1980—, pres., 1986—95; trustee Rebecca Kelly Dance Co., NYC, 1984—86; steward Power Ten, 1992—95. Mem. ABA (tax sect. com. on tax exempt financing 1985—), Nat. Assn. Bond Lawyers (lectr. 1985—), Securities Industry & Fin. Market Assn. (cons. 1985—), Practising Law Inst. (lectr. 1980, editor/author course materials 1980—), Bond Attys. Workshop (editor/author course material 1983—, lectr. 1983—), Princeton Club. Office: Goldman Sachs & Co 85 Broad St New York NY 10004-2456

MILLER, ARTHUR RAPHAEL, law educator; b. NYC, June 22, 1934; s. Murray and Mary (Schapin) Miller; m. Ellen Monica Joachim, June 8, 1958 (div. 1978); 1 child, Matthew Richard; m. Marilyn Tarmy, 1982 (div. 1988); m. Sandra L. Young, 1992 (div. 2001). Student, Bklyn. Coll., 1952-55, CCNY, 1955; AB in History, U. Rochester, 1955; LLB, Harvard U., 1958. Bar: NY 1959, US Supreme Ct. 1959, Mass. 1979. Assoc. Cleary, Gottlieb, Steen & Hamilton, NYC, 1958-61; assoc. dir. Columbia Law Sch. Project Internat. Procedure, NYC, 1961-62; lectr. Columbia Law Sch., NYC, 1961-62; assoc. prof. U. Minn. Law Sch., 1962-65; prof. U. Mich. Law Sch., 1965-72; vis. prof. Harvard Law Sch., Cambridge, Mass., 1971-72, prof., 1972-86, Bruce Bromley prof. law, 1986—2007; univ. prof. NYU Sch. Law, 2007—. Rsch. assoc. Mental Health Rsch. Inst., 1966-68; dir. project computer assisted instn. Am. Assn. Law Schools, 1968-75; spl. rapporteur State Dept. concerning chpt. II of Hague Conv., 1967; del. US-Italian Conf. Internat. Jud. Assistance, 1961, 62; chmn. task force external affairs Interuniv. Communications Coun., 1966-70; mem. law panel, com. sci. and tech. info. Fed. Coun. Sci. and Tech., Pres.'s Office Sci. and Tech., 1969-72; mem. adv. group Nat. Acad. Sci. Project on Computer Data Banks, 1970-78; mem. spl. adv. group to chief justice Supreme Ct. on Fed. Civil Litig.; mem. com. on automated personal data systems HEW, 1972-73; chmn. Mass. Security and Privacy Coun., Mass. Commn. on Privacy; mem. US Commn. New Technol. Uses Copyrighted Works, 1975-79; reporter US Supreme Ct.'s Adv. Com. on Civil Rules, 1978-86, mem. 1986-91; faculty Fed. Jud. Ctr.; reporter study on complex litig. Am. Law Inst.; bd. dirs. Rsch. Found. on Complex Litigations, 1975-80; bd. overseers Rand Inst. on Civil Justice, 1998-2002. Author: The Assault on Privacy: Computers, Data Banks, and Dossiers, 1971, Miller's Court, 1982; (with others) New York Civil Practice, 8 vols., Civil Procedure Cases and Materials, 7th edit., 1997, Federal Practice and Procedure: Civil, 47 vols., 1969—, CPLR Manual, 1967; host syndicated TV shows in Context, Miller's Law, Miller's Court, Headlines on Trial; legal expert Good Morning America. Served with AUS, 1958-59. Recipient Nat. Emmy award for The Constitution, That Delicate Balance. Mem. Am. Law Inst. Office: NYU Sch Law 40 Washington Square S, 409D New York NY 10012 Office Phone: 212-992-8147. Office Fax: 212-995-4590. E-mail: arthur.r.miller@nyu.edu.

MILLER, AUDREY THORNTON, retired vice principal; b. Glassboro, NJ, June 22, 1937; d. Aubrey and Rebecca Thornton; m. Kenneth C. Miller, Sr., Nov. 20, 1967; children: Yvette A. Rudd, Kenneth C. Jr. BS, Cheyney U., 1963; MEd, Rutgers U., 1974; EdD, Nova Southeastern U., 1998. Cert. prin., supr. N.J. Tchr. Camden (N.J.) Bd. Edn., 1963-74, asst. to prin., 1974-97, vice prin. H.C. Sharp Sch., 1997-2000; ret., 2000. Advisor Theta Chi City Wide chpt. Rowan U., 1980-85, Sharp Sch. Safety Patrol, Camden, 1991-95, Network III Drug Program, Camden, 1993-96; adv. bd. Carter's Psychol. Svc., Camden County, 1995—. Author: Using the Writing Process to Enchance Elementary Students Writing Proficiency and Teachers' Instructional Strategies, 1998. V.p. Garden City Alumnae of Delta Sigma Theta Sorority, Inc., Sicklerville, N.J., 1989-91; chair Career Women's Ministry, St. Matthews Bapt. Ch. Williamstown, N.J., 1993-96, chief ednl. svcs. comty. devel. ctr. programs SMCDC, 2003-07; mem. Camden County LWV. Recipient Set a Good Example award Gov. Christie Whitman, Trenton, 1994, Disting. Achievement award, Camden Bd. Edn., 1994, 96, Proclamation, Bd. Chosen Freeholders, Camden County, 2000, Cheyney U. Alumni Outstanding Service Award, 2003. Mem. NAACP, AFL-CIO, Black Women's Edn. Alliance (Educator's award 1992), Camden City Fedn. Sch. Adminstrs., N.J. State Fedn. Colored Women's Club (Outstanding Svc. in Edn. award 2000, Kappa Educators award 2007), Cheyney U. Alumni Assn. (life, area rep. S. Jersey chpt., 2000-02), Nova Southeastern U. Alumni Assn., Rutgers U. Alumni, Delta Sigma Theta (life, mem. ea. region leadership team 2005), Kappa Delta Pi, Kappa Alpha Psi (Edn. award 2006). Democrat. Avocations: interior decorating, travel, tennis. Home: 4 Pierson Pl Sicklerville NJ 08081-2006 Home Phone: 856-875-8671. Personal E-mail: milerau@aol.com.

MILLER, BARBARA KENTON, retired librarian; b. NYC, Sept. 21, 1934; d. Robert Alfred and Kathleen Hope (Levy) Kenton; m. John Arnold Miller, June 15, 1955; children: Valerie Ann Miller, Jennifer Karen Kraft. BA distinction, Finch Coll., 1960; MLS, C.W. Post, 1976. Cert. libr., N.Y. Libr., cons. archivist Coun. Fgn. Rels., NYC, 1977—2000; ret., 2000. Cons. archivist Coun. on Fgn. Rels. Mem. Spl. Librs. Assn., Beta Phi Mu. Avocations: dogs, golf. Office: Coun Fgn Rels 58 E 68 St New York NY 10021-5953 Personal E-mail: bkmiller55@aol.com.

MILLER, BARRY, researcher, psychologist; b. NYC, Dec. 25, 1942; s. Jack and Ida (Kaplan) M.; m. Susan Hallermeier; children: Eric, Arianne, Kristina, Barrie. BS in Psychology, Bklyn. Coll., 1965; MS in Psychology, Villanova U., 1967; PhD in Psychiatry, Med. Coll. Pa., 1971. Instr. psychology Villanova (Pa.) U., 1971-73; asst. dir. dept. behavioral sci., med. rsch. scientist Ea. Pa. Psychiatric Inst., Phila., 1971-73, sr. med. rsch. scientist, 1973-80; dir. Pa. Bur. Rsch. and Tng., Harrisburg, 1973-81; asst. prof. psychology U. Pa. Med. Sch., Phila., 1975-78, asst. clin. prof. psychology, 1978—; assoc. prof. psychiatry Med. Coll. Pa., Phila., 1981-90, rsch. assoc. prof. medicine, 1983-90, assoc. dean for rsch., 1981-90; dir. for rsch. devel. Albert Einstein Healthcare Network, Phila., 1990-95; dir. The Permanente Med. Group Rsch. Inst., Oakland, Calif., 1995-99; adj. assoc. prof. psychiatry Med. Coll. Pa., Phila., 1990—; rsch. assoc. prof. psychiatry Temple U. Sch. Med., Phila., 1990—; adminstrv. dir. rsch. ops. Divsn. Rsch., Oakland, Calif., 1999—. Mem. sci. and tech. task force Pa. Econ. Devel. Partnership, Harrisburg, 1987-88, adv. com. Clin. Rsch. Ctr. Psychopathology of Elderly, Phila., 1985-88; mem. cancer control prgram Pa. Dept. Health, 1994; vis. rsch. assoc. prof. Med. Coll. Pa., Phila., 1991—. Contbr. articles to profl. jours.; mem. editorial bd. Jour. Mental Health Adminstrn., 1988—, assoc. editor, 1989—. Bd. dirs. Community Mental Health Ctr. 6A, Phila., 1969-73, Northwest Jewish Youth Ctrs., Phila., 1974-75; mem. Lafayette Hill Civic Assn., 1973-86, Citizens Coun. Whitemarsh (Pa.) Twp., 1975-86; pres., bd. dirs. Golden Eagle Luxury Homeowners Assn., Pleasanton, Calif., 1995-97. Grantee HHS, NIH. Mem. AAAS, Am. Psychol. Assn., Assn. Mental Health Adminstrs., Assn. Univ. Tech. Mgrs., Soc. Rsch. Adminstrs., Calif. Psychol. Assn. Avocation: hiking. Office: Divsn Rsch 2000 Broadway Oakland CA 94612-3429 Office Phone: 510-891-3408. Business E-Mail: barry.x.miller@kp.org.

MILLER, BARRY RIXMANN, lawyer; b. Tempe, Ariz., Feb. 8, 1945; s. Ray E. and Dorothy (Rixmann) M.; m. Patricia A. Cunningham, Aug. 10, 1968; children: Christy, Brandy Ann. BS with honors, U. Ill., 1967; JD with honors, 1970. Bars: Ill. 1970, Tex. 1972, US Tax Ct. 1972. Mem. firm Andrews & Kurth, Houston, 1972-79, ptnr., 1979, mgmt. com., 1990-92, ptnr., co-head Tax Law Sect., Vinson & Elkins, LLP, 2003-05. Treas. Askew PTO, 1980. Served to 1st lt. US Army, 1970-72. Decorated Army Commendation medal. James scholar, 1963; recipient Bronze Tablet, U. Ill., 1967. Mem. Tex. Bar Assn., ABA (sect. on taxation), Order of the Coif, Beta Alpha Psi, Phi Alpha Mu, Sigma Chi. Republican. Contbr. articles to profl. jours. Office: Vinson & Elkins LLP First City Tower 1001 Fannin St, Ste 2300 Houston TX 77002 Office Phone: 713-758-4438. Business E-Mail: brmiller@velaw.com.

MILLER, BENJAMIN K., retired state supreme court justice; b. Springfield, Ill., Nov. 5, 1936; s. Clifford and Mary (Luthyens) M. BA, So. Ill. U., 1958; JD, Vanderbilt U., 1961. Bar: Ill. 1961. Ptnr. Olsen, Cantrill & Miller, Springfield, 1964-70; prin. Ben Miller-Law Office, Springfield, 1970-76; judge 7th jud. cir. Ill. Cir. Ct., Springfield, 1976-82, presiding judge Criminal div., 1977-81, chief judge, 1981-82; justice Ill. Appellate Ct., 4th Jud. Dist., 1982-84, Ill. Supreme Ct., Springfield, 1984-2001, chief justice, 1991-93, ret., 2001. Adj. prof. So. Ill. U., Springfield, 1974—; chmn. Ill. Cts. Commn., 1988-90; mem. Ill. Gov.'s Adv. Coun. on Criminal Justice Legis., 1977-84, Ad Hoc Com. on Tech. in Cts., 1985—. Mem. editorial rev. bd. Illinois Civil Practice Before Trial, Illinois Civil Trial Practice Pres. Cen. Ill. Mental Health Assn., 1969-71; bd. govs. Aid to Retarded Citizens, 1977-80; mem. Lincoln Legals Adv. Bd., 1988—. Lt. USNR, 1964-67. Mem. ABA (bar admissions com. sect. of legal edn. and admissions to bar 1992—), Ill. State Bar Assn. (bd. govs. 1970-76, treas. 1975-76), Sangamon County Bar Assn., Ctrl. Ill. Women's Bar Assn., Am. Judicature Soc. (bd. dirs. 1990-95), Abraham Lincoln Assn. (bd. dirs. 1988-98). Address: 100 E Bellevue PL Apt 29F Chicago IL 60611-5194 Office Phone: 312-840-7216.

MILLER, BENNETT, film director; b. 1967; Student, NYU. Dir.: over 200 commercials, (Documentary) The Cruise, 1998, New York Minute Video: A Film from 9/09/1999 at 9:09 A.M., 1999; (films) Capote, 2005 (Best First Film, NY Film Critics Circle, 2005). Avocations: chess, drawing, yoga. Office: c/o Endeavor Agency 9601 Wilshire Blvd 10th Fl Beverly Hills CA 90212 *

MILLER, BERNARD JOSEPH, JR., advertising executive; b. Louisville, July 31, 1925; s. Bernard J. Sr. and Myrtle (Herrington) M.; m. Jayne Hughes, Aug. 7, 1948 (div. Oct. 1970); children: Bernard J. III, Jeffrey, Janet Marie.; m. Brita Naujok, Nov. 24, 1970; 1 child, Brian. BS, Ind. U., 1949. Merchandising mgr. Brown-Forman Distillers, Inc., Louisville, 1949-54; v.p. Phelps Mfg. Co., Terre Haute, Ind., 1954-60; pres. Columbian Advt. Inc., Chgo., 1960-87, chmn., 1987—. 2d lt. USAF, 1943-46, PTO. Mem. Point of Purchase Advt. Inst. (dir. 1970-73), Saddle and Cycle Club (bd. dirs. 1987-90, 99—). Avocations: tennis, downhill skiing, collecting first edition autographed books.

MILLER, BETTY BROWN, freelance writer; b. Altus, Ark., Dec. 21, 1926; d. Carlos William and Arlie Gertrude (Sublett) Brown; m. Robert Wiley Miller, Nov. 15, 1953; children: Janet Ruth, Stephen Wiley. BS, Okla. State U., 1949; MS, U. Tulsa, 1953; postgrad., Am. U., 1966—68. Tchr. LeFlore (Okla.) H.S., 1947-48, Osage Indian Reservation H.S., Hominy, Okla., 1948-50, Jenks (Okla.) HS, 1950—51; lectr. Sch. Bus. U. Tulsa, 1950-51; tchr. Tulsa pub. schs., 1951-54; faculty mem. Burdette Coll., Boston, 1954-55; reporter Bethesda-Chevy Chase Tribune, Montgomery County, Md., 1970-73; freelance writer, contbr. newspapers and mags., 1973—. V.p. Kenwood Park (Md.) Citizens Assn., 1960; mem. Ft. Sumner Citizens Assn., editor newsletter, 1969; mem. Md. State PTA, editl. coord. leadership conf., 1973-74; founder, chair Montgomery County Forum Edn., 1970-75; trustee Friends Valley Forge Nat. Hist. Park; bd. dirs. Friends Curtis Inst. Music; active Nat. Mus. Women in the Arts, Musical Fund Soc. Phila.; trustee adv. Help the Aged Internat. Mem.: DAR, PEO, Union League Phila. (past mem. ladies com., mem. ladies adv. com.), The Nat. Gravel Soc., Internat. Platform Assn., Montgomery County Press Assn., Nat. Soc. Arts & Letters (past editor mag., bd. dirs. pub rels., past nat. corr. sec.), Huguenot Soc. Pa. (v.p. 1989—92, pres. 1993—95, past bd. dirs., hon. pres. 1997—), Nat. League Am. Pen Women (pasat nat. budget chmn., past nat. treas.), Soc. Descendants of Washington's Army at Valley Forge (past. nat. comdr. in chief, past inspector gen. Nat. Huguenot Soc., past. mem. gen. coun.), Acorn Club Phila., Sedgeley Club (pres. Phila. 1985—88), Washington Club, U.D.C., Adventures Unltd. (chmn. Washington chpt.), Capital Spkrs. Club Washington (past pres.), Melba T. Croft Music Club, Order Ea. Star (life). Republican. Address: PO Box 573 Valley Forge PA 19481-0573

MILLER, BEVERLY A(NN), reference librarian; b. Tulsa, Dec. 22, 1941; d. Buford Maxwell and Wilda (Durfee) M. BA, Thiel Coll., Greenville, Pa., 1964; MA in Libr. Sci., U. Denver, 1965; MA in History, Boise U., Idaho, 2003. Periodicals libr. Minot (N.D.) State Coll., 1966-67; asst. libr. Rocky Mountain Coll., Billings, Mont., 1967-68; circulation libr. Boise (Idaho) State Coll., 1968-71; reference and interlibr. libr. Boise (Idaho) State U., 1971—, bd. dirs., faculty advisor Women's Ctr., 1992-93. Bd. dirs. Higher Edn. Resource Svcs./West, Boise, 1991—. Book reviewer Libr. Jour., 1975-95; author, adv. bd. mem. Sage Woman Mag., 1980's; contbg. editor: Idaho Women in History, 1990. Mem. AAUP (bd. dirs. Boise State U. chpt. 1994-2003, treas.), NOW (bd. dirs. Boise 1978-79, Idaho 1979-80), Am. Fedn. Tchrs. (v.p. 1979-81 Boise State U.), Pacific N.W. Libr. Assn., Pacific N.W. Women's Studies Assn., Idaho Libr. Assn., Idaho Womens Network (bd. dirs. 1987-92), Snake River Alliance (bd. dirs. 1986). Avocations: women's history, dog sports. Home Phone: 208-343-5329; Office Phone: 208-426-1626. Business E-Mail: bmiller@boisestate.edu.

MILLER, BEVERLY WHITE, former college president, educational consultant; b. Willoughby, Ohio, 1923; d. Joseph Martin and Marguerite Sarah (Storer) White; m. Lynn Martin Miller, Oct. 11, 1945 (dec. 1986); children: Michaela Ann, Craig Martin, Todd Daniel, Cass Timothy, Simone Agnes. AB, Western Res. U., 1945; MA, Mich. State U., 1957; PhD, U. Toledo, 1967; LHD (hon.), Coll. St. Benedict, St. Joseph, Minn., 1979; LLD (hon.), U. Toledo, 1988. Chem. and biol. researcher, 1945-57; tchr. schs. in Mich., also Mercy Sch. Nursing, St. Lawrence Hosp., Lansing, Mich., 1957-58; mem. chemistry and biology faculty Mary Manse Coll., Toledo, 1958-71, dean grad. div., 1968-71, exec. v.p., 1968-71; acad. dean Salve Regina Coll., Newport, RI, 1971-74; pres. Coll. St. Benedict, St. Joseph, Minn., 1974-79, Western New Eng. Coll., Springfield, Mass., 1980-96, pres. emerita, 1996—. Higher edn. cons., 1996—; cons. U.S. Office Edn., 1980; mem. Springfield Pvt. Industry Coun./Regional Employment Bd., exec. com., 1982-94; mem. Minn. Pvt. Coll. Coun., 1974-79, sec., 1974-75, vice chmn., 1975-76, chmn., 1976-77; cons. in field. Author papers and books in field. Corporator Mercy Hosp., Springfield, Mass. Recipient President's citation St. John's U., Minn., 1979; also various service awards; named disting. alumna of yr. U. Toledo, 1998. Mem. AAAS, Am. Assn. Higher Edn., Assn. Cath. Colls. and Univs. (exec. bd.), Internat. Assn. Sci. Edn., Nat. Assn. Ind. Colls. and Univs. (govt. rels. adv. com., bd. dirs. 1990-93, exec. com. 1991-93, treas. 1992-93), Nat. Assn. Biology Tchrs., Assn. Ind. Colls. and Univs. of Mass. (exec. com. 1981-96, vice chmn. 1985-86, chmn. 1986-87), Nat. Assn. Rsch. Sci. Tchg., Springfield C. of C. (bd. dirs.), Am. Assn. Univ. Adminstrs. (bd. dirs. 1989-92), Delta Kappa Gamma, Sigma Delta Epsilon. Office: 6713 County Road M Delta OH 43515-9778

MILLER, BILL (WILLIAM H. MILLER III), diversified financial services company executive; BA, Washington and Lee U., 1972; attended, John Hopkins U. CFA 1986. Treas. J.E. Baker Co.; dir. rsch. Legg Mason, Inc., Balt., 1981—85, co-mgr. value trust fund, 1982—90, portfolio mgr., 1990—, CEO Legg Mason Capital Mgmt. Vice chmn. Santa Fe Inst., 2001—05, chmn., 2005—. Former military intelligence officer. Office: Legg Mason Cds Inv Serv PO Box 55214 Boston MA 02205-5214

MILLER, BLONDELL STEPHENSON, social worker, minister; b. Hartsville, SC; d. Johnnie and Marie Belvin Stephenson; m. James Lee Miller, Apr. 6, 1974; children: Taris Lydell, James Richard, Brandon Jerel. BA in History, Morris Coll., 1973; degree in Social Work, Winthrop U., 1980; student in Religious Edn., Duke U., 2004—05. Lic. pastor S.C. Conf. United Meth. Ch., 2003; LCSW S.C. Bd. Social Work, 1989. Tchr. Lee County Bd. Edn., Bishipville, SC, 1973—74; social worker Lee County Dept. Social Svc., Bishipville, 1974—2005; pastor Hartsville (S.C.) Dist. United Meth., 2000—. Chmn. bd. FEMA, Bishopville; bd. dir. Lee First Step, Bishopville, Waterse Head Start Program Health, Sumter, SC. Mem.: NAACP, Morris Coll. Alumni (sec.), Ea. Star (treas.), Delta Sigma Theta (chaplin 1986—). Meth. Avocations: cooking, reading, singing, travel, basketball. Home: 503 Pleasantview Dr Hartsville SC 29550 Office: Lee County Dept Social Svc 820 Brown St Bishopville SC 29010 Office Phone: 803-484-5376. Personal E-mail: blon1949@aol.com.

MILLER, BODE (SAMUEL BODE MILLER), professional skier; b. Easton, NH, Oct. 12, 1977; s. Woody and Jo Miller. Attended, Carrabassett Valley Acad. Mem. US Ski Team, 1996—2007. Co-author (with Jack McEnany): Bode: Go Fast, Be Good, Have Fun, 2005. Named Champion, FIS World Cup, 2005; recipient Six US Nat. Championship Medals, Two Silver-Medals, Winter Olympic Games, 2002, One Silver-Medal, Two Gold-Medals, World Championships, 2005, Super G Title, World Cup, 2005, 2006, US Alpine Championships, 2007. Achievements include first US skier in 22 yrs. to win World Cup overall championship, 2005. Office: US Ski and Snowboard Assoc Box 100 1500 Kearns Blvd Park City UT 84060 E-mail: bode@bodemillerusa.com.

MILLER, BONNIE SEWELL, marketing professional, writer; b. Junction City, Ky., July 24, 1932; d. William Andrew and Lillian Irene (McCowan) Sewell; m. William Gustave Tournade Jr., Nov. 5, 1950 (div. 1974); children: Bonnie Sue Tournade Zaner, William Gustave III, Sharon Irene Tournade Leach; m. Bruce George Miller, Nov. 15, 1981. BA, U. South Fla., 1968, MA, 1973. Cert. tchr., Fla. Chair dept. English Tampa Cath. H.S., Fla., 1972—78; tchr. Clearwater H.S., Fla., 1978—80; mgr. prodn. svcs. Paradyne Corp., Largo, Fla., 1980—83; freelance writer, cons. Tampa, 1983—84; mgr. product documentation PPS, Inc., Largo, 1984—86, mgr. mktg. comm., 1986—87; writer Nixdorf Computer Corp., Tampa, 1988—89; mktg. dir. Suncoast Schs. Fed. Credit Union, Tampa, 1989—98; co-owner, v.p., writer, cons. Need-A-Writer, Inc., Tampa, 1998—; instr. profl. and tech. writing and comm. for engrs. U. South Fla., 2004—. Instr. English, Hillsborough C.C., Tampa, Fla., 1975—87; cons. bus. writing Coronet Instrnl. Media Writing Project, 1976, Nat. Mgmt. Assn., 1981—87; adj. instr. profl. writing U. South Fla., 1993; adj. instr. tech. writing U. Tampa, 2002—, English instr., 2002—; adj. instr. profl. and tech. writing U. South Fla., 2004—. Author: Youth Financial Literacy, 1999, Effective Business Writing for Credit Unions, 2000, Meeting for a Lifetime, 2006; contbr. articles to profl. jours. Bd. dir. SERVE, Tampa, Credit Union Mktg. Assn. Coun., Sing Parent Displaced Homemakers Group; legis. chair Tampa PTA, 1965; judge speech contest Am. Legion, Tampa, 1976; vol. North Tampa Vol. Libr., 1988. NEH fellow, 1975. Mem. NAFE, Soc. Tech. Communicators, Am. Assn. Bus. Women, Kappa Delta Pi. Democrat. Methodist. Avocations: writing, sewing, gardening, travel, decorating. Home and Office: 516 2d Ave SE Lutz FL 33549 Business E-Mail: b.millerII@verizon.net.

MILLER, BRAD (RALPH BRADLEY MILLER), congressman; b. Fayetteville, NC, May 19, 1953; s. Nathan David and Margaret Virginia (Hale) Miller; m. Esther Susan Hall, Dec. 19, 1981. BS in Polit. Sci., U. NC Chapel Hill, 1975; MSc in Polit. Sci., London Sch. Econs., 1978; JD, Columbia U., 1979. Bar: NC 1979, US Dist. Ct. (ea. dist.) NC 1980, US Ct. Appeals (4th cir. 1980), US Dist. Ct. (mid. dist.) NC 1983. Law clk. to Hon. J. Dickson Phillips, Jr. US 4th Cir. Ct. Appeals, 1979-80; assoc. Allen, Steed & Allen, Raleigh, NC, 1980-82, Barringer, Allen & Pinnix, Raleigh, NC, 1982-84, LeBoeuf, Lamb, Leiby & MacRae, Raleigh, NC, 1985-88; prin. Nichols, Miller & Sigmon, Raleigh, NC, 1988-90; pvt. practice Raleigh, NC, 1991—; mem. NC State Ho. Reps., 1992—96, NC State Senate, 1997—2002, chmn. sen. jud. II com.; mem. US Congress from 13th NC dist., 2003—. Mem. fin. svcs. com. US Congress, mem. fgn. affairs com., mem. sci. and tech. com., chmn. subcommittee on investigations and oversight. Chmn. Wake County Dem. Com., 1985-87; mem. state exec. com. NC Dem. Com., 1985-89, 91-97; mem. NC Environ. Rev. Commn., 1994-95, mem. sentencing and policy adv. com. Mem. ATLA, NC Bar Assn., Wake County Bar Assn., NC Acad. Trial Lawyers, Am. Judicature Soc. Democrat. Episcopalian. Office: US House Reps 1722 Longworth House Office Bldg Washington DC 20515 Office Phone: 202-225-3032. Office Fax: 202-225-0181. *

MILLER, BRIAN DANIEL, music educator, organist; b. Charlotte, NC, Nov. 3, 1971; s. Vincent LaFollette and Jettie Rea Miller. BA in History, U. NC, 1994, B in Music Edn., 1995. Band tchr. Louisburg HS, NC, 1995—. Mem. NC Music Educators Conf., 1995—; fine arts dept. chair Louisburg HS, 1996—, mem. sch. planning team; mem. supt. dropout adv. team Franklin County Schs., 2004—05. Composer: The Louisburg March, 2001. Pianist Lions Club, Louisburg, NC, 2000—. Named Young Educator of Yr., Louisburg Jaycees, 2000, Tchr. of Yr., Franklin County Schs., 2000, Artist of Yr., Franklin County Arts Coun., 2001, Tchr. of Yr., Wal-Mart, 2002, 2003, 2004; recipient Never Stop Learning Educator award, WTVD-11. Mem.: Am. Theatre Organ Soc., Am. Guild Organists, Ctrl. Dist. Bandmasters Assn., James A. Johnson Masonic Lodge, Phi Mu Alpha Sinfonia, Phi Eta Sigma, Phi Beta Kappa. Republican. So. Baptist. Avocations: reading, collecting books and music, antique lamp repair, restoring typewriters and reed organs. Home: 102 Person St Louisburg NC 27549 Office Phone: 919-496-4722 ext. 225. Personal E-mail: bdmiller1935@aol.com.

MILLER, BRUCE ABRAHAM, lawyer; b. Bklyn., Oct. 11, 1927; s. Charles X. and Lydia Keyes (Barnett) M.; m. Edna Powell, Feb. 27, 1960; children: E. Powell, Ann L., Elizabeth D. JD, Wayne St. U., 1954. Bar: Mich. 1956. Former gen. coun. Metro-Detroit AFL-CIO; sp. counsel United Steelworkers Am., AFL-CIO-CLC, Am. Fed. Tchrs., AFL-CIO; atty. Miller Cohen, Detroit. Former officer-at-large Mich. Dem. Com.; treas. 13th Congl. Dist. Dem. Com.; chmn. Wayne County Dem. Com. With U.S. Army, 1946-48. Office: 600 W Lafayette Blvd 4th Fl Detroit MI 48226-3195 Home Phone: 248-540-8677; Office Phone: 313-964-4454. Business E-Mail: brucemiller@millercohen.com.

MILLER, BRYAN MICHAEL, music educator; b. Berwyn, Ill., Sept. 8, 1966; s. Donald Harold and Jean Ann Miller. BS in Music Edn., No. Ill. U., 1989; MusM, U. Notre Dame, 1991; diploma, Acad. Mil. Sci., 2000. Grad. asst. dir. bands U. Notre Dame, Ind., 1989—91; band dir. Reavis HS, Burbank, Ill., 1991—94; music dept. chair Leyden HS, Franklin Park, Ill., 1994—. Adj. faculty Vander Cook Coll., Chgo., 1999—2004; faculty Elmhurst Coll., Ill., 2005—; comdr. 566th Air Force Band, Peoria, Ill., 2000—; music dir. Ill. Ambassadors of Music, 2005—. Bd. dirs. Chgo. Youth Symphony Orch., 2002—; mem. leadership team Opus Chamber Music Camp, 2004—. Capt. USAF, 1998—. Decorated Achievement medal USAF, Ill. N.G., Commendation medal; recipient Citizen Soldier award, Acad. Mil. Sci., 2000. Mem.: Am. Fedn. Tchrs., Ill. Music Educators Assn., N.G. Assn., Moose, Am. Legion. Home: 5 S 738 Hummingbird Ln Naperville IL 60540 Office: Leyden High Sch 3400 N Rose St Franklin Park IL 60131

MILLER, BUFFY, dancer; b. Atlanta; Studies with, Patricia Bromley; student, New Ballet Sch. Mem. Feld Ballet Tech. Soc., 1986—97; with Ballet Tech., 1997—. Office: 108 High St 2 Portland ME 04101-3815

MILLER, C. ARDEN, physician, educator; b. Shelby, Ohio, Sept. 19, 1924; s. Harley H. and Mary (Thuma) Miller; m. Helen Meihack, June 26, 1948; children: John Lewis, Thomas Meihack, Helen Lewis, Benjamin Lewis. Student, Oberlin Coll., Ohio, 1942—44; MD cum laude, Yale U., New Haven, Conn., 1948. Intern, then asst. resident pediatrics Grace-New Haven Community Hosp., 1948—51; faculty U. Kans. Med. Center, 1951—66, dir. childrens rehab. unit, 1957—60, dean Med. Sch., dir., 1960—66; prof. pediatrics and maternal and child health U. N.C., Chapel Hill, 1966—98, emeritus, 1998—, vice chancellor health scis., 1966—71, chmn. dept. maternal and child health, 1977—87. Chmn. exec. com. Citizens Bd. Inquiry into Health Svcs. for Am., 1968—71. Mem. editl. bd.: Jour. Med. Edn., 1960—66; contbr. articles to profl. jours. Trustee Appalachian Regional Hosps., 1974—84, Planned Parenthood Fedn.; chmn. Alan Guttmacher Inst., 1978—84, 1986—. Recipient Robert H. Felix Disting. Svc. award, St. Louis U., 1977, Martha Mae Eliot award in pub. health, 1984, O. Max Gardner award, U. N.C., 1987; scholar Am. Markle scholar in med. scis., 1955—60. Fellow: Royal Soc. Health (hon.), Clare Hall Cambridge (Eng.) U. (life); mem.: APHA (chmn. action bd. 1972—75, pres. 1974—75, Sedgewick Meml. medal 1986), Inst. of Medicine NAS, Assn. Am. Med. Colls. (v.p. 1965—66), Soc. Pediat. Rsch., Delta Omega, Alpha Omega Alpha, Sigma Xi. Home: 350 Carolina Meadows Villa Chapel Hill NC 27517-7549

MILLER, CANDACE MARIE, healthcare educator; d. Raymond Bertrand and Daphne Anna Morin; m. Paul Miller, Aug. 23, 1997; 1 child, Alexandra. BA in Polit. Sci. & Journalism, Rutgers U., New Brunswick, NJ, 1992—95; MPH, Johns Hopkins U., Balt., 1997—99; ScD, Harvard U., Boston, 2001—05. Mgr. Ctr. for Alcohol & Other Drug Edn. George Wash. U., DC, 1999—2000; sr. trainer Ednl. Devel. Ctr., Newton, Mass., 2000—01; post doctoral fellow Harvard U., 2005—06; asst. prof. Boston U. Sch. Pub. Health, 2006—. Cons. UNICEF, NYC, 2005—06, Help Age Internat., London, 2005—06. Vol. US Peace Corps, Nkhotakota, Malawi, 1995—97. Avocation: running. Office: Boston Univ Sch Public Health 85 E Concord St 5th Fl Boston MA 02118

MILLER, CANDICE S., congresswoman; b. Clair Shores, Mich., May 7, 1954; m. Donald G. Miller; 1 child, Wendy Nicole. Student, Macomb County C.C., 1973—74, Northwood U., 1974. Sec., treas. D.B. Snider, Inc., 1972-79; trustee Harrison Twp., 1979-80, supr., 1980-92; treas. Macomb County, 1992-95; sec. of state State of Mich., Lansing, 1995—2003; mem. US Congress from 10th Mich. dist., 2003—. Mem. Lake St. Clair Blue Ribbon Commn. Chair John Engler for Gov. campaign, Macomb County; del. Rep. Nat. Conv., 1996; co-chair Rep. Platform Com., 1996, Dole/Kemp Presdl. Campaign, Mich., 1996, Bush/Cheney Presdl. Campaign, Mich., 2000; mem. Carehouse-Macomb County Child Adv. Ctr., Selfridge Air Nat. Guard Base Cmty. Coun., Detroit Econ. Club; mem. adminstrv. bd. Mich. State, mem. safety commn. Recipient Macomb Citizen of Yr. award, March of Dimes, 1997, Woman of Distinction award, Macomb County Girl Scouts, Adjutant General's Patriot award, Mich. Nat. Guard, 2002, GH award women in govt., Good Housekeeping mag., 2003, Econ. Excellence award, Macomb C. of C.; Paul Harris Internat. fellow. Mem.: Nat. Assn. Secretaries of State, Boat Town Assn. Republican. Presbyterian. Avocations: boating, yacht racing. Office: US Congress 228 Cannon HOB Washington DC 20515 also: District Office 48653 Van Dyke Ave Shelby Township MI 48317-2560 Office Phone: 202-225-2106, 586-997-5010. Office Fax: 202-226-1169, 586-997-5013. *

MILLER, CAROL, elementary school educator, counselor; b. Bklyn., Jan. 10, 1939; d. Maurice and Bess (Strauss) Shapiro; m. Stephen Herschel Miller (div.); children: Mark Alan, David Charles. BS in Elem. Edn., Ohio State U., Columbus, 1959; grad. work-edn., Queens Coll., Flushing, NY, 1959—61; MA in Counseling Psychology, Lewis & Clark Coll., Portland, Oreg., 1988. Cert. tchr. k-3 NY Bd. Edn., 1959, tchr. k-6 Calif. Bd. Edn., 1966, basic counselor Personnel Svcs., Oreg., 1988. Kindergarten tchr. Hampton St. Sch., Mineola, NY, 1959—61; tchr. (k-3) Roosevelt Elem. Sch., Santa Monica, Calif., 1961—66; elem. sch. tchr. Horace Mann Sch., Beverly Hills, 1966—67; substitute elem. sch. tchr. San Diego Sch. Dist., 1967—68, 1990—91; cancer support group facilitator Am. Cancer Soc., San Diego, 1992—99; breast cancer support group facilitator Scripps Meml. Hosp., LaJolla, 2000—02; adv. bd. mem. Am. Cancer Soc., San Diego, 1994—96; adv. bd. mem., breast cancer ctr. Scripps Meml. Hosp., LaJolla, 1999—2001; adv. bd. mem. St. Germaine Aux. for Child Abuse Prevention, San Diego, 1998—. Contbr. papers to profl. jours. and pubs. Leader Boy Scouts Am., Herhsey, Pa./Lake Oswego, Oreg., 1977—83; vol. Reach to Recovery, Pa., 1980—82, Oreg., 1982—88, Calif., 1988—; coord. Reach to Recovery Program, San Diego, Calif., 1991—93; vol. Polinsky Children's Ctr., San Diego, 1991—2005, U. Calif. San Diego, Moores Cancer Ctr., LaJolla, 2005—; com. mem. Citizen Involvement, Lake Oswego, Oreg., 1982. Recipient Terese Lasser award, Am. Cancer Soc., San Diego, 1993, Vol. of Yr., Health & Human Svcs., San Diego, 2002. Mem.: LWV, Psi Chi. Democrat. Jewish. Avocations: tennis, dance, reading, travel, writing. Home: 6555 Caminito Northland La Jolla CA 92037

MILLER, CAROLYN LYONS, microbiologist, military officer; b. Birmingham, Ala., June 28, 1955; d. John Henry and Annie Lois Lyons; m. Brian Lenny Miller, July 28, 1984; 1 child, Brian Lenny Miller, Jr. BS, U. Ala., 1977; MS, Ala. A&M U., 1979; PhD, Rutgers U., 1984; degree, Air U., 2000. Lic. medical technologist Am. Soc. Clin. Pathologists, 1984, cert. clin. lab. scientist Nat. Certification Agy, Lenexa, KS, 1984. Student asst. Dept. Biology and Microbiology U. Ala., Birmingham, Ala., 1973—77; rsch. asst. Dept of Biology and Food Sci. and Tech. Ala. A&M U., Normal, Ala., 1977—79; rsch. asst. Dept Pedodontics Sch. of Dentistry U. Ala., 1980; tchg. asst. biology and microbiology Cook Coll. Rutgers U., New Brunswick, NJ, 1980—83, asst. area coord. student life Douglass Coll., 1983—84; med. tech. intern Wilford Hall Med. Ctr., Lackland Air Force Base, Tex., 1985—86; chief quality control/epidemiology divsn. Air Force Sch. Aerospace Medicine, Brooks Air Force Base, Tex., 1986—89; comdr. 421st med. svc. squadron Wilford Hall Med. Ctr., Lackland Air Force Base, 1997—98; assoc. prof. Dept. Biology USAF Acad., Colorado Springs, Colo., 1989—93, exec. officer to the dean of the faculty, 1993—95; exec. officer to the comdr. Human Sys. Ctr., Brooks Air Force Base, Tex., 1995—97; ops. staff officer/dir., quality assurance & regulatory affairs 59th Med. Diagnostics and Therapeutics Group, Lackland Air Force Base, Tex., 1998—99; v.p. recruitment & diversity affairs Uniformed Svcs. U. Health Scis., Bethesda, Md., 1999—2002; pathology flight comdr. 375th Med. Group, Scott AFB, Ill., 2002—05; dep. med. support squadron comdr. 375th Med. Support Squadron, Scott Air Force Base, Ill., 2002—05; biomed. sci. corps exec. 375th Airlift Wing, Scott AFB, Ill., 2002—05; dir. chem., biol., nuc. and clin. surveilance Air Force Inst. for Operational Health, Brooks City AFB, Tex., 2005—. Faculty advisor for vol. cmty. med. clinic Med. Sch. Uniformed Svcs. U., Bethesda, 1999—2002; coach odyssey of the mind White Oaks Elem. Sch., Burke, Va., 2000—02; vol. instr. Incarnate Word Coll., San Antonio, 1995—97; chmn. parent adv. com. Child Devel. Ctr., Colorado Springs, Colo., 1991—95; mem., leadership coun. for cmty. svc. Alamo Fed. Exec. Bd., San Antonio, 1995—99; cons. in field. Contbr. articles to profl. jours. Cmty. mem. Alamo Fed. Exec. Bd., San Antonio, Tex., 1995—99; ch. med. vol. Emmanuel Ch., San Antonio, Tex., 1985—89; advisor to the bd. Uniformed Svcs Med. Sch., Bethesda, Md., 1999—2002; mil. deployment Mil., Overseas, Non-U.S., Classified, 2003—03. Col. USAF, 1985, Scott and various other Air Force Bases, over 20 years of service. Decorated Expeditionary Svc. Ribbon with Gold Border USAF, Air Force Outstanding Unit Award with Valor US; fellow, 81Rutgers U., 1984; Pell grant, U. of Ala., 1974—77. Master: Biomedical Scis. Corps (licentiate; licensure 1985, Chief Mastery badge 1995); mem.: Soc. Armed Forces Mil. Lab. Scientists (sr. mem. 1986, Best Rsch. Poster Presentation 1999), Am. Soc. Microbiologists (corr.; mem. 1978, Grad. Student award 1983), Assn.Mil. Surgeons of U.S. (corr.; mem. 1996), Am. Soc. Clin. Pathologists (assoc.; assoc. mem. 1990), Officers Club (assoc.; mem. 1986), Beta Beta Beta (hon.; honor mem. 1979), Zeta Phi Beta (corr.; pres. 1975—77, Cmty. Charity Supporter 1976). Achievements include research in converting urine to potable water to prevent discharge in space; development of medical laboratory in deployed location; first to tri-service military and federal medical school recruitment to help meet nation's need for physicians, women and minorities. Avocations: reading, horseback riding, running, walking, interior decorating. Home: 23003 Whisper Canyon San Antonio TX 78258-3211 Office: 2350 Gillingham Dr Brooks City-Base TX 78235 Home Phone: 210-481-9959; Office Phone: 210-536-8305. Personal E-mail: bbcmiller@earthlink.net. Business E-Mail: carolyn.miller@brooks.af.mil.

MILLER, CARROLL GERARD, JR., (GERRY MILLER), lawyer; b. San Antonio, Tex., Dec. 12, 1944; s. Carroll Gerard Sr. and Glyn (Roddy) M.; m. Sylvia Louise Mertins, Mar. 7 1971 (dec. 1982); children: Glyn Marie Bennett, Roddy Gerard, Gina Louise. AS, Del Mar Coll., 1965; BS, U. Houston, 1967; JD, Tex. Tech. U., 1970. Bar: Tex. 1970, Colo. 1987, D.C. 1989, U.S. Dist. Ct. (so. dist.) Tex. 1971, U.S. Ct. Appeals (5th cir.) Tex. 1973, U.S. Supreme Ct. 1974, U.S. Ct. Appeals (D.C. 1986); bd. cert. in criminal law. Assoc. Allison, Madden, White & Brin, Corpus Christi, Tex., 1970-71; asst. city atty. City of Corpus Christi, 1971; asst. dist. atty. Nueces County Dist. Attys. Office, Corpus Christi, 1971-73; asst. city atty. civil div. City of Corpus Christi, 1973-74; atty. Corpus Christi Police Dept.-City of Corpus Christi, 1974-77; pvt. practice Corpus Christi, 1973—. Adj. prof. Bee County Coll., Beeville, Tex., 1973-74, Tex. A & I U., Corpus Christi, 1975-76. Past treas. and diaconate First Presbyn. Ch., Corpus Christi; bd. dirs., incorporator Iron Curtain Outreach; 20/20 coun. Open Doors. Mem. SAR, SCV, Assn. Trial Lawyers Am., Tex. Criminal Def. Lawyers Assn., Nat. Criminal Def. Lawyers Assn., Coll. State Bar Tex., Sons of Republic Tex., Crime Stoppers, Inc. (past dir.), Bay Yacht Club (dir.). Republican. Avocations: sailing, scuba diving, photography, astronomy. Home: 609 Carmel Dr Sandia TX 78383 Office: 1007 Kinney St Corpus Christi TX 78401-3009 E-mail: lawgmiller@aol.com.

MILLER, CATHERINE H., nursing administrator, property manager; d. Lawrence James Gleason, Jr. and Arlene Joan Woolsey; m. Thomas Dewayne Keyser (div.); children: Kenneth James Keyser, Kerry Lee Keyser, Gary Wayne Keyser; m. James H. Miller, Dec. 14, 1996. Certificate acctg., Brown's Bus. Sch., Hempstead, NY, 1966; certificate cmty. health agt., certificate nursing asst., Dabney S. Lancaster C.C., Clifton Forge, Va., 1977, AAS, 1981. RN Va., 1981. Sec., bookkeeper Aluminum Specialties Home Improvement, Levittown, NY, 1960—76; cert. nursing asst. Liberty House Nursing Home, Clifton Forge, 1977—79, RN charge nurse, 1981—83, 1985—97, RN supr., 1997—2005; staff devel. dir. Alleghany Rehab./Health Care, Clifton Forge, 2006; RN supr. Beverly Health Care, Alleghany Rehab./Health Care, Clifton Forge, 2006—. Nurse, adult CPR instr. Am. Red Cross, Covington, Va., 1997—. Worthy matron Order of Ea. Star Martha chpt. 21, Covington, 1985. Named to Wall of Tolerance, Nat. Campaign for Tolerance, founding chair Rosa Parks, 2005. Avocation: painting. Office: Alleghany Highlands Cmty Svcs Adult Day Ctr 550 Pine St Clifton Forge VA 24422

MILLER, CHARLES ALLEN, politics educator; b. Washington, Oct. 27, 1937; BA, Swathmore Coll., Pa., 1959; MPA, Harvard U., 1962, PhD, 1968. Asst. prof. social sci. Clark Coll., Atlanta, 1967-70; asst. prof. politics Princeton (N.J.) U., 1970-74; assoc. prof., prof. politics Lake Forest (Ill.) Coll., 1974—. Author: The Supreme Court and the Uses of History, 1969, A Catawba Assembly, 1973, Jefferson and Nature, 1988; compiler: Isn't That Lewis Carroll?, 1984.

MILLER, CHARLES E., gynecologist; b. Iron Mountain, Mich., Aug. 18, 1953; s. Alfred and Muriel Miller; m. Laura Miller; children: Benjamin, Abagayle, Alec. BS in Medicine, Northwestern U., Chgo., 1975, MD, 1977. Diplomate Am. Bd. Ob-gyn., 1984. Dir. reproductive endocrinology and infertility Luth. Gen. Hosp., Park Ridge, Ill., 1983—85, dir. Ctr. for Advanced Reproduction for In-vitro Fertilization and Gamete Intrafallopian Transfer, 1989—95, dir. minimally invasive gynecol. surgery, 2005—; med. dir., med. dir. divsn. endoscopic surgery Ctr. for Human Reproduction, Schaumburg, Ill., 1995—99; dir. Ctr. for Minimally Invasive Gynecologic Surgery Glenbrook Hosp., Ill., 1997—2001; pvt. practice Arlington Heights, Ill., 1999—2001, Charles E. Miller, MD & Assocs., Arlington Heights and Naperville, Ill., 2001—. Cons. Ethicon Endo-Surgery, Cin., 2004—, Ethicon Women's Health and Urology, Somerville, NJ, 2004—, Galil Med., Ltd., Yokneam, Israel, 2006—, Serono, Rockland, Mass.; cons., mem. spkrs. bur. Smith & Nephew, Andover, Mass., 2005—; mem. spkrs. bur. Boston Sci., Natick, Mass., 2005—; clin. assoc. prof. dept. ob-gyn. U. Ill., Chgo., clin. assoc. dept. ob-gyn. Mem. adv. bd.: Jour. Minimally Invasive Gynecology, mem. editl. bd.: OB/GYN News; contbr. chapters to books, articles to profl. jours. Fellow: ACOG (cert. accreditation coun. for gynecologic endoscopy); mem.: Chgo. Assn. Gynecologic Endoscopists, Chgo. Assn. Reproductive Endocrinology, Soc. Reproductive Surgeons, Endometriosis Assn. (clin. adv. bd., bd. dirs. 2006), Am. Assn. Gynecologic Laparoscopists (pres. elect, sec. - treas. 2006), RESOLVE - The Nat. Fertility Assn. (clin. adv. bd. mem., Lifetime Achievement award 2005), Am. Soc. Reproductive Medicine (bd. mem.). Office: Charles E Miller MD & Associates 120 Osler Dr Naperville IL 60540 Home Phone: 847-436-6669; Office Phone: 630-361-1119. Office Fax: 630-428-0083. Business E-Mail: lmaki@charlesemillermd.org.

MILLER, CHARLES HAMPTON, lawyer; b. Southampton, NY, Jan. 25, 1928; s. Abraham E. and Ethel (Simon) M.; m. Mary Fried, Aug. 26, 1956; children: Cathy Lynn Castaneda, Steven Scott, Jennifer Lee Miller-Grady. BA, Syracuse U., 1949; LLB, Columbia U., 1952. Bar: N.Y. 1952, Republic of Korea 1954, U.S. Ct. Appeals (2d cir.) 1958, U.S. Supreme Ct. 1969, U.S. Ct. Appeals (3d cir.) 1972, U.S. Ct. Appeals (7th cir.) 1973, U.S. Ct. Appeals (9th cir.) 1995; cert. mediator (so. and ea. dists.) N.Y., mediator Supreme Ct. N.Y. County; arbitrator Ea. dist. N.Y. Asst. counsel Waterfront Commn., N.Y. Harbor, 1954-56; asst. atty. U.S. Atty. for So. Dist. N.Y., 1956-58; assoc. Cole & Deitz, NYC, 1958-61, Marshall Bratter Greene Allison & Tucker, NYC, 1961-64, ptnr., 1964-82, Hess Segall Guterman Pelz Steiner & Barovick, NYC, 1982-86, Loeb & Loeb LLP, NYC, 1986-2000, counsel, 2000—. Mem. faculty Continuing Legal Edn., Columbia U. Law Sch., 1976-82. With U.S. Army, 1952-54. Fellow: Am. Bar

Found.; mem.: ABA, Assn. of Bar of City of NY. Home: 171 Ralph Ave White Plains NY 10606-3813 Office: Loeb & Loeb LLP 345 Park Ave Fl 18 New York NY 10154-1895 Office Phone: 212-407-4910. Personal E-mail: marbuzz@msn.com.

MILLER, CHARLES LELAND, pediatrician; b. Elmira, NY, Nov. 21, 1929; s. Earle Leland and Winifred Suits (Boshart) Miller; m. Lois Iannotta Miller, June 12, 1954 (dec.); children: Deborah Clasry, Stephen, Randolph, Cynthia Mannis, Pamela Zorn, Jeffrey(dec.). AB, Hamiton Coll., Clinton, NY, 1951; MD, U. Pa., Phila., 1955. Cert. Am. Acad. Pediats. (Del. state chmn., Am. Acad. Asthma, Allergy and Immunology. Intern Del. Hosp., Wilmington, 1955—56, resident, 1958—60; pvt. practice pediats. Pediat. Assocs., Wilmington, 1960—96; med. missionary World Med. Mission (Samaritan's Purse), Boone, NC, 2000—. Clin. assoc., prof. pediats. Jefferson Med. Sch., Phila., 1973—; mem. Bd. Aid Internat. Medicine, Wilmington, 2001—07; courtesy staff emeritis Dupont Hosp. Children, Wilmington, Chirsitana Care Med. Ctr., Stanton, Del. Physician 17 mission trips World Med. Mission; elder, Stephen min. Westminister Presbyn. Ch., Wlimington, 1993—, mem. med. prayer team, 2002—. Capt. med. corp US Army, 1945—57. Recipient Vol. Yr., Habitat For Humanity, 2000, In Footsteps Of Great Physicians award, Samaritan's Purse, 2005. Fellow: Am. Assn. Allergy and Immunology; mem.: Del. State Acad. Medicine, New Castle County Med. Soc., Am. Acad., New Castle Pediat. Assn. (Cmty. Svc. award 2004).

MILLER, CHARLES P., lawyer; b. Charlestown, W.Va., May 14, 1961; BA cum laude, W. Va. Univ., 1983, JD, 1986. Bar: W. Va. 1986, Tex. 1987. Ptnr., Banking, Bus. Transactions, Securities practices, head Bus. Dept., mem. mgmt. com. Patton Boggs LLP, Dallas. Founder Dallas Private Equity Forum; mem. selection com. Tex. Investment Forum, 1997—2003. Named a Tex. Super Lawyer, Tex. Monthly Mag., 2003—04. Mem.: ABA, Dallas Bas Assn., Tex. Bankers Assn., Order of the Coif. Office: Patton Boggs LLP Suite 3000 2001 Ross Ave Dallas TX 75201-8001 Office Phone: 202-457-6000. Office Fax: 214-758-1550. Business E-Mail: cmiller@pattonboggs.com.

MILLER, CHARLES RICKIE, systems analyst, engineering executive; b. New Albany, Ind., Oct. 4, 1946; s. Marshall Christian and Thelma Virginia (Martin) M.; m. Janel Howell, Nov. 24, 1968; children: Kimberly, Brian, Audrey, Rachel. BA in Physics, DePauw U., 1969; postgrad., Rice U., 1969-70, U. Houston, 1972-76. Tech. editor ITT/Fed. Electric Corp., Houston, 1970-71, LTV/Svc. Tech. Corp., Houston, 1971; sys. safety engr. Boeing Aerospace Corp., Houston, 1971-76; thermal analyst space sys. divsn. Rockwell Internat. Corp., Houston, 1976-89; mgr. thermal and fluid sys. for space shuttle payloads Space Shuttle Program Office, NASA/L.B. Johnson Space Ctr., Houston, 1989—. Mem. editl. team Apollo 14, 15 preliminary sci. reports, 1971-72; mem. sys. integration negotiating team for Space Shuttle to Mir Space Sta. rendezvous and docking missions, 1993-98, chmn. negotiating team for Space Shuttle to Mir Space Sta. water preparation and transfer, 1994-98, space shuttle program co-chmn. for shuttle/internat. space sta. program joint tech. working groups for thermal control, environ. control and life support sys., 1996—. Bd. dirs. Space City Aquatic Team, Houston, 1990-91. Rector scholar DePauw U., 1964-68; Rice fellow Rice U., 1969-70. Mem. AIAA, ASME, Nat. Space Soc., Air Force Assn., Am. Inst. Physics, Planetary Soc., Sigma Pi Sigma. Avocations: children's sports, jogging, science fiction, military history. Home: 806 Walbrook Dr Houston TX 77062-4030 Office: NASA Mail Code MO2 LB Johnson Space Ctr Houston TX 77058 Office Phone: 281-483-1229. Business E-Mail: c.r.miller@nasa.gov.

MILLER, CHARLES T., prosecutor; b. Winslow, Wash., June 27, 1948; s. Charles Wilbur and Pharoeba H. (Good) M.; m. Rebecca Louise Campbell, Aug. 17, 1974; chidren: Angela Dawn, Emily Grace, Kathryn Louise. BS in Criminal Justice, W.Va. State Coll., 1973; JD, W.Va. U., 1977. Bar: W.Va. 1977, U.S. Ct. Appeals (4th cir.) 1977. Asst. prosecuting atty., Kanawha County, W.Va., 1977-82; assoc. and ptnr. E. F. Thaxton Attys., Charleston, 1982-84; 1st asst. US atty. (so. dist.) W.Va. US Dept. Justice, Charleston, 1984—93, 1994—, interim US atty., 1991—92, 1993, 2001, 2005—. With USN, 1966-69, Vietnam; maj. W.Va. Army Nat. Guard; lt. col. W.Va. Air Nat. Guard. Decorated Navy Achievement medal, Rep. of Vietnam Svc. medal, Rep. of Vietnam Campaign ribbon, Rep. of Vietnam Cross of Gallantry, Combat Action ribbon, Presdl. Unit citation. Presbyterian. Avocation: carpentry. Office: US Atty's Office PO Box 1713 Charleston WV 25326 *

MILLER, CHARLES WALLACE, historian, environmental geologist, educator; b. Phoenix, July 7, 1946; s. Charles W. and Emabel O. Miller; m. Connie Raschke, June 3, 1972; 1 child, Geoffrey Wallace. BA, U. Md., 1969; MA, U. Tex., 1970; BS, SUNY, Albany, 1978; PhD, Union Inst., 1990. Tchr. pub. schs., San Antonio, 1971-76; instr. San Antonio Coll., 1972-78, St. Mary's Univ., San Antonio, 1976-78, Cochise Coll., Sierra Vista, Az., 1989-90, Pima C.C., Tucson, 1998—; environ. geologist U.S. Geol. Survey, Metairie, La., 1978-80; field geologist U.S. Bur. Land Mgmt., Moab, Utah, 1980-84; historian U.S. Bur. Reclamation, Salt Lake City, 1990-94; environ. scientist USAF, Tucson, 1994—. Mineral cons., Tucson, 1984-89. Author: Stake Your Claim! The Tale of America's Enduring Mining Law, 1991, The Spirit of the Pioneers Still Rules, 1997, The Automobile Gold Rushes, 1998. Vol. East Tucson Bapt. Ch., Tucson, Boy Scouts Am.; group coord. Combined Fed. Campaign. Recipient Outstanding Alumni award, SUNY Albany (now Excelsior Coll.), 2005. Mem. SAR, Nat. Eagle Scout Assn., Mining History Assn., James Madison Brigade for Preservation of the U.S. Constn., Mensa, Hist. Soc., Golden Key, Phi Alpha Theta, Pi Sigma Alpha. Achievements include climbing two tallest peaks in the lower 48 and 13 others over 14,000 feet; rim-to-rim trek across Grand Canyon. Avocations: backpacking, scuba diving, photography, lifeguarding. Home: 136 S Shadow Creek Pl Tucson AZ 85748-3278 Office: USAF 355 CES CEVA Davis Monthan Afb AZ 85707

MILLER, CHRISTINE ODELL COOK, federal judge; b. Oakland, Calif., Aug. 26, 1944; m. Dennis F. Miller; 2 children. BA in Polit. Sci., Stanford U., 1966; JD, U. Utah, 1969. Bar: D.C., Calif. Law clk. to Hon. David T. Lewis US Ct. Appeals (10th cir.), Salt Lake City; trial atty. US Dept. Justice, US Ct. Claims; team leader atty. FTC; atty. Hogan & Hartson, Washington; spl. counsel Pension Benefit Guaranty Corp.; dep. gen. counsel US Rlwy. Assn.; ptnr. Shack & Kimball, Washington; judge US Ct. Fed. Claims, Washington, 1983—. Comment editor Utah law Rev. Scholar U. Utah Coll. Law. Mem. DC Bar Assn., Calif. State Bar, Order of Coif, Univ. Club, Cosmos Club. Avocation: genealogy. Office: US Ct Fed Claims 717 Madison Pl NW Ste 716 Washington DC 20005-1011

MILLER, CHRISTOPHER, science educator; BA in Physics, Swarthmore Coll.; PhD in Molecular Biology, U. Pa. NSF traineeship, 1969—70; NIH molecular biology tng. grant, 1972—74; NIH U. fellowship, 1970—72; Muscular Dystrophy Assn. postdoctoral fellowship, 1974—76; prof. biochemistry Brandeis U., Waltham, Mass. Investigator Howard Hughes Med. Inst., 1989—; adj. prof. molecular biology Mass. Gen. Hosp., Boston; Decade of the Brain lecture Soc. for Neuroscience, 1998; mem. nat. adv. com. Pew Scholars Program, 1999. Contbr. articles to profl. jours. Recipient K.S. Cole award in Membrane Physics, 1985—86, Alden W. Specer Neurobiology award, Columbia U. Coll. Physicians and Surgeons, 1994—95, MERIT (Method to Extend Rsch. in Time) award, NIH, 1996—2001. Mem.: Biophysical Soc. (pres. 2000—01), NAS. Office: Brandeis U 415 South St Waltham MA 02454-9110 Office Phone: 781-736-2340. Business E-Mail: cmiller@brandeis.edu. *

MILLER, CLAIRE ELLEN, editor, educator, writer; b. Milw., July 17, 1936; d. Emil George Benjamin and Phyllis Dorothy (Rahn) Holtzen; m. Gerald Ray Miller, June 21, 1958; children: Karin, Russell. BS in Edn., Concordia U., 1961. Tchr. Grace Episcopal Day Sch., Silver Spring, Md., 1971-77, The Norwood Sch., Bethesda, Md., 1977-79; writer Media Materials, Balt., 1980; project editor Ednl. Challenges, Alexandria, Va., 1981; asst. mng. editor Ranger Rick Mag., Nat. Wildlife Fedn., Vienna, Va., 1981-87, mng. editor, 1988-2001, contbg. editor, 2002—; propr. Claire Ellen Miller, Writer and Editor, Rockville, Md., 2001—. Author numerous activity books for presch. thru mid. sch., 1979-80; project editor 6 vocabulary books, 1981; author numerous children's mag. and newspaper stories and books, 1981—. Mem. Assn. Ednl. Pubs., Md. Ornithol. Soc. Democrat. Lutheran. Avocation: birding. Home and Office: 17501 Kirk Ln Rockville MD 20853-1033 Personal E-mail: clairemiller@erols.com.

MILLER, CLIFFORD ALBERT, merchant banker; b. Salt Lake City, Aug. 6, 1928; s. Clifford Elmer and LaVeryl (Jensen) M.; m. Judith Auten, Sept. 20, 1976; 1 child, Courtney; children by previous marriage, Clifford, Christin, Stephanie. Student, U. Utah, 1945-50, UCLA, 1956. Pres. Braun & Co., LA, 1955-82, chmn., 1982-87; exec. v.p. Gt. Western Fin. Corp., Beverly Hills, Calif., 1987-91; chmn. Clifford Group, Inc., bus. cons., 1992—; mng. dir. Shamrock Holdings, Inc., 1992—, Shamrock Capital Advisors, L.P., 1992—. Bd. dirs. Frontier Bank, Park City, Utah, Triad Broadcasting Co., Inc., Monterey, Calif.; cons. to White House, 1969—74. Trustee Harvey Mudd Coll., Claremont, Calif., 1974—, chmn. bd. trustees, 1991-98; chmn. bd. dirs. L.A. Master Chorale, 1989-93, chmn. emeritus, 1993; mem. chmn.'s coun. Music Ctr. Unified Fund Campaign; bd. trustees Keck Grad. Inst. Applied Life Scis., Claremont, 1997—. Mem. Calif. Club, Wilshire Country Club, Park Meadows Country Club, Pi Kappa Alpha. Office: Shamrock Holdings Inc 4444 W Lakeside Dr PO Box 7774 Burbank CA 91510-7774 Office Phone: 818-973-4297.

MILLER, CLIFFORD JOEL, lawyer; b. LA, Oct. 31, 1947; s. Eugene and Marian (Millman) M. BA, U. Calif., Irvine, 1969; JD, Pepperdine U., 1973. Bar: Calif. 1974, Hawaii 1974, U.S. Dist. Ct. Hawaii 1974. Ptnr. Rice, Lee & Wong, Honolulu, 1974-80, Goodsill Anderson Quinn & Stifel, Honolulu, 1980-89, McCorriston Miller Mukai MacKinnon, Honolulu, 1989—. Mem. ABA, Calif. Bar Assn., Hawaii Bar Assn., Am. Coll. Real Estate Lawyers. Avocations: sailing, volleyball, swimming, history. Office: McCorriston Miller Mukai MacKinnon 5 Waterfront Plz 500 Ala Moana Blvd Ste 400 Honolulu HI 96813-4920 Office Phone: 808-529-7300. Business E-Mail: cmiller@m4law.com.

MILLER, CONRAD S., emergency physician, writer; BS, Cornell U., Ithaca, NY, 1967; MD, NY Med. Coll., Valhalla, 1971. Diplomate Am. Bd. Emergency Medicine. Attending physician emergency rm. Southampton Hosp., NY, 1977—85, 2000, Brookhaven Meml. Hosp., Patchogue, NY, 1988—. Bd. dirs. LTV, Wainscott, NY. Host, prodr. (Nat. Pub. Radio program) The Nuclear Power Debate, 1991; author: The Most Important Issues Americans THINK They Know Enough About, 2004. Named NY State Grandmasters Surfing Champion, NY Staet Surfing Soc., 1991.

MILLER, CORBIN RUSSELL, investment company executive; b. Huntington, W.Va., Apr. 6, 1948; s. Corbin Russell and Ernestine (Thorne) M.; m. Kathryn Ann Anderson, Sept. 16, 1978. AB cum laude, Princeton U., NJ, 1971. Trainee Morgan Guaranty Trust Co., NYC, 1972-74, asst. treas., 1974-77; assoc. Wm. Sword & Co. Inc., Princeton, 1977-79; v.p. J. Henry Schroder Corp., NYC, 1979-83, J. Henry Schroder Bank & Trust, NYC, 1983-87; sr. v.p. IBJ Schroder Bank & Trust Co., NYC, 1987-90; chmn. Koala Techs. Corp., Pleasanton, Calif., 1990-91; mng. dir. Regent Ptnr. Inc., NYC and Denver, 1991-92; exec. v.p. S.N. Phelps & Co., Greenwich, Conn., 1992-95; exec. v.p., CFO, dir. Carey Internat., Inc., Washington, 1995-96; pres. Lombard North Am. Inc., San Francisco, 1997-99; sr. ptnr. Continuum Ventures LLC, NYC, 2000—. Bd. dirs. Met. Opera Guild, N.Y.C., 1994—. Mem. Am. Soc. Order St. John of Jerusalem (chancellor 1999-2002), Met. Opera Club (pres. 1992-94), Knickerbocker Club, Rockaway Hunting Club, Racquet and Tennis Club, The Brook. Republican. Episcopalian. Avocation: golf. Home: 1165 5th Ave New York NY 10029-6931 Office: Continuum Ventures LLC 300 Park Ave Fl 17 New York NY 10022-7402 E-mail: cm@corbinmiller.us.

MILLER, CRYSTAL ANN, respiratory therapist; b. San Diego, Apr. 18, 1979; d. Thomas Howard and Sharon Ann Miller; life ptnr. Robert Marshall Davis; 1 child, Jade Leinani. AA in Arts & Scis., Olympic Cmty. Coll., Bremerton, Wash., 1997; BA in Human Svcsi., Hawaii Pacific U., Kaneohe, 2000; AA in Sci. Respiratory, Tidewater Cmty. Coll., Va. Beach, 2001; MBA in Healthcare Mgmt., U. Phoenix, 2005. Cert. respiratory therapist NBRC, 2001, registered NBRC, 2005. Respiratory therapist Med. Staffing Network, Seattle, 2004—; respiratory theapist Overlake Hosp., Bellevue, Wash., 2004—. Respiratory agent on assignment, Seattle, 2005—. High priestess Druid, Lakebay, Wash., 1994—2007. Specialist US Army, 2001—02, Ft. Leonardwood, Mich. Recipient Employee Recognition award, Overlake Hosp., 2004—06. Mem.: Mensa (life). Achievements include research in medical instruction and education. Home: 221 195th Ave KP S Lakebay WA 98349 Office: Univ Wash 1925 Pacific St Seattle WA 98112 Personal E-mail: sweetc11@yahoo.com. Business E-Mail: mcrystal@u.washington.edu.

MILLER, DAN, information technology executive; m. Sheryl Miller; 2 children. BSBA, U. Colo., Boulder. Various product mktg., sales and mgmt. positions NBI, Inc., Colo.; dir. Reseller Channel Orgn. Sun Microsystems, Inc., dir. Telco Sales for US Western Market, various leadership positions in Global Sales Orgn. including v.p. US Telecom. Market Area, v.p. Global Svc. Provide Strategy Group, pres. Global Electric Motors Japan, sr. v.p. global systems practice. Office: Sun Microsystems Inc 4150 Network Cir Santa Clara CA 95054 Office Phone: 650-960-1300. *

MILLER, DANIEL RAYMOND, prosecutor; b. Evansville, Ind., Sept. 20, 1963; s. Daniel Edgar and Virginia Sue (Baumgart) M. BA magna cum laude, DePauw U., 1985; JD cum laude, Ind. U., 1989. Bar: Ind. 1989. Clk. to Hon. William I. Garrard, Ind. Ct. of Appeals, Indpls., 1989-90; dep. pros. atty. Vanderburgh County Pros.'s Office, Evansville, 1990—, dir. gun violence program, 2003—04, dir. drug law enforcement program, 2004—. Pres. Substance Abuse Coun. Vanderburgh County, 1997-98; chmn. pastoral coun. St. John Cath. Ch., Evansville, 1995-98; mem. Diocese of Evansville Pastoral Coun., 1997-2000; pres. 4-H Coun., 1999, 2003-2004, Nat. 4-H Leadership Trust, 2004-06. Mem.: Nat. Dist. Attys. Assn., Ind. Bar Assn., Vanderburgh County Coop. Ext. Svc. (bd. dirs. 2000—05), St. Vincent DePaul Soc. (pres. 1994, sec. conf. 1995—2003, pres. 2003—), 4-H Club Assn. (leader Energetics Club 1991—, bd. dirs. 1995—2001, treas. 2000—01, pres. Vanderburgh County 4-H Leaders 2001—02). Republican. Roman Catholic. Avocations: gardening, church choir. Home: 13521 N Green River Rd Evansville IN 47725-9769 Office: Vanderburgh Co Pros Office Rm 108 City County Adm Bldg Evansville IN 47708 Office Phone: 812-435-5118. E-mail: drmprosec@aol.com.

MILLER, DARCY M., publishing executive; b. Glen Ridge, NJ, June 17, 1953; d. Paul Richardson and Susan (Alling) Miller; m. James R. Donaldson III, Feb. 6, 1988 (div.); 1 child, Zoe Alling Donaldson; m. Richard G. Powers, Aug. 23, 2003. Co-founder, assoc. pub. Mus. Mag., NYC, 1979-83; pub. Crop Protection Chems. Ref., NYC, 1983-85; assoc. pub. Chief Exec. Mag., NYC, 1986-87, pub., 1987-89, exec. v.p., 1989-96; pub. Stagebill, NYC, 1996-97; group pub. Am. Baby Group, 1997-2000, pres., 2000—01; pres. corp. sales Primedia Inc., NYC, 2001—03; sabbatical, 2003—. Mem.: ASCAP, Advt. Women of N.Y. Democrat. Episcopalian.

MILLER, DAVID EDMOND, physician; b. Biscoe, NC, June 6, 1930; s. James Herbert and Elsie Dale (McGlaughon) M.; m. Marjorie Willard Penton, June 4, 1960; children: Marjorie Dale, David Edmond. AB, Duke U., 1952, MD, 1956. Diplomate Am. Bd. Internal Medicine (subspecialty bd. cardiovasular disease). Internmed. ctr. Duke U., Durham, N.C., 1956-57, resident in internal medicine, 1957-58, 59, 60, research fellow cardiovascular disease, 1958-59, 61, assoc. internal medicine and cardiology, 1963-79, clin. asst., prof. medicine cardiology, 1979-91; practice medicine specialising in internal medicine and cardiology Durham, 1964-2000; attending physician internal medicine div. cardiology Watts Hosp., Durham, 1964-76, chief medicine, 1975-76; attending physician cardiology divsn. internal medicine Durham Regional Hosp. (formerly Durham County Gen. Hosp.), 1976-2000, chmn. dept. internal medicine, 1976-82, pres. med. staff, 1980-81, ret., 2000. Adv. com. Duke Med. Ctr. Contbr. articles to profl. jours. Council clin. cardiology N.C. chpt. Am. Heart Assn., 1963—. Served to lt. comdr. USNR, 1961-63. Fellow ACP, Am. Coll. Cardiology, Royal Soc. Medicine, Royal Soc. Health; mem. AMA, So. Med. Assn., N.C. Med. Soc. (del. ho. of dels. 1981, 82, 83), N.C. Durham-Orange County Med. Soc., Am. Soc. Internal Medicine, N.C. Soc. Internal Medicine (exec. coun. 1984-92), Am. Fedn. Clin. Rsch. Clubs: Hope Valley Country, Carolina Yacht. Methodist. Home: 1544 Hermitage Ct Durham NC 27707-1680

MILLER, DAVID GROFF, insurance agent; b. Kansas City, Kans., Aug. 17, 1949; s. Vincent G. and Ruth (Whitton) M.; m. Marjorie Zwiers, 1979. BA, U. Kans., 1972. CLU. Press aide to U.S. Senator James B. Pearson, 1974-75; fed. grant adminstr. Kans. Gov. Robert Bennett, 1975-78; brokerage rep. Paul Revere Co., Overland Park, Kans., 1979-85; prin. Miller Agy., Inc., Eudora, 1985—. Rep. dist. 43 Kans. State Reps., 1981-91; chmn. Kans. State Rep. Party, 1995-98. Mem.: Ind. Ins. Agts., Omicron Delta Kappa. Methodist. Office: Miller Agy Inc PO Box 460 Eudora KS 66025-0460

MILLER, DAVID L., lawyer; b. Bklyn., Nov. 4, 1954; BA with distinction, George Washington U., 1976; JD magna cum laude, U. Mich., 1979. Bar: DC 1979, Va. 1986. Ptnr. Real Estate practice, mem. bd. dir., chmn. Legal Opinion com. Pillsbury Winthrop Shaw Pittman, McLean, Va. Bd. mem. Appleseed Found., Langley Sch., McLean, Va. Mem.: ABA (chmn. com. on legal opinions in real estate transactions), Am. Coll. Real Estate Lawyers (chmn. com. on legal opinions), Urban Land Inst., Nat. Assn. Industrial & Office Properties, Va. State Bar Assn., DC Bar Assn. (former vice chmn. steering com. sec.), Phi Beta Kappa, Order of the Coif. Office: Pillsbury Winthrop Shaw Pittman 1650 Tysons Blvd Mc Lean VA 22102-4859 Office Phone: 703-770-7925. Office Fax: 702-770-7901. Business E-Mail: david.miller@pillsburylaw.com.

MILLER, DAVID R., academic administrator; BS, U. Calif., Berkeley; PhD, Princeton U. Acting dean engrng. U. Calif. San Diego, La Jolla, assoc. dean engrng., assoc. vice chancellor, acting sr. vice chancellor, assoc. vice chancellor. Office: UCSD Office Sr Vice Chancellor Acad Affairs 9500 Gilman Dr Dept 0001 La Jolla CA 92093-0001 Business E-Mail: milleravc@ucsd.edu.

MILLER, DAVID WILLIAM, historian, educator; b. Coudersport, Pa., July 9, 1940; s. Arthur Charles and Kathryn Marie (Long) M.; m. Margaret Vick Richardson, Aug. 22, 1964; 1 child, Roberta Neal. BA, Rice U., 1962; MA, U. Wis., 1963; PhD, U. Chgo., 1968. Instr. history Carnegie Mellon U., Pitts., 1967-68, asst. prof., 1968-73, assoc. prof., 1973-80, prof., 1980—. Adj. prof. religious studies U. Pitts., 1998—. Author: Church, State and Nation in Ireland, 1898-1921, 1973, Queen's Rebels: Ulster Loyalism in Historical Perspective, 1978; editor: Peep o'Day Boys and Defenders: Selected Documents on the Disturbances in County Armagh, 1784-1796, 1990; co-editor: Piety and Power in Ireland, 1760-1960, 2000; assoc. editor: Oxford Dictionary of National Biography, 2004, Encyclopedia of Irish History and Culture, 2004; prin. developer: (interactive atlas) Great American History Machine, 1994. Sr. research fellow Inst. Irish Studies Queen's U., Belfast, Northern Ireland, 1975-76. Democrat. Presbyterian. Avocations: walking, singing. Office: Carnegie Mellon Univ Dept of History Schenley Park Pittsburgh PA 15213 Home Phone: 412-362-3953; Office Phone: 412-268-2953. Business E-Mail: dwmiller@cmu.edu.

MILLER, DAWN L., composition literature educator; d. John Merritt and Cora Armenda (LaRue) Hyndman; m. Louis J. Miller, June 11, 1966; 1 child, Daniel Louis. BS, St. Mary-of-the-Woods, 1963; MS in Edn., St. Francis U., 1971; MA, Ind. U., Ft. Wayne, 1994; cert. in organ, Notre Dame U., 2000. Profl. life tchg. lic. Ind. Tchr. St. Vincent Sch., Ft. Wayne, 1964—67, St. Joseph Sch., Garrett, Ind., 1974—90; tchr. Hebrew scriptures Bishop Luers H.S., Ft. Wayne, 1990—91; adj. faculty Ivy Tech. State Coll., Ft. Wayne, 1991—96; adj. faculty composition lit. Ind. U.-Purdue U., Ft. Wayne, 1992—. Nominee Ind. Tchr. of Yr., Diocese of Ft. Wayne-South Bend, 1990. Democrat. Roman Catholic. Avocations: piano, organ. Office: Ind Univ Purdue Univ English Dept 2101 Coliseum Blvd Fort Wayne IN 46805 Business E-Mail: millerd@ipfw.edu.

MILLER, DAWN MARIE, retired meteorologist; b. Hartford, Conn., Sept. 17, 1963; d. Eugene E. Miller and Audrey E. (Flagg) Laurel; m. Dennis James Miller, Sept. 9, 1989; children: Zackarey, Amanda. BS in Meteorology, SUNY, Oneonta, 1985. Customer support specialist WSI Corp., Bedford, Mass., 1985-87, from media TV mktg. to product mktg. specialist-data svcs. Billerica, Mass., 1987-97, sr. meteorologist, product mktg. specialist, 1997-99, sr. meteorologist, assoc. product mgr., 1999—2001, sr. meteorologist, media mktg. and promotion, 2001—03, ret., 2004; salon coord. Shear Class, LLC, Hudson, NH, 2005—. Mem.: Nat. Weather Assn., Am. Meteorol. Soc., Am. Hort. Soc., Nature Conservancy, Nat. Audubon Soc., Nat. Arbor Day Found., Oneonta Alumni Assn. Republican. Episcopalian. Avocations: meteorology, astronomy, photography, gardening, bird watching. Home: 37 Wren Dr Litchfield NH 03052-2540 Personal E-mail: dawn.miller@gmail.com.

MILLER, DEBORAH BREWSTER, educational consultant; b. Chgo., Mar. 26, 1933; d. Charles Tredick Brewster and Frances Merrill Holt; m. Marvin Robert Cowell, Aug. 10, 2002; children: Martha Miller Duvall, Andrew Holt; m. Michael Rudolph Miller, May 24, 1958 (div. Nov. 8, 1988). BA, Colo. Coll., Colo. Springs, 1955; M, Union Theol. Sem., NY, 1958. Cert. christian educator Assn. Presbyn. Ch. Educators, 1981. Ednl. cons. Monmouth Presbytery, Tennent, NJ, 1978—89; assoc. exec. Newton Presbytery, Randolph, NJ, 1989—2000. Mem. ruling body Raleigh Ct. Presbyn. Ch., chmn. worship com., libr. Mem.: Assn. Presbyn. Ch. Educators (life; staff adv. 1993—98, Lifetime Achievement award 2005). Home: 3523 Dogwood Ln SW Roanoke VA 24015 Home Phone: 540-343-8757.

MILLER, DECATUR HOWARD, lawyer; b. Balt., June 29, 1932; s. Lawrence Vernon and Katherine Louise (Baum) M.; m. Sally Burnam Smith, Nov. 23, 1963; 1 dau., Clemence Mary Katherine. BA, Yale U., 1954; LL.B., Harvard U., 1959. Bar: Md. 1959. Assoc. Piper & Marbury, Balt., 1959-62, 1963-66, ptnr., 1967-94, ptnr. emeritus, 1995—, mng. ptnr., 1974-87, chmn., 1987-94; Md. Securities commr., 1962-63. Bd. dirs. Mercantile Funds. Trustee Enoch Pratt Free Libr., 1975—2005, v.p., 1977—85, pres., 1985—89; trustee Calvert Sch., Balt., 1976—89, pres.,

1982—87; trustee Walters Art Gallery, Balt., 1987—91; bd. sponsors Sellinger Sch. Bus. and Mgmt. Loyola Coll., 1990—98; active Mayor's Bus. Adv. Coun., 1993—99; bd. vis. U. Md. Balt. County, 1994—2000; bus. sch. adv. coun. Morgan State U., 1994—96; chmn. Equal Justice Coun., 1999—2003; bd. dirs. Balt. Symphony Orch., 1970—, v.p., 1978—86, 1988—90, pres., 1990—92, life dir., 2002—; bd. dirs. United Way Ctrl. Md., 1988—91, The Leadership, 1990—93, Empower Balt. Mgmt. Corp., 1995—, Coll. Bound Found., 1990—2001, chmn., 1994—96; bd.dirs. Greater Balt. Com., 1988—96, chmn., 1992—94; bd. dirs. U. Md. Found., 2000—03. With US Army, 1954—56. Mem. Md. Bar Assn., Am. Law Inst., Am. Bar Found., Md. Bar Found., Century Assn., Elkridge Club, Ctr. Club, Elizabethan Club, Lawyers Round Table. Home: 3704 N Charles St Apt 1305 Baltimore MD 21218 Personal E-mail: dhm26@mindspring.com.

MILLER, DEMETRA FAY PELAT, elementary school educator, city official; b. Painesville, Ohio, June 15, 1933; d. William Anthony and Helen (Mimo) Pelat. Grad., Monticello Jr. Coll., Alton, Ill., 1953; BS in Edn., Kent State U., 1955, postgrad., 1957-63, John Carroll U., 1957-63. Tchr. Grant Elem. Sch., Cuyahoga Falls, Ohio, 1955-57, Benjamin Franklin Elem. Sch., Euclid, Ohio, 1957-58, Meml. Park Elem. Sch., Euclid, 1958-87, Lincoln Elem. Sch., Euclid, 1987—. Mem. Euclid City Coun., 1983—; sec. Citizens' Pet Responsibility Com., 1978—; trustee Shore Civic Cultural Ctr., 1988—; treas. Euclid Women's Caucus, 1978-79, v.p., 1981-83, pres., 1983; bd. dirs. YwCA-YMCA, Euclid, 1985—; mem. women's jr. bd., vol. Euclid Gen. Hosp., 1967—; mem. Euclid Devel. Corp., Euclid Recreation Commn., 1985—; former mem. citizens adv. bd. Regional Transit Authority; past mem. Euclid Charter Rev. Commn.; chmn. Euclid City Growth, Devel. and Zoning Commn., 1989—. Named Woman of Yr., Euclid Women's Caucus, 1985, Euclid Citizen of Yr., Am. Legion Post 343, 1986, cert. of appreciation YWCA-YMCA, 1989, One of Most Interesting People award Cleve. Mag., 1990. Mem. NEA (nat. del. 1978-89), Ohio Edn. Assn. (del. 1977—), Euclid Tchrs. Assn. (pres. 1978-79, 83-84, Outstanding Educator award 1979), Ednl. Coun. Cuyahoga County (pres. 1981-82), Coalition Major Ednl. Orgns., Delta Kappa Gamma. Greek Orthodox. Home: 25601 Zeman Ave Cleveland OH 44132-1816 Office: Euclid Bd Edn 651 E 222nd St Euclid OH 44123-2000

MILLER, DENNIS, comedian; b. Pitts., Nov. 3, 1953; m. Ali Espley, April 10, 1988; 2 children, Holden, Marlon. BA, Point Park Coll. Stand-up comic, cast mem. Saturday Night Live, 1985-91; prodr., writer, host Dennis Miller Show, 1992; exec. prodr., writer, host Dennis Miller Live, 1994—2002; announcer Monday Night Football, 2000—02; exec. prodr., host Dennis Miller, 2004—05; contbr., Hannity & Colmes Fox News, 2006—. HBO spls. include: Mr. Miller Goes to Washington (also exec. prodr.), 1988, host 13th Annual Young Comedians Show (also prodr., writer), 1989, Black & White, 1990, They Shoot HBO Specials, Don't They? (also exec. prodr.), 1993, Dennis Miller: Citizen Arcane (also exec. prodr.), 1996, Dennis Miller: The Millenium Special-1,000 Years, 100 Laughs, 10 Really Good Ones (also exec. prodr., writer), 1999, Raw Feed (also writer), 2003; host Freedomfest: Nelson Mandela's 70th Birthday Celebration, The America's Choice Awards, 1990, 43d Annual Primetime Emmy Awards Presentation, 1991; albums include The Off-White Album, 1989; actor (films) Disclosure, 1994, The Net, 1995, Tales From the Crypt Presents: Bordello of Blood, 1996, Murder at 1600 Pennsylvania Avenue, 1997, Joe Dirt, 2001; TV appearances include Sam Kinison: NewsRadio, 1995, Why Did We Laugh?, 1998, Saturday Night Live: The Best of Phil Hartman, 1998, The Best of Chris Farley, 1998, Bad Boys of Saturday Night Live, 1998; (video) The Best of Mike Myers, 1998, 25th Anniversary, 1999, SportsCenter, 2000, Primetime Glick, 2001, Boston Public, 2003, The View, 2004; author: The Rants, 1996, Ranting Again, 1998, I Rant Therefore I Am, 2000, The Rant Zone: An All-Out Blitz Against Bush League Politics, Twisted Child Stars, Soul-Sucking Jobs and People Who Eat Their Jobs, 2001. Recipient Best Writing Emmy award for a Variety/Music Program for Dennis Miller Live, 1994, 1995, 1996, 1998. Office: Fox New Network LLC 1211 Ave Americas New York NY 10036

MILLER, DENNIS EDWARD, health medical executive; b. Detroit, Dec. 21, 1951; m. Deborah Ann Keith, Feb. 12, 1977. BS, Austin Peay State U., 1973; MBA, U. South Fla., 1981. CPA. Chief exec. officer Hosp. Corp. of Am., Bennettsville, SC, 1976-84; div. v.p. Westworld Community Healthcare, Waco, Tex., 1984-86; group v.p. Nat. Healthcare, Inc., Dothan, Ala., 1986-87; COO Healthcare Connections, Brentwood, Tenn., 1988; cons. VHA Physician Svcs., Inc., Dallas, 1988-90; asst. adminstr., CFO Clarksville (Tenn.) Meml. Hosp., 1990; Franklin, Tenn., 1990; sr. v.p., COO Eastside Ventures, Inc., Birmingham, Ala., 1990-93; sr. v.p. Ea. Health System, Inc., Birmingham, 1993—2002; CEO Williamson Med. Ctr., Franklin, 2002—. Chmn. Minority Leadership Task Force, Ea. Health System, Inc., 1994-95. Sec. Ala. Health Svcs. Bd.; mem. Literacy Coun. Ala., Ala. Hosp. Assn. State Legis. Com., future directions com.; chmn. Birmingham Regional Healthcare Exec. Forum; chmn. friends of scouting campaign Boy Scouts Am., 1996; mem. Franklin Land Use Steering Com. subcom., Leadership Franklin, 2002, Franklin Tomorrow, Williamson 25, 2004, 05, Franklin Bus. Leadership Coun., 2006, Hosp. Alliance Tenn., 2006, Tenn. Hosp. Ass., 2006; chmn. Healthcare Exec. Forum Mid. Tenn., 2006; mem. coun. Boy Scouts Mid. Tenn., 2006; mem. archives and mus. com. Williamson County, 2006. Fellow Am. Coll. Healthcare Execs. (chmn diplomate credentials com., pres. mid. Tenn. chpt. 2006, Ala. Regent's award for exec. excellence 1995), Hosp. Fin. Mgmt. Assn. (Follmer Bronze Merit award for outstanding svc.); mem. AICPA, Tenn. Soc. CPAs, Ala. Soc. CPAs (chmn. state legis. com.), Ala. Hosp. Assn. (future directions com.), Birmingham C. of C. (chmn. memberhsip com.), Birmingham East Rotary Club (pres., chmn. membership com.), Leadership Franklin Class 2003, Franklin Noon Rotary Club, Mensa, Shriners, Masons, Birmingham Touchdown Club, Sigma Chi. Avocations: hunting, fishing, gardening, antiques. Office: Williamson Med Ctr 2021 Carothers Rd Franklin TN 37067 Home Phone: 615-599-0325; Office Phone: 615-435-5151.

MILLER, DENYCE KARLINA, tax specialist; b. Chgo., July 2, 1963; d. Sidney Miller, Vera Miller. BS in Commerce, DePaul U., 2001, M in Acctg., 2002; MBA, DePaul U., Chgo., 2007. CPA Ill. Tax cons. Denyce Miller Tax Svc., Bellwood, Ill., 2001—; postal employee devel. tng. technician USPS, Chgo., 1985—2005, auditor office inspector gen., 2005—. Mem. fin. com. Am. Postal Workers Union, Chgo., 2001—03. Author: Blind Love, 1996. Coord. hearing impaired Am. Postal Workers Union, Chgo., 1992—94, dir. clk. craft, 2001—03, coord. hearing impaired, 2001—03; combined fed. campaign key worker USPS, Chgo., 1989. Recipient Taekwondo First Dan award, Kukkiwon World Taekwondo Hdqs., 1996. Mem.: AICPA (Scholarship award 2001), Inst. Mgmt. Accts. (Scholarship award 2001), Ill. Cert. Pub. Accts. Soc. Democrat. Mem. Apostolic Ch. Avocation: Tae Kwon Do. Home: 1012 Marshall Bellwood IL 60104-2322 Home Phone: 708-544-6695; Office Phone: 708-268-1554. Home Fax: 708-544-8419. Personal E-mail: karlina2@yahoo.com, dmtaxes@hotmail.com.

MILLER, DIANE WILMARTH, retired human resources director; b. Clarinda, Iowa, Mar. 12, 1940; d. Donald and Floy Pauline (Madden) W.; m. Robert Nolen Miller, Aug. 21, 1965; children: Robert Wilmarth, Anne Elizabeth. AA, Colo. Women's Coll., 1960; BBA, U. Iowa, Iowa City, 1962; MA, U. No. Colo., Greeley, 1994. Cert. tchr., Colo.; vocat. credential, Colo.; cert. sr. profl. in human resources; lic. Colo. Ins. Prodr. Sec.-counselor U. SC Rep., Myrtle Beach AFB, 1968-69; instr. Coastal Carolina Campus U. SC, Conway, 1967-69; tchr. bus. Poudre Sch. Dist. R-1, Ft. Collins, Colo., 1970-71; travel cons. United Bank Travel Svc., Greeley, Colo., 1972-74; dir. human resources Aims C.C., Greeley, 1984—2001, ret., 2001. Instr. Aims CC, 1972—89; bd. dirs. U. No. Colo. Found., Greeley, 2003—, chair, 2007—. Bd. trustees 1st Congl. Ch., Greeley, 2005—. Mem.: Philanthropic Ednl. Orgn. (pres. 1988—89), Women's Investment Network (pres. 2007—), Women's Panhellenic Assn. (pres. 1983—84), Questers (pres. 2002—04), WTK Club (pres. 2006—07), Scroll and Fan Club (pres. 1985—86). Home: 3542 Wagon Trail Rd Greeley CO 80634-3405

MILLER, DON ROBERT, surgeon, educator; b. Highland, Kans., July 6, 1925; s. Pleasant V. and Lucy Anna (Hammond) M.; m. Geraldine Ellen Nelson, Sept. 6, 1947; children: Don R., Laurie, Todd, Marcia, Kristen, Felicia. AB, Westminster Coll., 1944; MD, U. Kans., 1948. Mem. faculty U. Kans., Kansas City, 1957-73, prof. surgery, 1970-73, U. Calif. Irvine, 1973-92, prof. emeritus, 1992—, vice chmn., chief dept. surgery, pres. med. staff, 1989-91. Dir. surgery Orange County (Calif.) Med. Center, 1973-77. Contbr. articles to profl. jours. Gov. 1988-92. Served with USNR, 1943-45, 50-52. Spl. research fellow Zurich, Switzerland, 1965-66 Fellow A.C.S., Am. Coll. Cardiology; mem. Am. Soc. Univ. Surgeons, Am. Surg. Assn., Soc. Vascular Surgery, Am. Assn. Thoracic Surgery, Am., Central, Western surg. assns., Internat. Cardiovascular Soc., Sigma Xi, Alpha Omega Alpha. Achievements include research on extracorporeal circulation, myocardial function. Home: 743 Louisiana St Lawrence KS 66044-2339

MILLER, DON WILSON, nuclear engineering educator; b. Westerville, Ohio, Mar. 16, 1942; s. Don Paul and Rachel (Jones) M.; m. Mary Catherine Thompson, June 25, 1966; children: Amy Beth, Stacy Catherine, Paul Wilson Thompson. BS in Physics, Miami U., Oxford, Ohio, 1964, MS in Physics, 1966; MS in Nuc. Engring., Ohio State U., 1970, PhD in Nuc. Engring., 1971. Rsch. assoc. Ohio State U., Columbus, 1966-68, univ. fellow, 1968-69, tchg. assoc., 1969-71, asst. prof. nuc. engring., 1971—74, assoc. prof., 1974-80, chmn. nuc. engring. program, 1977-97, prof., 1980—2004, dir. nuc. reactor lab., 1977—2002, prof. emeritus, 2004—, dir. Advanced Sys. and Safety, 2005—. Sec., treas. Cellar Lumber Co., Westerville, Ohio, 1972-84, 85—; cons. Monsanto Rsch. Corp., Miamisburg, Ohio, 1979, NRC, Washington, 1982-84, 99—, Scantech. Corp., Santa Fe, 1984-95, Neoprobe Corp., Columbus, 1990, Electric Power Rsch. Inst., Palo Alto, Calif., 1992-94; mem. adv. com. on reactor safeguards Nuc. Regulatory Commn., 1995-99. Patentee in field; contbr. articles to profl. jours. Mem. Westerville Bd. Edn., 1976-91, pres., 1977-78, 86-88; mem. Ohio Sch. Bd.'s Assn., Columbus, 1976-91; mem. fed. rels. com. Nat. Sch. Bd.'s Assn., Washington, 1984-86. With USAR, 1960-68. Named Tech. Person of Yr. Columbus Tech. Coun., 1979; named to All Region Bd. Ohio Sch. Bd's. Assn., 1981, 86, Westerville South H.S. Hall of Fame, 1996; recipient Achievement award Mid Ohio Chpt. Multiple Sclerosis Soc., 1988. Fellow Am. Nuc. Soc. (chmn. edn. divsn. 1986-87, bd. dirs. 1989-91, chair human factors divsn. 1993-94, v.p./pres. elect 1995-96, pres. 1996-97, Cert. Appreciation 1991); mem. IEEE (sr. mem.), Am. Soc. Engring. Edn. (chmn. nuc. engring. divsn. 1978-79, Glenn Murphy award 1989), Nuc. Dept. Heads Orgn. (chmn. 1985-86), Westerville Edn. Assn. (Friend of Edn. award 1992), Rotary (Courtright Cmty. Svc. award 1989), Kiwanis, Hoover Sailing Club, Alpha Nu Sigma (chmn. 1991-93). Avocations: American history, travel, amateur radio. Home: Friendship Village 5675 Ponderosa Dr Columbus OH 43231 Office: Ohio State U Dept Mech Engring Nuc Engring Program E430 Scott Lab 201 W 19th Ave Columbus OH 43210-1142 Home Phone: 614-891-1858; Office Phone: 614-292-7979. Business E-Mail: miller.68@osu.edu.

MILLER, DONALD EUGENE, lawyer; b. Providence, Mar. 20, 1947; s. Meyer Samuel and Beatrice (Wattman) M.; m. Deborah Neary Miller, Mar. 14, 1987. BA, Boston U., 1968; JD, U. Pa., 1972. Law clk. Assoc. Justice Alfred H. Joslin Supreme Ct., Providence, 1972-73; prin., lawyer Temkin, Merolla & Zurier, Providence, 1973-81, Temkin & Miller, Ltd., Providence, 1981-91; exec. v.p., gen. counsel, corp. sec. The Fairchild Corp., McLean, Va., 1991—. Author: (treatise) Buying and Selling a Small Business, 1987. Mem. RI Bar, Mass. Bar, DC Bar. Avocation: Shetland sheepdog breeding and exhibiting. Home: 10704 Riverwood Dr Potomac MD 20854-1332 Office: The Fairchild Corp 1750 Tysons Blvd Mc Lean VA 22102

MILLER, DONALD EUGENE, retired air traffic controller; b. Twin Falls, Idaho, Aug. 17, 1931; s. James Alonzo and Goldia Belle Miller; m. Betsy Jean Doty; children: Michelle Anne, Mileah Lynne. Studied, Aeronautical Acad., Okla. City, 1954—56. Lic. pilot FAA, 1977. Air traffic controller FAA, Des Moines, 1956—68, St. Louis, 1968—70; instr., air traffic control FAA Acad., Oklahoma City, 1970—74; automation specialist, air traffic control FAA Tower, Portland, Oreg., 1974—75, mgr., air traffic control Hillsboro, Oreg., 1975—77; liasion officer, air traffic control Marine Corps. Air Station, Yuma, Ariz., 1977—80; air traffic quality assurance FAA Regional Hdqs., LA, 1980—81, air traffic internat. br., 1985—90; air traffic mgr. FAA Radar Facility, Bakersfield, Calif., 1981—85; ret., 1990. Cons. Hughes Aircraft, Fullerton, Calif., 1991—. Author: (manual) Automated Radar Terminal System, 1971. County treas. Union County, Creston, Iowa, 1953—55. Staff sgt. USAF, 1949—52, Korea. Mem.: Air Traffic Control Assn. (bd. mem. 1980—82). Avocations: writing, golf, dance, travel. Home: 4963 Poseidon Way Oceanside CA 92056

MILLER, DONALD KENNETH, engineering consultant; b. St. Louis, Oct. 18, 1925; s. Henry Edward and Ernestine Elizabeth (Schmeer) M.; m. Arline Louise Heckman, Feb. 27, 1953; children: Garry Edwin, Kristine Louise Miller Morris. BSChemE, Mo. U., 1950. Registered profl. engr., Pa. Application engr. York (Pa.) Corp., St. Louis, Houston, York, 1951-62; mgr. quality control York divsn. Borg Warner Corp., 1962-65, chief engr., 1965-85; refrigeration specialist York Internat. Corp., 1985-88; pres. MDK Engring. Corp., York, 1988—. Author: (with others) Plant Engineering Handbook, 1959, ASHRAE Handbook, 1981-94, Applied Thermal Design, 1989; contbr. articles to ASHRAE Jour. and IIR/IIF Internat. Congress Procs.; inventor desuperheater control in a refrigeration apparatus. With USNR, 1944—46. Mem. NSPE, AIChE, ASHRAE (life mem., cen. Pa. chpt., sec. 1972-73, treas. 1973-74, v.p. 1974-75, pres. 1975-76, Disting. Svc. award 1992), Svc. Corps Ret. Execs. (past bd. mem., sec.), Rotary. Avocations: sketching, computers. Office Phone: 717-741-1199.

MILLER, DONALD LESESSNE, publishing executive; b. NYC, Jan. 10, 1932; s. John H. and Mamie (Johnson) M.; m. Ann Davie, Aug. 12, 1951 (div. 1981); children: Lynn, Mark; m. Gail Aileen Wallace, June 27, 1981. BA, U. Md., 1967; cert., Harvard Grad. Sch. Bus. Adminstrn., 1969. Enlisted U.S. Army, 1948, advanced through grades to maj., 1966, ret., 1968; spl. asst. to pres., mgr. corp. recruitment Inmont Corp., NYC, 1968-70; v.p. indsl. relations Seatrain Shipbldg. Corp., NYC, 1970-71; dep. asst. sec. def. U.S. Dept. Def., Washington, 1971-73; v.p. personnel mgmt. Columbia U., NYC, 1973-78; dir. personnel devel. and adminstrn. Internat. Paper, NYC, 1978-79; v.p. employee relations Consol. Edison N.Y., NYC, 1979-86, Dow Jones & Co., Inc., NYC, 1986-95; CEO, pub. Our World News. Author: An Album of Black Americans in the Armed Forces, 1969. Chmn. bd. emeritus Associated Black Charities, N.Y.C., 1982-94. Decorated Legion of Merit; decorated Army Commendation Medal; recipient Disting. Civilian Service medal Dept. Def., 1973, Disting. Alumnus award U. Md., 1977. Mem. Alpha Sigma Lambda, Pi Sigma Alpha, Phi Kappa Phi, Alpha Phi Alpha, Sigma Pi Phi.

MILLER, DONALD MUXLOW, accountant; b. Luverne, Minn., Feb. 21, 1924; s. Henry Clay and Mildred Eva (Muxlow) M.; m. Eunice Jean Gibson, Feb. 19, 1944 (dec. Feb. 17, 2004); children: SueRilla M., Donna Jean Eichten, Patsy Ann Pushee. Student, Metro State, St. Paul, 1973-84. CPA. Mgr. Hines & Paulus, CPA, Worthington, Minn., 1952-65; commandant Minn. Vets. Home, Mpls., 1965-68; prin. D.M. Miller, Acct., 1968-70, 76-78; asst. sec. Minn. State Senate, St. Paul, 1970-72; comptr. Western Oil Co., Mpls., 1972-76; commr. Dept. VA, State of Minn., St. Paul, 1978-81; pres. D.M. Miller & Assoc., Ltd., Mpls., 1981-97; chief exec. officer MARD, Inc., Mpls., 1985-95; v.p. Miller, Micketts & Assocs. Ltd., Mpls., 1993-96; pres. D.M. Miller Ltd., Worthington, 1997—2004. Trustee Heart Professorship Found., 1987-91; pres. Legionville Sch. Patrol Camp, Brainerd, Minn., 1963-64; pres. bd. govs. Big Island Vets. Camp, Mpls., 1986-88. 2d lt. USAAC, 1942—46, 1st lt. USAF, 1951—52. Recipient Volunteer of the Year award Kidney Found., 1975. Mem. VFW, Minn. Assn. Pub. Accts. (dist. dir. 2002—04), Nat. Assn. State Vets. Homes (hon. life mem., reg. v.p. 1967-68), Nat. Assn. State Dirs. Vets Affairs (reg. v.p. 1978-79), Minn. Gaming Assn. (exec. sec. 1987-92), Am. Legion (hon life mem., comdr. Minn. 1962-63, nat. com. chmn. 1980-84, pres. Minn. Found. Bd. 1990-91). Presbyterian.

MILLER, DONALD ROSS, management consultant; b. Huntington, NY, Aug. 5, 1927; s. George Everett and Ethel May (Ross) M.; m. Constance Higgins, 1948 (div. 1955); children: Donald Ross Jr., Cynthia Lynn, Candace Lee; m. Janet Heyman Behr, Apr. 15, 1965; children: Jeffrey Lawrence, Wendy Lorraine. BS/BEA, MIT, 1950. Cert. mgmt. cons. Inst. of Mgmt. Cons. Staff engr. Stop & Shop, Inc., Boston, 1950-56; v.p., dir. Cresap, McCormick and Paget, Inc., NYC, 1956-76; mng. dir. Donald R. Miller Mgmt. Cons., Palm Desert, Calif., 1977—2005. Pres., CEO Carl Fischer Inc., N.Y.C., 1996; chmn. bd. dirs. Nash Finch Co., Mpls., 1995-2000; bd. dirs. Michael Anthony Jewelers, Inc., Mt. Vernon, N.Y., Western Horizon Resorts, Inc., Gunnison, Colo. Author: Management Practices Manual, 3 vols., 1963, (booklet) Management of Managerial Resources, 1969. Bd. dirs. Queens Mus. Art, Flushing, N.Y., 1982-93, pres., 1988-92; pres. Lexington House, Forest Hills, 1984-2001; mem. MIT Alumni Adv. Coun., Cambridge, Mass., 1955-75; bd. govs. Alumni Ctr. N.Y.C., 1965-75, chmn., 1968-72; bd. dirs. Vol. Cons. Group, N.Y., 1969-79; trustee Queens Theatre in the Park, Flushing Meadow, N.Y., 1976-82; mem. vestry St. Margaret's Episcopal Ch., Palm Desert, Calif., 2003-05, sr. warden, 2004-05; trustee St. Margarets Episc. Sch., 2004-05. With U.S. Maritime Svc., 1945-46, ETO, U.S. Army, 1946-48. Mem. Nat. Assn. Corp. Dirs., Inst. Mgmt. Cons., Sky Club. Episcopal. Avocations: tennis, reading. Home and Office: 73850 Fairway Dr #10 Palm Desert CA 92260 Office Phone: 760-341-3503. E-mail: donmilleo@aol.com.

MILLER, DOROTHY ANNE SMITH, retired cytogenetics educator; b. NYC, Oct. 20, 1931; d. John Philip and Anna Elizabeth (Hellberg) Smith; m. Orlando Jack Miller, July 10, 1954; children: Richard L., Cynthia K., Karen A. BA in Chemistry magna cum laude, Wilson Coll., Chambersburg, Pa., 1952; PhD in Biochemistry, Yale U., 1957. Rsch. assoc. dept. ob-gyn Columbia U., NYC, 1964-72, from rsch. assoc. to asst. prof. dept. human genetics-devel., 1973-85; prof. dept. molecular biology and genetics Wayne State U., Detroit, 1985-94, prof. dept. pathology, 1985-96, prof. Ctr. for Molecular Medicine and Genetics, 1994-96. Vis. scientist clin. and population cytogenetics unit Med. Rsch. Coun., Edinburgh, Scotland, 1983-84; vis. prof. dept. genetics and molecular biology U. la Sapienza, Rome, 1988; vis. disting. fellow La Trobe U., Melbourne, Australia, 1992. Contbr. numerous articles to sci. jours. Grantee March of Dimes Birth Defects Found., 1974-93, NSF, 1983-84. Mem. Am. Soc. Human Genetics, Genetics Soc. Am., Genetics Soc. Australia, Phi Beta Kappa. Presbyterian. Home: 19365 Cypress Ridge Terr #817 Lansdowne VA 20176 Personal E-mail: damiller@smartneighborhood.net.

MILLER, DOROTHY ELOISE, education educator; b. Ft. Pierce, Fla., Apr. 13, 1944; d. Robert Foy and Aline (Mahon) Wilkes. BS in Edn., Bloomsburg U., 1966, MEd, 1969; MLA, Johns Hopkins U., 1978; EdD, Columbia U., 1991. Tchr. Cen. Dauphin East H.S., Harrisburg, Pa., 1966-68, Aberdeen (Md.) H.S., 1968-69; asst. dean of coll., prof. Harford C.C., Bel Air, Md., 1969—. Owner Ideas by Design, 1995—; mem. accreditation team Mid. States Commn., 1995—; statewide writing skills assessment com., statewide English stds. com. Md. Higher Edn. Commn. 1997-2001, English composition com., 1997—, English alignment com., 2002—; adj. prof. U. Balt., 2001. Editor: Renewing the American Community Colleges, 1984; contbr. articles to profl. jours. Pres. Harlan Sq. Condominium Assn., Bel Air, 1982, 90-96, Md. internat. divsn. St. Petersburg Sister State Com., 1993-2001; edn. liaison AAUW, Harford County, Md., 1982-92; cen. com. mem. Rep. Party, Harford County, 1974-78; crusade co-chair Am. Cancer Soc., Harford County, 1976-78; mem. faculty adv. com. Md. Higher Edn. Commn., 1993-96; people's adv. coun. Harford County Coun., 1994-2003. Recipient Nat. Tchg. Excellence award Nat. Inst. for Staff and Orgn. Devel., U. Tex.-Austin, 1992. Mem. Nat. Mus. Women in the Arts (charter). Republican. Methodist. Avocations: skiing, swimming, golf, reading, image consulting. Office: Harford Community Coll 401 Thomas Run Rd Bel Air MD 21015-1627 Business E-Mail: demiller@harford.edu.

MILLER, DOUGLAS LINN, lawyer; b. Reading, Pa., Nov. 17, 1950; BA, MA, Yale U., 1972; JD, Harvard U., 1975. Bar: Ga. 1975. Lawyer Troutman Sanders, Atlanta, 1975—99, mng. ptnr. having oversight of the Project Develop. and Fin. Practice Group Hong Kong, China, 1997—99; sr. v.p., gen. counsel, chief compliance officer Mirant Corp., Atlanta, 1999—2005. Miller acted as lead counsel in state regulatory rate case proceedings, as well as fuel cost recovery and demandside cost recovery riders, prudence reviews of nuclear power plant construction, nuclear power plant ops., fossil plant construction, and coal procurement practices. Mem. ABA, State Bar Ga. Office: Mirant Corp 1155 Perimeter Ctr W Atlanta GA 30338 Office Phone: 678-579-7924. Business E-Mail: douglas.miller@mirant.com.

MILLER, DUANE KING, health and beauty care company executive; b. NYC, Mar. 1, 1931; s. Henry Charles and Helen Marion (King) M.; m. Nancy L. Longley, June 6, 1954; children: Cheryl L., Duane L. AB in Econs. and Fin., NYU, 1951. V.p. mktg. Warner-Chilcott divsn. Warner Lambert Co., Morris Plains, NJ, 1970-72, pres. divsn., 1973-77; exec. v.p. Am. Optical div., pres. Am. Optical Internat div. Warner Lambert Co., Southbridge, Mass., 1978; pres. biol. and proprietary products divsn., v.p. Revlon Health Care Group, Revlon Corp., Tuckahoe, NY, 1978-80, pres. ethical, proprietary and vision care divsns., 1981-82, corp. v.p. parent co., 1982, pres. Revlon Health Care Group, 1983-92, corp. exec. v.p. parent co., 1984-92, pres. Revlon Health Beauty Care and Internat. Group, 1988-92, ret., 1992; pres. DKL Properties, health care cons., Promedex Techs., 1992—. Author: (with others) Marketing Planning for Chief Execs. and Planners, 1966. Mem. Rep. Nat. Com. Mem. Princeton Club NY, Masons, Shriners. Home: 9 Winding Way Greenville DE 19807

MILLER, DWIGHT MERRICK, archivist, historian; b. Keosauqua, Iowa, July 25, 1932; s. Leo Albert and Beryl Irene Miller; m. Frances Florine Olney, Nov. 19, 1961 (dec. Sept. 1977); 1 child, Dianne; m. Judith Spencer, 1979 (div. 1988); m. Pauline K. Leaverton, 1999. BA, U. Iowa, Iowa City, 1959; MA, Truman State U., Kirksville, 1961; attended, The American U., Washington, 1963-64. Asst. archivist Manuscript Divsn., Library of Congress, Washington, 1961-64; sr. archivist Herbert Hoover Presdl. Libr., West Branch, 1964-99. Compiler, asst. editor: The Public Papers of the Presidents: Herbert Hoover; 1929-1933 (6 vols.), 1974-77; co-editor: Herbert Hoover and Harry S. Truman: A Documentary History, 1992, Historical Materials in the Herbert Hoover Presidential Library, 1996, Herbert Hoover and Franklin D. Roosevelt: A Documentary History, 1998; editor: Laura Ingalls Wilder and the American Frontier: Five Perspectives, 2002. Co-chmn. Iowa Sesquicentennial Commn. Cedar Cty., Tipton, 1995-97. Mem. Herbert Hoover Presdl. Libr. Assn., Friends of the

Univ. of Iowa Libraries (adv. bd. 1976-81), Ft. Ticonderoga Assn. (adv. bd. 1991—). Presbyterian. Avocations: book collecting, historical Iowa pottery. Home: 10 Rita Lyn Ct Iowa City IA 52245-3504

MILLER, DWIGHT RICHARD, professional hair care industry executive, cosmetologist, consultant; b. Johnstown, Pa., Jan. 24, 1943; Grad., Comer & Doran Sch., San Diego; DSc (hon.), London Inst. for Applied Rsch., 1973. Cert. aromatherapist; lic. cosmetologist., instr.; Brit. Mastercraftsman. Styles dir. Marinello-Comer, Hollywood, Calif., 1965-67; expert Pivot Point Internat., Chgo., 1967-68; styles dir. Lapins, LA, 1969; dir. Redken, LA, 1970, Vidal Sassoon, London, 1971-74; world amb. Pivot Point, New Zealand and Australia, 1974-75, internat. artistic dir. Chgo., 1975-78; internat. dir., co-founder Hair Artists Inst. & Registry, 1978-81; internat. artistic dir. Zotos Internat., Darien, Conn., 1981-87, Matrix Essentials, Inc., Solon, Ohio, 1987-92; bd. dirs., founder, v.p. creative Anasazi Exclusive Salon Products, Inc., Dubuque, Iowa, 1992-96; pres. Anasazi Salon Sys., Santa Fe, 1996-98; cons., 1998—; pres. Sahag Products, 2004—06; owner Salon Sante Fe, 2004—06; internat. creative dir. Sudzz FX, 2006—; co-founder VLVT Acads., Savannah, Ga., Toronto, Seoul and Rome. Judge hairdressing competitions Norwegian Masters, Australian Nat. Championships, N.Am. Hairstyling Awards; pres. Intercrimpers, London, 1974-75; celebrity stylist Doris Day, Juliet Prowse, Cindy Crawford, Monica Seles; co-founder VLVT Acads., Savannah, Toronto, Seoul, Rome, 2007-; cons. in field. Author: Sculptic Cutting Pivot Point 75, Prismatics, 1983, Milady's Standard System of Salon Skills, 1998, Amos Master Cutting System, 2000; prodr.(and dir.): (documentaries, 15), (numerous tech. and industry videos); contbr. articles and photographs to popular mags.; mem. editl. bd.: Shades mag., Launchpad mag. With USMC, 1960—64. Named Artistic Dir. Yr. Am. Salon mag., Intercoiffure Educator of the Century; presented with Order of White Elephant, 1976; recipient London Gold Cup for Best Presentation London Beauty Festival, 1982, Dr. Everett G. McDonough award for Excellence in Permanent Waving, World Master award Art and Fashion Group, 1992, N.Am. Hairstylist of the Yr. award, 2000. Mem. Cercle des Arts et Techniques de la Coiffure, Intercoiffure, Haute Coiffure Franchaise, Soc. Cosmetic Chemists, Hair Artists Great Britain, Internat. Assn. Trichogists, Nat. Cosmetologists Assn. (HairAmerica, cert. instr.), Am. Soc. Phytotherapy and Aromatherapy, HairChicago (hon.), Art and Fashion Group (pres. 1993), 'Dressers MC (pres. 1990—), London's Alternative Hair Club (patron), Salon Assn., Am. Beauty Assn., Profl. Beauty Assn., Alternative Hair Club North Am. (hon. pres. 2003—). Achievements include development of several profl. product lines including Vidal Sassoon-London, Design Freedom, Bain de Terre, Ultra Bond, Vavoom!, Systeme Biolage, Anasazi, Sheer Blonde. Home and Office: 707 Don Gaspar Ave Santa Fe NM 87505-2629 Business E-Mail: dwight@dwightmiller.com.

MILLER, EDWARD DORING, anesthesiologist, hospital administrator, dean; b. Rochester, NY, Feb. 1, 1943; s. Edward D. and Natalie (Sidam) Miller; m. Leslie Coombs, June 15, 1968 (dec. Apr. 1987); children: Sara Davenport, Katherine Coombs; m. Lynne Root, Apr. 30, 1988; children: Lawrence Root, Elizabeth Root Fusco. AB, Ohio Wesleyan U., 1964; MD, U. Rochester, 1968. Diplomate Am. Bd. Anesthesiology, Am. Coll. Anesthesiology; cert. critical care medicine. Surg. intern Univ. Hosp., Boston, 1968-69; anesthesia resident Peter Bent Brigham Hosp., Boston, 1969-71; fellow in physiology Harvard Med. Sch., Boston, 1971-73; dir. anesthesia research Brooke Army Med. Ctr., Ft. Sam Houston, Tex., 1973-75; asst. prof. anesthesiology U. Va. Med. Ctr., Charlottesville, 1975-79, assoc. prof. anesthesiology, 1979-82, prof. anesthesiology, 1982-83, prof. anesthesiology, surgery, 1983-86; E.M. Papper prof. anesthesiology, chmn. dept. Columbia U. Coll. Physicians and Surgeons, NYC, 1986-94; Mark C. Rogers prof., chmn. dept. anesthesiology Johns Hopkins U., Balt., 1994—, interim dean med. faculty, v.p. medicine Sch. of Medicine, 1996-97, dean Sch. of Medicine, 1997—, CEO Sch. of Medicine, 1997—. Sr. scientist physiology, pharmacology Hosp. Necker, Paris, 1981-82; examiner Am. Bd. Anesthesiology; v.p. clin. faculty U. Va., 1983-85, pres. 1985-86. Editor Anesthesia and Analgesia, 1982-92; contbr. numerous articles to profl. jours. Pres. Barracks-Rugby-Preston Neighborhoods, Va., 1977-79; vestry Christ Episc. Ch., Va., 1985-86. Served to maj. M.C., U.S. Army, 1973-75. Recipient Rsch. Career Devel. award Nat. Inst. Gen. Med. Scis., 1978-83; NIH grantee, 1977-87, Inst. Nat. de la Sante et de la Recherche Medicale grantee, 1981-82. Mem. Assn. U. Anesthetists (sec. 1984-87), Am. Soc. Anesthesiologists, Am. Physiol. Soc., Internat. Anesthesia Research Soc. (trustee 1988—), Soc. Critical Care Medicine, Soc. Cardiovascular Anesthesiologists, Assn. Univ. Anesthesiologists (pres. 1990-92), Found. for Anesthesia Edn. and Rsch. (bd. dirs. 1986—), Up Med. Bd. Presbyn. Hosp. Office: Johns Hopkins U Sch Med Adminstrn 733 N Broadway Ste 100 Baltimore MD 21205-2196 Office Phone: 410-955-3180. Business E-Mail: emiller@jhmi.edu.

MILLER, ELIZABETH JOAN, artist, guidance counselor; b. Vienna, Austria, Nov. 2, 1925; arrived in U.S., 1941; d. Joseph Ronald Ehrlich and Martha Eleanor Lamm-Ehrlich; m. Alfred Abraham Miller; children: Mark M., Steven H. B in Chem. Engring., City Coll., NYC, 1947, MA in Math. Edn., 1965; MEd in Human Devel., Tchrs. Coll., Columbia U., NYC, 1977. Asst. to chief physicist Air Reduction Co., NYC, 1947—53; tchr. HS math. NYC Bd. Edn., 1960—77, guidance counselor, 1977—90; represented by High Studio Art Gallery, Moorpark, Calif., 2007, Twin Lakes Gallery, Mammoth, Calif., Gallery at the Landing, Westlake Village, Calif. One-woman shows include Camarillo Ctr. for Spiritual Living, Calif., 2006, 2007, Harbor Village Gallery, Ventura, Calif., 2006, 2007, Thousand Oaks Botanic Gardens, 2006, 2007, Leisure Village, 2007, Buena Ventura Art Gallery, Ventura, Calif., 2007, Westlake Libr., 2007—, Represented in permanent collections City of Oxnard. Mem. Westlake Village Art Guild, 1992—; pres. (sisterhood) Riverdale Temple, Bronx, NY, 1988—90; sec., then pres. Soc. Women Engrs., NE Region, 1950—56. Mem.: Buena Ventura Art Assn., Calif. Gold Coast Watercolor Soc., Peripheral Neuropathy Support (recording sec. 2000—06). Achievements include patents for visually learning mathematics operations with signed numbers. Home and Office: 2478 Chaucer Pl Thousand Oaks CA 91362 Office Phone: 805-493-2698. Personal E-mail: arliese@verizon.net.

MILLER, ELLEN S., marketing executive; b. Indpls., June 28, 1954; d. Harold Edward and Lilian (Gantner) M. BA, DePauw U., 1976; postgrad., Sch. Visual Arts, NYC, 1981-82. Editorial asst. Daisy mag., NYC, 1976-77; asst. dept. mgr., Christmas hiring mgr. Bloomingdale's, NYC, 1978; sales rep. Rosenthal USA Ltd., NYC, 1979, mktg. asst., 1980-81, dir. mktg. comms., 1982-90; mgr. consumer mktg. Creamer Dickson Basford, Providence, 1990, v.p., 1991-94; prin. E.S. Miller Comm., Providence, 1994—. Instr. Learning Connection. Editor Community Prep. Sch. newsletter, 1993. Trustee Cmty. Prep Sch., Providence, 1993—, mem. exec. com., 1997—. Recipient Bell Ringer award New Eng. Pub. Club, 1992, 93, Iris award N.J. chpt. Internat. Assn. Bus. Communicators, 1993, Silver Quill award Dist. I, 1993, Holland award Ctrl. Mass. Advt. Club, 1997. Mem. Pub. Rels. Soc. Am., Nat. Tabletop Assn. (com. chair 1989), Internat. Tabletop Awards (bd. dirs. 1989), Rotary Club. Republican. Presbyterian. Office Phone: 401-724-3773. Personal E-mail: ellensmiller@att.net.

MILLER, ELLIOTT CAIRNS, retired bank executive, lawyer; b. Cambridge, Mass., May 4, 1934; s. James Wilkinson and Mary Elliott (Cairns) M.; m. Mary Killion, July 2, 1960; children: Jonathan Vaill, Stephen Killion. AB, Harvard Coll., 1956; JD, U. Mich., 1961; LLM, Boston U., 1970. Bar: Conn. 1962. Assoc. Robinson & Cole, Hartford, Conn., 1961-66, ptnr., 1967-72; v.p., counsel Soc. for Savs., Hartford, Conn., 1972-73, sr. v.p., 1973-78, exec. v.p., 1978, pres., CEO, dir., 1979-90; pres., CEO Soc. for Savs. Bancorp Inc., 1987-90. Bd. dirs. nat. council Savs. Inst., Washington, 1984-88. Trustee, chmn. Kingswood-Oxford Sch., West Hartford, 1977-87; trustee Coordinating Coun. on Founds., 1987-90; bd. dirs. Downtown Coun., Hartford, 1975-90; trustee Greater Hartford Arts Coun., 1980-88; trustee Wadsworth Atheneum, 1990-99; trustee Hartford Stage Co., 1973-85, 1985—; corporator Hartford Hosp., Inst. of Living; mem. transition com. Conn. State Treas. Denise Nappier, 1998-99. With U.S. Army, 1956-58. Mem. Conn. Bar Assn., 21st Century Club (Hartford), Monday Evening Club (Hartford), Dauntless Club (Essex, Conn.), Ferrari Club Am., Bernese Mountain Dog Club. Methodist. Home: 9 Champlin Sq Essex CT 06426-1101 E-mail: soleoak@aol.com.

MILLER, EMILIE F., former state senator, consultant; b. Chgo., Aug. 11, 1936; d. Bruno C. and Etta M. (Senese) Feiza; m. Dean E. Miller; children: Desireé M., Edward C. BSBA, Drake U., 1958. Asst. buyer Jordan Marsh Co., Boston, 1958-60, Carson, Pirie, Scott & Co., Chgo., 1960-62; dept. mgr., asst. buyer Woodward & Lothrop, Washington, 1962-64; state labor coord. Robb Davis Daliles Joint Campaign; legis. aide Senator Adelard Brandt, Va., 1980-83; fin. dir. Saslaw for Congress, 1984; legis. cons. Va. Fedn. Bus. Profl. Women, 1986-87, 98-00; senator Va. Gen. Assembly, Richmond, 1988-92; cons. apptd. by Gov. Wilder to bd. dirs. Innovative Tech. Authority, 1992-94, Ctr. for Innovative Tech., 1992-94; sr. mgr. Thompson, Cobb, Bazilio & Assocs., 1999—2006. Bus. tng. seminars, Moscow, Nizhny Novgorod, Russia, 1993, Novgorod, St. Petersburg, 95; cons. in field. Guest editl. writer No. Va. Sun, 1981; host, prodr. weekly TV program, Channel 61. Active State Ctrl. Com. Dem. Party Va., Richmond, 1974—2005, steering com., 2000-05, chair 11th congrl. dist., 2001-05; mem. Fairfax County Dem. Com., 1968—, chair, 1976-80, 98-2000, Presdl. Inaugural Com., 1977, 1992 Dem. Nat. Platform Com., Va., Dem. Adv. Com. Robb-Spong Commn., 1978-79; chair 11th Congrl. Dist. Dem. Com., 2001—; founder, chair Va. Assoc. Dem. County and City Chmn., 1976-80; chmn. Fairfax County Dem. Com., 1976-80, 1998-00; security supr. 1980 Dem. Nat. Conv.; v.p. Va. Fedn. Dem. Women, 1992-94; bd. dirs. Stop Child Abuse Now, 1988, Ctr. Innovative Tech., 1992-94, Ct. Apptd. Spl. Advs., 1993-96; nat. alumni bd. J.A. Achievement, BRAVO adv. com. for the first Gov.'s Awards for Arts in Va., 1979-80; lay tchr. St. Ambrose Cath. Ch., 1963-80; del. to White House Conf. on Children, 1970; chair Va. Coalition for Mentally Disabled, 1992-94; com. of 100, Va. Opera Bd., 1994-99; bd. dirs. Social Action Linking Together. Recipient Disting. Grad. award Jr. Achievement, 1973, Woman of Achievement award Fairfax (Va.) Bd. Suprs. and Fairfax County Commn. for Women, 1982, Cmty. Svc. award Friends of Victims Assistance Network, 1988, Founders award Fairfax County Coun. of Arts, 1989, Mental Health Assn. of Northern Va. Warren Stambaugh award, 1991, Ann. Svc. award Va. Assn. for Marriage and Family Therapy, 1991, Psychology Soc. of Washington Cmty. Svc. award, 1993, pacesetter award So. Women in Pub. Leadership Conf., 1996. Mem. NOW, Nat. Mus. Women in the Arts, Va. Assn. Female Execs. (adv. bd., bd. dirs., v.p. 1992-99), Va. Assn. Cmty. Svc. Bds. (chmn. 1980-82), North Va. Assn. Cmty. Bds. (chmn. 1978-79, 95-98), Fairfax County Coun. Arts (v.p. 1980—, mem. exec. com. internat. children's festival, Founders award 1989), Fairfax County C. of C. (legis. com.), Greater Merrifield Bus. and Profl. Assn., Mental Health Assn. No.Va. (bd. dirs.), Ctrl. Fairfax C. of C., Falls Church C. of C., Bus. and Profl. Women's Fedn. Va., Mantua Citizens Assn. (exec. bd.), Bus. and Profl. Women's Club (pres. Falls Church chpt. 1994-96, 2007—, Woman of Yr. award 1990), Women's Nat. Dem. Club (past v.p., bd. govs.), Va. Assn. Female Execs. (bd. dirs. 1992-99), Phi Gamma Nu. Democrat. Roman Catholic. Avocations: tennis, art, baseball. Home: 8701 Duvall St Fairfax VA 22031-2711 Office Phone: 703-560-0291. Personal E-mail: emiliemiller@cs.com.

MILLER, ERNEST CHARLES, management consultant; b. Bronx, NY, July 14, 1925; s. Ernest Philip and Elizabeth (Hellwig) M.; m. Edith Grosvenor Porterfield, Nov. 11, 1947 (div. Oct. 3, 1963); children: Laura Lee, Marcy Rogers, Ernest Charles; m. Tung-fen Lin, Jan. 8, 1985. AB, Yale U., New Haven, 1945; MA, U. Pa., Phila., 1949. Lic. psychologist, N.Y. Instr. U. Pa., 1947-51, cons., 1950-53; br. mgr., bd. dirs. Richardson, Bellows, Henry & Co., Inc., 1953-55; mgr. personnel tech. Am. Standard, Inc., 1955-59; mng. prin. Hellwig, Miller & Assos., Westport, Conn., 1959-61; sr. assoc. Cresap, McCormick & Paget, Inc., NYC, 1961-63; with Am. Mgmt. Assns., NYC, 1964-83, pres. AMACOM div., 1978-81, group v.p. AMA Publs. Group, 1981-83; pres. Miller, Hellwig Assocs., 1984—. Author works in strategic planning, orgn. devel., human resources, exec. compensation and mgmt. Mem. Columbia U. All-Univ. Seminar, China Internat. Bus. Orgn. and Mgmt. NEH fellow, 1980 Mem. APA, Soc. Indsl. and Orgnl. Psychology. Episcopalian. Office: Miller Hellwig Assocs 150 W End Ave New York NY 10023-5713

MILLER, EUGENE, business educator, consultant; b. Chgo., Oct. 6, 1925; s. Harry and Fannie (Prosterman) M.; m. Edith Sutker, Sept. 23, 1951 (div. Sept. 1965); children: Ross, Scott, June; m. Thelma Gottlieb, Dec. 22, 1965; stepchildren: Paul Gottlieb, Alan Gottlieb. BS, Ga. Inst. Tech., 1945; AB magna cum laude, Bethany Coll., 1947, LLD, 1969; diploma, Oxford U., Eng., 1947; MS in Journalism, Columbia U., 1948; MBA, NYU, 1959; postgrad., Pace U., 1973—. Reporter, then city editor Greensboro (N.C.) Daily News, 1948-52; S.W. bur. chief Bus. Week mag., Houston, 1952-54, assoc. mng. editor NYC, 1954-60; dir. pub. affairs and communications McGraw-Hill, Inc., 1960-63, v.p., 1963-68; sr. v.p. pub. rels. and investor rels., exec. com. N.Y. Stock Exch., NYC, 1968-73; sr. v.p. CNA Fin. Corp., Chgo., 1973-75; chmn. Eugene Miller & Assos., Glencoe, Ill., 1975-77; v.p. USG Corp., Chgo., 1977-82, sr. v.p., 1982-85, mem. mgmt. com., 1982-91, exec. v.p., CFO, 1985-87, elected vice chmn., CFO, 1987-91, mem. exec. com., also bd. dirs.; prof., exec.-in-residence Coll. Bus. Fla. Atlantic U., Boca Raton, 1991—; chmn., CEO Ideon Group, Inc., Jacksonville, Fla., 1996. Campaign speechwriter Pres. Dwight Eisenhower, 1956; adj. prof. mgmt. NYU, 1963-65; prof. bus. adminstrn. Fordham U., 1969-75; prof. fin., chmn. dept. Northeastern Ill. U., 1975-78; lectr. to bus. and ednl. groups; bd. dirs. MRFI, Inc., Chgo., bd. dirs., mem. adv. bd. dirs. Nationwide Acceptance Corp., Chgo.; cons. to sec. Dept. Commerce, 1961-66; editor-in-residence U. Oreg., 1992; exec.-in-residence U. Ill., 1991, U. Wis., 1991, U. Toronto, 1992; exec.-in-residence, POHL fellow U. Wyo., 1992; mem. adv. bd. CFO mag., 1991-99; bd. dirs. The Strive Group, Chgo.; cons. Arthur Andersen & Co., Chgo., 1992-97; arbitrator NYSE, 2002—, NASD, 2005-. Author: Your Future in Securities, 1974, Barron's Guide to Graduate Business Schools, 1977, 15th edit., 2007; contbg. editor: Public Relations Handbook, 1988, Boardroom Reports, 1986—; writer syndicated bus. column., 1964-86; mem. editl. bd. IRQ mag., 1997—. Trustee Bethany Coll., 1970—; mem. alumni bd. Columbia U. Sch. Journalism. Comdr. USNR, World War II, ret. Recipient outstanding achievement award Bethany Coll., 1963, 50th anniversary award Sch. Journalism Columbia U., also honors award, 1963, Sch. Journalism Ohio U., 1964, disting. svc. award in investment edn. Nat. Assn. Investment Clubs, 1980, Roalman award Nat. Investor Rels. Inst., 1987; honored with Eugene Miller Bd. Rm. Bethany Coll., 1999, Eugene Miller Bd. Rm. Coll. Bus. Fla. Atlantic U., 2007. Fellow Pub. Rels. Soc. Am.; mem. Soc. Am. Bus. Editors and Writers (founder, Pres.'s award 2003), Fin. Execs. Inst., St. Andrew's Country Club, Sigma Delta Chi, Alpha Sigma Phi. Home: 7351 Ballantrae Ct Boca Raton FL 33496-1423 Office: Fla Atlantic U Coll Business 777 Glades Rd Boca Raton FL 33431-6424 Office Phone: 561-297-3630. Personal E-mail: Gene160@aol.com.

MILLER, EVAN, lawyer; b. Bklyn., Sept. 18, 1956; s. Richard and Lois Pearl (Hirsch) M. BA, Columbia U., 1978; JD, Georgetown U., 1981. Bar: N.Y. 1982, D.C. 1983, U.S. Dist. Ct. D.C. 1984, U.S. Ct. Appeals (D.C. and 11th cirs.) 1985. Law clk. to presiding justice U.S. Dist. Ct. (so. dist.) Ga., Brunswick, 1981-82; assoc. Pepper, Hamilton & Scheetz, Washington, 1982-88; ptnr. Johnson & Gibbs, Washington, 1988-94, Hogan & Hartson LLP, Washington, 1994—. Sr. editor Employee Benefits Law (BNA) 2d edit., 1999. Mem. ABA (co-chair employee benefits com. labor sect. 2003-05, employee benefits com. tax sect.) Office: Hogan & Hartson LLP 555 13th St NW Ste 800E Washington DC 20004-1161 Office Phone: 202-637-5776. Business E-Mail: emiller@hhlaw.com.

MILLER, EWING HARRY, retired architect; b. Toledo, Ohio, Oct. 5, 1923; s. Ewing Harry and Esther Alice (Graves) M.; children: Victoria Alice, Paul Ewing; m. Donna Barnard Ari. BA, U. Pa., 1947, MA, 1948. Draftsman Harbeson, Hough, Livingston & Larson, Phila., 1948; designer Nolen & Swinburne, Phila., 1950-52; project architect Gilboy & O'Malley, London, 1953-55; partner Miller, Vrydagh & Miller, Terre Haute, Ind., 1955-65; pres. Ewing Miller Partnership, Terre Haute, 1965-70, Archonics Corp., 1970-76, chmn. bd., 1976-79; sr. ptnr. for design Archonics Design Partnership, Indpls., 1979-84; assoc. ptnr. architecture eastern region U.S. Howard Needles, Tammen & Bergendoff, 1985-92; archtl. cons. Design & Bldg. Industry, 1992—2005; gen. ptnr. Lockerbie Devel. Co., 1978-86, Lockerbie Glove Devel. Co., 1983-86, East St. Devel. Co., 1979-86. Contbr. articles to profl. jours.; archtl. critic Indpls. Monthly Mag.; major archtl. works include: various bldgs. Ind. U., including grad. biology lab., Ind. State U., master plan and edn. bldgs., residence halls and sci. bldg., libr. and various classroom bldgs., Southwestern Ind. U., master plan and edn. bldgs., Ind. and Ohio Laborers Tng. Ctrs., master plan U. San Diego. Westin Conv. Hotel; various office parks, Indpls. Pub. Transp. Corp. facility, addition to Duesenberg Factory; master plan Ind. State Govt. Complex, State of Ind. and design of new state office bldg.; prin. in charge printing facility Ho. of Rep. Architect of the Capitol, prin. in charge of Mastser Plan for design and restoration of Old Exec. Office Bldg., Washington; master plan for remodeling The Pentagon, Washington; prin. in charge design for remodeling Dept. of State, Washington; client rep. for remodeling Midwest Direct Mktg. Ctr., B.M.G., Inc., N.Y. Mem. Ind. Gov.'s Commn. on Aging, 1959-62; pres. Gov.'s Commn. on Comprehensive Health Planning, Ind., 1970-75, Behavioral Research Found., 1965-85; bd. mgrs. Sheldon Swope Art Gallery, 1965-80, pres., 1965-73; bd. dirs. Center for Exploration of Values and Meaning, 1978-85, Herron Art Gallery, 1980-88; chmn. Indpls. Arts and Cultural Alliance, 1983; v.p. Am. Chestnut Land Trust, Port Republic, Md.; chmn. bd. Cove Point Natural Heritage Trust, Lusby, Md., 1995—, bd. mem. The Environmnental Fund of Maryland. Recipient design citation, biennial awards program Ind. Soc. Architects; Honor awards, triennial design awards East Central Region AIA; Nat. Archtl. award of excellence Am. Inst. Steel Constrn.; 1st Honor award and winner Internat. Competition for Housing, Indpls.; nat. award of excellence for univ. bldgs. Am. Sch. and Univ. Mag.; Ind. Soc. Architects Honor award restoration of Circle Theater, various office bldgs. Fellow AIA (mem. com. on design, chmn. com. on architecture for edn., mem. Vision 2000 study, architecture in coming decade), Downtown Neighborhood Assn. (bd. dirs. Washington chpt.), Lambda Alpha Hon. Soc. Home: 601 Pennsylvania Ave NW Apt 1202 Washington DC 20004-2644

MILLER, FLEMON MARSHALL, public works manager; b. LA, Sept. 15, 1942; s. Flemon Harris Miller and Claudia Marshall; m. Peggy Ann Torres, Mar. 14, 1992; children: Diane Barboza, Anthony Barboza; m. Louida Jarmon Penland (div.); 1 child, Marguet Marshall. Cert. course instr. in supplier diversity 2000, hazardous waste mgr. Dept. Transp. Warehouse man City of LA, 1969—75, auto parts storekeeper, 1975—77, storekeeper dept. water and power, 1977—89, sr. storekeeper dept. power and water supply supr., 1989—92, sr. storekeeper dept. power and water, 1992—99, sr. storekeeper dept. power and water and supr. investment recovery, 1999—; owner, operator The Miller Method Indsl. Metal Recyclers. Chmn. adv. coun. Normandie Ave. Elem. Sch., LA, 1972—77. Recipient Recycler of Yr., City of LA, 2006, Law Enforcement Hero award, Nat. Assn. Police Orgns., 2006. Office: Investment Recovery 11797 Truesdale St Sun Valley CA 91352 Office Phone: 818-581-8918.

MILLER, FORREST E., telecommunications industry executive; BS in acctg., Univ. So. Calif.; MBA, Stanford Univ. CPA. Acct. Coopers & Lybrand; sr. assoc. Marakon Assoc.; mgmt. positions through pres. Pacific Bell directory Pacific Telesis, 1984—97; pres., CEO SBC directory ops. SBC Comm., 1997—99, pres., CEO SNET, 1999, pres., CEO Southwestern Bell, group pres. corp. planning, group pres. external affairs & planning, 2004; group pres. AT&T Comm. Corp. AT&T Inc. (merger of SBC Comm. with AT&T Corp.), San Antonio, 2005—. Office: AT&T Inc 175 E Houston San Antonio TX 78205 Mailing: AT&T Inc PO Box 2933 San Antonio TX 78299-2933 *

MILLER, FRED HEINS, lawyer, retired law educator; s. Fred H. and Marian B. Miller; m. Marcia Henry, June 20, 1959; children: Frederick Clayton, Robert Henry. BA, U. Mich., Ann Arbor, 1959, JD, 1962. Bar: Ohio 1962, Okla. 1968. Assoc. Dunbar, Kienzle & Murphy, Columbus, Ohio, 1962—66; prof. U. Okla. Law Sch., Norman, 1966—2006, George L. Cross rsch. prof., 1989—2006, Kenneth McAfee chmn. law, centennial prof., 1991—2006; of counsel Phillips, McFall, McCaffrey, McVay & Murrah, Oklahoma City, 2006—. Pres. Nat. Conf. Com. Uniform State Laws, Chgo., 2003—05, cons. Fed. Res. Bd., Washington, 1975—76, mem. consumer adv. coun., 1983—85. Author: Truth in Lending, 2000, Law Modern Payment Systems, 2002; author, editor: Hawkland UCC Series, 2005—. Recipient Svc. award, Oklahoma City U., 2002. Mem.: ABA, Okla. Bar Assn., Am. Law Inst., Order of Coif, Phi Beta Kappa. Avocations: antiques, history. Office: U Okla Coll Law 300 Timberdell Rd Norman OK 73019

MILLER, FREDERICK EDWIN, JR., history professor, government agency administrator; b. Stamford, Conn., Jan. 27, 1939; s. Frederick Edwin and Florence Baker Miller; m. Louise Ellen Wood, July 20, 1985. B of Social Sci. in Edn. cum laude, Fairfield U., 1960; MA in History, Boston U., 1961; postgrad., NYU, 1965—67; JD, Fordham U., 1976. Tchr. dept. spl. pupil svcs. Stamford Pub. Schs., Conn., 1961—62; tchr. social studies Stamford Cath. High Sch., 1965—67; lectr. history and govt. CUNY, NYC CC, 1966—73; lectr. CUNY Queens Coll., 1968—69; state rep. Conn. Ho. Reps., Hartford, 1971—73; asst. clk. Superior Ct. Jud. Dist. Stamford-Norwalk, 1976—95; justice of peace Fairfield. Ajd. prof. Norwalk C.C., Concordia Coll., Bronxville, NY, Coll. New Rochelle, St. Basils Coll., Stamford, Fairfield U., Sacred Heart U.; incorporator Stamford Hosp., Stamford, Conn.; mem. bd. Drug Liberation Inc, Stamford, Conn., Stamford Forum for World Affairs, Stamford, Conn., South End Cmty. Ctr., Stamford, Conn., Spanish Internat. Ctr., Stamford, Conn.; mem. bd. trustees Catholic Charities, Diocese Bridgeport, Conn. Mem. adv. task force desegregation Stamford Pub. Schs., 1971—72; mem. Bd. Assessment Appeals, Fairfield, 1995—99, chmn., 1997—99; mem. Stamford Bd. Reps., 1967—77, pres., 1973—77. Mem.: AAUP, Am. Polit. Sci. Assn., Am. Cath. Hist. Assn., Am. Hist. Assn., Ancient Order Hibernians, KC 4th Degree, Fairfield U. Honor Soc., Phi Alpha Theta. Democrat. Roman Catholic. Home: 167 Rock Major Rd Fairfield CT 06824

MILLER, GALE TIMOTHY, lawyer; b. Kalamazoo, Sept. 15, 1946; s. Arthur H. and Eleanor (Johnson) M.; m. Janice Lindvall, June 1, 1968; children: Jeremy L., Amanda E., Timothy W. AB, Augustana Coll., 1968; JD, U. Mich., 1971. Bar: Mich. 1971, Colo. 1973, U.S. Dist. Ct. Colo. 1973, U.S. Ct. Appeals (10th cir.) 1979, U.S. Supreme Ct. 1997. Trial atty. FTC, Washington, 1971-73; assoc. Davis Graham & Stubbs LLP, Denver, 1973-77, ptnr., 1978—, chmn. exec. com., 1998—2001. Bd. dirs. Colo. Jud. Inst., 1999—, v.p., 2005—06, chair, 2006—, Colo. Lawyers Com., 1989—91, bd. dirs., 1987—2006, mem. exec. com., 2004—06. Recipient Cmty. Svc. award Colo. Hispanic Bar Assn., 1996: named Individual Lawyer of Yr. Colo. Lawyers Com., 1994. Mem. ABA (antitrust sect. task force on model civil antitrust jury instrns. 1985-87), Colo. Bar Assn. (mem.

bd. govs., 2007—, chair antitrust sect. 1996-98), Denver Bar Assn. Democrat. Lutheran. Office: Davis Graham & Stubbs LLP 1550 17th St Ste 500 Denver CO 80202 Home Phone: 303-399-2845; Office Phone: 303-892-7368.

MILLER, GARFIELD LANKARD, III, investment banker; b. Buffalo, Apr. 8, 1950; s. Garfield Lankard and Johanne (Cunningham) M.; m. Martha Ellen McGarry, Aug. 24, 1974; 1 child, Cornelia Lawton. BBA, Middlebury Coll., Vt., 1972; MBA, U. Pa., 1975. Account mgr. Citibank, N.A., NYC, 1975-79; ltd. ptnr. Bear, Stearns & Co., NYC, 1979-85; mng. dir. CS First Boston, Inc., NYC, 1985-91, Salomon Bros. Inc., NYC, 1991-94; pres. Aegis Energy Advisors Corp., NYC, 1994—. Office: Aegis Energy Advisors Corp 6th Fl 708 3rd Ave New York NY 10017-4119 Office Phone: 212-245-2552. E-mail: glmiller@aegisenergy.com.

MILLER, GARY C., lawyer; b. Little Rock, May 23, 1955; s. William Scott, Jr. and Margaret Imogene (Puckett) M.; m. Mary Catherine Miller, Oct. 23, 2000; children: Daniel, Sarah. BA in Econs. and Managerial Studies, Rice U., 1977; JD, U. Tex., 1980. Bar: Tex. 1980, U.S. Dist. Ct. (so. dist.) Tex. 1981, U.S. Dist. Ct. (no. and we. dists.) Tex. 1991, U.S. Dist. Ct. (ea. dist.) Tex. 1993, U.S. Ct. Appeals (5th cir) 1980, U.S. Supreme Ct. 1995. Atty. Wood, Campbell, Moody & Gibbs, Houston, 1980-83, Gibbs & Ratliff, Houston, 1983-85, Andrews & Kurth LLP and prececessor, Houston, 1985—. Contbr. articles to profl. jours. Chmn. Westminster Weekday Sch., Houston, 1993—96; chmn., bd. trustees Westminster United Meth. Ch., Houston, 1996—98; bd. dirs. Houston Vol. Lawyers Program, 2000—04, Houston Lawyer Referral Svc., 2004—05; co-chair HBA Legalines, 2002—03. Fellow Tex. Bar Found.; mem. ABA (bus. in bankruptcy com., bus. and corp. litigation com.), Houston Bar Assn., Order of Coif, Phi Beta Kappa. Office: Andrews & Kurth LLP 600 Travis Ste 4200 Houston TX 77002 Office Phone: 713-220-3829. Personal E-mail: gary8634@sbcglobal.net. Business E-Mail: garymiller@andrewskurth.com.

MILLER, GARY EVAN, psychiatrist, mental health services professional; b. Cleve., Aug. 19, 1935; s. Henry M. and Mollie (Price) M.; m. Karen Ann Marie Barrett, Sept. 16, 1972; children: Anna Charis, Rebecca Elizabeth. MD, U. Tex., Galveston, 1960. Diplomate in psychiatry, addiction psychiatry, and geriatric psychiatry Am. Bd. Psychiatry and Neurology. Intern Montefiore Hosp., NYC, 1960-61; resident in psychiatry U. Hosp. Cleve., 1961-62, Austin State Hosp., Tex., 1963-65; dep. commr. mental health services Dept. Mental Health and Mental Retardation, Tex., 1967-70; dir. Rio Grande State Ctr. for Mental Health and Mental Retardation, Dept. Mental Health, Harlingen, Tex., 1966-67; asst. commr., dir. Rochester regional office State Dept. Mental Hygiene, NY, 1970-72; clin. asst. prof. psychiatry U. Rochester Sch. Medicine and Dentistry, 1970-72; asst. clin. prof. psychiatry SUNY, Buffalo, 1970-72; cons. mental health Ga. Dept. Human Resources, Atlanta, 1972, dir. div. mental health, 1972-74; clin. prof. psychiatry Emory U. Sch. Medicine, Atlanta, 1972-74; vice chmn. Ga. State Planning and Adv. Coun. for Devel. Disabilities Services and Constrn., 1972-73; cons. mental health services orgn. and adminstrn., 1974-76; dir. mental health and devel. services State of NH Concord, 1976-82; commr. Tex. Dept. Mental Health and Mental Retardation Austin, 1982-88; clin. prof. psychiatry U. Tex. Health Sci. Ctr., Houston, adj. assoc. prof. psychiatry San Antonio, 1984-95; dir. profl. svcs. HCA Gulf Pines Hosp., Houston, 1988-94, chief of staff, 1993; clin. dir. adult psychiatry Cypress Creek Hosp., Houston, 1994-2000, med. dir., 2000—03, pres. med. staff, 1996; assoc. clin. psychiatry Post Oak Psychiatry Assoc., Houston, 1988-90; pres. Alternative Svc. Network, Houston, 1990—; chief of staff Kingwood (Tex.) Pines Hosp., 2003—04, dir. Psychiatric Svcs., 2004—. Dir. state alcoholism program in South Tex. region, 1966—67; dir. state alcoholism program in Ga., 1972—74; mem. faculty U. SC Sch. Alcohol and Drug Studies, 1975; mem. quality assurance com. Aetna US Healthcare Pharmacy, 1999—2001. Contbr. articles to profl. jours. Served as capt. M.C., US Army, 1962-63. Recipient Cert. of Recognition, Ga. Psychol. Assn., 1973. Fellow Am. Psychiat. Assn. (disting. life; cert. in adminstrv. psychiatry, com. on psychiat. adminstrn. and mgmt. 1999-2002); mem. AMA, Am. Soc. Clin. Psychopharmacology (cert.), Am. Soc. Addiction Medicine (cert. alcoholism and other drug dependencies), Am. Acad. Addiction Psychiatry, NH Psychiat. Soc. (pres. 1981-82), Nat. Assn. State Mental Health Program Dir. (bd. dir. 1984-88, sec. 1986-88), NH Med. Soc., Am. Acad. Psychiatry and the Law, Am. Assn. Psychiat. Adminstr. (pres. Tex. chpt. 1986), Tex. Med. Assn., Tex. Soc. Psychiat. Physicians (chair socioecons. com. 2006—), Mental Health Assn. Greater Houston (bd. dir. 1989-95, v.p. advocacy 1990-95, adv. coun. 1999—), Alpha Omega Alpha. Home: 5314 Westminister Ct Houston TX 77069-3338 Office: 530 Wells Fargo Dr Ste 110 Houston TX 77090-4026 Office Phone: 281-440-6899. Personal E-mail: gemhou@yahoo.com.

MILLER, GARY G., congressman; b. Huntsville, Ark., 1948; m. Cathy, 1972; 4 children. Student, Mt. San Antonio C.C. Founder G. Miller Devel. Co.; mem. U.S. Congress from 42nd Calif. dist., Washington, 1999—; mem. budget com., fin. svcs. com., sci. com. Bd. dirs. Sonrise Christian Sch., 1982; appointed to Diamond Bar (Calif.) Mcpl. Adv. Coun., 1988; elected to 1st Diamond Bar City Coun., 1989; mayor, 1992; elected to Calif. State Assembly, 1995 (chmn. budget com. and banking and fin. com., vice chmn. transp. com.). With U.S. Army. Republican. Achievements include proposing 24 bills signed into law, successfully negotiated funding of 1st class size reduction program, and produced balanced budget that reduced the bus. tax. to 1973 levels while maintaing a $310 million reserve. Office: US Ho Reps 1037 Longworth Ho Office Bldg Washington DC 20515-0542 *

MILLER, GARY H., lawyer; b. New Orleans, Mar. 11, 1957; s. Leo Jr. and Suzanne Robinowitz (Meltzer) M.; m. Ellen Baldwin Hoffman, Oct. 18, 1986; children: Matthew Hilliard, Katherine Elise. BA magna cum laude, New Eng. Coll., 1979; JD cum laude, Tulane U., 1982. Assoc. Jones Walker, New Orleans, 1982-89, ptnr., 1990—. Mem. moot ct. bd. Tulane U. Sch. Law, 1980-82; lectr in field. Bd. dirs. Golden Retriever Club Greater New Orleans, Inc., 1980, Burtheville Cmty. Assn., Inc., 1997—; class agt. New England Coll. Mem. La. Bar Assn. (treas. consumer protection, lender liability and bankruptcy sect. 1990-91, chmn. consumer protection, lender liability and bank sect. 1991-92), Phi Tau Beta. Democrat. Jewish. Avocations: retriever and obedience training, fishing, hunting, guitar. Office: PO Box 2599 Bryson City NC 28713 E-mail: fisher31157@msn.com, gmiller@joneswalker.com.

MILLER, GARY J., political economist; b. Urbana, Ill., Jan. 2, 1949; s. Gerald J. and Doris Elaine (Miner) M.; m. Anne Colberg, Jan. 29, 1971; children: Neil, Ethan. BA, U. Ill., 1971; PhD, U. Tex., 1976. Asst. prof. Calif. Inst. Tech., Pasadena, 1976-79; assoc. prof. Mich. State U., East Lansing, 1979-86; Taylor prof. polit. economy Washington U., St. Louis, 1986-97; assoc. dean for acad. affairs Olin Sch. Bus., St. Louis, 1995-96, prof. polit. sci. Author: Cities by Contract, 1981, Reforming Bureaucracy, 1987, Managerial Dilemmas, 1992. NSF grantee, 1981, 1983, 1992, 2003; recepient Herbert Simon award, 2004. Mem. Phi Beta Kappa, Phi Kappa Phi (Disting. Faculty award 1994). Democrat. Office: Washington U Dept Polit Sci 1 Brookings Dr Dept Polit Saint Louis MO 63130-4899 Home Phone: 314-822-9753; Office Phone: 314-935-5874. Business E-Mail: gjmiller@artsci.wustl.edu.

MILLER, GAY DAVIS, lawyer; b. Florence, Ariz., Dec. 20, 1947; d. Franklin Theodore and Mary Davis; 1 child, Katherine Alexandra BA, U. Colo., 1969; JD, Am. U., Washington, DC, 1975. Bar: DC 1975. Atty., spl. asst. to gen. counsel, sr. counsel corp. affairs Inter Am. Devel. Bank, Washington, 1975—78, 1983—2004; atty. Intelsat, Washington, 1978-80. Articles editor: Am. U. Law Rev., 1974—75, contbg. author: The Inspection Panel of the World Bank: A Different Complaints Procedure, 2001. Bd. dirs. Hist. Mt. Pleasant, Inc., Washington, 1985-86, Washington Bridle Trails Assn., 1992—2004. Mem.: ABA, Am. Soc. Internat. Law. E-mail: gaydavismiller@fone.net.

MILLER, GENEVIEVE, retired medical historian; b. Butler, Pa., Oct. 15, 1914; d. Charles Russell and Genevieve (Wolford) Miller. AB, Goucher Coll., Balt., 1935; MA, Johns Hopkins U., Balt., 1939; PhD, Cornell U., Ithaca, NY, 1955. Asst. in history medicine Johns Hopkins Inst. History of Medicine, Balt., 1943—44, instr., 1945—48, rsch. assoc., 1979—94; asst. prof. history of sci. Case Western Res. U. Sch. Medicine, Cleve., 1953-67, assoc. prof., 1967-79, assoc. prof. emeritus, 1979—; rsch. assoc. med. history Clevel. Med. Libr. Assn., 1953-62; curator Howard Dittrick Mus. Hist. Medicine, 1962-67, dir., 1967-79. Author: William Beaumont's Formative Years: Two Early Notebooks 1811-1821, 1946; The Adoption of Inoculation for Smallpox in England and France, 1957 (William H. Welch medal Am. Assn. History Medicine 1962), Bibliography of the History of Medicine of the U.S. and Canada, 1939-1960, 1964, Bibliography of the Writings of Henry E. Sigerist, 1966, Letters of Edward Jenner and Other Documents Concerning the Early History of Vaccination, 1983; assoc. editor Bull. of History of Medicine, 1944-48, acting editor, 1948, mem. adv. editl. bd., 1960-92; mem. bd. editors Jour. History of Medicine & Allied Scis., 1948-65; editor Newsletter Am. Assn. History of Medicine, 1986-96; contbr. articles to profl. jours. Alumna trustee Goucher Coll., Balt., 1966-69; trustee Judson Retirement Cmty., Clevel., 1993-99, Am. Coun. Learned Socs. fellow, 1948-50, Dean Van Meter fellow, Goucher Coll., 1953-54. Fellow Cleve. Med. Libr. Assn. (hon.); mem. Am. Assn. History Medicine (pres. 1978-80, mem. coun. 1960-63, Lifetime Achievement award 1999), Am. Hist. Assn., Internat. Soc. History of Medicine, Soc. Archtl. Historians, Phi Beta Kappa. Democrat. Home and Office: Judson Manor Apt 616 1890 E 107th St Cleveland OH 44106-2251

MILLER, GEOFFREY, child neurologist; b. Manchester, Eng., Feb. 1, 1947; came to U.S., 1988; s. Erwin and Cynthia Sarah Miller; m. Patricia Sarah Craigie, June 21, 1985; children: Joanne, Sally, Alethea. BA, MB, ChB, BAO, Trinity Coll., Dublin, Ireland, 1972, MA, 1982; MD, U. Western Australia, 1985; MPhil, U. Glasgow, Scotland, 2002. Diplomate Am. Bd. Psychiatry and Neurology, Am. Bd. Child Neurology, Am. Bd. Neurodevelopmental Disabilities. Fellow Royal Postgrad. Med. Sch., London, 1982-83; devel. pediatrician Princess Margaret Hosp. for Children, Perth, Australia, 1983-85; med. dir. Sir David Brand Ctr. for Cerebral Palsy, Perth, Australia, 1983-84; assoc. prof. pediat. Pa. State U., Hershey, 1988-92; co-dir. Muscular Dystrophy Assn. Clinic, Hershey, 1988-92, clinic physician Houston, 1998—; prof. pediat. & neurology Baylor Coll. Medicine, Houston, 1992—2004, chief devel. pediat. sect., 2000—02; dir. Meyer Ctr. Devel. Pediat., Tex. Childrens Hosp., 2000—02; prof. pediat. & neurology Yale U., 2004—. Vis. specialist West Australian Soc. for Crippled Children, Perth, 1983; investigator Neuromuscular Rsch. Inst., Perth, 1984-87; clin. dir. Child Neurology Svc. Yale U. Sch. Medicine, 2004—; mem. Yale Bioethics Ctr., 2004. Author: Extreme Prematurity. Practices, Bioethics, and Law, 2007; editor: Static Encephalopathies, 1992, Cerebral Palsies, 1998, Extreme Prematurity; contbr. articles to jours. in field. Capt. Royal Army Med. Corps, 1970-78. Elected and inducted into Am. Neurol. Assn., 1996. Fellow Royal Coll. Physicians, Royal Coll. Australasian Physicians; mem. Royal Coll. Physicians (London), Royal College of Paediatrics and Child Health, Child Neurology Soc. (membership com. 1996-97, internat. affairs com. 1997—, chmn. 2002-05, ethics com. 2005-), Internat. Child Neurology Soc., Soc. for Devel. Pediat., Am. Acad. Cerebral Palsy and Devel. Medicine (outcomes com. 2001—06, sci. selection com. 2006). Avocations: rugby, soccer. Business E-Mail: geoffrey.miller@yale.edu.

MILLER, GEORGE, congressman; b. Richmond, Calif., May 17, 1945; s. George and Dorothy (Rumsey) M.; m. Cynthia Caccavo, 1964; children: George, Stephen. BA, San Francisco State Coll., 1968; JD, U. Calif., Davis, 1972. Legis. counsel Calif. senate majority leader, 1969-73; mem. US Congress from 7th Calif. dist., 1975—, House Edn. and Labor Com., 1975—, chmn., 2007—; founding chmn. House Select Com. on Children, Youth and Families, 1983—91; chmn. House Natural Resources Com., 1991—94, House Dem. Policy Com., 2003—. Mem. Calif. Bar Assn. Democrat. Office: US Ho Reps 2205 Rayburn Ho Office Bldg Washington DC 20515-0507 *

MILLER, GEORGE, film director; b. Brisbane, Australia, Mar. 3, 1945; MD, U. NSW, Australia, 1970. Former physician St. Vincent's Hosp., Sydney, Australia. Films include: dir., writer: Violence in the Cinema, Part I, 1971, Mad Max, 1979, The Road Warrior-Mad Max II, 1982, Mad Max: Beyond the Thunderdome, 1985; dir., writer, prodr.: Lorenzo's Oil, 1992 (Acad. award nominee for best original screenplay 1992), 40,000 Years of Dreaming, 1996, Babe: Pig in the City, 1998, Happy Feet, 2006 (Best Animated Film award, LA Film Critics Assn. and NY Film Critics Circle, 2006, Animated Feature Film, British Acad. Film and TV Arts, 2007, Best Animated Feature, Acad. award, 2007); dir.: Devil in Evening Dress, 1973, Twilight Zone: The Movie, 1983, The Witches of Eastwick, 1987; editor Frieze, an Underground Film, 1973; assoc. prodr.: Chain Reaction, 1980; prodr.: The Year My Voice Broke, 1988, Dead Calm, 1989, Flirting, 1990, Video Fool For Love, 1996; prodr., writer: Babe, 1995 (Acad. award nominee for best film and for best screenplay 1996). Office: Kennedy Miller Prodns 30 Orwell St Kings Cross Sydney 2011 Australia also: Gang Tyre & Brown Inc c/o Jeff Mandell 132 S Rodeo Dr Beverly Hills CA 90212 *

MILLER, GEORGE ARMITAGE, psychologist, educator; b. Charleston, W.Va., Feb. 3, 1920; s. George E. and Florence (Armitage) M.; m. Katherine James, Nov. 29, 1939 (dec. Jan. 1996); children: Nancy, Donnally James. BA, U. Ala., 1940, MA, 1941; AM, Harvard U., 1944, PhD, 1946; PhD (hon.), U. Louvain, 1976; D Social Sci. (hon.), Yale U., 1979; DSc (hon.), Columbia U., 1980, U. Sussex, 1984, New Sch. Social Rsch., 1993; LittD (hon.), Charleston U., 1992; DSc (hon.), DSc (hon.), New Sch. Social Rsch., 1993, Princeton U., 1996, Williams Coll., 2000; DSc (hon.), Carnegie Mellon U., 2003. Instr. psychology U. Ala., 1941-43; rsch. fellow Harvard Psycho-Acoustic Lab., 1944-48; asst. prof. psychology Harvard U., 1948-51, assoc. prof., 1955-58, prof., 1958-68, chmn. dept psychology, 1964-67, co-dir. Ctr. for Cognitive Studies, 1960-67; prof. Rockefeller U., NYC, 1968-79, adj. prof., 1979-82; prof. psychology Princeton U., 1979-90, James S. McDonnell Disting. prof. psychology, 1982-90, James S. McDonnell Disting. prof. psychology emeritus, 1990—, program dir. McDonnell-Pew Program in Cognitive Neurosci., 1989-94; assoc. prof. MIT, 1951-55. Vis. Inst. for Advanced Study, Princeton, 1972-76, 82-83, mem., 1950, 70-72; vis. prof. Rockefeller U., 1967-68, MIT, 1976-79, group leader Lincoln Lab., 1953-55; fellow Ctr. Advanced Study in Behavioral Scis., Stanford U., 1958-59; Fulbright research prof. Oxford (Eng.) U., 1963-64; Sesquicentennial prof. U. Ala., 1981. Author: Language and Communication, 1951, (with Galanter and Pribram) Plans and the Structure of Behavior, 1960, Psychology, 1962, (with Johnson-Laird) Language and Perception, 1976, Spontaneous Apprentices, 1977, Language and Speech, 1981, The Science of Words, 1991; editor Psychol. Bulletin, 1981-82. Recipient Disting. Service award Am. Speech and Hearing Assn., 1976, award in behavioral scis. N.Y. Acad. Scis., 1982, Hermann von Helmholtz award Cognitive Neurosci. Inst., 1989, Nat. Medal Sci. NSF, 1991, Gold Medal Am. Psychological Found. 1990, Nat. Medal of Sci. 1991, Louis E. Levy medal Franklin Inst., 1991, John P. Govern award, Am. Assn. for Advancement of Sci., 2000; Guggenheim fellow, 1986, William James fellow Am. Psychological Soc., 1989; Fondation Fyssen Priz Internat. for cognitive sci., 1992. Fellow Brit. Psychol. Assn. (hon.); mem. NAS, AAAS (chmn. sect. J 1981, John P. McGovern award 2000), APA (pres. 1968-69, Disting. Sci. Contbn. award 1963, William James Book award divsn. gen. psychology 1993, Outstanding Lifetime Contbn. to Psychology award 2003), Eastern Psychol. Assn. (pres. 1961-62), Acoustical Soc. Am., Linguistic Soc. Am., Am. Statis. Assn., Am. Philos. Soc., Am. Physiol. Soc., Psychometric Soc., Soc. Exptl. Psychologists (Warren medal 1972), Am. Acad. Arts and Scis., Psychonomic Soc., Royal Netherlands Acad. Arts and Scis. (fgn.), Sigma Xi. Home: 16 Willow St Princeton NJ 08542-6923 Office: Princeton Univ Dept Psychology Green Hall Princeton NJ 08544

MILLER, GEORGE DAVID, retired military officer, not-for-profit executive; b. McKeesport, Pa., Apr. 5, 1930; s. George G. and Nellie G. (Cullen) M.; m. Barbara Aex; 1 child from previous marriage: George David Jr.; stepchildren: Jason Dunn, Elizabeth Dunn. BS, US Naval Acad., Annapolis, MD, 1953; MS in Aerospace Engring, Air Force Inst. Tech., Wright Patterson AFB, Dayton, Ohio, 1966; postgrad., Nat. War Coll., Fort Leslie J. McNair, Washington, 1970—71. Commd. 2d lt. US Air Force, 1953, advanced through grades to lt. gen., 1981; ops. officer, comdr. 22d Spl. Ops. Squadron, Nakhon Phanom Royal Thai AFB, Thailand, 1969—70; dep. comdr. for ops., vice comdr., comdr. 55th Strategic Reconnaissance Wing, Offutt AFB, Nebr., 1971-74; comdr. 17th Air div., 307th Strategic wing, U-Tapao Airfield, Thailand, 1974-75; comdr. 57th Air Div. Minot AFB, ND, 1975-76; asst. dep. chief staff ops. hdqrs. SAC, Offutt AFB, Nebr., 1976-77; dir. single integrated operational plan Joint Strategic Target Planning Staff, Joint Chiefs of Staff, 1977-79; dir. plans USAF, Washington, 1979-80, asst. dep. chief staff ops., plans and readiness, 1980-81; vice comdr.-in-chief SAC, Offutt AFB, Nebr., 1981-84; exec. dir., sec.-gen. U.S. Olympic Com., 1984-87; pres. exec. dir. Morris Animal Found., 1987—92; pres., CEO The Nat. Fire Protection Assoc., 1992—2002; pres. Miller Assocs. Consulting. Chmn. bd. dirs. RJA Group Inc.; bd. dirs. Target Safety Inc. Decorated Def. D.S.M., Air Force DSM, Legion of Merit, D.F.C. with 3 oak leaf clusters Air medal with 18 oak leaf clusters, others. Mem.: VFW, World Orgn. of Bldg. Ofcls. (pres. 2003—), Confedn. of Fire Protection Assns. Internat. (chmn. 1992—2005), Metro Fire Chiefs Assn., Nat. Fire Protection Assn. (pres. emeritus), Mil. Officers Assn., Air Force Assn., Daedalians, Shriners, Scottish Rite, Masons, Sojurners Am. Legion. Lutheran. Home: 20 Phillips Pond Natick MA 01760-5643 Office Phone: 508-380-9218. Business E-Mail: george.d.miller@comcast.net.

MILLER, GEORGE KEITH, lawyer; b. Washington, Mar. 6, 1954; s. Robert Hopkins and Catherine (Antoniades) M.; m. Andrea Ellen Kaliski, Mar. 7, 1981; 1 child, Daphne Kahn. BA magna cum laude, Yale U., 1975; JD, MPA, Harvard U., 1979. Bar: DC 1979, NY 1984, US Dist. Ct. (so. dist.) NY 1984. Assoc. Surrey & Morse, Washington, 1979-80, Paris, 1980-83, Simpson Thacher & Bartlett, NYC, 1983-88, ptnr., 1989—. Contbr. articles to profl. journs. Mem. ABA, NYC Bar Assn., NY State Bar Assn. (editl. bd., com. publ.), Internat. Bar Assn. Democrat. Greek Orthodox. Avocations: international economics, political issues. Office: Simpson Thacher & Bartlett 425 Lexington Ave Fl 15 New York NY 10017-3954 Office Phone: 212-455-7065. Office Fax: 212-455-2502. Business E-Mail: gmiller@stblaw.com.

MILLER, GEORGE W., federal judge, lawyer; b. Schenectady, NY, July 12, 1941; m. Mary Katherine, three children. BA magna cum laude, Princeton U., 1963; JD, Harvard U., 1966; LLM, George Washington U., 1968. Bar: N.Y. 1966, D.C. 1968, Va. 1978. Law clk. to Hon. Bruce M. Forrester US Tax Ct., 1966—67; assoc. Hogan & Hartson, 1970—77, spl. ptnr., 1977—79, ptnr., 1979—2004; judge US Ct. Fed. Claims, Washington, 2004—. Mem. US Ct. Fed. Claims Adv. Coun., 1994—2004; mem. Litig. Practice task force US Ct. Fed. Claims, 1995; mem. US Ct. Appeals DC cir. adv. com., 2002—04; mem. task force Racial Ethnic Bias & Adv. Com. DC Courts, 1990—92; mem. DC Ct. Appeals Bd. Prof. Responsibility, 1985—91, vice-chmn., 1988—89, chmn., 1989—91. Judge Adv. Gen. Corps USN, 1967—70 USNR, 1970—77. Mem.: US Ct. Fed. Claims Bar Assn. (bd. gov.). Office: US Ct Fed Claims 717 Madison Pl Washington DC 20005

MILLER, G(ERSON) H(ARRY), science administrator, mathematician, computer scientist, chemist; b. Phila., Mar. 2, 1924; m. Mary Alexa Heath, Jan. 28, 1961; children: Byron, Alexandra. BA, Pomona Coll., 1949; MEd in Counseling and Pers., Temple U., 1951; PhD. in Ednl. Psychology, U. So. Calif., 1957; MS in Math., U. Ill., 1982, postgrad., 1963-65. Jr. high sch. and jr. coll. instr. math. L.A. Sch. Dist., 1953-57; assoc. prof. Western Ill. U., Macomb, 1957-60; prof. Towson State U., Balt., 1960-61; prof. math. and edn. Parsons Coll., Fairfield, Iowa, 1961-65; prof. Tenn. Technol. U., Cookeville, 1966—68; prof. math. and computer sci. Edinboro (Pa.) U., 1968-71, 81-89, asst. dir. Institutional Rsch., 1972-80, emeritus prof., 1989—; dir. Studies On Smoking, Inc. and SOS Stop Smoking Clinic, Edinboro, 1972—. Dir. Nat. Study Math. Requirements for Scientists and Engrs., 1966-73; condr. Nat. Symposium for Am. Inst. Biol. Scis., Am. Chem. Soc. and Am. Soc. Engring. Educators, 1970-75; dir. Math. for Industry Confs.; spkr., presenter in field Contbr. numerous articles to profl. jours. Pres. Edinboro YMCA, 1972-83; bd. dirs. Common Cause, Harrisburg, Pa., 1975-80; Sgt. USAAF, 1943-46, PTO. Grantee U.S. Office Edn., 1968, 70, No Other World, 1973, NAS, 1980, ITT Life Ins. Corp., 1983, Erie County Found., 1987. Fellow Am. Inst. Chemists (cert. profl. chemist), AAAS; mem. APHA, Am. Assn. World Health, Am. Chem. Soc., Am. Soc. Engring. Edn., Internat. Assn. Pure and Applied Chemists, Internat. Soc. for Preventive Oncology, Math. Assn. Am., Am. Diabetes Assn., Sch. Sci. and Math. Assn., N.Y. Acad. Scis. (hon.), Acad. Sr. Profls. (hon.). Home (Summer): 25 Crescent Pl S Saint Petersburg FL 33711-5118 Home Phone: 727-867-8022. Personal E-mail: drghmiller@aol.com.

MILLER, GRAY HAMPTON, federal judge, lawyer; b. Houston, Dec. 9, 1948; Student, US Merchant Marine Acad.; BA, U. Houston, 1974, JD, 1978. Bar: Tex. 1978. Assoc. Fulbright & Jaworski LLP, Houston, 1978—86, head admiralty dept, 1996—2004, ptnr., 1986—2004, sr. ptnr., 2004—06; judge US Dist. Ct. (so. dist.) Tex., Houston, 2006—. Mem. ABA, Maritime Law Assn. U.S., State Bar Tex., Houston Bar Assn., Southeastern Admiralty Law Inst. (bd. dirs. 1989-91), Order of Barons. Office: US Dist Ct 515 Rusk Ave Houston TX 77002

MILLER, GREEN RUSSELL, economist, educator; b. Kenvir, Ky., Mar. 10, 1939; s. Clifford Wesley and Lorene (Farmer) M.; m. Carolyn Sue Blackburn, Oct. 7, 1966; children: Laura Marie, Russell Wesley. BA, U. Tex., El Paso, 1969; MA, U. Oreg., 1971; PhD, U. Ky., 1985. Instr. Transylvania U., Lexington, 1973—79; asst. prof. Sch. Pub. Affairs Ky. State U., Frankfort, 1977; prof. econs. Morehead State U., Ky., 1979—, dir. Ctr. for Econ. Edn., 1979—96. Bd. dirs. Ky. Coun. Econ. Edn., Louisville, 1979-96; cons. to various law firms, Ky., 1973—; supr. Cash-Fiscal Agy, El Paso Br. Fed. Reserve Bank of Dallas, 1959-1969; lectr. in field. Contbr. numerous articles to profl. jours. Coach Little League Baseball, Morehead, 1982-85, Youth Soccer League, 1985-86; bd. dirs. St. Albans Ch., Morehead, 1979-82, Gethsemane Luth. Ch., 1989-97; vol. One-on-One program Dept. of Corrections, Lexington, 1973-82, Morehead Cmty.Fed. Credit Union (treas. 1999-). With inf. U.S. Army, 1957-59. Mem. Midwest Econ. Assn., Ky. Econs. Assn., Internat. Bus. and Econ. Rsch. Assn. (Best Paper award, 2003), Mo. Valley Econ. Assn. (Jerome F. Schwier meritorious svc. award 1997), So. Econ. Assn., Ky. Assn. Ednl. Opportunity Program Pers., Joint Coun. on Econ. Edn., Nat. Assn. Econ. Educators, Ky. Coun. on Econ. Edn. (Outstanding Ctr. Dir. 1981-82), Assn. Ky. Econ. Educators (charter, original bylaws com., nominating com. 1985-93), Nat. Assn. Forensic Econs. (charter, bd. dirs. 1986-87, bus. editor Jour. Econs. 1990-97, chair acctg.-econs.-fin. 1988-2002), Southeastern Ky. Econ. Assn. (charter, chair

2004-06), Internat. Acad. Bus. and Pub. Rels. Adminstrn. Disciplines. Democrat. Lutheran-Episcopal. Avocations: hiking, reading. Home: 1240 Rodburn Hollow Rd Morehead KY 40351-9092 Office: Morehead State U UPO 1280 150 University Blvd Morehead KY 40351 Business E-Mail: g.miller@moreheadstate.edu.

MILLER, GREGORY JAMES, lawyer; b. New Bedford, Mass., Aug. 5, 1959; s. Martin. E. and Marjorie D. (Cohen) M. BA in History, Kalamazoo Coll., 1981; JD, N.Y. Law Sch., NYC, 1984. Bar: Conn. 1985, N.Y. 1985, U.S. Dist. Ct. Conn. (2d dist.) 1987. Assoc. Benenson & Kates, NYC, 1984-88, of counsel, 1988—2004; gen. counsel Gold Line Connector, Inc., West Redding, Conn., 1992—2004; of counsel Bainton McCarthy, LLC, Redding, Conn., 2004—. Bd. dirs. Command Security Corp., chmn. warrant com., mem. compensation and audit com., chmn. ind. dirs. com. Editor N.Y. Law Sch. Jour. of Human Rights, 1983-84. With U.S. Coast Guard, 2004—. Named Outstanding Young Man in Am. Jr. C. of C., 1984. Mem. N.Y. State Bar Assn., Conn. Bar Asn. Avocations: astronomy, Arabian horses, sailing. Home: 40 Great Pasture Rd West Redding CT 06896-2303 Office: Three Stamford Ave Stamford CT 06902-0500 Home Phone: 203-733-2887; Office Phone: 203-323-8080. E-mail: gmiller@gold-line.com.

MILLER, GREGORY KENT, structural engineer; b. Anaconda, Mont., July 6, 1951; s. Robert Bruce and Lois Patricia (Arvish) Miller. BS in Civil Engring./Engring. Mechanics, Mont. State U., 1973, MS in Engring. Mechanics, 1974. Project engr. U.S. Energy R&D Adminstrn., Idaho Falls, Idaho, 1974-77; structural engr. EG&G Idaho, Inc., Idaho Falls, 1977-93; supr. Lockheed Martin Idaho Technologies Co., Idaho Falls, 1994-99, BBWI, Idaho Falls, 1999—2005, Idaho Nat. Lab., Idaho Falls, 2005—. Contbr. articles to profl jours. Mem.: ASME (comt mem boiler and pressure vessel code sect III 1995—), Phi Kappa Phi (Sr of Yr 1973), Tau Beta Pi. Achievements include research in advanced modeling and analysis methods for evaluating failure of fuel particles in high-temperature gas-cooled reactors; contributed to technology for analyzing complex material behavior in pressure vessels; advanced methods for evaluating containers bearing nuclear materials for impact loads associated with accidental drop events. Office: Idaho Nat Lab Technologies Co PO Box 1625 Idaho Falls ID 83415-3855 Office Phone: 208-526-0360. Business E-Mail: gregoryk.miller@inl.gov.

MILLER, GREGORY R., prosecutor; BA, Drew U.; JD, Ohio No. U. Chief asst. US atty. (no. dist.) Fla. US Dept. Justice, Tallahassee, US atty. (no. dist.) Fla., 1993-98, asst. US atty. (no. dist.) Fla., 2000—02; US atty (no. dist.) Fla. US Dept Justice, Tallahassee, 2002—; assoc. Fowler, White, Gillen, Boggs, Villareal and Banker, PA, Tallahassee, 1998-2000. Office: US Attys Office 111 N Adams St Tallahassee FL 32301 Office Phone: 850-942-8430. Business E-Mail: gregory.miller@usdoj.gov. *

MILLER, H. TODD, lawyer; b. Buffalo, Sept. 19, 1947; s. Henry Opel and Irene Teresa (Hauck) M.; m. June Diehl Lancaster, Aug. 1, 1970; children: Catharine Maclay, Todd Lancaster, Peter Hanes. BA, SUNY, Buffalo, 1969; JD, Duke U., 1971. Bar: NC 1971, DC 1973. Jud. clerk to Hon. Charles R. Simpson US Tax Ct., Washington, 1971-73; assoc. atty. Hogan & Hartson LLP, Washington, 1973-78, ptnr., 1979—. Mem. Phi Beta Kappa, Order of the Coif. Episcopalian. Office: Hogan & Hartson Columbia Sq 555 13th St NW Ste 9W-312 Washington DC 20004-1161 Home Phone: 301-657-6223; Office Phone: 202-637-5667.

MILLER, HAROLD ARTHUR, lawyer; b. St. Marie, Ill., Aug. 18, 1922; s. Arthur E. and Luletta (Noé) M.; m. Michele H. Rogivue, Nov. 21, 1947; children: Maurice H., Jan Leland, Marc Richard. BS in Acctg., U. Ill., 1942, JD, 1950. Bar: Ill. 1950, U.S. Dist. Ct. Ill. 1950, U.S. Tax Ct. 1950, Fgn. svc. officer U.S. State Dept., Paris, France, 1945-48; ptnr. Filson, Williamson & Miller, Champaign, Ill., 1950-60, Williamson & Miller, Champaign, 1960-72, Miller & Hendren, Champaign, 1972—. Atty. Christie Clinic Found., Champaign, 1960—; atty. pub. schs. dists., Champaign & Vermilion Counties, Ill., 1960—; atty. for municipalities in Champaign County, Ill., 1970—. Author: Estate Planning for Doctors, 1961, Intervivos Trusts Alternative to Probate, 1996. Bd. dirs., officer Urbana Ill. Sch. Dist., 1957-69; chmn., trustee Parkland Coll., Champaign, 1971-91; founding bd. mem. CCDC Found., Champaign-Urbana Ednl. Found., Moore Heart Found., Christie Found.; life mem. PTA. With Spl. Svcs., U.S. Army, 1942-45, ETO. Mem. ABA, Am. Judicature Soc., Ill. and Local Bar Assns., Ill. Trial Lawyers Assn., Alpha Kappa Psi (trustee, atty.). Presbyterian. Office: Miller & Hendren Attys 30 E Main St #200 Champaign IL 61824-0980 Business E-Mail: ham@mhlawoffice.com.

MILLER, HAROLD EDWARD, retired manufacturing conglomerate executive, consultant; b. St. Louis, Nov. 23, 1926; s. George Edward and Georgenia Elizabeth (Franklin) M.; m. Lilian Ruth Gantner, Dec. 23, 1949; children— Ellen Susan, Jeffrey Arthur. BSBA, Washington U., St. Louis, 1949. Vice pres. Fulton Iron Works Co., St. Louis, 1968-71, pres., 1971-79, chmn. bd., 1979-90; v.p. Katy Industries Inc., Elgin, Ill., 1976-77, exec. v.p., 1978-90, also dir., to 1990; pres. HM Consulting, Palatine, Ill., 1990—. Internat. cons. Vigel Spa, Italy; v.p. Vigel U.S.A. Inc., 1996—. Served with U.S. Army, 1945-46. Mem. Barrington Tennis Club, Inverness Golf Club. Presbyterian. Office Phone: 847-991-7852. Personal E-mail: hmillercons84@sbcglobal.net.

MILLER, HARRIS N., educational association administrator; m. Deborah Miller, 1981; 2 children. BA summa cum laude, U. Pitts., 1972; MA, Yale U., 1975. Legis. asst. Subcom. on Immigration, Refugees and Internat. Law, Com. on Judiciary US Ho. of Reps., Washington; dep. dir. congl. rels. US Office of Personnel Mgmt.; legis. dir. for US Senator John A. Durkin US Senate; pres. Immigration Svcs. Assocs.; dir. govt. rels. Fragomen, Del Rey & Bernsen, PC; founder Harris Miller & Assocs.; pres. info. tech. Assoc. of Am., 1995—2005; pres. Info. Tech. Assn. Am., 1995, Career Coll. Assn. (CCA), Washington, 2007—. Bd. dirs. ITT Ednl. Svcs., Inc. Office: Career Coll Assn 1101 Connecticut Ave. NW Washington DC 20036 Office Phone: 202-336-6700. Office Fax: 202-336-6828. *

MILLER, HARRY FREEMAN, university administrator; b. Vallejo, Calif., Aug. 27, 1946; s. Theodore Harry and Grace (Eubank) M.; 1 child, Charissa Rainie. BA, Howard U., 1969; JD, U. Calif., Davis, 1972; cert., Harvard U., 1989, U. Chgo., 1998. Cert. fund raising exec. Grad. legal counsel Office of Calif. Atty. Gen., San Francisco, 1972—73; assoc. gen. sec. Stanford U., Palo Alto, Calif., 1973-79; asst. dean, lectr. law Syracuse (N.Y.) U., 1979-81; dir. devel. Georgetown U. Law Ctr., Washington, 1981-83; v.p. instnl. advt. Morgan State U., Balt., 1983-91; assoc. v.p., dir. planned giving U. South Fla., Tampa, 1991-95; assoc. v.p. devel. Tex. So. U., Houston, 1996—2000; dir. devel. Tex. A&M Inst. Bioscis. and Tech., Houston, 2001—. Host Lou Rawls Telethon for United Negro Coll. Fund, Syracuse, 1981, adv. com., Tampa, 1993-95; active Nat. Sports Festival Com., Syracuse, 1981; unit chmn. Tex. State Employees Charitable Campaign, 2003-06. Mem. Nat. Soc. Fund Raising Execs., Assn. Fund Raising Officers (bd. dirs. 1984-90), Assn. Fundraising Profls., Am. Inst. Parliamentarians, Assn. for Healthcare Philanthropy, Leadership Tampa, Tampa Urban League (bd. dirs. 1993-95), Phi Alpha Delta. Office: Texas A&M U System 2121 W Holcombe Blvd Houston TX 77030 Office Phone: 713-677-7559. Business E-Mail: hmiller@ibt.tamhsc.edu.

MILLER, HARVEY R., lawyer, bankruptcy reorganization specialist; b. Bklyn., Mar. 1, 1933; married AB, Bklyn. Coll., 1954; LLB, Columbia U. Law Sch., 1959. Bar: NY 1959, US Supreme Ct., US Ct. Appeals (2nd, 3rd, 4th, 5th and 9th cirs.), US Dist. Ct. (so. and ea. dists. NY). Positions up to sr. ptnr., chair bus. financing and restructuring grp. Weil, Gotshal & Manges, LLP, NYC, 1970—2002, 2007—; mng. dir., vice chmn. Greenhill & Co., 2002—07. Adj. assoc. prof. law NYU Law Sch., 1974—76, adj. prof. law, 1976—; vis. lectr. Yale Law Sch., 1983—84; lectr. law Columbia U. Sch. Law, 2000—. Bd. visitors Columbia U. Sch. Law. Fellow: Am. Bar Found., Am. Coll. Bankruptcy. Office: Weil Gotshal & Manges LLP 767 5th Ave Fl 29 New York NY 10153-0023 Office Phone: 212-389-1580, 212-310-8000. Office Fax: 212-389-1780, 212-310-8007. *

MILLER, HARVEY S. SHIPLEY, foundation trustee, philanthropist; b. Phila., Sept. 28, 1948; s. Frank Leroy and Betty Charlotte (Elfont) M. BA, Swarthmore Coll., 1970; JD, Harvard U., 1973, postgrad. Bar: N.Y. 1973. Assoc. Debevoise & Plimpton, NYC, 1973-75; curator and dir. dept. collections and spl. exhbns. Franklin Inst., Phila., 1975-81; v.p. Energy Solutions, Inc., NYC, 1982-84; pres., chief exec. officer, dir. Daltex Med. Scis., Inc., NYC, 1983-86, dir. exec. com., 1983-94, chief operating officer, vice chmn., 1986-91, pres., chief operating officer, 1991-93; trustee The Judith Rothschild Found., NYC, 1993—. Author: Milton Avery: Drawings and Paintings, 1976, It's About Time, 1979; author, editor: New Spaces: Exploring the Aesthetic Dimensions of Holography, 1979; co-author: Rapid Inactivation of Infectious Pathogens by Chlorhexidine-coated Gloves, 1992; contbr. articles to profl. jours. Mem. vis. com. on photography George Eastman House, Rochester, N.Y., 1976-78; trustee Milton and Sally Avery Arts Found., N.Y.C., 1983—, sec., 1996—; trustee The Franklin Inst., Phila., 1993-95, Phila. Mus. Art, 1985—, exec. com., 1993-96; assoc. trustee U. Pa., 1981-95; trustee Arcadia U., 2002-2005; bd. govs. Print Club, Phila., 1976-87; bd. overseers U. Pa. Sch. Nursing, 1981—, Edith C. Blum Art Inst. Bard Coll., 1984-87; bd. dirs., mem. corp. MacDowell Colony, N.Y.C., 1982-85; exec. bd. dirs. Fabric Workshop, Phila., 1976-86, hon. trustee, Miami Mu. Modern Art, 2004—; mem. prints and drawings and photographs trustees adv. com. Phila. Mus. Art, 1974—, trustee, 1985—, vice chmn., 2004—, investment com., 1989-95, exec., devel. and exhbn. coms., 1993-96, chair 125th ann. campaign, 1999-2002; mem. vis. com. 19th-century, modern, and contemporary art Met. Mus. Art, 1998—; bd. assocs. Swarthmore Coll. Librs., Phila., 1978-86; treas., dir. Arcadia Found., Norristown, Pa., 1981—; chmn. adv. bd. Inst. Contemporary Art U. Pa., 1982-84; trustee, vice chmn. coms. on instrn. Pa. Acad. Fine Arts, 1982-91, trustee emeritus, 1991—, chmn. collections and exhbns. com., 1985-87; trustee N.Y. Studio Sch., 1974-80, U. of the Arts, 1979-86; mem. exec. bd. Citizens for Arts in Pa., 1980; adv. bd. The Highlands Hist. Soc., 1999—; bd. dirs. Once Gallery, Inc., 1974-75, Wildlife Preservation Trust Internat., Inc., 1990-95; mem. Mayor's Cultural Adv. Coun., Phila., 1987-91; founding chair Mayor's Art-in-City Hall Program, Phila., 1992-94; trustees coun. Nat. Gallery Art, Washington, 1995-2000, 2001—06; mem. collections com. Hist. Soc. Pa., 1991-93, councilor trustee, 1992-93; mem. vis. com. photographs Met. Mus. Art, 1996—, vis. com. modern art, 1998—; mem. trustees' com. on drawings Mus. Modern Art, 1996—, trustee, 2003—, Prints and Illustrated Books, Museum of Modern Art, 2001—; mem. photography accessions com. San Francisco Mus. of Modern Art, 1997-2002; arts adv. com. Fund for the Waterworks, 1999-2001; founding mem., bd. trustees Maltz Jupiter (Fla.)Theatre, 2001—; bd. dirs. Am. Patrons of the Tate Gallery, 2003—; charter mem. The Drawings Group, L.A. County Mus. Art, 2003—; mem. drawings com. L.A. Mus. Contemporary Art, 2003—; bd. trustees Whitney Mus. Am. Art, 2004—; mem. Commn. on Drawing, 2005—, chmn. com. on drawings, 2004; bd. overseers Hammer Mus., L.A., 2004—; trustee Ursinus Coll., 2004—, Point Found., 2004—; collections com. Harvard U. Art Mus; bd. dirs. Salzburg Festival Soc., 2006—. Named 1st non-Russian recipient of Diploma of Merit, Russian Ministry of Culture, 2002; recipient Disting. Civic Svc. award, City Phila., 1997, Hon. Alumni award, U. Pa. Sch. Nursing, 2005. Fellow The Pierpont Morgan Libr., Coll. Physicians Phila.; mem. ABA, Assn. of Bar of City of N.Y., Athenaeum, Libr. Co. Phila., Am. Philos. Soc., Hist. Soc. Pa., Phila. Art Alliance, Union League of Phila., Harvard Club of N.Y.C., Swarthmore Club Phila., Palm Beach Yacht Club, Sunnybrook Golf Club, Phi Sigma Kappa. Republican. Home: Plumlyn 7036 Sheaff Ln Fort Washington PA 19034-2017 Office: 1110 Park Ave New York NY 10128-1201

MILLER, HARVEY WILLIAM, retired military officer; b. LaCrosse, Wis., Nov. 20, 1919; s. Carl William and Charlotte (Lumley) Miller; m. Marylin Buck Grindle, May 16, 1995; m. Daphne Olive Roddy, Dec. 29, 1942 (dec. Jan. 1995); children: Charlene, David, Peggy. BS with honors, U. Wis., Madison, 1941; MS, Mont. State Coll., Bozeman, 1942. Cert. tchr. history and bus. econs. grades 9-12 Va. Officer and pilot to lt. comdr. US Navy, 1943—65, prof. naval scis., 1955—58; mideast navy intelligence officer Morocco, 1959—61; intelligence officer USS Enterprise CVA(N) 65, 1961—63, Def. Intelligence Agy., Arlington, Va., 1963—65; indusl. intelligence CIA, Langley, Va., 1965—76. Mgr. officers club, Honolulu, 1947. Pres. Country Club Hills Civic Assn., Fairfax City, Va., 1968—74; mgr. Little League, Port Lyautey, Morocco, 1960—61; chmn. Hawaiian Island Luth. Evang. Inst.; mem. sch. bd. Lutheran Sch., Richfield, Minn., 1956—58; tchr. adult Bible sch. base chapel Port Lyautey, Morocco, 1959—61. Mem.: Mil. Officer Assn. Am., Nat. Active and Ret. Fed. Employees Assn. (pres. Va. Chpt. 1885 1985—, pres. Fla. Chpt. 583 2005—06). Democrat. Lutheran. Avocations: genealogy, square dancing, bowling, golf, softball. Home: 6332 Lomand Ave New Port Richey FL 34653 Personal E-mail: harlinmill@juno.com.

MILLER, HEIDI G., diversified financial company executive; b. 1951; married; 2 children. BA in History, Princeton U., 1974; PhD in History, Yale U., 1979. Various positions to mng. dir. emerging markets structured finance group Chemical Bank, 1979—92; joined as v.p. and asst. to the pres. Travelers Group, 1992, CFO, 1995—98, Citigroup (merger of Citibank and Travelers Group), NYC, 1998—2000; CFO, sr. exec. v.p. strategic planning and adminstrn. Priceline.com, Norwalk, Conn., 2000; vice chmn. Marsh & McLennan Co., Inc., NYC, 2001—02; exec. v.p. strategy and devel., CFO Bank One Corp., 2002—04; exec. v.p., CEO, treasury & securities div. J.P. Morgan Chase & Co. (merger of Bank One Corp. and J.P. Morgan Chase & Co.), NYC, 2004—. Bd. dirs. General Mills Inc., 1999—, Merck & Co., Inc., 2000—04, Bank One Corp., 2000—02, Local Initiatives Support Corp., 2004—. Trustee Princeton U., NYU Med. Sch. Named one of 50 Most Powerful Women in Bus., Fortune mag., 2006, 25 Most Powerful Women in Banking, US Banker, 2006. Avocation: yoga. Office: JP Morgan Chase & Co 270 Park Ave New York NY 10017 *

MILLER, HELEN ELIZABETH, art educator, adult education educator, artist; d. David Allen and Judith Busch (Stepmother), Ronald Raymond (Stepfather) and Christine Delores Mistarz; m. Todd Charles Miller, Aug. 8, 1998; 1 child, Samantha Alexandria. BA magna cum laude, Calumet Coll., 1995; MA, Ind. U., 1999; post-grad., U. Phoenix. Tchr. art Waukegan Sch. Sys., Ill., 2002—03, 2004—07, lead art tchr., 2005—; tchr. art Round Lake HS, Round Lake, 2003—04. Organizer clothing drive Carman Buckner Sch., Waukegan, Ill., 2004. Prin. works include 11 murals, Waukegan Sch. Sys. Grantee, Walmart, 2004. Green Party. Roman Catholic. Avocations: painting, drawing, scuba diving, bicycling, ceramics. Home: 330 Greenview Ln Lake Villa IL 60046 Office: Waukegan Sch Dist 60 Sheridan Rd Waukegan IL 60085 Office Phone: 847-360-5478. Personal E-mail: helenemiller@yahoo.com.

MILLER, HENRY FORSTER, architect; b. Sept. 16, 1916; s. Rutger Bleecker and Dorothy (Forster) M.; m. Maria Stockton Bullitt, Apr. 6, 1942; children: Maria, Andrew, Dorothy, Steven, Henry Jr. BA, Yale U., 1938, MArch, 1948. Registered architect, Conn., R.I., Mass. Instr. archtl. design Yale Sch. Architecture, New Haven, 1948-49; assoc. dir. facilities planning office Yale U., New Haven, 1974-90; assoc. Harold H. Davis Architect, New Haven, 1949-56; ptnr. Davis, Cochran & Miller, New Haven, 1956-69, Davis, Cochran, Miller, Baerman, Noyes, New Haven, 1969-74; pvt. practice Orange, Conn., 1990—. Pres. Conn. Bldg. Congress, 1957-58. Prin. works include Booth Meml. Boys Club Bldg. (Archtl. Design award 1971), Columbus Sch. New Haven (HUD Design Excellence award 1970), Orange Conn. residence (listed on Nat. Register of Historic Places 2001). Mem. bd. govs. New Haven Boys and Girls Club, 1956-93; v.p. Comty. Coun. Greater New Haven, 1964-66; apptd. mem. State Housing Commn., Conn., 1970-72; mem. Conn. Rev. Bd. for Nat. Register of Hist. Places, 1974-81; founding dir. Conn. Trust for Hist. Preservation, 1975-86, pres., 1975-77; bd. dirs. New Haven Preservation Trust. Maj. F.A. AUS, 1941-46, ETO. Decorated Bronze Star medal (2). Fellow AIA (Conn. state preservation coord. 1965-90, exec. com. 1967-69), Mory's Assn. Democrat. Roman Catholic. Avocations: drawing, painting.

MILLER, HENRY FRANKLIN, lawyer; b. Phila., May 19, 1938; s. Lester and Bessie (Posner) M.; m. Barbara Ann Gendel, June 20, 1964; children: Andrew, Alexa. AB, Lafayette Coll., 1959; JD, U. Pa., 1964. Bar: Pa. 1965. Law clk. U.S. Dist. Ct. Del., Wilmington, 1964-65; assoc. Wolf, Block, Schorr & Solis-Cohen LLP, Phila., 1965—71, ptnr., 1971—. Pres. Soc. Hill Synagogue, Phila., 1978-79, Big Brothers/Big Sisters Assn. of Phila., 1980-81, Jewish Family & Children's Agy., Phila., 1986-88. 1st lt. U.S. Army, 1959-60. Mem. Am. Coll. Real Estate Lawyers. Avocations: swimming, hiking, bicycling, reading. Office: Wolf Block Schorr & Solis-Cohen LLP 1650 Arch St Fl 21 Philadelphia PA 19103-2029 Home Phone: 215-925-6408; Office Phone: 215-977-2182. Business E-Mail: hmiller@wolfblock.com.

MILLER, HERBERT DELL, petroleum engineer; b. Oklahoma City, Sept. 29, 1919; s. Merrill Dell and Susan (Green) M.; m. Rosalind Rebecca Moore, Nov. 23, 1947; children: Rebecca Miller Wheeler, Robert Rexford. BS in Petroleum Engring., Okla. U., Norman, 1941. Registered profl. engr., Okla., Tex. Field engr. Amerada Petroleum Corp., Hobbs, N.Mex., 1947—48, Houston, 1948—49, dist. engr. Longview, Tex., 1949—57, sr. engr. Tulsa, 1957—62; petroleum engr. Moore & Miller Oil Co., Oklahoma City, 1962—78; owner Herbert D. Miller Co., Oklahoma City, 1978—. Maj., F.A. AUS, 1941—47, ETO. Decorated Bronze Star with oak leaf cluster, Purple Heart (U.S.); Croix de Guerre (France). Mem. AIME, Oklahoma City Golf. Republican. Episcopalian (pres. Men's Club 1973). Home and Office: 1819 W Wilshire Blvd Oklahoma City OK 73116-4115

MILLER, HERBERT ELMER, accountant; b. DeWitt, Iowa, Aug. 11, 1914; s. Elmer Joseph and Marian (Briggs) M.; m. Lenore Snitkey, July 1, 1938; 1 dau., Barbara Ruth. AB, State U. Iowa, 1936, MA, 1937; PhD, U. Minn., 1944; Dr. h.c., Free U. Brussels, 1982; D.H.L. (h.c.), De Paul U., 1983. C.P.A., Iowa. Acctg. prof. U. Minn., U. Mich., Mich. State U., 1938-70; ptnr. Arthur Andersen & Co., Chgo., 1970-78; dir. Sch. Acctg., U. Ga., Athens, 1978-83. Co-author: Finney-Miller accounting series, 1950-70; editor, contbr.: C.P.A. Rev. Manual, 1951-79. Mem. AICPA (bd. dirs. 1968-70), Am. Acctg. Assn. (pres. 1965-66), Federated Sch. Acctg. (pres. 1982), Beta Gamma Sigma, Beta Alpha Psi (nat. pres. 1961-62) Home: 145 S Stratford Dr Athens GA 30605-3025

MILLER, HERBERT H., lawyer; b. Balt., May 24, 1921; s. Louis Miller and Rebecca Platt; m. Irene R. Rosen, Aug. 27, 1944; children: Rose, Marjorie, Fran. JD cum laude, U. Balt., 1942; ABA in Acctg., Balt. Coll. of Commerce, 1947. Bar: Md. 1943, U.S. Dist. Ct. Md. 1944, U.S. Supreme Ct. 1986; notary pub. Md. Law clk. Rubenstein and Rubenstein, Balt., 1938-39, Joel J. Hochman, Balt., 1939-40, Feikin & Talkin, Balt., 1940-42; atty. Sherbow, Harris & Medwedeff, Balt., 1942-43, Harris & Medwedeff, Balt., 1943-45; pvt. practice Balt. and Towson, Md., 1946—. Mem. inquiry panel Atty. Grievance Com. Md., Balt. County, 1985—; panel chmn. Health Claims Arbitration, Balt., 1994—. Bd. trustees Balt. Coll. Commerce, 1948-52, Beth El Congregation, Balt. County, 1990-94; youth advisor B'nai B'rith, Balt., 1943-88, mem. B'nai B'rith Youth Orgn., pres., 1940-42. Mem. Md. State Bar Assn., Balt. City Bar Assn., Balt. County Bar Assn., Mensa Internat. (arbitrator Md.). Avocations: reading, handyman work, walking. Office: 200 E Joppa Rd Ste 205 Towson MD 21286-3107 Office Phone: 410-823-3340.

MILLER, HOLLY DARA, hospital administrator, physician; d. Algernon Maxwell and Constance Arlene (Becker) Miller; m. Allan Eric Siperstein, Nov. 12, 1995; children: Alden David Siperstein, Marion Alice Siperstein; m. Eric Albert Leon Meary, June 8, 1988 (div. 1995); 1 child, Aldea Marine Meary. MD, Albert Einstein Coll. of Medicine, NYC, 1987; Internship, St. Vincent's Hosp., NYC, 1989; MBA, ISA, Groupe HEC, Paris, 1994; Residency, Gen. Internal Medicine, U. Calif., San Francisco, 1996. Rsch. project mgr. Ciba-Geigy, Paris, 1990—92; staff physician On Lok Sr. Health Svcs., U. Calif., San Francisco, 1996—98; product mgr., mktg. dept. Oacis Healthcare Sys., San Rafael, Calif., 1998—99; mng. dir. The Cleve. Clinic, 1999—2007; v.p., chief med. info. officer Univ. Hosps., Shaker Heights, 2007—. Mem. editl. bd. MD Net Guide, Plainsboro, NJ, 2004—; mem. bd. dirs. Alpha - 1 Found., Fla., 2005—; mem. healthcare practice task force Nat. Gov.'s Assn., 2006; chair PHR steering com. Healthcare Info., Mgmt. Soc. Author: (articles) JAMIA. Grantee French-American Exch. Program, The French Govt., 1987, Rsch. in Healthcare Informatics, Robert Wood Johnson Found., 2004, Healthcare Informatics Rsch., Agy. for Healthcare and Rsch., 2004; scholar Josiah Macy Scholarship for Basic Sci. Rsch., Columbia U., 1982, Internat. Exch. Program, ISA, Groupe Hautes Etudes Commercials, 1993. Mem.: AMA. Achievements include research in ongoing funded research in Heathcare Informatics. Office: U Hosps MSC 8200 3605 Warrensville Ctr Rd Shaker Heights OH 44122 Office Phone: 216-767-8181.

MILLER, I. GEORGE, physician, educator, researcher; b. Chgo., Apr. 18, 1937; s. Irving George and Florence (Levy) M.; m. Arlette Goldmuntz, Mar. 25, 1962; children: Lisa, John, David. AB, Harvard U., 1958, MD, 1962. Intern Univ. Hosp., Western Res. U., Cleve., 1962-63; resident Univ. Hosp., Western Res., U., Cleve., 1963-64; epidemiology intelligence oficer Communicable Disease Ctr. USPHS, Atlanta, 1964-66; research fellow in medicine Harvard U. Med. Sch., Boston, 1966-69; asst. prof. pediatrics, epidemiology, biophysics and biochemistry Yale Sch. Medicine, New Haven, 1969-72, J.F. Enders prof., 1979—. Mem. exptl. virology study sect. NIH, 1974-77; mem. sci. adv. com. Damon Runyon Fund, 1979-85, dir., 1985-94; Leukemia Soc. Am., 1976-81. Contbr. numerous articles, chpts. to profl. publs.; editl. bd. Jour. Virology, 1981-87, Virology, 1982-86. Recipient epidemic Intelligence Service Alumni Assn. prize, 1967; Macy faculty scholar, 1977, Am. Cancer Soc. scholar, 1990; Howard Hughes Med. Inst. investigatorship, 1972-80 Fellow Infectious Diseases Soc. (Squibb award 1982, Enders award 1989); mem. Am. soc. Clin. Investigation, Am. Pediatric Soc., Am. Soc. Virology, Assn. Am. Physicians, Inst. Medicine. Jewish. Office: Yale U Sch Medicine Pediatrics Infectious Diseases PO Box 208064 New Haven CT 06520-8064 Home Phone: 203-389-6621; Office Phone: 203-785-4758. Business E-Mail: george.miller@yale.edu.

MILLER, ILANA DEBORAH, history professor; b. Santa Monica, Calif., Apr. 29, 1953; d. Sherman and Gloria Theresa Miller. MA, Pepperdine U., Malibu, Calif., 1988. Adj. prof. Pepperdine U., 1989—. Author: Reports from America, 2001, The Four Graces: Queen Victoria's Hessian Granddaughters, 2007; sr. editor: European Royal History Jour., 2003—. Independent. Jewish. Avocation: travel. Home Phone: 310-393-4062. Personal E-mail: ilanadeb@adelphia.net.

MILLER, IRVING FRANKLIN, chemical, biomedical engineer, academic administrator, educator; b. NYC, Sept. 27, 1934; s. Sol and Gertrude (Rochkind) M.; m. Baila Hannah Milner, Jan. 28, 1962; children: Eugenia Lynne, Jonathan Mark. BS in Chem. Engring., NYU, 1955; MS, Purdue U., 1956; PhD, U. Mich., 1960. Rsch. scientist United Aircraft Corp., Hartford, 1959-61; from asst. prof. to prof., head chem. engring. Poly. Inst. Bklyn., 1961-72; prof. bioengring., head bioengring. program U. Ill., Chgo., 1973-79, acting head sys. engring. dept., 1978-79, assoc. vice chancellor rsch., dean Grad. Coll., 1979-85, prof. chem. engring., head chem. engring., 1986-95, dir. Ctr. Advanced Edn. and Rsch., 1989-90, dir. Office Spl. Projects, 1990-92, dir. bioengring. program, 1992-95; dean Coll. Engring. U. Akron, Ohio, 1995-98, prof. biomed. engring., 1998-2000; dir. corp. ops. BioTechPlex Corp., 2002—06. Cons. to industry; cons. NAS, NIH; dir. distance learning programs Ohio Aerospace Inst., 1998—2000. Editor: Electrochemical Bioscience and Bioengineering, 1973; contbr. articles profl. jours. Mem. AIChE, AAAS, Am. Chem. Soc., Biomed. Engring. Soc., N.Y. Acad Scis. Home: 1746 N Larrabee St Chicago IL 60614-5634 Office Phone: 312-266-1728. Personal E-mail: ifmiller@sbcglobal.net. Business E-Mail: ifmiller@uic.edu.

MILLER, J. ALLEN, lawyer; b. July 21, 1951; BA cum laude, U. NH, 1972; JD, Cornell U., 1979. Bar: NY 1980. Ptnr., chmn. Corp. Dept. Chadbourne & Parke LLP, NYC, co-coord., Latin Am. Practice Group. Spkr. in field; contbr. articles to profl. jour.; note & comment editor Cornell Internat. Law Jour., 1978—79. Mem.: ABA, NY State Bar Assn. Office: Chadbourne & Parke LLP 30 Rockefeller Plz New York NY 10112 Office Phone: 212-408-5454. Office Fax: 212-541-5369. Business E-Mail: amiller@chadbourne.com.

MILLER, JACK (JOHN PETER MILLER), journalist; b. Aug. 3, 1928; s. Wesley and Margaret (Baker) M.; m. Helen DeMars, July 30, 1949 (dec.); children: Candice(dec.), Gregory(dec.). Student, Welland and Toronto. From sports page editor to front page editor Welland Evening Tribune, 1949—53; with Hamilton (Ont.) Spectator, 1953—71, radio and TV columnist, 1955—71; with Toronto Daily Star, 1971—91, radio and TV columnist, 1971—78, comm. editor, 1979—85, sci. columnist, 1982—85, sci. writer, 1985—89, sci. editor, 1989—91, sci. corr., 1991—95; prof. journalism Niagara Coll., 1996—99. Frequent TV and radio appearances. Contbr. stories to mags. Mem.: Can. Sci. Writers Assn. (2 writing awards 1985, writing award 1987, 2 writing awards 1988, writing award 1989). Office: 162 Martindale Rd Apt 501 Saint Catharines ON L2S 3S4 Canada E-mail: jackasinmiller@yahoo.com.

MILLER, JACK CONWAY, small business owner, landscape company executive; b. Collegeville, Pa., Jan. 23, 1924; s. John W. and Marguerite Blanche (Conway) Miller; m. Marguerite F. Martin, Feb. 10, 1948 (dec. Feb. 1978); children: Lynne, Craig, Mark(dec.), Susan; m. Carmen Aline Morin, Sept. 9, 1983. BSc, Phila. Coll. Pharmacy & Sci., 1944, MSc, 1948; PhD in Art Therapy (hon.), La. State U., 1988. Mgr. Ampul & Injection dept. McNeil Labs., Phila., 1948—52; sales mgr. Curtiss Breeding Svcs., Gary, Ill., 1952—71; co-founder Indoor Racket Complex Frog Hollow, Inc., Worcester, Pa., 1970—71; owner, operator Equity Semen Svcs., Inc., Trappe, Pa., 1970—76; co-owner, officer, operator Village Market, Inc., Boyertown, Pa., 1971—73; co-owner Equity Art Svcs., Collegeville, 1977—; creator, owner traditional Japanese moss garden Dans La Forêt, Collegeville, 1981—; owner Dans La Forêt Gardens & Nursery, Collegeville, 1981—; co-owner Morin-Miller Galleries, NYC, 1985—90; prin. Japanese Gardens Landscaper, 1991—. Cons. bamboo installation Phila. Mus. Art, 2000; writer, lectr., tchr. in field. Landscaper (prin. works) expansion Pagoda Gardens, Bala Cynwyd, 1992, Rosemont sect., Montreal, Que., Can., 1997, Japanese Zen Garden, Pagoda 100, Pagoda 10, 1999, creator, owner Kare san-sui Dnas La Foret, Collegeville, Pa., 1981—2000 (included in Archives of Am. Gardens, Smithsonian Instn.), creator Brown-Round granite sculpture, Biral Hill Farm, Ambler, Pa.; editor: Pa. Farm-O-Gram Dairy newsletter, 1965—71. Bd. dirs. Pa. All Am. Dairy Show, Harrisburg, 1970, 1971. Capt. inf. and combat engrs. US Army, 1944—46, ETO, PTO. Mem.: Rock Garden Soc., Pa. Horticultural Soc., Am. Rhododendron Soc. Achievements include having works included in Archives of Am. Gardens at the Smithsonian Inst., Washington. Avocations: music, reading, travel.

MILLER, JACK DAVID R., radiologist, physician, educator; b. Johannesburg, Apr. 15, 1930; s. Harold Lewis and Inez (Behrman) M.; m. Miriam Sheckter, Dec., 1988. B.Sc., M.B., Ch.B., U. Witwatersrand, Johannesburg, 1956. Diplomate: Am. Bd. Radiology. Intern Coronation Hosp., Johannesburg, 1957-58; resident in radiology Passavant Meml. Hosp., Chgo., 1959-62, Wesley Meml. Hosp., Chgo., 1959-62; fellow in radiology Northwestern U. Med. Sch., 1962-63; chmn. dept. radiology U. Hosp., Edmonton, Alta., Canada, 1971-83; radiologist, dept. radiology U. Alta Hosp., 1963—2004, head, dir. neuroradiology, 1984—92; prof. emeritus radiology U. Alta., 1997—. Clin. prof. radiology U. Alta., 1971—Fellow Royal Coll. Physicians Can., Am. Coll. Radiology. Personal E-mail: miribud@shaw.ca.

MILLER, JACQUELINE WINSLOW, library director; b. NYC, Apr. 15, 1935; d. Lynward Roosevelt and Sarah Ellen (Grevious) W.; 1 child, Percy Scott. BA, Morgan State Coll., 1957; MLS, Pratt Inst., 1960; grad. profl. seminar, U. Md., 1973. Cert. profl. libr. With Bklyn. Pub. Libr., 1957-68; head ext. svcs. New Rochelle (N.Y.) Pub. Libr., 1969-70; br. adminstr. Grinton Will Yonkers (N.Y.) Pub. Libr., 1970-75; dir. Yonkers Pub. Libr., 1975-96. Mem. adj. faculty grad. libr. studies Queens Coll., CUNY, 1989, 90. Mem. commr.'s com. Statewide Libr. Devel., Albany, N.Y., 1980; mem. N.Y. Gov.'s Commn. on Librs., 1990, 91; bd. dirs. Cmty. Planning Coun., Yonkers, N.Y., 1987; mem. Yonkers Black Women's Polit. Caucus, 1987; pres. bd. Literacy Vols. of Westchester County, 1991-92; mem. fair campaign practices com. LWV, 1996—. Recipient Yonkers Citizen award Ch. of Our Saviour, 1980, 2d Ann. Mae Morgan Robinson award Yonkers chpt. Westchester Black Women's Polit. Caucus, 1992, 3d Ann. Equality Day award City of Yonkers, 1992, African-Am. Heritage 1st award YWCA, 1994; named Outstanding Profl. Woman Nat. Assn. Negro Bus. and Profl. Women's Clubs Inc., 1981. Mem. ALA (councilor 1987-91), N.Y. State Libr. Assn., Pub. Libr. Dirs. Assn. (exec. bd.), N.Y. State Pub. Libr. Dirs. Assn., Westchester Libr. Assn., Yonkers C. of C. (bd. dirs. 1992-95), Educate the Girls, Inc. (bd. dirs., 2003—) Rotary (Yonkers chpt.). Personal E-mail: jacki@sprynet.com.

MILLER, JAMES CLIFFORD, III, economist; b. Atlanta, June 25, 1942; s. James Clifford and Annie (Moseley) M.; m. Demaris Humphries, Dec. 22, 1961; children: Katrina Demaris, John Felix, Sabrina Louise. BBA, U. Ga., 1964; PhD in Econs., U. Va., 1969; LLD (hon.), U. of Pacific, 1987; PhD (hon.), Kennesaw Coll., 1988. Asst. prof. Ga. State U., Atlanta, 1968-69; economist U.S. Dept. Transp., Washington, 1969-72; assoc. prof. econs. Tex. A&M U., College Station, 1972-74; economist U.S. Coun. Econ. Advs., Washington, 1974-75; asst. dir. U.S. Council Wage and Price Stability, Washington, 1975-77; resident scholar Am. Enterprise Inst., 1977-81; adminstr. Office Info. and Regulatory Affairs, Office Mgmt. and Budget and exec. dir. Presdl. Task Force on Regulatory Relief, Washington, 1981; chmn. FTC, Washington, 1981-85; dir. Office Mgmt. and Budget, Washington, 1985-88; disting. fellow, chmn., counsellor Citizens for a Sound Economy, 1988—2002; disting. fellow Ctr. for Study of Pub. Choice George Mason U., 1988—2002; sr. fellow Hoover Instn., 1988—. Pres., chmn. bd. Econ. Impact Analysts, Inc., 1978-02; chmn. or chmn. emeritus CapAnalysis Group of Howrey, 2002-06; bd. govs. US Postal Svc., 2003-, chmn., 2005-; sr. advisor Blackwell Sanders Peper Martin, 2006-. Author: Why the Draft?: The Case for a Volunteer Army, 1968, Economic Regulation of Domestic Air Transport: Theory and Policy, 1974, Perspectives on Federal Transportation Policy, 1975, Benefit-Cost Analyses of Social Regulation: Case Studies from the Council on Wage and Price Stability, 1979, Reforming Regulation, 1980, The Federal Trade Commission: The Political Economy of Regulation, 1987, The Economist as Reformer, 1989, Fix the U.S. Budget: Urgings of an "Abominable No-Man", 1994, Monopoly Politics, 1999. Candidate for Rep. nomination for U.S. Senate for Va., 1994, 96. Thomas Jefferson fellow, 1965-66, DuPont fellow, 1966-67, Ford Found. fellow, 1967-68. Mem. Am. Econ. Assn., Pub. Choice Soc., So. Econ. Assn. (exec. com. 1980-81, v.p. 1990-91), Adminstrv. Conf. U.S. (vice chmn. 1987-88). Republican. Baptist. Office: 750 17th St NW #1000 Washington DC 20006 Office Phone: 202-378-2302. Business E-Mail: jim@jimmiller.org.

MILLER, JAMES FORREST, lawyer; b. Sioux City, Ia., Jan. 28, 1952; AB magna cum laude, Dartmouth Coll., 1974; JD, Columbia Univ., 1977. Bar: DC 1978. Litigator, tax divsn. US Dept. Justice; sp. counsel US Dept. Treasury, 1989—93; ptnr., regulated industries, govtl. rels. Hunton & Williams LLP, Washington. Recipient Stone Scholar. Office: Hunton & Williams LLP 1900 K St NW Washington DC 20006-1109 Office Phone: 202-955-1934. Office Fax: 202-778-2201. Business E-Mail: jfmiller@hunton.com.

MILLER, JAMES GEGAN, research scientist; b. St. Louis, Nov. 11, 1942; s. Francis John and Elizabeth Ann (Caul) M.; m. Judith Anne Kelvin, Apr. 23, 1966; 1 child, Douglas Ryan. AB, St. Louis U., 1964; MA, Washington U., 1966, PhD, 1969. Asst. prof. physics Washington U., St. Louis, 1970-72, assoc. prof., 1972-77, prof. physics, 1977—, dir. lab. for ultrasonics, 1987—, rsch. asst. prof. medicine, 1976-81, rsch. assoc. prof. medicine, 1981-88, rsch. prof. medicine, 1988-2000, prof. biomed. engring., 1998—, Albert Gordon Hill prof. physics, 1999—, prof. medicine, 2000—. Contbr. articles to profl. jours.; patentee in field. Recipient I-R 100 award, Indsl. Research Devel. Mag., 1974, 1978, Merit award, NIH, 1998, Tchg. award, Emerson U., 2004; grantee, NIH, NASA. Fellow IEEE (sr., gov. com. Ultrasonics, Ferroelectrics and Frequency Control Soc. 1978-80,86-88, 92-94, Achievement award 2006), Am. Inst. Ultrasound in Medicine, Acoustical Soc. Am. (Silver medal 2004), Am. Inst. Med. and Biol. Engring.; mem. Am. Phys. Soc., Sigma Xi (nat. lectr. 1981-82). Office: Washington Univ St Louis Physics Dept CB 1105 One Brookings Dr Saint Louis MO 63130 Office Phone: 314-935-6229. Business E-Mail: james.g.miller@wustl.edu.

MILLER, JAMES H., electric power industry executive; BSEE, U. Del. Plant engr. Pub. Svc. Electric & Gas, Salem, NJ; various Delmarva Power & Light Co.; v.p. ops., constrn. and engring. ABB Resource Recovery Sys., pres., 1990-93, U.C. Oper. Svcs., 1993-94, ABB Envrion. Sys. Inc., Birmingham, Ala., 1994-95; exec. v.p. prodn., nuc. regulatory and environ. affairs USEC Inc., Bethesda, Md., 1995—99, exec. v.p., COO, 1999—2001; pres. PPL Generation PPL Corp., Allentown, Pa., 2001—04, exec. v.p., COO, 2004—05, pres., COO, 2005—06, chmn., pres., CEO, 2006—. With USN. Office: PPL Corp 2 N 9th St Allentown PA 18101-1179 *

MILLER, JAMES MONROE, lawyer; b. Owensboro, Ky., Apr. 20, 1948; s. James Rufus and Tommie (Melton) M.; m. Patricia Kirkpatrick, Nov. 28, 1975; children: Marian Elizabeth, James Graham. Student, George Washington U., 1966-67; BE, U. Ky., 1970, JD, 1973. Bar: Ky. 1973, U.S. Dist. Ct. Ky. 1973, U.S. Ct. Appeals (6th cir.) 1976, U.S. Supreme Ct. 1976. Law clk. to chief judge U.S. Dist. Ct. (we. dist.) Ky., Louisville and Owensboro, 1973-74; mng. ptnr. Sullivan, Mountjoy, Stainback & Miller, P.S.C., Owensboro, 1974—80, 2000—. Mem. Leadership Ky., 1988, Leadership Owensboro, 1986; bd. dirs. Leadership Ky. Found., 2002-; sec. Owensboro-Daviess County Indsl. Found., Inc. Mem. ABA, Ky. Bar Assn. (chmn. Law Day/Spkrs. Bur. com. 1989-91), Daviess County Bar Assn., Ky. Coun. on Higher Edn. (chmn. programs com. 1991-93, chmn. 1993-96), Coun. Postsecondary Edn., Gov.'s Higher Edn. Rev. Commn. (chmn. 1993), Gov.'s Task Force on Tchr. Edn. Democrat. Methodist. Avocations: fishing, hunting, hiking, golf, skiing. Home: 1920 Sheridan Pl Owensboro KY 42301-4525 Office: Sullivan Mountjoy Stainback & Miller PSC PO Box 727 100 Saint Ann St Owensboro KY 42303-4144 Office Phone: 270-926-4000. Business E-Mail: jmiller@smsmlaw.com.

MILLER, JAMES RUMRILL, III, finance educator; b. Phila., Dec. 21, 1937; s. James Rumrill and Elizabeth Pleasants (King) M.; m. Bettie M. Studer, May 1, 1989 (div. Jan. 2007); children from previous marriage: Elizabeth, Katharine, Kerry. AB, Princeton U., 1959; MBA (Woodrow Wilson fellow), Harvard U., 1962; PhD, MIT, 1966. Sys. analyst MITRE Corp., Bedford, Mass., 1962—67; asst. prof. bus. adminstrn. Stanford U., Calif., 1967—69, assoc. prof., 1970—73, prof., 1973—, Walter and Elise Haas prof. bus. adminstrn., 1977—97, assoc. dean Bus. Sch., 1974—76, Walter and Elise Haas prof. bus. adminstrn. emeritus, 1997—. Cons. in field. Author: Professional Decision Making, 1970; contbr. numerous articles to profl. jours. Mem. Phi Beta Kappa. Republican. Episcopalian. Office: 16641 W Loma Verde Trail Surprise AZ 85387 E-mail: mdmsinc@aol.com.

MILLER, JAMES VINCE, university president; b. Waynetown, Ind., July 16, 1920; s. J. Vince and Hazel B. (Spore) M.; m. Mildred Mae Hockersmith, June 13, 1943; children: Maryllyn Jean, Rachel Katherine. BA in Philosophy and English, U. Indpls., 1942; M.Div. in History and Lit., United Sem., Dayton, Ohio, 1945; postgrad., Earlham Coll., 1945-46; PhD in Philosophy, Boston U., 1955; LL.D. (hon.), Otterbein Coll., 1971, U. Indpls., 1979. Ordained to ministry Evang. United Brethren Ch., 1945; pastor Greensfork, Ind., 1944-46, Stow, Mass., 1946-48; faculty dept. philosophy and religion Bates Coll., Lewiston, Maine, 1950-64, prof., 1960-64, chmn. dept., 1958-64; acad. dean Otterbein Coll., Westerville, Ohio, 1964-68, v.p. for acad. affairs, acad. dean, 1968-71; pres. Pacific U., Forest Grove, Oreg., 1971-83, pres. emeritus, 1983—; pres. Nat. Coll. of Naturopathic Medicine, Portland, Oreg., 1989-93, pres. emeritus, 1993—. Adj. prof. Union Grad. Sch., 1970-78, San Francisco Theol. Sem., 1979-86; chmn. N.W. Assn. Pvt. Colls. and Univs., 1974-76; treas. Oreg. Ind. Coll. Assn., 1974-75, 76-78, chmn., 1978-79; adv. com. Oreg. Edn. Coordinating Commn., 1976-79; chmn. council for higher edn. United Ch. Bd. Homeland Missions, 1975-76; former mem. adv. com. Gov.'s Listening Post; former mem. spl. com. on future of edn. in Oreg., Oreg. Edn. Coordinating Commn.; former mem. Oreg. Bd. Optometry, 1988-92. Methodist. Address: 1633 Mowry Sq Richland WA 99354-2612

MILLER, JAN DEAN, metallurgy educator; b. Dubois, Pa., Apr. 7, 1942; s. Harry Moyer and Mary Virginia (McQuown) M.; m. Patricia Ann Rossman, Sept. 14, 1963; children: Pamela Ann, Jeanette Marie, Virginia Christine. BS, Pa. State U., University Park, 1964; MS, Colo. Sch. of Mines, Golden, 1966, PhD, 1969; D (hon.), U. Pretoria, South Africa, 2007. Rsch. engr. Anaconda Co., Mont., 1966; asst. prof. metallurgy U. Utah, Salt Lake City, 1968-72, assoc. prof., 1972-78, prof., 1978-2000, Ivor D. Thomas prof., 2000—, dept. chmn., 2002—; rsch. engr. Lawrence Livermore Lab., Calif., 1972. Cons. on processing of mineral resources to various cos. and govt. agys. Editor: Hydrometallurgy, Research, Development, and Plant Practice, 1983, others; contbr. over 425 articles to profl. jours.; 25 patents in field. Recipient Marcus A. Grossman award Am. Soc. Metals, 1974, Van Diest gold medal Colo. Sch. of Mines, 1977, Student award excellence in tchg. metall. engring. U. Utah, 1978, 82, 94, Extractive and Processing Lectr. award The Minerals, Metals and Materials Soc., 1992, Disting. Achievement medal Colo. Sch. of Mines, 1994, Best Paper award for fundamental rsch. 2000 TAPPI Recycling Symposium, 2000, Oustanding Tchg. award Coll. Mines and Earth Scis. U. Utah, 2000, J.D. Miller Symposium honor for innovations in resource processing, SME Annual meeting, Salt Lake City, 2005, Spl. Meritorious Recognition medal Gdansk U. Tech., Poland, 2005, Utah Govs. medal award for sci. and tech., 2006; Centennial fellow Coll. of Earth and Mineral Scis., Pa. State U., 1996. Mem. NAE, AIME (Henry Krumb lectr. 1987, Richards award 1991, Mineral Industry Edn. award 1997, Aplan award 2003), Soc. Mining, Metallurgy and Exploration (chmn. mineral processing divsn. 1980-81, Disting. Mem. award 1992, Antoine M. Gaudin award 1992), Am. Chem. Soc., Soc. Mining Engrs. (bd. dirs. 1980-83, program chmn. 1982-83, Taggart award 1986, 05, Stefanko award 1988, 02, symposium honoring J.D. Miller, 2005), Metall. Soc. (Extractive Metallurgy Tech. award 1988), Salt Lake Swim and Tennis Club, U. Utah Faculty Club. Baptist. Office: U Utah Metall Engring 135 S 1460 E Rm 412 Salt Lake City UT 84112-0114 Office Phone: 801-581-5160. Business E-Mail: jan.miller@utah.edu.

MILLER, JAN PAUL, lawyer, former prosecutor; b. Md. married; 2 children. BA in polit. sci., U. N.C., 1982; JD cum laude, Harvard U., 1985. Assoc. Christy & Viener LLP, 1985—86, Casner, Edwards & Roseman LLP, 1986—88, Gordon, Feinblatt, Rothman, Hoffberger & Hollander LLP, 1988—89; asst. U.S. atty. dist. Md US Dept. Justice, 1989—2002, U.S. atty. Ctrl. dist. Ill. Springfield, 2002—05; ptnr. Thompson Coburn LLP, Belleville, Ill., 2005—. Adj. prof. George Washington U. Recipient numerous commendations from law enforcement agencies, including FBI, U.S. Customs Svc., Drug Enforcement Adminstrn., U.S. Secret Svc., U.S. Postal Ins. Office: Thompson Coburn LLP 525 W Main St Belleville IL 62220 *

MILLER, JANEL HOWELL, psychologist; b. Boone, NC, May 18, 1947; d. John Estle and Grace Louise (Hemberger) Howell; m. C. Rick Miller, Nov. 24, 1968; children: Kimberly, Brian, Audrey, Rachel. BA, DePauw U., 1969; postgrad., Rice U., 1969; MA, U. Houston, 1972; PhD, Tex. A&M U., 1979. Lic. clin. psychologist, sch. psychologist Tex. Assoc. sch. psychologist Houston Ind. Sch. Dist., 1971-74; rsch. psychologist VA Hosp., Houston, 1972; assoc. sch. psychologist Clear Creek (Tex.) Ind. Sch. Dist., 1974-76; instr. psychology, counseling psychology intern Tex. A&M U., 1976-77; clin. psychology intern VA Hosp., Houston, 1977-78; coord. psychol. svcs. Clear Creek Ind. Sch. Dist., 1978-81, assoc. dir. psychol. svcs., 1981-82; pvt. practice Houston, 1982—. Faculty U. Houston-Clear Lake, 1984—; adolescent suicide cons., 1984—. DePauw U. Alumni scholar, 1965-69; NIMH fellow U. Houston, 1970-71. Mem. APA, Am. Assn. Marriage and Family Therapists, Soc. for Personality Assessment, Am. Coll. Forensic Examiners, Internat. Rorschach Soc., Tex. Psychol. Assn., Tex. Assn. Marriage and Family Therapists, Houston Psychol. Assn. (media rep. 1984-85), Houston Assn. Marriage and Family Therapists. Home: 806 Walbrook Dr Houston TX 77062-4030 Office: 16854 Royal Crest Dr Houston TX 77058-2529 Office Phone: 281-461-4098. Business E-Mail: shrinkskate@sbcglobal.net.

MILLER, JEANNE-MARIE ANDERSON (MRS. NATHAN J. MILLER), language educator, academic administrator; b. Washington, Feb. 18, 1937; d. William and Agnes Catherine (Johns) Anderson; m. Nathan John Miller, Oct. 2, 1960. BA, Howard U., 1959, MA, 1963, PhD, 1976. Instr. dept. English Howard U., Washington, 1963-76, asst. prof., 1976-79, assoc. prof., 1979-92, prof., 1992-97, prof. emeritus, 1997—, asst. dir. Inst. Arts and Humanities, 1973-75, asst. acad. planning, office v.p. for acad. affairs, 1976-90. Cons. Am. Studies Assn., 1972—75, Silver Burdett Pub. Co., NEH, 1978—; mem. adv. bd. D.C. Libr. for Arts, 1973—. Editor, Black Theatre Bull., 1977-86; Realism to Ritual: Form and Style in Black Theatre, 1983; assoc. editor Theatre Jour., 1980-81; contbr. articles to profl. jours., chpts. to books. Mem. Washington Performing Arts Soc., 1971—, Friends of Sta. WETA-TV, 1971—, Mus. African Art, 1971—, Arena Stage Assocs., 1972—, Washington Opera Guild, 1982—, Wolf Trap Assocs., 1982—, Drama League N.Y., 1995, Shakespeare Theatre, 2001—, Met. Opera Guild, 2002—, Solomon R. Guggenheim Mus., 2007—. Ford Found. fellow, 1970-72, So. Fellowships Fund fellow, 1973-74; Howard U. rsch. grant, 1975-76, 94-97, ACLS grant, 1978-79, NEH grant, 1981-84. Mem.: LWV, MLA, ACLU, AAUP, Nat. Archives Found., Folger Shakespeare Libr., Acad. Am. Poets, Am. Theatre and Drama Soc., Studio Mus. Harlem, Nat. Mus. Women in Arts, Nat. Bldg. Mus., Winterthur Guild, Hist. Soc. Washington, D.C. Preservation League, Nat. Trust Historic Preservation, Zora Neale Hurston Soc., Langston Hughes Soc., Ibsen Soc., Friends of Kennedy Ctr. for Performing Arts, Am. Assn. Higher Edn., Coll. Lang. Assn., Common Cause, Am. Assn. Higher Edn., Am. Studies Assn., Coll. English Assn., Nat. Coun. Tchrs. English, Sierra Club, Pi Lambda Theta. Democrat. Episcopalian. Home: 504 24th St NE Washington DC 20002-4818 E-mail: jmamiller@verizon.net.

MILLER, JEFF, congressman; b. St. Petersburg, Fla., June 27, 1959; m. Griswold Vicki Miller; 2 children. BA, U. Fla., 1984. Mem. Fla. Ho. of Reps., 1998—2002, U.S. Congress from 1st Fla. Dist., 2002—. Past chmn. Escambia County Legislative Del., 1999—2000. Mem. Fla. Hist. Soc., various areas of C. of C., Elizabeth Chapel United Meth. Ch., Chumuckla; mem. bd. dirs. Santa Rose County United Way; Pregnancy Resource Ctr. Milton Milton; Gulf Coast Coun. Boy Scouts Am.; Fla. FFA Found. Mem.: Coun. Ready Infrastructure, Com. on Rules, Ethics and Elections, Com. on Gen. Govt. Appropriations, Congl. Redistricting Com., Utilities and Telecommunications Com. (chmn.), Com. on Vet. Affairs, Ho. Armed Svcs. Com. Republican. Office: Congress 324 Cannon HOB Washington DC 20515-0901 *

MILLER, JENNIFER L., elementary school educator, small business owner; d. Frank L. and Patricia M. Warfel; m. Ryan G. Miller, July 2, 1994; children: Calleigh L., Garrett R., Trevor R. BA in Elem. Edn. (hon.), U. Portland, 1992. Cert. tchr. A-regular classroom Alaska, spl. edn. endorsement. Dir. summer recreation City of Wrangell, 1990—91; summer acad. tchr. geology; pvt. tutor Wrangell, 1991—92; 1st grade tchr. Wrangell City Schs., 1992—95, asst. coach h.s. girls basketball, 1993—94, multiage tchr. 1-2, 1995—96, multiage tchr. 2-3, 1996—2002; substitute tchr., 1998—92; multiage tchr. 1-2-3 Wrangell City Schs., 2002—03, multiage tchr. 2-3, 2003—04; tchr. 3rd grade Wrangell (Alaska) City Schs., 2004—; co-owner Clearwater Packing. Benchmark cut score com. dept. edn. State of Alaska, benchmark test bias com. edn. and early devel., stds. based assessment validation com., 2004—, content rev. com., 2005—, mem. dept. edn. data review com., 2006; adv. bd. Evergreen Elem., 2002—. Co-founder Evergreen Agtrl. Testing Site; leader Girl Scouts, Wrangell, 2002; active Friends of the Libr., Wrangell, Master Gardener's, Alaska; cmty. fair vendor Alaska, 1997; vol. Wrangell Little League, 2002, Alaskans for Drug Free Youth, Alaska, 1991, Hershey Track and Field, Alaska, 1990—91, Stikine River Rats Swim Team, Alaska, 1992; judge Wrangell H.S. Cheerleaders, Alaska, 1990—92. Recipient Youth Garden grant, Nat. Gardening Assn., 1999, Clay Muralist grant, Alaska Arts in Edn. Mem.: ASCD, NEA, NSTA, Alaska State Literacy Assn., Alaska Coun. Tchrs. Math., Internat. Reading Assn., Wrangell Tchr.'s Assn. (sec. 2000—, negotiations com., bldg. rep., Tchr. of Yr. 1997, 2001, 2006), Nat. Coun. Tchrs. English, Assn. for Childhood Edn. Internat., Juneau-Haines Reading Coun., Nat. Coun. Tchrs. Math., Elk. Home: PO Box 1899 25 Mile Zimovia Hwy Wrangell AK 99929 Home Phone: 907-874-3180. Home Fax: 907-874-3182. Personal E-mail: rjcgmill@aptalaska.net.

MILLER, JERRY HUBER, retired university chancellor; b. Salem, Ohio, June 15, 1931; s. Duber Daniel and Ida Claire (Holdereith) M.; m. Margaret A. Setter, 1958; children: Gregory, Joy, Carol, Beth, David. BA, Harvard U., 1953; MDiv., Hamma Sch. Theology, 1957; DD (hon.), Trinity Luth. Sem., 1981. Ordained to ministry Luth. Ch., 1957. Research assoc., intern Cornell U., Ithaca, NY, 1955-56; instr. Wittenberg U., Springfield, Ohio, 1956-57; parish pastor Ch. of Good Shepherd, Cin., 1957-62; asst. to pres.

Ohio Synod Luth. Ch. Am., 1962-66; sr. campus pastor, dir. campus ministry U. Wis., Madison, 1966-69; regional dir. Nat. Luth. Campus Ministry, Madison, 1969-76, exec. dir. Chgo., 1977-81; pres. Calif. Luth. U., Thousand Oaks, 1981-92, chancellor, 1992-94, pres. emeritus, 1994—; ret. Ventura County Maritime Mus., Channel Islands Harbor, Calif., 1993-95. Chmn. Los Robles Bank, Thousand Oaks, 1987-2000; mem. exec. com. Coun. Ind. Colls., Washington, Assn. Ind. Calif. Colls. and Univs., 1981-92, Coun. Luth. Colls., Luth. Ednl. Conf. N.Am., 1977-94; vice chair bd. behavioral sci. State Calif.; bd. dirs. Santa Barbara Bank and Trust. Editor: The Higher Disciplines, 1956; contbr. articles to profl. jours. Bd. dirs. Wittenberg U., Augustana Coll., Rock Island, Ill., United Way, Thousand oaks, Ventura County chpt. ARC, Thousand Oaks, YMCA; chmn. bd. dirs. Los Robles Hosp.; vice chair Stagecoach Inn Mus. Found., 1998—; bd. trustees Ventura County Maritime Mus., 1993—; bd. govs. Thousan Oaks Civic Arts Plaza, 2005—. Recipient Patrick Henry medal, Mil. Order of World Wars, 1992; named Man of Yr., Salem, 1975, Man of Yr. Conejo Valley, 1999; Siebert Found. fellow, 1975. Mem. Am. Assn. Higher Edn., Council Advancement and Support Edn., Harvard Alumni Assn., Western Coll. Assn. (bd. dirs.), Conejo Valley C. of C. (bd. dirs.), Conejo Symphony Orch. (bd. dirs.), Conejo Valley Hist. Soc. (bd. dirs. 1995—), Sr. Concerns Conejo Valley. Clubs: Harvard (Ill., Ohio, Wis., Calif.), YMCA (regional bd. dirs., vice chair 1996-99), Rotary. Avocations: skiing, golf, hiking, travel. Personal E-mail: msmjhm@aol.com.

MILLER, JO CAROLYN DENDY, family and marriage counselor, educator; b. Gorman, Tex., Sept. 16, 1942; d. Leonard Lee and Vera Vertie (Robison) Dendy; m. Douglas Terry Barnes, June 1, 1963 (div. June 1975); children: Douglas Alan, Bradley Jason; m. Walton Sansom Miller, Sept. 19, 1982. BA, Tarleton State U., Stephenville, Tex., 1964; MEd, U. North Tex., Denton, 1977; PhD, Tex. Woman's U., Denton, 1993. Tchr. Mineral Wells H.S., Tex., 1964-65, Weatherford Mid. Sch., Tex., 1969-74; counselor, instr. psychology Tarrant County Jr. Coll., Hurst, Tex., 1977-82; pvt. practice Dallas, 1982—. Author: (with Velma Baker, Jeannene Ward) Becoming: A Human Relations Workbook, 1981. Mem. ACA, Tex. State Bd. Examiners Profl. Counselors, Tex. State Bd. Marriage and Family Therapists, Tex. Counseling Assn., North Ctrl. Tex. Counseling Assn., Dallas Symphony Orch. League, Nat. Coun. Family Rels., Tex. Mental Health Counselors Assn., Internat. Assn. for Marriage and Family Counselors. Methodist. Office: 8222 Douglas Ave Ste 777 Dallas TX 75225-5938 Home Phone: 214-691-8980; Office Phone: 214-691-0400. Personal E-mail: jcdmphd@sbcglobal.net.

MILLER, JOEL STEVEN, inorganic and organic materials chemist, educator; b. Detroit, Oct. 14, 1944; s. John and Rose M.; m. Elaine J., Sept. 20, 1970; children: Stephen D., Mark A., Alan D. BS in Chemistry, Wayne State U., 1967; PhD, UCLA, 1971. Postdoctoral assoc. Stanford U., Calif., 1972; mgr. rsch. Occidental Rsch. Corp., Irvine, Calif., 1979-83; supr. rsch. Ctrl. R & D Lab. E. I. Du Pont Nemours & Co., Wilmington, Del., 1983-93; prof. chemistry U. Utah, 1993—, adj. prof. materials sci., 1994—2000. Disting. prof., assoc. Inorganic Synthesis Corp., Chgo.; vis. prof. U. Calif., Irvine, 1980, Weizmann Inst., Rehovot, Israel, 1985, U. Pa., Phila., 1988, U. Paris-Sud, 1991; Schmidt lectr. Weizmann Inst. Sci. Editor 16 books; mem. adv. bd. Jour. Materials Chemistry, 1991—2003, Advanced Materials, 1994—; mem. editl. bd. CrystEngComm, 1999-; mem. editl. adv. bd. Inorganic Chemistry, 2001-03, Chemistry-A European Jour.; contbr. over 450 articles to sci. jours. Indsl. fellow in material sci. Northwestern U., 1991-93; Wilhelm Manchot rsch. fellow 1996; fellow Japan Soc. Promotion Sci., 2000; recipient Disting. Rsch./Creative award, U. Utah, 2001, Gov. of Vt.'s medal for sci. and tech., 2004, James C. McGroddy prize for New Materials, Am. Phys. Soc., 2007. Mem. Am. Chem. Soc. (chmn. solid state subdiv. 1989, Utah award, 2003, Award Chemistry of Materials, 2000). Achievements include discovery and development of organic magnets and conductors. Office: Dept Chemistry U Utah Salt Lake City UT 84112 Home Phone: 801-273-9647; Office Phone: 801-585-5455. Office Fax: 801-581-8433. E-mail: jsmiller@chem.utah.edu. *

MILLER, JOHN, federal agency administrator, former news correspondent; married. Grad., FBI Nat. Exec. Inst. Correspondent WNEW-TV, 1973, WNBC-TV, 1988—94, ABCNEWS Law & Justice Unit, 1997—2002; co-anchor 20/20 ABC, 2002—03; dep. police commr., chief spokesman for commr. NYC Police Dept., 1994—95; bur. chief, counter-terrorism 7 criminal intelligence bur. LA Police Dept., 2003—05; asst. dir. pub. affairs FBI, Washington, 2005—. Co-author (with Michael Stone & Chris Mitchell): The Cell: Inside the 9/11 Plot, And Why the FBI and CIA Failed to Stop It, 2003. Recipient Emmy awards for broadcast journalist (9), Peabody awards (2), Dupont-Columbia award. Mem.: Internat. Assn. Police Chiefs, Internat. Assn. Bomb Technicians. Office: FBI 950 Pennsylvania Ave NW Washington DC 20535 *

MILLER, JOHN EDWARD, military officer, educational association administrator, information technology executive; b. Paragould, Ark., May 8, 1941; s. Wardlow Knox and Anna Mae (Danford) M.; m. Joan Carolyn Capano, Oct. 5, 1968; children: C. Claire, J. Andrew, JoAnna M., Mary Ellen. BS in Math., S.W. Mo. State U., 1963; MS in Ops. Rsch., Ga. Inst. Tech., 1971; postgrad., Yale U., 1991. Commd. 2d lt. U.S. Army, 1963, advanced through grades to lt. gen., 1993; student, then author, instr., grad. studies faculty mem. U.S. Army Command and Gen. Staff Coll., Ft. Leavenworth, Kans., 1974—77; bn. comdr. 4th Brigade, 4th Inf. Divsn., Wiesbaden, Germany, 1977—79; ops. and tng. officer 8th Inf. Div., Badkreuznach, Germany, 1979—81; student U.S. Army War Coll., Carlisle, Pa., 1982; divsn. chief Office Dep. Chief of Staff for Rsch. Devel. and Acquisition, Dept. Army, Washington, 1982—84; brigade comdr., chief of staff 9th Inf. Divsn., Ft. Lewis, Wash., 1984—87; asst. for combat devels. U.S. Army Tng. and Doctrine Command, Ft. Monroe, Va., 1987—88; asst. divsn. comdr. for ops. and tng. 8th Inf. Divsn., Baumholder, Germany, 1988—89; dep. comdt. U.S. Army Command and Gen. Staff Coll., Ft. Leavenworth, 1989—91; comdr. 101st Airborne Divsn., Ft. Campbell, Ky., 1991—93; comdt. U.S. army command, gen. staff coll. U.S. Army, Ft. Leavenworth, 1993—95; dep. comdg. gen. U.S. Army Tng. and Doctrine Command, Ft. Monroe, Va., 1995—97; exec. dir. learning solutions Oracle Corp., Reston, Va., 1997—2000, v.p. bus. develop, 2000—02, exec. dir. def. bus. ops., 2000—03, v.p. govt. ops., 2003—05, 2005—; pres., gen. mgr. Titan linguist ops. and tech. support L-3 Comms., Inc., 2005—. Apptd. mem. Am. U. MBA adv. bd., 1999; apptd. chair exec. bd. Nat. Academies, Army Sci. and Tech., 2001, Army Sci. Bd., 1999, Def. Sci. Bd., 2003; selected guest lectr. Def. Experts Exch., JFK Sch. Govt., Harvard U. and Peoples Liberation Army, China. Chair Army Distaff Found., 2003—. Decorated Disting. Svc. medal U.S. Army; recipient Outstanding Alumni award, S.W. Mo. State U., 1993. Mem. Assn. U.S. Army, Disabled Am. Vets Assn., 101st Airborne Divsn.Assn. Republican. Avocations: tennis, skiing, sailing. Office: 1900 Campus Commons Reston VA 20191 Office Phone: 703-390-7300. Personal E-mail: john.e.miller@l-3com.com.

MILLER, JOHN GRIDER, writer; b. Annapolis, Md., Aug. 23, 1935; s. John Stanley and Ruby Corinne (Young) M.; m. Susan Bradner Bailey, Oct. 26, 1974; children: Kerry, John, Alison. BA, Yale U., 1957. Commd. 2d lt. USMC, 1957, advanced through grades to col., inf./ops. advisor Vietnamese Marine Corps., 1970-71, prin. speechwriter for Commandant Washington, 1971-76, commd. officer Battalion Landing Team, 1977-78, asst. chief of staff ops. and plans III Amphibious Force Okinawa, 1982-83, dep. dir. Marine Corps History Washington, 1983-85, ret., 1985; mng. editor Procs. and Naval History U.S. Naval Inst., Annapolis, Md., 1985-2000. Author: The Battle to Save the Houston, 1985, (Pocket Books edit., 1992, Bluejacket edit., 2000), The Bridge at Dong Ha, 1989, (Dell edit. 1990, Bluejacket edit., 1996, Audiobook edit., 1997), Punching Out: A Guide to Post-Military Transition, 1994, The Co-Vans: U.S. Marine Advisors in Vietnam, 2000; contbf. author: The Marines, 1998, Commandants of the Marine Corps, 2004. Decorated Legion of Merit with gold star, Bronze Star with combat V, Cross of Gallantry, Vietnamese Marine Corps.; recipient Author of Yr. award Naval Inst., 1990, Alfred Thayer Mahan award Navy League of U.S., 2002. Mem. Marine Corps. Hist. Found. (bd. dirs., Gen. Wallace M. Greene Jr. Book award 1989, Disting. Svc. award 1998), Mil. Order of World Wars (past chpt. comdr., chmn. nat. mag. com.), Civitan Internat. (past chpt. pres.), Washington Naval and Maritime Corrs.' Cir., New Providence Club, Annapolis Chorale. Avocations: music, piano, choral singing, boating. Home: 21 Sands Ave Annapolis MD 21403-4426 E-mail: millerjohng@comcast.net.

MILLER, JOHN RIPIN, former federal agency administrator, former congressman; b. NYC, May 23, 1938; m. June Marion Hamula BA, Bucknell U., 1959; MA, JD, Yale U., 1964. Bar: Wash. Asst. atty. gen. State of Wash., 1965-68; practice law, 1968-72; pres. Seattle City Council, 1972-80; adj. prof. govt. law U. Puget Sound, 1981-84; mem. US Congress from 1st Wash. Dist., 1985—93, mem. budget com., fgn. affairs com.; dir. & sr. adv. Office to Combat Trafficking in Persons US Dept. State, Washington, 2002—04, dir. Office to Monitor & Combat Trafficking in Persons, 2004—06; rsch. prof. internat. affairs Eliot Sch. Internat. Affairs, George Washington U., Washington, 2007—. Bd. dirs. ATL Ultrasound, 1994—99; chmn. bd. dirs. Meridis, Inc., 2000—02; chmn. Discovery Inst., Seattle, 2001—02, sr. fellow, 2006—. Recipient Humanitarian award, Discovery Inst., 2004. Mem. Wash. State Bar Assn. Office: Eliot Sch Internat Affairs George Washington U 1957 E St NW Ste 501 Washington DC 20052 E-mail: jmiller4@gwu.com. *

MILLER, JOHN ROBERT, oil industry executive; b. Lima, Ohio, Dec. 28, 1937; s. John O. and Mary L. (Zickafoose) M.; m. Karen A. Eier, Dec. 30, 1961; children: Robert A., Lisa A., James E. BSChE with honors, U. Cin., 1960, D.Comml. Sc. hon., 1983. With Standard Oil Co., Cleve., 1960-86, dir. fin., 1974-75, v.p. fin., 1975-78, v.p. transp., 1978-79, sr. v.p. tech. and chems., 1979-80, pres., COO, bd. dirs., 1980—86; chmn., CEO TBN Holdings, Cleve., 1986—2000, Petroleum Ptnrs., Cleve., 2000—03; chmn. SIRVA, Inc., 2006—. Bd. dirs. Cambrex Corp., Eaton Corp.; chmn. Graphic Packaging Corp., 2006—; former chmn. Fed. Res. Bank, Cleve. Mem. Pepper Pike Club, The Country Club, Chagrin Valley Hunt Club, Tau Beta Pi. Office: 7511 Creek View Tr Chagrin Falls OH 44023 Office Phone: 440-543-2128. Business E-Mail: office@johnrmiller.com.

MILLER, JOHN RONALD, minister; b. LA, Jan. 4, 1938; s. Clarence Raymond and Yolanda Sarah (Capenaro) M.; m. Madelon Louise Tetaz, Mar. 26, 1966; children: Sarah Louise, John Ronald. BA, Southwestern Coll., 1960; MDiv, Drew U., 1963; MA, Rutgers U., 1966. Ordained to ministry United Meth. Ch., 1965, United Ch. Christ, 1966. Pastor Burden (Kans.) Meth. Ch., 1958-60; min. Wilson Meml. Union Ch., Watchung, NJ, 1961—. Mem. Consultation on Ch. Union, Princeton, N.J., 1982—, com. on disabled United Ch. of Christ, Montclair, N.J., 1982—. Chmn. Dorthea Dix Chapel Bldg. Program; pres. Trenton Psychiat. Hosp.-State of N.J., 1985; mem. N.J. State Bd. Human Svcs., 1996—. Southwestern Coll. scholar, 1960, Tipple scholar, 1960. Mem. Nat. Coun. Chs. of Jesus Christ (governing bd. 1985—), Internat. Coun. Community Chs. (moderator ecumenical commn. 1984—, regional trustee, exec. bd. 1987, v.p. exec. bd. 1991, pres. communion 1995-97), Optimists. Mem. United Ch. Of Christ. Office: Mary E Wilson Meml Union Ch 7 Valley Rd Watchung NJ 07069-6034 Office Phone: 908-755-5020.

MILLER, JOHN T., JR., lawyer, educator; b. Waterbury, Conn., Aug. 10, 1922; s. John T. and Anna (Purdy) M.; children: Kent, Lauren, Clare, Miriam, Michael, Sheila, Lisa, Colin, Margaret. AB with high honors, Clark U., 1944; JD, Georgetown U., 1948; Docteur en Droit, U. Geneva, 1951; postgrad., U. Paris, 1951. Bar: Conn. 1949 (inactive), D.C. 1950, U.S. Ct. Appeals (2d, 3d, 5th, 10th, 11th and D.C. cirs.), U.S. Supreme Ct. 1952. With Econ. Cooperation Adminstn. Am. Embassy, London, 1950-51; assoc. Covington & Burling, 1952-53, Gallagher, Connor & Boland, 1953-62; pvt. practice Washington, 1962—. Adj. prof. law Georgetown U. Law Ctr., Washington, 1959—; mem. Panel on Future of Internat. Ct. Justice. Co-author: Regulation of Trade, 1953, Modern American Antitrust Law, 1958, Major American Antitrust Laws, 1965; author: Foreign Trade in Gas and Electricity in North America: A Legal and Historical Study, 1970, Energy Problems and the Federal Government: Cases and Material, 8th edit., 1996, Deregulated Natural Gas and Electric Power Industries Seminar: Case Material, 5th edit., 2006; contbr. articles to profl. jours. Trustee Clark U., 1970-76, De Sales Sch. of Theology, 1993-97; mem. bd. advisors Georgetown Visitation Prep. Sch., 1978-94, trustee, 1994-96, emeritus trustee, 1996—; former fin. chmn. troop 46 Nat. Capital Area coun. Boy Scouts Am.; pres. Thomas More Soc. Am., 1996-97. 1st lt. U.S. Army, 1943-46, 48-49. Decorated Bronze Star; recipient 10 yr. teaching award, Nat. Jud. Coll., 1983. Mem. ABA (coun., chmn. adminstrv. law sect. 1972-73, ho. dels. 1991-93), AAUP, D.C. Bar Assn., Energy Bar Assn. (pres. 1990-91), Congl. Country Club, Army and Navy Club (bd. govs. 2000—), DACOR, Prettyman-Leventhal Am. Inn of Ct. (master 1988-99, pres. 1995-96), Sovereign Mil. Order of Malta (knight). Republican. Roman Catholic. Home: 4721 Rodman St NW Washington DC 20016-3234 Office: 1001 Connecticut Ave NW Washington DC 20036-5504 Office Phone: 202-331-1630. Personal E-mail: jtmillerjresq@verizon.net.

MILLER, JON PHILIP, marketing professional, pharmaceutical executive; b. Moline, Ill., Mar. 30, 1944; s. Clyde Sheldon and Alice Lenora (Taes) M.; m. Shirley Ann Hymes, Aug. 21, 1965; children: Melissa, Elizabeth. AB, Augustana Coll., 1966; PhD, St. Louis U., 1970; MBA, Pepperdine U., 1983. Rsch. assoc. to sr. biochemist ICN Pharm., Inc., Irvine, Calif., 1970—72, leader molecular pharmacology group, 1972—73, head molecular pharmacology/drug metabolism dept., 1973—76, dir. biology divsn., 1975—76; dir. SRI-NCI liaison group SRI Internat. (formally Stanford Rsch. Inst.), Menlo Park, Calif., 1976—78; sr. bioorganic chemist SRI Internat., Menlo Park, 1978—80, head medicinal biochemistry program, 1980—84, dir. biotech. rsch. dept., 1982—85, dir. biotech. and biomed. rsch. lab., 1985—92, assoc. dir. life scis. divsn., 1989—92; dir. bus. devel., strategic mktg. MDS Panlabs, Inc., Bothell, Wash., 1992—98; dir. pharm. mktg. Applied Biosys., Foster City, Calif., 1998—2001; dir. bus. devel. ACLARA Bioscis., Mountain View, Calif., 2001—03; pres. Miller & Co., Foster City, 2003—. Office: Miller & Co 1147 Blythe St Foster City CA 94404 Personal E-mail: jm330@sbcgobal.net.

MILLER, JONATHAN S., state official; b. Lexington, July 24, 1967; m. Lisa Miller; 2 children. BA, Harvard Coll., 1989; JD, Harvard Univ., 1992. Legis. dir. Congressman Jim Cape, 1994; dep. chief of staff US Dept. Energy, 1995—96; atty. Miller, Griffin, and Marks, 1997—99; with ETA Properties, 1999—; state treas. State of Ky., 1999—. Bd. dir. Lottery Corp., 2000—; vice chmn. State Investment Commn., 2000—; del. Nat.l Summit on Retirement Savings, 2002. Bd. dir. Lexington Urban League, 1999—, Ky. Teachers Retirement Sys., 2000—, Ky. Higher Edn. Assistance Authority, 2002—. Mem.: Ky. Bar Assn. Democrat. Office: State Treas Ste 100 1050 US Highway 127 S Frankfort KY 40601 also: 702 Capitol Ave Ste 183 Frankfort KY 40601 Office Phone: 502-564-4722. Office Fax: 502-564-6545. Business E-Mail: treasury.web@ky.gov. *

MILLER, JONATHAN WOLFE, theater and film director, physician; b. London, July 21, 1934; s. Emanuel Miller; m. Helen Rachel Collet, 1956; 3 children. Ed., St. John's Coll., Cambridge U.; MB Ch, Univ. Coll. Hosp. Med. Sch., London, 1959; DLitt (hon.), U. Leicester, 1981, Cambridge U., 1996; Dr. (hon.), Open U., 1983. Dir. Nottingham Playhouse, 1963-69; assoc. dir. nat. Theatre, 1973-75; mem. Arts Coun., 1975-76; artistic dir. Old Vic, 1988-90; lectr. Nat. Gallery, 1995, Met. Mus., NYC, 1995; curator major exhbn. Nat. Gallery, London, 1998. Vis. prof. drama Westfield Coll., U. London, 1977-78; lectr. wide variety of subjects. Co-author, actor in Beyond the Fringe, 1961-64; dir. Under Plain Cover Royal Ct. Theatre, 1962, The Old Glory, N.Y.C., 1964, Prometheus Bound, Yale Drama Sch., 1967, Oxford and Cambridge Shakespeare Co. prod. of Twelfth Night, on tour in U.s., 1969; dir. for Nat. Theatre, London: The Merchant of Venice, 1970, Danton's Death, 1971, The School for Scandal, 1972, The Marriage of Figaro, 1974; other prodns. include: The Tempest, London, 1970, Prometheus Bound, London, 1971, The Taming of the Shrew, Chichester, Eng., 1972, The Seagull, Chichester, 1973, The Malcontent, Nottingham, Eng., 1973, The Family in Love, 1974, The Importance of Being Earnest, 1975, All's Well That Ends Well, Measure For Measure, Greenwich Season, 1975, Three Sisters, 1977; dir. operas Arden Must Die, 1973, Sadler's Well Theatre, 1974, The Cunning Little Vixen, Glyndebourne, 1975, 77, Marriage of Figaro, Vienna State Opera, 1991, Robert Devereux, Monte Carlo, 1992, Die Gezeichnete, Zurich, 1992, Maria Stuarda, Monte Carlo, 1993, the Secret Marriage, Opera North, 1993; dir. for English Nat. Opera: The Marriage of Figaro, 1978, The Turn of the Screw, 1979, 91, Arabella, 1980, Othello, 1981, Rigoletto, 1982, 85 (alwo at Met. Opera, N.Y.C.), Fidelio, 1982, 83, Don Giovanni, 1985, The Magic Flute, 1986, Tosca, 1986, The Mikado, 1986, 88, The Barber of Seville, 1987, Cosi fan Tutte, 1995, Carmen, 1995; dir. for Kent Opera: Cosi Fan Tutte, 1975, Rigoletto, 1975, Orfeo, 1976, Eugene Onegin, 1977, La Traviata, 1979, 96, Falstaff, 1980, 81, Fiedlio, 1982, 83, 88; dir. for La Scala Milan: La Fanciulla del West, 1991, Manon Lescaut, 1992; dir. for Maggio Musicale, Florence: Don Giovanni, 1990, Cosí fan Tutte, 1991, 94, Marriage of Figaro, 1992, La Bohéme, 1994, La Bohéme, which transfered to La Bastille, 1995, dir., Strass Ariadne auf Naxos, 1997; dir. Met. Opera, N.Y.: Katya Kabanova, 1991, Pelléas et Mélisande, 1995; dir in co-prodn. with L.A. Music Ctr. and Houston Grand Opera House Der Rosenkavalier, 1994, King Lear at Lincoln Centre, N.Y., 2004; dir. Broadway play Long Day's Journey Into Night, 1986, The Taming of the Shrew at Royal Shakespeare Co., Stratford, 1987, Andromache, One Way Pendulum, Bussy D'Ambois, all at Vic, 1988, The Tempest, 1988, Turn of the Screw, 1989, Kimg Lear, 1989, The Liar, 1989, Cosi Fan Tutte at Lincoln Centre, N.Y., 2004; films include: Take a Girl Like You, 1969; TV films include: Whistle and I'll Come to You, 1967, Alice in Wonderland, 1967, The Body in Question Series, 1978, Henry the Sixth, part I, 1983, States of Mind Series, 1983, A Braief History of Disbelief Series, 2005; exec. prodr. Shakespeare TV series, 1979-81; author (TV) McLuhan, 1971, The Body in Question, 1978, States of Mind, The Facts of Life, Subsequent Performances, 1986, Who Cares, Born Talking, Museums of Madness, Anthropology, Opera Works; editor: Freud: The Man, His World, His Influence, 1972, The Don Giovanni Book, 1990; actor (TV) Jonathan Miller on Reflection, 1998, (TV mini-series) The Talk Show Story, 2000. Decorated Order of Brit. Empire; named Dir. of Yr., Soc. West End Theatre Awards, 1976; recipient Silver medal Royal TV Soc., 1981; fellow Univ. Coll. London; hon. fellow St. John's Coll., Cambridge U.; rsch. fellow in history of medicine Univ. Coll., London U., 1970-73. Fellow Royal Coll. Physicians (London and Edinburgh); mem. AAAS (fgn. mem.). Office: care IMG Artists 616 Chiswick High St London W45RX England Office Phone: 44 207957 5832. E-mail: cdyer@imgartists.com.

MILLER, JOSEF M., otolaryngologist, educator; b. Phila., Nov. 29, 1937; married, 1960; 3 children. BA in Psychology, U. Calif., Berkeley, 1961; PhD in Physiology and Psychology, U. Wash., 1965; MD (hon.), U. Göteborg, Sweden, 1987; MD (h.c.), U. Turku, Finland, 1995. USPHS fellow U. Mich., 1965-67, rsch. assoc., asst. prof. dept. Psychology Ann Arbor, 1967-68, prof., dir. rsch. dept. Otolaryngology, dir. Kresge Hearing Rsch. Inst., 1984—; asst. prof. depts. Otolaryngology, Physiology and Biophysics U. Wash., Seattle, 1968-72, rsch. affiliate Regional Primate Rsch. Ctr, 1968-84, assoc. prof., 1972-76, acting chmn. dept. Otolaryngology, 1975-76, prof., 1976-84; Lunn and Ruth Townsend prof. comm., 1996—. Mem. study sect. Nat. Inst. Neurol. and Communicative Disorders and Stroke, NIH, 1978-84, ad hoc bd. dirs. sci. counselors, 1988; sci. rev. com. Deafness Rsch. Found., 1978-83, chair, 1983—; mem. faculty Nat. Conf. Rsch. Goals and Methods in Otolaryngology, 1982; adv. com. hearing, bio-acoustics and biomechanics Commn. Behavioral and Social Scis. and Edn., Nat. Rsch. Coun., 1983—; hon. com. Orgn. Nobel Symposium 63, Cellular Mechanisms in Hearing, Karlskoga, Sweden, 1985; cons. Otitis Media Rsch. Ctr., 1985-89, Pfizer Corp., 1988; faculty opponent U. Gôteborg, Sweden, 1987; rsch. adv. com. Galludet Coll., 1987; chair external sci. adv. com. House Ear Inst., 1988-91; author authorizing legis. Nat. Inst. Deafness and Other Comm. Disorders, NIH, 1988, co-chair adv. bd. rsch. priorities com., bd. dirs. Friends adv. coun., 1989—, chair rsch. subcom., 1990-93, treas., bd. dirs., 1996—; grant reviewer Mich. State Rsch. Fund, NSF, VA; reviewer numerous jours. including Acta Otolaryngologica, Jour. Otology, Physiology and Behavior, Science. Mem. editorial bd. Am. Jour. Otolaryngology, 1981—, AMA, Am. Physiology Soc., Annals of Otology, Rhinology and Laryngology, 1980—, Archives of Oto-Rhino-Laryngology, 1985-93, Hearing Rsch., Jour. Am. Acad. Otolaryngology-Head and Neck Surgery, 1990—. Bd. dirs. Internat. Hearing Found., 1985—. Fellow U. Wash., 1962-65, Kresge Hearing Rsch. Inst., U. Mich., 1965-67; recipient award Am. Acad. Otolaryngology; grantee Deafness Rsch. Found., U. Wash., 1969-71; rsch. grantee NIH, 1969-73. Mem. AAAS, Am. Acad. Otolaryngology and Head and Neck Surgery (com. rsch. in otolaryngology 1971-82, continuing edn. com. 1975-79, NIH liaison com. 1988—, program steering com. jour. 1990, Pres. Citation 1997), Am. Auditory Soc., Am. Otological Soc., Am. Neurotological Soc., Am. Otologic Honor Soc., Acoustical Soc. Am. (com. rsch. psychol., physiol. acoustics 1969-78), Fedn. Am. Physiol. Soc., Fedn. Am. Socs. Exptl. Biology, Soc. Neurosci., Assn. Rsch. Otolaryngology (sec.-treas. 1979-80, pres. elect 1981, pres. 1982. program dir. mtg. 1983, award of merit com. 1985, 95-96, chair 1988, program dir., pres. symposium homeostatic mech. of inner ear 1993), Finnish Acad. Otolaryngology (hon.), Sigma Xi. Office: U Mich Kresge Hearing Rsch Inst 1301 E Ann St Rm R5032 Ann Arbor MI 48109-0506

MILLER, JOSEPH ARTHUR, manufacturing engineer, consultant, educator; b. Brattleboro, Vt., Aug. 28, 1933; s. Joseph Maynard and Marjorie Antoinette (Hammerberg) Miller; m. Ardene Hedwig Barker, Aug. 19, 1956; children: Stephanie L., Jocelyn A., Shana L., Gregory J. BS in Agrl., Andrews U., Berrien Springs, Mich., 1955; MS in Agrl. Mechs., Mich. State U., 1959; EdD in Vocat. Edn., UCLA, 1973. Constrn. engr. Thornton Bldg. & Supply, Inc., Williamston, Mich., 1959-63, C & B Silo Co., Charlotte, Mich., 1963-64; instr. and dir. retraining Lansing C.C., Mich., 1964-68; asst. prof./prog. coord./coop coord. San Jose State U., 1968-79; mfg. specialist Lockheed Martin Missiles and Space (and predecessor cos.), Sunnyvale, Calif., 1979-81, rsch. specialist, 1981-88, NASA project mgr., 1982-83, staff engr., 1988-96, rsch. staff engr., 1996-98, coord. flexible mfg. system simulation project, 1994-96, team mem. machining outsource initative project, AIMS agile mfg. project, 1995—97, coord. productivity improvement program, 1996—98; engring. and constrn. cons. Berry Creek, Calif., 1998—. Agrl. engring. cons. USDA Poultry Expt. Sta., 1960—62; computer numerical control cons. Dynamechtronics, Inc., Sunnyvale, 1987—90; machining cons. Space Sys. divsn. Lockheed, 1986—96; instr. computer numerical control DeAnza Coll., Cupertino, Calif., 1985—88, Labor Employment Tng. Corp., San Jose, Calif., 1988—93; career counselor Pacific Union Coll., Angwin, Calif., 1985—92; instr. computer-aided mfg. and non traditional machining San Jose State U., 1994—97; team leader pursuit of excellence machine tool project Lockheed Martin Missiles and Space, Sunnyvale, 1990—95, coord. safety award program, 1997—98, quality awareness program screening com., 1998. Author: Student Manual for CNC Lathe, 1990; contbr. articles to profl. jours. UCLA fellow, 1969—73. Mem.: Am. Soc. Indsl. Tech. (pres. 1980—81), Calif. Assn. Indsl. Tech. (pres. 1974—75, 1984—85), Nat. Assn. Indsl. Tech. (mem., chmn. accreditation visitation teams 1984—, pres. industry divsn. 1987—88, bd. cert. 1991—92), Soc. Mfg. Engr. (sr.; chmn. edn. com. local chpt. 1984—85, career guidance counselor 1986—88, fire safe coun. 2006—). Adventist. Avocations: violin, cabinet making, gardening, feeding hummingbirds. Home: PO Box 190 Berry Creek CA 95916-0190 Personal E-mail: jodenie@cncnet.com.

MILLER, JOYCE CATHERINE, chemistry professor, research scientist; d. Richard Norman and Gretna Mae Jones; m. John E. Miller, June 30, 1973. BA, Olivet Nazarene U., Kankakee, Ill., 1969—73; MA, Ball State U., Muncie, Ind., 1973—75; PhD, Ohio State U., Columbus, 1995—99. Cert. medical technologist Am. Soc. Clin. Pathologists, 1976. Rsch. technician in organic chemistry Ball Corp., Muncie, 1973—74; med. technologist Ball Meml. Hosp., Muncie, 1975—76; chemistry supr. Knox Cmty. Hosp., Mount Vernon, Ohio, 1976—78; evening supr. clin. lab. Bethesda Hosp., Zanesville, Ohio, 1978—81; clin. lab. dir. Joel Pomerene Meml. Hosp., Millersburg, Ohio, 1982—95; medical technologist Wooster Cmty. Hosp., Ohio, 1995—; tchg. asst. Ohio State U., 1996—98; assoc. prof. chemistry Mt. Vernon Nazarene U., Ohio, 1998—. Ch. pianist, Sunday sch. tchr. Loudonville Ch. Nazarene, Ohio, 1981—2006. Mem.: AAAS. Protestant. Avocations: golf, bicycling. Home: 874 Fairway Dr Howard OH 43028 Office: Mt Vernon Nazarene Univ 800 Martinsburg Rd Mount Vernon OH 43050 Home Phone: 419-651-2903. Business E-Mail: joyce.miller@mvnu.edu.

MILLER, JUDITH A. (JUDY MILLER), retired journalist; b. NYC, 1948; m. Jason Epstein, 1993. BA in Economics, Barnard Coll., 1969; MA, Princeton U., 1971. Corr. The Progressive, Nat. Pub. Radio; reporter, Washington Bur. NY Times, Washington, 1977, chief Cairo Bur. Egypt, 1983, Paris correspondent France, 1986—87, news editor and dep. bur. chief, Washington Bur., 1987—88, spl. correspondent to Persian Gulf crisis, 1990, spl. correspondent, Sunday Mag., 1990, sr. writer; ret., 2005. Lectr. in field. Author: One, By One, By One, 1990, God Has Ninety-Nine Names, 1996; co-author (with Laurie Mylroie): Saddam Hussein and the Crisis in the Gulf, 1990; co-author: (with William Broad and Stephen Engelberg) Biological Weapons & America's Secret War, 2002. Co-recipient Pulitzer Prize, explanatory journalism, 2002; recipient Emmy award, 2002, DuPont award, 2002. Achievements include first woman to be named chief of NY Times Cairo Bur. E-mail: miller@nytimes.com.

MILLER, JUDITH BRAFFMAN, writer; b. St. Louis, Feb. 21, 1947; d. William and Lorraine Shirley Braffman; m. Mark Ellis Miller, June 9, 1968. BA, U. Calif., Berkeley, 1969. Freelance writer, 1978—. Author: Wisps, Ashes, and Smoke. Active Amnesty Internat., NYC, 2002—, Am. Friends Svc. Com., 2005. Fellow: Royal Astron. Soc. Gt. Britain; mem.: AIAA, AAAS, ACLU, Am. Assn. Univ. Women, Royal Inst. Gt. Britan, Am. Assn. Variable Star Observers, Am. Assn. Variable Star Observers, Internat. Dark Sky Assn., Astron. Soc. of the Pacific, Nat. Space Soc., Planetary Soc., Am. Inst. Physics, Brit. Astron. Assn., Am. Astron. Soc., Am. Chem. Soc., NY Acad. Scis., Am. Soc. Journalists and Authors, Union Concerned Scientists. Avocations: naturalist, poetry, politics. Home and Office: 1149 Partridge Ave Saint Louis MO 63130 Office Phone: 314-725-7096. Personal E-mail: jbraffmanmiller@sbcglobal.net.

MILLER, JUDITH ELAINE, retired middle school educator, musician; d. Thomas Clifford and Beulah Mae Miller. BA in Math. with distinction, Ind. U., Bloomington, 1965, MAT in Math., 1968. Lic. life secondary math. tchr. Ind. Dept. Edn. Math. tchr. Greater Clark County Schs., Jeffersonville, Ind., 1965—2002, math. dept. chair Parkview Mid. Sch., 1975—84, team leader Parkview Mid. Sch., 1985—2002; ret., 2002. Co-sponsor Nat. Jr. Honor Soc.; coach Acad. Superbowl. Organist Corydon United Meth. Ch. Finalist Presdl. Award for Excellence in Math. and Sci. Tchg., State of Ind., 2002. Mem.: Ind. Ret. Tchrs. Assn., Nat. Coun. Tchrs. Math., So. Ind. Chpt. Am. Guild Organists (sec., corr. sec.), Fellowship United Meth. in Music and Worship, Ind. U. Alumni Assn. (life), Ind. Organists United, Jennie Gebhart Hedden Music Study Club (sec.), Delta Kappa Gamma (Beta Pi corr. sec.). Home: 470 Morris Ave Corydon IN 47112 Office Phone: 812-734-4502.

MILLER, JUDITH WOLFE COHEN, management consultant; b. Boston, Aug. 19, 1928; d. Benjamin and Charlotte Frances (Wolfe) Cohen; m. Sanford Arthur Miller, Aug. 17, 1958; children: Walie Jo, Debra Lauren. BS, Northeastern U., 1949. Research technician Mass. Gen. Hosp., Boston, 1949-51, NE Med. Ctr., Boston, 1951-52; spl. asst. MIT, Cambridge, 1952-61; v.p., treas. S.A. Miller and Assoc., Inc., San Antonio, Washington, 1987—. Cons. 9th internat. symposium on the U.S. Constitution Smithsonian Inst., Washington, 1987. Chmn. MIT Matrons, 1972, New Eng. Consevatory Prep. Sch. Parents' Assn., Boston, 1976, First Bicentennial '87 Symposium "The Constitution", Washington, 1985; Montgomery County chmn. Nat. Symphony Orch. Womens' Com., Washington, 1979-81; boutique chmn. Decorators' Showhouse Nat. Symphony Orch., Washington, 1981, 86; docent Nat. Archives Vols., Washington, 1979—; co-chmn. Am. Newspaper Pub. Assn. Found. Colloquium, Washington, 1985; pres. Nat. Archives Vols., Washington, 1983-84; vice-chmn. Constitution Study Group at Nat. Archives, Washington, 1982-87; docent Inst. Texan Culture, San Antonio, 1988-91; program chmn. U. Tex. Health Sci. Ctr. Club, San Antonio, 1988-89; White House vol. Presdl. Student Correspondence, 1996-2001. Mem.: Welcome to Washington. Home and Office: SA Miller & Assocs Inc 5450 Whitley Park Ter Apt 704 Bethesda MD 20814-2066 Office Phone: 301-897-3796. Office Fax: 301-897-0888.

MILLER, KAREN L., dean, nursing educator; BSN, Case Western Res. U.; MSN, U. Colo., PhD in Nursing. V.p. The Children's Hosp., Denver; assoc. prof. Coll. Nursing U. Colo. Health Scis. Ctr.; dean, prof. Sch. Nursing U. Kans., 1996—, dean Sch. Allied Health, 1998—. Mem. editl. bd. IMAGE: Jour. Nursing Scholarship. Grantee NIH, 1992. Fellow Am. Acad. Nursing; mem. ANA, ANA Coun. Nurse Rschrs., Am. Orgn. Nurse Execs., Coun. on Grad. Edn. for Nursing Adminstrn., Midwest Alliance in Nursing, Midwest Nursing Rsch. Soc., Sigma Theta Tau (collateral reviewer rsch. com.). Office: U Kans Sch Nursing 390 Rainbow Blvd Kansas City KS 66160-0001

MILLER, KARLA PATRICIA, elementary school educator; b. Takoma Park, Md., Apr. 6, 1968; d. James Roland and Patricia Melvin Miller. BS, U. Md., 1990, MEd, 1994, postgrad., 1997—2005. Advanced profl. cert. elem. grades and reading Md. State Dept. Edn., 2001. Tchr. 1st and 2d grade Montgomery County Pub. Schs., Olney, Md., 1991—95, reading specialist Silver Spring, 1995—98, tchr. 1st grade, 1998—2005. Mem. travel group observe best practices schs. Australia and New Zealand Montgomery County Pub. Schs., Rockville, 1993, first grade team leader, 1999—2000; mem. travel group observe schs. Australia and New Zealand, IRA's world congress Jr. Class Learning, Auckland, 2000; lect. Am. U., Washington, 2003; clin. supr. reading U. Md., College Park, 1997; cons. Md. State Dept. Edn., Balt., 1996—97. Participant Out of the Darkness Pallotta Teamworks, Washington, 2002. Mem.: IRA's Publ. Com., Internat. Reading Assn. (young author's chair Montgomery County coun. 1994—95, v.p. Montgomery County coun. 1995—96, pres.-elect Montgomery County coun. 1996—97, pres. Montgomery County coun. 1997—98, mem. internat. reading assn. pub. com. 1998—2000), Am. Edn. Rsch. Assn., Golden Key Nat. Honor Soc., Kappa Delta Pi, Phi Delta Kappa. Avocations: French, reading, writing. Office: Montgomery County Pub Schs 2111 Porter Rd Silver Spring MD 20910 Home Phone: 301-881-3619. Personal E-mail: kmiller4@umd.edu.

MILLER, KENDRA DANETTE, art services business owner; b. Jackson, Miss., Jan. 24, 1970; d. William Jerome Miller and Linda B. Walker. BA, Northwestern U., 1992; MA in Arts Adminstrn., Sch. of Art Inst. Chgo., 1997. Cert. fine and decorative art appraisal studies George Wash. U. Ctr for Profl. Devel., D.C., 2004. External affairs dir. Pinchot Inst. for Conservation, Wash., 2000—04; prin. Strata Fine Art Svcs., Silver Spring, Md., 2004—. Docent Nat. Mus. Women in the Arts, Wash., 2000—07; vol. Nativity Youth Ctr., Wash., 2004—05; adv. bd. McClinton Musical Theatre Arts Found., Bucharest, Romania, 2003—05; bd. mem. Woman Made Gallery, Chgo., 1997—99, treas., 1999; bd. mem. Imani Found. & Art Gallery, Kent, Ohio, Better Existence with HIV, Evanston, Ill., 1992—94. Scholar, Assn. Fundraising Profls., Greater N.Y. chpt., 2000, Nat. Capital Gift Planning Coun., 2002. Mem.: Am. Soc. Appraisers (assoc.). Conservative. Avocations: scuba diving, tennis, reading, art, travel. Office: Strata Fine Art Svcs LLC 8201 Schrider St Ste 4 Silver Spring MD 20910-4637 Office Phone: 240-271-5036. Business E-Mail: info@stratafineartservices.com.

MILLER, KENNETH EDWARD, sociologist, educator; b. NYC, June 17, 1929; s. Joseph F. and Irene (Edersheim) M.; m. Andrée Nora Barthelemy, Feb. 14, 1959 (div. Nov. 1984); children: Jennifer Andrée, Christopher Kenneth; m. Janet Sue Daniels, May 21, 1990. BA, U. Ala., 1953, MA, 1956; PhD, Duke, 1965; MS, Drake U., 1986. Asst. to pres., dir. devel. Jacksonville (Fla.) U., 1957-60; dir. Health Council, asso. dir. Community Planning Council, Birmingham, Ala., 1960-62; asst. prof. sociology Emory U., Atlanta, 1966-70, acting chmn. dept., 1969-70; prof. sociology Drake U., Des Moines, 1970-96, chmn. dept., 1970-79, 82-88, asst. to dean for grad. studies, 1991-92, prof. emeritus, 1996—. Research sociologist U. Ala., 1956-57; research asso. U.S. Civil Service Commn., summer 1968. Served with USN, 1946-48. Postdoctoral research fellow Duke, 1965-66. Mem. Midwest Sociol. Soc. Home: 2129 NW 140th St Clive IA 50325-8730

MILLER, KENNETH GREGORY, retired air force officer; b. Bryan, Tex., July 28, 1944; s. Max Richard and Catherine Mae (Sultzman) M.; m. Ann Marguerite Perpich, Nov. 25, 1966; children: Keith G., Deborah J., Craig S. BS in Aero. Engring., Purdue U., 1966; MS in Systems Mgmt., U. So. Calif., 1970; grad., Nat. War Coll., Washington, 1986; postgrad., U. Va., 1988. Commd. 2d lt. USAF, 1966, advanced through grades to brig. gen., 1995; with Office Sec. Def., Washington, 1980-81; various positions to dir. field ops. F-16 System Program Office, Wright-Patterson AFB, Ohio, 1981-86; chief engring. div. Sacramento Air Logistics Ctr., McClellan AFB, Calif., 1986-87; dir. materiel mgmt. Ogden Air Logistics Ctr., Hill AFB, Utah, 1987-89; vice comdr. Acquisition Logistics Div., Wright-Patterson AFB, 1989-90; comdr. Air Force Contract Mgmt. Divsn., Kirtland AFB, N.Mex., 1990; comdr. western dist. Def. Contract Mgmt. Command, LA, 1990-91; dir. C-17 Program Office, Wright-Patterson AFB, 1991-93; dep. asst. sec. for acquistion USAF, Washington, 1993-94, dir. supply hdqrs., 1994-95; v.p. for gulf ops. BDM Fed., 1995-96; group v.p. for advanced tech. svcs. group RJO Enterprises, Inc., 1997; sr. v.p. Dayton ops. CACI, Inc., 1997-99; group v.p. Air Force programs Anteon Corp., 1999—. Mem. engring. bd. visitors Purdue U. Decorated Disting. Svc. medal, Legion of Merit (2), Def. Superior Svc. medal; recipient award of merit Freedom Found; named Outstanding Aerospace Engr., Purdue U., Disting. Engring. Alumnus, Purdue U., 2001; named to ROTC Hall of Fame, 2001. Mem. Nat. Contract Mgmt. Assn. (bd. advisors 1990-92), Soc. Logistics Engrs., Nat. Def. Indsl. Assn. Office: 1560 Wilson Blvd Ste 800 Arlington VA 22209 Home: 9061 Daybreaker Drive Park City UT 84098 E-mail: kmiller@anteon.com.

MILLER, KENNETH LEE, counselor, educator; s. Arthur Jerome and Geraldine Marie Miller; m. Suellyn Mary Hetrick, May 28, 1983. BA in Sociology, Purdue U., 1979, MEd in Counseling, 1985, PhD, 1990. Diplomate Am. Bd. Med. Psychotherapists, 1988; profl. clin. counselor Ohio Counselor, Social Worker, and Marriage and Family Therapist Bd., 2002, nat. cert. counselor Nat. Bd. for Cert. Counselors, Inc./Va., 1988, approved clin. supr. Ctr. for Credentialing and Edn., Inc./N.C., 1998, life skills educator Teachers Coll., Columbia U., 1982. Co-dir. gender equity grant Purdue U., West Lafayette, Ind., 1987—89; asst. prof. Calif. State U., San Bernardino, 1990—92; asst. prof., capt. The Citadel, Charleston, SC, 1992—93; asst. prof. U. Hawaii at Manoa, Honolulu, 1993—95; assoc. prof. Youngstown (Ohio) State U., 2000—. Dir. U. Counseling Ctr./Cmty. Counseling Clinic Youngstown State U., 2000—04, dept. chair counseling, 2003—05; cons. Hunt County Dept. Mental Health, Greenville, Tex., 1995—95. Co-author: Gender-fair Counseling Strategies, 1988, Working for Change: Planning a Gender Equity Workshop, 1988; contbr. chapters to books, articles to profl. jours.; co-developer (videotape) A Model for Gender-fair Counseling, Freedom, Fairy Tale, Assembly Line, Your Choice/Your Future, Comedian, Obsolete, Inequality: A Subtle Disaster. Mem. San Bernardino County Mental Health Assn., 1990—92; adv. com. mem. Tri-County Child Advocacy Ctr., Youngstown, 2000—02; mem. bd. mgrs. John Will Anderson Boy's Club, Gary, Ind., 1983—83; sec. Hawaii Multicultural Counseling and Devel. Assn., Honolulu, 1994—95; com. mem. Multicultural Ethics Rev. Com., ACA, Honolulu, 1994—94; western divsn. rep. Nat. Orgn. for Human Svc. Edn., Seattle, 1991—92; judge Calif. Academic Decathlons, San Bernardino, Calif., 1990—91. Recipient Disting. Professorship award, Youngstown State U., 2001—02. Mem.: APA, ACA, Ohio Assn. for Counselor Edn. and Supervision, East Ohio Counseling Assn., Ohio Counseling Assn., Soc. for the Psychol. Study of Social Issues, Am. Coll. Counseling Assn., Assn. for Counselor Edn. and Supervision (Robert Frank Outstanding Counseling Program award 2002—03), Am. Ednl. Rsch. Assn., Kappa Delta Pi, Pi Lambda Theta, Chi Sigma Iota. Avocations: swimming, tennis, scuba diving. Office: Youngstown State Univ One University Plaza Youngstown OH 44555 Home Phone: 330-965-0508.

MILLER, KENNETH MICHAEL, electronics executive, director; b. Chgo., Nov. 20, 1921; s. Matthew and Tillie (Otto) M.; m. Dolores June Miller, Jan. 16, 1943 (dec. Dec. 1968); children: Barbara Anne Reed, Nancy Jeanne Hathaway, Kenneth Michael, Roger Allan; m. Sally J. Ballingham, June 20, 1970 (dec. Apr. 2002). Student, Ill. Inst. Tech., 1940-41, UCLA, 1961. Electronics engr. Rauland Corp., Chgo., 1941-48; gen. mgr. Lear, Inc., Santa Monica, Calif., 1948-59; v.p., gen. mgr. Motorola Aviation Electronics, Inc., Culver City, Calif., 1959-60; v.p., gen. mgr. instrument divsn. Daystrom, Inc., LA, 1961; gen. mgr. metrics divsn. Singer Co., L.A. and Bridgeport, Conn., 1962-65; v.p., gen. mgr. Lear Jet Corp., 1965-66; pres., dir. Infonics, Inc., 1967-68; v.p., gen. mgr. Computer Industries, Inc., 1968-69; dir. ops., tech. products group Am. Std. Corp., McLean, Va., also v.p., gen. mgr. Wilcox Elec. divsn. Kansas City, Mo., 1969-71; pres. Wilcox Elec., Inc. subs. Northrop Corp., Kansas City, 1971-72; v.p., dir. World Wide Wilcox, Inc. subs., McLean, 1971-72; pres., CEO, dir. Penril Corp., Rockville, Md., 1973-86; pres. K-M Miller and Assocs., Rockville, 1986—. Dir. George Mason Bank, NA, Washington, Palmer Nat. Bank, Washington. Mem. adv. bd. Washington Bus. Jour.; contbr. articles to profl. jours. Mem. regional planning coun. Cmty. Mental Health Svcs., Bridgeport, 1964; mem. Bridgeport Capital Fund Com.; trustee Park City Hosp.; vice dir. Montgomery County Arts Coun.; bd. dirs. U. Bridgeport; mem. Md. State Com. High Tech. Recipient Job Makers award Mfrs. Assn. Bridgeport, 1963. Fellow Radio Club Am. (dir., chmn grants-in-aid com.); mem. AIAA, IEEE, Aircraft Owners and Pilots Assn., Am. Mgmt. Assn., Armed Forces Comm. and Electronics Assn. (life), Electronic Industries Assn., Instrument Soc. Am. (life), Nat. Aero. Assn., Soc. Non-Destructive Testing, Soc. Automotive Engrs., Air Force Assn., Am. Radio Relay League (life), Amateur Satellite Corp. (life), Am. Def. Preparedness Assn. (life), Aero. Elec. Soc. (life), Nat. Capital DX Assn. (pres. 1987-88), Assn. Old Crows (life), Mfrs. Assn. Bridgeport (dir.), Bridgeport Engring. Inst., Bridgeport C. of C. (pres. 1964), Quarter Century Wireless Assn. (life, Disting. Svc. award 1994), Soc. Wireless Pioneers, Rolling Hills Country Club (Wichita), Algonquin Club (Bridgeport). Home and Office: 16904 George Washington Dr Rockville MD 20853-1128 Home Phone: 301-774-7709; Office Phone: 301-774-7709. Personal E-mail: kmm@prodigy.net.

MILLER, KENNETH W., lawyer; b. Chgo., Oct. 25, 1960; BS, U. Ill., 1982; JD magna cum laude, Northwestern U., 1985. Bar: Ill. 1985. Ptnr., chmn. pvt. equity practice Katten Muchin Rosenman LLP, Chgo. Mem.: ABA, Am. Inst. of CPAs. Office: Katten Muchin Rosenman LLP 525 W Monroe St Chicago IL 60661 Office Phone: 312-902-5261. Office Fax: 312-577-8747. Business E-Mail: ken.miller@kattenlaw.com.

MILLER, KERRY LEE, lawyer; b. West Palm Beach, Sept. 11, 1955; s. Clyde Howard and Alice (Hummel) M.; m. Myrna Patricia Garza, June 9, 1979; children: Alexander James, Eric Anthony. BA, George Mason U., 1977; JD, Cath. U., 1981. Bar: D.C. 1981, Va. 1982, U.S. Dist. Ct. (D.C. dist.) 1982, U.S. Ct. Appeals (D.C. and 4th cirs.) 1982, U.S. Ct. Appeals (fed. cir.) 1989, U.S. Ct. Claims 1989, U.S. Supreme Ct. 1989, U.S. Dist. Ct. (ea. and we. dists.) Va. 1993. Asst. gen. counsel Office Gen. Counsel U.S. Govt. Printing Office, Washington, 1981-87, assoc. gen. counsel contracts and procurement, 1987-99; adminstrv. law judge Bd. Contract Appeals U.S. Govt. Printing Office, 1999—2004, chief acquisition officer, 2004—06; asst. chief counsel Fed. Transit Admin., 2006—. Mem.: Fed. Bar Assn., Computer Law Assn., Contract Appeals Bar Assn. Business E-Mail: kerry.miller@dot.gov.

MILLER, KHADIJAH OLIVIA, education educator; d. Joseph Richard and Eunice Verdell Turner; m. L. Eric Miller, Oct. 26, 1997; children: Erin Kayla children: Ericka Olivia. BA in Print Journalism, NYU, 1993; MA in African Am. Studies, Temple U., 1995, PhD in African Am. Studies, 2001. Dir. women's studies program and women's ctr. Rosemont (Pa.) Coll., 2000—02; asst. prof. interdisciplinary studies. dept. head Norfolk State U., Va., 2002—. Recipient award for innovative excellence in tchg., learning and tech., 17th Internat. Conf. Coll. Tchg. and Learning, 2006; grantee, NEH, 2005. Mem.: AAUW, Am. Democracy Project (v.p. Norfolk State U. chpt. 2005—). Office: Norfolk State U 700 Park Avenue Norfolk VA 23504 Home Phone: 757-638-9580; Office Phone: 757-823-2864. Office Fax: 757-823-8602. Business E-Mail: komiller@nsu.edu.

MILLER, KLEBER C., lawyer; b. Austin, Tex., Aug. 11, 1924; LLB, Univ. Tex., 1951. Bar: Tex. 1951. Asst. dist. atty. Travis County, Tex., 1951; ptnr., litigation, energy practices Shannon Gracey Ratliff & Miller LLP, Fort Worth, Tex. Fellow: Am. Bar Found., Am. Coll. Trial Lawyers (past state chmn.), Tex. Bar Found. (life; chmn. of fellows); mem.: ABA, Am. Bd. Trial Advocates, Def. Rsch. Inst. (past state chmn.), Fedn. Def. & Corp. Counsel (v.p. 1966—68), Trial Lawyers Am., State Bar Tex. (bd. dir. 1976—79, chmn. 1978), Tex. Assn. Def. Counsel (bd. dir. 1973—76, pres. 1977), Fort Worth Tarrant County Bar Assn. (pres. 1967—68, Blackstone award 1992, Professionalism award 2000), Delta Sigma Rho. Office: Shannon Gracey Ratliff & Miller LLP Ste 3800 777 Main St Fort Worth TX 76102 Office Phone: 817-336-9333. Office Fax: 817-336-3735. Business E-Mail: kmiller@shannongracey.com.

MILLER, L. MARTIN, accountant, financial planner; b. NYC, Sept. 17, 1939; s. Harvey and Julia (Louis) M.; m. Judith Sklar, Jan. 21, 1962; children: Philip, Marjorie. BS, U. Pa., Phila., 1960; M in Taxation, Villanova U., Pa., 2001. CPA; CFP; accredited fin. planning specialist. Jr. acct. Deloitte, Haskins & Sells, NYC, 1960-62, sr. acct. Phila., 1962-64; mng. ptnr. Morison Cogen LLP, Phila., 1964—2005. Treas. Coronet Container Co., Inc., Phila., Val Mar Realty Corp., NYC; dir. Penn Internat. Trading Co., Phila.; mng. dir. CPA Tax Forum, 1966-69; underwriting mem. Lloyds of London, 1978-95, chmn. Mid-Atlantic region, 1991-92; faculty Wharton Sch. U. Pa., 1992-2004, Villanova U., 2003—; MBA program faculty LaSalle U., 2003—; continuing edn. faculty AICPAs, 2006; lectr. in field. Author: Accountants Guide to S.E.C. Filings, 1968, Salaries, Penn. Non-Profit Report, 1997, Worker Compensation, Practical Tax Strategies, 2000; contbr. articles to profl. jours. Mem. Phila. Rep. Com., 1963-67, treas. Daerr-Bannon for state rep. com., 1997; chmn. Lower Merion Twp. scholarship fund, 1975-78; bd. dirs. Main Line Br. ARC, 1997-2000; bd. dirs. Penn Valley Civic Assn., 1973-79, Gladwyne Civic Assn., 1992-95; mem. Lower Merion Planning Commn., 1978-82, Gov.'s Tax Study Commn.; pres. Mensa Edn. and Rsch. Found., 1984-86; mem. SEC Forum on Small Bus. Capital Formation, 1983, Pa. Impact, 1995; apptd. to Pa. State Bd. Accountancy, 1985-94, chmn., 1990-91; elected sch. bd. dir. Lower Merion Twp., 1993-97, also chmn. fin. com. Served with U.S. Army, 1961-62. Recipient Outstanding Achievement award Germantown Civic Assn., 1965. Mem. Nat. Assn. Securities Dealers (industry arbitrator 2005—)Pa. Inst. CPAs (edn. com. 1975-78, bd. dirs. 1979-81, by-laws chmn. 1980-83, mem. non-profit orgns. com. 1995-99, fin. planning com. 2002-2003), Nat. Assn. State Bds. Accountancy (edn. com. 1987, nominating com. 1989, experience com. 1990, continuing edn. com. 1995—), Am. Arbitration Assn. (mem. comml. panel, 2002—), Cert. Fin. Planner (bd. ethics 1995-97), AICPAs (nat. tax commn. 1979-82, exec. com. self regulation divsn. for CPA firms 1984-87, acctg. and rev. svcs. com., long range planning com., ethics divsn. 1985-88, specialization bd. 1989-90, ethics exec. com. 1990-93, mem. curriculum and acctg. edn. 1993-96, chmn. fin. assistance task force 1995, bd. dirs. Estate Planning Coun. 1998-2004, nomination com. 1999, discussion leader continuing edn. 2005), Little 10 Acctg. Assn. (edn. chmn. 1980-84), Main Line C. of C. (govt. affairs com. 1991-99), Mensa (internat. fin. officer 1970-74), Masons (past master), Plays and Players Club (treas. 1978-79), Beta Alpha Psi. Home: 204 Dove Ln Haverford PA 19041-1902 Office: Morison Cogen LLP 150 Monument Rd Bala Cynwyd PA 19004-1702

MILLER, LARRY G., professional sports team executive; b. Phila. BBA in Acctg., Temple U., Phila., 1982; MBA, La Salle U., Phila., 1987. Exec. v.p., contr. Jantzen, Inc., Portland, Oreg., pres., 1992—97, Portland Trail Blazers, 2007—; v.p. USA apparel Nike, Inc., Oreg., 1997—99, pres. Brand Jordan, 1999—2006, v.p., gen. mgr. basketball, 2006—07. Bd. mem. Urban League Portland, Portland Sports Authority. Office: Portland Trail Blazers One Center Ct Ste 200 Portland OR 97227 *

MILLER, LARRY H., professional sports team owner, auto dealer, broadcast executive; b. Salt Lake City; m. Gail Miller; 5 children. LLD (hon.), U. Utah, 1991; degree (hon.), Utah Valley State Coll., Salt Lake Cmty. Coll. With auto parts bus., Denver and Salt Lake City; owner auto dealerships, Salt Lake City, Albuquerque, Denver and Phoenix; part-owner NBA Utah Jazz, Salt Lake City, 1985—86, owner, 1996—, Larry H. Miller Grp., Salt Lake City, KJZZ-TV, Salt Lake City, 1993—. Office: Utah Jazz 301 W South Temple Salt Lake City UT 84101-1216 also: Larry H Miller Group 5650 S State St Murray UT 84107-6131 *

MILLER, LAURA ARIANE, lawyer; b. NYC, Apr. 26, 1954; d. Walter Hamilton and Phoebe Therese (Adil) M.; m. Glenn Richard Reichardt, Sept. 10, 1977 (div. Dec. 1984). BA, U. Mich., 1974; MPP, Harvard U., 1976; JD, Yale Law Sch, 1988. Bar: Va. 1988, DC 1989, US Dist. Ct. (ea. dist.) Va. 1989, US Dist. Ct. DC 1990, US Ct. Appeals (4th and DC cirs.) 1990. Assoc. ICF, Inc., Washington, 1976-77; special asst. Sec. HEW, Washington, 1977-79; depty commr. U.S. Adminstrn. Children, Youth, Families, Washington, 1979-81; pres. The Delta Corp., Washington, 1981-85; law clk. to Hon. Byron White U.S. Supreme Ct., Washington, 1988-89; assoc. Cacheris & Towey, Washington, 1989; ptnr. Nixon Peabody, Washington. Com. mem. Fairfax County (Va.) Democrats; del.

Va. State Democratic Conv., 1982; mem. Govs. Adv. Com. Children, Va., 1984-85. Named one of The 50 Most Influential Women Lawyers in Am., Nat. Law Jour., 2007. Mem. ABA (co-chair criminal litig. com., mem. governing coun. litig. sect.), Am. Inn of Ct., Va. Women Attys. Assn., DC Women's Bar Assn., DC Bar Assn., Commonwealth of Va. Bar Assn., Am. Trial Lawyers Assn., Lawyers Club of DC, Yale Law Sch. Assn. Washington (treas. 1990). Avocations: tennis, racquetball, opera. Office: Nixon Peabody 401 9th St NW Ste 900 Washington DC 20004 Office Phone: 202-585-8313. Office Fax: 866-947-3685. *

MILLER, LAURA M., former mayor, journalist; b. Balt., Nov. 18, 1958; m. Steven Wolens; children: Alex, Lily, Maxwell. BA, U. Wis., Madison, 1980. Mem. city coun. City of Dallas, 1998—2002, mayor, 2002—07. Columnist, investigative reporter Dallas Observer, metro columnist Dallas Times Herald, New York Daily News, The Dallas Morning News, The Miami Herald; freelance writer: The Miami Herald. Recipient H.L. Mencken Writing award, Balt. Sun, 1995, 6 Katie awards, Dallas Press Club, 2 Tex. Headliner awards, 2 Philbin awards, Dallas Bar Assn., cert. of merit, ABA. *

MILLER, LEE I., lawyer; b. Nov. 16, 1947; BSBA, Georgetown U., 1969, JD, 1973. Bar: Md. 1973, Ill. 1976. Ptnr., Real Estate practice Rudnick & Wolfe, Chgo., mng. ptnr., 1992—99; ptnr, co-chmn. Piper Marbury Rudnick & Wolfe, Chgo., 1999—2004; ptnr., joint CEO DLA Piper Rudnick Gray Cary, Chgo., 2005—. Bd. dir. Griffindor Capital Ptnrs. LLC. Editorial asst. Tax Lawyer, 1972-73. Bd. visitors Georgetown Univ. Law Ctr.; mem. adv. bd. Georgetown Univ. Corp. Counsel Inst. Recipient Judge Learned Hand Human Rels. award, Am. Jewish Com., 2001. Mem.: Ill. State Bar Assn., Chgo. Bar Assn., Am. Coll. Real Estate Lawyers, Real Estate Roundtable (pres. club mem.), Phi Alpha Delta. Office: DLA Piper Rudnick Gray Cary Suite 1900 203 N La Salle St Chicago IL 60601-1293 Office Phone: 312-368-4029. Office Fax: 312-236-7516. Business E-Mail: lee.miller@dlapiper.com.

MILLER, LEROY PAUL, JR., language educator; b. Holyoke, Mass., Feb. 21, 1949; s. Leroy Paul Sr. and Rose Marie (Danehey) Miller. AA, Northampton Jr. Coll., Mass., 1972; BA, U. New. Eng., Biddeford, Maine, 1974; MEd, Springfield Coll., Mass., 1977; postgrad., Am. Internat. Coll., Springfield. Cert. elem. tchr., English tchr., history tchr., guidance counselor Mass. Sch. adjustment counselor Holyoke Pub. Schs., 1978-79, edni. programmer, 1979-80, tutor Chpt. I, 1980-81; tutor Amherst (Mass.) Pub. Schs., 1982-84; tchr. West Springfield (Mass.) Pub. Schs., 1985-86; tchr. English Springfield Pub. Schs., 1986—. Fundraiser M. Marcus Kiley Mid. Sch.; alumni counselor U. New Eng., 1977—. Mem. NEA, ASCD, Nat. Coun. Tchrs. English, Mass. Tchrs. Assn., Springfield Edn. Assn. (faculty rep. 1986—), U. New Eng. Alumni Assn. (v.p. 1990—), Elks, Psi Chi. Democrat. Roman Catholic. Avocations: reading, bowling. Home: 2 Gerard Way Holyoke MA 01040-1204 Office: M Marcus Kiley Mid Sch 180 Cooley St Springfield MA 01128-1108 Office Phone: 413-787-7240. Personal E-mail: lmill55169@aol.com.

MILLER, LESLIE ANNE, lawyer; b. Franklin, Ind., Nov. 4, 1951; d. G. Thomas and Anne (Gaines) Miller; m. Richard B. Worley, Feb. 14, 1987. AB cum laude, Mt. Holyoke Coll., 1973; MA in Polit. Sci., Rutgers U., 1974; JD, Dickinson Sch. Law, 1977; LLM with honors, Temple U., 1994; LLD (hon.), Thomas Jefferson U. Coll. Health Profls., 2002; HHD (hon.), Wilson Coll., 2001. Bar: Pa. 1977, U.S. Dist. Ct. (ea. dist.) Pa. 1977, U.S. Ct. Appeals (3d cir.) 1980, U.S. Dist. Ct. (ea. dist.) Pa. 1987. Assoc. LaBrum & Doak, Phila., 1977—81, ptnr., 1982—86, Goldfein & Joseph, Phila., 1986—95, McKissock & Hoffman, P.C., Phila., 1995—2003; gen. counsel Gov. Pa., 2002—. Bd. dirs. WHYY-TV, 1996—; del. Third Circuit Jud. Conf., 1981, 82, 85; mem. Jud. Inquiry and Rev. Bd., 1990-94, chair, 1993-94; mem. faculty trial advocacy program Dickinson Sch. Law, 1992, 94; mem. hearing com., disciplinary bd. Supreme Ct. Pa., 1996—; mem. faculty Acad. Advocacy Temple U., 1994—; judge pro tem Ct. of Common Pleas; interm pres. Kimmel Ctr. for the Performing Arts, 2001-02 Mem. acad. ball com. Phila. Orch., 1986-87, 89-91, 95-96, mem. acad. music com. 1998—; mem. Open Space Task Force Com., Lower Merion Twp., Pa., 1990, bd. dirs., 1990-94, mem. counsel, 1990, Lower Merion Conservancy, 1995-97, 00-, others; bd. dirs. Med. Coll. Pa., 1985-96, sec., 1987-92, chair presdl. search com., 1993, chair presdl. inauguration, 1987, chair com. on acad. affairs, 1989-95, chair dean's search com., 1994-95, chair nomenclature com., 1996; bd. dirs. Med. Coll. Hosps., 1991-96, Allegheny Health Edn. and Rsch. Found., 1993-96, Hahnemann U. Med. Sch., 1994-96, Pa. Ballet, 1994—, St. Christopher's Hosp. for Children, 1991-94, vice chair, 1990-94; bd. dirs. Phila. Free Libr., 1997—, bd. dirs. Kimmel Ctr. for the Performing Arts, 1999—, interim pres., 2001-02, vice chair bd. dirs., 2002—; hon. chair Pa. Breast Cancer Coalition, 2003, exec. v.p. Pa. chpt., 2005; bd. trustees Mt. Holyoke Coll., 2000—, chair, 2005—; bd. govs. Dickinson Sch. Law, Pa. State U., 2001-; mem. bd. dirs. Free Libr. Phila. Found., 2005-. Recipient Mary Lyon award Mt. Holyoke Alumni Assn., 1985, Alumnae Medal of Honor, 1988, Hon. Alumnae award, 1989, Pres.'s award Med. Coll. Pa., 1993, Sylvia Rambo award Dickinson Sch. of Law, 1997, Star award Forum of Exec. Women, 1998, Ann Alpern award PBA Women in the Profession, 1999, Sandra Day O'Connor award Phila. Bar Assn., 1999, Outstanding Leadership in Support of Legal Svcs. award Pa. Legal Svcs., 1999, Women Making History Nat. Assn. of Women Bus. Owners, 2002, Women of Distinction award, Phila. Bus. Jour., 2001, Internat. Women's Forum "Women Who Make a Difference" award, 2003, Pink Ribbon award Pa. Breast Cancer Coalition, 2003, Woman One award Drexel U. Inst. for Women's Health and Leadership, 2004, Pa. Meritorious Svc. medal, 2005; named to Pa. Honor Roll of Women, 1996; named Disting. Dau. of Pa., Gov. of Pa., 1999. Fellow Am. Bar Found., Pa. Bar Found.; mem. ABA, Phila. Bar Assn. (exec. com. divsn. young lawyers 1982-85, bicentennial com. 1986-87, bd. govs. 1990-93, gender bias task force 1993-97, chair com. on jud. selection and retention 1987-89, vice chair 1985-87, investigative divsn. 1982-85, chair Andrew Hamilton Ball 1989, trustee Phila. Bar Found. 1990-97, co-chair century three commn. 1995-97, others), Pa. Bar Assn. (found. ho. dels. life fellow, bd. govs. 1980-83, 84-87, 91-93, chair young lawyers divsn. 1982-83, long range planning com. 1985-87, com. on professionalism, 1987-91, vice chmn. jud. inquiry and rev. bd. study com. 1989-91, sec. 1984-87, chair ho. dels. 1991-93, chair commn. on women in the profession 1993-95, v.p. 1996-97, pres. 1998-99, immediate past pres. 1999—, apptd. mem. ct. jud. discipline 1999), Pa. Bar Inst. (faculty, course planner), Phila. Assn. Def. Counsel (exec. coun. 1987-90, 94, joint trial demonstration with Phila. Trial Lawyers Assn. 1993), Def. Rsch. Inst. (spkr. toxic torts seminar 1983), Phila. Bar Edn. Advocacy Women Litigators (course planner, faculty 1995), Women's Assn. Women's Alternatives (bd. dirs. 1983-94, vice chair 1985-94), Phila. Forum Exec. Women, Pa. Women's Forum (pres. 2002-04), Com. of Seventy, Mt. Holyoke Alumnae Assn. (bd. dirs. 1986-89, 1999—). Democrat. Lutheran. Avocations: collecting American antiques, gardening, running. Office: Governors Office of Gen Counsel 225 Main Capitol Bldg Harrisburg PA 17120 Office Phone: 610-940-5325. Personal E-mail: millesq@aol.com.

MILLER, LINDA B., political scientist; b. Manchester, NH, Aug. 7, 1937; d. Louis and Helene (Chase) M. AB cum laude, Radcliffe Coll., 1959; MA, Columbia U., 1961, PhD, 1965. Asst. prof. Barnard Coll., 1964-67; rsch. assoc. Princeton U., 1966-67, Harvard U., 1967-71, 76-81, lectr. polit. sci., 1968-69; assoc. prof. Wellesley (Mass.) Coll., 1969-75, prof. polit. sci., 1975—2004, chmn. dept., 1985-89. Vis. prof. rsch. Watson Inst., Brown U., 1997, adj. prof. internat. rels., 1998—2000, 2003—, sr. fellow, 2000—03; vis. prof. polit. sci. Brown U., 1997. Author: World Order and Local Disorder: The United Nations and Internal Conflicts, 1967, Dynamics of World Politics: Studies in the Resolution of Conflicts, 1968, Cyprus: The Law and Politics of Civil Strife, 1968; co-author, co-editor: Ideas and Ideals: Essays on Politics in Honor of Stanley Hoffmann, 1993, Argentia, 2007—; editor Internat. Studies Rev., 1999-2002; contbr. articles to profl. jours. Internat. Affairs fellow Coun. Fng. Rels., 1973-74, Rockefeller Found. fellow, 1976-77, Oceanographic Instn. sr. fellow, 1979-80, 82-83, NATO social sci. rsch. fellow, 1982-83. Mem. Inst. Strategic Studies, Internat. Studies Assn., Coun. Fgn. Rels., Phi Beta Kappa. Home: PO Box 415 South Wellfleet MA 02663-0415 Office: Watson Inst Brown U PO Box 1970 Providence RI 02912-1970 Office Phone: 401-863-1598. Business E-Mail: Linda_Miller@brown.edu.

MILLER, LINDA KAREN, retired secondary school educator, social studies educator, law educator; b. Kansas City, Jan. 22, 1948; d. Bennie Chris and Thelma Jane (Richey) M. B of Secondary Edn., U. Kans., 1970; M of Secondary Edn., U. Va., 1978, EdD, 1991. Tchr. social studies Pierson Jr. H.S., Kansas City, 1970—72; substitute tchr. Fairfax Pub. Schs., Va., 1972—73; reading aide Lake Braddock Secondary Sch., Burke, Va., 1973—74; tchr. social studies Mark Twain Intermediate Sch., Alexandria, Va., 1974—75, Herndon Intermediate Sch., Va., 1975—78, Fairfax H.S., 1978—86, 1987—2002; ret., 2002. Instr. Sch. Law Cmty. Coll. So. Nev., Las Vegas, 2003; del. People to People, China, 2005; cons. in field. Pres. Nev. Women's History Project; Nev. coord. Nat. Coun. for History Edn., 2005. Named Pre-Collegiate Tchr. of Yr., Orgn. Am. Historians, 1996, Secondary Tchr. of Yr., Nat. Coun. for Social Studies, 1996, U. Va., 1997, Outstanding Secondary Tchr., Va. Hist. Soc., 1998, Va. Geography Tchr. of Yr., 1999, Global Technet Tchr. of Yr., Nat. Peace Corps Assn., 1999, Nat. Peace Educator, 2002; recipient George Washington medal, Valley Forge Freedom Found., 1988, Excellence in Tchg. award, U. Kans. Sch. Edn., 1999, Celebrating Tchg. Excellence award, Am. Coun. Tchrs. Russian, 1998, World History Tchg. prize, World History Assn., 2002, Humanities Leadership award, NEH, 2003; fellow, Korean Soc., 2000, 2004, Am. Revolution fellow, NY Hist. Soc., 2001. Mem. Nat. Coun. Social Studies (curriculum com. 1991-94), Am. Legal History Soc., Orgn. Am. Historians, Nat. Coun. for History Edn., Nev. Coun. Social Studies, U. Va. Alumni Assn., Rotary (pres. So. Nev. women's project). Republican. Episcopalian. Avocation: doll collecting.

MILLER, LISA ANN, lawyer; b. Bayshore, NY, Dec. 23, 1959; d. Harold Douglas and Joan Marie Miller; m. Michael E. Millhoan (div.); children: Shane E. Millhoan, Clayton W. Perry. BA in Polit. Sci., Ohio No. Coll., Ada, 1998; JD, U. Toledo, Toledo, Ohio, 2002. Bar: Ohio, Ohio (Supreme Ct.) 2002. Asst. to advertising dir. Good Housekeeping Mag., NY, 1985—88; asst. mktg. dir. Family Circle Mag., NY Times, NY, 1988—90; assoc. atty. Wise & Dorner LLC, Toledo, 2000—03; staff atty. Seneca County Dept. Family Svcs., Tiffin, Ohio, 2003—04; pvt. practice Findlay, Ohio, 2004—. Pres. Seneca County Bar Assoc., Tiffin, Ohio, 2006, v.p., 2004—05; law libr. trustee Seneca County Law Libr. Assoc., Tiffin, Ohio, 2004—06. Atty. advisor St. Wendelin HS Mock Trial Team, Fostonia, Ohio, 2006; voting rights staff Voter Protection Program, Fostonia, Ohio, 2004. Mem.: Southern Poverty Law Ctr., Ohio Assn. Criminal Defense Atty., Ohio State Bar Assn. Office Phone: 419-424-5553.

MILLER, LORING ERIK, insurance agent, broker; b. NYC, Apr. 6, 1951; s. Martin and Frances (Kaufman) M.; m. Ilene Jane Cook, Dec. 18, 1983; children: Justin, Jennifer, Mallory. Student, L.I. U., 1968—72; diploma, GM Sch. Dealership Mdse./Mgmt., 1977. Treas. Dial Chevrolet Inc., Westbury, NY, 1970—77, v.p., owner, 1977—88; pres. Mid. Country Brokerage Inc., Westbury, 1984—87, Loring E. Miller Agy. Inc., Mineola, NY, 1978—, ALLCOPS Consulting Group LLC, 2006—. Bd. dirs., pres. Nassau County Police Res. Assn., 1985—; chmn. bd. dirs., founder Suffolk County Police Res., 1997—; NY's Finest Found.; state trustee, lodge pres. NY State Fraternal Order of Police.; bd. dirs., Suffolk County Crime Stoppers; scoutmaster Boy Scouts Am., 1994-97; hon. mem. Nassau County Police Dept.; dir. NY Law Enforcement Found.; main bd. dirs., peace officer, dir. spl. ops. divsn. law enforcement Nassau County Soc. Prevention Cruelty to Animals, 2003; mem. Nassau County Law Enforcement Explorer Adv. Bd., 2006—. Mem.: Chiefs of Police Assn. Suffolk County, Profl. Ins. Agts. NY. Office: 398 Willis Ave Mineola NY 11501-1819

MILLER, LOUIS H., lawyer; b. Lampeter, UK, Apr. 22, 1945; m. Diane Matuszewski, Dec. 31, 1973; children: Margaret, Anthony. BA in History, Rutgers U., 1967; JD, Temple U., 1970. Bar: NJ 1970, US Dist. Ct. NJ 1970, US Supreme Ct. 1996. Law clk. to Judge Thomas Beetel Hunterdon County Ct., Flemington, NJ, 1970-71; law clk. to Judge Baruch Seidman Superior Ct. NJ Chancery, Trenton, NJ, 1971-72; assoc. Jefferson, Jefferson & Vaida, Flemington, 1972-75; ptnr. Vaida & Miller, Flemington, 1975-78; pvt. practice Flemington, 1978-81, 88—; judge Superior Ct. NJ, Flemington, 1981-88; of counsel Levinson Axelrod Wheaton & Grayzel, Flemington, 1990-97. Spl. dep. atty. gen. NJ Hunterdon County Prosecutor Office, Flemington, 1972-73; condemnation commr. Appt. Superior Ct. NJ, Flemington, 1988—, NJ Assembly spkrs. commr.; commr. NJ State Commn. Investigation, Trenton, 1993-97; arbitrator US Fed. Dist. Ct. NJ, 1989—. Twp. committeeman Alexandria Twp. Com., R.D. Milford, NJ, 1978-81. Mem. Am. Judges Assn., Am. Judicature Soc., NJ State Bar Assn. (mem. dist. ethics com. 1980-81, mem. mcpl. ct. practice com. 1996—), Hunterdon County Bar Assn., Consular Law Soc., Welsh Am. Geneal. Soc., Welsh North Am. C. of C. (bd. dirs.), USF Constellation Mus. (mem. bd. trustees 2003-). Republican. Avocations: paleontology, travel, hiking. Office: PO Box 850 40 Main St Flemington NJ 08822-1411 Office Phone: 908-782-1818. Personal E-mail: millerlh@earthlink.net.

MILLER, LOUIS HOWARD, biologist, researcher; b. Balt., Feb. 4, 1935; s. David and Daisy (Arenson) Miller; m. Susan K. Pierce; 1 child, Jennifer. BS, Haverford Coll., 1956; MD, Washington U., St. Louis, 1960; MS in Parasitology, Columbia U., 1964. Asst. prof. then assoc. prof. Coll. of P & S, Columbia U., NYC, 1967—71; head malaria sect. NIAID, NIH, Bethesda, Md., 1971—92, chief lab. parasitic diseases, 1992—. Contbr. articles to profl. jours. Capt. US Army, 1965—67. Recipient Paul Ehrlich/Ludwig Darmstaedter prize, 1989, Award for Disting. Achievement in Infectious Disease Rsch., Bristol-Myers Squibb, 1996, Commonwealth award in sci. and invention, 1999. Fellow: ACP, Queensland Inst. Med. Rsch., Royal Soc. Tropical Medicine and Hygiene; mem.: Assn. Am. Physicians, Inst. of Medicine, NAS, Am. Soc. Tropical Medicine and Hygiene (pres. 1988). Office Phone: 301-435-2177.

MILLER, LYNN FIELDMAN, lawyer; b. Newark, Oct. 9, 1938; d. George Martin and Helene G. (Friedman) Fieldman; m. Arthur Harold Miller, Aug. 24, 1958; children: Jennifer Lyn, Jonathan Daniel. BA in English, Barnard Coll., NYC, 1959; MLS, Rutgers U., New Brunswick, NJ, 1971, MA in Theater Arts, 1977; JD, Rutgers U., Newark, 1990. Bar: N.J. 1990, U.S. Dist. Ct. N.J. 1990, U.S. Ct. Appeals (3d cir.) 1992. Head libr. Alma White Coll., Zarapheth, N.J., 1971; reference libr. Douglas Coll., New Brunswick, N.J., 1971-79; media libr. Rutgers U., New Brunswick, 1979-87; intern Hon. Anne E. Thompson Fed. Dist. Ct., Trenton, NJ, 1988; assoc. Wilentz, Goldman & Spitzer, Woodbridge, NJ, 1989, Greenbaum, Rowe, Smith, Woodbridge, 1990-91, Miller & Littman, New Brunswick, 1991-93; ptnr. Miller & Miller, New Brunswick, 1993-2001, Miller, Miller & Tucker, P.A., 2001—. Editor in chief: (jour.) Women's Rights Law Reporter, 1989-90. Active Highland Park (NJ) Environ. Commn., 1991-97, Supreme Ct. Com. on Women in the Cts.; trustee Middlesex County Bar Found., 2002—. Mem. NJ State Bar Assn. (trustee 2000-06, individual rights com. 1989-95, chair individual rights com. 1995-97, dir. entertainment and arts law sect. 1992-96, bd. trustees Women in the Profession sect. 1997-98, sec. 1998-99, chmn. 2000-01, chair spl. com. consumer protection law 2002-2004), Middlesex County Bar Assn. (chair women lawyers sect. 1995-96, bd. trustees 1996-2002, treas. 2003-04, 2d v.p. 2004-05, 1st v.p. 2005-06, pres.-elect 2006—). Avocations: walking, bicycling. Office: 96 Paterson St New Brunswick NJ 08901-2109 Office Phone: 732-828-2234. Business E-Mail: lmiller@millerandmiller.com.

MILLER, MALCOLM HENRY, manufacturing sales executive, real estate developer; b. Elgin, Ill., Feb. 6, 1934; s. Carl Theodore and Alice Lucy (Garbisch) M. BA, U. Wis., Madison, 1957; postgrad., Am. Inst. Fgn. Trade, 1961, U. N.Mex., Albuquerque, 1963. Sales engr. Fairbanks Morse Corp., Beloit, Wis., 1962; pvt. practice real estate Albuquerque, 1964-75; supt., v.p. Walworth Foundries, Inc., Darien, Wis., 1959-61, exec. v.p. sales, co-owner, 1975—; v.p. sales, co-owner Waukesha Specialty Co., Inc., Darien, 1975—. Treas. Fastcast, Inc., Albuquerque, 1993—. Loan advisor, developer Community Assn. for Sr. Housing, Albuquerque, 1967-70; Rep. candidate for state senator N.Mex., 1970; active fin. com. Bernalillo County Reps., N.Mex., 1970-80, Walworth County Reps., Wis., 1976-77; mem. Congressman Ryan's 1st Dist. Small Bus. Adv. Com. Served to 1st lt. US Army, 1957-59. Mem. Am. Foundrymen's Assn., Dairy Food Industries Supply Assn., Dairy Food Industries Supply Assn. (bd. dir. 1992-95), Santa Fe Opera Guild, Big Foot Country Club, Nat. "W" Club, Masons, The Madison Club, Sigma Alpha Epsilon. Republican. Episcopalian. Avocations: exercise, films, opera, fly fishing. Home: 223 Fremont St PO Box 37 Walworth WI 53184-0037 Office: Walworth Foundries Inc PO Box 160 Hwy 14 and I-43 Interchange Darien WI 53114

MILLER, MARGERY, psychologist, educator, speech pathology/audiology services professional, mental health services professional; m. Donald F. Moores; children: Kip Lee, Tige Justice. BA, Elmira Coll., 1971; MA, NYU, 1972; EdS, MS, SUNY, Albany, 1975; MA, Towson State U., 1987; PhD, Georgetown U., 1991. Lic. speech pathologist Md., psychologist Md.; cert. tchr. nursery-6th grades, spl. edn. N.Y., nationally cert. sch. psychologist. Speech and lang. pathologist Mental Retardation Inst. Flower and Fifth Ave. Hosp., NYC, 1971—72; cmty. speech/lang. pathologist, dir. speech and hearing svc. NY State Dept. Mental Hygiene, Troy, 1972—74; instr. comm. disorders dept. Coll. St. Rose, Albany, NY, 1975—77; clin. supr. U. Md., College Park, 1978; speech/lang. pathologist Md. Sch. for Deaf, Frederick, 1978—84; auditory devel. specialist Montgomery County Pub. Schs., Rockville, Md., 1984—87; coord. Family Life program Nat. Acad. Gallaudet U., Washington, 1987—88, interim dir., 1988—89; dir. Counseling and Devel. Ctr. N.W. Campus, Washington, 1989—93; prof. psychology, coord. psychology internship program, dir. undergrad. psychology program Gallaudet U., Washington, 1993—; lic. practicing psychologist Bethesda, Md., 1998—. Instr. sign-lang. program Frederick CC; dance instr. for deaf adolescents; diagnostic cons. psychology and speech pathology; presenter at confs.; profl. coaching, Md., Fla., 2002—. Author: It's O.K. to be Angry, 1976; co-author: Cognition, Education and Deafness: Directions for Research and Instruction, 1985; mem. editl. rev. com. Gov.'s Devel. Disabilities Coun., Md.; contbr. articles to profl. jours. Vol., choreographer Miss Deaf Am. Pageant, 1984. Office Edn. Children's Bur. fellow, 1971. Mem.: APA, Montgomery County Md. Mental Health Assn., Am. Assn. Higher Edn., Nat. Assn. Sch. Psychologists, Nat. Assn. Deaf, Am. Speech, Lang. and Hearing Assn. (cert. clin. competence in speech/lang. pathology). Office: Gallaudet U 800 Florida Ave NE Washington DC 20002-3660 Office Phone: 202-651-5540. Business E-Mail: margery.miller@gallaudet.edu.

MILLER, MARILYN LEA, library and information scientist, educator; AA, Graceland Coll., 1950; BS in English, U. Kans., 1952; AMLS, U. Mich., 1959, PhD of Librarianship and Higher Edn., 1976. Bldg.-level sch. libr. Wellsville HS, Kans., 1952-54; tchr.-libr. Arthur Capper Jr. HS, Topeka, 1954-56; head libr. Topeka HS, Topeka, 1956-62; sch. libr. cons. State of Kans. Dept. of Pub. Instrn., 1962-67; from asst. to assoc. prof. Sch. Librarianship Western Mich. U., Kalamazoo, 1967-77; assoc. prof. libr. sci. U. NC, Chapel Hill, 1977-87, prof., chair dept. libr. and info. studies Greensboro, 1987-95, prof. emeritus, 1996—. Vis. faculty Kans. State Tchrs., Emporia, 1960, 63, 64, 66, U. Minn., Mpls., 1971, U. Manitoba, Winnipeg, Can., 1971; vis. prof. Appalachian State U., Boone, NC, 1987; adv. bd. sch. libr. media program Nat. Ctr. for Ednl. Stats., 1989, user rev. panel, 1990; chair assoc. dean search com. Sch. Edn., 1988, coord. Piedmont young writers conf., 1989-94, 97-99, chair race and gender com., 1990-93, SACS planning and evaluation com., 1990-91, learning resources ctr. adv. com., 1991-93; hearing panel for honor code U. NC Greensboro, 1988-91, assn. women faculty and administrv. staff, 1987-95, faculty coun., 1987-95, chair, 1994-95, univ. libr. com., 1987-88, com. faculty devel. in race and gender scholarship, 1990-92; lectr. and cons. in field. Editor: Pioneers and Leaders in Library Service to Youth, 2003; mem. editl. bd. The Emergency Librarian, 1981-97, Collection Building: Studies in the Development and Effective Use of Library Resources, 1978-96; contbr. chpt. to books, articles to profl. jour. Children's libr. specialists to visit Russian sch. and pub. libr., book publs., Moscow, Leningrad, Tashkent, 1979; hon. del. White House Conf. on Libr. and Info. Svcs., Washington, 1991; head del. Romanian Summer Inst. on Librarianship in U.S., 1991; citizen amb. People to People Internat. Program, People's Republic of China, 1992, Russian and Poland, 1992, Russia, 1994, Barcelona, 1995; exec. bd. dirs. Friends of Greensboro Pub. Libr., 1996-99, chair gift shop and coffee shop adv. com., 1996-2002, v.p., 2003-05, pres. 2005—; chair Citizens Materials Adv. com., 1999-; chair Citizens Strategic Long Range Planning com., 1994-95, 2001-03, chair, 2003, 06, Sch. Pub. Libr. com., 2002—, chair, 2003—; pub. libr. trustee, 2005-, NC State Libr. Commn., 2006-. Recipient Freedom Found. medal, 1962, Disting. Svc. to Sch. Librs. award Kans. Assn. Sch. Librs., 1982, Disting. Svc. award Graceland Coll., 1992, Disting. Alumnus award Sch. Libr. and Info. Studies, U. Mich., 1988, Contribution to Libr. Info. Sci. award Assn. Libr. Info. Sci., 1999; Delta Kappa Gamma scholar, 1972. Mem.: ALA (awards com. 1971—72, chair Chgo. conf. resolutions 1972, chair 1973—75, resolutions com. 1976—78, adv. com. Nat. Ctr. Ednl. Stats. 1984, standing com. libr. edn. 1987—91, yearbook adv. com. 1988—90, chair 1989—90, pres. 1992—93, exec. dir. 1994, chair rsch. com., chair search com., Disting. Svc. award Am. Assn. Sch. Librs. 1993), Friends of N.C. Pub. Librs. (bd. dirs. 2000—), So. Assn. Colls. and Schs. (accreditation team 1988), Southeastern Libr. Assn. (chair libr. educators sect. 1990—92), N.C. Assn. Sch. Librs. (Disting. Svc. award 2004), Assn. Libr Svc. to Children (bd. dirs. 1976—81, pres. 1979—80, rsch. com. 1982—85, chair 1984—85, Disting. Svc. award 2005), Assn. Ednl. Comms. and Tech., Am. Assn. Sch. Librs. (nominating com. 1980, pub. com. 1981—82, chair search com. exec. dir. 1985, v.p., pres.-elect 1985—86, pres. 1986—87, coord. coms. nat. stds. vision and implementation 1995—98), N.C. Libr. Assn. (life; edn. libr. com. 1978—80, 1982—86, bd. dirs. 1987—99, exec. bd. status women roundtable 1989—2003, chmn.-elect 1995—97, chmn. 1997—99, commn. on status of sch. librs. 1999—2000). Personal E-mail: marilynl@bellsouth.net.

MILLER, MARK A., information technology training executive; B in Bus. Adminstrn., U. Mich. V.p. Nutri/System, Inc., sr. v.p., pres.; founder, pres. Foxboro Group; chmn., CEO Signature Plastic Surgery, Inc., 1997—2000; group exec. v.p. Ea. U.S. Right Mgmt. Cons., Inc.; CEO New Horizons Worldwide, Inc., 2006—. Office: New Horizons Worldwide Inc 1900 South State Coll Blvd Ste 200 Anaheim CA 92806-6135 Office Phone: 714-940-8000. Office Fax: 714-938-6002.

MILLER, MARK KARL, journalist, editor; b. Meadville, Pa., Aug. 5, 1953; s. Richard Karl and Ellener Louise (Zimber) M. BA in Comms. and Journalism, Shippensburg U. of Pa., 1975. Editl. asst. Broadcasting mag., Washington, 1975, staff writer, 1976—77, asst. editor, 1977—80, sr. news editor, 1980—87, asst. mng. editor, 1987—91; mng. editor Broadcasting & Cable mag., Washington, 1991—98, Digital TV mag., Washington, 1999; freelance editor, writer, photographer, rschr., 2000—; dep. editor TVNewsday.com, 2006—. Mem. editl. adv. bd. Shippensburg U. of Pa., 1989-94, mem. profl. adv. bd. comm./journalism dept., 1994-96. Recipient Outstanding Alumnus award Shippensburg U., 1992. Mem. Soc. Profl. Journalists, Art Deco Soc. of Washington (bd. dirs., publs. chair 1986-97), Nat. Press Club. Home and Office: 2425 Valley Way Cheverly MD 20785-2956 Office Phone: 301-773-0058. E-mail: mkmiller@comcast.net.

MILLER, MARSHALL LEE, lawyer; b. Chattanooga, Tenn., Oct. 18, 1942; BA, Harvard U., 1964; student, Oxford U., Eng., Heidelberg U., Germany; JD, Yale U., 1970. Bar: D.C. 1971, U.S. Supreme Ct. 1979. Spl. asst. to adminstr. U.S. EPA, 1971-73; assoc. dep. atty. gen. U.S. Dept. Justice, 1973-74; asst. sec. labor (acctg.), dep. adminstr. OSHA, 1975-76; ptnr. Baise & Miller, Washington. Bd. editors: Yale Law Jour.; Soviet Mil. editor: Armed Forces Jour., 1983-87; author books internat. and environ. topics. Bd. dirs. Bulgarian-Am. Enterprise Fund, Electronic Warfare Assocs., Am. Coun. of Internat. Living, Am. Assn. Advancement Sci. Home: PO Box 1311 Bethany Beach DE 19930-1311 Office: Baise Miller Pc PO Box 14368 Washington DC 20044-4368

MILLER, MARY HELEN, retired state government administrator; b. Smiths Grove, Ky., June 30, 1936; d. Walter Frank and Lottie Belle (Russell) Huddleston; m. George Ward Wilson, Sept. 12, 1958 (div. Sept. 1973); children: Ward Glenn, Amy Elizabeth Huddleston; m. Francis Guion Miller Jr., June 6, 1981. BA, Western Ky. U., 1958. Tchr. Fayette County Schs., Lexington, Ky., 1958-60, Seneca High Sch., Louisville, 1960-63, Shelby County High Sch., Shelbyville, Ky., 1963-69; rsch. analyst Legis. Rsch. Com., Frankfort, Ky., 1973-79, asst. dir., 1979-83, 90-91; chief exec. asst. Office Gov., Frankfort, 1983-87, 93-95, legis. liaison, 1991-93; cabinet sec. Natural Resources and Environ. Protection Cabinet, Frankfort, 1987-88; sales assoc. W. Wagner, Jr. Comml. Real Estate, Louisville, 1989-91; ret., 1996. Author: (constl. revision) Citizens Guide To/Perspective, 1978, (booklet) A Look at Kentucky General Assembly, 1979, A Guide to Education Reform, 1990, (handbook) Gubernatorial Transition in Kentucky, 1991. Mem. Leadershi Ky. Alumni, Frankfort, 1986, Waterfront Devel. Corp. Bd., Louisville, 1986—87, Greater Louis Partnership Econ. Devel., 1988—92, Shelbyville 2000 Found. Bd., 1991—92; mem., sec. Regional Airport Authority Bd., Louisville, 1986—89; mem. Shelby County Cmty. Theatre Bd., Shelbyville, 1978—83, 1988—91, treas., 1979—83, pres., 1989—91; chair Shelby County Cmty. Found., 1995—2000; mem. Ky. Long Term Policy Bd., 1992—99, chair, 1995; mem. Ky. Hist. Properties Commn., 1995—99; exec. com. Ky. Hist. Soc., 2002—, v.p., 2004—; mem. Shelby Devel. Found., 2003—05. Recipient Vic Hellard Jr. Pub. Svc. in Ky. award, 1999; named Shelbyville Citizen of Yr., 1998. Mem. Caryatid Book Club (pres. 1999), Women's Initiative Networking Groups (pres. 1998), Western Ky. U. Alumni Assn. (bd. dirs. 1992-95). Democrat. Episcopalian. Avocations: reading, theater, gardening, antiques. Home: 1116 Main St Shelbyville KY 40065-1420 E-mail: mhm1116@aol.com.

MILLER, MAX DUNHAM, JR., lawyer; b. Des Moines, Oct. 17, 1946; s. Max Dunham and Beulah (Head) M.; m. Melissa Ann Dart, Jan. 10, 1969 (div. July 1975); 1 child, Ann Marie Victoria; m. Caroline Jean Armendt, Sept. 19, 1981 (div. Dec. 2001); children: Alexander Bradshaw, Benjamin Everrett; m. Marion Beall Nadolny, June 27, 2004. BS with high honors, Mich. State U., 1968; postgrad., George Washington U., 1970-71; JD, U. Md., 1975. Bar: Md. 1976, U.S. Dist. Ct. Md. 1976, U.S. Ct. Appeals (4th cir.) 1981, U.S. Supreme Ct. 1982. Engr. U.S. Dept. of Def., Aberdeen Proving Ground, Md., 1968-72; law clk. to presiding judge Md. Cir. Ct., Higinbothom in Bel Air, Md., 1975-76; asst. county atty. Harford County, Bel Air, 1976-79; assoc. Lentz & Hooper P.A., Balt., 1979-81; ptnr. Miller, Olszewski & Moore, P.A., Bel Air, 1981-94; prin. Law Offices of Max D. Miller, P.A., 1994—. County atty. Harford County, Md., 1983-88. Mem. Md. Bar Assn., Assn. Trial Lawyers Am., Md. Trial Lawyers Assn., Harford County Bar Assn., Phi Kappa Phi, Phi Eta Sigma. Avocations: golf, sailing, canoeing, bicycling. Office: 5 S Hickory Ave Bel Air MD 21014-3732 Office Phone: 410-879-3300.

MILLER, MAXINE LYNCH, retired home economist, retired interior designer, educator; b. Ellensburg, Wash., Feb. 15, 1921; d. Ralph A. Lynch and Bertha Sorenson; m. Harlan LeRoy Miller, Aug. 29, 1950 (div. June 1965). BA in Home Econs., Wash. State U., Pullman, 1942; MA in Home Econs., U. Wash., Seattle, 1959. Asst. prof. to prof. Calif. State U., LA, 1955—80; prof. emeritus, 1980. Chair program accreditation team, nat. treas. Interior Design Educators Coun., Inc. Recipient Interior Design Educators Coun. Emeritus Letter of Commendation award, Found. Interior Design Edn. Rsch., 1959; scholar, Am. Soc. Interior Design, 1968. Mem.: Nat. Soc. DAR. Avocations: genealogy, photography, art, crafts. Home: 913 Chamith Ln Ellensburg WA 98926

MILLER, MAYNARD MALCOLM, geologist, educator, science administrator, former state legislator; b. Seattle, Jan. 23, 1921; s. Joseph Anthony and Juanita Queena (Davison) M.; m. Joan Walsh, Sept. 15, 1951; children: Ross McCord, Lance Davison. BS magna cum laude, Harvard U., 1943; MA, Columbia U., 1948; PhD, St. John's Coll., Cambridge U., 1957; student, Naval War Coll., Air War Coll., Nat. Def. U., Oak Ridge Inst. Nuc. Sci.; DSc (hon.), U. Alaska, 1990. Registered profl. geologist, Idaho. Asst. prof. naval sci. Princeton U., NJ, 1946; organizer, dir. Office Naval Rsch., Juneau Icefield Rsch. project Am. Geog. Soc., NYC, 1946—55, rsch. assoc., 1948—55; geologist Gulf Oil Co., Cuba, 1947; staff scientist Swiss Fed. Inst. for Snow and Avalanche Rsch., Davos, 1952—53; instr. dept. geography Cambridge U., 1953—56; assoc. prodr., field project dir. film Seven Wonders of the World Cinerama Corp., Europe, Asia, Africa, Mid. East, 1954—55; rsch. assoc. Lamont Geol. Obs., NYC, 1955—59; sr. scientist dept. geology Columbia U., NYC, 1957—59; asst. prof. geology Mich. State U., East Lansing, 1959—61, assoc. prof., 1961—63, prof., 1963—75; dean Coll. Mines and Earth Resources U. Idaho, Moscow, 1975—88, dean emeritus, prof. geology, dir. Glaciological and Arctic Scis. Inst., 1975—; dir., state geologist Idaho Geol. Survey, 1975—88, dir. emeritus; rep. Legislature of State of Idaho, Boise, 1992—2000. Geophys. cons. Nat. Park Svc., NASA, USAF, NAS; mapping expdn. Brady Icefield and Glacier Bay, Alaska, 1940-41; leader Mt. St. Elias Expdn. USAF-Harvard Mountaineering Club, Alaska, 1946; geologist Am. Mt. Everest Expdn., Nepal, 1963; dir. Nat. Geog. Soc. Alaskan Glacier Commemorative Project, 1964—; organizer leader Nat. Geog. Soc. Joint U.S.-Can. Mt. Kennedy Yukon Meml. Mapping Expdn., 1965; leader Muséo Argentino de Ciencias Naturales, Patagonian expdn. and glacier survey for Inst. Geologico del Peru and Am. Geog. Soc., 1949-50; adv. missions People's Republic of China, 1981, 86, 88, 98; geol. expdns. Himalaya, Nepal, 1963, 84, 87; USAF ice survey mission to Ellesmere Land, North Pole and Polar Sea, 1951; organizer, ops. officer USN-LTA blimp geophysics flight to Ice Island T-3 and North Pole area Office Naval Rsch., 1958; ONR-LTA coord. SS Nautilus First Transit North Pole; prin. investigator U.S. Naval Oceanog. Office sea and pack ice rsch. Ice Island T-3 Polar Sea, 1967-68, 70-73; dir. lunar field sta. project Mt. Rainier summit simulation USAF-Boeing Co., 1959-60; prin. investigator Nat. Geog. Soc. 30 Yr. Remap of Lemon, Taku and Cathedral Massif Glaciers, Juneau Icefield, 1989-2005; dir. Found. for Glacier and Environ. Rsch., Pacific Sci. Ctr., Seattle, 1955-95, 97—, chmn., 1992—, pres., 1955-85, trustee, 1960—, cons. Dept. Hwys. State of Alaska, 1965; chmn., dir. World Ctr. for Exploration Found., NYC, 1968-71; dir., adv. bd. Idaho Geol. Survey, 1975-88; chmn. nat. coun. JSHS program U.S. Army Rsch. Office and Acad. Applied Sci., 1982-90; sci. dir. U.S. Army Rsch. Office and DOD Nat. Sci. and Humanities Symposia programs, 1991—; disting. guest prof. China U. Geoscis., Wuhan, 1981—, Changchun U. Earth Scis., People's Republic of China, 1988—; adj. prof. U. Alaska, 1986-. Author: Field Manual of Glaciological and Arctic Sciences; co-author books on Alaskan glaciers and Nepal geology; contbr. articles to profl. jours., chpts. to books. Past mem. nat. exploring com., nat. sea exploring com. Boy Scouts Am.; past mem. nat. adv. bd. Embry Riddle Aero. U.; bd. dirs. Idaho Rsch. Found.; pres. state divsn. Mich. UN Assn., 1970-73; mem. Centennial and Health Environ. Commns., Moscow, Idaho, 1987—. With USN, 1943-46, PTO. Decorated 11 campaign and battle stars; Fulbright scholar Cambridge U., 1951-53; named Leader of Tomorrow Seattle C. of C. and Time mag., 1953, one of Ten Outstanding Young Men U.S. Jaycees, 1954; recipient commendation for lunar environ. study USAF, 1960, Hubbard medal Nat. Geog. Soc., 1963, Elisha Kent Kane Gold medal Geog. Soc. Phila., 1964, Karo award Soc. Mil. Engrs., 1966, Franklin L. Burr award Nat. Geog. Soc., 1967, Nat. Commendation Boy Scouts Am., 1970, Disting. Svc. plaque UN Assn. U.S., Disting. Svc. commendation State of Mich. Legis., 1975, Outstanding Civilian Svc. medal U.S. Army Rsch. Office, 1977, Outstanding Leadership in Minerals Edn. commendations Idaho Mining Assn., 1985, 87, Nat. Disting. Tchg. award Assn. Am. Geographers, 1996; grantee NSF, Nat. Geog. Soc., NASA, ARO, M.J. Murdock Trust, Dept. of Interior, others, 1948—. Fellow Geol. Soc. Am., Arctic Inst. N.Am., Explorers Club; mem. AAAS (councilor, Pacific divsn. 1978-88), AIME, ASME (hon. nat. lectr.), Am. Geophys. Union, Internat. Glaciological Soc. (past councilor), Assn. Am. State Geologists (hon.), Am. Legis. Exch. Coun., Am. Assn. Amateur Oarsmen (life), Am. Alpine Club (hon., life), Fulbright Assn., Alpine Club (London), Appalachian Club (hon. corr.), Brit. Mountaineering Assn. (hon., past v.p.), The Mountaineers (hon.), Cambridge U. Mountaineering Club (hon.), Himalyan Club (Calcutta), English Speaking Union (nat. lectr.), Naval Res. Assn. (life), Dutch Treat Club, Circumnavigators Club (life), Adventurers Club N.Y. (medalist), Am. Legion, VFW, Harvard Club (N.Y.C. and Seattle), Sigma Xi, Phi Beta Kappa (past pres. Epsilon chpt.), Phi Kappa Phi. Republican. Methodist. Avocations: skiing, mountaineering, photography. Home: 514 E 1st St Moscow ID 83843-2814 Office: Univ Idaho Coll Sci Moscow ID 83844-3022 Address: Found Glacier & Environ Rsch 4470 N Douglas Hwy Juneau AK 99801-9403 Office Phone: 208-882-1237. Office Fax: 208-882-6207. Business E-Mail: jirp@uidaho.edu.

MILLER, MERRILL ANTHONY, JR., energy executive; b. Burlington, Iowa, July 4, 1950; s. Merrill Anthony Sr. and Florence Mae (Douglas) M.; m. Diana Sue Wagner, June 17, 1972; 1 child, Paul. BS in Engring., U.S. Mil. Acad., 1972; MBA, Harvard U., 1980. Team mgr. Procter & Gamble, Mehoopany, Pa., 1977-78; asst. to pres. Helmerick & Payne, Tulsa, 1980-82, v.p. and gen. mgr. no. div. Okla. City, 1982; with Nat. Oilwell Varco, Houston, 1996—, pres., 2000—, COO, 2000—05, CEO, 2001—, chmn., 2002—. Bd. dirs. Internat. Computer Exchange, Inc., Boulder, Colo. Mem. Internat. Assn. Drilling Contractors (bd. dirs. 1985—, chmn. midcontinent chpt. 1986-87). Roman Catholic. Avocations: sports, reading. Office: National Oilwell Varco 10000 Richmond Ave Houston TX 77042-4200 *

MILLER, MERRY, educational association administrator; b. Mesquite, Tex., 1970; Sr. programming dir. Learning Annex, NYC, 2002—. Named one of 40 Under 40, Crain's NY Bus., 2007. Office: Learning Annex 7th Fl 48 W 37th St New York NY 10018 Office Phone: 212-371-0280. Office Fax: 212-290-2430. *

MILLER, MICHAEL, physician, educator; b. Queens, NY, June 19, 1957; s. Irving Maltz and Lenore (Goldstein) Miller; m. Lisa L. Miller; children: Avery Lauren, Ilana Frieda, Myles Solomon. BA, Rutgers U., 1979; MD, Robert Wood Johnson Med. Sch., 1983. Diplomate Am. Bd. Internal Medicine, Am. Bd. Cardiovascular Disease, Nat. Bd. Med. Examiners. Intern dept. medicine Med. Ctr. U. Cin., 1983-84, resident internal medicine, 1984-86; lipoprotein metabolism fellow Sch. Medicine Johns Hopkins U., Balt., 1986-89, cardiovascular disease fellow, 1988-91; dir. ctr. preventive cardiology U. Md. Med. Sys., Balt., 1991—; assoc. prof. medicine divsn. cardiology Sch. Medicine U. Md., Balt., 1991—; asst. prof. medicine divsn. cardiology Sch. Medicine Johns Hopkins U., Balt., 1991—; adj. asst. prof. dept. medicine Baylor Coll. Medicine, Houston, 1992—. Tchr. Sch. Medicine U. Md., 1994—, Johns Hopkins U., 1993—, Balt. Pub. Sch. Sys., 1991—; lectr. in field. Author: The Practice of Coronary Disease Prevention, 1996, The Cholesterol Planner, 3d edit., 2004, 5th edit., 2006; contbr. chpts. to books and articles to profl. jours.; reviewer numerous jours.; featured in ednl. recordings, 1990—. Mem. Gov.'s Task Force Cardiovasc. Disease Prevention. Grantee NIH/Am. Heart Assn., 1989—, Bristol-Myers Squibb, 1991-93, Sandoz, 1992-93, Pfizer, 1992—, Merck, 1997—; recipient Robert Galbraith award, 1979, William F. Grupe award, 1983, Samuel Kaslev award, 1994. Fellow Am. Coll. Cardiology (co-author Preventive Cardiology, 1998—), Am. Heart Assn. Coun. Arteriosclerosis; mem. AAAS, Am. Soc. Preventive Cardiology (past pres. 2007), Am. Heart Assn. Coun. Epidemiology, Phi Beta Kappa. Jewish. Avocations: skiing, tennis, hiking. Home: 5 Green Heather Ct Baltimore MD 21208 Office: U Md Divsn Cardiology 22 S Greene St Baltimore MD 21201-1544 Office Phone: 410-328-6299. E-mail: mmiller@medicine.maryland.edu.

MILLER, MICHAEL DOUGLAS, lawyer; b. Tucson, Dec. 25, 1948; s. Robert Friend and Mary (Fawcett) M.; m. Jennifer Louise Hunter, Dec. 23, 1960; 1 child, Hunter Douglas. BS, U. Ariz., 1973, JD, 1976. Bar: Ariz. 1977. Pvt. practice, Tucson, 1977—. Mem. Ariz. Bar Assn., Ariz. Trial Lawyers Assn., Pima County Bar Assn. Avocations: fishing, camping, outdoor activities. Office: 2830 N Swan Rd Ste 140 Tucson AZ 85712-6301 Office Phone: 520-327-3801. E-mail: mdm1@mdmlaw.net.

MILLER, MICHAEL JEFFREY, editor, columnist; b. Chgo., Dec. 10, 1958; s. Kenneth Maynard and Joan (Callner) Miller; m. Joan A. Slobin, Oct. 18, 1987. BS in Computer Sci., Rensselaer Poly., Troy, NY, 1979; MS in Journalism, Northwestern U., Evanston, Ill., 1980. Sr. editor Bldg. Design and Constrn., Chgo., 1980—83; west coast bur. chief Popular Computing, San Francisco, 1983—85; exec. editor InfoWorld, Menlo Park, Calif., 1985—89, editor, 1989—90, editor-in-chief, 1991, PC Mag., NYC, 1991—2005; exec. v.p., editl. dir. Ziff-Davis Pub., 1997—2005; chief content officer Ziff-Davis Media, 2005—06; sr. v.p. tech. strategy Ziff Brothers Investments, 2006—. Mem.: Soc. Profl. Journalists, Am. Soc. Technion. Office: Ziff Davis Media Inc 28 E 28th St New York NY 10016-7930

MILLER, MICHAEL JON, survey engineer; b. Parkers Prairie, Minn., Mar. 17, 1950; s. Buford Kenneth and Gretchen Cena (Sharp) M.; m. Terry Lynn Peck, May 20, 1972; children: Livia Mica, David Peter. BS, U. Wis., Platteville, 1972; M of Pub. Adminstrn., Ariz. State U., 1988. Cert. profl. land surveyor, Wis., Ariz., soil tester, Wis. Chief of surveys Hovelsrud Cons. Assn., Richland Ctr., Wis., 1972-78; ops. mgr. Tech, Advisors, Inc., Phoenix, 1978-82; profl. surveyor Coe and Van Loo, Inc., Phoenix, 1982-83; survey engr. City of Phoenix, 1983—. Land surveyor mem. Ariz. Bd. Tech. Registration, 1989-97, emeritus mem., 1997—, sec., 1990-91, vice chmn., 1991, chmn., 1991-92, vice chmn. 1993-94, chmn. 1994-95; mem. Enforcement Adv. Com., 1997—. Content editor The Ariz. Surveyor; contbr. articles to profl. jours. Dep. registrar Dem. Party of Ariz., Phoenix, 1983-94; clk. Phoenix Friends Meeting, 1985-86; recording clk. Intermountain Yearly Meeting of Religious Soc. of Friends, 1984-85. Fellow Am. Congress on Surveying and Mapping (membership chmn. 1987-88); mem. Nat. Soc. Profl. Surveyors (gov. for Ariz. 1985-89), Western Fedn. Land Surveyors (state del. 1988-89), Ariz. Profl. Land Surveyors (sec. 1983-84, pres. 1985-86, Outstanding award 1981, life mem. award 1996), Nat. Coun. Examiners for Engrs. and Surveyors (chmn. western zone nominating com. 1998), Am. Pub. Works Assn., Am. Soc. for Pub. Adminstrn. (bd. dirs. Ariz. chpt. 2000—, pres.-elect 2003, pres. 2004-05, comm. dir. sect. for historic, artistic and reflective expression, chair 2005-), World Clown Assn., Internat. Jugglers Assn., Greater Ariz. Bicycle Assn. Democrat. Avocations: history, writing, juggling, bicycling. Home: 4026 E Campbell Ave Phoenix AZ 85018-3709 Office Phone: 602-495-2050. Personal E-mail: piman4449@qmail.com. Business E-Mail: michael.miller@phoenix.gov.

MILLER, MICHAEL PATIKY, lawyer; b. Huntington, NY, Apr. 16, 1944; s. George J. and Alida (Patiky) Miller; m. Dorothy Denn, Dec. 25, 1966; children: Lauren M. Golubtchik, Jonathan M., Rachel Miller Lazarus. AB, Rutgers U., 1965; JD, NYU, 1968. Bar: N.J. 1968, U.S. Dist. Ct. N.J. 1968, Calif. 1975, U.S. Dist. Ct. (no. dist.) Calif. 1975, U.S. Tax Ct. 1977, U.S. Ct. Appeals (9th cir.) 1977, U.S. Ct. Appeals (fed. cir.) 1984, U.S. Dist. Ct. (cen. dist.) Calif. 1982, U.S. Supreme Ct. 1983, U.S. Claims Ct. 1986. Chief of procurement and admin. law U.S. Army, 1973—74; atty. Electric Power Rsch. Inst., Palo Alto, Calif., 1974—77; assoc. Weinberg, Ziff & Kaye, Palo Alto, 1977—78; ptnr. Weinberg, Ziff & Miller, Palo Alto, 1978—, mng. ptnr., 1990—98; lectr. on tax and estate planning U. Calif. Extension, 1980—. Author: Creditor Rights in Proceedings Outside Estate Adminstrn., 1995, rev., 1999, Estate Planning for Foreign Nationals in Silicon Valley, 2000, Death, Debts and Taxes 2000, rev. 2006, Building A Better Boiler, Doing the Math in Estate Planning, 2006, Don't Make Mistakes with Judicial Council Forms, 2006; co-author: Decedents Estate Practice, 2001, rev. annually, Trust Administration, 2d edit., 2001—; contbg. author: California Wills and Trusts, 1991, Estate Planning for Unmarried Couples, 1998, Doing the Math of Estate Planning, 1999, Trust and Estate Litigation, 2004; contbr. chpts. in books and articles to profl. jours. Treas. No. Calif. region United Synagogue Am., 1985-89, pres., 1992-95. Capt. U.S. Army, 1969-74, Vietnam, Ethiopia. Recipient Lion of Judah award, 1984, Cert. Merit U. Judaism, 1992. Mem. ABA (chmn. region VI pub. contract law sect. 1975-78, commn. tax practice in small law firms, com. on taxation of trusts, estates, taxation sect. 1986—), N.J. State Bar, State Bar of Calif. (commr. tax law adv. commn. 1989-92, 93-95, chair 1994-95, mem. bd. legal specialization 1994-95, chair probate sect. 1982), Silicon Valley Bar Assn. (pres. 2000-02, trustee 2002—, treas. 2006—). Office: Weinberg Ziff & Miller 400 Cambridge Ave Palo Alto CA 94306-1507 Home Phone: 408-732-1868; Office Phone: 650-329-0851. Business E-Mail: mpmiller@taxattorney.com.

MILLER, MICHELLE D., lawyer; b. 1952; BA cum laude, Boston Univ., 1974; JD magna cum laude, Boston Coll., 1979. Bar: Mass. 1979. Law clk. Judge Paul J. Liacos, Supreme Judicial Ct. Mass., 1979—80; assoc. to ptnr. Wilmer Cutler Pickering Hale & Dorr, Boston, 1980—, vice chmn. Litigation dept., vice chmn. Antitrust & Competition dept., mem. exec. com. Contbr. articles to profl. jours. Named one of Top 50 Female Mass. Lawyers, Boston Mag., 2004. Mem.: ABA, Boston Bar Assn. (former co-chmn. Antitrust com.), Order of the Coif. Office: Wilmer Cutler Pickering Hale & Dorr 60 State St Boston MA 02109 Office Phone: 617-526-6116. Office Fax: 617-526-5000. Business E-Mail: michelle.miller@wilmerhale.com.

MILLER, MILTON ALLEN, lawyer; b. LA, Jan. 15, 1954; s. Samuel C. and Sylvia Mary Jane (Silver) Miller; m. Mary Ann Toman, Sept. 10, 1988; 1 child, Mary Ann. AB in Econs. with distinction and honors, Stanford U., 1976; JD with honors, Harvard U., 1979. Bar: Calif. 1979, U.S. Ct. Appeals 9th cir.) 1979, U.S. Supreme Ct. 1989, Calif. (U.S. Dist. Ct. (cen., no. and so. dists.)) 1981. Law clk. U.S. Ct. Appeals (9th cir.), Sacramento, 1979—80; assoc. Latham & Watkins, LA, 1979—87, ptnr., 1987—. Chmn. ethics com. Latham & Watkins, LA, 1986—. Author: (non fiction) Attorney Ethics, 1993; editor: (articles) Harvard Law Rev., 1978—79; contbr. articles to profl. jours. Mem.: ATLA, ABA, L.A. County Bar Assn. (chmn. profl. responsibility and ethics com.), Calif. State Bar Assn. (mem. com. on profl. responsibility), Harvard Club (Boston and NY), Phi Beta Kappa. Office: Latham & Watkins Ste 4000 633 W 5th St Los Angeles CA 90071-2005 Office Phone: 213-485-1234. Business E-Mail: milt.miller@lw.com. *Notable cases include Medavoy vs. Klein and Raquel Welch vs. MGM Corp.; served as trial and insurance counsel in San Juan Dupont Plaza Hotel Fire litigation.*

MILLER, MONTE BALDWIN, retired internist; b. Independence, Mo., Sept. 4, 1930; s. Marshall Baldwin and Frances Lee Miller; m. Christine Faye Vielguth, Sept. 6, 1953; children: Mitchell, Mark, Michelle. BA, U. Kans., 1951; MD, U. Kans., Kansas City, 1955. Bd. cert. internal medicine. Intern Tacoma (Wash.) Gen. Hosp., 1955—56; commd. USAF, 1956, advanced through grades to lt. gen., 1988, flight surgeon Williams AFB, Ariz., 1956—58; pvt. practice Garnett, Kans., 1958—62; resident internal medicine Wilford Hall USAF Med. Ctr., Lackland AFB, Tex., 1962—65; asst. for tng. dept. medicine David Grant USAF Med. Ctr., Travis AFB, Calif., 1965—67, chmn. dept. medicine, 1968—73, dir. hosp. svcs. and dep. comdr., 1973—75, comdr., 1975—77; chief of medicine 12th USAF Hosp., Cam Rahn Bay, 1967; asst. clin. prof. Dept. Medicine Calif., Davis, 1968—78; med. directorate br. chief Hdqrs. Air Force Inspection and Safety Ctr., Norton AFB, Calif., 1978—79, chief med. inspection divsn., 1979—80; comdr. Malcolm Grow USAF Med. Ctr., Andrews AFB, DC, 1980—81; command surgeon Mil. Airlift Command, Scott AFB, Ill., 1981—85; comdr. Wilford Hall USAF Med. Ctr., Lackland AFB, Tex., 1985—86; command surgeon Hdqrs. U.S. European Command, Stuttgart, Germany, 1986—88; surg. gen. USAF, 1988—91; med. dir. Birch and Davis Internat. Project King Abdulaziz U., Saudi Arabia. Cons. internal medicine USAF Surgeon Gen., Washington, 1970—88. Contbr. articles to profl. jours. Bd. mem. Meth. Ch., Winchester, Tenn., 1994—98, Franklin County Adult Activity, Winchester, 2000—; bd. mem., past pres. Timsford Coun., Winchester, 2000—. Fellow: ACP (Air Force gov. 1985, Laureate award); mem.: U. Kans. Med. Alumni (Disting. Alumni 1990), AMA (bd. govs. 1988—91, ho. dels. 1988, mem. reference com. on med. edn. 1991), Phi Beta Kappa. Republican. Avocation: bass fishing. Home: 306 Cooper Ln Winchester TN 37398-4316

MILLER, MORRIS HENRY, lawyer; b. Thomasville, Ga., June 14, 1954; s. Gibbes Ulmer and Marianne (Morris) M.; m. Anita Carol Payne, Mar. 23, 1985; children: Morris Payne, Rose Elizabeth, David Gibbes, Paul Louis Henry, John Henry. BS in Acctg. summa cum laude, Fla. State U., 1976; JD, U. Va., 1979. Bar: Fla. 1979. Assoc. Holland & Knight, Tampa, Fla., 1979-84, ptnr. Tallahassee, 1984—, chmn. health law practice, 1989—2001, knowledge mgmt. ptnr., 2001—04, CLE ptnr., 2004—05. Of counsel Seminole Boosters, Inc., 2006—. Dist. fin. chmn. Gulf Ridge coun. Boy Scouts Am., 1988-89, mem. pack com., cubmaster Pack 23, Suwannee River Area coun., 1995-98, scoutmaster Troop 182, 1997-99, scoutmaster Troop 10, 2000-01, asst. scoutmaster, 2002-06, scoutmaster Troop 50, 2006—, dist. nominating com., exec. bd., 2005-; mem. Leadership Tampa, 1986, Leadership Tampa Bay, 1989; bd. dirs. John G. Riley House Mus. Ctr. for African-Am. History and Culture, 1998-99, Tallahassee YMCA, 1994-2002, chmn. long range planning com., 1997; founder, chmn. Tampa Bus. Com. for Arts, Inc., 1988-89; elder Presbyn. Ch. Mem. ABA (health and bus. law sects.), Fla. Bar (chmn., vice chmn. computer law com. 1983-89, Fla. corp. law revision com. 1986-89, health and bus. law sects.), Tallahassee Bar Assn. Office: Holland & Knight 315 S Calhoun St Ste 600 Tallahassee FL 32301-1897 Home Phone: 850-668-4193; Office Phone: 850-425-5655. Business E-Mail: morris.miller@hklaw.com.

MILLER, NANCY ELLEN, computer scientist, consultant; b. Detroit, Aug. 30, 1956; d. George Jacob and Charlotte M. Miller. BS in Computer and Comm. Scis., U. Mich., 1978; MS in Computer Scis., U. Wis., 1981. Product engr. Ford Motor Co., Dearborn, Mich., 1977; computer programmer Unique Bus. Sys., Inc., Southfield, Mich., 1978; tchg. asst. U. Wis., Computer Scis. Dept., Madison, 1978—82; computer scientist Lister Hill Nat. Ctr. Biomed. Commns., Nat. Libr. Medicine, NIH, Bethesda, Md.,

1984—88; pvt. practice West Bloomfield, Mich., 1993—. *Nancy E. Miller's professional interests in the field of artificial intelligence include: knowledge representation, expert systems, default logic, planning, knowledge-based systems, case-based reasoning, logic programming, agents, fuzzy logic, neural networks, and genetic programming. She is also interested in object-oriented programming and design. Ms. Miller is highly skilled in the following computer languages, systems, and tools: Lisp, Prolog, C++, C, Pascal, UNIX, Windows, Framekit, HTML, etc. She has used rapid prototyping and structured programming methodologies. Ms. Miller has worked in many facets of computer science, from research and development to end-user applications, in academia, government and industry, and on all sizes of computers.* Recipient Jour. of Am. Soc. for Info. Sci. Best Paper award, 1988. Mem. Assn. for Computing Machinery (sec. S.E. Mich. spl. interest group on artificial intelligence 1993-94), Am. Assn. for Artificial Intelligence, Assn. for Logic Programming, U. Wis. Alumni Assn. (life), U. Mich. Alumni Assn. (life), Am. Contract Bridge League, Nat. Women's Polit. Caucus, NARAL Pro-Choice Am., Jewish Fedn. Met. Detroit, Planned Parenthood Fed. Am., Hadassah: The Women's Zionist Orgn. Am. (life). Democrat. Jewish. Address: PO Box 4224 Southfield MI 48037-4224

MILLER, NANCY K., literature educator; PhD, Columbia U. Faculty mem. French Dept. Columbia U.; prof. Women's Studies Dept. Bernard Coll.; prof. English Dept. Lehman Coll.; disting. prof. comparative lit., English and French CUNY, NYC, 1999—. Contbr. articles to profl. jours.; editor: Poetics of Gender, 1985, Extremities: Trauma, Testimony, and Community, 2001; author: (memoir) Out of Breath, The Heroine's Text: Readings in the French and English Novel, 1980, Subject to Change: Reading Feminist Writing, 1989, Bequest and Betrayal: Memoirs of a Parent's Death, 1995, But Enough about Me: Why We Read Other People's Lives, 2001. Office: CUNY Grad Ctr PhD Program in Eng 365 5th Ave New York NY 10016-4309 E-mail: nmiller@gc.cuny.edu. *

MILLER, NANCY LOIS, senior pastor; b. Lancaster, Pa., July 20, 1954; d. William Martin and Dorothy DeBoer Miller. BA, Lebanon Valley Coll., 1976; MDiv, Garrett-Evangelical Theol. Sem., 1980. Cert. deacon Ea. Pa. Ann. Conf. United Meth. Ch., 1977, elder Ea. Pa. Ann. Conf. United Meth. Ch., 1981, basic quarter clin. pastoral edn. Rush Presbyn. St. Luke's Med. Ctr., Ill., 1979. Student asst. pastor Cmty. Ch. Wilmette, Ill., 1977—78; vesper intern Vesper Soc., San Leandro, Calif., 1978—79; sr. pastor Milton Grove United Meth. Ch., Mount Joy, Pa., 1980—82, Bellegrove United Meth. Ch., Annville, Pa., 1992—94, Water Works United Meth. Ch., Cleona, Pa., 1992—94, Radnor United Meth. Ch., Rosemont, Pa., 1994—98, Coventryville United Meth. Ch., Pottstown, Pa., 1998—2003, Messiah United Meth. Ch., Lafayette Hill, Pa., 2003—; assoc. in resident svs., assoc. chaplain Cornwall Manor Retirement Cmty., Pa., 1983—84; founding pastor Faith United Meth. Ch., Lititz, Pa., 1984—92. Mem. dist. com. min. Lancaster Dist. United Meth. Ch., Pa., 1981—83; chairperson Evaluation Com. Conf. Coun. on Mins. of The Ethnic Minority Local Ch. Task Force, Valley Forge, Pa., 1982—82; chairperson, mem. commn. Comission on Status & Role Women Ea. Pa. Ann. Conf. The United Meth. Ch., Valley Forge, Pa., 2000—; mem. United Meth. Ch. Camp Pocono Plateau Site Com., Cresco, Pa., 1981—85; co-chair Harry Hosier Dist. Ministerium of The United Meth. Ch., Phila., 1994—96; chair worship com. & retreat com., mem. of steering com. Women of Faith (sub-com. The Met. Christian Coun. of Phila.), 1994—98. Actor: (plays) Musical Carnival. Founding pastor Faith United Methodist Ch. Mem.: EPA Conf. United Meth. Ch. Women Profl. Ministry, Conshohocken Bus. and Profl. Women, Whitemarsh Twp. Bus. Assn. Democrat. Avocations: travel, camping, needlework, singing, piano. Office: Messiah United Meth Ch 527 Ridge Pike Lafayette Hill PA 19444 Home Phone: 610-825-6455; Office Phone: 610-828-0118. Personal E-mail: nancylmiller@verizon.net.

MILLER, NATHANIEL GREGORY, mathematics professor; b. Berkeley, Calif., Sept. 5, 1972; s. Douglas Edward and Eleanor Goudsmit Miller. AB, Princeton U., NJ, 1994; PhD, Cornell U., Ithaca, NY, 2001. Instr. Cornell U., Ithaca, 1994—2001; asst. prof. math. scies. U. No. Colo., Greeley, 2001—. Contbr. articles to profl. jours. Mem.: Math. Assn. Am. Avocations: cello, hiking. Home: 464 Morrison Alley Boulder CO 80302 Office: University of Northern Colorado Ross Hall Greeley CO 80631 Home Phone: 970-302-6315; Office Phone: 970-351-2297. Business E-Mail: nat@alumni.princeton.edu.

MILLER, NEIL STUART, advertising executive; b. NYC, July 30, 1958; s. Irving Israel Maltz and Lenore (Goldstein) M.; m. Karen Joyce Salomon, Nov. 22, 1987; children: Lindsay Alexandra, Jacqueline Olivia, Sara Allison. BS, SUNY, Buffalo, 1980; MBA, SUNY, Binghamton, 1982. CPA, N.Y. Staff auditor Peat Marwick Mitchell & Co., NYC, 1982-83; ops. auditor Gulf & Western Industries, NYC, 1983-84; spl. projects acct. Mickelberry Comms., NYC, 1984-86; v.p. fin. Ptnrs. & Shevack Inc. (subs. Mickelberry Comms. Inc.), NYC, 1986-87, sr. v.p. fin., 1987-89, exec. v.p., CFO, 1989-96, exec. v.p., COO, 1996-98; sr. v.p., fin. dir. McCann Erickson New York (subs. Interpublic Group of Cos.), NYC, 1998-2000; CFO N.Am. MindShare (subs. WPP Group PLC), NYC, 2000; COO TN Media (subs. True North Comm./Interpublic Group of Cos.), NYC, 2000—01; CFO N.Am. Foote, Cone & Belding (subs. Interpub. Group of Cos.), NYC, 2001—04; exec. v.p., CFO N.Am. McCann Erickson, NYC, 2004—. Mem. AICPA, N.Y. State Soc. CPAs (past mem. com. CFOs and advt.). Avocations: skiing, motorcycling, golf. Home: 594 W Saddle River Rd Upper Saddle River NJ 07458-1115 Office: McCann Erickson 622 Third Ave New York NY 10017 Office Phone: 646-865-2255. Business E-Mail: Neil.Miller@mccann.com.

MILLER, NICOLE, art columnist; Arts Beat columnist Washington Post, visual arts columnist for Sunday Source. Office: Washington Post 1150 15th St NW Washington DC 20071 Business E-Mail: millern@washpost.com.

MILLER, NICOLE JACQUELINE, fashion designer; b. Ft. Worth, Mar. 20, 1951; d. Grier Bovey and Jacqueline (Mahieu) M. BFA, RISD, 1973; cert. de coursspeciale, École de la Chambre Syndicale de la Couture Parisienne, Paris, 1971. Opened boutique Gamine, Stockbridge, Mass., 1973—74; asst. designer Clovis Ruffin, NYC, 1974; designer Raincheetahs, NYC, 1974—75, P.J. Walsh, NYC, 1975-82, Nicole Miller, NYC, 1982—, millergirl sportswear line, 2003—, Nicole by Nicole Miller, J.C. Penney, 2005—. Mem. Sports Commn. of NY, Commn. of Status of Women; bd. trustees RI Sch. of Design. Bd. dirs. Smith's Food and Drug. Recipient Dallas Fashion award, 1991, Earnie award for children's wear, Michael award for fashion. Mem. Fashion Group, Fashion Roundtable, Coun. Fashion Designers of Am., NY Athletic Club. Avocations: skiing, ice skating, waterskiing, wind surfing. Office: 525 7th Ave Fl 20 New York NY 10018-4901 *

MILLER, NORMAN CALVIN, economist; b. Greensburg, Pa., May 28, 1939; s. Harold C. and Helen (Kovaleski) M.; m. Patricia Luan, Dec. 27, 1977; children: Doug, Scott, Craig, Pamela, Joshua. BS, St. Vincent Coll., 1961; MA, U. Pitts., 1964, PhD, 1966. Asst. prof. econs. Bowling Green (Ohio) U., 1966-67, Carnegie-Mellon U., Pitts., 1967-71; cons. U.S. Treasury Dept., Washington, 1971-72; prof. econs. U. Pitts., 1972-85; Lange prof. econs. and Am. enterprise Miami U., Oxford, Ohio, 1985—. Author: Macroeconomics, Balance of Payments and Exchange Rate Theories; editor: Open Economy Macroeconomics, International Reserves in Developing Countries; contbr. more than 30 scholarly articles to profl. jours. Grad. fellowship NSF, 1963-66, grantee NSF, 1967-69, U.S. State Dept., 1972. Mem. Am. Econ. Assn. Office: Miami U Laws Hall Oxford OH 45056-3628 Home Phone: 513-774-8523; Office Phone: 513-529-2836. E-mail: millernc@muohio.edu.

MILLER, NORMAN CHARLES, JR., editor, reporter; b. Pitts., Oct. 2, 1934; s. Norman Charles and Elizabeth (Burns) M.; m. Mollie Rudy, June 15, 1957; children— Norman III, Mary Ellen, Teri, Scott. BA, Pa. State U., 1956. Reporter Wall Street Jour., San Francisco, 1960-63, reporter NYC, 1963-64, bur. chief Detroit, 1964-66, Washington corr., 1966-72, Washington Bur. chief, 1973-83; nat. editor Los Angeles Times, 1983-97; lectr. journalism U. So. Calif., 1997—2001; ret., 2001. Author: The Great Salad Oil Swindle, 1965 Served to lt. (j.g.) USN, 1956-60. Recipient Disting. Alumnus award Pa. State U., 1978; George Polk Meml. award L.I. U., 1963; Pulitzer Prize, 1964 Mem.: Gridiron (Washington). Roman Catholic. Avocation: tennis.

MILLER, NORMAN RICHARD, lawyer; b. Oak Ridge, Tenn., Apr. 4, 1948; s. Francis J. and Sylvia R. Miller; m. Carol Golden, Aug. 15, 1971; children: Russell, Adam, Jordan. BA with distinction, Northwestern U., 1970; JD, Harvard U., 1973. Bar: Tex. Law clk. to Judge Latham Castle U.S. Ct. Appeals (7th cir.), Chgo., 1973-74; ptnr. Akin, Gump, Strauss, Hauer & Feld, Dallas, 1980-90, Cox & Smith Inc., San Antonio, 1990-93, Kirkpatrick & Lockhart LLP, Dallas, 1995, Patton Boggs LLP, Dallas. Trustee Temple Shalom, 1982-84; mem. bd. student adv. Harvard Law Sch. Hon. Woodrow Wilson fellow. Mem. ABA (task force securities law Opinions, com. fed. regulation securities, com. negotiated acquisitions), State Bar Tex. (securities com.), Dallas Bar Assn.; fellow Tex. Bus. Law Found., Phi Beta Kappa. Office: Patton Boggs LLP 2001 Ross Ave Ste 3000 Dallas TX 75201 Office Phone: 214-758-6630. Office Fax: 214-758-1550. E-mail: nmiller@pattonboggs.com.

MILLER, ORLANDO JACK, obstetrician, gynecologist, educator, geneticist; b. Okla. City, May 11, 1927; s. Arthur Leroy and Iduma Dorris (Berry) M.; m. Dorothy Anne Smith, July 10, 1954; children: Richard Lawrence, Cynthia Kathleen, Karen Ann. BS, Yale U., 1946, MD, 1950. Intern St. Anthony Hosp., Okla. City, 1950-51; asst. resident in obstetrics and gynecology Yale-New Haven Med. Center, 1954-57, resident, instr., 1957-58; vis. fellow dept. obstetrics and gynecology Tulane U. Service, Charity Hosp., New Orleans, 1958; hon. research asst. Galton Lab., Univ. Coll., London, 1958-60; instr. Coll. Physicians and Surgeons Columbia U., NYC, 1960, asso. dept. obstetrics and gynecology, 1960-61, asst. prof., 1961-65, asso. prof., 1965-69, prof. dept. human genetics and devel., dept. obstetrics and gynecology, 1969-85; asst. attending obstetrician, gynecologist Presbyn. Hosp., NYC, 1964-65, assoc., 1965-70, attending obstetrician and gynecologist, 1970-85; prof. molecular biology, genetics and ob-gyn. Wayne State U. Sch. Medicine, Detroit, 1985-94, prof. Ctr. for Molecular Medicine and Genetics, 1994-96, prof. emeritus, 1996—, chmn. dept. molecular biology and genetics, 1985-93, dir. Ctr. for Molecular Biology, 1987-90. Bd. dirs. Am. Bd. Med. Genetics, 1983-85, v.p., 1983, pres., 1984, 85. Author: (with E. Therman) Human Chromosomes, 2000; editor Cytogenetics, 1970-72; assoc. editor: Birth Defects Compendium, 1971-74, Cytogenetics and Cell Genetics, 1972-97; mem. editl. bd. Cytogenetics, 1961-69, Am. Jour. Human Genetics, 1969-74, 79-83, Gynecologic Investigation, 1970-77, Teratology, 1972-74, Cancer Genetics and Cytogenetics, 1979-84, Jour. Exptl. Zoology, 1989-92, Chromosome Rsch., 1994-99; mem. editl. bd. com. Genomics, 1987-93, assoc. editor, 1993-96; mem. adv. bd. Human Genetics, 1978-98; cons. Jour. Med. Primatology, 1977-94; consulting editor McGraw-Hill Yearbook of Sci. and Tech., 1995—, Encyclopedia of Science and Technology, 1997—; contbr. chpts. to textbooks and articles to med. and sci. jours. Mem. sci. adv. com. on rsch. Nat. Found. March of Dimes, 1967-96, mem. sci. com., 1996—; mem. sci. rec. com. Basil O'Connor starter grants, 1973-77, 86-94; mem. human embryology and devel. study sect. NIH, 1970-74, chmn., 1972-74; mem. com. for study of inborn errors of metabolism NRC, 1972-74; mem. sci. adv. com. virology and cell biology Am. Cancer Soc., 1974-78, mem. sci. adv. com. cell and devel. biology, 1986-90; mem. human genome study sect. NIH, 1991-94; U.S. rep. permanent com. Internat. Congress of Human Genetics, 1986-91. With AUS, 1951-53. James Hudson Brown Jr. fellow Yale U., 1947-48; NRC fellow, 1953-54; Population Council fellow, 1958-59; Josiah Macy Jr. fellow, 1960-61; NSF sr. postdoctoral fellow U. Oxford, 1968-69; vis. scientist U. Edinburgh, 1983-84; Disting. vis. fellow, Fogarty Internat. fellow LaTrobe U., Melbourne, Australia, 1992; recipient Pres. Disting. Scientist award Soc. for Gynecol. Investigation, 1999. Fellow AAAS; mem. AAAS, Am. Soc. Human Genetics (bd. dirs. 1970-73, 86-90), Genetics Soc. Am., Acad. Scholars, Wayne State U. (life, pres. 1996-97), Sigma Xi. Home: 19365 Cypress Ridge Terr # 817 Lansdowne VA 20176 Office: 540 E Canfield St Detroit MI 48201-1928 E-mail: ojmiller@smartneighborhood.net.

MILLER, PAMELA GUNDERSEN, retired mayor; b. Cambridge, Mass., Sept. 7, 1938; d. Sven M. and Harriet Adams Gundersen; m. Ralph E. Miller, July 7, 1962; children: Alexander, Erik, Karen. AB magna cum laude, Smith Coll., 1960. Feature writer Congl. Quar., Washington, 1962-65; dir. cable TV franchising Storer Broadcasting Co., Louisville, Lexington, Ky., 1978—80; mem. 4th dist. Lexington Fayette County Urban Coun., 1973-77; councilwoman-at-large, 1982-93; vice mayor, 1984-86, 89-93; mayor, 1993—2003. Dep. commr. Ky. Dept. Local Govt., Frankfort, 1980-81; pres. Pam Miller, Inc., 1984-94, Cmty. Ventures Corp., 1985-95. Mem. Fayette County Bd. Health, 1975—77, Downtown Devel. Commn., 1975—77; bd. dirs. YMCA, Lexington, 1975—77, 1985—90, Fund for the Arts, 1984—93, Coun. of Arts, 1978—80, Sister Cities, 1978—80; chmn. Prichard Com. for Acad. Excellence, 2004—; treas. Planned Parenthood, 2003—, Fayette Edn. Found., 2005—07; pres. Lexington Opera Soc., 2007—; alt. del. Dem. Nat. Com., 1976; bd. dirs. Lexington Opera Soc., 2003—; chair Fund for Arts Campaign, 2003—04. Named woman of achievement YWCA, 1984, outstanding Woman of Blue Grass AAUW, 1984. Mem. LWV (dir. 1970-73), Profl. Women's Forum. Home: 140 Cherokee Park Lexington KY 40503-1304

MILLER, PATRICIA A., music educator, opera and concert artist; b. Washington, June 16; d. Robert Lee and Bernice (Echols) Miller. MusB, Boston U.; MusM, New Eng. Conservatory; artist's diploma, Accademia di Santa Cecilia, Rome; postdoctoral diploma, Mozarteum, Salzburg. Artist Thea Dispeker Artist's Mgmt., Inc., NYC, 1981—95; assoc. prof. music, artist-in-residence U. Mo., Columbia, 1983—85; prof. music, dir. vocal studies, artist-in-residence George Mason U., Fairfax, Va., 1991—, disting. univ. prof., 2007—; prof. voice Oberlin Coll. Conservatory, Oberlin, Ohio, 2000—01. Dir. vocal studies George Mason U., 1995—, prodr. opera theater, 2000—, dir. Inst. Vocal Arts, 2004—; lectr. Smithsonian, Wash., DC, 2000—02. Performer: (Operas) ERCOLE Amante, 1986, Carmen, 1985, Porgy & Bess, 1996,; concert/recital artist Kennedy Ctr., Washington, 2000, Kiev, 2002, Austrian Embassy, 2003, Salzburg, Austria, 2004, Kaynon Concert Hall, Seoul, Korea, 2005; performer (soloist): Schloss Leopololskron Great Hall, 2004, Kiev Philharmonic Orch., 2004, New Strathmore Music Ctr., 2005, Nat. Philharmonic Orch. and Chorus, 2005, 2007, Moscow State U., 2006, Pushkin Mus. and Concert Hall, 2006, Schloss Leopoldskron, 2006, Internat. Conf. on Edn., Health, Culture, Pub. Opinion, 2006. Mem. opera panel Nat. Endowment Arts, 2003—04, 2006; mem. panel Va. Commn. for the Arts, 2004—05. Recipient Shining Star Cmty Svc. award, Nat. Urban League, Sojourner Truth Leadership award, George Mason U., 2004; grantee, Am. Embassy, 2002; Fulbright scholar, Rome. Mem.: Fulbright Assn. (bd. dirs. Nat. Capitol area), Nat. Assn. Tchrs. Singing (state bd. dirs.), Sigma Alpha Iota (Alumni Artistry Leadership award 2004, Outstanding Artist award 2004). Methodist. Avocations: travel, walking, swimming, cooking. Office: George Mason Univ Dept Music MSN-3E3 4400 University Dr Fairfax VA 22030-4444 Office Phone: 703-993-1382. Personal E-mail: labellavoce1@aol.com. Business E-Mail: pmilleb@gmu.edu.

MILLER, PATRICIA LOUISE, state legislator, nurse; b. Bellefontaine, Ohio, July 4, 1936; d. Richard William and Rachel Orpha (Williams) M.; m. Kenneth Orlan Miller, July 3, 1960; children: Tamara Sue, Matthew Ivan. RN, Meth. Hosp. Sch. Nursing, Indpls., 1957; BS, Ind. U., 1960. Staff nurse Cmty. Hosp., Indpls., 1958, Meth. Hosp., Indpls., 1959; office nurse A.D. Dennison, MD, 1960-61; rep. State of Ind. Dist. 50, Indpls., 1982-83; senator State of Ind. Dist. 32, Indpls., 1983—, chair senate health and provider svcs. com., 1999—; mem. labor and pension com., 1985—94; mem. edn. com., 1989—92; legis. appt. and elections com., chmn. interim study com. pub. health and mental health Ind. Gen. Assembly, 1986; chair Senate Environl. Affairs, 1990—91; health and environ affairs, 1992—; mem. election com., 1992—; mem. budget subcom. Senate Fin. Com., 1995—. Mem. Bd. Edn. Met. Sch. Dist., Warren Twop., 1974-82, pres., 1979-80, 80-81; mem. Warren Twp. Citizens Screening Com. for Sch. Bd. Candidates, 1972-84, Met. Zoning Bd. Appeals, Divsn. I, apptd. mem. City-County Coun. on Aging, Indpls. 1977-80; mem. State Bd. Vocat. and Tech. Edn., 1978-82, sec., 1980-82; mem. gov.'s Select Adv. Commn. for Primary and Secondary Edn., 1983; precinct committeeman Rep. Party, 1967-74, ward vice-chmn., 1974-78, ward chmn., 1978-85, twp. chmn., 1985-87; vice chmn. Marion County Rep., 1986-2000; sgt. at arms, 1982, mem. platform com., 1984, 88, 90, 92, co-chmn. Ind. Rep. Platform Com., 1992; rep. Presdl. Elector Alternate, 1992; active various polit. campaigns; bd. dirs. PTA, 1967-81; pres. Grassy Creek PTA, 1971-72; state del. Ind. PTA, 1978; mem. child car adv. com. Walker Career Ctr., 1976-80, others; bd. dirs. Ch. Fedn. Greater Indpls., 1979-82, Christian Justice Ctr., Inc., 1983-85, Gideon Internat. Aux., 1977, Ctrl. Ind. Coun. Aging; mem. United Meth. Bd. Missions Aux. Indpls., 1974-80, v.p., 1974-76, mem. nominating com., 1977; bd. dirs. Lucille Raines Residence, Inc., 1977-80; exec. com. S. Ind. Conf. United Meth. Women, 1977-80, lay del. s. Ind. Conf. United Meth. Ch., 1977—, fin. and adminstrn. com., 1979-88, planning and rsch. com., 1980-88, co-chmn. law adv. com., chmn. health and welfare, conf. coun. ministries, also mem. task force, bd. ordained ministry, also panel, chmn. com. on dist. superintendency, dist. coun. on ministries; sec. Indpls. S.E. Dist. Council on Minstries, 1977-78, pres. 1982; chmn. council on ministries Cumberland United Meth. Ch., 1969-76; chmn. stewardship com. Old Bethal United Meth. Ch., 1982-85, fin. com., 1982-85, adminstrv. bd., mem. council on ministries, 1981-85; co-chair Evangelism Com., 1994—; jurisdictional del. United Meth. Ch., 1988, 92, 96-2000; alternate del. United Methodist Ch. Gen. Conf., 1988, del. 1992; mem. adv. com. Warren Fine Arts Found., 1991—; mem. adv. bd. St. Francis Hosp., 1992-2005; mem. health and human svcs. com. Midwest Legis. Conf., 1995; del rep. various confs. and convs. Recipient Lambda Theta Honor for Outstanding contbr. in fiedl of end., 1976; named Woman of Yr. Cumberland Bus. and Profl. Women, 1979; Ind. Vocat. Assn. citation award, 1984, others. Mem. Indpls. dist. Dental Soc. Women's Aux., Ind. Dental Assn. Women's Aux., Am. Dental Assn. Women's Aux., Coun. State Govt. (intergovtl. affairs com.), Nat. Conf. State Legis. (vice chmn. health com. 1994—), Warren Twp. Rep., Franklin Rep., Lawrence Rep., Center Twp. Rep., Fall Creek Valley Rep, Marion County Coun. Rep. Women (3rd v.p. 1986-89), Ind. Women's Rep. (legis. chair 1988-89), Nat. Fedn. rep. Women, Beech Grove Rep., Perry Twp. Rep., Indpls. Women's Rep. Club (3rd v.p. 1989—), Indpls. Press Club. Office Phone: 317-232-9400. Business E-Mail: s32@in.gov.

MILLER, PATRICK DWIGHT, JR., religious studies educator, minister; b. Atlanta, Oct. 24, 1935; s. Patrick Dwight and Lila Morse (Bonner) M.; m. Mary Ann Sudduth, Dec. 27, 1958; children: Jonathan Sudduth, Patrick James. AB, Davidson Coll., 1956; BD, Union Theol. Sem., Va., 1959; PhD, Harvard U., 1964. Ordained to ministry Presbyn. Ch., 1963. Pastor, minister Trinity Presbyn. Ch., Traveler's Rest, S.C., 1963-65; asst. prof. Bibl. studies Union Theol. Sem., Richmond, Va., 1966-68, assoc. prof., 1968-73, prof., 1973-84, dean of faculty, 1979-83; Charles T. Haley prof. of Old Testament Theology Princeton (N.J.) Theol. Sem., 1984—. Author: The Divine Warrior in Early Israel, 1973, The Hand of the Lord, 1977, Sin and Judgment in the Prophets, 1982, Interpreting the Psalms, 1986, Deuteronomy, 1990, They Cried to the Lord, 1994, The Religion of Ancient Israel, 2000, Israelite Religion and Biblical Theology, 2000; editor: Theology Today, 1990-2005 Mem. Soc. of Bibl. Lit. (sec.-treas. 1987-88, pres. 1998), Rev. Std. Version Translation Com. Democrat. Presbyterian. Office: Princeton Theol Sem PO Box 821 Princeton NJ 08542-0803

MILLER, PATRICK WILLIAM, research scientist, educator; b. Toledo, Sept. 1, 1947; s. Richard William and Mary Olivia (Rinna) M.; m. Jean Ellen Thomas, Apr. 5, 1974; children: Joy, Tatum, Alex. BS in Indstrl. Edn., Bowling Green State U., 1971, MEd in Career Edn. and Tech., 1973; PhD in Indstrl. Tech. Edn., Ohio State U., 1977; Master's cert. Govt. Contract Adminstrn., George Washington U., 1995. Tchr. Montgomery Hills Jr. High Sch., Silver Spring, Md., 1971-72, Rockville (Md.) High Sch., 1973-74; asst. prof. Wayne State U., Detroit, 1977-79; assoc. prof., grad. coord. indstrl. edn. and tech. Western Carolina U., Cullowhee, NC, 1979-81; assoc prof. U. No. Iowa, Cedar Falls, 1981-86; dir. grad. studies practical arts and vocat.-tech. edn. U. Mo., Columbia, 1986-89; devel. editor Am. Tech. Pubs., Homewood, Ill., 1989-90; proposal mgr. Nat. Opinion Rsch. Ctr. U. Chgo., 1990-96; dir. grants & contracts Cty Colls. Chgo., 1996-99; assoc. v.p. acad. affairs Prairie State Coll., 1999—2001, also dean workforce devel. and career edn., 1999—2001; prof. Govs. State U., University Park, Ill., 2001—. Pres. Patrick W. Miller and Assocs., Munster, Ind., 1981—; presenter, cons. in field Author: Nonverbal Communication: Its Impact on Teaching and Learning, 1983, Teacher Written Tests: A Guide for Planning, Creating, Administering and Assessing, 1985, Nonverbal Communication: What Resarch Says to the Teacher, 1988, How To Write Tests for Students, 1990, Nonverbal Communication in the Classroom, 2000, Nonverbal Communication in the Workplace, 2000, Grant Writing: Strategies for Developing Winning Proposals, 2d edit., 2002, Test Development: Guidelines, Practical Suggestions and Examples, 2001, Body Language: An Illustrated Introduction for Teachers, 2005, Body Language on the Job, 2006; mem. editl. bd. Jour. Indsl. Tchr. Edn., 1981-88, Am. Vocat. Edn. Rsch. Jour., 1981-85, 94—, Tech. Tchr., 1982-84, Jour. Indsl. Tech., 1984—, Jour. Vocat. and Tech. Edn., 1987-90, Human Resource Devel. Quar., 1989-93; contbr. articles to profl. jours. Sec. U. No. Iowa United Faculty, Cedar Falls, 1983-84, pres., 1984-86. Lance cpl. USMC, 1966-68, Vietnam. Named one of Accomplished Grads. of Coll. Tech., Bowling Green State U., 1995; recipient editl. recognition award, Jour. Indsl. Tchr. Edn., 1984, 1986, 1988. Mem. ASTD, Am. Edn. Rsch. Assn., Assn. for Career and Tech. Edn., Am. Vocat. Edn. Rsch. Assn., Nat. Assn. Indsl. Tech. (chmn. rsch. grants 1982-87, pres. industry divsn. 1991-92, chmn. exec. bd. 1992-93, past pres. 1993-94, Leadership award 1992, 93), Nat. Assn. Indsl. and Tech. Tchr. Educators (pres. 1988-89, past pres. 1989-90, trustee 1990-93, Outstanding Svc. award 1988, 90), Internat. Tech. Edn. Assn., Coun. Tech. Tchr. Edn., Epsilon Pi Tau, Phi Delta Kappa. Personal E-mail: patrickwmiller@sbcglobal.net.

MILLER, PAUL AUSBORN, adult education educator; b. East Liverpool, Ohio, Mar. 22, 1917; s. Harry A. and Elizabeth (Stewart) M.; m. Catherine Spiker, Dec. 9, 1939 (dec. Dec. 1964); children— Paula Kay, Thomas Ausborn; m. Francena Lounsbery Nolan, Jan. 15, 1966. BS, U. W.Va., 1939; MA, Mich. State U., 1947, PhD, 1953. County agrl. agt. in, W.Va., 1939-42; extension specialist sociology and anthropology Mich. State U., East Lansing, 1947-55, asst. prof., 1947-52, assoc. prof., 1953, prof., 1953-61, dir. coop. ext. svc., 1954-58, provost Morgantown, 1959-61; pres. W.Va. U., Morgantown, 1962-66; asst. sec. for edn. HEW,

Charlotte, 1966-68; disting. prof. edn., dir. univ. planning studies U. N.C., Charlotte, 1966-68; prof. adult edn. N.C. Sate U. at Raleigh, 1668-69; pres. Rochester (N.Y.) Inst. of Tech., 1969-79, pres. emeritus, 1979—, prof., 1979-83. Sr. program cons. W.K. Kellogg Found., 1979-83; adj. prof. rural sociology U. Mo.-Columbia, 1994—. Author: Community Health Action, 1953; co-author: Patterns for Lifelong Learning, 1973; contbr. to publs. in field. Mem. Colombian Commn. Higher Edn., 1960-61. Served as 1st lt. USAAF, 1942-46. Named to the Internat. Adult and Continuing Edn. Hall of Fame. Fellow Am. Sociol. Assn.; mem. Rural Sociol. Soc., Phi Kappa Phi, Epsilon Sigma Phi. Home: 1909 Walden Ct Columbia MO 65203-5407 Personal E-mail: millerpau@missouri.edu.

MILLER, PAUL DAVID, aerospace transportation executive, retired admiral; BA, Fla. State U.; MBA, U. Ga. Commd. USN, advanced through grades to four star adm.; comdr.-in-chief U.S. Atlantic Command; supreme allied comdr.-Atlantic NATO; with Litton Marine Sys., 1995-99; pres. Sperry Marine Inc.; CEO Alliant Techsystems, Inc., Hopkins, Minn., 1999—2004, chmn., 1999—2005.

MILLER, PAUL DEAN, breeding consultant, geneticist, educator; b. Cedar Falls, Iowa, Apr. 4, 1941; s. Donald Hugh and Mary (Hansen) M.; m. Nancy Pearl Huser, Aug. 23, 1965; children: Michael, Steven. BS, Iowa State U., 1963; MS, Cornell U., 1965, PhD, 1967. Asst. prof. animal breeding cornell U., Ithaca, N.Y., 1967-72; v.p. Am. Breeders Svc., De Forest, Wis., 1972-95; exec. dir. Nat. Dairy Herd Improvement Assn., 1996—2003; pres. Windsor (Wis.) Park Inc., 1985—. Adj. prof. U. Wis., Madison, 1980—, sr. scientist, 2003—; dir. Internat. Com. on Animal Recording, 1998-2003. Contbr. articles to profl. jours. Mem. Beef Improvement Fedn. (disting. svc. award 1980), Am. Soc. Animal Sci., Am. Dairy Sci. Assn., Nat. Assn. Animal Breeders (dir. 1983-92, v.p. 1986). Republican. Office: Univ Wis 446 Animal Sci Bldg 1675 Observatory Dr Madison WI 53706-1284 Home: 6301 Fox Run Sun Prairie WI 53590-9357 E-mail: pdmil@aol.com, pdmiller2@wisc.edu.

MILLER, PAUL J., lawyer; b. Boston, Mar. 27, 1929; s. Edward and Esther M.; children— Robin, Jonathan; m. Michal Davis, Sept. 1, 1965; children— Anthony, Douglas BA, Yale U., 1950; LL.B., Harvard U., 1953. Bar: Mass. 1953, Ill. 1957. Assoc. Miller & Miller, Boston, 1953-54; assoc. Sonnenschein Nath & Rosenthal, Chgo., 1957-63, ptnr., 1963—; bd. dirs. Oil-DriCorp. Am., 1975—2004. Trustee Latin Sch. of Chgo., 1985-91. 1st lt. JAGC, U.S. Army, 1954-57. Fellow Am. Bar Found.; mem. Tavern Club, Saddle and Cycle Club, Law Club, Phi Beta Kappa. Avocation: gardening. Office: Sonnenschein Nath & Rosenthal 233 S Wacker Dr Ste 8000 Chicago IL 60606-6491 E-mail: pjm@sonnenschein.com.

MILLER, PAUL J., orthopedist, surgeon; b. NYC, July 19, 1927; s. Murray and Kitty Miller; m. Nanci Franco; children: Jimmy, Andrew, Michael. BA, Columbia U., 1947; MD, NYU, 1951. Orthop. surgeon, pvt. practice, Queens, NY, 1958—. Attending orthopedist LI Jewish Hosp., New Hyde Park, NY, 1962—. Capt. USAF, 1953—55, Germany. Fellow: ACS, AMA, Internat. Coll. Surgeons, Am. Acad. Orthopedic Surgeons. Avocations: golf, travel. Home: 101 Brook St Garden City NY 11530 Office: Mishkin Miller Forman PC 238-25 Hillside Ave Bellerose NY 11426 Office Phone: 718-464-7376.

MILLER, PAUL SAMUEL, lawyer; b. Paterson, NJ, Apr. 8, 1939; s. Louis and Etta (Wolff) M.; m. Carol Plesser, Mar. 26, 1961; children: Nicole F., Margo H., Jason E. BA, Rutgers U., 1960, JD magna cum laude, 1962. Bar: N.Y. 1963. Assoc. Kaye, Scholer, Fierman, Hayes & Handler, NYC, 1962-63, Rubin, Baum & Levin, NYC, 1964; ptnr. Fishman, Miller & Zimet, NYC, 1964-70; counsel Leasing Cons., Inc., Rosyln, N.Y., 1970-71; with Pfizer Inc., NYC, 1971—2002, assoc. gen. counsel, v.p., gen. counsel, 1986-92, sr. v.p., gen. counsel, 1992-99, exec. v.p., gen. counsel, 1999—2002; spl. counsel Kaye Scholer LLP, NYC, 2002—. Ofcl. corr. Pharm. Mfrs. Assn., mem., chmn. exec. com. law sect., 1989-90. Mem. United Jewish Appeal Com., Essex County, 1981-83, co-chmn. Livingston sect., 1982; former chmn. bd. dirs. Citizens Crime Commn. of N.Y.C., Inc.; bd. dirs. Am. Israel Pub. Affairs Com., Am. Jewish Congress, Jewish Theol. Sem., U.S. C. of C., chmn. Nat. Chamber Litigation Coun.; mem. bus. adv. coun. Touro Law Sch.; mem. bd. overseers Inst. Civil Justice, RAND. Albert Einstein Coll. Medicine, Jaffee Inst. Strategic Studies at Tel Aviv U. Recipient Jerusalem Humanitarian award, Shaare Zedek Medical Ctr., 1999, Louis Marshall Award, Jewish Theological Seminar, 2001. Mem. ABA (antitrust law sect., corp. banking and bus. law sect., natural resources law sect., sci. and tech. sect., mem. health law forum com.), N.Y. State Bar Assn. (antitrust law sect., food and drug law sect.). Office: Kaye Scholer LLP 425 Park Ave New York NY 10022 Business E-Mail: pmiller@kayescholer.com.

MILLER, PAULA J., library director; m. Jay Miller; children: Jason, Jon, James. BA in Psychology, Kent State U.; MLIS, U. Md. Positions including head circulation, reference libr., children's asst. and administrv. coord. Kent Free Libr., Ohio; dir. Dover Pub. Libr., Del., Westlake Porter Pub. Libr., Ohio, 1992—2006; adminstr. Eastern Shore Regional Libr., Md.; exec. dir. Pikes Peak Libr. Dist., Colorado Springs, 2006—. Office: Pikes Peak Libr Dist PO Box 1579 Colorado Springs CO 80901 Office Phone: 719-531-6333 ext. 2010.

MILLER, PEGGY GORDON ELLIOTT, retired academic administrator; b. Matewan, W.Va., May 27, 1937; d. Herbert Hunt and Mary Ann (Renfro) Gordon; m. Robert Lawrence Miller, Nov. 23, 2001; stepchildren: Rohn J., Robert K.;children from previous marriage: Scott Vandling Elliott III, Anne Gordon Elliott. BA, Transylvania Coll., 1959; MA, Northwestern U., 1964; EdD, Ind. U., 1975; degree (hon.), Transylvania U., 1993, Chungnam Nat. U., Korea, 2000; D in Pub. Svc., SD State U., 2006. Tchr. Horace Mann H.S., Gary, Ind., 1959-64; instr. English Am. Inst. Banking, Gary, 1969-70, Ind. U. N.W., Gary, 1965-69, lectr. Edn., 1973-74, asst. prof. edn., 1975-78, assoc. prof., 1978-80, supr. secondary student tchg., 1973-74, dir. student tchg., 1975-77, dir. Office Field Experiences, 1977-78, dir. profl. devel., 1978-80, spl. asst. to chancellor, 1981-83, asst. to chancellor, 1983-84, acting chancellor, 1983-84, chancellor, 1984-92; pres. U. Akron, Ohio, 1992-96, SD State U., 1998—2006, pres. emeritus, 2006—. Sr. fellow Nat. Ctr. for Higher Edn., 1996-97; vis. prof. U. Ark., 1979-80, U. Alaska, 1982; bd. dirs. Lubrizol Corp., A. Schulman Corp., Commn. on Women in Higher Edn., SD Mus. Art, Akron Tomorrow, Ohio Aerospace Consortium, Ohio Super Computer Com., Brookings C. of C.; holder VA Harrington disting. chair in edn., 1994-96, Charles G. Herbrich chair in leadership mgmt., 1996—; chmn. Growth partnership Rsch. Pk. Author: (with C. Smith) Reading Activities for Middle and Secondary Schools: A Handbook for Teachers, 1979, Reading Instruction for Secondary Schools, 1986, How to Improve Your Scores on Reading Competency Tests, 1981, (with C. Smith and G. Ingersoll) Trends in Educational Materials: Traditionals and the New Technologies, 1983, The Urban Campus: Educating a New Majority for a New Century, 1994, also numerous articles. Bd. dirs. Am. Humanics Meth. Hosp., N.W. Ind. Forum, N.W. Ind. Symphony, S.D. Art Mus., Boys Club N.W. Ind., Akron Symphony, NBD Bank, John S. Knight Conv. Ctr., Inventure Pl., Akron Roundtable, Cleve. Com. Higher Edn., 4-H Found., S.D. Art Mus., S.D. Value. Recipient Disting. Alumni award Northwestern U., UA Disting. Alumni award, 1994, Dist. Alumni award, Ind. U., 2004, Disting. Hon. Alumni, S.D. State U.; numerous grants; Am. Council on Edn. fellow in acad. adminstrn. Ind. U., Bloomington, 1980-81. Mem. Assn. Tchr. Educators (nat. pres. 1984-85, Disting. Mem. 1990), Ind. Assn. Tchr. Educators (past pres.), North Ctrl. Assn. (mem. commn. at large), Am. Assn. State Colls. and Univs. (acting v.p. divsn. acad. and internat. programs 1997, bd. dirs., treas., chmn. global priorities commn.), Am. Coun. Edn. (bd. dirs., exec. com.), Leadership Devel. Coun. ACE, Office Women Higher Edn. (mem. emerita of exec. bd), Am. Humanics (bd. dirs.), Ohio Inter Univ. Coun. (chairperson), Internat. Reading Assn., Akron Urban League (bd. dirs.), P.E.O., Cosmos Club, Phi Delta Kappa (Outstanding Young Educator award), Delta Kappa Gamma (Leadership/Mgmt. fellow 1980), Pi Lambda Theta, Pi Kappa Phi, Chi Omega. Episcopalian. Avocation: music. Home: 4834 Sweet Meadow Cir Sarasota FL 34238 Office Phone: 605-691-7391.

MILLER, PENELOPE ANN (PENOLOPE ANDREA MILLER), actress; b. LA, Jan. 13, 1964; d. Mark Miller and Beatrice Ammidown; m. Will Arnett (div.); m. James Huggins May 28, 2000; 1 child Elosia May. Studies with Herbert Berghof. Appeared in (plays) The People From Work, 1984, Biloxi Blues, 1984-85, Moonchildren, Our Town (Tony Award nom.); (TV series) The Guiding Light, 1984, As the World Turns, 1984; (films) Adventures in Babysitting, 1987, Biloxi Blues, 1988, Big Top Pee-Wee, 1988, Miles From Home, 1988, Dead-Bang, 1989, Downtown, 1990, Flashback, 1990, The Freshman, 1990, Kindergarten Cop, 1990, Awakenings, 1990, Other People's Money, 1991, Year of the Comet, 1992, The Gun in Betty Lou's Handbag, 1992, Chaplin, 1992, Carlito's Way, 1993 (Golden Globe nom.), The Shadow, 1994, The Relic, 1997, Little City, 1997, Breakup, 1998, Outside Ozona, 1998, Chapter Zero, 1999, Forever Lulu, 2000, Along Came a Spider, 2001, Funny Money, 2006, The Messengers, 2007; (TV films) Our Town, 1989, Witch Hunt, 1994, The Hired Heart, 1997, Merry Christmas George Bailey, 1997, Rhapsody in Bloom, 1998, Ruby Bridges, 1998, Rocky Marciano, 1999, All-American Girl: The Mary Kay Letourneau Story, 2000, Killing Moon, 2000, Dodson's Journey, 2001, A Women's a Helluva Thing, 2001, Dead in a Heartbeat, 2002, Scared Silent, 2002, Rudy: The Rudy Giuliani Story, 2003, Thanksgiving Family Reunion, 2003, Carry Me Home, 2004, Personal Effects, 2005; (TV miniseries) The Last Don, 1997; guest appearances Tales from the Darkside, 1985, The Facts of Life, 1987, Family Ties, 1987, The Popcorn Kid, 1987, Miami Vice, 1987, St. Elsewhere, 1987, The Closer, 1998, CSI:NY, 2005, Desparate Housewives, 2005, Vanished, 2006. Mem. Actors' Equity Assn., AFTRA. *

MILLER, PETER C., lawyer; b. 1965; BA, Marquette U., 1987; JD, DePaul U., 1990. Bar: Ill. 1990. Ptnr. Seyfarth Shaw LLP, Chgo., chmn. Employee Benefits Practice Group. Mem.: Employee Stock Ownership Plans (ESOP) Assn., Ill. State Bar Assn., ABA. Office: Seyfarth Shaw LLP 55 East Monroe St Ste 4200 Chicago IL 60603 Office Phone: 312-269-8513. Office Fax: 312-269-8869. Business E-Mail: pmiller@seyfarth.com.

MILLER, PETER KARL, music educator; b. York, Pa., Sept. 11, 1959; s. Paul Wilson and Gertrud Dorothea Miller; m. Mary Elizabeth Feldmann, Oct. 16, 1982; children: Emily Elizabeth, Christina Anna, Marissa Allison. BS in music edn., Ind. U. Pa., 1981; MusM in vocal performance, Cleve. Inst. Music, 1983, MusM in organ performance, 1994. Cert. state tchr. Ohio, 1994, Ill., 2006. Dir. of music St. Ignatius of Antioch Ch., Cleveland, Ohio, 1983—91; organist, choir dir. Temple Emanu-El, University Heights, Ohio, 1983—96; dir. of music ministries St. Dominic Ch., Shaker Heights, Ohio, 1991—96; min. of music Grace United Meth. Ch., Decatur, Ill., 1996—2001; asst. adj. prof. of music Millikin U., Decatur, 1999—2002; elem. string tchr. Decatur Pub. Sch. Dist. 61, Decatur, Ill., 2001—02; asst. prof. of music Ind. Wesleyan U., Marion, Ind., 2002—. Music faculty Cuyahoga CC, Cleve., 1983—87; artistic dir. Sacred Madrigal Singers, Decatur, Ill., 1996—. Musician: various faculty recitals, 2003—; sr. recital vocal coach, accompanist:; dir.(musician): Sacred Madrigal Singers Feast of Christmas Past and Present. Dir. Sons of Harmony Barbershop Chorus, Marion, Ind.; pianist, worship leader, choir dir., soloist Imboden Creek Gardens United Meth. Worship. Svc.; supply organist St. John's Episcopal Ch., Decatur, Ill.; guest choral dir. St. Cecelia Mass Gethsemane Episcopal Ch., Marion, Ind., 2006; guest musician, organ dedications, recitals at various chs. Ohio. Mem.: Soc. for Preservation and Encouragement of Barbershop Quartet Singing in Am., Music Tchrs. Nat. Assn., Am. Guild of Organists (assoc.), Music Educators Nat. Conf. (assoc.), Nat. Assn. of Tchrs. of Singing (assoc.), Decatur Running Club, Phi Mu Alpha. Conservative. Luth. Avocations: running, bicycling, numismatics, philatelics, travel. Home: 413 W Decatur St Decatur IL 62522 Office: Ind Wesleyan U 4201 S Washington St Marion IN 46953 Home Phone: 217-233-2996; Office Phone: 765-677-2162. Office Fax: 765-677-2620. Personal E-mail: pmmiller@insightbb.com. Business E-Mail: peter.miller@indwes.edu.

MILLER, PETER M., lawyer; b. 1959; BA magna cum laude, Miami U., 1982; JD cum laude, Georgetown U., 1985. Bar: Ill. 1985, Mass. 1988. Ptnr., Trusts & Estates Sect. & Tax Sect. Mintz Levin Cohn Ferris Glovsky & Popeo PC, Boston. Office: Mintz Levin Cohn Ferris Glovsky & Popeo PC One Financial Ctr Boston MA 02111 Office Phone: 617-348-1726. Office Fax: 617-542-2241. Business E-Mail: pmiller@mintz.com.

MILLER, PETER N., historian, educator; b. NYC, Dec. 13, 1964; BA, Harvard Coll.; MA, Harvard U.; PhD, U. Cambridge. Rsch. fellow U. Cambridge, 1990—93; Mellon instr. in social scis. U. Chgo., 1993—96; asst. prof. U. Md., 1998—2001; prof. cultural history Bard Grad. Ctr., NY, 2001—, chair academic programs. Author: Defining the Common Good: Empire, Religion and Philosophy in Eighteenth-Century Britain, 1994, Peiresc's Europe: Learning and Virtue in the Seventeenth-Century, 2000; co-author: The Song of the Soul: Understanding Poppea, 1992; contbr. articles to profl. jours. Fellow, NEH, John D. and Catherine T. MacArthur Found., Wissenschaftskolleg zu Berlin, Warburg Inst., John Simon Guggenheim Meml. Found., 2003. Office: Bard Grad Ctr 18 W 86th St New York NY 10024

MILLER, PHILIP EFREM, librarian; b. Providence, Feb. 18, 1945; s. Jacob and Natalie (Rouslin) M.; m. Zenia Weiner, Dec. 20, 1969; 1 son, Paul Jeremy. BSL., Georgetown U., 1967; MS, U. Mich., 1968, A.M.L.S., 1973; PhD, NYU, 1984. Asst. libr. Hebrew Union Coll., NYC, 1973-76, acting libr., 1976-78, librarian, 1978—. Author: Karaite Separatism in 19th Century Russia, 1993. Mem.: Assn. Jewish Librs. (pres. 1982—84). Home: 56 Truman Dr Marlboro NJ 07746-1122 Office: Hebrew Union Coll-Jewish Inst of Religion Klau Libr 1 W 4th St New York NY 10012-1186 E-mail: pmiller@huc.edu.

MILLER, PHILIP JAY, plastic surgeon; b. Hazelton, Pa., Sept. 11, 1963; BA in Biology, Wesleyan U., 1985; MD, U. Mass. Sch. Medicine, 1989. Diplomate Am. Bd. Facial Plastic & Reconstructive Surgery, Am. Bd. Otolaryngology, Nat. Bd. Med. Examiners. Intern & resident, gen. surgery NYU Med. Ctr., NYC, 1989—91, tchg. asst., surgery, 1990—91, tchg. asst., otolaryngology, 1991—95, asst. prof., dept. otolaryngology, 1997—, instr., dept. otolaryngology, 1997; resident, otolaryngology/head & neck surgery NYU Sch. Medicine, NYC, 1991—95; fellow, facial plastic & reconstructive surgery Oreg. Health Sci. U., Portland, 1995—96, instr., facial plastic surgery, dept. otolaryngology, 1995—96; private practice NYC. Guest examiner Am. Bd. Otolaryngology; vis. prof. US and Eng.; presenter in field. Contbr. articles to profl. jours., chapters to manuscripts; guest editor Facial Plastic Surgery, Clinics of Facial Plastic Surgery, featured on Today Show, NBC, Frank Field Report, featured in Elle, Health Mag., Women's World. Treats female victims of domestic violence. Named one of Top Surgeon, Consumer Rsch. Coun. Am. Fellow: ACS, Am. Acad. Otolaryngology/Head & Neck Surgery, Am. Acad. Facial Plastic Surgery & Reconstructive Surgery (bd. dir.); mem.: Phi Beta Kappa. Office: 60 E 56th 3rd Fl New York NY 10022 Address: NYU Medical Ctr 530 First Ave Ste 7U New York NY 10016 Office Phone: 212-750-7100. Office Fax: 212-263-2044. *

MILLER, PHILIP JOHN, insurance agent, consultant; b. Yonkers, NY, Apr. 28, 1945; s. Arnold Norris and Shirley Miller; m. Violet Ann Miller, Oct. 6, 1968; 1 child, Andrea Marie. BA, LI U., 1966; M, CCNY, 1967. Lic. property/casualty/health ins. broker. V.p. Montgomery and Montgomery, NYC, 1970—77; sr. v.p. Kornreich Orgns., NYC, 1977—95; pres. Creative Resources Group, Hauppauge, NY, 1995—2000, Prosulting Inc., Northport, NY, 2000—. Cons. ins. fraud FBI, 1995—; cons. U.S. Govt., Washington, 2000—; established and managed specialized insurance programs for food industry, hazardous material trucking, non-profit organizations, and geriatric cmty. Author: Serious on Safety, 2002; co-author: Food Equipment Facts, 1988; author: Onwards and Upwards, 2003, Onwards and Upwards, Book II, 2006; guest appearances for various topics on insurance for Fox Five and CNBC, guest spkr. Dr. Bernard Meltzer show, 1990; author: Arbitration Insurance - the Need to Know, 2006. Mem. Presdl. Roundtable, Washington, 2000—, Senatorial Inner Cir., Washington, 2001—, Senatorial Inner Cir. Commn., Washington, 2005, Senatorial Trust, Washington, 2001—, Presdl. Task Force Commn. of Accomplishment, 2005. Capt. spl. ops. US Army, 1962—67. Nominee medal of Freedom; named Businessman of Yr., NRCC, Washington, 2005, 2006. Mem.: Associated Risk Mgrs. Achievements include discovery of computer eye strain caused by computer overuse in the workplace is a compensatory disease under the worker's compensation insurance law in the state of New York. Avocations: martial arts, architecture, writing. Office: Prosulting Inc 111 Soundview Ter Northport NY 11768 Office Phone: 631-757-6152. Office Fax: 631-757-9458.

MILLER, PHILLIP EDWARD, environmental scientist; b. Waterloo, Iowa, May 29, 1935; s. Joe Monroe and Katherine Elva (Groom) Miller; m. Cathy Ann Love, Sept. 15, 1962; children: Eric Anthony, Bryan Edward, Stefan Patrick, Gregory Joseph. BA Sci. Edn., U. No. Iowa, 1961; MA Sci. Edn., U. Iowa, 1964; postgrad., U. Wis., 1966—68. Tchr. physics and chemistry Millersburg Cmty. H.S., Iowa, 1961—62; supervising tchr. NSF Insvc. Inst. U. Iowa, Iowa City, 1962—64; instr. biology, area coord. OEO We. Ky. U., Bowling Green, 1964—66; sci. editor, journalism instr.-sci. and tech. writing Mich. State U., East Lansing, 1968—74; asst. prof. agr., forestry and home econs. U. Minn., St. Paul, 1974—77; sr. editor atomic energy divsn. E.I. du Pont de Nemours and Co., Aiken, SC, 1977—89; sr. scientist environ. protection dept. Westinghouse Savannah River Co., Aiken, 1989—99; pres. Agy. Book Authors, Collectors and Understanding Sci., Aiken, 1994—2004. Radiol. air and drinking water program owner environ./govt. group Morrison Knudsen Corp., Aiken, 1999—2000; prin. scientist Washington Group Internat., Inc., Aiken, 2000—03; panelist 26th Internat. Tech. Comm. Conf., LA, 1979; participant Dept. Energy/Westinghouse Sch. Environ. Excellence, Cin., 1991; invited contbr. to procs. 1st Tatarstan Symposium Energy, Environment and Econs., Kazan, Russia, 1992; cert. pilot U.S. Power Squadrons, 2004—. Mem. publs. com. Ctrl. Assn. Sci. and Math. Tchrs., Iowa City, 1969—72; editor: Nat. Task Force Agrl. Energy R & D, 1976; editor, contbr.: Minn. Sci. Mag., 1974—77; contbr. articles to profl. jours. Judge speech Optimist and 4-H Club Contests, Aiken, 1985—86. Sgt. US Army, 1955—58. Recipient Disting. Marksman Badge Gold medal, 1st pl. Sci. Writing, Argonne Labs. Assn., 1973, Profl. Achievement Permanent Profl. cert., Iowa State Bd. Pub. Instrn., 1974, Blue ribbon, Am. Assn. Agrl. Coll. Editors, Tex. A&M, 1976. Achievements include the discovery that low-zinc root environment causes delay of development and acceleration of senescence in tobacco plants; research in the causes and timing of pre-adolescent initial interest in science.

MILLER, R. CHARLES, lawyer; BA cum laude, Harvard U., 1980; JD cum laude, U. Pa., 1985. Bar: D.C. 1989, US Supreme Ct. Law clk. Judge Spottswood W. Robinson III, US Ct. Appeals (D.C. cir.), Chief Justice William H. Rehnquist, US Supreme Ct.; spec. counsel Office of the Gen. Counsel, SEC, Washington, 1992—95; regional atty. Dole presidential campaign, 1996; adminstrv. ptnr. & mem. mgmt. com. Kirkpatrick & Lockhart Nicholson Graham LLP, Washington. Editor (in chief): Univ. Pa. Law Rev.; co-author: Mutual Fund Regulation - An A to Z Workshop; contbr. articles to profl. jours. Mem.: Am. Law Inst., Order of the Coif.

MILLER, R. TERRY, lawyer; b. San Jose, Calif., Feb. 28, 1947; BA, U. Calif., Berkeley, 1968; JD, So. Meth. U., 1971. Bar: Tex. 1971. Sr. ptnr. Fulbright & Jaworski LLP, Dallas; now ptnr., co-chair real estate and fin. practice group and mem. mgmt. com. Akin Gump Strauss Hauer & Feld LLP, Dallas. Mem. ABA, State Bar Tex., Dallas Bar Assn., Phi Alpha Delta. Office: Akin Gump Strauss Hauer & Feld LLP ste 4100 1700 Pacific Ave Dallas TX 75201-4675 Office Phone: 214-969-4237. Office Fax: 214-969-4343. Business E-Mail: tmiller@akingump.com.

MILLER, R. WARBURTON, psychologist, farmer; b. Bellefonte, Pa., Nov. 23, 1921; s. Joseph Frederick and Mary (Warburton) Miller; m. Joyce Larayne Miller; children: Pamela Joyce, Page Layne. AB, Pa. State U., 1942; MA, U. Redlands, Calif., 1951; PhD, U. So. Calif., 1957; postgrad., San Bernardino Valley Coll., Calif., Columbia U., NYC, U. Mich., U. Minn., LA State Coll., U. Internat., Saltillo, Coah, Mex., Inst. Mex. Cultura Internat.; JD, Loma Linda Coll. Law, 1985. Lic. clin. psychologist, marriage, family and child counselor, clin. speech pathologist. Capt. USN, 1942—44, 1951—53; officer USNR, 1942—74; staff psychologist San Bernardino County Med. Ctr., 1968—74; forensic psychologist/clin. psychologist; pvt. practice with Dr. Joyce Miller. Mem. psychology examining com. State Bd. Med. Examiners, 1970—74; dir. Mojave Valley Coordinating Coun. Family Mental Health, 1971—72; lectr. U. So. Calif., U. Redlands, Loma Linda U.; bd. dirs., v.p. E. Pioneer Mut. Water Co.; expert witness in forensic psychology; chmn. bd. dirs. AVORA Corp. Author (with Joyce Miller): Dealing with the Behavioral Problems in the Elementary School, 1968, A Layman's Handbook for Aphasic Rehabilitation, 1973; contbr. articles to profl. jours. Bd. dirs. State of Calif. Psychologists Polit Action Com.; past pres. Carriage Club, Civic Light Opera Assn., San Bernardino chpt. City of Hope Hosp. # 434, San Bernardino County Navy League; bd. dirs., past pres. Goodwill Industries Inland Counties; pres. San Bernardino Libr. Found., 1995—. Recipient George Washington medal, Freedoms Found. Valley Forge, 1970, 1972, 1973, honor cert., 1974, Disting. citizens Lifetime Achievement award, Calif. Inland Empire Coun., Boy Scouts Am., 2000. Fellow: Am. Assn. Marriage Counselors; mem.: SAR (nat. trustee 1970—74, chmn. nat. soc. Ind. Day com. 1971—73, v.p. gen. nat. soc. we. dist. 1972—74, nat. exec. com. 1973—74, sec. gen. nat. soc. 1974—76, past pres. So. Calif. chpt. Riverside, past pres. State of Calif.), Inland So. Calif. Soc. Clin. Psychologists, Calif. Sate Psychol. Assn., San Bernardino Area C. of C. (bd. dirs., pres. 1999), Naval Res. Assn., Rotary (Paul Harris award), Hon. Order Ky. Cols., Masons, Kappa Sigma, Pi Delta Sigma, Tau Kappa Alpha. Avocation: travel. Home and Office: 6836 Palm Ave Highland CA 92346-2513 Office Phone: 909-881-2786.

MILLER, RAYMOND EDWARD, computer science educator; b. Bay City, Mich., Oct. 9, 1928; s. Martin Theophil and Elizabeth Charlotte (Zierath) M.; m. Marilyn Lueck, June 18, 1955; children: Patricia Ann, Laura Jean, Donna Lyn, Martha Eileen. BS in Mech. Engring., U. Wis., 1950; BEE, U. Ill., 1954, MS in Math., 1955, PhD in Elec. Engring., 1957. Design engr. IBM, Endicott, Poughkeepsie, NY, 1950—51, mem. rsch. staff Yorktown Heights, NY, 1957—81; dir., prof. Ga. Inst. Tech., Atlanta, 1980—89, prof. emeritus, 1989—; dir. Ctr. Excellence in Space Data and Info. Scis. NASA, Greenbelt, Md., 1988—93; prof. U. Md., College Park, 1989—2001, prof. emeritus, 2002—. Pres. Computing Scis. Accreditation Bd., N.Y.C., 1985-87. Author: Switching Theory, Vols. I and II, 1965; editor: (with J.W. Thatcher) Complexity of Computer Computation, 1972; patentee in field. Lt. USAF, 1951-53. Fellow, Computing Sci. Accreditation

Bd., 2003. Fellow AAAS, IEEE; Assn. for Computing Machinery, IEEE Computer Soc. (v.p. edn. acts 1991-92). Lutheran. Avocations: tennis, fishing. Office: U Md Dept of Computer Sci A V Williams Bldg College Park MD 20742-0001

MILLER, RAYMOND JARVIS, agronomy educator; b. Claresholm, Alta., Can., Mar. 19, 1934; came to U.S., 1957, naturalized, 1975; s. Charles Jarvis and Wilma Macy (Anderson) M.; m. Frances Anne Davidson, Apr. 28, 1956; children: Cheryl Rae, Jeffrey John, Jay Robert. BS, U. Alta., Edmonton, 1957; MS, Wash. State U., 1960; PhD, Purdue U., 1962; Doctorate (hon.), Moscow State Agro Engring. U., 2000. Mem. faculty N.C. State U., 1962-65, U. Ill., 1965-69; asst. dir., then assoc. dir. Ill. Agrl. Expt. Sta., 1969-73; dir. Idaho Agrl. Expt. Sta., 1973-79; dean U. Idaho Coll. Agr., 1979-85, v.p. for agr.; dean Coll. Agr. and Coll. Life Sci. U. Md., College Park, 1986-89, vice chancellor agr. and natural resources, 1989-91; pres. Md. Inst. for Agrl. and Natural Resources, 1991-93, prof. agronomy, 1986—, dir. internat. program agrl. natural resources, 1998—. Internat. expert in areas of agrl. sci. and edn. with spl. emphasis on Russia, former Soviet Union, East Europe, China, L.Am. and the Pacific Rim. Author numerous papers in field. Pres. Idaho Rsch. Found., 1980-85; bd. govs. Agrl. Rsch. Inst., 1979-80; chmn. legis. subcom. Expt. Sta. Com. on Policy, 1981-82; chmn. bd. divsn. agr. Land Grant Assn., 1985-86; co-chmn. Nat. Com. Internat. Sci. Edn. Joint Coun., USDA, 1991-94; bd. dirs. C.V. Riley Found., 1985-93; chmn. budget com. Bd. Agr., Nat. Assn. State Univs. and Land Grant Colls., 1993; mem. U.S./Russian Subcom. on Agrl. Rsch., Edn. and Ext., 1996—. Fed. Provincial grantee U. Alta., 1954-56, Dan Baker scholar U. Alta., 1954-56; grantee Internat. Congress Soil Sci., 1960, Purdue U. Rsch. Found., summers 1960, 61 Fellow AAAS, Am. Soc. Agronomy, Soil Sci. Soc. Am.; mem. Internat. Soc. Soil Sci., Clay and Clay Minerals Soc., Am. Chem. Soc., Am. Soc. Plant Physiolotists, Elks, Lions, Sigma Xi, Phi Kappa Phi, Gamma Sigma Delta, Alpha Zeta. Office: Symons Hall Univ Md College Park MD 20742 Office Phone: 301-405-1316. E-mail: millerrj@umd.edu.

MILLER, RAYMOND VINCENT, JR., lawyer; b. Providence, July 1, 1954; s. Raymond Vincent and Mary Eunice (Mullen) M.; m. Elizabeth Ann White, May 31, 1980; children: Travis, Charles. BA, U. R.I., 1976; JD cum laude, U. Miami, 1981. Bar: Fla. 1981, U.S. Dist. Ct. (so. dist.) Fla. 1981, U.S. Ct. Appeals (11th cir.) 1986, U.S. Dist. Ct. (mid. dist.) Fla. 1987. Area supr. job devel. and tng. div. R.I. Dept. Econ. Devel., Providence, 1977-78; assoc. Thornton & Herndon, Miami, Fla., 1981-83, Britton, Cohen et al, Miami, 1983-85, Edward A. Kaufman, P.A., Miami, 1985-88; ptnr. Kaufman, Miller, Dickstein & Grunspan, Miami, 1988-2000; shareholder Gunster, Yoakley & Stewart, P.A., 2000—. Mem. ABA, Fla. Bar Assn., Nat Order Barristers, Soc. Bar and Gavel. Office: Gunster Yoakley & Stewart PA 2 S Biscayne Blvd Ste 3400 Miami FL 33131 Office Phone: 305-376-6048. E-mail: RMiller@gunster.com.

MILLER, REUBEN GEORGE, retired economics professor; b. Phila., Mar. 28, 1930; s. George and Edna (Fuchs) M.; m. Sylvia Raigla, June 9, 1955. BA, LaSalle Coll., 1952; diploma, U. Stockholm, 1954; MA, U. Mont., 1956; PhD, Ohio State U., 1966. Asst. instr. Ohio State U., 1954-57; acting asst. prof. Oberlin (Ohio) Coll., 1957-58; asst. prof. U. Mass., Amherst, 1959-67; assoc. prof. econs. Smith Coll., Northampton, 1967-70; Charles A. Dana prof. econ., chmn. dept. Sweet Briar Coll., Va., 1970—2004, chmn. div. social scis., prof. emeritus, 2004—. Mem. adv. staff Computer Sci. Corp., Washington; cons. Dept. Def.; Fulbright-Hayes lectr. econs. Coll. Law, Nat. Taiwan U., Republic China, 1965-66 Contbr. articles to profl. jours. Am.-Scandinavian Found. fellow, 1952-53; Research Tng. fellow Social Sci. Research Council, 1958-59 Mem. Am. Econ. Assn., Am. Fin. Assn., Royal Econ. Soc. Office: Sweet Briar Coll Dept Econs Sweet Briar VA 24595 Business E-Mail: miller@sbc.edu. E-mail: rsmiller@uscyber.net.

MILLER, RICHARD ALAN, retired economist, educator; b. Springfield, Ohio, Feb. 25, 1931; s. Ross and Beatrice Miller; m. Joan Taylor Walton, July 7, 1956; children: Carol Elizabeth, Jean Anne, Eric Ross. BA, Oberlin Coll., 1952; MA, Yale U., 1957; MA (hon.), Wesleyan U., 1972; PhD, Yale U., 1962. Mem. faculty Wesleyan U., Middletown, Conn., 1960—2006, chmn. dept. econs., 1968-69, 71-73, 75-76, 92-94, Andrews prof., 1995-98, Woodhouse/Sysco prof., 2002—06, Woodhouse/Sysco prof. emeritus, 2006—. Vis. lectr. Yale U., New Haven, 1961-62, vis. assoc. prof., 1967-68, vis. prof., 1973, 83, 85, 95; vis. assoc. prof. U. Calif., Berkeley, 1969-70; vis. prof. U. Adelaide, Australia, 1981; vis. lectr econs. U. Conn., Storrs, 1983; economist Econ. Policy Office, Antitrust Div., U.S. Dept. Justice, Washington, 1973-74, cons., 1974-75; cons. antitrust sect. State Conn., 1980, 82; dir. Kawanhee, Inc., Maine, 1975-81, 82-86 Contbr. articles on indsl. orgn. and antitrust econs. to profl. jours. Mem. cert. adv. coun. Dept. Edn., State Conn., 1982-86; mem. coms. Bd. for State Acad. Awards. State Conn., 1978-97; dean faculty of Cons. Examiners., 1985-87; trustee Conn. Joint Coun. Econ. Edn., 1982-85. Served to lt. (j.g.) USNR, 1952-55. Ford Found. fellow Yale U., 1958-59; NSF fellow MIT, 1964-65, Wesleyan U., 1965-69; Shelby Cullom Davis Found. grantee Wesleyan U., 1979-82; Fulbright fellow N.Z. Inst. Econ. Research, 1986, 88. Mem. Am. Econs. Assn., Indsl. Orgn. Soc. Congregationalist. Home: 83 Paterson Dr Middletown CT 06457-5138 Office Phone: 860-685-2354. E-mail: ramiller@wesleyan.edu.

MILLER, RICHARD ALLEN, lawyer; b. East Chgo., Ind., Nov. 22, 1945; s. Ernest R. and Sophie D. (Kurmis) M.; m. Patricia Annette Bratton, July 26, 1969 (div. May 1974); 1 child, Jason Todd; m. Kathleen Patrice Sills, Jan. 3, 1976; children: Andrew Christian, Caroline Grace. BS, Ind. U., 1967; JD, Valparaiso U., 1973. Bar: Ind. 1974, U.S. Dist. Ct. (no. dist.) Ind. 1974, U.S. Supreme Ct. 1985, U.S. Ct. Appeals (7th cir.) 1987, U.S. Claims Ct. 1990. Assoc. Owen W. Crumpacker & Assocs., Hammond, Ind., 1974-76, Benjamin, Greco & Gouveia, Gary, Ind., 1976-77; ptnr. Greco, Gouveia, Miller & Pera, Gary, 1978-79, Greco, Gouveia, Miller, Pera & Bishop, Merrillville, Ind., 1979-85, Gouveia & Miller, Merrillville, 1985—2004, Richard A. Miller & Assocs., Merrillville, Ind., 2004—. Spl. counsel City of Hammond, 1974-76; trial counsel Ind. Toll Rd. Com., South Bend, 1981-82, Ind. Dept. Highways Toll Rd. Div., Granger, 1982-87; spl. asst. U.S. Rep. Peter J. Visclosky, Gary and Washington, 1985-86. Author: Indiana Rules of Evidence Applying to Expert Testimony, 1991. Campaign mgr. Visclosky for U.S. Congress, 1st Congl. Dist., Ind., 1983-88; dist. coordinator Nat. Bicentennial Competition on U.S. Constitution and Bill of Rights, 1st Congl. Dist., Ind., 1987-88. Mem. Ind. Bar Assn., Assn. Trial Lawyers Am., Ind. Trial Lawyers Assn. Democrat. Lutheran. Avocations: fly fishing, walking dog. Office: Law Offices Richard A Miller & Assocs 370 W 80th Pl Merrillville IN 46410-6173 Home: 1018 Sterling Ct Crown Point IN 46307-2686 Office Phone: 219-756-9390. Business E-Mail: ram@ramalaw.com.

MILLER, RICHARD HARRY, philosopher, educator; b. Akron, Ohio, Feb. 28, 1944; m. Nola Gould, Aug. 20, 1966; 1 child, Benjamin. PhD, Columbia U., NY, 1971. Tchr. philosophy and history of ideas NC Sch. Arts, Winston-Salem, 1972—, interim dean undergraduate academic and grad. programs, 2006—. Leader soup kitchen team Samaritan Inn, Winston-Salem, 1985—2007. Recipient Excellence in Tchg. award, U. NC Bd. Govs., 1991. Office: NC Sch Arts 1533 S Main St Winston Salem NC 27117 Office Phone: 336-770-3241. Business E-Mail: millerr@ncarts.edu.

MILLER, RICHARD JACKSON (RICK MILLER), lawyer; b. Milw., July 17, 1946; s. Wayne D. and Margarite M. (Von Sitany) Miller; m. Irene Nikki Tsacoyeanes, May 28, 1972; children: Nicole Elizabeth, Andrew James, Katherine M., Penelope Constance. BA, U. N.C., 1968; JD, U. Va., 1971. Bar: NY 1973, US Dist. Ct. (so. dist.) NY 1975, US Ct. Appeals (2nd cir.) 1975, Fla. 1988. Assoc. Brown and Wood, NYC, 1971-78, Wood and Dawson, NYC, 1978-82; ptnr. Alexander and Green, NYC, 1982-86, Mudge, Rose, Guthrie, Alexander & Ferdon, West Palm Beach, Fla., 1986-95, Edwards, Angell, Palmer and Dodge, LLP, West Palm Beach, Fla., 1995—. Contbr. articles to jours., chpts. to books; co-author: State and Local Govt. Debt Financing. Capt. USAR, 1972-79. Mem. Fla. Bar Assn., NY State Bar Assn., Univ. Club, NYC. Episcopalian. Avocations: golf, tennis. Office: Edwards Angell Palmer and Dodge 1 N Clematis St Ste 400 West Palm Beach FL 33401 E-mail: rmiller@eapdlaw.com.

MILLER, RICHARD KEITH, academic administrator, engineering educator; b. Fresno, Calif., June 12, 1949; s. Albert Keith and Gloria Mae (Pittman) M.; m. Elizabeth Ann Parrish, July 10, 1971; children: Katherine Elizabeth, Julia Anne. BS in Aerospace Engring., U. Calif., Davis, 1971; MS in Mech. Engring., MIT, 1972; PhD in Applied Mechanics, Calif. Inst. Tech., Pasadena, 1976. Asst. prof. mech. engring. U. Calif., Santa Barbara, 1975-79; assoc. prof. civil engring. U. So. Calif., LA, 1979-85, prof., 1985-92, assoc. dean engring., 1989-92; prof., dean Coll. Engring., U. Iowa, 1992-99; founding pres., prof. mech. engring. Franklin W. Olin Coll. Engring., Needham, Mass., 1999—. Cons. Astro Aerospace Corp., The Aerospace Corp., Jet Propulsion Lab. Contbr. numerous articles to sci. and profl. jours. Mem. AIAA, ASME, ASCE, Am. Soc. Engring. Edn. Office: Franklin W Olin Coll Engring Office of Pres Olin Way Needham MA 02492-1200 Office Phone: 781-292-2301. Office Fax: 781-292-2314. E-mail: richard.miller@olin.edu.

MILLER, RICHARD KIDWELL, artist, actor, educator; b. Fairmont, W.Va., Mar. 15, 1930; s. Maurice Entler and Lillian (Reed) M.; m. Teresa Marie Robinson, Apr. 27, 1957. Student, Pa. Acad. Fine Arts, 1948-49; BA, Am. U., 1953; MFA, Columbia U., 1956. Asst. prof. Kansas City Art Inst., 1968-69; instr. painting Scarsdale (N.Y.) Community Sch., 1970-75. Participated extensively in profl. theater as actor and singer including roles in Broadway Prodn. Baker Street, Oliver, Funny Girl, Wonderful Town, Illya, Darling, Indians, Rise and Fall of the City of Mahogonny; actor stock cos. including Fiddler on the Roof; one-man art shows include Trans-Lux Gallery, Washington, 1951, Bader Gallery, Washington, 1954, Balt. Mus. Art, 1955, Graham Gallery Ltd., N.Y.C., 1960, 62, 65, Argas Gallery, Madison, N.J., 1966, Jefferson Place Gallery, Washington, 1966, Albrecht Kemper Mus. Art, St. Joseph, Mo., 1969, L.I. U., 1973, Aaron Berman Gallery N.Y.C., 1983, Westbeth Gallery, N.Y.C., 1982, John Jay Gallery, N.Y.C., 1998, 2000, JCC of Mid-Westchester, 2001, Retrospective Exhbn., U. W.Va., 2004, John Jay Gallery, N.Y.C., 2006; group shows include Corcoran Gallery Art., 1950-51, 53, Pa. Acad. Fine Arts, 1951, 64, Carnegie Internat., 1961, Salon de National, Paris, 1954, Whitney Mus., 1958, U. Nebr., 1963, Martha Jackson Gallery, N.Y.C., 1973, Nat. Acad. Design, N.Y.C., 1996, 2002, 04, Art of the Northeast, New Caanan, Conn., 1996, Nat. Acad. Mus., N.Y.C., 2007, others; represented in permanent collections Albrecht Kemper Mus. of Art, St. Joseph, Mo., Hirshorn Mus. and Sculpture Garden, Washington, Phillips Collection, Washington, Rochester Mus. Art, U. Ariz. Mus. of Art, Tucson, Watkins Gallery Collection, Washington, U. W.Va., Morgantown, NAD Mus., also numerous private collections; featured in Jan. edit. Am. Artist Mag., 1988, Christian Sci. Monitor, 1990, World Artists (Claude Marks), 1991. Washington Times Herald scholar, 1944, 45, 46; Gertrude Whitney scholar, 1948-53, 55-56; Fulbright fellow, 1953-54 Mem.: Nat. Acad. Design Mus. Address: 222 W 83d St Apt 8C New York NY 10024-4913 Office Phone: 914-472-3300. *I have an insatiable need to express myself— I suppose I was born with it. I was given more than one talent to satisfy this need, and for that I thank God. I have endeavored to use these talents to the absolute best of my ability. I can do no more than that. Some times I have succeeded, and many times I have failed, but the real joy and meaning is in the doing. All the pain has been worth it.*

MILLER, RICHARD N., former medical association administrator; b. Jan. 27, 1938; m. Janet Olin, 1966; children: Margaret, Julia. Grad., Loras Coll.; MD, U. Iowa, 1963; MPH, Harvard U., 1967. Diplomate Am. Bd. Preventive Medicine. Intern Washington Hosp. Ctr., 1963-64; resident Walter Reed Army Inst. Rsch., Washington, 1967-69; pub. health officer Third Civil Affairs Detachment U.S. Army, Canal Zone, Republic of Panama, 1964-66, chief preventive medicine activity USARSUPTHAL Bangkok, 1970-72, chief preventive medicine activity USAMEDDAC Frankfurt, Germany, 1972-75, regional preventive medicine cons. Ft. McPherson, Ga., 1975-79; dir. divsn. preventive medicine Walter Reed Inst. Rsch., Washington, 1979-93, dir. residency program in gen. preventive medicine, 1979-88, 91-93, dir. WRAIR ann. tropical medicine course, 1979-93; asst. prof. preventive medicine and biometrics USUHS, Washington, 1981-93; dir. Med. Follow-up Agy. Inst. of Medicine, Washington, 1993—2001. Contbr. articles to profl. jours. Mem. Am. Coll. Epidemiology, Am. Soc. for Tropical Medicine and Hygiene, Soc. for Epidemiology Rsch., Infectious Disease Soc. Am. Office: Inst Med Med Follow-up Agy 2101 Constitution Ave NW Washington DC 20418-0007

MILLER, RICHARD SHERWIN, law educator; b. Boston, Dec. 11, 1930; s. Max and Mollie Miller; m. Doris Sheila Lunchick, May 24, 1956 (dec. April 23, 2005); children: Andrea Jayne Armitage, Matthew Harlan. BSBA, Boston U., 1951, JD magna cum laude, 1956; LLM, Yale U., New Haven, Conn., 1959. Bar: Mass. 1956, Mich. 1961, Hawaii 1977. Pvt. practice law, Boston, 1956—58; assoc. prof. law Wayne State U., Detroit, 1959—62, prof., 1962—65; prof. law Ohio State U., Columbus, 1965—73, dir. clin. and interdisciplinary programs, 1972—73; prof. U. Hawaii, Honolulu, 1973-95, prof. emeritus, 1995—, dean, 1981-84, dir. summer externship program, 2006—. Vis. prof. law USIA/U. Hawaii, Hiroshima U. Affiliation Program, Japan, 1986, Victoria U., Wellington, New Zealand, 1987; del. Hawaii State Jud. Conf., 1989-92 Author: Courts and the Law: An Introduction to our Legal System, 1980; editor: (with Roland Stanger) Essays on Expropriations, 1967; editor-in-chief: Boston U. Law Rev., 1955-56; contbr. articles to profl. jours. Mem. Hawaii Substance Abuse Task Force, 1994-95; mem. Hawaii Patients Rights Task Force, 2005-06; arbitrator Hawaii Ct. Annexed Arbitration Program, 1995-99; bd. dirs. Drug Policy Forum Hawaii, 1996—, Kokua Coun., 2007—; mem. Save our Star-Bulletin Com., 1999-2001, Citizens for Competitive Air Travel, 2002, Citizens Against Gasoline Price Gouging, 2003-; cons. Hawaii Coalition for Health, 1997-. 1st Lt. USAF, 1951—53. Sterling-Ford fellow Yale U., 1958-59; named Lawyer of Yr. Japan-Hawaii Lawyers Assn., 1990; recipient Cmty. Svc. award Hawaii Med. Assn. Alliance, 1999. Mem. ABA, Hawaii State Bar Assn., Hawaii ACLU, Am. Inn of Ct. IV (emeritus founding mem., master of the bench), Am. Law Inst., Honolulu Cmty.-Media Coun. (chair 1994-89, treas. 2000-02, vice chair 1998-2000), Yale Club of Hawaii. Democrat. Office: U Hawaii Richardson Sch Law 2515 Dole St Honolulu HI 96822-2328 Business E-Mail: rmiller@aya.yale.edu.

MILLER, RICHARD STANLEY, music educator; b. Allentown, Pa., Mar. 16, 1938; s. Elwood Stanley and Ella Loretta Miller; m. Janet Elizabeth Taylor, Oct. 15, 2005; m. Andrea Kay Matter, Sept. 6, 1961 (dec. Oct. 2003); children: Donna Cooper, Deborah Burg, Richard Jr. BS in Music Edn., Lebanon Valley Coll., Annville, Pa., 1960; M in Music Edn., Pa. State U., State College, 1963, postgrad., Temple U., Phila. Dir. bands, orchs. and instrumental music East Juniata Sch. Dist., Cocolamus, Pa., 1960—63, West Phila. H.S., 1963—64, Springfield Twp. Sch. Dist., Pa., 1964—93, Drexel U., Phila., 1988—2003; ret., 2003. Part-time dir. bands, orchs. and instrumental music Widner U., Chester, Pa., 1969—70; supr. student tchrs. West Chester U., 1965—93, Immaculata U., 2004—05; guest condr. and adjudicator, Pa., NJ, Del.; guest condr. in field. Author: P Trigger Trombone for Beginners, 1973, Use of FpH for Beginning Trombones, 1975. Participant Cancer Walk for Life, 2005—07; active Townwatch for Malvern Area. Master sgt. USAF, 1960—91. Mem.: NEA, Pa. Music Educators Assn. (sec. dist. R, Citation of Excellence 1985), Music Educators Nat. Conf., Nat. Band Assn. (Citation of Excellence 1977, 1983), Pa. State Edn. Assn. (life), Phi Mu Alpha, Phi Beta Mu (past pres., Outstanding Bandmaster's award 1996). Avocations: model railroading, gardening, woodworking. Home: 26 Hickory Ln Malvern PA 19355-2866

MILLER, RICHARD STEVEN, lawyer; b. Mt. Vernon, NY, Dec. 5, 1951; s. Norman and Mildred (Curtis) M. BA, U. Pa., 1974; JD, NYU, 1977. Bar: N.Y. 1978, U.S. Dist. Ct. (so. and ea. dists.) N.Y. 1978, U.S. Ct. Appeals (2d cir.) 1978. Asst. dist. atty. Kings County, NY, 1977-79; with Hahn & Hessen, NYC, 1979-82, Levin & Weintraub & Crames, NYC, 1982-87; counsel, then ptnr. Rogers & Wells, NYC, 1987-91; ptnr. Dewey Ballantine LLP, NYC, 1991-2001; prin. shareholder Greenburg Traurig LLP, NYC, 2001—, and co-chmn. nat. reorgn., bankruptcy and restructuring practice, 2001—. Mem. ABA, Internat. Bar Assn., Am. Bankruptcy Inst. Office Phone: 212-801-6767. Office Fax: 212-805-5567. Business E-Mail: millerr@gtlaw.com.

MILLER, RICHARDS THORN, naval architect, engineer; b. Jan. 31, 1918; s. Herman Geistweit and Helen Buckman (Thorn) M.; m. Jean Corbat Spear, Sept. 13, 1941 (dec.); children: Patricia (Mrs. Charles G. Fishburn), Linda (Mrs. John X. Carrier); m. Alice Johnson Houghton, May 19, 1984. BS in Naval Arch. and Marine Engring., Webb Inst. Naval Arch., Glen Cove, NY, 1940; Naval Engr., MIT, Boston, 1951. Registered profl. engr. Commd. ensign USN, 1940, advanced through grades to capt., 1960; head preliminary design br. Bur. Ships, 1960-63; dir. Mine Def. Lab., Panama City, Fla., 1963-66; dir. ship design Naval Ship Engring. Ctr., 1966-68; specialized work design oceanographic rsch. ships, mine sweepers, torpedo boats, destroyers; ret., 1968. Mgr. ocean engring. Oceanic divsn. Westinghouse Electric Corp., 1969-75, adv. engr., 1975-79; cons. naval arch. and engr., 1968—; arbitrator admiralty and ship bldg. contract cases, 1978—; mem. com. naval arch. Am. Bur. Shipping, 1960-63, mem. tech. com., 1978-92; mem. ship structure com., 1966-68. Author: (with R.G. Henry) Sailing Yacht Design, 1963, (with K.L. Kirkman) Sailing Yacht Design—A New Appreciation, 1990; also sects. in books, articles. Decorated Navy Legion of Merit; recipient William Selkirk Owen award Webb Alumni Assn., 1983. Fellow Soc. Naval Archs. and Marine Engrs. (chmn. S.E. sect. 1965-66, chmn. marine sys. com. 1970-77, chmn. tech. and rsch. steering com. 1977-78, chmn. small craft com. 1983-87, v.p. tech. and rsch. 1979-81, hon. life v.p. 1981—, mem. coun. 1976—, mem. exec. com. 1977-81, Capt. Joseph H. Linnard prize 1964, Disting. Svc. award 1988); mem. Am. Soc. Naval Engrs. (mem. coun. 1976-78), U.S. Naval Inst., Christie Soc., Md. Bd. for Profl. Engrs., N.Y. Yacht Club, Annapolis Yacht Club, Sailing Club of the Chesapeake, Sigma Xi. Home and Office: BayWoods of Annapolis 7101 Bay Front Drive Apt 316 Annapolis MD 21403-3701

MILLER, RITA, personnel consultant, diecasting company executive; b. Bklyn., Jan. 15, 1925; d. Joseph and Etta M.; BA, Bklyn. Coll., 1947; MA, Boston U., 1949; children: Erika Greenwald, Roy Barnet Glickman. Personnel officer, sec. to pres. Marine Elec. Corp., Bklyn., 1943-47; script writer Song Debut, Boston, 1949-50; dir. Writers' Workshops, interviewer pub. opinion surveys, New Rochelle, N.Y., 1962-64; dir. pers. and indsl. rels. Dynacast divsn. Coats & Clark, Inc., Yorktown Heights, 1966-89. Mem. Am. Soc. Personnel Adminstrn., Westchester Personnel Mgmt. Assn. (dir.), Personnel Council New Rochelle, Bus. and Profl. Women U.S.A., Nat. Sociology Hon. Soc. Editor: The Management Consultant (George Kenning), 1965; contbr. articles to profl. jours. Home and Office: 29-I Windsor Ct Keene NH 03431 Office Phone: 603-352-7636.

MILLER, ROBERT, advertising executive; b. NYC, June 2, 1923; s. Samuel and Adele (Elswit) M.; m. Frances Fitzgerald, June 10, 1944 (dec. 1978); children: Marc Robert, William Fitzgerald, Daniel Bates, Ellen Minette (Mrs. John Meyer); m. Sandra Gold, 1980; 1 child, Richard Scott. Student, NYU, 1940-42, Syracuse U., 1943. Newsroom employee N.Y. Daily Mirror, 1942; with Miller Advt. Agy., Inc., NYC, 1946—, v.p., 1948-54, chmn. bd., 1954-57, pres., 1958—, Miller Advt. Service Corp., 1956-62, Miller Advt. Agy. Ill., Inc., 1965-73, also bd. dirs. Bd. dirs. Hereford Ins. Co., Inc., 1988-94. Author: Clash of Cultures, 2003; Contbg. editor Madison Avenue mag., 1975-78. Bd. govs. Roslyn Democratic Club, 1957-61, 68-73; mem. Nassau County Dem. Com., 1958-61, 68-73; Bd. dirs. Shalom Peace Found., 1970-89. Served to 1st lt. USAAF, 1942-46. Mem.: VFW, Jewish War Vets., Am. Legion. Home: 301 E 52nd St New York NY 10022-6319 also: 17 Shelly Dr Ellenville NY 12428-1809 Office: Miller Advt Agy Inc 71 Fifth Ave New York NY 10003-3004

MILLER, ROBERT CHARLES, retired physicist; b. State College, Pa., Feb. 2, 1925; s. Lawrence P. Miller and Eva Mae (Gross) Wiedemann; m. Virginia Callaghan, Aug. 30, 1952; children: Robin Miller Storey, Jeffrey Lawrence Miller, Lauren Miller Lynch. AB, Columbia U., 1948, MA, 1952, PhD, 1956. Staff mem. Johns-Manville Research Ctr., Finderne, NJ, 1948-49; teaching asst. in physics Columbia U., NYC, 1949-51, lectr. in physics, 1951-53; mem. tech. staff Bell Telephone Labs., Murray Hill, NJ, 1954-63, head solid state spectroscopy research dept., 1963-67; staff mem. Inst. Defense Analyses, Arlington, Va., 1967-68; head optical elec. research dept. Bell Telephone Labs., Murray Hill, 1968-77; mem. tech. staff AT&T Bell Labs., Murray Hill, 1977-84, disting. mem. tech. staff, 1984-88, ret., 1988. Cons. Office of Sec. Def., Arlington, Va., 1968-75. Inventor (with Dr. J.A. Giordmaine) Optical Parametric Oscillator, 1965 (co-recipient R.W. Wood prize, 1986); contbr. articles to profl. jours. Served with U.S. Army, 1943-46, ETO. RCA predoctoral fellow Columbia U., 1953-54. Fellow Am. Phys. Soc.; mem. AAAS, N.Y. Acad. Scis., Sigma Xi. Avocations: sailing, sports cars, tennis. Home: 65 Eaton Ct Cotuit MA 02635-2908 E-mail: rvcmiller@prodigy.net.

MILLER, ROBERT FRANK, retired electronics engineering educator; b. Milw., Mar. 30, 1925; s. Frank Joseph and Evangeline Elizabeth (Hamann) M.; m. La Verne Boyle, Jan. 10, 1948 (dec. 1978); children: Patricia Ann, Susan Barbara, Nancy Lynn; m. Ruth Winifred Drobnic, July 26, 1980. BSEE, U. Wis., 1947, MSEE, 1954, PhD in Elec. Engring., 1957. Profl. engr., Wis. Instr. physics Milw. Sch. Engring., 1949-53; sr. engr. semicondr. Delco Electronics/GMC, Kokomo, Ind., 1957-67, asst. chief engr., 1967-70, mgr. product assurance, 1970-73, dir. quality control, 1973-85; asst. prof. elec. engring. tech. Purdue U., Kokomo, Ind., 1986—2005, ret., 2005. Ind. cons., Kokomo, 1990—; mem. Ind. Microelectronics Commn., Indpls., 1987—. Author tech. papers; co-author lab. manuals. Bd. dirs. Howard Community Hosp. Found., Kokomo, 1974—, particpating in med. end. support; trustee YMCA, Kokomo, 1990—, bd. dirs., 1967-90. Named Disting. Alumnus U. Wis., Madison, 1980, 90. Mem. IEEE (life), Am. Soc. Quality Control (bd. dirs. sect. 0918, advisor Cen. Ind. sect. bd. 1988—), Sigma Xi, Tau Beta Pi, Phi Kappa Phi, Eta Kappa Nu. Presbyterian. Achievements include active in local medical and scientific education. Home: 3201 Susan Dr Kokomo IN 46902-7506

MILLER, ROBERT G., drug store chain company executive; b. 1944; With Albertson's Inc., 1961-89, exec. v.p. retail ops., 1989-91; chmn. bd., pres., CEO Fred Meyer Inc., Portland, Oreg., 1991—98, vice chmn. bd., CEO, 1998—99; vice chmn., COO Kroger Co., Cin., 1999; CEO Rite Aid Corp., Camp Hill, Pa., 1999—2003, chmn., 1999—2007. Dir. Harrah's Entertainment Inc., 1999—, Wild Oats Markets Inc. Office: Rite Aid Corp 30 Hunter Ln Camp Hill PA 17011-2410 *

MILLER, ROBERT HAROLD, otolaryngologist, educator; b. Columbia, Mo., July 2, 1947; s. Harold Oswald and Ruth Nadine (Ballew) M.; m. Martha Guillory, Apr. 18, 1981 (div.); children: Morgan Guillory, Reed

Thurston. BS in Biology, Tulane U., 1969, MD, 1973, MBA, 1996. Diplomate Am. Bd. Otolaryngology. Resident otolaryngology, head/neck surgery UCLA, 1978; from asst. prof. to assoc. prof. otolaryngology-head and neck surgery Baylor Coll. Medicine, Houston, 1978—87; prof., chmn. otolaryngology-head and neck surgery Tulane Sch. Medicine, New Orleans, 1987—98, vice-chancellor for clin. affairs, 1997—99; dean U. Nev. Sch. Medicine, 1999—2001, prof., 1999—2002; prof. otolaryngology-head and neck surgery Tulane Sch. Medicine, New Orleans, 2002—03; exec. dir. Am. Bd. Otolaryngology, Houston, 2004—. Bd. dirs. Am. Bd. Otolaryngology; chief of staff Tulane Hosp., 1995-96; vis. prof. otolaryngology Baylor Coll. Medicine, Houston, Tex., 2004—. Mem. editl. bd. Archives of Otolaryngology, 1986-05, Head & Neck Surgery, 1987-03, Laryngoscope, 1996-, ENToday, chmn., 2006-. Named Outstanding Young Man, Houston C. of C., 1980; Robert Wood Johnson Health Policy fellow, 1996-97. Fellow ACS, Am. Soc. Head & Neck Surgery, Am. Acad. Oto-Head & Neck Surgery (Disting. Svc. award 1994, Honor award 1991), Triological Soc. (exec. sec. 1992-97, treas. 1997-2004). Avocations: tennis, computers. Home: 2616 Wroxton Rd Houston TX 77005 Office: Am Bd Otolaryngology 5615 Kirby Dr 600 Houston TX 77005 Office Phone: 713-850-0399. Business E-Mail: rmiller@aboto.org.

MILLER, ROBERT J., lawyer; BS, Ctrl. Mich. U., 1982; MBA, U. Okla., 1986, JD, 1990. Bar: Ariz., US Dist. Ct., Dist. of Ariz. 1990. Ptnr., group dep. Bankruptcy, Restructuring and Creditors' Rights Bryan Cave LLP, Phoenix. Office: Bryan Cave LLP 1 Renaissance Square Two N Ctrl Ave, Ste 2200 Phoenix AZ 85004 Office Phone: 602-364-7043. E-mail: rjmiller@bryancave.com.

MILLER, ROBERT J., lawyer; b. 1949; married; 2 children. BA, Bklyn. Coll., CUNY, 1971; JD, Georgetown U., 1974. Bar: NY 1975, US Supreme Ct. 1978. Ptnr. Blutrick, Falcone & Miller LLP, NYC, Blutrich, Herman & Miller LLP, NYC, Parker Duryee Rosoff & Haft (combined with Reed Smith in 2002), NYC, 1996—2002, mng. ptnr.; ptnr. Reed Smith LLP, NYC, 2002—, NY/NJ practice group leader litig. group. Pro-bono counsel Fedn. of Italian-Am. Organizations of NY. Mem.: Assn. of the Bar of the City of NY (mem. litig. com., mem. arbitration com.). Office: Reed Smith LLP 599 Lexington Ave 29th Fl New York NY 10022 Office Phone: 212-549-0249. Office Fax: 212-521-5452. Business E-Mail: rmiller@reedsmith.com.

MILLER, ROBERT JAMES, educational association administrator; b. Mansfield, Ohio, Jan. 27, 1926; s. Dennis Cornelius and Mabel (Snyder) M.; m. Jerri Ann Burran, June 5, 1952; children: Robert James Jr., Dennis Burran. Student, Heidelberg Coll., 1946-47; BS, U. N.Mex., 1950, MA, 1952; postgrad., Miami U., Oxford, Ohio, 1951-55; MBA, Fla. Atlantic U., 1978. Asst. exec. sec. Phi Delta Theta Hdqrs., Oxford, Ohio, 1951—54, adminstrv. sec., 1954—55, exec. v.p., 1955—91, historian, 2006—; pres. Phi Delta Theta Found., Oxford, 1984—96, historian, 2006—; bus. mgr. The Scroll, Oxford, 1955—91; cons., 1997—. Editor: Phikeia—The Manual of Phi Delta Theta, 1951, 19 edits., 1989, Phis Sing, 1958, Constitution and General Statutes of Phi Delta Theta, Fraternity Education Foundations, 1962, Directory of Phi Delta Theta, 1973. Chmn. United Appeal, Oxford, 1960; bd. dirs. Interfrat. Found., 1995—, Oxford Cmty. Arts Ctr., 2005-06; bd. dirs. Knolls Oxford, 2007—; pres. Miami U. Art Mus., 1993-94, McCullough-Hyde Hosp., Oxford, 1966, chmn. endowment adv. com., 1988-89; vol. leader Boy Scouts Am., Oxford, 1966-79; historian Phi Delta Theta Found., 2006—. Named Citizen of Yr., City of Oxford, 1968; recipient citation Theta Chi, 1967, Order of Interfrat. Svc. Lambda Chi Alpha, 1994, Interfrat. Leadership award Sigma Nu, 1994, accolate for intrafraternity svc. Kappa Alpha, Meritorious Svc. award Boy. Scouts Am., 1977, others; Interfrat. Inst. fellow Ind. U., 1988. Mem. Nat. Intrafraternity Conf. (com. mem. 1954-96, Gold medal 1992), Am. Soc. Assn. Execs. (cert.), Cin. Soc. Assn. Execs., Fraternity Execs. Assn. (pres. 1962-63, Disting. Svc. award 1991), Edgewater Conf. (pres. 1978-79), Summit Soc., Country Club Oxford (bd. dirs.), Work Devel. Assn. (pres. 1999—), Order of Symposiarchs, Order of Omega, Rotary (founder Oxford club 1965, pres. 1966, Merit award 1974, dist. gov. S.W. Ohio 1978-79, study group exch. leader South Africa 1992), Blue Key, Phi Delta Kappa, Omicron Delta Kappa Home: 15 Woodcrest Way Oxford OH 45056-9485 Office: Phi Delta Theta Ednl Found 2 S Campus Ave Oxford OH 45056-1801 Office Phone: 513-523-6966.

MILLER, ROBERT JOSEPH, lawyer, former governor; b. Evanston, Ill., Mar. 30, 1945; s. Ross Wendell and Coletta Jane (Doyle) Miller; m. Sandra Ann Searles, Oct. 17, 1949; children: Ross, Corrine, Megan. BA in Polit. Sci., U. Santa Clara, 1967; JD, Loyola U., 1971. First legal advisor Las Vegas (Nev.) Met. Police Dept., 1973—75; justice of the peace Las Vegas Twp., 1975—78; dep. dist. atty. Clark County, Las Vegas, 1971—73, dist. atty., 1979—86; lt. gov. State of Nev., 1987—89, gov., 1989—98; sr. ptnr. Jones Vargas, Las Vegas, 1999—2005; prin. Dutko Worldwide, Las Vegas, Nev., 2005—. Bd. dir. Newmont Mining Corp., Zenith Nat. Ins. Corp., Wynn Resorts Ltd. Chmn. Nev. Commn. on Econ. Devel., Carson City, 1987—91, Nev. Commn. on Tourism, Carson City, 1987—91; mem. Pres. Reagan's Task Force on Victims of Crime, 1982; chmn. Nev. divsn. Am. Cancer Soc., 1988—90. Mem.: Nev. Dist. Attys. Assn. (pres. 1979, 1983), Nat. Govs. Assn. (vice chmn. exec. com. 1995—96, chmn. 1996—97, past chmn. com. on justice and pub. safety, chmn. legal affairs com. 1992—94, lead gov. on transp. 1992—), Western Govs. Assn. (chmn. 1993—94), Nat. Dist. Attys. Assn. (pres. 1984—85). Democrat. Roman Catholic. Office Phone: 702-240-0831.

MILLER, ROBERT L., JR., (BOB MILLER), federal judge; b. 1950; m. Jane Woodward. BA, Northwestern U., 1972; JD, Ind. U., 1975. Law clk. to Hon. Robert A. Grant U.S. Dist. Ct. (no. dist.) Ind., 1975; judge St. Joseph Superior Ct., South Bend, Ind., 1975-86, chief judge, 1981-83; judge US Dist. Ct. (no. dist.) Ind., South Bend, Ind., 1985—, chief judge, 2003—. Mem. US Jud. Panel on Multidistrict Litig., 2003—. Office: US Dist Ct 325 Robert A Grant Fed Bldg 204 S Main St South Bend IN 46601-2122

MILLER, ROBERT LOUIS, dean, chemistry professor; b. Chgo., Jan. 26, 1926; s. Sam P. and Ida (Reich) M.; m. Virginia Southard, Oct. 26, 1947 (dec. Sept. 1973); children: Ruth, Stephen, Martin, Andrew; m. Bonnie Seay Berard, Nov. 28, 1975; children: Edouard, Derek. PhB, U. Chgo., 1947, BS, 1949, MS, 1951; PhD, Ill. Inst. Tech.; PhD (NSF Sci. faculty fellow), 1963. Mem. faculty U. Ill. Chgo. Circle Campus, 1953-67, asst. dean Coll. Liberal Arts and Scis., 1963-65, assoc. dean Coll. Liberal Arts and Scis., 1965-67; prof. chemistry U. NC, Greensboro, 1968—98, dean arts and scis., 1968—85, acting dean Grad. Sch., 1989—91, spl. asst. to provost, 1993—94, 1996—97, acting assoc. provost, 1994—96, interim head dept. math. scis., 2001—03, interdepartmental head computer scis., 2006—07. Am. Coun. Edn. adminstrv. intern SUNY-Binghamton, 1967-68. Mem. exec. com. of com. environ. affairs Piedmont Council Govts., 1971-76; mem. Greensboro Task Force on Energy; chmn. residential and transp. subcom Greensboro Energy Commn.; mem. Bd. Edn., Oak Park, Ill., 1965-66; bd. dirs. Hospice at Greensboro, 1981-87, pres., 1982-84, vol. 1988-89; vol., mem. bd. dirs. Cities in Schs., 1988-92; bd. dirs. Gilbert Pearson Audubon Soc., Greensboro Civil Liberties Union, Weatherspoon Gallery, 1981-85. Served with AUS, 1944-46, ETO. Mem. AAAS, Sigma Xi (treas. chpt.). Home: 4020 Watauga Dr Greensboro NC 27410-4502 Office: Dept Computer Sci Univ NC Greensboro NC 27412 Personal E-mail: rmill07@bellsouth.net. Business E-Mail: rlmiller@uncg.edu.

MILLER, ROBERT NOLEN, lawyer; b. Monmouth, Ill., May 30, 1940; s. Robert Clinton and Doris Margaret (Nolen) M.; m. Diane Wilmarth, Aug. 21, 1965; children: Robert Wilmarth, Anne Elizabeth. BA, Cornell Coll., Mt. Vernon, Iowa, 1962; JD, U. Colo., 1965. Bar: Colo. 1965. Assoc. firm M. Quiat, Denver, 1965-66, Fischer & Beaty, Ft. Collins, Colo., 1969-70; dist. atty. Weld County Dist. Atty's. Office, Greeley, Colo., 1971-81; U.S. atty. U.S. Dept. Justice, Denver, 1981-88; chief counsel litigation and security US West Inc., Englewood, Colo., 1988-93; of counsel Patton, Boggs & Blow, Denver, 1993-94; ptnr., head litig. LeBoeuf, Lamb, Greene & Mac Crae, Denver, 1994—2003; mng. ptnr. Perkins Coie, Denver, 2003—. Instr. bus. law Am. U., U. SC, Myrtle Beach, 1966-69; mem. Gov.'s Commn. for Columbine and Civil Justice Reform, 1999—; mem. Supreme Ct. Nominating Commn., 1999-2005. Co-author: Deathroads, 1978 Bd. dirs. Boys Club, Greeley, 1974-78, 1st Congl. Ch., Greeley, 1975-78; Rep. candidate for atty. gen. Colo., 1977-78. Capt. USAF, 1966-69. Recipient Citizen of Yr. award Elks Club, Greeley. Mem. Fed. Bar Assn. (pres. Colo. chpt. 1983-84), Colo. Dist. Atty's Coun. (pres. 1976-77), Colo. Bar Assn., Weld County Bar Assn., Rotary (pres. local chpt. 1980-81). Republican. Avocations: fishing, hunting, reading. Office: Perkins Coie 1899 Wynkoop Ste 700 Denver CO 80202-1043 Office Phone: 303-291-2313. Business E-Mail: rmiller@perkinscioe.com.

MILLER, ROBERT RAYMOND, JR., biology professor; s. Robert Raymond and Evelyn Louise Miller; m. Linda Sue Fannin, Sept. 7, 1956. BS, Elmhurst Coll., Ill., 1975; MS, Ill. State U., Normal, 1977; PhD, U. Iowa, Iowa City, 1989. Assoc. prof. Knox Coll., 1989—94, Grand View Coll., Des Moines, 1994—97, Hillsdale Coll., Mich., 1997—2000, prof. biology, 2000—. Vis. asst. prof. Knox Coll., 1989—91. Contbr. articles to profl. jours. Mem.: Am. Chemistry Soc., NY Acad. Scis., Rsch. Soc. Alcoholism, Teratology Soc., Genetics Soc. Am. Achievements include research in alcohol and homocysteine-induced embryonic death; membrane composition and cryogenic freezing. Office: Hillsdale College 278 N West St Hillsdale MI 49242-1205 Office Phone: 517-607-2393. Office Fax: 517-609-2252. Business E-Mail: bob.miller@hillsdale.edu.

MILLER, ROBERT SCOTT, clinical social worker, psychiatric hospital surveyor; b. Seattle, Dec. 12, 1947; s. Bert Lester and Carol Theresa (Gustafson) M.; m. Karen Ann Staake, Nov. 12, 1977; children: Sarah, Megan, Emily. BA in Sociology cum laude, Seattle Pacific U., 1970; AM in Social Work, U. Chgo., 1972; MA in Human Resources Mgmt., Pepperdine U., Malibu, Calif., 1977; diploma in life skills coaching, Stonebridge Associated Colls., UK, 2002; DBA, Calif. Pacific U., Escondido, 2006. LCSW. Br. supr. Wash. State Dept. Social and Health Svcs., Oak Harbor and Anacortes, 1975—78, supr. casework Everett, 1973—75; lectr., coord. rural cmty. mental health project U. Wash., Seattle, 1978—83; exec. dir. Armed Svcs. YMCA, Oak Harbor, 1984—86; area dir. United Way of Island County, 1986—88, exec. dir., 1988—92, Saratoga Cmty. Mental Health, Coupeville, 1992—93; outpatient therapist, attention-deficit/hyperactivity disorder mental health specialist Cath. Cmty. Svcs. Northwest, Oak Harbor, 1993—96; dir. Cath. Cmty. Svcs. NW, 1996—2001, Mount Vernon, 1996—99, clin. dir. Everett, 1998—2004; privacy officer Health Ins. Portability and Accountability Act, 2001—04; pvt. practice counselor, 2001—; psychiat. hosp. surveyor, quality control reviewer Ascellon Corp., Balt., 2004—; supr., mgr. skill cert. Rutgers U., 2007, project mgr. skill cert., 2007. Internship supr. counseling program, Seattle U., 1998-99, Bastyr U., 2000-01; instr. sociology and psychol. Chapman U. Naval Air Sta. Whidbey Island, Orange, Calif., 1988-95, 2004; practicum instr. sch. social work Ea. Wash. U., 2003. *Robert Miller researched with J. Ray: Rural Community Mental Health: The Scope of Practice, Worker Satisfaction, and Implications for Training, University of Washington (1982). He presented paper The Role Transition of Professionals Moving to Rural Locales, NATO Symposium on Role Transitions, University Wisconsin, 1982. He designed first crisis nursery in Washington (1983). One of first two male presidents of a Business & Professional Women's club (1986). He received McDonald's Program Achievment Awards for YMCA latchkey program, and community indoctrination tour for Whidbey Island Naval Air Station personnel (1986).* Contbr. articles to profl. jours. Pres. Wash. Assn. Social Welfare, 1975-76; bd. dir. Puget Sound chpt. Huntington's Disease Soc. Am., 1989-93, pres., 1991, fund-raising chmn., 1989-91, v.p., 1990; adv. bd. United Ways Wash., 1991-92; chmn. Island County bd. emergency food and shelter program Fed. Emergency Mgmt. Agy.; vice chmn. Cmty. Resource Network, Oak Harbor, 1991; steering com. Greater Oak Harbor Econ. Summit, 1991; strategic planning com. Whidbey Gen. Hosp., Coupeville, 1992-93; exec. com. Mt. Baker coun. Boy Scouts Am., 1993; bd. dir. Opportunity Coun., Bellingham, 1993-94, Concerts on the Cove, Coupeville, 1993-96, v.p., 1994-95; active Oak Harbor Citizen's Comprehensive Plan Task Force, 1994, Readiness to Learn Coupeville Cmty. Team, 1996; risk mgmt. subcom. chair Assoc. Provider Network, 1997-98; child study team Island County, 1996-99, child protective team, 1997-99; health adv. bd. Head Start, Mt. Vernon, Wash., 1999-2002. Recipient outstanding svc. award Armed Svcs. YMCA of US, Dallas, 1985, two program merit awards McDonald's Corp., Oak Harbor, 1986; named Alumni of a Growing Vision, Seattle Pacific U., 1991, Diplomat of Yr. Greater Oak Harbor C. of C., 1991, Celebrating Excellence award, Ascellon Corp., 2005. Mem. NASW (bd. dirs. Wash. chpt. 1982-85), Acad. Cert. Social Workers, Greater Oak Harbor C. of C., Soc. Mayflower Descendants. Democrat. Roman Catholic. Avocations: kayaking, genealogy, fishing, 3rd degree mason. Home: 2450 Rocky Way Coupeville WA 98239-9610 Office: Ste B206 275 SE Cabot Dr Oak Harbor WA 98277

MILLER, ROBERT STEVENS, JR., (STEVE MILLER), automotive company executive; b. Portland, Oreg., Nov. 4, 1941; s. Robert Stevens and Barbara (Weston) Miller; m. Margaret Rose Kyger, Nov. 9, 1966 (dec. Aug. 11, 2006); children: Christopher John, Robert Stevens, Alexander Lamont. AB with distinction, Stanford U., 1963; LLB, Harvard U., 1966; MBA, Stanford U., 1968. Bar: Calif. 1966. Fin. analyst Ford Motor Co., Dearborn, Mich., 1968-71, spl. studies mgr. Mexico City, 1971-73; dir. fin. Ford Asia-Pacific, Inc., Melbourne, Australia, 1974-77, Ford Motor Co., Caracas, Venezuela, 1977-79; v.p., treas. Chrysler Corp., Detroit, 1980-81, exec. v.p. fin., 1981-90, vice chmn., 1990-92; sr. ptnr. James D. Wolfensohn, Inc., NYC, 1992-93; chmn. Morrison Knudsen, 1995—96; chmn., CEO Waste Management, 1997—99, Fed. Mogul Corp., Smithfield, Mich., 1999—2000, 2004—05, non exec. chmn., 2001; chmn., CEO Bethlehem Steel Corp., Pa., 2001—03, Delphi Corp., Troy, Mich., 2005—06, exec. chmn., 2007—. Office: Delphi Corp 5725 Delphi Dr Troy MI 48098 *

MILLER, ROBERTA DORIS, elementary school educator; b. Lynn, Mass., May 14, 1940; d. Morris and Lorraine Miller. BS in Edn. cum laude, Lesley Coll., Cambridge, Mass., 1961; M in Edn., Salem Coll., Mass., 1964; postgrad., Boston U. Tchr. Brookline (Mass.) Pub. Schs., 1968—. Pilot math. programs Ednl. Devel. Corp., Newton, Mass., 1988-89; pilot sci. programs TV series 3! 2! 1! Contact!, 1991; developer curriculum materials in math. and lang. arts Brookline Pub. Schs., 1969—; participant Math for Tomorrow program NSF, 1994; faculty Suffolk U., Boston, 2000—; presenter in field. Coord. presentation of programs to nursing homes and vets. hosps.; coord. fundraising victims and schs. of Hurricane Andrew, 1992; chair, coord. fundraising for victims of the Midwest floods, 1993. Mem.: MATSOL (Mass. Assn. Tchrs. of Speakers Other Langs., Inc.), NEA, Mass. Tchrs. Assn. Avocations: travel, reading, music. Personal E-mail: bobdorrob@yahoo.com.

MILLER, RONALD, journalist, critic; b. Santa Cruz, Calif., Feb. 28, 1939; s. Fred Robert and Evelyn Lenora Miller; m. Darla-Jean Irene Rode, Nov. 2, 1963. AA, Monterey Peninsula Coll., 1958; BA, San Jose State U., 1961. Reporter Santa Cruz (Calif.) Sentinel, 1959-62; reporter, chief news bur. San Jose (Calif.) Mercury News, 1962-77, editor T.V., 1977-99; syndicated TV columnist Knight Ridder Syndicate, 1978-99. Commentator, critic Sta. KLOK, San Jose, 1981-83; nat. judge Cableace awards, 1987; adj. instr. Whatcom C.C., Bellingham, Wash., 2001-04, Western Wash. U., 2003—. Author: (foreword) Les Brown's Encyclopedia of Television, 1992; co-author: Masterpiece Theatre, 1995, Author: Mystery! A Celebration, 1996 (Agatha, Anthony, and Macavity award nominee 1996-97); columnist, mng. editor The Columnists.com website, 1999—; mystery columnist Alibris.com. website, 2000, PBS mystery.com website, 2001-2002; program host Am. Mus. Radio and Electricity, 2003; TV columnist Mystery Scene Mag., 2004-. Recipient Nat. Spot News Photo award Sigma Delta Chi, 1961, Outstanding Alumnus award San Jose State U. Dept. Journalism and Mass Comm., 1985, Nat. Headline award Press Club Atlantic City, 1994. Democrat. Home and Office: 5437 Canvasback Rd Blaine WA 98230

MILLER, RONALD ALFRED, family physician; b. Orange, Calif., Sept. 27, 1943; s. Alfred Casper and Inez Geraldine (Gunderson) M.; m. Jean Ilene Andrews, June 18, 1966; children: Jon, Lauri, Bryan. BA, Pacific Luth. U., 1965; MD, U. Wash., 1969. Diplomate Am. Bd. Family Practice (bd. dirs. 1985-90, pres. bd. 1989-90). Intern in medicine Parkland Meml. Hosp., Dallas, 1969-70; gen. practice residency USPHS Gallup Indian Med. Ctr., Gallup, N.Mex., 1970-72; prin. Medical Doctor Glacier Med Assocs., Whitefish, Mont., 1972—. Clin. prof. U. Wash., Seattle, 1975—; coord. community clin. unit in family medicine, U. Wash., Whitefish, 1975—; bd. dirs. Utah Med. Ins. Assn., Salt Lake City, 1987—. Bd. dirs. Whitefish Housing Authority, 1977-82; mem. alumni bd. Pacific Luth. U., Tacoma, 1976-81, pres., 1979-80; mem. Glacier Community Chorale, Whitefish, 1984—, bd. dirs., 1990-92. Lt. comdr. USPHS, 1970-72. Mem. Am. Acad. Family Physicians (com. on continuing med. edn. 1977-81, com. on edn. 1984-89, Mead Johnson award Grad. Edn. in Family Practice 1972), Mont. Acad. Family Physicians (bd. dirs., sec./treas, v.p., pres. 1982-83, del. nat. congress 1978-84), Rotary, Alpha Omega Alpha. Republican. Lutheran. Avocations: hunting, fishing, skiing, backpacking, singing. Home: 1046 7th St W Whitefish MT 59937-3227 Office: 1111 Baker Ave Whitefish MT 59937-2905

MILLER, RONALD BAXTER, language educator, writer; b. Rocky Mount, NC, Oct. 11, 1948; s. Marcellus Cornelius and Elsie (Bryant) M.; m. Jessica Garris, June 5, 1971 (div. Dec. 1998); 1 child, Akin Dasan; m. Diana L. Ranson, Sept. 3, 2000. BA magna cum laude, N.C. Ctrl. U., 1970; AM, Brown U., 1972, PhD, 1974. Asst. prof. English Haverford Coll., Haverford, Pa., 1974-76; assoc. prof. English, dir. Black lit. program U. Tenn., Knoxville, Tenn., 1977-81, prof. English, dir. Black lit. program, 1982-92, Lindsay Young prof. liberal arts and English, 1986-87; prof. English, dir. Inst. for African Am. Studies U. Ga., Athens, 1992—2006, prof. English, African Am. studies, 2006—. Instr. summer sch. Roger Williams Coll., Bristol, R.I., 1973; lectr. SUNY, Oneonta, 1974; Mellon prof. Xavier Univ., New Orleans, 1988; Irvine Found. visiting scholar Univ. San Francisco, 1991. Author: (reference guide) Langston Hughes and Gwendolyn Brooks, 1978, The Art and Imagination of Langston Hughes, 1989, 2d. edit., 2006 (Am. Book award, 1991); editor, contbr.: Black American Literature and Humanism, 1981, Black American Poets Between Worlds, 1940-60, 1986; co-author, co-editor: Call and Response The Riverside Anthology of African American Literary Tradition, 1998, ed., "The Short Stories", Collected Works of Langston Hughes 15, 2002; mem. editl. bd. Tenn. Studies in Lit., 1991-93, Black Fiction Project (Yale-Cornell-Duke-Harvard), 1985—, U. Ga. Press, 1994-97; contbr. articles to profl. jour. Recipient award Am. Coun. of Learned Soc., 1978, Golden Key Faculty award Nat. Golden Key, 1990, 95, Alpha award for disting. svc. U. Ga. Athens, 1993, Am. Book award, 1991; Sr. Tchg. fellow U. Ga. Athens, 1994, Langston Hughes prize, 2001, Outstanding Tchg. award Student Govt. Assn., 2005-06; Nat. Rsch. Coun. sr. fellow, 1986-87, NDEA fellow, 1970-72, Ford Found. fellow, 1972-73, NEH fellow, 1975; Nat. Fellowships Fund dissertation grant, 1973-74, ACLS Conf. grantee, 1978. Mem. MLA (exec. com. Afro-Am. Lit. Discussion Group 1980-83, chair 1982-83, mem. del. assembly 1984-86, 97-99, com. on langs. and lits. of Am. 1993-97, chair 1996), Langston Hughes Soc. (pres. 1984-90, exec. editor Langston Hughes Review 1993—). Office: U Ga Inst African Am Studies Athens GA 30602 Business E-Mail: rbmiller@uga.edu.

MILLER, RONALD D., medical educator, researcher; Prof. cellular & molecular pharmacology Univ. Calif., San Francisco, chmn. Dept Anesthesia and Perioperative Care. Office: Univ Calif Dept Anesthesia C-450 Box 0648 521 Parnassus St San Francisco CA 94143-0648 E-mail: millerr@anesthesia.ucsf.edu.

MILLER, RONALD H., energy executive; With Texaco, 1971—81; sr. mktg., logistics and devel. positions Aventine Renewable Energy Holdings, 1981—99, pres., CEO Aventine Renewable Energy, Inc. subs., 2000—, pres., CEO, 2003—, mem. Class III bd. dirs. Chmn. Renewable Fuels Assn., 1995—2001, 2005—, vice chmn., 2001—05. Office: Aventine Renewable Energy Inc PO Box 10 Pekin IL 61555-0010 Office Phone: 309-347-9200. Office Fax: 309-346-0742. *

MILLER, RONALD K., real estate broker, educator; b. Penn Yan, Ny, Apr. 8, 1948; s. Harold and Helen Miller; m. Marguerite Miller, July 16, 2001; children: Jennifer McKay, Kristoffer; m. Jane Miller, Jan. 2, 1970 (div. May 1, 2001). BA, MacMurray Coll., Jacksonville, Illinois, 1970; MA, Elmira Coll., Elmira, NY, 1975. Educator Canandaigua Schools, Canandaigua, NY, 1970—71, Dundee Schools, Dundee, NY, 1972—. Assoc. broker Finger Lakes Properties, Penn Yan, NY, 1992—. Choir dir. First Presbyn. Ch., Penn Yan, NY, 1970—2002. Avocations: gardening, woodworking. Office: Dundee Central School 55 Water Street Dundee NY 14837 Home Phone: (315) 536-2505.

MILLER, RONALD LYNN, director; b. Pitts., Sept. 1, 1950; s. Calvin John and Virginia (Ricca) Miller; children: Veronica Lynn, Maria Eileen. B, Westminster Coll., 1972; M in religion, Pitts. Theol. Sem., 1975; vis. scholar, U. Oxford, 1990—92; PhD in sociology and internat. studies, U. Pitts., 1994. Prof., sociology U. Pitts., 1980—88, prof., religion, 1988—92, prof., global studies, 1992—96; founder to dir. Ctr. Global Studies Internat. Interdisciplinary, Pitts., 1995—. Lectr. various Universities. Author: Introduction to Global Studies, 2003, Revolution in Japan and England, 1996, Individual Identity Formation, 1984. Mem.: Somatics Soc., Somatics Soc., World Hist. Assn., Am. Sociol. Assn., Am. Acad. of Religion, Assn. for Psychol. Sci., Am. Polit. Sci. Assn., Am. Phys. Soc., Am. Philos. Assn., Internat. Neural Network Soc., Assn. for the Study of Ethnicity and Nationalism, Am. Musicolog. Soc., Am. Math. Soc., Linguistics Soc. Am., Law and Soc. Assn., Modern Lang. Assn., Internat. Studies Assn., Am. Hist. Assn., Geol. Soc. Am., Internat. Geog. Union, Assn. Am. Geographers, Coun. for European Studies, Am. Econ. Assn., Econ. Soc. Am., Communal Studies Assn., Internat. Soc. for Comparative Study of Civilizations, Internat. Union of Pure and Applied Chemistry, Am. Chem. Soc., Genetics Soc. of Am., Am. Soc. for Micro., Am. Astron. Soc., Assn. for Asian Studies, Am. Assn. for Artificial Intelligence, Am. Anthrop. Assn., Am. Studies Assn., African Studies Assn. Achievements include patents pending for a module for doing global studies at the university level. Office: Ctr Global Studies Internat Interdisciplinary 40 Beltzhoover Ave Pittsburgh PA 15210 Office Phone: 412-381-3753. Business E-Mail: ronaldlynnmiller@centerforglobalstudies.com.

MILLER, RONALD MELLADO, education educator; b. El Paso, Texas, Nov. 3, 1970; s. Donald Hale and Corina Mellado Miller; m. Patricia Marie Addicks, Feb. 4, 1995; children: Hannah Aurora, Gideon McKay, Shiloh Marie, Eve Asenath. MS, Purdue Univ., 1997—99, PhD, 2000—03. Sci. rschr. Purdue Univ., West Lafayette, Ind., 1997—2003; prof. Brigham Young Univ., Laie, Hawaii, 2003—. Statis., human factors engring. cons. Miller Consulting, West Lafayette, Ind., 1995; human factors engring.

cons. Purdue Univ. Human Factors in Aviation Rsch. Group, West Lafayette, Ind., 1998—; statis., human factors engring. cons. Miller Consulting, Laie, Hawaii, 2003—. Internat. cmty. activist Purdue Univ., West Lafayette, Ind., 1998—2003, Brigham Young U., Hawaii, Laie, Hawaii, 2003. Grantee Rsch. Grant, Purdue U., 2002; scholar Mosell-Watt Bell Scholarship, Brigham Young U., 1995—97; Grad. Fellowship, Purdue Univ., 1997—2003. Mem.: APA, Psychonomic Soc., Am. Statis. Assn., Human Factors and Ergonomic Soc. Lds Ch. Achievements include research in refuting the fundamental theoretical difference between pavlovian and instrumental conditioning; co-author of the only current theory how mental chunking operates. Avocations: travel, swimming, surfing. Office: Brigham Young Univ Hawaii 55-220 Kulanui St BYUH Box #1970 Laie HI 96762 Home: 55-457 Moana St Laie HI 96762 Office Phone: 808-293-3831. Business E-Mail: millerr@byuh.edu.

MILLER, ROSILAND, retired art history educator, writer; b. NY, Oct. 4, 1932; d. John and Gloria Smonian; m. Colemon Miller; 1 child, Susan J. Miller Woods. BA in Art, Balt. Inst. Art, 1954; M in Art History, U. Md., 1975. Assoc. prof. art history, chair fine arts dept. U. Balt., 1969-78; assoc. prof. art history N.Y.C. C.C., 1979-83; rschr. Smithsonian Inst., Washington, 1985-87; ret., 1987. Lectr. Met. Mus. Art, N.Y.C., and Balt. Mus., 1979-88, St. Petersburg (Fla.) Jr. Coll., 1987—, Corcoran Gallery, Tampa Mus. Art, St. Petersburg Mus. Fine Arts.; instr. Loyola Coll., Md.; dir. art gallery Johns Hopkins U., Balt., 1984. Author: Magic, Myths and Religions of Primitive Societies, 1985; sculptor bronze works exhibited at N.Y. galleries, Met. Mus., Balt. Art Mus.; contbr. articles to profl. jours. Lectr. Pinellas County Sch. Sys., 1993, 94. Recipient Outstanding Contbn. to Women in Arts award Internat. Women's Yr., 1975, Humanitarian award Md. Humanitarian Affairs Soc., 1985. Mem. AAUW, AAUP. Home: 5955 30th Ave S Apt 105 Gulfport FL 33707-5337

MILLER, ROSS HAYS, retired neurosurgeon; b. Ada, Okla., Jan. 30, 1923; s. Harry and Helen (Rice) M.; m. Catherine Railey, May 2, 1943; children— Terry Hays, Helen Stacy. BS, East Central State Coll., Ada, 1943; MD, U. Okla., 1946; MS in Neurosurgery, U. Minn., 1952. Diplomate: Am. Bd. Neurol. Surgery (chmn. exam. com. 1978-84). Intern St. Luke's Hosp., Cleve., 1946-47; fellow in neurosurgery Mayo Clinic, Rochester, Minn., 1950-54; instr. in neurosurgery Mayo Med. Sch., 1954-63, asst. prof. neurosurgery, 1963-73, asso. prof., 1973-75, prof., chmn. dept. neurosurgery, from 1975, now ret. Vis. prof. neurol. surgery Med. Coll. Ga., Augusta Contbr. articles to profl. jours. Trustee East Central State U. Found. Served as capt., M.C. U.S. Army, 1947-49, Korea. Named to Okla. Hall of Fame, 1977, Athletic Hall of Fame, East Central U. Okla., 1977; recipient Disting. Alumnus award East Central U. Okla., 1974, Mayo Found. Disting. Alumnus award, 1992. Mem. AMA, ACS, Am. Assn. Neurol. Surgeons (chmn. com. profl. practice 1976-79, dir. 1976-79, v.p. 1979, rep. to Council Med. Splty. Socs. 1980-84), Congress Neurol. Surgeons (exec. com. 1963-65), Minn. Soc. Neurol. Scis., Neurosurg. Soc. Am. (v.p. 1975), Soc. Neurol. Surgeons (v.p. 1983), Sigma Xi.

MILLER, ROSS JAMES, state official, prosecutor; b. Las Vegas, Mar. 26, 1976; s. Bob and Sandy Miller; m. Lesley Miller; 1 child, Cameron Elise. BA in English, Stanford U., Calif., 1999; student, Monterrey Technol. Inst., Mex.; JD/MBA, Loyola Marymount U., LA, 2002. Dep. dist. atty. Clark County, Nev.; sec. state State of Nev., Carson City, 2007—. Past pres. Citizen Alert, Nev.; bd. mem. HELP of So. Nev.; bd. mem. Legacy Soc. Boys and Girls Clubs. Democrat. Office: Office Sec State 101 N Carson #3 Carson City NV 89701 Office Phone: 775-684-5708. Business E-Mail: sosexec@sos.nv.gov.

MILLER, RUANE, artist, educator; d. Edward F. and Helen B. Miller; children: Rian Bogle, Adrea Bogle. BFA, Tyler Sch. Art, Phila., 1962—65; MFA, Tyler Sch. Art, Rome, 1966—68, Rochester Inst. Tech., NY, 1984—86. Asst. prof. art history & fine arts Lycoming Coll., Williamsport, Pa., 1977—78; instr. silkscreen SUNY, Albany, 1981—81; instr. drawing & painting Rochester Inst. Tech., NY, 1985—86; vis. artist & lectr. digital art UCLA, 1986—87; prof. digital & fine arts Coll. NJ, Ewing, 1986—. Computer graphics chairman Coll. NJ, 1986—94; juried paper presenter, panel discussant natl. conf. on liberal arts & edn., Sch. Visual Arts, NYC, 1988; juried workshop participant Siggraph's Internat. Conf., 1990; chmn. Coll. NJ, Ewing, NJ, 1994—97, fine arts chmn., 1998—2002, digital arts chmn., 2002—04. Exhibitions include William Penn Mem. Mus., Harrisburg, PA, 1980, Middlesex County Mus., Piscataway, NJ, 1990, Lycoming Coll., Williamsport, Pa., 1990, Condesco-Lawler gallery, NYC, 1995, Silvermine Guild, New Canaan, Conn., 1996, Art Inst. Phila., 1997, Lycoming Coll., 2000, Newark Mus. Art, Newark, NJ, 2002, Hunterdon Mus. Art, Clinton, NJ, 2003, Bristol-Myers Squibb gallery, 2005, State Mus., Trenton, NJ, 2006, Princeton U., NJ, 2006, Represented in permanent collections Phila Mus. Art, Mus. Art San Francisco, US Embassy, Rome, Mercer County Cultural & Heritage Com. Recipient Dodge Fellowship award & partial residency grant, Vt. Studio Ctr., 1996, Artist Residency fellowship, Ucross Found., 1998, Sustained Rsch. awards, Coll. NJ, 1998—; scholar NCGEF Ednl. Scholarship award, Natl. Computer Graphics Assn., 1989; Ednl. Resource grant, Siggraph's Internat. Conf., 1987, Computers in Curriculam grant, Dept. Higher Edn., NJ, 1988. Mem.: Nat. Assn. Schs. Art & Design, Am. Print Alliance, So. Graphics Coun., Princeton Artist's Alliance (co-pres. 2003—05). Office: Coll NJ Dept Sch Art Media & Music PO Box 7718 Trenton NJ 08628-0718 Personal E-mail: ruane@ruanemiller.com.

MILLER, RUBY SILLS, retired gerontologist; b. Montpelier, Ind., July 7, 1919; d. Elijah Bert and Alma (Beeks) Sills; m. Glenn Kenneth Miller, Mar. 26, 1966. BS in Edn., Ball State Tchrs. Coll., 1957; MBA, U. Wis., 1958; MPS, New Sch. Social Rsch., 1983; post-masters cert., Hunter Brookdale Ctr. on Aging, 1988. Reporter Montpelier Herald, 1937-41; soc. editor, reporter Hartford City News-Times, Ind., 1941-44, bus. office supr., 1945-57; asst. to dean, instr. U. Wis. Sch. Bus., 1958-60; exec. dir. Nat. Fedn. Bus. and Profl. Women's Clubs, 1960-64; asst. to nat. exec. dir. Girl Scouts U.S.A., NYC, 1964-66, spl. asst. to nat. exec. dir., 1972-74; dir. exptl. project for adminstrv. trainees Camp Fire Girls, Inc. and Girl Scouts U.S.A., 1966-68; dir. regional confs. Nat. Assembly for Social Policy and Devel., Inc., 1968-71; project dir. Nat. Ctr. for Vol. Action, 1971-72; cons. Nat. Coun. for Homemaker-Home Health Aide Svc., Inc., 1972, 76; asst. dir. Gustavus Adolphus Cmty. Lounge Sr. Ctr., 1977-78; cmty. program officer Queens County NYC Dept. Aging, 1978-89; ret., 1989; gerontologist cons., 1989—. Sec. Hartford City Retailers Assn., 1951-54 Mem. bd. life mem. Bellevue Day Care Ctr., 1979—, pres., 1980—82; bd. mem. Bellevue Hosp. Adv. Coun., 1978—82, 1991—97; region 1 field rep. NY State Wide Sr. Action Coun., 1989—91, bd. trustees, 1992—2002, region 1 pres., 1996—98, state pres., 1996—98; coord. vol. nat. study guardianship system NY Older Women's League and Ctr. Social Gerontology, Ann Arbor, Mich., 1990—91; pres. Ind. Bapt. Youth Fellowship, 1944—46; supt. Sunday sch. 1st Bapt. Ch. in Montpelier Bapt. Ch., 1949—51; bd. trustees Cmty Ch., Unitarian-Universalist, 1987—92, 1998—2003, vice chair, 1999—2002. Mem.: State Soc. Aging NY. Home: 165 E 32nd St Apt 5G New York NY 10016-6009 Personal E-mail: rmiller7030@aol.com.

MILLER, RUSH GLENN, JR., library director; b. Atlanta, Mar. 13, 1947; s. Rush Glenn and Gene (Ramsey) M.; m. Katherine Graves Miller, 2004; children: Lisa, Glenn, John, Edward; stepchildren: Hart, Megan. BA in History, Delta State Coll., Cleveland, Miss., 1969; MA in History, Miss. State U., 1971, PhD in Medieval History, 1973; MLS, Fla. State U., 1974. Asst. prof. U. Miss., Oxford, 1974-75; dir. libr. svcs. Delta State U., 1975-82; dir. libr. Sam Houston State U., Huntsville, Tex., 1982-86; dean librs. Bowling Green State U., 1986-94; dir. univ. libr. sys. U. Pitts., 1994—. Del. White House Conf. Librs., Washington, 1979; users coun. del. Online Computer Libr. Ctr., Inc., Dublin, Ohio, 1992-94; bd. mem. Assn. Rsch. Librs., 2003-06. Co-author: Beyond Survival: Managing Academic Libraries in Transition, 2007; contbg. author: Diversity and Multiculturalism in Libraries, 1994, others; editor: Miss. Librs., 1982-84; mem. editl. bd. Jour. Academic Leadership; contbr. articles to profl. jours. Recipient Past President's award Miss. Libr. Assn., 1976. Mem. ALA (various coms. 1976—), Southeastern Libr. Assn. (exec. bd. 1976-82), Acad. Libr. Assn. Ohio. Republican. Methodist. Avocations: golf, reading. Office: U Pitts Hillman Libr 3960 Forbes Ave Pittsburgh PA 15260 Office Phone: 412-648-7710, 412-648-7747. Office Fax: 412-648-7887. Business E-Mail: rgmiller@pitt.edu. *

MILLER, RYAN, professional hockey player; b. East Lansing, Mich., July 17, 1980; Attended, Mich. State U., 1999—2002. Goalie Rochester Americans, 2002—05, Buffalo Sabres, 2003—. Player NHL YoungStars Game, 2003. Recipient Hobey Baker Meml. Award, 2001, Baz Bastien Meml. Trophy, Am. Hockey League, 2005. Office: Buffalo Sabres HSBC Arena One Seymour H Knox III Plaza Buffalo NY 14203-3096 *

MILLER, SABRINA WARES, librarian; d. Margaret Ann Bonds and Edson Brigham Wares; children: Adrian Matthew, Brandon Thomas. BA, Sul Ross State U., Alpine, Tex., 1992; MLS, NC Ctrl. U., Durham, 2000. Cert. health info. profl. Med. Libr. Assn., 2005. Med. libr. intern Laupus Libr., East Carolina U. Sch. of Medicine, Greenville, NC, 2000—00; edn. ctr. libr. Mid-Am. Cancer Ctr., Springfield, Mo., 2000—01; pub. svcs. med. libr. John B. Coleman, M.D., Health Scis. Libr., Houston CC, 2001—06; tech. libr. Champion Techs., Fresno, Tex., 2006—. Accreditation cons. Acad. of HealthCare Professions, Houston, 2004—. Vol. Poe Elem. Sch., Houston, 2003; vol. charity work Salvation Army. Bedichek Faculty Devel. grant, Houston C.C. Sys., 2001, 2003. Mem.: Spl. Libr. Assn., Mensa Internat., Acad. Health Info. Profls., Tex. Med. Ctr. Health Scis. Libr. Consortium, Med. Libr. Assn. Democrat. Office: PO Box 450499 Houston TX 77245 Home Phone: 713-807-7947; Office Phone: 281-431-2561.

MILLER, SAM SCOTT, lawyer; b. Ft. Worth, July 26, 1938; s. Percy Vernon and Mildred Lois (MacDowell) M.; m. Mary Harrison FitzHugh, May 10, 1969. BA, Mich. State U., 1960; JD, Tulane U., 1964; LLM, Yale U., 1965. Bar: La. 1965, N.Y. 1966, Minn. 1969. Assoc. Simpson Thacher & Bartlett, NYC, 1965-68; sr. counsel Investors Diversified Services, Mpls., 1968-73; ptnr. Ireland Gibson Reams & Miller, Memphis, 1973-74; gen. counsel Paine Webber Group, Inc., NYC, 1974-87, sr. v.p., 1976-87; ptnr. Orrick, Herrington & Sutcliffe, NYC, 1987—. Adj. prof. NYU Law Sch., 1986-90; vis. lectr. Yale Law Sch., 1980-85, Inst. Internat. Econs. and Trade, Wuhan, China, 1983, U. Calif., 1986; trustee Omni Mut., Inc., 1988-90, Charles Schwab & Co., 1991-. Contbr. articles to profl. jours.; editor-in-chief: Tulane Law Rev, 1964-65; bd. editors Securities Regulation Law Jour., 1982—. Bd. dirs. Guthrie Theatre Found., Mpls., 1971-74; bd. dirs. Minn. Opera Co., 1971-74, Yale U. Law Sch. Fund., 1981—; bd. govs. Investment Co. Inst., 1980-87. Fellow Fgn. Policy Assn.; mem. ABA (chmn. subcom. market regulation 1985-93, vice chmn. com. fed. regulation securities 1995-98, chmn. subcom. electronic comm. 1999-02), Assn. Bar City NY (treas. and mem. exec. com. 1994-96, chmn. broker-dealer investment co. and regulations subcom. 1982-83), Internat. Bar Assn., Securities Industry Assn. (chmn. fed. regulation com. 1976-78), Down Town Assn., Knickerbocker Club, Order of Coif, Omicron Delta Kappa. Democrat. Baptist. Office: Orrick Herrington & Sutcliffe 666 5th Ave Rm 203 New York NY 10103-1798

MILLER, SCOTT D., lawyer; b. Redondo Beach, Calif., 1961; BSE, Ariz. State U., 1982; JD, Columbia U., 1985. Bar: Calif. 1987. Law clk. William A. Norris, US Ct. of Appeals (9th cir.), 1985—86; assoc. Sullivan & Cromwell, Palo Alto, ptnr., and co-head, tech. practice specialty group. Named one of 12 "Dealmakers of the Yr.", The American Lawyer, 2003—04. Office: Sullivan & Cromwell 1870 Embarcadero Rd Palo Alto CA 94303-3308 Office Phone: 650-461-5620. Office Fax: 650-461-5700. Business E-Mail: millersc@sullcrom.com.

MILLER, SCOTT R., plastic surgeon; MD, U. Calif Irvine Coll. Medicine, 1991. Cert. San Diego Internat. Plastic Surgery Soc., Calif. Med. Bd., AMA, Am. Soc. Plastic Surgery, Am. Bd. Plastic Surgery. Intern, then resident in surgery U. Calif., Irvine Coll. Medicine/U. Calif. Med. Ctr., Dept. Surgery, Irvine, 1991—95; resident in plastic & reconstructive surgery U. Calif, San Diego, 1995—97; Bruce Connell fellow of aesthetic cosmetic surgery, 1997; attending surgeon Scripps Meml. Hosp., La Jolla, Calif., pvt. practice, dir., Miller Cosmetic Surgery Ctr.; vol. clin. prof. plastic surgery U. Calif., San Diego. Active in Interface Internat. Surgery Program; mem. instructional coarse com. Plastic Surgery Ednl. Found.; San Diego physician instr. Contour Thread Lift Cert. Course; hosp. affiliations Scripps Meml. Hosp., La Jolla, Scripps Hosp., Encinitas, Children's Hosp., San Diego, Mission Viejo Regional Med. Ctr. Mem. editl. adv. bd. Radius; contbr. chapters to books. Recipient Outstanding Contbn. award, Am. Soc. Aesthetic Plastic Surgery, Hatfield Surg. Excellence award, U. Calif. Irvine. Fellow: ACS; mem.: AMA, Calif. Med. Assn., Am. Soc. Aesthetic Plastic Surgeons (Outstanding Contbn. award), San Diego County Med. Soc., San Diego Internat. Plastic Surgery Soc., Calif. Soc. Plastic Surgeons, Am. Soc. Plastic Surgeons. Office: Miller Cosmetic Surgery Ctr 9834 Genesee Ave La Jolla CA 92037 Office Phone: 858-453-3133, 866-338-9444. E-mail: info@millercosmeticsurgery.com. *

MILLER, SHANNON, Olympic athlete; b. Rolla, Mo., Mar. 10, 1977; Student, Boston Coll. Gymnist U.S. National Gymnastic Team, 1990—97. Named Female Athlete of Yr., Nat. March of Dimes Found., 1993; named to U.S. Olympic Hall of Fame, 2005, Internat. Gymnastics Hall of Fame, 2006. Achievements include most decorated gymnast in US history; won a total of 58 International and 49 National Competition medals; won 9 World Championship medals including 2 back to back All-Around Gold medals; won a Silver All-Around and Silver medal for the balance beam at the Barcelona Olympic Gymnastics in 1992; was a member of the Bronze Team for winning the Bronze medal for floor exercise and uneven bars at the Barcelona Olympic Gymnastics in 1992; was a member of the Gold Team for winning the Gold medal for the balance beam at the Olympics in 1996.

MILLER, SIENNA, actress; b. NYC, Dec. 28, 1981; d. Ed and Jo Miller. Attended, Lee Strasberg Inst. Rep. advertising campaign Tod's fashion house, 2007. Actor: (films) South Kensington, 2001, High Speed, 2002, Layer Cake, 2004, Alfie, 2004, Casanova, 2005, Interview, 2007, Stardust, 2007; (TV series) Bedtime, 2002, Keen Eddie, 2003; guest appearance Late Night with Conan O'Brien, 2003. Office: c/o Endeavor Talent Agency 9701 Wilshire Blvd, 3rd Fl Beverly Hills CA 90212 *

MILLER, STEPHANIE, radio personality; b. Lockport, NY, Sept. 29, 1961; BA Theatre, U. So. Calif. Stand up comedian Laugh Factory; talk show host radio station WLVL, WCMF, Brother Wease Show, Rochester, NY, 1985, WCKG, Chgo., KFI, LA, 1993—95; late night TV talk show host The Stephanie Miller Show, Buena Vista TV, 1995; talk show host KTZN, KABC, LA, 1997; co-host Equal Time, CNBC, 1997—2000; game show host I've Got a Secret, Oxygen cable TV network, 2000—01; co-host Pure Oxygen, Oxygen cable TV network, 2001—04; host The Stephanie Miller Show, 2004—. Frequent panelist PAX-TV, Balderdash. Avocations: dogs, stand up comedy. Office: Jones Radio Networks Inc 133 Ave Americas 11th Fl New York NY 10036 E-mail: stephanie@stephaniemiller.com. *

MILLER, STEPHEN HERSCHEL, surgeon, educator; b. NYC, Jan. 12, 1941; s. Morris Louis and Mildred Lily (Beller) M.; children: Mark, David. MD, UCLA, 1964; MPH, San Diego State, 1996. Diplomate Am. Bd. Surgery, Am. Bd. Plastic Surgery (mem. exec. com. 1985—, chmn. written examination sect. 1985—, bd. dirs. 1984—, chmn. 1989-90). Asst. prof. surgery U. Calif., San Francisco, 1973-74; from assoc. prof. to prof. surgery Milton S. Hershey Med. Ctr., Hershey, Pa., 1974—78; chief div. plastic surgery Oreg. Health Scis. U., Portland, 1979-88, Staff Scripps Clinic, La Jolla, Calif., 1988—98; clin. prof. surgery U. Calif., San Diego, 1989—98; adj. prof. surgery Northwestern U., Evanston, Ill., 1998—; pres., CEO Am. Bd. Med. Specialities, Evanston, Ill., 2004—. Bd. dirs. Edn. Commn. for Foreign Med. Grads. Editor-in-chief Yearbook of Plastic, Reconstructive and Aesthetic Surgery, 1988-95, 2007. Physician advisor Boy Scouts Am., dist. chmn. scoutmaster exec. coun., 1983-84; bd. dirs. Temple Beth Israel, Portland, 1984-86. Recipient Physician Recognition award, 1976; grantee Med. Rsch. Found. of Oreg., 1980, Oreg. Health Scis. U., 1980. Mem. ACS (chmn. program com. 1983-87), Am. Soc. Plastic and Reconstructive Surgery (bd. dirs. 1980-89, v.p. 1985-86, pres.-elect 1986-87, pres. 1987-88, grantee 1976), Am. Assn. Plastic Surgeons (chmn. rsch. com. 1983-84, trustee 1988-91, sec. 1990-93, pres. 1994-95), Assn. Acad. Chmn. Plastic Surgery (sec./treas. 1985—); Am. Bd. Med. Specialites (sect., exec. v.p., 1998). Avocations: reading, golf. Home: 808 Judson Ave Apt 4D Evanston IL 60202-2456 Address: Am Bd Med Specialities 1007 Church St Ste 404 Evanston IL 60201-5913 Office Phone: 847-491-9091. Fax: 847-328-3596.

MILLER, STEPHEN RALPH, lawyer; b. Chgo., Nov. 28, 1950; s. Ralph and Karin Ann (Olson) Miller; m. Sheila L. Krysiak, Feb. 2, 1998; children from previous marriage: David Williams, Lindsay Christine. BA cum laude, Yale U., 1972; JD, Cornell U., 1975. Bar: Ill. Assoc. McDermott, Will & Emery, Chgo., 1975-80, income ptnr., 1981-85, equity ptnr., 1986—2006, mgmt. com. mem., 1992-95, counsel, 2006—. Mem. spl. task force on post-employment benefits Fin. Acctg. Stds. Bd., Norwalk, Conn., 1987—91. Contbr. articles to profl. jours. Trustee Police Pension Bd., Wilmette, Ill., 1992—98; mem. Chgo. Coun. Fgn. Rels., 1978—, mem. devel. com., 1997—2002, chair devel. subcom., 1999—2002, mem. external rels. com., 2002—03, mem. pres.'s cir. steering com., 2005—; trustee Seabury Western Theol. Sem., Evanston, Ill., 1994—2002, chancellor, 1996—97, 2004—05, chair trusteeship com., 2000—02; mem. Seabury Coun., 2004—. Mem.: ABA, Hundred Club Cook County, Cornell Club Chgo., Lawyers' Club Chgo., Yale Club Chgo. Avocations: sailing, water-skiing, cross country skiing. Office: McDermott Will & Emery 227 W Monroe St Ste 4700 Chicago IL 60606-5096 Office Phone: 312-984-7634. Business E-Mail: smiller@mwe.com.

MILLER, STEPHEN WILEY, lawyer; b. Washington, Feb. 27, 1958; s. Robert Wiley and Betty Ruth (Brown) M.; m. Andrea Brill, Feb. 12, 1982; children: Ashley, Craig, Kevin. BA, Denison U., 1980; JD, U. Va., 1984. Bar: Va. 1984, U.S. Dist. Ct. (ea. dist.) Va. 1987, U.S. Ct. Appeals (4th cir.) 1984. Assoc. Hunton & Williams, Richmond, Va., 1984-87; asst. U.S. atty. U.S. Atty.'s Office, U.S. Dept. Justice, Richmond, 1987—. Contbr. articles to profl. jours. Mem. ABA, Va. State Bar, Va. Bar Assn., Phi Alpha Delta (chpt. pres. 1982-83, state coordinator 1986—, outstanding svc. award 1983). Office: US Attys Office 600 E Main St Richmond VA 23219-2441

MILLER, STEVEN, medical administrator; Grad., U. Mo., Kansas City. Hosp. staff, faculty Wash. U., 1990—, nephrology fellow, 1988, asst. prof., 1991—97, assoc. prof., 1997—, dir. hypertension clinic divsn. nephrology; med. dir. systemwide renal network Barnes-Jewish Hosp.; chief med. officer Wash. U. Sch. Medicine-Barnes Jewish Hosp., 1999—2005; now v.p. of rsch. Express Scripts Inc., St. Louis. Mem.: Internat. Soc. Nephrology, ACP. Office: Express Scripts Inc 13900 Riverport Dr Maryland Heights MO 63043

MILLER, STEVEN E., professor of international affairs; b. North Hollywood, Calif. m. Deborah K. Louis; children: Jonathan, Nicholas. B, Occidental Coll., LA; MA in Law and Diplomacy, Fletcher Sch. Law and Diplomacy, PhD in Internat. Relations. Sr. rsch. fellow Stockholm Internat. Peace Rsch. Inst.; tchr. defense and arms control studies Dept Polit. Sci. MIT; dir. Internat. Security Program Belfer Ctr. Sci. and Internat. Affairs Harvard U., Mass., co-prin. investigator Mass. Editor-in-chief Internat. Security jour.; co-chmn. US Pugwash Com.; mem. Coun. Internat. Pugwash; mem. adv. com. Stockholm Internat. Peace Rsch. Inst.; mem. scientific com. Landau Network Centro Volta, Italy; coun. mem. Internat. Inst. Strategic Studies; steering com. Kokkalis Program on Southeastern and East-Central Europe John F. Kennedy Sch. Govt. Harvard U., steering com. Ukrainian Project. Editor: The Rise of China, 2000, Nationalism and Ethnic Conflict, 2001, The Russian Military: Power and Policy, 2004, Offense, Defense, and War, 2004; co-author: (monograph) War with Iraq: Costs, Consequences, and Alternatives, 2002; contbr. to Nezavisimaya Gazeta. Mem.: Am. Acad. Arts and Sciences (com. internat. security studies, fellow 2006). Office: Belfte Ctr Sci and Internat Affairs Littauer 378 79 John f Kennedy St Cambridge MA 02138 Office Phone: 617-495-1411. Office Fax: 617-495-8963. E-mail: steven_miller@harvard.edu.

MILLER, STEVEN H., museum director; b. Phila., 1947; m. Jane McClure Pelson; children: Andrew Steven, Katherine Ann. BA, Bard Coll., 1970. Cert. in Conservation Sci. Internat. Ctr. for the Study of Preservation and Restoration of Cultural Property, Rome, 1978. Asst. to sr. curator Mus. of City of N.Y., NYC, 1971-72, asst. curator paintings, prints and photographs, 1973-77, curator prints and photographs, 1977-79, curator, dept. head fine art collections, history and spl. collections, 1979-85, sr. curator, 1985-87; asst. dir. Maine State Mus., 1987-91; dir. of mus. Western Res. Hist. Soc., Cleve., 1991-95; exec. dir. The Bennington (Vt.) Mus., 1995—2001, Morris Mus., Morristown, NJ, 2001—; exec. v.p. Morris Mus. Found., Morristown, NJ, 2001—. Adj. prof. mus. studies Case Western Res. U., 1991—94, Seton Hall U., 2001—; lectr. NYU, 1978—87, Columbia U., NYC, 1981, 82, New Sch. for Social Rsch., NYC, 1978, 83, Maine State Mus., 1987—91. Author catalogs; contbr. articles to profl. jours. Charter and former mem. hist. preservation com. City of Gardiner, Maine; mem. Williamstown Art Conservation Ctr.; bd. trustees ArtPride, NJ; bd. govs. Bard-St. Stephen's Alumni Assn.; bd. trustees Hist. Deerfield, Mass.; past bd. dirs. Vt. Mus. and Gallery Alliance; former mem. landmarks preservation com. Shaker Heights, Ohio; former mem. adv. com. Blaine House Restoration, Maine; former mem., art adv. com. Gracie Mansion Conservancy, NYC; former mem. adv. coun. Mus. Moving Image, Astoria, NY; trustee ARTPride, NJ. Mem.: NARAS (assoc.), Century Assn., Maine Assn. Mus. (co-founder, charter coun. mem.), Am. Assn. Mus. (mem. mus. advocacy team, mem. mus. accreditation vis. com.), Park Ave. Club (Morristown). Home: 45 Washington Ave Morristown NJ 07960-5622 Office Phone: 973-971-3702.

MILLER, STEVEN MAX, humanities educator; b. Portland, Ind., Feb. 9, 1950; s. J. Max and Belva Kathryn (Kitty Booher) M.; m. Fran Felice Koski, May 30, 1985 (div. 1992). BA in English with high honors, Coll. of William and Mary, 1972; MA in English Lang. and Lit., Ind. U., 1975, PhD in English Lang. and Lit., 1985. Sr. libr. asst. cataloger rare books and spl. collections Lilly Libr., Bloomington, Ind., 1972-76; prof. English Millersville U., Pa., 1985—, dir. univ. honors program, 1999-2001, dir. Honors Coll., 2001—06. Cons. women writers project Brown U., Providence, 1990-95. Contbr. articles to profl. jours. Grantee NEH, 1991, 92. Mem. MLA, John Donne Soc. Am., Spenser Soc. Episcopalian. Avocations: gardening. Office: Millersville U Dept English PO Box 1002 Millersville PA 17551-0302 Office Phone: 717-872-3121.

MILLER, STUART A., construction executive; s. Leonard and Sue Miller. Grad., Harvard U.; JD, U. Miami, 1982. Various positions homebuilding divsn. Lennar Corp., Miami, Fla., v.p., 1988—97, bd. dirs., 1990—, pres. homebuilding divsn., 1991—97, pres. prin. real estate and mgmt. divsn., 1995—97, pres., CEO Miami, Fla., 1997—; chmn. bd. Riley Property Holdings, LLC (formerly LNR Property Corp.), 1997—2005. Bd. dirs. Union Bank Fla.; mem. Harvard U. Joint Ctr. Housing Studies Policy Adv. Bd. Named one of 50 Most Generous Philanthropists, BusinessWeek, 2005. Office: Lennar Corp 700 NW 107th Ave Ste 400 Miami FL 33172-3154 Office Phone: 305-559-4000. *

MILLER, STUART A., lawyer; b. Suffern, NY; BA, Hamilton Coll., 1994; JD, Bklyn. Law Sch., 1997. Bar: NY 1997, NJ 1998, Fla. 1998, US Dist. Ct. Ea. Dist. NY, US Dist. Ct. So. Dist. NY, US Dist. Ct. Dist. NJ. Ptnr. Wilson, Elser, Moskowitz, Edelman & Dicker LLP, NYC. Mem.: NY State Bar Assn., Def. Rsch. Inst., Assn. of the Bar of the City of NY. Office: Wilson Elser Moskowitz Edelman & Dicker LLP 23rd Fl 150 E 42nd St New York NY 10017-5639 Office Phone: 212-490-3000 ext. 2403. Office Fax: 212-490-3038. Business E-Mail: millers@wemed.com.

MILLER, SUE, information technology executive; Owner Sue Miller & Assoc., Atlanta. Leadership roles Tech. Assn. Ga.; leadership roles exec. com. Digital Ball. Mem.: Women in Tech. (pres. 2000, v.p. 1999, pres. found. 2006—, dir. 1996—98, 2001—05). Office: Women in Tech Ste A Box 473 4780 Ashford Dunwoody Rd Atlanta GA 30338-5504 Office Phone: 678-234-7329. Personal E-mail: witmiller@yahoo.com.

MILLER, SUSAN ANN, retired school system administrator; b. Cleve., Nov. 24, 1947; d. Earl Wilbur and Marie Coletta (Hendershot) M. BS in Edn., Kent State U., 1969; MEd, Cleve. State U., 1975; PhD, Kent State U., 1993. Cert. supt.; cert. elem. prin., cert. elem. supervisor; cert. Learning Disabled/Behavior Disabled tchr.; cert. tchr. grades 1-8; cert. sch. counselor; lic. counselor. Tchr., guidance counselor, interim prin. North Royalton City Schs., Ohio, 1969-84; dir. elem. and spl. edn., acting supt., asst. supt. Ednl. Svc. Ctr. of Cuyahoga County, Valley View, Ohio, 1984—. Contbr. articles to profl. jours. Grantee Latchkey Program, State Dept. Edn., North Coast Leadership Forum, Peer Assistance and Rev., Entry Yr. Program, Alt. H.S. Mem. ASCD, Coun. Exceptional Children, Phi Delta Kappa. Home: 7236 Morning Star Trail Sagamore Hills OH 44067 Personal E-mail: sumrtoi47@yahoo.com.

MILLER, SUSAN CALABRESE, lawyer, consumer products company executive; b. Groton, Conn., June 5, 1959; AB summa cum laude, Duke Univ., 1980; JD, Harvard Univ., 1984. Bar: Pa. 1984, Calif. 1985. Assoc. Latham & Watkins, LA; sr. counsel Avery Dennison, Pasadena, Calif., 1991—95, sr. counsel Asia Pacific Hong Kong, 1995—98, asst. gen. counsel Pasadena, Calif., 1998—2007, v.p., gen. counsel, 2007—. Mem.: ABA, LA County Bar Assn., Phi Beta Kappa. Office: Avery Dennison Corp 150 N Orange Grove Blvd Pasadena CA 91103 *

MILLER, SUZANNE MARIE, library director, educator; b. Feb. 25, 1954; d. John Gordon and Dorothy Margaret (Sabatka) M.; 1 child, Altinay Marie. BA in English, U. S.D., 1975; MA in Library Sci., U. Denver, 1976, postgrad. in law, 1984. Librarian II Law Sch. U. SD, Vermillion, 1977-78; law libr. U. LaVerne, Calif., 1978-85, law instr., 1980-85; asst. libr. tech. svcs. McGeorge Sch. Law, Calif., 1985-99, prof. advanced legal rsch., 1994-99; libr. SD State Library, Pierre, 1999—2004, Minn. State Libr. Svcs. and Sch. Tech., Roseville, 2004—. Co-author (with Elizabeth J. Pokorny) U.S. Government Documents: A Practical Guide for Library Assistants in Academic and Public Libraries, 1988; contbr. chapters to book, articles to profl. jours. Pres. Short Grass Arts Coun., 2001—03; bd. dirs. Black Hills Playhouse Bd., 1999—2004, S.D. Ctr. for the Book Bd., 2002—04. Recipient A. Jurisprudence award Bancroft Whitney Pub. Co., 1983. Mem.: ALA, Minn. Ednl. Media Orgn., Minn. Libr. Assn., Western Coun. State Librs. (sec. 2001—02), Chief Officers of State Libr. Agys. (sec. 2002—04, chair Rsch. & Stats. com. 2004—06), Western Pacific Assn. Law Librs. (sec. 1990—94, pres. elect 1994—95, pres. 1995—96, local arrangements chair 1997), No. Calif. Assn. Law Librs. (mem. program com., inst. 1988), Mt. Plains Libr. Assn. (S.D. rep. to exec. bd. 2001—04), So. Calif. Assn. Law Librs. (arrangements com. 1981—82), Am. Assn. Law Librs., S.D. Libr. Assn. Roman Catholic. Office: Minn Dept Edn 1500 Hwy 36 West Roseville MN 55113-4266 Office Phone: 651-582-8251. Business E-Mail: suzanne.miller@state.mn.us.

MILLER, TED ROBERT, management consultant; b. Sept. 17, 1947; s. Marvin Lester and Carolyn Ruth Miller; m. Valerie Sue Nelkin. BS in Engring., Case Western Res. U., 1968; MS in Ops. Rsch., U. Pa., 1971, M in City Planning, 1970, PhD in Regional Sci., 1975. Ops. rsch. analyst U.S. Dept. Commerce, Nat. Bur. Stds. and HEW, Washington, 1971-75; staff dir. task force on Nat. Blood Data Ctr. Am. Blood Commn., Rosslyn, Va., 1975-77; asst. dir. urban and econ. devel. Nat. Inst. Advanced Studies, Washington, 1977-78; v.p. Granville Corp., Washington, 1978-84; sr. rsch. assoc. Urban Inst., Washington, 1984-93; dir. Children's Safety Network Econ. and Ins. Rsch. Ctr., 1992—. V.p. Nat. Pub. Svcs. Rsch. Inst., Calverton, Md., 1993-96, pres., 1997-2002; prin. rsch. scientist Pacific Inst. Rsch. and Evaluation, Calverton, 1997—. Mem. editl. bd. Jour. Safety Rsch., 1991—, Jour. Forensic Econs., 1991-2004, Acc. Analysis and Prevention, 1993—, Inj. Prev., 2002-; contbr. articles to profl. jours. Mem. Bd. Proprs. Ea. N.J., 1974-98; pres. Adelphi Ter. Condo. Assn., 1979-81. Recipient Nationwide on Your Side Hwy. Safety award, 1996, State and Territorial Injury Prevention Dirs. Assn. Vision award, 2005. Fellow Assn. Advt. Automotive Medicine, Am. Inst. Cert. Planners; mem. AAAS, APHA (Excellence in Sci. award injury control sect. 1999), So. Regional Sci. Assn. (exec. coun. 1990-92), Am. Econ. Assn., Pi Delta Epsilon. Democrat. Office: 11701 Beltsville Dr Ste 300 Beltsville MD 20705

MILLER, TERRY ALAN, chemistry professor; b. Girard, Kans., Dec. 18, 1943; s. Dwight D. Miller and Rachel E. (Detjen) Beltram; m. Barbara Hoffmann, July 16, 1966; children: Brian, Stuart. BA, U. Kans., 1965; PhD, Cambridge U., Eng., 1968. Disting. tech. staff Bell Telephone Labs, 1968-84; vis. asst. prof. Princeton U., 1968-71; vis. lectr. Stanford U., 1972; vis. fgn. scholar Inst. Molecular Sci., Okazaki, Japan, summer 1983; Ohio eminent scholar, prof. chemistry Ohio State U., Columbus, 1984—. Chair Molecular Spectroscopy Symposium, Columbus, 1992—. Mem. editl. bd. Jour. Chem. Physics, 1978-81, Laser Chemistry, 1986—, Rev. of Sci. Instruments, 1986-89, Jour. Phys. Chemistry, 1989-95, Jour. Optical Soc. Am., 1989-95, Chemtracts, 1989-90, Ann. Revs. Phys. Chemistry, 1989-94, Jour. Molecular Structure, 1996-; mem. editl. bd. Jour. Molecular Spectroscopy, 1982-87, editor 2005-; contbr. articles to profl. jours. Recipient Bourke medal Royal Soc. Chemistry, 1998; Marshall fellow Brit. Govt., 1965-67, NSF fellow, 1967-68. Fellow Optical Soc. Am. (Meggars award 1993), Am. Phys. Soc. (H.P. Broida award 1999), AAAS; mem. Am. Chem. Soc. (councilor), Coblentz Soc. (Bomen-Michaelson award 1995). Office: Ohio State U 120 W 18th Ave Columbus OH 43210-1106

MILLER, TERRY MORROW, lawyer; b. Columbus, Ohio, Mar. 11, 1947; s. Robert E. and Elizabeth Jane (Morrow) M.; m. Martha Estella Johnson, Mar. 20, 1976; 1 child, Timothy. BS, Ohio State U., 1969, JD, 1975. Bar: Ohio 1975, U.S. Ct. Appeals (6th cir.) 1979, U.S. Supreme Ct. 1980. Asst. atty. gen. State of Ohio, Columbus, 1975—77; ptnr. Miller & Noga, Columbus, 1977—81; assoc. Vorys, Sater, Seymour and Pease, Columbus, 1981—85, ptnr., 1986—. Trustee Columbus Lit. Coun., 1997—2004. Sgt. U.S. Army, 1969-71, Okinawa. Mem. Am. Bankruptcy Law Forum, Columbus Bar Assn., Lakes Golf and Country Club, Rattlesnake Ridge Golf Club. Avocations: golf, Ohio history. Home: 288 E North Broadway Columbus OH 43214-4114 Office: Vorys Sater Seymour et al PO Box 1008 52 E Gay St Columbus OH 43216-1008 Home Phone: 614-263-7670; Office Phone: 614-464-5645. Business E-Mail: tmmiller@vssp.com.

MILLER, THEODORE NORMAN, lawyer; b. Chgo., Oct. 9, 1942; s. Alexander Hyman and Bertha Helen (Swidler) M.; m. Marylyn Sue Zax, June 21, 1964; children— Henry, Amy. B.A., U. Mich., 1964; LL.B., Yale U., 1967. Bar: Ill. 1967, Calif. 1991, U.S. Dist. Ct. (no. dist.) Ill. 1967, U.S. Ct. Appeals (7th cir.) 1968, U.S. Supreme Ct. 1972. Law clk. U.S. Ct. Appeals (7th cir.), 1967-68; assoc. Sidley & Austin, Chgo., 1968-73, ptnr., 1973—, now mng. ptnr, NYC office, and vice chmn., mgmt. com. and mem. exec. com. Mem. ABA, Chgo. Bar Assn., Chgo. Council Lawyers, Phi Beta Kappa, Order of Coif. Office: Sidley Austin Brown & Wood LLP 787 Seventh Ave New York NY 10019-6018 Office Phone: 212-839-5886. Office Fax: 212-839-5599. Business E-Mail: tmiller@sidley.com.

MILLER, THEODORE T., radiologist; b. NYC, Mar. 1, 1961; BA, U. Pa., 1983; MD, Vanderbilt U., 1987. Diplomate Am. Bd. Radiology, 1993. Intern N.Y. Hosp., NYC, 1987—88; resident Mt. Sinai Hosp., NYC, 1988—92; fellow Hosp. Spl. Surgery, 1992—93; attending radiologist Columbia Presbyn. Med. Ctr., 1993—96, North Shore U. Hosp., Manhasset, 1996—2006; staff radiologist Hosp. Spl. Surgery, NYC, 2006—. Dir. North Shore Imaging Assocs., Great Neck, NY, 1996—; chief musculoskeletal imaging North Shore U. Hosp., Manhasset, 2000—; assoc. prof. radiology NYU Sch. Medicine, 2001—06, Weill Med. Coll., Cornell U., 2006—; v.p. NY Roentgen Soc., 2006. Mem. editl. bd.: Radiology, Skeletal Radiology, Seminars Musculoskeletal Radiology, Radiographics, 2005; author: (textbook) Diagnostic Musculoskeletal Imaging, 2005. Recipient Pres.'s medal, Internat. Skeletal Soc., 2006. Fellow: Am. Coll. Radiology; mem.: NY Roentgen Soc. (v.p.), Soc. Skeletal Radiology, Internat. Skeletal Soc., Radiol. Soc. N.Am. (editl. bd. mem. 2003, Editl. fellow 2001). Achievements include patent for Temporary vena cava filter. Office: Hosp Spl Surgery 535 E 70th St New York NY 10021 Office Phone: 212-606-1127. Business E-Mail: millertt@hss.edu.

MILLER, THOMAS EUGENE, lawyer, writer; b. Bryan, Tex., Jan. 4, 1929; s. Eugene Adam and Ella Lucille (Schroeder) M. BA, BS, Tex. A&M U., 1950; MA, U. Tex., 1956, JD, 1966; postgrad., U. Houston, 1956-58, U. Calif., 1983. Bar: Tex. 1966. Rsch. technician M.D. Anderson Hosp., Houston, 1956-58; claims examiner trainee Social Security Adminstrn., New Orleans, 1964; trademark examiner U.S. Patent and Trademark Office, Washington, 1966; editor Bancroft-Whitney Co., San Francisco, 1966-92; ret., 1992. Author: (under pseudonym Millard Thomas) Home From 7-North, 1984; contbr. to numerous legal publs. Mem. Dem. Nat. Com., 1981—; mem. Celebrate Bryan Com., chmn. Bryan Med. Heritage Com. Mem. ABA, World Lit. Assn., World Inst. Achievement, United Writers Assn. India, Nat. Trust for Hist. Preservation, Tex. Bar Assn., U. Tex. Sch. of Law, Non-practicing Alumni Adv. Coun., African Wildlife Found., World Wildlife Fund, Internat. Platform Assn., Nat. Writers Assn., Scribes, Acad. Polit. Sci., Press Club, Commonwealth Club, Westerners Internat., Rotary Club (Paul Harris fellow, Found. fellow), Menninger Soc., Tex. A&M U. Club, Phi Kappa Phi, Psi Chi, Phi Eta Sigma. Methodist. Home: 101 N Haswell Dr Bryan TX 77803-4848 *Personal philosophy: Use your experience and abilities not only to understand life and to succeed, but also to help others' journeys through life.*

MILLER, THOMAS J., state attorney general; b. Dubuque, Iowa, Aug. 11, 1944; s. Elmer John and Betty Maude (Kross) Miller; m. Linda Cottington, Jan. 10, 1981; 1 child, Matthew. BA, Loras Coll., Dubuque, 1966; JD, Harvard U., 1969. Bar: Iowa 1969. With VISTA, Balt., 1969—70; legis. asst. to US Rep. John C. Culver, 1970—71; legal edn. dir. Balt. Legal Aid Bur., part-time faculty U. Md. Sch. Law, 1971—73; pvt. practice McGregor, Iowa, 1973—78; city atty., 1973—79, Marquette, Iowa; atty. gen. State of Iowa, 1978—90, 1994—; ptnr. Faegre & Benson, Des Moines, 1991—95. Chmn. Microsoft case exec. com.; co-chmn. Airline Competition Working Grp.; pres. 2nd Dist. New Dem. Club, Balt., 1972. Mem.: ABA, Nat. Assn. Attys. Gen. (pres. 1989—90, chmn. consumer protection, ins., budget, and antitrust coms., Wyman award 1990), Iowa Bar Assn., Common Cause. Democrat. Roman Catholic. Office: Office of Atty Gen Hoover State Office Bldg 1305 E Walnut St Des Moines IA 50319-0112 Office Phone: 515-281-5164.

MILLER, THOMAS J., former ambassador; b. Chgo., 1948; m. Bonnie Miller; 2 children. BA in Polit. Sci., U. Mich., 1969, MA in Asian Studies and Polit. Sci., 1973, PhD in Polit. Sci., 1975. Various to sr. fgn. svc./min. counselor U.S. Dept. State, 1976—, analyst for Vietnam, Laos, & Cambodia, 1976—77, spl. asst. to under sec. polit. affairs, 1977—79; dep. prin. officer U.S. Consulate, Chiang Mai, Thailand, 1979—81; dep. chief of mission U.S. Embassy, Athens, 1994-97; spl. coord. for Cyprus (amb.) U.S. Dept. State, 1997-99, U.S. amb. to Bosnia and Herzegovina, 1999—2001, U.S. amb. to Greece Athens, 2001—04. Lectr. in field; initiator Model UN programs at three Washington high schs. Recipient numerous awards in field. Avocations: speaks greek, spanish, thai, indonesian, japanese.

MILLER, THOMAS WILLIAM, psychologist; b. Rochester, NY, Feb. 7, 1943; s. William J. Miller and Evelyn A. Weber; m. Jean Alderson, June 17, 1967; children: David T., Jeanine M. BS, St. John Fisher, Rochester, 1965; MS, U. Scranton, 1967; PhD, SUNY, Buffalo, 1971. Lic. clin. psychologist Ky., Mich., Pa., Conn. Psychologist Buffalo Psychiat. Ctr., 1965-70; asst. prof. Rosary Hill Coll., Williamsville, N.Y., 1970-74; v.p. student affairs Daemen Coll., Amherst, N.Y., 1974-75; psychologist VA Med. Ctr., Buffalo, 1975-80, chief psychology svc. Lexington, Ky., 1980-96; prof. dept. psychiatry U. Ky., Lexington, 1980—; prof. Murray (Ky.) State U., 1996—, U. Conn. Sch. Allied Health, 2000—. Vice-chmn. State Psychology Bd., Frankfort, Ky., 1983-86. Author: Stressful Life Events, 1989, Chronic Pain, 1990, Manual of Sexual Abuse, 1991, Clinical Handbook of Child Abuse, 1995, Theory and Assessment of Stressful Life Events, 1996, Clinical Disorders and Stressful Life Events, 1997, Children of Trauma, 1998, Clinical Handbook of Adult Exploitation and Abuse, 1998. Bd. dirs. Nat. Kidney Found., Lexington, 1982—, Big Bros. Big Sisters Calloway County; mem. exec. bd. Bluegrass coun. Boy Scouts Am., Lexington, 1983; nat. and state legis. chair NARFE. Named Outstanding Alumnus, SUNY, Buffalo, 1988; recipient recognition award Ky. Dept. Human Resources, 1993, RHR Internat. award, 1996, Outstanding Psychologist award, 1997, Disting. VA Rsch. award, 1997, Rsch. Excellence award, 2000, Disting. Contbn. to the Sci. of Psychology award, 2004. Fellow APA (pres. dvsn. psychology in pub. svc., Pub. Svc. award 2004), Am. Psychol. Soc., Conn. Psychol. Assn.; mem. Ky. Psychol. Assn. (pres. 1986), Assoc. VA Chief Psychologists (pres. 1985-89). Home: 3237 Saxon Dr Lexington KY 40503

MILLER, THORMUND AUBREY, lawyer; b. Pocatello, Idaho, July 14, 1919; s. Roy Edmund and Lillian (Thordarson) Miller; m. Hannah A. Flansburgh, Feb. 10, 1946 (dec. Jan. 2003); children: Karen Lynette Van Gerpen, Christine Alison Westall; m. Barbara Cornell Singelyn, May 8, 2004. BA, Reed Coll., 1941; LLB, Columbia U., 1948; grad., Advanced Mgmt. Program, Harvard Bus. Sch., 1961. Bar: Calif. 1949, D.C. 1951, U.S. Supreme Ct. 1960. Assoc. McCutchen, Thomas, Matthews, Griffiths & Greene, San Francisco, 1948-50; atty. So. Pacific Transp. Co., Washington, 1950-56, asst. gen. atty., 1956-59, gen. atty., 1959—66, sr. gen. atty. San Francisco, 1966—75, gen. solicitor, 1975—79, gen. commerce counsel, 1979—83, dir., mem. exec. com., 1983—87, v.p., gen. counsel, 1983—89; gen. counsel So. Pacific Comms. Co., San Francisco, 1970—79, dir., 1970—81. Pres. Wood Acres Citizens Assn., Bethesda, Md., 1955-56; exec. com. Holbrook Palmer Recreation Park Found., 1979—, pres., 1982-84; bd. dirs. Atherton Civic Interest League, 1981—, pres., 1992-94; mem. Atherton Park and Recreation Commn., 1991-95, Atherton Waste Reduction Commn., 1999-2005, San Mateo Civil Grand Jury, 1997; alumni bd. Reed Coll., 1971-72, trustee, 1987-2002, campaign com., 1995-2000; joint donor Thormund A. Miller/Walter Mintz chair in econ. history; bd. dirs. Assocs. U. Calif. Press, 1994—2006. Lt. USNR, 1942-46. Mem.: ABA, Calif. Bar Assn. Presbyterian.

MILLER, TIMOTHY ALDEN, plastic and reconstructive surgeon; b. Inglewood, Calif., Dec. 11, 1938; s. Henry Bernard and Florence Algena (Maddock) M.; 1 child, Matthew Christopher. Student, U. Calif., Berkeley; MD, UCLA, 1963. Diplomate Am. Bd. Surgery, Am. Bd. Plastic Surgery (dir. 1991-97). Intern Vanderbilt U. Hosp., Nashville, 1963-64; resident in surgery, dept. surg. pathology UCLA, 1966-67, resident, then chief resident gen. and thoracic surgery, 1967-69, acting asst. prof., 1969-70, prof. surgery, 1981—; asst. surg. resident John Hopkins Hosp., 1967; fellow plastic and reconstructive surgery U. Pitts., 1970-72; chief plastic surgery West Wadsworth VA Med. Ctr., 1973—; prof., chief plastic and reconstructive surgery UCLA Sch. Medicine, 2002—. Author: (novel) Practice to Deceive, 1991; assoc. editor Jour. Plastic & Reconstructive Surgery, 1987-93, co-editor, 1994-99. Trustee Children's Inst. Internat., 1995-2000. Capt. U.S. Army, 1964-66, Vietnam (Bronze Star, 1966, Vietnam Spl. Forces Parachute award, 1966). Recipient Thomas Symington award Pitts. Acad. Medicine, 1971, Ralph Goldman Rsch. award, 1996, 1999. Mem. Am. Soc. for Plastic Surgery (co-editor Jour. Plastic and Reconstructive Surgery), Am. Soc. for Aesthetic Plastic Surgery (bd. dirs. 1990-95), Am. Soc. Surgery of Hand, Am. Soc. Maxillofacial Surgeons, Plastic Surgery Ednl. Found. (bd. dirs. 1991-95), Plastic Surgery Rsch. Coun.; Phi Beta Kappa. Office: UCLA Med Ctr 200 UCLA Med Plz Ste 465 Los Angeles CA 90095-8344 Office Phone: 310-825-5644. Business E-Mail: tmiller@mednet.ucla.edu. *

MILLER, TONI M. ANDREWS, critical care nurse; b. Webb City, Mo., July 20, 1949; d. John F. and Gettius M. (Short) Henry; div.; children: Bradley Ardrey, Mischa Andrews, Paul Andrews. ADN, Mo. So. Coll., Joplin, 1973, BSN, 1995. Cert. ACLS, TNCC, PALS. Asst. insvc. dir. Kirksville (Mo.) Osteo. Hosp., 1975-76; charge nurse, unit program supr. St. Louis Devel. Disabilities Treatment Ctr., 1983-85; clin. supr. ICU Oak Hill Osteo. Hosp., Joplin, 1986-95; emergency room/ICU nurse Fitzgibbon Hosp., Marshall, Mo., 1997, 1998, 2000—, 1998-2000; ICU nurse Bothwell Hosp., Fitzgibbon Hosp., Marshall, Mo., 2000—02, Bothwell Hosp., Sedalia, 2002—. Recipient Joseph P. Kennedy award, 1966. Mem. AACN. Home: 2010 Annie Baxter Ave Joplin MO 64804-0323

MILLER, VALERIE CAROL, journalist; b. Chgo. d. V. Heinz and Arlene Elizabeth Miller. A in Gen. Studies, C.C. So. Nev.; BA Comms., U. Nev., 1998. Travel coord. Great Escape Travel, Las Vegas, 1996—97; staff writer, reporter U. Nev. Las Vegas Rebel Yell Students Newspaper, 1997—98; travel coord. World Travel and Accessories, Las Vegas, 1998—2000; reporter, freelance writer, intern Las Vegas Sun Newspaper, 1998—2000; broadcaster, disk jockey Sta. KLAV AM 1230, Las Vegas, 1997—; reporter, staff writer Las Vegas Bus. Press Newspaper, 2000—; staff writer Las Vegas Sr. Press. Host radio show Valerie's Music Magic. Vol. Shade Tree Shelter, Las Vegas, 2002; vol. writer Nev. Times Newspaper, Las Vegas, 1995, 1997. Nominee Journalist of Merit award, Nev. Press Assn., 2002, 2003, Small Bus. Journalist of Yr., Nev. Small Bus. Adminstrn., 2003; recipient Best Feature Story award third prize, Nev. Press Assn., 2001, Small Bus. Journalist of Yr. award for Nev., U.S. Small Bus. Assn., 2002, Merit award for news writing, Internat. Assn. Bus. Comm., 2003, Merit award for series writing, 2003, 2005, Best Bus. Story award, Nev. Press. Assn., 2002, 2004. Fellow: Soc. for the Advanced Placement of Materials, Working in Comms., Soc. Profl. Journalists, 3rd Wave Nev., Tortois Group; mem.: Phi Lambda Eta. Avocations: travel, writing poems and song lyrics, movies. Office: Las Vegas Bus Press 1385 Pama Ln Ste 111 Las Vegas NV 89119 Office Phone: 702-871-6780 ext. 331. Personal E-mail: millerv52@hotmail.com. Business E-Mail: vmiller@lvpress.com.

MILLER, VERNE WILLIAM, computer engineer, consultant; b. Chgo., Mar. 22, 1953; s. Fritz Henry and Dorothy Ruth Miller. BS Computer Engring. cum laude, DeVry U., 2005. Registered: State of Ill. (Police Officer) 1983, lic.: Glock, Inc. (Glock Armorer & Instr.) 1996; cert. CPR instr. ARC, 1995, emergency first aid instr. ARC, 1995, lic. emergency rescue technician State of Ill., 1987, controlled Substance Class I and II State of Ill., 1989. Mech. engr. Sheldons Mfg. Corp., Elgin, Ill., 1973—76; law enforcement officer Chgo. Union Sta. R.R. Police, 1982—87, Amtrak Police Dept., Chgo., 1987—2001; cons., rschr. LETCON, Harwood Heights, Ill., 1990—. Cons. U.S. Dept. Justice, Office Justice Stats., Washington, 1990—94; adv. bd. mem. Nat. Tactical Officers Assn., 1992—94; cons., trainer Midwest Tactical Tng. Inst., Freeport, Ill., 1989—91. Author: (book) Police Identification Guide to Street Gangs; Volumes I & II; contbr. articles to profl. jours. Spkr. - anti-drug edn. Bartlett Sr. Citizens Groups, Ill., 1989—91. Mem.: IEEE, NRA (life), Clan Kincaid Scottish Heritage Soc., Ill. State Rifle Assn., Law Enforcement Alliance Am., North Am. Hunting Club (life), Alpha Chi, Tau Alpha Pi (Nu Delta chpt. v.p. 2003—04, Nu Delta chpt. pres. 2004—05). Republican. Lutheran, Mo. Synod. Avocations: photography, writing. Home: 5654 W Gunnison St Chicago IL 6060-3216 E-mail: vernemiller@sbcglobal.net.

MILLER, VIRGINIA LOUISE, director; b. Meadville, Pa., Dec. 13, 1941; d. Don and Virginia Haven; m. Edward S. Malc, 1962 (dec. 1992); m. William Russell Miller, Nov. 20, 1998; 1 child, Elizabeth Malc-Dwyer. BS in Elem. Edn., Edinboro U., Pa., 1962, MS in Elem. Edn., 1969. Cert. reading specialist Edinboro U., 1973, reading supr. Edinboro U., 1975, elem. sch. adminstrn. Edinboro U., 1982, edn. in therapy for Dyslexia L1 Internat. Multisensory Structured Lang. Edn. Coun., 2005. Reading tchr. various sch. dists., Pa., 1962—72; reading specialist Sch. Dist., Conneaut Lake, Pa., 1972—99, acting prin., 1984; dir. 32d Degree Masonic Learning Ctr. for Children, Erie, Pa., 2004—. Adj. faculty Pa. State Univ., State College, 2005—. Apptd. spl. advisor Erie County Ct., Erie, Pa., 2001—03. Mem.: Internat. Dyslexia Assn. Methodist. Home: 3218 Georgian Ct Erie PA 16506 Office: 32d Degree Masonic Learning Ctr for Children 4701 Old Zuck Rd Erie PA 16506-4963 Office Phone: 814-838-2405. E-mail: read4701@yahoo.com.

MILLER, W. KIEVIT, writer; b. Bklyn., Mar. 5, 1950; d. Walter Benedict Miller and Gladys Christina Marie Swadba; children: Cove Kievit, Brook Kievit. BA in Environ. studies, Fla. Internat. U., Tamiami, 1984; D candidate in natural health, Clayton Coll. Dist. coord. Broward Soil and Water Conservation Dist., Davie, Fla., 1985; tchr. Mus. of Discovery and Sci., Fort Lauderdale, Fla., 1984, 1993; head guide Seminole Tribe of Fla., Big Cypress Reservation, 1999; founder, CEO BIOKIND Tours, LLC, Venus, Fla., 2000—. Author: (book) BIOKIND Rhetoric for a New Paradigm, A Field Guide for the Future, 2000, BIOKIND Tracks, Traces of & Whispers for (and from) the Soul, 2003, The BIOKIND Body, A Naturapathic Approach to Health and Fitness, 2005. Capt. USCG. Scholar, Audubon Soc., 1984, Art of Living Found., 1996. Home Phone: 863-441-1301; Office Phone: 863-531-0093. Business E-Mail: biokindtours@biokind.com.

MILLER, W. TIMOTHY, lawyer; b. Indpls., May 13, 1967; B in Music, DePauw U., 1989; JD, Cornell U., 1992. Bar: Ohio 1992. Named one of Ohio's Rising Stars, Super Lawyers, 2005, 2006; named to Best Lawyers in Am., Woodward/White Inc., 2006. Mem.: Tri-State Assn. for Corp.

Renewal, Am. Bankruptcy Inst., ABA, Ohio State Bar Assn., Cin. Bar Assn. Office: Taft Stettinius & Hollister LLP 425 Walnut St Ste 1800 Cincinnati OH 45202-3957 Office Phone: 513-381-2838. Office Fax: 513-381-0205.

MILLER, WAENARD LIVINGSTON, cardiologist; b. Greenville, SC, Mar. 1, 1947; s. Waenard Livingston and Margaret Evelyn (Burns) M.; m. Sheila McLawhorn, Dec. 20, 1969; children: Waenard Livingston III, Bernyrd Carlysle. BS in Physics, Clemson U., 1969; MS in Nuclear Physics, U. Tenn., 1970; MS in Biology, Wright State U., 1974; MD, Med. U. S.C., 1978; MS in Med. Mgmt., U. Tex., 2000. Diplomate Am. Bd. Internal Medicine, subspecialty of cardiovascular disease. Intern in internal medicine Southwestern Med. Sch., Dallas, 1978-79, resident in internal medicine, 1979-81, fellow in cardiology, 1981-83; pvt. practice cardiology Plano, Tex., 1983—. Lab. dir. HCA Med. Ctr., Plano, 1994. 1st lt. USAF, 1971-74. Fellow Am. Coll. Cardiology, Am. Coll. Cardiology (councilor Tex. divsn., 2004-05), Am. Heart Assn. (pres. Plano divsn., 1986, affiliate faculty 1990-). Avocations: travel, golf. Office: Legacy Heart Ctr 6601 Preston Rd Plano TX 75024 Office Phone: 469-326-3400. Business E-Mail: wmiller@legacyheartcenter.com.

MILLER, WALKER DAVID, judge; m. Susanne Hauk; 3 children. LLB, U. Colo., 1963; M in Comparative Law, U. Chgo., 1965. Bar: Colo. 1963, U.S. Dist. Ct. 1965, U.S. Ct. Appeals 1971, U.S. Supreme Ct. 1970. Asst. prof. Sch. Law, U. Kans., Lawrence, 1966-69; ptnr. Miller & Ruyle, Greeley, Colo., 1969, Miller, Ruyle, Steinmark & Shade, Greeley, 1970-74; solo practice, Greeley, Colo., 1974-92; ptnr. Karowsky, Witwer, Miller and Oldenburg, Greeley, 1992-96; judge U.S. Dist. Ct. Colo., Denver, 1996—. Office: US Dist Ct Colo 901 19th St Rm A938 Denver CO 80294-1929 Office Phone: 303-844-2468. E-mail: walker_d_miller@cod.uscourts.gov.

MILLER, WALTER JAMES, retired literature educator, writer; b. McKee City, NJ, Jan. 16, 1918; s. Walter Theodore and Celestia Anna (Simmons) Miller; m. Mary T. Hume; children: Naomi, Jason, Robin, Jared, Elizabeth. BA, CUNY, 1941; MA, Columbia U., 1952. Instr. English Poly. Inst. Bklyn., 1946—53, asst. prof., 1953—55; asst. prof. English and modern langs. Colo. State U., Ft. Collins, 1955—56; assoc. prof. English NYU, 1958—66, prof. English, 1966—84, prof. emeritus, 1984—. Dir. Summer Writers Conf. Hofstra U., Hempstead, NY, 1972—79, NYU, NYC, 1983—85. Author: Engineers as Writers, 1953, Making an Angel: Poems, 1977, 1001 Ideas for English Papers, 1994, Love's Mainland: New and Selected Poems, 2001, Joseph in the Pit: A Verse Drama, 2002, Essential Vonnegut: Interviews Conducted by Walter Miller, CDI, 2006; author, translator: Annotated Jules Verne, 1995; editor, translator: Verne's 20,000 Leagues Under the Sea, 1993, The Meteor Hunt, 2006, Essential Vonnecut: Interviews, 2006; contbg. editor Simon and Schuster, 1969-97. Pub. relations officer US Infantry, 1943—46. Recipient Spl. award, Engrs. Coun. Profl. Devel., 1966, Charles Angoff award, The Lit. Rev., 1983, Gt. Tchr. award, NYU Alumni Assn., 1980, Fisher Second Harvest award, CUNY Alumni Assn., 1997; fellow, Ruttenberg Found., 1999—2006. Business E-Mail: wjm2@nyu.edu.

MILLER, WALTER LUTHER, pediatrician, educator; b. Alexandria, Va., Feb. 21, 1944; s. Luther Samuel and Beryl (Rinderle) M. SB, MIT, 1965; MD, Duke U., 1970. Diplomate Am. Bd. Pediatrics. Intern, then resident Mass. Gen. Hosp., Boston, 1970-72; staff assoc. NIH, Bethesda, Md., 1972-74; sr. resident U. Calif., San Francisco, 1974-75, rsch. fellow, 1975-78, asst. prof. pediatrics, 1978-83, assoc. prof., 1983-87, prof., 1987—, dir. Child Health Rsch. Ctr., 1992—2003, faculty biomed. scis. grad. program, 1982—, faculty genetics grad. program, 1998—, dir. pediat. endocrinology tng. program, 1994—, chief divsn. endocrinology, 2000—, assoc. prof. metabolic rsch. unit, 1983-87, prof., 1987—. Bd. scientific counselors Nat. Inst. of Child Health & Human Devel., 2004—. Editor DNA and Cell Biology Jour., 1983—; mem. editl. bds. numerous sci. jours.; contbr. articles to profl. jours., chpts. to books. Del. Dem. Nat. Conv., N.Y.C., 1976. Served with USPHS, 1972-74. Recipient Nat. Rsch. Svc. award NIH, 1975, Clin. Investigator award, 1978, Albion O Bernstein award NY Med. Soc., 1993, Clin. Endocrinology Trust medal Brit. Endocrine Soc., 1993, Henning Andersen prize European Soc. Pediatric Endocrinology, 1993, Samuel Rosenthal Found. prize for excellence in acad. pediatrics, 1999. Fellow: AAAS, Molecular Medicine Soc.; mem.: Androgen Excess Soc. (founding mem., bd. dirs. 2002—05), Am. Soc. Biochem. Molecular Biology, Lawson Wilkins Pediat. Endocrine Soc. (edn. com. 1992—96, coun. 1995—96, corp. adv. bd. 1998—2002, program dirs. com. 2004—), Am. Soc. Clin. Investigation, Am. Soc. Human Genetics, Endocrine Soc. (fin. com. 1999—2002, annual meeting steering com. 2005—, Edwin B. Astwood lecture award 1988, Clin. Investigator Lectr. award 2006), European Soc. for Paediatric Endocrinology (hon.), Japanese Soc. for Pediat. Endocrinology (hon.), We. Soc. Pediat. Rsch. (Ross Rsch. award 1982), Soc. Pediat. Rsch., Am. Pediat. Soc., Am. Acad. Pediats., Assn. Am. Physicians, Am. Soc. for Microbiology, Theta Delta Chi. Achievements include patents in field; published in over 300 pubs. Office: U Calif Med Ctr Dept Pediat Rm 672 S San Francisco CA 94143-0978

MILLER, WALTER NEAL, insurance company consultant; b. NYC, Nov. 26, 1929; s. Morton and Kathryn (Gersten) M.; m. Nancy Louise Clapp, Sept. 11, 1954; children— Scott, Timothy, David, Kathryn Wallace, Amy Tully. BA, Swarthmore Coll., 1951. With N.Y. Life Ins. Co., NYC, 1951-86; sr. v.p., actuary Prudential Ins. Co., Newark, 1986-93; sr. v.p., chief actuary Prudential Preferred Fin. Svcs., Liberty Corner, NJ, 1993-94; pvt. practice cons., 1994—. Author: (with others) Analysis of Actuarial Theory for Variable Life Insurance, 1969; contbr. articles to profl. jours. Mem. Soc. Actuaries (bd. dirs.), Am. Acad. Actuaries (bd. dirs., v.p.), Actuarial Stds. Bd. (chmn.), Estuary Coun. Srs. (pres. bd. dirs.). Home: 48 Eagle Ridge Dr Essex CT 06426-1370 Personal E-mail: walterm746@aol.com.

MILLER, WARREN LLOYD, lawyer; b. Bklyn., July 18, 1944; m. Jana Morris. BA, Am. U., Washington, 1966; JD with honors, George Washington U., Washington, 1969. Bar: Va., 1969, DC, 1969, various US Dist. Cts., US Ct. Appeals (various US cirs.), US Supreme Ct. 1981. Law clk. to Hon. Edward A. Beard Superior Ct. D.C., 1968-69; asst. U.S. atty. for D.C., 1969-74; ptnr. Stein, Miller & Brodsky, 1974-85; pres. Warren L. Miller, P.C., 1986—; of counsel Reed, Smith, Shaw & McClay, 1986-93. Lectr. Am. U., 1972-73; mem. Jud. Conf. DC Cir., 1984-96; pres. Asst. US Attys. Assn. DC, 1983-84; spkr. Nat. Press Club, 2004. Contbr. articles to profl. jours. Parliamentarian credentials and rules coms. Rep. Nat. Conv., 1984; mem. D.C. Law Revision Commn., 1987-91 (apptd. by Pres. Reagan), mem. US Commn. Preservation Am.'s Heritage Abroad, 1992— (apptd. by Pres. Bush, reapptd. by Pres. Clinton 1996, 99), now chmn. (apptd. by Pres. Bush), 2001—; bd. dirs. Found. for Buchenwald and Mittelbau-Dora Memls., 1994—; spkr. ceremonies commemorating 50th anniversary of liberation of Buchenwald Concentration Camp, Buchenwald, Germany, 1995, Ceremony Dedicating Little Camp Meml., Buchenwald, Germany, 2002; spkr. US Holocaust Meml. Mus., 1995, 2002; fundraiser for Rep. Nat. Com. and Pres. Bush, 1988-92; co-chmn. dinner for V.P. Bush, 1988; vice-chmn. Pres.'s Dinner, 1989; co-chmn. Pres.'s Club, Washington, 1990-92; chmn. fundraiser for US Senator Christopher Bond, 1992, 97, 01; chmn., fundraiser US Senator John Warner, 1996, 2001; vice-chmn., fundraiser Senator Bob Dole, 1996; co-chmn., fundraiser Gov. George W. Bush Presdl. Exploratory Com., 1999, honoring Pres. George W. Bush, 2003; mem. host com., fundraiser for Gov. George W. Bush, 2000, Gov. Jeb Bush, 2002, v.p. Dick Cheney, 2003; co-leader US Del. to Internat. Conf., Warsaw, Poland, 2002 (apptd. by Sec. State Colin Powell); spkr. Warsaw Ghetto Uprising Commemoration, Poland, 2002, 60th Anniversary of Liberation of DORA Concentration Camp, Nordhausen, Germany, 2005, Kielce Program, 60th Anniversary, Poland, 2006. Decorated Order of Three Stars Pres. of Latvia, comdr.'s cross Order of Merit Poland, Order of Morning Star Pres. Croatia; recipient Univ. Student Achievement award, Am. U. Mem. Congl. Country Club (Bethesda, Md.), Phi Delta Phi, Omicron Delta Kappa, Pi Gamma Mu. Achievements include negotiating and concluding bi-lateral agreements on behalf of the US with the following governments: Bosnia and Herzegovina, Latvia, Lithuania, Bulgaria, Macedonia, Estonia, Czech Republic, Germany, Austria, Hungary, Poland, Armenia, Albania, Serbia and Croatia. Fax: 703-848-1841.

MILLER, WENDY A., elementary school educator; b. NC; BA in Spl. Edn., Univ. NC; MA in Curriculum/Adminstrn., E. Carolina Univ. Cert. Nat. Bd. Tchg. Standards 2002. Tchr., 1987—, James W. Smith Elem. Sch., Cove City, NC, 1998—. Featured in (TV spl.) Heroes in the Classroom, ABC, 2003, spl. guest (Wayne Brady Show) Salute to America's Best Teachers, 2003. Named Craven County Schs.' Tchr. of Yr./Tchr. Ambassador, 2004, SE Region Tchr. of Yr., 2005, NC Tchr. of Yr., 2006; recipient Disney Am. Tchr. of Yr. Honoree, 2003. Mem.: Internat.Reading Assn., Coun. for Exceptional Children, NC Assn. Educators. Office: James W Smith Elem Sch 150 Koonce Town Rd Cove City NC 28523 Business E-Mail: wendy.miller@craven.k12.nc.us. *

MILLER, WENTWORTH, actor; b. Chipping Norton, Eng., June 2, 1972; BA, Princeton U., 1995. Actor: (films) Romeo and Juliet, 2000, Room 302, 2001, The Human Stain, 2003, Underworld, 2003, (voice) Stealth, 2005,: (TV miniseries) Dinotopia, 2002; (TV series) Prison Break, 2005—. Office: c/o Peter Kiernan Mgmt 360 9111 Wilshire Blvd Beverly Hills CA 90210

MILLER, WILBUR HOBART, retired management consultant; b. Boston, Feb. 15, 1915; s. Silas Reuben and Muriel Mae (Greene) Miller; m. Harriett I. Harmon, June 20, 1941; children: Nancy Iber Miller Harray, Warren Harmon, Donna Sewall Miller Davidge. BS, U. N.H., 1936, MS, 1938; PhD, Columbia U., 1941. Rsch. chemist Am. Cyanamid Co., Stamford, Conn., 1941—49, Washington tech. rep., 1949—53, dir. food industry devel., 1953—57, tech. dir. products for agr. Cyanamid Internat. NYC, 1957—60; sr. scientist Dunlap & Assocs., Darien, Conn., 1960—63; sr. assoc. Dunlap & AssocCs., Darien, 1963—66; coord. new product devel. Celanese Corp., NYC, 1966—67, mgr. comml. rsch., 1967—68, dir. corp. devel., 1969—84; ret., 1984. Lectr. bus. and soc. Western Conn. State Coll., 1977—79; pres.'s coun. U. NH, 1982—; internat. fellow U. Bridgeport, 1985—88; cons. in field. Contbr. scientific papers to profl. jours.; patentee in field. Chmn. Stamford Forum World Affairs, 1954—87, hon. chmn., 1987—; adv. bd. Ctr. Study Presidency, 1980—99; bd. dirs. Stamford Symphony, 1974—80, v.p., 1978—80; bd. dirs. Stamford Hist. Soc., 1988, v.p., 1991—92, pres., 1993—95; bd. dirs. Coun. Continuing Edn., Stamford, 1960—70, pres., 1963; bd. dirs. Stamford Sr. Ctr., 1997—, vice chmn., 2002—03, chmn., 2003—04, trustee, 2005—; elder United Presbyn. Ch., nominating com., 1960—63; pres. Interfaith Coun. Stamford, 1973. Recipient Am. Design award, 1948, Outstanding Achievement award, Coll. Tech., U. N.H., 1971, Golden Rule award, J.C. Penney & Co., 1986; Univ. fellow, Columbia U., 1940—41. Fellow: AAAS, Am. Inst. Chemists (councillor N.Y. chpt. 1984—85); mem.: Am. Acad. Polit. and Social Scis., Soc. Internat. Devel., Inst. Food Tech., Société de Chimie Industrielle (v.p. fin. Am. sect. 1980—84, bd. dirs. 1984—, chmn. edn. com. 1997—), N.Y. Acad. Scis., Am. Chem. Soc. (news svc. adv. bd. 1948—53), Chemists Club (treas. 1982—84), Sigma Xi, Phi Kappa Phi, Alpha Chi Sigma. Home: 122 Palmers Hill Rd #1111 Stamford CT 06902-2134

MILLER, WILBUR RANDOLPH, academic administrator; b. Elsberry, Mo., Nov. 12, 1932; s. Charles Clifton and Pauline Jean (Dryden) M. Student, SE Mo. U., 1951-53; BEd, U. Mo., 1954, MEd, 1955, EdD, 1960. Cert. secondary tchr., Mo. Tchr. indsl. arts Hazelwood Sch. Dist., St. Louis, 1955-56, U. Lab. Sch., Columbia, Mo., 1956-60; indsl. tchr. educator Purdue U., West Lafayette, Ind., 1960-63; asst. prof. U. Mo., Columbia, 1963-67, assoc. prof. and chmn. dept. coll. edn., 1967-76, prof. and assoc. dean coll. edn., 1976-86, dean coll. edn., 1986-91, prof., dean emeritus, 1992; cons. Rep. of Turkey, 1993, 94; assoc. v.p. devel. Auburn U., Ala., 1996—2007; ret., 2007. Chmn. adv. coun. Fed. Rsch. Ctr. in Vocat. Edn., Ohio State U., Columbus, 1981-84; internat. edn. cons. 1992—; edn. adv. bd. DeVry Inc., Oakwood Terrace, Ill., 1986—; mem. pvt. post-sec. tech. sch. accreditation commn. Accrediting Commn. Career Schs. and Colls. Tech., 1994-98. Author: Teaching Children Through Construction Activities, 1985, Instructors and Their Jobs, 1998, 3d edit., 2005, The Golf Primer, 1991, Handbook for College Teaching, 1997, 2d edit., 2003; editor: (series) Basic Industrial Arts, 1978; contbr. more than 40 articles to profl. jours. Pres., bd. dirs. Lenoir Inc., Columbia, 1977-84; mem. Woodhaven Sch. Bd., Columbia, 1982-83. With USNR, 1955-63. Recipient U. Mo. Faculty/Alumni award, 1985. Mem. Nat. Assn. Indsl. Tchr. Educators (pres., officer 1965-74), Am. Indsl. Arts Assn. (v.p. 1980), Mo. Vocat. Assn. (pres. 1974-75), Mo. Assn. Colls. for Tchr. Edn. (pres. 1987-90), Am. Vocat. Assn. (Outstanding Svc. award 1979), U. Mo. Faculty Club (officer 1977-82), Kiwanis. Mem. Christian Ch. (Disciples Of Christ). Avocations: golf, travel, home maintenance. Office: PO Box 2683 Auburn AL 36831-2683 Office Phone: 334-844-1139.

MILLER, WILLIAM ALVIN, clergyman, author, lecturer; b. Pitts., Jan. 1, 1931; s. Christ William and Anna Ernestine (Wilhelm) M.; m. Marilyn Mae Miller, Aug. 8, 1953; children: Mark William, Eric Michael. BA, Capital U., 1953; MDiv, Luth. Theol. Sem., Columbus, Ohio, 1957; MST, Andover Newton Theol. Sch., Newton Centre, Mass., 1958, D of Ministry, 1974. Ordained to ministry Luth. Ch.; lic. marriage & family therapist, Minn.; cert. chaplain Assn. of Profl. Chaplains. Pastor St. James Luth. Ch., Balt., 1958—66; chaplain Fairview Hosp., Mpls., 1966—73, dir. dept. religion & health, 1973—87; instr. Fairview Sch. Nursing, Mpls., 1967—75, Luther Northwestern Theol. Sem., St. Paul, 1973—85; pres. Woodland Pub. Co., Wayzata, Minn., 1979—2000; dir. Woodland Pastoral Assocs., Mpls., 1987—96; assoc. pastor Ctrl. Luth. Ch., Mpls., 1989—94. Chair bd. dirs. Luth. Social Svcs. Md., Balt., 1963-65; adminstr. Dialogue 88, Mpls., 1987-88; marriage & family therapist emeritus, Minn. Author: Why Do Christians Break Down?, 1973, Big Kids' Mother Goose, 1976, When Going to Pieces Holds You Together, 1976, You Count, You Really Do!, 1976, Mid Life, New Life, 1978, Conversations, 1980, Make Friends With Your Shadow, 1981, Prayers at Mid Point, 1983, The Joy of Feeling Good, 1986, Your Golden Shadow, 1989, 91, Meeting the Shadow, 1991; assoc. editor Jour. Pastoral Care, Decatur, Ga., 1984-88, editl. cons., 1988—; contbr. articles to profl. jours. Chaplain, Jr. C. of C., Randallstown, Md., 1962-64; bd. dirs. Am. Protestant Health Assn., Schaumburg, Ill., 1983-89; clin. mem. Am. Assn. Marriage & Family Therapy, 1989-96, Minn. Assn. Marriage & Family Therapy, 1989-96. Fellow Coll. Chaplains (pres. 1985-87), Assn. Mental Health Clergy (Anton T. Boisen award 1989); mem. Assn. Clin. Pastoral Edn. (supr. emeritus 2000—), Am. Assn. Marriage and Family Therapy, Minn. Assn. Marriage and Family Therapy. Avocations: woodworking, publishing, construction. Home and Office: 2005 Xanthus Ln N Minneapolis MN 55447-2053

MILLER, WILLIAM CHARLES, theological educator, minister; b. Mpls., Oct. 26, 1947; s. Robert Charles and Cleithra Mae (Johnson) M.; m. Brenda Kathleen Barnes, July 24, 1969; children: Amy Renee, Jared Charles. BA, Ind. Wesleyan U., 1968; MLS, Kent State U., 1974, PhD, 1983; postgrad., U. Kans., 1984; MA in Religious Studies, Ctrl. Bapt. Theol. Sem., 1988; MBA, MidAm. Nazarene U., 1997; STM, Nashotah House, 2001. Ordained to ministry Ch. of Nazarene, 1986, received into communion and ordained Episcopal Ch., 2006, cert. ordained deacon Episcopal Ch., 2006, ordained priest Episcopal Ch., 2007. Libr. technician Kent State U., 1972—74; catalog libr. Mt. Vernon Nazarene Coll., Ohio, 1974—76, libr. catalog and acquisitions, 1976—78; dir. libr. svcs., prof. theol. bibliography Nazarene Theol. Sem., Kansas City, Mo., 1978—2005, dean adminstrn., 1996—98, 1999—2005; dir. accreditation Assn. Theol. Schs., Pitts., 2005—. Adj. rsch. assoc. U. Kans., 1984-85; adj. prof. MidAm. Nazarene U., Olathe, Kans., 1994-2000, Ind. Wesleyan U., 2005, Nazarene Theol. Sem., 2005-07; bd. dirs. Small Libr. Computing Inc.; pres. Mo. Libr. Network Corp., St. Louis, Mo., 1998-2001. Author: Holiness Works: A Bibliography, 1986; editor TUG Newsletter, 1984-87, bd. dirs., 1985-88; editor Jour. Religious and Theol. Info., 1990-98. With U.S. Army, 1968-72. Mem. Assn. Study Higher Edn., Am. Theol. Libr. Assn. (bd. dirs. 1985-88), Wesleyan Theol. Soc., Ch. Eng. Record Soc., Beta Phi Mu. Home: 18290 W 155th Ter Olathe KS 66062-6718 Office: Assn Theol Schs 10 Summit Park Dr Pittsburgh PA 15275-1103 Office Phone: 412-788-6505. Business E-Mail: miller@ats.edu.

MILLER, WILLIAM CHARLES, lawyer; b. Jacksonville, Fla., Aug. 6, 1937; s. Charles and Mary Elizabeth (Kiger) M.; m. Hadmut Gisela Larsen, June 10, 1961; children: Monica Lee, Charles Andreas. BA, Washington and Lee U., 1958, LLB, 1961; LLM, NYU, 1963; postgrad., Harvard U., 1978. Bar: Fla. 1961, Calif. 1984, Ind. 1987, US Supreme Ct. 1968. Counsel to electrochem., elastomers and internat. depts. E.I. duPont de Nemours & Co., Wilmington, Del., 1963-66; counsel S. Am. ops. Bristol-Myers Co., NYC, 1967-69; internat. counsel Xerox Corp., Stamford, Conn., 1969-79, assoc. gen. counsel, 1979-80; v.p., gen. counsel, sec. Max Factor & Co., Hollywood, Calif., 1981-85, Boehringer Mannheim Corp. (now Roche Diagnostics), Indpls., 1985-92; v.p., gen. counsel Collagen Corp., Palo Alto, Calif., 1992-95, GenProbe Inc., San Diego, 1995-96, Safeskin Corp., San Diego, 1996-98; exec. v.p. Lipomatrix Inc., Neuchatel, Switzerland, 1998-99; gen. counsel Turbostar Comm. Corp., 2000—02, exec. v.p., gen counsel, 2002—03; exec. v.p., dir., gen. counsel Aesthetic and Reconstructive Techs., Inc., 2002—. Bd. dirs. Southwestern Legal Found., 1975-85. Fulbright scholar, 1959-60; Ford Found. fellow, 1961-62; Hague Acad. fellow, 1963; German Govt. grantee, 1962-63; Kappa Sigma scholar, 1959. Mem. Internat. Bar Assn., ABA, Calif. Bar Assn., Fla. Bar Assn., Ind. Bar Assn., Masons, Elks, Phi Beta Kappa, Phi Eta Sigma, Delta Theta Phi. Republican. Mem. Christian Ch. Home: 4521 Randag Dr North Fort Myers FL 33903-4731 Personal E-mail: wcmesq@comcast.net.

MILLER, WILLIAM CHARLES, academic administrator, retired naval officer; b. LA, Dec. 1, 1940; s. John Benjamine and Marianne Georgette (Lyons) M.; m. Barbara Jean Leach, June 8, 1962; children: Linda, William, Julie, James, Marianne. BS, U.S. Naval Acad., 1962; MSEE, Stanford U., 1965, PhDEE, 1967. Commd. ensign USN, 1962, advanced through grades to rear adm.; instr. elec. engring. U.S. Naval Acad., Annapolis, Md., 1975-76, exec. asst. to supt., 1976-79; comdg. officer USS Cushing (DD-985), 1979-81; exec. asst. Office Asst. Sec. Navy, Washington, 1981-83; program mgr. Office Naval Tech., Washington, 1983-86; comdg. officer Naval Rsch. Lab., Washington, 1986-87; div. dir. Office Chief Naval Ops., Washington, 1987-90; chief naval rsch. Dept. Navy, Washington, 1990—93; assoc. provost W.Va. Univ., 1993—97; exec. dir., vice chmn. W.Va. Univ. Rsch. Corp., 1993—97; academic dean U.S. Naval Acad., Annapolis, 1997—. Dir. Joint Counter Low Observables Office, Washington, 1989-90; keynote speaker 18ty Internat. Symposium on Naval Hydrodynamics, 1990. Decorated Legion of Merit with 3 oak leaf clusters. Mem. IEEE (keynote speaker Ocean Engring. Systems symposium OCEANS 1990, Internat. Conf. on Neural Networks 1991). Roman Catholic. Avocations: fishing, boating. Office: US Naval Academy Office of Academic Dean 121 Blake Rd Annapolis MD 21402-5000

MILLER, WILLIAM CHARLES, architect, educator; b. San Francisco, May 11, 1945; s. Francis Leland and Ethel Lorene (Britt) M.; m. Beverly Jean McConnell, Dec. 22, 1968; children: Britt A., David A. BArch, U. Oreg., 1968; MArch, U. Ill., 1970. Cert. arch. Nat. Coun. Archtl. Registration Bds., Ariz., Kans., Utah. Asst. prof. Coll. Architecture U. Ariz., Tucson, 1970—77; assoc. prof. dept. architecture Kans. State U., Manhattan, 1977-86, prof., 1986-92, head dept., 1990-92; prof. Coll. of Architecture and Planning U. Utah, Salt Lake City, 1992—, dean, 1992—2002; architect various firms. Guest lectr. in field; presenter numerous profl. socs. and orgns.; dir. west ctrl. region Assn. Collegiate Schs. Architecture, 1988-91, chair theme paper sessions ann. meeting, San Francisco, 1990, chair regional paper sessions ann. meeting, Washington, 1991, co-chair adminstrv. conf., Milw., 1995; bd. dirs. Nat. Archtl. Accrediting Bd., 1996-99; mem. Utah Architects Lic. Bd., 2000—; chair edn. com. NCARB, 2005—; vis. disting. prof. U. Ill., Urbana Champain, 2003; mem. nomenclature commn., NAAB, 2003. Author: Alvar Aalto: An Annotated Bibliography, 1984; co-editor: The Architecture of the In-Between, 1990, Architecture: Back to Life, 1991; contbr. over 60 articles to profl. jours., chpts. to books. Bd. dirs. Assist, Inc., 1992-2002, Artspace, Inc., 1997-2002, Contemporary Arts Group, 1992-96, Salt Lake City Art Design Bd., 1995-2003. Recipient Disting. Prof. award Assn. Collegiate Schs. Architecture, 2004, Svc. awards Nat. Coun. Archtl. Registration Bds., Nat. Archtl. Accrediting Bd. Fellow AIA (pres-elect Flint Hills, treas. Utah, exec. com., treas., exec. com. Western Mountain region, elected coll. of fellows 1997, adv. com. 2007—); mem. Am.-Scandinavian Found., Soc. for Advancement Scandinavian Studies, Educator/Practioner Network, Tau Sigma Delta. Office: U Utah Coll Architecture & Planning Salt Lake City UT 84112 Office Phone: 801-581-8254. Business E-Mail: miller@arch.utah.edu.

MILLER, WILLIAM FREDERICK, research and development company executive, educator, financial consultant; b. Vincennes, Ind., Nov. 19, 1925; s. William and Elsie M. (Everts) M.; m. Patty J. Smith, June 19, 1949; 1 son, Rodney Wayne. Student, Vincennes U., 1946-47; BS, Purdue U., 1949, MS, 1951, PhD, 1956; DSc (hon.), 1972. Mem. staff Argonne Nat. Lab., 1955-64, assoc. physicist, 1956-59, dir. applied math. div., 1959-64; prof. computer sci. Stanford U., Palo Alto, Calif., 1965-97, Herbert Hoover prof. pub. and pvt. mgmt. emeritus, 1997—, assoc. provost for computing, 1968-70, v.p. for rsch., 1970-71, v.p., provost, 1971-78; mem. Stanford Assocs., 1972—; pres emeritus., CEO SRI Internat., Menlo Park, Calif., 1979-90; chmn. bd., CEO SRI Devel. Co., Menlo Park, David Sarnoff Rsch. Ctr., Inc., Princeton, NJ, 1987—90. Chmn. emeritus bd. dirs. Borland Software, Sentius Corp.; founder, chmn. Nanostellar, Inc.; professorial lectr. applied math. U. Chgo., 1962-64; vis. prof. math. Purdue U., 1962-63; vis. scholar Ctr. for Advanced Study in Behavioral Scis., 1976; mem. adv. coun. BHP Internat., 1990-97; computer sci. and engring bd. NAS, 1968-71; mem. Nat. Sci. Bd., 1982-88; corp. com. computers in edn. Brown UU., 1971-79; mem. policy bd. EDUCOM Planning Coun. on Computing in Edn., 1974-79, chmn., 1974-76; mem. ednl. adv. bd. Guggenheim Meml. Found., 1976-80; com. postdoctoral and doctoral rsch. staff NRC, 1977-80, computer sci. and telecom.; dir. Fund Am., 1977-91, Fireman's Fund Ins., 1977-91, Wells Fargo Bank and Co., 1996-97, Varian Assocs. Inc., 1973-96. Mem. editl. bd. Pattern Recognition Jour, 1968-72, Jour. Computational Physics, 1970-74. Served to 2d lt. F.A. AUS, 1943-46. Recipient Frederic B. Whitman award United Way Bay Area, 1982, Sarnoff Founders medal, 1997, David Packard Civic Entrepreneurship Team award, 1998, Robert K. Jaedicke Silver Apple award Stanford U. Bus. Sch. Alumni, 1998, The Dongbaeg medal Order of Civil Merit, The Rep. of Korea, 2000, The Okawa prize, The Okawa Found. for Info. and Telecoms., 2000, Most Mentor award Internat. Angel Investors, 2002; named to Silicon Valley Engring. Hall of Fame, 2001, Jr. Achievement Bus. Hall of Fame, 2002. Fellow IEEE (life), Am. Acad. Arts and Scis., AAAS; mem. Soc. Indsl. and Applied Math., Assn. Computing Machinery, Nat. Acad. Engring., Sigma Xi, Tau Beta Pi (Eminent Engr. 1989). Office: Stanford U Grad Sch Bus Stanford CA 94305

MILLER, WILLIAM GREEN, former ambassador; b. NYC, Aug. 15, 1931; m. Suzanne Lisle; 2 children. BA, MA, Oxford U., UK; postgrad., Harvard U. Tutor Winthrop House Harvard U., 1956-59; with Fgn. Svc., 1959; vice consul, polit. officer Isfahan, Iran, 1959-62; polit. officer Tehran, Iran, 1962-64; line officer, exec. secretariat Dept. of State, 1965-66; mem. Sr. Interdepartmental Group, 1966-67; spl. asst. fgn. affairs and def. Senator John Sherman Cooper, 1967-73; staff dir. Senate Select Com. Emergency Powers, 1973-75, Senate Select Com. to Study Govtl. Ops. with Respect to Intelligence Communities, 1975-76, Senate Select Com. Intelligence, 1976-81; assoc. dean, adj. prof. internat. politics Fletcher Sch. Law and Diplomacy, 1981-83, rsch. assoc., 1983-85; faculty assoc. Harvard Ctr. Middle Eastern Studies, 1983-86; pres. Am. Com. U.S.-Soviet Rels., 1986-92; U.S. amb. to Ukraine, 1993-98. Cons. D.H. Sawyer and Assocs., Ltd., N.Y.C., 1985; bd. dirs. Internat. Found., pres. 1986-92; pres. Com. Am.- Russian Rels., cons. Catherine T. MacArthur Found., 1992-93. Contbr. articles to profl. jours. Bd. mem. UN Assn., 2002—; co-chmn. bd. Myiv-Mohyla U. Found., 2002—; bd. dirs. The Andrei Sakharov Found., 1998—, Inst. Soc. Action and Renewal in Eurasia, 1998—; bd. mem. US - Ukraine Found., 2002—. Rsch. fellow Harvard Ctr. Sci. and Internat. Affairs, 1984-86, John F. Kennedy Sch. of Govt. fellow Harvard U., 1986. Fellow Rsch. Inst. of Politics; mem. Nat. Acad. Pub. Diplomacy, Nat. Acad. Pub. Adminstrn., Internat. Inst. Strategic Studies, Coun. Fgn. Rels., Children of the 21st Century, Middle East Inst., Soc. Iranian Studies, Search For Common Ground. Office: Woodrow Wilson Internat Ctr Scholars 1 Woodrow Wilson Plaza 1300 Pennsylvania Ave NW Washington DC 20004-3002 Office Phone: 202-691-4000. Business E-Mail: wmiller@igc.org.

MILLER, WILLIAM HUGHES, theoretical chemist, educator; b. Kosciusko, Miss., Mar. 16, 1941; s. Weldon Howard and Jewel Irene (Hughes) M.; m. Margaret Ann Westbrook, June 4, 1966; children: Alison Leslie, Emily Sinclaire. BS, Ga. Inst. Tech., 1963; AM, Harvard U., 1964, PhD, 1967. Jr. fellow Harvard U., 1967-69; NATO postdoctoral fellow Freiburg (Germany) U., 1967-68; asst. prof. chemistry U. Calif., Berkeley, 1969-72, assoc. prof., 1972-74, prof., 1974—, dept. chmn., 1989-93, chancellor's prof., 1998—2001, Kenneth S. Pitzer disting. prof., 1999—. Fellow Churchill Coll., Cambridge (Eng.) U., 1975-76; hon. prof. Shandong U., People's Republic of China, 1994. Alfred P. Sloan fellow, 1970-72; Camille and Henry Dreyfus fellow, 1973-78; Guggenheim fellow, 1975-76, Christensen fellow St. Catherine's Coll., Oxford, 1993; recipient Alexander von Humboldt-Stiftung U.S. Sr. Scientist award, 1981-82, Ernest Orlando Lawrence Meml. award, 1985, Hirschfelder prize in theoretical chemistry, U. Wis., 1996, Alumni Achievement award Ga. Inst. Tech., 1997, Spiers medal Faraday divsn. Royal Soc. Chemistry, London, 1998. Fellow AAAS, Am. Acad. Arts and Scis., Am. Phys. Soc. (Irving Langmuir award 1990); mem. NAS, Am. Chem. Soc. (Theoretical Chemistry award 1994, Ira Remsen award 1997, Peter Debye award 2003), Internat. Acad. Quantum Molecular Sci. (Ann. prize 1974, Herschbach award in chem. dynamics 2007, Weld award in chemistry 2007). Office: U Calif Dept Chemistry Berkeley CA 94720-0001

MILLER, WILLIAM IAN, law educator; b. 1946; BA, U. Wis., 1969, M of Philosophy, 1973, PhD, 1975; JD, Yale U., 1980. Bar: Wis. 1980. Assoc. prof. U. Houston, 1981-85; prof. U. Mich. Law Sch., Ann Arbor, 1984—, Thomas G. Long Prof. Law. Vis. assoc. prof. U. Mich., An Arbor, 1984-85; vis. prof. Yale U., fall 1988. Author: Bloodtaking and Peacemaking: Feud, Law, and Society in Saga Iceland, 1990, Humiliation, 1993, The Anatomy of Disgust, 1997, The Mystery of Courage, 2000, Faking It, 2003, An Eye for an Eye, 2006. Mem. Law and Soc. Assn., Am. Soc. Legal History, Am. Hist. Assn. Office: U Mich Law Sch 411 Hutchins Hall 625 S State St Ann Arbor MI 48109-1215 Office Phone: 734-763-9014. Office Fax: 734-763-9375. E-mail: wimiller@umich.edu.

MILLER, WILLIAM IRWIN, finance company executive; b. Columbus, Ind., Apr. 30, 1956; s. Joseph Irwin and Xenia Ruth (Simons) M.; m. Lynne Marie Maguire, Oct. 29, 1983; children: Katherine Maguire, Laura Marie, Emily Elizabeth. BA, Yale U., 1978; MBA, Stanford U., 1981. Sect. mgr. Cummins Engine Co., Inc., Charleston, SC, 1978-79; assoc. Warburg Pincus Capital Corp., NYC, 1981-83; pres. Irwin Mgmt. Co., Inc., Columbus, 1984-90, also bd. dirs.; chmn. Irwin Fin. Corp., Columbus, 1990—. Chmn. Irwin Mgmt. Co. and Tipton Lakes Co., Columbus, 1984—; bd. dirs. Cummins Inc., Irwin-Sweeney-Miller Found., Columbus, New Perspective Fund, LA, New World Fund, LA. Trustee The Taft Sch., Watertown, Conn., 1979-2006, Christian Theol. Sem., Indpls., 1988-94, Europacific Growth Fund, L.A., 1992—, Yale U., New Haven, 2005—; bd. dirs. Cummins Found., Columbus, Ind., 1989—, Irwin Fin. Found., Columbus, 1991—, Tennant Co., 1993-2005, The Heritage Fund of Bartholomew County, Columbus, 1998-2006, John D. and Catherine T. MacArthur Found., 2005—; mem. investment com. Yale U., New Haven, 1995-99, 2000—; mem. Ctrl. Ind. Corp. Partnership, Indpls., 1999—, Nat. Bldg. Mus., 2001-06. Office: Irwin Fin Corp 500 Washington St PO Box 929 Columbus IN 47202-0929 Office Phone: 812-376-1641.

MILLER, WILLIAM NAPIER CRIPPS, lawyer; b. Long Branch, NJ, June 7, 1930; adopted s. Julia (Erwin) M.; m. Carolyn Anderson, Jan. 19, 1951 (div. 1963); children: Bruce Douglass, Jennifer Erwin; m. Hannelore Steinbeck, Dec. 4, 1970 AA, Coll. Marin, 1949; student, U. Calif.-Berkeley, 1949-51, JD, 1955. Bar: N.Y., Calif. 1956, U.S. Supreme Ct. 1983. Assoc. Mudge, Stern, Baldwin & Todd, NYC, 1955-58, Pillsbury, Madison & Sutro, San Francisco, 1959-65; ptnr. Pillsbury, Winthrop Shaw Pittman LLP, San Francisco, 1966—; staff NYU Law Sch., 1957-58; ct. adv. com. Calif. State Assembly Judiciary Com., 1979-80. Author: Long Pig, 2002. Bd. dirs. Laguna Honda Hosp., San Francisco, 1966—; bd. visitors U. Calif.-Hastings Law Sch. Served with USAF, 1951-52. Served USAF, 1950—52. Recipient Bur. Nat. Affairs award U. Calif.-Hastings, 1955; recipient Thurston Soc. award, 1953. Fellow Am. Coll. Trial Lawyers; mem. ABA, San Francisco Bar Assn., Order of Coif, St. Francis Yacht Club. Home: 16 George Ln Sausalito CA 94965-1890 Office: Pillsbury Winthrop Shaw Pittman LLP PO Box 7880 San Francisco CA 94120-7880 Home Phone: 415-332-6665; Office Phone: 415-983-1464. Business E-Mail: william.miller@pillsburylaw.com.

MILLER, WILLIAM RICHEY, JR., lawyer; b. Oklahoma City, Apr. 4, 1947; s. William Richey and Edna Rosalind (Nielsen) M.; m. Susan Hammond, Aug. 2, 1970; children: Brooke, Karen. BA, Pomona Coll., Claremont, Calif., 1969; MA, Claremont Grad. Sch., 1972; JD, Lewis and Clark Coll., 1975. Bar: Oreg. 1975, U.S. Dist. Ct. Oreg. 1976, U.S. Ct. Appeals (9th cir.) 1976. Staff atty. Oreg. Ct. Appeals, Salem, 1975-76; with firm Griffith, Bittner, Abbott & Roberts, Portland, Oreg., 1976-83; ptnr. Davis Wright Tremaine, Portland, 1983—. Adj. prof. Lewis and Clark Law Sch., 1975-78. Bd. dirs. Portland Civic Theatre, 1988-91, Am. Lung Assn. Oreg., Portland, 1985-88, Oreg. Bus. Com. for the Arts, Portland, 1991-93. Mem. Oreg. State Bar (sect. chair 1990-91), Comml. Fin. Assn., Oreg. Bankers Assn., Lewis and Clark Alumni Assn. (bd. dirs. 1989-92). Presbyterian. Home: 843 Lakeshore Rd Lake Oswego OR 97034-3704 Office: Davis Wright Tremaine 1300 SW 5th Ave Ste 2300 Portland OR 97201-5682 Office Phone: 503-778-5304.

MILLER, WILMA HILDRUTH, education educator; b. Dixon, Ill., Mar. 8, 1936; d. William Alexander and Ruth Karin (Hanson) M. BS in Edn., No. Ill. U., DeKalb, 1958, MS in Edn., 1961; DEd, U. Ariz., 1967. Cert. reading specialist. Elem. tchr. Dist. 170, Dixon, Ill., 1958-63, Dist. 1, Tucson, Ariz., 1963-64; asst. prof. edn. Wis. State U., Whitewater, 1965-68; assoc. prof. edn. Ill. State U., Normal, 1968-72, prof., 1972-98, prof. emeritus, 1998—. Author: Diagnosing and Correcting Reading Difficulties in Children, 1988, Reading Comprehension, 1990, Complete Reading Disabilities Handbook, 1993, Alternative Assessment Techniques in Reading and Writing, 1995, Reading and Writing Remediation Kit, 1997, The Reading Teacher's Survival Kit, 2001, Reading Skills Problem Solver, 2002, Survival Reading Skills for Secondary School Students, 2003, 101 Ways for Developing Emergent Literacy, 2004, others; contbr. over 225 articles to profl. jours. Altar Guild, usher, greeter, communion asst. Our Saviour Luth. Ch., Normal, 1990—. Recipient Outstanding Contbn. to Edn. award No. Ill. U., 1998. Mem. Internat. Reading Assn. (parent and reading com. 1972-74, editl. adv. bd. 1995-98, Outstanding Dissertation award 1968), Mid-State Reading Coun. (editl. adv. bd. 1991-98), Alpha Upsilon Alpha (advisor Reading chpt. 1993-98), Pi Lambda Theta, Kappa Delta Pi, Phi Delta Kappa. Avocations: travel, writing, reading, antiques. Home: 302 N Coolidge St Normal IL 61761-2435 Personal E-mail: whmille@ilstu.edu.

MILLER, ZELL BRYAN, former senator, governor; b. Young Harris, Ga., Feb. 24, 1932; s. Stephen Grady and Birdie (Bryan) M.; m. Shirley Carver, Jan. 14, 1954; children: Murphy Carver, Matthew Stephen. Student, Young Harris Coll., 1951; AB in History, U. Ga., 1957, MA in History, 1958. Dir. Ga. Bd. Probation, 1965-66; dep. dir. Ga. Dept. Corrections, 1967-68; exec. sec. to gov. Ga., 1968-71; mem. State Bd. Pardons and Paroles, Atlanta, 1973-75; lt. gov. State of Ga., 1975-90, gov., 1990-98; prof. polit. sci. and history U. Ga., 1999; U.S. senator from Ga., 2000—05; sr. advisor McKenna Long & Aldridge LLP, Atlanta, 2005—. Prof. Young Harris Coll., 1959-64, Emory U., Young Harris Coll., U. Ga.; bd. dirs. various corps., including Overseas Pvt. Investment Corp. (OPIC), Ga. Power, Gray Comms., Ezgov.com, Post Properties, Kollmann USA; keynote speaker Democratic Nat. Convention, NYC, 1992, Republican Nat. Convention, NYC, 2004; retired Jan. 2005; commr., Am. Battle Monuments Commn., 2005-, part-time commentator, Fox News Channel, 2005-. Author: The Mountains Within Me, 1985, Great Georgians, 1983, They Heard Georgia Singing, 1996, Corps Values: Everything You Need to Know I Learned in the Marines, 1996, Listen to this Voice: Selected Speeches of Governor Zell Miller, 1998, A National Party No More: The Conscience of a Conservative Democrat, 2003, Deficit of Decency, 2005. Mem. Ga. Senate, 1960-64; mayor Young Harris, 1959; exec. dir. Democratic Com. Ga., 1971-72; pres. Coun. State Govts., 1991; vice chmn. So. Gov.'s Assn., 1991; bd. dirs. Towns County Hosp. Authority. Served with USMC, 1953-56. Mem. Ga. Sch. Food Services Assn. (life), Ga. Peace Officers Assn. (life), Gridiron Soc. U. Ga., Blue Key, Lions Club. Democrat. Meth. Office: McKenna Long & Aldridge LLP 303 Peachtree St NE Ste 5300 Atlanta GA 30308 also: Am Battle Monuments Commn 2300 Clarendon Blvd Ste 500 Arlington VA 22201

MILLER, ZOYA DICKINS, civic worker, consultant; b. Washington, July 15, 1923; d. Randolph and Zoya Pavlovna (Klementinovska) Dickins; m. Hilliard Eve Miller, Jr., Dec. 6, 1943; children: Jeffrey Arnot, Hilliard Eve III. Grad., Stuart Sch. Costume Design, Washington, 1942; student, Cochran Galleries of Fine Arts, 1942, Sophie Newcomb Coll., 1944, New Eng. Conservatory Music, 1946, Colo. Coll., 1965; grad., Internat. Sch. Reading, 1969; student, Cochran Galleries of Fine Arts, 1942. Lic. pvt. pilot. Instr. Stuart Summer Sch. Costume Design, Washington, 1942; fashion coord. Julius Garfinckel, Washington, 1942-43; fashion coord., cons. Mademoiselle mag., 1942-44; star TV show Cowbelle Kitchen, 1957-58, Flair for Living, 1958-59; model mags. and comml. films, also nat. comml. recs., 1956-80; dir. rsch. devel. Webb-Waring Inst. Cancer, Aging and Antioxidant Rsch., Denver, 1973—2006, devel. cons., 2006—. Contbr. articles, lectrs. on health care sys. and fund raising. Mem. exec. com., bd. dirs. El Paso County chpt. Am. Lung Assn. Colo., 1965—84, bd. dirs., 1965—87, chmn. radio and TV coun., 1963—70, mem. med. affairs com., 1965—70, pres., 1965—66, procurer found. funds, 1965—70; developer nat. radio ednl. prodns. for internat. use Am. Lung Assn., 1963—70, coord. statewide pulmonary screening programs Colo., other states, 1965—72; chmn. benefit fund raising El Paso County Cancer Soc., 1963; co-founder, coord. Colorado Springs Debutante Ball, 1967—; coord. Nat. Gov.'s Comprehensive Health Planning Coun., 1967—74, chmn., 1971—72, Colo. Chronic Care Com., 1969—73, chmn. fund raising, 1970—72, chmn. spl. com. conl. studies on nat. health bills, 1971—73; mem. Colo.-Wyo. Regional Med. Program Adv. Coun., 1969—73, Colo. Med. Found. Consumers Adv. Coun., 1972—78; mem. decorative arts com. Colorado Springs Fine Arts Ctr., 1972—75; founder, state coord. Nov. Noel Pediat. Benefit Am. Lung Assn., 1973—87; founder, chmn. bd. dirs. Newborn Hope, Inc., 1987—; mem. adv. bd. Wagon Wheel Girl Scouts, 1991—94; mem. cmty. adv. coun. Beth-El Nursing Sch., 1998—; chmn. Colo. Festival World Theatre Gala, 2005; gala chmn. Colorado Festival World Theatre, 2005; maj. donor devel. dir. Meml. Health Sys., Colorado Springs, 2006—; bd. dirs. Episcopal Columbarium Assn., 2001, The Family Attachment Ctr., Inc., Meml. Hosp. Found., Colo. Springs, Colo., 2004; hon. bd. mem. KCME 88.7 FM, Colorado Springs, Colo., 2004; gala chmn. Colo. Festival of World Theatre, 2005; maj. donor devel. dir. Meml. Health Sys., Colo. Springs, 2006—. Zoya Dickins Miller Vol. of Yr. award established Am. Lung Assn. of Colo., 1979; recipient James J. Waring award Colo. Conf. on Respiratory Disease Workers, 1963, Nat. Pub. Rels. award Am. Lung Assn., 1979, Gold Double Bar Cross award, 1980, 83, Jefferson award Am. Inst. Pub. Svc., 1991, Thousand Points of Light award The White House, 1992, Recognition award So. Colo. Women's C. of C., 1994, Silver Spur Cmty. award Pikes Peak Range Riders, 1994, Silver Bell award Assistance League Colorado Springs, 1996, Svc. to Mankind award Centennial Sertoma Club, 1997, Help Can't Wait award Pikes Peak chpt. ARC, 1997, Cmty. Weaver award The Independent News, 1997, Apgar award Colo. March of Dimes, 1998; named Humanitarian of Yr., Am. Lung Assn. of Colo., 1987, El Pomar Found. award for Excellence, Russell Tutt Leadership award, 2004. Mem.: Nat. Soc. Fund Raising Execs., Denver Round Table for Planned Giving, Colo. Assn. Fund Raisers, Nat. Soc. Colonial Dames, The Family Attachment Ctr., Nat. Cowbell Assn. (El Paso county pres. 1954, TV chmn., chmn. nat. Father of Yr. contest Colo. 1956—57), Broadmoor Garden Club, Garden of the Gods Club, Cheyenne Mountain Country Club. Home: 74 W Cheyenne Mountain Blvd Colorado Springs CO 80906-4336 E-mail: hope4455@adelphia.net.

MILLER-ENGEL, MARJORIE, foundation administrator, commissioner, small business owner; d. David Harry Siegel and Ruth Joan Gord; m. Robert Alan Engel, May 4, 1984; 1 child, Liana Laura Engel. BA, Syracuse U. Cert. interior design cons. NY Sch. Interior Design. Assoc. dir. devel. Planned Parenthood Fedn., NYC; account exec. Harold Oram Consulting, NYC; pres., owner Marjorie Miller Pub. Rels., NYC; founder, chmn. Life Ctr. Youth, Inc., Santa Fe, 1982—; pres., owner M. M. Designs, Inc., Santa Fe, 1989—. Co-owner Greenkey Property Investments, Santa Fe, 1989—. Commr. N.Mex Commn. Status Women, 2003—. Mem.: Intl. Women's Forum. Office: Life Ctr Youth Inc PO Box 8718 2725 Agua Fria St Santa Fe NM 87504

MILLER-LANE, BARBARA See LANE, BARBARA

MILLER-LERMAN, LINDSEY, state supreme court justice; b. LA, July 30, 1947; BA, Wellesley Coll., Mass., 1968; JD, Columbia U., NYC, 1973; LHD (hon.), Coll. St. Mary, Omaha, 1993. Bar: NY 1974, US Dist. Ct. (so. dist.) NY 1974, US Ct. Appeals (2d cir.) 1974, Nebr. 1976, US Dist. Ct. (ea. dist.) NY 1975, US Dist. Ct. Nebr. 1976, US Ct. Appeals (8th cir.) 1979, US Supreme Ct. 1982, US Ct. Appeals (6th cir.) 1984, US Ct. Appeals (10th cir.) 1987. Law clk. U.S. Dist. Ct., NYC, 1973-75; from assoc. to ptnr. Kutak Rock, Omaha, 1975-92; judge Nebr. Ct. Appeals, Lincoln, 1992-98, chief judge, 1996-98; justice Nebr. Supreme Ct., 1998—. Contbr. articles to profl. jours. Office: Nebr Supreme Ct State Capitol Rm 2222 Lincoln NE 68509 Office Phone: 402-471-3734. Business E-Mail: lmiller-lerman@nsc.state.ne.us.

MILLER-SYDNEY, AUDREY YVONNE, music educator; d. Joseph Horace Miller and Edith Mae Gibson-Miller. BA, Va. State U., Petersburg, 1960; MusM, Manhattan Sch. Music, NYC, 1966. Cert. tchr. NY. Choral and music instr. Irving N. Taylor Jr. HS, Danville, Va., 1960—62, NYC Pub. Schs., NYC, 1963—65; vocal and instrumental tchr. Union Settlement Music Sch., NYC, 1963—67; music tchr. Joan of Arc Jr. HS, NYC, 1967—68; project coord. Salem Crescent Learning Ctr., NYC, 1979—80; chmn. music, magnet coord. Dr. Alfred M. Franko Magnet Sch., Mt. Vernon, NY, 1978—97; adj. prof. music appreciation Coll. New Rochelle, NY, 2002—. Home: Apt 4B 730 Riverside Dr New York NY 10031-2444 E-mail: amsydney02@verizon.net.

MILLER UDELL, BRONWYN, judge; b. Danbury, Conn., Aug. 7, 1972; BA, Barnard Coll., Columbia U., 1994; JD, U. Miami, 1997. Bar: (Fla.) 1997. Asst. state atty. State of Fla., Miami, 1997—2005; judge Dade County, 2005—. Adj. faculty Fla. Internat. U., 2001—02; mem. Witness Justice Adv. Bd. Active Cmtys. in Schs. Miami Mentoring Program, Coral Gables Sr. HS PTA, Take Stock in Children; co-chair Expert Corps. Vol.; adv. bd. Jewish Vol. Ctr. Mem.: League of Prosecutors (bd. dir.), Fla. Assn. Women Lawyers, Fla. Pros. Attys. Assn., Federalist Soc. Lawyer's Divsn., Elephant Forum, Coconut Grove C. of C., Phi Delta Phi. Office: 73 W Flager St Ste 418 Miami FL 33130 Office Phone: 305-349-7148. Business E-Mail: bmiller@judl.flcourts.org.

MILLET, T. KELLEY, securities trader; b. 1960; Various positions including analyst, global head capital markets and syndicate J.P. Morgan, 1982—2001; sr. mng. dir., co-head global credit trading ops. Bear Stearns, 2001—06; pres. MarketAxess Holdings, Inc., 2006—. Office: Market-Axess Holdings Inc MarketAxess Corp 140 Broadway 42d Fl New York NY 10005 *

MILLETT, STEPHEN MALCOLM, futurist, consultant, historian; b. NYC, Feb. 22, 1947; s. John David and Catherine (Letsinger) Millett; m. Patricia McBurney, 1970; children: Jennifer Jane, Ann E.; m. Sherry Richards, Aug. 2, 1989. AB, Miami U., Oxford, Ohio, 1969; MA, Ohio State U., 1970, PhD, 1972. Rschr. Battelle, Columbus, Ohio, 1979—2006; founder Futuring Assoc. LLC, Columbus, 2007. Mgr. tech. forecasts incl. Strategic Technologies 2005, Strategic Technologies 2020, Innovations in War on Terrorism. Author: Manager's Guide to Technology Forecasting, 1991, Scottish Settlers of America, 1996; pub. and editor U.S. Scots, 1992-97. Mem. at large State Bd. Edn. Ohio, 2003—. Capt. USAF, 1973—79. Mem. World Futures Soc., Assn. of Profl. Futurists (founding mem.), Phi Delta Theta. Home: 3673 Tillbury Ave Columbus OH 43220 Personal E-mail: smillett@columbus.rr.com.

MILLGATE, MICHAEL (MICHAEL HENRY MILLGATE), retired literature educator; b. Southampton, Eng., July 19, 1929; arrived in Can., 1964; s. Stanley and Marjorie Louisa Millgate; m. Jane Barr, Feb. 27, 1960. BA, Cambridge U., 1952, MA, 1956; postgrad., U. Mich., Ann Arbor, 1956-57; PhD, U. Leeds, 1960. Tutor Workers' Ednl. Assn., Eng., 1953-56; lectr. English lit. U. Leeds, 1958-64; prof., chmn. dept. English York U., Ont., Can., 1964-67; prof. English U. Toronto, 67-94, univ. prof., 87-94, univ. prof. emeritus, 1994—. Carpenter lectr. Ohio Wesleyan U., 1978; vis. scholar Meiji U., 1985. Author: William Faulkner, 1961, American Social Fiction, 1964, The Achievement of William Faulkner, 1966, Thomas Hardy: His Career as a Novelist, 1971, Thomas Hardy: A Biography, 1982, Testamentary Acts: Browning, Tennyson, James, Hardy, 1992, Faulkner's Place, 1997, Thomas Hardy: A Biography Revisited, 2004; editor: Tennyson: Selected Poems, 1963, Thomas Hardy: The Life and Work of Thomas Hardy, 1985, William Faulkner Manuscripts, 20 (4 vols.), 21 (2 vols.), 22 (4 vols.), 23 (2 vols.), 1986, New Essays on Light in August, 1987, Thomas Hardy: Selected Letters, 1990, Letters of Emma and Florence Hardy, 1996, Thomas Hardy's Public Voice, 2001; co-editor: Transatlantic Dialogue, 1966, Lion in the Garden, 1968, The Collected Letters of Thomas Hardy, Vol. I, 1978, Vol. II, 1980, Vol. III, 1982, Vol. IV, 1984, Vol. V, 1985, Vol. VI, 1987, Vol. VII, 1988, Thomas Hardy's Studies, Specimens, Etc. Notebook, 1994. Mem. ednl. adv. bd. John Guggenheim Meml. Found., 1994—2005. Can. Coun. leave fellow, 1968-69, S.W. Brooks fellow U. Queensland, 1971; Killam sr. rsch. scholar, 1974-75; John Simon Guggenheim Meml. fellow, 1977-78, Connaught sr. fellow, 1979-80; Social Sci. and Humanities Rsch. Coun. Can. leave fellow, 1981-82, grantee, 1977—2006; Can. Coun. grantee, 1973-77; Killam rsch. fellow, 1986-88. Fellow Royal Soc. Lit., Royal Soc. Can. (Pierre Chauveau medal 1999); mem. MLA (adv. com. Ctr. for Edit. Am. Authors 1971-74, com. on scholarly edits. 1985-89), Victorian Studies Assn. Ont. (pres. 1970-72), Thomas Hardy Soc. (v.p. 1973—), Tennyson Soc. Home: 1 Balmoral Ave Apt 809 Toronto ON Canada M4V 3B9 E-mail: michael.millgate@utoronto.ca.

MILLIAN, JOHN C., lawyer; b. Jan. 30, 1958; BA in Econ., Univ. Calif., Berkeley, 1980; JD, Yale Univ., 1983. Bar: Wash. 1984, Calif. 1987, DC 1988. Law clk. Judge Gerhard A Gesell US Dist. Ct., Washington, 1983—84; ptnr. litig. dept. Gibson Dunn & Crutcher LLP, Washington, 1991—, former ptnr.-in-charge DC office. Pro bono atty. Wesley Theol. Sem.; bd. dir. Wesley Sem. Found.; former mem. exec. com. Gibson Dunn & Crutcher. Mem.: ABA, Coun. for Ct. Excellence (bd. dir.). Office: Gibson Dunn & Crutcher LLP 1050 Connecticut Ave NW Washington DC 20036 Office Phone: 202-955-8213. Business E-Mail: jmillian@gibsondunn.com.

MILLICAN, ELLIOT STEPHEN, mechanical engineer; b. Little Rock, Ark., Feb. 20, 1978; s. Leslie Wayne Millican and Stella Pukpillo Walker, Benjamin Whitfield Walkjer (Stepfather); m. Amanda Mae Franklin, Mar. 20, 2004; 1 child, Preston Stephen. BS, Tex. A&M U., Coll. Station, 2001. Cert. profl. engr., Tex., 2006. Assoc. E&C Engrs. & Cons. Inc., Houston, 2001—. Welcom ctr. greeter Houston's First Bapt. Ch., 2006—07. Mem.: Am. Soc. Heating, Refrigeration and Air Conditioning Engrs. Home: 3615 Parkshire Dr Pearland TX 77584 Office: E&C Engrs & Cons Inc 1010 Lamar Houston TX 77002

MILLICHAP, JOSEPH GORDON, neurologist, educator; b. Wellington, Eng., Dec. 18, 1918; came to U.S., 1956, naturalized, 1965; s. Joseph P. and Alice (Flello) M.; m. Mary Irene Fortey, Feb. 25, 1946 (dec. Oct. 1969); children: Martin Gordon, Paul Anthony; m. Nancy Melanie Kluczynski, Nov. 7, 1970 (dec. Apr. 1995); children: Gordon Thomas, John Joseph. MB Surgery honors, St. Bartholomew's Med. Coll., U. London, 1946, MD Internal Medicine, 1951, diploma child health, 1948. Diplomate Am. Bd. Pediat., Am. Bd. Neurology and Child Neurology, Am. Bd. Electroencephalography. Intern, resident St. Bartholomew's Hosp., 1946—49, Hosp. Sick Children, London, 1951—53, Mass. Gen. Hosp., Boston, 1958—60; pediat. neurologist NIH, 1955—56; USPHS fellow neurology Mass. Gen. Hosp., Boston, 1958—60; cons. pediat. neurology Mayo Clinic, 1960—63; pediat. neurologist Children's Meml. Hosp., Northwestern Med. Ctr., Chgo., 1963—; prof. neurology and pediat. Northwestern U. Med. Sch., 1963—. Cons. surgeon gen. USPHS; mem. med. adv. bds. Ill. Epilepsy League, Muscular Dystrophy Found., Cerebral Palsy Found., 1963—; vis. prof. Gt. Ormond St. Hosp., U. London, 1986-87 Author: Febrile Convulsions, 1967, Pediatric Neurology, 1967, Learning Disabilities, 1974, The Hyperactive Child with MBD, 1975, Nutrition, Diet and Behavior, 1985, Dyslexia, 1986, Progress in Pediatric Neurology, 1991, Vol. II, 1994, Vol. III, 1997, Environmental Poisons in Our Food, 1993, A Guide to Drinking Water, Hazards and Health Risks, 1995, Attention Deficit Hyperactivity and Learning Disorders, 1998, (with G.T. Millichap) The School in a Garden, 2000; editor Jour. Pediatric Neurology Briefs; contbr. articles to profl. jours., chpts. to books Chmn. rsch. com. med. adv. bd. Epilepsy Found., 1965—. Served with RAF, 1949-51 Named New Citizen of Year in

Met. Chgo., 1965; recipient Americanism Medal DAR, 1972, Brennemann award Chgo. Pediat. Soc., 1998; USPHS rsch. grantee, 1957 Fellow Royal Coll. Physicians; mem. AMA, Am. Neurol. Assn., Am. Pediat. Soc., Am. Soc. Pediat. Rsch., Am. Acad. Neurology, Am. Soc. Pharmacology and Exptl. Therapeautics, Soc. Exptl. Biology and Medicine, Am. Bd. Psychiatry and Neurology (asst. examiner 1961—) Episcopalian. Office: Children's Meml Hosp Box 51 2300 N Childrens Plz Chicago IL 60614-3394 Home Phone: 312-943-1719.

MILLIGAN, CYNTHIA HARDIN, dean, lawyer; BA, U. Kans., 1967; JD, George Washington U., 1970. Bar: D.C. 1970, Nebr. 1977. Assoc. Arent, Fox, Kintnor, Plotkin & Kahn, Washington, 1970-77; ptnr. Rembolt, Ludtke, Milligan & Berger, Lincoln, Nebr., 1977-87; dir. Nebr. Dept. Banking and Fin., Lincoln, 1987-91; pres. CMA, Lincoln, 1991-98; dean U. Nebr. Coll. Bus. Adminstrn., Lincoln, 1998—. Bd. dirs. Wells Fargo & Co., San Francisco, Gallup Orgn., Princeton, N.J., Calvert Funds, Bethesda, Md. Trustee, bd. chmn. W.K. Kellogg Found., Battle Creek, Mich. Fellow Nebr. Bar Found.; mem. Nebr. Bar Assn. Office: U Nebr Coll Bus Adminstrn PO Box 880405 Lincoln NE 68588-0405

MILLIGAN, JOHN DRANE, historian, educator; b. NYC, Oct. 11, 1924; s. Carl Glover and Hazel Gray (Drane) M.; m. Joyce Mary Jervis, Nov. 16, 1946; children: Jacqueline M., Paula J., Mary M., Elizabeth Y. BA, U. Mich., 1952, MA, 1953, PhD, 1961. Tchg. asst. U. Mich., 1951-52, tchg. fellow, 1954-56; from asst. prof. to prof. history SUNY, Buffalo, 1962-2000, dir. grad. programs in history, 1963-68, 94-95, dir. undergrad. programs in history, 1979-86, acting dept. chmn., summers, 1977, 78-80, 88, prof. emeritus, 2000. Vis. prof. McMaster U., Hamilton, Ont., Can., 1964, 69-70 Author: Gunboats Down the Mississippi, 1965, From the Fresh-Water Navy, 1861-1864, 1970; also chpts. in books, articles in jours., encys. Mem. Ann Arbor chpt. NAACP, exec. bd., 1956-61; mem. ACLU, exec. bd., 1959-61; mem. campaign coms. for various candidates for local and nat. office, 1960-76; mem. Buffalo NAACP, Buffalo Housing Opportunities Made Equal, Citizens Council on Human Relations, Physicians for Social Responsibility, Common Cause, Amnesty Internat.; faculty chmn. United Fund dr., 1977; active Foster Parents Plan, 1955-70; adoptive parent Internat. Social Services; founder charitable trust for minority coll. scholarships. Served with USAAF, 1943-46, USAFR, 1946-56. James B. Angell scholar U. Mich.; grantee Rsch. Found. SUNY, US Naval Inst.; Citation of Civil War Round Table; Moncado Award of Am. Mil. Inst. Mem.: Soc. Civil War Historians, Afro-Am. Hist. Soc., Buffalo and Erie County Hist. Soc., So. Hist. Assn., Assn. Am. Historians, Am. Hist. Assn., SUNY Buffalo Founders' Soc., Buffalo Coun. for Responsibility in Fgn. Policy, SUNY Buffalo Pres.'s Assocs., Civil War Round Table, Silver Wings Assn., Cambria Flying Soc., Niagara Soaring Club, Aircraft Owners and Pilots Assn., Soaring Soc. Am., Exptl. Aircraft Assn., Phi Alpha Theta, Phi Kappa Phi, Tau Sigma Delta. Home: 21 Allenhurst Rd Buffalo NY 14214-1201 *If an individual cannot influence for the better the course of humankind, one can sometimes influence for the better the life of another individual.*

MILLIGAN, SISTER MARY, theology studies educator, consultant; b. LA, Jan. 23, 1935; d. Bernard Joseph and Carolyn (Krebs) M. BA, Marymount Coll., 1956; Dr. de l'Univ., U. Paris, 1959; MA in Theology, St. Mary's Coll., Notre Dame, Ind., 1966; STD, Gregorian U., 1975; D. honoris causa, Marymount U., 1988. Tchr. Cours Marymount, Neuilly, France, 1956-59; asst. prof. Marymount Coll., Los Angeles, 1959-67; gen. councillor Religious of Sacred Heart of Mary, Rome, 1969-75, gen. superior, 1980-85; asst. prof. Loyola Marymount U., Los Angeles, 1977-78, provost, 1986-90, prof., 1990—96, dean liberal arts, 1992-97, provincial superior, 1997—2003; prof. St. John's Sem., 2003—. Pres. bd. dirs. St. John's Sem., Camarillo, Calif., 1986-89; mem. exec. com. Internat. Union Superiors Gen., Rome, 1983-85; mem. planning bd. spiritual renewal program Loyola Marymount U., Los Angeles, 1976-78. Author: That They May Have Life, 1975; compiler analytical index Ways of Peace, 1986; contbr. articles to profl. jours. Vis. scholar Grad. Theol. Union, Berkeley, 1986. Mem. Coll. Theology Soc., Cath. Biblical Assn. Democrat. Roman Catholic. Business E-Mail: mmilligan@stjohnsem.edu.

MILLIGAN, VICTOR, consulting engineer; b. Belfast, No. Ireland, Nov. 11, 1929; arrived in Can., 1956; s. Albert and Margaret (Walker) M.; m. Mary Ann Pelikan, July 20, 1955 (dec. 1988); children: Jeffrey, Michael; m. Audrey Morrow, Oct. 9, 1990 (dec. Oct 2003). BS, Queen's U., No. Ireland, 1951, MS, 1952, DSc (hon.), 1993; D Engring. (hon.), Waterloo U., Ont., Can., 1990. Registered profl. engr. Ont., Alta., Nfld. Asst. engr. James Williamson & Ptnrs., Glasgow, Scotland, 1952-54; rsch. fellow Purdue U., Lafayette, Ind., 1954-55; tech. officer Imperial Chem. Industries Ltd., Cheshire, England, 1955-56; from dist. to asst. chief engr. Geocon, Ltd., Toronto, Ont., Canada, 1956-60; prin. Golder Assocs., Toronto, 1960-74, pres., CEO, chmn., 1974-84, sr. prin., chmn., cons., 1984-94. Mem. faculty engring. sci. adv. com. U. Western Ont., 1973-76; adj. prof. dept. geol. engring. U. Toronto, 1980-83; pres. Consulting Engrs. Ont., 1982-83; chmn. assoc. com. on geotechnical rsch. NRC, 1984-89. Co-author: Stability in Open Pit Mining, 1971, Geotechnical Practice in Open Pit Mining, 1972; founding editor Can. Geotechnical Jour., 1963-68; contbr. over 50 sci. papers. King George VI Meml. Rsch. fellow 1954-55; recipient Engring. Excellence medal Assn. Profl. Engrs. Ont., 1988, Beaubien award Assn. Consulting Engrs. Canada Outstanding Excellence, 1997; fellow Can. Acad. Engring., 1994. Fellow ASCE, Instn. Civil Engrs. (hon.), Geol. Soc. Can., Engring. Inst. Can. (Julian C. Smith medal 1991, Sir John Kennedy medal, 2005), Royal Acad. Engring.; mem. Can. Geotech. Soc. (R.F. Legget award 1973), Internat. Soc. Soil Mechanics and Geotech. Engring.

MILLIGRAM, STEVEN IRWIN, lawyer; b. NYC, July 16, 1953; s. Harry William and Judith Edith (Soffen) M.; m. Evan L. Greenberg; children: David Michael, Brian Harry; stepchildren: Caitlin Anderson, Kyle Smith. BA, SUNY, Buffalo, 1976; JD, Pace U., 1981. Bar: N.Y. 1982, U.S. Dist. Ct. (ea. and so. dists.) N.Y. 1982, N.J. 1982, U.S. Dist. Ct. N.J. 1982, U.S. Dist. Ct. (no. dist.) N.Y. 1993, U.S. Supreme Ct. 1998. Asst. dist. atty. County of Bronx, N.Y., 1982-86; assoc. Meiselman, Farber, Packman & Eberz, Poughkeepsie, N.Y., 1986-91, Drake, Sommers, Loeb, Tarshis and Catania, P.C., Newburgh, NY, 1991—96; ptnr. Drake, Sommers, Loeb, Tarshis, Catania and Liberth PLLC, Newburgh, NY, 1996—2006, Tarshis, Catania, Liberth, Mahon & Milligram PLLC, 2006—. Founding atty. Bedford (N.Y.) Mt. Kisco Youth Ct., 1984—85; lectr. Nat. Bus. Inst., 1991—92, Practising Law Inst., 1993. Contbg. author: Trial Advocacy in New York, 1991, Civil Trial Procedures in New York, 1991, Winning the Slip and Fall Case, 1993. Mem. N.Y. State Trial Lawyers Assn., N.Y. State Bar Assn., Pace U. Alumni Assn., Orange County Bar Assn. (bd. dirs. 2000—, sec. 2004-05, v.p. 2005—, chmn. law day com.). Jewish. Home: 178 Rye Hill Rd Monroe NY 10950-3023 Office: Tarshis Catania Liberth Mahon & Milligram PLLC One Corwin Ct Newburgh NY 12550 Office Phone: 845-565-1100. Business E-Mail: smilligram@tclmm.com.

MILLIKAN, CLARK HAROLD, physician; b. Freeport, Ill., Mar. 2, 1915; s. William Clarance and Louise (Chamberlain) M.; m. Gayle Margaret Gross, May 2, 1942 (div. Apr. 1966); children: Terri, Clark William, Jeffry Brent; m. Janet T. Holmes, July 21, 1966 (div. Dec. 1987); m. Nancy Futrell, Dec. 28, 1987. Student, Parsons Jr. Coll., Kans., 1935; MD, U. Kans., 1939. Diplomate Am. Bd. Psychiatry and Neurology. Intern St. Luke's Hosp., Clev., 1939-40, asst. resident medicine, 1940-41; from resident neurology to asst. prof. neurology State U. Iowa, Iowa City, 1941-49; staff Mayo Clinic, Rochester, Minn., 1949—, cons. neurology, 1958—; dir. Mayo Center for Clin. Rsch. in Cerebrovascular Disease; prof. neurology Mayo Sch. Medicine; physician-in-chief pro tem Cleve. Clinic, 1970; prof. neurology U. Utah Sch. Medicine, Salt Lake City, 1976-87, U. Miami (Fla.) Sch. Medicine, 1987-88; scholar in residence, dept. neurology Henry Ford Hosp., Detroit, 1988-92; prof. neurology Sch. of Medicine Creighton U., Omaha, 1992-94; clin. prof. neurology Med. Coll. Ohio, Toledo, 1994-97; dir. acad. affairs Intermountain Stroke Rsch. Found., Salt Lake City, 1997—. Asst. chmn., editor trans. 2d Princeton Conf. Cerebrovascular Disease, 1957, chmn. confs., 1961, 64; chmn. com. classification and nomenclature cerebrovascular disease USPHS, 1955-69; mem. council Nat. Inst. Neurologic Diseases and Blindness, NIH, USPHS, 1961-65, div. regional med. program, 1965-68; A.O.A. lectr. Baylor U., Waco, Tex., 1952; James Mawer Pearson Meml. lectr., Vancouver, B.C., Can., 1958; Conner Meml. lectr. Am. Heart Assn., 1961; Peter T. Bohan lectr. U. Kans., 1965, 73 Editor: Jour. Stroke, 1970-76, assoc. editor, 1976—. Recipient Outstanding Alumnus award, U. Kans., 1973. Fellow ACP, Am. Acad. Neurology (founding chmn. sect. on stroke and vascular neurology 1994), Royal Soc. Medicine; mem. AMA, AAUP, AAAS, Assn. Rsch. Nervous and Mental Disease (pres. 1961), Am. Neurol. Assn. (1st v.p. 1969-70, pres. 1973-74), Minn. Med. Assn., Four County Med. Soc. South Minn., Cen. Neuropsychiat. Assn., N.Y. Acad. Sci., Am. Heart Assn. (chmn. coun. cerebrovascular disease 1967-68, Gold Heart award 1976, Spl. Merit award 1981), Nat. Stroke Assn. (pres. 1986, editor Jour. Stroke and Cerebrovascular Disease 1990—), Sigma Xi. Office Phone: 801-263-0611. Office Fax: 801-263-9141.

MILLIKAN, LARRY EDWARD, dermatologist; b. Sterling, Ill., May 12, 1936; s. Daniel Franklin and Harriet Adeline (Parmenter) M.; m. Jeanine Dorothy Johnson, Aug. 27, 1960; children: Marshall, Rebecca. BA, Monmouth Coll., 1958; MD, U. Mo., 1962. Intern Great Lakes Naval Hosp., Ill., 1962-63; housestaff in tng. U. Mich., Ann Arbor, 1967-69, chief resident, 1969-70; asst. prof. dermatology U. Mo., Columbia, 1970-74, assoc. prof., 1974-81; chmn. dept. dermatology Tulane U., New Orleans, 1981—, chair/prof. emeritus, 2006—. Cons. physician Charity Hosp., New Orleans, Tulane U. Hosp., New Orleans, Riley Hosp., Anderson Hosp., Rush Hosp., all Meridian, Miss.; mem. bd. trustees Sulzberger Inst. for Dermatological Edn., 1995-99; chmn. cont. med. edn. com. La. State Med. Soc., 1994-97. Assoc. editor Internat. Jour. Dermatology, 1980-99, Clinics in Dermatology, 1999—; mem. editl. bd. Current Concepts in Skin Disorders, Am. Jour. Med. Scis.; mem. editl. bd. Clinics in Dermatology, 1985—, assoc. editor, 1999—; contbr. articles to med. jours. Bd. dirs. Women's Dermatol. Assn., 1994-99. With USN, 1960-67. Recipient Andres Bello awrd Govt. of Venezuela, 1989, citation of merit Sch. Medicine, U. Mo., 1993, Faculty Alumnus award U. Mo., 1997; named Disting. Alumnus, Monmouth Coll., 1990; Nat. Cancer Inst. grantee, 1976-84. Fellow ACP; mem. AAAS, AMA, Am. Acad. Dermatology (bd. dirs. 1986-90), Am. Dermatol. Assn., Am. Dermatol. Soc. for Allergy and Immunology (pres., bd. dirs.), Soc. for Investigative Dermatology (past pres. South sect.), So. Med. Assn. (vice chmn. dermatology sect. 1984, chmn. 1994), Coll. Physicians Phila., Assn. Profs. Dermatology (bd. dirs. 1984-86), Orleans Parish Med. Soc., La. Med. Soc., Pan Am. Med. Assn., Internat. Soc. Dermatology (dep. sec. gen. 1989-99), Mo. Allergy Assn. (past pres.), Am. Coll. Cryosurgery, Assn. Acad. Dermatol. Surgeons, Internat. Soc. Dermatol. Surgery, Internat. Acad. Cosmetic Dermatology (sec. gen. 1996-), Dermatol. Found. Leaders Soc. (state chmn. 1993-97). Office: Tulane Univ Sch Medicine Dept of Dermatology 1430 Tulane Ave TB36 New Orleans LA 70112-2699

MILLIKEN, DOUGLAS GORDON, financial consultant, municipal official; b. Denver, June 13, 1957; s. J. Gordon and Marie (Machell) M. M in Acctg. and Fin. Mgmt., U. Denver, 1980; M in Taxation, U. Denver Law Sch., 2005. CPA, 1980. Ind. fin. cons., Centennial, Colo., 1990—. Mem. fin., acctg., intergovtl. rels. com. Nat. League Cities, 2002—; elected. treas. City of Centennial, 2001. Bd. mem., Colo. Legal Initiatives Project, Denver, 1993-96. Mem. Colo. Soc. CPAs, Rocky Mountain Wrestling Club (founding mem. 1994). Avocation: amateur wrestling. Home: 5315 S Nepal Way Centennial CO 80015-2143 Office: City of Centennial Ste 200 12503 E Euclid Dr Centennial CO 80111-6400 E-mail: doug@dougmilliken.com.

MILLIKEN, JOHN GORDON, research economist; b. Denver, May 12, 1927; s. William Boyd and Margaret Irene (Marsh) M.; m. Marie Violet Machell, June 13, 1953 (dec. 2004); children: Karen Marie, Douglas Gordon, David Tait, Anne Alain. BS, Yale U., 1949, BEng, 1950; MS, U. Colo., 1966, PhD, 1969. Registered profl. engr., Colo. Engr. U.S. Bur. Reclamation, Denver, 1950-55; asst. to plant mgr. Stanley Aviation Corp., Denver, 1955-56; prin. mgmt. engr., dept. mgr. Martin-Marietta Aerospace Divsn., Denver, 1956-64; mgmt. engr. Safeway Stores, Inc., Denver, 1964-66; sr. rsch. economist, prof., assoc. div. head U. Denver Rsch. Inst., 1966-86; pres. Univ. Senate, 1980-81; prin. Milliken Chapman Rsch. Group, Inc., Littleton, Colo., 1986-88, Milliken Rsch. Group, Inc., Littleton, 1988—. Vis. fellow sci. policy rsch. unit U. Sussex, Eng., 1975-76; cons. mgmt. engr. Author: Aerospace Management Techniques, 1971, Federal Incentives for Innovation, 1974, Recycling Municipal Wastewater, 1977, Water and Energy in Colorado's Future, 1981, Metropolitan Water Management, 1981, Technological Innovation and Economic Vitality, 1983, Water Management in the Denver, Colorado Urban Area, 1988, Benefits and Costs of Oxygenated Fuels in Colorado, 1990, Water Transfer Alternatives Study, 1994, Colorado Springs Water Resources Plan Alternative Assessment Study, 1995, Colorado Springs Utilities Wastewater Infrastructure Alternatives Study, 1998; contbr. articles to profl. jours. Bd. dirs. S.E. Englewood Water Dist., 1963—, South Englewood San. Dist., 1965—; bd. dirs. South Suburban Pk. and Recreation Dist., 1971-96, chmn., 1990-92; v.p. South Suburban Land and Facilities Corp., 2001—; chmn. Dem. Com. of Arapahoe County, 1969-71, 5th Congl. Dist. Colo., 1972-73, 74-75; mem. exec. com. Colo. Faculty Adv. Coun., 1981-85; mem. Garrison Diversion Unit Commn., 1984; trustee Colo. Local Govt. Liquid Asset Trust, 1986-2005, chmn., 1991-93; bd. dirs. Colo. Spl. Dist. Assn. Property and Liability Pool, 1989-2006, pres. 1997-98. With M.C., U.S. Army, 1945-46. Decorated WWII Vietnam medal; recipient Adlai E. Stevenson Meml. award, 1981, cert. of Appreciation for svc. to Nation, U.S. Sec. Interior, 1984, hon. title "Amicus Universitatis," U. Denver, 1994, Disting. Svc. award Spl. Dist. Assn. Colo., 1995; Milliken Park named in his honor for svcs. to Littleton/Centennial Cmty., 1996. Mem. Acad. Mgmt., Nat. Assn. Bus. Economists, Yale Sci. and Engring. Assn., Am. Water Works Assn., Sigma Xi, Tau Beta Pi, Beta Gamma Sigma, Sigma Iota Epsilon. Congregationalist. Home and Office: 6502 S Ogden St Centennial CO 80121-2561 Personal E-mail: jgordonmil@aol.com.

MILLIKEN, MARY SUE, chef, television personality, writer; Former mem. staff Le Perroquet, Chgo., Restaurant d'Olympe, Paris; formerly chef, co-owner City Cafe, LA; chef, co-owner CITY, LA, 1985—94, Border Grill, LA, 1985—91, Santa Monica, 1990—, Las Vegas, 1999—, Ciudad, LA, 1998—. Co-host (TV series) Too Hot Tamales, 1995—, Tamales' World Tour, (radio show) Good Food; co-author: City Cuisine, 1989, Mesa Mexicana, 1994, Cantina, 1996, Cooking with Too Hot Tamales, 1997, Mexican Cooking for Dummies; guest appearances (TV series) Oprah Winfrey Show, Maury Povich, Today Show, Sabrina the Teenage Witch, featured in USA Today, People Mag., Entertainment Weekly. Active Scleroderma Rsch. Found. Named Chef of Yr., Calif. Restaurant Writers, 1993. Mem.: Chef's Collaborative 2000, Women Chefs and Restaurateurs. Office: Border Grill 1445 4th St Santa Monica CA 90401 *

MILLIKEN, ROGER, textile/chemical company executive; b. NYC, Oct. 24, 1915; s. Gerrish and Agnes (Gayley); m. Justine V. R. Hooper, June 5, 1948 (dec.); children: Justine, Nancy, Roger, David, Weston. AB, Yale U., New Haven, Conn., 1937; LLD (hon.), Wofford Coll., Spartanburg, SC, Rose-Hulman Inst. Tech., Terre Haute, Ind., Phila. Coll. Textiles and Sci., Brenau U., Gainsville, Ga., The Citadel, Charleston, SC; D. Textile Industry (hon.), Clemson U., SC; DHL (hon.), Converse Coll., Spartanburg; D. Bus. Adminstrn. (hon.), U. SC, Spartanburg; LLD (hon.), LaGrange Coll., Ga., Furman U., Greenville, SC; HHD (hon.), Presbyn. Coll., Clinton, SC. Bd. dirs. Milliken & Co. (formerly Deering Milliken), Spartanburg, SC, 1941—, pres., 1947-83, chmn., CEO, 1983—2005, chmn., 2006—. Chmn. bd. Inst. Textile Tech., 1948—97, chmn. emeritus, 1997—; bd. dirs. S.C. Textile Mfrs. Assn. Chmn. Greenville-Spartanburg Airport Commn.; trustee Wofford Coll., SC. Named Businessman of Yr., SC C. of C., 1981, Citizen of the Carolinas, NC C. of C., 1991, Leader of the Century, Textile World Mag., 1999; named to SC Bus. Hall of Fame, 1985, SC Hall of Fame, 1998, Nat. Bus. Hall of Fame, 2000; recipient Neville Holcombe Disting. Citizenship Award, Spartanburg Area C. of C., 1985, Lifetime Achievement Award, No. Textile Assn., 1999, Buck Mickel Leadership award, Greenville C. of C., 2006. Mem.: AIA (hon.), Am. Soc. Landscape Architects (hon.), Garden Club Am. (mem.-at-large), Yeamans Hall, Augusta Nat. Golf Club, Links, Union League. Office: Milliken & Co PO Box 3167 Spartanburg SC 29304

MILLIMET, ERWIN, lawyer; b. NYC, Oct. 7, 1925; s. Maurice and Henrietta (Cohen) Millimet; children: Robert, James, Rachel, Sarah. BA magna cum laude, Amherst Coll., 1948; LLB cum laude, Harvard U., 1951. Bar: NY 1952. Formerly sr. ptnr., chmn. exec. com. Stroock & Stroock & Lavan, NYC; ret., 1991. Mem. faculty Grad. Sch. Mgmt., U. Mass. Mem. bd. visitors U. San Diego Law Sch.; mem. Five Coll. LIR (learning in retirement), Northhampton, Mass.; active Nat. Support Group for Africa; founder Citizens for Am., Washington, 1984; mem. Rep. Presdl. Task Force, 1948. Fellow, Amhurst Coll., Boston Globe. Mem. NY State Bar Assn., Assn. of Bar of City of NY, Fed. Bar Assn., Rep. Club (NYC and Washington), Phi Beta Kappa. E-mail: emill@gis.net.

MILLIN, LAURA JEANNE, museum director; b. Elgin, Ill., June 11, 1954; d. Douglas Joseph and Patricia Ruth (Feragen) M. BA in Interdisciplinary Studies, The Evergreen State Coll., 1978. Dir. On The Boards, Seattle, 1979; art dir. City Fair Metrocenter YMCA, Seattle, 1980; dir. Ctr. on Contemporary Art, Seattle, 1981; co-owner Art in Form Bookstore, Seattle, 1981-89; co-dir. 3d internat festival of films by women dirs. Seattle Art Mus. & 911 Contemporary Arts, 1988; auction coord. Allied Arts of Seattle, 1989; dir. Missoula (Mont.) Mus. of the Arts, 1990—. Dir. Visual AIDS Missoula Mus. of the Arts, 1989; curator Radio COCA, Ctr. on Contemproary Art, Seattle, 1986, co-curator, 1981, 83; lectr. in field. Co-editor: Another (ind. feminist newspaper), Seattle, 1989, editor: (exhibition catalog) James Turrell: Four Light Installations, 1981. Bd. dirs. Internat. Festival of Films by Women Dirs., Seattle, 1987, 89, Nine One One Contemporary Arts Ctr., Seattle, 1981-87, bd. chmn. 1981-85; bd. advisors REFLEX (art mag.), Seattle, 1988-89, Ctr. on Contemporary Art, Seattle, 1983-86; state vis. Mont. Arts. Coun., Missoula, 1991, NEA, Mpls., 1988, Chgo., 1987;; panelist Mont. Arts Coun., Helena, 1990; cons. Seattle Arts Commn., 1989, juror, 1985. Home: 1721 S 9th St W Missoula MT 59801-3432

MILLING, BERT WILLIAM, JR., judge; b. Mobile, Ala., Mar. 5, 1946; s. Bert William and Marjorie Ann (Smith) M.; m. Priscilla Pitman, Apr. 15, 1966; children: Brooks Pitman, Jesery Bacon, Maran Celeste. AB in Philosophy, The Coll. of William and Mary, 1968; JD, U. Ala., 1971. Bar: Ala. 1971. Legal officer 212th Arty. Group, Fort Lewis, Wash., 1971-72; legal asst. officer Judge Advocate Gen.'s Office, Ft. Sill, Okla., 1972-74; spl. asst. atty. gen. Dist. Atty.'s Office, Mobile, 1974-75, asst. dist. atty., 1977-78; assoc. Sintz, Pike, Campbell & Duke, Mobile, 1975-77; ct. referee Juvenile Div. of Cir. Ct., Mobile, 1978-81; counsel U.S. Senate Com. on Jud., Subcom. on Security & Terrorism, Washington, 1981-83; asst. U.S. atty. Justice Dept., Mobile, 1983-86; U.S. magistrate judge U. S. Dist. Ct. So. Dist. Ala., Mobile, 1986—. Mem. Adminstrv. Office U.S. Cts.; mem. adv. group Magistrate Judges and Tech. Facilities Adv. Coun., 2005—. Capt. U.S. Army, 1971-74; maj. N.G., USAR, 1975-87. Mem. Ala. Bar Assn., Mobile Bar Assn., Fed. Magistrate Judges Assn. (budget and fin. com. 2005-07), Christian Legal Soc. Anglican. Avocations: photography, music, reading, exercising. Office: US Courthouse 113 Saint Joseph St Mobile AL 36602-3606

MILLING, R(OSWELL) KING, bank executive, lawyer; b. New Orleans, Aug. 7, 1940; s. Robert E. and Claudia (Pipes) M.; m. Anne McDonald, June 20, 1964; children— Roberts Clay II, Roswell King Jr., Michael Delery BA, Washington and Lee U., 1962; LLB, Tulane U., 1965. Bar: La. 1965, U.S. Dist. Ct. (ea. dist.) La. 1965, U.S. Ct. Appeals (5th cir.) 1965, U.S. Sup. Ct. 1979, U.S. Ct. Appeals (11th cir.) 1981. Assoc. Milling, Saal, Saunders, Benson & Woodward (now Milling Benson Woodward LLP), New Orleans, 1965-69, ptnr., 1969-84; pres. Whitney Nat. Bank, New Orleans, 1984—, also bd. dirs.; pres. Whitney Holding Corp., New Orleans. Past pres. Bur. Govtl. Rsch., New Orleans, Downtown Devel. Dist.; mem. Met. Area Com., La. Civil Svc. League; past chmn. Upper Pontalba Bldg. Commn.; trustee Dillard U.; bd. dirs. L.A. Civil Svc. League, New Orleans Ctr. for Creative Arts; chmn. Gov.'s Adv. Commn. on Coastal Restoration and Conservation. Mem. La. State Bar Assn., New Orleans Bar Assn., ABA. Office: Whitney Nat Bank 228 Saint Charles Ave Ste 228 New Orleans LA 70130-2628

MILLIS, ROBERT LOWELL, astronomer, science observatory director; b. Martinsville, Ill., Sept. 12, 1941; m. Julia Drean, 1965; children: David, Daniel. BA, Ea. Ill. U., 1963; PhD in Astronomy, U. Wis., 1968. Staff astronomer Lowell Obs., Flagstaff, Ariz., 1967—86, assoc. dir., 1986—90, acting dir., 1989—90, dir., 1990—. Bd. dir. Mus. of No. Ariz., United Way of No. Ariz. Mem. Am. Astron. Soc., Internat. Astronomy Union, Divsn. Planetary Sci. (sec.-treas. 1985-88, chmn. 1994-95). Achievements include discovery of the Rings of Uranus (with J.L. Elliot); research in planetary satellites and ring systems; the occultation studies of solar system objects; comet and Kuiper belt objects. Office: Lowell Observatory 1400 W Mars Hill Rd Flagstaff AZ 86001-4499 Business E-Mail: rim@lowell.edu.

MILLIS-HORTON, CYNTHIA MARIE, art educator; d. Orson Everett Millis and Kareen Lillian Nelson Millis; m. Richard Doyle Horton, Jan. 12, 1981. MusB in Edn., Yankton Coll. Conservatory Music, SD, 1971; A in Applied Sci.-Comm. Art/Media Prodn., Houston C.C., 1985; MLA in Art History, U. St. Thomas, Houston, 1991; postgrad., Tex. Tech U., Junction, 1996—2007. Asst. chair for art, prof., fine arts & speech dept. Houston C.C. Southwest, Stafford, Tex., 1983—. Presenter Cancer Counseling Houston, 2003—07. Grantee Reading Popular Cartography grant, NEH, 2004. Mem.: Women's Caucus Art (pres.-elect 2000—02). D-Liberal. Avocations: art, travel. Office: Houston Cmty Coll SW 9910 Cash Rd Stafford TX 77477 Office Phone: 713-718-6913. Business E-Mail: cynthia.millis@hccs.edu.

MILLISOR, KENNETH RAY, lawyer; b. Belle Center, Ohio, Jan. 31, 1937; s. Darrel R. and Clara Sue (Miller) M.; m. Annette M. Seifert Ross, June 7, 1985. BA, Ohio Wesleyan U., 1959; JD, Ohio State U., 1960. Bar: Ohio 1960, U.S. Dist. Ct. (no. dist.) Ohio, 1965, U.S. Ct. Appeals (6th cir.) 1965, U.S. Ct. Appeals (D.C. cir.) 1975, U.S. Supreme Ct. 1970. Ptnr. Poetzel & Andress, Akron, Ohio, 1960-74, Millisor & Nobil, Akron and Cleve., 1975—. Past v.p. Akron Area coun. Boy Scouts Am.; active United Way. Mem. ABA, Ohio Bar Assn., Cleve. Bar Assn., Order of Coif, Shoreby Club (pres. 2000-03). Democrat. Home: 864 Beach Rd Lakewood OH 44107 Office: Millisor & Nobil Co 9150 S Hills Blvd Ste 300 Cleveland OH 44147-3599 Home Phone: 216-226-4868; Office Phone: 440-838-8800. E-mail: KMillisor@millisor.com.

MILLMAN, BRUCE RUSSELL, lawyer; b. Bronx, NY, June 4, 1948; s. Meyer and Garie (Solomon) M.; m. Lorrie Jan Liss, Aug. 12, 1973; children: Noemi, Avi. AB, Princeton U., 1970; JD, Columbia U., 1973. Bar: N.Y. 1974, U.S. Dist. Ct. (ea. and so. dists.) N.Y. 1975, U.S. Ct. Appeals (2d dir.) 1978, U.S. Supreme Ct. 1978. Assoc. Rains & Pogrebin and predecessors, Mineola, NY, 1973-79, ptnr., 1980—2004; prin. Grotta, Glassman & Hoffman, P.A., NYC, 2004—. Arbitrator Nassau County Dist. Ct., Mineola, 1981-83. Contbr. New York Employment Law, 1995, Labor and Employment Law for the Corporate Counselor and General Practitioner, 1994, Updating Issues in Employment Law, 1986, Public Sector Labor and Employment Law, 1988. Bd. dirs. West Side Montessori Sch., N.Y.C., 1984-90, sec., 1985-87, pres., 1987-90. Harlan Fiske Stone scholar Columbia U. Law Sch., N.Y.C., 1971, 73. Mem. ABA, N.Y. State Bar Assn. (chair labor and employment law sect. 1997-98), Nassau County Bar Assn., Indsl. Rels. Rsch. Assn. (bd. dirs. L.I. chpt. 1984—, pres. 1995-96). Home: 60 Riverside Dr New York NY 10024-6108 Office: 532 Broadhollow Rd Melville NY 11747 also: Littler Mendelson PC 885 Third Ave 16th Fl New York NY 10022-4834 Home Phone: 212-595-9444; Office Phone: 212-283-2677. Business E-Mail: bmillman@littler.com.

MILLMAN, JODE SUSAN, lawyer, writer; b. Poughkeepsie, NY, Dec. 28, 1954; d. Samuel Keith and Ellin Sadenberg (Bainder) M.; m. Michael James Harris, June 20, 1982; children: Maxwell, Benjamin. BA, Syracuse U., 1976, JD, 1979; MA, Ea. Mich. U., 2005. Bar: N.Y. 1980, Mich. 2001, U.S. Dist. Ct. (so. and ea. dists.) N.Y. 1982, U.S. Supreme Ct. 1983. Asst. corp. counsel City of Poughkeepsie, 1979-81; assoc. Law Office of Lou Lewis, Poughkeepsie, 1981-85; pvt. practice Poughkeepsie, 1985—; pres. Seats Pub. Co., 2001—. Staff counsel City of Poughkeepsie Office of Property Devel., 1990—; gen. mgr. WCZX-Comms. Corp.; adj. prof. U. Detroit Mercy Law Sch., 2005—, Manst Coll., 2006—. Author: (novels) (children's books) Birthday Wishes and Rock'n Roll Dreams, The Firebird Ballet, Goldie Lox and the Three Behrs, (non-fiction) SEATS: New York (150 Seating Plans to Metro N.Y. Theatres, Concert Halls and Stadiums), SEATS: Chicago (125 Seating Plans to Metro Chgo./Millw. Theatres, Concert Halls and Sports Stadiums); contbg. author: Kaminstein Legislative History of the Copyright Law, 1979. Pres. Dutchess County (N.Y.) Vis. Bur., 1980—82; mem. assigned counsel program Dutchess County Family Ct.1985, 1985—; trustee Greater Poughkeepsie Libr. Dist., 1991—94, Poughkeepsie Day Sch., 1995—2002; chmn. Millman, Harris, Romano Found., Inc., 2001—; bd. dirs. Poughkeepsie Ballet Theater, 1982, Jewish Cmty. Ctr., 1988. Mem.: Washtenaw County Bar Assn., Mich. Bar Assn., Dutchess County Bar Assn. (grievance com. 1994—2001), N.Y. State Bar Assn. Democrat. Jewish. Home: 10 Circular Rd Poughkeepsie NY 12601 Office: 97-99 Cannon St Poughkeepsie NY 12601 Personal E-mail: jodem54@aol.com.

MILLMAN, LAURA DIANE, federal official; b. NYC, Apr. 23, 1946; BA cum laude, City Coll., 1966; MA, Lehman Coll., 1969; JD cum laude, Fordham U., 1976. Bar: NY 1977, DC 1978, Md. 1987. Honors prog. trial atty. US Dept. Justice, NYC, Washington, 1976-88; ptnr. West & Galebach, Gaithersburg, Md., 1988-91; spl. master US Ct. Fed. Claims, Washington, 1991—. Avocations: synchronized swimming, walking. Office: Office Spl Master US Ct Fed Claims 717 Madison Pl NW Washington DC 20005

MILLMAN, RICHARD GEORGE, architect, educator; b. St. Johns, Mich., Feb. 12, 1925; s. Harold Fildew and Elizabeth Hill (Van Deusen) M.; m. Mary Louise Manley, June 17, 1950; childen: John Richard, Ruth Barbara. BArch, U. Mich., 1951, MArch, 1962. Registered arch., Mich., Ohio, Ala. Job capt. Smith Hinchman & Grylls, Detroit, 1951-52; designer assoc. Eliot Robinson, AIA, Birmingham, Mich., 1952-55; designer Eero Saarinen Assocs., Bloomfield Hills, Mich., 1955-56; assoc. Chas. W. Lane Assocs. Inc., Ann Arbor, Mich., 1956-59; prin. Kainlauri, MacMullan, Millman, Ann Arbor, 1959-62; assoc. prof. Ohio U., Athens, 1962-68; prof. Auburn (Ala.) U., 1968—, head architecture dept., 1968-73, 84-85, head indsl. design dept., 1988-89. Prof. Mid. East Tech. U., Ankara, Turkey, 1966-67, King Faisal U., Dammam, Saudi Arabia, 1979-81. One man shows include Dhahran Art Group, Saudi Arabia, 1981, Peet Gallery, Auburn U., 1983, 91, Heritage Hall Mus., Talladega, Ala., 1998; author: Washtenaw Community College, 1962, Auburn U. Tour Guide, 1990. With U.S. Army, 1943-46, ETO, PTO. Decorated Bronze Star; recipient Cert. of Honor Ala. Hist. Commn., 1977; Alumni scholar U. Mich., 1961; Fulbright lectr. Exch. Com., Mid. East Tech. U., 1966. Mem. AIA (treas. Ala. coun. 1969, v.p. 1970, pres. 1972, emeritus 1990, Auburn chpt. pres. 1970, emeritus), Nat. Coun. Archtl. Registration Bd. (cert.), Auburn Arts Assn., Ga. Watercolor Soc. (signature mem.), Watercolor Soc. Ala. (signature mem.; pres. 2003), So. Watercolor Soc. (signature mem.). Avocations: painting, photography. Home: 736 Brenda Ave Auburn AL 36830-6038 Office Phone: 334-887-6428. E-mail: millmmm@charter.net.

MILLNER, F. ANN, academic administrator; BS, Univ. Tenn.; MS, Southwest Tex. State Univ.; EdD, Brigham Young Univ. Assoc. dean, asst. v.p., dir. outreach edn. Weber State Univ., Ogden, Utah, 1982—93, v.p. univ. rels., 1993—2002, pres., 2002—. Trustee Intermountain Health Care; past pres. Ogden/Weber C. of C. Recipient Athena award, Ogden/Weber C. of C. Mem.: Am. Assn. State Colleges and Universities (mem. Coun. State Representatives), Phi Kappa Phi. Office: Weber State Univ President's Office 3850 University Circle Ogden UT 84408 *

MILLOY, FRANK JOSEPH, JR., surgeon; b. Phoenix, June 26, 1924; s. Frank Joseph and Ola (McCabe) M. BS, Notre Dame U., 1946; MS, Northwestern U., 1949, MD, 1948. Diplomate Am. Bd. Surgery and Thoracic Surgery. Intern Cook County Hosp., Chgo., 1947-49, resident, 1953-57; practice medicine, specializing in surgery Lake Forest, Ill., 1958—. Hon. attending staff Presbyn.-St. Lukes Hosp.; former mem. attending staff Cook County Hosp.; mem. staff U. Ill. Rsch. Hosp.; clin. assoc. prof. surgery, U. Ill. Med. Sch.; assoc. prof. surgery Rush Med. Sch. Contbr. articles to profl. jours., chapters to books. Cons. West Side Vet. Hosp. Served as apprentice seaman USNR, 1943-45; lt. M.C., USNR, 1950-52; PTO. Mem.: ACS, Soc. Med. History Chgo. (pres.), Cook County Hosp. Surg. Alumni Assn., Karl Meyer Surg. Soc. (sec.), Warren Cole Surg. Soc. (past sec.), Ill. Thoracic Surg. Soc. (past pres.), Soc. Thoracic Surgeons, Am. Coll. Chest Physicians, Internat. Soc. Surgery, Chgo. Surg. Soc., Univ. Club (Chgo.), Met. Club, Knights of Malta, Phi Beta Pi. Home: 574 Jackson Ave Glencoe IL 60022-2036

MILLS, BARRY, academic administrator, lawyer; b. Providence, Sept. 8, 1950; m. Karen Gordon Mills. BA in Biochemistry and Govt. cum laude, Bowdoin, 1972; PhD, Syracuse U., 1976; JD, Columbia U., 1979. Bar: N.Y. 1980. Mem. Debevoise & Plimpton, NYC, 1979—86, ptnr., 1986—2001; pres. Bowdoin Coll., Brunswick, Maine, 2001—. Bd. trustees Bowdoin Coll., Brunswick, Maine, 1994—2000. Harlan Fiske Stone scholar, Columbia Law Sch., 1979. Mem. Assn. of Bar of City of N.Y. Office: Bowdoin Coll Hawthorne-Longfellow Hall 5700 College Station Brunswick ME 04011-8448 Office Phone: 207-725-3221. *

MILLS, BELEN COLLANTES, early childhood education educator; b. Philippines; d. Ricardo and Epifania (Tomines) C.; children: Belinda Mills Keiser, Roger A. BSE, Leyte Normal Coll., Tacloban, Leyte, Philippines, 1954; MS in Edn., Ind. U., 1955, EdD, 1967. Asst. prof. Fla. State U., Tallahassee, 1968—74, assoc. prof., 1974—89, prof. early childhood edn., 1989—98, prof. emerita, 1998—. Author books on early childhood edn., phonics-based children's books and acad. readiness computer programs; contbr. articles to profl.jours. Smith-Mundt Fulbright scholar. Mem. Nat. Assn. for Edn. of Young Children, Nat. Assn. Early Childhood Tchr. Edn., World Coun. for Curriculum and Instrn., Assn. Childhood Edn. Internat. Home: PO Box 20023 Tallahassee FL 32316-0023 Office Phone: 850-576-2251.

MILLS, BOB, member of Canadian parliament; b. Young, Sask., Can. m. Nicole Mills; children: Ken, Kari Anne, Melinda, Rosanno, Ric, Amanda. BA in Sci. and Edn., U. Sask. Tchr. biology Lindsay Thurber Comprehensive H.S., 1965-79; founder Mills Travel, Ltd., 1979—; elected to House of Commons, Red Deer, Alta., Canada, 1993—. Parliamentary activities include mem. steering com. on fgn. affairs and internat. trade, Ofcl. Opposition Fgn. Affairs Critic, Opposition Health Critic, 2000—, mem. standing com. on health, chief environ. critic. gen., 2001-06. Mem. Am. Express Network (recipient Travel Hall of Fame award 1992). Avocations: farming, gardening, photography, travel. Office: 534-N Centre Ottawa ON Canada K1A 0A6 Office Phone: 613-995-0590. Business E-Mail: millsb@parl.gc.ca.

MILLS, BRAD, computer technician; b. Beckley, W.Va., Apr. 4, 1971; s. Wallace and Cheryl Mills; m. Martha Lynn Keaton, Jan. 15, 1994; children: Katherine Elaine, Andrew Archer. BS, W.Va. Tech., Montgomery, 1994. Systems integrator IBM, Research Triangle Park, NC, 1995—98; technician Siemens, Berlin, 1998—2007; info. tech. specialist Mountaineer Gas Co., Charleston, W.Va., 2007—. Webmaster Nat. Scrabble Assoc. Club 620, Charleston, W.Va., 2005—, Nat. Scrabble Assoc. Club 352, Pitts., 2007—. Contbr. comedy troupe. Mem.: Am. Mensa Ltd., Nat. Scrabble Assn. (dir. local club, tournament 2005—), Pi Kappa Phi. Home: 3607 Naylor Dr Charleston WV 25302 Home Phone: 304-345-0484.

MILLS, BRADFORD, merchant banker; b. NYC, Dec. 16, 1926; s. Dudley Holbrook and Louise (Morris) M.; m. Cheryl Ann Di Paolo; children: Elizabeth Lee, Bradford Alan, Barbara Louise, Ross Dudley. BA cum laude in Econs, Princeton U., 1948; postgrad., Oxford U., Eng., 1950-51. Asst. to dir. overseas pers. divsn. ECA, Paris, 1948-50; assoc. corp. fin. dept. F. Eberstadt & Co., NYC, 1954-62, ptnr., 1960-62; mng. ptnr. N.Y. Securities Co., 1962-70; chmn., dir. Specialized Svcs., Inc., Atlanta, 1968-85; pres., CEO Overseas Pvt. Investment Corp., Washington, 1971-73, dir., 1971-75; chmn. bd., dir. F. Eberstadt & Co. Internat., 1973-74; mng. ptnr. Bradford Assocs., 1974-92; ltd. ptnr. Bradford Investment Ptnrs. Ltd., 1992-96. Past chmn. Diamond Glass, MMX Corp., HWC Corp., Chgo. Stock Tab Corp., O.S. Kelly Co., Filtration Scis., Overseas Pvt. Investors Ltd., Overseas Pvt. Equities, Overseas Equity Investors, Inc., Specialized Svcs., Inc., U.S. Precision Glass, Inc., Amwell Valley Conservancy, Bradford Ventures, Stonecare Internat.; chmn. Bradford Investment Group, HDMR Discovery Inc., Wordsmith Media Ventures LLC; bd. dirs. The Princeton Packet, Pulsed Instruments, TF Instruments, Inc. Pres. Mills Found.; trustee, vice chmn. Millbrook Sch., NY, 1978-05; sec., trustee, mem. exec. fin., investment and strategic planning coms., 1995-, Princeton Healthcare Sys.; trustee SAVE/Friends of Homeless Animals, 2006-. Mem. Coun. Fgn. Rels., Blooming Grove Club (Pa.), Links Club, Leash Club, Anglers Club N.Y., Nassau Club (trustee 1998-04), Bedens Brook Club, Amwell Valley Conservancy, Inc., Amwell Conservancy Found. (chmn.), TPC at Jasna Polona. Office: 2ND FL 92 Nassau St Princeton NJ 08542-4519 Office Phone: 609-921-3880. Personal E-mail: patchesteddy@msn.com.

MILLS, CHARLES N., healthcare supplies and products company executive; b. Sept. 30, 1961; BS, MBA, Cornell U. With IBM; then joined Medline Industries, Mundelein, Ill., 1986, pres. textile divsn., 1991—97, CEO, 1997—.

MILLS, CHRISTOPHER JAMES, neurophysiologist, electroneurodiagnostic technologist; b. Ontario, Calif., Mar. 15, 1975; s. James Shultz Mills and Patricia Ann Patterson-Foged. BS in Biology, Calif. State U., San Marcos, 1998; ScD, Buxton Coll. Pub. Health, Vancouver, B.C., Can., 2004. Cert. clin. neurophysiologist Am. Coll. Surg. Neurophysiologists. Rsch. assoc. Oreg. Health and Sci. U., Portland, 2000—03, polysomnography technologist, 2001—04; neurophysiologist VSL Neuro Labs, Palm Beach Gardens, Fla., 2005—. Bd. dirs. Physicians Health Orgn., Miami. Fund raiser Physicians Health Orgn., Miami, 2004—. Fellow: Am. Coll. Neurophysiologists; mem.: Am. Soc. Neurophysiol. Monitoring, Am. Soc. Electroneurodiagnostic Technologists (licentiate). Liberal. Achievements include research in neurophysiological function during acute osmotic stimulation; role of vasopressin in regulation of blood pressure and oxytocin release. Avocations: golf, private pilot, travel, painting. Office: Neurosurg Diagnostics PA 3355 Burns Rd Ste 200 Palm Beach Gardens FL 33410 Home: 406 Victory Circle Boynton Beach FL 33436 also: 1015 S K St Lake Worth FL 33460 Business E-Mail: millscj@neuroiom.net. E-mail: cmills@neurosed.us.

MILLS, CORINNE C., music educator; d. William P. and Cynthia L. Channon; children: Kristen Danielle, Pamela Dawn. MusB, Hartt Sch., West Hartford, Conn., 1977; MS in Ednl. Leadership, Ctrl. Conn. State U., 2005. Cert. Conn. Dept. Edn., adminstrn. cert. Conn. State U., 2007. Traffic coord. Fafair Bearing Co., New Britain, Conn., 1980—82; cello tchr. U. Conn. Cmty. Sch. Arts, Storrs, 1990—93; music tchr. Hartford (Conn.) Pub. Sch., 1995—2001, dist. music coach, 2001—; cello tchr., ensemble coach Hartford Conservatory, 1992—2000. Tchr., coach, dir. summer program Hartford Conservatory, Conn., 1992—2000. Musician (asst. prin. cellist): Ea. Conn. Symphony Orch., 1982—; musician: (cellist) Chevrolet Music Theater, 1991—, Andrea Bocelli Am. Tour, 2001—; co-author: Teaching Music in the Urban Classroom: A Guide to Survival, Success and Reform, 2006. Bd. trustees Hartford Conservatory, 2007—. Mem.: Music Educators Nat. Conf., Am. Orff Schulwerk Assn., Am. Fedn. Tchrs., Am. Fedn. Musicians, Alpha Chi. Democrat. Avocation: gardening. Office: Hartford Pub Sch 960 Main St Hartford CT 06103 Personal E-mail: corrinnemills@sbcglobal.net. Business E-Mail: millcoo1@hartfordschools.org.

MILLS, DALE DOUGLAS, journalist; b. Seattle, Oct. 4, 1930; d. Donald Emery and Antoinette (Kinleyside) Douglas; m. William Russell Mills, Aug. 13, 1955; children: Lida Susan, William Tad Jr., Peter Donald, Jane Douglas. BA, U. Wash., Seattle, 1952. Reporter Seattle Times, 1954-55, 74-83; asst. libr. Harvard U., 1955-56; editor Puget Soundings mag., 1968-71. Author: Deliver Us From Squid Roe, 1995. Mem. com. sign control Seattle City Coun., 1970-72; rsch. dir. City Coun. campaign; bd. mgrs. King County Juvenile Ct.; trustee Allied Arts Seattle; bd. dirs. King County Coun. for Prevention of Child Abuse and Neglect. Recipient awards for excellence in journalism Wash. Press Assn., Nat. Fedn. Press Women, Allied Daily Newspapers, C.B. Blethen Meml. award for disting. investigative reporting, Excellence award Soc. Profl. Journalists/Sigma Delta Chi; named Disting. Alumnus Lakeside-St. Nicholas Sch., 1984. Mem.: Jr. League Seattle, Helen T. Bush Children's Hosp Guild, Earthjustice, Sunset Club, Seattle Yacht Club, Kappa Kappa Gamma. E-mail: ddmills@comcast.net.

MILLS, DANIEL QUINN, business educator, consultant, author; b. Houston, Nov. 24, 1941; s. Daniel Monroe and Louise (Quinn) M.; children: Lisa Ann, Leandra, Shirley Elizabeth, Eliza Day, Sargent; m. Elizabeth Moore. BA, Ohio Wesleyan U., 1963; MA, Harvard U., 1965, PhD, 1968. Prof. MIT, Cambridge, 1968-75, Harvard Bus. Sch., Boston, 1976—. Impartial umpire Plan to Settle Disputes in Constrn., 1973-79, Trans-Alaska Pipeline, 1975-78, AFL-CIO Internal Disputes Plan, 1975-82; commr. Nat. Commn. on Employment Policy, Washington, 1982-86. Author: Industrial Relations in Construction, 1971, Labor, Government and Inflation, 1975, Labor-Management Relations, 1978, 5th edit., 1993, The New Competitors, 1985, Not Like Our Parents: The Baby-Boom Generation, 1987, The IBM Lesson, 1988, The Rebirth of the Corporation, 1990, The GEM Principle, 1994, Broken Promises: What Went Wrong at IBM, 1996, e-Leadership, 2000, Buy, Lie and Sell High: How Investors Lost Out on Enron and The Internet Bubble, 2002, Wheel, Deal and Steal: Deceptive Accounting, Deceitful CEO's and Ineffective Reforms, 2003, Having It All, 2004, How to Lead-How to Live, 2005, Principles of Management, 2005, Masters of Illusion, 2006. Mem. Am. Econ. Assn., Indsl. Rels. Rsch. Assn., Phi Beta Kappa Office: Harvard U Harvard Bus Sch Soldiers Field Rd Allston MA 02163 Office Phone: 617-495-6206. Business E-Mail: dmills@hbs.edu.

MILLS, DAVID HARLOW, psychologist, professional society administrator; b. Marshalltown, Iowa, Dec. 26, 1932; s. Harlow Burgess and Esther Winifred (Brewer) M.; m. Janet Louise Anderson, June 15, 1957 (div. 1984); children: Ross Harlow, Anne Louise; m. Susan S. Greene, Aug. 3, 1984. BS, Iowa State U., 1955, MS, 1957; PhD, Mich. State U., 1964. Postdoctoral fellow USPHS U. Ill., Champaign, 1964-65; from asst. prof. psychology to assoc. prof. Iowa State U., Ames, 1965-69, asst. dir. counseling ctr., 1967-69; faculty U. Md., College Park, 1969-81, prof. psychology, 1972-81, asst. dir. counseling center, 1969-81; adminstrv. officer Am. Psychol. Assn., Washington, 1981-86; pvt. practice Bangor, Maine, 1989—, Blue Hill, Maine, 1990—. Cons. Iowa Women's Reformatory, 1966-69, VA, Rockwell City, Iowa, 1966-69; rsch. assoc. Nat. Register Health Svcs. Providers in Psychology; mgmt. cons. Ctr. Creative Leadership U. Md., 1980—; mem. Maine Bd. Psychologists; mem. exam com. Assn. State and Provincial State Psychology Bds., 1995-98; mem. Maine State Bd. Examiners Psychologists, 1994-2003, cons., 20030172., chair, 1996-99. Contbr. articles to profl. jours. Pres. Woodmoor-Pinecrest Citizens Assn., Silver Spring, Md., 1973-74; mem. com. higher edn. Allied Civic Group Montgomery County, 1974, sr. fellow Consortium of Univs. of the Washington D.C. Met. Area., 1987—; mem. diocesan rev. bd. Portland (Maine) Roman Cath. Diocese, 1997-2002. Served with U.S. Army, 1957-61. Fellow APA (chair ct. on profl. stds., 1988-1989. ethics 1981-1989, ethics cons. 1990—); mem. Internat. Assn. Counseling Svcs. (accrediting bd. 1972-74, v.p. 1975-77, pres. 1977-79). Democrat. Unitarian Universalist. Office: PO Box 108 Little Deer Isle ME 04650-0108 E-mail: bigskye@acadia.net.

MILLS, DAVID MICHAEL, ophthalmologist, plastic surgeon; s. Michael Mills and Donna Mills-Ratkiewicz, Robert Ratkiewicz (Stepfather); m. Elizabeth Ann Hoover, Jan. 29, 2000; children: Lauren, Ashley, Haley. MD, U. Mich., Ann Arbor, 2000. Diplomate Am. Bd. Ophthalmology, 2005. Attending physician Nicolitz Eye Cons., Jacksonville, Fla., 2004—. Contbr. articles to profl. jours., chapters to books. Recipient Sr. Biochemistry award, Am. Inst. Chemists Found., 1992—96, Wheaton Found. award, 1994—96; fellow, Albany Med. Ctr., Lions Eye Inst., Ophthalmic Plastic Surgery, 2005—; scholar, Wheaton Coll., 1993—96; Presdl. scholar, 1992—96, Balfour scholar, 1992—96. Fellow: ACS (assoc.), Am. Acad. Cosmetic Surgery (assoc.); mem.: AMA, Am. Soc. Cataract and Refractice Surgery, Fla. Soc. Ophthalmology, Am. Acad. Ophthalmology, Fla. Med. Assn., Phi Beta Kappa. Achievements include research in quntifying the effect of horizontal tightening on upper eyelid position; a national study of the microbiological spectrum of acute and chronic dacryocystitis. Office: Nicolitz Eye Consultants 7051 Southpoint Pkwy Jacksonville FL 32216 Home Phone: 518-334-0954; Office Phone: 904-398-2720.

MILLS, DON HARPER, pathology and psychiatry educator, lawyer; b. Peking, China, July 29, 1927; came to U.S., 1928; s. Clarence Alonzo and Edith Clarissa (Parrett) M.; m. Lillian Frances Snyder, June 11, 1949; children: Frances Jo, Jon Snyder. BS, U. Cin., 1950, MD, 1953; JD, U. So. Calif., 1958. Diplomate Am. Bd. Legal Medicine. Intern L.A. County Gen. Hosp., 1953-54, admitting physician, 1954-57, attending staff in pathology, 1959—; pathology fellow U. So. Calif., LA, 1954-55, instr. pathology, 1958-62, asst. clin. prof., 1962-65, assoc. clin. prof., 1965-69, clin. prof., 1969—, clin. prof. psychiatry and behavioral sci., 1986—. Asst. in pathology Hosp. Good Samaritan, LA, 1956-65, cons. staff, 1962-72, affiliate staff, 1972-91; dep. med. examiner Office of Los Angeles County Med. Examiner, 1957-61; instr. legal medicine Loma Linda U. Sch. Medicine, Calif., 1960-66, assoc. clin. prof. humanities, 1966-95; cons. HEW, 1972-73, 75-76, Dept. Def., 1975-80; trustee Am. Bd. Legal Medicine, Inc., Chgo., 2004—; med. dir. Profl. Risk Mgmt. Group, 1989-2001, Octagon Risk Svcs., Inc., 2001-07, Sedgwick Caronia, 2007—. Column editor Newsletter of the Long Beach Med. Assn., 1960-75, Jour. Am. Osteo. Assn., 1965-77, Ortho Panel, 1970-78; exec. editor Trauma, 1964-88, mem. editl. bd., 1988-2006; mem. editl. bd. Legal Aspects of Med. Practice, 1972-90, Med. Alert Comms., 1973-75, Am. Jour. Forensic Medicine and Pathology, 1979-87, Hosp. Risk Control, 1981-96; contbr. numerous articles to profl. jours. Bd. dirs. Inst. for Med. Risk Studies, 1988—; mem. adv. bd. Pacific Ctr. for Health Policy and Ethics, 1997—, chmn., 1999—. With USN, 1946—47. Recipient Ritz Heerman award Calif. Hosp. Assn., 1986, Disting. fellow Am. Acad. Forensic Scis., 1993, Genesis award Pacific Ctr. for Health Policy and Ethics, 1993, Founder's award Am. Coll. Med. Quality, 1994. Fellow Am. Coll. Legal Medicine (pres. 1974-76, bd. govs. 1970-78, v.p. 1972-74, chmn. malpractice com. 1973-74, jour. editl. bd. 1984—, gold medal 1999), Am. Acad. Forensic Sci. (gen. program chmn. 1966-67, chmn. jurisprudence sect. 1966-67, 73-74, exec. com. 1971-74, 84-88, v.p. 1984-85, pres. 1986-87, ethics com. 1976-86, 91-2001, chmn. ethics com. 1994-2001, long-term planning com. 1990—2004, jour. editl. bd. 1965-79); mem. AMA (jour. editl. bd. 1973-77), AAAS, ABA, Am. Coll. Med. Quality (hon. life), Calif. Med. Assn., Los Angeles County Med. Assn., Los Angeles County Bar Assn., Am. Health Lawyers Assn., Calif. Soc. Hosp. Attys. Home: 700 E Ocean Blvd Unit 2606 Long Beach CA 90802-5039 Office: 5000 Airport Plaza Dr Ste 250 Long Beach CA 90815-4959 Office Phone: 562-420-5987.

MILLS, DOROTHY ALLEN, investor; b. New Brunswick, NJ, Dec. 14, 1920; d. James R. and Bertha Lovilla (Porter) Allen; m. George M. Mills, Apr. 21, 1945; children: Dianne Adele McKay, Dorothy Louise Sphatt. BA, Douglass Coll., New Brunswick, NJ, 1943. Investment reviewer Ctrl. Hanover Bank, NYC, 1943-44; asst. to dir. of admissions and sec. undergrad. yrs. Douglass Coll., New Brunswick, 1944-45; sec., regional dir. O.P.A., Ventura, Calif., 1945-46; corp. sec. George M. Mills Inc., Highland Park, NJ, 1946-75; pvt. investor N. Brunswick, 1975—. Sr. v.p. Children Am. Revolution, N.J., 1965; active alumni com. Douglass Coll., 1990—. Recipient Douglass Alumni award, 1992. Mem. AAUW, New Brunswick Hist. Soc., DAR, English Speaking Union, Rutgers Alumni Faculty Club, Woman's League of Rutgers U., Princeton-Douglass Alumni Club, N. Brunswick Women's Club, Auxiliary Robert Wood Johnson Hosp. and Med. Sch. Republican. Mem. Dutch Reformed Ch. Avocations: travel, gardening, bridge. Home: 1054 Hoover Dr New Brunswick NJ 08902-3244

MILLS, DOROTHY JANE (DOROTHY Z. SEYMOUR), writer, editor, consultant; b. Cleve., July 5, 1928; d. Henry Zander and Katherine Helen Reinert; m. Harold Seymour, May 21, 1949 (dec. Sept. 25, 1992); m. Roy Elburt Mills, Feb. 15, 1995. Student, Cleve. State U., 1946—49; BS, Case-Western Res. U., 1950, MA, 1952. Cert. elem. and H.S. tchr. Ohio, N.Y. Tchr. Cleve. Pub. Schs., 1950—54, Parma Heights (Ohio) Pub. Schs., 1955—57, Pelham (N.Y.) Pub. Schs., 1957—63, Warwick (N.Y.) Pub. Schs., 1963—66; sr. editor Ginn & Co., Pubs., Boston, Lexington, Mass., 1967—73, Lexington, 1979—81; freelance writer, editor, cons., 1981—; owner Patrician Publs., Naples, Fla., 1998—. Cons. Stillpoint Pub., Walpole, NY, 1987—; freelance editor, 1987—95; lectr. in field. Author: (children's textbooks) Bill and the Fish, 1965, Brad and Nell, 1965, Stop

Pretending, 1965, Ballerina Bess, 1965, Ann Likes Red, 1965, The Rabbit, 1965, The Tent, 1965, The Sandwich, 1965, Big Beds and Little Beds, 1965, (edn. text) Toad Charts, 1987, (novels) The Sceptre, 1998, 1999, The Labyrinth, 2003, The Treskel, 2005, (cookbook) Meatless Meat: A Book of Recipes for Meat Substitutes, 2001; co-author, editor: Fear Not to Sow Because of the Birds, 1988;; co-author (with Harold Seymour): Baseball: The Early Years, 1960, Baseball: The Golden Age, 1971, Baseball: The People's Game, 1990; author: (autobiography) A Woman's Work: Writing Baseball History with Harold Seymour, 2004; co-author: (edn. text) Word Recognition, 1987, author short stories; contbr. articles to publs. Mem.: NASSH, SABR, AAUW. Democrat. Unitarian Universalist. Avocations: piano, singing, travel. Home: 6935 Carlisle Ct Apt C 207 Naples FL 34109 Office Phone: 239-596-2842. Personal E-mail: dorothyjanemills@comcast.net.

MILLS, DOUGLAS L., physics professor; b. Berkeley, Calif., Apr. 2, 1940; s. Eli J. and Bruna G. Mills; m. Sandra Ann Thrall, June 18, 1961; children: Scott Alan, Sherylle Mills Englander. PhD, U. Calif., Berkeley, 1965. Postdoctoral fellow U. Paris, Orsay, France, 1965—66; asst. prof. physics U. Calif., Irvine, 1966—69, assoc. prof. physics, 1969—83, prof. physics, 1983—2005, rsch. prof. physics, 2005—. Co-author with H. Ibach (textbook) Electron Energy Loss Spectroscopy and Surface Vibrations; author: (textbook) Non Linear Optics; Basic Concepts; contbr. scientific papers. Staff commodore Bahia Corinthian Yacht Club, Newport Beach, Calif., 1995—96. Fellow: Am. Phys. Soc. Home Phone: 949-824-5148; Office Phone: 949-824-5148. Business E-Mail: dlmills@uci.edu.

MILLS, EDWARD WARREN, corporation executive; b. NYC, Apr. 7, 1941; m. Maria Parascandolo, Sept. 19, 1971; children: Edward Warren, Foy Fitzhugh, Joseph V.O. BS, Washington and Lee U., 1962; MBA, Hofstra U., 1974; JD, NY Law Sch., 1977. Bar: NY 1977, DC 1978. Acct., Wasserman & Taten, NYC, 1962-69; exec. v.p. L.H. Keller, Inc. and Hugo P. Keller, Inc., NYC, 1969-74; pres. Gen. Ruby & Sapphire Co., 1974-94, Qualistar Corp., 1974-94, EWM Gen. Corp., 1993—. Mem. ABA, NY State Bar Assn., DC Bar Assn. Office: 7700 Massachusetts Ave New Port Richey FL 34653-3024 Home: PO Box 610 New Port Richey FL 34656-0610 Home Phone: 727-376-8466. Business E-Mail: genrus73@aol.com.

MILLS, EDWIN SMITH, economics professor; b. Collingswood, NJ, June 25, 1928; s. Edwin Smith and Roberta (Haywood) M.; m. Barbara Jean Dressner, Sept. 2, 1950; children: Alan Stuart, Susan Dorinda; m. Margaret M. Hutchinson, Jan. 22, 1977. BA, Brown U., 1951; PhD, U. Birmingham, Eng., 1956. Asst. lectr. Univ. Coll. North Staffordshire, Eng., 1953-55; instr. MIT, 1955-57; mem. faculty Johns Hopkins, Balt., 1957-70, prof. econs., 1963-70, chmn. dept. econs., 1966-69; prof. econs. and pub. affairs, Gerald L. Phillippe prof. urban studies Princeton U., 1970-75, prof. econs., 1975-87, chmn. dept., 1975-77; Gary Rosenberg prof. real estate and fin. Kellog Sch. Mgmt. Northwestern U., Evanston, Ill., 1987—96, emeritus prof., 1996—. Vis. rsch. fellow Cowles Found., Yale, 1961; sr. profl. staff Coun. Econ. Advisers, 1964—65. Author: Urban Economics, 1972, The Burden of Government, 1986; editor: Jour. Urban Econs., 1973—90; contbr. articles to profl. jours. 2d lt. US Army, 1946—48. Recipient numerous rsch. grants and contracts, 1960—95. Mem.: Am. Econ. Assn., Phi Beta Kappa. Home: 1 Calvin Cir Apt A413 Evanston IL 60201-1953 Office: Northwestern U Ctr Real Estate Rsch Kellogg Graduate School 2001 Sheridan Rd Evanston IL 60208-2001 Office Phone: 847-491-8340. Business E-Mail: e_mills@kellogg.northwestern.edu.

MILLS, ELIZABETH SHOWN, historical writer, genealogist; b. Cleve., Miss., Dec. 29, 1944; d. Floyd Finley Shown and Elizabeth Thulmar (Jeffcoat) Carver; m. Gary B. Mills, 1963; children: Clayton Bernard, Donna Rachal, Daniel Garland. BA, U. Ala., Tuscaloosa, 1980. Cert. genealogist, geneal. lectr. Hist. writer, educator, 1972—; editor Nat. Geneal. Soc. Quar., Arlington, Va., 1987—2002. Faculty Samford U. Inst. of Genealogy and Hist. Rsch., Birmingham, Ala., 1980—; contract dir., cons. U. Ala., 1985-92; faculty Nat. Inst. of Geneal. Rsch., 1985-97. Author, editor, translator Cane River Creole Series, 6 vols.; author: Evidence: Citation and Analysis for the Family Historian, 1997, Professional Genealogy: A Manual for Researchers, Writers, Editors, Lecturers, and Librarians, 2001, Isle of Canes: A Historical Novel, 2004, QuickSheet: Citing Online Historical Resources, Evidence Style, 2005, Evidence Explained: Citing History Sources from Artifacts to Cyberspace, 2007; contbr. articles to profl. jours. Trustee Nat. Bd. Certification Genealogists, 1984—, v.p., 1989-94, pres., 1994-96; trustee Assn. Profl. Genealogists, 1984-90, 92-94, regional v.p., 1988-89; trustee Assn. Promotion Scholarship in Genealogy, 1984-90 Named Outstanding Young Women of Am. Jaycees, Gadsden, 1976, Outstanding Alumna award U. Ala. New Coll., Tuscaloosa, 1990. Fellow Am. Soc. Geneal. (sec. 1992-95, v.p. 1995-98, pres. 1998-2001), Nat. Geneal. Soc. (councilor 1987-92), Utah Geneal. Assn., Grady McWhiney Rsch. Found. (sr.); mem. Assn. Profl. Genealogists (Smallwood Svc. award, 1989). Republican. Roman Catholic.

MILLS, EUGENE SUMNER, academic administrator; b. West Newton, Ind., Sept. 13, 1924; s. Sumner Amos and Lela (Weatherly) M.; m. Dorothy Frances Wildman, Oct. 22, 1945; children: David Walden, Sara Anne. AB, Earlham Coll., 1948; MA, Claremont Grad. U., 1949, PhD, 1952; Spl. Postdoctoral Auditor, Harvard, 1958-59; LLD (hon.), So. NH U., 1979, U. N.H., 1988; LHD (hon.), Earlham Coll., 1987. From instr. to prof. psychology Whittier (Calif.) Coll., 1950—60, prof., 1960—62, chmn. dept. psychology, 1952—62; pres. Whittier (Calif.) Coll. and Whittier Coll. Sch. of Law, 1979-89; prof. psychology Whittier (Calif.) Coll., 1979-89, emeritus prof. psychology, pres. emeritus, 1989—; faculty U. NH, Durham, 1962—79, dean Grad. Sch., 1963—67, dean Coll. Liberal Arts, 1967—70, acad. v.p., 1970—71, provost, 1971—74, pres., 1974—79. Vis. prof. U. Victoria, B.C., 1958, 60; bd. dirs. Elderhostel, Inc., 1977-97, chmn., 1984-90, vice chmn., 1996-97; vice chmn., bd. dirs. Fedco Inc., 1996-98; interim pres. Earlham Coll., 1996-97; mem. NH Psychol. Assn., 1962-79, pres., 1969-70, bd. dirs., 1967-70; trustee Earlham Coll., 1966-69, 96-97, hon. lifetime trustee, 1997—. Author: George Trumbull Ladd: Pioneer American Psychologist, 1969, The Story of Elderhostel, 1993; contbr. articles to profl. jours. Bd. dirs. LA County coun. Boy Scouts Am., 1981—89; bd. dirs. Fedco Charitable Found., 2001—, UNHART Gallery, 2004—. Danforth Found. grantee; NSF grantee. Fellow Am. Psychol. Assn.; mem. Western Psychol. Assn., Sigma Xi, Phi Kappa Phi., Omicron Delta Kappa Mem. Soc. Of Friends. E-mail: dottymills25@yahoo.com.

MILLS, FREDERICK VANFLEET, art educator, watercolorist; b. Bremen, Ohio, June 5, 1925; s. Frederick William and Juanita Ellen (VanFleet) M.; m. Lois Jean Rademacher; children: Mark Steven (dec.), Michael Sherwood, Mollie Sue, Merre Shannon, Randal Dean, Susan Lynn, Todd Patrick, Shondra Marie. BS, Ohio State U., 1949; MS, Ind. U., 1951, EdD, 1956; postgrad., U.S. Army Staff and Command Coll., 1973-76. Tchr. art, supr. Celina (Ohio) Pub. Schs., 1949-51; instr. univ. h.s. Ind. U., 1951-55, prof. art, art edn., chmn. dept. art edn. Bloomington, 1959-65; vis. prof. U. Tex.-Austin, 1965; chmn. dept. related arts, crafts and interior design U. Tenn., Konxville, 1966-68; prof. art, chmn. dept. art Ill. State U., 1968-85, prof. emeritus, 1985—; dist. prof. art Lincoln Coll., Normal, 1986—. Rsch. reader humanities HEW, 1968-69; resource person arts, edn. and Ams. panel Rockefeller Report Am Coun. Arts in Edn., 1977-78; cons. Latin Am. Fulbright Scholarship Program Harvard U., 1981-82; mem. com. Ill. Fine Arts Rev. for Capital Devel. Bd., 1987—, planning com. Nat. Inst. Advanced Studies in Art and Design and Archives of Am. Art Sch., 1988—, rsch. com. Nat. Sch. Art and Design. One-man shows include McLean County Arts Ctr., Bloomington, Ill., Lincoln (Ill.) Coll., Ill. Agriculture Assn. Credit Union Art Exhbn. Series, Bloomington, Suzette Schochet Gallery, Newport, R.I.; represented in permanent collections Ill. State U. Credit Union, Normal, Ill. State U. Computer Lab., Normal, Mid-Ill. Credit Union, Bloomington, I Wonderlin Gallery, Normal, Ill., State Farm Ins. Co., Kemper Fin. Securities/Kemper Fin. Fund, First of Am. Bank, Ill., Diamond Star Motors Corp., Easter Seal Assn., City of Vladimir, Russia, City of Asahikawa, Hokkaido, Japan, County of McLean, City of Bloomington, Town of Normal; author, editor: The Status of the Visual Arts in Higher Education, 1976, New Perspectives in Visual Arts Administration, 1977, Issues in the Administration of Visual Arts, 1978, Politics and the Visual Arts, 1979, The Visual Arts in the Ninth Decade, 1980; editor Western Arts Bull., 1958-62; featured in 12 part ser. As An Artist Sees local pub. access; contbr. to profl. jours. Pres. Ill. Alliance Art Edn., 1975-77, Ill. Task Force for Arts Edn. in Gen. Edn., 1976-77; mem. Tenn. Arts Commn., 1967-68, Nat. Alliance Arts Edn./Kennedy Ctr., 1975-77; charter trustee Ill. Summer Sch. for Arts, v.p., v.p. Found. Bd., 1988-94; bd. dirs., co-founder Sugar Creek Arts Festival, Normal, 1985—; chair major gifts com. Normal Theater Restoration Project, 1992—; bd. dirs., v.p. McLean County Arts Ctr., Bloomington, 1980-90, sponsor Skilled Crafts award, 1968—. Served to maj. USAR; Col. Ill. Militia. Recipient Recognition award Alliance for Arts Edn., 1984, Outstanding Svc. award Ill. Alliance Arts Edn., 1984, 1994 Ornament of Yr./Artist of Yr. award, Ill. State U. Alumni Assn. Svc. Awd.; subject articles, TV interviews Mem. Nat. Council Art Adminstrs. (charter, sr. rsch. editor bd. dirs. 1973-81), Nat. Assn. Schs. Art (instnl. del. 1974-84, nominating com. 1977-78, rsch. com. 1976-77), Western Arts Assn. (pres. 1962-64), Coll. Art Assn., Nat. Art Edn. Assn. (dir. 1964-66), Scabbard and Blade, Phi Delta Kappa, Delta Tau Delta, Delta Phi Delta. Clubs: Rotary Internat. Home: 25306 Arrowhead Lne Hudson IL 61748-9414 *As I reflect on my life and career up to this point, I feel that consistency and humaneness are two words that come to mind. It seems extremely important to be consistent when a person relates to others, and if that is coupled with humaneness and consideration of the value of others, being aware of their strengths and weaknesses, their likes and dislikes, it becomes easier to relate to them in this most complex world of ours.*

MILLS, GEORGE MARSHALL, financial consultant; b. Newton, NJ, May 20, 1923; s. J. Marshall and Emma (Scott) M.; m. Dorothy Lovilla Allen, Apr. 21, 1945; children: Dianne (Mrs. Thomas McKay III), Dorothy L.A. (Mrs. Edward Sphatt). BA, Rutgers U., 1943; MA, Columbia U., 1951. CLU, CPCU; chartered fin. cons.; cert. govt. fund mgr. Pres. George M. Mills Inc., North Brunswick, NJ, 1946—75; pres. CORECO, Inc., Newark, 1960-78; risk mgr. N.J. Hwy. Authority, Woodbridge, 1976-95; pres. Assoc. Risk Mgmt., North Brunswick, NJ, 1995—. Cons. Govs.'s Com. on Bus. Efficiency in Pub. Schs., 1979-80; cons. Risk Mgmt. Ins., Real Estate. Bd. dirs. Alpha Chi Rho Ednl. Found., vice-chmn. 1991-95; workshop Easter Seal Soc.; mem. Gov.'s Task Force on Sound Mcpl. Govt., 1981-82; pres. Nat. Interfrat. Conf., 1979-80. With USNR, 1943-46. Recipient Congl. Order of Merit, 1946—47, Congl. Distinction Medal, 2006, Mem. Congl. Bus. Adv. Coun. (chmn. 2003-, co-chair Presdl. Inauguration Com.), Am. Coll. Life Underwriters, Am. Coll. Property Liability Underwriters, Internat. Bridge Tunnel and Turnpike Assn. (chmn. risk mgmt. com. 1980-95, bus. ins. risk mgmt. bd. 1988-95, chair Congress Bus. Adv. Coun. 2003-06, co-chair presdl. inaugeration com. 2005, Matthew J. Lenz Jr. medal 1989, Paul K. Addams award 1992, Businessman of Yr. 2003-06, Ronald Reagan Gold medal 2005-06, Presdl. Ronald Reagan Gold medal 2006, Congl. Order of Merit 2006), New Brunswick Hist. Soc., English Congl. Speaking Union, Rutgers Club (trustee), Alpha Chi Rho (nat. councillor 1964-70, nat. pres. 1970-73, nat. treas. 1975-78), Kappa Kappa Psi, Tau Kappa Alpha, Phi Delta Phi. Mem. Reformed Ch. Am. Home: 1054 Hoover Dr New Brunswick NJ 08902-3244 Office Phone: 732-828-2700.

MILLS, HELENE AUDREY, retired education educator; b. Oct. 6, 1933; d. Paul Albert and Mabel Meister; m. Ray Mills, Apr. 17, 1954; children: Keith, Katherine(dec.), Kevin. BS in Family Life Edn., Wayne State U., Detroit, 1954; MEd in Human Resources, Wayne State U., 1965, EdD in Gen. Adminstrn., 1980. Supr., instr. Wayne State Coll. Edn., 1958-67; tchr. life studies, health edn. Seaholm HS, Birmingham, Mich., 1967-72, 74-77, asst. to prin., 1974-77, asst. prin., 1978-79, prin., 1990-97, Derby Mid. Sch., Birmingham, 1980-90; asst. prof. Oakland U., Rochester Hills, Mich., 1997—2002; ret., 2002. Adj. prof. Oakland U., Rochester, 1985—89, Wayne State U., Detroit, 1989—91; consulting editor Clearing Ho., 1985—97. Contbr. articles to profl. jours. Mem. steering com. Meadowbrook Leadership Acad., 1984—87; mem. Detroit Strategic Planning Task Force, 1986—88; mem. exec. bd. Oakland County Youth Assistance, 1987—90; v.p. Cmty. Ho. Sr. Women's Club, Birmingham, Mich., 2004—; program chairperson women's group Northbrooke Ch., 1997—99, mem. adult ministries purpose com., 1998—99. Recipient PTSA Coun. Pres. award, 1982, Celebration of Women award, Greater Detroit Coun. NA'AMAT U.S., 1986, Exemplary Secondary Sch. award, State of Mich., 1991. Mem.: NASCD, Oakland County Secondary Prins. Assn. (pres. 1983—85, Prin. of the Yr. 1991), Mich. Secondary Prins. Assn., Mich. Coun. Family Rels., Mich. Assn. Supervision and Curriculum Devel., Nat. Secondary Prins. Assn., Nat. Staff Devel. Assn., Birmingham Area Sr. Citizens Assn. (bd. mem., program chair 2003—), Phi Delta Kappa (chmn. mem. Oakland br. 1998—2002).

MILLS, JERRY WOODROW, lawyer; b. Springfield, Mo., July 17, 1940; s. Woodrow Wilson and Billie Louise M.; m. Marion Cargile, Mar. 27, 1964; children: Eric E., Brendon W. BSEE, Tex. A&M U., 1963; JD, Georgetown U., 1967. Bar: Tex. 1967, U.S. Patent & Trademark Office 1967, US Ct. Fed. Claims, US Dist. Ct. No. Tex., US Ct. Appeals 5th 10th 11th & Fed. Cir. Ptnr. Richards, Harris & Hubbard, Dallas, 1970-82, Baker, Mills & Glast, Dallas, 1982-90; sr. ptnr., chmn. intellectual property dept. & mem. exec. com. Baker Botts LLP, Dallas, 1990—. Adj. prof. So. Meth. U. Law Sch., 1994-97. Bd. dirs. Dallas Legal Svcs. Project, 1972-75, Entrepreneurs Found. No. Tex., trustee & sec. Dallas Theater Ctr., mem. external adv. & develop. council Tex. A&M Univ. Named a Texas Super Lawyer, Texas Monthly mag. & Law & Politics mag., 2003—04. Fellow Tex. Bar Found., Dallas Bar Found.; mem. ABA, Tex. State Jr. Bar Assn. (treas. 1975, dir.), Dallas Jr. Bar Assn. (pres. 1971, Outstanding Young Lawyer award 1975), Dallas Bar Assn. (bd. dirs. 1983-85), Eta Kappa Nu, Phi Eta Sigma, Phi Kappa Phi, Tau Beta Pi. Methodist. Office: Baker Botts LLP 800 Trammell Crow Ctr 2001 Ross Ave Ste 900 Dallas TX 75201-2980 Office Fax: 214-661-4665. Business E-Mail: jerry.mills@bakerbotts.com.

MILLS, JON, dean emeritus, law educator; b. Miami, Fla., July 24, 1947; s. Herb J. and Marguerite (Sweat) M.; m. Beth Bechard; children: Marguerite St. Amand, Elizabeth Buchanan Mills. BA in Economics, Stetson U., 1969, LLD (hon.), 1986; JD with honors, U. Fla., 1972. Bar: U.S. Ct Appeals (11th Cir.). Jud. clerk 2nd Dist. Ct. Appeals, Fla., 1972; spl. asst. State Atty. Rolling vs. State, 1990; ptnr. McGalliard, Mills, DeMontomollin, Smith, Monaco & Sieg, 1980—86; mem. Fla. Ho. of Reps., 1978-88, majority leader, 1985—86, speaker, 1987-88; mem. faculty U. Fla., Gainesville, 1973—80; prof. law U. Fla., Coll. Law, Gainesville, 1995—, founding dir., Ctr. for Governmental Responsibility, 1973—80, 1988—, dir., Ctr. for Governmental Responsibility, 2003—, interim dean, 1999—2001, dean, 2001—03, dean emeritus, 2003—. Mem. Fla. Constitution Revision Commn., 1987—88, Commn. on the Future of the South, State Comprehensive Plan Com., 1985, Fla. Motion Picture, TV, and Recording Industry Bd.; adv. coun., bd. dir. State Legis. Leaders Found.; chair Fla. Coun. on Far East R&D; spkr. in field. Co-author: Voting Rights and Democracy: The Law and Politics Districting, 1996; prodr., moderator, Florida Forum, 1989; exec. prodr., moderator, Sunshine Showdown, 1991; co-editor, moderator, Common Ground, 1995 (recipient 1998 Suncoast Regional Emmy award for Common Ground TV program "Whose Water Is It Anyway?"; contbr. articles to profl. jours. Del., Dem. Nat. Convention, 1984; chair, State Dem. Convention, 1987; founding chmn., Fla. Chpt. Dem. Leadership Coun., 1987; pres., Fla. Chpt. Dem. Leadership Coun., 1993-; mem. Coun. Internat. Administrative Units, Office of Internat. Studies and Programs, Governor's Growth Mgmt. Adv. Com., 1993, U. Fla. Found. Investment Com., 1998-2002; founding pres. bd. dirs., So. Legal Coun., Fla. Arts Celebration; former mem. exec. com. Fla. Dem. Party; chair, U. Fla. President's External Rels. Com.; trustee, Fla. Nature Conservancy Bd., 1988-; bd. dir. U. Fla. Ctr. for Performing Arts, Save our Everglades, 1996-, Internat. Computer and Automated Rsch. 1st lt. USAR. Decorated Order of Coif; recipient Allen Morris award, 1979-80, 1985-86, Outstanding Legis. award Fla. Health Care Assn., 1982, Legis. award, Fla. Audubon Soc., 1983, Sierra Club Fla. Chpt., 1983, 1984, Fla. C.ofC. Legis. award for Leadership in Quality of Life Legislation, 1984, Dept. Health and Human Services Commissioner's award for Outstanding Leadership Services in Prevention of Child Abuse and Neglect, 1985, League of Women Voters Outstanding Elected Official, 1985, Nature Conservancy Pub. Svc. award, 1986, President's 1997 Conservationist of Yr. award, Fla. Audubon Soc., 1998, Spl. Recognition award, Fla. Assn. Countries for outstanding work as a mem. of the Constitution Revision Commn., 1998, Conservation Civic Leader of Yr., Fla. Wildlife Fedn., 1998, Bd. Regents Disting. Cmty. Svc. award, 1998; named Rep. of Yr. Assn. Retarded Citizens Fla., 1981, Most Effective Mem. of the House, 1985, 1986, Gainesville Sun 1998 Person of Yr. for Govt., 1998, Most Valuable Mem., Fla. Constitutional Revision Commn., 1998. Fellow Am. Bar Found.; mem. ABA, Fla. Bar Assn., Fla. Supreme Ct. Hist. Soc., Pi Kappa Alpha, Fla. Blue Key, Fla. Supreme Ct. Professionalism Commn. Methodist. Avocations: flying, scuba diving, skiing, photography, Karate. Home: 2727 NW 58th Blvd Gainesville FL 32606-8516 Office: U Fla Coll Law 230 Bruton-Geer Hall Gainesville FL 32611 also: PO Box 117625 Gainesville FL 32611 Office Phone: 352-273-0835. Office Fax: 352-392-1457.

MILLS, KEVIN LEE, computer scientist, researcher; b. Frederick, Md., Oct. 21, 1951; s. John Lee and Doris Jean (Comer) M.; m. Karen June Davis, Dec. 30, 1972; children: Colin Walter, Elizabeth Anne. BS in Polit. Sci. and Econs., Frostburg State U., Md., 1973; MS in Tech. Mgmt., Am. U., 1979; PhD in Info. Tech., George Mason U., 1996. Sr. computer analyst System Devel. Corp., McLean, Va., 1976-81; project mgr. Tesdata Systems Corp., McLean, 1981-82; computer scientist Nat. Bur. of Stds., Gaithersburg, Md., 1982-84, group leader, 1984-87; divsn. chief Nat. Inst. Stds. and Tech., Gaithersburg, 1987-95; program mgr. Def. Advanced Rsch. Projects Agy., Arlington, Va., 1996-98; adj. prof. George Mason U., 1996—2006; divsn. chief Nat. Inst. Standards & Technology, Gaithersburg, Md., 1999-2001, sr. rsch. scientist, 2001—. Cons. in field, 1980-82. Contbr. articles to jours. With USMC, 1972—78. Mem. IEEE (sr.). Avocations: hiking, writing, reading, photography. E-mail: kmills@nist.gov.

MILLS, KEVIN PAUL, lawyer; b. Detroit, Oct. 1, 1961; s. Raymond Eugene and Helene Audrey M.; m. Holly Beth Fechner, June 15, 1986. BA, Oberlin Coll., 1983; JD, U. Mich., 1987. Bar: Mich. 1988. High sch. tchr., asst. dir. summer environ. inst. The Storm King Sch., Cornwall-on-Hudson, N.Y., 1983-84; staff atty. E. Mich. Environ. Action Coun., Birmingham, Mich., 1987-90; assoc. Tucker & Rolf, Southfield, Mich., 1988-89; sr. atty., pollution prevention program dir. Environ. Def., Washington, 1990—. Low-level radioactive waste cons. State Mich., Lansing, 1988; founder Pollution Prevention Alliance, 1991, co-founder Great Printer's Project, 1992, co-founder Clean Car Campaign, 1999, staff to co-chair eco-efficiency Pres. Coun. Sustainable Devel., 1993-95, Auto Pollution Prevention adv. group, 1994-98, EPA Auto Mfr. CSI, 1994-97; mem. adv. bd. Nat. Pollution Prevention Roundtable, 1996-2003; mem. adv. com. Working Group on Cmty. Right-to-Know, 1997-2004; mem. Nat. Adv. Coun. on Environ. Policy and Tech., 1997-2002; bd. dirs. Inst. Market Tranformation to Sustainability, 2001—; bd. dirs. Senate Employees Child Care Ctr., 2003-04, v.p., 2004. Bd. dirs., v.p. Ea. Mich. Environ. Action Coun., Birmingham, 1985-87; pres. Environ. Law Soc., Ann Arbor, Mich., 1986-87; exec. com. Takoma PTA, 2005—. Recipient Outstanding Achievement award Environ. Def., 2000, Nominating Com. Soc. Auto Engrs. environ. Excellence in Transp. award, 2000-03. Mem.: State Bar Mich. Office: Environ Def 1875 Connecticut Ave NW Washington DC 20009-5728

MILLS, MARGARET H., linguist; b. Davenport, Iowa, Jan. 8, 1954; d. Oliver Wendell and Elizabeth Barrett Hill; m. Marcus M. Mills, May 22, 1976; children: Olivia Lauren, Hillary Barrett, Caroline Manning. BA; MA, U. Iowa; PhD in Slavic Linguistics, U. Mich., 1985; MPH, U. Iowa, 2005. Instr., asst. prof. Russian Ill. State U., Normal, 1984—86; asst. prof. Russian Georgetown U., Washington, 1986—89, U. Iowa, Iowa City, 1989—93, assoc. prof. Russian, 1993—2000, prof. Russian, 2000—. Author: Topics in Colloquial Russian, 1990, UI Neonatology Handbook, 1997, Slavic Gender Linguistics, 1999, Medical Issues and Health Care Reform in Russia, 1999; contbr. articles to profl. jours. Grantee, Nat. Rsch. Coun., 1997, Social Sci. Rsch. Coun., 1996—98, NIH, 2000, Eurasia Found., Washington and Moscow, 2000, Am. Coun. Internat. Edn., Moscow, 2001. Office: U Iowa Dept Russian Iowa City IA 52242

MILLS, MICHAEL PAUL, judge; b. Charleston, South Carolina, Aug. 25, 1956; s. Paul H. and Shirley (Dulaney) M.; m. Mona (Robinson), Aug. 2, 1976; children: Alysson, Chip, Rebekah, Penn. AA, Itawamba Cmty. Coll., Fulton, Miss., 1976; BA, U. Miss., 1978, JD, 1980; LLM, U. Va., 2001. Bar: Miss., 1980; U.S. Ct. Appeals (Fed. Cir.), 1986; U.S. Ct. Appeals (5th cir.), 1980; U.S. Supreme Ct., 1990. Pvt. practice, Miss., 1980-95; legis. Miss. Ho. of Reps., Jackson, Miss., 1983-95; mem. Nat. Conf. Commr. on Uniform State Laws, 1993—; justice Miss. Supreme Ct., Jackson, Miss., 1995—2001; judge US Dist. Ct. (no. dist.), Miss., Oxford, 2001—. Adj. prof. law U. Miss. Office: Fed Bldg Rm 335 911 Jackson Ave Oxford MS 38655 Office Phone: 662-234-1538. Office Fax: 662-234-1447.

MILLS, MIKE, popular musician; b. Calif., Dec. 17, 1958; 1 child, Julian. Student, U. Ga. Bass guitarist R.E.M., 1980—. Rec. albums include Chronic Town, 1982, Murmur, 1983 (Rolling Stone Album of Yr. 1983), Reckoning, 1984, Fables of the Reconstruction, 1985, Life's Rich Pageant, 1986, Dead Letter Office, 1987, Document, 1987, Eponymous, 1988, Green, 1988, Out of Time, 1991 (Group Grammy award, Best Alternative Music Performance, 1992), Automatic for the People, 1993 (4 Grammy nominations), Monster, 1994, Murmur, 1995, New Adventures in Hi-Fi, 1996, Up, 1998, Reveal, 2001, Around the Sun, 2004; songs include The One I Love, Orange Crush (MTV Video Music award for Best Post Modern Video, 1990), Losing My Religion, 1991 (6 MTV Video Music Awards, 1991, 2 Grammy awards: Best Group Pop Vocal Performance, Best Short Form Music Video, 1992), Everybody Hurts, 1992 (4 MTV Video Music Awards, 1994), Man on the Moon, The Great Beyond, Imitation of Life, It's the End of the World As We Know It; appeared on Robbie Robertson's album, Storyville, 1991, Backbeat soundtrack, 1994, Man on the Moon soundtrack, 1999. Named to Rock & Roll Hall of Fame, with R.E.M., 2007; recipient Top Modern Rock Artist, Top World Album awards, Billboard Music Awards, 1991, 3 Grammy awards for Best Group Pop Vocal Performance, Best Alternative Music Performance, and Best Short Form Music Video, 1992, Best Internat. Group, Brit Awards, 1992, 1993, Patrick Lippert award, Rock the Vote, 1994, Video Vanguard award, MTV Video Music Awards, 1995. Office: REM PO Box 8032 Athens GA 30603-8032 *

MILLS, OLAN, II, photography company executive; b. 1930; married. Grad., Princeton U., 1952. With Olan Mills, Inc., Chattanooga, 1955—, now chmn. Office: Olan Mills Inc Gen Offices 4325 Amnicola Hwy Chattanooga TN 37406-1014

MILLS, RICHARD HENRY, federal judge; b. Beardstown, Ill., July 19, 1929; s. Myron Epler and Helen Christine (Greve) M.; m. Rachel Ann Keagle, June 16, 1962; children: Jonathan K., Daniel Cass. BA, Ill. Coll., 1951; JD, Mercer U., 1957; LLM, U. Va., 1982. Bar: Ill. 1957, U.S. Dist. Ct. Ill. 1958, U.S. Ct. Appeals 1959, U.S. Ct. Mil. Appeals 1963, U.S. Supreme Ct. 1963. Legal advisor Ill. Youth Commn., 1958-60; state's atty. Cass County, Virginia, Ill., 1960-64; judge Ill. 8th Jud. Cir., Virginia, 1966-76, Ill. 4th Dist. Appellate Ct., Springfield, Ill., 1976-85, U.S. Dist. Ct. (cen. dist.) Ill., Springfield, 1985—. Adj. prof. So. Ill. U. Sch. Medicine, 1985-06; mem. adv. bd. Nat. Inst. Corrections, Washington, 1984-88, Ill. Supreme Ct. Rules Com., Chgo., 1963-85. Contbr. articles to profl. jours. Pres. Abraham Lincoln coun. Boy Scouts Am., 1978-80. With U.S. Army, 1952-54, Korea, col. res.; maj. gen. Ill. Militia. Recipient George Washington Honor medal Freedoms Found., 1969, 73, 75, 82, Disting. Eagle Scout Boy Scouts Am., 1985. Fellow Am. Bar Found.; mem. ABA, Nat. Conf. Fed. Trial Judges (chmn. 1999-00), Ill. Bar Assn., Chgo. Bar Assn., Cass County Bar Assn. (pres. 1962-64, 75-76), Sangamon County Bar Assn., 7th Cir. Bar Assn., Am. Law Inst., Fed. Judges Assn., Army and Navy Club (Washington), Sangamo Club, Masons (33 degree), Lincoln-Douglas Am. Inn of Ct. 150 (founding, pres. 1991-93). Republican. Office: US Dist Ct 600 E Monroe St Ste 117 Springfield IL 62701-1659 Office Phone: 217-492-4340.

MILLS, RICHARD PAUL, school system administrator; b. Paris, Nov. 28, 1944; m. Judith Mills. BA with honors, Middlebury Coll., 1966; MA in Am. History, Columbia U., 1967, MBA, 1975, EdD, 1977. Tchr. history Dalton Sch., NYC, 1967—71; creator with others Elizabeth Seeger Sch., NYC, 1971—73; planning assoc. N.J. Dept. of Edn., 1975-78, dir. policy analysis, 1978-80, dep. asst. commr., 1980-82, spl. asst. to the commr., 1982-84; spl. asst. to Gov. Thomas H. Kean of N.J., 1984-88; commr. of edn. State of Vt., 1988-95, State of N.Y., 1995—; pres. Univ. of the State of N.Y., 1995—. Adj. asst. prof. Columbia Univ. Tchrs. Coll., 1977; adj. assoc. prof. Rider Coll., N.J., 1979; cons. task force to oversee fiscal reform in Newark, 1975; tchr. The Dalton Sch., N.Y.C., 1967-71, Elizabeth Seeger Sch., N.Y.C., 1971-73; mem. Carnegie Task Force on Learning in the Primary Grades; chair mgmt. group Nat. Alliance for Restructuring Edn.; bd. New Stds. Project; mem. bd. Nat. Ctr. on Edn. and the Economy. Contbr. articles to profl. jours. U.S. rep. to standing com. European Ministers of Edn., 1987. Office: NY State Edn Dept 111 Edn Bldg 89 Washington Ave Albany NY 12234-4909 *

MILLS, STEPHANIE ELLEN, writer; b. Berkeley, Calif., Sept. 11, 1948; d. Robert C. and Edith (Garrison) M.; m. Philip Thiel (div. 1990). BA, Mills Coll., 1969. Campus organizer Planned Parenthood, Alameda, San Francisco, Calif., 1969-70; editor in chief Earth Times, San Francisco, 1970; story editor Earth, San Francisco, 1971; conference facilitator Mills Coll., Oakland, 1973-74; writer family planning program Emory Univ., Atlanta, 1974; dir. outings program Friends of the Earth, San Francisco, 1975-76, dir. membership devel., 1976-78; fellow Found. for Nat. Progress, San Francisco, 1978-80; from asst. editor to editor CoEvolution Quar., Sausalito, Calif., 1980-82; editor in chief, rsch. dir. Calif. Tomorrow, San Francisco, 1982-83; dir. devel. World Coll. West, San Rafael, Calif., 1983-84; freelance writer, lectr., 1984—; adj. prof. Grand Valley State Univ., Traverse City, Mich., 2002. V.p. Earth First! Found., 1986-89; pres. No. Mich. Environ. Action Coun., 1987-88; mem. planning com. Great Lakes Bioregional Congress, 1991; pres. bd. dirs. Oryana Natural Foods Coop., 1992-93; mem. adv. coun. Earth Island Inst., mem. adv. bd. Orion Soc., mem. Am. for Maine Woods, Nat. Park Adv. com., Northwoods Wilderness Recovery. Author: In Service of the Wild: Restoring and Reinhabiting Damaged Land, 1995, Whatever Happened to Ecology?, 1989, Epicurean Simplicity, 2002; editor: Turning Away from Technology: A New Vision for the Twenty-first Century, 1997 (Utne Visionary award 1996); editor, contbr. In Praise of Nature, 1990; corr. Wild Earth; editor-in-chief Not Man Apart newsletter from Friends of the Earth, 1978; editl. adv. E; contbr. to Ency. Brit. Book of Yr., 1998; contbr. articles to popular mags. Bd. dirs. Planned Parenthood Fedn. Am., 1970-76. Recipient award Mademoiselle, 1969, Friends of UN Environ. Program, 1987; grantee Point Found., 1972, IRA-HITI Found., 1992; resident Blue Mountain Ctr., 1983, 86. Avocations: swimming, cooking. Office: care Katinka Matson Brockman Inc 5 E 59th St New York NY 10022-1027

MILLS, STEPHEN, performing company executive; Prin. dancer Ballet Austin, 1987, choreographer, 1988, resident choreographer, 1992, assoc. artistic dir., 1999—, artistic dir., 2002—. Instr. Internat. Theatrical Inst., Cyprus; master tchr. Booker T. Washington H.S. for the Performing Arts, Dallas, Va. Sch. of the Arts, New Orleans Ctr. for Creative Arts, Stephens Coll., Mo., Point Park Coll., Pitts., Ballet Austin. Choreographed works have been shown at Ballet Builders at Lincoln Ctr., 1998, Rencontres Chorégraphiques Internat. des Seine-Saint-Denis, Paris, Cuballet, Havana, The Dayton Ballet, The Sarasota (Fla.) Ballet, Ballet Pacifica, Dallas Black Dance Theatre, Dance Kaleidoscope, Ontario Ballet Theatre, Toronto, Icelandic Ballet Co., Reykjavik; performing mem. Harkness Ballet, Am. Dance Machine, Cin. Ballet, Indpls. Ballet Theatre, Balanchine Repertoire. Bd. trustees Dance USA. Office: Ballet Austin 3002 Guadalupe St Austin TX 78705-2818 *

MILLS, STEPHEN G., lawyer; BA summa cum laude, U. Mich., 1980, JD magna cum laude, 1984. Bar: NY. Tax ptnr. King & Spaulding LLP, NYC; ptnr. Goodwin Procter LLP, NYC, 2007—. Office: Goodwin Procter LLP 559 Lexington Ave New York NY 10022 Office Phone: 212-813-8911. E-mail: smills@goodwinprocter.com.

MILLS, STEVEN A., information technology executive; Sales trainee, mktg. rep. IBM, NYC, 1974—80, mem. bus. planning staff divsn. data processing, 1981—82, mgr. bus. planning staff, 1982—84, adminstrv. asst. to v.p. and asst. group exec. plans and controls, 1984—85, dir. planning info. sys. and comm. group, 1985—88, dir. fin. planning, 1988—89, dir. ops. programming sys., 1989—90, asst. gen. mgr. fin. and planning, 1990—92, gen. mgr. Santa Teresa lab., 1992—95; gen. mgr. software group strategy and solutions IBM Software Group, 1995—2000, sr. v.p., group exec., 2000—. Mem. ops. com. IBM, mem. worldwide mgmt. coun., mem. corp. tech. com. Office: IBM 1133 Westchester Ave White Plains NY 10604 *

MILLS, SUSAN WILSON, music educator; b. Louisville, Nov. 12, 1962; d. William Johnson II and Linda Lee Wilson; m. Dennis Richard Mills, Oct. 25, 1997. BA, Rollins Coll., Winter Park, Fla., 1984; MA, U. Ctrl. Fla., Orlando, 1990, EdD, 1999. Cert. profl. educator, music Fla., 1989. Dir. sch. music St. Margaret Mary Sch., Winter Park, 1990—98; vis. asst. prof. U. Ctrl. Fla., Orlando, 1999—2000; assoc. chair performing arts Frostburg State U., Md., 2000—06; assoc. prof., coord. music edn. Appalachian State U., Boone, NC, 2006—. Mem. exec. bd. Md. Music Educators Assn., Balt., 2003—06; grant reviewer Md. Arts Coun., Balt., 2003—04. Contbr. chapters to books; performer: Master Musicians Festival, 2003. Grantee Umcolo: The Kimberley Project, Eastman Sch. Music, 2001; Summer Music fellow, Northwestern U., 1994, Appalachian Music fellow, Berea Coll., 2006. Mem.: Coll. Music Soc., Music Educators Nat. Conf., NC Music Educators Assn. Avocations: sailing, swimming, dance, reading, cooking. Office: Appalachian State U Hayes Sch Music ASU Box 32096 Boone NC 28608 Office Phone: 828-262-6441.

MILLS, WILLIAM HAROLD, JR., construction executive; b. St. Petersburg, Fla., July 24, 1939; s. William Harold and Caroline (Bonfoey) M.; m. Sylvia Ludwig, Jan. 4, 1962 (div. 1975); children— William Harold III, Robert Michael, Leslie Anne; m. Kimberly Keyes, May 4, 1985 (div. 1988); m. Gigi Alice Schmidt, Aug. 1, 1990. Grad., Woodberry Forest Sch., 1954-57; BS in Civil Engring., U. Fla., 1961. Cert. Class A gen. contractor, Fla. V.P. bus. devel. Mills & Jones Constrn., St. Petersburg, Fla., 1964-68; v.p. Wellington Corp., Atlanta, 1968-71; exec. v.p. Mills & Jones Constrn., St. Petersburg, Fla., 1971-79; pres., chmn. Federal Constrn. Co., St. Petersburg, 1979-88, vice chmn., 1988—; pres., chair Univ. Housing Svcs., Inc., St. Petersburg. Mem. adv. com. St Petersburg Port, 1993—. Pres. St. Petersburg Progress, Inc., 1986-87; active mem. Suncoasters, St. Petersburg, 1974—, St. Anthony's Devel. Found., St. Petersburg, 1983-86; past chmn. Pinellas Marine Inst., St. Petersburg, Blue Ribbon Zoning Com., City of St. Petersburg; mem. Tony Janus Award Com.; former mem. Pinellas County Constrn. Licensing Bd., Tampa Bay Aviation Adv. Com., United Fund Pinellas County; former mem. U. South Fla. Campus Adv. Bd. Served with USPHS, 1962-64. Named Hon. Royal Navy Liaison officer Her Majesty's Royal Navy, 1984. Mem. ASCE, NSPE, Am. Mgmt. Assn., Mensa, St. Petersburg Area C. of C. (bd. govs. 1983-85), Fla. Sports Adv. Coun., Order of Salvador/Salvador Dali Mus., St. Petersburg Yacht Club, Dragon Club, Les Ambassadeurs Club (London), Annabel's Club (London), Useppa Island Club (past bd. govs.), Sigma Alpha Epsilon, U.S. Croquet Assn., Univ. Fla. Pres.'s Coun. (life). Republican. Episcopalian. Home: 1260 Brightwaters Blvd NE Saint Petersburg FL 33704-3728 E-mail: wmillsjr@uhsi.com.

MILLS, WILLIAM HAYES, lawyer; b. Gordo, Ala., Mar. 30, 1931; s. Early S. and Bama (Cameron) M. LLB, U. Ala., 1956. Bar: Ala. 1956. Pvt. practice, Birmingham, Ala.; ptnr. Rogers, Howard, Redden & Mills, 1961—79, Redden, Mills & Clark, 1979—. Arbitrator Fed. Mediation and Conciliation Svc., Am. Arbitration Assn. Served with AUS, 1948-50, 50-51. Mem. ABA, Ala. Bar Assn., Birmingham Bar Assn. Baptist. Home: 2105 Williamsburg Way Birmingham AL 35223-1740 Office: Redden Mills & Clark 940 Financial Ctr Birmingham AL 35203 Home Phone: 205-870-4139; Office Phone: 205-322-0457. Business E-Mail: whm@rmclaw.com.

MILLS, WILLIAM JAMES, JR., orthopedist, surgeon, researcher; b. San Francisco, Calif., July 7, 1918; s. William James Mills and Rose Lena Conrad; m. Elaine Mary Nagelvoort, Aug. 23, 1952; children: Sarah, Janet, William, Martha, Mary, John, Matthew. BA, U. Calif., 1942; MD, Stanford U., 1950; LittD (hon.), U. Alaska, 2003; DSc (hon.), U. Man., 2006. Cert. Am. Coll. Surgery, Am. Acad. Orthopedic Surgery, Am. Orthopedic Assn., Arctic Inst. N. Am. Intern U. Mich. Hosp., Ann Arbor, Mich., 1949—51, resident, 1951—54; pvt. practice orthopaedist Anchorage, 1955—66; pvt. practice orthop. surgeon, 1968—; surgeon US Naval Hosp., DaNang, Vietnam, 1966—67; asst. prof. Vanderbilt U. Hosp., Nashville, 1967—68. Founder, dir. Alaska Arctic Med. Rsch. Found., Anchorage, 1978—; adj. prof. U. Alaska, Anchorage, 1980—; clin. prof. dept. orthop. surgery U. Wash. Editor-in-chief: Alaska Medicine Jour., 1959; contbr. scientific articles, photographs to jours. Rear admiral USNR, 1942—78, WWII, Vietnam, ret. USNR, 1978. Recipient Dr. Helen Whaley award, Alaska Treatment Ctr., Alpine Team medal, City of Lecco, Italy, 1961, Disting. Achievement award, U. Mich., 2002, Jack Hildes medal, Circumpolar Health Soc., 2003, Disting. Achievement, U. Mich., 2001. Fellow: ACS, Am. Orthop. Assn., Am. Acad. Orthop. Surgeons. Avocations: camping, fly fishing, reading, stamp collecting/philately, gardening. Home and Office: 1544 Hidden Lane Anchorage AK 99501

MILLSAP, GINA J., library director; m. Ried Millsap; 1 child, Nick. MLS, U. Mo., Columbia, 1977. Intern Daniel Boone Regional Libr., Columbia, Mo., head reference, computer svcs.; exec. dir. Ames Pub. Libr., Iowa, 1996—2005, bd. dirs. Iowa; dir. Topeka Shawnee County Pub. Libr., Kans., 2005—. Named one of the Movers & Shakers, Libr. Jour., 2007. Mem.: Iowa Libr. Assn. (former pres., former chair, govt. affairs com.), ALA. Office: Topeka & Shawnee County Pub Libary 1515 SW 10th Ave Topeka KS 66604 Office Phone: 785-580-4400.

MILLSAPS, WILLIAM HOBART, JR., retired editor; b. Chattanooga, July 1, 1942; s. William Hobart and Myra Sue (Bryant) M.; m. Nancy Dickenson Hurt; children: Katherine Gail Millsaps Renick, Camerian Sue. Student, U. Tenn., 1960-66. Sports writer The Knoxville (Tenn.) Jour., 1963-66, Richmond (Va.) Times-Dispatch, 1966-71, assoc. sports editor, 1972, exec. sports editor, 1973-76, sports editor, 1977-91, mng. editor, 1992-93, exec. editor, 1994—2005; ret., 2005. Pres. U.S. Basketball Writers Assn., 1986, AP Sports Editors, 1980; pres. Leadership Metro Richmond Alumni Assn., 1995. Named to, U.S. Basketball Writers Assn. Hall of Fame, media wing Va. Sports Hall of Fame, Va. Comm. Hall of Fame; recipient 11 Va. Sports Writer of Yr. awards, Nat. Sportscasters and Sportswriters Assn. Mem. Willow Oaks Country Club (Richmond) Presbyterian. Avocations: reading, golf.

MILLSON, RORY OLIVER, lawyer; b. Capetown, Republic of South Africa, Nov. 26, 1950; s. Harry E. and Fay Leonard (Liesching) M.; m. Linda Ellen Rodd, June 15, 1985; children: Helen Fay, John Rodd, Henry Francis. BA, Yale U., 1973, JD, 1977; MA, Oxford U., Eng., 1975. Bar: N.Y. 1978, U.S. Dist. Ct. (so. and ea. dists.) N.Y. 1978, U.S. Ct. Appeals (D.C. cir.) 1990, U.S. Ct. Appeals (2d cir.) 1991, U.S. Supreme Ct. 1991. With Cravath, Swaine & Moore, NYC, 1976—, ptnr., litig., 1984—. Office: Cravath Swaine & Moore 825 8th Ave Fl 38 New York NY 10019-7475 Office Phone: 212-474-1672. Office Fax: 212-474-3700. Business E-Mail: rmillson@cravath.com.

MILLSPAUGH, MARTIN LAURENCE, real estate developer, consultant; b. Columbus, Ohio, Dec. 16, 1925; s. Martin Laurence and Elisabeth (Park) M.; m. Meredith Plant, May 10, 1952; children: Elisabeth, M. Laurence, Meredith, Thomas. AB summa cum laude, Princeton U., 1949. Reporter, columnist Richmond News Leader, Va., 1949-53; urban affairs writer Balt. Evening Sun, 1953-57; asst. commr. Urban Renewal Adminstrn., Washington, 1957-60; dep. gen. mgr. Charles Ctr., Balt., 1960-65; pres., chmn., CEO Charles Ctr.-Inner Harbor Mgmt., Inc., 1965-85; exec. v.p., pres., vice chmn. Enterprise Devel. Co., Columbia, Md., 1985—2005; pres. Enterprise Internat. Devel. Co., Columbia, 1988-91, vice chmn., 1991—2005, Enterprise Real Estate Svcs., Inc., 1996—2005; pvt. practice Balt., 2005—. Conducted seminars in Nagasaki and Kagoshima, Japan, 1991-92; lectr. Columbia U., Princeton U., Johns Hopkins U., U. Md., U. New Orleans, NYU, Acad. Polit. Sci., AAAS, Lambda Alpha Internat. Urban Land Inst., 1985-95, U.K. Inst. Travel and Tourism, 1993, Can. Water Resources Assn., 1991, Nat. Bldg. Mus., 1995, Internat. Property Market, Cannes, 1996, others; appeared on USIA Worldnet TV Dialogue, Montevideo, Uruguay, 1990, Recife and Rio de Janeiro, 1995; cons. in field. Author: (with others) The Human Side of Urban Renewal, 1958; author (newspaper series) Design for Living (hon. mention Heywood Broun award 1957); profl. appearances include VOA, 1994, CBS Sunday News, 1994; contbr. articles to profl. jours. Trustee Enoch Pratt Free Libr., Balt., 1965-85, Gilman Sch., 1975-80, Bryn Mawr Sch. for Girls, 1978-81; bd. dirs. Planned Parenthood Assn. Md., 1962-65, Roland Park Civic League, 1962-64, sec., 1963-64, Blue Cross of Md., Inc., 1970-80, Balt. Symphony Orch. Assn., 1974-78, YMCA Greater Balt. area, 1977-81; Md. Internat. Coun., Balt., 1992-96, mem. long range planning com., 1994-96, sec., 1995-96; chair nominating com. World Trade Ctr. Inst., 1996-01; task force Twentieth Century Fund, NYC, 1984-85; adv. coun. real estate devel. program Columbia U. Grad. Sch. Architecture and Planning, 1985-94; bd. advisors Fight-Blight Fund, Balt., 1961-62, Waterfront Ctr., Washington, 1987-90; adv. bd. Nat. Aquarium, Balt., 1988-2001, Sch. Bus. Mgmt. Morgan State U., 1993-94, Real Estate Inst., Sch. Profl. and Bus. Studies Johns Hopkins U., 1994-2006, chair, 2000-2002; pres.'s adv. bd. U. Md. Balt. County, 1989-94; adv. bd. Ctr. for Balt. Studies/U. Balt., 2001-02; adv. panel Ctr. Strategic and Internat. Studies, Washington, 1993-94; mem. Md. Transp. Real Estate Adv. Group, 1996; mem. U.S. Senate Productivity Award Selection Com. for Md., 1987. Sgt. USAF, 1944-46, PTO. Recipient Disting. Svc. award U.S. Housing and Home Fin. Agy., Washington, 1960, Excellence award Urban Land Inst., 1980, Civic Accomplishment award Greater Balt. Comm., 1981, Urban Planning award The Waterfront Ctr., 1995, Prix d'Excellence Awd. Internat. Real Estate Fedn., 1997. Mem. Urban Land Inst. (hon., exec. group internat. coun., 1989-97, vice chmn. internat. coun. 1995-96, chair adv. panel for city of Harrisburg, Pa., 1984, internat. com. 1987-88, Balt. dist. coord. 1987-91, vice-chmn. dist. coun. com. 1991-94, Balt. dist. coun. exec. com. 1992—, adv. panel for Oklahoma City, 1995, chair Project Analysis Chattanooga, 1999, awards com. 1995-97), Internat. Real Estate Fedn. (Greater Balt. com. 2005), urban affairs coun. 1982-87), Coun. on Urban Econ. Devel., Internat. Downtown Assn., Internat. New Town Assn. (adv. panel for waterfront devel. for City of Malmo, Sweden 1987), Phi Beta Kappa, Lambda Alpha. Clubs: Center, Balt., 14 W Hamilton St (Balt.); Ivy (Princeton, NJ). Democrat. Episcopalian. Home: 203 Ridgewood Rd Baltimore MD 21210-2538 E-mail: mmillsii@aol.com.

MILLSTEIN, IRA M., lawyer, educator; b. NYC, Nov. 8, 1926; s. Harry M. and Birdie E. (Rosenbaum) M.; m. Diane G. Greenberg, July 3, 1949; children: James Eliot, Elizabeth Jane. BS, Columbia U., 1947, LL.B., 1949. Bar: NY 1949, US Supreme Ct. 1973. Atty. antitrust div. Dept. Justice, Washington, 1949-51; assoc. firm Weil Gotshal & Manges LLP, NYC, 1951-57, ptnr., 1957—. Fellow faculty govt. John F. Kennedy Sch. Govt., Harvard U., 1983-87; Yale Sch. Mgmt. sr. assoc. dean for corp. governance 2005-, Eugene F. Williams Jr. vis. prof. in competetive enterprise and strategy 1996—; chmn. pvt. sector adv. group of Global Corp. Governance Forum sponsored by World Bank/OECD-Paris, Washington, 1999-2005, chmn. emeritus 2005-; counsel, bd. dirs. Lower Manhattan Devel. Corp., 2002-05; bd. mem. World Trade Ctr. Meml. Found.; chmn. NY State Commn. Pub. Authority Reform, 2004-06. Author: (with Katsh) The Limits of Corporate Power, 1981, (with MacAvoy) The Recurrent Crisis in Corporate Governance, 2003; contbr. articles to profl. jours. Mem. Nat. Commn. on Consumer Fin., 1969-72, chmn., 1971-72; chmn. exec. com. bd. overseers Albert Einstein Coll. Medicine, Yeshiva U., Bronx, NY, 1981—, chmn., 2004-07; chmn. bd. trustees Cen. Pk. Conservancy, 1990-99; co-chair NYSE, NASD Blue Ribbon com. on improving audit coms., 1999. Decorated chevalier Nat. Order of Merit, France. Named one of 100 Most Influential Lawyers, Nat. Law Jour., 2006. Mem. Am. Acad. Arts and Scis. (elected), ABA (chmn. antitrust law sect. 1977-78), NY State Bar Assn. (chmn. antitrust law sect. 1967-68), Nat. Assn. Corp. Dirs. (bd. dirs. 1994—2004, 2007-, governance coun. 2004-07), Met. Club, Quaker Ridge Golf Club. Home: 1240 Flagler Dr Mamaroneck NY 10543-4601 Office: Weil Gotshal & Manges LLP 767 5th Ave Ste 3201 New York NY 10153-0023 Business E-Mail: ira.millstein@weil.com.

MILLSTEIN, JAMES ELIOT, lawyer; s. Ira M. Millstein; m. Carolyn Whitney MacIver, July 10, 1993. Grad., Princeton U., NJ; MS in Polit. Sci., U. Calif., Berkeley; JD, Columbia U., NYC. Ptnr., head corp. restructuring practice grp. Cleary, Gottlieb, Steen & Hamilton; mng. dir., co-head restructuring grp. Lazard. Mailing: 17 Woodbine Ave Larchmont NY 10538-3610 Office: Lazard 30 Rockefeller Plz New York NY 10020 Home Phone: 914-834-8715. *

MILLSTEIN, LINCOLN, media company executive; BA in Polit. Sci., U. Conn.; postgrad., Stanford U., 1980—81. Reporter, editor The Hartford Courant, 1973—83, bus. editor, 1981—83; varous editor positions The Globe, 1983—85; v.p. new media The Boston Globe, 1995—99; CEO Boston.com, 1998—99; group v.p., pub. N.Y. Times Digital, N.Y. Times Co., NY, 1999—2000, exec. v.p. NY, 2000—04; sr. v.p., dir. digital media Hearst Newspapers, 2005—. Profl. Journalism fellow, NEH, 1980—81. Achievements include development of and introduction of The Globe 100 list of the top companies in Massachusetts in 1989. Office: Hearst 250 W 55th St New York NY 10019-5201

MILLSTONE, DAVID JEFFREY, lawyer; b. Morgantown, W.Va., 1946; AB, Johns Hopkins U., 1968; JD, W.Va. U., 1971. Bar: Ohio 1971. Ptnr. Squire, Sanders & Dempsey LLP, Cleve. Co-author: Wage Hour Law--How to Comply, 2001; editor: Ohio and Fed. Employment Law Manual, 2001; contbr. chapters to books. Past chair regional bd., nat commr., nat. exec. com. mem., chair edn. com. Anti-Defamation League, 2002—05. Mem.: ABA, Ohio Mgmt. Lawyers Assn., Cleve. Bar Assn. Office: Squire Sanders & Dempsey 4900 Key Tower 127 Public Sq Ste 4900 Cleveland OH 44114-1304 Office Phone: 216-479-8574. E-mail: dmillstone@ssd.com.

MILMAN, NATALIE BORDELON, education educator; BA in English and Spanish, Tulane U., 1991; MA in Multicultural Edn., Calif. State U., Dominguez Hills, 1994; PhD in Instructional Tech., U. Va., Charlottesville, 2000. Tchr. Long Beach (Calif.) Unified Sch. Dist., 1991—96; asst. prof. George Washington U., Washington, 2001—. Author: The Digital Teaching Portfolio Handbook: A How-To Guide for Teachers, 2003, What Every School Leader Should Know About Digital Teaching Portfolios, 2003, The Digital Teaching Portfolio Workbook: Understanding the Digital Teaching Portfolio Process, 2005, Digital teaching portfolios: Catalysts for Fostering Authentic Professional Development, 2005. Named Luminary, Gelman Libr., George Wash. U., 2005; recipient Outstanding Grad. Tchg. Asst. award, U. Va., 1999; Curry Ctr. for Tech. and Tchr. Edn. fellow, 1997—2000. Mem.: Am. Ednl. Rsch. Assn. (chmn. spl. interest group 2005—). Office: George Washington U 2134 G St NW Washington DC 20052 Office Phone: 202-994-1884.

MILMED, PAUL KUSSY, lawyer; b. Newark, Oct. 15, 1944; s. Leon Sidney and Bella (Kussy) M.; m. Debra R. Anisman, Oct. 23, 1988; children: Laura, Julia. AB, Amherst Coll., 1966; MSc, U. London, 1968; EdM, Harvard U., 1969; JD, NYU, 1975. Bar: N.J. 1975, N.Y. 1976, U.S. Ct. Appeals (2d cir.) 1975, U.S. Dist. Ct. N.J. 1975, U.S. Dist. Ct. (so. dist.) N.Y. 1976, U.S. Dist. Ct. (ea. dist.) N.Y. 1994. Law clk. Hon. Alan B. Handler N.J. Superior Ct. Appellate Divsn., Newark, 1975-76; assoc. Weil, Gotshal & Manges, NYC, 1976-83; asst. U.S. atty. U.S. Atty.'s Office, So. Dist. N.Y., NYC, 1983-93, chief environ. protection unit, 1990-93; of counsel White & Case, NYC, 1993—. Ct.-apptd. mediator U.S. Dist. Ct., So. Dist. N.Y., 1996—. Rsch. editor NYU Rev. of Law and Social Change, 1974-75; editl. adv. bd. Fordham Environ. Law Jour., 1993—; contbr. articles to profl. jours. Mem. bd. trustees The Town Sch., NYC, 1997-06. Mem. Assn. Bar City of N.Y. Avocation: photography. Home: One Gracie Terr New York NY 10028 Office: White & Case 1155 Avenue Of The Americas New York NY 10036-2787 Office Phone: 212-819-8751. E-mail: pkm@post.harvard.edu.

MILMOE, J. GREGORY, JR., lawyer; b. White Plains, NY, Nov. 16, 1947; AB, Cornell U., 1970; JD, Fordham U., 1975. Bar: NY 1976. Joined Skadden, Arps, Slate, Meagher & Flom, NYC, 1971—, mailroom asst., 1971, ptnr., co-leader corp. restructuring. Lectr. on fiduciary and restructuring issues for legal and business audiences. Articles editor Fordham Law Rev., 1974—75. Named a Dealmaker of Yr., Am. Lawyer mag., 2007. Office: Skadden Arps Slate Meagher & Flom 4 Times Sq New York NY 10036 Office Phone: 212-735-3770. Office Fax: 917-777-3770. Business E-Mail: jmilmoe@skadden.com. *

MILNE, CHRISTOPHER, photographer, journalist, educator; b. NYC, June 6, 1934; s. C. Lee Wilmoth and Helen Milne; m. Vesta Seymour Fulton, Jan. 6, 1999; children: Bruce, Milne, Geoffrey, David, James, Kevin. BA, Geneva Coll., 1956; postgrad., U. Pitts., 1957—59, Boston U., 1968, U. Fla., 1984, Wheaton Coll., 1988; studied color photography, Roman Vishniak, Montreal, 1973. Writer U.S. Steel, Pitts., 1957-61; owner Interprel Corp., Pitts., 1961—; photographer Robert F. Kennedy Funeral Train, 1968; writer, corr. U.P.I., Washington, 1968—94; pub., editor Ea. Shore Echo, Halifax, 1976-77; founder Marine Gallery and Mus., Canada, 1978; instr. various colls., 1988—; publ. Safe Harbour Press, Crescent, Pa., 1989—; CEO, Milne Inst., Crescent, 1999—. Spl. investigator Scranton commn. investigating killings Kent State U., 1971; mem. speaker's bureau Ethics in Journalism. Editor: RR Stations of Pennsylvania, 1967; author: Ethics for Journalists, 2000; contbr. articles & photographs to Official Railway Guide, 1978-79; photographer traveling exhibit A Brutal Season, Northern Ireland, 1988-, When Trains Were King, 1992—; asst. editor Can. Nat. Rlwys., 1978; official photographer CPR, 1974. Counselor House Trailer Com. on Aging, 1970; spl. investigator Agy. for Social Concerns of United Meth. Ch., 1970 Mem. SAR, VFW, Nat. Geog. Soc. (life), Soc. Profl. Journalists, Train Collectors Assn., Profl. Photographers Am., Nat. Multiple Sclerosis Soc., N.H. Art Assn., Newburyport (Mass.) Art Assn., Pitts. History and Landmarks Found. (docent), Scottish Rite Masonic Orders Achievements include one of three official news photographers on Robert F. Kennedy funeral train. Address: Safe Harbour Studios PO Box 233 Sewickley PA 15143 Business E-Mail: cmmilne@geneva.edu.

MILNER, CHARLES FREMONT, JR., manufacturing executive; b. Durham, NC, July 21, 1942; s. Charles Fremont and Eloyse Sargent Milner; m. Molly Franc Wakefield, Aug. 28, 1965; children: Bernadette Ann Milner Gardner, Eloyse Lee Milner Ellerman. BA, Guilford Coll., 1963; MBA, Harvard U., 1965. Asst. to comptroller Harvard U., 1965-66; instr. Northeastern U., Boston, 1965-66; with Burlington Hosiery Co. divsn. Burlington (N.C.) Industries, 1966-71, asst. v.p., 1970-71; exec. v.p. Parklane Hosiery Co., Inc., New Hyde Park, N.Y., 1971-74; pres. Rudin & Roth, Inc. divsn. NCC Industries, NYC, 1974-75; v.p. apparel group M. Lowenstein and Sons, NYC, 1975-76; pres., CEO BBC, Inc. and Camp Industry divsns. Genesco, Inc., 1976-80; gen. mgr. Johnston and Murphy Shoe Co. divsn., 1979—82; gen. mgr. footwear mktg. and mfg. Genesco, Inc., 1980-81, v.p., 1981-82; pres., CEO Hope Hosiery Mills and C.M. Industries, Inc., Denver, Pa., 1983—. Trustee Friends Acad., Locust Valley, NY, 1974-79, Guilford Coll., 1982-97, vice chmn., 1989, chmn., 1990-97; mem. class chief fund agt. Harvard Bus. Sch., 1986-91, 40th reunion co-chmn. 2005, alumni bd., 1992-2001, v.p., 1995-97, pres., 1997-99, past pres., 1999-2001. Mem. Nat. Assn. Hosiery Mfrs. (dir. 1978-82, 87—, exec. com. 1989-93, 99—, 2d vice-chmn. 1991-92, vice-chmn. 1992, chmn. 1993), Lancaster Country Club (bd. govs. 2004—), Hamilton Club, Moselem Springs Golf Club. Home: 158 Hamilton Rd Lancaster PA 17603-4734 Office: 205 Washington St Denver PA 17517 E-mail: mmilner@socksmyway.com.

MILNER, CLYDE A., II, historian; b. Durham, NC, Oct. 19, 1948; s. Charles Fremont and Eloyse (Sargent) M.; m. Carol Ann O'Connor, Aug. 14, 1977; children: Catherine Carol, Charles Clyde. AB, U. N.C., 1971; MA, Yale U., 1973, MPhil, 1974, PhD, 1979. Admissions counselor Guilford Coll., Greensboro, NC, 1968-70; acting instr. Yale U., New Haven, 1974-75; research fellow McNickle Ctr., Chgo., 1975-76; instr. Utah State U., Logan, 1976-79, asst. prof., 1979-82, assoc. prof., 1982-88, prof., 1988—2002; dir. Mountain West Ctr. for Regional Studies, 1997-2000; dir. PhD program in heritage studies Ark. State U., 2002—, prof., 2002—. Reader of manuscripts History Book Club, Inc., 1986—; exec. dir. Am. Studies program Utah State U., 1997-2000, vis. prof. Yale U., 2006-07, sr. rsch. fellow Beinecke Libr., 2006-07. Author: With Good Intentions, 1982; editor: Major Problems in the History of the American West, 1989, co-editor 2d edit., 1997; editor: A New Significance: Re-envisioning the History of the American West, 1996; assoc. editor The Western Hist. Quar., 1984-87, co-editor, 1987-89, editor, 1990-97, exec. editor, 1998-2002; co-editor: Churchmen and the Western Indians, 1985, Trails: Toward a New Western History, 1991, Oxford History of the American West, 1994 (Western Heritage award for non-fiction Nat. Cowboy Hall of Fame 1994, Caughey Western History Assn. award for best book on history of Am. West 1995). Recipient Paladen Writing award The Montana Mag. Western History, 1987, Faculty Svc. award Associated Students Utah State U., 1987, Outstanding Social Science Researcher award Utah State U., 1983, (with Carol A. O'Connor) Charles Redd prize Utah Acad. Scis., Arts and Letters, 1996; fellowship fund established in his honor Western Hist. Quar. Utah State U., 2002, Grad. Editl. Assistantship in his honor with Anne M. Butler, 2004. Mem. Western History Assn., Orgn. Am. Historians (Disting. lectr. 2004—, adv. bd. newsletter 2005—), Phi Alpha Theta, Phi Beta Kappa. Mem. Soc. Of Friends. Home: 1306 E Country Club Terr Jonesboro AR 72401-4325 Office: Ark State U Heritage Studies PhD Program PO Box 69 State University AR 72467 Office Phone: 870-972-3509. Business E-Mail: cmilner@astate.edu.

MILNER, HAROLD WILLIAM, hotel executive; b. Salt Lake City, Nov. 11, 1934; s. Kenneth W. and Olive (Schoettlin) Milner; m. Susan Emmett, June 19, 1959 (div. 1976); children: John Kenneth, Mary Sue; m. Lois Friemuth, Aug. 14, 1977; 1 child, Jennifer Rebecca. BS, U. Utah, 1960; MBA, Harvard, 1962. Instr. Brigham Young U., Provo, Utah, 1962-64; v.p. Gen. Paper Corp., Mpls., 1964-65; dir. finance Amalgamated Sugar Co., Ogden, Utah, 1965-67; corp. treas. Marriott Corp., Washington, 1967-70; pres., chief exec. officer, trustee Hotel Investors, Kensington, Md., 1970-75; pres., CEO Americana Hotels Corp., Chgo., 1975-85, Kahler Corp., Rochester, Minn., 1985-97, Kensington Co., Salt Lake City, 1997—. Trustee Baron Asset Funds, 1987—. Author: A Special Report on Contract Maintenance, 1963. Lt. US Army, 1960. Mem.: Minn. Bus. Partnership (bd. dirs. 1991—). Mem. Lds Ch. Office: The Kensington Co 2293 Morning Star Dr Park City UT 84060-6725 Office Phone: 435-640-1129. Personal E-mail: hmilner@aol.com.

MILNER, IRVIN MYRON, retired lawyer; b. Cleve., Feb. 5, 1916; s. Nathan and Rose (Spector) M.; m. Zelda Winograd., Aug. 15, 1943 AB cum laude, Western Res. U. (now Case Western Res. U.), 1937, JD, 1940, LL.M., 1970. Bar: Ohio 1940, U.S. Dist. Ct. (no. dist.) Ohio 1946. Pvt. practice, Cleve., 1946—2005; ret., 1996. Exec. sec., counsel Men's Apparel Club Ohio, Cleve., 1947-48; adj. instr. Sch. Law, Case Western Res. U., 1965-66; spl. counsel Ohio Office Atty. Gen., 1960-70; legal counsel Korean Am. Assn. Greater Cleve., 1973-95. Mem. Cleve. Fgn. Consular Corps., 1970-96, hon. consul Rep. of Korea for Cleve., 1970-96; bd. dirs. Internat. Human Assistance Programs, Inc., 1973-79, voting corp. mem., 1980-88; mem. Republican Nat. Com. Served with U.S. Army, 1941-45, ETO. Decorated Order Diplomatic Svc. Merit-Heung-in medal (Republic of Korea), 1975; named to Disting. Alumni Hall of Fame, Cleveland Heights (Ohio) High Sch., 1983. Fellow Internat. Consular Coll., Ohio Bar Found.; mem. ABA (small bus. com., corp. bus. law sect. 1971-74), Greater Cleve. Bar Assn., Cuyahoga County Bar Assn. (pres. 1975-76, co-chmn. jud. standards com. 1987-88, life trustee, award of Special Merit 1976, Pres.' award 1988), Ohio State Bar Assn. (coun. dels., 1976-86, com. on legal ethics and profl. conduct 1984-97), Cuyahoga County Bar Found. (sec.-treas. 1980-84, bd. dirs. 1984—), Cuyahoga County Coun. Ohio VFW (comdr. 1958, Merit award 1958), Am. Security Coun. (nat. adv. bd.), Cleve. Coun. on World Affairs, Greater Cleve. Vets. Coun. (pres. 1957), Western Res. Coll. Alumni Assn. (bd. dirs. 1982-88), Cleve. City Club, Masons (32 deg.), Tau Epsilon Rho (chancellor Cleve. Grad. chpt. 1987-88), Delta Phi Alpha. Jewish.

MILNER, RICHARD GERARD, physicist; b. Cork, Ireland, Dec. 2, 1956; s. William and Maura (McGrath) M.; m. Eileen Troy, June 21, 1980; children: William, Samuel, David. BS with honors, Univ. Coll. Cork, 1978, MS, 1979; PhD, Calif. Inst. Tech., 1985. Rsch. assoc. Calif. Inst. Tech., 1985-88, rsch. scientist, 1988; asst. prof. MIT, Cambridge, 1988-93, assoc. prof., 1993-98, prof., 1998—, dir. Bates Linear Accelerator Ctr., 1998—. Mem. medium energy physics group MIT Lab. Nuc. Sci. Contbr. articles to profl. jours. Recipient Presdl. Young Investigator award NSF, 1989. Office: MIT Dept Physics Rm 26-447 77 Massachusetts Ave Cambridge MA 02139-4301 E-mail: milner@mitlns.mit.edu.

MILNES, ARTHUR GEORGE, electrical engineer, educator; b. Heswall, Eng., July 30, 1922; came to U.S., 1957, naturalized, 1964; s. George and Marion (Teasdale) M.; m. Mary Laverne Wertz, Dec. 4, 1955; children: Sheila Rae, Brian George, John Teasdale. BSc, U. Bristol, Eng., 1943, MSc, 1947, DSc, 1956. With Royal Aircraft Establishment, 1943-57, prin. sci. officer, 1952-57; mem. faculty Carnegie-Mellon U., Pitts., 1957-87, prof. elec. engring., 1960-87, assoc. head dept., 1966-69, Buhl prof., 1973-87, prof. emeritus Pitts., 1987—. Cons. to industry on semiconductor devices, 1957 Author: Transductors and Magnetic Amplifiers, 1957, (with D.L. Feucht) Heterojunctions and Metal-Semiconductor Junctions, 1972, Deep Impurities in Semiconductors, 1973, Semiconductor Devices and Integrated Electronics, 1979; contbr. articles to profl. jours. FOA rsch. fellow NAS-Royal Soc. London, 1954. Fellow IEEE (J.J. Ebers award 1982, van der Ziel award 1993), Am. Phys. Soc., Instn. Elec. Engrs. (London). Home: 1417 Inverness St Pittsburgh PA 15217-1157 Personal E-mail: arthurmilnes@worldnet.att.net.

MILNOR, HAZEL, nurse; b. Marble, Ark., Apr. 2, 1921; d. Andrew Jackson and Laura Jane (Davis) Spencer; m. John Champion Milnor, June 21, 1951 (dec. Aug. 1989); children: Mary Christine, Jean Ann Laura. RN, Calif., Hawaii. Nurse pvt. duty, Calif., 1942—; surg. nurse Queen's Hosp., Hawaii, 1944-46; flight attendant United Airlines, San Francisco, 1946-51. Author: Entertaining in Hawaii, 1977, (poetry) As Angels Watch, 1997. Founder, founding pres. Spl. Angels Ministry, Hawaii; chair develop. com. Spl. Angels. Recipient Disting. Svc. award ARC Hawaii, 2005, Kapuna award Bishop of Hawaii Episc. Diocese, 2005; inducted Internat. Poetry Hall of Fame Mem. ARC US, Clipped Wings (mem.-at-large), Honolulu Acad. Arts, Internat. Soc. Poets (disting.), Oahu Country Club, Hawaii Polo Club. Republican. Episcopalian. Avocations: collecting angels, travel.

MILNOR, JOHN WILLARD, mathematician; b. Orange, NJ, Feb. 20, 1931; AB, U. Princeton, 1951, PhD, 1954; DSc (hon.), Syracuse U., 1965, U. Chgo., 1967. Mem. faculty Princeton U., 1953—62, prof., 1960—62, Henry Putman chair, 1962; prof. math., dir. Inst. Math. Scis. SUNY, Stony Brook, NY, 1988—. Editor: Annals of Mathematics, 1962—, Morse Theory, Characteristic Classes, —, Dynamics in One Complex Variable, —, Singular Points of Complex Hypersurfaces, —, Topology from the Differentiable Viewpoint, —. Recipient Fields medal, Internat. Congress Math. in Stockholm, 1962, Nat. medal of Sci., 1967, Leroy P. Steele prize, 1982, Wolf prize in math., Wolf Found., Israel, 1989; Henry Putman fellow, 1949, 1950, Alfred P. Sloan fellow, 1955—59. Mem.: NAS, Russian Acad. Scis. (fgn. mem.), Am. Math. Soc. (Steele prize 2004), Am. Philos. Soc., Am. Acad. Arts and Sci. Achievements include proof that a 7-dimensional sphere can have several differential structures; research in holomorphic dynamics. Office: SUNY Inst Math Sci Math Bldg 5D 148 Stony Brook NY 11794-3660

MILNOR, WILLIAM ROBERT, physician; b. Wilmington, Del., May 4, 1920; s. William Robert and Virginia (Sterling) Milnor; m. Gabriella Mahaffy, Aug. 19, 1944; children: Katherine Alexander, William Henry. AB, Princeton U., 1941; MD, Johns Hopkins U., 1944. Diplomate Am. Bd. Internal Medicine. Intern, resident Johns Hopkins Hosp., 1944-46; rsch. fellow Nat. Heart Inst., 1949-51; physician-in-charge heart sta. Johns Hopkins Hosp., 1951-60, physician, 1952—; mem. faculty Johns Hopkins Med. Sch., 1951—, prof. physiology, 1969—. Vis. fellow St. Catherine's Coll. Oxford U., England, 1968; mem. med. adv. panel Am. Inst. Biol. Scis., 1971—; assessor Nat. Med. Rsch. Coun. Australia, 1976—. Author: Hemodynamics, 1989, Cardio-vascular Physiology, 1990; contbr. articles to med. textbooks and med. jours. Capt. med. corps USAAF, 1946—48. Fellow: ACP; mem.: Heart Assn. Md., Am. Heart Assn. (chmn. rsch. com. 1966), Biomed. Engring. Soc., Am. Fedn. Clin. Rsch., Am. Physiol. Soc.

MILONAS, E. LEO, lawyer, former state judge; b. Oct. 23, 1936; BA, CCNY, 1957; LLB, Bklyn. Law Sch., 1960. Bar: NY 1960. Judge, Criminal Ct. City of NY, 1973—76, supervising judge, Bronx County Criminal Ct., 1973—74, supervising judge, NY County Criminal Ct., 1974—77; justice, Supreme Ct. State of NY, 1978—82, dep. chief adminstrv. judge, 1979—81, assoc. justice, appellate div., 1982—98, chief adminstrv. judge, 1993—95; ptnr., Litigation practice Pillsbury Winthrop Shaw Pittman, NYC, 1998—. Mem. NY State Commn. on Judicial Nomination, 2000—, Governor's Departmental Judicial Screening Com., 2000—, Commn. on Fiduciary Appointments; chmn. First Dept. Pre-Argument Conf. Appellate div. NY State Supreme Ct.; co-chmn. Comml. Courts Task Force NY State. Bd. dir. Legal Aid Soc., 2001—, Fund for Modern Courts, 2000—, Nat. Ctr. for State Courts, 1974, 1980, 2002—; bd. dir. & mem. exec. com. Nat. Urban League, 1990—; bd. dir. Judges & Lawyers Breast Cancer Alert, co-pres., 1997—99; bd. dir. Fund for the City of NY. Fellow: ABA (mem. Ho. Del. 2000—); mem.: Assn. Bar City of NY (v.p. 2000—01, pres. 2002—04), NY State Bar Assn. (mem. Council on Judicial Assns. 1978—). Office: Pillsbury Winthrop Shaw Pittman 1540 Broadway New York NY 10036 Office Phone: 212-858-1615. Office Fax: 212-858-1500. Business E-Mail: eleo.milonas@pillsburylaw.com.

MILONAS, MINOS, artist; b. Heraklion, Crete, Greece, Apr. 28, 1936; arrived in USA, 1964, naturalized, 1968; s. Stavros and Maria (Kaplantzis) M.; m. Arlene Watson, Dec. 23, 1963 (div. 1970); m. Sarah Brown, Dec. 1973 (div. 1974); m. Elaine Mauceli, May 26, 1988. BA, Calif. State U., Northridge, 1970; MFA, U. Wash., Seattle, 1972. Freelance writer and poet, Athens, 1960-64; freelance artist LA, 1964-66; instr. U. Wash., 1971-72, Studio Milonas, Seattle, 1972-76, artist NYC, 1977—, textile designer, 1984-94. One man shows include Second Story Gallery, Seattle, 1971, Henry Art Gallery, Seattle, 1972, Polly Friedlander Gallery, Seattle, 1973, Stavrakakis Gallery, Crete, Greece, 1977, West Broadway Gallery, N.Y.C., 1979, 81, 82, Heraklion Art Gallery, Crete, 1983, Kreonides Gallery, Athens, 1983, 84, Doma Gallery, N.Y.C., 1988, Hellenic Cultural Ctr., N.Y., 1990, 93, Cypriot Consulate, N.Y.C., 1990; exhibitions in group shows at Calif. State U., Northridge, 1968-69, Mcpl. Art Gallery, L.A., 1969, U. Wash. Libr., Seattle, 1971, 72, Panaca Gallery, Bellevue, Wash., 1973, Mercer Island Art Gallery, Seattle, 1973, Henry Art Gallery, Seattle, 1973, Tacoma Art Mus., 1973, 75, N.W. Watercolor Soc., 1974, Gordon Woodside Gallery, Seattle, 1974, Coll. of the Cisciyous, Calif., 1975, Laguna Gloria Art Mus., Austin, Tex., 1975, Redmonds (Wash.) Arts Festival, 1975, Univ. Dist. Arts Festival, Seattle, 1976, Bellevue Art Mus., 1976, Sunne Savage Gallery, Boston, 1976, Cretan Artists, Stavrakakis Gallery, Heraklion, Crete, 1978, Internat. Drawing Biennale, Cleveland, Eng., 1981-82, Bowes Mus., Barnard Castle, Eng., 1982, Shipley Art Gallery, Gateshed, Eng., 1982, House of Commons, London, 1982, Haggin Mus., Stockton, Calif., 1985-86, U. N.D., Grand Forks, 1987, Greek Cultural Ctr., Springfield, Mass., 1987, 89, Del Bello Gallery, Toronto, Ont., Can., 1987, Ball State U., Muncie, Ind., 1989, Morin-Miller Galleries, N.Y.C., 1989-90, Columbia (Md.) Coll., 1989, Grand Prospect Hall, Bklyn., 1990, Kenneth Raymond Gallery, Boca Raton, Fla., 1993-96, Pan Cretan Art Exhbn. Rethymnon Mcpl. Art Gallery, Crete, Greece, 2003—, Melina Merkouri Cultural Ctr., Athens, 2003; author: The Small Caravan, 1962, short stories; author 20 books of poetry in Greek, From A to Z, Poems in English, 2003, Look At Manhattan, Poems in English, 2004, Autobiography, in Greek, 2005, Poems from April, Bilingual Poems in English and Greek, 2005, For Her, Bilingual Poems in English and Greek, 2005, Florida, Bilingual Poems in English and in Greek, 2006; videos include Multimedia Artist, 1988, 500 Definitions--Art Is, 1991; donated paintings to various orgns. Recipient 4 Sculpture awards Summer Art Festivals, 1970-76, 2 Merit awards Greek Cultural Ctr., 1987; U. Wash. grantee, 1970; U. Wash. scholar, 1971. Mem.: Poets House, Greek-Am. Writers Assn. Democrat. Home and Office: 790 11th Ave Apt 39A New York NY 10019-3521

MILONE, FRANCIS MICHAEL, lawyer; b. Phila., Pa., June 18, 1947; s. Michael Nicholas and Frances Theresa (Fair) Milone; m. Maida R. Crane, Nov. 25, 1991; children: Michael, Matthew. BA, LaSalle Coll., 1969; MS, Pa. State U., 1971; JD, U. Pa., 1974. Bar: Pa. 1974, U.S. Dist. Ct. (ea. dist.) Pa. 1974, U.S. Dist. Ct. (mid. dist.) Pa. 1979, U.S. Dist. Ct. (ea. dist.) Mich. 1983, U.S. Ct. Appeals (3d cir.) 1978, U.S. Ct. Appeals (4th and 5th cirs.) 1979, U.S. Supreme Ct. 1979. Assoc. Montgomery, McCracken, Walker & Rhoads, Phila., 1974—77; ptnr.,firm chmn., chmn. firm mgmt. com. Morgan, Lewis & Bockius, Phila., 1981—. Mem.: ABA (labor and litig. sects.), Phila. Bar Assn., Pa. Bar Assn. Office: Morgan Lewis & Bockius 1701 Market St Philadelphia PA 19103-2903 Office Phone: 215-963-5670. Office Fax: 215-963-5001. E-mail: fmilone@morganlewis.com.

MILONE, LYDIA, lawyer; b. Bklyn., Sept. 24, 1956; d. Joseph F. and Natalie C. Milone; m. John Kevin Wrynn, June 7, 2003. BA, CUNY, NYC, 1979; JD, Fordham U., NYC, 1989. Bar: Conn. 1989, NY 1990. Assoc. Bender & Bodnar, White Plains, NY, 1989—93, Gassman, Fisher & Fass, Garden City, NY, 1993—95, Reisman, Pierez, et al., Garden City, 1995—97, Hoffinger Friedland Dobrish & Stern, NYC, 1997—2000; ptnr. Bodnar & Milone LLP, White Plains, 2000—. Author: Internat. Law Jour. Fordham U. Sch. Law, 1988—89; editor in chief: Domestic Law Rev.; contbr. articles to profl. jours. Fellow: Am. Acad. Matrimonial Lawyers; mem.: Westchester County Bar Assn. (exec. com. mem. 2002, lectr.), NY State Bar Assn. (lectr.), Westchester County Women's Bar Assn., Assn. Collaborative Lawyers Rockland-Westchester (pres. 2005—07, v.p. 2004—05, founding mem.). Office: Bodnar & Milone LLP 140 Grand St Ste 401 White Plains NY 10601 Office Phone: 914-997-2500.

MILORO, PROTOPRESBYTER FRANK, religious organization administrator, theology studies educator; b. Wilmington, Del., Jan. 26, 1947; m. Constance Ann Evanisko, Apr. 20, 1969; children: Alexandra, Stephanie, Christopher. Grad. summa cum laude, Saviour Sem., 1969; grad. with high honors, St. Vincent Coll., 1972; attended, U. Pitts. Ordained to Diaconate and Priesthood, 1969. Assigned St. John's Ch., Ligonier, Pa., 1969-72, St. Stephen's Ch., Latrobe, Pa., 1969-72, St. John's Ch., Rahway, NJ, 1972-76; dir. Camp Nazareth, diocesan dir. youth, 1976-86; dean Christ the Saviour Sem.; elevated to dignity of Very Rev., 1985; sec. to bishop; instr. homiletics and parish administrn.; diocesan chancellor Am. Carpatho-Russian Orthodox Diocese, 1990—; dean Christ the Savior Cathedral, 1997—. Chaplain Ea. Orthodox residents Polk Ctr., Commonwealth Pa., established chapel. Assoc. editor The Ch. Messenger. Russian Orthodox. Office: 312 Garfield St Johnstown PA 15906-2122

MILSOM, ROBERT CORTLANDT, banker, director; b. Butler, Pa., Dec. 15, 1924; s. Robert C. and M. Ethel (Leyland) M. BS, John Carroll U., 1948. With PNC Bank (formerly Pitts. Nat. Bank), 1948-90; asst. sec., asst. cashier customer relations div. PNC Bank, 1953-56, asst. v.p. loan div., 1956-60, v.p. charge comml. loan group, 1960-65, sr. v.p. charge comml. banking div., 1965-68, exec. v.p., 1968-72, pres., 1972-85, chmn., CEO, 1985-90, also bd. dirs., 1972—; vice chmn., dir. PNC Bank Corp, 1972-90. Bd. dirs. PNC Bank N.A., PNC Equity Mgmt. Corp., Exec. Svc. Corps., Foxwall Med. Svc.; chmn. bd. trustees Mercy Hosp. Pitts., 1994—. Bd. dirs. Pitts. Mercy Health System, Inc., Pitts. Ballet Theatre, Regional Indsl. Devel. Corp.; hon. trustee John Carroll U., Cleve.; mem. adv. bd. Mon Valley Renaissance program California U. Pa. Mem. Duquesne Club of Pitts., Fox Chapel Golf Club of Pitts., Laurel Valley Golf Club, Rolling Rock Club. Office: PNC Bank NA Two PNC Plz 2-PTPP-20-2 620 Liberty Ave Pittsburgh PA 15222-2719 Office Phone: 412-762-2251.

MILSON, BERTRAM IRVING, surgeon; b. Green Bay, Wis. s. Louis and Marion Milson; m. Patti Salscheider, Jan. 30, 1991; children: Michael, Debra, James. BS, Northwestern U., 1952; MD, Marquette Med. Coll., 1956. Diplomate Am. Bd. Surgery. Surgeon Dousman Clinic, Green Bay, 1961—2005. Med. advisor N.W. Tech. Sch., Green Bay, Wis. Col. USAR, 1957—94. Fellow: Am. Coll. Emergency Physicians, Am. Coll. Surgeons. Republican. Jewish. Office: Dousman Clinic 1745 Dousman Green Bay WI 54303

MILSTEAD, TERRY LEE, secondary school educator; d. Lee Clyde and Rosa Jean Milstead. AA in Gen. Liberal Edn., Alvin CC, Tex., 1981; BA in History, U. Houston Clear Lake, 1983, BS in Psychology, 1983, MS in Spl. Edn. with honors, 1990; PhD in Ednl. Adminstrn., Lacrosse U., Bay St. Louis, Miss., 2007. Cert. secondar history tchr. Tex. Edn. Agy., 1983, secondary psychology tchr. Tex. Edn. Agy., 1983, spl. edn. Tex. Edn. Agy., 1990. Spl. edn. tchr. Houston Ind. Sch. Dist., IM Terrell Mid. Sch., 1986—90, Houston Ind. Sch. Dist., FS Key Mid. Sch., 1990—97, Houston Ind. Sch. Dist., Bellaire HS, 1998—99; history tchr. Houston Ind. Sch. Dist., WI Stevenson Mid. Sch., 1999—. Radiology U. Tex. Med. Br., Galveston, 1980—86; spl. edn. dept. chmn. Houston Ind. Sch. Dist., FS Key Mid. Sch., 1997—98. Finalist Secondary Tchr. of Yr. award, Houston ISD, 2003—04; recipient Tchr. of Month award, IM Terrell Mid. Sch., 1988, FS Key Mid. Sch., 1991—92, Tchr. of Yr. award, 1996, WI Stevenson Mid. Sch., 2000—02, 2003—04, SE Region Tchr. of Yr. award, Houston ISD, 2003—04, Tchr. award, Oustanding Am. Tchrs. Nat. Honor Roll, 2005—06. Mem.: ASCD (assoc.), Tex. Fedn. Tchrs. (assoc.), Houston Area Fedn. Tchrs. (assoc.), Houston Area Coun. Social Studies (assoc.), Tex. State Coun. Social Studies (assoc.), Nat. Coun. Social Studies (assoc.), Kappa Delta Pi (life). Avocations: gardening, sewing, piano, clarinet, saxophone. Office: WI Stevenson Mid Sch 9595 Winkler Houston TX 77017 Business E-Mail: tmilstea@houstonisd.org.

MILSTED, AMY, biomedical educator; BSEd, Ohio State U., 1967; PhD, CUNY, 1977. Lectr. Hunter Coll./CUNY, 1970-76; instr. Carnegie-Mellon U., Pitts., 1976-77; postdoctoral fellow Muscular Dystrophy Assn./Carnegie-Mellon U., Pitts., 1978-79; rsch. assoc. Case Western Res. U., Cleve., 1979-82; rsch. chemist VA Med. Ctr., Cleve., 1982-87; project staff The Cleve. Clin. Found., 1987-89; asst. staff dept. brain and vascular rsch. Cleve. Clinic Found., 1989-93; grad. faculty Sch. Biomed. Scis. Kent (Ohio) State U., 1995—; assoc. prof. dept. biology U. Akron, Ohio, 1993-2000, prof. biology, 2000—. Contbr. articles to profl. jours. Fellow Am. Heart Assn.; mem. AAAS, Inter-Am. Soc. Hypertension, Am. Chem. Soc., Endocrine Soc., Assn. Women in Sci. Office: Univ Akron Dept Biology Asec 279 Akron OH 44325-3908 E-mail: milsted@uakron.edu.

MILSTEIN, ELLIOTT STEVEN, lawyer, educator, academic administrator; b. Oct. 19, 1944; s. Samuel M. and Mildred K. Milstein; m. Bonnie Myrun, Oct. 1, 1967 (div. Oct. 1992); 1 child, Jacob. BA, U. Hartford, 1966, LLD (hon.), 1997; JD, U. Conn., 1969; LLM, Yale U., 1971; LLD (hon.), Nova Southeastern U., 2001. Bar: conn. 1969, D.C. 1972, U.S. Dist. Ct. Conn. 1969, U.S. Ct. Appeals (D.C.) 1972. Lectr. law U. Conn. Clin. Program, 1969-70; staff counsel New Haven Legal Assistance Assn., 1971-72; asst. prof. law, dir. clin. programs Washington Coll. Law Am. U., 1972-74, assoc. prof., dir. clin. programs, 1974-77, prof., dir. clin.

programs, 1977-88, interim dean, 1988-90, dean, 1990—. Prof. law, Washington Coll. Law Am. U., 1995—; co-dir. Nat. Vets. law Ctr., 1978-84; cons. Calif. Bar Bd. of Bar Admissions, Nat. Conf. Bar Examiners, law tng. Practising Law Inst., N.Y.C.; chmn. D.C. Law Students in Ct. Program, 1982-83; mem. Law Tchrs. for Legal Svcs. Bd. dirs. Alliance for Justice, 1996-97. Ford Urban Law fellow, 1971-72; recipient The Lever award for expanding legal svcs. to the poor DC Law Students in Ct. Program, 2006. Mem. ABA (skills tng. com. 1983-85, govt. rels. com. 1992—), ACLU, Soc. Am. Law Tchrs., Assn. Am. Law Schs. (chmn. sect clin. edn. 1982, accreditation com. 1984-86, chmn. standing com. clin. edn. 1993—, exec. com. 1996-2001, pres.-elect 1999, parliamentarian, 2004—, pres. 2000, William Pincus award for outstanding contbns. to clin. legal edn. 1992, Lever award 2006). Democrat. Home: 3216 Brooklawn Ct Bethesda MD 20815-3941 Office: Am U Washington Coll Law 4801 Massachusetts Ave NW Washington DC 20016-8196

MILSTEIN, HOWARD P., bank executive; b. May 15, 1951; BA, Cornell U., 1973; MBA, JD, Harvard U., 1977. Co-chmn., pres., CEO Emigrant Savings Bank, NY Pvt. Bank & Trust; mng. ptnr. Milstein Properties; founding chmn. FriedbergMilstein; chmn. MB Real Estate. Mem. Nat. Bd. Smithsonian Inst.; trustee Cornell U.; mem. bd. overseers Weill Cornell Med. Coll., 1989—; mem. bd. trustees Thomas Jefferson Found., Inc., 2006—. Named one of Forbes' Richest Americans, 2006. Home: NY Pvt Bank & Trust 5 E 42nd St #7 New York NY 10017

MILSTEIN, LAURENCE BENNETT, electrical engineering educator, researcher; b. Bklyn., Oct. 28, 1942; s. Harry and Sadie (Kaplan) M.; m. Suzanne Barbara Hirschman, Oct. 3, 1969; children: Coreen Roxanne, Renair Marissa. BEE, CUNY, 1964; MSEE, Poly. Inst. Bklyn., 1966, PhD in Elec. Engring., 1968. Mem. tech. staff Hughes Aircraft Co., El Segundo, Calif., 1968-69, staff engr., 1969-72, sr. staff engr., 1972-74; asst. prof. Rensselaer Poly. Inst., Troy, NY, 1974-76, U. Calif.-San Diego, La Jolla, 1976-79, assoc. prof., 1979-82, prof. elec. engring., 1982—, chmn. dept., 1984-88, Ericsson endowed chair, 2005. Cons. Hughes Aircraft Co., Culver City, Calif., 1976—78, Lockheed Missiles and Space Co., Sunnyvale, Calif., 1978—93, Motorola Satellite Comm., 1992—96, InterDigital Comm. Corp., 1992—96, Golden Bridge Tech., 1995—99; cons. various govt. agys., pvt. cos., 1975—. Contbr. articles to profl. jours.; co-editor: Tutorials in Modern Communications, 1983, Spread Spectrum Communications, 1983. Recipient Outstanding Tchr. award Warren Coll., U. Calif.-San Diego, La Jolla, 1982, Disting. Tchg. award, 1999; grantee Army Rsch. Office, 1977-84, 86-89, 91-2001, Office of Naval Rsch., Arlington, Va., 1982-05, TRW, San Diego, 1983-89, 92-97, NSF, 1993-04, 2006—. Fellow IEEE (Millennium medal 2000, Edwin Armstrong Achievement award 2000, MILCOM long term tech. achievement award 1998, F.W. Ellersick MILCOM prize paper award 2002), IEEE Coms. Soc. (bd. govs. 1983, 85-87, 93-95, v.p. for tech. activities 1990-91), IEEE Info. Theory Soc. (bd. govs. 1989-94). Jewish. Office: U Calif San Diego Dept Elec Computer Engring La Jolla CA 92093 Office Phone: 858-534-3096. Business E-Mail: milstein@ece.ucsd.edu.

MILSTEIN, MONROE GARY, retail executive; b. NYC, Jan. 14, 1927; s. Abe Herman and Ann Ethel (Isaacs) M.; m. Henrietta Haas, Dec. 22, 1949; children— Lazer, Andrew, Stephen BS, NYU, 1946. Pres. Monroe G. Milstein Inc., NYC, 1947—; chmn. bd., pres., chief exec. officer Burlington Coat Factory Warehouse Corp., NJ, 1972—2007; dir. Fidelity Bank & Trust Co. of N.J., 1972—. Trustee, pres. bd. Long Beach Pub. Library, N.Y., 1967-76; pres. bd. trustees Nassau Library System, Roosevelt Field, N.Y., 1971-73 Recipient Man of Yr. awards Coat and Suit Buyers Assn., 1984, Long Beach C. of C., Youth Service award B'nai B'rith Mem. Am. Gen. Mdse. Assn., U.S. C. of C. Clubs: Dads (Long Beach) (pres. 1969). Lodges: B'nai B'rith (v.p. 1960-62). Jewish. Avocations: fishing, reading, music.

MILSTEIN, PAUL, real estate developer; b. NYC, 1923; s. Morris Milstein; m. Irma Milstein; 4 children. Student, NYU Sch. Architecture. Pres. Circle Floor Co. Inc., NYC, 1961; founder & pres. Milstein Properties, NYC. Former chmn. bd. Starrett Corp.; co-chmn. Emigrant Savings Bank. Donates to NY Pub. Library; Cornell U.; life trustee NY Presbyn. Hosp., NYC; trustee Am. Mus. Natural Hist., NYC. Named one of 400 Richest Americans, Forbes, 2006—, World's Richest People, Forbes mag., 2007. Office: Emigrant Bank 5 E 42nd St New York NY 10017-6994 *

MILSTEIN, RICHARD CRAIG, lawyer; b. NYC, July 16, 1946; s. Max and Hattie (Jacobson) Milstein; children: Brian Matthew, Rachel Helanie. AA with hons., Miami-Dade Jr. Coll., 1966; AB cum laude, U. Miami, Fla., 1968; JD, U. Miami, 1973. Bar: Fla. 1974, US Dist. Ct. (so. dist.) Fla. 1974, US Ct. Appeals (5th cir.) 1974, US Ct. Appeals (11th cir.) 1982, U.S. Supreme Ct. 1977. Assoc. August, Nimkoff & Pohlig., Miami, Fla., 1974—76; mng. ptnr. Jepeway, August, Gassen & Pohling, Miami, 1976—78, August, Pohlig & Milstein, P.A., Coral Gables, Fla., 1980—83; sr. ptnr. Milstein & Wayne, Coral Gables, 1983—85; ptnr. Tescher & Milstein, PA, Coral Gables, 1986—90, Akerman, Senterfitt & Eidson, P.A., 1990—. Named to U. Miami Iron Arrow Hon. Soc., U. Miami, 1998—; recipient Extraordinary Voices Award, Mothers' Voices S. Fla., 2000, Establishment of the Richard C. Milstein Excellence Award, Dade County Bar Assoc., 1999, Outstanding Alumnus Award, U. Miami Sch. of Law, 1999, Tobias Simon Pro Bono Service Award, FL Supreme Ct., 1996, John Minor Wisdom Professional and Public Service Award, American Bar Association Section of Litigation, 1996, Pro Bono Service Award for the Eleventh Judicial Circuit, FL Bar Pres., 1996, Pro Bono awards, 1986, Pro Bono Service Award for the Eleventh Judicial Circuit, FL Bar Pres., 1986. Mem.: U. Miami Law Alumni, Fla. Bar Assn., Coral Gables Bar Assn., Dade County Bar Assn., Am. trial Lawyers Assn., ABA, Nat. Coun. Aging, Nat. Acad. Elder Law, Am. Coll. Trust and Estate Counsel, Dade County Cultural Alliance, U. Miami, South Fla. Inter-Profl. Council Inc., South Fla. Mediation Ctr., Ops. SafeDrive, Met. Dade County Ind. Rev. Panel, Acad. Fla. Trial Lawyers, Miami Coalition Inc., Ptnr. for Youth, Metro Dade County Cultural Affairs Coun., Dade County Vol. Lawyers for Arts, Bet Shira Congregation, Dance Umbrella Inc., Zeta Epsilon Nu, Alpha Kappa, Phi Kappa Phi, Delta Pi, Phi Alpha Theta, Omicron Delta Kappa, Delta Theta Mu, Phi Theta Kappa. Democrat. Office: Akerman Senterfitt & Eidson One SE 3rd Ave Fl 28 Miami FL 33131

MILSTEIN, RICHARD SHERMAN, lawyer; b. Westfield, Mass., May 9, 1926; s. Abraham and Sarah (Yudman) M. BA, Harvard U., 1948; JD, Boston U., 1952. Bar: Mass. 1952, U.S. Supreme Ct. 1959. Ptnr. Ely & King, Springfield, Mass., 1954-95, Chaplin & Milstein, Boston, 1984-91; sr. counsel Robinson, Donovan, Madden & Barry P.C., Springfield, 1995-98. Dir. Mass. Continuing Legal Edn., 1969-80; founding dir., 1980-. Commr. Springfield Parking Authority, 1984—90; trustee Cmty. Music Sch., Springfield, 1994—96, Springfield Symphony Orch., 1995—99, Springfield Libr. Mus. Assn., 1990—2000, Baystate Hosp. Found., 2001—03; overseer Mass. Supreme Jud. Ct. Hist. Soc., 1995—, Boston Lyric Opera, 1999—; trustee Baystate Hosp., v.p., 1995—97; vice chmn. Westfield Acad., 1980—99; chmn. Horace Smith Fund, 1977—93; bd. dirs. Boston Ctr. for Adult Edn., 1998—, v.p., 1998—2003; bd. overseers Huntington Theater, Boston, 1999—; mem. vis. com. Mus. Fine Arts, Boston, 2002—; bd. dirs. Friends of Boston U. Libraries, 2005—; life trustee Sta. WGBY Pub. TV, Springfield, former chmn. bd. trustees. Lt. comdr. USCGR, 1952—64. Recipient Am. Law Inst.-ABA Harrison Tweed Spl. Merit award for contbn. to CLE, 1997, Mass. Bar Cmty. Svc. award, 1998, William Pynchon award for Cmty. Svc. City of Springfield, 1999. Fellow Am. Coll. Trust and Estate Counsel, Mass. Bar Found. (life); mem. Am. Law Inst. (life), Am. Bar Found. (life), Soc. Four Arts Palm Beach. Home: 300 Boylston St Boston MA 02116-3923 also: Mass Continuing Legal Edn 10 Winter Pl Boston MA 02108-4751 Home (Winter): 330 S Ocean Blvd Apt 2E Palm Beach FL 33480 Office Phone: 617-350-7006 ext. 1241. Personal E-mail: rsmilstein@aol.com, rsmilstein_ab@post.harvard.edu.

MILTON, CATHERINE HIGGS, entrepreneur; b. NYC, Jan. 6, 1943; d. Edgar Homer and Josephine (Doughty) Higgs; m. A. Fenner Milton (div.); m. Thomas F. McBride, Aug. 25, 1974 (dec. Oct. 31, 2003); children: Raphael McBride, Luke McBride. BA, Mt. Holyoke Coll., 1964, PhD (hon.), 1992. Reporter, travel writer Boston Globe, 1964-68; with Internat. Assn. Chiefs Police, Washington, 1968-70; asst. dir. Police Found., Washington, 1970-75; spl. asst. US Treasury Dept., Washington, 1977-80; project staff Spl. Com. Aging/Senate, Washington, 1980-81; spl. asst. to pres., founder/exec. dir. Stanford U. Haas Ctr. for Public, Calif., 1981-91; exec. dir. Commn. for Nat. and Cmty. Svc., Washington, 1991-93; v.p. Corp. for Nat. Svc., Washington, 1993-95; exec. dir. Presidio Leadership Ctr., 1995-96; exec. dir. US Programs Save the Children, Westport, Conn., 1996—2002; pres. Friends of the Children, Portland, Oreg., 2002—05. Mem. US Atty. General's Task Force on Family Violence, 1981-82; chair nat. forum Kellogg Found., 1990; bd. dirs. Inst. Higher Edn. Policy, Generation United. Author: Women in Policing, 1972, Police Use of Deadly Force, 1976; co-author: History of Black Americans, 1965, Team Policing, Little Sisters and the Law, 1970. Bd. dirs. Youth Svc. Calif., L.A., 1986-91, Trauma Found., San Francisco, 1982-90, Generation United, 1985-, Inst. Higher Edn. Policy, 1985-; spl. advisor Campus Compact, 1986-91. Nat. Kellogg Found. fellow, Battle Creek, Mich., 1985-88; recipient Dedication and Outstanding Efforts award Bd. Suprs., Santa Clara, Calif., 1989, Outstanding Vol. Contbn. award Strive for Five, San Francisco, 1991, Dinkelspiel award Stanford U., 1991; named Outstanding Campus Adminstr. COOL, 1987. Avocations: backpacking, skiing, hiking, travel. Home: 3652 SE Oak St Portland OR 97214

MILTON, CHAD EARL, lawyer; b. Brevard County, Fla., Jan. 29, 1947; s. Rex Dale and Mary Margaret (Peacock) M.; m. Ann Mitchell Bunting, Mar. 30, 1972; children: Samuel, Kathleen, Kelsey. BA, Colo. Coll., 1969; JD, U. Colo., 1974; postgrad., U. Mo., 1976-77. Bar: Colo. 1974, Mo. 1977, U.S. Dist. Ct. Colo. 1974, U.S. Dist. Ct. (we. dist.) Mo. 1977. Counsel Office of Colo. State Pub. Defender, Colo. Springs, 1974-76; pub. info. officer, counsel Mid-Am. Arts Alliance, Kansas City, Mo., 1977-78; claims counsel Employers Reinsurance Corp., Kansas City, Mo., 1978-80; sr. v.p. Media/Profl. Ins., Kansas City, Mo., 1981-2000; sr. v.p. nat. practice leader, intellectual property & media Marsh, Kansas City, Mo., 2000—. Reporter, photographer, editor Golden (Colo.) Daily Transcript, 1970; investigator, law clk. Office of Colo. State Pub. Defender, Denver, Golden, 1970-74; participant Annenberg Project on the Reform of Libel Laws, Washington, 1987-88; adj. prof., comm. and advt. law Webster U., 1989-93; lectr. in field. Pres. bd. dirs. Folly Theater, 1992-94, Kans. City Chamber Orch., 1995—. Mem. ABA (chair intellectual property law com. of the torts and ins. practice sect., forum com. on comm. law, ctrl. and Ea. European law initiative), Mo. Bar Assn., Kansas City Met. Bar Assn., Libel Def. Resource Ctr. (editorial bd., exec. com.). Avocations: tennis, golf, skiing, sailing, antique maps. Home: 8821 Alhambra St Shawnee Mission KS 66207-2357 Office: Marsh 2405 Grand Blvd Kansas City MO 64108-2510 Office Phone: 816-556-4365. E-mail: chad.e.milton@marsh.com.

MILTON, JOHN CHARLES DOUGLAS, nuclear physicist, researcher; b. Regina, Sask., Can., 1924; s. William and Frances Craigie; m. Gwendolyn Margaret Shaw, Oct. 10, 1953; children: Bruce F., Leslie J.F., Neil W.D., Theresa M. A.M. in Music, U. Man., 1943, B.Sc. with honors, 1947; MA, Princeton U., 1949, PhD in Physics, 1951. Asst. rsch. officer Atomic Energy Can., Ltd., Chalk River, Ont., 1951-57, assoc. rsch. officer, 1957-62, sr. rsch. officer, 1962-70, prin. rsch. officer, 1970-91, head nuclear physics br., 1967-83, dir. physics div., 1983-85, v.p. physics and health scis., 1986-90, researcher emeritus, 1990-97. Vis. scientist Lawrence Berkeley Lab., 1960-62, Centre de Recherches, Strasbourg & Bruyeres-le-Chatel, 1975-76; chmn. nuclear physics grants Natural Sci. and Engring. Research Council, 1977-82; adv. bd. TRIUMF 1984-92; bd. dirs. Can. Fusion Fuels Tech., 1986-90, Tokamak de Varennes, 1986-90. Pres. Deep River Hort. Assn., 1997-98; mem., bd. gov. Deep River and Dist. Hosp., 2004-. Fellow: Royal Soc. Can., Am. Phys. Soc.; mem.: Can. Assn. Physicists (pres. 1992). Avocations: gardening, music, skiing. Home: 3 Alexander Pl Deep River ON Canada K0J 1P0 E-mail: dmilton@magma.ca.

MILTON, JOSE, real estate development company executive; b. Cuba; arrived in US, 1962; Architect, Cuba, Miami; founder J. Milton & Associates, Coral Gables, Fla., 1962—. Office: J Milton & Associates Ste 301 3211 Ponce De Leon Blvd Coral Gables FL 33134 Office Fax: 305-447-6760.

MILTON, JOSEPH PAYNE, lawyer; b. Richmond, Oct. 24, 1943; s. Hubert E. and Grace C. Milton; children: Michael Payne, Amy Barrett, David King; m. Cela Cabler Milton, Apr. 8, 1989. BS in Bus. Adminstrn., U. Fla., 1967, JD, 1969. Bar: Fla. 1969, U.S. Ct. Appeals (5th cir.) 1971, U.S. Supreme Ct. 1972, U.S. Ct. Appeals (11th cir.) 1981. Assoc. Toole, Taylor, Moseley & Gabel, Jacksonville, 1969-70; ptnr. Toole, Taylor, Moseley, Gabel & Milton, Jacksonville, 1971-78, Howell, Liles, Braddock & Milton, Jacksonville, 1978-89; sr. ptnr. Milton, Leach, Whitman, D'Andrea, Cherek & Milton, P.A., Jacksonville, 1990—. Mem. jud. nominating commn. Fla. Supreme Ct., 2002, chmn., 2005—06. Mem. Mayor's Blue Ribbon Task Force; mem. Law Ctr. Coun., U. Fla. Coll. Law, 1972-78, mem. alumni coun., 1995—; campaign chmn. N.E. Fla. chpt. March of Dimes, 1973-74, v.p., 1974-75; pres. Willing Hands, 1974-75; chmn. attys.' divsn. United Way, 1977; pres. Civic Round Table of Jacksonville, 1980-81; mem. exec. com. Jacksonville Area Legal Aid, Inc., 1982-83; chmn. pvt. bar involvement com. Legal Aid Bd. Dirs., 1982-83; mem. Hist. Soc. Fla. Supreme Ct., membership chmn. N. Fla. US Supreme Ct. Hist. Soc. Recipient Outstanding Svc. award for individual contbns. in support of legal svcs. for the poor, 1981; named Superlawyer of Fla., 2006, 2007, Million Dollar Advocates Forum. Fellow: Soc. Lawyers for Pub. Svc., Southeastern Admiralty Law (com., dir. Port, Jacksonville 1996—99), Am. Bar Found., Internat. Soc. Barristers; mem.: ATLA, Nat. ABOTA Found. (treas. 2004—05, pres. 2006—), Am. Judicature Soc., Acad. Fla. Trial Lawyers, Maritime Law Assn. U.S. (mem. com. professionalism 1996—), Nat. Assn. R.R. Trial Counsel (exec. com. 1979—2004, v.p. southeastern region 1984—86, pres. 1990—91), Jacksonville Assn. Def. Counsel (pres. 1981—82, lectr. CLE programs, guest lectr. U. Fla. Nat. Assn. R.R. Trial Counsel), Fla. Coun. Bar Assn. Pres. (exec. com. 1982—88, v.p. 1984, pres. 1985—86, Outstanding Past Bar Pres. award 2001), Fla. Bar (grievance com. 1975—77, chmn. grievance com. 1976, 4th jud. cir. nominating commn. 1980—82, voluntary bar liaison com. 1982—83, mem. exec. coun. for trial sect. 1982—89, chmn. 1987, 1988, bd. govs. 1988—90, charter mem. admirality and maritime law bd. cert. 1996—2000, chmn. 1998, chmn. 4th jud. cir. professionalism com. 1998—, bd. cert civil trial lawyer, bd. cert. admiralty and maritime law, mem. Hist. Soc. for 11th cir., recipient Outstanding Professionalism Program 1999, 2001), Jacksonville Bar Assn. (young lawyers sect. 1974—75, pres. 1980—81, Lawyer of Yr. award 1999), Am. Bd. Trial Advs. (pres. Jacksonville chpt. 1997, FLABOTA bd. mem. 1997—, treas. 1999, nat. bd. mem. 1999—, pres.-elect 2000, treas. 2004, charter, chpt. selected as Best in Nation 1997, Jacksonville chpt. Trial Lawyer of Yr. 2000, selected as Fla. Trial Lawyer of Yr. 2000, named Master In Trial Master of Yr. 2003), Country Club Sapphire Valley (NC), Gulf Life Tower Club, Univ. Club, San Jose Country Club. Republican. Home: 4655 Corrientes Cir N Jacksonville FL 32217-4329 Office: Milton Leach Whitman D'Andrea Charek & Milton PA 815 S Main St Ste 200 Jacksonville FL 32207-8181 Office Phone: 904-346-3800. Personal E-mail: jmilton@miltonleach.com.

MILTON, MICHAEL ANTHONY, minister, writer; b. New Orleans, Feb. 26, 1958; s. Jessie Ellis Milton and adopted s. Mary Eva Turner; m. Mae S. Slow, June 8, 1985; 1 child, John Michael Ellis. Diploma, Def. Lang. Inst., Monterey, Calif., 1977; BA, MidAm. Nazarene U., Olathe, Kansas, 1989; MDiv, Knox Theol. Sem., Ft. Lauderdale, Fla., 1993; PhD, U. Wales, Lampeter, 1998. Ordained min. Presbyn. Ch. Am., 1993. Founder Westminster Acad., Overland Park, Kans., 1993; founding pastor Redeemer Presbyn. Ch., Overland Park, 1993—97; adminstr. Knox Theol. Sem., Fort Lauderdale, Fla., 1997—98; founding pastor Kirk O' the Isles Presbyn. Ch., Savannah, Ga., 1998—2002; adj. prof. Erskine Theol. Sem., Due West, SC, 1998—; sr. min. First Presbyn. Ch., Chattanooga, 2001—. Adj. prof. Knox Theol. Sem., Ft. Lauderdale, 1998—, dir. Composer (singer/musician): (musical album) He Shall Restore; author: (book) Leaving a Career to Follow a Call: A Vocational Guide to the Ordained Ministry, 2000, The Demands of Discipleship: Expository Messages from Daniel, 2005, Authentic Christianity and the Life of Freedom: Expository Messages from Galatians, 2005, Oh, The Deep, Deep Love of Jesus, 2007, (booklet) Giving as an Act of Worship, 2006, Following Ben: Expository Preaching as the Power for Frail Followers of Pulpit Giants, 2007. Adminstrv. com. Presbyn. Ch. Am.; chmn. strategic planning Knox Theol. Sem., Ft. Lauderdale, 2005; bd. dirs. Cherokee coun. Boy Scouts of Am., Chattanooga, 2004; contbg. editor Preaching Jour., Franklin, Tenn., 2005. Maj. USAR, 1992—. Recipient Leadership award, MidAm. Nazarene U., 1989, award for systematic theology, Knox Theol. Sem., 1993, award for preaching, 1993. Mem.: Evang. Theol. Soc., Navy League Am. (chaplain 2004—), Res. Officer Assn. (life). Republican. Presbyterian. Avocations: travel, reading, gardening, painting, drawing. Home: 3806 Chestnut Ridge Ln Signal Mountain TN 37377 Office: First Presbyn Ch 554 McCallie Ave Chattanooga TN 37402 Home Phone: 423-886-7722; Office Phone: 423-648-7919. Office Fax: 423-237-1208. Business E-Mail: mikemilton@1stpresbyterian.com.

MILTON, PETER WINSLOW, artist; b. Lower Merion, Pa., Apr. 2, 1930; s. William Hammond and Lois (Preston) M.; m. Edith Hanna Cohn, June 3, 1961; children: Jeremy Lawrence, Naomi Helen. BFA, Yale U., 1954, MFA, 1962. Tchr. art Md. Inst., Balt., 1961-68, Yale Summer Sch. of Music and Art, 1970; artist-in-residence Dartmouth Coll., winter 1983, Rockefeller Found., Bellagio, Italy, 1990, Pasadena (Calif.) City Coll., 1999, Weber State U., Ogden, Utah, 2004. Guest lectr. J. Paul Getty Mus., 1999. Exhibited in over 80 one-man shows including, Balt. Mus., 1965, De Cordova Mus., Lincoln, Mass., 1970, Phillips Exeter Acad., 1971, 83, The Franz Bader Gallery, Washington, 1967, 71, 80, 82, 86, 87, 88, 89, 91, Museo La Tertulia, Cali, Colombia, 1972, Corcoran Gallery Art, Washington, 1972, Asso. Am. Artists, N.Y.C., 1975, Galerie Georges Bernier, Paris, 1975, Biblioteca Luis Angel Arango, Bogota, Colombia, 1975, Galerie Petites Formes, Osaka, Japan, 1979, Francis Kyle Gallery, London, 1980, 88, 91, 94, 06, Bklyn. Mus., 1980, 88, Hood Mus., Dartmouth Coll., 1983, Louis Newman Galleries, Beverly Hills, Calif., 1984, 87, 94, Graystone Gallery, San Francisco, 1985, Edith Caldwell Gallery, San Francisco, 1992, 94, Mary Ryan Gallery, N.Y.C., 1993, Currier Mus. Art, Manchester, N.H., 1997, De Young Mus., San Francisco, 1998, Jack Rutberg fine Arts, Los Angeles, 2001, Ayle Gallery, 2006; 2 traveling exhbns. to 40 Am. cities, 1977-81; exhibited in numerous group shows; represented in numerous permanent collections. Yale traveling fellow, 1954; Louis Comfort Tiffany Found. grantee, 1964; recipient numerous nat. and internat. awards and prizes including Medal of Honor Interprint Exhbn., Lvov, USSR, 1990, awards exequo Internat. Triennial Graphics Arts, Crocow, Poland, 1991, 94, 03, 04, Commendary award Miniprint Exhbn., Finland, 1998, Hon. award Internat. Biennial, Varna, Bulgaria, 1997, Internat. Triennial Graphic Arts, Poland, 2003, Miniprint Exhbn., Finland, 2004, Spl. Jury award Internat. Biennial, Varna, 2005. Subject of: Peter Milton: Complete Etchings 1960-1976, 1977, The Jolly Corner, 21 etchings (Henry James) 1980, The Primacy of Touch: The Drawings of Peter Milton, 1993, The Aspern Papers, 18 drawings, 1 etching (Henry James) 1993, Peter Milton: Complete Prints, 1960-96, Chronicle Books, 1996. Home: PO Box 237 Francestown NH 03043-0237 Personal E-mail: petermilton@earthlink.net.

MILTON-JONES, DELISHA, professional basketball player; b. Riceboro, Ga., Sept. 11, 1974; d. Beverly Milton; m. Roland Jones, June 30, 2003. BA in Sports Mgmt., U. Fla., Gainesville, 1997. Forward Am. Basketball League Portland Power, 1997—99, WNBA LA Sparks, 1999—2004, WNBA Washington Mystics, 2005—. Forward EuroLeague Ekaterinburg team, Russia, 2002; mem. USA Basketball Women's Sr. Nat. Team, 2004. Named to Western Conf. All-Star Team, WNBA, 2000, Ea. Conf. All-Star Team, 2007; recipient Gold Medal, US Olympic Festival, 1994, World Univ. Games, 1997, World Championships, 1998, 2002, US Olympic Cub, 1999, Olympic Games, 2000. Mailing: Washington Mystics 627 N Glebe Rd Ste 850 Arlington VA 22203 *

MILUNAS, J. ROBERT, health care organization executive; b. Aug. 7, 1947; s. Joseph John M.; m. Glenetta Graham; children: Amy, Joseph, Anna Kate. BS, Tulane U., 1969; postgrad., Samford U., 1973; MBA, Ga. State U., 1977. Mgr. internal and govt. reporting, corp. contr.'s staff Arvin Industries Inc., Columbus, Ind., 1977-80; mgr. consol. acctg., corp. contr.'s staff Mattel Inc., Hawthorne, Calif., 1980-82; asst. contr. Times Mirror Cable TV Inc., Irvine, Calif., 1982-83; Western Divsn. contr. SCA, Santa Ana, Calif., 1983-84; v.p., corp. contr. Tchrs. Mgmt. Investment Corp., Newport Beach, Calif., 1984-86; v.p., CFO Beech St. Inc., Irvine, 1987-89; v.p. fin. and adminstrn. ConsumerHealth Inc., Newport Beach, Calif., 1989-93; pres. Aegis Consulting Svcs., Dana Point, Calif., 1993—. 1st lt. U.S. Army Transp. Corps., 1969-71. Decorated Bronze Star. Roman Catholic. Office Phone: 404-321-4232. Personal E-mail: milunas@gmail.com. *Life is a precious gift to be nurtured daily through interaction with friends and family and helping others achieve their potential.*

MILUNSKY, AUBREY, geneticist, pediatrician, educator; b. Johannesburg, Nov. 3, 1936; came to U.S., 1969; 1 child, Jeffrey M. MB, BCh, U. Witwatersand, Johannesburg, 1960, DSc, 1982; postgrad., Gt. Ormond St. Hosp., London, 1965. Diplomate Am. Bd. Pediatrics, Am. Bd. Med. Genetics. Intern Johannesburg Gen. Hosp./Baragwanath Hosp., Johannesburg, 1961; resident in internal medicine and pediat. Baragwanath Hosp., 1961-64; pediat. registrar Queen Mary's Hosp. for Children, Surrey, Eng., 1965-66; asst. pediatrician New England Med. Ctr. Tufts U., Boston, 1966-70, from instr. to asst. prof. pediat. Sch. Medicine, 1966-70; rsch. fellow and assoc. in neurology Mass. Gen. Hosp./Harvard Med. Sch., Boston, 1969-70; dir. Birth Defects and Genetics Clinic Mass. Gen. Hosp., Boston, 1971-73, asst. pediatrician, 1971-82, assoc. dir. Cystic Fibrosis Clinic, 1975-79; asst. prof. pediatrics Harvard Med. Sch., Boston, 1971-81; prof. pediatrics and ob-gyn. Sch. Medicine, dir. Ctr. for Human Genetics, assoc. physician Univ. Hosp. Boston U., 1981—, prof. pathology, 1985—, Endowed chair human genetics, 1991—; pediatrician Boston City Hosp., 1981—. Mem. Mass. State Genetics Adv. Bd., 1983-84; profl. adv. bd. Nat. Tuberous Sclerosis Assn., 1990-93; quality assurance com. New England Regional Genetics Group, 1990-96. Author: The Prenatal Diagnosis of Hereditary Disorders, 1973, Know Your Genes, 1977, How to Have the Healthiest Baby You Can., 1987, Choices, Not Chances: An Essential Guide to your Heredity and Health, 1989, Heredity and Your Family's Health, 1992, Your Genetic Destiny: Know Your Genes, Secure Your Health, Save Your Life, 2001; editor: Clinics in Perinatology, Vol. II, 1974, The Prevention of Genetic Disease and Mental Retardation, 1975, Genetic

Disorders and the Fetus: Diagnosis, Prevention and Treatment, 1979, 5th edit., 2004, Coping with Crisis and Handicap, 1981, (with G.J. Annas) Genetics and the Law I, 1976, Genetics and the Law II, 1980, Genetics and the Law III, 1986, (with E.A. Friedman and L. Gluck) Advances in Perinatal Medicine, 1981, Vol. II, 1982, Vol. III, 1983, Vol. IV, 1985, Vol. V, 1986; mem. editl. bd. Am. Jour. Law and Medicine, 1974-93, Am. Jour. Med. Genetics, 1977-94, Bioethics Digest, 1977-78, Prenatal Diagnosis, 1980-90, 92—, Intelligence Reports in Ob-Gyn., 1982-88, Fetal Therapy, 1986—; peer reviewer New England Jour. Medicine, Pediatrics, Am. Jour. Med. Genetics, Am. Jour. Ob-Gyn., Am. Jour. Law and Medicine, Am. Jour. Pub. Health, Prenatal Diagnosis, Fetal Therapy, Ob-Gyn., Epidemiology, Jour. Pediatrics; contbr. over 300 articles to profl. jours. Recipient First Place Film award Nat. Coun. Family Rels. Media Awards Co., 1990, Tinsley Harrison award So. Soc. for Clin. Investigation, 1991; Aubrey Milunsky Endowed Chair in Human Genetics named in his honor Boston U., 1991. Fellow Am. Coll. Med. Genetics (founding), Royal Coll. Physicians (diploma in child health 1965); mem. Am. Pediat. Soc., Am. Soc. Human Genetics (social issues com. 1983-87), Am. Soc. Law and Medicine (v.p. 1982-83, pres.-elect 1983-85, pres. 1985-86, bd. dirs. 1986-88, 90-93), Soc. for Pediat. Rsch., Mass. Med. Soc. Office: Boston U Sch Medicine Ctr for Human Genetics 715 Albany St Boston MA 02118-2307

MIMMS, THOMAS BOWMAN, JR., lawyer; b. Atlanta, Oct. 11, 1944; s. Thomas Bowman and Alice Buehl Mimms; m. Alison Hayward, July 22, 1967; children: Karen Mimms Swift, Christina Mimms Couret. BA, U. N.C., 1965; JD, Columbia U., 1969. Bar: Fla. 1969, Ga., 1999, U.S. Supreme Ct. 1973, U.S. Ct. Appeals (11th cir.) 1981 Ga. Supreme Ct., 2000, U.S. Dist. Ct. (no. dist.) Ga. 2002. Assoc. atty. Fleming O'Bryan, Fort Lauderdale, Fla., 1969-72; shareholder Macfarlane Ferguson & McMullen, Tampa, Fla., 1972-99. Fellow Am. Bar Found.; mem. Fla. Bar Assn. (exec. coun. bus. law sect. 1987-99, chair bus. law legislation com. 1995-99, chair bus. law bankrupty/UCC com. 1988-89, chair fin. instns. com. 1993-94), Tampa Bay Bankruptcy Bar Assn. (pres. 1992-93), Columbia U. Alumni Club (dir. 1991-99). Democrat. Episcopalian. Office: Malon D Mimms Co 85A Mill St Ste 100 Roswell GA 30075-4952 Home Phone: 770-509-9157; Office Phone: 770-518-1100. E-mail: legal@mimms.org.

MIMS, WILLIAM CLEVELAND, lawyer; b. Harrisonburg, Va., June 20, 1957; s. David Lathan and Lurleen Shirley (Stovall) M.; m. Jane Ellen Rehme, Dec. 20, 1980; children: Katherine Grace, Emily Anne, Sarah Joy. AB, Coll. of William & Mary, 1979; JD, George Washington U., 1984; LLM, Georgetown U., 1986. Bar: Va. Legis. asst. Congressman Paul Trible, Washington, 1981-82; dep. legis. dir. Senator Paul Trible, Washington, 1983-85; chief of staff Congressman Frank Wolf, Washington, 1986-87; atty. Hazel & Thomas, P.C., Leesburg, Va., 1987-91, Worcester, Mims & Atwill, P.C., 1993—2002, Mims, Atwill & Leigh, P.C., Leesburg, 2002—05; mem. Va. Gen. Assembly, Richmond, 1991—2006, del., 1992-98, senator, 1998—2005; chief deputy Va. Atty. Gen., Richmond, 2006—. Adj. prof. law George Mason U., 2002-05; mem. Va. Housing Commn., 1994-2005, chmn. 2000—2003; mem. Va. Code Commn., 2000, 05, chmn., 2003—. Bd. dirs. Dulles Area Transp. Assn., Herndon, Va., 1994-2005, Marshall Home Preservation Fund, Leesburg, 1992-2005, Youth for Tomorrow, 1995-97; treas., bd. dirs. Loudoun Bar Assn., Leesburg, 1988-89; active Nat. Eagle Scout Assn., 1992--. Flemming fellow, 1995-96. Mem. Va. Bar Assn. (Boyd-Graves Conf. 1996—, bd. govs. 2002—), Va. Trial Lawyers Assn., Christian Legal Soc., No. Va. Transp. Assn. Republican. Episcopalian. Office: Va Atty General Office 900 E Main St Richmond VA 23219

MIN, BALSHIK, pathologist; b. Seoul, Republic of Korea, Jan. 15, 1942; s. Young-Ock and Yang-Hee (Kim) Min; m. Jungsoon Ahn, Apr. 25, 1970; children: James, Susan. MD, Seoul Nat. U., 1966. Pathologist Faxton-St. Luke's Healthcare, Utica, NY, 1978—2005, dir. labs., 1984—2005; pathologist Centrex Clin. Labs., New Hartford, NY, 1978—, dir. labs., 1990—96; pathologist Rome Meml. Hosp., NY, 2005—, dir. labs., 2005—07. Capt. Republic of Korea Army, 1966—70. Fellow: Coll. Am. Pathologists; mem.: AMA, Ctrl. NY Acad. Medicine, Nat. Soc. Histotechnology, Am. Soc. Clin. Pathology. Avocations: reading, classical music, gardening, golf. Office: Rome Meml Hosp 1500 N James St Rome NY 13440 Home Phone: 315-793-3238; Office Phone: 315-338-7045.

MIN, DAVID BYONG, chemist, educator, research scientist; b. Seoul, Republic of Korea, Sept. 12, 1942; arrived in U.S.A, 1965; s. Yun S. Min and Sun D. Yoon; m. Hyung Ok Lee, Aug. 1, 1963; children: Peter K., Stephen K. BS, Seoul Nat. U., Republic of Korea, 1965; MS, U. Minn., Mpls., 1968; PhD, Rutgers U., New Brunswick, NJ, 1973. Mgr. CP, Best Foods Rsch. Ctr., Union, NJ, 1976—79; prof. Ohio State, Columbus, 1979—. Hon. prof. Rutgers U., 1976—79; cons. Ministry of Agr., Seoul, 2001—; sci. editor Jour. of Food Sci., Chgo., 2001—. Author: Flavor Chemistry of Foods, 1998, Chemistry of Food Lipids, 2002. Pres. Korean Cath. Ch., Columbus, Ohio, 2000—02. Recipient Rsch. Achievement award, Inst. of Food Technologists, 1995, Disting. Sr. Faculty Rsch. award, Ohio State, 1999, Rsch. award, Korean Soc. of Food Sci. and Tech., 2002; fellow, Am. Oil Chemicals Co., 2001, Inst. of Food Technologists, 2002. Roman Catholic. Achievements include development of singlet oxygen oxidation of foods; research in oxygen quenching to improve flavor stability of foods; mechanism of light sensitivity of riboflavin. Avocations: golf, travel. Home: 1306 Lakeside Pl Worthington OH 43085 Office: Ohio State Univ 2015 Fyffe Rd Columbus OH 43210 Office Phone: 614-292-7801. Personal E-mail: min.2@osu.edu.

MIN, JANICE BYUNG, editor-in-chief; b. Atlanta, 1969; m. Peter Sheehy, 1997; 2 children. BA in Journalism, Columbia U., NYC, 1990. Reporter, Westchester County, NY, 1990—92; writer to sr. editor People mag., NYC, 1992—97; with Life mag., NYC, 1997—98; asst. mng. editor In Style mag., NYC, 1998—2001; exec. editor Us Weekly mag., NYC, 2002—03, editor-in-chief, 2003—. Named one of 40 Under 40, Crain's NY Bus., 2006; recipient Editor of Yr., AdWeek mag., 2005. Office: Us Weekly 1290 Ave of Americas New York NY 10104-0298 Office Phone: 800-283-3956. Office Fax: 212-651-7890. *

MIN, SANG HEE, internist, researcher; b. Seoul, Republic of Korea, Mar. 11, 1976; d. Seung Il Min and Jung Hwa Lee. MD, U. Buenos Aires, 2002. Lic. physician Calif., 2007. Internist, Med. Scientist Pathway resident Albert Einstein Coll. Medicine-Jacobi Med. Ctr., Bronx, NY, 2003—. Mem.: ACP (assoc.), AMA (assoc.), Am. Assn. Cancer Rsch. (assoc.). Achievements include discovery of transporter protein responsible for the absorption of folates and the molecular basis of hereditary folate malabsorption. Office: Albert Einstein Coll Medicine 1300 Morris Park Ave Chanin Bldg 628 Bronx NY 10461 Home Phone: 917-361-1614; Office Phone: 718-430-2595.

MIN, SOO BONG, bank executive; b. Hwanghae Province, Korea, 1938; BA in Economics, Seoul U. Various positions including COO, pres. Comml. Bank Korea, Seoul, Republic of Korea, 1959—94; pres., CEO Hanmi Bank, 1995—99; pres., CEO, dir. Wilshire Bancorp, LA, 1999—. Office: Wilshire Bancorp Inc 3200 Wilshire Blvd Los Angeles CA 90010 Office Phone: 213-387-3200. Office Fax: 213-427-6584. *

MINA, JOHN LOUIS (IVAN MINEA), religious studies educator, archivist; b. Nancy, France, Jan. 31, 1950; came to U.S. 1951; s. Albert and Mila (Koenig) M. BA with highest honors, U. Calif., Santa Barbara, 1972; MA, U. Calif., Berkeley, 1974, PhD, 1979. Lectr. Centre D'Etudes Russes, Meudon, France, 1984—85; vis. asst. prof. U. Ky., Lexington, 1987—88; prof. Sts. Cyril and Methodius Sem., Pitts., 1990—95; archivist Met. Archdiocese of Pitts., Byzantine Rite, 1997—. Contbr. articles to profl. jours. Mem. Cath. Hist. Soc. West Pa., Pitts.; rep. theol. com. Christian Assocs. S.W. Pa. Recipient Dobro Slovo, U. Calif., Berkeley, 1980; U. Calif. Regents scholar, 1968; Fulbright fellow, 1972. Mem. Assn. Cath. Diocesan Archivists, KC (4th degree), Phi Beta Kappa. Byzantine Catholic. Avocations: travel, foreign affairs. Home: 318 Park Ave Clairton PA 15025-1758 E-mail: ivanmina@msn.com.

MINA, RICHARD T., apparel executive; Pres. Footlocker Europe Footlocker Inc., 1996—99, pres., CEO Champ Sports, 1999—2003, pres., CEO, 2003—. Office: Footlocker Inc 112 W 34th St New York NY 10120

MINAHAN, DANIEL FRANCIS, lawyer, retired manufacturing executive; b. Orange, NJ, Dec. 3, 1929; s. Alfred A. and Katherine (Kelly) M.; m. Mary Jean Gaffney, May 2, 1953; children: Daniel F. Jr., John A. AB magna cum laude, U. Notre Dame, 1951; JD magna cum laude, U. Conn., 1964; grad., Advanced Mgmt. Program, Harvard, 1975. Bar: Conn. 1964, U.S. Supreme Ct 1969, U.S. Ct. of Appeals (2d cir.), U.S. Dist. Ct. Conn. 1971. Mgr. indsl. engring. Uniroyal, Inc., Naugatuck, Conn., 1952-59, mgr. indsl. relations, 1959-64, dir. labor relations NYC, 1964-66; v.p. indsl. relations and labor counsel Phillips Van Heusen Corp., NYC, 1966-69; v.p. personnel-adminstrn. Broadway-Hale Stores, Inc., LA, 1969-70; v.p. employee relations, sec. Magnavox-N.Am., Philips Corp., 1970-73, v.p. ops., group exec., 1973-83, sr. v.p. adminstrn., 1984-89, exec. v.p., 1989-93, vice-chmn., 1991-93; vice-chmn. nat. found. bd. Robert Anderson Sch. Mgmt., U. N.Mex., 1993-98; pvt. practice, 1998—. Trustees adv. coun., Fairfield U., mem. dean's coun. Grad. Sch. Bus. Co-author: The Developing Labor Law, 1971. Chmn. bd. Internat. Fedn. Keystone Youth Orgns., London and Chgo., 1984-88; vice-chmn. nat. found. bd. Anderson Sch. Mgmt., U. N.Mex., 1993-98. With USMC. Mem. The Forum for World Affairs, Conn. Bar Assn., Harvard Club, Club Internat. (Chgo.).

MINAHAN, JOHN P., academic administrator; BA in Philos., Canisius Coll.; PhD in Philos., Georgetown U. With Xavier U., U. North Fla., SUNY Buffalo; dean, coll. liberal arts and sciences Western Oreg. U., Monmouth, Oreg., 1986—98, prof. philos., 1986—98, provost, 1998—2004, interim pres., 2005—06, pres., 2006—. Office: Office of President Western Oreg University 345 N Monmouth Ave Monmouth OR 97361 Office Phone: 503-838-8888. Business E-Mail: president@wou.edu. *

MINAR, PAUL G., interior designer, consultant; b. Phoenix, July 12, 1932; s. Aaron Crowther and Ione Anna (Schmid) Mortensen. Student, Ariz. State U., 1950-54, John F. Kennedy U., 1978-80, Antioch West U., 1980. Sound effects technician, TV stage mgr. Sta. KHJ-AM-TV, LA, 1955-63; displayer W.&J. Sloane Furniture Co., Beverly Hills, Calif., 1963-66, Bullock's Dept. Store, LA, 1966-68, Macy's Dept. Store, San Francisco, 1968-70; interior designer Lloyd's Furniture Co., San Diego, 1970-71, Bonynge's Furniture Co., Oakland, Calif., 1971-72, Breuner's Furniture Co., Oakland, 1972-74; design cons. The Other Artist, San Francisco, 1974—. Archival rschr. and conservation Petaluma Hist. Mus., 1994—; cons. Human Svcs. Dept., Oakland, Calif., 2003—; profl. numerologist; lectr. in onomatology. Author: Numbers: The Energy Force in Your Name, 2006; writer, producer (documentary) The Modern Nursing Home, 1959. Vol. talent agt. San Francisco Symphony Black and White Ball, 1983; mem. Fine Arts Mus. of San Francisco. Mem. Inst. Noetic Scis., Petaluma Mus. Assn., Assn. Internationale de Numerologues, Calif. Soc. Psychical Study. Democrat. Roman Catholic. Avocations: wilderness exploration, tennis, classical music, parapsychology, world history. Office: The Other Artist 3200 Buchanan St San Francisco CA 94123-3517 E-mail: numbers@paulminar.com.

MINARDI, ANN SEGURA, lawyer, musician; d. William A. and Mary Louise Segura; m. John Christopher Minardi, June 10, 1983; children: Christine Ann, Angela Rose. BA, U. Mich., 1980; JD, Boston U., 1984. Bar: Md. 1988, U.S. Ct. Internat. Trade 1988, U.S. Ct. Appeals (fed. cir.) 1988, U.S. Supreme Ct. 1989. Atty. Office of Regulations and Rulings, Washington, 1988—. Musician: (professional flutist) Friday Morning Music Club, 1998—. Recipient Academic award, U. Mich., 1980. Mem.: Customs Lawyers Assn. (chair, program com. 2004—05). Avocation: equestrian sports. Office: Customs and Border Protection 1300 Pennsylvania Ave NW Washington DC 20229 Home Phone: 301-570-1569.

MINARDI, RICHARD A. (RICK), JR., lawyer; b. Mobile, Ala., Aug. 15, 1943; s. Richard A. and Martha F. (Beck) Minardi; m. Frances Archer Guy, Oct. 21, 1989. BA, Yale U., 1965, LLB, 1968. Bar: Va. 1969. Assoc. McGuire Woods & Battle, Richmond, Va., 1968-71; ptnr. Staples, Greenberg Minardi & Kessler, Richmond, 1971-86, Mays & Valentine, Richmond, 1986-2000; ptnr., mem. exec. com. Troutman Sanders LLP, Richmond, 2001—. Mem.: ABA, Richmond Bar Assn., Va. Bar Assn. Office: Troutman Sanders LLP Troutman Sanders Bldg 1001 Haxall Point Richmond VA 23219 Office Phone: 804-697-1252. Office Fax: 804-698-5128. Business E-Mail: rick.minardi@troutmansanders.com.

MINARIK, CAROL T., elementary school educator; b. Chgo., Aug. 2, 1949; d. Roman Richard and Estelle Therese Dluski; m. Richard James Minarik, June 24, 1983; children: Jessica, Melissa, Jeffrey. BS in Edn., Chgo. State U., 1970. Tchr. Oak Lawn-Hometown Sch. Dist., Ill., 1971—84, St. Linus Sch., Oak Lawn, 1994—. Mem.: Nat. Coun. Tchrs. Math. Avocation: music. Home: 10729 S Long Ave Oak Lawn IL 60453 Office: St Linus Sch 10400 S Lawler Oak Lawn IL 60453 Office Phone: 708-425-1656.

MINARIK, ELSE HOLMELUND (BIGART MINARIK), author; b. Aarhus, Denmark, Sept. 13, 1920; d. Kaj Marius and Helga Holmelund; m. Walter Minarik, July 14, 1940 (dec.); 1 child, Brooke Ellen; m. Homer Bigart, Oct. 3, 1970 (dec.). BA, Queens Coll., 1942. Tchr. 1st grade, art Commack (N.Y.) Pub. Schs., 1950-54. Author children's books: Little Bear, 1957, Father Bear Comes Home, 1959, Little Bear's Friend, 1960, Little Bear's Visit, 1961, No Fighting, No Biting, 1958, Cat and Dog, 1960, The Winds That Come From Far Away, 1960, The Little Giant Girl and the Elf Boy, 1963, A Kiss for Little Bear, 1968, What If, 1987, Percy and the Five Houses, 1988, It's Spring, 1989, The Little Girl and the Dragon, 1991, Am I Beautiful, 1992. Mem. PEN Club. Home: 30 Gebig Rd Nottingham NH 03290 Office: care Greenwillow Books 1350 Ave Americas New York NY 10019

MINARIK, STEPHEN JOSEPH, III, communications executive, former political organization administrator; b. Rochester, NY, Jan. 2, 1960; s. Stephen Joseph Jr. and Eleanor Emily (Synkowski) M.; m. Patricia Williams, 1987 (div. Aug. 1996); 1 child, Stephen J. IV.; m. Renee; children: Stephanie, Kathleen, Christopher BA in Polit. Sci., U. Rochester, 1982. Asst. dep. clk. Monroe County Legis., Rochester, 1988-89, legis. dir., 1989-90; exec. dir. Monroe County Rep. Com., Rochester, 1990—2005, chmn., 1991—2005; ptnr. Impact Comm. LLC, Rochester, 1997—; chmn. NY Rep. State Com., Albany, 2005—06. Mgr. Rochester Youth Hockey, 1996-97; coach Webster (N.Y.) Soccer League, 1997. Roman Cath. Avocations: golf, hockey, lacrosse.

MINAYA, OMAR, professional sports team executive; b. Valverde Mao, Dominican Republic; Scout Tex. Rangers, 1985—97, dir. pers. and internat. scouting, 1995—97; sr. asst. gen. mgr. N.Y. Mets, 1997—2002; v.p. Montreal (Can.) Expos, 2002—04, gen. mgr., 2002—04; exec. v.p. baseball operations, gen. mgr. New York Mets, 2004—. Recipient Hispanic Heritage in Sports award, Hispanic Heritage Found., 2003. Office: c/o New York Mets Shea Stadium 123-01 Roosevelt Ave Flushing NY 11368 *

MINC, HENRYK, mathematics professor; b. Lodz, Poland, Nov. 12, 1919; s. Izrael and Haja (Zyngler) M.; m. Catherine Taylor Duncan, Apr. 16, 1943; children: Robert Henry, Ralph Edward, Raymond. MA with honors, Edinburgh U., Scotland, 1955, PhD, 1959. Tchr. Morgan Acad., Dundee, Scotland, 1956-58; lectr. Dundee Tech. Coll., 1957-58, U. BC, Vancouver, Canada, 1958-59, asst. prof., 1959-60; assoc. prof. U. Fla., Gainesville, 1960-63; prof. U. Calif., Santa Barbara, 1963-90, prof. emeritus, 1990—. Vis. prof. Technion Israel Inst. Tech., Haifa, 1969-80. Author: A Survey of Matrix Theory and Matrix Inequalities, 1964, Russian translation, 1972, Chinese translation, 1990, Introduction to Linear Algebra, 1968, Spanish translation, 1968, Modern University Algebra, 1966, Elementary Linear Algebra, Spanish translation, 1971, New College Algebra, 1968, Elementary Functions and Coordinate Geometry, 1969, Algebra and Trigonometry, 1970, College Algebra, 1970, College Trigonometry, 1971, Integrated Analytic Geometry and Algebra with Circular Functions, 1973, Permanents, 1978, Russian translation, 1980, Chinese translation, 1991, Nonnegative Matrices, 1988, Chinese translation, 1991; contbr. over 80 rsch. articles to math. jours., 9 rsch. papers to archaeol. and ancient numismatic jours., 12 articles to Burns Chronicle; referee and reviewer math. jours. 2nd lt. Polish Army, 1940-48, France, UK. Recipient Lester Ford award Math. Assn. Am., 1966, rsch. contract Office Naval Rsch., 1985-88, Air Force Office Sci. Rsch. grantee, 1960-83, Lady Davis fellow, 1975-78. Fellow: Soc. Antiquaries of Scotland; mem.: Friends of Ellisland, Robert Burns Assn. N.Am., Saltire Soc., Scots. Lang. Soc., Scottish Soc. Santa Barbara (past chieftain), Robert Burns World Fedn. (hon. pres.), Am. Math. Soc. Democrat. Home: 4076 Naranjo Dr Santa Barbara CA 93110-1213 Office: U Calif Dept Math Santa Barbara CA 93106 Personal E-mail: hmincburns@cox.net.

MINCE, CAROL KIRKHAM, history educator; b. Clarksville, Tenn., Aug. 1, 1961; d. Lawrence Ray and Mary Virginia Cox; m. John William Mince Jr., Apr. 23, 1992. BS, Austin Peay State U., 1982, MA in Edn., 1984. Cert. tchr. Tenn. Asst. mgr. Kelley's Food City, Clarksville, 1980—93; social studies tchr. New Providence Mid. Sch., Clarksville, 1993—2005; world history tchr. Montgomery Ctrl. HS, Cunningham, Tenn., 2005—06, Am. govt. and world geography tchr., 2006—. Named Tchr. of Yr. at Bldg. Level, Tenn. Dept. Edn., 2000, 2004. Mem.: NEA, ASPCA, Tenn. Geog. Alliance, Nat. Coun. Social Studies., Clarksville-Montgomery County Edn. Assn. (Disting. Classroom Tchr. award 2000, 2004), Tenn. Edn. Assn., Nat. Humane Edn. Soc., Am. Humane Assn., Humane Soc. US, Phi Kappa Phi. Avocations: reading, hiking, antiques, photography. Office: Montgomery Ctrl HS 3955 Hwy 48 Cunningham TN 37052 Business E-Mail: carol.mince@cmcss.net.

MINDELL, DAVID A., engineering educator; BA in Elec. Engring., Yale U., 1988, BA in Lit., 1988; PhD, Mass. Inst. Tech., 1996. Ocean engr. deep submergence lab. Woods Hole Oceanographic Instn., 1990—95; grad. fellow NSF, 1993—95, Dibner Inst. History Sci. and Tech., 1995—96; asst. prof. Mass. Inst. Tech., 1996—2000, Frances and David Dibner prof. history engring. and mfg., 2000—, prof. engring systems. Tech. cons. Hermetic Scis. Co., 1986—; vis. investigator deep submergence lab. Woods Hole Oceanographic Instn., 1996—; vis. rsch. fellow Smithsonian Instn., 1999; adj. rschr. Inst. Exploration, Mystic, Conn. Editor: Technology, Archaeology, and the Deep Sea; author: (book) War, Technology and the Experience Aboard the USSS Monitor, 2000, Between Human and Machine: Feedback, Control, and Computing before Cybernetics, 2002; contbr. articles to profl. jours., chapters to books. Recipient Sally Hacker Prize, Soc. History Tech. for War, 2001, Abbott Payson Usher Prize, 1998; MacVicar faculty fellow, Mass. Inst. Tech, 2001—. Fellow: Explorer's Club; mem.: IEEE, History Sci. Soc., Soc. History Tech. Office: Mass Inst Tech 77 Massachusetts Ave Bldg E51-185 Cambridge MA 02139 Office Phone: 617-253-0221. Office Fax: 617-258-8118. Business E-Mail: mindell@mit.edu.

MINDELL, EUGENE ROBERT, surgeon, educator; b. Chgo., Feb. 24, 1922; s. Leon and Tillie (Rosenthal) M.; m. June A. Abrams, Sept. 19, 1945; children: Barbara, Ruth, David, Douglas. BS, U. Chgo., 1943, MD, 1945. Diplomate Am. Bd. Orthopaedic Surgery (bd. dir. 1977-84, pres. 1983-84). Resident in orthopaedic surgery U. Chgo. Clinics, 1948-52; instr. U. Chgo., 1952; mem. faculty dept. orthopaedic surgery Sch. Medicine SUNY, Buffalo, 1953—, prof. Sch. Medicine, 1964—; chmn. dept. SUNY Sch. Medicine, Buffalo, 1964-88, dir. orthopaedic oncology Sch. Medicine, 1988—. Mem. bd. mgrs. Erie County Med. Ctr., 1990-96. Assoc. editor Jour. Bone and Joint Surgery, 1984-88, trustee, 1991—; dep. editor Clin. Orthopaedics and Related Rsch. representing Musculoskeletal Tumor Soc., 1997—; contbr. articles to profl. jours. Lt. (j.g.) M.C. USNR, 1946-48. Eugene R. Mindell Endowed Chair of Orthopaedic Surgery established in his honor SUNY, Buffalo, 1996; recipient Disting. Svc. award Alumni U. Chgo. Sch. Medicine, 1990, award for achievement in health care D'Youville Coll., 2002, Lifetime Acheivement Excellence in Tchg. award, SUNY Buffalo Dept. Orthop. Surgery, 2002; NRC fellow, 1949-50. Fellow ACS; mem. Am. Acad. Orthopaedic Surgeons (bd. dirs. 1991-92), Am. Orthopaedic Assn. (v.p. 1990-91), Assn. Orthopaedic Chmn., Am. Assn. Surgery of Trauma, Am. Orthopaedic Rsch. Soc. (pres. 1972-73, residency rev. com. 1985-91), Musculoskeletal Tumor Soc. (pres. 1989-90), Coun. Musculoskeletal Specialty Socs. (chmn. elect 1991, chmn. 1992). Jewish. Office: 100 High St Buffalo NY 14203-1126 Home: 290 Kingstown Way Duxbury MA 02332 Business E-Mail: emindell@kaleidehealth.org.

MINDICH, DAVID T.Z., journalist, educator; m. Barbara Richmond; 2 children. Student, Univ. Coll. London, 1983—84; BA in English and Am. Lit., Brandeis U., Waltham, Mass., 1985; MA in Am. Civilization, NYU, 1989, PhD in Am. Studies, 1996. Prodn. asst. CNN, NYC, 1985, assignment editor, 1986—87; freelance, 1987—; asst. prof. St. Michael's Coll., Colchester, Vt., 1996—2000, assoc. prof., 2000—05, chair journalism & mass communication dept., 2000—06, prof. journalism & mass communication, 2005—. Instr. Morehouse Coll., Atlanta, 1989—90; instr. expository writing prog. NYU, 1990—93, adj. prof. journalism dept., 1994, LI U., 1993. Contbr. articles to mainstream publs., chapters to books; author: Just the Facts: How "Objectivity" Came to Define American Journalism, 1998, Tuned Out: Why Americans Under 40 Don't Follow the News, 2005; mem. editl. bd.: Journalism Hist., 2005—, Communication Methodologies and Measures, 2005—. Recipient US Prof. of Yr. award, Carnegie Found. for Advancement of Tchg. and Coun. for Advancement and Support of Edn., 2006. Mem.: Am. Journalism Historians Assn., Assn. Edn. in Journalism and Mass Communication (head hist. divsn. 1998—99, Krieghbaum Under-40 award for Outstanding Achievement in Rsch., Tchg. and Pub. Svc. 2002), Kappa Tau Alpha. Office: Journalism & Mass Communication Dept St Michaels Coll One Winooski Park Colchester VT 05439 Office Phone: 802-654-2637. Office Fax: 802-654-2560. E-mail: dmindich@smcvt.edu.

MINDICH, ERIC, investment company executive; b. 1967; BA in Economics, summa cum laude, Harvard U., 1988. Mem. equities arbitrage dept. Goldman Sachs Group Inc., 1988—92, head dept., 1992—2000, sr. exec., ptnr., 2000—04, co-head equities divsn.; founder Eton Pk. Capital Mgmt., 2004—. Leadership coun. New Am. Found.; trustee Whitney Mus. Am. Art, Mt. Sinai Med. Ctr. Inc.; bd. dirs. Havard Mgmt. Co., 1996—2004, Horace Mann Sch., Lincoln Ctr. Theatre. Mem.: Phi Beta Kappa. Office: Eton Park Captial Mgmt 825 Third Ave New York NY 10022 Office Phone: 212-593-0766, 212-756-5300. *

MINDLIN, PAULA ROSALIE, retired reading educator; b. NYC, Nov. 27, 1944; d. Simon S. and Sylvia (Naroff) Bernstein; m. Alfred Carl Mindlin, Aug. 14, 1965; 1 child, Spencer Douglas. BA in Edn., Bklyn. Coll., 1965; MS in Edn., Queens Coll., 1970, Specialist Sch. Adminstrn, 1973. Tchr. Dist. 16 Pub. Sch., Bklyn., 1965—68; reading tchr. Dist. 29 Pub. Sch. and Dist. 16, Bklyn., 1968—85; instr. insvc. courses Cmty. Sch. Dist. 29, Queens Village, NY, 1984—93, reading coord. Reading/Comm. Arts Program, 1985—90, dir. reading, 1990—94. Adj. lectr. York Coll., 1989; dir. Chpt. 1 Program (Nat. Recognition 1994, U.S. Sec. of Edn.); curriculum cons., 1997—98. Recipient svc. award N.Y. State Reading Assn. Coun., 1996. Mem. Queensboro Reading Coun. (pres. 1994-96, Educator of Yr. award 1994). Avocations: reading, gardening, travel.

MINEHAN, CATHY ELIZABETH, retired bank executive; b. Jersey City, Feb. 15, 1947; d. Harry Manford Jones and Rita Jane (Decora) Jones Leary; m. Gerald Paul Minehan, July 18, 1970; children: Melissa Jane, Brian Patrick. BA, U. Rochester, 1968; MBA, NYU, 1977. Various positions to sr. v.p. Fed. Res. Bank NY, NYC, 1968—75, ops. analysis officer, 1975, mgr. mgmt. info. dept., 1976—78, asst. v.p., 1979—82, v.p., 1982—87, sr. v.p., 1987—91; COO Fed. Res. Bank Boston, 1991-94, pres., 1994—2007. Cons. IMF, Washington, 1990-91; bd. dirs. Boston Mcpl. Rsch. Bur., Park St. Corp., The New Eng. Coun.; mem. Gov.'s Coun. Econ. Growth and Tech. Bd. dirs. Boston Pvt. Industry Council, Boston Mcpl. Rsch. Bur., Jobs for Mass., New Eng. Council, Boston Pub. Libr. Found.; mem. Mass. Women's Forum, Boston, 1991—; bd. advisors Caroll Sch. Mgmt. Boston Coll.; trustee Bentley Coll., 1992—; trustee coun. U. Rochester, 1993—. Mem. Pub. Securities Assn. (ex officio, govt. ops. com. 1986-91), Beta Gamma Sigma. Democrat. Roman Catholic. Avocations: golf, skiing, jogging. *

MINEHART, JEAN BESSE, retired tax accountant; b. Cleve., Nov. 8, 1937; d. Ralph and Augusta Besse; m. Ralph Conrad Minehart, Aug. 28, 1959; children: Patricia Minehart Miron, Deborah Minehart Rust, Elizabeth Minehart Biedermann, Stephen. BA, Wellesley Coll., Mass., 1959; MEd, U. Va., Charlottesville, 1971. Rsch. assoc. Age Ctr. of New Eng., Boston, 1959-61; substitute tchr. Charlottesville Sch. Sys., Va., 1976-81; tax acct. H&R Block, Charlottesville, 1982-94, Huey & Bjorn, Charlottesville, 1994—2006; ret., 2006. Past pres. Ephphatha Village Housing for the Deaf, Charlottesville, 1984-87; bd. dirs. Tues. Evening Concert Series, Charlottesville, 1990-94; sec., bd. dirs. Family Svc., Inc., Charlottesville, 1987-91; bd. dirs. Westminster Organ Concert Series; elder Westminster Presbyn. Ch., 1979-81, 94-96, trustee, 2005— Scholar, Wellesley Coll. scholar. Mem. LWV (v.p., treas. 1991-95) Blue Ridge Wellesley Club (pres. Charlottesvillechpt. 1989-91, dorm rep. 1996-2004). Avocations: reading, music. Home: 1714 Yorktown Dr Charlottesville VA 22901

MINEKA, SUSAN, psychology professor; b. Ithaca, NY, June 2, 1948; d. Francis Edward and Muriel Leota (McGregor) M. BA in Psychology magna cum laude, Cornell U., 1970; PhD, U. Pa., 1974. Lic. psychologist Ill. Prof. psychology U. Wis., Madison, 1974-85, U. Tex., Austin, 1986-87; prof. Northwestern U., Evanston, Ill., 1987—. Co-dir. Panic Treatment Ctr., Evanston Hosp., 1988—99; co-dir. Anxiety and Panic Treatment Clinic Northwestern U., 2001—; mem. NIH Panic Consensus Panel, 1991. Editor: Jour. Abnormal Psychology, 1990—94; assoc. editor Emotion, 2003—06; contbr. articles to profl. jours. Fellow, Ctr. for Advanced Study in the Behavioral Scis., Stanford, Calif., 1997—98; grantee, NSF and NIMH, 1978—. Fellow APA (bd. sci. affairs 1992-94, chair 1994, pres. divsn. 12, sect. 3 1995), Am. Psychol. Soc. (bd. dirs. 2001-04); mem. Assn. for Advancement Behavior Therapy, Midwestern Psychol. Assn. (pres. 1996-97), Soc. for Rsch. in Psychopathology (mem. exec. bd. 1992-94, 2000-03), Soc. for Sci. of Clin. Psychology (Disting. Scientist award 2007), Phi Beta Kappa, Sigma Xi. Democrat. Office: Northwestern U Psychology Dept Evanston IL 60208-0001 E-mail: mineka@northwestern.edu.

MINER, BRAD C., secondary school educator; s. Jon and Freda Miner; m. Melissa Blustone, Aug. 18, 1990; children: Seth, Shane, Sarabeth. BS in Edn., Calif. U. Pa., 1989. Tchr. Brownsville Area Sch. Dist., Pa., 1995—. Avocations: running, exercise, bicycling. Office: Brownsville Area High Sch 1 Falcon Dr Brownsville PA 15417

MINER, JACQUELINE, political consultant; b. Dec. 10, 1936; d. Ralph E. and Agnes (McGee) Mariani; m. Roger J. Miner, Aug. 11, 1975; children: Laurence, Ronald Carmichael, Ralph Carmichael, Mark. Ind. polit. cons., Hudson, NY; instr. history and polit. sci. SUNY, Hudson, 1974—79. Mem. nat. steering com. Fund for Am.'s Future, 2d cir. Hist. Com.; mem. White House Outreach Working Group on Central Am.; candidate for Rep. nomination U.S. Senate, 1982; co-chair N.Y. state steering com. George Bush for Pres. campaign, 1986—88; del. Rep. Conv., 1992, GOP Conv., 1992; Rep. county committeewoman, 1958—76; vice chmn. N.Y. State Ronald Reagan campaign, 1980, N.Y. State Rep. Com., 1991—93; co-chmn. N.Y. State Reagan Roundup Campaign, 1984—86; chmn. Coll. Consortium for Internat. Studies. Mem.: PEO, U.S. Supreme Ct. Hist. Soc. Address: 1 Merlins Way Hudson NY 12534-4157

MINER, JAMES ROSS, emergency physician, educator; b. Minneola, NY, Jan. 11, 1970; MD, Mayo Med. Sch., Rochester, Minn., 1996. Lic. physician MN, 1997. Assoc. prof. of emergency medicine U. of Minn. Med. Sch., Mpls., 1999—. Assoc. editor Acad. Emergency Medicine, 2003—06. Fellow: Am. Coll. of Emergency Physicians. Achievements include research in pain management. Office: Hennepin County Medical Center 701 Park Ave S Minneapolis MN 55415 Office Phone: 612-873-8791. E-mail: jimminer@hotmail.com.

MINER, JOHN BURNHAM, industrial relations educator, writer; b. NYC, July 20, 1926; s. John Lynn and Bess (Burnham) M.; children by previous marriage: Barbara, John, Cynthia, Frances; m. Barbara Allen Williams, June 1, 1979; children: Jennifer, Heather. AB, Princeton U., 1950, PhD, 1955; MA, Clark U., 1952. Lic. psychologist, N.Y. Rsch. assoc. Columbia U., 1956-57; mgr. psychol. svcs. Atlantic Refining Co., Phila., 1957-60; mem. faculty U. Oreg., Eugene, 1960-68; prof., chmn. dept. orgnl. sci. U. Md., College Park, 1968-73; rsch. prof. Ga. State U., Atlanta, 1973-87, Disting. prof., 1974; pres. Orgnl. Measurement Systems Press, Eugene, Oreg., 1976—; prof. human resources SUNY, Buffalo, 1987-94, chmn. dept. orgn. and human resources, 1989-92; profl. practice Eugene, Oreg., 1995—. Cons. McKinsey & Co., N.Y.C., 1966-69; vis. lectr. U. Pa., Phila., 1959-60; vis. prof. U. Calif., Berkeley, 1966-67, U. South Fla., Tampa, 1972; researcher on orgnl. motivation, theories of orgn., human resource utilization, bus. policy and strategy, entrepreneurship. Author: Personnel Psychology, 1969, Personnel and Industrial Relations, 1969, 1973, 1977, 1985, The Challenge of Managing, 1975; author: (with Mary Green Miner) Policy Issues Personnel and Industrial Relations, 1977; author: (with George A. Steiner) Management Policy and Strategy, 1977; author: (with M.G. Miner) Employee Selection Within the Law, 1978; author: Theories of Organizational Behavior, 1980, Theories of Organizational Structure and Process, 1982, People Problems: The Executive Answer Book, 1985, The Practice of Management, 1985, Organizational Behavior: Performance and Productivity, 1988, Industrial-Organizational Psychology, 1992, Role Motivation Theories, 1993; with Donald P. Crane Human Resource Management: The Strategic Perspective, 1995; author: The 4 Routes to Entrepreneurial Success, 1996; author: (with Michael H. Capps) How Honesty Testing Works, 1997; author: A Psychological Typology of Successful Entrepreneurs, 1997, Organizational Behavior: Foundations, Theories and Analyses, 2002, Organizational Behavior: Essential Theories of Motivation and Leadership, 2005, Organizational Behavior: Essential Theories of Process and Structure, 2006, Organizational Behavior: Historical Origins, Theoretical Foundations, and the Future, 2006, Organizational Behavior: From Theory To Practice, 2007, many other books and monographs; contbr. numerous articles, papers to profl. jours. With US Army, 1944—46, ETO. Decorated Bronze Star, Combat Infantryman's badge. Fellow APA, Acad. of Mgmt. (editor Jour. 1973-75, pres. 1977-78), Soc. for Personality Assessment, Am. Psychol. Soc.; mem. Soc. for Human Resource Mgmt., Inst. Operations Rsch. Mgmt. Sci., Am. Sociolog. Assn., Indsl. Rels. Rsch. Assn., Internat. Coun. for Small Bus., Strategic Mgmt. Soc., Internat. Pers. Mgmt. Assn., Human Resource Planning Soc. Republican. Home and Office: 34199 Country View Dr Eugene OR 97408-9440 Office Phone: 541-484-2715.

MINER, ROGER JEFFREY, federal judge; b. Apr. 14, 1934; s. Abram and Anne M. Miner; m. Jacqueline Mariani; 4 children. BS, SUNY; LLB cum laude, NY Law Sch., 1956; postgrad., Bklyn. Law Sch., Judge Advocate Gen.'s Sch., U. Va.; LLD (hon.), NY Law Sch., 1989, Syracuse U., 1990, Albany Law Sch./Union U., 1996; attended, Emory U. Bar: NY 1956, US Ct. Mil. Appeals 1956, Republic of Korea 1958, US Dist. Ct. (so. and ea. dists.) NY 1959. Ptnr. Miner & Miner, Hudson, NY, 1959—75; corp. counsel City of Hudson, 1961—64; asst. dist. atty. Columbia County, 1964, dist. atty., 1968—75; justice NY State Supreme Ct., 1976—81; judge US Dist. Ct. (no. dist.) NY, 1981—85; sr. judge US Ct. Appeals (2d cir.), Albany, NY, 1997—. Adj. assoc. prof. criminal law State U. Sys., NY, 1974—79; adj. prof. law NY Law Sch., 1986—96, Albany Law Sch. Union U., 1997—2002; faculty assoc. Ariz. State U. Coll. Law, 2004; lectr. state and local bar assns.; lectr. SUNY, Albany, 1985; with NY Law Sch. Bd. Trustees, 1991—96; hon. trustee NY Law Sch. bd. trustees, 1996—; chmn. 2d Cir. Com. on Hist. and Commemorative Events, 1989—94; mem. jud. coun. 2d Cir., 1992—96; with No. Dist. Hist. Com., 1981—85, State, Fed. Jud. Coun. of N.Y., 1986—91, Cameras in the Courtoom Com., 1993—96; chmn. Jud. Conf. on US com. on fed.-state jurisdiction, 1987—92, State, Fed. Jud. Coun. of N.Y., 1990—91; trustee Practicing Law Inst., 1995—2002. Mng. editor: NY Law Sch. Law Rev.; contbr. articles to law jours. 1st lt. JAGC US Army, 1956—59, capt. USAR, ret. Named Columbia County Man of Yr., 1984; recipient Dean's medal for disting. profl. svc., NY Law Sch., Disting. Alumnus award, Charles W. Froessel award for Valuable Contbn. to Law, Albany Jewish Fedn. award, Abraham Lincoln award, Cmty. Svc. award, Kiwanis, others, Ellis Island medal of honor. Mem.: ATLA, ABA, Columbia County Magistrates Assn., Am. Soc. Writers on Legal Subjects, Fed. Bar Coun., Fed. Judges Assn., Am. Judicature Soc., Am. Law Inst., Columbia County Bar Assn., Assn. of Bar of City of NY, NY State Bar Assn., B'nai Brith, NY Law Sch. Alumni Assn. (hon.; bd. dirs.), Supreme Ct. Hist. Soc., Columbia County Hist. Soc., Elks (past exalted ruler). Jewish. Office: US Ct Appeals 445 Broadway Ste 414 Albany NY 12207-2926 *

MINER, THOMAS HAWLEY, entrepreneur; b. Shelbyville, Ill., June 19, 1927; s. Lester Ward and Thirza (Hawley) M.; m. Lucyna T. Minciel, July 22, 1983; children: Robert Thomas, William John. Student, U.S. Mil. Acad., 1946—47; BA, Knox Coll., 1950; JD, U. Ill., 1953. Bar: Ill. 1954. Counsel Continental Ill. Nat. Bank & Trust Co., Chgo., 1953—55; pres. Harper-Wyman Internat. S.A., Venezuela and Mex., 1955—58, Hudson Internat. S.A., Can. and Switzerland, 1958—60, Thomas H. Miner & Assoc., Inc., Chgo., 1960—; chmn. Miner, Fraser & Gabriel Pub. Affairs, Inc., Washington, 1982—88, Miner Sys., Inc., 1981—; internat. dir. Urban Retail Properties Inc., 2005—; chmn., CEO Ill. Global Partnership, Inc., 2005—; dir. US-China C. of C., 2007—. Bd. dirs. Lakeside Bank, Worldschool, Bright Oceans Internat. Corp.; chmn. Ill. dist. export coun. U.S. Dept. Commerce, 1971—; sec. Consular Corps. Chgo., 1986—88; chmn. Mid-Am. China Mgmt. Tng. Ctr., Global Software Source, Geo Vision, Inc., U.S.-Iraq Bus. Alliance. Chmn. bd. dirs. Sch. Art Inst. Chgo., 1977-81; bd. govs., life mem., sustaining fellow Art Inst. Chgo.; former chmn. UN Assn., Chgo.; founder, chmn. Mid-Am. Com., 1968—; former mem. bd. dirs. UNICEF, NAM, Internat. Trade Policy Com. and Working Group on Commonwealth of Ind. States and Ea. Europe; trustee 4th Presbyn. Ch., Chgo., Roosevelt U., Chgo., 1996; bd. advisors Mercy Hosp.; vice chmn. Chgo. Sister Cities; mem. adv. bd. Internat. Inst. Edn.; bd. dirs. Internat. Sister Cities. With USNR, 1945-46; mem. Pres. Coun. U. Ill. Found.; dir. Internat. Urgan Retail Properties Co.; chmn. Ill. Global Partnership, Inc. Capt. U.S. Army, 1946-47. Decorated comdr. Crown of the Kingdom of Belgium, 2003, commendatore Ordine al Merito della Repubblica Italiana; recipient Alumni Achievement award Knox Coll., 1974, Gold Medallion award Internat. Visitors Ctr. Chgo., 1989; named One of Chgo.'s 10 Outstanding Young Men, 1962, Chicagoan of Year Chgo. Assn. Commerce and Industry, 1968, Alumni of Month Coll. Law U. Ill., Nov. 1970, Aug. 1984; hon. consul Republic of Senegal, 1970-88. Mem. Am. Mgmt. Assn., Chicagoland C. of C., Mid-Am. Arab C. of C. (founder, former pres.), Chgo. Bar Assn., Chgo. Com., Chgo. Coun. Fgn. Rels. (past dir.), Coun. of the Ams., Internat. Trade Club (past dir., pres.), Japan-Am. Soc., Nat. Coun. U.S.-China Trade, Nat. Acad. Scis. (pres. coun.), English Speaking Union (dir., past chmn.) Trade and Econs. Coun. USA-CIS (dir.), U.S.-Russia Bus. Coun., Mus. Contemporary Art, Newcomen Soc. N.Am., U.S.-China Bus. Coun., U.S.-Arab C. of C. (bd. dirs.), U.S.-Mex. C. of C. (bd. dirs.), Thomas Minor Soc., Chgo. Club, Econ. Club, Grant Park Concerts Soc., Chgo. Farmers Club, Mid-Am. Club, Univ. Club (Washington), Univ. Club (Milw.), Hillsboro Club (Fla.), Tryall Golf and Beach Club (Jamaica), Rotary, Phi Delta Phi, Phi Gamma Delta. Office: 900 N Michigan Ave Ste 1300 Chicago IL 60611 Home Phone: 312-944-2453; Office Phone: 312-915-3336. Personal E-mail: ltminer@aol.com. Business E-Mail: minert@urbanretail.com.

MINER, TRACY A., lawyer; b. 1958; BA in Psych., U. Notre Dame, 1980; JD summa cum laude, Boston Coll., 1985. Bar: Mass. 1985, US Ct. Appeals (DC cir.). Atty., chair white collar def. grp. Mintz, Levin, Cohn, Ferris, Glovsky & Popeo, P.C., Boston. Bd. advs. Sentencing Project Am. Law Inst.; mem. adv. com. US Ct. Appeals (1st cir.). Contbr. chapters to books. Named a Mass. Super Lawyer, 2004. Mem.: Boston Bar Assn. (mem. criminal law steering com.), Mass. Assn. Criminal Def. Lawyers (bd. dirs., past pres.), NACDL. Office: Mintz Levin Cohn Ferris Glovsky & Popeo PC 1 Financial Ctr Boston MA 02111 Office Phone: 617-348-1694. Office Fax: 617-542-2241. E-mail: taminer@mintz.com.

MINES, MICHAEL, retired lawyer; b. Seattle, May 4, 1929; s. Henry Walker and Dorothy Elizabeth (Bressler) M.; m. Phyllis Eastham, Aug. 24, 1957; children: Linda Mines Elliott, Sandra, Diane Paull, Michael Lister. BA, U. Wash., 1951, JD, 1954. Bar: Wash. 1954, U.S. Dist. Ct. (we. dist.) Wash. 1957, U.S. Dist. Ct. Mont. 1970, U.S. Ct. Appeals (9th cir.) 1961, U.S. Supreme Ct. Assoc. Skeel, McKelvy, Henke, Evenson & Uhlman, Seattle, 1956-66, ptnr., 1966-68, Hullin, Roberts, Mines, Fite & Riveland, Seattle, 1968-75, Skeel, McKelvy, Henke, Evenson & Betts, Seattle, 1975-79, Betts, Patterson & Mines, 1978—2004; ret., 2004. Moderator Wash.-No. Idaho conf. United Ch. of Christ, 1975-76; trustee Plymouth Housing Group, 1991-97; chair adult edn. bd. Plymouth Congl. Ch., Seattle, 1998-2001. With U.S. Army, 1954-56. Mem. ABA (hon.), Wash. State Bar Assn., Seattle-King Bar Assn., Am. Coll. Trial Lawyers (state chair 1984-85), Internat. Acad. Trial Lawyers (bd. dirs. 1991-96), U. Wash. Law Sch. Alumni Assn. (trustee, pres. bd. dirs. 1995-97). Home: 2474 Crestmont Pl W Seattle WA 98199-3714 Personal E-mail: mpmines@aol.com. Business E-Mail: mmines@bpmlaw.com.

MINETA, NORMAN YOSHIO, management consultant, former secretary of transportation; b. San Jose, Calif., Nov. 12, 1931; s. Kay Kunisaku and Kane (Watanabe) M.; m. Danealia; children: David, K., Stuart S.; stepchildren: Robert M. Brantner, Mark Brantner. BS, U. Calif.-Berkeley, 1953; D of Pub. Svc., Santa Clara U., 1989; HHD (hon.), Rust Coll., 1993. Agt./broker Mineta Ins. Agy., San Jose, 1956-89; mem. adv. bd. Bank of Tokyo, Calif., 1961-75; mem. city coun. City of San Jose, 1967-71, vice mayor, 1969-71, mayor, 1971-75; mem. US Congress from 13th (now 15th) Calif. dist., 1975-95; subcom. surface transp., 1989-92; former dep. Dem. whip; ranking minority mem. transp. and infrastructure com.; sr. v.p., mng. dir. transp. sys. & srvs. Lockheed Martin, Washington, 1995-2000; sec. US Dept. Commerce, Washington, 2000-2001, US Dept. Transp., Washington, 2001—06; vice chmn. global comm. consultancy Hill & Knowlton Inc., Washington, 2006—. Chmn. fin. com. Santa Clara County (Calif.) Council Chs., 1960-62; commr. San Jose Human Relations Commn., 1962-64, San Jose Housing Authority, 1966-67; bd. dirs. Nat. RR Passenger Corp.(AMTRAK), 2001-, AECOM Tech. Corp. 2007-; mem. adv. bd. Carolinks 2006- Precinct chmn. Community Theater Bond Issue, 1964; mem. spl. gifts com. Santa Clara County council Boy Scouts Am., 1967; sec. Santa Clara County Grand Jury, 1964; bd. dirs. Wesley Found., San Jose State Coll., 1956-58, Pacific Neighbors, Community Council Cen. Santa Clara County, Japan Soc., San Francisco, Santa Clara County chpt. NCCJ, Mexican-Am. Community Services Agy.; mem. exec. bd. No. Calif.-Western Nev. dist. council Japanese Am. Citizens League, 1960-62, pres. San Jose chpt., 1957-59; bd. regents Smithsonian Instn., 1979-95; chmn. Smithsonian vis. com. for Freer Gallery, 1981-95; mem. bd. regents Santa Clara U.; chmn. Nat. Civil Aviation Rev. Commn., 1997; mem. Smithsonian Nat. Bd., 1996—. Served to lt. AUS, 1954-56. Recipient Golden Plate award, Acad. Achievement, 2005, Presdl. Medal of Freedom, 2006. Mem. Greater San Jose C. of C., Nat. Assn. Indsl. Ins. Agts., Calif. Assn. Indsl. Ins. Agts., San Jose Assn. Ind. Ins. Agts. (dir. 1960-62), North San Jose Optimists Club (pres. 1956-58), Jackson-Taylor Bus. and Profl. Assn. (dir. 1963). Democrat. Meth. Office: Hill & Knowlton Inc Ste 601 600 New Hampshire Ave NW Washington DC 20037 *Personal philosophy: My two greatest responsibilities are accountability and accessibility to everyone I represent, and to anyone who comes to me for help.* *

MINETREE, JAMES LAWRENCE, III, retired military officer, educator; b. Balt., Feb. 21, 1937; s. James Lawrence and Rhoda (Blossom) M.; m. Martha Milling, Apr. 9, 1983; children: James Lawrence IV, Peter Milling, Jennifer Grace, Margaret Warner; stepchildren: Rachael, Aubrilyn. B, U. Nebr., Omaha, 1971; MA, U. So. Calif., LA, 1973. Commd. 2d lt. U.S. Army, 1964, advanced through grades to lt. col., 1979; mem. Nat. Intelligence Coun. CIA, Langley, Va., 1979-82; ret. U.S. Army, 1982; with GE Aerospace Sys., Reston, Va., 1982-85; sr. cons. Fed. Emergency Mgmt. Agency, 1985; dir. Crisis Mgmt. Info. Sys. BDM, Tysons Corner, Va., 1985-86; pres. Analytical Scis. Inc., Vienna, Va., 1986-90; founder Nat. Inst. for Urban Search and Rescue, Santa Barbara, Calif., 1982—; adj. prof. U. Md. U. Coll., College Park, 1992—; founder, pres. Wilson Inst. for Humanitarian Assistance, Springfield, Va., 1998—. Trustee Nat. Assn. Search and Rescue, Fairfax, Va., 1984—88; mem. nat. adv. bd. Congl. Fire Svcs. Inst., Washington, 1990—96; designated army strategist. Author. U.S. Govt. rep. European Coun., Athens, Greece, 1990; conceived U.S. Nat. and Internat. Urban Search and Rescue Teams, 1987; disaster mgmt. officer Fed. Emergency Mgmt. Agy., Washington, 1993—2000. With USCG Res., 1954—58. Decorated Legion of Merit (2), Bronze Star (2), Air medal, Meritorious Svc. medal, Army Commendation medal (3), Vietnam Cross of Gallantry, Civic Action medal, others, Dominican Republic and Republic of Vietnam; recipient Presdl. citation Pub. Svc. The White House, Washington, 1995. Mem. VFW, Nat. Def. Exec. Res., Bath County C. of C. (bd. dirs.), Assn. U.S. Army, Am. Legion. Republican. Episcopalian. Home: Grace Hill Farm 5425 Mill Creek Rd Millboro VA 24460 E-mail: peteminetree@mgwnet.com.

MINEUR, YANN SÉBASTIEN, neuroscientist; b. Lons-le-Saunier, Jura, France, Feb. 27, 1977; s. Jean-Pierre Henri and Françoise Micheline Mineur; m. Elizabeth Klaiber, Oct. 9, 2005. B in Biology, U. Orléans, France, 1997, lic. in population and organismal biology, 1998, M in Molecular Genetics and Physiology with honors, 1999; postgrad. diploma with honors, U. Paris V, 2000; PhD in Neuroscis. summa cum laude, U. Paris VI, 2004; PhD, U. Mass., Worcester, 2004. Rschr. Yale U. Sch. Medicine, New Haven, 2004—. Recipient Travel award, Internat. Soc. on Psychiat. Genetics, 2000, Internat. Behavioral Neurosci. Soc., 2001, Fedn. European Neurosci. Soc., 2002, Internat. Behavioral and Neural Genetics Soc., 2003, Outstanding Young Scientist award, 2006; fellow, European Union, 2001, Internat. Behavioral and Neural Genetics Soc., 2006. Achievements include patents pending for use of nicotinic acetylcholine receptors partial agonists as potential antidepressants. Office: Yale Univ Sch Medicine 34 Park St New Haven CT 06519 Home Phone: 203-737-2042; Office Phone: 203-737-2042.

MING, JENNY J., former retail executive; b. Canton, China, 1955; arrived in US, 1964; married; 3 children. BA in Clothing Merchandising, San Jose State U. Mdse. mgr. brand activewear Gap Inc., 1986—89, v.p., divsn. mdse. mgr., 1989—94, sr. v.p. merchandising, Old Navy, 1994—96, exec. v.p. merchandising, Old Navy, 1996—99, pres., Old Navy, 1999—2006, mem., sr. oper. com., 1999—2006. Bd. dirs. Epiphany, Inc., 2001—. Bd. dirs. Big Brothers Big Sisters, San Francisco; mem. Com. of 100. Named one of 50 Most Powerful Women in Am. Bus., Fortune mag., 2003; recipient Award for Leadership in Bus. & Community Svc., Merage Found. for the American Dream, 2006. *

MING, SI-CHUN, pathologist, educator; b. Shanghai, Nov. 10, 1922; arrived in US, 1949, naturalized, 1964; s. Sian-Fan and Jan-Teh (Kuo) M.; m. Pen-Ming Lee, Aug. 17, 1957; children: Carol, Ruby, Stephanie, Michael, Jeffrey, Eileen. MD, Nat. Ctrl. U. Coll. Medicine, China, 1947. Resident in pathology Mass. Gen. Hosp., Boston, 1952-56; assoc. pathologist Beth Israel Hosp., Boston, 1956-67; asst. prof. pathology Harvard U. Med. Sch., 1965-67; assoc. prof. U. Md., 1967-71; prof. Temple U., Phila., 1971-93, prof. emeritus, 1993—, acting chmn. dept. pathology, 1978-80, dep. chmn. dept. path., 1980-86. US rep. WHO Collaborating Ctr. for Primary Prevention, Diagnosis and Treatment of Gastric Cancer, 1984-98; hon. prof. Tianjin Med. Coll., Shanghai Second Med. U., Fourth Mil. Med. U., China, 1988—. Author: Tumors of the Esophagus and Stomach, 1973, supplement, 1985, Precursors of Gastric Cancer, 1984, Pathology of the Gastrointestinal Tract, 1992, 2d edit., 1998; mem. editl. bd. World Jour. Gastroenterology, 1998-05, Gastric Cancer, 1998-05. Nat. Cancer Inst. sr. fellow Karolinska Inst. Stockholm, 1964-65. Mem. AAAS, US Canadian Acad. Pathology, Am. Soc. Investigative Pathology, Am. Gastroenterol. Assn., NY Acad. Scis. Achievements include development of classification method for stomach carcinoma based on the growth pattern of the cancer; establishment of pathological criteria for the diagnosis of premalignant lesions of the digestive tract. Office: 3401 N Broad St Philadelphia PA 19140-5104 Business E-Mail: ming@temple.edu.

MING, XUE, pediatrician, pediatric neurologist, neuroscientist, pharmacologist; b. Wenzhou, Zhejiang, China; MD, Shanghai Med. U., 1984; PhD, U. Medicine and Dentistry NJ Med. Sch., 1991. Pediatrics resident SUNY-Upstate Med. Ctr.; fellow, pediatric neurology John Hopkins Med. Inst., Balt., 1994—97; pediatric neurologist, neuroscientist, dept. neuroscience U. Medicine and Dentistry NJ, Univ. Hosp., Newark, 1997—; assoc. prof., dept. neurology & neuroscience U. Medicine and Dentistry NJ-NJ Med. Sch. Contbr. articles to profl. jours. Office: Dept Neurology & Neurosciences 90 Bergen St DOC 8100 Newark NJ 07101 Address: UMDNJ NJ Med Sch Behavioral Health Sciences Bldg F-Level 183 South Orange Ave Newark NJ 07103 Office Phone: 973-972-5204. Office Fax: 973-972-2369. Business E-Mail: mingxu@umdnj.edu.

MING, YAO, professional basketball player; b. Shanghai, Sept. 12, 1980; s. Yao Zhie Yuan and Fang Feng Di; m. Ye Li, Aug. 6, 2007. Student, Shanghai Phys. & Sport Technic Edn. Inst., Shanghai Fgn. Lang. Inst. Player Shanghai Sharks, Chinese Basketball Assn., 1997—2002, Houston Rockets, NBA, 2002—. Mem. Chinese Olympic Basketball Team, Athens,

2004; ctr. NBA Western Conf. All-Star Team, 2003, 04, 05, 06, 07. Author: Yao: A Life in Two Worlds, 2004; film appearances The Year of the Yao, 2004, guest appearances (voice TV series) The Simpsons, 2005. Named NBA All-Rookie First Team, 2002; named one of 100 Most Influential People, People mag., 2004; recipient Laureus World Newcomer of Yr. award, 2003. Achievements include being 1st player to be #1 overall pick to come from an international basketball league; appeared on covers of Sports Illus., The Sporting News, ESPN the Mag. SLAM, Inside Stuff and Basketball Digest; featured in Visa, Apple Computer and Gatorade TV commercials. Avocation: computer games. Office: Houston Rockets 1510 Polk St Houston TX 77002-1099 *

MINGER, TERRELL JOHN, public administration and natural resource institute executive; b. Canton, Ohio, Oct. 7, 1942; s. John Wilson and Margaret Rose M.; m. Judith R. Arnold, Aug. 7, 1965; 1 child, Gabriella Sophia. BA, Baker U., 1966; MPA, Kans. U., 1969; postgrad., MIT, 1975; Loeb fellow, Harvard U., 1976-77; postgrad, Stanford U., 1979; MBA, U. Colo., 1983. Asst. dir. admissions Baker U., 1966-67; asst. city mgr. City of Boulder, Colo., 1968-69; city mgr. City of Vail, Colo., 1969-79; pres., CEO Whistler Village Land Co., Vancouver, B.C., Can., 1979-81; v.p., gen. mgr. Cumberland S.W. Inc., Denver, 1981-83; exec. asst. dep. chief of staff to Gov. Colo., 1983-87; pres., CEO Sundance Inst. for Resource Mgmt., Utah, 1986—, Sundance Enterprises Ltd., 1988-91. Adj. prof. grad. sch. pub. affairs U. Colo., 1983—, Sch. Bus. U. Denver, 1992—; bd. dirs. Colo. Open Lands, Inc.; participant UN Conf. on Environment and Devel., Rio de Janeiro, 1992; chmn. environ. adv. bd. Wal-Mart, Inc., 1990—; co-chmn. task force sustainable consumption World Bus. Coun. Sustainable Devel.; co-chmn. N.Am. Telecom./Environ. Taskforce; dir. Stapleton Found. Sustainable Cities, 2000-; chmn. Environ. Excellence Task Force Telecomm. Industry; environ. advisor Salt Lake City Olympic Com.; bd. chmn. Three Sisters Mountain Village, Canmore, Aberta, 2002-. Editor: Greenhouse/Glasnost-The Global Warming Crisis, 1990, Val Symposium Papers, 1970-79; author, editor: Growth Alternatives for Rocky Mountain West, 1976, Future of Human Settlements in the West, 1977. Spl. del. UN Habitat Conf. Human Settlements, spl. rep. to UN Environ. Program, 1992, coord. UN Global Youth Forum, 1993-94, co-chmn. conf. on environ. and mktg., N.Y.C., 1993; founder Vail Symposium, advisor UN Environ. Program Telecom. Charter, Nairobi, Kenya, 1999; co-founder, bd. dirs. Colo. Park Found., 1985—; chair World Alpine Championship Conf., Vail, Colo., 1999; founding mem. Greenhouse/Glasnost U.S./USSR Teleconf. with Soviet Acad. Scis., 1989—; mem. pres. task force Commn. on Sustainable Devel., 1994—; co-chmn. Golf and Environ. Conf., Pebble Beach, Calif., 1995; founder, pres. Western Rendezvous, 1995—; bd. dirs. Piton Found., 1996; co-chair UN Sustainability Roundtable for Europe and No. Am., 2002. Nat. finalist White House Fellowship, 1978; recipient Colo. Soc. Landscape Arch. award, 1999, Sacred Mountain Gold medal, Taos, N.Mex., 2005; named one of B.C.'s Top Bus. Leaders for the '80s, 1980. Mem. Urban Land Inst., Colo. Acad. Pub. Adminstrn. (charter, founding mem. 1988), Colo. City Mgmt. Innovation award 1974-76), Western Gov.'s Assn. (staff coun., chmn. adv. com. 1985-86), Flatirons Athletic Club, Lewis and Clark Nat. Bicentennial Commn. (commr. 2000-2005). Home: 785 6th St Boulder CO 80302-7416 Office: Ctr for Resource Mgmt 1030 13th St Ste 100 Boulder CO 80302 Business E-Mail: tminger@crm.org.

MINGLE, JAMES JOHN, lawyer; m. Barbara O'Neil; children: Christina, Jonathan. AB in English, St. Joseph's Coll., Phila., 1968; JD, U. Va., 1973. Bar: Md. 1974, Va. 1990, N.Y. 1996. Asst. to pres. Frostburg State Coll., 1973-77, adj. prof. bus. law, 1975-77; asst. atty. gen. State of Md., 1977-89; chief counsel Md. State Univ. and Coll. Sys., U. Md., Md. Pub. TV, 1981-89; gen. counsel U. Va., Charlottesville, 1989-95, lectr. law, 1994-95; gen. counsel, sec. corp., adj. prof. law Cornell U., Ithaca, NY, 1995—. Adj. prof. law U. Md., 1984-88; asst. to bus. mgr. Phila. 76ers NBA Club, 1968-69; city atty. City of Frostburg, Md., 1974-76; joint adv. bds., Cornell Med. Coll., Qatar, 2001. Mem.: Cornell-Nanyang Inst. Hospitality Mgmt., Nat. Assn. Coll. and U. Attys. Office Phone: 607-255-3903. Business E-Mail: jjm19@cornell.edu.

MINGLE, JOHN ORVILLE, engineer, educator, lawyer, consultant; b. Oakley, Kans., May 6, 1931; s. John Russell and Beulah Amelia (Johnson) M.; m. Patricia Ruth Schmitt, Aug. 17, 1957; children: Elizabeth Lorene, Stephen Roy. BS, Kans. State U., Manhattan, 1953, MS, 1958; PhD, Northwestern U., 1960; JD, Washburn U., 1980. Bar: Kans., Wyo., U.S. Patent Office; registered profl. engr., Kans. Tng. engr. Gen. Electric Co., Schenectady, 1953-54; mem. faculty Kans. State U., 1956-90, prof. nuclear engring., 1965-90, prof. emeritus, 1990—, Black & Veatch Disting. prof., 1973-78; dir. Inst. Computational Research Engring., 1969-88; exec. v.p., patent counsel Kans. State U. Research Found., 1983-88. Instr. Northwestern U., 1958-59; vis. prof. U. So. Calif., 1967-68; cons. govt. and industry; engring. legal cons. 1990—. Author: The Invarient Imbedding Theory of Nuclear Transport, 1973; also articles. Bd. dirs. Laramie Regional Airport, 1994-97. Officer AUS, 1954—56, lt. US Army, 1954—56. Mem. ABA (chairperson sci. and tech. phys. scis. com. 1982-92), NSPE (sect. exec. com. 1985-87, chmn. 1985-86), Am. Nuclear Soc. (sect. pres. 1976-77), Am. Inst. Chem. Engrs. (profl. devel. com. 1982-95), Am. Soc. Engring. Edn. (chmn. Midwest sect. 1985-86, exec. com. 1984-87), Profl. Engrs. in Edn. (vice chmn. 1978-80, workshop chairperson 1983), Kans. Engring. Soc. (past chpt. pres.), Kans. Bar Assn., Licensing Execs. Soc., Sigma Xi (past chpt. pres., lectr.), Soc. Univ. Patent Adminstrs. (exec. com. 1985-87, v.p. cen. region 1985-87). Home: 1409 Downey St Laramie WY 82072-1867 Office Phone: 307-742-0171. *In times past workaholic behavior produced prudent contributions. Now in our world of paradox, the philosophy has been turned on its head, and an iota of "wisdom work" often overshadows everything else.*

MINICHELLO, DENNIS, lawyer; b. Cleve., June 9, 1952; s. Ernest Anthony and Mary Theresa (Rocci) M.; m. Janine Stevens, Feb. 14, 1987. BA in Econs., MA in Econs., Ohio U., 1974; JD, Northwestern U., 1978. Bar: U.S. Dist. Ct. (no. dist.) Ill., U.S. Ct. Appeals (7th cir.), Supreme Ct. Ill., U.S. Supreme Ct. Assoc. Haskell & Perrin, Chgo., 1978-84; ptnr. Tribler & Marwedel, Chgo., 1984-89, Keck, Mahin & Cate, Chgo., 1989—97; shareholder Marwedel, Minichellot & Reeb, P.C., 1997—. Contbr. articles to profl. jours. Bd. dirs. Great Lakes Naval and Maritime Mus. Fulbright scholar, 1974-75. Mem. ABA, Ill. State Bar Assn., Chgo. Bar Assn. (mem. transp. com.), Maritime Law Assn. (proctor), Ohio U. Alumni Assn. (bd. dirs.), The Propeller Club US (pres. 1983-84), Port Chgo., Transp. Lawyers Assn., Conf. Freight Counsel, Midwest High Speed Rail Coalition (pres. 2000—), Def. Rsch. Inst., Leading Lawyers Network. Roman Catholic. Avocations: reading, exercise. Office: Marwedel Minichello & Reeb PC 10 S Riverside Plz Ste 720 Chicago IL 60606-3709 Office Phone: 312-902-1600 ext. 5065. Business E-Mail: dminichello@mmr-law.com.

MINICK, MICHAEL, publishing executive; b. Albany, NY, Mar. 26, 1945; s. Jason and Ruth Isabelle (Solomon) M. Student, U. Va., 1963-66; BA in History, L.I. U., 1968. Editorial dir. Mag. Mgmt., NYC, 1969-73; mng. editor Gentlemen's Quarterly, NYC, 1975-76; pub., ptnr. Beauty Digest, NYC, 1978-90; pub. Pa. Ofcl. Wine and Liquor Quar., NYC, 1985—, Ohio Liquor Quar., 1990—. Adj. prof. NYU Sch. Journalism. Author: The Kung Fu Exercise Book-Health Secrets of Ancient China, 1974, The Wisdom of Kung Fu, 1974; contbr. numerous articles to popular mags. Mem.: Pa. Wine and Spirit Assn., Sir Harold Actors Soc., 25 Yr. Club of Ind. Distbrs. Democrat. Home: 440 W 22nd St New York NY 10011-2526

MINICUCCI, RICHARD FRANCIS, lawyer, former hospital administrator; b. NYC, Jan. 16, 1947; s. Daniel Michael and Marie Felice (Trotta) M.; m. Nancy Jean Moran, Aug. 16, 1969; children: Jonathan, Elizabeth, Richard. BA, Rutgers U., 1969; MHA, Duke U., 1971; JD, Memphis State U., 1976. Bar: Tenn. 1977, N.Y. 1978. Adminstrv. asst. Duke Hosp., Durham, NC, 1971; health planner Mid-South Med. Ctr. Coun., Memphis, 1971-73; dir. adminstrn. Memphis & Shelby County Hosp. Authority, 1973-77; assoc. Hayt Hayt & Landau, Great Neck, NY, 1977-81, ptnr., 1981-89, Nixon Peabody LLP (Nixon Hargrave Devans & Doyle, LLP), Garden City, NY, 1989—. Lectr. various health law assns. Editor: New York Environmental Law Handbook, 2d edit.; author: Residency Training Program Accreditation, 1st-5th edits., Mastering the Accreditation Process, 1999; editor-in-chief Accreditation Alert, Trouble in Academia: Ten Years of Litigation in Medical Education, 2003; contbr articles to profl. jours. Co-chmn. fund raising Luth. High Sch., Brookville, N.Y., 1991. Capt. U.S. Army, 1971-79. Mem. Am., Nassau Bar Assn., Am. Health Lawyers Assn. Republican. Roman Catholic. Avocations: tennis, skiing, hockey, travel. Office: Nixon Peabody LLP 990 Stewart Ave Ste 350 Garden City NY 11530-4838

MINIER, LEE N., funeral director; b. Utica, NY, Feb. 17, 1950; s. Hugh B. and Ann D. Minier; m. Meredith L. Leigh, July 7, 1974; 1 child, Marissa. AB, Ill. Coll., Jacksonville, 1972; MS, SUNY, Brockport, NY, 1974; PhD, U. Colo., Denver, 1979. Lic. funeral dir. N.Y. Postdoctoral fellow Nat. Multiple Sclerosis Soc., Richmond, Va., 1979—81; rsch. assoc. U. Colo. Health Sci. Ctr., Denver, 1981—83; v.p., funeral dir. Christopher-Mitchell Funeral Homes, Inc., Albion, NY, 1990—. Contbr. articles to profl. jours. Pres., bd. dirs. Oak Orchard Cmty. Health Ctr., Albion, NY, 1990—92, Brockport, NY, 1990—92; bd. dirs. Ea. Orleans Red Cross, Albion, 1993; campaign chairperson United Way, Orleans County, NY, 2000, 2002. Mem.: Soc. for Vertebrate Paleontology, Nat. Ctr. for Sci. Edn. Avocations: weightlifting, canoeing, bicycling. Office: Christopher-Mitchell Funeral Homes Inc 21 West Ave Albion NY 14411 Office Phone: 585-589-4471.

MINIKES, STEPHAN MICHAEL, ambassador, lawyer, banker; b. Berlin, Aug. 29, 1938; came to U.S., 1949; naturalized, 1957; married; 1 child. BS, Cornell U., 1961; JD, Yale U., 1964. Bar: N.Y. State 1965, U.S. Ct. Appeals 2nd Circuit, 1967, U.S. Supreme Ct. 1972, U.S. Ct. Mil. Appeals, 1973, D.C. 1977. Assoc. firm Milbank, Tweed, Hadley & McCloy, NYC, 1964-68, Borden & Ball, NYC, 1968-72; counsel to spl. cons. for energy Pres. U.S., 1973; counsel to chief Naval Ops., Washington, 1972-74; sr. v.p. Export-Import Bank of U.S., Washington, 1974-77; resident mng. partner firm Butler & Binion, Houston and Washington, 1977-84, Thelen Reid & Priest, NY, LA, San Francisco, and Wash., 1984—2001; amb. Org. Security and Coop. in Europe, Vienna, 2001—05; chmn. global affairs and pub. policy Xenophon Strategies, San Francisco, 2006—, Wash., 2006—. Contbr. articles to profl. jours. Mem. exec. com. Yale U. Law Sch., 1979-82, 86-89, 93-97; trustee, chmn. fin. com. Washington Opera, 1979-84. Mem. ABA, Fed. Bar Assn., D.C. Bar Assn., Assn. of Bar of City of N.Y., Am. Soc. Internat. Law, Am. Coun. Germany (bd. dirs., 1994-2001), Cornell U. Alumni Assn., Yale U. Alumni Assn. (law sch. rep. 1981-83, 86-90), Yale Law Sch. (Exec. Com., 1986-90), Internat. Rep. Inst. Clubs: Yale (Washington), Metropolitan (Washington). Home: 419 Walker Rd Great Falls VA 22066 Office Phone: 202-957-7727.

MINKEL, HERBERT PHILIP, JR., lawyer; b. Boston, Feb. 11, 1947; s. Herbert Philip and Helen (Sullivan) M. BA, Holy Cross Coll., 1969; JD, NYU, 1972. Bar: Mass. 1973, US Dist. Ct. Mass. 1973, NY 1976, US Dist. Ct. (so. dist.) NY 1978. Law clk. U.S. Dist. Ct. Mass., Boston, 1972-73; assoc. Milbank, Tweed, Hadley & McCloy, NYC, 1973-79; ptnr. Fried, Frank, Harris, Shriver & Jacobson, NYC, 1979-94; mem. adv. com. on bankruptcy rules Jud. Conf. U.S., 1987-93; sr. ptnr. Minkel and Assoc., NYC and Boston, 1994—. Adj. assoc. prof. NYU Law Sch., 1987-94. Contbg. author: American Bankers Assn. Bankruptcy Manual, 1979; contbg. editor: Collier on Bankruptcy, 15th edit., 1979-96; contbr. articles to profl. jours. Bd. advisors Internat. Yacht Restoration Sch., Newport, R.I., nat. bd. advisors, Mystic Seaport, Conn. Root-Tilden scholar NYU, 1969-72. Mem. ABA, Nat. Bankruptcy Conf., Assn. Bar City of N.Y. Home: 68 Bumps River Rd Osterville MA 02655-1525 Office: Minkel and Assocs 131 E 62d St New York NY 10021 Office Phone: 212-319-2797. Business E-Mail: hminkel@nyc.rr.com.

MINKEL, JUSTIN, elementary school educator; s. Dan and Julie M.; m. Karen Minkel. BA, Cornell Univ.; MA, Univ. Calif., Berkeley. Former tchr. Teach for Am., NY, Calif., Texas, Senegal, W. Africa; tchr. Harvey Jones Elem. Sch., Springdale, Ark., 2003—. Finalist Nat. Tchr. of Yr., 2007; named Ark. Tchr. of Yr., 2007. Achievements include being fluent in Spanish, French, two African languages. Office: Jones Elem Sch 900 S Powell St Springdale AR 72764 Business E-Mail: justinmink@yahoo.com. *

MINKER, JACK, computer scientist, educator; b. Bklyn., July 4, 1927; s. Harry and Rose (Lapuck) M.; m. Rita Goldberg, June 24, 1951 (dec. Oct. 11, 1988); children: Michael Saul, Sally Anne; m. Johanna Cartee Weinstein, Jan. 19, 1997. BA cum laude with honors in Math., Bklyn. Coll., 1949; MS in Math., U. Wis., 1950; PhD in Math., U. Pa., 1959. Grad. teaching asst. U. Wis., 1949-50; tchr. math. Erasmus Hall HS, Bklyn., 1950-51; engr. Bell Aircraft Corp., Buffalo, 1951-52; mgr. info. tech. sect. RCA, Bethesda, Md., 1952-63; dir. tech. staff Auerbach Corp., Washington, 1963-67, tech. cons., 1967-72; mem. Faculty NIH Grad. Sch., 1965-66; vis. mem. faculty U. Md., 1967-68, assoc. prof. computer sci., 1968-71, prof., 1971-98, prof. emeritus, 1998—, 1st chmn. dept. computer sci., 1974-79; cons., speaker, lectr. in field; cons. NSF, 1979-82, chmn. adv. bd. on computer sci., 1980-82. Prof. Inst. Advanced Computer Studies, 1986—; vice-chmn. Com. Concerned Scientists, 1973—; past mem. US Nat. Com. for Fedn. Info. Documentalists. Author: (with H. Gallaire and J.M. Nicolas) Logic and Data Bases a Deductive Approach, 1984; editor: (with H. Gallaire and J.M. Nicholas) Advances in Data Base Theory, vol. 1, 1980, vol. 2, 1984, (with H. Gallaire) Logic and Data Bases, 1978, Foundations of Deductive Databases and Logic Programming, 1988, (with J. Lobo and A. Rajasekar) Foundations of Disjunctive Logic Programming, 1992; editor: Logic-Based Artificial Intelligence, 2000; founding editor-in-chief Theory and Practice of Logic Programming, 2000-2001; contbr. articles to profl. jours.; publs. reviewer; mem. editl. bd. numerous jours. With US Army, 1945—46. Recipient U. Md. Presdl. medal, 1996, Allen Newell award ACM/AAAS, 2005; named Disting. Scholar-Tchr. U. Md., 1997-98, fellow Acad. Excellence in Tchg. and Learning, 2002—. Fellow: IEEE (editl. bd. Expert Info.Sys. jour.), ACM, AAAS, Am. Assn. Artificial Intelligence; mem.: Assn. Computing Machinery (chmn. nat. program com. 1968—69, vice chmn. com. on sci. freedom and human rights 1979—89, founding, Outstanding Contbn. award 1985). Jewish. Office: U Md Dept Computer Sci Dept and Inst Advanced Computer College Park MD 20742-0001 Office Phone: 301-405-2676. Business E-Mail: minker@cs.umd.edu.

MINKOFF, JACK, retired economics professor; b. NYC, Jan. 29, 1925; s. Isidore and Yetta (Fine) M.; m. Anne B. Johnson, June 19, 1948; children— Ellen, Paul. AB, Cornell U., 1948; A.M., Columbia U., 1950, PhD (Ford Found. fellow), 1960. Instr. econs. Western Res. U., 1952-53; instr. econs. Sarah Lawrence Coll., 1959-60; prof. econs., chmn. dept. social sci. Pratt Inst., Bklyn., 1960—, acting dean Sch. Liberal Arts and Scis., 1985-86, dean, 1986-93, acting provost, 1993-95, prof. econs., 1996—2002, ret., 2002. Served with USAAF, 1943-45. Social Sci. Rsch. Coun. fellow, 1950-51. Mem. Phi Beta Kappa. Home: 57 Ruxton Rd Great Neck NY 11023-1528

MINKOFF, JOHN, mathematician, educator; b. Bklyn. s. Alvin Minkoff and Mollie Schwartz; m. Susan Alder, Nov. 19, 1966; 1 child, John. BSEE, Columbia U., 1962, MSEE, 1963, PhD, 1967. Rsch. engr. Columbia U., NYC, 1964-67, rsch. assoc., 1967-73; mgr. analysis activities Riverside Rsch. Inst., NYC, 1973-77; mem. tech. staff Bell Tel. Labs., Whippany, NJ, 1977-86; disting mem. tech. staff ATT/Lucent Techs. Bell Labs., Whippany, 1986—2001; staff scientist space sys. divsn. ITT, 2001—. Adj. prof. elec. engring. Polytech. U. NY, 1989-90; adj. prof. applied math. NYU, NYC, 1990-95. Author: Signals Noise and Active Sensors, 1992, Signal Processing Fundamentals and Applications for Communications and Sensing Systems, 2002; contbr. articles to profl. jours. Music dir. Hawthorne (NJ) Symphony Orch. NSF grantee, 1975. Mem. Am. Phys. Soc. Jewish. Avocation: music. Home: 578 Jones Rd Englewood NJ 07631 Office Phone: 973-284-2011. Office Fax: 973-284-1893. Business E-Mail: john.minkoff@itt.com.

MINKOVA, DONKA, language educator; b. Sofia, Bulgaria; d. Lubomir Zhekov and Kalina Zavoeva-Zhekova; m. Robert P. Stockwell; children: Dimo Diakov, Lubomir Diakov. PhD, U. Sofia, 1983. Lectr./sr. lectr. in English lang. U. Sofia, 1969—83; prof. English lang. UCLA, 1983—. Author: History of Final Vowels in English, 1991; author: (with Robert Stockwell) English Words: History and Structure, 2001; author: Alliteration and Sound Change in Early English, 2003; co-editor: Studies in the History of the English Language: A Millennial Perspective, 2002, Chaucer and the Challenges of Medievalism, 2003. Fellow Pres.'s Rsch. fellow in the humanities, U. Calif., 1994—95, John Simon Guggenheim Found., 2000—01; hon. fellow, Inst. Advanced Studies in Humanities, U. Edinburgh, Scotland, 1980—81. Office: English Dept UCLA 149 Humanities Bldg Los Angeles CA 90095 E-mail: minkova@humnet.ucla.edu.

MINKOWITZ, MARTIN, lawyer, former state government official; b. Bklyn., 1939; s. Jacob and Marion Minkowitz; m. Carol L. Ziegler; 1 son from previous marriage, Stuart Allan. AA, Bklyn. Coll., 1959, BA, 1961; JD, Bklyn. Law Sch., 1963, LLM, 1965. Bar: NY 1963, US Supreme Ct. 1967, US Tax Ct. 1974, all four US Dist. Cts. NY. Ptnr. Minkowitz, Hagen & Rosenbluth, NYC, 1964—76; gen. counsel State of N.Y. Workers' Compensation Bd., 1976—81; dep. supt. and gen. counsel State of N.Y. Ins. Dept., 1981—88; instr. CUNY, 1975; ptnr. Stroock & Stroock & Lavan, 1988—. Cons. City Coun. NYC 1969; hearing officer NYC Transp. Dept., 1970-75; adj. prof. law NY Law Sch., NYC, 1982—; adv. bd. Coll. Ins., 1987-90; lectr. ABA, NY C. of C., Practicing Law Inst., NY State Bar Assn., Nat. Assn. Ins. Commrs., Nat. Conf. Ins. Legis. Author: West's New York Workers' Compensation, 2003-; (with others) Rent Stabilization and Control, 1973, Handling the Basic Workers' Compensation Law Case, 1996, West's New York General Practice; co-author: Workers Compensation, Insurance and Law Practice-The Next Generation, 1989; commentaries to McKinney's Consol. Laws, 1982—; mem. editl. bd. Jour. Occupl. Rehab. U. Rochester, 1991—; contbr. articles to profl. jours. Bd. dir., sec. Kingsbay YM-YWHA, Bklyn., 1978-99, elected dir. emeritus, 1999—; pres. bd. dir. Shore Terrace Co-op., Bklyn., 1982-83; co-chmn. exec. bd., met. coun., nat. v.p. Am. Jewish Congress, N.Y.C., 1983-91; bd. dir. Met. Coord. Coun. on Jewish poverty, 1993—, Nat. Conf. Cmty. and Justice (bd. dir. N.Y. divsn. 1994-2001, nat. bd. trustees 1995-2001, chair N.Y. divsn. 1998-2001); bd. Am. Soc. Workers Compensation, 2003—. Recipient cert. meritorious svc. Bklyn. Law Sch., Outstanding Pub. Svc. award Ind. Ins. Agt. Assn., citation outstanding performance State of N.Y. Workers' Compensation Bd., Disting. Leadership award N.Y. Claims Assn., City of Peace award State of Israel Bonds, Brotherhood award NCCJ, 2003, Man of Yr. awards Congregation B'Nai Avraham, Bklyn., 2003, Kingsbay YM-YWHA, 2005. Fellow NY State Bar Found. (life, mem. fed. bar coun., com. on 2d cir.); mem. NY County Lawyers Assn. (chmn. unlawful practice of law com. 1982-86, mem. profl. ethics com. 1985-91, chair worker's compensation com. 1988-91, bd. dir. 1997-2006, chair profl. ethics com. 2001-2006, bd. dir., exec. bd. 2003-05, 2006-07), NY State Bar Assn. (mem. house of dels. 1999-2003, 2004—, chmn. unlawful practice of law com. 1981-83, mem. com. on profl. ethics 1981-84, chmn. com. profl. discipline, mem. com. on jud. nominations, editor One on One publ. 2001—, Sustaining Mem. of Yr. award 1995), Soc. Ins. Receivers, Bklyn. Law Sch. Alumni Assn. (v.p. bd. dir. 1984-92, pres. elect 1993-94, pres. 1995-96). Office: Stroock Stroock & Lavan 180 Maiden Ln Fl 17 New York NY 10038-4937 Office Phone: 212-806-6256. Business E-Mail: mminkowitz@stroock.com.

MINKOWYCZ, W. J., mechanical engineering educator; b. Libokhora, Ukraine, Oct. 21, 1937; came to U.S., 1949; s. Alexander and Anna (Tokan) M.; m. Diana Eva Szandra, May 12, 1973; 1 child, Liliana Christine Anne BS in Mech. Engring., U. Minn., 1958, MS in Mech. Engring., 1961, PhD in Mech. Engring, 1965. From asst. prof. to James P. Hartnett prof. U. Ill., Chgo., 1966—2006, James P. Hartnett prof., 2006—. Cons. Argonne Nat. Lab, Ill., 1970-82, U. Hawaii, Honolulu, 1974-94. Founding editor-in-chief (jour.) Jour. Numerical Heat Transfer, 1978—; editor-in-chief: Internat. Jour. Heat and Mass Transfer, 1968-, Rheologically Complex Fluids, 1972, Internat. Comms. in Heat and Mass Transfer Jour., 1974-, 1988, Handbook of Numerical Heat Transfer, 2006; editor: (book series) Computational and Physical Processes in Mechanics and Thermal Sciences, 1979—, Advances in Numerical Heat Transfer, 1996—, Vol. 1, 1997, Vol. 2, 2000; contbr. articles to profl. jours. Recipient Silver Circle for Excellence in Teaching, U. Ill.-Chgo., 1975, 76, 81, 86, 90, 94, Harold A. Simon award Excellence in Teaching, 1986, Ralph Coats Roe Outstanding Tchr. award Am. Soc. Engring. Edn., 1988, U. Ill. Disting. Tchr. award, 1989. Fellow: ASME (Heat Transfer Meml. award 1993, Classic Paper award 2006); mem.: Pi Tau Sigma, Sigma Xi. Republican. Ukrainian Catholic. Office: U Ill Dept Mech Engring Mail Code 251 842 W Taylor St Chicago IL 60607-7021 Office Phone: 312-996-3467. Business E-Mail: wjm@uic.edu.

MINNA, ANTHONY JOSEPH, financial planner, lawyer; b. Toronto, Ont., Can., Aug. 13, 1964; s. Antonio and Anne (Capicciotti) M. Student, Johannes-Gutenberg U., Mainz, Germany, 1985—86; BA with honours, U. Toronto, 1987, LLB, 1991; LLM with distinction, U. Brussels, 1992. Bar: NY 1992, Ont. 1994. Articling student Siskind, Cromarty, Ivey & Dowler, London, Ont., 1992-93; lawyer Copeland, McKenna, Toronto, 1995, Walch & Schurti, Vaduz, Liechtenstein, 1996-99; compliance officer, company sec. Clariden Trust Mgmt., Zurich, Switzerland, 1999—2002; wealth planner UBS Ltd., Nassau, The Bahamas, 2003—. Avocations: bicycling, swimming, golf. Office Phone: 242-394-9311. Business E-Mail: anthony.minna@ubs.com.

MINNAUGH, MARK J, food products/retail grocery executive; Grad., Gannon Univ., 1981. Sr. v.p., then exec. v.p., CFO Giant Eagle, Inc., Pitts. Trustee Gannon Univ., Erie, Pa. Office: Giant Eagle Inc 101 Kappa Dr Pittsburgh PA 15238-2833 *

MINNELLI, LIZA, singer, actress; b. Los Angeles, Mar. 12, 1946; d. Vincente and Judy (Garland) M.; m. Peter Allen, Mar. 3, 1967 (div. June 24, 1972); m. Jack Haley Jr., Sept. 15, 1974 (div. 1979); m. Mark Gero, Dec. 4, 1979 (div. 1992); m. David Gest, Mar. 16, 2002 (div. 2003). Appeared in Off-Broadway revival of Best Foot Forward, 1963; appeared with mother at London Palladium, 1964; nightclub debut at Shoreham Hotel, Washington, 1965; appeared in Flora, the Red Menace, 1965 (Tony award), The Act, 1977 (Tony award), The Rink, 1984, Victor Victoria; films include Charlie Bubbles, 1967, The Sterile Cuckoo, 1969, Tell Me That You Love Me, Junie Moon, 1970, Cabaret, 1972 (Oscar award), That's Entertainment, 1974, Lucky Lady, 1975, A Matter of Time, 1976, Silent Movie, 1976, New York, New York, 1977, Arthur, 1981, Rent A Cop, Arthur on the Rocks, 1988, Stepping Out, 1991, The OH in Ohio, 2006; recorded You Are For Loving, 1963, Tropical Nights, 1977, Liza Minnelli at Carnegie Hall, 1987, Results, 1989, Maybe This Time, 1996, Gently, 1996, Minnelli on Minnelli, 2000, (with Herbie Hancock, Johnny Mathis, Donna Summer), Liza's Back!, 2003; (TV films) Parallel Lives, 1994, The West Side Waltz, 1995, Jackie's Back!, 1999; appeared on TV in own spl. Liza With a Z, 1972 (Recipient Emmy award); other TV appearances include Goldie and Liza Together, 1980, Baryshnikov on Broadway, 1980, The Princess and the Pea, Showtime, 1983, A Time to Live, 1985, Sam Found Out, 1988, Liza Minnelli Live from Radio City Music Hall, PBS (Emmy nomination, Music Program Performance, 1993), The Wonderful World of Oz: 50 Years of Magic, 1990, A Century of Cinema, 1994, My Favorite Broadway: The Leading Ladies, 1999, (TV series) Arrested Development, 2003-05; guest appearance Law & Order: Criminal Intent, 2006; internat. tour with Frank Sinatra, Sammy Davis Jr., 1988. Awarded the Brit. equivalent of the Oscar for Best Actress, 1972, Italy's David di Donatello award (twice), the Valentino award. Address: Capitol Records Inc 1750 Vine St Hollywood CA 90028-5209 also: Angel EMI Guardian Records 304 Park Ave S New York NY 10010-5339

MINNEMAN, KENNETH PAUL, pharmacology educator; b. Sacramento, Calif., Sept. 1, 1952; s. John Jesse and Esther Annette Minneman; children: Jennifer, Rebecca, Jeffrey. BS, MIT, 1974; PhD, U. Cambridge, England, 1977. Asst. prof. pharm. Emory U., Atlanta, 1980-85, assoc. prof. pharm., 1985-90, prof. pharm, 1990-2000, Charles Howard Candler prof. pharm., 2000—. Editor: Brody's Human Pharmacology: Molecular to Clinical, 2005 Undergraduate Fellowship, Nat. Sci. Found., 1970-74; biomed. rsch. grantee NIH, 1981-2005; postdoctoral fellow U. Colo. Med. Ctr., Denver, 1977-80; John Jacob Abel award, 1986, Award for Excellence in Basic Pharmacology, PhRMA Found., 2000. Mem. AAAS, Am. Soc. Pharm. & Exptl. Therapeutics (exec. coun. 1999-02, pres.-elect 2006-07, pres. 2007—), Soc. Neurosci., Internat. Soc. Neurochem. Office: Emory U 1510 Clifton Rd Atlanta GA 30322 Office Phone: 404-727-5985. Fax: 404-727-0365. Business E-Mail: kminneman@pharm.emory.edu.

MINNER, RUTH ANN, governor; b. Melford, Del., Jan. 17, 1935; m. Frank Ingram (dec. 1967); 3 children; m. Roger Minner (dec. 1991). Student, Del. Tech. and Community Coll. Office receptionist to Gov, State of Del., Dover, 1972—74; mem. Del. Ho. of Reps., Dover, 1974—82, Del. State Senate, Dover, 1982—92; lt. gov. State of Del., Dover, 1993—2001, gov., 2001—. Mem.: Dem. Nat. Com. Democrat. Office: Office Gov William Penn St Tatnall Bldg 3d Fl Dover DE 19901 Office Phone: 302-744-4101. Office Fax: 302-739-2775. *

MINNERLY, ROBERT WARD, retired headmaster; b. Yonkers, NY, Mar. 21, 1935; s. Richard Warren and Margaret Marion (DeBrocky) M.; m. Sandra Overmire, June 12, 1957; children: Scott Ward, John Robert, Sydney Sue. AB, Brown U., Providence, 1957; MAT, U. Tex., Arlington, 1980. Tchr., coach Rumsey Hall Sch., Washington, Conn., 1962—64, Berkshire Sch., Sheffield, Mass., 1964—70, asst. head, 1969—70, headmaster, 1970—76; dir. Salisbury Summer Sch. Reading and English, Conn., 1970; prin. upper sch. Ft. Worth Country Day Sch., 1976—86; headmaster Charles Wright Acad., Tacoma, 1986—96; ednl. cons. The Edn. Group, 1996—2000; interim dir. Harold E. LeMay Mus., 2001—02; exec. dir. R. Merle Palmer Minority Students Scholarship Found., 2004—06. Cons. Tarrant County Coalition on Substance Abuse, 1982-84; mayor's task force Tacoma Edn. Summit, 1991-92; bd. dirs. World Cultural Interaction, Gig Harbor, Wash. Contbr. articles to profl. jours. Bd. dirs. Tacoma/Pierce County Good Will Games Art Coun., 1989, Multicare Found., Tacoma, 2002, Tacoma Baseball Found., 2003—; mem. exec. com. Am. Leadership Forum, 1991-95; bd. dirs. Broadway Ctr. for Performing Arts, Tacoma, 1988-94, 96-98, mem. exec. com., 1990-93; elected Wash. State Bd. Edn., 1996-2001; bd. dirs. Tacoma Youth Choir, 2000-03. Named Adminstr. of Yr. Wash. Journalism Edn. Assn., 1991; recipient Columbia award, Wash. Fedn. Ind. Schs., 2000. Mem. Pacific N.W. Assn. Ind. Schs. (chmn. long-range planning com. 1989-92, exec. com. 1990-92, 91, v.p. 1994). Presbyterian. Home: 6204 Waterview Dr Arlington TX 76016 Personal E-mail: bobmin7309@sbcglobal.net.

MINNERS, HOWARD ALYN, federal agency administrator, researcher, preventive medicine physician; b. Rockville Center, NY, Sept. 1, 1931; s. Howard A. and Marie Henriette (Soberski) M.; m. Gretchen Paffenbarger, Oct. 25, 1958; children: Todd, Bradford. AB, Princeton U., 1953; MD, Yale U., 1957; MPH, Harvard U., 1960. Diplomate Am. Bd. Preventive Medicine, Nat. Bd. Med. Examiners. 2d. lt. USAF, 1956; intern Wilford Hall USAF Hosp., San Antonio, 1957-58; resident Sch. of Aerospace Medicine, USAF, Brooks AFB, Tex., 1960-62; advanced through grades to maj. USAF, 1966; advanced through grades to rear adm. USPHS, ret., 1987; dir. office rsch. promotion and devel. WHO, Geneva, Switzerland, 1977-80; dir. Office of Sci. Advisor Agy. Internat. Devel., Washington, 1981-91; dep. dir. Office Internat. Health USPHS and Asst. Surgeon Gen., 1980-81. Assoc. dir. NIH NIAID, 1966-77; astronaut flight surgeon NASA, Houston, 1962-66; mem. Dean's Coun. Yale Med. Sch., 2007-. Pres. Model A Ford Found., 1994-2000. Fellow World Acad. Art and Sci., Am. Coll. Preventive Medicine; mem. AAAS, Internat. Found. Sci. Stockholm (pres., chmn. bd. trustees 1991-97), Yale Med. Alumni Fund (chmn. bd. trustees 2003-06, trustee 2006—). Avocations: Model A Ford restoration, history.

MINNEY, MICHAEL JAY, lawyer; b. Lancaster, Pa., Aug. 15, 1948; s. Jay W. and Mary Jane (Erisman) M.; m. Barbara Ann Dunlap, June 28, 1975; 1 child, Michael Jayson. Student, U.S. Mil. Acad., 1967; BA, Ohio Wesleyan U., 1970; JD, Villanova U., 1973. Bar: Pa. 1973, U.S. Dist. Ct. (ea. dist.) Pa. 1974, U.S. Supreme Ct. 1977, U.S. Ct. Appeals (3d cir.) 1979. Ptnr. Minney, Mecum & Kohr, Lancaster, 1975-78, 1978-84; sole practice Lancaster, 1973-75, 84—. Regional coun. Govs. Justice Commn., Harrisburg, Pa., 1975—78; commr. Pa. Commn. on Sentencing, Harrisburg, Pa., 1979—81; chmn. bd. arbitration Court of Common Pleas, Lancaster County, Pa. Candidate U.S. House of Reps., 16th Dist., Pa., 1974, 76; bd. dirs. United Cerebral Palsy, Lancaster, 1976-84, pres. 1983-84; mem., prin. Bring Back Baseball to Lancaster. Named one of Outstanding Young Men of Am., 1976. Mem. Lancaster County Bar Assn., Pa. Bar Assn., James Buchannan Found. for the Preservation of Wheatland (treas, 1998-99, v.p. 2001, pres. 2002—), Elks, Conestoga Country Club (Lancaster). Republican. Lutheran. Avocations: running, golf, photography. Office: 145 E Chestnut St Lancaster PA 17602-2740 Office Phone: 717-299-5649.

MINNICH, DIANE KAY, legal association administrator; b. Iowa City, Feb. 17, 1956; d. Ralph Maynard Minnich and Kathryn Jane (Obye) Tompkins. BA in Behavioral Sci., San Jose State U., 1978. Tutorial program coord./instr. Operation SHARE/La Valley Coll., Van Nuys, Calif., 1979-81; field exec. Silver Sage Girl Scout Coun., Boise, Idaho, 1981-85; continuing legal edn. dir. Idaho State Bar/Idaho Law Found. Inc., Boise, 1985-88, dep. dir., 1988-90, exec. dir., 1990—. Sec.-treas. Western States Bar Conf., 2001-2005; bd. dirs. Atty. Liability Protection Soc.--A Fmily of Profl. Svc. Cos.; mem. adv. bd. legal asst. program Boise State U. Mem. Assn. CLE Adminstrs., Chgo., 1985-90; bd. dirs. Silver Sage coun. Girl Scouts, Boise, 1990-93, 99-2001, mem. nominating com., 1990-94, 97-2001, chair nominating com., 1991-92; mem. legal asst. program adv. bd. Boise State U.; bd. dirs. Boise Schs. Found., 2004—. Named one of Outstanding Young Women in Am., 1991. Mem. ABA (standing com. on pub. edn. adv. commn. 2004—07), Nat. Orgn. Bar Execs. (membership com. 1992-97, chair 1996-97), Zonta Club Boise (pres. 1991-92, bd. dirs. 1989-93), Rotary Club Boise (chair mem. com. 1994-97, bd. dirs. 1996-97, 99—2005, pres. 2003-04). Avocations: jogging, golf. Office: Idaho State Bar Idaho Law Found PO Box 895 525 W Jefferson St Boise ID 83702-5931 Home: 1118 Harrison Blvd Boise ID 83702-3448 Office Phone: 208-334-4500. E-mail: dminnich@isb.idaho.gov.

MINNICK, BRUCE ALEXANDER, lawyer; b. New London, Conn., Apr. 16, 1943; s. Robert Wood Minnick and Nedra Louise (Alexander) Wiesman; m. Judith Anita Saxon, Sept. 23, 1967 (div. 1981); children: Audra Anne, Lisa Michelle; m. Charlotte Ann Springfield, Apr. 10, 1983 (div. 1991); 1 child, Matthew Alexander; m. Debra C. Williams, July 3, 1997; 1 stepchild, Brandy Michelle Williams. AA, Broward Community Coll., 1970; BS with honors, Fla. State U., 1971, JD, 1977. Bar: Fla. 1978, U.S. Dist. Ct. (no. dist.) Fla. 1979, U.S. Dist. Ct. (mid. and so. dists.) Fla. 1982, U.S. Supreme Ct. 1981, U.S. Ct. Appeals (11th cir.) 1982, U.S. Tax Ct. 1983, U.S. Ct. Claims 1983, U.S. Dist. Ct. (ea. dist.) Mich. 1990; cert. Expert in Labor and Employment Law, The Fla. Bar, 2003. Asst. v.p., asst. comptroller Pan Am. Bank Miami, 1971—74; staff dir., counsel rules com. Fla. Ho. Reps., Tallahassee, 1976-78; v.p., gen. counsel Fla. Credit Union League, Tallahassee, 1978-80; asst. atty. gen. dept. legal affairs State of Fla., Tallahassee, 1981-86; ptnr. Mang, Rett & Collette, P.A., Tallahassee, 1986-93, Mang, Rett & Minnick PA, Tallahassee, 1994-95; pvt. practice Bruce A. Minnick PA, Tallahassee, 1996—; resident ptnr. Kahn & Assocs., LLC, Cleve., 2005—. Chief advocate Fla. Commn. on Ethics, 1985—86; lectr. state agys., 1982—, Fla. Bar, 1986—; pres. Civil Rights Dispute Resolution Ctr., 2002—. Mem. Leon County Dist. Adv. Com., 1980—82, 1992—94; mem. exec. com. Leon County Dems., 1984—2000, 2001—05. Mem.: ABA (labor sect., local govt. and law sect.), Fed. Bar Assn. (pres.-elect Tallahassee chpt. 1995, pres. 1996), Fla. Women Lawyers Assn., Fla. Govt. Bar Assn., Tallahassee Bar Assn., Fla. Bar Assn. (chmn. com. labor sect. 1987—91, exec. coun. labor sect. 1989—93, founding chmn. Fed. Ct. practice com. 1990—92, del. to 11th Cir. Jud. Conf. 1990—92, rep. mem. pub. rels. com. 1991—93, com. chmn. govt. lawyer sect. 1991—2000, ann. meeting com. 2004—06), Golden Eagle Country Club, Univ. Ctr. Club, Phi Alpha Delta. Christian Scientist. Avocations: golf, astronomy, writing. Home: 9017 Eagles Ridge Dr Tallahassee FL 32312-4046 Office: 2815 Remington Cir Ste 200 PO Box 15588 Tallahassee FL 32317 Home Phone: 850-893-4441; Office Phone: 850-386-9444. Fax: 850-385-8414. Personal E-mail: baminnick@earthlink.net. Business E-Mail: bruce@minnicklaw.com.

MINNICK, MALCOLM DAVID, lawyer; b. Indpls., July 5, 1946; s. Malcolm Dick and Frances Louise (Porter) M.; m. Heidi Rosemarie Klein, May 24, 1972. BA, U. Mich., 1968, JD, 1972. Bar: Calif. 1972, U.S. Dist. Ct. (ctrl. dist.) Calif. 1972, U.S. Ct. Appeals (9th cir.) 1984, U.S. Dist. Ct. (no. dist.) Calif. 1986, U.S. Supreme Ct. 1986. Assoc. Lillick McHose & Charles, LA, 1972-78; ptnr. Lillick & McHose, LA, 1978-91, Pillsbury Winthrop Shaw Pittman LLP, San Francisco, 1991—. Group mgr. Creditors Rights and Bankruptcy Group, 1993-98; panelist Calif. Continuing Edn. of Bar, LA, 1982-86, 88, San Francisco, 2005, Practicing Law Inst., 1992, 93, 94, Banking Law Inst., 1999, 2000; bd. govs. Fin. Lawyers Conf., LA, 1981-84; mem. exec. com. Lillick & McHose, 1982-85. Co-author: Checklist for Secured Commercial Loans, 1983. Pres. Ross Sch. Found., 1997-98. Mem. ABA (corp., banking and bus. law sect.), Am. Bankruptcy Inst., Calif. Bar Assn. (Uniform Comml. Code com. 1983-86), LA County Bar Assn. (exec. com. comml. law and bankruptcy sect. 1987-90), Bar Assn. San Francisco (comml. law and bankruptcy sect., panelist 2004), LA Country Club, Univ. Club (bd. dirs. 1983-86, pres. 1985-86). Avocation: golf. Office: Pillsbury Winthrop Shaw Pittman LLP 50 Fremont St San Francisco CA 94105-2230 Office Phone: 415-983-1351. Business E-Mail: dminnick@pillsburylaw.com.

MINNICK, MARY E., investment company executive, former beverage company executive; b. Evanston, Ill., Nov. 27, 1959; BS in Bus., Bowling Green St. U., 1981; MBA, Duke U., 1983. With fountain sales, bottle/can divsn. Coca-Cola USA; asst. v.p., dir non-carbonated beverages The Coca-Cola Co., 1993—95, v.p., Middle & Far East mktg., 1996—97, pres. South Pacific divsn., 1997—2000, pres., Coca-Cola Japan, 2000—01, pres., COO, Asia Group, 2001—05, exec. v.p., 2002—07, pres. mktg., strategy & innovation, 2005—07; ptnr. Lion Capital, London, 2007—. Mem. Dean's Coun. John F. Kennedy Sch. Bus., Harvard U.; bd. visitors Fuqua Sch. Bus. Named one of 50 Most Powerful Women in Bus., Fortune mag., 2005, 2006, 100 Most Powerful Women in World, Forbes mag., 2005, 25 Masters of Innovation, BusinessWeek, 2006, 50 Women to Watch, Wall St. Jour., 2006, Next 20 Female CEOs, Pink Mag. & Forté Found. 2006. Office: Lion Capital 21 Grosvenor Place London SW1X 7HF England Office Phone: +44 (0) 20 7201 2200. Office Fax: +44 (0) 20 7201 2222. *

MINNIGH, JOEL DOUGLAS, library director; b. Greenville, Pa., Apr. 9, 1949; s. Wendell Ellsworth and Frances Alene (Hyde) M.; m. Margaret Beth Crowther, Dec. 26, 1972; children: Bradley Dean, Douglas Knox. BA, Allegheny Coll., 1971; MLS, U. Pitts., 1975. Cert. libr., Pa. Asst. libr. Wilkinsburg (Pa.) Pub. Libr., 1976-77, head libr., 1977—. Bd. dirs. Goodwill Industries Pitts., 1980-90, Mulberry Sr. Citizens Ctr., Wilkinsburg, Pa., 2001--; vice chmn. bd. dirs. Bach Choir Pitts., 1984-87; sec., bd. dirs. United Meth. Ch. Union, Pitts., 1987-88; elder, deacon Fox Chapel Presbyn. Ch., 1987—, soloist, 1998—. Recipient honor Goodwill Industries Pitts., 1990, citation Pa. Senate, 1991. Mem. Pa. Libr. Assn. (treas. S.W. chpt. 1988-89, 2004-05), Allegheny County Libr. Assn. (pres. librs. adv. coun. 2001-02, bd. dirs. 2002-05), Wilkinsburg C. of C. (dir. 1998-03, sec. 1999-2003). Republican. Avocations: travel, cooking, gardening, music, reading. Home: 1009 Blackridge Rd Pittsburgh PA 15235-2719 Office: Wilkinsburg Pub Libr 605 Ross Ave Pittsburgh PA 15221-2145

MINNIX, BRUCE MILTON, television and theatre director; b. Hendersonville, NC, Apr. 26, 1923; s. Bruce Milton and Jane Irene (Leverett) M.; m. Corinne McClure, Aug. 5, 1950; 1 child, Tracy Logue. BA, U. N.C., 1948. Mem. faculty New Sch., N.Y.C., 1977-80; adj. prof., Bklyn., 1985; AT&T sales tng. program, 1987. Dir. numerous TV shows including: U.S. Steel Hour, 1961-63; Shakespeare in Central Park- Merchant of Venice, 1962—, Anthony and Cleopatra, 1963—, Hamlet, 1964; Essay on Doors, 1963, Never Too Young, 1965-66, Galileo Oratorio, 1967 (Emmy nomination) On Being Black, 1969, The Haggadah Oratorio, 1981, Search for Tomorrow, 1968-74, All My Children, 1978-79, Another World, 1981, Texas, 1981-82, Body Talk, 1983, As the World Turns, 1985-86; The Cradle Will Rock, 1986 (Emmy nomination). Minolta Tng. series Minolta Info. Network, 1980-81; dir. Citibank, 1984, N.J. Bell (AT&T), 1985; writer, dir. Victorian Cape May A Video Visit to a Town out of Time, 1988 (medal Houston Film Festival), dir. Ricardo Muti and the Future of the Philadelphia Orchestra, 1988, Pitney Bowes Copier Intro 1992, Time Warner Cable 1991, Rain, 2005; producer, writer: Mt. Washington Valley, A Video Visit in Four Seasons, 1990; Actor: Music Video by Little Texas What Might Have Been, 1993, The New York Idea, 2002-03 Mayor, City of Cape May, N.J., 1972-76; founding mem., 3-term pres. Mid-Atlantic Center for Arts. Served with USN, 1943-45. Recipient award, NJ Film Festival, 2006. Mem. Dirs. Guild Am. Achievements include earning the designation of National Historic Landmark for City of Cape May, 1986. Office Phone: 609-884-7365.

MINOGUE, JOHN P., academic administrator, educator, priest; b. Chgo., Jan. 1946; B in Philosophy, St. Mary of the Barrens; MDiv, Deandreis Inst. Theology, 1972; M in Theology, DePaul U., 1975; PhD in Ministry, St. Mary of the Lake Sem., 1987. Ordained Vincentian priest, 1972. Vincentian priest Congregation of the Mission; instr. theology, dir. clin. pastoral placement programs St. Thomas Sem., Denver, 1972-76; instr. grad. theology, asst. then acad. dean DeAndreis Inst., 1976-83; pres. DePaul U., Chgo., 1993—. Trustee DePaul U., 1991—; bd. dirs. DePaul U. Corp., 1981-91; adj. prof. Sch. New Learning DePaul U., 1984—, instr. law and med. ethics Coll. Law DePaul U., 1989—; asst. prof. clin. ob.-gyn. Northwestern U.; instr. health care ethics St. Joseph Coll. Nursing, Joliet, Ill., Northwestern Sch. Nursing, Chgo.; cons. nat. health care ethics, patient decision-making, mem. Congregation of the Missions Bd. mem. Children's Meml. Hosp. Mem.: NASA (bd. mem.). Office: De Paul U Office of the Pres 55 E Jackson Blvd 22nd Fl Chicago IL 60604-2287

MINOGUE, ROBERT BROPHY, retired nuclear engineer; b. Covington, Ky., Jan. 31, 1928; s. Joseph and Catherine Ann (Brophy) M.; m. Marie Joan Clarke, June 12, 1954; children: Patrick, Margaret, Marie, Francis. BS, Thomas More Coll., 1949; MS, U. Cin., 1951; grad., Oak Ridge Sch. Reactor Tech., 1952. Nuclear engr., then head nuclear tech. sect. naval reactors br. AEC, Washington, 1952-56; head research reactor design and enngring., then head nuclear power plant engring. sect. Gen. Atomic div. Gen. Dynamics Corp., 1957-67; chief spl. projects br. div. reactor standards AEC, Washington, 1967-72, asst. dir., then dep. dir. regulatory standards, 1972-74; dir. office standards devel. Nuclear Regulatory Commn., Washington, 1975-80, dir. office research, 1980-86; pvt. practice Temecula, Calif., 1986—. U.S. mem. sr. adv. group Safety Standards IAEA, 1974-86; mem. Com. on Interagy. Radiation Research and Policy Coordination, 1982-86. Author: Reactor Shielding Design Manual, 1956; patentee: Triga Research Reactor. Served with AUS, 1946-48. Recipient Bernard F. Langer award, ASME, 1982. Roman Catholic. Home and Office: 29743 Marhill Cir Temecula CA 92591-1809

MINOR, EDWARD COLQUITT, paper company executive, lawyer; b. Balt., Dec. 1, 1942; s. Edward Essau and Mary Newell (Schultz) Minor; m. Joan Slade, Aug. 29, 1964; 1 child, Elizabeth Colquitt. AB in Econ., Western Md. Coll., 1964; LLB cum laude, Boston U., 1967. Bar: Md. 1967, Ga. 1972, Va. 1974, U.S. Supreme Ct. Assoc, Semmes Bowen & Semmes, Balt., 1967-68; judge adv. U.S. Army, Savannah and Vietnam, 1968-72; assoc. Connerat Dunn & Hunter, Savannah, 1972-73; sr. atty. Kraft Paper Union Camp Corp., Savannah, 1973, asst. gen. counsel, asst. sec Fine Paper Franklin, Va., 1974-85, assoc. gen. counsel, asst. sec. Fine Paper, 1985-99, mgr. Fine Paper, 1988-95, divsn. procurement mgr. purchasing Fine Paper, 1995-99; pvt. practice, 2003—; m2 consulting Fed. Contracting. Mem. citizens adv. bd. Va. Dept. Environ. Qualtiy; energy cons., 2001—02. Mem. Gov.'s Commn. Efficiency, 1988; chmn. Franklin Constl. Bicentennial Commn.; chmn. bd. dirs. Southampton Acad., Courtland, Va., 1985—88; dep. mem. Va. Bus. Coun., 1985—88; chmn. citizens adv. bd. Va. Dept. Air Pollution Control, 1992, mem., 1993—99, Roundtable Environ. Standing, 1991; mem. exec. bd. Diocese S.E. Va., Episcopal Ch., 1985—89; vestryman Emmanual Episcopal Ch., Franklin, 1985, 1987, 1991; bd. dirs. Tidewater Heart Assn., Norfolk, Va., 1980—86, Future of Hampton Rds., Inc., Rawles Mus. Arts, 1992—93. Decorated Bronze Star. Fellow: Royal Soc. Encouragement Arts Am.; mem.: Ga. Bar Assn., Md. Bar Assn., Va. Bar Assn. (co-chmn. corp. counsel sect. 1990—92, bd. govs. adminstrv. law sect., jud. com. 1997—, bd. govs. corp. counsel sect. 1998—2000), Va. State Bar (chmn. environ. sect. 1990—91), Courtland Ruritan Club (pres. 2003), Town Point Club, Norfolk Yacht Club, Rotary (pres. Franklin 1992—93). Home: 23456 Thomas Cir Courtland VA 23837-1336 Personal E-mail: ecminor@verizon.net.

MINOR, ELIZABETH COLQUITT, chemistry professor; b. Ga., 1971; d. Edward C. and Joan S. Minor; m. Jay Alan Austin, 1999; 1 child, Benjamin Thomas Austin. PhD in Chem. Oceanography, MIT, Cambridge, 1998. Asst prof. Old Dominion U., Norfolk, Va., 2000—05; assoc. prof. U. Minn., Duluth, 2005—. Assoc editor Limnology & Oceanography Methods, 2005—; presenter in field. Contbr. articles to profl. jours. Founding mem., young adults group St. Andrew's Episc. Ch., Norfolk, Va., 2002—05. Grantee, ACS Petroleum Rsch. Fund, 2001—03; grants, NSF Chem. Oceanography, 2003—. Mem.: Am. Soc. Limnology and Oceanography, Am. Geophys. Union, European Assn. Organic Geochemists, Am. Chem. Soc. Office: LLO Univ Minn Duluth 2205 East 5th St Duluth MN 55812 Office Phone: 218-726-7097.

MINOR, GEORGE GILMER, III, drug and hospital supply company executive; b. 1940; married. BA, Va. Mil. Inst., 1963; MBA, U. Va., 1966. With Owens & Minor, Inc., Richmond, Va., 1963—, mgr. sales Acme Candy Co. div., 1966-68, mgr. retail mktg., 1968-73, div. mgr. wholesale drug br., 1973-77, v.p., 1977-80, exec. v.p., 1980-81, pres., 1981—99, CEO, 1984—2005, chmn., 1994—. Bd. dir. SunTrust Banks Inc. Bd. dir. Va. Biotechnology Rsch. Park Authority, Richmond Renaissance; v.p. bd. vis. Va. Mil. Inst.; chmn. bd. trustees Va. Health Care Found.; mem. adv. bd. Univ. Va. Sch. Nursing. Named Va. Industrialist of the Year, 2001; named to Greater Richmond Bus. Hall of Fame, 2003. Office: Owens & Minor Inc 9120 Lockwood Blvd Mechanicsville VA 23116 *

MINOR, HALSEY, multimedia company executive; married; 3 children. BA in Anthropology, U. Va., 1987. Investment banker Merrill Lynch Capital Markets, San Francisco, 1987—89; founder, CEO Global Publishing Corp., 1989—90; cons. Russell Reynolds Associates, 1991—92; founder, chmn., CEO CNET: The Computer Network, San Francisco, 1992—2000; chmn. emeritus CNET Networks, Inc., 2000—; founder, chmn., CEO Grand Central Communications, 2000—. Founding investor Listen.com (acquired by Real Media and Salesforce.com); bd. dirs. salesforce.com, Inc. Office: Grand Central Communications 50 Fremont St 16th Fl San Francisco CA 94105 Office Phone: 415-344-3200. Office Fax: 415-344-3250.

MINOR, JOSEPH EDWARD, civil engineer, educator; b. Corpus Christi, Tex., June 2, 1938; s. William Smoot Jr. and Irene (Schiller) M.; m. Treva Ann Edmiston, Sept. 3, 1960; children: Joseph Edward Jr., Sharon Diane. BSCE, Tex. A&M U., 1959, M of Engring., 1960; PhD, Tex. Tech U., 1974. Registered profl. engr., Tex., Mo., Fla. Sr. rsch. engr. Southwest Research Inst., San Antonio, 1962-69; P. Whitfield Horn prof. Tex. Tech U., Lubbock, 1969-88; Thomas Reese prof., chmn. dept. civil engring. U. Mo., Rolla, 1988-93, rsch. prof., 1993—. Pres. Insulating Glass Cert. Council, N.Y., 1986-89; vis. prof. Tex. A&M U., Kingsville, 2003-. Contbr. articles to profl. jours. Served with USAR. Recipient Disting. Engr. award Tex. Tech U., 1989, Disting. Svc. award Nat. Hurricane Conf., 1999; Nat. Def. fellow, 1959-60; Fulbright scholar, 1978. Fellow ASCE (pres. Tex. sect. 1984-85, award of honor 2003); mem. NSPE, Tex. Soc. Profl. Engrs. (Engr. of Yr. Nueces chpt. 2006). Presbyterian. Avocation: fishing. Office: Joseph E Minor PE Consulting Engineer PO Box 603 Rockport TX 78381-0603 E-mail: josephminor@sbcglobal.net.

MINOR, RICKEY, composer, television producer, music director; Musical dir. (TV series) Am. Idol, 2005—, NAACP Image Awards, Grammy Eve part, Disney's High Sch. Musical Tour; prodr.: (TV series) Don't Forget the Lyrics, American's Got Talent, 2006, Celebrity Duets, 2006, VHI Divas, Superbowl XXXVIII, Superbowl XXXIX; worked with Alicia Keys, Beyonce, Black Eyed Peas, Britney Spears, Marc Anthony, Mary J. Blige, Whitney Houston, Dixie Chicks, Jamie Foxx, Justin Timberlake, Aretha Franklin, Sting, Ray Charles, Jennifer Hudson, Heather Headley, Celine Dion. Office: Minor Productions Inc 1040 N Las Palmas Ave Bungalow E Los Angeles CA 90038 Office Phone: 323-860-6700. Office Fax: 323-860-6767. E-mail: info@rickeyminor.com. *

MINOR, ROBERT ALLEN, lawyer; b. Washington, Oct. 20, 1948; s. Robert Walter and Joan (Allen) M.; m. Sue Ellyn Blose, June 13, 1981; children: Robert Barratt, Sarah Allen. AB in English, Duke U., 1970; JD, Ohio State U., 1975. Bar: Ohio 1975, US Dist. Ct. (so. dist.) Ohio 1976, DC 1979. Assoc. Vorys, Sater, Seymour & Pease, LLP, Columbus, Ohio, 1975-82, ptnr., 1982—. Author seminar articles. With U.S. Army, 1970-72. Mem. Ohio Bar Assn., Columbus Bar Assn., Athletic Club Columbus,

Scioto Country Club. Republican. Presbyterian. Office: Vorys Sater Seymour & Pease LLP PO Box 1008 52 E Gay St Columbus OH 43215-3161 Office Phone: 614-464-6410. Business E-Mail: raminor@vssp.com.

MINOR, RONALD RAY, minister; b. Aliceville, Ala., Nov. 3, 1944; s. Hershel Ray and Minnie Ozell (Goodson) M.; m. Gwendolyn Otella Newsome, July 25, 1970; 1 child, Rhonda Davis. BA in Ministerial, Southeastern U., 1971, BA in Secondary Edn., 1973; DDiv, So. Bible Coll., 1984. Ordained to ministry Pentecostal Ch. of God, 1968. Gen. sec. Pentecostal Ch. of God, Joplin, Mo., 1979—2005, dist. supt. Miss., 1975-79, pastor LaBelle, Fla., Bartow, Fla., Orient Park Tabernacle, Tampa, Fla., Lafayette (Ind.) Pentecostal Ch. of God. Pres. Pentecostal Young People's Assn., Fla. and Miss.; sec. Gen. Bd. Pentecostal Ch. of God, Joplin, 1979-2005; bd. dirs. Nat. Assn. Evangs., Wheaton, Ill., 1981-96; adv. coun. Am. Bible Soc., N.Y.C., 1979-2003; sec. Commn. Chaplains, Washington, 1991-95. Office: Pentecostal Ch of God 3511 S 9th St Lafayette IN 47909 Home Phone: 765-477-9803. E-mail: ronaldminor@insightbb.com.

MINOR, STERLING ARTHUR, lawyer; b. Sioux City, Iowa, July 1, 1952; s. Harold DeForrest and Mary Ruth (Thompson) M.; children: Elizabeth Anne, Lauren Camille; m. Ellen L. Luby, June 28, 1998. BS, Duke U., 1974; JD, So. Meth. U., 1977. Bar: Tenn. 1977, Tex. 1982, U.S. Ct. Appeals (6th cir.) 1978, U.S. Ct. Appeals (D.C. cir.) 1978, U.S. Ct. Appeals (5th cir.) 1982; bd. cert. bus. bankruptcy law Tex. Bd. Legal Specialization. Ptnr. Martin & Cochran, Nashville, 1977-81; participating assoc. Sheinfeld, Maley & Kay, Houston, 1981-86; ptnr. Bracewell & Zeluff, 1986—88; mem. Baker, Brown, Sharman & Parker, Houston, 1989-91; pvt. practice Houston, 1991—. Spkr. in field. Reviewing editor: Guide to Asset Protection Planning, 1998, 99; columnist Legal Minutes, West U Mag., The Mag. River Oaks, Meml./Villages Mag., Tanglewood Mag., Bellaire Mag., Downtown Voice, 1993-95; contbr. numerous articles on bus. entities, asset protection and bankruptcy to profl. jours. Chmn. Zoning Bd. Adjustment, City West University Place, Tex., 1987-97; adminstrv. bd. mem. West University United Meth. Ch., 1988-90, 96-98; bd. mem. West University Elem. Sch. PTA, 1989-92, Rotary Club West University, 1995-96, The Sentinel Club, Inc., 1996-97; pres. Art League Houston, 1998-2000. Fellow Houston Bar Found.; mem. Coll. State Bar Tex. Office: 808 Travis St Ste 1418 Houston TX 77002-5734 Office Phone: 713-223-8585. Office Fax: 713-223-4324. Business E-Mail: sminor@sterlingminor.com.

MINOT, WINTHROP GARDNER, lawyer; b. Greenwich, Conn., Jan. 27, 1951; s. William Amory Gardner Minot and Molly (Cummings) Cook; children: Hilary Russell, Amory Cummings, Constance Gardner. AB magna cum laude, Harvard U., 1973, MPA, JD magna cum laude, 1979; MA, University Coll., Oxford, Eng., 1975. Bar: Mass. 1979. Assoc. Ropes & Gray, Boston, 1979-87, ptnr., 1987—. Bd. dirs. Beacon Hill Civic Assn., Boston, 1981-88; trustee Mass. Eye and Ear Infirmary, Boston, 1987—, Boston Chamber Music Soc. Mem. ABA, Boston Bar Assn., Phi Beta Kappa. Editor Harvard U Law Rev., 1978-79. Office: Ropes & Gray 1 International Pl Fl 4 Boston MA 02110-2624 Office Phone: 617-951-7364. Office Fax: 617-235-0076. Business E-Mail: winthrop.minot@ropesgray.com.

MINOW, JOSEPHINE BASKIN, civic volunteer; b. Chgo., Nov. 3, 1926; d. Salem N. and Bessie (Sampson) Baskin; m. Newton N. Minow, May 29, 1949; children: Nell, Martha, Mary. BS, Northwestern U., Evanston, Ill., 1948. Asst. to advt. dir. Mandel Brothers Dept. Store, Chgo., 1948-49; tchr. Francis W. Parker Sch., Chgo., 1949-50; vol. in civil and charitable activities, 1950—; bd. dirs. Juvenile Protective Assn., Chgo., 1958—, pres., 1973-75. Bd. dirs. Parnham Trust, Beaminster, Dorset, England. Author: Marty the Broken Hearted Artichoke, 1997. Founder, coord. Children's divsn. Hospitality and Info. Svc., Washington, 1961-63; mem. Caucus Com., Glencoe, Ill., 1965-69; co-chmn. spl. study on juvenile justice Chgo. Cmty. Trust, 1978-80; chmn. Know Your Chgo., 1980-83; bd. dirs. Chgo. Coun. Fgn. Rels., 1977-2003, hon. life mem., 2003; trustee Chgo. Hist. Soc., Ravinia Festival Assn.; mem. women's bd. Field Mus., U. Chgo.; founding mem., v.p. women's bd. Northwestern U., 1978; bd. govs. Chgo. Symphony, 1966-73, 76-; mem. Citizens Com. Juvenile Ct. of Cook County, 1985-96; exec. com. Northwestern U. Libr. Coun., 1974-96; co-chair grandparents' adv. com. Chgo. Children's Mus., 1999; bd. dirs. Jane Addams Juvenile Ct. Found.; dir. Abraham Lincoln Presdl. Libr. and Mus., 2005—. Recipient spl. award Chgo. Sch. and Workshop for Retarded, 1975, Children's Guardian award Juvenile Protective Assn., 1993. Mem. Hebrew Immigrant Aid Soc. (bd. dirs. 1977-98, award 1988), Friday Club, The Arts Club. Democrat. Jewish. Office: Chgo Hist Museum Clark St at North Ave Chicago IL 60614 Personal E-mail: ojmarmie@aol.com.

MINOW, NEWTON NORMAN, lawyer, educator; b. Milw., Jan. 17, 1926; s. Jay A. and Doris (Stein) Minow; m. Josephine Baskin, May 29, 1949; children: Nell, Martha, Mary. BS, Northwestern U., 1949, JD, 1950, LLD (hon.), 1965, U. Wis., Brandeis U., 1963, Columbia Coll., 1972, Govs. State U., 1984, De Paul U., 1989, RAND Grad. Sch., 1993, U. Notre Dame, 1994, Roosevelt U., 1996, Barat Coll., 1996, Santa Clara U. Sch. Law, 1998, Cath. Theol. Union, 2001. With firm Mayer, Brown & Platt, Chgo., 1950-51, 53-55; law clk. to chief justice U.S. Supreme Ct., 1951-52; asst. counsel to Ill. Gov. Stevenson, 1952-53; spl. asst. to Adlai E. Stevenson in presdl. campaign, 1952, 56; ptnr. firm Stevenson, Rifkind & Wirtz, Chgo., NYC and Washington, 1955-61; chmn. FCC, Washington, 1961-63; exec. v.p., gen. counsel, dir. Ency. Brit., Chgo., 1963-65; ptnr. Sidley Austin LLP, Chgo., 1965—91, sr. counsel, 1991—. Former trustee, past chmn. bd. dirs., adv. trustee Rand Corp.; past chmn. Chgo. Ednl. TV; chmn. pub. rev. bd. Arthur Andersen & Co., 1974—83; trustee Carnegie Corp. N.Y., 1987—97, chmn. bd. trustees, 1993—97; Annenberg prof. comm. law and policy Northwestern U., 1987—2003, prof. emeritus, 2003—, hon. trustee, 2007—; dir. Annenberg Washington Program, 1987—96; chmn. tech. and privacy adv. com. Sec. Def., 2003—04. Author: (book) Equal Time: The Private Broadcasters and the Public Interest, 1964; co-author: Presidential Television, 1973, Electronics and the Future, 1977, For Great Debates, 1987, Abandoned in the Wasteland: Children, Television, and the First Amendment, 1995, As We Knew Adlai. Bd. govs. Pub. Broadcasting Svc., 1973—80, chmn. bd. dirs., 1978—80; vice chmn. presdl. debates LWV, 1976, 1980, 1993—; chmn. bd. overseers Jewish Theol. Sem., 1974—77; trustee Notre Dame U., 1964—77, 1983—96, life trustee, 1996; trustee Mayo Found., 1973—81, Northwestern U., 1975—87, life trustee, 1987—. With US Army, 1944—46. Named one of Am.'s 10 Outstanding Young Men, 1961; recipient George Foster Peabody Broadcasting award, 1961, Ralph Lowell award, 1982, Lifetime Achievement award, Am. Lawyer, 2004, Woodrow Wilson award for Pub. Svc., 2006, Legal Legend award, Am. Constitution Soc., 2006, Lifetime Achievement award, Common Sense Media, 2006, Paul Simon award for Pub. Svc., 2006. Fellow: Am. Acad. Arts and Scis., Am. Bar Found.; mem.: Northwestern U. Alumni Assn. (medal 1978), Century Club (N.Y.C.), Chgo. Club, Comml. Club (pres. 1987—88). Democrat. Office: Sidley Austin LLP One S Dearborn St Chicago IL 60603 Office Phone: 312-853-7555. Business E-Mail: nminow@sidley.com.

MINSHALL, GREG, computer programmer; b. Carmel, Calif., Apr. 21, 1952; s. Glenn Almon and Martha Jane (Hardesty) M.; m. Maria Concepción Gonzalez, Dec. 30, 1976 (div. Jan. 1984); children: Matthew, Cecilia; m. Carol Ann Mendel, Oct. 4, 1987 (div. Feb. 1992); children: Oriana, Jacob. BA in Math., U. Calif., Berkeley, 1985. Computer programmer Stanford Linear Accelerator Ctr., Menlo Park, Calif., 1969-70, 72-73; computer programmer/engr. Inst. for Advanced Computation, Sunnyvale, Calif., 1978-80; computer programmer U. Calif., Berkeley, 1980-88; cons., 1984-88; computer programmer Novell, Inc., Walnut Creek, Calif., 1988-95, Ipsilon Networks, Inc., Mountain View, Calif., 1995—97; founder Siara Sys., 1998—2002; mem. tech. adv. bd. Netillion, 2004—05. Bd. dirs. Kronos Quartet. Mem. Assn. for Computing Machinery, Usenix

MINSINGER, WILLIAM ELLIOTT, orthopedist, surgeon; b. Quincy, Mass., Aug. 3, 1950; s. Oscar Jacob and Helga Katherine Minsinger; m. Linda Jean Walch, Feb. 14, 1957; children: William, Keith, Kristopher. MD, Boston U., 1978. Pres. Blue Hill Obs., East Milton, Mass., 1984—2006; chief surgery Gifford Med. Ctr., Randolph, Vt., 2000—06. Author: (historical work) The 1938 Hurricane An Historical and Pictorial Summary, (historical book) Hurricane Bob, The 1944 Hurricane, The 1927 Flood in Vermont & New England, The 1955 Floods Hurricnaes Connie & Diane. Vice chair Orange County Rep. Com., Vt., 2005—06. Mem.: New Eng. Orthop. Soc. (pres. 2006—), Vt. Civil War Hemlocks. Avocation: weather. Home: Box 256 Randolph Center VT 05061 Office: Hitchcock Assocs Randolph 3 Maple St Randolph VT 05060 Home Phone: 802-728-5895; Office Phone: 802-728-2455. Office Fax: 802-728-4239; Home Fax: 802-728-5895. Personal E-mail: minsinger@adelphia.net. E-mail: william.minsinger@hitchcock.org.

MINSKOFF, EDWARD, architectural firm executive; s. Leo Minskoff and Isabelle; m. Julie Minskoff. Grad., Mich. State U.; MBA, U. Calif., LA. CEO Olympia & York; founder, chmn. Edward J. Minskoff Equities Inc. Chair endowment, pediatric oncology NYU Med. Ctr. Trustee NYU Med. Ctr.; bd. dirs. NYU Med. Ctr. Cancer Inst.; vice chmn. bd. trustee NYU Sch. Medicine Found. Named one of Top 200 Collectors, ARTnews Mag., 2006. Mem.: Assn. for a Better NY (exec. com.), Real Estate Bd. NY (gov.). Avocations: squash, golf, exercise. Office: 1325 Ave of Americas 53rd St New York NY 10019

MINTER, DAVID LEE, English literature educator; b. Midland, Tex., Mar. 20, 1935; s. Kenneth Cruse and Frances (Hennessy) M.; m. Cynthia Caroline Sewell, Dec. 22, 1957; children: Christopher Sewell, Frances Elizabeth. BA, N. Tex. State U., 1957, MA, 1959; BD, Yale U., 1961, PhD, 1965. Univ. lectr. Hamburg (W. Ger.) U., 1965-66; lectr. Yale U., 1966-67; asst. prof. Rice U., Houston, 1967-69, assoc. prof., 1969-74, prof., 1974-80; prof. English Emory U., Atlanta, 1981-89, Asa G. Candler prof. Am. lit., 1989-90, dean Coll. Arts and Scis., 1981-90, v.p. arts and scis., 1984-90; Libbie Shearn Moody prof. English Rice U., Houston, 1990-99, interim vice provost, univ. libr., 1995-96, interim provost, 1999-2000, Bruce and Elizabeth Dunlevie prof. English, 1999—2002. Author: The Interpreted Design as a Structural Principle in American Prose, 1969, William Faulkner: His Life and Work, 1980, 82, 91, 97, French edit., 1984, Korean edito., 1999, A Cultural History of the American Novel: Henry James to William Faulkner, 1994, 96, Faulkner's Questioning Narratives: Fiction of the Major Phase, 2001, 04; editor: Twentieth-Century Interpretations of Light in August, 1969, The Norton Critical Edit. of The Sound and the Fury, 1987, 93; co-editor: The Harper American Literature, 1986, 93, 96, 97, The Columbia Literary History of the United States, 1987 (Italian edit. 1990, Chinese edit. 1994, Japanese edit. 1997); also articles and revs. Fulbright Travel fellow, 1966; Nat. Endowment for Humanities fellow, 1969-70; Am. Council Learned Socs. grantee, 1975; Fred Harris Daniels fellow, 1980 Mem. MLA, Am. Lit. Group, Am. Studies Assn., Phi Beta Kappa. Methodist. Home: 2145 Swift Houston TX 77030-1215 E-mail: dcmint@rice.edu.

MINTER, JERRY BURNETT, electronics executive; b. Ft. Worth, Oct. 31, 1913; s. Claude Joe and Roxie (Ayers) M.; m. Monica Rose Hanlon, Mar. 2, 1940; children: Claude, Mark (dec.), Byron, Claire, Maureen. BSEE, MIT, 1934. Engr. Boonton (N.J.) Radio Corp., 1935-36, Ferris Instruments Co., Boonton, 1936-39; v.p., chief engr. Measurements Corp., Boonton, 1939-53; pres. Components Corp., Denville, NJ, 1946—. Contbr. articles to tech. jours. Pilot CAP, Morristown, N.J., 1947-50. Fellow IEEE (life, past chmn. No. N.J. sect.), Audio Engring. Soc. (past pres.), Radio Club Am. (life, pres. emeritus, past pres., Armstrong medal 1968); mem. AIAA, Am. Soc. Metals (life), N.Y. Acad. Scis., Soc. Motion Picture and TV Engrs. (life), Internat. Soc. Photo-Optical Instrumentation Engrs., Quiet Birdmen. Achievements include 26 patents in field. Home: 48 Normandy Heights Rd Morristown NJ 07960-4613 Office: Components Corp 6 Kinsley Pl Denville NJ 07834 Office Phone: 973-627-0290.

MINTER, PHILIP CLAYTON, retired communications company executive; b. Sydney, Aug. 9, 1928; came to U.S., 1957; s. Roy Dixon and Adeline Claire (Bradly) M.; m. Mary Bashford Schettler, Jan. 24., 1959 (dec. July 1999); children: Elizabeth C., Margaret S. BSc with honours, U. Sydney, 1951; MS, U. Wyo., 1958; PhD, U. Wis., 1960. Tchr. King's Sch., Parramatta, Australia, 1951-57; mng. dir. Motivational Rsch. Assocs., Sydney, 1960-62; dir. rsch. Nat. Fund Raising Coun., Sydney, 1962-65; project dir. USDA, Ft. Collins, Colo., 1965-67; chief info. pesticides program USPHS, Atlanta, 1967-68; mgr. data bases div. Pa. Rsch. Assocs., Phila., 1968-70; pres. Ednl. Communications Inc., King of Prussia, Pa., 1970-94; v.p. Medication Mgmt. Systems Internat., LLC, 2001—; dir. Unmaned Ocean Vehicles, 2005—. Pres. Svc. Tng. Ltd., Kenilworth, Eng., 1976-88; cons. Westinghouse Learning Corp., 1972. Author: Handbook for Pesticide-Chemicals Program Coordinators, 1967. Recipient Terry Magill award Australia Soc., N.Y., 1994. Mem. Soc. Automotive Engrs., Sci. Rsch. Soc. Am., Royal Heritage Soc. (bd. dirs.), U. Wis. Alumni Assn. (bd. dirs. Delaware Valley br.), Australian/Am. C. of C. Phila. (pres.), Union League, Brit. Officers Club Phila. (pres. 1992-93), The Order of Autralia, Sigma Xi. Republican. Episcopalian. Home: 1576 Stapler Dr Yardley PA 19067-4214 Personal E-mail: aacc@comcast.net. E-mail: pminter@comcast.net.

MINTON, JENNIFER, computer software company executive; Various positions audit divsn. Arthur Andersen, LLP, 1983; various fin. positions including asst. corp. contr. Oracle Corp., Redwood City, Calif., 1989—98, v.p., 1995—2000, corp. contr., 1998—2001, sr. v.p., 2000—01, sr. v.p. fin. and ops., 2001—. Office: Oracle Corp 500 Oracle Pky Redwood City CA 94085 Office Phone: 650-506-7000. Office Fax: 650-506-7200. *

MINTON, JERRY DAVIS, lawyer, consultant, retired banker; b. Ft. Worth, Aug. 13, 1928; s. Robert Bruch and Anna Elizabeth (Davis) M.; m. Martha Drew Fields, Nov. 28, 1975; children: Marianne, Martha, John Morgan. BBA, U. Tex., Austin, 1949, JD, 1960; grad. cert., Nat. Trust Sch., Northwestern U., 1960. Of counsel Michener, Larimore, Swindle, Whitaker, Flowers et al., 1991—96; adv. dir. Kanaly Trust Co., Houston, 1992-2000. Vice chmn. 1st Nat. Bank Ft. Worth, 1982-84; chmn., CEO 1st City Nat. Bank Ft. Worth, 1986-91. Pilot USAF, 1951-55, pilot Tex. Air N.G., 1955-57; capt. USAFR Ret. Decorated D.F.C., Air medal with 3 oak leaf clusters. Mem. Air Force Assn., State Bar Tex., Tarrant County Bar Assn., Soc. Descs. of Washington's Army at Valley Forge, SAR, SCV, Mil. Order Stars and Bars, Mil. Order World Wars, D.F.C. Soc., Ft. Worth Air Power Coun., Order Quiet Birdmen, Order of Daedalians, River Crest Country Club, Breakfast Club, Wildcatters Club, Sigma Iota Epsilon, Phi Delta Phi. Episcopalian. Home: 5404 El Dorado Dr Fort Worth TX 76107-3236

MINTON, JOHN D., JR., state supreme court justice; m. Susan Lenell Page. BA in English & History, Western Ky. U., 1974; JD, U. Ky. Coll. of Law, 1977. Atty., priv. practice Bowling Green, Ky., 1981—95; chief administrative judge Green River Region, Ky., 1996—2003; circuit judge Warren County, Ky., 1992—2003; judge Second Appellate Dist. Ky. Ct. of Appeals, 2003—06; justice Ky. Supreme Ct., 2006—. Leader Ky. Conf. of United Methodist Church; bd. mem. Student Life Found. Western Ky. U. Office: Ky Supreme Ct Warren Cty Justice Ctr 1001 Ctr St 2nd Fl Rm 204 Bowling Green KY 42101 Office Phone: 270-746-7867 ext. 103. *

MINTON, JOSEPH PAUL, retired safety organization executive; b. Houston, Oct. 20, 1924; s. Joseph Marion and Stella (Fite) M.; m. Nancy Fettig, June 19, 1948; children: Joan M., Michael J., Jean A., Mary B., John E., Diane C. BS in Air Transp., Purdue U., 1949; Grad., U.S. Air Force Air Command and Staff Coll., 1958. Commd. 2d lt. USAF, 1944, advanced through grades to col., 1966, combat Burma, World War II, assigments in crew, staff and command, ret., 1967; v.p. Purdue Airlines Inc., Lafayette, Ind., 1967-68, pres., CEO, 1969-71; mng. dir., chief exec. officer Saber Air Ltd., Singapore, 1971-73; sr. v.p. Brit. Caledonian Airways, NYC, 1974-76; mng. dir. Nat. Transp. Safety Bd., Washington, 1977-78; exec. dir. Nat. Safety Coun., Washington, 1978-88. Decorated D.F.C. with oak leaf cluster, Air medal with 3 oak leaf clusters, 3 battle stars, Air Force Commendation medal with oak leaf cluster. Roman Catholic. Address: 1720 Lake Shore Crest Dr Apt 15 Reston VA 20190-3243

MINTON, KENT W., lawyer; b. Independence, Mo., May 16, 1955; s. Roy V. and Donabelle M. Minton; m. Karen S. MacDonald, Oct. 21, 1989; children: Kathy, Megan, Abby. BS, Ctrl. Mo. State U., 1976; postgrad., U. Tulsa, 1979-80; JD, U. Mo., Kansas City, 1982. Bar: Mo. 1982, U.S. Dist. Ct. (we. dist.) Mo. 1982, U.S. Ct. Claims 1986. Assoc. Paxton, Block et al, Independence, 1982-83, Holliday & Holliday, Kansas City, 1983-85; ptnr. Raymond, Raymond & Minton, Kansas City, 1985-96, Stewart, Cook, Constance, Stewart, Minton & Wight LLC, Independence, 1996—. Bd. dirs. Comprehensive Mental Health Svcs. Found., Independence. Contbr. chpt. to book. Mem. Mo. Bar (trust law revision subcom.), Kansas City Metro Bar Assn. (probate com.). Office: Stewart Cook Constance Stewart Minton & Wight LLC 501 W Lexington Ave Independence MO 64050-3648

MINTON, YVONNE FAY, mezzo-soprano; b. Sydney; d. Robert Thomas and Alice Violet M.; m. William Barclay, Aug. 24, 1965; children—Malcolm Alexander, Alison Elizabeth. Student, Sydney Conservatorium Music, 1960-61. Mezzo-soprano with all maj. orchs. in, Australia, 1958-61; moved to, London, 1961, joined, Royal Opera House, Covent Garden, 1965-70, guest artist, Cologne (Germany) Opera, 1969—, U.S. debut as Octavian in Der Rosenkavalier, 1970; appeared, with Lyric Opera, Chgo., 1970, Met. Opera, N.Y.C., 1973, San Francisco Opera, 1974, Paris Opera, 1974, Bayreuth, 1974, Salzburg, 1978; sang regularly with maj. symphony orchs. throughout world, 1968—; recs. include The Knot Garden, 1970, Cosi Fan Tutte, 1971, Lulu, 1979; maj. vocal works include Mahler songs with, Chgo. Symphony; condr. master classes across Europe and vocal coach in London. Comdr. Order Brit. Empire, 1980 Hon. mem. Royal Acad. Music. Office: care Ingpen & Williams 7 St Georges Ct 131 Putney Bridge Rd London SW15 2PA England

MINTZ, ALBERT, lawyer; b. New Orleans, Oct. 19, 1929; s. Morris and Goldie (Goldblum) M.; m. Linda Barnett, Dec. 19, 1954; children— John Morris, Margaret Anne Easthope. BBA, Tulane U., 1948, JD, 1951. Bar: La. 1951; cert. tax specialist, estate and adminstrn. specialist. Since practiced in, New Orleans; ptnr. Montgomery, Barnett, Brown, Read, Hammond & Mintz, Hurwitz-Mintz Realty Cos., New Orleans. Bd. dirs. Strauss Distbrs., Avrico, Inc. Mem. editl. bd. Tulane Law Rev. Adv. bd. Law Sch. Tulane U.; chmn., dir. adv. bd. Tulane Summer Lyric Theater; bd. dirs. Tulane Ctr. Stage Talent and Shakespearean Theatre; bd. dirs. Jewish Cmty. Ctr., New Orleans, 1965-72, Jewish Fedn., 1968-, Home for Jewish Aged, 1968-71, Jewish Family Svc., New Orleans, 1968-72; trustee, bd. mgrs. Touro Infirmary Hosp. and Found.; trustee Jewish Endowment Found.; charter mem. La. Hist. Assn.; bd. trustees, mem. Temple Sinai. Recipient Judah Touro Society Award, 1999, Tulane Outstanding Alumnus award, Class of 1951, 2001, Outstanding Vol. award Tulane U., 2003, Role Model award Young Leadership Com., 2004, Young Profl. Excellence and LAdership award, 2005. Mem. ABA, La. Bar Assn. (lectr., publ. on corp., tax, real estate law), New Orleans Bar Assn. (exec. com. 1971-74), Am. Law Inst., U.S. Hist. Assn., New Orleans C. of C. (chmn. com. civic affairs and state legis. 1968-69), Tulane Emeritus Club (chmn. exec. com., pres. 2004), Phi Delta Phi, Omicron Delta Kappa, Zeta Beta Tau. Jewish. Home: 1915 State St New Orleans LA 70118-6251 Office: 3200 Energy Ctr 1100 Poydras St New Orleans LA 70163-1101 Business E-Mail: amintz@monbar.com.

MINTZ, JACK MAURICE, think tank executive, economics educator; b. Edmonton, Alta., Can., Mar. 6, 1951; s. David Benjamin and Clara (Abramovich) M.; m. Eleanor Janice Schwartz, Aug. 31, 1975; children: Avi Ilan, Gaela Lana. B.A. with honors, U. Alta., Edmonton, 1973; M.A., Queen's U., Kingston, Ont., Can., 1974; Ph.D., U. Essex, Colchester, Eng., 1980. Cons. Econ. Council Can., Ottawa, Ont., 1974-75; assoc. prof. econs. Queen's U., Kingston, 1978-89; prof. J.L. Rotman Sch. Mgmt., U. Toronto, 1989-; pres., CEO, C.D. Howe Inst.; bd. dirs. Brascan, Ont. Financing Authority, CHC Ltd. Author: Most Favored Nation, 2001 (Donner prize, Davis prize); contbr. articles to profl. jours. Royal Ont. Mus. Found. Commonwealth fellow, Eng., 1975-78; postdoctoral fellow Social Sci. and Humanities Rsch. Coun. Can., 1981-82, Inst. Mgmt., 1984. Mem. Can. Econs. Assn., Am. Econs. Assn., Am. Fin. Assn., Nat. Stats. Coun. Lodge: B'nai B'rith Youth Orgn. (internat. pres. 1969-70, exec. mem. 1983-84). Avocations: running, squash. Office: CD Howe Inst 67 Yonge St Toronto ON M5E 1J8 Canada Office Phone: 416-865-1904.

MINTZ, JEFFRY ALAN, lawyer, mediator; b. NYC, Sept. 15, 1943; s. Aaron Herbert and Lillian Betty (Greenspan) M.; m. Susan Politzer, Aug. 22, 1979; children: Jennifer, Melanie, Jonathan. AB, Tufts U., 1964; LLB, Rutgers U., 1967; postgrad., U. Pa. Law Sch., 1968-70. Bar: D.C. 1968, N.Y. 1970, U.S. Supreme Ct. 1972, N.J. 1973, Pa. 1983; registered mediator, N.J.; cert. civil trial atty. N.J. Supreme Ct. Law clk. to judge U.S. Ct. Appeals, New Orleans, 1967-68; asst. defender Defender Assn. Phila., 1968-70; asst. counsel NAACP Legal Def. and Ednl. Fund, NYC, 1970-74; dir. Office Inmate Advocacy, N.J. Dept. Pub. Adv., Trenton, 1974-81; pvt. practice Haddonfield and Medford, N.J, 1982; ptnr. Stein & Shapiro, Medford, 1982-83, Cherry Hill, N.J., 1983-84, Mesirov, Gelman, Jaffe, Cramer & Jamieson, Cherry Hill, Phila., 1984-90, Schlesinger, Mintz & Pilles, Mt. Holly, N.J., 1990-92; pvt. practice Mt. Holly, 1992—. Trustee Congregation M'kor Shalom, Cherry Hill, 1990-97; mem. Burlington County and Mt. Laurel Dem. Coun. Com., 1993-95, 2002-05; chair Moorestown Dem. Com., 1995-2001. Mem. NJ Bar Assn. (del., gen. coun. 1986-88, 89-91), Burlington County Bar Assn. (trustee 1989-92, chair ADR com. 2005-), Dist. Fee Arbitration Com. (vice chmn. 1999-2000, chmn. 2000-01), NJ Assn. Profl. Mediators, Burlington County C. of C. Jewish. Home: 22 Lexington Ct Mount Laurel NJ 08054-3701 Office: 129 High St Mount Holly NJ 08060-1401 Home Phone: 856-235-5363; Office Phone: 609-267-5400. Personal E-mail: mhlaw1@verizon.net.

MINTZ, JOEL ALAN, law educator; b. NYC, July 24, 1949; s. Samuel Isaiah and Eleanor (Streichler) M.; m. Meri-Jane Rochelson, Aug. 25, 1975; children: Daniel Rochelson, Robert Eli. BA, Columbia U., NYC, 1970, LLM, 1982, JSD, 1989; JD, NYU, 1974. Bar: N.Y. 1975, U.S. Dist. Ct. (so. and ea. dists.) N.Y. 1982, U.S. Ct. Appeals (2d cir.) 1982. Atty. enforcement divsn. EPA, Chgo., 1975—76, chief atty. case devel. unit, 1977—78, policy advisor to regional adminstr., 1979; sr. litig. atty. Office Enforcement, EPA, Washington, 1980—81; asst. prof. environ. law Nova U. Law Ctr., Ft. Lauderdale, Fla., 1982—85, assoc. prof., 1985—87, prof., 1987—. Author: State and Local Government Environmental Liability, 1994, Enforcement At the EPA: High Stakes, 1995; author: (with others) Environmental Law, 4th edit., 2000, State and Local Taxation and Finance

In A Nutshell, 3d edit., 2007, Environmental Enforcement: Cases and Materials, 2007; contbr. articles to legal jours. and treatises. Mem. ABA, Environ. Law Inst. Assocs., Fla. Bar (assoc.), Internat. Coun. Environ. Law, Internat. Union for Conservation of Nature (commn. on environ. law), Assn. Am. Law Schs. (exec. com., state and local govt. law sect.), Ctr. for Progressive Reform (scholar), Phi Alpha Delta. Avocations: reading, fitness walking, canoeing. Home: 2060 NE 209th St Miami FL 33179-1628 Office: Nova Southeastern U Law Ctr 3305 College Ave Fort Lauderdale FL 33314-7721 Home Phone: 305-932-6011; Office Phone: 954-262-6160. Business E-Mail: mintzj@nsu.law.nova.edu.

MINTZ, M. J., lawyer; b. Phila., Oct. 29, 1940; s. Arthur and Lillian (Altenberg) Mintz; m. Judith E. Held; children: Robert A., Christine L. BS, Temple U., 1961, JD, 1968. CPA Pa., D.C.; bar: D.C. Atty. adv. to judge U.S. Tax Ct., Washington, 1968-70; asst. gen. counsel Cost of Living Coun. Exec. Office of Pres., Washington, 1971-73; ptnr. Dickstein, Shapiro & Morin, Washington, 1973—2005, M.J. Mintz, P.C., Washington, 2006—. Adj. prof. George Mason U. Law Sch., Va., 1974—78; advisor U.S. Sec. Labor, Employee Ret. Income Security Act, 1974, Adv. Coun., Washington, 1982—85. Contbr. articles to profl. jours. Apptd. by Pres. Ronald Reagan to adv. com. Pension Benefit Guaranty Corp., 1987, reapptd. and designated chmn. by Pres. George Bush; apptd. by Gov. George Allen of Va. Bd. Va. Pub. Bldg. Authority, 1996—2001, reapptd. by Gov. James Gilmore, 2001—06; Rep. candidate Fairfax County Bd. Suprs., 1971. Fellow: Nat. Assn. Watch & Cook Collectors (star), Freeman of the Worshipful Co. of Clockmakers (London); mem.: AICPA, ABA, Antiquarian Horological Soc. (London), Naval Club (London), Chappaquiddick Beach Club, Met. Club (Washington), Belle Haven Country Club, Cosmos Club. Avocation: antiquarian horologist.

MINTZ, MARILYN D., artist, writer; b. Phila., Mar. 18; d. Milton A. and Mildred L. Mintz. Attended, U. Calif., Santa Barbara, 1968—70; BFA in Theater, Calif. Inst. of Arts, 1972; MA in Film and TV, U. Calif., LA, 1975. Founder, pres., CEO M.D.M. Co., Studio City, Calif., 1981, Sweetheart Arts Co., Inc., Los Gatos, Calif., 1990—. Actor: Calif. Shakespeare Festival, 1970; author: (play) A Man (adaptation of Shakespeare's Julius Caesar), 1972, The Martial Arts Films, 1978, 2nd edit., 1983; scriptwriter, creator: Cartoon Pictures, 1979, The Cartoonist, 1980, columnist: Images, 1967—68. Achievements include patents for doll and associated products. Office: The Sweetheart Arts Co Inc PO Box 1411 Los Gatos CA 95031

MINTZ, MARSHALL GARY, lawyer; b. Detroit, May 28, 1947; BA, UCLA, 1968, JD, 1971. Bar: Calif. 1972. Law clk. appellate dept L.A. County Superior Ct., 1971-72; ptnr. Kelly Lytton Mintz & Vann, LLP, LA, Calif., 1995-2001; of counsel Sidley & Bell LLP, LA, 2001—03; mem. Mintz & Werner, LA, 2003—. Moderator, panelist Calif. Continuing Edn. of the Bar, 1980—; mem. arbitration adminstrv. com. L.A. County Superior Ct., 1979, mem. 1984 Olympics spl. settlement panel; mem. arbitration panel L.A. Superior Ct., 1999—; lectr. Lorman Ednl. Seminars, 2002-. Mem. ABA, State Bar Calif., L.A. County Bar Assn. (arbitrator arbitration and client rels. com. 1978-99), Assn. Bus. Trial Lawyers (bd. govs. 1976-77, program chmn. 1976). Office: 1801 Century Park E Ste 2400 Los Angeles CA 90067-2326 Home Phone: 310-446-9440; Office Phone: 310-556-9692. E-mail: mgmintz@earthlink.net.

MINTZ, MORTON ABNER, writer, reporter; b. Ann Arbor, Mich., Jan. 26, 1922; s. William and Sarah (Solomon) M.; m. Anita Inez Franz, Aug. 30, 1946; children— Margaret Ruth, Elizabeth Diane (dec.), Roberta Joan, Daniel Robert. AB in Econs, U. Mich., 1943. Reporter St. Louis Star-Times, 1946-50; reporter, asst. city editor St. Louis Globe-Democrat, 1951-58; reporter Washington Post, 1958-88. Former chair Fund for Investigative Journalism; sr. advisor niemanwatchdog.org; dir. Project on Govt. Oversight, 1997—. Author: The Therapeutic Nightmare, 1965, By Prescription Only, 1967, The Pill: An Alarming Report, 1969, At Any Cost: Corporate Greed, Women, and the Dalkon Shield, 1985, (with Jerry S. Cohen) America, Inc.: Who Owns and Operates the United States, 1971, Power, Inc.: Public and Private Rulers and How to Make Them Accountable, 1976, (with others) In the Name of Profit: Profiles in Corporate Irresponsiblity, 1972, More Bucks, Less Bang: How the Pentagon Buys Ineffective Weapons, 1983. Recipient Heywood Broun, Raymond Clapper, George Polk awards for journalism, 1962, A.J. Liebling award, 1974, Worth Bingham Meml. award, 1976, Columbia Journalism award, 1983, Hugh M. Hefner First Amendment award for lifetime achievement, 1996. Mem.: Com. Concerned Journalists. E-mail: mintzm@earthlink.net.

MINTZ, NORMAN NELSON, investment banker, educator, retired academic administrator; b. NYC, Sept. 18, 1934; s. Alexander and Rebecca (Nelson) M.; m. Marcia Lynn Belford, Aug. 27, 1960; children: Geoffrey Belford, Douglas Nelson. AB, Bucknell U., Lewisburg, Pa., 1955; PhD, NYU, NYC, 1966. Asst. gen. mgr. Ross Products Inc., NYC, 1957-59; media analyst Benton & Bowles Inc., NYC, 1960; asst. prof. fin. Syracuse (N.Y.) U., 1965-69; asst. prof. econs. Columbia U., NYC, 1968-72, assoc. dean Grad. Sch. Arts and Scis., 1972-77, dep. provost, 1977-80, acting provost, 1978-79, sr. v.p., 1980-82, exec. v.p. for acad. affairs, 1982-89, exec. v.p., ret., 1990—; mng. dir. Loeb Ptnrs. Corp., 1990—. Economist U.S.-P.R. Commn. on Status of P.R., 1965-66; bd. dirs. Loeb Holding Corp., Loeb Ptnrs. Corp., Sr. Network, Inc., KmX Corp., Evare, L.L.C., Intersections, Inc., Loeb Arbitrage Fund., Ultramercial, LLC, Virtualscopics, Inc. Author: Monetary Union and Economic Integration, 1970; contbr. articles to profl. jours. Dir. Citizens Budget Commn., Conf. on Jewish Social Studies, 1975—94, N.Y.C. Coun. on Econ. Edn., 1993—. 1st lt. Signal Corps. US Army, 1955—57. Earhart Found. fellow, 1963-65. Mem. Am. Econ. Assn., Am. Fin. Assn., Royal Econ. Soc., India House Club, Phi Beta Kappa, Omicron Delta Epsilon. Office: care Loeb Ptnrs 61 Broadway New York NY 10006-2701 Home Phone: 212-749-8043; Office Phone: 212-483-7041. E-mail: nmintz@loebpartners.com.

MINTZ, SAMUEL ISAIAH, language educator, writer; b. NYC, Nov. 20, 1923; Nathan and Anna (Sheinkman) M.; m. Eleanor Streichler, Mar. 2, 1947; children: Joel Alan, Jonathan. BA, Bklyn. Coll., 1948; MA, Columbia U., 1949, PhD, 1958. Prof. City Coll. N.Y., NYC, 1948-86, prof. doctoral faculty, 1965-86, prof. emeritus, 1986—, CUNY Grad. Ctr., NYC, 1986—. English faculty Cambridge U., Eng., 1964-65; vis. prof. Columbia U., N.Y.C., 1969-70, Barnard Coll., N.Y.C., 1987-89; vis. fellow Wolfson Coll. Oxford U., 1973. Author: The Hunting of Leviathan, 1962, 2d edit., 1996; editor: From Smollett to Henry James, 1980; founder, editor History Ideas Newsletter, N.Y.C., 1954-60; contbr. articles to profl. jours. With Army Air Force, 1943—46. Fulbright fellow Cambridge U., 1956-57, rsch. scholar, 1964-65, Guggenheim fellow, 1964. Office: City U NY Grad Sch 365 5th Ave New York NY 10016-4309

MINTZES, JOEL J., biology professor, researcher; b. LA, Dec. 13, 1947; s. Herbert and Shirley Mintzes; m. Susan S. Solomon, June 22, 1969; 1 child, Aaron Lewis. BS, U. Ill., 1970, MS, 1971; PhD, Northwestern U., Evanston, Ill., 1974. Asst. prof. U. Ill., Chgo., 1974, U. Windsor, Ontario, Canada, 1974—79; assoc. to full prof. biology U. NC, Wilmington, 1979—. Vis. prof. sci. edn. Tata Inst. Fundamental Rsch., Bombay, 2003; vis. ecology scholar Providence U., Taichung, Taiwan, 2004. Editor: Handbook of College Science Teaching; contbr. scientific papers. Mem. B'nai Israel Congregation, Wilmington, NC, 1990—95. Recipient Sci. Edn. Award Merit, Editl. Bd., Sci. Edn., 1984; Fulbright-Technion fellow, Israel Inst. Tech., Haifa, 2004. Mem.: NSTA, Nat. Assn. Rsch. in Sci. Tchg. Achievements include research in conceptual development and cognitive processes in biology; environmental education. Home: 2305 N Lumina Av Wrightsville Beach NC 28480 Office: U NC 601 S College Road Wilmington NC 28403 Home Phone: 910-256-3005; Office Phone: 910-962-3437. Office Fax: 910-962-4066; Home Fax: 910-962-4066. Business E-Mail: mintzes@uncw.edu.

MINTZ-HITTNER, HELEN ANN, physician, researcher; b. Houston, Aug. 12, 1944; d. Bert and Jeanette (Haydis) Mintz; m. David Hittner, Sept. 8, 1968 (div. May 11, 1989); children: Miriam Annette Hittner Tondera, Susan Michelle Hittner, George Jacob Hittner. BA, Rice U., 1965; MD, Baylor Coll. Medicine, 1969. Lic. Tex. Bd. of Med. Examiners, 1969. Intern pediat. Baylor Affiliated Hosps., Houston, 1969—70, resident ophthalmology, 1970—73; fellow pediat. ophthalmology Tex. Children's Hosp., Houston, 1973—74; pediat. ophthalmologist Houston, 1974—95; Alfred W. Lasher III prof. pediat. ophthalmology U. Tex. Houston Med. Sch., 1995—. Author: several rsch. reports and jour. articles. Fellow: Am. Acad. Ophthalmology (Honor award 1986, Sr. Honor award 2005); mem.: N.Y. Acad. Medicine, N.Y. Acad. Sci., Ciba Found., Soc. Heed Fellows (life), Assn. Rsch. in Vision and Ophthalmology, Am. Assn. Pediat. Ophthalmology and Strabismus, Phi Beta Kappa (life), Alpha Omega Alpha (life). Liberal. Jewish. Achievements include discovery of Primary etiology of retinopathy of prematurity; research in Genetic linkage of aniridia to chromosome 11p13 (PAX6); Genetic identification of anterior segment dysgenesis on chromosome 10q25 (PITX3); Genetic identification of anterior segment dysgenesis on chromosome 1p32 (FOXE3); Genetic identification of anterior segment dysgenesis on chromosome 20p11.2 (VSX1). Home: 2400 N Braeswood Blvd #125 Houston TX 77030-4357 Office: U of Tex-Houston Med Sch 6410 Fannin St #920 Houston TX 77030-5204 Personal E-mail: mintzhittner@aol.com. Business E-Mail: Helen.A.Mintz-Hittner@uth.tmc.edu.

MINUDRI, REGINA URSULA, librarian, consultant; b. San Francisco, May 9, 1937; d. John C. and Molly (Halter) M. BA, San Francisco Coll. for Women, 1958; MLS, U. Calif., Berkeley, 1959. Reference libr. Menlo Park (Calif.) Pub. Libr., 1959-62; regional libr. Santa Clara County (Calif.) Libr., 1962-68; project coord. Fed. Young Adult Libr. Svcs. Project, Mountain View, Calif., 1968-71; dir. profl. svcs. Alameda County (Calif.) Libr., 1971, asst. county libr., 1972-77; libr. dir. Berkeley Pub. Libr., 1977-94; city libr. San Francisco Pub. Libr., 1997-2000. Lectr. U. San Francisco, 1970-72, U. Calif., Berkeley, 1977-81, 91-93, San Jose State U., 1994-97; cons., 1975-90; mem. adv. bd. Miles Cutter Ednl., 1992-98. Author: Getting It Together, A Young Adult Bibliography, 1970; contbr. articles to publs. including Sch. Libr. Jour., Wilson Libr. Bull. Bd. dirs. No. Calif. ACLU, 1994-96, Cmty. Memory, 1989-91, Berkeley Pub. Libr. Found., 1996-99; bd. dirs. Berkeley Cmty. Fund, 1995-99, chair youth com., 1994-96; mem. bd. mgrs. ctrl. br. Berkeley YMCA, 1988-93. Recipient proclamation Mayor of Berkeley, 1985, 86, 94, Citation of Merit, Calif. State Assembly, 1994; named Woman of Yr., Alameda County North chpt. Nat. Women's Polit. Caucus, 1985, Outstanding Alumna, U. Calif. Sch. Libr. and Info. Scis., Berkeley, 1987, Lifetime Achievement award Berkeley Cmty. Fund, 2001. Mem. ALA (pres. 1986-87, exec. bd. 1980-89, coun. 1979-88, 90-94, Grolier award 1974), Calif. Libr. Assn. (pres. 1981, coun. 1965-69, 79-82), LWV (dir. Berkeley chpt. 1980-81, v.p. comm. svcs. 1995-97). Home and Office: Reality Mgmt 836 The Alameda Berkeley CA 94707-1916

MINZNER, PAMELA BURGY, state supreme court justice; b. Meridian, Miss., Nov. 19, 1943; BA cum laude, Miami U., 1965; LLB, Harvard U., 1968. Bar: Mass. 1968, N.Mex. 1972. Pvt. practice, Mass., 1968—71, Albuquerque, 1971—73; adj. prof. law U. N.Mex., Albuquerque, 1972—73, asst. prof., 1973—77, assoc. prof., 1977—80, prof. law, 1980—84; judge N.Mex. Ct. Appeals, Albuquerque, 1984—94, chief judge, 1993—94; justice N.Mex. Supreme Ct., Santa Fe, 1994—, chief justice, 1999—2001. Mem. faculty Inst. Preparativo Legal U., N.Mex. Sch. Law, 1975, 79; participant NEH Summer Seminars for Law Tchrs. Stanford Law Sch., 1982, U. Chgo. Law Sch., 1978. Author (with Robert T. Laurence): A Student's Guide to Estates in Land and Future Interests: Text, Examples, Problems & Answers, 1981, 2d edit., 1993. Mem.: ABA, State Bar N.Mex. (co-editor newsletter 1979—83, bd. dirs. 1978—79, 1983—84, sect. on women's legal rights and obligations), Gamma Phi Beta. Democrat. Avocations: reading, bridge, movies. Office: Supreme Ct NMex PO Box 848 Santa Fe NM 87501-0848 *

MIOTKE, ANNE ELIZABETH, artist, educator; b. Milw., Aug. 31, 1943; d. Hubert August and Dorothy Margaret Miotke. BA in Art, English, Mt. Mary Coll., Milw., 1965; MS in Painting, U. Wis., Milw., 1970; MFA in Painting, 1973. Instr. Mt. Mary Coll., Milw., 1970—72, 2005—; tchg. asst. U. Wis., Milw., 1972—73, adj. prof. fine arts, 2002—03; instr. Layton Sch. Art & Design, Milw., 1973—73; prof. fine arts Art Acad. Cin., 1974—92; adj. prof. fine arts Milw. Inst. Art & Design, 1992—2005; instr. Milw. Area Tech. Coll., 2004—. Grad. fellow summer U. Wis., Milw., 1972; guest curator Kohler Arts Ctr., Sheboygan, 1979; vis. specialist Milw. Art Mus., 1975—79; featured artist inaugural web site Wis. Acad. Arts & Letters, Madison, 1999; lectr. in field; represented by Grace Chosy Gallery, Madison, Edgewood Orchard Galleries, Fish Creek, Tory Folliard Gallery, Milw. One-woman shows include Dorothy Bradley Galleries, Milw., 1974, 1978, 1981, 1983, 1985, 1988, 1989, 1991, Emery Galleries Xavier U., Cin., 1984, Northern Ky. U., Highland Heights, 1986, Doris Ulmann Galleries Berea Coll., Ky., 1987, Jay County Ctr. Arts, Portland, Ind., 1987, Toni Birckhead Gallery, Cin., 1988, Mt. Mary Coll., Milw., 1988, 2001, Carnegie Arts Ctr., Covington, Ky., 1989, Cummings Gallery Mercyhurst Coll., Erie, Pa., 1989, Tory Folliard Gallery, Milw., 1993, 1995, 1997, 1999, 2001, 2005, 2007, Yeiser Art Ctr., Paducah, Ky., 1996, Indpls. Art Ctr., 1997, Leu Gallery Belmont U., Nashville, 1997, Artspace Kohler Arts Ctr., Wis., 1998, Charles Allis Art Mus., Milw., 2004, major commissions, Paine Art Ctr. and Arboretum, Oshkosh, Wis., 1992, Young Pres.'s Orgn., Milw., 1993, U. Hosp., Cleve., 1993, Profl. Dimensions, Inc., Milw., 1996, exhibited in group shows at Jan Cicero Gallery, Chgo., 1989, 1990, 1992, exhibitions include Charles A Wustum Mus. Fine Arts, Racine, Wis., 1969, 1971, 1972, 1973, 1991, 1993, 1994, 1995, 1996, 1997, 1998, 1999, 2000, 2001, 2002, 2003, 2004, 2005, 2006, Wis. Painters and Sculptors Competitions, 1971, 1972, 1973, 1974, 1993, 1996, Springfield Art Mus., Mo., 1977, 1980, 1982, 1983, 1989, Contemporary Arts Ctr., Cin., 1984, Zaner Gallery, Rochester, NY, 1984, Fine Arts Galleries U. Wis., Milw., 1985, Ind. U. East, Richmond, 1986, Arts Consortium, Cin., 1986, Evansville Mus. Arts and Scis., Ind., 1986, 1987, 1988, 1990, Coll. Mt. St. Joseph, Cin., 1987, 1992, Contemporary Arts Ctr. South Australia, Adelaide, 1988, Naracoorte Art Gallery, South Australia, 1988, Riverland Regional Cultural Trust, 1988, Dorothy Bradley Galleries, Milw., 1990, Edgewood Orchard Galleries, Fish Creek, Wis., 1990, 1994, 1998, 2004, 2006, Jan Cicero Gallery Navy Pier, Chgo., 1990, Contemporary Still Life, Rockford, Ill., 1991, Contemporary Art Ctr., Cin., 1991, Rahr-West Mus., Manitowoc, Wis., 1991, Paine Art Ctr. and Arboretum, Oshkosh, Wis., 1991, Art Acad. Cin., 1992, Tom Folliard Galery, Milw., 1994, Chgo. Botanic Gardens, Glencoe, Ill., 1996, Grace Chosy Gallery, Madison, Wis., 1998, 2001, 2003, 2005, Represented in permanent collections Alverno Coll., Milw., Am. Bank, Beechwood, Ohio, Am. Nat. Bank, Springfield, Mo., Bristol-Myers US Pharmaceutical Group, Evansville, Ind., Bright Future, Inc., Cin. Art Mus., Ctrl. Trust Bank, Cin., Cin. Bell, Cin. Bell Info. Sys., Cin. Gas and Electric, Citizen's Bank of Sheboygan, Wis., City of Cin. Dept. Health, Deloitte, Haskins & Sells, Federated Dept. Stores Corporate Hdqs., Fidelity Investments, Cin., G.E.M. Savings, Dayton, Ohio, Gilberts Commonwealth Assn., Reading, Pa., Harris Bank, Hinsdale, Ill., Heritage Ins., Sheboygan, Wis., Hyatt Regency Hotel, Louisville, IBM, LA, Jansen Group, Inc., Milw., Kemper Group, Long Grove, Ill., Liberty Nat. Bank, Louisville, Miller Art Mus., Sturgeon Bay, Wis., Miller Brewing Co., Milw., Milw. Inst. Art and Design, Mt. Mary Coll., Milw., Northwestern Mutual Life Ins., Ohio Nat. Bank, Columbus, Paine Art Ctr. and Arboretum, Oshkosh, Wis., Prudential Life Ins., Newark, Racine Art Mus., Wis., Rahr-West Art Mus., Manitowoc, Wis., St. Norbert's Coll., DePere, Wis., Scripps Howard Corporate Hdqs., Cin., Smith and Schnacke, State Bank of East Troy, Wis., Sterling Tool and Mfg. Co., Milw., U. Wis., Madison, Milw., Waukesha, Union Bank and Trust, Lancaster, Wis., U. Hosp., Cleve., Wehr Corp., Milw., Winter's Nat. Bank Atrium I, Cin., Yeiser Art Ctr., Paducah, Ky. Recipient Profl. Excellence award, Mt. St. Mary Coll. Alumni Assn., 1982, Sacajawea award, Profl. Dimensions, Inc., 1996; fellow, Ohio Arts Coun., 1980—81, 1988—89; grantee, Nat. Endowment Arts, 1975, 1979. Mem.: Phi Kappa Phi. Roman Catholic. Avocation: travel. Home: 4791 N Elkhart Ave Whitefish Bay WI 53211-1002 Office Phone: 414-332-2720.

MIQUELON, MIRIAM F., former prosecutor, lawyer; b. Elmhurst, Ill. children: Aaron, Rachel. Grad., U. Ariz., 1975, DePaul U., 1978; LLM in Taxation, Chgo.-Kent Coll. Law; postgrad. in Taxation, DePaul U.; postgrad. in History, Northwestern U. Lawyer, Houston, Stone, McGuire, Benjamin & Kocoras, Miquelon and Assocs., 1981—88, Keck, Mahin & Cate, Chgo., 1988—91; asst. U.S. atty. Ea. Dist. N.Y., Bklyn., 1991—93, So. Dist. Ill., 1993—99; asst. spl. counsel to Spl. Counsel John C. Danforth, 1999—2000; asst. U.S. atty. So. Dist. Ill., 2000—02, U.S. atty., 2002—03. Adj. prof. law Washington U. Sch. Law, St. Louis; adj. faculty Northwestern U. Coll. Law, Chgo. Recipient Chief Postal Inspector's award, U.S. Postal Inspection Svc., 2001, Spl. commendations, FBI, Drug Enforcement Adminstrn., U.S. Customs Svc., IRS. Avocations: volunteering, sports activities.

MIQUELON, WADE D., food products executive; Fin. dir. SE Asian Beauty Care bus. Procter & Gamble, CFO Thailand, Myanmar, Cambodia and Laos subsidiaries, CFO, sr. dir. ASEAN, Australia and India region Singapore, 2001—03, CFO Western European bus. Geneva, 2003—06; exec. v.p., CFO Tyson Foods, Springdale, Ark., 2006—. Office: Tyson Foods 2210 W Oaklawn Dr Springdale AR 72762-6999 Office Phone: 479-290-6111. Office Fax: 479-757-7984. *

MIR, ALEKSANDRA, artist; b. Lubin, Poland, 1967; Communication & Media studies, Schillerska/Gothenburg U., Gothenburg, 1986—87; BFA in Media Arts, Sch. Visual Arts, NY, 1992; Grad. Faculty Cultural Anthropology, New Sch. Social Rsch., NY, 1994—96. One-man shows include Life is Sweet in Sweden, Trixter, Gothenburg, 1995, Pick UP (oh baby), Lyd/Galerie, Copenhagen, 1997, City Forest (prototype), Tompkins Sq. Pk., NY, 1998, Conspiracy Night, Swiss Inst., NY, 1999, Gavin Brown's enterprise, NY, 2001, Corp. Mentality, Lukas & Sternberg, NY, 2002, Naming Tokyo (part II), Swiss Inst., NY, 2003, Happy Holidays, The Wrong Gallery, NY, 2003, The Big Umbrella (NY), PS1 Contemporary Art Ctr., NY, 2004, New Commission, Fundacion NMAC, Montenmedio, 2005, exhibited in group shows at Empires without States, Swiss Inst., NY, 1999, Democracy!, Royal Coll. Art, London, 2000, COPY, Roth Horowitz Gallery, NY, 2002, The Twentieth Anniversary Show, Gavin Brown's enterprise, NY, 2003, Sandwiched, Jacob Fabricius, NY, 2003, Power, Corruption & Lies, Roth Horowitz, NY, 2004, Calif. Earthquakes, Daniel Reich Gallery, NY, 2004, Whitney Biennial, Whitney Mus. Am. Art, 2004. Mailing: c/o Andrew Roth 160 A East 70th St New York NY 10021 E-mail: aleksandra_mir@hotmail.com.

MIRABELLO, FRANCIS JOSEPH, lawyer; b. Ft. Lauderdale, Fla., Mar. 2, 1954; s. Frank Guy and Mary (Sorce) M.; m. Marianna Hay O'Neal, Aug. 5, 1978; children: Diana H., A. Paul. BS in Civil Engring., Princeton U., 1975; JD, Harvard U., 1978. Bar: Calif. 1978, Pa. 1981, Fla. 1983. Assoc. Irell & Manella, Los Angeles, 1978-81; ptnr. Morgan, Lewis & Bockius, Phila., 1981—, mng. personal law practice group. Lectr. law Villanova (Pa.) U. Law Sch., adj. prof. law U. Pa., Phila. Mem. ABA, Merion Cricket Club, St. Davids Gold Club, Ford Plantation Club. Avocations: tennis, golf. Office: Morgan Lewis & Bockius 1701 Market St Philadelphia PA 19103-2903 Office Phone: 215-963-5248. Office Fax: 215-963-5001. Business E-Mail: fmirabello@morganlewis.com.

MIRABILE, THOMAS KEITH, lawyer; b. May 11, 1948; s. Joseph Anthony and Marie Johanna (Reynolds) M.; m. Pamela S. Brogan, Sept. 5, 2002; children: Adrian, Joseph, Paul, Neil; stepchildren: Paul and Neil Brogan. BA, No. Ill. U., 1972; MA, Northeastern Ill. U., 1974; JD, Oklahoma City U., 1975; LLM, DePaul U., 2003. Bar: Okla. 1976, Ill. 1977, U.S. Dist. Ct. (we. dist.) Okla. 1976, U.S. Dist. Ct. Ariz. 1992, U.S. Dist. Ct. (no. dist.) Ill. 2002, U.S. Ct. Appeals (10th cir.) 1980, U.S. Tax Ct. 1977, U.S. Supreme Ct. 1983, U.S. Ct. of Claims 1985. Prof. sociology Oklahoma City U., 1976-77; prof. bus. Edmond, Okla., 1977-82; ptnr. Mirabile and Assocs. P.C., Oklahoma City, 1977—95; prof. Sch. Law, Grad. Sch. Bus. Oklahoma City U., 1986-95; prof. Grad. Sch. Webster U., 1991—. Vis. faculty DePaul U., Chgo. Mem. Ill. Bar Assn., Okla. Bar Assn.

MIRABITO, ANTHONY JASON, lawyer, educator; b. NYC, Jan. 29, 1948; s. Anthony Joseph Mirabito and Jean Theresa (Cultrone) Mirobito; m. Marjorie Rose Berger, July 7, 1974; children: Katherine Rose, Andrew. BS in Engring. Physics, NYU, 1965—69; JD, Am. U., 1973; LLM in Patent/Internat. Law, Georgetown U., 1975. Bar: Pa. 1974, DC 1975, Mass. 1981, registered: US Patent & Trademark Office 1977. Patent examiner, atty. US Patent & Trademark Office, Arlington, Va., 1969—75; atty. US Dept. Commerce, Washington, 1975—77, US Internat. Trade Commn., Washington; in-house counsel Westinghouse Electric Co., Pitts., 1979—80; legal cons. Mass. computer & software cos., Boston area, 1980—; of counsel Gaston Snow & Ely Bartlett, Boston, 1984, head, patent dept.; ptnr., Intellectual Property Law Wolf, Greenfield & Sacks; founding ptnr., co-chmn., Intellectual Property Law Sect. Mintz Levin Cohn Ferris Glovsky & Popeo PC, Boston. Assoc. prof. law Suffolk U. Law Sch., Boston, 1980—; lectr. in field. Contbr. articles to law reviews; editor: Foreign Investment in US, 1977. Mem.: Pa. Bar Assn., Mass. Bar Assn., ABA, DC Bar Assn. (Internat. Law Sect.), Boston Bar Assn., Small Bus. Assn. of New Eng., Boston Patent Law Assn. (former pres.), Winchester Boat Club (Mass.). Achievements include patents in field. Office: Mintz Levin Cohn Ferris Glovsky & Popeo PC One Financial Ctr Boston MA 02111 also: Suffolk U Law Sch 41 Temple St Boston MA 02114-4241 Office Phone: 617-348-1805. Office Fax: 617-542-2241. Business E-Mail: jmirabito@mintz.com.

MIRACLE, DORIS JEAN, retired medical/surgical nurse; b. Louisville, July 23, 1931; d. Bernard Louis and Catherine Federle; m. Earl Miracle, Aug. 31, 1951; 1 child, David. Surg. nurse Norton Hosp., Louisville, 1951, Norton-Children's Hosp., Louisville, 1969—86; ret., 1986. Poetry (albums) Sounds of Poetry, 2003; author: numerous poems; contbr. articles to profl. jours. Recipient Editors Choice award, 2003, 2006. Mem.: Wilderness Rd. Writers, Gaslight Writers, Ky. Writers Coalition, Internat. Soc. of Poets, Soc. Children's Book Writers and Illustrators, Louisville Astronomical Soc. Avocations: reading, poetry, astronomy, art, music. Personal E-mail: doriskitm@aol.com.

MIRACLE, GORDON ELDON, advertising educator; b. Olympia, Wash., May 28, 1930; s. Gordon Tipler and Corine Adriana (Orlebeke) M.; m. Christa Stoeter, June 29, 1957; children: Gary, Gregory, Glenn. BBA, U. Wis., 1952, MBA, 1958, PhD, 1962. Case officer, civilian intelligence analyst U.S. Army, Fed. Republic Germany, 1955-57; instr. commerce U. Wis. Grad. Sch. Bus., Madison, 1958-60; instr., then asst. prof. mktg. U. Mich., Ann Arbor, 1960-66; assoc. prof. advt. Mich. State U., East Lansing, 1966-70, chmn. PhD program in mass media, 1973-74, chmn. dept., 1974-80, prof. advt., 1970-99, prof. emeritus, 1999—. Vis. prof. mktg.

mgmt. N. European Mgmt. Inst., Oslo, 1972-73; cons., lectr. in field. Author: Management of International Advertising, 1966; co-author: International Marketing Management, 1970, Advertising and Government Regulation, 1979, Instructor's Manual for International Marketing Management, 1971, European Regulation of Advertising: Supranational Regulation of Advertising in the European Economic Community, 1986, Voluntary Regulation of Advertising: A Comparative Analysis of the United Kingdom and the United States, 1987, (in Korean) Cultures in Advertising: Advertising in Cultures, 1990; contbr. articles to scholarly and profl. jours.; editor: Marketing Decision Making: Strategy and Payoff, 1965, Sharing for Understanding, Proc. Ann. Conf. Am. Acad. Advt., 1977. Served with AUS, 1952-55. Recipient first Biennial Excellence in Advt. award, U. Ill., 1995; Ford Found. fellow, 1961-62, 64, Am. Assn. Advt. Agys. fellow Marsteller, Inc., 1967, Advt. Ednl. Found. fellow McCann-Erickson Hakuhodo, 1985, Fulbright rsch. fellow Waseda U., Tokyo, 1985; recipient numerous grants; recipient Viktor-Mataja medal Austrian Advt. Rsch. Assn., Vienna, 1999. Fellow: Am. Acad. Advt. (treas., exec. com. 1978—79); mem.: Internat. Advt. Assn., Internat. Advt. Assn. ((ednl. accreditation com. 1993—95, internat. advt. edn. group 1996—2001), Am. Mktg. Assn., Acad. Internat. Bus. (sec., exec. com. 1973—75), Adcraft Club Detroit. Home: 10025 Oak Island Dr Laingsburg MI 48848-8718 Office: Mich State U Dept Advt East Lansing MI 48824 Business E-Mail: miracle@msu.edu.

MIRACLE, NANCY, foundation administrator, writer; Acting student with Lee Strasberg, Carnegie Hall Studios, NYC, 1955—62; tutored in classical lit. and writing, NYC, 1963—66; student, Manhattan C.C., NYC, 1965—69; student, creative writing, New Sch. for Social Rsch., NYC, 1971—76; MFA in Creative Writing, Goddard Coll., Plainfield, Vt., 1979; tutored, Ibiza, Spain, 1979—80. Lectr. Marymount Coll., NYC, 1979; tutor CUNY, NYC, 1983; condr. workshops Women's Internat. Writing Group, NYC, 1976—82; tchr. YMCA Writing Workshops, Honolulu, 1988—89, St. Louis Sch., Honolulu, 1993—94; tutor U. Hawaii, Honolulu, 1990—2000; pres. and founder Marilyn Monroe Found., Honolulu, NYC, 1985—. Actor(lead): 2 plays, 1955—58; author: (novels) Lesser Sins, 1979, Venus Oh So Bright, 1994, Here I Am Mother, The Real Story of Marilyn Monroe, 1985, (play) Here I Am Mother, 2004 (Am. Book award, 1985). Mem.: Dramatists Guild. Office Phone: 212-560-7505. Personal E-mail: marilynmonroefoundation@yahoo.com.

MIRAKIAN-ESCOBAR, RACHEL ANN, language educator; b. Cleve., July 21, 1966; d. Nazar Mirakian and Mary Hazarian, Lucy Baboyan (Stepmother); m. Ebert Eduardo Escobar, Jan. 22, 2005. Bachelor, SUNY, Purchase, 2005. Tchg. asst. Souther Westchester Boces, Valhalla, NY, 1996—99; freelance writing tutor self-employed, New Rochelle, NY, 1996—2005; English lang. instr. Pace U., Pleasantville, NY, 2006—; adj. instr. Westchester CC, Valhalla, NY, 2006—. Student workshop devel. Westchester CC, 2003—06, editor/proofreader ann. report, 2005, author student devel. handouts, 2005—06. Designer (computer game) Symmetry;, author short stories. Mem. United Ch. Christ, Pelham, NY, 2005—, Empty Hand Zen Ctr., New Rochelle, 2006. Mem.: Avant Guard, Bookbuilders, Purchase Alumni Assn., Mensa. Liberal. Christian-Buddhist. Avocations: writing, meditation, reading, films, travel. Office: Pace U 861 Bedford Rd Pleasantville NY 10570 Office Phone: 914-923-2600. Personal E-mail: rme580@optonline.net.

MIRAN, PATRICIA MARIE, art educator; b. Seattle, Apr. 6, 1951; d. Robert Glenroy Hancock and Bernice Iris Brisky; m. Maynard Alvin Miran, May 1, 1983; children: Maxwell, Jacob, Emma. Diploma in fine arts illustration, Art Students League, NYC, 1974; BS cum laude, Excelsior Coll., 2001. Childrens story hr. dir. Sayre Libr., 1989—95; exec. dir. Lincoln Acad., Waverly, NY, 1998—2004; tchr. Jewish Cmty. Sch., Elmira, NY, 1999—. Libr. dir. Cady Libr., Nichols, NY, 1996; tutor, remedial reading M-G Edn., Elmira, 2001—; commr. Commn. Rehab., 2001—06; instr. Elmira Bus. Inst., 2005, pvt. painting lessons, 2006—. Rep. 4-H Cornell Coop. Ext., Owego, NY, 1989—2001; active Tioga County Coun. on the Arts. Grantee, N.Y. State Coun. on Arts, 1994—96; scholar, Calif. Coll. Arts and Crafts, 1969—70, Art Student League, 1971. Mem.: Arnot Art Mus. Avocations: gardening, birdwatching, hiking, canoeing, painting. Home and Studio: 21 Lincoln St Waverly NY 14892 Office: Jewish Cmty Sch PO Box 3087 1008 W Water St Elmira NY 14905 Office Phone: 607-732-7410. Personal E-mail: mmiran@stny.rr.com.

MIRANDA, CARLOS SA, food products company executive; b. Fall River, Mass., Nov. 16, 1929; s. Carlos Sa and Annette (Pratt) M.; m. Natalie Cardoso, Jan. 5, 1949; children: Carla, Lucy, John. BS in Mech. Engring., Marquette U., 1956. With internat. divsn. Kellogg Co., Battle Creek, Mich., 1964—65; gen. mgr. Kellogg Co. Brazil, 1965—80; v.p. Kellogg Internat., Battle Creek, 1980—89; gen. mgr. Kellogg's Spain, 1983—84; country dir. internat. exec. svc. corps. Costa Rica, 1990—91; mediator Fla. County Cts., 1994—. Recipient Pero Vaz Caminha award, Brazil, 1976; conferred title Comdr. of Legion of Honor of Marshal Rondon, Brazil, 1971. Mem. ASME. Independent. Roman Catholic. Home: 8949 Wildlife Loop Sarasota FL 34238

MIRANDA, HERMES, school counselor; b. LA, Aug. 24, 1958; s. Henrietta Collins; m. Patricia Salazar, Feb. 4, 1971; children: Naomi Ruth Cross, Isaac Keith. MS, LI U., NY, 1996. Cert. sch. counselor NY, 1997. Enlisted US Army, 1976, advanced to master sgt., 1995, ret., 1997; counselor Newburgh Enlarged Sch. Dist., NY, 1997—. Decorated Meritorious Svc. medal with Oak Leaf Cluster US Army. Mem.: Newburgh Tchrs. Assn., Orange County Counselor's Assn. (assoc.). Republican. Home: 9 Princeton Dr Walden NY 12586 Home Phone: 845-778-8525; Office Phone: 845-563-7018.

MIRANDA, M. JEANNE, psychiatrist; BS, Idaho State U., 1976; MA, U. Kansas, 1983, PhD, 1986. Asst. clin. prof. psychology U. Calif. San Francisco (UCSF), 1988—95, asst. prof. in residence in psychology, 1992—95; assoc. prof. psychology Georgetown U., Washington, 1995—2001; assoc. prof. biobehavioral sciences & psychiatry UCLA Neuropsychiatric Inst., 2001—, assoc. dir. Health Svcs. Rsch. Ctr. Sr. scientific editor Mental Health: Culture, Race, & Ethnicity, 2001. Recipient Interdisciplinary Achievement award, LPPI-UCSF Alumni-Faculty Assn., 1986, R.E. Harris award, UCSF, 1986; fellow, Rehabilitation Svc. Adminstrn., 1980—84; NIMH Clin. Svcs. Rsch. Fellowship, 1986—88. Mem.: Inst. Medicine. Office: Health Svcs Rsch Ctr UCLA Wilshire Ctr Ste 300 10920 Wilshire Blvd Los Angeles CA 90024-6505 Office Phone: 310-794-3710. E-mail: mirandaj@ucla.edu.

MIRANDA, ROBERT NICHOLAS, publishing executive, director; b. Bklyn., July 9, 1934; m. Marilyn H. Pils, May 25, 1958; children: Marilyn, Robert, Susan, Lori, Jennifer. AA in Acctg. and Bus. Adminstrn., SUNY, Farmingdale, 1967. Pres. Pergamon Press, Inc., Elmsford, NY, 1965—92; chmn., CEO Cognizant Communication Corp., Elmsford, 1992—; owner Miranda Press, 2002. Bd. dirs., exec. v.p., vice chmn. Soc. and Assoc. Svc. Corp., McLean, Va., 1979-82; bd. dirs., chmn. electronics com. Copyright Clearance Ctr., 1984-93. Pub. Acupuncture and Electro Therapeutics Rsch., Analgesia, Bird Behavior, Cancer Prevention Internat., Cell Transplantation, Festival Mgmt. and Event Tourism, Gene Expression, Info. Tech. and Tourism, Life Support and Biosphere Sci., Oncology Rsch., Tourism Analysis, Technology: Jour. of Regulatory Sci., Failure and Lessons Learned in Info. Tech., Pacific Tourism Rev., Tourism, Culture and Comm., Tourism Dynamic Book Series, Tourism in Marine Environments, Habitation: An Internat. Jour., Revs. in Analgesia, Event Mgmt., Tourism Rev. Internat., Info. Tech. in Hospitality. Served with USNR, 1954-59. Mem. Internat. Soc. Intelligent Sys. (founder, bd. dirs., fin. dir. 1992—). Avocations: hunting, fishing, horseback riding. Office: Cognizant Comm Corp 3 Hartsdale Rd Elmsford NY 10523-3701 Office Phone: 914-592-7720. Personal E-mail: cogcomm@aol.com.

MIRANDA-LEVI, JASON, film producer, writer; arrived in US, 1939, naturalized, 1957; s. Jose Antonio Miranda and Mercedes Bertolin-Levi; m. Maria L Maria Luisa Echaurren, Nov. 24, 1962; 1 child, Mychele Lita Ohre. BS, Fordham U., 1954—58; JD, St. Johns U., 1958—61. Lic.: NY (Attorney) 1963. Pvt. law practice, NYC, 1964—74. Prodr.: (film and telvision) Han Matado a Un Cadaver; (TV series) Cara a Cara; author: (novels) The Spanish Enigma, Dancer in the Dark; exhibitions include Photographic Surrealism, Toledo Art Mus., Ohio. Lance cpl. USMC, 1951—53, Korea. Recipient Dama del Paraguas, City of Barcelona, Spain, 1973, La Font de Canaletas, City Coun. of the City of Barcelona, Spain, 1973, Medal of San Jordi, Province of Barcelona, Barcelona, Spain, 1976, Font de Canaletas, City Coun. of Barcelona, Spain, 1975. Mem.: SAG, NY Bar. Republican. Jewish. Avocations: antique watch collector, travel, reading, haute cuisine, flute. Personal E-mail: jmlevi@sbcglobal.net.

MIRANTE, THOMAS ANTHONY, retired secondary education educator; b. Utica, NY, Oct. 11, 1931; s. John and Catherine (Cerro) M.; m. Lucy Fiore, Aug. 11, 1962; children: Anne Catherine, Mary Jo. BS in Music, SUNY, Potsdam, 1954; MS in Music, Ithaca Coll., 1955; postgrad., Colgate U., 1964; studies with Earl George, David Diamond. Cert. music tchr., guidance counselor, N.Y. Pianist 6th Infantry div. Band U.S. Army, Ft. Ord, Calif., 1955-56; choral dir. 1st Infantry div. Post Chapel U.S. Army, Ft. Riley, Kans., 1956-57; tchr. music Port Leyden (N.Y.) Cen. Sch., 1957-60; dir. music, tchr. Oneida (N.Y.) City Schs., 1960-92. Music critic Oneida Dispatch, 1972; composer: Piano Sonata, 1964, Symphony 1, 1968, Viola Concerto, 1971, numerous other works, 1968-87; author: Voices Amid the Thunder, 1989, Song of Evil, 1996; contbr. articles to profl. jours. Trustee Canastota (N.Y.) Library Bd., 1986. Rockefeller grantee Am. Music Ctr., 1975, grantee N.Y. State Council of Arts, 1975. Mem. BMI, Madison County Music Tchrs. Assn. Democrat. Roman Catholic. Avocation: walking. Home: 208 N Main St Canastota NY 13032-1033

MIRE, WELDON J., oil industry executive, human resources specialist; B of Fgn. Lang., U. La., 1971; postgrad., U. Costa Rica. Joined Halliburton, Houston, 1978, sr. shared svcs. mgr., 1998—99, dir. bus. devel., global dir. strategic bus. devel., 1999, sales mgr. Asia Pacific sales, 1999—2001, divsn. v.p., country v.p. for Indonesia, 2001—02, v.p. human resources, 2002—. Office: Halliburton 10200 Bellaire Blvd Houston TX 77020-5299 Office Phone: 281-575-3000. E-mail: weldon.mire@halliburton.com.

MIRELS, HAROLD, aerospace engineer; b. NYC, July 29, 1924; s. Hyman and Lily (Efron) M.; m. Nell Segal, Oct. 4, 1953; children: Lily, Laurence Franklin, Jeremy Mark. BSME, Cooper U., 1944; MSME, Case Inst. Tech., 1949; PhD in Aero. Engring., Cornell U., 1953. Sect. head NACA, Cleve., 1944-57; br. chief NASA, Cleve., 1957-61; dept. head Aerospace Corp., El Segundo, Calif., 1961-78, assoc. dir., 1978-84, prin. scientist, 1984-93; cons., 1993—. Co-inventor continuous wave chem. laser. Recipient Tech. Achievement award Cleve. Tech. Socs., 1960. Fellow AIAA (Fluid and Plasmadynamics award 1988), Am. Phys. Soc.; mem. Nat. Acad. Engring. Home: 3 Seahurst Rd Palos Verdes Peninsula CA 90274-3700

MIRENBURG, BARRY LEONARD, publishing executive, educator; b. NYC, Feb. 16, 1952; s. Fred and Mildred (Solomon) M. BS, Mercy Coll., 1979; BFA, Cooper Union, 1980; MBA, N.Y. Inst. of Tech., 1983; MA, Columbia U., 1983, postgrad., 1983—; MFA, Syracuse U., 1990; postgrad., Columbia U. Tchrs. Coll., 1997. Pres., pub. Barlenmir House, NYC, 1972—; pres., owner Barlenmir House Theatres, Inc., NYC, 1978—; head Design Graphics N.Y. Inst. of Tech., NYC, 1979—; pres., creative dir. The Corp. Communications Group, NYC, 1985—, Mirenburg & Co., NYC, 1985—. Instr. unranked Parsons Sch. of Design, N.Y.C., 1979—, coord. computer graphics, 1990-91; asst. prof. Fashion Inst. of Tech., N.Y.C., 1979-81; corp. art dir. Music Sales/Quick Fox, N.Y.C., 1982-85; adj. assoc. prof. Grad. Sch. Coll. of New Rochelle, N.Y., 1985—; founder, exec. dir. Am. Health and Fitness Alliance, 1998—. Recipient more than 125 awards and honors for art and design; Fulbright scholar, 1991. Mem. AAUP, Nat. Coun. Art Adminstrs., Am. Inst. Graphic Arts, Soc. Publ. Designers, Am. Ctr. for Design, Art Dirs. Club, Soc. Indsl. Designers, Coll. Art Assn., Mensa. Home and Office: 404 E 79th St New York NY 10021

MIRENGOFF, PAUL E., lawyer, political blogger; married; 2 children. AB summa cum laude, Dartmouth Coll., 1971; JD, Stanford Law Sch., 1974. Lawyer with Office of Gen. Counsel Equal Opportunity Commn., 1976—81; with Hunton & Williams, Washington, 1981—99; ptnr. Akin Gump Strauss Hauer & Feld LLP, Washington, 1999—. Contbr. (book) Employment Discrimination Law, (book) Sexual Harassment in Employment Law, articles to profl. jours.; published a column about affirmative action Washington Post; author: (blog website) powerlineblog.com, 2002—. Mem.: DC Bar. Office: Akin Gump Strauss Hauer & Feld LLP Robert S Strauss Bldg 1333 New Hampshire Ave NW Washington DC 20036-1564 Office Phone: 202-887-4354. Office Fax: 202-887-4288. Business E-Mail: pmirengoff@akingump.com. E-mail: powerlinefeedback@gmail.com. *

MIRICK, JOHN O., lawyer; b. Worcester, Mass., Nov. 27, 1946; s. Richard W. and Margaret (Whittemore) M.; m. Diane Kay Lohman, Aug. 2, 1969; children: Christopher R., Seth H. BA magna cum laude, Amherst Coll., Mass., 1968; MA, University Coll., London, 1969; JD cum laude, Harvard U., 1972. Bar: Mass. 1972, U.S. Dist. Ct. Mass. 1973, U.S. Ct. Appeals (1st cir.) 1974, U.S. Ct. Appeals (2nd cir.) 1979, U.S. Supreme Ct. 1980, U.S. Ct. Appeals (fed. cir.) 2006. Assoc. Hale & Dorr, Boston, 1972-76; ptnr. Mirick, O'Connell, DeMallie & Lougee, Worcester, Mass., 1976—. Trustee Mass. Continuing Legal Edn., 1988-92. Trustee Dynamy, Inc., Worcester, 1979—89, Mass. Bd. Bar Overseers, 1999—2002, chair, 2001—02; mem. Mass. Jud. Nominating Commn., 2003—06. Fulbright scholar, 1969. Mem. ABA, Mass. Bar Assn, Mass. Acad. Trial Attys., Assn. Trial Lawyers Am., Am. Antiquarian Soc., Phi Beta Kappa. Office: Mirick O'Connell DeMallie & Lougee 100 Front St Worcester MA 01608 Office Phone: 508-791-8500. Business E-Mail: jomirick@modl.com.

MIRIPOL, JERILYN ELISE, poet, writer, writing therapist; b. Chgo., Jan. 22; d. Albert and Janice (Tuchin) M.; m. Richard Palmer Van Duyne, Dec. 30, 1986. BA in English Lit., Northeastern Ill. U., 1974. Writing therapist Northshore Retirement Hotel, Evanston, Ill., 1983; creative writing tchr. Oakton Community Coll., Evanston, 1985—; writing therapist St. Francis Hosp., Evanston, 1989—. Artist-writer-in-residence Dawes Sch., Evanston, 1985; artist-in-residence Evanston Twp. High Sch., 1988; writing facilitator for individual students, Chgo., 1987—; tchr. writing therapy to mental health profls. and caregivers U. Wis., Milw., 1989; presenter writing therapy workshop, 1990, Nat. Assn. Poetry-Therapy, Chgo., 1991. Author: Discovering Self-Awareness Through Poetry, 1987, (poetry) The Sounds Were Distilled, 1977; author numerous poems; contbr. articles to profl. jours. Vol. Ridgeview Nursing Home, Evanston, 1982-83; advocate of children of abuse, human and civil rights. Talent scholar in creative writing Northeastern Ill. U., Squaw Valley Community Writers scholar, 1980, Radgale Found. scholar, 1985, Aspen Writer's Workshop Breadloaf Writer's Conf. scholar; Danforth fellow nominee; Dawes Sch. grantee, 1987. Mem. NOW, PEN, UNICEF, ACLU, Nat. Assn. Poetry Therapy, Women's Internat. League for Peace, Humanitas Internat. (human rights com.), Amnesty Internat., Am. Acad. Poets, Ill. Alliance of Arts, Pan Pacific Southeast Asia Women's Assn. (v.p.), 11th Ann. Poetry Therapy Conf. (keynote speaker), Greenpeace, Death Penalty Foes. Avocations: music, dance, art, reading, drama, films. Home: 1520 Washington Ave Wilmette IL 60091-2417 Home Phone: 847-251-6721; Office Phone: 847-251-6721. Personal E-mail: jmiripol@webtv.net.

MIRK, JUDY ANN, retired elementary school educator; b. Victorville, Calif., June 10, 1944; d. Richard Nesbit and Corrine (Berghoefer). BA in Social Sci., San Jose State U., Calif., 1966, cert. in teaching, 1967; MA in Edn., Calif. State U., Chico, 1980. Cert. elem. edn. tchr. Calif. Profl. psychology trainee John F. Kennedy U., Orinda, Calif., 1997—99; tchr. Cupertino (Calif.) Union Sch. Dist., 1967-95; lead tchr. lang. arts Dilworth Sch., San Jose, 1988-90, mem. supt.'s adv. team, 1986-90, mem. student study team, 1987-95; ret. Mem. student study team, 1987-95; mem. Dilworth Sch. Site Coun., 1981-95. Mem.: The Commonwealth Club of Calif., Phi Mu. Independent. Avocations: photography, natural history, watercolors. Personal E-mail: jmirk@aol.com.

MIRKIN, GABE BARON, physician, medical educator, writer, radio personality; b. Brookline, Mass., June 18, 1935; s. Mitchell and Vera (Baron) M.; children: Gene, Jan, Jill, Geoffrey, Kenny; m. Diana Purdie Rich, 1998. BA, Harvard U., 1957; MD, Baylor U., 1961. Diplomate Am. Bd. Pediatrics, Sub Bd. Allergy, Am. Bd. Allergy and Immunology, Am. Bd. Sports Medicine. Resident in pediatrics Mass. Gen. Hosp., Boston, 1961-63; fellow allergy, immunology, dermatology Johns Hopkins Hosp., Balt., 1963-65; allergy, immunology, dermatology, sports medicine pvt. practice, Silver Spring, Md., 1966—. Tchg. fellow pediat. Harvard Med. Sch., 1962-63; tchg. fellow allergy and immunology Johns Hopkins Med. Sch., 1963-65; asst. prof. dept. phys. edn. U. Md., College Park, 1976-83; assoc. clin. prof. dept. pediat. Georgetown U. Sch. of Medicine, 1984—. Author: The Sportsmedicine Book, 1978, Getting Thin, 1983, Dr. Gabe Mirkin's Fitness Clinic, 1986, The Complete Sportsmedicine Book for Women, 1985, 2d rev. edit. 1991; (with Shangold) Women and Exercise, 1988, Dr. Gabe Mirkin's Fatfree, Flavorfull Book, 1995; (with Diana Mirkin) The 20 Gram Diet, 1995, The 20/30 Fat and Fiber Diet Plan, Dr. Gabe Mirkins Pocket Guide to Fitness & Sports; (with Rich) The Whole Grains Cookbook, 1997, The Good Food Book, 2001, Healthy Heart Miracle, 2004; author (newsletter) The Mirkin Report, 1990—; columnist: N.Y. Times, 1978-89, United Features, 1989-94, Washington Post, 1976, Singer Media Corp., 1994-99; appearances on P.M. Mag. WDVM-TV, Washington, 1979, House Party, NBC TV, 1990, The Learning Channel; host internationally syndicated radio talk show, 1996-2003; daily radio spots on fitness and nutrition, CBS Radio Stations News Svc., 1979—; host talk show on health fitness and nutrition, KMOX Radio, St. Louis, 1972-89, 98; nightly talk show host NBC Washington, WRC, 1982-84, 87—, WNTR, 1984-86; weekly spots for Physicians Radio Network, 1984-85; daily talk show syndicated by Sun Radio Network, 1992; weekly talk show WEEI, Boston, 1993-94, others; columnist and contbg. editor to health and fitness mags.; contbr. articles to profl. jours., chpts. to books. Major USAF, 1968-70. Fellow Am. Coll. Allergists, Am. Assn. Cert. Allergists, Am. Assn. for Clin. Immunology and Allergy, Am. Acad. Pediatrics, Am. Acad. Allergy and Immunology. Avocation: bicycle tandem racing. Office: 10901 Connecticut Ave Kensington MD 20895-1645 Office Phone: 301-942-7900. Business E-Mail: gabe@drmirkin.com.

MIRKIN, MICHAEL V., chemistry professor; b. Alma-Ata, Kazakhstan, USSR, May 18, 1961; s. Vulf and Ninel Mirkin; m. Marina Gert, May 5, 1960; 1 child, Alexander. BS, MS in Chemistry, Kazakh State U., Alma-Ata, Kazakhstan, 1982, PhD, 1987. Postdoctoral assoc. chemistry U. Tex., Austin, 1990—93; asst. prof. chemistry Queens Coll., CUNY, Flushing, 1993—98, assoc. prof. chemistry, 1998—2004, prof. chemistry, 2004—. Co-editor (co-editor): (monograph) Scanning Electrochemical Microscopy, 2001. Mem.: Soc. Electroanalytical Chemistry, Electrochem. Soc., Am. Chem. Soc. Office: Dept Chemistry Queens Coll 65-30 Kissena Blvd Flushing NY 11367 Home Phone: 212-254-9831; Office Phone: 718-997-4111. Office Fax: 718-997-5531. Business E-Mail: mmirkin@qc.cuny.edu.

MIRKOW, FRANK J., lawyer; b. Bogota, Colombia, Feb. 4, 1965; s. Italo and Cristina Mirkow; m. Andrea C. Frank, May 26, 2001; children: Hamilton Kennan, Harrington Frank. BA, U. Md., 1987; MPA, Harvard U., 1990; JD, Cornell U., 2000. Cons. Price Waterhouse, LLP, Washington and Riyadh, Saudi Arabia, 1990—93; sr. cons. Arthur Andersen, LLP, Washington and Moscow, 1993—97; assoc. Shaw Pittman, LLP, Washington, 2000—02, Hale and Dorr, LLP, Washington, 2002—04, Haynes and Boone, LLP, Washington, 2004—06; assoc. gen. counsel Maximus Corp., 2006—. Bd. dirs. Fgn. Policy Discussion Group, Washington, 2000—; corp. sec. Internat. Ctr. for Religion and Diplomacy, Washington, 2000—. Fgn. policy intern Sen. Edward M. Kennedy, Washington, 1987—88; term mem. Coun. of Fgn. Rels., Washington, 2000—05; adj. fellow Ctr. for Strategic and Internat. Studies, Washington, 1993—98. Mem.: ABA, Am. Soc. Internat. Law, Phi Kappa Phi, Phi Alpha Theta, Phi Beta Kappa. Home: 4831 Alton Pl NW Washington DC 20016 E-mail: fjm5@yahoo.com.

MIRMAN, JOEL HARVEY, lawyer; b. Toledo, Dec. 3, 1941; s. Benjamin and Minnie Mirman; children: Lisa, Julie, Benjamin. BBA, Ohio U., 1963; JD, Ohio State U., 1966. Bar: Ohio 1966, U.S. Dist. Ct. (so. dist.) Ohio 1966, U.S. Supreme Ct. 1972. Ptnr. Topper, Alloway, Goodman, DeLeone & Duffey, Columbus, Ohio, 1966-85, Benesch, Friedlander, Coplan & Aronoff, 1986-93; shareholder Buckingham, Doolittle & Burroughs, Columbus, 1994—2003; ptnr. Gamble Hartshorn, LLC, Columbus, 2004—. Lectr. Ohio CLE Inst., Columbus, 1972—; former mem. Supreme Ct. of Ohio Commn. on Certification of Specialists. Author direct examination CLE materials; contbr. articles to profl. jours. Mem. Ohio Elections Commn., 1976-80, vice-chmn. 1980. Named Ohio Super Lawyer, 2007; named one of Best Lawyers in Am., 2003—04, 2004—05, 2005—06, 2006—, Ohio's Top 100 Super Lawyers, 2004, Top 50 Lawyers in Columbus, Ohio Super Lawyers, 2005. Mem. Ohio State Bar Assn. (coun. of dels.), Worthington Hills Country Club, Worthington Hills Civic Assn. (pres. 1992-93). Office: Gamble Hartshorn LLC 1 E Livingston Ave Columbus OH 43215 Home Phone: 614-985-5588; Office Phone: 614-324-5985. Business E-Mail: mirman@gamblehartshorn.com.

MIRON, ALEXANDER, research scientist; b. Bucharest, Romania, Dec. 3, 1963; s. Stefan Dinu and Stela Miron; m. Penelope Lyn Davis; children: David Arthur, Robert Stefan. BA, Duke U., Durham, NC, 1986, PhD, 1992. Postdoctoral fellow NIH, 1993—95; asst. rsch. prof. Duke U. Med. Ctr., Durham, NC, 1996—98; instr. Harvard Med. Sch., Boston, 1998—. Contbr. articles to profl. jours. Mem.: Am. Assn. Cancer Rsch., Am. Soc. Human Genetics. Achievements include patents pending for a blood test for breast cancer; method for DNA sequencing (Exon Grouping Analysis); protein fractionation chromatography apparatus. Avocations: tennis, swimming, travel, golf. Home: 291 Beverly Rd Chestnut Hill MA 02467 Office: Dana Farber Cancer Inst 44 Binney Boston MA 02115 Home Phone: 617-323-9345; Office Phone: 617-632-5176. Office Fax: 617-632-3709. Business E-Mail: alexander_miron@dfci.harvard.edu.

MIRONER, MERRIL A., lawyer; b. Gloversville, NY, Dec. 28, 1940; BS with honors, Union Coll., 1962; JD cum laude, Columbia U., 1965. Bar: NY 1966, US Dist. Ct., No. Dist. NY, US Dist. Ct., So. and Ea. Dists. NY, US Ct. Appeals, 2nd Cir. Confidential legal asst. Appellate Div. of Supreme Ct., Third Dept., 1965—67; ptnr. Katten Muchin Rosenman, NYC. Mem.: NY State Bar Assn. Office: Katten Muchin Rosenman 575 Madison Ave New York NY 10022 Office Phone: 212-940-8910. Office Fax: 212-940-8776. E-mail: merril.mironer@kattenlaw.com.

MIROWSKI, PHILIP EDWARD, economics professor; b. Jackson, Mich., Aug. 21, 1951; s. Edward and Elizabeth Mirowski. BA, Mich. State U., 1973; MA in Econs., U. Mich., 1976, PhD in Econs., 1979. Asst. prof. U. Santa Clara, Calif., 1978-81, Tufts U., Medford, Mass., 1981-84, assoc. prof. econs., 1984-90; Carl Koch prof. econs. and history and philosophy of sci. U. Notre Dame, Ind., 1990—. Vis. assoc. prof. Yale U., New Haven, 1987-88; vis. prof. Tinbergen Inst., Erasmus U., Rotterdam, Holland, 1991, U. Paris, 1997, U. Modena, Italy, 1998, Santa Fe Inst., 2001; Fulbright sr. fellow, 2003, Internat. Ctr. for Advanced Studies, NYU, 2004. Author: Reconstruction of Economic Theory, 1986, Against Mechanism, 1988, More Heat Than Light, 1989, Machine Dreams, 2002, Science Bought and Sold, 2002, Effortless Economy of Science, 2004; editor: Natural Images in Economics, 1994, Edgeworth on Chance, 1994, Collected Works of William Thomas Thornton, 1999, Agreement on Demand, 2006; mem. editl. bd. History Polit. Econ., Duke U., 1986—, Social Concept, 1988-94, Jour. Instnl. Econs., 2004—, Jour. History of Econ., 2001—; contbr. articles to profl. jours. Mem. AAAS, Am. Econs. Assn., History Sci. Soc., History Econs. Soc., Soc. for Social Studies of Sci. (Ludwig Fleck prize 2006), Philosophy of Sci. Assn. Office: U Notre Dame 400 Decio Hall Notre Dame IN 46556 E-mail: mirowski.1@nd.edu.

MIRRA, SUZANNE SAMUELS, pathologist; BA, Hunter Coll., 1962; MD, SUNY, Bklyn., 1967. Instr. pathology Yale U. Sch. Medicine, New Haven, 1971-73; staff pathologist Atlanta VA Med. Ctr., Decatur, Ga., 1973-97; asst. prof. pathology Emory U. Sch. Medicine, Atlanta, 1973-80, assoc. prof. pathology, 1981-93, prof. pathology, 1993-97; prof., chair dept. pathology SUNY Health Sci. Ctr., Bklyn., 1997—. Dir., prin. investor Emory Alzheimer's Disease Ctr., Atlanta, 1991—97. Mem. editl. bd. Arch Pathol. Lab. Med., 1988-2000, Jour. Neuropathology Exptl. Neurology, 1991-95, Brain Pathology, 1995-99, Alzheimer's Disease Reviews, 1995-2000. Recipient Albert E. Levy Sci. Faculty Rsch. award Emory U., 1987, Disting. Alumnus Achievement award SUNY, 1992; named to Hunter Coll. Hall of Fame, 1996. Fellow Coll. Am. Pathologists (Presdl. award 1987,89, Herbert Lansky award 1990, chair neuropathology commn. 1992-95); mem. Am. Assn. Neuropathologists (v.p. profl. affairs 1992-97, pres. 1999-2000, Meritorious Contributions to Neuropathology award, 2005), Alzheimer's Assn. (bd. dir. Atlanta chpt. 1987-97, nat. bd. dir. 1997-05), Alpha Omega Alpha. Office: SUNY Health Sci Ctr 450 Clarkson Ave Brooklyn NY 11203-2056 Business E-Mail: suzanne.mirra@downstate.edu.

MIRREN, HELEN (ILYNEA LYDIA MIRONOFF), actress; b. London, 1946; d. Basil and Katherine M.; m. Taylor Hackford, Dec. 31, 1997; First appeared with Nat. Youth Theatre; appeared as Cleopatra in Antony and Cleopatra, Old Vic, 1965; joined Royal Shakespeare Co., 1967; appeared as Castiza in The Revenger's Tragedy and Diana in All's Well That Ends Well; other roles include: Cressida in Troilus and Cressida, Royal Shakespeare Co., Stratford, Eng., 1968; Hero in Much Ado About Nothing, Stratford, 1968; Win-the-Fight Littlewit in Bartholomew Fair, Aldwych, 1969; Lady Anne in Richard III, Stratford, Ophelia in Hamlet, Julia in The Two Gentlemen of Verona, Stratford, 1970 (last part also at Aldwych); Tatyana in Enemies, Royal Shakespeare Co., Aldwych, 1971; title role in Miss Julie, Elynae in The Balcony, The Place, 1971; with Peter Brook's Centre Internationale de Recherches Theatrales, Africa and U.S., 1972-73; Lady Macbeth, Royal Shakespeare Co., Stratford, 1974, and Aldwych, 1975; Maggie in Teeth 'n' Smiles, Royal Ct., 1975; Nina in The Seagull and Ella in The Bed Before Yesterday, Lyric for Lyric Theatre Co., 1975, Antony and Cleopatra, The Roaring Girl, Henry VI-Parts 1, 2, 3, 1977-78, Measure for Measure, 1979, The Duchess of Malfi, 1980-81, Faith Healer, 1981, Royal Shakespeare Co., Barbican, 1983, Extremities, 1984, Madame Bovary, 1987, Two Way Mirror, 1988, Sex Please We're Italian, 1991, A Month in the Country, 1994 (Tony nominee - Lead Actress in a Play, 1995); actor (films) Herostratus, 1967, A Midsummer Night's Dream, 1968, Red Hot Shot, 1969, Age of Consent, 1969, Miss Julie, 1972, Savage Messiah, 1972, O Lucky Man!, 1973, Hamlet, 1976, The Quiz Kid, 1979, Caligula, 1979, The Hussy, 1980, The Fiendish Plot of Dr. Fu Manchu, 1980, The Long Good Friday, 1980, Excalibur, 1981, Cal, 1984 (Best Actress award Cannes Film Festival 1984), 2010, 1984, White Nights, 1984, Coming Through, 1985, Heavenly Pursuits, 1985, The Mosquito Coast, 1986, Pascali's Island, 1987, When The Whales Came, 1988, The Cook, The Thief, His Wife, and Her Lover, 1989, Bethune, The Making of a Hero, 1990 The Comfort of Strangers, 1990, Where Angels Fear to Tread, 1991, The Gift, 1991, The Hawk, 1991, The Prince of Jutland, 1991, The Madness of King George, 1994 (Acad. award nominee for Best Supporting Actress), (voice only) The Snow Queen, 1995, Some Mother's Son, 1996, Critical Care, 1997, (voice only) Prince of Egypt, 1998 Teaching Mrs. Tingle, 1998, Greenfingers, 2000, The Pledge, 2001, No Such Thing, 2001, Last Orders, 2001, Gosford Park, 2001, Calendar Girls, 2003, The Clearing, 2004, Raising Helen, 2004, Shadowboxer, 2005, (voice only) The Hitchhiker's Guide to the Galaxy, 2005, The Queen, 2006 (Volpi award for Best Actress, Venice Film Festival, 2006, Best Actress, NY Film Critics Circle award & LA Film Critics Assn., 2006, Best Actress Nat. Bd. Review, 2006, Best Actress Fla. Film Critics Cir., 2006, African-American Film Critics Assn., 2006, Nat. Soc. of Film Critics, 2007, 2006 Best Actress Critics Choice award, Broadcast Film Critics Assn., 2007, Best Performance by an Actress in a Motion Picture-Drama, Golden Globe award, Hollywood Fgn. Press Assn., 2007, Outstanding Performance by Female Actor in a Leading Role & Outstanding Performance by a Female Actor in a TV Movie or Miniseries, SAG, 2007, Actress in a Leading Role, British Acad. Film and TV Arts, 2007, Acad. award best actress in a leading role, 2007); actor, dir. (films) Happy Birthday, 2001; actor (TV movies) Bellamira, 1974, Caesar and Claretta, 1974, The Philanthropist, 1975, The Collection, 1976, As You Like It, 1978, S.O.S. Titanic, 1979, Mrs. Reinhardt, 1981, A Midsummer Night's Dream, 1981, Cymbeline, 1982, Soft Targets, 1982, Faerie Tale Theatre, 1987, Red King White Knight, 1988, Prime Suspect, 1991 (Best Actress award BAFTA 1991), Prime Suspect 2, 1992, (Best Actress award BAFTA 1992), Prime Suspect 3, 1993 (Best Actress award BAFTA 1994), Prime Suspect 4: The Lost Child, 1995 (Emmy award Best Actress 1996), PrimeSuspect 4: Inner Circles, 1995, Prime Suspect 4: Scent of Darkness, 1995, Losing Chase, 1995, Prime-Suspect 5: Errors of Judgment, 1996, The Passion of Ayn Road, 1999, Onthe Edge, 2001, Georgetown, 2002, Door to Door, 2002, The Roman Spring of Mrs. Stone,2003, (voice only) Pride, 2004, Prime Suspect 6: The Last Witness, 2003,(voice only) Pride, 2004, Elizabeth I (Emmy award for Outstanding Lead Actress in a miniseries or movie, 2006, Best Performance by an Actress in a Mini-Series or Motion Picture Made for TV, Golden Globe award, Hollywood Fgn. Press Assn., 2007), 2005, Prime Suspect 7: The Final Act, 2006; actor (miniseries) Cousin Bette, 1971, Oresteia, 1979, Painted Lady, 1997; (TV appearances) Thriller, 1974, Play of the Month, 1974, '75, '77, Play for Today, 1979, '82, The Hidden Room, 1993,Tracey Takes On, 1998, French and Saunders, 1999, Frasier, 2004, Third Watch, 2005; Named Dame Brit. Empire, 2003, recipient Distinction in Theatre award Geffen Playhouse, 2007; Mem. PTO. Office: Internat Creative Mgmt Inc 4-6 Soho Sq London W1D 3PZ England *

MIRRLEES, SIR JAMES ALEXANDER, economics professor; b. Minnigaff, Scotland, July 5, 1936; s. George Barlas MacNab and Nan Lindsay (Purdie) M.; m. Gillian Marjorie Hughes, July 29, 1961 (dec. 1993); children: Catriona, Fiona; m. Patricia Wilson, May 12, 2001. MA, Edinburgh U., Scotland, 1957; BA, Cambridge U., Eng., 1959, PhD, 1963; DLitt (hon.), Warwick U., Eng., 1982, Portsmouth U., 1997, Brunel U., 1997, Edinburgh U., Scotland, 1997, Oxford U., 1998. Lectr. in econ. U. Cambridge, England, 1963-68; Edgeworth prof. econs. U. Oxford, England, 1968-95; prof. polit. economy U. Cambridge, 1995—2003, emeritus prof. polit. economy, 2003—, fellow Trinity Coll., 1995—; disting. prof.-at-large Chinese U. of Hong Kong, 2002—; hon. prof. Peking U.; vis. eminent scholar faculty economics and commerce U. Melbourne, Australia, 2005—. Vis. prof. MIT, 1968, 70, 71, 76, U. Calif., Berkeley, 1986, Yale U., 1989. Co-author: (with Little) Project Appraisal and Planning for Developing Countries, 1974; contbr. articles to profl. publications. Recipient Nobel Prize in Econ. Sciences, 1996; Knighted for contributions to econ. sci., Eng., 1997. Fellow Brit. Acad., Roy. Soc. of Edinburgh, Econometric Soc. (pres. 1983-84); mem. NAS (fgn. mem.), Royal Econ. Soc. (pres. 1989-92), Am. Econ. Assn. (hon.), Am. Acad. Arts and Sci., Assn. Univ. Tchr. Econ. (chmn. 1983-87). Office: Trinity Coll CB2 ITQ Cambridge England Office Phone: +44 1223 339 516, +852 2609 7831.

MIR-SEPASI, M. HOSSEIN, cardiac thoracic surgeon; b. Mar. 12, 1942; BS, Washington U., St. Louis, 1963; MD, The Johns Hopkins Sch. Medicine, Balt., 1967. Chair, cardio thoracic surgery Am. Hosp. Tehran, Iran, 1976—97; chair surgical med. coun. Iranian Med. Inst., Tehran, 1981—97; cardio thoracic surgery Pvt. Practice, 1997—. Fellow: Am. Coll. Cardiology, ACS. Home: 4658 Kilarney Cir Santa Rosa CA 95403

MIRSKI, SARA, real estate developer; B. summa cum laude, U. Minn.; MS Real Estate, NYU Sch. Continuing & Profl. Studies, 2003. Mng. dir. devel. Leviev Boymelgreen Developers, Bklyn., 2003—. Named one of 40 Under 40, Crain's NY Bus., 2007; recipient award, Better Homes & Gardens, 1997. Office: Leviev Boymelgreen 752 Pacific St Brooklyn NY 11238 Office Phone: 718-398-3200. Office Fax: 718-398-3222. E-mail: info@boymelgreendevelopers.com. *

MIRSKY, ARTHUR, retired geologist, educator; b. Phila., Feb. 8, 1927; s. Victor and Dorothy M.; m. Patricia Shorey, Dec. 22, 1961; 1 dau., Alexis Catherine. Student, Bklyn. Coll., 1944, student, 1946—48; BA, U. Calif., 1950; MS, U. Ariz., 1955; PhD, Ohio State U., 1960. Cert. geologist, Ind. Field uranium geologist AEC, S.W. U.S., 1951-53; cons. uranium geologist Albuquerque, 1955-56; asst. dir. Inst. Polar Studies, Ohio State U., 1960-67; adj. asst. prof. geology Ohio State U., 1964-67; from asst. prof. geology to prof. Ind. U.-Purdue U., Indpls., 1967-94, prof. emeritus, 1994—, coord. geology, 1967-69, chmn. dept. geology, 1969-93. Contbr. articles to profl. jours. Served with USN, 1944-46. Mem. AAAS, AAUP, Am. Inst. Profl. Geologists, Geol. Soc. Am., Nat. Assn. Geosci. Tchrs., Am. Geol. Inst., Soc. Sedimentary Geology, Ind. Acad. Sci., Sigma Xi. Office: Indiana U-Purdue U Dept Earth Scis 723 W Michigan St Indianapolis IN 46202-5132 Office Phone: 317-278-0229. E-mail: amirsky@iupui.edu.

MIRVAHABI, FARIN, lawyer; b. Tehran, Iran; d. Ali and Azar Mirvahabi; m. Richard C. Powell; children: Bobby Naemi, Jimmy Naemi. Degree in Law, Tehran U., Iran, 1968; M of Comparative Law, Georgetown U., 1972; LLM, George Washington U., 1976; JSD, NYU, 1978; diploma, The Hague Acad. Internat. Law, 1983. Bar: Va. 1989, U.S. Dist. Ct. (ea. and we. dists.) Va. 1990, D.C. 1990, U.S. Dist. Ct. D.C. 1990, U.S. Supreme Ct. 1997. With Gold & Cutner, NYC, 1979-80; in-house counsel IRA Engring. and Constrn., Tehran, London, 1981-82; legal advisor Bank Markazi, Tehran, 1981-82; practiced law The Hague, The Netherlands, 1982-87; arbitrator Iran Air-Pan Am Arbitration Tribunal, Paris, 1984-87; legal cons. Rooney, Barry & Fogerty, Washington, 1987-88; atty. sole practice, Washington, 1989—. Law prof. No. Va. Law Sch., Alexandria, 1989-90; instr. Paralegal Inst., Arlington, Va., 1988-89; prof. Tehran U., 1982; panelist Am. Arbitration Assn.; guest speaker in field; life dep. gov. Am. Biog. Inst. Rsch. Assn., 19995—. Contbr. numerous articles to profl. jours. Named Maxplank fellow Maxplank Inst. of Internat. Law, 1986; recipient Clyde Eagleton award NYU, 1977, Woman of Yr. medallion honoring Cmty. Svc. and Profl. Achievement, 1995, Spl. Merit award DC Bar, 2005. Mem. ABA, Internat. Bar Assn., Arbitration Forum Inc., D.C. Bar Assn. (panelist client-atty. arbitration bd. 1990—), D.C. Bar & Lawyers Assn., Trial Lawyers Assn., Va. Bar Found., Am. Soc. Internat. Law, Am. Film Inst. The Kennedy Ctr. Avocations: reading, writing, Broadway shows, picnic, swimming. Office: 1629 K St NW Ste 300 Washington DC 20006 Office Phone: 703-534-6677.

MIRVIS, THEODORE NEAL, lawyer; b. Hampton, Va., July 28, 1951; s. Allan and Lena Gelman (Sear) M.; m. Ruth Lynn Tershel, July 1, 1973; children: Jason Stephen, Michelle Beth, Eric Sear. BA summa cum laude, Yeshiva Coll., 1973; JD magna cum laude, Harvard U., 1976. Bar: N.Y. 1978. Law clk. to hon. Henry J. Friendly U.S. Ct. Appeals (2d cir.), NYC, 1976-77; assoc. Wachtell, Lipton, Rosen & Katz, NYC, 1977-82, ptnr., 1982—. Co-author: New York Practice Under CPLR, 1986. Mem.: Tulane Corp. Law Inst. (planning com.), Am. Law Inst. Office: Wachtell Lipton Rosen & Katz 51 W 52nd St Fl 29 New York NY 10019-6150 Office Phone: 212-403-1204. Office Fax: 212-403-2204. Business E-Mail: tnmirvis@wlrk.com.

MIRZA, LEONA LOUSIN, elementary school educator, director; b. Chgo., July 1, 1944; d. Max B. and Opal Lousin; m. David B. Mirza; children: Sara Anush, Elizabeth Ann. BA in Math., North Park Coll., Chgo., 1965; MA in Edn., Western Mich. U., Kalamazoo, 1967, EdD in Edn., 1972; cert. in computer studies, North Park Coll., 1983. Specialist in elem. curriculum and adminstrn. Tchr. Kalamazoo Pub. Schs., 1965-69; prof. math. edn. North Park U., Chgo., 1969-2001, asst. acad. dean, 1999—2001, chair dept. stats., 2004—; dir. Inst. for Internat. and Cultural Studies, 2001—06. Editor The Ill. Math. Tchr., 1992-95; contbr. articles to profl. jours. Chmn. adv. com. on edn. in Ill., 1975-77. Mem. Nat. Coun. Tchrs. Math., Ill. Coun. Tchrs. Math., Ill. Assn. Colls. of Tchr. Edn., Ill. Assn. Tchrs. Edn. in Pvt. Colls. (officer 1974-86). Home: 5241 N Sawyer Ave Chicago IL 60625-4715 Office: 3225 W Foster Ave Chicago IL 60625-4823 Office Phone: 773-244-5731. Business E-Mail: lmirza@northpark.edu.

MIRZA, ZAKIR HUSSAIN, aerospace company consultant; b. Jullundar, India, Dec. 15, 1947; arrived in Can., 1971; came to US, 1977, naturalized, 1984. s. Mohammad Hussain and Kaniz Fatima Mirza; m. Naveeda J. Mirza, Aug. 26, 1977; children: Noreen, Hassan, Nadeem. BSc in Physics/Maths., U. Panjab, Lahore, Pakistan, 1968, MSc in Physics, 1970. Cert. pvt. pilot FAA, in project mgmt. Calif. Inst. Tech. Test engr. Bendix Corp., Windsor, Ont., Can., 1971-79; mgr. instrumentation engring. Nat. Tech. Sys., Saugus, Calif., 1979-82; sr. instrumentation engr. Wyle Labs., Norco, Calif., 1982-84; sr. test engr. Rohr Corp., Chula Vista, Calif., 1984-87; cons. various clients Hughes Space and Comm., El Segundo, Calif.; cons. Ledtronics, Torrance, Calif., Teledyne Continental Motors, Muskegon, Mich., FMC Corp., San Jose, Calif., Stewart and Stevenson, Houston, Thiokol Corp., Brigham City, Utah, 1987—2001; sr. staff engr. Boeing Satellite Devel. Ctr., El Segundo, 2001—. Fellow AIAA (assoc., past chmn. LA chpt.), Inst. Advancement Engring. Dfl. Muslim. Avocations: flying fixed wing aircraft, swimming.

MIRZAIE, IDA A., economics professor; b. Tehran, Iran; PhD, U. Wis., Milw., 1999. Faculty Ohio State U., Columbus, 2000—. Office: Ohio State U 410 Arps Hall 1945 N High St Columbus OH 43210 Business E-Mail: mirzaie.1@osu.edu.

MIRZAKHANI, MARYAM, mathematician; b. Tehran, Iran, May 1977; BS in Math., Sharif U. Tech., Tehran, Iran, 1999; PhD in Math., Harvard U., Cambridge, Mass., 2004. Postdoctoral rschr. dept. math. Harvard U., Cambridge, Mass.; rsch. fellow Clay Math. Inst., Cambridge, Mass., 2004—; asst. prof. math. Princeton U., NJ. Contbr. articles to profl. jours. Named one of Brilliant 10, Popular Sci. mag., 2005. Office: Dept Math Princeton U 904 Fine Hall Princeton NJ 08544 Office Phone: 609-258-4236. E-mail: mmirzakh@princeton.edu. *

MISA, KENNETH FRANKLIN, management consultant; b. Jamaica, NY, Sept. 24, 1939; s. Frank J. and Mary M. (Soszka) M. BS in Psychology cum laude, Purdue U., 1963; PhD in Psychology, St. John's U., 1966. Cert. mgmt. cons.; lic. psychologist, Calif. Staff psychologist Rohrer, Hibler & Replogle, LA, 1966-67; assoc. A.T. Kearney, Inc., LA, 1968-71, sr. assoc., 1972-74, prin., 1975-78, v.p., ptnr., 1979-86; pres. HR Cons. Group, 1987—. Mem. APA, Am. Psychol. Soc., Calif. State Psychol. Assn., Soc. for Human Resources Mgmt., Human Resources Planning Soc., Indsl. Rels. Rsch. Assn., Soc. for Indsl. and Orgnl. Psychology, World Affairs Coun. L.A., Town Hall So. Calif., Glendale C. of C., Jonathan Club. Republican. Roman Catholic. Home: One Bristol Ct Rancho Mirage CA 92270 Office: HR Cons Group 100 N Brand Blvd Ste 200 Glendale CA 91203-2642 Office Phone: 818-241-0060. Home Fax: 323-254-8553. Personal E-mail: kfmhrcg@aol.com.

MISAKIAN, JO ELLEN PRIEST, school librarian, dean; d. Frederick and Velma Priest; m. John L. Misakian, Nov. 3, 1956; children: Johnny Lee, Jeffrey Dale, James Kevin. BS, N.Y. Inst. Tech., NYC, 1992; MLS, San Jose State U., 1993; cert. in tchg., Nat. U., Fresno, Calif., 1994; cert. in libr. media svc., San Jose State U., 1994. Libr. technician Sanger (Calif.) Unified Sch. Dist., 1970—94; libr. media coord. Fresno County Office of Edn., 1994—99; libr. media program dir. Fresno Pacific U., 9999—, interim dean Sch. Edn., 2005—. Mem. adv. bd. Infopeople, Calif., 2002—, Ame Nixon Ctr. for Study of Children's Lit., Fresno, 2002—. Mem. adv. bd.: Tchr. Libr. Jour., 2002—; author: The Essential School Library Glossary, 2004; contbr. articles to profl. jours. Chair Ctrl. Valley Libr. Com., 2000—, Fresno Reads Roundtable, 2001—04; ex-dir. Heartland Regional Libr. Network, 2002—, William Saroyan Soc. Bd., 2006—. Mem.: ALA, Calif. Sch. Libr. Assn. (pres. 2000—01, chair libr. standards task force 2002—04, Profl. Svc. award 2005). Republican. Protestant. Home: 253 N DeWolf Fresno CA 93727 Office: Fresno Pacific Univ Sch Edn 1717 S Chestnut Fresno CA 93702 Office Phone: 559-453-2291. Office Fax: 559-453-7168. Business E-Mail: jmisakian@fresno.edu.

MISCAVIGE, DAVID, head of religious order; b. Phila., 1960; s. Ron and Loretta Miscavige; m. Shelly Barnett, 1981. Mem. Sea Orgn. and Commodore's Messenger Orgn. Ch. of Scientology, 1976, asst. to L. Ron Hubbard; chmn. bd. Religious Tech. Ctr., 1987—. Scientologist. Avocations: photography, snorkeling, motorcycling. Office: Religious Tech Ctr Internat 1710 Ivar Ave, Ste 1100 Los Angeles CA 90028 Office Phone: 323-663-3258. Office Fax: 323-667-0960.

MISCELLA, MARIA DIANA, humanities educator; b. NYC, July 11, 1929; d. Nicola and Giovanna (Tangorra) Torelli; m. Emilio Miscella, Feb. 27, 1954 (dec. Sept. 30, 1996); children: Delia, Marisa, Giuliana. Tchr. Degree, Istituto Magistrale, Lecce, Italy, 1946; postgrad., U. Naples, 1946-48; BA, Hunter Coll., 1954, MA, 1972. Cert. secondary educator NY. English corr. GE Co., Rome, 1950-51; corr. Spanish & French Pettinos Import & Export Co., NYC, 1952-53; tchr. Italian Harrison (N.Y.) H.S., 1967-87, St. John's U., Queens, NY, 1987-89; lectr. Italian various orgsn., NY, 1987—; lectr. Italian lit. and history various colls. and univs., NY, 1987—. Moderator of club Harrison (N.Y.) H.S., 1967-87. Mem. Little Neck (N.Y.) Civic Assn., 1970-95, Am. Assn. Ret. People, Douglaston, N.Y., 1994—; founder, treas. Italian Am. Women's Ctr., 1997—. Recipient scholarship Columbia U., 1954, Letter of Commendation, Bd. Regents, Albany, N.Y., 1980, Cert. Recognition and Gratitude for Contbn. to the Arts and Dedication to Cmty., N.Y.C. Coun., 2004, Spl. Lit. Contest prize The Salt Queen Found., 2005; named Woman of Yr., Consortium of L.I. Italian Am. Orgns., 1992. Mem. AAUW (hostess, v.p. 1990-93, cert. of commendation 1996), Am. Assn. Tchrs. of Italian (sec. Societa Onoraria Italica 1979-91), Ams. Italian Heritage (bd. mem. 1982—, Women of the Yr. 2004), Sons of Italy (John Marino Lodge cultural com. mem 1994—, Merit award 1995), Assn. Italian Am. Educators (dir./historian by-laws com. 2000), N.Y. State United Tchrs., Am. Fedn. Tchrs., Nat. Italian Am. Found., Douglaston Women Club, Retirees Club. Roman Catholic. Avocations: reading, writing, travel, going to theatre, playing bridge.

MISCHEL, WALTER, psychology professor; b. Vienna, 1930; BA in psychology, NYU, 1951; MA in psychology, City Coll. NY, 1953; PhD in psychology, Ohio State U., 1956, DSc (hon.), 1997. Asst. prof., dept. psychology Harvard U., 1958—62, Stanford U., 1962—83; Niven prof. psychology, dept. psychology Columbia U., 1983—. Author: Introduction to Personality, 2004, Personality and Assessment, 1996, numerous other works. Recipient Merit award, Nat. Inst. Mental Health, 1989. Fellow: Am. Psychological Assn. (Disting. Sci. Contribution award 1982), Am. Acad. Arts and Scis.; mem.: NAS. Office: Columbia U 401A Schermerhorn Hall New York NY 10027 Business E-Mail: wm@paradox.psych.columbia.edu.

MISCHKA, JAMES, fashion designer; b. Burlington, Wis., Dec. 23, 1960; BA in Mgmt. and Art Hist., Rice Univ., Houston, 1982; BFA in Fashion Design, Parsons Sch. Design, NYC, 1985. Apprenticeship with Yves St. Laurent, Paris; apprenticeship with Willi Smith NYC, 1985—88; co-founder, ptnr. Badgley Mischka, NYC, 1985—; ptnr. Badgley Mischka Dress, NYC. Named one of Top 10 American Designers, Vogue; recipient Mouton Cadet Young Designers award, 1989, Dallas Internat. Apparel Rising Star award, 1992. Office: 525 7th Ave Fl 18 New York NY 10001-4901 *

MISCHKE, CARL HERBERT, retired religious association executive; b. Hazel, SD, Oct. 27, 1922; s. Emil Gustav and Pauline Alvina (Polzin) M.; m. Gladys Lindloff, July 6, 1947; children: Joel, Susan Mischke Blahnik, Philip, Steven. BA, Northwestern Coll., Watertown, Wis., 1944; M.Div., Wis. Luth. Sem., Mequon, 1947. Ordained to ministry Evang. Lutheran Ch. Parish pastor Wis. Synod, 1947-79; pres. Western Wis. Dist. Evang. Luth. Ch., Juneau, 1964-79; v.p. Wis. Luth. Synod, Milw., 1966-79, pres., 1979-93; retired, 1993. Lutheran.

MISCHKE, FREDERICK CHARLES, retired manufacturing executive; b. Benton Harbor, Mich., Sept. 21, 1930; s. Fred William and Clara Adeline (Ruhno) M.; m. Kathleen Ann Schultz, Nov. 19, 1955 (dec. Aug. 1980); children: Stephanie Ann, Michael Frederick (dec. Oct. 12, 1996), Eric William; m. Lori Ann Leonard, Dec. 23, 1983. AA, Lake Mich. Coll., 1956; BBA, Western Mich. U., 1958. CPA, Ind., Mich. Staff acct. Lybrand, Ross Bros. & Montgomery, Chgo., 1958-63, supr. acctg. Niles, Mich., 1963-65; v.p., treas. Skyline Corp., Elkhart, Ind., 1965-91, ret., 1991. Vol. Svc. Corps. Ret. Execs., 1992-2007, local v.p., 1993-99, treas. 2000-2006; chmn. Meml. Endowment Fund Luth. Ch., 1995-2006. Mem. AICPA, Ind. Assn. CPAs (Civic Achievement award, 1976), Mich. Assn. CPAs, Fin. Execs. Inst. (Michiana chpt. pres. 1974-75), Elcona Country Club (pres. 1975), Rotary (local pres. 1976-77). Republican. Lutheran. Avocations: photography, boating, golf. Home: 23322 Greenleaf Blvd Elkhart IN 46514-4508 Personal E-mail: freddycm@aol.com.

MISE, JESSE SHERDEN, structural engineer, consultant; b. Jonesville, Va., July 13, 1933; s. Clabe Moss and Gladys Elizabeth (Orr) M.; m. Betty Joy Curtiss, July 8, 1984; children: Nancy Miller, Linda Andrews, Doug Hinshaw. BS in Math., Tenn. Tech., 1957. Registered profl. engr., Tenn., Mo. Road designer Va. Dept. Hwys., Petersburg, 1958-64; structural designer various archtl., engring. firms, 1964-67; structural engr. Combustion Engring., Windsor, Conn., 1967-72, Tenn. Eastman, Kingsport, 1973-76, TVA, Knoxville, 1976-87, ABB Environ., Knoxville, 1988-91; cons. Jesse S. Mise, P.E., Knoxville, 1992—; chief engr. James Thomas Engring., Knoxville, 1992—. Author: Engineers Guide to Unusual Opportunities, 1972. Mem. Patriots of East Tenn., Knoxville, 1996—. Mem. ASCE, Nat.

Coun. of Examiners for Engring. and Surveying, 1993—. Home and Office: 5704 Melstone Rd Knoxville TN 37912-4629 Personal E-mail: alt2000tec@aol.com, jessemise@aol.com.

MISELSON, ALEX J. (JACOB MISELSON), portfolio manager, securities analyst, investment theorist; b. NYC, Feb. 23, 1926; s. Aaron and Bertha (Guskin) M. BS in Social Sci. with honors in History, CCNY, 1947; MA in History, Columbia U., 1950; MA in Econs., Queens Coll., 1975. Instr. dept. history CCNY, 1949—55; tchr. Kearny (N.J.) HS, 1955—57, Uniondale HS, LI, NY, 1957—76; reg. rep. Herzfeld and Stern, NYC, 1977—81, Haas Securities Corp., NYC, 1981—83, Fahnestock and Co., NYC, 1983—85, Dominick and Dominick, NYC, 1985; dir. rsch. A.T. Brod and Co., Inc., NYC, 1986—94, Investors Assocs., NYC, 1994—96, Paragon Capital Markets, NYC, 1996—2003, dir. investment strategy, 2000—03; sr. v.p., investment strategist View Trade Securities, Jersey City, 2003—. Instr. econs. Nassau CC, 1969-75; head coach basketball Kearny HS, NJ, 1955-57; asst. coach basketball C.W. Post Coll., Greenvale, L.I., 1958-59; spl. guest TV talk shows; commentator in fin. field, 1988—. Contbr. Dick Davis Digest; contbr. articles to profl. jours., interviewed by talk shows with appearances on host Joe Franklins radio show in NYC, 2000-04. Active LI Coun. for Econ. Edn., Hofstra U., Hempstead, NY, 1968-75. With US Army, 1944-45. Mem. Phi Delta Kappa, Phi Alpha Theta, Phi Beta Kappa. Avocations: reading, writing, theater. Office Phone: 800-839-9706 ext. 208.

MISER, ANN, retired government researcher; b. Balt., Jan. 29, 1935; d. Robert and Lucile Miser; 1 adopted child, Janna. BS in Fine Arts and Edn., U. NC, Chapel Hill, 1956; student, Earlham Coll., Richmond, 1952—54, Johns Hopkins U., Balt., 1960. Art tchr. Md. State Dept. Edn., Balt., 1958—60, NY State Dept. Edn., NYC, 1961—62; owner Lady Baltimore Temporary Agy. and Miss Liberty Inc., London, 1963—75; US govt. rschr. Commerce Dept., Phila., 1975—2005; ret., 2005. Mem.: U. NC Alumni Assn., Multiple Myaloma Soc. Democrat. Mem. Soc. Of Friends. Avocations: travel, reading, sports. Home: 6101 Allwood Ct Baltimore MD 21210

MISHAAN, EMILIO, transplant surgeon, educator; b. Guatemala, Guatemala, Aug. 20, 1960; s. Ezra Mishaan and Ivonne Smeke; 1 child, Isabella. BS, U. del Valle, Guatemala, 1981; MD, U. Francisco Manoquin, Guatemala, 1985. Chief resident surgery Hosp. San Juan de Dios, Guatemala, 1989—90, emergency surgeon, 1992—94; gen. surgeon Hosp. Militar, Guatemala, 1990—99; prof. surgery U. Francisco Marroquin, Guatemala, 1992—; transplant surgeon Hosp. San Juan de Dios, 1994—. CEO Venoclinic, Guatemala, 2001—06, Guatemala Laser Inst. Fellow: ACS, SAGES. Jewish. Avocations: running, hunting, fishing. Home: Km 19 9 Carretera El Salvador Guatemala City Guatemala Office: Gae 3-22 Z10 of 403 CMII Guatemala City Guatemala Personal E-mail: emishaans@yahoo.com

MISHELEVICH, DAVID JACOB, medical products executive; b. Pitts., Jan. 26, 1942; s. Benjamin and Sarah (Bachrach) M.; m. Bonnie Gray McKim, Dec. 6, 1981; 1 child, Cory Jane. BS in Physics, U. Pitts., 1962; MD, Johns Hopkins U., 1966, PhD in Biomed. Engring., 1970. Lic., Md., Tex. Intern in medicine Balt. City Hosps. (now The John Hopkins Bayview Med. Ctr.), 1966-67; active duty USPHS, 1967—69, inactive reserve, 1969—; staff assoc. Nat. Inst. Neurol. Diseases and Stroke, NIH, Bethesda, Md., 1967-69; exec. v.p. Nat. Ednl. Consultants, Balt., 1971-72; prof., dept. chairperson, dir. med. computing resources ctr. U. Tex. Health Sci. Ctr., Dallas, 1972-82; attending physician/sr. attending physician internal med. Dallas County Hosp., Dist. Parkland Meml. Hosp., 1973-82; v.p. computer and software tech. EAN-TECH, Mountain View, Calif., 1983-84; CEO Garden Gate Software, Cupertino, Calif., 1984-86; dir., then v.p. and gen. mgr. applications and rsch. divsn. IntelliCorp, Inc., Mountain View, 1986-89; v.p. mktg. and sales Viewpoint Engring., Mountain View, 1989-90; v.p. engring. AirWays Med. Techs., Inc., Palo Alto, Calif., 1991-93; dir., then v.p. R&D, chief tech. officer Circadian, Inc., San Jose, Calif., 1993-95, v.p., gen. mgr. AirWays Asthma Ctrs. divsn., 1995-96; CEO Sterling Healthcare Outcomes, Inc., Cupertino, 1996—2002, Playa del Rey, Calif., 2002—; founder, exec. v.p., chief tech. officer QENM.com, 1999-2001; chief tech. officer HealthShore, Inc., 2001—04; lead technologist Outbreak! Music Sys., 2002—; chief tech. officer TeleCath, 2003—. Pres. Mishelevich Assocs., Dallas, 1982-83, Cupertino, 1990-91, cons. prof. of neurosurgery Stanford U. Sch. Medicine, 2003-; dir. biomed. engring. and med. affairs Aubrey Group, Inc., Irvine, Calif., 2005—; mem. biomed. libr. rev. com. NIH-Nat. Libr. Medicine, 1978-82; cons. in field. Former tech. reviewer IBM Sys. Jour., Jour. of AMA; rev. IEEE computer Soc. Internet, 2001-03; contbr. numerous articles to profl. jours.; patentee in field. V.p. Dallas chpt. Am. Jewish Congress, 1980-84, Am. Jewish Fund, 1980-81; pres. Westport Bch. Club Villas, Homeowners Assn., 2003-06. Fellow Am. Coll. Med. Informatics; mem. AAAS, IEEE, IEEE Computer Soc. (exec. bd. tech. com. on computational medicine 1981-83), Am. Assn. for Artificial Intelligence, Assn. for Computing Machinery (chair Dallas chpt. 1974-75), Am. Med. Informatics Assn., Internat. Tandem Users Group (past pres.), Model T Ford Club of Am., Am. Radio Relay League (life), Phi Beta Kappa, Omicron Kappa. Democrat. Jewish. Home and Office: 7301 Vista del Mar #B111 Playa Del Rey CA 90293 Office Phone: 310-305-2791. E-mail: david@mishelevich.com. *Working with computers for some forty-five years has made me particularly sensitive to human needs and productivity. Two principles in which I believe are the human resources principle (maximize people's strengths and minimize or neutralize their weaknesses so they perform personally and professionally better than they would otherwise expect of themselves), and the optimality principle (I would rather do a 92% job in two weeks than a 97% job in 2 years).*

MISHKIN, BARBARA FRIEDMAN, lawyer; b. Phila., Feb. 19, 1936; d. Maurice Harold and Gertrude (Sanders) F.; m. Martin S. Thaler, Mar. 22, 1958 (div. 1970); children: Diane Sanders, Paul Sanders, David Emile, Amy Suzanne; m. Mortimer Mishkin, May 27, 1971. AB, Mount Holyoke Coll., 1957; MA, Yale U., 1958; JD, Am. U., 1981. Bar: D.C. 1982, U.S. Supreme Ct. 1989, U.S. Ct. Appeals (4th cir.) 1995. Rsch. psychologist NIMH, Bethesda, Md., 1968-69; spl. asst. to chief judge U.S. Ct. Appeals (D.C. cir.), Washington, 1970-71; spl. asst. to scientific dir. Nat. Inst. Child Health, Bethesda, 1971-74; asst. staff dir. Nat. Commn. for the Protection of Human Subjects, Washington, 1974-78; staff dir. Ethics Adv. Bd. HEW, Washington, 1978-80; dep. dir. Pres.' Commn. on Ethics in Medicine and Rsch., Washington, 1980-83; assoc. Hogan and Hartson, Washington, 1983-89, counsel, 1990-93, ptnr., 1994—2006, of counsel, 2006—. Cons. Ctr. for Law and Health Scis., Boston, 1970-73; cons., lectr. Johns Hopkins U. Sch. of Medicine, Balt., 1971-73; bd. dirs. Bon Secours Health Systems, Inc., Columbia, Md., 1984-90. Contbr. numerous articles on health law, med. ethics and biomed. research to jours. in field. Mem. policy bd. Legal Counsel for the Elderly, Washington, 1984-88, vice chair, 1988-90; trustee Mt. Holyoke Coll., 1985-90; mem. Mayor's Adv. Task Force on Hospice Licensure, Washington, 1985-87; bd. dirs. Hebrew Home Greater Washington, 1987-91. Recipient Lifetime Achievement award, Health Improvement Inst., 2004. Mem. ABA (chair sect. on health and environment 1988-92, chair com. on regulating rsch. 1996-98), D.C. Bar Assn. (subcom. rights of the elderly and the handicapped 1985-92, Pro Bono Atty. Yr. 1988), AAAS (com. on sci. freedom and responsibility 1986-92, AAAS/ABA Nat. Conf. Lawyers and Scientists 1992, ABA co-chair 1993-97), Am. Soc. Law, Medicine and Ethics (bd. dirs. 1995-98). Home: 5610 Wisconsin Ave Apt 402 Chevy Chase MD 20815-4429 Office: Hogan & Hartson Columbia Sq 555 13th St Washington DC 20004-1109 Home Phone: 301-652-0490; Office Phone: 202-637-5680. Business E-Mail: bfmishkin@hhlaw.com.

MISHKIN, FREDERIC STANLEY, federal official, economics educator; b. NYC, Jan. 11, 1951; s. Sidney and Jeanne (Silverstein) M.; m. Sally A. Hammond; children: Matthew, Laura. Student, Oxford U., Eng., 1971-72; BS in Economics, MIT, 1973, PhD in Economics, 1976. Tchg. asst. MIT, 1974—76; asst. prof. U. Chgo., 1976-81, assoc. prof., 1981-83; vis. assoc. prof., dept. economics and dept. fin., Kellogg Grad. Sch. Mgmt. Northwestern U., Evanston, Ill., 1982-83; faculty rsch. fellow Nat. Bur. Econ. Rsch., Cambridge, Mass., 1979—80, rsch. assoc., 1980—; prof. econs. Columbia U. Grad. Sch. Bus., NYC, 1983-91, A. Barton Hepburn prof. econs., 1991—99, Alfred Lerner prof. Banking and Fin. Institutions, 1999—; exec. v.p. and dir. rsch. Fed. Res. Bank NY, NYC, 1994—97; mem. bd. govs. Fed. Res. Sys., Washington, 2006—. Economist, bd. govs., Fed. Res. System, Washington, 1977, acad. cons. bd. govs., 1993, vis. scholar, Divsn. Internat. Fin., bd. govs., 1993; mem. Conf. on Income and Wealth, 1984-; vis. scholar, Inst. for Fiscal and Monetary Policy, Ministry of Fin., Japan, Tokyo, 1986, Res. Bank of Australia, 1994, Bank of Eng., 2001; mem. Brookings Panel on Econ. Activity, Washington, 1977-78; mem. acad. adv. panel Fed. Res. Bank of N.Y., NYC, 1990-94, 1997-, academic cons., 1997-; vis. prof. Princeton U., 1990-91; mem., Ctr. for Latin Am. Economics, Fed. Res. Bank Dallas, 1996-; Harry Johnson Lecture, Money Macroeconomics and Finance Rsch. Group Annual Conf., 1993; hon. prof. Renmin (Peoples) U. China, 1999; Homer Jones Lecture, 2000; Henry George Lecture, Univ. Scranton, 2004; John Kuszczak Meml. Lecture: Bank of Can., 2005; JMCB-FDIC invited lecture, 2005; chmn., External Evalution Com. for Rsch. Activities, Internat. Monetary Fund, 1999; advisor, Inst. Contemporary Fin., Shanghai Jiao Tong U., 2000-, Bank of Korea, Inst. for Monetary and Econ. Rsch., 2005-06; mem. Financial Economists Roundtable, 2001-04; mem. internat. adv. bd., financial supervisory svc., S. Korea, 2000-01; vis. rsch. fellow, The World Bank, 2000-01; sr. fellow, FDIC Ctr. for Banking Rsch., 2003-. Author: A Rational Expectations Approach to Macroeconometrics, 1983, The Economics of Money, Banking and Financial Markets, 1986, 4th edit. 1995, Money, Interest Rates and Inflation, 1993, Financial Markets, Institutions and Money, 1995, also articles; mem. editl. bd. American Economic Review, 1982-85, journal of International Money and Finance, 1992-, Fianance India, 1999-, Ctrl. Bank of Chile Series, Central Banking Analysis, and Economic Policy, 2001-; assoc. editor Journal of Business and Economic Statistics, 1986-93, Journal Applied Econometrics, 1985-2000, Journal Money, Credit and Banking, 1992-, Journal Economic Perspectives, 1994-2004; mem. adv. bd. International Finance, 1997-, Macroeconomics and Monetary Economics Abstracts, 1996-; editor Fed. Res. Bank NY, Economic Policy Review, 1994-97, mem. editl. bd., 1997-. NSF Grad. Fellowship, 1973—76, Alfred P. Sloan Found. Fellowship, 1982—86. Mem. Am. Econ. Assn., Am. Fin. Assn., Ea. Econ. Assn. (v.p., 2002-03, pres.-elect, 2003-04, pres. 2004-05), Phi Beta Kappa, Sigma Xi. Avocations: sailing, cross country skiing, long distance cycling, reading. Office: Fed Res Sys 20th St & Constitution Ave NW Rm 2010 Washington DC 20551 Business E-Mail: fsm3@columbia.edu. *

MISHKIN, MICHAEL LAWRENCE, psychologist, educator; b. Staten Island, NY, Feb. 24, 1951; s. Arthur E. and Arlene Rubinstein Mishkin. BS in Psychology, U. Fla., Gainesville, 1972; MS in Psychology, U. Ala., Birmingham, 1978; EdS in Sch. Psychology, U. Fla., Gainesville, 1981, PhD in Sch. Psychology, 1987. Lic. psychologist Fla., cert. Fla., nat. cert. sch. psychologist. Ednl. diagnostician Marion County Pub. Schs., Ocala, Fla., 1976, 1978—80, sch. psychologist, 1980—; pvt. practice psychologist NCS Counseling and Devel. Ctr., Tavares, Fla., 2005—. Adj. prof. Argosy U., Sarasota, Fla., 2005—. Homeless children's tutor Marion County Pub. Schs., 2002—; mem. leadership coun. Take Stock in Children, Ocala, 1997—; pres. bd. dirs. Cornerstone Sch., Ocala, 1990. Named Student Svcs. Worker of Yr., Marion County Sch. Sys., 1980. Mem.: Internat. Assn. Sch. Psychologists, Nat. Assn. Sch. Psychologists, Fla. Assn. Sch. Psychologists, Marion Counseling Assn. (sec., treas. pres., Sch. Psychologist of Yr. 1986—87). Republican. Jewish. Avocations: reading, games, theater. Home: 2325 SE 19th Cir Ocala FL 34471 Office: Marion County Pub Schs 1517 SE 30th Ave Ste 5 Ocala FL 34471

MISHKIN, MORTIMER, neuropsychologist; b. Fitchburg, Mass., Dec. 13, 1926; AB, Dartmouth Coll., 1946; MA, McGill U., Montreal, Can., 1949, PhD, 1951; DSc (hon.), McGill U., 2004. Asst. in research and physiology and psychiatry Yale U. Med. Sch., New Haven, 1949-51; research assoc. Inst. of Living, Hartford-Conn. and NYU Bellevue Med. Ctr., NYC, 1951-55; research psychologist, sect. on neuropsychology NIMH, Bethesda, Md., 1955-75, research physiologist, Lab. of Neuropsychology, 1976-78, chief sect. cerebral mechanisms Lab. of Neuropsychology, 1979-80, chief Lab. of Neuropsychology, 1980-97, assoc. dir. basic rsch. DIRP, 1994-97, chief sect. cognitive neuroscience, 1997—, acting chief, lab neuropsychology, 2005—. Part-time instr. psychology Howard U., 1956-58; vis. scientist Nencki Inst. Exptl. Biology, Warsaw, Poland, winter 1958, 68, Tokyo Met. Inst. Neuroscis., summer 1978, Oxford U. Dept. Exptl. Psychology, summer 1979, Inst. Child Health U. Coll. London, 1993, vis. prof., 2000-; mem. psychol. scis. panel NIH, 1959-61, exptl. psychology study sect., 1965-69; mem. NIMH Assembly of Scientists Council, 1962-64, 72-74; mem. NIMH Scientist Promotion Rev. Com., 1984-86; mem. adv. com. Cognitive Neurosci. Inst., 1982-86; mem. NIH Fogart Internat. Scholars-in-Residence Adv. Panel, 1985-89, McDonnell Found. Study panel, 1987-89; adv. bd. McDonnell-Pew Program Cognitive Neurosci., 1989-94; cons. Developmental Cognitive Neurosci. Unit, Inst. Child Health, U. Coll. London, 1990—, vis. prof., 2000—; active Human Frontier Sci. Program, 1992-94, chmn. 1993; adv. bd. Ctr. for the Neural Basis of Cognition, U. Pitts. and Carnegie Mellon U., 1994-96, chair, 1999, 2004; adv. bd. La. State U. Neurosci. Ctr., 1994-96, Frontier Rsch. Program, RIKEN, Japan, 1994-96, Zanvyl Krieger Mind-Brain Inst., Johns Hopkins U., 1994-2000, Cognitive and Behavioral Neurosci. Panel, SUNY, Stony Brook, 1996, Mental Health and Neurosci. Clin. Rsch. Ctr., U. N.C., Chapel Hill, 1996-98, Krasnow Inst., George Mason U., Fellow Mentor Program, 1997-2002. Cons. editor Jour. Comparative and Physiol. Psychology, 1963-73, Exptl. Brain Rsch., 1965—, Brain Rsch., 1974-78, Neuropsychologia, 1963-92, Human Neurobiology, 1981-87, Jour. Cognitive Neurosci., 1989—, Jour. NIH Rsch., 1989-97, Cerebral Cortex, 1990-95, Advances in Neurobiology, 1990—, Handbook Behavioral Neurology, 1991—, Current Opinion in Neurobiology, 1991—, Neurobiology of Learning and Memory, 1992—, Learning and Memory, 1993—, Jour. Internat. Neuropsychol. Soc., 1995-99, Internat. Encyclopedia of the Social and Behavioral Scis., 1998-2002; reviewing editors Sci., 1985-93; assoc. editor Neuroreport, 1990-2000; contbr. numerous articles to profl. jours., also abstracts and book revs. Served to lt. (j.g.) USNR. Recipient U.S. Presdl. Disting. Rank award, 1992, Karl Spencer Lashley prize Am. Philos. Soc., 1996, Found. Ipsen Neuronal Plasticity prize, 1995, Med. Rsch. award Met. Life Found., 2000. Fellow AAAS (chair-elect 1990-91, chair 1991-92, past chair 1992-93), APA Assn. (officer, divsn. 6 mem. at large 1964-66, coun. rep. 1967-69, pres. 1968-69, Disting. Scientific Contribution award, 1985); mem. NAS (officer, sect. 52 chmn. 1989-92), Ea. Psychol. Assn., Internat. Brain Research Orgn. (officer, rep.-at-large governing coun. 1993-98), Internat. Neuropsychol. Soc., Internat. Neuropsychol. Symposium, Internat. Primatological Soc., Internat. Soc. Neuroethology, Cognitive Neuroscience Soc. (Hermann von Helmholtz award, 1989) Soc. Exptl. Psychologists (Howard Crosby Warren medal 1998), Soc. Neurosci. (officer, pres.-elect 1985-86, pres. 1986-87, past pres. 1987-88), Inst. Medicine, Brazilian Acad. Sci., Sigma Xi, Phi Beta Kappa. Achievements includes research in behavioral and cognitive neuroscience in primates. Office: NIMH Lab Neuropsychology 49 Convent Dr Msc 4415 Bldg 49 Bethesda MD 20892-0001 Business E-Mail: mishkinm@mail.nih.gov.

MISHKIN, PAUL J., lawyer, educator; b. Trenton, NJ, Jan. 1, 1927; s. Mark Mordecai and Bella (Dworetsky) M.; m. Mildred Brofman Westover. 1 child, Jonathan Mills Westover. AB, Columbia U., 1947, JD, 1950; MA (hon.), U. Pa., 1971. Bar: N.Y. State bar 1950, U.S. Supreme Ct. bar 1958. Mem. faculty Law Sch. U. Pa., Phila., 1950-72; prof. law U. Calif., Berkeley, 1972-75, Emanuel S. Heller prof., 1975—2000, Emanuel S. Heller prof. emeritus, 2000—. Cons. City of Phila., 1953; reporter study div. jurisdiction between state and fed. cts. Am. Law Inst., 1960-65; mem. faculty Salzburg Seminar in Am. Studies, 1974; Charles Inglis Thompson guest prof. U. Colo., 1975; John Randolph Tucker lectr., 1978, Owen J. Roberts Meml. lectr., 1982; vis. fellow Wolfson Coll., Cambridge U., 1984; vis. prof. Duke U. Law Sch., 1989. Author: (with Morris) On Law in Courts, 1965, (with others) Federal Courts and the Federal System, 2d edit, 1973, 3d edit, 1988; contbr. articles to profl. jours. Trustee Jewish Publ. Soc. Am., 1966-75, Ctr. for Law in the Pub. Interest, 2001-04; mem. permanent com. Oliver Wendell Holmes Devise, 1979-87. With USNR 1945-46. Rockefeller Found. rsch. grantee, 1956; Center for Advanced Study in Behavioral Scis. fellow, 1964-65; recipient Russell Prize for Excellence in Teaching, 1996. Fellow Am. Acad. Arts Scis., Am. Bar Found.; mem. Am. Law Inst., Order of Coif, Phi Beta Kappa. Home: 91 Stonewall Rd Berkeley CA 94705-1414 Office: U Calif Sch Law Boalt Hall Berkeley CA 94720 Business E-Mail: pjm@law.berkeley.edu.

MISHLER, CLIFFORD LESLIE, publisher; b. Vandalia, Mich., Aug. 11, 1939; s. Nelson Howard and Lily Mae (Young) M.; m. Sandra Rae Knutson, Dec. 21, 1963 (dec. July 8, 1972); m. Sylvia M. Leer, Feb. 27, 1976; children: Sheila, Sharon, Susan. Student, Northwestern U., 1957-58. Author, pub. ann. edits. Ann. Studies U.S. and Can. Commemorative Medals and Tokens, 1958-63; assoc. editor Numismatic News, Krause Publs., Iola, Wis., 1963-64, editor, 1964-66, numismatic editor all publs., 1966-75, exec. v.p., pub. all numismatic publs., 1975-78, exec. v.p., pub. all products, 1978-88, sr. v.p., pub. all Numismatic products, 1988-89, sr. v.p. ops., 1989-90; pres. Krause Publs., Iola, Wis., 1991-99, chmn. bd. dir., 2000—02, numismatic cons., 2002—05; dir. numismatic devel. Whitman Pub., 2005—. Bd. dirs. First State Bank Iola, 1972-83, Scandinavia Telephone Co., 1981-97, TDS Telecom cmty. bd., 1997-2000; mem. coins and medals adv. panel Am. Revolution Bicentennial Commn., 1970-75; mem. ann. assay commn. U.S. Mint, 1973. Co-author: Standard Catalog of World Coins, ann. 1972-2005; contbr. articles New Book Knowledge, ann. 1969-81. Co-founder Iola Old Car Show, Inc., 1972, ex-officio dir., 1985—2003; mem. Wis. Commemorative Quarter Coun., 2001—03; bd. dirs. William R. Higgins, Jr. Found., 1991—; chmn. fund drive Iola-Scandinavia Cmty. Fitness and Aquatic Ctr., 1999—2001. Recipient The Internat. Vreneli Preistrager: The "Friendly Prize" for lifetime numismatic achievements, Munzen-Revue, Basel, Switzerland, 2001, Numis. Amb. award, Numis. News/Balt., Md., 2003. Fellow Am. Numismatic Soc. (life, coun. mem. 1997-2003, trustee 2003—); mem. Am. Numismatic Assn. (life, bd. govs. 2007—, Merit medal 1983, Farran Zerbe Meml. Disting Svc. award 1984, Glen Smedley meml. dedicated svcs. award 1991, Lifetime Achievement award 1997, named Numismatist of Yr. 2002, named to Hall Fame 2004, Burnett Anderson Meml. award for Excellence in Numismatic writing, 2005), Token and Medal Soc. (life, pres. 1976-78, editor jour. 1964-68, Disting. Svc. award 1966, 80), Numismatists of Wis. (life, pres. 1974-76, Meritorious Svc. award 1972), Soc. Internat. Numismatics (award of excellence 1981), Blue Ridge Numismatic Assn. (life, hall of fame 1994), Tex. Numismatic Assn. (life, hall of fame 1993), Ind. State Numismatic Assn. (life, founders award 1993), Ctrl. States Numismatic Soc. (life, medal of merit 1984), Iola Lions (Melvin Jones fellow 1996). Home: 100 Island Dr Iola WI 54945-9485 Office: 105 N Main St Iola WI 54945-0001 Office Phone: 715-445-5050. Personal E-mail: mish@athenet.net.

MISHLER, JOHN MILTON (YOCHANAN MENASHSHEH BEN SHAUL), science educator, artist; b. Cairo, Ill., Sept. 25, 1946; s. John Milton and Mary Jane (Woodbury) Mishler; m. Mary Therese Stember, Apr. 15, 1972 (div. Nov. 1981); m. Sigrid Ruth Elizabeth Fischer, Dec. 15, 1981; 1 child, Joshua Evan. AA with honors, Orange Coast Coll., Costa Mesa, Calif., 1966; AB in Molecular Biology, U. Calif., San Diego, 1969, ScM in Engring. Scis., 1971; DPhil in Immunohematology, St. John's Coll., Oxford U., 1978. Cert. cmty. coll. instr. Calif. Clin. coord. McGaw Labs., Costa Mesa, 1972-78; rsch. fellow Royal Postgrad. Med. Sch., Eng., 1977-78, Med. U., Cologne, Fed. Republic Germany, 1978-80; br. chief Nat. Heart, Lung and Blood Inst. NIH, Bethesda, Md., 1980-82; prof. med., basic life scis. and pharmacol. U. Mo., Kansas City, 1983-89, asst. vice chancellor, 1983-85, dir. div. basic med. scis., 1985-86, assoc. vice chancellor, 1985-89; prof. nat. scis. U. Md. Ea. Shore, Princess Anne, 1989-94, dean grad. studies and rsch., 1989-91; prof. biology Delaware Valley Coll. Sci. and Agrl., Doylestown, Pa., 1994—, dean of Coll., 1994-95. Frequent nat. and internat. lectr.; chmn. 13 nat. and internat. meeting sects. Author: Pharmacology of Hydroxyethyl Starch. Use in Therapy and Blood Banking, 1982; mem. editl. bd. Jour. Soc. Rsch. Adminstrs., 1987-91; book rev. editor Grants Mag., 1987-89; contbr. over 100 articles to profl. jours. Bd. dirs. Ctr. for Bus. Innovation, Inc., 1987, Bucks Assn. for Retarded Citizens, 1995-96; v.p. Artsbridge, 1999-2000. Sr. rsch. fellow Alexander von Humboldt Foun. (Germany), 1978-80; recipient Outstanding Adminstrn. Svc. award U. Mo., Kansas City, 1987, Excellence award Soc. Rsch. Adminstrn., 1989, Cert. Appreciation, 1991, Silver and Bronze awards Artist Guild of Delaware Valley, 1998, Second prize Chester County Art Assn., 1998, Bd. Dirs. award Gtr. Norristown Art League, 1998, Award of Merit Westmoreland Art Nats., 1998, Perkins Ctr. for Arts, 2000, Robert Ransley Outstanding Talent award, 1999, 2d prize drawing Ctr. for the Creative Arts, 1999, 1st prize graphics Perkiomen Valley Art Ctr., 1999, 2d prize, 2002, Wayne Art Supply award Wayne Art Ctr., 2002, Pres.'s award Salmagundi Club, 2002, Best of Show/1st Pl. award Louisville Art Assn., 2003, Jerry's Artarama award Montana Watercolor Soc., 2003, honorable mention Associated Artists Southport, 2004, Franklin Square Gallery, 2004, hon. mention Taos Nat. Watercolor Soc., 2004, Winston Churchill award Mo. Watercolor Soc., 2005, Ursus Abstract award Tubac Ctr. of Arts, 2006, 3rd prize Conneaut Cmty. Ctr. for Arts, 2006. Fellow Internat. Soc. Haematology, Royal Coll. Pathologists; mem. Am. Soc. Hematology, German Soc. Hematology, Nat. Coun. Univ. Rsch. Adminstrn., Nat. Assn. State Univs. and Land-Grant Colls. (mem. exec. com. coun. on rsch. policy and grad. edn. 1990-91), Coun. Grad. Schs., N.Y. Acad. Scis., Sigma Xi. Jewish. Avocations: reading, abstract art painting, writing, music. Home: 475 North St Apt 6F Doylestown PA 18901-3863 Office: Delaware Valley Coll 700 E Butler Ave Doylestown PA 18901-2607 Office Phone: 215-489-2351. Business E-Mail: mishlerj@devalcol.edu.

MISIOROWSKI, ELISE BESSON, museum director; b. NYC, Jan. 17, 1947; d. John Case Besson and Louise Katrina Foot; m. Robert Alan Misiorowski, June 10, 1966; 1 child, Rebecca Alexis. Student, Knox Coll., 1966; diploma in gemology, Gemol. Inst. Am., 1981. Diamond grader Gemol. Inst. Am. Gem Trade Lab., Santa Monica, Calif., 1979—82; rsch. libr. Gemol. Inst. Am. Libr., Santa Monica, 1984—97; mus. dir. Gemol. Inst. Am. Mus., Carlsbad, Calif., 2001—. Faculty Antique, Period Jewelry and Gem Conf., Maine, 1994, Maine, 98, RI, 97, RI, 99; lectr. Gemol. Inst. Am. Alumni Assn., Basel, Switzerland, 1998, Hong Kong, 99. Contbr. articles to profl. jours., column to Profl. Jeweler's Mag. Vol. Peace Corps, Honduras, 1966—69. Mem.: Am. Soc. Jewelry Historians, Soc. Jewellery Historians, Women's Jewelry Assn. Democrat. Episcopalian. Avocations: jewelry fabrication, pearl stringing, crocheting, book collecting. Office: Gemological Inst Am Robert Mollawad Campus 5345 Armada Dr Carlsbad CA 92008 Office Phone: 760-603-4073.

MISKIMEN, THERESA MARIE, psychiatrist, educator; b. Mayaguez, P.R., Sept. 5, 1964; d. George William and Carmen M. (Rivera) M.; m. Juan Carlos Ortiz. BS in Biology magna cum laude, U. P.R., 1986, MD, 1990. Diplomate Am. Bd. Psychiatry and Neurology. Instr. psychiatry U. Medicine and Dentistry N.J., Newark, 1994-97, asst. prof. psychiatry, 1997—2000; assoc. prof. psychiatry RWJ Med. Sch., Piscataway, 2000—. Mem. pharmacy and therapeutic com. U. Medicine and Dentistry U. Hosp., Newark, 1995-99; lectr. Acad. Medicine N.J., Princeton, 1999-; med. dir., acute inpatient unit, UBHC, 2004-, v.p., med. svcs., 2006-. Resident column editor N.J. Psychiat. News, 1993. Active Nat. Hispanic Mentor Recruitment Network, Interamerican Coll. Physicians and Surgeons, Newark, 1996-99. Am. Assn. Med. Colls. fellow, 1997. Fellow Am. Psychiat. Assn. (disting., chairperson early career psychiatry com. 1997-98); mem. N.J. Psychiat. Assn. (treas. 2004-06, v.p. 2006-), Beta Beta Beta. Business E-Mail: miskimtm@umdnj.edu.

MISKUS, MICHAEL ANTHONY, electrical engineer; b. East Chicago, Ind., Dec. 10, 1950; s. Paul and Josephine Miskus. BS, Purdue U., 1972, AAS in Elec. Engring. Tech., 1972; cert. mgmt., Ind. U., 1972, Ind. Ctrl. Coll., 1974; MA in Orgnl. Mgmt., U. Phoenix, 1996, postgrad., 1997; PhD in Orgnl. Behavior, Columbia U., 1998. Cert. plant engr. IIPFE; registered environ. assessor REA, Calif. Svc. engr. Reliance Electric & Engring. Co., Hammond, Ind., 1972-73; maintenance supr., maintenance mgr. Diamond Chain Co./AMSTED Industries, Indpls., 1973-76; primary and facilities elec. engr. Johnson & Johnson Baby Products Co., Park Forest South, Ill., 1976-81; prin. Miskus Cons., indsl./comml. elec. cons., 1979—; plant and facilities engring. mgr. Sherwin Williams Co., Chgo. Emulsion Plant, 1981-85; with Miscon Assocs., Riverside, Calif., 1985—; acting dir. plant and facilities engring. Bourns Inc., 1982-90; facility mgr. Cardiovascular Devices Inc., 3M Healthcare, 1990—; mgr. Metrology and Corp. Metrology Lab. & ISO 9000, 3M, St. Paul; facilities ops. mgr. Press Enterprise, Riverside, 1997-2001; dir. facilities and plant engring. Shell Solar Industries LP, Camarillo, Calif., 2001—; project mgr. Devel. mktg. svcs. tng. sales tools Siemens, Power Conversion Divsn., NYC, 2002—. Instr., lectr. EET program Moraine Valley CC, Palos Hills, Ill., 1979; instr. cert. program plant engring. U. Calif.; lectr. energy engring., bldg. automation sys. Prairie State Coll., Chicago Heights, Ill., 1980—; mem. adj. faculty, faculty adv. bd. Orange Coast Coll., Costa Mesa, Calif.; bd. dirs., v.p. adminstrn. Internat. Inst. Plant & Facilities Engring.; commr., chmn. Riverside Energy Commn., 1988—; mem. Elec. Industry Evaluation Panel; siemens project mgr. Siemens Energy and Automation LD Motors, 2002—; chief cons. Miscon Cons. Productivity, Improvement Sys. Self Elec. Use Sys. Author: (text) The New Business Society. Mem. faculty adv. bd. Moraine Valley CC, 1980—. Mem. IEEE, Am. Inst. Plant Engrs. (pres. Pomona chpt. 1989—, chmn. western region VI membership, chmn. nat. coun. stds. labs. region II Twin Cities sect. 1995—), Assn. Facility Engrs. (pres. Inland Empire chpt. III 1997—), Assn. Energy Engrs. (sr., So. Calif. chpt.), Assn. Profl. Energy Mgrs. (bd. dirs. Orange County chpt. 1992), Internat. Inst. Plant and Facilities Engring. (dir. tech. 1999—), Illuminating Engring. Soc. N.Am., Internat. Platform Assn., Riverside C. of C., Purdue Alumni Orgn. LA (v.p. Inland chpt.), Purdue Club LA (v.p. Inland Empire sect.). Personal E-mail: columbia303@yahoo.com, jakeyboy@ez2.net.

MISLOW, KURT MARTIN, chemist, educator; b. Berlin, June 5, 1923; came to U.S., 1940, naturalized, 1946; s. Max and Ida (Bingen) M.; m. Jacqueline Ford, 1966; children: Christopher, John. BS, Tulane U., 1944, DSc (hon.), 1975; PhD, Calif. Inst. Tech., 1947; Doctorate (hon.), Free U., Brussels, 1974, Uppsala U., 1977, Düsseldorf U., 1994, Zurich U., 2004. Instr. NYU, 1947-51, asst. prof., 1951-56, asso. prof., 1956-60, prof., 1960-64; Hugh Stott Taylor prof. chemistry Princeton, 1964-88, chmn. dept. chemistry, 1968-74, prof. emeritus, 1988—. Vis. prof. Stanford U., 1960, Calif. Inst. Tech., 1994; M.S. Kharasch vis. prof. U. Chgo., 1989; Univ. lectr. U. London, 1965; J.A. McRae Meml. lectr. Queen's U., 1967; H.A. Iddles lectr. U. N.H., 1972; Solvay lectr. and medalist Free U. Brussels, 1972; E.C. Lee lectr. U. Chgo.; A.A. Vernon lectr. Northeastern U., 1976; PPG lectr. Ohio U., 1977; J. Musher Meml. lectr. Hebrew U. Jerusalem, 1978; North Country lectr., 1978; Honor lectr. Ariz. State U., 1981; E. Ritchie meml. lectr. Sydney U., 1983; Fuson lectr. U. Nev., 1983; Research Scholar lectr. Drew U., 1983; McGregory lectr. Colgate U., 1984; Sandia lectr. U. Alta., 1984; Purves lectr. McGill U., 1985; Arnold lectr. So. Ill. U., 1985; Bergmann lectr. Yale U., 1986; H.C. Brown lectr. Purdue U., 1988; Irvine lectr. U. St. Andrews, 1988; Eyring lectr. Ariz. State U., 1989; Disting. Scientist lectr. Bard Coll., 1991; Syntex Disting. lectr. Colo. State U., 1991; Disting. scientist lectr. Bard Coll., 1991; J.W.T. Spinks lectr. U. Saskatchewan, 1992; Bristol-Myers-Squibb disting. lectr. Syracuse U., 1992; Churchill fellow Cambridge U., 1974-75; mem. adv. panel chemistry NSF, 1963-66; mem. panel medical and organic chemistry NIH, 1963-66. Author: Introduction to Stereochemistry, 1965; also numerous articles; bd. editors: Jour. Organic Chemistry, 1965-70; mem. editl. adv. bd. Monatshefte für Chemie, Topics in Stereochemistry, Accounts of Chem. Rsch., Chem. and Engring. News, Bull des Sociétés Chimiques Belges, Symmetry, Jour. Math. Chemistry. Recipient Solvay medal Free U. Brussels, 1972, Prelog medal, ETH Zurich, 1986, W.H. Nichols medal, 1987, Sci. Achievement award medal CCNY, 1988, Disting. Alumni award Calif. Inst. Tech., 1990, Chirality medal, 1993, Sesquicentennial medal Tulane U., 1997, Arthur C. Cope Scholar award Am. Chem. Soc. 1995; Guggenheim fellow, 1957-58, 74-75, Alfred P. Sloan fellow, 1959-63, Sherman Fairchild disting. scholar Calif. Inst. Tech., 1990, 91, 94. Fellow AAAS, Am. Acad. Arts and Scis.; mem. NAS, AAUP, Am. Chem. Soc. (James Flack Norris award 1975), Academia Nazionale dei Lincei (fgn. mem.), Phi Beta Kappa, Sigma Xi. Personal E-mail: kmislow@princeton.edu.

MISNER, CHARLES WILLIAM, physics professor; b. Jackson, Mich., June 13, 1932; s. Francis deSales and Madge B. (Mee) M.; m. Susanne Elisabeth Kemp, June 13, 1959; children: Benedicte Elisabeth, Francis Frithjof, Timothy Charles, Christopher Kemp. BS, U. Notre Dame, 1952; MA, Princeton U., 1954, PhD, 1957. Instr. Princeton U., NJ, 1956-59, asst. prof. NJ, 1959-63; assoc. prof. physics U. Md., College Park, 1963-66, prof., 1966-2000, assoc. chair physics dept., 1995-99, prof. emeritus, sr. rsch. scientist, 2000—. Vis. fellow Inst. for Theoretical Physics, U. Calif., Santa Barbara, 1980-81, All Souls Coll., Oxford, Eng., 1973, Max Planck-Albert Einstein Inst., Potsdam, Germany, 2000, 02, 05; vis. faculty Calif. Inst. Tech., 1972, Princeton U., 1969 Author: (with Wheeler and Thorne) Gravitation, 1973, (with Patrick J.Cooney) Spreadsheet Physics, 1991; contbr. articles to profl. jours. Recipient Sci. Centennial award U. Notre Dame, 1965, Dannie Heineman prize (with R. Arnowitt and S. Deser) for math. physics Am. Phys. Soc., 1994; NSF sr. postdoctoral fellow, 1966-67; Guggenheim fellow, 1972-73; Einstein Centennial lectr., 1979. Fellow Am. Phys. Soc., Royal Astron. Soc., Am. Acad. Arts and Scis., Am. Assn. Advancement Sci; mem. Philosophy of Sci. Assn., Am. Math. Soc. Fedn. Am. Scientists. Democrat. Roman Catholic. Office: U Md Dept Physics College Park MD 20742-4111 E-mail: misner@physics.umd.edu.

MISNER, CHARLOTTE BLANCHE RUCKMAN, retired community organization administrator; b. Gifford, Idaho, Aug. 30, 1937; d. Richard Steele and Arizona (Hill) Ruckman; m. G. Arthur Misner, Jr., Aug. 29, 1959; children: Michelle, Mary, Jennifer. BS in Psychology, U. Idaho, 1959. Vol. numerous orgns., India, Mexico, The Philippines, 1962-70; sec., v.p., pres., trustee St. Luke's Hosp., Manila, 1970-84; founding mem., 3d v.p., pres. Am. Women's Club of Philippines, 1980-84; exec. dir. Friends of Oakland (Calif.) Parks and Recreation, 1986-2000, ret., 2000. Active Lincoln Child Ctr., Oakland, 1984—. Recipient Vol. Svc. award Women's Bd. St. Luke's Hosp., 1977, Mid. Sch. Vol. award Internat. Sch.-Manila, 1980. Me. Alpha Gamma Delta (alumnae treas., pres. East Bay 1985-89, province dir. alumnae 1989-98, bd. dirs. alumni devel. 1998-2005, mem. steering com. centennial capital campaign 1999—), Cum Laude Soc. (hon.).

MISNER, JEFFREY J., air transportation executive; b. 1954; married; 3 children. BA, San Deigo State Univ. With Kenneth Leventhal and Co., Newport, Calif., 1979—81; tax & bus. cons. Ernst & Young, Orange County, Calif., 1981—91; v.p. treas. ops. Continental Airlines Inc., Houston, Utah, 1995—2000, sr. v.p., CFO, 2001—04, exec. v.p., CFO, 2004—. With USMC, 1971—75. Office: Continental Airlines Inc PO Box 4607 Houston TX 77210-4607 *

MISRA, RAGHUNATH PRASAD, physician, educator; b. Calcutta, West. Bengal, India, Feb. 1, 1928; came to U.S., 1964; s. Guru Prasad and Anandi M.; m. Therese Rettenmund, Sept. 13, 1963; children: Sima, Joya, Maya, Tara. BSc honors, Calcutta U., 1948; MBBS, Med. Coll., Calcutta, 1953; PhD, McGill U., Montreal, Que., 1965. Diplomate Am. Bd. Anat. and Clin. Pathology. Asst. prof., dir. kidney lab. U. Louisville Sch. Medicine, 1964—68; assoc. investigator and dir. kidney lab Mt. Sinai Hosp., Cleve., 1968—73; asst. prof. Case We. Res. Med. Sch., Cleve., 1973—76; asst. prof., dir. kidney lab. Sch. Medicine La. State U., Shreveport, 1976—80, assoc. prof. Sch. Medicine, 1990—96, prof. Sch. Medicine, 1986—98, emeritus prof. Sch. Medicine, 1998—. Cons. VA Med. Ctr., Shreveport, 1977-98, EA Conway Meml. Hosp., Monroe, La., 1980-98; dir. Ocular Pathology Lab. Sch. Medicine La. State U., Shreveport, 1988— Author: Atlas of Skin Biopsy, 1983 Pres. India Assn. of Shreveport, 1979, 81 Tallisman fellow Mt. Sinai Hosp., 1970-73. Fellow Am. Coll. Pathologists, Am. Soc. Clin. Pathologists, Am. Coll. Internat. Physicians, U. Calcutta Med. Alumni Assn. Am. (pres. 1992-93), Sigma Xi (pres. 1987-89) Democrat. Hindu. Avocations: photography, travel. Office: La State U Sch Medicine 1501 Kings Hwy Shreveport LA 71103-4228 Home Phone: 318-865-9092; Office Phone: 318-675-5012. Business E-Mail: rmisra@lsuhsc.edu.

MISRACH, RICHARD LAURENCE, photographer; b. LA, July 11, 1949; s. Robert Laskin and Lucille (Gardner) M.; m. Debra Bloomfield, Jan. 18, 1981 (div. 1987); 1 son, Jacob Luke; m. Myriam Weisang, Apr. 17, 1989. AB in Psychology, U. Calif., Berkeley, 1971. Instr. Assoc. Students Studio, U. Calif., Berkeley, 1971-77; vis. lectr. U. Calif.-Berkeley, 1982; lectr. U. Calif.-Santa Barbara, 1984. Juror Nat. Endowment Arts, 1986; lectr. Calif. Inst. for Arts, 1990. Exhbns. include Whitney Biennial, 1981, 91, Musée d'Art Moderne, Paris, 1979, Mus. Modern Art, N.Y.C., 1978, Grapestake Gallery, San Francisco, 1979, 81, Young-Hoffman Gallery, Chgo., 1980, Oakland Mus., 1982, 87, San Franciso Mus. Modern Art, 1983, Centre Georges Pompidou, Paris, 1983, L.A. County Mus. Art, 1984, Fraenkel Gallery, San Francsico, 1985, 89, 91, 95, 97, 99, Min Gallery, Tokyo, 1975-87, Univ. Art Mus., Berkeley, Curt Marcus Gallery, 1995, 96, 97, 2000, James Danziger Gallery, 1995, Robert Mann Gallery, N.Y., 1999, Melbourne Internat. Festival, Australia, 1995, G. Gibson Gallery, 2000, High Mus. Art, Atlanta, 2000, Froenhel Gallery, 2002, 04, 06, Grant/Selwyn Fine art, 2003, Pace MacGill Chelsea, 2004, 06, Marc Selwyn Fine Art, 2005, others; one person exhbns. at Art Inst. Chgo., 1988, Milw. Art Mus., 1988, Carpenter Ctr., Harvard U., 1988, Fotomann, Inc., N.Y., 1989, 91, Photographers Gallery, 1990, Parco Gallery, Tokyo, 1990, Arles Festival, France, 1990, Jan Kesner Gallery, 1990, 91, 94, 2000, Houston Mus. Fine Arts, 1996, Ctr. Creative Photography, Tucson, 1996, Mus. Contemporary Art, Chgo., 1997, Contemporary Mus. of Art Art, Hawaii, 1997, San Jose Mus. of Art, 1998, Diputacion de Granada, Spain, 1999; art commn. cover Time mag., July 4, 1988; books include Telegraph 3 A.M., 1974, Grapestake Gallery, 1979, (A Photographic Book), 1979, Hawaii portfolio, 1980, Graecism dye-transfer portfolio, 1982, Desert Cantos, 1987, (Internat. Ctr. of Photography award 1988), Bravo 20: The Bombing of the American West, 1990 (Pen Ctr. U.S. A. West award for nonfiction 1991), Richard Misrach, Minn. Gallery, 1988, Violent Legacies, Aperture, 1992, Crimes and Splendors, 1996, Cantos del Desierto, Di putacion de Granada, 1999, The Sky Book, 2000, Richard Misrach: Golden Gate, 2001, Pictures of Paintings, 2002, Chronologies, 2005. Guggenheim fellow, 1978; Ferguson grantee, 1976; NEA grantee, 1973, 77, 84, 92; AT&T comm., 1979; Eureka fellow, 1991; recipient Koret Israel prize, 1992. *Photographs are the shadows of reality much like dreams. On the one hand, they appear to literally transcribe the real world, while on the other, they defy our linear concept of time and meaning. Because the primary illusion of photography is fact, it is the most powerful art medium of our time.*

MISSAN, RICHARD SHERMAN, lawyer, educator; b. Oct. 5, 1933; s. Albert and Hannah (Hochberg) Missan; m. Aileen Louise Missan; children: Hilary, Andrew, Wendy. BA, Yale U., 1955, JD, 1958. Bar: NY 59, US Dist. Ct. (so. and ea. dists.) NY 79, US Ct. Appeals (2d cir.) 93. Assoc. Kaye, Scholer, Fierman, Hays & Handler, NYC, 1962—67; ptnr. Schoenfeld & Jacobs, NYC, 1968—78, Walsh & Frisch, NYC, 1979—80, Gersten, Savage & Kaplowitz, NYC, 1980—87; v.p., gen. counsel Avis, Inc., 1987—88; pvt. practice NYC, 1988—. Spl. prof. law Hofstra U., 1988—; mem. panel mediators U.S. Dist. Ct. (ea. dist.) NY, 1997—, U.S. Bankruptcy Ct. (so. dist. NY), 2003—. Revision author: Corporations, New York Practice Guide (Business and Commercial). Mem.: ABA, Assn. Bar City NY (mem. com. corrections, chmn. subcom. legis., chmn. subcom. juvenile facilities, mem. com. atomic energy, mem. com. mcpl. affairs, mem. com. housing urban devel.), Fed. Bar Coun., NY State Bar Assn., Yale Club.

MISSAR, CHARLES DONALD, retired librarian; b. Cleve., July 16, 1925; s. Charles Frank and Genevieve Catherine (Buechele) M.; m. Margaret Mary du Fief, Feb. 17, 1962 (dec.); children: Charles David, Stephen du Fief. Student, Sacred Heart Sem., Detroit, 1943-45, St. Mary's Sem., Cleve., 1945-49; BA, John Carroll U., 1951; MLS, Cath. U. Am., 1960. Referral specialist Libr. of Congress, Washington, 1963-66; ERIC info. specialist U.S. Office Edn., Washington, 1966-72; head Ednl. Reference Ctr. Nat. Inst. Edn., Washington, 1973-78, supervisory libr., 1978-85; sr. libr. U.S. Dept. Edn., 1985-86; sr. editor Computer Scis. Corp. Profl. Svcs. Group, 1986-94, Missar Assocs., Washington, 1994—2001. Agy. rep. Fed. Libr. Com., Washington, 1978-86; ann. lectr. Fed. Libr. Resources Workshop, Catholic U. Am., Washington, 1981-96. Editor: Management of Federally Sponsored Libraries: Case Studies and Analysis, 1995; compiler, author: A Checklist of Ohio Imprints From 1821 to 1825, 1960; editor monthly jour. Tech. Abstract Bull., 1958-60; mem. editl. bd. Online Mag., 1977-80 Bd. dirs. Shrine of the Most Blessed Sacrament St. Pius X Libr., 1995—. Recipient Superior Svc. Group award U.S. Office Edn., 1968, Superior Performance award Nat. Inst. Edn., 1974, 84; inductee Spl. Libraries Assn. Hall of Fame, 1991. Mem. ALA, D.C. Libr. Assn. (treas. 1972-74), Spl. Librs. Assn. (chmn. edn. divsn. 1980-81, chmn. 1989-90), Am. Soc. Info. Sci. (chmn. info. svcs. for edn. group 1984-86), John Carroll Soc., Cleve. Club, Serra Club (pres. 1992-93, 94-96), Arimathean Club, Ohio Soc., Cosmos Club. Roman Catholic. Home: 5617 32nd St NW Washington DC 20015-1622 Personal E-mail: cdmissar@aol.com.

MISSETT, JUDI SHEPPARD, dancer, jazzercise company executive; b. Iowa; BA in Theater, Radio/TV, Northwestern U., Chgo., 1966. Profl. dancer, Chgo., 1966-77; jazzercise instr., choreographer, tchr. Calif., 1977—; pres. worldwide dance-fitness franchise orgn. Jazzercise, Inc., Carlsbad, Calif.; prin. JM TV Prodns.; prin. mail-order catalog bus. Jazzertogs. Instr. convs., children's fitness progs. Author: (comprehensive nutrition prog.) The Jazzercise Know More Diet; author weekly fitness column for Los Angeles Times Syndicate; performer, prodr. home exercise videos. Mem. Calif. Gov.'s Coun. on Phys. Fitness & Sports; bd. dirs. San Diego Inner-City Games; contbr. millions of dollars for charities by leading spl., large-scale workout classes. Recognized for contbns. to growth and advancement of fitness industry by Pres. Reagan in his White House Conf. on Women in Bus., 1986, Aerobics and Fitness Assn. Am., Am. Coun. on Exercise, Pres.' Coun. on Phys. Fitness & Sports; named Entrepreneur of Year, Working Woman Mag., 1988; recipient Lifetime Achievement award Internat. Assn. Fitness Profls., 1991, Women Who Mean Bus. award San Diego Bus. Jour., 1995, A Woman of Accomplishment award Soroptimist Internat. of San Diego, 1996; inducted into Internat. Assn. Fitness Profls. Hall of Fame, 1992. Mem. Nat. Fitness Leaders Assn. (exec. dir., Charles Bucher Meml. award 1996). Office: Jazzercise Inc 2460 Impala Dr Carlsbad CA 92008-7226

MISSIMER, THOMAS MICHAEL, geologist; b. Lancaster, Pa., Mar. 10, 1950; s. Jacob M. and Lorraine L. (Bilodeau) M. AB in Geology, Franklin and Marshall Coll., 1972; MS in Geology, Fla. State U., 1973; PhD in Marine Geology and Geophysics, U. Miami, Fla., 1995. Registered profl. geologist, Fla., Ga., Ind., Va., Tex. Hydrologist U.S. Geol. Survey, Ft. Myers, Fla., 1973-75; rsch. assoc. sedimentology U. Miami, Coral Gables, 1975-76; pres. Missimer & Assocs., Inc., Cape Coral, Fla., 1976-92; vice chmn. ViroGroup, Inc., Cape Coral, 1991-93; pres. CDM Missimer, Ft. Myers, 1993-99; v.p. Camp, Dresser & McKee, Inc., Ft. Myers, 1994—2004, CDM Missimer, Ft. Myers, 1999—2004; pres. Missimer Groundwater Sci., Inc., Ft. Myers, 2004—07; v.p. Schlumberger Water Svcs. USA, Inc., 2007—. Mem. Bd. Fla. Profl. Geologists, 1991-97, avice chmn., 1993, chmn., 1994; apptd. by Gov. J. Bush to the Fla. Forever Adv. Coun., 1999—2003; mem. tech. adv. com. Gov.'s Com. for a Substantial South Fla., 1995-98, chmn., 1996-98. Author Water supply development for membrane water treatment facilities, 1994, Lender's Guide to environmental liability management, 1996; contbr. articles to profl. jours. Mem. citizens planning adv. com. Bd. Lee County (Fla.), 1981-82, chmn., 1982-83. Recipient Best Paper award, Internat. Desalination Assn., D.C. World Conf. on Desalination, 1991, Acad. Merit award U. Miami, 1997, Thomas A. Philpolt Excellence Presentation award, Gulf Coast Assn. Geol. Sci., 2004. Mem. Geol. Soc. Am., Am. Inst. Profl. Geologists (cert. profl. geol. scienitst), Am. Water Resources Assn., Am. Water Works Assn., AAAS, Am. Inst. Hydrology (cert. profl. hydrogeologist), Am. Groundwater Assn. (cert. Hydrogeologist), Fla. Acad. Scis. (chmn. earth and planetary sci. sect. 1973-74, 95), Internat. Desalination Assn., Southeastern Geol. Soc., S.E. Desalting Assn. (bd. dirs. 1996-98). Republican. Achievements include research in hydrogeological and geological studies of Southeastern U.S. Home: 3214 Mcgregor Blvd Fort Myers FL 33901-6723 Personal E-mail: missimertm@aol.com.

MISTACCO, VICKI E., foreign language educator; b. Bklyn., Nov. 18, 1942; d. Anthony Sebastian and Lucia (Lalli) M. BA, NYU, 1963; MA, Middlebury Coll., 1964; M of Philosophy, Yale U., 1968, PhD, 1972. Instr. French Wellesley Coll., Mass., 1968-72, asst. prof. French, 1972-78, assoc. prof. French, 1978-84, prof. French, 1984—, chmn., 1978-81. Nat. adv. bd. Sweet Briar Jr. Yr. in France, Va., 1978—. Author: Women and Literary Tradition: Anthology from The Middle Ages to the Present, 2006, vol. 2, 2007; contbr. articles to profl. jours. Fulbright fellow, 1963-64, Woodrow Wilson fellow, 1964-67; NEH fellow, 1983-84, 94-95. Mem.: North East MLA, MLA, Soc. Internat. pour l'Etude des Femmes de l'Ancien Régime, Women in French, Am. Assn. Tchrs. French, Phi Beta Kappa. Democrat. Roman Catholic. Avocations: photography, travel. Office: Wellesley Coll Dept French 106 Central St Wellesley MA 02481-8268 Office Phone: 781-283-2406. Business E-Mail: vmistacco@wellesley.edu.

MISTICK, BARBARA KNAUS, library director; b. Little Rock, May 1, 1955; d. William Anton and Georgianna (Barbarich) Knaus; m. Joseph Sabino Mistick; children: Sloane V. Berrent, Victoria, Adriana. BBA, Carlow Coll., 1990; MBA, U. Pitts., 1992; D in Mgmt., Case Western Res. U., Cleve. Mgr. limo svcs. Checker Cab Co., Tulsa, Okla., 1973—74; sales rep. Nat. Industries Mut., Denver, 1975—76; gen. mgr. Colonial Taxi & Paratransit Svcs., Pitts., 1976—82; pres. Mobility, Inc., Pitts., 1981—88; entrepreneur Stash & Store Inc., Pitts., 1987; gen. mgr. Western Pa. Laidlaw Transit, Pitts., 1988—89; dir. Nat. Edn. Ctr. for Women in Bus. Seton Hall U., 1995; disting. svc. prof. entrepreneurship and pub. policy Carnegie Mellon U., 2003; dir. Girls Math and Sci. Initiative, Carnegie Libr. Pitts., 2005—. Mem. paratransit com. TRB, NAS, Washington, 1978-90; mem. adv. com. Pa. Chamber/Unemployment Co., Harrisburg, 1985-90. Co-author: The Adventure to Entrepreneurship, A Journey to Self Discovery for Young Women; contbr. articles to profl. jours. Bd. mem. South Side Local Devel. Co., Pitts., 1987-89; pres. bd. trustees St. Edmunds Acad., Pitts., 1987—; bd. mem. YWCA of Pitts., 1989—, investment com. chair, 1991—; bd. mem. Pitts. Opera, 1990—, mktg. com., 1991—; mem. Leadership Pitts., 1986-87. Named one of Pitts. Top 50 Bus. Leaders, Pitts. Post-Gazette; recipient Women's Bus. Adv. award, US Small Bus. Adminstrn., Supporter of Entrepreneurship award, Ernst & Young, Women of Spirit award, Carlow Coll., 2003, Vectors Edn. award, 2003. Mem. Internat. Taxicab Assn. (bd. dirs. 1984-88), Pa. Sch. Bus. Assn. (bd. dirs. 1984-88). Office: Carnegie Libr Pitts 4400 Forbes Ave Pittsburgh PA 15213 Office Phone: 412-622-3114.

MISTRAL, JACQUES, economist; b. Toulouse, France, Sept. 22, 1947; s. Léon and Lucienne (Bataillard) M.; m. Bernadette Tricou, July 1, 1970; 3 children. D Econ. Sci., U Paris, 1976; diploma, Ecole Polytechnique, Paris, 1969. Economist French Ministry of Fin., Paris, 1970—76; prof. econs. U. Paris, 1977—81; rsch. officer Centre D'Etudes Prospectives et D'Economie Mathematique, 1980—84; dep. dir. Nat. Sch. Stats. and Econ. Adminstrn., Paris, 1984—88; econ. adviser Prime Minister of France, Paris, 1988—91; exec. v.p. Axa Group, Paris, London, Beijing, Melbourne, 1992—2000; spl. advisor to Minister of Economy, Fin. and Industry Paris, 2000—01; minister, counselor for econ. and fin. affairs Embassy of France, Washington, 2001—. Bd. dirs. Ctr. d'Etudes Prospectives et d'Economie Internationale. Notre Etat, 2000, Etat t'urgence, 2004, La raison du plies tort, 2004. Lt. arty., French armed forces, 1969. Fellow, Harvard U., Kennedy Sch. Govt., 2005—06. Mem.: Le Cercle des Economistes, Le Siècle. Office: Embassy of France 4101 Reservoir Rd NW Washington DC 20007-2130 Office Phone: 202-944-6380. E-mail: jacques_mistral@ksg.harvard.edu.

MISTRY, PERCY SHIAVAK, investment banker; b. Bombay, July 22, 1947; arrived in UK, 1987; s. Shiavak P. and Banoo S. (Engineer) M.; m. Pauline Earnshaw, Oct. 15, 1969. B of Tech. with honors, Loughborough U., Eng., 1969; MBA, U. Toronto, 1970, MPhil, 1971. Sr. advisor to exec. v.p. Internat. Fin. Corp., Washington, 1977-78; mng. dir. SGV-SUN Hung Kai Corp. Fin., Hong Kong, 1978-81; dir., sr. fin. advisor The World Bank, Washington, 1981-87; sr. fellow Oxford (Eng.) U., 1987-92; chmn. Oxford Internat. Assoc., 1988—, Oxford Internat. Fin., 1992-97; CEO Synergy Power Corp., 1998-2000, Acad. Coun. Willon Park, 1999—2004. Chmn. Ukraine Fin. Corp., 1995-98, D.C. Gardner & Co., London, 1992-93; bd. dirs. Indsl. Credit & Investment Corp. India, Bombay, 1993-97, Forum on Debt & Devel., The Hague, Holland, 1988-98, Synergy Power Corp., Hong-Kong, 1987-2003, Small Enterprises Assistance Funds; columnist The Banker, 1987-91; advisor DBSA, UN-ECA, 1999—, Commonwealth Secretariat on Internat. Fin. Svcs., 2005, Govt. of Mauritius, 2005-06; chmn. high-level expert com. on making Mumbai an IF Ctr., 2006. African Debt: The Case for Relief, 1988, African Debt Revisited: Procrastination or Progress?, 1991, Inflation in Ethiopia, 1992, Economic Integration in Southern Africa, 1993, The Financial Condition of the African Development Bank, 1993, Multilateral Debt: An Emerging Crisis, 1994; author: Multilateral Development Banks, 1995, Resolving Africa's Multilateral Debt Problem, 1996, Regional Integration and Economic Development, 1996, Adjustment, Investment and Development Finance in Southern

Africa, 2000, Role of the Commonwealth in International Negotiations, 2001, Mobilizing Support and Resources for the UN, 2001, Financing for Development, 2001, Regulation of International Financial Service in Mauritices: Cost/Benefit Study, 2006, Mitigating Risks for Foreign Investments in Least Developed Countries, 2003, Cost-Benefit Study of AML-CFT Regulations in Commonwealth Countries, 2006, Making Mumbai an International Financial Center, 2007; co-author: Development Finance in Southern Africa, 1989, Zambia: Exchange Rate Policy, 1989, Financing the Multilateral System, 1991, The Conversion of Official Bilateral Debt, 1992, Adjusting Privatization, 1992 (Acad. Book of Yr., 1993). Dir. US-Caresbac, Atlanta, 1988-92; trustee The P.C. Mistry Found., Bombay, 1987—, F.S. Mistry Found. Mem. The Reform Club, The Willingdon Club, Cricket Club of India, The Royal Western India Turf Club. Avocations: thoroughbred racehorse owning and breeding, swimming, squash, tennis, reading. Office Phone: 4419 9383 1567. Personal E-mail: OxfordIntluk@aol.com, percysmistryuk@aol.com.

MISUREC, RUDOLF, physician, surgeon; b. Dobre Pole, Czechoslovakia, June 27, 1924; came to U.S., 1967; s. Gustav and Hilda (Safar) M.; m. Miluse Kisil, 1951 (div. 1978); children: Peter Clyde, Rudolph Carl; m. Stanislava Coufal, 1978. MD, Masaryk's U., Brno-Czechoslovakia, 1950. Diplomate Am. Bd. Urology, gen. surgery (Czechoslovakia), thoracic surgery (Czechoslovakia). Intern U. Ill., Chgo., 1967-68, resident in urology, 1968-71, clin. asst. prof. urology, 1975—. Mem. Rep. Presdl. Task Force, 1984, Rep. Presdl. Legion of Merit, 1992. Capt. Czechoslovakia Army, 1950-55. Recipient Cert. of Achievement U.S. Army, 1967, Letter of Appreciation, 1967. Fellow ACS, Internat. Coll. Surgeons, Am. Urol. Assn.; mem. AMA, Chgo. Med. Soc., N.Y. Acad. Scis., Czechoslovak Soc. Arts and Scis. (U.S.). Roman Catholic. Office: 3340 Oak Park Ave Berwyn IL 60402-3420

MITAU, LEE R., lawyer, bank executive; b. Oct. 17, 1948; AB cum laude, Dartmouth Coll., 1969; JD magna cum laude, U. Minn., 1972. Bar: Minn. 1972, NY 1973. Law clk. to Hon. George E. MacKinnon US Ct. Appeals (DC cir.), 1972-73; assoc. Cleary, Gottlieb, Steen & Hamilton, 1973—79; ptnr. Oppenheimer, Wolff & Donnelly, 1979—83, Dorsey & Whitney, Mpls., 1983—95, mem. policy com., 1988—99, chmn. corp. dept., 1989—95; exec. v.p., gen. counsel US Bancorp, Mpls., 1995—. Adj. prof. law William Mitchell Coll. Law, 1982—83; bd. dirs. H.B. Fuller Co., St. Paul, 1996—, Graco Inc., Mpls., 1990—, chmn., 2002—. Trustee Mpls. Inst. Arts, Minn. Pvt. Coll. Coun.; bd. govs. Mpls. Club. Office: US Bancorp US Bancorp Ctr 800 Nicollet Mall Minneapolis MN 55402 *

MITCH, WILLIAM EVANS, nephrologist; b. Birmingham, Ala., July 22, 1941; s. William Evans and Mary Elizabeth (Ackerman) Mitch; m. Frances Alexandra Fisher, Aug. 21, 1965; children: Eleanor Baylor, William Armistead. BA, Harvard Coll., Cambridge, Mass., 1963; MD, Harvard Med. Sch., 1967. Cert. internal medicine and nephrology Am. Bd. Internal Medicine. Intern Brigham & Women's Hosp., Boston, 1967-68, resident, 1968-69, 1973—74, Johns Hopkins Hosp., Balt., 1972-73; clin. assoc. NIH, Bethesda, Md., 1969-72; from asst. prof. to assoc. prof. dept. pharmacology Johns Hopkins U., Balt., 1974-78; assoc. prof. medicine Harvard Med. Sch., Boston, 1978-87; prof. Emory U. Sch. Medicine, Atlanta, 1987—2002; disting. prof. U. Tex., Galveston, 2002—04; prof. Baylor Coll. Medicine, Houston, 2004—. Mem. study sect. NIH, 1988—92, mem. nat. adv. com., Nat. Inst. Diabetes, Digestive and Kidney Diseases, 2007—. Editor: The Progressive Nature of Renal Disease, 1986, 2d edit., 1992, Nutrition and the Kidney, 1988, 5th edit., 2005. Pres. region II Nat. Kidney Found., 1990—92, chmn. sci. adv. bd., 1996—98; chmn. exec. coun. kidney Am. Heart Assn. Grantee, NIH, 1979—, Merit award, 2004—. Mem.: Internat. Soc. Nephrology (treas. 1997—2003), Am. Soc. Nephrology (pres. 2004), Am. Clin. and Climatol. Assn., Assn. Am. Physicians, Am. Soc. Clin. Investigation. Office: Baylor Coll Nephrology Divsn MS Alkek N-520 1 Baylor Plz Houston TX 77030 Office Phone: 713-798-8350. Business E-Mail: mitch@bcm.edu.

MITCHAM, JULIUS JEROME, accountant; b. Pine Bluff, Ark., Jan. 2, 1941; s. James Vernon and Bertha Lee (Robertson) M.; m. Janet Claire Berry, Mar. 31, 1970 (div. Sept. 1981); m. Marsha Lee Henderson, Oct. 22, 1983; 1 child, Timothy John. BBA, U. Cen. Ark., 1971. CPA Ark., Okla.; cert. healthcare fin. mgr. Br. mgr. Comml. Nat. Bank, Little Rock, 1961-66; auditor, acctg. supr. Ark. Blue Cross and Blue Shield, Little Rock, 1971-77; contr. Riverview Hosp., Little Rock, 1977-81; pvt. practice acctg. Little Rock, 1981-82; contr. Henryetta (Okla.) Med. Ctr., 1982-83; fin. report supr. Am. Med. Internat., Inc., Houston, 1983; dir. corp. acctg. Ft. Myers (Fla.) Cmty. Hosp., 1984-86; contr. Med. Ctr. of Southeast Okla., Durant, 1986-87; CFO Gulf Coast Cmty. Hosp./Qualicare of Miss., Inc., 1987-88; asst. adminstr. fin. S.W. Gen. Hosp., San Antonio, 1988-89; pvt. practice San Antonio, 1989-90; CFO Bapt. Meml. Hosps. of Mississippi County, Blytheville, Ark., 1991-94, Med. Arts Hosp., Texarkana, Tex., 1994-96, Healthsouth Rehab. Hosp., Texarkana, Tex., 1997-98; pres. Mitcham & Assocs., 1998—2001; CFO Muscogee (Creek) Nation Divsn. Health Adminstrn., Okmulgee, Okla., 2002—04, Booneville (Ark.) Meml. Hosp., Ark., 2004—05, Okmulgee Meml. Hosp., 2005—. With USN, 1959—61. Mem. AICPA, Ark. Soc. CPAs, Healthcare Fin. Mgmt. Assn. (cert. fellow), Lions (sec. 1985-86, 2d v.p. 1995-96), Masons. Republican. Baptist. Home: PO Box 277 Okmulgee OK 74447 Office: PO Box 1038 Okmulgee OK 74447 Office Phone: 918-758-3102. Personal E-mail: jmitch41@aol.com.

MITCHARD, JACQUELYN, writer; b. 1953; H.S. English tchr., 1974—76; mng. editor, reporter Pioneer Press, Chgo., 1976—79; reporter The Capital Times, Madison, Wis., 1979—84; metro reporter, columnist Milw. Jour., 1984—88; speechwriter for Donna Shalala, 1989—93. Author: Mother Less Child, 1985, Jane Addams: Pioneer in Social Reform and Activist for World Peace, 1991, Jane Addams: Peace Activist, 1992, The Deep End of the Ocean, 1996, The Rest of Us: Dispatches from the Mothership, 1997, The Most Wanted, 1998, A Theory of Relativity, 2001, Twelve Times Blessed, 2003, Christmas Present, 2003, Starring Prima!, 2004, Baby Bat's Lullaby, 2004, The Breakdown Lane, 2005, Cage of Stars, 2006.

MITCHELL, ALICE JOYCE, retired secondary school educator, retired dietician; b. W.Va., Jan. 27, 1936; d. Edgar Dunbar and Mildred Edna Jones; m. Ernest Lopez Mitchell. BS in Home Econs., W.Va. State Coll., Institute, 1957; degree in Higher Edn. Adminstrn., N.Y.U., Hofstra U. Dietician Kings County Hosp., Bklyn., 1957—58, Montefiore Hosp., Bronx, 1958—66; substitute tchr. home econs. Bd. Edn. Bronx, 1966—68; tchr. home econs. NYC Bd. Edn., 1968—91; ret., 1991. Chairperson home econs. dept. Jr. HS 117, Bklyn., 1971—75, Bklyn., 1979—85, dean of girls, 1976—79; tchr. mentor 117 Intermediate Sch., Bklyn., 1989—91. Served Coast Guard Aux., 1977—78, Bayside, N.Y. Named Master Tchr., Prin. 117 Bklyn., 1971, 1972, 1973, 1974, 1975, 1979, 1980, 1981, 1982, 1985. Mem.: Sr. Coalition, TREA Sr. Citizens League, W.Va. State U. Alumni Club, Acorn, 55+ Club. Republican. Catholic. Avocations: sewing, gardening, travel. Home: 572 S Main St Freeport NY 11520

MITCHELL, ALISON N., newspaper reporter, editor; b. Bay Shore, NY, May 2, 1954; d. Sidney L. and Audrey (Auerhahn) M. BA, Radcliffe Coll., 1976. Reporter The Record, Bergen County, NJ, 1976-77; reporter Newsday, Melville, NY, 1977-81, Capital bur. chief, 1981-84, Congl. corr., Capital Bureau chief, fgn. correspondent Washington & Moscow, 1985—91; reporter, White House correspondent, Washington bureau chief New York Times, Washington & NYC, 1991—2003, dep. nat. editor, 2003; edn. editor New York Times. Recipient Walter Brown award for coverage of state govt., Legis. Corr. Assn., 1983, Everett McKinley Dirksen award, Nat. Press Found., 1999. Mem. N.Y. Legis. Corr. Assn. Office: New York Times 229 W 43d St New York NY 10036 Office Phone: 212-556-7356. Office Fax: 212-556-7614. *

MITCHELL, ALLAN EDWIN, lawyer; b. Okemah, Okla., May 13, 1944; m. Neva G. Ream; children: Brian E. Mitchell, Amy E. Harrison. BA in Mass. Comm., Northwestern Okla. State U., Alva, 1991; JD, U. Okla., 1994. Bar: Okla. 1994, U.S. dist. ct. (we. and no. dists.) 1994. Asst. state mgr. Oklahomans for Right to Work, Oklahoma City, 1967-68; exec. dir. London Sq. Village, Oklahoma City, 1968-73; dist. mgr. Farmland Ins. Svc., Oklahoma City, 1974-80, Nat. Farmers Union, Oklahoma City, 1980-85; dist. agt. Prudential Ins., Cherokee, Okla., 1985-89; atty. Hughes & Grant, Oklahoma City, 1994-96, Collins & Mitchell, Cherokee, Okla., 1996—2000; asst. dist. atty Woods County, Okla., 1996—. Mem. Cherokee Bd. Edn., 1985-90; mem. fin. com. Rep. Party of Okla., 1995, state com., 1997X; scoutmaster, 1981-86, bd. mem. Great Salt Plains Coun. Boy Scouts Am.; adult advisor Girl Scouts Am.; pres. United Way Cherokee, 1984; mem. Okla. Sch. Bd. Mems. Legis. Network, 1985-90, state com. Okla. Rep. Party, 1997; vol. Okla. Spl. Olympics, 1996, 97; lay min. Ch. of the Nazarene. Avocations: public speaking, politics, civic activities. Office: Office of Dist Atty Woods County Courthouse Alva OK 73717 Office Phone: 580-327-2171.

MITCHELL, ANDREA, journalist; b. NYC, Oct. 30, 1946; d. Sydney and Cecile Mitchell; m. Alan Greenspan, Apr. 6, 1997. BA in English Literature, U. Pa., 1967. Polit. reporter KYW Newsradio, Phila., 1967-76; polit. corr. Sta. KYW-TV, Phila., 1972-76; corr. Sta. WTOP-TV, Washington, 1977-78; gen. assignment and energy corr. NBC News, Washington, 1978-81, White House corr., 1981-88, chief congl. corr., 1989-92, chief White House corr., 1993-94, chief fgn. affairs corr. Washington, 1995—. Substitute host Meet the Press, 1988-; host MSNBC The Mitchell Report, Decision 2000. Author: (book) Talking Back: ...to Presidents, Dictators, and Assorted Scoundrels, 2005. Trustee U. Pa., 1995—. Recipient award for pub. affairs reporting Am. Polit. Sci. Assn., 1969, Pub. Affairs Reporting award AP, 1976, AP Broadcast award, 1977; named Communicator of the Yr., Phila. chpt. Women in Comms., 1976, Woman of the Yr., Phila. chpt. Am. Women in Radio and TV, 1989, Lucretia Mott award Woman's Way, 1991, Welles Hangen award superior achievement journalism, Brown U., 2003, Lifetime Achievement award RTNDA, 2004, Harvard U. Goldsmith Career Achievement prize, 2005. Office: NBC News 4001 Nebraska Ave NW Washington DC 20016-2733

MITCHELL, ANGELA CAROL, elementary school educator; b. Carbondale, Ill., June 26, 1980; d. Samuel Everett Childers and Carol Ann (Jacobs) Mitchell. BS, Vanderbilt U., Nashville, 2002, M in Edn., 2004. Cert. tchg. Tenn. Tchg. aide U. Sch. Nashville, 2003—04; tchr. Jones Paideia Magnet Sch., Met. Nashville Pub. Sch., 2004—05, Oak Hill Sch., Nashville, 2005—. Mem.: NEA, Student Tenn. Edn. Assn. (v.p. 1999—2002), Kappa Delta Pi, Kappa Delta Epsilon, Gamma Beta Phi, Phi Eta Sigma, Alpha Lambda Delta, Pi Lambda Theta, Psi Chi (life). Independent. Avocations: writing, reading, travel. Office: Oak Hill Sch 4815 Franklin Rd Nashville TN 37220 Home Phone: 615-556-6332; Office Phone: 615-297-6544. Business E-Mail: mitchella@oakhillschool.org.

MITCHELL, ARTHUR, dancer, choreographer, performing company executive, educator; b. NYC, Mar. 27, 1934; s. Arthur and Willie Mae Mitchell. Student, Sch. Am. Ballet.; D. Arts (hon.), Columbia Coll., Chgo., 1975; cert. of competence, Peter U., 1978; DFA (hon.), City Coll., CUNY, 1979, N.C. Sch. Arts, 1981, L.I. U. Sch. Bus. Pub. Adminstrn., 1982, Fordham U., 1983, Princeton U., 1986, Williams Coll., 1986, Juilliard Sch., 1990; DHS (hon.), Urbana Coll., 1979; DA (hon.), Harvard U., 1987. With William Dollar's Ballet Theatre Workshop, 1954, John Butler Co., 1955; prin. dancer NYC Ballet, 1955-72; artistic dir., founder Am. Negro Dance Co., NYC, 1966—; founder, dir., choreographer Dance Theatre of Harlem, NYC, 1969—; former resident choreographer, artistic dir. Nat. Ballet Co., Brazil. Tchr. dance Karel Shook Studio, Melissa Hayden Sch., Cedarhurst, L.I., Jones-Haywood Sch. Ballet, Washington. Dancer Kiss Me Kate, Orpheus, Carmen Jones, Allegro, Creation of the World, Episodes, House of Flowers, choreographer with Rod Alexander Newport Jazz Festival, Rhythmetron, 1971, Ode to Otis, 1969, Lil' Gal, 1969, Tones, 1970, Biosfera, 1970, Fun and Games, 1970, Holberg Suite, 1970, Manifestations, 1975, Concerto for Jazz Band and Orch., 1971, Fête Noire, 1971, Spiritual Suite: Dance In Praise of His Name, 1976, Breezin', 1977, The Greatest, 1977, El Mar, 1977, Doin' It, 1978, Porgy and Bess, 1985, Phoenix Rising, 1987, John Henry, 1988, Ribbon in the Sky, 1990, Bach Passacaglia, 1993; co-choreographer Broadway prodn. Shinebone Alley, dancer, choreographer, actor Spoleto Festival of Two Worlds, 1960; dancer tv prodns. A Streetcar Named Desire, PBS dance prodn. Songs of Mahler, Dance in America: Dance Theatre of Harlem, Stravinsky's Firebird, NBC prodn. Creole Giselle, A&E prodn. Fall River Legend. Active Nat. Conf. on Social Welfare, 1973, U.S. Dept. State Dance Adv. Panel; pres. Task Force on Arts and Humanities, 1981; mem. Commn. for Cultural Affairs, NYC, 1982; mem. adv. bd. Arts and Entertainment, NYC; mem. Partnership, Inc., 1983, Nat. Coun. Arts, 1987, Pres. Commn. on White House Fellowships, 1991. Named to Hall of Fame, NAACP Image Awards, 1986; recipient Changers award, Mademoiselle Mag., 1970, award, North Shore Commn. Arts Ctr., 1980, Capezio Dance award, 1971, Ann. Excellence award, John F. Kennedy Ctr. for Performing Arts, 1980, award, Am. Dance Guild, 1982, Am. Black Achievement award, Ebony Mag., 1983, Pres.'s Cabinet award, U. Detroit, 1982, Paul Robeson award, Actors Equity Assn., 1986, Lion of the Performing Arts award, NY Pub. Libr., 1986, Arnold Gingrich Meml. award, 1987, Banquet of Golden Plate, 1989, Harkness Disting. Artist award, Adelphi U., 1990, Disting. Svc. to Arts award, Am. Acad. Arts and Letters, 1994, Zenith award for Fine Arts, 1994, Handel Medallion, NYC, 1993, Barnard Medal of Distinction, Barnard Coll., 1994, Lifetime Achievement award, Sch. Am. Ballet, 1995, Nat. Medal of Arts, Nat. Endowment Arts, 1995, Living Landmarks award, NY Landmarks of Conservancy, 1995; grantee Fletcher Fellowship, Fletcher Found.; Conroy fellow, St. Paul's Sch., Concord, N.H., 1982, MacArthur fellow, 1994. Office: Dance Theatre Harlem 466 W 152nd St New York NY 10031-1896 *

MITCHELL, BETTY JO, publishing executive, writer; b. May 2, 1931; d. Edith Darrah McWilliams. BA, S.W. Mo. State U., Springfield, 1952; MSL, U. So. Calif., 1967; MBA, PhD, Calif. Coast U., 2002. Asst. acquisitions libr. Calif. State U., Northridge, 1967—69, libr. for pers. and fin., 1969-71, acting assoc. libr. dir., 1971-72, assoc. dir. univ. librs., 1972-81; mgr. info. sys. City Santa Monica Rent Control, Calif., 1984-93; owner Viewpoint Press, Tehachapi, Calif. Cons. We. Interstate Commn. for Higher Edn. USOE Inst. for Tng. in Staff Devel. Problem Solving; participant workshops in field; spkr. at profl. confs. in field; bd. dirs. Tehachapi Cmty. Orch. Author: ALMS: A Budget Based Library Management System, 1982, The Secret of Hilhouse: An Adult Book for Teens, 1993, The Huckenpuck Papers: The Tale of a Family's Secret and a Young Girl's Search for Self-Esteem, 2001, Seeds of Violence, 2005; co-author: Cost Analysis of Library Functions: A Total System Approach, 1978, How to See the U.S. on $12 a Day; contbr. writings to profl. publs.; editor Staff Development column in Spl. Librs., 1975-76. Bd. dirs. San Fernando Valley coun. Girl Scouts U.S., 1974-77, employed pers. com., 1979-81; bd. dirs. Bear Valley Springs Condominium Owners Assn., 1978, Empyrean Found., 1978-81, Tehachapi Cmty. Orch. Found., 1998—, Tehachapi Performing Arts Ctr. Found., 2003—, Tehachapi Heritage League, 2005—. Mem. AAUP, AAUW, ALA (chmn. various coms.), Assn. Women in Computing (bd. dirs. 1987-89), Nat. Libr. Assn., Author's Guild, Calif. Libr. Assn., Assn. Calif. State U. Profs. (sec., exec. com. 1971-72), Phi Beta Chi, Alpha Mu Gamma. Office: PMB 400 785 Tucker Rd Ste G Tehachapi CA 93561-2523 Personal E-mail: joie99@aol.com.

MITCHELL, BEVERLY SHRIVER, hematologist, oncologist, educator; b. Balt., May 14, 1944; m. John Robert Pringle; children: Robert Mitchell, Elizabeth Greene. AB summa cum laude in Biochemistry, Smith Coll., 1965; MD, Harvard U., 1969. Hematology fellow U. Mich., Ann Arbor, 1975-77, from instr. to asst. prof. internal medicine, 1977-81, assoc. prof., 1981-87, prof. internal medicine and pharmacology, 1987-91, U. N.C., Chapel Hill, 1991—, divsn. chief hematology/oncology, 1994—2003; assoc. dir. Lineberger Cancer Ctr., Chapel Hill, 1994—2005; deputy dir. Stanford Cancer Ctr., Stanford U., 2005—. Mem. bd. sci. counselors Cancer Treatment divsn. Nat. Cancer Inst. Vice chair med. and sci. affairs Leukemia and Lymphoma Soc., 2003—05. Recipient Stohlman award Leukemia Soc., 1988. Mem. Am. Soc. Hematology (treas. 1991-96, v.p. 1998, pres. 2000), Phi Beta, Inst. Medicine. Achievements include research in nucleotide metabolism and the development of novel therapies for hematologic malignancies. Office: Stanford Cancer Ctr 800 Welch Rd Stanford CA 94305-5796 Office Phone: 650-736-7716. Business E-Mail: bmitchell@stanford.edu.

MITCHELL, BRENDA KING, training services executive; b. NYC, Jan. 9, 1943; d. William Franklin and Ola Mae (Ross) K.; divorced; 1 child, Corrie Nelson. BA, Fordham U., 1973; MA, Hunter Coll., 1977; PhD in Pub. Adminstrn., Nova U., 1981. Dir. manpower planning Addictive Disease Agy., NYC, 1973-77; project and contract mgr. Pub./Pvt. Ventures Corp., Phila., 1978-80; exec. dir. Econ. Devel. Corp., Phila., 1980-84; bus. mgr. Control Data Corp., Mpls., 1984-87; dep. sec. Pa. Dept. Comm., 1987—91; spl. asst. to Gov. of Pa. in community econ. devel. initiatives, 1989—91; sec. Commonwealth of Pa., Harrisburg, 1991-94; pres., CEO African Am. Delaware Valley Port Corp., Phila., 1993—94, Mgmt. & Environ. Tech. Inc., Phila., 1995—; co-founder, mng. ptnr. Cmty Leadership Devel. Inst., Allegheny County, Pa., 1999—. Sole propr. bus. in real estate devel. & property mgmt., Phila., Harrisburg, adv. coun. US Dept. Commerce Industry sector, 1994-, bd. dir. Penns Landing Corp, 2001-, adv. bd. Benjamin Franklin Tech. Ptnrs., 2002-. Author: They Crossed Together, 1975. Recipient citation for Outstanding Leadership in Econ. Devel., City of Phila. Mayor's Office, 1987; named for Outstanding Leadership, People United to Serve Humanity, Inc., 1991, Disting. Alumni, Nova U., 1992, Policy Advocate of Yr., Nat. Assn. Bus. Women Owners, 1992. Mem. NAACP (life), Nat. Congress of Black Women, Nat. Forum Black Pub. Adminstrs. (pres. 1987), Forum Exec. Women, Black Women's Leadership Conf. Home: 5204 Overbrook Ave Philadelphia PA 19131-2409 Office: Mgmt & Environ Tech Inc Ste 1108 1315 Walnut St Philadelphia PA 19107 Office Phone: 215-546-7991. Office Fax: 215-546-7995.

MITCHELL, BRIAN CHRISTOPHER, academic administrator; b. Lowell, Mass., Feb. 23, 1953; s. Christopher Joseph and Doris Katherine (McEvoy) M.; m. Maryjane Murphy, June 28, 1975; children: Jeffrey Ryan, Patrick Joseph. BA, Merrimack Coll., 1974; MA, U. Rochester, 1976, PhD, 1981. Chair history dept. Anna Maria Coll., Paxton, Mass., 1982-85; program officer Nat. Endowment Humanities, Washington, 1985-91; pres. Commn. Ind. Colls. and Univs. Pa., Harrisburg, 1991-98, Washington and Jefferson Coll., Washington, Pa., 1998—2004, Bucknell U., Lewisburg, Pa., 2004—. Instr. U. Mass., Lowell, 1977-85; adj. prof. George Mason U., Fairfax, Va., 1988-91; cons. Lowell Nat. Hist. Park, 1977-81, Lowell Heritage State Park, 1977-78. Author: The Paddy Camps: The Irish of Lowell, 1821-1861, 1988, On The North Bank, 1984; editor: Building the American Catholic City, 1986; contbg. author: From Paddy to Studs, 1986. Mem. Pa. Humanities Coun.; mem. Pa. Hist. and Mus. Commn.; chair Pa. selection com. Rhodes Scholarship Trust. Grantee Am. Coun. Learned Socs., 1985, NEH. Mem. Am. Hist. Assn. (Albert J. Beveridge award), Orgn. Am. Historians, Nat. Assn. Ind. Colls. and Univs. Roman Catholic. Office: Off of President Bucknell U Box A0527 Lewisburg PA 17837 Office Phone: 570-577-1511. E-mail: bmitchel@bucknell.edu. *

MITCHELL, BRIAN STOKES, actor; b. Seattle, Oct. 31, 1958; s. George Thomas and Lillian (Stokes) M. Prin. actor 12th Night Repertory Co., San Diego, 1977-80; co-star Roots: The Next Generations, LA, 1980, Trapper John, M.D., LA, 1980-86, The Good War, LA, 1987, The Fresh Prince of Bel Air, 1993, In the House, 1996, Crossing Jordan, 2002, Frasier, 2002—03; co-star Mail Kennedy Ctr., Washington, The Music Box Theatre, Broadway, N.Y.C., and Pasadena, Calif., 1987-88; star David Merrick's Broadway play Oh Kay Richard Rodgers Theatre, 1990. Guest tchr., speaker San Diego Jr. Theater, 1984; guest star The White Shadow, 227, Houston Knights, Alf, Night Court, L.A., 1987; voice-over actor, series reg. California Raisins, New Kids on the Block, Kid 'n Play, 1988—; trustee Actor's Fund, 1999—, pres. 2004-07; mem. honors artist com. Kennedy Ctr., 2001, 02, 04; pres. Actors Fund Am., 2004; mem. artist's com. Ams. for the Arts, 2004. Appeared in Broadway prodn. Jelly's Last Jam, 1992, Kiss of the Spider Woman, 1994-95, Ragtime, Ford Theater for Performing Arts, 1996 (Drama League Disting. Performance award, Can.'s Dora award, Drama League award), Shubert Theatre, L.A., 1997 (L.A. Critics award), Kiss Me Kate, 1999-2001 (Tony Award, 2000, Drama Desk award, Outer Critics Circle award), Do Re Mi, 2000, Carnival, 2001, King Hedley II, 2001, Sweeney Todd, 2002, South Pacific, 2005; appeared in National Theater prodn. Man of La Mancha, 2002 (Helen Hayes award), National Symphony Orchestra Pops: An Evening with Brian Stokes Mitchell, 2005; composer: (symphonic suite) 3 Scenes for Clipper Ships, 1983; (Trapper John, M.D. TV scores) The Wunderkind, Friends and Lovers, I Only Have Ice For You, 1984; film work includes Ghost Dad, 1990, (voice) The Prince of Egypt, 1998, Ruby's Bucket of Blood, 2000, Call me Clause, 2001; composer (CD) Brian Stokes Mitchell, 2006. Ambassador March of Dimes, U.S. Tour, 1984-85; performer USO, European Tour, 1984, Far East/Middle East Tour, 1985, Calif. Orgn. of Police and Sheriffs, L.A., 1986. Recipient Best Pop Song and Composer of Yr. awards Los Angeles Songwriters Showcase, 1986, Drama League Distinguished Performance Award, 1998, Nightlife award, outstanding cabaret male vocalist in a major engagement, 2006. Mem. Acad. of TV Arts and Scis. (blue ribbon panelist 1987), ASCAP, Screen Actors' Guild, AFTRA, Actors Equity Assn. Avocations: flying, skiing, composing.

MITCHELL, BRUCE TYSON, lawyer; b. San Francisco, Nov. 6, 1928; s. John Robert and Lorraine C. (Tyson) M.; m. Adrienne Means Hiscox, Oct. 14, 1951; 1 son, Mark Means. AB with great distinction, Stanford U., Calif., 1949, JD, 1951. Bar: Calif. 1952, US Dist. Ct. (no. dist.) Calif 1952, US Ct. Appeals (9th cir.) 1952, US Supreme Ct. 1971. Estate adminstr. Crocker Nat. Bank, San Francisco, 1955-57; atty. Utah Internat. Inc., San Francisco, 1957-87, sec., 1974-87, sr. counsel, 1961—87, ret., 1987; pvt. practice securities arbitrator. Mem. non-securities panel arbitrators NY Stock Exch., NASD Bd. Arbitrators; mem. adv. bd. archaeology, Stanford U. Chmn. San Mateo County Rep. Ctrl. Com., 1964-70; mem. Calif. Rep. Ctrl. Com., 1964-74, 77-83; alt. del. Rep. Nat. Conv., 1968; co-chmn. San Mateo (Calif.) County Pres. Ford Com., 1976; mem. bd. visitors sch. law Stanford U., 1980-83; exec. v.p., bd. dirs. San Francisco Jr. C. of C., 1961; bd. dirs. No. Calif. chpt. Arthritis Found., 1972-85, 1987-92, St. Francis Hosp. Found., San Francisco, 1992-98, 99—, hon. dir., 1998-99—. Lt. (j.g.) USNR, 1952-55, Japan. Mem. ABA, Calif. Bar Assn., San Francisco Bar Assn., Am. Judicature Soc., Am. Soc. Corp. Secs. (v.p. 1976-77, dir. 1976-79), Assn. Former Intelligence Officers, Commonwealth Club of Calif. (pres. San Francisco 1973), Stanford Assocs., Pacific Union Club, Olympic Club, Capitol Hill Club, Travelers Century Club, Masons. Congregationalist. Home: 165 Redwood Dr Hillsborough CA 94010-6971 Office: 225 Bush St Fl 16 San Francisco CA 94104-4213 Office Phone: 415-439-8801.

MITCHELL, BURLEY BAYARD, JR., lawyer; b. Oxford, NC, Dec. 15, 1940; s. Burley Bayard and Dorothy Ford (Champion) M.; m. Mary Lou Willett, Aug. 3, 1962; children: David Bayard (dec.), Catherine Morris. BA with honors, N.C. State U., 1966, DHL (hon.), 1995; JD, U. N.C., 1969; LLD (hon.), Campbell U., 1998. Bar: N.C. 1969, U.S. Ct. Appeals (4th cir.) 1970, U.S. Ct. Appeals (3d cir.) 2002, U.S. Supreme Ct. 1972. Asst. atty. gen. State of N.C., Raleigh, 1969-72, dist. attys., 1973-77, judge Ct. Appeals, 1977-79, sec. crime control, 1979-82; justice Supreme Ct. N.C., Raleigh, 1982-94; chief justice Supreme Ct. of N.C., Raleigh, 1995-99; ptnr. Womble Carlyle Sandridge and Rice, Raleigh, 1999—. Served with USN, 1958-62, Asia. Recipient N.C. Nat. Guard Citizen Commendation award, 1982 Mem. ABA, VFW, N.C. Bar Assn., Mensa, Am. Legion, Phi Beta Kappa. Democrat. Methodist. Home: 4301 City of Oaks Wynd Raleigh NC 27612-5316 Office: Wacovia Capital Ctr 150 Fayetteville St Mall Ste 2100 PO Box 831 Raleigh NC 27602-0831 Office Phone: 919-755-8166.

MITCHELL, CAROL ANN, nursing educator; b. Portsmouth, Va., Aug. 31, 1942; d. William Howell and Eleanor Bertha (Wesarg) M.; m. David Alan Friedman, June 17, 1971 (div. 1988). Diploma, NYU, 1963; BS, Columbia U., 1968, MA, 1971, EdM, 1974, EdD, 1980; MS, SUNY, Stony Brook, 1990. Charge nurse Nassau County Med. Ctr., East Meadow, N.Y., 1963-65; staff nurse Meml. Hosp., NYC, 1965-68; head nurse, supr. Cmty. at Glen Cove (N.Y.), 1969-71; assoc. prof. dept. nursing Queensborough C.C. CUNY, Bayside, 1971-80; assoc. prof. Marion A. Buckley Sch. Nursing Adelphi U., Garden City, N.Y., 1981-88; ednl. cons. Nat. League for Nursing, NYC, 1980-81; prof. sch. nursing SUNY, Stony Brook, 1988-92, chmn. adult nursing, 1988-92; prof. chair Coll. Nursing East Tenn. State U., 1992-95, mem faculty, 1995-96; geriat. nurse practitioner, dir. geriat. evaluation unit Vet. Affairs Med. Ctr., Mountain Home, Tenn., 1997—. Mem. faculty Regents Coll. degrees in nursing program USNY, Albany, 1978-91, cons., 1978—; faculty cons. geriats. Montefiore Med. Ctr., 1991-93. Editor emeritus: Scholarly Inquiry in Nursing Practice, 1983—; contbr. articles to profl. jours. Robert Wood Johnson clin. nurse scholar postdoctoral fellow U. Rochester (N.Y.), 1983-85. Mem.: Am. Geriatrics Soc., Am. Nurses Assn. Avocations: reading, gardening, bicycling, travel, cooking.

MITCHELL, CAROL ANN, lawyer; b. New Bedford, Mass., Sept. 2, 1957; d. John E. and Edith A. (Mogensen) M. AB, Vassar Coll., 1979; JD, William and Mary Coll., 1982. Bar: D.C. 1983, U.S. Ct. Appeals (Fed. cir.) 1988, U.S. Ct. Internat. Trade 1986. Atty.-advisor Benefits Rev. Bd., Washington, 1982-83; import compliance specialist Internat. Trade Adminstrn. U.S. Dept. Commerce, Washington, 1983-85; assoc. Collier, Shannon & Scott, Washington, 1985-90, Akin, Gump, Strauss, Hauer & Feld, Washington, 1990-91, Dewey, Ballantine, Washington, 1991-94; of counsel Steptoe & Johnson, Washington, 1994—2002.

MITCHELL, CATHY (C.C.) CHRISTINE, art educator; b. Phoenixville, Pa., 1954; d. William Douglas and Christine (Donshietz) Mitchell. AA, Cuyahoga C.C., Parma Heights, Ohio, 1975; BFA, Sch. of the Art Inst. Chgo., 1987, MA in Art Edn., 1994. Cert. art tchr. grades K-12 Ill., 1987, Ohio, 1998. Dir./arts coord. Howland Sch. Arts, Chgo. Pub. Schs., 1987—98; interim coord. dept. edn. Wexner Ctr. for the Arts, Columbus, Ohio, 1998—2000; arts educator - visual art Columbus (Ohio) Pub. Schs., 2000—. Mem. adv. bd. Art Inst. Chgo., 1991—98; mem. edn. bd. Mus. Contemporary Art, Chgo., 1997—99; adj. faculty dept. art edn. Elmhurst (Ill.) Coll., 1997. Co-prodr., writer (video) School Improvement Planning, Chicago Public Schools. Mem. Cliff Dwellers, Chgo., 1997; com. chair Columbus Arts Festival, 1998—; trustee Parkview NE Condominium Assn., Lewis Center, Ohio, 2001—; active Joel Hall Dance Co., Chgo., 1997—2001. Recipient Nat. Grand prize, Tchr.-Student Photography, Canon Photography with USA Today, 1997, Outstanding Svc. in Arts Edn. for the State of Ill. award, Ill. Alliance for the Arts, 1997, Art Tchr. of Yr., Ill. Alliance for Arts, 1997. Mem.: NEA (assoc.), Ohio Edn. Assn. (assoc.), Nat. Art Edn. Assn. (assoc.). Office: CC Mitchell PO Box 1674 Powell OH 43065-1674 Home Phone: 614-888-1897. Personal E-mail: box1674@ameritech.net.

MITCHELL, CONNIE, director; m. George Mitchell, Sr.; children: Carlata, George Jr. Tchr. adv. Office Adminstrv./Instrnl. Pers. Detroit Pub. Schs. Dir. Ednll. Enrichment Acad.; mem. bd. dir. Nat. Bd. Profl. Tchg. Standards, 1995—2003. Active Meth. Children's Home Soc. Named Middle Sch. Tchr. of Yr., Newsweek Mag./WDIV-TV, 1994, Tchr. of Yr., Detroit Pub. Schs., 1994; recipient Golden Apple Tchr. award, Wayne County Regional Edn. Svc. Agy. Mem.: Nat. Bd. for Profl. Tchg. Stds. (bd. mem.), Alpha Kappa Alpha. Office: Detroit Pub Schs Schs Ctr Bldg 3031 W Grand Blvd Detroit MI 48202

MITCHELL, DAVID BENJAMIN, lawyer, arbitrator, mediator; b. Miami Beach, Fla., Nov. 3, 1950; s. Quintus Eugene and Gertrude (Ziegler) M.; m. Lynn Stewart, Dec. 11, 1993. BA, U. Miami, Coral Gables, Fla., 1973; JD, Stetson U., 1978. Bar: Fla. 1979, U.S. Dist. Ct. (so. dist.) Fla. 1979, U.S. Tax Ct. 1987, U.S. Supreme Ct. 2004; cert. family mediator; cert. arbitrator; cert. ins. mediator. Assoc., sr. assoc. Semet, Lickstein, Morgenstern & Berger, P.A., Coral Gables, 1987-90; pres. David B. Mitchell, P.A., Coral Gables, 1990—. Pres. South Fla. Mediation Assocs., Inc., Coral Gables, 1990-92. Author: Magna Carta: It's American Legacy, 2005. Active Coral Gables Cmty. Found., 1996—; grad. Leadership Miami, 1987; bd. dirs. Ponce de Leon Devel. Assn., pres., 1992-93; bd. dirs. Internat. Zen Found. of Fla., 1997—, Coral Gables Citizens Crime Watch, 1998-2006, pres., 2001-03; vice chmn. Coral Gables City-Wide Anti-Crime Com., 2002-05, chmn., 2005-06; active Coral Gables Emergency Ops. Dept., 2005; chmn. Coral Gables Pub. Safety Com., 2006—. Recipient Key to the City of Coral Gables, 1993, 2006. Mem. The Fla. Bar (family law sect.), Dade County Bar Assn. (family law com., county cts. com., vice chair, 2004, Cert. of Appreciation 1994-95), Coral Gables Bar Assn. (law day com. 1996, scholarship com. 1996, bd. dirs. 1997-2005, pres. 2003-04), Fla. Acad. Profl. Mediators, U. Miami Alumni Club of Greater Miami (sec., dir. 1996-98), Republican Nat. Lawyers Assn., Federalist Soc., SAR (chpt. pres., 2005-06), Jamestown Soc., Soc. Descs. of Knights of the Garter, Order of Crown of Charlemagne, Baronial Order of Magna Carta, Rotary Club Coral Gables (dir. 2001-03, pres.-elect 2006—), Royal Soc. St. George, Mil. Order Crusades, Order Mergovinian Dynasty, Order Founders and Patriots Am., Son Confederate Vets, Mil. Order of the Stars and Bars. Republican. Buddhist. Office Phone: 305-461-5015. Personal E-mail: mitchellesq@aol.com.

MITCHELL, DAVID LANCASTER, research educator; b. LA, Dec. 13, 1954; s. Eugene M. and Elizabeth B. Mitchell. BS in Chemistry, Calif. Poly. State U., San Luis Obispo, 1981; PhD, U. Nev., 1995. Rsch. scientist Desert Rsch. Inst., Reno, 1989—95, asst. rsch. prof., 1995—2000, assoc. rsch. prof., 2000—. Cons. Atmospheric and Environ. Rsch., Inc., Lexington, Mass., 2000—01. Contbr. articles to profl. jours. Pres. Divine Mission USA, Reno, 2002—. Recipient Peter B. Wagner medal of excellence, Desert Rsch. Inst., 2000; grantee, Dept. Energy, NOAA, NSF. Mem.: Am. Meteorol. Assn. (chmn. com. on cloud physics 2000—06). Achievements include research in accurate analytical treatment of ice particle-radiation interactions; dependence of North American monsoon on sea surface temperatures; satellite remote sensing of atmospheric ice mass. Avocation: teaching meditation and yoga. Office: Desert Rsch Inst 2215 Raggio Pky Reno NV 89512-1095 Home Phone: 775-746-5448; Office Phone: 775-674-7039. Office Fax: 775-674-7007. E-mail: mitch@dri.edu.

MITCHELL, DAVID WALKER, lawyer; b. Oakland, Calif., Nov. 11, 1935; s. Theodore Boyd and Helen Louise (Walker) M.; m. Carolyn Hilliard Graves, July 29, 1961; children: Sarah, Betsy. AB in History, Stanford U., 1957; JD, Harvard U., 1960. Bar: Calif. 1961. Assoc. Kindel & Anderson, LA, 1961-65, Weir, Hopkins, Donovan, San Jose, Calif., 1965-68; ptnr. Hopkins, Mitchell & Carley, San Jose, 1968-87, McCutchen, Doyle, Brown & Enersen, San Jose, 1987-93, Hoge, Fenton, Jones & Appel, San Jose, 1993-2000, of counsel, 2001—. Bd. dirs. Peninsula Open Space Trust, Menlo Park, Calif., 1982—2005, pres., 1984-92; bd. dirs. Cmty. Found. Silicon Valley., San Jose, 1977-94, 99-2003; chair bd. trustees United Way Santa Clara County, 1983-85. Fellow Am. Bar Found., Am. Leadership Forum (sr.); mem. Santa Clara County Bar Assn. (trustee 1972-75), San Jose C. of C. (bd. dirs. 1975-80). Mem. United Ch. of Christ. Avocations: music, hiking. Office: Hoge Fenton Jones Appel 60 S Market St Ste 1400 San Jose CA 95113-2396 Office Phone: 408-287-9501. Business E-Mail: dwm@hogefenton.com.

MITCHELL, DENNIS ANTHONY, dentist, educator; b. Port of Spain, Trinidad and Tobago, May 1, 1962; s. Victor O'Reilly Mitchell and Ulyth Lamour Lewis, Cyril Theodore Lewis (Stepfather) and Maria Mitchell (Stepmother); m. Bridgette Vanera Joyner, July 8, 2001; children: Angelique Victoria children: Danielle Lindsey. BA, Cornell U., 1984; DDS, Howard U., 1989; MPH, Columbia U., 1996. Gen. practice dental resident Harlem Hosp. Ctr., NYC, 1989—90, chief resident, 1990—91; clin. instr. Columbia U. Sch. Dental and Oral Surgery, NYC, 1991—94, dental pub. health resident, 1994—96, dir. cmty. dentcare network Harlem, 1996—2002, asst. dean diversity and multicultural affairs, 2004—; cmty. health services fellow Columbia U. Ctr. Cmty. Health Partnerships, NYC, 2002—04. Cons. HIV dental standards of care com. NY State Dept. Health AIDS Inst., NYC, 1995—2002; cons. NY State oral cancer control partnership workgroup com. NY State Dept. Health, Bur. Dental Health, NYC, 2001—04, cons. NY State oral health planning com., Albany, 2004—; cons. Ctr. Health and Health Care in Schs. Robert Wood Johnson Found., Lawrenceville, NJ, 2001—04, cons. pipelines, profession and practice, community-based dental edn., 2002—. Named to Disting. African Americans in Dentistry Calendar, Aetna Inc., 2004; recipient Cmty. Svc. award, Harlem Cmty. Dental Soc., 1991, Chief Resident award, Harlem Hosp. Ctr. Dept. of Dentistry, 1991, Nat. Rsch. Svc. award, Nat. Inst. Allergy and Infectious Diseases, 1994, Outstanding Achievement award, Nat. Dental Assn., 1997, Cmty. Leadership award, 2002, Disting. Alumni award, Howard U. Coll. Dentistry, 2002, Leadership award, West Harlem Group Assistance, 2004; grantee Minority Clin. Assoc. Physician's award, Nat. Inst. Craniofacial Rsch., 1998, Nat. Inst. Dental and Craniofacial Rsch., 2001. Mem.: APHA, Am. Dental Edn. Assn., Greater Met. NY Dental Soc. (pres. 1998—2000), Internat. Assn. of Dental Rsch., Am. Assn. Pub. Health Dentistry, Nat. Dental Assn. (trustee 1993—99, Cmty. Leadership award and Outstanding Achievement Award 1997, 2002), Omicron Kappa Upsilon, Alpha Phi Alpha. Democrat. Achievements include first to dental service network for children and adults in Harlem, New York; research in oral manifestations of HIV disease in injecting drug users; dental caries experience in Northern Manhattan adolescents; effects of periodontal therapy intervention on preterm birth. Avocations: reading, travel, golf. Home: 190 Cherry Ln Teaneck NJ 07666 Office: Columbia U Coll Dental Medicine P& S Bldg Box 20 630 West 168th St New York NY 10032 Home Phone: 201-357-8693; Office Phone: 212-342-3714. Office Fax: 212-305-1034; Home Fax: 212-305-1034. Personal E-mail: dml48@columbia.edu.

MITCHELL, EARL NELSON, physicist, researcher; b. Centerville, Iowa, Aug. 30, 1926; s. Earl Nelson and Nina (Swank) M.; m. Marlys Marie Panning, July 23, 1955. AB magna cum laude, U. Iowa, 1949, MS, 1951; PhD, U. Minn., 1955. Research scientist Sperry Rand Corp., St. Paul, 1955-58; asst. prof., then assoc. prof. physics U. N.D., Grand Forks, 1958-62; vis. assoc. prof., then assoc. prof. and prof. physics U. N.C., Chapel Hill, 1962-91, prof. emeritus, 1991—, asst. chmn. dept., 1968-76. Lectr. Hamline U., 1956, 57; cons. Sperry Rand Corp., 1958-62 Contbr. articles to profl. jours.; author textbooks. Mem. Chapel Hill Planning Bd., 1970-71; pres. Chapel Hill Concert Series, 1967-70; mem. bd. for missions to deaf Luth. Ch. Mo. Synod, 1958-64. Served in USNR, 1945-46. Mem.: Am. Soc. Enologists (bd. dirs. ea. sect. 1984—91, pres.-elect 1988, pres. 1989, past pres. 1990), Am. Phys. Soc., N.C. Wine Growers Assn. (pres. 1994—98, past pres. 1998—2003), Phi Eta Sigma, Sigma Xi, Phi Beta Kappa. Democrat. Office: U NC Dept Physics Chapel Hill NC 27599-0001

MITCHELL, EARL WESLEY, clergyman; b. Excelsior Springs, Mo., Mar. 16, 1931; s. Earl Van and Ora Leah (Butterfield) M.; m. Mary Lou Bell, June 8, 1956; children: Susan Yvonne, Randall Bruce. Ordained to ministry Christian Union Ch., 1971. Min. Vibbard (Mo.) Christian Union Ch., 1962-69, Liberty (Mo.) Christian Ch., 1969—77, Barwick Christian Union Ch., Cameron, Mo., 1977-80, Independence (Mo.) Christian Union Ch., 1980—95; assoc. pastor Flack Meml. Christian Union Ch., Excelsior Springs, Mo., 1995—. Former mem. state exec. bd. Christian Union Mo., 1995-98; area rep. Mo. Christian Union USA; former mem. gen. exec. bd., former editor C.U. Witness. Sgt. USAF, 1951-55. Avocations: music, woodworking, painting, photography. Home and Office: 618 Henrie St Excelsior Springs MO 64024-2022

MITCHELL, EDWARD JOHN, economist, retired educator; b. Newark, Aug. 15, 1937; s. Edward Charles and Gladys (Werner) M.; m. Mary Josephine Osborne, June 14, 1958; children: Susan, Edward. BA summa cum laude, Bowling Green State U., 1960; postgrad., Oxford U., Eng., 1963-64; PhD in Econs., U. Pa., Eng., 1966. Lectr. in econs. Wharton Sch., U. Pa., 1964-65; economist Rand Corp., 1965-68; mem. Inst. Advanced Study, Princeton, NJ, 1968-69; sr. economist Pres.'s Council Econ. Advs., Washington, 1969-72; vis. assoc. prof. econs. Cornell U., 1972-73; assoc. prof. bus. econs. U. Mich., 1973-75, prof., 1975-88, prof. emeritus bus. econs. and pub. policy, 1988—; pres. Edward J. Mitchell Inc., Ann Arbor, 1977—94. Dir. nat. energy project Am. Enterprise Inst., 1974-76; pres. Fountainhead Investment Co., 1984—94. Author: U.S. Energy Policy: A Primer, 1974, Dialogue on World Oil, 1974, Financing the Energy Industry, 1975, Vertical Integration of the Oil Industry, 1976, The Deregulation of Natural Gas, 1983; contbr. articles to profl. jours. Home: 310 Penny Ln Santa Barbara CA 93108-2601 Office: Grad Sch Bus U Mich Ann Arbor MI 48109 Personal E-mail: ejmitchell@xtra.co.nz.

MITCHELL, ELIZABETH MARELLE, family practice nurse practitioner, medical/surgical nurse, nursing educator; b. Bemis, Tenn., Dec. 2, 1937; d. William Columbus and Ruth Marelle (Wadley) Latham; m. Thomas Alton McNatt, June 20, 1953 (dec. Mar. 1984); children: Glenn McNatt, Craig McNatt, Chris McNatt; m. Charles Leon Mitchell, Sept. 7, 1985; stepchildren: Melanie Campbell, Mike, Allyson Webb. AA in Nursing, Union U., 1965; BSN, U. Tenn., Martin, 1994; MSN, FNP, U. Tenn., Memphis, 1996. RN Tenn., cert. nurse, operating room, BCLS, BCLS instr., BCLS instr. trainer, ACLS, ACLS instr., family nurse practitioner, ANCC. Staff nurse med.-surg. units Jackson-Madison County Gen. Hosp., Tenn., 1965-66; physician 1st asst. Jackson Clinic Surgeons, 1966-74; nursing instr. Jackson Area Vo-Tech Sch., 1974-78, nursing instr. supr., 1978-81; supr. oper. rm. Jackson Splty. Hosp. (acquired by Jackson-Madison County Gen. Hosp. 1983), 1981-85; instr. nurse edn. Jackson-Madison County Gen. Hosp., 1985-96; family nurse practitioner Perry County Med. Ctr., 1996—. Nursing adv. bd. mem. Jackson Area Vo-Tech Sch., 1987—96; task force nursing asst. curriculum devel. mem. State of Tenn., Nashville, 1992; clin. skills judge Health Occupations Student Assn. Tenn. State Competition, Nashville, 1992. Tchr. Sun. sch. Malesus Bapt. Ch., Malesus, Tenn., 1975—86. Mem.: ANAA, West Tenn. Healthcare Edn. and Tng. Conf. Group (pres. 1987, regional rep. 1988, sec. 1994), Tenn. Nursing Assn., Am. Soc. Healthcare Edn. and Tng. (svc. rep. West Tenn. 1988, Outstanding Regional Rep. Tenn. chpt. 1988), Assn. Oper. Rm. Nurses (program com. 1993, 1994), Am. Acad. Nurse Practitioners, U. Tenn. Martin Nursing Honor Soc., Sigma Theta Tau, Phi Theta Kappa. Avocations: reading, swimming, crafts. Home: 4963 Hwy 412 w Linden TN 37096-5611 Office: Perry County Med Ctr 115 E Brooklyn St Linden TN 37096

MITCHELL, ERIC EHRMAN, photographer, stock broker; b. Phila., Nov. 24, 1954; s. Ehrman Burkman and Hermine (Strickler) M.; m. Leslie Ann March, Aug. 18, 1984; children: Meredith Hermine, Lauren Calder. BS in Photography and Bus., Skidmore Coll., 1977. Accredited asset mgmt. specialist. Head photographer Phila. Mus. Art, 1978-86; freelance photographer St. Peters, Pa., 1986-94; stockbroker Montanto Securities, Bluebell, Pa., 1994-95, Boenning & Scattergood, Inc., Pottstown, Pa., 1996—, v.p., 1996—. Photographs have appeared in various books, catalogues and mags. worldwide. Planning commr. South Coventry Twp., Chester County, Pa., 1990-96, 2001—, supr., 1992-98; mem. Fedn. No. Chester County Cmtys., Pa., 1992-2003; bd. dirs. Pottstown Meml. Med. Ctr., 2003—, Kimberton Waldorf Sch. 2006-; bd. dirs., pres. Pottstown Rotary Cmty. Endowment Fund, 2006—. Fellow Paul Harris, 2002. Mem.: Am. Soc. Media Photographers, St. Andrews Soc., Pottstown Club (pres. 2005—06), Rotary. Avocations: skiing, hiking, woodland management, technical analysis of the stock market. Office: Boenning & Scattergood 601 High St Pottstown PA 19464 Office Phone: 610-327-0600.

MITCHELL, GARY EARL, physicist, researcher; b. July 5, 1935; s. Earl Raymond and Delma Kathlene (Lockard) Mitchell; m. Carolyn Fey Stutz, Aug. 4, 1957; children: Scott Frederick, Karen Lee(dec.). BS, U. Louisville, 1956; MA, Duke U., 1958; PhD, Fla. State U., 1962. Rsch. assoc. Columbia U., NYC, 1962—64, asst. prof., 1964—68; assoc. prof. NC State U., Raleigh, 1968—74, prof. physics, 1974—, assoc. head physics dept., 1982—97; assoc. dir. Triangle Univs. Nuclear Lab., 1992—. Sr. scientist Alexander von Humboldt Found., Bonn, Germany, 1975, Bonn, 97. Contbr. numerous articles to sci. pubs. Recipient Alumni Disting. Prof. award, NC State U. Fellow: Am. Phys. Soc. (Jesse Beams award 1997); mem.: numerous sci. assns. Avocation: history. Home: 2913 Harriman Rd Durham NC 27705-5423 Office: NC State U Dept Physics PO Box 8202 Raleigh NC 27695-0001 Office Phone: 919-660-2638. Business E-Mail: mitchell@tunl.duke.edu, gary_mitchell@ncsu.edu.

MITCHELL, GEORGE CHARLES, diplomat, international consultant, mediator, educator, writer; b. Aug. 6, 1920; s. Charles Peter and Athena N. (Kapotas) Mitchell; m. Nina Catherine Chaconas, Oct. 22, 1955; children: Martina, Melinda, Marlena. BS, U. Nebr., Kearney, 1941; postgrad., U. Nebr., Lincoln, 1941-42; cert., Oxford U., 1947; MA, Georgetown U., 1947; cert., Acad. Internat. Law, The Hague, The Netherlands, 1948; PhD summa cum laude, Sorbonne U., Paris, 1949; postgrad., Inst. d'Etudes Politiques, Paris, 1947-49, George Washington U. Law Sch., 1959-61, Fgn. Svc. Inst., 1962, postgrad., 1969, U. Pitts., 1974, U.S. Army War Coll., 1980, U.S. Naval War Coll., 1981. News corr., Washington and Western Europe, 1946-49; polit. analyst U.S. Dept. State, Washington, 1951-54, specialist, 1954-55; dep. prin. officer, econ. com. officer, consul Am. Consulate Gen., Belfast, No. Ireland, 1955-58; fgn. rels. officer, UNESCO rels. staff U.S. Dept. State, Washington, 1958-62; prin. officer, polit. officer, consul Am. Consulate, Arequipa, Peru, 1962-67; dean Consular Corps, 1965-66; polit.-mil. officer, 1st sec. Am. Embassy, Santo Domingo, Dominican Republic, 1967-68; prin. officer, polit.-econ. officer, consul Am. Consulate, San Luis Potosi, Mex., 1968-71; chief Speakers Bur. U.S. Dept. State, Washington, 1971-72, plans officer Bur. Pub. Affairs, 1971-72; exec. dir. World Affairs Coun. Pitts., 1973-91; internat. con., mediator Pitts., 1989—; exec. dir. internat. mgmt. tng. Lang. Ctr., Pitts., 1990-91. Adj. prof. grad. internat. bus. mgmt. Point Pk. U., 1991—2003; internat. mgr. U.S. Arbitration and Mediation, Pa., 1992—93; bd. dirs. Stas. KGFW and KQKY, Kearney, Stas. KKAR and KQKQ, Omaha, Stas. KXNP-KODY, North Platte, 1954—96; leader del. to China World Affairs Coun., 1978; leader del. to Taiwan and Philippines Nat. Coun. World Affairs, 1988. Author: (book) Matthew B. Ridgway: Soldier, Statesman, Scholar, Citizen, 1999; editor: World Affairs Coun. newsletter, Nat. Coun. World Affairs Orgns. newsletter; co-editor: (book) Asian/Pacific Dynamics-Economic, Political, Security, 1984; radio interviewer on internat. affairs, judge (TV series) Battle of Wits; contbr. articles to U.S. govt. publs., profl. jours., newspapers. Founder Prescott Sch., Arequipa, 1965; mem. Western Pa. Dist. Export Coun., Pitts., 1979—92; founder, pres. Atheneum Soc., Washington, 1952; founder Am. Soc. Arequipa, 1963. Lt. (j.g.) USNR, 1942—45, ETO. Recipient Meritorious Honor award, U.S. Dept. State, 1966, Disting. Svc. award, U. Nebr., 1972, 1988; scholar AHEPA, 1939; Paul Harris fellow, Rotary Found., 2004, scholar, U. Nebr., 1941. Mem.: Am. Arbitration Assn., Midwest Conf. World Affairs (adv. coun. 1988—90), Assn. Conflict Resolution, Internat. Exec. Svc. Corps, Fgn. Affairs Rels. Corps, Nat. Coun. World Affairs Orgns. (v.p. 1985—87, pres. 1987—89, bd. dirs., exec. com. 1974—91), Com. Present Danger (founding, bd. dirs.), Am. Fgn. Svc. Assn., Rotary, Mortar Bd. Avocations: reading, writing, public speaking, antiques, travel. Home and Office: 3416 Brookdale Dr Upper Saint Clair Pittsburgh PA 15241-1558

MITCHELL, GEORGE ERNEST, JR., zoology educator; b. Duoro, N.Mex., June 7, 1930; s. George Ernest and Alma Thyrza (Hatley) M.; m. Billie Carolyn McMahan, Mar. 14, 1952; children: Leslie Dianne, Karen Leigh, Cynthia Faye. BS, U. Mo., 1951, MS, 1954; PhD, U. Ill., 1956. Asst. prof. animal sci. U. Ill., 1956-60; assoc. prof. U. Ky., Lexington, 1960-67, prof., 1967-98, prof. emeritus, 1998—, dir. grad. studies in animal scis., 1964-96, coord. beef cattle and sheep, 1974-90. Contbr. articles to profl. jours. Served with USAF, 1951-53. Fulbright research scholar New Zealand, 1973-74; Rsch. scholar Japan Soc. for Promotion of Sci., Japan, 1989 Mem. Am. Soc. Animal Sci. (sec. 1969-70, v.p. 1970-71, pres. So. sect. 1971-72, rsch. fellow 1989, Disting. Svc. award 1994), Am. Dairy Sci. Assn., Am. Inst. Nutrition, AAAS, Council for Agrl. Sci. and Tech., Sigma Xi, Alpha Zeta, Gamma Sigma Delta, Omicron Delta Kappa. Democrat. Methodist. Home: 690 Hill N Dale Rd Lexington KY 40503-2164 Office: U Ky 809 W P Garrigus Bldg Lexington KY 40546-0001 Personal E-mail: gmitchel@earthlink.net.

MITCHELL, GEORGE JOHN, entertainment company executive, lawyer, former senator; b. Waterville, Maine, Aug. 20, 1933; s. George J. and Mary (Saad) M.; m. Heather MacLachlan; children: Andrea, Andrew, Claire. BA, Bowdoin Coll., 1954; LL.B., Georgetown U., 1960. Bar: Maine 1960, D.C. 1960. Trial atty. anti-trust divsn. US Dept. Justice, Washington, 1960-62; exec. asst. to Senator Edmund Muskie US Senate, 1962-65; ptnr. Jensen, Baird, Gardner & Henry, Portland, Maine, 1965-77; US atty. Dist. Maine US Dept. Justice, 1977-79; judge US Dist. Ct. Maine, 1979-80; US Senator from Maine, 1980-95; majority leader, 1988-95; mem. environ. and pub. works com., 1980-95; mem. vet. affairs com., fin. com., 1981-95; mem. nat. ocean policy study group, arms control observer group; ex officio mem. intelligence com.; chmn. Dem. Senatorial Campaign Com., 1984-86; spl. counsel Verner, Liipfert, Bernhard, McPherson and Hand, Washington, 1996—2002, Preti, Flaherty, Beliveau, Pachios & Haley, Portland, Maine, 1997—2005; ptnr. Piper Rudnick, Washington, 2002—04; ptnr., chmn. global bd., co-chmn. Govt. Controversies practice group DLA Piper, 2005—; chmn. The Walt Disney Co., Burbank, Calif., 2004—06. Chmn. Maine Democratic Com., 1966-68; nat. committeeman, Maine, 1969-77; dep. dir. Edmund S. Muskie presdl. campaign, 1968, 1972; asst. county atty. Cumberland County, 1971; spl. adv. to Pres.& Sec. of State for Econ. Initiatives in Ireland, 1995-2000; chmn., Sharm el-Sheikh Internat. Fact-Finding Com. to Examine Crisis in Middle East, 2000-01; head, Investigation of Steroid Abuse in Major League Baseball, 2006-; bd. dirs. The Walt Disney Co., 1995-2007. Author: World on Fire: Saving an Endangered Earth, 1990, Not For America Alone: The Triumph of Democracy and The Fall of Communism, 1997, Making Peace, 1999; co-author (with William S. Cohen): Men of Zeal: A Candid Inside Story of the Iran-Contra Hearings, 1988. Served with U.S. Army, 1954-56; overseer Red Cross 9-11 Disaster Fund. Recipient Phila. Liberty medal, 1998, Presdl. Medal of Freedom, 1999, Truman Inst. Peace Prize, German Peace Prize, UNESCO Peace Prize, Harry Hopkins medal. Chaired Northern Ireland peace talks which led to the Good Friday Agreement, 1998. Office: DLA Piper 1251 Ave of the Americas New York NY 10020-1104 Business E-Mail: george.mitchell@dlapiper.com.

MITCHELL, GEORGE PHYDIAS, gas and petroleum company executive; b. Galveston, Tex., 1919; m. Cynthia BS, Tex. A&M U., 1940. Exploration engr., geologist Amoco Prodn. Co., 1940-41, cons. geologist, engr., 1940-41; pres. Mitchell Energy & Devel. Corp., 1947-72, chmn. bd. dirs., CEO, 1972—. With Mitchell Energy & Devel. Corp., The Woodlands, Tex., 1947—, chmn., pres., 1972—, chief exec. officer, from 1972, also bd. dirs.; pres. George Mitchell & Assocs. Served to maj. U.S. Army, 1942-46. Recipient Michel T. Halbouty Human Needs award, Am. Assn. Petroleum Geologists 1994; named one of Forbes' Richest Americans, 2006.

MITCHELL, HARRY E., congressman, former state legislator; b. Tempe, July 18, 1940; s. Harry Casey and Irene Gladys (Childres) M.; m. Marianne Prevratil, May 5, 1962; children: Amy, Mark. BA, Ariz. State U., 1962, MPA, 1981. Tchr. Tempe (Ariz.) H.S., 1964—; city councilman City of Tempe, 1970—76, vice mayor, 1976—78, mayor, 1978—94; mem. Ariz. State Senate, 1999—2006, US Congress from 5th Ariz. dist., 2007—, mem. sci. & tech. com., transp. & infrastructure com., vets affairs com. Chmn., Ariz. Dem. Party, 2005-06; Bd. dirs. Tempe Sister City; trustee Tempe St. Lukes Hosp., Rio Salado Devel. Dist.; state rep. Sister Cities Internat., Washington; mem. Ariz. State U. Liberal Arts Alumni Adv. Bd., Adv. Council Ctr. Pub. Affairs, Ariz. Commn. Post Secondary Edn.; mem. Nat. League Cities Resolutions Com.; exec. com. League Ariz. Cities; bd. dirs. Ariz. Mcpl. Water Users. Recipient Disting. Svc. award Tempe Jaycees, Pub. Programs Disting. Achievement award, Ariz. State U. Mem. Ariz. State U. Alumni Bd. (chmn.), Ariz. State U. Advanced Pub. Exec. Program. Democrat. Roman Catholic. Office: 2434 Rayburn House Office Bldg Washington DC 20515 also: 7201 E Camelback Rd Ste 335 Scottsdale AZ 85253 *

MITCHELL, J. BARRY, corporate financial executive; m. Beth Mitchell; 3 children. BBA, Lehigh Univ., 1970, MBA, 1971. With PECO Energy Co., 1971—2000, v.p., treas., 1994—2000, Exelon Corp. (formed by merger of PECO Energy & Unicom Corp.), Chgo., 2000—02; sr. v.p., treas. Exelon Corp., Chgo., 2002—03, sr. v.p., treas., bus. unit CFO, 2003—05, sr. v.p., treas., CFO, 2005—. Bd. dir. Energy Ins. Mutual; mem. adv. bd. Factory Mutual Ins. Co. Mem. exec. com. Juvenile Diabetes Rsch. Found.; trustee Merit Sch. Music. Office: Exelon Corp 10 S Dearborn St Chicago IL 60603 also: Exelon Thermal Technologies 200 W Jackson Blvd Ste 1310 Chicago IL 60606-6941

MITCHELL, JAMES ANDREW, education educator; b. Fort Campbell, Ky., Feb. 16, 1953; s. James Andrew and Joyce Anne (Smith) M.; 1 child, Magdalena Amelie. AB, Vassar Coll., 1975; MA, Princeton U., 1979, PhD, 1985. Instr. Princeton U., Princeton, NJ, 1981—82; asst. prof. Haverford Coll., Pa., 1981—82, U. Redlands, Calif., 1982—85; escort/interpreter U.S. Dept. State, Washington, 1983—86; project mgr. Delphi Internat. Group, Washington, 1986—89; asst. prof. Mt. Vernon Coll., Washington, 1990—94; assoc. prof. Calif. State U., Northridge, 1994—2003, prof., 2003—. Vis. faculty fellow Am. U. in Kygyzstan, 2001, U. Bucharest, 2001; bd. dirs. South East European Inst. of Internat. Affairs; Am. fgn. policy adv. bd. Dushkin Publ., 2006—. Contbr. articles to profl. jours. Mem. African policy issues group George Bush for Pres. Campaign, Washington, 1988. J. William Fulbright fellow CIES and USIA, U. Bucharest, 1977, NEH fellow, Washington, 1989, John Parker Compton pre-doctoral fellow Ctr. for Internat. Studies, Princeton U., 1981; Rsch. grantee Woodrow Wilson Sch., Princeton U., 1989 Mem.: Princeton Club of N.Y. Avocations: exercise, aerobics. Office: Dept Polit Sci/Calif State 18111 Nordhoff St Northridge CA 91330-0001 Office Phone: 818-677-3488. Business E-Mail: james.mitchell@csun.edu.

MITCHELL, JAMES EDWARD, physician, educator; b. Chgo., June 19, 1947; s. James Edward and Elizabeth Latimer M.; m. Karen Antrim, June 14, 1969; children: James, Katherine. BA, Ind. U., 1968; MD, Northwestern U., 1972. Diplomate Am. Bd. Psychiatry Neurology. Intern Indpls. U., Mpls., 1972—73; resident U. Minn., Mpls., 1973—76, from asst. prof. to prof., 1979-90, prof., 1990-96; prof., chmn. dept. neuroscience sch. medicine & health sci. U. N.D., Fargo, 1996—. Pres., scientific dir. Neuropsychiat. Rsch. Inst., Fargo, 1996—. Named Tchr. of Yr., N.D. Psychiat. Residents Assn., 1997-98, 98-99. Fellow Am. Psychiat. Assn., Am. Assn. Social Psychiatry; mem. Acad. Eating Disorders (pres. 1999-2000), Eating Disorders Rsch. Soc. (sec.-treas. 1995—). Avocations: canoeing, art, travel. Office: Neuropsychiat Rsch Inst PO Box 1415 700 1st Ave S Fargo ND 58107 Office Phone: 701-293-1335. Fax: 701-293-3226. E-mail: mitchell@medicine.nodak.edu.

MITCHELL, JAMES KENNETH, civil engineer, educator; b. Manchester, NH, Apr. 19, 1930; s. Richard N. and Henrietta (Moench) M.; m. Virginia D. Williams, Nov. 24, 1951; children: Richard A., Laura K., James W., Donald M., David K.; m. Holly R. Taylor, May 19, 2007. BBCE, Rensselaer Poly. Inst., 1951; MS, MIT, 1953, DSc, 1956. Mem. faculty U. Calif., Berkeley, 1958-93, prof. civil engring., 1968-89, chmn. dept., 1979-84, Edward G. and John R. Cahill prof. civil engring., 1989-92, Edward G. and John R. Cahill prof. civil engring. emeritus, 1993—; Via prof. civil engring. Va. Poly. Inst. and State U., Blacksburg, 1994-99, Univ. Disting. prof., 1996-99, Univ. Disting. prof. emeritus, 1999—. Geotech. cons., 1960—. Author: Fundamentals of Soil Behavior, 1976, 3d edit., 2005; contbr. articles to profl. jours. Asst. scoutmaster Boy Scouts Am., 1975-82; mem. Moraga (Calif.) Environ. Rev. Com., 1978-80. Served to 1st lt. AUS, 1956-58. Recipient Exceptional Sci. Achievement medal NASA, 1973, Berkeley citation, 1993, Chief of Engrs. Outstanding Svc. award U.S. Army Corps Engrs., 1999, Rensselaer Alumni Assn. Fellows award, 2006, Dept. of Army Outstanding Civilian Svc. medal, 2007. Mem. ASCE (hon., Huber prize 1965, Middlebrooks award 1962, 70, 73, 01, Norman medal 1972, 95, Terzaghi lectr. 1984, Terzaghi award 1985, H. Bolton Seed medal 2004, Outstanding Projects and Leaders award in edn., 2006, pres. San Francisco sect. 1986-87), NAS, Nat. Acad. Engring. (vice chair civil engring. sect. 2001-03, chair 2003-05), Am. Soc. Engring. Edn. (We. Electric Fund award 1979), NRC (geotech. bd. chmn. 1990-94, bd. on infrastructure and constrn. environ. 1994-96, transp. rsch. bd. exec. com. 1983-87, mem. water sci. and tech. bd. 2005—), Internat. Soc. Soil Mechanics and Geotech. Engring. (v.p. N.Am. 1989-94, Kevin Nash Gold medal 2001), Earthquake Engring. Rsch. Inst., Japanese Geotech. Soc. (internat. hon. mem.), Brit. Geotech. Soc. (Rankine lectr. 1991), Sigma Xi, Tau Beta Pi. Office: Va Tech Dept Civil Engring Blacksburg VA 24061-0105 Office Phone: 540-231-7351. Business E-Mail: jkm@vt.edu.

MITCHELL, JAN L., advocate, writer; d. Milton Bennington and Frances J. Mitchell (Stepmother). Ins. agy. mgr. Malcolm Ins. Group, Canton, Ohio, 1994—2002; pvt. disability adv., motivational spkr. and writer Canton, Ohio, 2004—. Gov. appointee Ohio Govs. Coun. on People with Disabilities, Columbus, 2006—. Exhibitions include A Modern Day Betsy Ross (First Pl. Amazing Design, 2003), Goldilocks Revisited (Third Pl., 2002). Ms. Wheelchair Ohio Ms. Wheelchair Am., Washington, 2007—. Recipient Mayor's Proclamation and Key to the City, Canton, 2007. Mem.: Aultman Hosp. Womans Bd., Internat. Assn. Assistance Dog Ptnrs. (scholar 2003), Congress Lake Country Club, Glenmoor Country Club, Canton Woman Club, Jr. League Canton (Exceptional Merit award 2000). Avocations: travel, animals. Home: 4614 Preserve Dr NW Canton OH 44708 Home Phone: 330-478-1437. Personal E-mail: mswheelchairohio@aol.com.

MITCHELL, JASON WAYNE, radiologist; b. Passaic, NJ, Dec. 29, 1976; s. William Steven and Diane Lee (Brum) Mitchell; m. Amy Michelle Morin, July 10, 1999. BS, Boston Coll., Chestnut Hill, 1994—98; MD, UMDNJ-NJMS, Newark, 2000—04. Intern & chief resident transitional program St. Barnabas Med. Ctr., Livingston, NJ, 2004—05; chief resident diagnostic radiology UMDNJ, 2005—. Pres., NJMS resident coun. UMDNJ, 2005—06. Mem.: AMA, Soc. Interventional Radiology, Radiologic Soc. N.Am., Am. Coll. Radiology, Am. Mensa. R-Consevative. Roman Cath. Achievements include research in diagnostic and interventional radiology with a focus in hepatic pathology and the treatment of hepatocellular carcinoma. Avocations: chess, poker. Home: 19 Elinora Dr Wanaque NJ 07465 Office: UMDNJ 150 Bergen St C-320 Newark NJ 07103 Home Phone: 973-839-0810. Personal E-mail: mitchejn@gmail.com. Business E-Mail: j.mitchell@umdnj.edu.

MITCHELL, JERRY, choreographer, actor; Choreographer (Broadway plays) Jerome Robbins' Broadway, 1989, Three Men on a Horse, 1993, Grease, 1994, You're a Good Man, Charlie Brown, 1999, The Full Monty, 2000, The Rocky Horror Picture Show, 2000, Hairspray, 2002, Imaginary Friends, 2002, Gypsy, 2003, Never Gonna Dance, 2003, La Cage aux Folles, 2004 (Tony award, best choreography, 2005, Drama Desk award, outstanding choreography, 2005, Outer Critics Circle award, outstanding choreography, 2005), Dirty Rotten Scoundrels, 2005, Catch Me If You Can, 2005, choreographer & dir. Legally Blonde, 2007, conceiver and dir. Broadway Bares (annual charity event), choreographer (films) Scent of a Woman, 1992, Jeffrey, 1995, In & Out, 1997, Drop Dead Gorgeous, 1999, Hedwig and the Angry Itch, 2001, Camp, 2003, Marci X, 2003, dance consultant Meet Joe Black, 1998, choreographer (TV series) The Drew Carey Show, 1995, (TV films) Geppetto, 2000, art dir. The New Gladiators, 1983; actor: The Secret of the Purple Reef, 1960. *

MITCHELL, JERRY, reporter; b. Texarkana, Tex., 1959; BA, Harding U., Ark., 1982; MA, Ohio State U., Columbus, 1997. Spl. projects reporter Clarion-Ledger, Jackson, Miss., 1986—. Author: The Preacher & the Klansman, 1998; cons. (documentaries) Killed by the Klan, 1999. Finalist Pulitzer Prize, 2006; recipient Kennedy Ctr. honors, ADL, 1998, Heywood Broun award for disting. journalism, 1999, Outstanding Alumnus award, Harding U., 1999, Nat. Assn. Black Journalists award, 1999, newspaper award, Sidney Hillman Found., 1999, Sigma Delta Chi award for pub. svc. in journalism, Soc. Professional Journalists, 1999, 2 Best of Gannett awards, 1999, Silver Em award, U. Miss. Dept. Journalism, 2000, Outstanding Achievement Award of Excellence, Gannett Co., 2002, John Chancellor award for Excellence in Journalism, Columbia U., 2005, Pres.'s medal, CUNY Queen's Coll., 2005, Vernon Jarrett award, NC Agricultural & Technical State U. Inst. Advanced Journalism Studies, 2006, Tom Renner medal for outstanding crime reporting, Investigative Reporters & Editors, 2006, George Polk award for justice reporting, 2006. Achievements include investigative reporting leading to the prosecution and conviction of white supremacists who had committed murders in the 1960s; including the murders of civil rights activists in Mississippi and the 1963 bombing of a church in Birmingham that killed four girls. Office: Clarion-Ledger PO Box 40 Jackson MS 39205 Office Phone: 601-961-7064. Office Fax: 601-961-7211. E-mail: jmitchell@clarionledger.com.

MITCHELL, JOAN LAVERNE, research scientist; b. Palo Alto, Calif., May 24, 1947; d. William Richardson and Doris LaVerne (Roddan) M. BS in Physics, Stanford U., 1969; MS in Physics, U. Ill., 1971, PhD in Physics, 1974. Rsch. staff mem. T.J. Watson Rsch. Ctr. IBM, Yorktown Heights, NY, 1974-88, 96-98, mgr. T.J. Watson Rsch. Ctr., 1979-88, image tech. cons. mktg. White Plains, NY, 1989-91, rsch. staff mem. T.J. Watson Rsch. Ctr. Hawthorne, NY, 1991-94, mgr. T.J. Watson Rsch. Ctr., 1992-94, supplemental employee Burlington, NY, 1994-96; vis. prof. U. Ill., Urbana, 1996; with IBM Printing Systems Divsn., Boulder, Colo., 1999—2007, IBM fellow, 2001—07; InfoPrint Solutions Co. fellow InfoPrint Solutions Co., 2007—. Del. CCITT Study Group XIV, 1978-79, ISO JPEG Com., 1987-94, ITU-T Study Group 16 Working Party 3, 2005—. Co-author: JPEG Still Image Data Compression Standard, 1993, MPEG Video Compression Standard, 1997; contbr. articles to profl. jours. Recipient U. Ill. Coll. Engring. Disting. Alumni Svc. award, 2006, Leadership award Internat. Multimedia Telecoms. Consortium, 2006; Xerox Indsl. fellow, 1970-71. Fellow IEEE; mem. NAE, Am. Phys. Soc., Soc. for Imaging Sci. and Tech., Sigma Xi (chpt. sec. 1976, v.p. 1977, pres. 1978), Phi Beta Kappa, Phi Kappa Phi. Democrat. Achievements include co-inventor on numerous patents. Home: 1172 Fall River Cir Longmont CO 80501 Office: InfoPrint Solutions Co 6300 Diagonal Hwy MS004N Boulder CO 80301-9270 Office Phone: 303-924-4271. Business E-Mail: joanm@us.ibm.com.

MITCHELL, JOHN CHARLES, marketing professional; b. Bedford, Ind., May 25, 1947; s. John Lewis and Mary Ellen (Rowe) M.; m. Marie Elizabeth Bruland, Aug. 21, 1971; 1 child, Allison Anne. BA in Econs., Va. Mil. Inst., 1969; MBA, JD, Ind. U., 1975. Bar: Ind., 1975, Fed. Cts., 1975. Brand mgr. Procter and Gamble Co., Cin., 1975-82; group product mgr. RJR/Del Monte, San Francisco, 1982-84; dir. mktg. RJR/Nabisco, Parsippany, NJ, 1984-87, v.p. mktg., 1987-88, v.p., gen. mgr., 1988-90, pres. sales and logistics co., 1991-94, pres. Planters, Lifesavers co. Winston-Salem, NC, 1994-96; pres. bus. printer divsn. Lexmark Internat., Inc., Lexington, Ky., 1997-99; founder Collaborative Leaders, Inc., Chapel Hill, NC, 2001—. 1st lt. US Army, 1969-71. Inductee Va. Mil. Inst. Sports Hall of Fame, 1981. Republican. Methodist. Avocations: golf, skiing. E-mail: jandmmitchell@nc.rr.com.

MITCHELL, JOHN DANIEL, taxonomist, ecologist; b. NYC, Nov. 30, 1957; s. John Dietrich and Miriam (Pitcairn) M.; m. Beth Ann Trowbridge, Aug. 4, 1979; children, George Trowbridge, Charles Arthur. BS in Biology, Muhlenberg Coll., 1979. Wildlife mgr. Pennypack Watershed Assn., Huntingdon Valley, Pa., 1979-80; hon. rsch. assoc. N.Y. Bot. Garden, Bronx, NY, 1983-95, hon. curator, 1995—; chmn. bd., exec. sec. Beneficia Found. Bd. dirs. Beneficia Found., Jenkintown, Pa.; mem. bot. scis. com. N.Y. Bot. Garden. Sr. author: The Cashew and Its Relatives, 1987; co-author: Topic-Plant Ecology, 1986; illustrator: Search for Style, 1982, MacBeth Unjinxed, 1985; co-author: Guide to the Vascular Plants of Central French Guiana, 1997, Part 2, 2002; contbr. articles to profl. jours. Bd. dirs. N.J. Nature Conservancy, 2000—, Am. Bird Conservancy, 1999—, Wildlife Trust, 2000—. Fellow Linnean Soc. London; mem. Internat. Assn. Plant Taxonomists, Ecol. Soc. Am., AAAS, BAT Conservation Internat. (vice-chmn. 1987—), Pennypack Watershed Assn. (bd. dirs. 1981-90), Inst. for Advanced Studies in the Theatre Arts (adv. bd. 1987-95), Phila Bot. Club, New Eng. Bot. Club, Explorers' Club, Orgn. for Flora Neotropica. Democrat. Avocations: birdwatching, hiking, photography, travel, sketching.

MITCHELL, JOHN GERALD, educational administrator; b. Cadiz, Ky., Oct. 8, 1936; s. John Carter and Mary Cicero (Terrell) M.; m. Barbara Jane Hayes, Dec. 18, 1960; children: David Terrell, Angela Carol. AA, Bethel Coll., Hopkinsville, Ky., 1960; BA in English Edn., Western Ky. U., 1962; BD, So. Bapt. Theol. Sem., 1966, PhD in Bibl. Lang., 1970; PhD in Edn. Leadership, Vanderbilt U., 1984. Cert. secondary sch. tchr., Ky. Dir. admissions Bethel Coll., 1963; vocat. guidance cons. Bapt. Sunday Sch. Bd., Nashville, 1970-72; pres., exec. dir. Edn. Corp. Am., Nashville, 1972-76; acad. dean Truett McConnell Coll., Cleve., 1976-80; asst. acad. v.p. Wayland Bapt. U., Plainview, Tex., 1982, asst. to pres.-planning, 1990; exec. dir. XL Learning, Nashville, 1991—; seminar leader U. Geneva, 1975-76; adj. prof. edn. Austin Peay State U., 1993-, interin dean sch. edn., 2003-06 presenter in field; cons. U. Calif., Riverside, 1975. Author: Re-Visioning Educational Leadership Garland Publishing, Inc., 1990; co-author: The Church Covenant, 1971; contbr. articles to profl. jours. Exec. com. Ga. Mountain Program on Aging, Cleveland, Ga., 1977-78; ednl. adv. com. U.S. Congressman Edward Jenkins, Ga., 1978-79; careers com. N.Ga. Tech. Sch., Clarkesville, 1979. With US Army, 1956-58. Recipient Tchg. Excellence and Campus Leadership award Sears-Roebuck Found., 1990, Outstanding Academic Book award Am. Libr. Assn., 1992. Mem. Plainview C. of C. (gov. affairs com. 1985-87), Internat. Platform Assn., World Future Soc., Am. Conf. Acad. Deans, Soc. Educators and Scholars, Am. Assn. Sch. Adminstrs., Tex. Edn. Assn., Am. Assn. for Higher Edn. Democrat. Baptist. Clubs: Internat. Relations Bethel Coll. (pres. 1958-59), Grad. So. Bapt. Theol. Sem. (v.p. 1968-69). Avocations: flying; fishing; camping; gardening. Office: XL Learning 4285 Trenton Rd Clarksville TN 37040-5643 Personal E-mail: jmitchell1231@charter.net.

MITCHELL, JOHN LAURIN AMOS, biological science educator; b. Lincoln, Nebr., July 18, 1944; s. William A. and Ruth Chilla (Cobbey) M.; m. Gail Ann Kurtz, July 13, 1968; children: Jill, Todd. BA, Oberlin Coll., 1966; PhD, Princeton U., 1970. Postdoctoral fellow McArdle Inst. Cancer Rsch., Madison, Wis., 1970-73; asst. prof. No. Ill. U., DeKalb, 1973-78, assoc. prof., prof., 1983—; dir. Ctr. Biochem. Biophys. Rsch., 1997—. Inventor in field; contbr. articles to profl. jours.

MITCHELL, JOHN NOYES, JR., retired electrical engineer; b. Pownal, Maine, Dec. 16, 1930; s. John Noyes and Frances (Small) M.; m. Marilyn Jean Michaelis, Sept. 1, 1956 (dec.); children: Brian John, Cynthia Lynn Mitchell Tumbleson, Stephanie Lee Mitchell Judson; m. Jacqueline A. Starr, Sept. 10, 1999. BSEE, Milw. Sch. Engring., 1957. Registered profl. engr., Ohio. Elec. rsch. engr. Nat. Cash Register Co., Dayton, Ohio, 1957—65; sr. engr. Xerox Corp., Rochester, NY, 1965—70, mgr. area, 1970—73, Dallas, 1973—76, El Segundo, Calif., 1976—79, mgr. tech. program, 1979—85, mgr. competitive benchmarking, 1985—92, mgr. quality, 1992—97. With USN, 1949—53. Mem.: IEEE, Shriners, Masons. Republican. Episcopalian. Home: 5545 Downham Meadow Sarasota FL 34235-0971 Personal E-mail: jnmitch3@comcast.net.

MITCHELL, JON CEANDER, music educator, conductor; b. Chgo., June 18, 1949; s. James William and Violet Linnea Mitchell; m. Ester Morales, Dec. 22, 1973; children: Monica Mitchell Finn, Lydia, David. MusB, Millikin U., Decatur, Ill., 1971; MS in Music Edn., U. Ill., 1972, EdD in Music Edn., 1980. Asst. prof. music Hanover Coll., Ind., 1982—87; condr. wind ensemble Carnegie Mellon U., Pitts., 1987—91; asst. prof. music U. Ga., Athens, 1991—92; prof. music U. Mass., Boston, 1992—96, chair dept., 1996—. Music dir. North Pitts. Civic Symphony, Pitts., 1988—92; guest conducting various bands and orchs. Author: From Kneller Hall to Hammersmith, 1990, A Comprehensive Biography of Gustav Holst, 2001, The Braunschweig Scores: Felix Weingartner and Erich Leinsdorf on Beethoven's First Four Symphonies, 2005; condr.: CD Beethoven: Piano Concerto in D, Op. 61, Concerto in D, 2004, The Youthful Beethoven, 2005, Beethoven: Piano Concerto in E Flat, Wio.0.4, 2005; condr. (CD) Gustav Holst: Composer as Arranger, 2007; contbr. articles to profl. jours. Mem.: Coll. Band Dirs. Nat. Assn., Music Educators Nat. Conf., World Assn. Symphonic Bands and Ensembles (asst. editor newsletter 2000, editor WASBE jour. 1994), Condrs. Guild, Phi Kappa Phi. Avocations: travel, model railroading, coaster collecting. Office: Dept Performing Arts U Mass 100 Morrissey Blvd Boston MA 02125-3393

MITCHELL, JONI (ROBERTA JOAN ANDERSON), singer, songwriter, artist; b. Ft. Macleod, Alta., Can., Nov. 7, 1943; d. William A. and Myrtle M. (McKee) Anderson; m. Chuck Mitchell (div.); m. Larry Klein, Nov. 21, 1982. Student, Alta. Coll. Albums Song to a Seagull, Clouds, Ladies of the Canyon, Blue, For the Roses, Court and Spark, 1974, Miles of Aisles, The Hissing of Summer Lawns, 1975, Hejira, 1976, Don Juan's Reckless Daughter, 1979, Mingus, 1979 (Jazz Album of Year and Rock-Blues Album of Year, Downbeat mag., 1979), Shadows and Light, 1980, Wild Things Run Fast, 1982, Dog Eat Dog, 1985, Chalk Mark in a Rainstorm, 1988, Night Ride Home, 1991, Turbulent Indigo, 1994, Hits, 1996, Taming the Tiger, 1998, Both Sides Now, 2000, Travelogue, 2002, screenwriter/actor (films) Love, 1982; contbr. album dog Eat Dog/Wild Things Run Fast, 1996; co-creator (Operas) The Fiddle and the Drum, 2007; exhibitions include Green Flag Song, 2006, Flag Dance, 2007. Named to Rock and Roll Hall of Fame, 1997; recipient Grammy award for Best Folk Performance, 1969, Grammy award for Best Arrangement Accompanying Vocalists (with Tom Scott), 1974. Address: care Reprise Records 3300 Warner Blvd Burbank CA 91505-4632 *

MITCHELL, JOSEPH PATRICK, architect; b. Bellingham, Wash., Sept. 29, 1939; s. Joseph Henry and Jessie Delila (Smith) Mitchell; m. Marilyn Ruth Jorgenson, June 23, 1962; children: Amy Evangeline, Kirk Patrick, Scott Henry. Student, Western Wash. State Coll., 1957-59; BA, U. Wash., 1963, BArch, 1965. Assoc. designer, draftsman, project architect Beckwith Spangler Davis, Bellevue, Wash., 1965-70; prin. J. Patrick Mitchell, AIA & Assocs./Architects/Planners/Cons., Kirkland, Wash., 1970—. Del. various internat. confs.; charter mem. Northshore Bapt. Ch., 1969, elder, 1984—90; bd. ext. and ctrl. com. Columbia Bapt. Conf., 1977—83, vice-moderator, 1995—96, moderator, 1996—97, overseer ch. ministries bd., pres., 1997—99; charter mem. Cascade Cmty. Ch., 1997—; trustee Bakke Libr./Cultural Ctr., 1994—96; chmn. long range planning com. Lake Retreat Camp, 1965—93; active Deming Hist. Cemetery Assn., 1997—. Recipient Internat. Archtl. Design award, St. John Vianney Parish, 1989. Mem.: AIA, Christian Camp and Conf. Assn., Wash. Farm Forestry Assn., Internat. Conf. Bldg. Ofcls., Nat. Coun. Archtl. Registration Bds., Nat. Fedn. Bus., Interfaith Forum Religion, Art, and Architecture (arch. edn. tour Finland, St. Petersburg, Russia 1998, Japan 2000, edn. tour China 2001, Spain, Portugal, Scandanavia, Estonia, Russia 2002, Switzerland, France 2004, Eng., Scotland, Ireland 2005, France 2006, Peru, Equador, Costa Rica 2007), Constrn. Specification Inst., Woodinville C. of C. Office: 12620 120th Ave NE Ste 208 Kirkland WA 98034-7511

MITCHELL, KAREN FRANCES, artist, jewelry designer; b. Denver, Aug. 24, 1953; d. Harry Francis and Mary Jane Margrete (Jensen-Borg) Mitchell. BFA, U. Colo., Boulder, 1975; postgrad., Gemological Inst. Am., NYC, 1986, Kulicke Jewelry Arts Inst., 1988, Cecilia Bauer Studio, 1992, Fashion Inst. of Tech., 1993, Nat. Acad. Design, 1994. Cert. tchr., art specialist. Jewelry designer, pres. Karen Mitchell Design, Aspen, Colo., 1978—; cultural rschr., cons. various Italian newspapers and mags., NY., Colo., 1992-94, Italian Consulate Cultural Inst., NY, 1992—94. Instr. workshops design and goldsmithing technique; apprentice Van der Schoot Disegno e Fabricazione, Milan, 1989—91. Co-designer, co-author (book) World Gold Coun. Jewelry Trend Book, 1991—95; exhibitions include World Gold Coun., Aaron Faber Gallery, N.Y.C., Yaw Gallery, Mich., SOFA, Chgo., NY, J. Cotter Gallery, Cindy Griem Fine Jewels, Somerhill Gallery, N.C., Facere Gallery, Wash., Concepts Gallery, Calif., Greene & Greene Gallery, NJ, Yann Gallery, Chgo., Master's Showcase Park Ave., N.Y.C., Fall Crafts Park Ave., The Artful Hand Gallery, Boston, Works Gallery, N.Y.C., Am. Craft Coun. Shows, Balt., Am. Craft Coun., San Francisco, Positive Images Gallery, Austin, Tex., Telluride Gallery, Colo. Vol. chmn. benefit com. Aspen Art Mus.; co-chmn. benefit com. Aspen Music Festival; mem. Les Dames d'Aspen; vol. Profl. Women's Orgn., Milan, Am. Craft Mus., NY, 1993, Coun. Fashion Designers Am., NY, Internat. Design Conf. of Aspen, Screening Com. Aspen Film Fest, Soprano, Aspen Choral Soc.; vol. benefit Aspen Ski Club/U.S. Olympic Equestrian Team, 1995; trustee Aspen Snowmass Coun. Arts. Named Vol.

of the Yr., Aspen Art Mus., 2001. Mem.: Jewelry Design Profl.'s Network, Am. Craft Coun., Soc. N.Am. Goldsmiths. Address: PO Box 4885 Aspen CO 81612-4885 E-mail: kmdaspen@hotmail.com.

MITCHELL, KENNETH DAVID, physiologist, educator; b. Musselburgh, Scotland, Mar. 5, 1959; children: Elaine J., Fraser K., Keith J. BSc with upper 2d class honors, U. Edinburgh, Scotland, 1981, PhD in Physiology, 1986. Physiology tutor Univ. Med. Sch., Edinburgh, 1981-84; rsch. assoc. dept. physiology and biophysics Nephrology Rsch. and Tng. Ctr. U. Ala., Birmingham, 1984-86, postdoctoral rsch. fellow, 1986-87, rsch. instr., 1987-88, scientist I, 1987-88; asst. prof. dept. physiology Tulane U. Sch. Medicine, New Orleans, 1988-95, assoc. prof., 1995—. Contbr. articles to profl. jours. Fellow Am. Heart Assn. (fellow Coun. High Blood Pressure Rsch. 1993—, Established Investigator award 1995-2000), Am. Soc. Nephrology; mem. Am. Physiol. Soc., Internat. Soc. Nephrology. Office: Tulane U Sch Medicine Dept Physiology SL39 1430 Tulane Ave New Orleans LA 70112-2699 Office Phone: 504-988-2593. Business E-Mail: kdmitch@tulane.edu.

MITCHELL, LEE MARK, private equity investor, executive; b. Albany, NY, Apr. 16, 1943; s. Maurice B. and Mildred (Roth) M.; m. Barbara Lee Anderson, Aug. 27, 1966; children: Mark, Matthew. AB, Wesleyan U., 1965; JD, U. Chgo., 1968. Bar: Ill. 1968, D.C. 1969, U.S. Supreme Ct. 1972. Assoc. Leibman, Williams, Bennett, Baird & Minow, Chgo. and Washington, 1968-72, Sidley & Austin, Washington, 1972-74, ptnr., 1974-84, 92-94; exec. v.p. and gen. counsel Field Enterprises, Inc., Chgo., 1981-83, pres., CEO, 1983-84, Field Corp., 1984-92; prin. Golder, Thoma, Cressey, Rauner, Inc., Chgo., 1994-98; mng. ptnr. Thoma Cressey Bravo, Inc., Chgo., 1998—. Chmn. Chgo. Stock Exch., Inc., 2000—04. Author: Openly Arrived At, 1974, With the Nation Watching, 1979; co-author: Presidential Television, 1973. Bd. visitors U. Chgo. Law Sch., 1984—86, Medill Sch. Journalism, Northwestern U., 1984—91; pres. bd. govs. Chgo. Met. Planning Coun., 1988—91; mem. midwest regional adv. bd. Inst. Internat. Edn., 1987—99; trustee Ravinia Festival Assn., 1989—97, Northwestern U., Northwestern Meml. Hosp.; U.S. del. Brit. Legis. Conf. on Govt. and Media, Ditchley Park, England, 1974; adv. com. LWV Presdl. Debates, Washington, 1979—80, 1982; vice chair Chgo. Met. Planning Coun., 1999—2005, chair, 2005—. Mem.: Econ. Mid-Am. Club, ABA, Comml. Club Chgo. Home: 135 Maple Hill Rd Glencoe IL 60022-1252 Office: Thoma Cressey Bravo Inc Sears Tower Ste 9200 233 S Wacker Dr Chicago IL 60606-6331 Business E-Mail: lmitchell@tcb.com.

MITCHELL, LUCILLE ANNE, retired elementary school educator; b. Dayton Corners, Ill., Oct. 19, 1928; d. Roy Rollin and Edna May (Whitehouse) Sheppard; m. Donald L. Mitchell; children: David, Diane, Barbara, Patricia. BS in Edn., Augustana Coll., 1966; MS in Edn., Western Ill. U., 1972, Edn. Specialist, 1974. Tchr. Carbon Cliff (Ill.) Elem. Sch., 1962-65, Moline (Ill.) Bd. Edn., 1967-92. Mem. textbook selection com. Moline Bd. Edn., 1967-84, rep. Moline Bd. Edn., Ill. Network Sch. Devel., 1973. Author: numerous poems. Counselor to pastor Cmty. of Christ, 2001—02, 2007—, elder in priesthood, 1991—. Named Ill. Master Tchr., State of Ill., 1984; recipient Internat. Peace prize United Cultural Convention, 2005. Mem. Ill. Edn. Assn. (com. mem.), Moline Edn. Assn. (com. mem.), Delta Kappa Gamma (program chmn. 1978-79, rec. sec. 1980-81) Avocations: organ, piano, painting, poetry, teaching Bible study classes. Personal E-mail: donnlucy@mchsi.com.

MITCHELL, MARCIA JEANNE, writer; b. San Jose, Calif., Feb. 20, 1932; d. Eugene Lewis Wilcox and Gladys Delphine Shoemaker; m. John Alexander Donnan (div. June 1, 1975); children: Alan James Donnan, Kristen Elizabeth Donnan; m. Thomas Francis Mitchell, June 29, 1985. Student, Colo. State U., 1965—67; BA, Norwich U., Vt. Coll., 1989. Writer, editor Rapid City (S.D.) Jour., 1968—73; cabinet officer, sec. labor S.D. State Govt., Pierre, SD, 1973—75; sr. exec. Corp. for Pub. Broadcasting, Washington, 1975—80; assoc. dir. Am. Film Inst., Washington & L.A., 1980—85; freelance writer, prodr., 1988—. Lectr., seminar leader mgmt. strategies for women, 1980—82; lectr. Crystal Cruise Lines, 1999, Cunard QE2, 2001; motivational sem. spkr. Prodr.: world premieres of maj. motion pictures, 1980—86, A Daughter's Tribute to Fred Astaire, 2001; author: Cosmetics from the Kitchen, 1972, Raindance to Research, 1977, Management Strategies for Women, 1980, 1981, The Spy Who Seduced America: Lies and Betrayal in the Heat of the Cold War, 2002. Past sec. Nat. Assns. Commns. on Women; vice chair Montserrat Found. for Charitable Giving, West Indies, 1995—2001; chair spl. events Hill City (S.D.) Arts Coun., 2001; mem. Montserrat Nat. Trust, Montserrat, 2001; past chair grants com. State Fine Arts Coun., SD; past mem. State Commn. on Status of Women, SD; mem. S.D. Humanities Found. Bd., 2005—06; past bd. dirs. Women's Equity Action League, NYC; past chair TV broadcasting com. PBS Sta. WETA-TV, Washington. Recipient 1st pl. feature writing, S.D. Press Women, 1995, Counter-Intelligence Book of Yr., Assn. Former Intelligence Officers, 2002, 1st pl., Non-fiction Books, 2003. Mem.: Nat. Fedn. Press Women (Top Press Woman of Yr. 1972—73). Roman Catholic.

MITCHELL, MARY JENKINS, public health service officer; b. Rochester, NY; d. Hudson and Clara May Jenkins; m. Floyd Mitchell, Aug. 24, 1991; 1 child, Derek Scot. B Cmty. Health, St. Joseph's Coll., Bklyn., 1984; MPA, LI U., Bklyn., 1999. Cert. non-profit mgmt. Columbia U., 1986. Asst. to pres. Bklyn. Borough Pres.' Office, 1987—95; dir., health careers inst. LI U., 1995—2000; regional v.p. Am. Cancer Soc., Bklyn., 2000—03; exec. dir. MSI Area Health Edn. Ctr., NYC, 2004—. Adj. prof. LI U., Brooklyn, NY, 1998—2000; student cons. Pub. Svc. Commn., Pretoria, South Africa, 1998. V.p. Justice Works Cmty., Inc., Bklyn., 1995—2000; deaconess Flatbush Tompkins Congl. Ch., Bklyn., 1997—2004; bd. dirs. NY Women's Found., NYC, 1993—95. Recipient Ability, Accomplishment and Cmty. Svc. award, Outstanding Young Women Am., 1986, Cmty. Leadership award, Bklyn Exec. Bus. Women's Assoc., 2004. Mem.: Pi Alpha Alpha (life). Office: Manhattan-State Area Health Educ Ctr 43 Central Park North New York NY 10026 Home Phone: 718-287-8992; Office Phone: 212-534-2432. Personal E-mail: mljm1@exeite.com. Business E-Mail: mary@msiahec.org.

MITCHELL, MELVIN CLIFFORD, music educator; b. Talihina, Okla., Dec. 1, 1942; s. Lem Granville Mitchell and Evelyn Irene Gale, J. E. Gale (Stepfather); m. Joyce Elaine Anglin, June 23, 1962; children: Matthew Clark, Daniel Dale. MusB in Edn., Okla. State U., 1964; MEd, Southwestern Okla. State U., 1975. Cert. vocal music dir. K-12 Okla. State U. Vocal music dir. Shelbyville (Mo.) Sch. Sys., 1964—65, Littleton (Colo.) Sch. Dist., 1965—66, Lone Wolf (Okla.) Pub. Sch. Sys., 1967—70, Woodward (Okla.) Pub. Sch. Sys., 1970—75; chmn. and vocal music dir. Ea. Okla. State Coll., Wilburton, 1975—83; vocal music dir. Lewisville (Tex.) Ind. Sch. Dist, 1986—. Musical cast mem. and soloist Okla. State U., Stillwater, 1961—64; contest chmn. N.W. Okla Vocal Music Dist., Woodward, 1970—75; vocal music adjudicator/clinician, Okla., 1970—83; mem. all-state music com. Okla. Music Educators Assn., Oklahoma City, 1972—75; dir. sweepstakes choirs Woodward choral orgns., Enid, Okla., 1973—75; dir. musicals Woodward Pub. Schs., 1973—75; vocal music dir. Okla. State 4-H Round-Up, Stillwater, 1975—79; dir. musicals Ea. Okla State coll., 1975—83; vocal choral arranger Griffin Mid. Sch. A cappella Choir, The Colony, Tex., 1998—. Fellow: Phi Delta Kappa (assoc.; found. rep. 1998—2004); mem.: Tex. Choral Dirs. Assn. (assoc.), Tex. Music Educators Assn. (assoc.), Am. Choral Dirs. Assn. (life). Republican. Baptist. Avocation: golf. Home: 2216 Swallow Ln Lewisville TX 75077 Office: Griffin Mid Sch 5105 N Colony Blvd The Colony TX 75056 Home Phone: 972-317-2463; Office Phone: 469-713-5973 x 2960. Home Fax: 972-317-9863. Business E-Mail: mitchellmc@lisd.net.

MITCHELL, MEMORY FARMER, retired communications executive; b. Raleigh, NC, Jan. 21, 1924; d. James S. and Foy Johnson Farmer; m. Thornton W. Mitchell, Sept. 7, 1963 (dec.); children: James Thornton, David Wingate. BA, Meredith Coll., 1944; LLB, JD, U. N.C., 1946, MA in History, 1949. Bar: N.C. 1947. Staff mem. Inst. Govt., Chapel Hill, NC, 1946—47; instr. in history Meredith Coll., Raleigh, NC, 1949—50; asst. state archivist N.C. Divsn. Archives and History, NC, 1956—61; adminstrv. asst. N.C. State Bd. Pub. Welfare, Raleigh, 1950—54; judge Cabarrus County Domestic Rels. Ct., Concord, NC, 1954—56; hist. pubs. adminstr. N.C. Divsn. Archives and History, 1961—82, ret., 1982. Pres. Hist. Soc. N.C., 1973—74. Author: Legal Aspects of Conscription and Exemption in North Carolina, 1861-1865, 1965; editor: Messages and Address of Governors Terry Sanford, Daniel K. Moore, Robert W. Scott, James Holshouser Jr., James B. Hunt, 5 vols., 1966—82; mem. editl. bd.: Am. Archivist, 1972—74. Pres. Meredith Coll. Alumnae Assn., 1982—84; dir. Carolina Charter Corp., 1970—, Wake County Resources for Srs., NC, 1992—98; active Pullen Meml. Bapt. Ch., Raleigh, NC, 1st Bapt. Ch., Raleigh. Named Tar Heel of Wk., News and Observer, Raleigh, N.C., Oct. 1, 1961; recipient Outstanding Alumna award, Meredith Coll. Alumnae, 1978. Mem.: So. Hist. Assn. (coun. 1977—79), N.C. Soc., N.C. Lit. and Hist. Assn. (sec.-treas. 1976—77, Christopher Crittenden award 1981), Friends of the Archives (dir.). Democrat. Baptist. Avocations: reading, travel, cooking, embroidery, crocheting. Home: 2431 Medway Dr Raleigh NC 27608

MITCHELL, MOZELLA GORDON, language educator, minister; b. Starkville, Miss., Aug. 14, 1936; d. John Thomas and Odena Mae (Graham) Gordon; m. Edrick R. Woodson, Mar. 20, 1951 (div. 1974); children: Cynthia LaVern, Marcia Delores Woodson Miller. AB, LeMoyne Coll., 1959; MA in English, U. Mich., 1963; MA in Religious Studies, Colgate-Rochester Divinity Sch., 1973; PhD, Emory U., 1980. Instr. in English and Speech Alcorn A&M Coll., Lorman, Miss., 1960-61; instr. English, chmn. dept. Owen Jr. Coll., Memphis, 1961-65; asst. prof. English and religion Norfolk State Coll. U. Norfolk, Va., 1965—81; assoc. prof. U. South Fla., Tampa, 1981—93, prof., 1993—, chmn.-elect religious studies dept., 2005—, chair religious studies dept., 2006—; pastor Mount Sinai AME Zion Ch., 1982—89; presiding elder Tampa dist. AME Zion Ch., 1988—; pastor, founder Love of Christ AME Zion Tabernacle, Branden, 1993—; candidate for bishop AME Zion Ch., 2003—04, presiding Elder, 1998—2004. Vis. assoc. prof. Hood Theol. Sem., Salisbury, N.C., 1979-80, St. Louis U., 1992-93; vis. asst. lectr. U. Rochester, N.Y., 1972-73; co-dir. Ghent VISTA Project, Norfolk, 1969-71; cons. Black Women and Ministry Interdenominational Theol. Ctr; lectr. Fla. Humanities Coun., 1994-95; Meml. lectr. Mordecai Johnson Inst., Colgate Rochester Div. Sch., 1997. Author: Spiritual Dynamics of Howard Thurman's Theology, 1985, Howard Thurman and the Quest for Freedom, Proc. 2d Ann. Howard Thurman Convocation (Peter Lang), 1992, African American Religious History in Tampa Bay, 1992;, New Africa in America: The Blending of African and American Religious and Social Traditions Among Black People in Meridian, Mississippi and Surrounding Counties (Peter Lang), 1994, Crucial Issues in Caribbean Religions (Peter Lang), 2006, Crucial Issues in Caribbean Religion, 2006; editor: Martin Luther King Meml. Series in Religion, Culture and Social Devel.; editorial bd. Cornucopia Reprint Series; contr. articles and essays in field. Mem. Tampa-Hillsborough County Human Rels. Coun., 1987—; founder Women at the Well, Inc.; del. 7th assembly World Coun. Chs., Canberra, Australia, 1991, 17th World Meth. Coun., Rio de Janiero, 1996; del. 18th World Meth. Coun., Brighton, England, 2001; mem. connectional coun. A.M.E. Zion Ch., Charlotte, 1984—, staff writer Sunday sch. lit., 1981—, mem. jud. coun., candidate for bishop, 2002—04; pres. Fla. Coun. Chs., Orlando, Fla., 1988—90, pres.-elect, 1998—, pres. exec. bd., 2000. Recipient ecumenical leadership citation Fla. Coun. Chs., 1990, Inaugural lectr. award Geddes Hanson Black Cultural Ctr. Princeton Theol. Sem., 1993; fellow Nat. Doctoral Fund, 1978-80; grantee NEH, 1981, Fla. Endowment for Humanities, 1990—, U. South Fla. Rsch. Coun., 1990—. Mem. Coll. Theology Soc., Am. Acad. Religion, Soc. for the Study of Black Religion (pres. 1992-96), Joint Ctr. for Polit. Studies, Black Women in Ch. and Soc., Alpha Kappa Alpha. Phi Kappa Phi. Democrat. Methodist. Avocations: piano, poetry, tennis, bicycling, Scrabble. Office: Univ South Florida Religious Studies Dept CPR 107 Tampa FL 33620 Office Phone: 813-974-1852. Personal E-mail: mozellam@aol.com. Business E-Mail: mmitchel@acas.usf.edu. *In my estimation, people are people, whatever the race, class or status. Between the front yard and the back porch of each individual dwells the real person, to whom I like to direct my approach.*

MITCHELL, ORLAN E., clergyman, academic administrator; b. Eldora, Iowa, Mar. 13, 1933; s. Frank E. and Alice G. (Brown) M.; m. Verlene J. Huehn, June 10, 1952; children: Jolene R., Stephen M., Nadene A., Timothy M., Mark E. BA, Grinnell Coll., 1955; B.D., Yale U., 1959, M.Div., 1965; D.Min., San Francisco Theol. Sem., 1976. Ordained to ministry United Ch. of Christ, 1959; pastor chs. Sheridan Twp., Iowa, 1954-55, New Preston, Conn., 1956-59, Clarion, Iowa, 1959-69, Yankton, SD, 1969-77; pres. Yankton (S.D.) Coll., 1977-96; conf. minister Iowa Conf. United Ch. Christ; ret., 1996. Cons. in field. Mem. Sch. Bd., Clarion, Iowa, 1965-69, mem., Yankton, S.D., 1973-77, pres., 1976; bd. dirs. Lewis and Clark Mental Health Center. Mem. S.D. Found. Pvt. Colls., S.D. Assn. Pvt. Colls., Colls. of Mid-Am. Lodges: Kiwanis; Masons. Democrat. Mem. United Ch. Of Christ. Office: 725 Park St Grinnell IA 50112-2235 Personal E-mail: orlanm@pcpartner.net.

MITCHELL, PATRICIA EDENFIELD, broadcast museum administrator; b. Swainsboro, Ga., Jan. 20, 1943; d. James Otis and Bernice Tucker Edenfield; m. Jay Addison Mitchell, Aug. 20, 1964 (div. June 1970); 1 child, Mark Addison. BA magna cum laude, U. Ga., 1964, MA, 1965. English instr. U. Ga., Athens, 1965—69; English, drama instr. Va. Commonwealth U., Richmond, 1969—70; researcher, writer LOOK Mag., NYC, 1970; cons., speech writer Garth Assocs., NYC, 1970—71; TV prodr., reporter WB2-TV, Boston, 1971—77; anchor, talk show host WTTG-TV, Washington, 1977—79; corr. NBC-TV Today, NYC, 1984—89, CBS-TV Sunday Morning, NYC, 1989—90; exec. prodr., writer documentaries VU Prodns., LA, 1990; pres. CNN Prodns. and Time Inc. TV TBS, 1992—2000; pres., CEO PBS, 2000—06; pres. Mus. TV & Radio, 2006—. Creator, prodr., host, owner Woman to Woman (nationally syndicated program), LA, 1983—; spkr., conf. leader on women's issues, 1973—; bd. trustees Sundance Inst.; former mem. exec. com. TBS, Inc., CNN Exec. Com.; bd. mem. Internews, 2002—. Mem. adv. com. Nat. Coun. on Rsch. on Women, NYC, 1990—92; mem. adv. bd. Schlesinger Libr. on History of Women, Radcliffe Coll., Cambridge, Mass., 1985—92; media com. Hollywood Women's Polit. Com., LA, 1989—92; former trustee Metro Atlanta YMCA, High Mus. Art, Atlanta; mem. adv. bd. Santa Barbara Sch. Comm. U. Calif.; pres. Global Green USA (Am. affiliate Mikhail Gorbachev's worldwide conservation orgn.); nat. bd. mem. Girls Inc. Named One of the 100 Most Powerful Women in Television, The Hollywood Reporter; recipient Emmy for Best Daytime Program, TV Acad., 1984, Emmy for Best Host-Daytime, 1971, numerous film festival awards, 1989—92, Women in Cable & Broadcasting Woman of the Year, CINE Golden Eagle for Lifetime Achievement, Sandra Day O'Connor award for Leadership. Avocations: hiking, bicycling, horseback riding, reading. Office: Mus TV & Radio 25 W 52nd St New York NY 10019 Office Phone: 212-621-6800.

MITCHELL, PATRICK E., lawyer; b. Oconomowoc, Wis., June 6, 1957; BS, Christian Bros. Coll., 1979; JD, U. Va., 1982. Bar: Tex. 1982. Shareholder, tax practice group Jenkens & Gilchrist, P.C., Dallas, v.p. bd. dirs. Mem.: ABA, Dallas Bar Assn. Office: Jenkens & Gilchrist PC 1445 Ross Ave Ste 3200 Dallas TX 75202-2799 Office Phone: 214-855-4363. Office Fax: 214-855-4300. Business E-Mail: pmitchell@jenkens.com.

MITCHELL, PATSY MALIER, religious school founder, administrator; b. Greenwood, Miss., Aug. 28, 1948; d. William Lonal and Lillian (Walker) Malier; m. Charles E. Mitchell, Apr. 20, 1970; children: Christopher, Kara, Angela. BS in Edn., Delta State U., 1970, MEd, 1974, Edn. Specialist, 1979; MA in Ch. Ministries, Ch. of God Sch. Theology, 1990; PhD in Psychology and Counseling, La. Bapt. U., 1994; D in Edn. Christian Sch. Adminstrn., Baptist Christian U., 1992. Cert. sch. adminstr. Youth, Christian edn. dir. Ch. of God, Minter City, Miss., 1975—, teen talent dir., 1983—, missions rep., 1975—, dist. Christian edn. dir. Cleveland, Miss., 1983-85, sch. adminstr., 1985—. Del. Ch. of God Edn. Leadership, Cleveland, Tenn., 1990; del., spkr. Christian Sch. Internat., Chattanooga, 1991. Prodr.: (TV and radio program) Maranatha Live, 1994; contbr. articles to profl. jours. Dir. St. Jude Children's Hosp., Memphis, 1991; vol. 4-H Club, Greenwood, Miss., 1985—91. Named Outstanding Young Women of Am., 1983, Top 10 of 50 Leading Bus. Women in Miss., 2001; recipient Cmty. Pride award, Chevron, 1988, Internat. Woman of Yr. award, 1993, One of One Thousand Greatest Ams., 2004, Top 100 Educators in the World, 2005—06, Internat. Educator of Yr., 2004, 2005, 2006. Mem.: NAFE, Ch. of God Edn. Assn., Christian Schs. Internat., Christian Sch. Adminstrs., Gospel Music Assn., Ch. of God Sch. of Theology Alumni assn., Delta State Alumni Assn. Republican. Home: 5642 County Rd 544 Minter City MS 38944 Office Phone: 662-299-4592. *The greatest gift that God has given mankind is the capacity to love and encourage others. It is God's gift to us and our gift to others.*

MITCHELL, PAULA RAE, nursing educator, dean; b. Independence, Mo., Jan. 10, 1951; d. Millard Henry and E. Lorene (Denton) Gates; m. Ralph William Mitchell, May 24, 1975. BS in Nursing, Graceland U., Lamoni, Iowa, 1973; MS in Nursing, U. Tex., 1976; EdD in Ednl. Adminstrn., N.Mex. State U., 1996. RN, Tex., Mo. Instr. nursing El Paso C.C., Tex., 1979-85, dir. nursing Tex., 1985—2003, acting divsn. chmn. health occupations Tex., 1985-86, divsn. dean Tex., 1998-99, dean health occupations Tex., 1999-2000, curriculum facilitator Tex., 1984—85, dean health occupations, math and sci., campus dean Rio Grande, 2000—. Ob-gyn. nurse practitioner Planned Parenthood, El Paso, 1981-86, med. com., 1986-98; cons. in field, army med. dept. officer Acad. Health Scis.Ft. Author: (with Grippando) Nursing Perspectives and Issues, 1989, 93; contbr. articles to profl. jours. Founder, bd. dirs. Health-CREST, El Paso, 1981—85; mem. pub. edn. com. Am. Cancer Soc., El Paso, 1983—84, mem. profl. activities com., 1992—93; mem. El-Paso City-County Bd. Health, 1989—91; mem. Govt. Applications Rev. Com. Rio Grande Coun. Govts., 1989—91; mem. collaborative coun. El Paso Magnet H.S. for Health Care Professions, 1992—94; co-chair health and human svcs. task force Unite El Paso Health, 1996—98, mem. steering com., 1999—2000; co-chair health taskforce El Paso Cmty. Legis. Agenda, 1997—99; mem. adv. com. Ctr. for Border Health Rsch., Paso del Norte Health Found., 1998—2004; mem. Leadership El Paso, 1999; mem. health profl. shortage task force Greater El Paso C. of C., 2001—, mem. health care coun., 2002—; mem. star adv. com. Canutillo Tex. Ind. Sch. Dist., 2003—05; mem. El Paso County Civil Svc. Commn., 2006—; mem. civil svc. commn. City El Paso, 2006—; coord. West Tex. Med. Res. Corps, 2006—; bd. dirs. Border Health Inst., El Paso, 2001—, sec.-treas., 2003—; mem. cmty. adv. bd. Victory Warriors Drill and Dance Acad., El Paso, 2001—; mem. governing bd. Mesa Hills Specialty Hosp., 2002—. Capt. US Army, 1972—78, capt. USAR, 1978—98, ret. USAR, 1998. Decorated Army Commendation medal, Meritorious Svc. medal; named to Women's Hall Fame, El Paso Commn., 1999; named Outstanding Alumni, N.Mex. State U. Dept. Edn. Mgmt. and Devel., 2002-03; recipient Unite El Paso Legacy award 1997, Merit and Svc. cert. Victory Warriors Drill and Dance Acad., 2003, Outstanding Cmty. Svc. award, 2003, Appreciation and Cmty. Responsibility cert., 2005, Appreciation cert., 2006. Mem. Nat. League Nursing (resolutions com. Assocs. Degree coun. 1987-89, accreditation site visitor, AD coun. 1990—, Tex. edn. com. 1991-92, Tex. 3d v.p. 1992-93, Tex. 1st v.p. 1997-99, nominating com. 1999-2000), Am. Soc. Psychoprophylaxis Obstetrics (cert. childbirth educator 1978), Nurses Assn. Am. Coll. Ob-Gyn. (cert. in ambulatory women's healthcare, 1983, chpt. coord. 1979-83, nat. program rev. com. 1984-86, corr. 1987-89), Advanced Nurse Practitioner Group El Paso (coord. 1980-83, legis. com. 1984), Am. Phys. Therapist Assn. (comm. on accreditation, site visitor for phys. therapist asst. programs 1991-), Orgn. Assoc. Degree Nursing (Tex. membership chmn. 1985-89, chmn. goals com. 1989-2004, nat. bylaws com. 1990-95), Am. Vocat. Assn., Am. Assn. Women Cmty. and Jr. Colls., Tex. Orgn. Nurse Execs., Nat. Coun. Workforce Edn. (articulation task force 1986-89, program standards task force 1991-93), Nat. Coun. Instrnl. Adminstrs. (coord. med. res. corps. West Tex. chpt. 2006—), Tex. Soc. Allied Health Profls. (sec. 2004-2007), Tex. Nurses Assn. (pres.-elect dist. one 2002-03, pres. 2003-05, past pres. 2005-06), Am. Soc. Allied Health Profls. (edn. com. 1993-96), El Paso C. of C. (healthcare coun. 2001-05), El Paso Commn. for Women (treas. 2007—), Am. Legion, Mil. Order World Wars (staff officer 2007—), Sigma Theta Tau, Phi Kappa Phi. Mem. Christian Ch. (Disciples Of Christ). Home: 4616 Cupid Dr El Paso TX 79924-1726 Office: El Paso C C PO Box 20500 El Paso TX 79998-0500 Office Phone: 915-831-4030. Business E-Mail: paulam@epcc.edu.

MITCHELL, PETER KENNETH, educational consultant; b. Bklyn., June 12, 1949; s. Peter Kenneth and Joan Marie (Hayes) Mitchell; 1 child, Elyse Alexandra. Cert. in French lang. proficiency, U. de Neuchatel, Switzerland, 1969; BA, SUNY, Geneseo, 1970; MS in French, L.I. U., 1975. Tchr. French, Spanish and English Mid. Country Sch. Dist., Selden, NY, 1972-81; tech. asst. to dir. internat. affairs dept. Am. Fedn. Tchrs., Washington, 1981—90; asst. to gen. sec. Internat. Fedn. Free Tchrs. Unions, Amsterdam, Netherlands, 1986—91; exec. dir. Internat. Reading Assn., Newark, Del., 1990-91; owner Insights Out Assocs., Newark, Del., 1992—97. Dir. mktg. Jr. Achievement Del., 1994—99. Contbr. articles to profl. jours. Recipient Father of the Yr. award, Nat. Multiple Sclerosis Soc., 1998. Mem.: Amnesty Internat., Washington U. Club, Blue and Gold Club. Avocations: reading, music. Home and Office: Insights Out Assocs 5702 Vicky Dr Newark DE 19702

MITCHELL, REBECCA, library director; BLS, U. Miss.; MLS, U. Ala. Dir. Talladega Pub. Libr., Gadsden Pub. Libr., Ala., 1989—2001, Ala. Pub. Libr. Svc., Montgomery, 2002—; medical libr. Bapt. Meml. Hosp.; bibliographic instr. Houston Cole Libr., Jacksonville State U. Mem. Chief Officers of State Libr. Agencies, sec., 2006—08; mem. project adv. com. This Good Land, Ala. Literary Landscape. Formerly involved with Gadsden Chamber of Commerce, United Way, Metro Arts Coun., Woman's Club. Mem.: Ala. Libr. Assn. Office: Alabama Public Library 6030 Monticello Dr Montgomery AL 36130 Office Phone: 334-213-3902. Office Fax: 334-213-3993. *

MITCHELL, REGINALD EUGENE, mechanical engineering educator; b. Houston, May 16, 1947; s. Clifford Eugene and Juanita Beatrice (Thomas) M.; 1 child, Erika Gene; m. Shirley Ann Myers, Nov. 9, 1990. BS in Chem. Engring., U. Denver, 1968; MS in Chem. Engring., N.J. Inst. Tech., Newark, 1970; ScD in Chem. Engring., MIT, 1975. Mem. tech. staff Sandia Nat. Labs., Livermore, Calif., 1975-89, disting. mem. tech. staff, 1989-91; assoc. prof. mech. engring. dept. Stanford (Calif.) U., 1991—. Recipient Outstanding Tchr. award Tau Beta Pi, 1994. Mem.: Nat. Orgn. Black Chemists and Chem. Engrs. (Percy Julian award 1987), Combustion

Inst., Sigma Xi. Avocations: board games, card games, tennis. Home: 6143 Viewcrest Dr Oakland CA 94619-3728 Office: Stanford U Mech Engring Dept Bldg 520 Rm 520C Stanford CA 94305-3032 Business E-Mail: remitche@stanford.edu.

MITCHELL, RICHARD BOYLE, security firm executive; b. St. Louis, June 20, 1947; s. Samuel West and Blair (Boyle) M.; m. Sallie Jean Gear, Dec. 4, 1999; children: Rebecca, Jessica. BS in Mktg., NYU, 1969. Account exec. D.L. Blair Corp., NYC, 1967—70, NW Ayer Advt. Agy., NYC, 1970-74; sr. account exec. Ted Bates Agy., NYC, 1974-75; sr. v.p. DKG Advt., NYC, 1975-81, McCaffrey/McCall, NYC, 1981-86; pres., CEO Marshall Jaccoma Mitchell, NYC, 1986-96; sr. ptnr. Modem Media, NYC, 1996-97; mng. dir., mgmt. cons. MJM Cons., NYC, 1997—2001; pres. 911 Consulting, Wilton, Conn., 2001—. Commr. Wilton (Conn.) Police Dept., 1984-01. Served with USAR, 1969-74. Mem.: Wilton Riding. Democrat. Roman Catholic. Avocations: military history, running, weight-lifting. Home: 20 Indian Hill Rd Wilton CT 06897-1319 Office Phone: 203-563-9999. E-mail: bomitchell@911consulting.net.

MITCHELL, RICK, journalist, writer; b. San Jose, Calif., Nov. 27, 1952; s. Maurice Dale Mitchell and Mary Margaret (Woody) Gron; m. Lori Sumako, May 3, 1987; 1 child, Chelsea Pearl. BA in Am. Studies, Calif. State U., Fullerton, 1974. Music critic Oreg. Jour., Portland, 1978-82, Willamette Week, Portland, 1983, The Oregonian, Portland, 1984-85; music critic, sports columnist Willamette Week, 1986; freelance writer LA, 1987; arts and entertainment reporter The Bakersfield Californian, 1988; music critic Houston Chronicle, 1989-99. Author: Garth Brooks: One of A Kind, Workin' on A Full House, 1993. Mem. Houston Zen Cmty.; artistic dir. Houston Internat. Festival, 2000—. Mem. Amnesty Internat. Avocations: athletics, reading, music. E-mail: mitchako@msn.com.

MITCHELL, RIE ROGERS, psychologist, counselor, educator; b. Tucson, Feb. 1, 1940; d. Martin Smith and Lavaun (Peterson) Rogers; m. Rex C. Mitchell, Mar. 16, 1961; 1 child, Scott Rogers. Student, Mills Coll., 1958-59; BS, U. Utah, 1962, MS, 1963; postgrad., San Diego State U., 1965-66; MA, PhD, UCLA, 1969. Diplomate Am. Bd. Psychology; registered play therapist, supr.; cert. sandplay therapist. Tchr. Coronado (Calif.) Unified Sch. Dist., 1964-65; sch. psychologist Glendale (Calif.) Unified Sch. Dist., 1968-70; psychologist Glendale Guidance Clinic, 1970-77; asst. prof. ednl. psychology Calif. State U., Northridge, 1970-74, assoc. prof., 1974-78, prof., 1978—. Chmn. dept. ednl. psychology, 1976-80, 2000—06, acting exec. asst. to pres. Calif. State U., Dominguez Hills, 1978-79; cons. to various Calif. sch. dists.; pvt. practice psychology, Calabasas, Calif. Author: Sandplay: Past Present & Future, 1994; contbr. numerous articles to profl. jours. Recipient Outstanding Educator award Maharishi Soc., 1978, Woman of Yr. award U. Utah, 1962, Profl. Leadership award Western Assn. Counselor Edn., 1990, Disting. Tchg. award Calif. U. Northridge, 1994. Mem. APA, Calif. Assn. Counselor Edn., Supervision and Adminstrn. (dir. 1976-77), Western Assn. Counselor Edn. and Supervision (officer 1978-82, pres. 1980-81), Assn. Counselor Edn. and Supervision (dir. 1980-81, program chmn. 1981-82, treas. 1983-86, Presdl. award 1986, Leadership award 1987), UCLA Doctoral Alumni Assn. (pres. 1974-76), Am. Ednl. Rsch. Assn., Calif. Women in Higher Edn. (pres. chpt. 1977-78), Calif. Concerns (treas. 1984-86), Sandplay Therpists of Am. (fin. officer 1996-2000, bd. mem. 1993—, exceptions com. chair, 1995-96), Internat. Soc. Sandplay Therapy (bd. mem., 2004-, v.p., 2006-), Pi Lambda Theta (pres. chpt. 1970-71, chairwoman nat. resolutions 1971-73). Home: 4503 Alta Tupelo Dr Calabasas CA 91302-2516 Office: Calif State U Counselor Edn Dept Northridge CA 91330-0001 Office Phone: 818-677-4976. Business E-Mail: rie.mitchell@csun.edu.

MITCHELL, ROBERT DALE, engineer, consultant; b. Worthington, Minn., Aug. 2, 1910; s. Karl V. and Margaret Dumont (Steigleder) M.; m. Carol Sherman Northrop, June 17, 1939; children: Constance Remington, Robert Brown. BS, SD State U., Brookings, 1932; S.M. (grad. fellow), Harvard U., Cambridge, Mass., 1939. Engr. J. Emberg, Madison, SD, 1932-35; instr. S.D. State U., 1935-37; engr. Malcolm Pirnie Engrs., NYC, 1939-42, project engr., ptnr., 1945-70; sr. v.p., sec., chief engr. Malcolm Pirnie, Inc., 1970-75; cons. Malcolm Pirnie Engrs., 1975—. Served to maj. San. Corps AUS, 1942-45. Recipient Disting. Engr. award SD State U., 1977 Fellow Am. Coun. Engring. Cons.; mem. ASCE (life), Am. Water Works Assn., New Eng. Water Works Assn. (Commemorative award 1963) Office: 104 Corporate Park Dr White Plains NY 10604-3804 Home: 795 Wash Rd Rye NH 03870-2204

MITCHELL, ROGER LOWRY, retired agronomy educator; b. Grinnell, Iowa, Sept. 13, 1932; s. Robert T. and Cecile (Lowry) M.; m. Joyce Elaine Lindgren, June 26, 1955; children: Laura, Susan, Sarah, Martha. BS in Agronomy, Iowa State Coll., 1954; MS, Cornell U., 1958; PhD in Crop Physiology, Iowa State U., 1961. Mem. faculty Iowa State U., 1959-69, prof. agronomy, 1966-69, prof. charge farm operation curriculum, 1962-66; prof. agronomy, chmn. dept. U. Mo., Columbia, 1969-72, 81-83, emeritus prof., 1998—, dean agr., dir. expt. sta., 1983-98, dean extension, 1972-75, emeritus dean, 1998—; v.p. agr. Kans. State U., Manhattan, 1975-80; exec. dir. Mid-Am. Internat. Agrl. Consortium, 1981; ret., 1998. Exec. bd. divsn. agr. Nat. Assn. State Univs. and Land Grant Colls., 1978-80, 85-90, chmn., 1988-89; mem. bd. agr. NRC/NAS, 1983-86. Author: Crop Growth and Culture, 1970; co-author: Physiology of Crop Plants, 1985 Served to 2d lt. USAAF, 1954-56. Danforth fellow, 1956-61; Acad. Adminstrn. fellow Am. Council Edn., 1966-67; recipient Henry A. Wallace award Iowa State U., 1993, Sec.'s Honor award USDA, 1998. Fellow AAAS (chmn. sect. O 1980-81), Am. Soc. Agronomy (pres. 1979-80), Crop Sci. Soc. (pres. 1975-76); mem. Soil Sci. Soc. Am., Coun. Agrl. Sci. and Tech., Sigma Xi, Gamma Sigma Delta, Alpha Zeta, Phi Kappa Phi. Home: 502 W Lathrop Rd Columbia MO 65203-2804 Business E-Mail: mitchellrj@missouri.edu.

MITCHELL, RONNIE MONROE, lawyer, educator; b. Clinton, NC, Nov. 10, 1952; s. Ondus Corneilus and Margaret Ronie (Johnson) M.; m. Martha Cheryl Coble, May 25, 1975; children: Grant Stephen, Mitchell, Meredith Elizabeth Mitchell. BA, Wake Forest U., 1975, JD, 1978. Bar: N.C. 1978, U.S. Dist. Ct. (ea. dist.) N.C. 1978, U.S. Ct. Appeals (4th cir.) 1983, U.S. Supreme Ct. 1984. Assoc. atty. Brown, Fox & Deaver, Fayetteville, NC, 1978-81; ptnr. Harris, Sweeny & Mitchell, Fayetteville, 1981-91, Harris, Mitchell & Hancox, 1991-96, Harris & Mitchell, 1997-98, Harris, Mitchell, Burns & Brewer, 1998-2000, Mithchell, Brewer, Richardson, Adams, Burns and Boughman, 2000—. Adj. prof. law Norman Adrian Wiggins Sch. of Law, Campbell U; bd. dirs. Mace, Inc. Contbr. chpts. to books. Chmn. Cumberland County Bd. Adjustment, 1985-92, Cumberland County Rescue Squad, 1986-93; bd. dirs. Cumberland County Rescue Squad, Fayetteville, 1983-91. Recipient U.S. Law Week award Bur. Nat. Affairs, 1978. Mem. ABA, ATLA, Twelfth Judicial Dist. Bar Assn. (pres. 1988-89), N.C. Bar Assn. (councillor Young Lawyers divsn. 1982-85), N.C. Legis. Rsch. Commn. (family law com. 1994), Cumberland County Bar Assn. (mem. family law com., N.C. State Bar Bd. legal specialization), N.C. Acad. Trial Lawyers, Fayetteville Ind. Light Infantry Club, Dem. Men's Club (pres. 1993-94), Moose, Masons. Home: 1901 Water Oaks Dr Fayetteville NC 28301-9125 Office Phone: 910-678-7100.

MITCHELL, ROSS EDWARD, research scientist, educator; s. Douglas Earl and Tedi Kurtz Mitchell; m. Constance Leilani Cunningham, July 27, 1991; children: Kevin Douglas, Timothy Ian. BS in Chemistry, U. Calif., Riverside, 1986; MS in Phys. Chemistry, U. Chgo., 1989; PhD Edn., Adminstrn. and Policy, U. Calif., Riverside, 2001. Cert. phys. sci. tchr. State of Calif. Commn. on Tchr. Credentialing, 1993. Sci. tchr. Houston Ind. Sch. Dist., 1991—92, San Bernardino (Calif) City Unified Sch. Dist., 1992—97; rsch. fellow Calif. Ednl. Rsch. Coop., Riverside, 1997—2001; rsch. scientist Gallaudet Rsch. Inst., Washington, 2001—. Expert witness Gallaudet Rsch. Inst., Washington, 2001—05; adj. assoc. prof. Gallaudet U., Washington, 2003—04; curriculum coord. CPEC Eisenhower Summer Inst. for Am. Indians, U. Calif., Riverside, 1997. Contbr. articles to profl. jours., chapters to books. Coach and referee Am. Youth Soccer Orgn., Riverside, Calif., 1998—2001; den and pack leader Cub Scout Pack 1756, Montgomery Village, Md., 2003—05; adult Sunday sch. tchr. St. Luke's Luth. Ch., Derwood, Md., 2004—05. Named to All Tournament, First Team, Highlander Classic Water Polo Tournament, 1985; recipient varsity letter water polo, U. of Calif., Riverside, 1985—86; fellow lab. grad. participant, Argonne Nat. Lab., 1988—89; grantee, U. of Calif., Riverside, 1985—86, Inst. on Statis. Analysis for Edn. Policy, Am. Ednl. Rsch. Assn., 2004; Naval Res. Officer Tng. Corps scholar, USN, 1982—83, Rosemary S. J. Schraer fellow, U. of Calif., Riverside, 1999—2000, Sci. of Learning Ctr. Catalyst grantee, NSF, 2004—, Proctor & Gamble rsch. fellow, U. of Minn., 1990, Coffman alumni scholar, 1991, fellowship grantee, U. of Calif., Riverside, 1997—98, CERC rsch. fellow, 1997—2001. Mem.: Nat. Soc. for Study of Edn., Am. Sociol. Assn., Am. Ednl. Rsch. Assn., Phi Delta Kappa. Lutheran. Office: Gallaudet Rsch Inst 800 Florida Ave NE Washington DC 20002-3695 Home Phone: 301-869-7591; Office Phone: 202-651-5576. E-mail: ross.mitchell@gallaudet.edu.

MITCHELL, ROY SHAW, lawyer; s. Malcolm Douglas and Ruth Landon (Holland) M.; m. Nancy Elizabeth Bishop, Aug. 27, 1955; children: Mark E., Jeffrey B., Jennifer R. BS, Cornell U., 1957; JD with honors, George Washington U., DC, 1959. Bar: DC 1959, Ohio 1960, Va. 1967, US Ct. Fed. Claims 1963, US Supreme Ct. 1965. Atty. Hudson & Creyke, Washington, 1961-67, Lewis, Mitchell & Moore, Vienna, Va., 1967-87, Morgan, Lewis & Bockius LLP, Washington, 1987-99; pres., CEO constrn. claims group Hill Internat., Inc., Washington, 1999—2004; mediator, arbitrator, neutral, 2004—. Vice-chmn. Ameribanc Savs. Bank, Annandale, Va., 1980-95; trustee Ameribanc Investors Group, Annandale, 1980-95; chmn. The Ctr. Mgmt. Devel. and Tng., Inc., 2004—. Co-author: (with others) Handbook of Construction Law and Claims, 1982, 89; contbr. numerous articles to profl. jours. Fellow ABA (former nat. chmn.; pub. contract law sect.), Am. Coll. Construction Lawyers, Va. Bar Assn., DC Bar Assn. Presbyterian. Avocation: boating. Home: 5 Jefferson Run Rd Great Falls VA 22066-3200 Home Phone: 703-759-0109; Office Phone: 571-435-7191. E-mail: roysmitchell@aol.com.

MITCHELL, RUTHIE YVETTE, human services administrator, director; b. Harrisburg, Pa., Nov. 14, 1960; d. Jerry Mitchell and Nina Walters; children: Edmond Vincent, Sharrow, Tyrone, DeAndre Diggs. B in Human Svcs., M in Human Svcs., Lincoln U., 2004; student, Capella U., Mpls., Minn., 2004—. Armed correctional officer supr. DC Dept. Corrections, Lorton, Va., 1985—90; campus police officer Howard U., Washington, 1998—2002; preventive case mgmt. counselor Us Helping Us, Washington, case mgr., 2000—, transitional discharge planner, project mgr., 2002—; exec. dir. Jewel In the Night, Washington. Facilitator Dept. Corrections Tng. Acad., 1985, Fed. Protective Svc. Divsn. Acad., 1998, Ct. Svcs. Offender Supervision Agy., Washington, 2004. Editor: (book) So This Is Nina, 2004. Vol. substance abuse counselor Pilgrim Rest Bapt. Therapeutic Svcs., Washington, 1998—. Recipient Outstanding Performance Duty, HUH Security Divsn., 2000. Mem.: Pi Gamma Mu. Avocations: writing, ballet. Home: 5802 Southern Ave Washington DC 20019 Office: Jewel in Night 5802 Southern Ave Washington DC 20019 Office Phone: 202-446-1105. Office Fax: 202-204-0808. Personal E-mail: ruthiemitchell2002@yahoo.com.

MITCHELL, SAM, professional basketball coach; b. Sept. 2, 1963; m. Anita Mitchell; children: Morgann, Maya, Rhagan, Rhana. Student, Mercer U. Draft pick NBA Houston Rockets, 1985; player Continental Basketball Assn. Rapid City Thrillers, SD, 1985—87; profl. basketball player France, 1987—89, NBA Minn. Timberwolves, 1989—92, 1995—2002, NBA Ind. Pacers, 1992—95; asst. coach NBA Milw. Bucks, 2002—04; lead asst. coach NBA Charlotte Bobcats, 2004; head coach NBA Toronto Raptors, 2004—. Named NBA Coach of Yr., 2007. Office: Toronto Raptors Air Canada Ctr 40 Bay St Toronto ON M5J 2X2 Canada *

MITCHELL, SCOTT PATRICK, advertising executive, Internet company executive; b. Orland Park, Ill., June 7, 1971; s. William Lee and Patricia Ann Mitchell; m. Kristine Eileen Woodlock, Sept. 26, 1992; children: William Lee, Kaitlyn Eryn, Mackenzie Lauren. BS in Econs., Ill. State U., Normal; MBA in Fin., Benedictine U., Lisle, Ill., MS in Organizational Behavior. Ceo WCI, Clearwater, Fla., 2002—04, Think Partnership, Clearwater, 2004—. Avocations: jogging, swimming, boating, travel. Office: Think Partnership 28050 US 19 N Ste 509 Clearwater FL 33761 Home Phone: 727-776-5390; Office Phone: 727-796-0255. Business E-Mail: scott@thinkpartnership.com.

MITCHELL, SHAWNE MAUREEN, author; b. Tacoma, Wash., Jan. 09; d. F. King and Nona Margaret Burnside (Hayes) M.; m. J.D. Cook, Spt. 4, 1982; children: Travis, Austin. BA, U. Wash.; postgrad., U. Santa Monica, 1997—. CEO Adventures of the Spirit, Santa Barbara, Calif., 1994—; author, spkr. Soul Style, 1995—; columnist Feng Shui-Soul Style, Calif., 1996—. Cons. real estate, Wash., Calif., 1980—; dir. Small Luxury Hotels, L.A., 1986-87; internat. spkr., author on subject of higher consciousness; internat. spkr. on Feng Shui. Author: Soul Style, 1997, Exploring Feng Shui, Ancient Secrets and Modern Insights, 2001, Creating Home Sanctuaries with Feng Shui, 2002, Simple Feng Shui, 2004; editor: Home Sanctuaries mag.; contbr. articles to profl. jours. Bd. dirs. Montecito (Calif.) Ednl. Found., 1997-99, Los Positas Park Found., Santa Barbara, 1995. Mem.: Womens Exec. Network, Santa Barbara Polo Club. Avocations: boating, hiking, travel, music, art. Office: Adventures of the Spirit Inc PO Box 5765 Santa Barbara CA 93150-5765 Office Phone: 805-565-8885. E-mail: shawne@shawnemitchell.com.

MITCHELL, STACY MARIE, medical transcriptionist; b. Lakewood, Calif., June 11, 1973; d. Jerry Layne and Mary Anne Barbour; m. Sean Thomas Mitchell, Aug. 12, 2000; children: Marshal Sean, Molly Marie. BS in Office Adminstrn., Bob Jones U., Greenville, SC, 1991—95. Sr. mktg. specialist World Class Promotions/Internat., Englewood, Colo., 1995—2000; dist. compression adminstr. J-W Oper. Co., Wray, Colo., 2000—01; phys. therapy sec. Melissa Meml. Hosp., Holyoke, Colo., 2001—05; freelance med. transcriptionist Holyoke, 2005—07, Sterling, Colo., 2007—. Mem.: Am. Assn. Med. Transcriptionist, Nat. Assn. Self-Employed. Conservative-R. Non-Denominational. Avocations: walking, reading. Home and Office: 1171 Westview Dr Sterling CO 80751 Office Fax: 970-522-2418. Personal E-mail: jeepmom812@yahoo.com.

MITCHELL, STEPHEN MILTON, investment company executive; b. Atlanta, Oct. 23, 1943; s. Judge Stephenson and Elizabeth Ruth (Morgan) M.; m. Carolyn Docia Goss, June 29, 1968; children: William Stephenson, Scott Milton, Gregory Stephen. B of Indsl. Engring. with honors, Ga. Inst. Tech., 1965, MS in Indsl. Engring., 1966. Registered profl. engr., Ga. Sr. engr. Lochkeed-Ga. Corp., Marietta, 1966-70; mgr. material control Snapper Power Equipment, McDonough, Ga., 1970-73; pres. Atlanta Processing Co., Conley, Ga., 1973-86; sr. v.p., gen. mgr. Norcom, Inc., Norcross, Ga., 1986-93; chmn., CEO Atlanta Processing B, Inc., Tucker, Ga., 1993-94; CEO Internat. Processing Corp., Atlanta, 1994, Sertec Corp., Atlanta, 1995—, also bd. dirs. Bd. dirs. Atlanta Processing Co., Conley, Ga., Norcom, Inc., Norcross, APB Inc., Tucker, Ga., IPC, Atlanta; mem. exec. com., chmn., bd. dirs. Clairmont Oaks, Inc., 1988—. Bd. dirs., treas. Common Cause, Ga., 1989—; active First Bapt. Ch. of Decatur, Ga., 1968—, chmn. bd. deacons, 1993, 95. Mem. Young Presidents Orgn., World Presidents Orgn., Ga. Tech. Alumni Assn. (trustee 1981-87). Republican. Home: 5268 Browning Way SW Lilburn GA 30047-7029 Office: Sertec Corp 2100 Powers Ferry Rd NW Ste 200 Atlanta GA 30339-5014

MITCHELL, STEVE HAROLD, psychologist; b. Madison, Tenn., Nov. 28, 1954; s. Ralph and Doris Mitchell. BS, Tenn. Tech. U., 1977; MS, U. Ala., 1978; PhD, OH State U., 1983. Assoc. prof. psychology Cumberland Coll., Williamsburg, Ky., 1986-92; asst. prof. Ball State U., Muncie, Ind., 1983-86; behavior specialist, 1989-99; assoc. prof. psychology Somerset CC, Ky., 1999—. Author: Conception Through Adolecence: Research, Theories, and Applications (Who's Who Among America's Teachers); contbr. articles to profl. jours. Mem.: Soc. Rsch. Child Devel., Coun. Children Behavior Disorders, Coun. Exceptional Children, Lions (pres. Somerset chpt. 2002—05). Achievements include research in sexual attitudes of college students in the 21st Century.

MITCHELL, STUART, medical entomologist, consulting physician; m. Martha Mitchell. BS in Physics, Iowa State U., Ames, 1981; MS in Pest Mgmt., Purdue U., 1999; PhD in Entomology, Trinity Coll., Metairie, La., 2000, PhD in Zoology, 2002, PhD in Biology, 2003, PhD in Naturopathy, 2005, D of Naturopathy; DSc (hon.), Breyer State U., 2005; DSc in Osteo. Medicine, Belford U., 2005. Bd. cert. entomologist, cert. in homeland security, wildlife control profl., trainer in food safety Nat. Environ. Health Assn., med. investigator, in traditional naturopathy. Cons. physician, med. entomologist Springer Svcs., Des Moines, 1996—. Tchr., food mgr. NSF Internat., Des Moines, 2002—, tchr. HACCP, 2002—; cons. Whitmire Micro-Gen Labs., 2003. Author: (pest mgmt. tng. manual) Guidelines On Training; contbr. articles to profl. jours. Developer The Springer Inst.; mem. Des Moines Parks Bd., 2002—03; bd. dirs. Blank Pk. Zoo, Des Moines, 2002—03, Des Moines Bot. Ctr., 2002—03. Mem.: AAAS, Entomol. Soc. Am., Am. Inst. Baking, Phi Chi Omega. Democrat. Lutheran. Avocations: science, walking. Office: Springer Svcs 5360 NE 14th Str Ste A Des Moines IA 50313-2002 Office Phone: 515-262-9229, 800-793-1833. Office Fax: 515-262-9149. Personal E-mail: docmitchell@hotmail.com.

MITCHELL, SUSAN ELAINE, pharmacist; b. Texas City, Tex., Sept. 20, 1962; d. John Wayne and Dixie Davenport Mitchell. BA in Psychology, U. Tex., Austin, 1984; BS in Pharmacy, U. Houston, 1993; PharmD, U. Fla., Gainesville, 2001. Clk., typist U. Tex. Med. Br., Galveston, 1986—90, pharmacist, 1993—; unit sec. Hermann Hosp., Houston, 1990—93. Dir. children/youth handbell choir; mem. adult handbell choir; music sec. Chancel Choir. Mem.: TPA, TSHP, ASHP, Galveston Hist. Found., Lions Club Internat. (tail twister 2005—06, sec. 2006—, Lion of Yr. 2004). Methodist. Avocations: photography, animal advocacy, needlecrafts, music. Home: 2417 34th Ave N Texas City TX 77590

MITCHELL, TEDDY LEE, physician; b. Columbia, La., Feb. 24, 1962; s. Oliver Clayton nad Mary Elizabeth (Johnston) M.; m. Janet Luisa Tornelli, Apr. 9, 1988; children: Mary Katherine, Oliver Charles, Christopher Tornelli. BS in Biology, Stephen F. Austin State U., 1983; MD, U. Tex. Med. Br., 1987. Diplomate Am. Bd. Internal Medicine, Cert. of Added Qualification-Sports Medicine. Intern U. Tex. Med. Br., Galveston, 1987-88, resident, 1988-90, 90-91; med. dir. wellness program Cooper Aerobics Ctr., Dallas, 1991—2006, pres., med. dir., 2006—. Mem. Rep. Sen. Inner Cir., Washington, 1993, Heritage Found., Washington, 1993. Capt. U.S. Army Res. Med. Corps, 1988-96. Fellow ACP (cert. Merit 1990), Am. Coll. Sports Medicine; mem. AMA, Tex. Med. Assn., Dallas County Med. Soc. Methodist. Avocations: exercise, travel, music. Home: 3224 Lovers Ln Dallas TX 75225-7626 Home Phone: 214-750-1278; Office Phone: 972-560-2667.

MITCHELL, THEODORE REED, educational association administrator, former academic administrator; b. San Rafael, Calif., Jan. 29, 1956; s. Theodore Robert and Genevieve Dolores (Doose) Mitchell; m. Christine M. Beckman, July 8, 1995; children: Caroline Mitchell Beckman, Theo Beckman. BA, Stanford U., 1978, MA, 1980, PhD, 1983. Asst. prof. Dartmouth Coll., Hanover, NH, 1981—86, assoc. prof., 1986—87, chair dept. edn., 1987—91; dep. to pres. and provost Stanford U., Calif., 1991—92; dean Sch. Edn. and Info. Studies UCLA, 1992—96, vice chancellor, 1996—98; v.p. for edn. and strategic initiatives The J. Paul Getty Trust, 1998—99; pres. Occidental Coll., 1999—2005; CEO NewSchools Venture Fund, San Francisco, 2005—. Trustee Stanford U., 1985—90, Thetford Acad., Vt., 1989—91; bd. dirs. L.A. Edn. Partnership, L.E.A.R.N. Author: Political Education, 1985, Sociology of Education, 1998. Bd. dirs. Children Now, Oakland, Calif., 1994—, Gateway Learning Corp., 1996—. Office: NewSchools Venture Fund 49 Stevenson St, Ste 575 San Francisco CA 94105 Office Phone: 415-615-6860. Fax: 415-615-6861. *

MITCHELL, THOMAS EDWARD, JR., communications cabling executive; b. Sacramento, Apr. 12, 1946; s. Thomas Edward and Violet Mae (Southall) M.; m. Terri Kathleen Vance, Apr. 20, 1969; children: Anthony E., Brian C. BA, Nat. U., 1987, MBA, 1988. Enlisted USMC, 1966, advanced through grades to maj., 1980, retired, 1989; sr. exec. Nat. Decision Sys., Encinitas, Calif., 1989-90, Equifax Mktg. Decision Sys., San Diego, 1990—94; exec. v.p. Holocom Networks, Carlsbad, Calif., 1994—2002; pres. Holocomm Sys. Inc., San Diego, 1994—2002. Bd. dirs. Cal-Pacific Steel Structure Inc., Hawaii, Calif., Holocomm. sys. Inc., San Diego, Calif., Holocom Networks, Carlsbad, Calif.; instr. bus. mgmt. San Diego (Calif.) Golf Acad., 2003—. Contbr. articles to profl. jours.; patentee in field. Dir. Toys for Tots, L.A./ORange Counties, Calif., 1974-77. Recipient Silver Star medal U.S. Pres., 1968, Meritorious Svc. medal, Joint Chiefs of Staff Commendation medal, others. Mem. World Trade Assn. (assoc. 1989—), Am. Legion, Internat. Platform Assn. Avocations: restoring old cars, racquetball, golf, history. Home: 3264 Chase Ct Oceanside CA 92056-3809 Office: San Diego Golf Acad 1910 Shaowridge Dr Ste 111 Vista CA 92083

MITCHELL, TIMOTHY LYNN, music educator; b. Maysville, Ky., Sept. 4, 1959; s. Charles Harrison and Gwendell Mae Mitchell. BA in Music, No. Ky. U., Highland Heights, 1982, MusB Edn., 1982; MA in Edn., Georgetown Coll., Ky, 1993. Min. of music Main St. Bapt. Ch., Alexandria, Ky., 1985—92; gen. music tchr. Kelly Elem. Sch., Burlington, Ky., 1990—. Tchr. rep. Kelly Sch. Site-Based Coun., Burlington, 1994—96; sch. tech. coord. Kelly Elem. Sch., Burlington, 2005—. Mem.: NEA, Ky. Edn. Assn., Ky. Music Educators Assn., Nat. Assn. for Music Edn. Avocations: writing plays and musicals, travel. Home: 2265 West Horizon Dr Hebron KY 41048-9577 Office: Kelly Elem Sch 6775 McVille Rd Burlington KY 41005-8659 Home Phone: 859-283-0934; Office Phone: 859-334-4450.

MITCHELL, WAYNE LEE, retired health facility administrator; b. Mar. 25, 1937; s. Albert C. and Elizabeth Isabelle (Nagel) M.; m. Marie Galletti. BA, U. Redlands, Calif., 1959; MSW, Ariz. State U., 1970, EdD, 1979. Social worker various county, state, and fed. agys., 1962-70; social worker Bur. Indian Affairs, Phoenix, 1970-77, USPHS, 1977-79; asst. prof. Ariz. State U., 1979-84; with USPHS, Phoenix, 1984—2003, ret., 2003; pvt. practice cons. Phoenix, 2003—. Lectr. in field. Contbr. articles to profl. jours. Bd. dirs. Phoenix Indian Cmty. Sch., 1973-75, ATLATL, 1994-98, Partnership for Cmty. Devel. Ariz. State U.-West, 1996-99, Cen. Ariz. Health Sys. Agy., 1982-85; mem. Phoenix Area Health Adv. Bd., 1975, Cmty. Behavioral Mental Health Bd., 1976-80, Fgn. Rels. Com., Phoenix; trustee Heard Mus. Anthropology, Phoenix, 1996; apptd. Ariz. State Bd. Behavioral Health Examiners, 2000-2002. With USCG, 1960-62. Named in Voices and Faces, 2003; recipient Comty. Svc. award, Ariz. Temple of Islam, 1980, Ariz. State U., 1996, Dir. Excellence award, Phoenix Area IHS Dir., 1992, 1993, Nat. IHS Dir.'s award for outstanding svc., 2001, NARD Lifetime Achievement award, 2005. Mem. NASW (Lifetime Achievement award 2003), Fgn. Rels. Coun., U.S.-China Assn., Kappa Delta Pi, Phi Delta Kappa, Chi Sigma Chi. Democrat. Congregationalist. Home: PO Box 9592 Phoenix AZ 85068-9592 Personal E-mail: drwlmitch@cox.net.

MITCHELL, WILFRID BEDE, librarian, library association executive; b. Bloomington, Ind., Nov. 5, 1953; s. W. Bede and Barbara Plumb Mitchell; m. Carrie N. Cornejo, May 30, 1992. BA in Philosophy, U. Mich., 1975, MLS, 1977; EdD, Mont. State U., 1989. Circulation and reserve libr. Mont. State U., Bozeman, 1978-85; head circulation libr. U. N.C., Greensboro, 1985-90; assoc. univ. libr. Appalachian State U., Boone, N.C., 1990-99; dean libr. Ga. So. U., Statesboro, 1999—. Contbr. articles to profl. jours. Mem. ALA, Assn. Coll. and Rsch. Librs. (chair acad. status com. 1995-96, chair instnl. priorities and faculty rewards task force, 1996-98, bd. dirs. 2002—06), Libr. Adminstrn. Mgmt. Assn. (chair publs. and bibliography com. sys. and svcs. sect. 1997-98, strategic planning implementation com. 2001-03, pres.-elect, 2006-07, pres. 2007—), Ga. Libr. Assn. (chmn. academic libr. divsn. 2001-02, chmn. adminstrv. svcs. com. 2003), Southeastern Libr. Assn. (chmn. legis com. 2005-06). Office: Ga So U Henderson Libr PO Box 8074 Statesboro GA 30460-8074 Office Phone: 912-681-5115. Office Fax: 912-681-0093.

MITCHELL, WILLIAM EDMUND, electronics executive; b. LA, Mar. 13, 1944; s. John Stewart and Helen (Fine) M.; m. Jan Marie Scheyer, Feb. 16, 1969; children: Alden, Amanda, Alyssa. BS in Engring., Princeton U., NJ, 1966; MS in Engring., U. Mich., Ann Arbor, 1967. Analyst Exxon Corp., NYC, 1969-72, dept. mgr. Baton Rouge, 1972-73; ops. mgr. Raychem. Corp., Menlo Park, Calif., 1973-76; regional mgr. Raychem Internat., Menlo Park, Calif., 1977-85, v.p., 1985-88; sr. v.p. Raychem Corp., Menlo Park, 1988-93; pres., CEO Nashua Corp., NH, 1993—95; chmn., pres., CEO Sequel Inc., 1995—99; pres. Solectron Global Svcs., 1999—2002; v.p. Solectron Corp., 1999—2002; pres., CEO Arrow Electronics Inc., Melville, NY, 2003—, chmn., 2006—. Bd. dirs. Rogers Corp., Conn. Mem. Orgn. Corp. Growth, Am. Electronics Assn. (bd. dirs. 1993—), Ladera Oaks Club. Republican. Avocations: swimming, tennis, literature. Office: Arrow Electronics Inc 50 Marcus Dr Melville NY 11747-4210 Office Phone: 631-847-2000. *

MITCHELL, WILLIAM GRAHAM CHAMPION, lawyer, corporate officer; b. Raleigh, NC, Dec. 24, 1946; s. Burley Bayard and Dorothy Ford (Champion) Mitchell; children: William Graham, Margaret Scripture. AB, U. N.C., 1969, JD with highest hons., 1975. Bar: N.C. 1975, U.S. Dist. Ct. (ea., mid., and we. dists.) N.C. 1976, U.S. Ct. Appeals (4th cir.) 1978. Ptnr. Womble, Carlyle, Sandridge & Rice, Winston-Salem, 1975-87; sr. v.p. for external affairs RJR Nabisco, Atlanta, 1987-89; exec. v.p. R.J. Reynolds Tobacco Co., Winston-Salem, 1988-89; ptnr. Howrey & Simon, Washington, 1990-94; spl. counselor to chmn. bd. True North Comm., Inc., Chgo., 1996; chmn. bd., CEO Global Exch. Carrier Co., Leesburg, Va., 1997-00; pres., CEO Global Comms. Techs. Inc., Reston, Va., 1999-2000; chmn. bd., CEO Convergence Equipment Co., Manassas, Va., 1999-2000; chmn. bd. Qfactor Inc., Bethesda, Md., 2000-01; exec. v.p., gen. mgr. Verisign Inc., Mountainview, Calif., 2001—03; chmn. bd., CEO Network Solutions, Inc., Dulles, Va., 2003—. Bd. dirs. Fed. Agrl. Mortgage Corp., Washington. Mem. Pres.'s Adv. Com. Trade Policy and Negotiations, Indsl. Policy Adv. Com., Washington, 1991—; bd. dirs. Washington Performing Arts Soc., 1988—92; founding trustee Prog. Policy Inst., 1988—; bd. advisors Dem. Leadership Coun., 1988—; vice chmn. fin. Bush Campaign; mem. exec. com. Nat. Assn. Mfrs., Washington, 1988—89, Nat. Fgn. Trade Coun., 1988—89; chmn. Tobacco Inst., Washington, 1988—89. Mem.: ABA (vice chmn. antitrust sect., pvt. litigation com. 1987—89, chmn. FTC com. 1986), Forsyth Country Club, City Club Washington, Georgetown Club, Order of Coif. Personal E-mail: champ@champmitchell.com. Business E-Mail: cmitchell@networksolutions.com.

MITCHEM, ALLEN P., lawyer; b. Burley, Idaho, Oct. 30, 1918; s. James Edgar and Adah Elizabeth (Allen) Mitchem; m. Katherine I. Webber, Aug. 21, 1993; children: Allen P., James E., Lowell E. AB, Ft. Hays State U., Kans., 1940; JD magna cum laude, Washburn U., Kans., 1947; LLM, Columbia U., NYC, 1948. Bar: Kans. 1947, Colo. 1949, US Supreme Ct. 2004. Assoc. prof. Coll. Law, U. Denver, 1948—53; pvt. practice law Denver, 1953—60, 1963—; minority counsel interior and insular affairs com. U.S. Senate, Washington, 1961—62. Vis. lectr. Sch. Law U. Colo., Boulder, 1954, 57, 59; lectr. Coll. Law U. Denver, 1953—63; arbitrator, Denver, 1965—. Contbr. articles to legal rev. Dist. gov. Civitan Internat., 1957—58, judge adv., 1958—59; pres. Denver Execs. Club, 1986—88; chmn. gen. bd. Ctrl. Christian Ch., 1963—65, 1975—76; trustee Endowment Assn. Ft. Hays State U., 1968—78; dir. Colo. Christian Home, Denver, 1974—80; pres. Denver Civitan Club, 1955—56; dir. Denver Area Coun. Chs., 1955, 1957. Capt. USMC, 1942—45. Recipient Alumni Achievement award, Ft. Hays State U., 1970. Mem.: ABA, Denver Bar Assn., Colo. Bar Assn. Home: 420 S Marion Pkwy Apt 2002 Denver CO 80209-5526 Personal E-mail: apmitchem@msn.com.

MITCHINSON, MILLIAM J., social studies educator; s. George Wayne and Barbra Lee (Cody) Mitchinson; m. Sara Irene Dorothy, Jan. 28, 1995; children: Benjamin, Jilliam, Allison. BA in Hist., U. Iowa, Iowa City, 1992; MA in Edn. Leadership, Aurora U., Ill., 1998. Social studies tchr. West Aurora High Sch., 1993—, social studies dept. chair, 2001—. Baseball coach West Aurora High Sch., 1994—. Mem.: Ill. Coun. Social Studies, Nat. Coun. Social Studies. Avocations: baseball, fishing, basketball, reading, music. Office: W Aurora High Sch 1201 W NY St Aurora IL 60506 Business E-Mail: bmitchinson@sd129.org.

MITGANG, LEE DAVID, journalist, writer, educator, foundation administrator; b. NYC, Nov. 12, 1949; s. Herbert and Shirley (Kravchick) Mitgang; m. Gina Saporito, June 17, 1979; 1 child, Caroline. BA in Polit. Sci., U. Mich., Ann Arbor, 1971; MS in History of Polit. Thought, London Sch. Econ., 1972. Corr. bus. and Wall Street, UPI, NYC, 1972-74; bus. writer AP, NYC, 1974-76, urban affairs writer, 1976-80, nat. edn. writer, 1980-91; sr. fellow Carnegie Found. for Advancement of Tchg., Princeton, NJ, 1992-97; pvt. practice cons., journalist Ridgewood, NJ, 1997-2000; dir. comm. Wallace Found., NYC, 2000—, dir. editl. svcs., 2002—. Asst. dir. Hechinger Inst. Edn. and Media Tchrs. Coll., Columbia U., 1999—2000. Co-author: Building Community: A New Future for Architecture Education and Practice, 1996; prin. author: School Choice, 1992; author: Big Bird and Beyond: The New Media and The Markle Foundation, 2000; contbg. editor: Archtl. Record Mag., 1997—2001; mem. editl. bd. Reaching Today's Youth Jour., 1996—. Recipient John Hancock award for Excellence in Bus. Journalism, 1976, Gerald Loeb award for Disting. Bus. and Fin. Journalism, 1977, Sci.-in-Soc. award, Nat. Assn. Sci. Writers, 1989, Disting. Achievement award, Ednl. Press Assn., 1991. Mem.: Edn. Writers Assn. Home and Office: 216 Doremus Ave Ridgewood NJ 07450-4240 Office Phone: 212-251-9780. Business E-Mail: lmitgang@wallacefoundation.org.

MITRA, ASOKE NATH, retired physicist, educator; b. Rajshahi, India, Apr. 15, 1929; s. Jatindra Nath and Rama Rani (Bose) M.; m. Anjali Ghosh, Nov. 27, 1956; children: Bani, Gargi. BA with honors in Math., Ramjas Coll., Delhi, 1947, MA in Math., 1949; PhD in Physics, Delhi U., 1952, Cornel U., 1955. Lectr. physics U. Delhi, 1949-52; ctrl. states scholar Govt. India, Cornell U., Ithaca, N.Y., 1952-55; reader in physics Aligarh Muslim U., India, 1955-60, Delhi U., 1960-62; vis. prof. physics Ind. U., Bloomington, 1962-63; prof. physics Delhi U., 1963-69, sr. prof., 1969-89; Einstein rsch. prof. U. Delhi, 1989—94; freelance writer-rschr., 1996—. Profl. cons. Rutherford Lab., 1968; vis. scientist UCLA, 1967, CERN, 1968, 83, 85, U. Tex.-Austin, 1971, Bonn, 1974, U. Paris, 1977, Deutsche Elektronen Synchrotron, 1979, Internat. Ctr. for Theoretical Physics, Trieste, 1962, 65, 67, 68, 69, 70, 71, 74, 77, 83, Tubingen, 1985, Ind U., Bloomington, 1986; nat. lectr. Univ. Grants Commn., India, 1973; vis. prof. U. Ill., Chgo., 1986-87, Nat. Inst. Adv. Studies, Bangalore, 1995; vis. lectr. Nuffield Found., Australia, 1973; mem. internat. adv. coms. for successive internat. conf. series on few body problems in nuc. and particle physics and other internat. confs.; convenor, organizer 7th Internat. Conf. on Few Body Problems, Delhi U., 1975-76; sr. exch. visitor U.S. univs., Indo-U.S. Joint Program, 1976; sr. exch. visitor Brit. univs., Indian Nat. Sci. Acad. Royal Soc. Exch. Programme, 1979. Editor: Few Body Dynamics, 1976, Niels Bohr-A Profile, 1985, Quantum Field Theory, 2000, India in the World of Physics: Then and Now, 2007; bd. editors: Few Body Systems, 1985-2000; contbr. over 220 articles to revs. to profl. jours. Mem. physics panel Univ. Grants Commn., India, New Delhi, 1974-76, 80-82; mem. coun. Raman Rsch. Inst., Bangalore, India, 1978-88; mem. Nat. Bd. for Higher Maths., Bombay, 1982-88; mem. phys. adv. com. dept. sci. and tech. Govt. India, 1982-87; mem. physics coms. Coun. for Sci. and Indsl. Rsch., New Delhi, 1974-78, 81-91; mem. nat. accelerator com. Dept. Atomic Energy, India, 1979-83. Recipient S.S. Bhatnagar award Coun. for Sci. and Indsl. Rsch. India, New Delhi, 1969, Megh Nad Saha award Univ. Grants Commn., New Delhi, 1975, S.K. Mitra Birth Centenary medal Indian Sci. Congl. Assn., 1999; nat. fellow Univ. Grants Commn., 1975-78; assoc. Internat. Ctr. for Theoretical Physics, Trieste, 1967-70, sr. assoc., 1972-77, hon. assoc., 1978-83. Fellow Third World Acad. Scis., Indian Nat. Sci. Acad. (sec. 1975-79, editor publ. 1983-86, Albert Einstein rsch. prof. 1989-94, S.N. Bose medal 1986), Indian Acad. Sci. (coun. 1975-78), Am. Phys. Soc., Nat. Acad. Sci. India. Avocations: stamp collecting/philately, philosophy of science. Home: 244 Tagore Park Delhi 110009 India Office Phone: 91-11-27446153. Personal E-mail: ganmitra@nde.vsnl.net.in.

MITRA, SANJIT KUMAR, electrical and computer engineering educator; b. Calcutta, West Bengal, India, Nov. 26, 1935; came to U.S., 1958; MS in Tech., U. Calcutta, 1956; MS, U. Calif., Berkeley, 1960, PhD, 1962; D of Tech. (hon.), Tampere U., Finland, 1987; Academician, Acad. Finland, 2000; D in Tech. (hon.), Bucharest U., Romania, 2004. Asst. engr. Indian Statis. Inst., Calcutta, 1956-58; from teaching asst. to assoc. Univ. Calif., Berkeley, 1958-62; asst. prof. Cornell U., Ithaca, NY, 1962-65; mem. tech. staff Bell Telephone Labs., Holmdel, NJ, 1965-67; prof. U. Calif., Davis, 1967-77, prof. elec. and computer engring. Santa Barbara, 1977—, chmn. dept. elec. and computer engring., 1979-82; dir. Ctr. for Info. Processing Rsch., 1993-96. Cons. Lawrence Livermore (Calif.) Nat. Lab., 1974-95; cons. editor Van Nostrand Reinhold Co., N.Y.C., 1977-88; mem. adv. bd. Coll. Engring. Rice U., Houston, 1986-89; mem. adv. coun. Rsch. Inst. for Math. and Computing Sci., U. Groningen, The Netherlands, 1995—; mem. adv. bd. Internat. Signal Processing Ctr., Tampere U. of Tech., Finland, 1997—; external assessor Faculty of Engring., U. Putra Malaysia, Serdang, 1997—2000; hon. prof. No. Jiatong U., Beijing, China, 1985, Tech. U. Cluj-Napoka, 2005. Author: Analysis and Synthesis of Linear Active Networks, 1969, Digital and Analog Integrated Circuits, 1980; co-editor: Modern Filter Theory and Design, 1973, Two-Dimensional Digital Signal Processing, 1978, Miniaturized and Integrated Filters, 1989, Multidimensional Processing of Video Signals, 1992, Handbook for Digital Signal Processing, 1993, Digital Signal Processing: A Computer-Based Approach, 1997, 3d edit., 2005, Nonuniform Discrete Fourier Transform and Its Signal Processing Applications, 1998, Digital Signal Processing Laboratory Using MATLAB, 1999, Nonlinear Image Processing, 2000. Named Disting. Fulbright Prof., Coun. for Internat. Exch. of Scholars, 1984, 1986, 1988, Disting. Sr. Scientist, Humboldt Found., 1989; recipient F.E. Terman award, 1973, award, AT&T Found., 1985, Edn. award, Am. Soc. Eng. Edn., 1988, U. medal, Tech. U. Slovakia, 2005. Fellow: IEEE (Tech. Achievement award 1996, Mac Van Valkenburg award 1999, Millennium medal 2000, McGraw-Hill/Jacob Millman award 2001, Best Paper award 2002, James H. Mulligan Jr. Edn. medal 2006, Soc. award 2006, Edn. award 2006), AAAS, Internat. Soc. Optical Engring. (Tech. Achievement award 2005); mem.: India NAS, Indian Nat. Acad. Engring., IEE UK (Blumlein-Browne-Wilans premium 2000), Acad. Engring. Mex., US Nat. Acad. Engring., Norwegian Acad. Technol. Scis., Croatian Acad. Arts and Scis., Acad. of Finland, European Assn. for Signal Processing (Tech. Achievement award 2001). Achievements include patents for two-port networks for realizing transfer functions; non-reciprocal wave translating device; discrete cosine transform-based image coding and decoding method; method and apparatus for multipath channel shaping; method for embedding and extracting digital data in images and videos. Office: Univ Calif Dept Elec and Computer Engring Santa Barbara CA 93106-9560

MITROPHANOV, ALEXANDER YURYEVICH, mathematician, researcher; b. Novosibirsk, Russia, Apr. 24, 1976; s. Yuri Ivanovich Mitrophanov and Lydia Dmitriyevna Mitrophanova. MS with highest distinction, Saratov State U., Russia, 1998, MS with highest distinction, 2001, PhD, 2002. Cert. profl. translator Gymnasium 3, Saratov, Russia, 1993. Jr. rsch. scientist Saratov State U., Russia, 2001—02, mathematician, 2002—04, sr. rsch. scientist, 2003—04; postdoctoral fellow Ga. Inst. Tech., Atlanta, 2004—06; postdoctoralrsch. assoc. Washington U. Sch. Medicine, St. Louis, 2006—. Jour. reviewer Zentralblatt MATH, 2003—06; jour. referee Briefings in Bioinformatics, 2005—06, BMC Bioinformatics, 2004—06, Bioinformatics, 2006. Contbr. articles to profl. jours. Participant, Freedom Support Act Future Leaders Exch. Program U.S. Govt., 1993—94, A. M. Bogomolov scholar, Saratov State U., 1995—98. Mem.: Internat. Soc. Computational Biology. Achievements include development of modern sensitivity theory for Markov chains; novel approach to the quantitative analysis of signal transduction/transcriptional regulatory systems in bacteria; first to develop inequality-based sensitivity theory for hidden Markov models; research in theory and biological applications of birth-death processes. Office: Washington Univ Sch Medicine Dept Molecular Microbiology Campus Box 8230 660 S Euclid Ave Saint Louis MO 63110-1093 Office Phone: 314-362-3691. Business E-Mail: alex@borcim.wustl.edu.

MITSAKOS, CHARLES LEONIDAS, education educator, consultant; b. Lowell, Mass., Oct. 17, 1939; s. Leonidas A. and Vasiliki (Sampatakakis) M.; m. Stella Martakos, June 23, 1963; children: Charles L. Jr., Andria Estelle. BS in Edn., Lowell State Coll., 1961; EdM, Boston U., 1963, EdD, 1977. Tchr., team leader, social studies curriculum specialist Lexington (Mass.) Pub. Schs., 1961-67; social studies coord., cons. Chelmsford (Mass.) Pub. Schs., 1967-78; asst. supt. of schs. Andover (Mass.) Pub. Schs., 1978-83; supt. of schs. Winchester (Mass.) Pub. Schs., 1984-92; clin. faculty supr. Sch. Edn., Boston Coll., Chestnut Hill, Mass., 1992-93; prof. edn., chair divsn. edn. Rivier Coll., Nashua, NH, 1993—. Ednl. cons. to schs. and sch. dists. in 15 states, U.S. V.I., U.S. Dept. Def. Dep. Schs. and Ministries of Edn., 1970—; facilitator Sch. Adminstrs. Leading with Tech. (SALT), Bill and Melinda Gates Found. funded project, 2002-05; dir. Mid. Sch. Staff Devel. Inst. for Social Desegregation Program, Fairfield County, S.C., 1972; mem. staff, lectr. in team tchg. and social studies edn. NSF Insts., Stanford U., Ind. U., SUNY, Geneseo, Xavier U., U. NC, Boston U., 1968-75; sr. lectr. sch. adminstrn. and curriculum devel. Sch. Grad. Studies, Rivier Coll., 1977-93, numerous others. Author, gen. editor: (multimedia program for elem. sch.) The Family of Man Social Studies Program, 1971-77; co-author: (textbooks) America! America!, 1977, revised 2d edit., 1987, Ginn Social Studies, 1987; author: (workbook) America! America! Workbook, 1982, (textbook) Earth's Geography and Environment, 1991, others. Mem. Coun. Tchr. Edn. NH Dept. Edn.,; mem., bd. dirs., treas., past pres. Social Sci. Edn. Consortium, Fin. Com. and Steering Com. So. NH Sch. to Careers Partnership; past chmn. task force on teenagers and religious edn. Greek Orthodox Archdiocese of North and South Am.; former trustee U. Lowell; chairperson affirmative action com., chairperson com. to oversee U. Lowell Rsch. Found.; former mem. ad hoc budget com. Town of Winchester; former mem. bd. dirs., chairperson nominating com. and search com. for resident dirs. Andover Com. for A Better Chance; fund-raising chairperson, mem. edn. com., former trustee, newsletter editor local ch. Recipient Disting. Alumni award U. Lowell, Coll. of Edn., 1987. Democrat. Greek Orthodox. Avocations: writing, mosaic iconography, travel, reading. Office: Rivier Coll 420 S Main St Nashua NH 03060-5086 Home Phone: 978-256-9663; Office Phone: 603-897-8582. E-mail: cmitsakos@rivier.edu.

MITSCHER, LESTER ALLEN, chemist, educator; b. Detroit, Aug. 20, 1931; s. Lester and Mary Athelda (Pounder) M.; m. Betty Jane McRoberts, May 29, 1953; children: Katrina, Kurt, Mark. BS, Wayne U., 1953, PhD, 1958. Rsch. scientist, group leader Lederle Labs., Pearl River, NY, 1958-67; prof. Ohio State U., Columbus, 1967-75, U. Kans., Lawrence, 1975—, chmn. dept. medicinal chemistry, 1975-92; intersearch prof. Victorian Coll. of Pharmacy, Monash U., Melbourne, Australia, 1975—. Author: (with D. Lednicer) The Organic Chemistry of Drug Synthesis, Vol. 1, 1976, Vol. 2, 1980, Vol. 3, 1984, Vol. 4, 1990, The Chemistry of the Tetracycline Antibiotics, 1978; co-author: The Green Tea Book, 1997; editor-in-chief Medicinal Research Reviews, 1995-99; contbr. over 250 articles to profl. jours. Recipient Disting. Alumnus award Sch. Pharmacy, Wayne State U., 1980, 97, Rsch. Achievement award Acad. Pharm. Scis., 1980, 97, Volweiler Rsch. award Am. Assn. Colls. Pharmacy, 1985, Higuchi-Simmons award U. Kans., 1986. Fellow AAAS; mem. Am. Soc. Pharmacognosy (pres. 1992-93, Rsch. Achievement award 2007), Am. Chem. Soc. (former chmn. councilor medicinal chemistry divsn., Bristol-Myers Smissman rsch. award 1989, Med. Chemistry award 2000, Medicinal Chemistry Hall of Fame medicinal chemistry divsn. 2007), Japanese Antibiotics Assn., Soc. Heterocyclic Chemistry, Internat. Orgn. for Chemistry in Developing Countries (steering com.). Presbyterian. Office: Dept Medicinal Chemistry U Kans Lawrence KS 66045 Office Phone: 785-864-4562. Business E-Mail: lmitscher@ku.edu.

MITSEFF, CARL, lawyer; b. Detroit, Nov. 16, 1928; s. Frank H. and Katherine (Schaffer) M.; m. Phyllis Schlitters, June 28, 1952; children: C. Randall, Bradley Scott, Julie, Emily, Faye. BS, Wayne State U., 1952, LL.B., 1955. Bar: Mich. 1956. Practiced in Detroit, 1956—; staff atty. Burroughs Corp., 1955-60; mem. firm LeVasseur, Mitseff, Egan & Capp, 1960-80, Mitseff & Baril, 1980-85, Fitzgerald, Hodgman, Cox, Cawthoren & McMahon, 1986-90, Cox & Hodgman, 1990—. Spl. asst. atty. gen. State of Mich.; lectr. in field. Named to Mich. Workers Compensation Hall of Fame, 2000. Mem. ABA, State Bar Mich., Internat. Assn. Ins. Counsel, Internat. Assn. Indsl. Accident Bds. and Commns., Detroit Athletic Club (bd. dirs.), Beavers (pres.), Exec. Club (pres.), Bus. Round Table (chmn.), Lochmoor Club, Grosse Pointe Yacht Club, Pi Kappa Alpha, Delta Theta Phi. Home: 612 N Brys Dr Grosse Pointe Woods MI 48236-1247 Office: 1001 Woodward Ave Ste 1000 Detroit MI 48226-1904 Office Phone: 313-963-3210. Personal E-mail: c.mitseff@aol.com.

MITTEL, JOHN J., diversified financial services company executive, economist; b. L.I., NY; s. John and Mary (Leidolf) M.; 1 child, James C. BBA, CUNY. Rschr. econs. dept. McGraw Hill & Co., NYC; mgr., asst. to pres., Indsl. Commodity Corp., J. Carvel Lange Inc., and J. Carvel Lange Internat., Inc., NYC, 1956-64, corp. sec., 1958-86, v.p., 1964-80, exec. v.p., 1980-86; pres. I.C. Investors Corp., NYC, 1972—, I.C. Pension Adv., Inc., NYC, 1977—. Bd. dir. several corps.; plan adminstr., trustee Combined Indsl. Commodity Corp. and J. Carvel Lange Inc. Pension Plan, 1962-86, J. Carvel Lange Internat. Inc. Profit Sharing Trust, 1969-86, Combined Indsl. Commodity Corp. and J. Carvel Lange Inc. Employees Profit Sharing Plan, 1977-86. Co-author: How Good a Sales Profit Are You, 1961, The Role of the Economic Consulting Firm. Mem. grad. adv. bd. Bernard M. Baruch Coll., CUNY, 1971-72. Mem. Conf. Bd., Am. Statis. Assn., Newcomen Soc. N.Am., Union League (N.Y.C.). Office: 10633 Saint Andrews Rd Boynton Beach FL 33436-4714

MITTELSTAEDT, ROBERT E., JR., dean; married; 3 children. BS in Mech. Engring., Tulane U., 1965; MBA, U. Pa., 1971. Founder, pres. Intellego, Inc., 1985—89; mem. faculty Wharton Sch. of U. Pa., Phila., 1973—2004, vice dean exec. edn., 1990—2004, vice dean Wharton West, 2000—01; dean Ariz. State U. W.P. Carey Sch. Bus., Tempe, Ariz., 2004—. Bd. dirs. Lab. Corp. of Am., 1996—, HIP Found., Inc., 1997—, IS&S Inc., 1988—, chmn., 1988—97. Served USN, 1965—70. Office: Ariz State U WP Carey Sch Bus Main Campus PO Box 873506 Tempe AZ 85287-3506 Office Phone: 480-965-2468. Office Fax: 480-965-5539. E-mail: Robert.Mittelstaedt@asu.edu.

MITTEMEYER, BERNHARD THEODORE, urology and surgery educator; arrived in U.S., 1944, naturalized; BS in Biology, Moravian Coll., 1952, LLD (hon.), 1982; MD, Temple U., 1956; DSc, William Jewell Coll., 1985. Diplomate Am. Bd. Urology, Am. Bd. Quality Assurance and Utilization Rev. Physicians. Rotation intern Santa Barbara (Calif.) Cottage and County Hosps., 1956—57; advanced through grades from capt. to lt. gen. U.S. Army, 1957—81; resident in gen. surgery Fitzsimons Army Med. Ctr., Denver, 1959—61; resident in urol. surgery Tripler Army Med. Ctr., Honolulu, 1962—65; asst. chief urol. surgery svc. urol. residency tng. program Walter Reed Army Med. Ctr., Washington, 1965—68, 1971—74, chief urol. surgery svc. and urol. residency tng. program, 1974—77, chief dept. surgery, 1976—77, comdg. gen., 1980—81; surgeon gen. Dept Army, Washington, 1981—85; ret., 1985—86; sr. v.p., corp. med. dir. Whittaker Health Svcs., LA, 1985—2002; prof. urology and surgery Tex. Tech U., Lubbock, 1986—, exec. v.p. Health Scis. Ctr., 1986—96; interim dean Tex. Tech U. Sch. Medicine, Lubbock, 1988—90, 1995—96, nterim dean; provost Tex. Tech U., Lubbock, 1988—96. Clin. assoc. prof. urology George Washington U. Sch. Medicine, Washington, 1974—85; clin. prof. surgery Uniformed Svcs. U. Health Scis., Bethesda, Md., 1976—; vis. prof., guest lectr. urology U. Mo., U. Pitts., Korea U., Pa. State U., U. Mass., U. Va., Wake Forest U., Armed Forces Inst. Pathology, Walter Reed Army Inst. Rsch., 1975—; ctrl. com. of pub.-acad. liaison Tex. Dept. Mental Health and Mental Retardation, 1990—; managed health care adv. com. ex. Dept. Criminal Justice, 1993—96; presenter in field. Contbr. articles to profl. jours. Trustee Moravian Coll., 1982—86; bd. dirs. Sci. Spectrum, Lubbock, 1988—, Lubbock Symphony Orch., 1989—92, Lubbock Conv. and Visitors Bur., 1991—93. Decorated D.S.M., Legion of Merit with oak leaf cluster, DFC, Bronze Star with V device, Air medal with oak leaf cluster; recipient Comenius award, Moravian Coll., 1978, Founders medal, Assn. Mil. Surgeons, 1978, Alumni Achievement award in health policy, Temple U. Sch. Medicine, 1988. Fellow: ACS, Am. Coll. Quality Assurance and Utilization Rev. Physicians, Am. Coll. Physician Execs.; mem.: AMA (ho. of dels. 1981—85), South Ctrl. Sect. Am. Urol. Assn., Lubbock-Crosby-Garza County Med. Soc. (armed svcs. com. 1988—96), Tex. Med. Assn. (cons. coun. on med. edn. 1987—96), Assn. U.S. Army, Soc. Med. Cons. to Armed Forces, Am. Acad. Med. Dirs., Uniformed Svcs. U. Surg. Assocs., Soc. U. Urologists, Soc. Govt. Svc. Urologists, Am. Urol. Assn., Lubbock C. of C. Office: Texas Tech Univ Sch Medicine Rm 2B450 3601 4th St MS 6207 Lubbock TX 79430 Office Phone: 806-743-3000. Office Fax: 806-743-3021. E-mail: bmittemeyer@cox.net, Bernhard.Mittemeyer@ttuhsc.edu.

MITTEN, DAVID GORDON, classical archaeologist; b. Youngstown, Ohio, Oct. 26, 1935; s. Joe Atlee and Helen Louise (Boyd) M.; children: Claudia Antonia Sabina, Eleanor Elizabeth. BA, Oberlin Coll., 1957; MA in Classical Archaeology, Harvard U., 1958, PhD in Classical Archaeology, 1962. From instr. dept. fine arts to assoc. prof. Harvard U., Cambridge, Mass., 1962-69, James Loeb prof. classical art and archaeology, 1969—;

curator ancient art Harvard U. Art Mus., Cambridge, 1976-96, George M.A. Hanfmann curator ancient art, 1996—2005, curator emeritus, 2006—. Assoc. dir. Harvard-Cornell Sardis Expdn., 1976—; Whitehead vis. prof. archaeology Am. Study of Classical Studies, Athens, Greece, 1990-91. Author: (with S.F. Doeringer) Master Bronzes from the Classical World, 1967; Classical Bronzes: Mus. Art, RISD, 1975, (with Arielle P. Kozloff) The Gods Delight: The Human Figure in Classical Bronze, Cleve. Mus. Art, 1988. Woodrow Wilson fellow Harvard U., 1958; Fulbright fellow Am. Sch. Classical Studies at Athens, 1959-60; Archaeol. Inst. Am. Olivia James fellow, 1969-70; John Simon Guggenheim Found. fellow, 1976-77. Mem. Archaeol. Inst. Am., Assn. Field Archaeology (co-founder), Am. Schs. Oriental Rsch., Brit. Sch. Archaeology (Athens, Greece), Am. Numismatic Soc. Office: Sackler Mus 316 Harvard Univ 485 Broadway Cambridge MA 02138-3845 Office Phone: 617-495-3355. E-mail: mitten@fas.harvard.edu.

MITTEN, L. RUSSELL, lawyer, former telecommunications industry executive; BA, Southeast Mo. State U.; JD, Wash. U., St. Louis. Bar: Conn., Mo., Tex., Wash., Hawaii, US Supreme Ct., US Ct. of Appeals, U.S. Dist. Ct. Gen. counsel Missouri Public Service Commn., Gen. Telephone Co. of Southwest, Gen. Telephone Co. of Northwest, GTE Service Corp.; v.p., gen. counsel, sec. GTE Hawaiian Telephone; gen. counsel Citizens Communications, 1990—91, v.p., gen. counsel, asst. sec., 1991—2000, v.p., gen. counsel, sec., 2000—02, sr. v.p., gen. counsel, sec., 2002—06; atty. Brydon, Swearengen & England PC, Jefferson City, Mo., 2006—. Office: Brydon, Swearengen & England PC 312 E Capitol Ave PO Box 456 Jefferson City MO 65102 Office Phone: 573-635-7166 160. Office Fax: 573-635-0427. E-mail: rmitten@brydonlaw.com.

MITTEN, MATTHEW JOHN, law educator, lawyer; b. Tiffin, Ohio, Apr. 26, 1959; BA in Econs., Ohio State Univ., 1981; JD magna cum laude, Univ. Toledo, 1984. Bar: Ga. 1984. Atty. antitrust and intellectual property law Kilpatrick Stockton LLP, Atlanta, 1984—89; prof. law So. Tex. Coll. Law, Houston, 1990—99; prof. law, dir. Nat. Sports Law Inst. Marquette U. Law Sch., Milw., 1999—, assoc. dean academic affairs, 2002—04. Sr. fellow U. Melbourne Law Sch., 2005—06; faculty, comparative sports law TC Beirne Sch. Law, Univ. Queensland, Brisbane, Australia; vis. prof. Univ. Toledo Coll. Law; vis. lectr., sports medicine Univ. Tenn. Grad. Sch. Medicine; spkr. in field; cons. in field. Note and comment editor U. Toledo Law Review; contbr. articles i profl. jours. and chapters in books; co-author: Sports Law and Regulation-Cases, Materials and Problems, 2005. Chair NCAA Com. Competitive Safeguards and Med. Aspects Sports, 2002—05. Mem.: ABA (entertainment and sports law), Ct. Arbitration Sport, Am. Assn. Law Sch. (past chmn., sect. Law & Sports), Sports Lawyers Assn. (bd. dir.), Order of the Coif. Office: Marquette University Law School Sensenbrenner Hall PO Box 1881 Milwaukee WI 53201-1881 Office Phone: 414-288-7494. Business E-Mail: matt.mitten@marquette.edu.

MITTENDORF, KIMBERLY ANN, secondary school educator, real estate consultant; d. K. A. and Jo Mittendorf. BS in Edn., Murray State U., 1980, MA in Edn., 1987. Cert. career and tech. edn. Nat. Bd. Tchr. Certification, 2004, lic. real estate Paducah C.C., 1990. Tchr. McCracken County Pub. Schs., Paducah, Ky., 1982—; real estate specialist Prudential Real Estate, Paducah, 1990—99. Mem. Paducah Bd. Realtors, 1990—2001; mem. edn. com. Challenger Learning Space Ctr., Paducah, 2001—03; mem. fed. res. economics edn. com. Fed. Res., Louisville, 2005—. Affiliate Hon. Order of Ky. Cols., Louisville, 1996—; inductee Paducah C. of C. Leadership Class, 1995—96; mem. Paducah C. of C., 1995—98; mem. funds distbn. com. United Way, Paducah, 1996—97. Recipient Invitation to China, People to People Amb. -Edn. Del. to China, 2005. Mem.: NEA (assoc.), Ky. Edn. Assn. (assoc.), Ky. Assn. Career and Tech. Edn. (assoc.), Pi Lambda Theta. Avocations: literature, architecture and design, fitness, cuisine. Office: McCracken County Pub Schs 435 Berger Rd Paducah KY 42001 Business E-Mail: kim.mittendorf@mccracken.kyschools.us.

MITTERAND, HENRI C., literature educator, writer; b. Vault-De-Lugny, Yonne, France, Aug. 7, 1928; arrived in U.S., 1989; s. Joseph and Helene (Dangauthier) Mitterand; m. Helene T. D'Afflitto, Dec. 24, 1955; children: Marie-Helene, Jacques-Olivier. Lic., U. Paris, 1969, Maitrise, 1950, Agregation, 1951, PhD, 1969; degree (hon.), U. Athens, 1997. From asst. to assoc. prof. U. Besancon, France, 1957-65; assoc. prof. U. Reims, France, 1965-68; prof. in French lit. U. Paris 8, 1968-78; prof. U. Paris 3, 1978-90, Columbia U., NYC, 1990—2004, prof. emeritus, 2004—. Vis. prof. Stanford U, 1966, U. Toronto, Canada, 1970—93, U. Pa., 1999; editl. cons., Paris, 1971—; mem. numerous adv. bds. in field; lectr. in field. Editor: (book) Zola, 5 Vols., 1959—67 (award, 1968), Zola, 15 Vols., 1970; author: Le Discours du roman, 1980, L'Illusion réaliste, 1994, Zola et le Naturalisme, 1986, Le Regard et le Signe, 1987, Le Roman á l'oeuvre, 1998, Zola I, 1999, Zola II, 2001, Zola III, 2002. Decorated officer Palmes Academiques France, chevalier Legion d'Honneur, comdr. Order Arts and Letters; recipient Prix de l'Academie Française, Grand Prix de la Ville de Paris, 2000. Mem.: Soc. Fellows/Columbia U., Acad. du Morvan, Inst. Pierre Larousse, Soc. des Amis de Zola (pres. 1990—), Royal Soc. Can. Avocations: sailing, music, films, reading. Office: Columbia U Broadway/116th St W New York NY 10027 E-mail: hm12@columbia.edu.

MITTERMILLER, JAMES JOSEPH, lawyer; b. Washington, Apr. 13, 1953; s. Jack and Alice Marie (Froeba) M.; m. Elizabeth Gaillard Simons, June 23, 1979; children: Samuel Stoney, Paul Andrew, Laurie Alice, Claire Mary. Student, U. Heidelberg, 1973-74; BA, Claremont McKenna Coll., 1975; JD, U. Calif. Berkeley, 1978. Bar: Calif., U.S. Dist. Ct. (so., ctrl. and ea. dists.) Calif., U.S. Ct. Appeals (9th cir.), U.S. Supreme Ct. Assoc. Sheppard, Mullin, Richter & Hampton, LA, 1978-86, ptnr., 1986—. Panelist Calif. Continuing Edn. of Bar, L.A. and San Diego, 1984—. Dir. Legal Aid Soc. of San Diego, 1990—, pres., 1998-2000; bd.dirs., LaJolla YMCA, 2001-04. Recipient Wiley Manuel Pro Bono award Calif. State Bar, 1992, 2001. Mem. Assn. Bus. Trial Lawyers (bd. dirs. 1998-2001), Am. Inns of Ct., Claremont McKenna Coll. Alumni Assn. San Diego (bd. dirs.). Avocations: swimming, surfing. Office: Sheppard Mullin Richter & Hampton 501 W Broadway Fl 19 San Diego CA 92101-3536

MITTLEBERG, ERIC MICHAEL, pharmaceutical executive; b. NYC, Nov. 7, 1951; s. Irving Ralph and Rose (Schnieder) M.; m. Jane Susan Baumoehl, Dec. 25, 1977; children: Scott, Alyson, Lauren. BS in Pharmacy, St. Johns U., Jamaica, NY, 1974, MS in Ind. Pharmaceutics, 1978, PhD in Pharmaceutics, 1982. Registered pharmacist, N.Y. Assoc. scientist Hoffmann-LaRoche Inc., Nutley, NJ, 1974-78; dept. head process improvement Lederle Labs, Pearl River, NY, 1978-83; mgr. mfg. devel. Key Pharm., Miami, Fla., 1983-86; dir. prodn. and tech. svcs. Schering Labs, Miami, 1986-89; sr. dir. pharm. devel. and tech. svcs. worldwide R.W. Johnson Pharm. Rsch. Inst., Raritan, NJ, 1989-97; v.p. sci., med. affairs Ivax Corp., 1997—2006; exec. v.p. pharm. R&D Par Pharm., Inc., Spring Valley, NY, 2006—. Mem. Internat. Soc. Pharm. Engrs., Acad. Pharm. Sci., Am. Pharm. Assn. Office: Par Pharm Inc 2 Ram Ridge Rd Spring Valley NY 10977 Office Phone: 845-573-5599. Business E-Mail: emittleberg@parpharm.com.

MITTLER, DIANA (DIANA MITTLER-BATTIPAGLIA), music educator, pianist; b. NYC, Oct. 19, 1941; d. Franz and Regina (Schilling) Mittler; m. Victor Battipaglia, Sept. 5, 1965 (div. 1982). BS, Juilliard Sch., 1962, MS, 1963; DMA, Eastman Sch. Music, 1974. Choral dir. William Cowper Jr. H.S. and Springfield Gardens Jr. H.S., Queens, NY, 1963-68; coord. music Flushing H.S., Queens, 1968-79; asst. prin. music Bayside H.S., Queens, 1979-86; assoc. prof. music Lehman Coll., CUNY, 1986-87, prof., 1987—, choral dir., 1986—. Cons. ednl. projects New World Records, 1987—; ednl. cons. Flushing Coun. on Culture and the Arts; cons. Sta. WNET; assoc. condr. Queens Borough-Wide Chorus, 1964-70; pianist, founder Con Brio Chamber Ensemble, 1978; faculty So. Vt. Music Festival, 1979-83; soloist with N.Y. Philharm., 1956; examiner NYC Bd. Edn. Bd. Exams., 1985—. Author: 57 Lessons for the H.S. Music Class, 1983, Franz Mittler: Austro-American Composer, Musician and Humorous Poet, 1993; contbr. articles to profl. jours.; performance Internat. Summer acad. Mozarteum, Salzburg, Austria, 1995, Weill Recital Hall, 1996, Merkin Hall, 1997, Herbert von Karajan Centrum, Vienna, Austria, 1998; rec. Franz Mittler., Preiser Records, Trio and Piano Pieces, 2003; featured in Last Stop, Kew Gardens, 2007; featured on Study with the Best Series, CUNY TV, 2005. Choral dir., accompanist various charitable, religious, mil., civic holiday functions. N.Y. State Regents scholar, 1958-62; scholarships Juilliard Sch. and Eastman Sch. Music; recipient Excellence in Tchg. award, 1993, Prism award, 1996. Mem. Am. Choral Dirs. Assn., Music Edn. Nat. Conf., Golden Key Soc. Democrat. Home: 10857 66th Ave Forest Hills NY 11375-2247 Office: Lehman Coll Music Dept Bedford Pk Blvd W Bronx NY 10468 Office Phone: 718-960-7795. Personal E-mail: dianamittler@aol.com.

MITTON, MICHAEL ANTHONY, environmental technology company executive; b. Bremen, Germany, Mar. 13, 1947; came to U.S., 1948 (parents Am. citizens); s. Ralph Walter and Aniela (Pilarz) M.; m. Lisa Van der Veer, Mar. 7, 1986 (div. 1991); m. Marilyn Kay Bowen, Sept. 18, 1993. BS, U. Wyo., 1970. Asst. mgr. ops. Moller Steamship Co., NYC, 1970-72; investment analyst Moller Industries, NYC, 1972-73; internal auditor Corning (N.Y.) Glass Works, 1973-75, supr. acctg., 1975-76; dir. acctg. Autotrain Corp., Washington, 1977-78; pres. RMA Ltd., Ft. Collins, Colo., 1978-81; contr. Purecycle Corp., Boulder, Colo., 1981-83; pres., chief exec. officer, treas. Synthetech Inc., Albany, Oreg., 1983-90, bd. dirs., chmn., 1990-95; ret., 1995; pres., CEO Chemical Biosensors, Inc., Beaverton, Oreg., 1992-95; technology entrepreneur, founder environ. tech. co., 1995—. Co-chmn. Oreg. Biotech. Industry Coun., 1989-90. Mem. Gov.'s Task Force Tech. Transfer, 1992-94. Fellow Am. Leadership Forum; mem. Soaring Soc. Am., Oreg. Biotech. Assn. (bd. dirs., chmn. 1990-91, pres. 1991-92), Multnomah Athletic Club. Avocations: flying, squash, skiing, sailing. Home: PO Box 4275 Incline Village NV 89450-4275

MITWELL, JILL, television director; married. BA, Bucknell U.; MA in TV and Film, Boston U. Dir.: (TV series) Guiding Light, As the World Turns, One Life to Live (Outstanding Directorial Achievement in Daytime Serials, Dirs. Guild Am., 1993, 2000, 2007). Office: c/o One Life to Live ABC Daytime 56 W 66th St New York NY 10023 *

MITYAS, SHERIF, management consultant; V.p., Midwest region AT Kearney, Inc., Chgo., also mng. ptnr., Midwest region. Mem.: Am. Lung Assn. (Jr. Achievement), Comml. Club (mem. civic com.). Office: AT Kearney Inc 222 W Adams St Chicago IL 60606

MITZNER, KENNETH MARTIN, electrical engineer, consultant; b. Bklyn., May 7, 1938; s. Louis Bernard and Dora (Sandler) Mitzner; m. Ruth Maria Osorio, Dec. 26, 1968; children: Camille Lorena Mitzner Zeiter, Esther Jeannette Mitzner Lin, Sharon Michelle Mitzner Mentkowski. BS, MIT, 1958; MS, Calif. Inst. Tech., 1959, PhD, 1964. Mem. tech. staff Hughes Aircraft, Malibu, Calif., 1959-64; prin. engr. B-2 divsn. Northrop Corp., Pico Rivera, Calif., 1964-94; owner Mitzner Sci. and Tech., Oceanside, Calif., 1995—. Instr. U. Calif., Santa Barbara, 1964—65; lectr. in field. Author: (handbook) Demonstrations Against Abortion & Death Selection, 1970; contbr. chapters to books, articles to profl. jours. Bd. dirs. Nat. Right to Life Com., 1980—81; pres. Mobilization for Unnamed, Oceanside, 1970—; bd. dirs. Ams. United for Life, 1971—94; sec. Calif. Pro Life Coun., Sacramento, 1972; mem. Los Angeles County Select Citizens Com. Life Support Policies, LA, 1983—85; bd. dirs. Jewish Life Issues Com., Solana Beach, 1983—. Named Patron of Life, Calif. Pro Life Coun., 1976; recipient Pres.'s award, 1979; Howard Hughes fellow, 1959—64, Fulbright Found. grantee, Govt. of Italy, 1961—62. Fellow: IEEE (life); mem.: Electromagnetics Acad., U.S. Nat. Commn. Internat. Union Radio Sci. (del. 20th gen. assembly). Jewish. Avocations: history, stamp collecting/philately, birdwatching. Personal E-mail: kmitzner@aol.com.

MIURA, MASAKO KUSAYANAGI, retired dermatologist; b. Pasadena, Calif., June 29, 1914; d. Takejiro Kusayanagi and Matsu Hoshizaki; m. Kiyoshi Miura, June 29, 1955; m. James Mitsuo Goto (div.); children: Denise Goto Kodani, Hans Masaji Goto. AB, U. So. Calif., LA, 1936, MD, 1941. Resident dermatology LA County Hosp., 1941—42, 1945—49; physician War Relocation Authority, Manzanar, 1942—43, Topaz, 1943—45; sch. physician LA Bd. Edn, 1951—54; physician US Army, Oakland, 1954—55, Monterey, 1955—81; ret., 1981; supervising physician Project Scout, Santa Cruz County, 1983—88. Fellow: Pacific Dermatology Assn. (nominating com. 1987); mem.: Internat. Soc. Dermatology, San Francisco Dermatol. Soc., Nat. Assn. Ret. Fed. Employees (program chair 2000), Half-Century Club, Japanese Am. Citizens League, 4-H (10 year gold pin for tchg. frgn. foods), Phi Kappa Phi, Phi Beta Kappa. Methodist. Home: 2917 Crocker Ct Aptos CA 95003

MIURA, ROBERT MITSURU, mathematician, researcher, educator; s. Richard Katsuki and Frances Yoneko Miura; m. Kathryn Bannai; children: Derek Katsuki, Brian Robert, Jared Bannai Nagae, Sean Takeo. BS, U. Calif.-Berkeley, 1960, MS, 1962; MA, Princeton U., 1964, PhD, 1966. Rsch. assoc. Princeton U. Plasma Physics Lab., 1965-67; assoc. rsch. scientist Courant Inst. Math. Sci., NYC, 1967-68; asst. prof. math. NYU, 1968—71; assoc. prof. math. Vanderbilt U., Nashville, 1971—75; assoc. prof. to prof. math. U. BC, Vancouver, Canada, 1975—2001; prof. math. sci. and biomed. enging. NJ Inst. Tech., Newark, 2001—. Assoc. chmn. math. sci. NJ Inst. Tech., 2003—05, dir. divsn. biol. scis., 2004—05, acting chmn. math. sci., 2005—06; co-program dir., program in Quantitative Neurosci. Howard Hughes Med. Inst., 2006—. Editor: Backlund Transformations, 1976, Nonlinear Phenomena in Physics and Biology, 1981, Some Mathematical Questions in Biology-Neurobiology, 1982, Muscle Physiology, 1986, DNA Sequence Analysis, 1986, Plant Biology, 1986; mem. editl. bd. Can. Applied Math. Quar., 1991—; co-editor-in-chief: Analysis and Applications, 2000—, mem. editl. bd.: Integrative Neurosci., 2001—06; contbr. articles to profl. jours. Mem. steering com. Ctr. Math. Rsch., U. Montreal, 1990-94; mem. sci. adv. panel Fields Inst., Toronto, 2002-06, mem. sci. nominating com., 2003. John Simon Guggenheim fellow, 1980-81; U. B.C. hon. Killam fellow, 1980-81. Fellow AAAS (nominating com., math. sect.), Royal Soc. Can.; mem. Am. Math. Soc. (Leroy P. Steele prize-Seminal Contribution to Rsch., 2006), Soc. Indsl. and Applied Math. (chmn. joint com. on math. in life scis. 1981-84; vice chair, chair, activity group on the life scis. 2005-06, 2007-), Can. Math. Soc. (internat. affairs com.), Soc. Math. Biology (bd. dirs. 1995-98, nominating com. 1998), Pacific Inst. Math. Sci. (interim exec. bd. 1996), Sigma Xi. Office: NJ Inst Tech Dept Math Sci Univ Hgts Newark NJ 07102 Business E-Mail: miura@njit.edu.

MIXON, AARON MALACHI, III, medical products executive; b. May 22, 1940; m. Barbara Weber; 2 children. BA, Harvard U., 1962, MBA, 1968. CEO, chmn. Invacare Corp., Elyria, Ohio, 1979—. Chmn. bd. trustees Cleve. Clinic Found. Office: Invacare Corp 1 Invacare Way PO Box 4028 Elyria OH 44036-2125 Office Phone: 440-329-6000. Office Fax: 440-366-9008.

MIXON, KENNETH WAYNE, history professor, department chairman; b. Winnsboro, SC, Aug. 19, 1945; s. Cornelius Burch and Lucille Daughtry Mixon; m. Frances Frazier Mixon, Feb. 10, 1967; children: Phillip Eldridge, Eleanor Mixon Attwood. BA, U. SC, 1967, MA, 1970; PhD, U. NC, 1974. Asst. prof. history U. So. Miss., Natchez, 1975—77; from asst. to full prof. dept. history Mercer U., Macon, Ga., 1977—96; prof., chair dept. history Augusta (Ga.) State U., 1996—. Author: Southern Writers and the New South Movement, 1980, The People's Writer, 1995; editor: My Young Master, 1987; contbr. more than 25 articles to profl. jours. Neighborhood fundraiser Am. Cancer Soc., Augusta, 2001—, Am. Heart Assn., Augusta, 2001—. Served with US Army, 1967—69, Korea. Mem.: MLA (South Atlantic divsn.), So. Hist. Assn., Am. Hist. Assn. Democrat. Presbyterian. Avocation: running. Office: Augusta State U Dept History Augusta GA 30904

MIXSON, ARCHIBALD JAMES, research scientist, internist, endocrinologist; b. Louisville, Oct. 25, 1952; s. James Goodwin and Loraine Lyle Mixson; m. Nancy Ruth Gavin, Oct. 3, 1981; children: Claire Loraine, James Gavin. BA in Math., Vanderbilt U., Nashville, 1974; MD, Emory Sch. Medicine, Atlanta, 1979. Lic. internal medicine ACP, 1983. Post-doctoral fellow NIH, Bethesda, Md., 1986—89, sr. staff fellow, 1989—95; rsch. asst. prof. U. Md., Balt., 1995—98, asst. prof., 1998—2006, assoc. prof., 2006—. Named to America's Top Physicians, Consumer's Rsch. Coun. of Am., 2003—07; grantee, NIH, Nat. Cancer Inst., 1997—2002, 2004—, Md. Indsl. Partnerships, 2002—04. Achievements include patents for carrier: DNA complexes containing DNA ecoding anti-angiogenic peptides and their use in gene therapy; histidine copolymers and methods for using same; branched histidine copolymers and methods for using same; cationic vehicle: DNA complexes and their use in gene therapy. Avocations: tennis, travel. Office: U Md 10 South Pine St Bldg MSTF Rm 759 Baltimore MD 21201 Office Phone: 410-706-3223.

MIXTER, CHRISTIAN JOHN, lawyer; b. Basel, Switzerland, Mar. 13, 1953; s. Keith Eugene and Beatrice Maria (Ruf) M.; m. Linna M. Barnes, Dec. 17, 1977; children: Sara Elizabeth Barnes Mixter, Laura Ellen Barnes Mixter. BA, Ohio State U., 1974; JD, Duke U., 1977. Bar: N.Y. 1978, D.C. 1981. Assoc. Davis Polk & Wardwell, NYC and Washington, 1977-87; assoc. counsel Office Ind. Counsel (Iran/Contra), Washington, 1987-91; asst. chief litigation counsel Enforcement divsn. SEC, Washington, 1991-97, chief litigation counsel, 1997-2000; ptnr. Morgan, Lewis & Bockius LLP, Washington, 2000—. Mem. ABA (bus. law and litig. sects.), Assn. Bar City N.Y., Phi Beta Kappa, Order of the Coif. Office: Morgan Lewis & Bockius LLP 1111 Pennsylvania Ave NW Washington DC 20004 E-mail: cmixter@morganlewis.com.

MIYAGAWA, CHIORI, theater educator, playwright; life ptnr. Hap Tivey. MFA, CUNY, 1989. Asst. lit. mgr. Actors Theatre of Louisville, 1990—91; lit. mgr. Arena Stage, Washington, 1991—92; assoc. artist Pub. Theater, NYC, 1992—93; artistic assoc. N.Y. Theatre Workshop, NYC, 1993—2000; assoc. prof. theater Bard Coll., Annandale-on-Hudson, NY, 2001—. Playwritht-in-residence Yale Sch. Drama, New Haven, 1996—2000; bd. dir. Alliance of Resident Theatre, NYC, 2003—. Author (plays) America Dreaming, 1995 (Rockefeller Mulit-Artist Prodn. award, 1994), Nothing Forever (Rockefeller Mulit-Artist Prodn. award, 1995), Yesterday's Window, FireDance, 1997, Jamaica Avenue, 1998, Broken Morning, 1998 (TCG Extended Collaboration grant, 1998), Awakening, 1999 (Japan Found. award, 2000), Woman Killer, 2001, Antigone's Red, 2002, Antigone Project/Red Again, 2004; author: (plays) Leaving Eden, 2005. Recipient, Ensemble Studio Theatre/Alfred P. Sloan Found., 2002; fellow, N.Y. Found. for Arts, 1994, Van Lier Playwriting fellow, N.Y. Theatre Workshop, 1997, Asian Cultural Coun., 1999, MacDowell Colony, 2002—03; McKnight Playwriting fellow, Playwrights Ctr., 1998. Democrat. Buddhist. Office: Bard Coll Theater Dept Annandale On Hudson NY 12504 Office Phone: 845-758-7938. E-mail: miyagawa@bard.edu.

MIYAGAWA, GEORGE ROBERT, retired military officer; b. Kalamazoo, Mich., July 30, 1932; s. George Yoshio Miyagawa and Myra Eva Nielsen Miyagawa; m. Ellen Jane Brooks Miyagawa, Sept. 24, 1955 (dec.); children: John James, Kay Elizabeth Miyagawa Ennis. BA in Econs., Kalamazoo Coll., 1950; MA in Ops. Mgmt., U. So. Calif., LA; postgrad., US Naval Postgrad. Sch., Monterey, Calif., 1960—61, US Naval War Coll., Newport, RI, 1965—66. Lic. aviator US Naval Air Tng. Command, 1956. Commd. 2 lt. USN, 1956, advanced through grades to capt., 1976, pilot land based squadron Whidbey Island, Wash., 1956—60, pilot carrier based squadron Quonset Point, RI, 1963—65, command squadron (air control) Virginia Beach, Va., 1973—74, command air group (air control), 1976—78. Mem., chmn. Econ. Devel. Commn., Fluvanna County, Va., 1980—84. Recipient Howard prize in econs., Kalamazoo Coll., 1954. Methodist. Avocations: blacksmithing, antebellum restoration, tree farming. Home Phone: 434-842-3378.

MIYAGAWA, HIROAKI, materials scientist, researcher; b. Sendai, Japan, Aug. 13, 1972; arrived in US, 2000; s. Kazuhiko and Emiko Miyagawa. BS, Nagoya U., Japan, 1996; MS, Tokyo Inst. Tech., 1998, PhD, 2000. Postdoctoral rsch. assoc. Ctr. Intelligent Processing Composites Northwestern U., Evanston, Ill., 2000—01; vis. rsch. assoc. Composite Materials and Structures Ctr. Mich. State U., East Lansing, Mich., 2002—04, vis. rsch. assoc. Sch. of Packaging, 2004—05; sci. rschr. Nitto Denko Tech. Corp., Oceanside, Calif., 2006—. Contbr. articles to profl. jours. Vol. train operator Fox River Trolley Mus., South Elgin, Ill., 2001—05, Orange Empire Rlwy. Mus., Perris, Calif., 2006. Mem.: ASME, Materials Rsch. Soc., Soc. Advancement Material and Process Engring. (1st Pl. Outstanding Tech. Paper award 2001), The Japan Soc.Mech. Engrs. Achievements include patents pending for biobased epoxy, their nanocomposites and methods for making those. Home: 3760 North Way Oceanside CA 92056 Office: Nitto Denko Technical Corporation 501 Via Del Monte Oceanside CA 92054 Home Phone: 760-231-9108. Personal E-mail: hiroaki.miyagawa@gmail.com.

MIYAGAWA, ICHIRO, physicist; b. Hiratsuka, Kanagawa, Japan, Mar. 5, 1922; s. Shigejiro and Tsuma (Itoh) M.; m. Mitsuko Yamada, Feb. 10, 1950; children: Shigeru, Haruyo, Mari. BS, Nagoya U., Japan, 1945; DSc, U. Tokyo, 1954. Asst. prof. U. Tokyo, 1959-62; vis. asst. prof. Duke U., Durham, NC, 1963-65; asst. prof. physics U. Ala., Tuscaloosa, 1965-66, assoc. prof., 1966-70, prof., 1970-80, Univ. Research prof. physics, 1980-92, prof. emeritus, 1992—. Contbr. articles to profl. jours. Recipient Samuel Ullman award, 1998; USPHS grantee; EPA grantee; NIH grantee. Fellow Am. Phys. Soc.; mem., AAAS, Sigma Xi. Home: 6434 Misty Ridge Dr Birmingham AL 35235- *Finding truth in any work or in any matter, however simple, is rewarding, although painful in many cases. Successful people in every spectrum of society are master discoverers of truth.*

MIYAKE, ISSEY, fashion designer; b. Hiroshima, Japan, Apr. 22, 1938; BA in Graphic Design, Tama Art U., Tokyo, 1959—64; studies at, La Chambre Syndicale de la Couture Parisienne, Paris, 1965—68. Began making clothing, 1962; presented first collection in, 1963; asst. designer Guy Laroche, Paris, 1965—68, Hubert de Givenchy, Paris, 1968-69; designer Geoffrey Beene, NYC, 1969-70; founder Miyake Design Studio, NYC, 1970—, Issey Miyake, Inc., NYC, 1971—. Started working on the pleats series, 1988; launched the line Pleats Please Issey Mikake, 93; presented A-POC line (A Piece of Cloth), 98; established Mikake Issey Found., 2004. Exhbns. of work include: exhbns. in NY and Paris in 1971-73, Issey Miyake and a Piece of Cloth Seibu Mus. Art, Tokyo, 1977, East Meets West, Internat. Design Conf., Apsen, Colo., 1979, Musee des Arts Decoratifs, Paris, 1978, Costumes for Maurice Béjart's ballet, Casta Diva, performed at IRCAM, Centre Pompidou, Paris in collaboration with

Tomio Mohri, 1980, MIT, Cambridge, 1982, San Francisco Mus. Modern Art, 1983, Issey Miyake Bodyworks, Victoria and Albert Mus., London, 1985, Energies exhbns. Stedelijk Mus., Amsterdam, 1990, Touko Mus. of Contemporary Art, Tokyo, 1990, Costume for the Loss of Small Details William Forsythe & Frankfurter Ballet, 1991, Issey Miyake Making Things exhbn., found. Cartier pour l'art contempo-rain Paris, ACE Gallery, NY, Mus. Contemporary Art, Tokyo, 1998-2000, A-POC Making Issey Miyake & Dai Fujiwara exhbn. Vitra Design Mus. Berlin, 2001, Big Bang exhbn. Centre Pompidou Paris, 2005; represented in permanent collections: Met. Mus. Art, NYC, Victoria and Albert Mus., London. Author: Issey Miyake: East Meets West, 1978, Issey Miyake: Bodyworks, 1983. Named Person of Cultural Merit, Japan Govt., 1998; recipient Japan Fashion Editor's Club award, 1974, Mainichi Design award, 1977, 1984, 1996, Pratt Inst. NY award for Creative Design, 1980, Internat. award, Coun. Am. Fashion Designers, 1984, Neiman-Marcus award, 1984, Best Collection presented by a Fgn. Designer award of Les Oscars 1985 de la Mode, Paris, 1985, award of the Japanese mag. for the textile industry Senken Shimbun, 1986, Asahi award, 1992, Chevalier de l'ordre Nat. de la Légion d'Honneur, 1993, Georg Jensen award, Denmark, 1999, Wexner prize, U. Ohio, 2004, Praemium Imperiale award for sculpture, Japan Art Assn., 2005, Kyoto prize (Arts and Philosophy Category), Inamori Found., 2006. Office: Issey Miyake USA Corp 3 W 18th St Fl 7 New York NY 10011-4610 Address: Miyake Design Studio 1-23 Ohyama-cho Shibuya-ku Tokyo 151 Japan

MIYAKE, STEPHANIE ANN, psychology professor, director, marriage and family therapist; b. Tulsa, Okla., Feb. 8, 1953; d. Thomas Wayne and Thelma Ann Shank; m. Thomas Masami Miyake, Mar. 19, 1988; children: Jan, Amber, Diann, Chris, Lance. BA, U. Ark., 1988; MA, Phillips Grad. Inst., 1994. Lic. marriage and family therapist Calif., Tex. Bus. mgr., therapist Angeles Cmty. Counseling Ctr., Monrovia, Calif., 1994—2002; marriage and family therapist self employed, 1994—; PsyD program admin. Azusa Pacific U., Azusa, Calif., 1999—2003, dir. MA clin. psych. program, 2001—05, dir. clin. training, 2005—07, PsyD adminstrv. faculty, 2007—. Trea., bd. mem. Angeles Cmty. Counseling Ctr., Monrovia, Calif., 1998—2002; adv. So. Calif. Consortium of Marriage and Family Therapist Educators, Encino, Calif., 2002—. Editor: Skilled Empathy, 2004; author: Clinical Placement Manual, 2000. Chairperson Claremont HS Grad. Night 2000, Claremont, Calif., 1999—2000; bd. pres. San Gabriel Valley Choral Co., Monrovia, Calif., 1997—99, bd. sec., 2000—03; 1st. v.p. Parent Faculty Assn., Claremont, Calif., 1998—99. Recipient Pres. award, Phillips Grad. Inst., 1994. Mem.: Tex. Assn. of Marriage and Family Therapists, Calif. Assn. of Marriage and Family Therapists, Am. Assn. of Marriage and Family Therapists, Phi Kappa Phi. Achievements include built MA program to be nationally recognized in a 3 year period. Avocations: gardening, singing. Office: Azusa Pacific U Dept of Grad Psych 701 E Foothill Blvd Azusa CA 91702 Office Fax: 628-815-5015. Business E-Mail: smiyake@apu.edu.

MIYAKE, YASUJI, computer science educator; b. Nagoya, Aichi Pref, Japan, Nov. 28, 1936; m. Sugako Yamada, Apr. 29, 1971; 1 child, Shigemitsu. B in Engring., Nagoya U., 1960, M in Engring., 1962, DEng, 1968. Rsch. assoc. Nagoya U., 1965-68, asst. prof., 1968-69, assoc. prof., 1969-78; prof. engring. Mie U., Japan, 1978-2000, prof. emeritus, 2000—; prof., computer sci. dept. engring. Chubu U., Japan, 2000—07, chairperson computer sci. dept. engring., 2000—03, chairperson computer sci. dept. Grad. Sch., 2004—07, vis. prof., 2007—. Dir. Computation Ctr. Mie U., 1982-87, senator, 1997-99. Inventor, patentee in field; contbr. articles to profl. jours. Recipient 1st prize Inst. for character recognition technique contests, Inst. Posts and Telecom., Ministry of Posts and Telecom. Japan, 1992, 93, 94, commendation from dir. Tokai Elec. Comm. Control, 1997. Mem. Inst. Electronics, Info. Comm. Engrs. Japan, Info. Processing Soc. Japan, Japanese Soc. Med. Electronics Biol. Engring. Buddhist. Avocations: photography, collecting cameras, driving. Office: Chubu U 1200 Matsumoto-cho Kasugai 487-8501 Japan Personal E-mail: y-miyake@u01.gate01.com. Business E-Mail: miyake@cs.chubu.ac.jp.

MIYAMOTO, RICHARD TAKASHI, otolaryngologist; b. Feb. 2, 1944; s. Dave Norio and Haruko (Okano) Miyamoto; m. Cynthia VanderBurgh, June 17, 1967; children: Richard Christopher, Geoffrey Takashi. BS cum laude, Wheaton Coll., 1966; MD, U. Mich., 1970; MS in Otology, U. So. Calif., 1978; D Engring. (hon.), Rose Hulman Inst. Tech., 2001. Diplomate Am. Bd. Otolaryngology. Intern Butterworth Hosp., Grand Rapids, Mich., 1970—71, resident in surgery, 1971—72; resident in otolaryngology Ind. U. Sch. Medicine, Indpls., 1972—75; fellow in otology and neurotology St. Vincent Hosp. and Otologic Med. Group, LA, 1977—78; asst. prof. Ind. U. Sch. Medicine, Indpls., 1978—83, assoc. prof., 1983—88, prof., 1988—, chmn., 1987—, chief otology and neurotology dept. otology, head and neck surgery, 1982—, chmn. dept. otolaryngology, 1987—, Arilla DeVault prof. otolaryngology, 1991; chief otolaryngology, head and neck surgery Wishard Meml. Hosp., 1979—2002. Mem. editl. bd.: Laryngoscope, Am. Jour. Otology, Otolaryngology - Head and Neck Surgery, European Archives of Oto-Rhino-Laryngology, Anales de Otorrinolaringologia Mexicana; contbr. articles tto profl. jours. Mem. adv. coun. Nat. Inst. Deafness and other Commication Disorders, 1989—94, 2002—; mem. adv. bd. Alexander Graham Bell Assn. for the Deaf, The Ear Found., St. Joseph Inst. Deaf, chmn., 2004—. Maj. USAF, 1975—77. Fellow: ACS, Am. Auditory Soc. (mem. exec. com. 1985—2003), Am. Otological, Rhinological and Laryngological Soc. (v.p. mid. sect. 2002—03), Am. Acad. Otolaryngology (gov. 1982—); mem.: Assn. Acad. Depts. in Otolaryngology-Head and Neck Surgery (sec.-treas. 2002—04, pres.-elect 2004—06), Deafness Rsch. Inst. (bd. dirs., pres. Centurion group, comm. com.), Inst. of Medicine of NAS, Am. Neurotology Soc. (pres.-elect 1999—2000, pres. 2000—01), Collegium Oto-Laryntologicum Amecitiae Sacrum, Royal Soc. Medicine London, Assn. Rsch. Otol. (pres.-elect 2000—01, pres. 2001—), Am. Otol. Soc. (coun. 1992—), Otosclerosis Study Group (coun. 1993—), NY Acad. Scis., Am. Acad. Pediats., Marines Meml. Assn., Cosmos Club of Washington, Alpha Omega Alpha (pres. Ind. chpt. 2003—), Wheaton Coll. Scholastic Honor Soc., Psi Iota Xi. Office: Ind U Sch Med 702 Barnhill Dr Indianapolis IN 46202-5128

MIYASAKI, GEORGE JOJI, artist; b. Kalopa, Hawaii, Mar. 24, 1935; BFA, Calif. Coll. Arts and Crafts, 1957, MFA, 1958. Asst. prof. art Calif. Coll. Arts and Crafts, Oakland, 1958-64; mem. faculty dept. art U. Calif., Berkeley, 1964-94, prof. emeritus, 1994—. Grantee John Hay Whitney fellow, 1957—58; Tamarind printing fellow, 1961, Guggenheim fellow, 1963—64, Nat. Endowment for Arts fellow, 1980—81, 1985—86. Mem.: NAD. Home: 2844 Forest Ave Berkeley CA 94705-1309

MIYASAKI, SHUICHI, lawyer; b. Paauilo, Hawaii, Aug. 6, 1928; s. Torakichi and Teyo (Kimura) M.; m. Pearl Takeko Saiki, Sept. 11, 1954; children: Joy Michiko, Miles Tadashi, Jan Keiko, Ann Yoshie. BSCE, U. Hawaii-Honolulu, 1951; JD, U. Minn., 1957; grad., Army War Coll., 1973. Bar: Minn. 1957, Hawaii 1959, U.S. Supreme Ct. 1980. Examiner U.S. Patent Office, 1957-59; dep. atty. gen. State of Hawaii, 1960-61; mem., dir., sec./treas. Okumura Takushi Funaki & Wee, Honolulu, 1961-90; pvt. practice Honolulu, 1991—; atty. Hawaii Senate, 1961, chief counsel ways and means com., 1962, chief counsel judiciary com., 1967-70; civil engr. Japan Constrn. Agy., Tokyo, 1953-54; staff judge adv., col. USAR, Ft. DeRussy, Hawaii, 1968-79. Local legal counsel Jaycees, 1962; lectr. Nat. Assn. Pub. Accts. Hawaii Chpt. Ann. Conf., 1990, 94, Mid Pacific Inst. Found., Honolulu, 1990, Econ. Study Club of Hawaii, 1990, Meiji Life Ins. Co. Japan, 1992, Cent. YMCA, 1992, City Bank Honolulu, 1997. Legis. chmn. armed services com. C. of C. of Hawaii, 1973; instnl. rep. Aloha council Boy Scouts Am., 1963-78; exec. com., sec., dir. Legal Aid Soc. Hawaii, 1970-72; state v.p. Hawaii Jaycees, 1964-65; dir., legal counsel St. Louis Heights Community Assn., 1963, 65, 73, 91—; dir., legal counsel Citizens Study Club for Naturalization of Citizens, 1963-68; advisory bd. Project Dana Honolulu, 1991—, vice chair, 1991, 92; bd. dirs. Omote Senke Found., 1999—; life mem. Res. Officers Assn. U.S. Served to 1st lt. AUS, 1951-54. Decorated Meritorious Service medal with oak leaf cluster. Mem. ABA, Hawaii Bar Assn., U.S. Patent Office Soc., Hawaii Estate Planning Council, Waikiki Rotary Club (pres., 2005-06), Central YMCA Club, Waikiki Athletic Club, Army Golf Assn., Elks, Phi Delta Phi. Office: 1001 Bishop St Ste 1030 Honolulu HI 96813-3408 *Personal philosophy: Study hard, work hard, play hard, love hard, have time for nonsense, help others and be fair to all concerned.*

MIYATA, SACHIKO, social scientist, researcher; d. Yoko Miyata. PhD, U. Tokyo, 2002. Rsch. fellow U. Tokyo, 2002—05; postdoctoral fellow Internat. Food Policy Rsch. Inst., Washington, 2005—. Cons. World Bank, Washington, 2005. Ambassadorial scholar, Rotary Found. Internat., 1993—94, rsch. fellow, Japan Soc. Promotion of Sci., 2002—05, Sci. Rsch. grantee, Ministry Edn., Govt. Japan, 2002—05. Home Phone: 202-657-5066; Office Phone: 202-862-5666. Office Fax: 202-467-4439.

MIZE, GERALD L., JR., lawyer; b. Atlanta, Aug. 14, 1958; Student, Phillips Universität, Marburg an der Lahn, W. Germany, 1978, Ludwig Maximillans Universität, Munich, 1979; AB in Polit. Sci. and German, Univ. Ga., 1980, JD, 1984. Bar: Ga. 1984. Ptnr. in charge, internal comm. Alston & Bird LLP, Atlanta, co-chair, bus. devel. com. Office: Alston & Bird LLP One Atlantic Ctr 1201 W Peachtree St NW Atlanta GA 30309-3424 Office Phone: 404-881-7579. Office Fax: 404-881-7777. Business E-Mail: gmize@alston.com.

MIZE, JOE HENRY, industrial engineer, educator; b. Colorado City, Tex., June 14, 1934; s. Kelly Marcus and Birtie (Adams) M.; m. Betty Bentley, Mar. 16, 1966; 1 dau., Kelly Jean. BS in Indsl. Engring, Tex. Tech. Coll., 1958; MS (Research Found. grantee) in Indsl. Engring, Purdue U., 1963, PhD, 1964. Registered profl. engr., Ala., Okla. Indsl. engr. White Sands Missile Range, N.Mex., 1958-61; grad. research asst. Purdue U., Lafayette, Ind., 1961-64; asso. prof. engring. Auburn (Ala.) U., 1964-69; dir. Auburn (Ala.) U. (Computer Center), 1965-66; prof. engring. Ariz. State U., Tempe, 1969-72; prof., head Sch. Indsl. Engring. and Mgmt. Okla. State U., Stillwater, 1972-80, dir. Univ. Ctr. for Energy Research, 1980-83, Regents prof., 1982-94; v.p. Hong Kong U. of Sci. and Tech., 1994-98; prof., v.p. Hong Kong U. Sci. & Tech., 1994-98; rsch. affiliate engring. sys. divsn. MIT, 1998—. Cons. to Air War Coll., 1968-69, U.S. Army, Ops. Analysis Standby Unit, U. N.C., 1965-69, various mfg. firms, 1964—; program adv. Office of Mgmt. and Budget, Exec. Office of the President, Washington, 1974-79; adv. to NSF, 1974-94, Nat. Center for Productivity and Quality of Work Life, 1973-78; chmn. tech. adv. council So. Growth Policies Bd., 1975-77; accrediting visitor Engrs. Council for Profl. Devel., 1973-80 Author: (with J.G. Cox) Essentials of Simulation (translated into Japanese 1970), 1968, Prosim V.: Instructor's Manual, 1971, Student's Manual, 1971, (with C.R. White and George H. Brooks) Operations Planning and Control, 1971, (with J.L. Kuester) Optimization Techniques with Fortran, 1973, (with W.C. Turner and K.E. Case) Introduction to Industrial and Systems Engineering, 3d edit., 1993 (named Book of Yr., Am. Inst. Indsl. Engrs. 1979), Guide to Systems Integration, 1991; contrbr. articles to profl. jours., more. Recipient Disting. Engring. Alumnus award Purdue U., 1978 Mem. Am. Inst. Indsl. Engrs. (exec. v.p. 1978-80, pres. 1981-82, H.G. Maynard Innovative Achievement award 1977, Gilbreth Indsl. Engring. award 1990), Am. Soc. for Engring. Edn. (sec. govt. rels. com. 1975-76), Nat. Soc. Profl. Engrs., Okla. Soc. Profl. Engrs. (Outstanding Engring. Achievement award 1977, Outstanding Engr. in Okla. 1981), Inst. Mgmt. Scis., Coun. Indsl. Engring. Acad. Dept. Heads (chmn. 1975-76), NAE, Nat. Rsch. Coun., Sigma Xi, Tau Beta Pi, Alpha Pi Mu. Office: Oklahoma State U Dept Indsl Engring Stillwater OK 74078-0001

MIZEL, LARRY A., housing construction company executive; b. 1942; married. BA, U. Okla., 1964; JD, U. Denver, 1967. Founder, dir. MDC Holdings Inc., Denver, 1972—, pres., 1996—99, chmn. bd., CEO, 1999—. Past trustee Marsico Investment Fund; dir. Richmond Am. Homes. Chmn. bd. Simon Weisenthal Ctr., 2003—. Office: MDC Holdings Inc 4350 S Monaco St Denver CO 80237-1867 *

MIZGALA, HENRY F., physician, consultant, retired medical educator; b. Montreal, Can., Nov. 28, 1932; s. Louis and Mary (Ropeleski) M.; m. Pauline Barbara Delaney, Oct. 26, 1957; children: Paul Stephen, Cynthia Louise, Liane Mary Mizgala Sizemore, Melanie Frances Mizgala Dressler, Nancy Elizabeth Mizgala Lewis. BA magna cum laude, Loyola Coll., Montreal, 1953; MD, CM, McGill U., 1957. Rotating intern, then resident in medicine St. Mary's Hosp., Montreal, 1957—59, asst. physician, 1963—66; resident in medicine Royal Victoria Hosp., Montreal, 1959—60; Dazian fellow cardiology Mt. Sinai Hosp., NYC, 1960—61, USPHS fellow cardiology, 1961—62; resident in cardiology Montreal Gen. Hosp., 1962—63, assoc. physician, 1966—74; asst. physician, cons. cardiology Lachine Gen. Hosp., Que., 1964—80; mem. faculty McGill U. Med. Sch., Montreal, 1968—74, assoc. prof. medicine, 1973—74; assoc. prof., then prof. Montreal U. Med. Sch., 1974—81; cardiologist Montreal Heart Inst., also dir. CCU, 1974—80; prof. medicine U. B.C., 1980—87, prof. medicine, head divsn. cardiology, 1980—87, prof. medicine emeritus, 1998—; hon. attending med. staff, cardiologist Vancouver Hosp. and Health Scis. Ctr. Cons. Centre Hosp. Baie des Chaleurs, Gaspe, Que., 1975—80, B.C. Cancer Agy., Vancouver, 1981—; cons. staff Univ. Hosp., U. B.C. site, 1981—94; hon. cons. Montreal Heart Inst., 1980—. Mem. editl. bd. Can. Jour. Cardiology, 1988-99, Jour. Am. Coll. Cardiology, 1992-95; contbr. articles to profl. jours. Fellow Royal Coll. Physicians and Surgeons Can., Am. Coll. Cardiology, Am. Heart Assn. (coun. clin. cardiology); mem. Can. Med. Assn., Can. Cardiovasc. Soc. (treas. 1974-90), Que. Med. Assn., B.C. Med. Assn., B.C. and Yukon Heart and Stroke Found. (bd. dirs., sr. bd. dirs.), Alpha Omega Alpha. Office: U BC Divsn Cardiology Dept Med 865 W 10th Ave Vancouver BC Canada V5Z 1L7 Home Phone: 604-261-6224; Office Phone: 604-875-4755. Business E-Mail: mhenry@interchange.ubc.ca.

MIZRAHI, ABRAHAM MORDECHAY, retired health products executive, pediatrician; b. Jerusalem, Apr. 16, 1929; came to U.S., 1952, naturalized, 1960; s. Solomon R. and Rachel (Haliwa) M.; m. Suzanne Eve Glasser, Mar. 15, 1956; children: Debra, Judith, Karen. BS, Manchester Coll., 1955; MD, Albert Einstein Coll. Medicine, 1960. Diplomate: Am. Bd. Pediatrics, Nat. Bd. Med. Examiners. Intern U. N.C., 1960-61; pediatric resident Columbia-Presbyn. Med. Center, NYC, 1961-63, NIH fellow in neonatology, 1963-65; assoc. dir. Newborn Service Mt. Sinai Hosp., NYC; also dir. Newborn Service Elmhurst Med. Center, 1965-67; staff physician Geigy Pharm. Corp., NYC, 1967-69, head cardio-pulmonary sect., 1969-71; sr. v.p. corp. med. affairs USV Pharm. Corp., Tuckahoe, NY, 1971-76; v.p. health and safety Revlon, Inc., NYC, 1976-89, sr. v.p. human resources, 1989-94; ret., 1994. Assoc. in pediatrics Columbia U., 1963-67; cons. in neonatology Misericordia-Fordham Med. Ctr., 1967-89; clin. affiliate N.Y. Hosp.; clin. asst. prof. Cornell U. Med. Coll., 1982—. Contbr. articles to profl. jours. Trustee Westchester (N.Y.) Jewish Center. Mem. AMA, N.Y. State and County Med. Soc., Am., N.Y. acads. medicine, Am. Soc. Clin. Pharmacology and Therapeutics, Am. Pub. Health Assn., Am. Occupational Med. Assn. Home: 7 Jason Ln Mamaroneck NY 10543-2108 *The principles that have guided my life are old Biblical concepts. Firstly, that God had created Adam and Eve and all Men are, therefore, brothers and sisters. Secondly, God created Man and, therefore every human being has a spark of God in him. It, therefore, follows that killing diminshes God's presence on earth and saving of a human being increases His presence.*

MIZRAHI, EDWARD ALAN, allergist; b. Tyler, Tex., Aug. 24, 1945; BS in Econs., U. Pa., 1967; MD, U. Fla., 1972. Diplomate Am. Bd. Internal Medicine, Am. Bd. Allergy and Immunology. Intern Med. Coll. Ga., Augusta, 1972-73, resident, 1973-75; fellow Nat. Jewish Hosp., U. Colo., Denver, 1975-77; pvt. practice Jacksonville, Fla., 1977—. Physician Bapt. Med. Ctr., Jacksonville, Meml. Med. Ctr., Jacksonville, St. Luke's Med. Ctr., Jacksonville, St. Vincent's Med. Ctr., Jacksonville, Meth. Hosp., Jacksonville, Orange Park (Fla.) Med. Ctr. Mem. Am. Coll. Allergy, Asthma and Immunology, Am. Acad. Allergy, Asthma and Immunology, Fla. Med. Assn., Fla. Allergy, Asthma and Immunology Soc., Duval County Med. Soc., Southeastern Allergy Assn. Office: Ste A3 3636 University Blvd S Jacksonville FL 32216-4223

MIZRAHI, ISAAC, fashion designer; b. Bklyn., Oct. 14, 1961; s. Zeke and Sarah M. Attended, Parsons Sch. Design, 1982. Design asst. Perry Ellis, 1982-84, Jeffrey Banks, 1984-85, Calvin Klein, 1985-87; founder, ready-to-wear line Isaac Mizrahi, 1987—98, added menswear line, added eyewear, 1990—98; designer, Isaac Mizrahi for Target Target Corp., 2002—; designer, Isaac By Isaac Mizrahi. Subject: (documentaries) Unzipped, 1995; costume designer: Twyla Tharp's Ballet Brief Fling, Am. Ballet Theatre.; costume designer The Women, Roundabout Theatre Co., 2002 (Costume Design, Drama Desk award, 2002), Barefoot In the Park, Cort Theatre, NYC, 2006, The Threepenny Opera, Roundabout Theatre Co., 2006, English National Opera's-King Arthur, 2006, creator (series of comic books) The Adventures of Sandee the Supermodel, 1997, one man show (off broadway) Les Mizrahi, host The Isaac Mizrahi Show, Oxygen Network, 2001—03, Isaac, Style Network, 2005—. Recipient Perry Ellis new fashion talent award Coun. Fashion Designers Am., 1989; named Best Womenswear Designer 1989 Coun. Fashion Designers Am., 1990. Office: 876 Centennial Ave Piscataway NJ 08854-3917 *

MIZRUCHI, MARK SHELDON, sociology professor, business administration professor; b. New Haven, Dec. 10, 1953; s. Ephraim Harold and Ruth M.; m. Katherine Teves, June 1981 (div. June 1995); 1 child, Joshua; m. Gail Schulman, Nov. 2006. BA, Washington U., 1975; MA, SUNY, Stony Brook, 1977, PhD, 1980. Statis. analyst Albert Einstein Coll. of Medicine, Bronx, NY, 1980-83, asst. prof. psychiatry, 1981-87, supr. statis. svcs., 1983-87; asst. prof. sociology Columbia U., NYC, 1987-89, assoc. prof. sociology, 1989-91; prof. sociology and bus. adminstrn. U. Mich., Ann Arbor, 1991—. Author: The American Corporate Network, 1904-1974, 1982, The Structure of Corporate Political Action, 1992; editor (with M. Schwartz) Intercorporate Relations, 1987. Recipient Presdl. Young Investigator award NSF, 1988-93, Excellence in Edn. award U. Mich., 2004; grantee NSF, 1987-88, 93-95, 99-2000, 2002-03; invited fellow Ctr. for Advanced Study in the Behavioral Scis., 1989. Mem. Am. Sociol. Assn., Acad. Mgmt., Internat. Network for Social Network Analysis, Sociol. Rsch. Assn. Office: Dept Sociology Univ Mich Ann Arbor MI 48109-1382 Office Phone: 734-764-7444. Office Fax: 734-763-6887. Business E-Mail: mizruchi@umich.edu.

MIZUMURA, MEGUMI, conservator; b. Tokyo, May 4, 1968; BA in Conservation, Camberwell Coll. Arts, London, 1998; MA in Conservation of Fine Art, Northumbria U., Newcastle upon Tyne, UK, 2000. Paper conservator Tokyo Restoration and Conservation Ctr., 2000—01; asst. conservator Nishio Conservation Studio, Washington, 2001—04; paper conservator Bergen Art Mus., Norway, 2004; Kress intern paper conservator NE Document Conservation Ctr., Andover, Mass., 2004—05; Mellon fellow paper conservator Conservation Ctr. Art and Hist. Artifacts, Phila., 2005—06; asst. conservator Fairclough & Harrison, Ltd., Bristol, England, 2006—07; conservator Far East painting Brit. Mus., London, 2007—. Spkr. workshops Suleymaniye Libr., Istanbul, Turkey, 2007. Contbr. articles to profl. jours. Fellow, Kress Found., 2004—05. Mem.: Inst. Conservation, Japan Soc. Conservation Cultural Property. Home: 2 Downs Ln London E5 8QD England Home Phone: 07726101006. Personal E-mail: megumimizumura@aol.com.

MKRYAN, SONYA, geophysicist, educator, research scientist; b. Beyrouth, Lebanon, Mar. 1, 1935; arrived in U.S., 1979; d. Vahram and Marie (Topalian) Faradjian; m. Karapet Mkryan, Apr. 11, 1970; children: Marine, Anahit, Lusine. MS in Physics, Pedagogical Inst., 1956; PhD in Tech. Scis., Tbilicy State U., 1970. Physics, math. tchr. HS, Ghaltakchi, 1956-57; libr. Ores Dept., Leninakan, Armenia, 1957-60; geophysicist, rschr. Inst. Geophysics Engring. Seismology, Leninakan, 1960-70; assoc. prof. physics Polytech. Inst., Kirovakan, Armenia, 1970-79; mech. insp. Robertshaw Co., Anaheim, Calif., 1980-82; tchr. Pasadena (Calif.) Sch. Dist., 1983-86; eligibility worker, acting supr. Dept. of Pub. Svcs., Glendale, Calif., 1986-97; social worker home supportive svcs. Glendale, 1997—. Author: (poetry) Ups and Downs of Life, 1987, Incessant Melodies, 1992, Light and Darkness, 1997, (novels) Eternities Travelers, 1998, Man and Its Time, 2006, Paradoxical Reality and My Heartbeats, 2006; one-woman shows include Tekeyan Gallere, Pasadena, Calif., 1989, Pasadena Union of Marash Armenians Hall, 1982—95, exhibited in group shows at Altadena, Pasadena, Downey, Glendale, Ambassador Hotel, L.A. (2d prize, 1987), Wilshir Ebel, 1988. Bd. dirs. Sahag-Mesrob Armenian Christian Sch. Mem.: Armenian Radio and TV Com., Armenian Allied Arts Assn. (1st prize 1982, 1984, 1985, 1987, 1991), Nat. Libr. Poets, Internat. Soc. Poets, Armenian Writers Union Calif. Avocations: writing, walking, reading, cooking, dance. Home: 2723 N Lake Ave Altadena CA 91001-1903

MLAY, MARIAN, retired government official; b. Pitts., Sept. 11, 1935; AB, U. Pitts., 1957; postgrad., Princeton U., 1969-70; JD, Am. U., 1977. Mgmt. intern HEW, Washington, 1961-70, dep. dir. Chgo. region, 1971-72, dir. divsn. consol. funding, 1972-73; dep. dir. office policy devel. and planning USPHS, Washington, 1973-77; dir. program evaluation EPA, Washington, 1978-9, dep. dir. office of drinking water, 1979-84, dir. office of ground water protection, 1984-91, dir. oceans and coastal protection, 1991-95; sr. rsch. assoc. Nat. Acad. Pub. Adminstrn., 1995-97; ret., 1997. Contbr. articles to profl. jours., chpts. to books. Bd. dirs. DC United Fund, 1979-80, New Dominion Chorale, 2001-04, Davis Meml. Goodwill Book Com., 1999-02; mem. Woman's Nat. Dem. Club, 2005, sec. bd. govs., 2007. Princeton U. fellow, 1969-70; recipient Career Edn. award Nat. Inst. Public Affairs, 1969. Mem. ABA, DC Bar Assn. (co-chair steering com. energy, environ. and natural resources sect., Best Section award, 1986-87). Achievements include development of a ground-water protection strategy for EPA establishing a national program to support related state and local efforts and to define a common ground-water protection policy for EPA. Home: 3146 Gracefield Rd Apt 417 Silver Spring MD 20904 Home Phone: 301-890-8525. Personal E-mail: mlayma@aol.com.

MLSNA, KATHRYN KIMURA, lawyer; b. Yonkers, NY, Apr. 23, 1952; d. Eugene T. and Grace Kimura; m. Timothy Martin Mlsna; 3 children. BA, Northwestern U., 1974, JD, 1977. Bar: Ill. 1977, U.S. Dist. Ct. (no. dist.) Ill. 1977. Mng. counsel McDonald's Corp., Oak Brook, Ill., 1977—. Speaker in field. Contbr. author to 2 ABA books. Bd. dirs. Japanese Am. Svc. Com.; mem. adv. bd. intellectual property DePaul U. Sch. Law, 1999—; chair Coun. of One Hundred, 2002-04. Mem.: ABA, Promotion Mktg. Assn. (v.p. 1988—92, chmn., pres. 1992—93, chmn. integrated mktg. com. 1993—94, chmn. assn. alliance com., co-chair legal and govtl. affairs com.), Asian Am. Bar Assn. (bd. dirs. 1996—98), Chgo. Bar Assn., Ill. Bar Assn., Girl Scouts Prairie Winds (bd. dirs. 2003—), Northwestern U. Alumni Assn. (bd. dirs. 1994—98, 2002—04, officer). Office: McDonald's Corp 2915 Jorie Blvd Oak Brook IL 60523-1911

MNUCHIN, ALAN GEOFFREY, investment banker; b. 1960; s. Robert Mnuchin and Elaine Terner Cooper; m. Kimberly Kassel, Feb. 11, 1995. BS, U. Pa., 1982; MBA, U. Chgo., 1984. Various positions to v.p., comm., media, tech. divsn. Goldman Sachs, NYC, 1984—96; sr. mng. dir. Bear Stearns Co., NYC, 1996—99; co-head, media banking Lehman Brothers, NYC, 1999—2003; founder, mng. dir. AGM Ptnrs. LLC, NYC, 2003—. Named a Top Dealmaker, Dealmaker mag., 2006. Office: AGM Ptnrs LLC 767 5th Ave New York NY 10153 Office Phone: 212-812-7878. *

MNUCHIN, STEVEN T., investment company executive; m. Heather Mnuchin. BA, Yale Univ. Various mgmt. positions Goldman Sach, 1985—2001, exec. v.p., chief info. officer, 2001—02; vice chmn. ESL Investments Inc., 2003; CEO SFM Capital Mgmt. LP, 2003—04; chmn., co-CEO Dune Capital Mgmt. LP, 2004—. Mem. Yale Devel. Bd.; trustee Whitney Mus. Am. Art, Hirshhorn Mus. & Sculpture Garden, Riverdale Country Sch.; bd. dir. Kmart (now Sears Holding Corp.); bd. trustees NY Presbyn. Med. Ctr., 2004—. Office: Dune Capital Mgmt LP 30th Fl 623 Fifth Ave New York NY 10022

MO, LUKE WEI, physicist, researcher; b. Shangtung, China, June 3, 1934; s. Si-leng and Shu-feng (Lo) M.; m. Doris Chang, Dec. 31, 1960; children: Curtis L., Alice. BSEE, Nat. Taiwan U., 1955; MS in Physics, Nat. Tsinghua U., 1959; PhD, Columbia U., 1963. Rsch. assoc. Columbia U., NYC, 1963—64; rsch. physicist Stanford Linear Accelerator, Calif., 1965—69; asst. prof. physics U. Chgo., 1969—76; prof. physics Va. Poly. Inst. and State U., Blacksburg, 1976—. Contbr. articles to profl. jours. Served with Taiwan Air Force, 1955-56. Recipient Alumni Research Excellence award Va. Poly. Inst. and State U., 1980, Guggenheim fellow, 1981. Fellow Am. Phys. Soc. Office: Va Poly Inst Dept Physics Blacksburg VA 24061-0435 Business E-Mail: lmo@vt.edu.

MOAG, RODNEY FRANK, language educator, country and bluegrass singer, musician, record producer; b. Warsaw, NY, Oct. 15, 1936; s. Hugh Alexander and Imogene (Hodges) Moag; m. Rachel Ann Foley, Feb. 9, 1964 (div. Aug. 1974); children: Robin Gray, Hugh Daniel, Jeffrey Lee. BS, Syracuse U., 1961; MA, U. Wis., 1966, PhD, 1973. Instr., asst. prof. U. Mo., Columbia, 1968—74, dir. college preparatory program for visually impaired, 1974; vis. Fulbright prof. U. S. Pacific, Suva, Fiji, 1975-78; vis. assoc. prof. U. Mich., Ann Arbor, 1978-80, adj. prof., 1981, vis. assoc. prof., 1982; sr. lectr. U. Tex., Austin, 1981, 83-90, assoc. prof., 1990—2004, prof. emeritus, 2004—. Author: (reference grammar) Fiji Hindi, 1977, Malayalam, 1986, singer (country music artist) 6 albums. Mng. dir. Amateur Radio Repeaters Washtenaw, 1984—86; pres. Mich. Repeater Coun., 1985—88; vol. programmer KO-OP, 1995—. Mem.: Austin Repeater Orgn., Tex. VHF FM Soc., Ctrl. Tex. Bluegrass Assn., Austin Amateur Radio Club (v.p. 1993—94). Avocations: amateur radio, music. Home: 6909 Miranda Dr Austin TX 78752-3119 Office Phone: 512-467-6825. Personal E-mail: rodmoag@texas.net.

MOATES, (G.) PAUL, lawyer; b. May 26, 1947; s. Guy Hart and Virginia Rose (Mayolett) Moates; m. Constance A. Sadler. BA cum laude, Amherst Coll., 1969; JD, U. Chgo., 1975. Bar: Ill. 1975, DC 1976, US Ct. Appeals (DC cir.) 1976, US Supreme Ct. 1980, US Ct. Appeals (6th cir.) 1984, US Ct. Appeals (3d cir.) 1991, US Ct. Appeals (7th cir.) 1993. Assoc. Sidley & Austin (now Sidley Austin Brown & Wood LLP), Washington, 1975—82; ptnr. and head transp. practice Sidley Austin LLP, 1982—, mem. exec. com. and worldwide co-chair acctg. and fin. com. Contbr. articles to profl. jours. With White House Comm. Agy. US Army, 1971—73, Washington, DC. Mem.: ABA, DC Bar Assn., Ill. Bar Assn. Office: Sidley Austin LLP 1501 K Street NW Washington DC 20005 Office Phone: 202-736-8175. Office Fax: 202-736-8711. E-mail: pmoates@sidley.com.

MOAVENZADEH, FRED, engineering educator; BS, Teheran U., 1958; MS, Cornell U., 1960; PhD, Purdue U., 1962. Asst. prof. MIT, Cambridge, Mass., 1965—66, assoc. prof., 1966—72, prof., 1972—, dir. tech. & devel. program, 1973—, dir. Ctr. for Tech., Policy & Indsl. Devel., 1998—, James Mason Crafts prof. systems engring. Cons. in field; mem. rsch. ctr. coun. CII, 1992—. Author: (book) Future Cities: Dynamics and Sustainability, 2002, Global Construction and the Environment: Strategies and Opportunities, 1994; author: (with David Geltner) Transportation, Energy and Economic Development: A Dilemma in the Developing World, 1984; author: over 300 profl. publs. and reports; editor: Concise Encyclopedia of Building & Construction Materials, 1990, Proceedings of the Conference on Science, Technology and Development in Latin America, 1986; editor-in-chief: Construction Business Review, mem. editl. bd.: Jour. Urban Tech. Recipient deFleury Medal, U.S. Army Corps Engrs., 2001. Mem.: NAE (Transp. Rsch. bd., Bldg. Rsch. Inst.), ASCE (mem. editl. bd. Jour. Infrastructure Systems), AAAS, Soc. Internat. Devel. Sci. Office: MIT Bldg E40-231 77 Massachusetts Ave Cambridge MA 02139-4307 also: MIT 1-175 77 Massachusetts Ave Cambridge MA 02139-4307 Office Phone: 617-253-8973. Office Fax: 617-253-7140. Business E-Mail: ctpidcom@mit.edu.

MOAZED, KHOSROW L., retired engineering educator; b. Meshed, Iran, Sept. 14, 1930; arrived in U.S., 1943; s. Mohammed and Forough Moazed; m. Carolyn Turner Green, Nov. 14, 1953; children: David Charles, Steven Darius, Elizabeth Ashraf, Maryam Leela. BSc, Rensselaer Poly., 1953, MSc, 1956, Carnegie Mellon U., 1958, PhD, 1959. Registered profl. engr., N.C. Rsch. assoc. Rensselaer Poly. Inst., Troy, NY, 1953—56; GE fellow Carnegie-Mellon U., Pitts., 1956—59; asst. prof. Ohio State U., Columbus, 1959—65, assoc. prof., 1965—68; prof. N.C. State U., Raleigh, 1968—91, prof. emeritus, 1991—, chmn. faculty senate, 1982—83. Prin. sci. officer Nat. Phys. Lab., Teddington, England, 1966; vis. prof. Naval Ocean Sys. Ctr., San Diego, 1985—90. Contbr. scientific papers to profl. jours. Capt., mission pilot CAP, 1995—2002. Grantee, NSF, USAF Office Sci. Rsch., U.S. Army Rsch. Office, Office Naval Rsch. Avocations: flying, art, writing, skiing.

MOBLEY, CUTTINO RASHAWN, professional basketball player; b. Sept. 1, 1974; Student, U. R.I. Guard Houston Rockets, 1998—2004, Orlando Magic, 2004—05, Sacramento Kings, 2005, LA Clippers, 2005—06. Participant Schick Rookie Challenge, 2000. Named to Schick All-Rookie Second Team, 1998-99; named Atlantic 10 Player of Yr., 1997-98. Office: LA Clippers Staples Center 1111 S Figueroa St Los Angeles CA 90015

MOBLEY, EMILY RUTH, library director, educator, dean; b. Valdosta, Ga., Oct. 1, 1942; d. Emmett and Ruth (Johnson) M. AB in Edn., U. Mich., 1964, AM in Libr. Sci., 1967, postgrad., 1973-76. Tchr. Ecorse (Mich.) Pub. Schs., 1964-65; adminstrv. trainee Chrysler Corp., Highland Park, Mich., 1965-66, engring. libr., 1966-69; libr. II Wayne State U., Detroit, 1969-72, libr. III, 1972-75; staff asst. GM Rsch. Labs. Libr., Warren, Mich., 1976-78, supr. reader svcs., 1978-81; libr. dir. GMI Engring. & Mgmt. Inst., Flint, Mich., 1982-86; assoc. dir. for pub. svcs. & collection devel., assoc. prof. libr. sci. Purdue U. Librs., West Lafayette, Ind., 1986-89, acting dir. librs., assoc. prof. libr. sci., 1989, dean librs., prof. libr. sci., 1989—2004; Esther Ellis Norton Disting. Prof. Libr. Sci. Purdue U., West Lafayette, Ind., 1997—. Adj. lectr. U. Mich. Sch. Libr. Sci., Ann Arbor, 1974-75, 83-86; grants reader Libr. of Mich., 1980-81; project dir. Mideastern Mich. Region Libr. Cooperation, 1984-86; cons. Libr. Coop. of Macomb, 1985-86, Clark-Atlanta U., 1990-91; search com. for new dir. of libr. Smithsonian Instn., 1988; mem. GM Pub. Affairs Subcom. on Introducing Minorities to Engring.; presenter in field. Author: Special Libraries at Work, 1984; mem. editl. bd. Reference Svcs. Rev., 1989-2004, Infomanage, 1993-97. Corp. vis. com. for librs. MIT, 1990-2004, Carnegie-Mellon U., 1998—; mem. Ind. Statewide Libr. Automation Task Force, 1989-90; state tech. strategy subcom. on info. tech. and telecomms. Ind. Corp. for Sci. & Tech., 1989; nat. adv. com. Libr. of Congress, 1988; trustee Libr. of Mich., 1983-86, v.p., 1986, long range plan com., 1979-82, task force on document access and delivery, 1977-79; info. project mem. Rep. Nat. Conv., 1980; bd. dirs. Small Farms Assn., Southfield, Mich., Lafayette Symphony Orch., YWCA. Recipient Bausch & Lomb award, 1960, Cert. for Outstanding Performance in Acad. Achievement State of Mich. Ho. of Reps., 1976, Spl. Tribute for Outstanding Contbns. Libr. of Mich. Bd. Trustees, 1986, Disting. Alumnus award U. Mich. Sch. Info. & Libr. Studies, 1989; U. Mich. Regents Alumni scholar, 1960-64; CIC doctoral fellow in libr. sci., 1973-76. Mem. ALA (com. on accreditation, subcom. to rev. 1972, standards for accreditation 1988-89, OLOS minority internship com. 1988-89, nominating com. 1992-93, mem. coun. resolutions com. 1993-97), Assn. Coll. & Rsch. Librs. (task force on libr. sch. curriculum 1988-89, com. on profl. edn. 1990-92), Libr. Adminstrn. & Mgmt. Assn., Assn. Rsch. Librs. (bd. dirs. 1990-93), Spl. Librs. Assn. (pres. 1987-88, fellow 1991, com. mem.), Alpha Kappa Alpha, Phi Kappa Phi, Sigma Xi, Iron Key. Office: Purdue U Librs Stewart Ctr Lafayette IN 47907 Business E-Mail: emobley@purdue.edu.

MOBLEY, JOHN HOMER, II, lawyer; b. Shreveport, La., Apr. 21, 1930; s. John Hinson and Beulah (Wilson) Mobley; m. Sue Lawton, Aug. 9, 1958; children: John Lawton(dec.), Anne Davant. AB, U. Ga., 1951, JD, 1953. Bar: Ga. 1952, U.S. Dist. Ct. D.C. Ptnr. Kelley & Mobley, Atlanta, 1956-63, Gambrell & Mobley, Atlanta, 1963-83; sr. ptnr. Sutherland Asbill & Brennan, Atlanta, 1983—. Founding chmn. Cmtys. in Schs. of Ga.; bd. dirs. Nat. Cmtys. in Schs.; former mem. bd. visitors Emory U.; trustee emeritus Canterbury Ct. Episcopal Retirement Home of Atlanta; trustee Episcopal Diocese of Atlanta Fund; twice sr. warden All Saints Episcopal Ch. Capt. JAGC USAF, 1953—55. Recipient Disting. Svc. Scroll, U. Ga. Law Sch., 2003. Mem. ABA, D.C. Bar, State Bar Ga., Atlanta Bar Assn., Am. Judicature Soc., Atlanta Lawyers Club, Atlanta Athletic Club, Atlanta Country Club, Commerce Club, Piedmont Driving Club, Georgian Club, N.Y. Athletic Club, Met. Club of Washington, Phi Delta Phi. Home: 4348 Sentinel Post Rd NW Atlanta GA 30327-3910 Office: Sutherland Asbill & Brennan 999 Peachtree St NE Ste 2300 Atlanta GA 30309-3996 Office Phone: 404-853-8128. Business E-Mail: john.mobley@sablaw.com.

MOBLEY, KAREN RUTH, art director; b. Cheyenne, Wyo., Aug. 26, 1961; d. David G. and Marlene G. (Franz) M. BFA, U. Wyo., 1983; MFA, U. Oka., 1987. Sales assoc. Morgan Gallery, Kansas City, Mo., 1984-85; grad. asst. U. Okla. Mus. Art, Norman, 1985-87; dir. Univ. Art Gallery N.Mex. State U., Las Cruces, 1988-93; exec. dir. Nicolaysen Art Mus., Casper, Wyo., 1993-96; dir. Spokane Arts Com., 1997—. Guest artist Oklahoma City C.C., 1986. Exhbns. include Phoenix Triennial, 1990, New Am. Talent, Laguna Gloria Art Mus., Austin, Tex., 1992, Adair Margo Gallery, El Paso, 1992-94, Wyo. Arts Coun. Gallery and Casper Coll., 1995, Mont. State U., 1996, Whitworth Coll., 2004, Good Works Gallery, 2005 Trustee Westminster Congl. Ch.; bd. dirs. Spokane Pub. Radio. Wyo. Arts Coun. Individual Artist grantee 1994, Lit. fellow, 1995-96; named Outstanding Young Women Am. Mem. Am. Assn. Mus., Coll. Art Assn., Wash. State Arts Alliance, Rotary 21, Phi Beta Kappa, Phi Kappa Phi. Office: Spokane Arts Com 808 W Spokane Falls Blvd Spokane WA 99203 Office Phone: 509-625-6050. Business E-Mail: kmobley@spokanecity.org.

MOBLEY, NANCY ELIZABETH, artist, educator; b. San Angelo, Tex, July 29, 1940; d. William Carl and Mary Elizabeth Fox; m. Billy Jack Wimberley, Aug. 2, 1958 (div. 1972); children: Billy Carl, John Wayne, James Bryan; m. Thomas Howard Mobley, Sept. 28, 1974. BA, Angelo State U., San Angelo, 1990. Draftsman Gen. Tele. Co., San Angelo, 1965-68, William E. Fox & Assoc., San Angelo, 1970-74; draftsman, archtl. estimator Burk Constrn. Co., San Angelo, 1974-76; illustrator Helenikon Air Base, Athens, Greece, 1977-80, Bitburg Air Base, Germany, 1980-82, publicity writer, editor, 1982-83; jewelry designer Jeweler's Workshop, San Angelo, Tex., 1985-87; part-time artist, art tchr. San Angelo, Tex., 1976—. Vol. art tchr. Children's Art Mus., San Angelo, 1995-98; tchr. watercolor Kendall Gallery, San Angelo, 2004—. One-woman shows include Athens Art Gallery, 1979, Bitburg (Germany) Am. Express Bank, 1980, Houston Harte U. Ctr. Gallery, San Angelo, Tex., 1984-85, 88, 96, 2007, Tom Green County Libr., San Angelo, 2000, 04, Houston Harte U. Ctr. Gallery, 2007; exhibited in group shows at Tom Green County Libr., San Angelo, 1984, Breckenridge (Tex.) Fine Arts Ctr., 1996-99, Soc. Watercolor Artists, Ft. Worth, 1997, Watercolor Art Soc. Houston, 1998, Shannon Hosp., San Angelo, 1999; paintings in J.Walker Gallery, San Angelo, Tex., 2001—, Gallery One Fine Arts, Brownwood, Tex., 2004, 05; represented in pub. and pvt. collections. Docent San Angelo Mus. Fine Art, San Angelo, 1995-99; bd. dirs. Hospice of San Angelo, 2004—. Bertha B. Becton scholar Angelo State U., San Angelo, 1988, Charles Wendell Art scholar Angelo State U., San Angelo, 1990, Carr acad. scholar Angelo State U., San Angelo, 1988-90, 1st pl. watercolors Breckenridge (Tex.) Arts Nat. Competition, 1996, 1st pl. alumni art competition Angelo State U. Alumni Assn., San Angelo, 1998, Best of Show Zeta Phi's 2nd Internat. Art Competition, San Angelo, Tex. 1st pl. Marcia Williams Art Comp., 2003, 1st pl. watercolors Fine Arts of Coleman, 2003, Russel C. Myers competition, 2004, others. Mem. San Angelo Art Club (3rd v.p. 1997-98, 2006—, 1st v.p. 1998-99, 2nd v.p. 1999-02, Artist of Yr. 1998).mem. Friends Book Club, 2000—.chmn. of Art Auction to benfit Hospice of San Angelo,2003 Baptist. Avocations: reading, writing, exercising, collecting antiques. Home: 106 Churchill Blvd San Angelo TX 76903-8613 Personal E-mail: nancymobley@cox.net.

MOBLEY, STACEY J., lawyer, chemicals executive; b. Chester, Pa., Nov. 19, 1945; s. James Otis and Retha B. (Hollis) M.; m. Joan Thompson, Aug. 28, 1970; children: Michele. BS in Pharmacy, Howard U., 1968, JD, 1971. Bar: Pa. 1972, D.C. 1979, U.S. Supreme Ct. 1979; registered pharmacist. Sr. v.p., chief admin. officer, gen. counsel DuPont Co., Wilmington, Del., 1972—83, dir. fed. affairs Washington, 1983—86, v.p. fed. affairs, 1986—92, sr. v.p. comm. in external affairs Wilmington, Del., 1992—99, chief admin. officer, gen. counsel, 1999—, sr. v.p., 2001—. Bd. dirs. Wilmington Trust Co. State chmn. Del. United Way campaign, 1998; chair Del. Strategic Econ. Coun., 2001. Named one of Am. Top Black Lawyers, Black Enterprise mag., 100 Most Influential Lawyers, Nat. Law Jour., 2006; recipient LexisNexis Corp.egal Times Disting. Legal Svc. award, Alumni award for disting. postgrad. achievement in law, Howard U., 2002, Gerald Kandler Award, Am. Civil Liberties Union of Del, 2006, Award for Excellence in Corp. Practice, Assn. of Corp. Counsel, 2006. Mem. Wilmington Club, Carlton Club. Avocations: tennis, golf. Office: DuPont Co 1007 Market St Wilmington DE 19898-0001 *

MOBLEY, TONY ALLEN, foundation administrator, former dean, recreation educator; b. Harrodsburg, Ky., May 19, 1938; s. Cecil and Beatrice (Bailey) M.; m. Betty Weaver, June 10, 1961; 1 child, Derek Lloyd. BS, Georgetown Coll., 1960; MS, Ind. U., 1962, D Recreation, 1965; MRE, So. Sem., Louisville, 1963. Chmn. dept. recreation and pks. Western Ill. U., Macomb, 1965-72, Pa. State U., University Park, 1972-76; prof., chmn. recreation and pks., dean Sch. Health, Phys. Edn. and Recreation Ind. U., Bloomington, 1976—; exec. dir. Ind. U. Found., Bloomington, 2002—. Chair health adv. coun. White River Park Commn., State of Ind., 1979—; v.p Ind. Sports Corp., Indpls., 1983-89; bd. dirs. Nat. Inst. for Fitness and Sport, Indpls., 1984-93; J.B. Nash scholar, lectr. Am. Assn. Leisure and Recreation, Reston, Va., 1985. Contbr. over 50 articles to profl. jours. Bd. dirs. Monroe County YMCA, Bloomington, 1984-88, United Way, Bloomington, 1994—; mem. Gov.'s Coun. for Phys. Fitness and Sport, 1991—. Am. Coun. Edn. adminstrv. internship fellow, N.C. State U., 1970-71. Fellow Am. Acad. Pk. and Recreation Adminstrn. (pres. 1985-86); mem. Nat. Recreation and Pk. Assn. (pres. 1978-79, Nat. Disting. Profl. award 1981), Assn. Rsch., Adminstrn., Profl. Couns. and Socs. (pres. 1986-87, award 1987), Am. Alliance Health, Phys. Edn., Recreation and Dance (Coll. and Univ. Adminstrs. Coun. Honor award 1986, R. Tait McKenzie award 1996), Soc. Pk. and Recreation Edn. (pres. 1974-75, award 1978), Ind. Pk. and Recreation Assn. (Outstanding Profl. award 1985). Avocations: golf, travel. Office: Ind U Found PO Box 500 Bloomington IN 47402

MOBLEY, WILLIAM C., neuroscientist; PhD, Stanford U., 1974, MD, 1976. Prof. neurology & neurological sciences Stanford U. Sch. Medicine, prof. pediatrics, chair neurology & neurological sciences, 1997—, dir. Neuroscience Inst., 2003—; co-dir. Stanford Brain Rsch. Inst. Named Derek Denny Brown scholar, Am. Neurological Assn., 1991. Fellow: Royal Coll. Physicians; mem.: Assn. Univ. Profs. Neurology (pres.), Am. Soc. Exptl. Neurotherapeutics, Alzheimer's Assn. (Zenith award, Temple award), Inst. Medicine. Office: Stanford Med Sch Mail Code 5489 MSLS P205 Stanford CA 94305-5489 Office Phone: 650-723-6424. Office Fax: 650-498-6262. E-mail: ngfv1@stanford.edu.

MOBLEY, WILLIAM HODGES, management consultant, educator, writer, researcher; b. Akron, Ohio, Nov. 15, 1941; BA, Denison U., 1963; PhD, U. Md., 1971. Registered psychologist, Hong Kong. Mgr. employee rels. rsch. PPG Industries, Pitts., 1971-73; prof. U. S.C., Columbia, 1973-80; head dept. of mgmt. Tex. A&M U., College Station, 1980-83, dean. Coll. of Bus. Adminstrn., 1983-86, exec. dep. chancellor, 1986-88, pres., 1988-93; chancellor Tex. A&M U. Sys., College Station, 1993-94; prof. mgmt. Tex. A&M U., College Station, 1980-96, China Europe Internat. Bus. Sch., Shanghai, 2002—; pres. Mobley Group Pacific Ltd., Shanghai, 2001—. Vis. fellow Cornell U., 1994, vis. prof. Hong Kong U. Sci. and Tech., 1995-97, U. Hong Kong, 1998; prof. mgmt. China Europe Internat. Sch., Shanghai, 2002—. Author: Employee Turnover, 1982, Advances in Global Leadership, vol. I, 1999, vol. II, 2001, vol. III, 2003, vol. IV, 2006. Bd. dirs. Internat. Food and Agrl. Devel. and Econ. Coop., U.S. AID, 1992-94; mem. tri-lateral task force on N.Am. Higher Edn. Coop., USIA, 1993-95; trustee SIOP Found., 1998-2001, AMMA Found., Denison U., 2000-2002; mem. Pres. Bush's Commn. on Minority Bus. Devel., 1990-92, U.S. Com. of the Pacific Econ. Coop. Coun., 1995—. Sr. Fulbright scholar Found. for Scholarly Exchange, Republic China, 1978-79; recipient DAAD, Rep. Germany, 1984; Fellow NDEA U.S. Dept. of Edn., 1968-71. Fellow APA, Am. Psychol. Soc. Business E-Mail: williamm@mobleygrouppacific.com.

MOCEANU, DOMINIQUE, retired Olympic athlete; b. Hollywood, Calif., Sept. 30, 1981; Mem. Nat. Team, 1992—93, 1993—94, 1995—96, 1999; coach Gymnastics World, Ohio, 2002—. Competitions include U.S. Classic, 1991, 92, 93, U.S. Gymnastics Championships, 1992, Am. Classic, 1993, U.S. Olympic Festival, 1993, Coca-Cola Nat. Championships, 1993, 94, 95, 96, Am. Classic/World Championships, 1994, Am. Classic/Pan Am. Games, 1995, World Team Trials, 1995, U.S. Olympic Trials, 1996, John Hancock U.S. Gymnastics Championships, 1997, 98; mem. U.S. Olympic Team, Sydney, 2000. Named 1st pl. balance beam, U.S. Classic, Salt Lake City, 1991, 2d pl. in balance beam jr. divsn., U.S. Gymnastics Championships, Columbus, 1992, 2d pl. in all around, 1st team vault, uneven bars and floor exercise, Jr. Pan Am. Games, 1992, 1st pl. in team and balance beam, 3d pl. in uneven bars, Internat. Tournament of Jr. Women's Gymnastics, Charleroi, Belgium, 1993, 1st pl. in all around, vault and team floor exercise, 3d in uneven bars and balance beam jr. divsn., Coca-Cola Nat. Championships, Nashville, 1994, 1st pl. in team all around, 1st pl. in vault, 3d pl. in balance beam and floor exercise, Am. Classic-Pan Am. Games Trials, Oakland, Calif., 1995, 1st pl. in all around, 2d pl. in floor exercise, 3d pl. in vault, Coca-Cola Nat. Championships, New Orleans, 1995, 1st pl. in all around, World Team Trials, Austin, 1995, 1st pl. in uneven bars, 3d pl. in balance beam, Reese's Internat. Gymnastics Cup, Portland, 1995, 1st pl. in all around, team and floor exercise, 3d pl. in vault and balance beam, 2d pl. in uneven bars, Visa Challenge, Fairfax, Va., 1995, 3d pl. all around for team, 2d pl. team balance beam, World Championships, Sabae, Japan, 1995, ISOC SportsWoman of Month (2), 1995, individual all-around finalist, World Championship Team, 1997; recipient Silver and Bronze medals, World Championships, 1995, Gold medal team competition, Atlanta Olympic Games, 1996, Gold medal, Goodwill Games, 1998. Avocations: swimming, reading, music. Office: Gymnastics World 6630 Harris Rd Cleveland OH 44147

MOCHIDA, PAULA T., library director; Reference libr. to head Sinclair Libr. U. Hawaii, Manoa, 1974—98, assoc. univ. libr. adminstrn. and pub. svcs., 2006, interim univ. libr.; spl. asst. distance learning U. Hawaii Sys., 1998—2005. Mem. adv. bd. U. Hawaii Libr. and Info. Sci. prog. Editor: Ke Kukini Library Newsletter. Office: U Hawaii Manoa Libr 2550 McCarthy Mall Honolulu HI 96822 Office Phone: 808-956-2472. E-mail: paula@hawaii.edu.

MOCK, BEVERLY A., geneticist, researcher; children: Alex, Chris; m. Douglas Lowy. MS, U. Md., 1980, PhD in zoology, 1983. Studies on the genetics of susceptibility to parasitic diseases Dept. Immunology Walter Reed Army Inst. Rsch.; assoc. dir. sci. programs Ctr. Cancer Rsch., Nat. Cancer Inst., 1999—2007, chief Lab. Genetics, 2004—06, dep. chief Lab. Cancer Biology and Genetics. Office: Lab Cancer Biology and Genetics 37 Convent Dr Bldg 37 Rm 3146 Bethesda MD 20892-4258 Office Phone: 301-496-2360. Office Fax: 301-402-1031. E-mail: bev@helix.nih.gov.

MOCK, DAVID CLINTON, JR., internist; b. Redlands, Calif., 1922; s. David Clinton and Eithel (Benson) Mock; m. Marcella Enriqueta Fellin, 1952. AB, U. So. Calif., 1944; MD, M.H.D., Hahnemann Med. Coll., 1948. Intern Hahnemann Hosp., Phila., 1948-49; resident San Mateo (Calif.) County Hosp., 1949-51, 54, VA Hosp., Oklahoma City, 1954-55; research fellow in exptl. therapeutics U. Okla., Oklahoma City, 1956-57, L.N. Upjohn fellow, 1958, dir. exptl. therapeutics unit, 1959-62; dir., preceptorship program, 1968-76; assoc. prof. medicine U. Okla., Oklahoma City, 1963-72, prof., 1972-84, prof. emeritus medicine, 1984—, assoc. dean med. student affairs, 1970-76, assoc. dean postdoctoral edn., 1976-82, dir. continuing med. edn., 1980-83, dir. Transitional Yr. program, 1980-84, dir. History of Medicine program, 1982-84. Chief med. svc., Navajo Base Hosp., Ft. Defiance, Ariz., 1951-53; assoc. faculty homeopathy Royal London Homeopathic Hosp. Capt. USPHS, 1951-99, res.; now ret. Fellow: ACP; mem.: N.Y. Acad. Scis., Am. Fedn. Medical Rsch. Unitarian Universalist. Home: 570 Alameda Blvd Coronado CA 92118-1617

MOCK, FRANK MACKENZIE, lawyer; b. South Bend, Ind., May 17, 1944; s. Frank Carlton and Julia (Baughmann) M.; m. Virginia Johns, Dec. 31, 1974 (div. Feb. 1991); children: Shannon, John, Bridget; m. Christine Mall, June 1995; 1 child, Mackenzie Ann. BA, Duke U., 1966, JD, 1969. Bar: Fla. 1969. Assoc. Mahoney, Adams, Criser, Jacksonville, Fla., 1969-74, ptnr., 1977-92; gen. counsel Builders Investment Group, Valley Forge, Pa., 1974-77; ptnr. Baker & Hostetler, Orlando, Fla., 1992—2006, Ruden McClosky, Orlando, Fla., 2006—. Mem. ABA, Am. Coll. Mortgage Lawyers, Duval County Bar Assn., Orange County Bar Assn., Dade County Bar Assn., Palm Beach County Bar Assn., Turnaround Mgmt. Assn. Republican. Episcopalian. Avocations: hiking, fishing, reading. Home: 2147 Santa Antilles Rd Orlando FL 32806-1533 Home Phone: 407-894-6402; Office Phone: 407-244-8001. Business E-Mail: frank.mock@ruden.com.

MOCK, JOAN BODET, music educator; b. Houston, Dec. 3, 1937; d. Edward Bodet and Dorothy Crawford; m. Donald P. Garrett, 1966 (dec. 1985); children: William Clifford Garrett, Christopher Paul Garrett; m. Raymond Cecil Mock, July 7, 2002; 1 child from previous marriage, Charles H. Edwards II. B Music Edn., Ind. U., 1960; postgrad., U. N.Mex. Cert. tchr. N.Mex. Tchr. Espanola (N.Mex.) H.S., 1963—66, Hope H.S.,

Albuquerque, 1978—79; tchr. group piano lessons Piano Store Orgn., Colorado Springs, 1969—70; pvt. tchr. Garrett's Sch. Piano and Voice, Albuquerque; substitute tchr. Albuquerque Pub. Schs. Soloist for Ed Sullivan, Houston, 1956. Performer: Houston Little Theater, 1954—56, Acola Theater, 1970—79, The Ballad Hunter TV Program, 1954—56; dir.: O.P.E.R.A., 1978; contbr. poems to lit. publs. Soloist Christ Unity Ch., Albuquerque, 1988—92. Inst. Work scholar, Ind. U., 1957—60. Mem.: Albuquerque Music Tchrs. Assn., Nat. Music Tchrs. Assn., Nat. Fedn. Music Clubs. Home and Office: 10401 Crosscut Dr NW Albuquerque NM 87114 Office Phone: 505-350-7612.

MOCK, THEODORE JAYE, finance educator; b. Traverse City, Mich., May 28, 1941; s. Raymond Doris and Georgeann (Lardie) M.; m. Mary Jo Icenhower, Mar. 25, 1962; children: Christopher, Cameron BS in Math., Ohio State U., 1963, MBA in Fin., 1964; PhD in Bus. Adminstrn., U. Calif.-Berkeley, 1969. Dir. AIS Research Ctr. UCLA, 1969-73; dir. Ctr. Acctg. Research, Arthur Andersen Alumni prof. acctg. U. So. Calif., 1982—. Vis. prof. Norwegian Sch. Econs. and Bus., Bergen, 1988, Bond U., Gold Coast, Australia, 1990, 92, So. Cross U., Lismore, Australia, 1994, Australia Nat. U., 2002-; adj. prof. U. Maastricht, The Netherlands, 1991—; hon. prof. Hong Kong City U., 1995-98; bd. dirs. Maastricht (The Netherlands) Acctg. Rsch. Ctr., U. Limburg, 1991—; Shaw prof. Nanyang Tech. U., Singapore, 1997, Tang Peng Yeu; vis. prof. Nat. U. Singapore, 2000. Author: (monographs) Risk Assessment, 1985, Internal Accounting Control (Am. Acctg. Assn. Wildman medal), 1983, Measurement and Accounting Information Criteria, 1976, Impact of Future Technology on Auditing, 1988, Auditing and Analytic Review, 1989, Belief Functions in Business Decisions, 2002; mem. editorial bd. Auditing: A Jour. of Practice & Theory, 1983-86, 88-93, 99—, editor, 1993-96; mem. editorial bd. The Acctg. Rev., 1972-78, Internat. Jour. Auditing, 1998—. Recipient CPA Faculty Excellence award Calif. CPA Found. for Edn. and Rsch., 1983; Fulbright scholar U. Otago, Dunedin, New Zealand, 1988, U. Limburg, Maastricht, The Netherlands, 1993. Mem. Acctg., Orgns. and Soc. (editorial bd. 1978-93), Am. Acctg. Assn. (dir. rsch. 1982-84, acad. vice chmn. auditing sect. 1990-91, chair auditing sect. 1991-92, Collaboration award with AICPA, 1998, Outstanding Auditing Educator award 2003). Office: U So Calif Sch Acctg Los Angeles CA 90089-0001

MOCKAPETRIS, PAUL V., computer scientist, information technology executive; BS in Physics and Elec. Engring., MIT, 1971; PhD in Info. and Computer Sci., U. Calif., Irvine, 1982. Rschr. Info. Scis. Inst., U. So. Calif., dir. High Performance Computing and Comm. Div.; program mgr. networking Advanced Rsch. Projects Agency (ARPA); with @Home, Software.com (now OpenWave), Fiberlane (now Cisco), Siara (now Redback Networks); chmn., chief scientist Nominum Inc., Redwood City, Calif. Chair Internet Engring. Task Force, 1994—96; mem. adv. bd. Staccato Comms., 2005—. Mem.: NAE. Achievements include invention of Domain Name System (DNS). Office: Nominum, Inc 2385 Bay Rd Redwood City CA 94063

MOCKER, HANS WALTER, physicist; b. Teplice, Czech Republic, Feb. 22, 1929; came to U.S., 1960; s. Emil and Marie (Schubert) M.; m. Carol Virginia Vines, Feb. 13, 1981; children: Peter, Nancy. MS in Physics, Inst. Tech., Darmstadt, Germany, 1954; PhD in Physics, U. Innsbruck, Austria, 1959. Sr. rsch. scientist rsch. dept. Honeywell, Mpls., 1960—65, prin. rsch. scientist sys. and rsch., 1965—69, sect. chief sys. and rsch., 1969—78, prin. rsch. fellow sys. and rsch., 1978—93; fellow Tech. Ctr. Alliant Tech. Sys., Mpls., 1991—93; cons. Electro-Optics Laser Sys., Dothan, Ala., 1994—. Physicist Farbenfabriken Bayer, Krefeld, Germany, 1959-60; mem. advanced group on electronic devices Undersec. of Def., Washington, 1977-78; presenter in field. Co-author: Design of Infrared and Laser Systems, 1981; contbr. articles to profl. jours. including Laser Focus, Applied Optics, Applied Physics Letters, IEEE Jour. Quant. Electr. Coach Minn. Soccer Assn., Mpls., 1981-83. Recipient H.W. Sweatt award, 1968, ir-100 award Indsl. Rsch. Mag., 1969, 77, Excellence in Oral Presentation, Soc. Automotive Engrs., 1993; named one of 7 Wonders of Engring., Minn. Soc. Profl. Engrs., 1970. Achievements include patents for apparatus for supervising proportion of magnetically active component in a fluid, for ring laser biased to permit two equal intensity transition frequencies to be generated in opposite directions, for optical system for laser doppler homodyne detection, for relaxation laser synchronizer for pulsed laser operation, for rapidly tunable laser, for method and means for removing claddings from optical fibers, for rapid wavelength switching of IR lasers with Bragg Cells, for laser doppler velocimeter using stable semiconductor or solid-state lasers, for scanning laser helmet mounted sight, for laser cavity helmet mounted sight, for solid-block homodyne interferometer, for look-ahead windshear detector by filtered Raleigh-scattered light. Home: 5290 Juniper Ct Golden CO 80403

MOCKLER, ESTHER JAYNE, state senator; b. Jackson, Wyo., Sept. 21, 1957; d. Franklin and Nancy (Fisher) Mockler. BA in Polit. Sci., Wellesley Coll., 1980. Legal asst., 1981-84; legal adminstr., 1984-87; rschr., cons., 1987—; exec. dir. Wyo. Dem. Party, 1993-95; mem. from Dist. 44 Wyo. Ho. of Reps., Cheyenne, 1992—96; mem. from Dist. 8 Wyo. Senate, Cheyenne, 1996—. Mem. Audubon Wyo. Bd. Office: PO Box 1857 Cheyenne WY 82003-1857 Home Phone: 307-632-5883; Office Phone: 307-632-5883.

MOCKLER, JOLEE MARIE, art educator; b. Kenosha, Wis., June 21, 1957; d. Frank A. and Josephine (Pavelich) Bobusch; m. John R. Mockler, Feb. 20, 1982. BA in Art Edn., Carthage Coll., 1979; MS in Secondary Edn., U. Wis., 2000. Lic. Art Edn. K-12 Wis. Elem. art tchr. Kenosha Unified Sch., Kenosha, Wis., 1979—80; adj. prof. Edgewood Coll., Art Edn. Dept., Madison, Wis., 2003—; art instr., chairperson Reedsburg Area HS, Wis., 1988—; bus. owner Homeworks Furniture and Accents, Reedsburg, Wis., 1991—98. Supr. student tchrs. Edgewood Coll., Madison, Wis., 1996—; art dept. chairperson Reedsburg Sch. Dist., Reedsburg, Wis., 1998—; supr. student tchrs. Luther Coll., Decorah, Iowa, 2000; judge art shows Sauk County Art Assn., Baraboo, 2006; liason US Army recruiter Reedsburg Area HS, 2006—. Co-author: Reedsburg Sch. Dist., K-12 Art Curriculum, 1988—89. Judge for rep. Tammy Baldwin's Congressional Art Competition 2nd Congressional, Madison, Wis., 2003; active Sauk County Basset Hound Rescue. Recipient Top Notch Tchr. award, Wis. TV Channel 3, 2003, Excellence in Edn. award, Reedsburg BOE, 1999, Tchr. of Month award, Reedsburg Area HS, 1998, 2003, 2007, Outstanding Am. Tchrs. award, Nat. Honor Roll, 2005—06. Mem.: NEA, Sauk County Art Assn., Reedsburg Edn. Assn., Wis. Edn. Assn. Home: PO Box 243 La Valle WI 53941 Office: Reedsburg Area HS 1100 S Albert Ave Reedsburg WI 53959 Office Phone: 608-524-4327 ext. 1134. Business E-Mail: jmockler@rsd.k12.wi.us.

MOCKO, GEORGE PAUL, minister; b. Little Falls, NY, Feb. 15, 1934; s. George and Anna (Swancara) M.; m. Elizabeth Carol Davidson, Sept. 2, 1956 (dec); children: David (dec.), Paul, Kristopher, Elissa; m. Delores Hay, Oct. 16, 2004. BA, Hartwick Coll., 1956; BD, Phila. Sem., 1959, STM, 1972; DD (hon.), Gettysburg Coll., 1978. Ordained to ministry Evang. Luth. Ch. in Am., 1959. Pastor Jacob's and Outwood Chs., Pine Grove, Pa., 1959-62; assoc. pastor St Mark's Ch., Wilmington, Del., 1962-65, sr. pastor, 1965-78, Ascension Evang. Luth. Ch., Towson, Md., 1978-91; bishop Del.-Md. Synod Evang. Luth. Ch. in Am., Towson, 1991-2000, ret., 2000. Author books; contbr. articles to profl. jours. Mem. Evang. Luth. Ch. Home: 501 Sussex Rd Baltimore MD 21286-7609 Personal E-mail: GPmocko@aol.com. *Colossians speaks of Christ as the one in whom "all things hold together". I know that Christ is the one who holds me together. Proclaiming and living his life, the church holds our society together.*

MOCUMBI, PASCOAL MANUEL, former prime minister of Mozambique; b. Maputo, Mozambique, Apr. 10, 1941; m. Adelina Mocumbi; 4 children. Grad. in medicine, U. Lausanne, Switzerland. Founding mem., head info. and propaganda dept. FRELIMO, 1963; elected to Mozambique People's Assembly, mem. ctl. com., 1983; provincial health dir., prin. physician Sofala Province, 1976-80; min. health Govt. of Mozambique, Maputo, 1980-87, min. for fgn. affairs, 1987-94, prime min., 1994—2004; high rep. European & Developing Countries Clin. Trials Partnership, The Hague, Netherlands, 2004—. Mem. bd. Internat. Women's Health Coalition, Medicines for Malaria Venture, African Med. & Rsch. Found.; mem. WHO, Commn. on Social Determinants of Health. Mem.: Inst. Medicine (assoc.). Office: EDCTP PO Box 93015 2509 AA The Hague Netherlands

MODABBER, ZIA F., lawyer; b. Jan. 9, 1962; BA, U. Calif., Berkeley, 1984; JD, Loyola Law Sch., 1988. Bar: Calif. 1988, U.S. Dist. Ct. (ctrl. dist.) Calif., U.S. Dist. Ct. (no. dist.), U.S. Ct. Appeals (9th cir.). Assoc. Wyman Bautzer Kuchel & Silbert, LA; ptnr. Katten Muchin Zavis Rosenman, LA. Mem.: ABA, LA County Bar Assn., St. Thomas More Law Honor Soc. Office: Katten Muchin Rosenman Ste 2600 2029 Century Park E Los Angeles CA 90067 Office Phone: 310-788-4627. Office Fax: 310-712-8462. Business E-Mail: zia.modabber@kattenlaw.com.

MODANO, MIKE, professional hockey player; b. Livonia, Mich., June 7, 1970; Center Minn. North Stars, 1988—93, Dallas Stars, 1993—. Mem. Team USA, Canada Cup, 1991, Team USA, World Cup of Hockey, 1996, 2004, US Olympic Hockey Team, Nagano, Japan, 1998, Salt Lake City, 2002, Torino, Italy, 06. Named to NHL All-Star Game, 1993, 1998—2000, 2003, 2004. Achievements include being the first overall draft pick in NHL entry draft, 1988; being a member of World Cup Champion Team USA, 1996; being a member of Stanley Cup Champion Dallas Stars, 1999; being a member of silver medal winning USA Hockey Team, Salt Lake City Olympics, 2002; being captain of USA Olympics Hockey Team, 2006; being the second US-born player to score 500 goals, 2007. Office: c/o Dallas Stars 2601 Avenue of the Stars Frisco TX 75034 *

MODE, CHARLES J., mathematician, educator; b. Bismarck, ND, Dec. 29, 1927; s. Charles and Fannie E. (Hansen) M.; m. Eleanore L. Perdelwitz; 1 dau., Martha Lisa. BS in Genetics, N.D. State U., 1952; MS in Genetics, Kans. State U., 1953; PhD in Genetics, U. Calif., Davis and Berkeley, 1956; postgrad. in stats. (Univ. fellow), N.C. State U., 1956-57. Asst. prof. math. Mont. State U., 1957-59, asso. prof., 1960-62, prof., 1963-66, mem. genetics group, 1957-66; asso. prof. math. stats. SUNY, Buffalo, 1966-70; prof. math. Drexel U., 1970—. Cons. to industry. Author: (books) Multitype Branching Processes - Theory and Applications, 1971, Stochastic Processes in Demography and Their Computer Implementation, 1985, Stochastic Processes in Epidemiology, HIV/AIDS, Other Infectious Diseases and Computers, 2000; contbr. articles to profl. pulbs.; editor (assoc.): (jour.) Math. Bioscis., 1975—. Mem. Inst. Math. Stats., Biometric Soc., Am. Math. Soc., AAAS, Population Assn. Am., Sigma Xi, Phi Kappa Phi, Pi Mu Epsilon. Lutheran. Office: Drexel U Dept Math Philadelphia PA 19104 Home: 422 Freedom Blvd Coatesville PA 19320 Business E-Mail: cmode@math.drexel.edu.

MODELL, JEROME HERBERT, anesthesiologist, educator; b. St. Paul, Sept. 9, 1932; s. William and Frieda (Singer) M.; m. Shirley Graves, Nov. 25, 1977; children— Charles, Jack, Julie. BA, U. Minn., 1954, BS, MD, U. Minn., 1957; DSc (hon.), U. Fla., 2004. Intern U.S. Naval Hosp., St. Albans, NY, 1957-58, resident, 1958-60; practice medicine specializing in anesthesiology Gainesville, Fla., 1969—; attending staff U.S. Naval Hosp., St. Albans, 1960-61, chief anesthesiology Pensacola, Fla., 1961-63; asso. prof. dept. anesthesiology U. Miami (Fla.) Sch. Medicine, 1963-69; prof., chmn. dept. anesthesiology U. Fla. Coll. Medicine, Gainesville, 1969-92, sr. assoc. dean clin. affairs, 1990-95, exec. assoc. dean, 1996-97, interim dean, 1997; assoc. v.p. U. Fla. Health Sci. Ctr. Affiliations, 1992-96. Assoc. v.p. U. Fla. Health Sci., 1998-2000, emeritus prof. 2000—, courtesy prof. large animal scis., 1999—. Author: The Pathophysiology and Treatment of Drowning and Near-Drowning, 1971, (with others) Introduction to Life Support, 1973; also numerous scientific articles. Served to lt. comdr. USN, 1957-63. Recipient Rsch. Career Devel. award, NIH, 1967—69, Lifetime Achievement award, Am. Soc. Critical Care Anesthesiologists, 1991. Mem. AMA, AAAS, Assn. U. Anesthetists, Am. Soc. Anesthesiologists (Disting. Svc. award, 2005), N.Y. Acad. Scis., Am. Coll. Chest Physicians. Home: PO Box 14347 Gainesville FL 32604-2347 Office: U Fla Coll Medicine PO Box 100254 Gainesville FL 32610-0254 Home Phone: 352-591-2220; Office Phone: 352-265-8076.

MODELL, STEPHEN MARK, medical researcher, educator; b. Detroit, June 22, 1958; s. Richard Martin and Sola Jane (Hamburger) M.; m. Wanpen Prasoptham, Jan. 14, 1988; 1 child, Marrisa Lynne. AB in Philosophy, Stanford U., 1980; MD, Med. Coll. Ohio, 1984; MS in Clin. Rsch. Design/Statis. Analysis, U. Mich., 1991. Asst. coord. The Resource for Pub. Health Policy U. Mich. Sch. Pub. Health, Ann Arbor, 1987-89; rsch. asst., dept. psychiatry U. Mich., Ann Arbor, 1989-90, Genome Ethics Com. rsch. assoc., 1992-94, Coun. Genetics and Soc. rsch. assoc. dept. health mgmt. and policy, 1995-98, rsch. dir. genetics policy dept. health mgmt. and policy, 1999—2001; dir. dissemination Mich. Ctr. for Genomics and Pub. Health, 2001—. Mem. pres.'s coun. Med. Coll. Ohio, 1992—. Genome studies sect. editor Ultimate Reality and Meaning, 1995—; editor Studies in Biophilosophy, 1997, Studies in Medicine and Health, 2006. Recipient honorable mention Nellie Westerman prize competition in clin. rsch. ethics, Am. Fedn. Clin. Rsch., 1995. Mem. AMA, Am. Fedn. Med. Rsch., N.Y. Acad. Scis., Maimonides Soc., Internat. Soc. Study of Human Ideas on Ultimate Reality and Meaning (bd. dirs. 1994—, treas. 1999-2000, v.p. 2001-02, pres. 2003-04), Rotary (hon.). Avocations: book discussion groups, water sports, jogging, hiking, travel. Office: U Mich Sch Pub Health 2675 CBPH SPH-I Tower 109 S Observatory St Ann Arbor MI 48109-2029 E-mail: mod@umich.edu.

MODEN, JOLEEN, communications executive; B in Bus. Adminstrn. and Acctg., Kans. State U. CPA. Ptnr. Coopers & Lybrand; v.p., CFO, treas. Signature Home Care Grp.; dir. corp. audit PepsiCo Inc.; asst. contr. internal audit GTE, 1998—2000; sr. v.p. internal auditing Verizon Comm. Inc., NYC, 2000—. Office: Verizon Comms Inc Verizon Ctr VC44E227 One Verizon Way Basking Ridge NJ 07920-1997 E-mail: joleenmoden@verizon.com.

MODERACKI, EDMUND ANTHONY, music educator, conductor; b. Hackensack, NJ, July 18, 1946; s. Edmund Joseph and Helen Theresa (Fisher) Moderacki; m. Brenda Wing Moderacki. BA, Montclair State Coll., 1968, postgrad., 1970—71; MA, Hunter Coll., 1970, postgrad., 1970—72, Newark State Coll., 1969—70, Seton Hall U., 1970, Rutgers U., 1976—78, Ctr. for Understanding Media, 1973. Tchr. music pub. schs., River Vale, NJ, 1968—; asst. condr. Ridgewood Symphony Orch., NJ, 1969—, trustee, pres., 1986—87, 1994—95; artistic dir. Ridgewood Symphony, 2001—; asst. condr. Adelphi Chamber Orch., 1994—95; condr. Project Symphony, 2003. Tuba soloist Rutherford Cmty. Band, Ridgewood Village Band, Waldwick Band, Ridgewood Concert Band, 1978—, trustee, 1985-2000, guest condr., 1985, 86, 88, 93; mgr. All Bergen High Sch. Band, 1994; condr. All Bergen County High Sch. Band, 2001 Author: Images of America: River Vale. Town historian River Vale, 2002; mem. steering com. Bergen County Teen Arts, 1991—; mem. River Vale Hist. Preservation Commn., 2004—. Recipient County Exec. Vol. award, 1991, Tchr. Recognition award Gov. of State of N.J., 1990; Bergen County PTA fellow, 1976. Mem. NEA, Music Educators Nat. Conf., N.J. Orch. Assn. (trustee 1981-85), N.J. Edn. Assn. (alt. del. assembly 1983-93, mem. state membership com. 1986—), Music Educators Bergen County (bd. mem. at-large 1995-97, treas. 1997-2000, pres.-elect 2000-02, pres. 2002-04, treas. 2004—), River Vale Edn. Assn. (pres. 1981-83, 88-91, 2000-03), Brigade Am. Revolution (bd. dirs. at large 1991-95, info. officer 1989-95, adj. 1996-2000, editor Brigade Press 2002-05), Phi Mu Alpha Sinfonia, Kappa Delta Pi. Home: 740 White Birch Rd Township Of Washington NJ 07676 Office: Woodside Sch Rivervale NJ 07675 Office Phone: 201-358-4000 ext. 2801.

MODERY, RICHARD GILLMAN, retired marketing and sales executive; b. Chgo., Sept. 20, 1941; s. Richard Gustave Modery and Betty Jane (Gillman) Modery Perok; m. Kay Francis Whitby, July 31, 1966 (div. July 1977); children: Stacey Lynn, Marci Kay; m. Anne-Marie Lucette Arsenault, Feb. 27, 1979. Student, Joliet Jr. Coll., 1959—61, Aurora Coll., 1963—64, Davenport Bus. Coll., 1969—71, Northwestern U., 1987. Engr., projects engr., projects mgr., mktg. products mgr. Rapistan, Inc., Grand Rapids, Mich., 1964—75; mgr. estimating, project mgmt., customer svc. E.W. Buschman Co., Cin., 1975—78; v.p. distbg. sales, v.p. engring. and sales, exec. v.p. Metzgar Conveyor Co., Grand Rapids, 1979—84; mng. dir. Metzco Internat (Ctrl. and S.Am.), Grand Rapids, 1981—84, Transfer Technologies, Inc., Grand Rapids, 1984—87; gen. ptnr., pres., CEO Nat. Monument Co., Grand Rapids, 1986—89; v.p. Translogic Corp., Denver, 1987—88; corp. officer, v.p. mktg., field ops. and sales S.I. Handling Systems, Inc., Easton, Pa., 1988—91; v.p. mktg., sales and engring. Integrated Material Handling Co., Oshkosh, Wis., 1991—93; pres. Handling Concepts, Inc., Chgo., 1993—2006, Modery Sys., Inc., Chgo., 1997—2005; ret., 2005. Agt. Muratic-Murata Automated Sys., Inc., 1997—2000. Bd. dirs. Naperville Humane Soc., Ill., 2001—05, mem. fin. and revenue generating com.; commr. Traffic Commn. City of East Grand Rapids, Mich., 1983—86. With U.S. Nat. Guard, 1963—69. Mem. Internat. Material Mgmt. Soc., Am. Mgmt. Assn., Material Handling Inst. Am., Material Handling Inst. (spkr. nat. confs.), Am. Mktg. Assn., Conveyor Equipment Mfrs. Assn., Material Handling Equipment Distbrs. Assn., Mason (32 degree). Achievements include patents in field. Avocations: golf, photography, power walking, computers. Home: 2255 Palmer Cir Naperville IL 60564-5672

MODESITT, LELAND EXTON, JR., (L.E. MODESITT JR.), consultant, writer, poet; b. Denver, Oct. 19, 1943; s. Leland Exton and Nancy Lila (Evans) M.; m. Virginia Dale Eschenburg, Sept. 16, 1964 (div. 1977); m. 2d, Christina Alma Gribben, Oct. 22, 1977 (div. 1991); children— Leland Exton, Susan Carnall, Catherine Grant, Nancy Mayo, Elizabeth Leanore, Kristen Linnea; m. Carol Ann Janes Hill, Jan. 4, 1992; step-children: Lara Beth Hill, Kevin L. Hill. BA, Williams Coll., 1965; postgrad. U. Denver, 1970-71. Rsch. analyst C.A. Norgren Co., Littleton, Colo., 1969-70; assoc. Koelbel & Co., Denver, 1970-72; rsch. dir. Armstrong for Congress, Aurora, Colo., 1972; legis. asst. US Rep. William Armstrong, Washington, 1973-78; adminstrv. asst. US Rep. Ken Kramer, Washington, 1979-81; dir. legislation US EPA, Washington, 1981-84, spl. asst. external affairs, 1984-85; mem. Multinat. Bus. Svcs., 1985—91; instr. Georgetown U., 1980-81; lectr. Plymouth State U., 1990-93. Author: (novels) The Fires of Paratime, 1982 (main selection Sci. Fiction Book Club, May, 1982), The Hammer of Darkness, 1985, The Ecologic Envoy, 1986, Dawn For a Distant Earth, 1987, The Silent Warrior, 1987, In Endless Twilight, 1988, The Magic of Recluce, 1991, The Towers of the Sunset, 1992, The Magic Engineer, 1994, The Order War, 1995, The White Order, 1998, Scion of Cyador, 2000, Legacies, 2002, Scepters, 2004, Flash, 2004, Wellspring of Chaos, 2004, Ordermaster, 2005, Alector's Choice, 2005, The Eternity Artifact, 2005, Cadmian's Choice, 2006, Soarer's Choice, 2006, The Elysium Commission, 2007, Natural Ordermage, 2007; author short stories and poetry; contbr. articles to profl. jours. With USN, 1965-69, SE Asia. Republican. Home: 255 Sunnyview Rd Cedar City UT 84720-2897 Personal E-mail: lmodesitt@aol.com.

MODIN, FREDRIK, professional hockey player; b. Sundsvall, Sweden, Oct. 8, 1974; Left wing Brynas IF, Toronto Maple Leafs, 1996—99, Tampa Bay Lightning, 1999—2006, Columbus Blue Jackets, 2006—. Player NHL All-Star Game, 2001. Achievements include being a member of Stanley Cup Champion Tampa Bay Lightning, 2004; being a member of gold medal winning Swedish Hockey Team, Torino Olympics, Italy, 2006. Office: Columbus Blue Jackets Nationwide Arena 200 W Nationwide Blvd Columbus OH 43215

MODISETT, JEFFREY A., lawyer, former state attorney general; b. Windfall, Ind., Aug. 10, 1954; s. James Richard and Diana T. Modisett; m. Jennifer Ashworth, June 9, 1990; children: Matthew Hunter Ashworth, Haden Nicholas. BA, UCLA, 1976; MA, Oxford U., Eng., 1978; JD, Yale U., 1981. Bar: Ind., Calif., D.C. Clk. to Hon. R. Peckham U.S. Dist. Ct. (no. dist.) Calif., San Francisco, 1981—82; asst. U.S. atty. Office U.S. Atty. (ctrl. dist.) Calif., LA, 1982—88; issues dir. Evan Bayh for Gov., Indpls., 1988; exec. asst. to gov. State of Ind., Indpls., 1988—90; prosecutor Marion County, Indpls., 1991—94; sr. counsel Ice Miller Donadio & Ryan, Indpls., 1995—96; atty. gen. State of Ind., 1997—2000; dep. CEO, gen. counsel Dem. Nat. Conv., 2000; co-CEO TechNet, Palo Alto, Calif., 2000—01; ptnr. Manatt Phelps & Phillips LLP, 2001—02; mng. ptnr. Bryan Cave LLP, LA, 2002—. Chmn. Gov. Commn. for Drug Free Ind., Indpls., 1989—, Gov. Coun. on Impaired and Dangerous Driving, Indpls., 1989—; pres. Family Advocacy Ctr., Indpls., 1991—94, Hoosier Alliance Against Drugs, Indpls., 1993—96; dir. Cmty. Couns. of Indpls., 1991—93; chmn. Ind. Criminal Justice Inst., Indpls., 1989—90, dir., 1989—; vice chmn. Juvenile Justice and Youth Gang Study Com., Indpls., 1992—94; legal analyst Sta. WTHR-TV, Indpls., 1995—96. Author: Prosecutor's Perspective, 1991—94; editor-in-chief: Yale Jour. Internat. Law, 1980—81. Co-chair Ind. State Dem. Coordinated Campaign, Indpls., 1996. Named Top Lawyer, Indpls. Monthly mag., 1993; named to Sagamore of Wabash, State of Ind., 1995; recipient Spl. Enforcement award, U.S. Customs, 1988, Child Safety Adv. award, Automotive Safety for Children, 1997, STAR Alliance Impact award, 1998, Spirit of Ind. award, Am. Lung Assn., 1999. Mem.: Indpls. Bar Assn., Ind. Bar Assn. Democrat. Avocation: bicycling. Office: Bryan Cave LLP 120 Broadway, Ste 300 Santa Monica CA 90401 Office Phone: 310-576-2370. Office Fax: 310-576-2200. E-mail: jamodisett@bryancave.com.

MODJTABAI, AVID, bank executive; b. 1961; BS in Indsl. Engring., Stanford U.; MBA in Fin., Columbia U. With McKinsey & Co.; exec. vice-pres., dir. internet svcs. Wells Fargo, San Francisco, head online personal fin. svcs., exec. vice-pres., dir. HR, 2005—. Named one of 25 Most Powerful Women in Banking, US Banker, 2004, 25 Women to Watch, 2006, 100 Most Influential Women in Bay Area Bus., San Francisco Bus. Times, 2004—05. Office: Wells Fargo 420 Montgomery St San Francisco CA 94104 *

MODLIN, HOWARD S., lawyer; b. NYC, Apr. 10, 1931; s. Martin and Rose Modlin; m. Margot S. Modlin, Oct. 18, 1956; children: James, Laura, Peter. AB, Union Coll., Schenectady, 1952; JD, Columbia U., 1955. Bar: N.Y. 1956, D.C. 1973. Assoc. Weisman, Celler, Spett & Modlin, P.C., NYC, 1956-61, ptnr., 1961-76, mng. ptnr., 1976-95, pres., 1996—. Chmn. bd. dirs., sec. Gen. DataComm Industries, Inc., Naugatuck, Conn.; bd. dirs. Am.-Book-Stratford Press, Inc., NYC, Fedders Corp., Liberty Corner, NJ, Trans-Lux Corp., Norwalk, Conn. Chmn. bd. dirs. Daus. of Jacob Geriat. Ctr., Bronx, N.Y. Mem. ABA, Assn. of Bar of City of N.Y., D.C. Bar Assn. Office: Weisman Celler Spett & Modlin PC 445 Park Ave New York NY 10022-2606 Office Phone: 212-371-5400.

MODNY, CYNTHIA JEAN, dermatologist; b. Jan. 23, 1945; d. Michael Theodore and Mary (Tabaka) M. BA, Mt. Holyoke Coll., 1967; MD, U. Va., Charlottesville, 1971. Diplomate Am. Bd. Dermatology. Intern Lenox

Hill Hosp., NYC, 1971-72; resident N.Y. Hosp./Cornell Med. Ctr., NYC, 1972-75, instr. dermatology, 1976—81; practice medicine specializing in dermatology Montclair, N.J., 1976-92, Phoenix, 1994—. Pvt. practice cons. undersea medicine, Montclair, 1982-92; clin. instr. dermatology Skin and Cancer Unit, NYU Med. Ctr., N.Y.C., 1981-92; participant Physicians' Undersea Medicine Tng., NOAA, Miami, Fla., 1982; dir. Skin Cancer Inst., Montclair, 1984. Med. editor Dive Travel Report (monthly), 1983-92; contbr. article to Skin Diver mag. Bd. dirs. Montclair Sr. Citizens, 1984. Fellow Am. Acad. Dermatology; mem. Undersea Med. Soc., Am. Soc. Dermatologic Surgery, Princeton Club, Mt. Holyoke Club (N.Y.C.).

MODRICH, PAUL L., biochemistry professor; b. Raton, N.Mex., June 13, 1946; BS in Biology, MIT, 1968; PhD in Biochemistry, Stanford U., 1973; postgrad., Harvard U., 1973-74. Asst. prof. chemistry U. Calif., Berkeley, 1974; asst. prof. biochemistry Duke U., 1976, assoc. prof. biochemistry, 1980, prof. biochemistry, 1984, dir. program in genetics, 1989-92, investigator Howard Hughes Med. Inst., 1994—, James B. Duke prof. biochemistry. Contbr. articles to profl. jours.; assoc. editor: Biochemistry, 1992-94, mem. editl. adv. bd., 1986-91, 95—; mem. editl. bd. Nucleic Acids Rsch., 1980-82, Jour. Biol. Chemistry, 1982-83. Recipient award in enzyme chemistry Pfizer, 1983, NAS, 1993, Mott prize in cancer rsch. GM, 1996, Medal of Honor for basic rsch., Am. Cancer Soc., 2005, Pasarow Found. award in cancer rsch. Fellow: Am. Acad. Arts & Sci.; Mem. NIH (mem. biochemistry study sect. 1980-84, NIH NIGMS merit award 1986), Am. Soc. Biochemistry and Molecular Biology (councillor 1989-92, 97—, mem. publs. com. 1995-97), Inst. Medicine. Office: Department of Biochemistry Nanaline H Duke Box 3711 DUMC Durham NC 27710 Office Phone: 919-684-2775.

MODRUSON, FRANK B., information technology executive; m. Lynne Modruson. BS, Dickinson Coll.; MS, Pa. State Univ. With Accenture Ltd., NYC, 1987—97, ptnr., 1997—, chief info. officer. Mem. Cingular Wireless BMG Bd. Adv. Bd. dir. Lyric Opera, Chgo. Named one of Top 25 Chief Tech. Officers, InfoWorld mag., 2006. Office: Accenture Ltd 1345 Ave of the Americas New York NY 10105

MOE, ANDREW IRVING, veterinarian; b. Tacoma, Jan. 2, 1927; s. Ole Andrew and Ingeborg (Gordham) M.; m. Dorothy Clara Becker, June 25, 1950 (dec. Nov. 30, 2001); children: Sylvia Moe McGowan, Pamela Moe Barker, Joyce. BS in Biology, U. Puget Sound, 1949; BA, Wash. State U., 1953, DVM, 1954. Meat cutter Art Hansen, Tacoma, 1943—48; gen. practice as vet. Baronti Vet. Hosp., Eugene, Oreg., 1956-57; vet. regulatory Calif. Animal Health br., resident vet. II Calif. Dept. Food & Agr., Modesto, 1957-64, acting vet.-in-charge Modesto Dist. office, vet. III, 1976-77, ret., 1990—. Watersafety instr. ARC, 1958-61. Capt. Vet. Corps., 1954-56, 62; lt. col. Biomed Scis. Corps. USAF, ret., 1982. Recipient Chief Vet. badge, 1975. Mem. VFW (life, comdr. post 4144 1998-2001, quartermaster 2000-02, trustee post 3199, 2004-07), No. San Joaquin Vet. Med. Assn. (pres. 1979), Calif. Acad. Vet. Medicine (charter), Mil. Officers Assn. of Am. (charter), Res. Officers Assn. (life), Ret. Officers Assn. (life), Assn. Mil. Surgeons U.S. (life), Sons of Norway, Am. Legion (life), Shriners (bd. dirs. Modesto Shrine 1995), Masons (life), (Illustrious Master Modesto chpt. 1983, Allied Masonic degrees, pres. Modesto Masonic Luncheon Club 1991, 98, Meritorious Svc. medal 1992, Man of Yr. award 1999), Scottish Rite (life, pres. Ctrl. Valley 1997, bd. dirs. 1998-2006), Presido Yacht Club Sausalito, Theta Chi, Alpha Psi. Lutheran. Home: 161 Norwegian Ave Modesto CA 95350-3542

MOE, JANET ANNE, elementary school educator, church organist; b. Sacramento, May 24, 1946; d. Joseph Robert and Virginia Lou (Jones) Mangan; m. Edward Earl Moe, Aug. 23, 1969 (dec. Aug. 2002); children: Erik John, Erin Jean Moe Mitchell. BA, Calif. Luth. U., 1968; std. secondary tchg. credential, Calif. State U., Sacramento, 1969, crosscultural, lang. and acad. devel. cert. (CLAD), 1996; cert. in Orff Schulwerk Levels I, II and III, U. Calif. Santa Cruz, 1987; MS, Nat. U., Sacramento, 2001, preliminary adminstrv. credential, 2001. Elem. tchr. Gloria Dei Luth. Sch., Sacramento, 1969—73; elem. music specialist Sacramento City Unified Sch. Dist., 1982—. All-city elem. choir coord. Sacramento City Unified Sch. Dist., 1999—2001; chorus dir. Sierra Mt. Music Camp, 2001; facilitator Calif. dept. edn. model arts project Sacramento City Unified Sch. Dist. Singer: Sacramento City Coll. Choir, including touring choir, 1998—2006. Touring choir So. Calif. and Hawaii Calif. Luth. U., 1967—68; task force to restore music and the fine arts Sacramento City Unified Sch. Dist., 1999—2000; organist Gloria Dei Luth. Ch., 1970—2002, Luth. Ch. of Good Shepherd, 2003—. Recipient Hon. Svc. award, PTA Bear Flag Sch., Sacramento, 1992, VH1 Save the Music grant, 2002, 2005. Mem.: NEA, Sacramento Cmty. Concerts Assn. (bd. dirs. 2006—), Calif. Music Educators Assn. (bd. dirs. 2001—04, elem. rep., mem. bd. Capitol Sect., Outstanding Music Educator award 1996, 2003), Nat. Audubon Soc. Republican. Lutheran. Avocations: birdwatching, travel, yoga, reading, hiking. Home: PO Box 109 Elk Grove CA 95759-0109

MOE, LONN ANDRE, state revenue official; b. Springfield, Minn., Nov. 18, 1958; s. Roy Melvin and Margaret Joy Moe. BS in Agrl. Econs. and Agrl. Bus. Adminstrn., U. Minn., St. Paul, 1981, MS in Agrl. Bus. Mgmt., 1984. Rsch. analyst Minn. Dept. Revenue, St. Paul, 1985—87, rsch. analyst intermediate, 1987, rsch. analyst specialist, 1987—92, rsch. analyst specialist sr., 1992—99, revenue ops. specialist, 1999—. Study leader Grace Ch. Roseville, Minn., 1988—. Recipient Achievement award, Minn. Dept. Revenue, 1989, 1995, 2005, 2007. Mem.: Landscape Plant Devel. Ctr. Avocations: horticulture, horseback riding. Office Phone: 651-556-6144.

MOE, RICHARD PALMER, lawyer; b. Duluth, Minn., Nov. 27, 1936; s. Russell James and Virginia Mary (Palmer) M.; m. Julia Neimeyer, Dec. 26, 1964; children— Eric Palmer, Andrew Neimeyer, Alexandra Julia. BA, Williams Coll., 1959; LL.B., U. Minn., 1966. Bar: Minn. 1967, D.C. 1979, N.Y. 1991. Adminstrv. asst. to mayor, City of Mpls., 1961-62; to lt. gov. Minn., 1963-66; fin. dir. Minn. Democratic Farmer-Labor Party, 1967-69, chmn., 1969-72; adminstrv. asst. to Sen. Walter F. Mondale of Minn., Washington, 1972-76; chief of staff Vice Pres. Walter F. Mondale, 1977-81; counsel Davis Polk & Wardwell, Washington, 1981-85, ptnr., 1985-92; pres. Nat. Trust for Hist. Preservation, Washington, 1992—. Trustee Ford Found., 1998—. Office: Nat Trust for Hist Preservation 1785 Massachusetts Ave NW Washington DC 20036-2117

MOE, RONALD CHESNEY, public administration researcher; b. San Diego, May 28, 1937; s. Chesney R. and L. Bernice (Weston) M.; m. Carolyn Carr, May 18, 1962 (div. Feb. 1974); children: Steven, Cynthia; m. Grace Tyler, Apr. 30, 1976. BA, Claremont Coll., 1959; MA, Columbia U., 1962, PhD in Pub. Law and Govt., 1968. Asst. prof. San Diego State U., 1967-70; sr. policy advisor Office of Econ. Opportunity, Exec. Office of the Pres., Washington, 1970-71, Cost of Living Coun., Exec. Office of the Pres., Washington, 1971-73; specialist govt. orgns. and mgmt. Congl. Rsch. Svc. Libr. of Congress, Washington, 1973—2002. Cons. OECD, Paris, 1996—. Brookings Instn., Washington, 2003-, Congl. Rsch. Svc., 2003-; adj. prof. George Washington U., 2003-. Contbr. chpts. in books, articles to profl. jours. Mem. exec. bd. Congregational. Chs. of Am., Milw., 1985-89. Capt. U.S. Army Res., 1961-63. Ctr. Study of Am. Govt. fellow Johns Hopkins U., Washington, 1993—; recipient ASPA Louis Brownlow award, 1988, 91, 95-96. Fellow Nat. Acad. Pub. Adminstrn.; mem. Acad. Polit. Sci., Cosmos Club (Washington), Phi Beta Kappa. Republican. Home: 4700 Connecticut Ave NW Apt 407 Washington DC 20008-5609 Office: Congl Rsch Svc Libr Of Congress Washington DC 20540-0001 E-mail: rmoe@crs.loc.gov.

MOE, STANLEY ALLEN, architect, consultant; b. Fargo, ND, May 28, 1914; s. Ole Arnold and Freda Emily (Pape) Moe; m. Doris Lucille Anderson, July 25, 1937 (dec. 2000); children: Willa Moe Crouse, Myra Moe Galther; m. Reiko Izuno, Nov. 11, 2001. BArch, U. Minn., Mpls., 1936; DEng (hon.), U. ND, Grand Forks, 1993. lic. arch. several states; cert. Nat. Coun. Archtl. Registration Bds. Project arch. various firms, 1936—42, U.S. Army Corps Engrs., Africa, 1942—43; ptnr. H.S. Starin, Archs. & Engrs., Duluth, Minn., 1943—47; sr. ptnr. Moe & Larsen, Archs. & Engrs., LA, 1947-54; ptnr., gen. mgr., exec. v.p. Daniel, Mann, Johnson & Mendenall, LA, 1954-71, corp. v.p., 1972-79; prin. Stanley A. Moe, AIA, LA, 1979—. Dir. design of major mil. projects in Eritrea, Sudan, Egypt, Yemen for Allied Forces, 1942-43; chmn. control com. DMJM & Assocs., dir. design prototype, tng. & operational facilities Titan I Intercontinental Ballistic Missiles Program USAF, 1958-63; project dir. Space Shuttle facilities Kennedy Space Ctr., 1973; project dir. for design of aircraft maintenance complex Iranian Aircraft Industries, 1978; project mgr. for design of major med. facility program Min. of Def. and Aviation, Saudi Arabia, 1975-76; project mgr. design of Boufarik Internat. Airport, Algeria, 1983. Pres. San. Fernando Valley Young Reps., 1952, Van Nuys (Calif.) Jaycees, 1950. Recipient Disting. Svc. award for cmty. svc., Van Nuys Jaycees, 1949, Sioux award, U. ND Alumni Assn., 1985, Trustees Soc. award, U. Minn., 1992; inducted into ND Entrepreneur Hall of Fame, 2000. Mem. AIA (Calif. coun.), Rotary, Delta Tau Delta. Republican. Presbyterian. Avocations: world travel, hunting, fishing, historic restoration, woodworking. Home and Office: 447 S Plymouth Blvd Los Angeles CA 90020-4706 E-mail: stanmoe@sbcglobal.net.

MOECKEL, STEVEN, concertmaster; b. Germany, 1978; Studied, Ind. U. Co-concertmaster Ulm Philharmonic; concertmaster Tucson Symphony Orch., 2002—. Mem., master class and recital Greater Oro Valley Arts Coun. Fundraiser uninsured cancer patients; mem. Tucson Arthritis Support League. Named one of 40 Under 40, Tucson Bus. Edge, 2006. Office: Tucson Symphony Center 2175 N Sixth Ave Tucson AZ 85705-5606 Office Phone: 520-792-9155.

MOEDDEL, MICHAEL J., lawyer; b. Cin., Apr. 6, 1978; BA, Ohio State U., 1999; JD, U. Cin. Coll. Law, 2002. Bar: Ohio 2002, US Dist. Ct. Southern Dist. Ohio 2002. Instr., Pre-Law Elder High Sch.; assoc. Keating Muething & Klekamp PLL, Cin. Commr. Cin. Recreation Commn.; mem., Caddie Classic Com. Evans Scholars; mem., Bd. Dirs. Greater Cin. Sports Corp. Named one of Ohio's Rising Stars, Super Lawyers, 2006. Mem.: Ohio State Bar Assn., Cin. Bar Assn., ABA, Order of Coif. Office: Keating Muething & Klekamp PLL One E Fourth St Ste 1400 Cincinnati OH 45202 Office Phone: 513-579-6400. Office Fax: 513-579-6457.

MOEHLMAN, MICHAEL SCOTT, lawyer; b. Columbus, Ohio, Apr. 11, 1938; s. Arthur Henry and Marguerite Caroline M.; m. Carol Jean Shafer, Sept. 28, 1963; 1 son, Matthew. BA, Harvard U., 1960; LLB, U. Tex., 1963. Bar: Tex. 1963. With Strasburger & Price, Houston. Bd. dirs. St. Martin's Episcopal Children's Ctr. Fellow Tex. Bar Found.; mem. ABA (com. bank securities), Internat. Bar Assn., Tex. Bar Assn. (com. revision corp. law), Houston Bar Assn. (judicature com.), Tex.-Mex. Bar Assn., Am. Judicature Soc., Houston Bar Found. (chmn. bd. dirs.), Phi Delta Phi. Clubs: Houston (chmn. fin. com., bd. dirs., pres.), Houston Racquet, Houston Yacht, Harvard (Boston), Harvard (NYC), St. Charles Bay Hunting. Episcopalian. Office: Strasburger & Price 1401 McKinney St Ste 2200 Houston TX 77010-4035 Office Phone: 713-951-5684. Business E-Mail: michael.moehlman@strasburger.com.

MOEHRING, AMANDA J., geneticist; b. Calif. d. Carl J. and M. Christine Moehring; m. Thomas E. Winkeler; 1 child, Emma M. Winkeler. BS, Pacific U., Oreg., 1997; PhD, NC State U., 2003. Postdoctoral scholar Duke U., Durham, NC, 2004—. Contbr. articles to profl. jours. Mentor young girls Women and Math, Raleigh, 2001—02; vol. Habitat for Humanity, Quetzaltenango, Guatemala, 1994—94; chair policy Duke U. Postdoctoral Assn., 2006—07; mentoring program Pacific U., Forest Grove, Oreg., 1994—97. Fellow, NIH, 2001—03, 2005—, NC State U., Raleigh, 2003—04; scholar, Pacific U., 1993—97; W. M. Keck Behavioral Biology fellow, NC State U., 1999—2003. Office: Duke U Biology Box 90338 Durham NC 27708 Home Phone: 919-544-9921; Office Phone: 919-613-8193.

MOEHRING, FRED ADOLF, wholesale distribution executive; b. Bklyn., Nov. 4, 1935; s. Fred Henry Christian and Elsa Marta (Klein) M.; m. Marilyn Agnes Rieber, June 7, 1958; 1 child, Donna. Grad. H.S., Jamaica, NY. Salesman Miller-Charles and Co., Mineola, NY, 1956-63, Century Fasteners Corp., Elmhurst, NY, 1963-65; gen. mgr. Stewart Air Industries, Syosset, NY, 1965-70; salesman Supreme Lake Mfg. Co., Plantsville, Conn., 1971, Allmetal Screw Products Inc., Garden City, NY, 1971-72; cab driver Scull's Angels, Flushing, NY, 1972-74; gen. mgr. Empire Fasteners, Long Island City, NY, 1974-83, Mar-Lin Sales, Bklyn., 1983-97, Fred A. Moehring, Inc., Bklyn., 1998—. Mem. ASME, ASTM, NRA, ASM Internat., Soc. Automotive Engrs., Met. Fastener Distbrs. Assn. (pres. 1991-92), Steuben Soc. Am., United German-Am. Com. of U.S.A., Inc., German-Am. Steuben Parade Com. Republican. Lutheran. Avocations: golf, travel. Office: Fred A Moehring Inc 208 N 8th St Brooklyn NY 11211-2008 Office Phone: 718-963-2220. Personal E-mail: fred35@iwon.com. Business E-Mail: famsales@usa.com.

MOEHRINGER, J. R., writer; b. NYC, Dec. 7, 1964; BA in History, Yale Coll., 1986. News asst. NY Times, 1986—90; gen. assignment reporter Rocky Mountain News, Denver, 1990—94; reporter, Orange County edit. Los Angeles Times, 1994—97, bur. chief Atlanta, 1997, corr. Denver. Author: (memoir) The Tender Bar, 2005. Finalist Pulitzer Prize for Feature Writing, 1998; named Scripps Howard Nat. Non-Deadline Writer of Yr., 1992; recipient Feature Writing award, AP News Exec. Coun., 1997, Lit. award, Penn Ctr. USA West, 1997, Livingston award for Young Journalists, 1997, Pulitzer Prize for Feature Writing, 2000; grantee Niemann Fellow, Harvard Univ. Home: Denver CO Office: c/o Mort Janklow Janklow & Nesbit Assoc 13th fl 445 Park Ave New York NY 10022

MOELHMAN, AMY JO, social worker; b. Lafayette, Ind., Mar. 18, 1954; d. Charles and Marian (Young) Moelhman. BS, Ball State U., 1976; MSW, U. Denver, 1979. Lic. clin. social worker, Ind. Social worker Adolescent Crisis Team, Adams County Social Svc., Denver; counselor adolescent boys prog. Pleasant Run Children's Home, Indpls.; group therapist Mothers of Victims of Sexual Abuse, Mid-Town Mental Health, Indpls.; supr. foster care and counseling prog. Children's Bur., Indpls.; mgr. Family Connection Ctr., 1989-90; dir. family programs Vis. Nurse Svc., Indpls., 1990-96; dir. Holy Family Svcs., Cath. Social Svcs., Indpls., 1996—2001; cons. Brown County Family Access Ctr., 1999—; supr. cmty. programs Indpls. Transition Ctr. Casey Family Programs, 2001—03; exec. dir. Ind. Alliance Human Svcs., Indpls., 2004—. Chair Ind. Coalition of Family-based Svcs., 1992-94; co-chair family preservation com. Marion County Stepahead; part-time faculty masters in social work program Ind. U.-Purdue U., Indpls. Contbr. articles to profl. jours. Mem. NASW, Acad. Cert. Social Workers. Home: 818 E 53rd St Indianapolis IN 46220-3104 Office Phone: 317-603-6866. Personal E-mail: amoelhman@aol.com.

MOELING, WALTER GOOS, IV, lawyer; b. Quantico, Va., Feb. 16, 1943; s. Walter Goos III and Dorothy M.; m. Nell Frances Askew, Aug. 27, 1965; children: Charles H., Christine E. BA, Duke U., 1965, JD, 1968. Bar: Ga. 1968. Assoc. Powell Goldstein, Atlanta, 1968-75, ptnr., 1975—. Bd. dirs. So. Banking Law and Policy Conf., 1989-96, Southeastern Conf. for Bank Dirs., 1996—, Children's Rehab. Ctr., Atlanta, 1982—, Gatchell Home, Atlanta, 1983-99; bd. dirs. Frazer Ctr., 1989—, chmn. bd. dirs., 1993. Mem. ABA (mem. banking com. 1986—), Ga. C. of C. (bd. dirs. 1998-2000), Ga. Bar Assn., Ga. Bankers Assn. (assoc., chairperson bank counsel sect. 1992-95, bd. dirs. 1998-2000), Cmty. Bankers Assn. (assoc.), Capital City Club, Willow Point Country Club. Democrat. Unitarian Universalist. Avocations: golf, fly fishing. Office: Powell Goldstein LLP One Atlantic Ctr 1201 W Peachtree St Atlanta GA 30309-1740 Office Phone: 404-572-6629. Business E-Mail: wmoeling@pogolaw.com.

MOELLEKEN, BRENT RODERICK WILFRED, surgeon; b. Vancouver, BC, Can., Apr. 19, 1960; BA, Purdue U., 1979; MD, Yale U., 1985; postgrad., Harvard U., 1980-81. Diplomate Am. Bd. Surgery, Am. Bd. Plastic Surgery. Intern U. Calif., San Francisco, 1985-86, resident in gen. surgery, 1986-92, rsch. fellow in plastic surgery, 1988-90, resident in plastic surgery, 1992-94; fellow in aesthetic surgery UCLA, 1994-95; pvt. practice Beverly Hills, Calif., 1995—, Santa Barbara, Calif., 1995—. Attending surgeon UCLA Hosp., Cedars-Sinai Hosp., L.A.; asst. clin. prof. UCLA; surgeon ABC-TV Extreme Makeover. Plastic surgery before and after lead surgeon: (TV series) Discovery Health Channel; contbr. over 120 articles to profl. jours.; appeared in: over 60 TV shows. Fellow ACS; mem. Am. Soc. Plastic Surgeons, Am. Soc. Aesthetic Plastic Surgery. Achievements include invention of livefill graft; superficial cheek lift operation; hybrid alidominoplasty 360 facelift. Office: 120 Spalding Dr Ste 340 Beverly Hills CA 90212 Office Phone: 310-273-1001. Business E-Mail: info@drbrent.com. E-mail: drbrent@drbrent.com.

MOELLER, AUDREY CAROLYN, retired energy company executive, corporate secretary; b. Pitts., May 10, 1935; d. Nicholas William and Edith Tecla (Russman) M. Grad. high sch., Pitts. Legal sec. Equitable Resources Inc., Pitts., 1955-72, asst. corp. sec., 1972-80, corp. sec., 1980-86, v.p., corp. sec., 1986-99; also corp. sec. Equitable Resources Inc. subs.; ret., 1999. Com. mem. United Way Allegheny County, Pa., 1978, United Way Southwestern Pa., 1984. Mem.: Pa. Assn. Notaries, Am. Soc. Corp. Secs. (chmn. membership and asst. sec. Pitts. chpt. 1995, treas. 1996, v.p. and program chmn. 1997, pres. 1998), Loyal Christian Benefit Assn. (nat. coun. 1993, pres. br. 331 2000, nat. auditor 2001—04). Democrat. Roman Catholic. Avocations: singing, golf, travel. Home: 1003 Cherry Hill Dr Presto PA 15142

MOELLER, DADE WILLIAM, environmental engineer, educator; b. Grant, Fla., Feb. 27, 1927; s. Robert A. and Victoria (Bolton) M.; m. Betty Jean Radford, Oct. 7, 1949 (dec. Oct. 1998); children: Garland Radford, Mark Bolton, William Kehne, Matthew Palmer, Elisabeth Anne. BSCE, Ga. Inst. Tech., 1947, MS in Environ. Engring., 1948; PhD in Nuc. Engring., N.C. State U., 1957. Commd. jr. asst. san. engr. USPHS, 1948, advanced through grades to san. engr. dir., 1961; rsch. engr. Los Alamos (N.Mex.) Sci. Lab., 1949-52; staff asst. Radiol. Health Program, Washington, 1952-54; rsch. assoc. Oak Ridge Nat. Lab., 1956-57; chief radiol. health tng. Taft San. Engring. Ctr., Cin., 1957-61; officer charge Northeastern Radiol. Health Lab., Winchester, Mass., 1961-66; assoc. dir. Kresge Ctr. Environ. Health, Harvard Sch. Pub. Health, 1966-83, prof. engring. in environ. health, head dept. environ. health scis., 1968-83, dir. Office of Continuing Edn., 1982-84, assoc. dean continuing edn., 1985-93; environ. cons., 1993—; pres. Dade Moeller & Assocs., Inc., 1993—2003, chmn. bd., 2005—; prof. emeritus Harvard Sch. Pub. Health, 2006—. Cons. radiol. health. Author: (textbook) Environmental Health, 3rd edit., 2005; contbr. articles to profl. jours. Chmn. Am. Bd. Health Physics, 1967-70; mem. com. 4 Internat. Commn. on Radiol. Protection, 1978-85; chmn. nat. air pollution manpower devel. adv. com. U.S. EPA, 1972-75; mem. adv. com. reactor safeguards U.S. NRC, 1973-88, chmn., 1976, chmn. adv. com. nuc. waste, 1988-93; chmn. sci. and tech. rev. panel Office of Civilian Radioactive Waste Mgmt., U.S. Dept. Energy, 2003-. Named to Ga. Inst. Tech. Engring. Hall of Fame, 1999; recipient Disting. Engring. Alumnus award, N.C. State U., 2001, Disting. Prof. Emeritus award of merit, Sch. Pub. Health, Harvard U., 2006. Fellow Am. Pub. Health Assn., Am. Nuc. Soc.; mem. AAAS, Am. Acad. Environ. Engrs., Nat. Coun. Radiation Protection and Measurements (hon.), NAE, Am. Acad. Health Physics Soc. (pres. 1971-72, Robley D. Evans Commemorative medal 2003, William McAdams Outstanding Svc. award 2005). Home and Office: 257 River Island Rd New Bern NC 28562-3669

MOELLER, FLOYD DOUGLAS, lawyer; b. Safford, Ariz., Aug. 16, 1949; s. Floyd Albert and Helen Lou (Posey) M.; m. Tyra Brown, Dec. 18, 1970; children: Kristin, Sam, John, Susan. BS in Police Sci., Brigham Young U., 1972, JD, 1977; MS in Mgmt., Lesley Coll., 1985, MA in Counseling Psychology, 1987; LLM in Tax, Washington Sch. Law, 1987, D of Juridicial Sci., 2001. Bar: N.Mex. 1978, U.S. Dist. Ct. N.Mex. 1978, U.S. Dist. Ct. Ariz. 1978, U.S. Ct. Appeals (10th cir.) 1979, U.S. Tax Ct. 1981, U.S. Supreme Ct. 1981, Navajo Nation, Hopi Tribe, Jicarilla Apache Tribe, White Mountain Apache Tribe, So. Ute Tribe, Ute Mountain Tribe, So. Paiute Coun., Ft. Belknap Indian Ct., Gila River Indian Ct., Mescalaro Apache Ct., S.W. Inter Tribal Ct. Appeals, Zuni Tribal Ct. Assoc. Wade Beavers & Assocs., Farmington, N.Mex., 1978-79; ptnr. Nunn & Moeller, Farmington, 1979; sole practice Farmington, 1979—80; ptnr. Moeller & Burnham, Farmington, 1980-87; sole practice, 1987—. Mem. exec. com. Better Bus. Bur. of 4 Corners, 1978, bd. dirs., 1978—; bd. dirs. Farmington Pub. Library Bd., 1979-86, San Juan Med. Found., 1985-04, San Juan Pub. Library Found., Halvorson House; chmn. local troop coms. Boy Scouts Am., Farmington, 1985—. Capt. USMC, 1972-75. Named diplomat Nat. Bd. Trial Advocacy, 1986. Mem. ABA, J. Reuben Clark Law Soc., Nat. Panel Consumer Arbitrators, Am. Arbitration Assn., N.Mex. Trial Lawyers Assn., N.Mex. State Bar Assn. (CLE, fee arbitration coms. 1985, pres. trial practice sect. 1988), Navajo Nat. Bar Assn., San Juan County Bar Assn. (pres. 2006—), 4 Corners Inn of Ct. Republican. Mem. Lds Ch. Avocations: reading, poetry, gardening, knot tying. Office: PO Box 15249 Farmington NM 87401-5249 Office Phone: 505-327-7456. Fax: (505) 362-0818. E-mail: dmoeller@advantas.net.

MOELLER, JOSEPH W., forest products company executive; b. Holdenville, Okla., 1943; m. Mary Moeller; 3 children. BS in Bus. Adminstrn., Aarhus U., Denmark; Degree in Petroleum Mktg., Tulsa, 1966. Joined Koch Industries, Wichita, Kans., 1966, v.p. refined products group, 1980, pres. petroleum group, 1992—95, pres. Koch Industries Internat., 1995—98, pres. Koch Ventures, 1998—99, pres., COO, 1999—2005, also bd. dirs.; pres., CEO Georgia-Pacific Corp., Atlanta, 2005—, also bd. dir., 2005—, chmn., 2006—. Trustee U. Tulsa; mem. 25 Yr. Club Petroleum Industry. Named Outstanding Alumnus, U. Tulsa Coll. Bus. Adminstrn., 1995—96. Office: Georgia-Pacific 133 Peachtree Street NE Atlanta GA 30303 Office Phone: 404-652-4000.

MOELLER, LAURA LEE, retired retail executive, library and information consultant; b. St. Louis, Feb. 20, 1927; d. Edwin Charles and Henrietta Maude (Schelp) Luedde; m. Gerald Herbert Moeller, June 25, 1949; children: Dereck John, Dori Lee, Merry Cay. AB, Harris Tchrs. Coll., St. Louis, 1948; sch. libr. cert., Washington U., St. Louis, 1965. Elem. tchr. Howard Sch., St. Louis, 1948-50, Bay View Sch., Norfolk, Va., 1951; libr. East Ladue Jr. High Sch., St. Louis, 1965-77; mgr., buyer Wornall House Mus. Shop, Kansas City, Mo., 1978-79; co-owner Crabtree & Evelyn London on Plaza, Kansas City, 1979—94. V.p. Women's Coun. U. Mo., Kansas City, 1984—85; coord. libr. Second Presbyn. Ch., 1989—2005. Mem.: DAR (treas. Westport chpt. 1992—94, vice regent 1994—96, regent 1996—98), AAUW, Plaza Mchts. Assn. (nominating com. 1981, bd. dirs. 1991—94), Mo. Assn. Sch. Librs. (pres. 1976—77), Nat. Soc. Magna Charta Dames and Barons, Rotary Aux., Conservative Capitalists Investment Club (sec. 2002—03), Carriage Club. Presbyterian. Avocations: reading, tai chi, line dancing. Home: 6247 Rosewood St Shawnee Mission KS 66205 Personal E-mail: lmoeller@kc.rr.com.

MOELLER, PHILIP D., commissioner; BA, Stanford U. Staff coord. com. energy, utilities and telecom. Washington State Senate; energy policy advisor to Senator Slade Gordon U.S. Senate, 1997—2000; dir. fed. rels. Capline Corp., Wash.; commr. Fed. Energy Regulatory Commn., Washington, 2006—. Head fed. office Alliance Energy Corp. Office: Fed Energy Regulatory Commn 888 First St NE Washington DC 20426 Office Phone: 202-502-8852. Office Fax: 202-502-6400.

MOELLERING, JOHN HENRY, aviation maintenance company executive; b. Ft. Wayne, Ind., Feb. 4, 1938; s. Robert Charles and Irene Pauline (Nolde) M.; m. Karla Louise Fritzsche, Dec. 21, 1963; children: John Henry, Matthew C., Ann Elizabeth. BS, U.S. Mil. Acad., 1959; MS, U. Calif., Berkeley, 1962; postgrad., Army Command and Gen. Staff Coll., 1971-72, Army War Coll., 1976-77. Registered profl. engr., La. Commd. 2d lt. U.S. Army, 1959, advanced through grades to lt. gen., 1985; aide de camp Combat Devel. Command, 1961-63; command and staff 24th Inf. Div., Fed. Republic Germany, 1964-67; ops. officer Engr. Group, Vietnam, 1967-68; instr. civil engring., asst. prof. history U.S. Mil. Acad., 1968-71; with Office Army Chief of Staff, Pentagon, 1972-73; White House staff, 1973-74; bn. comdr. 101st Airborne Div., 1974-76; dist. engr. Vicksburg, Miss., 1977-79; exec. to Army Chief of Staff, Pentagon, 1979-81; asst. div. comdr. 9th Inf. Div., Ft. Lewis, Wash., 1981-82; commandant West Point, NY, 1982-84; comdg. gen. Ft. Leonard Wood, Mo., 1984-85; asst. to chmn. Joint Chiefs of Staff, Pentagon, Washington, 1985-87; corp. v.p. Automatic Data Processing, Inc., San Ramon, Calif., 1987-90; pres., chief exec. officer Lear Siegler Mgmt. Svcs. Corp., Oklahoma City, 1990-93; pres. UNC Aviation Svcs., Annapolis, Md., 1993-97; pres., CEO Lear Siegler Svcs., Inc., Annapolis, Md., 1997—2002, JM Assocs., Chapel Hill, NC, 2002—. Bd. dirs. USAA Ins. Co., Lear Sigeler Svcs., Inc., Indsl. Coll. of the Armed Forces; frequent lectr. Nat. Def. U.; mem. adv. bd. Sch. Bus. Adminstrn. The Citadel; adj. faculty Kenan-Flagler bus. sch. U. NC, 2006—. Editor, contbr.: Evolution of Modern Warfare, 1969, Battalion Commanders Speak Out, 1977. Mem. Sci. Def. Bd., The Pentagon; chmn. Class of '59 fund com. U.S. Mil. Acad., 1984—89. Decorated Def. DSM, Army DSM, Legion of Merit, Bronze Star; White House fellow, 1973-74. Mem.: Nat. Def. Indsl. Assn. (bd. dirs.), Phi Kappa Phi. Office: 50130 Manly Chapel Hill NC 27517-8565 Personal E-mail: johnmoellering@hotmail.com.

MOELLERING, ROBERT CHARLES, JR., internist, educator; b. Lafayette, Ind., June 9, 1936; s. Robert Charles and Irene Pauline (Nolde) M.; children: Anne Elizabeth, Robert Charles, Catherine Irene; m. Mary Jane Ferraro, July 11, 1987. BA, Valparaiso U., 1958, DSc, 1980; MD cum laude, Harvard U., 1962; DPH (hon.), St. Elizabeth U., 2005. Diplomate: Am. Bd. Internal Medicine. Intern Mass. Gen. Hosp., Boston, 1962-63, resident, 1963-64, postdoctoral fellow in infectious diseases, 1967-70, resident, 1966-67, mem. infectious disease unit and asst. physician, 1970-76, assoc. physician, 1976-83, hon. physician, 1983—, cons. bacteriology, 1972-87; instr. medicine Harvard U. Med. Sch., Boston, 1970-72, asst. prof., 1972-76, assoc. prof., 1976-80, prof., 1980—; chmn. dept. medicine, physician-in-chief New Eng. Deaconess Hosp., 1981-96; pres., CEO Deaconess Profl. Practice Group, 1995-98; Shields Warren-Mallinckrodt prof. rsch. Harvard U. Med. Sch., Boston, 1981-89, Shields Warren-Mallinckrodt prof. med. rsch., 1989-99, 2005—, Herrman Blumgart prof. medicine, 1999—2005; assoc. physician-in-chief Beth Israel Deaconess Med. Ctr., 1996—98, physician-in-chief, 1998—2005, pres., CEO, Harvard Med. Faculty physician, 1998—2003, chmn. bd. dirs., pres., trustee, 2003—05. Mem. subcom. on susceptibility testing Nat. Com. for Clin. Lab. Standards, 1976-88; mem. subcom. on antimicrobial agts. and chemotherapy, 1978-80; subcom. on antimicrobiol disc. diffusion susceptibility testing, 1980-88; chmn. data safety monitoring bd. Nat. Inst. Allergy and Infections Disease, NIH, 1997—2002; trustee Caregroup, 1998-2005, BIDMC, 1998-2005; bd. dirs. NanoBio Corp., Nabriva Therapeutics Forschungs GmBH. Mem. editl. bd. Antimicrobial Agts. and Chemotherapy, 1977-81, editor, 1981-85, editor-in-chief, 1985-95; editor European Jour. Clin. Microbial Infectious Diseases, 1990—; consulting. editor Infectious Disease Clinics N.Am., 1986—; editor Les Infections, 1983; editl. bd. New Eng. Jour. Medicine, 1977-81, European Jour.Clin. Microbiology, 1981—, Jour. Infectious Diseases, 1981-85, 89-93, Infectious Disease Alert, 1981-92, Pharmacotherapy, 1982—, Antimicrobial Agts. Ann., 1984-87, Zentralblatt Fur Bacteriologie, Microbiologie and Hygiene, 1984—, Jour. of Infection, 1986—, Innovations, 1986-90, Residents Forum in Internal Medicine, 1988-90, Diagnostic Microbiology and Infectious Disease, 1989-90, Internat. Jour. Antimicrobial Agts., 1990—, Infectious Diseases in Clin. Practice, 1991-92, Jour. Infection and Chemotherapy, 1995—, Clin. Infectious Disease, 1999-2004. Served with USPHS, 1964-66. Grantee USPHS, NIH. Master ACP, Am. Acad. Microbiology, Infectious Diseases Soc. Am. (v.p. 1988-89, pres. elect 1989-90, pres. 1990-91, past pres. 1991-92); fellow Royal Coll. Physicians (hon.); mem. Am. Soc. Microbiology, Am. Clin. and Climatol. Assn., Internat. Soc. Chemotherapy, Am. Soc. Clin. Investigation, Assn. Am. Physicians, European Soc. Clin. Microbiology, Am. Fedn. Clin. Rsch., Assn. Profs. Medicine, Roxbury Clin. Records Club, Mass. Med. Soc. (councilor), Brit. Soc. Antimicrobial Chemotherapy, Coun. Biology Editors, Alpha Omega Alpha, Phi Kappa Psi. Home: 49 Longfellow Rd Wellesley MA 02481-5220 Office: Beth Israel Deaconess Med Ctr Dept Medicine 110 Francis St Boston MA 02215-5501 E-mail: rmoeller@bidmc.harvard.edu.

MOELY, BARBARA E., psychologist, educator; b. Prairie du Sac, Wis., July 17, 1940; d. John Arthur and Loretta Ruth (Giese) M.; children: John Jacob Moely Wiener, David Andrew Moely Wiener. Student, Carroll Coll., 1958-60; BA, U. Wis., 1962, MA, 1964; PhD, U. Minn., 1968. Asst. prof. U. Hawaii, Honolulu, 1967-71; rsch. psychologist UCLA, 1971-72; asst. prof. Tulane U., New Orleans, 1972-75, assoc. prof. psychology, 1975-85, prof., 1985—2004, prof. emerita, 2004—, dept. chmn., 1992-96, dir. Office of Svc. Learning, 1999—2004. Contbr. articles to profl. jours. Grantee U.S. Office Edn., Handicapped Pers. Preparation, 1977-80, Tulane U., 1973, 75, 77-78, 83-84, Inst. for Mental Hygiene, City of New Orleans, 1983-84, 2000, Nat. Inst. Edn., 1983-84, La. Edn. Quality Support Fund, 1988-89, 91-92, 96, HUD, 1997-2003, Annenberg, 1997, HHS, 1997-2002, US Dept. Edn., 1999-2002, Fund for Improvement Post-Secondary Edn., 2000-03, Corp. Nat. and Cmty. Svc., 2003-. Mem. AAUP (v.p. La. conf. 1992-93, sec. 1993-97, v.p. 1998-2000, pres. Tulane 1992-94), Am. Ednl. Rsch. Assn., Southwestern Soc. for Rsch. in Human Devel. (pres. 1986-88), Phi Beta Kappa (pres. Alpha chpt. La. 1981-82, sec. 1995-99) Office: Tulane U Ctr Pub Svc 327 Gileson Hill New Orleans LA 70118 Business E-Mail: moely@tulane.edu.

MOERBEEK, STANLEY LEONARD, lawyer; b. Toronto, Ont., Can., 1951; arrived in U.S., 1953; s. John Jacob and Mary Emily Moerbeek; m. Carol Annette Mordaunt, Apr. 17, 1982; children: Sarah, Noah. BA magna cum laude, Calif. State U., Fullerton, 1974; student, U. San Diego-Sorbonne, Paris, 1977; JD, Loyola U., 1979. Bar: Calif. 1980; cert. in internat. bus. transactions, bankruptcy and bus. rehab., and civil trial practice. From law clk. to assoc. McAlpin Doonan & Seese, Covina, Calif., 1977-81; assoc. Robert L. Baker, Pasadena, Calif., 1981-82, Miller Bush & Minnott, Fullerton, 1982-83; prin. Law Office of Stanley L. Moerbeek, Fullerton, 1984—. Notary pub. lt. gov. 9th cir. law student divsn. ABA, 1979; judge pro tem Orange County Superior Ct., 1984—96. Mem. Heritage Found., Washington, 1989—. Recipient plaque of Appreciation, Fullerton Kiwanis, 1983; Calif. Gov.'s Office scholar, 1970. Mem.: Orange County Bar Assn. (Coll. Trial Advocacy 1985), Calif. Assn. Realtors (referral panel atty. 1985—), Phi Kappa Phi. Roman Catholic. Avocations: history, politics, sports. Office: 1370 N Brea Blvd Ste 210 Fullerton CA 92835-4128 Office Phone: 714-773-5396. Personal E-mail: slmlaw@sbcglobal.net.

MOERDLER, CHARLES GERARD, lawyer; b. Paris, Nov. 15, 1934; came to the U.S., 1946, naturalized, 1952; s. Herman and Erna Anna (Brandwein) M.; m. Pearl G. Hecht, Dec. 26, 1955; children: Jeffrey Alan, Mark Laurence, Sharon Michele. BA, L.I.U., 1953; JD, Fordham U., 1956. Bar: NY 1956, U.S. Supreme Ct. 1962. Assoc. Cravath, Swaine & Moore, NYC, 1956-65; spl. counsel coms. City of N.Y. and judiciary N.Y. State Assembly, 1960-61; commr. bldgs. City of N.Y., 1966-67; sr. ptnr., chmn. litigation dept. Stroock & Stroock & Lavan, NYC, 1967—. Bd. dirs., gen. counsel, dir. N.Y. Post Co., Inc., 1987-92; cons. housing, urban devel. and real estate to Mayor of N.Y.C., 1967-73; mem. com. on character and fitness of applicants for admission to Bar, Appellate divsn. 1st Dept., N.Y., 1977—, vice chmn. 1998—; mem. disciplinary com. appellate divsn. 1st Dept., N.Y., 1998—2004, 06—, commr. N.Y. State Ins. Fund, 1978-97, vice chmn., 1986-94, chmn., 1995-97; mem. Mayor's Com. on Judiciary, 1994-2001; mem. N.Y.C. Housing Devel. Corp., 1997—; bd. dirs. N.Y.C. Residential Mortgage Ins. Corp., 1997—; chmn. bd. dirs. Bank Austria Creditanstalt LLC, 1999-2001; mem. N.Y.C. Bd. Collective Bargaining, 2000—. Mem. editorial bd. N.Y. Law Jour., 1985—; assoc. editor Fordham Law Rev., 1956. Asst. dir. Rockefeller nat. presdl. campaign com., 1964; adv. bd. Sch. Internat. Affairs Columbia U., 1977-80; bd. govs. L.I.U., 1966, trustee, 1985-91; chmn. Cmty. Planning Bds. 8 and 14, Bronx County, 1977-78; sr. v.p., mem. exec. com. Am. Jewish Congress, 2005—; bd. overseers Jewish Theol. Sem. Am., 1993-95; trustee St. Barnabas Hosp., Bronx, N.Y., 1985—. Recipient Walker Metcalf award L.I. U., 1966, Castle award Manhattanville Coll., 2005. Mem. Am. Bar Assn., N.Y. State Bar Assn., N.Y. County Lawyers Assn., Internat. Bar Assn., Assn. of Bar of City of N.Y., Free Sons of Israel, Metro. Club. Home: 7 Rivercrest Rd Bronx NY 10471-1236 Office: Stroock Stroock & Lavan 180 Maiden Ln New York NY 10038 Home Phone: 718-884-5303; Office Phone: 212-806-5648. Business E-Mail: cmoerdler@stroock.com.

MOERNER, WILLIAM ESCO, physical chemist, educator; b. Pleasanton, Calif., June 24, 1953; s. William Alfred and Bertha Frances M.; m. Sharon Judith Stein, June 19, 1983; 1 child, Daniel Everett. BS in Physics and Elec. Engring., Washington U., St. Louis, 1975, AB in Math., 1975; MS in Physics, Cornell U., 1978, PhD in Physics, 1982. Langsdorf engring. fellow Washington U., St. Louis, 1971-75; NSF grad. fellow Cornell U., Ithaca, N.Y., 1975-78, rsch. asst., 1978-81; mem. rsch. staff IBM Almaden Rsch. Ctr., San Jose, Calif., 1981-88, mgr. Laser-Materials Interactions, 1988-89, rsch. staff mem. and photorefractive polymer project leader, 1989-95; prof. and disting. chair phys. chemistry and biochemistry U. Calif., San Diego, 1995-98; prof. chemistry Stanford U., Calif., 1998—, Harry S. Mosher prof. chemistry Calif., 2002. Gen. chair Topical Meeting on Persistent Spectral Hole-Burning, 1991; Samuel L. McElvain lectr., dept. chemistry, U. Wis., 1993; Ehrenfest Colloquium lectr., U. Leiden, The Netherlands, 1994; vis. guest prof., lab. for phys. chemistry, Swiss Inst. Tech., Switzerland, 1993-94; A.D. Little Lectr., Dept. Chemistry, MIT, 1995; Robert Burns Woodward vis. prof. Harvard U., 1997-98. Author, editor: Persistent Spectral Hole-Burning: Science and Applications, 1988, Single Molecule Optical Detection, Imaging, and Spectroscopy, 1997; guest edito, spl. issue, Accounts of Chem. Rsch. on Single Molecules and Atoms, 1996; adv. editor Chemical Physics Letters; contbr. articles to tech. publs. Tenor San Jose Symphonic Choir, 1983-91, Stanford Symphonic Chorus, 2000—; ofcl. observer Am. Radio Relay League, Santa Clara Valley, Calif., 1987-88, asst. tech. coord., 1990-95, asst. emergency coord., 2000—. NSF Grad. Fellow, Cornell U., 1975-79; named Wilkinson Outstanding Young Elec. Engr. award, Nat. Winner Eta Kappa Nu, 1984; recipient IBM Outstanding Technical Achievement awards for Photon-Gated Persistent Spectral Hole-Burning, 1988, Single-Molecule Detection and Spectroscopy, 1992, Earle K. Plyler prize for molecular spectroscopy, 2001. Fellow Am. Phys. Soc.(symposium organizer, laser sci. topical group, 1992, March mtg., 1993), Optical Soc. Am.(chair fundamental and applied spectroscopy technical group, 1992-94, gen. chair and founder, adv. chair topical conf. on persistent spectral hole-burning sci. and applications, 1991, 1993, 1994, co-editor), Am. Acad. Arts and Scis., AAAS, Geoffrey Frew Fellow Australian Acad. Scis.,; mem. IEEE (sr. mem., asst. treas. Lasers and Electro-Optics Soc. ann. meeting 1988, 1989, symposium organizer, ann. mtg. 1989), Am. Chem. Soc. (organizer, symposium on chemistry of single molecules, 1997), Biophys. Soc., IBM Amateur Radio Club W6YX (pres. 1987-88), Materials Rsch. Soc. (symposium organizer, 1991), Soc. Photo-Optical Instrumentation Engrs. (mem. program com., 1996-98), NAS. Achievements include being a patentee in strain-sensitive spectral features detection method, device, photorefractive polymers. Office: Dept Chemistry, M/C 5080 Stanford Univ 375 N-S Mall Stanford CA 94305-5080 Office Phone: 650-723-1727. Office Fax: 650-725-0259. Business E-Mail: w.e.moerner@stanford.edu, moerner@stanford.edu. *

MOESER, JAMES CHARLES, academic administrator; b. Colorado City, Tex., Apr. 3, 1939; s. Charles Victor and Virginia (James) M.; m. Jesse Kaye Edwards, Jan. 26, 1963 (div. July 1984); children: James Christopher, Kathryn Carter; m. Susan Kay Smith Dickerson, June 21, 1987. B.Mus., U. Tex., 1961, M.M., 1964; postgrad. (Fulbright grantee), Hochschule fur Musik, Berlin, 1961-62; D.MA (Univ. fellow), U. Mich., 1966. Chmn. dept. organ, asst. prof. organ U. Kans., 1966-69, assoc. prof., 1969-74, prof., 1974-86, dean Sch. Fine Arts, 1975-86, Carl and Ruth Althaus disting. prof. organ, 1985-86; organist, choirmaster Plymouth Congl. Ch., Lawrence, Kans., 1967-86; organist nat. conf. Music Tchrs. Nat. Assn., Portland, Oreg., 1972, LA, 1974; dean Coll. Arts and Architecture, Pa. State U., State College, 1986—91; v.p., academic affairs & provost U. SC, 1991—96; chancellor U. Nebr., Lincoln, Nebr., 1996—2000, U. NC, Chapel Hill, 2000—. Concert organist, on tour, W. Ger., 1977, Lisbon (Portugal) Festival, 1978, 81, recitals for, Musica Festiva da Costa Verde, Portugal, 1981; organist concerts, W. Ger., 1982, 86, 87; world premier Paul Creston's 3d Symphony for Organ and Orchestra, Kennedy Ctr., Washington, 1982. Bd. govs. Josephson Inst. Ethics, 1998-2002; trustee N.C. Symphony Soc., Inc., 2001—; mem. vis. com. Meml. Ch., Harvard U. Recipient Palmer Christian award U. Mich., 1981, Disting. Alumnus awrd Grad. Sch. U. Tex., 2001; Kent fellow Danforth Found.; Danforth Assoc. Mem. Am. Guild Organists (past dean chpt., nat. dir. student groups 1973-75, nat. chmn. com. on profl. edn. 1983—, chmn. 2d nat. conf. on organ pedagogy 1984, 3d nat. conf. 1986, v.p. 1986—); fellow Am. Acad. Arts & Scis. Episcopalian. Home: 1000 Raleigh Rd Chapel Hill NC 27517-4415 Office: UNC Office of the Chancellor PO Box 9100 Chapel Hill NC 27599-0001 Office Phone: 919-962-1365. E-mail: james_moeser@unc.edu. *

MOFFAT, MARYBETH, consulting company executive; b. Pitts., July 25, 1951; d. Herbert Franklin and Florence Grafe (Knerem) M.; m. Brian Francis Soulier, Nov. 30, 1974 (div.). BA, Carroll Coll., Waukesha, Wis., 1973. Indsl. engring. technician Wis. Centrifugal Co., Waukesha, Wisc., 1976-77; indsl. engr. Utility Products, Inc., Milw., 1977-79; mgr. indsl. engring. Bear Automotive (divsn. SPX Corp.), Bangor, Pa., 1980-90; program mgr. Toyota Johnson Controls, Inc. Automotive Systems Group, 1990-2001; pres., CEO Moffat Enterprises, Inc., 2001—. Group home house parent Headwaters Regional Achievement Ctr., Lake Tomahawk, Wis., 1974. Mem. Am. Inst. Indsl. Engrs., MTM Assn. for Standards Rsch., Indsl. Mgmt. Soc., Alpha Gamma Delta (standards chmn. 1971-72). Republican. Methodist. Avocations: skiing, horseback riding, swimming, reading. Personal E-mail: m.moffat@insightbb.com.

MOFFAT, ROBERT W., JR., information technology executive; BS in Econs., Union Coll.; MBA in Mgmt. Info. Sys., Iona Coll. Various mgmt. positions including gen. mgr. personal sys. group, gen. mgr. fin., planning, and bus. sup. IBM Europe IBM, 1978—, sr. v.p., integrated supply chain, 2002—. IBM ptnr. exec. Bell South, Aetna, Carolina Power & Light, Ingram Micro, Progress Energy, CDW, Insight Direct. Office: IBM 1133 Westchester Ave White Plains NY 10604 *

MOFFAT, JOYCE ANNE, performing company executive; b. Grand Rapids, Mich., Jan. 3, 1936; d. John Barnard and Ruth Lillian (Pellow) M. BA in Lit., U. Mich., 1957, MA in Theatre, 1960; HHD (hon.), Profl. Sch. Psychology, San Francisco, 1991. Stage mgr., lighting designer Off-Broadway plays; costume, lighting and set designer, stage mgr. stock cos., 1954-62; nat. subscription mgr. Theatre Guild/Am. Theatre Soc., NYC, 1965-67; subscription mgr. Theatre, Inc.-Phoenix Theatre, NYC, 1963-67; cons. NYC Ballet and NYC Opera, 1967-70; asst. house mgr. NY State Theater, 1970-72; dir. ticket sales City Ctr. of Music and Drama, Inc., NYC, 1970-72; prodn. mgr. San Antonio's Symphony/Opera, 1973-75; gen. mgr. San Antonio Symphony/Opera, 1975-76, 55th St. Dance Theater Found., Inc., NYC, 1976-77, Ballet Theatre Found., Inc./Am. Ballet Theatre, NYC, 1977-81; v.p. prodn. Radio City Music Hall Prodns., Inc., NYC, 1981-83; artist-in-residence CCNY, 1981—; propr. mgmt. cons. firm for performing arts NYC, 1983—; exec. dir. San Francisco Ballet Assn., 1987-93; mng. dir. Houston Ballet Assoc., 1993-95; gen. mgr. Chgo. Music and Dance Theater, Inc., 1995—2004. Cons. Ford Found., NY State Coun. on Arts, Kennedy Ctr. Performing Arts., Lensic Performing Arts Ctr., Santa Fe, Bloomington Cultural Dist., Ill., Sheboygan Theater Found., Wis., The Arts Partnership Spartanburg, SC; mem. dance panels NY State Coun. on Arts, 1979-81; mem. panels for Support to Prominent Orgns. and Dance, Calif. Arts Coun., 1988-92. Appointee San Francisco Cultural Affairs Task Force, 1991; chmn. bd. dir. Tex. Inst. Arts in Edn., 1994—; trustee Internat. Alliance of Theatrical Stage Employees Local 16 Pension and Welfare Fund, 1991-94; bd. dir. Rudolf Nureyev Dance Found., Chgo., 1998—. Mem. Assn. Theatrical Press Agts. and Mgrs., Actors Equity Assn., United Scenic Artists Local 829, San Francisco Visitors and Conv. Bur. (bd. dirs.), Argyle Club (San Antonio). Office Phone: 864-457-4575.

MOFFATT, KATY (KATHERINE LOUELLA MOFFATT), musician, lyricist, vocalist; b. Ft. Worth, Nov. 19, 1950; d. Lester Huger and Sue-Jo (Jarrott) M. Student, Sophie Newcomb Coll., 1968, St. John's Coll., 1969-70. Rec. artist Columbia Records, 1975-79, Permian/MCA Records, 1982-84, Enigma Records, LA, 1985, Wrestler Records, LA, 1987-88, Red Moon Records, Switzerland, 1988-93, Philo/Rounder Records, 1989-96, Round Tower Music, U.K., Ireland, Europe, 1993-96, Watermelon Records, U.S., 1994-96, Panther City Records, New Zealand, 1998, Hightone/HMG Records, 1998-2001, Western Jubilee/Dualtone Records, 2001—, Demon/Westside Records, 2002, Fuel Records/Universal Records, 2005. Folksinger, Ft. Worth, 1967-68; musician, vocalist, songwriter, rec. artist: (films) Billy Jack, 1970, Hard Country, 1981, The Thing Called Love, 1993; prodn. asst. film, Sta. KIII-TV, Corpus Christi, 1970, audio engr., Sta. KRIS-TV, Corpus Christi, 1970; musician, vocalist in blues band, Corpus Christi, 1970; receptionist, bookkeeping asst., copywriter, announcer, Sta. KFWT, Ft. Worth, 1971, musician, vocalist, songwriter, Denver, 1971-72, on tour, 1973, 75—, Denver, 1974, on tour, 1976-79, European tour, 1977, Can. tour, 1984-85, on tour in Europe, U.S., Can., Asia and Australia, 1985—; albums include Katy, 1976, Kissin' In The California Sun, Am. release, 1977, internat. release, 1978, A Town South of Bakersfield, 1985, Walkin' on the Moon, European release, 1988, U.S. release, 1989, Child Bride, 1990, (duet album with brother Hugh) Dance Me Outside, 1992, (Switzerland only) Indoor Fireworks, 1992, The Greatest Show On Earth A.K.A. The Evangeline Hotel, 1994, Hearts Gone Wild, 1994, Tulare Dust, 1995, (duet album with Kate Brislin) Sleepless Nights, 1996, Midnight Radio, 1996, Angel Town, 1998, Loose Diamond, 1999, Cowboy Girl, 2001, (reissue on CD) Katy/Kissin' in the California Sun, 2002, Up Close & Personal, 2005; songs include The Magic Ring, 1971; Gerry's Song, 1973, Kansas City Morning, 1974, Take Me Back To Texas, 1975, (Waitin' For) The Real Thing, 1975, Didn't We Have Love, 1976, Kissin' in the California Sun, 1977, Walkin' on the Moon, 1989. Recipient Record World Album award, 1976; named one of 4 Top New Female Vocalists, Cashbox Singles Awards, 1976; nominee for Top New Female Vocalist, Acad. Country Music, 1985; winner best singer-songwriter category Ft. Worth Weekly Mag. Music awards, 1997. Mem. AFTRA, SAG, NARAS, Am. Fedn. Musicians.

MOFFATT, MICHAEL ALAN, lawyer; b. Indpls., Feb. 22, 1964; s. James L. Kelso and Peggy A. Tackett; children: Patricia Margaret, Michael Alan, Nicole Elizabeth, Michelle Ann. BA in Polit. Sci., Depauw U., 1986; JD, Ind. U., 1989. Bar: Ind. 1989, U.S. Dist. Ct. (so. and no. dists.) Ind. 1989, U.S. Ct. Appeals (7th cir.) 1991, U.S. Supreme Ct., 1999. Law clk., assoc. White & Raub, Indpls., 1987-94; assoc. Wooden McLaughlin & Sterner, Indpls., 1994-95, Barnes & Thornburg, Indpls., 1995-2000, ptnr., 2001; shareholder Ogletree Deakins, Nash, Smoak and Stewart, P.C., 2001—06, Littler Mendelson P.C., 2006—. Lectr. litigation, paralegal program, Ind. U./Purdue U., Ind. CLE Forum & labor/employmemt seminars. Contbr. articles to legal jours. Co-chmn. Keep Am. Beautiful, Greencastle, Ind., 1986, bd. dirs., sec., 1990—94; tournament chair Fall Creek Little League, 2002, v.p., 2003, pres., 2004, 2005; mem. devel. control com. Geist Harbors Property Owner's Assn., Indpls., 1993—94, cons., 1994, pres., 1997—99; cons. pediatric ethics com. Meth. Hosp., Indpls., 1990—92. Mem.: ABA (bd. dirs., sec. labor and employment sect.), Indpls. Bar Assn. (exec. coun. labor law sect. 1999, vice chmn. 2000, chmn. 2001), Ind. Bar Assn. (mem. exec. coun. labor law sect. 2002—), Fed. Bar Assn., U.S. Auto Club (sec. 2004—05, 2nd v.p. 2006, bd. dirs., 1st v.p. 2007, Winners Cir.), Exch. Club (pres.-elect 1997—98, pres. 1998—99, past pres. 1999—2000). Avocations: golf, basketball, softball. Office: Littler Mendelson PC First Ind Plz Ste 1500 135 N Pennsylvania St Indianapolis IN 46204 Office Phone: 317-287-3522.

MOFFETT, J. DENNY, lawyer; b. Atlanta, Sept. 20, 1947; s. James Denny Moffett Jr. and Dorothy (Mckenzie) McCall; m. Mary F. Ray, June 6, 1987; children: David, Jenny. BA, U. Okla., 1969; JD with honors, George Washington U., 1972, LLM in Taxation, 1974. Bar: Okla. 1972, U.S. Tax Ct. 1973, Wyo. 2001. Legis. asst. U.S. Senate, Washington, 1973-74; ptnr. Conner & Winters, Tulsa, 1974-90, McKenzie, Moffett, Elias & Books, Tulsa, Oklahoma City, 1990-97, Moffett & Assocs., P.C., Tulsa, 1997—, Jackson, Wyo., 2001—. Adj. faculty U. Tulsa Law Sch., 1978; arbitrator Nat. Assn. Securities Dealers. Commr. Ark.-Okla. River Compact Commn., 1990-94; pres. Nicholas Club Tulsa, 1984; endowment com. Trinity Episcopal Ch., 1990—. 2d lt. U.S. Army, 1972-74; bd. dirs. Am. Cancer Soc., 1991-94. Mem. Am. Arbitration Assn., Tulsa Tax Club (pres. 1981, 94). Republican. Home: 2132 E 32nd Pl Tulsa OK 74105-2222 Office: Moffett & Assocs PC 1722 S Carson Ave Ste 3203 Tulsa OK 74119 also: Moffett & Assocs PC PO Box 4797 215 S Willow St Jackson WY 83001 Office Phone: 307-733-8734, 918-587-5700. E-mail: jdmofflaw@aol.com.

MOFFETT, JAMES ROBERT, mining executive; b. Houma, La., Aug. 16, 1938; s. Robert E. and Mary G. (Pollack) M.; m. Louise C. Hohmann, June 5, 1960; children: Crystal Louise, James R. BS, U. Tex., 1961; MS, Tulane U., 1963. Cons. geologist oil and gas industry, New Orleans, 1964-69; v.p. founding ptnr. McMoRan Exploration Co., New Orleans, 1969-74; pres., chief exec. officer McMoRan Oil & Gas Co., New Orleans, 1974-81, 81-85, chmn., chief exec. officer, 1985—97, dir., from 1974; vice-chmn. Freeport McMoRan Inc., New Orleans, 1981-85, chmn., chief exec. officer, 1984—97, chmn., 1997—; co-chmn. McMoRan Exploration Co. Mem. Nat. Petroleum Council, Washington, 1979, Commn. on the

Future of South, 1986; bd. dirs. La. Energy Nat. PAC, Metairie, La., 1979, World Trade Ctr., New Orleans, Am. Cancer Soc. Greater New Orleans, Bus. Task Force Edn., Inc.; chmn. bd. La. Coun. Fiscal Reform; chmn. bus. coun. New Orleans and River Region, 1985-87. 2nd lt. U.S. Army, 1961-68, capt. Res. ret. Recipient T award Ex Students Assn. U. Tex., 1960, Hornblower Yr. award Pub. Relations Soc. Am., 1986, Vol. Yr. award Urban League Greater New Orleans, 1987; Minnie Stevens Piper Found. scholar U. Tex., 1960, Jacques E. Yenni, S.J. award Loyola U. of New Orleans for Outstanding Community Svc., Jr. Achievement Bus. Hall of Fame award, 1987, Loyola U. of New Orleans' Integritas Vitae award, 1988; named One of Ten Outstanding Persons of 1985 Inst. for Human Understanding, New Orleans Mem. All Am. Wildcatters, New Orleans Geol. Soc., Petroleum Club New Orleans, Greater New Orleans Mktg. Com. (exec. com. 1987), Geology Found U. Tex. (adv. council 1972-85), Devel. bd. U. Tex., La. Ind. producers Royalty Owners Assn. South La. Mid-Contintent Oil Gas Assn. (v.p.), Dinner Steering Com. (Disting. Citizen award 1983, 85 Boy Scouts Am. New Orleans div.), Green Wave Club. Republican. Mailing: Freeport-McMoRan Copper & Gold Co PO Box 61119 New Orleans LA 70161 *

MOFFETT, SUSAN L., information technology manager; b. Pitts., May 14, 1972; d. Kenneth E. and Peggy S. Sponagle; m. James C. Moffett, Mar. 9, 1996; 1 child, Abigail S. BA in Comm., U. Wis., Stevens Pt., 1994; MS in Orgnl. Mgmt., Capella U., Mpls., 2006. Desktop pub., adminstrv. asst. Robert W. Baird & Co., Tampa, Fla., 1996—2001; info. tech. mgr. Focus Mgmt. Grp., Tampa, 2001—; info. teeh. sys. technician USN Res., Tampa, 2002—. Mng. ptnr. JSM Consulting, LLC, Wesley Chapel, Fla., 2006—. Vol. Spl. Olympics, Tampa, 1998—2007; Sunday sch. tchr. St. Andrew Presbyn. Ch., Tampa, 2006—07. E-5 USN, 2002—07, Tampa. Decorated Achievement medal USN and USMC, Bluejacket of Quarter award Navy Operational Support Ctr. Mem.: Alpha Sigma Alpha (life). R-Conservative. Presbyterian. Avocations: rock climbing, mountain biking. Office: Focus Mgmt Grp 5001 W Lemon St Tampa FL 33609 Business E-Mail: s.moffett@focusmg.com.

MOFFITT, BRENDA A., lawyer; b. 1969; BA cum laude, US Internat. U., 1990; JD, Boston Sch. Law, 1998. Bar: Mass. 1998. Assoc. McCarter & English, Boston, Sullivan & Worcester, Boston. Mem.: Boston Bar Assn., ABA. Office: Sullivan & Worcester 1 Post Office Sq Boston MA 02109 Office Phone: 617-338-2972. Office Fax: 617-338-2880. Business E-Mail: bmoffitt@sandw.com.

MOFFITT, CHARLES WILLIAM, art gallery director; b. Altoona, Pa., Mar. 24, 1932; s. Charles William and Beatrice Jeanette (Shellenberger) Moffitt; m. Virginia Colyer, July 26, 1956 (dec.); m. Marianne Foley Potter, May 23, 1980 (dec.); children: Michelle Ann Hunt, Charles William III, Deborah K. Moffitt Russell; m. Mary Lou Herold, Nov. 24, 2001; stepchildren: Sherry Marshall, Heather Clayton, Kristin Pfauser. BA, Pa. State U., 1957. Examiner Pa. R.R., Buffalo, 1957-62; asst. to pres. White Cross Stores, Inc., Monroeville, Pa., 1962-65, sec., 1965-70, v.p. adminstrn., sec., 1970-72; dir. labor relations and legal affairs Revco D.S., Inc., Cleve., 1972-75, asst. v.p. personnel, 1974-75; pres. Fashion Wearhouse, Inc., Altoona, Pa., 1975-87; dir., ptnr. Servello Gallery Art, 2002—. Owner Omega Advt. Co.; pres. Olympus I, Inc., 1980-87; agt. Prin. Fin. Group, 1988-90, Variable Annuity Life Ins. Co., 1990-2001. Co-author: Mince-meat Cartoons, Altoona Mirror Newspaper. Bd. dirs. Bedford Springs Music Festival, 1984-87, Blair County Arts Found., 1987-91, Blair Concert Chorale, 2005-07. Republican. Roman Catholic. Home: RR 5 Box 2324 Altoona PA 16601 Office Phone: 814-946-8922. E-mail: monkmoffitt@hotmail.com.

MOFFITT, WILLIAM BENJAMIN, lawyer; b. NYC, Jan. 16, 1949; s. William Benjamin and Victoria Lucinda Moffitt; 1 child, Pilar. BA, U. Okla., 1971; JD, Am. U., 1975. Bar: Va. 1976, US Dist. Ct. (ea. dist.) Va. 1976, US Ct. Appeals (4th cir.) 1980, US Ct. Appeals (5th cir.) 1981, US Ct. Appeals (11th cir.) 1982, US Ct. Appeals (6th cir.) 1988, US Ct. Appeals (1st cir.) 1991, US Dist. Ct. Md. 1994, US Ct. Appeals (3rd cir.) 1994. Ptnr. Lowe, Mark & Moffitt, Alexandria, Va., 1976-81, Mark & Moffitt, Alexandria, Va., 1981-85, Moffitt, Keats & Jones, Alexandria, Va., 1985-87, Moffitt & Jones, Alexandria, Va., 1987-89, William B. Moffitt & Assocs., Alexandria, Va., 1989-91, Moffitt, Zwerling & Kemler, Alexandria, Va., 1991-96, Asbill, Junkin & Moffitt, Chartered, Washington, 1996—2004; ptnr., criminal def. Asbill Moffitt & Boss (acquired by Cozen O'Connor), Washington, 2004—. Mem. Legal Svcs. Bd. No. Va., 1982; pres. Va. Coll. Criminal Def. Lawyers, 1983. Contbr. article to profl. jour. Bd. dirs. ACLU, 1981. Named one of Am. Top Black Lawyers, Black Enterprise Mag., 2003. Fellow Am. Bd. Criminal Lawyers; mem. Alexandria Bar Assn., Nat. Assn. Criminal Def. Lawyers (bd. dirs. 1988—, strike force chair 1993, nat. sec. 1994, nat. treas. 1995, second v.p. 1996, first v.p. 1997-98, pres.-elect 1998-99, pres. 1999-2000); Internat. Assn. Criminal Def. Lawyers, Va. Assn. Criminal Def. Lawyers. Office: Cozen O Connor Ste 500 1667 K St NW Washington DC 20006 Office Phone: 202-912-4816, 800-540-1355. Office Fax: 202-912-4830. Business E-Mail: wmoffitt@cozen.com.

MOFFLY, JOHN WESLEY, IV, magazine publishing executive; b. Phila., Aug. 5, 1926; s. John W. III Moffly and Audrey (Kane) Chancellor; m. Donna Jeannette Clegg, July 11, 1959; children: Jonathan Wesley, Audrey Kane Klotz. BA, Woodrow Wilson Sch., Princeton U., 1949. NY advt. mgr. House & Home Mag. Time Inc., NYC, 1962-66, NY advt. exec. LIFE Mag., 1967-73, v.p. selling areas mktg. divsn., 1973-87; pres., owner Moffly Publs., Inc., 1987—; pubs. Greenwich, Westport, New Canaan-Darien and At Home mags., Fairfield County. Bd. dirs. Boys and Girls Club Greenwich, United Way, Greenwich Emergency Med. Svc., Greenwich Adult Day Care; mem. Amb.'s Round Table-Forum, World Affairs. With USAAF, 1944-45. Mem. Greenwich C. of C. (chmn. bd. dirs. 1999-00, Small Businessman of Yr. 1991), Riverside Yacht Club, Cruising Club Am., Indian Harbor Yacht Club, Greenwich Rotary Club (Citizen of Yr. 2006). Republican. Episcopalian. Avocations: sailing, tennis, clay bird shooting, skiing, international studies. Home: 100 Meadow Rd Riverside CT 06878-2520 Office: Greenwich Mag 39 Lewis St Greenwich CT 06830-5558

MOFFORD, ROSE, former governor of Arizona; b. Globe, Ariz., June 10, 1922; m. T.R. Mofford (div.). Attended pub. schs. Sec. to Joe Hunt, Ariz. State Treas., 1941-43, Ariz. State Tax Commr., 1943-54, Wesley Bolin, Ariz. Sec. of State, 1954-55; asst. sec. of state State of Ariz., Phoenix, 1955-75, asst. dir. of revenue, 1975-77, sec. of state, 1977-88, governor, 1988-90; Ariz. elector for John Kerry US Presdl. Election, 2004. Democrat. Address: 330 W Maryland Ave # 104 Phoenix AZ 85013-1340 *

MOGABGAB, ROSE-WARREN BERRYMAN, academic administrator, writer; b. Richmond, Va., Mar. 13, 1940; d. Maynard Warren Berryman and Bessie Virginia Edwards; m. William Joseph Mogabgab, July 15, 1988 (dec.); children: Robert Mogabgab Berryman, William Joseph Mogabgab Berryman. AB, Randolph-Macon Woman's Coll., 1962. From mgr. lab. Sch. Medicine to rsch. assoc. Tulane U., New Orleans, 1965—81, rsch. assoc. Sch. Medicine, 1981—92; freelance med. writer and cons. New Orleans, 1993—. Presenter in field. Contbr. articles to profl. jours. Recipient 25 Yr. Svc. award, Tulane U. Sch. Medicine, 1980, Civc award, Mayor New Orleans, 1982. Mem.: Women for a Better La., Randolph Macon Woman's Coll. Alumnae (pres. New Orleans chpt. 1990—2001), Kingsmill Yacht Club, Kappa Alpha Theta. Avocations: antiques, gardening, travel. Home: 1220 Brookhaven Park Pl NE Atlanta GA 30319

MOGEL, WILLIAM ALLEN, lawyer; b. NYC, Mar. 7, 1942; s. Harry H. and Therese M.; m. Judith; children: Elisabeth, Andrew. BA cum laude, Hobart Coll., 1963; LLB, U. Pa., 1966. Bar: D.C. 1967, Md. 1971. Ptnr. Saul Ewing, 2005. Adj. instr. Am. U., Washington, 1982—; active Washington Bd. Trade. Author: Transportation & Marketing of Natural Gas, 1985, 86, Natural Gas: Current Federal and State Developments, 1987; editor: Natural Gas Yearbook, 1988-92; co-editor: Energy Law & Transactions; editor-in-chief Energy Law Jour., 1980—; contbr. articles to profl. jours. Trustee Hobart Coll., 1983-88. Capt. U.S. Army, 1966-69. Mem. Fed. Energy Bar Assn. Home: 5812 Madaket Rd Bethesda MD 20816-3201 Office: Saul Ewing 1025 Thomas Jefferson Pl Washington DC 20007 Office Phone: 202-295-6612. Business E-Mail: wmogel@saul.com.

MOGENSEN, CHARLES RAY, JR., retired food service executive; b. Elizabeth, NJ, May 7, 1946; s. Charles Ray, Sr. and Helen Oakley (Holland) Mogensen; m. Linda Diane Friezer, Apr. 25, 1970; children: Charles Ray III, Jason C., Eric S., Lindsey H. Student, Middlesex County Vocat. Coll., 1972. Cert. food exec., lic. real estate agt. NJ. Chef St. Elizabeth Hosp., Elizabeth, N.J., 1969-70; dir. food svcs. Cornell Hall Conv. Ctr., Union, N.J., 1970-96; dir. food svc. Corrections Corp. Am., Elizabeth Detention Ctr., 1996—2006; ret., 2006. Pres. C.R.M. Food Enterprises, Ltd., Kenilworth, NJ, 1971—89; real estate agt. Real Estate Cons., Short Hills, NJ; owner C.R. Mogensen Antiques, Ltd., Red Bank, NJ; cons. in field. Author: (recipes) Escargots Without Shells, 1979 (citation merit, 1979). Mem. adv. bd. Episcopalian Program Homeless, Elizabeth, 1990, Union County Coalition Homeless, NJ, 1991; mem. Rep. Nat. Com., Washington, 1988. With USMC, 1964—68, Vietnam. Named N.Y. Dist. winner, Gen. Foods Corp., 1981; recipient cert. of Appreciation, Roselle Park (N.J.) First Aid Squad, 1986, award of Merit, USNR, 1990, citation and medal commemorating Vietnam War Svc., State of N.J. Mem.: VFW, Am. Correctional Food Svc. Assn., Internat. Food Svc. Exec. Assn. (pres. 1977, 1979, 1985, 1986, bd. dirs. 1989—91, Royal Order of Skillet 1987, Humanitarian award 1987, Disting. Svc. medal N.J. 2004, Fed. Exec. Bd. Disting. Svc. award 2004), Asia Soc., Masons, Am. Legion (cert. of appreciation 1999), Vets. Vietnam War (life). Avocations: antiques; coin collecting/numismatics, oriental art. Home: The Harbour Club 708 Sunshine Ct Parlin NJ 08859 E-mail: mogen708@verizon.net.

MOGG, JIMMY W., gas industry executive; b. Hydro, Okla., 1949; m. Freda Mogg; 2 children. B in Math., Southwestern Okla. State U., 1971; grad. advanced mgmt. program, Harvard U. With gas supply dept. Panhandle Ea. Pipe Line Co., Liberal, Kans., 1973—80; mgr. forcasting and ops. Panhandle Ea., Kansas City, 1980—86; gen. mgr. gas supply Trunkline Gas Co., Houston, 1986—88; gen. mgr. contracts and ops., gas supply Panhandle Ea., Trunkline, 1988; v.p. gas supply Panhandle Ea., Trunkline, Tex. Ea. Transmission Corp., 1989—91; sr. v.p. Panhandle Ea., 1991; pres. Centana Energy Corp., 1992—94; pres., CEO Duke Energy Field Svcs. LP, Denver, NC, 1994—99, chmn., pres., CEO, 1999—2004; group v.p. Duke Energy, Charlotte, NC, 2004—06, chief devel. officer, 2004—06, advisor to chmn., 2006; chmn. DCP Midstream Partners, 2005—. Chmn. bd. dirs. TEPPCO Ptnrs. LP, 1997—2005. Bd. dirs. Rocky Mountain chpt. Jr. Achievement. Mem.: Gas Processors Assn. (past pres.), Soc. Petroleum Engrs. Office: DCP Midstream Partners 370 17th St Ste 2775 Denver CO 80202 *

MOGGE, HARRIET MORGAN, educational association executive; b. Cleve. d. Russell VanDyke and Grace (Wells) Morgan; m. Robert Arthur Mogge (dec.); 1 child, Linda Jean. BME, Northwestern U.; postgrad., Ill. State U. Instr. piano, Evanston, Ill., 1954-58; instr. elem. music pub. schs., Evanston, 1959; editl. asst. archivist Summy-Birchard Co., Evanston, 1964-66, asst. to editor-in-chief, 1966-67, cons., 1968-69, ednl. dir., 1969-74, also historian, 1973-74; supr. vocal music jr. high sch., Watseka, Ill., 1967-68; asst. dir. profl. programs Music Educators Nat. Conf., Reston, Va., 1974-84, dir. meetings and convs., 1984-94, mgr. direct mktg. svc., 1981-89; sr. cons. Conv. Cons. Svc., 1993—2003, ret., 2003—. Mng. editor Am. Suzuki Jour., 1972-74, Gen. Music Today, 1987-91; mgr. display advt. Model T Times, 1971—2006; vice chair editl. bd. Exposition Mgmt., 1991-93. Active various cmty. drives; parish bd. clerk, United Christian Parish, 2001—; sec., bd. dirs. Reston Cmty. Orch., 2006-. Mem. Music Educators Nat. Conf., Am. Choral Dirs. Assn., In and About Chgo., Music Educators Assn. (bd. dirs.1973-74), Suzuki Assn. Ams. (exec. sec. 1972-74, Disting. Svc. award 1996), Internat. Assn. Exposition Mgmt. (cert., mem. edn. com. 1979-88, chmn. edn. com. 1985-87, bd. liaison edn. com. 1987-88, bd. dirs. Washington chpt. 1983-85, nat. bd. dirs. 1986-91, nat. v.p. 1989, nat. pres. 1990, Disting. Svc. award 1996), Bus. and Profl. Women's Club Watseka (bd. dirs. 1968-70), Antique Automobile Club (registrar ann. meeting 1961-86), Model T Ford Club Internat. (v.p. 1971-72, 76-77, pres. 1981, treas. 1983-87, bd. dirs. 1971-87), Mu Phi Epsilon, Kappa Delta (province pres. 1960-66, 72-76, regional chpts. dir. 1976-78, nat. dir. scholarship 1981-84). Republican. Presbyterian. Home and Office: 1919A Villaridge Dr Reston VA 20191-4824 Office Phone: 703-201-1281.

MOGK, JOHN EDWARD, law educator, association executive, consultant; b. Detroit, Feb. 10, 1939; s. Clifford Anthony and Evelyn Lenore (Paselk) M.; m. Lylas Heidi Good, Aug. 23, 1964; children: Marja, Tenley, Matthew. BBA, U. Mich., 1961, JD with distinction, 1964; diploma in comparative law, U. Stockholm, 1965. Bar: N.Y. 1966, Mich. 1970. Assoc. atty. Shearman & Sterling, NYC, 1964-68; mem. faculty Wayne State U. Sch. Law, 1968—, dir. grad. studies, 1990-95. Pres. MERRA Rsch. Corp., 1974-94; cons. econ. and urban devel., arbitrator; vis. prof. U. Utrecht, The Netherlands, 2000. Editor Michigan International Lawyer and Utilities Law Rev.; contbr. articles to profl. jours. Chmn. Mich. TOP Task Force, 1972; vice chmn. Mich. Constrn. Code Commn., 1973; mem. exec. com. Southeastern Mich. Coun. Govts., 1970; chmn. Detroit Sch. Boundary Commn., 1970, Downtown Detroit Vacant Bldg. Com., 1991-93; mem. Detroit Bd. Edn., 1970; mgr. Detroit Empowerment Zone Proposal, 1994; project exec. New Detroit Stadium, 1995; pres. Habitat for Humanity Detroit, 1999-2006. Named Outstanding Wayne State U. Assoc. Prof., 1971, Outstanding Wayne Law Sch. Prof., 1977, 83, 93, 97, 2003, Outstanding Young Man in Detroit, 1972, One of Ten Outstanding Young Men in U.S., 1973, One of Four Outstanding Vols. in U.S., 1974; recipient Presdl. citation Wayne State U., 1977, State of Mich., 1988, 94; Am.-Scandinavian fellow, 1965; vis. fellow U. Warwick, Eng., 1985-86. Mem. ABA, Mich. Bar Assn. (Outstanding Achievement award Internat. Law Sect. 2001). Home: 1000 Yorkshire Rd Grosse Pointe Park MI 48230-1432

MOGLEN, EBEN, law educator; b. New Haven, July 13, 1959; s. Sig and Helene (Rosenbaum) M. AB with High Honors, Swathmore Coll., Pa., 1980; MPhil, JD in History with Honors, Yale U., 1985, PhD with Distinction in History, 1993. Bar: NY 1988, US Supreme Ct., 1993. Programmer, analyst, programming language, R&D IBM Corp., San Jose, Calif., 1979—84, assoc. corp. counsel Armonk, NY, 1983; assoc. Cravath, Swaine & Moore, NY, 1984; law clk. to Hon. Judge Edward Weinfeld US Dist. Ct, So. Dist. NY, 1985-86; law clk. to Justice Thurgood Marshall US Supreme Ct., Washington, 1986-87; assoc. prof. law to prof. law Columbia U., NYC, 1987—94, prof. law, 1994—; founding dir., counsel, chmn. Software Freedom Law Ctr., NYC, 2005—. Mem., gen. counsel Free Software Found., 1993—2006; vis. prof., faculty of law Tel-Aviv U., 1991; vis. prof. U. Va. Law Sch., 1993, Harvard Law Sch., 1994—95; spkr. in field. Contbr. articles to profl. jours.; host of web blog emoglen.law.columbia.edu. Recipient Electronic Frontier Found. Pioneer award, 2003. Mem. ABA, Am. Soc. for Legal History, Phi Beta Kappa. Office: Columbia U Law Sch 435 W 116th St, Rm 642 New York NY 10027-7297 also: Software Freedom Law Ctr 1995 Broadway (68th St) Fl 17 New York NY 10023 Office Phone: 212-854-8382. Office Fax: 212-854-7946. E-mail: moglen@columbia.edu. *

MOGLEWER, SARAH ANNE, music educator; b. Canoga Park, Calif., July 12, 1958; d. Sidney and Edna Moglewer. MusB in Performance, Cath. U. Am., 1982, MM in Performance, 1984. Cert. tchr. music Nat. Bd. Profl. Tchg. Stds. Pvt. piano tchr., Torrance, Calif., 1987—2002, Prescott, Ariz., 2002—; substitute tchr. Prescott Schs. & tri-city area, 2002—. Recitalist, Calif., Ariz., Colo. Editor: (book) Etudes for Piano-Louise Farrenc, 2002; contbr. articles to profl. jours. Mem.: Music Tchrs. Assn. Calif., Ariz. Music Tchrs. Assn., Music Tchrs. Nat. Assn., Sigma Alpha Iota (sec. 1981).

MOGLIA, JOSEPH H., brokerage house executive; m. Amy Jardine; 4 children from previous marriage. BA, Fordham U., 1971; MA, U. Del., 1974. Def. coord. Dartmouth Coll. football team, 1981—83; with Merrill Lynch, 1983—97, head global fixed income inst. sales, head mcpl. div., sr. v.p., head investment performance & product group, 1997—2001; CEO Ameritrade Holding Corp., 2001—. Author: Perimeter Attack Offense, 1981. Bd. dir. Creighton Univ., Nat. Italian Am. Found., 2005—, AXA Fin., 2002—. Office: Ameritrade Holding Corp 4211 S 102nd St Omaha NE 68127-1031 Mailing: Ameritrade Holding Corp PO Box 2760 Omaha NE 68103-2760 Office Phone: 402-331-2744. Business E-Mail: jmoglia@ameritrade.com. *

MOGREN, PAUL ANDREW, librarian; b. Fort Collins, Colo., Aug. 31, 1950; s. Edwin W. and Arle Mae (Arnason) M.; m. Ann Marie Breznay, Aug. 16, 1980; 1 child, Christian Andrew. BA, Colo. State U., 1972; MA, U. Denver, 1973; PhD, U. Utah, 1980. Reference libr. Marriott Libr., U. Utah, Salt Lake City, 1973-82, head of reference, 1982-96, collection specialist, 1996—. Cons. Gov.'s Mansion Libr., Salt Lake City, 1995—, Dixie Coll. Libr., St. George, Utah, 1990; adj. prof. Emporia (Kans.) State U., 1996—; mem. Ogden Union Sta. Libr., 1997—. Mem. AAUP (pres. U. Utah chpt. 1986-89), ALA (coun. 1992-96, RUSA History Libr. of Yr. award 2000), Utah Libr. Assn. (pres. 1988-89). Avocations: gardening, travel. Office: U Utah Marriott Libr 295 S 15th East Salt Lake City UT 84112-0860 Business E-Mail: paul.mogren@utah.edu.

MOHAJER, DINEH, cosmetics company executive; b. Bloomfield Hills, Mich., Sept. 2, 1972; d. Reza and Shahnaz Mohajer. B in Pre-medicine, U. So. Calif. Founder, CEO Hard Candy, Inc., Beverly Hills, Calif., 1996—. Office: Hard Candy 729 Farad St Costa Mesa CA 92627-4304 *

MOHAMED, JOSEPH, SR., real estate broker, developer, farmer; b. Omar, W.Va., Mar. 19, 1928; s. Mose and Minnie Elizabeth (Martin) M.; m. Shirley Ida Medeiros; children: Joseph Jr., John W., James R., Leslie Louise. BBA Personnel, Sacramento State U., 1952; postgrad., U. Pacific, U. Calif., Davis, Am. River Coll. Farmer, 1949—; founder comml. trucking operation Calif., 1949-52; founder Mexican Co. of Agr. and Livestock Ltd., Ensenada, Baja, Calif., Mexico, 1953-57; owner Quintair, Inc., Calif., 1954—; contractor, real estate developer, 1949—; owner Joseph's Landscape Svc., Sacramento, 1952—, Joseph Mohamed Enterprises, 1971—. Pest control adviser, Calif., 1970—. Mem. Rep. Nat. Com., Rep. Presdl. Task Force, 1965—, Govs.' Emergency Drought Task Force, 1977, Civil Affairs Assn., Calif. Rental Assn., 1975—, Sacramento Apartment Assn., Calif. Apt. Assn., Nat. Apt. Assn.; dir. McClellan Aviation Museum Found., Sacramento County Sheriff's Mounted Posse, 1961—; pres. First Spiritual Enlightenment Ctr., 1994-. With US Army, 1946—48, col. USAR, 1978, ret. Decorated Legion of Merit; recipient Master Aviator Badge. Mem. Sacramento U. Alumni Assn., Sacramento State U. Horseman's Assn., Calif. State Horseman's Assn., Sacramento Metro. C. of C., Navy League of U.S., Res. Officer's Assn., Assn. of U.S. Army, Mil. Civil Affairs Assn., Sacramento Bd. Realtors, Calif. Assn. Realtors, Nat. Assn. Realtors, Masons, Shriners.

MOHAMMED, JABY, engineering educator; arrived in US, 2002; s. Thazhethudiyil M. and Laila Mohammed; m. Shama Korattiparambil, Dec. 25, 2002; 1 child, Jenna. BS in Mech. Engring., U. Kerala, India, 1997; PhD in Engring., U. Louisville, 2006. Project engr. NeST R&D Ctr., Cochin, 1998—2001; tchg. asst. U. Louisville, 2001—06; asst. prof. Morehead State U., Ky., 2006—. Mem.: SME (faculty advisor 2002, scholar 2003), IIE (life), Ky. Acad. Sci. (life), ASQ (life), NAIT (life), POMS (life), Informs (life), Golden Key Honor soc. (life). Achievements include design of new marerial innovation for die casting molds using laser cladding process. Home: 145 Lois Ln # 5 Morehead KY 40351 Office: Morehead State U 215 A Lloyd Cassity Bldg Morehead KY 40351 Home Phone: 502-262-4899; Office Phone: 606-783-2417. Home Fax: 606-783-5030. Business E-Mail: j.mohammed@moreheadstate.edu.

MOHAMMED, NAZR, professional basketball player; b. Sept. 5, 1977; BA, Univ. Ky., 1999. Center Phila. 76ers, Pa., 1999—2001, Atlanta Hawks, Ga., 2001—03, New York Knicks, NY, 2003—04, San Antonio Spurs, Tex., 2004—05. Achievements include member, NBA Championship Team. Office: San Antonio Spurs One SBC Ctr San Antonio TX 78219

MOHAMOUD, YUSUF MOHAMED, agricultural engineer; s. Mohamed Mohamoud Guled and Halima Younis; m. Kaha M. Barre, 1989. BSc, Somali Nat. U., Mogadishu, Somalia, 1981; M Agrl. Engring., U. Mo., Columbia, 1985; D Agrl. Engring. in Water Resources, U. Ill., Urbana-Champaign, 1989. Registered profl. engr., Va. Hydrologist Internat. Inst. Tropical Agr., Ibadan, Nigeria, 1990—93; water resources engr. Engring. Cons., Abidjan, Cote d'Ivoire, 1993—96; rsch. scientist U. Ariz., Tucson, 1996—99; environ. engr. Ga. Environ. Protection Divsn., Atlanta, 2000—02; rsch. hydrologist US EPA, Athens, Ga., 2003—. Cons. water resources engr., Atlanta, 1999—2000. Recipient Bronze medal, US EPA, 2005. Office: US EPA 960 College Rd Athens GA 30605 Home Phone: 770-495-0026; Office Phone: 706-355-8109. Office Fax: 706-355-8109. Business E-Mail: mohamoud.yusuf@epa.gov.

MOHAN, DINESH, research scientist; b. Bijnor, Uttar Predesh, India, July 4, 1968; s. Shur Vir Singh and Vidya Devi; m. Surekha Mohan, Feb. 9, 2001; 1 child, Ishan. MSc in Chemistry, U. Roorkee, India, 1990, PhD in Chemistry, 1994. Sr. rsch. fellow Indian Inst. Tech. Roorkee, U. Roorkee, 1993—95, rsch. assoc., 1995—97; vis. prof. U. San Luis Potosi, Mexico, 1997—97; postdoctoral rsch. assoc. dept. energy and geo-environ. engring. Pa. State U., State College, 1997—99; lectr. Ctr. Mining Environment Indian Sch. Mines, Dhanbad, Jharkhand, India, 2000—00; scientist Indsl. Toxicology Rsch. Ctr., Lucknow, 2000—. Contbr. articles to profl. jours. Mem.: Indian Network For Soil Contamination Rsch. (life). Hindu. Achievements include research in Acid Mine Drainage Treatment; development of low cost adsorbents from waste materials; research in Removal and recovery of valuable metals from wastewater; development of Low Cost Activated Carbons From Various Waste Materials; research in Pressure filtration behaviour of dispersed and floculated alumina salrries at high percent solids; development of adsorbent media for arsenic removal; research in Removal of VOCs using adsorption; Soil Remediation. Avocations: reading, writing, travel, cricket. Home: 4/41 2nd Fl Vivek Khand 4 Gomti Nagar Lucknow 226001 India Office: Indsl Toxicology Rsch Ctr Mahatama Gandhi Marg Post Box 80 Lucknow 226001 India Home Phone: 0091-522-303547; Office Phone: 0091-522-508916. Office Fax: 0091-522-228227;228471. Personal E-mail: dm_1967@hotmail.com.

MOHAN, JOHN J., lawyer; b. St. Louis, May 22, 1945; s. John Joseph and Virginia Loretta (Durkin) M.; m. Elaine Bronwyn Lipe, May 29, 1982; children: Bryn Elizabeth, John Burke. BS Indsl. Engring., St. Louis U., Sch. Engring. and Earth Scis., 1967; JD, St. Louis U., 1971. Bar: Mo. 1971, Ill. 1971, U.S. Dist. Ct. (we. dist.) Mo. 1971, U.S. Dist. Ct. (ea. dist.) Mo. 1980, U.S. Dist. Ct. (so. dist.) Ill. 1981, U.S. Ct. Appeals (8th cir.) 1987. Asst. prosecuting atty. St. Louis County, 1971-72; asst. cir. atty. St. Louis Cir. Atty's. Office, 1972-74; spl. asst. state's atty. St. Clair County Atty's. Office, Belleville, Ill., 1974—; assoc. Lashley, Caruthers, Theis, Rava & Hamel, St. Louis, 1979-80; ptnr. Schreiber, Tueth & Mohan, Clayton, Mo., 1981-83, Danis, Reid, Murphy, Tobben, Schreiber & Mohan, Ladue, Mo., 1983-87, Hinshaw & Culbertson, St. Louis, 1987-97, Blackwell, Sanders, Peper, Martin, St. Louis, 1998-2000, Tueth, Keeney, Cooper, Mohan & Jackstadt, P.C., 2000—; mcpl. judge City Wildwood, Mo., 2004—. Mem. U. Mo. Law Sch. Found. Scholarship. Mem. ABA, Am. Arbitration Assn. (cert. mediator, arbitrator 1988—), Ill. State Bar Assn., Mo. Bar, Bar Assn. Met. St. Louis, St. Clair County Bar, St. Louis County Bar, Def. Rsch. Inst., Mo. Orgn. Def. Lawyers, Pinnacle Arbitration and Mediation Svcs. (cert. mediator, arbitrator 1997—), Phi Delta Phi. Home: 529 Big Horn Basin Ct Wildwood MO 63011-4818 Office: Tueth Keeney Cooper Mohan Jackstadt PC Ste 600 34 N Meramec Clayton MO 63105

MOHAN, SAMEER VIJAY, lawyer; b. NYC, May 15, 1974; BA, U. Tex., Austin, 1996; JD, U. Houston Law Ctr., 1999. Bar: Tex. 1999. Assoc. Baker Hostetler, Houston. Bd. mem. West Tex. Dist. Export Coun., 2005. Alumni rels. editor: Houston Jour. Internat. Law, 1998—99, contbg. editor: Hosp. Contracts Manual. Named a Rising Star, Tex. Super Lawyers mag., 2006. Mem.: Houston Young Lawyers Assn., ABA, Houston Bar Assn., Brazil-Tex. C. of C. Office: Baker Hostetler 1000 Louisiana St Ste 2000 Houston TX 77002 Office Phone: 713-646-1309. E-mail: smohan@bakerlaw.com. *

MOHAN, TUNGESH NATH, television and film producer, film educator; b. Lucknow, India, Oct. 30, 1949; arrived in U.S., 1979; s. Bhola Shambu and Saraswati P. (Devi) Nath; m. Annette Gonsalves Mohan; 1 child, Lathika. BS, Kalyani U., India, 1969; diploma in Cinema, Film and TV Inst. India, Poona, 1972; MA, Andrews U., 1980. Prodr. Bombay TV, 1972-75, 77-79; asst. prof. Film and TV Inst. India, Poona, 1975-77; TV prodr. 700 Club, Virginia Beach, Va., 1980-82; prodr. spl. projects Christian Broadcasting Network, Virginia Beach, 1982-86, Christian Broadcasting Network Cable Prodns., Inc., Virginia Beach, 1986-87; dir. Internat. CBN Prodrs. Group, 1987-89, Internat. NorthStar Entertainment Group, LA, 1989-92; mgr. Adventist Comm. Network, Silver Spring, Md., 1992-93; pres. TriAngel Media Corp., Thousand Oaks, Calif., 1992-94; dir. Digital Video Ctr., Samford U., Birmingham, Ala., 2005—. Adj. prof. Film and TV Inst. India, Poona, 1975—79, Spicer Coll., Poona, 1975—79, Hampton U., Va., 1980—92; pres. Prodrs. Unit One, Virginia Beach, 1982—, L.I.F.E. Inc., 1993—; cons. Global Comm. Assocs., Virginia Beach, 1987—88, Global TV Syndication, 1998—; dir. Telecom. Ctr., Huntsville, Ala., 1998—2000. Prodr., dir.: (films) Even So, 1972; Dishantar, 1975 (cert. Proficiency, 1975); Raktajeevee, 1977 (Golden Lion award, 1977); (documentaries) Afghanistan: Under the Iron Claw, 1982; Here I Stand, 2001; In the Footsteps of Martin Luther, 2001; Revolution of Conscience, 2001; prodr., dir., writer: (films) U-Turn, 1973 (Garima award, 1973); exec. prodr.: Stand at Ease, 1989—90, A Father of Preachers, 2001; co-exec. prodr.: Rin Tin Tin K-9 Cop, 1988—89; prodr.: Touching the Supernatural, 1992, Midnight Cry, 1994, Master Control, 1994, The Way We Were, 1995, Bought at a Price, 1996, Hanged on a Twisted Cross, 1996 (Chris award for best film, Bronze medal for screenplay Columbus Film Festival, 1996), Inn Keeper, 1996, The Invitation, 1997, The Gift, 1997 (Bronze Plaque for 2d pl. Columbus Internat. Film Fest, 1997), (dir.): Reaalizing the Vision, 2001, The Hymnmaker, 2002, For One English Officer, 2002, The Dawning, 2002, Thank You, Mr. Hodges, 2003, The Invitation, 2003, Truth to Tell, 2003, Christianity & Islam: A Dialogue, 2004, The 51st State, 2006, Born With a Wooden Spoon, 2006, Life is Calling, 2007, Called, 2007. Mem.: NATAS, Dirs. Guild Am., Writers Guild Am., Lions. Mem. Seventh-Day Adventist. Avocation: Avocations: collecting stamps, music, camping, travel, tennis. Home Phone: 256-852-4054. E-mail: lifeincva@aol.com.

MOHANTY, DILLIP K., chemistry professor, researcher; b. Baripada, Orissa, India, Nov. 13, 1956; s. Nabakishore and Subarna Mohanty; m. Padmashree Roy-Choudhray, Sept. 17, 1988; children: Ankita, Arpita. BS, Ravenshaw Coll., Cuttack, India, 1974; MS, Indian Inst. Tech., Kharagpur, India, 1976, Diploma in Rubber Tech., 1977; MS, Stony Brook U., NY, 1979; PhD, Va. Tech, Blacksburg, 1983. Sr. rsch. scientist Air Products, Allentown, Pa., 1983—85; rsch. scientist Va. Tech, 1985—88; asst. prof. Ctrl. Mich. U., Mt. Pleasant, 1988—93, prof. chemistry, 1997—, assoc. prof., 1993—97. Rschr. Ctrl. Mich. U., 1988—. Donations to charitable orgns. Salvation Army, Doctors without Borders, Mt. Pleasant, 1989—2006. Decorated Army Rsch. Office, Mich., USN; grantee, Petroleum Rsch. Fund, Nat. Inst. of Health, Army Rsch. Office, State of Mich., USN, 1989, 1992, 2002, 2003, 2004, 2005, 2006, NIH. Mem.: Am. Soc. Microbiology, Am. Soc. Materials. Achievements include discovery of new reaction; vicarious Michael additions; patents for plasticization of poly (vinyl alcohol); cross linking of poly (ary ether phosphine oxides); patents pending for inert polymers; pegylation; vicarious Michael reaction; dendrimer cores; cross linking of poly(phenylene sulfide)s; polymeric vasodialtor. Avocations: gardening, reading, walking. Office: Ctrl Mich U Dow 254 Mount Pleasant MI 48859 Home Phone: 989-772-7207; Office Phone: 989-774-6445. Office Fax: 989-774-3883. Business E-Mail: mohan1dk@cmich.edu.

MOHAPATRA, SURYA N., laboratory executive; PhD in Med. Physics, U. London; MS electrical engring., Sambalpur Univ., India. Sr. v.p. Picker Internat., 1981—99; sr. v.p., COO Quest Diagnostics, Teterboro, NJ, 1999, pres., COO, 1999—2004, chmn., pres., CEO, 2004—. Bd. dirs. Vasogen Inc., 1999—. Contbr. articles to profl. jours. Mem.: Royal Coll. Surgeons Eng. (hon.). Achievements include patents in field. Office: Quest Diagnostics One Malcolm Ave Teterboro NJ 07608 *

MOHIELDIN, AHMED NADER, electrical engineer; b. Cairo, Feb. 23, 1974; arrived in US, 1999; s. Nader Mohieldin Rizk and Inas Hassan Abuzaid; m. Marwa Aly Mahmoud Aly, Sept. 24, 2003; 1 child, Abdelrahman Ahmed Nader. BS, Cairo U., 1996, MS, 1998; PhD in Elec. Engring., Tex. A&M U., 2003. Tchg. asst. Cairo U., 1996—98; rsch. asst. Tex. A&M U., Coll. Sta., Tex., 1999—2003; integrated circuits design engr. Tex. Instruments Inc., Dallas, 2003—. Reviewer Transactions on Cirs. and Sys., 2001—06. Contbr. articles to profl. jours. Mem.: IEEE. Achievements include patents pending for digital compensation of continuous-time sigma-delta converter; digital blockers detection for wireless receiver; patents for high frequency tunable filter. Home Phone: 972-234-5936; Office Phone: 214-480-3817. Personal E-mail: anader2000@yahoo.com.

MOHIUDDIN, SYED MAQDOOM, cardiologist, educator; b. Hyderabad, India, Nov. 14, 1934; came to US, 1961, naturalized, 1976; s. syed Nizamuddin and Amat-Ul-Butool Mahmoodi Mohiuddin; m. Ayesha Sultana Mahmoodi, July 16, 0961; children: Sameena J., Syed R., Kulsoom S. MB, BS, Osmania U., 1960; MS, Creighton U., Omaha, 1967; DSc, Laval U., Que., Can., 1970. Diplomate in internal medicine and cardiovasc. disease Am. Bd. Internal Medicine. Intern Altoona Gen. Hosp., Pa., 1961-62; resident in cardiology Creighton Meml. Hosp., also St. Joseph Hosp., Omaha, 1963-65, mem. staff, 1965—; prof. adjoint Laval U. Med. Sch., 1970; practice medicine specializing in cardiology Omaha, 1970—; prof. Creighton U. Med. Sch., 1977—, assoc. dir. div. cardiology, 1983-96; prof. pharmacy practice Creighton U. Sch. Pharmacy, 1986—, dir. divsn. cardiology, 1996—2007, assoc. chair for acad. affairs dept. medicine, 1998—2007, Richard W. Booth MD prof. cardiology, 2005—, chair dept. medicine, 2007—. Cons. Omaha VA Hosp. Rsch. fellow Med. Rsch. Coun. Can., 1968; grantee Med. Rsch. Coun. Can., 1970, NIH, 1973, 2000-03. Fellow ACP, Am. Coll. Cardiology (gov. for Nebr. 1987-90), Am. Coll. Clin. Pharmacology, Am. Coll. Chest Physicians; mem. AAAS, Am. Heart Assn. (fellow coun. clin. cardiology, bd. dirs. 1973-75), Am. Fedn. Clin. Rsch., Nebr. Heart Assn. (chmn. rsch. com. 1974-76, dir. 1973—), Gt. Plains Heart Com. (Nebr. rep. 1976-84, pres. 1977-78), N.Y. Acad. Scis., Nebr. Cardiovasc. Soc. (pres. 1980-81), Creighton Med. Assn. (v.p. 2005—). Democrat. Muslim. Home: 12531 Shamrock Rd Omaha NE 68154-3529 Office: Cardiac Ctr Creighton U 3006 Webster St Omaha NE 68131-2027 Office Phone: 402-280-4566. Business E-Mail: smm@cardiac.creighton.edu.

MOHLER, BRIAN JEFFERY, diplomat; b. Niskayuna, NY, May 28, 1948; s. Donald and Rosemary (Brown) M. BA, Johns Hopkins U., 1970, MA, 1972. Economist Congl. Rsch. Svc. Libr. of Congress, Washington, 1973-74; commd. fgn. svc. officer U.S. Dept. State, 1974, staff asst. Bur. Econ. Affairs Washington, 1974-76, economist Bur. Econ. Affairs, 1979-82, desk officer European cmty. affairs Bur. European Affairs, 1982-84, desk officer Japanese affairs Bur. East Asian and Pacific Affairs, 1984-86, dep. dir. of econs. for Japanese affairs Bur. East Asian and Pacific Affairs, 1993-95, dir. econ. sanctions policy Bur. Econ. Affairs, 1999-2001, dir. Japanese affairs Bur. East Asian and Pacific Affairs, 2001—03, sr. adviser for Iraq Econ. Reconstrn. Bur. Econ. Affairs, 2003—04, sr. insp. Office of the Insp. Gen., 2004—05; consul Am. Consulate Gen., Strasbourg, France, 1976-78; petroleum attache Am. Embassy, Riyadh, Saudi Arabia, 1986-88, counselor for econ. affairs, 1988-90, dep. chief of mission Abu Dhabi, United Arab Emirates, 1990-93; counselor for econ. affairs Am. Embassy, Tokyo, 1995-99; minister counselor econ. affairs Am. Embassy, Ottawa, Canada, 2005—. 2d lt. U.S. Army, 1972, capt. USAR, 1972-85. Recipient Superior Honor award Dept. of State, 1993, 98, 2003, 04, Meritorious Honor award, 1987, 2004, award Sec. of Transp., 1998. Mem.: Japan-Am. Soc. of Washington DC, Am. Fgn. Svc. Assn., Can. Club Ottawa, Sigma Nu. Roman Catholic. Home: 18 Maple Lane Ottawa ON K1M 1G7 Canada Office Phone: 613-688-5214. Personal E-mail: bjmohler@hotmail.com. Business E-Mail: mohlerbj@state.gov.

MOHLER, RICHARD ALBERT, JR., academic administrator, theologian; b. Lakeland, Fla., Oct. 9, 1959; s. Richard Albert Sr. and Janet Rae (Johnson) M.; m. Mary Ann Kahler, July 16, 1983; children: Mary Katherine, Christopher Albert. BA magna cum laude, Samford U., 1980; MDiv, So. Bapt. Theol. Sem., Louisville, 1983, PhD, 1989; postgrad., St. Meinrad Sch. Theology, 1985, Oxford U., Eng., 1986. Ordained min. So. Bapt. Ch. Pastor Union Grove Bapt. Ch., Bedford, Ky., 1982-87; asst. to pres., coord. found. support, dir. capital funding So. Bapt. Theol. Sem., Louisville, 1983-89, pres., 1993—; editor The Christian Index, Atlanta, 1989-93, prof. christian theology, 1996—, Joseph Emerson Brown prof. Christian theology, 2005—. Assoc. dir. The So. Sem. Found., 1983-89; rsch. fellow Ethics and Religious Liberty Commn., 1998—; bd. dirs. Focus on the Family; lectr. in field. Assoc. editor Preaching, 1985-93, contbg. editor, 1993—; gen. editor: The Gods of the Age of the God of the Ages?, 1993; editor-in-chief The So. Bapt. Jour. Theology, 1997—; columnist Religion News Svc., 1998—; sr. corr. World Mag., 1997—; mem. editl. bd. Salem Broadcasting, 1999—; host (radio programs) Truth On the Line, 2001—, The Albert Mohler Program; author daily Crosswalk Commentaries; contbr. articles to profl. jours. Pres., chmn. Coun. of Sem. Pres. of So. Bapt. Conv., 1996—, chmn., Greater Louisville Billy Graham Crusade, 2001. Named one of 40 Rising Evang. Leaders, Christianity Today, 1996, one of 96 Southerners to Watch, Atlanta Jour. and Constitution, 1996, one of 50 Young Leaders Under 40 years of age TIME Mag., one of Emerging Leaders in Edn. CHANGE Mag., 1998. Mem. Am. Acad. Religion, Soc. Biblical Lit., Evang. Theol. Soc., Evang. Philos. Soc., So. Bapt. Hist. Soc., Bapt. Pub. Rels. Assn., So. Bapt. Press Assn., Evang. Press Assn., Nat. Assn. Evangs., Ga. Bapt. Hist. Soc., Rotary Internat., Phi Kappa Phi, Omicron Delta Kappa. Achievements include being named one of 50 young leaders under 40 years of age TIME Mag. Office: So Bapt Theol Sem 2825 Lexington Rd Louisville KY 40280-0001 Home Phone: 502-897-4121; Office Phone: 502-897-4121. Personal E-mail: mail@albertmohler.com. Business E-Mail: presoffice@sbts.edu, mohler@sbts.edu.

MOHLER, RONALD RUTT, electrical engineering educator; b. Ephrata, Pa., Apr. 11, 1931; s. David Wealand and Elizabeth (Rutt) M.; m. Nancy Alice Strickler, May 6, 1950; children: Curtis Gene, Pamela Louise, Susan Lynn, Anita Marie, John Scott, Andrew Thomas, Jennifer Lee, Lisa Nancy. BS (scholarship), Pa. State U., 1956; MS, U. So. Calif., 1958; PhD, U. Mich., 1965. Designer, trainee Textile Machine Works, Rockwell Internat. Corp., Reading, Pa., 1949-56; staff mem. Hughes Aircraft Co., Culver City, Calif., 1956-58, Los Alamos Sci. Lab., 1958-65; asso. prof. elec. engring. U. N.Mex., Albuquerque, 1965-69; prof. elec. engring./aerospace, mech. and nuclear engring. U. Okla., 1969-72, prof., chmn. info. and computing scis., 1970-72; dir. Systems Research Center, 1969-72; adj. prof. elec. engring. and nuclear engring. U. N.Mex., Los Alamos Grad. Center, 1959-65; cons. Sandia Corp., Albuquerque, 1966-69, Aerojet-Gen. Corp., Sacramento, 1966; vis. assoc. prof. system sci. UCLA, 1968-69; cons. community health project OEO, Oklahoma City, 1970-71; prof. elec. and computer engring. Oreg. State U., Corvallis, 1972-98, prof. emeritus, 1998—, head dept., 1972-79, 90; pres. Pace Tech., Inc., 1982-97. Vis. prof. U. Rome, 1973, 75, Imperial Coll., London, 1978-79, U.S. Naval Postgrad. Sch., 1983-85, Australian Nat. U., 1988, Sydney U., 1995, 98; cons. Optimization Software, L.A., 1973—, Bonneville Power Adminstrn., 1975—, Internat. Inst. Applied Systems Analysis, 1988—. Author: Optimal Control of Nuclear Reactors, 1970, Bilinear Control Processes, 1973, Nonlinear Systems: Dynamics and Control, vol. 1, 1991, Applications to Bilinear Control, vol. II, 1991, Disease Dynamics, 1993; editor: Theory and Application of Variable Structure Systems, 1972, Variable Structure Systems with Application to Biology and Economics, 1975, Recent Developments in Variable Structure Systems, Economics and Biology, 1979, Nonlinear Time Series and Signal Processing, 1988, assoc. editor Annals of Nuclear Energy, 1973-97; contbr. jours. Chmn. St. Stephens Sch. Bd., Norman, 1970-72. Recipient NATO award, 1979; rsch. grantee NSF, 1966-99, Sandia Labs., 1966-68, 96-97, ONR, 1981-92, NASA, EPRI, BPA, 1990-97; AEC fellow, 1961-65, Hughes fellow, 1956-58; Acad. Sci. exch. scientist to USSR and China, 1980, US-CIS (USSR) Commn. on Engring. Edn., 1991—. Fellow IEEE (life, local chmn. 1975); mem. Control System Soc., Sigma Xi, Tau Beta Pi, Pi Tau Sigma. Democrat.

MOHLER, STANLEY ROSS, preventive medicine physician, educator; b. Amarillo, Tex., Sept. 30, 1927; s. Norton Harrison and Minnie Alice (Ross) M.; m. Ursula Luise Burkhardt, Jan. 24, 1953; children: Susan Luise, Stanley Ross, Mark Hallock. BA, MA, U. Tex., 1953, MD, 1956. Diplomate Am. Bd. Preventive Medicine. Intern USPHS Hosp., San Francisco, 1956-57; med. officer Center Aging Research, NIH, Bethesda, Md., 1957-61; dir. Civil Aeromed. Rsch. Inst., FAA, Oklahoma City, 1961-66, chief aeromed. applications divsn. Washington, 1966-78; prof., vice chmn. dept. community medicine, dir. aerospace medicine Wright State U. Sch. Medicine, Dayton, Ohio, 1978—. Rsch. assoc. prof. preventive medicine and pub. health U. Okla. Med. Sch., 1961—; vice-chmn. Am. Bd. Preventive Medicine, 1978—, sec.-treas., 1980—. Co-editor: Space Biology and Medicine (5 vols.), 1995 (Life Scis. Book award Internat. Acad. Astronautics); contbr. articles to profl. jours. Bd. dirs. Sr. Citizens Assn. Oklahoma City, 1962—, Flying Physicians Assn., 1961—. Served with AUS, 1946-48. Recipient Gail Borden Rsch. award, Boothby award Aerospace Med. Assn., 1966, FAA Meritorious Svc. award, 1974, Cecil A. Brownlow Publ. award Flight Safety Found., 1998, Marie Marvingt award French Soc. Aerospace Medicine and Aerospace Med. Assn., 2006; co-recipient Life Scis. Book award in space, biology and medicine Internat. Acad. Astronautics, 1995. Fellow Geriatrics Soc., Aerospace Med. Assn. (pres. 1983, Harry G. Moseley award 1974, Lyster award 1984, Louis H. Bauer Founders award 1998), Am. Coll. Preventive Medicine, Gerontol. Soc.; mem. AMA, Aircraft Owners and Pilots Assn. (Sharples award 1984, Hubertus Strughold award 1991), Alpha Omega Alpha. Home: 6539 Reigate Rd Dayton OH 45459-3214 Office: Wright State U Sch Medicine PO Box 927 Dayton OH 45401-0927 Office Phone: 937-775-1400.

MOHLING, CHARLOTTE, middle school educator; BA in Home Econ. Edn., ND State Univ. Tchr. Wessington Springs (SD) Sch. Dist., 1975—. Bd. visitors ND State Univ. Named ESA Region 3 Tchr. of Yr., 2007, SD Tchr. of Yr., 2007; named to USA 2004 All-USA Tchr. Team; recipient Wessington Springs Disting. Svc. award (three times). Mem.: Nat. Coalition of Family and Consumer Sci., Assn. Edn. Comm. and Tech. Project, Assn. Career and Technical Edn. (pres., Family & Consumer Sci. Divsn.). Office: Wessington Springs Sch Dist 301 Dakota North PO Box 449 Wessington Springs SD 57382 Business E-Mail: charlotte.mohling@k12.sd.us. *

MOHN, LOUIS, publishing executive; b. 1956; married; 2 children. BA, Miami Univ., Oxford, Ohio. Acct. mgr., dir. mktg. McGraw-Hill Cos., Pitts.; various sr. level positions including v.p. sales BusinessWeek (a McGraw-Hill pub.), NYC; sr. v.p. Real Names Corp.; pres. consumer auto group Primedia pub., NYC, 2001—06; pub. Playboy mag., NYC, 2006—; and v.p., pub. group Playboy Enterprises, NYC, 2006—. Office: Playboy Enterprises 730 Fifth Ave New York NY 10019 Office Phone: 212-261-5000.

MOHN, MELVIN PAUL, anatomist, educator; b. Cleve., June 19, 1926; s. Paul Melvin and Julia (Jacobik) M.; m. Audrey Faye Lonergan, June 28, 1952; children— Shorey Faye, Andrew Paul AB, Marietta Coll., 1950; Sc.M., Brown U., 1952, PhD in Biology, 1955. Instr. SUNY Downstate Med. Ctr., Bklyn., 1955-59, asst. prof., 1959-63; asst. prof. anatomy U. Kans. Sch. Medicine, Kansas City, 1963-65, assoc. prof., 1965-72, prof., 1972-89, prof. emeritus, 1989—. Cons. Nat. Med. Audiovisual Ctr., Atlanta, 1972; vis. lectr. U. Miami Sch. Medicine, Fla., 1966. Bd. dirs. U. Kans. Med. Ctr. Credit Union, 1968-77, Kansas City Youth Symphony, 1972-77; mem. U.S. Pony Club, 1964-71, Med. Arts Symphony, 1965-71, 90—, Spring Hill Chorale, 1990-96, Spring Hill Hist. Soc., 1997—. Served with USN, 1944-46, PTO. McCoy fellow, 1950, Arnold biology fellow, 1954 Fellow AAAS; mem. Am. Soc. Zoologists, Am. Assn. Anatomists, Am. Inst. Biol. Sci., Masons, Lions, Rotary, Ruritan, Olathe Trail Riders, Phi Beta Kappa, Sigma Xi, Beta Beta Beta. Republican. Methodist. Home: Yankee Bit Farm 23595 W 223rd St Spring Hill KS 66083-4029 Office: U Kans Med Ctr Dept Anatomy 39th and Rainbow St Kansas City KS 66103

MOHON, EARLENE MANN, counselor; b. Jackson, Tenn., Sept. 22, 1939; d. German Earl and Lillie Frances (Graves) Mann; m. Robert Troy Mohon, Apr. 21, 1961; children: David, Chad. BS, Miss. U. for Women, 1960; MEd in Counseling and Guidance, Miss. Coll., 1968; student, Miss. State U., U. So. Miss., E. Tex. U., Stephen Austin U., So. Methodist U., U. Ala., Birmingham. Tchr. Natchez Pub. Schs., Miss., 1960-61, Leesville Pub. Schs., La., 1961-62, Chapel Hill Pub. Schs., Tex., 1962-63, Judson Pub. Schs., Longview, Tex., 1963-65, Jackson Pub. Schs., Miss., 1965-69; substitute tchr. Mountain Brook Pub. Schs., Ala., 1981-83; counselor Birmingham City Schs., Ala., 1987—2003; ret. Recipient citation for drug free program Mayor of Birmingham, citation for drug free progam in elem. sch. Birmingham Sch. Bd. Mem. NEA, Am. Assn. for Counseling and Devel., Ala. Assn. for Counseling and Devel., Ala. Edn. Assn., Birmingham Edn. Assn., Chi Sigma Iota (sponsor Just Say No Club Ala., 1989), Pi Tau Chi. Republican. Baptist. Avocations: painting, needlecrafts. Home: 3516 Crest Brook Rd Birmingham AL 35223-1510 Office: 3136 Norwood Blvd Birmingham AL 35234-2123

MOHR, ANTHONY JAMES, judge; b. LA, May 11, 1947; s. Gerald Leonard and Rita Lenore (Goldstein) Mohr. BA in Govt. cum laude with honors, Wesleyan U., 1969; JD, Columbia U., 1972; diploma with honors, Internat. Faculty for Comparative Law, 1975. Bar: Calif. 1972, US Dist. Ct. (ctrl. dist.) Calif. 1973, US Ct. Appeals (9th cir.) 1974, DC 1976, US Supreme Ct. 1981. Law clk. to judge US Dist. Ct. (ctrl. dist.) Calif., 1972-73; assoc. Alschuler Grossman, 1973-75; pvt. practice LA, 1976-94; judge LA Mcpl. Ct., 1994-97, LA Superior Ct., 1997—. Faculty atty. asst. tng. program UCLA, 1982—97, bd. dirs. internat. student ctr., 1986—2007; bd. dirs. Performing Tree, 1997—2002. Mem. editl. bd. Calif. Bar Jour., 1979—80, LA Lawyer Mag., 1989—94; contbr. articles to profl. jours. Mem. nat. adv. coun. Ctr. Study of Presidency, 1974—99; del. White House Conf. Youth, 1971; faculty Ctr. Jud. Edn. and Rsch., 1997—; bd. dirs. Pacific SW Anti-Defamation League, 2007—; mem. LA Dist. Atty.'s Adv. Coun., 1976—82; hearing officer LA County Employees Ret. Assn., 1986—94. Mem.: ABA, LA County Bar Assn., Am. Judicature Soc. (bd. dirs. 1982—83), Barristers Beverly Hills Bar Assn. (pres. 1979—80), Assn. Bus. Trial Lawyers (bd. govs. 2001—03), Beverly Hills Bar Assn. (bd. govs. 1975—80, chmn. litig. sect. 1983—85, chair resolutions com. 1991—92, ex officio bd. dirs. 1998—99, 2002—, Disting. Svc. award 1992), Calif. Judges Assn. (mem. ethics com. 2001—04), Phi Beta Kappa, Phi Delta Phi. Office: LA Superior Ct 600 S Commonwealth Ave Los Angeles CA 90005 Office Phone: 213-351-8590. Business E-Mail: amohr@lasuperiorcourt.org.

MOHR, BENJAMIN JOHN, engineering educator; s. John Orlando and Barbara Jane Mohr; m. Kathryn Elizabeth Larson, July 5, 2003. BS in Civil Engring., U. Del., Newark, 2001; MS in Civil Engring., Ga. Inst. Tech., Atlanta, 2002, PhD, 2005. EIT Del., 1997. Asst. prof. Tenn. Technol. U., Cookeville, 2005—. ASCE faculty advisor Tenn. Technol. U., Cookeville, 2006—. Reviewer: Cement and Concrete Rsch. Recipient Ralph E. Powa Jr. Faculty Enhancement award, Oak Ridge Associated Univs., 2007, Sigma Xi award, Tenn. Technol. U., 2007; grantee, NSF, 2006—, Fed. Hwy. Adminstrn., 2006—; Pres. fellow, Ga. Inst. Tech., 2002—05. Mem.: ASCE (corr.; reviewer Jour. Materials in Civil Engring.), Am. Soc. Engring. Edn., Internat. Union Labs. and Experts in Constrn. Materials, Sys. and Sturctures (corr.), Am. Ceramic Soc. (corr.; cements divsn.), Am. Concrete Inst. (corr.), Chi Epsilon (life), Tau Beta Pi (life), Sigma Xi (life). Achievements include invention of wood-derived materials for internal curing of cement-based materials. Office: Tennessee Technological University 1020 Stadium Dr Cookeville TN 38505-0001 Office Phone: 931-372-3546. Office Fax: 931-372-6239. Business E-Mail: bmohr@tntech.edu.

MOHR, CHRISTINA, retired economist; b. San Diego, Calif., June 1, 1949; d. Lloyd Crowell and Joan Watkins, Oliver Watkins (Stepfather); m. Peter Joseph Mohr, July 13, 1989; stepchildren: Robert, Tracie 1 child, Oliver Wise. BS in Polit. Sci, U. Pa., Phila., 1971; MA in Internat. Affairs, George Washington U., Washington, DC, 1979; PhD in Econs., U. Md., College Park, 1993. Cons. World Bank, Washington, 1982; analyst sci. resource Nat. Sci. Found., Washington, 1983—86, speech writer for dir., 1987—93; sci. diplomacy fellow US Agy. Internat. Devel., Washington, 1994—95; sr. analyst Nat. Sci. Found., Washington, 1996—2001; ret., 2001. Commr. People with Disabilities Commn., Montgomery County, Md., 1994—96. Home: 2932 Woodstock Ave Silver Spring MD 20910 Personal E-mail: mohr@nist.gov.

MOHR, JAY, comedian, actor; b. Verona, NJ, Aug. 23, 1970; m. Nicole Chamberlain, 1998 (div. 2004); 1 child, Jackson; m. Nikki Cox, Dec. 29, 2006. Actor: (films) For Better or Worse, 1996, Jerry Maguire, 1996, The Brave Little Toaster to the Rescue, 1997, Picture Perfect, 1997, Suicide Kings, 1997, Paulie, 1998, Small Soldiers, 1998, Jane Austen's Mafia!, 1998, Playing By Heart, 1998, 200 Cigarettes, 1999, Go, 1999, Cherry Falls, 2000, Pay It Forward, 2000, Speaking of Sex, 2001, The Adventures of Pluto Nash, 2002, Simone, 2002, Seeing Other People, 2004, Are We There Yet?, 2005, King's Ransom, 2005, Even Money, 2006, The Groomsmen, 2006, Lonely Street, 2006; (TV films) The Barefoot Executive, 1995, Olive, the Other Reindeer, 1999, Black River, 2001, Community Service, 2006, A Salute to the Troops and USO, 2006, Christmas Do-Over, 2006; (TV series) Saturday Night Live, 1993—95, Local Heroes, 1995—96, The Jeff Foxworthy Show, 1996, From the Earth to the Moon, 1998, Ghost Whisperer, 2006; guest appearances (TV series) Action, 1999, The Simpsons, 2000, Nights Visions, 2001, Scrubs, 2003, Fastlane, 2003, CSI: Miami, 2003, The West Wing, 2004, Las Vegas, 2005, Family Guy, 2000, 2005. Mailing: c/o NY Entertainment Ste 2010 1776 Broadway New York NY 10019 E-mail: jay@jaymohr.com. *

MOHR, JAY PRESTON, neurologist, educator; b. Mar. 5, 1937; s. John G. and Marguerite F. Mohr; m. Joan L. Seal, Mar. 10, 1962; children: Thea, Gregory. AB, Haverford Coll., 1958; MS, MD, U. Va., 1963. Diplomate Am. Bd. Neurology and Psychiatry. Intern then asst. resident Mary Imogene Bassett Hosp., Cooperstown, NY, 1963-65; asst. resident N.Y. Neurol. Inst., Columbia-Presbyn. Med. Ctr., NYC, 1965-66; instr. neurology Johns Hopkins U. Med. Sch., U. Md. Med. Sch., 1969-71; assoc. neurologist Mass. Gen. Hosp., Boston, 1972-78; asst. prof. Harvard U. Med. Sch., 1972-78; prof. neurologi, chmn. dept. U. South Ala. Med. Sch., Mobile, 1978-83; Sciarra prof. clin. neurology Columbia U. Coll. Physicians & Surgeons, NYC, 1983—. Dir. cerebrovascular research N.Y. Neurol. Inst., N.Y.C., 1983—; dir. Doris and Stanley Tananbaum Stroke Ctr., 2003—. Contbr. articles to med. jours. Mag. M.C., U.S. Army, 1969-72. Neurology fellow Mass. Gen. Hosp., 1966-69. Fellow Am. Acad. Neurology; mem. Am. Neurol. Assn., Am. Heart Assn. (Stroke coun.), Sigma Xi. Democrat. Mem. Soc. Of Friends. Office: Doris & Stanley Tananbaum Stroke Ctr NY Neurol Inst 710 W 168th St New York NY 10032-2603 also: Presbyn Hosp Columbia-Presbyn Med Ctr New York NY 10032-3784 Office Phone: 212-305-8033. Business E-Mail: jpm10@columbia.edu.

MOHR, JOHN LUTHER, biologist, environmental consultant; b. Reading, Pa., Dec. 1, 1911; s. Luther Seth and Anna Elizabeth (Davis) M.; m. Frances Edith Christensen, Nov. 23, 1939; children: Jeremy John, Christopher Charles. AB in Biology, Bucknell U., 1933; student, Oberlin Coll., 1933-34, Marine Biol. Lab., Woods Hole, Mass., 1934; PhD in Zoology, U. Calif., Berkeley, 1939; postgrad., Am. U., 1963. Research asso. Pacific Islands Research, Stanford, 1942-44; rsch. assoc. Allan Hancock Found., U. So. Calif., 1944-46, asst. prof., 1946-47, asst. prof. dept. biology, 1947-54, asso. prof., 1954-57, prof., 1957-77; chmn. dept., 1960-62; prof. emeritus, 1977—; vis. prof. summers U. Wash. Friday Harbor Labs., 1956, '57. Rsch. assoc. history and philosophy of sci., NSF, Am. U., 1963, vertebrate zoology Natural History Mus., Los Angeles County, 1996-2003; marine borer and pollution surveys harbors So. Calif. Dept. of Fish and Game, 1948-51, arctic marine biol. rsch., 1952-71; chief marine zool. group U.S. Antarctic rsch. ship Eltanin in Drake Passage, 1962, in South Pacific sector, 1965. Mem. Biol. Stain Commn., 1948-80, trustee, 1971-80, emeritus trustee, 1981—, v.p., 1976-80; bd. dirs. Calif. Natural Areas Coord. Coun., 1981-90. Guggenheim fellow, 1957-58. Fellow AAAS (coun. 1964-73, Sr. Scientists and Engrs. Nat. Network), So. Calif. Acad. Scis., Sigma Xi (life, exec. com. 1964-67, 68, 69, chpt.-at-large bd. 1968-69); mem. Marine Biol. Assn. Eng. (life). Achievements include research in problems with American English leading to dyslexia. Home: 3819 Chanson Dr Los Angeles CA 90043-1601 Office Phone: 323-295-5664. Personal E-mail: jmohr10000@aol.com.

MOHR, LAWRENCE CHARLES, physician; b. S.I., NY, July 8, 1947; s. Lawrence Charles Sr. and Mary Estelle (Dawsey) M.; m. Linda Johnson, June 14, 1970; 1 child, Andrea Marie. AB with highest honors, U. N.C., 1975, MD, 1979. Diplomate Am. Bd. Internal Medicine. Commd. 2d lt. U.S. Army, 1967, advanced through grades to col., 1989; med. intern Walter Reed Army Med. Ctr., Washington, 1979-80, resident in medicine, 1980-82, chief resident, 1982-83, attending physician, 1984-86, pulmonary fellow, 1986-87; command surgeon 9th Inf. Div., Ft. Lewis, Wash., 1983-84; med. cons. Madigan Army Med. Ctr., Tacoma, 1983-84; White House physician Washington, 1987-93; asst. prof. medicine Uniformed Svcs. U. of the Health Scis., Bethesda, Md., 1984-91; assoc. prof. medicine Uniformed Svcs. U. Health Scis., Bethesda, Md., 1991-94; assoc. clin. prof. medicine George Washington U., Washington, 1990-94; prof. medicine Med. U. S.C., Charleston, 1994—, dir. environ. bioscis. program, 1995—. Attending physician Med. U. Hosp., Charleston, 1994—, Charleston Meml. Hosp., 1994—; mem. Working Group on Disability in U.S. Presidents, 1995—. Editor: International Case Studies in Risk Assessment and Magagement, 1997, Biomarkers, Medical and Workplace Applications, 1998; contbr. articles to profl. jours. and books. Bd. dirs. Internat. Lung Found., Washington; mem. adv. bd. Nat. Mus. Health and Medicine, Washington; mem. sci. adv. bd. Consortium in Environ. Risk Evaluation; prin. investigator Consortium in Molecular Epidemiology and Biomarker Rsch. Decorated Silver Star, Bronze Star with 2 V devices and 3 oak leaf clusters, Purple Heart, Meritorious Svc. medal with oak leaf cluster, Air medal, Army Commendation medal with oak leaf cluster, D.S.M.; recipient Erskine award Walter Reed Army Med. Ctr., 1982; named Outstanding Med. Resident, 1982. Fellow ACP, Am. Coll. Chest Physicians; mem. AMA, Army and Navy Club, Order Mil. Med. Merit, Harbour Club, Phi Beta Kappa. Episcopalian. Avocations: mountain climbing, skiing. Home: 673 Lake Francis Dr Charleston SC 29412-4345 Office: Med U S C Environ Bioscis Program 171 Ashley Ave Charleston SC 29425-0001

MOHR, MICHAEL ARTHUR, lawyer; b. 1950; BSME, Tex. A&M Univ.; JD, Georgetown Univ., 1977. Bar: Mich. 1977. V.p., gen. counsel Alticor Inc. Office: Alticor Inc Legal Dept 7575 E Fulton Rd Ada MI 49355 Office Phone: 616-787-8457. Office Fax: 616-787-4000.

MOHR, ROGER JOHN, retired advertising agency executive; b. Milw., Sept. 8, 1931; s. Reinhold and Clara (Meissner) M.; m. Pauline Spicuzza, Oct. 18, 1958; children: Gregory, Mary Margaret, Kristin, Thomas, Kathleen. BS in Speech, Marquette U., 1953; postgrad. radio and TV, Northwestern U., 1955-56. Staff announcer radio sta. WBKB, West Bend, Wis., 1952, WCAN, Milw., 1952-54; with Arthur Meyerhoff Assos., Inc., Chgo., 1956-80, pres., 1965-80, BBDO, Chgo., 1980-82, chmn., 1982-90, vice chmn. internat., 1991-93; ret., 1993. Chmn. Lake Bluff (Ill.) Plan Commn., 1972-75; mem. Lake Forest (Ill.) Plan Commn., 1994-2000, chmn., 1999-2000; bd. dirs. Chgo. City Ballet, 1982-84, Off the Street Club, 1976-78; mem. adv. coun. Marquette U. Sch. Comm., 1993-99; alderman Lake Forest City Coun., 2000-06; mem. Lake Forest Sr. Resources Commn., 2006—. Served with AUS, 1954-55. Mem. Am. Assn. Advt. Agys. (chmn. Chgo. coun. 1966-67, sec., treas., nat. bd. dirs. 1976-77), Evans Scholars Alumni Assn. (pres. 1964-65), Western Golf Assn. (bd. dirs. 1980-2000, v.p. 1994-2000, trustee 2000—), Knollwood Club (bd. govs. 1980-85, 89-92), Tavern Club (bd. govs., v.p. 1988-94). Home: 2000 Knollwood Rd Lake Forest IL 60045-1137 Personal E-mail: rjpmmohr@sbcglobal.net.

MOHRAZ, ALI, engineering educator; b. Tehran, Iran, May 16, 1974; s. Behzad Mohraz and Mahram Dorri. BSc in Chem. Engring., Azad U., Tehran, Iran, 1996; M in Chem. Engring., CUNY, 1999; PhD, U. Mich., Ann Arbor, 2004. Rsch. assoc. U. Ill., Urbana-Champaign, 2004—06; asst. prof. U. Calif., Irvine, 2006—. Rackham fellow, U. Mich., 2003—04. Mem.: AIChE, Am. Chem. Soc., Materials Rsch. Soc. Office: University of California 916 Engineering Tower Irvine CA 92697 Home Phone: 949-466-5667; Office Phone: 949-824-2028. Office Fax: 949-824-2541. Personal E-mail: amohraz@gmail.com. E-mail: mohraz@uci.edu.

MOHRAZ, JUDY JOLLEY, foundation administrator; b. Houston, Oct. 1, 1943; d. John Chesler and Mae (Jackson) Jolley; m. Bijan Mohraz; children: Andrew, Jonathan. BA, Baylor U., 1966, MA, 1968; PhD, U. Ill., 1974. Lectr. history Ill. Wesleyan U., 1972-74; asst. prof. history So. Meth. U., Dallas, 1974-80, coord. women's studies, 1977-81, assoc. prof. history, 1980-94, asst. provost, 1983-88, assoc. provost for student academics, 1988-94; pres. Goucher Coll., Towson, Md., 1994-2000, Virginia G. Piper Charitable Trust, Scottsdale, Ariz., 2000—. Cons. Ednl. Testing Svc., Princeton, NJ, 1984-93, Nat. Park Svcs., Seneca Falls, NY, 1992-93; bd. dirs. Balt. Equitable Soc., 1996-00, The Assocs. First Capital, 1999-00, Coun. Foundations, 2005-; bd. visitors US Naval Acad., 1996-01. Trustee St. Mark's Sch. Tex., 1993-94; adv. bd. U. Tex. Southwestern Med. Sch., 1992-94; active Leadership Dallas, 1994; bd. dirs. Nat. Assn. Ind., The Balt. Cmty. Found., Coun. of Founds., 2005—; pres. Ariz. Grantmakers Forum, 2003-05; mem. Ariz. State Sch. Readiness Bd., 2003-07; bd. dirs. Greater Phoenix Leadership, 2005—. Recipient Disting. Alumni award Baylor U., 1993; named Woman of Merit, Omicron Delta Kappa, 1993. Office: Virgina G Piper Charitable Trust 6720 N Scottsdale Rd Ste 350 Scottsdale AZ 85253 Home Phone: 602-957-9433; Office Phone: 480-948-5853. Business E-Mail: jmohraz@pipertrust.org.

MOHRFELD, RICHARD GENTEL, marketing professional; b. Camden, NJ, Dec. 30, 1945; s. Herbert Henry and Elizabeth Weldon (Gentel) M.; m. Ann Bacon, June 20, 1971 (div. 1975); m. Janice Lee Strickland, July 1, 1978; children: Kathryn Elizabeth, Christopher Hall. BSc in Geology, Dickinson Coll., 1971. Staff geologist Temple U., Phila., 1971-74; pres. Mohrfeld Inc., Collingswood, NJ, 1974—2002; sr. mktg. exec. Quest Environ. & Enging. Svcs., Inc., Clinton, 2002—05; environ. specialist Salem County Health Dept., 2006—. Bd. dirs. South Jersey Savs. & Loan Assn., Turnersville, N.J., 1984-2000. Bd. dirs. Boy Scouts Am., Camden County, N.J., 1985—; trustee Knight Park Trustees, Collingswood, 1986-2006, Health Care Support Found., Inc., 1994-2006. Sgt. USAF, 1969-71. Mem. ASHRAE, Air Conditioning Contractors Am. (pres. 1986-88), Fuel Mchts. Assn. N.J. (pres. 1992-94), Rotary (pres. Collingswood 1980-81). Episcopalian. Avocations: travel, photography. Home and Office: 314 Auburn Rd Pilesgrove NJ 08098-2602 Office Phone: 856-935-7510. Personal E-mail: m-fuel@comcast.net.

MOHRMAN, HENRY JOE, JR., lawyer, investment manager; b. St. Louis, Jan. 28, 1948; s. Henry Joseph and Mavis Claire (Lynch) M.; m. Mary Beth Mohrman, Aug. 26, 1969; children: Aaron Henry, Anna Rose. BA, Yale U., 1969; JD, U. Chicago, 1973. Bar: Mo. 1973, Ill. 1974, U.S. Supreme Ct. 1997. Assoc. Greenfield & Davidson, St. Louis, 1973-76; asst. gen. counsel LaBarge, Inc., St. Louis, 1976-77; tax mgr. Ernst & Young, St. Louis, 1977-81; pvt. practice St. Louis, 1982—. Gen. counsel Miss. Valley Equipment Co., St. Louis, 1982—, MKT Mfg., Inc., St. Louis, 1986—, Ronald Coase Inst., 2000—, Whisler Farms LLC, 2002—; prin. Mohrmanlaw LC, 2004—. Mem. ABA, U. Chicago Law Sch. Alumni Assn. (pres. St. Louis chpt. 1986-2005). Avocations: horsemanship, literature, theater, mathematics. Office: 7751 Carondelet Ave Ste 805 Clayton MO 63105-3369 Office Phone: 314-721-3626.

MOHRMAN, KATHRYN J., academic administrator; BA, Grinnell Coll., 1967; MA, U. Wis., 1969; PhD, George Washington U., 1982. Dean undergrad. studies U. Md., College Park, 1988—93; pres. The Colo. Coll., Colorado Springs, 1993—2002; exec. dir. Hopkins-Nanjing Ctr. for Chinese and Am. Studies, Johns Hopkins U., 2003—. Office: 1619 Massachusetts Ave NW Washington DC 20036 Office Phone: 202-663-5801.

MOIR, CHRISTOPHER ROBERT, surgeon; b. Montreal, Can., Jan. 5, 1954; came to U.S., 1994; BS, U. Brit. Columbia; MD, U. Brit. Columbia, Vancouver, B.C., Can., 1979. Diplomate Am. Bd. Surgery, Am. Bd. Surg. Critical Care, Am. Bd. Ped. Surgery. Intern, general surgery Dalhousie U. Program, 1979-80; resident, pediatric surgery U. Brit. Columbia, Vancouver, BC, Canada, 1980-86; fellow, pediatric surgery McGill U., Montreal, QC, Canada, 1986-88; divsn. chmn. surgery Mayo Found., Mayo Clinic Coll. Medicine, Rochester, Minn., 1994—; assoc. prof., surgery Mayo Clinic Coll. Medicine, Rochester, Minn., 1994—. Contbr. articles to profl. jours. Fellow Royal Coll. Surgeons (Can.); mem. ACS, Royal Coll. Pediatric Surgeons Can., Physicians and Surgeons B.C. (Can.), Am. Pediatric Surgeons Assn. lead surgeon for a team of doctors who separated conjoined twin girls in 2006. Office: Mayo Clinic Dept Ped Surg 200 First St SW Rochester MN 55905 Business E-Mail: moir.christopher@mayo.edu.

MOIZE, JERRY DEE, lawyer, federal official; b. Greensboro, NC, Dec. 19, 1934; s. Dwight Moody and Thelma (Ozment) M.; m. Margaret Ann Wooten, Aug. 13, 1976; 1 child, Jerry Dee Jr. AB cum laude, Elon Coll., NC, 1957; JD, Tulane U., New Orleans, 1960; diploma, Army Command & Gen. Staff Sch., USAR, 1981. Bar: Colo. 1961, US Dist. Ct. Colo. 1961, US Ct. Mil. Appeals 1962, US Supreme Ct. 1965, NC 1965. Legal clk. Air Def. Commd., Colo. Springs, Colo., 1960-61, assistance officer, 1962-63; chief legal assistance divsn. 2nd Army, Ft. Meade, Md., 1964-65; staff JAG, Indiantown Gap Mil. Reservation, 1965; law clk. to hon. Eugen Gordon U.S. Dist. Ct. (mid. dist.) NC, Winston-Salem, 1965-66; dir. Legal Aid Soc. Forsyth County, Winston-Salem, 1966-69; exec. dir. Forsyth Bail Project, Winston-Salem, 1968-69, Lawyer Referral Svc. of Bar of 21st Jud. Dist., Winston-Salem, 1968-69; staff atty. office of gen. counsel FAA, Washington, 1969-70, acting chief admin. & legal resources, 1970-71; staff atty. office of gen. counsel Dept. HUD, Washington, 1971, counsel Jackson area office Miss., 1971-83, chief counsel Jackson field office Miss., 1983-94, acting dir. Jackson field office, 2006, acting sr. advisor to dep. regional dir. Region IV Atlanta, 2006; chief counsel Office Gen. Counsel Miss., Jackson, 1994—; HUD del. Miss. Fed. Exec. Assn., 1997—2000. Lectr. U. W.Va. Conf. on Poverty Law, 1968; HUD program svc. adviser, 2000—. Editor NC Legal Aid Reporter, 1968-69, NC Legal Aid Directory, 1968, Avlex Legal Index (2nd supplement), 1971, developed Miss. low income housing financing mechanism 1975-76; contbr articles to profl. jours., articles to splty. mags. Dem. candidate NC Ho. of Reps., Guilford County, 1964; mem. mil. com. Forsyth County NC Red Cross, 1967-68; pack leader Andrew Jackson coun. Boy Scouts Am., 1986-92; active Project Adv. Group US Office Econ. Opportunity Legal Svc. Program, 1968-69, Adv. Com. on Housing & Urban Devel., Miss., Law Rsch. Inst., 1980-81, Pilot Mountain Preservation & Park Com., Winston-Salem, 1968-70; mem. Race Com. Whitworth Hunt Races, 1973-76; Am. Master of Foxhounds Assn., 1976-79; adv. Order DeMolay, 1997—; sec. Miss Scottish Games, 1999, v.p. 2000, pres. 2001. Capt. AUS, 1960-65; ret. lt. col. USAR, 1966-87. Decorated Meritorious Svc. medal, Army Commendation medal with oak leaf cluster, Army Res. Forces Achievement medal with three oak leaf clusters, Nat. Def. Svc. medal, Armed Forces Res. medal; named Hon. Knight Mason, 1999; recipient Legion of Honor, Order of De Molay, 2000. Mem.: KT, SCV, NRA, Miss. Opera Assn., NC State Bar, Fed. Bar Assn., Caledonian Soc. Miss., The Austin Hunt (joint master of foxhounds 1976—79), Iron Bridge Hunt (v.p. 1964—65), Miss. Hist. Assn., Miss. Track Club, Whitworth Hunt (founder, master of foxhounds 1975—76), Capital Club (Jackson, Miss.), Rosicrucian, Masons (32 degree), Shriners, Order Ea. Star, Pi Gamma Mu. Republican. Episcopal. Avocations: running, book collecting. Office: Miss State Dept Housing & Urban Devel Fed Bldg 100 W Capitol 9th Flr Jackson MS 39269 Home: 120 Highland Cove Ridgeland MS 39157-4719 Home Phone: 601-605-3453; Office Phone: 601-965-4700 ext. 2325.

MOJER-TORRES, LISA NAN, lawyer; b. Queens, NY, Dec. 1, 1956; d. Joseph Raymond and Gwendolyn Emma Mojer; m. Rolando Torres, Oct. 24, 1987; children: Matthew Roland Torres, Liam Joseph Torres. BA, Boston U., 1978; JD, NYU, 1991. Bar: N.J. 1994, N.Y. 1994. Atty. at law Lisa Mojer-Torres, Esq., Lawrenceville, NJ, 1994—; spl. svcs., consumer adv. State of NJ, Dept. HHS, Divsn. of Addiction Svcs., Trenton, 2005—. Coun. mem. Dept. HHS, SAMHSA, Ctr. for Substance Abuse Treatment Nat. Adv. Coun., Rockville, Md., 1999—2001; com. mem. Dept. HHS, FDA, Ctr. for Drug Evaluation and Rsch. Drug Abuse Adv. Com., Rockville, Md., 1993—96; cons., expert witness, atty., consumer adv. Lisa Mojer-Torres, Esq., Lawrenceville, NJ, 1995—; panel mem. and expert witness nat. treatment plan initiative of the ctr. for substance abuse treatment Dept. HHS, SAMHSA, Ctr. for Substance Abuse Treatment, Rockville, Md.; nat. policy panelist JoinTogether (Boston U. Sch. of Pub. Health) in collaboration with the ABA (Standing Com. on Substance Abuse), Washington, 2002—03. Mem. editl. bd. Jour. Maintenance in the Addictions; author (rschr.): NJ Gov.'s Study Commn. on Discrimination in Pub. Contracting. Recipient Pub. Svc. award, Nat. Inst. of Drug Abuse, 1995. Mem.: NY Bar Assn., NJ Bar Assn. Democrat-Npl. Avocation: figure skating. Home: 9 Whitemarsh Dr Lawrenceville NJ 08648 Office: NJ DHS Divsn of Addiction Svcs PO Box 362 Trenton NJ 08648 Home Phone: 609-671-1995; Office Phone: 609-292-5050. Office Fax: 609-292-3816; Home Fax: 609-671-1994. Personal E-mail: rtorres605@aol.com. Business E-Mail: lisa.mojer-torres@dhs.state.nj.us.

MOJIRI, AHMAD, mathematics professor; s. Jalil Mojiri Andani and Aghdas Ghadarkhah. BSc, Isfahan U. Tech., 1995, MSc, 1997; PhD, U. Ottawa, Canada, 2003. Asst. prof. math. Wilfrid Laurier U., Waterloo, Ont., Canada, 2003—04, Southwestern Coll., Winfield, Kans., 2005—06, Tex. A&M U., Texarkana, 2006—. Author: On Uniserial Modules in the Auslander-Reiten Quiver. Vol. Amnesty Internat., Ottawa, 2001—02. Scholar, Isfahan U. Tech., 1995—96; Doctoral Rsch. scholar, U. Ottawa, 1999—2003. Mem.: Math. Assn. Am., Am. Math. Soc. Avocations: bicycling, jogging, travel, movies. Office: Texas A&M U 2600 N Robison Rd Texarkana TX 75505 Office Phone: 903-223-3028.

MOJTABAI, ANN GRACE, author, educator; b. NYC, June 8, 1937; d. Robert and Naomi (Friedman) Alpher; m. Fathollah Mojtabai, Apr. 27, 1960 (div. 1966); children: Chitra, Ramin. BA in Philosophy, Antioch Coll., 1958; MA in Philosophy, Columbia U., 1968, MS in Libr. Sci., 1970. Lectr. philosophy Hunter Coll., CUNY, 1966-68; libr. CCNY, 1970-76; fellow Radcliffe Inst. Ind. Study, Cambridge, Mass., 1976-78; Briggs-Copeland lectr. on English Harvard U., 1978-83; writer-in-residence U. Tulsa, 1983—2005, Yaddo Found., Saratoga, NY, 1975, 76. Author: Mundome, 1974, The 400 Eels of Sigmund Freud, 1976, A Stopping Place, 1979, Autumn, 1982, Blessed Assurance, 1986, Ordinary Time, 1989, Called Out, 1994, Soon: Tales From Hospice, 1998. Recipient Richard and Hinda Rosenthal award Am. Acad. and Inst. Arts and Letters, 1983, Lillian Smith award So. Regional Coun., 1986, Lit. Acad. award AAAL, 1993; Guggenheim fellow, 1981-82 Mem.: PEN, Mark Twain Soc., Tex. Inst. Letters, Phi Beta Kappa. Home: 2329 Woodside Drive Amarillo TX 79124-1036 Personal E-mail: agmojtabai@aol.com.

MOK, CARSON KWOK-CHI, structural engineer; b. Canton, China, Jan. 17, 1932; came to U.S., 1956, naturalized, 1962; s. King and Chi-Big (Lum) M.; m. Virginia Wai-Ching Cheng, Sept. 19, 1959. BSCE, Chu Hai U., Hong Kong, 1953; M.C.E., Cath. U. Am., 1968. Registered profl. engr., Md., D.C. Structural designer Wong Cho Tong, Hong Kong, 1954-56; bridge designer Michael Baker Jr., Inc., College Park, Md., 1957-60; structural engr., chief design engr., assoc. Milton A. Gurewitz Assocs., Washington, 1961-65; ptnr. Wright & Mok, Silver Spring, Md., 1966-75; owner Carson K.C. Mok, Cons. Engr., Silver Spring, 1976-81, pres., 1982—. Facility engring. cons. Washington Met. Area Transit Authority, 1985-86; pres. Transp. Engring. and Mgmt. Assocs., P.C., Washington, 1986-2002; adj. asst. prof. Howard U., Washington, 1976-79, adj. assoc. prof., 1980-81. Contbr. articles to profl. jours. Bd. dirs. U.S. Pan Asian Am. C. of C. Sec.; N.Am. trustee China Grad. Sch. Theology, Wayne, Pa., 1972-74, pres., 1975-83, v.p., 1984-91, dir., 1992—; elder Chinese Bible Ch. Md., Rockville, 1978-80; chmn. Chinese Christian Ch. Greater Washington, 1958-61, 71, elder, 1972-76; dir. Evergreen Family Friendship Svc., Inc., A Pub. Benefit Corp., Colorado Springs, 1993—. Recipient Outstanding Std. of Tchg. award Howard U., 1980, Nat. Merit award U.S. Dept. Transp., 2000. Mem. ASCE, ASTM, Nat. Assn. Corrosion Engrs., Concrete Reinforcing Steel Inst., Am. Inst. Steel Constrn., Am. Concrete Inst., Am. Welding Soc., Prestressed Concrete Inst., Post-Tensioning Inst., Soc. Exptl. Mechanics, Internat. Assn. Bridge and Structural Engring., Pui Ching Mid. Sch. Alumni Assn. (pres. nation's capital chpt. 1991-97). Home: 4405 Bestor Dr Rockville MD 20853-2137 Office: 9001 Ottawa Pl Silver Spring MD 20910-2257 Office Phone: 301-587-3448. E-mail: ckm9001@aol.com.

MOK, SAMUEL TINSING, federal agency administrator; m. Nancy Mok; 2 children. BS in Acctg., Fordham U., 1968; MA in Auditing, Cath. U., Washington, 1982; grad., US Army Inst. of Administration, Fort Benjamin Harrison, US Foreign Svc. Inst., Rosslyn, Va. Cert. Internal Auditor, Govt. Fin. Mgr. Dir. acctg. Time-Life Books, 1976—82; corp. treasurer U.S. News & World Report, 1982—86; foreign svc. officer Bureau of East Asian and Pacific Affairs, U.S. Dept. of State, 1986; mem. fed. sr. exec. svc., CFO, comptr. U.S. Treasury Dept., 1988—92; CEO GL Assocs., 1992—96; mng. mem. Condor Cons., LLC, 1996—2002; chief fin. officer U.S. Dept. Labor, Washington, 2002—. With US Army. Decorated Meritorious Unit Citation, Meritorious Svc. medal. Office: US Dept Labor 200 Constitution Ave NW Washington DC 20210 Business E-Mail: mok-samuel@dol.gov.

MOKRASCH, LEWIS CARL, neurochemist, educator; b. St. Paul, May 9, 1930; s. Lewis and Anna (Dvorak) M.; m. Jane Carolyn Church, Apr. 20, 1974. BS magna cum laude, Coll. St. Thomas, 1952; PhD, U. Wis., 1955. Rsch. assoc. dept. psychiatry and neurology La. State U. Med. Center, New Orleans, 1956-57, assoc. prof. dept. biochemistry, 1971-76, prof., 1976-92, prof. emeritus, 1992—, acting head dept., 1978-79. Instr. medicine U. Kans. Med. Center, Kansas City, 1957-59, assoc. in medicine, dir. neurochemistry lab., 1959-62; asst. biochemist McLean Hosp., Belmont, Mass., 1960-64, assoc. biochemist, 1964-71; assoc. dept. biol. chemistry Harvard Med. Sch., Boston, 1964-67; asst. prof., 1967-71; adj. assoc. prof. biology Hellenic Coll., Brookline, Mass., 1969-71; staff scientist Neurosciences Rsch. Program, Brookline, 1970-71; vis. prof. neurology Duke U. Med. Ctr., 1981-82; bd. adv. Alzheimer Care Ctr., Winston-Salem; grant reviewer neurological diseases and blindness NIMH, 1969-92; lectr. in field Co-author: Myelin, 1971; contbr. articles to profl. jours.; reviewer: jours. Sci., FASEB. Pres. Belmont Preservation Soc., 1969; candidate Bd. Selectman, Belmont, 1969; active Forsyth County Adult Care Home Cmty. Adv. Com., Hospice, Sr. Fin. Care, Winston-Salem, Sr. Svcs. Program, Winston Salem, Citizens Quality Nursing Home Care, New Orleans, 1991-92; sr. leader Duke Long Term Care Program Edn. Com.; edn. com. Shepherd Ctr.; bd. adv. Williams Alzheimer Care Ctr., Winston-Salem, Reynolda Ho. Mus. Am. Art, Reynolda Gardens. Grantee NIMH, 1973-74, Nat. Inst. Neurol. Disability and Blindness, 1957-90, Schlieder Found., 1971-72, 83-84, La. Bd. Regents, 1986-88. Fellow Am. Assn. Clin. Chemists; mem. Am. Soc. Neurochemistry (local chmn. 1974), Am. Soc. Biol. Chemists, Soc. Neurosci. (founder, pres. local chpt. 1974-75), Soc. Rsch. Adminstrs. (membership chmn. New Eng. sect.), Nat. Citizens

Coalition Nursing Home Reform, Am. Assn. Individual Investors (founder, past pres., sec. Piedmont chpt.). Libertarian. Achievements include first demonstration of adaptive enzyme regulation in animals and allosteric control of fructose bisphosphatase, of incorporation of hydrouracil into transfer RNA, of thermogenic mechanism for arousing hibernators, of metabolic control in hibernation, of altered hydrophobic proteins in neurological disorders, of biosynthesis of hydrophobic proteins and mitochondrial proteins in brain in vitro, of altered transport processes in cells of neurological disease victims, of defective transport of acetylcholine precursors into cells of Alzheimer's victims and that such transport is modulatable; development of coestimation method for ketoses, aldoses, and pentoses; first isolation in pure form of receptor hydrophobic proteins from mammalian brain. Home: 2711 Pilgrim Ct Winston Salem NC 27106 Personal E-mail: drlewmokasch@aol.com. *Before I entered Science, I regarded it as a Priesthood of individuals dedicated to the service of humanity, whose common goal was the enhancement of human life and the remedying of its ills. After 50 years in Science, I hold this thesis more strongly and have found many colleagues who agree with it. I am certain now that the failures and abuses of Science derive from the use of it for the goals of wealth, fame and power.*

MOKRZECKI, LECH MARIAN, history of education educator; b. Warsaw, Apr. 5, 1935; s. Justyn and Irena (Druhowino) M.; m. Aleksandra Maria Horbowska, Aug. 20, 1983. MA, U. Toruń, Poland, 1956; dipl. cellist, Acad. Music, Gdańsk, Poland, 1962, MA, 1964; PhD, Higher Sch. Pedagogy, Gdańsk, Poland, 1967; DrHabil, U. Gdańsk, Poland, 1975; PhD (hon.), Linköping U., 1998. From asst. to prof. extraordinary Gdańsk U., Poland, 1966, prof. ordinary, 1993—2006. Author: Three Centuries of Gdansk Learning, 1969, 2d edit., 1976, The Study of the Teaching of History, 1973, In the Sphere of the Work of Gdansk Historians in XVII Century, 1974 (Min. of Edn. award 1976), The Beginning of the Knowledge of the Sea in the Former Kingdom of Poland, 1983, The Fortress Vistulamouth, 1978, Traditions of Teaching History to the Close of XVI Century-Selected Countries and Problems, 1992 (Min. of Edn. award 1993), From the Tradition of Teaching History to the End of 16th Century, 1992, Science and Education in Polish Lithuanian Commonwealth, 2001, The History of Gdansk University, 2006; co-author, editor: In the Sphere of Culture, Music, Ballet, 1971 (Min. of Culture award 1972), Scientific Copy Books of Gdansk University, Pedagogy History of Education, 1993, 97; co-author: A Significant Social Revolution, 1994. Head, History of Social Sci. Commn., Policy Acad. Sci. Mem. Assn. Internat. pour History of Edn. Belgium, Com. Internat. Scis. History, Commn. History of Historiography Italy, Polish Acad. Scis. (History of Sci. and Tech. com.). Roman Catholic. Avocations: travel, reading poetry. Home: Biała 6-28 80-435 Gdansk Poland Office: Gdansk Higher Pedagogie School Biskupia 24A 80-875 Gdansk Poland

MOL, GRETCHEN, actress; b. Deep River, Conn., Nov. 8, 1972; d. Janet Mol; m. Tod Williams, June 1, 2004. Grad., Am. Musical & Dramatic Acad. Actor: (films) Girl 6, 1996, The Funeral, 1996, Donnie Brasco, 1997, The Last Time I Committed Suicide, 1997, The Deli, 1997, Bleach, 1998, Too Tired to Die, 1998, Rounders, 1998, New Rose Hotel, 1998, Celebrity, 1998, Finding Graceland, 1998, Music from Another Room, 1998, The Thirteenth Floor, 1999, Cradle Will Rock, 1999, Sweet & Lowdown, 1999, Forever Mine, 1999, Just Looking, 1999, Attraction, 2000, Get Carter, 2000, The Shape of Things, 2003, Heavy Put-Away, 2004, The Notorious Bettie Page, 2005, Puccini for Beginners, 2006, Trainwreck: My Life as an Idiot, 2007, The Ten, 2007; (TV films) Calm at Sunset, 1996, Subway Stories: Tales from the Underground, 1997, Picnic, 2000, Freshening Up, 2002, The Magnificent Ambersons, 2002; (TV miniseries) Dead Man's Walk, 1996; (TV series) Girls Club, 2002. Office: c/o William Morris Agy 1 William Morris Pl Beverly Hills CA 90212 Office Phone: 310-859-4000. *

MOLAISON, ELAINE FONTENOT, dietician, nutritionist, educator; BS, U. Southwestern La., Lafayette, 1994; MS, La. Tech U., Ruston, 1996; PhD, U. So. Miss., Hattiesburg, 2000. Registered dietician Ill., 1995. Asst. prof. La. Tech U., 2000—04, U. So. Miss., 2004—. Mem.: Am. Dietetic Assn. (Found. New Rschrs. award 2000). Avocation: aerobics. Office Phone: 601-266-6548.

MOLANO, CHARLES HERNANDO, Spanish professor, consultant; b. Cali, Departamento del Valle, Colombia, Jan. 5, 1962; s. Hernando and Aleida Beatriz Molano; m. Kimberly Briggs, Apr. 9, 1986; children: Brenden Charles, Francesca Lauren, Jeron Hernando, Erica Fernanda. MA, Ariz. State U., Tempe, 2001. Tchr. asst. Ariz. State U., 1995—97; prof. Spanish, Ctrl. Ariz. Coll., Apache Junction, 1998—2002, Mesa CC, Ariz., 1999—2002; asst. prof. Spanish, Dodge City CC, Kans., 2002—03; asst. prof. fgn. langs. Lehigh Carbon CC, Schnecksville, Pa., 2003—. Cons. owner Molano Enterprises Consulting, Interpreting, and Translations, Alburtis, Pa., 1996—. Mem. Latino Rep. Com., Allentown, Pa., 2004; Melchizedek Priesthood elder LDS Ch., 1980—. Presdl. scholarship, Mesa CC, 1991-1992, Marron and Gold scholar, Ariz. State U., 1992-1993, Los Diablos scholarship, 1993-1994. Mem.: ACTFL. Conservative. Mem. Lds Ch. Avocations: traveling, history, geography, religion, wood burning. Home: 199 Maple Ct Alburtis PA 18011 Office: Lehigh Carbon CC 4525 Education Park Dr Schnecksville PA 18078 Home Phone: 610-966-7202; Office Phone: 610-799-1724. Office Fax: 610-799-1529. Personal E-mail: chmolano@netscape.net. Business E-Mail: cmolano@lccc.edu.

MOLAY, HILARY S., lawyer; b. 1954; BA, Brandeis U.; JD, U. Miami. Bar: 1980. Law clerk to Judge Rita C. Davidson Md. Ct. of Appeals; trial atty. civil div. US Dept. Justice, Washington; assoc. Shank, Irwin & Conant, Finley, Kumble, Wagner, Heine, Underberg, Manley, Myerson & Casey; counsel J.C. Penney Co., Inc.; v.p., gen. counsel, sec. Zale Corp., Irving, Tex., 2000—05, sr. v.p., gen. counsel, corp. sec., 2005—. Mem. adv. bd. corp. counsel symposium Southern Methodist U., 2004; mem. gen. counsel forum Nat. Retail Federation. Mem.: ABA, Am. Soc. of Corp. Secretaries (mem. corp. practices comm.). Office: Zale Corp 901 W Walnut Hill Ln Irving TX 75038 *

MOLDENHAUER, SUSAN, museum director, curator; BFA, No. Ill. U., 1974; MFA, Pa. State U., 1982. Gallery mgr. Sch. Visual Arts, Pa. State U.; exec. dir. Second Street Gallery, Charlottesville, Va.; curator mus. progs. U. Wyo. Art Mus., Laramie, 1991—96, asst. dir., 1996—2000, interim dir., 2000—02, dir., chief curator, 2002—. Office: U Wyo Art Mus 2111 Willett Dr Laramie WY 82071-3807 Office Phone: 307-766-6620. E-mail: uwartmus@uwyo.edu.

MOLDENHAUER, WILLIAM CALVIN, soil scientist; b. New Underwood, SD, Oct. 27, 1923; s. Calvin Fred and Ida (Killam) M.; m. Catherine Ann Maher, Nov. 26, 1947; children— Jean Ann, Patricia, Barbara, James, Thomas BS, S.D. State U., 1949; MS, U. Wis., 1951, PhD, 1956. Soil surveyor S.D. State U., Brookings, 1948-54; soil scientist U.S. Dept. Agr., Big Spring, Tex., 1954-57, Ames, Iowa, 1957-72, Morris, Minn., 1972-75; rsch. leader Nat. Soil Erosion Rsch. Lab., Agrl. Rsch. Svc. U.S. Dept. Agr., West Lafayette, Ind., 1975-85; prof. dept. agronomy Purdue U., West Lafayette, 1975-85, prof. emeritus, 1985—. Contbr. articles to profl. jours. Served with U.S. Army, 1943-46 Fellow Am. Soc. Agronomy, Soil Sci. Soc., Soil Conservation Soc. Am. (pres. 1979), World Assn. Soil and Water Conservation (pres. 1983-85, exec. sec. 1985-2003). Home and Office: 2400 Sunrise Ridge Cir #107 Brookings SD 57006 E-mail: moldwcm@yahoo.com.

MOLEN, JOHN KLAUMINZER, lawyer; b. Gary, Ind., June 13, 1952; s. Franklin B. and Jane Anne (Klauminzer) M.; m. Susan Wilson Blair, Aug. 10, 1985; children: Mary Wilson, Elisabeth Blair. AB with honors, U. NC, 1974, MBA, 1978, JD with honors, 1978. Bar: Ala. 1978. Assoc. Bradley Arant Rose & White LLP, Birmingham, Ala., 1978-84, ptnr., 1984—. Mem. Rotary Club Birmingham-Sunrise. Presbyterian. Avocations: sailing, swimming. Office: Bradley Arant Rose & White LLP One Federal Pl 1819 5th Ave N Birmingham AL 35203-2104 Office Phone: 205-521-8238. Business E-Mail: jmolen@bradleyarant.com.

MOLER, EDWARD HAROLD, retired lawyer; b. Oklahoma City, May 26, 1923; s. Harold Stanley and Rosemary (Callahan) M.; m. Donna Blocksom Cram, Sept. 12, 1964; children: John Frederick, Shelley Elizabeth, Christopher Bryan. BA, U. Okla., 1947, LLB, 1948. Bar: Okla. 1948, U.S. Supreme Ct. 1951. Pvt. practice law, Oklahoma City, 1948-52, 61—; asst. mcpl. counselor, 1952-59; mcpl. counselor, 1959-61; spl. justice Okla. Supreme Ct., 1977. Trustee Oklahoma City Mcpl. Improvement Authority, 1960-61, Dolese Found, 2007-; bd. dirs. Mummers Theatre, Inc., 1969—; bd. dirs. Greater Oklahoma City YMCA, 1981-91. 2d lt. USAAF, 1943-45. Mem. ABA, Okla. Bar Assn., Oklahoma County Bar Assn. (bd. dirs. 1963-67, pres. 1968), Rotary, Phi Delta Phi, Phi Gamma Delta (pres. local chpt. 1946, pres. Nu Omega Housing Assn. 1963-65). Home: 2540 NW Grand Blvd Oklahoma City OK 73116-4110 E-mail: demoler@cox.net.

MOLER, ELIZABETH ANNE, utilities executive; b. Salt Lake City, Jan. 24, 1949; d. Murray McClure and Eleanor Lorraine (Barry) M.; m. Thomas Blake Williams, Oct. 19, 1979; children: Blake Martin Williams, Eleanor Bliss Williams. BA, Am. U., 1971; postgraduate student, Johns Hopkins U., Balt., 1972; JD, George Washington U., 1977. Bar: DC 1978. Chief legis. asst. Senator Floyd Haskell, Washington, 1973-75; law clk. Sharon, Pierson, Semmes, Crolius & Finley, Washington, 1975-76; profl. staff mem. com. on energy and natural resources US Senate Com. on Energy and Natural Resources, Washington, 1976—77, counsel, 1977—86, sr. counsel, 1987-88; mem. FERC, Washington, 1988-93, chair, 1993-97; dep. sec. Dept. Energy, Washington, 1997-98, acting sec., 1998; ptnr. Vinson & Elkins, Washington, 1999; sr. v.p. govt. affairs and policy Unicom Corp. (now Exelon Corp.), 2000—02, exec. v.p., 2002; exec. v.p. govt. and environ. affairs and pub. policy, mem. strategy and policy com. Exelon Corp., Washington. Bd. dirs. Henry M. Jackson Found. Recipient Disting. Svc. award, Nat. Energy Resources Orgn., Energy Daily Ann. Pub. Policy Leadership award, Woman of Yr. award, Women's Coun. Energy and the Environment. Mem. ABA, DC Bar Assn. Democrat. Office: Exelon Corp Suite 400 East 101 Constitution Ave NW Washington DC 20001 Office Phone: 202-347-7500.

MOLHO, EMANUEL, publisher; b. NYC, Jan. 27, 1936; s. Isaac Emanuel and Alvira (Altchek) M.; m. Brenda Nadel, Sept. 25, 1965; children— Deborah Rochelle, Brian Emanuel. BA, NYU, 1957; MBA, Wharton Sch., U. Pa., 1960. Pres. French & European Publs., Inc., NYC, 1961—, French & Spanish Book Corp., 1967—. Pres. Librairie de France, Inc., 1961—. Recipient Orden de Merito Civil Spain, 1975 Mem. Am. Booksellers Assn., French-Am. C. of C. in U.S. (exec. com.), Paris Am. Club. Office: Librairie de France Rockefeller Center Promenade 610 5th Ave New York NY 10020-2497 E-mail: livresny@aol.com.

MOLHOEK, KERRINGTON RAMSEY, research scientist; d. Carlton Lee and Linda Ford Ramsey; m. Charles Conrad Molhoek, June 12, 2004. PhD, U. Va., Charlottesville, 2004. Rsch. faculty U. Va. Sch. Medicine, Charlottesville, 2004—. Mem.: U. Va. Alumni Assn. (life), Colonnade Club (life), Nat. Soc. Collegiate Scholars (life), Delta Delta Delta (life). Office: U Va 409 Lane St MR-4 Rm 3038 Charlottesville VA 22908 Business E-Mail: klr5w@virginia.edu.

MOLHOLM, KURT NELSON, retired federal agency administrator; b. Denver, June 24, 1937; s. Ervin Maurice and Helen Pauline (Nelson) M.; m. Sonja Dell Williams, Aug. 17, 1967; children: Kevin William, Paul Nelson. BS, U. Oreg., 1959; MS, George Washington U., 1974; grad., Indsl. Coll. Armed Forces, 1974. Computer specialist D.L.A. Adminstrv. Support Ctr., Alexandria, Va., 1963-65; with Hdqrs. Def. Logistics Agy., Alexandria, 1965-85, chief planning and policy office, 1975-76, chief ADP/T tech. div., 1984-85; adminstr. Def. Tech. Info. Ctr., Alexandria, 1985—2005; ret., 2005. Pres. Nat. Fedn. Abstracting and Info. Svcs., Phila., 1993-94, treas., 1990-93; del. Va. Govs. Conf. Librs. Info. Svcs., 1990, Fed. Libr. Pre-White House Conf. On Librs. Info. Sci., 1990; vice chmn. Fed. Libr. and Info. Ctr. Com., 1992-93, 2002-03; chmn. CENDI Group, 1991-94, 99-2001; mem. NATO Agard Tech. Info. Panel, 1985-91, Internat. Coun. Sci. and Tech. Info., 1993—, treas., 1998-2001, chair editl. bd., 1999-2001, pres. 2001—04; mem. Info. Infrastructure Task Force, 1993-97; chair panel 2 U.S. Nat. Commn. on Librs. and Info. Sci. Comprehensive Assessment of Pub. Info. Dissemination, 2000; mem. Handle Sys. Adv. Com., 2001-; NFAIS Conrad Meml. lectr., 2003; cons. in field, 2006-. 1st lt. U.S. Army, 1960-63. Recipient Meritorious award William A. Jump Meml. Found., 1973, Civilian Svc. award, Def. Logistics Agy., 1991, Exceptional Civilian Svc. award, DLA, 1985, Exceptional Civilan Svc. award, Def. Info. Systems Agy., 2005. Methodist. Personal E-mail: kmolholm@verizon.net. E-mail: kurt@molholm.com.

MOLINA, ALFRED, actor; b. London, May 24, 1953; m. Jill Gascione, 1985; 2 children. Grad., Guildhall Sch. Music and Drama. Film appearances include Raiders of the Lost Ark, 1981, Meantime, 1983, Number One, 1984, Eleni, 1985, Ladyhawke, 1985, Water, 1985, Letter to Brezhnev, 1986, Prick Up Your Ears, 1987, Manifesto, 1988, Not Without My Daughter, 1991, Enchanted April, 1992, American Friends, 1993, The Trial, 1993, Meverick, 1994, White Fang 2: Myth of the White Wolf, 1994, The Steal, 1994, Species, 1995, Scorpoin Spring, 1995, Hideaway, 1995, Dead Man, 1995, Drowning in the Shallow End, 1989, When Pigs Fly, 1993, White Fang II: Myth of the White Wolf, 1994, Maverick, 1994, The Steal, 1994, Hideaway, 1995, The Perez Family, 1995, Dead Man, 1995, Species, 1995, Nervous Energy, 1995, Before and After, 1996, Mojave Moon, 1996, Anna Karenina, 1997, Scorpion Spring, 1997, Further Gesture, 1997, Boogie Nights, 1997, The Man Who Knew Too Little, 1997, Impostors, 1998, The Treat, 1998, Pete's Meteor, 1998, Dudley Do-Right, 1999, Magnolia, 1999, Chocolat, 2000, Texas Rangers, 2001, Frida, 2002, Plots with a View, 2002, Ape, 2002, My Life Without Me, 2003, Identity, 2003, Coffee and Cigarettes, 2003, Luther, 2003, Chronicles, 2004, Spider-Man 2, 2004, (voice) Steamboy, 2004, Sian Ka'an, 2005, The Da Vinci Code, 2006, As You Like It, 2006, The Hoax, 2006, Orchids, 2006, The Moon and the Stars, 2007; (TV films) The Accountant, 1990, Virtuoso, 1991, Angels, 1992, Ashenden, 1992, A Year in Provence, 1993, The Marshal, 1993, Requiem Apache, 1994, The Place of Lions, 1997, Rescuers: Stories of Courage: Two Couples, 1998, Miracle Maker (voice), 2000, Murder on the Orient Express, 2001; (Broadway shows) Art, 1998, Fiddler on the Roof, 2004 (Tony nom. best actor in a musical, 2004); other stage appearances include Destiny, 1977, Troilus and Cressida, 1977, Bandits, 1977, The Bundle, 1977, Frozen Assets, 1977, That Good Between Us, 1977, King Lear, 1977, Dingo, 1978, Irish Eyes and English Tears, 1978, Willie, 1978, Accidental Death of an Anarchist, 1979 (Plays and Players award for most promising new actor), Destry Rides Again, 1982, Dreyfus, 1982, Viva, 1985, The Night of the Iguana, 1992, Molly Sweeney, 1995 (Theatre World award, 1996, Drama Desk award, 1996), True West, 2001, The Cherry Orchard, 2002, Howard Katz, 2007. Office: William Morris Agy 151 S El Camino Dr Beverly Hills CA 90212-2775 *

MOLINA, GLORIA, municipal official; b. Montebello, Calif., May 31, 1948; d. Leonardo and Concepcion Molina; m. Ron Martinez, 1 child, Valentina Student, East L.A. Coll., 1968, Calif. State U., LA, 1968-70. Staffing specialist Office Presdl. Pers., Washington, 1977-79; dir. intergovtl and congl. affairs region IX US Dept. Health & Human Services, San Francisco, 1979-81; So. Calif chief dep. Calif. State Rep. Willie L. Brown Jr., 1981; mem. Calif. State Assembly, 1982—86, L.A. City Coun., 1987—91, L.A. County Bd. Supervisors, 1991—, chair, 2005—. Mem. Revenue & Taxation, Labor & Employment, Utilities & Comm. Coms., Select Com. on Small Bus., 1982—, Consumer Protection, 1984—; chairwoman Subcom. Mental Health & Devel. Disabilities, 1984—. Named Hispanic of the Yr. Caminos mag., 1982, Dem. of the Yr. L.A. County Dem. Ctrl. Com., 1983, Woman of the Year Mexican-Am. Opportunity Found., 1983, MS mag, 1984, Woman of the Yr. Hispanic Bus. mag., 2006 Mem. Comision Femenil Mexicana Nacional. Office: LA County 500 W Temple St Ste 856 Los Angeles CA 90012-2723

MOLINA, GUSTAVO, engineering educator, researcher; b. Cordoba, Argentina; B in Mech. and Elec. Engring., Nat. U. Cordoba, Argentina, 1986; MSc in Mech. Engring., U. Ottawa, Ontario, Can., 1994; PhD in Mech. Engring., Va. Tech, Blacksburg, Va., 2000. Asst. prof. Ga. So. U., Statesboro, Ga., 2000—06, assoc. prof., 2006—. R&d engr. CIMM-INTI, Cordoba, Argentina, 1986—96. Mem.: Adhesion Soc. Achievements include research in pioneer work on triboemission phenomena. Office: Ga So Univ Technology Building Forest Dr Statesboro GA 30460-8045 Office Phone: 912-681-0125.

MOLINA, JOSEPH MARIO (MARIO MOLINA), medical administrator; b. Long Beach, Calif., May 16, 1958; s. C. David and Mary R. (Salandini) M.; m. Therese Ann Flynn; children: Carley, Colleen, David, Mary Clare. BA, Calif. State U., Long Beach, 1980; MD, U. So. Calif., 1984. Diplomate Am. Bd. Internal Medicine. Intern and residency Johns Hopkins U., 1984—87; assoc. investigator VA, San Diego, 1988-90; asst. clin. prof. U. So. Calif., LA, 1990-91; med. dir. Molina Healthcare, Inc., Long Beach, 1991-94, v.p. HMO, 1994—96, chmn., pres., CEO, 1996—. Bd. dirs. New Am. Alliance. Nat. trustee Boys and Girls Club Am. Named one of Top 10 Latinos in Healthcare, LatinoLeaders mag., 2004, 25 Most Influential Hispanics, Time Mag., 2005; named to Hall of Fame, Long Beach Cmty. Coll., 2002; recipient Ernst & Young Gr. L.A. Entrepreneur of Yr. award, 2002. Mem. ACP, Am. Diabetes Assn., Calif. Med. Assn. Avocation: collecting antique medical books. Office: Molina Healthcare Inc 1 Golden Shore St Long Beach CA 90802-4202 Office Phone: 562-435-3666. Business E-Mail: mario.molina@molinahealthcare.com.

MOLINA, KEVIN, social studies educator; b. Miami, Fla., Aug. 17, 1971; s. Jose and Lilia Molina. BS in Social Studies Edn., Fla. Internat. U., Miami, 1995. Cert. social sci. tchr. 6-12 Fla., 1996. Social sci. tchr. Glades Mid. Sch., Miami, 1995—96, Conchita Espinosa Acad., Miami, 1996—2000, Archbishop Coleman F. Carroll HS, Miami, 2000—04; social studies tchr. St. Brendan HS, Miami, 2004—. Non-Partisan. Roman Catholic.

MOLINA, MARIO JOSE, physical chemist, educator; b. Mexico City, Mar. 19, 1943; arrived in U.S., 1968; s. Roberto Molina-Pasquel and Leonor Henríquez; m. Alvarez Guadalupe, Feb. 11, 2006; 1 child, Felipe. Bachillerato, Acad. Hispano Mexicana, Mexico City, 1959; Ingeniero Químico, U. Nacional Autónoma de México, 1965; postgrad., U. Freiburg, Fed. Republic Germany, 1966—67; PhD, U. Calif., Berkeley, 1972. Asst. prof. U. Nacional Autónoma de México, 1967—68; research assoc. U. Calif.-Berkeley, 1972—73, U. Calif.-Irvine, 1973—75, asst. prof. phys. chemistry, 1975—79, assoc. prof., 1979—82; sr. rsch. scientist Jet Propulsion Lab., 1983—89; prof. dept. earth, atom and planet sci., dept. chemistry MIT, Cambridge, 1989—96, Martin prof. atmospheric chemistry, 1997—2004, Inst. prof., 1997—2004; prof., chemistry and biochemistry Univ. Calif., San Diego, 2004—; faculty, Ctr. for Atmospheric Sci. Scripps Inst. of Oceanography, 2004—. Bd. dirs. MacArthur Found. Named a Trailblazer in Sci., Sci. Spectrum Mag., 2005; named one of 50 Most Important Hispanics in Govt., Edn., Hispanic Engineer and Info. Tech. mag., 2005; recipient Tyler Ecology award, 1983, Esselen award for chemistry in pub. interest, 1987, Max-Planck-Forschungs-Preis, Alexander von Humboldt-Stiftung, 1994, Nobel Prize in Chemistry, 1995, Sasakawa prize, UNEP, 1999. Mem.: NAS, Pontifical Acad. Sci., Inst. of Medicine, Am. Geophys. Union (Pres.'s Com. on Advisors on Sci. and Tech. 1994—2000), Am. Phys. Soc., Am. Chem. Soc. Achievements include discovery of the theory that fluorocarbons deplete ozone layer of stratosphere. Office: Dept Chem & Biochem UCSD 3050-E 9500 Gilman Dr La Jolla CA 92093-0356 Office Phone: 858-534-1696. *We have to understand our environment to find out if we are tampering with it. One of our accomplishments has been to call attention to society's potential altering of the atmosphere.*

MOLINA, RAFAEL EVENCIO, retired urologist; b. Havana, Cuba, July 6, 1923; came to U.S., 1961; s. Joseph M. and Maria H. Molina; m. Maria T. Rodriguez (div.); children: Louis R., Maria T., Manuel E., Rafael E. BA, BS, Colegio de Belen, Havana, 1941; MD, U. Havana, 1949. Diplomate Am. Bd. Urology. Resident U. Miami, Fla., 1963-66; physician Hoffman Urol., Huntington, W.Va., 1966—2002; ret., 2004. Contbr. articles to med. jours. Mem. AMA, ACS, Am. Urodynamic Soc., Am. Urol. Assn., Am. Soc. Nephrology, Cuban Med. Soc. in Exile, Rotary Club, Elks Club, Huntington Area C. of C. Republican. Roman Catholic. Avocation: tennis. Home: PO Box 7052 Huntington WV 25774-7052 also: 170 Woodland Dr Huntington WV 25705-1346

MOLINA, TANYA E., school librarian; b. Hamilton, New Zealand, June 2, 1971; arrived in U.S., 1973; d. Cyril Alfred and Karen Dawn Call; 1 child, Christian Michael. BS, No. Ariz. U., 1997, MEd, 1998; MA, U. Ariz., 2000. Tchr. Safford (Ariz.) Unified Sch. Dist., 1997—2001; libr. King City (Calif.) Elem. Sch. Dist., 2001—02; libr. media specialist Avondale (Ariz.) Elem. Sch. Dist., 2002—. Cons. in field. Mem.: ALA, Internat. Reading Assn., Ariz. Libr. Assn. Republican. Lds Ch. Avocations: writing, reading, scrapbooks. Office: Centerra Mirage Sch Goodyear AZ 85338

MOLINARI, SUSAN, former congresswoman; b. Staten Island, NY, Mar. 27, 1958; d. Guy V. and Marguerite (Wing) Molinari; m. Bill Paxon; 2 children. BA, SUNY, Albany, 1980, MA, 1982. Former intern for State Senator Christopher Mega; former rsch. analyst N.Y. State Senate Fin. Com.; former fin. asst. Nat. Rep. Gov.'s Assn.; ethnic community liaison Rep. Nat. Com., 1983-84; minority leader N.Y.C. Council, 1986-90; mem. 101st-104th Congresses from 14th (now 13th) N.Y. dist., 1990-97, vice-chair House Rep. Conf.; anchor CBS News Sat. Morning, NYC, 1997-98; Chairman, CEO The Washington Group, 2001—. Author: (book) Representative Mom: Balancing Budgets, Bill and Baby in the U.S. Congress, 1998. Roman Catholic. Office: c/o The Washington Group 1401 K Street NW Ste 1000 Washington DC 20005

MOLINARO, JOSEPH DANIEL, dentist, director; b. Phila., May 4, 1969; s. Daniel Joseph and Antoinette Marie (Napolio) Molinaro; m. Ellen Catherine Frank, June 14, 2003. BS in Biology, Villanova U., Pa., 1991; DMD, Temple U., Phila., 1995; MS in Oral Biology, George Washington U., Washington, 2001. Diplomate Fed. Svcs. Bd. Gen. Dentistry, 2002, Am. Bd. Gen. Dentistry 2002. Gen. dentist U.S. Naval Dental Ctr. USN, Agana, Guam, 1995—97, dental clinic divsn. officer, 1996—97, gen. dentist USS George Washington CVN 73 Norfolk, Va., 1997—99, dental clinic divsn. officer, 1998—99, resident, comprehensive dentistry Nat. Naval Dental Ctr. Bethesda, Md., 1999—2001, comprehensive dentist, dental clinic dept. head dental annex br. Indian Head, Md., 2001—04, dep. sr. dental surgeon pers. exch. program Portsmouth, England, 2004—06; operative dentistry dept. head Dental Clinic MC Recruit Depot, 2006—. Contbr. articles to profl. jours. Lt. comdr. Dental Corps USN, 1995—, Dental Corps. Decorated Navy and Marine Corps Commendation medal, Navy and Marine Corps Achievement medal, Humanitarian Svc. medal USN; recipient Martin I. Munin award, Temple U. Sch. Dentistry, 1995, Comdg. Officer's award for excellence, Nat. Naval Dental Ctr., 2000, Chief of the Dental Corps award, 2001; Health Profls. scholar, USN, 1994—95. Fellow: Acad. Gen. Dentistry; mem.: ADA, Acad. Operative Dentistry, Edward C. Penick Endodontic Study Club. Roman Catholic. Achievements include completed a study comparing the influence of various dental restorative materials on tooth cusp stiffness. Avocations: travel, reading, sports. Personal E-mail: joeandellen@molinaro.us.

MOLINARO, SAMUEL L., JR., diversified financial services company executive; b. Binghamton, NY, Dec. 30, 1957; m. Lisa Melino; children: Danielle Anne, Alexa Nicole. BBA in Acctg., St. Bonaventure U., Olean, NY, 1980. CPA, NY. Mgr. Price Waterhouse, NYC, 1980-86; sr. v.p. fin. Bear Stearns Companies Inc., NYC, 1986-96, sr. v.p., CFO, 1996—2001, exec. v.p., CFO, 2001—07, exec. v.p., CFO, COO, 2007—. Office: Bear Stearns 383 Madison Ave New York NY 10179 *

MOLINARO, THOMAS J., lawyer; b. Cleve., June 4, 1952; s. Albert J. and Marilyn Molinaro; children: Daniel, Paul, Marisa, Anna. BS, U. Wis., 1976; JD, U. Wis. Law Sch., 1979. Bar: Wis., U.S. Dist. Ct. (we. and ea. dists.) Wis. Law clk. Wis. Ct. Appeals, Waukesha, 1979-80; assoc. Crooks, Law & Connell, Wausau, 1980-83; ptnr. Brady, Hoover & Molinaro, Wausau, 1983-85, Brady & Molinaro, Wausau, 1986-92; sole practice law Wausau, 1993—2002; ptnr. Grischke, Molinaro & Laughlin, LLSC, Wausau, 2003—. Bd. dirs. Marathon Civic Corp., Wausau, 1988-94, Wausau Area Youth Soccer Assn., 1990-94; membership com. YMCA, Wausau, 1988-90. Mem. ATLA, Wis. Bar Assn., Marathon County Bar Assn. Avocations: antique collecting and restoration, skiing, soccer.

MOLINA-WALTERS, DEBI ANN, education educator; b. Antioch, Calif., Aug. 16, 1959; d. Joe Guererro and Dorothy Mildred Molina; m. Daniel Wade Walters, Sept. 6, 1997. AA, Los Medanos Jr. Coll., Pittsburg, Calif., 1979; BA, Sonoma State U., Rohnert Park, Calif., 1983; MS, Hayward State U., Calif., 1995; MA, Chapman U., Concord, Calif., 1997; EdD, U. of the Pacific, Stockton, Calif., 2004. Adminstrv. credential Chapman U., PPS - sch. counseling credential Chapman U., elem. tchr. credential Sacramento State U., astronomy Sonoma State U. Tchr. 6th grade elem. sch. Marsh Elem. Sch., Antioch, 1989—91; tchr. mid. sch. sci. and leadership Pk. Mid. Sch., Antioch, 1991—2000; lectr. Chapman U., Concord, 1998—2004; tchr. h.s. sci. Antioch H.S., 2000—01; tchr. 6th grade sci. and leadership Bidwell Elem., Antioch, 2001—03; lectr. Hayward State U., 2002—04; mid. sch. sci. tchr. Dallas Ranch Mid. Sch., Antioch, Calif., 2003—04; clin. asst. prof. Ariz. State U., Mesa, 2004—. Chair sci. dept. Antioch Unified Sch. Dist., 1998—2004, mem. leadership team, 1998—2004, mentor tchr., 1992—2004; sci. club adviser Pk. Mid. Sch., Antioch, 1991—2000; cons. Antioch Unified Sch. Dist., 1998—2004. Contbr. articles to profl. jours. Named Tchr. of Yr., 1991Contra Costa County Jaycees, 1991; recipient Tchg. Recognition award, Ariz. State U., 2004, Svc. award, PTSA, 1991. Mem.: ASCD, Am. Soc. Quality, Ariz. Assn. for Environ. Edn., No. Am. Assn. for Environ. Edn., Nat. Sci. Educators Leadership Assn., Calif. Sci. Tchrs. Assn., Am. Edn. Rsch. Assn., Ariz. Sci. Teachers Assn., Nat. Sci. Tchr. Assn. (assoc.), Phi Delta Kappa. Office: Ariz State Univ Bldg 140 7001 E Williams Field Rd Mesa AZ 85212 Home Phone: 480-748-6562; Office Phone: 480-727-1510. Office Fax: 480-727-1964. E-mail: drmo@asu.edu.

MOLINDER, JOHN IRVING, engineering educator, consultant; b. Erie, Pa., June 14, 1941; s. Karl Oskar and Carin (Ecklund) M.; m. Janet Marie Ahlquist, June 16, 1962; children: Tim, Karen. BSEE, U. Nebr., 1963; MSEE, Air Force Inst. Tech., 1964; PhD EE, Calif. Inst. Tech., 1969. Registered profl. engr., Calif. Project officer Ballistic Systems Div., Norton AFB, Calif., 1964-67; sr. engr. Jet Propulsion Lab., Pasadena, Calif., 1969-70; prof. engring. Harvey Mudd Coll., Claremont, Calif., 1970—; prin. engr. Qualcomm Inc., 1996-97; contractor Boeing Satellite Systems, 2000—02. Part-time lectr. Calif. State U., L.A., 1970-74; mem. tech. adv. panel Kinemetrics, Pasadena, 1985-86; part-time mem. tech. staff Jet Propulsion Lab., Pasadena, 1974-97, rep. NASA Hdqrs., Washington, 1979-80; vis. prof. elec. engring. Calif. Inst. Tech., 1982-83. Contbr. articles to profl. jours. Served to capt. USAF, 1963-67. Mem.: IEEE (sr.). Avocations: bicycling, reading, computers. Office: Harvey Mudd Coll Dept Engring 301 Platt Blvd Claremont CA 91711-5901 Home Phone: 909-593-0982. Business E-Mail: John_Molinder@hmc.edu.

MOLINE, JENNIFER M., consumer products company executive; Various positions up to v.p., treas. Tupperware Corp., 1989—2000; v.p. acctg. svcs. ANC Rental Corp., 2000—03; v.p. US fin. ops., dir. fin. integration DHL Express, 2003—06; sr. v.p., contr. Office Depot, Inc., Delray Beach, Fla., 2006—. Office: Office Depot Inc 2200 Old Germantown Rd Delray Beach FL 33445 *

MOLINEAUX, CHARLES BORROMEO, lawyer, arbitrator, columnist, poet; b. NYC, Sept. 27, 1930; s. Charles Borromeo and Marion Frances (Belter) M.; m. Patricia Leo Devereux, July 2, 1960; children: Charles, Stephen, Christopher, Patricia, Peter, Elizabeth. BS cum laude, Georgetown U., 1950; JD, St. Johns U., 1959. Bar: N.Y. 1959, Mass. 1981, D.C. 1988. From assoc. to ptnr. Nevius, Jarvis & Pilz and successor firms, NYC, 1959-77; ptnr. Gadsby & Hannah, NYC, 1978-80; v.p., gen. counsel Perini Corp., Framingham, Mass., 1980-87; pvt. practice Washington, 1987—. Adj. faculty Internat. Law Inst., Washington, 1989—. Author numerous poems. Mem. adv. bd. Inst. for Transnat. Arbitration; committeeman Rep. Party, Nassau County, NY, 1965—71, mem. exec. com., committeeman Fairfax County, Va., 1989. 1st lt. US Army, 1954—56. Fellow Am. Bar Found.; mem. ASCE, Am. Arbitration Assn. (constrn. ADR task force 1994—), Chartered Inst. Arbitrators, Fedn. Internat. Engrs.-Conseils (Assoc. Gen. Contractors del. constrn. contract com., Louis Prangey award for svc. to profession cons. engring. 1996), Soc. Constrn. Arbitrators London, Del. Hist. Soc., London Ct. Internat. Arbitration, Fellowship Cath. Scholars. Roman Catholic. Home: 8321 Weller Ave Mc Lean VA 22102-1717 Office: 1660 International Dr Ste 400 Mc Lean VA 22102 Office Phone: 703-287-4232. Personal E-mail: cmlnx@aol.com.

MOLITERNO, DAVID J., cardiologist, educator; b. Flint, Mich., Oct. 29, 1960; s. Donald G. and Betty J. Moliterno; m. Judith Ann Delp; children: Nathaniel, Benjamin. BS with honors, U. Mich., 1982; MD, Med. Coll. Va., 1987. Diplomate Am. Bd. Internal Medicine, Am. Bd. Cardiovascular Medicine, Am. Bd. Interventional Cardiology, lic. physician Ohio. Intern Vanderbilt U. Hosps., Vanderbilt U. Med. Ctr., Nashville, 1987—88; resident Vanderbilt U. Hosps. and Nashville VA Med. Ctr., 1988—90; fellow Parkland Meml. Hosp. and Dallas VA Med. Ctr., U. Tex. Southwestern Med. Ctr., 1990—93; fellow in interventional cardiology dept. cardiovascular medicine, sect. interventional cardiology The Cleve. Clinic Found., 1993—94, staff physician sect. interventional cardiology dept. cardiovascular medicine, 1994—2003; asst. prof. medicine dept. cardiology Cleve. Clinic Health Sci. Ctr., The Ohio State U., 1994—99; vice chmn., internal medicine, chief, divsn. cardiology, Jefferson M. Gill prof. cardiology Univ. Ky., 2003—. Med. dir. Cleve. Clinic Cardiology Investigators' Assn., 1999—; lectr. in field. Contbr. numerous articles to profl. jours.; reviewer: jours. in field, sect. editor: Jour. Thrombosis and Thrombolysis, med. editor: Cardiac Consult, mem. editl. bd.: Current Controlled Trials in Cardiovascular Medicine, Jour. Am. Coll. Cardiology. Named one of Best Doctors in Am., 2007. Fellow: ACP, European Soc. Cardiology (thrombosis working group), Am. Coll. Cardiology; mem.: AMA, Am. Heart Assn. (arteriosclerosis and thrombosis coun., clin. cardiology coun.). Office: Gill Heart Inst UK HealthCare 800 Rose St Lexington KY 40536 *

MOLITOR, GRAHAM THOMAS TATE, lawyer; b. Seattle, Apr. 6, 1934; s. Robert Franklin and Louise Margaret (Graham) M.; m. Carlotta Jean Crate, July 30, 1960; children: Graham Thomas Tate, Anne Therese, Christopher Robert. BS, U. Wash., 1955; LLB, Am. U., 1963. Bar: D.C. 1963. Rsch. asst. U. Wash., Seattle, 1957; bailiff U.S. Criminal Ct. D.C., 1958-59; legis. counsel U.S. Ho. of Reps., Washington, 1961-63; dir. candidate rsch. Rockefeller for Pres. Com., 1963-64, 68; D.C. counsel, asst. dir. govt. rels. Nabisco, Inc., Washington, 1964-70; dir. govtl. rels. Gen. Mills, Inc., Washington, 1970-77; pres., CEO Pub. Policy Forecasting, Inc., Potomac, Md., 1977—2004; prin. ptnr. Pub. Policy Communicators, 1989-91. Prin., ptnr. Pub. Policy Action Inst., Potomac; adv. bd. Creative Bus. Strategies, Inc.; adj. prof. Grad. Sch. Bus. Am. U., Washington, 1969—75, Washington, 1979—85, Montgomery Coll., Rockville, Md., 1987—88; dir. rsch. White House Conf. on Indsl. World Ahead, 1971—72; mem. White House Adv. Com. on Social Indicators, 1975—76; chmn. Commn. on the Future of Montgomery County, 1986—88; guest lectr. numerous univs.; mem. White House Confs. on Food, Nutrition and Health, 1969—71, White House Conf. on Youth, 1970; bd. dirs. First Global Conf. on the Future, Inc., Can., 1980—; organizing com. Found. for the Future, 1997—, bd. advisors, 1999—, mem. scholar adv. bd., 2001—. Contbg. editor Food Tomorrow Newsletter, 1976-77; co-editor, chmn. editl. bd. Ency. of the Future, 1991-96; cons. editor Hist. Guide to Am. Govt., 1995-97, McMillan Compendium of the Twenty-First Century, 1998-99; editl. adv. bd. Technol. Forecasting and Social Change, 1999—; chmn. editl. bd. Future Survey, 1995-97, World Ency. of Police Forces and Correctional Systems, 2003-05; mem. editl. bd. Hudson Inst. Study of World Food Problems, 1975-77, bd. Bus. Tomorrow Newsletter, 1977-79, Jour. Futures Studies, 2001—; bd. advisors New Mktg. Techs. Monitor, 1983-85; polit. editor On the Horizon, 1993-95; contbr. articles to profl. jours. Mem. Food Adv. Bd., N.Y.C., 1980-86. Served to 1st lt. U.S. Army, 1958-61. Recipient Disting. Service award Grocery Mfrs. Am., 1973-74, Disting. Service award Nat. Consumer Info. Center, 1974, Disting. Service award Am. Mgmt. Assn., 1975. Fellow: World Acad. Art and Sci. (exec. com. 2000—, chmn. com. on yr. 3000 2001—, bd. trustees); mem.: World Future Soc. (gen. chmn. 2d Gen. Assembly 1975, v.p., dir. 1981—94, v.p., legal counsel 1994—2004, Disting. Svc. award 1975, 2004), E.D. Export Coun., Washington Indsl. Roundtable, Washington Bus.-Govt. Rels. Coun., Univ. Club, Phi Alpha Delta, Phi Kappa Sigma. Republican. Presbyterian. Home and Office: 6343 Saucon Valley Dr Fayetteville PA 17222-9242 E-mail: gmolitor@earthlink.net.

MOLITOR, MICHAEL A., entrepreneur, consultant; b. Bklyn., Nov. 7, 1965; s. Henry J. and Janet A. (Monti) M.; m. Michele A. Emery, July 8, 1995; 1 child, Michael. BS, Siena Coll., 1987; MBA, Columbia U., 2000. CFP. Fin. aid counselor Janet's Coll. Tuition Aid, Massapequa Park, N.Y., 1987-92; income tax acct. Michael A. Molitor, Massapequa, N.Y., 1988—; owner, fin. aid counseling svc. Molitor Coll. Aid Counseling, Massapequa, 1992—; money mgr. Molitor Money Mgmt., Massapequa, 1992—. Cons. Alive-To-Thrive, Inc., Westchester, N.Y., 1992—, cons., adv. bd. Orphan's Aid Soc., Douglaston, N.Y., 1994—; cons. in field. Author: You Can Afford A College Education, 1992; contbr. articles to profl. jours., various TV talk shows. Con. to Guidance Dept. Massapequa Sch. Dist., Massapequa, 1995-98, mem. Long Island Assn., Hauppauge, N.Y., 1990-92. Recipient Top Producer-Pres. Club Transamerica Funds, Houston, 1993-94, mem. signature Club Oppenheimer Funds, Denver, 1995. Mem. Internat. Assn. Fin. Planning, N.Y. Fin. Air Adminstr. Assn., NAt. Assn. Fin. Aid Adminstr., BMW Car Club Am., Porsche Club Am. Mem. Christian Ch. Avocations: golf, drumming, track driving.

MOLITOR, STEVEN JOHN, lawyer; b. May 19, 1962; BA, Franklin and Marshall Coll., 1984; JD, Cornell U., 1987. Bar: N.Y. 1988, Pa. 1996. Assoc. Morgan, Lewis & Bockius LLP, NYC and Phila., 1992-95, ptnr., 1995—2004; ptnr. fin. and real estate practice group Dechert LLP, Phila., 2004—. Home: 1701 Market St Philadelphia PA 19103-2903 Office: Dechert LLP Cira Centre 2929 Arch St Philadelphia PA 19104-2808 Office Phone: 215-994-2777. Office Fax: 215-994-2222. E-mail: steven.molitor@dechert.com.

MOLITORIS, BRUCE ALBERT, nephrologist, educator; b. Springfield, Ill., June 26, 1951; s. Edward and Joyce (Tomasko) M.; m. Karen Lynn Wichterman, June 16, 1973; children: Jason, Jared, Julie. BS, U. Ill., 1973, MS in Nutrition, 1975; MD, Wash. U., 1979. Resident Sch. Medicine U. Colo., Denver, 1979-81, nephrology fellow, 1981-84, asst. prof. medicine, 1984-88, assoc. prof. medicine, 1988-93, prof., 1993; dir. nephrology Ind. U. Med. Sch., Indpls., 1993—; vis. scientist U. Colo., MCDB, Boulder, 1989-90, Max Planck Inst., Federal Republic of Germany, 1984-85; dir. Ind. Ctr. Biol. Microscopy, 2002—. Dir. home dialysis Denver VA Ctr., 1984-93; vis. scientist dept. molecular biology Colo. State U., Ft. Collins, 1998; founding mem. INphoton LLC, med. dir. pharmacophotonics. Assoc. editor: Jour. Investigative Medicine, 1994-99; reviewer: NIH, 1991-94; mem. editl. bd. Am. Jour. Physiology, 1989-2000, Am. Jour. Kidney Diseases, 1991-; contbr. articles to profl. jours. Pres. Cherry Creek Village South Homeowners Assn., 1989-90, Pickwick Commons Home Owners Assn., 1999; v.p. Our Father Luth. Ch., Denver, 1989-90; coun. mem. King of Glory Luth. Ch., Indpls., 1999-2002; coach Cherry Creek Soccer Assn., Greenwood Village, 1988-91, Centennial Little League Titans Basketball; bd. dirs. CSSA, 1993. Recipient Upjohn Achievement award, 1979, Liberty Hyde Bailey award, 1973. Mem. Am. Assn. Physicians, Am. Soc. Nephrology (program chmn. 2002-03, chair acute kidney disease adv. group 2005-), Internat. Soc. Nephrology, NY Acad. Sci., Am. Soc. Clin. Investigation, Am. Fedn. Clin. Rsch. (nat. counselor 1991-94), Western Assn. Physicians. Avocations: bridge, fishing, antiques, hiking. Office: Indiana U Med Ctr R-2 202C 950 W Walnut St Indianapolis IN 46202-5135

MOLL, DAVID CARTER, civil engineer; b. Ames, Iowa, Aug. 5, 1948; s. Dale Curtis and Virginia (Carter) Moll; m. Margaret E. Newman (div. 1989); 1 child, Megahn Elizabeth; m. Melanie G. Harding, 2004 (div. 2006). BSCE, Iowa State U., 1971; cert. advanced study, Am. Grad. Sch. Internat. Mgmt., 1983; MBA with distinction, U. Mich., 1984; advanced masters cert. in project mgmt., George Washington U., 2006. Engr. in tng., Iowa; field engr. Chgo. Bridge & Iron Co., 1971; subcontract supr., field engr. Morrison-Knudsen Internat. Co., Inc., Surinam and Panama, 1976; site supt. engring., asst. supt. constrn. Fluor Corp., Saudi Arabia, 1977-82; group mgr. Cummins Engine Co., Columbus, Ind., 1984-85; mgr. spl. projects Kerr-McGee Coal Corp., Oklahoma City, 1985-88; project mgr. Kerr-McGee Corp., Oklahoma City, 1989, 1993—98, London, 1989-90, Saudi Arabia, 1990—92, Kerr-McGee Environ. Mgmt. Corp., Oklahoma City, 1998—2004; pres. Integrated Solutions Inc., 2005—. Lt. USN, 1971—75. Mem.: AGSIM (leadership cir.), ASCE, Project Mgmt. Inst. (Red Earth chpt. dir. fin., cert. project mgmt. profl.), NY Acad. Scis., Am. Soc. Quality Control (mem. constrn. tech. com.), Civil Engr. Corps (Meritorious Svc. medal), Marston Club, Order of the Knoll (Campanile Guild), Am. Legion, Chi Epsilon. Avocations: cross country skiing, jogging, golf, travel.

MOLL, DEBORAH ADELAIDE, lawyer; b. Wilmington, Del., Jan. 19, 1946; BA, St. John's Coll., Annapolis, Md., 1969; MA, U. Tex., 1972, JD, 1975. Bar: N.Mex 1977. Law clk. Tex. Ct. Criminal Appeals, Austin, 1975-76, U.S. Ct. Appeals (10th cir.), Santa Fe, 1977-78; asst. atty. gen. N.Mex Atty. Gen., Santa Fe, 1978-84; asst. appellate defender N.Mex Pub. Defender Dept., Santa Fe, 1984-87; staff atty. N.Mex Taxation and Revenue Dept., Santa Fe, 1987-92; shareholder Kemrer-Hayes & Moll, P.A., Albuquerque, 1992; gen. counsel N.Mex Gen. Svcs. Dept., Santa Fe, 1993—. Mem.: N.Mex. State Bar (bd. dirs. bankruptcy sect. 1992, adv. opinion com. 1993—96, bd. dirs. pub. law sect. 1996—, chair pub. law sect. 1997—98, bd. dirs. employment law sect. 1999—2003, chair ad hoc com. 2001, com. establish legal specialization constrn. and pub. contracts 2002—). Avocation: photography. Office: NMex Gen Svcs Dept 715 Alta Vista St Santa Fe NM 87505-4108 Office Phone: 505-827-2000. E-mail: Deborah.Moll@state.nm.us.

MOLL, GEORGE WILLIAM, pediatrician, educator; b. Milw., Nov. 23, 1947; s. George William, Sr. and Laverne Delores (Klein) M.; m. Susana Valdez Ramos, June 24, 1978; children: Christina, Teresa. BA in Chemistry cum laude, Carleton Coll., 1969; PhD in Biochemistry, U. Chgo., 1975, MD, 1977. Diplomate Nat. Bd. Med. Examiners; diplomate in pediatrics and pediat. endocrinology Am. Bd. Pediatrics; cert. PALS, CPR. Pediatric resident Mott Children's Hosp., U. Mich., Ann Arbor, 1977-79; pediatric endocrinology fellowship Wyler Children's Hosp., U. Chgo., 1979-81; asst. prof. pediatrics U. Chgo., 1981-85, Emory U. Sch. Medicine, Atlanta, 1985-87; assoc. prof. pediatrics U. Miss. Med. Ctr., Jackson, 1987-93, prof. pediatrics, 1993—; assoc. staff pediatric endocrinology Little Co. of Mary Hosp., Evergreen Park, Ill., 1981-85, The Meth. Hosps., Gary and Merrillville, Ind., 1981-85; staff pediatric endocrinologist The Emory Clinic, Atlanta, 1985-87, Henrietta Egleston Hosp. for Children, Atlanta, 1985-87, Grady Meml. Hosp., Atlanta, 1985-87; staff Emory Univ. Hosp., 1987, dir. pediatric endocrinology; staff U. Miss. Med. Ctr., Jackson, 1987—. Contbr. articles to profl. jours. Active Diabetes Found. of Miss., Inc., 1998, Juv. Diabetes Found. Internat., 1998, Filipino-Am. Assn. of Miss., 1990—, Chronic Disease Coalition of Miss., 1996—. Recipient med. scientist NIH scholarship/grant U. Chgo., 1970-77, Andrew Mellon Found. fellowship, 1981-82, Med. Excellence award So. Med. Assn., 1995; grantee Am. Lung Assn., 1987-89, Eli Lilly Co., Mobil Oil Co., 1991, Diabetes Rsch. and Edn. Found., Inct., 1992, Pharmacia & Upjohn, 1998, others. Fellow Am. Acad. Pediatrics, Am. Coll. Endocrinology; mem. AAAS, Nat. Bd. Med. Examiners (comprehensive task force for reprodn./endocrinology 1989-90), Chgo. Endocrine Club (sec. 1984-85), N.Y. Acad. of Sci., Am. Fedn. for Med. Rsch., Lawson Wilkins Soc. for Pediat. Endocrinology, Midwest and So. Soc. for Pediatric Rsch., Miss. State Med. Assn., Cen. Miss. Med. and Pediatric Soc., The Endocrine Soc. (regional rep. U.S. Pharmacopeia Quinquennial), Am. Diabetes Assn., Juv. Diabetes Found., Sigma Xi, others. Achievements include isolation of a bovine brain protein kinase and establishment of a protein kinase assay employing a novel PEI-cellulose thin-layer system as part of a PhD Biochemistry; established a novel modified flow-dialysis system for steady state hormone action studies; assisted the delineation of a LH-receptor defect related to precocious puberty and a novel genetic mutation in thyroid binding globulin in males; novel genetic mutation in succinate dehydrogenase subunit B gene for malignant paraganglioma. Avocations: carpentry, general handicrafts, electronics, computer repair work. Office: Univ Miss Med Ctr 2500 N State St Jackson MS 39216-4500 Business E-Mail: gmoll@ped.umsmed.edu.

MOLL, JOHN LEWIS, retired electronics engineer; b. Wauseon, Ohio, Dec. 21, 1921; s. Samuel Andrew and Esther (Studer) M.; m. Isabel Mary Sieber, Oct. 28, 1944; children: Nicolas Josef, Benjamin Alex, Diana Carolyn. B.Sc., Ohio State U., 1943, PhD, 1952; Dr. h.c., Faculty Engring., Katholieke U. Leuven, (Belgium), 1983. Elec. engr. RCA Labs., Lancaster, Pa., 1943-45; mem. tech. staff Bell Telephone Labs., Murray Hill, N.J., 1952-58; mem. faculty Stanford U., 1958-69, prof. elec. engring., 1959-69; tech. dir. optoelectronics Fairchild Camera and Instrument Corp., 1969-74; dir. integrated circuits labs. Hewlett-Packard Labs., Palo Alto, Calif., 1974-80, dir. IC structures research, sr. scientist, 1980-87, dir. Superconductivity Lab., 1987-90, mem. tech. staff, 1990-96; ret., 1996. Author: Physics of Semi Conductors, 1964; co-author Computer Aided Design and VLSI Device Development, 1985, rev. edit., 1988; inventor (with Ebers) first analytical transistor model, 1953, still valid and useful for circuit design. Recipient Howard N. Potts medal Franklin Inst., 1967, Disting. Alumnus award Coll. Engring., Ohio State U., 1970, Benjamin C. Lamme medal Coll. Engring., Ohio State U., 1988, Vladimir Karapetoff award Eta Kappa Nu, 1995; Guggenheim fellow, 1964, C&C Award, NEC Fund Integration Comm. and Computers, 1997. Fellow IEEE (Ebers award 1971, Thomas A. Edison medal 1991), Am. Acad. Arts and Scis.; mem. Am. Phys. Soc., Nat. Acad. Engring., Nat. Acad. Scis. Home: 600 Sand Hill Rd Apt 201H Palo Alto CA 94304-2635

MOLL, LLOYD HENRY, retired bank executive; b. Reading, Pa., June 26, 1925; s. Lewis J. and Katie (Rothermel) M.; m. Luise G. Keiper, Oct. 25, 1947; children: Lloyd E., Darryl M. BA, Albright Coll., Reading, 1952. Aircraft engine installer War Dept., 1942-47; tire inspector Firestone Tire & Rubber Co., Pottstown, Pa., 1947-48; asst. mgr. Household Fin. Corp., Reading, Pa., 1952—57; v.p. Meridian Asset Mgmt. Inc. and Meridian Trust Co. (formerly Am. Bank & Trust Co. of Pa.), Reading, 1957—94; v.p. sales and mktg. Investors Trust Co., Wyomissing, Pa., 1995—2005; ret., 2005. Co-founder, past dir. Estate Planning Council of Berks County. Served with AUS, 1945-47. Mem. Am. Inst. Banking. (dir., chmn. bank relations Berks County chpt., pres. 1972-73), Toastmasters (pres. Reading club 1992), Optimists (pres. Reading club 1978-79). Democrat. *Although it has been known to fail me on occasion I try to live by my understanding of the "Golden Rule". When it does fail me I'm usually able to discount such failure by recounting in my mind the many times it has been a two-way street or by convincing myself that I didn't try hard enough in this particular instance. All too often it comes to me much later that the other fellow's interpretation of the "Golden Rule" was far superior to mine. When this happens I have added to my learning. When it does not happen, it forces me to try that much harder to avoid "PERFECTION".*

MOLL, MARYANN ELIZABETH, education educator; b. Buffalo, Apr. 1, 1943; d. Bernard J. and Jean Moll; children: Mark D. Szczepanik, Nancy J. Szczepanik. AA in Paralegal with honors, Erie C.C., Buffalo, 1998; BA in Legal Studies and History, SUNY, Buffalo, 2000; MEd with honors, Ottawa U., Phoenix, 2007. Cert. social studies tchr. Ariz., 2001, endorsed ESL tchr. Ariz., 2006. Copyright asst. U. Buffalo Law Sch., 1998—2000; sub. tchr. Mesa Pub. Schs., Ariz., 2001—03; tchr., ESL coord. Ombudsman Ednl. Svcs., Phoenix, 2004—. Vol. Make A Difference, Phoenix, 2003—. Roman Catholic. Avocations: embroidery, sewing, reading, crocheting.

MOLLAND, MARIA U., Internet company executive; b. 1974; BA, Northwestern U.; MBA, Harvard U. With Disney Internet Group, Volpe Brown Whelan; bus. devel. mgr. Yahoo Finance, 2002—05; gen. mgr. MarketWatch, Inc. Dow Jones & Co., San Francisco, 2005—.

MOLLARD, JOHN DOUGLAS, engineering and geology executive; b. Regina, Sask., Can., Jan. 3, 1924; s. Robert Ashton and Nellie Louisa (McIntosh) M.; m. Mary Jean Lynn, Sept. 18, 1952; children: Catherine Lynn, Jacqueline Lee, Robert Clyde Patrick. BCE, U. Sask., 1945; MSCE, Purdue U., 1947; PhD, Cornell U., 1952; LLD (hon.), U. Regina, 1995. Registered profl. engr., profl. geologist Sask., Alta. and B.C., Can. Resident constrn. engr. Sask. Dept. Hwys. and Transp., 1945; grad. asst. Purdue U., West Lafayette, Ind., 1946-47; rsch. engr. sch. civil engring. Cornell U., Ithaca, NY, 1950-52; air surveys engr., soil and water conservation and devel. Prairie Farm Rehab. Adminstrn., Govt. of Can., 1947-50, chief, airphoto analysis and engring. geology divsn. Regina, 1953-56; pres. J.D. Mollard and Assocs. Ltd., Regina, 1956—. Aerial resource mapping surveys tech. adv. Colombo plan, Govts. Ceylon and Pakistan, 1954-56; adv. Shaw Royal Commn. on Nfld. Agr.; lectr. in field. Author: Landforms and Surface Materials of Canada, 8 edits.; co-author: Airphoto Interpretation and the Canadian Landscape, 1986; contbr. over 100 articles to profl. publs. Organizer, canvasser United Appeal campaigns; bd. dirs. Regina

Symphony Orch., 2002; gov. gen. Can. Adrian Clarkson Rideau Hall. Decorated officer Order of Can.; named to Engring. Alumni Wall of Distinction, U. Sask., 2000; recipient First Meritorious Achievement award, Lt. Gov. Sask., 2002, Engring. Achievement award, Assn. Profl. Engrs. Sask., 1984, Massey medal, Royal Can. Geog. Soc., 1989, Allied Arts medal, Royal Archtl. Inst. Can., 1998, Sask. Geotech. Achievement award, Sask. Geotech. Group, 2002, Sask. Centennial medal, Govt. of Sask., 2005, Roger Brown award, Can. Geotechnical Soc., 2006. Fellow: ASCE, Engring. Inst. Can. (Keefer medal 1948, Julian C. Smith medal 1999), Internat. Explorers Club, Can. Acad. Engring., Geol. Soc. Can., Geol. Soc. Am., Am. Soc. Photogrammetry and Remote Sensing (award for contbns. airphoto interpretation and remote sensing 1979); mem.: Can. Soc. Petroleum Engrs., Geol. Soc. Sask., Regina Geotech. Soc., Can. Geotech. Soc. (1st R.M. Hardy Meml. Keynote lectr. 1987, Thomas Roy award with engring. geology divsn. 1989, R.F. Legget award 1992, Rogert J.E. Brown award 2006), Assn. Cons. Engrs. Can., Regina YMCA (former dir.), Rotary (former dir. Regina club). Mem. United Ch. of Can. Avocations: jogging, reading, golf, tennis, nature study. Office: 810 Avord Tower 2002 Victoria Ave Regina SK Canada S4P 0R7 Office Phone: 306-352-8811 8855. Office Fax: 306-352-8820. Business E-Mail: mollard@jdmollard.com.

MOLLEN, EDWARD LEIGH, pediatrician, allergist, clinical immunologist; b. Richmond, Va., May 13, 1946; s. Irving Roth and Ruth (Damsky) M.; m. Mary Viola Jeffrey, Dec. 14, 1975; children: Shawn, Michael, Eric, Christopher. BS in Chemistry, Coll. William and Mary, 1968; MD, Med. Coll. Va., 1972. Diplomate Am. Bd. Pediatrics, Am. Bd. Allergy and Immunology. Resident in pediatrics Med. Coll. Va., Richmond, 1972-75, fellow in allergy and immunology, 1975-77; practice allergy and pediatric allergy and clin. immunology Allergy Assocs. of Richmond, 1977-85; pvt. practice allergy/pediatric allergy and clin. immunology Richmond, 1985—. Fellow Am. Acad. Allergy, Asthma and Immunology, Am. Acad. Pediatrics; mem. Med. Soc. Va., Richmond Acad. Medicine, Asthma and Allergy Soc. Va. Avocations: bicycling, running, gardening. Office: 5855 Bremo Rd Ste 702 Richmond VA 23226-1926 Home Phone: 804-353-8353; Office Phone: 804-288-5216. E-mail: elmollenmd@aol.com.

MOLLENAUER, LINN FREDERICK, retired physicist, writer; b. Washington, Pa., Jan. 6, 1937; B of Engring. Physics, Cornell U., 1959; PhD in Physics, Stanford U., 1965. Asst. prof. physics U. Calif., Berkeley, 1965—72; rsch. staff Bell Labs./Lucent Techs., Holmdel, NJ, 1972—2003; ret., 2003. Author (with J.P. Gordon): Solitons in Optical Fibers: Fundamentals and Applications, 2006; co-editor (with J.C. White): Tunable Lasers, 1987. Recipient Ballantine medal, Franklin Inst., 1986, Rank prize in Photonics, 1991; fellow, Bell Labs., 2000. Fellow: IEEE (LEOS Disting. Lectr. award 1991, LEOS Quantum Electronics award 2001), AAAS, Optical Soc. Am. (R.W. Wood prize 1982, Charles Hard Townes award 1997); mem.: NAE. Achievements include first to demonstrate optical soliton propagation, leading to the realization of soliton-based, ultra-high-capacity lightwave communication. Personal E-mail: linnm@optonline.net.

MOLLENKOTT, VIRGINIA RAMEY, English literature and language educator, writer, guest lecturer; b. Phila., Jan. 28, 1932; d. Robert Franklin and May (Lotz) Ramey; m. Frederick H. Mollenkott, June 17, 1954 (div. July 1973); 1 child, Paul F. BA, Bob Jones U., 1953; MA, Temple U., 1955; PhD, NYU, 1964; D in Ministries (hon.), Samaritan Coll., 1989. Chair English dept. Shelton Coll., Ringwood, NJ, 1955—63, Nyack Coll., NY, 1963—67; prof. English William Paterson U. N.J., Wayne, 1967—97, chair English dept., 1972—76, prof. emeritus, 1997—. Asst. editor Seventeenth Century News, NYC, 1965-75; stylistic cons. New International Version of the Bible, Am. Bible Soc., 1970-78; translation com. An Inclusive Language Lectionary, Nat. Coun. Chs., 1980-88; bd. dirs. Pacem in Terris, Warwick, NY, Kirkridge Conf. Ctr., Bangor, Pa., 1980-91, Upper Room AIDS Ministry, Harlem, NYC, 1989-94; adv. bd. Program on gender and soc. Rochester Divinity Sch., NY, 1993—; manuscript evaluator Jour. Feminist Studies in Religion, Cambridge, Mass., 1994—; contbg. editor The Witness, 1994-2000, 2002-03, The Other Side, 2003-05; lectr. in field. Author: Adamant and Stone Chips, 1967, In Search of Balance, 1969, Women, Men and the Bible, 1977 1st rev. edit. 1988, Korean translation, 1981, Speech, Silence, Action, 1980, (with others) Is the Homosexual My Neighbor? A Positive Christian Response, 1978, rev. edit. 1994 (Integrity award 1979), The Divine Feminine: Biblical Imagery of God as Female, 1983, in German 1985, French, 1990, Italian, 1993; (with others) Views from the Intersection, 1984, Godding: Human Responsibility and the Bible, 1987, Sensuous Spirituality: Out from Fundamentalism, 1992, rev. edit., 2007, Omnigender: A Trans-Religious Approach, 2001 (Lambda Literary award 2002, Ben Franklin award 2002), rev. edit., 2007, (with others) Transgender Journeys, 2003; editor: Women of Faith in Dialogue, 1987, Adam Among the Television Trees, 1971; editl. bd. Studies in Theology & Sexuality, 1997—. Recipient Lifetime Achievement award, Svcs. and Advocacy for Gay, Lesbian, Bisexual and Transgender Elders, 1999, NJ Lesbian and Gay Lifetime Achievement award, 1992. Mem. MLA (exec. com. religion and lit. 1976-80), Women's Inst. for Freedom of Press (assoc.), Milton Soc. Am. (exec. com. 1974-76). Democrat. Episcopalian. Avocations: travel, gardening. Home and Office: 11 Yearling Trl Hewitt NJ 07421-2510 Home Phone: 973-853-4287; Office Phone: 973-853-4287. Business E-Mail: jstvrm@warwick.net.

MOLLER, JAMES HERMAN, pediatrician, educator; b. Fresno, Calif., Aug. 12, 1933; s. Leonard Hansen and Eloise Jean (Hunter) M.; m. Carol Suzanne Eymann, Sept. 8, 1957; children: James, Elizabeth. AB, Stanford U., 1954, MD, 1958. Instr. pediat. U. Minn., Mpls., 1965-66, asst. prof., 1966-70, assoc. prof., 1970-73, prof., 1973—, Dwan prof., 1975—2005, interim head pediat., 1976-78, 97-99, chief pediat., 1976-78, head pediat., 1999—2003; chief of staff U. Minn. Hosp., Mpls., 1984-89. Vis. prof. Nat. Heart & Lung Inst., London, 1989-90, Inst. Child Health, London, 1989-90. Contbr. over 200 sci. articles to profl. jours. Bd. dirs. U. Minn. Hosp., 1984-89, Mpls. Children's Health Ctr., 1975-78, Children's Hosp., St. Paul, 1975-78, Minn. Assn. Pub. tchg. Hosps., Mpls., 1984-89, Variety Club Heart Assn., Mpls., 1980-83. Capt. U.S. Army, 1961-63. Fellow Am. Acad. Pediat. (exec. bd. 1991-92, dist. chmn. 1991-92, alternate dist. chmn. 1985-91, Ross Edn. award 1989), Am. Coll. Cardiology; mem. Am. Heart Assn. (pres. 1993-94, v.p. 1986-91, bd. dirs. 1986-95, award of Merit 1989), Am. Fedn. Clin. Rsch., Am. Pediatric Soc., Am. Bd. Pediat. Nat. Bd. Med. Examiners, Midwest Soc. Pediatric Cardiology Soc., Minn. Med. Assn. (intersplty. coun. 1979-82, resource group child health 1980-82), Minn. Acad. Medicine, Mpls. Met. Pediatric Soc., No. Pediatric Cardiology Soc. (pres. 1978-79), Midwest Soc. Pediatric Rsch. Soc. Pediatric Rsch., Hennepin County Med. Soc. (bd. dirs. 1986-89), Irish Am. Paediatric Soc., British Paediatric Cardiac Assn., Coun. Med. Splty. Socs. (bd. dirs., 1991—), Sub-bd. Pediatric Cardiology (chmn. 1992-94), Internat. Heart Found. (pres. 1997-98), World Heart Fedn. (bd. dirs. 1999). Independent. Congregationalist. Avocations: gardening, travel, oriental carpets, reading. Home: 4816 Sheridan Ave S Minneapolis MN 55410-1917 Office: U Minn 420 Delaware St SE Minneapolis MN 55455-0374 Office Phone: 612-626-2790. Business E-Mail: molle002@umn.edu.

MOLLICA, JOSEPH A., pharmaceutical executive; b. 1940; Various positions, sr. v.p. drug devel. Ciba-Geigy, Ardsley, NY, 1966—86; v.p. med. products E.I. Du Pont De Nemours & Co., Inc., Wilmington, Del., 1987—90; CEO Du Pont Merck Pharm. Co., Wilmington, Del., 1991—93; CEO, chmn. Pharmacopeia, Princeton, NJ, 1994—2004, chmn., 2004—. Office: Pharmacopeia Inc Po Box 5350 Princeton NJ 08543-5350 Business E-Mail: mollica@pcop.com.

MOLLICK, ANDRE VARELLA, economics professor, researcher; b. Natal, Brazil, June 9, 1967; arrived in US, 1996, permanent resident, 2005; s. Hildebrando and Maria das Gracas Varella Mollick; m. Carolina Avila Campos, Apr. 13, 1996; children: Sofia, Isabella. BA in Econs., U. Brasilia, Brazil, 1987; MSc in Econs., U. Tsukuba, Japan, 1994, PhD in Econs., 1996. Fgn. exch. and funds trader Bank of Tokyo-Mitsubishi, Miami, Fla., 1997—98; treasury mgr. SONY Capital Corp., NYC, 1998—2000; asst. prof. Monterrey's Tech. Inst., Monterrey, Nuevo Leon, Mexico, 2000—03, assoc. prof., 2003—04, U. Tex. - Pan Am., Edinburg, 2004—. Presenter in field. Contbr. articles to profl. jours. Scholar Undergraduate Sch., Brazilian Ministry Edn. and Culture, 1985—87, Japanese Govt. (Monbusho), 1989—96. Mem.: Am. Econ. Assn. Avocations: swimming, reading. Office: University of Texas - PanAm Economics 1201 W University Dr Edinburg TX 78541-2999 Home Phone: 956-383-9224.

MOLLIS, RALPH (A. RALPH MOLLIS), state official, former mayor; b. Providence, May 24, 1961; s. Joseph Gregory Jr. and Gloria Louise (Stone) Mollis; children: Michael, Angelo, Briana; m. Laurie Ranaldi; 1 stepchild Gian Piscione. BA in Polit. Sci., St. Anselm Coll., 1983; student, So. New Eng. Sch. Law, 1983—85. Registered investment adv. 1996. V.p., dir. office ops. LAMCO Pension and Investment Adv. Firm, Worwick, RI, 1983—94; acting mayor Town of North Providence, RI, 1994, mayor RI, 1997—2007; bus. mgr. AAT Restaurant Corp., Providence, 1994-95; inst. & investment rep. NY Life, Providence, 1995-96; asst. property mgr., budget cons. Ferland Property Mgmt., RI, 1996; sec. state State of RI, Providence, 2007—. Coun. mem. Town of North Providence, 1986-96, coun. pres., 1992-94, HS bldg. com., 1991—. Recipient Environ. Merit award, US EPA, 2000, Giovanni Da Verrazzano award for Outstanding Svc. to RI Cmty., 2002, Portuguese Am. Citizens Com. of RI Govt. award, 2005. Mem. Lions, Italia-Am. Club (Outstanding Pub. Svc. award 2000), Sons of Italy. Democrat. Roman Catholic. Avocations: coaching, golf. Office: Office Sec State 82 Smith St State House Rm 217 Providence RI 02903 *

MOLLMAN, JOHN PETER, publishing executive; b. Belleville, Ill., Feb. 8, 1931; s. Kenneth John and Maurine (Farrow) M.; m. Carol J. Piper, Apr. 4, 1998; children: Sarah Chase Underhill, Eric Cleburne. BA, Washington U., St. Louis, 1952. Advt. specialist Gen. Electric Co., Schenectady and Boston, 1952-54; mgr. Enterprise Printing Co., Millstadt, Ill., 1956-66; dir. prodn. Harper & Row Pubs., NYC, 1967-74; pub. Harper's Mag. Press, NYC, 1971-74; v.p. prodn. Random House Inc., NYC, 1974-81; sr. v.p. World Book-Childcraft Inc., Chgo., 1981-88; pres. World Book Pub., 1988-91; pub. cons., 1991-92; dir. intellectual property devel. Multimedia Publishing Microsoft, 1992-96; cons. in electronic pub. Carmel, Calif., 1996—. Mem. vis. com. Washington U.; mem. pub. com. Art Inst. Chgo.; bd. dirs. Yerba Buena Ctr. for the Arts, San Francisco; pres. Internat. ebook Award Found., N.Y. Mem. Golf Club at Quail Lodge, Phi Delta Theta, Sigma Delta Chi, Omicron Delta Kappa. Unitarian Universalist. Home: 25340 Vista Del Pinos Carmel CA 93923-8804 Office Phone: 831-622-7532. Personal E-mail: pmollman@msn.com.

MOLLOFF, FLORENCE JEANINE, speech and language therapist; b. St. Louis, Aug. 28, 1959; d. Lawrence Allan and Rietta Gertrude (Fiegenbaum) M. BS, Fontbonne Coll., St. Louis, 1983; MEd summa cum laude, Nat. Louis U., St. Louis, 1989; student, Project ACCESS Inst., 1992, Judevine Ctr. Autistic Children Tng., 1992. Cert. speech correctionist, Mo. Intern St. Louis State Sch. for Profoundly Retarded, 1983-84; speech therapist St. Louis Pub. Schs., 1984—; Judvine Ctr. for Autistic Children Tng., 1992; speech/lang. therapist St. Louis Pub. Schs./Autism Program, 1992-93, 97—; speech/lang. therapist Michael Sch. Medically Fragile and Multiply Handicapped Michael Sch. Medically Fragile and Multiply Handicapped, 1993-96; speech and lang. pathologist autism program Buder, 1996—, Buder and Fanning, 1997—2000. Speech, lang. therapist St. Louis Pub. Schs./Michael Sch. for Medically Fragile and Multiply Handicapped, 1993—; ednl. cons. program devel. Mo. Coalition for Environ., St. Louis, Columbia, Kansas City, 1990—; cons., trainer in puppetry Kids on the Block, St. Louis Pub. Schs., 1988—; vol. grant writer West End Restoration Corp.; speech/lang. therapist Mid. Sch. for Medically Fragile and Multiply Handicapped, 1993-96. Author: (pseudonym F.J. Molotschnikov) 91 Seconds to Armageddon, 1999; author, creator transition curriculum: Consultative Resource Program, 1989; creator puppet program: Save Our Astonishing Planet, 1990; ednl. cons. program devel. young St. Louis audiences (adapted program for severe to profoundly handicapped children "Arabian Nights", 1994; editor: Strides Newsletter, St. Louis, 1996-98; contbr. artist St. Louis Internat. Jazz Mus.; vol. grant writer West End Restoration Corp. Educator, lobbyist Coalition for the Environ., St. Louis, 1990, newsletter editor, 2000-01; activist, lobbyist Housing Now, St. Louis, 1989; foster parent Christian Children's Fund, 1986—; activist Habitat for Humanity Internat., 1994—; fundraiser Gateway I Have a Dream Found., 1995—; hon. nat. steering com. Pres. Clinton's Re-election, 1995; contbg. mem. Dem. Nat. Com., 1995—; vol. grant writer West End Restoration Corp.; active Emily's List, Cross-Cultural Solutions Project, New Delhi, India, 1998, World Affairs Coun., St. Louis, Mo., 2002 Mem. AAUW, ASCD, Coun. Exceptional Children (state rep. Mo. divsn. for children with communicative disorders 1988-89, presenter nat. conv. 1989), Internat. Platform Assn., Am. Fedn. Tchrs. (bldg. rep. 1992), Nat. Arbor Day Found., Nat. Parks and Conservation Assn., Nat. Women's Polit. Caucus, Mo. Assn. for Augmentative Comm. Systems, Met. St. Louis Women's Polit. Caucus, Emily's List, Am. Med. Writers Assn., Soc. for Tech. Com., NEA (editor Strides newsletter 1996-97, grantee Internet project, sec. St. Louis 1997-99), Mo. NEA, Amnesty Internat., World Affairs Coun. St. Louis. Independent. Avocations: puppetry, international affairs, running, films. Home: 10116 Thorpe Ave Saint Louis MO 63114 Office Phone: 314-353-1349. Personal E-mail: jeanine.molloff@yahoo.com. Business E-Mail: fmolloff@slps.org.

MOLLOHAN, ALAN BOWLBY, congressman; b. Fairmont, W.Va., May 14, 1943; s. Robert H. and Helen (Holt) Mollohan; m. Barbara Whiting, Aug. 7, 1976; children: Alan, Robert, Andrew, Karl, Mary Kathryn. AB in Polit. Sci., Coll. William and Mary, 1966; JD, W.Va. U. Coll. Law, 1970. Assoc. law firm, 1970-82; mem. US Congress from 1st W.Va. dist., 1983—, mem. appropriations com., ranking minority mem. sci., state, justice, commerce and related agencies subcommittee. Served in USAR, 1970—83. Mem.: ABA, W.Va. Bar, Elks, Moose. Democrat. Baptist. Office: US Ho Reps 2302 Rayburn Ho Office Bldg Washington DC 20515-0001 Office Phone: 202-225-4172. *

MOLLOY, DAVID SCOTT, JR., labor relations educator; b. Providence, Aug. 17, 1946; s. David Scott and Miriam Virginia (Handy) Molloy; children: Kelsey Allende Molloy, Cady Larkin Molloy. BA, RI Coll., Providence, 1970; MA, U. NH, Durham, 1972; PhD, Providence Coll., 1991. Bus driver RI Pub. Transit Authority, Providence, 1973-81; bus. agt. Amalgamated Transit Union, Providence, 1981-84; chief-of-staff US Congressman Schneider, Cranston, RI, 1984-86; prof. U. RI, Kingston, 1986—. Lectr. various labor unions, 1980—; intern dir. Labor Rsch. Ctr., U. RI, Kingston, 1986—; radio commentator Voice of America, Washington, 1992—. Author: (book) Trolley Wars, 1996; contbr. articles to profl. jours.; contbg. editor: Two-Volume Historical Encyclopedia of American Labor, 2004. Mem. exec. bd. Providence Heritage Commn., 1982—92, Leadership RI, Providence, 1987—90, RI Heritage Hall of Fame, 1998—, v.p., 2005; bd. dirs. RI State Humanities Coun., Providence, 1985—95; chmn. Libr. RI Hist. Soc., Providence, 1987—93. Named RI Prof. of Yr., Carnegie Found. and CASE, 2005; recipient Achievement medal, City of Providence, 1986, Scott Molloy Labor Collection award, Smithsonian Instn., 1990, Tchg. Excellence award, Indsl. Rels. Rsch. Assn., 2000, Inst. Labor Studies, 2001. Mem.: AAUP (U. RI chmn. PAC 1994—96), Inst. Labor Studies (bd. dirs. 1987—), RI Indsl. Rels. Assn. (pres. 1995—96), Am. Fedn. Labor and Congress of Indsl. Orgn. (RI adv. exec. bd. 1981—84, Achievement award 1995), RI Irish Famine Meml. (edn. dir. 1996—), Blackstone Valley Heritage Corridor (commr. 1988—98), RI Labor History Soc. (founder, 1st pres. 1987—2000). Avocations: collecting labor and industrial artifacts, weightlifting. Home: 550 Usquepaugh Rd West Kingston RI 02892-1924 Office: Labor Rsch Ctr 36 Upper College Rd Kingston RI 02881-2005 Office Phone: 401-874-2569. Business E-Mail: molloy@uri.edu.

MOLLOY, DONALD WILLIAM, federal judge, lawyer; b. Butte, ID, July 18, 1946; BA, U. Mont., 1968, JD with honors, 1976. Bar: Mont. 1976, U.S. Dist. Ct. Mont. 1976, U.S. Ct. Appeals (9th cir.) 1977, U.S. Supreme Ct. 1984. Law clk. to Hon. James F. Battin U.S. Dist. Ct., Billings, Mont., 1976-78; ptnr. Berger, Anderson, Sinclair & Murphy, Billings, Mont., 1978-81, Anderson, Edwards & Molloy, Billings, Mont., 1981-90, Anderson & Molloy, Billings, Mont., 1990-91; ptnr., sr., owner The Molloy Law Offices, Billings, Mont., 1991-96; judge US Dist. Ct. Mont., Missoula divsn., 1996—, chief judge, 2001—. Lawyer rep. 9th Cir. Jud. Conf., San Francisco, 1989-92. Aviation lt. USNR, 1968—72. Mem. ABA, Yellowstone County Bar Assn. (pres. 1984-95), Mont. Trial Lawyers Assn. (Trial Lawyer of Yr. 1993), Am. Trial Lawyers, Am. Bd. Trial Advocates, Am. Judicature Soc., Mont. Bar Assn., Pa. Trial Lawyer's Assn., Tex. Trial Lawyers Assn., Am. Law Inst. Roman Catholic. Avocations: aviation, pilot. Office: US Dist Ct Dist Mont PO Box 7309 Missoula MT 59807-7309

MOLLOY, SYLVIA, language educator; b. Buenos Aires, Aug. 29, 1938; came to U.S. 1967; d. Herbert Edward and Margarita Berta (Chasseing) M. Licence es Lettres, U. Paris, 1960, Diplome D'Etudes Superieures, 1961, Doctorat de U. Paris, 1967. Asst. prof. Spanish SUNY, Buffalo, 1967-69; asst. prof. Spanish Vassar Coll., Poughkeepsie, NY, 1969-70, Princeton U., Princeton, NJ, 1970-73, assoc. prof., 1973-81, Emory L. Ford prof., 1981-86; prof. Spanish Yale U., New Haven, 1986-90; Albert Schweitzer prof. of Humanities NYU, 1990—. Author: La Diffusion de la Litterature Hispanoamericaine en France, 1972, Las Letras de Borges, 1979, En Breve Carcel, 1981, At Face Value: Autobiographical Writing in Spanish America, 1991; co-author Women's Writing in Latin America, 1991, Hispanisms and Homosexualities, 1998, El Común Olvido, 2002, Varia Imaginación, 2003; author short stories and contbr. articles to profl. jours.; cons., editorial bd. Revista Iberoamericana, 1979-81, 1985-89, Latin Am. Literary Rev., 1985—, Revista de Filología, Buenos Aires, 1985— Fellow Am. Philos. Soc., 1970, NEH, 1976; Social Sci. Research Council grantee, 1983; Guggenheim Found. fellow, 1986-87 Mem. MLA (pres.), Asociacion Internacional de Hispanistas, Instituto Internacional de Literatura Iberoamericana

MOLNAR, MICHAEL J., artist, educator; b. Aug. 13, 1948; Student, Luzerne County C.C., Nanticoke, Pa., 1968—70; BFA, Md. Inst. Art, Balt., 1975; studied with Vincent Civiletti, Orange, Pa., 1977; studied with Joseph Sheppard, Md. Inst. Coll. Art, Balt., 1970—75; postgrad., Schuler Sch. Fine Art, Balt., 1990—91. Asst. to Leonard Behr, Md. Inst. Coll. Art., Balt., 1973; pvt. tchr., rschr. Old Masters techniques, 1977—80; prof. painting and illustration Luzerne County CC, 1980—. Exhibitions include Woodson Art Mus., Wis., 2003, Phil Brook Mus., Tulsa, 2004, Indian Hills CC, Iowa, 2005, Hagin Mus., Calif., 2005, Huntsville Mus. Art, Ala., 2005, Longmont Mus., Colo., 2006, Krasi Art Ctr., St. Joseph, Mich., 2006, Montgomery Mus. Fine Art, Ala., 2006, Colgate U., Hamilton, NY, 2006, Tex. A&M U., 2006, Jule Collins Smith Mus. Art, Auburn, Ala., 2006—07, numerous others, exhibited in group shows at Van de Griff Gallery, N.Mex., 2002—03, Eleanor Ettinger Gallery, NY, 2003, 2005, Rittenhouse Fine Art Gallery, 2003, Phoenix Mus., 2003, Moore Gallery, Pa., 2003, Principle Gallery, Va., 2004, 20 North Gallery, Ohio, 2004, Vanier Gallery, Ariz., 2004, John Pence Gallery, Calif., 2004, others. Recipient Best in Show award, Bald Eagle Art League, Pa., 1977, Salmagundi Club, NY, 1988, Scottsdale Artist Sch., 1989, Lycoming County Hist. Mus., Williamsport, Pa., 1991, Bianco Gallery, Buckingham, Pa., 1998, Windsor & Newton Corp. award, Bald Eagle Art League, Pa., 2001, 1st Pl. award, Pa. Coll. Tech., 2002, 3d Pl. Portrait award, Portrait Arts Festival Met. Mus., 2003. Mem.: Am. Soc. Portrait Artists, Knickerbocker Artist, Allied Artists Am. (John Young award 2000, Gary Erbe award 2005), Am. Soc. Classical Realism. Home: 1772 Hudson Dr Weatherly PA 18255

MOLNAR, VIOLET, mental health nurse; b. Budapest, Hungary; arrived in U.S., 1960; d. Janos Molnar and Erzsebeth Krekacs. ADN, Atlantic Union Coll., 1967; BSN, Walla Walla Coll., Wash., 1973. RN Mass., Calif. Staff nurse New Eng. Meml. Hosp., Stoneham, Mass., 1968—70; IV therapist Loma Linda U. Med. Hosp., Calif., 1970—72; psychiat. nurse St. Bernardines Med. Ctr., San Bernardino, Calif., 1974—89, Corona Regional Med. Ctr., San Bernardino, 1990—. Pub. spkr. Pres. Lady's Club Friendly Cir., Loma Linda, 1997—99, pres., 2006—; elder, deaconess, greeter Seventh Day Adventist Ch. Loma Linda U., 1975—. Mem.: Rotary Club San Bernardino/Highland (Paul Harris fellow 2001). Avocations: travel, reading, church activities. Home: 11422 Benton St Loma Linda CA 92354 Personal E-mail: imolnar@juno.com, lbimolnar@verizon.net.

MOLNAU, CAROL L., lieutenant governor, former state legislator; b. Waconia, Minn., Sept. 17, 1949; m. Steven F. Molnau; 3 children. Attended, U. Minn. Mem. Chaska City Coun., 1989—92, Minn. Ho. of Reps., 1992—2003; commr. Minn. Dept. Transportation; lt. gov. State of Minn., St. Paul, 2003—. Active Corn Growers, Farm Bur., Soybean Growers, Norseland Ch. Mem. Agrl. Com., Econ. Devel., Infrastructure & Regulation Fin.-Transportation Fin. Divsn., Fin. Inst. & Ins.: Internat. Trade & Economic Devel. Republican. Office: Office Lt Governor 130 State Capitol 75 Rev Dr Martin Luther King Jr Blvd Saint Paul MN 55155 Office Phone: 651-296-3391. Office Fax: 651-296-2089.

MOLOFF, ALAN LAWRENCE, retired military officer, physician; b. Bklyn., Sept. 29, 1954; s. Louis and Muriel Moloff. BS, U. Vt., 1976; DO, U. NJ, 1983; MPH, Harvard U., 1988; student, U.S. Army Command/Gen. Staff Course, 1994-95. Fellow Am. Bd. Preventive Medicine, bd. cert. aerospace medicine, bd. cert. undersea medicine. Commd. platoon leader U.S. Army, 1976, advanced through grades to col., 1999; intern Fitzsimons Army Med. Ctr., Aurora, Colo., 1983—84; med. officer 1st Battalion 10th Spl. Forces Group, Bad Tolz, Germany, 1984—87; resident in aerospace medicine Harvard U., Boston, 1987—89; chief spl. ops. forces divsn. Acad. Health Scis., San Antonio, 1989—92; command surgeon Spl. Forces Command, Ft. Bragg, NC, 1992—93; dep. surgeon U.S. Army Spl. Ops. Command, Ft. Bragg, 1993—94; with command and gen. staff coll. U.S. Army, 1994—95; dep. surgeon 30th Med. Brigade, Heidelberg, Germany, 1995—96; SETAF surgeon, 1995—97; dep. U.S. Army Europe Fwd Surgeon, Hungary, 1995—96; surgeon V Corps, Germany, 1996—97; comdr. 212th M.A.S.H., Wiesbaden, Germany, 1997—99; fellow environ. policy inst. Army War Coll., 1999—2000; comdr. U.S. Army Aeromed. Ctr., 2000—02, Def. Med. Readiness Tng. Inst., 2002—06; ret., 2006. Founding mem. Bd. Disaster Medicine; prof. emergency medicine Med. Coll. Ga.; faculty Ctr. for Disaster Medicine and Humanitarian Assistance, U. South Fla.; lectr. in field; instr. Advanced Trauma Life Support; instr. Disaster Life Support. Contbr. articles to profl. jours. Active in civic activities. Decorated Def. Superior Svc. medal, Legion of Merit, Meritorious Svc. medal with 4 oak leaf clusters, Joint Svc. Commendation medal, S.W. Asian Svc. medal, Army Commendation medal with oak leaf cluster, Joint Army Achievement medal, Armed Forces Svc. medal, Armed Forces Expeditionary medal, NATO medal, Kuwait Liberation medal, Kosovo Campaign medal, German Paratrooper badge, Pathfinder badge, Expert Field Med. badge, Order of Mil. Med. Merit,

Master Parachutist award, Ranger, Spl. Forces Qualified Master Flight Surgeon badge, Navy Dive Med. Officer badge, Order of Aeromed. Merit. Fellow: Aerospace Med. Assn., Am. Coll. Preventive Medicine; mem.: Spl. Ops. Med. Assn. (pres.), Soc. U.S. Army Flight Surgeons (life), Assn. Mil. Osteo. Physicians and Surgeons, Assn. Mil. Surgeons U.S. Avocations: skiing, scuba diving, weightlifting, military history, rock climbing. Personal E-mail: moloffa@hotmail.com.

MOLONEY, DANIEL M., electronics executive; BSEE, U. Mich.; MBA in Mgmt., U. Chgo. Joined Gen. Instrument Corp. (merged with Motorola), 1983; sr. v.p., gen. mgr. IP sys. group Motorola, Inc., Schaumburg, Ill., 2000—02, exec. v.p., pres., CEO broadband comm. sector, 2002—05, exec. v.p., pres. connected home solutions Horsham, Pa., 2005—. Contbr. articles to profl. jours. Office: Motorola Inc 1295 E Algonquin Rd Schaumburg IL 60196 also: Motorola Inc 101 Tournament Dr Horsham PA 19044-3603 *

MOLONEY, THOMAS E., lawyer; b. Rockville Ctr., NY, Jan. 9, 1949; BS, U. Dayton, 1971; JD, U. Notre Dame, 1974. Bar: Ohio 1974. Prin. Am. Energy Svcs., Inc., Columbus, Ohio. Office: Am Energy Svcs Inc 1105 Schrock Rd Ste 602 Columbus OH 43229-1174 Office Phone: 614-885-1901. E-mail: amtem@sbcglobal.net.

MOLONEY, THOMAS JOSEPH, lawyer; b. Bklyn., Oct. 14, 1952; s. Thomas J. and Grace (Nelson) M.; m. Molly K. Heines, Dec. 26, 1976. AB, Columbia U., 1973; JD cum laude, NYU, 1976. Bar: NY 1977, US Dist. Ct. (so. dist.) NY 1977, US Dist. Ct. (ea. dist.) NY 1978, US Ct. Appeals (2d cir.) 1981, US Dist. Ct. (no. dist.) NY 1988, US Ct. Appeals (4th cir.) 1989, US Supreme Ct. 1991. Assoc. Cleary, Gottlieb, Steen & Hamilton, NYC, 1976—84, ptnr., 1984—. Bd. dirs. NY Lawyers for Pub. Interest, NYC, 1986-91; mediator US Bankruptcy Ct. for So. Dist. NY, 1995. Asst. counsel Gov.'s Jud. Nominating Com., NYC, 1981-85; chmn. bus. adv. coun. Washington Irving High Sch., 1994—. Mem. ABA, Am. Bankruptcy Inst., Assn. of Bar of City of NY (bankruptcy, corp. reorganization coms. 1983-86, chair com. legal assistance 1995-97), Order of Coif. Avocations: chess, golf, dance, travel, wine. Office: Cleary Gottlieb Steen & Hamilton 1 Liberty Plz Fl 38 New York NY 10006-1470

MOLONEY, THOMAS WALTER, management consultant; b. NYC, Feb. 8, 1946; s. Thomas Walter and Anne (Heney) M. BA, Colgate U., 1967; MA, Columbia U., 1970, MPH, 1973, MBA, 1975. Program dir. Nat. Ctr. for Deaf-Blind, New Hyde Park, N.Y., 1971-72; spl. asst. to dir. and dean N.Y. Hosp., NYC, 1973-74; asst. v.p. Robert Wood Johnson Found., 1975-80; sr. v.p. The Commonwealth Fund, NYC, 1980-92; dir. pub. policy and health programs The Inst. for Future, 1992-99; ptnr., owner S/B Futures Inc., Palm Beach, Fla., 1997—. Vis. lectr. Princeton (N.J.) U., 1975-80; bd. dirs. Grantmakers in Health, N.Y.C., 1984—, chmn. bd., 1984-88; mem. health adv. com. GAO, 1987—; mem. health adv. coun. Johns Hopkins U. Sch., Hygiene and Pub. Health, Balt., 1989-91; bd. dirs. Found. Health Svcs. Rsch., Washington, 1985-92; mem. bd. visitors Med. Sch., U. Calif. at Davis, 1988—; mem. vis. com. Grad. Sch. Mgmt. and Urban Policy New Sch. for Social Rsch., N.Y.C., 1988-92; mem. Nat. Bd. Examiners, 1986-90; mem. sr. adv. bd. global leadership program U. Mich. Grad. Sch. Bus., Ann Arbor, 1988—; mem. pres. com. The N.Y. Acad. Scis., 1987-90; policy scholar The Eisenhower Ctr. Columbia U., N.Y.C., 1992—. Inst. Health Policy Studies U. Calif., San Francisco, 1992—. Author books; editor: New Approaches to the Medicaid Crisis, 1983; contbr. articles to profl. jours. Bd. dirs. New Eng. Med. Ctr., Boston, 1982-89. Policy scholar Inst. Health Policy Studies U. Calif., San Francisco, 1992—, Eisenhower Ctr. Columbia U., 1992—. Fellow AAAS; mem. Inst. Medicine, Nat. Acad. Scis., Nat. Acad. Social Ins., N.Y. Acad. Medicine, N.Y. Acad. Scis. (pres'. com. 1987-90). Office: S/B Futures Inc Fl 8 1170 N Ocean Blvd Palm Beach FL 33480-3244

MOLONEY, WILLIAM J., school system administrator; BA in History and Polit. sci., MA in History and Polit. sci., Harvard U.; PhD in Ednl. Mgmt., Harvard U., Cambridge, Mass.; postgrad. studies in Slavic History, Oxford and U. of London. Served as a tchr., asst. prin., prin. Prin., headmaster, asst. supt., & supt. Mass., RI, NY, Pa. and Md.; dir. Am. Sch., London; supt. Calvert county pub. schools, Prince Frederick, Md., 1993—97; commr. edn. Colo. Dept. Edn., Denver, 1997—; sec. Colo. Bd. Edn., 1997—. Chmn. Edn. Leaders Coun., Washington; adj prof. Various Univs.; bd. dirs. Bds. of the Ctr. for Workforce Preparation, Ednl. Excellence Network; spkr. in field; cons. in field. Co-author: (Books) The Content of America's Character, Education Innovation: An Agenda to Frame the Future; newspaper columnist:. Office: Colo Dept Education 201 E Colfax Ave Rm 500 Denver CO 80203 Office Phone: 303-866-6646. Office Fax: 306-866-6938. E-mail: moloney_w@cde.state.co.us.

MOLSON, ERIC H., brewery company executive; b. Montreal, Sept. 16, 1937; s. Thomas Henry Pentland and Celia Frances (Cantlie) Molson; m. Jane Mitchell, Apr. 16, 1966; 3 children. AB in Chemistry, Princeton U., 1959. With Molson Inc., Montreal, 1960—, chmn. bd., 1988—2005; chmn. Molson Coors Brewing Co., Denver, 2005—; chancellor Concordia U., Montreal, 1993—. Bd. dirs. Montreal Gen. Hosp. Corp. and Found., Canadian Irish Studies Found., Vie des Arts. Office: Molson Coors Brewing Co 1555 Notre Dame St E Montreal PQ Canada H2L 2R5 also: Molson Coors Brewing Co 1225 17th St Denver CO 80202 Office Phone: 514-521-1786. *

MOLTENI, AGOSTINO, pathology educator; b. Como, Lombardy, Italy, Nov. 12, 1933; came to U.S., 1963; s. Enrico and Antonia (Signorini) M.; m. Loredana Brizio, Sept. 5, 1963; children: Claudio Enrico, Ronald Stephen. MD, U. Milan, Italy, 1957; PhD in Pathology, SUNY, Buffalo, 1970. Lic. Italian Bd. Internal Medicine, 1963. Intern and resident in internal medicine U. Milan (Italy), 1957-62; asst. prof. U. Milan, 1957-63; chief rsch. sect. Farmitalia Drug Co., Milan, 1963-65; rsch. assoc. SUNY, Buffalo, 1965-69, asst. prof., 1969-71; assoc. prof. U. Kans., Kansas City, 1971-76; prof. pathology Northwestern U., Chgo., 1976-96, prof. emeritus, 1996—; prof. pathology and pharmacology U. Mo., Kansas City, 1996—, adj. prof. basic med. scis. Vis. prof. Harvard U., 1983-84; dir. med. students rsch. program U. Mo. Kansas City, 2004-; adj. prof. anesthesia, U. Mo., Kansas City, 2007-. Editor, author: Endocrinology and Thermal Trauma, 1990, Menopause Update, 1992; exec. editor Current Pharmaceutical Design, 2000—, Nutrition Rsch., 2003, PPAR Rsch., 2005; contbr. articles to profl. jours., chpts. to books. Recipient Sharer in Lasker award Lasker Found., N.Y.C., 1983, Rsch. Career Devel. award NIH, Washington, 1970, award Am. Heart Assn., Chgo., 1982. Fellow Am. Acad. Clin. Biochemistry; mem. Am. Acad. Pathology, Am. Soc. Investigative Pathology, Clin. Chemistry Soc., Endocrine Soc. (emeritus), Am. Assn. Clin. Chemistry (emeritus). Achievements include patent for captopril as a cancer chemopreventive agent; research on hypertension and hormonal regulation of cancer. Office: U Mo Truman Med Ctr 2301 Holmes St Kansas City MO 64108-2640 Office Phone: 816-235-5604. Business E-Mail: moltenia@umkc.edu.

MOLTZ, JAMES EDWARD, brokerage house executive; b. Williamsport, Pa., July 25, 1932; s. George N. and Margaret L. (Abell) M.; m. Barbara Vance, Sept. 8, 1956; children: George Wilson, James Clay, John Thomas. BS, Williams Coll., 1954; MBA, Wharton Sch., U. Pa., 1956. Chartered fin. analyst. Cyrus J. Lawrence Inc., NYC, 1957-62, rsch. dir., 1962-64, gen. ptnr., 1964-71, mng. ptnr., 1971-73; chmn., pres. C.J. Lawrence/Deutsche Bank Securities Corp., NYC, 1973-95; chief investment officer Deutsche Bank Securities, 1996-99; vice chmn. ISI Inc., NYC, 1999—. Mem. fin. com. Williams Coll.; trustee Sterling and Francine Clark Art Inst.; chmn. Woods Hole Oceanographic Inst.; trustee Rockefeller Bros. Fund, Edna McConnell Clark Found Mem. Fin. Analysts Fedn., N.Y. Soc. Security Analysts (former dir.), Union League Club (N.Y.C.), Wee Burn Country Club (Darien), Windsor Club (Vero Beach), The Links (N.Y.C.), The Blind Brock Club Home: 29 Indian Spring Trl Darien CT 06820-2109 Office: ISI Inc 40 W 57th St New York NY 10019 E-mail: jmoltz@isimgt.com.

MOLYNEAUX, DAVID GLENN, newspaper travel editor; b. Marion, Ind., Oct. 16, 1945; s. Glenn Ingersol and Barbara Wingate (Draudt) M.; children: Miles David, Rebecca Susan; m. Judi Dash, May 15, 1994. BS in Econs., Miami U., Oxford, Ohio, 1967. Reporter The Plain Dealer, Cleve., 1967-75, city editor, 1976-78, assoc. editor, 1979-80, editorial page editor, 1980-82, travel editor, 1982—. V.p. bd. trustees Soc. Am. Travel Writers Found., 2002—04, pres. bd. trustees, 2004—. Editor: 75 Years-An Informal History of Shaker Heights, 1987. Trustee Shaker Heights Pub. Libr., 1987—95. With U.S. Army, 1968-70. Mem. Cleve. Press Club. Office: Plain Dealer 1801 Superior Ave E Cleveland OH 44114-2198 Office Phone: 216-999-4560. E-mail: travel@plaind.com.

MOLZ, CAROL JEAN, elementary school educator; d. Wayne J. and Neva M. Madill; 1 child from previous marriage, Ellie Catherine DeHaven. BE, Pitts. State U., Kans., 1974, EdM, 1991. Phys. edn. tchr. Haysville Jr. HS, Kans.; sec. Madill Carbide, Inc., Wichita; tchr. Unified Sch. Dist. 265, Goddard. Mem. profl. adv. com. Unified Sch. Dist. 265, Goddard, Kans., 1999—2003; grade level dept. head Clark Davidson Elem. Sch.; presenter Character Edn. State Conf., Wichita, 2002; bd. dir. Madill Carbide, Inc. Contbr. articles to profl. jours. Mem. Unified Sch. Dist. 265 PTO, 1998—; chmn. defribrillator fund raising com. Unified Sch. Dist. 265, Kans., chmn. humane society fund raisers; bldg. rep. Susan G. Koman Found.; chmn. Clark Davidson sch. Ronald McDonald Pop-Top Dr. Recipient Tookie Cmty. Svc. award, KDFI FM, Golden Apple award, KAKE TV, Cmty. Svc. award, Goddard Police Dept. Home: 1 Tonjo Ct Goddard KS 67052-9101

MOLZ, REDMOND KATHLEEN, public affairs educator; b. Balt., Mar. 5, 1928; d. Joseph T. and Regina (Barry) M. BS, Johns Hopkins U., Balt., 1949, MA, 1950; MALS, U. Mich., Ann Arbor, 1953; DLS, Columbia U., NYC, 1976. Librarian I and II Enoch Pratt Free Library, Balt., 1953-56; pub. relations officer Free Library of Phila., 1958-62; editor Wilson Library Bull. H.W. Wilson Co., Bronx, NY, 1962-68; chief planning staff Bur. Libraries and Learning Resources U.S. Office Edn., Washington, 1968-73; prof. library sci. Sch. Library Service Columbia U., NYC, 1976-80, Melvil Dewey prof., 1980-93; prof. pub. affairs Sch. Internat. and Pub. Affairs, Columbia U., NYC, 1993-99, prof. emeritus, 2000—. Cons. U.S. Nat. Commn. Librs. and Info. Sci., Washington, 1974-75, U.S. Adv. Commn. Intergovtl. Relations, Washington, 1979-80; mem. nat. adv. coun. The Sheridan Librs., Johns Hopkins U., 1997—. Author: Federal Policy and Library Support, 1976 (Ralph R. Shaw award 1977), National Planning for Library Service, 1935-75, 1984, Library Planning and Policy Making: The Legacy of the Public and Private Sector, 1990, The Federal Roles in Support of Public Library Services, 1990, The Federal Roles in Support of Academic and Research Libraries, 1991; co-author (with Phyllis Dain) Civic Space/Cyberspace: The American Public Library in the Information Age, 1999; co-editor: The Metropolitan Library (anthology), 1972; author TV script Portraits in Print, 1959. Recipient Leadership Tng. award Fund for Adult Edn., 1956-57; recipient Disting. Alumnus award Sch. Library Sci. U. Mich., 1969, George Virgil Fuller award Columbia U., 1975, Johns Hopkins U. scholar, 1949-50, Horace H. Rackham fellow U. Mich., 1952-53, Columbia U. scholar, 1974-76, Tangley Oaks fellow, 1975-76; Council Library Resources Inc. Officers' grantee, 1974 Mem. ALA (councilor 1972-74, 76-80, exec. bd. 1976-80, chmn. legis. com. 1985-86), Freedom to Read Found. (dir. 1972-79, pres. 1977-79) Business E-Mail: rkm2@columbia.edu.

MOMAH, ETHEL CHUKWUEKWE, retired women's health nurse; b. Iyi-Enu, Ogidi, Nigeria, May 28, 1934; arrived in US, 1978; d. Zaccheus C. and Victoria U. (Orizu) Obi; m. Christian Chike Momah, Nov. 21, 1959; children: Chukwudi, Adaora, Azuka. SRN, Harrow Hosp., Middlesex, UK, 1956; SCM, Mothers Hosp., London, 1957; MTD, Midwife Tchrs. Coll., Surrey, UK, 1964; BS, Upsala Coll., 1988. Cert. inpatient obstetric nurse Nat. Cert. Corp. Nurse-midwife Guy's Hosp., London, 1959; nursing sister, head nurse labor/delivery Univ. Coll. Hosp., Ibadan, Nigeria, 1960-62; midwife tutor Lagos Island Maternity Hosp., Nigeria, 1963-66; nurse-midwife Brit. Hosp., Paris, 1966, Hosp. Cantonal, Geneva, 1967-78; staff nurse St. Peters Med. Ctr., New Brunswick, NJ, 1980—85, patient care coord., 1985-90, antenatal testing nurse, 1990—2005; ret., 2005; substitute sch. nurse Arlington Ind. Sch. Dist., Tex., 2006—. Recipient Disting. Svc. award, NNEWI Union NY Tri-State Inc., 2000, Cultural Performance award, Anambra Enugu States Assn. N.J., 2001, Disting. Svc. award, Anambia Enugu States Assn., 2002, Cmty Leadership award, Assocs. Mental Health Devel. Disabilities, NJ, 2004, Legion of Honor award, Chapel of Four Chaplains, 2005, Courageous Leadership award, Anambra State Assn. N.J., 2006, Invaluable and Devoted Svc. award, Nnewi N.Y. Tri-State, 2006. Mem.: Nnewi USA, Inc. (v.p. 2003—), Assn. Women's Health, Obstetric and Neonatal Nurses, Umunne Women's Assocs. Dallas, Anambra-Enugu States Assn. N.J., Nne-Egwu (dance mother 1990—2006). Personal E-mail: nnanne@sbcglobal.net.

MOMBAERTS, PETER, biology professor; b. Leuven, Belgium, Sept. 27, 1962; s. Leon Mombaerts and Daisy Kortleven. MD, Cath. U. of Leuven Belgium, 1987; PhD in Biology, MIT, 1992. Postdoctoral fellow Columbia U., NY, 1993—95; from asst. prof. biology to assoc. prof. Rockefeller U., NYC, 1995—2003, prof., 2003—. Recipient Presdl. early career award for scientists and engrs. Pres. of U.S., 1997, career scientist award Irma T. Hirschl Trust, 1997-2000, Takasago award for rsch. in olfaction Assn. for Chemoreception Scis., 2001, Firmenich Fragrance award, 2001; Searle scholar, 1996-99, Basil O'Connor starter scholar March of Dimes Birth Defects Found., 1997-99, scholar Rita Allen Found., 1998-2001; Alfred P. Sloan rsch. fellow, 1997-99, Klingenstein fellow in neuroscis., 1997-2000, McKnight scholar in neurosci., 1997-2000, Guggenheim fellow, 1998-99. Office: Rockefeller U 1230 York Ave New York NY 10021 Fax: 212-327-7310. Business E-Mail: peter@rockefeller.edu.

MOMBOULI, SERGE, ambassador; b. Pointe-Noire, Republic of Congo, 1959; married; 6 children. Corp. sales Air Afrique, Paris; v.p. A.W.E. Grp., Houston; v.p. internat. ops. and project devel. Transworld Consortium Corp., Houston, 1995—97; Congolese presdl. spokesman in US, 1997; chargé d'affaires Embassy of Republic of Congo, 1997—2001; Congolese amb. to the US, 2001—. Office: Embassy of Republic of Congo 4891 Colorado Ave NW Washington DC 20011 Home Phone: 301-765-5931; Office Phone: 202-726-5500. E-mail: smombouli@hotmail.com.

MOMENI, REZA, plastic surgeon; BA, Haverford Coll., 1990—94; MD, Med. Coll. of Pa., 1994—98. Diplomate Am. Bd. Plastic Surgery. Resident in gen. surgery Yale U., New Haven, 1998—2001, resident in plastic surgery, 2001—04, chief resident in plastic surgery, 2003—04; plastic, reconstructive, & hand surgeon Summit Med. Group, Summit, NJ, 2004—. Cons. MedSN.com, Santa Monica, Calif., 1998—2000; sci. reviewer Med. Sci. Monitor, Old Westbury, NY; med. illustration J/B Woolsey, Conshohocken, Pa., 1998—99. Nat. splty. rep. Am. Assn. of Med. Colleges - Orgn. of Resident Representatives, Washington, 2003—. Recipient 1st Pl., US Pharmacopeia Competition, 1996, Alpha Omega Alpha, Med. Coll. of Pa., 1998, Phi Beta Kappa, Haverford Coll., 1994, Nat. Pathology Honor Soc., Med. Coll. of Pa., 1996; scholar Class of 1934 scholarship, Haverford Coll., 1992; Yale Plastic Surgery Scholastic award, Yale Univ., 2002, William Goldman scholarship, William Goldman Found., 1996—98, Howard Hughes Med. Inst. Rsch. scholarship, Howard Hughes Inst., 1993, Med. Coll. of Pa., Haverford Coll., 1995, Class of 1910 scholarship, Med. Coll. of Pa., 1995, Huldah Kerner scholarship, 1996, Ruth Weil Meml. scholarship, 1997, Weston Ellsworth scholarship, 1997. Mem.: AMA, NJ Soc. Plastic Surgeons, NY Regional Soc. Plastic Surgery, Am. Soc. Plastic Surgeons (amb. surgeon 2007—), Union County Med. Soc., NJ Med. Soc., Phi Beta Kappa, Alpha Omega Alpha, Yale Surg. Soc. Achievements include research in cranial reconstruction after dural complications; pulse oximetry in melanoma sentinel node dissection may be false; frontal sinus fractures: an institutional review. Avocations: travel, sailing, skiing, snowboarding. Office: Summit Plastic Surgery 1 Diamond Hill Rd Berkeley Heights NJ 07922 Office Phone: 908-277-8759.

MOMIN, SHAMIM, curator; Grad., Columbia U. Assoc. curator Whitney Museum Am. Art, NYC, 2003—; curator 2004 Whitney Biennial Curator, 2008 Whitney Biennial Curator. Co-author: Alex Katz: Small Paintings, 2001, Sue De Beer, 2005, Zak Smith: Pictures Of Girls, 2005, Ellen Harvey: Mirror, 2006, Terence Koh, 2007. Office: Whitney Museum 945 Madison Ave New York NY 10021 *

MOMMSEN, KATHARINA, retired literature and language professor, foundation administrator; b. Berlin, Sept. 18, 1925; came to U.S., 1974, naturalized, 1980; d. Hermann and Anna (Johannsen) Zimmer; m. Momme Mommsen, Dec. 23, 1948. DPhil, U. Tübingen, 1956; Dr. habil., Berlin Free U., 1962. Collaborator Acad. Scis., Berlin, 1949—61; assoc. prof. Free U., Berlin, 1962—70; prof. German Carleton U., Ottawa, Canada, 1970—74; Albert Guerard prof. lit. Stanford U., 1974—94, ret., 1995. Vis. prof. U. Giessen, Tech. U. Berlin, 1965, State U. N.Y., Buffalo, 1966, U. Calif., San Diego, 1973; pres. Mommsen Found. Author over 200 publs. on 18th-20th century German and comparative lit.; editor: Germanic Studies in America. Mem. Goethe Soc. Home: 980 Palo Alto Ave Palo Alto CA 94301-2223 Business E-Mail: katmom@stanford.edu. E-mail: k.mommsen@comcast.net.

MONACELLI, GIANFRANCO, publishing executive; b. Milan; came to U.S., 1965; s. Rodolfo and Isabella (Paolillo) M.; m. Eugenia Hyman; children: Nurit, Fausto, Alexander. Dr., U. Turin, Italy, 1963, Acad. Santa Cecilia, 1964; BS, Mannes Coll., 1967; postgrad., Columbia U., 1969. Gen. mgr. Rizzoli Internat. Bookstore, NYC, 1969-72, v.p., 1972-75; exec. v.p. Rizzoli Internat., Milan, 1975-78; pres., chief exec. officer Rizzoli Internat. Publs., Inc., NYC, 1975-93, Rizzoli Internat. Bookstores, Inc., NYC, 1975-92, Rizzoli Editore Corp., NYC, 1975-89; sr. v.p. RCS Rizzoli Corp., NYC, 1989-93; pres. USITAL Ltd., NYC, 1993—, The Monacelli Press, Inc., NYC, 1994—; v.p. Epikos Security Printing S.A., NYC, 1997—. Trustee Mannes Coll., N.Y.C., 1979-81; pres. Weathersfield Music Festival, Vert., 1993—; mem. vis. com. U. Miami, Coral Gables, Fla., 1988-89. Recipient Met. Home Design 100 award, 1997, collaborative achievement award AIA, 1999; named Pub. of Yr., AIA, 1996. Mem. Century Assn., Am.-Italy Soc. (pres. 1993-94).

MONACH, ANDREW E., lawyer; b. Schenectady, NY, Jan. 28, 1954; BA with honors, Stanford U., 1976; JD, Yale U., 1979. Bar: Calif. 1979. Assco. Morrison and Foerster, San Francisco, 1979—84; dep. pub. defender San Francisco Pub. Defender's office, 1984—85; ptnr. Morrison and Foerster, San Francisco, 1985. Lectr. in field. Named No. Calif. Super Lawyers, San Francisco mag., 2006. Mem. Phi Beta Kappa. Office: Morrison & Foerster 425 Market St San Francisco CA 94105 Office Phone: 415-268-7588. Office Fax: 415-268-7522. Business E-Mail: amonach@mofo.com.

MONACO, ANTHONY JOHN, retired health facility administrator, writer; b. Steubenville, Ohio, Oct. 26, 1926; s. Antonio Monaco and Maria Concetta Di Crescentis; m. Wilna Mae Dellinger, Apr. 11, 1953; children: Gregg Anthony, Carol Ann Dawley, Susan Lorraine. BS, Duquesne U., 1949; MPH, U. Pitts., 1958. Exec. dir. So. Ill. Med. Ctr., Mt. Vernon, 1972—79; pres., CEO Healthcare Coun. Nca, Washington, 1980—96. Adminstr. Berwick Hosp., Pa., 1956—72. Author: The Songs And Wisdom Of David And Solomon, 2003, Scriptures From The Orient, 2003, The Spirit Is in the Form, 2003, The Challenge of Moses, 2004, The Mission of Jesus and John, 2004, The Recitations of Mohammed, 2004, The Testimony of the Major Prophets, 2004, The Truth of Nanak and the Sikhs, 2004, The Real Holy Grail, 2004, Living in the Light Above the Line, 2005, God The Intelligent Designer Man The Intelligent Design, 2006, 10 Steps to God, 2006. With US Army, 1944—45. Home: 13062 Gorham Way Woodbridge VA 22192-2948 Home Phone: 703-492-8396. Personal E-mail: therealholygrail@yahoo.com.

MONACO, DANIEL JOSEPH, lawyer; b. Easton, Pa., May 12, 1922; s. Federico and Maria (Romano) M.; m. Marian P. Monaco, June 26, 1953 (div.); children: Denise E., Mimi D. AB with honors, Lafayette Coll., 1943; postgrad., U. Mich., 1944—45; MA, U. Chgo., 1946; JD, Stanford U., 1950. Bar: Calif. 1951, US Dist. Ct. (no. dist.) Calif. 1951, US Supreme Ct. 1961. Mem. faculty U. Miami, Fla., 1946-47; founder, of counsel Monaco, Anderlini & Finkelstein, San Mateo, Calif., 1953—; probate judge State of Calif., 1963-67. Real estate broker, Calif., 1957-67; judge pro tem Calif. Mcpl. and Superior Cts. Chmn. San Mateo County Dem. Ctrl. Com., 1960-61, Citizen World Ct.; mem. Calif. State Dem. Exec. Bd.; founder, pres. Circlon Internat., 1978-81; chmn. World Peace Through Law Ctr. com. to establish a Citizens' World Ct.; pres. peninsula com. UN Ednl. Sci. & Cultural Orgn., 1955-59; mem. No. Calif. Coun. Fgn. Affairs; San Mateo County Hosp. Found. Bd. With US Army, 1943-46, lt. USAR, 1946-50. Recipient Gentry Mag. Cmty. Stars award, 1997. Mem. ABA, ATLA, UN Assocs.-USA (pres. San Mateo County chpt. 1958-65), Calif. State Bar Assn., Calif. Trial Lawyers Assn. (bd. govs.), San Mateo County Trial Lawyers Assn. (pres.), World Jurist Assn. (2d v.p. 1995-97, 1st v.p. 1997-99, pres. 1999-2001, hon. pres. 2003—), Am. Bd. Trial Advs., Internat. Law Assn. World Citizens, Gorbachev Found., The Commonwealth Club, Peninsula Golf and Country Club, U. Chgo. dist. speaker series, 2004. Democrat. Avocations: travel, international law. Office Phone: 650-348-0102. Office Fax: 650-348-0962. Personal E-mail: dukemonaco@aol.com.

MONACO, REB LEON, county official; s. Lewis Frank Monaco and Sara Marie Mancuso; m. Jill Marie Isaia, Aug. 15, 1965; children: Theran, Laura. BA, San Jose State U., Calif., 1968, MA, 1971. Tchg. credentials Calif. Spl. edn. tchr. Hollister Sch. Dist., Calif., 1968—2000; county supr. San Benito County, Hollister, 2003—. Adj. health educator Gavilan Coll., Gilroy, Calif., 1989—2000; mem. San Benito County Drug Adv. Bd., Hollister, 1996—2000, San Benito County Grand Jury, Hollister, 1998. Founding mem. Calif. Blacksmith Assn., San Jacinto, 1977; vol. docent, blacksmith Calif. State Park, San Juan Bautista, 1998; chmn. San Benito County Bd., Hollister, 2005. Mem.: Calif. Ret. Tchrs. Assn., Am. Mensa, Ltd., San Benito Lodge 211 Masons (master 1978). Democrat. Avocations: blacksmithing, bicycling, reading. Home: 6991 Southside Rd Hollister CA 95023 Office: San Benito County 481 Fourth St Hollister CA 95023

MONACO, ROBERT ANTHONY, radiologist; b. NYC, July 5, 1945; s. Edmond V. and Jean M.; m. Susan Margaret Thompson; children: Kevin, Robert, Christopher, Sarah. BS, Siena Coll., 1967; MD, N.J. Coll. Medicine, 1971. Diplomate Am. Bd. Radiology, Am. Bd. Nuclear Medicine. Radiology resident N.J. Coll. Medicine, Newark, 1971-75; fellow in nuclear medicine med. ctr. NYU, NYC, 1975-76; attending radiologist Med. Ctr. Ocean County, Point Pleasant, NJ, 1976-87, dir. dept. radiology, 1987—, sec. med. staff, 1998-2000. Gen. ptnr Point Pleasant Radiology Group, 1987—; sec. bd. dirs. Found. Med. Ctr. Ocean County, Mid-Coastal

IPA, 1997; mng. ptnr. Open MRI of Wall, 1999—. Capt. USAR, 1972-76. Mem. Am. Coll. Radiology, Am. Coll. Nuc. Medicine, Radiol. Soc. NJ (exec. com. 2005-). Roman Catholic. Avocations: tennis, fishing, swimming. Home: 13 Bretwood Dr Colts Neck NJ 07722 Office: Open MRI of Wall Rt 34 Wall NJ 07719 Office Phone: 732-974-8060. Personal E-mail: rammdo1@aol.com.

MONAGHAN, CRAIG THOMAS, former retail and automotive executive; b. Phila., Feb. 16, 1957; m. Mary Lou Murphy, Jul. 25, 1981; children: Shannon, Connor, Rand. BS industrial engr., Lehigh U., 1980; MBA in fin., Wharton U. Pa., 1985. Cert. mgmt. acct. Financial analyst General Motors Corp., NYC, 1985-87, mgr. overseas fin., 1987-88; dir. corp. fin. Squibb, Princeton, NJ, 1988-90; dir. internat. fin. Bristol-Myers Squibb, NYC, 1990-91; asst. treas. Reader's Digest, Pleasantville, NY, 1991-92, controller europe, 1992—98; CFO iVillage.com, 1998-2000; exec. v.p., CFO AutoNation, Inc., Fort Lauderdale, Fla., 2000—06; CFO Sears Holdings Corp., Hoffman Estates, Ill., 2006—07. Capt. US Army, 1980—83. Mem.: Inst. Mgmt. Accts. Avocations: fishing, golf, reading.

MONAGHAN, DOMINIC, actor; b. Berlin, Dec. 8, 1976; Actor: (TV series) Hetty Wainthropp Investigates, 1996—98, Lost, 2004— (Outstanding Performance by an Ensemble in a Drama Series, Screen Actors Guild award, 2006); (TV films) Hostile Waters, 1997, This Is Personal: The Hunt for the Yorkshire Ripper, 2000; (TV miniseries) Monsignor Renard, 2000; appeared: I Love the 90's, 2005; I Love the 90's: Part Deux, 2005; actor: (films) The Lord of the Rings: The Fellowship of the Ring, 2001, The Lord of the Rings: The Two Towers, 2002, The Lord of the Rings: The Return of the King, 2003, An Insomniac's Nightmare, 2003, Spivs, 2004, The Purifiers, 2004, Shooting Livien, 2005. Office: c/o ABC 77 W 66th St New York NY 10023

MONAGHAN, PETER GERARD, lawyer; b. Belfast, Ireland, July 12, 1949; came to U.S., 1961; s. William Liam and Elizabeth (Eccles) M.; m. Barbara Marion Farrenkopf, Sept. 24, 1972; children: Brian Patrick, Kevin James, Allison Mary. BS, Fordham U., 1970; JD, St. John's U., Jamaica, NY, 1977. Bar: N.Y. 1978, U.S. Dist. Ct. (so. dist.) N.Y. 1978, U.S. Dist. Ct. (ea. dist.) N.Y. 1979, U.S. Supreme Ct. 1986. Claims examiner Royal Ins. Co., NYC, 1970-76; assoc. Kroll, Edelman, Elser and Dicker, NYC, 1976, Bower and Gardner, NYC, 1977-83, ptnr., 1984-91, Bartlett, McDonough, Bastone & Monaghan, LLP, Mineola, N.Y., 1992—. Cubmaster Boy Scouts Am., Bayside, N.Y., 1985-89. Capt. U.S. Army Res., 1970-78. Mem. ATLA, ABA, Queens County Bar Assn., N.Y. State Bar Assn. (trial lawyers sect. com. on med. malpractice 1988—), Assn. Bar City N.Y. (com. on med. malpractice 2002-05), Nassau County Bar Assn. Office: Bartlett McDonough Bastone & Monaghan LLP 300 Old Country Rd Mineola NY 11501-4198 Office Phone: 516-877-2900.

MONAGHAN, THOMAS STEPHEN, philanthropist; b. Ann Arbor, Mich., Mar. 25, 1937; m. Marjorie Zybach, Aug. 25, 1962; children—Mary, Susan, Margaret, Barbara Student, Ferris State Coll., U. Mich.; PhD (hon.), Cleary Coll., 1982, Madonna Coll., 1983, Eastern Mich. U., 1984, So. Fla. U., 1985. Ptnr. Dominick's Pizza, Ypsilanti, Mich., 1960-65; pres., chmn. bd., founder, CEO Domino's Pizza, Inc., Ann Arbor, Mich., 1960-98; ret., 1998; founder Ave Maria Sch. Law, 2000—, Ave Maria Univ., Fla., 2003—. Owner Detroit Tigers, 1983-92. Author: (autobiography) Pizza Tiger. Founder Mater Christi Found. (now Ave Maria Found.), 1983—; bd. dirs. Cleary Coll., Ypsilanti, Henry Ford Hosp., Detroit, U. Steubinville, Ohio, St. Joseph's Hosp. Devel. Bd., Ann Arbor. Served USMC, 1956—59. Named Entrepreneur of Yr. Harvard U. Bus. Sch., 1984, Pizzaman of Yr. Nat. Assn. Pizza Owners, 1984; recipient Golden Plate award Am. Acad. Achievement, 1984, Golden Chain award Multi Unit Franchise Svc. Orgn., 1986, Horatio Alger award, 1986, Restaurant Bus. Leadership award, 1986, Pope John Paul II Family Fidelity award 1988, Pine Mission's Knights of Charity award, 1990, Semper Fidelis award USMC, 1990. Mem. Internat. Franchise Assn. (Entrepreneur of Yr. 1986), Nat. Restaurant Assn. (Silver Plate award 1985), Mich. Restaurant Assn., Ypsilanti C. of C., U. Mich. Pres.'s Club, Ann Arbor Pres.'s Assn., Missionary Vehicle Assn. (bd. dirs.), AIA (hon.), Mich. Soc. Architects (hon.). Clubs: Barton Hills Country (Ann Arbor). Lodges: K.C. Roman Catholic. Avocations: collecting Frank Lloyd Wright furniture and memorabilia, classic cars. Office: Ave Maria Univ 1025 Commons Circle Naples FL 34119

MONAHAN, JOHN MICHAEL, lawyer; b. Syracuse, Mar. 2, 1969; d. James Paul Monahan Sr. and Linda Lou Monahan; m. Gena Marie Mattiaccio, Sept. 4, 2004. Student, U. Sheffield, Eng., 1989; BA in Polit. Sci. (hon.), Hobart Coll., Geneva, NY, 1991; JD, George Mason U., Arlington, Va., 1996. Bar: N.Y. 1997, U.S. Dist. Ct. (we. dist.) N.Y. 2001, U.S. Dist. Ct. (we. dist.) N.Y. 2003. Intern White House, Washington, 1991; clk. to Hon. William F. O'Brien III N.Y. Supreme Ct., Madison County, 1996—2000; atty. Hancock & Estabrook, LLP, Syracuse, NY, 2000—03, Phillips Lytle LLP, Buffalo, 2003—04, Jaeckle Fleischmann & Mugel, LLP, Buffalo, 2004—. Spkr. in field. Contbr. articles to profl. jours. Mem.: ABA, Soc. Human Resources, Erie County Bar Assn., N.Y. State Bar Assn. Republican. Roman Catholic. Avocations: golf, guitar, travel. Home: 57 5th Ave Williamsville NY 14221 Office: Jaeckle Fleischmann & Mugel LLP 12 Fountain Plaza Buffalo NY 14202 Office Phone: 716-856-0600, 716-856-0432. Business E-Mail: jmonahan@jaeckle.com.

MONAHAN, JOHN T., law educator, psychologist; b. NYC, Nov. 1, 1946; s. John Joseph and Dorothy (King) M.; m. Linda Costa, Aug. 24, 1969; children: Katherine, John. BA, SUNY, Stony Brook, 1968; PhD, Ind. U., 1972; LLD (hon.), CUNY, 1997. Asst. prof. social ecology U. Calif., Irvine, 1972—78, assoc. prof., 1978—80; prof. U. Va. Sch. Law, Charlottesville, 1980—, now Henry L. and Grace Doherty Charitable Found. prof. law, Class of 1941 rsch. prof., prof. psychology and psychiat. medicine. Dir. mental health law MacArthur Found., Chgo., 1988-98, dir. Rsch. Network on Mandated Cmty. Treatment, 2000-. Editor: Who is the Client? The Ethics of Psychological Intervention in the Criminal Justice System, 1980; co-editor: Prevention in Mental Health: Research, Policy and Practice, 1980, Mentally Disordered Offenders: Perspectives from Law and Social Science, 1983, Children, Mental Health, and the Law, 1984, Violence and Mental Disorder: Developments in Risk Assessment, 1994, Coercion and Aggressive Community Treatment: A New Frontier in Mental Health Law, 1996, Mental Disorder, Work Disability, and the Law, 1997, Research in Community and Mental Health, Vol. 10: Coercion in Mental Health Services - International Perspectives, 1999; author: The Clinical Prediction of Violent Behavior (reprinted as Predicting Violent Behavior: An Assessment of Clinical Techniques), 1981; co-author: Social Science in Law: Cases and Materials, 1985, 1990, 1994, 1998, 2002, Rethinking Risk Assessment: The MacArthur Study of Mental Disorder and Violence, 2001, Adjudicative Competence: The MacArthur Studies, 2002. Recipient Disting. Contbn. to Rsch. in Pub. Policy Award, APA, Washington, 1990, Isaac Ray Award, APA, NY, 1996; Ind. U. Fellow, Harvard U., 1976-77; fellow Stanford U., 1978-79, Oxford U., 1992. Mem. APA (founding pres. divsn. psychology and law), Inst. of Medicine Office: U Va Sch Law 580 Massie Rd Charlottesville VA 22903-1789 Office Phone: 434-924-3632. E-mail: jmonahan@virginia.edu.

MONAHAN, THOMAS PAUL, accountant; b. Pitts., Feb. 27, 1951; s. Thomas Andrew and Patricia (Tompkins) M.; m. Ellen McKeithan Easterby, Aug. 2, 1975; children: Kelley Kathleen, Thomas Patrick, Kyle Easterby, Tessa Elizabeth. BS in Acctg., U. S.C., 1073. CPA SC. Staff acct. Rogers, Brigman, Peterson & Co., Columbia, S.C., 1972-75, ptnr., 1975-82; chmn., treas., prin. GMK Assocs., Columbia, 1982—. Chmn., bd. dirs., treas. Devel. Properties, Inc.; trustee, pres. Town Theater Trust, 2000—. Mem. bus. coun. S. Dems., 1986—; bd. dirs. Cultural Coun. of Richland and Lexington Counties; pres. Town Theatre Trust; active Com. of 100. Mem. AICPA, S.C. Assn. CPAs, Columbia Stage Soc. (trustee, bd. dirs.), Spring Valley Country Club, Capital City Club, Palmetto Club, Zeta Beta Tau (trustee emeritus). Home: 1117 Adger Rd Columbia SC 29205-1942 Office: GMK Assoc Ste 2100 1201 Main St Columbia SC 29201-3263 Office Phone: 803-256-0000. Business E-Mail: tmonahan@gmka.com.

MONAJEMI, PEZHMAN, electrical engineer; s. Ahmad and Mehrangiz Monajemi. BS in Elec. Engring., Sharif U., Tehran, Iran, 1994; MS in Elec. and Computer Engring., Ga. Inst. Tech., Atlanta, 2003; PhD in Elec. and Computer Engring., Ga. Inst. Tech., Atlanta, 2006. Micro electro-mech. sys. engr. Silicon Clocks, Inc., Fremont, Calif.; sr. RF design engr. Jacket Micro Devices, Inc., Atlanta, 2005—. Trainer Ga. Inst. Tech., Atlanta, 2002—05. Contbr. scientific papers in MEMS engring. Recipient Best Trainer award, Microelectronics Rsch. Ctr., Atlanta, 2003. Mem.: IEEE (Sensor Conf. Best Paper award 2004). Achievements include development of wafer-level metal-organic MEMS packaging using decomposable polymers. Office: Silicon Clocks Inc 39141 Civic Ctr Dr Ste 450 Fremont CA 94538 Office Phone: 510-742-5625. Personal E-mail: monajemi@gmail.com.

MONAT, WILLIAM ROBERT, university official; b. Biwabik, Minn., Oct. 9, 1924; s. William Stephen and Milda Aleta (Sundby) M.; m. Josephine Ann Sclafani, Sept. 9, 1951; children: Lise Ann, Kathryn, Margaret, William Michael, Eric. AA, Virginia Jr. Coll., Minn., 1947; BA magna cum laude, U. Minn., 1949, PhD, 1956; postgrad., Wayne U., 1949-50. Asst. prof. Wayne U., 1954-57; exec. asst. to Gov. Mich., 1957-60; asso. prof. Pa. State U., 1960-65, prof. polit. sci., 1965-69; asso. dir. Inst. Pub. Adminstrn., 1962-69; majority budget dir. Pa. Ho. of Reps., 1968-69; prof., chmn. dept. polit. sci. No. Ill. U., De Kalb, 1969-71, provost, 1976-78, Regency prof., 1986-92; Regency prof. emeritus, 1992—; pres. No. Ill. U., De Kalb, 1978-84; chancellor Ill. Bd. Regents, 1984-86; prof., dean faculties Baruch Coll., City U. N.Y., 1971-74, v.p. acad. affairs, 1974-76. Cons. USPHS, 1958, Office of Sec. Dept. Labor, 1963-64, Bur. Labor Stads., 1966, Office of Gov. Pa., 1968; bd. dirs. 1st Nat. Bank DeKalb, Castle Bancgroup, Inc. Author: Labor Goes to War, 1965, The Public Library and its Community, 1967, Politics, Poverty and Education, 1968; Editor: Public Adminstration in Era of Change, 1962, The Achieving Institution, 2000; contbr. articles to profl. jours. Mem. Gov.'s Commn. on Sci. and Tech., 1983-87; trustee Grad. Sch. Polit. Mgmt., NY, 1986-95; chmn. City of Dekalb Plan Commn.; trustee DeKalb Sanitary Dist., 2005. With AUS, 1943-46. Recipient Outstanding Achievement award U. Minn., 1981; decorated Bronze Star medal. Mem. Am. Polit. Sci. Assn., Am. Soc. Pub. Adminstrn., Phi Beta Kappa. Home: 1605 Mayflower Dr Dekalb IL 60115-1723 Business E-Mail: wmonat@niu.edu.

MONATH, NORMAN, publishing company executive; b. Toronto, Ont., Can. came to U.S., naturalized, 1944; m. Pauline K. Farber, Aug. 30, 1952 (dec. Feb. 1972); children— Richard, Robert, Bruce. Dir. subsidiary rights Simon & Schuster, Inc., 1957-59; now cons.; founding pres. Cornerstone Library, Inc., NYC, 1960—. Composer (with Walt Kelly) Songs of the Pogo, 2003; author: Know What You Want And Get It!, rev. edit., 2002; How To Play Popular Piano, 1984, How To Play Popular Guitar, 1994, (with William Cole) Folk Songs of England, Ireland, Scotland and Wales; editor (with Bobby Short) unpublished songs of Cole Porter; songwriter with Hal David, Sammy Cahn; recs. by Dionne Warwick, Supremes, Mitch Miller, Jerry Vale, Burns and Allen, Burl Ives. With signal corps U.S. Army, 1942-45. Mem. ASCAP. Inventor Bali word game, 1954. Home: 3545 S Ocean Blvd Apt 101 Palm Beach FL 33480-5716 E-mail: monathn@bellsouth.net.

MONATH, THOMAS PATRICK, physician; b. Hewlett Harbor, NY, Aug. 13, 1940; s. Paul E. and Elizabeth (Burger) M.; m. Jennifer Sanderson Mills, Sept., 25, 1964 (div. 1981); 1 child, Andrea; m. Margaret Blake Garvan, June 25, 1988; 1 child, Nicholas. AB, Harvard U., 1962, MD, 1966. Diplomate Am. Bd. Internal Medicine. Intern, resident Peter Bent Brigham Hosp., Boston, 1966-68, 73-74; med. officer Ctr. Disease Control, Atlanta, 1968-72, dir. div. Vector-Borne Diseases Ft. Collins, Colo., 1974-88; chief virology div. U.S. Army Med. Rsch. Inst. Infectious Diseases, Frederick, Md., 1988-92; chief sci. officer Acambis Inc., Cambridge, Mass., 1992—2006; ptnr. Kleiner Perkins Caufield & Byers, Menlo Park, Calif., 2006—. Cons. WHO, Geneva, 1974—; chmn. panel on virus diseases Am. Inst. Biol. Scis., Washington, 1978-88; mem. U.S.-Japan Coop. Med. Sci. Program, 1974-78; vis. rsch. fellow U. Ibadan, Nigeria, 1970-72; sr. sci. and tech. adv. to dir. CIA, 1998—. Author, editor: St. Louis Encephalitis, 1980, The Arboviruses, 1988, Field's Virology, 1990, 95, The Flaviviruses, 2003; assoc. editor Human Vaccines, Vector-Brose, Zoonotic Diseases, Acta Tropica, Jour. Virol. Methods; contbr. more than 350 articles to sci. jours. Capt. USPHS, 1968-88, col. U.S. Army, 1988-92. Recipient Presidential Citation, Med. Amateur Radio Coun., 1974, Nat. Young Meml. award Am. Com. on Anthropod-Borne Viruses, 1986, Meritorious Svc. medal UPSHS, 1978. Fellow ACP, Royal Soc. Tropical Med. Hygiene; mem. Am. Soc. Tropical Med. Hygiene (councillor 1976-80, pres. 2004-05, Richard M. Taylor award, 2002, Walter Reed medal 2002), Am. Com. on Arthopod-Borne Viruses (chmn. 1980-82), Am. Soc. Virology, Internat. Soc. Infectious Diseases. Democrat. Home: 21 Finn Rd Harvard MA 01451-1925 Office Phone: 978-456-3290. Business E-Mail: tmonath@kpcb.com.

MONCK, MAUREEN F., psychoanalyst; b. NYC, Dec. 12, 1938; d. Lawrence Finnerty and Mary Henrietta Crean-Lynch; m. Robert A. Monck, June 16, 1962 (dec. Jan. 1983); children: Merritt Monck-Rowley, Erinna Monck Bernstein, Caitlin Monck-Marcellino. BS, Georgetown U., 1960; PhD, NYU, 1968; MA in Art History, Cooper Hewitt-New Sch., 1999; postdoctoral cert. in adult psychoanalysis, Derner Inst.; postdoctoral cert. in child and adolescent psychotherapy, Adelphi U. Pvt. practice psychoanalyst, Oyster Bay, NY, 1968—; pres. Oyster Bay (N.Y.) Hist. Soc., 2004; supr. of psychotherapy Metro. Ctr. for Mental Health, NYC, 1997—; dir. psychotherapy tng. program L.I. Inst. for Psychoanalysis, East Meadow, NY, 1985—93; dir. nursing program C.W. Post - L.I. U., Brookville, NY, 1972—75. Office Phone: 516-922-6125.

MONCREIFF, ROBERT P., lawyer; b. Evanston, Ill., Mar. 26, 1930; s. W. Philip and Maxine E. M.; m. Elisabeth M.; children: Anne, Philip, Jane. BA, Yale U., 1952; MA, Oxford U., Eng., 1954; LLB, Harvard U., 1957. Bar: Mass. 1957. Assoc. Palmer & Dodge, Boston, 1957-62; ptnr. Edwards Angell Palmer & Dodge, Boston, 1993—95, of counsel, 1995—. City councillor, Cambridge, Mass., 1970-74. Office: Edwards Angell Palmer Dodge LLP 111 Huntington at Prudential Ctr Boston MA 02199-7613 Office Phone: 617-239-0290. Business E-Mail: rmoncreiff@eapdlaw.com.

MONCRIEF, JACQUELINE C., retired state agency administrator; b. Cin., Ohio, Apr. 27, 1940; d. John L. Craddock and Novella D. Noble; children: David, Vanessa, Orlando. Student, Cen. State U., Wilberforce, Ohio, 1958—61; BA, Capital U., Columbus, Ohio, 1991. Cert. Gospel Lighthouse Sch. Ministry, lic. missionary Bishop Ross, Friendstone Ch. Monetary supr. Ohio Bur. Employment Svcs., Columbus, 1974—2001, initial claims supr., 1974—2001; compliance auditor Ohio Dept. Job and Family Svcs., Columbus, 1974—2001; ret. Mem. various planning teams ODJFS, Columbus. Vol. United Way; tutor, mentor Adopt-a-Sch. program Starling Sch., 1996—99; tutor, mentor Ohio Reads program Sedalia Sch., 1999—2000. Recipient Outstanding Svc. award and trophy, GMWA, 1988, plaque, Luth. Social Svcs., 1985. Mem.: Gospel Music Workshop of Am. Baptist. Avocations: singing in choir, dance, travel, games. Home: 1858 Riverdale Rd Columbus OH 43232

MONCRIEF, MICHAEL JOSEPH, mayor, former state legislator; b. Houston, Sept. 5, 1943; s. Richard Barto Sr. and Mary Daisy (Wiley) M.; m. Rosemary Brewer, Dec. 31, 1980; children: Troy L., Mitchell K. BS, Tarleton State U., 1968. Ind. oil prodr., Ft. Worth, 1969—; mem. Tex. Ho. of Reps., 1971—72, mem. appropriations com., 1970-72; judge Tarrant County, Tex., 1974—86; mem. Tex. State Senate, 1991—2003; pres. pro tempore Tex. Senate, 2001; mayor City of Ft. Worth, 2003—. Past mem. Tarrant County Drug Abuse Bd., Lone Star Transp. Authority, N. Central Tex. Council of Govts., Appropriations Com.; mem. Gov.'s Blue Ribbon Commn. on Criminal Justice, many other groups. Bd. dirs. Assn. Retarded Citizens (hon. chmn.), chmn. Neighborhood Resources Devel. Coun., Tarrant County Med., Edn. and Rsch. Found., Tarrant County Mental Health Assn., Drug Treatment Ctr., Tarrant County Juvenile Bd., Ft. Worth State Sch., Inst. Pub. Svc. Tarleton State U., Tex. Affiliate Adv. Com., AHA, Alliance for Children (hon.), Paul Quinn Coll., Tex. Preservation Bd., US Olympic Com., and several others; pres. Neighborhood Health Horizons; past bd. dirs. Gill Children Svcs., Inc., Ft. Worth Libr. Bd., Longhorn Coun. Boy Scouts Am., Tex. Soc. for Prevention of Blindness, North Tex., many others; dir. North Tex. Commn., 2003-; affiliated with Ft. Worth C. of C., Tex. Arts Alliance, Muscular Dystrophy Assn., Inc. and several others. Named Outstanding Cmty. Leader Am., 1970, Outstanding Young Man Am., 1971, Newsmaker of Yr., 1974, 78, Freshman Legislator of Yr., Tex. Legislature, 1971, AARP award, 1997, Common Cause Star of Tex. Pub. Svc. award, 2000, Kiwanis Club ' Community Builder" award, 2002, many other honors. Mem. Tarleton Alumni Assn. (Disting. Alumni 1977), Ind. Petroleum Assn. Am., Am. Judicature Soc., Nat. Coll. Probate Judges, Ft. Worth Res. Police Officers, other profl. orgns. Avocations: skiing, tennis, golf, hunting rattlesnakes and alligators. Office: Office of Mayor 1000 Throckmorton St Fort Worth TX 76102 Business E-Mail: Mayor@fortworthgov.org. *

MONCRIEF, WILLIAM ALVIN, JR., oil and gas producer; b. Little Rock, Mar. 27, 1920; d. William Alvin and Elizabeth (Bright) Moncrief; m. Deborah Beggs, Jan. 30, 1947; children: William A. III, R.W., C.B., T.O. BS in Petroleum Engring., U. Tex., Austin, 1942. Registered profl. engr., Tex. Ptnr. Moncrief Oil, Ft. Worth, 1945—; dir. First Republic Bank, Dallas. Regent, U. Tex. sys. Served to ensign USNR, 1944-45, PTO. Named Disting. Engring. Grad. U. Tex.-Austin, 1983; named one of 400 Richest Ams. Forbes mag., 2006. Mem.: Shady Oaks of Ft. Worth (pres.); Eldorado (Indian Wells, Calif.); Brookhollow (Dallas). Republican. Episcopalian. Office: Moncrief Oil Moncrief Bldg 950 Commerce St at 9th Fort Worth TX 76102

MONCURE, ASHBY CARTER, surgeon, educator; b. Richmond, Va., Dec. 27, 1934; s. Powhatan and Maude Leah (Carley) M.; m. Patricia Juanita Leighton, June 21, 1960 (dec. Oct. 2001); children: Diana, Ann Marie, Ashby, Elizabeth; m. Margot Graham Lord, June 19, 2004. MD, U. Va., 1960. Diplomate Am. Bd. Surgery, Am. Bd. Thoracic Surgery, Am. Bd. Vascular Surgery. Intern Mass. Gen. Hosp., Boston, 1960-61, resident, 1961-62, 64-68; practice medicine specializing in surgery Boston, 1969—. Instr. surgery Harvard Med. Sch., Boston, 1969-71, asst. prof. surgery, 1971-77, asst. clin. prof. surgery, 1977-86, assoc. clin. prof. surgery, 1986—2000, clin. prof. surgery, 2000-03, clin. prof. surgery emeritus, 2003; assoc. vis. surgeon Mass. Gen. Hosp., Boston, 1973-79, vis. surgeon, 1980—2003, sr. surgeon, 2003—. Editor: MGH Textbook of Emergency Medicine, 1978, 2d edit., 1983, 3d edit., 1989, Complex Operations at the Mass. Gen. Hospital, 1983. Capt. U.S. Army, 1962-64. Fellow ACS; mem. New Eng. Surg. Soc. (pres. 2000), Ea. Surg. Soc. (pres. 2004), Am. Surg. Assn., Soc. Thoracic Surgeons, Internat. Cardiovascular Soc., Am. Assn. Thoracic Surgery, Soc. Vascular Surgery, Boston Surg. Soc. (pres. 1995). Clubs: Union Boat, Weston Golf. Episcopalian. Home: 3 Glen Oak Dr Wayland MA 01778

MONCURE, JOHN LEWIS, lawyer; b. Houston, Nov. 4, 1930; s. Walter Raleigh Daniel and Margaret (Atkins) M.; m. Norma Steed, Dec. 29, 1954 (dec. June 1982); children: John Carter, Michael Lewis, Douglas Lee, Stuart Richard, Mary Margaret; m. Margaret Edmonston, Nov. 12, 1983. BBA, U. Houston, 1953; JD, U. Tex., 1956. Bar: Tex. 1956. Assoc. Butler, Binion, Rice, Cook & Knapp, Houston, 1956-68; ptnr. Prappas, Moncure & Eidman, Houston, 1969-86, John L. Moncure and Assocs., Houston, 1987—. Lectr. bus. law U. Houston, 1958-59, 68-69 Mem. sch. bd. St. Thomas Episcopal Sch., Houston, 1965-78; mem. vestry St. Thomas Episc. Ch., 1975-78. Named Distinguished Alumni Coll. Bus., U. Houston, 1968 Fellow Am. Coll. Probate Counsel; mem. Am., Tex., Houston bar assns., Assn. Christian Schs. (trustee), Coll. Bus. Alumni Assn. U. Houston (pres., dir.), U. Houston Alumni Fedn. (treas., dir.), Sigma Alpha Epsilon. Republican. Home: 1220 W Clay Houston TX 77019 Office: 1200 River Oaks Tower 3730 Kirby Dr Houston TX 77098-3905 Home Phone: 713-528-9870; Office Phone: 713-831-6821.

MONDALE, JOAN ADAMS, wife of former Vice President of United States; b. Eugene, Oreg., Aug. 8, 1930; d. John Maxwell and Eleanor Jane (Hall) Adams; m. Walter F. Mondale, Dec. 27, 1955; children— Theodore, Eleanor Jane, William Hall. BA, Macalester Coll., 1952. Asst. slide librarian Boston Mus. Fine Arts, 1952-53; asst. in edn. Mpls. Inst. of Arts, 1953-57; weekly tour guide Nat. Gallery of Art, Washington, 1965-74; hostess Washington Whirl-A-Round, 1975-76; ambassador to Japan, 1993-96. Author: Politics in Art, 1972, Letters from Japan, 1998. Bd. govs. Women's Nat. Dem. Club; hon. chmn. Fed. Coun. on Arts and Humanities, 1978-80; bd. dirs. Associated Coun. of Arts, 1973-75, Reading Is Fundamental, Am. Craft Coun., NYC, 1981-88, J.F.K. Ctr. Performing Arts, 1981-90, Walker Art Ctr., Mpls., 1987-93, 97-03, Minn. Orch., Mpls., 1988-93, 97-2003, St. Paul Chamber Orch., 1988-90, Northern Clay Ctr., 1988-93, St. Paul, 1988-93, Nancy Hauser Dance Co., Mpls., 1989-93, Minn. Landmarks, 1991-93; trustee Macalester Coll., 1986—00; mem. commn. Nat. Portrait Gallery, 1997—; chair Hiawatha Light Rail Transit Pub. Art and Design com., 2000-04; active Walker Art Ctr., 2003—07, Minn. Orch., 1997—; citizen's stamp adv. com. US Postal Svc., 2005— Mem.: Phi Beta Kappa Epsilon. Democrat. Presbyterian. Home: 2116 Irving Ave S Minneapolis MN 55405-2541 E-mail: joan.mondale@mac.com.

MONDALE, WALTER FREDERICK, lawyer, former Vice President of United States; b. Ceylon, Minn., Jan. 5, 1928; s. Theodore Sigvaard and Claribel Hope (Cowan) M.; m. Joan Adams, Dec. 27, 1955; children: Theodore, Eleanor, William. BA cum laude, U. Minn., 1951, LLB cum laude, 1956. Bar: Minn. 1956. Law clk. Minn. Supreme Ct.; pvt. practice law, 1956-60; atty. gen. State of Minn., 1960-64; US Senator from Minn., 1964-77; v.p. U.S., 1977-81; mem. NSC, 1977-81; mem. firm Winston & Strawn LLP, 1981-87; US amb. to Japan US Dept. State, Tokyo, 1993-96, presdl. envoy to Indonesia, 1998; ptnr. Dorsey & Whitney LLP, Mpls., 1987—93, ptnr., internat. corp. practice group, sr. counsel, 1997—. Chmn. Nat. Democratic Inst. for Internat. Affairs, 1986—93. Author: The Accountability of Power*Toward a Responsible Presidency, 1975; mem. Minn. Law Rev. Dem. nominee for Pres. U.S., 1984. With U.S. Army, 1951-53. Named Disting. Univ. Fellow in law and pub. affairs, Hubert H. Humphrey Inst. of Pub. Affairs, Univ. Minn. Presbyterian. Democrat. Office: Dorsey & Whitney 50 S 6th St Ste 1500 Minneapolis MN 55402-1498 Office Phone: 612-340-2600. Office Fax: 612-340-2868. *

MONDAVI, ROBERT GERALD, winery executive; b. Virginia, Minn., June 18, 1913; s. Cesare and Rosa (Grassi) Mondavi; m. Marjorie Declusin, 1940 (dec.); children: Robert, Timothy, Marcia; m. Margrit Biever, 1980. BA in Econs. & Bus. Adminstrn., Stanford U., 0196; Hon. Degree, Cornell U., 1995; Degree in Fine Arts Honoris Causa, Calif. Coll. Arts & Crafts, 2002. Dir. Sunny St. Helena Wine Co., St. Helena, Calif.,

1937—45; v.p., gen. mgr. Charles Krug Winery, St. Helena, 1943—66; pres. Robert Mondavi Winery, Oakville, Calif., 1966—91; chmn. bd. Robert Mondavi Winery (acquired by Constellation Brands), Oakville, Calif., 1991—2004. Chmn. Wine Inst. Author: (autobiography) Harvests of Joy: My Passion for Excellence, 1998. Benefactor Copia: The Am. Ctr. for Wine, Food and the Arts, 2001—. Named Winemaker of Yr., Am. Wine Soc., 1982, Commandeur de Bordeaux, Grand Conseil du Vin de Bordeaux, 1983, Man of Yr., Wines and Vines mag., 1986, Decanter mag., 1988, Wine & Spirits Profl. of Yr., James Beard Found., 1990, Beverage Industry's Man of Yr., Christerman Found., 1991, Hon. Master of Wine, Inst. of Masters of Wine, 1993, Bus. Leader of Yr., Harvard Bus. Sch. Assn. No. Calif., 1997, US House Reps, Disting. Hon. Mem. of the Agrl. Leadership Alumni, 2003; named to Nat. Bus. Hall of Fame, Jr. Achievement, Inc., 1991, Bay Area Bus. Hall of Fame, Bay Area Coun., 1995, Internat. Food & Beverage Hall of Fame, Doctor of Oenology, Honoris Causa, Bd. Trustees, Johnson & Wales U., 2000, Hall of Fame-Distinguished Restaurants of N.Am., 2000; recipient Hall of Fame award, Calif. Restaurant Assn. Ednl. Found., 1988, Merit award, Am. Soc. of Enology and Viticulture, 1990, Ambassador and Master of Aesthetics of Gastronomy award, Culinary Institute of Am., 1991, Calif. State Fair Lifetime Achievement award, 1997, Wine Spectator's Reader's Choice award, 1997, Internat. Achievement award, World Trade Club, 1997, Lifetime Achievement award, European Wine Coun., 1998, Patron of the Arts award, Songwriter's Hall of Fame, NYC, 1999, Ellis Island Family Heritage award, Statue of Liberty-Ellis Island Found., Inc., 2005, F. Norman Clark Entrepreneur of Yr. award, Calif. Travel Industry Assn., 2000, Wine Industry Integrity award, 2000, Lifetime Achievement Recognition from:, Calif. State Assembly, 2002, Am. Food and Entertainment award by Bon Appetit mag. and TV Food Network and Wine Enthusiast mag. Wine awards, 2002, Presdl. Citation, U. Calif. Davis, 2002, Order of Merit of the Republic of Italy, Govt. Italy, 2002, Award of Merit-Winemaker of the Century, Confrerie de la Chaine des Rotisseurs, 2003, Legion d'Honneur award, Govt. France, 2003, Lifetime Achievement award, Vinexpo, 2003. Mem.: Am. Inst. of Wine and Food, Calif. State Polytechnic U. Pomona (hon. life chmn. 1992, Winemaker of Yr. 1992), Cornell Soc. of Hotelman (assoc.). Achievements include donated gift with wife to the Univ. of Calif. to establish the Robert Mondavi Inst. for Wine and Food Science and to name in honor of Robert and Margrit Mondavi Ctr. for the Performing Arts; torch bearer International Olympic Committee in 1996. Office: Robert Mondavi Winery PO Box 106 Oakville CA 94562-0106 Address: Robert Mondavi Winery Hwy 29 Oakville CA 94562

MONDELLO, JOHN PAUL, financial consultant; b. NYC, Aug. 9, 1948; s. Salvatore Carmelo and Mary (Monaco) M.; m. Catherine Mary Seyfried, Sept. 12, 1970; children: Lynn Marie, Timothy. BA in Econs., LeMoyne Coll., Syracuse, NY, 1971; MS in Fin. Svcs., Am. Coll., Bryn Mawr, Pa., 1986. CLU, Chartered Fin. Cons. Fin. cons. Signator Advisory Group, Westbury, NY, 1972—. Instr. estate planning Am. Soc. CLU & ChFC, Garden City, 1990-96, Empire State Coll., 1997-02. 1st lt. US Army N.G., 1971-77. Mem. LI Assn. Ins. and Fin. Advisors (Victor Goldberg Svc. award 1989), John Hancock Chmn.'s Coun., Million Dollar Round Table (life), John Hancock Pres.'s Cabinet, John Hancock Hall of Fame. Avocations: golf, reading, spectator sports. Office: Signator Adv Group 1025 Old Country Rd Ste 325 Westbury NY 11590 Office Phone: 516-794-9696 ext.13. Business E-Mail: jmondello@jhnetwork.com.

MONDELLO, JOSEPH N., political organization administrator; b. Bklyn., Feb. 13, 1938; s. Joseph and Rose Martin Mondello; m. Linda Elisabeth Crabtree; children: Joseph, Elizabeth, Lisa. BA, Hofstra Coll.; JD, New England Sch. of Law; DA (hon.), Five Towns Coll., 1995. Ptnr. Flaum, Imbarrato & Mondello, Levittown, N.Y., 1975-87; councilman Town of Hempstead, N.Y., 1979-87; vice chmn. Nassau County Bd. of Suprs., Mineola, N.Y., 1987-93; presiding supr. Town of Hempstead, 1987-93; Rep. nat. committeeman NYC, 1992—, Washington, 1992—; chmn. Nassau County Rep. com., Westbury, 1983—2006, NY Rep. State Com., Albany, 2006—. Counsel Law Firm of Certolman, Balin, Adler & Hyman, East Meadow, 1997—. Maj. gen. N.Y. Guard, Albany. Mem. Knights of the Holly Sepulcher, KC, Order of Sons of Italy, Levittown Kiwanis Club, Am. Vets., Am. Legion. Republican. Roman Catholic. Avocations: fishing, tennis. Office: NY Rep State Com 315 State St Albany NY 12210

MONDELLO, LISETTE MCSOUD, federal agency administrator; BA, Trinity Coll. Dir. comm. office of Sen. Alfonse D'Amato U.S. Senate, Washington, dir. comm. office of Sen. Kay Bailey Hutchison; sr. advisor office comm. and outreach US Dept. Edn.; asst. sec. pub. & intergovernmental affairs US Dept. Veterans Affairs, 2005—. Office: US Dept Veterans Affairs 810 Vermont Ave NW Rm 900 Washington DC 20420 Office Phone: 202-273-5750. Office Fax: 202-273-5717.

MONDINO, BARTLY J., ophthalmologist; b. Sacramento, May 24, 1945; married; children: Kara, Kristen. BA in Med. Scis., Stanford U., 1967, MD, 1971. Diplomate Am. Bd. Ophthalmology. Intern Stanford (Calif.) U. Hosp., 1971-72; ophthalmology resident N.Y. Hosp., Cornell U., NYC, 1972-75; fellow in cornea, external disease U. Pitts. Sch. Medicine - Eye and Ear Hosp., Pitts., 1975-76, asst. prof. ophthalmology, 1976-79, assoc. prof. ophthalmology, 1979-82; dir. Charles T. Campbell Microbiology Lab. Eye and Ear Hosp., Pitts., 1978-82; assoc. prof. ophthalmology UCLA - Jules Stein Eye Inst., LA, 1982-83, prof. ophthalmology, 1983—, Wasserman Endowed chair dept. ophthalmology, 1988—; chief cornea-external disease divsn. UCLA, 1991-99, chmn. dept. ophthalmology, 1994—; dir. UCLA - Jules Stein Eye Inst., 1994—; with exec. program for acad. healthcare mgmt. The John E. Anderson Grad. Sch. Mgmt./UCLA, 1992. Bd. dirs. Charles R. Drew U. of Medicine and Sci., L.A., Braille Inst., L.A.; mem. adv. com. Rsch. Study Club, Murrieta, Calif., 1994—, scientific adv. panel on ophthalmology Calif. Med. Assn., San Francisco, 1994—. Editl. bd.: Am. Jour. Ophthalmology, Chgo., 1992—, ophthalmic Surgery and Lasers, 1995—, Ophthalmology Times, 1996—, Ophthalmic Practice (Can.), 1996—; editor-in-chief: EYE Newsletter, 1994—; co-chair corneal diseases program planning panel of Nat. Eye Inst.'s Vision Rsch. Program Planning Subcom., Bethesda, md., 1997—, others. Recipient scholarship Stanford U. Sch. Medicine, Rsch. to Prevent Blindness Manpower award 1983-84, Rsch. to Prevent Blindness Sr. Scientific Investigator's award 1994, various lectureships, others. Mem. AMA, Assn. for Rsch. in Vision and Ophthalmology, Assn. Univ. Profs. of Ophthalmology, Am. Acad. Ophthalmology, Calif. Assn. Ophthalmology, Calif. Cornea Club, Calif. Med. Assn., Contact Lens Assn. of Ophthalmologists, Eye Bank Assn. of Am., L.A. County Med. Assn., L.A. Soc. Ophthalmology, Ophthalmology Rsch. Found., Ophthalmic Surgery and Laser Therapy, Rsch. Study Club. Office: 100 Stein Plz # 2-142 Los Angeles CA 90095-7000 Business E-Mail: mondino@jsei.ucla.edu.

MONDLIN, MARVIN, publisher, appraiser, consultant; b. Bklyn., July 1, 1927; s. Samuel and Thelma (Schultz) M.; m. Phyllis Grossman, Oct. 23, 1962 (div. 1968); 1 child, Gerri; m. Irene Szmulewicz, Sept. 4, 1970. Student, Cornell U., 1945; student of Aesthetic Realism, with Eli Siegel, 1945—68; student, CCNY, 1948, Bklyn. Coll., 1969—71. Ptnr. Amory Books, NYC, 1953-59; clk. Strand Book Store, NYC, 1951, estate book buyer, 1959-71, 74-76, sr. exec. v.p., 1976—2004; proprietor Am. Sunbeam Pub., NYC, 1996—. Bus. mgr. Definition Press., NYC, 1957; cataloger U. Cath. de Louvain, Belgium, 1972. Author: Appraisals: A Guide for Bookmen, 1997; co-author: Book Row, An Anecdotal and Pictorial History of the Antiquarian Book Trade, 2003; proofreader, copy editor Dover Publs., NYC, 1958; editor Yearbook of Internat. Assocs., 1974; pub. Robert Clairmont's Quintillions, 2006. Mem.: Typophiles, Ephemera Soc. Am., European Soc. History of Phtography, Am. Photog. Hist. Soc., Bibliog. Soc. London, Bibliog. Soc. Am., Appraisers Assn. Am., Camera Club. Avocation: photography. Home Phone: 212-982-8189; Office Phone: 212-982-8189. E-mail: marvinmondlin@verizon.net.

MONDRY, DIANE, secondary school educator; b. Reginas, Sask., Can. 3 children. Career and tech. edn. tchr. Cmty. H.S., Grand Forks, ND. Part-time instr. dept. info. sys. and bus. edn. U. N.D. Recipient Outstanding Tchr. award, Nat. Assn. Vocat. Edn. Spl. Needs Pers. Mem.: NEA, Assn. for Career and Tech. Edn. (immediate past pres. 2001—02), Nat. Bd. for Profl. Tchg. Stds. (bd. mem.). Office: Cmty High Sch 500 Stanford Rd Grand Forks ND 58203-2748

MONDRY, LAWRENCE N., automotive executive; V.p., nat. mdse. mgr. Highland Superstones, Inc., 1983-88, 88-90; sr. v.p., gen. mdse. mgr. CompUSA, Inc., Dallas, 1990-93, exec. v.p. merchandising, 1993—2000, pres., COO, 2000—03, CEO, 2003—06; pres., CEO CSK Auto Inc., Phoenix, 2007—. Bd. dir. Micron Technology, Golfsmith Inc. Office: CSK Auto Inc 645 E Missouri Ave Phoenix AZ 85012 *

MONDUL, DONALD DAVID, patent lawyer; b. Miami, Fla., Aug. 24, 1945; s. David Donald and Marian Wright (Heck) M.; children: Alison Marian, Ashley Megan; m. Anna Marie Towle, Oct. 12, 1996. BS in Physics, U.S. Naval Acad., 1967; MBA, Roosevelt U., 1976; JD, John Marshall Law Sch., 1979. Bar: Ill. 1979, Fla. 1980, Tex. 1998; U.S. Patent Office 1980; U.S. Ct. Appeals (fed. cir.) 1982; U.S. Supreme Ct. 1990. Commd. ensign USN, 1967, advanced through grades to comdr., 1977; mktg. rep. Control Data Corp., Chgo., 1977-79; patent atty. Square D Co., Palatine, Ill., 1979-81; group patent counsel Ill. Tool Works Inc., Chgo., 1981-87; assoc. Cook, Wetzel & Egan, Chgo., 1987-89; ptnr. Foley & Lardner, Chgo. and Milw., 1989-95; sr. patent atty. IBM, East Fishkill, NY, 1995-96; gen. patent counsel Ericsson, Inc., Richardson, Tex., 1996-99; pvt. practice Dallas, 1999—. Comdr., USNR, 1967-87. Achievements include patents for Electrical Encoding Device; Method and Apparatus for Determining the Product of Two Numbers; Apparatus for Providing Power to Selected Portions of a Multiplying Device; Method and Apparatus for Multiplying a Plurality of N Numbers; Method and for Establishing an Operating Parameter for a Power Supply Device; Apparatus and Method for Locating Objects in a Three-Dimensional Space; Air Baffle Apparatus. Home and Office: 3060 Bonsai Dr Plano TX 75093 Personal E-mail: dmondul@aol.com.

MONE, MICHAEL EDWARD, lawyer; b. Brockton, Mass., May 15, 1942; s. Edward Patrick and June Elizabeth (Kelliher) M.; m. Margaret E. Supple, Sept. 11, 1965; 1 child, Michael Edward. BA, Middlebury Coll., 1964, LLB (hon.), 2000; JD, Boston Coll., 1967; LLB (hon.), Suffolk U., 1999. Bar: Mass. 1967, U.S. Dist. Ct. Mass. 1968, U.S. Ct. Appeals (1st cir.) 1968. Trial atty. Schneider & Reilly, Boston, 1967-73, ptnr., 1969-73; trial lawyer Esdaile, Barrett & Esdaile, Boston, 1973—, ptnr., 1976—. Instr. Boston Coll. Law Sch., 1981, U.S. Supreme Court, 1996. Chmn. Zoning Bd. Appeals, Brockton, 1976-78. Fellow Am. Coll. Trial Lawyers (bd. regents 1995-2001, sec. 1997-98, pres. 1999-2000); mem. ABA, ATLA (bd. govs. 1975-78), Mass. Bar Assn. (pres. 1993-94), Mass. Acad. Trial Lawyers (pres. 1981-84, joint bar com. on jud. nominations 1986-90). Office: Esdaile Barrett & Esdaile 75 Federal St Boston MA 02110-1913 Office Phone: 617-482-0333. Business E-Mail: mone@ebelaw.com.

MONEY, DAVID R., lawyer, information technology executive; BS, MBA, U. Utah, Salt Lake City; student, U. Oreg. Sch. Law; JD, U. Utah, Salt Lake City. Ptnr. Jones, Waldo, Holbrook and McDonough, Salt Lake City; dep. gen. counsel First Data Corp., Greenwood Village, Colo., 2004—07, exec. v.p., gen. counsel, sec., 2007—. Mem.: Utah Bar Assn., Colo. Bar Assn. Office: First Data Corp 6200 S Quebec St Greenwood Village CO 80111 Office Phone: 303-488-8000. *

MONEY, ROBERT MCGUFFEY, history professor; b. Madison, Ind., Nov. 8, 1930; s. C.V. and Esther McGuffey Money; m. Margaret Sarah Niemetta, May 30, 1964; children: Thomas Andrew, Elizabeth Anne. BA in History and Geography, No. Mich. U., Marquette, 1953; MA, U. Mich., Ann Arbor, 1958; postgrad., Mich. State U., 1958—62. Grad. asst. Sch. Journalism Mich. State U., East Lansing, 1959—62, grad. asst. dept. history, 1960—62; tchr. history Alma Coll., Mich., 1962—64; instr. humanities Mich. State U., East Lansing, 1965—67; tchr. history Lake Superior State U., Sault St. Marie, Mich., 1969—. Pres. Sault Hist. Sites, Sault St. Marie, 1970—72; chmn. City Hist. Commn., Sault St. Marie, 1980—85; lectr. in field. Moderator Presbytery Mackinaw, Presbyn. Ch. USA, Petoskey, Mich., 1991—92, moderator Mackinaw Presbytery, 2002—03. Cpl. US Army, 1953—56. Recipient Distinguished Tchr. award, Lake Superior State U., 1986. Mem.: VFW (life), Mich. Oral History Soc. (bd. dirs. 1994—), Hist. Soc. Mich. (bd. dirs. 1992—2006), Chippewa County Hist. Soc. (pres. 1971—74, bd. dirs. 1971—), Ohio Hist. Soc. (assoc.), Co. Mil. Historians (assoc.), One Rm. Schoolhouse Assn. (life), Soc. Bayonnet Collectors (assoc.). Democrat. Presbyterian. Avocations: antiques, 19th century education, travel, refinishing furniture. Home: 409 W Easterday Ave Sault Sainte Marie MI 49783 Home Phone: 906-632-6659; Office Phone: 906-635-2327.

MONEYPENNY, EDWARD WILLIAM, retail executive; b. Long Branch, NJ, Jan. 28, 1942; s. Edward Henry and Eleanor Kathleen (O'Hagan) M.; m. Connie Wills, Feb. 19, 1966; children: Matthew, Jonathan, Christopher. BS in Acctg., St. Joseph's U., 1964; MS in Acctg. Sci., U. Ill., 1967. CPA, Pa. Audit mgr. Coopers & Lybrand, Phila., 1970-76; mgr. corp. acctg. Sun Co., Inc., Radnor, Pa., 1976-78; v.p. fin. adminstrn. Sun Prodn. Co., Dallas, 1978-81; v.p. fin., CFO Oryx Energy Co. (formerly Sun Exploration and Prodn. Co.), Dallas, 1981-91; sr. v.p. fin., CFO Oryx Energy Co., Dallas, 1992-94, exec. v.p. fin., CFO, bd. dirs., 1994-99; sr. v.p. fin., CFO Fla. Progress Corp., St. Petersburg, Fla., 1999-2000; exec. v.p. fin., CFO Covanta Energy Corp., Fairfield, NJ, 2001; sr. v.p. fin., CFO 7-Eleven, Inc., Dallas, 2002—05. Chmn. dean's bus. coun. U. Ill. Sch. Bus., 2000-01, mem. exec. com., dean's bus. coun., 2002-; bd. dirs., mem. audit com. The Timberland Co., Stratham, NH, 2006—, NY and Co., N.Y.C., 2006—. 1st lt. U.S. Army, 1967-70. Home: 4712 Stonehollow Way Dallas TX 75287-7524

MONG, ROBERT WILLIAM, JR., publishing executive; b. Fremont, Ohio, Jan. 22, 1949; s. Robert William and Betty (Dwyer) M.; m. Carla Beth Sweet, July 25, 1975 (div. 1979); m. Diane Elizabeth Reischel, Jan. 23, 1988; children: Eric Robert, Elizabeth Diana. BA, Haverford Coll., Pa., 1971; graduate exec. bus. program, Stanford U., 1997. Reporter Cin. Post, 1973-75, Capital Times, Madison, Wis., 1975-77; city editor Madison Press Connection, 1977-79; asst. city editor Dallas Morning News, 1979-80, bus. editor, 1980-81, projects editor, 1981-83, asst. mng. editor, 1983-88, dep. mng. editor, 1988-90, mng. editor, 1990-96; pub. Owensboro Messenger-Inquirer, 1996-97; exec. v.p. A.H. Belo Corp., Dallas, 1997-98; pres., gen. mgr. The Dallas Morning News, Dallas, 1998-2001, pres., editor, 2001—. Recipient J.B. Buck Marryat award for meritorious svc., Dallas Press Club, 2005. Mem. Am. Soc. Newspaper Editors, Newspaper Assn. Am., Southern Newspaper Pubs. Assn., Am. Press Inst. (bd. dirs.). Office: The Dallas Morning News PO Box 655237 508 Young St Dallas TX 75202-4828 Home Phone: 214-521-1952; Office Phone: 214-977-8222. Business E-Mail: bmong@dallasnews.com.

MONGA, MANOJ, medical educator; b. Belfast, Northern Ireland, May 4, 1965; s. Trilok Nath and Uma Monga Monga; m. Mary McGinnis, May 29, 1995; children: Nathan Joseph, Miles Manoj, Natalie Marie. BS with honors, Queen's U., Kingston, Ont., 1986; MD, Chgo. Med. Sch., 1990. Asst. prof. U. Calif., San Diego, 1997—2001; assoc. prof. U. Minn., Mpls., 2001—04, prof., 2004—. Dir. urology residency program U. Minn., Mpls., 2005—; co-dir., Ctr. Systematic Reviews Urologic Surgery VAHCS Mpls., Mpls., 2005—; dir. endourology & urologic laparoscopy fellowship U. Minn., 2002—, mem. biomedical engring. inst., 2002—. Contbr. articles to profl. jours., chapters to books. Vol. surg. missions Internat. Volunteers Urology, Bhopal, India, 2002. Recipient Disting. Alumni award, Chgo. Med. Sch., 2006. Fellow: ACS, Am. Urol. Assn.; mem.: R.O.C.K. Soc., Endourologial Soc. Achievements include patents for percutaneous plug; guide wire engaging ureteroscope; 4 patents pending in medical devices. Office: U Minn 420 Delaware St SE MMC 394 Minneapolis MN 55455 Office Phone: 612-625-7486. E-mail: monga002@umn.edu.

MONGAN, JAMES JOHN, healthcare system administrator; b. San Francisco, Apr. 10, 1942; s. Martin and Audrey Vera (Cunningham) M.; m. Jean Trotter Holmes, Apr. 22, 1972; children: John Holmes, Sarah Holmes. Student, U. Calif., Berkeley, 1959-62; BA, Stanford U., 1963, MD, 1967. Intern Kaiser Found. Hosp., San Francisco, 1967-68; med. officer USPHS, Denver, 1968-70; profl. staff mem. U.S. Senate Fin. Com., Washington, 1970-77; dep. asst. sec. for health HEW, Washington, 1977-79; assoc. dir. human resources Domestic Policy Staff, White House, 1979-81; asst. surgeon gen. USPHS, 1979-81; exec. dir. Truman Med. Center, U. Mo., Kansas City, 1981-96; dean sch. medicine U. Mo., Kansas City, 1987-96; pres. Mass. Gen. Hosp., 1996—2002; pres., CEO Partners HealthCare Sys. Inc, Boston, 2003—. Prof. healthcare policy, prof. medicine Harvard Med. Sch.; mem. com. on consequences of uninsured Inst. Medicine; chair adv. com. Commonwealth Fund Task Force; mem. Kaiser Commn. on Medicaid and the Uninsured. Trustee Kaiser Family Found., 1993—2001; chmn. Greater Boston C. of C., 2004—. Mem. NAS, Inst. Medicine (coun. mem. 2006-), Am. Hosp. Assn. (trustee 1988-91), Am. Assn. Teaching Hospitals (bd. dirs. coun. tchg hospitals. 1984-90). Office: Partners HealthCare Sys Inc Prudential Tower 800 Boylston St Ste 1150 Boston MA 02199-8001 *

MONHEIT, ALAN GOODMAN, obstetrician, gynecologist; b. Phila., Apr. 5, 1949; s. Richard S. and Jane G. Monheit; children: Robin, Jeffrey, Daniel. BSc, Muhlenberg Coll., 1971; MD, U. Pa., 1975. Intern U. Calif., San Diego, 1975-76, resident physician dept. ob-gyn., 1975-79, fellow, maternal/fetal medicine, 1979-81; attending physician U. Hosp., Stony Brook, 1981—; clin. assoc. prof. SUNY, Stony Brook, 1981—. Tchr. medicine, specialist in high risk pregnancy SUNY, Stony Brook, 1981—. Contbr. articles to profl. jours. Recipient Tchg. award Coun. on Resident Edn. in Ob-gyn., 1997. Mem. ACOG, Assn. Profs. Ob-Gyn., Soc. Perinatal Obstetricians (poster prize 1987), Suffolk County Ob-Gyn. Soc., Phi Beta Kappa. Avocations: bicycling, hiking, space exploration, meteorology. Office: SUNY Dept Obstetrics Gynecology HSC T-9 Stony Brook NY 11794 Office Phone: 631-444-7650.

MONHEIT, MOLLY JANE, artist; b. Yakima, Wash., Aug. 5, 1922; d. Laurel LaVergne and Edna (Bracewell) Lugar; m. John Palmer Ruckel (dec. 1952); children: Gail Ruckel, Andrew Ruckel; m. George Monheit, Dec. 7, 1952; 1 child, William. Student, Art Ctr. Sch., Calif., 1942; BA magna cum laude, Wash. State U., 1944; MA, Mills Coll., 1947. Clk., artist, cons. Papyrus, Lafayette, Calif., 1976-97; ret., 1997. Exhibited paintings in Wash., Tex., and Calif.; prin. works represented in permanent collections in pvt. homes and museums in 38 countries; contbr. articles to Bird Watchers Digest. Precinct chmn. Reps., Lafayette, 1954-70; social chmn. Valley View Estates, Lafayette, 1954-80. Recipient fellowship Aurelia Reinhart, 1945-47. Mem. Soc. Western Artists, Am. Women Artists, East Bay Watercolor Soc., Audubon Soc., Am. Field Svc. (pres. 1970), Diablo Art Assn. (pres.), Alpha Gamma Delta. Presbyterian. Avocations: birding trips, track and field.

MONIS, JOHNNY, chef; b. 1980; Attended, Johnson & Wales Culinary Sch. Chef McCrady's Restaurant, Charleston, SC; exec. chef Chef Geoff's Downtown, Washington, 2003; owner, exec. chef Komi, Washington, 2003—. Named one of Best New Chefs, Food and Wine Mag., 2007. Office: Komi 1509 17th St Washington DC 20036 Office Phone: 252-332-9200. Office Fax: 252-332-9201. *

MONISMITH, CARL LEROY, civil engineering educator; b. Harrisburg, Pa., Oct. 23, 1926; s. Carl Samuel and Camilla Frances (Geidt) M. BSCE, U. Calif., Berkeley, 1950, MSCE, 1954; D of Engring. (hon.), Carleton U., Ottawa, 2004. Registered civil engr., Calif., 1961. From instr. to prof. civil engring. U. Calif., Berkeley, 1951—, chmn. dept. civil engring., 1974-79, Robert Horonjeff prof. civil engring., 1986—, prof. emeritus, 1996. Cons. Chevron Rsch. Co., Richmond, Calif., 1957-93, U.S. Army CE Waterways Expt. Sta., Vicksburg, Miss., 1968-00, B.A. Vallerga, Inc., Oakland, Calif., 1980-98, ARE, Austin, Tex. and Scotts Valley, Calif., 1978-92; cons. Bechtel Corp., San Francisco, 1982-86. Contbr. numerous articles to profl. jours. Served to 2d lt. C.E., U.S. Army, 1945-47. Recipient Rupert Myers medal U. NSW, 1976; named Henry M. Shaw Lectr. in Civil Engring., N.C. State U., 1993, First Paul Kraser Kent lectr. dept. civil and environ. engring. U. Ill., Urbana-Champaign, 2007; sr. scholar Fulbright Found., U. NSW, 1971, Nat. Asphalt Pavelent Assn. R.D. Kenyon Rsch. and Edn. award for Outstanding Contbns. for Hot Mix Asphalt Tech., 2002, Hall of Fame, 2005; named Disting. Engring. Alumnus, Coll. Engring., U. Calif., Berkeley, 1996 Fellow: AAAS; mem.: ASTM, NAE, NRC (assoc.), NAS (assoc.), ASCE (hon.; pres. San Francisco sect. 1979—80, ednl. activities com. 1989—91, State of Art award 1977, James Laurie prize 1988), Nat. Assn. of the Nat. Acads., Asphalt Inst. (Roll of Honor 1990), Calif. Asphalt Pavement Alliance (award 2002), Am. Soc. Engring. Edn., Internat. Soc. Asphalt Pavements (hon.; chmn. bd. dirs. 1988—90, Disting. Lectr. 2004), Assn. Asphalt Paving Technologists (hon. W.J. Emmons award 1961, 1965, 1985), Transp. Rsch. Bd. (assoc.; chmn. pavement design sect. 1973—79, K.B. Woods award 1972, 1st disting. lectureship 1992, Roy W. Crum award 1995). Avocation: stamp collecting/philately. Office: U Calif Dept Civil Engring 215 Mclaughlin Hall Berkeley CA 94720-1712 Home Phone: 510-234-7835; Office Phone: 510-665-3560. Business E-Mail: clm@maxwell.berkeley.edu.

MONIZ, ERNEST JEFFREY, physics professor; b. Fall River, Mass., Dec. 22, 1944; s. Ernest Perry and Georgina (Pavao) M.; m. Naomi Hoki, June 9, 1973; 1 child, Katya BS, Boston Coll., 1966; PhD, Stanford U., 1971. Prof. physics MIT, Cambridge, 1973-97, dir. Bates Linear Accelerator Ctr. Middleton, 1983-91, head physics dept., 1991-95, 97; under sec. U.S. Dept. Energy, Washington, 1997—2001; prof. physics and engring. systems MIT, 2001—. Cons. Los Alamos Nat. Lab., 1975-95; assoc. dir. for sci. Office of Sci. and Tech. Policy, Exec. Office of the Pres., 1995-97. Contbr. articles to profl. jours. Fellow: AAAS, Am. Phys. Soc., Humboldt Found. Office: 77 Massachusetts Ave Bldg E40-451 Cambridge MA 02139-4307 Office Phone: 617-253-7517. E-mail: ejmoniz@mit.edu.

MONJAN, ANDREW ARTHUR, neuroscientist; b. NYC, Feb. 9, 1938; s. Victor Momjian and Sonia (Sherinian) Dardarian; m. Susan Vollenweider, July 1961 (div. Nov. 1965); m. Usha Bose, Aug. 14, 1969; children: Matthew, Vanessa. BSc, Rensselaer Poly. Inst., 1960; PhD, U. Rochester, 1965; MPH, Johns Hopkins U., 1970. Rsch. asst. Sterling-Winthrop Rsch. Inst., Rensselaer, NY, 1960; USPHS rsch. fellow Ctr. for Brain Rsch. U. Rochester, NY, 1964-66; asst. prof. depts. psychology and physiology U. Western Ont., London, Canada, 1966-69; from asst. prof. to assoc. prof. dept. epidemiology Sch. Hygiene and Pub. Health Johns Hopkins U., Balt., 1971-83; expert epidemiology extramural programs br. NIH, Bethesda, Md., 1983-85, chief neurobiology/immunology programs physiology aging br., 1985-87, acting assoc. dir., 1987, chief neurobiology, 1987—; exec. sec. Nat. Commn. on Sleep Disorders Rsch., 1990-92. Presenter in field. Contbr. articles to profl. jours. N.Y. State Regents scholar, 1955-59; N.Y.

State Regents Grad. Tchg. fellow, 1960-62, USPHS rsch. fellow, 1962-64, 69-70. Office: Nat Inst Aging 7201 Wisconsin Ave Msc9205 Ste 350 Bethesda MD 20892-9205 Office Phone: 410-496-9350. Business E-Mail: am39m@nih.gov.

MONK, ALLAN JAMES, baritone; b. Mission City, BC, Can., Aug. 19, 1942; m. Marlene Folk; 3 children. Student, Elgar Higgin and Boris Goldovsky. Operatic debut in Old Maid and the Thief, San Francisco, 1967; joined touring co., later main co. San Francisco Opera; appeared with Tulsa Opera, Pitts. Opera, Edmonton Opera, Vancouver Opera, So. Alta. Opera, Chgo. Opera, Balt. Opera, Miami Opera, Colo. Opera, Mont real Opera, Hawaii Opera Theatre, Portland Opera.;, 1976. Met. Opera debut as Schaunard in La Boheme, 1976, sang title role in Wozzeck, Wolfram in Tannheuser, Dr. Malatesta in Don Pasquale, Rodrigo in Don Carlo, Sharpless in Madame Butterfly, Herald in Lohengrin; sang with Can. Opera Co. as Abelard in Heloise and Abelard, Macbeth, Rigoletto, Belcore in L'Elisir D'Amoure, Jago in Otello, as Ford in Falstaff, four villains in Les Contes d'Hoffman; with Nat. Arts Ctr. Opera Festival, Ottawa, Ont., Can., title role in Don Giovanni, Almaviva in Le Nozze Di Figaro, gulielmo in Cossi Fan Tutti, Tomsky in Pique Dame, Marcello in La Boheme; Carnegie Hall debut as Vladislav in Dalibor, 1977; European debut as Wozzeck, 1980; solo recitalist; toured with Nat. Arts Ctr. Orch. in USSR, Poland, Italy, 1973; movie debut as Baron Douphol in La Traviata, 1983. Named Artist of Yr. Can. Music Council, 1983, laureat Order of Can., 1985. Office: 14415 Parkland Blvd SE Calgary AB Canada T2J 4L5 Home Phone: 403-281-9640; Office Phone: 403-281-9640.

MONK, CARL COLBURN, legal association and academic administrator, lawyer; b. Sept. 11, 1942; BA in Polit. Sci., Okla. State U., 1965; JD, Howard U., 1971. Bar: DC 1971, NY 1973. Assoc. Simpson, Thacher & Bartlett, NYC, 1971—74; asst. prof. to assoc. prof. Washburn U., Topeka, 1974—78, assoc. dean to dean, prof., 1976—88, disting. prof. law, 1988—. Dep. dir. Assn. Am. Law Schs., Washington, 1988-90, exec. dir., 1992—; vis. scholar Bklyn. Law Sch., 1985-86; vis. prof. law W.S. Richardson Sch. Law U. Hawaii Manao, 1990-91; lit. cons. Contbr. articles to profl. jours. Bd. dirs. Kans. Civil Liberties Union. Office: Assn Am Law Schs Ste 800 1201 Connecticut Ave NW Washington DC 20036-2717 Office Phone: 202-296-1526. Office Fax: 202-296-8869. E-mail: cmonk@aals.org. *

MONK, DEBRA, actress; b. Middletown, Ohio, Feb. 27, 1949; Grad., Frostburg State U. Stage appearances include (Broadway) Ah, Wilderness!, Steel Pier Company, Nick & Nora, Prelude to a Kiss, Pump Boys and Dinettes (also co-author), Redwood Curtain (Tony award featured actress in play 1993), Picnic (Tony nomination featured actress 1994), (theatre) Death Defying Acts, 3 Hotels (Helen Hayes award leading actress 1994), Assassins, Oil City Symphony (co-author, Drama Desk award Best Ensemble 1988), Laughing Wild, 2005, Chicago, 2005, Curtains, 2006 (Drama Desk award outstanding featured actress in a musical, 2007); TV appearances include Women & Wallace, 1990, Loving, 1994, Redwood Curtain, 1995, Ellen Foster, 1997, NYPD Blue, 1998-2001 (Emmy award for Outstanding Guest Acress in a Drama Series 1999), The Music Man, 2003, Eloise at the Plaza, 2003, Eloise at Christmastime, 2003, Show People, 2006; films include: Prelude to a Kiss, 1992, For Love or Money, 1993, Fearless, 1993, Quiz Show, 1993, Reckless, 1995, Bridges of Madison County, 1995, Jeffrey, 1995, First Wives Club, 1996, Bed of Roses, 1996, Mrs. Winterbourne, 1996, Substance of Fire, 1996, Devil's Advocate, 1997, Extreme Measures, 1996, In and Out, 1997, Bulworth, 1998, Center Stage, 2000, Briar Patch, 2003, Milwaukee, Minnesota, 2003, Palindromes, 2004, Dark Water, 2005. *

MONK, DIANA CHARLA, small business owner; b. Visalia, Calif., Feb. 25, 1927; d. Charles Edward and Viola Genevieve (Shea) Williams; m. James Alfred Monk, Aug. 11, 1951; children: Kiloran, Sydney, Geoffrey, Anne, Eric. Student, U. Pacific, Stockton, Calif., 1946-47, Sacramento Coll., 1947-48, Calif. Coll. Fine Arts, San Francisco, 1948-51, Calif. Coll. Arts & Crafts, Oakland, 1972. Art tchr. Mt. Diablo Sch. Dist., Concord, Calif., 1958-63; pvt. art tchr. Lafayette, Calif., 1963-70; gallery dir. Jason Aver Gallery, San Francisco, 1970-72; owner, mgr. Monk & Lee Assocs., Lafayette, 1973-80; stable owner, mgr. Longacre Tng. Stables, Santa Rosa, Calif., 1989—. One-person shows include John F. Kennedy U., Orinda, Calif., Civic Arts Gallery, Walnut Creek, Calif., Vallery Art Gallery, Walnut Creek, Sea Ranch Gallery, Gualala, Calif., Jason Aver Gallery, San Francisco; exhibited in group shows at Oakland (Calif.) Art Mus., Crocker Nat. Art Gallery, Sacramento, Le Salon des Nations, Paris. Chair bd. dirs. Walnut Creek (Calif.) Civic Arts, 1972-74, advisor to dir., 1968-72; exhibit chmn. Valley Art Gallery, Walnut Creek, 1977-78; juror Women's Art Show, Walnut Creek, 1970, Oakland Calif. Art. Home and Office: Longacre Tng Stables 1702 Willowside Rd Santa Rosa CA 95401-3922 Home Phone: 707-544-7030; Office Phone: 707-544-7030. Personal E-mail: longacrestables@msn.com.

MONK, MEREDITH JANE, artistic director, composer, choreographer, filmmaker; b. NYC, Nov. 20, 1942; d. Theodore G. and Audrey Lois (Zellman) Monk. BA, Sarah Lawrence Coll., 1964; ArtsD (hon.), Bard Coll., 1988, U. of the Arts, 1989, Juilliard Sch. Music, 1997, San Francisco Art Inst., 1998, Boston Conservatory, 2001, Bennington Coll., 2002, Cornish Coll. Arts, 2002. Artistic dir., founder Ho. Found. Arts, NYC, 1968—. Bd. dirs. Am. Music Ctr., The Kitchen. Prin. works include 16 Millimeter Earrings, 1966, Vessel, 1971, Quarry, 1976, Recent Ruins, 1979, Turtle Dreams, 1983, The Games, 1983, Book of Days, 1988, Facing North, 1990, Atlas, 1991, Three Heavens and Hells, 1992, Volcano Songs, 1994, American Archeology, 1994, The Politics of Quiet, 1996, Magic Frequencies, 1998, Mercy, 2001, Possible Sky, 2003, Impermanence, 2004, Stringsongs, 2005, Basket Rondo, 2007, exhibitions include Libr. of Performing Arts, Lincoln Ctr., 1996, Walker Art Ctr., Mpls., 1998, Whitney Mus. Art, 2002, Exit Art, 2002. Recipient Obie award, Village Voice, 1972, 1976, 1985, Creative Arts award, Brandeis U., 1974, Villager award, 1980, 1983, Deutches Kritiker preis, 1981, 1986, Bessie award, 1985, Nat. Music Theatre award, 1986, Dance Mag. award, 1993, John D. and Catherine T. MacArthur award, 1995, Sarah Lawrence Disting. Alumna award, 1996, Samuel Scripps award, 1996, Sigma Phi Omega award, 1987; fellow Guggenheim, 1972, 1982, Norton Stevens, 1993—94, MacDowell Colony. Fellow: Am. Acad. Arts and Scis. (USA Artist award 2006); mem.: ASCAP (award 1980—2000, Concert Music award 2005, Bessie award 2005, Classical Music award 2006). Office: House Found for Arts 306 W 38th St Ste 401 New York NY 10018

MONK, SUSAN MARIE, pediatrician, educator; b. York, Pa., May 7, 1945; d. John Spotz and Mary Elizabeth (Shelly) M.; m. Jaime Pacheco, June 5, 1971; children: Benjamin Joaquin, Maria Cristina. AB, Colby Coll., 1967; MD, Jefferson Med. Coll., 1971. Diplomate Am. Bd. Pediatrics. Pediatrician Children's Med. Ctr., Dayton, Ohio, 1975—; asst. clin. prof. pediat. Wright State U., Dayton, 1976—83, assoc. clin. prof. pediat., 1983—2000, asst. prof. pediatrics, 2000—. Mem. bd. dirs. Children's Med. Ctr., Dayton, 1991-96, chief-of-staff, 1992-94. Mem. Am. Acad. Pediatrics, We. Ohio Pediatric Soc., Pediatric Ambulatory Care Soc. Avocations: reading, gardening, travel, movies, theater. Office: Childrens Health Clinic 730 C Valley St Dayton OH 45404-1845 Office Phone: 937-641-5355.

MONMONIER, MARK, geographer, writer; b. Balt., Feb. 2, 1943; s. John Carroll and Martha Elizabeth (Mason) M.; m. Margaret Janet Kollner, Sept. 4, 1965; 1 child, Jo Kerry. BA, Johns Hopkins U., 1964; MS, Pa. State U., 1967, PhD, 1969. Asst. prof. U. Rhode Island, Kingston, 1969-70, SUNY, Albany, 1970-73; assoc. prof Syracuse U., NY, 1973-79, prof. NY, 1979-98, Disting. prof. geography NY, 1998—. Cons. N.Y. State, Albany, 1974-93, Nat. Geog. Soc., 1987, Microsoft Corp., 1993-99, Belmont Rsch., 1995, AT&T Rsch., 1996-97, George Philip Ltd., England, 1996-97; rsch. geographer U.S. Geol. Survey, Reston, Va., 1979-84; dep. dir. N.Y. Ctr. for Geographic Info. and Analysis, 1989-90; Robinson vis. fellow George Mason U., 1985; Ida Beam Disting. vis. prof. U. Iowa, 1985; mem. adv. bd. GIS Law and Policy Inst., 1994-98; adv. bd. Philip Lee Philips Soc.; cons. and expert witness various law firms, 1995—; co-editor History of Cartography in the Twentieth Century, 1999-2004, editor 2004-; mem. mapping sci. com. NRC, 2000—05, mem. com. on planning for catastrophe, 2005-06; mem. coastal elevations and sea level rise advisory com. US EPA, 2006— Author: Maps, Distortion and Meaning, 1977, Computer-assisted Cartography, 1982, Technological Transition in Cartography, 1985, Maps with the News, 1989, How to Lie with Maps, 1991, French edit., 1993, Japanese edit., 1995, 2nd edit., 1996, German edit., 1996, Korean edit., 1998, Czech edit., 2000;: Mapping it Out, 1993, Drawing the Line, 1995, Cartographies of Danger, 1997, Air Apparent, 1999, Bushmanders and Bullwinkles, 2001, Spying with Maps, 2002, Rhumb Lines and Map Wars, 2004, 2006, From Squaw Tit to Whorehouse Meadow, 2006; co-author: The Study of Population: Elements, Patterns, Processes, 1982; assoc. editor The American Cartographer, Falls Church, Va., 1977—82, 1982—84; co-editor, co-author: Map Appreciation, 1988; co-editor: History of Cartography Project, 1997; editor: The American Cartographer, 1982—84; assoc. editor: Mapping Sciences and Remote Sensing, 1987—97; contbg. editor Cartographica, 1984—, mem. editl. adv. bd. Mercator's World, 1997—2003. Statistician, Police Dept, Syracuse, NY, 1978-80. Fellow John Simon Guggenheim Meml. Found., 1984, centennial fellow Pa. State U. Coll. Earth & Mineral Scis., 1996; recipient Chancellor's citation for Disting. Acad. Achievement, 1993, Disting. Geographer award Pa. Geog. Soc., 2000, O.M. Miller Cartographic medal Am. Geog. Soc., 2001, Excellence in Grad. Edn. Faculty Recognition award, 2005. Fellow: Am. Geogl. Soc., Am. Congress on Surveying and Mapping; mem.: Philip Lee Phillips Soc., N.Am. Cartographic Info. Soc. (editl. bd. 1998—2001), Can. Cartographic Assn. (Award of Distinction 2002), Authors Guild, Am. Cartographic Assn. (pres. 1983—84), Assn. Am. Geographers (Media Achievement award 2000, Globe Book award 2004), Tau Beta Pi, Pi Tau Sigma, Sigma Xi (pres. Syracuse chpt. 2001—02). Roman Catholic. Home: 302 Waldorf Pky Syracuse NY 13224-2240 Office: Syracuse U Dept Geography Syracuse NY 13244-1020 Business E-Mail: mon2ier@maxwell.syr.edu.

MONOD, PAUL KLEBER, history professor; b. Montreal, Quebec, Can., June 25, 1957; s. Kléber Michel Louis Monod and Joan Donovan; m. Jan Maria Albers, Aug. 11, 1984; 1 child, Evan Albers. BA, Princeton U., 1978; MA, Yale U., New Haven, 1979; PhD, Yale U., New Haven, Conn., 1985. Prof. Middlebury Coll., Vt., 1984—, Barton Hepburn prof. history, 2005—. Author: (historical study) Jacobitism and the English People, 1688-1788., 1989 (John Ben Snow Prize, North Am. Conf. on Brit. Studies, 1991), The Power of Kings: Monarchy and Religion in Europe, 1589-1715, 1999, The Murder of Mr. Grebell: Madness and Civility in an English Town, 2003. Pres. John Graham Emergency Shelter, Vergennes, Vt., 2006—. Fellow, NEH, 2007—; Leverhulme vis. fellow, U. Sussex, 1990—91, vis. fellow, Harris Manchester Coll., Oxford U., 2001—02. Mem.: New Eng. Hist. Assn. (pres. 2003—04). Home: 30 Field Days Rd Weybridge VT 05753 Office: Middlebury Coll History Department Middlebury VT 05753 Office Phone: 802-443-5041. Business E-Mail: monod@middlebury.edu.

MONOSSON, IRA HOWARD, physician; b. NYC, Mar. 23, 1937; adopted s. Henry M.; s. I. Easer Rosenfield and Yetta Malvin; m. Aviva May Sokol, Sept. 20, 1970; children: Elana, Danielle, Ari. BA, Stanford U., 1959, MD, 1962. Diplomate Am. Bd. Preventive Medicine; cert. in occupational medicine. Intern Montefiore Hosp., Bronx, NY, 1962—63; resident L.A. County Gen. Hosp., 1963-64, Cedars of Lebanon Hosp., LA, 1964-65; fellow Scripps Clinic and Rsch. Found., La Jolla, Calif., 1965-66; resident U. Calif., Irvine, 1976-77; pvt. practice San Diego, 1966-68, Southington, Conn., 1968-69, Ctrl. Med. Group, LA, 1969-71; prin., owner Mid-City Med. Group, LA, 1971-73; ptnr., physician Foley Med. Group, LA, 1973-74; pub. health physician City of L.A., 1975; chief pub. health med. officer Calif. State Divsn. Occupational Safety & Health, LA, 1976-82; pvt. practice various, Calif., 1982—. Asst. clin. prof. medicine UCLA Sch. Medicine; asst. clin. prof. preventive medicine U. So. Calif. Sch. Medicine; mem. UCLA Inst. Biosafety Com., 1982—; adv. bd. Hazardous Substances Task Force, City of L.A., Calif. State Divsn. Indsl. Accidents, 1984-86, Occupl. Medicine Calif. Med. Assn., 1985-88; cons. in field; mem. state regulatory bd. Calif. Indsl. Med. Coun., 1990—2003, chmn. 1990-93. Mem. Environ. Occupl. Health com. Am. Lung. Assn. Calif., 1986-89; steering com. of L.A. 2000 project, 1980-81; adv. com. Del Amo/Montrose Superfund Site, 1995—, Permanent Disability Study, Calif. State Commn. Health and Safety and Workers Compensation; mem. L.A. Unified Sch. Dist. Bd. Edn. Ind. Commn. regarding The Belmont Learning Ctr., 1999—. Author: (with others) A Practical Approach to Occupational and Environmental Medicine, 1994; contbr. articles to profl. jours. Fellow Am. Coll. Preventive Medicine, Am. Coll. Occupl. Environ. Medicine (bd. dirs. 1993-95), Royal Soc. Medicine, Am. Acad. Occupl. Medicine; mem. AMA, Calif. Soc. Indsl. Medicine and Surgery (pres. 1995, bd. dirs.). Office: Ste 300 7230 Med Ctr Dr West Hills CA 91307 Office Phone: 818-704-0886. Personal E-mail: imonosson@gmail.com.

MONROE, CARL DEAN, III, lawyer; b. Birmingham, Ala., Sept. 15, 1960; s. Carl D. and Martha Jo M. BA, Birmingham-So. Coll., 1982; JD, Georgetown U., Washington, DC, 1985. Bar: Ala. 1986, US Ct. Appeals (11th cir.) 1988. Scheduler Siegelman for Atty. Gen., Montgomery, 1986; legal rsch. aide Office of Sec. of State State of Ala., Montgomery, 1986; asst. atty. gen., adminstrv. asst. Office of Atty. Gen., Montgomery, 1987-89; atty.-advisor Office Gen. Counsel US Dept. Energy, Washington, 1989—. Mem. panel of judges Georgetown Law Ctr. Moot Ct., 1991, 92, CIA Environ. Roundtable; lectr. waste mgmt. Johns Hopkins U., natural resources George Washington U. Mem. panel of judges Ala. YMCA Youth Legislature, Montgomery, 1979, 87, 88, 89; office coord. blood dr. ARC, Montgomery, 1987, 88; com. mem. Georgetown Alumni Admissions, Washington, 1986-91; mem. Nat. Trust for Hist. Preservation, Beahrs Environ. Leadership Seminar, U. Calif.-Berkeley, 2001. Mem. ABA (author environ. law sect. newsletter Looking Ahead), Acad. Polit. Sci., Ala. Bar Assn., Birmingham-So. Alumni (alumni leader 1986—), Phi Beta Kappa. Democrat. Presbyn. Avocations: water-skiing, tennis, horseback riding. Home: 2400 M St NW 1001 Washington DC 20037 Business E-Mail: dean.monroe@hq.doe.gov.

MONROE, CRAIG, professional baseball player; b. Texarkana, Tex., Feb. 27, 1927; Outfielder Tex. Rangers, 2001, Detroit Tigers, 2002—. Office: Detroit Tigers Comerica Pk 2100 Woodward Ave Detroit MI 48201

MONROE, EVELYN JONES, retired librarian; d. Freeman B. Jones Sr. and Emma Bush Jones; m. Ralph B. Benbow (div.); m. Robert Aaron Monroe, June 6, 1966; 1 child, Cheryl Denise. BS, Ala. State Coll., Montgomery, 1955; MS in Libr. and Info. Scis., U. Wis., Madison, 1964. Cert. life and health ins. agt. Va., 1995. Tchr., libr. Mobile County Sch. Bd., Mobile, Ala., 1955—66; sch. libr. Norfolk Pub. Sch. Sys., Va., 1966—67; adminstrv. libr. Fleet Combat Direction Sys. Support Activity, Virginia Beach, Va., 1967—84; tech. libr. Virginia Beach, 1984—94; benefit coord. Benefit Assn., Virginia Beach, 1995—96; asst. instr. Donovan Agy., Virginia Beach, 1996—97; asst. registrar Portsmouth, Va., 1999—2000; ret., 1994. Chmn., tng. coord. Coun. Navy Sci. and Tech. Librs., Dept. Navy, 1987—92; counselor, coord. FCDSSA, Virginia Beach, 1976—86; supr. tech. writers, editors Computer Program Documentation for Delivery to Ship and Shore Activities, 1984—94. Chmn. bd. trustees Hist. Third Bapt. Ch., Portsmouth, Va., 2003—. Recipient Excellence award, Naval Sea Sys. Command, 1984. Mem.: Am. Contract Bridge League, Am. Bridge Assn. (club point coord. 1987—2006), Delta Sigma Theta. Democrat. Avocation: bridge. Home: 37 Lantern Way Portsmouth VA 23703 Personal E-mail: gniemarobinson@hotmail.com. E-mail: monroeejn@aol.com.

MONROE, FREDERICK FALES, geologist, oceanographer; b. Washington, May 3, 1936; s. Sheldon McKinley and Fredericka Fales Monroe; m. Lori Rose Farquharson, June 11, 1988; m. Patricia Ann Lynch, July 11, 1971 (dec.); m. Sue Ellen Reeves, Oct. 7, 1963 (div. Oct. 7, 1970); children: Elizabeth Carmela, Patricia Alexis(dec.), Calli Grace, Victoria Michelle, John Scott, Lisa Diane Buyan, Christina Lee. BA, Amherst Coll., 1958; MS, The Am. U., 1970; MA, U. Miami, 1977; PhD, The Am. U., 1989. Profl. geologist Va., 1983. Geologist King & Gavaris, Cons. Engrs., NYC, 1960—62; phys. sci. aide US Geol. Survey, Denver, 1962; oceanographer US Army Corps Engrs., Washington, 1962—67; ass't. prof ocean engrng. Fla. Atlantic U., Boca Raton, 1967—71; oceanog. cons. Arthur Strock, Inc., 1971—75; fgn. affairs officer US Dept. State, Washington, 1975—. Adj. asst. prof. No. Va. CC, Alexandria, 2002—05; professorial lectr. The Am. U., Washington, 1989—93. Recipient Meritorious Honor award, US Dept. State, 1983, Career Achievement medal, 2001. Fellow: The Explorers Club; mem.: Marine Tech. Soc. (founding). Achievements include research in marine resource potential of US Exclusive Economic Zone; co-founded US Army Corps of Engrs. Coastal Engring Rsch. Ctr. Underwater Ops. Group; provided tech. support on deep seabed mining to US delegation to the UN Law of the Sea Convention; wrote Coastal State Control and the Global Ocean Harvest UMI, Ann Arbor, 1989. Office Phone: 202-663-2171. Personal E-mail: ffmonroe@hotmail.com.

MONROE, HASKELL MOORMAN, JR., chancellor emeritus, retired history professor, dean; b. Dallas, Mar. 18, 1931; s. Haskell M. and Myrtle Marie (Jackson) Monroe; m. Margaret Joan Phillips, June 15, 1957; children: Stephen, Melanie, Mark, John. BA, Austin Coll., Tex., 1952, MA, 1954; PhD, Rice U., Houston, 1961; D (hon.), Austin Coll., 1984. From instr. to prof. Tex. A&M U., 1959-80, asst. dean Grad. Sch., 1965-68, asst. v.p. acad. affairs, 1972-74, dean faculties, 1974-80, assoc. v.p. acad. affairs, 1977-80, dean faculties emeritus College Station, 1997—; pres. U. Tex., El Paso, 1980-87; chancellor U. Mo., Columbia, 1987-91, prof. history, 1987-97, chancellor emeritus, prof. history, 1997—. Instr. Schreiner Inst., Kerrville, Tex., 1959; vis. lectr. Emory U., 1967, 72; faculty lectr. Tex. A&M U., 1972; alumni lectr. Austin Coll., 1980; bd. dirs. City Nat. Bank, Southwestern Bell Corp., Boone County Nat. Bank, SBC Comms., Inc.; history adv. com. Sec. Air Force, 1987; orientation com. Dept. Def.-Joint Chiefs, 1986. Contbr. articles, revs. to profl. jours.; editor: Papers of Jefferson Davis, 1964—69; adv. editor: Texana, 1964—71; mem. bd. editl. advisers Booker T. Washington Washington Papers, 1965—85. Bd. dirs. Brazos Valley Rehab. Ctr., 1975-77, Salvation Army, El Paso, 1984-87, Columbia, Mo., 1988-97, Crime Stoppers of El Paso, United Way Columbia, 1988-94, Keep Brazos Beautiful, 1999-2003, Washington-on-the-Brazos State Park Assn., 2002-; trustee Bryan Hosp., 1976-79, chmn., 1979; bd. ch. visitors Austin Coll., 1977-78; deacon First Presbyn. Ch., Bryan, 1961-63, elder, 1965-67, 69-71, 73-74, clk. of session, 1973-74, chmn. pulpit nominating com., 1971-72; mem. presbytery's coun. Presbytery of Brazos, 1969-71, mem. resources for the 80s steering com., 1978-80; elder 1st Presbyn. Ch., El Paso, 1984-87, 1st Presbyn. Ch., Columbia, 1994-96; mem. exec. bd. Great Rivers coun. Boy Scouts Am., 1990-97; mem. Pres. Coun. NCAA, 1986-87; chmn. Jefferson Davis award com. Confederate Mus., 1996-97; bd. dirs. Salvation Army, 1989-97, Schreiner U., 1999--. Recipient Citation of Appreciation, LULAC, 1982, Honor award Salvation Army, 1997, Faculty Disting. Achievement award Tex. A&M U., 1964, U. Mo. Alumni award for tchg., 1995, also numerous achievement awards; grantee Social Sci. Rsch. Coun., Tex. A&M U., Huntington Libr., Intrafraternity and Sorority Outstanding Tchr. award, 1997; named Ky. Col., 1967; named to Legends of Aggieland, 1998. Mem. Am. Hist. Assn., Orgn. Am. Historians, So. Hist. Assn. Hist. Found. Presbyn. and Reformed Chs. (pres. 1970-72), Coll. Football Assn. (chmn. bd. 1989-90, bd. dirs.), Truman Scholarship Panel, Soc. Conf. Deans Faculties and Acad. V.P.s (pres. 1978), Rotary (El Paso, hon. Columbia, Mo., Bryan, Tex., Paul Harris fellow 1986, 2000). Home: 1005 Sonoma Cir College Station TX 77845-7907 Office: Tex A&M U 6B15 Evans Libr College Station TX 77843 Office Phone: 979-324-4546. Business E-Mail: hmonroe@tamu.edu.

MONROE, JAMES WALTER, retired corporate financial executive; b. Fairfax, SD, Feb. 13, 1936; s. Sherman William and Frances (Burnett) M.; m. Dorothy Lou Gillette, Apr. 1, 1961; children— Steven James, David Walter, Melody Anne, Andrew Scott. Student, Huron Coll., SD, 1954-56, U. Nebr., 1956-57; BA, Nebr. Wesleyan U., 1960. Mgr. Belleville (Kans.) C. of C., 1960-61, Concordia (Kans.) C. of C., 1961-62; asst. chief Div. Nebr. Resources, 1962-65; dir. S.D. Indsl. Devel. Expansion Agy., 1965-67, Nebr. Dept. Econ. Devel., 1967-71; sec. Nebr. Resources Found., 1967-71; exec. dir. Omaha Econ. Devel. Council, 1971-76; pres. Kansas City (Mo.-Kans.) Area Devel. Council, 1976-90; pres., chief exec. officer New Orleans and the River Region C. of C., 1990-96, Metrovision Found., Econ. Devel. Coun. Metro, New Orleans; ret., 1996. Mem. Am. Indsl. Devel. Council, 1965—, chmn. certification bd., 1981-82; sec. labor mgmt. council Greater Kansas City, 1979-90; mem. exec. com. Gov.'s Econ. Devel. Adv. Council, 1979-81. Bd. dirs. Am. Econ. Devel. Coun., 1992—. Served with AUS, 1957-59. Independent. Congregationalist. Home: 19015 84th Ave W Edmonds WA 98026

MONROE, JANE D., federal agency administrator; Probation officer; police officer; spl. agt. FBI, Abuquerque, 1985, Tampa, Fla., Washington; spl. agt. criminal divsn. FBI Hdqs., Washington; spl. agt. behavioral sci. unit FBI Acad., Quantico, Va.; supr. white collar crime and pub. corruption squad FBI, San Diego, 1995, coord. hostage negotiation and evidence response teams, 1995—99, asst. spl. agt. in charge Denver, 1999, spl. agt. in charge LA, 2002, asst. dir. cyber divsn. Washington, 2002—. Office: Fed Bur Investigation J Edgar Hoover Bldg 935 Penn Ave NW Washington DC 20535-0001

MONROE, JOSEPH M., oil industry executive; B in Chem. Engring., NC State U.; M in Chem. Engring., U. Calif., Berkeley; MBA, U. So. Calif. V.p. pipelines and terminals, pres. Unocal Pipeline Co. Unocal Corp., 1999—2002; sr. v.p. supply and distbn. Tesoro Refining and Mktg. Co. Tesoro Corp., San Antonio, 2002—04, sr. v.p. strategic planning and bus. devel., sr. v.p. orgnl. effectiveness, sr. v.p. bus. intergration & analysis, sr. v.p. corp. devel., sr. v.p. bus. devel. & logistics. Office: Tesoro Corp 300 Concord Plz San Antonio TX 78216-6999 Office Phone: 210-283-2000.

MONROE, KENDYL KURTH, retired lawyer; b. Clayton, N.Mex., Sept. 6, 1936; s. Dottis Donald and Helen (Kurth) Monroe; m. Barbara Sayre, Sept. 12, 1956; children: Sidney, Dean, Loren. AB, Stanford U., Calif., 1958, LLB, 1960. Bar: NY 1961, Calif. 1961. Assoc. Sullivan & Cromwell, NYC, 1960-67, ptnr., 1968-94; ret., 1994. Chmn. TEB Charter Svcs., Inc., Teterboro, NJ, El Valle Escondido Ranch Ltd. Co., Seneca, N.Mex., Eklund Assn. Clayton, N.Mex. Chmn. adv. coun. Mandala Ctr., Des Moines, N.Mex.; mem. adv. com. Cornerstones Cmty. Partnerships, Santa Fe; v.p., bd. dirs. Clan Munro Assn., Great Falls, Va.; chmn. Union County Med. Found., Clayton, N.Mex., Union County Water Bd., Clayton; bd. dirs. N.Mex. Water Dialogue, Corrales, N.Mex. Heritage Preservation Alliance, Santa Fe, NY Chamber Soloists, NYC. Mem.: Assn. Bar City of NY, State Bar Calif., Met. Club. Home: 189 Sayre Rd Seneca NM 88415 Office Phone: 505-451-7454. Personal E-mail: kkmonroe@bacavalley.com.

MONROE, ROBERT RAWSON, national security consultant; b. Oakland, Calif., Sept. 25, 1927; s. Robert Ansley and Muriel Estelle (Burnham)

M.; m. Charlotte Boies Anderson, Oct. 16, 1951; children: Robert Anderson, Nancy Lynn Monroe Sims, Susan Leslie Monroe Gordon. BS in Naval Sci., U.S. Naval Acad., 1950; MA in Internat. Rels., Stanford U., Calif., 1962. Commd. ensign USN, 1950, advanced through grades to vice-admiral, 1977; dir. Navy Systems Analysis, 1972-73; comdr. South Atlantic Force, 1973-74; comdr. Operational Test and Evaluation Force USN, 1974-77; dir. Def. Nuclear Agy., 1977-80; dir. Navy Rsch., Devel., Test and Evaluation, 1980-83; ret., 1983; joined Bechtel Nat., Inc., San Francisco, 1984, mgr. def. and space, 1984-89, v.p., 1985, sr. v.p., ptnr., 1987, mgr. mktg. and govt. ops., 1989-91, mgr. spl. projects, 1992-93, mgr. govt. ops. Washington, 1993—2002, sr. counselor, 2002—05; ret., 2005; nat. security cons., 2006—. Mem. nat. security adv. bd. Los Alamos (N.Mex.) Nat. Lab., 1983—88; mem. tech. evaluation panel U.S. Dept. Energy, 1983—88; mem. engring. adv. com. Oak Ridge Nat. Lab., 1986—89, Rensselaer Poly. Inst., 1990—91; mem. bd. advisors Office Tech. Assessment, Washington, 1987—89, Nat. Contract Mgmt. Assn., 1986—91; mem. task forces Def. Sci. Bd., Washington, 1983—89; corp. mem. Charles Stark Draper Lab., Cambridge, Mass., 1983—; affiliate mem. Ctr. for Internat. Security and Cooperation, Stanford U., 1989—93; chmn. space transp. subcom. NASA's Adv. Coun., 1995—2001; mem. strategic adv. bd. Nev. Test Site, 1995—99; mem. Nat. Security adv. panel Sandia Nat. Labs., 1996—; mem. threat reduction adv. com. (nuc. panel) Dept. Def., 1998—; mem. Enhanced Test Readiness External Rev. Group, 2002—03; mem. threat reduction adv. com. (sci. & tech. panel) Dept. Def., 2004—, mem. U.S. Nuc. Strategy Forum, 2004—; mem. mil. com. Ctr. for Security Policy, 2004—; mem. adv. bd. arms control and nonproliferation State Dept., Washington, 2005—06, chmn. task force on nat. strategy to combat weapons of mass destruction, 2006—07, mem. internat. security adv. bd., 2006—. Decorated DSM, Def. DSM, Legion of Merit, Bronze Star medal with combat device, Joint Svcs. Commendation medal, USN Commendation medal with combat device; Legion of Honor (France). Avocations: tennis, golf, hiking, reading. Home: 2313 Sawdust Rd Vienna VA 22181-3044 Personal E-mail: rrmonroe@cox.net.

MONROE, STEPHANIE JOHNSON, federal agency administrator; BA, U. Md., 1980; JD, U. of Baltimore, 1985. Legis. asst. to senator of NH US Senate; chief counsel, staff dir. Com. on Labor & Human Resources, Children, Families, Drugs & Alcoholism Subcommittee, US Senate, 1989—2001; chief counsel Com. on Health, Education, Labor & Pensions, US Senate, 2001—05; profl. staff mem. US Senate Budget Com.; asst. sec. Office for Civil Rights US Dept. Edn., Washington, 2005—. Head Start Quality & Expansion adv. com. US Dept. Health & Human Svcs., 1993—. Office: Office for Civil Rights US Dept Education Potomac Ctr 6th Fl 550 12th St SW Washington DC 20202-1100 Office Phone: 202-245-6700. Office Fax: 202-205-9862. *

MONROE, THOMAS EDWARD, business and financial executive; b. Ironton, Mo., Nov. 19, 1947; s. Donald Mansfield and Edwina Frances (Carr) M.; children: Thomas Edward II, Katherine Jenna. BA, Drury U., 1969; postgrad., Washington U. Sch. Bus. Adminstrn., St. Louis, 1970. Acctg. mgr., asst. contr. Am. Transit Corp., St. Louis, 1970-74; mgr. corp. devel., asst. treas. Chromalloy Am. Corp., St. Louis, 1974-77, v.p. fin., 1977-78, exec. v.p., 1978-82; dir. Chromalloy Fin. Corp., 1976-82, Am. Universal Ins. Co., 1978-82; chmn. Capital Assocs. Corp., 1982—, Fed. Air Ambulance, The Safe Deposit Co., CompuVault, Inc., James Flying Svc., Inc., Lindbergh Leasing, Inc., Vault II, LLC. Trustee Kingsbury Pl. Assn.; former trustee 2d Presbyn. Ch. With USMC, 1969—75, with USMC, 1969—75. Mem. Algonquin Club. Presbyterian. Office: Capital Assocs Corp 515 S Lindbergh Blvd Saint Louis MO 63131-2731 Office Phone: 314-991-3130.

MONROE, WILLIAM LEWIS, human resources executive; b. Detroit, May 11, 1941; s. Lewis Stewart and Ada Jeanette (Williams) Monroe; m. Sharon Lynne Kahal, June 30, 1967; children: Andrea M. Dunk, William J. BA, Western Mich. U., 1963, MA, 1964. Rsch. analyst Chrysler Corp., Detroit, 1965-72, labor economist, 1972-77, mgr. retirement, savs. and unemployment benefit plans, 1977-81; dir. employee benefits W. R. Grace & Co., NYC, 1981-87, v.p. human resources, 1987-2001, bd. trustee, v.p. coun. on employee benefits, 1989-2001, pres. coun. on employee benefits, 1995-96; cons. AON Cons./ASA, Boca Raton, 2001—02. Adj. prof. mgmt. FAU Univ., Boca Raton, 2001; corp. bd. dirs. Internat. Found. Employee Benefits, 1986—88; mem. bus. rsch. adv. coun. U.S. Dept. Labor/Bur. Labor Stats., 1987—96; mem. Human Resources Policy Inst. Boston U., 1993—96. Co-chmn. closing com. PTSA Sch., Birmingham, Mich., 1977; chmn. pers. com. Wilton Presbyn. ch., Wilton, Conn., 1982—86; officer, bd. dirs. Forest Hills Property Owners Assn., Birmingham, 1974—80; mem. exec. bd. Gulf Stream coun. Boy Scouts Am., 1993—99. Served USAR, 1965—71. Mem.: Soc. for Human Resources & Mgmt., Boca Raton Resort and Club. Republican. Presbyterian. Avocation: Avocations: tennis, golf. Personal E-mail: bmonroe10@aol.com.

MONROY, GLADYS H., lawyer; d. Henry B. and Leonora E. (Low) Chu; m. Jaime L. G. Monroy (div.); m. C. Lawrence Marks, Nov. 29, 1980. BA, Hunter Coll., NYC, 1957; MS, NYU, 1968, PhD, 1973; JD, U. San Francisco, 1986. Bar: Calif.; registered U.S. Patent and Trademark office. Lab. technician Sloan-Kettering Inst., NYC, 1957-60, Pub. Health Rsch. Inst., NYC, 1960-63, rsch. asst., 1963-68; post doctoral fellow Albert Einstein Coll. Medicine, Bronx, NY, 1973-77; asst. prof. N.Y. Med. Coll., Valhalla, 1977-79; acquisitions editor Acad. Press, Inc., 1979-81; reseach assoc. U. Calif., San Francisco, 1981-83; atty. Irell & Manella, Menlo Park, Calif., 1986-90, ptnr., 1990-91, Morrison & Foerster, Palo Alto, Calif., 1991—. Co-chair I.P. Group, 1997—2005, Life Scis. Group, 1997-2002; treas. Silicon Valley Intellectual Property Assn., 1993, sec., 1994, v.p., 1995, pres., 1996; bd. dir. Calif. State Bar Intellectual Property Sect., 1997-99; co-chair IP HIV Vaccine Enterprise, 2002-. Contbr. articles to profl. jours. Mem. bd. dirs. Project Hogar De Los Ninos, Menlo Park, Calif., 1987, 89, mem. Profl. Women's Network, San Francisco, 1988—90; mem. bd. dirs. Child Advocates of Santa Clara and San Mateo Counties, 1995—99. Named one of Best Lawyers in Am., 2004-07; named Leading Lawyer in Silcon Valley, 2002-2007; elected to Patent Hall of Fame, Global Practice Law Co. Mem. ABA, Am. Intellectual Property Law Assn., Am. Soc. Human Genetics, Am. Chem. Soc., Calif. Bar Assn., San Francisco Intellectual Property Law Assn. (chair patent com. 1992-94), Peninsula Patent Law Assn. (program chair 1993-94, treas. 1994-95, sec. 1995-96, v.p. 1996-97, pres. 1997—98), Am. Soc. Microbiology, Phi Alpha Delta. Avocations: swimming, bicycling, skiing, reading, opera. Office: Morrison & Foerster LLP 755 Page Mill Rd Palo Alto CA 94304-1018 Office Phone: 650-813-5600. Office Fax: 650-494-0792. Business E-Mail: gmonroy@mofo.com.

MONSELL, THOMAS OLIVER, secondary school educator, writer; b. Greenport, NY, Aug. 26, 1933; s. Harry Monroe and Amy Adelle Monsell. BA, Ithaca Coll., 1952—56; MS, SUNY, Albany, 1959—60. Prodn. asst. Robbins Music Corp., NYC, 1957—58; English tchr., drama coach, libr. Lindenhurst Pub. Sch., NY, 1960—88. Founder, dir. Stirling Players Cmty. Theater, Greenport, NY, 1972—; textbook contbr. Henry Holt & Co., Harcourt, Brace, NY, 1989—94; film & theater critic New York Guardian, 1993—96. Author: (explication) Shakespeare in Perf: Hamlet, 1990, (media criticism) Nixon on Stage and Screen, 1998; co-author (with Antonia Booth): (regional history) Greenport, 2003. Village historian (with James Monsell) City of Greenport, NY, 2000—. Mem.: Shaw Soc., Ibsen Soc. Am., Eugene O'Neill Soc., James Jones Lit. Soc., Soc. Mayflower Descendants. Avocations: reading, writing, travel, theater, directing plays for charity benefits. Home: 525 First St Greenport NY 11944

MONSEN, ELAINE RANKER, nutritionist, educator, editor; b. Oakland, Calif., June 6, 1935; d. Emery R. and Irene Stewart (Thorley) Ranker; m. Raymond Joseph Monsen, Jr., Jan. 21, 1959; 1 dau., Maren Ranker Grainger-Monsen. BA, U. Utah, 1956; MS (Mead Johnson grad. scholar), U. Calif., Berkeley, 1959, PhD (NSF fellow), 1961; postgrad. NSF sci. faculty fellow, Harvard U., 1968-69. Dietetic intern Mass. Gen. Hosp., Boston, 1956-57; asst. prof. nutrition, lectr. biochemistry Brigham Young U., Provo, Utah, 1960-63; mem. faculty U. Wash., 1963—, prof. nutrition, adj. prof. medicine, 1976-84, prof. nutrition and medicine, 1984—2004, prof. emeritus, 2004—, chmn. div. human nutrition, dietetics and foods, 1977-82, dir. grad. nutritional scis. program, 1994-99, mem. Council of Coll. Arts and Scis., 1974-78; chmn. Nutrition Studies Commn., 1969-83. Vis. scholar Stanford U., 1971-72; mem. sci. adv. com. food fortification Pan-Am. Health Orgn., São Paulo, Brazil, 1972; tng. grant coordinator NIH, 1976-97. Editor-in-chief Jour. Am. Dietetic Assn., 1983-2003; Editor Emeritus, Jour. Am. Dietetic Assn., 2003—; mem. editorial bd. Coun. Biology Editors, 1992-96; author rsch. papers on lipid metabolism, iron absorption. Bd. dirs. A Contemporary Theatre, Seattle, 1969-72; trustee, bd. dirs. Seattle Found., 1978-95, vice chmn., 1987-91, chmn., 1991-93; pres. Seattle bd. Santa Fe Chamber Music Festival, 1984-85; mem. Puget Sound Blood Ctr. Bd., 1996-99. Grantee Nutrition Found., 1965-68, Agrl. Rsch. Svc., 1969-84; recipient Disting. Alumnus award U. Utah, F. Fischer Meml. Nutrition Lectr. award, 1988, L.F. Cooper Meml. Lectr. award, 1991, L. Hatch Meml. Lectr. award, 1992, Goble Lectr. award Purdue U., 1997. Fellow: Am. Soc. Clin. Nutrition (sec. 1987—90), Am. Inst. Nutrition; mem.: Wash. Heart Assn. (nutrition coun. 1973—76), Am. Soc. Parenteral and Enteral Nutrition, Soc. Nutriton Edn., Am. Dietetic Assn. Office: U Wash PO Box 353410 Seattle WA 98195-3410

MONSKY, JOHN BERTRAND, investment company executive; b. Montgomery, Ala., May 17, 1930; s. Harry and Belle (Golding) M.; m. Joan Gilbert, June 8, 1952; children: Leslie Joy, John Richard, Harry Robert. BA, Yale, 1952; MBA, Harvard, 1954. Sec. Devoe & Raynolds Co., Inc., Louisville, Ky., 1956-65; v.p., dir. Universal Marion Corp., Jacksonville, Fla., 1965-69, pres., chmn. bd., chief exec. officer, 1969-71, cons., 1971—; vice chmn. ServAmerica, Inc., Jacksonville, 1972-74, co-chmn. bd. dirs., 1974-80, chmn. bd. dirs., 1980—; pres., chmn. bd. dirs. First Fla. Capital Corp., 1985—. Dir. Fla. Wire & Cable Co., Jacksonville, 1975-82 Past pres. bd. trustees Jacksonville Country Day Sch.; bd. dirs. Jacksonville Art Mus.; trustee Bolles Sch., Jacksonville, Jacksonville Symphony Assn. Served with USAF, 1954-56. Mem. Jacksonville Area C. of C. (com. of 100), Jackson County Citizen Involvement Clubs, Harvard Bus. Sch. Club of Ky. (exec. com. 1964-65), Phillips Acad. Andover Alumni Club of Ky. (pres. 1963-64), Epping Forest Cmty. Master Assn. (bd. dirs. 1994—), Yale Club N.E. Fla. (bd. dirs. 1987—), Yale Club of NYC, Harvard Club (Jacksonville), Assn. Yale Alumni (del. 1996—, schs. com.), River Club, Ponte Vedra Club, Epping Forest Yacht Club, Harvard Bus. Sch. Alumni Club (Jacksonville, bd. dirs.) Home: Epping Forest 7015 Gaines Ct Jacksonville FL 32217-2672 Office: 300 Wharfside Way # B Jacksonville FL 32207-8153 Office Phone: 904-396-0348. Personal E-mail: jbmonsky@aol.com. Business E-Mail: jbmonsky@firstfloridacapital.com.

MONSON, CAROL LYNN, osteopath, psychotherapist; b. Blue Island, Ill., Nov. 3, 1946; d. Marcus Edward and Margaret Bertha (Andres) Monson; m. Frank E. Warden, Feb. 28, 1981. BS, No. Ill. U., 1968, MS, 1969; D.O., Mich State Coll. Osteo. Medicine, 1979. Lic. physician Mich., diplomate Am. Bd. Osteo., Am. Bd. Family Physicians, Am. Bd. Osteo. Gen. Practice. Expeditor-psychotherapist H. Douglas Singer Zone Ctr., Rockford, Ill., 1969—71; psychotherapist Tri-County Mental Health, St. Johns, Mich., 1971—76; pvt. practice psychotherapy East Lansing, Mich., 1976—80; intern Lansing Gen. Hosp., Mich., 1979—80, residency dir. family practice, 1988—97; pvt. practice osteo. medicine Lansing, 1980—2002; mem. staff Ingham Regional Med. Ctr., chmn. family practice, 1987—89. Field instr. Sch. Social Work U. Mich., 1973—76; clin. instr. Ctrl. Mich. Dept. Psychology, 1974—75; clin. prof. Mich. State U., 1980—88, asst. prof., 1988—2003, assoc. prof., 2003—06, prof., 2006—, tng. supr. family medicine residency, 1988—97, faculty devel. fellow, 1994—95, chair dept. family and cmty. medicine, 2005—, residency dir. family medicine, 1994—97; mem. adv. bd. Substance Abuse Clearinghouse, Lansing, 1983—85, Kelly Health Care, Lansing, 1983—85, Americor Health Svcs., Lansing, 1984—88, Lansing Home Care, Lansing, 1988—94. Fellow: Am. Coll. Family Practice (osteo.); mem.: Coun. Med. Splty. Socs. (mem. conjoint com. 2005—), Am. Coll. Family Physicians (residency insp. 1991—), Mich. Assn. Osteo. Family Physicians (pres.-elect 1994, pres. 1995—96), Nat. Assn. Career Women (conv. com. 1984—), Ingham County Osteo. Assn. (pres. 1993—95, 1996—97), Mich. Osteo. Assn. (program com. 1992—, governance coun. 1996—97, bd. trustees 1997—2004, pres.-elect 2001—02, pres. 2002—03), Internat. Transactional Analysis Assn., Am. Acad. Family Practice, Am. Osteo. Assn. (del. 1994—, health policy fellow 1997—98, bd. trustees 2003—, chair membership 2004—), Mich. Coun. Grad. Med. Edn. (appointee 1998—, pres. 1999—2002), Lansing Assn. Career Women, Soc. Tchrs. of Family Medicine, Zonta (chmn. service com. Mid Mich. Capital Area chpt.). Avocations: gardening, orchid growing, antique collecting. Office: 8201 E W Fee Hall East Lansing MI 48824-1316 Office Phone: 517-355-4730.

MONSON, DAN, men's college basketball coach; b. Spokane, Wash., Oct. 6, 1961; BS in Math., U. Idaho, 1985; MS in Athletic Adminstrn., U. Ala., 1988. Asst. coach Oregon City HS, 1985—86; grad. asst. U. Ala., Birmingham, 1986—88; asst. coach Gonzaga U., Spokane, 1988—94, assoc. head coach, 1994—97, head coach, 1997—99, U. Minn., 1999—2006, Long Beach State U., Calif., 2007—. Dir. Gopherball Basketball Camp, Mpls.; asst. coach World Univ. Games, 1999, USA Basketball's 20-and-under team, 2004. Named Coach of Yr., 1998, Nat. Rookie Coach of Yr., Basketball Times, 1998. Achievements include coaching the West Coast Conf. Champions, 1998; reached NCAA Sweet 16, 1998-99. Office: Long Beach State U Mens Basketball Athletic Dept 1250 Bellflower Blvd Long Beach CA 90840 *

MONSON, DAVID CARL, school system administrator, state legislator, farmer; b. Langdon, ND, July 30, 1950; s. Carl Arthur and Shirley Jean (Klai) M.; m. Mary Kathryn Greutman, July 8, 1972; children: Cordell Carl, Cale David, Jared Arthur. Cert. tchr., adminstr., N.D. Sci. tchr. Hankinson (N.D.) Pub. Sch., 1972-75; tchr. Nekoma (N.D.) Pub. Sch., 1975-76; tchr., prin. NeKoma (N.D.) Pub. Sch., 1976-79; tchr., supt. Nekoma (N.D.) Pub. Sch., 1979-80; tchr., prin. Milton (N.D.)-Osnabrock H.S., 1981-84; supt. Adams (N.D.) Pub. Schs., 1984-88; ins. agt. N.Y. Life, Fargo, ND, 1988-95; self-employed ins. agt., Osnabrock, 1988—2003; farmer, 1975—; mem. N.D. Ho. of Reps., Bismarck, 1993—, asst. majority leader, 1998—; supt. Edinburg (N.D.) Pub. Schs., 1995—. Dir. Cavalier County Mut. Ins. Co., Osnabrock, N.D., 1990-98, Northeast Mut. Ins. Co., Cando, N.D., 1998–, N.Am. Indsl. Hemp Coun., 1999—. Leader Bobcats 4-H Club, 1988—2001; pres. Dovre Luth. Ch., Osnabrock, 2002—; mem. sch. bd. dirs. Osnabrock Sch. Bd., 1989—2001. Mem. N.D. Farm Bur., N.D. Coun. Sch. Adminstrs., Eagles, KP (grand sec. N.D. and Sask. 1985-93, award 1990). Republican. Lutheran. Avocations: skiing, gardening, hunting, coin collecting/numismatics. Business E-Mail: dmonson@nd.gov.

MONSON, DIANNE LYNN, literacy educator; b. Minot, ND, Nov. 24, 1934; d. Albert Rachie and Iona Cordelia (Kirk) M. BS, U. Minn., 1956, MA, 1962, PhD, 1966. Tchr. Rochester (Minn.) Pub. Schs., 1956-59, U.S. Dept. Def., Schweinfurt, West Germany, 1959-61, St. Louis Park (Minn.) Schs., 1961-62; instr. U. Minn., Mpls., 1962-66; prof. U. Wash., Seattle, 1966-82; prof. literacy edn. U. Minn., Mpls., 1982-97, prof. emeritus, 1997—. Chmn. curriculum and instrn. U. Minn., 1986—89. Co-author: Scott Foresman Reading, 2000, New Horizons in the Language Arts, 1972, Children and Books, 6th edit., 1981, Experiencing Children's Literature, 1984, Language Arts: Teaching and Learning Effective Use of Language, 1988, Reading Together: Helping Children Get A Good Start With Reading, 1991; assoc. editor: Dictionary of Literacy, 1995; mem. editl. bd. Five Owls Mag., 1997-2005. Bd. adv. Kerlan Collection, 2001—04, Minn. Humanities Commn., 2004—05; bd. dirs. Friends of Kerlan Collection, 2000—04. Recipient Outstanding Educator award U. Minn. Alumni Assn., 1983, Alumni Faculty award U. Minn. Alumni Assn., 1991. Fellow Nat. Conf. Rsch. in English (pres. 1990-91); mem. ALA, Nat. Coun. Tchrs. English (exec. com. 1979-81), Internat. Reading Assn. (dir. 1980-83, Arbuthnot award 1993, Reading Hall of Fame 1997), U.S. Bd. Books for Young People (pres. 1988-90). Lutheran. Home: 515 S Lexington Pkwy # 604 Saint Paul MN 55116 Business E-Mail: monso001@tc.umn.edu.

MONSON, JAMES EDWARD, electrical engineer, educator; b. Oakland, Calif., June 20, 1932; s. George Edward and Frances Eleanor M.; m. Julie Elizabeth Conzelman, June 25, 1954; children: John, Jamie, Jennifer BSEE, Stanford U., 1954, MSEE, 1955, PhD in Elec. Engring., 1961. Mem. tech. staff Bell Telephone Labs., Murray Hill, NJ, 1955-56; devel. engr. Hewlett-Packard Co., Palo Alto, Calif., 1956-61; Robert C. Sabini prof. engring. emeritus Harvey Mudd Coll., 1961—. Governing bd. Claremont Unified Sch. Dist., 1966—71, pres., 1969—70, Claremont Civic Assn., 1974—75; bd. dirs. Claremont YMCA, 1978—82, Coastal Health Alliance, 1999—2006, West Main Sr. Svcs., 2007—. Fellow NSF, 1954-55, Japan Soc. Promotion Sci., 1984; Fulbright Rsch. grantee, 1975-76; Fulbright sr. lectr., 1980. Fellow IEEE (life); mem. Phi Beta Kappa, Sigma Xi. Home: PO Box 1029 Point Reyes Station CA 94956-1029 Office: Harvey Mudd Coll 301 E 12th St Claremont CA 91711-5901 Personal E-mail: j.monson@ieee.org.

MONSON, JOHN RUDOLPH, lawyer; b. Chgo., Feb. 4, 1941; s. Rudolph Agaton and Ellen Louise (Loeffler) M.; m. Susan Lee Brown, May 22, 1965; children: Elizabeth Louisa, Christina Lee, Donald Rudolph. BA with honors, Northwestern U., 1963; JD with distinction, U. Mich., 1966. Bar: Ill. 1966, N.H. 1970, Mass. 1985. Atty. assoc. Chapman & Cutler, Chgo., 1966-68, Levenfeld, Kanter, Baskes & Lippitz, Chgo., 1968-70, Nighswander, Martin & Mitchell, Laconia, NH, 1970-71; mem., ptnr. Wiggin & Nourie, PA, Manchester, NH, 1972—, pres., 1991—94. Sec., gen. counsel Rock of Ages Corp., 1996-2000. Mem. N.H. Fish and Game Commn., Concord, 1980-94, chmn., 1983-93; sr. bd. dirs. Brown-Monson Found., 1991—; incorporator Cath. Med. Ctr., 1988-95, Optima Health, 1994-99; commr. N.H. Land and Cmty. Heritage Commn., 1998-2000. Fellow Am. Coll. Trust and Estate Counsel, Safari Club Internat. (v.p. 1999-2001, dir.-at-large 1997-99, treas. 2001-02, pres. elect 2002-04, pres. 2004—05). Republican. Avocations: skiing, hunting, running. Home: 24 Wellesley Dr Bedford NH 03110-4531 Office: Wiggin & Nourie PA 670 N Commerical St Ste 305 Manchester NH 03105 Office Phone: 603-669-2211.

MONSON, LARRY LEE, music educator; b. Grand Island, Nebr., Oct. 17, 1942; s. Owen H. and Glenna Imojene Monson; m. LaVonne Elise Havekost, Mar. 21, 1964; children: Martin Laurence, Ann Elise, Eric Lee. BA, Midland Luth. Coll., 1965; MA, U. Iowa, 1966. Cert. tchr. Iowa. Dir. music 1st Luth. Ch., Cedar Rapids, Iowa, 1964—67; dir. music and youth Kountze Meml. Ch., Omaha, 1967—69; dir. music 1st Luth. Ch., Sioux Falls, SD, 1969—72, St. Paul Luth. Ch., Davenport, Iowa, 1972—79; choral dir. City HS, Iowa City, 1979—89; dir. choral activities Doane Coll., Crete, Nebr., 1989—, ret. prof. choral music, 2004. Chair music cert. Nebr. State Edn., Lincoln, 1990—93. Bd. dirs. Polley Music Libr., Lincoln, 1989—95. Recipient Outstanding Alumni Achievement award, Midland Luth. Coll., 2001. Mem.: Soc. Preservation and Encouragement of Barbershop Quartet Singing, Internat. Fedn. Choral Music, Am. Choral Dirs. Assn. Avocations: biking, travel, coaching quartets, gardening. Home: 611 W Water St Decorah IA 52101 Home Phone: 563-382-6255. E-mail: larry.monson@doane.edu.

MONSON, ROBERT JOSEPH, education educator; b. St. Paul, July 2, 1947; s. Robert Joseph and Lorraine (Pieruccioni) M.; m. Tracey Monson, Dec. 18, 1970 (dec. 1986); 1 child, Ashley Taylor. BA, St. Thomas Coll., St. Paul, 1969, MA, 1971; PhD, St. Louis U., 1975. Tchr. St. Bernards Schs., St. Paul, 1969-71; asst. prin. Mamaroneck (N.Y.) High Sch., 1975-78; prin. Chapel Hill (N.C.) High Sch., 1978-81; asst. sch. supt. Sch. Dist. South Orange-Maplewood (N.J.), 1981-85; supt. schs. Beachwood (Ohio) pub. schs., 1985-87, Westwood (Mass.) pub. schs., 1987-94, Mendota Heights, Minn., 1994-99; sr. lectr. Lesley Coll., 1990-2000; assoc. prof. Tchrs. Coll. Columbia U., NYC, 1999—. Rsch. cons. NSF, 1975. Contbr. articles to profl. jours. Named Educator of Yr., AGPA, 1981; postdoctoral fellow Harvard U., 1977. Mem. Prins Ctr. Harvard U. (bd. dirs. 1989-91). Roman Catholic. Home: 957 Lake Ave Greenwich CT 06831 Office: 525 W 120th St Box 67 New York NY 10027 Office Phone: 212-678-8118. Business E-Mail: rjm210@columbia.edu.

MONSON, THOMAS SPENCER, religious organization administrator, retired publishing executive; b. Salt Lake City, Aug. 21, 1927; s. George Spencer and Gladys (Condie) M.; m. Frances Beverly Johnson, Oct. 7, 1948; children— Thomas L., Ann Frances, Clark Spencer. BS with honors in mktg, U. Utah, 1948; MBA, Brigham Young U., 1974, LLD (hon.), 1981; D in Bus. (hon.), U. Utah, 2007. With Deseret News Press, Salt Lake City, 1948-64, mgr., 1962-64; mem. Coun. Twelve Apostles, Ch. of Jesus Christ of Latter-day Saints, 1963-85, bishop, 1950-55; pres. Canadian Mission, 1959-62; mem. first presidency Ch. of Jesus Christ of Latter-day Sts., 1985—; chmn. bd. Deseret News Pub. Co., 1977-96. Vice chmn. Deseret Mgmt. Corp.; pres. Printing Industry Utah, 1958; bd. dirs. Printing Industry Am., 1958-64; mem. Utah exec. bd. U.S. West Communications. Mem. Utah Bd. Regents; mem. nat. exec. bd. Boy Scouts Am.; trustee Brigham Young U. With USNR, 1945-46. Recipient Recognition award, 1964, Disting. Alumnus award U. Utah, 1966; Silver Beaver award Boy Scouts Am., 1971; Silver Buffalo award, 1978; Bronze Wolf award World Orgn. of the Scout Movement, 1993. Mem. Utah Assn. Sales Execs., U. Utah Alumni Assn. (dir.), Salt Lake Advt. Club, Alpha Kappa Psi. Clubs: Exchange (Salt Lake City). Mem. Lds Ch. Office: LDS Ch 47 E South Temple Salt Lake City UT 84150-9701

MONTAG, JOHN JOSEPH, II, librarian; b. Omaha, Jan. 8, 1948; s. John Joseph and Ruth Helen (Johnston) M.; m. Linda Kay Lubanski, Apr. 8, 1971; children: Nicole Elizabeth, Megan Kristine. BA, Midland Luth. Coll., 1970; postgrad., Wash. State U., 1970-74; MA, U. Iowa, 1976; postgrad., U. Nebr., 1982-84. English tchr. pub. schs., Nebr., Iowa, 1972-75; reference libr. Concordia Coll., Moorhead, Minn., 1976-81; asst. prof. libr. sci. U. Nebr., Lincoln, 1981-84; dir. Office of Info. State Libr. Iowa, Des Moines, 1984-86, state libr., 1986-87; dir. Thomas Libr. Wittenberg U., 1987-95, Cochrane-Woods Libr. Nebr. Wesleyan U., Lincoln, 1995-97, dir. libr. and computer svcs., 1997-99, univ. libr., 1999—. Trustee Bibliog. Ctr. for Rsch., Denver, 1986-87; adv. bd. No. Lights Libr. Network, Detroit Lakes, Minn., 1980-81; chair Southwest Ohio Consortium Higher Edn. Libr. Coun., 1991-94; mem. exec. com. Nebr. Inst., 1998—; cons. U.S. Dept. of Edn. Contbr. articles to profl. jours. Co-founder Nebr. Found. for Oral History, 2001—. Univ. Found. libr. improvement grantee, U. Nebr., 1983; Challenge grantee NEH, 1992; Tchg. Am. History grantee Lincoln Pub. Schs., 2002, 04. Mem. ALA, Assn. Coll. and Rsch. Librs., Nebr. Ind. Coll. Libr. Consortium (chmn. libr. dirs.

2000—). Office: Cochrane Woods Libr Nebr Wesleyan U 5000 Saint Paul Ave Lincoln NE 68504-2760 Home Phone: 402-489-2418; Office Phone: 402-465-2401. E-mail: jmontag@nebrwesleyan.edu.

MONTAGUE, BRIAN JOHN, consulting company executive; b. Washington, Oct. 9, 1951; s. H.C. and Dorothy (Brand) M.; m. Kathryn Valente, Oct. 2, 1993. BA, Bridgewater Coll., 1973; student, St. Mary's Coll., Md., 1975, George Washington U., 1980, Miss. State U., 1981. Toxicology technician Hazelton Labs., Vienna, Va., 1973-74; asst. mgr. Chesapeake Sea Farms, Ridge, Md., 1974-76; tng. instr., program coord. Natural Resources Dept., Annapolis, Md., 1976-77; fishery biologist Nat. Aquarium, U.S. Fish and Wildlife Svc., Washington, 1977-82, curator aquarium, 1982-88; pres. Aquatic Images, Annapolis, 1989—. Lectr. local interest groups, 1990—; fisheries biologist, ecol. risk assessment specialist U.S. EPA, Washington. Office: Aquatic Images 3527 Jamestown Rd Davidsonville MD 21035-2009

MONTAGUE, DROGO K., urologist; b. Alpena, Mich., Dec. 11, 1942; s. Frank Wright and Susan Alice (Kidder) M.; children: Mark Andrew, Lisa Joy. Student, U. Mich., 1960—63, MD cum laude, 1968. Diplomate Am. Bd. Urology. Intern Cleve. Clinic Hosp., 1968-69, resident in gen. surgery, 1969-70, resident in urology, 1970-73; assoc. staff urologist Cleve. Clinic Found., 1973-75, staff urologist, 1975—, head sect. prosthetic surgery, 1981—, urology residence program dir., 1985—2006, dir. Ctr. for Sexual Function, 1987—; prof. surgery Cleve. Clinic Lerner Coll. Medicine Case Western Res. U., 2004—. Trainee cardiovascular rsch. tng. program NIH, 1962-68; trustee Am. Bd. Urology, 1989-95, mem. examination com., 1975-80, examiner cert. exam., 1980-88, rep. to Am. Bd. Med. Specialties, 1989-95. Reviewer various publs. in field; contbr. numerous articles to profl. publs., chpts. to books; editor: Disorders of Male Sexual Function, 1988, Surgical Treatment of Erectile Dysfunction, 1993; author audiovisual tapes in field; mem. editl. bd. Jour. Urology. James B. Angell scholar, 1961, 62, Nat. Found. scholar, 1963-68; recipient Russell and Mary Hugh Scott Edn. award, 1989, Iowa Rsch. award, 1967. Fellow ACS; mem. Am. Urolog. Assn. (chmn. sci. exhibits com. North Cen. sect. 1977, mem. residency edn. com. 1979-83, vice chmn. audio visual com. 1989-95, mem. various coms., editor Am. Urolog. Assn. Video Libr. 1995-2000, chmn. audio visual com. 1996-2002, chmn. erectile dysfunction guidelines panel 1999—), Am. Assn. Genitourinary Surgeons, Cleve. Urolog. Soc. (sec.-treas. 1978-80, v.p. 1980-81, pres. 1981-82, 94-95), Soc. for Study of Impotence (pres. 1995). Office: Cleve Clinic Found Glickman Urol Inst A/100 9500 Euclid Ave Cleveland OH 44195-0001 Home Phone: 216-831-9937; Office Phone: 216-444-5590. Business E-Mail: montagd@ccf.org.

MONTAGUE, EDGAR BURWELL, III, (MONTY MONTAGUE), industrial designer; b. Charlotte, NC, Aug. 6, 1958; s. Edgar B. Jr. and Mary Sue (Calhoun) M.; m. Nancy Oliver Stallworth, Feb. 25, 1984; children: Nancy Lea, Edgar Eubank. B Environ. Design cum laude, N.C. State U., 1980. Indsl. designer Design/Joe Sonderman, Inc., Charlotte, 1980-85; design prin. Bolt (formerly Machen Montague, Inc.), Charlotte, NYC, 1985—, BOLT, Charlotte, 1994—. Holder over 15 design and/or utility patents; work published in Product Design 1-6, Design for Humanity. Designer corp. identity program Habitat for Humanity, Charlotte, 1987 (logo design now used throughout world). Recipient ann. design award Internat. Design mag., 1988-93, ID-40 ID Mag., 1994, Disting. Alumni award N.C. State U., 1999. Mem. Indsl. Designer Soc. Am. (co-founder Carolina chpt., program chmn. 1981-83, vice chmn. 1984, 93, Kudo award for chpt. svc. 1982, Indsl. Design Excellence awards 1989-94). Avocations: travel, art, coaching soccer. Office: BOLT 1415 S Church St Ste S Charlotte NC 28203-4124 Office Phone: 704-372-2658. Business E-Mail: monty@boltgroup.com.

MONTAGUE, ROBERT LATANE, III, lawyer; b. Washington, Sept. 18, 1935; s. Robert Latane and Frances Breckinridge (Wilson) M.; m. Prudence Darnell, June 20, 1964; children: Anne Steele Mason Montague Bavin, Robert Latane IV. BA, U. Va., 1956, LLB, 1961. Bar: Va. 1961, D.C. 1966, U.S. Supreme Ct. 1966. Asst. atty. gen., Ky., 1961-64; pres. Historic Alexandria Found., 1968-70; chmn. Alexandria Environ. Policy Commn., 1970-74; pres. Conservation Coun. Va., 1978-80; chmn. Alexandria Commn. on Bicentennial of U.S. Constitution, 1987-91, Alexandria Historical Restoration and Preservation Commn., 1988—2001; trustee Assn. for Preservation of Va. Antiquities, 1990-96. Chmn. Bd. of Vis. of Gunston Hall, 1987-92; del. Moscow Conf. on Law and Econ. Coop., 1990. Comdr. USNR, 1956-79. Mem. Va. Bar Assn., Va. State Bar (chmn. environ. law sect. 1973-74), Alexandria Bar Assn. Office: 1007 King St Alexandria VA 22314-2922

MONTALTO, PAUL, academic administrator; m. Audrey Transill, May 22, 1982. Grad., Culinary Inst. Am., Hyde Park, NY, Nassau County Bd. Coop. Edn. Studies, Westbury, LI. Cert. Exec. Chef. Caterer In Good Taste, Locust Valley, NY; chef instr. Conn. Culinary Inst., Suffield, 1996—, dir. edn., 2004—. Recipient Gold medal, Am. Culinary Fedn. 2004 Nat. Convention, tallow sculpture competition, Orlando, Best in Show award, First Place award. Mem.: Conn. Chefs Assn. (1st v.p. pub. rels.). Home: 33 Indian Run Enfield CT 06082 Office: Conn Culinary Inst 1760 Mapleton Ave Suffield CT 06078 Home Phone: 860-749-5410; Office Phone: 866-672-4337. *

MONTALVO, EILEEN, communications executive; b. 1973; Exec. v.p., Sales and Mktg. GolTV, 2005—06; dir., Mktg. and Comm. Discovery Networks US Hispanic Grp., 2006—. Named one of 40 Executives Under 40, Multichannel News, 2006. Office: Discovery Communications Inc 1 Discovery Pl Silver Spring MD 20910

MONTANEZ-JOHNER, NANCY, federal agency administrator; With profl. ptnrs. program region III behavioral health svcs. Health and Human Svcs. Sys. State of Nebr., 1995—99, adminstr. S.W. svc. area, 1999—2001, CEO We. svc. area, 2001—04, dir., 2004—06; under sec. agr. food, nutrition & consumer services USDA, Washington, 2006—. Bd. dirs. Commodity Credit Corp. USDA, 2006—. Office: USDA Whitten Bldg 1400 Independence Ave SW Rm 240-E Washington DC 20250 Office Phone: 202-720-7711. Office Fax: 202-690-3100.

MONTAVON, VICTORIA A., university librarian, dean; b. Cin. m. James M. Myers; 3 children. Libr. Rider U., Temple U., Lindenwood Coll., Carlow Coll., Notre Dame Coll., Ohio, St. Joseph 's U., Phila., 1990—96, Wright State U., 1996—2001; dean, libr. U. Cin., 2001—. Recipient Pres. Quality Svc. award, 2003. Office: U Cin U Librs PO Box 210033 Cincinnati OH 45221-0033 Office Phone: 513-556-1515. E-mail: Victoria.Montavon@uc.edu. *

MONTE, BONNIE J., performing arts company executive, director, educator; b. Stamford, Conn., Nov. 27, 1954; d. Eugene N. and Ruth M. (Thompson) M. BA, Bethany Coll., 1976; diploma, Hartman Conservatory, Stamford, 1978; LHD (hon.), Drew U., 2005. Assoc. artistic dir. Williamstown (Mass.) Theatre Festival, 1981-89; casting dir. Manhattan Theatre Club, NYC, 1989-90; artistic dir. The Shakespeare Theatre of NJ, Madison, 1990—. Mem. faculty Drew U., 1991-96; guest artist-in-residence U. Notre Dame, The New Sch.-Eugene Lang. Coll., U. S.C. Recipient Nat. Soc. of Arts and Letters award, N.J., 1997, Alumni Achievement award for arts mgmt. Bethany Coll., 1999; grantee Lotte Crabtree Found., Boston, 1977. Democrat. Avocations: bicycling, archery, writing, travel. Office: Shakespeare Theatre NJ 36 Madison Ave Madison NJ 07940-1434

MONTEDONICO, JOSEPH, lawyer; b. Washington, May 30, 1937; s. Joseph and Linda (Love) M.; m. Lynne Morrell, Nov. 12, 1979; 1 child, Maria. BA, U. Md., 1962, JD, 1965. Bar: Md. 1965, DC 1965, admitted to practice: U.S. Dist. Ct. DC 1965, U.S. Dist. Ct. Md. 1965, U.S. Supreme Ct. Law clk. to justice, Rockville, Md., 1965-66; assoc. Donahue, Ehrmantraut Mitchell, Rockville, 1966-78; ptnr. Donahue, Ehrmantraut, Montedonico, Washington, 1978-88, Montedonico & Mason, Rockville, 1988-91, Montedonico, Hamilton & Altman, PC, Chevy Chase, Md., 1991—2001, Montedonico, Belcoure & Tazzara, Washington, 2001—. Cons., lectr. in field. Author: Medical Malpractice and Health Care Care, 1987, Legal Consideration of Outpatient Anesthesia, Anesthesiology Clinics, 1987, Medical and Legal Principles of Surgical Pathology, Textbook of Surgical Pathology, 1989. With U.S. Army, 1956-58. Named one of Best Lawyers in Am., Washingtonian Mag., 1989—96, Best 75 Lawyers in Washington, 2002. Mem.: Nat. Italian Am. Found., Internat. Acad. Trial Lawyers, Am. Bd. Trial Advocates, Montgomery County Bar Assn., ABA, DC Bar Assn., Md. Bar Assn., Internat. Acad. Trial Lawyers, Am. Bd. Trial Lawyers (pres. DC chpt.), Omicron Delta Kappa, Phi Alpha Delta, Inns of Ct. Republican. Avocations: scuba, skiing, photography. Office: Montedonico Belcoure & Tazzara PC 1020 19th St NW Ste 420 Washington DC 20036 Office Phone: 202-296-1322. Office Fax: 202-296-0985. E-mail: Joseph.Montedonico@mbt_legal.com.

MONTEIRO, GEORGE, language educator, writer; b. Cumberland, RI, May 23, 1932; s. Francisco José and Augusta (Temudo) M.; m. Lois Ann Hodgins, Aug. 14, 1958 (div. 1992); children: Katherine, Stephen, Emily; m. Brenda Murphy, Mar. 25, 1995. AB, Brown U., 1954; AM, Columbia U., 1956; PhD, Brown U., 1964; DHL (hon.), U. Mass., Dartmouth, 1993. From instr. to assoc. prof. Brown U., Providence, 1961-72, prof. English, 1972-99, prof. Portuguese, 1984-99, adj. prof., 1999—; prof. U. Mass., Dartmouth, 2006. Vis. prof. Providence Coll., 1967-68; Fulbright prof. Am. lit. U. Sao Paulo, 1969-71. Author: Henry James and John Hay: The Record of a Friendship, 1965, The Coffee Exchange: Poems, 1982, Robert Frost and the New England Renaissance, 1988, Double Weaver's Knot: Selected Poems, 1989, The Presence of Camões, 1996, The Presence of Pessoa, 1998, Stephen Crane's Blue Badge of Courage, 2000, Fernando Pessoa and Nineteenth-Century Anglo-American Literature, 2000; editor: The Man Who Never Was: Essays on Fernando Pessoa, 1982, The Correspondence of Henry James and Henry Adams, 1877-1941, 1992, Critical Essays on Ernest Hemingway's Farewell to Arms, 1994, Conversations with Elizabeth Bishop, 1996; translator: In Crete with the Minotaur and Other Poems, 1980, The Sea Within, 1983, Fernando Pessoa: Self Awareness and Thirty Other Poems, 1988, A Man Smiles at Death with Half a Face, 1991, Iberian Poems, 2005. Decorated Order of Prince Henry the Navigator (Portugal). Office: Brown U Portuguese & Brazil Studies Providence RI 02912-0001 Office Phone: 401-863-3042. Personal E-mail: georgemonteiro23@yahoo.com.

MONTEIRO, MARISTELA GOLDNADEL, physician, researcher; b. Niteroi, Brazil, May 15, 1960; s. Christiano Jorge and Myriam (Goldnadel) Monteiro. MD, Escola Paulista de Medicina, 1983, PhD, 1986. Asst. prof. Escola Paulista de Medicina, Sao Paulo, Brazil, 1986—87, adj. prof., 1987—; med. officer WHO, Geneva, 1994—95, scientist, 1996—99, coord. intervention R & D substance abuse dept., 1999—2000, coord. mgmt. substance dependence, 2000—03; regional advisor alcohol, substance abuse Pan Am. Health Orgn., 2004—. Postdoctoral fellow U. Calif. San Diego, 1987-89; advisor Am. Psychiat. Assn. Task Force on Substance Use Disorders, 1989-93; advisor WHO/PSA, Geneva, 1993-94. Editor: Brazil-United States Binational Drug Abuse Research, 1993; contbr. over 100 articles to profl. jours. Mem. Internat. Soc. for Biomed. Rsch. on Alcoholism. Jewish. Avocation: scuba diving. Office: Pan Am Health Orgn 525 23rd St NW Washington DC 20037 Home Phone: 301-871-5782. Business E-Mail: monteirm@paho.org.

MONTEITH, LARRY KING, chancellor emeritus; b. Bryson City, NC, Aug. 17, 1933; s. Earl and Essie (King) M.; m. Nancy Alexander, Apr. 19, 1952; children: Larry, Carol, Steve. BSEE, N.C. State U., 1960; MSEE, Duke U., 1962, PhD in Elec. Engring., 1965. Registered profl. engr., N.C. Mem. tech. staff Bell Tel. Labs., Burlington, NC, 1960-62, Rsch. Triangle Inst., Raleigh, NC, 1962-66, group leader rsch. sect., 1966-68; adj. asst. prof. elec. engring. N.C. State U., Raleigh, 1965-68, assoc. prof., 1968-72, prof., 1972—, head dept. elec. engring., 1974-78, dean of engring., 1978-89, interim chancellor, 1989-90, chancellor, 1990-98, chancellor emeritus, 1998—. Contbr. articles to profl. jours. With USN, 1952-56. Recipient Disting. Engring. Alumnus award Duke U., 1984, Outstanding Engring. Achievement award N.C. Soc. Engrs., 1990, Disting. Engring. Alumnus award N.C. State U., 1999. Fellow IEEE, Am. Soc. for Engring. Edn.; mem. NSPE (edn. adv. group), Raleigh C. of C. (bd. dirs.), Rotary Internat. (Paul Harris fellow Rotary Found. 1997), Phi Beta Kappa, Sigma Xi, Sigma Iota Rho, Phi Kappa Phi, Eta Kappa Nu, Tau Beta Pi, Sigma Beta Delta. E-mail: lmonteith@nc.rr.com.

MONTELEONE, PATRICIA L., dean; MD, St. Louis U., 1961; MBA, MHA. V.p. med. affairs Cardinal Glennon Children's Hosp., 1986—93; prof. pediatrics St. Louis U. Sch. Medicine, 1967—, dean, 1994—. Office: St Louis U Sch Medicine 1402 S Grand Blvd Saint Louis MO 63104-1004

MONTELONGO, MICHAEL D., marketing executive, former civilian military employee; b. NYC, Aug. 20, 1955; m. Debra Tenison; 1 child, Amanda. BS in Gen. Engring., U.S. Mil. Acad., 1977; MBA in Corp. Strategy and Fin., Harvard U., 1988; grad., Command and Gen. Staff Coll., 1992. Commd. 2d lt. U.S. Army, 1977, advanced through grades to lt. col.; asst. prof. social scis. dept. U.S. Mil. Acad., West Point, NY, 1988; adv., spl. asst. to comdr.-in chief U.S. So. Command, 1989; bn. exec. officer, bn. and brigade ops. officer U.S. Army, 1993—94, spl. asst. to chief of staff, 1994—95; legis. asst. U.S. Senate, 1995—96; dir. BellSouth Small Bus. Svcs., 1996—98; sales exec. and cons. Cap Gemini Ernst & Young, 1998—2001; asst. sec. for fin. mgmt. & comptr., Dept. of Air Force U.S. Dept. Def., Washington, 2001—05; sr. v.p. for strategic mktg. Sodexho Inc., Gaithersburg, Md., 2005—. Bd. dirs. Denny's Corp., 2005—. Trustee Unite El Paso, 1993; mem. Leadership El Paso Program, 1999. U.S. Army Advanced Civil Schooling fellow, 1986, Inter-Univ. Seminar on Armed Forces and Soc. fellow, 1990, Congl. Hispanic Caucus Inst. fellow, 1992, Army Congl. fellow, 1995. Mem.: Am. Soc. Mil. Comptrollers (pres. 2004), Nat. Soc. Hispanic MBAs (sec.), Assn. West Point Grads. (minority outreach com. 1999—, bd. dirs. Ga. Hispanic voter registration campaign 2000). *

MONTEMAYOR, CARLOS RENE, advertising agency executive; b. San Antonio, Nov. 21, 1945; s. Raul Martin and Mary (Lyall) M.; m. Marina Cara Cook, Sept. 21, 1967 (div. Dec. 1978); m. Barbara Kay Volmer, Dec. 23, 1979; 1 child, Justin Norman. BBA in Mktg., U. Tex., 1967; MS in Journalism, Northwestern U., 1968. Account exec. Campbell-Ewald Co., Detroit and Cin., 1968-72, Ross Roy Inc., Detroit, 1972-74, Pitluk Group, San Antonio, 1974-76; v.p. GSD&M Advt., San Antonio, 1976-78; mktg. mgr. Church's Fried Chicken, San Antonio, 1978-81; v.p. Ed Yardang & Assocs., San Antonio, 1981-83; pres. Montemayor y Asociados, San Antonio, 1983—2002, vice chmn., 2002—05, Global Hue, 2002—05; v.p. strategic devel. Meximerica Media, San Antonio, 2006—. Bd. dirs. USAA Fed. Savs. Bank; past pres. Fiesta San Antonio, Ray Feo XLVII Fiesta, 1995; mem. bd. govs. Cancer Therapy and Rsch. Ctr.; mem. bd. govs., exec. com. S.W. Found.; mem. bd. dirs. ACCION Tex. 2d Lt. USAR, 1968-74. Mem.: Argyle Club, Govs. Club. Republican. Roman Catholic. Avocations: collecting classic cars, travel. Home: 61 Granburg Cir San Antonio TX 78218-3030 Office: Meximerica Media 115 E Travis 8th Fl San Antonio TX 78205 Home Phone: 210-822-0897; Office Phone: 210-581-3694. Business E-Mail: carlos.montemayor@diamiosrumbo.com.

MONTER, E. WILLIAM, retired history professor; b. Cin., Sept. 22, 1936; s. Edward W. and Florence S. Monter; m. Barbara Heldt, June 18, 1963 (div. Aug. 2, 1976); children: Andrea, Gustav C. Heldt, Elizabeth A. Heldt(dec.); m. Rosellen E. Engstrom, July 22, 1978. BA, Wabash Coll., Crawfordsville, Ind., 1958; PhD, Princeton U., 1963. Prof. of history Northwestern U., Evanston, Ill., 1972—2002, prof. emeritus, 2002—. Sec., program on cultural exch. in Europe, 1400-1700 European Sci. Found., Strasbourg, 1997—2004; cons. 2000 papal jubilee Office of Papal Theologian, Vatican City, 1998; mem. editl. bd. Ency. of Witchcraft ABC-Clio Pub., Santa Barbara, Calif., 1999—; vis. prof. history U. Chgo., 2005—06. Author: Calvin's Geneva (also Japanese ed.), 1967, (book) Witchcraft in France and Switzerland, 1976, Ritual, Myth and Magic (also Italian ed.), 1983, Frontiers of Heresy (Spanish ed.), 1990, Judging the French Reformation, 1999, Bewitched Duchy: Lorraine, 2007. Fellow, NEH, 1974-75, 1992-93, 1999-2000, Camargo Found. (France), 1994, 2001; grantee, Am. Coun. of Learned Societies, 1969, 1972;, Social Sci. Rsch. Coun., 1966—67, Guggenheim fellow, 1994, Richardson fellow, Inst. for Advanced Study, 1987—88, CIES (Fulbright) fellow, CCHN, Spain, 1985—86. Mem.: Am. Hist. Assn. (com. on coms. 1984—87), Am. Soc. for Reformation Rsch. (pres. 1980), Soc. d'Histoire de Genève (corr.). Home: 829 Linden Ave Wilmette IL 60091 Home Phone: 847-256-4585. Personal E-mail: monter@northwestern.edu.

MONTERO, SYLVIA, pharmaceutical executive; b. PR; BA, Columbia U. Barnard Coll., 1972; MA, CUNY Queens Coll., 1976. HS tchr. Spanish and bilingual studies, NYC; prof. lit. Interamerican U., PR; with Pfizer Puerto Rico, 1978—82, Pfizer, Inc., NYC, 1982—, v.p. human resources Animal Health Grp., 1994, sr. v.p. human resources Global Rsch. and Devel., 2003, sr. v.p. human resources, 2005, head worldwide talent devel. and human resources, head human resources leadership team. Bd. mem. Grand St. Settlement. Named one of Top 50 Hispanic Bus. Women, Hispanic Bus. Mag., 2001, 80 Elite Women, 2002, 20 Corp. Elite in US, 2006; recipient Orgullo Latino award, 100 Hispanic Women orgn., 2005. Mem.: Hispanic Fedn. Office: Pfizer Inc 235 E 42nd St New York NY 10017

MONTES, LEOPOLDO FELICIANO, dermatologist, educator; b. Buenos Aires, Nov. 22, 1929; came to U.S., 1955, naturalized, 1974; s. Leopoldo A. and Celia (Gaztambide) M.; m. Maria Mercedes Pfeiffer, Nov. 25, 1961; children: Carolina, Mercedes, Ana, Leopoldo, Teresa, William. MD, U. Buenos Aires, 1954; MS, U. Mich., 1959. Intern City of Buenos Aires Hosps., 1954-55; resident in dermatology Pa. Hosp., Phila., 1955-56; resident in dermatology, then instr. U. Mich. Med. Center, Ann Arbor, 1956-60; practice medicine specializing in dermatology Buenos Aires, 1960-63, 82—, Houston, 1963-66, Birmingham, Ala., 1966-81; dermatologist U. Ala., Eye Found.; asst. prof. Baylor U. Coll. Medicine, Houston, 1963—66; mem. faculty U. Ala. Med. Ctr. and Med. Coll. Ala., Birmingham, 1966—, prof. dermatology, 1969—81, assoc. prof. microbiology, 1968—91, prof. emeritus, 1982—; dermatologist Birmingham Dermatology Ctr., 1985—; clin. prof. dermatology U. South Ala., 2002—03; dermatologist Inst. Argentino de Diagnostico & Tratamiento, 1995—. Adj. prof. anatomy Coll. Medicine, U. South Ala., Mobile, 1981-89; adj. prof. large animal surgery and medicine Auburn U. Sch. Veterinary Medicine, 1977—; dir. Dermatology Rsch. Structural Rsch. Ctr., Mobile, 1990—, Vitiligo Unit, 1990; cons. Johnson & Johnson, Del-Ray Lab., Procter & Gamble, Upjohn Co., Delbay Co., Bayer, Warner, Lambert, Westwood Pharms., Tex. Pharm., Alcon, Owen Lab., Hoffman-La Roche, 1963—; CEO Westhoven Press. Author: Atlas of Skin Diseases of the Horse, 1983, Vitiligo-Nutritional Therapy, 1999, Scanning Electron Microscopy of Normal and Abnormal Skin, 1985, Vitiligo-Current Knowledge and Nutritional Therapy, 2006; founding editor Jour. Cutaneous Pathology, 1973-83. Mem. internat. adv. bd. Nat. Vitiligo Found., 2002—. Recipient Rsch. Career Devel. award USPHS, 1965-70; grantee USPHS, NSF, Kresge Found., John A. Hartford Found., NASA. Fellow Am. Acad. Dermatology, Am. Acad. Microbiology, Royal Coll. Physicians and Surgeons Can. (life); mem. AAAS, Am. Soc. Microbiology, Soc. Investigative Dermatology, Histochem. Soc., Am. Soc. Cell Biology, Am. Fedn. Clin. Rsch., Electron Microscope Soc. Am., Internat. Soc. Tropical Dermatology (Asst. sec. gen. 1969-74), Am. Dermatol. Assn., Am. Soc. Dermatopathology, Nat. Acad. Medicine Buenos Aires (life), Jockey Club Argentina (life), Sigma Xi. Achievements include patents in field. Home: Suipacha 1308 1011 Buenos Aires Argentina Office: Paraguay 2302 1121 Buenos Aires Argentina also: Structural Rsch Ctr 120 Novatan Rd Mobile AL 36608 Office Phone: 011-5411-4962-4684. Fax: 011-5411-4314-4328. E-mail: leopoldo_montes@hotmail.com. *While taking care of a patient I always considered it indispensable to study and research as much as I could about the disease I was treating, to feel I was perhaps the only one in a position to help, to put myself-as Lord Lister said- in the patient's place.*

MONTGOMERIE, COLIN STUART, professional golfer; b. Glasgow, Troon, Ayrshire, Scotland, June 23, 1963; children: Olivia Rose, Venetia, Cameron. Mem. Walker Cup Team, 1985, 87, Ryder Cup Team, 1991, 93, 95, 97, 99, 2002, Dunhill Cup Team, 1988, 91-2000, World Cup Team, 1988, 91-93, 97-99, UBS Cup Team, 2003. Decorated European Order of Merit; winner Scottish Stroke Play, 1985, Scottish Amateur Championship, 1987, European Tour Rookie of Yr., 1988, Portuguese Open, 1989, Scandinavian Masters, 1991, 99, 2001, Heineken Dutch Open, 1993, Volvo Masters, 1993, 2002, Spanish Open, 1994, English Open, 1994, Volvo German Open, 1994-95, Alfred Dunhill Cup, 1995, Trophee Lancome, 1995, Dubai Desert Classic, 1996, Murphy's Irish Open, 1996-97, 2001, Canon European Masters, 1996, Million Dollar Challenge, 1996, Compaq European Grand Prix, 1997, World Cup Individual, 1997, Andersen Cons. World Champion, 1997, King Hassan II Trophy, 1997, Brit. Masters, 1998, German Masters, 1998, Benson & Hedges Internat. Open, 1999, BMW Internat. Open, 1999, Std. Life Loch Lomond, 1999, Volvo PGA Championship, 1998-2000, Cisco World Matchplay Championship, 1999, The Skins Game (USA), 2000, Novotel Perrier Open de France, 2000, Ericsson Australian Masters, 2001, European Open, 2007; 2d pl. US Open, 1994, 97, TCL Classic 2002, Macau Open, 2003, Caltex Singapore Masters, 2004, Hong Kong Open, 2005, Smurfit Kappa European Open, 2007; leader European Tour Merit, 1993-99, Ryder Cup Team, 2004, 2006, UBS Cup Team, 2004 Avocations: music, cars, films. Mailing: PGA Tour 112 PGA Tour Blvd Ponte Vedra Beach FL 32082

MONTGOMERY, ANN D., federal judge, educator; b. Litchfield, Minn., May 9, 1949; m. Theodore Smetak; 2 children; 1 stepchild. BS, U. Kans., 1971; JD, U. Minn., 1974. Bar: Minn. 1974, US Dist. Ct. Minn., US Ct. Appeals (8th cir.), US Supreme Ct. Law clk. DC Ct. Appeals, Washington, 1974-75; asst. US atty. Dist. Minn., Mpls., 1976-83; mcpl. judge Hennepin County, 1983-85; judge Hennepin County Dist. Ct., 1985-94, US Magistrate Ct., 1994-96; federal judge US Dist. Ct., Mpls., 1996—. Adj. prof. U. Minn. Law Sch., Mpls., 1988—; steering com. mem., dir. criminal divsn. Minn. Jud. Coll., 1990-94. Recipient Trial Judge of Yr. award Am. Bd. Trial Advocates, 1996. Mem. FBA, Minn. Dist. Judges Assn., Minn. Bar Assn., Minn. Women Lawyers (Myra Bradwell award 2000), Hennepin County Bar Assn. (Professionalism award 1993), Eighth Cir. Dist. Judges Assn. (pres. 2003-04). Office: US Dist Ct 300 S 4th St Minneapolis MN 55415-1320 Fax: 612-664-5097. E-mail: admontgomery@mnd.uscourts.gov.

MONTGOMERY, ANNA FRANCES, elementary school educator; b. Spokane, Wash., Nov. 5, 1945; d. Carl Jacob and Edna Frances (Evans) Kuipers; m. William Lee Montgomery Jr., Oct. 7, 1989. AA, Mid. Ga. Coll., 1965; BS Elem. Edn., Woman's Coll. Ga., 1966; MEd, Ga. Coll., 1969, specialist Edn., 1973; studied Brit. ednl. sys., London, 1978. Cert. elem. tchr., Ga. Classroom tchr. Muscogee County Sch. Dist., Columbus, Ga., 1966—2002, reading summer tchr. Title 1 tutorial program, 1975, instr. staff devel. program, 1977—80; lead tchr. social sci. Wesley Heights Elem. Sch., Columbus, 1992—2002, chmn. mgmt. team, 1997—98; ret., 2002. Instr. tennis and athletics Camp Tegawitha, Tobyhanna, Pa., 1970; judge Columbus Regional Social Sci. Fair, 1977, 93-96; presenter in field Editor: Muscogee County School District's Handbook for Beginning Teachers, 1979 Vol. Med. Ctr. Aux., Columbus, 1975-79; pres. pastor's Bible study class St. Luke United Meth. Ch., 1993-94, 96-98, mem. Sarah Cir. 2, 11, 1969-71, 78-80, co-chmn., 1974-76, chmn., 1976-78; mem. Bessie Howard Ward Handbells Choir. Recipient Valley Forge Tchrs. medal Freedoms Found. at Valley Forge, 1975, Outstanding Tchr. of Yr. award Wesley Hts. Elem. Sch., 1975, Muscogee County Sch. Dist., 1979; named Very Important Lady award Girl Scouts U.S., Columbus, 1976, Outstanding Young Woman Am., 1982 Mem. AAUW (devel. chmn. Ga. state centennial fellowship com. Columbus br. 1973-75), NEA, Ga. PTA (hon. life), Profl. Assn. Ga. Educators (life, bldg. rep. Muscogee County chpt. 1983-2002, sec. 1992-94, treas. 1994-98, pres.-elect 1998-2000, Muscogee County's sys. rep. to the state 2000-02, social chmn. 2002-03), Nat. Coun. Social Studies (hostess and registration coms. ann. meeting 1975), Ga. Coun. Social Studies, Ga. Sci. Tchrs. Assn., Atlanta Alumni Club, Valley Area Sci. Tchrs. (corr. sec. 1996-98), Ga. Coll. Alumni Assn., Mid. Ga. Coll. Alumni Assn., Order of Amaranth (charity 1991-93, 95, truth 1994, assoc. conductress 1996, conductress 1997, assoc. matron 1998, royal matron 1999), Scottish Rite Ladies Aux., Ga. Ret. Educators Assn., Muscogee Ret. Educators Assn., Alpha Delta Kappa (Rho chpt., sec. 1975-76, pres.-elect 1976-78, pres. 1978-80, chaplain, 1996-98, 2006—, chmn. ways and means com. 2005—), Delta Kappa Gamma (Beta Xi chpt., pres. 1980-82, chmn. pubs. and publicity 1976-78, chmn. profl. affairs 1978-80, chair nominations com. 1980-82, chmn. world fellowship and fund raising 1984-86, 96-2004, chmn. fin. 1990-92, chmn. membership 1994-96, 2000-04), Order Internat. Fellowship in Edn. (life), Wesley Heights Elem. Sch. PTA (treas. 1983-86), Wynn House, Phi Delta Kappa, Phi Theta Kappa (life). Avocations: reading, gardening, travel, fishing, clarinet. Home: 5134 Stone Gate Dr Columbus GA 31909-5573

MONTGOMERY, BETTY DEE, former state attorney general, retired state legislator; b. Apr. 3, 1948; BA, Bowling Green State U.; JD, Coll. Law U. Toledo, 1976. Criminal clk. Lucas County Common Pleas Ct.; asst. pros. atty. Wood County, Ohio, 1977—78, pros. atty. Ohio, 1980—88, City of Perrysburg, Ohio, 1978—81; mem. Ohio State Senate, Columbus, 1988—95; atty. gen. State of Ohio, Columbus, 1994—2002, auditor, 2002—06. Bd. dirs. Dominion Homes, Inc., 2007—. Mem. bd. dirs. Ohio Sch. Bd. Atty. Assn. Recipient Women of Achievement award, Toledo Women in Comms., 1984, Govt. Leaders Against Drunk Drivers, MADD, 1990, Senator of the Year, Ohio Hospice Assn., 1991, Disting. Svc. award, Ohio State Bar Assn., 1992, Ohio Women Hall of Fame award, 1996, Public Svc. award, Ohio Assn. of Big Brothers/Big Sisters, 1999, Advocacy award, Ohio Soc. Healthcare Consumer Advocacy, 1999, Child Adv. of the Year, Ohio Ct. Appointed Spl. Advs./Guardian Ad Litem Assn., 1999, Toledo YWCA Milestones award, Women in Govt., 2001, Presdl. award for Pro Bono Svc., The Ohio Legal Assistance Found., 2002, ABA Pro Bono award, to the Office of the Atty. Gen., 2002, Disting. Alumnus award, Bowling Green State Univ., 2003. Mem.: Ohio Prosecuting Atty. Assn. (mem. 1984), Legis. Com., Internat. Prosecutors Assn., Wood County Bar Assn., Alternative Edn. Adv. Com. (former chmn.), Wood County Child Abuse & Neglect Adv. Bd. (former vice-chmn., chmn.), Sexual Abuse Prevention Project, Wood County Sch. (mem. 1981—), Bowling Green C. of C. Republican. *

MONTGOMERY, C. MICHAEL, lawyer; b. Radford, Va., Jan. 7, 1947; s. Carl Ford and Margaret Painter Montgomery; children: Michael A., Jennifer M. McLees, Alexander S., Catherine R. BA, U. Va., Charlottesville, 1969; JD, U. Va., 1972. Bar: Va. 1972, Colo. 1984, Wyo. 1991. Atty./ptnr. Seawell McCoy Winston & Dalton, Norfolk, Va., 1972—84; ptnr., shareholder Montgomery, Green & Jarvis, Denver, 1984—96; ptnr. Montgomery Kolodny, 1996—. Mem.: ABA, Assn. Def. Trial Attys., Am. Bd. Trial Advocates, Colo. Def. Lawyers Assn (pres. 1989—90). Avocations: golf, skiing, guitar, banjo. Office: Montgomery Kolodny et al 1775 Sherman St 21st Fl Denver CO 80203

MONTGOMERY, CHARLES BARRY, lawyer; b. Latrobe, Pa., Apr. 17, 1937; BA cum laude, Muskingum Coll., 1959; JD, U. Mich., 1962. Bar: Ill. 1962, U.S. Dist. Ct. (no. dist.) Ill. 1982, U.S. Supreme Ct. 1971. Atty. Jacobs & McKenna, 1962-67; founder, ptnr. Jacobs, Williams and Montgomery, Ltd., 1967-85; sr. ptnr., comml. and class action litig. and profl. liability litig. Williams Montgomery & John Ltd., Chgo., 1985—. Instr. advocacy inst. U. Mich., Ann Arbor, 1985, advanced program Nat. Inst. Trial Advocacy, 1986, trial acad. Internat. Assn. Def. Counsel, 1987, law inst. program Def. Rsch. Inst; pub. spkr. litigation. Contbr. articles to profl. jours. Fellow Internat. Acad. Trial Lawyers, Internat. Soc. Barristers; mem. ABA (vice-chair medicine and law com. 1989-90), Am. Bd. Trial Advs., Am. Arbitration Assn., Chgo. Bar Assn., Def. Rsch. Inst., Ill. Assn. Def. Trial Counsel, Ill. Assn. Hosp. Attys., Ill. State Bar Assn., Internat. Assn. Def. Counsel, Soc. Trial Lawyers, Legal Club of Chgo., Trial Lawyers Club of Chgo. Office: Williams Montgomery & John Ltd Ste 2100 20 N Wacker Dr Chicago IL 60606-3094 Office Phone: 312-443-3200. Office Fax: 312-630-8542. Business E-Mail: cbm@willmont.com.

MONTGOMERY, CHARLES HARVEY, lawyer; b. Spartanburg, SC, Jan. 28, 1949; s. Dan Hugh and Ann Louise (Gasque) M.; m. Renée Jean Gubernot, Mar. 27, 1971; children: Charles Scott, Marie Renée. BA, Duke U., 1971; JD, Vanderbilt U., 1974. Bar: N.C. 1974, U.S. Dist. Ct. (ea. dist.) N.C. 1974, U.S. Supreme Ct. 1979, U.S. Dist. Ct. (mid. dist.) N.C. 1991; cert. family law specialist, N.C., 1995. Assoc. Jordan Morris & Hoke, Raleigh, NC, 1974-75; atty. Wake County Legal Svcs., Raleigh, 1975-76; pvt. practice, Raleigh, 1977; ptnr. Montgomery & Montgomery, Cary, NC, 1978-79, Sanford Adams McCullough & Beard, Raleigh, 1979-86, Adams McCullough & Beard, Raleigh, 1986-88, Toms Reagan & Montgomery, Cary, 1989-92, Toms & Montgomery, Cary, 1992-93; pvt. practice, Cary, 1993—. Bd. dirs. Br. Bank and Trust, Cary; pres. Family Law Mediation, Inc. Councilman Town of Cary, 1977-81, 83-87; vice-chmn. Wake County Dem. party, Raleigh, 1991-92; commr. Wake County, Raleigh, 1992; bd. dirs. East Cen. Cmty. Legal Svcs., Inc., 1997-2003, State Capitol Found., 1994—. Mem.: ABA, Cary Bar Assn. (organizer 1993—), N.C. Acad. Trial Lawyers (chair family law sect. 1996—98), Wake County Bar Assn. (bd. dirs. 1999—2001), N.C. Bar Assn. (chmn. pub. info. com. 1994—96, dir. family law coun. 1994—97, 2006—). Methodist. Avocation: sailing. Office: PO Box 1325 Cary NC 27512-1325 also: 590 New Waverly Pl Ste 110 Cary NC 27512-1325 Office Phone: 919-816-9002. Business E-Mail: charles@montylaw.com.

MONTGOMERY, CHARLES HOWARD, retired bank executive; b. Bloomington, Ill., Mar. 23, 1930; s. Dewey H. and Madeline (Wonderlin) M.; m. Diane Dickerson Cohen, Aug. 30, 1978 (dec. Oct. 1996); children: Alison, Douglas; m. Katharine Yang, Oct. 4, 1997. AB, Ill. Wesleyan U., 1951; MS, U. Ill., 1960. CPA, Ill. Auditor Lybrand Ross Bros. & Montgomery, Rockford, Ill., 1955-59; with Abbott Labs., North Chicago, Ill., 1959-67, controller, 1965-67; v.p. finance Anchor Coupling Co., Libertyville, 1967-69; v.p., comptroller First Nat. Bank Chgo., 1969-73, sr. v.p., 1973-75, exec. v.p., 1976-88, comptroller, 1973-88, First Chgo. Corp.; ret. Past chmn. Inter-Assn. Com. Bank Acctg. With US Army, 1952—53. Mem. Fin. Execs. Inst., AICPA, Ill. Soc. CPAs, Tau Kappa Epsilon, Phi Kappa Phi, Univ. Club (Chgo.) Address: 6321 N Avers Ave Chicago IL 60659-1001 Home: 824 Georgia St Key West FL 33040 Personal E-mail: chmonty@att.net.

MONTGOMERY, CLEOTHUS, minister; b. Henderson, Tex., Dec. 6, 1926; s. Lewis and Amanda (Waters) M.; m. Emma Agusta Tinch (dec. Aug. 23, 1987); children: Michael Dennis, Debra Marie, Pamela Key, Diane Renea, Anthony Cleothus (dec.). BS in Drafting, Calif. Coll., 1951; B in Theology, Union Bapt. Theol. Sem., 1962; M in Theology, Inter Bapt. Theol. Sem., 1965, DD, 1973; D in Sacred Theol. (hon.), Mt. Hope Bible Coll., 1973; M in Ministry, Trinity Theol. Sem., 1990, D in Ministry, 1993. Cert. christian counselor, Tex. Minister Northside Missionary Bapt. Ch., Houston, 1962—. Counselor Chemical Dependency, Houston, 1989-97, Internat. Christian Isnt., 1990-97; invited pastor by Campus for Christ to Israel, 1987, Africa, 1990, Russia, 1995-97. Pres. World Christian Tng. Ctr., Houston, 1985-90, Houston Minister Christian Fellowship, 1992-97; chmn. Minister Network Life Gift, Houston, 1988-90, Ministers Against Crime, Houston, 1989-97; treas. Life Investment for Tng., Houston, 1990-97; v.p. Ministerial Adv. to Mayor, Houston, 1995-97; trustee bd. of regency, adv. bd. Coll. of Biblical Studies. With U.S. Army, 1945-46. Mem. NAACP, Am. Assn. Christian Counselors (chemical dependency counselor 1993-97). Democrat. Baptist. Avocations: reading, devotional writings, bowling, travel, jogging. Home: 1407 Laurentide St Houston TX 77029-3411 Office: Northside Missionary Bapt Ch 3202 Bennington St Houston TX 77093-9222

MONTGOMERY, CLIFF WILSON, journalist, writer, researcher; b. Cumberland, Md., Aug. 13, 1965; s. Clifford Ray and Elizabeth Ann Montgomery. European Lit. (hon.), Ed. by pvt. tutor, Charlotte, NC, 1983—91, Am. Lit. (hon.), 1994—98. East coast polit. corr. 3 A.M. Mag., Kirkland, Wash., 2000—; editor, pub. The Am. Spark, 2006—. Media cons. Sierra Club, Charlotte, NC, 1998. *One of the first journalists to debunk the principal rationale behind the second Iraq War, showing the country no longer possessed stores of chemical and biological weapons or their weapon agents, and was not an immediate nuclear threat. Believes it is the job of any journalist to, "tell truth to power," however unpopular the truth.* Freelance journalist Washington Spectator, In These Times, Working for Change, Alternet and Political Affairs. Active Nat. Trust for Hist. Preservation, 1996—99, Archaeol. Inst. Am., 1999—2000; activist Amnesty Internat., 1992—96; active Pub. Concern Found., 1994—. Independent. Avocations: history, travel, motorcycling. Personal E-mail: clifmn@aol.com. Business E-Mail: cmont@americanspark.com.

MONTGOMERY, DAVID BRUCE, marketing educator; b. Fargo, ND, Apr. 30, 1938; s. David William and Iva Bernice (Trask) Montgomery; m. Toby Marie Franks, June 11, 1960; children: David Richard, Scott Bradford, Pamela Marie. BSEE, Stanford U., 1960, MBA, 1962, MS in Stats., 1964, PhD in Mgmt. Sci., 1966; D honoris causa, Limburgs U. Centrum, Belgium, 1998. Asst. prof. mgmt. MIT, 1966-69, assoc. prof., 1969-70; assoc. prof. mktg. and mgmt. sci. Stanford U., 1970-73, prof., 1973-78, Robert A. Magowan prof. mktg., 1978-92, Sebastian S. Kregge prof. mktg. strategy, 1992-99, prof. emeritus, 1999—; dean Sch. Bus. Singapore Mgmt. U., 2003—05. Prin. MAC Group, Inc., 1969-91; adv. bd. LEK Partnership, London; sci. adv. bd. Univ. Connection, Bonn, Germany; acad. trustee Mktg. Sci. Inst., 1994-2000, exec. dir., 1995-97. Author: (with Glen L. Urban) Management Science in Marketing, 1969, (with Massy and Morrison) Stochastic Models of Buying Behavior, 1970, (with Day et al) Planning: Cases in Computer and Model Assisted Marketing, 1973, (with others) Consumer Behavior: Theoretical Sources, 1973, (with G. J. Eskin) Data Analysis, 1975; editor 5 books; cons. editor Jour. Internat. Mktg., 2000-03; mem. editl. bd. Mgmt. Sci., Jour. Mktg., Jour. Mktg. Rsch., Mktg. Sci., Jour. acad. of Mktg. Sci., Jour. Internat. Mktg.; contbr. more than 100 articles and tech. reports to sci. and profl. jours. Trustee Family Service Assn. of Mid Peninsula, 1972-73. Recipient citation for outstanding contbns. to use of computers in mgmt. edn. Hewlett Packard, 1977, Best Paper award Strategic Mgmt. Soc., 1996. Mem.: Am. Mktg. Assn. (Contribution to Mktg. Strategy award 2002), Inst. Mgmt. Scis., Tau Beta Pi. Presbyterian. Home: 960 Wing Pl Stanford CA 94305-1028 Office: Stanford U Grad Sch Bus Stanford CA 94305 Business E-Mail: montgomery_david@gsb.stanford.edu.

MONTGOMERY, DAVID CAMPBELL, retired physics professor; b. Milan, Mo., Mar. 5, 1936; s. Merrill Edward and Ruth E. (Campbell) Montgomery; m. Shirley Arlene Imig, July 20, 1957; children: Kathleen Montgomery Sutton, Elizabeth. Student, U. Mo., 1953-55; BS, U. Wis., 1956; MA, Princeton U., 1958, PhD, 1959; D honoris causa (hon.), Eindhoven U. Tech., The Netherlands, 1996. Research assoc. Princeton U., 1959-60; instr. U. Wis., 1961-62; asst. prof. U. Md., 1962-65; assoc. prof. U. Iowa, Iowa City, 1965-70, prof., 1970-77; prof. physics Coll. William and Mary, Williamsburg, Va., 1977-84; prof. Dartmouth Coll., Hanover, NH, 1984—2004, rsch. prof., prof. emeritus, 2004—. Vis. prof., rschr. U. Colo., 1966, U. Alaska, 1968, U. Calif., Berkeley, 1969—70, Bell Labs., 1971; lectr. Internat. Summer Sch. Theoretical Physics, Les Houches, France, 1972, U. Wis., Madison, 1973, vis. prof., rschr., 89; vis. prof. Hunter Campus CUNY, 1973—74, U. Nagoya, Japan, 1983, Columbia U., NYC, 1985, Tech. U., Eindhoven, Netherlands, 1992; vis. scientist Nat. Ctr. Atmospheric Rsch., Boulder, Colo., 1975—76, Boulder, 1979, Boulder, 87, Boulder, 2002, Boulder, 2004—06, Riso Nat. Lab., Roskilde, Denmark, 2001; cons. NASA Hdqs., Washington, 1977—82, JET Joint Undertaking, Culham, England, 1991; vis. rsch. prof. U. Md., 1977—84; vis. staff Los Alamos Sci. Lab., 1977—81, 1986, 1991—92, 1994, cons., collaborator, vis. staff; former cons. Oak Ridge Nat. Lab., NASA; vis. rschr. Los Alamos Nat. Lab., 1987—88, cons., 1998—2000; J. M. Burgers prof. Eindhoven Tech. U., Netherlands, 1995—98, Netherlands, 2000—01, U. Md., 1997; vis. rschr. Courant Inst. NYU, 1997. Former assoc. editor: Physics of Fluids, Internat. Jour. Engring. Sci.; contbr. articles to profl. publs. and monographs. Fellow: Am. Phys. Soc.; mem.: NY Acad. Scis., Sigma Xi, Phi Beta Kappa, Phi Mu Alpha, Pi Mu Epsilon. Achievements include introduction of modern fluid turbulence methods into space and controlled fusion theory; development of maximum entropy, or "most probable" states, method of describing coherent structures achieved as a product of turbulent relaxation. Office: Dartmouth College Physics Dept Hanover NH 03755 Office Phone: 603-646-3219.

MONTGOMERY, DENISE KAREN, nurse; b. NYC, Dec. 23, 1951; d. Thomas Cornell and Dorothy Marie (Castine) Simons; m. Timothy Bruce Montgomery, July 19, 1974 (div. Feb. 1981); m. Joseph Samuel Montgomery, Aug. 20, 1983. A in Nursing, San Jacinto Coll., 1971. RN, Tex. Charge nurse Aarons Womens Clinic, Houston, 1977; rsch. asst. dept. ob-gyn. Baylor Coll. Medicine, Houston, 1977-81, nursing supr., 1979-81, program coord. population control program, 1979-81; nurse Dr. Eric J. Haufrect, Houston, 1982-83; office mgr., supr. Dr. Samuel Law, Houston, 1983-84, Dr. J.S. Montgomery III, 1987—. Contbr. articles to profl. jours. Recipient Disting. Pub. Svc. award Am. Heart Assn., 1976; numerous rsch. grants. Mem. Nat. Assn. Coll. Ob-Gyn, Republican. Mem. Christian Ch. Home: 8202 N Tahoe Dr Houston TX 77040-1256 Office Phone: 281-955-5330. E-mail: denmnt@hotmail.com.

MONTGOMERY, DILLARD BREWSTER, musician, educator; b. Memphis, Jan. 1, 1936; s. Mary Joyce Montgomery; m. Joyce Helena Beale, Dec. 9, 1965; 1 child, Lisa Jenean. BS, Tenn. State U., 1962, MA, 1968. Profl. musician Nashville Assn. Musicians, 1958—; band dir., keyboardist The New Imperials, Nashville, 1962—; tchr. Met. Nashville Schs., 1962-94, ret., 1994; asst. prin. W.A. Bass Middle Sch., 1984-93, prin., 1993-94. Choir dir. John Wesley United Meth. Ch., Nashville, 1958—, Dixon United Meth. Ch., 1970-71, Braden United Meth. Ch., 1985-2002; profl. model Terrance Hurd Agy., 1999—. Served with USAF, 1955-58. Mem. NEA, Tenn. Edn. Assn., Met. Nashville Edn. Assn., Nat. Musicians Union, Tenn. State U. Alumni Assn. (life), Alpha Phi Alpha (life). Democrat. Methodist. Avocations: computers, collecting old music, collecting old movies, recording and transferring old albums and tapes to CD, recording old movies to video and DVD. Home: 638 W Nocturne Dr Nashville TN 37207 Office Phone: 615-650-3232. E-mail: dmontgo1@bellsouth.net.

MONTGOMERY, HENRY IRVING, financial planner; b. Dec. 18, 1924; s. Harry Biggs and Martha Grace (Wilkinson) Montgomery; m. Barbara Louise Hook, Aug. 14, 1948; children: Priscilla Ann, Barbara Ruth, Michael Henry, Kelly Anne, Andrew Stuart. Student, U. Iowa, 1942-43, 47-48; BBA, Tulane U., 1952; postgrad., U. Minn., 1976. CFP Colo. Field agt. OSS, SSU, CIG, CIA, Cen. Europe, 1945-47; pres. Nehi Bottling Co., Decorah, Iowa, 1952-64; prin. Montgomery Assocs., Mktg. Cons., Trieste, Italy and Iowa, 1965-72; pres. Planners Fin. Svcs., Inc., Mpls., 1972-95, chmn., 1992—2005. Prin. Montgomery Investment Mgmt., 1992—. Author: Race Toward Berlin, 1945. With US Army, 1943—46, ETO. Decorated Bronze Star; recipient P. Kemp Fain Profl. Svc. award, 1998. Mem.: VFW, DAV, Twin Cities Soc. CFPs, Twin City Fin. Planners (pres. 1975—78), Met. Tax Planning Group (pres. 1984—87), Mpls. Estate Planning Coun., Investment Co. Inst. (investment adviser com. 1982—), Internat. Assn. Fin. Planning (internat. dir. 1976—81, govt. rels. com. 1991—2005), Nat. Assn. Securities Dealers (dist. 8 com. 1988—91, vice-chmn. 1990), Inst. CFPs (bd. dirs. 1977—82, pres. 1980—81, chmn. 1981—82, chmn. fin. products stds. bd. 1984—88), Elks, Am. Legion, Beta Gamma Sigma. Avocation: languages (Italian, German). Office: Planners Fin Svcs Inc 7710 Computer Ave Ste 100 Minneapolis MN 55435-5417 Office Phone: 952-835-9000.

MONTGOMERY, HUBERT THERON, JR., physician, health care administrator; b. Birmingham, Ala., July 29, 1935; s. Hubert Theron and Edna M. (Morrison) M.; m. Sarah Diane Bryans, Sept. 19, 1969; children: Alfred Peter, Melanie Anne, Laurel Elaine, Amy Diane. AB, Birmingham So. Coll., 1957; MD, Tulane U., 1961. Diplomate Am. Bd. Surgery, Am. Bd. Plastic Surgery. Rotating intern St. Vincent Hosp., Birmingham, 1961-62; resident surgery Lloyd Noland Hosp., Fairfield, Ala., 1964-68; pvt. practice, Montgomery, Ala., 1968-73, 75—; resident plastic surgery U. Tenn., Memphis, 1974-75; pres., CEO Med One Inc., Montgomery, 1983—96; exec. v.p., chief exec. officer Central Ala. Preferred Provider, Inc., Montgomery, 1984-96; sec.-treas. Montgomery Surg. Ctr., Inc., 1984-85; pres. Bodegas de Mendoza, Inc., 2001—; pres., CEO Crux Imports, Inc., 2005—. Sect. chief plastic surgery Bapt. Med. Ctr., Montgomery, 1976-78, St. Margaret's Hosp., Montgomery, 1987-89. Sec.-treas. Ala. Soc. Plastic Surgeons, 1990-92, pres. 1994-96; mem. Hitchcock Award Com., Montgomery, 1985. Maj. U.S. Army, 1963-69. Named New Bus. of Yr., Ala. Bus. Rev., Montgomery, 1985. Fellow: ACS; mem.: Soc. Latin Am. Plastic Surgeons (treas. 1997—98, v.p. 1999—2001, pres. 2002—04), Am. Cancer Soc. (dir. Montgomery chpt. 2002—), Newcomen Soc. N.Am., Wynn Lakes Country Club, Montgomery Country Club, Capitol City Kiwanis (dir. 1987—88). Baptist.

MONTGOMERY, JAMES FISCHER, savings and loan association executive; b. Topeka, Nov. 30, 1934; s. James Maurice and Frieda Ellen (Fischer) M.; m. Diane Dealey; children: Michael James, Jeffrey Allen, Andrew Steven, John Gregory. BA in Acctg., UCLA, 1957. With Price, Waterhouse & Co., C.P.A.'s, LA, 1957-60; controller Conejo Valley Devel. Co., Thousand Oaks, Calif., 1960; asst. to pres. Gt. Western Fin. Corp., Beverly Hills, Calif., 1960-64; fin. v.p., treas United Fin. Corp., LA, 1964—69, exec. v.p., 1967—74, pres., 1974—75; chmn., CEO Great Western Financial Corp., Chatsworth, Calif., 1975-96, chmn. bd. dirs., 1996—97; founder, CEO Frontier Bank, Park City, Utah, 1998—2002, chmn., 1998—. Pres. Citizens Savs. & Loan Assn., Los Angeles, 1970-75. Served with AUS, 1958-60. Office: Frontier Bank 1245 Deer Valley Dr PO Box 981180 Park City UT 84098-1180

MONTGOMERY, JOEL ROBERT, communications executive, consultant; b. Lexington, Sept. 9, 1946; s. Joseph Gwinn and Lucille O'Hair Montgomery. AA, U. Fla., 1966; BA, Fla. State U., 1968; MEd, EdD, Fla. Internat. U., 1992. Cert. group leader educator MATC, 1978, orgnl. develop. MATC, 1979. Mgmt. cons. Coopers & Lybrand (now Price Waterhouse Coopers), LA, 1979—80; regional cons. interaction mgmt. Develop. Dimensions Internat., LA, 1981—82; pres., cons. coach Resources Inst., Hollywood, Fla., 1982—93; mgr. learning arch. Andersen Cons. (now Accenture), St. Charles, Ill., 1993—98; sr. lead bus. cons. orgnl. change Origin Tech. in Bus. (now Atos-Origin), Dallas, 1999—2000; CEO, performance coach MetaLearning.com, LLC, Geneva, Ill., 2000—02; pres. Meta Corp., 2001—; bilingual educator East Aurora H.S., Aurora, Ill., 2004—05; author, pub., on-line educator, cons. Joelmonty.net, Geneva, 2005—; bilingual educator Kimball Mid. Sch., Elgin, Ill., 2006—. With Internat. Inst. Develop. of Human Resources, Bogota, Colombia, 1982; adj. instr. Fla. Internat. U., Miami, 1989—90; performance coach, spkr., cons. Practical Bus. Assessments, Geneva, 2001—02; rep. Primerica Fin. Svcs., Carol Stream, Ill., 2002—; bilingual educator Larkin HS, Elgin, Ill., 2003, Meadowdale Elem. Sch., Carpentersville, Ill., 2003—04, East Aurora (Ill.) H.S., 2004—05; pub., on-line educator, cons. Joelmonty.net, Geneva, 2005—. Author: (book) Catalog of Workshop-Seminar Materials for The Resources Institute and INDER-HU, 1983, Human Relations Workbook--The Human Side of Teaching, 1990, (Book) The Development, Application and Implications of a Strategy for Reflective Learning from Experience, 1992; contbr. articles to profl. jours. Mem. ARC, Washington, 1964—, chmn. bd. dirs. Fox River chpt. St. Charles, 1993—96, bd. dirs. Broward County chpt. Ft. Lauderdale, 1990—92. Capt. US Army, 1969—79. Recipient Joint Svc. Commendation medal, U.S. Army, 1975. Mem.: Ednl. Soc. Resource Mgmt., Am. Soc. Tng. & Develop., Orgnl. Develop Network, Internat. Found. Action Learning (leadership team U.S. chpt. 1995—2002), Acad. Human Resources Develop. (bd. dirs. 1997—99). Avocations: swimming, travel. Office: 717 Anderson Blvd Geneva IL 60134-1246 Office Phone: 630-208-0988. Personal E-mail: joelmonty@usa.net.

MONTGOMERY, JOHN A., physicist; b. Memphis, Jan. 2, 1944; s. John and Mary Emma (Pittman) Montgomery; m. Cathi Montgomery. B in Physics, North Tex. State U., 1967, M in Physics, 1969; PhD, Catholic U. Am., 1982. Rsch. physicist advanced techniques br. electronic warfare divsn. Naval Rsch. Lab., 1968—80, head off-board countermeasures br., 1980—85, superintendent Tactical Electronic Warfare Divsn. (TEWD), 1985—2002, dir. rsch, 2002—. U.S. nat. leader Tech. Cooperation Program Multinat. Group on Electronic Warfare, 1987—. Mem.: Sr. Exec. Svc. (Presdl. Rank Meritorious Exec. award 1988, Presdl. Rank. Disting. Exec. award 1991, Presdl. Rank Meritorious. Exec. award 1999, Presdl. Rank. Disting. Exec. award 2002), Sigma Xi. Achievements include development of new electronic warfare technologies; more than 80 systems approved for operational use by the Navy and other services. Office: Naval Rsch Lab 4555 Overlook Ave SW Washington DC 20375

MONTGOMERY, JOHN HAROLD, environmentalist; b. San Francisco, Mar. 16, 1955; s. Lloyd Cecil Montgomery and Liane Claire (Klein) Malinofsky; m. Patricia Elizabeth Keim, Sept. 13, 1986; 1 child, Kelly Elizabeth. AS in Chemistry, Brookdale C.C., Lincroft, NJ, 1978; BS in Geology, Stockton State Coll., Pomona, NJ, 1984. Lic. profl. geologist, Tenn., Pa.; lic. subsurface evaluator, NJ; cert. lay spkr. Lab. technician Seals Eastern, Inc., Red Bank, NJ, 1977-78, Inter-Polymer Rsch. Corp.,

Farmingdale, NJ, 1978-79; rsch. technician CPS Chem. Co., Old Bridge, NJ, 1979-80; reporter Asbury Park Press, Neptune, NJ, 1974-86; rsch. chemist Union Carbide Corp., Bound Brook, NJ, 1985-86; prin. geologist NJ Dept. Environ. Protection, Trenton, 1986-90; corp. prin. hydrologist Groundwater & Environ. Svcs. Inc., Neptune, NJ, 1990—95, 1996—; project hydrogeologist T&M Assocs., Middletown, NJ, 1995-96. Author: Groundwater Chemicals Desk Reference, 1990, 7th edit., 2007, Groundwater Chemicals Desk Reference- Vol. 2, 1991, 3d edit., 2000, Agrochemicals Desk Reference, 2d edit., 1997. Mem. Nat. Ground Water Assn., Geol. Assn. NJ, Marina View Homeowner's Assn. (v.p. 1986-87). Republican. Methodist. Achievements include research in quantitative structure phys. relationships in determining aqueous solubilities of organic compounds, fate and transport of organics in groundwater. Office: GES Inc 1340 Campus Pky Neptune NJ 07753 Office Phone: 732-919-0100. Personal E-mail: jhmontyite1@comcast.net. Business E-Mail: jmontgomery@gesonline.com.

MONTGOMERY, JOHN HAROLD, psychiatrist; s. Joseph and Jane Montgomery; m. Heather Montgomery, July 17, 1999; children: Abigail, Blake, Zachary. DO, Nova Southeastern U., 1998. Diplomate Psychiatry and Forensic Psychiatry, Am. Bd. Psychiatry and Neurology. Forensic psychiatrist Miss. State Hosp., Whitfield, 2003—, svc. chief female line, 2004—. Asst. clin. prof. dept. psychiatry U. Miss. Med. Ctr., Jackson, 2003—. Contbr. articles to profl. jours. Recipient Young Investigator award, Am. Acad. of Psychiatry and the Law, 2003, Rosner award, Am. Acad. Forensic Scis., 2004; Steinberg Fellowship in Psychiatry and the Law, U. Rochester Sch. Medicine and Dentistry, 2002—03. Office: MS State Hospital Whitfield MS 39193 Home Phone: 601-454-7538; Office Phone: 601-351-8000. Personal E-mail: jmontgo651@yahoo.com. Business E-Mail: montgjo@msh.state.ms.us.

MONTGOMERY, JOHN T., lawyer; BA, U. Mich., 1969; JD, Boston Coll., 1975. Bar: Mass. 1975, US Dist. Ct. (Mass., ea. Mich.), US Ct. Appeals (1st, 2d, 3d, 4th & D.C. cir.). Asst. atty. gen. Commonwealth of Mass.; assoc. Ropes & Gray, Boston, 1982—85, ptnr. litigation dept., 1985—90; first asst. atty. gen. Commonwealth of Mass., 1990—92; ptnr. litigation dept. Ropes & Gray, Boston, 1992—, mng. ptnr. & mem. mgmt. com. Named one of Top Ten Lawyers, Mass. Lawyers' Weekly, 1998. Fellow: Am. Coll. Trial Lawyers; mem.: New England Legal Found. (dir.). Office: Ropes & Gray 1 International Pl Boston MA 02110-2624 Office Phone: 617-951-7565. Office Fax: 617-951-7050. Business E-Mail: john.montgomery@ropesgray.com.

MONTGOMERY, JOHN WARWICK (BARON OF KILTARTAN AND LORD OF MORRIS, COMTE DE ST. GERMAIN DE MONTGOMMERY), law educator, theologian; b. Warsaw, NY, Oct. 18, 1931; s. Maurice Warwick and Harriet (Smith) M.; m. Lanalee de Kant, Aug. 26, 1988; 1 adopted child, Jean-Marie. AB in Philosophy with distinction, Cornell U., 1952; BLS, U. Calif., Berkeley, 1954, MA, 1958; BD, Wittenberg U., 1958, MST, 1960; PhD, U. Chgo., 1962; Docteur de l'Université, mention Théologie Protestante, U. Strasbourg, France, 1964; LLB, LaSalle Extension U., 1977; diplôme cum laude, Internat. Inst. Human Rights, Strasbourg, 1978; MPhil in Law, U. Essex, Eng., 1983; Dr. (hon.), Inst. Religion and Law, Moscow, 1999; LLM, Cardiff U., Wales, 2000; LLD, Cardiff U., 2003. Bar: Va. 1978, Calif. 1979, D.C. 1985, Wash. 1990, U.S. Supreme Ct. 1981, Eng. 1984, Paris 2003; lic. real estate broker Calif.; cert. law librarian; advanced cert. Heraldry Soc.; diplomate Med. Library Assn.; ordained to ministry Luth. Ch., 1958. Librarian, gen. reference service U. Calif. Library, Berkeley, 1954-55; instr. Bibl. Hebrew, Hellenistic Greek, Medieval Latin Wittenberg U., Springfield, Ohio, 1956-59; head librarian Swift Libr. div. and Philosophy, mem. federated theol. faculty U. Chgo., 1959-60; assoc. prof., chmn. dept. history Wilfred Laurier U. (formerly Waterloo Luth. U.), Ont., Can., 1960-64; prof., chmn. div. ch. history, history of Christian thought, dir. European Seminar program Trinity Evang. Div. Sch., Deerfield, Ill., 1964-74; prof. law and theology George Mason U. Sch. Law (formerly Internat. Sch. of Law), Arlington, Va., 1974-75; theol. cons. Christian Legal Soc., 1975-76; dir. studies Internat. Inst. Human Rights, Strasbourg, France, 1979-81; founding dean, prof. jurisprudence, dir. European program Simon Greenleaf U. Sch. Law, Anaheim, Calif., 1980-88; lic. disting. prof. theology and law, dir. European program Faith Evang. Luth. Sem., Tacoma, 1989-91; from prin. lectr. to reader in law Bedfordshire U., England, 1991-93, prof. law and humanities, dir. Ctr. Human Rights, 1993-97, emeritus prof., 1997—; disting. prof. apologetics, law, and history of Christian thought, v.p. acad. affairs U.K. and Europe Trinity Coll. and Theol. Sem., Newburgh, Ind., 1997—2007; disting. prof. law Regent U., Va., 1997-99; sr. counsel European Ctr. Law and Justice, 1997-2001; founding dir. Internat. Acad. of Apologetics, Evangelism and Human Rights, Strasbourg, France, 1997—; disting. rsch. prof. philosophy and Christian thought Patrick Henry Coll., Purcellville, Va., 2007—. Vis. prof. Concordia Theol. Sem., Springfield, Ill., 1964-67, DePaul U., Chgo., 1967-70, Concordia U., Irvine, Calif., 2006; hon. fellow Revelle Coll., U. Calif., San Diego, 1970; rector Freie Fakultaten Hamburg, Fed. Republic Germany, 1981-82; lectr. Rsch. Scientists Christian Fellowship Conf. St. Catherines Coll., Oxford U., 1985, Internat. Anti-Corruption Conf., Beijing, China, 1995; Pascal lectr. on Christianity and the Univ., U. Waterloo, Ont., Can., 1987; A. Kurt Weiss lectr. biomed. ethics U. Okla., 1997; adj. prof. Puget Sound U. Sch. Law, Tacoma, 1990-91; founding dir. Internat. Acad. Apologetics, Evangelism and Human Rights, Strasbourg, France, 1997—; Worldwide Adv. Conf. lectr. Inns of Ct. Sch. Law, London, 1998; law and religion colloquium lectr. U. Coll. London, 2000; hon. chmn. academic bd. Internat. Inst. Religious Freedom, World Evangel. Fellowship, 2005- . Author: The Writing of Research Papers in Theology, 1959, A Union List of Serial Publications in Chicago Area Protestant Theological Libraries, 1960, A Seventeenth-Century View of European Libraries, 1962, 1962, Chytraeus on Sacrifice: A Reformation Treatise in Biblical Theology, 1962, The Shape of the Past: An Introduction to Philosophical Historiography, 1962; author: (rev. edit.), 1975; author: The Is God Dead Controversy, 1966; author: (with Thomas J.J. Altizer) The Altizer-Montgomery Dialogue, 1967; author: Crisis in Lutheran Theology, 2 vols., 1967; author: (rev. edit.), 1973; author: Es confiable el Christianismo?, 1968, Ecumenicity, Evangelicals, and Rome, 1969, Where is History Going?, 1969, (Romanian edit.) 2004, History and Christianity, 1970, Damned Through the Church, 1970, The Suicide of Christian Theology, 1970, Computers, Cultural Change and the Christ, 1970, In Defense of Martin Luther, 1970, La Mort de Dieu, 1971; author: (with Joseph Fletcher) Situation Ethics: True or False?, 1972; author: The Quest for Noah's Ark, 1972; author: (rev. edit.), 1974; author: Verdammt durch die Kirche, 1973, Christianity for the Toughminded, 1973, Cross and Crucible, 2 vols., 1973, Principalities and Powers: The World of the Occult, 1973, (rev. edit.), 1975, (Romanian edit.), 2004, How Do We Know There is a God?, 1973, Myth, Allegory and Gospel, 1974, God's Inerrant Word, 1974, Jurisprudence: A Book of Readings, 1974; author: (4th edit.), 1992; author: The Law Above the Law, 1975, Cómo Sabemos Que Hay un Dios?, 1975, Demon Possession, 1975, The Shaping of America, 1976, Faith Founded on Fact, 1978, Law and Gospel: A Study for Integrating Faith and Practice, 1978; author: (3rd edit.), 1994; author: Slaughter of the Innocents, 1981, The Marxist Approach to Human Rights: Analysis & Critique, 1984, Human Rights and Human Dignity, 1987, (Romanian edit.) 2004, Wohin marschiert China?, 1991, Evidence for Faith: Deciding the God Question, 1991, Giant in Chains: China Today and Tomorrow, 1994, Law and Morality: Friends or Foes?, 1994, Jésus: La Raison Rejoint L'Histoire, 1995; author: (with C.E.B. Cranfield and David Kilgour) Christians in the Public Square, 1996; author: Conflicts of Law, 1997, The Transcendent Holmes, 2000, The Repression of Evangelism in Greece, 2001, Tractatus Logico-Theologicus, 2002, Christ Our Advocate, 2002, History, Law and Christianity, 2002, Heraldic Aspects of the German Reformation, 2003, The Church: Blessing or Curse?, 2004; editor: Lippincott's Evangelical Perspectives, 7 vols., 1970-72, 1970—72, International Scholars Directory, 1973, Simon Greenleaf Law Rev., 7 vols., 1981—88, Global Jour. Classical Theology, 1998—; contbg. editor: Christianity Today, 1965—84, New Oxford Review, 1993—95; author: (films) Is Christianity Credible, 1968, In Search of Noah's Ark, 1977, Defending the Biblical Gospel (11 videocassette series), 1985, (TV series) Christianity on Trial, 1987—93; contbr. articles to acad., theol., legal encys. and jours., chapters to books . Nat. Luth. Ednl. Conf. fellow, 1959-60; Can. Council postdoctoral sr. research fellow, 1963-64; Am. Assn. Theol. Schs. faculty fellow, 1967-68; recipient Angel award Nat. Religious Broadcasters, 1989, 90, 92, Patriarch's Medal, Romanian Orthodox Church, 2003. Fellow Trinity Coll. (Newburgh, Ind.), Royal Soc. Arts (Eng.), Victoria Inst. (London) (hon. v.p.; essay prize 2003-04), Soc. Advanced Legal Studies (U.K.), Acad. Internat. des Gourmets et des Traditions Gastronomiques (Paris), Am. Sci. Affiliation (nat. philosophy sci. and history sci. commn. 1966-70); mem. ALA, European Acad. Arts, Scis. and Humanities (corr. mem., Paris), Acad. Lit. France (titulary mem.), Lawyers' Christian Fellowship (hon. v.p. 1995—), Nat. Conf. U. Profs., Calif. bar Assn. (human rights commn. 1980-83), Internat. Bar Assn., World Assn. Law Profs., Mid. Temple and Lincoln's Inn (barrister mem.), Am. Soc. Internat. Law, Union Internat. des Avocats, Nat. Assn. Realtors, Tolkien Soc. Am., N.Y. C.S. Lewis Soc., Am. Hist. Assn., Soc. Reformation Rsch., Creation Rsch. Soc., Tyndale Fellowship (Eng.), Stair Soc. (Scotland), Presbyn. Hist. Soc. (North Ireland), Heraldry Soc. (advanced cert.), Soc. Genealogists, Irish Geneaol. Soc., Am. Theol. Libr. Assn., Bibliog. Soc. U. Va., Evang. Theol. Soc., Internat. Wine and Food Soc., Soc. des Amis des Arts (Strasbourg), Chaîne des Rôtisseurs (commandeur), Athenaeum (London), Players' Theatre Club (London), Sherlock Holmes Soc. London, Soc. Sherlock Holmes de France (hon.), Club des Casseroles Lasserre (Paris), Club Prosper Montagné (Paris), Ordre des chevaliers du Saint-Sepulcre Byzantin (commandeur), Freeman of City of London, Freeman and Liveryman of Scriveners' Co., Phi Beta Kappa, Phi Kappa Phi, Beta Phi Mu. Mailing: 2 rue de Rome 67000 Strasbourg France Office: No 9 4 Crane Ct Fleet St London EC4A 2EJ England Home Phone: 33-3-88867370; Office Phone: 33-3-88610882. Office Fax: 33-3-88057294. Personal E-mail: 106612.1066@compuserve.com.

MONTGOMERY, JOSEPH WILLIAM, financial consultant; m. Linda Montgomery; children: Joseph, Madeline. BBA, Coll. William and Mary, Williamsburg, Va., 1974. CFP; cert. portfolio mgr. Account exec. Wheat, First Securities, Inc., Lynchburg, Va., 1975-79, Williamsburg, Va., 1979-81, v.p., investment officer, 1981-82, sr. v.p., investment officer, 1982-90; mng. dir. investments Wachovia Securities, Williamsburg, Va., 1990—, head Optimal Svc. Group. Mem. nat. nominating com. Outstanding Young Am. Program, 1998; bd. dirs. Future Hampton Roads, Inc., 1995—; mem. nat. campaign steering com. Campaign of 4th Century, William & Mary, 1992, United Way Williamsburg, 1993-95; bd. vis., 1995-99; mem. commn. tercentenary observanced Coll. William & Mary, 1992; sec. William & Mary Endowment Assn., 2000-05; mem. nat. campaign steering com. William & Mary, 2001; mem. adv. coun. Peninsula White Sox, 1986; bd. dirs. Nat. Conf. Christians & Jews, peninsula chpt., 1986-91; mem. Williamsburg Cmty. Health Found., 1998; dir., treas. Franklin & Gladys Clark Found.; mem. Greater Williamsburg Cmty. Trust, 1999-; mem. Jamestown Yorktown Found., 1999-, v.p., 2000, sr. v.p., 2001; bd. trustees Hamptons Rds. Acad., 2003-; mem. nat. adv. coun. Colonial Williamsburg, 2006-; mem. adv. com. Va. Retirement System, 2001-05. Named one of Top 300 Fin. Advisors in Country, Worth Mag., 1998, Top 100 Fin. Advisors, Worth Mag., 1999-, Top 10 Ace Advisers, Ticker Mag., 2000, Nation's 100 Most Exclusive Wealth Advisors, 2004, Top Ranked Teams in Am. Rsch. Mag., 2004, 05, Top 100 Brokers Barron's Mag., 2004-, Top 100 Wealth Advisors Worth Mag., 2005; named to Broker Hall of Fame, Rsch. mag., 1996, The Chancellor's Cir., Coll. William and Mary, 1998; recipient Best Brokers in Am. award Reg. Rep. Mag., 2002, Am. Top 50 Brokers award Reg. Rep. Mag., 2003; named State of Va. Top Fin. Advisor Va. Bus. Mag., 2005-06; featured advisor The Winner's Cir. Book, 2002, Winner's Cir. IV Book, 2005. Mem. Internat. Assn. Fin. Planning, Inst. Cert. Fin. Planners, Investment Mgmt. Cons. Found., 1998, Soc. of Alumni William & Mary (pres. 1992, treas. 1991, sec. 1990, bd. dirs. 1989, Alumni Medallion 1996, Wachovia Way award, 2004). Office: Wachovia Securities 275 McLaws Cir Williamsburg VA 23185 Office Phone: 757-220-1782. *

MONTGOMERY, JULIE-APRIL, lawyer; b. Chgo., June 17, 1957; d. Constance Louise Montgomery. BS, U. San Francisco, 1978; MBA, Roosevelt U., 1979; JD, NYU, 1983, LLM in Taxation, 1985. Bar: Ill. 1983, U.S. Dist. Ct. (no. dist.) Ill. 1983, N.Y. 1990, U.S. Supreme Ct. 1995. Legis. advisor Ill. State Senator Charles Chew, Chgo., 1983-84; staff atty. Ill. Indsl. Comm., Chgo., 1984; sole practice Chgo., 1985-86; asst. corp. counsel City of Chgo. Office of Corp. Counsel, 1986—. Co-author Ill. Inst. Cont. Legal Edn. States and Local handbook, 1990; contbr. articles to profl. jours. Instr. Minority Legal Edn. Resources Inc., Chgo., 1983—; vol. March of Dimes Chgo., 1995—; shelter vol. children's program Chgo. Christian Indsl League, 1996—. Mem. ABA, Ill. State Bar Assn. (state local tax sect. 1996—), Ill. Cert. Pub. Accts. Soc. (state and local tax sect. 1995—), Chgo. Bar Assn. (state and local tax sect. 1986—, chmn. com. 1994-95), Phi Alpha Delta, Phi Chi Theta, Alpha Sigma Nu. Lutheran. Avocations: cross-stitching, collecting betty boop, puzzles, movies, history. Office: City of Chgo Corp Counsel 30 N La Salle St Ste 1040 Chicago IL 60602-2503

MONTGOMERY, KATHRYN SUZAINNE, elementary school educator; b. Meridian, Miss., Nov. 23, 1978; d. Manuel Lee and Suzainne Frederick Montgomery. BS in Elem. Edn., Miss. State U., Meridian, 2002, M in Elem. Edn., 2007. Tchr. 5th grade West Lauderdale Mid. Sch., Collinsville, Miss., 2002—. Mem.: Houghton Mifflin Tchr.'s Club. Home: 15330 Hwy 486 Philadelphia MS 39350

MONTGOMERY, KEITH NORRIS, SR., insurance agent, military officer; b. Natchez, Miss., Sept. 22, 1951; s. Charles Norris Jr. and Miriam (Marron) M.; m. Joan Marie Bishop (div.); children: Keith Jr., Mason, Brenton BBA, U. Miss., 1974. Sales rep. Boyle-Midway, Monroe, La., 1975-77, Am. Nat. Ins., Jackson, Miss., 1977-79; owner Exec. Benefits, Clinton, Miss., 1979—; state rep. Miss. Ho. of Reps., Jackson, 1993—2003; asst. inspector gen. US Army, 2005—. City councilman City of Clinton, 1985-93. Master sgt. USNG, 1972— Mem.: Clinton C. of C. Republican. Methodist. Home: 104 Countrywood Cir Clinton MS 39056-5717 Personal E-mail: montykn@yahoo.com.

MONTGOMERY, LANI LYNN, art educator; b. Oceanside, NY, Sept. 24, 1950; d. Warren Andrew and Lucy Marie; m. Bruce Montgomery, Dec. 18, 1976; children: Colin, Kirstin, Kerrin. AA, Suffolk County C.C., NY, 1972; BA, Dowling Coll., Oakdale, NY, 1976; MA, Montclaire State U., NJ, 1997. Tchr. art Bridgewater-Raritan Schs., NJ, Abington Sch. Dist., Pa. Recipient Disting. Tchr. award, Bridgewater-Raritan Schs., 2003, Golden Apple award, 1990, 1993. Fellow: Nat. Art Edn. Assn., NJ Art Edn. Assn.; mem.: NEA, Am. Canoe Assn. (instr. 1999—). Episcopalian. Avocations: kayaking, white-water rafting, cross country skiing, bicycling, hiking.

MONTGOMERY, LARRY (R. LAWRENCE MONTGOMERY), retail executive; b. 1949; BS in Math., Ferris State U., Mich. Pres., CEO Black's divsn. Allied Store Corp., 1985-87; sr. v.p., dir. stores, gen. mdse. mgr. Softlines, L.S. Ayres divsn. May Dept. Stores, 1987-88; sr. v.p., dir. stores Kohl's Corp., Menomonee Falls, Wis., 1988-93, exec. v.p., 1993-96, vice chmn., 1996—2000, CEO, 1999—, chmn., 2002—. Bd. dirs. Kohl's Corp., 1994—. Office: Kohls Corp N56 W17000 Ridgewood Dr Menomonee Falls WI 53051-5660 Office Phone: 262-703-7000. *

MONTGOMERY, LYNN MARIE, educational consultant; b. Faribault, Minn., July 13, 1955; d. Wilford C. and Marian Margaret Campbell; m. Daniel Dale Montgomery, June 12, 1976; children: Kristi Lynn, Ryan Lee. BS, Coll. of St. Benedict, St. Joseph, Minn., 1976; MA, U. St. Thomas, St. Paul, 1994. Elem. tchr. Anoka-Hennepin # 11, Coon Rapids, Minn., 1977-98; exec. dir. Assn. Tchr. Educators, Reston, Va., 1998—2003; tchg. and learning specialist Anoka-Hennepin, Coon Rapids, Minn., 2003—. Greater Minn. facilitator Destination Imagination, 1999-2000, Odyssey of the Mind, 1986-98; chair Adams Environ. Edn. Com., Minn., 1994—. Mem. AAUW, ASCD, Assn. Tchr. Educators (pres. 1998-99, Disting. Clinician 1995, Pres.'s Svc. award 1997), Minn. Assn. Tchr. Educators (bd. dirs. 1990-2000), Anoka-Hennepin Edn. Found. (bd. dirs. 1995-2000). Office: Anoka Hennepin 11 11299 Hanson Blvd Minneapolis MN 55433

MONTGOMERY, MATTHEW L., lawyer; b. 1977; BBA in Mgmt., Tex. A&M U., 2000; JD, Baylor U. Sch. Law, 2003. Bar: Tex. 2003, US Dist. Ct. (no. dist. Tex.) 2003. Assoc. def. atty. Walters, Balido & Crain, Dallas. Named a Rising Star, Tex. Super Lawyers mag., 2006. Mem.: Dallas Assn. Young Lawyers, Dallas Bar Assn. Office: Walters Balido & Crain 900 Jackson St Founders Sq Ste 600 Dallas TX 75202 Office Phone: 214-749-4805. E-mail: matt.montgomery@wbclawfirm.com. *

MONTGOMERY, MICHAEL DAVIS, research and development company executive, real estate investor; b. San Luis Obispo, Calif., June 4, 1936; s. Harold Ray and Elva Dee (Davis) M.; m. Rita Martin, Dec. 28, 1957 (div. Sept. 1975); children: Jeanne, Gwen, Michele. MSEE, Stanford U., 1959; PhD, U. N.Mex., 1967. Group leader Max Planck Inst. for Astrophysics, Munich, 1974-76; group leader advanced concepts Los Alamos (N.Mex.) Nat. Labs., 1976-83; program mgr. for simulation Maxwell Labs. Inc., San Diego, 1983-84, dep. for DNA programs, 1984-85, v.p. rsch. and devel., 1986-91, sr. v.p. applied tech., 1991-92, sr. cons., 1992—97; owner Casa Del Mar Inn, Santa Barbara, Calif., 1991-97; real estate investor Montgomery Investments, LLC, 1997—. Owner and cons. All Santa Fe Reservations Assoc., 1999—2005. Assoc. editor Jour. Geophys. Research; contbr. articles to sci. jours. Served to lt. comdr. USN, 1959-62. Recipient (charter) Sr. Scientist award Alexander Von Humboldt Found., 1972. Mem. AAAS, Am. Phys. Soc., Phi Beta Kappa, Sigma Xi, Tau Beta Pi. Avocations: amateur radio, w5mgt. Home and Office: 872 Muirfield Dr Oceanside CA 92058 Personal E-mail: mikedmont@cox.net.

MONTGOMERY, MIKE, professional basketball coach; b. Long Beach, Calif., Feb. 27, 1947; m. Sarah Montgomery; children: John, Anne. BA in Phys. Edn., Calif. State U., Long Beach, 1968; MS in Phys. Edn., Colo. State U., 1976. Coach U. Fla., The Citadel, Colo. State U., USCG Acad.; asst. coach Boise State U.; head basketball coach U. Mont., Missoula, 1978-86, Stanford U., Calif., 1986—2004, asst. to athletic dir., 2007—; head coach Golden State Warriors, 2004—06. Named Head Coach of Yr. USA Men's 22 and Under Select Team, U.S. Basketball Men's Collegiate Com., 1996, U.S. Basketball Devel. Coach of Yr., 1996, U.S. Olympic Com. Basketball Devel. Coach of Yr., 1996. Office: Stanford U Dept Athletics Arrillaga Family Sports Ctr 641 E Campus Dr Stanford CA 94305-6150

MONTGOMERY, REX, biochemist, educator; b. Halesowen, Eng., Sept. 4, 1923; came to U.S., 1948, naturalized, 1963; s. Fred and Jane (Holloway) M.; m. Barbara Winifred Price, Aug. 9, 1948 (dec.); children: Ian, David, Jennifer, Christopher. BSc, U. Birmingham, Eng., 1943, PhD, 1946, DSc, 1963. Rsch. assoc. U. Minn., 1951-55; mem. faculty U. Iowa, Iowa City, 1955—2005, prof. biochemistry, 1963—2005, assoc. dean U. Iowa Coll. Medicine, 1974-95, v.p. rsch., 1989-90, prof. emeritus, 2005—. Vis. prof. Nat. Australian U., 1969-70; mem. physiol. chemistry study sect. NIH, 1968-72; mem. drug devel. contract rev. com., 1975-87; chmn. com. biol. chemistry NAS, 1961-64; pesticide and fertilizer adv. bd. Iowa Dept. Agr., 1990-91; bd. dirs. Wallace Tech. Transfer Found., 1989-93; chmn. bd. dirs. Neurotron Inc., 1990-95; mem. rsch. com. Iowa Corn Promotion Bd., 1995-2001; rsch. dir. Biotech. Byproducts Consortium, 1989—; cons. in field. Author: Chemical Production of Lactic Acid, 1949, Chemistry of Plant Gums and Mucilages, 1959, Quantitative Problems in Biochemical Sciences, 2d edit., 1976, Biochemistry: A Case-Orientated Approach, 6th edit., 1996; mem. editl. adv. bd. Carbohydrate Rsch., 1968-80; mem. editl. bd. Molecular Biotherapy, 1988-92; contbr. articles to profl. jours. Postdoctoral fellow Ohio State U., 1948-49; fellow Sugar Research Found., Dept. Agr., 1949-51 Fellow: Royal Soc. Chemistry. Home: 701 Oaknoll Dr Iowa City IA 52246-5168 Office: U Iowa Coll Medicine Dept Biochemistry Iowa City IA 52242 Business E-Mail: rex-montgomery@uiowa.edu.

MONTGOMERY, ROBERT MOREL, JR., lawyer; b. Birmingham, Ala., June 9, 1930; s. Robert Morel and Ella Bernice (Smith) M.; m. Mary Lemerle McKenzie, Mar. 6, 1953; 1 child, Courtnay Elizabeth. BS, U. Ala., 1952; LL.B., U. Fla., 1957. Bar: Fla. 1957; diplomate Acad. Fla. Trial Lawyers. With Howell & Kirby Attys at Law, Jacksonville, Fla., 1957-59; ptnr. Howell, Kirby, Montgomery, Sands & D'Aiuto, Jacksonville, Fla., 1959-66, Howell, Kirby, Montgomery, D'Aiuto, Dean & Hallowes, West Palm Beach, Fla., 1966-75, Montgomery, Lytal, Reiter, Denny & Searcy, West Palm Beach, Fla., 1976-85, Montgomery Searcy & Denny, West Palm Beach, Fla., 1986-89; sr. ptnr. Montgomery & Larson, LLP, West Palm Beach, Fla., 2001—05, Robert M. Montgomery Jr. & Assocs. PL, 2006—. Civil trial adv. Nat. Bd. Trial Advocacy; lectr. Princeton U., U. Oxford Law Sch. Chmn. Palm Beach Opera; chmn. emeritus Palm Beach Cultural Coun.; co-chmn. Children's Place at Home Safe, Inc.; trustee Nat. Pub. Radio. 1st lt. AUS, 1952-54. Named Alumnus of Yr. U. Fla. Law Rev., 1983, Philanthropist of Yr. Nat. Assn. Fund Raising Execs., 1990, Honoree for Yr. City of Hope, 1991, Victim Adv. of Yr., Palm Beach County Sheriff's Office, 1997, Child Advocate of the Yr., 1996; recipient Learned Hand award Am. Jewish Com., 1985, Humanitarian award Albert Einstein Coll., 1990, Pub.'s award honor contbg. most to improving quality of life in Broward and Palm Beach counties, 1992, Great Am. Traditions award B'nai B'rith, 1996, Humanitarian award Albert Einstein Coll. Medicine, 1999, Haym Solomon award Anti-Defamation League, 2000, Palm Beach C.C. Leadership award, 2002, Man of Yr. award Lake Worth Cultural Spotlight Com., 2002, Heartland award Lawton Chiles Found., 2003, Fla.'s Children First!, Inc. award, 2003, Dr. Martin Luther King Jr. Disting. award NAACP, 2004, Lifetime Achievement award Urban League, 2005, Disting. Cmty. Svc. award Alexis de Toqueville Soc. Palm Beach United Way, 2006, Muse award Palm Beach County Cultural Coun., 2007. Mem. ABA, Fla. Bar Assn. (lectr. continuing edn.), Palm Beach County Bar Assn., Trial Lawyers Assn. Am., Inner Circle Advs. Home: 1800 S Ocean Blvd Palm Beach FL 33480-5104 Office: PO Box 3086 West Palm Beach FL 33402-3086 Office Phone: 561-832-2880. Business E-Mail: rmm@rmmjr.com.

MONTGOMERY, ROY DELBERT, retired gas industry executive; b. Indpls., Apr. 24, 1926; s. Lloyd Sipes and Nona Mae (Brummett) M.; m. Barbara Ann Reno, Apr. 21, 1946; children: Stephanie, Rebecca, Jeffrey, Laura. Student, Purdue U., 1950-51; M.E., Internat. Corr. Schs., 1953; A.S. in Mgmt. and Adminstrn., Ind. U., 1973. Registered profl. engr. Ind. Engr. Citizens Gas & Coke Utility, Indpls., 1952-59, supt., 1959-60, dir., 1960-73, exec. dir., 1973-78, v.p., 1978-82, sr. v.p., 1982-86, cons., 1986-88. Mem. adv. bd. AdvancedMgmt. Conf., I.U. Grad. Sch. Bus., 1974—78. Contbr. articles to profl. jours. V.p. exploring Crossroads Am. Coun. Boy Scouts Am., Ind., 1978; corp. rep. Jr. Achievement Ind., 1970-82; pres. Fairway Trace at Pendia I, 1994—, Fairway Trace Home Owners Assn., 1995-99. Recipient Bronze Big Horn award Boy Scouts Am. Explorer Div., Ind., 1978 Mem. Am. Gas Assn. (merit award 1966), Ind. Gas Assn., Scientec Club Ind., Kiwanis. Republican. Avocations: painting, golf, genealogy. Personal E-mail: roydmon@comcast.net.

MONTGOMERY, SUSAN BARBIERI, lawyer; b. New Haven, Nov. 11, 1949; BFA, RISD, 1971, MAE, 1978; JD, Northeastern U., 1986. Bar: Mass. 1986, U.S. Dist. Ct. Mass. 1987, U.S. Ct. Appeals (D.C. cir.) 1988. Tchr., dept. chmn. Westport (Mass.) Pub. Schs., 1976-83; freelance artist Westport, 1971—; law clk. to Justice J. Harold Flannery Mass. Superior Ct., Boston, 1986; assoc. Foley Hoag LLP, Boston, 1986-94, ptnr., 1995—. Adj. prof. Suffolk U. Law Sch., 1999—; advisor in field. Co-editor: Worldwide Trademark Transfer, 1992—2006. Trustee Vol. Lawyers for Arts, Boston, 1992—; chmn. bldg. com. Westport Arts Group, Inc.; advisor Am. Law Inst. Mem. ABA (chair elect IPL sect., mem. UCITA working group, past chair bus. baw & IPL sect. joint task force), Mass. Bar Assn. (coms. 1987—), Boston Bar Assn. (coms. 1987—), Internat. Trademark Assn. (chmn. publs. com., dir. 1995-97), Copyright Soc. (com. mem. 1991—), Lex Mundi (chair intellectual property practice group). Office: Foley Hoag LLP Seaport World Trade Center West 155 Seaport Blvd Boston MA 02210-2600 Office Phone: 617-832-1222. Business E-Mail: smontgomery@foleyhoag.com.

MONTGOMERY, THEODORE ASHTON, physician; b. LA, Oct. 27, 1923; s. Wayne A. and Hazel (Osmer) M. MD, U. So. Calif., 1947; MPH cum laude, Harvard U., 1955. Diplomate: Am. Bd. Preventive Medicine, Am. Bd. Pediatrics. Intern Los Angeles County Gen. Hosp., 1946-48; intern L.A. Children's Hosp., 1948, resident, 1950-51, St. Louis Children's Hosp., 1951-52; asst. in pediatrics Washington U., St. Louis, 1951-52; instr. pediatrics U. So. Calif., 1952-55; practice medicine specializing in pediatrics, LA, 1952-54; lectr. pub. health U. Calif., Berkeley, 1960-83. Cons. child health Calif. Dept. Pub. Health, 1954-60, chief maternal and perinatal health, 1960-61, acting chief bur. maternal and child health, 1961-63, asst. chief div. preventive med. services, 1963-66, chief, 1966-68, chief preventive medicine program, 1968-69, dep. dir. of Dept., 1969-73; mem. mental retardation projects rev. com. USPHS, 1965-66, charter mem. surgeon gen.'s adv. com. on immunization practices, 1964-66; mem. task force on alcoholism, drug and narcotic abuse Calif. Commn. on Criminal Justice, 1968-70; chief div. disease control Alameda County Health Care Svcs. Agy., 1973-74; cons. maternal and child health Calif. Dept. Health, Berkeley, 1974-78; chief maternal and child health br. No. Calif. Regional Office, Calif. Dept. Health Svcs., 1978-83; WHO fellow med. care adminstrn., Europe, 1966; co-chmn. Calif. Inter-agy. Council on Tb, 1966-72; vice chmn. Calif. Drug Rsch. Adv. Panel, 1969-70; participant White House Conf. Mental Retardation, 1963, White House Conf. on Mental Retardation Cmty. Ctrs., 1965; Gov's. chmn. Calif. Regional Hemodialysis Rev. Com., 1968-73; exec. sec. Gov.'s Population Study Commn., 1966; mem. com. on Tb, Calif. Lung Assn., 1973-74 Author: (with others) Standards and Recommendations for Public Prenatal Care, 1960, Guide to Hearing Testing of School Children, 1961; contbr. articles to med. jours. Bd. dirs. Calif. Interagy. Coun. on Family Planning, 1970-73; chmn. Calif. State Interdepartmental Com. on Food and Nutrition, 1977-79, pres. Clan Montgomery Soc. Internat., 1981-84, regional commr., 1985-91. With M.C. AUS, 1948-50. Fellow Am. Acad. Pediatrics (chmn. Calif. com. on Indian health 1973-76, mem. nat. com. on Indian health 1963-79, vice chmn. 1977-79), Am. Pub. Health Assn. (chmn. task force on population policy 1971-72); mem. Alpha Epsilon Delta, Delta Omega. Home: 85 Wildwood Gdns Piedmont CA 94611-3831 E-mail: tmontgo458@aol.com.

MONTGOMERY, THOM MATHEW, health program administrator, counselor; b. Delaware, Okla., Dec. 30, 1942; s. Francis Thomas and Ellen Grace (Whelan) M.; m. Dinah Lee Hicks, Feb. 4, 1961 (div. 1964); children, Laura Diane, Raymond Hunter; m. A.N.D. Miller. Degree, Highlands U., 1966; student, Tulsa U., 1961-64, U. Calif., Irvine, 1980-81, Glenn U., Dublin, Ireland, 1993—2002. Brokerage mgr. John Hancock Life Ins. Co., Boston, 1964-70; mng. editor Renown Publs., Reseda, Calif., 1970-77; publs. dir. Am. Pub. Health Found., Corona Del Mar, Calif., 1977-79; program adminstr. Life Plus Martin Luther Hosp., Anaheim, Calif., 1979-92; dir. rsch. Brookside Inst., Irvine, Calif., 2001—. Pres. Montgomery Counseling Assocs., Fullerton, 1986—. Author: Ennobled Blood: The Heiresses of Monkstown Castle, 2002, Naltrexone: Pulling Back the Curtain, 2004; contbr. articles to profl. jours. Founding mem. Task Force on Alcohol & Drug Abuse for Disabled, Orange County, 1981, Sobriety Faire, Orange County, 1982; bd. dirs. Mid Valley Cmty. Police Coun., San Fernando Valley Employee Assistance Programs. Fellow Am. Pub. Health Found.; mem. Nat. Assn. Alcohol and Drug Abuse Counselors, Internat. Assn. Alcohol and Drug Abuse Counselors, Calif. Assn. Alcohol and Drug Abuse Counselors. Republican. Presbyn. Avocations: chess, hiking, swimming, poetry, drama. Home: 35167 El Diamante Dr Wildomar CA 92595 Office: 213 N Pomona Fullerton CA 92832 Office Phone: 310-413-4672.

MONTGOMERY, WILL S., lawyer; b. Dallas, Jan. 8, 1958; BA, Stanford U., 1980, MA, 1981; JD, U. Chgo., 1984. Bar: Tex. 1984. Shareholder Jenkens & Gilchrist, P.C., Dallas, 1992—2007, firm leader litig. practice group; ptnr. Hunton & Williams LLP, Dallas, 2007—. Mem.: ABA, Dallas Bar Assn., Tex. State Bar. Office: Hunton & Williams LLP Ste 3700 1445 Ross Ave Dallas TX 75202 Office Phone: 214-468-3361. Office Fax: 214-468-3599. Business E-Mail: wmontgomery@hunton.com.

MONTGOMERY, WILLIAM ADAM, lawyer; b. Chgo., May 22, 1933; s. John Rogerson and Helen (Fyke) Montgomery; m. Jane Fauver, July 28, 1956 (div. Dec. 1967); children: Elizabeth, William, Virginia; m. Deborah Stephens, July 29, 1972; children: Alex, Katherine. AB, Williams Coll., 1955; LLB, Harvard U., 1958. Bar: D.C. 1958, Ill. 1959, U.S. Ct. Appeals (7th cir.) 1959, U.S. Supreme Ct. 1977. Atty. civil divsn., appellate sect. Dept. Justice, Washington, 1958—60; assoc. Schiff Hardin LLP, Chgo., 1960—68, ptnr., 1968—93, 1999—; v.p., gen. counsel State Farm Ins. Cos., Bloomington, Ill., 1994—97, sr. v.p., gen. counsel, 1997—99. Author: (39 corp. practice series) Tying Arrangements, 1984; co-author: Insurance Antitrust and Unfair Trade Practices Law, 2002; contbr. articles to profl. jours. Fellow: Am. Coll. Trial Lawyers; mem.: ABA (coun. antitrust sect. 1989—92), Seventh Cir. Bar Assn. (pres. 1988—89), Chgo. Bar Assn., Lawyers Club Chgo. Avocations: skiing, woodturning. Office: Schiff Hardin LLP 6600 Sears Tower Chicago IL 60606 Business E-Mail: wmontgomery@schiffhardin.com.

MONTGOMERY, WILLIAM LAYTON, music educator, educator, musician; b. Waco, Tex., Mar. 28, 1934; s. Layton Edmond and Fey Ruth (Fomby) M.; children: Layton Howard, Scott Lewis, Claudia Cathleen. B Mus. Edn., Cornell Coll. Iowa, 1953; postgrad., Curtis Inst. Music, 1953-54; MusM, Cath. U. Am., Washington, 1957, PhD, 1975. Prin. flutist Nat. Gallery of Art Orch., Washington, 1965-88, Theater Chamber Players of Kennedy Ctr., Washington, 1968—2004; prof. music U. Md., College Park, 1964, chair instrumental, wind and percussion divsns., 1972—91, dir. grad. studies, 1991—99, mem. univ. senate exec. com., 2005—07, chair univ. senate core com., 2005—07, chair univ. senate, 2006—07. Bd. advisors Flute Talk Mag., Northbrook, Ill., 1982-95, Instrumentalist Mag., Northbrook, 1978-95; adv. cons. Libr. Congress, Music Div., Washington, 1978, 79, 84; mem. Fulbright selection com. in music, 1995-98. Mem. U.S. Marine Band, 1954-63. Mem. Nat. Flute Assn. (pres. 1976-77), Flute Soc. Washington (pres. 1978-80, 82-84), Arts Club Washington (music chmn. 1990—, prodr. weekly Friday noon concert series 1992—). Home: 4614 Harvard Rd College Park MD 20740-3753 Office: Univ Md Sch Music College Park MD 20742-0001 Business E-Mail: wlm@umd.edu.

MONTGOMERY LINMAN, SINA JO, pediatric nurse practitioner; b. Ida Grove, Iowa, Apr. 2, 1953; d. John Albert Jr. and Grace Ione Montgomery; children: Bradley John Linman, Nissa Marie Linman, Mindi Sue Megan Linman. BSN, U. Iowa, Iowa City, 1975, cert. pediat. nurse practitioner, 1989. Cert. pediat. nurse practitioner, Pediat. Nursing Cert. Bd., 1988. Surg. nurse Mercy Hosp., Iowa City, 1975—78; nurse mgr. outpatient clinic Drs. Luhman, Hesse, Greenwald and Johnson, Iowa City, 1978—80; ICU nurse U. Iowa Hosps. and Clinics, Iowa City, 1980—81; clin. nursing instr. St. Joseph Sch. Nursing, Sioux City, Iowa, 1981—82, Morningside Coll., Sioux City, 1982—83; staff nurse Horn Meml. Hosp., Ida Grove, Iowa, 1983—85; vis. nurse Buena Vista County and Ida County Pub. Health Depts., Storm Lake and Ida Grove, Iowa, 1985—90; pediat. nurse practitioner Iowa State Dept. Health, 1989—90, USAF, Dept. Def., Offutt Air Force Base, Meth. Health Sys., Council Bluffs, Iowa, 1996—. Spkr. in field. Assoc. mem. Josyln Art Mus., Omaha, 1998—, Lauritson Bot. Gardens, Omaha, 2006—; docent Friends of Joslyn Castle, Omaha, 2007—. Maj. USAF, 1989—96. Recipient Preceptor of the Yr. award, USAF Physician's Asst. Students, Offutt AFB, 1990. Fellow: ANA, Nat. Assn. Pediat. Nurses and Practitioners (local treas. 2005—); mem.: Internat. Assn. Forensic Nurses, So. Clin. Neurol. Assn. (assoc.), Flying Physician's Assn., Sigma Theta Tau. Avocations: running, travel, cooking. Office: Meth Physicians Clinic 1 Edmonson Pl Site 310 Council Bluffs IA 51503 Home Phone: 402-291-3905; Office Phone: 712-396-4310. Office Fax: 712-396-4217.

MONTI, PAOLO, research scientist; b. Novara, Italy, May 12, 1973; s. Mario Monti and Ileana Bogogna. Laurea, Politecnico di Torino, Italy, 2001; PhD, U. Tex. Dallas, Richardson, 2005. Rsch. engr. Boston Comm. Networks (BCN), Inc., Dallas, 1999—2000; rsch. asst. U. Tex. Dallas, Richardson, 2001—05, rsch. assoc., 2006—. Contbr. articles to profl. jours. Mem.: IEEE. Home: 4750 Pear Ridge Dr #7310 Dallas TX 75287 Office: U Tex Po Box 830688 - M/S Ec33 Richardson TX 75083 Home Phone: 1 972 931 9432; Office Phone: 1 972 883 4621. Office Fax: 1 972 883 2710. Personal E-mail: paolo.monti@gmail.com. Business E-Mail: paolo.monti@ieee.org.

MONTIE, JEFFREY W., food products executive; b. Cleve., Ohio, July 1, 1961; BA in Bus., Cedarville U., Ohio; MBA, Ohio State U. Brand mgr. Kellogg Co., 1987—95; v.p. global innovation Kellogg Europe, 1995—99; v.p., gen. mgr. ready-to-eat cereal bus. Kellogg USA, 1999—2000, sr. v.p., gen. mgr. ready-to-eat cereal bus., 2000, pres. morning foods div., 2000—02; sr. v.p. Kellogg Co., 2002—03; pres. morning foods div. Kellogg N. Am., 2003; exec. v.p. Kellogg Co., 2003—; pres. Kellogg N. Am., 2004—. Office: Kellogg Co 1 Kellogg Sq Battle Creek MI 49016 *

MONTO, ARNOLD SIMON, epidemiology educator; b. Bklyn., Mar. 22, 1933; s. Jacob and Mildred (Kaplan) M.; m. Ellyne Gay Polsky, June 15, 1958; children: Sarah D. Monto Maniaci, Jane E., Richard L., Stephen A. BA in Zoology, Cornell U., Ithaca, NY, 1954; MD, Cornell U., NYC, 1958. Diplomate Am. Coll. Epidemiology. Intern, asst. resident in medicine Vanderbilt U. Hosp., Nashville, 1958—60; USPHS postdoctoral fellow in infectious disease Stanford U. Med. Ctr., Palo Alto, Calif., 1960—62; mem. staff virus diseases sect. mid. Am. rsch. unit Nat. Inst. Allergy and Infectious Disease, Panama, 1962—65; assoc. prof. U. Mich. Sch. Pub. Health, Ann Arbor, 1965—76, prof., 1976—, chmn. dept. population planning and internat. health, 1993—97, dir. Ctr. for Population Planning, 1993—97, dir. U. Mich. Bioterrorism Preparedness Initiative, 2002—04. Vis. scientist Clin. Rsch. Ctr., Northwick Park Hosp., Harrow, Eng., 1976; scholar-in-residence bd. on sci. and tech. for internat. devel. NAS and Inst. Medicine, Washington, 1983-84; vis. scientist div. communicable diseases WHO, Geneva, 1986-87; mem. pulmonary diseases adv. com. Nat. Heart, Lung and Blood Inst., Bethesda, Md., 1979-83; mem. nat. adv. coun. Nat. Inst. Allergy and Infectious Diseases, Bethesda, 1989-93; mem. WHO Influenza Pandemic Task Force, 2006—. Contbr. articles to med. jours. Recipient career devel. award NIH. Fellow Am. Coll. Epidemiology, Infectious Diseases Soc. Am.; mem. APHA (governing coun. 1978-80), Am. Epidemiol. Soc. (pres. 2004-05). Achievements include research on respiratory viral infections in the community; demonstration of effectiveness of influenza vaccine in severe disease in the elderly; prevention of spread of influenza virus and treatment of illness, occurrence, causes and treatment of common cold. Office: U Mich Sch Pub Health I 109 Observatory St Ann Arbor MI 48109-2029 Office Phone: 734-764-5453. Business E-Mail: asmonto@umich.edu.

MONTONI, RICHARD A., management consultant; BS, Boston U.; MS, Northeastern U. Audit ptnr. KPMG LLP; CFO, exec. v.p. CIBER, Inc., Englewood, Colo., 1996—2000, Managed Storage Internat., Inc., Broomfield, Colo., 2000—01; CFO, treas. MAXIMUS, Inc., Reston, Va., 2002—06, CEO, 2006—. Office: MAXIMUS Inc 11410 Sunset Hills Rd Reston VA 20190-5207 Office Phone: 703-251-8500. Office Fax: 703-251-8240.

MONTOYA, DELILAH MARIE, artist, educator; b. Ft. Worth, Dec. 10, 1955; d. John Louis Merriman and Amalia Maria Garcia; 1 child, Lucianna Trujillo. MFA, U. N.Mex, Albuquerque, 1994. Vis. prof. Hampshire Coll., Amherst, Mass., 1997—99, Calif. State U., LA; Harnish vis. prof. Smith Coll., Northhampton, Mass., 1998—2000; assoc. prof. U. Houston, 2001—. Photo documentary publication, Women Boxers: The New Warriors, fotofest installaton, The Trail of Thirst, video day of the dead installation, San Sebastiana; Angel de la Muerte, photographic digital installation, Guadalupe en Piel, photographic installation, La Guadalupana, collotype prints, El Sagrado Corazon. Mem. Fotofest, Houston, Tex., 2001—07. Mem.: Coll. Arts Assn. (Profl. Devel. fellow 1992—94). Democrat. Roman Catholic. Avocations: cross country skiing, travel. Office: U Houston Dept Art 100 Fine Arts Bldg Houston TX 77204-4019 Home Phone: 505-256-9290; Office Phone: 832-723-3636. Business E-Mail: dmontoy2@mail.uh.edu.

MONTOYA, JUAN PABLO, professional race car driver; b. Bogota, Colombia, Sept. 20, 1975; m. Connie Montoya; 1 child, Sebastian. CART (Championship Auto Racing Teams) driver, 1999—2001; with Team McLaren Mercedes, 2006, Target Chip Ganassi Racing, 2006—. Named Rookie of Yr. in CART (Championship Auto Racing Teams) Racing, 1999; winner: Indy 500, 2000, Monaco Gran Prix, 2003, Telcel Motorola 200, 2007, NASCAR Nextel Cup Toyota/Save Mart 350, 2007; 7 Career Formula One Grand Prix Wins, 29 podium appearances. Office: c/o Target/Chip Ganassi Racing 7777 Woodland Dr Indianapolis IN 46278-1794 *

MONTOYA, MALAQUIAS, art educator, artist; b. Albuquerque, N.Mex., June 21, 1938; BA with hon., Univ. Calif. Berkeley, 1970. Comml. artist, silkscreener, 1962—68; foreman silkscreen dept. Circo Inc., 1963—66; art instr. Laney Coll., Berkeley, 1969—70, Contra Costa Coll., Richmond, Calif., 1971; art workshop dir. Alameda Co. Neighborhood Arts Program, 1974—81; lectr., Chicano Studies Dept. Univ. Calif, Berkeley, 1960—74, full prof., 1990—, now cooperating faculty, 1996—. Spkr. in field. Exhibitions include several galleries and mus. including Whitney Mus. Am. Art, NYC, 2006. Office: PO Box 6 Elmira CA 95625

MONTOYA, REGINA T., association executive, lawyer; b. Tucumcari, N.Mex., Dec. 25, 1953; d Fred and Rosa (Meraz) M.; m. Paul E. Coggins, June 12, 1976; 1 child, Jessica. BA, Wellesley Coll., 1975; JD, Harvard U., 1979. Bar: Tex. 1979. Law clk. to U.S. Dist. Judge Sarah T. Hughes, Dallas, 1979-80; ptnr. Akin, Gump, Strauss, Hauer & Feld, Dallas, 1980-90; shareholder Godwin, Carlton & Maxwell, Dallas, 1990-93; asst. to pres., dir. Office of Intergovernmental Affairs, Washington D.C., 1993; v.p. Westcott Comm., 1994—95; panelist Between the Lines KERA-TV, 1994; public delegate UN Gen. Assembly, 1998; pres. WORKRules, 1995—2005; CEO New Am. Alliance, 2005—. Bd. dirs. Wash. Mut., 2006-. Trustee Wellesley Coll., 1990—; bd. dirs. Dallas Theater Ctr., 2004—, Parkland Found., 2005—. Mem. Student Loan Mktg. Assn. (bd. dirs. 1994-2001). Democrat. Roman Catholic. Office Phone: 202-772-1872. Business E-Mail: rmontoya@naaonline.org.

MONTOYA, RUDY, JR., volunteer; b. Austin, Tex. m. Carol Montoya; 2 children. BS, Texas A&M U., 1989. With Atty. Gen.'s Office, 1988—, head info. tech. divsn., 2006—; mem. Austin Ind. Sch. Dist. Bd. Trustees, Tex., 1996—2006, trustee for dist. 2 Tex., 1999—2006, v.p. Tex. Bd. dirs. Tex. Assn. Sch. Bds., 1998—2005, sec./treas., 2005—; chair Tex. Purchasing Coop. Recipient Austin Under 40 award for Edn. & Austinite of Yr. award, 2006. Office: Austin Ind Sch Dist 1111 W 6th St Austin TX 78703 also: Office of the Atty Gen PO Box 12548 Austin TX 78711-2548

MONTOYA, VELMA, economist, consultant; b. LA, Apr. 9, 1938; d. Jose Gutierrez and Consuelo (Cavazos) Montoya; m. Earl A. Thompson; 1 child, Bret L. Thompson. BA in Diplomacy and World Affairs, Occidental Coll., 1959, MA in Internat. Rels., 1960; MS in Econs., Stanford U., 1965; PhD in Econs., UCLA, 1977. Asst. prof. econs. Calif. State U., LA, 1965-68; vis. assoc. prof. U. So. Calif., 1979; instr. UCLA, 1981-82; staff economist The Rand Corp., Santa Monica, Calif., 1973-82; asst. dir. for strategy, White House Office of Policy Devel. Exec. Office of the Pres., 1982-83; expert economist Office Regulatory Analysis, OSHA, U.S. Dept. of Labor, 1983-85; dir. of Studies in Pub. Policy and Assoc. Prof. of Political Economy, Sch. of Bus. Mgmt. Chapman U., 1985-87; adj. prof. Sch. Bus. Mgmt. Pepperdine U., 1987-88; pres. Hispanic-Am. Pub. Policy Inst., 1984-90; assoc. prof. fin. Sch. Bus. Adminstrn., Calif. State Poly. U., Pomona, 1988-90; mem. Occupl. Safety and Health Rev. Commn., 1990-97; cons. on regulatory and econ. policy, 1997—. Cons. Urban Inst., 1974, Mexican-Am. Study Project UCLA, 1966, Grad. and Profl. Fellowships to the Office of Post Secondary Edn., U.S. Dept. Edn.; editl. referee Contemporary Policy Issues, Economic Inquiry, Policy Analysis, Jour. Econ. Lit.; discussion leader Am. Assembly on Rels. Between the U.S. and Mex.; pres. del. White House Conf. on Aging, 1981; reader of 1988 proposals for the U.S. Dept Edn. for the Improvement and Reform of Schs. and Tchg.; rsch. participant U.S. Dept. Edn. Delphi Assessment of Drug Policies for Use in Minority Neighborhoods, 1989; mem. Hispanic adv. panel Nat. Commn. for Employment Policy, 1981-82; lectr. Brookings Inst. Seminars for U.S. Bus. Leaders; bd. adv. Close-Up Found., 1982-83; discussant Western Econ. Assn. Meetings, 1985, 93; bd. adv. Nat. Rehab. Hosp., 1991-94; nat. exec. adv. bd. Harvard Jour. Hispanic Policy, 1993-95; reader proposals for Hispanic Serving Instns., U.S. Dept. Edn., 2001-2004; regional panel to select White House Fellows, 2002—, hon. coun. U. Calif. Press, 2007-. Mem. census adv. com. on hispanic population for 1990 census, 1988—93; mem. adv. com. Senate Rep. Conf. Task Force on Hispanic Affairs, Washington, 1991—; bd. regents U. Calif., 1994—2005; program rev. com. Los Alamos (N.Mex.) Nat. Lab.; mem. steering com. GetSmarter.org, 1998—99; mem. outreach adv. bd. U. Calif., 1998—2005, mem. coun. friends Bancroft Libr. Berkeley, 2005—; commr. Calif. Postsecondary Edn. Commn., 2000—01, 2004—05; mem. Am. Coun. Trustees and Alumni, Inst. Effective Governance Adv. Bd., 2003—, White Ho. Fellows Regional Selection Panel, 2002—; mem. Calif. state adv. com. US Commn. Civil Rights, 2007—. Named One of the 100 U.S. Hispanic Influentials Hispanic Bus. Mag., 1982, 90, 97, Woman of the Yr. Mex.-Am. Oportunity Found., 1983, The East L.A. Com. Union, 1979, one of 80 Elite Hispanic Women, Hispanic Bus. Mag., 2002, 03; recipient Freedom Found. at Valley Forge Honor Econ. Edn. Excellence Cert., 1986, Profl. Achievement award S.E. L.A. Lincoln Club, 2002, Hispanic Leadership award Minorities in Bus. Mag., 2001; Univ. fellow Stanford U., Internat. Rels. fellow Calif. PTA, John Hay Whitney Opportunity fellow; Calif. State Univ. Found. Faculty Rsch. grantee; Marshall scholar, Fulbright scholar. Mem. ASTM (com. on rsch. and tech. planning 1985-87), Am. Econ. Assn. (session chair ann. meetings 1995), Nat. Coun. Hispanic Women (pres. 1997—), Am. Soc. Hispanic Econimists, State Bar of Calif., Calif. State Bar Ct. (exec. com. 1987-89, disciplinary bd. 1986-89), Western Econ. Assn., Indsl. Rsch. Inst. for Pacific Nations (adv. bd. 1988-89), Salesian Boys and Girls Club (bd. dirs. 1989—), Vets. in Com. Svc. (adv. com. 1989-94), Women's Club Hollywood, Phi Beta Kappa, Omicron Delta Epsilon, Phi Alpha Theta. Home: 6970 Los Tilos Rd Los Angeles CA 90068-3107 Office Phone: 213-427-8048. Personal E-mail: velmamontoya@earthlink.net.

MONTPETIT, JEFFREY M., lawyer; b. St. Paul, 1972; BA, St. John's U., Collegeville, Minn., 1995; JD, William Mitchell Coll. Law, St. Paul, 1998. Bar: Minn. 1999, US Dist. Ct. (dist. Minn.) 1999, US Ct. Appeals (8th cir.) 1999. Atty. Sieben, Grose, Von Holtum & Carey, Ltd., Mpls., 1998—. Named a Rising Star, Minn. Super Lawyers mag., 2006. Mem.: Wis. Bar Assn., Hennepin County Bar Assn., ABA, Fed. Bar Assn., Minn. Trial Lawyers Assn., Assn. Trial Lawyers of Am., Minn. State Bar Assn. Office: Sieben Grose Von Holtum & Carey Ltd 900 Midwest Plz East Bldg 800 Marquette Ave Minneapolis MN 55402 Office Phone: 612-333-9762. E-mail: jeffrey.montpetit@knowyourrights.com. *

MONTRONE, PAUL MICHAEL, former scientific instruments company executive; b. Scranton, Pa., May 8, 1941; s. Angelo H. and Beatrice M. (Giancini) M.; m. Sandra G. Gaudenzi, May 30, 1963; children: Michele Marie Cogan, Angelo Henry, Jerome Lawrence. BS in Accounting magna cum laude, U. Scranton, 1962; PhD in Fin., Econs. and Ops. Research, Columbia U., 1965. Ops. analyst Office Sec. Def., Washington, 1965-67; exec. v.p., chief fin. officer Wheelabrator-Frye Inc., Hampton, NH, 1970-83; exec. v.p. Signal Cos., Inc., La Jolla, Calif., 1983-85, pres. Engineered Products Group Hampton, NH, 1983-85; exec. v.p. fin. and adminstrn. AlliedSignal Inc., Morristown, NJ, 1985-86; pres. The Henley Group Inc., Hampton, NH, 1986-92, bd. dirs.; chmn., CEO Wheelabrator Techs. Inc., Hampton, NH, 1987-90; pres., co-owner The Gen. Chem. Group Inc., 1989-94, chmn. bd., 1994-96; vice chmn. Abex Inc., 1992-95; pres. Fisher Sci. Internat., Inc., Hampton, NH, 1991—98, CEO, 1991—2006, chmn., 1998—2006. Bd. dirs. Waste Mgmt.; mem. adv. bd. Sintokogio, Ltd. Pres. emeritus Met. Opera Assn.; bd. dir. Wang Ctr. for Performing Arts; dir. & treas. Found. for NIH; trustee Healthcare Leadership Council; mem. bd. overseers The Bus. Roundtable, Bus. Sch. Columbia U., N.Y.C.; adv. com. Consumer Protection and Quality in the Health Care Industry, Washington. Capt. U.S. Army, 1965-67. Mem.: Brook, University (N.Y.C.); Bald Peak Colony (Melvin Village, N.H.); Lyford Cay (Nassau, Bahamas). Roman Catholic. *

MONZON, CARLOS MANUEL, physician; s. Carlos Manuel and Amparo (Letona) Monzon; children: Carlos Rodolfo, Juan Pablo. MD, U. San Carlos, Guatemala, 1976; MSc, U. Minn., 1982. Diplomate Am. Bd. Pediat., Am. Bd. Pediat. Hematology and Oncology. Resident in pediat. U. San Carlos, 1976-77, U. Mo., Columbia, 1977-80; fellow in pediat. hematology and oncology Mayo Grad. Sch. Medicine, Rochester, Minn., 1980-82; instr. pediat. U. Mo., Columbia, 1982-83, asst. prof. child health, 1983-89; clin. asst. prof. in pediatrics Kansas U. Sch. Medicine, Kansas City, 1992—. Contbr. articles to med. jours. Recipient Fritz Kenny Meml. award in pediat. rsch. Midwest Soc. Pediat. Rsch., 1981. Fellow Am. Acad. Pediat. Home: 14201 Melrose St Overland Park KS 66221 Office: 20375 W 151st St Olathe KS 66061-7218

MOOD, FRANCIS P., JR., lawyer, utilities executive; BA, The Citadel, 1960, LLD (hon.), 1985; LLB, U. Va., 1963; LLD (hon.), U. SC, 2004. Bar: SC 1963. Ptnr. Haynsworth Sinkler Boyd, Columbia, SC, 1967—2004, pres., 1984—92; sr. v.p., gen. counsel, asst. sec. SCANA Corp., Columbia, SC, 2005—. Permanent mem. Judicial Conf., US Ct. Appeals (4th cir.); interim dean Univ. SC Sch. Law, 2003; chmn. SC Bd. Law Examiners, 1973—82. Mem. bd. vis. The Citadel, 1973—79, 1994—2000, chmn.,

1997—2000; bd. dir. The Citadel Develop. Found., 1980—88, 1990—94, 2001—, pres., 1982—86; mem. Univ. SC Sch. Law Partnership Bd., 1991—94, pres., 1991—93; mem. Ctrl. Carolina Cmty. Found., 1992—98, pres., 1995—97; bd. dir. Liberty Fellowship, 2004—, Columbia Urban League. Served US Army, 1964—66. Mem.: ABA, State Bar SC, Richland County Bar Assn. Office: SCANA Corp 1426 Main St Columbia SC 29218 *

MOOD, GIRISH RUDRA NAIK, physician; b. Bangalore, India, Sept. 30, 1971; s. Rudra Naik and Rukmini Bai; m. Archana Ramanaik, Nov. 17, 2004. MBBS, Bangalore Med. Coll., 1995; MD, CWRU, Cleve., 2005. House physician Wockhardt's Heart Inst., Bangalore, 1996—97, Chase Farm Hosp., Enfield, England, 1999—2000, Queen Mary Hosp., Sidcup, England, 2000—01, Guy's & St. Thomas Hosp., London, 2001—02; resident St. Vincent Charity Hosp., Cleve., 2002—05; assoc. staff Cleve. Clinic, 2005—. Contbr. articles to profl. jours. Nat. Merit scholar, India, 1987—89. Mem.: Med. Coun. India, Am. Bd. Med. Specialtists, Am. Heart Assn., Royal Coll. Surgeons Galsgow. Avocations: white-water rafting, cricket, gourmet cooking. Office: Cleve Clinic 9500 Euchid Ave Cleveland OH 44195

MOODY, DIXON MCGUIRE, radiologist; b. Tyler, Tex., Jan. 12, 1937; s. Dwight Lyman Moody and Helen Blaine McGuire; m. Lucinda L. Blitz, Aug. 15, 1964; children: Abigail Ann (Moody) Sinwell, Susan Eloise (Moody) Prieto, Sarah Katherine (Moody) Bialas. MD, U. of Tex. Southwestern, Dallas, 1963. Diplomate Diagnostic Radiology Am. Bd. of Radiology, 1971, Neuroradiology Am. Bd. of Radiology, 1995. Resident physician Stanford U. Sch of Medicine, Palo Alto, Calif., 1963—70; asst. physician Cornell U. Sch of Medicine, NYC, 1970—71; asst. prof. U. of N.Mex Sch Medicine, Albuquerque, 1971—73; prof. and chief of neuroradiology Wake Forest U. Sch. Medicine, Winston-Salem, NC. Mem. Nat. Adv. Coun. NINDS, NIH, Bethesda, Md., 1994—97, Ctr. for Sci. Rev., NIH, Bethesda, Md., 1998—2004; mem., sci. program com. Radiol. Soc. of N.Am., Oak Brook, Ill. Capt. US Army, 1966—67. Decorated Bronze Star Medal US Army; recipient Established Investigator, Clin. Sci. Award, Wake Forest U. Sch. of Medicine, 2002; grantee Jacob K Javits Neurosci. Investigator, NIH, 1984—2004, Clin. Hypotheses in Neuroscience Imaging Rsch., Charles A Dana Found., 1996-1999. Fellow: Am. Coll. of Radiology; mem.: Am. Soc. of Neuroradiology (Outstanding Contributions in Rsch. award 2005), Soc. for Neurosci., Radiol. Soc. of N.Am. (Outstanding Rschr. award 2005), Forsyth Country Club, Hillsboro Club, Alpha Omega Alpha. Achievements include research in Brain injury during heart surgery due to fat emboli; brain hemorrhage in neonates due to rupture of veins; dementia due to obstruction of veins and loss of capillaries; significant vascular disease in Alzheimer's brains; cause and prevention of brain injury during cardiopulmonary bypass. Avocation: tennis. Office: Wake Forest University School Medicine Medical Center Blvd Winston Salem NC 27157-1088 Office Phone: 336-716-2485. Business E-Mail: dmmoody@wfubmc.edu.

MOODY, GENE BYRON, engineering executive, small business owner, minister; b. Calhoun, Ga., Aug. 29, 1933; s. Denzel Elwood and Mary Edna (Hughes) M.; m. Willie Earline Chauncey, Sept. 1, 1955; children: Byron Eugene, Iva Marie Levy. BSCE, U. Tenn., 1956. Registered profl. engr., Ala., Ark., Ga., La., Miss., Tex. V.p. S.I.P. Engrng. Corp., Baton Rouge, 1968-70; project engr. S.I.P., Inc., Houston, 1970-73; dir. of engrng. Jacus Assoc., Mpls., 1972-73; dir. of civil engrng. Barnard & Burk, Baton Rouge, 1973-79; project mgr. Process Svcs., Baton Rouge, 1979-80, Salmon & Assoc., Baton Rouge, 1980-81; chief engr. Minton & Assoc., Lafayette, La., 1982; mgr. Assoc. Engr. Cons., Baton Rouge, 1982-86; owner Gene B. Moody, P.E., Baton Rouge, 1986—. Author: Deliverance Manual, 1989; contbr. articles to profl. jours. Tchr. Lake Hamilton Bible Camp, Hot Springs, Ark., 1981—. With U.S. Army, 1957. U. Chattanooga scholar, 1951, U. Tenn. scholar, 1953. Fellow ASCE; mem. Am. Soc. Safety Engrs., La. Soc. Profl. Surveyors, Soc. Automotive Engrs., Inst. Transp. Engrs., La. Engrng. Soc., Transp. Res. Rsch. Bd., others. Home and Office: 14930 Jefferson Hwy Baton Rouge LA 70817-5217 Home Phone: 225-755-8870. E-mail: gbmoody@bellsouth.net.

MOODY, JACQUELINE ELAINE, music educator; d. Roberta Anita Foster; m. Christopher Moody, Dec. 29, 1981; children: Dominique Elaine, Crystal Simone. BS, Fisk U., Nashville, 1978; MusM, Boston Conservatory of Music, 1980; EdS, U. of Miami, Coral Gables, Fla., 1992. Tchr. Fla. Dept. of Edn. Music instr. Elaine Sch. of Music, Miami, 1988—; music tchr. Perrine Elem., Miami, 1997—; music prof. Miami Dade Coll., Miami, 2006—. Singer Conn. Opera Co., Hartford, 1982—88, Fla. Grand Opera, Miami, 1989—90. Vol. Sweet Home Missionary Bapt., Perrine, Fla., 2003—06. Named Educator of Note, Young Patronessess of the Opera, 2000, Outstanding Educator, Delta Sigma Theta, 2000; recipient Presdl. scholarship, Fisk U., 1974—75, Minority scholarship, U. of Miami, 1988—89, Champion of the Arts award, Nat. Bus. and Profl. Women, 2005. Mem.: Jack and Jill of Am., Inc (corr.; chaplain, chairperson for children's cluster 2002—), Sigma Alpha Iota (corr.; corr. sec. 1999—2000), Delta Sigma Theta (corr. Outstanding Educator 2000). Democrat. Baptist. Avocations: playing the piano, singing, cooking, travel, sewing. Office: Perrine Elem Sc 8891 SW 168 St Miami FL 33157 Home Phone: 305-258-5337; Office Phone: 305-235-2442.

MOODY, ROBERT ADAMS, neurosurgeon; b. Swampscott, Mass., Oct. 1, 1934; s. George F. and Florence P. M.; m. Claudia; children: Robert Adams, II, Cathy, Paul, Lisa, Sherri. BA, U. Chgo., 1955, BS, 1956, MD, 1960. Intern Royal Victoria Hosp., Montreal, Que., Canada, 1960-61; resident in neurosurgery U. Vt. Affiliated Hosps., 1961-66; fellow Lahey Clinic, Boston, 1963-64; asst. prof. neurol. surgery U. Chgo. Med. Sch., 1966-71; sr. clin. instr., then asst. clin. prof. Tufts U. Med. Sch., 1972-74; prof. neurosurgery Abraham Lincoln Med. Sch., U. Ill., Chgo., 1975-81; chmn. div. neurosurgery Cook County Hosp., Chgo., 1974-81, assoc. chmn. dept. surgery, 1976-81; clin. prof. neurosurgery SUNY-Binghamton, 1983—2005; chmn. neurosurgery Guthrie Clinic, Sayre, Pa., 1981-95; ret., 1995. Contbr. articles med. jours. USPHS fellow, 1957-58 Mem. ACS, Am. Assn. Neurol. Surgeons, Pa. Neurosurg. Soc. (councillor 1986-87, pres.-elect 1988, pres. 1989), Mid-Atlantic Neurosurg. Soc., Ctrl. Neurosurg. Soc. (pres. 1978-79), Alumni Assn. Lahey Clinic Found., Sigma Xi. Office: Guthrie Clinic Guthrie Sq Sayre PA 18840 Business E-Mail: rcmoody@cqservices.com.

MOODY, ROBERT LEE, insurance company executive; b. 1936; Chmn., chief exec. officer Nat. Western Life Ins. Co., Austin, Tex., also bd. dirs.; pres. Am. Nat. Ins. Co., Galveston, Tex., 1995—2000, chmn., CEO, 2000—, also bd. dirs.; also pres. Moody Bankshares, Inc., Galveston, Tex. Pres. Moody Investments, Galveston. Office: Am Nat Ins Co 1 Moody Plz Galveston TX 77550 *

MOODY, RON, actor, writer; b. London, Jan. 8, 1924; s. Bernard and Kate (Ogus) Moodnick. BSc in Econs., U. London, 1953. Appeared in plays: 6 Years Revue, 1959, Candide, 1960, Oliver, as Shylock in Merchant of Venice, 1967, as Polonius in Hamlet, 1972, as Richard in Richard III, 1978, Iago in Othello, 1981, as Harpagon in Moliere's The Miser, Peter Pan, 2000, 05, The Sunshine Boys, 2001, Comedians, 2001, Oliver, 2003, Peter Pan, Malvern, 2005, Scrooge in A Christmas Carol, 2006-07; (films) Oliver, 1967, Twelve Chairs, 1970, Dogpound Shuffle, 1973, Wrong is Right, 1981, Where is Parsifal?, 1983, Ghost in Monte Carlo, 1989, Kid in King Arthur's Court, 1995, The Three Kings, 1999, Paradise Grove, 1999, Chopsticks, 2000, Steps, 2000, Revelation, 2001, Lost Dogs, 2004, Moussaka and Chips, 2005, The Lizard Boy, 2006, The Legion of Fire, 2007; stage musicals: USA tour HMS Pinafore, 1987, Sherlock Holmes, 1989, Streets of Dublin, 1992, Bertie, 1993, Peter Pan, 1995, The Canterville Ghost, 1998; on TV as Inspector Hart in Nobody's Perfect, ABC-TV, 1980, Dial M for Murder, 1981, Keen Eddie, 2003, The Bill, 2003, Holby City, 2005, Celebration of Oliver, 2005; dir. (play) Kafka In Love, 1991; author-composer musical comedies Joey, 1966, Saturnalia, 1970, Move Along Sideways, 1971, The Showman, 1976, Nine Lives, 1991; touring Move Along Sideways, 1991, Monologues, 2003; author: (books) The Devil You Don't, 1980, Very Very Slightly Imperfect, Off the Cuff, 1987, The Amazon Box, 1998. Served with RAF, 1943-48. Recipient Golden Globe award, 1968, Moscow Golden Bear award as best actor, 1970, Coco Trophy award, Clowns Internat., 1999; nominated Oscar, 1968. Mem. Am. Acad. Motion Picture Arts and Scis., Variety Club of Great Brit., Actors Equity, Screen Actors Guild, Clowns Internat. (life pres.), Performing Rights Soc. Writers, Soc. Authors. Home: Ingleside 41 The Green Southgate London N14 6EN England Office: Eric Glass Ltd 25 Ladbroke Crescent Notting Hill London WII IP5 England also: The Barry Freed Co 468 N Camden Dr Ste 201 Beverly Hills CA 90210 Office Phone: 0207 229 9500.

MOODY, WILLARD JAMES, SR., lawyer; b. Franklin, Va., June 16, 1924; s. Willie James and Mary (Bryant) M.; m. Betty Glenn Covert, Aug. 21, 1948; children: Sharon Paige Moody Edwards, Willard J. Jr., Paul Glenn. AB, Old Dominion U., 1946; LLB, U. Richmond, 1952. Bar: Va. 1952. Pres. Moody, Strople Kloeppel & Basilone Inc., Portsmouth, Va., 1952—. Commr. Chancery, Portsmouth, 1960—, Accounts, 1960—. Del. Va. Ho. of Reps., Portsmouth, 1956-68; senator State of Va., 1968-83; chmn. Portsmouth Dems., 1983—. Recipient Friend of Edn. award Portsmouth Edn. Assn., 1981. Mem. ABA, Va. Bar Assn., Portsmouth Bar Assn. (pres. 1960-61, lectr. seminars), Va. Trial Lawyers Assn. (pres. 1968-69), Hampton Roads C. of C. (bd. dirs. 1983-86), Portsmouth C. of C. (bd. dirs. 1960-61), Inner Circle Advs., VFW, Cosmopolitan Club, Moose. Home: 120 River Point Cres Portsmouth VA 23707-1028 Office: Moody Strople Kloeppel & Basilone Inc 500 Crawford St Portsmouth VA 23705 Office Phone: 757-393-4093.

MOOERS, CHRISTOPHER NORTHRUP KENNARD, physical oceanographer, educator; b. Hagerstown, Md., Nov. 11, 1935; s. Frank Burt and Helen (Miner) M.; m. Elizabeth Eva Fauntleroy, June 11, 1960; children: Blaine Hanson MacFee, Randall Walden Lincoln. BS, U.S. Naval Acad., 1957; MS, U. Conn., 1964; PhD, Oreg. State U., 1969. Postdoctoral fellow U. Liverpool, Eng., 1969-70; asst. prof. U. Miami, Fla., 1970-72, assoc. prof., 1972-76, U. Del., Newark, 1976-78, prof., 1978-79; prof., chmn. dept. oceanography Naval Postgrad. Sch., Monterey, Calif., 1979-86; dir. Inst. for Naval Oceanography, Stennis Space Ctr., Miss., 1986-89; sci. advisor to dir. Inst. for Naval Oceanography, 1989; rsch. prof. U. N.H., Durham, 1989-91; prof., chmn. divsn. applied marine physics U. Miami, 1991-93, dir. Ocean Pollution Rsch. Ctr., 1992—2002, dir. Ocean Prediction Exptl. Lab., 1993—. Coord. Coastal Ocean Sci. Program, 1991—; chmn. modeling and analysis steering team Integrated Ocean Observing Sys., 2006—. Editor Jour. Phys. Oceanography, 1991-96; mng. editor Coastal and Estuarine Studies, 1978-99. With USN, 1957-64. NSF fellow, 1964-67; NATO fellow, 1969-70; Sr. Queen Elizabeth fellow, 1980 Mem.: AAAS, Estuarine Res. Fedn., Marine Tech. Soc., Am. Meteorol. Soc. (chmn. sci.and tech. com. meterology and oceanography of Coastal Zone 1996—2002), U. Nat. Oceanog. Lab. Sys./Fleet Improvement Com. (chair 1994—97), U.S. Nat. Com. Internat. Union Geodesy and Geophysics (chmn. 1995—99), Ea. Pacific Oceanic Conf. (chmn. 1979—86), Am. Geophys. Union (pres. ocean sci. sect. 1982—84), The Oceanography Soc. (interim councilor 1987—88), Sigma Xi (U. Miami chpt. pres. 2006—). Achievements include pioneering direct observation of transient coastal ocean currents and fronts plus mesoscale and coastal ocean prediction rsch. Home: 2521 Inagua Ave Coconut Grove FL 33133-3811 Office: U Miami Divsn Applied Marine Physics OPEL/RSMAS 4600 Rickenbacker Causeway Miami FL 33149-1031 Office Phone: 305-421-4088. Business E-Mail: cmooers@rsmas.miami.edu. *My central goal is to understand the ocean as a physical system by combining the interpretation of observations with dynamical theory and numerical models. Special emphasis has been on the dynamics of coastal oceans (continental shelf regions), now the scientific basis for practical mesoscale ocean prediction applied to coastal oceans and semi-enclosed seas and pioneering the development of operational oceanography.*

MOOG, MARY ANN PIMLEY, lawyer; b. Havre, Mont., May 29, 1952; d. Orville Leonard and Della Mae (Cole) Pimley; children: Eric John, Keith Cole, Trygg Orville. BS, Mont. State U., 1975; JD, U. Mont., 1981; LLM, NYU, 1983. Bar: Mont. Law clk. Mont. Supreme Ct., Helena, 1981-82; assoc., ptnr., staff atty. Bosch, Kuhr, Dugdale, Martin & Kaze, Havre, 1984—. Recipient Am. Jurisprudence Book award Lawyers Coop. Publ. Co., 1980-81, Tax award Prentice Hall, Inc., 1981, Northwestern Union Trust Co. award, 1981. Mem. ABA, Mont. Bar Assn., 12th Jud. Bar Assn. (pres. 1987-88), Phi Delta Phi. Democrat. Roman Catholic. Avocations: sports, arts and crafts, photography. Home: 925 Wilson Ave Havre MT 59501-4331 Office: Bosch Kuhr Dugdale Martin & Kaze PO Box 7152 Havre MT 59501-7152 Office Phone: 406-265-6706.

MOOG, MATTHEW, Internet company executive; b. 1970; s. Robert A. and Shirleigh Moog; m. Lucy Morton Herman, Sept. 11, 1994. Grad. cum laude, George Washington U. Bus. devel. exec. Microsoft Corp., 1992—96; v.p. sales CoolSavings, Inc., Chgo., 1996—98, exec. v.p. sales, mktg., 1998—2001, pres., 2001—, COO, 2001, now CEO, 2001—. Named one of 40 Under Forty, Crain's Bus. Chgo., 2005. *

MOOK, SARAH, retired chemist; b. Bklyn., Oct. 29, 1929; d. Wong and Lie Won (Woo) M. BA, Hunter Coll., NYC, 1952; postgrad., Columbia U., NYC, 1954—57, postgrad., 1962—65, U. Hartford, Conn., 1958—59; grad., N.Y.C. Citiznes Police Acad., 2001. Cartographic aide U.S. Geol. Survey Dept. of Interior, Washington, 1952-54; rsch. asst. Mineral Beneficiation Lab. Columbia U., NYC, 1954-57; analytical chemist nuc. divsn. Combustion Engrng., Inc., Windsor, Conn., 1957-59; rsch. scientist Radiations Applications Inc., Long Island City, NY, 1959-62; chemist Marks Polarized Corp., Whitestone, NY, 1962-64; sr. chemist NRA Inc. subs. Nuc. Rsch. Assocs., Inc., New Hyde Park, NY, 1964-75; clin. chemist Coney Island Hosp., Bklyn., 1974-84, cmty. bd., 1978-80; assoc. chemist Bellevue Hosp. Ctr., 1984-89, prin. chemist, 1989-95; ret., 1995. Instr. ESL Homecrest Cmty. Svcs., Inc., Bklyn., 1999—2005, Jay Sr. Ctr., Bklyn., 2006—; patient safety com. Coney Island Hosp., NY, 2007—. Contbr. articles to profl. jours. Mem. adv. com. to state assemblyman State of NY, 1970-72; trustee Park Ave. Christian Ch., 1973-82, sec., 1973-80, vice-chair, 1980-81, chair bd. trustees, 1981-82, pres. Christian Women's Fellowship, 1962-65, elder, 1982—; mem. Neighborhood Adv. Bd. for Cmty. Devel., 1996—, sec., 1996-99, chair 2000-02; mem. Cmty. Bd., 2002-04; mem. cmty. adv. bd. Coney Island Hosp., 2004—. Named Woman of Yr., N.Y.C. Coun., 2004; recipient Margaret M. McCord Woman of Yr. Meml. award, Sheepshead Bay Hist. Soc., 2004, Woman of Yr. Humanitarian award, NY State Senate, 2004, Disting. Leadership in Cmty. award, NYC Office of Comptr. Mem. Am. Assn. Clin. Chemistry (sec. NY Met. sect. 1999—), AAAS, Am. Chem. Soc., NY Acad. Sci., Van Slyke Soc., Citizens Police Acad. Alumni Assn. (publicity com. 2004—). Republican. Home: 2042 E 14th St Brooklyn NY 11229-3314

MOON, BONGKI, computer scientist, educator; b. Kunsan, Republic Of Korea; m. Chungin Moon. BS, Seoul Nat. U., Republic of Korea, 1983; PhD, U. Md., College Park, 1996. Assoc. prof. U. Ariz., Tucson, 1997—. Grantee Career award, NSF, 1999. Mem.: Assn. Computer Machinery (Svc. award 2003). Office: U Ariz 1040 E 4th St Tucson AZ 85721-0077 Office Phone: 520-621-4326. Office Fax: 520-621-4246. Business E-Mail: bkmoon@cs.arizona.edu.

MOON, CRAIG A., publishing executive; b. Jamestown, NY; m. Patricia Moon; children: Kelly, Jeffrey, Taylor. Student, St. Petersburg Coll., U. South Fla. Mgmt. positions in adv. and circulation Tampa Tribune, Phila. Inquirer, Yakima Herald-Republic, Wash.; advt. dir. Modesto Bee, Calif.; v.p. advt. The Cin. Post, 1985—88, The Cin. Enquirer, 1985—88; pres. & pub. The News-Press, Ft. Myers, Fla., 1988—89, Ark. Gazette, Little Rock, 1989—91; pres. The Tennessean, Nashville, 1991—2002, pub., 1992—2002; pres. Piedmont Newspaper Group Gannett Co., Inc., 1999—2002, exec. v.p. Newspaper Divsn. McLean, Va., 2002—03, pres. & pub., USA Today, 2003—. Office: USA Today 7950 Jones Branch Dr Mc Lean VA 22108 *

MOON, DEOK HYUN, research scientist, educator; arrived in U.S., 1991; s. Dae Ju Moon and Chun Ja Go; m. Mun Jung Kang, Aug. 4, 1968. BE in Environ. Engrng., Chosun U., 1991; ME in Environ. Engrng., Stevens Inst. Tech., 1994; PhD, Stevens Inst. Tech., 2003. Postdoctoral rsch. assoc. Stevens Inst. Tech., Hoboken, 2003—06, rsch. asst. prof., 2006—. Office: Stevens Inst Tech Ctr for Environ Sys Castle Point on Hudson Hoboken NJ 07030 Home Phone: 201-321-7691; Office Phone: 201-216-8097. Office Fax: 201-216-8212. E-mail: dmoon@stevens.edu.

MOON, HOJIN, mathematical statistician, educator; m. Elizabeth K. Hyunju; children: Mark (Ki Sung), Christopher K. PhD, SUNY, Stony Brook, 1999. Instr. U. Tex., M. D. Anderson Cancer Ctr., Houston, 1999—2003; math. statistician Nat. Ctr. for Toxicological Rsch., U.S. FDA, Jefferson, Ark., 2003—07; assoc. prof. Calif. State U.- Long Beach, 2007—. Scientist Instl. Animal Care and Use Com., Nat. Ctr. for Toxicological Rsch., US FDA, Jefferson, Ark., 2004—07. Contbr. articles to profl. jours., chapters to books. Recipient Academic Excellence award, Han Yang U., 1987, Disting. Student Paper award, Internat. Biometric Soc., Ea. NAm. Region, 1999, award, US FDA, 2004, Outstanding Svc. award, 2004, 2006. Mem.: Soc. for Risk Analysis, Am. Statis. Assn. (Ctrl. Ark. chpt. rep. 2004—), FDA Statis. Assn. (ctr. rep. 2005—), Am. Assn. for Cancer Rsch., Internat. Biometric Soc. Presbyterian. Achievements include research in attribution of tumor lethality for occult tumors in the absence of cause-of-death information; development of improved survival-adjusted tests for animal carcinogenicity/tumorigenicity data; estimation of lag time between onset of and death from an occult tumor via attribution of tumor lethality; dose-response modeling for microbial risk assessment; optimal tree-based ensemble methods for class prediction and classification by ensembles from radom partitions; high-dimensional biomarkers in personalized medicine. Office: Calif State U- Long Beach 1250 Bellflower Blvd Long Beach CA 90840 Business E-Mail: hmoon623@yahoo.com.

MOON, IL-JU, marine biologist, educator; b. Busan, Busansi, Republic Of Korea, May 20, 1968; s. Hong-Rae Moon and In-Sik Kim; m. Hyunjoo Lee; 1 child, Hannah. PhD, Seoul Nat. U., Korea, 2000. Postdoctoral rsch. scientist U. RI, Narragansett, 2000—03, marine rsch. assoc., 2003—05. Contbr. articles to profl. jours. Grantee Rsch. grant, NSF, 2004—07, Ctr. Atmospheric Sci. & Earthquake Rsch., 2006—07. Mem.: Korean Meteorol. Soc. (jour. editor 2006—), Korean Oceanogrphy Soc. (life). Achievements include development of coupled hurricane-wave-ocean model; new momentum flux parameterization under strong wind speeds.

MOON, JAMES RUSSELL, retired technology education educator; b. St. Cloud, Minn., Apr. 12, 1950; s. Glenn Howard and Audrey Katherine (Berg) M.; m. Corrine Mae St. Aubin, July 14, 1978; children: Sheri Ann, Brian Michael. BS, St. Cloud State U., 1972; MS, Bemidji State U., 1975. Tech. edn. tchr. Minnetonka Pub. Schs., Minn., 1972—2005, dist. dept. chmn. tech. edn., 1993-95; ret., 2006. Voc. standards com. Minn. Dept. Edn., 1995; mem. State Planning Com., 1989-2005. Designer/engr.: Row Crop Tractor, 1975; contbr. articles to profl. jours. Recipient Anchor award Minn. Pub. Schs., 1991, Tchr. Excellence award Internat. Tech. Edn. Assn., 1994, Disting. Tech. Educator Citation, 2002, Minnetonka Co-curricular Advisor of Yr., 2001, Tchr. of Yr. Optimist Club of Glen Lake, 2005; named Disting. Tech. Educator, Internat. Tech. Edn. Assn., 2002. Mem. Minn. Valley Tech. Edn. Assn. (sec. 1974), Minn. Tech. Edn. Assn. (mem. supermileage state competition com. 1989-2005, Tech. Edn. Tchr. of Yr. 1993, Disting. Svc. award 1991, 92, 94, Joyce Gustafson Meml. award, 2003). Presbyterian. Avocations: auto restoration, outdoor activities. Home: 2037 20th St SE Buffalo MN 55313-4813 Home Phone: 763-682-3679.

MOON, JOHN ELLIS VAN COURTLAND, retired historian; b. Geneva, Oct. 25, 1929; arrived in US, 1940; s. Carlyle van Courtland and Marie Edmée (Choisy) Moon; m. Palma Roberge (div.); children: John Albert van Courtland, Margaret Hames, Laurelle Conte; m. Joan Mary Farrell, July 24, 1971. AB in History and Lit., Harvard U., 1952, PhD in Am. Civilization, 1968; MA in English and Comparative Lit., Columbia U., 1953. Instr. English Merrimack Coll., North Andover, Mass., 1953—55, Boston U., 1957—58; from instr. to prof. history Boston State Coll., 1958—82; prof. Fitchburg State Coll., Mass., 1982—93, prof. emeritus, 1993—. Chmn. com. Coun. Pres., Mass. State Coll. Sys., 1990; vis. prof. Kings Coll., U. London, 1994—95; presenter in field. Author: Confines of Concept: American Strategy in World War II, 1988; co-editor: Biological and Toxin Weapons: Research, Development and Use from the Middle Ages to 1945, 1999; contbr. articles to profl. jours. Grantee, John Kittredge Fund, 1994, John D. and Catherine MacArthur Found., 1994. Mem.: Mass. State Coll. Assn. (pres., Boston State Coll. chpt. 1980—82), Am. Assn. Univ. Profs. (pres., Boston State Coll. chpt. 1970—72, pres. Mass. state conf. 1982—84, William S. Tacey award 1998). Avocations: mountain climbing, book collecting, trekking, travel. Home and Office: 11 Monmouth Ct Brookline MA 02446 Office Phone: 617-739-5475. Personal E-mail: jevcm@comcast.net.

MOON, JOHN HENRY, SR., banker; b. Van Buren, Ark., Aug. 19, 1937; s. B.R. and Alma (Witte) M.; m. Agnes Rose Dickens, Aug. 16, 1958; children: John Henry, Randall Allen. AA, Delmar Coll., Corpus Christi, Tex., 1956; BBA cum laude, Tex. A&M U., Kingsville, 1958. Sr. acct. Tex. Eastern Transp. Co. and subs., 1958-63; exec. v.p., dir. Houston Rsch. Inst., 1963-68; sr. v.p., asst. to chmn. bd., dir. Main Bank, 1968—69; vice chmn. bd., dir. N.E. Bank, 1969; CEO, chmn. bd., dir. Pasadena Nat. Bank, Tex., 1970-81; gen. ptnr. Moon and Assocs., Ltd., 1977—. Chmn. bd., pres. Interservice Life Ins. Corp., Phoenix, Cmty. Bank, Houston, 1975-81, Interstate Bank, Houston, 1977-81, Moon Credit Corp., Pasadena, 1975—, Peoples Bank, Houston, 1983-93; chmn. bd. Cmty. Nat. Bank, Friendswood, Tex., 1981-93, Peoples Nat. Bank, Pasadena, Tex., 1984-93; chmn., pres. Sam Houston Pky. Transp. Corp., 1991-93; bd. dirs. Quality Wire Rope Corp., chmn., 1999-2005; pres. Sure Found. Inc., 1987—. Past bd. dirs. Pasadena Heart Assn., Salvation Army, Tex. Assn. Prevention of Blindness; past chmn. City of Pasadena Bd. Devel.; past chmn. adv. bd. Pasadena Civic Ctr.; past dir. S.E. Econ. Devel., Inc.; bd. dirs. San Jacinto Coll. Found., 2000-03, chmn., 2002-03. Named Outstanding Young Man of Yr., Pasadena Jr. C. of C., 1973; named to Pasadena Hall of Fame, 1988. Mem. AICPA, Pasadena C. of C. (bd. dirs. S.E. Econ. Devel., "C" Club, Citizen of Yr. 1994), Tex. Soc. CPAs, Tex. Bankers Assn., Rotary (pres. Pasadena Rotary found. 2001—). Home: 310 Del Monte Dr Friendswood TX 77546 Office: PO Box 3487 Pasadena TX 77501 Office Phone: 713-943-7777. Business E-Mail: jhmoon@mooncapitalcorp.com.

MOON, KATHLEEN K., language arts educator; m. Gary F. Moon. BA in Elem. Edn. with honors, Georgian Ct. Coll., Lakewood, NJ, 1971. Cert. reading recovery Rutgers U., New Brunswick, 2002. Tchr. grade 3 John Adams Elem. Sch., North Brunswick, 1973—74; tchr. grade 1 Parsons Elem. Sch., North Brunswick, 1971—73, 1974—2001, tchr. reading recovery, 2001—02, tchr. lang. arts academic support, 2002—. Chair TV-Turn-Off Week, NBTEA scholarship com. Parsons Elem. Sch. Mem. Literacy Vols. Am., 1991—; vol. Elijah's Promise Soup Kitchen, New Brunswick; usher Ch. of the Assumption, New Egypt, NJ, 2005—, St. Thomas Acquinas Ch., Beach Haven, NJ, 2007—. Recipient and honored, Gov.'s Tchr. Recognition Program, 2003. Mem.: NEA, NJEA, NBTEA, North Brunswick Twp. Ednl. Assn., Middlesex County Ednl. Assn., N.J. Reading Assn., Middlesex Reading Assn., NTEA, NEA, Georgian Ct. U. Alumni Assn., Delta Tau Kappa, Phi Delta Phi. Avocations: reading, walking, boating, cross stitch, kayaking. Office: Parsons Elem Sch 899 Hollywood St North Brunswick NJ 08902

MOON, KIMBERLE IRENE, voice educator; b. Dayton, Ohio, Feb. 3, 1952; d. Cratty Andrew and E. Janell Moon; m. Robert Bruce McKee, May 8, 1981; children: Marcus Allen, Maison Andrew. MusB, Ohio U., 1974, MusM, 1976, D of Music, 1984. French tchr. Miamisburg H.S., Ohio, 1977—78; german tchr. Dayton Stebbins H.S., Dayton, 1978—79; theater dir. Chipola Jr. Coll., Marianna, Fla., 1980—81, voice instr., 1986—; singing voice specialist Tallahasse Profl. Voice Clinic, 1997—; voice prof. Bapt. Coll. Fla., Graceville, 1998—. Pres., treas. Tallahassee Cmty. Chorus, 1993—98. Trustee Tallahassee CC, 2005—, vice chair dist. bd. trustees, 2006—07. Named Tchr. of Yr., vice chair dist. bd. trustees Tallahassee CC, 2006—07. Mem.: Voice and Speech Trainers Assn., Nat. Assn. Teachers of Singing, Phi Kappa Phi. Office: Bapt Coll Fla 5400 Coll Dr Graceville FL 32440 Office Phone: 850-263-3261 ext 468.

MOON, LORETTA MARIE, recreational therapist; b. Spokane, Wash., Jan. 22, 1952; d. George Edmond and Eva Louise Moon; m. William Roy Rose, 1976 (div. 1989); children: Charlie Ann Rose, Julie Lynn Rose, Jennifer Rene Rose, Nicolle Louise Rose. AS, AA, Big Bend C.C., Moses Lake, Wash., 1974; BA in Recreation Adminstrn., Ea. Wash. U., Cheney, 1976. Cert. recreation therapist Nat. Coun. Therapeutic Recreation, 1989. Lifeguard Spokane County Parks Dept., Wash., 1971—76; recreation leader 2 Interlake Sch. Severe and Profound, Medical Lake, 1989—92; instr. adult swimming class YWCA, Spokane, 1990—92, coord. adaptive aquatic, 1992—94; recreation therapist geriatric unit Ea. State Hosp., Medical Lake, 1992—94; recreation therapist, aquatic therapy specialist Ea. State Hosp./ Wash. State Therapy Pool, 1994—; lifeguard, instr. water safety YWCA, 2002—05; nurse asst. Carol's Adult Family Home, Nine Mile Falls, 2004—06. Mem., pres. Med. Lake Mid. Sch., 2001—02; leader, outdoor chmn. Inland North West Campfire, Spokane, 1983—91; tchr. LDS Ch., 1980—. Mem.: US Water Fitness Assn. (Top 100 Aquatic Dirs. US 1997—2006, Top Aquatic Therapy Ctr. US 2003—06), Am. Assn. Phys. Activity (master tchr. 2000—), Am. Therapeutic Recreation Assn. Mem. Lds Ch. Avocations: swimming, embroidery, crocheting, gardening. Home: 5732 N D St Spokane WA 99205 Home Phone: 509-328-8527; Office Phone: 509-299-4283. Personal E-mail: recreationrose@aol.com.

MOON, MARC R., cardiac surgeon; MD, Wayne State U., Detroit, 1988. Cert. in gen. surgery/thoracic surgery Bd. Surgery/Bd. Thoracic Surgery, 1996. Prof. surgery Wash. U., Saint Louis, Mo., 1998—2006. Editl. bd. Jour. Thoracic and Cardiovascular Surgery. Office: Washington Univ Sch Medicine 3108 Queeny Tower Saint Louis MO 63110-1013 Office Phone: 314-362-0993. Office Fax: 314-362-0328.

MOON, MARILYN LEE, economist; b. El Dorado, Kans., July 7, 1947; d. Jesse Morris and Shirley Lois M.; m. Douglas Gomery, Jan. 13, 1973. BA in Econs., Colo. Coll., 1969; MS in Econs., U. Wis., 1972, PhD in Econs., 1974. Rsch. assoc. Inst. for Rsch. on Poverty U. Wis., Madison, 1973-74; asst. prof. econs. U. Wis., Milw., 1974-80, assoc. prof. econs., 1980-81; sr. analyst human resources and cmty. devel. divsn. The Congl. Budget Office, Washington, 1981-83; sr. rsch. assoc. Health Policy Ctr. The Urban Inst., Washington, 1983-86; dir. pub. policy inst. AARP, 1986-89; sr. rsch. assoc. The Urban Inst., 1989-94, sr. fellow, 1994—2003; v.p. Am. Insts. for Rsch., 2003—, dir. health program. Cons. The Pepper Commn., 1989. Author: The Meaurement of Economic Welfare: Its Application to the Aged, 1977, Medicare Now and in the Future, 1993, 2d edit., 1996, Medicare: A Policy Primer, 2006; co-author: Balancing Access, Cost and Politics: The American Context for Health System Reform, 1991, Entitlements and the Elderly: Protecting Promises, Recognizing Realities, 1995; editor: Economic Transfers in the United States, vol. 49, 1984; co-editor: Improving Measures of Economic Well-Being, 1977; columnist The Washington Post, 1993-00; contbr. articles to profl. jours. Pub. trustee social security and Medicare trust funds, 1995-00. Ford Found. fellow, 1971-73. Mem. Nat. Acad. Social Ins. (bd. dirs. 1993-00, pres. 2005-), Medicare Rights Ctr. (bd. dirs. 1998, pres. 2005-), Inst. Medicine, Phi Beta Kappa. Avocations: photography, hiking, reading. Office: Am Insts for Rsch 10720 Columbia Pike Silver Spring MD 20901 Home Phone: 301-951-4385; Office Phone: 301-592-2101. E-mail: mmoon@air.org.

MOON, NORMAN K., judge; BA, U. Va., 1959, JD, 1962, LLM, 1988. Bar: (Va.) 1962. With firm Edmunds & Williams (formerly Williams, Robertson & Sackett), Lynchburg, Va., 1962—74; judge 24th Jud. Cir., 1974—84, chief judge, 1982—85; judge Ct. of Appeals of Va., 1985—93, chief judge, 1993—97; judge U.S. Dist. Ct. (we. dist.) Va., 1997—. Vis. lectr. U. Va. Law Sch., Charlottesville, 1975—88. Office: PO Box 657 Lynchburg VA 24505-0657

MOON, RONALD T.Y., state supreme court chief justice; b. Sept. 4, 1940; m. Stella H. Moon. B in Psychology and Sociology, Coe Coll., 1962, LLD (hon.), 2001; LLB, U. Iowa, 1965; LLD (hon.), Inha U., Incheon, Korea, 2003. Bailiff, law clk. to Chief Judge Martin Pence U.S. Dist. Ct., 1965-66; dep. prosecutor City and County of Honolulu, 1966-68; assoc. Libkuman, Ventura, Ayabe, Chong & Nishimoto (predecessor firm Libkuman, Ventura, Moon & Ayabe), Honolulu, 1968-72, ptnr., 1972-82; judge 9th div. 1st cir., Cir. Ct., State of Hawaii, Honolulu, 1982-90; assoc. justice Hawaii Supreme Ct., Honolulu, 1990-93, chief justice, 1993—. Bd. dirs. Nat. Consortium on Racial and Ethnic Fairness in Ctr., 2004—; adj. prof. law U. Hawaii, 1986—88; lectr., guest spkr. numerous events. Recipient Disting. Svc. award, Nat. Ctr. for State Cts., 2003, Grand Prize award, Kyungmin Mission Schs., Korea, 2003. Mem. ATLA, ABA (Pursuit of Justice award tort, trial and ins. practice sect. 2006), Hawaii Bar Assn. (Golden Gavel award 2001), Am. Bd. Trial Advocates (pres. 1986-93, nat. sec. 89-91), Am. Inns of Cts. IV (bencher 1983—, bd. trustees 2004—), Am. Judicature Soc., Hawaii Trial Judges' Assn., Conf. Chief Justices (bd. dirs.). Office: Supreme Ct Hawaii 417 S King St Honolulu HI 96813-2902 Office Phone: 808-539-4700. Business E-Mail: ronald.t.moon@courts.state.hi.us.

MOON, WARREN, professional football player; b. Los Angeles, Nov. 8, 1956; Graduated, Univ. Wash. Quarterback houston oilers, 1984—93, Minn. Vikings, 1994—96, Seattle Seahawks, 1997—98, Kansas City Chiefs, 1999—2000. Named to NFL Pro Bowl, 1988—95, 1997, NFL Pro Football Hall of Fame, 2006. Office: c/o Pro Football Hall of Fame 2121 George Halas Dr NW Canton OH 44708

MOONEY, BETH, bank executive; BA, U. Tex.; MBA, So. Meth. U. Sec. First Republic Bank, Dallas, bank mgr., 1980, Citicorp; head banking group AmSouth Bank, Tenn., No. La., 2000—04, sr. exec. v.p., CFO Birmingham, 2004—06; vice chairwoman KeyCorp, 2006—. Bd. dir. United Way Met. Nashville, 2001—, Vanderbilt Univ. Med. Ctr. Named one of 25 Most Powerful Women in Banking, US Banker, 2005, Top 10 CFOs in Banking, 2006, 25 Women to Watch, 2006. Office: KeyCorp 127 Public Sq Cleveland OH 44114 Office Phone: 615-748-2214. Office Fax: 205-326-4072. *

MOONEY, HAROLD ALFRED, plant ecologist; b. Santa Rosa, Calif., June 1, 1932; s. Harold Walter and Sylvia Anita Stefany; m. Sherry Lynn Gulmon, Aug. 15, 1974; children— Adria, Alyssa, Arica. AB, U. Calif., Santa Barbara, 1957; MA, Duke U., 1958, PhD, 1960. Assoc. prof. UCLA, 1960—68, Stanford U., Calif., 1968—75, prof. biology, 1975—, Paul S. Achilles prof. environ. biology, 1976—, sr. fellow, Inst. Internat. Studies, 2000—03. Author: Mediterranean-type Ecosystems, 1973, Convergent Evolution in Chile and California, 1977, Components of Productivity of Mediterranean Climate Regions, 1981, Disturbance in Ecosystems, 1983, Physiological of Plants in the Wet Tropics, 1984, Physiological Ecology of North American Plant Communities, 1985, Ecology of Biological Invasions of North America and Hawaii, 1986, Biological Invasions, A Global Perspective, 1989, Biodiversity and Ecosystem Function, 1993, Seasonally Dry Tropical Forests, 1995, CO2 and Terrestrial Ecosystems, 1995, Functional Roles of Biodiversity, 1996, Principles of Terrestrial Ecology, 2002. Served with AUS, 1953-55. Recipient Humboldt award, 1989, Max Planck Forsgungs Preis award Alexander von Humboldt Soc., 1992, Inst. Ecology prize, 1990, Nev. Medal of Sci. award, 2000, Blue Planet prize, 2002; Guggenheim fellow, 1974, Nat. Acad. Scis. fellow, 1982. Fellow AAAS, Am. Acad. Arts and Scis., Am. Philos. Soc.; mem. Ecol. Soc. Am. (pres. 1988-89, Mercer award 1961, Eminent Ecologist 1996), Brit. Ecol. Soc. (hon. mem.), Am. Inst. Biol. Scis. (pres. 1994), Internat. Coun. Sci. Unions (sec. gen. 1996-2002), Botanical Soc. Am. (Merit award, 1983). Office: Dept Biol Scis Stanford Univ Stanford CA 94305-1926 Office Phone: 650-723-1179.

MOONEY, JAMES DAVID, JR., aerial photographer; b. Anderson, Ind., May 20, 1921; s. James David and Jane (Watson) M.; m. Christine Mott, Dec. 29, 1944 (div. 1957); children: Barbara, James II, Richard; m. Gloria van Bomel Schoninger, Dec. 8, 1972. Student, U.S. Naval Acad., 1940-43; naval aviator, USN Flight Sch., 1943; BS in Engring., Princeton U., 1947. Cert. protection profl. Am. Soc. for Indsl. Security; lic. comml. pilot FAA. Supply mgr. Willys-Overland Motors, Inc., Maywood, Calif., 1947-50; contr. F.L. Jacobs Co. Inc., Detroit, 1953-55; spl. rep. U.S. Steel Export Co., Washington, 1956-61; mgr. internat. ops. Armour Rsch. Found., Chgo., 1962-65; v.p. CDC Sys., Elizabeth, N.J., 1972-74; pres. Cash Control Corp., Mineola, N.Y., 1974-77; cons. J.D. Mooney Assoc., Oyster Bay, N.Y., 1978-98; pres. Aerial Photos by JDM, Inc., 1998—. Author: Long Range Planning, 1967. Police commr. Village of Centre Island, Oyster Bay, 1979-83, mayor, 1983-89. Lt. USN, 1940-45, 51-53. Mem.: N.Y. State Conf. Mayors, Internat. Assn. Chiefs of Police, Aircraft Owners and Pilots Assn., Seawanhaka Corinthian Yacht Club, Piping Rock Club. Roman Catholic. Avocations: tennis, sailing. Home: 527 Centre Island Rd Oyster Bay NY 11771-5015

MOONEY, JAMES F., telecommunications industry executive; With IBM Corp., 1980—99; COO Baan Co.; CEO, COO Tradeout Inc.; exec. v.p., COO Nextel Comms.; non-exec. chmn. Virgin Media Inc., NYC, 2003—. Bd. dir. NTL Europe. Office: NTL Europe Inc 22 Suffolk St London SW1Y 4HG England also: Virgin Media Inc Ste 2863 909 3rd Ave New York NY 10022 *

MOONEY, JOHN BRADFORD, JR., oceanographer, engineer, consultant; b. Portsmouth, NH, Mar. 26, 1931; s. John Bradford and Margaret Theodora (Akers) M.; m. Martha Ann Huntley, Dec. 25, 1953 (dec. May 1990); children: Melinda Jean, Pamela Ann, Jennifer Joan; m. Jennie Marie Duca, Nov. 24, 1990. BS, U.S. Naval Acad., 1953; postgrad., George Washington U., 1970, 71, 76; grad. sr. execs. nat./internat. security, Harvard U., 1980. Commd. ens. USN, 1953, advanced through grades to rear adm., 1979; chief staff officer Submarine Devel. Group 1, 1971-73; commdr. Bathyscaphe Trieste II, 1964-66, Submarine Menhaden, 1966-68; comdg. officer Naval Sta., Charleston, SC, 1973-75; dep. dir. Deep Submergence Systems Div., Office Chief Naval Ops., Washington, 1975-77; comdr. Naval Tng. Ctr., Orlando, Fla., 1977-78; dir. Total Force Planning Div., Office Chief Naval Ops., Washington, 1978-81; oceanographer USN, 1981-83, chief naval rsch., 1983-87, ret., 1987; pres. Harbor Br. Oceanographic Instn., Inc., Ft. Pierce, Fla., 1989-92, marine bd., 1991-94. Mem. marine programs adv. coun. Grad. Sch. Oceanography, U. R.I., Narragansett, 1989—; chmn. study panel on undersea vehicles and nat. needs NRC, 1993—96, mem. adv. com. for postdoctoral and sr. rsch. associateship programs, 1995—2001; mem. panel to visit the former Soviet Union to evaluate undersea tech. for U.S. govt., 1993; chair, 95. At controls of Trieste II when hull of Thresher was found on floor of Atlantic, 1964; coordinated deep search and recovery of hydrogen bomb lost off coast of Spain, 1966; condr. recovery operation from depth of 16,400 feet in Mid-Pacific, 1972. Decorated Legion of Merit with 1 gold star; recipient spl. citation Armed Forces Recreation Assn., 1975, Dist. Eagle Scout award, 1986. Fellow Marine Tech. Soc. (pres. 1991-93), Explorers Club; mem. NAE, Am. Soc. Naval Engrs., Soc. Naval Architects and Marine Engrs., U.S. Naval Inst., Nat. Geog. Soc., Smithsonian Assocs., Masons, Shriners, Order of DeMolay (Legion of Honor), Tau Beta Pi. Avocations: swimming, grandchildren. Home and Office: 2313 Windswept Dr Austin TX 78738 Office Phone: 512-263-2799. Personal E-mail: jbradmooney@prodigy.net.

MOONEY, JOHN JOSEPH, chemical engineer; b. Paterson, NJ, Apr. 6, 1930; s. Denis and Mary Ellen (Hegarty) M.; m. Claire Josephine Ververs, Dec. 19, 1954; children: John, Mary Beth, Noreen, Susan, Kathleen, Elizabeth. BS in Chemistry, Seton Hall U., 1955; MS in Chem. Engring., Newark Coll. Engring., 1960; MBA in Mktg., Fairleigh Dickenson U., 1991. Project engr. Engelhard Corp., East Newark, 1960-64, chief process engr. Newark, 1965-70, sect. head auto rsch., 1970-72, mgr., 1972-74, tech. dir. Menlo Park, NJ, 1974-81, new ventures mgr., 1981-84, mgr. tech. svc., 1984-90, mgr. technology and new applications Iselin, NJ, 1991—2003; pres., founder Environ. and Energy Tech. Policy Inst., 2002—. Pres. Mfrs. of Emissions Controls Assn. (MECA), 1999—2002. Contbr. articles to profl. jours. With U.S. Army, 1954-56. Recipient Nat. Medal Tech., US Dept. Commerce, 2002. Fellow Soc. Automotive Engrs. Democrat. Roman Catholic. Achievements include patents in combustion and automobile emission catalysts, polyfunctional catalysts and methods of use which describe the catalysts introduced on the 1977 Volvo and now are used on all U.S. passenger cars and light trucks.

MOONEY, JUSTIN DAVID, motel executive, consultant; b. Kansas City, Mo., Feb. 21, 1932; s. J.L. and Phoebe (Lighton) M.; m. Alayne I. Kohn, June 15, 1958; children: Jo Ann, David Alan. BBA, U. Mich., 1954, MBA, 1957. Cert. hotel administr. Mich. State U., 1982, advacned hotel administr. Am. Hotel and Lodging Sch., Fla., 1991. Mgr. Woolf Bros., Kansas City, 1958-66, asst. to pres., 1967-70; pres. Mission Inn Motel, Inc., Overland Park, Kans., 1970-90, J & A Ventures, Inc., Leawood, Kans., 1990—. Bd. dirs. Nat. Fedn. of Ind. Bus., 1989-95, vice chmn. State of Kans., 1994-95. Mem. C. of C., Greater Kans. City, 1965-71, life mem. 1968-70, chmn. membership dept., 1970-71; chmn. Hwy. 56 Bus. Dist., 1984-87, bd. dir., 1984-90; bd. dir. hospitality divsn. Johnson County C.C., 1982-2005, chmn. bd., 1986-2005; bd. dir. Overland Park Conv. and Visitors Bur., 1983-90, v.p., 1987-90; bd. dir. Temple B'nai Jehudah, 1972-83, 86-93, hon. bd. dir. 1995-, pres. Men's Club, 1972-74; bd. dir. 1965-90, pres. Catalina Bay, 1990-95, bd. dir. 1987-95, Heart Am. Jewish Hist. Soc., 1991-93, treas., 1991-93; bd. dir., exec. com., pres. Spindrifter, 1990-95; bd. mem. Pavilions Property, 2000-06, treas 2005-06; exec. bd., treas. Nat. Coun. Jewish Women, 2003-07. With Army Intelligence US Army, 1954—56. Recipient Lifetime award Jewish Chautauqua, 1979, Hannah G. Solomon award Nat. Coun. Jewish Women, 2003; named to Men's Club Hall of Fame, 1978. Mem. Am. Hotel and Motel Assn. (bd. dirs. 1983-88, small properties adv. com., 1985-88, chmn. small properties adv. com., 1988-89, exec. com. 1987-89, vice-chmn. small properties adv. coun. 1985-88, chmn. 1988-89), Kansas City C. of C. (Hall of Fame Man of Yr. 1971), Kans. Hotel Motel Assn. (bd. dirs. 1972-84, pres. 1982-84, Hotel Man of Yr. 1981, 82), Greater Kans. City Hotel/Lodging Assn. (bd. dirs. 1973—, pres. 1982-84, chair 1985, Life Time Achievement award 1998), Greater Kansas City Hotel and Lodging Found. (bd. dir. 2000—), Kans. Lodging Assn. (bd. dir. 1983-1990, Hotel Man of Yr. 1981, 82, 83, 84, chmn. bd. 1985-86), Kansas City Athletic Club (treas. 1971-72, bd. dirs. 1969-72), Temple Sisterhood (life). Avocations: antiques, sports. Home and Office: J&A Ventures Inc 14701 Delmar Leawood KS 66224-9545

MOONEY, KENNETH FRANK, design educator; b. Peterboro, NH, Feb. 7, 1961; s. Frank Ernest and Anita Catherine Mooney. BFA, Ctrl. Conn. State U., New Britain, 1986; MFA, U. Tex., Austin, 1989. Asst. prof. Mass. Coll. of Liberal Arts, North Adams, 1997—2003, Cen. Conn. State U., New Britain, 2003—. Dir. of prodn. Oldcastle Theatre Co., Bennington, Vt., 1989—2004. Costume design, La Ronde (nat. finalist Am. Coll. Theatre Festival, 1986), Revenge of the Space Pandas (nat. finalist Am. Coll. Theatre Festival, 1988); artist, theatrical designer (Broadway): Wicked-The Musical (Tony award for costume design, 2004); How To Succeed in Business, Night of the Iguana, The Red Shoes. Recipient study grant for scene painting technique, Cen. Conn. State U., 2005. Avocations: tennis, travel. Office: Cen Conn State U 1615 Stanley St New Britain CT 06050 Home Phone: 860-384-9576; Office Phone: 860-832-3154. E-mail: mooneyk@ccsu.edu.

MOONEY, KRISTA MICHELE, academic administrator; b. Tallahassee, Fla., Jan. 4, 1973; d. Dennis Robert and Mary Ann Mooney. Student, Auburn U., 1990—91; AA, Tallahassee CC, 1990, AA, 1992; BA in Psychology, Fla. State U., 1995, JD, 1998, PhD in Higher Edn., 2005; Cert. of Completion law program, Oxford U., Eng., 1996. Head coach all-star squad Fla. Cheer Gyms, Inc., Tallahassee, 1993—94; instr. Nat. Cheerleaders Assn., Tallahassee, 1993—95; Fla. Supreme Ct. cert. legal intern Leon County Attorney's Office, Tallahassee, 1997; dir. alumni devel. Fla. State U. Coll. Law, Tallahassee, 1998—99; rsch. asst., academic and student affairs, bd. regents State U. Sys. Fla., Tallahassee, 1999—2000, sr. ednl. policy analyst, academic student affairs, bd. govs., 2003—06, assoc. dir. bd. gov., 2006—; cons. MGT Am., Inc., Tallahassee, 2000—02; sr. ct. analyst Office of State Courts Adminstr., Supreme Ct. Fla., Tallahassee, 2002—03. Participant and grad. Opportunity Tallahassee, 2005—05; vol. Guardian ad Litem, Tallahassee, 1995—99, Ronald McDonald Ho., Tallahassee, 1992—2002, Habitat for Humanity, Tallahassee, 1992—98, Meals on Wheels, Tallahassee, 1992—2002, Children's Miracle Network, Tallahassee, 1992—95; sec. Tallahassee 25, 2004—05, internat. v.p., 2005—06, tutoring/mentoring chmn., 2003—04, pres., 2006—; vol. fundraiser and booster Seminole Boosters, Tallahassee, 1992—2006. Named one of Top Twenty-Five Instr., Nat. Cheerleaders Assn., 1993—94; recipient Follow the Leader Leader Vol. of the Yr., Tallahassee 25, 2004, Disting. Pro Bono Svc. award, Fla. State U. Coll. Law, 1998; scholar, Auburn U., 1990—94. Mem.: ASTD, So. Assn. Coll. Student Affairs, Nat. Assn. Student Pers. Adminstrs., Nat. Assn. Grad.-Profl. Students, Hardee Ctr. Women in Higher Edn., Edn. Law Assn., Am. Ednl. Rsch. Assn., Fla. State U. Alumni Assn. (life), U. Ctr. Club, Capital Tiger Bay Club, Fla. State U. Varsity Club (life), Seminole Torchbearers (life), Alpha Delta Pi Alumni Assn., Phi Alpha Delta. Home: 2958 Foxcroft Dr Tallahassee FL 32309 Office: Florida Bd Govs 325 West Gaines Street Suite 1601-A Tallahassee FL 32399-0400 Home Phone: 850-878-7181; Office Phone: 850-245-9700. Personal E-mail: fsujdphd@aol.com.

MOONEY, LORI, county official; b. Atlantic City, Aug. 22, 1929; d. Joseph Aloysius and Alice Marie Inemer; m. Charles H. Calvi (div.); children: Joseph P., Stephen C., Christina L.; m. Thomas Christopher Mooney; children: Thomas C., Timothy C. Svc. rep. Bell Telephone Co., Atlantic City, 1950-58; sr. evaluator U.S. Census Bur., NJ, 1960-63; coord. Nat. Sml. Bus. Com. for Johnson and Humphrey, Washington, 1964; owner, mgr. Lori Mooney & Co., Realtors, Atlantic County, NJ, 1965-77; commr. Atlantic County Bd. Elections, 1970—, also chmn., 5 yrs; county clk. County of Atlantic, Mays Landing, 1978-96. Mem. Active Corps Execs., Nat. SBA; chmn. county clk. liaison com. N.J. Supreme Ct., 1984-86. Del. Dem. Nat. Conv., 1972, 76, 84, 88, 96; mem. congl. liaison com. Acad. for State and Local Govts., 1989—; mem. U.S. Senator Bill Bradley's Citizen Adv. Com. Del. Dem. Nat. Conv., 1976, 84, 88, 92, 96, 2000. Recipient Woman of Achievement award N.J. Fedn. Bus. and Profl. Women, 1985, Role Model award The Sun Newspaper, 1989; inducted into Atlantic County Women's Hall of Fame, 2000, Holy Spirit H.S. Inaugural Hall of Fame, 2000. Mem. Internat. Assn. Clks., Recorders, Election Ofcls. and Treas. (N.J. dir. 1988—), Atlantic County Realtors Assn., Bus. and Profl. Women Atlantic County (scholarship chmn. 1982-85), County Officers Assn. N.J. (bd. dirs. 1978-96, pres. 1991-92, 92-93), N.J. Assn. County Clks. (chmn. 1984-86), N.J. Assn. Realtors, Nat. Assn. Realtors, Nat. Assn. Counties, N.J. League Municipalities, Assn. Records Mgrs. and Administrs., Atlantic City Women's C. of C. Home: 100 Carol Rd Linwood NJ 08221-2502 Office: Atlantic County Clks Office Main St Mays Landing NJ 08330-1702

MOONEY, MARILYN, lawyer; b. Pitts., July 29, 1952; d. James Russell and Mary Elizabeth (Cartwright) M. BA summa cum laude, U. Pa., 1973, JD, 1976. Bar: Mass. 1977, D.C. 1985, Pa. 1990, U.S. Dist. Ct. D.C. 1985, U.S. Ct. Appeals (D.C. cir.) 1985, U.S. Supreme Ct. 1986. Atty. E. I. du Pont de Nemours & Co., Wilmington, Del., 1976-84, Washington, 1985; assoc. Fulbright & Jaworski L.L.P., Washington, 1985—89, ptnr., 1990—, ptnr. in charge corp. and securities practice Washington Office, 2005—. Contbr. articles to profl. jours. Mem.: ABA (fed. regulation securities com.), D.C. Bar (corp. fin. and securties law and internat. sections), Internat. Bar Assn. (issues and trading in securities com.), Am. Soc. Corp. Secs. (securities law com.). Office: Fulbright & Jaworski LLP 801 Pennsylvania Ave NW Washington DC 20004-2615 Home Phone: 202-468-7070; Office Phone: 202-662-4678. E-mail: mmooney@fulbright.com.

MOONEY, MATTHEW THOMAS, engineering executive; b. Columbus, Ohio, Feb. 23, 1976; s. Richard Paul and Joung Mooney; m. Mi-Jung Kim Mooney, July 7, 2001. B in Mech. Engring., U. Minn., Mpls., 1999, MBA, 2005. Registered profl. engr., Minn., Ill., Mich., Wis. Mech. engr. Wold Archs. & Engrs., St. Paul, 1999—2005, COO, 2006—. Mem.: ASHRAE, Am. Soc. Plumbing Engrs. Office: Wold Archs & Engrs 305 St Peter St Saint Paul MN 55102

MOONEY, MICHAEL EDWARD, lawyer; b. Beloit, Wis., Jan. 21, 1945; s. William C. and Edith (Slothower) M. BA in Econs., St. Norbert Coll., 1966; JD, Boston Coll., 1969. Bar: Mass. 1969, Maine 1969, US Tax Ct. 1975, US Ct. Internat. Trade 1986. Assoc. Nutter, McClennen & Fish, LLP, Boston, 1969—77, sr. ptnr., 1978—, now mng. ptnr. V.p., exec. dir. Fed. Tax Inst. New Eng.; spkr., lectr. numerous seminars. Co-editor: Considerations in Buying or Selling a Business, 1985; mem. bd. editors Accounting and Financial Planning for Law Firms, 1988—. Co-chmn. Metro One Divsn. United Way, 2003—06; chmn. Artery Bus. Com.; bd. dirs. Filene Found., Music Lives, Jobs for Mass. Fellow Am. Coll. Tax Counsel; mem. Boston Bar Assn. (chmn. tax highlights com. 1986-95, fin. com. 1990-92, founder, chmn. summer jobs program, co-chair Diversity Task Force 2007),

Boston Tax Forum. Office: Nutter McClennen & Fish World Trade Ctr West 155 Seaport Blvd Boston MA 02210-2604 Office Phone: 617-439-2000. Personal E-mail: mmooney@nutter.com.

MOONEY, MICHAEL JOSEPH, university professor; b. Evansville, Ind., Dec. 15, 1942; s. Joseph Thomas and Marie Louise (DeJean) Mooney; children: Susanne, Julia. AB summa cum laude, St. Meinrad Coll., 1964; STL magna cum laude, Univ. Innsbruck, Austria, 1968; M in Philosophy, Columbia U., NYC, 1973, PhD, 1982; DHL (hon.), Kyoto U. Fgn. Studies, 1991, Waseda U., Japan, 1999. Lectr. dept. religious studies, St. Mary's U., Halifax, Nova Scotia, Canada, 1968-70; project coord. Columbia U., NYC, 1973-74, preceptor dept. religion, 1975-76, spl. asst. to exec. v.p. for acad. affairs, 1976-77, asst. provost, 1977-79, assoc. provost, 1979-82, dep. provost, 1982-89; pres. Lewis and Clark Coll., Portland, Oreg., 1989—2003; prof. Waseda U., Tokyo, 2003—. Bd. dirs. Reid Hall, Inc., NYC and Paris, 1977—89, v.p., 1983—89; trustee Jour. Philosophy, 1982—; bd. dirs. Roothbert Fund, 1980—92; visitor Inst. for Advanced Study, Princeton, NJ, 1984; trustee Oreg. Ballet Theater, 1992—2004; mem. Portland Opera Assn., 1992—93; bd. dirs. Nat. Assn. Ind. Colls. and Univs., 1995—99, mem. exec. com., 1997—99, sec., 1998—99; mem. commn. on internat. edn. Am. Coun. Edn., 1993—95, mem. com. women in higher edn., 1997; mem. Truman Scholarship Finalists Selection Com., 2001—04; bd. adv. Music Performance Trust Fund, 2002—04. Author: Vico in the Tradition of Rhetoric, 1985 (Gottschalk prize Am. Soc. 18th Century Studies 1985); editor: Renaissance Thought and Its Sources, 1979; co-editor: Toward a Theology of Christian Faith: Readings in Theology, 1968, Vico and Contemporary Thought, 1976, Small Comforts for Hard Times: Humanists on Public Policy, 1977. Trustee Scuola d'Italia, NYC, 1986—89, World Affairs Coun., Oreg., 1992—2001, pres., 1999—2000. Recipient Rome prize Am. Acad. in Rome, 1989, Internat. Citizen award Oreg. Consular Corps., 2002; Roothbert Fund fellow, 1972, Kent fellow Danforth Found., 1972, Woodrow Wilson fellow, 1972, Presdl. fellow Columbia U., 1972, F.J.E. Woodbridge Disting. fellow Columbia U., 1973; NEH grantee, 1984; Cavaliere Ufficiale, Order Merit, Republic of Italy, 1991. Fellow Italian Acad. for Advanced Studies in Am. (sr.); mem. Phi Beta Kappa (hon.).

MOONEY, RICHARD EMERSON, writer; b. Plainfield, NJ, Mar. 31, 1927; s. Wandell M. and Alice (Joy) M.; m. Elizabeth B. Coleman, Oct. 30, 1954; children: James C., Stephen E., John B. BA, Yale U., 1947; postgrad. (Nieman fellow), Harvard U., 1955-56. Writer United Press, NYC, 1948-51, econ. reporter Washington, 1951-56, N.Y. Times, Washington, 1957-63, European econ. correspondent Paris, 1963-67, econ. reporter NYC, 1967, asst. to exec. editor, 1968, asst. to mng. editor, 1969, dep. fgn. editor, 1970-72, asst. fin. editor, 1972-76, mem. editl. bd., 1982-95; contbg. editor, 1995-96; v.p. Hartford Courant, 1976-81, exec. editor, 1976-81, dir., 1977-81. Author: (with Edwin L. Dale, Jr.) Inflation and Recession, 1959. Trustee Hartford Courant Found., 1977-81. Served with USNR, 1944-48. Mem. Soc. Silurians (bd. govs. 1998-2004), Yale Club, The Coffee House, Century Assn., Cosmopolitan Club. Home and Office: 130 E 67th St New York NY 10021-6136 Personal E-mail: remooney@aol.com.

MOONEY, TED (EDWARD COMSTOCK MOONEY), editor, art critic, writer; b. Dallas, Tex., Oct. 19, 1951; s. Booth and Elizabeth (Comstock) M. Student, Columbia U., 1969-71; BA, Bennington Coll., 1973. Mng. editor Fiction mag., NYC, 1975-77; sr. editor Art in Am. mag., NYC, 1977—. Author: (novels) Easy Travel to Other Planets, 1981 (Sue Kaufman prize for 1st fiction AAAL 1981), Traffic and Laughter, 1990, Singing Into the Piano, 1997, The Same River Twice, 2007; contbr. short stories in Esquire, Am. Rev., Granta, articles to L.A. Times, Vogue, Harper's Bazaar, Artforum; lectr. in field. Fellow Creative Artists Pub. Svc. Award, 1977, Ingram Merrill Found., 1978, 80, Guggenheim fellow, 1983. Fellow N.Y. Inst. for Humanities; mem PEN Am. Center. Democrat. Episcopalian. Office: Art in Am 575 Broadway New York NY 10012-3230 Office Phone: 212-941-2800. Office Fax: 212-941-8885.

MOONEY, THOMAS ROBERT, lawyer; b. Montclair, NJ, June 16, 1933; s. Thomas Edward and Ruth Evelyn (Meurling) M.; m. Mary Frances Davis, Aug. 23, 1958; children: Terrance Kevin, Rebecca Lee Poyner, Thomas Edward. BA in Econs., Fla. So. Coll., Lakeland, 1956; LLB, JD, Stetson U., St. Petersburg, Fla., 1961. BAr: Fla. 1961, Ga. 1962, U.S. Dist. Ct. (mid. dist.) 1964, U.S. Supreme Ct. 1965. Claims adjuster State Farm Mut. Ins. Co., Atlanta, 1961-63; atty. Maguire, Voorhis & Wells, P.A., Orlando, Fla., 1963-64, Meyers & Mooney, P.A., Orlando, 1964-94, Meyers, Mooney Stanley & Hollingsworth, Orlando, 1994—. Chair Workers Compensation Edtl. Conf., Fla., 1980-81. Chmn. bd. dirs. Epilepsy Assn. Ctrl. Fla., Orlando, 1964-67; bd. dirs. Children's Home Soc., Orlando, 1970-75, chmn., 1970-72. 1st lt. U.S. Army, 1956-58, Korea. Mem. ATLA, ABA, Fla. Bar Assn., Ga. Bar Assn., Acad. Fla. Trial Lawyers (chair workers compensation sect. 1985), Fla. Workers Advocates (bd. dirs. 1992—). Democrat. Methodist. Avocations: skiing, golf, travel, hiking, rafting.

MOONEY, THOMAS T., history educator, geography educator; b. Albany, NY, Sept. 12, 1954; s. Donald J. and Marguerite A. Mooney; m. Deborah Schneider, 1988; 1 child, Leilah; m. Virginia Rhodes (div.); 1 child, Ruairi Rhodes. BA, Antioch Coll., 1973. Cert. comprehensive social studies tchg. cert. Ohio, 1973. Tchr. Cin. Pub. Schs., 1974—79; pres. Cin. Fedn. Tchrs., 1979—2000; v.p. Am. Fedn. Tchrs., Washington, 1992—; pres. Ohio Fedn. Tchrs., Columbus, 2000—. Bd. dirs. Albert Shanker Inst., Washington, 1998—, Holmes Partnership, Waco, 1996—2000, Nat. Bd. Profl. Tchg., Arlington, 2000—. Mem. Cincinnatus Assn., Cin., Gay, Lesbian, Straight Educators Network, Washington. Democrat. Avocations: travel, music, Irish, Latin Am. and Caribbean history.

MOONEY, TIMOTHY, playwright, actor, theater director; b. Elgin, Ill., Nov. 4, 1959; s. James Arthur and Shirley Louise Mooney; 1 child, Isaac Arthur. BA, So. Ill. U., 1981; MFA, U. Nebr., 1985. Editor, founder The Script Rev., Arlington Heights, Ill., 1989—94; artistic/exec. dir. Stage Two, Waukegan, Ill., 1993—98; author, adaptor Moliere for the People, Prospect Heights, Ill., 1998—; author, actor, dir. Timothy Mooney Repertory Theatre, Prospect Heights, 2004—. Guest dir. U. Wis., Whitewater, 2001—, The Beck Ctr., 2005. Author: Tartuffe, The Imaginary Invalid and Thirteen Other Plays, 2005; author: (actor, dir.) (plays) Moliere Than Thou (Best Adapted Work award San Francisco Fringe Festival, 2004), Criteria (Artistic Picks Finalist, Seattle Fringe Festival, 2003), Karaoke Knights, a One-Man Rock Opera. Mem.: AFTRA. Office: Timothy Mooney Repertory Theatre PO Box 638 Prospect Heights IL 60070 Home Phone: 847-757-3648; Office Phone: 847-757-3648. E-mail: tim_mooney@earthlink.net.

MOONEY, WILLIAM PIATT, actor; b. Bernie, Mo., May 2, 1936; s. Lowell E. and Louise S. M.; m. Valorie Shaw Goodall, Jan. 13, 1962; children: Sean Goodall, William Norvell. Student Am. theater wing, U. Colo., Boulder, Doctorate (hon.). Pres. William Mooney Assocs., cons. to industry for exec. presentations. Appeared in continuing role of Paul Martin on TV series All My Children, 1972-85 (2 Emmy nominations); one-man show Half Horse, Half Alligator, 1964, Damn Everything But the Circus, 1980, They All Wanted in the Act (The Lindbergh Kidnapping and Trial), 2004, Tonight! Buffalo Bill!, 2006; stage appearances: Brownsville Raid, We, A Man for All Seasons, 1965,Lolita, 1981; films: The Next Man, Network, A Flash of Green, Beer, Second Sight, C.A.T. Squad; author/star mus. play Banjo Reb and the Blue Ghost; co-author: ASAP-The Fastest Way to Create a Memorable Speech, 1992, Ready-to-Tell Tales, 1994, A Storyteller's Guide, 1995, Spiders in the Hairdo, 1999, (Grammy nominee 1998), (PBS) With a Dog's Eyes, 1997; recording artist: Why the Dog Chases the Cat, 1997 (ALA Notable Parent's Choice Gold and Naird awards), Spiders In The Hairdo, 1997, More Ready-To-Tell Tales From Around The World, 2000, The Exploding Toilet, 2004. Dir. jazz mus. Jam, 8 yrs. Colo. Univ. Opera Theater, others. Nominee Grammy award, 1995, 1998; recipient Regents' Disting. Svc. award, U. Colo., Boulder, 2007. Address: 2879 Shadow Creek Dr #105 Boulder CO 80303 E-mail: bmooney303@aol.com.

MOONEYHAM, BOBBY R., educational association administrator; D, U. Okla., 1975. Tchr., Yukon, Okla.; dir. Beaver County Cooperative Guidance Prog., Okla.; supt. Corn Pub. Schs., Okla., Okemah Pub. Schs., Okla.; exec. dir. Okla. State Sch. Bds. Assn., 1975—2000, Nat. Rural Edn. Assn., 2002—; adj. instr. dept. edn. leadership and policy studies U. Okla., Norman. Creator Okla. Edn. Coalition, 1998. Named a Friend of Edn., Okla. Edn. Assn., 2004; named to Okla. Educators Hall of Fame, 2000. Office: U Okla 112 Fourth St Box 2 Norman OK 73019 Office Phone: 405-325-7959. E-mail: bmooneyham@ou.edu. *

MOONVES, LESLIE, broadcast executive; b. NYC, Oct. 6, 1949; s. Herman and Josephine (Schleifer) Moonves; m. Nancy Wiesenfeld, Dec. 17, 1978 (div.); children: Adam, Sara, Michael; m. Julie Chen, Dec. 23, 2004. BA, Bucknell U., Lewisburg, Pa., 1971. Devel. exec. Catalina Prodns., Burbank, Calif., 1980—81; v.p. devel. Saul Ilson Prodns. Columbia Pictures TV, Burbank, 1981—82; v.p. movies and mini-series 20th Century Fox, LA, 1982—85, Lorimar, Inc., Culver City, Calif., 1985—88; exec. v.p. creative affairs Lorimar-Telepictures, Culver City, 1988—90; pres. Lorimar TV, Burbank, 1989—93, Warner Bros. TV, Burbank, 1993—95, CBS Entertainment, LA, 1995—97; exec. v.p. CBS/Broadcast Group, 1995—97; pres., CEO CBS TV, 1998—2003, chmn., CEO, 2003—04; co-pres., co-COO Viacom Inc., NYC, 2004—06; pres., CEO CBS Corp., 2006—. Bd. dirs. KB Home, 2004—. Developer, prodr. (TV series) Dallas, Dark Justice, Guns of Paradise, Knots Landing, Midnight Caller, Sisters, Family Matters, Full House, Perfect Strangers, Family Man, I'll Fly Away, Reasonable Doubts, Step by Step, Hangin' with Mr. Cooper, The Jackie Thomas Show, Crossroads, Homefront, Going to Extremes, Shaky Ground, It Had To Be You, Time Trax, Against the Grain, Lois & Clark: The Adventures of Superman, Cafe Americain, How'd They Do That, Living Single, Family Album, Getting By. Bd. dirs. LA Free Clinic; co-chair LA bd. govs. Mus. TV and Radio; bd. trustees Entertainment Industries Coun.; trustee Nat. Coun. for Families and TV, Am. Film Inst.; mem. adv. bd. NCAA. Named Showman of Yr., Variety, Most Powerful Man in Hollywood, Entertainment Weekly; recipient Gold Medal award, Internat. Radio and TV Soc., 2003, Career Achievement award, Casting Soc. Am., Sherrill Corwin award, Am. Jewish Com. Mem.: NATAS (exec. com.), Hollywood Radio & TV Soc. (bd. dirs. 1988—91, pres. 1991). Democrat. Jewish. Office: CBS Corp 51 W 52nd St New York NY 10019-6188 Office Phone: 212-975-4321. *

MOONWALKER, TU, minister, counselor, artist; b. Feb. 9, 1948; BA, Calif. State U., Sacramento, 1972; BS, U. Calif., Davis, 1973; MA, Tex. Tech. U., 1978, MS, 1979; postgrad., So. Meth. U., 1979. Chef Fairmont Hotel, San Francisco, 1971—72; rsch. and biopsy technician Tex. Tech. U. and Med. Ctr., Lubbock, 1974—78; Native Am. artist Santa Fe, 1979—87; cons. Am. Indian art Wheelwright Mus., Santa Fe, 1984—87; spiritual counselor, tchr. Ctr. for Universal Beingness, Moriarty, N.Mex., 1988—; min., canon Brigade of Light Ch., Cedar Mountain, NC, 1991—. Tech. advisor Am. Playhouse PBS Spl., Crestone, Colo., 1987; chmn. bd. dirs. Crystal Found., Denver, 1988—92, Profit from the Sun, Moriarity, 1999—2001; co-founder Ctr. for Universal Beingness; cons., spkr. in field. Dir.(writer): Karen Lee Dance Theater, 2000—02. Chairperson bd. dirs. Ednl. Opportunity Program Calif. State U., Sacramento, 1971; mem. art com. chair, bd. dirs. YWCA, Lubbock, 1976—77; coun. mem. Sacramento Indian Ctr., 1971; vol. Talking Talons Youth Group, Tijeras, N.Mex., 2000. Named Outstanding Young Woman Am., 1982; recipient Humanitarian award, Friends for Life, Albuquerque, 1996; Wetlands Devel. Fed. grant, U.S. Wildlife, N.Mex., 1999. Mem.: Inst. Noetic Scis., Astron. Soc. Pacific, N.Y. Acad. Scis., Defenders of Wildlife (Wildlife Guardian), Acad. Am. Poets. Avocations: crafts, woodworking, stained glass, poetry, writing. Office: 30-A Steeldust Ave Moriarty NM 87035

MOOR, CARL H., lawyer; b. Evanston, Ill., Mar. 22, 1961; BA with high honors in Polit. Sci., Swarthmore Coll., 1983; JD, Yale U., 1988. Bar: Calif. 1988. Clk. to Judge Mariana R. Pfaeizer US Dist. Ct. (ctrl. dist. Calif.), 1988—89; civil litigator Hall & Phillips, LA, 1989—94; asst. US atty. criminal divsn., major frauds sect. Ctrl. Dist. Calif., 1994—2001; atty. Munger, Tolles & Olson, 2001—. Henry Luce Found. scholar, Tokyo, 1986—87. Mem.: Phi Beta Kappa. Office: Munger Tolles & Olson LLP 35th Fl 355 S Grand Ave Los Angeles CA 90071-1560 Office Phone: 213-683-9247. Office Fax: 213-683-4047. E-mail: Carl.Moor@mto.com. *

MOOR, ROB, professional sports team executive; b. Geneva; came to US, 1966; Grad., U. Calif., Irvine. Distbn. staff MGM Studios; mem. staff royalties, licensing and profits 20th Century Fox Studios; exec. v.p. NHL LA Kings; pres. Minn. Timberwolves, 1994—2005, CEO, 2005—; pres. Midwest Entertainment Grp. Bd. mem. Greater Mpls. Conv. and Visitors Assn., Downtown Coun. Mem. Greater Mpls. C. of C. (bd. dirs.). Office: Minn Timberwolves 600 First Ave N Minneapolis MN 55403-1416 *

MOORADIAN, ARSHAG DERTAD, internist, educator; b. Aleppo, Syria, Aug. 20, 1953; arrived in U.S., 1981; s. Dertad and Araxi (Halajian) Mooradian; m. Deborah Lynn Miles, June 25, 1985; children: Arshag Dertad, Jr., Ariana Araxie. BS, Am. U., Beirut, 1976, MD, 1980. Diplomate Am. Bd. Internal Medicine. Asst. prof. medicine UCLA, 1985-88; assoc. prof. U. Ariz., Tucson, 1988-91; prof. St. Louis U., 1991—2006; prof. medicine, chmn. dept. medicine U. Fla., 2006—. Contbr. articles to profl. jours. Grantee VA, 1985—97. Mem.: Am. Diabetes Assn. (chmn. task force micronutrients 1990—91, chmn. coun. nutrition and metabolism 2000—02), Endocrine Soc., Gerontol. Soc. Am., Am. Fedn. Clin. Rsch., Phi Kappa Phi, Alpha Omega Alpha. Mem. Armenian Orthodox Ch. Achievements include identification of a potential biomarker of aging; research in on age-related changes in the blood-brain barrier; on age-related changes in thyroid hormone action; on diabetes related changes in the central nervous system. Office: U Fla Coll Medicine Dept Medicine 653-1 West Eighth St Jacksonville FL 32209 Business E-Mail: arshag.mooradian@jax.ufl.edu.

MOORADIAN, GEORGE T., lawyer; BA with high distinction, U. Mich., 1976; JD, U. Mich. Law Sch., 1978; LLM, NYU, 1980. Bar: DC 1979, Mich. 1979, Calif. 1983. Ptnr.-in-charge Baker & Hostetler, Costa Mesa, Calif., coord., tax, personal planning and employee benefits. Office: Baker & Hostetler 600 Anton Blvd Ste 900 Costa Mesa CA 92626-7221

MOORE, ALBERT CUNNINGHAM, lawyer, insurance company executive; b. Miami, Fla., May 31, 1931; s. Elias Richard and Virginia Adelaide (Thompson) Moore; m. Anne Cambreleng Bonynge, Aug. 24, 1957; children: Emily Robinson French, Barbara Raffield, Catherine Anne Bonynge Wells. AB, U. N.C., 1953; JD, U. Va., 1959. Bar: N.Y. 1960. Atty. White & Case, NYC, 1959-69; corporate sec. Studebaker-Worthington, Inc., NYC, 1969-72; sr. v.p., gen. counsel Crum & Forster, 1973-87. Former trustee N.J. Shakespeare Festival; former bd. dirs. DeBordieu Property Owners Assn., DeBordieu Arch. Rev. Bd. With USNR, 1953—56. Mem.: Wilton Ctr. Tennis Club (NH), Chi Phi, Phi Alpha Delta. Home: 529 Cedar Club Cir Chapel Hill NC 27517

MOORE, ALECIA B. See PINK

MOORE, AMANDA LEIGH See MOORE, MANDY

MOORE, AMY NORWOOD, lawyer; b. Durham, NC, Sept. 24, 1953; AB summa cum laude, Mt. Holyoke Coll., 1976; MA in English, U. Va., 1978, JD, 1983. Bar: DC 1984, registered: US Ct. Appeals, DC 1985, US Ct. Appeals (6th cir.) 1985, US Tax Ct. 1998. Law clk. to Frank M. Coffin, U.S. Ct. Appeals (1st cir.), 1983-84; ptnr., Employee Benefits Practice Group Covington & Burling, Washington. Articles editor Va. Law Rev., 1982—83. Mem.: Phi Beta Kappa. Office: Covington & Burling 1201 Pennsylvania Ave NW Washington DC 20004-2401 Office Phone: 202-662-5390. Office Fax: 202-662-6291. Business E-Mail: anmoore@cov.com.

MOORE, ANDREW TAYLOR, JR., banker; b. Tarboro, NC, June 17, 1940; s. Andrew Taylor and Mary Dare (Allsbrook) M. BA in History, Duke U., 1962; LLB, U.Va., Charlottesville, 1965. Asst. sec. Signet Banking Corp., Richmond, 1965-71, asst. v.p., corporate sec., 1971-75, v.p., corporate sec., 1975-82, sr. v.p., corporate sec., 1982-94. Bd. dirs. Theatre IV, Richmond, Va., 1981-97, Va. State YMCA adv. coun., Lynchburg, 1988—; trustee Hist. Richmond Found., 1993-98; mem. presidents coun. Va. Hist. Soc., 1996-2004. Presbyterian (elder 1996—). Avocations: jogging, gardening, travel. Home: 2011 Hanover Ave Richmond VA 23220-3539 Office Phone: 804-353-5039. Personal E-mail: atmjr01@aol.com.

MOORE, ANN ROY, school system administrator; b. Florence, Ala. BA, Hampton U., Va.; MA, EdS, U. No. Ala.; EdD in Curriculum Leadership Pers. and Early Childhood Edn., Vanderbilt U., 1986; cert. in ednl. adminstrn., 1986, cert. in ednl. adminstrn., 1987; cert. supt., Ala. A&M, 1992. Former tchr. pre-sch. and elem. sch. Huntsville (Ala.) City Schs., curriculum specialist, 1978—80, former prin., mgr. elem. edn., dep. supt., 1999—2001, supt., 2001—; former asst. supt. Florence Sch. Sys. Office: Huntsville City Schs 200 White St Huntsville AL 35801

MOORE, ANN S., publishing executive; b. McLean, Va., 1950; d. Monty and Bea Sommovigo; m. Donovan Moore; 1 son, Brendan. BA in Polit. Sci., Vanderbilt U., 1971; MBA, Harvard U., 1978. With Time, Inc., NYC, 1978—; gen. mgr. Sports Illustrated, 1983—89; founding publisher Sports Illustrated for Kids, 1989-91; publisher People mag., 1991—93, pres., 1993—98, People Mag. Group (renamed People/In Style Mag. Group, 2001), 1998—2001; exec. v.p. Time Inc., 2001—02, chmn., CEO, 2002—. Bd. dirs. Avon Products Inc., 1993; public spkr. bus. and women's issues. Hon. bd. mem. Gilda's Club, NYC; founder Time to Give Back; bd. dirs. Wallace Found. Named Pub. Exec. of Yr., Adweek, 1998, 2004 Bus. Statesman, Harvard Bus. Sch.; named one of The 50 Most Powerful Women in Am. Bus., Fortune mag., 100 Most Powerful Women, Forbes mag., 2005—06, 50 Women to Watch, Wall Street Journal, 2005, 50 Most Powerful Women in Bus., Fortune mag., 2006, Next 20 Female CEOs, Pink Mag. & Forté Found., 2006; recipient AOL Time Warner Civic Leadership award, 2003. Achievements include guiding People magazine to spin off several popular titles including In Style (domestic and international), Teen People, People en Español, and Real Simple. Office: Time Warner Cable 1 Time Warner Ctr New York NY 10019-6038 *

MOORE, ANNE, physician; b. NYC, Apr. 28, 1944; d. John D.J. and Mary Foote Moore; m. Arnold L. Lisio, Sept. 6, 1969; children: Philip Moore, Mary Foote. BA, Smith Coll., 1965; MD, Columbia U., 1969. Diplomate Am. Bd. Internal Medicine, Am. Bd. Hematology (chmn. 1996), Am. Bd. Oncology. Intern dept. medicine N.Y. Hosp., NYC, 1969-73, assoc. attending physician, 1981-95, attending physician, 1996—; postdoctoral fellow Rockefeller U., 1972-73, hematology-oncology fellow, 1973-75; asst. prof. medicine Cornell U. Med. Coll., NYC, 1975-91, assoc. prof. clin. medicine, 1981-95, prof. clin. medicine, 1996—. Cons. Strang Cancer Prevention Ctr.; lectr., cons., in field. Author: Patient's Guide to Breast Cancer Treatment, 1992, rev. edit., 1997; ad hoc reviewer Am. Jour. Clin. Oncology, 1994, New Eng. Jour. Medicine, 1994, 96, 97; contbr. articles to profl. jours., chpts. to books. Trustee St. David's Sch., 1983-89, HealthCare Chaplaincy, Inc., 1991—; bd. dirs. Camilli Found., 1990—, Cure Myeloma Fund, 1988-98, N.Y. Community Trust. Recipient award SHARE, 1992, Wholeness of Life award Hosp. Chaplaincy, 1992, Alumnae award Oak Knoll Sch., 1994, Eileen Dreyer Meml. Lectureship award Sass Found. for Med. Rsch., 1996, Commendation award Office of Exec. Nassau County, 1996, award Artists for Breast Cancer Survival, Inc., 2000. Mem. Am. Bd. Internal Medicine (bd. dirs. 1996—), Am. Soc. Hematology, Am. Soc. Clin. Oncology, N.Y. Acad. Scis., Soc. for Study of Blood (membership chmn. 1979-80), N.Y. Met. Breast Cancer Group (membership chmn. 1992-93, sec.-treas. 1993-95, v.p. 1995-96, pres. 1997-99), Soc. for Study of Breast Disease, N.Y. Cancer Soc., N.Y. Acad. Medicine (trustee 1998-2006). Office: Weill-Cornell Med Ctr 428 E 72nd St New York NY 10021-4635

MOORE, BARRY M., architect, educator; Sr. assoc. Gensler Archs., Houston. Adj. assoc. prof. U. Houston; founding dir. Workshop for Hist. Architecture. Bd. mem. Houston Mod. Recipient Tau Sigma Delta Silver medal for Tchg., 1994. Fellow: AIA (Houston chpt., AIA Houston Educator award 2004). Office: Gensler Archs 711 Louisiana St Ste 300 Houston TX 77002 Office Phone: 713-844-0000. Office Fax: 713-844-0001. *

MOORE, BEATRICE, religious organization administrator; b. Somerville, Mass., Oct. 6, 1928; d. George and Christina Turner; m. Wendell Moore, May 9, 1953; children: Karl C., Linda Moore Flewelling, Diane Pearl, Larry. BA in Theology and English, Berkshire Christian Coll., Lenox, Mass., 1950. Pres. The Woman's Home and Foreign Mission Soc., Loudon, NH, past nat. pres. Charlotte, NC, 1987—96, nat. spiritual life chmn., 1997—2005. Sunday sch. tchr., deaconess Loudon Ridge Family Bible Ch.; chair Concord Christian Women's Club, 2002-03, 05-06; prayer coord. Ladies Bible Study leader, 1998-05, Concord Christian Women's Club, 2003-04; active Women's Home and Fgn. Mission Soc., Loudon, past pres. NH Soc., past pres. ea. region; hostess, contact chmn., prayer adv., Bible club guide Stonecroft Ministries, Friendship Bible Study Guide; past leader 4-H Club. Mem.: Concord Christian Womens Club (chair 2005—). Office: Woman's Home & Foreign Mission 845 Loudon Ridge Rd Loudon NH 03307-1712

MOORE, BETTY JO, legal assistant; b. Medicine Lodge, Kans., July 10, 1921; d. Joseph Christy and Helen Blanche (Hubbell) Sims; m. Harold Frank Moore, June 19, 1941 (dec.); children: Terrance C., Harold Anthony, Trisha Jo. Cert., U. West L.A., 1978; student, Wichita U., Kans., 1940-41. Cert. legal asst./escrow officer. Sec. UCLA, 1949-59; escrow officer Security Pacific Nat. Bank, LA, 1959-62, Empire Savs. & Loan Assn., Van Nuys, Calif., 1962-64; escrow supr. San Fernando Valley Bank, Van Nuys, 1964; escrow officer Heritage Bank, Westwood, Calif., 1964-66; escrow coord. Land Sys. Corp., Woodland Hills, Calif., 1966-67; escrow officer/asst. mgr., real estate lending officer Security Pacific Nat. Bank, LA, 1967-80; real estate paralegal Pub. Storage, Pasadena, 1980-81; asst. mgr. escrow dept. First Beverly Bank, Century City, Calif., 1982-84; escrow trainer/officer Moore's Tng. Temps Inc., Canoga Park, Calif., 1984—92, legal asst., 1992—. Participant People to People Amb. Program/Women in Mgmt. to USSR, 1989; observer Internat. Fedn. Bus. and Profl. Women's Congress, Washington, 1965, 81, Nassau, Bahamas, 1989, Narobi, Kenya, 1991, Havana, Cuba, 2004. Adv. bd. escrow edn. Pierce Coll., Woodland Hills, Calif., 1968-80. Recipient Cert. of Appreciation, Pierce Coll., 1979, Calif. Fedn. Bus. and Profl. Women, 1989, Nat. Women's History Project, 1995. Mem. Nat. Fedn. Bus. and Profl. Women's Clubs, Calif. Fedn. Bus. and Profl. Women (pres. dist. 1987-88, Calif. Found. chmn. 1988-89, internat. concerns chmn. 1996-97, 2003), Woodland Hills Bus. and Profl.

Women ((pres. 1991-92, 94-95), Valley/Sunset Dist. BPW (v.p. legislation/pub. policy 1997-98, 2001-02, 03, Cert. of Appreciation 2002), Tri Valley Dist. Bus. and Profl. Women (legis. chair 1992-93, exec./corr. sec. 1993-94, 94-95), Internat. Fedn. Bus. and Profl. Women, Nat. Women's Polit. Caucus (coord., sec. San Fernando Valley caucus 1986-87, sec. 1990-2003, legis. co-chair 1991-93), Women's Orgn. Coalition San Fernando Valley (exec. com. L.A. Women's Equality Day 1995, pres. 2002—), San Fernando Valley Escrow Assn. (bd. dirs. 1962-64), L.A. Women's Family Equity Coalition, U. West L.A. Alumni Assn., Rotary, U.N. Assn. (v.p. San Fernando Valley), League of Women Voters. Democrat. Methodist. Avocations: reading, musical theater.

MOORE, BETTYJANE, elementary school educator; b. Belleville, Ill., Dec. 26, 1945; d. TeryeRacin and BettyJane (Miles) Rasmussen; m. William Allen Moore, July 10, 1966; children: Gretchen S., Chad A. BS, Wichita State U., Kansas, 1968; MEd, Southwestern Coll., Kansas, 1991. Cert. reading specialist elem. Educator Paul B. Cooper Elem., Derby, Kans., 1968—72, Oxford Elem. Sch., Kans., 1974—. Pres., co-owner Lifeslider, Inc. Ch. clerk Slate Valley Bap. Ch., Oxford, 1985—; sec. Sumner County Hist. Geneological Soc., Wellington, Kans., 1995—. Named Elem. Tchr. of Yr., Oxford Sch. Dist., 2002—03. Mem.: Nat. Edn. Assn. Home: 1201 S Oxford Rd Geuda Springs KS 67051 Personal E-mail: bjmoore@kanokla.net.

MOORE, BOB STAHLY, communications executive; b. Pasadena, Calif., July 3, 1936; s. Norman Hastings and Mary Augusta (Stahly) M. Student, U. Mo., 1954-58, MIT, 1958-62. Dir. news WPEO, Peoria, Ill., 1958—60, KSST, Davenport, Iowa, 1960—62, WIRE, Indpls., 1962—64, WCFL, Chgo., 1964—67; White House corr. Metromedia, Inc., Washington, 1967—71; dir. news Gateway Comm., Altoona, Pa., 1972—74; chief Washington Bur. MBS, 1974—76, v.p. news Arlington, Va., 1976—78, White House corr., 1978—81; dir. comm. Fed. Home Loan Bank Bd., Washington, 1981—85; spl. asst. to bd. govs. Fed. Res. Sys., Washington, 1985—. Active ARC. Served with USAF, 1961-63. Recipient profl. awards Ind. News Broadcasters, 1963, Ill. News Broadcasters, 1965, UPI, 1960, 63, 65, AP, 1956, 58, 61, 65, 67, Mo. News Broadcasters, 1956, 61. Mem. Radio and TV News Dirs. Assn. (Profl. award), White House Corrs. Assn., State Dept. Corrs. Assn., Radio-TV Corrs. Gallery (U.S. Capitol), Chgo. Coun. on Fgn. Rels., Pub. Rels. Soc. Am., Nat. Press Club, Washington Press Club, Chgo. Press Club, Mo. C. of C., Ill. C. of C., Sigma Delta Chi. Presbyterian. Home: 114 W Arlington Ave Vandalia MO 63382 Office: 20th And Constitution NW Washington DC 20551-0001

MOORE, C. BRADLEY, chemistry professor; b. Boston, Dec. 7, 1939; s. Charles Walden and Dorothy (Lutz) Moore; m. Penelope Williamson Percival, Aug. 27, 1960; children: Megan Bradley, Scott Woodward. BA magna cum laude, Harvard U., 1960; PhD, U. Calif., Berkeley, 1963. Predoctoral fellow NSF, 1960-63; asst. prof. chemistry U. Calif., Berkeley, 1963-68, assoc. prof., 1968-72, prof., 1972-2000, vice chmn. dept., 1971-75, chmn. dept. chemistry, 1982-86, dean Coll. Chemistry, 1988-94, prof. grad. sch., 2000—; v.p. rsch. Ohio State U., Columbus, Disting. prof. math. and phys. sci., prof. chemistry, 2000—03, prof. emeritus, 2003—; prof. chemistry Northwestern U., 2003—, v.p. rsch., 2003—. Assoc. prof. Faculty Scis., Paris, 1970, 75; Miller Rsch. Prof. U. Calif., Berkeley, 1972-73, 87-88; vis. prof. Inst. for Molecular Sci., Okazaki, Japan, 1979, Fudan U., Shanghai, 1979, adv. prof., 1988—; vis. fellow Joint Inst. for Lab. Astrophysics, U. Colo., Boulder, 1981-82; faculty sr. scientist (Chemical Sci. Div.) Lawrence Berkeley Nat. Lab., 1974-2000, divsn. dir., 1998-2000: mem. editl. bd. Jour. Chem. Physics, 1973-75, Chem. Physics Letters, 1980-85, Jour. Phys. Chemistry, 1981-87, Laser Chemistry, 1982—; mem. Basic Energy Scis. adv. com. Office Sci. U.S. Dept. Energy, 2000-03. Editor: Chemical and Biochemical Applications of Lasers; assoc. editor Annual Review of Physical Chemistry, 1985-90; contbr. articles to profl. jours. Trustee Sci. Svc., 1995—, Sci. and Tech. Campus, 2000-03; mem. bd. govs. Ohio Supercomputer Ctr., 2000-03; rsch. officer Coun. of Ohio Bd. of Regents, 2000-03; pres., chmn. bd. Ohio State U. Rsch. Found., 2000-03; mem. governing bd. Argonne Nat. Lab., 2005—, mem. sci. policy coun., 2005—. Recipient Coblentz award, 1973, E.O. Lawrence Meml. award U.S. Dept. Energy, 1986, Lippincott award, 1987, 1st award Inter-Am. Photochem. Soc., 1988; nat. scholar Harvard U., 1958-60; fellow Alfred P. Sloan Found., 1968, Guggenheim Found., 1969, Humboldt Rsch. award for Sr. U.S. Scientists, 1994. Fellow AAAS, Am. Acad. Arts and Scis., Am. Phys. Soc. (Plyler award 1994); mem. NSF adv. com. for education and human resources directorate, chair subcom. policy and planning 1997-99, NAS (chmn. com. undergrad. sci. edn. 1993-97, class I membership com., 1998-2000, 2002, 2000 nominating com.), Am. Chem. Soc. (past chmn. divsn. phys. chemistry, Calif. sect. award 1977). Avocation: bicycling. Office: Northwestern U Crown 2-223 633 Clark St Evanston IL 60208 Office Phone: 847-491-3485. E-mail: moorecb@northwestern.edu.

MOORE, CARLETON BRYANT, geochemistry educator; b. NYC, Sept. 1, 1932; s. Eldridge Carleton and Mabel Florence (Drake) M.; m. Jane Elizabeth Strouse, July 25, 1959; children: Barbara Jeanne, Robert Carleton; m. Diane Beets, Apr. 23, 2000. BS, Alfred U., 1954, DSc (hon.), 1977; PhD, Cal. Inst. Tech., 1960. Asst. prof. geology Wesleyan U., Middletown, Conn., 1959-61; mem. faculty Ariz. State U., Tempe, 1961—; nat. rsch. coun. rsch. assoc. NASA Ames Rsch. Ctr., 1974; prof., dir. Ctr. for Meteorite Studies Ariz. State U., Regents' prof., 1988—. Vis. prof. Stanford U., 1974; Prin. investigator Apollo 11-17; preliminary exam. team Lunar Receiving Lab., Apollo, 12-17. Author: Cosmic Debris, 1969, Meteorites, 1971, Principles of Geochemistry, 1982, Grundzügeder Geochemie, 1985; editor: Researches on Meteorites, 1961, Jour. Meteoritical Soc.; contbr. articles to profl. jours. Asteroid 5046 named Carletonmoore in his honor, 2000. Fellow Am. Geophys. Union, Ariz.-Nev. Acad. Sci. (pres. 1979-80), Meteoritical Soc. (life hon., pres. 1966-68), Geol. Soc. Am., Mineral. Soc. Am., AAAS (council 1967-70); mem. Geochem. Soc., Am. Chem. Soc., Am. Ceramic Soc., Sigma Xi. Office: Ariz State U Ctr Meteorite Studies Tempe AZ 85287-2504 Address: PO Box 26137 Tempe AZ 85285 Home Phone: 480-838-3353; Office Phone: 480-965-3576. Business E-Mail: cmoore@asu.edu.

MOORE, CAROL A., academic administrator; b. Newark, Dec. 8, 1945; d. James Clifford and Helen Mohan Brierley; m. Thomas Eric Moore, Nov. 25, 1967; 1 child, Kimberly Ann. BS in Biology, Montclair St. Coll., NJ, 1967; MA in Biology, Monclair State Coll., NJ, 1972; PhD in Biology, Northeastern Univ., Boston, Mass., 1981. Sci. tchr. H.S. and Jr. H.S., 1967—71; asst. prof. biology Massasoit C.C., Brockton, Mass., 1972—83, divsn. chairperson sci. and tech., asst prof. biology, 1979—83, asst. dean academic affairs, asst. prof. biology, 1983—84; dean academic affairs, chief acadamic officer, prof. biology Lasell Coll., Newton, Mass., 1984—88; dean undergraduate sch., chief acadminc officer, prof. biology Lesley Coll., Cambridge, Mass., 1988—91; provost & v.p. academic affairs, chief academic officer, prof. biology Mercy Coll., Dobbs Ferry, NY, 1992—98; pres. Lyndon State Coll., Lyndonville, Vt., 1998—. Vis. scientist Marine Sci. Inst., Northeastern Univ., Nahant, Mass., 1991—. Contbr. scientific papers to numerous conf., chapters to books, articles to profl. jour. Mem., Vt. higher edn. coun. rep. New Eng. Higher Edn. Bd., 1991—; mem., adv. bd. Vt. Telecom Advancement Ctr. USDA Grant, 2002—, Office of Nursing Workforce Rsch., Planning and Develp., Univ. Vt., 2001—; mem., Vt. bd. dirs. Girl Scout Coun., 2001—; mem. Am. Coun. Edn. Commn. on Women in Higher Edn., 2002—03; mem. Vt. Higher Edn. Coun., 1998—; rep. New Eng. Bd. of Higher Edn., 2002—, pres., 2001—02, v.p., 2000—01, exec. com., 1999—, sec.-treas., 1999—2000, com. on cert. & accreditation, 1998—; bd. dirs. Northeastern Vt. Devel. Assn., 2000—, Northeast Kingdom Learning Svc., 2000—. Grantee Title III Retention Grant, 1995, AAC Cirriculm. Devel. Grant, 1990, NSF, 1983. Mem.: Soc. of Devel. and Comparative Immunology, Soc. for Invertebrate Pathology, Nat. Shellfisheries Soc., Am. Soc. of Zoologists (travel award), New Eng. Estuarine Rsch. Soc., Nat/ Assn. for Women Deans, Adminstr., and Counselors, Assn. of Tchr. Educators, Am. Coun. of Edn./ Nat. Identification Program, Nat. Assn. of Academic Affairs Adminstr., Sigma Xi, Phi Sigma. Office: Lyndon State Coll PO Box 919 1001 Coll Rd Lyndonville VT 05851

MOORE, CAROLE IRENE, librarian; b. Berkeley, Calif., Aug. 15, 1944; AB, Stanford U., 1966; MLS, Columbia U., 1967. Reference libr. Columbia U., NYC, 1967-68, U. Toronto, Can., 1968-80, head cataloging, 1980-85, assoc. libr., 1985-86, chief libr., 1986—. Mem. nat. adv. bd. Nat. Libr. Can., Ottawa, 1991-94; bd. dirs. Rsch. Librs. Group. 1994-2000, U. Toronto Press, 1994—. Recipient Disting. Alumni award Columbia U., 1989. Mem. ALA, Can. Libr. Assn., Can. Assn. Rsch. Librs. (pres. 1989-91, bd. dirs. 1996-98). Avocation: gardening. Office: U Toronto Libr 130 Saint George St Toronto ON Canada M5S 1A5

MOORE, CASSANDRA CHRONES, real estate broker; b. Oneonta, NY, June 14, 1935; d. Constantine John and Antonia (Laskaris) Chrones; m. Thomas Gale Moore, Dec. 28, 1958; children: Charles Godwin, Antonia Laskaris. BA summa cum laude, Radcliffe Coll., Cambridge, Mass., 1956; MA, Harvard U., 1958; PhD, U. Mich., 1975. Lic. real estate broker Calif. Lectr. Duquesne U., Pitts., 1962-65, Mich. State U., East Lansing, 1966-68; broker, owner Moore Assocs., Palo Alto, Calif., 1983-85; dir. state and mcpl. legislation Nat. Assn. Realtors, Washington, 1985-87; exec. dir. Fed. Interagy. Coun. on Homeless, Washington, 1987-89; adj. scholar Competitive Enterprise Inst., Washington, 1989—, mem. adv. bd., 1995—; adj. scholar Cato Inst., Washington, 1996—. Author: Haunted Housing, 1997. Co-chmn. Radcliffe Alumnae Lectureship Com., Palo Alto and San Francisco, 1984-2000; mem. nat. com. Radcliffe Alumnae Professorship Fund, 2001-02. Recipient Fulbright fellowship U.S. Govt., Washington, 1956-57. Mem.: Calif. Assn. Scholars (mem. adv. bd. 2005—), Palo Alto Bd. Realtors (dir. 1984, 1985), Tsintzinian Soc. (bd. mem. 1999—, alt. bd. mem. 2001—02), Am. Assn. Small Property Owners (bd. mem. 1997—), Radcliffe Club Peninsula (pres. 1980—82), Phi Beta Kappa. Avocations: hiking, swimming, skiing. Office: 415 Cambridge Ave Palo Alto CA 94306 Office Phone: 650-853-0798. Personal E-mail: ccmassoc@comcast.net.

MOORE, CHARLES HEWES, JR., manufacturing executive; b. Coatesville, Pa., Aug. 12, 1929; s. Charles Hewes and Jane Richards (Scott) M.; m. Judith L. McClellan, June 23, 1971; children: Charles Hewes III, James, David, Susan, Kevin, Christopher, Margery, Brian, Amanda. BME, Cornell U., 1952. With Lenape Forge Co. div. Gulf & Western Industries, West Chester, Pa., 1952-73; pres. Lapp div. Interpace Corp., Le Roy, NY, 1973—78; pres., chief exec. officer Allied Thermal Corp. subs. Interpace, 1978-79; sr. v.p., dir. Interpace, 1979-80; exec. v.p., dir. Interpace Corp., Parsippany, NJ, 1980-81; pres., chief exec. officer, dir. Clevepak Corp., 1981-83, 84-86, chief exec. officer, vice chmn. bd., dir., 1983-84; mng. dir. Peers & Co., 1987-88; chief exec. officer Peers Mgmt. Resources, Inc., 1987-88; pres., chief exec. officer Ransburg Corp., Indpls., 1988-92; pres. ITW Finishing Systems and Products, Indpls., 1990-92; exec. v.p. Ill. Tool Works Inc., Glenview, 1991-92; vice-chmn. Advisory Capital Ptnrs., Inc., Greenwich, Conn., 1992—94; chmn. bd. dirs. Xpander Pak Inc., 1994—2000; dir. athletics Cornell U., 1994—99. Dep. to chairs Com. Encouraging Corp. Philanthropy, NY, 1999—2000, exec. dir., NY, 2000—; mem. Pres. Coun. on Phys. Fitness and Sports, 2002—. Commr. Smithsonian Am. Art Mus., 2000—; chmn. audit com., pub. sector dir. U.S. Olympic Com., 1992—2000; mem. nat. bd. Smithsonian Instn., 2001—06. Recipient Gold medal in 400 meter hurdles, 1952 Olympics, Herbert Adams Meml. award for advancement of Am. sculpture, Nat. Sculpture Soc., 1985. Mem. Pine Valley Golf Club (N.J.), Royal and Ancient Golf Club St. Andrews (Scotland), Blind Brook Golf Club (N.Y.). Republican. Episcopalian. Office: Com Encouraging Corp Philanthropy 110 Wall St Ste 2-2 New York NY 10005 Office Phone: 212-825-1254.

MOORE, CHARLES LOYD, lawyer; b. El Paso, Tex., Aug. 14, 1944; s. Charles McKinney and Alice Adeline (Loyd) M.; m. Peggy Jo Ball, Dec. 20, 1969; children: Kirk, Julie. BS in Mil. Engring., US Mil. Acad., West Point, NY, 1966; MSME, Calif. Inst. Tech., Pasadena, 1968; JD summa cum laude, So. Meth. U., Dallas, 1975. Bar: N.Mex. 1975, US Dist. Ct. 1975. Commd. 2d. lt. US Army, 1966, advanced through grades to capt., 1968, resigned, 1972; assoc. Keleher & McLeod, P.A., Albuquerque, 1975-79, mem. firm, 1979—2005; assoc. gen. counsel PNM Resources, Inc., Albuquerque, 2005—. Contbr. articles to profl. jours. Dist. co-chmn. ann. fund campaign McMurry U., Abilene, Tex., 1988, trustee, 1989—92, Hatton W. Sumners Found., Dallas, 1999—; co-vice chmn. Hatton W. Summers Found., Dallas, 2006—; dir. Robert O. Anderson Schs. Mgmt. Found. Bd., U. N.Mex., Albuquerque, 2003—05; co-chair N.Mex. Lawyers for Gen. Wesley Clark for Pres. campaign, Albuquerque, 2003—04. Decorated Vietnam Svc. medal, Vietnam Campaign medal, Bronze Star, Joint Svc. Commendation medal; named N.Mex. Bus. Lawyer of Yr., 2005; named one of Best Lawyers of Am., 1989—90, 1991—92, 1993—94, 1995—96, 1997—98, 1999—2000, 2001—02, 2003—04. Mem. ABA, State Bar of N.Mex. (v.p. young lawyers divsn. 1977-78, chair bus. law sect. 2001, N.Mex. Bus. Lawyer of Yr. 2005), Albuquerque Bar Assn., Phi Delta Phi (Internat. Grad. of Yr. Biennial Conv. 1975), Phi Kappa Phi. Avocations: running, reading. Office: PNM Resources Inc Alvarado Sq MS 1200 Albuquerque NM 87158 Business E-Mail: cmoore1@pnm.com.

MOORE, CHERYL (MILKES) JEROME, lawyer; b. Dallas, Jan. 10, 1951; d. Dean and Marjorie (Wolens) Milkes; m. Edward Jerome, Aug. 21, 1976 (div. 1986); 1 child, Elizabeth Milkes; m. David Moore, Feb. 25, 1995. Student, Tulane U., 1969-70; BA and BSW, Syracuse U., 1972, JD, 1976. Bar: N.Y. 1977, Tex. 1978, U.S. Dist. Ct. (no. dist.) N.Y., U.S. Dist. Ct. (all dists.) Tex., U.S. Ct. Appeals (5th cir.). Law clk. Bogart & Andrews, Syracuse, NY, 1975-76; assoc. Law Office Louis Tarantelli, Horseheads, NY, 1976-78, Glast, Miller & Allen, Dallas, 1985-86; sr. planner, adminstrn. asst. County of Dallas, 1977—78, chief commr. fraud, Dist. Atty.'s Office, 1979-85; ptnr. Hewitt, Jerome & Armstrong, Dallas; ptnr., Securities, Oil & Gas Law, Comml. & Transactional Litigation Patton Boggs LLP, Dallas, dep. chmn. litigation dept., mem. mgmt. com. Adj. prof. So. Meth. U. Coll. Law, Dallas, 1986-2000; tchg. staff Nat. Inst. Trial Advocacy. Contbr. articles to profl. jours. Bd. dirs. Cmty. Homes Adults, Inc., Dallas, 1987-2004; bd. dirs. Jewish Fedn. Dallas; chair Legacy Sr. Communities Inc., 2004—. Mem. N.Y. Bar Assn., Tex. Bar Assn., Dallas Bar Assn. Democrat. Jewish. Office: Patton Boggs LLP Suite 3000 2001 Ross Ave Dallas TX 75201-8001 Office Phone: 214-758-3504. Office Fax: 214-758-1550. Business E-Mail: cmoore@pattonboggs.com.

MOORE, CHRISTOPHER, writer; b. Toledo, 1957; Author: (novels) Practical Demonkeeping, 1992, Coyote Blue, 1994, Bloodsucking Friends, 1995, Island of the Sequined Love Nun, 1997, The Lust Lizard of Melancholy Cove, 1999, Lamb: The Gospel According to Biff, Christ's Childhood Pal, 2002, Fluke: or I Know Why the Winged Whale Sings, 2003, The Stupidest Angel: A Heartwarming Tale of Christmas Terror, 2004, A Dirty Job, 2006 (The Quill Award for General Fiction, 2006), You Suck, 2007. Office: HarperCollins 10 E 53rd St New York NY 10022 *

MOORE, CHRISTOPHER HUGH, writer; b. Stoke-on-Trent, Eng., June 9, 1950; arrived in Can., 1954; s. M. Vincent and Kathleen A. (Lennox) M.; m. Louise A. Brophy, May 7, 1977; children: Elizabeth, Kate. BA with honors, U. B.C., Vancouver, 1971; MA, U. Ottawa, Ont., Can., 1977. Staff historian Nat. Historic Pks. Svc., Louisbourg, N.S., Can., 1972-75; sec. to bd. Heritage Can. Found., Ottawa, 1977-78; writer, historian Toronto, Ont., 1979—; dir. Access Copyright Licensing Agy., 2001—07. Author: Louisbourg Portraits, 1982, 2000, The Loyalists, 1984, 94, Eighteen Sixty-Seven, 1997, The Big Book of Canada, 2002; co-author: Illustrated History of Canada, 1987, The Story of Canada, 1992, Canada: Our Century, 1999. Recipient Gov. Gen.'s Lit. award Can., 1983, Sec. of State Prize Govt. Can., Ottawa, 1985, Mr. Christie's Prize Christie-Brown Ltd., Toronto, 1993. Mem. Writers' Union of Can. (chair contracts com. 1990-94, mem. nat. coun. 1995-97, nat. chair, 1999-00), Can. Hist. Assn. Office: 70 Woodside Ave Toronto ON Canada M6P 1M1 E-mail: cmed@sympatico.ca.

MOORE, CHRISTOPHER M., lawyer; b. LA, Oct. 12, 1938; s. Prentiss Elder and Josephine (French) M.; m. Gillian Reed, Sept. 29, 1965; children: Stephanie Kia Conn, Carrie Christine McKay. AB, Stanford U.; JD, Harvard U. Dep. county counsel L.A. County Counsel, 1965-66; ptnr. Burkley & Moore, Torrance, Calif., 1969-74; pvt. practice Law Offices of Christopher Moore, Torrance, 1974-81; ptnr. Burkley, Moore, Greenberg & Lyman, Torrance, 1981-90; prin. Christopher M. Moore & Assoc., Torrance, 1990-2000, Moore, Bryan & Schroff, Torrance, 2000—. Mem. bd. edn. Palos Verdes (Calif.) Peninsula Unified Sch. Dist., 1972—77. Fellow: Am. Acad. Matrimonial Lawyers, Am. Coll. Trust and Estate Counsel; mem.: Palos Verdes Golf Club, L.A. Yacht Club. Avocations: sailing, golf. Office: Moore Bryan & Schroff Ste 490 21515 Hawthorne Blvd Torrance CA 90503-6525 Home Phone: 310-375-4967; Office Phone: 310-540-8855. E-mail: chris@mbslawcorp.com.

MOORE, CORI, lawyer; b. Seattle, Mar. 28, 1973; BSFS, Georgetown Univ., 1995; JD, Seattle Univ., 1998. Bar: Wash. 1998. Assoc. atty., comml. litig. Perkins Coie LLP, Seattle. Contbr. articles to numerous profl. jours. Named Wash. Rising Star, SuperLawyer Mag., 2006. Mem.: ABA, Wash. Bar Assn. Office: Perkins Coie LLP Ste 4800 1201 Third Ave Seattle WA 98101-3099

MOORE, CORNELL LEVERETTE, financial services executive, lawyer; b. Tignall, Ga., Sept. 18, 1939; s. Jesse Lamar and Luetta (Leverette) M.; m. Wenda Lee Weekes, June 27, 1965; children: Lynne M., Jonathon C. Meredith L. AB, Va. Union U., 1961; JD, Howard U., 1964. Bar: Minn. 1964, U.S. Dist. Ct. Minn. 1977. Atty. U.S. Treasury, various locations, 1965-68; asst. v.p., legal officer N.W.N. Bank, Mpls., 1968-70; pres. Leverette, Weekes, Mpls., 1970—; exec. v.p. Shelter Mfg. Co., Mpls., 1970-74; pres., chief exec. officer Lease Moore Equipment, Inc., Mpls., 1977-86; sr. v.p., gen. counsel Miller and Shroeder Fin. Inc., Mpls., 1987—. Bd. dirs. Golden Valley (Minn.) Bank, Ward & Assocs., Inc., Atlanta. Trustee Mpls. Soc. Fine Arts, 1986, Va. Union U., Richmond, 1986, Dunwoody Inst., Mpls. 1986, chmn. bd. vis., John H. Johnson Sch. Comm. Howard Univ. Democrat. African Methodist Epicopal. Club: Minneapolis.

MOORE, DANIEL ALTON, JR., retired state supreme court justice; b. 1933; BBA, U. Notre Dame, 1955; JD, U. Denver, 1961. Dist. ct. magistrate judge, Alaska, 1961-62; pvt. practice law, 1962-80; judge 3d Jud. Dist. Superior Ct., 1980-83; justice Alaska Supreme Ct., Anchorage, 1983-92, chief justice, 1992-95; ret., 1995. Mediator for J.A.M.S./Endispute, 1996—.

MOORE, DANIEL CHARLES, retired anesthesiologist; b. Cin., Sept. 9, 1918; s. Daniel Clark and May (Strebel) M.; m. Betty Maxine Tobias, Aug. 5, 1945 (div. 1988); children: Barbara, Nancy, Daniel, Susan. Grad., Amherst Coll., Mass., 1940; MD, Northwestern U., 1944. Diplomate Am. Bd. Anesthesiologists. Intern Wesley Meml. Hosp., Chgo., 1944, resident, 1945; dir. anesthesia Va. Mason Hosp., Seattle, 1947-72; anesthesiologist (Mason Clinic), 1947-72, sr. cons. in anesthesia, 1972-83. Clin. prof. U. Wash. Sch. Medicine, 1963—89. Author: Regional Block, 1953, Stellate Ganglion Block, 1954, Complications of Regional Anesthesia, 1955, Anesthetic Techniques for Obstetrical Anesthesia and Analgesia, 1964, also papers. Served as capt. M.C. AUS, 1945-47. Recipient Ralph M. Waters award Ill. Soc. Anesthesiologists, Carl Koller Gold medal European Soc. Regional Anaesthesia, 1995, Eagle Scout, 1930. Mem. Am. Soc. Anesthesiologists (1st v.p. 1953-54, 2d v.p. 1954-55, pres. 1958-59, distinguished service award 1976), AMA (sec. anesthesiology sect. 1956-58), Am. Acad. Anesthesiology, Am. Soc. Regional Anesthesia (adv. bd., Gaston Labat award 1977), Wash. Soc. Anesthesiologists (pres. 1949-50), Wash. Med. Soc., King County Med. Soc., Faculty Anaesthetists Royal Coll. Surgeons (hon.), Northwest Forum, Beta Theta Pi, Nu Sigma Nu. Home: Madison Park Pl # 103 2000 43rd Ave E Seattle WA 98112-2704 Office: PO Box 900 Seattle WA 98111-0900 Home Phone: 206-726-9832; Office Phone: 206-223-6980. Fax: 206-223-6982. E-mail: daniel.moore@vmmc.org.

MOORE, DAVID GENE, academic administrator; b. Tonasket, Wash., Oct. 2, 1938; s. Leonard W. and Peggy (Furst) M.; m. Diane Russell, June 15, 1965 (div. 1984); children: John, Kathy, Alan, m. Kathryn Welsch, Nov. 24, 1999. BA in Polit. Sci., Seattle U., 1960; MBA, U. Puget Sound, 1973; MS in Computer Sci., Kans. State U., 1978; postgrad., U. Mich., 1978—. Commd. 2d lt. U.S. Army, 1960, advanced through grades to col., 1979, ret., 1980; dean mgmt. info. systems Mott Community Coll., Flint, Mich., 1980-82, dean mgmt., 1982-84, pres., 1985-92; pres DeVry Inst. Tech., Los Angeles, Calif., 1992-94; pres. Nat. Edn. Centers, Inc., 1994-95; founder, chmn., pres and CEO Corinthian Colleges, Inc., Santa Ana, 1995—. Bd. dirs. Greater Flint Edn. Consortium. Contbr. articles to profl. jours. Mem. exec. com. Orange County Performing Arts Ctr., Opera Pacific. Decorated Silver Stars (2), Legion of Merit (2); recipient numerous civic and profl. awards. Mem. Soc. Automotive Engrs. (chmn. robotics sect. 1986—), Data Processing Mgmt. Assn. Avocations: skiing, woodworking. Office: Corinthian Colleges Inc 6 Hutton Centre Dr Ste 400 Santa Ana CA 92707-5764 E-mail: dmoore@cci.edu.

MOORE, DEMI (DEMI GUYNES, DEMETRIA GENE GUYNES), actress; b. Roswell, N.Mex., Nov. 11, 1962; d. Danny and Virginia Guynes; m. Freddy Moore, 1980 (div. 1984), m. Bruce Willis, Nov. 21, 1987 (div. 2000); 3 daughters: Rumer Glenn, Scout LaRue, Tallulah Belle; m. Ashton Kutcher, Sept. 24, 2005. Studies with Zina Provendie. Owner Moving Pictures. Actress: (feature films) Choices, 1981, Parasite, 1981, Young Doctors in Love, 1982, Blame it on Rio, 1984, No Small Affair, 1984, Master Ninja 1, 1984, St. Elmo's Fire, 1985, About Last Night..., 1986, Wisdom, 1986, One Crazy Summer, 1987, The Seventh Sign, 1988, We're No Angels, 1989, Ghost, 1990, Mortal Thoughts, 1991 (also co-producer), The Butcher's Wife, 1991, Nothing But Trouble, 1991, A Few Good Men, 1992, Indecent Proposal, 1993, Disclosure, 1994, The Scarlet Letter, 1995, Now and Then, 1995 (also prodr.), Undisclosed, 1996, Striptease, 1996, The Juror, 1996, G.I. Jane, 1997 (also prodr.), Deconstructing Harry, 1997, Passion of Mind, 2000, Charlie's Angels: Full Throttle, 2003, Half Light, 2006, Bobby, 2006, Mr. Brooks, 2007; (TV series) General Hospital, 1982-83; (TV movies) If These Walls Could Talk, 1996 (also exec. prodr.), (voice) The Magic 7, 2006; (voice) Beavis and Butt-Head Do America,1996, The Hunchback of Notre Dame, 1996, The Hunchback of Notre Dame II, 2002; Producer: Austin Powers: International Man of Mystery, 1997, Austin Powers: The Spy Who Shagged Me, 1999, Austin Powers in Goldmember, 2002; guest appearances on Saturday Night Live (host), 1988, Moonlighting, 1989, Tales of the Crypt, 1990, Will & Grace, 2003. Named one of 50 Most Beautiful People in the World, People, 1996. Office: Creative Artists Agy Inc 9830 Wilshire Blvd Beverly Hills CA 90212-1825 *

MOORE, DENNIS, congressman; b. Anthony, Kans., Nov. 8, 1945; m. Stephene; 7 children. BS, U. Kans., 1967; JD, Washburn U., 1970. Bar: Kans. 1970. Asst. atty. gen. State of Kans., 1971-73; pvt. practice, 1973-76; dist. atty. Johnson County, 1977-89; ptnr. Erker & Moore, LLC, 1991-98, Smith, Gill, Fisher & Butts, 1989-91; mem. U.S. Congress from 3d Kans. dist., 1999—, mem. com. on fin. svcs. and the budget. Elected to Johnson County C.C. bd. trustees, 1993; re-elected, 1997; bd. dirs. Johnson County Safehome, Coalition for Prevention of Child Abuse, Kans. Child Abuse Prevention Coun., CASA (Ct. Appointed Spl. Advocate), United Cmty. Svcs., Cmty. Corrections Adv. Bd.; unsuccessful Dem. candidate for state atty. gen., 1986. With U.S. Army, U.S. Army Res. Democrat. Achievements include personally prosecuting more than 25 felony jury trials; led Consumer Protection Divsn. in the investigation and successful prosecution of a nat. oil co. charged with rigging gas pumps to cheat consumers; established a victim assistance unit; was cited by an ind. cons. hired by the Johnson County Bd. Commrs. as running the most efficient office in Johnson County govt.; served as pres. Kans. County and Dist. Atty.'s Assn. Office: US Ho Reps 1727 Longworth Ho Office Bldg Washington DC 20515-1603

MOORE, DONALD EMERSON, III, zoological park administrator, curator, wildlife biologist; b. Syracuse, NY, Jan. 9, 1954; s. Donald Emerson and Ruth Hodge (Steinhilber) M.; m. Adrienne Rose Whiteley (div.); children: Jessie Rose, Caitlin Grace; m. Suzanne L. Daley. BS in Environ. Sci. and Forestry, SUNY, Syracuse, 1976; MPA, Syracuse U., 1990; PhD, SUNY, Syracuse, 2001. Cert. biologist. Edn. asst. Burnet Park Zoo, Syracuse, 1976-77, technician animal care, 1977-79, zoologist, 1980-83, curator mammals, 1984-93; dir. Thompson Park Conservancy, 1993-95; curator Wildlife Conservation Soc., NYC, 1997—2002, dir., 2003—06; vis. assoc. prof. Hunter Coll. Animal Behavior and Conservation Focus, 2005—07; assoc. dir. Smithsonian Nat. Zoo, 2006—. Sci. adviser Thompson Park Zoo, Watertown, N.Y., 1984-2006; mem. master plan team A New Breed of Zoo, 1980-86, Springdale Farm Park, 1985-88; exploring adviser, 1989-96. Author: (mgmt. format) Species Mgmt. Plan, 1978, Disney's Wonderful World of Animals, 2006; contbr. articles to sci. jours. Instr. ARC, Syracuse, 1978-87; mem. master plan team Millbrook Sch., 1988-89. Fellow: Am. Zoo and Aquarium Assn. (prof.); mem.: NY Acad. Sci., Internat. Soc. Behavioral Ecology, Soc. Conservation Biology, Internat. Union Conservation Nature and Natural Resources (deer specialist group, mustelid/viverrid specialist group, reintroduction specialist group), Wildlife Soc., Am. Soc. Mammalogists, Explorers Club (resident fellow), Sigma Xi. Presbyterian. Avocations: skiing, hiking, canoeing, canning jams and jellies, photography. Office: Smithsonian Nat Zoo 3001 Connecticut Ave NW Washington DC 20010 Office Phone: 202-633-3241.

MOORE, DONALD WALTER, retired academic administrator; b. Culver City, Calif., June 9, 1942; s. Raymond Owen and Jewel Elizabeth (Young) M.; m. Dagmar Ulbrich, Mar. 28, 1968; 1 child, Michael. AA, L.A. Valley Coll., 1967; BA in History, Calif. State U., Northridge, 1970; MA in Learning Disability, Calif. State U., 1973; MLS, U. So. Calif., 1974. Asst., adj. prof. L.A. Pierce Coll. Libr., 1974—; instr. reading L.A. Trade Tech. Coll., 1978—80, pres.'s staff asst., 1983—87; instr. learning skills L.A. City Coll., 1987—88, dir. amnesty edn., 1988—92, dir. English and citizenship program, 1992—2003, ret., 2003. Adj. instr. computer sci. L.A. (Calif.) Trade-Tech. Coll., 1983—. Author: A Guidebook to US Army Dress Helmets, 2000, Custer's Ghosts and Custer's Gold, 2007; contbr. fiction, articles, revs. to various publs. Mem. Little Big Horn Assn., The Co. Mil. Historians, Horror Writers Assn., Mystery Writers Am. Republican. Roman Catholic. Avocations: writing, collecting military memorabilia, reading. Personal E-mail: writer99@ca.rr.com. *Personal philosophy: To survive in this world you must believe in yourself and know what's worth fighting for and what's not. But never despair, despair is the greatest sin.*

MOORE, DUNCAN THOMAS, optics scientist, educator; b. Biddeford, Maine, Dec. 7, 1946; s. Thomas Fogg Moore and Virginia Robinson Wing; m. Gunta Liders, July 1995. BA in Physics, U. Maine, 1969, DSc (hon.), 1995; MS in Optics, Rochester U., NY, 1970, PhD in Optics, 1974. Asst. prof. U. Rochester, 1974-78, assoc. prof., 1978-86, prof., 1986—, Kingslake prof., 1993—, dean engring. and applied sci., 1995-97, prof. biomed. engring., 2001—, prof. bus. adminstrn., 2005—, vice provost entrepreneurship, 2007; pres. and founder Gradient Lens Corp., Rochester, 1980—97; dir. N.Y. State Ctr. Advanced Optical Tech., Rochester, 1987—94; assoc. dir. technology White House Office Sci. & Technology Policy, Washington, 1997—2000; CEO Infotonics Tech. Ctr. Inc., 2002—04. Vis. scientist Nippon Schlumberger, Tokyo, 1983; Congl. fellow Am. Phys. Soc., Washington, 1993—94; sci. advisor Sen. John D. Rockefeller IV, W.Va., 1993—94; exec. dir. Univ. Industry and Govt. Partnership Advanced Photonics, 2001—02; mem. environ. and energy svc. rev. com. Idaho Nat. Engring. and Environ. Lab., 2001—02; mem. bd. assessment for Nat. Inst. Stds. and Tech. programs NRC, 2001—05, mem. panel for physics, 2001—05, chmn. panel for physics, 2002—05, chmn., 2002—05, mem. adv. coun. US commn. optics, 2006—, mem. com. sci., tech. and law, 2006—; mem. engring. vis. com. NASA-Goddard Space Flight Ctr., 2002—06, chair applied engring. and tech. directorate vis. com., 2002—06, mem. James Webb Space Telescope product integrity team, 2002—; mem. nat. innovation initiative Coun. on Competitiveness, 2004; lectr. in field. Contbr. articles to profl. jours. Chmn. Hubble Ind. Rev. Panel, 1990—91. Named Engr. of the Yr., Rochester Engring. Soc., 1999; recipient Disting. Inventor of Yr. award, Rochester Intellectual Property Law Assn., 1993, Grin Optics award, Japanese Applied Physics Soc., 1993, Sci. and Tech. award, Greater Rochester C. of C., 1992, Gold medal, Internat. Soc. Optical Engring., 2006. Mem.: AAAS (mem. com. sci. engring. and pub. policy 2005—), NAE, IEEE Lasers and Electro-Optics Soc. (govt. fellows selection com. 2005—), Am. Inst. Physics (state dept. fellowship selection com. 2001—02), Coalition Photonics and Optics (chair 1996—97), Forum Physics and Soc. (exec. com. 1996—97), Coun. Sci. Soc. (co-chair govt. affairs com. 1996—97), Materials Rsch. Soc., Am. Assn. Engring. Soc. (bd. govs. 1995—97, Nat. Engring. award 1999), Optical Soc. Am. (bd. dirs. 1987—89, editor Applied Optics 1990—92, bd. dirs. 1992—97, v.p. 1994, pres. 1996, adv. coun. homeland security 2004—, Leadership award 2001), Am. Soc. Precision Engring., Am. Ceramic Soc. (Edward Orton, Jr. Meml. lectr 2002). Achievements include patents in field. Home: 4 Claret Dr Fairport NY 14450-4610 Office: The Inst Optics University of Rochester Rochester NY 14627-0186 Office Phone: 585-275-5248. Business E-Mail: moore@optics.rochester.edu.

MOORE, EDWARD WARREN, lawyer; b. Odessa, Tex., July 21, 1959; s. Edward Warren and Gloria (Schroeter) M.; m. JoAnne Bisso; children: Peggy, Barbara. BA in Econs., Princeton U., 1981; JD, So. Meth. U., 1984. Bar: Tex. 1984, US Dist. Ct. (no. dist.) Tex. 1984, US Dist. Ct. (we. dist.) Tex. 2003, US Ct. Appeals (5th cir.) 1984, US Ct. Appeals (10th cir.) 1985. Assoc. Ravkind, Kuehne & Biesel, Dallas, 1984-85; ptnr. Kuehne & Moore, Dallas, 1984-96; pvt. practice, 1996—; mng. ptnr. Moore & Anderson, 2000—03; v.p., gen. counsel Tissue Gen, Inc. Dir. Rsch. Group Tex., Inc.; mentor North Tex. Enterprise Ctr. for Med. Tech.; expert witness N. Mex. State Senate. Mem. Princeton U. Class Alumni Giving Com.; mem. auction com., auction host, annual convention Safari Club Internat.; chmn. exhbitor registration com. Dallas Safari Club. Fellow Am. Bar Found.; mem. AAAS, ABA (litigation sect., bus. law sect. and com., intellectual property sect.), State Bar Tex., Dallas Bar Assn., Dallas Country Club, Safari Club Internat. (life), Dallas Safari Club (life), DSC 100 (vol.), Order of Flags. Roman Catholic. Home: 7044 Turtle Creek Blvd Dallas TX 75205-1254 Home Phone: 214-369-2636; Office Phone: 214-706-9040. Business E-Mail: eddymoore@ewmpllc.net.

MOORE, EDWIN J.T., retired obstetrician, gynecologist; b. Holyoke, Mass., Aug. 19, 1924; s. Edwin Aloysius and Mary Hartnett Moore; m. Bernice Deady, June 10, 1950; children: Ned, Bill, Terry(dec.), Mary Alice, Maureen, Kevin, Dennis, Kathleen, Timothy(dec.), Brendan(dec.). Student, Wesleyan U., Middletown, Conn., 1972—73, Washington U., St. Louis, 1943—44; MD, Tufts U., Boston, 1948. Diplomate Am. Bd. Ob-Gyn. Internship St. Francis Hosp., Hartford, Conn., 1948—49; residency Brady Maternity Hosp., Albany, NY, 1949—50; chief obstetrics resident NY Poly Clinic Hosp., 1953—54; chief gynecology resident Coney Island Gen. Hosp., 1954—55; chief ob-gyn St. Mary's Hosp., Waterbury, Conn., chief of staff. With US Army, 1943—46, World War II, lt. Med. Corps USN, 1950—53, Republic of Korea. Fellow: ACS, ACOG (chmn. Conn. sect.); mem.: Conn. Soc. Am. Bd. Ob-Gyn. (pres.), Hartford Ob-Gun. Soc. (pres.), New Eng. Ob-Gyn. Soc. (pres.). Roman Catholic. Avocations: golf, walking. Home: 234 Watch Hill Rd Westerly RI 02891

MOORE, EMMETT BURRIS, JR., physical chemist, educator; b. Bozeman, Mont., June 14, 1929; s. Emmett Burris and Iris Marie (Brown) M.; m. Diane Elizabeth Girling, Oct. 1, 1960; children: Karen Elizabeth, Robin Diane. BS in Chemistry with honors, Wash. State U., 1951; PhD in Phys. Chemistry (Shell fellow), U. Minn., 1956. Teaching asst. U. Minn., Mpls., 1951-55, asst. prof. physics Duluth, 1957-59; staff scientist Boeing Sci. Research Labs., Seattle, 1959-73. Lectr. chemistry Seattle U., 1973; dir. power plant siting Minn. Environ. Quality Bd., St. Paul, 1973-76; gen. mgr. Richland (Wash.) Divsn. Olympic Engring. Corp., 1976-78; staff scientist Pacific N.W. Nat. Lab., 1978-96; mem. environ. engring. rev. panel EPA, 1989-95; alt. mem. Hanford Adv. Bd., 1995-2000, 2007; adj. prof. environ. sci. Wash. State U., 1990—. Author: (book) The Environmental Impact Statement Process and Environmental Law, 1997, 2d edit., 2000, An Introduction to the Management and Regulation of Hazardous Waste, 2000, 2nd edit., 2007; contbr. articles to profl. jours. Trustee Mid-Columbia Symphony Soc., 1978-85, v.p., 1980-81, pres., 1981-83; trustee Richland Light Opera Co., 1984-88, bus. mgr., 1984-88. Recipient Land Grant Faculty Excellence award Wash. State U., 1999. Fellow AAAS; mem. Am. Phys. Soc., Am. Chem. Soc. (chmn. Pauling award com. 1971, sec. Puget Sound sect. 1971-73, mem. energy panel of com. on chemistry and pub. affairs 1983-86), Am. Assn. Physics Tchrs. (v.p. Wash. sect. 1965-66, pres. 1966-67), Phi Beta Kappa, Phi Kappa Phi, Phi Eta Sigma, Alpha Chi Sigma, Phi Lambda Upsilon, Sigma Alpha Epsilon (v.p. province 1972-73) Episcopalian (vestryman 1967-69, 76-79, 91, sr. warden 1969, del. diocesan conv. 1969-72). Home: 2323 Greenbrook Blvd Richland WA 99352-8427 Office: Wash State U 2710 University Dr Richland WA 99354-1671 Office Phone: 509-372-7276. Business E-Mail: ebmoore@wsu.edu.

MOORE, ERNEST CARROLL, III, lawyer; b. Honolulu, Oct. 24, 1944; s. Ernest Carroll Jr. and Frances (Miller) M.; children: Tiffany Meredith, Alyssa Judi. BA, Dartmouth Coll., 1967; JD, So Meth. U., 1974. Bar: Hawaii 1974, U.S. Dist. Ct. Hawaii 1974, U.S. Ct. Appeals (9th cir.) 1974. Ptnr. Torkildson, Katz, Fonseca, Moore & Hetherington, Honolulu, 1974—. Bd. dirs. Hawaii chpt. ARC, Honolulu, 1979, trustee La Pietra-Hawaii Sch. for Girls, 1998—, 1st v.p., 2005; bd. dirs. Outrigger Duke Kahanamoku Found., 1999—, pres., 2005; bd. govs. The Pacific Club, 2002, sec. 2005-06, 2d v.p., 2006, 1st v.p., 2007. Mem. Am. Acad. Hosp. Attys., Nat. Health Lawyers Assn., Indsl. Relations Research Assn., Soc. for Human Resources Mgmt., Order of Coif, Pacific Club (bd. govs.), Outrigger Canoe Club. Republican. Episcopalian. Avocations: tennis, photography. Office: Torkildson Katz Fonseca Jaffe Moore & Hetherington 700 Bishop St Fl 15 Honolulu HI 96813-4187 Office Phone: 808-523-6000. Business E-Mail: ecm@torkiloson.com.

MOORE, ERNEST EUGENE, JR., surgeon, educator; b. Pitts., June 18, 1946; s. Ernest Eugene Sr. and Mary Ann (Burroughs) M.; m. Sarah Van Duzer, Sept. 2, 1978; children: Hunter Burroughs, Peter Kitrick. BS in Chemistry, Allegheny Coll., 1968; MD, U. Pitts., 1972. Surg. resident U. Vt., Burlington, 1972-76; chief of trauma Denver Health Med. Ctr., 1976—, chief dept. surgery, 1984—. Prof. surgery, vice chmn. dept. U. Colo., 1984—; dir. facilities Colo. Trauma Inst., 1984-95. Editor: Critical Decisions in Trauma, 1987, Trauma, 1988, rev. edits., 1991, 96, 00, 05, 07, Early Care of the Injured, 1989, Surgical Secrets, 1996, rev. edit., 2002, 05, Trauma Manual, 2003, World Jour. Emergency Surgery; assoc. editor Jour. Trauma, Am. Jour. Surgery, World Jour. Surgery, Surgery-Problem Solving Approach, 2d edit., 1994, others; patentee retrohepatic vena cava shunt. Fellow ACS (com. on trauma, vice chair 1990), Soc. Univ. Surgeons (pres. 1989), Am. Assn. Surgery of Trauma (pres. 1993), Internat. Assn. Surgery of Trauma and Surg. Intensive Care (pres. 1998-99), Pan Am. Trauma Assn. (pres. 1991), Southwestern Surg. Congress (pres. 1998), Western Trauma Assn. (pres. 1989). Republican. Avocations: skiing, mountaineering, hunting, ultramarathons, fishing. Home: 2909 E 7th Avenue Pky Denver CO 80206-3839 Office: Denver Health Med Ctr Dept Surgery Denver CO 80204 Office Phone: 303-436-6558. Business E-Mail: ernest.moore@dhha.org.

MOORE, FAY LINDA, systems engineer; b. Houston, Apr. 7, 1942; d. Charlie Louis and Esther Mable (Banks) Moore; m. Noel Patrick Walker, Jan. 5, 1963 (div. 1967); 1 child, Trina Nicole Moore. Student, Prairie View Agrl. and Mech. Coll., 1960-61, Tex. So. U., 1961, Our Lady Lake U., 1993, U. Phoenix, 2003. Cert. ISO 9001 Internal Auditor, 1994-97. Instr. Internat. Bus. Coll., Houston, 1965; keypunch operator IBM Corp., Houston, 1965-67, sr. keypunch operator, 1967-70, programmer technician, 1970-72, asst. programmer, 1972-73, assoc. programmer, 1973-74, sr. assoc. programmer, 1984-87, staff programmer, 1987-92, staff sys. analyst, 1992-96; sr. software quality engr. Loral Space Info. Sys., Houston, 1994—96; owner, pres. AFT Co., Houston, 1993—; sr. software quality engr. Lockheed Martin Corp., Houston, 1996-97; software quality engr. Motorola, Inc., Austin, 1998-2001, quality sys. rev. assessor, 1998-2001, info. tech. quality engr., 2000-2001; prin. sys. engr. L-3 comms. Titan Corp., Houston, 2001—, ISO 9001 lead internal auditor, 2005—; software quality engr. Software Engring. Inst. Space shuttle flight support team IBM, 1985—92, mem. space sta. team, 1992—93. Recipient Apollo Achievement award, NASA, 1969, Quality and Productivity award, 1986, 1992, Cert. of Recognition, NASA Office of Space Flight, 2004. Democrat. Roman Catholic. Avocation: personal computing.

MOORE, FAYE HALFACRE, jewelry manufacturer; b. Granville, Tenn., Oct. 16, 1941; d. Benton Mack and Dora Mai (Carter) Halfacre; m. Travis Edward Halford, Jan. 2, 1965; children: Kristi Faye, Trent Edward; m. Charles Harold Moore, Jan. 23, 1989. BSBA, Tenn. Technol. U., 1963. Exec. sec. E.I. du Pont de Nemours, Old Hickory, Tenn., 1963-65, Amoco, New Orleans, 1965-66; adminstrv. asst. Thompson & Moss, Atlanta, 1967-72; founder, owner Strictly Natural, Ltd., Atlanta, 1975—, Elegant Accessories, Internat., Atlanta, 1980—. Pres. Sandy Springs Arts and Heritage Soc., Atlanta, 1986; founding dir. Leadership Sandy Springs, 1987; bd. dirs. Lindsey-Wilson Coll., Columbia, Ky., 1989, Cardinal Hill Hosp., Lexington, 1989, Ky. Ednl. TV Authority, vice chmn. 1992; bd. dirs. Ky. Literacy Commn., Ky. Literacy Found., chmn. 1991; bd. dirs. Lexington Philharm. Found., 1989, chmn. 1991—; adv. bd. Marco Cmty. Banks, 2003-; trustee Tenn. Technol. U., 2005—. Named Citizen of Yr. Sandy Springs Jr. Women's Club, 1976. Mem. Women Bus. Owners, Assn. Women Entrepreneurs (founder), Women's Commerce Club, Marco Island Woman's Club (pres., 2003), Remax, 100% Club, Rotary. Democrat. Avocations: harp, piano, reading, painting, gardening. Home: 5900 Russell Cave Rd Lexington KY 40511-8441 Office: 847 N Collier Blvd Marco Island FL 34145 Home: 840 S Collier Marco Island FL 34145 Personal E-mail: marcofaye@aol.com.

MOORE, GARETH, human resources specialist; b. Harrogate, North Yorkshire, England, Oct. 2, 1977; arrived in US, 1994; m. Heather Moore, July 8, 2000; 1 child, Liam. BA in English, St. Mary's Coll. of Md., 2000. Cert. sr. profl. in human resources Human Resources Cert. Inst., 2006. Human resources generalist Nutra Mfg., Greenville, SC, 2001—04; dir. human resources Jarden Plastic Solutions, Greer, 2004—. Mem.: Soc. Human Resources Mgmt., Mensa. Office: Jarden Plastic Solutions 103 S Batesville Rd Greer SC 29650 Home Phone: 864-918-5567. Business E-Mail: gmoore@jardenplasticsolutions.com.

MOORE, GEORGE CRAWFORD JACKSON, lawyer; b. Tenn. BA, U. Fla., 1963; PhB in Soviet Law, U. St. Andrews, Scotland, 1966; MA in English Law with honors, Cambridge U., Eng., 1968, LLM in Internat. Law, 1969. Bar: Eng. (Barrister, Inner Temple) 1970, Jamaica 1971, Fla. 1973, Turks & Caicos Islands 1974, U.S. Supreme Ct. 1976, Antigua and Barbuda, Brit. V.I., Grenada, Montserrat, St. Lucia 1977, Anguilla 1999. Legis. asst. to U.S. sen., Washington, 1970-72; asst. pub. defender Palm Beach County, Fla., 1973; pvt. practice West Palm Beach, Fla., 1973—. Founding pres. World Trade Coun. of Palm Beach County, 1981—; chmn. Fla. Coun. Internat. Devel., 1983—84, 2000—03, Fla. Gov.'s Conf. on World Trade and Investment, 1989, Fla. Export Coun. of U.S. Dept. Commerce, 1991—92, Free Trade Agreement of Americas. Editor spl. issues Fla. Bar Jour., 1982, 87, chmn. editorial bd., 1988-89; mem. editorial bd. The Internat. Lawyer jour. of ABA, 1979-84; contbr. articles to profl. jours. Chmn. Fla. Econ. Growth and Internat. Devel. Commn., 1989-90. Fellow: Ctr. Internat. Legal Studies, Soc. Internat. Bus. Fellows (v.p.); mem.: ABA, Fla. Bar (chmn. internat. law sect. 1994—95, bd. cert. specialist in internat. law 1999—, chmn. internat. law cert. bd. 2004—). Office: 105 S Narcissus Ave Ste 812 West Palm Beach FL 33401-5530 also: 11 King's Bench Walk, Temple London EC4Y 7EQ England Office Phone: 561-833-9000, 44-20-7632-8500. Business E-Mail: barrister@barrister.law.com.

MOORE, GEORGE EMERSON, JR., geologist, educator; b. Lebanon, Mo., Jan. 2, 1914; s. George Emerson and Dorothea Louisa (Niewohner) M.; m. Wilma Corrine Leonard, May 20, 1939; children: George E. III, Dana Corinne, Craig G. AB, U. Mo., 1936, MA, 1938; PhD, Harvard U., 1947. Instr. U. Mo., 1938-39; teaching asst. Harvard U., 1940-42, 1946-47; geologist A.P. Green Fire Brick Co., Mexico, Mo., 1942-46; instr. Ohio State U. at Columbus, 1947-48, asst. prof., 1948-57, assoc. prof., 1957-64, prof., 1964-84, prof. emeritus, 1984—. Geologist U.S. Geol. Survey, 1952-83 Fellow Geol. Soc. Am.; mem. Phi Beta Kappa, Sigma Xi. Home: 58 Mulberry Dr Wakefield RI 02879-1416

MOORE, GORDON E., electronics executive, researcher; b. San Francisco, Jan. 3, 1929; s. Walter Harold and Florence Almira (Williamson) Moore; m. Betty I. Whittaker, Sept. 9, 1950; children: Kenneth, Steven. BS in Chemistry, U. Calif., Berkeley, 1950; PhD in Chemistry and Physics, Calif. Inst. Tech., 1954. Tech. staff Shockley Semicondr. Lab., 1956—57; mgr. engring. Fairchild Camera & Instrument Corp., 1957—59, dir. R & D, 1959—68; co-founder Intel Corp., Santa Clara, Calif., 1968, exec. v.p., 1968—75, pres., CEO, 1975—79, CEO, 1979—87, chmn., 1979—97, chmn. emeritus, 1997—. Bd. dirs. Varian Assocs. Inc., Transamerica Corp., Gilead Sciences, Inc. Founder, chmn. Gordon & Betty Moore Found.; bd. trustee Calif. Inst. Tech., 1995—2001, sr. trustee, 2001—. Named one of Forbes' Richest Americans, 1999—, World's Richest People, Forbes mag., 2001; recipient Nat. Medal Tech., President George Bush, 1990, Fellow award, Computer History Mus., 1998, Bower award for Bus. Leadership, Franklin Inst., 2002, Perkin medal, Soc. Chem. Industry, 2004. Fellow: IEEE (Founders medal 1977); mem.: Am. Phys. Soc., NAE. Achievements include having a pygmy owl named after him for his donations to environ. rsch. Avocations: fishing, golf. Office: Intel Corp 2200 Mission College Blvd Santa Clara CA 95054-1549 also: Betty & Gordon Moore Library Wilberforce Rd Cambridge CB3 0WD England *

MOORE, GREGORY E., lawyer; b. Annapolis, Md., Mar. 4, 1952; SB, MIT, 1973; JD, Harvard Univ., 1976. Bar: Mass. 1977. Assoc. Ropes & Gray, Boston, 1976—85, ptnr. corp. dept., 1985—, co-head venture capital & emerging companies practice group. Chmn. MIT Alumni Fund Bd., 2000—02; mem. MIT Corp., 2003—; bd. dir. Lexington Montessori Sch. Mem.: ABA (chmn. Com. on Tech. & Intellectual Property 1988—92), Mass. Bar Assn., Boston Bar Assn., Computer Law Assn. (former bd. dir.). Office: Ropes & Gray 1 International Pl Boston MA 02110-2624 Office Phone: 617-951-7370. Office Fax: 617-951-7050. Business E-Mail: gregory.moore@ropesgray.com.

MOORE, GREGORY L., editor; b. Cleve., Sept. 16, 1954; m. Nina Henderson Moore; children: Michael Langston, Jasmine Henderson. B. Journalism & Polit. Sci., Ohio Wesleyan U., 1976. Reporter Dayton Journal Herald, 1976—80, Cleveland Plain Dealer, 1980—83, political editor, 1983—86; asst. metro editor Boston Globe, 1986—94, mng. editor, 1994—2002; editor Denver Post, 2002—. Mem. Pulitzer Prize Bd., 2004—; mem. bd. trustees Ohio Wesleyan U. Named Journalist of Yr., New Eng. ch., Nat. Assn. Black Journalists, 1996. Mem.: Am. Soc. Newspaper Editors, Nat. Assn. Black Journalists. Office: Denver Post 101 W Colfax Ave Denver CO 80202 Office Phone: 303-820-1400. E-mail: gmoore@denverpost.com. *

MOORE, GUY WILL, retired public information officer, historian, writer; b. Retta, Okla., June 19, 1922; s. Guy Thomas Moore and Pearl Grace Glasgow; m. Hazel Avenell Cartwright, Aug. 31, 1948 (dec. June 18, 1986); children: Anne Elizabeth Tarquinio, March Victoria Dodge. BA in Journalism, U. Okla., 1950, MA in History, 1952. News writer Office of the Army Surgeon Gen., Washington, 1956—57, info. specialist, 1957—59; info. specialist (first) U.S. Army Rsch. and Devel. Command, Washington, 1959—60; dep. info. officer, divsn. gen. med. scis. NIH, Bethesda, Md., 1960—61, staff asst., office of dir. pub. affairs, 1961—64, chief pub. info. sect. office of rsch info., chief supervisory pub. info. specialist, news br., office of comm., 1967—79; ret., 1979. Chmn. pub. info. intern recruitment tng. com. NIH, 1961—79, spkr. grants assoc. seminar, 1971—72; spkr. Am. Coll. Pub. Rels. Assn., Washington, 1970. Author: The Case of Mrs. Surratt, 1954, The NIH: How it Works, 1981; contbg. author: The Surratt Society's In Pursuit of..., 1990; contbr. articles to astronomy jours. Contr. project feeder watch Cornell Lab of Ornithology, 1987—. Mem.: No. Va. Astronomy Club, Nat. Capitol Astronomers, Surratt Soc. Avocations: astronomy, birdwatching. Home: 224 N Nelson St Arlington VA 22201

MOORE, GWENDOLYNNE S. (GWEN MOORE), congresswoman; b. Racine, Wis., Apr. 18, 1951; 3 children. BA in Polit. Sci., Marquette U., Milw., 1978. Mem. Wis. State Assembly, 1989—92, Wis. State Senate from 4th dist., Madison, 1992—2004, US Congress from 4th Wis. dist., 2005—, mem. small bus. com., mem. fin. svcs. com. Named one of Most Influential Black Americans, Ebony mag., 2006. Democrat. Office: US House Reps 1408 Longworth House Office Bldg Washington DC 20515-4904 Office Phone: 202-225-4572. *

MOORE, HAL G., mathematician, educator; b. Vernal, Utah, Aug. 14, 1929; s. Lewis Henry and Nora (Gillman) M.; m. D'On Empey, July 20, 1956; children: David, Nora (Mrs. Bret C. Hess), Alison (Mrs. Samuel M. Smith). BS, U. Utah, 1952, MS, 1957; PhD, U. Calif., Santa Barbara, 1967. Tchr. Salt Lake City Pub. Schs., 1952-53; instr. math. Carbon Jr. Coll., also Carbon H.S., Price, Utah, 1953-55, Purdue U., Lafayette, Ind., 1957-61, adminstrv. asst. dept. math, 1960-61; from asst. prof. math. to assoc. prof. math. Brigham Young U., Provo, Utah, 1961-71, prof., 1971-95, prof. emeritus, 1995—, assoc. chmn. dept. math., 1986-89. Author: Precalculus

Mathematics, 2d edit, 1977, (with Adil Yaqub) Elementary Linear Algebra With Applications, 1980, College Algebra and Trigonometry, 1983, A First Course in Linear Algebra, 1992, 3d edit., 1998; contbr. articles to profl. jours. Mem. High Coun., LDS Ch., 1985-91, MTC br. pres., 1991-94, Bishop, 1958-61, 78-82. NSF faculty fellow, U. Calif., Santa Barbara, 1964—66. Mem. Am. Math. Soc., Math. Assn. Am. (bd. govs. 1989-92), Utah State Math. Coalition (planning dir. 1990, bd. dir. 1991-92), Sigma Xi (dir. 1974-80, 82-85, com. chmn. 1982-90), Phi Kappa Phi. Home and Office: 631 W 650 S Orem UT 84058-6027 Home Phone: 801-225-7125. Personal E-mail: mooreh@math.byu.edu. *Revelation and reason can work together to bring human beings closer to the truth of their existence and place in the universe. But charity and love and dedication are as necessary to the success of this union as they are to all others.*

MOORE, HERFF LEO, JR., management educator; b. San Antonio, Jan. 24, 1937; s. Herff Leo Moore Sr. and Constance (Benesh) Wold; m. Cheryll Burkett, Aug. 18, 2007; children: Terri Lynne, Christopher Scott, Kimberly Anne. BSBA, Ohio State U., Columbus, 1964; MBA, U. Tex., Austin, 1968; MS in Cmty. Svcs., U. Rochester, 1976; PhD, U. Tex., Arlington, 1980. Cert. sr. profl. in human resources (life). Prodn. mgmt., quality assurance officer Sacramento Air Logistics Ctr. USAF, 1964—67; pers. mgmt., adminstrv. cons. Aero. Sys. Divsn. Wright-Patterson AFB, Dayton, Ohio, 1968—73; pers. mgmt. and quality assurance cons. Defense Contract Adminstrv. Svcs. Dist. Hdqrs., Rochester, NY, 1973—76; lectr. in mgmt. and doctoral student U. Tex. Arlington, 1976—79; asst. prof. bus. adminstrn. Ea. Ky. U., Richmond, 1979—81; assoc. prof. mgmt. East Tex. State U. Texarkana, 1981—83, Saint John Fisher Coll., Rochester, 1983—85, U. Ctrl. Ark., Conway, 1985—99, ret., 1999. Pres. H.M.C.C. Mgmt. Group, Conway, 1988-2005, H.M. Merchandising Internat., Inc., 2006; CEO B&B Better Books, 2007; participant Leadership Texarkana Leadership Tng., 1981-82; mgmt. cons., devel. trainer, Calif., NY, Ark., Ohio, NJ, Fla., Ga., Tex., 1964—. Author: (with others) Language, Customs and Protocol: A Guidebook for International Students and Employees, 1992; contbr. numerous articles to profl. jours. Capt. USAF, 1964—76. Recipient Significant Performance Contbr. award Def. Supply Agy., 1975; Nat. scholar Phi Kappa Phi, 1968; named Honor Grad. USAF Officers Tng. Sch., 1964. Mem. Soc. for Human Resource Mgmt. (tng. and devel. com. 1989-94, select panel on edn. 1989-91, coll. rels. com. 1989-92, bd. dirs. area IV 1987-91, sec., treas. Ark. coun. 1986-87), Ark. Human Resources Assn. (pres. 1991-92, bd. dirs. 1991-93), Acad. Mgmt., Soc. Human Resource Mgmt. (superior merit awards student chpt. U. Ctrl. Ark. 1985-90, 93), Alpha Kappa Psi, Phi Kappa Phi, Sigma Iota Epsilon. Mem. Assembly Of God Ch. Avocations: golf, chess, political buttons. Home: 1422 Autumncrest Dr Arlington TX 76002-3591 Personal E-mail: herffmoore@hotmail.com.

MOORE, HUBERT, JR., retired addictions counselor, consultant; b. Oklahoma City, Jan. 2, 1932; s. Hubert and Goldie Edith Moore; m. Mary Alene Jarnet, Dec. 9, 1958 (div. Oct. 1959); 1 child, LeAnne; m. Shirley M. Mumchuck, Apr. 1978 (dec. Nov. 8, 1985); children: Peggy, JoAnn, Lisa, Sharon. AA in Counseling, U. Alaska, 1986, BA in Human Svcs., 1992, BA in Psychology, 1992, BA in Sociology, 1996; MA in Anthropology, U. Mindanao, Philippines, 1998. Cert. addictions counselor II Alaska, Nat. Assn. Alcohol and Drug Abuse Counselors, master forensic counselor and criminal justice specialist Nat. Assn. Forensic Counselors, Nat. Register Addiction Counselors, Calif. Registry Addiction Specialists. Substance abuse counselor II No. Regional Ctr. for Addictions, Fairbanks, Alaska, 1977—85; forensic counselor Fairbanks Correction Facility, 1995—96; addictions cons. Soldotna, Alaska, 1991—2005; owner, operator (daycare ctr.) Papa's Playhouse, Soldotna, 1998—2006; ret., 2006. Campaign vol. Rep. Caucus, Soldotna, 1991—. Republican. Muslim. Avocations: philosophic studies, demographic research, motorcycling, moutain climbing, social research. Home and Office: PO Box 1057 Soldotna AK 99669 Business E-Mail: altcounselingconsult@lycos.com.

MOORE, HUGH JACOB, JR., lawyer; b. Norfolk, Va., June 29, 1944; s. Hugh Jacob and Ina Ruth (Hall) M.; m. Jean Garnett, June 10, 1972; children: Lela Miller, Sarah Garnett. BA, Vanderbilt U., Nashville, 1966; LLB, Yale U., New Haven, Conn., 1969. Bar: Tenn. 1970, US Dist. Ct. (mid. dist.) Tenn. 1970, US Dist. Ct. (ea. dist.) Tenn. 1973, US Dist. Ct. (we. dist.) Tenn. 1982, US Ct. Claims, US Ct. Appeals (6th cir.) 1973, US Ct. Appeals (fed. cir.) 1999, US Supreme Ct. 1972. Law clk. US Dist. Ct. (mid. dist.) Tenn., Nashville, 1969-70; trial atty. civil rights divsn. US Dept. Justice, Washington, 1970-73; asst. U.S. atty. Eastern Dist. of Tenn., Chattanooga, 1973-76; assoc. Witt, Gaither & Whitaker, PC, Chattanooga, 1976-77, shareholder, 1977—2002, also bd. dirs.; shareholder Shumacker, Witt, Gaither & Whitaker, PC, Chattanooga, 2002—06, Chambliss, Bahner & Stophel, PC, Chattanooga, 2006—. Mem. Commn. Women and Minorities Profession Law, 1995-97; mem. hearing com. Bd. Profl. Responsibility Supreme Ct. Tenn., 1996-2002; mem. mediation and arbitration panel US Dist. Ct. (ea. dist.) Tenn.; cert. arbitrator, cert. mediator Tenn. Rule 31, Nat. Assn. Securities Dealers; cert. artbitrator NY Stock Exch., Nat. Arbitration Forum; mem. adv. commn. on rules of civil and appellate procedure Tenn. Supreme Ct., chmn., 1999—. Contbr. articles to profl. jours. Bd. dirs. Adult Edn. Coun., Chattanooga, 1976-81, pres., 1977-79; bd. dirs. Chattanooga Symphony and Opera Assn., 1981-87, Riverbend Fesitval, 1983-85, 91—, pres., 1995-97, Landmarks Chattanooga, 1983-84, Cornerstones, 1995-98, Orange Grove Sch., 1996-, pres., 2005-07; mem. alumni coun. McCallie Sch., 1980-85; trustee St. Nicholas Sch., 1983-89, chmn., 1986-88. Master Am. Inns of Ct. (Brock-Cooper Inn); fellow Am. Coll. Trial Lawyers, Tenn. State Com., Tenn. Bar Found., Chattanooga Bar Found, Am. Bar Found.; mem. ABA (mem. bd. editors jour. Litigation News 1983-90), Tenn. Bar Assn., Chattanooga Bar Assn. (mem. bd. govs. 1985-87), Am. Arbitration Assn. (mem. roster neutrals), Mountain City Club, Rotary, Yale Club NY. Methodist. Home: 101 Ridgeside Rd Chattanooga TN 37411-1830 Office Phone: 423-756-3000. Business E-Mail: hmoore@cbslawfirm.com.

MOORE, J. STROTHER, computer scientist, educator; s. J. Strother and Jessie Louise Moore; m. Jo Anne O'Neil; children: Lisa, Jonathan, Chris. BS in Math., MIT, Cambridge, 1970; PhD in Computational Logic, U.Edinburgh, 1973. Programmer dept. computational logic U. Edinburgh, Scotland, 1971—72, rsch. fellow, 1973; rsch. mathematician computer sci. lab. Xerox Palo Alto Rsch. Ctr., Calif., 1973—76, SRI Internat., Menlo Park, Calif., 1976—78, sr. rsch. mathematician, 1979—81, staff scientist, 1981; assoc. prof. dept. computer scis. U. Tex., Austin, 1981—84, Gottesman Family Centennial prof., 1985—88, Adm. B.R. Inman prof. computing theory, 1997—, chair dept. computer scis., 2001—; founder, bd. dirs. Computational Logic, Inc., Austin, 1987—, chief scientist, 1987—96. Lectr. in field. Contbr. articles to profl. jours.; co-author: (software) Boyer-Moore Theorem Prover, 1971, A Computational Logic, 1979, A Computational Logic Handbook, 1988, Computer-Aided Reasoning: An Approach, 2000; co-editor: The Correctness Problem in Computer Science, 1981; mem. editl. bd.: Jour. Automated Reasoning, Formal Methods in Sys. Design. Co-recipient John McCarthy prize for Prog. Verification, 1983, Current prize in Automatic Theorem Proving, Am. Math. Soc., 1991, Herbrand award, Conf. on Automated Deduction, 1999. Fellow: Assn. Computing Machinery (Software Sys. award 2005), Am. Assn. Artificial Intelligence; mem.: NAE. Avocation: rock climbing. Office: Dept Computer Scis U Tex Austin Taylor Hall 4 140A Austin TX 78712-1188 Office Phone: 512-471-9590. Office Fax: 512-471-8885. E-mail: moore@cs.utexas.edu. *

MOORE, JACKSON WATTS, bank executive; b. Birmingham, Ala., Nov. 2, 1948; s. Joseph Watts and Shellye Louise (Jackson) M.; m. Elizabeth Wilson, June 12, 1971; children: Jackson Jr., Wilson, Shellye. BS, U. Ala., 1970; JD, Vanderbilt U., 1973. Assoc. Martin, Tate, Morrow and Marston, Memphis, 1973-77; mng. ptnr. Wildman, Harrold, Allen, Dixon and McDonnell, Memphis, 1977-89; pres., COO Union Planters Corp., Memphis, 1989, also bd. dirs., chmn., CEO, 2000—04; pres. Regions Financial Corp., 2004—, CEO, 2005—06, exec. chmn., 2006—. Bd. dirs. Union Planters Nat. Bank, Mid-South Pub. Comms. Network, Memphis Devel. Found., PSB Bancshares, Clanton, Ala. Bd. dirs. Boy Scouts Am., Memphis Emmaus Comty.; trustee Vanderbilt Univ.; chmn. bd. Vanderbilt Law Sch.; bd. trustees pres.'s cabinet U. Ala. Capt. U.S. Army, 1973. Mem. Memphis Country Club, Memphis Hunt and Polo Club. Republican. Methodist. Avocations: golf, tennis, reading. Office: Regions Financial Corp 417 N 20th St Birmingham AL 35202 *

MOORE, JACQUELYN CORNELIA, retired labor union administrator, editor; b. Dec. 25, 1929; d. James C. and Harriette I. Thomas; m. Clarence Carbin Moore, Jan. 19, 1947 (dec. Feb. 1970); children: Clarence Joseph, Janet Elizabeth Moore Marshall. Mail clk. U.S. P.O., Phila., 1966—93; editor Local 509 Newsletter Nat. Alliance of Postal and Fed. Employees, Washington, 1969—74, editl. newsletter chmn., 1969—74, sec. dist. 5, 1972—74, nat. editor Nat. Alliance, 1974—2004, mem. exec. bd., 1974—, union photographer, 1974—2005, ret., 2004. Dir. 202 Housing for Elderly Corp. bds., Chattanooga, New Orleans, 1981—2004, Atlanta, 1988—2004; sec. supervisory com. Nat. Fed. Credit Union, 1977—82, 1984—94, chair, 1994—. Vol. D.C. Voting Rights Corp., Washington, 1979—2004; sustaining mem. Dem. Nat. Com., 1977—2004. Mem.: Nat. Alliance Postel and Fed. Employees. Roman Catholic. Home: 1640 11th St NW 202 Washington DC 20001 E-mail: jacmar5362@aol.com.

MOORE, JAMES CONKLIN, lawyer; b. Albany, NY, Dec. 20, 1939; s. James Alexander and Doris Virginia (Conklin) M.; m. Shirley Jean Mitchell, June 17, 1961; children: James, Jennifer, David, Eliza. BS, Cornell U., 1961, LLB, 1964. Bar: NY 1964, U.S. Dist. Ct. (we. dist.) NY 1966, U.S. Dist. Ct. (mid. dist.) Pa. 1981, U.S. Dist. Ct. (no. dist.) NY 1980, U.S. Ct. Mil. Appeals 1965. Assoc. Wiser, Shaw, Freeman, Van-Graafeiland, Harter & Secrest, Rochester, NY, 1966-74; ptnr. Harter, Secrest & Emery, Rochester, 1974—2003, mediator, arbitrator, counsel, 2004—. Bd. dirs. Empire Justice Ctr., chmn., 2007—. Contbr. articles to profl. jours., chapters to books. Trustee, pres. Friends of Rochester (N.Y.) Pub. Libr., 1993—98; trustee Nat. Equal Justice Libr., 2006—; bd. dirs., vice chmn. Geva Theater, Inc., 2002—06; pres. Legal Connection, Inc., 2002—04; coun. mem. Cornell U., 1997—2002; bd. dirs. Monroe County Bar Found., 2002—04; chmn. bd. trustees NY Lawyer Assistance Trust, 2001—04. Capt. US Army, 1964—66, Vietnam. Adv. bd. Rochester Area Ednl. TV, 1981-87; elder, trustee Third Presbyn. Ch., Rochester. Fellow: ABA (ho. of dels. 1998—, standing comm. on legal assistance to indigent defendants), N.Y. Bar Found. (bd. dirs. 1997—2000), Am. Coll. Trial Lawyers; mem.: Union Internat. Advocate (US pres. 2005—07), Am. Arbitration Assn., Nat. Conf. Bar Pres. (exec. com. 1999—2002), Monroe County Bar Assn. (chmn. judiciary com. 1982—85, trustee 2004—06, chmn. com. on lawyer advt. 2006), N.Y. State Bar Assn. (chmn. ins. sect. 1984—85, ho. del. 1984—87, chmn. task force on liability ins. 1986—87, 1986—87, chmn. com. ins. programs 1988—94, exec. com. 1992—2000, ho. del. 1993—, v.p. 1994—97, pres. 1998—99, chmn. nominating com. 2001, chmn. com. on ADR 2006—, com. on jud. nominations 2006—), Am. Inst. Law (elected). Avocations: history, restoring old furniture. Home: 251 Windemere Rd Rochester NY 14610-1342 Office: Harter Secrest & Emery 1600 Bausch & Lomb Pl Rochester NY 14604-2711 Office Phone: 585-231-1124. Business E-Mail: jmoore@hselaw.com.

MOORE, JAMES E., state supreme court justice; b. Laurens, SC, Mar. 13, 1936; s. Roy Ernest and Marie (Hill) M.; m. Mary Alicia Deadwyler, Jan. 27, 1963; children: Erin Alicia, Travis Warren. BA, Duke U., 1958, JD, 1961; D of Humanities (hon.), Lander Univ., 1997. Bar: S.C. 1961, U.S. Dist. Ct. S.C. 1961. Pvt. practice, Greenwood, S.C., 1961-76; mem. SC Ho. of Reps., Columbia, SC, 1968—76; cir. judge 8th Jud. Cir. SC, Greenwood, 1976-91; assoc. justice SC Supreme Ct., 1992—. Supreme ct. liaison S.C. Bd. of Law Examiners, Bd. of Commn. on Jud. Conduct, Bd. of Commn. on Atty. Conduct; chmn. Chief Justice's Commn. on Profession. Recipient Outstanding Contribution to Justice award, S.C. Trial Lawyers Assn., 1996. Mem. S.C. Bar Assn., ABA, Am. Judicature Soc.; First Baptist Church of Greenwood. Baptist. Home: 148 Amherst Dr Greenwood SC 29649-8901 Office: SC Supreme Ct PO Box 11330 Columbia SC 29211 Office Phone: 864-942-8559.

MOORE, JAMES R., lawyer; b. Longview, Wash., Sept. 14, 1944; s. James Carlton and Virginia (Rice) M.; m. Patricia Riley, Aug. 25, 1967 (div. 1978); 1 child, Katherine M.; m. Christine M. Monkman, July 14, 1979 (div. 1996); stepchildren: Amy McKenna, John McKenna; 1 foster child, Zia Sunseri; m. Kathryn Lindquist, Aug. 26, 1996; stepchildren: Matthew Elggren, Adam Elggren, Erin Elggren, David Heilner. BA, Whitman Coll., 1966; JD, Duke U., 1969. Bar: Wash. 1970, U.S. Ct. Appeals (4th cir.) 1972, U.S. Supreme Ct. 1973, U.S. Ct. Appeals (9th cir.) 1974, D.C., 1995. Law clk. to Hon. J. Barnes U.S. Ct. Appeals (9th cir.), LA, 1969-70; trial atty. pollution control, land/natural resources div. U.S. Dept. Justice, Washington, 1970-74; asst. U.S. atty. U.S. Atty.'s Office, Seattle, 1974-82; regional counsel U.S. EPA Region 10, 1982-87; counsel Perkins Coie, 1987-88, ptnr., 1989-98; sr. environ. counsel, v.p. Huntsman Corp., Salt Lake City, 1999—; dep. gen. counsel Huntsman Internat., 2002—04, Huntsman LLC, Salt Lake City, 2004—, Huntsman Corp., Salt Lake City, 2005—. Spkr. in field. Contbr. articles to profl. jours. Bd. dirs. Environ. Law Inst., 1995-2000; chmn. audit com. Whitman Coll., 1994-2007, bd. overseers 2003—; mem. Athlete's Hall of Fame Com., 2003—; ethics com. Bd. Environ. Auditors Cert., 1998— Mem. ABA (sect. environ., energy and resources 1987—, vice chmn. in-house counsel com., 2003-04, chmn. 2004-06), Wash. State Bar Assn. (environ. and land use sects. 1974—, spl. dist. coun. 1988-95). Democrat. Office: Huntsman Corp 500 Huntsman Way Salt Lake City UT 84108-1235 Home Phone: 801-583-0830; Office Phone: 801-584-5828. Business E-Mail: jim_moore@huntsman.com.

MOORE, JANE ROSS, librarian, educator; b. Phila., Apr. 24, 1929; d. John William and Mary M. Ross; m. Cyril Howard Moore, Jr., June 1, 1956 (div. Mar. 1967). AB, Smith Coll., 1951; MLS, Drexel U., 1952; postgrad., Columbia U.; MBA with distinction, NYU, 1965; PhD, Case Western Res. U., 1974. Cataloguer Yale U. Libr., 1952-54; chief tech. processes libr. Lederle Labs., Am. Cyanamid Co., Pearl River, NY, 1954-58; chief serials catalog libr. Bklyn. Coll. Libr., 1958-65, asst. prof., chief catalog divsn., 1965-70, assoc. prof., chief catalog divsn., 1971-73, asso. prof., assoc. libr. adminstrv. svcs., 1973-76; prof., chief libr. Mina Rees Libr., Grad. Ctr., CUNY, 1976-91, prof., chief libr. emerita, 1991—. Lectr. Syracuse U. Grad. Sch. Libr. Sci., 1967, 69, Queens Coll. Grad. Sch. Libr. and Info. Studies, 1967—69, adj. assoc. prof., 1974—76, adj. prof., 1977—86; HEW Title IIB fellow Case Western Res. U. Sch. Libr. Sci., 1970—72; mem. chancellor's task force librs. CUNY, 1979—81; trustee N.Y. Met. Reference and Rsch. Libr. Agy., 1984—93, 2d v.p., 1985—88, v.p., 1988—90, treas., 1991—93. Elder Presbyn. Ch., clk. session, pres. corp.; bd. dirs. Vis. Nurse Assn. Bklyn., 1984—2006, mem. exec. com., 1987—2006, vice chmn., 2001—06; bd. dirs., mem. exec. com., sec. Vis. Nurse Regional Health Care Sys., Inc., 2001—06. Mem.: AAUW, AAUP, ALA (life; membership com. 1967—71, chmn. coun. regional groups, resources and tech. svcs. divsn. 1968—69, dir. divsn. 1968—70, 1975—76, chmn. divsn. cataloging and classification sect. 1975—76), The Typophiles (sec.-treas. 1996—2006), N.Y. Tech. Svcs. Librs. (pres. 1963—64), Spl. Librs. Assn., Am. Printing History Assn., OCLC Users Coun. (SUNY del. 1981—85), Assn. Coll. and Rsch. Librs. (chmn. univ. librs. sect. 1983—84), N.Y. Libr. Assn. (pres. resources and tech. svcs. sect., councilor 1966—67, sec.-treas. acad. and spl. librs. sect. 1973—75, councilor 1975—76, 1978—81, pres. 1979—80), Chartered Inst. Libr. and Info. Profl. Gt. Britain (life), NYU Grad. Sch. Bus. Adminstrn. Alumni Assn. (rec. sec. 1967—69, dir. 1969—70, 1975—79), Princeton Club N.Y., Smith Coll. Club Bklyn. (pres. 1966—68, class treas. 1976—81), N.Y. Libr. Club (sec. 1964—66, coun. 1966—70, 1973—77, 1979—82, pres. 1980—81), Smith Coll. Club N.Y., Archons of Colophon, Phi Kappa Phi. Home: 103 Kendal Dr Oberlin OH 44074-1905

MOORE, JEAN E., social worker, academic administrator, educator, radio personality; d. Hugh Huriel and Theodora H. Buchanan Campbell; m. Robert M. Moore, Jr.; children: Robert M. III, Doreen R. Moore Closson. BA, Hunter Coll., 1947; M of Social Svc., Bryn Mawr Coll., 1949; EdD, Temple U., 1978. Cert. social worker Acad. Cert. Social Workers, LCSW Pa., 1989. Social worker Children's Svc., Inc., Phila., 1949—52; asst. chief clin. social work svcs. Region 10 U.S. VA, Phila., 1952—60; social work specialist Ctrl. Relocation Bur., Phila. Redevel. Authority, 1962—67; social work/human svcs. adviser for Model Cities Region III U.S. Dept. Housing and Urban devel. for 6 states and D.C., 1967—69; assoc. prof., grad. faculty, dir. new career ladders Temple U., Phila., dir. program devel. Office of Rsch. and Program Devel., 1969—89, assoc. prof. emerita, 1989—; exec. asst. to pres. Cheyney U. of Pa., 1985—91; v.p. instnl. advancement U. Md. Ea. Shore, Princess Anne, Md., 1991—97; host, exec. prodr. Univ. Forum Temple U. Pub. Radio, Phila., 1997—. Mem. internat. bd. advisors Radio for Peace Internat.; bd. dirs., club dir. Gundaker Found., Inc.; cons., spkr., presenter, lectr. Contbr. articles to profl. publs. Past bd. trustees Lackawanna Jr. Coll., C.C. of Phila.; past pres. Fair Housing Coun. Suburban Phila.; chair vis. accreditation teams Mid. States Assn. Colls. and Schs. Commn. on Higher Edn.; past bd. pres. Spectrum Health Svcs., Inc.; chair State Bd. Pvt. Corresp. Schs.; elder Lansdowne First Presbyn. Ch.; bd. dirs. Children's Svc., Inc. Named Paul Harris fellow, Rotary Found., 2005, Guy Gundaker fellow, Gundaker Found. Rotary Internat. Dist. 7450, 2006; named to Hall of Fame, Hunter Coll., 1999; recipient Documentary Gold award, Internat. Assn. Audio Visual Commns., 1999, Crystal awards of Excellence, The Communicator Awards, 1999, 2000, 2002, 2003, 2004, 2005, 2006, 1st pl. radio/ednl., Broadcast Edn. Assn., 2000, Documentary award, 2000, Achievement in Radio award, March of Dimes, 2000—04, Gold Cindy award, Internat. Assn. Audio Visual Communicators, 2000, 2002, 2003, Undoing Racism award, Radnor Twp., 2002, Media award, Kelly Anne Dolan Meml. Fund, 2003, Martin Luther King Jr. Humanitarian award, Upper Merion, 2004, Mayor's Fire Prevention medal, City of N.Y., Outstanding Contbn. in Edn. award, Theta Nu Sigma, Image award, Black Women in Sport Found., Radio Program awards, Best Coverage Maternal Health Issues/Problems Risk Pregnancies, numerous academic awards. Mem.: NASW (Golden Membership Disting. Svc. award 2005), Broadcast Pioneers of Phila., Inc., Pa. Abolition Soc. (bd. mgrs.), Rotary Club Upper Darby-Lansdown (bd. dirs. 2001—05), Phi Delta Kappa, Alpha Chi Alpha, Phi Beta Kappa, Delta Sigma Theta. Avocations: international travel, writing, poetry. Office Phone: 215-204-4376.

MOORE, JERRY A., III, lawyer; b. Washington, Dec. 1, 1946; BA, Univ. Minn., 1968; MA, Univ. Wis., 1970; JD, Georgetown Univ., 1975. Bar: DC 1975. Law clerk, Hon. Barrington D. Parker US Dist Ct, 1975—76; dir., programs Greater Washington Bd. of Trade; ptnr., real estate practice group Venable LLP, Washington. Past trustee Nat. Urban League; chmn. of bd. Washington Urban League; vice chmn. of bd, treas. Children's Hospital; chmn. (two terms) DC United Way. Lt. USN, 1968—73. Office: Venable LLP 575 Seventh St NW Washington DC 20004 Office Phone: 202-344-4763. Office Fax: 202-344-8300. Business E-Mail: jamoore@venable.com.

MOORE, JERRY JAY, sales executive, retired archaeologist; b. Ft. Sam Houston, Tex., Jan. 29, 1960; s. Richard Vernal and Irmgard Ludwiga Ottilia (Bennewitz) Moore. Student, Ea. Ill. U., 1980—83. Lab. asst. Archaeol. Investigations Ctr. So. Ill. U., Carbondale, 1979; field/lab. technician Ill. State Mus. Soc., Springfield, 1980; asst. lab. supr. Ill. State Mus. Soc., Dickson Mounds Mus., Havana, 1980—81, Am. Resources Group, Ltd., Carbondale, 1983—86; archaeol. technician Midwestern Archaeol. Rsch. Ctr. Ill. State U., Normal, 1986—93; archaeol. asst. U. Ill., Urbana, 1993—94; archaeol. asst. Inst. Archaeology and Anthropology U. S.C., Columbia, 1993—94; merchandising asst. J.C. Penney Co., Champaign, Ill., 1994—2000; sales profl. Bergner's/Saks Inc., Urbana, 2000—02, Dick's Sporting Goods, Inc., Champaign, 2002—. Co-author: monographs; contbr. articles to profl. jours. Founding mem. Nat. Campaign for Tolerance, Civil Rights Meml. Ctr., Wall of Tolerance, Montgomery, Ala., 2004; founding sponsor Martin Luther King Jr. Nat. Meml., Washington, 2006. Named to Wall Tolerance, So. Poverty Law Ctr. Civil Rights Meml. Ctr., 2004; scholar, State of Ill., 1978—82. Mem.: SAR, Soc. Collegiate Journalists, Iroquois County Hist. and Geneal. Soc., Soc. of the War of 1812 (U.S. Army Mil. Uniform Ft. Dearborn, Ill. Project 1999—2000, sgt. at arms 2000—), Sons of the Revolution, Sons of Union Vets. of the Civil War (dept. of Ill. genealogist 1998—, Ill. dept. ordnance assessment 2004—05), Phi Theta Kappa. Republican. Roman Catholic. Avocations: history, antiques, genealogy. Home: 590 S Park St Paxton IL 60957 Office: 2113 N Prospect Ave Champaign IL 61822 Office Phone: 217-352-4173.

MOORE, JOHN EDDY, former lieutenant governor; b. Charleston, W.Va., July 13, 1943; s. George Roy and Alvaretta (Hoskins) M.; m. Martha Clay Spangenberg, Aug. 7, 1966; children— Brian Clay, Stacia Hoskins BS in Comemrce, Washington and Lee U., 1965; JD, U. Ky., 1968. Group dir. Rockwell Internat., Cedar Rapids, Iowa, 1974-80, v.p. Dallas, 1980-81; v.p., ptnr. Korn/Ferry Internat., Dallas, 1981-82; sr. v.p. Cessna Aircraft, Wichita, Kans., 1982—2002; lt. gov. State of Kansas, 2003—07. Dir. Health Care Plus, Wichita, Kans., Riverside Hosp., Wichita; former mem. Spl. Commn. on Pub. Agenda for Kans.; sec. Kans. Foodbank Warehouse, Wichita; bd. dirs. Booth Meml. Residence, Wichita Mem. Midwest Aerospace Indsl. Relations Council, Machinery and Allied Products Inst. (human resources council), Wichita C. of C. (chmn. state legis. com.), Kans. C. of C. and Industry (bd. dirs.) Republican. Methodist. Avocation: golf.

MOORE, JOHN HAMPTON, academic administrator; b. Grand Forks, ND, Apr. 19, 1935; s. Charles Harold and Marie (Lindberg) M.; m. Barbara Sue Corbett, Feb. 23, 1963; children: John Randolph, Matthew Corbett BS in Engring., U. Mich., 1958, MBA, 1959; PhD in Econs., U. Va., Charlottesville, 1966. Rsch. chemist Procter & Gamble Co., 1959-63; asst. prof. econs. U. Va., Charlottesville, 1966-70, assoc. prof. econs., 1970-77; assoc. dir., rsch. prof. Law and Econs. Ctr. U. Miami, Fla., 1977-80; assoc. dir., prof. econs. Law and Econs. Ctr. Emory U., Atlanta, 1981; assoc. dir., sr. fellow Hoover Instn. Stanford U., Calif., 1981-85, acting dep. dir. Hoover Instn. Calif., 1983-84; dep. dir. NSF, Washington, 1985-89; dir. Internat. Inst., George Mason U., Washington, 1990-95, Disting. Svc. prof., 1995-96; pres. Grove City (Pa.) Coll., 1996—2003. Sr. assoc. St. Antony's Coll. Oxford (Eng.) U., 1973; mem. Nat. Sci. Bd., Washington, 1982-85; dir. George C. Marshall Inst., 1993—. Author: Growth With Self-Management: Yugoslav Industrialization, 1952-75, 80; co-translator, co-editor: Stalinist Planning for Economic Growth, 1933-52, 1980; editor: To Promote Prosperity, 1984, Legacies of the Collapse of Marxism, 1994; contbr. articles to profl. jours. Bd. dirs. Thomas Jefferson Ctr. Found., 1972-85, Civilian R&D Found., 1995—, George C. Marshall Inst., 2002-; chmn. standing fin. com. Internat. Coun. Sci. Unions, 1992-96; trustee Earhart Found., 1993—, Am. Council Science Health, 2000—; mem. sci. bd. Internat. Basic Scis. Program, UNESCO, 2005—. NASA fellow, 1963-66, Hoover Instn., Stanford U. fellow, 1975-76. Mem. AAAS, Am. Econ. Assn., Mont Pelerin Soc. (bd. dirs. 1992-96, v.p. 1994-96), Raven Soc., So. Econ. Assn., Phila. Soc., (bd. dirs. 2003—, dir., 2004-), Sigma Xi (chmn. internat. com. 1991-97, exec. com. 1995-2000, pres. 1998-99), Phi Eta Sigma, Tau Beta Pi, Omicron Delta Kappa. Home: 7254 Marlow Pl Bradenton FL 34201 Personal E-mail: jhmoore1@comcast.net.

MOORE, JOHN HARTWELL, anthropology educator, consultant; b. Williston, ND, Feb. 27, 1939; s. William Andrew and Mary Montgomery Moore; m. Shelley Ann Arlen, June 6, 1981; children: Jeremiah, Jessica, Alexandra. BS, U. of Ark., Fayetteville, AR, 1962; Ph. D, NYU, New York, NY, 1974. Anthropology educator U. Okla., Norman, 1977—93, U. Fla., Gainesville, 1993—. Cons. Native Am. Rights Fund, Boulder, Colo., 1979—, Sand Creek Massacre Descendants Trust, Anadarko, Okla., 1991—, Sawridge Indian Band, Slave Lake, Alberta, Canada, 1992—; pres. U. Fla. Faculty, 2006—. Author: (book) The Cheyenne; editor: Political Economy of North American Indians, Interstellar Travel and Multi-Generation Space Ships; editor-in-chief: Macmillan Ency. Race and Racism. Del. to state conv. Dem. Party, Oklahoma City, 1991—91; chpt. pres. Vietnam Veterans Against the War, West Orange, NJ, 1968—69; state com. Rainbow Coalition, Oklahoma City, 1987—93. Second Lt. US Army, 1962—64, East Asia. Decorated UN Peacekeeping Medal, Armed Forces Expeditionary Medal US Army, US Nat. Def. medal, Korea Nat. Def. medal; recipient Governor's Cmty. Svc. Award, State of Okla., 1990. Fellow: Ctr. for Advanced Study in the Behavioral Sciences, Am. Assn. for the Advancement of Science (chair of anthropology sect. 1997—98); mem.: Human Genome Diversity Project (chair north am. cmty. 1998). Democrat. Ethical Culture. Achievements include research in role of ethnogenesis in human evolution; rates of gene flow from ethnic intermarriage; demographic requirements for interstellar space travel. Home: 3328 North West 18 Avenue Gainesville FL 32605 Office: University of Florida 1112 Turlington Gainesville FL 32611 E-mail: moojohn@anthro.ufl.edu.

MOORE, JOHN NORTON, lawyer, educator, diplomat; b. NYC, June 12, 1937; s. William Thomas and Lorena (Norton) M.; m. Barbara Schneider, Dec. 12, 1981; children: Victoria Norton, Elizabeth Norton. AB in Economics, Drew U., 1959; LLB with honors, Duke U., 1962; LLM, U. Ill., 1965; postgrad., Yale U., 1965-66. Bar: Fla. 1962, Ill. 1963, Va. 1969, D.C. 1972, U.S. Supreme Ct. 1972. Tchg. fellow U. Ill., 1962—63; asst. prof. U. Fla., 1963—65, assoc. prof., 1965—66, asst. dean, 1964—66; assoc. prof. U. Va. Sch. Law, Charlottesville, 1966—69, prof., 1969—76, Walter L. Brown prof. law, 1976—, dir. grad. program, 1968—93, dir. Ctr. Oceans Law and Policy, 1976—, dir. Ctr. Nat. Security Law, 1984—. Counselor on internat. law Dept. State, Washington, 1972-73; chmn. Nat. Security Coun. Task Force on Law of Sea and dep. spl. rep. of Pres. and amb. Law of Sea Conf., 1973-76; fellow Woodrow Wilson Internat. Ctr. for Scholars, Washington, 1976; adj. prof. Georgetown Law Ctr., 1978—; mem. Nat. Adv. Com. on Oceans and Atmosphere, 1984-85; mem. U.S. del. Conf. Security and Coop. in Europe, 1984; spl. counsel, dep. agt. for U.S. to World Ct.; former cons. to the Pres.'s Intelligence Oversight Bd., Arms Control and Disarmament Agy., U.S. Info. Agy.; chmn. bd. dirs. U.S. Inst. Peace, 1985-91; co-chmn. with the U.S. dep. atty. gen. Moscow Seminar on the Rule of Law, 1990; legal advisor during Gulf crisis Kuwait's Amb. to U.S., Kuwait Rep. to UN Boundary Commn., 1991-94. Author: Law and the Indo-China War, 1972 (Phi Beta Kappa award); editor: Law and Civil War in the Modern World, 1976, Readings in International Law, 1979, The Arab-Israeli Conflict, 3 vols., 1976, 4th vol., 1991, Nat. Security Law, 1990, 2d edit., 2005, Crisis in the Gulf, 1992, Nat. Security Law Documents, 1995, Treaty Interpretation, The Constitution and the Rule of Law, 2001, The National Law of Treaty Implementation, 2001, Solving the War Puzzle, 2003; editor: The Real Lessons of the Vietnam War, 2002, Civil Litigation Against Terrorism, 2003; mem. editl. bd. Am. Jour. Internat. Law; contbr. articles to profl. jours. Sesquicentennial assoc. Ctr. Advanced Studies, U. Va., 1971-72; adv. bd. law of sea State Dept., 1977-80, adv. bd. internat. law, 1982; chmn. bd. dirs. U.S. Inst. Peace, 1986-89, 89-91; chmn. oceans policy com. Rep. Nat. Com.; com. on exploration of the seas Nat. Acad. Nat. Rsch. Coun., 2002; active Consortium on Intelligence. Recipient Alumni award in arts Drew U., 1976; Compass Disting. Achievement award for significant contbns. to art and sci. of oceanography and marine tech., 1994; NIH fellow Yale U., 1965-66. Mem. ABA (past vice-chmn. sect. internat. law, past 5-term chmn. com. on law and nat. security), Am. Law Inst., Am. Oceanic Orgn. (past exec. coun.), Marine Tech. Soc. (past exec. coun.), Rhodes Acad. Oceans Law and Policy (founding dir.), Coun. Fgn. Rels., Order of Coif, Cosmos Club, N.Y. Yacht Club, Freedom House (bd. dirs.), Phi Beta Kappa. Republican. Episcopalian. Office: U Va Sch Law 580 Massie Rd Charlottesville VA 22903-1789 Office Phone: 434-924-7441. E-mail: jnm9s@virginia.edu. *Life offers opportunity to pursue many worthwhile interests. In selecting among them it has seemed most useful to focus on those issues of sufficiently broad general significance as to justify the efforts of a lifetime. For me that has meant focus on promoting democracy and the rule of law, improving the functioning of government, controlling and reducing war, and the policy choices of the ocean frontier.*

MOORE, JOHN PLUNKETT DENNIS, publisher; b. Mexico, Mo., Mar. 2, 1931; s. Dennis Talmage and Vona Mae (Vance) M.; m. Lydia Benz Ahern, Aug. 15, 1959; children: Alison Ahern, Lydia Benz, John Talmage, Maude Ahern, Meredith Coleman. Student, Princeton U., 1948-51, U.S. Naval Acad., 1951-53; BA, U. Mo., Columbia, 1953; postgrad., Harvard Law Sch., 1955-56. Coll. traveler The Dryden Press, Inc., NYC, 1957-59; coll. traveler The Macmillan Co., NYC, 1959-60, editor, 1960-67; assoc. exec. editor Columbia U. Press, NYC, 1968-74, editor in chief, 1974-80, pres., 1980-97, also bd. dirs. Bd. dirs., pres. Columbia U. Music Press; bd. dirs. Univ. Presses of Calif., Columbia and Princeton, Chichester, West Sussex, Eng., 1979-97, chmn., 1981-83, 85-87, 96-97; trustee Composer's Recordings, Inc., 1984-97. Author: Columbia University Press: A Historical Sketch, 1893-1993; mem. editl. bd. N.Y. Acad. Scis., 1993-01. Bd. dirs. Greenwich (Conn.) Health Assn., 1970-75; bd. dirs. assoc. Family Ctr., Greenwich, Stamford, 1975—; trustee Princeton Libr. in N.Y.C., 1984—; mem. vestry St. Barnabas Ch., Greenwich, 1995-98. With U.S. Army, 1953-55. Mem. Assn. Am. Univ. Presses (chair internat. com. 1994-96, bd. dirs. 1996-97). Clubs: Publishers Lunch (admissions com. 1996-99), Princeton Club NY (mem. svcs. com. 2006—, Faculty House Columbia U., Century Assn.; Nassau, the Book Table, The Ch. Club N.Y., Princeton Club So. Calif., The English Speaking Union, The Mystery Club (pres. 2006-07, mem. exec. com. Princeton class 1952). Episcopalian. Home: 321 Riversville Rd Greenwich CT 06831-3228 Home (Winter): 1912 Kelton Ave Los Angeles CA 90025 E-mail: jdm123@aol.com.

MOORE, JOHN RONALD, manufacturing executive; b. Pueblo, Colo., July 12, 1935; s. John E. and Anna (Yesberger) M.; m. Judith Russelyn Bauman, Sept. 5, 1959; children: Leland, Roni, Timothy, Elaine. BS, U. Colo., 1959; grad. advanced mgmt. program, Harvard Grad. Sch. Bus., 1981. Mgmt. trainee Montgomery Ward & Co., Denver, 1960-65; distbn. mgr. Midas Internat. Corp., Chgo., 1965-71; v.p., gen. mgr. Midas, Can., Toronto, Ont., 1972-75; pres. Auto Group Midas Internat. Corp., Chgo., 1976-82, pres., chief exec. officer, 1982-98; ret., 2005. Bd. dirs. Keystone Automotive Industries, Inc. Bd. dirs. Lake Forest Grad. Sch. Mgmt., U. Colo. Found.; dir. Chgo. Crime Commn.; trustee U. Colo. Found. Mem. Harvard Bus. Sch. Alumni Assn., U. Colo. Alumni Assn., Chgo. Coun. Global Affairs, Econ. Club Chgo., Comml. Club Chgo. Republican. *There is very little we accomplish in our lifetime that results from effort we alone expend. All of us should have the wisdom to express our appreciation to our families and associates who have helped us attain our goals and accomplishments— for failure to do so tarnishes our successes and breeds selfishness.*

MOORE, JON ALISTAIR, biology professor, researcher; b. Boonton, NJ, Mar. 20, 1959; s. John Richard Moore and Ruby Jane Thow; m. Susan Lynn Richardson, May 16, 1987; children: Kathleen Joy, Scott Landstreet. BS in Geoscis., U. Ariz., Tucson, 1983, BS in Ecology and Evolutionary Biology, 1983; PhD in Biology, Yale U., New Haven, 1993. Lectr., dir. undergraduate studies program in organismal biology Yale U., 1994—97; vis. scientist Nat. Marine Fisheries Svc., Woods Hole, Mass., 1998—2000; asst. prof. biology Fla. Atlantic U., Wilkes Honors Coll., Jupiter, 2000—05, assoc. prof. biology, 2005—. Curatorial affiliate Peabody Mus. of Natural History, Yale U., 1994—; guest investigator Woods Hole Oceanog. Instn., 2000—01. Co-editor (symposium proceedings) Symposium on Deep-Sea Fisheries, 2003; contbr. more than 40 articles to profl. jours. Bd. dirs. Loggerhead Marinelife Ctr. Juno Beach, 2000—. Office: Florida Atlantic U 5353 Parkside Dr Jupiter FL 33458 Home Phone: 772-562-4098; Office Phone: 561-799-8025. Office Fax: 561-799-8602. Business E-Mail: jmoore@fau.edu.

MOORE, JOYCE KRISTINA, financial planner, director; b. Phila., June 19, 1955; d. Oscar Herbert Hariu and Virginia Wilson (Guss) Leas; m. William Burns Moore, June 20, 1980 (div. 1990); children: William Patrick, Kristofer Sean. Student, Beloit Coll., 1973-74, U. Pa., 1974-75, Lafayette Coll., 1984-88, Am. Coll., 1991—. ChFC. Photographer Clair Pruett Studios, Drexel Hill, Pa., 1977-80; photographic cons. Dan's Camera City, Allentown, Pa., 1980-81; contr., co-founder BioService, Inc., Bethlehem, Pa., 1985-89; contr. Mega Video Inc., Easton, Pa., 1989-91; spl. rep. John Hancock Fin. Svcs., Allentown, 1990—91; prin. Joyce Moore Fin. Svcs., Macungie, Pa., 1991—. Co-editor: Estate Planning Success for Pennsylvania Residents, 2002. Bd. dirs. Spring Garden Children's Sch., Easton; den leader Cub Scout Pack 31, Williams, Pa., 1991—95, scout leader, 1995—97; trustee United Friends Sch., Quakertown, Pa., 2004—; councilwoman Glendon Borough, 1992—97, coun. v.p., 1996—97; overseer Religous Soc. Friends, 1986—92. Mem.: LWV (bd. dirs. Easton area 1987—91, pres. 1989—90), Greater Phila. Sustainable Bus. Network, Nat. Assn. Ins. Fin. Advisors (bd. dirs. Lehigh Valley chpt. 1995—, pres. Lehigh Valley chpt. 2000—01, bd. dir. Pa. chpt. 2002—), First Affirmative Fin. Network, Progressive Asset Mgmt., Social Investment Forum. Avocations: needlecrafts, folk music, canoeing. Office: Joyce Moore Fin Svc PO Box 175 Macungie PA 18062-0175 Office Phone: 610-966-6127. Business E-Mail: joyce@jmfs.com.

MOORE, JUEL ANN, retired elementary school educator; d. Lucy Mae Giddens; m. Gene Paul Moore, Mar. 31, 1962; children: Dr. Gina LuChrista Moore-Sanders, Richard Vernon. BA, Fisk U.; PhD, San Diego State U. and Claremont U., 1998. Cert. reading specialist Calif. Tchr. Met. Nashville, 1962—67, Travis Unified Schs., Fairfield, Calif., 1967, San Diego City Schs., 1969—81, prin. coach, 1981—2002, literacy cons. Charter Sch., 2002—. Author: (book chpt.) Black English. Recipient Svc./Cmty. award, Women's Inc., 2003. Master: Assn. African Am. Educators (pres. 2002—03). Presbyterian. Achievements include research in Language Registers of African Americans. Avocations: travel, reading, writing, research, discussion groups. Home Phone: 619-286-8769. Personal E-mail: gpjamoore@yahoo.com.

MOORE, JULIANNE (JULIE ANNE SMITH), actress; b. Fayetteville, NC, Dec. 3, 1960; m. Sundar Chakravarthy, Nov. 21, 1983 (div. Oct. 12, 1985); m. John Gould Rubin, May 3, 1986 (div. Aug. 25, 1995); m. Bart Freundlich, Aug. 23, 2003; 2 children. BFA, Boston Univ. With The Guthrie Theater, 1988-89. Actress: (theatre) Serious Money, 1987, Bone-the-Fish, 1988, Ice Cream with Hot Fudge, 1990, Uncle Vanya; (Broadway) The Vertical Hour, 2006; (TV soap operas) As the World Turns (Emmy award outstanding ingenue in daytime drama series 1988), The Edge of Night; (TV films) Money, Power, Murder, 1989, Lovecraft, 1991; (feature films) The Hand That Rocks the Cradle, 1992, The Gun in Betty Lou's Handbag, 1992, Body of Evidence, 1993, Benny & Joon, 1993, The Fugitive, 1993, Short Cuts, 1993, Vanya on 42nd Street, 1994, Roommates, 1995, Nine Months, 1995, Safe, 1995, Assassins, 1995, Surviving Picasso, 1996, The Myth of Fingerprints, 1997, The Lost World: Jurassic Park, 1997, Hellcab, 1997, Boogie Nights, 1997, Chicago Cab, 1998, The Big Lebowski, 1998, Psycho, 1998, Map of the World, 1999, Magnolia, 1999, Cookie's Fortune, 1999, An Ideal Husband, 1999, The End of the Affair, 1999, Hannibal, 2001, Evolution, 2001, The Shipping News, 2001, Far From Heaven, 2002, The Hours, 2002, Marie and Bruce, 2004, Laws of Attraction, 2004, The Forgotten, 2004, The Prize Winner of Defiance, Ohio, 2005, Freedomland, 2006, Children of Men, 2006, Next, 2007. Office: Creative Artists Agy care Kevin Huvane 9830 Wilshire Blvd Beverly Hills CA 90212-1825 *

MOORE, JUSTIN EDWARD, information technology executive; b. West Hartford, Conn., June 17, 1952; s. Walter Joseph and Victoria Mary (Calcagni) M. BS in Mgmt. Sci., Fla. Inst. Tech., 1974. Systems assoc. Travelers Ins., Hartford, Conn., 1974-77; data processing programmer R.J. Reynolds Inc., Winston-Salem, NC, 1977-78; programmer/analyst Sea-Land Svc., Elizabeth, NJ, 1978-79, mgr. market analysis Oakland, Calif., 1979-82; asst. v.p., dir. application systems Fox Capital Mgmt. Corp., Foster City, Calif., 1982-86; mgr. bus. svcs. dept mktg. and pricing Am. Pres. Cos., Ltd., Oakland, 1987-88, dir. mktg. and pricing systems, 1988-89; dir. systems devel. The Office Club, Concord, Calif., 1989-91; dir. MIS Revo, Inc., Mountain View, Calif., 1992-93; account mgr. Imrex Computer Sys., Inc., South San Francisco, 1993-94; project mgr. Affiliated Computer Svcs., Inc., San Ramon, Calif., 1994—. Republican. Roman Catholic. Avocations: golf, personal computing, investment mgmt. Home: 5214 Jomar Dr Concord CA 94521-2343 Office: Affiliated Computer Svcs Inc 4000 Executive Pky Ste 275 San Ramon CA 94583-4257 Office Phone: 925-866-1692. Business E-Mail: justin.moore@acs-inc.com. *Personal philosophy: Strive always to do the right things, at the right time, the right way for the right reasons.*

MOORE, KAREN NELSON, judge; AB magna cum laude, Radcliffe Coll., 1970; JD magna cum laude, Harvard U., 1973. Bar: DC 1973, Ohio 1976, US Ct. Appeals (DC cir.) 1974, US Supreme Ct. 1980, US Ct. Appeals (6th cir.) 1984. Law clk. to Hon. Malcolm R. Wilkey US Ct. Appeals (DC Cir.), Washington, 1973—74; law clk. to Hon. Harry A. Blackmun US Supreme Ct., Washington, 1974—75; assoc. Jones, Day, Reavis & Pogue, Cleve., 1975—77; asst. prof. Case Western Res. Law Sch., Cleve., 1977—80, assoc. prof., 1980—82, prof., 1982—95; judge US Ct. Appeals (6th cir.), Cleve., 1995—. Vis. prof. Harvard Law Sch., 1990—91. Mem. Harvard Law Rev., 1971—73; contbr. articles to profl. jours. Trustee Lakewood Hosp., Ohio, 1978—85, Radcliffe Coll., Cambridge, 1980—84. Fellow: Am. Bar Found.; mem.: Harvard U. Alumni Assn. (bd. dirs. 1984—87), Am. Law Inst., Phi Beta Kappa. Office: US Ct Appeals 6th Cir Carl B Stokes US Courthouse 801 W Superior Ave Cleveland OH 44113-1831 *

MOORE, KENNETH CAMERON, lawyer; b. Chgo., Oct. 25, 1947; s. Kenneth Edwards and Margaret Elizabeth (Cameron) M.; m. Karen M. Nelson, June 22, 1974; children: Roger Cameron, Kenneth Nelson, Kristin Karen. BA summa cum laude, Hiram Coll., 1969; JD cum laude, Harvard U., 1973. Bar: Ohio 1973, U.S. Dist. Ct. Md. 1974, U.S. Ct. Appeals (4th cir.) 1974, D.C. 1975, U.S. Dist. Ct. (no. dist.) Ohio 1976, U.S. Ct. Appeals (6th cir.) 1977, U.S. Ct. Appeals (D.C. cir.) 1979, U.S. Supreme Ct. 1980. Law clk. to judge Harrison L. Winter U.S. Ct. Appeals (4th cir.), Balt., 1973-74; assoc. Squire, Sanders & Dempsey LLP, Washington, 1974—75, Cleve., 1975-82, ptnr., 1982—, profl. ethics ptnr., 1996—, mem. fin. com., 1990—, chair profl. ethics com., 2003—. Chmn. Ohio Fin. Com. for Jimmy Carter presdl. campaign, 1976; del. Dem. Nat. Conv., 1976; chief legal counsel Ohio Carter-Mondale Campaign, 1976; trustee Hiram Coll., 1997—, mem. exec. com., 1999, vice chair bd. trustees, 2000—, mem. bd. Laurel Sch., mem., 2005-, exec. com., 2006-, sec., 2006-, vice chair, 2007—. With AUS, 1970—76. Mem. ABA, Fed. Bar Assn., Ohio Bar Assn., Cleve. Bar Assn., Cleve. City Club. Home: 15602 Edgewater Dr Cleveland OH 44107-1212 Office: Squire Sanders & Dempsey LLP 4900 Key Ctr 127 Public Sq Ste 4900 Cleveland OH 44114-1304 Office Phone: 216-479-8500.

MOORE, KENNETH JAMES, agronomist, educator; b. Phoenix, June 6, 1957; s. George Taylor and Barbara Joyce (Amy) M.; m. Gina Marie McCarthy Aug. 11, 1979; children: Ellyn Elizabeth, David Taylor, Mark Daniel. BS in Agr., Ariz. State U., 1979; MS in Agronomy, Purdue U., 1981, PhD in Agronomy, 1983. Asst. prof. agronomy U. Ill., Urbana, 1983-87; assoc. prof. N.Mex. State U., Las Cruces, 1988-89; rsch. agronomist Agrl. Rsch. Svc., USDA, Lincoln, Nebr., 1989-93; prof. Iowa State U., Ames, 1993—. Adj. assoc. prof. U. Nebr. Lincoln, 1989-93, prof., 1993-96; sr. rsch. fellow Ag Rsch. Grasslands, New Zealand, 1998; dir. MS in Agronomy Distance Edn. program Iowa State U., 1995—, dir. Crop Advisor Inst., 2000—. Founding editor Crop Mgmt., 2001-02; assoc. editor Agronomy Jour., 1989-93, tech. editor, 1994-97; assoc. editor Crop Sci., 1994; editor: Forages: An Introduction to Grassland Ag, 2003, Forages: The Science of Grassland Agriculture, 2007, Native-Warm Season Grasses: Research Trends and Issues, 2000, Post-Harvest Physiology and Preservation of Forages, 1995; contbr. chpts. to books. Bd. dirs. Lincoln Children's Mus., 1991-93, Children's Svcs. of Ctrl. Iowa, 1996-97; bd. dirs. Children's Mus. Ctrl. Iowa, 1997-2002, pres., 2000-01; mem. mgmt. com. N.E. YMCA, Lincoln, 1991-93; mem. youth policy forum Lincoln YMCA, 1991-92. Recipient Point of Light award USDA, 1991. Fellow Am. Soc. Agronomy (bd. dirs. 2002-05 06—, pres.-elect 2007), Crop Sci. Soc. Am. (divsn. chmn. 1990-92, pres. 2003-04, exec. com. and bd. dirs. 2002-05, Young Crop Scientist award 1993); mem. Am. Forage and Grassland Coun. (Outstanding Young Scientist award 1982, merit award 1991). Independent. Methodist. Avocations: swimming, fishing, music. Office: Iowa State U Agronomy Dept 1571 Agronomy Hall Ames IA 50011-0001 Office Phone: 515-294-5482. Business E-Mail: kjmoore@iastate.edu.

MOORE, KIMBERLY ANN, federal judge; b. Baltimore, Md., June 15, 1968; BS in Electrical Engring., MIT, 1990, MS, 1991; JD, Georgetown U., 1994. Bar: Md. 1995, DC. Assoc. Kirkland & Ellis LLP, DC & L.A., 1994—95; law clk. to Hon. Glenn L. Archer Jr. US Ct. Appeals (Fed. Cir.), 1995—97; asst. prof. law Chgo.-Kent Coll. Law, 1997—99, assoc. dir., Intellectual Property Law Program, 1998—99; asst. prof. law U. Md. Sch. Law, 1999—2000; counsel Morgan, Lewis & Bockius LLP, 2000—03; assoc. prof. law George Mason U. Sch. Law, 2000—04, prof. law, 2004—06; judge US Ct. Appeals (Fed. cir.), Washington, 2006—. Assoc. editor Fed. Cir. Bar Journ., 1997—98, editor-in-chief, 1998—2006. Named one of 100 Most Influential Lawyers, Nat. Law Jour., 2006. Office: US Ct Appeals Fed Cir 717 Madison Pl NW Washington DC 20439 *

MOORE, LAURENCE JOHN, business educator; b. Greeley, Colo., May 7, 1938; s. John Harold and Ruth Anderson M.; m. Nancy Kay Hibbert, Aug. 31, 1963 (div. Apr. 1996); children: Rebecca Ann, John Andrew, Stefani Ruth. BA in Econs., Monmouth Coll., Ill., 1962; MS in Econs., Ariz. State U., 1965, DBA in Mgmt. Sci., 1970. Dist. mktg. rep. Standard Oil Co. (Ind.), Chgo., 1962-63; sr. analyst long range and capital planning, 1964-66; head quantitative studies Continental Ill. Bank, Chgo., 1966-67; mem. faculty dept. mgmt. sci. Coll. Bus. Va. Poly. Inst. and State U., Blacksburg, 1970—, prof. Coll. Bus., 1977-85, C&P Disting. prof. bus., 1985-96, head dept. Coll. Bus., 1976-83, dir. univ. fin. planning and analysis, 1983-84, dir. univ. planning, 1988-89, Bell Atlantic-Va. prof. of bus., 1996—2002, Verizon prof. bus., 2002—. Cons. in field. Author: (with S.M. Lee, B.W. Taylor) Management Science, 1981, 4th edit., 1993, (with S.M. Lee) Introduction to Decision Sciences, 1975, (with E.R. Clayton) GERT Modeling and Simulation: Fundamentals and Applications, 1976. Served with U.S. Army, 1957-59. Recipient Disting. Service award SE region Am. Inst. Decision Scis., 1977 Fellow Am. Inst. Decision Scis. (pres. 1983-84, Disting. Svc. award 1986); mem. Inst. Mgmt. Sci. (Disting. Svc. award SE region), Inst. for Ops. Rsch. and Mgmt. Sci., Alpha Iota Delta, Beta Gamma Sigma, Omicron Delta Epsilon, Sigma Iota Epsilon. Presbyterian. Home: 1013 Chateau Ct Blacksburg VA 24060-3676 Office: Va Poly Inst and State U Dept Bus Info Tech 1007 Pamplin Hall Blacksburg VA 24061-5102 Office Phone: 540-231-5887. Business E-Mail: ljmoore@vt.edu.

MOORE, LEON, JR., social studies educator; b. Seoul, Apr. 2, 1970; arrived in U.S., 1970; s. Leon Sr. and Suk Hyon Moore. BA, Wichita State U., Kans., 1993, EdM, 2004. Cert. tchr. comprehensive social studies Kans. Tchr. social studies Unified Sch. Dist. 259, Wichita, Kans., 1993—2006; adult edn. inst. Butler County CC, El Dorado, Kans., 2007—. Volleyball coach Wichita Cath. Diocese, 2003—05. Mem.: Butler Workforce Ctr. Democrat. Roman Catholic. Avocations: reading, writing. Home: 1951 N Burns Wichita KS 67203

MOORE, LINDA A., art dealer, curator; b. Janesville, Wis., Aug. 2, 1947; d. Evert August Frederick and Helen Marilyn Anderson; m. Terry Douglass Moore, Mar. 22, 1969; children: Adrienne Jean, Craig William. Fgn. study program, U. Madrid, 1968; BA magna cum laude, U. of Calif., Santa Barbara, 1969; MA, Stanford U., Palo Alto, 1970; MHA, U. of Wash., 1976. Adminstr. U. of Calif. Student Health Svc., Irvine, 1972—75; v.p. Children's Hosp. and Health Ctr., San Diego, 1976—78; asst. hosp. adminstr. Kaiser Permanente, San Diego, 1978—83, asst. med. group adminstr., 1983—88; owner Linda Moore Gallery, San Diego, 1983—. Bd. dirs. Mus. of Photographic Arts, San Diego; adv. bd. Lux Art Inst., San Diego, 2004—; mem. Latin Am. arts com. San Diego Mus. of Art, 1990—. Contbr. book; author: (exhbn. catalogue) Iturria (Best Art Catalogue, Cleo Design award, 1992), Drowned Ophelia, Lo Maravilloso; editor: DEfining A Vision, 2006. Mem. Presidio Pk. Adv. Coun., San Diego, 2004—07, Patrons of the Prado, Balboa Pk., San Diego, 2005—07. Recipient TWIN - honoring Women Profls. award, YWCA, 1979, Top Women Hosp. Adminstrs., Calif. Hosp. Forum Mag., 1980, grad. study grant, Kellogg Found., 1975—76; fellow, Ford Found., 1969—70. Mem.: Francis Parker Sch. (bd. mem., chair ann. fund 1988—89), Young Hosp. Adminstrs. of San Diego (pres. 1981—82), Am. Coll. of Health Care Adminstrs. (chair young adminstrs. forum 1980—81), Jeanie Anderson Meml. Fund (bd. mem. 1972—2006), LEAD San Diego (bd. mem. 1986—87), ZLAC Rowing Club, Jr. League of San Diego (bd. mem. 1984—85, Best Project Video Employer Sponsored Child Care Project award 1986), Rotary Club 33 of San Diego, Phi Beta Kappa. Avocations: travel, writing, bridge. Office: Linda Moore Gallery 4244 Altamirano Way San Diego CA 92103 Home Phone: 619-291-0828; Office Phone: 619-260-1101. Personal E-mail: lmooregal@aol.com.

MOORE, LOIS JEAN, health science facility administrator; married; 1 child. Grad., Prairie View Sch. Nursing, Tex., 1957; BS in Nursing, Tex. Woman's U., 1970; MS in Edn., Tex. So. U., 1974. Nurse Harris County (Tex.) Hosp. Dist., 1957—; pres., chief exec. officer Harris County Hosp.; adminstr. Jefferson Davis Hosp., Houston, 1977-88, exec. v.p., chief ops. officer, 1988—2001; chief adminstr. U. Tex. Harris County Psychiat. Hosp., Houston, 2001—. Mem. adv. bd. Tex. Pub. Hosp. Assn. Contbr. articles to profl. jours. Mem. Mental Health Needs Council Houston and Harris County, Congressman Mickey Leland's Infant Mortality Task Force, Houston Crack-down Com., Gov.'s task force on health care policy, 1991; chairperson Tex. Assn. Pub. and Nonprofit Hosps., 1991, subcom. of Gov.'s task force to identify essential health care svc., 1992; bd. dirs. ARC, 1991—, Greater Houston Hosp. Coun., March of Dimes, United Way. Recipient Pacesetter award North-East C. of C., 1991; named Nurse of Yr.

Houston Area League Nursing, 1976-77, Outstanding Black Achiever YMCA Century Club, 1974, Outstanding Women in Medicine YWCA, 1989. Mem. Am. Coll. Hosp. Adminstrs., Tex. Hosp. Assn. (chmn. pub. hosp. com.), Young Hosp. Adminstrs., Nat. Assn. Pub. Hosps. (bd. dirs., mem. exec. com. Tex. assn.), License Vocat. Nurses Assn., sigma Theta Tau. Home: 3730 S Macgregor Way Houston TX 77021-1506 Office: Univ Texas Harris County Psychiatric Ctr 2800 S Macbryor Way Houston TX 77021 Office Phone: 713-741-7803.

MOORE, LORRIE, writer, English professor; b. Glens Falls, NY, Jan. 13, 1957; BA summa cum laude, St. Lawrence U., 1978; MFA, Cornell U., 1982. Now prof. English, U. Wis., Madison. Author: Self-Help, 1985, Anagrams, 1986, The Forgotten Helper, 1987, Like Life, 1990, Who Will Run the Frog Hospital?, 1994, Birds of America, 1998 (Nat. Book Critics Cir. award finalist, Irish Times Internat. Prize for Lit.); editor: I Know Some Things: Stories About Childhood by Contemporary Writers, 1992, The Best American Short Stories 2004; contbr. fiction reviews and essays to NY Times, NY Review of Books, Harper's, Paris Rev., New Yorker, others. Recipient Nat. Endowment Arts award, 1989, award, Irish Times, 1999, Rea award achievement in short story, 2004, PEN/Malamud award short fiction, 2005; Guggenheim fellow, 1991, Lannan Found. fellow, 2001. Mem.: Am. Acad. Arts and Letters. Office: 7187 Helen C White Hall Univ Wis Dept English 600 N Park St Madison WI 53706

MOORE, MALCOLM FREDERICK, manufacturing executive; b. Kankakee, Ill., Sept. 19, 1950; s. Robert Dunham and Josephine Frances (Jones) M.; m. Patricia Claudine Bennert, June 13, 1971; children: Michael Dunham, Emily Woodhull, Marjorie Nicoll. BSBA, Am. U., 1972; M of Mgmt., Northwestern U., 1982. Internat. mktg. mgr., product mgr. FMC Corp., Chgo., 1973-84, mktg. and engring. mgr., 1985-90; cons. Frank Lynn & Assoc., Chgo., 1984-85; v.p., gen. mgr. Lindberg unit of Gen. Signal, Watertown, Wis., 1990-93; pres. Abar Ipsen Industries, Inc., Bensalem, Pa., 1993-96, Centorr Vacuum Industries, Nashua, NH, 1993-96, Linac Holdings, Inc., Rockford, Ill., 1994-96; pres., CEO Pangborn Corp., Hagerstown, Md., 1996-98; pres., COO Gehl Co., West Bend, Wis., 1999—. Bd. dirs. Twin Disc, Inc. Inventor material handling equipment. Episcopalian.

MOORE, MANDY (AMANDA LEIGH MOORE), actress, singer; b. Nashua, NH, Apr. 10, 1984; d. Don and Stacy Moore. Host MTV show, Mandy, 2000. Actor: (films) Street Rats, 1996, Magic Al and the Mind Factory, 2000, (voice only) Dr. Doolittle 2, 2001, The Princess Diaries, 2001, A Walk to Remember, 2002 (MTV Movie award breakthrough performance-female, 2002, Teen Choice awards choice breakout performance-actress, with Shane West Teen Choice awards choice chemistry, 2002), Try Seventeen, 2002, How to Deal, 2003, Chasing Liberty, 2004, Saved!, 2004, (voice only) Racing Stripes, 2005, Romance & Cigarettes, 2005, American Dreamz, 2006, Southland Tales, 2006, (voice only) Brother Bear 2, 2006, Dedication, 2007, Because I Said So, 2007, License to Wed, 2007; (TV films) Summer Music Mania 2001, 2001, (TV appearances) Touched by an Angel, 1997, Entourage, 2005, Scrubs, 2006, (voice only) The Simpsons, 2006; singer: (albums) So Real, 1999, I Wanna Be With You, 2000, Mandy Moore, 2001, Coverage, 2003, The Best of Mandy Moore, 2004, Candy, 2005, Wild Hope, 2007. Office: William Morris Agy One William Morris Pl Beverly Hills CA 90212 *

MOORE, MARC ANTHONY, retired academic administrator, writer, retired military officer; b. Dallas, July 15, 1928; s. Edward Clark and Mary Cathrine (Spake) M.; m. Mary Joan Donahue, Sept. 5, 1953; children—Daniel, Mary Ellen, Virginia, Andria. BA, So. Meth. U., 1951; MA, George Washington U., 1970; grad., Amphibious Warfare Sch., 1960, Nat. War Coll., 1974; LHD (hon.), Philippine Women's U., 1987. Enlisted man U.S. Marine Corps, 1946-48, commd. 2d lt., 1951, advanced through grades to maj. gen., 1978; regtl. comdr. Camp Pendleton, Calif., 1971; regtl. exec. officer, infantry bn. comdr. Vietnam, 1970; with Joint Chief Staff Ops., Washington, 1977-78; asst. dir. Marine Command and Staff Coll., 1972-73; dir. div. English and history U.S. Naval Acad., 1974-76; comdg. gen. 4th Marine Div., New Orleans, 1978-80; chief of staff U.S. Forces, Japan, from 1980, now ret.; former chancellor San Diego campus, v.p. for devel. Nat. U., 1990-91. Teaching asst. dept. psychology George Washington U., 1974; instr. dept. behavioral sci. U.S. Naval Acad., 1975-76; adj. faculty Nat. U., 1983 Co-founder Leadership 2000; mem. pres. council Calif. State U., San Marcos, 1993-96, 98-2000; mem. bd. advisors Marine Mil. Acad., 1983-95; founder and council advisors mem., Command Mus. and Warfare Leadership Ctr., Marine Recruit Depot, San Diego, 1984—. Decorated Def. Superior Svc. medal, Legion of Merit with combat V, Bronze Star with combat V with oak leaf cluster, Air medal, Def. Meritorious Svc. medal, Order Sacred Treasure (Japan); recipient Disting. Alumni award So. Meth. U., 1981. Mem. Marine Corps Assn., Phi Delta Theta. Roman Catholic. Home: 3611 Lago Sereno Escondido CA 92029-7902

MOORE, MARION E., retired mathematics professor; s. Floyd O. and Bobbie E. Moore; m. Cleta J. Sappenfield, Jan. 24, 1953; 1 child, Leslie Ann Finlayson. BS, West Tex. State Coll., Canyon, Tex., 1957; MS, Tex. Tech U., Lubbock, Tex., 1960; PhD, U. N.Mex, Albuquerque, 1968. Instr. West Tex. State Coll., Canyon, 1958—61, U. N.Mex, Albuquerque, 1961—66; prof. U. Tex., Arlington, Tex., 1966—2001; ret.; prof. emeritus U. Tex., 2002—. Dir. History Math. Conf., Arlington, 1976—76; presenter in field; dir. numerous masters theses and PhD dissertations. Contbr. articles to profl. jours. Cpl. inf. US Army, 1953—55, Germany. Mem.: Am. Men Sci., Math. Assn. Am., Am. Math. Soc. Home: 3207 Canongate Dr Arlington TX 76015-2213 Office: Univ Tex 701 S Nedderman Dr Arlington TX 76019-0408 Home Phone: 817-465-3658; Office Phone: 817-272-3429. Business E-Mail: moore@uta.edu.

MOORE, MARK HARRISON, criminal justice and public policy educator; b. Oak Park, Ill., Mar. 19, 1947; s. Charles Eugene and Jean (McFeely) M.; m. Martha Mansfield Church, June 15, 1968; children—Phoebe Sylvina, Tobias McFeely, Gaylen Williams. Student, Phillips Acad., 1962-65; BA, Yale U., 1969; M.Public Policy, Harvard U., 1971, PhD, 1973. Teaching fellow, instr. public policy J.F. Kennedy Sch. Govt., Harvard U., Boston, 1971-73, asst. prof., 1973-74, 75-76, assoc. prof., 1976-79, Guggenheim prof. criminal justice policy and mgmt., 1979—; dir. Hauser Ctr. Non-Profit Orgns. Harvard U., 1998—. Spl. asst. to adminstr., chief planning officer Drug Enforcement Adminstrn., U.S. Dept. Justice, Washington, 1974-75; cons. U.S. Dept. Justice, 1975-76, 81 Author: Buy and Bust: The Effective Regulation of an Illicit Market in Heroin, 1977, Creating Public Value: Strategic Management in Government, 1995, (with others) Dangerous Offenders, 1985, From Children to Citizens: Vol. 1, The Mandate for Juvenile Justice, 1987, (with Malcolm K. Sparrow) Ethics in Government, 1990, (with Malcolm K. Sparrow and David Kennedy) Beyond 911: A New Era for Policing, 1991; editor: (with Joel Fleishman and Lance Leibman) Public Duties, 1980, (with Dean Gerstein) Alcohol and Public Policy, 1981. Dir. Hauser Ctr. for Non Profit Orgns. Mem. Assn. Schs. Public Policy and Mgmt., Phi Beta Kappa Home: 331 Waverley St Belmont MA 02478-2418 Office: JF Kennedy Sch Govt Harvard U 79 Jfk St Cambridge MA 02138-5801 Office Phone: 617-795-1113. Business E-Mail: mark_moore@harvard.edu.

MOORE, MARVELENE C., music educator; b. Franklin, Tenn., Sept. 13, 1944; d. Frank and Sadie Gibson Moore. BA, Talladega Coll., 1966; M in Music Edn., George Peabody Coll., 1970, edn. specialist, 1971; PhD, U. Mich., 1977. Music specialist Decatur Pub. Sch., Ala., 1966—69; prof., music edn. U. Tenn., Knoxville, 1978—; asst. prof., music edn. Savannah State Coll., Ga., 1977—78; admin. asst. U. Mich., Ann Arbor, 1974—77. Chair, music in sch. and tchr. edn. Internat. Soc. for Music Edn., Nedlands, Australia, 2004—; mem. Jour. for Arts Edn., Hong Kong. Author: Making Music Series, 2002—05, The Music Connection Series, 1995—, Making Music with Movement and Dance, 2005—, Classroom Managment in the General Choral and Instrumental Programs, 2002—. Instr., children's classes in movement U. Tenn., Knoxville, 1985—95; min. of music United Methodist Ch., Knoxville, 1980—87, Redemption Internat. Ctr., Knoxville, 1987—95; adv. bd. Tenn. Alliance for Arts Edn., Nashville. Recipient James A. Cox Endowed Chair, U. Tenn., 2002—05, Hall of Fame, Tenn. Music Edn. Assn., 2005. Mem.: Internat. Assn. Jazz Edn. Resource Team, Music Educators Nat. Conf. (gen. music chair 1998—2000). Presbyterian. Home: 1256 Halifax Rd Knoxville TN 37922 Office: U Tenn 1741 Vol Blvd Knoxville TN 37922 Office Phone: 865-974-7515. Business E-Mail: mmoore7@utk.edu.

MOORE, MARY FRENCH (MUFFY MOORE), potter, advocate; d. John and Rhoda French; m. Alan Baird Minier, 1982; children: Jonathan Corbet, Jennifer Corbet, Michael Corbet. BA cum laude, Colo. U., 1964. Ceramics mfg., Wilson, Wyo., 1969-82, Cheyenne, Wyo., 1982—. Commr. County Teton (Wyo.), 1976-83, chmn. bd. commrs., 1981, 83, mem. dept. pub. assistance and social svc., 1976-82, mem. recreation bd., 1978-81, water quality adv. bd., 1976-82. Bd. dirs. Teton Sci. Sch., 1968-83, vice chmn., 1979-81, chmn., 1982; bd. dirs. Grand Teton Music Festival, 1963-68, Teton Energy Coun., 1978-83, Whitney Gallery of Western Art, Cody, Wyo., 1995—, Opera Colo., 1998—, Opera Colo. Found., 2005-06; mem. water quality adv. bd. Wyo. Dept. Environ. Quality, 1979-83; Dem. precinct committeewoman, 1978-81; mem. Wyo. Dem. Ctrl. Com., 1981-83; vice chmn. Laramie County Dem. Ctrl. Com., 1983-84, Wyo. Dem. nat. committeewoman, 1984-87; chmn. Wyo. Dem. Party, 1987-89; del. Dem. Nat. Conv., 1984, 88, mem. fairness commn. Dem. Nat. Com., 1985, vice-chair western caucus, 1986-89; chmn. platform com. Wyo. Dem. Conv., 1982; mem. Wyo. Dept. Environ. Quality Land Quality Adv. Bd., 1983-86; mem. Gov.'s Steering Com. on Troubled Youth, 1982, dem. nat. com. Compliance Assistance Commn., 1986-87; exec. com. Assn. of State Dem. Chairs, 1989; mem. Wyo. Coun. on the Arts, 1989-95, chmn., 1994-95, Dem. Nat. Com. Jud. Coun., 1989—; legis. aide for Gov. Wyo., 1985, 86; project coord. Gov.'s Com. on Childrens' Svcs., 1985-86; bd. dirs. Wyo. Outdoor Coun., 1984-85; polit. dir., dep. mgr. Schuster for Congress, 1994-95; adminstrv. dir. Freudenthal for Gov., 2002, pers. coord., 2002; mem. pres.' adv. com. on the performing arts John F. Kennedy Ctr. for the Performing Arts, 1999-2001. Recipient Woman of Yr. award Jackson Hole Bus. and Profl. Women, 1981, Dem. of Yr. Nellie Tayloe Ross award Wyo. Dems., 1990. Mem. Alden Kindred of Am., Jackson Hole Art Assn. (bd. dirs., vice chmn. 1981, chmn. 1982), Assn. State Dem. Chairs, Soc. Mayflower Descendents, Pi Sigma Alpha. Home: 8907 Cowpoke Rd Cheyenne WY 82009-1234 Home Phone: 307-501-2236.

MOORE, MARY JOHNSON, retired community health nurse; b. West Point, NY, Feb. 8, 1940; d. Robert Phillip and Edith Virginia (Carr) Johnson; m. Prentis Monroe Moore, Dec. 28, 1960 (dec. Jan. 1990); children: Carol Edith, Tracey Marie. Diploma, Boston City Hosp. Sch. Nursing, 1960. RN. Clinic nurse in pediat. and obstetrics Harris County Health Dept./Lyons Clinic, Houston, 1982—85; clinic nurse Tex. Sch. for Deaf, Austin, 1986—87; staff nurse pediat. Ben Taub Hosp., Houston, 1989—92; telephone triage nurse, ob-gyn. McGregor Clinic, Houston, 1992—93; staff nurse pediat. Grant Hosp., Chgo., 1994—96; clinic nurse Columbus-Maryville Hosp., Chgo., 1996—2002; travel nurse Star-Med Profl. Staffing, 2002—03; case mgr. Brockton Neighborhood Health Ctr., Mass., 2003—04; ret., 2004. Active Sr. Chorus Massasoit C.C., 2006—; mem. vol. choir St. Chrysostoms Episcopal Ch., 1997—2002; lay reader Trinity Episcopal Ch., Brockton, 2006—. George Monks Meml. scholar, 1960. Democrat. Avocations: art, music, poetry, collecting unicorns, angels and lighthouses. Home: 72 Pine St Brockton MA 02302 Personal E-mail: mryjrn@yahoo.com.

MOORE, MARY TYLER, actress; b. Bklyn., Dec. 29, 1936; d. George and Marjorie Moore; m. Richard Meeker, 1955 (div. 1961); 1 child, Richard (dec.); m. Grant Tinker, 1963 (div. 1981); m. Robert Levine, 1983. Chmn. bd. MTM Enterprises, Inc., Studio City, Calif. Stage appearances include (Broadway debut) Breakfast at Tiffany's, 1966, Whose Life Is It, Anyway?, 1980, Sweet Sue, 1988, The Players Club Centennial Salute, 1989, Rose's Dilemma, 2003; appeared in TV series Richard Diamond, Private Eye, 1957-59, Dick Van Dyke Show, 1961-66, Mary Tyler Moore Show, 1970-77, Mary, 1978, Mary Tyler Moore Hour, 1979, Mary, 1985, Annie McGuire, 1988, New York News, 1995, Mary and Rhoda, 1998; miniseries Gore Vidal's Lincoln, 1988, New York News, 1995; in TV movies Love American Style, 1969, Run a Crooked Mile, 1969, First You Cry, 1978, Heartsounds, 1984, Finnegan Begin Again, 1984, The Last Best Year, 1990, Thanksgiving Day, 1990, Stolen Babies, 1993 (Emmy award, Outstanding Supporting Actress in a Miniseries or Special, 1993), Payback, 1997, Mary and Rhoda, 2000, Like Mother, Like Son: The Strange Story of Sante and Kenny Kimes, 2001, Miss Lettie & Me, 2002, The Gin Game, 2003, Blessings, 2003; films: X-15, 1961, Thoroughly Modern Millie, 1967, Don't Just Stand There, 1968, What's So Bad About Feeling Good?, 1968, Change of Habit, 1969, Ordinary People, 1980 (Acad. Award nominee for best actress 1981), Six Weeks, 1982, Just Between Friends, 1986, Keys to Tulsa, 1996, Flirting with Disaster, 1996, Reno Finds Her Mom, 1997, Labor Pains, 1999; appeared on Broadway in Whose Life Is It Anyway?, 1980, Sweet Sue, 1987, Labor Pains, 2000, Cheats, 2002; in TV spl. How to Survive the Seventies, 1978, How To Raise a Drug Free Child; author: After All, 1995. Chair Juvenile Diabetes Found., 1985—. Recipient Emmy award Nat. Acad. TV Arts and Scis. 1964-65, 73-74, 76, Golden Globe award 1965, 81, Star on the Hollywood Walk of Fame, 1992; named to TV Hall of Fame, 1985. Office: William Morris Agy care Betsy Berg 151 S El Camino Dr Beverly Hills CA 90212-2775

MOORE, MCPHERSON DORSETT, lawyer; b. Pine Bluff, Ark., Mar. 1, 1947; s. Arl Van and Jesse (Dorsett) M. BS, U. Miss., 1970; JD, U. Ark., 1974. Bar: Ark. 1974, Mo. 1975, U.S. Patent and Trademark Office 1977, U.S. Dist. Ct. (ea. dist.) Mo. 1977, U.S. Ct. Appeals (8th, 10th and fed. cirs.). Design engr. Tenneco, Newport News, Va., 1970-71; assoc. Rogers, Eilers & Howell, St. Louis, 1974-80; ptnr. Rogers, Howell, Moore & Haferkamp, St. Louis, 1981-89, Armstrong, Teasdale, Schlafly & Davis, St. Louis, 1989-95, Polster, Lieder, Woodruff & Lucchesi, St. Louis, 1995—. Engr. City of Ladue, Mo., 1998-2000; mem. intellectual property adv. bd. Washington U. Bd. dirs. Legal Svcs. Ea. Mo.; mem. Ladue Zoning and Planning Commn., 1989—; chmn. St. Michael's Houses, Ch. St. Michael and St. George. With USAR, 1970-76. Mem. ABA, Bar Assn. Met. St. Louis (chmn. young lawyers sect. 1981-82, sec. 1984-85, v.p. 1985-86, chmn. trial sect. 1986-87, pres. 1988-89), Ark. Bar Assn., St. Louis Bar Found. (sec. 1984-85, v.p. 1988-89, pres. 1989-90), The Mo. Bar (chmn. patent, trademark and copyright law com. 1992-94, co-chmn. 1994-95), St. Louis County Bar Assn., Women Lawyers Assn., Am. Intellectual Property Law Assn., Mound City Bar Assn., Phi Delta Theta Alumni (treas. St. Louis chpt. 1987-88, sec. 1988-89, v.p. 1989-90), Racquet Club (St. Louis). Home: 3 Mayfair Rd Saint Louis MO 63124 Office: Polster Lieder Woodruff & Lucchesi Ste 200 12412 Powers Ct Dr Saint Louis MO 63131-3615 Office Phone: 314-238-2400.

MOORE, MECHLIN DONGAN, communications executive, management consultant; b. NYC, May 21, 1930; s. Albere Ethier and Pamela (Robinson) M.; m. Elizabeth Ann Tonkin, Feb. 11, 1956 (dec. 1992); children: Lansing, Pamela; m. Valery Ann Shields, July 14, 1995. AB, Harvard U., 1952. Reporter Washington Post, 1955-59; dir. build Am. better com. Nat. Assn. Real Estate Bds., D.C., 1960-64; dir. info. Urban Land Inst., D.C., 1964-66; exec. v.p. Ctrl. Assn. Seattle, 1966-70; asst. to pres. United Airlines, Inc., Chgo., 1971-72, sr. v.p. external affairs, 1972-74, group v.p. mktg., 1975-76, sr. v.p. pub. affairs, 1976-79; pres. Ins. Info. Inst., NYC, 1979-91; chmn., CEO Informatrix Worldwide SuperSite Devel., 1996-98; pvt. practice Naples, Fla., 1991—; advisor Vertical Net, Inc., 1998-2001; project planning dir. Fla. Gulf Coast Univ. Found., 2004—05. Pres. Eagles Mere Water Co., 1993-96; bd. electors Ins. Hall of Fame. Author publs. Nat. Assn. Real Estate Bds.; assoc. editor Jour. Property Mgmt. Adv. bd. mem. Traffic Inst. Northwestern U.; past mem. St. George's Vestry, N.Y.C. 1st lt. U.S. Army, 1952-54. Recipient Commendation Ribbon with Metal Pendant U.S. Army, 1954, Disting. Svc. award Central Assn. Seattle, 1972 Mem. Univ. Club, Shenorock Shore Club. Republican. Episcopalian. Home: 750 Vistana Cir Naples FL 34119 Office Phone: 239-777-1595. E-mail: mmoore7412@aol.com.

MOORE, MEGAN M., mathematics educator, department chairman; d. James R. and Elizabeth F. Moore. BA in Math., Mills Coll., Oakland, Calif., 1994—98; MA in Math., San Francisco State U., 2001—04. Math dept. chair Convent Sacred Heart HS, San Francisco, 2005—. Mem.: Nat. Coun. Tchrs. Math. Office: Convent Sacred Heart 2222 Broadway San Francisco CA 94115 Home Phone: 415-553-8187. Business E-Mail: mmoore@sacredsf.org.

MOORE, MICHAEL, film director, writer; b. Flint, Mich., Apr. 23, 1954; m. Kathleen Glynn; 1 stepchild, Natalie. Studied Journalism, U. Mich.-Flint. Former editor Flint Voice, Mich. Dir., writer, prodr. Roger and Me, 1989 (Ten Best Films of Yr. list), 1992 Bowling for Columbine, 2002 (Academy award Best Documentary Feature, 2003), Fahrenheit 9/11, 2004 (Palme d'Or, Cannes Film Festival, 2004), Sicko, 2007; actor, dir. prodr., writer Canadian Bacon, 1994; dir., creator, host TV Nation, 1994-1995 (Outstanding Informational Series Emmy award, 1995); dir.: (films) Two Mikes Don't Make a Wright, 1992, The Big One, 1997, (TV) The Awful Truth, 1999; Actor only: EdTV, 1999, Lucky Numbers, 2000, The Fever, 2004; Author: Downsize This! Random Threats from Unarmed America, 1996, Adventures in a TV Nation, 1998, Stupid White Men and Other Sorry Excuses for the State of the Nation!, 2002, Dude, Where's My Country?, 2003, Will They Ever Trust Us Again? Letters From the War Zone, 2004, The Official Fahrenheit 9/11 Reader, 2004. Named one of Time Mag. 100 Most Influential People, 2005. Office: Creative Artists Agy c/o David Tenzer 9830 Wilshire Blvd Beverly Hills CA 90212-1804

MOORE, MICHAEL ROBERT, music educator, band director; s. Michael Ruben and Rosa Lee Moore; m. Janie Lynn Creech, June 12, 1993. MusB in Edn., Bowling Green State U., 1994. Cert. tchr. K-12 Dept. Edn., Ohio. Instr. marching band Hamilton (Ohio) H.S. Marching Band, 1988—2001; dir. of music Stephen T. Badin H.S., Hamilton, 2001—. Deacon West Side Bapt. Ch., Hamilton, 2003—07, chair structure reform com., 2003—04, tchr. adult theology, 2002—07, tchr. team kids, 2002—07. Recipient Educator of Distinction award, Nat. Soc. H.S. Scholars, 2004. Mem.: Music Educator's Nat. Conf. Republican. Southern Baptist. Avocations: model railroading, photography, music. Office: Stephen T Badin H S 571 New London Rd Hamilton OH 45013 Home Phone: 513-988-0207; Office Phone: 513-863-3993. Business E-Mail: mmoore@mail.badinhs.org.

MOORE, MICHAEL WATSON, musician, educator; b. Cin., May 16, 1945; s. Clarence Watson and Jeannette Elizabeth (Gardner) M.; m. Renee Allyn White, Oct. 23, 1993; children: Benjamin Butler, Matthew Satyavan. Attended, Cin. Coll. Conservatory of Music, 1964-65. Bass instr. Summer Stage Bank Clinic, 1969, Eastman Sch. of Music, Rochester, NY, 1974-87, U. Bridgeport, Bridgeport, Conn., 1981-83, L.I. U., Bklyn., 1993-96, William Patterson U., Wayne, NJ, 1994-95. String bass player with Cal Collins Trio, Cin., 1965, Woody Evans Trio, Cin., 1965, Woody Herman Band, USO, Africa, Ea. Europe, 1966-67, Marion McPartland Trio, N.Y.C., 1968, Freddie Hubbard Quintet, N.Y.C., 1969-70, Jack Wilkins Trio, N.Y.C., 1971, Chet Baker Quartet, N.Y.C., 1972-73, Phil Woods Quartet, N.Y.C., 1972, Gene Bertoncini Duo, N.Y.C., 1972—, Stan Getz Quartet, N.Y.C., 1973, Tony Bennett, N.Y.C., 1973, Ruby Braff, George Barnes Quartet, N.Y.C., 1973-75, Gerry Mulligan Quartet, N.Y.C., 1974, Benny Goodman Sextet, N.Y.C., 1974-76, Lee Konitz Quartet, N.Y.C., 1975, Teddy Wilson Duo, N.Y.C., 1977, Jim Hall Trio, N.Y.C., 1977, Bill Evans Trio, N.Y.C., 1978, Bob Brookmeyer Quintet, N.Y.C., 1978, Mike Abene, Michael Moore Quintet, N.Y.C., 1978, Zoot Sims Quartet, N.Y.C., 1979, Gary Burton Quartet, N.Y.C., 1981-82, Louis Belson Quartet, N.Y.C., 1982, Roger Kellaway Duo and Trio, N.Y.C., 1980s, Jimmy Rowles Duo, N.Y.C., 1980s, Jon Scoffield Duo and Quartet, N.Y.C., 1980s, Lew Tabackin Trio, N.Y.C., 1980s, Hank Jones Trio, N.Y.C., 1980s, Shelly Mann Trio, N.Y.C., 1980s, Pepper Adams Quartet, N.Y.C., 1980s, Lou Levy Duo, N.Y.C., 1980s, Al Cohen Trio, N.Y.C., 1980s, Jake Hanna Quartet, N.Y.C., 1980s, Rosemary Clooney, N.Y.C., 1987-88, Louis Stewart Trio, Ireland and U.K., 1990, Howard Alden Trio, N.Y.C., 1990s, Warren Vache Trio, N.Y.C., 1990s, Harry Allen Trio, N.Y.C., 1990s, Ken Peplowski Trio, N.Y.C., 1990s, Charlie Byrd Quartet, N.Y.C., 1990s, Dave Brubeck Quartet, 2001—; co-leader duo with Rufus Reid, 1995, with Chris Potter, 1995; leader duo with Bill Charlap, 1995; tour Japan with Harry Allen, 1997; leader trio with Ken Peplowski and Tom Melito, 1998-, Dave Brubeck Quartet, 2001—; composer: Rio Pindare, 1986, Wake Me When It's Over, 1988, The Lilter, 1989, The Old New Waltz, 1992, Zoot's Suite, 1995, Just Me, Just Me, 1995, When I Wage Battle Next, 1999, Moon Dog, 1999; recs. Michael Moore Trio Plays Gershwin, 1993, Michael Moore/Bill Charlap, 1995 (One of the Best Jazz CDs of 95, The New Yorker, 1996), Michael Moore/Rufus Reid Doublebass Delights, 1996 (One of the Best Jazz CDs of 96, The New Yorker, 1997), Michael Moore/Rufus Reid The Intimacy of the Bass, 1999, Michael Moore and His Trio The History of Jazz: Vol. 1, 2000, The Michael Moore Trio The History of Jazz Vol. 2 Dedication, 2002 (One of Best Jazz CDs of 2002, The New Yorker), Video with Rufus Reid, 1998; author: Melodic Improvising in the Thumb Position: Method for Improvisation for the String Bass, 1986, (with Clem Derosa) The Michael Moore Bass Method, 2002; performer: (with Weslia Whitfield) The White House, 1996. Councilman Borough of Bangor, Pa., 1987-88. Mem. ASCAP. Avocation: piano. Home and Office: 5 E 22d St Apt 15M New York NY 10010-5325

MOORE, MIKE (MICHAEL C.), lawyer, former state attorney general; b. Pascagoula, Miss. m. Tisha R. Moore; 1 child, Kyle. Grad., Jackson County Jr. Coll., 1972; BA, U. Miss., 1974, JD, 1976. Asst. dist. atty. State of Miss., Jackson, Miss., 1977—78, dist. atty., 1979, atty. gen., 1988—2004; gen. counsel Phelps Dunbar LLP, Jackson, Miss., 2004—; pvt. practice Mike Moore Law Firm. Chmn. Partnership for a Greater Miss. Named Lawyer of Yr., Nat. Law Jour., 1998; named one of Ten Most Outstanding Young Americans, Young Jaycees, 1992; recipient Wyman award. Democrat. *

MOORE, MILO ANDERSON, banker; b. Orange, NJ, Aug. 26, 1942; s. Milo H. and Helen M.; m. Judith J. Colosimo, May 4, 1968; children: Milo Robert, Matthew Wiley, Marykate Bartlett BS, Ithaca Coll., 1964; MBA, Rutgers U., 1971. Traffic supt. N.Y. Tel. Co., NYC, 1964-71; trust officer Midlantic Nat. Bank, Newark, 1971-76; v.p. Shearson Loeb Rhoades, NYC, 1976-80; sr. v.p. Donaldson Lufkin & Jenrette, NYC, 1980-85; sr. mng. dir. Bear, Stearns & Co., 1985-92; v.p. JP Morgan Pvt. Bank, Morristown, NJ, 1992—2004. Advisor Jr. Achievement, Bronx, N.Y., 1967-68; pres. Chatham Jaycees, N.J., 1974; big bros. Morris County Big Bros., Morristown, 1971-81; pres. Stanley Congl. Ch., Chatham, N.J., 1995-97; trustee SAGE Solutions, 1994-2004, pres., 2002. Mem. Securities Industry Assn. (tax shelter com. 1982-85), Glenburnie Club (pres. 1989—),

Canoe Brook Country Club (Summit, N.J.), Beta Gamma Sigma. Office: JP Morgan Chase Pvt Banking 225 South St Morristown NJ 07960-5336 Office Phone: 973-285-2256. E-mail: milo.moore@jpmorgan.com.

MOORE, MITCHELL JAY, lawyer, educator; b. Lincoln, Nebr., Aug. 29, 1954; s. Earl J. and Betty Marie (Zimmerlin) M.; m. Sharon Lea Campbell, Sept. 5, 1987. BS in Edn., U. Mo., Columbia, 1977, JD, 1981. Bar: Mo. 1981, U.S. Dist. Ct. (we. dist.) Mo. 1981, Tex. 1982, U.S. Ct. Appeals (8th cir.) 1998. Tchr. Clinton Mid. Sch., 1978; sole practice Columbia, Mo., 1981—. Coordinating atty. student legal svcs. ctr. U. Mo., Columbia, 1983-89. Mem. Columbia Substance Abuse Adv. Commn., 1989—; bd. dirs. Planned Parenthood of Ctrl. Mo., Columbia, 1984-86, Opportunities Unltd., Columbia, 1984-86, ACLU of Mid-Mo., 1991-98; Libertarian candidate for Atty. Gen. of Mo., 1992, 2000, for 9th congl. dist. U.S. Ho. of Reps., 1994, 96, for Mo. State Rep. 23d dist., 1998, mem. Probation and Parole Citizens Adv. Bd., 1997-99. Mem.: Boone County Bar Assn., Phi Delta Phi. Unitarian Universalist. Avocations: softball, camping, Tae Kwon Do. Office: 1210 W Broadway Columbia MO 65203-2126 Home Phone: 573-443-2642; Office Phone: 573-449-3318. Personal E-mail: mmoore259@mchsi.com.

MOORE, NANCEY FAY, history educator; d. George Thomas and Mildred Fay Moore. BA in Polit. Sci., U. Charleston, W.Va., 1979, BA in European History, 1979; MA in Am. History., NC State U., Raleigh, 1994. Cert. PPI Inc., NC, 1998. History instr. Wake Tech CC, Raleigh, 1994—; computer instr. Durham Tech CC, NC, 2001—02. Mem. polit. sci. search com. Wake Tech CC, 2005—05; com. rep. U. Ulster, Raleigh, 2006. Election return rep. WCHS TV sta., Charleston, W.Va., 1980—80. Mem.: Am. Assn. Women in CC's, So. Assn. Women Historians (life), Phi Alpha Theta (life; pres. 1975—79), Pi Gamma Mu (life; v.p. 1975—79). Democrat. Baptist. Office: Wake Tech CC 9101 Fayetteville Rd Raleigh NC 27603 Office Phone: 919-866-5247. Business E-mail: nfmoore@waketech.edu.

MOORE, OLIVER SEMON, III, publishing executive, consultant; b. Jersey City, July 26, 1942; s. Oliver S. and Ann Loy (Spies) M.; m. Dina Downing DuBois, Feb. 23, 1961 (div. 1974); 1 child, Deborah; m. Christine Laine Meyers, May 12, 1990; 1 child, Kathryn Laine. BA, U. Va., 1964. Chief bur. Richmond (Va.) Times-Dispatch, 1964-66; corr. Time mag., NYC, 1966-67, contbg. editor, 1967-68; assoc. editor Newsweek, NYC, 1969-71; freelance writer, 1972-75; mng. editor Motor Boating and Sailing, NYC, 1976-78, editor, 1980-82; exec. editor US Mag., N.Y. Times Co., 1978-80; dep. editor Town & Country Mag., NYC, 1982-84; editor Sci. Digest Mag., NYC, 1984-86; pub. dir. Yachting Mag., NYC, 1986-95; editorial dir. Outdoor Life, NYC, 1993-95; v.p. The Outdoor Co., NYC, 1994-95; editor-at-large Motor Boating & Sailing, 1995—2001; pres. Alamo Pub. Svcs., Inc., Detroit, 1995—. Co-founder, chmn. bd. Corp! (Mag.), 1998. Author: (poems) Voices International, 1969; contbg. editor Sports Afield, 1996—; photographer (mags.) Motor Boating and Sailing, Yachting, Working Woman Corp! (books) Lines to a Little Girl, Rancho Paradiso. Recipient Merit award Art Dirs. Club, 1981, award of merit Soc. Publ. Designers, 1981, Excellence in Media award Nat. Arbor Day Found., 1985. Mem. Am. Soc. Mag. Editors, Mag. Pubs. Assn. (nat. mag. award 1995), N.Y. Yacht Club, Grosse Pointe (Mich.) Club, Bayview (Mich.) Yacht Club, Wyndemere Country Club (Fla.). Republican. Episcopalian. Avocations: sailing, antique cars. Personal E-mail: omoore@comcast.net.

MOORE, PAMELA GAY, retired music educator; b. Eugene, Oreg., Dec. 31, 1945; d. John Robert and Alta Rachel Wetzel; m. Glen Eugene Moore; children: Sean Eugene, Connemara Heather Pursley. BA in Music, Seattle Pacific U., 1968; MA in Edn., U. Wash., Seattle, 1971. Cert. tchr. Wash., Yamaha Music Sch., Wash. Profl. musician, entertainer, Port Angeles and Seattle, Wash.; tchr.'s asst. Sharples Jr. HS, Seattle, 1971—72; preschool music tchr. Yamaha Music Sch., Seattle and Port Angeles, 1972—82; tchr. parent presch. coop. Peninsula Coll., Port Angeles, 1975—76; pvt. piano tchr. Seattle and Port Angeles, 1973—85; elem. gen. music tchr. Port Angeles Pub. Schs., 1977—85, mid. sch. choral tchr. gen. music, 1985—97, k-5 elem. gen. music tchr., 1997—2007; ret., 2007. Music entertainer, Oregon, Washington, Idaho, 1979—; choral dir. Holy Trinity Luth. Ch., Port Angeles, 1980—81; coord., dir. mid. sch. mass choir North Olympic Music Educators, Wash., 1986—88; music dir. musicals Port Angeles Cmty. Players, 1985—; site team mem. Franklin Elem. Sch., Port Angeles, 2003—. Composer scripts, musical arrangements, musicals for children, adult scripts, arrangements, songs; developer: curriculum in group music education, music composition. Women's retreat music dir. Holy Trinity Luth., Sequim Cmty. Ch., Port Angeles and Sequim, Wash., 1987—2006; mem. contemporary svc. worship team Sequim Cmty. Ch., 2002—06. Grantee, Port Angeles Pub. Schools, 1996; scholar, Seattle Pacific U., 1964. Mem.: Delta Kappa Gamma. Democrat. Avocations: painting, music synthesizers, reading, travel, sports.

MOORE, PAT HOWARD, engineering and construction executive, educator; b. Laredo, Tex., Sept. 16, 1930; s. Howard Warren and Odette Evelyn (Bunn) M.; m. Elsie Mae Crossman, Mar. 23, 1954; children: Linda Marie Ford, Margaret Ann, Andrew Patrick. BA, Rice U., Houston, 1952, BS in Civil Engring., 1953; postgrad., Tulane U., New Orleans, 1956-58. Registered profl. engr., Tex., La. Div. engr. McDermott Inc., Morgan City, La., 1956-58; pres., dir. Navasota Tel. Co., Tex., 1958-63; project mgr. Brown & Root, Inc., Houston, 1963-67, exec. v.p., dir., 1990-95; pres., dir. Fluor Ocean Svcs., Houston, 1968-80; sr. v.p. Raymond Internat., Inc., Houston, 1980-86; pres., dir. Martin Moore Inc., Bellaire, Tex., 1986-90; mgmt. cons. Bellaire, 1996—2003. Adv. dir. Tex. Commerce Bank, Houston, 1979-86, Third Tech. Inc., Ft. Worth, 2004-06; bd. govs. Rice U., 1984-88, lectr. ethics 1996-03, adj. prof. civil and environ. engring., 2003-; bd. dirs. SGB, Inc., Houston, 1986-90, Charter Builders, Inc., Dallas, 1988-90, Versar, Inc., Springfield, Va., 1998-02, XServ, Inc., Houston, 1997-2007. Spl. investigator US Army Counter Intelligence, 1954—56, hon. discharge, 1962. Named Outstanding Engring. Alumnus, Rice U., 2005. Fellow ASCE(life mem. 1995); mem. Chi Epsilon (hon. mem. 1995), Kiwanis (pres. 1960). Methodist. Home: 124 Chuckwagon Trail Georgetown TX 78633-4598 Business E-Mail: moore@rice.edu.

MOORE, PATRICK J., paper company executive; b. Sept. 7, 1954; m. Beth Moore; 3 children. BSBA, DePaul U., Chgo. Asst. treas. Jefferson Smurfit Corp., St. Louis, 1987-90, treas., 1990-93, v.p., treas., 1993-94; v.p., gen. mgr. Indsl. Packaging divsn. Indsl. Packaging divsn., St. Louis, 1994-96; v.p., CFO Jefferson Smurfit Corp., St. Louis, 1996—98, Smurfit-Stone Container Corp., Chgo., 1998—2002, pres., CEO, 2002—03, chmn., pres., CEO, 2003—06, chmn., CEO, 2006—. Serves on NASDAQ CEO Coun.; bd. dir. Am. Forest & Paper Assn., JP Morgan Nat. Adv. Bd., Intern. Corrugated Case Assn., Archer Daniels Midland. Mem. Civic Progress, St. Louis, Comml. Club, Chgo., Wash. U. John M. Olin Sch. Bus. Nat. Coun.; bd. dir. Met. YMCA, St. Louis, Boys Hope/Girls Hope, Big Shoulders Fund, Chgo. Office: Smurfit-Stone Container Corp 150 N Michigan Ave Chicago IL 60601-7568 *

MOORE, PATSY SITES, food service consultant; b. San Marcos, Tex., Mar. 29, 1939; d. Sam W. and Hilda (Wiede) Sites. BS in Home Econs. Edn., S.W. Tex. State U., 1970. Owner, operator Westover Kindergarten and Nursery Sch., San Marcos, 1965-68; food svc. dir. San Marcos Consol. Ind. Sch. Dist., 1975-97; cons. to food svc. industry, San Marcos, 1997—. Cons. in field., 1997—. Mem. steering com. Play Scape/Children's Park, San Marcos, 1992, co-chair Hays County Parks Meml. tree program, 2005-; mem. Hays County Pks. Adv. Bd., City of San Marco Sr. Citizens Adv. Coun.; sr. adv. bd. City of San Marcos, 2000—; adv. bd. Hays County Parks, 1998—; vice chmn. Hays Rep. Club, 2001-2002, sec., 2003, pres. 2006. Mem. Am. Sch. Food Svc. Assn., Tex. Sch. Food Svc. Assn., Ctrl. Tex. Sch. Food Svc. Dir. Assn. (founder, past pres.), Heritage Assn. (mem. bd. dir. 2003-), Order Eastern Star, San Marcos Fedn. Rep. Women (pres.), Pres. Hays Rep. Club, Spring Lake Garden Club (sec. 1999, 2000, pres. 2002-03). Lutheran. Avocations: gardening, painting, lapadary. Home and Office: 285 Hilliard Rd San Marcos TX 78666-8905 Personal E-mail: pmoore@sanmarcos.net.

MOORE, PEARL B., retired nursing educator; b. Pitts., Aug. 25, 1936; d. Hyman and Ethel (Antis) Friedman; 1 child, Cheryl. BS in Nursing, U. Pitts., 1968, M in Nursing, 1974. Staff nurse Allegheny Gen. Hosp., Pitts., 1957-60; instr. Liliane S. Kaufman Sch. Nursing, Pitts., 1960-70, asst. dir., 1970, dir., 1970-72; cancer nurse specialist Montefiore Hosp., Pitts., 1974-75; coord. Brain Tumor Study Group, Pitts., 1975-83; adj. asst. prof. U. Pitts., 1983—2007; ret., 2007. Contbr. articles in field to profl. publs. Fellow Am. Acad. Nursing; mem. ANA, Oncology Nursing Soc. (exec. dir. 1983—, CEO 1999, Disting. Svc. award 1995), Am. Soc. Clin. Oncology, Am. Soc. Assn. Execs., Nurses Alumnae U. Pitts., Sigma Theta Tau. Home: 5701 Centre Ave Pittsburgh PA 15206

MOORE, PETER, interactive entertainment software company executive; b. Liverpool, Eng., 1955; B, Keele U., United Kingdom; M, Calif. State U., Long Beach. Pres. Patrick U.S.A.; sr. v.p. SEGA; pres., COO SEGA Am.; corp. v.p., interactive entertainment bus., entertainment and device divsn. Microsoft Corp., Redmond, Wash., 2003—07; pres. EA Sports Electronic Arts Inc., 2007—. Office: Electronic Arts Inc 209 Redwood Shore Pkwy Redwood City CA 94065 *

MOORE, PHILIP NICHOLAS, author; b. Atlanta, Nov. 29, 1957; s. Nicholas George and Addy Marie (Todd) M. DDiv, Immanuel Bapt Theol. Sem., 1998. Pres. Rams Head Press Inc., Atlanta, 1995—. Author: The End of History—Messiah Conspiracy, 1996, Nightmare of the Apocalypse, 1997, Eternal Security for True Believers, 1997, A Liberal Interpretation of the Prophecy of Israel-Disproved, 1997, What if Hitler Won the War, 1998. Avocations: reading, writing, researching, travel to israel, study of hebrew. Home: 2995 Slaton Dr NW Atlanta GA 30305-2005 Fax: 1-404-816-9994. Personal E-mail: thecon@aol.com.

MOORE, POWELL ALLEN, former federal agency administrator; b. Milledgeville, Ga., Jan. 5, 1938; s. Jere N. and Sarah (Allen) Moore; m. Pamla Hill Prochnow, Sept. 29, 2001; children: Frances Moore Preston, Powell Allen Jr. BA in Jounalism, U. Ga., 1959. Press sec. to Senator Richard Russell US Senate, Washington, 1966-71; dep. dir. pub. info. US Dept. Justice, Washington, 1971-72; dep. spl. asst. to Pres. for legis. affairs The White House, Washington, 1973-75, cons. pub. affairs, 1975-81, dep. asst. to Pres. for legis. affairs, 1981-82; asst. sec. for congl. rels. US Dept. State, Washington, 1982-83; v.p. legis. affairs Lockheed Corp., Washington, 1983-85, Ginn, Edington, Moore and Wade, Washington, 1985-90; pres. ASL Internat., Washington, 1990-93; sr. prin., mng. dir. Capitoline, MS&L, Washington, 1993-98; chief of staff to Senator Fred Thompson US Senate, Washington, 1998-2001; asst. sec. for legis. affairs US Dept. Def., Washington, 2001—05; mng. dir., fed. govt. relations McKenna Long & Aldridge LLP, Washington, 2005—. Dir. press Com. to Re-elect the Pres., Washington, 1972; cons. Pres. Ford Com., 1976, Reagan-Bush Com., 1980. Served to capt., inf. U.S. Army, 1959-62. Recipient Def. Dept.'s medal for Disting. Pub. Svc., 2005. Mem. Belle Haven Country Club, Met. Club. Republican. Episcopalian. Office: McKenna Long & Aldridge LLP 1900 K St NW Washington DC 20006 E-mail: pmoore@mckennalong.com.

MOORE, RACHEL SUZANNE, performing company executive, dancer; b. Davis, Calif., Feb. 19, 1965; d. Charles Vincent and Patricia (Dudley) M. BA, Brown U., 1992; MA, Columbia U., 1994. Dancer Am. Ballet Theatre II, NYC, 1982-84, 1984—88; devel. officer Nat. Cultural Alliance, Wash., 1994—95; dir., coord. Center for Cmty. Devel. & Arts Americans for the Arts, Wash., 1995—97; mng. dir. Ballet Theater of Boston, Boston, 1998; exec. dir. Project STEP, Boston, 1998—2001; dir. Boston Ballet Center for Dance Ed., Boston, 2001—04; exec. dir. Amer. Ballet Theatre, NYC, 2004—. Adjunct dance prof. Emerson Coll., Boston U. Presidential scholar U.S. Dept. of Edn., Washington, 1982. Mem. Am. Guild of Mus. Artists. Democrat. Unitarian Universalist. Office: Am Ballet Theatre 890 Broadway Fl 3D New York NY 10003-1211

MOORE, RANDALL CHARLES, biology professor; b. Columbus, Tex., June 21, 1954; s. Doyle Liles and Tillie Mae (Spross) M.; m. Kris Collum, May 20, 1989. BS in Biology, Tex. A&M U.; MS in Botany, U. Ga., 1977; PhD in Biology, UCLA, 1980. Asst. prof. Baylor U., Waco, Tex., 1980—83, assoc. prof., 1983—88; prof., chmn. biology dept. Wright State U., Dayton, Ohio, 1988—93, asst. dean to assoc. dean Coll. Sci. and Math., 1990—93; prof. biology, dean Buchtel Coll. Arts and Sci. U. Akron, Ohio, 1993; with U. Louisville; faculty mem. to prof. biology Post Secondary Tchg. and Learning U. Minn., Twin Cities, 2000—. Sci. and tech. writer SciWrite, Waco and Dayton, 1983; corres. prof. Pontificia Universidad Catolica de Chile, Santiago, 1986. Editor: Compatibility Responses in Plants, 1982; author: Biology Laboratory Manual, 1985, 2nd edit. 1989, 3rd edit. 1992, The Living Desert, 1991, Writing to Learn Biology, 1992; mem. editl. bd.: Jour. Coll. Sci. Tchg., Issues in Writing, Jour. Biol. Edn. Sci. educator Trotwood Madison Sch. Dist., 1990. Fulbright scholar, 1988; named Most Outstanding Prof. Baylor U., 1986, Wright State U., 1993; grantee NSF, 1990, NASA, 1991; recipient Tchr. Exemplar award Soc. Coll. Sci. Tchrs., 1993, US Prof. of Yr. award, Carnegie Found. for Advancement of Tchg. and Coun. for Advancement and Support of Edn., 2006. Mem. AAAS, Am. Soc. Plant Physiologists, Bot. Soc. Am. (editor The Am. Biology Tchr., 1983-2002), Nat. Assn. Biology Tchrs. (hon.). Avocations: music, writing, running, movies, reading. Office: U Minn Post Secondary Tchg and Learning 374 Appleby Hall 128 Pleasant St SE Minneapolis MN 55455 Office Phone: 612-626-4458. Office Fax: 612-625-0709. E-mail: rmoore@umn.edu. *

MOORE, RICHARD ALAN, landscape architect; b. St. Louis, Jan. 17, 1930; s. Ira Mack and Helen Adoline (Fakes) M.; m. Patricia Ruth Burke, Mar. 15, 1952 (div. 1967); children: Sheryl Louise, Richard Dennis, Sara Lynn, Sandra Lee. BS, U. Mo., 1951; MLA, U. Oreg., 1957. Registered landscape architect, Calif., Hawaii. Asst. prof. landscape architecture Calif. State Poly. Coll., Pomona, 1957-61; assoc. prof., head dept. landscape architecture N.C. State U., Raleigh, 1962-67; pvt. practice landscape architecture Pomona, Calif., 1957-61; dir. land devel. and planning Oceanic Properties Inc., Honolulu, 1967-69; pvt. practice Honolulu, 1969-70, 79—; dir. ops. Eckbo, Dean, Austin & Williams, Honolulu, 1970-71, v.p. ops., 1971-73; pres. EDAW, Inc., San Francisco, 1973-76, chmn. bd., 1976-78; prof. landscape architecture Tex. A&M U., Bryan, 1977-79. Prin. works include Whispering Pines Motor Lodge, N.C., 1964 (award of merit N.C. chpt. AIA 1964), North Shore Devel. Plan, Kauai, Hawaii, 1973, Comprehensive Zoning Ordinance, County of Kauai, 1973 (Am. Soc. Landscape Architects honor award 1973, HUD honor award 1974), Lihue Devel. Plan, Kauai, 1975, Koloa, Poipu, Kalaheo Devel. Plan, Kauai, 1978, Gen. Plan Update, Kauai, 1982, Mililani Town Devel. Plan, 1967-69 (Am. Soc. Landscape Architects merit award 1970), Lanai Land Mgmt. and Devel. Study, 1969 (Am. Soc. Landscape Architects merit award 1970), Wailea Master Devel. Plan, 1971, Kukuiula Devel. Plan, 1983, Lanai Project Dist. Master Plan, 1983-89, Maliu Ridge Devel. Plan, North Kohala, 1985, Mililani Mauka Devel. Plan, 1988, Devel. Plan, Lanai City Comml. Dist., 1990, Dandan Golf Course, Guam, 1991. Fst lt. U.S. Army, 1951-53, Korea. Fellow Am. Soc. Landscape Architects; mem. Masons. Avocations: sports, drawing, painting.

MOORE, RICHARD CARROLL, JR., physician; b. Balt., Nov. 24, 1946; s. Richard Carroll and Virginia Mae (Clark) M.; m. Jeremy Pierson, Jan. 27, 1973; children: Peter Gregory, Laura Alexandra. BA, Johns Hopkins U., 1968, MPH, 1981; MD, UCLA, 1972. Diplomate Am. Bd. Family Practice. Intern South Balt. Gen. Hosp., 1972-73; commd. med. officer USPHS, 1976, dir. health unit 1, 1988-97, ret., 1997; chief med. div. aviation tng. ctr. USCG, Mobile, Ala., 1976-80, chief med. ops. Washington, 1981-86, sr. med. officer Yard Curtis Bay, Md., 1986-88; staff physician Piedmont Prime Care, Danville, Va., 1997-98; med. dir. Carilion Occupl. Medicin, Roanoke-Salem Ctr., 1999—2001; med. dir. occpl. health svcs. Valley Health System, 2001—06; pres., med. dir. Premier Health Resources, 2006—. Mem. exec. bd. Emergency Med. Svcs. Coun., Mobile County, 1979, Med. and Chirurg. Faculty Md.; clin. asst. prof. family medicine U. Va., 1999—2002; med. dir. Roanoke Elec. Steel, 2000—02. Mem. editl. bd. MD Med. Jour., 1995-97. Bd. dirs. Midway Fed. Credit Union, 1989-96, pres., 1991-96. With USN, 1973-76. Mem. Aerospace Med. Assn., So. Med. Assn, Soc. US Naval Flight Surgeons, Johns Hopkins U. Alumni Assn., Med. Soc. of Va., UCLA Alumni Assn., Alpha Omega Alpha, Sigma Phi Epsilon. Republican. Home: Hobby Horse Hill 3223 Browntown Rd Front Royal VA 22630-7647 Office: Premier Health Resources 1849 Plaza Dr Ste 200 Winchester VA 22601 Office Phone: 540-450-0233. Office Fax: 540-450-0235. Business E-Mail: rcmmd@premhealth.com.

MOORE, RICHARD HANCOCK, lawyer, state official; b. Oxford, NC, Aug. 30, 1960; s. Graham Tingley and Lucy Landis (Hancock) M.; m. Noel Crook, May 18, 1985; 3 children. Student, Harvard U., 1981; BA cum laude, Wake Forest U., 1982, JD, 1986; postgrad. degree, London Sch. Econs and Polit. Sci., 1984. Bar: NC 1986, DC 1987, US Claims Ct. 1988, US Dist. Ct. DC 1988. Clk. to presiding justice U.S. Dist. Ct. (so. dist.) Tex., Corpus Christi, 1986-87; assoc. Finley, Kumble, Wagner, Washington, 1987-88, Laxalt, Washington, Perito & Dubuc, Washington, 1988; chief exec. Dept. Crime Control and Public Safety, 1996; atty. Zolicoffer and Long Law; fedl. prosecutor Ea. NC; state treas. State of NC, 2000—. Chief counsel, bd. dirs. Morlow Inc., San Marcos, Tex., 1986; NC State Ho. of Reps., 1992-94. Co-author: Faces from the Flood: Hurricane Floyd Remembered Mem. ABA, N.C. Bar Assn., D.C. Bar Assn., Order of Barristers, Phi Alpha Theta. Democrat. Episcopalian. Avocations: golf, basketball, travel. Office: State Treas 325 N Salisbury St Raleigh NC 27603-1385 Office Phone: 919-508-5176. Office Fax: 919-508-5167. *

MOORE, RICHARD KERR, electrical engineering educator; b. St. Louis, Nov. 13, 1923; s. Louis D. and Nina (Megown) M.; m. Wilma Lois Schallau, Dec. 10, 1944 (dec. 1999); children: John Richard, Daniel Charles. BS, Washington U. at St. Louis, 1943; PhD, Cornell U., 1951. Test equipment engr. RCA, Camden, NJ, 1943-44; instr. and rsch. engr. Washington U., St. Louis, 1947-49; rsch. assoc. Cornell U., 1949-51; rsch. engr., sect. supr. Sandia Corp., Albuquerque, 1951-55; prof., chmn. elec. engring. U. N.Mex., 1955-62; Black and Veatch prof. U. Kans., Lawrence, 1962-94; prof. emeritus, 1994—; dir. remote sensing lab. U. Kans., 1964-74, 84-93. Pres. Cadre Corp., Lawrence, 1968-87; cons. cos., govt. agys. Author: Traveling Wave Engineering, 1960; co-author: (with Ulaby and Fung) Microwave Remote Sensing, Vol. I, 1981, Vol. II, 1982, Vol. III, 1986; contbr. to profl. jours. and handbooks. Lt. (j.g.) USNR, 1944-46. Recipient Achievement award Washington U. Engring. Alumni Assn., 1978, Outstanding Tech. Achievement award IEEE Geosci. and Remote Sensing Soc., 1982, Louise E. Byrd Grad. Educator award U. Kans., 1984, Irving Youngberg Rsch. award U. Kans., 1989, Australia prize, 1995. Fellow AAAS, IEEE (sect. chmn. 1960-61, Outstanding Tech. Achievement award coun. oceanic engring. 1978); mem., NAE, AAUP, Am. Soc. Engring. Edn., Am. Geophys. Union, Internat. Sci. Radio Union (chmn. U.S. commn. F 1984-87, internat. vice chmn. commn. F 1990-93, chmn. 1993-96), Kiwanis, Sigma Xi, Tau Beta Pi. Presbyterian (past elder). Achievements include research in submarine communications, radar altimetry, radar as a remote sensor, radar oceanography; patent for polypanchromatic radar. Home: 1712 Carmel Dr Lawrence KS 66047-1840 Office: U Kans R S & Remote Sensing Lab 2335 Irving Hill Rd Lawrence KS 66045-7612 Personal E-mail: rmoore@sunflower.com.

MOORE, RICHARD LAWRENCE, structural engineer, consultant; b. Rocky Ford, Colo., Feb. 7, 1934; s. Lawrence and Margaret Kathryn (Bolling) M.; m. Donna St. Clair, Mar. 26, 1972 (div. 1983); 1 child, Andrew Trousdale; m. Margaret Ann Guthrie, May 4, 1984. BSCE, U. Colo., 1957; MS, Princeton U., 1963; PhD, Calif. Western U., Santa Ana, 1975. Registered profl. engr., Mass., Maine, Colo., Pa., Iowa, Nebr., N.Mex., Wyo., Ill., Ark., Mo., ND, Mich., Okla., Mont., N.H. Structural engr. Cameron Engrs., Denver, 1964-66; v.p. Moore Internat., Jeddah, Saudi Arabia, 1967-78; asst. to pres. C.H. Guernsey Co., Oklahoma City, 1979-82; pres. R.L. Moore Co., Boston, 1983—; v.p., dir. Isolink Ing., Basel, Switzerland, 1990—. Nat. chmn. Roof Cons. Inst., Raleigh, N.C., 1988-92; prof. Episcopal Sch. Theology, Denver, 1967-71. Patentee in field. Member Mound City (Mo.) Libr. Bd., 1963-64; pres. Dist. Rep. Party, Boston, 1988—; sr. warden St. John Chrysostom Epis. Ch., Denver, 1966-71. Danforth Found. scholar, 1962. Mem. ASCE, NSPE, Am. Concrete Inst., Nat. Forensic Ctr. Avocations: golf, travel, antique pocket watch collecting. Home and Office: RL Moore Co 534 E Broadway Boston MA 02127-4407

MOORE, RICHARD WAYNE, electric power industry executive, former prosecutor; b. Bartow, Fla., Dec. 5, 1952; s. James Ferrell and Mary Etta (Carlisle) M.; m. Elizabeth Ann Mitchell, Sept. 1, 1984; children: Michaelan Susan, John Mark. BS summa cum laude, Spring Hill Coll., 1974; JD, Samford U., 1977. Bar: Ala. 1977, U.S. Dist. Ct. Ala. 1977. Assoc. Marr & Friedlander, Mobile, Ala., 1977-79; ptnr. Sherling, Drinkard & Moore, Mobile, Ala., 1979-81; assoc. Gibbs & Craze, Cleve., 1981-85; sr. litigation counsel U.S. Atty.'s Office, Mobile, 1985—2003; insp. gen. TVA, Knoxville, Tenn., 2003—. Atlantic fellow in Pub. Policy U.K., Oxford, Eng., 1997. Mem. Mobile County Bar Assn., Paul Brock Mobile Inn of Ct. Anglican. Avocation: hunting. Office: TVA E Tower 400 W Summit Hill Dr Rm 4C Knoxville TN 37902 Office Phone: 865-632-4120.

MOORE, ROBERT HENRY, writer, editor, communications consultant; b. Madisonville, Ky., Sept. 16, 1940; s. William Lee Moore and Robbie (Pritchett) Ruby; m. Diana Churchill, Aug. 17, 1963 (div. 1978); children: Randall Lee, Robin Churchill; m. Patricia Mary George, Oct. 4, 1981; 1 child, Christopher Robert. BA, Davidson Coll., NC, 1962; MA, U. N.C., 1964; PhD, U. Wis., 1972. Asst. dir. admissions Davidson Coll., 1963-64; teaching asst. U. Wis., Madison, 1965-68; staff and faculty U.S. Mil. Acad., West Point, NY, 1968-70; lectr., asst. prof. U. Md., College Park, 1970-76, assoc. prof., 1976; cons. U.S. Congress, Washington, 1976-77; emerging issues coordinator The Conf. Bd., NYC, 1977-79; dir. govt. relations Benefacts, Inc., Washington, 1977-78; v.p. Alexander & Alexander, Inc., Washington, 1978-81, Alexander & Alexander Svcs. Inc., NYC, Washington, 1981-85, sr. v.p. corp. rels., 1985-95, sr. v.p. (inactive), 1995-97; chmn., pres. A & A Govt. and Industry Affairs Inc., Washington, 1990-94, Aon Corp., Vienna, Va., 1997—2005. Del. Nat. Security Affairs Conf., Washington, 1978-82; mem. adv. bd. Career Opportunities Inst., U. Va., Charlottesville, 1982-86, Ctr. for New Am. Work Force, 1992-96; mem. corp. adv. bd. Queens Coll., CUNY, 1985-96; mem. V.P.'s Forum, 1989-94; mem. coun. Conf. Bd. Corp. Comm. Execs., 1990-94; mem. Pub. Rels. Sem., 1993-97; editl. advisor Ctr. for Mind-Body Medicine, Washington, 1998-2000; adv. coun. Mindfulness Practice Ctr. of Fairfax, 1998—; bd. visitors Dictionary of Am. Regional English, 1999—; adv. to chmn. NEH, 1999-2001. Co-author: (with others) School for Soldiers: West Point and the Profession of Arms, 1974 (NYT award 1974), Spreading the Risks: Insuring the American Experience, 2003 (Washington Book Pubs. award

2003), Risk Management, 2004 (Book of the Year), Revised Edit., 2005; contbr. articles to profl. jours,; contbr. interviews to nat. mags., newspapers, radio and TV. Mem. kitchen cabinet Points of Light Found., 1991-95. With U.S. Army, 1968-70, capt. USAR, 1970-72. Ops. Crossroads Africa fellow, 1960; U. Md. rsch. grantee, 1972, 76. Mem. Nat. Assn. Ins. Brokers (exec. com., bd. dirs., pres. 1985-86, chmn. past presidents adv. coun. 1989-93).

MOORE, ROBERT LOWELL, JR., (ROBIN MOORE), author; b. Boston, Oct. 31, 1925; s. Robert Lowell Sr. and Eleanor (Turner) M.; m. Barbara Luther, 1948 (div.1949); 1 child, Lacy; m. Joan Friedman, Sept. 15, 1952 (div. 1955); 1 child, Margo Joan; m. Mary Olga Troshkin, Feb. 17, 1973 (dec. April 2, 2005); m. Helen Edelston, June 29, 2005. AB, Harvard U., 1949. European corr. Boston Globe, 1947; ind. TV prodr. NYC, 1949-52; dir. pub. rels. Sheraton Corp. Am., Boston, 1952- 54, dir. advt. and pub. rels., 1954-56, bd. dirs., 1954-62. Author: Pitchman, 1956, The Devil to Pay, 1961, The Green Berets, 1965, The Country Team, 1967, Fiedler, 1968, The French Connection, 1969, Court Martial, 1970, The Khaki Mafia, 1971, The Fifth Estate, 1974, Compulsion, 1982; (with Xaviera Hollander) The Happy Hooker, 1972, The Treasure Hunter, 1975, Dubai, 1976, Mafia Wife, 1977, The Banksters, 1977, Rhodesia, 1978, The Big Paddle, 1978, Search and Destroy, 1978, The Washington Connection, 1979; (with Milt Machlin) The Family Man, 1985, Force nine, 1987, The Man Who Made It Snow, 1990, The White Tribe, 1991, The Moscow Connection, 1994, the Hunt for Bin Laden (N.Y.Times Bestseller), 2003, Hunting Down Saddam, 2004; co-author: (with Raymond Flynn) Accidental Pope, 2000; screenwriter: The Green Berets, 1967, The French Connection, 1971, The Happy Hooker, 1973, Inchon, 1979, Hoffa, 1985, The Sparrowhook Curse, 1996. With USAAF, 1944-46, ETO. Decorated Air medal with two bronze oak leaf clusters. Mem.: Spl. Ops. Assn., Spl. Forces Assn., Spl. Forces Club (London), Dutch Treat Club (NYC), Met. Club (NYC). Achievements include developing pvt. TV closed circuit network for hotels. Personal E-mail: rmoore31@aol.com.

MOORE, ROBERT MADISON, food products executive, lawyer; b. New Orleans, June 21, 1925; s. Clarence Greer and Anna Omega (Odendahl) M.; m. Evelyn Eileen Varva, Apr. 11, 1953; children: Eileen Alexandria Moore Wynne, John Greer. BBA, Tulane U., 1947; JD, U. Va., 1952; LLM (Food Law Inst. fellow), NYU, 1953. Bar: La. 1956, Calif. 1972. Asst. to pres., gen. counsel Underwear Inst., NYC, 1953-55; pvt. practice law New Orleans, 1955-56; asst. gen. atty., dir. Legal services, sec. and gen. atty. Standard Fruit & Steamship Co., New Orleans, 1957-72; v.p., gen. counsel Castle & Cooke Foods, 1972-81, Castle & Cooke, Inc., 1973-81, sr. v.p. law and govt., 1981-82; pres. Internat. Banana Assn., 1983-98; acting exec. dir. Pan Am. Devel. Found., 1999. Dir. Ferson Optics of Del., Inc., 1958-69, Baltime Securities Corp., Pan American Devel. Found. Asst. atty. gen., La., 1960-66. Served with AUS, 1943-46. Mem. ABA, Calif. Bar Assn., La. Bar Assn., SAR (sec. 1960-61), KM, Cosmos Club, Phi Delta Phi, Alpha Tau Omega. Democrat. Roman Catholic. Home: 3323 R St NW Washington DC 20007-2310 E-mail: rmevmoore@aol.com.

MOORE, ROBERT WILLIAM, professional organization executive; b. Claysburg, Pa., June 4, 1924; s. Frank B. and Sarah A. (Edelbute) M.; m. Helen Lingenfelter, July 17, 1948; children: Thomas R., Priscilla Jane. BA, Pa. State U., 1948. With Price Waterhouse & Co., Pitts., 1948-62, mgr., 1955-62; asst. contr. Con-Gas Svc. Corp., Pitts., 1962-65, Consol. Natural Gas Svc. Co., Inc., Pitts., 1966-72, contr., 1972-78, Consol. Natural Gas Co., Pitts., 1972-78; pres. Fin. Execs. Inst., Morristown, NJ, 1978-89, pres. emeritus, 1989—. Mem. Fin. Acctg. Standards Adv. Coun., 1978-89. Bd. dirs. Central Blood Bank, Pitts., 1960-78, treas. corp., 1962-68, chmn. finance com., 1962-68, chmn. bd., 1969-72; mem. exec. bd. Pa. State U. Alumni Council, 1975-83; mem. exec. com. Campaign for Pa. State U., bd. vis.; pres. Pa. State Coll. Bus. Adminstrn. Soc., 1981-83. Served with AUS, 1943-45. Named to Inaugural Class of Fin. Execs. Inst. Hall of Fame. Mem. Am., Pa. insts. C.P.A.s, Inst. of Mgmt. Acct., Fin. Execs. Inst., Pa. State U. Alumni Assn., Pa. Soc., Beta Alpha Psi (nat. forum), Delta Tau Delta. Clubs: University (dir., pres. 1975-76), Valley Brook Country (dir. 1968-70, v.p. bd. 1970), Duquesne (Pitts.), St. Clair Country. Episcopalian. E-mail: rmooropgh@msn.com.

MOORE, ROBERT YATES, neuroscience educator; b. Harvey, Ill., Dec. 5, 1931; s. Raymon Irwin and Marie Louise (Fischer) M.; children: Elizabeth Allen, Matthew McCormick, Joshua Gilbert, Thomas Douglas. BA magna cum laude, Lawrence U., 1953; MD with honors, U. Chgo., 1957, PhD, 1962; MD (hon.), Lund U., Sweden, 1974. Diplomate: Am. Bd. Psychiatry and Neurology. Intern Univ. Hosp., Ann Arbor, Mich., 1958-59; resident U. Chgo., 1959-64, asst. prof. neurology and anatomy, 1964-66, assoc. prof., 1966-70, prof., 1970-74; prof. neurosci. U. Calif., San Diego, 1974-79; prof., chmn. dept. neurology SUNY, Stony Brook, 1979-90; prof. psychiatry, neurology and neurosci. U. Pitts., 1990—, chmn. dept. neurology, 1992-2000. Cons. Contbr. numerous articles to profl. jours. Recipient numerous grants. Fellow Am. Acad. Neurology; mem. Am. Neurol. Assn., Soc. Neurosci., Internat. Brain Research Orgn., Am. Assn. Anatomists. Office: U Pitts Dept Neurology 3471 5th Ave Ste 811 Pittsburgh PA 15213-3232

MOORE, ROGER ADDISON, pediatrician, anesthesiologist; b. Portsmouth, Va., 1948; MD, U. Va., 1973. Diplomate Am. Bd. Pediatrics, Am. Bd. Anesthesiology. Intern Colo. Affil. Hosps., Denver, 1974-75, resident in pediatrics, 1975-77; resident in anesthesiology Hosp. U. Pa., Phila., 1977-79; fellow in pediat. anesthesiology, CCM Children's Hosp., Phila., 1979; chmn. anesthesiology dept. Deborah Heart - Lung Ctr., Browns Mills, NJ, 1993—2005, chair emeritus, 2005—; assoc. prof. anesthesiology U. Pa., 1988-97, clin. assoc. prof. anesthesiology, 1998—. Mem. AMA, Am. Assn. Pediatrics, Am. Soc. Anesthesiologists (first v.p. 2006—), Soc. Cardiovasc. Anesthesiologists (pres. 2001-03), Alpha Omega Alpha, others. Office: Deborah Heart & Lung Ctr Browns Mills NJ 08015 Address: Soc Cardiovascular Anesthesiologists PO Box 11086 Richmond VA 23230-1086 Office Phone: 609-893-6611. Personal E-mail: rogermoore435@yahoo.com.

MOORE, ROY DEAN, retired judge; b. Chickasha, Okla., Jan. 15, 1940; s. Frank B. and Delia Pauline (Morgan) M.; m. Carolyn Kaye Wood, Aug. 10, 1962; children— Darla Kaye, Jared Dean, Amy Darise. BA, Central State U., 1962, M. Teaching, 1966; JD, Oklahoma City U., 1970; grad., Nat. Coll. State Trial Judges, 1972. Bar: Okla. 1970. Coach debate, instr. dramatics Kingfisher (Okla.) High Sch., 1962-67; instr. English and journalism, head dept. lang. arts. Jarman Jr. High Sch., Midwest City, Okla., 1967-70; pros. atty. City of Lawton, Okla., 1970; spl. dist. judge 5th Jud. Dist. Okla., 1971-72; pvt. practice law Lawton, 1973-90; dist. judge 5th Jud. Dist. Okla., 1990—2002. Pres. Swinney PTA, 1975-76; Editor: Problems in Teaching in the Secondary School, 1966. Pres. Comanche County Mental Health Assn., 1973-74, bd. dirs., 1972-76; co-chmn. Kingfisher County Reps. for Congressman James V. Smith, 1966; mem. state exec. com. Okla. Republican Com., 1973-74, chmn. auditing com., 1977-78; del. Rep. Nat. Conv., 1976; chmn. cts. com. Assn. South Central Okla. Govts. Crime Commn.; chmn. Comanche County Reps. for Reagan for Pres., 1973-83; mem. adv. bd. Jim Taliferro Mental Health Center, 1977-78; del. Nat. Mental Health Assn. Conv., 1975; bd. dirs. Lawton Campfire Girls; elder N.W. Ch. of Christ, 1977—; dir. Back to Bible Campaigns, 1976-2002. Named Outstanding Dist. Judge in State of Okla., Okla. Trial Lawyers Assn., 1999. Mem. Am., Okla., Comanche County bar assns., Okla. Trial Lawyers Assn., Lawton Antique Auto Club, Ford Retractible Club Am., Alpha Psi Omega, Delta Theta Phi. Republican. Mem. Ch. of Christ (elder). Clubs: Fraternal Order of Police, Lion. Home: 2114 NW Atlanta Ave Lawton OK 73505-3923 Personal E-mail: voka1@sbcglobal.net.

MOORE, RYAN NATALIE, creative director; b. Redlands, Calif., Sept. 14, 1977; d. Robert Willard Moore and Cynthia Moon. BA, U. Calif., San Diego, 1998. Assoc. writer, prodr. KGTV, McGraw-Hill Broadcasting Group, San Diego, 1997—2000; dir. creative svcs. Disney-ABC Domestic TV, Burbank, Calif., 2000—. Mem.: PROMAX, Acad. TV Arts Scis., Mensa. Office: Disney ABC Domestic TV 500 S Buena Vista St Burbank CA 91521-4220 Home Phone: 818-729-7984; Office Phone: 818-460-7607. Personal E-mail: ryannatalie@earthlink.net.

MOORE, SALLY FALK, anthropology educator; b. NYC, Jan. 18, 1924; d. Henry Charles and Mildred (Hymanson) Falk; m. Cresap Moore, July 14, 1951; children: Penelope, Nicola. BA, Barnard Coll., 1943; LL.B., Columbia U., 1945, PhD, 1957. Asst. prof. U. So. Calif., Los Angeles, 1963-65, assoc. prof., 1965-70, prof., 1970-77, UCLA, 1977-81; prof. anthropology Harvard U., Cambridge, Mass., 1981—, Victor Thomas prof. anthropology, 1991—, dean Grad. Sch. Arts and Scis., 1985-89. Author: Power and Property in Inca Peru, (Ansley Prize 1957), 1958, Law as Process, 1978, Social Facts and Fabrications, 1986, Moralizing States, 1993, Anthropology and Africa, 1994, Law and Anthropology, 2005. Trustee Barnard Coll., Columbia U., 1991—92; master Dunster House, 1984—89. Grantee Social Sci. Rsch. Coun., 1968-69, NSF, 1972-75, 79-80, Wenner Gren Found., 1983; Guggenheim fellow, 1995-96. Fellow Am. Acad. Arts & Scis., Am. Anthrop. Assn., Royal Anthrop. Inst. (Huxley medallist, lectr. for 1999); mem. Am. Philos. Soc., Assn. Polit. and Legal Anthropology (pres. 1983), Am. Ethnological Soc. (pres. 1987-88), Assn. Africanist Anthropologists (pres.-elect 1995, pres. 1996-98), Law and Soc. Assn. (Kalven prize 2005) Democrat. Office: Harvard U 350 William James Hall Cambridge MA 02138

MOORE, SHEMAR, actor; b. Oakland, Calif., Apr. 20, 1970; B in communications, Santa Clara Univ. Actor: (TV series) Living Single, 1995, The Jamie Foxx Show, 1996, Arli$$, 1997, Chicago Hope, 1998, Moesha, 1999, For Your Love, 1999, Malcolm & Eddie, 1999, The Young and the Restless, 1994—2002 (Outstanding Supporting Actor Daytime Emmy award, 2000), 2004—05 (Outstanding Actor in Daytime Drama Series, NAACP Image award, 2006), Birds of Prey, 2003, Half & Half, 2004, Criminal Minds, 2005—; (TV films) Mama Flora's Hope, 1998, How To Marry a Billionaire: A Christmas Tale, 2000, Reversible Errors, 2004; (films) Hav Plenty, 1997, Butter, 1998, Box Marley, 2000, The Brothers, 2001, Motives, 2004, The Seat Filler, 2004, Greener, 2004, Diary of a Mad Black Woman, 2005. Mailing: c/o CBS Television City 7800 Beverly Blvd Los Angeles CA 90036

MOORE, SHERRY MILLS, lawyer; b. 1951; m. Tim Moore; 2 children. BA, Beloit Coll.; JD, Univ. ND, 1979. Bar: ND 1979. Pvt. practice, Bismarck, ND. Bd. mem. Mental Health Assn. of ND, Prevent Child Abuse ND; pres. Bismarck Library Bd.; chair Mayor's Task Force on Methamphetamine. Named Vol. Lawyer of Yr., Big Muddy Bar Assn., 2000. Mem.: State Bar Assn. ND (pres. 2004). Avocations: photography, reading, jetskiing. Office: Atty-at-Law 300 N 4th St PO Box 4144 Bismarck ND 58502-4144 Office Phone: 701-222-4777. Office Fax: 701-222-8502. *

MOORE, STANLEY WAYNE, retired political science professor; b. Camden, NJ, Feb. 11, 1937; s. Frank Stafford and Alma Beatrice (Law) M.; m. Nancy Joan Crawford, Sept. 1, 1961; children: David Crawford, Andrea Katrina, Stanley Edward Stafford Moore, Sonia Elizabeth. AB magna cum laude, Wheaton Coll., 1959; MA and PhD in Govt., Claremont Grad. U., 1971. Asst. prof. polit. sci. Calif. State U.-Stanislaus, Turlock, 1967—69, Monterey Inst. for Internat. Studies, Calif., 1969—72; vis. assoc. U. Redlands, Calif., 1972—73; assoc. prof. Pepperdine U., Malibu, Calif., 1973—79, prof. polit. sci., 1979—, emeritus prof. polit. sci. Pres. Calif. Ctr. for Edn. in Pub. Affairs, Inc., 1991-2002. Author: A Child's Political World: A Longitudinal Perspective, 1985; contbr. articles to profl. jours. Scoutmaster troop 761 Boy Scouts Am., 1981-92, adv. bd. LA Area Coun., 1993—, chair advancement com., 1994-98; vice chmn. Ventura County Air Pollution Control Bd., 1981-92; mem. Ventura County Beyond the Yr. 2000 Commn., 1988-90, Nat. Dem. Com., Calif. Dem. Com., Christians in Polit. Sci.; bd. dirs. Calif. Bicentennial Found. for US Constn., 1987-91; moderator Camps and Conf. Ministry Bd., 1998-2004; bd. dirs. LA chpt. Christians for Biblical Equality, Staff of Hope, Christians Empowering for Reconciliation with Justice; elder Presbyn. Ch., USA, del. Gen. Assembly, 2000; elected to Hist. Highland Pk. Neighborhood Coun., 2002—, treas. 2006—; mem. Senate Congress LA Neighborhood Couns., 2006—, Dept. Water and Power Oversight Com., 2006-. Recipient Medal of Honor, Boy Scouts Am., 1989; grantee Spencer Found. Chgo., 1979, 81. Fellow Am. Sci. Affiliation; mem. Am. Polit. Sci. Assn., We. Polit. Sci. Assn., So. Calif. Polit. Sci. Assn. (pres. 1988-2002), So. Calif. Soc. for Internat. Devel. (pres. 1988-98), Coun. Soc. for Internat. Devel., Sierra, Aubudon Soc., Nat. Wildlife Fedn., Highland Pk. C. of C. (bd. dirs., sec. 2005—), Kiwanis (bd. dirs. 2003—). Presbyterian (elder). Avocations: backpacking, fishing, photography, reading, ch. activities.

MOORE, STEPHEN JAMES, lawyer; b. Kansas City, Mo., Aug. 9, 1947; s. James Andrew and Frances Clare (Kennedy) M. BSBA, Rockhurst U., 1969, BA, 1975; JD, U. Mo., Kansas City, 1977, LLM, 1997. Bar: Mo. 1978, U.S. Dist. Ct. (we. dist.) Mo. 1978, U.S. Ct. Appeals (8th cir.) 1980, U.S. Ct. Appeals (10th cir.) 1981, U.S. Ct. Fed. Claims 1991, U.S. Ct. Appeals (6th cir.) 1997. Law intern Mo. Atty. Gen.'s Office, Kansas City, 1976-77, asst., 1978; assoc. Popham, Conway, Sweeny, Fremont & Bundschu PC, Kansas City, 1978-84, Freilich, Leitner & Carlisle, PC, Kansas City, 1985, Herrick, Feinstein, Kansas City, 1985-86, Freilich, Leitner, Carlisle & Shortlidge, Kansas City, 1986-90; ptnr. Freilich, Leitner & Carlisle, Kansas City, Dallas, L.A., 1987-2000, Aspen, Colo., 1997-2000, Peters, Moore & Jones, LLC, Kansas City, Mo., 2001—02, Peters & Moore, L.L.C., 2002—04; pvt. law firm Stephen J. Moore, PC, 2005—. Adj. prof. law U. Mo., Kansas City, 1995—. Mem. Friends of Art, Nelson-Atkins Mus. Art, Kansas City, 1988—, Smithsonian Inst., Washington, 1985—, Nat. Trust for Historic Preservation, Washington, 1988—, Libr. of Congress Assocs., The Federalist Soc., Nat. Audubon Soc. Mem. ABA, Assn. Trial Lawyers Am., Kansas City Metro Bar Assn., Sports Car Club Am., Am. Mus. Nat. History, Porsche Club Am., Lake Ozarks Yacht Assn., Boat Owners Assn. U.S., Ancient Order of Hibernians, Delta Theta Phi, Tau Kappa Epsilon. Roman Catholic. Avocations: vintage sportscars, boating. Home: 5840 McGee St Kansas City MO 64113-2132 Office: 1500 Traders on Grand Bld 1125 Grand Ave Kansas City MO 64106 Office Phone: 816-777-1012. Business E-Mail: stephen@moorelandlaw.com.

MOORE, STEVEN E., energy executive; Various positions including gen. counsel, v.p., sr. v.p. law & pub. affairs, bd. dirs. OGE Energy Corp., Oklahoma City, 1974—95, pres., COO, 1995-96, chmn., pres., CEO, 1996—2007, chmn., CEO, 2007—. Bd. dir. BOK Fin. Corp., Integris Health. Office: Okla Gas and Elec Co 321 N Harvey Oklahoma City OK 73102 *

MOORE, SUZAN E., lawyer; b. Richlands, Va., Apr. 27, 1960; d. Farrell Ray Moore and Sandra R. Campbell; m. Scott W. Mullins, Dec. 23, 1989. BA with highest honors, U. Tenn., 1982; JD, U. Va., 1985. Bar: Va. 1985, Ky. 1991, W.Va. 1991, US Dist. Ct. (we. dist. Va.) 1985, US Dist. Ct. (so. dist. W. Va.) 1991, US Dist. Ct. (ea. dist. Va.) 1996, US Ct. Appeals (4th cir.) 1985. Assoc. Penn, Stuart, Eskridge & Jones, Abingdon, Va., 1985—89; assoc. gen counsel Westmoreland Coal Co., Big Stone Gap, 1989—91, asst. gen. counsel, 1991—95; assoc. gen. counsel Pittston Coal Mgmt. Co., Lebanon, 1995—2002, Alpha Natural Resources, LLC, 2003—, asst. v.p. legal, 2003—; assoc. counsel Alpha Natural Resources, Inc., 2005—. Moot ct. explorer post leader Boy Scouts Am., 1988; team diabetes fundraising mem. Walt Disney World Marathon, 2003; bd. dirs. S.W. Va. Legal Aid Soc., 1987—89, United Way S.W. Va., 1992—93, Client Centered Legal Svcs., 1995—2001; bd. trustees William King Regional Arts Ctr., 2004—, sec., 2005—. Mem.: ABA, Va. State Bar, Energy & Mineral Law Found. Avocations: fly fishing, mountain biking, hiking, canoeing, skiing. Office: Alpha Natural Resources Inc PO Box 2345 One Alpha Pl Abingdon VA 24212 Home: 385 Brushey Ridge Rd Nora VA 24272

MOORE, T. JUSTIN, III, lawyer; b. Richmond, Va., Nov. 26, 1956; BA cum laude, Princeton U., 1979; MBA, JD, U. Va., 1983. Co-head, Global Capital Markets, Mergers, Acquisitions Team Hunton & Williams LLP, Richmond, Va., 1983—91, ptnr., 1991—, mem. exec. com., 2004—. Bd. dir. Valentine Mus., 1999—; chmn., prof. divsn. United Way, Richmond, 1997—98; bd. trustees Historic Richmond Found., 1984—95, pres., 1991—93; bd. gov. St. Christopher's Sch., 1992—, chmn., 2002—. Mem.: ABA, Va. Bar Assn. Office: Hunton & Williams LLP Riverfront Plz East Tower 951 E Byrd St Richmond VA 23219-4074 Office Phone: 804-788-8464. Office Fax: 804-788-8218. Business E-Mail: jmoore@hunton.com.

MOORE, THOMAS A., lawyer; b. Waterford, Ireland, May 2, 1942; STL, Cath. U., 1968; JD, Fordham U., 1972. Bar: N.Y. 1973, U.S. Dist. Ct. (so. and ea. dists.) N.Y. 1973, U.S. Supreme Ct. 1991. Atty. Kramer, Dillof, Livingston & Moore, NYC, 1973—, sr. ptnr. Lectr. in field. Mem.: ATLA (nat. bd. dirs. 1992), Am. Bd. Trial Advs., N.Y. State Trial Lawyers Assn. Office: Kramer Dillof Livingston & Moore 217 Broadway New York NY 10007

MOORE, THOMAS ANDREW, biotechnology executive; b. Cambridge, Mass., Jan. 28, 1951; s. Leo B. and Christine (Banios) M.; m. Avril Barton, Nov. 8, 1975; children: Thomas, Diana, Juliet. BA in History, Princeton U., 1973. Brand asst. Procter & Gamble Co., Cin., 1973-84, advt. mgr. Beauty Care, 1984-86, gen. mgr. Vidal Sassoon LA, 1986-88, v.p. Health Care Cin., 1988-91; pres. Procter & Gamble Can., Toronto, Ont., Can., 1991-92; pres. Health Care Procter & Gamble USA, Cin., 1992-96; group v.p. Procter & Gamble Co., Cin., 1992-96; pres., CEO Nelson Communications, 1996—2002; CEO Biopure Corp., Cambridge, Mass., 2002—04; chmn., CEO Advaxis Corp., New Brunswick, NJ, 2006—. Bd. mem. Alteon Inc., 2001—07, El Dorado Mktg., 2004—, MD Offices Inc., Kingston, NY, 2006—; chmn. of bd. Ashanti Vineyards, Paarl, South Africa, 2005—, Mayan Pigments Inc., El Paso, Tex., 2006—. Treas. Alliance Drug Free Can., Toronto, 1991, 92; chmn. Cin. Ballet Co., 1986-91; bd. dirs. Am. Health Found., NYC, 1989-2004, Mercy Hosp., Anderson, Ohio, 1993-96, D&R Greenway Land Trust, 2000-06, Nat. Pub. Radio Found., 2002-06, Sound Portraits Prodn., 2004-. Mem. Non Prescription Drug Mfrs. Assn. (vice chmn. 1992—96), Princeton Club, Union Club, Jasna Polana. Avocations: fly fishing, wine collecting, consumption. Office Phone: 617-331-4872. Business E-Mail: mooringsllc@aol.com.

MOORE, THOMAS DAVID, academic administrator; b. Rochester, NY, July 26, 1937; s. Robert Franklin and Hilda (Kennedy) M.; m. Virginia Muller, June 13, 1959; children: Kathleen Mary, Michael David, Thomas David. BSS, St. John Fisher Coll., 1959; MS, SUNY, Brockport, 1962; EdD, Rutgers U., 1966. Tchr. Rochester City Schs., 1959-62; grad. asst. Rutgers U., New Brunswick, NJ, 1963-65; from asst. to full prof. Kent (Ohio) State U., 1965-93, asst. v.p. acad. affairs, 1976-83, v.p. faculty affairs and personnel, 1984-86, provost, v.p. acad. and student affairs, 1987-91, prof. emeritus ednl. philosophy, 1991—; provost, v.p. acad. affairs Ctrl. Washington U., 1993-97, prof. edn. and philosophy, 1997—. Roman Catholic. Avocations: sports, films, public affairs, music. Office Phone: 330-524-0688. Personal E-mail: vmoore4860@sbcglobal.net.

MOORE, THOMAS EDWIN, biologist, educator, museum director; b. Champaign, Ill. s. Gerald E. and Velma (Lewis) M.; m. E. Eleanor Sifferd, Feb. 4, 1951; children: Deborah S., Melinda S. BS, U. Ill., 1951, MS, 1952, PhD, 1956. Tech. asst. Ill. Natural History Survey, Urbana, 1950-56; instr. zoology U. Mich., Ann Arbor, 1956-59, asst. prof. zoology, 1959-63, assoc. prof. zoology, 1963-66, prof. biology, 1966—2000, curator insects, 1956—2000, dir. exhibit mus., 1988-93. Vis. prof. Orgn. Tropical Studies, San Jose, Costa Rica, 1970, 72; bd. dir. Orgn. Tropical Studies, San Jose, 1968-79; mem. steering com. tropical biome US Internat. Biol. Program, 1969-72; mem. conf. planning com. Nat. Inst. Environment, 1991-92; mem. steering com. Univ. Colloquium on Environ. Rsch. and Edn., 1991-93, grievance com. U. Mich., 1997-98, faculty handbook com., 1997-98. Co-editor: Lectures on Science Education, 1991, 92, 93; Cricket Behavior and Neurobiology, 1989; author movie 17-Year Cicadas, 1975, TV, 1998; co-author: Singing Insects of N.Am. Website, 2003—. County rep. Huron River Watershed Coun., Ann Arbor, 1987-95; mem. Mich. H.S. Accreditation Adv. Com., Ann Arbor, 1988-92; mem. U. Mich. Senate Adv. Com. on Univ. Affairs, 1993-96, vice chair, 1995-96; mem. U. Mich. Acad. Freedom Lecture Fund, 1995—, treas., 1995-98; vol. Kempf House Ctr. for Local History, Ann Arbor, Mich.; cons. NSF Visual Tech. in Environ. Curricula, 1994-97; cons. Misery Bay exhibits ParksCanada, 2003-07. Rsch. grantee NSF, 1963-66, 66-69, 96-97, rsch. equipment grantee, 1984-86, rsch. grantee Def. Advanced Rsch. Project Agy./Office of Naval Rsch. 1998—. Fellow AAAS, AAUP (pres. U. Mich. chpt. 1996-99, exec. bd. Mich. conf. 1996-98), Royal Entomol. Soc. London, Linnaean Soc. London; mem. Assn. Tropical Biology (pres. 1973-75), Sigma Xi (pres. U. Mich. chpt. 1994-96, coun. 1993-98) Home: 4243 N Delhi Rd Ann Arbor MI 48103-9485 Office: Mus of Zoology U Mich Ann Arbor MI 48109-1079 Office Phone: 734-764-0471. Business E-Mail: temoore@umich.edu.

MOORE, THOMAS GALE, economist, educator; b. Washington DC, Nov. 6, 1930; s. Charles Godwin and Beatrice (McLean) M.; m. Cassandra Chrones, Dec. 28, 1958; children: Charles G., Antonia L. BA, Geroge Washington U., 1957; MA, U. Chgo., 1959, PhD, 1961. Fgn. research analyst Chase Manhattan Bank, NYC, 1960-61; asst. prof. econs. Carnegie Inst. Tech., 1961-65; assoc. prof., then prof. econs. Mich. State U., East Lansing, 1965-74; sr. staff economist Council Econ. Advisers, 1968-70; hon. research fellow Univ. Coll., London, 1973-74; adj. scholar Am. Enterprise Inst., 1971—, CATO Inst., 1982—; sr. fellow Hoover Inst. on War, Revolution and Peace-Stanford U., 1974—, dir. domestic studies program, 1974-85; mem. Council Econ. Advisers, Washington, 1985-89. Mem. Nat. Critical Materials Council, 1985-89; mem. econ. adv. bd. Dept. Commerce, 1971-73; mem. adv. com. RANN, 1975-77, NSF, 1975-77; cons. Dept. Transp., 1973-74, 81-83; mem. adv. panel Synthetic Fuels Corp., 1982; mem. adv. bd. Reason Found., 1982—; dir. Stanford Savs. & Loan, 1979-82, chmn., 1982. Author: The Economics of American Theater, 1968, Freight Transportation Regulation, 1972, Trucking Regulation: Lessons from Europe, 1976, Uranium Enrichment and Public Policy, 1978, Climate of Fear: Why We Shouldn't Worry About Global Warming, 1998; co-author: Public Claims on U.S. Output, 1973; contbr. articles to profl. jours. Served with USN, 1951-55, Korea. Fellow Earhart Found., 1958-59; fellow Walgreen Found., 1959-60, Hoover Instn., 1973-74 Mem. Am. Econ. Assn., Mont. Pelerin Soc., Chevy Chase Club. Home: 3766 La Donna Ave Palo Alto CA 94306-3150 Office: Stanford U Hoover Instn Stanford CA 94305 Office Phone: 650-723-1411. Business E-Mail: moore@hoover.stanford.edu.

MOORE, THOMAS JOSEPH, finance company executive; b. Kalamazoo, Jan. 5, 1943; s. John Joseph and Bernita (Ryan) M.; m. Laura Leigh Johnson, Aug. 1, 1975; children: Ryan Michael, Janelle Marie, Darcie Kathleen. BBA, Western Mich. U., 1965; MBA, So. Meth. U., 1990. Various sales and mktg. positions IBM Corp., Southfield, Mich., 1968-79; exec. v.p., owner Carsonville (Mich.) Metal Products Corp., 1976-79; assoc. prof. Oakland Coll., Farmington Hills, Mich., 1977-78; group mgr.

industry mktg. Recognition Equipment Inc., Dallas, 1979-81; mgmt. cons. APC Skills div. Alexander Proudfoot Co., Palm Beach, Fla., 1982-83; pres., chief exec. officer Lumentech of Am., Inc., Dallas, 1983-85; v.p., prin. Capital Alliance Corp., Dallas, 1985-2001; ptnr. EquiCap Ptnrs., LLC, Dallas, 2001—; mgr. EquiCap Investments, LLC, Dallas, 2003—; ptnr. Cunningham Partnership LLP, Houston, 2003—. Chmn., CEO, Laura Leigh Stores, Inc., Plano, Tex., 1993-2006; chmn. Luxury Baths by Arrow, Houston, 2003—; vis. lectr. Baylor U., Waco, Tex., 1986-89, sponsor, CEO roundtable, 1989-93; bd. dirs. MJ Designs, Inc., Coppell, Tex., 1997-98; co-CEO Arrow Marble LLC, Houston, 2003—, Designer Bath and Kitchen, LLC, 2005—07, Luxury Baths of San Antonio, LLC, 2005—, Luxury Baths of Dallas, LLC, 2005—. Pres. Bent Tree Homeowners Assn., Dallas, 1981-83; co-chair Jesuit Coll. Prep. Sch. Challenge Dr., 1992-95; chair car raffle Ursuline Acad. of Dallas, chmn. maj. donor campaign, 1994-95, co-chair bridge the gap campaign, 1995-96, chair underwriting, 1996; chmn. adv. coun., chmn. fin. com. John Paul II H.S., Plano, Tex., 2004-2006. Mem. So. Meth. U. Exec. MBA Alumni Assn. (bd. dirs. 1990-92), Legatus, Serra Club Dallas. Republican. Roman Catholic. Avocations: running, reading, racquetball, cooking, wine tasting. Office: EquiCap Ptnrs LLC Park Central III Ste 514 12700 Park Central Dr Dallas TX 75251 Home: 5418 Westgrove Dallas TX 75248-2039 Office Phone: 972-233-8282. Business E-Mail: tmoore@equicappartners.com.

MOORE, THOMAS LLOYD, library director; b. Springfield, Ill., Oct. 4, 1942; s. Edward Joseph and Dorothy A. (Menezes) M.; m. Ann Mary Walsh, Aug. 29, 1971; children: Sean Christopher, Martin Thomas, Kathleen Adele. AA in Liberal Arts, Springfield Coll., 1963; BA in Philosophy, Cardinal Glennon Coll., St. Louis, 1968; MLS, Rosary Coll., River Forest, Ill., 1973. Tchr. 4th grade Little Flower Parochial Sch., Springfield, 1963-66; paraprofessional br. mgr. Lincoln Libr. Sys., Springfield, 1970—72; head adult svcs. Elk Grove Village Pub. Libr., Ill., 1973—74; dir. Northlake Pub. Libr. Dist., Ill., 1974—75, Danville Pub. Libr., Ill., 1975—78, Wake County Pub. Libr. Sys., Raleigh, NC, 1981—; adminstrv. libr. Palatine Pub. Libr. Dist., Ill., 1978—81; trainer Roger Schwarz & Assocs., Chapel Hill, NC, 1998—. Adj. instr. NC Ctrl. U. Sch. Libr. and Info. Sci., 1992, 94, 2007. Bd. dirs. Commit to a Healthier Region, 1991-93, Planned Parenthood of the Capital & Coast, 1993-97, sec., 1994; bd. dirs. Pirates Cove Homeowners Assn., 1992-97, v.p., 1993-94, pres., 1995-96; mem. Libr. Power Adv. Com., 1993-95, Facilitators Orgnl. Devel. Group, 1995—, ASSIST Wake to Health Coalition, 1992-94. Mem. ALA, NC Libr. Assn. Democrat. Roman Catholic. Office: Wake County Pub Libr 4020 Carya Dr Raleigh NC 27610-2913 Office Phone: 919-250-1212. E-mail: tmoore@co.wake.nc.us.

MOORE, THOMAS PAUL, retired broadcast executive; b. Danville, Ill., Feb. 29, 1928; s. Lester Rufus and Mabel Ellen (Jackson) M.; m. Jean LaVonne Sather, Aug. 31, 1952; children: Randyl Ellen, Patricia Kay, Gregory Sather. BA, North Cen. Coll., Naperville, Ill., 1952; postgrad., Denver U., 1952-53. Newscaster Sta. KFEL-AM-FM-TV, Denver, 1952-54; sales rep. Sta. KGMC, Englewood, Colo., 1954-56; sales mgr. Sta. KDEN-AM-FM, Denver, 1956-62; pres. Stas. WBCO, WQEL, Bucyrus, Ohio, 1962-98; ret., 1998. Hon. dir. First Fed. Cmty. Bank, 2001—. Lay leader, mem. program coun. Ohio Sandusky Conf., United Meth. Ch., 1966-69 (pres. gen. laity bd. and laymen's found. 1968-72); mem. Gen Coun. on Ministries, 1980-84, N.W. Ohio Water Devel. Adv. Com., 1967-69, Sandusky River Basin Water Pollution Study Com., 1968-69; v.p., bd. mgrs. EUB Men, Evang. United Brethren Ch., 1958-68; pres. Rocky Mountain Conf., 1957-61; mem. gen. bd. Nat. Coun. Christian Chs. Am., 1968-72; charter pres. Bucyrus Bratwurst Festival, Inc., 1968; adv. bd. Bucyrus Salvation Army, 1964-68; mem. planning com. East Ohio Conf., 1972-76 (chmn. commn. on minimum salaries, 1968-72, lay leader, 1972-76); vice chmn. coun. ministries, mem. episcopal com., 1972-76, head. del. to gen. conf., Portland, Oreg., 1976, Balt., 1984; head del. to Jurisdictional Conf., Sioux Falls, 1976, Duluth, Minn., 1984; pres. United Meth. Comms., 1972-76, mem. gen. coun. fin. and adminstrn., 1976-80; mem. comms. commn. Nat. Coun. Chs., 1972-76; mem. comms. con. Ohio Coun. Chs.; mem. Episc. com., chmn. New Vision Task Group, both East Ohio Conf., North Cen. Jurisdiction, United Meth. Ch.; mem. exec. com. Coun. on Ministries, 1980-86; mem. World Meth. Coun., 1986-91, World Meth. Conf., 1996; trustee United Theol. Sem., 1972-80; trustee Ohio No. U., 1986-2007, life trustee, 2007-, mem. exec. com., 1991-2003, chair student affairs com., 1991-95, chair, 1995-2007; mem. exec. com. East Ohio del. to United Meth. Gen. Conf. and Jurisdictional Conf., 1987-91; sec. Cmty. Improvement Corp., Bucyrus, 1989-91; mem. Overall Econ. Devel. Com. of Crawford County, 1992-96; chmn. Crawford County Traffic Safety Coun., 1979-89, 96-98; pres. Crawford County Econ. Devel. Adv. Coun., 1992-96; mem., sec. Crawford County Devel. Bd., Inc., 1997-2000; mem. exec. com. of del. to 1988 Gen. Conf. United Meth. Ch., St. Louis; bd. dirs. Bucyrus Cmty. Hosp., 1992, mem. fin. com., 1993-96, chmn., 2004-2007, chmn. nominating com., 1993-96, campaign dir., chair fundraising com., 1993-96, v.p. bd. dirs., 1994-96; chmn. North Ctrl. Ohio Health Sys., 1996-98; mem. Crawford County Rep. Ctrl. Com., 1998-2001; mem. City of Bucyrus Bd. of Zoning Appeals, 1998-2001; pres. Crawford County Devel. Bd., 2000—; chmn. City of Bucyrus Bd. Zoning Appeals, 2000-01; sec. Bucyrus Pub. Libr Bd., 2004—. Served with USN, 1946-48. Named a Civic Leader of Am., 1968. Mem. Nat. Assn. Broadcasters (legis. liaison 1984-91, mem. small market radio com.), Ohio Assn. Broadcasters (pres. 1982-85), North Ctrl. Ohio Broadcasters Assn. (pres. 1983-84, 96-98, v.p. 1985-96), Bucyrus Area C. of C. (chmn. airport study com. 1967-68, bd. dirs. 1964-67, pres. 1989-91), Rotary (pres. Bucyrus chpt. 1992-93). Office Phone: 419-562-6023. Personal E-mail: tommoore@wavelinc.com, ccdbinc@wavelinc.com.

MOORE, THOMAS RONALD (LORD BRIDESTOWE), lawyer; b. Duluth, Minn., Mar. 27, 1932; s. Ralph Henry and Estelle Marguerite (Hero) M.; m. Margaret C. King, Sept. 10, 1955 (dec. May 10, 2003); children: Willard S., Clarissa, Charles R.H. BA magna cum laude, Yale U., 1954; JD, Harvard U., 1957. Bar: N.Y. 1958, U.S. Supreme Ct. 1965. Instr. Harvard Law Sch., 1956-57; with Dewey Ballantine, NYC; ptnr. Breed, Abbott & Morgan, NYC, Law Offices of Thomas R. Moore, NYC. Lectr. Harvard U. Law Sch., Cornell Law Sch., NYU Law Sch., Practising Law Inst., NYC, Las Vegas, New Orleans; lectr. Oxford U. Author: Plantagenet Descent, 31 Generations from William the Conqueror to Today, 1995; co-author: Estate Planning and the Close Corporation; editor-in-chief: Gastronome, bd. editors: The Tax Lawyer; contbr. articles to profl. jours.; numerous interviews in popular press and TV commentaries. Bd. dirs. exec. com. Citymeals on Wheels; pres. bd. dirs. Nat. Soc. to Prevent Blindness; sec.-treas., trustee A.D. Henderson Found., Del., trustee, Fla.; bd. dirs. Phoenix Theatre Inc., Inst. Aegean Prehistory, Found. Future of Man, Am. and Internat. Friends of Victoria and Albert Mus., London; conservator NY Pub. Libr.; trustee Found. for Renaissance of St. Petersburg (Russia), Malcolm Wiener Found.; pres. bd. dirs. Laurence Levine Charitable Fund., Inc.; vice chmn. NY Hist. Soc.; bd. dirs. Gov.'s Commn. on Scholastic Achievement; constl. advisor to Pres. George Bush; advisor to King Michael of Romania. Decorated Knight, Queen Elizabeth II; named Class Marshall, Yale; recipient Coat of Arms, Queen Elizabeth II, Order of Crown of Charlemagne, Order of Plantagenet, Order of Barons of Magna Charta, Order of Descendants Knights of the Garter, Thomas R. Moore Disting. Pub. Servant award, Nat. Soc. to Prevent Blindness; Scholar of House, Yale. Mem.: St. Andrews Soc., St. George Soc., Confrerie de la Chaine des Rotisseurs (nat. pres., dir., exec. com. world coun. Paris), Robert Burns Soc., Nat. Wine Coalition (bd. dirs.), Chevalier du Tastevin, The Pilgrims, Church Club, Univ. Club, Delta Sigma Rho. Republican. Episcopalian. Office: 590 Madison Ave Ste 2100 New York NY 10022 Office Phone: 212-333-8630.

MOORE, THOMAS SCOTT, lawyer; b. Portland, Oreg., Nov. 17, 1937; s. Harry Alburn and Geraldine Elizabeth (Scott) M.; m. Saundra L. Wagner, Sept. 7, 1957 (div. 1974); children: Cindy, Kristin, Thomas, Victoria, Wendy; m. Alice H. Zeisz, Nov. 5, 1976; 1 child, Alice G. BA, Willamette U., 1959, JD cum laude, 1962. Bar: Oreg. 1962, Wash. 2002. Pvt. practice, Portland, 1962—. Contbr. articles to law jours. Republican. Avocation: tennis. Office: Ste 230 5901 SW MacAdam Ave Portland OR 97239-3621

MOORE, THURSTON ROACH, lawyer; b. Memphis, Dec. 10, 1946; s. Richard Charlton Moore and Halcyon Hall (Roach) Lynn; m. Corell Luckhardt Halsey, Sept. 26, 1998. BA with distinction, U. Va., 1968, JD, 1974. Bar: Va. 1974. Rsch. analyst Scudder, Stevens & Clark, NYC, 1968—71; ptnr. Hunton & Williams LLP, Richmond, Va., 1974—91, mng. partner, 1991—2006, chmn., 2006—. Mem.: ABA (chmn. ptnrs. com. 1992—96, bus. law sect., fed. regulation security com., bus. law coun.), Richmond Bar Assn., Va. State Bar, Va. Bar Assn., Va. Commwealth U. Sch. Bus. Found. (trustee, bd. dirs.), Mary Morton Parsons Found. (trustee, bd. dir.), Nature Conservancy Va. (chmn., trustee, bd. dir.), Va. Mus. Fine Arts (trustee), Va. Found. Ind. Coll. (trustee, bd. dirs.), Met. Bus. Found. (pres. 1995—2001, dir.), Phi Beta Kappa. Office: Hunton & Williams Riverfront Plz E Tower 951 E Byrd St Richmond VA 23219-4074 Office Fax: 804-788-8218. Business E-Mail: tmoore@hunton.com.

MOORE, TIM, lawyer; b. Lafayette, La., Sept. 4, 1957; BS in geology, Stephen F. Austin State U., 1979; JD summa cum laude, U. Houston, 1990. Bar: Tex. 1990. Geologist Placid Oil Co., New Orleans, 1980—84, Jackson, Miss., 1980—84; regional geologist Gulf Coast Kaiser Energy Inc., New Orleans, 1984—87; assoc. Weil, Gotshal & Manges, Houston, 1990—94; gen. counsel - corp. TransTex. Gas Corp., 1994—2000; v.p., gen. counsel, sec. Plains Resources, 2000—01, Plains All Am. Pipeline, Houston, 2000—. Mem.: Am. Corp. Counsel Assn., State Bar Tex., Order of the Barons, Order of the Coif, Omicron Delta Kappa. Office: Plains All Am Pipeline 333 Clay St Ste 1600 PO Box 4648 Houston TX 77210-4648 *

MOORE, TIM J., lawyer; b. Wichita, Kans., June 1, 1964; s. Dennis F. and Mary Jane (O'Malley) M.; m. Kelly S. Belford, June 4, 1993; children: Henry, Charlotte. AB magna cum laude, Brown U., 1986; JD cum laude, Harvard U., 1989. Bar: Kans. 1989, US Dist. Ct. Kans. 1989, US Dist. Ct. (no. dist.) Tex. 1994, US Ct. Appeals (10th cir.) 1992, US Ct. Appeals (5th cir.) 1999. Ptnr. Morris, Laing, Evans, Brock & Kennedy, Chartered, Wichita, 1989—. Mem. bd. editors Wichita Barometer, 1989—; contbr. articles to profl. jours. Pres.& bd. dir. Wichita Pub. Libraries, v.p. Wichita Pub. Library Found., bd. dirs. Law and Pub. Policy Magnet Sch., Wichita, 1992-93; dist. rep. Boy Scouts Am., Wichita, 1993-95; state chair Nat. Alumni Schs. Program, Wichita, 1994—, mem. Kans. Library Trustee Assn., Brown Alumni Sch. Com., Kans., Boy Scouts of Am., Blackbear (advancement com.). Recipient Ratcliffe Hicks award Brown U, 1985, 86. Mem. Wichita Bar Assn. (bd. govs. 1998—, bd. of govs.), Wichita Young Lawyers Assn. (pres. 1992-93), ABA, Kans. Bar Assn., Am. Intellectual Property Law Assn., Kansas, Am. Trial Lawyers. Democrat. Roman Catholic. Sr. editor Harvard Jour. of Law and Pub. Policy. Office: Morris Laing Evans Brock & Kennedy Chartered Old Town 300 N Mead St Ste 200 Wichita KS 67202-2745 Office Phone: 316-262-2671. Office Fax: 316-262-6226.

MOORE, TIRIN, neuroscientist, educator; b. Oakland, Calif., June 12, 1969; s. Walter Peter Moore and Mary Lucille Salmon; m. Giovanna Ceserani, June 21, 2003; 1 child, Emilia T. PhD, Princeton U., NJ, 1995. Asst. prof. neurobiology Stanford U., Calif., 2003—. Recipient Nat. Rsch. Svc. award, NIH, 1999—2002, Early Career award, NSF, 2006—; scholar, Pew Charitable Trust, 2004—, McKnight Endowment Fund Neurosci., 2006—; NSF fellow, 1990—93, MIT fellow, 1995—99, Princeton U. fellow, 1999—2003, Alfred P. Sloan Found. fellow, 2004—06. Mem.: Soc. Neurosci. Achievements include research in neurophysiology of vision, movement and cognition. Avocations: travel, movies. Home Phone: 650-283-0188; Office Phone: 650-725-8712.

MOORE, VERNON JOHN, JR., pediatrician, consultant, lawyer; b. Chgo., Mar. 18, 1942; s. Vernon John Moore; m. Rutheva deVera Dizon, Feb. 27, 1979; children: Christopher, Joseph. BS, Loyola U., Chgo., 1964, JD, 1986; MD, U. Ill.-Chgo., 1968. Bar: Ill. 1986, U.S. Dist. Ct. (no. dist.) Ill. 1986. Intern St. Joseph Health Care Ctrs. and Hosp., Chgo., 1968-69, resident in pediat., 1971-74, chief resident, 1972-74, mem. med. staff, 1974-76, 78-86; pvt. practice Chgo., 1974-76, 97—; mem. med. staff Naval Hosp. Great Lakes, 1976-78; med. officer Chgo. Mil. Entrance Processing Sta., 1996—2002, Midwest Ctr. for Youth and Families, Kouts, Ind., 1997—2006; mem. med. staff Ill. Masonic Med. Ctr., Chgo., 1997—2005, Swedish Covenant Hosp., Chgo., 1998—2005, Luth. Gen. Hosp., Park Ridge, Ill., 1998—2005, Alexian Bros. Med. Ctr., Elk Grove Village, Ill., 2000—02. Asst. dir. pediat. edn. St. Joseph Health Care Ctrs. and Hosp., 1974—76, co-dir., 1978—86, acting chmn. dept. pediat., 1985—86; clin. assoc. prof. pediat. Loyola U., Maywood, Ill., 1981—87; med. cons. CNA Ins. Cos., Chgo., 1987—94; pediat. med. cons. Hartgrove Hosp., Chgo., 1996—2007, Alexian Bros. Behavioral Health Hosp., Hoffman Estates, Ill., 1999—2001. Part-time staff Senator Everett M. Dirksen, Chgo., 1961—64. With med. corps USNR, 1969—2002, ret. as capt. USNR, 2002. Mem.: U. Ill. Pres. Coun., Alumni Assn. Coll. Medicine U. Ill. (alumni councillor 1989—92), U. Ill. Alumni Assn. (bd. dirs. 1983—89). Republican. Roman Catholic. Home: 146 Park Ave River Forest IL 60305-2040

MOORE, VIRGINIA BRADLEY, librarian; b. Laurens, SC, May 13, 1932; d. Robert Otis Brown and Queen Esther (Smith) Bradley; m. David Lee Moore, Dec. 27, 1957 (div. 1973). BS, Winston-Salem State U., 1954; MLS, U. Md., 1970. Cert. in libr. sci. edn. Tchr. John R. Hawkins H.S., Warrenton, NC, 1954-55, Happy Plains H.S., Taylorsville, NC, 1955-58, Young and Carver elem. schs., Washington, 1958-65; libr. Davis and Minor elem. schs., Washington, 1965-72, Ballou Sr. H.S., Kramer Jr. H.S., Washington, 1972-75, 78-80, Anacostia Sr. H.S., Washington, 1975-77, 80-95; libr. I, adult svcs. Greenbelt (Md.) Br. Libr., 1997—. Dir. ch. libr. workshops Asbury United Meth. Ch., Washington, 1972—74, 1976; spkr., presenter Ch. and Synagogue Libr. Assn., 1975, 80, 83, spkr. spring workshop, 99, presenter, 2000; mem. serials com. Prince George's County Meml. Libr. Sys., 2000—05; chair-competency based curriculum D.C. pub. schs., 1978—93; chair local arrangements launching Nat. Sch. Libr. Media Month U.S. Capitol, 1985; mem. 1st libr. and info. sci. del. to People's Republic China, 1985; mem. faculty 1st established pub. svc. acad. in nation Anacostia Sr. H.S., 1990—95; coord. Nat. Libr. Week workshop Greenbelt Libr. Prince George's County Meml. Libr. Sys., 2002; presenter in field; host ch. chair spring workshops Ch. and Synagogue Libr. Coun., Nat. Capital Area, 2004. Author: (bibliography) The Negro in American History, 1619-1968, 1968; (with Helen E. Williams) Books By African-American Authors and Illustrators for Children and Young Adults, 1991; TV script for vacation reading program, 1971, sound/slide presentation D.C. Church Librs.' Bicentennial Celebration, 1976; video script and tchr.'s guide for Nat. Libr. Week Balloon Launch Day, 1983; bibliography Black Literature/Materials, 1987; contbr. articles to profl. jours. Co-chmn. nat. libr. involvement com. Martin Luther King, Jr. Fed. Holiday Commn., 1990—99, chmn., 1996—99; trustee LeRoy C. Merritt Humanitarian Fund, 2002—06; libr. Mt. Carmel Bapt. Ch., Washington, 1984, chair ch. libr. com., 2000—05, ad hoc com. for churchwide programs, 2001—05, libr. Sunday Sch. Mother's Day coord., 1990—94, jr. ch. pianist, 1994—97, Sunday Sch. adult dept. pianist, 1984—, co-chmn. African-Am. History Mo. commn., 1996—2005, chmn. publicity com., 1996—99, com. renovation of Rev. Arthur H. Pace Libr. Multipurpose Rm., vice-chair publicity liaison com., 1999—2005, soprano sanctuary choir, 1995—, soprano soloist women's day and tribute commemoration, 1998, music com., 1998—2005; chmn. social responsibilities roundtable Martin Luther King Jr. holiday task force Am. Libr. Assn., 1999—; rec. sec. Washington Pan-Hellenic Coun., 1975. Named outstanding educator, Mt. Carmel Bapt. Ch., 1984; recipient Outstanding Congl. Libr., Ch. and Synagogue Libr. Assn., 2001, certs. of award, D.C. Pub. Libr., 1980, D.C. Pub. Schs., 1983; fellow Grad. fellow, U. Md., 1969; scholar NDEA scholar, Central State Coll., Edmond, Okla., 1969, U. Ky., 1969, Ball State U., 1969. Mem. ALA (councilor-at-large 1983-91, 96—, com. on coms. 2005, Freedom to Read Honor Roll, 1999), LWV (sec. Prince George's County, Md. 1997-99, v.p. 1999-2000, pres. 2000-05, mem. lobby corps. 2004-, nominations chair Nat. Capital area 2005—2006), AARP, Internat. Assn. Sch. Librs., NEA (life), Am. Assn. Sch. Librs. (coms. 1973-83, 1987—), D.C. Assn. Sch. Librs. (pres. 1971-73, citation 1973, newsletter editor 1971-75, 83), Intellectual Freedom Com. (chmn. 1983-99), Freedom to Read Found., Soc. Sch. Librs. Internat. (charter), Intellectual Freedom Roundtable (bd. dirs. exec. com. 1989-91), D.C. Libr. Assn., Md. Libr. Assn., Md. Ednl. Media Orgn., Internat. Platform Assn., S.E. Neighbors Club, Am. First Day Cover Soc., Nat. Coun. Negro Women, Zeta Phi Beta (v.p. chpt. 1972-74), Delta Kappa Gamma (v.p. Alpha chpt. 1990-92, pres. 1992-95, Nu State D.C. membership chmn. 1991-92, 2002-, rec. sec. 1994-95, v.p. 1995-97, liaison U.S. Forum 1995-97, 99—, spkr., state pres. 1997-99, steering com. spkr. Soc. Internat. Legis. seminar 1998, D.C. state del. Nat. Legis. Seminar 2006). Democrat. Achievements include being First Lady Laura Bush's guest at White House to launch Nat. Libr. Week, 2003. Home: 2100 Brooks Dr Apt 721 Forestville MD 20747-1016 Office: Prince Georges County Meml Libr Sys Greenbelt Br Libr 11 Crescent Rd Greenbelt MD 20770-1891 E-mail: vbmoore_99@yahoo.com.

MOORE, VIRGINIA LEE SMITH, elementary school educator; b. Middletown, NY, May 13, 1943; d. James William and Anna Van Alst (Suydam) Smith; m. Thomas J. Moore, Oct. 16, 1965 (div. Apr. 1980); 1 child, Christian Thomas. AA in Liberal Arts, Orange County C.C., 1963; BA in Sociology magna cum laude, SUNY, Buffalo, 1965; MS in Edn., SUNY, New Paltz, 1980; MS in Edn. of Gifted, Coll. New Rochelle, 1990, cert. elem. edn., staff devel., 1994; cert. sch. adminstrn., 1994. Cert. elem. tchr., N.Y. Spl. edn. tchr. The Devereux Found., Glen Loch, Pa., 1965-66; elem. tchr. Harris Sch., Coatesville, Pa., 1967, Pine Bush (N.Y.) Cen. Schs., 1967-70, 78-00, substitute tchr., 1970-71; nursery sch. tchr. Olivet Meth. Nursery Sch., Coatesville, Pa., 1976-78; profl. devel. coord. Pine Bush Sch. Dist., 1998. Participant math., sci. and tech. on elem. level program NSF, 1997—2000; presenter ednl. workshops in various sch. dists. and for orgns. and instns. Contbr. articles to profl. jours. Pres. Redtown Residents' Assn., Middletown, 1988—. Recipient Dean's Acad. Excellence award Coll. of New Rochelle, 1991, Orange County Conservation Tchr. of Yr., 1993, NY State Conservation Tchr. of Yr., 1993, Presdl. award for excellence in math. and sci. tchg. NY State, 1997; Partnership in Edn. grantee Area Fund Orange County, NY, 1991, Energy grantee Orange and Rockland Utilities, 1995, Tech. grantee Mid-Hudson Tchr. Ctr., 1997-98, Energy grantee NY State Electric and Gas, 1998. Mem. NSTA, DAR, Internat. Tech. Edn. Assn. (N.Y. State Elem. Sch. Tchr. Excellence award 1998-99), N.Y. State United Tchrs., Sci. Tchrs. Assn. N.Y. State (Outstanding Sci. Tchr. award 1992, Excellence in Sci. Tchg. award 1995), N.Y. State Tech. Edn. Assn. (Tech. grantee 1999), Orange County Geneal. Soc., Phi Beta Kappa. Bapt. Achievements include development of interactive science museum exhibits and historical preservation. Avocations: piano, reading, genealogy, history. Home: 177 Benedict Rd Montgomery NY 12549

MOORE, WARD WILFRED, medical educator; b. Cowden, Ill., Feb. 12, 1924; s. Cecil Leverett and Velma Leona (Frye) M.; m. Frances Laura Campbell, Jan. 29, 1949; children— Scott Thomas, Ann Gail, Brian Dean, Kevin Lee. AB, U. Ill., 1948, MS, 1951, PhD, 1952; DSc (hon.), Mahidol U., Bangkok, 2001. Instr., rsch. assoc. U. Ill., 1952-54; asst. prof. Okla. State U., Stillwater, 1954-55, Ind. U., Bloomington, 1955-59, assoc. prof., 1959-66, prof. physiology, 1966-89, prof. physiology and biophysics emeritus, 1989—, acting chmn. dept. anatomy, 1971-73, assoc. dean basic med. scis., 1971-89, assoc. dean, dir. med. scis. program, 1976-89. Vis. prof. Postgrad. Med. Center, Karachi, Pakistan, 1963-64; staff mem. Rockefeller Found., 1968-71; vis. prof., chmn. dept. physiology, faculty sci. Mahidol U., Bangkok, Thailand, 1968-71 Served with U.S. Army, 1943-46. Mem. Am. Physiol. Soc., Endocrine Soc., Am. Soc. Nephrology, Soc. Study Reproduction, Am. Assn. Anatomists, Soc. Exptl. Biology and Medicine, Am. Assn. Med. Colls., AAAS, Am. Inst. Biol. Scis., AAUP, Ind. Acad. Sci., Ind. Hist. Soc., Shelby County (Ill.) Hist. Soc., Monroe County (Ind.) Hist. Soc., Soc. Sons of Am. Revolution, Sigma Xi, Phi Sigma. Home: 3500 E Bradley St Bloomington IN 47401-4201 Office: Indiana U Jordan Hall # 105 Bloomington IN 47405 Business E-Mail: moorew@indiana.edu.

MOORE, WAYLAND D., artist; b. Belton, SC, Sept. 8, 1935; s. James H. and Sara E. Moore; m. Debeased Moore; children: Wayland, Frankie, Patsy, Herbert, Cyndi. Cert., Ringling Sch. Art. and Design, Sarasota, Fla., 1957. Art dir. Sta. WIS-TV, Columbia, SC, 1958—61; illustrator Greenville, SC, 1961—62, Atlanta, 1969—70; editl. cartoonist Sarasota Herald Tribune, 1962—68; graphics dir. Atlanta Braves, 1970—74; sports artist Felicie Edits., NYC, Paris, 1974—80; worldwide landscape painter Versatility, Inc., Atlanta, 1980—. Instr. Emory U., 1970—2007; trustee Ringling Coll. Art and Design. Author: (poetry) Brush Strokes of Poetry, 2006. With USAF, 1960—64. Nominee Pulitzer Prize for Editl. Cartooning, 1965; named Artist of the Yr., Nat. League Pen Women, 1985; recipient commendation, White Ho. Home and Studio: 2124 Azalea Cir Decatur GA 30033

MOORE, WILLIAM B., energy executive; m. Shelly Moore; 2 children. BBA, Wichita State U., 1974. Fin. asst. Westar Energy, Inc., Topeka, 1978, v.p. fin., 1985, exec. v.p., CFO, treas, 1998—2000, exec. v.p., COO, 2002—06, pres., COO, 2006—07, pres., CEO, 2007—; sr. mng. dir., sr. adv. Saber Ptnrs., LLC, 2000—02. Chmn. bd., v.p. electric divsn. KGE. Mem. exec. bd. Wichita Area C. of C.; chair Goodwill Industries, Easter Seals Kans., United Way Plains, 2004; mem. exec. com. of bd. dirs. Wichita State U. Found.; bd. dirs. Kans. Sports Hall of Fame, Intrust Fin. Corp., Shocker Athletic Scholarship Orgn., Wichita Insight. Office: Westar Energy Inc 818 S Kansas Ave Topeka KS 66612 Office Phone: 785-575-6300. *

MOORE, WILLIAM GROVER, JR., management consultant, retired military officer; b. Waco, Tex., s. William Grover and Annie Elizabeth (Pickens) Moore; m. Marjorie Y. Gardella, Jan. 18, 1943; 1 child, Allyson. Student, Kilgore Coll., Tex., 1937—39, Sacramento State Coll., 1951, George Washington U., 1962; grad., Air War Coll., Air U., 1957, Nat. War Coll., 1962. Enlisted U.S. Army Air Force, 1940, commd. 2d lt., 1941, advanced through grades to gen., 1977; comdr. 777th Squadron, 15th AF, Italy, 1944—45, 3535th Maintenance and Supply Group, Mather AFB, Calif., 3d Bomb Group, Korea, 1952; chief bases and units divsn. Hdqrs. USAF, 1952—56; asst. dep. chief of staff ops. Hdqrs. USAF Europe, 1957—61; comdr. 314th Troop Carrier Wing, Stewart AFB, Tenn., 1962—63, 839th Air Divsn., 1963—65; asst. J3 U.S. Strike Command, 1965—66; comdr. 834th Air Divsn., Vietnam, 1966—67; dir. operational requirements Hdqrs. USAF, 1967—70; comdr. 22d AF, 1970—73, 13th AF, 1973; chief of staff Pacific Command, 1973—76; asst. vice chief of staff Hdqrs. USAF, 1976—77; comdr. in chief Mil. Air Lift Command, 1977—79; ret., 1979; pres., COO Emery Air Freight Corp., Wilton, Conn., 1981—83; bus. cons., 1983—. Pres. Met. Nashville Airport Authority, 1984—. Decorated Def. D.S.M. with 2 oak leaf clusters, D.S.M. with 2 oak leaf clusters, Legion of Merit with 4 oak leaf clusters, Silver Star, D.F.C. with oak leaf cluster, Air Medal with 9 oak leaf clusters, Air Force Commendation medal with 10 oak leaf clusters (U.S.), Croix de Guerre with palm France, Armed Forces Honor medal 1st class Vietnam, Republic of China Cloud and Banner, Legion of Honor Republic of the Philippines; named to Minuteman Hall of Fame, 1979; recipient L. Mendel Rivers award of excellence; fellow Jimmy Doolittle fellow in aerospace edn., 1978. Mem.: Am. Ordnance Assn., Nat. Def. Transp. Assn., Air Force Assn. Home: 932 W Main St Franklin TN 37064-2730 Office: Nashville Internat Airport 1 Terminal Dr Ste 501 Nashville TN 37214-4110

MOORE, WILLIAM HENRY, radiologist; b. Pompton, NJ, Dec. 6, 1973; m. Rebecca Anne Case, May 30, 1999; 1 child, Charlotte Catherine. MD, Albany Med. Coll., NY, 1999. Diplomate Am. Bd. Radiology. Intern Albany Med. Ctr., 1999—2000; resident in radiology U. Hosp., Stony Brook, NY, 2000—04, chief thoracic imaging, 2004—; vis. fellow thoracic imaging NYU, NYC, 2003—04. Contbr. articles to profl. jours. Named Tchr. of Yr., 2005, Outstanding Tchr., Stony Brook Med. Sch., 2006; recipient Roentgen Rsch. award, 2003. Mem.: Soc. Thoracic Radiologist (sr.), Alpha Omega Alpha, A3CR2 (assoc.; vice chair problem solving 2002—03). Home Phone: 631-751-3566; Office Phone: 631-444-7955. Office Fax: 631-444-7538. Business E-Mail: william.moore@stonybrook.edu.

MOORE, WILLIAM LEROY, JR., career officer, internist; b. Savannah, Ga., June 1, 1934; s. William Leroy Sr. and Helen Louise (Robbins) M.; m. Anna Elizabeth Ballard, Mar. 15, 1958; children: William L., Christopher A., Mary Beth. Student, Ga. Inst. Tech., 1951-52; AB, Emory U., 1955; MD, Med. Coll. Ga., 1959; postgrad. mil. tng. courses, 1962-94. Diplomate Am. Bd. Internal Medicine, Am. Bd. Infectious Diseases. Commd. capt. U.S. Army, 1962, advanced through grades to maj. gen., 1991; intern Floyd Hosp., Rome, Ga., 1959-60; pvt. practice Rome, 1960-61; resident in internal medicine Brooke Gen. Hosp., Ft. Sam Houston, Tex., 1965-68; rsch. fellow in infectious diseases U. Tex. Southwestern Med. Sch., Dallas, 1968-70; resident in internal medicine Parkland Meml. Hosp., Dallas, 1968-70; gen. med. officer Martin Army Hosp., Ft. Benning, Ga., 1962, 5th Spl. Forces Group, Spl. Warfare Ctr., Ft. Bragg, N.C., 1962-63; gen. internist, group surgeon, commdg. officer 1st Spl. Forces Group, Spl. Action Force, Okinawa, Japan, 1963-65; asst. chief to chief infectious disease svc. Brooke Gen. Hosp., Ft. Sam Houston, Tex., 1970-74; chief internal medicine svc., chief dept. medicine, chief profl. svcs. Eisenhower Army Med. Ctr., Ft. Gordon, Ga., 1978-83; comdr. Frankfurt (Germany) Army Regional Med. Ct., 97th Gen. Hosp., 1983-86; project mgr. Office of Surgeon Gen., Washington, 1986-88; adj. faculty Nat. Def. U., Ft. Lesley J. McNair, Washington, 1986-88; vice comdr. Joint Mil. Med. Command, Randolph AFB, Tex., 1988-91; comdr. Brooke Army Med. Ctr., Ft. Sam Houston, Tex., 1988-91, U.S. Army Med. Dept. Ctr. & Sch., Ft. Sam Houston, Tex., 1991-94; state epidemiologist, dir. communicable & environ. disease Tenn. Dept. Health, 1995-2001; prof. medicine divsn. infectious diseases Vanderbilt U. Sch. Medicine, Nashville, 1994—; chief of staff VA Med. Ctr., Nashville, 2001—02; dir. bur. epidemiology Nashville Davidson Met. Health Dept., 2002—. Clin. assoc. in medicine U. Tex. Southwestern Med. Sch., 1969-70; clin. assoc. prof. medicine U. Tex. Med. Sch., 1970-74; chief. sect. of infectious diseases Med. Coll. Ga., 1974-75, assoc. prof., 1974-78, clin. prof., 1978-83; prin. investigator infectious disease rsch. VA Hosp., Augusta, Ga., 1974-78, asst. chief med. svc., 1974-75, dir. clin. microbiology lab., 1974-78, epidemiologist, 1974-78; head intenal medicine infectious disease 97th gen. Hosp., Frankfurt, 1983-86, Walter Reed Army Med. Ctr., 1986-88; clin. prof. medicine U. Tex. Health Sci. Ctr., San Antonio, 1989-94; mem. ref. panel on Am. Hosp. Formulary Svc. of Am. Soc. Hosp. Pharmacists, 1974-78; faculty Advisor Lane-Walker AMSA Free Clinic, Augusta, 1975-78; mem. various coms. and bds., VA Hosp., Augusta, 1974-78. Contbr. articles to profl. jours. Mem. Army Comty. Coun. San Antonio, 1988-94; dir., bd. dirs. Army Med. Dept. Mus. Found. Inc., 1989-94; bd. dirs. San Antonio Area chpt. ARC, 1989. Decorated Army Commendation medal, Meritorious Svc. medal (3), Legion of Merit with three oak leaf clusters, Disting. Svc. medal Army Med. Dept. Regiment, 1994, Order of Mil. Med. Merit; recipient Scholastic Excellence award C.V. Mosby Co., 1959, Laureate award, Am. Coll. Physician, 1996, Dirs. Commendation VA Hosp., Augusta, 1978, Surgeon Gen.'s A Profl. Designer for Internal Med., 1982. Fellow ACP, Infectious Diseases Soc. Am.; mem. NAS (nat. rsch. coun. 1995-96), Assn. Mil. Surgeons U.S. (mem.-at-large exec. coun. Alamo chpt. 1989), Soc. Med. Cons. to Armed Forces (chmn. com. on cons. activities 1977-79), Am. Heart Assn. (bd. dirs. San Antonio divsn. 1988-89), San Antonio Rsch. Club (sec., pres. 1970-74), Tenn. Med. Assn., Nashville Acad. Medicine, Tenn. Pub. Health Assn., Coun.State and Territorial Epidemiologists. *Strict adherence to moral and ethical principles, willingness to work hard, use all of one's talents to benefit others and take advantage of all of the opportunities one finds to improve one's self while serving others are the elements of success in this life.*

MOORE, WILLIAM THEODORE, JR., federal judge; b. Bainbridge, Ga., May 7, 1940; s. William T. and Mary (Talbert) M.; m. Jane Hodges, July 18, 1964; children: Sarah S., Mary T. William T III. AA, Ga. Mil. Coll., 1960, Law (hon.), 1978; JD, U. Ga., Athens, 1964; LLM, U. Va., Charlottesville, 2001. Bar: Ga. 1964, US Dist. Ct. (so. dist.) Ga. 1964, US Ct. Appeals (5th and 11th cirs.) 1979, US Supreme Ct. 1980. US atty. US Dist. Ct. (So. Dist.) Ga., Savannah, 1977-81; ptnr. Corish, Smith, Remler & Moore, Savannah, 1967-77, Sparkman, Harris & Moore, Savannah, 1981-87, Oliver Maner & Gray, Savannah, 1988-94; judge US Dist. Ct. (So. Dist.) Ga., Savannah, 1994—2004, chief judge, 2004—. Atty. Savannah-Chatham County Bd. Pub. Edn., 1975-77, mem. U.S. Atty. Gen's. Adv. com. D.C. 1978-81. Recipient Spl. Appreciation award Ga. Bur. of Investigation, 1980, US Dept. Treasury Bur. of Alcohol, Tobacco & Firearms, D.C., 1980; Extraordinary Svc. award Savannah Chapt. Fed. Bar Assn., 1980. Fellow Am. Bd. Criminal Lawyers (pres. 1993); mem. NACDL, Nat. Assn. Former US Attys. (bd. dirs. 1984—), Jud. Conf. US (com. on criminal law, sentencing subcomittee, 11th cir. jud. coun.), Ga. Assn. Criminal Def. Lawyers (v.p. 1986—), Ga. Bar Assn. Democrat. Episcopalian. Avocations: jogging, weight training, golf, reading. Office: US Dist Courthouse 125 Bull St PO Box 10245 Savannah GA 31412-0445 Office Phone: 912-650-4173.

MOORE, WISTAR, cardiovascular surgeon; b. Feb. 16, 1959; BA, U. N.C., 1981, MD, 1985. Bd. cert. gen. surgery, thoracic surgery. Gen. surgery resident Mass. Gen. Hosp., 1985-90; cardiothoracic resident The Emory Clinic, 1990-93; cardiovasc. surgeon Watson Clinic, Lakeland, Fla., 1993-2000; chief divsn. cardiovasc. thoracic surgery Lakeland Regional Med. Ctr., 1996-2000; cardiovasc. surgeon Cardiovasc. Surgeons, Orlando, Fla., 2000—04, Leesburg-Ocala Heart Inst., 2004—. Fellow ACS, Am. Coll. Chest Physicians; mem. Fla. Soc. Thoracic and Cardiovasc. Surgeons, So. Thoracic Surg. Assn., Soc. Thoracic Surgeons. Office: 700 Doctors Ct Leesburg FL 34748 Office Phone: 352-787-9830.

MOORE-BECKHAM, ROSALIND ELIZABETH, retired social worker; d. Claude R. Hardrick and Marion Lucretia Whaley-Hardrick; m. George W. Moore (dec.); 1 child, Markus Moore; m. William Henry Beckham, Sept. 29, 1984. BS in Edn., U. Hartford, West Hartford, Conn., 1975; MSW, U. Conn., West Hartford, 1981. Sales clk. G. Fox & Co., Hartford, 1949—60; headstart tchrs. aide Bd. Edn., Hartford, 1965—72; outreach coord. Inst. of Living, Hartford, 1972—78; social worker Cath. Family Svcs., Hartford, 1980—93; program dir. My Sisters' Place, Inc., Hartford, 1993—99; social worker, tutor Asian Family Svcs., Hartford, 2001—05; ret. Author: With A Psalm in My Heart, 2001. Deacon Union Bapt. Ch., Hartford. Avocations: walking, aerobics, bicycling, quilting. Home: PO Box 400156 Hartford CT 06140-0156

MOOREHEAD, DONALD V., lawyer; b. Balt., Apr. 10, 1943; BA, Univ. Va., 1965; JD with honors, George Washington Univ., 1968. Bar: DC 1968, Calif. 1982, U.S. Ct. Appeals, DC cir. 1969, U.S. Tax Ct. 1971. Chief Rep. counsel U.S. Senate Fin. Com., 1975—76; v.p. & gen. counsel Kaiser Aluminum & Chem. Corp., 1981—84; ptnr., Public Policy, Tax Law, Bus. Tranactions practices, mem. exec. com. Patton Boggs LLP, Washington. Adj. prof. Georgetown Univ. Law Sch., 1974—80. Mem.: ABA. Office: Patton Boggs LLP 2550 M St NW Washington DC 20037-1350 Office Phone: 202-457-5212. Office Fax: 202-457-6315. Business E-Mail: dmoorehead@pattonboggs.com.

MOORE-VICULIN, CHARLOTTE ANNE, artist, musician; d. Harry and Virginia Longworth (Dyer) Moore; m. Richard Jerry Viculin, Oct. 15, 1977. Grad., Detroit Conservatory of Music; BFA, postgrad., Wayne State U. Self-employed portrait artist, mural painter; tchr., performer piano, vocalist Detroit, Livonia and Plymouth, Mich.; music arranger, profl. music judge. Fundraiser Plymouth Symphony League, 1980—95; bd. dirs., former sec. Plymouth Symphony, 1991—96. Named Nat. Career Woman of Yr., Nat. Assn. Career Women, 1991. Mem. Am. Soc. Portrait Artists, Portrait Soc. Am., Nat. Guild Piano Tchrs., Nat. Music Tchrs. Assn., Mich. Music Tchrs. Assn., Nat. Fedn. Music Clubs, Mich. Fedn. Music Clubs (officer), Ann Arbor Area Piano Tchrs. Guild (officer), Livonia Area Piano Tchrs. Forum (officer) Home: 27265 Canfield Dr W Dearborn Heights MI 48127-1044 Office: Charlotte Moore-Viculin Studios of Music and Art 352 N Main St Ste 4 Plymouth MI 48170-1270 Office Phone: 734-459-1112.

MOORE-WLEKLINSKI, PATRICIA MARIE, secondary school educator; b. Syracuse, NY, Oct. 10, 1956; d. John William and Mary Jane Moore; m. John Joseph Wleklinski, Aug. 18, 1984; 1 child, Alyssa Jane Wleklinski. BS in Elem. Edn., SUNY, Cortland, 1978, MEd, 1990. Cert. elem. tchr. NY. Elem. tchr. St. Ann's Sch., Syracuse, 1982—85; English tchr. Christian Bros. Acad., Syracuse, 1985—2005. Varsity cheerleading coach West Genesee Sr. HS, Camillus, NY, 1978—85; majorette instr. Liverpool HS, NY, 1975—78, Cicero-North Syracuse HS, Cicero, NY, 1978—81, Syracuse U., 1981—83, Genesee Alumni Bd., 2001, 06. Basketball support chmn. Empire State Games, Syracuse, 1982—2006; religious edn. tchr. St. Joseph's Ch., Camillus, 2001—06, eucharistic min. and lector, 2001—04. Recipient Outstanding Educator for a Merrill Presdl. scholar, Cornell U., 2005, Coach's Achievement award, Onondaga HS League, 1994. Mem.: Nat. Cath. Educators Assn., NY State English Coun., Nat. Coun. Tchrs. English. Roman Catholic. Avocations: reading, music, puzzles, twirling. Home Phone: 315-488-2526. Personal E-mail: pmmw10@twncy.rr.com.

MOORHEAD, GERALD LEE, architect; b. Davenport, Iowa, Feb. 18, 1947; s. Wayne Lee and Marilou (George) M. BA, Rice U., 1969, BArch, 1971. Arch. Middleton & Statton, El Paso, Tex., 1967, MA Floyd Assocs., Houston, 1968, CRS Design Inc., Houston, 1969-70, Phillips & Peterson AIA, Houston, 1969-73; arch., v.p. Charles Tapley Assocs., Houston, 1973-83; propr. Lloyd Jones Fillpot Assocs., 1986-87, Gerald Moorhead, Arch., 1983-98; sr. assoc. Bailey Archs., 1998—. Photography exhibited in group shows at Galveston Arts Coun., Tex., 1976, Jewish Cmty. Ctr., Houston, 1977, Cronin Gallery, Houston, 1977; one-man photog. exhbns. include Autry Ho. Gallery, Houston, 1979; editor, photographer: Houston Architectural Guide, 1999, Buildings of Texas; editor: Houston Architectural Ballade, 2000; contbg. editor Tex. Arch., Arthtl. Record; contbr. articles on architecture to profl. publs.; exhbn. curator Houston Mus. Natural Sci., 1990, Mus. Fine Arts, Houston, 1991, FotoFest, Houston, 1996. Treas. Houston Ctr. for Photography, 1985-87. Recipient Spl. award Houston AIA/Houston Home & Garden, 1979, Internat. prize Union Archs. Kazakstan, 1991; named Arch. Laureate of Kazakstan, 1992. Fellow AIA (Honor award Houston chpt. 1979, Young Arch. award Houston chpt. 1985); mem. Soc. Archtl. Historians, Nat. Trust for Hist. Preservation, Tex. Soc. Archs. (1st Honor award 1976, Interiors award 1986, Flowers Journalism award 1995), Rice Design Alliance. Home: 1755 W Main Ave Houston TX 77098-3607

MOORHEAD, LUCY GALPIN, writer; b. NYC, Jan. 24, 1926; d. Perrin Comstock and Stephanie (English) Galpin; children: William S., Lucy Perrin M. Grayson, Stephen G., James B. BA, Vassar Coll., Poughkeepsie, NY, 1946. Author: Entertaining in Washington, 1978, Dolly Appleton, (a novel) In the Town and In the Country (a memoir), 2004. Mem. Chevy Chase Club, Cosmopolitan Club. Episcopalian. Avocations: fox-hunting, painting.

MOORHEAD, ROLANDE ANNETTE REVERDY, artist, educator; b. Périgueux, France; d. RémyJean and Andrée Marcelle (Lavollée) Reverdy; m. Elliott Swift Moorhead, III, Sept. 30, 1960; children: Edward Marc, Roland Elliott, Rémy Bruce. Degree in liberal arts, Coll. Technique, Nice, France, 1954. Bi-lingual sec., France, 1957-58, French Embassy, Washington, 1959-60, 68-70; chmn. exhibit com. Lauderdale-By-The-Sea Art Guild, Ft. Lauderdale, Fla., 1972-75, v.p., 1972-74, founder group 5 Women Artists; exhibit com. Broward Art Guild, Ft. Lauderdale, Fla., 1976; treas., dir. Alliance Francaise, Miami, Fla., 1973-75. Juror, lectr. in field; invited guest artist Franco-Am. Art Show, Curemonte, France, 1996-97. One-woman shows include Ocean Club Art Gallery, Ft. Lauderdale, 1971-74, Pier 66 Gallery, Ft. Lauderdale, 1973, 75, 76, Ft. Lauderdale City Hall, 1974, 77-78, 81-88, 91-2000, St. Basil Orthodox Ch., North Miami Beach, 1977, Galerie Vallombreuse, Biarritz, France, 1977, Gallerie Mouffe, Paris, 1978, Gallerie du Palais des Fêtes, Périgueux, 1978, 88, Le Club Internat., Ft. Lauderdale, 1979, Leonard Gallery, Ft. Lauderdale, 1990-92, Tallahassee Capitol Bldg., 1990, Lighthouse Pt. Gallery, Fla., 1990, Hollywood Art and Cultural Ctr., Fla., 1987, 89-91, 93, 95, Ft. Lauderdale Arts Inst., 1991, 93-95, Dover Gallery, Boca Raton, Fla., 1992; Galerie Mouffe, Paris, 1978, Glass Gallery, Pembroke Pines, Fla., 2001; exhibited in group shows at Broward Art Guild, 1971, 73-74, Point of Am. Gallery, Ft. Lauderdale, 1971, 73, Internat. Festival, Miami, 1976, Internat. Salon, Biarritz, 1977, Internat. Summer Salon, Paris, 1977, Fine Art Gallery Show and Competition, Long Galleries, Ft. Lauderdale, 1979, Pembroke Pines City Hall, Fla., 1982, Hollywood City Libr., 1982, Bailey Hall Art Gallery BCC Campus, Davie, Fla., 1990-92, Coral Ridge Presbyn. Ch., Ft. Lauderdale, 1998, Schacknow Mus. Plantation, Fla., 1998, 2000, Art Serve Gallery Ft. Lauderdale, 1998-2001, 06-07, BonnettHouse Gallery, Ft. Lauderdale, 1999, 2001-02, Tamarac City Hall Gallery, Fla., Ft. Lauderdale Mus. Art, 2000, Gallery YES, Wilton Manors, Fla., 2001, Webber Art Ctr., Ocala, Fla., 2003, Artists Haven Fine Art Gallery, Ft. Lauderdale, 2003, Sunrise Civic Ctr. Gallery, Fla., 2006; represented in permanent collections Ft. Lauderdale City Hall, DAV Hdqrs., Washington, Associated Aircraft Co., Ft. Lauderdale, March of Dimes Bldg., Ft. Lauderdale, Oakland Pk. City Libr., Fla., St. Josephs Convent, St. Augustine, Fla., US Air Force Mus., Ohio, Main Line Fleets, Inc., Palm Beach, Fla., Creditreform, Dusseldorf, Germany, St. Front Cathedral, Périgueux, St. Sacerdoce Cathedral, Sarlat, France, Club Med, Fla. and Caribbean, also numerous pvt. collections US and Europe; author art manual for Broward Arts Coun., Fla., 1986 Recipient Best in Show award Internat. Salon, Biarritz, 1977; named artist in residence Broward County Sch., 1985. Mem. Am. Soc. Portrait Artists, Nat. Assn. Women Artists, Fla. Watercolor Soc., Palm Beach Watercolor Soc., Nat. League Am. Penwomen (pres. chpt. 1994-96), Art 24, Périgueux, Internat. Soc. Marine Painters, Am. Watercolor Soc., Nat. Mus. Women in Arts, Nat. Mus. Am. Indian, Gold Coast Water Color Soc. (pres. 1984-87), 2+3 The Artist Orgn., Union des Francais de l'Etranger. Home: PO Box 8692 Fort Lauderdale FL 33310-8692

MOORHEAD, SYLVESTER ANDREW, retired education educator; b. Denver, Feb. 23, 1920; s. Ray Rodney and Cora Margaret (Payne) M.; m. Katherine May Schlessman, July 21, 1945; children: Rodney A., Sylvia Kay, Kent A., Pamela Ann. BA, U. No. Colo., 1942; PhD, Stanford U., 1950. Tchr. secondary sch., Redwood City, Calif., 1947-48, Sunnyvale, Calif., 1948-49; mem. faculty U. Miss., 1949—, prof. edn., 1955—, dean U. Sch. Edn., 1961-85, dean emeritus, 1985—. Contbr. articles profl. jours. Served with USAAF, 1942-45. Mem. NEA (life), Kappa Delta Pi, Phi Delta Kappa. Lodges: Rotary. Baptist. Home: 211 Vivian St Oxford MS 38655-2719

MOORING, F. PAUL, physics editor; b. Pitt County, NC, Feb. 6, 1921; s. Benjamin Arthur and Amanda Elizabeth (Congleton) M.; m. Jean Louise Carpenter, Aug. 28, 1948; children: Cecily Hamm, Carol Larson, Margaret Calderon. BA, Duke U., 1944; PhD, U. Wis., 1951. Instr. Duke U., Durham, NC, 1943-46; teaching asst. U. Wis., Madison, 1946-50, rsch. asst., 1950-51; physicist Argonne (Ill.) Nat. Lab., 1951-83; editor, cons. Am. Inst. Physics, Argonne, 1983—. Adj. prof. St. Louis U., 1966-83. Contbr. articles to profl. jours. Pres. The Ill. Prairie Path, Wheaton, Ill., 1971-93, Ill. Audubon Soc., Wayne, Ill., 1978-81. Fulbright Rsch. fellow U. Helsinki, 1962-63. Mem. AAAS, Am. Phys. Soc, DuPage County Environ. Commn. Democrat. Home: 295 Abbotsford Ct Glen Ellyn IL 60137-4803 E-mail: fmooring@aol.com.

MOORMAN, CHARLES W., transportation executive; b. Hattiesburg, Miss. Grad., Ga. Tech. Univ., Harvard Bus. Sch. With Norfolk Southern Corp., 1970—, v.p. employee rels., 1992—93, v.p. info. tech., 1993—99; pres. Thoroughbred Tech. & Telecommunications, 1999—2003; sr. v.p. corp. planning & svc. Norfolk Southern Corp., 2003—04, pres., 2005—, CEO, 2005—, chmn., 2006—. Office: Norfolk Southern Corp 3 Commercial Pl Norfolk VA 23510-2191 *

MOORMAN, DONALD WAYNE, surgeon, healthcare administrator; b. Leon, Iowa, Aug. 16, 1951; s. Virgil Glen and Dorothy Ann (Coon) Moorman. BS, Iowa State U., Ames, 1973; MD, U. Iowa, Iowa City, 1976. Diplomate Am. Bd. Surgery, cert. investigator Nat. Cancer Inst. Intern in surgery Akron Gen. Med. Ctr., Ohio, 1976—77, resident in surgery, 1976—81; ICU rotation Jackson Meml. Hosp., Miami, Fla., 1979; patient safety leadership fellow Health Forum, 2003—04; clin. instr. surgery Northeastern Ohio U. Coll. Medicine, Rootstown, 1980—83, assoc. prof., 1986—91, prof., 1991—93; sr. staff dept. surgery Akron Gen. Med. Ctr., 1981—92, surgery clerkship dir., 1981—89, program dir. gen. surgery residency program, 1987—92, dir. nutritional support team, 1982—92; dir. clin. divsn., sr. staff scientist, chmn. Human Gene Therapy Rsch. Inst., 1993—2000; sect. chief dept. surgery Iowa Meth. Med. Ctr., Des Moines, 1998—2000; vice chair edn., assoc. surgeon in chief Beth Israel Deaconess Med. Ctr., Boston, 2000—, program dir. residency in gen. surgery, 2000—01, acting chief surgery, 2001, attending trauma surgery, dir. Trauma Ctr., 2003—04, faculty dir. Clin. adv. bd. Critical Care Am., 1983—88; clin. assoc. prof. U. Iowa, Iowa City, 1993—2000, mem. adv. com., 1996—2000; collaborating prof. zoology and genetics Iowa State U., Ames, 1993—; lectr. surgery Harvard Med. Sch., 2000—01, assoc. prof., 2000—; gen. surgery cons. VA Med. Ctr., Des Moines, mem. dean's com.; mem. courtesy gen. surgery staff Iowa Luth. Hosp., Des Moines; mem. gen. staff Broadlawns Med. Ctr., Des Moines; dir. surg. edn. Iowa Meth. Med. Ctr., Des Moines, dir. clin. divsn. Human Gene Therapy Rsch. Instn., chief sect. gen. surgery, chair surgery edn. com., mem. med. staff, ATLS instr.; sr. scholar Carl J. Shapiro Inst. Edn. and Rsch. Harvard Med. Sch. and Beth Israel Deaconess Med. Ctr., 2000—; mem. anatomical gift pub. awareness adv. com. State of Iowa Dept. Pub. Health, 1997—, team leader physician Iowa trauma sys. verification, 2000—. Contbr. articles to profl. jours. Named Tchr. of the Yr., Akron Gen. Med. Ctr., 1986, Disting. Alumni, 2005, Surgery Tchr. of the Yr., Iowa Meth. Med. Ctr., 2000; named to Hall of Distinction, Indianola HS, Iowa, 2005; recipient Dean's Spl. award, Northeastern Ohio U. Coll. Medicine, 1992, Harold Benloff award Humanism in Edn., Beth Israel Deaconess Med. Ctr., 2001, 2003. Fellow: ACS (chair Iowa dist. #2 1996—99, chair patient safety subcom., co-chair patient safety and quality improvement subcom.); mem.: AMA, Eastern Cooperative Oncology Group, Iowa Oncology Rsch. Assn. (v.p., bd. dirs. 1994—), Polk County Med. Soc. (pres. elect 1999, pres. 2000), Boston Surg. Soc., Ctrl. Surg. Assn., Iowa Acad. Surgery (chair resident rsch. competition, mem. program com. ann. meeting), Assn. Hosp. Med. Edn. (mem. project adv. panel 1988—89), Soc. Critical Care Medicine, Assn. Program Dirs. Surgery (mem. edn. com. 1992, bd. dirs. 1994—99), Midwest Surg. Assn. (treas. 1998—2001, pres. elect 2002—03, pres. 2003—04, chair nominating com. 2004—06), Phi Eta Sigma, Alpha Omega Alpha. Office: Beth Israel Deaconess Med Ctr 110 Francis St 9B Boston MA 02215

MOORMAN, JOHN A., librarian; b. Humboldt, Nebr., Sept. 15, 1947; m. Ileen Mary Geiger, Dec. 20, 1968; children: Johanna, Jessica Trinoskey, John A. Moorman Jr. AB, Guilford Coll., Greensboro, NC, 1969; MSLS, U. N.C., 1972; postgrad., U. N.C., Greensboro, 1974-75; PhD, U. Ill., 2002. Pub. svcs. and circulation libr. Guilford Coll., 1972-75; dir. Elbert Ivey Meml. Libr., Hickory, NC, 1975-80, Brazoria County Libr. System, Angleton, Tex., 1980-86, Oak Lawn (Ill.) Pub. Libr., 1986-88; exec. dir. Cumberland Trail Libr. System, Flora, Ill., 1989-92; city libr. Decatur (Ill.) Pub. Libr., 1992-2000; dir. Williamsburg (Va.) Regional Libr., 2000—. Adj. faculty Cath. U., 2003—. Author: Managing Small Library Collections in Businesses and Community Organizations: Advice for Non-Librarians, 1989, Running a Small Library: A How-To-Do-It Manual, 2006. Grad. Decatur Leadership Inst., 1993, Leadership Hist. Triangle, 2003. Mem.: ALA, Va. Libr. Assn. (legis. com.). Mem. Soc. Of Friends. Avocations: travel, reading, woodworking, sports. Home: 8216 Old Mill Ln Williamsburg VA 23188-1135 Office: Williamsburg Regional Libr 7770 Croaker RD Williamsburg VA 23188 Office Phone: 757-259-7777. E-mail: jmoorman@mail.wrl.org.

MOORMAN, RICHARD HAL, IV, lawyer; b. Waco, Tex., Mar. 2, 1950; s. George R. and Billie (Scoggin) M.; m. Lucy Baker, May 24, 1974; children: Theodore Clark, Lydia Anne, Peter Baker. BCE, MIT, 1971; JD, So. Meth. U., 1976. Bar: Tex. 1976, U.S. Dist. Ct. (so. dist., we. dist., ea. dist.) Tex. 1976, U.S. Ct. Appeals (5th cir.) 1976; Bd. Cert. Civil Trial Law and Estate Planning and Probate Law, Tex. Bd. of Legal Specialization. Engr. Turner Collie & Braden, Houston, 1971-72, P.G. Bell Co., Houston, 1972-73; ptnr. Moorman Tate Moorman Urquhart & Haley L.L.P., Brenham, Tex., 1976—. Bd. dirs. Washington County Abstract Co., Brenham; bd. mem. Trinity Med. Ctr. Hosp.; past examiner (2002) Tex. Bd. of Legal Specialization; course dir. State Bar of Tex. Advanced Estate Planning and Probate Seminar. Editor: Real Property Probate and Trust Law Jour. Mem. Tex. Air Control Bd., Austin, 1980-86; past pres. Washington on Brazos State Pk. Assn., Brenham, Brenham Downtown Assn. Named one of Tex. Superlawyers. Fellow Am. Coll. Trust and Estate Counsel, Tex. Bar Found.; mem. ABA (estate gift tax com.), State Bar of Tex. (coun. mem. real estate probate and trust sect.), Washington County C. of C. (pres.); Main Street Bd, Elder: Brenham Bible Ch. Avocations: antiques, hunting, fishing, theology. Office: Moorman Tate Moorman Urquhart Haley LLP 207 E Main St Brenham TX 77833-3754 Office Phone: 979-836-5664. Business E-Mail: hmoorman@moormantate.com.

MOORMAN, WILLIAM A., federal judge, retired career military officer; b. Chgo. BA in History and Econs., U. Ill., 1967, JD, 1970; Grad., Air Command. & Staff Coll., Maxwell AFB, 1980; student Nat. War Coll., 1988—89. Commd. 2d lt. USAF, 1970, advanced through grades to maj. gen., 1999, ret., 2002; chief of contracts Air Force Comm. Svc., Richards-Gebaur AFB, Mo., 1971—74; chief of claims 475th Air Base Wing and 5th

Air Force, Yokota AB, Japan, 1974-77; dep. staff judge advocate then staff judge advocate 31st Tactical Fighter Wing, Homestead AFB, Fla., 1977-79; staff judge advocate 832nd Air Divsn., Luke AFB, Ariz., 1980-83; chief preventive law and legal air group, then chief Office of the Judge Advocate Gen., Washington, 1983-88; staff judge advocate 12th Air Force/U.S. Southern Command Air Forces, Bergstrom AFB, Tex., 1989-91; dep. staff judge advocate Strategic Air Command, Offutt AFB, Nebr., 1991-92, staff judge advocate, 1992-93, Hdqrs. USAF Europe, Ramstein AB, Germany, 1993-95; comdr. Air Force Legal Svcs. Agy., Bolling AFB, D.C., 1995-96; staff judge advocate Hdqs. Air Combat Command, Langley AFB, Va., 1996—99; judge JAG Hdqs., USAF, Washington, 1999—2003, US Ct. Appeals Vets. Claims, Washington, 2004—. Decorated Legion of Merit with oak leaf cluster. Office: US Ct Appeals Vets Claims 625 Indiana Ave NW Ste 900 Washington DC 20004 *

MOOS, H. WARREN, physicist, educator, astronomer, director; b. NYC, Mar. 26, 1936; s. Henry H. and Dorothy E. (Warren) M.; m. Doris Elaine McClure, July 13, 1957; children: Janet, Paul, Daniel, David. BS, Brown U., 1957; MA, U. Mich., 1959, PhD, 1962. Rsch. assoc. Stanford (Calif.) U., 1961-63; acting asst. prof. Johns Hopkins U., Balt., 1963-64, asst. prof., 1964-68, assoc. prof., 1968-71, prof., 1971—, dir. Ctr. for Astrophys. Scis., 1988-93, chmn. Physics & Astronomy, 1993-96. Cons. in field; mem. com. on planetary and lunar exploration NRC/Nat. Acad. Sci., Washington, 1982-86; mem. space and earth sci. adv. com. NASA, Washington, 1984-87; vis. fellow Joint Inst. for Lab. Astrophysics, 1972-73, 80-81. Co-editor Optical Properties of Ions in Crystals, 1967, Coalition, Astrophysics in the Far Ultraviolet: Fives Years of Discovery with Fuse, 2006; contbr. over 300 articles to profl. jours. Trustee Associated Univs., Inc., 2002—, chair bd. trustees, 2004—. Sloan Found. fellow, 1965-69. Fellow Am. Phys. Soc.; mem. Am. Astron. Soc., Internat. Astron. Union. Achievements include prin. investigatorof far ultraviolet spectroscopic explorer; co-investigator of Apollo 17 ultraviolet spectrometer, of Hopkins Ultraviolet Telescope, of Voyager ultraviolet spectrometer, of space telescope imaging spectograph; research on ultraviolet astronomy and fusion plasma diagnostics. Office: Johns Hopkins U Dept Physics & Astronomy 34th & Charles Sts Baltimore MD 21218

MOOS, RUDOLF H., psychologist, researcher; b. Berlin, Sept. 10, 1934; s. Henry R. and Herta M. (Ehrlich) M.; m. Bernice Schradski, June 9, 1963; children: Karen, Kevin. BA in Psychology, U. Calif., Berkeley, 1956, PhD, 1960. Mem. faculty psychiatry Stanford (Calif.) U., 1962—, dir. psychiatry research tng. program, 1967-92, prof. psychiatry, 1972—, dir. social ecology lab., 1967-92; sr. rsch. career scientist VA Med. Center, Palo Alto, Calif., 1981—, dir. Ctr. for Health Care Evaluation, 1984—2002, dir. Program Evaluation and Resource Ctr., 1990-99. Vis. prof. Inst. Psychiatry, also Maudsley and Royal Bethlem Hosp., London, 1969-70 Author: Issues in Social Ecology, 1974, Evaluating Treatment Environments, 1974, Health and the Social Environment, 1974, Evaluating Correctional and Community Settings, 1975, Human Adaptation Coping with Life Crises, 1976, The Human Context, 1976, Environment and Utopia, 1977, Coping with Physical Illness, 1977, Evaluating Educational Environments, 1979, Coping with Physical Illness: New Perspectives, 1984, Coping with Life Crises: An Integrated Approach, 1986, Alcoholism Treatment: Content, Process and Outcome, 1990, Group Residential Facilities for Older Adults, 1994, Evaluating Residential Facilities, 1996; mem. editl. bd. Jour. Behavioral Medicine, 1984-04, Internat. Jour. Therapeutic Cmtys., Prevention in Human Svcs., Psychosomatic Medicine, Evaluation and Program Planning, 1977-99, Jour. Personality and Social Psychology, 1985-91, Health Psychology: An Internat. Jour., 1985-97, Violence, Agression, and Terrorism, 1985-94, Jour. Substance Abuse, 1986-2001, Jour. Applied Gerontology, 1988-2005, Jour. Cmty. and Applied Social Psychology, Psychology and Aging, 1986-91, Environ. and Behavior, 1987-91, Indian Jour. Clin. Psychology, 1996-2002, Jour. Studies Alcohol, 1997, Am. Jour. Cmty. Psychology, 1998—, Pakistan Jour. Psychol. Rsch., 2005, Internat. Jour. Clin. and Health Psychology, 2006; assoc. editor: Ency. of Psychological Assessment. Fellow APA, Acad. Clin. Psychology, Acad. Behavioral Medicine, Soc. Behavioral Medicine, Am. Orthopsychiat. Assn., Nat. Inst. on Alcohol Abuse and Alcoholism (mem. coun.); mem. Am. Sociol. Assn., Am. Psychosomatic Assn. (mem. coun.). Home: 25661 W Fremont Rd Los Altos CA 94022-1600 Office: Stanford U Dept Psychiatry MC 5550 Palo Alto CA 94305

MOOS, WALTER HAMILTON, pharmaceutical company executive; AB in Chemistry cum laude, Harvard U., 1976; PhD in Chemistry, U. Calif., Berkeley, 1982. Scientist Parke-Davis Rsch. Divsn. Warner Lambert Co., Ann Arbor, Mich., 1982-83, sr. scientist, 1984, rsch. assoc., 1984-86, sr. rsch. assoc., 1986-87, sect. dir. chemistry, 1987-89, dir. chemistry, 1989, sr. dir. chemistry, 1990, v.p. neuroscis. and biol. chemistry, 1990-91; v.p. rsch. devel. Chiron Corp., Emeryville, Calif., 1991-97; chmn., CEO MitoKor, San Diego, 1997—2004; v.p. bioscience div. SRI Internat., Menlo Park, Calif., 2005—. Adj. asst. prof. dept. medicinal chemistry Coll. Pharmacy, U. Mich., 1990, adj. assoc. prof., 1990-91; adj. prof. dept. pharm. chemistry U. Calif., San Francisco, 1992—; bd. dirs. Migenix, Rigel Pharm., Biotech. Industry Orgn., Alnis, Anterion, Axiom, Keystone Symposia, Mimotopes, Oncologic, Onyx; presenter to numerous sci. confs. Co-editor: Drug Discovery Technologies, 1990, Cognitive Disorders: Pathophysiology and Treatment, 1991; editor-at-large Medicinal Chemistry, 1988-2004; cons. editor Bio-Organic and Medicinal Chemistry Letters. Mem. Am. Peptide Soc. (charter mem.), U. Mich. Enzyme Discussion Group (co-founder), ACS Divsn. Medicinal Chemistry (chmn. membership com. 1989, councilor 1990), Am. Chem. Soc. Office: SRI Internat 333 Ravenswood Ave Menlo Park CA 94025

MOOSHAGIAN, MARK NISHAN, education educator; b. Worcester, Mass., Dec. 8, 1960; s. Madieros and Mary Mooshagian; 1 child, John Samuel. BS, U.S. Naval Acad., Annapolis, 1982; MA, U. R.I., Kingston, 2006. Cert. Secondary Math. Tchr. R.I., 1998, Commonwealth of Mass., 2003. Owner, operator Subway Sandwiches, Bristol, RI, 1994—97; math tchr. Commonwealth of Mass., Fall River, 2001—05, Newport (R.I.) Pub. Schs. Mem. Friends of Sheffield PTO, Newport, RI, 2005—06. Lt. USN, 1982—93. Decorated Surface Warfare Officer USN, Armed Forces Expeditionary medal, Nat. Def. Svc. medal, Master Tng. Specialist. Mem.: Mensa, VFW (life), DAV (life), Nat. Honor Soc., U.S. Naval Acad. Alumni Assn. (life). Conservative. Armenian Apostolic. Home: 3 Bedlow Pl Newport RI 02840 Office: Home 3 Bedlow Pl Newport RI 02840 Home Phone: 401-847-9549; Office Phone: 401-847-9549. Business E-Mail: mooshagian@teachers.org.

MOOSSA, A. R., surgeon, educator; b. Port Louis, Mauritius, Oct. 10, 1939; s. Yacoob and Maude (Rochecoute) M.; m. Denise Willoughby, Dec. 28, 1973; children: Pierre, Noel, Claude, Valentine. BS, U. Liverpool, Eng., 1962, MD (hon.), 1965; postgrad., Johns Hopkins U., 1972—73, U. Chgo., 1973—74. Intern Liverpool Royal Infirmary, 1965—66; resident United Liverpool Hosps. and Alder Hey Children's Hosp., 1966—72; from asst. prof. surgery to assoc. prof. U. Chgo., 1975-77, prof., dir. surg. rsch., chief gen. surgery svc., vice chmn. dept., 1977-83; chmn. dept. surgery U. Calif.-San Diego Med. Ctr., 1983—2004, prof., surgery, emeritus chmn., assoc. dean, spl. counsel for clin. affairs, 2004—. Litchfield lectr. U., Oxford, Eng., 1978; praelector in surgery U. Dundee, Scotland, 1979; Hampson Trust vis. prof. U. Liverpool, 1992, G.B. Ong. vis. prof. U. Hong Kong, 1993, Philip Sandblon vis. prof. U. Lund, Sweden. Editor: Tumors of the Pancreas, 1982, Essential Surgical Practice, 1983, 4th edit., 2000, Comprehensive Textbook of Oncology, 1985, 2d edit., 1991, Gastrointestinal Emergencies, 1985, Problems in General Surgery, 1989, Operative Colorectal Surgery, 1993. Fellow Royal Coll. Surgeons (Hunterian prof. 1977); mem. ACS, Am. Surg. Assn., Soc. Univ. Surgeons, Am. Soc. Clin. Oncology, European Surg. Assn. Office: U Calif San Diego Thornton Hosp 9300 Campus Point Dr 7212 La Jolla CA 92037 Office Phone: 858-657-6112. Business E-Mail: amoossa@ucsd.edu.

MOOSSY, JOHN, neurologist, consultant, pathologist; b. Shreveport, La., Aug. 24, 1925; s. John Yazbeck and Rose (Ferris) M.; m. Yvonne Reese, Mar. 15, 1951; children: John Jefferson, Joan Marie. MD, Tulane U., 1950. Intern Charity Hosp. of New Orleans, 1950-51, neurology resident, 1951-53; neuropathology fellow Columbia U. Coll. of Physicians and Surgeons, NYC, 1953-54; assoc., lectr. in neuropathology Tulane U. Sch. Medicine, New Orleans, 1954-57; asst. to prof. in pathology, neurology La. State U., New Orleans, 1957-65; prof. pathology, grad. faculty U. Pitts., 1965-67; prof. pathology neuropathology Bowman Gray Sch. of Medicine, Winston-Salem, NC, 1967-72; prof. pathology and neurology, dir. div. neuropathology U. Pitts., 1972-93, emeritus prof., 1993—. Dir. Cerebrovascular Disease Study, World Fedn. of Neurology, Antwerp, Belgium, 1960-61; cons. Armed Forces Inst. of Pathology, Washington, 1977—, mem. sci. adv. bd., Washington, 1984-86. Editor: Cerebral Vascular Disease Seventh Conference, 1970, Cerebrovascular Diseases 12th Research Conference, 1981; editor-in-chief Jour. Neuropathology and Exptl. Neurology, 1981-91; mem. editorial bd. Archives Neurology, 1982-92. Recipient Excellence in Teaching award U. Pitts. Sch. of Medicine, 1987-88; named Commencement Speaker U. Pitts. Sch. of Medicine, 1989. Mem. Am. Acad. Neurology (sec.-treas. 1963-655), Am. Neurol. Assn. (v.p. 1977-78), Am. Assn. Neuropathologists (pres. 1974-75, Neuropathology award 1992), Internat. Soc. Neuropathology, Coun. Biology Editors.

MOOT, JOHN S., lawyer; BA, St. Lawrence U., 1983; JD cum laude, Am. U., 1988. Bar: DC, Md. Assoc. Verner, Liipfert, Bernhard, McPherson & Hand; atty. Skadden, ARps, Slate, Meagher & Flom LLP, 1992—2005, ptnr.; gen. counsel Fed. Energy Regulatory Commn., Washington, 2005—. Office: Federal Energy Regulatory Commn 888 First St NE Washington DC 20426

MOOTE, A. LLOYD, history professor; b. Hamilton, Ont., Can., Mar. 22, 1931; s. Stanley Alanson and Esther Grace (Wood) M.; m. Barbara Brown, Dec. 27, 1956 (div. 1982); children: Karen, Peter, Daphne, Robert; m. Dorothy Carter May, May 30, 1986. BA, U. Toronto, 1954; MA, U. Minn., Mpls., 1956, PhD, 1958. Tchg. asst. U. Minn., Mpls., 1955-58; lectr. U. Toronto, 1958-61; asst. prof. U. Cin., 1961-62; from asst. prof. to prof. history U. So. Calif., LA, 1962-92, prof emeritus, 1993—. Vis. prof. Queen's U., Kingston, Ont., 1965-66; chmn. gen. edn. program U. So. Calif., 1978-81; mem. Inst. Advanced Study, Princeton, 1988-89; affiliated prof. Rutgers U., 1994—. Author: The Seventeenth Century, 1970, The Revolt of the Judges, 1971, The World of Europe: The Seventeenth Century, 1973, 2d edit., 1979, Louis XIII: The Just, 1989, paperback edit., 1991, (with Dorothy C. Moote) The Great Plague: The Story of London's Most Deadly Year, 2004, paperback edit., 2006 (nominated Pulitzer prize); co-editor, contbr. issue of French hist. studies on biography, 1996; mem. editl. bd. French Hist. Studies, 1971-74; internat. adv. bd. European History Quar., 1983—. Founder, convener So. Calif. Early Modern French Studies Group, 1980-93, Rutgers, Princeton and Phila. Early Modern History Group, 1994—. Recipient William Koren prize Soc. French Hist. Studies, 1962, creative scholarship award U. So. Calif. Assocs., 1973, faculty book award U. So. Calif. chpt. Phi Kappa Phi, 1990; younger scholar NEH, 1969; grantee Am. Philos. Soc., 1962, Haynes Found., 1973, Wellcome Inst. for History Medicine, 1993-94, Burroughs-Wellcome Fund, 1996; Guggenheim fellow, 1976, fellow U. Essex, Eng., 1993-94, Rutgers Ctr. for Hist. Analysis, 1995-97. Mem. Am. Hist. Assn., Soc. French Hist. Studies (pres. 1984-85), Soc. for Study French History (U.K.), Sixteenth-Century Studies Conf. Home: 149 Meaowbrook Dr Princeton NJ 08540-3664 Personal E-mail: dlmoote@verizon.net.

MOOTHA, VAMSI KRISHNA, biomedical researcher, educator; BS, Stanford U., 1993; MD, Harvard U, 1998; internship and residency in Internal Med., Brigham and Women's Hospital, 1998—2001; postdoctoral fellowship, Whitehead and Broad Institutes, 2004. Asst. prof. sys. biology Harvard Med. Sch., Boston; also asst. prof. med. Mass. Gen. Hosp., Boston. Author: numerous articles in jour. such as Proceedings of the Nat. Acad. of Sci. USA, Cell, and Nature Genetics. Named a MacArthur Fellow, 2004. Achievements include pioneering powerful, adaptable computational strategies for mining data collected in laboratories throughout the world, as well as for fundamental insights in seritochondrial biology. Office: Dept Systems Biology Broad Inst 2 Cambridge Ctr Cambridge MA 02142-1401 Address: Ctr for Human Genetic Rsch Simches Rsch Bldg 185 Cambridge St Boston MA 02114 Office Phone: 617-252-1672. Office Fax: 617-252-1902. E-mail: vamsi@hms.harvard.edu.

MOOTY, JOHN WILLIAM, lawyer; b. Adrian, Minn., Nov. 27, 1922; s. John Wilson and Genevieve (Brown) M.; m. Virginia Nelson, June 6, 1952 (dec. 1964); children: David N., Bruce W., Charles W.; m. Jane Nelson, Jan. 15, 1972. BSL, U. Minn., 1943, LLB, 1944. Bar: Minn. 1944. Ptnr. Gray, Plant, Mooty & Bennett, Mpls., 1945—. Bd. dirs. Internat. Dairy Queen, Inc., Bur. of Engraving, Inc., Riverway Co. and subs.; chmn. Rio Verde Svcs., Inc., Ariz. Author (with others): Minnesota Practice Methods, 1956. Chmn. Gov.'s Task Force on Edn., 1981; pres. Citizens League Mpls., 1970; acting chmn. Republican Party of Minn., 1958. Named to Minn. Bus. Hall of Fame, 2003. Mem. ABA, Minn. Bar Assn., Hennepin County Bar Assn., U. Minn. Alumni Assn. (pres. 1982), Tonto Verde Country Club, Minikahda (Mpls.) Club, Mpls. Club. Home: 8106 Highwood Dr Apt Y232 Bloomington MN 55438-1054 Office Phone: 612-632-3200. Business E-Mail: john.mooty@gpmlaw.com.

MORA, ALBERTO J., retail executive, lawyer; b. Boston, 1952; BA with honors, Swarthmore Coll., 1974; JD, U. Miami, 1981. Bar: Fla., D.C. Fgn. svc. officer US Dept. State, 1975—78; gen. counsel USIA, 1989—93, mem. broadcasting bd. govs., 1995—2001; counsel internat. law Greenberg Traurig LLP, Washington; gen. counsel, Dept. of Navy US Dept. Def., Washington, 2001—05; v.p., gen. counsel, internat. divsn. Wal-Mart Stores, Inc., 2006—. Bd. dirs. Nat. Coun. for Internat. Visitors, Radio Free Asia, Radio Free Europe/Radio Liberty. Editor-in-chief: Law of the Ams.: U. Miami Jour. of Internat. Law. Recipient Profile in Courage award, John F. Kennedy Library Found., 2006; fellow, Orgn. of Am. States. Mem.: Coun. Fgn. Rels. Office: Wal-Mart Stores Inc 702 SW 8th St Bentonville AR 72716 Office Phone: 479-204-9027.

MORA, ANTONIO GONZALEZ, III, broadcast journalist; b. Havana, Cuba, Dec. 14, 1957; came to U.S., 1960; s. Antonio Gonzalez Jr. and Natalia (Sandoval) M.; m. Julie Good, Aug. 27, 1994; children: Clara, Antonio Daniel. JD, U. Catolica Andres Bello, Caracas, Venezuela, 1980; LLM, Harvard U., Cambridge, Mass., 1981; DHL, Our Lady of Holy Cross, New Orleans, 2000; PhD (hon.), Ursinus Coll., 2001. Assoc. Debevoise & Plimpton, NYC, 1981-88; anchor Sta. WXTV, Secaucus, NJ, 1990-91, Sta. WNJU, Teterboro, NJ, 1991; anchor Nightside NBC, Charlotte, NC, 1992; reporter, anchor Sta. WTVJ-TV, Miami, 1992-93; host Good Day LA Tv Sta. KTTV, LA, 1993—94; host Good Morning America Sunday ABC, NYC, 1994-95; correspondent ABC News, NYC, 1995-99; news anchor Good Morning America ABC, NYC, 1999—2002; evening news anchor TV Sta. WBBM, Chgo., 2002—. Recipient Nat. Emmy award, 2000, Peabody award, 2000-01, Edward R. Murrow award, 2000, 5 Local Emmy awards, 2004-05. Mem.: Coun. Fgn. Rels.

MORA, ELIZABETH, comptroller, academic administrator; B, U. Calif. Berkeley; MBA, Simmons Grad. Sch. Mgmt. CPA. Mgr. nat. regulatory cons. Coopers & Lybrand (now PricewaterhouseCoopers), 1987—97; dir. cost analysis and compliance Harvard U., 1997—2000, dir. office sponsored programs, 2000—04, assoc. v.p. for sponsored programs, 2004—06, acting v.p. fin., 2006, v.p. fin., CFO, 2006—. Office: Harvard U Massachusetts Hall Harvard Yard Cambridge MA 02138 E-mail: elizabeth_mora@harvard.edu. *

MORA, JIM (JAMES LAWRENCE MORA), professional football coach; b. Los Angeles, Nov. 19, 1961; s. James Earnest and Connie Beatrice Mora; m. Shannon Mora; children: Cole, Lillia, Ryder, Trey. Grad., U. Wash., 1983. Asst. coach U. Wash., 1984; pro. pers. San Diego Chargers, 1985, asst. coach, 1986—91; secondary coach New Orleans Saints, 1992—96; asst. coach San Francisco 49ers, 1997—2003; head coach Atlanta Falcons, Flowery Br., Ga., 2004—07; asst. head coach/secondary Seattle Seahawks, 2007—. Office: Seattle Seahawks 11220 NE 53rd St Kirkland WA 98033 *

MORA, PAT, writer, speech professional; b. El Paso, Tex., Jan. 19, 1942; d. Raul Antonio and Estella (Delgado) M.; m. William H. Burnside, July 27, 1963 (div. Aug. 1981); children: William Burnside, Elizabeth Burnside, Cecilia Burnside; m. Vernon L. Scarborough, May 25, 1984. BA, Tex. Western Coll., 1963; MA, U. Tex., El Paso, 1967. Lectr. English U. Tex., El Paso, 1979-81, asst. to v.p. for acad. affairs, 1981-89, mus. dir., asst. to pres., 1987-89; cons. W.K. Kellogg Found., Battle Creek, Mich., 1989-91. Advisor Kellogg Nat. Fellowship Program, 1991-93. Author: (poetry) Chants, 1984 (SW Book award 1985), Borders, 1986 (SW Book award 1987), Communion, 1991, Agua Santa: Holy Water, Aunt Carmen's Book of Practical Saints, 1997; (nonfiction) Nepantla: Essays from the Land in the Middle, 1993, House of Houses, 1997; (children's books) Confetti: Poems for Children, Uno, Dos, Tres: One, Two, Three, Listen to the Desert: Oye al Desierto, The Race of Toad and Deer, The Gift of the Poinsettia: El regalo de la flor de nochebuena, The Desert Is My Mother: El desierto es mi madra, Agua, Agua, Agua, Pablo's Tree, A Birthday Basket for Tía, 1992 (SW Book award 1993), Tomás and the Library Lady, 1997, A library for Juana: The World of Sor Juana Inés, 2002 (Tomás Rivera Mexican American Children's Book award, 2002), Dona Flor: A Tall Tale About a Giant Woman with a Great Big Heart, 2005 (Am. Libr. Assn. Pura Belpre Author Honor Book, 2006). Kellogg nat. fellow W.K. Kellogg Found., 1986; Nat. Endowment Arts Creative Writing fellow, 1994; recipient poetry award Conf. Cin. Women, 1990; named to El Paso Herald Post Writers Hall of Fame, 1988. Mem Tex. Inst. Letters, Acad. Am. Poets, Nat. Coun. Tchrs. English, Soc. Children's Book Writers, Poetry Soc. Am. Democrat. Avocations: reading, walking, travel.

MORA, PHILIPPE, screenwriter, producer, director, painter; b. Paris, Aug. 8, 1949; s. Georges and Mirka Madeleine (Zelik) M.; m. Pamela Mai Krause, Aug. 1, 1980; children: Madeleine Mai, Georges Ritchie Maximillian, Dominic Marceau. Student, La Trobe U., Melbourne, Australia, 1967. Screenwriter, dir., producer, 1969—. Founder Cinema Papers mag., Melbourne, 1967. Dir., writer, prodr. (films) Trouble in Molopolis, 1969, The Howling III: The Marsupials, 1987, Snide and Prejudice, 1997, According to Occam's Razor, 1999, Project 65, 2002, Gertrude Stein, 2006, Dali, 2007; co-writer (film) Double Headed Eagle, 1971; dir., writer (films) Swastika, 1972 (Blue Ribbon award 1974), Brother Can You Spare a Dime, 1975, Mad Dog, 1976 (John Ford Meml. award 1976), According to Occam's Razor, 2000, Gertrude Stein, 2006; dir. (films) The Beast Within, 1980, The Return of Captain Invincible, 1981, A Breed Apart, 1983, The Howling II, 1984, Death of a Soldier, 1985, Back in Business, 1996; dir. prodr. Communion, 1990, Art Deco Detective, 1994, Pterodactyl Woman from Beverly Hills, 1994, Precious Find, 1995, Burning Down the House, 1996, Thick and Thin, 1997, Joseph's Gift, 1999, The Times They Ain't A Changin', 2005, The Vatican Tapes, 2005; dir., prodr. (film) Hamlet, 2001; exhibited in one-man and group shows at Argys Gallery, Melbourne, 1967, Clytie Jessop Gallery, London, 1968-71, Sigi Kraus Gallery, London, 1970-71, Camden Arts Centre, London, 1970, Richard Demarco Gallery, Edinburgh, 1971, Tolarno Gallery, Melbourne, 1971, Watters Gallery, Sydney, Australia, 1972, William Mora Gallery, Melbourne, 1987, Caz Gallery, L.A., 1990, Larrikins in London, 2003, Coll. Fine Arts, Sydney, 2003; represented in permanent collection Nat. Gallery Collection, Canberra, Australia, 1982, Mus. Modern Art Australia; English Lit. exhbn. Victorian Edn. Authority, Victoria, Australia, 1966; contbr. articles to mags.; contbr. columns to newspapers. Mem. Dirs. Guild Am., Acad. Motion Picture Arts and Scis., Australian Film Dirs. Assn. Office: Michael Blaha Esq 2530 Wilshire Blvd Santa Monica CA 90403-4616 Personal E-mail: moracyber@juno.com.

MORADI, AHMAD F., software company executive; b. Tehran, Persia, Mar. 21, 1955; arrived in US, 1973; s. Akbar and Afsar (Mokaram) M.; m. Lourdes Pernas; l child, Aimee. AS, Broward Community Coll., 1978; BA, Fla. Atlantic U., 1980; PhD, LaSalle U., 1989. Advisor restaurant industries, Miami, Fla., 1974-78; pres. Octa-8, Inc., Ft. Lauderdale, Fla., 1980-82; mgmt. cons. MGI-MCG, Boca Raton, Fla., 1982-83; dir. ops. Datamation, Hollywood, Fla., 1983-85; pres. Software Intelligence Corp., Ft. Lauderdale, 1985—; with ARM Financial Corp., 1987-89; MIS dir., CIO Churchill Tech., Inc., Davie, Fla., 1992—; MIS dir. Westmack Group Holding Co., Delray Beach, 1995—; prin. G4, Inc., Ft. Lauderdale, 1992—; CEO Futuretrak Internat. OTC BB:FTRK, 1998-99, Worldcast Interactive Inc.; with Biomed. Rsch. Techs., 1997—, Interchange Med., Inc., 1999—, Maxwell Rand Inc., 1999—, Netstairs.com, 2000—. Lectr. South Fla. Bus. Jour., 1984-85, Victoria Hosp., Miami, Fla., 1985, Mt. Sinai Hosp., Miami, Fla., 1985, U. Miami, Fla., 1986, Chiropractic Today, 1989; cons., bus., mktg., internat. mktg. and telemarketing mgmt. Software Intelligence Corp., 1985—; systems analyst Softway, Inc., Ft. Lauderdale, 1986; hon. co-chmn. bus. adv. coun. Nat. Leadership Coun.and Nat. Rep. Bus. Commn.; hon. chmn. U.S. Presdl. Bus. Commn., 2002. Named Businessman of Yr., U.S. Presdl. Bus. Commn., 2003; recipient Gold medal, 2002. Mem. Data Processing Mgmt. Assn., Small Bus. Inst. Office Phone: 954-229-0900. E-mail: amoradi@g41.com.

MORAHAN-MARTIN, JANET MAY, psychologist, educator; b. NYC, Jan. 13, 1944; d. William Timothy and May Rosalind (Tarangelo) Morahan; m. Curtis Hermon Martin, June 2, 1979; l child, Gwendolyn May. AB, Rosemont Coll., Pa., 1965; MEd, Tufts U., 1968; PhD, Boston Coll., 1978. Asst. mkt. rsch. analyst Compton Advt. Co., NYC, 1965-67; mkt. rsch. analyst Ogilvy & Mather Advt., NYC, 1967; ednl. rsch. asst. Tufts U., Medford, Mass., 1968-69; counselor Psychol. Inst. Bentley Coll., Waltham, Mass., 1971-72; dir. counseling svcs. Bryant U., Smithfield, RI, 1972-75, psychology instr., 1972—76, asst. prof. psychology, 1976—81, assoc. prof. psychology, 1981—91, prof. psychology, 1991—, chair dept. applied psychology, 2007—. Bd. dirs. Multi-Svc. Ctr., Newton, Mass., 1980-82. Contbr. articles to profl. jours., chpts. to books; reviewer APA Conv., 1985—, Teaching of Psychology Jour., 1988—, Collegiate Micro-Computer Jour., 1991, 93, Nat. Soc. Sci. Jour., 1991; mem. editl. bd., spl. edit. editor Cyber Psychology and Behavior. Bd. dirs. Wellesley (Mass.) Community Children's Ctr., 1986-90, Coun. for Children, Newton, Mass., 1984-86. NIMH fellow, 1967-68; NSF grantee, 1974-76, U.S. Office Edn. grantee, 1980. Mem. APA, Mass. Audubon Soc., Internat. Soc. for Online Mental Health (founding mem.), Soc. for Tchg. of Psychology, Soc. Computers in Psychology. Avocations: photography, antiques, gardening, literature. Home: 17 Fuller Brook Rd Wellesley MA 02482-7108 Office: Bryant U 1150 Douglas Pike Smithfield RI 02917-1291 Business E-Mail: jmorahan@bryant.edu.

MORALES, CARLOS M., lawyer; b. NY, 1953; JD, Columbia Law Sch., NYC. Bar: NY 1980. With Mktg. Regulation Divsn. SEC; with Merrill Lynch & Co., NYC, 1986—, mem., Equity Trading Counsel Grp., 1989—92, mem., Debt and Equity Markets Counsel Grp., 1992; sr. v.p., assoc. gen. counsel Merrill Lynch Internat., NYC; chief legal officer, dir. Merrill Lynch Pierce, Fenner & Smith. Co-founder Merrill Lynch Hispanic Employee Network. Mem. bd. dirs. Hispanic Fedn. Named one of Corp. Elite, Hispanic Bus. Mag., 2007. Office: Merrill Lynch & Co 222 Broadway 4th Fl New York NY 10038 Office Phone: 212-236-1000. Office Fax: 212-670-4446. *

MORALES, DIANE K., former federal agency administrator; b. Houston, July 11, 1946; d. Arthur Clement and Helen Mary (Araiza) Morales, Louie Welch (Stepfather); m. James Neal Glerum. BA, U. Tex.-Austin, 1968. Account exec. Goodwin, Dannenbaum, Littman & Wingfield, Houston, 1968—70; pub. rels. rep. Gittings, Inc., Dallas, 1970—71; asst. buyer, mgr. Neiman-Marcus, Dallas, 1971—80; sr. assoc., mktg. mgr. 3/D Internat., Houston, 1980—81; dep. asst. sec. policy U.S. Dept. Interior, Washington, 1981—83; bd. dirs. CAB, Washington, 1983—86; v.p. govt. rels. Earth Tech. Corp., Washington, 1986—88; pres. Morales Consulting Svc. Co., Washington, 1988—90; dep. asst. sec. def. for logistics U.S. Dept. Def., Washington, 1990—93, dep. under sec. logistics and material readiness, 2001—04; pres. DMS, Inc., Washington, 1993—2001, DMG Enterprises, LLC, Washington, 2004—. Mem. logistics mgmt. com. Nat. Def. Industry Assn., 1995—2001. Pres. Downtown Rep. Women's Club, Dallas, 1975-80; bd. dirs. Dallas County Men's Rep. Club, 1978-80, Dallas Coun. Women's Rep. Club, 1978-80, Houston Interam. C. of C., 1980-81, Christian Embassy, 1990-93, Am. Cancer Soc./NOVA, 2000-04, Wolf Trap Found., 2005—, Nat. Job Corps Assn., 2005—; Project Nehemiah, 1996—, Tex. State Soc., 1996-2001; mem. Rep. Women's Fed. Forum, Rep. Nat. Hispanic Assembly, Conservative Rep. Network, 1985-89. Mem.: Women in Def. Industry. Republican. Presbyterian.

MORALES, GRISEL, language educator; b. Bronx, NY, Dec. 31, 1962; d. Ernesto Morales and Carmen Medina; m. Waldemar Martinez, Dec. 28, 1985; children: Erika Jaleesa Martinez, Katayra Andrea Martinez. BA in Secondary Edn., U. Interamericana, San German, PR, 1996; MA in Ednl. Adminstrn., U. Phoenix, 2006. Cert. English tchr. NJ, 1999, adminstr. NJ, 2007, supr. NJ, 2007. Fin. analyst Prudential Ins. Co., Newark, 1998—2000; English tchr. Essex County Vocat. and Tech. High Schs., Newark, 2000—. Mem.: NJ Coun. Tchrs. English. Office: Essex County Vo-Tech High Schs 300 N 13th St Newark NJ 07107 Home Phone: 908-687-3024; Office Phone: 973-483-5466.

MORALES, HECTOR E., JR., bank executive, lawyer; BA, Columbia Coll.; JD, U. Tex. Pvt. practice Graves, Dougherty, Hearon & Moody, Austin, Tex., Crain, Caton, & James, Houston; atty. internat. law Reliant Energy, Houston, 1993—97; pres., gen. mgr. Reliant Energy Argentina, 1997—2000; sr. v.p. Viamericas Corp.; fin. svcs. cons.; alt. exec. dir. U.S. Inter-Am. Devel. Bank, 2003, acting exec. dir., 2003—04, exec. dir., 2004—. Office: US Dept Treasury 1300 NY Ave NW Rm NE1101 Washington DC 20577 Office Phone: 202-623-1075. Office Fax: 202-623-3096.

MORALES, JULIO K., lawyer; b. Havana, Cuba, Jan. 17, 1948; arrived in US, 1960; s. Julio E. and Josephine (Holsters) M.; m. Suzette M. Dussault, May 31, 1970 (div. 1978); children: Julio E., Karel A.; m. Barbara A. Miller, July 14, 1979 (div. 1988); 1 child, Nicolas W. BA, Carroll Coll., 1969; JD, U. Mont., 1972. Bar: Mont. 1972, U.S. Dist. Ct. Mont. 1972, U.S. Ct. Mil. Appeals 1972, U.S. Ct. Appeals (9th cir.) 1980. Law clk. to presiding justice Mont. Supreme Ct., Helena, 1972; sole practice Missoula, Mont., 1973-78, 88—; sr. ptnr. Morales & Volinkaty, Missoula, 1978-88; pvt. practice law Morales Law Office, 1988—. Author: Estate Planning for the Handicapped, 1975. Pres. Rockmont, Inc., Missoula, 1985-2001. Served to 2d lt. U.S. Army, 1972. Named Boss of the Yr., Missoula chpt. Mont. Assn. Legal Secs., 1988. Mem. ABA (dist. rep. 1975-79, exec. coun. young lawyer divsn. 1977-79), Mont. Bar Assn. (chmn. law day 1974, 75, 77), Am. Judicature Soc., ATLA, World Assn. Lawyers, Missoula Soccer Assn. (pres. 1983-85), Mont. Sailing Assn. (bd. dirs. 1994—), Nat. Exch. Club (bd. dirs. Yellowstone dist. 1987-88, pres. 1990-91), Missoula Exch. Club, Elks (officer 1999-2001, exalted ruler 2001-02), Phi Delta Phi. Roman Catholic. Avocations: sports, coaching youth, boating, skiing, golf. Office: PO Box 9311 430 Ryman St Missoula MT 59802-4249 Office Phone: 406-728-6005. Business E-Mail: jmorales@jmoraleslaw.com.

MORALES, TOMÁS D., academic administrator, educator; m. Evy Morales; 3 children. BA cum laude, SUNY, New Paltz, 1975; MA, SUNY, Albany, 1978, PhD in Ednl. Adminstrn. and Policy Studies, 1998. Counselor Ednl. Opportunity Program SUNY, New Paltz, 1975—77, dir. Office of Spl. Admissions and Ednl. Opportunity Program, 1981—94, asst. v.p. student affairs, 1987—94, asst. dean Sch. Edn., 1991—94; asst. dir. state programs Cornell U., 1977—79; assoc. dir. Advancement on Individual Merit (AIM) Program SUNY, Stony Brook, 1979—81; v.p. student affairs, dean students City Coll., CUNY, NYC, 1994—2001; prof. Dept. Edn. Calif. State Poly. U., Pomona, 2001—07, v.p. student affairs, 2001—03, interim v.p. academic affairs, 2003, provost, v.p. academic affairs, 2003—07; pres. Coll. Staten Island, CUNY, 2007—. Bd. dirs. AmeriChoice Health Svcs. NY, Inc. Contbr. articles to profl. jours. Bd. dirs. Los Padres Found. Recipient Peggy Champagne Meml. Leadership Award for Outstanding Svc., SUNY, 1990, Exemplary Model of Adminstrv. Leadership Award, Am. Assn. Univ. Adminstrs., 2003; fellow Inst. Ednl. Leadership, 1982—83. Mem.: Am. Assn. Higher Edn. Office: Coll Staten Island Office of Pres 2800 Victory Blvd Staten Island NY 10314 *

MORALES-RAMOS, JUAN ALFREDO, entomologist, researcher; s. Alfredo Morales and Hortencia Ramos De Morales; m. Maria Guadalupe Rojas, Sept. 15, 1985. BS, Autonomous U. Nuevo Leon, Mex., 1977; MS, Higher Coll. of Tropical Agr., Mex., 1982; PhD, Tex. A&M U., 1991. Rschr., lectr. Colegio Superior de Agricultura Tropical, Cardenas, Tabasco, Mexico, 1978—84; rsch. technician Tex. A&M U., Coll. Sta., Tex., 1985—86; rsch. entomologist US Dept. Agrl.-Agrl. Rsch. Svc. Subtropical Agrl. Rsch. Ctr., Weslaco, Tex., 1992—98, US Dept. Agrl.-Agrl. Rsch. Svc. So. Regional Rsch. Ctr., New Orleans, 1998—2004, US Dept. Agrl.-Agrl. Rsch. Svc. Nat. Biol. Cont. Lab., New Orleans, 2004—. Author: Natural Enemies and Pest Control: An Integrated Pest Management Concept, 2003; mem. editl. bd.: Biopesticides Internat., 2006—; contbr. articles to prof. jours. Recipient Scientist of the Yr. award, US Dept. Agr., 2002, Excellence in Tech. Transfer award, Fed. Lab. Consortium, 2004. Mem.: Fla. Entomol. Soc., Am. Inst. of Biol. Scis., Soc. Mex. de Control Biologico, Entomol. Soc. of Am., The Mars Soc., The Planetery Soc. Achievements include research in mass propagation an release technology of the boll weevil parasitoid Catolaccus grandis; development of artificial diet for the boll weevil parasitoid Catolaccus grandis; patents for artificial diet for Ectoparsitoid Insects; first to first biological control of a primary insect pest (the boll weevil) in an annual crop (cotton); first biological control of a primary insect pest by mass propagating a natural enemy using an artificial diet; patents for bait matrix for control of subterranean termites; first to the use of chemical analysis of food sources for the development of artificial diets and baits for beneficial insects and pests; 5 US patents; development of nutritionally based bait matrixes to deliver toxics to socialinsect pests such as termite and ants. Avocations: astronomy, music. Office: USDA-Agrl Rsch Svc Nat Biol Control Lab 59 Lee Rd Stoneville MS 38776 Business E-Mail: jmorales@msa-stoneville.ars.usda.gov.

MORALEZ, JOSELYN HOPE, special education educator; b. Lordsburg, N.Mex., July 7, 1966; d. Mary Lou Chavez. BS, N.Mex. State U., 1988. Instr. elem. spl. edn. Animas Pub. Schs., N.Mex., 1988—90, Lordsburg Pub. Schs., 1990—. Mem. Coun. Exceptional Children, Delta Kappa Gamma. Office: Southside Elem Sch 200E 9th St Lordsburg NM 88045 Home Phone: 505-542-3778; Office Phone: 505-542-9473. E-mail: jmoralez@lmsed.org.

MORAN, ANNE E., lawyer; b. Rockville Centre, NY, July 9, 1953; BA, Wellesley Coll., 1975; JD, Harvard U., 1978. Bar: DC 1978, NY 1979, US Ct. of Fed. Claims. Law clk. to Hon. Philip Nichols US Ct. Appeals (Fed. cir.); ptnr. Miller & Chevalier Chartered, Washington, Steptoe & Johnson LLP, Wash. Mem. ERISA adv. coun. US Dept. Labor, 1992-94; tax counsel fin. com. US Senate, 1983-86; adj. prof. LLM prog. Georgetown U. Contbr. Recipient Best Lawyers of Am., 2007. Mem. ABA (chmn. joint com. on employee benefits 1989-90), DC Bar (chmn. com. on employee benefits), Phi Beta Kappa, spkr. in feilds. Office: Steptoe & Johnson 1330 Connecticut Ave NW Washington DC 20036-1704 Office Phone: 202-429-6449. Office Fax: 202-429-3902. E-mail: amoran@steptoe.com. *

MORAN, BARBARA BURNS, librarian, educator; b. Columbus, Miss., July 8, 1944; d. Robert Theron and Joan (Brown) Burns; m. Joseph J. Moran, Sept. 4, 1965; children: Joseph Michael, Brian Matthew. AB, Mount Holyoke Coll., S. Hadley, Mass., 1966; MLS, Emory U., Atlanta, 1973; PhD, SUNY, Buffalo, 1982. Head libr. The Park Sch. of Buffalo, Snyder, NY, 1974-78; prof. Sch. Info. and Libr. Sci. U. N.C., Chapel Hill, 1981—, asst. dean, 1987-90, dean, 1990-98, prof. and dir. internat. programs, 1999—. Bd. govs. U. N.C. Press, 1998—; Fulbright sr. specialist Charles U., Prague, 2006; participant various seminars; evaluator various edn. progs.; cons. in field. Author: (book) Academic Libraries, 1984; author: (with Robert D. Stueart) Library Information Center Management, 2007; author: Continuity and Change: The Integration of Oxford University's Libraries, 2005; contbr. articles to profl. jours., chapters to books; mem. editl. bd.: Jour. Acad. Librarianship, 1992—94, Coll. and Rsch. Librs., 1996—2002, Jour. Edn. Info. and Libr. Sci., 2001—06. Mem. Chapel Hill Public Libr. Bd., 2004—. Grantee Univ. Rsch. Coun., 1983, 1989, Coun. Libr. Resources, 1985, ALISE/H.W. Wilson Scholar, State Acad. Culture, St. Petersburg, Russia, 1996, IMLS, 2004; others, Fulbright sr. specialist, Charles U., Prague, 2006. Mem.: ALA, N.C. Libr. Assn., Assn. Libr. And Info. Sci. Edn., Soc. for History of Authorship, Reading, and Publishing, Popular Culture Assn., Beta Phi Mu. Home: 1307 Leclair St Chapel Hill NC 27517-3034 Office: Univ NC Sch Info & Libr Sci Chapel Hill NC 27599-0001 Office Phone: 919-962-8067. Business E-Mail: moran@ils.unc.edu.

MORAN, CHARLES A., security firm executive, educator; b. Chgo., Feb. 7, 1943; s. Charles W. and Rose B. M.; m. Donna L. Orbach, Sept. 3, 1967; children: Scott Alan, Erin Lizabeth. AB, Princeton U., 1964; JD, U. Mich., 1967; postgrad. advanced mgmt., Harvard U., 1982. CFP CFP Bd. Stds., 1996, cert. employee benefit specialist Internat. Found. and Wharton Sch. U Pa., 2003. With Chase Manhattan Bank, NYC, 1967-70; pension trust officer, adminstrv. officer, officer in charge new bus. devel., pension div. Mfrs. Hanover Trust Co., NYC, 1970-87, sr. v.p., officer-in-charge employee benefit trust div., 1979-80; chmn. bd., pres., CEO, MH/Edie Investment Counsel (formerly Lionel D. Edie & Co.), NYC, 1980-82, officer-in-charge corp. trust div., 1982-83, officer in charge-global securities group, 1983-87; pres. Govt. Securities Clearing Corp., NYC, 1987-96, Strategic Fin. Adv., Montclair, NJ, 1996—; asst. prof., faculty fellow, faculty senate Coll. of NJ, Trenton, 1996—99; prof. Harvard U., Cambridge, Mass., 1997—; asst. prof., residential coll. adv. bd. Bucknell U., 1999—2003; prof. dir. fin. planning program SUNY, Cobleskill, 2003—; dir. Ctr. for Collaborative Sustainability NYU, 2006—. Chmn. bd. dirs. Inform, Inc.; cons. Urban Vol. Cons. Group, Inc.; adv. coun. US Dept. Labor; adv. bd. BNA Pension Reporter; mem. Employees Retirement Income Security Act of 1974 Roundtable; industry adv. com. Future Electronic Funds Payments Svcs. Fed. Res.; cons. Cmty. Ptnrs., Harvard Bus. Sch. Club NY; fin. planning assn., bd. dir., chair, govt. relations com., chair ethics com.; lectr. in field. Adv. bd. mem., Jour. Fin. Planning; contbr. articles to profl. jours. Mem. Am. Inst. Banking, Am. Employee Benefits Inst. (treas. 1976-79), NY State Bankers Assn. (employees trust com.), Assn. Pvt. Pension and Welfare Plans (dir., mem. exec. com.), ERISA Industry Com. (pres., dir., mem. exec. com., treas.), Am. Bankers Assn. (chmn. employee benefit trust com. 1977-82), Internat. Found. Pension and Welfare Plans, Bank Adminstrn. Inst. (mem. tech. commn.), NY C. of C. (task force on pub. pensions), Fin. Planning Assn. (dir., chmn. govt. rels. com., chmn. ethics com.), The Inst. of Cert. Fin. Planners (bd. dirs., com. on career devel.), NJ Soc. Inst. Cert. Fin. Planners (bd. dirs., sec., treas.), World Future Soc., Internat. Soc. Cert. Employee Benefit Specialists, Am. Acad. Mgmt., Am. Soc. Fin. Svcs. Profls., Strategic Mgmt. Soc., Internat. Soc. Cert. Employee Benefit Specialist, Princeton Club, Harvard Bus. Sch. Club NY-Cmty. Ptnrs. (cons.).

MORAN, CHRISTIAN J., federal official; b. Milford, Conn. m. Megan Moran; 2 children. Grad. with honors, Coll. of the Holy Cross, Worcester, Mass., U. Conn. Sch. Law. Law clk. Conn. Superior Ct.; law clk. to Judge Edward J. Damich US Ct. Fed. Claims, spl. master Washington, 2006—; assoc. Spinella & Jaffe, P.C., Hartford, Conn.; trial atty. comml. litig. br. US Dept. Justice Civil Divsn. Full-time vol. house parent Boys Hope. Office: Office of Spl Masters US Ct Fed Claims 717 Madison Pl NW Washington DC 20005 *

MORAN, CHRISTOPHER JOHN, radiologist, educator; b. Detroit, Apr. 2, 1948; s. Frank William and Susan T. Moran; m. Eleanor M. Maldeon, Sept. 5, 1969; children: Christopher John Jr., William Joseph, Mary Catherine. BS, U. Notre Dame, South Bend, Ind., 1970; MD, St. Louis U., 1974. Diplomate Am. Bd. Radiology in diagnostic radiology, 1978, cert. neuroradiology Am. Bd. Radiology, 95. Prof. radiology, neurol. surgery Washington U., St. Louis, 2003—. Mem. sci. adv. bd. Stereotaxis Inc., St. Louis, 1999—. Assoc. editor: Radiology, 2002—04, cons. to editor:, 2005—06. Bd. dirs. Injured Marine Semper Fi Fund, 2005—. Fellow: Am. Coll. Radiology; mem.: Am. Soc. Interventional and Therapeutic Neuroradiology (sr.), Am. Soc. Neuroradiology (sr.). Achievements include patents in field. Home: 12559 Amersham Ct Saint Louis MO 63141 Office: Washington U 510 S Kingshighway Saint Louis MO 63110 Office Phone: 314-362-5949.

MORAN, EILEEN A., utilities executive; BSBA, Seton Hall U., South Orange, NJ; M in Econs., D in Econs., Fordham U., NY; grad. Mgmt. Devel. Program, Harvard Grad. Sch. Bus. Adminstrn. With Pub. Svc. Electric. & Gas Co., 1977, various fin. and investment positions including asst. treas.; v.p. investments PSEG Resources, 1986—90, pres., 1990—, Enterprise Group Devel. Corp., 1997—; mem. exec. officers group Pub. Svc. Enterprise Group Inc., 1997—. Bd. mem. Duff & Phelps Utility and Corp. Bond Trust, Duff & Phelps Utilities Tax Free Income Fund, Phoenix Duff & Phelps Instnl. Mut. Funds. Mem. adv. bd. Benedictine Acad. Office: PSEG PO Box 570 Newark NJ 07101 Office Phone: 973-430-7000. *

MORAN, JAMES BYRON, federal judge; b. Evanston, Ill., June 20, 1930; s. James Edward and Kathryn (Horton) M.; m. Janet Remen; children: John, Jennifer, Sarah, Polly; stepchildren: Katie, Cynthia, Laura, Michael, Susan, Carol, Peggy, Tom, Lee. AB, U. Mich., 1952; LLB magna cum laude, Harvard U., 1957. Bar: Ill. 1958. Law clk. to judge U.S. Ct. of Appeals (2d cir.), 1957-58; assoc. Bell, Boyd, Lloyd, Haddad & Burns, Chgo, 1958-66, ptnr., 1966-79; judge U.S. Dist. Ct. (no. dist.) Ill., Chgo., 1979—. Dir. Com. on Ill. Govt., 1960-78, chmn., 1968-70; vice chmn., sec. Ill. Narcotic Drug Adv. Coun., 1967-74; dir. Gateway Found., 1969—; mem. Ill. Ho. of Reps., 1965-67; mem. Evanston City Council, 1971-75. Served with AUS, 1952-54. Mem. Chgo. Bar Assn., Chgo. Council Lawyers, Lawyers Club, Phi Beta Kappa. Home: 117 Kedzie St Evanston IL 60202-2509 Office: US Dist Ct 219 S Dearborn St Chambers 1846 Chicago IL 60604-1800 Home Phone: 847-475-3422; Office Phone: 312-435-5572. Personal E-mail: jbm117@aol.com.

MORAN, JAMES JOSEPH, JR., insurance company executive; s. James J. and Marilyn A. (Sullivan) M.; m. Mary Therese Stevens, Oct. 6, 1979; children: Sean M., James E., Matthew S. AB cum laude, Boston Coll., 1975, JD, 1978. Bar: Mass. 1978, U.S. Ct. Appeals (1st cir.) 1979, U.S. Dist Ct. Mass. 1979, U.S. Tax Ct. 1979, U.S. Supreme Ct. 1982; CPCU; Assoc. in reins. Assoc. Haussermann, Davison & Shattuck, Boston, 1978-84, Morrison, Mahoney & Miller, Boston, 1984—87, ptnr., 1988—98; pres. Eastern Casualty Ins. Co., Marlborough, Mass., 1998—2001; sr. v.p, sec., gen. counsel Quincy (Mass.) Mutual Fire Ins. Co., 2001—. V.p., gen. counsel Ind. Property-Casualty Insurers Mass. Inc., 1991-98; bd. dirs. R.I. Insurers Insolvency Fund, 2003-06; bd. dirs. Mass. Insurers Insolvency Fund, 2004—; counsel Mass. Assn. Ins. Agts., 1985-96; ins. broker, Mass.; New Eng. regional regulatory counsel Alliance Am. Insurers, 1994-98; trustee New Eng. Coll. Fin., 1998-2000. Bd. dirs. (gubernatorial appointee) Mass. Pollution Liability Reinsurance Corp., 1988-90. Recipient Econ. Leadership award Orgn. New Equality, 1997. Mem. Internat. Assn. Def. Coun., CPCU Soc. (pres. Boston chpt. 1993-94), Fedn. Ins. Corp. Coun., Ins. Libr. Assn. Boston (trustee 1983-2004, pres. 1989-90), Liquor Liability Joint Underwriting Assn. Roman Catholic. Home: 15 Bramel Cir Walpole MA 02081-2043 Office: Quincy Mutual Fire Ins Co 57 Washington St Quincy MA 02169-9155

MORAN, JAMES MICHAEL, JR., astronomer, educator; b. Plainfield, NJ, Jan. 3, 1943; s. James Michael and Martha (Algermissen) M.; m. Barbara Putney Smith, Nov. 30, 1974; children: Susan Harrison, Michael Putney. BS, U. Notre Dame, 1963; SM, MIT, 1965, PhD, 1968. Mem. staff MIT Lincoln Lab., Lexington, 1968-70; sr. radio astronomer Smithsonian Astrophys. Obs., Cambridge, Mass., 1970—; prof. practice of astronomy Harvard U., Cambridge, 1979-89, Donald H. Menzel prof. astrophysics, 2001—, chmn. astronomy dept., 2006—; assoc. dir. Harvard-Smithsonian Ctr. Astrophysics, Cambridge, 1987-92, dir. Submillimeter Array Project, 1996—2005. Jansky lectr. Nat. Radio Astronomy Obs., 1996; trustee N.E. Radio Obs. Corp., Cambridge, 1983—. Contbr. numerous articles on radio astronomy to profl. publs. Co-recipient Rumford prize Am. Acad. Arts and Scis., 1971; recipient Sr. award Alexander von Humboldt Soc., 1993. Fellow AAAS, IEEE; mem. NAS, Am. Astron. Soc. (Pierce prize 1978), Explorers Club. Achievements include development of technique of very long baseline interferrometry; research in study of black holes. Home: 93 Anson Rd Concord MA 01742-5704 Office: Harvard-Smithsonian Center for Astrophysics 60 Garden St Cambridge MA 02138-1516 Office Phone: 617-495-7477. Business E-Mail: moran@cfa.harvard.edu.

MORAN, JEFFREY W., JR., county surrogate; b. Winfield Park, NJ, Dec. 23, 1946; m. Patricia Kennedy, 1969; children: Collenn, Tricia. BA, Alma White Coll., Newark State Coll., 1970, MA. Assemblyman dist. 9 N.J. State Assembly, 1986—2003; Ocean county surrogate, 2003—. Councilman Beachwood, N.J.; chmn. higher edn. & regulated profls. com. N.J. State Assembly, mcpl. govt. com., sr. citizens com., tourism com., N.J. Hist. Commn.; asst. dir. handicapped svcs. Toms River (N.J.) Sch. Planning bd. Beachwood City Coun.; mem. utilities authority Ocean County, N.J.; mem. Selective Svc. Bd.; trustee New Lisbon Devel. Ctr. Awarded Nat. Def. Medal. Mem. Beachwood Civic Improvement Assn., Taxpayers Assn., N.J. State Sch. Prins. Assn., Ocean County Sch. Prins. Assn. Office: PO Box 2191 Toms River NJ 08754-2191

MORAN, JERRY, congressman; b. Great Bend, Kans., May 29, 1954; m. Robba A. Moran; 2 children. BS, Kansas U., 1976, JD, 1981. Senator dist. 37 State of Kans., 1989—96, sen. majority leader, 1994—96; mem., asst. majority whip US Congress from 1st Kans. dist., 1997—, mem. agr., transp., infrastructure, vets. affairs coms., chmn. subcom. on gen. commodities; chmn. Rural Health Care Coalition. Republican. Office: US House Reps 1519 Longworth House Office Bldg Washington DC 20515-1601 Office Phone: 202-225-2715. Office Fax: 202-225-5124. *

MORAN, JIM (JAMES PATRICK MORAN JR.), congressman, stock broker; b. Buffalo, May 16, 1945; s. James Patrick and Dorothy (Dwyer) Moran; m. Mary Craig, Dec. 27, 1967 (div. 1974); children: Jimmy, Mary; m. Mary Howard; children: Michael, Patrick, Dorothy. BA in Econs., Coll. Holy Cross, Worcester, Mass., 1967; postgraduate student, CUNY, 1967-68; MPA, U. Pitts., 1970. Comptr., budget analyst US Dept. Health, Edn. and Welfare, Washington, 1968—74; budget and fiscal policy specialist Congl. Rsch. Svc. Libr. Congress, Washington, 1974-76; sr. staff mem. appropriations com. US Senate, Washington, 1976-79; investment broker A.G. Edwards & Sons, Alexandria, Va., 1979; mem. City Coun., Alexandria, Va., 1979—82; vice mayor Alexandria, Va., 1982-84; mayor, 1985—90; mem. US Congress from 8th Va. dist., 1991—, mem. appropriations com. Chmn. No. Va. Transp. Bd., 1988, United Way, 1977-79; vice chmn. Mental Health Retard and Substance Abuse Bd., 1976-78, vice chmn. D.E.O., 1976-78; dir. Met. Area Coun. Govts., dir. No. Va. Transp. Commn., 1985. Recipient Outstanding Citizenship award, YMCA, 1983. Mem. C. of C. (dir. 1985-86). Democrat. Roman Catholic. Office: US House Reps 2239 Rayburn House Office Bldg Washington DC 20515-4608 Office Phone: 202-225-4376. *

MORAN, JOHN BERNARD, retired government official; b. Saginaw, Mich., Nov. 26, 1936; s. Leo Lewis and Marie Katherine (Langley) M.; m. Diann Marie Markey, May 20, 1963 (div.); m. Barbara Jane Livingston, Aug. 18, 1978; children— Leslie Marie, Leanne Rene, Jeffrey John BS in Metall. Engring., Ill. Inst. Tech., 1959. Sr. automotive specialist Dow Chem. Co., Midland, Mich., 1962-71; program dir. research EPA, Research Triangle Park, N.C., 1971-75, dir. monitoring tech. div. Washington, 1975-76; dir. div. safety research Nat. Inst. for Occupational Safety and Health, Ctrs. for Disease Control, USPHS, HHS, Morgantown, W.Va., 1976-77, 83-88; dir. research and devel. safety products div. Am. Optical Corp., Southbridge, Mass., 1977-80; v.p., dir. ops. Geomet, Inc., Rockville, Md., 1980-83; program dir. Hartford Engring. Tech., Inc., Windsor, Conn., 1988; assoc. dir. health and safety laborers Associated Gen. Contractors, 1988-89; dir. safety and health Laborers Health and Safety Fund, 1989-95; spl. asst. to dep. asst. sec. Worker Health and Safety U.S. Dept. Energy, Washington, 1995; dir. policy OSHA, U.S. Dept. Labor, Washington, 1996; expert cons. to asst. sec. OSHA, Washington, 1996—; expert cons. to CDC Chem./Bioagts., 1996-99, ret.; now cons. in field. Mem. Nat. Mine Health Rsch. Adv. Com., Atlanta, 1980-84; govt. del. ILO, Geneva, 1985; mem. Nat. Adv. Com. on Constrn. Safety and Health, 1985-88, 92-95, Bur. Labor Stats. Rsch., 1991-95, hazardous material transp. info. com. NAS, 1991-93, Hazardous Materials Control Rsch. Inst.; chmn. lead subcom. Bldg. Constrn. Trades Dept., 1991-95; adj. asst. prof. mech. engring. W.Va. U., 1985-88; vis. ext. prof. U. Conn., Storrs, 1988-90; mem. Fed. Facilities Environ. Restoration Com., constrn. com. A 10 Am. Nat. Stds. Inst.; co-chair EPA-Labor Superfund Task Force, 1990-95, 96—; mem. nat. lead task force HUD, 1993-95; cons., expert witness. Patentee; contbr. articles to profl. jours, chpts. to books. Mem. Task Force on Hazardous Materials, Rockville, Md., 1983. chmn. Nat. Tech. Workshops on Safety and Health Issues. Served to capt. USMC, 1959-65 Recipient Bronze medal for commendable service EPA, 1974, Commitment to Life award Nat. Safe Workplace Inst., 1988. Mem. Internat. Soc. Respiratory Protection (pres. 1985-87, bd. dirs. 1987-89), Am. Conf. Govtl. Indsl. Hygienists. Roman Catholic. Home: 107 Galemist Ct Brunswick GA 31523-7143

MORAN, JOHN FRANCIS, cardiologist; b. Chgo., Sept. 5, 1938; MD, Loyola U., Stritch Sch. Medicine, 1964. Cert. cardio. disease 1973. Office: Loyola U Med Ctr 2160 S 1st Ave Maywood IL 60153

MORAN, JON S., humanities educator; b. Rock Island, Ill., Nov. 11, 1941; s. John P. and Betty L. Moran; m. Sonia Spargnapani, May 31, 1965; children: Ian M., McKenna Bellamy, Tecia Guista. BS in Philosophy, St. Louis U., 1963; PhD in Philosophy, Tulane U., New Orleans, 1972. Asst. prof. St. Ambrose Coll., Davenport, Iowa, 1968—73; prof. Mo. State U., Springfield, 1973—. Head dept. philosophy Mo. State U., 1991—2003. Contbr. articles to profl. jours. Bd. dirs. Assn. Retarded Citizens Mo., Jefferson City, 1980—85, pres., 1984—85. Avocation: running. Office: Mo State Univ Philosophy Dept 901 S National Springfield MO 65804 Office Phone: 417-836-5650. Business E-Mail: jonmoran@missouristate.edu.

MORAN, KIMBERLY DIANNE, secondary school educator, artist; b. Kingsport, Tenn., Apr. 3, 1959; d. Talmadge Atlee and Alma Irene Archer; m. M. G. Moran, May 26, 1990; 1 child, Nathaniel T.; 1 child, Jamie C. BS, East Tenn. State U., 1981. Bank teller First Atlanta Bank, 1984—87; art tchr. Sullivan County Schs., Kingsport, Tenn., 1987—89, Crestview HS, Fla., 1989—95, W.C. Pryor Mid. Sch., Fort Walton Beach, Fla., 1995—2006, Fort Walton Beach HS, 2006—. Tchr. adult and children Sunday Sch.; art coord. Okaloosa Dist. Art Show. Named Tchr. of Yr., Pryor Middle Sch., 1999—2000. Mem.: Okaloosa County Edn. Assn., Nat. Edn. Assn., Nat. Art Edn. Assn. Republican. Presbyn. Avocations: reading, walking, sewing, board games, painting, drawing, working with clay. Home: 210 Baker Ave Fort Walton Beach FL 32548-4318 Office: Fort Walton Beach HS 400 Hollywood Blvd Fort Walton Beach FL 32548

MORAN, MARK J., air transportation executive; married; 4 children. B in Engring., Marquette U., Milw., 1979. Registered profl. engr. Design engr. Boeing Co., 1979; with Piedmont Airlines; dir. engring. US Airways; with Continental Airlines, Inc., Houston, 1994—, sr. v.p. tech. ops. and purchasing, exec. v.p. ops., 2004—. Office: Continental Airlines Inc PO Box 4607 Houston TX 77210 *

MORAN, MARTIN JOSEPH, fundraising company executive; b. Bklyn., Nov. 3, 1930; s. Dominick and Mary (Lydon) Moran; m. Mary Therese Schofield, June 5, 1954; children: Martin Joseph, John P., Maureen M., Thomas S., Robert P., William M., Maria M. BA, St. John's U., 1952. Profl. fundraising cons., 1956—; founder Martin J. Moran Co., Inc., NYC, 1964, pres., 1964—74, chmn. bd., 1974—. Mem. Am. Revolution Bicentennial Commn., Oyster Bay, NY, Massapequa Park Ethics Commn., 1969—72; trustee Notre Dame Coll., SI, NY, 1969—72, La Salle Acad., NYC, 1971—87; mem. pres.'s coun. Cath. U. P.R., Ponce, 1966—71; mem. Cardinal's Com. for Edn., NYC, 1970—79, Cardinal's Com. for Laity Archdiocese NY, 1979—98, Massapequa Park (NY) Bd. Zoning Appeals, 1972—84, chmn., 1978—84; bd. councilors, sec., treas. Equestrian Order Holy Sepulchre of Jerusalem, 1990—, sec.-treas., 1990—93, pres., 1993—. Served as aviator USNR, 1952—56. Decorated knight Grand Cross Order Holy Sepulchre, Pope Paul VI, Knight of Malta Pope Paul VI, papal Knight of Order of St. Gregory the Gt. Pope John Paul II, knight comdr.; recipient Pietas medal, St. John's U., NY, 1988. Mem.: Am. Assn. Fundraising Counsel (bd. dirs. 1970—75), Navy Hist. Assn., Navy League, Friendly Sons of St. Patrick, Nassau County Hist. Soc., St. John's U. Alumni Assn. (pres. 1987—94), Old Port Yacht Club, Lost Tree Club (N. Palm Beach, Fla.), KC. Home: 1300 Lakeshore Dr Massapequa Park NY 11762-1764 Office: Martin J Moran Company 11 Penn Plz Fl 5 New York NY 10001-2003 Personal E-mail: mjmmarty@aol.com.

MORAN, MARY (MOLLY) HURLEY, English language educator; b. Boston, May 1, 1947; d. William Thomas and Mary Cecilia (Lynch) Hurley; m. Michael George Moran, Aug. 14, 1977; 1 child, Alison Emily. BA, Brown U., 1969; MA, U. N.Mex., 1975, PhD, 1980. Asst. prof. English Clemson (S.C.) U., 1982-86; tech. writer, editor Analysis & Technology, Middletown, R.I., 1987-88; instr. English U. Ga., Athens, 1988-91, from asst. prof. to prof. devel. English, 1991—2006, prof. to prof. devel. English, 2006—. Author: Margaret Drabble: Existing Within Structures, 1983, Penelope Lively, 1993, Finding Susan, 2003; contbr. articles to profl. jours. Mem. NCTE. Home: 193 Mell St Athens GA 30605-1311 Office Phone: 706-542-0469. Business E-Mail: mhmoran@uga.edu.

MORAN, MITCH, lawyer; b. Houston; BA, Northwestern U.; JD, Miss. Coll., 1996. Farmer, La.; atty. Tribal Chief Phillip Martin Miss. Band of Choctaw Indians, 1996; solo practice Moran Law Firm, Carthage, Miss., 1998—. Achievements include defense atty. for Edgar Ray Killen, convicted of the 1964 manslaughter of 3 civil rights workers, Andrew Goodman, James Chaney and Michael Schwerner in June 2005. Office: Moran Law Firm 119 N Pearl St Carthage MS 39051 Office Phone: 601-298-2000.

MORAN, NANCY A., ecologist, educator; b. Dallas, Dec. 21, 1954; BA in biology, U. Tex., 1976; MS in zoology, U. Mich., 1978, PhD in zoology, 1982. Asst. prof. entomology U. Ariz., 1986—91, assoc. prof. ecology and evolutionary biology, 1991—96, prof. ecology and evolutionary biology, 1996—2001, regent's prof. ecology and evolutionary biology, 2001—. NSF postdoctoral fellow, No. Ariz. U., 1984-1986, NAS postdoctoral fellow, Inst. Entomology, Czech, 1984, MacArthur Fellow, John D. and Catherine T. MacArthur Found., 1997. Mem. NAS, Soc. Study Evolution (pres. 2002), Am. Naturalists Soc. (v.p. 2001, Pres. award, 1988); fellow Am. Acad. Arts & Sciences Office: U Ariz Dept Ecology and Evolutionary Biology PO Box 210088 Biosciences W 310 1041 E Lowell St Tucson AZ 85721 Office Phone: 520-621-3581. Office Fax: 520-621-9190. E-mail: nmoran@email.arizona.edu.

MORAN, PAUL JAMES, journalist, columnist; b. Buffalo, July 20, 1947; s. Paul James and Frances (Sciortino) M.; m. Kim Maldiner, Mar. 17, 1975 (div. July 1979); m. Colette Stass (div. Jan. 1997). Student, SUNY, Buffalo, 1965-67, Millard Fillmore Coll., 1971-73. Sports editor Tonawanda News, North Tonawanda, NY, 1972-75; writer/columnist Fort Lauderdale (Fla.) News/Sun Sentinel, 1975-85, N.Y. Newsday, Melville, 1985—. Cons. Green Country Racing Assn., Tulsa, 1983-85. Author: (with others) Crown Jewels of Thoroughbred Racing; contbr. articles to mags. and newspapers. Sgt. USAF, 1967-71. Recipient Eclipse award Thoroughbred Racing Assn., 1985, 90, Disting. Writing award Am. Soc. Newspaper Editors, 1990, Deadline Writing award Soc. Silurians, 1990, Deadline Reporting award L.I. Press Club, 1991, Disting. Sports Writing award N.Y. Newspaper Pubs. Assn., 1992, (with others) Journalism collection Best Newspaper Writing 1991, Media award L.I. Vet. Med. Assn., 1997, excellence in continuing feature Fla. Mag. Assn., 1999, Best of Manhattan award N.Y. Press, 2002. Mem. N.Y. Turf Writers' Assn. (pres. 1990-92, sec.-treas. 1992-94), Nat. Turf Writers' Assn. (bd. dirs. 1987-90). Republican. Avocations: photography, art collecting. Home: 40 Carnation Ave Floral Park NY 11001-1730 Office: Newsday 235 Pinelawn Rd Melville NY 11747-4250 Personal E-mail: pmoran1686@aol.com.

MORAN, PHILIP DAVID, lawyer; b. Lynn, Mass., June 3, 1937; s. J. Francis and Margaret M. (Shanahan) M.; m. Carole A. Regan, May 12, 1962; children: Maura F., Philip David. AB, Holy Cross Coll., 1958; EdM, Salem State Coll., 1961; JD, Suffolk U., 1968. Bar: Mass. 1968, US Dist. Ct. Mass. 1972, US Supreme Ct. 1988, US Ct. Appeals (1st cir.) 1993, US Ct. Appeals (fed. cir.) 2006. House counsel Viatron Computer Systems Corp., Burlington, Mass., 1968-71; ptnr. Kane & Moran, Lynn, Mass., 1972-78; pvt. practice law Salem, Mass., 1978—; propr. Law Offices of Philip D. Moran P.C., 1993—. Asst. dist. atty. Essex County (Mass.), 1974-78; mem. pres.'s coun. Holy Cross Coll., 1985—, Nat. Inst. Trial Advocacy U. Colo., 1973; gen. chmn. bicentenary com. Maynooth Coll., Boston, 1994-96. Contbg. author: Encyclopedia of Biomedical Policy, 1995. Bd. dirs. Nat. Right to Life Inc., 1977-83, 87—, treas., 1981-83; bd. dirs. Mass. Citizens for Life, 1973—, pres. 1979-80, chmn. 1991-93; chmn. Salem Con Con, 1982-89; active Salem Bd. Voter Registration, 2005; pastoral coun. Archdiocese Boston, 2006—; bd. dirs. Cath. Citizenship, 2004-, treas., 2004-. With US Army, 1960—66. Recipient Ignatius O'Connor Pro Life award, 1994, Gold medatl St. Patrick Maynooth Coll., Irelnd, 1996, Knight of Malta, 1997, Family, Faith and Freedom award Family Rsch. Coun., 1997, Citizenship award Mass. Family Inst., 1997, Leadership award, Nat. Rep. Cong. Com., 2003. Mem. Mass. Bar Assn., Salem Bar Assn., Lynn Bar Assn., Am. Trial Lawyers Assn., Nat. Acad. Elder Law Attys., Murray Inn of Ct., Pro Life Legal Def. Fund (pres. 1997), Hibernian Civil Rights Coalition (bd. dirs. 1997, pres. 1997), Irish Am. Partnership, Nat. Coalition of Pro Life Dems. (bd. dirs., treas. 1999-2001), Dem State Com., Catholic Alliance (bd. dirs., gen. coun. 1999-2001), Internat. Soc. Photographers. Roman Catholic. Avocations: swimming, reading, gardening, boating, photography. Home: 415 Lafayette St Salem MA 01970-5337 Office: 265 Essex St Salem MA 01970-3419 Office Phone: 978-745-6085. Personal E-mail: philipmoranesq@aol.com.

MORAN, RACHEL, law educator; b. Kansas City, Mo., June 27, 1956; d. Thomas Albert and Josephine (Portillo) Moran. AB, Stanford U., 1978; JD, Yale U., 1981. Bar: Calif. 1984. Assoc Heller, Ehrman, White & McAuliffe, San Francisco, 1982-83; prof. law U. Calif., Berkeley, 1984—, Robert D. and Leslie-Kay Raven prof. law, 1998—. Vis. prof. UCLA Sch. Law, 1988, 2002, Stanford (Calif.) U. Law Sch., 1989, NYU Sch. Law, 1996, U. Miami Sch. Law, 1997, U. Tex. Law Sch., 2000, Fordham Law Sch., 2005; chair Chicano/Latino Policy Project, 1993—96; dir. Inst. for Study Social Change, 2003—. Contbr. articles to profl. jours. Recipient Disting. Tchg. award, U. Calif. Mem.: ABA, Calif. Bar Assn., Am. Law Inst., Phi Beta Kappa. Democrat. Unitarian Universalist. Avocations: jogging, aerobics, reading, listening to music. Office: U Calif Sch Law Boalt Hall Berkeley CA 94720 Home Phone: 510-420-0992; Office Phone: 510-643-6351. Business E-Mail: moran@law.berkeley.edu.

MORAN, TERRY, news correspondent; BA, Lawrence U., 1982. Writer New Republic; reporter, asst. mng. editor Legal Times; corr., anchor Court TV, 1992—97; joined ABC News, 1997, corr. assigned to US Supreme Ct., 1998—99, chief White House corr. Washington, 1999—, anchor World News Tonight Sunday, 2004—, co-anchor Nightline, 2005—. Contbr. NY Times, Washington Post. Recipient Lucia R. Briggs Disting. Achievement Award, Lawrence U., 2003, Merriman Smith award, White House Corrs. Assn., 2006. Office: ABC News Nightline 1717 Desales St NW Washington DC 20036 Office Phone: 202-222-7700. Office Fax: 202-222-7686. E-mail: terry.moran@abc.com.

MORAN, THOMAS HARRY, retired academic administrator; b. Milw., Oct. 21, 1937; s. Harry Edward and Edna Agnes Moran; m. Barbara Ellen Saklad, June 10, 1969; children: David Thomas, Karen Ellen. BS, U. Wis., Madison, 1964, MA, 1972, PhD, 1974. Dir. capital budgeting Wis. Dept. Adminstrn., 1962-64; exec. dir. Wis. Higher Ednl. Aids Bd., 1964-69; spl. cons. tax policy Wis. Dept. Revenue, 1973-74; dep. dir. Wis. Manpower Coun., Office of Gov., 1974-76; v.p. bus. and fin., treas. U. Detroit, 1976-78; exec. assoc. v.p. health affairs U. So. Calif., LA, 1979-87, v.p. bus. affairs, 1988—2002, v.p. emeritus, 2002—. USN fellow, 1957-59, U.S. Office Edn. rsch. fellow, 1973. Mem. Am. Assn. Higher Edn., Phi Kappa Phi. Personal E-mail: moranthm@aol.com.

MORAN, THOMAS J., insurance company executive; BS in Math., Manhattan Coll.; JD (hon.), Nat. Univ. Ireland. Pension underwriter through exec. v.p. Mutual of America Life Ins. Co., NYC, 1975—90, pres., COO, 1992—94, pres., CEO, 1994—. Bd. dir. Life Ins. Coun. NY, Genovese Drug Stores. Bd. mem. Manhattan Coll., United Way NYC, Nat. Ctr. for Disability Services, Nat. Com. on American Fgn. Policy, Univ. Coll. Dublin Graduate Sch. Bus. Recipient Medal of Honor, Cavalry Hospital, Humanitarian Award, NYC Fire Dept., Concern Worldwide, Ellis Island Medal of Honor, Terence Cardinal Cooke award. Office: Mutual of America Life Ins Co 320 Park Ave New York NY 10022 Office Phone: 212-224-1600. Office Fax: 212-224-2539. *

MORAN, WENDI K, biology educator; d. Walter Paul and Karen Gay Wolfram; m. Gerald Raymond Moran, Jan. 27, 1997; 1 child, Matthew Tyler. BS in biology, Hardin-Simmons U., Abilene, Texas, 2002, MS in Environ. Mgmt., 2004. Adj. prof. and biology lab coord. Hardin-Simmons U., 2002—. Exec. dir., founder Conservation Tng. Rsch. Edn. Ctr., Abilene, 2005—. Spl. events com. chair PDBC Women's Ministry, Abilene, Tex., 2004—06; sec. U. Women, Abilene, 2004—06. Recipient Grad. Dean's Award of Excellence - Nominee, Hardin-Simmons U., 2004, Travel award, Tex. Acad. of Sci., 2004; Rsch. grant, 2005, Grad. Dean scholarship, Hardin-Simmons U., 2002—04. Mem.: Am. Soc. of Mammologists, Tex. Acad. of Sci. Bapt. Avocations: reading, outdoor recreation, wildlife photography. Personal E-mail: wkmoran@aol.com.

MORAN, WENDY JACQUELINE, music educator, musician; b. Chappaqua, NY, Jan. 16, 1952; d. Edward Albert and Gladys (Dildarian) Hamilton; m. Brian Vincent Moran, Aug. 5, 1979; children: Melissa Kathleen, Kevin William. Attended, U. N.C., Greensboro, 1970—72; MusB Edn., Westminster Choir Coll., Princeton, NJ, 1975; grad. student in Musicology, NYU, 1978—80. Cert. music specialist Pre-K-12 Dept. Edn. Mass., 2000, N.J., 1975. Music specialist Westminster Choir Coll. (Conservatory divsn.), Princeton, 1975; pvt. instrn. (voice/flute/recorder/eurhythmics) Holliston, Mass., 1975—; music specialist Montessori Children's Rm., Armonk, NY, 1975—83, various Montessori schs., music schs., pub. schs., pvt. schs., Md., Mass., and NY, 1983—89, Christian Family Montessori Sch., Holliston, 1989—2006, Hopkinton Pub. Schs., Mass., 1996—. Flute soloist in field, 1975—; soprano soloist in field, 1975—; student Kodaly Music Tchrs. Workshops, Princeton, 1975; participant/student Music Educator Workshops/Chamber Music Workshops:Dalcroze Sch. of Music/Mannes Coll. of Music, NYC, 1978—89; participant master class with Jean-Pierre Rampal, NYC, 1979, Montessori Music Teacher's Workshop Whitby Sch., Greenwich, Conn., 1980; flutist Southeastern Mass. Concert Band, Medway, Mass., 1990—; singer Berkshire Choral Inst., Sheffield, Mass., 1996—; profl. devel. mgr., exec. bd. New Eng. chpt. Am. Orff-Schulwerk Assn., Lexington, Mass., 1999—2003; singer Heritage Chorale, Framingham, 1999—, chorus rep. bd. dirs., 2003—; singer/flutist Composer's Conf.: Chamber Music Ctr. and Singer's Workshop, Wellesley, Mass., 2003—. Author (co-author): (guidebook) Curriculum Guide for Hopkinton, Mass. Dept. Music; singer: (concerts) choral concerts under the direction of Leonard Bernstein, Pierre Boulez, Antal Dorati, (concert) under Robert Shaw in Mostly Mozart Festival, Lincoln Ctr. Music specialist, volunteered classes in music to support funding for town playground Town of Annapolis, Md., 1988; membership chmn. Medway Newcomer's Club, Mass., 1988—89. Recipient numerous monetary awards given to Hopkinton Edn. Found. in name of Ms. Moran for fostering excellence in edn., Hopkinton, Mass., 1999 - 2005. Mem.: Gone with the Winds woodwind quintet, Cmty. Orch., Arundel Vocal Arts Soc. (Md.), Westchester Choral Soc., Somer's Chorale, Bach Choral Soc., Pleasantville Cantata Singers (N.Y.), Broadmoor Chamber Singers. Achievements include developing a system for music education based upon Kodaly/Orff/Dalcroze methods; researching and developing methods for ear-training and pitch understanding for young children; thirty years of studying and implementing creative approaches of music education based upon the Dalcroze, Kodaly, Orff methods of music learning. Avocations: yoga, swimming, cross-country skiing, hiking, dance. Home: 267 Norfolk St Holliston MA 01746 Office: Hopkinton Public Schools Haydn Rowe St Hopkinton MA 01748 Home Phone: 508-429-1949. Personal E-mail: wenmora@aol.com. Business E-Mail: wmoran@hopkinton.k12.ma.us.

MORANO, GERARD JOHN, marketing executive; b. Mount Vernon, NY, Oct. 23, 1944; s. Gerard Anthony and Pauline (Ungaro) M.; m. Allison Lenore Folz, June 28, 1975; 1 child, Steven Christopher. BS in Fin., CUNY, 1974; BA in Mktg., Pace U., Pleasantville, NY, 1981; MBA, Pace U., White Plains, NY, 1982. From fin. planner to mgr. sales promotion ITT Continental, Rye, NY, 1968—84; from dir. mktg. to sr. v.p. mktg. and comm. Quality Bakers Am., Greenwich, Conn., 1984—2000; exec. v.p. QBA, Advt., Inc., Greenwich, Conn., 1992—2000, Solutions Mktg. LLC, Darien, Conn., 2001—06; pres. Cygone Prodns., 2006—. Alumni mentor Pace U., 1988—; fundraiser Vietnam Vets. Meml. Com., Washington, 1980-82; bd. dirs. Vets. Bus. Network, 2001—. With U.S. Army, 1966-68, Vietnam. Decorated Bronze Star; recipient Conspicious Silver Svc. Star and Order of Merit, State of NY, 2001. Mem.: Promotional Mktg. Assn., Am. Film Inst., 199th Inf. Assn., Ellis Island Found., Vietnam Vets. Am., Wildlife Conservation Soc. Avocations: photography, videography. Personal E-mail: jmorano2000@aol.com.

MORANT, BRENDA WHITE, publishing executive, small business owner, investor; b. Balt., May 5, 1944; BS, U. Md., 1973; MPA, Cen. Mich. U., 1974. Founder, chief exec. officer Women's Econ. Enterprises, 1988—; publisher Networking Mag., 1990—; bus. devel. The BES Co., 1988—; owner Market Rsch. Cons., Atlanta, 1994—. Cons. U.S. Air Force, Oscoda, Mich., 1977, Greater Mt. Calvery Bapt. Ch., Jackson Miss., 1991—, Options & Opportunities Career Ctr., Greenville, N.C., 1991—. Inventor electro thermo engineered insulated refrigeration container system for heat sensitive products. Organizer Battered Women's Ctr., 1979, Juneteen Celebration in Miss., 1980, Commn. on Women, 1986, Industrial Energy Soc., 1984. With USMC, 1962-64. Named 1st Businesswoman on the front Cover of Miss. Official State Mag., 1987; recipient Innovation award U.S. Dept of Energy, 1985, Governor Miss., 1985. Mem.: NAFE, Alumni Assn. Ctrl. Mich. U. (pres. Atlanta chpt.), Assn. Female Vets. (bd.). Avocations: dance exercising, boating, travel, painting, reading. Office: BES Techs PO Box 162125 Atlanta GA 30321-2125

MORANT, RICARDO BERNARDINO, psychology professor; b. New Britain, Conn., Feb. 13, 1926; s. J. Ramon and Rosario (Ciscar) M.; m. G. Francisca Giner, Dec. 26, 1955; children— Ramon, Francisca, Dolores, Ricardo. AB, Harvard, 1948; postgrad., Wesleyan Coll., Middletown, Conn., 1948-49; MA, Clark U., 1950, PhD, 1952. From faculty to prof. Brandeis U., Waltham, Mass., 1952—91, Minnie and Harold L. Fierman prof. psychology, 1991—2005, prof. Volen Nat. Ctr. for Complex Sys., 1994—2005, prof. emeritus, 2005—. Prin. investigator NIMH, Spencer Found., Rothman Found. 1960—; spl. research space perception, body orientation. Bd. dirs. Coun. Pub. Schs., 1970-73; mem. steering com. Sensory Aid Eval. and Devel. Ctr., MIT, 1963-67; chmn. bd. trustees Hiatt Ednl. Programs, 1982-94. Served with USNR, 1946-48. Fellow APA; mem. Psychonomic Soc. Home: 35 Cliff Rd Wellesley MA 02481-3001 E-mail: morant@brandeis.edu.

MORARI, MANFRED, chemical engineer, educator; b. Graz, Austria, May 13, 1951; came to U.S., 1975; s. Manfred and Hilde M.; m. Marina Korchynsky, May 12, 1984. Diploma Chem. Engring., Eidgenoessische Technische Hochschule, Zurich, Switzerland, 1974; PhD in Chem. Engring., U. Minn., 1977; Dr h c, Babes Bolyai U., 2003. Asst. prof. U. Wis., Madison, 1977-81, assoc. prof., 1981-83; prof. chem. engring. Calif. Inst. Tech., Pasadena, 1983-94, McCollum-Corcoran prof., 1991-94, exec. officer, 1990-93, prof. control and dynamical sys., 1993-94; exec. officer, 1993-94; head automatic control lab. ETH. Gulf vis. prof. chem. engring. Carnegie Mellon U., 1987. Contbr. articles to profl. jours. Recipient D.P. Eckman award Am. Automatic Control Coun., 1980, J.R. Ragazzini award Am. Automatic Control Coun., 2007. Fellow: NAE, AIChE (A.P. Colburn award 1984, Profl. Progress award 1995, Computing in Chem. Engring. award 2002), IEEE (George S. Axelby Outstanding Paper award 1990, Control Sys. Field award 2005), Am. Soc. Engring. Edn. (Curtis W. McGraw rsch. award 1989), Am. Chem. Soc. Home: Laerchentobelstrasse 22 CH-8700 Kusnacht Switzerland Office: Automatic Control Lab ETH-Z ETL I 29 CH-8092 Zurich Switzerland Business E-Mail: morari@control.ee.ethz.ch.

MORATH, MAX EDWARD, entertainer, composer, writer; b. Colorado Springs, Colo., Oct. 1, 1926; s. Frederic Palmer and Gladys Hester Nancy (Ramsell) M.; m. Norma Loy Tackitt, Oct. 23, 1953 (div. 1992); children: Kathryn, Christine, Frederic; m. Diane Fay Skomars, May 24, 1993. BA in English, Colo. Coll., 1948; postgrad., Stanford NBC-Radio-TV Inst., Palo Alto, Calif., 1951; MA in Am. Studies, Columbia U., 1996. Touring nationally in concerts and theater, 1961-2005; writer, host (radio series WFMT Radio) Ragtime to the Max, 2006; recs. on Epic, RCA, Vanguard, SoloArt, Omega, Premier; author: The Road to Ragtime, 1999, The NPR Curious Listener's Guide to Popular Standards, 2002; playwright, prodr., composer (musical play) Trust Everybody...But Cut the Cards, 2003. Mem. Broadcast Music, Inc. Home and Office: 463 Hartley Place Duluth MN 55803 Office Phone: 218-724-5886. Personal E-mail: rathmo@gmail.com.

MORAWETZ, CATHLEEN SYNGE, mathematician; b. Toronto, Ont., Can., May 5, 1923; arrived in U.S., 1945, naturalized, 1950; d. John Lighton and Elizabeth Eleanor Mabel (Allen) Synge; m. Herbert Morawetz, Oct. 28, 1945; children: Pegeen Morawetz Rubinstein, John Synge, Lida Morawetz Jeck, Nancy. BA, U. Toronto, 1945; SM, MIT, 1946; PhD, NYU, 1951; degree (hon.), Ea. Mich. U., 1980, Smith Coll., 1982, Brown U., 1982, Princeton U., 1986, Duke U., 1988, N.J. Inst. Tech., 1988, U. Waterloo, 1993, U. Dublin, 1996, U. Toronto, 1996. Research assoc. Courant Inst., NYU, 1952—57, asst. prof. math., 1957—60, assoc. prof., 1960—65, prof., 1965—, assoc. dir., 1978—84, dir., 1984—88. Chmn. bd. Sch. Theoretical Physics Dublin Inst. for Advanced Studies, 1995—2000. Contbr. articles to profl. jours. Trustee Princeton U., 1973—78, Sloan Found., 1980—94. Recipient Nat. medal of Sci., NSF, 1998; fellow Guggenheim, 1967, 1979; grantee Office of Naval Rsch., 1975—90. Fellow: AAAS, Royal Soc. Can.; mem.: NAS, London Math. Soc., Royal Irish Acad., Soc. Indsl. and Applied Math., Am. Philos. Soc., Am. Acad. Arts and Scis., Am. Math. Soc. (term trustee 1975—85, pres. 1995—97, George David Birkhoff prize in Applied Math. (awarded jointly by Am. Math. Soc. and Soc. for Indsl. and Applied Math.) 2006, Steele prize 2004). Achievements include research in applications of partial differential equations, especially transonic flow and scattering theory. Office: CIMS 251 Mercer St New York NY 10012-1110 Office Phone: 212-998-3297. Business E-Mail: morawetz@cims.nyu.edu.

MORD, IRVING CONRAD, II, lawyer; b. Mar. 22, 1950; s. Irving Conrad and Lillie Viva (Chapman) M.; m. Julia Ann Russell, Aug. 22, 1970 (div. Apr. 1980); children: Russell Conrad, Emily Ann; m. Kay E. McDaniel, Aug. 31, 1985; children: Kurt August, Clayton Troy. BS, Miss. State U., 1972; JD, U. Miss., 1974. Bar: Miss. 1974, U.S. Dist. Ct. (no. dist.) Miss. 1974, U.S. Dist. Ct. (so. dist.) Miss. 1984. Counsel to bd. suprs. Noxubee County, Miss., 1976-80, Walthall County, Miss., 1980—, Bd. Edn., Walthall County, 1982—. County pros. atty. Noxubee County, Macon, Miss., 1974—80, Walthall County, Tylertown, Miss., 1982—88, Tylertown, 1991—96. Bd. dirs. East Miss. Coun., Meridian, 1978-80, Trustmark Nat. Bank, Tylertown, 1986—, chmn., 2002-; v.p. Macon coun. Boy Scouts Am., 1978, mem. coun., 1979; county crusade chmn. Am. Cancer Soc., Macon, 1976-78, county pres., 1979; chmn. fund dr. fine arts complex Miss. State U., Macon, 1979; Walthall County family master, 1996—, Walthall County Youth referee, 1996—; mem. Local Workforce Investment Bd., 2000—. Recipient Youth Leadership award Miss. Econ. Coun., 1976. Mem. Miss. Assn. Bd. Attys. (v.p. 1985, pres. 1986), Miss. Assn. Sch. Bd. Attys., Miss. State Bar, Am. Judicature Soc. (Torts award 1972), Nat. Fed. Ind. Bus., Miss. State U. Alumni Assn., Walthall County

C. of C., Phi Kappa Tau (bd. govs. 1976-80, grad. coun. 1972—, pres. grad. coun. 1977-80, pres. house corp. 1977-80, Alumnus of Yr. Alpha Chi chpt. 1979), Rotary (sec.-treas. 1977, v.p. 1978, pres. Macon 1979, pres. Tylertown club 1986-87), Phi Delta Phi. Office: 729 Beulah Ave Tylertown MS 39667-2709 Office Phone: 601-876-2611. E-mail: icmord@bellsouth.net.

MORDEN, ANNETTE SONJA KNUDSON, retired education educator; b. Phoenix, Mar. 17, 1940; d. Maynard Wold and Mertie Lucille Knudson; m. Robert Dean Morden, Aug. 5, 1962; children: Kristina, Shauna. BA, U. No. Iowa, 1962, MA in edn., 1966. Math tchr. Rockford Roosevelt, Ill., 1962—65; benthic biologist U. Wis., 1972, 1975, sr. lectr. and dir. math tutoring lab, 1982—2005. Unit leader and budget, audit and fin. com. League of Women Voters, 1971—73; brownie and girl scout leader Girl Scouts Am., 1963—64, 1977—82; bd. dirs. and exec. bd. YMCA, 1976—81; mem. founding com. and exec. bd. Habitat for Humanity, 1991—94. Mem.: Assn. U. Wis. Profls. Lutheran. Avocations: reading, travel, snorkeling. Home: 1422 N 21st St Superior WI 54880

MORDEN, JOHN REID, security-business intelligence consultant; b. Hamilton, Ont., Canada, June 17, 1941; s. Warren Wilbert and Isabelle Gemmell (Reid) M.; m. Margaret Keens, June 27, 1964; children: Michael, Geoffrey. BA, Dalhousie U., 1962; postgrad., Dalhousie Law Sch., 1962-63; LLD (hon.), Dalhousie U., 2003. With Can. Dept. External Affairs, various worldwide cities, 1963-84; asst. dep. min. native claims Dept. Indian & Northern Devel., Canada, 1984-85; trade and econ. policy Can. Dept. External Affairs, 1985-86; asst. sec. to cabinet Fgn. and Def. Affairs, Can., 1986-87; dir. Can. Security Intelligence Svc., 1987-91; dep. min. fgn. affairs Govt. Can., 1991-94; pres, CEO, Atomic Energy of Can., Ltd., Ottawa, Ont., Canada, 1994-98; mng. dir. Kroll Asocs. Can., Toronto, 1999-2000; chmn. KPMG Corp. Intelligence Inc., Toronto, 2000—02; pres. RM & A, Inc., 2002—; exec. dir. Independent Inquiry UN Iraq Oil for Food Programme, 2004—06. Mem. Can. com. Coun. Security and Cooperation in Asia and Pacific; security advisor CARE Can.; adv. bd. Homeland Security Alliance, 2003—05. Chair bd. govs. Trent U.; mem. internat. adv. coun. York U., 1993—2006; chair Coun. Chairs Ont. Univs., 2004—06; bd. dirs. Nat. Assn. Univ. Bd. Chairs, 2007—. Decorated Order of Can.; Order of So. Cross (Brazil); recipient Ian L. Macrae award, 1998. Fellow: Can. Def. and Fgn. Affairs Inst.; mem.: Nat. Assn. U. Bd. Chmns. (bd. dirs.), Nat. Club, Toronto Hunt Club. Avocations: photography, music, ballet, reading. Office Phone: 416-486-3520. Business E-Mail: reidmorden@rogers.com.

MORDEN, ROBERT DEAN, biology professor; b. Jefferson, Iowa, Mar. 16, 1939; s. Bert E. and Ruth Agnus Morden; m. Annette Sonja Knudson, Aug. 5, 1962; children: Kristina Kay, Shauna Suzanne. BA, U. Northern Iowa, Cedar Falls, 1962, MA, 1966; PhD, U. Ill., Champaign, 1971. Lic. med. technologist AMA, 1977. Chmn. dept. sci. Dysart HS, Iowa, 1962; sci. tchr. Auburn HS, Rockford, Ill., 1962—65; fellow U. Northern Iowa, 1965—66, U. Ill. Nat. Inst. Health, Urbana, 1966—71; faculty U. Wis., Superior, 1971—, chmn. dept. biology and med. tech., 1989—92. Mem. clin. faculty St. Lukes Hosp., Duluth, Minn., 1977—83. Contbr. articles to profl. jours. Recipient Tchg. Excellence award, Regents of Wis., 1993—94, Chancellor's Exemplary Advising award, 1996—97, 1997—98, Faculty Achievement award, Burlington Northern Found., 1996—97. Business E-Mail: rmorden@uwsuper.edu.

MORDINO, JOSEPH T., lawyer; b. Buffalo, Feb. 27, 1971; BA, St. Lawrence University, 1992; JD, U. Cin., 1995. Bar: Ohio 1995, US Dist. Ct. Southern Dist. Ohio 1995, Ky. 2002, US Dist. Ct. Northern Dist. Ohio 2006, US Ct. of Appeals Sixth Cir. Ptnr. Faulkner & Tepe LLP, Cin. Named one of Ohio's Rising Stars, Super Lawyers, 2006. Mem.: Ky. Acad. Trial Attorneys, Def. Rsch. Inst., Ohio Assn. Civil Trial Attorneys, Ky. Bar Assn., Ohio State Bar Assn., Cin. Bar Assn., Phi Beta Kappa. Office: Faulkner & Tepe LLP 2200 Fourth and Vine Tower 1 W Fourth St Cincinnati OH 45202-3606 Office Phone: 513-421-7500. Office Fax: 513-421-7502.

MORDY, JAMES CALVIN, retired lawyer; b. Ashland, Kans., Jan. 3, 1927; s. Thomas Robson and Ruth (Floyd) M.; m. Marjory Ellen Nelson, Nov. 17, 1951; children: Jean Claire Mordy Jongeling, Rebecca Jane Mordy King, James Nelson. BA in Chemistry, U. Kans., 1947; JD, U. Mich., 1950; postgrad., George Washington U., 1952—53. Bar: Kans. 1950, Mo. 1950, cert.: Am. Bankruptcy Bd. (in bus. bankruptcy law). Assoc., Morrison, Hecker, Buck, Cozad & Rogers, Kansas City, Mo., 1950—59; ptnr. Morrison & Hecker LLP, Kansas City, 1959—96, sr. counsel, 1996—97, of counsel, 1997—2000; ret., 2000. Mem. Mich. Law Rev., 1948-49; contbg. author: Missouri Bar Insurance Handbook, 1968, Missouri Bar Bankruptcy Handbook, 1991, also supplements; contbr. articles to profl. jours. Chmn. bd. Broadway United Meth. Ch., Kansas City, 1964-70, chmn. bd. trustees, chmn. fin. com., 1988-90, 94, 2000-2002; bd. dirs. Broadway Child Enrichment Ctr., 1980-2006; bd. dirs., exec. com. Della Lamb Neighborhood House, Kansas City, 1973-80; bd. dirs., treas. Friends of Sacred Structures, Kansas City, 2000—; coun. mem. St. Paul Sch. Theology, Kansas City, 1986-; bd. dirs. Kingswood Sr. Living Cmty., Kansas City, 2004—, vice chmn., 2005-; del. 17th World Meth. Conf., Rio de Janeiro, 1996; ranger Rocky Mountain Nat. Park, 1948-1949. With USN, 1945-46, 51-53, comdr. USNR, ret. Recipient Shepherd of the Lamb award, Della Lamb Neighborhood House, 1980; Summerfield scholar, 1943—47. Fellow Am. Coll. Bankruptcy, Am. Bar Found. (life); mem. ABA, Am. Judicature Soc., Am. Bankruptcy Inst., Mo. Bar Assn., Kansas City Met. Bar Assn., Lawyers Assn. Kansas City, Workout Profs. Assn. Kansas City, Univ. Club (v.p., bd. dirs. 1983, 86), Barristers Soc., Phi Beta Kappa, Delta Tau Delta (pres. Kansas City alumni chpt. 1965-72, pres. U. Kans. House Corp. 1966-72), Alpha Chi Sigma, Phi Alpha Delta. Avocations: travel, geography (maps), history, music, theology. Home: 8741 Ensley Ln Leawood KS 66206-1615 Office: Stinson Morrison Hecker LLP 1201 Walnut St Kansas City MO 64106-2150

MORE, DONNA, lawyer; d. Mordecai More; m. Harry "Hud" Englehart; 1 child, Maizey. Grad., Georgetown U., 1983. Prosecutor Cook County State's Atty.'s Office, Chgo., 1983—89; asst. U.S. atty. No. Dist. Ill., 1989—90; chief legal counsel Ill. Gaming Bd., 1990—94; with Freeborn & Peters, 1994—2000; pvt. practice More Law Group, 2000—04; with Greenberg Traurig, 2004—06; gen. counsel, v.p., sec. Columbia Entertainment, 2006—. Office: Columbia Sussex Corp 207 Grandview Dr Fort Mitchell KY 41017

MORE, DOUGLAS MCLOCHLAN, lawyer; b. NYC, Apr. 21, 1926; s. Morgan Berkeley and Lucinda (Bateson) M.; m. Pamela Bennett Marr, Aug. 6, 1954; children— Robin Maclachlan More Eddy, Alison Marr More Davies. Grad., Phillips Exeter Acad., 1943; BA, Harvard U., 1947; LL.B., Columbia U., 1950. Bar: N.Y. State bar 1950, Conn. bar 1981, Fla. bar 1983. With N.Y. Trust Co., 1950-51; asso. firm Bigham, Englar, Jones & Houston, NYC, 1951-53; fin. analyst Johns-Manville Corp., 1953-54; assoc. firm Kissam & Halpin, NYC, 1954-59; assoc. counsel Hooker Chem. Corp., 1959-63, gen. counsel, 1963-72, v.p., 1967-72; v.p. law Airco, Inc., 1972-75; gen. counsel Beker Industries Corp., 1975-81, v.p., 1975-78, sr. v.p., 1978-81; ptnr. firm More Phillips & Duncan, P.C., Greenwich, Conn., 1981-88, of counsel, 1988—. Served to lt. (j.g.) USNR, 1943-46. Mem. ABA, Conn. Bar Assn., Greenwich Bar Assn., Phi Delta Phi, Phoenix S-K Club, Hasty Pudding Inst. 1770 (Harvard). Home and Office: 27 Skylark Rd Greenwich CT 06830-4624 Office Phone: 203-869-0663.

MORE, JOSÉ, photojournalist; Bur. chief United Press Internat., Kans., Mo.; chief photographer Palm Beach Post, Fla.; photographer Chgo. Tribune, 1980—, chief photographer, 1991—94. Co-recipient George Polk award for internat. reporting, 2006. Office: Chicago Tribune 435 N Michigan Ave Chicago IL 60611 E-mail: jmore@tribune.com.

MORE, PHILIP HARVEY BIRNBAUM, business administration educator; b. San Diego, Jan. 21, 1944; s. Louis and Ruth Laureen (Bay) B.; m. Marlin Sue Van Every, Dec. 26, 1964; 1 child, Brian Philip. BA, U. Calif., Berkeley, 1965; PhD, U. Wash., 1975. Internal cons./analyst Los Angeles County Civil Svc. Commn., 1965-67; tchg. assoc. U. Wash., Seattle, 1972-74; asst. prof. bus. adminstrn. Ind. U., Bloomington, 1975-80, assoc. prof., 1980-85, prof., 1986—. Resident dir. J.F.K. Int., Tiburg U., The Netherlands; vis. scholar Polish Acad. Scis., Hungarian Acad. Scis., Tokyo U., SDA Bocconi, Milan, Italy, Seoul Nat. U., Korea, Dartmouth Coll. Co-author: Organization Theory: Structural and Behavioral Analysis, Modern Management Techniques for Engineers and Scientists, International Research Management: Studies in Interdisciplinary Methods From Business, Government and Academics, 1990; assoc. editor IEEE Transaction on Engring. Mgmt. jour.; contbr. articles to profl. jours., book revs., chpts. to books. With USAF, 1967—71. NSF fellow, 1974-75, NY Acad. Scis. fellow, 1981; U. Hong Kong Sr. Fulbright scholar, 1981-82. Mem. Acad. Mgmt. (pres. tech. and innovation mgmt. divsn. 1989-90), Engring. Mgmt. Soc., Inst. Ops. Rsch. and Mgmt. Scis., Internat. Assn. for Study of Interdisciplinary Rsch., Beta Gamma Sigma, Beta Alpha Psi, Sigma Iota Epsilon, Sigma Chi. Methodist. Office: Univ So Calif Marshall Sch Bus Los Angeles CA 90089-0808 Office Phone: 213-740-0744.

MOREAN, WILLIAM D., manufacturing executive; s. William E. Morean and Audrey Peterson; m. Kelly Morean; 4 children. Student in Aviation, Western Mich. U. With Jabil Circuit, St. Petersburg, Fla., 1977—, v.p., pres., bd. dirs., 1978—, chmn. bd. dirs., 1988—, CEO, 1988—2000. Bd. dirs. Eagle's Wing Found., St. Petersburg. Named one of 400 Richest Ams., Forbes mag., 2006. Office: Jabil Circuit 10560 Dr Martin Luther King Jr St N Saint Petersburg FL 33716

MOREFIELD, MICHAEL THOMAS, financial executive; b. Chgo., Aug. 13, 1956; s. Preston Thomas and Geraldine Judith Morefield BA in Acctg., Lewis U., Romeoville, Ill., 1978; M of Fin., Loyola U., Chgo., 1987. Mgr. gen. acctg. Gen. Binding Corp., Northbrook, Ill., 1980, dir. corp. acctg., 1981—83, dir. corp. fin. planning, 1983, asst. corp. contr., 1984—86, corp. contr., 1986—88; sr. v.p. fin. and adminstrn., CFO Toyoda Machinery USA, Inc., Arlington Heights, Ill., 1988—93; v.p. fin., CFO Schmalbach-Lubeca Holdings, Inc., Downers Grove, Ill., 1993—99; v.p., CFO United Plastics Group, Inc., Westmont, Ill., 1999—2002; v.p. fin., CFO Exelon Svcs. Inc., Westchester, Ill., 2002—03; sr. exec. v.p., CFO Portola Packaging, Inc., Batavia, 2004—. Bd. dirs. Cap Snap Europe. Mem. Friars Civic Orgn., Romeoville, Ill., 1976-78. Mem. Nat. Machine Tool Builders Assn. (fin. com. 1988-90), Arlington Heights C. of C Avocations: scuba diving, music, skiing, basketball, baseball. Home: 6836 Bantry Ct Darien IL 60561-3688 Office: 951 Douglas Rd Batavia IL 60510 Office Phone: 630-326-2074.

MOREHEAD, RICHARD SCOTT, medical educator; b. Miami, Fla., Aug. 31, 1962; MD, Oral Roberts U., Tulsa, Okla. Assoc. prof. medicine U. Ky. Coll. Medicine, Lexington, 1994—.

MOREHOUSE, LAWRENCE GLEN, veterinarian, educator, academic administrator; b. Manchester, Kans., July 21, 1925; s. Edwy Owen and Ethel Merle (Glenn) M.; m. Georgia Ann Lewis, Oct. 6, 1956; children: Timothy Lawrence, Glenn Ellen. BS in Biol. Sci., Kans. State U., 1952, DVM, 1952; MS in Animal Pathology, Purdue U., 1956, PhD, 1960. Lic. vet. medicine. Veterinarian County Animal Hosp., Des Peres, Mo., 1952-53; supr. Brucellosis labs. Purdue U., West Lafayette, Ind., 1953-60; staff veterinarian lab. svcs. USDA, Washington, 1960-61; discipline leader in pathology and toxicology, animal health divsn. USDA Nat. Animal Disease Lab., Ames, Iowa, 1961-64; prof., chmn. dept. vet. pathology U. Mo. Coll. Vet. Medicine, Columbia, Mo., 1964—69, 1969—86, dir. Vet. Med. Diagnostic Lab., 1968-88, prof. emeritus, 1986—. Cons. USDA, to comdg. gen. U.S. Army R&D Command, Am. Inst. Biol. Scis., NAS, to Surg. Gen., Miss. State U., St. Louis Zoo Residency Tng. Program, Miss. Vet. Med. Assn., Okla. State U., Pa. Dept. Agr., Ohio Dept. Agr. Co-editor: Mycotoxic Fungi, Mycotoxins, Mycotoxicoses: An International Encyclopedic Handbook, 3 vols., 1977; contbr. articles on diseases of animals to profl. jours. Active Trinity Presbyn. Ch., Columbia, 1964-2002; bd. dirs. Mo. Symphony Soc., Columbia, 1989-92. Pharmacists mate second class USNR, 1943-46, PTO; 2d. lt. U.S. Army, 1952-56. Recipient Outstanding Svc. award USDA, 1959, merit cert., 1963, 64, Disting. Svc. award U. Mo. Coll. Vet. Medicine, 1987, Dean's Impact award, 1996, Kans. State U. Alumni award, 2004. Fellow Royal Soc. Health London; mem. AAAS, Am. Assn. Vet. Lab. Diagnosticians (E.P. Pope award 1976, chmn. lab. accreditation bd. 1972-79, 87-90, pres. 1979-80, sec.-treas. 1983-87), World Assn. Vet. Lab. Diagnosticians (bd. dirs. 1984-94, dir. emeritus 1994—), N.Y. Acad. Sci., U. S. Animal Health Assn., Am. Assn. Lab. Animal Sci., Mo. Soc. Microbiology, Am. Assn. Avian Pathologists, N.Am. Conf. Rsch. Workers in Animal Diseases, Mo. Univ. Retirees Assn. (pres. 1996-99). Presbyterian. Avocations: classic cars, boating, genealogy. Home: 916 Danforth Dr Columbia MO 65201-6164 Office: U Mo Vet Med Diagnostic Lab PO Box 6023 Columbia MO 65205-6023 Office Phone: 573-442-7069. Personal E-mail: gmoreho@att.global.net. Business E-Mail: lmorehou@coin.org.

MOREHOUSE, SARAH MCCALLY, retired political science professor; b. Boston, Jan. 15, 1927; d. Ralph Dewey and Eugenia Whitehead (Norris) Powell; m. W. Bradley Morehouse, Nov. 8, 1969 (div. Nov. 1986); children: Richard, John, Catherine, David; m. Malcolm Edwin Jewell, Dec. 28, 1991. BA in Polit. Sci., Wellesley Coll., 1948; PhD in Polit. Sci., Yale U., 1964. Instr. Conn. Coll., New London, 1964-66; lectr. Hunter Coll., Bronx, NY, 1966—69; assoc. prof. Manhattanville Coll., Purchase, NY, 1969—75; prof. U. Conn., Stamford, 1976-92, prof. emerita, 1992—. Univ. senator U. Conn., 1982-85, assoc. dir., 1990-91. Author: State Politics, Parties and Policy, 1981, The Governor as Party Leader, 1998; contbr. various articles to profl. jours. Sec. Charter Revision Commn. Fairfield, Conn., 1960, mem., 2006; chmn. Ethics Commn., Fairfield, 1984-88; pres. LWV, 1996-98; state LWV sec. bd. dirs. 1998-2001. Vis. professorship for women NSF, 1991; fellow Danforth Found., 1960; rsch. grantee Russell Sage Found., 1983; vis. scholar U. Calif, Berkeley, 1991-92. Mem. Wellesley Club. Home: 242 Somerset Ave Fairfield CT 06824-4935 Personal E-mail: macsarahj@worldnet.att.net.

MOREHOUSE, VALERIE JEANNE, librarian; b. Taft, Calif., Jan. 30, 1947; d. Gordon Stanley and Cloe Ozelle (Reed) Hogue; m. Keith Herbert Morehouse, Aug. 22, 1968 (div. 1994); 1 child, Gordon. AA, Taft Coll., 1966; AB in English, U. Calif., Berkeley, 1968; MSLS, Simmons Grad. Sch. Libr. Sci., 1977. Cert. profl. librarian, Mass. Asst. libr. dir. Plymouth (Mass.) Pub. Librs., 1977—82; asst. exec. dir. Southeastern Librs. Coop., Rochester, Minn., 1982—84; libr. automation cons. N.D. State Libr., Bismarck, 1984—89; dist. libr. media dir. Bismarck Pub. Sch. Dist., 1989—97; sys. adminstr. MARINet, San Rafael, Calif., 1997—2000; libr. Temple Isaiah of Contra Costa County, Lafayette, 2001—. Adv. panelist for literature Mass. Coun. on Arts and Humanities, Boston, 1980-82. Editor, writer Libr. A Word to the Wise, 1995-97; author: Anthology: A Collection of Cape Cod Poets, 1974. Legis. chair, membership chair N.D. Libr. Assn., 1987-93; mem. N.D. Gov.'s Adv. Libr. Vision 2004 Com., Bismarck, 1995-96; mem. Ctrl. Dakota Libr. Network Bd., Bismarck, 1992—. Recipient Capewide 1st prize for poetry Provincetown Assn. for Living Arts, 1972, Spl. Recognition award COSMEP, 1977, Pres.' award for svc. to librs. N.D. Libr. Assn., 1994. Mem. ALA (chair publs. com. 1985-87, columnist, reviewer The Book List 1977-79), Calif. Libr. Assn., Beta Phi Mu. Avocations: gardening, travel. Office: Temple Isaiah Libr 3800 Mt Diablo Blvd Lafayette CA 94549 E-mail: valmorehouse@earthlink.net.

MORELAN, PAULA KAY, choreographer; b. Lafayette, Ind., Nov. 24, 1949; d. Dickie Booth and Marian Maxine (Fetterhoff) M.; m. Kerim Sayan, Aug. 10, 1974. Student, U. Utah, 1968-69; BFA, Tex. Christian U., 1972; postgrad., El Centro Coll., 1969-70. Tchr. Rosello Sch. Ballet, Dallas, 1972-74; mgr., tchr. Ballet Arts Ctr., Dallas, 1974-76; owner, tchr. Ballet Classique, Garland, Tex., 1976-87, Garland Ballet Acad., 1977-87; resident choreographer Garland Civic Theatre, 1988—, lifetime mem., 1998. Asst. to Mythra Rosello Tex. Civic Ballet, Dallas, 1972—74; assoc. artistic dir. Dance Repertory Theatre Dallas, 1974—75, artistic dir., 1975—76, Garland (Tex.) Ballet Assn., 1977—90, Classical Ballet Acad., Performing Arts Sch., 1987—90; artistic dir. musical theatre dept. KD Actors Conservatory, 2005—; founder, chairperson Act IV Guild, 2002—05. Bd. dirs. Garland Civic Theatre, 2000—05. Nominee Best Choreography award, 2006, Best Choreographer award, 2006; recipient Leon Rabin award Best Choreography, Dallas Theatre League, 1996, 1998, 2000—01, 2004, Choreographer of Yr. award, 2001—04, Best Choreographer award, 2003, Column award, 2004. Personal E-mail: pkm@worldnet.att.net.

MORELAND, DONALD EDWIN, physiologist; b. Enfield, Conn., Oct. 12, 1919; s. Albert Sinclair and Ruth (Cowan) M.; m. Verdie Brown Stallings, Nov. 6, 1954; 1 child, Donna Faye; stepchildren: Frank C., Paul Ziglar. BS in Forestry, N.C. State U., 1949, MS in Plant Physiology, 1950, PhD in Plant Physiology, 1953. Plant physiologist SUNY Coll. Forestry, Syracuse, 1952-53, USDA-Agrl. Rsch. Svc., Raleigh, NC, 1953-71, rsch. leader, 1972-78, sr. exec., 1979-95, collaborator, 1996—; asst. prof. to prof. N.C. State U., Raleigh, 1953-95, prof. emeritus, 1996—. Mem. toxicology study sect. NIH, USPHS, Bethesda, Md., 1963-67. Editor: Biochemical Responses Induced by Herbicides, 1982; mem. editorial bd. Pesticide Biochemistry and Physiology, 1971-97, Pesticide Sci., 1987-96; contbr. articles to profl. jours. 1st lt. U.S. Army, 1941-46. AEC predoctoral fellow, 1950-52. Fellow AAAS, Weed Sci. Soc. Am. (outstanding rsch. award 1973); mem. Am. Chem. Soc., Plant Growth Regulator Soc. Am., Am. Soc. Plant Physiologists, So. Weed Sci. Soc., Sigma Xi. Avocations: woodworking, surf fishing, square dancing. Home: 1508 Pineview Dr Raleigh NC 27606-2562 Office: NC State U USDA-Agrl Rsch Svc Dept Crop Sci 3127 Ligon St Raleigh NC 27607-5376

MORELAND, RICHARD PAUL, musician, educator; b. Hastings, Nebr., Aug. 15, 1946; s. Robert Howard Moreland and Marjorie Ellen Musick-Moreland; m. Marian Hope Snyder, Aug. 24, 1968; children: Laurel Ann Moreland-Graves, Randall Scott. BS in Music Edn., Bob Jones U., Greenville, SC, 1969. Cert. tchr. Mich. Tchr. Covert Pub. Schs., Mich., 1969—70, Swartz Creek Pub. Schs., Mich., 1970—97; dir. music United Meth. Ch. of Swartz Creek, 1972—. Part-time tchr. Montrose Cmty. Schs., Mich., 2002—06; chmn. divsn. interpretation Bd. Diaconal Ministry, Mich., 1986—94; ann. conf. choir dir. United Meth. Ch., Mich., 2005. Composer choral anthems; author: (children's plays) The Not-So-Silent Night, 1998—, Wee Three Kings, 1999—; orchestrator: online orchestrations cokesbury.com. Avocations: model railroading, hiking.

MORELL, WILLIAM NELSON, JR., retired foreign trade association executive, government agency administrator; b. July 13, 1920; s. William N. and Louise (Cox) M.; m. Patricia Leonhard, Apr. 3, 1943; 1 child, Lynn Noble. Student, Coll. William and Mary, 1938—40; AB, George Washington U., 1942; MA, U. Pa., 1948; postgrad., Am. U., 1950—51; grad., Nat. War Coll., 1956. Jr. economist Bur. Labor Stats., 1941; asst. to prof. fin. George Washington U., 1941; naval mem. U.S. mil. mission to Moscow, 1944-46; asst. prof. Drexel Inst. Tech., 1946-48; instr. U. Pa., 1947-48; with CIA, 1949-68, staff mem. Office Nat. Est., 1950-52, mng. dir. U.S. econ. intelligence com., 1955-65, chmn., 1966-67; chmn. spl. study group NSC Planning Bd., 1960; econ. counselor Am. Embassy, Moscow, 1960-61; dep. dir. office rsch. and reports CIA, 1962-66, dir. Office Econ. Rsch., 1966-67, mem. U.S. econ. def. adv. com., adv. com. export policy, 1966-67; lectr. on Communist econs., 1960-68; faculty Nat. War Coll., 1968; econ. counselor Am. Embassy, Taipei, Taiwan, 1968-73, spl. asst. to sec. treasury, 1973-77; treasury mem. U.S. Nat. Intelligence Bd., 1973-77; mng. dir. USA-ROC Econ. Coun., Crystal Lake, Ill., 1977-78, pres., 1979-90; cons. U.S. Taiwan Trade, 1979-94, ret., 1994. Author, lectr. on Taiwan economy. Eucharistic min. Episc. ch. Lt. USNR, 1942-46. Decorated Order Brilliant Star Taiwan, Order Brilliant Star with Violet Grand Cordon; recipient Superior Achievement award, medal of merit CIA, Exceptional Svc. medal Treasury Dept., U.S. Nat. Intelligence Disting. Svc. award, Taiwan Econ. Ministry medal. Mem. Artus, Econ. Soc. (hon.). Home: 340 S Berkshire Dr Lake Forest IL 60045-4823

MORELLA, CONSTANCE ALBANESE, ambassador, former congresswoman; b. Somerville, Mass., Feb. 12, 1931; d. Salvatore and Mary Christine (Fallette) Albanese; m. Anthony C. Morella, Aug. 21, 1954; children: Paul, Mark, Laura; guardians of: Christine, Catherine, Louise, Rachel, Paul, Ursula. AA, Boston U., 1950, AB, 1954; MA, Am. U., 1967, D of Pub. Svc. (hon.), 1988, Norwich U. and Dickinson Coll., 1989, Mt. Vernon Coll., 1995, U. Md. U. Coll., 1996, USUHS, 1997, U. Md., 1997, Elizabethtown Coll., 1999. Tchr. Montgomery County (Md.) Pub. Schs., 1956-60; instr. Am. U., 1968-70; prof. Montgomery Coll., Rockville, Md., 1970-86; mem. Md. Ho. Dels., Annapolis, 1979-86, U.S. Congress from 8th Md. dist., 1987—2003; mem. sci. com., tech. subcom., basic rsch. subcom., govt. reform com., chair D.C. subcom., mem. civil svc. subcom.; visiting fellow Kennedy School, Harvard, 2003; U.S. permanent rep. to Orgn. for Econ. Co-operation & Devel. U.S. Dept. State, Paris, 2003—. Mem. civil svc., adv. bd. Am. Univ., Washington Mem. adv. coun. Montgomery County Hospice Soc.; hon. bd. mem. Nat. Kidney Found; active Human Rights Caucus; Congressional Women's Caucus, Older Ams. Caucus, Population and Devel. Caucus; mem. Bd. Cafritz Found. Named Glamour Woman of Yr. Glamour mag. 1995, Washingtonian of Yr. 1991; named to Md. Women's Hall of Fame, Md. Women's Hall of Fame, 1994. Republican. Avocations: theater, tennis, reading. Home: USOECD PSC 116 APO AE 09777

MORELLO, CANDIS MARGUERITE, pharmacist, educator; b. Lynwood, Calif., May 5, 1969; d. Albert James and Darcy Lovgren Pavich (Stepmother), Keith R. (Stepfather) and Claire Barragan Kerr; m. Christopher Salvatore Morello; children: Joseph Salvatore, Lucas Sebastian. BA, U. Calif., Davis, 1991; PharmD, U. Calif., San Francisco, 1996. Cert. Diabetic educator Nat. Cert. Bd. Diabetes Educators, 1999. Ambulatory care pharmacist specialist Vets. Affairs San Diego Healthcare Sys., 1997—99; ambulatory care pharmacist specialist Spectrum Healthcare Resources Naval Med. Ctr. San Diego Ambulatory Care Clinics, 1999—2002; affiliate faculty mem. dept. pharmacy Idaho State U., Pocatella, 1999—2002; clin. asst. prof. Sch. Pharmacy Western U. Health Scis., Calif., 1999—2002; asst. clin. prof. Sch. Pharmacy U. Calif., San Francisco, 2000—, asst. prof. clin. pharmacy Skaggs Sch. Pharmacy and Pharm. Scis. San Diego, 2002—. Co-author: A Process Guide for Pharmacists, 3rd ed.; contbr. articles to profl. jours. Clin. pharmacist vol. Various Cmty. Outreach Projects, San Diego, 1996—, Taking Control of Your Diabetes, San Diego, 1996; clin. pharmacist vol. Free Med. Clinic Project U. Calif, San Diego, 2000—; co-chair and coord., Ask a Pharmacist session Taking Control of Your Diabetes Conf., San Diego, 2002—; clin. pharmacist vol., Project Stand Down Vetrans Village, San Diego, 2002—03. Recipient Faculty Excellence award, U. Calif., San Diego, 2003, Excellence in Tchg. award, 2005, 2006. Fellow: Calif. Soc. Health-Sys. Pharmacists (assoc.; del. 1997, co-chair continuing edn. com. 1998—99, faculty student liason 2003—, Practitioner Recognition Program award 2003); mem.: Am. Pharm. Assn. (assoc.), Am. Soc. Health-Sys. Pharmacists (assoc.; student faculty liason 2003—05), San Diego Soc. Health-Sys. Pharmacists (assoc.; sec., mem. cmty. outreach com. 1998—2001, del. seminar meetings 1999—2005, bd. dirs. 2002—05, Pharmacist of the Yr. 2002, Dena L. Barker Meml. award 2002), Am. Coll. Clin. Pharmacy (assoc.), Am. Assn. Colls. Pharmacy (assoc.), Phi Lambda Sigma (assoc.), Rho Chi (assoc.), Phi Delta Chi (assoc.; v.p. 1993—94). Office: U Calif San Diego Skaggs Sch Pharmacy, PharmSci 9500 Gilman # 0719 La Jolla CA 92093-0719 Office Phone: 858-822-5586. Office Fax: 858-822-5624. Business E-Mail: candismorello@ucsd.edu.

MORELLO, CELESTE ANNE, historian, criminologist; b. Norristown, Pa., July 22, 1958; d. Ann M. Morello. Student, Loyola U., Rome, 1978; BA in Classics cum laude, BA in Art History magna cum laude, Chestnut Hill Coll., Phila., 1980; MS in Criminology, St. Joseph's U., Phila., 1994; MA in History, Villanova U., Pa., 2000; grad., Civilian Police Acad., Phila., 2000. Tchr. history, social studies, sci. Archdiocese of Phila., 1977-84; lectr. on ancient history of Sicily, 1982—; cons. criminologist in Mafia and LCN history Phila. Police and U.S. Atty.'s Office, 1993—. Pioneer in criminal and Mafia history; petitioner, originator over 25 Phila. hist. marker sites Pa. Hist. and Mus. Commn. Hist. Marker Program, 1993—; lectr. in field. Author: Beyond History: The Times and Peoples of St. Paul's R.C. Church, 1843-1993, 1992; writer, dir. History of the Mafia and LCN in Philadelphia 1880-1959 for Dept. of Justice, FBI, Phila., 1997, History of South Philadelphia, Introduction, Institute for Service Learning, 1996, Survey of Illicit Narcotics Use in Philadelphia 1900-45 for Dept. of Justice, High Intensity Drug Traffic Area, Philadelphia/Camden, The Phenomenon of the Mafia, 1997, Oral Histories of Three Men: All Mafiosi Before 1930, 1998, The Early Sicilian American Mafia Before 1930, 1998, Case Study of A Western Sicilian Colony in Suburban Philadelphia, 1998, The Philadelphia Italian Market Cookbook, 1999, Before Bruno: The History of Philadelphia's Mafia, Book I 1880-1931, 1999, Book II 1931-1946, 2001, Book III 1946-1959, 2005, The Philadelphia Police's Homicide Records: The First Decades of Investigating and Advancement, 2003, Philadelphia's Italian Foods: A History of Over 200 Years with Recipes from the City's Best Italian Cooks, 2006; contbr. articles to profl. jours., chpts. to books. Founder Sicilian Culture Collection, Hist. Soc. Pa., Phila. Mem. Moyamensing Hist. Soc. (founder), Pa. Hist. Assn. Roman Catholic. Home and Office: 1234 S Sheridan St Philadelphia PA 19147-4820 Office Phone: 215-334-6008.

MORELLO, JOSEPH ALBERT, musician, educator; b. Springfield, Mass., July 17, 1928; s. Joseph Charles and Lilia (LaPalme) M.; m. Jean Ann Mehnert. Grad. high sch., Springfield. Ind. drummer, Springfield, 1945-49; drummer Gil Melé, Stan Kenton, Tal Farlow, Johnny Smith, NYC, 1953-55, Dave Brubeck Quartet, touring worldwide, 1955-68; clinician Selmer Ludwig Drum Co., Elkhart, Ind., 1957-92; leader Joe Morello Quartet, 1979—; clinician DW Drums, Oxnard, Calif., 1993—; rec. artist Digital Music Products Inc., 1993—. Rec. artist Savoy, Capitol, Norgran, Blue Note, Columbia, RCA labels; innovator finger control in jazz drumming; author: Joe Morello Drum Method, The Natural Approach to Technique, 1993, Joe Morello Drum Method 2, 1994, also New Directions in Rhythm, Rudimental Jazz, Off the Record, Master Studies, Master Studies II, 2006; releases include (with Joe Morello Quartet) Going Places, 1993, Morello's Standard Time, 1994, Marion Mc Partland's Hickory House Trio, 1999, Marion McPartland Trio with Joe Morello, 2002, Rufus Reid Live at Shanghai Jazz, 2002. Named to Hall of Fame, Modern Drummer mag., 1988, Percussive Arts Soc. Hall of Fame, 1993, Am. Jazz Hall of Fame, 2001, Trumpets Jazz Hall of Fame, 2002; recipient New Star award, Downbeat mag., 1955, Melody Maker mag. award, 1963—67, Jazz mag. award, 1964—67, Thomas A. Edison Lifetime Achievement award, 1990, Lifetime Achievement award, Jersey Shore Jazz and Blues Found., 1996, Recognition of Outstanding Leadership award, Kosa Internat. Percussion Workshops, 2002, Lifetime Achievement award, Montreal Drum Festival, 2002, poll winner, Downbeat mag., 1963—65, Playboy mag., 1963—67, Lifetime Achievement award, Sabian Ltd., 2003. Mem.: N.J. Jazz Soc. Avocation: photography.

MORELLO, STEVEN JOHN, lawyer; b. Saginaw, Mich., Sept. 17, 1952; m. Francia S. Morello, Apr. 8, 1978; children: Steven Jr., Rebecca. BS in Fgn. studies, Georgetown U., 1974; JD, U. Detroit Mercy Sch. Law, 1977; MBA, Boston Coll. Law Sch., Heidelberg, Fed. Republic Germany, 1980; MA in Pastoral studies, Sacred Heart Major Seminary. Bar: Mich. 1977, Ill. 1984; cert. profl. contracts mgr., Nat. Contract Mgmt. Assn. (Fellow). Staff asst. U.S. Senator Philip A. Hart, Washington; mng. atty. regional offfice Digital Equipment Corp., Arlington Heights, Ill., 1984; atty. contract Northrop Corp. Def. Sys. Divsn., Rollings Meadows, Ill., 1982-84; v.p., gen. counsel Prechter Holdings Inc., Southgate, Mich.; gen. counsel, Dept. Army U.S. Dept. Def., Washington, 2001—05; gen. counsel Sault Ste. Marie Tribe of Chippewa Indians. Mem. Sault Ste. Marie Tribe of Chippewa Indians. Capt. JAGC US Army, 1978—85, trial counsel 21st Support Command, first mem. Trial Def. Svc., Karlsruhe, Germany, legal asst., adminstrv. law officer, Berlin Recruting Command, Ft. Sheridan, Ill., contract atty., 86th Army Reserve Command USAR, Ft. Sheridan, Ill. Fellow Nat. Contract Mgmt. Assn. (pres. Chgo. chpt. 1985-86). Office: Sault Tribe Legal Dept 523 Ashmun St Sault Sainte Marie MI 49783

MORELLO, TOM, musician; b. NYC, May 30, 1964; s. Mary Morello and Ngethe Njoroge. B in polit. sci., Harvard Coll. Band mem. Lock Up; guitarist Rage Against the Machine, 1991—2001, Audioslave, 2001—; solo artist (as The Night Watchman), 2007—. Played at Lollapalooza, 1992, Latinpalooza, 1994, Tibetan Freedom Concert, San Francisco, 1996, Lollapalooza, 1996, Tibetan Freedom Concert, East Troy, Wis., 1999, Woodstock 99, Coachella Festival, Indio, Calif., 1999, Indio, 2007. Musician: (albums) (with Lock Up) Something Bitchin' This Way Comes, 1989, (with Rage Against the Machine) Rage Against the Machine, 1992, Evil Empire, 1996, The Battle of Los Angeles, 1999, Renegades, 2000, Live at the Grand Olympic Auditorium, 2003, (with Audioslave) Audioslave, 2002, Out of Exile, 2005, Revelations, 2006, (as The Nightwatchman) One Man Revolution, 2007, (songs) (with Rage Against the Machine) Tire Me, 1996 (Grammy award for Best Metal Performance, 1997), Guerilla Radio, 2000 (Grammy award for Best Hard Rock Performance, 2001); actor: (films) Made, 2001, Berkeley, 2005. Co-founder Axis of Justice; co-host Axis of Justice Radio Network. Named one of 100 Greatest Guitarists of All Time, Rolling Stone, 2003; recipient Best Guitarist award, Calif. Music Awards, 1997—2001. *

MORELOCK, JASMINE CRAWFORD, artist; b. Boise, June 30, 1925; d. Graydon Clemson and Doris Cecile (Dinwiddie) Crawford; m. Max Maurice Morelock, Apr. 8, 1950; 1 child, Maurice Max. AA, Stephens Coll., Columbia, Mo., 1945; BA, La. State U., 1948; MA, La. Sch. Tech., 1979; MFA cum laude, Inst. Allende, San Miguel Allende, Guanajuato, Mexico, 1978. Cert. tchr. speech and art, La. Advtsg. writer programming dept. KRMD Radio Sta., Shreveport, La., 1946—47; with Bozell and Jacobs Nat. Advt. Agy., 1949—50; with comml. design Glen Mason Advt. Agy.; asst. prof. fine arts La. State U., Baton Rouge, 1948-49; head art dept. Southfield Sch., Shreveport, La., 1972-74; tchr. portrait classes Bossier C. C., Bossier City, La., 1989-91; tchr. art Caddo Parish Sch. Bd., Shreveport, La., 1975-80; represented by Gallery on the Green, Lexington, Mass., Juleaux Gallery of Fine Arts, Kansas City, WLR Design Co., Shreveport, La., Lytle's, Shreveport, La., Riverwalk Gallery, New Orleans. Presenter workshops Barnwell Art Ctr., Shreveport, La., J&M Studio Groups, Shreveport, Women's Dept. Club, Shreveport, Springhill Art Assn., La., 1993. One woman exhbns. include La. State U. Shreveport Gallery, 1992, Cambridge Club, Shreveport, 1993, The Glen Gallery, Shreveport, 1995, Shreve Meml. Libr., Shreveport, 1995, numerous others; group exhbns. include Valerie Originals, KJ's Antiques and Silks, Hot Springs, Ark., 1986, Women Artists of La., Baton Rouge, 1987, Boots Pharmaceutical Co., Cambridge Club, Shreveport, La., 1988, 90, 92, Stoner Arts Ctr., Shreveport, 1989, 90, Gallery on the Green, Lexington, Mass., 1989, Simmers Gallery, Shreveport, 1989, La. Artist Group Show, 1990, Barksdale Air Base, 1990, Turner Art Ctr., 1990, Artport, Shreveport, 1990, 92, 93, 94, Riverside Galleries, Shreveport, Southwestern Watercolor Soc., 1992, 94, Nat. Mus. Art, Washington, 1993, Still River Artists, Danbury, Conn., 1993, Okla. 12th Annual Juried Show, 1995, Shreveport Art Port, 2004-06, 2007-, Northwest La. Triennial Competition, Meadows Mus., 2006, numerous others; represented in pvt. and pub. collections La. State U. Ctr., St. Luke's Hosp., St. Vincent's Acad., U. Club, Seagull Cos., McGoldrick Oil Co., numerous others; featured in (cover) (Goodloe Stuck) The Shreveport Madam, 1986, Boots Pharm. Art Catalogue, 1990, Behold, I Make All Things New, 1991, Artists of La. Catalogue, 1991, (t.v. show) Focus on the Arts, The Shreveport Times, 1995. Recipient Special Selection award Ark. Arts Ctr., Little Rock, 1984, First Purchase Prize Izora and Thilo Steinschulte Meml. award First Meth. Ch. Alexandria (La.), 1984, First Place Ark-La-Tex-Okla Competition First Meth. Ch., Shreveport, 1984. Mem. Nat. Watercolor Soc., Nat. Assn. Women Artists, Southwestern Watercolor Soc. (Elizabeth Shanon Meml. award 1991), La. Watercolor Soc. Soc. Exptl. Artists, Hoover Watercolor Soc. (v.p., First Place 1984, H.M. award 1993), Registry of La. Artists, La. Artists, Inc., Southeastern Ctr. for Contemporary Art, Coalition of Women's Art (nat., Dallas). Home: 427 Monrovia St Shreveport LA 71106-1607 Office Phone: 318-861-3773. Personal E-mail: jcmore@bellsouth.net.

MORENCY, PAULA J., lawyer; b. Oak Park, Ill., Mar. 13, 1955; AB magna cum laude, Princeton U., 1977; JD, U. Va., 1980. Bar: Ill. 1980, U.S. Dist. Ct. (no. dist.) Ill. 1980, U.S. Ct. Appeals (7th cir.) 1981, U.S. Ct. Appeals (5th cir.) 1990, U.S. Dist. Ct. (ctrl. dist.) Ill. 1999, U.S. Dist. Ct. (ea. dist.) Wis. 2000. Assoc. Mayer, Brown & Platt, Chgo., 1980-86, ptnr., 1987-94, Schiff Hardin LLP, Chgo., 1994—. Adj. prof. trial advocacy Northwestern U. Sch. Law, Chgo., 1997—; faculty Midwest Regional, Nat. Inst. for Trial Advocacy, 1988—; mem. pres.'s coun. Dominican U., 1998-2002. Author: Cross-Examination of a Franchise Executive, 1995, Insurance Coverage Issues in Franchise and Intellectual Property Litigation, 1996, Re-Emergence of Franchise Class Actions, 1997, Judicial and Legislative Update: ABA Forum on Franchising, 1999, How to Find, Use and Defend Against the Expert Witness, 2000, Dealing With System Change in a High-Tech World, 2001, A Decade After Daubert, 2004. Mem. ABA (forum franchising, governing com. 2001-04, litig. sect., antitrust sect., intellectual property sect.), Chgo. Coun. of Lawyers (bd. govs. 1989-93), Constnl. Rights Found. Chgo. (chair 2001). Office: Schiff Hardin LLP 6600 Sears Tower Chicago IL 60606 Office Phone: 312-258-5549.

MORENO, ALBERT F., lawyer, former apparel executive; b. Dec. 1943; BA in economics, San Diego State U., 1966; M in L.Am. econ. studies, U. Madrid, 1967; JD, U. Calif., Berkeley, 1970. Bar: Calif. 1970. Regional dir. Legal Svcs. Corp., San Francisco; asst. gen. counsel Levi Strauss & Co., San Francisco, 1978—81, assoc. gen. counsel, 1981—85, dep. gen. counsel, 1985—94, chief counsel Levi Strauss N.Am., 1994—96, sr. v.p., gen. counsel, 1996—2006. Bd. dirs. New Century Energies Inc., 1999—2000, Xcel Energy Inc., 2000—. Dean's adv. coun. San Diego State U. Coll. Arts and Letters; chmn. bd. trustees Rosenberg Found., 2003—. Recipient Monty Alumni Award, San Diego State U., 2001. Office: Board of Directors c/o Xcel Energy 414 Nicollet Mall Minneapolis MN 55401-1993 *

MORENO, ARTURO (ARTE MORENO), major league baseball team owner, former advertising executive; b. Tucson, Aug. 1947; m. Carol Moreno, 1986; 3 children. BS in Mktg., Univ. Ariz., 1973. With Eller Outdoor, 1973—84; pres., COO Outdoor Systems Inc., 1984—99; former owner Salt Lake Trappers minor league baseball club; former minority owner Arizona Diamondbacks baseball club, Phoenix Suns basketball club; owner & pres. Los Angeles Angels of Anaheim baseball club, 2003—. Bd. dir. Nelnet. Cofounder (with Carol Moreno) Moreno Family Found. Served US Army, 1966—68, Vietnam. Named one of Forbes' Richest Americans, 2006. Office: Los Angeles Angels of Anaheim 2000 Gene Autry Way Anaheim CA 92806

MORENO, BARRY, historian, writer; b. LA; s. Rafael Salvarote and Eva Maria Moreno. BA in History, Calif. State U., LA, 1985. Libr., historian Statue of Liberty and Ellis Island, NYC, 1988—. EEO counselor Nat. Park Svc., NYC, 1988—96. Author: The Statue of Liberty Encyclopedia, 2000, Italian Americans, 2003, Images of America: Ellis Island, 2003, Encyclopedia of Ellis Island, 2004, Images of America: The Statue of Liberty, 2004, Children of Ellis Island, 2005, Manhattan Street Scenes, 2006, Castle Garden and Battery Park, 2007, (forewards) Ellis Island Interviews, 1997, The Holy Spark: Rogel and the Goddess of Liberty, 2006, (bibliography) Statue of Liberty Revisited, 1994; cons. for, appeared on numerous film, TV and radio documentaries introducing Ellis Island: Everyone's Monument, 1991, On the Inside: The Statue of Liberty, 1999, Building a Colossus: The Statue of Liberty, 2001, The Sweetest Sound, 2001, Lady by the Sea: The Statue of Liberty, 2004, How to Start Your Own Country, BBC, 2005; contbr. chapters to books, articles to profl. jours. Recipient EEO Counseling award Statue of Liberty Nat. Monument, 1994. Mem. Mus. Coun. N.Y., Am. Immigration and Ethnic History Soc., Calif. Hist. Soc., Monarchist League, Am. Vaudeville Soc., English-Speaking Union, Orgn. Am. Historians. Roman Catholic. Avocations: writing, studying foreign languages, reading. Office: Museum Svcs Divsn Ellis Island New York NY 10004 E-mail: barry_moreno@nps.gov.

MORENO, CARLOS R., state supreme court justice; b. LA, Nov. 4, 1948; m. Christine Moreno; children: Keiko, Nicholas. BA in Polit. Sci., Yale U., 1970; JD, Stanford U., 1975. Dep. city atty. L.A. City Atty.'s Office; atty. with Mori & Ota (now known as Kelley, Drye & Warren), 1979; apptd. justice Mncpl. Ct., 1986—93; justice L.A. County Superior Ct., 1993—97, US Dist. Ct. (ctrl. dist.) Calif., 1998—2001; assoc. justice Supreme Ct. Calif., 2001—. Bd. visitors Stanford Law Sch.; bd. govs. Assn. Yale Alumni; dir. Arroyo Vista Family Health Ctr. Recipient Criminal Justice Superior Ct. Judge of Yr. award, L.A. County Bar Assn., 1997, For God, For Country and For Yale award, Yale U., 2001. Mem.: Municipal Ct. Judges Assn., Presiding Judges Assn., Calif. Judges Assn., Mexican Am. Bar Assn. (past pres.). Avocations: theater, opera, crossword puzzles. Office: Calif Supreme Ct 350 McAllister St San Francisco CA 94102-4783 *

MORENO, DONNA MARIE, communications executive; b. Amesbury, Mass., July 25, 1957; d. Robert and Marie Doris (Lucier) Menzigian; m. Carlos Moreno, Nov. 17, 1999. BS Math., U. Lowell, 1979, MBA Ops., 1983. Analyst material control AVCO Corp., Wilmington, Mass., 1979—81; analyst ops. Blue Cross & Blue Shield, Boston, 1981—83, analyst risk, 1983—84; analyst sys. Bell Atlantic Corp., Bethesda, Md., 1984—86, cons. internal, 1986—89, mgr. project, 1989—91, mgr. new tech. strategic planning, 1992—97, sr mgr. sales channel devel., 1997—2001; sr. mgr. mktg. Verizon, 2001—04, sr. cons. sales incentive compensation, 2004—. Spkr. FUSE Nat. and Regional Confs., 1988, 91; mem. Verizon Hispanic Orgn Inventor (software) User-assisted Adhoc Reporting, 1988, Natural English Report Access, 1988 Vol. Montgomery County Vol. Assn., Md., 1983—, PALS Montgomery County, 1984—; chair spl. events New Mem. Svcs. John F. Kennedy Ctr. Performing Arts, Washington, 1985—, vol. adv. com., 1991-92; chair vol. adv. com. Kennedy Ctr., 1992—; bd. dirs. Sister City Corp., Rockville, v.p., 1993-95, pres.-elect, 1994-95, pres., 1995—; Geissenbier mem. Jr. Chamber Internat. Found., 1996—; Geissenbier mem. US Jr. C. of C. Found., 1997—; mem. Montgomery County Ethnic Affairs Commn., 2005—; bd. dirs. US Jaycees Found., sec., 2003-04, dir. 2005—; dir. Women's Assn. Verizon Employees Mid Atlantic Mentoring Program, 2003-04, Mid Suburban Program, 2005— Recipient Internat Tng. Fellow, JCI, 2001—. Mem. NAFE, Ops. Rsch. Soc., Intelligent Computer Rsch. Inst., Focus User Group (co-chmn. artificial intelligence group 1989, leader, coord. spl. interest groups for Nat. Com., 1989, nat., regional spkr. 1988, 91), Women's Assn. Verizon Employees (bd. dirs.), Native Am. People of Verizon (local pres. 2006, nat. pres. 2007), Rockville Jr. C. of C. (sec. 1992-93), Md. Jr. C. of C. (program mgr. internat. involvement 1992-93, dist. dir. 1993-94, cmty. devel. v.p. 1994-95, US Jr. C. of C. internat. affairs commn. 1995-98, JCI individual devel. commn. 1996, spl. asst. to world pres. 1997—), Internat. Spkrs. Platform, Jr. C. of C Republican. Roman Catholic. Avocations: photography, travel. Office: Verizon 13100 Columbia Pike Silver Spring MD 20902 Personal E-mail: dmenzigian@aol.com.

MORENO, JAIME, professional soccer player; b. Santa Cruz, Bolivia, Jan. 19, 1974; Grad., Tahuichi Acad., Santa Cruz. Mem. Middlebrough, English Premier League, 1995—96, DC United Major League Soccer, 1996—2002, NY/NJ MetroStars, Major League Soccer, 2003; forward DC United, Washington, 2004—, Bolivia Nat. Soccer Team, 1999—. Named Most Valuable Player, Major League Soccer, 1999, AT&T Best XI, 1999. Mem., DC United, Major League Soccer Cup Champions, 1996, 1997, & 1999; mem. DC United, Major League Soccer, US Open Cup Champions, 1996; mem. DC United, Major League Soccer, CONCACAF Champions Cup Winners, 1998; Winner, Golden Boot award, Major League Soccer (16 goals), 1997. Mailing: RFK Stadium 2400 East Capital St, SE Washington DC 20003

MORENO, JONATHAN, bioethicist; b. Poughkeepsie, NY, June 11, 1952; B., Hofstra U., 1973, PhD (hon.), 1998; PhD, Washington U., 1977. Prof. Swarthmore Coll., Pa., U. Tex., Austin, George Washington U., Washington, U. Penn., Philadelphia, 1995—97, Health Sci. Ctr., SUNY Brooklyn, 1997—98; Emily Davie and Joseph S. Kornfeld prof. Biomedical Ethics U. Va., Charlottesville, 1998—, dir. Ctr. for Biomedical Ethics; sr. fellow Ctr. for Am. Progress, Washington. Faculty affiliate Kennedy Inst. Ethics, Georgetown U.; adv. bd. Howard Hughes Med. Inst.; bd. Health Sciences Policy Inst. Medicine, com. on prison rsch.; com. biodefense analysis & countermeasures Nat. Academies; accredidation coun. Assn. Accreditation of Human Rsch. Protection Programs; sr. cons. Nat. Bioethics Adv. Commn.; sr. policy & rsch. analyst President's Adv. Com. on Human Radiation Experiments, Washington; ethics commentator ABCNews.com. Author: Ethics in Clinical Practice, 1994, Deciding Together: Bioethics & Moral Consensus, 1995, Arguing Euthanasia, 1995, Undue Risk: Secret State Experiments on Humans, 2001, In the Wake of Terror: Medicine & Morality in a Time of Crisis, 2003, Ethical & Regulatory Aspects of Clinical Research, 2003, Is There an Ethicist in the House?, 2005; contbr. articles, chapters to books. Fellow: NY Acad. Medicine, Hastings Ctr.; mem.: Am. Soc. Bioethics & Humanities (former pres.), Inst. Medicine ((in conjunction w/NRC) mem. adv. com. Human Embryonic Stem Cell Rsch. 2006—). Office: Ctr Biomedical Ethics UVA PO Box 800758 Charlottesville VA 22908 Office Phone: 434-924-8274. E-mail: jdm8n@virginia.edu.

MORENO, LUIS ALBERTO, bank executive; m. Gabriela Febres-Cordero; children: Nicolas, Natalia. B in Bus. Adminstrn. and Econs., Fla. Atlantic U., 1975; MBA, Thunderbird U., 1977. Divisional mgr. Praco, 1977—82; exec. prodr. TV Hoy, 1982—90; pres. Instituto de Fomento Industrial, Colombia, 1991—92; min. econ. devel., 1992—94; chair Andres Pastrana presdl. campaign, 1994; sr. advisor Luis Carlos Sarmiento Orgn., 1994—97; rep. for Andean Region WestSphere Capital, 1997—98; Colombian amb. to the US, 1998—2005; pres. Inter-Am. Devel. Bank, Washington, 2005—. Recipient King of Spain prize for journalism, Orden al Mérito Civil Ciudad de Bogotá, en el Grado de Gran Cruz, Mayor of Bogotá, 1990, Orden al Mérito Industrial — José Gutiérrez Gómez, Colombian Nat. Bus. Assn., 2002, Orden de Boyacá en el Grado de Gran Cruz, Pres. of Colombia, 2002. Office: Inter-Am Devel Bank 1300 New York Ave NW Washington DC 20577 *

MORENO, PATRICIA FRAZIER, lawyer; b. Lebanon, Pa. d. Joseph James and Cariella Agnes (Rothermel) Frazier; m. Camille Quijada Moreno, Dec. 4, 1982; children: William David, Helen Grace, Camille Fitzcarraldo. Student, Millersville U., 1969-71, Cochise Coll., 1992-93; BA in Polit. Sci., U. Ariz., Sierra Vista, 1997; JD, U. Ariz., 2001. Cert.: Nat. Assn. Legal Secs. (profl. legal sec.), Nat. Assn. Legal Assts. (legal asst.), bar: Ariz. 2002. Law clerk John F. Kelliher, Jr. PC, Sierra Vista, Ariz., 1999-2001, assoc., 2002—04; spl. asst. atty. gen. State of Ariz., 2005. Assoc. faculty Cochise Coll., Sierra Vista, 1996—97, U. Ariz. S., 2003—; with Policy-Studies, Inc., 2005. Mem. human rels. commn. City of Sierra Vista, 1982—83; mem. adv. bd. Salvation Army, Sierra Vista, 1988—92. Named Sec. of the Yr., S.E. Ariz. Legal Secs. Assn., 1993, Lawyer of the Yr., Ariz. Vol. Lawyers Program, Alumnus of the Yr., U. Ariz. S., 2006; named one of Top 50 Pro Bono Lawyers, Ariz. Legal Svcs. Found., 2005. Mem.: ACLU, Borderline Mensa (officer 1987—93, scholar 1992). Democrat. Avocations: cyberculture, film history, politics, writing. Office: Child Support Svcs Ariz 7 Bisbee Rd Bisbee AZ 85603 Office Phone: 520-432-3161. Business E-Mail: patricia.moreno@azbar.org.

MORENO, RITA (ROSITA DOLORES ALVERIO), actress; b. Humacao, PR, Dec. 11, 1931; m. Leonard I. Gordon, June 18, 1965; 1 child, Fernanda Luisa. Spanish dancer since childhood, night club entertainer; appeared on Broadway in The Sign in Sidney Brustein's Window, 1964-65, Gantry, 1969-70, The Last of the Red Hot Lovers, 1970-71, The National Health, 1974, The Ritz, 1975, Wally's Cafe, 1981, The Odd Couple, 1985; (off Broadway) After Play, 1995, (London prodn.) Sunset Blvd., 1996; motion picture debut, 1950, and appeared in numerous films including West Side Story, Carnal Knowledge, The King and I, Singing in the Rain, The Four Seasons, I Like It Like That, 1994, Angus, 1995, Wharf Rat, 1995, Slums of Beverly Hills, 1998, Carlo's Wake, 1999, Blue Moon, 2000, Pinero, 2001, King of the Corner, 2004, Lolo's Cafe, 2006, Play It By Ear, 2006, (TV) The Rockford Files: If It Bleeds...It Leads, 1999, Strong Medicine, 2003, The Guardian, 2003, Copshop, 2004, Law and Order, 2005, (series) American Family, 2002. Recipient Acad. Award for best supporting actress, 1962; Grammy award for best rec., 1973, Antoinette Perry award for best supporting actress Broadway play, 1975, Emmy award, 1977, 78, award Nat. Osteoporosis Found., 2000, Presdl. Freedom medal, 2005. Achievements include being in the Guinness Book of World Records as the only female performer to win Acad., Grammy, Tony and Emmy awards. Address: care Agency for Performing Arts 9200 W Sunset Blvd Los Angeles CA 90069-3502

MORENO-ASPITIA, ALVARO, physician, researcher; s. Ricardo Moreno-Azorero and Susana Aspitia; m. Maga; children: Sebastian, Camila, Pablo. MD, U. Nacional de Asuncion, Paraguay, 1991. Diplomate Internal Medicine Am. Bd. of Internal Medicine, PA, 1997, Medical Oncology Am. Bd. of Internal Medicine, 2000, Hematology Am. Bd. of Internal Medicine, 2000, Pediatrics Am. Bd. of Pediat., 1997, Am. Bd. of Pediat., 2004. Resident internal medicine/pediat. Scott and White Hosp. Tex. A&M Coll. of Medicine, Temple, Tex., 1993—97, chief resident, 1996—97; fellow Mayo Clinic Grad. Sch. Medicine, Jacksonville, Fla., 1997—2000; cons., asst. prof. medicine Mayo Clinic and Mayo Grad. Sch. of Medicine, Jacksonville, Fla., 2000—. Assoc. dir. clin. studies unit Mayo Clinic, Jacksonville, Fla., 2001—, assoc. dir. multidisciplinary breast clinic, 2005—; assoc. program dir. hematology & oncology fellowship Mayo Grad. Sch. of Medicine, Jacksonville, Fla., 2005—. Contbr. scientific papers. Recipient, Alpha Omega Alpha Honor Med. Soc., 1997, Sr. yr. gold medal, Coll. Internat., 1985, 2000 Shahin Award for Rsch., DCMS, 2000, Tchr. of the Yr. (Hematology/Oncology), Dept. of Internal Medicine, 2004; scholar Oncology Fellow Scholarship Methods in Clin. Cancer Rsch., AACR-ASCO, 1998. Fellow: ACP, Am. Acad. of Pediat.; mem.: Am. Assn. for Cancer Rsch., Am. Soc. of Hematology, Am. Soc. of Clin. Oncology, Alpha Omega Alpha Honor Med. Soc. Achievements include research in Clinical trials in the treatment of hematologic and solid malignancies. Office: Mayo Clinic 4500 San Pablo Rd Jacksonville FL 32224

MORENO-CABRAL, CARLOS EDUARDO, cardiac surgeon; b. Zacatecas, Mex., Nov. 4, 1951; s. Manuel Julio Moreno and Dominga Cabral; m. Elaine Nakamura; children: Rodrigo, Iza, Daniel. MD, Nat. U. Mex., 1976. Diplomate Am. Bd. Thoracic Surgery. Resident in gen. surgery U. Hawaii, 1977-80, Mich. State U., 1980-82; fellow in cardiac surgery Stanford (Calif.) U., 1982-84, 86-88; tng. in thoracic surgery SUNY, Bklyn., 1984-86; dir. cardiac transplant program St. Francis Hosp., Honolulu, 1989—. Author: Postoperative Management in Adult Cardiac Surgery, 1988. Fellow ACS; mem. Soc. Thoracic Surgeons, European Assn. Cardio-Thoracic Surgery. Avocation: photography. Office: 1380 Lusitana St Ste 912 Honolulu HI 96813-2448 E-mail: cemoreno@aol.com.

MORÉTEAU, OLIVIER, law educator; DEA in Comparative Law, Université Jean Moulin, 1978, DEA in French Pvt. Law, 1981, PhD summa cum laude, 1990. Tchg. and rsch. asst. Université Jean Moulin, Lyon, France, 1980—90, dir. internat. rels., 1993—95, v.p. internat. rels., 1997—99, assoc. dir. Edouard Lambert Institute of Comparative Law, 1985—2000, dir., 2000—05, assoc. prof., 1990—98, prof. comparative law, 2000—05; prof. pvt. law Université Pierre Mendes, Grenoble, France, 1998—2000; prof. law, Russell B. Long Eminent Scholars Academic Chair, dir. Ctr. of Civil Law Studies La. State U., Baton Rouge, 2005—. Vis. prof. U. Minn., 1992, Boston U., 1993—2000, 2002—04, U. Melbourne, 2002, 04. Contbr. articles to profl. jours. Mem.: Am. Law Inst., Société de Législation comparée, European Centre of Tort and Insurance Law, European Group on Tort Law, Internat. Acad. Comparative Law. Office: La State U Paul M Herbert Law Ctr W323 Law Ctr Baton Rouge LA 70803-1000 Office Phone: 225-578-0067. Office Fax: 225-578-3677. E-mail: moreteau@lsu.edu.

MORETTI, AUGUST JOSEPH, pharmaceutical executive, lawyer; b. Elmira, NY, Aug. 18, 1950; s. John Anthony and Dorothy M. (De Blasio) M.; m. Audrey B. Kavka, Nov. 8, 1981; children: David Anthony, Matthew Alexander. BA magna cum laude, Princeton U., 1972; JD cum laude, Harvard U., 1975. Assoc. Heller, Ehrman, White and McAuliffe, San Francisco, 1976-82, ptnr., 1982-2000; CFO, gen. counsel Surro Med, Inc., 2001—05; CFO Alexza Pharms., 2005—. Lectr. bus. adminstrn. U. Calif. Berkeley, 1977-79; bd. dirs. AviGenics. Bd. dirs. Ann Martin Children's Ctr.; mem. adv. panel U. Calif. Berkeley Entrepreneur Program. Mem. ABA.

MORETTI, FRANCO, professor of comparative literature; Ed., Universita' di Roma Laurea, 1972. Prof. Ctr. for Study of the Novel, Stanford U., 2000—, Danily C. and Laura Louise Bell prof., prof. English and Comparative Lit. Calif. Scientific adv. Ministry of Rsch., France; lectr. Gauss seminars Princeton U.; lectr. Beckman lectr. UCLA, Berkeley. Author: Signs Takes for Wonders, 1983, The Way of the World, 1987, Modern Epic, 1996, Atlas of the European Novel 1800-1900, 1998, Graphs, Maps and Trees, 2005; chief editor The Novel, 2006; contbr. articles New Left Rev. Fellow: Wissenschaftskolleg zu Berlin; mem.: Am. Acad. Arts and Sciences. Office: Dept Comparative Lit Stanford Univ Margaret Jacks Hall Bldg 460 Rm 417 Stanford CA 94305-2087 Office Phone: 650-723-4590. Office Fax: 650-725-0755. E-mail: moretti@stanford.edu.

MOREWITZ, STEPHEN JOHN, behavioral scientist, consultant, sociologist, educator; b. Newport News, Va., May 14, 1954; s. Burt M. and Ruth (August) M., Lora Friedman (stepmother). BA, Coll. William and Mary, 1975, MA, 1978; PhD, U. Chgo., 1983. Rsch. asst. Michael Reese Hosp., Chgo., 1979-84; asst. social scientist Argonne (Ill.) Nat. Lab., 1984-85; asst. to dean, asst. prof. U. Ill., Chgo., 1988-92, sr. rsch. splst., 1991-92; vol. rsch. staff San Francisco Gen. Hosp., 1993-97; pres. S. Morewitz, PhD & Assocs., Chgo. and Buffalo Grove, Ill., 1988—, San Francisco, 1992—. Part-time sociology faculty DePaul U., Chgo., 1985—; mem. faculty St. Elizabeth's Hosp., 1987—88; assoc. prof. Calif. Coll. Podiatric Medicine, 1997—2000, prof., rsch. dean, 2000—02; adj. prof. Calif. Sch. Podiatric Medicine, 2003—; cons. in field; lectr. Calif. State U., 2004. Co-author: Medical Malpractice, 1996; author: Sexual Harassment and Social Change, 1996, Stalking and Violence, 2003, Domestic Violence and Maternal Child Health, 2004; contbr. articles to profl. jours., chapters to books. Vol. docent Garfield Farm Mus., LaFox, Ill., 1979—; curator Saving of S.S. Quanza, Chgo., 1991—. Mem. Am. Pub. Health Assn. (Top 10 Injury Poster award 2000), Am. Diabetes Assn. (profl. sect.), Assn. for Behavioral Scis. and Med. Edn., Am. Sociol. Assn. (cert., nat. finalist med. sociology), Soc. Behavioral Medicine, Generalist in Med. Edn., Sociol. Practice Assn., Soc. Study Social Problems (divsn. chmn., Outstanding Scholar award 2003). Avocations: theater, museum design, swimming, environmental preservation, farming. Office: S Morewitz PhD & Assocs PMB M858 28 E Jackson Blvd 10 Fl Chicago IL 60604

MOREY, CARL REGINALD, musicologist; b. Toronto, Ont., Can., July 14, 1934; s. Reginald Donald and Julia Beatrice (Mabey) M.; m. Lorna Ann Dalton, June 2, 1960 (dec.); 1 child, Rachel Adriana MusB, U. Toronto, 1957; MusM, Ind. U., 1961, PhD, 1965. Asst. prof. Wayne State U., Detroit, 1962-63; assoc. prof. U. Windsor, Ont., 1964-70; prof. music U. Toronto, 1970-2000, dean faculty of music, 1984-90, Jean A. Chalmers prof., dir. Inst. for Can. Music, 1991-2000. Author: Music in Canada: A Research and Information Guide, 1997; MacMillan On Music, 1997, An Opera Sampler, 1998, Opera Viva, 2000; editor: (musical) Works of Glenn Gould (Schott), 1995, 96, 97, 99, 2004. Avocation: swimming. Office: U Toronto Faculty of Music Toronto ON Canada M5S 2C5 Home: 907 77 Carlton St Toronto ON Canada M5B 2J7 Business E-Mail: carl.morey@utoronto.ca.

MOREY, CHARLOTTE ANN, elementary school educator, music educator; b. Dickinson, ND, Dec. 1, 1949; d. Clarence William Hartman and Catherine Sills; m. Michael Scott Morey, June 19, 1971; children: Christopher Michael, Melissa Kay. BS, Dickinson State Coll., 1971. Elem. music specialist Slope County Schs., Amidon, ND, 1971—72, New England Pub. Schs., 1972—75, 1980—80; jr. high sch. music specialist McKenzie County Pub. Schs., Watford City, 1976—78; elem. music specialist Hettinger Pub. Schs., 1985—2000, Lincoln Elem. Sch., Fargo, 2000—. Contbr. articles to profl. jours. Flutist cmty. bands, Hettinger, Bismark, Fargo, 1981—; organist Luth. Ch., Regent, New England, Watford City, Hettinger, 1965—2000. Named N.D. Music Educator of Yr., 2001; recipient Disting. Svc. award, Internat. Misic Camp, 1999, Alumni Fellows award, Dickinson State U., 2004. Mem.: Music Educators Assn. N.D. (clinician & adjudicator 1971—), Orgn. Am. Kodaly Educators (clinician 1995—, pres. North Plains chpt.), N.D. Music Educators Assn. (state chair, bd. dirs., exec. bd., Music Educator of Yr. 2001), N.D. Am. Choral Dirs. Assn. (state pres. 2001—, past repertoire & stds. chair). Avocations: cross stitch, gardening, cooking, reading. Office: Lincoln Elem Sch 2120 9th St S Fargo ND 58103

MOREY, DARYL, professional sports team executive; m. Ellen Morey; children: Karen, Scott. B in Computer Sci., Northwestern U.; MBA, MIT, 2000. Statis. cons. STATS, Inc.; prin. cons., dir. knowledge mgmt. Parthenon Grp.; tech. lead MITRE Corp.; sr. v.p. ops. and info. Boston Celtics, 2003—06; asst. gen. mgr. Houston Rockets, 2006—. Tchr. MIT Sloan Sch. Mgmt. Contbr. articles to profl. publs. Office: Houston Rockets Toyota Ctr 1510 Polk St Houston TX 77002 *

MOREYRA, ABEL E., medical educator; b. Mar del Plata, Argentina, Dec. 2, 1941; came to U.S., 1972; s. Genaro and Emilia (Basso) M.; m. Maria Elena Moreyra; children: Maria Eugenia, Maria Evelina, Fernando Abel. MD, U. Nacional de La Plata, Argentina, 1967. Fellow Cleve. Clinic Found., 1972-75; asst. prof. medicine UMDNJ-Robert Wood Johnson Med. Sch., New Brunswick, NJ, 1975-83, assoc. prof., 1983-95, prof., 1995—. Fellow ACP, Am. Coll. Cardiology; mem. Am. Coll. Angiology. Office: UMDNJ-RW Johnson Med Sch CN-19 Rm 582A New Brunswick NJ 08903 Office Phone: 732-235-7851. E-mail: moreyrae@umdnj.edu.

MORFOPOULOS, V., metallurgical engineer, materials engineer; b. Athens, Greece, Oct. 22, 1937; BS, Purdue U., 1958; MS, Columbia U., 1961, ScD in Engring. Sci., 1964. Rsch. assoc. metall. engring. Purdue U., 1957-60; rsch. engr. U.S. Steel Corp., 1961; instr. chem. CUNY, 1961-63; rsch. engr. Argonne Nat. Lab., 1963, Am. Iron & Steel, Columbia U., 1964-65, sr. metall. sci., 1965-66; tech. dir. R&D testing Am. Standards Testing Bur., 1966—. Mem. Int. Commn. Chem. Thermodyn. & Kinetics; mem. Transp. Rsch. Bd., Nat. Rsch. Coun.; cons. in field. Mem. AAAS, Am. Inst. Mining, Metall. Petroleum Engrs., Am. Soc. Engr. Edn., Assn. Cons. Chemists and Chem. Engrs., N.Y. Acad. Sci. Achievements include research in corrosion and oxidation phenomena. low and high temperature thermodynamics, liquid metals and compounds, surface phenomena, electrometallurgy and electrode phenomena, electrical and magnetic properties of matter, failure and stress analysis, metal finishing, joining and working. Office Phone: 212-943-3160. Personal E-mail: worldteck@aol.com.

MORFORD, CRAIG S., federal agency administrator, prosecutor; b. Schenectady, NY, Feb. 10, 1959; BA, Hope Coll., 1981; JD, Valparaiso U. Sch. Law, 1984. Trial atty. Office Chief Counsel IRS, 1984—87; trial atty. organized crime prosecution US Dept. Justice, 1986—89, asst. US atty. (no. dist.) OH, mem. organized crime strike force, 1989—2002, interim US atty. (ea. dist.) Mich., 2004—05, spl. atty. to US atty. gen. heading investigation into first major US post Sept. 11th trial, 2004, 1st. US atty. (no. dist.) Ohio, 2005—06, interim US atty. (mid. dist.) Tenn., 2006—07, acting dep. atty. gen., 2007—. Recipient Atty. Gen.'s award for Disting. Svc. (2), US Dept. Justice. Office: US Dept Justice 950 Pennsylvania Ave NW Washington DC 20530 *

MORFORD, JOANN (JOANN MORFORD-BURG), state senator, investment company executive; b. Miller, SD, Nov. 26, 1956; d. Darrell Keith Morford and Eleanor May Morford-Steptoe. BS in Agrl.-Bus., Comml. Econs., S.D. State U., 1979; cert. in personal fin. planning, Am. Coll., 1992. CLU; chartered fin. cons. Agrl. loan officer 1st Bank System, Presho, SD, 1980-82, Wessington Springs, SD, 1982-86, Am. State Bank, Wessington Springs, 1986; investment rep. ARM Fin. Svcs. Inc., Wessington Springs, 1986-96, Capital Financial Svcs., Inc., Miller, 1997—; mem. S.D. State Senate, Wessington Springs, 1990-96, majority whip, 1993-94, minority whip, 1995-96, mem., 1990-97, Miller, 1997-98; ins. agt. Western Fraternal Life Assn., 2001—03. Mem. transp. com., commerce com., taxation com. S.D. State Senate, Pierre, 1990—92, mem. appropriations com., 1993—98, chair ops. and audit com., 1993—94, mem. ops. and audit com., 1995—98; mem. fed. issues environ. com. Nat. Conf. State Legislators' Assembly, 1994—98, vice chair, 1996—97. Mem. midwestern-Can. task force Midwest Conf., 1990—94; treas. twp. bd. Wessington Springs, 1990—92; active Wessington Springs Sch. Improvement Coun., 1992—95; bd. dirs. Nyoda Coun. Girls Scouts U.S.; mem. fin. com. United Meth. Ch., Miller, 2001—04. Fleming fellow, Ctr. Policy Alternatives, 1996. Mem.: S.D. Farmers Union, Bus. and Profl. Women (2nd v.p. 2002), Alumni Coun. Young Polit. Leaders (China delegation 1996, host El Salvador delegation 1999), Future Farmers Am. (adv. bd. Wessington Springs chpt. 1984—96), S.D. State U. 4-H Alumni Assn., Order Ea. Star (various offices 1980—). Democrat. Home and Office: 1510 N Parkview Pl Miller SD 57362-0021

MORFORD, MARIE ARLENE, insurance company executive; b. Wichita, Oct. 21, 1929; d. George and Bertha (Wear) Bachman; divorced; children: Stephen, Cheryl, Phillip. Clk. McKesson Robbin Drug, Wichita, 1948-49, Safeway Offices, Wichita, 1952-55; ins. sec. Benfer Ins., Newton, Kans., 1955-70, Ctrl. Agy., Newton, 1970-87; patient admitting operator Halstead (Kans.) Hosp., 1988-90; ins. rep., office mgr., lic. rep. State Farm, Newton, Kans., 1990—. Dir. religious edn. St. Mary's Ch., Newton, 1988, advisor adult religious edn., 1996, eucharistic minister, 1982; rep. Mother to Mother Ministry, Newton, 1988, Harvey County Citizens for Life, Newton, 1989; regent Daus. of Isabella St. Joseph's Cir., Kans., 1993-97, 2005-, treas., 1995—, state vice regent, 1999—; pres. Wichita Diocesan Coun. of Cath. Women, 1993-95; adv. bd. Wichita Diocesan Religious Edn. Mem. Daus. of Isabella (state vice regent 1999-2001, state auditor 2001, regent 2005—, state trustee, 2000—). Home: 1206 Harrison PO Box 135 Newton KS 67114-0135 Office Phone: 316-282-0459.

MORGAN, ALAN VIVIAN, geologist, educator; b. Barry, Glamorgan, Wales, Jan. 29, 1943; emigrated to Can., 1964, naturalized, 1977; s. George Vivian Williams and Sylvia Nesta (Atkinson) M.; m. Marion Anne Medhurst, June 14, 1966; children: Siân Kristina, Alexis John. B.Sc. with honors in Geology and Geography, U. Leicester, Eng., 1964; M.Sc. in Geography, U. Alta., Calgary, Can., 1966; PhD in Geology, U. Birmingham, Eng., 1970. Postdoctoral fellow U. Western Ont. and U. Waterloo, Ont., Canada, 1970-71; asst. prof. earth scis. and man-environ. studies U. Waterloo, 1971-78, assoc. prof. earth scis., 1978-85, prof., 1985—, assoc. dir. Quaternary Scis. Inst. Ont., Canada, 1992-97, dir. Quaternary Scis. Inst., 1997—2004. Mem. Brit. Schs. Exploring Soc. Ctrl. Iceland Expdn., 1960; rep. Can. Geosci. Coun., 1977-83, exec. dir., 1988-94, adminstrv. dir., 1996-2001, edn. dir., 2003-06; mem. com. on global change Royal Soc. Can., 1988-91, mem. com. on pub. awareness of sci., 1989-94; coord. global change Geol. Survey Can., 1990-92; sr. officer Internat. Geosci. Edn. Orgn., 2000—, sec.-treas., 2003—; dir. Can. Prize Awards Found., 2000—, Can. Prize Found., 2001-; chair Can. Geosci. Edn. Network, 2003-06. Author 6 field guides; editor What On Earth, 1987—; assoc. editor Geosci. Can., 2000—; editor newsletter OYEZ, 1990-94; contbr. articles to numerous profl. publs.; dir., prodr. documentary film The Heimaey Eruption, 1974. Recipient award for MS thesis Can. Soc. Petroleum Geologists, 1967, Bancroft award Royal Soc. Can., 1994, John H. Moss award Nat. Assn. Geology Tchrs., 1995, J. Willis Ambrose medal Geol. Assn. Can., 1997. E.R.W. Neale medal Geol. Assn. Canada, 1998, Civic award City of Waterloo, 2004; Charles Lapworth scholar, 1970; grantee Nat. Scis. and Engring. Rsch. Coun. Can., 1971-2005. Fellow Geol. Assn. Can. (hon. life, sec.-treas. 1975-83, disting. fellow), Geol. Soc. Am.; mem. Am. Quaternary Assn. (pres. 1990-92), Can. Quaternary Assn. (pres. 1987-89), Brit. Quaternary Rsch. Assn., Internat. Union Quaternary Rsch. (sec. gen. XII congress 1983-87). Office: U Waterloo Dept Earth Scis Waterloo ON Canada N2L 3G1 Home Phone: 519-747-4049; Office Phone: 519-888-4567 ext. 3029. Business E-Mail: avmorgan@uwaterloo.ca.

MORGAN, ALFRED VANCE, management consulting company executive; b. Liberal, Kans., Apr. 13, 1936; s. Forest Francis and Gertrude Irene (Henning) M.; m. Peggy Ann Riley, June 29, 1960; children: Trudie Marie, Vance Riley, Allen Forest, Bradley Augustus, Kelly James. BBA, U. Kans., 1958; MBA, U. So. Calif., 1966; postgrad., Am. Inst. Banking, 1965. Asst. mgr. Fruehauf Trailer Co., LA, Calif., 1960-61; asst. mktg. dir. Security Pacific Nat. Bank, 1961-65; mktg. exec. Doyle, Dane, Bernbach Advt., 1965-66; cons. Harbridge House, Inc., Boston, 1966-71; pres. Morgan Bus. Assocs., Inc., Santa Barbara and Boston, 1971—; instr. bus. L.A. City Coll., 1971-72; instr. mgmt. Santa Barbara City Coll., 1973. Pres. Exptl. in Internat. Living, 1980-81. Contbr. articles to profl. publs. Mem. Lobero Theatre Bd., 1984-88; mem. vestry All Saints Espiscopal Ch., 2003—, jr. warden, 2006; v.p. El Escorial Condo Assn., 2003—. With AUS, 1958-60. Mem. ASTD, Am. Mktg. Assn. L.A., Am. Soc. Profl. Cons., U. So. Calif. Grad. Sch. Bus. Alumni Assn. Office: Morgan Bus Assocs 8096 Puesta del Sol Carpinteria CA 93013 Office Phone: 805-684-6191. Fax: 805-684-6116. Personal E-mail: almorgan@morganba.com.

MORGAN, ANNE MARIE G., broadcast journalist, educator; b. Paducah, Ky., Apr. 23, 1955; d. Ralph Edward and Vera Christine Gill; m. Michael William Morgan, Nov. 19, 1977; children: Deborah, Jon, James. BA in Govt. and Psychology, Coll. William and Mary, 1976; MA in Polit. Sci., U. Richmond, 1997; postgrad. in Pub. Policy, Va. Commonwealth U., 1998. HS tchr. James-City County Sch., Williamsburg, Va., 1977, Colonial Hts. Sch., Va., 1977-79; TV and radio journalist Capitol News, Richmond, Va., 1984—, Va. Pub. Broadcasting, Richmond, Va., 1987—, WRIC-TV, Richmond, 1994—96, WTVR-TV, Richmond, 1996—2000; broadcast news anchor Va. News Network, Richmond, Va., 2000—02; journalist WVTF Radio, Roanoke, 2002—, Va. Pub. Radio, 2002—. Assoc. prof. polit. sci. U. Richmond, Va., 1998—. Author: (with others) Controversies in American Public Polity, 1999, Opposing Viewpoints Series, 1991. Sec. Parents' Guidance/Pupil Pers. Guidance Com., Powhatan, Va., 1996—98; state bd. dirs. Va. Pub. Broadcasting, Richmond, 2000—02; bd. dirs. Va. Adv. Coun. Adult Edn. and Literacy, Richmond, 1999—2002, Coun. Child Care and Early Childhood Devel., Richmond, 1995—96; chair bd. dirs. State Bd. for Cmty. Colls., Richmond, 1997—2002; chair Va. Coun. Status of Women, Richmond, 1994—2002. Recipient Meritorious award, Va. Assoc. Press Broadcasters, 2002, Disting. Faculty award, U. Richmond Sch. Contg. Studies, 2005, 1st Pl. award, Nat. Fedn. Press Women, 2005; Gov. proclamation Anne Marie Morgan Day in Commonwealth Va., Gov. Va., 1997. Mem.: Soc. Profl. Journalists, Soc. Profl. Journalists (Va. profl. chpt.), Nat. Fedn. Press Women (1st Pl. Prepared Radio Report award 2005), Va. Press Women (1st Pl. award 2005, 1st Pl. award on the scene report radio 2006, 1st Pl. award spl. radio programming 2007, 1st Pl. award prepared radio report 2007), Capitol Corrs. Assn., Am. Polit. Sci. Assn., Pi Sigma Alpha. Avocations: music, singing, mentoring.

MORGAN, ARDYS NORD, school improvement consultant; b. South Bend, Ind., Nov. 1, 1946; d. Arthur August and Janet Ardis (Eide) Nord; children: Elizabeth Elayne, Matthew Richard. BS in Elem. Edn., Ind. U., Bloomington, 1968; MS in Elem. Edn., Ind. U., Indpls., 1972; reading cert., Ind. U., South Bend, 1982; EDS, Ind. U., Bloomington, 1992; adminstr. lic., Ind. U.-Purdue U., Indpls., 1989; EdD in Curriculum and Sch. Adminstrn., Ind. U., 1994. Tchr., South Bend, 1968-69, 73-87; adminstr. dept. instrn. and curriculum, 1987-90; tchr. Indpls., 1969-70; resident lectr. Ind. U./Purdue U., Indpls., 1970-73, adminstr., 1989; mem. adj. faculty Ind. U., South Bend, 1985-90, acting program dir. elem. and secondary edn., 1990-92; asst. supt. schs. Michigan City (Ind.) Area Schs., 1992-94; supt. Union North United Schs. Corp., 1994-96; ednl. cons., tech. and staff devel. in curriculum Lightspan Partnership, San Diego, 1997-99; pres. Sch. Improvement Partnership, Inc., Granger, Ind., 1999—. Cons. in field. Recipient Disting. Alumni award div. edn. Ind. U., South Bend, 1990. Lilly Endowment fellow, 1987. Home: 51550 Stratton Ct Granger IN 46530-8342 Office: Sch Improvement Partnership 51550 Stratton Ct Ste 300 Granger IN 46530-8342

MORGAN, ARLENE NOTORO, university administrator; b. Phila., July 27, 1945; d. James Vincent and Mary Rose (Actis-Grande) Notoro; m. David J. Morgan, Mar. 3, 1948; children: Elizabeth, Lauren. BS in Journalism, Temple U., 1967. Reporter Delaware County Daily Times, Chester, Pa., 1967-69, Phila. Inquirer, 1969—, dep. metro editor, 1990-91, sr. editor, asst. mng. editor, 1991-2000, reader advocate columnist, 1998-2000; assoc. dean prizes and programs Columbia U. Grad. Sch. Journalism, NYC, 2000—05; treas. Scattergood Behavioral Health Found., Phila., 2005—. Author: The Authentic Voice: The Best Reporting on Race and Ethnicity, 2006. Bd. dirs. Friends Hosp., Phila., 1978—2005, Scattergood Behavioral Health Found., 2005—; mem. adv. bd. Temple U., La. State U.; mem. diversity com. Am. Soc. Newspaper Editors; dir. Columbia Race Project; mem. centennial com. Corpus Christi Ch., Manhattan. Recipient Phila. Newspapers Inc. Employee Recognition award, 1987, Excellence in Diversity award Knight Ridder, 1995; Media Studies Ctr. fellow Freedom Forum, 1996-97. Mem. Soc. Profl. Journalists., Newspaper Assn. Am. (diversity com.). Roman Catholic. Avocations: ballet, travel, opera and art appreciation, advocate to the mentally ill. Office Phone: 212-854-5377. E-mail: am494@columbia.edu.

MORGAN, BARBARA M., psychotherapist, educator; b. Biloxi, Miss., June 18, 1960; m. Franklyn C. Morgan, Dec. 15, 1991; children: Rachel E. McCauley, Erin L. McCauley, Brittany N. McCauley. PhD, Coll. of William and Mary, 1998. Lic. profl. counselor Va., 1998, marriage and family therapist Va., 1998, cert. counselor Nat. Bd. for Cert. Counselors, 1998. Prof. of psychology Richard Bland Coll., Petersburg, Va., 1997—; pvt. practice psychotherapist Barbara M. Morgan, Ph.D., Colonial Heights, Va., 1998—; pres. Relationship Intelligence, LLC, Colonial Heights, Va., 2005—. Contbr. articles to profl. jours. Adult edn. leader Christ and Grace Episcopal Ch., Petersburg, Va., 2000—06; pres. Va. Assn. of Marriage and Family Counselors, Charlottesville, 1998—99; bd. mem. Southside Regional Med. Ctr. Ethics Bd., Petersburg, Va., 1999—2006, Coll. of William and Mary Sch. of Edn. Adv. Bd., Williamsburg, Va., 2005—06. Recipient Acad. award, Va. Commonwealth Univ. Coll. of Humanities and Scis., 1994, Helen C. Hopper Meml. scholarship for family counseling, Coll. of William and Mary, 1995, Dean's award for student scholarship on women, 1996—98, Award of excellence, Coll. of William and Mary Sch. Edn., 1998. Mem.: Va. Assn. of Marriage and Family Counselors, Va. Counselors Assn., Am. Counselors Assn. Avocations: running, horseback riding, gardening, playing the piano. Office: Barbara M Morgan PhD 320C Charles Dimmock Pky Colonial Heights VA 23834 Home Phone: 804-712-3974; Office Phone: 804-520-4166. Office Fax: 804-520-6475; Home Fax: 804-520-6475. Personal E-mail: barbmorgan@rcn.com.

MORGAN, BARBARA R., astronaut; b. Fresno, Calif., Nov. 28, 1951; m. Clay Morgan; 2 children. BA in Human Biology with distinction, Stanford U., 1973; tchg. credential, Coll. Notre Dame, Belmont, Calif., 1974. Tchr. remedial reading and math Flathead Indian Reservation Arlee (Mont.) Elem. Sch., 1974; tchr. remedial reading/math McCall-Donnelly Elem. Sch., Idaho, 1975—78, tchr., 1975—78, 1979—85, 1986—98; tchr. elem. English and sci. Colegio Americano de Quito, Ecuador, 1978—79; astronaut, educator mission specialist candidate NASA, Johnson Space Ctr., Houston, 1998—. Backup candidate for Tchr. in Space Program NASA, 1985, mem. edn. divsn., office human resources and edn.; mem. fed. task force for women and minorities in sci. and engring. NSF; worked with NASA, speaking to ednl. organizations throughout the country, 1986; crew mem. STS-118 mission (Endeavour), 2007. Recipient Citizen of Yr. award, USA Today, 1986, Edn. award, Women in Aerospace, 1991, Wright Bros. "Kitty Hawk" Sands of Time Edn. award, L.A. C. of C., 1991, Space Pioneer award for edn., Nat. Space Soc., 1992, Pres.'s Medallion award, U. Idaho, 1998, Idaho Fellowship award, 1998, Women in Aerospace award, 2003. Mem.: NEA, Challenger Ctr. for Space Sci. Edn. (Challenger 7 award 1995), Internat. Tech. Edn. Assn. (Lawrence Prakken Profl. Cooperation award 1996), Internat. Reading Assn., Nat. Sci. Tchrs. Assn., Nat.

Coun. Tchrs. Math., Idaho Edn. Assn., Nat. PTA (hon.; hon. life mem.), Phi Beta Kappa. Avocations: playing the flute, reading, hiking, swimming, skiing. Office: Astronaut Office/CB NASA Johnson Space Ctr Houston TX 77058 *

MORGAN, BETHANYE BRANCH, biology professor; d. James and Elizabeth Branch; 1 child, Jokwon Bagby. MS, Prairie View A & M U., Tex. Asst. prof. biology Tarrant County Coll., Arlington, Tex., 1996—, dept. chair life sciences, 2004—07. Author: (lab manual) General College Biology Laboratory Manual, A Comparative Analysis of AIDS Awareness Among Male and Female African-American Leaders at the Southwestern Black Student Leadership Conference. Recipient Excellence award, Nat. Inst. Staff and Orgnl. Devel., 2005. Master: Women Sci.; mem.: Tex. C.C. Tchrs. Assn., Tex. Assn. Black Pers. Higher Edn. Business E-Mail: bethanye.morgan@tccd.edu.

MORGAN, BETSY STELLE, lawyer; b. Terre Haute, Ind., Mar. 15, 1963; BA, DePauw U., 1985; JD, John Marshall Law Sch., 1988. Bar: Ill. 1989. With Baker & McKenzie, Chgo., 1988—, counsel, 1997—2002, ptnr., 2002—. Co-chair N.Am. Pro Bono Initiative Baker & McKenzie, Chgo. Author: United States Business Immigration Manual, 2003. Office: Baker and McKenzie One Prudential Plz 130 E Randolph Dr Chicago IL 60601

MORGAN, BEVERLY CARVER, pediatrician, educator; b. NYC, May 29, 1927; d. Jay and Florence (Newkamp) Carver; children: Nancy, Thomas E. III, John E. MD cum laude, Duke U., 1955. Diplomate Am. Bd. Pediat. (oral examiner 1984-90, mem. written examination com. 1990—), Nat. Bd. Med. Examiners. Intern, asst. resident Stanford U. Hosp., San Francisco, 1955-56; clin. fellow pediat., trainee pediatric cardiology Babies Hosp.-Columbia Presbyn. Med. Ctr., NYC, 1956-59; rsch. fellow cardio-vasc. diagnostic lab. Columbia-Presbyn. Med. Ctr., NYC, 1959-60; instr. pediat. Coll. Physicians and Surgeons, Columbia U., NYC, 1960; dir. heart sta. Robert B. Green Meml. Hosp., San Antonio, 1960-62; lectr. pediat. U. Tex., 1960-62; spl. rsch. fellow in pediatric cardiology Sch. Medicine, U. Wash., Seattle, 1962-64, from instr. to prof. pediat., 1962-73, chmn. dept. pediat., 1973-80; mem. staff U. Wash. Hosp., chief of staff, 1975-77; mem. staff Harborview Med. Ctr., Children's Orthop. Hosp. and Med. Ctr., dir. dept. medicine, 1974-80; prof., chmn. dept. pediat. U. Calif., Irvine, 1980-88, prof. pediat. and pediatric cardiology, 1980—; pediatrician in chief Children's Hosp. Orange County, 1988. Mem. pulmonary acad. awards panel Nat. Heart and Lung Inst., 1972-75; mem. grad. med. edn. nat. adv. com. to sec. HEW, 1977-80; mem. Coun. on Pediatric Practice; chmn. Task Force on Opportunities for Women in Pediat., 1982; mem. nursing rev. com. NIH, 1987-88. Contbr. articles to profl. jours.; mem. editl. bd. Clin. Pediat., Am. Jour. Diseases of Children, Jour. of Orange County Pediatric Soc., Jour. Am. Acad. Pediat., LA Pediatric Soc. Recipient Women of Achievement award Matrix Table, Seattle, 1974; Disting. Alumnus award Duke U. Med. Sch., 1974; Ann. award Nat. Bd. Med. Coll. Pa., 1977; Career Devel. award USPHS, 1966-71; Moseby scholar, 1955. Mem. Am. Acad. Pediat. (chmn. com. on pediat. manpower 1984-86), Am. Coll. Cardiology, Soc. for Pediat. Rsch., Am. Fedn. Clin. Rsch., Am. Pediat. Soc., Assn. Med. Sch. Pediat. Dept. Chmn. (sec.-treas. 1981-87), Western Soc. for Pediat. Rsch., Alpha Omega Alpha. Office: U Calif Irvine Med Ctr Dept Pediatrics 101 The City Dr S Orange CA 92868-3201 Home Phone: 949-675-5361; Office Phone: 714-456-6483. Business E-Mail: bcmorgan@uci.edu.

MORGAN, BEVERLY HAMMERSLEY, secondary school educator, artist; b. Wichita Falls, Tex. d. Vernon C. and Melba Marie (Whited) Hammersley; m. Robert Lewis Morgan, Sept. 21, 1957 (div. 1972); children: Janet Claire, Robert David. BA, So. Meth. U.; MA, U. Ala., 1980, AA certification, 1982; postgrad., U. Tex., 1991—. Cert. art tchr., Tex., Ala.; cert. elem. tchr., Ala. Tchr. art Ft. Worth Pub. Schs., 1955-60; tchr. English, Lincoln County Schs., Fayetteville, Tenn., 1961-62; elem. tchr. Huntsville (Ala.) Pub. Schs., 1960-61, 62-68, tchr. art, 1972-92, 93-94. One-woman shows include U. Ala., 1980, Huntsville Art League, 1981, and various other art gallerys, art shows and exhbns. Mem. HAL Gallery, Huntsville, Madison County Sr. Art Gallery. Mem. Huntsville Mus. Art, Am. Contract Bridge League. Republican. Avocations: bridge, travel, collecting Hammersley English bone china. Home: 12027 Chicamauga Trl SE Huntsville AL 35803-1544

MORGAN, BRUCE RAY, management consultant; b. LA, Oct. 29, 1932; s. Francis Raymond and Rose Hall (Black) M.; m. Bette Jeanne Moore, Oct. 7, 1957; children: Michael John, Brian Leo, Jeanne Anne. AA, Sacramento Jr. Coll., 1952; BS, U. Calif.-Berkeley, 1954, LL.B., 1957. Bar: Calif. 1957. Judge adv. USAF, Saudi Arabia and Morocco, 1958-61; atty. firm Thelen, Marrin, Johnson & Bridges, San Francisco, 1961-67; dep. dir. Peace Corps, Nepal, 1967-68, dir, 1968-70; exec. dir. Center Research and Edn., Denver, 1971-75; dir. U.S. representation to Saudi Arabia-U.S. Joint Commn. on Econ. Coop., Riyadh, 1975-76; pres. Bruce Morgan Assocs., Inc., Washington, 1976—. Editor: Calif. State Bar Jour. Legis. Rev, 1957. Served with USAF, 1958-61. Mem. U.S., Calif. bars. Office: Bruce Morgan Assocs 4201 Cathedral Ave NW Apt 823W Washington DC 20016 Home Phone: 202-362-4194. Business E-Mail: bmorgan@bmainc.com.

MORGAN, CATHERINE MARIE, psychologist, writer; b. Duluth, Minn., Mar. 27, 1947; m. Ralph Morgan, 1967; 1 child, Andrew. BS, U. Nebr., 1968; MEd, U. Okla., 1973; PhD, Okla. State U., 1987; postgrad. Menninger Found., Psychotherapy Tng. Program, 1987-89. Child devel. specialist Southwest Guidance Ctr., Wheatland, Okla., 1973-74; pvt. practice Family Counseling Assocs., San Antonio, 1974-75; psychol. asst. Edmond Guidance Ctr., Okla., 1975-82; psychol. asst. supr. Southeast Guidance Ctr., Del City, Okla., 1982-86; psychol. intern Cleve. County Health Dept., Moore, Okla., 1986-87; psychologist Cen. State Hosp., Norman, Okla., 1987-89; pvt. practice assocs. in psychology Edmond, Okla.; vice chair bd. mgrs. Integris Mental Health; pres. Assocs. in Psychology, 1988—. Mem. AAUW, APA, Okla. Psychol. Assn., Am. Bus. Women's Assn., P.E.O., Kappa Delta Pi. Avocations: writing, reading, knitting, racquetball. Office: 9636 N May Ave Ste 200 Oklahoma City OK 73120

MORGAN, CLYDE NATHANIEL, dermatologist; b. Bell County, Tex., Nov. 2, 1923; s. Xenophen William and Rhoda Ella (Deck) M.; m. Birdie Joyce Rich, Mar. 3, 1951; children: Clyde Nathaniel Jr., Reinette Jean, Nancy Elaine. *Dr. Morgan is a descendant of Morgan ap Morgan, the first white settler in West Virginia, of Captain David Morgan, Indian fighter and Captain in the American Revolution, and of James Morgan who assisted in establishing American independence while acting in the capacity of private and Indian spy under Captain James Brenton and Colonel John Evans in 1778. Family tradition has it that Captain David Morgan taught George Washington how to survey. Wife, Birdie Morgan, was a delegate to the Republican National Convention in 1984.* BS, Abilene Christian Coll., 1948; MD, U. Tex., Galveston, 1953. Cert. Bd. of Am. Acad. Cryosurgery, 1978. Assoc. prof. biology Abilene (Tex.) Christian Coll., 1954-56; pvt. practice Abilene, 1954-67; dermatologist, 1969—. *Presented research papers on the development of special techniques in the cryosurgical treatment of benign and malignant lesions of the skin before the American College of Cryosurgery meetings in New Orleans and New York City; before the Southern Medical Association meeting in San Antonio; before the World Congress of cryosurgery meetings in San Remo, Italy, and Manila, Philippines; and before the Indian Cryogenics Council in Calcutta. Invited guest lecturer at the Jadavpur University Medical School in Calcutta, India.* Contbr. articles to profl. jours. Chmn. Taylor County Republican Party, 1965—70; delegate Republican Nat. Convention, 1968, 1980, alt. delegate, 1976. 1st lt. air corps US Army, 1943—46. Named Disting. Pres., Greater Abilene Kiwanis Club, 1979; recipient Med. Econs. award, 1963. Fellow Am. Acad. Family Practice; mem. AMA, SAR (chpt. pres. 1997-99, past pres. Big Country chpt., award 1995), Am. Coll. Cryosurgery, Internat. Soc. Cryosurgery, Tex. Med. Assn., So. Med. Assn., Tex. Dermatologic Soc., Taylor-Jones-Haskell County Med. Soc., Indian Coun. on Cryogenics (hon. fellow). Republican. Mem. Ch. Of Christ. Avocations: golf, fishing, hunting, cryogenics research. Home: 1718 Cedar Crest Dr Abilene TX 79601-3228 Office: 1166 Merchant St Abilene TX 79603-5014 Office Phone: 325-673-4242. Personal E-mail: cnmorgan@cox.net, clybird@juno.com.

MORGAN, COLBY SHANNON, JR., lawyer; b. Marshalltown, Iowa, Mar. 29, 1949; s. Colby Shannon and Elizabeth Perkinson (Robertson) M.; m. Leslie Marmon, Apr. 5, 1975; children: Colby Shannon III, Jeffrey Michael, Sarah Elizabeth. AB cum laude, Dartmouth Coll., 1971; JD, Vanderbilt U., 1974. Bar: NY 1975, US Dist. Ct. (so. and ea. dists.) NY 1976, Tenn. 1977, US Dist. Ct. (we. dist.) Tenn. 1978, US Ct. Appeals (6th cir.) 1980, US Dist. Ct. (ea. and we. dists.) Ark. 1983, US Ct. Appeals (8th cir.) 1987, US Dist. Ct. (no. dist.) Calif. 1994, US Ct. Appeals (3d cir.) 1995, US Ct. Appeals (9th cir.) 1996, US Ct. Appeals (4th cir.) 1996, US Supreme Ct. 1998, US Dist. Ct. (no. dist.) NY 1998, US Dist. Ct. (we. dist.) Mich. 2001, US Dist. Ct. (ctrl. and no. dists.) Ill. 2001, US Ct. Appeals (2d cir.) 2004. Assoc. Crowe, McCoy, Agoglia & Zweibel, Mineola, N.Y., 1974-78, Rosenfield, Borod & Kremer, Memphis, 1978-83, Apperson, Crump, Duzane & Maxwell, Memphis, 1983-86, Shuttleworth, Smith, Young & Webb, Memphis, 1986; sr. atty. Holiday Inns, Inc., Memphis, 1986-91; assoc. Petkoff & Lancaster, Memphis, 1991-92; sr. counsel Fed. Express Corp., Memphis, 1992. Chancellor, bd. dirs. Memphis Boys Town, 1979-86; chmn. Memphis Civil Svc. Commn., 1980-83; bd. dirs., chmn. bd. dirs. Memphis Emmaus Cmty., 1983—; bd. dirs. Christ Meth. Adminstrv. Bd., Memphis, 1984-86; Leadership Memphis, 1984—; cub-master Pack 241 Boy Scouts Am., Memphis, 1992-93; treas., bd. dirs. Memphis Symphony Chorus, 1981-85. Recipient FedEx Five Star award, 1997, Campaign Leadership award, United Way of the Mid South, 2000. Mem. ABA, FBA, Assn. Corp. Counsel, Dartmouth Lawyers Assn., Federalist Soc., Order of the First Families of Tenn., Gen. Soc. Colonial Wars, NY Sons of the Revolution, Mil. Order of the Stars and Bars (lt. comdr. 1994—), Tenn. Geneaol. Soc., Jamestowne Soc., Hereditary Order of Families of the Presidents, Clan Donnachaidh Soc., Mensa, SAR (chancellor, past pres. Memphis soc., v.p. West Tenn. 1992—, pres.-elect, past registrar, past chancellor, bd. govs. Tenn. chpt. 1994—), Scottish Rite. Republican. Methodist. Avocations: genealogy, marathon runner, tennis, golf, reading. Home: 5521 Fiesta Dr Memphis TN 38120-2826 Office: Fed Express Corp 3620 Hacks Cross Rd Memphis TN 38125 Office Phone: 901-434-8545. E-mail: csmorgan@fedex.com.

MORGAN, DANIEL LOUIS, lawyer, educator; b. Newark, Oct. 17, 1952; s. A. Henry and Eunice (Neubauer) M. BA in History, Tufts U., 1974; JD, U. Conn., 1977; LLM, Georgetown U., 1981. Bar: Conn. 1977, D.C. 1978. Atty., advisor, chief counsel IRS, Washington, 1977-81; assoc. Tucker, Flyer & Lewis P.C., Washington, 1981-85, prin., 1985-99; ptnr., bus. planning, employment law Venable, LLP, Washington, 2000—. Adj. prof. Cath. U. Law Sch., Washington, 1984-96; profl. lectr. in law George Washington U. Law Sch., 1997-2000; charter fellow Am. Coll. Employee Benefits Counsel. Co-author: The 401(K) Handbook, 1991, Employees and Independent Contractors, 1990; contbr. articles to profl. jours. Fellow Am. Coll. Employee Benefits Counsel (charter); mem. ABA (chmn. tax sect. com. on employment taxes 1986-88), D.C. Bar Assn. (sect. taxation and employee benefits com., chmn. employee benefits com. 1998-2000). Office: Venable LLP 575 7th St NW Washington DC 20004-1601 Office Phone: 202-344-8550. Office Fax: 202-344-8300. Business E-Mail: dlmorgan@venable.com.

MORGAN, DAVID FORBES, minister; b. Toronto, Ont., Can., Aug. 3, 1930; came to U.S., 1954; s. Forbes Alexander and Ruth (Bamford) M.; m. Delores Mae Storhaug, Sept. 7, 1956; children: Roxanne Ruth, David Forbes II. BA, Rocky Mt. Coll., 1960; ThB, MDiv, Coll. of the Rockies, 1970; postgrad., Bishop's Sch. Theology; LittD (hon.), N.D. Nat. Coll., 1954, D.C. Nat. Coll., 1954, Temple Coll., 1956. Ordained priest. Pres. Coll. of the Rockies, Denver, 1960-73; founder, rector Prior Order of Christ Centered Ministries, Denver, 1973—; canon pastor St. John's Cathedral, Denver, 1982-96, canon at large, 1996—. Bd. dirs. Internat. Contemplative Outreach, Ltd., mem. internat. faculty. Author: Christ Centered Ministries, A Response to God's Call, 1973, Songs with a Message, 1956. Mem.: Oratory of the Good Shepherd, Toronto. Home: 740 Clarkson St Denver CO 80218-3204 Office: 740 Clarkson St Denver CO 80218-3204 Personal E-mail: occmine@earthlink.net.

MORGAN, DENNIS RICHARD, lawyer; b. Jan. 3, 1942; s. Benjamin Richard and Gladys Belle (Brown) Morgan. BA, Washington and Lee U., 1964; JD, U. Va., 1967; LLM in Labor Law, NYU, 1971. Bar: Ohio 1967, Va. 1967, U.S. Ct. Appeals (4th cir.) 1968, U.S. Ct. Appeals (6th cir.) 1971, U.S. Supreme Ct. 1972. Law clk. to chief judge U.S. Dist. Ct. (ea. dist.) Va., 1967—68; mem. Marshman, Snyder & Seeley, Cleve., 1971—72; dir. labor rels. Ohio Dept. Adminstrv. Svcs., 1972—75; asst. city atty. Columbus, Ohio, 1975—77; dir. Ohio Legis. Reference Bur., Columbus, 1979—81; assoc. Clemans, Nelson & Assocs., Columbus, 1981; pvt. practice Columbus, 1978—92. Lectr. in field; guest lectr. Cen. Mich. U., 1975; judge moot ct. Ohio State U. Sch. Law, 1981, 83, grad. divsn., 73, 74, 76; guest lectr. Baldwin-Wallace Coll., 1973; legal counsel Dist. IV Comms. Workers Am., 1982—88; pers. dir. Pub. Utilities Commn., Ohio, 1989—91; asst. atty. gen. State of Ohio, 1991—2003. Negotiator Franklin County United Way, 1977—81; regional chmn. ann. alumni fund-raising program U. Va. Sch. Law; mem. Greater Hilltop Area Commn., 1989—2006; pres. Woodbrook Village Condominium Assn., 1985—2005, v.p., 2005—; vice-chmn. Franklin County Dem. Party, 1976—82; dem. com. person Ward 58, Columbus, 1973—2006; chmn. rules com. Ohio State Dem. Conv., 1974; co-founder, trustee Greater West Side Dem. Club; bd. dirs. Hilltop Civic Coun., Inc., 1997—99. Capt. US Army, 1968—70. Recipient Am. Jurisprudence award, 1967; scholar Robert E. Lee Rsch., 1965. Mem.: Am. Judicature Soc., Fed. Bar Assn., Indsl. Rels. Rsch. Assn., Pi Sigma Alpha. Roman Catholic. Home: 21320 Lancaster Run Unit 1116 Estero FL 33928 Personal E-mail: wahoos1967@yahoo.com.

MORGAN, DEREK, chef; BA in Polit. Sci., U. Ga.; grad., Art Inst. Atlanta. Line cook Villa Christina, Atlanta, 1995, sous chef, Boulevard Bistro, Atlanta, 1998, Woodside restaurant, Brentwood, Calif., The Ranch on Camelback Mountain, 1999; exec. chef Royal Palms Resort and Spa, Phoenix; owner, exec. chef D. Morgan's Restaurant and Wine Bar, Cartersville, Calif. Guest chef Celebrity Chef Tour, 2006; mem. James Beard Found., Am. Culinary Fedn. Named Best Hotel Chef in Am., James Beard Found., 2003; recipient Best Hotel Restaurant in World award, Hideaway Report, 2001. Office: D Morgan's 28 W Main St Cartersville GA 30120 Office Phone: 770-383-3535. Office Fax: 770-383-9396. Business E-Mail: derek@dmorgans.com. *

MORGAN, DONALD CRANE, lawyer; b. Detroit, Sept. 17, 1940; s. Donald Nye and Nancy Morgan; m. Judith Munro, June 23, 1962; children: Wendy, Donald. BA, Ohio Wesleyan U., 1962; JD, U. Mich., 1965. Bar: Mich. 1966, U.S. Dist. Ct. (ea. dist.) Mich. 1966, U.S. Ct. Appeals (6th cir.) 1967, U.S. Supreme Ct. 1971. Ptnr. Kerr, Russell and Weber, Detroit, 1965-87; of counsel Draugelis & Ashton, Plymouth, Mich., 1988-93; pvt. practice Plymouth, Mich., 1993—. Twp. atty. Plymouth Twp., 1970-85, Northville Twp., 1972-85; city atty. City of Plymouth, 1995-98; commr. Home Rule Charter Review Commn., City of Plymouth, 2005—. Chmn. Wayne County II congl. Dist. Rep. Party, 1979-81; bd. dirs. Growth Works, Inc., 1999—, treas., 1992-95, pres. 1995-99, dir. 2000—; ruling elder 1st Presbyn. Ch., Plymouth, 1976-79, 90-93; local bd. 222 mem. U.S. Selective Svc. Sys.; mem. home rule charter rev. com, City of Plymouth, 2002-04; elder commr. Detroit Presbytery. Paul Harris fellow, 1980. Mem. ABA, State Bar of Mich. (rep. assembly 1979-85, 89-95, 2003—, chmn. medicolegal problems com. 1995-96), Detroit Assn. Def. Trial Counsel, Plymouth Rotary (pres. 1985-86), Plymouth Rotary Found., Inc. (sec. 1996-98, dir. 1995, 99-2002), Phi Alpha Delta, Sigma Alpha Epsilon, Pi Sigma Alpha. Republican. Presbyterian. Avocations: reading, travel, sports. Home: 1440 Woodland Pl Plymouth MI 48170-1569 Office: 134 N Main St Plymouth MI 48170-1236 Office Phone: 734-453-8888. Personal E-mail: morganlaw48170@aol.com.

MORGAN, DONNA EVENSEN, lawyer; b. Bklyn., Feb. 28, 1957; d. Edward Ivar and Judith (Larsen) Evensen; m. Charles S. Morgan, Sept. 3, 1988. BA, Colgate U., 1979; JD, U. Mich., 1984. Bar: Ill. 1985. Assoc. Chapman and Cutler, Chgo., 1985-86, Kirkland and Ellis, Chgo., 1987-89, Mayer Brown Rowe & Maw LLP, Chgo., 1989—. Office: Mayer Brown Rowe & Maw LLP 71 S Wacker Dr Chicago IL 60606-4637 Home Phone: 630-887-0192; Office Phone: 312-701-7138. Business E-Mail: dmorgan@mayerbrownrowe.com.

MORGAN, EDMUND SEARS, retired history professor; b. Mpls., Jan. 17, 1916; s. Edmund Morris and Elsie Sears (Smith) M.; m. Helen Theresa Mayer, June 7, 1939; children: Penelope, Pamela; m. Marie Caskey, June 22, 1983. AB, Harvard U., 1937, PhD, 1942. Instrument maker Radiation Lab., MIT, 1942-45; instr. U. Chgo., 1945-46; asst. prof. Brown U., 1946-49, asso. prof., 1949-51, prof., 1951-55, acting dean grad. sch., 1951-52; prof. Yale U., 1955-65, Sterling prof., 1965-86, prof. emeritus, 1986—. Rsch. fellow Huntington Libr., 1952-53; Johnson rsch. prof. U. Wis., 1968-69 Author: The Puritan Family, 1944, Virginians at Home, 1953; author: (with Helen M. Morgan) The Stamp Act Crisis, 1953; author: The Birth of the Republic, 1956, The Puritan Dilemma, 1958, The Gentle Puritan, 1962, Visible Saints, 1963, Roger Williams, 1967, So What About History, 1969, American Slavery American Freedom, 1975, The Challenge of the American Revolution, 1976, The Meaning of Independence, 1976, The Genius of George Washington, 1980, Inventing the People, 1988, Benjamin Franklin, 2002, The Genuine Article, 2004, Not Your Usual Founding Father, 2006; mem. editl. bd.: N.E. Quar.; contbr. articles and revs. to hist. jours. Trustee Smith Coll., 1984-89. Recipient Nat. Humanities medal, 2000, Pulitzer citation, 2006. Mem.: Am. Acad. Arts and Scis., Orgn. Am. Historians (pres. 1971—72), Royal Hist. Soc., Brit. Acad., Am. Philos. Soc., Am. Antiquarian Soc., Mass. Hist. Soc., Colonial Soc. Mass.

MORGAN, ELAINE R., hematologist, oncologist, medical educator; b. Phila., May 22, 1946; d. Bernard and Sadie Jean (Blackman) Morgan; children: Brandon, Kerry David, Ari, Erin, Katelyn. BA, U. Pa., Phila., 1967, MD, 1971; cert. in Clin. Bioethics, Med. Coll. Wis., Milw., 2001. Cert. hosp. palliative medicine 2006. Resident pediat. Children's Hosp. of LA, 1971—74; fellow pediat. oncology Children's Hosp. Med. Ctr., Boston, 1974—75; attending physician Children's Meml. Hosp., Chgo., 1976—. Co-dir. pediat. hospice Palliative Care North Shore, Evanston, Ill., 1999—, Horizon Hospice Midwest Palliative Care Ctr.; med. advisor Make A Wish Found., Ill.; med. dir. Parent to Parent Children's Meml. Hosp., Chgo., 1995—; mem. faculty Feinberg Sch. Medicine, Northwestern U., 1978—, prof. pediat., 2005—. Contbr. articles to profl. jours. Recipient Tchr. of Yr., Children's Meml. Hosp., 1987; grantee, Leukemia Rsch. Found., 1978—79. Fellow: Am. Acad. Pediat.; mem.: Am. Soc. Bioethics and Humanities, Am. Acad. Pediat. Hematology-Oncology, Am. Soc. Clin. Oncology, Am. Soc. Hematology, Phi Beta Kappa. Avocations: reading, children's issues, crafts. Office: Children's Meml Hosp 2300 Children's Plz Chicago IL 60614 Office Phone: 773-880-4562. Business E-Mail: emorgan@northwestern.edu.

MORGAN, ELIZABETH, plastic surgeon; b. Washington, July 9, 1947; d. William James and Antonia (Bell) Morgan; 1 child, Elena. BA magna cum laude, Harvard U., 1967; postgrad. (fellow), Oxford U., 1967-70; MD, Yale U., 1971; PhD in Psychology, U. Canterbury, Christchurch, New Zealand, 1995. Diplomate Am. Bd. Surgery, Am. Bd. Plastic Surgery. Intern Yale-New Haven Hosp., 1971-72, resident, 1972-73, 76-77, Tufts-New Eng. Med. Center, Boston, 1973-76, Harvard-Cambridge Hosp., Mass., 1977-78; columnist Cosmopolitan mag., 1973-80; pvt. practice specializing in cosmetic plastic surgery Washington, 1978-87, McLean, Va., 1998—2006, Chevy Chase, Md., 1998—2006; chief plastic surgery Beverly Hills Physicians, Calif., 2006—07; asst. clin. prof. dept. plastic surgery UCLA, 2006—. Faculty dept. psychology U. Md., 1995; assoc. faculty dept. law, justice and soc. Am. U., 1998. Author: The Making of A Woman Surgeon, 1980, Solo Practice, 1982, Custody, A True Story, 1986, The Complete Book of Cosmetic Surgery for Men, Women and Teens, 1988. Fellow: ACS, Am. Soc. Plastic Surgeons; mem.: APA. Episcopalian. Office: 333 S Doheny Dr 202 Los Angeles CA 90048-3527 Home Phone: 310-858-1561; Office Phone: 818-817-0600. E-mail: morgan52650@gmail.com.

MORGAN, ELIZABETH ANN, lawyer; d. Cyril Charles and Ann Howard Morgan; m. Matthew J. Bokor, May 1984 (div. Feb. 1999). BA, U. Fla., 1979; JD, Emory U., 1990. Bd. cert. bus. litigation: Fla. 1997. Ptnr. Powell Goldstein Frazer & Murphy LLP, Atlanta, 2000—03, Hunton & Williams LLP, Atlanta, 2003—06, Epstein Becker and Green PC, Atlanta, 2006—. Vice chair litigation com. U.S. Intellectual Property Owners Assn., Washington, 2006—07; vice chair bus. litig. certification com. Fla. Bar, Tallahassee, 1998—2005; mem. Fla. Bar Standing Com. on Professionalism, 1993—2002. Mem. Leadership Atlanta, 2002; dir. ACLU of Ga., Atlanta, 2003—05. Named one of Top 50 Women Attys. in Atlanta, Atlanta Mag. and Ga. Super Lawyers Mag., 2005, Ga.'s Legal Elite, Ga. Trend Mag., 2003, 2004, 2005, Top 5% Ga. Intellectual Property Litig. Attys., Atlanta Mag. and Ga. Super Lawyers Mag., 2004, 2005, 2006, 2007. Master: Bleckley Inn of Ct.; mem.: FBA, ATLA (chair bus. torts 2005—06), ABA, Fla. Assn. for Women Lawyers (pres. Miami chpt. 1995), Internat. Trademark Assn. (chair U.S. legis.subcom. 2002—03, chair polit. action com. 2003—, mem. USPTO subcom. 2004—), Licensing Execs. Soc., Nat. Assn. for Women Lawyers, Ga. Assn. for Women Lawyers, Atlanta Bar Assn., Copyright Soc. of U.S., Am. Intellectual Property Law Assn. (vice chair trademark legis. com., women in intellectual property law com.), Acad. of Fla. Trial Lawyers, Atlanta Lawyer's Club. Office: Epstein Becker and Green PC Resurgens Plaza 945 E Paces Ferry Rd Ste 2700 Atlanta GA 30326-1380 Office Phone: 404-869-5315, 404-923-9000. Office Fax: 404-869-5415, 404-923-9099. Business E-Mail: eamorgan@ebglaw.com.

MORGAN, ELIZABETH K., retired critical care nurse; b. Lansdowne, Pa., Feb. 18, 1951; d. Charles Knight and Marian Swope (Wing) Morgan; m. James Tracy Grey III, Dec. 27, 1980 (div. 2002); children: Michael Grey, James Tracy IV Grey, Joshua S. Grey. AA, Elmira Coll., NY, 1976; grad. in practical nursing, Upper Bucks Voc-Tech, Perkasie, Pa., 1979; AA in Nursing, Bucks County Community Coll., Newtown, Pa., 1989; student, LaSalle U., 1992—96. Cert. health profl. paramedic, Pa.; cert. CPR, ACLS, TNCC. Paramedic Warminster Ambulance, Pa., 1986; staff practical nurse Warminster Gen. Hosp., 1986—89; ICU/CCU staff nurse Nazareth Hosp., Phila., 1989—96, coord. cardiac rehab., 2001—02, staff to charge nurse telemetry stroke fl., part-time nurse IV team, 2002—. Mem. Warrington Ambulance Corps. Mem. AACN.

MORGAN, EVAN, retired chemist; b. Spokane, Wash., Feb. 26, 1930; s. Evan and Emma Anne (Klobucher) M.; m. Johnnie Lu Dickson, Feb. 14, 1959; 1 child, James. BS, Gonzaga U., 1952; MS, U. Wash., 1954, PhD, 1956. Staff chemist IBM Corp., Poughkeepsie, NY, 1956-60; group supr. Olin Mathieson Co., New Haven, 1960-64; assoc. prof. chemistry High Point Coll., NC, 1964-65; sr. rsch. chemist Reynolds Metals Co., Richmond, Va., 1965-72; chemist Babcock & Wilcox, Lynchburg, Va., 1972-95, Lynchburg Tree Steward, Lynchburg, 1995. Mem. Am. Chem. Soc. Home: 5128 Wedgewood Rd Lynchburg VA 24503-4208 Personal E-mail: emorgan@worldnet.att.net.

MORGAN, FRANK, mathematics professor; BS, MIT, 1974; MA, Princeton U., 1976, PhD, 1977; ScD (hon.), Cedar Crest Coll., 1995. Moore instr. to assoc. prof., Green prof. MIT, Cambridge, 1977-87; chmn. Dept. Math. Williams Coll., 1988—94, Meenan 3d Century prof., chmn. dept. math., 1997—2003. Vis. prof. Rice U., Houston, 1982-83, Stanford U., 1986-87; mem. Inst. Advanced Study, Princeton, N.J., 1990-91; vis. prof. disting. tchg. Princeton U., 1997—; adj. prof. U. Mass., 1992—. Author: Geometric Measure Theory, 1988, 3d edit., 2000, Riemannian Geometry, 1993, revised edit., 2001, Calculus Lite, 1995, 2d edit., 1997, The Math Chat Book, 2000; contbr. over 100 articles to profl. jours. Recipient Haimo award for disting. coll. or univ. tchg. of math. Math. Assn. Am., 1993; grantee NSF, 1977—. Mem.: Math. Assn. Am. (2d v.p. 2000—02). Office: Williams College Dept of Mathematics Williamstown MA 01267

MORGAN, FRANK EDWARD, II, corporate financial executive; b. Burlington, Vt., May 16, 1952; s. Robert Griggs and Ruth (Jepson) M. First Class Cert. Merit, U. Edinburgh, Scotland, 1973; AB with honors, Brown U., 1974; LLM, Cambridge U., Eng., 1976; JD, U. Va., 1978. Bar: Mass. 1978, N.Y. 1990. Assoc. Gaston & Snow, Boston, 1978—82; v.p., gen. counsel Madison Fund, Inc. and Adobe Resources Corp., NYC, 1982—87; ptnr. Gaston & Snow, NYC, 1987—91, Mayer, Brown & Platt, NYC, 1991—96, Dewey Ballantine, NYC, 1996—2003; pres., COO Coller Capital, Inc., NYC, 2003—. Bd. mem. ABS Ventures, Annex Capital, Capitol Health Ptnrs., New Venture Ptnrs. and Washington and Congress, Cambridge in Am. Republican. Congregationalist. Home: 14 Sutton Pl S New York NY 10022-3071 Office: Coller Capital Inc 410 Park Ave Ste 740 New York NY 10022 Office Phone: 212-644-8500. Business E-Mail: frank.morgan@collercapital.com.

MORGAN, GARY LORIN, systems engineer, director, researcher; b. Balt., Oct. 23, 1948; s. Lorin C. and Pearl C. (Dise) Morgan; m. Kathleen Marie Lamm, Dec. 6, 1986; children: Ashley, Lauren. BS in Engring. Sci., Johns Hopkins U., 1975. Level II cert. program mgmt., Def. Acquisition Workforce Improvement Act, 2006. Rsch. assoc. Johns Hopkins U., Balt., 1966-75; sr. rsch. scientist Pfizer Med. Systems, Columbia, Md., 1976-84; quality assurance mgr. U.S. Design Corps., Lanham, Md., 1984-88; dir. R&D Pacific Sci. Co., Silver Spring, Md., 1988-93; chief rsch. scientist Triton Thalassic Tech., Ridgefield, Conn., 1994—2002; prin. Ship Point Rsch. Lab, Elkridge, Md., 2003—. Contbr. articles to profl. jours. Pres., dir. Marshallee Civic Assn. Achievements include patents for particle detecting instrument with sapphire detecting cell; particle measurement system with sonically measured flow rate; sterilization of opaque liquids with ultraviolet radiation; lamp for generating high power ultraviolet radiation. Avocations: boating, fishing. Office: Ship Point Rsch Lab 5821 Bellanca Dr Elkridge MD 21075 Personal E-mail: glmorga@verizon.net.

MORGAN, GEORGE ARTHUR, psychologist; b. Chgo., Aug. 20, 1936; s. George Arthur and Josephine Read Morgan; m. Hildegarde Swanson, June 9, 1962; children: Arthur Swanson, Lisa Morgan Heimer. BA, DePauw U., Greencastle, Ind., 1958; MA, Harvard U., Cambridge, Mass., 1959; PhD, Cornell U., Ithaca, N.Y., 1965. Instr. psychology Washington and Jefferson Coll., Washington, Pa., 1959—61; human factors psychologist IBM Space Guidance Ctr., Owego, NY, 1962—62; asst. prof. psychology Hiram Coll., Ohio, 1964—71; health scientist adminstr. Nat. Inst. Child Health and Human Devel., Bethesda, Md., 1971—73, rsch. psychologist, 1973—76; asst. acad. v.p. and assoc. prof. psychology Coll. Charleston, SC, 1976—79; prof. human devel. and family studies Colo. State U., Fort Collins, 1979—2001, prof., sch. edn., 1992—2001, prof. emeritus edn. and human devel., 2001—. Asst. dir. Upward Bound project Hiram Coll., Ohio, 1966—69, asst. dean, dir. instl. rsch., 1967—71; assoc. dean Colo. State U., Fort Collins, 1979—84, head dept. of design, merchandising and consumer scis., 1984—92, coord. Sch. Edn., Office Rsch. Support, 2001—; clin. prof. psychiatry U. Colo. Sch. Medicine, Denver, 1999—. Editor (author): (scholarly book) Mastery Motivation: Origins, Conceptualizations, and Applications; author: (text book) Research Methods in Applied Settings: An Integrated Approach to Design and Analysis, 2000, SPSS for Intermediate Statistics: Use and Interpretation (2nd ed), 2007, Understanding and Evaluating Research in Applied and Clinical Settings, 2006, SPSS for Introductory Statistics: Use and Interpretation (3rd ed), 2007; contbr. over 60 articles to profl. jours. Chair Western Home Econs. Rsch. Administrs., 1983—85; bd. mem. Colo. Home Econs. Assn., 1984—85; resource allocation panel Ft. Collins United Way, Colo., 1984—86; treas. Friends of Gustafson Gallery, Fort Collins, Colo., 1986—91; textiles com. Gov.'s Execs. for Econ. Opportunity, Colo., 1990—92; cons. Larimer County Index of Cmty. Well-Being Project, Fort Collins, Colo., 2002—02. Recipient Scholarly Excellence award, Coll. Applied Human Scis., Colo. State U., 2000; fellowship, Woodrow Wilson Found., 1958-1959, Grad. fellowship, Danforth Found., 1958-1964, Acad. Adminstrn. fellow, Am. Coun. Edn., 1969-1970, Curriculum Evaluation grant, US Office of Edn., 1969-1971, Curriculum Devel. grant, NEH, 1969-1971, Faculty Devel. grant, Lilly Endowment, 1978-1979, Rsch. on Mastery Motivation grant, Devel. Psychobiology Rsch. Group, 1979-2000, Mastery Motivation Rsch. grant, MacArthur Found. Rsch. Network, 1982-1987. Mem.: APA (life), Devel. Psychobiology Rsch. Group (exec. com. 1997—2004), Phi Beta Kappa. Achievements include research in mastery motivation in infants and toddlers; development of dimensions of mastery questionnaire. Avocations: visited 380+ national park service sites, family genealogy. Home: 4824 Regency Dr Fort Collins CO 80526-3810 Office: Colo State Univ 233 Edn Bldg Fort Collins CO 80523-1588 Home Phone: 970-223-3493; Office Phone: 970-491-0608. Personal E-mail: gmorgan@lamar.colostate.edu. Business E-Mail: gmorgan@cahs.colostate.edu.

MORGAN, GEORGE HENRY, patent agent, consultant; s. George Nathaniel and Helen Henrietta (Weis) Morgan; m. Lubov Nicholovena Uvarova, Oct. 15, 2004; children: George Dominiic, Christopher Donald, Robert Andrew, Anne Michaelene, James Patrick, Thomas Henry. BS in Mech. Engring., La. State U., Baton Rouge, 1958; MS in Mech. Engring., Mo. Sch. Mines & Metallurgy, Rolla, 1959. Registered profl. engr., La., 1958. Pres. George H. Morgan, P.E., Patent Agt., Evansville, Ind., 1973—; sales mgr. White Hydraulics, Hopkinsville, Ky., 1987—93. Author: You Might Be An Inventor If, 2002. Commr. Pub. Housing Authority, South Bend, Ind., 1966—71. With US Army, 1953—55. Decorated Ind. Commendation award State of Ind. Mem.: Ill. Mining Inst., Soc. Automotive Engrs. (com. chmn. 1973—2000, MacFarland award 1990). Achievements include patents for brakes, clutch, jacks, hydraulic drives. Office: George H Morgan PE Patent Agent 401 Tyler Ave Evansville IN 47715-3243 Office Phone: 812-476-4065. Office Fax: 812-476-4065. Business E-Mail: patagent@evansville.net.

MORGAN, GREGORY PAUL, financial investment advisor; b. Cocoa Beach, Fla., Sept. 9, 1958; s. Paul Leo and Mickey Maxine (Cooper) M. BS in Psychology magna cum laude, Pepperdine U., 1980. Cert. fin. planner. Fin. analyst Williams & McCombs, Inc., Arlington, Tex., 1980-83; fin. advisor Balanced Fin., Dallas, 1983-86; ptnr. Strategic Fin. Group, Arlington, 1986—. Chmn. coun. Lowry Fin. Svcs.; pres. Strategic Fin.Mgmt., 1989; lectr. numerous orgns. Big Bros. Am. United Way, Dallas, 1986—. Named Best Fin. Planners, Dallas Mag., 2003, 2004, 2005; named to Bloomberg Top 200 Wealth Mgrs., 2003, 2004, 2005, 2006. Mem.: Fin. Planners Assn. Avocations: tennis, running, snow-skiing. Office: 5310 Harvest Hill Rd Ste 226 Dallas TX 75230-5893 Home: 403 Rockcrest Dr Coppell TX 75019 Office Phone: 972-960-6460 Ext.2. Business E-Mail: gmorgan@sfmgadvisors.com.

MORGAN, HENRY COKE, JR., judge; b. Norfolk, Va., Feb. 8, 1935; s. Henry Coke and Dorothy Lea (Pebworth) M.; m. Margaret John McGrail, Aug. 18, 1965; children: A. Robertson Hanckel Jr., Catherine Morgan Stockwell, Coke Morgan Stewart. BS, Washington and Lee U., 1957, JD, 1960; LLM in Jud. Process, U. Va., 1998. Bar: Va. 1960, US Dist. Ct. (ea. dist.) Va. 1961, US Ct. Appeals (4th cir.) 1964. Asst. city atty. City of Norfolk, 1960-63; ptnr. Pender & Coward, Virginia Beach, Va., 1963-92; vice chmn., gen. counsel Princess Anne Bank, 1986-92; judge U.S. Dist. Ct. (ea. dist.) Va., 1992—2004, sr. judge, 2004—. Served with US Army, 1958-59. Episcopalian. Office: US Dist Ct Eastern Dist Va Walter E Hoffman US Courthouse 600 Granby St Ste 307 Norfolk VA 23510-1915 E-mail: henry_morgan@vaed.uscourts.gov.

MORGAN, HUGH JACKSON, JR., retired bank and energy executive; b. Nashville, Aug. 10, 1928; s. Hugh Jackson and Robert Ray (Porter) M.; m. Ann Moulton Ward, Aug. 28, 1954; children— Ann, Grace, Caroline, Hugh AB, Princeton U., NJ, 1950; LL.B., Vanderbilt U., Nashville, 1956; A.M.P., Harvard Bus. Sch., 1976. Bar: Tenn. 1956. Practice law Miller & Martin, Chattanooga, 1956-60; atty. So. Natural Gas Co., Birmingham, Ala., 1961-65, gen. atty., 1966-70, v.p., 1971-78, pres., 1982-84, chmn. bd., 1984-87; v.p. Sonat Inc., Birmingham, Ala., 1973-78, sr. v.p., 1979-84, exec. v.p., 1984, vice chmn. bd., 1984-87; vice chmn. Nat. Bank of Commerce, Birmingham, Ala., 1987-90, chmn., 1990—2003. Bd. dirs. Atrion Corp. Chmn. Birmingham Airport Authority, 1986-2000; trustee Children's Hosp. Ala., Birmingham, 1974—. Served to lt. (j.g.) USN, 1950-53. Recipient Bennett Douglas Bell Meml. prize Vanderbilt Law Sch., 1956 Mem. Order of the Coif. Clubs: Mountain Brook (pres. 1972), Redstone, (Birmingham); Belle Meade (Nashville); Linville Golf (N.C.). Lodges: Rotary. Home: 3121 Brookwood Rd Birmingham AL 35223-2016 Office: 1927 1st Ave N Birmingham AL 35203-4058

MORGAN, JACQUI, illustrator, painter, art educator, writer; b. NYC, Feb. 22, 1939; d. Henry and Emily (Cook) Morganstern; m. Onnig Kalfayan, Apr. 23, 1967 (div. 1972); m. Tomás Gonda, Jan. 1983 (dec. 1988). BFA with honors, Pratt Inst., Bklyn., 1960; MA, CCNY, 1978. Textile designer M. Lowenstein & Sons, NYC, 1961-62, Fruit of the Loom, NYC, 1962; stylist-design dir. Au Courant, Inc., NYC, 1966—; assoc. prof. Pratt Inst., Bklyn., 1977—, Fashion Inst. Tech., NYC. Guest lectr. U. Que., Syracuse U., Warsaw TV & Radio, Poland, NYU, Parsons Sch. Design, N.Y.C., Sch. Visual Arts, N.Y.C., Va. Commonwealth U., Fashion Inst. of Tech., others; mem. profl. juries; curator Tomás Gonda retrospective exhbn.; condr. workshops. One-person shows include Soc. Illustrators, NYC, 1977, 2005, Art Dirs. Club, NYC, 1978, Gallerie Nowe Miasto, Warsaw, 1978, Gallerie Baumeister, Munich, 1978, Hansen-Feuerman Gallery, NYC, 1980, Krannert Mus./U. Ill., 1998, Art Gallery at Marywood U., Scranton, Pa., 1998, Spring Studio, 2006; group shows include Mus. Contemporary Crafts, NYC, 1975, Smithsonian Instn., Washington, 1976, Mus. Warsaw, 1976, 78, Mus. Tokyo, 1979, Nat. Watercolor Soc., 1989, Salmagundi Club, 1990, New Eng. Watercolor Soc. Open, 1990, Miss. Watercolor Grand Nat., 1990, Illustration West 29, 1990, Adirondack Nat., 1990, Die Verlassenen Schuhe, 1993, N.Y. restaurant Sch., 1994, Lizan-Tops Gallery, 1996, 2005, The Art Club, 2000, Mus. at Fashion Inst. Am., 2003, Soc. Illustrators, NYC, 2004, The Hopper Ho., 2006; represented in permanent collections: Smithsonian Instn., Mus. Warsaw; author, illustrator: Watercolor for Illustration; produced 3 instrnl. watercolor videos; series of prints pub., 1995; series of plates publ., 1995; co-curator Tomas Gonda Retrospective, Va. Commonwealth U., Rutgers U., Carnegie Mellon U., others in U.S., Mus. Modern Art, Buenos Aires, Ulmer Mus., Ulm, Germany; illustrator Lights Along the Path, 1999, The Healing Garden, 1999; contbr. articles to profl. jours. Recipient more than 200 awards from various orgns. including Soc. Illustrators, Fed. Design Coun., Comm. Arts Mag., Am. Inst. Graphic Arts, N.Y. Art Dirs. Club, Print Design Ann. Mem.: Graphic Artists Guild (dir. 1975—79), Soc. Illustrators, Women Artists of the West, Pa. Watercolor Soc. Studio: 6940 Yellowstone Blvd 515 Forest Hills NY 11375-3400 *I understand that it's the pleasure of the process and the satisfaction of improvement that gives satisfaction.*

MORGAN, JAMES C., manufacturing executive; b. 1938; BSME, MBA, Cornell U.; DEng (hon.), De Anza Coll., 1994. Corp. staff Textron Inc., 1963—72; sr. ptnr. West Ven Mgmt., San Francisco, 1972—76; pres. Applied Materials, Inc., Santa Clara, Calif., 1976—87, CEO, 1977—2003, chmn., 1987—. Apptd. by Pres. Clinton to Commn. U.S.-Pacific Trade and Investment Policy, 1996; mem. Nat. Adv. Com. Semiconductors, 1988—92; bd. dirs. Cisco Sys.; apptd. to U.S.-Japan Sector Govt. Commn., 2002; adv. bd. mem. Ctr. Sci. Tech. &: Soc. Santa Clara U., Calif.; vice-chmn. Presdl. Export Council, 2003—. Co-author: Cracking the Japanese Market: Strategies for Success in the New Global Economy. Bd. gov. Nature Conservancy; trustee Nature Conservancy Calif. Named Internat. Citizen of Yr., World Forum of Silicon Valley, 1995; named to Jr. Achievement Hall of Fame, 1991; recipient Cmty. Svc. award, NCCJ, 1995, Nat. Medal of Tech., Pres. Clinton, 1996, Global Humanitarian Award, Tech. Mus. Innovation, Cmty. Svc. Award, Nat. Conf. Cmty. & Justice. Mem.: Semiconductor Equipment and Materials Internat. (dir. emeritus, past pres.), Pacific Basin Econ. Coun. (chmn.'s circle), Coun. Competitiveness, Nat. Ctr. Asia-Pacific Econ. Cooperation (bd. dirs.), Congrl. Econ. Leadership Inst. (bd. dirs.), World Presidents Orgn., Semiconductor Equipment and Materials Internat./SEMATECH (past bd. dirs., Global Pioneer Award), Am. Electronics Assn. (past bd. dirs.). Office: Applied Materials Inc 3050 Bowers Ave Santa Clara CA 95054-3298 *

MORGAN, JAMES DURWARD, retired computer company executive; b. NYC, Sept. 10, 1936; s. Durward Field and Harriet (Airey) M.; m. Ruth Ann Dobson, Jan. 14, 1967; children: Jennifer, Andrew. BEE, Yale U., 1961, MEE, 1962. Systems engr. Calspan Corp., Buffalo, 1962-68; v.p. Comptek Rsch. Inc., Buffalo, 1968—83, 1990—2001, also bd. dirs.; v.p. Barrister Info. Systems Corp., Buffalo, 1983-90, also bd. dirs., 1983—. Former mem. adv. coun. Erie C.C., Amherst, N.Y., 1985-2000, past chmn.; bd. dirs. Yale Alumni Bd., Buffalo, 1987-2001. Served with USN, 1959-61. Mem.: IEEE, ACM.

MORGAN, JAMES JOHN, environmental engineering educator; b. NYC, June 23, 1932; s. James and Anna (Treanor) M.; m. Jean Laurie McIntosh, June 15, 1957; children— Jenny, Johanna, Eve, Michael, Martha, Sarah BCE, Manhattan Coll., 1954; MSCE, U. Mich., 1956; postgrad., U. Ill., 1956-60; PhD, Harvard U., 1964; ScD (hon.), Manhattan Coll., 1989. Instr. civil engring. U. Ill., Urbana, 1956-60; assoc. prof. U. Fla., Gainesville, 1963-65, Calif. Inst. Tech., Pasadena, 1965-69, prof. environ. engring., 1969-87, Marvin L. Goldberger prof. environ. engring. sci., 1987—, dean of students, 1972-75, dean grad. studies, 1981-84, v.p. student affairs, 1980-89; exec. officer environ. engring. sci., 1993-96. Mem. environ. studies bd., NRC, 1974-80, Abel Wolman lectr., 2004; chmn. Acid Deposition Sci. Adv. Com., Calif., 1983-98; chmn. Gordon Rsch. Conf. on Environ. Sci.; Water, 1970. Author: (with Werner Stumm) Aquatic Chemistry, 1970, 2d edit., 1981, 3rd edit. 1996; editor Environ. Sci. and Tech., 1966-74; contbr. articles to profl. jours. Recipient Stockholm Water prize, 1999, Clarke Water prize, 1999. Mem. ASCE (award 1997), Am. Chem. Soc. (award 1980), AAAS, Am. Soc. Limnology and Oceanography (editorial bd. 1977-80), Nat. Acad. Engring., Assn. Environ. Engring. Profs. (award 1981, 83, 94), Am. Water Works Assn. (award 1963), Sigma Xi, Chi Epsilon. Democrat. Roman Catholic. Avocations: tennis, music. E-mail: morgan_j@caltech.edu.

MORGAN, JAMES PHILIP, pharmacology and cardiology educator; b. Cin., Jan. 13, 1948; s. James Weldon and Dorcas Adele (Meyer) M.; m. Kathleen Greive, Dec. 22, 1973; children: James Patrick, Jonathan Michael. BS, U. Cin., 1970, PhD, 1974, MD, 1976. Diplomate Am. Bd. Internal Medicine, Am. Bd. Cardiovascular Disease. Fellow internal medicine Mayo Clinic, Rochester, Minn., 1976—79, fellow cardiovascular disease, 1979—83; asst. medicine Beth Israel Hosp., Boston, 1983—. Instr. pharmacology U. Cin., 1975—76; asst. prof. pharmacology, instr. medicine Mayo Clinic, 1981—83; asst. prof. medicine Harvard U., Boston, 1983, assoc. prof., 1988—96, Herman Dana prof. medicine, 1996—2005; affiliate faculty, dept. pharmacology Harvard Med. Sch., 1986—2000; chief and prgram dir. cardiovascular divsn. Beth Israel Hosp., 1994—2001, vice chmn. medicine, 2000—05; chief cardiovasc. medicine St. Elizabeth's Med. Ctr., Boston, 2005—, dir. Caritas Christi Cardiovasc. Ctr., 2005—; chief cardiovasc. medicine Caritas Carney Hosp. Contbr. articles to profl. jours. Recipient Young Investigators award Am. Coll. Cardiology, 1982, Balfour award Mayo Clinic, 1983, Advanced Cardiac Life Support Spl. Recognition award Mayo Clinic, 1983, Rsch. Career Devel. award NIH, 1985-90. Mem. AMA, Am. Heart Assn., Biophys. Soc. Am. Soc. Pharmacology and Exptl. Therapeutics, Masons. Avocation: philatelics. Office: Caritas St Elizabeth's Med Ctr 736 Cambridge St Boston MA 02135-2997 Office Phone: 617-789-2226. Business E-Mail: james.morgan@caritachristi.org.

MORGAN, JANE HALE, retired library director; b. Dines, Wyo., May 11, 1926; d. Arthur Hale and Billie (Wood) Hale; m. Joseph Charles Morgan, Aug. 12, 1955; children: Joseph Hale, Jane Frances, Ann Michele. BA, Howard U., 1947; MA, U. Denver, 1954. Staff Detroit Pub. Libr., 1954-87, exec. asst. dir., 1973-75, dep. dir., 1975-78, dir., 1978-87; ret., 1987. Mem. Mich. Libr. Consortium Bd.; exec. bd. Southeastern Mich. Regional Film Libr.; vis. prof. Wayne State U., 1989—. Trustee New Detroit, Inc., Delta Dental Plan of Mich., v.p. Delta Dental Fund, Delta Dental Plan of Ohio; v.p. United Southwestern Mich.; pres. Univ.-Cultural Ctr. Assn.; bd. dirs. Rehab. Inst., YWCA, Met. Affairs Corp., Literacy Vols. Am., Detroit, Mich. Ctr. for the Book, Interfaith Coun.; bd. dirs., v.p. United Comty. Svcs. Met. Detroit; chmn. Detroiters for Adult Reading Excellence; chmn. adv. coun. libr. sci. U. Mich.; mem. adv. coun. libr. sci. U. Mich., mem. adv. coun. libr. sci. Wayne State U.; dir. Met. Detroit Youth Found.; chmn. Mich. LSCA adv. coun.; mem. UWA Literacy Com., Attys. Grievance Com., Women's Commn., Mich. Civil Svc. Rev. Com.; vice-chair Mich. Coun. for Humanities; v.p. Commn. for the Greening of Detroit; adv. com. Headstart; mem. Detroit Women's Com., Detroit Women's Forum, Detroit Exec. Svc. Corps.; sec., treas. Delta Dental Fund, pres., 1999. Recipient Anthony Wayne award Wayne State U., 1981, Summit award Greater Detroit C. of C.; named Detroit Howardite of Year, 1983 Mem. ALA, AAUW, Mich. Libr. Assn., Women's Nat. Book Assn., Assn. Mcpl. Profl. Women, NAACP, LWV, Women's Econ. Club (bd. dirs.), Sorosis Club (v.p.), Alpha Kappa Alpha (pres.). Democrat. Episcopalian.

MORGAN, JOE LELAND, physician, psychiatrist; b. Augusta, Ga., June 5, 1955; s. Robert Leland and Jozette Morgan; m. Debra Baily Morgan, July 10, 1993; children: Robert, David 1 stepchild, Tonya. BS, Valdosta State Coll., Valdosta, Ga., 1976; MS, Univ. Ga. Vet Sch., Athens, Ga., 1979; MD, Med. Coll. of Ga., Augusta, Ga., 1987. Cert. Am. bd. of Psychiatry and Neurology, 1993. Rsch. asst. Med. Coll. of Ga., Augusta, Ga., 1979—83, med. sch., 1983—87, med. resident, 1988—89, psychiatry resident, 1989—90, chief resident psychiatry, 1990—91, asst. prof. psychiatry, 1991—95; pvt. practice Valdosta Psychiatric Assoc., Valdosta, Ga., 1995—. Chief psychiatry svc. South Ga. Med. Ctr., Valdosta, Ga., 2000—, Parkwood Devel. Ctr., Valdosta, Ga., 1999—. Contbr. chapters to books, articles pub. to profl. jour. Recipient Vet. Adminstrn. Special Performance Award, 1993; grantee Dean's Summer Rsch. Grant, Med. Coll. og Ga., 1984. Mem.: APA, Med. Ass. of Ga., Ga. Psychiatric Physicians Assn. (v.p. 2007, Psychiatrist of Yr. 2004). Republican. Meth. Avocations: fishing, tennis, snorkeling, scuba diving, baseball. Office: Valdosta Psychiatric Asso PO Box 3229 Valdosta GA 31604-3229 Office Phone: 229-244-4200. Business E-Mail: 244200@bellsouth.net.

MORGAN, JOHN DAVIS, government agency administrator, consultant; b. Newark, Feb. 14, 1921; s. John Davis and Caroline Frommel (Schaller) M.; m. Leta Maude Bretzinger, June 27, 1953; children: John Davis III, Bret Zinger. BS, Pa. State U., 1942, MS, 1947, PhD, 1948, E.M., 1950; grad. extension course, Indsl. Coll. of Armed Forces, Washington, 1953. Asst. for materials and stockpile policies Nat. Security Resources Bd., Washington, 1948-51; dir. materials rev. div. DPA, Washington, 1951-53; materials expert ODM, Washington, 1953-56; mem. staff President's Cabinet Com. on Mineral Policy, 1953-54; cons. bus. and def. problems in metals, minerals and fuels Washington, 1956-71; mem. nat. def. exec. res. for ODM, 1956-58, OCDM, 1958-61, Office Emergency Planning, 1961-71, Emergency Minerals Adminstrn., 1972-95; mem. spl. stockpile advisory com. to ODM, 1957-58; com. on scope and conduct of materials research NAS, 1959-60, then, mem. com. on mineral sci. and tech., 1966-70; mem. Interagy. Adv. Com. on Mining and Mineral Research, 1977-95. Head dept. sci. and math. Daytona Beach C.C., Fla., 1961-71; asst. dir. mineral position analysis U.S. Bur. Mines, Dept. Interior, Washington, 1971-74, acting dir. bur., 1973-74, 77-78, assoc. dir. mineral and materials supply/demand analysis, 1974-79, chief staff officer, 1979-95, Interior Dept. liaison to Com. Internat. Econ. Policy Staff, 1973-77, to Econ. Policy Bd. Staff, 1974-77, to Dept. Def. Materials Steering Group, 1975-78, to FPA-FEMA Stockpile Com., 1975-88, to Winter Energy Emergency Planning Group of Dept. of Energy, 1977-81; alt. Interior rep. Trade Policy Rev. Group, 1975-81; chmn. minerals rev. com. Non-Fuel Minerals Policy Study, 1978; chmn. materials supply task force NSC Stockpile Study, 1983-87; liaison to Dept. Def. Stockpile Com., 1988-95; mem. Def. Logistics Agy. Market Impact Com., 1988-95; mem. Def. Dept. Adv. Com. Operation and Modernization of Stockpile, 1993-95; U.S. rep. UN Sci. Conf. on Resources, 1949; lectr. numerous univs. including Nat. Def. U., War Coll., Indsl. Coll., Def. Intelligence Coll., Army War Coll., 1949—; hon. prof. Indsl. Coll., 1983—; invited spkr. nat. meetings sci. and engring. socs., 1949—. Author: Domestic Mining Industry of the U.S. in World War II, 1949; corr.: Mining Ann. Rev., London, 1958-95; contbr. articles to profl. jours. Served from 2d lt. to maj. Corps Engrs. AUS, 1942-46. Decorated Bronze Star; recipient Distinguished Service gold medal Interior Dept., 1976; named Meritorious Exec. Sr. Exec. Service, 1983 Fellow Soc. Am. Mil. Engrs.; mem. Sci. Research Soc. Am., Soc. Mining Engrs. (Disting. mem.), AIME (nat. Krumb lectr. 1973, Legion of Honor 1989), Sigma Xi, Tau Beta Pi, Sigma Tau, Pi Mu Epsilon, Phi Lambda Upsilon, Phi Kappa Phi, Phi Eta Sigma, Sigma Gamma Epsilon. Clubs: Cosmos (Washington). Home: 5013 Worthington Dr Bethesda MD 20816-2748

MORGAN, JOHN DERALD, SR., electrical engineer, educator, writer, researcher; b. Hays, Kans., Mar. 15, 1939; s. John Baber and Avis Ruth (Wolf) M.; m. Elizabeth June McKneely, June 23, 1962; children: Laura Elizabeth, Kimberly Ann, Rebecca Ruth, John Derald. BSEE, La. Tech. U., Ruston, 1962; MS, U. Mo., Rolla, 1965, Degree (hon.) in Elec. Engring., 1987; PhD in Engring., Ariz. State U., Tempe, 1968. Registered profl. engr. Mo., N.Mex., Ala., SC; bd. cert. engr. in forensic engring. Elec. engr. Tex. Eastman div. Eastman Kodak Co., 1962-63; instr. U. Mo., Rolla, 1963-65,

Ariz. State U., 1965-68; asso. prof. elec. engring. U. Mo., Rolla, 1968-72, Alcoa Found. prof. elec. engring., 1972-75, chmn. elec. engring., 1978-85, assoc. dir. Ctr. Internat. Programs, 1970-78, Emerson Electric prof., 1975-85; dean engring. N.Mex. State U., 1985-99; v.p. univ. advancement U. Ala. in Huntsville, 1999—; exec. sec. U. Ala. Huntsville Found., 1999—; pres. J. Derald Morgan and Assoc., Inc.; ptnr. Morgan-Morris Devel. Co. LLC; mng. ptnr. Morgan Travel, LLC. Nat. adv. com. Engring. Exploring; cons. to industry. Author: Power Apparatus Testing Techniques, 1969, Computer Monitoring and Control of Electric Utility Systems, 1972, Control and Distribution of Megawatts Through Man-Machine Interaction, 1973, Electromechanical and Electromagnetic Machines and Devices, 1986, Wolf Brethren, 2003, Macy Friends, vols. I and II; also articles; mem. editl. bd. McMillan Publishers Engring. Divsn. Pres. bd. trustees First United Meth. Ch., Rolla, 1971-73, pres. adminstrv. bd., 1978-79; v.p., mem. bd. adminstrn. People to People, 1976; bd. dirs., cubmaster Ozarks dist. Boy Scouts Am., 1968-79, asst. dist. commr., 1971-73, cubmaster Yucca coun., 1986-90, coun. commr., 1989-90, asst. scout master, 1990-99, dist. com. Sunshine Dist., dist. chmn. Meramec dist., 1978-80, engring. exploring nat. com.; chmn. Creek Dist., 2000—05, bd. dirs. Greater Ala. Coun. No. Svc. Dist., 2000—; bd. dirs. Mo. Ptnrs. of the Americas; external adv. com. mem. for engring. rsch., Wash. U., St. Louis; adv. bd. Nat. Pollution Prevention Ctr.; mem. tech. com. NASULGC; coord. 27th Nat. Engring. Deans' Inst.; mem. Engrs. Club St. Louis; treas. Mo. Incutech Found. (bd. dir., founding mem.); mem. tech. adv. com. N. Mex. Rsch. Devel. Inst.; com. mem. N. Mex. Commn. Higher Edn.; mem bd. dir. N. Mex. INC, Quatro, MESA, ASEE (by-laws com. mem.), US West; task force mem. EDC/NSPE; bd. dir. Order of the Engr. Recipient Scouters Key award and Scouter Tng. award Ozarks coun., Boy Scouts Am., 1971, Dist. award of merit 1977, Silver Beaver award, 1982, Cub Leader award, Webelos Leader award, Dist. Com. Key award, James West Soc. award, Sunshine Dist. Yucca coun.; T.H. Harris scholar, 1959-61; John H. Horton scholar, 1961-62; Exec. of Yr. Messila Valley Profl. Sec. Assn.; Pres. Svc. award, N. Mex. State U., 1990; Disting. Engr. award, N.Mex. Engring. Found.; Engr. Yr., NMSPE, 1993. Fellow: IEEE (chmn. internat. practices subcom. 1972—79, chmn. ednl. resources subcom. 1973—78, chmn. 1979—85, sec. PSE com., vice chmn., mem. power sys. engring. standards com., PES ednl. com., midwest power symposium adv. bd., v.p. midwest power symposium advisory bd. 1973—74, chmn. internat. practices subcom., chmn. ednl. resources subcom., sec. power sys. engring. com., chmn. power sys. engring. com., mem. standards com. on dielectric testing, Centennial award 1984, award of Merit St. Louis sect., Educators award St. Louis sect., honor award St. Louis sect.), Nat. Acad. Forensic Engrs.; mem.: PSI, ASTM, Nat. Soc. Engring. Profls. (mem. com., vice chair, edn. adv. group, nomination com., edn. found. fin. devel., PEE mem. com. chair, bd. dir., nat. dir., PEE chair), Order of the Engr. (nat. bd. govs. 1996—, sec.), Am. Soc. Engring. Edn. (chair bylaws com. 1999—2001), N.Mex. Soc. Profl. Engrs. (N.Mex. Engr. of Yr. 1993), NSPE (bd. govs., nat. dir., vice chmn., S.W. chmn. Profl. Engrs. in Edn. v.p., mem. Steinman Coun.), SAR (Tenn. Valley chpt. sec.), Rotary Internat. (Paul Harris fellow 1997), Phi Kappa Phi, Omicron Delta Kappa, Eta Kappa Nu, Tau Beta Pi, Sigma Xi, Epsilon Gamma (grand master, grand procurator), Kappa Sigma (faculty and alumni advisor, Hall of Fame Beta Cptr.). Republican. Methodist. Achievements include patents in field. Home: 113 Lansdowne Dr Madison AL 35758-7613 Office: U Ala in Huntsville Alumni House 102 Huntsville AL 35899-0001 Office Phone: 256-824-6127. Personal E-mail: jdm@knology.net.

MORGAN, JOHN RICHARD, writer, publishing executive; b. Torrington, Conn., Sept. 28, 1953; s. John Brechin Morgan and Alice May (Getchell) Morris; m. Barbara Ann Walsh, Oct. 5, 2002; 1 child, John Ashworth. BA in English Lit., U. Conn., Storrs, 1978; MAT English, Brown U., Providence, 1981. Mgr. real estate test devel. Assessment Svcs., Inc., Bala Cynwyd, Pa., 1994—98, database mgr. and test specialist ins. programs Phila. and Bala Cynwyd, 1991—94; owner Morgan Testing Svcs., New London, Conn., 1998—. Instr. mythology and Shakespeare, The Am. Sch. in Switzerland, Thorpe, Surrey, England, 1981—83; editor, writer SAT/AP programs Ednl. Testing Svcs., Princeton, NJ, 1986—90; rhetoric instr. U. Iowa, Iowa City, 1986—87; real estate sales Coldwell-Banker, Tucson, 1990—91. Author: Real Estate Exam Prep (Promissor), Real Estate Exam Prep: Connecticut Regs, Real Estate Exam Prep: Conn Combo, Bermuda Real Estate, Real Estate Exam Prep (PSI). Founder and donor Getchell Legacy scholarship fund Lyme Acad. Coll. Fine Arts, Old Lyme, Conn., 2004—. With USCGR, 1979—86, Pt. Judith, RI and Nashville. Grantee Nashville's Parthenon's East & West Pediments Mythology Rsch., Nashville Coun. on the Arts, 1983. Mem.: Real Estate Educators Assn., Assn. Real Estate Lic. Law Ofcls. (assoc.), Mensa, Mystic Seaport, Am. Legion. Achievements include 17 marathons completed nationwide. Home: Box 231 Waterford CT 06385 Office: Morgan Testing Services Box 1982 New London CT 06320 Office Phone: 860-857-4936. Office Fax: 860-447-0757. Business E-Mail: jmorgan@morgantestingservices.com.

MORGAN, JOYCE KAYE, social worker; b. Acme, Pa., July 17, 1941; d. Jesse Gray and Lillian (Kubick) Hoyman; m. James Edward Morgan, Oct. 13, 1967 (dec. Nov. 2, 1996). BS in Secondary Edn., Calif. State Coll., 1963; MSW, W.Va. U., 1967. Cert. social worker; lic. social worker, Pa.; bd. cert. diplomate social work. Tchr. Scottdale (Pa.) Jr.-Sr. High Sch., 1963-64, Hempfield Jr. High, Greensburg, Pa., 1966; social worker, supr. Rosewood State Hosp., Owings Mills, Md., 1967-72, Latrobe (Pa.) Area Hosp., 1974-79; pvt. practice Mt. Pleasant, Pa., 1987-2000. Mem. Multi Disciplinary Team Child Abuse, Greensburg, Pa., 1978-79; sec. adv. bd. Westmoreland County Children's Bur., Greensburg, 1979-83. Avocations: gardening, crafts, painting. Home: Happy Hill Farm 113 Sunset View Ln Mount Pleasant PA 15666-8927

MORGAN, KATHRYN DIANE, criminology educator; b. Cameron, Tex., Aug. 14, 1953; children: Moya Elyse, Bria Kathryn. PhD, Fla. State U., Tallahassee, 1991. Assoc. prof. U. Ala., Birmingham, 1991—. Mem. bd., site-based coun. Tuscaloosa City Schs. PTSA, 2000. Patricia Harris fellow, 1986—91. Mem.: Acad. Criminal Justice Scis., Am. Soc. Criminology, Phi Kappa Phi. Baptist. Avocations: cooking, reading. Home: 4714 7th Ct E Tuscaloosa AL 35405 Office: U Ala 210 University Blvd Office Bldg Birmingham AL 35294-4562 Home Phone: 205-758-2162; Office Phone: 205-934-2069. Office Fax: 205-934-2067; Home Fax: 205-934-2067. Personal E-mail: kmorgan0853@comcast.net. Business E-Mail: kmorgan@uab.edu.

MORGAN, KERMIT JOHNSON, lawyer; b. Wales-Henderson, Iowa, Feb. 13, 1914; s. Samuel Jr. and Jennie Amelia Morgan; m. Georgina R. Morgan, Oct. 21, 1940 (dec. 1958); children: Georgina Morgan Street, Wilson S.; m. Ortrud Impol, Dec. 9, 1960. BA, U. Iowa, 1935; JD, U. So. Calif., 1937. Bar: Calif. 1939. Pvt. practice, LA, 1940—45, 1958—65, 1971—80, 1991—; ptnr. McBain & Morgan, LA, 1945—58, McBain, Morgan & Roper, 1965—71, Morgan & Armbrister, LA, 1980—91. Mem. ABA, Am. Bd. Trial Advs. (diplomate, nat. pres. 1973, pres. LA 1972, Inaugural Lifetime Achievement award local chpt. 2004, Nat. Lifetime Achievement award 2005), Assn. Def. Trial Attys. (bd. dirs. 1982-85), Internat. Assn. Ins. Counsel, Hon. Order of Blue Goose, Calif. State Bar, Assn. So. Calif. Def. Counsel (bd. dirs. 1966-67), LA Bar Assn. Republican. Congregationalist. Avocation: golf. Home: 2108 Stradella Rd Los Angeles CA 90077-2325 Office: 3420 Ocean Pk Blvd Santa Monica CA 90405 Home Phone: 310-472-8328; Office Phone: 310-314-4764. E-mail: lamarb@cableone.net.

MORGAN, LARRY RONALD, minister; b. Springhill, La., Mar. 12, 1936; s. Woodrow Wilson Morgan and Alma Elizabeth (Dunn) Burch; m. Elizabeth Dianne Baker, May 24, 1958; children: Elizabeth Denise Morgan Davis, Dennis Kevin. ADiv, Bapt. Missionary Assn. Theol. Sem., Jacksonville, Tex., 1990. Ordained to ministry Bapt. Ch., 1971. Clk., carrier U.S. P.O., Springhill, La., 1956-71; assoc. pastor Webb Chapel Bapt. Ch., Dallas, 1971-72, pastor, 1972-99, First Bapt. Ch., Springhill, La., 1999—. Clk., trustee Bapt. Missionary Assn. Sem., Jacksonville, 1983-86; chmn. bd. trustees Bapt. Progress, Dallas, 1984-87. Pres. PTA Browning Elem. Sch., Springhill, 1969-70. With USAR, 1959-66. Mem. Bapt. Missionary Assn. Am. (v.p. hdqrs. Little Rock 1985-86, pres. 1986-88, v.p. Am. 1996-98, pres. 1998-2000), Dallas County Bapt. Assn. (moderator 1982-84), Bapt. Missionary Assn. of La. (moderator 2000—), Springhill Baptist Assn. (moderator 2001-). Baptist. Home: 611 Butler St Springhill LA 71075-2519 Office Phone: 318-539-2610. Personal E-mail: ronaldmorgan1@cmaaccess.com.

MORGAN, LEON ALFORD, retired utilities executive; b. Washington, Dec. 29, 1934; s. Albert Lewis and Alice Viets (Alford) M.; children: David Richard, Sherry Alice; m. Jacqueline Jamieson, Feb. 14, 1993. BSEE, Worcester Poly. Inst., Mass., 1957. Registered profl. engr., Conn. With United Illuminating Co., New Haven, 1957-94, gen. ops. mgr., then v.p. ops., 1973-76, exec. v.p., 1976-83, sr. v.p. fin., 1984-94. Episcopalian. Home: 43 Forest Brook Rd Guilford CT 06437-2245

MORGAN, LINDA GAIL, theater producer; b. Tallahassee, May 14, 1952; d. Thomas Mitchell Morgan Sr. and Helen Frances (Rives) Stokes. BS, Fla. State U., 1974. Prodn. mgr. Valley Forge Ballet-5th World Peace Youth Culture Festival, Honolulu, 1985, Salute to Lady Liberty, Madison Square Gardens, 1986, US Constn. 200 Yr. Anniversary Parade, Phila., 1986-89, Columbus Day Parade, NYC, 1988, Gift of the White Bird Parade-Landmark Entertainment, Oita, Japan, 1990-91, 1996 Olympic Opening and Closing Ceremonies-Centenniel Events, Inc., Olympic Stadium, Atlanta, 1996, Super Bowl XXXI Half Time Show, New Orleans, 1997, NY Jets Halftime Show, Meadowlands Stadium, NJ, 1997; prodn. state mgr. Walt Disney Bus. Prodns., 1998; coordinating prodr. (musical) This Is America, The New World, Freedom Music, Santa Monica, Calif., 1989, California Traditional Music Festival, Human Rights Lectr. Series, Soka U. Am., LA, 1992-95, The Genius and the Great, LA, 1993, Every Child Deserves a Chance, LA, 1994, A Tribute to Burt Reynolds, LA, 1994, Celebrate the Garnet and Gold IV Honoring Charles Nelson Reilly, LA, 1995, Leisure Quest Internat./Entertainment Devel. Group, Burbank, Calif., 1997; artist agt., co. gen. mgr. Zoli Mgmt., Inc., NYC, 1986-89; orch. prodn. mgr. All Am. Gen. Meeting, Spectrum, Phila., 1987; asst. prodn. mgr. 8th World Peace Culture Festival, Fukuoka, Japan, 1987, This Is America, Madison Square Gardens, 1988, 1991 Olympic Festival Opening Ceremonies Radio City Spl. Events, Dodger Stadium, LA, 1991; prodn. staff Inauguration Mayor of Atlanta, Civic Ctr., Atlanta, 1998; event mgr. Coke on Ice World of Coca Cola, Atlanta, 1997-98, Disney Events Productions, 1998-2003, Tribeca Film Fest., 2004; prodr. Anheuser-Bush Creative Svcs., 2001-; prodn. mgr. Eventsful, NYC, 2007. Mem. Soka Gakkai Internat. (arts divsn. culture dept. 1995-), Fla. State U. So. Calif. Alumni Assn. (bd. dirs. 1991-95, Garnet Gold award 1995), Internat. Spl. Event Soc., Alpha Chi Omega. Democrat. Buddhist. Avocations: arts, needlepoint, antiques, piano, gardening. Personal E-mail: lgailmorgan@cs.com.

MORGAN, LINDA JOAN, former federal agency administrator, lawyer; b. Chester County, Pa., May 19, 1952; m. Michael E. Karam; 1 child, Meredith Lyn. AB in Hispanic Studies, Vassar Coll., 1973; JD, Georgetown U., 1976; postgrad., Harvard U., 1991. Bar: DC 1976. Assoc. Welch & Morgan, Washington, 1976-78; staff counsel US Senate Com. on Commerce, Sci. and Transp., 1978-86, gen. counsel, 1987-94; mem. ICC, Washington, 1994-96, chmn., 1995-96, Surface Transp. Bd., Washington, 1996—2003; ptnr. Covington & Burling, Washington, 2003—, chmn., Trasp. Practice Group. Named Alumna of Yr., Georgetown U. Law Ctr., 1999, Person of Yr. in Transp., Robert H. Smith Sch. Bus., U. Md., 2003; named one of 5 People to Watch, Washington Post, 1998; recipient Woman of Yr. award, Women's Transp. Seminar. Mem.: Women's Transp. Seminar, Women's Bar Assn., Bar Supreme Ct. US, DC Bar Assn. Democrat. Office: Covington & Burling 1201 Pennsylvania Ave NW Washington DC 20004-2401 Office Phone: 202-662-6291, 202-662-5214. Business E-Mail: lmorgan@cov.com.

MORGAN, LUCY WARE, news correspondent, journalist; b. Memphis, Oct. 11, 1940; d. Thomas Allin and Lucile (Sanders) Keen; m. Alton F. Ware, June 26, 1958 (div. Sept. 1967); children: Mary Kathleen, Andrew Allin; m. Richard Alan Morgan, Aug. 9, 1968; children: Lynn Elwell, Kent Morgan AA, Pasco Hernando C.C., New Port Richey, Fla., 1975; student, U. South Fla., 1976-80. Reporter Ocala Star Banner, Fla., 1965-68, St. Petersburg Times, Fla., 1967-86, capitol bur. chief, 1986—2006, sr. corr., 2006—. Assoc. editor and bd. dirs. Times Pub. Co., 1991—2006. Recipient Paul Hansel award Fla. Soc. Newspaper Editors, 1981, First in Pub. Service award Fla. Soc. Newspaper Editors, 1982, First Place award in pub. service Fla. Press Club, 1982, Pulitzer award for investigative reporting Columbia U., 1985, First Place award in investigative reporting Sigma Delta Chi, 1985; named to Kappa Tau Alpha Hall of Fame, 1992, Fla. Women's Hall of Fame, 2006; named Fla. Senate Press Gallery in Morgan's honor, 2005. Home: 7030 Spencer Dr Tallahassee FL 32312-3548 Office: St Petersburg Times 336 E College Ave Tallahassee FL 32301-1551 Home Phone: 850-668-8817; Office Phone: 850-224-7263. Personal E-mail: lucytimes@aol.com.

MORGAN, LYLE WARNER, II, medical educator; b. Fremont, Nebr., Apr. 5, 1947; s. Lyle W. and Ione E. Morgan. AB, Doane Coll., 1969; MEd, Fla. Christian U., 1970; MA, Wayne State Coll., Nebr., 1973, MS in Edn., 1976; PhD, U. Nebr., 1980; D in Homeopathic Medicine, Internat. U., Brussels, Belgium, 1984. Prof. Pittsburg State U., Kans., 1984—, chmn. pre-medicine & health scis. program, 2000—04. Dir. composition Pittsburg State U., 1984—, dir. English edn., 1984—; sachem Tribe of Mic-O-Say, 1980; chieftain Tribe of Lone Bear, Mo., 2005. Author: Homeopathic Treatment of Sports Injuries, 1988, Homeopathic Medicine: First-Aid & Emergency Care, 1989, Treating Sports Injuries the Natural Way, 1990, Homeopathy and Your Child, 1992. Mem. Ozark Trails Coun. Boy Scouts of Am., Springfield, Mo., 1984—, exec. bd. mem., v.p., 1994—. Recipient Vigil Honor award, Order of the Arrow, 1979, Silver Beaver award, Boy Scouts Am., 1983, Distinguished Eagle Scout award, 1995, Silver Antelope award, 1997; fellow, Coll. Preceptors, UK, 1993. Mem.: SAR, Commn. Religious Counseling and Healing (licentiate), Rockefeller Family and Assocs. Republican. Office: Pitts State U 1701 S Broadway Pittsburg KS 66762-7515 Home Phone: 620-231-4641; Office Phone: 620-235-4691.

MORGAN, M. JANE, computer systems consultant; b. Washington, July 21, 1945; d. Edmond John and Roberta (Livingstone) Dolphin (dec.); 1 child, Sheena Anne. Student, U. Md., 1963-66, Montgomery Coll., 1966-70; BA in Applied Behavioral Sci with honors, Nat.-Louis Univ., 1987, MS in Mgmt., 1991; postgrad. diploma in info. resource mgmt, Am. U., 1995; cert., USDA Grad. Sch., 2000; postgrad. diploma, State U. Calif., Northridge, 2002. With HUD, Washington, 1965-84, computer specialist, 1978-84; pres., CEO Systems and Mgmt. Assocs., 1983-91; dir. systems engring. Advanced Tech. Systems, Inc., Vienna, Va., 1984-86, sr. cons., 1989; chief tech. staff Tech. and Mgmt. Svcs., Inc., 1986-89; sr. computer scientist Integrated Systems divsn. Computer Scis. Corp., 1989-90; computer systems specialist gen. svcs. adminstrn. U.S. Govt., 1991—2001; divsn. dir. U.S. Gen. Svcs. Adminstrn., 2001—06. Mgmt. cons. Author: Rapid Identification of Critical Staff, 1991. Bd. dirs. PL Active. Mem. Federally Employed Women (life, webmaster, 1996-, nat. exec. v.p. 1998-2000), Order Eastern Star. Episcopalian. Personal E-mail: webwoman@jmorgan.net.

MORGAN, MARABEL, writer; b. Crestline, Ohio, June 25, 1937; d. Howard and Delsa (Smith) Hawk; m. Charles O. Morgan, Jr., June 25, 1964; children— Laura Lynn, Michelle Rene. Student, Ohio State U. Pres. Total Woman, Inc., Miami, Fla., 1970—. Pub. speaker. Author: The Total Woman, 1973, Total Joy, 1976, The Total Woman Cookbook, 1980, The Electric Woman, 1985, The Home on the Range Cookbook, 1995. Office: c/o Total Woman Inc 1300 NW 167th St Ste 3 Miami FL 33169-5738

MORGAN, MARIANNE, corporate professional; b. Muncie, Ind., Oct. 13, 1940; d. Clarence Wilson and Mary Estle (Shafer) M. BA, Calif. State U., Long Beach, 1962; MS, U. So. Calif., 1968. Lic. real estate salesperson, Fla. Lab. technician Ball Meml. Hosp. Pathology Lab, Muncie, 1956-61; sr. libr. asst. Anaheim (Calif.) Pub. Libr., 1963-68; coll. libr. Orange Coast Coll., Costa Mesa, Calif., 1968-73; exec. v.p. Brady Products, Inc., Clearwater, Fla., 1973—. Bd. dirs. Brady Products, Inc., Clearwater, Suncoast Fluid Power, Inc., Clearwater. Fiction book reviewer, Libr. Jour., 1969-73; photography pub. in Irvine mag., 1973. Named Alice Miriam Kitselman Scholar, Kitselman Estate, Muncie, 1958. Mem. Nat. Water Well Assn., Boat Owners of the U.S., U.S. Tennis Assn., Crescent Oaks Country Club. Avocations: boating, tennis, photography, travel, raising akc bull-dogs.

MORGAN, MARSHALL T., emergency physician; s. Tad Martin and Daisy Morgan; m. Jean Campbell. BA, Princeton U., NJ, 1964; student, U. Paris, France, 1964; MD, U. Chgo., Ill., 1968. Diplomate Am. Bd. Internal Medicine, Am. Bd. Emergency Medicine. Physician Hazard Clin., Ky., 1969—70; med. dir. Emergency Dept. U. Calif. LA, Santa Monica, 1977—81, Emergency Medicine U. Calif. LA, LA, 1982—, Medstar Air Ambulance U. Calif. LA, 1983—91; clin. prof. medicine Sch. Medicine U. Calif. LA, 1991—; chief, divsn. emergency med. Med. Ctr. U. Calif. LA, 1991—, chief staff, 2006—. Fellow: Am. Coll. Physicians, Am. Coll. Emergency Physicians; mem.: AMA, Calif. Med. Assn. Democrat. Office: U Calif LA 924 Westwood Blvd Ste 300 Los Angeles CA 90024 Office Phone: 310-794-0578. Business E-Mail: mmorgan@mednet.ucla.edu.

MORGAN, MARY ANN, lawyer; b. Orlando, Fla., Mar. 12, 1955; d. Charles Clayburn and Eileen Louise (Mutzbauer) M.; m. Patrick Thomas Burke, Dec. 12, 1992. BS in Criminology, Fla. State U., 1978, JD, 1986. Bar: Fla. 1986, U.S. Dist. Ct. (mid. dist.) Fla. 1986, U.S. Supreme Ct. Investigator Auditor Gen.'s Office State of Fla., Orlando, 1979-83; staff analyst criminal justice com. Fla. Ho. of Reps., Tallahassee, 1985-86; ptnr. Billings, Cunningham, Morgan & Boatwright, Orlando, 1986—2005, mng. ptnr., 2005—. Chmn. renovation com. Orange County Hist. Mus., Orlando, 1995—; spkr. Physician/Lawyer Drug Awareness Program, Orange County Schs., Orlando, 1997. Mem. ABA, ATLA, Fla. Bar Assn. (spkrs. bur. 1997, chair grievance com. 1993-96, vice chair 9th jud. cir. fee arbitration com.), Orange County Bar Assn. (exec. coun. 1991—, chmn. renovation com. 1995—, del. ABA 1989, 90, pres. young lawyers sect. 1990-91, pres. 2001-02), Acad. Fla. Trial Lawyers, Ctrl. Fla. Assn. for Women Lawyers (bd. dirs. 1990-92), Fla. State U. Alumni Assn. (bd. dirs. 1996—), Orange County Legal Aid Soc. (bd. dirs. 1997—, pres.-elect 1998-99, pres. 1999-2000), Nat. Assn. Women Lawyers, Am. Inns of Ct., Tiger Bay Club, Million Dollar Advs. Club. Avocations: waterskiing, golf, boating. Office: Billings Morgan Boatwright & Herandez LLC 399 Carolina Ave Winter Park FL 32789 Office Phone: 407-679-9900. Business E-Mail: maryann@billingslawfirm.com.

MORGAN, MARY DAN, librarian; b. Tallulah, La., Nov. 30, 1943; d. Daniel Boone and Mary Louise (McLeod) M.; m. William Jefferson Day (div. Dec. 1995); 1 child, Forrest Jefferson Day. BA, La. Coll., 1965; MLS, La. State U., 1968; MA Edn., Murray State U., 1976; MSW, U. Louisville, 1992. Cert. social worker, Ky., Ind. Libr. Ascension Parish Schs., Donaldsonville, La., 1966—68, Jefferson County Schs., Louisville, 1968—75; tchr. Webster County Schs., Dixon, Ky., 1975—79, Hardin County Schs., Elizabethtown, Ky., 1979—82, dir. media ctr., 1982—87, tchr. day and residential juvenile facilities, 1987—91, tchr. mid. and sr. high alt. schs., 1991—93; social worker Hospice of Ctrl. Ky., Elizabethtown, 1993—2000, Gentiva Health Svcs., Louisville, 1995, Lincoln Trail Dist. Home Health, Elizabethtown, 1997—98; libr. Luther Luckett Correctional Complex, La Grange, Ky., 2000—. Pres. Webster County Tchrs. Assn., Dixon, Ky., 1977-78; sec. Ky. Libr. Network Bd., Frankfort, 1986-87. Mem.: ALA, AAUW, NASW, NEA (life), Filson Hist. Soc. Office: Luther Luckett Correctional Complex PO Box 6 La Grange KY 40031 Office Phone: 502-222-0363.

MORGAN, MARY E., publishing executive; married; 1 child. B, SUNY Binghamton. Adv. dir. Fitness Mag., 1992—94; assoc. group pub. Parents and Child Mag., 1994—95; assoc. pub. Ladies Home Journal, 1995—97; v.p., pub. Health Mag., 1997—2003, Redbook, 2003—. Mem. editl. bd. Pharmaceutical Executive Magazine. Mem.: Nat. Assn. of Chain Drug Stores, Cosmetic Exec. Women (philanthropy com.), Advt. Women of N.Y. (mem. bd. dirs.), Advt. Club of N.Y. Office: Redbook 224 West 57th St New York NY 10019 Home: Chatham MA Office Phone: 212-649-3450. *

MORGAN, MARY JO, school system administrator; b. West Point, NY, Aug. 19, 1948; d. William Burbridge and Phyllis VanderFehr Yancey; m. Joe Howard Morgan, Nov. 25, 1976; children: Phyllis Ruthann(dec.), Marian Amanda, Elizabeth Darbonne. Master's degree, George Wash. U., 1972; PhD, U. ND, 1993. H.s. prin. Norman County West Schs., Halstad, Minn., 1993—98; chief ops. officer Little Falls (Minn.) Cmty. Schs., 1999—. Asst. dir. Bur. of Ed Rsch., U. N.D., Grand Forks, 1990—93. Mem.: AAUW (pres. 2004), ASCD, Soc. for Human Resource Mgmt. Dfl. Roman Catholic. Avocation: community theater. Home: 1109 Celebration Dr Sartell MN 56377 Office: Little Falls Cmty Schs 1001 5th Ave SE Little Falls MN 56345 Home Phone: 320-252-0279; Office Phone: 320-632-2005. Office Fax: 320-632-2010; Home Fax: 320-632-2010. Business E-Mail: mjmorgan@lfalls.k12.mn.us.

MORGAN, MARY LOU, retired education educator, volunteer; b. Chgo., Mar. 5, 1938; d. William Nicholas and Esther Lucille (Galbraith) Wanmer; m. James Edward Morgan, May 30, 1963. BA in Bus. Edn. and Econs., Wichita State U., Kans., 1971, MEd in Student Pers. and Guidance, 1974; postgrad., Kans. State U., Manhattan, 1986. Cert. bus. tchr., Kans. Reservationist Braniff, Wichita, Kans., 1961—62; stenographer, fin. analyst, clk.-typist Boeing Co., Wichita, 1962—68, tng., pers. and records positions, 1979—93; pers. cons. Rita Pers. Svc., Wichita, 1974—75; adminstrv. aide, manpower specialist, job developer City of Wichita, 1975—76; account exec., employment counselor Mgmt. Recruiters, 1976—77; pers. mgr., patient cons. Women's Clinic, 1977; vocat. rehab. counselor State of Kans., Parsons, 1977—79; pvt. detective Investigation Svcs., Wichita, 1981—84; instr. career devel. Wichita State U., 1988—90. Paralegal asst. Turner & Hensley, Wichita, 1975. Coord. funding Women's Crisis Ctr., Wichita, 1975; docent Carver Mus., Hoover Mus.; vice chmn. Hist. Preservation Commn.; founder, coord. Ann. Women's Chautauqua; Precinct committeewoman Wichita Dem. Com., 1992—94; pres. Jasper County-Newton County Dems., 1998; sub., co-chair then chmn. precinct walkers voter registration Grover Beach Dems., 2004—, assembly dist. mem., 2005—07, chmn. equal rights com., del. to state; mem. 22,000 Club Calif. State Dem. Coun., 2006—07; vol. Dem. Party, San Luis Obispo; bd. dir. City of Wichita Commn. on Status of Women, 1988—91. Mem.:

AARP, NOW (founder, 1st pres. and v.p. program chmn. Wichita chpt. 1969—93, asst. state coord. polit. action com. Wichita chpt. 1993—95, at-large state bd. Joplin chpt. 1994—95, 1997—98, 1999—2000, at-large state mem. 2001—04, del. nat. convention 2006), AAUW (bd. dir. edn., equity, women's issues Joplin br. 1999—2000, pres. Grover Beach br. 2002—04, mem. state pub. policy com. 2003—04, br. pub. policy chair 2004—05, v.p. membership 2004—06), LWV (v.p. issues study Joplin area league 1998—2000, Grover Beach league 2001—06, off board dir. 2002—03, bd. dir. 2003—04), Alliance Ret. Persons, Dem. Women United, Century Club. Avocations: water-skiing, boating, travel.

MORGAN, MARY LOUISE FITZSIMMONS, fund raising executive, lobbyist; b. NYC, July 22, 1946; d. Robert John and Mary Louise (Gordon) Fitzsimmons; m. David William Morgan, Aug. 7, 1971; children: Mallory Siobhan, David William. BA, Marquette U., 1964; MA, Cath. U., 1966; postgrad., Columbia U., 2005. Asst. prof. Monmouth U., West Long Branch, NJ, 1966-69; campaign dir. United Way, NYC, 1969-80; pres. Morgan Communications, NYC, 1980-82; capital campaign dir. YMCA of Greater NY, 1982-85; dir. devel. NY Med. Coll., Valhalla, 1985-88; counsel Challenger Ctr., Va., 1988-89; v.p. Ctr. Molecular Medicine & Immunology, Newark, 1989-92, Garden State Cancer Ctr., Newark, 1989-92; chief devel. and pub. affairs officer Mental Health Assn., White Plains, NY, 1993-95; dir. external affairs St. Vincents Svcs., 1996—, mng. dir., 2006—. Adj. prof. Iona Coll., New Rochelle, NY, 1994-95; dir. Meth Ch. Home for Aged, Riverdale, NY, Casita Maria Inc., NYC, 1975-95; pres., founding dir. Achievement Rewards for Coll. Scientists Inc., 1978-80. Sec. Darien (Conn.) Dem. Town Com., 1984—, vice chmn. Darien nominating com. 1986—. Recipient 50th Anniversary award Casita Maria Inc., N.Y.C., 1984, Iris award Bus. Communicators of Am., 1991, Nat. Depression Awareness Campaign award NMHA, 1994, Am. Graphic Design award, 2002. Mem. Nat. Soc. Fund Raising Execs., Nat. Soc. Hosp. Adminstrn., Spring Lake (NJ) Bath and Tennis Club. Democrat. Roman Catholic. Avocations: golf, gardening, tennis. Office: 66 Boerum Pl Brooklyn NY 11201-5705 Home Phone: 203-356-1212; Office Phone: 718-422-2255. E-mail: MaryL.Morgan@svs.org.

MORGAN, MICHAEL BREWSTER, publishing executive; b. LA, Dec. 30, 1953; s. Brewster Bowen and Eleanor (Boysen) M.; m. Debra Hunter, July 20, 1986. BA, Conn. Coll., 1975. Coll. sales rep. Addison Wesley Pub. Co., Chapel Hill, NC, 1977—81, sponsoring editor Reading, Mass., 1981—84; CEO Morgan Kaufmann Pubs., San Francisco, 1984—2002, Morgan and Claypool Pubs., San Rafael, Calif., 2002—. Mem. Am. Assn. Artificial Intelligence, Assn. Computing Machinery. Office: Morgan and Claypool Pubs 40 Oak View Dr San Rafael CA 94903 Home Phone: 415-492-9415. Business E-Mail: morgan@morganclaypool.com.

MORGAN, MICHAEL DAROLD, academic administrator; b. Lufkin, Tex., 1959; s. L. B. and Esta Lee Morgan; m. Terry Jean Smith, 1994. BBA, Baylor U., Waco, Tex., 1982; MA, Southwestern Bapt. Theol. Sem., Ft. Worth, 1985; PhD, U. North Tex., Denton, 1992. Asst. dean Baylor U. George W. Truett Theol. Sem., Waco, 1996—2003; v.p. univ. rels. Samford U., Birmingham, Ala., 2003—. Trustee Birmingham Regional C. of C., 2005, Bapt. U. of the Americas, San Antonio, 2001. Mem.: Assn. Fundraising Profls. Democrat. Baptist. Office: Samford University 800 Lakeshore Dr Birmingham AL 35229 Office Phone: 205-726-2011.

MORGAN, M(ILLETT) GRANGER, electrical engineering educator, researcher; b. Hanover, NH, Mar. 7, 1941; s. Millett G. M. and Eleanor (Walbridge) M.; m. Elizabeth Nichols, Aug. 10, 1963; children: Kristiana L., Frederick M. AB, Harvard U., 1963; MS, Cornell U., 1965; PhD, U. Calif., San Diego, 1969. Rsch. asst., grad. rsch. asst., NASA fellow Dartmouth Coll., Jicamarca Radar Obs./Cornell U./Arcibo Obs. and U. Calif.-San Diego, 1959—69; dir. computer jobs thru tng. project U. Calif., San Diego, 1969—72, lectr., 1970—71, acting asst. prof., 1971—72; assoc. prog. dir., prog. dir. divsn. computer rsch. NSF, Washington, 1972—74; vis. assoc. physicist Brookhaven Nat. Lab., Upton, NY, 1974; from asst. prof. elec. engring.-engring. and pub. policy, coord. grad. program in EEP to prof. Carnegie-Mellon U., Pitts., 1974—81, prof. engring., 1981—, head dept. engring. and pub. policy, 1980—, Lord chair prof. engring., 1996—, univ. prof., 2003—. Chmn. sci. adv. bd. EPA; chmn. adv. bd. Elec. Power Rsch. Inst.; environ. tech. adv. bd. Alcoa; chmn. sci. and tech. coun. Internat. Risk Governance Coun.; assoc. Nat. Acad., 2002—; cons. in field. Author: (with Max Menrion) Uncertainty: A Guide to Dealing with Uncertainty in Quantitative Risk and Policy Analysis, 1990, paperback edit., 1992; (with others) Risk Communication: A Mental Model Approach, 2002; (with John Peha) Science and Technology Advice for Congress, 2003; contbr. articles to profl. jours. Fellow IEEE, AAAS, Soc. Risk Analysis (editl. bd., Disting. Achievement award 1995); mem. Am. Geophys. Bioelectromagnetics Soc., Sci. Am. (bd. advisors), NAS, Sigma Xi. Office: Carnegie Mellon U Dept Engring and Pub Policy Baker Hall 129 Pittsburgh PA 15213 Office Phone: 412-268-2672. E-mail: granger.morgan@andrew.cmu.edu. *My primary professional objective is to improve education and practice related to policy research on problems that involve science and technology.*

MORGAN, OWAIN DAVID, investment company executive; b. Bristol, Gloucestershire, England, Jan. 4, 1971; s. David Morgan and Helen Frances Bates. MA in Physics with honors, St. John's Coll. Oxford U., Eng., 1992. Pvt. pilot cert. Head trading rsch. JP Morgan, London, 1994—98, head core European strategy rsch., 1996—98, emerging markets proprietary trader, 1998—99, proprietary credit investment mgr. NYC, 1999—2002; dir. risk mgmt. The Rohatyn Group, 2002—. Editor rsch. Global Markets Outlook and Strategy. Editor. Mem.: Global Assn. Risk Mgmt. Professionals. Home Phone: 212-791-3565; Office Phone: 212-984-2933. E-mail: owain.morgan@rohatyngroup.com.

MORGAN, RAYMOND F., plastic surgeon; b. Pitts., Apr. 24, 1948; s. Edwin J. and Alberta (Hirt) M.; m. Sue Ann; children: Ryan Frederic, Alexander Evan, Elizabeth Anne. BS, U. Pitts., 1969, MEd, DMD, U. Pitts., 1972; MD, W.Va. U., 1976. Diplomate Am. Bd. Plastic Surgery, Am. Bd. Hand Surgery. Intern Johns Hopkins U. Hosp., Balt., 1976-77, resident surgery, 1977-80, resident plastic surgery, 1980-82; resident hand surgery Union Meml. Hosp., Balt.; staff U. Va. Health Scis. Ctr., Charlottesville, M.T. Edgerton prof., chmn. dept. plastic surgery, 1988, prof. plastic maxilofacial surgery, clin. orthopedic surgery, and chair, dept. plastic maxillofacial surgery. Fellow ACS, Soc. Univ. Surgeons, So. Surg. Assn., Am. Soc. for Surgery of the Hand, Am. Assn. Plastic Surgeons. Office: U of Va Dept Of Plastic Surgery PO Box 800376 Charlottesville VA 22908-0376 Business E-Mail: rfm9u@virginia.edu. *

MORGAN, RAYMOND FRANKLIN, education educator; b. Crisfield, Md., Dec. 19, 1943; s. Raymond Franklin and Anna Marie (Evans) M.; m. Susan Morgan, July 1, 1978; children: Jonathan, Christopher. BA, Randoph-Macon Coll., 1966; MEd, U. Va., 1970, EdD, 1974. Tchr. English and reading Chesterfield Pub. Schs.; English tchr. York Acad. and Miller Sch. of Albemarle; asst./assoc. prof. grad. program dir. in reading, then prof. edn. Old Dominion U., Norfolk, Va., 1974—. Presenter, spkr., cons. in field. Co-author: Reading to Learn in the Content Areas, 6th edit., 2006, others; co-author: The Psychology of Human Development, 2d edit., 1985, 3rd edit., 1993, Critical Reading-Thinking Skills for the College Student, 1985, 2d edit., 1986; mem. editl. bd. Reading in Va., Reading Improvement; contbr. over 60 articles to profl. jours Recipient Tonelson award Darden Coll. Edn.; NSF grantee. Mem.: Nat. Soc. for the Study of Edn., Coll. Reading Assn., Assn. Lit. Scholars Critics, Phi Kappa Phi. Avocation: golf. Home: 5298 W Valleyside Ct Virginia Beach VA 23464-2606 Office Phone: 757-683-4181. Personal E-mail: rmorgvbva@aol.com. Business E-Mail: rmorgan@odu.edu.

MORGAN, RAYMOND VICTOR, JR., mathematics professor; b. Brownwood, Tex., May 10, 1942; s. Raymond Victor and Lovey Lucile (Tate) M.; m. Mary Jane Folks, Aug. 13, 1967; children: Jason Wesley (dec.), Jeremy Victor. BA, Howard Payne U., 1965; MA, Vanderbilt U., 1966; PhD, U. Mo., 1969. Asst. prof. So. Meth. U., Dallas, 1969-75; assoc. prof. Sul Ross State U., Alpine, Tex., 1975-82, math. dept. chmn., 1976-85, prof., 1982—, dean of scis., 1979-86, exec. asst. pres., 1985-90, pres., 1990—. Author textbook: Agricultural Mathematics, 1978; author articles. Bd. dirs. Texas Rural Cmtys., 1998-2006, chair, 2003—04, Marfa Pub. Radio, 2005-, Tex. Internat. Edn. Consortium; founder regional commr. Alpine Soccer League, 1984; v.p. coach Alpine Baseball League, 1983; pres. Alpine PTA, 1982-83; founder, pres. So. Meth. U. Faculty Club, 1973-75; mem. exec. com. Tex. Assn. Coll. and Univ. Student Pers. Adminstrs., 1990-92; commr. So. Assn. Colls. and Schs., 1999-2003, mem. commn. on colls. class of 2003, 2003. NSF grantee, 1979. Mem. Am. Assn. Higher Edn., Tex. Assn. Coll. Tchrs. (chpt. v.p. 1978-79), Math. Assn. Am. (chmn. Tex. sect. 1985-86), Chihuahuan Desert Rsch. Inst. (bd. dirs.), Lions Club (pres. 1979-80, Lion of Yr. 1980, 83), Alpine Country Club. Republican. Mem. Ch. Of Christ. Avocations: motorcycling, golf, hunting, sports. Home: PO Box 1341 Alpine TX 79831-1341 Office: Sul Ross State U E Highway 90 PO Box C114 Alpine TX 79831-0114 Home Phone: 432-837-8245; Office Phone: 432-837-8032. Business E-Mail: rvmorgan@sulross.edu.

MORGAN, RICHARD GREER, lawyer; b. Houston, Dec. 23, 1943; s. John Benjamin (Stepfather) and Audrey Valley (Brickwede) Haus; children: Richard Greer, Jonathan Roberts. AB in History, Princeton U., 1966; JD, U. Tex., 1969. Bar: Tex. 1969, DC 1970, Minn. 1976, U.S. Ct. Appeals (5th and 9th cirs., temporary emergency ct. appeals) 1976. Atty., advisor to commr. Lawrence J. O'Connor, Jr. Fed. Power Commn., Washington, 1969—71; assoc. Morgan, Lewis & Bockius, Washington, 1971—75; ptnr. O'Connor & Hannan, Washington, 1975—89, Lane & Mittendorf, Washington, 1989—97; mng. ptnr. Shook, Hardy & Bacon, L.L.P., Houston, 1997—2003, Fridge & Resendez, Houston, 2004—. Bd. dirs. Hexagon, Inc.; instr. law seminars; lectr. in field. Author: Gas Lease and Royalty Issues, Natural Gas Yearbook, 1989—92, 2002; contbr. articles to profl. jours. Bd. dirs. Mighty Spl. Music Makers, U. Tex. Law Sch. Found. Mem.: ABA, Energy Law Found. (pres.), DC Bar Assn., Energy Bar Assn. (bd. dirs.), Fed. Bar Assn., Princeton Alumni Assn. Houston, Princeton Alumni Coun. Office: Fridge & Resendez Ste 800 405 Main St Houston TX 77002 Office Phone: 713-226-9100. Business E-Mail: rmorgan@fridge-resendez.com.

MORGAN, RICHARD J., dean, law educator; JD, UCLA, 1971. Bar: Calif. Assoc., ptnr. Krueger & Marsh, LA, 1972-80; dean, prof. U. Wyo. Coll. Law, 1987-89; assoc. dean Ariz. State U. Coll. Law, Tempe, 1983-87, dean, prof., 1990-97; dean, prof. William S. Boyd Sch. Law U. Nev., Las Vegas, 1997—. Office: U Nev William S Boyd Sch Law 4505 S Maryland Pkwy Las Vegas NV 89154-9900 Office Phone: 702-895-3671. E-mail: morgan@ccmail.nevada.edu.

MORGAN, ROBERT, writer, poet, educator; b. Hendersonville, NC, 1944; BA, U. N.C., 1965; MFA, U. N.C., Greensboro, 1968; LittD (hon.), U. N.C., Chapel Hill, 2006. Tchg. asst. U. N.C., Greensboro, 1967—68; instr. Salem Coll., Winston-Salem, NC, 1968—69; lectr. Cornell U., Ithaca, NY, 1971—73, asst. prof., 1973—78, assoc. prof., 1978—84, prof. English, 1984—, Kappa Alpha prof. English, 1992—. Author: Boone: A Biography, 2007, (poetry) Zirconia Poems, 1969, The Voice in the Crosshairs, 1971, Red Owl, 1972, Land Diving, 1976, Trunk and Thicket, 1978, Groundwork, 1979, Bronze Age, 1981, At the Edge of the Orchard Country, 1987, Sigodlin, 1990, Green River: New and Selected Poems, 1991, Topsoil Road, 2000, The Strange Attractor: New and Selected Poems, 2004, (novels) The Blue Valleys, 1989, The Mountains Won't Remember Us, 1992, The Hinterlands, 1994, The Truest Pleasure, 1995, Gap Creek, 1999 (So. Book award), This Rock, 2001, Brave Enemies: A Novel of the American Revolution, 2003, (essays) Good Measure, 1993. Recipient N.C. award for lit., James G. Hanes Poetry award, Jacaranda Rev. Fiction prize, Enniu Tictjcus prize, 1979, O. Henry award, 1997, Acad. award in lit., Am. Acad. Arts and Letters, 2007; fellow, Nat. Endowment for the Arts, 1968, 1974, 1981, 1987, Guggenheim Found., 1988—89; Bellagio fellow, Rockefeller Found. Mem.: Fellowship of So. Writers. Office: Goldwin Smith Hall Dept English Cornell U Ithaca NY 14853 also: c/o Algonquin Books PO Box 2225 Chapel Hill NC 27515-2225 Office Phone: 607-255-3503. Business E-Mail: rrm4@cornell.edu.

MORGAN, ROBERT HALL, lawyer; b. San Jose, Calif., Oct. 14, 1950; s. William Robert and Willa June (Hall) M.; children: Robert Scott, Ryan William, Cory Benjamin, Nathan Thomas, Katherine Linn; m. Susan Parks Morgan. BA, U. Oreg., 1974; MBA, U. Santa Clara, 1975, JD summa cum laude, 1978. Bar: Calif. 1978, U.S. Dist. Ct. (no. dist.) Calif. 1978. Legal extern Supreme Ct. Calif., San Francisco, 1978; pvt. practice law, 1978—; counsel Better Bus. Bur. Santa Clara Valley, Ltd., San Jose, 1980-86. Bd. dirs. Youth Sci. Inst., 1987-92, pres. 1990-92; bd. dirs. Triton Mus. of Art, 1998-; prin. Morgan Law Offices; bd. dirs. Nat. Mus. of The Morgan Horse, 2002—. Mem. Santa Clara County Bar Assn. Democrat. Office: Morgan Law Offices 1501 The Alameda San Jose CA 95126-2311 Office Phone: 408-971-3233. E-mail: RHM@Morganlawoffices.com.

MORGAN, ROBERT MARION, educational research educator; b. Ponca City, Okla., Feb. 5, 1930; s. Perry Harrison and Velma Beatrice (Stowe) M.; m. Constance Louise Claus, Jan. 3, 1963; children— Stephen, Melayne. BS, Okla. State U., 1955, MS, 1956; PhD, Ohio State U., 1958; LLD, Dongah U., Pusan, Korea. Asst. prof. U. N.M., 1958-62; pres. Gen. Programmed Tchg. Corp., Palo Alto, Calif., 1961-64; v.p. Ranchers Corp., Albuquerque, 1962-64; dir. ednl. systems Litton Industries, College Park, Md., 1964-66; dep. dir. divsn. vocational rsch. U.S. Office Edn., Washington, 1966-68; prof., head dept. ednl. rsch. Fla. State U., Tallahassee, 1968-74; dir. Center for Ednl. Tech., 1968-75, Learning Systems Inst., 1975—2003, prof. emeritus, 2003. Lectr. Catholic U. Am., 1966-68, Seoul (Korea) Nat. U., 1970-71; cons. AID, Republic of Brazil, Korea, Italian Air Force, Navy Dept., U.S. Naval Acad.; Chmn. Fla. R & D, Council, 1969—; sch. bd. U. Sch., Tallahassee, 1969-74. Author: Programmed Instruction-A Concept of Learning, 1963, An Educational Systems Analysis for the Republic of Korea, 1970; contbr. articles to profl. jours. Bd. dirs. U.S. Coalition for Edn. for All, 1992—; trustee Aerospace Ednl. Found. With AUS, 1949-52. Fellow Royal Soc. Arts; mem. Am. Ednl. Research Assn., Am. Psychol. Assn., Nat. Soc. for Programmed Instrn., Am. Mgmt. Assn., Rotary, Sigma Xi. Republican. Presbyterian. Office: Fla State Univ C4605 University Ctr Tallahassee FL 32306 Home: 144 Bellevalley Ln Columbia SC 29223 Home Phone: 803-788-1981. E-mail: rmorgan32@sc.rr.com.

MORGAN, ROBIN EVONNE, poet, writer, journalist, editor; b. Lake Worth, Fla., Jan. 29, 1941; 1 child, Blake Ariel. Grad. with honors, The Wetter Sch., 1956; student, pvt. tutors, 1956-59, Columbia U.; DHL (hon.), U. Conn., 1992. Free-lance book editor, 1961-69; editor Grove Press, 1967-70; editor, columnist World column Ms. Mag., NYC, 1974-87, editor in chief, 1989-93, cons. editor, 1993—, columnist, 2003—04, global editor, 2004—. Vis. chair and guest prof. women's studies New Coll., Sarasota, Fla., 1973; disting. vis. scholar, lectr. Ctr. Critical Analysis of Contemporary Culture, Rutgers U., 1987, U. Canterbury, Christchurch, New Zealand, 1989, U. Denver Grad. Sch. Internat. Affairs, 1996-97; invited spl. cons. UN com. UN Conv. to End All Forms Discrimination Against Women, Sao Paulo and Brasilia, Brazil, 1987; adv. bd. ISIS (internat. network women's internat. cross-cultural exch.); spl. advisor gen. assembly conf. on Gender UN Internat. Sch., 1985-86; free-lance journalist, lectr. cons., editor, 1969—; presenter, spkr. in field Author, compiler, editor: Sisterhood Is Powerful: An Anthology of Writings from the Women's Liberation Movement, 1970, Swedish edit., 1972, Sisterhood Is Global: The International Women's Movement Anthology, 1984, U.K. edit., 1985, Spanish edit., 1994, Feminist Press edit., 1996, Sisterhood Is Forever:The Women's Anthology for A New Millennium, 2003; author: (nonfiction) Going Too Far: The Personal Chronicle of a Feminist, 1978, German edit., 1978, The Anatomy of Freedom: Feminism, Physics and Global Politics, 1982, 2d edit., 1994, fgn. edits. UK, 1984, Germany, 1985, Argentina, 1986, Brazil, 1992, The Demon Lover: On the Sexuality of Terrorism, 1989, UK edit., 1989, Japanese edit., 1992, Italian edit., 1998, rev. US edit., 2002, The Word of a Woman: Feminist Dispatches 1968-91, 1992, 2d edit., 1994, UK edit., 1992, Chinese edit., 1996, A Woman's Creed, English, Arabic, French, Italian, Sanskrit, Hindi, Russian, Spanish, Portuguese, Chinese and Persian edits., 1995, Saturday's Child: A Memoir, 2000, Fighting Words: Combating the Religious Right, 2006, (fiction) Dry Your Smile: A Novel, 1987, UK edit., 1988, The Mer-Child: A New Legend, 1991, German edit., 1995, Korean edit., 2000, The Burning Time, 2006, UK edit., 2007, (poetry) Monster: Poems, 1972, Lady of the Beasts: Poems, 1976, Death Benefits: Poems, 1981, Depth Perception: New Poems and a Masque, 1982, Upstairs in the Garden: Selected and New Poems, 1968-88, 1990, A Hot January: Poems 1996-1999, 1999, (plays) In Another Country, 1960, The Duel, 1979; editor: The New Woman: Anthology, 1969; author numerous poems; contbr. articles to profl. jours Mem. 1st women's liberation caucus CORE, 1965, Student Nonviolent Coordinating Com., 1966; organizer 1st feminist demonstration against Miss Am. Pageant, 1968; founder, pres. Sisterhood is Powerful Fund, 1970, NY Women's Law Ctr., 1970; founder NY Women's Ctr., 1969; co-founder, bd. dirs. Feminist Women's Health Network, Nat. Battered Women's Refuge Network, Nat. Network Rape Crisis Ctr.; bd. dirs. Women's Fgn. Policy Coun.; adv. trustee Nat. Women's Inst. Freedom of Press; founding mem. Nat. Mus. Women in Arts; founder Sisterhood is Global Inst., 1984, officer, 1989-97, chair adv. bd., 1997-2004, pres., 2004—; co-founder Nat. Women's Media Ctr., 2005, Greenstone Radio Network, 2006; co-organizer, U.S. mem. ofcl. visit Coalition of Philippines Women's Movement, 1988; chair NY state com. Hands Across Am. Com. for Justice and Empowerment, 1988; adv. bd. Global Fund for Women, Equality Now Recipient Front Page award for disting. journalism, Wonder Woman award for internat. peace and understanding, 1982, Feminist of Yr. award Fund for Feminist Majority, 1990; Human Rights Activism Award from Equality NOW, 2002, Feminist Press award, 2003; writer-in-residence grantee Yaddo, 1980; grantee Nat. Endowment for Arts, 1979-80, Ford Found., 1982-84 Mem. Nat. Mus. Women in Arts, Feminist Writers' Guild, Media Women, N.Am. Feminist Coalition, Pan Arab Feminist Solidarity Assn. (hon.), Israeli Feminists Against Occupation (hon.). Personal E-mail: info@robinmorgan.us.

MORGAN, RONALD BRIAN, retired aerospace engineer, advocate, writer, lecturer; b. Jamaica, NY, Nov. 12, 1935; s. Raymond Edward and Gladys Irene Morgan; m. Eileen Marie Crowley, Dec. 19, 1959 (dec.); children: Glen, Genevieve, Mary, Mark, Brian. EE, Manhattan Coll., Bronx, NY, 1955. Design engr. Douglas Aircraft Co., Santa Monica, Calif., 1955—68; lead engr. and group leader McDonnell Douglas Corp., Kennedy Space Ctr., Fla., 1968—75; supr. Planning Rsch. Corp., Cocoa Beach, 1975—83; sec.-treas. Exec-Invest, Inc., 1979—83; prin. engr. McDonnell Douglas Corp., Merritt Island, 1983—93; author and lectr. self-employed, Cocoa Beach, 1998—2001; owner and pres. Ronald B. Morgan Publ., Merritt Island, 2001—; founder, pres. Am. Millennium Found., Inc., 2004—. Bd. dirs. McDonnell Douglas Mgmt. Assn., Kennedy Space Ctr., 1969—74; co-founder and 2nd pres. PRC Mgmt. Assoc., Cocoa Beach, Fla., 1975—82; co-founder and by-laws chmn. Profl. Business-men's Assn., 1970—72; bd. mem. Brevard County Bicentennial Com., 1973—76. Author: The Am. Spirit in the New Millenium, 2001, (play) No Time for Planners, 1970—72. Senate pres. Fla. Silver-Haired Legislature, Merritt Island, Fla., 2001—, CEO, 2004; chmn. Brevard County Pub. Guardianship Funding Task Force, 2004—05; bd. dirs. commn. on aging Brevard County, 2005—; dept. elder affairs adv. coun. Sate of Fla., 2005—; bd. dirs. Joe Realino Meml. Fund, Cocoa Beach, Fla., 2001—, Sr. Resource Alliance Advocacy Coun., 2000—, chmn., 2005; bd. dirs. Brevard County TRIAD, Inc., 2005; chmn. bd. dirs. Found. Indigent Guardianship, Inc., 2005—; adv. coun. Dept. Elder Affairs, Fla., 2005—. Recipient Apollo Program Honoree, NASA, 1969, Space Shuttle Return to Flight Group Achievement award, NASA, Kenedy Space Ctr., 1989, Congressional Record citation, 2001. Mem.: AARP Avocacy Team (Fla. coord. 2002—03), Brevard Tomorrow/Leadership Brevard (mem. govt. working group 2000—04). Roman Catholic. Achievements include invention of electrical "T" connector; design of first aircraft emergency lighting system used on commercial aircraft; first series of hand-held elec./electronic test equipment for commercial aircraft; first integrated logistics system for all NASA Kennedy Space Ctr. facilities, systems and equipment; integrated logistics system for the mirror fusion project at the Lawrence Livermore Labs; first integrated data system used for configuration mgmt. of Spacelab payloads flown on the Space Shuttle at Kennedy Space Ctr. Avocations: historical research, law research, legislative bills, senior issues.

MORGAN, RUTH PROUSE, academic administrator, educator; b. Berkeley, Calif., Mar. 30, 1934; d. Ervin Joseph and Thelma Ruth (Prcesang) Prouse; m. Vernon Edward Morgan, June 3, 1956; children: Glenn Edward, Renée Ruth. BA summa cum laude, U. Tex., 1956; MA, La. State U., 1961, PhD, 1966. Asst. prof. Am. govt., politics and theory So. Meth. U., Dallas, 1966-70, assoc. prof., 1970-74, prof., 1974-95; prof. emeritus, 1995—; asst. provost So. Meth. U., Dallas, 1978-82, assoc. provost, 1982—86, provost ad interim, 1986-87, provost, 1987-93, provost emerita, 1993—; v.p. Chem. Abatement Tech., Inc., 1995—. Tex. state polit. analyst ABC, N.Y.C., 1972-84. Author: The President and Civil Rights, 1970, Governance By Decree: The Impact of the Voting Rights Act in Dallas, 2004; mem. editl. bd. Jour. of Politics, 1975-82, Presdl. Studies Quar., 1980-2006; contbr. articles to profl. jours. Active Internat. Women's Forum, 1987—, City of Dallas Redistricting Commn., 2001, Greater Dallas Planning Coun. 1997—; trustee Hockaday Sch., 1988-94, Kilby Awards Found., 1993-95; bd. dirs. United Way, Met. Dallas, 1993-99; adv. com. US Army Command and Gen. Staff. Coll., 1994-97; founder Archives of Women of the Southwest, 1992, chmn. adv. com. 1995-99; mem. Dallas Women's Found.; adv. bd. Cary M. Maguire Ctr. for Ethics and Pub. Responsibilty, 1998—. Mem. Am. Polit. Sci. Assn., So. Polit. Sci. Assn. (exec. coun. 1979-84), Southwestern Polit. Sci. Assn. (pres. 1982-83, exec. coun. 1981-84), The Dallas Assembly, The Dallas Forum of Internat. Women's Forum (pres. 1996-97), Charter 100 Club (pres. 1991-92), Ctr. for the Study of the Presidency, The Women's Mus (charter), Dallas Summit Club (pres. 1992-93), Phi Beta Kappa, Pi Sigma Alpha, Phi Kappa Phi, Theta Sigma Phi. Avocations: photography, travel. Home Phone: 214-691-5944; Office Phone: 214-691-5944. Personal E-mail: morgan_ruth@yahoo.com.

MORGAN, SAMUEL P(OPE), physicist, applied mathematician; b. San Diego, July 14, 1923; s. Samuel Pope and Beatrice Marie (Summers) M.; m. Mary Caroline Annin, Jan. 23, 1948; children: Caroline Gail, Lesley Anne, Alison Lee, Diane Elizabeth. BS, Calif. Inst. Tech., 1943, MS, 1944, PhD in Physics, 1947. Mem. tech. staff AT&T Bell Labs., Murray Hill, NJ, 1947-59, head dept. math. physics, 1959-67, dir. computing tech., 1969-70, dir. computing sci. research center, 1967-82, disting. mem. tech. staff, 1982-95, Lucent Tech./Bell Labs., 1996-98, ret., 1998. Research, publs. on electromagnetic theory, applied math., queueing theory; patentee in field. Fellow IEEE (life); mem. AAAS, Am. Phys. Soc., Sigma Xi. Home: 4113 Fellowship Rd Basking Ridge NJ 07920-3906

MORGAN, STEPHEN CHARLES, academic administrator; b. Upland, Calif., June 2, 1946; s. Thomas Andrew and Ruth Elizabeth (Miller) M.; m. Ann Marie McMurray, Sept. 6, 1969; 1 child, Kesley Suzanne. BA, U. La Verne, 1968; MS, U. So. Calif., 1971; EdD, U. No. Colo., 1979. Devel. officer U. La Verne, Calif., 1968-71, asst. to pres. Calif., 1971-73, dir. devel. Calif., 1973-75, v.p. devel. Calif., 1975-76, pres. Calif., 1985—; dir. devel. U. So. Calif., LA, 1976-79; exec. dir. Ind. Colls. No. Calif., San Francisco, 1979-85. Dir. Ind. Colls. So. Calif., L.A., 1985—. Bd. dirs. Mt. Baldy United Way, Ontario, Calif., 1988-98, McKinley Children's Ctr., San Dimas, Calif., 1989-99, LeRoy Haynes Ctr. for Family and Children's Svcs., 2000—; chair nat. com. on higher edn. Ch. of Brethren, Elgin, Ill., 1988-90; dir. Pomona Valley Hosp. Med. Ctr., 1992-98, 99—, Inter Valley Health Plan, 1992-97, PFF Bank and Trust, 2001—. Mem. Assn. Ind. Calif. Colls. and Univs. (exec. com. 1989—, vice-chmn. 1996-2000, chmn. 2000-2002), L.A. County Fair Assn. (bd. dirs., chmn. 2002—), Western Coll. Assn. (exec. com. 1992-98, pres. 1996-98), Western Assn. Schs. and Colls. (sr. accrediting commn. 1996-2001), Pi Gamma Mu. Avocations: orchid culture, gardening, travel. Home: 2518 N Mountain Ave Claremont CA 91711-1579 Office: U LaVerne Office Pres 1950 3rd St La Verne CA 91750-4401 E-mail: morgans@ulv.edu.

MORGAN, SUANN LEE, information technology manager, consultant; b. New Brunswick, NJ, June 25, 1954; d. George and Helen Mahilo; 1 child, Melanie Morgan Thumm. Grad. H.S., Somerville, NJ. Project mgr. AT&T, NYC, 2001—. Office: AT&T 225 Liberty St New York NY 10080 Business E-Mail: suann_morgan@ml.com.

MORGAN, THOMAS I., manufacturing executive; With Genuine Parts Co., 1975—97; CEO U.S. Office Products Co., Washington, 1997—99, Value America, 1999, enfoTrust Networks, 2000—01; pres., COO Hughes Supply Inc., Orlando, Fla., 2001—03, pres., CEO, 2003—. Office: Hughes Supply Inc Corp Office One Hughes Way Orlando FL 32805

MORGAN, THOMAS ROWLAND, retired marine corps officer; b. Allentown, Pa., Jan. 6, 1930; s. Harry Campbell and Olwen (Pierce) M.; m. Barbara A. Croze, June 29, 1957; children— Lynn A., Susan E., Beth E. BA in History, Colgate U., 1952; student, Marine Corps Command and Staff Coll., 1965-66; MA in Edn., U. Va., 1973. Commd. 2d lt. USMC, 1952, advanced through grades to gen., 1986; naval aviator Naval Air Sta., Pensacola, Fla., 1953-54; asst. maintenance officer 3d Marine Aircraft Wing, El Toro, Calif., 1954-55; personnel officer Marine Aircraft Group Western Pacific, 1954-55; aide to comdg. gen. 1st Marine Aircraft Wing, Pacific, 1955; asst. ops. officer Marine Aircraft Group, Kaneohe Bay, Hawaii, 1956-57; squadron pilot, ground tng. officer Marine Attack Squadron, Hawaii, 1957-59; flight instr. Naval Air Sta., Olathe, Kans., 1959; personnel officer, aircraft maintenance officer Marine Fighter Squadron, Beaufort, SC, 1959-61; exec. officer Hdqrs. and Maintenance Squadron, Atsugi, Japan, 1961-62; fleet liaison officer Marine Corps Air Sta., Yuma, Ariz., 1962-65; comdr. Marine Fighter Attack Squadron, Beaufort, 1966-67; group ops. officer, officer-in-charge DaNang DASC, Vietnam, 1968-69; exec. officer Marine Corps Air Sta., Quantico, Va., 1969-71; exec. officer Naval ROTC unit U. Va., 1971-73; chief war plans br. J-5 U.S. European Command Hdqrs., Stuttgart, Fed. Republic Germany, 1973-76; asst. to dep. chief of staff requirements and programs Hdqrs. U.S. Marine Corps, Washington, 1976-77; asst. div. comdr. 3d Marine Div., Okinawa, Japan, 1977-78; asst. chief of staff C-5 Combined Forces Command, Seoul, 1978-80; dep. comdr. FMF Pacific, Camp Smith, Hawaii, 1980-81; dep. chief of staff for requirements and programs Hdqrs. Marine Corps, Washington, 1981-85, dep. chief staff for plans, policies and ops., acting Chief of Staff, 1985-86, asst. commandant, 1986-88, ret. Decorated D.S.M., Def. Superior Service medal, Legion of Merit, Bronze Star medal, Meritorious Service medal, Air medal; Order of Nat. Security medal, Cheonsu medal (Korea) Mem. Am. Legion Avocations: golf, skiing, water sports. E-mail: tmorgva@cox.net.

MORGAN, TIMI SUE, lawyer; b. Parsons, Kans., June 16, 1953; d. James Daniel and Iris Mae (Wilson) Baumgardner; m. Rex Michael Morgan, Oct. 28, 1983; children: Tessa Anne, Camma Elizabeth. BS, U. Kans., 1974; JD, So. Meth. U., 1977. Bar: Tex. 1977, U.S. Dist. Ct. (no. dist.) Tex. 1978, U.S. Ct. Appeals (5th cir.) 1979, U.S. Tax Ct. 1980; cert. tax law specialist. Assoc. Gardere & Wynne, Dallas, 1977-79, Akin, Gump, Strauss, Hauer & Feld, Dallas, 1979-83, ptnr., 1984-86; of counsel Stinson, Mag & Fizzell, Dallas, 1986-88; sole practice Dallas, 1988—. Adj. lectr. law So. Meth. U., 1989-90, 92-98. Bd. dirs. Dallas Urban League Inc., 1987-91. Mem. State Bar Tex. (mem. taxation sect.), Dallas Bar Assn., So. Meth. U. Law Alumni Coun. (sec. 1985-86), Order of Coif, Beta Gamma Sigma. Republican. Episcopalian. Personal E-mail: tsmorganpc@aol.com.

MORGAN, VICTORIA, performing company executive, choreographer; BFA, U. Utah, 1973, MFA magna cum laude, 1976. Prin. dancer Ballet West, 1969-78, San Francisco Ballet, 1978-87; resident choreographer San Francisco Opera, 1987—97; artistic dir. Cin. Ballet, 1997—. Dancer with lead roles in numerous classical, neoclassical and modern ballets including works by George Balanchine, Forsythe, and Kudelka, lead roles for TV and films, choreographer creating over 40 works for 20 ballet and opera cos. across U.S. including Utah Ballet, Pacific Northwest Ballet, Glimmerglass Opera, N.Y.C. Opera and Cin. Opera; creator, prodr. Ballet CD-ROM, choreography featured in documentary The Creation of O.M.O. Office: Cincinnati Ballet 1555 Central Pkwy Cincinnati OH 45214-2863 *

MORGAN, VIRGINIA MATTISON, judge; b. 1946; BS, Univ. of Mich., 1968; JD, Univ. of Toledo, 1975. Bar: Mich. 1975, Federal 1975, U.S. Ct. Appeals (6th cir.) 1979. Tchr. Dept. of Interior, Bur. of Indian Affairs, 1968-70, San Diego Unified Schs., 1970-72, Oregon, Ohio, 1972-74; asst. prosecutor Washtenaw County Prosecutor's Office, 1976-79; asst. U.S. atty. Detroit, 1979-85; magistrate judge U.S. Dist. Ct. (Mich. ea. dist.), 6th circuit, Detroit, 1985—. Mem. bd. Fed. Jud. Ctr., 1997-2001; mem. jud. conf. U.S. Com. on Long Range Planning, 1993-96. Recipient Spl. Achievement award Dept. of Justice, Disting. Alumni award U. Toledo, 1993. Fellow Mich. State Bar Found.; mem. FBA (chpt. pres. 1996-97), Fed. Magistrate Judges Assn. (pres. 1995-96). Office: US Courthouse 231 W Lafayette Blvd Detroit MI 48226-2700

MORGAN, WILLIAM BRUCE, naval architect; b. Fairfield, Iowa, Dec. 20, 1926; s. Orville Burns and Mary Verle (Balderson) M.; m. Mary Maxine Gillam, June 21, 1950; children: Margaret Ann, Ann Elise. BS in Marine Engring., U.S. Mcht. Marine Acad., 1950; MS in Hydraulic Engring., U. Iowa, 1951; DEng in Naval Architecture, U. Calif., 1961. Hydraulic engr. David Taylor Model Basin, Bethesda, Md., 1951-52, naval architect, 1952-58, naval architect supr., 1958-62, head propeller br., 1962-70; head hydromechanics div. David Taylor Naval Ship R&D Ctr. (formerly David Taylor Model Basin), Bethesda, 1970-79, head hydromechanics directorate, 1979—2001; ret. Chmn. exec. com. Am. Towing Tank Conf., 1983-86; mem. exec. com. Internat. Towing Tank Conf., 1984-90. Co-inventor ventilated propeller, supercavitating propeller with air ventilation; contbr. articles to profl. jours. Recipient Navy Disting. Civilian Svc. award USN, 2000, Navy Superior Civilian Svc. award, 1974, Navy Meritorious Svc. award, 1967, Meritorious Exec. award Office of Pres., 1987, William Froude medal Royal Instn. Naval Architects, 1989, Capt. Robert Dexter Conrad award USN, 1993, Gibbs Bros. medal NAS, 1997; named to U. Iowa Disting. Engring. Alumni Acad., 1999. Fellow Soc. Naval Architects and Marine Engrs. (hon. life; exec. com. 1985—, Davidson medal 1986), ASME (chmn. fluids engring. div. 1981-82); mem. NAE, Schiffbautechnische Gesellschaft, Am. Soc. Naval Engrs. (Gold Medal award 1993), Chinese Soc. Naval Architects and Marine Engrs. (hon.), Sigma Xi. Presbyterian. Home: 110 Upton St Rockville MD 20850-1836 Personal E-mail: wbmorgan@erols.com.

MORGAN, WILLIAM J., retired accounting company executive; b. Bklyn., Jan. 12, 1947; s. William J. and Emma T. (Kraft) M.; m. Patricia A. Maltz, Mar. 23, 1968; children: Michele, Jennifer. BS, St. John's U., 1968. CPA, NY Conn., NJ. Ind. dir. Barnes Group Inc., PGT Inc.; ptnr. KPMG LLP, Stamford, Conn., audit staff, 1968—72, audit supr., 1972—74, audit mgr., 1974—77, ptnr.-in-charge pvt. bus. adv. svc. NYC, 1977—79, nat. office, ptnr.-in-charge recruiting, 1979—82, ptnr. comml. health care practice Short Hills, NJ, 1982—91, ptnr.-in-charge N.J. audit practice, 1989—91, mng. ptnr. Fairfield/Westchester counties practice, 1991—94, ptnr. in charge met. N.Y. area mfg., retail and distbn. practice, 1993—96, ptnr. in charge global accts., 1996—98, mng. ptnr. Stamford office, 1996—2003, chmn. audit quality coun., mem. audit and risk adv. svcs. leadership team, 2004—06; ret., 2006. Mem. Bus. Unit Planning Task Force, 1987—90, compensation com., 1990—91, chmn. profit distbn. com., 1991—95, future direction com., 1991—93, pension task force, 1991—92, chmn. compensation com., 1997—2003, bd. process com., 1997—2002, nominating com., 2002—03, independence disciplinary com., bd. dirs. KPMG LLP, 1991—2003, KPMG Americas, 1997—2003, Barnes Group, Inc., PGT, Inc. Acctg. adv. bd. Grad. Sch. Bus. Fordham U., 1979—82; standardization com. Nat. Retail Mchts. Assn., 1979; trustee Tri County Scholarship Fund, 1984—91; v.p., exec. com., adv. bd. Fairfield coun. Boy Scouts Am., 1993—95; bd. dirs. Stamford Symphony, 1995—99; bd. dirs., chmn. bus. ops. com. heritage affiliate Am. Heart Assn., 1997—2000; chmn. Fairfield County Info. Exch., 1992—94; chmn. bd. SACIA, the Bus. Coun. of Fairfield Co., 2001—03, bd. dirs., 1993—2004, Inroads Fairfield and Westchester County chpt., 1992—95; Ambs. Roundtable Bus. Execs. for Nat. Security, 1995—99; exec. com. Conn. Policy and Econs. Coun., 1995—99. Recipient Stamford Good Scout award, 1999, Walter H. Wheeler Disting. Leadership award, 2000, KPMG-Walter E. Hanson Lifetime Achievement award, 2004. Mem. AICPA (small bus. devel. com. 1979-81, acctg. lit. awards com. 1983-86), N.J. Soc. CPA (chmn. acctg. and auditing stds. com. 1988-90, trustee 1990-92, pub. rels. task force, 1987, subcom. health care acctg. 1983-86), N.Y. State CPA (retail acctg. com. 1975-78, com. on edn. in coll. and univs. 1978-82), Nat. Assn. Accts. (dir. manuscripts 1975-77, v.p. N.Y. chpt. 1977-81, pres. NY chpt. 1981-82, nat. publs. com. 1982-83, com. acad. rels. 1983-84, nat. dir. 1983-86, Disting. Svc. award 1975), Health Care Fin. Mgmt. Assn. (NJ chpt. chmn. auditing com. 1982-83, legis. task force com. 1985-86, chmn. joint ventures com., 1987-88), Swedish Am. C. of C. (bd. dirs., exec. com. 1993—), Fairmount Country Club (bd. govs., treas. 1987-90), Woodway Country Club, Conn. Golf Club (bd. govs. 2003-06). Roman Catholic.

MORGAN, WILLIAM JASON, geophysics educator; b. Savannah, Ga., Oct. 10, 1935; married; 2 children. BS, Ga. Inst. Tech., 1957; PhD in Physics, Princeton U., 1964. Rsch. assoc. Princeton U., 1964-66, from asst. prof. to assoc. prof., 1966-77, prof. geophysics, 1977—. Recipient Japan prize, 1990, co-Recipient James b. Macelwane Young Investigator medal Am. Geophysical Union, 1995, Nat. Medal of Science award, 2002. Mem. NAS, 1982-, Am. Geophys. Union, European Union Geol. Sci. Achievements include research in mantle convention, heat flow, plate tectonics, marine geophysics. Office: Princeton U Dept Geosciences 417 Guyot Hall Princeton NJ 08544-0001 E-mail: wjmorgan@princeton.edu.

MORGAN, WILLIAM NEWTON, architect, educator; b. Jacksonville, Fla., Dec. 14, 1930; s. Thomas and Kathleen (Fiske) M.; m. Bernice E. Leimback, July 31, 1954; children: William Newton, Dylan Thomas. AB magna cum laude, Harvard Coll., 1952, MArch Grad. Sch. of Design, 1958. Pres. William Morgan Architects, P.A., Jacksonville, Fla., 1961—. Critic various archtl. schs.; lectr. in field; adj. prof. of art history, Jacksonville U., 1995-96, U. North Fla., 1997; Beinecke-Reeves Disting. Prof. Architecture, U. Fla., 1998-99. Prin. works include Fla. State Mus., Jacksonville Police Meml. Bldg., Pyramid Condominium, Ocean City, Md., Fed. Cts. and Offices, Ft. Lauderdale, Fla., Westinghouse World Hdqs., Orlando, Fla., Neiman-Marcus store, Ft. Lauderdale, 1st Dist. Ct. Appeal, Tallahassee, Fla., Conf. Ctr., Tallahassee, U.S. Embassy, Khartoum, Sudan, U.S. Courthouse, Tallahassee; author: Prehistoric Architecture in the Eastern United States, 1980, Prehistoric Architecture in Micronesia, 1988, Ancient Architecture of the Southwest, 1994, Precolumbian Architecture in Eastern North America, 1999. Subject of The Architecture of William Morgan (Paul Spreiregen) 1987, Images Master Architect Series: William Morgan (Robert McCarter), 2002; Fulbright grantee to Italy, 1958-59; grantee Graham Found. Advanced Studies Arts, 1973; Lehman fellow Harvard U., 1957, Wheelwright fellow 1964-65, fellow NEA, 1991; Sam Gibbons Eminent scholar Fla. A&M U. and U. South Fla.; recipient numerous nat. and regional awards for excellence in design. Fellow AIA (past chmn. com. design) AIA Inst. honor for rsch. into the beginnings of archtl. creativity 1998, Fla. 2000 Millenium award honor for design 2000). Office: William Morgan Architects 220 E Forsyth St Jacksonville FL 32202-3328 Office Phone: 904-356-4195. Personal E-mail: wnmorgan@aol.com.

MORGAN, WILLIAM RICHARD, mechanical engineer; b. Cambridge, Ohio, Mar. 27, 1922; s. Wilbur Alfred and Treva Beatrice (Minto) M.; m. Marjorie Eleanor Stevens, Feb. 17, 1946; children: Carol M. Morgan Dingledy, William R., Jr. BSME, The Ohio State U., 1944; MSME, Purdue U., 1950, PhD in Mech. Engring., 1951. Registered profl. engr., Ohio. Power plant design engr. Curtiss Wright Corp., Columbus, Ohio, 1946-47; instr., rsch. fellow Purdue U., West Lafayette, Ind., 1947-51; supr. exptl. mech. engring. GE, Cin., 1951-55, mgr. controls analysis, devel. Aircraft Gas Turbine Divsn., 1955-59, mgr. XV5A vertical take-off and landing aircraft program, 1959-65, mgr. acoustic engring. Flight Propulsion Divsn., 1965-69, mgr. quiet engine program Flight Propulsion Divsn., 1969-71; pres. Cin. Rsch. Corp., 1971-73; v.p., COO SDRC Internat., Cin., 1973-79; engring. and mgmt. cons. Cin., 1979—. Contbr. articles to profl. jours. Lt. j.g. USNR, WWII. Westinghouse Rsch. fellow Mem. ASME, Masons, Sigma Xi (emeritus), Pi Tau Sigma, Pi Mu Epsilon. Achievements include patents in Humidity Detection and Indicating Instrument, Stall Prevention/Acoustic Tip Treatment, Acoustic Treatment, Inlet Noise Reduction Configuration; research in geometric configuration factors in radiant heat transmission. Home and Office: 312 Ardon Ln Cincinnati OH 45215-4102

MORGAN-PRAGER, KAROLE, lawyer, publishing executive; b. Redding, Calif., 1962; BA in Jour., Univ. Nevada, Reno, 1984; JD, UCLA, 1987. Bar: Calif. 1987, US Dist. Ct. Ctrl. Dist. Calif. 1989. Assoc. Morrison & Foerster, LA, 1987—92; assoc. gen. counsel Times Mirror Co., 1992—95; gen. counsel, corp. sec. McClatchy Co., Sacramento, 1995—, also v.p., 1998—. Copywright agent StarTribune Co. Office: McClatchy Co Legal Dept 2100 Q St Sacramento CA 95818-6899

MORGANROTH, MAYER, lawyer; b. Detroit, Mar. 20, 1931; s. Maurice Jack Morganroth and Sophie (Reisman) Blum; m. Sheila Rubinstein, Aug. 16, 1958; children: Lauri, Jeffrey, Cherie. JD, Detroit Coll. Law, 1954. Bar: Mich. 1955, US Dist. Ct. Mich. 1955, Ohio 1958, US Dist. Ct. (no. dist.) Ohio 1958, US Dist. Ct. DC 2002, US Ct. Appeals (6th cir.) 1968, US Supreme Ct. 1971, NY 1983, US Dist. Ct. NY 1985, US Tax Ct. 1985, US Ct. Appeals (4th cir.) 1985, US Ct. Claims 1986, US Ct. Appeals (2d cir.) 1986, US Ct. Appeals (fed. cir.), US Ct. Appeals (8th cir.) 1994, US Dist. Ct. Wash. DC, 2002. Sole practice, Detroit, 1955—, NYC, 1983—; ptnr. Morganroth & Morganroth, PLLC, 1989—. Cons. to lending instns.; lectr. on real estate NYU, 1980—, bus. entities and structures Wayne State U., 1981—; trial atty. in fed. and state jurisdictions, nationwide. Served with USN, 1948-50. Mem. ATLA, ABA, FBA, NY State Bar Assn., Southfield Bar Assn., Oakland Bar Assn., Assn. Trial Lawyers Mich., Am. Judicature Soc., US Supreme Ct. Hist. Soc., Nat. Assn. Criminal Def. Attys., West Bloomfield (Mich.) Club, Fairlane Club (Dearborn, Mich.), Knollwood Country Club, Edgewood Athletic Club (pres. 1963-65). Democrat. Jewish. Office: 3000 Town Ctr Ste 1500 Southfield MI 48075-1186 also: 156 W 56th St Ste 1101 New York NY 10019-3800 Office Phone: 248-355-3084. Business E-Mail: mmorganroth@morganrothlaw.com.

MORGANSTERN, JAMES, art history educator; b. Pitts., Oct. 16, 1936; s. Richard R. and Anita F. Morganstern; m. Sara Anne McGee, June 5, 1966. BA, Williams Coll., Mass., 1958; MA, NY U., NYC, 1964, PhD, 1973. Asst. prof. U. Wis., Milw., 1970—73; asst. prof. to prof. Ohio State U., Columbus, 1973—. Vis. lectr. U. Va., Charlottesville, 1987. Contbr. articles to profl. jours.; co-author (editor): The Fort at Dereagzi and Other Material Remains in Its Vicinity: From Antiquity to the Middle Ages, 1993. Avocations: tennis, walking, music, films. Home: 70 Webster Park Ave Columbus OH 43214 Office: Ohio State Univ History of Art 108 N Oval Mall Columbus OH 43210

MORGANTE, JOHN-PAUL, human resources specialist; b. Yonkers, NY, June 26, 1962; s. Enzo and Teresa (DellaToffola) M.; m. Ellen Rothberger, May 26, 1984; children: Camden Anne, Bethany Nicole, Hailee Marie. BA, U. So. Calif., LA, 1984; MBA, Open U. Bus. Sch., England, 2004. Ordained to ministry Christian Ch., 1987; cert. profl. in human resources; sr. profl. human resources. Adminstrv. dir. MCM Internat., Lomita, Calif., 1984-87; dir. human resources, 1987-91; exec. dir. Champions for Christ, Austin, Tex., 1991-93; pres. Annimar Assocs., Austin, 1991—95; OD and tng. officer Tex. Dept. Health, Austin, 1995-97; mgr. human resources The TFE Group, Augusta, Ga., 1997-99, sr. mgr., 2000; corp. human resources mgr. Morris Comms. Corp., Augusta, Ga., 2000—01, asst. dir. corp. human resources, 2001—03; dir. human resources and adminstrn. Talla-Com Industries, Tallahassee, 2003—. Contbr. articles to profl. jours. Ctrl. com. Orange County (Calif.) Reps., 1988-89; intern U.S. Rep. Robert Badham, Washington, 1983, campaign worker, 1984; intern Assemblyman Curt Pringle, Garden Grove, Calif., 1988; campaign worker U.S. Senator Chic Hecht, 1982, U.S. Rep. Robert Dornan, 1984, Reagan-Bush, 1984, Tex. State rep. Terry Keel, Austin, 1996, Leadership Austin program Austin C. of C., 1994; solicitation bd. City of Austin, 1996-97; del. Dist. 14 Rep. Conv., Austin, 1996; nat. nominating com. Outstanding Young Ams., 1996-2001; peer moderator Nat. Issues Conv., Phila., 1996; campaign work George W. Bush, 2000; moderator, Mayor's Initiative on Race, Tallahassee, 2003. Recipient Rep. Presdl. Legion Merit, Mfg. Tng. Inst., 2006, Presdl. Commemorative Honor Roll, 1991, Staff Mem. of Yr., 1987; commd. Hon. Texan by Gov. George Bush, 1995. Mem. ASTD, Soc. for Human Resource Mgmt. (Area II bd. dirs. 2002-03), Augusta-Aiken Soc. for Human Resource Mgmt. (sec. 2000, pres. elect, 2001, pres. 2002), Big Bend Soc. Human Resource Mgmt. (exec. bd. 2004, sec. 2005-), Acad. Mgmt., World at Work, Human Resource Planning Soc., Human Capital Inst., Rotary Club Tallahassee, Sister City Com. Tallahassee. Avocations: golf, travel, contemporary jazz. Office: Talla-Com Industries 1721 W Paul Dirac Dr Tallahassee FL 32310 Business E-Mail: jpmorgante@annimar.com.

MORGENROTH, EARL EUGENE, entrepreneur; b. Sidney, Mont., May 7, 1936; s. Frank and Leona (Ellison) M.; m. Adrienne Smith; children: Dolores Roxanna, David Jonathan, Denise Christine BS, U. Mont., Missoula, 1961. From salesman to gen. mgr. Sta. KGVO-AM Radio, Missoula, Mont., 1958-65; sales mgr. Stas. KGVO-TV, KTVM-TV and KCFW-TV, Missoula, Butte, Kalispell, Mont., 1965-66, gen. mgr., 1966-68, Sta. KCOY-TV, Santa Maria, Calif., 1968-69; v.p., gen. mgr. Western Broadcasting Co., Missoula, 1966-69, gen. mgr., pres., 1969-81, numerous cos. in Mont., Calif., Idaho, PR, Ga., 1966-84; pres., chmn. Western Broadcasting Co., Missoula, 1981-84, Western Comm., Inc., Reno, 1984-90; prin. Western Investments, Reno, 1984—. Chmn. Western Fin., Inc., Morgenroth Music Ctrs. Inc., Mont. Band Instruments, Inc., E&B Music Inc., Times Square, Inc., Rio Plumas Ranches, LLC; mem. presdl. adv. coun. U. Mont., 1994—, mem. biol. scis. adv. coun., 1999—. Mem. Mont. Bank Bd., Helena; commencement spkr. U. Mont., 1988, mem. pres.' adv. coun., 1992—, mem. biol. scis. adv. coun., 2001—; bd. dirs. U. Mont. Found., 1985-95. With. US Army, 1954-57. Named Boss of Yr. Santa Maria Valley J.C.s, 1968, Alumnus of the Yr., U. Mont. Bus. Sch., 1998. Mem. U. Mont. Century Club (pres.), Missoula C. of C. (pres.), Rocky Mountain Broadcasters Assn. (pres.), Craighead Wildlife-Wildlands Inst. (bd. dirs. 1991-97), Boone and Crockett Club (pres. 2001-02), Grizzly Riders Internat. (bd. dirs., v.p. 1991—, pres. 2005-), Bldg. A Scholastic Heritage (bd. dirs. 1987-97). Republican. Methodist.

MORGENS, WARREN KENDALL, retired lawyer; b. Oklahoma City, May 25, 1940; s. Alvin Gustav and Helen Alene (McFarland) M. Student, Westminster Coll., Fulton, Mo., 1958-60; BSBA, Washington U., St. Louis, 1962, JD, 1964. Bar: Mo., 1964, U.S. Supreme Ct. 1968, D.C., 1981. Atty., gen. counsel's office SEC, Washington, 1968-69; asst. atty. gen. State of Mo., St. Louis, 1969-72; ptnr. Park, Craft & Morgens, Kansas City, Mo., 1973-76; pvt. practice law Kansas City, 1976-81; mng. atty. Hoskins, King, McGannon & Hahn, Washington, 1981-85; spl. ptnr. Barnett & Alagia, Washington, 1985-89; of counsel Anderson, Hibey, Nauheim & Blair, Washington, 1989-93; pvt. practice Washington, 1993—2003; property trustee Va., 2001—03; cons. trustee Ariz. and Calif., 2003—. Patron Nat. Symphony, Washington, 1966-68, 81-85, Washington Performing Arts Soc., 1989—93, Kansas City Philharm., 1974-80, Supreme Ct. Hist. Soc., Washington, 1982—93, The Williamsburg (Va.) Found., 1982—93. Named one of Outstanding Young Men Am., 1977. Mem. Mo. Bar Assn., D.C. Bar Assn., Univ. Club (St. Louis). Republican. Presbyterian. Avocations: hiking, sailing, fishing, golf. Home: 5221 La Jolla Hermosa Ave La Jolla CA 92037 Personal E-mail: mogues@att.net.

MORGENSEN, JERRY LYNN, construction company executive; b. Lubbock, Tex., July 9, 1942; s. J. J. and Zelline (Butler) Morgensen; m. Linda Dee Austin, Apr. 17, 1965; children: Angela, Nicole. BS in Civil Engring., Tex. Tech U., 1965. Area engr. E.I. Dupont Co., Orange, Tex., 1965-67, div. engr. La Place, La., 1967-73; project mgr. Hensel Phelps Constrn. Co., Greeley, Colo., 1973-78, area mgr., 1978-80, v.p., 1980-85, pres., CEO, 1985—, chmn. bd. Mem. bd. trustees UNC; Member Constn. Indus. Devel. Coun. CSU; mem. Tex. Tech. Civil Engring. Acad. Office: 420 6th Ave Greeley CO 80631-2332

MORGENSON, GRETCHEN C., reporter; b. State College, Pa., Jan. 2, 1956; married; 1 child. BA in English and History, Saint Olaf Coll., Northfield, Minn., 1976. Asst. editor to writer, fin. columnist Vogue Mag., 1976—81; stock broker Dean Witter Reynolds, NYC, 1981—84; staff writer Money Mag., 1984—86; editor, investigative bus. writer Forbes Mag., 1986—93, press sec. for Forbes for President campaign, 1995—96, asst. mng. editor, 1996—98; exec. editor Worth Mag., 1993—95; asst. bus. and fin. editor NY Times, NYC, 1998, now Market Watch columnist, Sunday Money and Bus. section. Author: Forbes Great Minds of Business, 1997; co-author: The Woman's Guide to the Stock Market, 1981; author: (with Campbell R. Harvey) The New York Times Dictionary of Money and Investing: The Essential A-to-Z Guide to the Language of the New Market, 2002; co-author: (with Allen R. Myerson (editor), Floyd Norris) The New Rules of Personal Investing: How to Prosper in a Changing Economy, 2001. Recipient Gerald Loeb award, 1998, 2002, Pulitzer Prize for beat reporting, 2002, TJFR Group/MasterCard Internat. Bus. News Luminaries award, 2003, Fin. Journalism prize for lifetime achievement, Women's Econ. Round Table, 2003. Office: NY Times 229 W 43d St New York NY 10036

MORGENSTEIN, WILLIAM, shoe company executive; b. Bklyn., Jan. 11, 1933; s. Samuel and Jeanne Marie (Mittentag) M.; m. Sylvia Dove, June 8, 1952; children: Lee Brian, David Barry. BS in Fin., U. Ala., 1955. Salesman Greenwald Shoe Co., Birmingham, Ala., 1954-56; sr. buyer Melville Shoe Corp., NYC, 1958-67; pres. Kitty Kelly Shoe Co., NYC, 1967-70; exec. v.p. A.S. Beck Shoes, NYC, 1970-71, Sandia Internat., Englewood Cliffs, NJ, 1971-75; pres., chief exec. officer Marquesa Internat. Corp., Englewood, NJ, 1975-95; sr. acct. mgr. Signature Group divsn. Montgomery Ward, 1995—99; v.p. Advanceme.com Inc., 1999—; sr. v.p., nat. sales dir. Sterling Funding Corp., 2005—. Internat. cons. footwear exporting, 1965—. Served with U.S. Army, 1956-58. Mem. Footwear Distbrs. and Retailers Am. (vice-chmn., bd. dirs., exec. com.), Internat. Footwear Assn. (vice-chmn., exec. com. 1986—, chmn. 1989—, pres.), 210 Assn. (Pres.' Circle 1987), Toastmasters (past pres. Teaneck, NJ chpt.). Republican. Jewish. Avocations: history, golf. Office Phone: 866-486-5638 ext. 1161. Personal E-mail: bmorgens@aol.com. Business E-Mail: bill.morgenstein@sterlingfunding.com.

MORGENSTERN, JOE, film critic; b. NYC, Oct. 3, 1932; s. Mark E. and Mollie (Fisch) M.; m. Rosetta Jacobs, Jan. 21, 1962 (div. Apr. 1981); 1 child, Anna. BA in English magna cum laude, Lehigh U., 1953. Film critic Newsweek mag., NYC, 1965-72; columnist LA Herald Examiner, 1982-87; film critic Wall Street Jour., NYC, 1995—. Co-founder Nat. Soc. Film Critics. Author: World Champion, 1968 (TV scripts) Boy in the Plastic Bubble, Law & Order, 10,000 Black Men Named George. Recipient Pulitizer Prize for criticism, 2005. Mem. Phi Beta Kappa, NY Film Critics Cir., LA Soc. Film Critics. Office: Wall Street Jour PO Box 1946 Santa Monica CA 90406-1946 E-mail: joe.morgenstern@wsj.com.

MORGENSTERN, LEON, surgeon; b. Pitts., July 14, 1919; s. Max Samuel and Sarah (Master) M.; m. Laurie Mattlin, Nov. 27, 1967; 1 son, David Ethan. Student, CCNY, 1936—37; BA magna cum laude, Bklyn. Coll., 1940; MD, N.Y. U., 1943. Diplomate: Am. Bd. Surgery. Intern Queens Gen. Hosp., Jamaica, NY, 1943—44, fellow, asst. resident in pathology, 1947—48, resident in surgery, 1948—52; practice medicine, specializing in surgery LA, 1953—, Bronx, NY, 1959—60; dir. surgery Cedars of Lebanon Hosp., LA, 1960—73, Cedars-Sinai Med. Ctr., LA, 1973—88, emeritus dir. surgery, 1989—, dir. bioethics program, 1995—; prof. surgery UCLA Sch. Medicine, 1973-90, prof. surgery emeritus, 1990—. Asst. prof. surgery Albert Einstein Coll. Medicine, N.Y.C., 1959-60; adj. prof. bioethics U. Judaism, L.A., 1996—; dir. Ctr. Health Care Ethics Cedars-Sinai Med. Ctr., 1998-2004, emeritus dir. 2004-. Assoc. editor Mount Sinai Jour. Medicine, 1984-88, Surg. Innovation, 2004-; contbr. articles to profl. publs. Served to capt. M.C. U.S. Army, 1944-46. Mem. Soc. for Surgery Alimentary Tract, Soc. Am. Gastrointestinal Endoscopic Surgeons (hon.), Am. Gastroent. Assn., L.A. Surg. Soc. (pres. 1977), ACS (sec.-treas. 1976-77, pres. 1978, bd. dirs. So. Calif. chpt. 1976-84, gov.-at-large), Internat. Soc. Surgery, Western Surg. Assn., Pacific Coast Surg. Assn., AMA, Calif. Med. Assn., L.A. County Med. Assn., Am. Surg. Assn., others. Home: 5694 Calpine Dr Malibu CA 90265-3812 Office Phone: 310-423-1630. Business E-Mail: morgenstern@cshs.org.

MORGENSTERN, ROBERT TERENCE, lawyer; b. NYC, Aug. 23, 1944; s. Carl G. and Jean C. (Madden) M.; m. Nancy G. Golden, June 29, 1968; children: Cynthia, John, Kathryn, Brian. BA, Villanova U., 1966, JD, 1969. Bar: N.J. 1969, U.S. Supreme Ct. 1986; cert. civil trial atty. Assoc. Dolan & Dolan, Newton, N.J., 1969-74, officer, dir., 1975—. Mem. ABA, Assn. Trial Lawyers Am., N.J. Fedn. Planning Officials, Sussex County Bar Assn. (v.p.), N.J. State Bar Assn., Rotary. Roman Catholic. Home: 44 Deire Dr Sparta NJ 07871-1134 Office: Dolan & Dolan PA 53 Spring St & 1 Legal Ln PO Box D Newton NJ 07860-0605 Home Phone: 973-729-8788; Office Phone: 973-383-1600.

MORGENSTERN, SHELDON JON, symphony orchestra conductor; b. Cleve., July 1, 1938; s. Irwin Arthur and Harriet Sue Morgenstern; m. Patricia Lou Bradshaw; 1 child, Sali Sharpe Hagan. MusB, Northwestern U., 1961; MusM, New Eng. Conservatory, 1966; DMA (hon.), Greensboro Coll., NC, 1986. Mem. conducting staff New Eng. Conservatory, 1965-66; music dir. Greensboro Symphony Orch., 1967-74; prin. guest condr. Betica Philharm., Seville, Spain, 1978-82, Polish Radio Orch., Warsaw, 1990—. Music advisor Miss. Symphony Orch., 1985-86; bd. mem. Istanbul Internat. Festival, Turkey, 1975—, Company for Televised Theatre; mus. cons. U.S. Dept. Interior for Wolf Trap Farm Park, 1972; mem. adv. bd. Avery Fisher Award, 1978—; music dir. Ea. Music Festival, Greensboro, 1962-98, music dir. emeritus, 1998—; artistic adv. Arts Sans Frontieres, 2005-; adv. coun. mem. Kent/Blossom Music Festival, 2006-. Author: No Vivaldi in the Garage, 2001. Mem. adv. bd. Blossom Cleve. Orch. Festival, 2006—. Recipient O'Henry award City of Greensboro, 1980, Long Leaf Pine award State N.C., 1989, Nat. Alumni award Northwestern U., 1990. Home: Airans/Farges Ch des Charmys 01550 Collonges France E-mail: shellymorgenstern@yahoo.fr.

MORGENTHALER, DAVID TURNER, venture capitalist; b. Chester, S.C., Aug. 5, 1919; s. Henry W. and Elizabeth (Taylor) M.; B.S. in Mech. Engring., M.S., Mass. Inst. Tech., 1941; m. Lindsay Anne Jordan, May 17, 1945; children— David T., Gary J., Todd W., Gaye Elizabeth. Sales mgr. Ervite Corp., 1945-47; mech. engr. Copes Vulcan div. Blaw-Knox Co., 1947-50; v.p., dir. sales Delavan Mfg. Co., Des Moines, 1950-57; pres. Foseco, Inc., Cleve., 1957-68; chmn. bd. Foseco Technik Ltd., Birmingham, Eng., 1964-68; chmn. bd. API Instruments Co., 1968-70, dir., 1963-70; chmn. bd. Mfg. Data Systems, Inc., Ann Arbor, Mich., 1969-81; chmn. exec. com., dir. LFE Corp., Waltham, Mass., 1970-85; founding ptnr. Morgenthaler Assos.; mng. ptnr. Morgenthaler Ventures, 1981—; dir. Hauserman, Inc., Cleve., Tartan Labs., Inc., Pitts., Three Phoenix Co.; bd. dirs., Ribozyme Pharmaceuticals, 1992-02, chmn., 1995-02; ons. Brentwood Assocs.; trustee Cleve. Clinic Found.; bd. overseers Case Western Res. U. Served to capt., AUS, 1941-45. Mem. Nat. Venture Capital Assn. (past pres.), Chief Execs. Orgn., Inc. (past pres.), Young Pres. Orgn. (sr. v.p., bd. dirs.), Sigma Nu. Clubs: Westwood Country, Union, Pacific Union, Lyford Cay. Home: 13904 Edgewater Dr Cleveland OH 44107-1416 Office: 50 Public Sq Ste 2700 Cleveland OH 44113

MORGENTHALER-LEVER, ALISA, lawyer; b. St. Louis, June 3, 1960; d. Gerald Thomas and Mary Louise (Neece) M. BA, S.W. Mo. State U., 1982; JD, Cornell U., 1985. Bar: N.Y. 1986, D.C. 1988, Calif. 1990. Law clk. City of Springfield, Mo., 1981; atty. bd. govs. Fed. Res. Sys., Washington, 1984, staff atty., 1985-86; assoc. Kirkpatrick & Lockhart, Washington, 1986-88, Stroock & Stroock & Lavan, Washington, 1988-89; ptnr. Christensen, Glaser, Fink, Jacobs, Weil & Shapiro, LLP, LA, 1989—. V.p., sec., bd. dirs. L.A. Retarded Citizens Found.; v.p., bd. dirs. Malibu Riviera III Homeowners Assn., 2000—04. Named one of So. Calif. Super Lawyers, 2006, 2007, Top 50 Women Lawyers So. Calif., 2007. Mem. ABA, Calif. Bar Assn. (del. to com. on adminstrn. justice), DC Bar Assn., NY Bar Assn., LA County Bar Assn. (jud. appts. com., jud. profile com.), Beverly Hills Bar Assn., Century City Bar Assn., Women Lawyers Assn. of LA (bd. dirs.), 3019 Third St. Owners Assn. (v.p. bd. dirs. 1991-00), Order of Omega, Phi Alpha Delta, Rho Lambda, Phi Kappa Phi, Pi Sigma Alpha, Gamma Phi Beta. Office: Christensen Glaser Fink Jacobs Weil & Shapiro LLP 10250 Constellation Blvd 19th Fl Los Angeles CA 90067-5010 Business E-Mail: amorgenthaler@chrisglase.com.

MORGENTHAU, ROBERT MORRIS, prosecutor; b. NYC, July 31, 1919; s. Henry Jr. and Elinor (Fatman) M.; m. Martha Pattridge (dec.); children: Joan, Anne, Elinor, Robert P., Barbara; m. Lucinda Franks, Nov. 19, 1977; children: Joshua, Amy. BA, Amherst Coll., 1941, LLD (hon.), 1966; LLB, Yale U., 1948; LLD (hon.), NY Law Sch., 1968, Syracuse Law Sch., 1976, Albany Law Sch., 1982, Colgate U., 1988. Bar: N.Y. 1949. Assoc. firm Patterson Belknap & Webb, NYC, 1948-53, ptnr., 1954-61; U.S. atty. So. Dist. N.Y., 1961-62, 62-70; dist. atty. New York County, 1975—. Former pres. N.Y. State Dist. Attys. Assn.; lectr. London Sch. Econs., 1993. Chmn. Police Athletic League; trustee Baron de Hirsch Fund; chmn. Gov.'s Adv. Com. on Sentencing, 1979; counsel N.Y. State Law Enforcement Coun.; chmn. A Living Meml. to the Holocaust-Mus. of Jewish Heritage; Dem. candidate for Gov. of N.Y., 1962; trustee Temple Emanu-El, NYC; bd. dirs. P.R. Legal Def. and Edn. Fund. Lt. comdr. USNR, 1940—45. Recipient Emory Buckner award Fed. Bar Coun., 1983, Yale Citation of Merit, 1982, Fordham-Stein prize, 1988, Thomas Jefferson award in law U. Va., 1991, Brandeis medal U. Louisville, 1995, Omanut award Yeshiva U., 1995, Trumpeter award Nat. Consumers League, 1995, Frank S. Hogan award N.Y. State Dist. Atty's. Assn., 2000, Lone Sailor award USN Meml. Found., 2000; named Man of Yr., Fed. Law Enforcement Assn. Found., 2004; Matheson-Morgenthau Disting. Professorship in Law named in his honor, Va. Law Sch. Fellow Am. Bar Found.; mem. ABA, N.Y. State Bar Assn. (award for Excellence in Pub. Svc. 2001), Assn. of the Bar of the City of N.Y., N.Y. County Lawyers Assn. (Disting. Pub. Svc. award 1993), Amherst Alumni Assn. (hon. pres. 2001), Phi Beta Kappa. Office: Office Dist Atty 1 Hogan Pl New York NY 10013-4311

MORGISON, F. EDWARD, investment broker; b. Clay Center, Kans., Oct. 4, 1940; s. Fred and Lena Edna (Chaput) M.; m. Karen Lorene Herdman, Nov. 21, 1964; 1 child, Diana Michelle. BA in Math., Emporia State U., 1963; MSBA, U. Mo., Columbia, 1964; postgrad., U. Mo., Kansas City. Cert. purchasing mgr.; registered securities agt., Mo., Kans., Ill., 2001. Computer programmer U. Mo. Med. Ctr., Columbia, 1964-65; adminstrv. and budget analyst Urban Renewal Project, Independence, Mo., 1965-66; acct. exec., bank broker Stifel Nicolaus & Co., Kansas City, Mo., 1966-73; pres., CEO Will-Mor Investment Sys., Kansas City, Mo., 1973-75; br. mgr. Edward Jones & Co., Kansas City, 1975; editl. and exec. asst. to Morgan Maxfield for U.S. Congress, Kansas City, 1976; sr. acct. exec., merger and acquisitions specialist Rowland & Co., Kansas City, 1976-77; chmn. bd., pres., CEO Mo. Securities, Inc., Kansas City, 1977-78; v.p., regional mgr. Charles Schwab & Co., Kansas City, 1978-79; v.p. Profl. Assistance, Kansas City, 1979-81; exec. v.p. J. Penner & Assocs., Kansas City, 1981-82; pres. J. Penner & Co., Kansas City, 1982-83; acct. exec., registered broker Lowell H. Listrom & Co., 1981-84; pres., CEO First Allen Securities, Inc., 1983-89, Venture House, Kansas City, 1989—. Agt. Offerman & Co., Kansas City, 1979-81, CEO Morgison & Assoc., Kansas City, 1979-81; fiscal dir. Housing Authority of Kansas City, 1981; dir., sec. Hubach Group, Inc., 1987-88; treas. Skytrader Corp., 1986-89, Emergency Sys. Svcs., 1986-87, Internat. Tex. Industries, Inc., San Antonio, 1986-88; chmn. bd., treas. Masters Mark, Inc., 1986-89; CFO Am. Utilicraft Corp., 1992-97, v.p. purchasing, 1997-2005; acct. exec. N.Y. Stock Exch., Am. Exch., 1965-89. Recipient Bausch and Lomb Sci. award, 1959, Sci. award Lambda Delta Lambda, 1962. Mem. NRA (life), U. Mo. Alumni Assn. (life), Emporia State U. Alumni Assn. (life), U.S. Chess Fedn. (life), Mensa (life). Home: 1000 NE 96th Ter Kansas City MO 64155-2145

MORGNER, AURELIUS, economist, educator; b. NYC, May 23, 1917; s. Oscar A. and Anna G. (Hoffmeister) M. BS in Bus. Adminstrn., U. Mo., 1938, MA in Econs., 1940; PhD, U. Minn., 1955. Investigator Dept. Labor, 1941; project dir. Employment Stblzn. Research Inst., 1941-42; instr. bus. adminstrn. U. Minn., 1942-46; lectr. Northwestern U., 1946-47; assoc. prof. Tex. A&M U., 1947-56, prof., 1956-58; vis. prof. U. São Paulo, Brazil, 1958-60, dir. grad. social studies, 1959-60; prof. econs. U. So. Calif., LA, 1960—, chmn. dept., 1962-69; prof. internat. econs. Sch. Internat. Relations, 1960—. Pub. panel mem. Chgo. Regional War Labor Bd., 1943-45; pub. rep. minimum wage com. Dept. Labor, 1942,43; cons. Govt. Eucador, 1965-68, Govt. Guyana, 1968, state Nev., 1970, Philippines, 1971-72, Yemen Arab Republic, 1974-75; U.S. State Dept. vis. lectr., Brazil, summer 1966 Co-author: Local Labor Markets, 1948, Problems in Economic Analysis, 1948, Problems in the Theory of Price, 1954 (trans. Spanish 1965, Portuguese 1967). Ford faculty fellow Columbia U., 1954-55 Mem. So. Calif. Econ. Assn. (pres. 1965-66), Am. Econs. Assn., Western Econ. Assn., Am. Arbitration Assn., Internat. Studies Assn. Office: U So Calif Dept Econs Los Angeles CA 90089-0001

MORGRIDGE, JOHN P., computer systems network executive; b. Elmhurst, Ill., July 23, 1933; m. Tashia F. Morgridge; three children. BBA in Mktg. & Fin., U. Wis., 1955; MBA, Stanford U., 1957; DSc (hon.), U. Wis., 1994; LLD (hon.), Carleton U., 2002; LHD, Lesley Coll., No. Ill. U. Mktg. profl. Honeywell Info. Systems, 1960-80; v.p. mkgt., sales and svc. Stratus Co., Inc., 1980-86; pres., chief ops. officer GRiD Systems (now part of Tandy Corp.), 1986-88; pres., CEO Cisco Systems, Inc., San Jose, Calif., 1988-95, chmn., 1995—2006, chmn. emeritus, 2006. Lectr. Stanford U. Bus. Sch., 1997—. Bd. dirs. Coun. on Competiveness, CARE, The Cisco Found., The Cisco Learning Inst., Interplast, The Nature Consevancy, Wis. Alumni Rsch. Found.; trustee Stanford U., 2002—. Capt. USAF, 1957—60. Recipient Leadership in Tech. award Tech. Corps, 1988, Ernest C. Arbuckle award, Stanford U., 1998, Philanthropist of the Yr., Ctr. for Excellence in Nonprofits, 1999, Deveneck Hamanitarian award, Hidden Villa, 1999; named one of 400 Richest Americans, Forbes, 2006. Office: Cisco Systems Inc 170 W Tasman Dr San Jose CA 95134-1700 *

MORHAIME, MIKE, video game company executive; Grad., UCLA. Co-founder, pres. Blizzard Entertainment (originally Silicon & Synapse), Irvine, Calif., 1991—. Prodr.: (video games) The Lost Vikings, 1992, Orcs & Humans, 1994, The Death and Return of Superman, 1994, BlackThorne, 1994, Warcraft II: Tides of Darkness, 1995, Justice League Task Force, 1995, Diablo, 1996, Warcraft II: The Dark Saga, 1997, Norse by Norse West: The Return of the Lost Vikings, 1997, StarCraft: Brood War, 1998, StarCraft, 1998, Warcraft II: Battle.net Edition, 1999, StarCraft 64, 2000, Diablo II, 2000, Diablo II: Collector's Edition, 2000, Diablo II: Lord of Destruction, 2001, Warcraft III: Reign of Chaos, 2002, Warcraft III: The Frozen Throne, 2003, Rock 'n Roll Racing, 2003, World of Warcraft, 2004. Named one of 50 Who Matter Now, CNNMoney.com Bus. 2.0, 2006. Office: Blizzard Entertainment PO Box 18979 Irvine CA 92623 *

MORHOUSE, SANFORD W., lawyer; b. Keene Valley, NY, Dec. 13, 1944; BA, Williams Coll., 1966; JD, Columbia Univ., 1969. Bar: N.Y. 1969, US Dist. Ct. so. N.Y. Assoc. to ptnr. Dewey Ballantine LLP, NYC, 1969—, co-chmn. mgmt. com., mem. exec. com. & chmn. private equity group. Dir. Damon Runyon Cancer Rsch. Found., Broad Hollow Estates Inc. Mem.: ABA, N.Y. State Bar Assn., Assn. of the Bar City of N.Y., Am. Coll. Real Estate Lawyers. Office: Dewey Ballantine LLP 1301 Ave of the Americas New York NY 10019-6092 Office Phone: 212-259-8400. Office Fax: 212-259-8499. Business E-Mail: smorhouse@dbllp.com.

MORI, ALLEN ANTHONY, academic administrator, consultant; b. Hazleton, Pa., Nov. 1, 1947; s. Primo Philip and Carmella (DeNoia) M.; m. Barbara Epoca, June 26, 1971; 1 child, Kirsten Lynn. BA, Franklin and Marshall Coll., Lancaster, Pa., 1969; MEd, Bloomsburg U. Pa., 1971; PhD, U. Pitts., 1975. Spl. edn. tchr. White Haven (Pa.) State Sch. and Hosp., 1969-70, Hazleton Area Sch. Dist., 1970-71, Pitts. Pub. Schs., 1971-74; supr. student tchrs. U. Pitts., 1974-75; prof. spl. edn. U. Nev., Las Vegas, 1975-84; dean coll edn. Marshall U., Huntington, W.Va., 1984-87; dean coll. edn. Calif. State U., LA, 1987—2003, provost, v.p. acad. affairs Dominquez Hills, 2003—. Hearing officer pub. law 94-142 Nev. Dept. Edn., Carson City, 1978—; mem. Nev. Gov.'s Com. on Mental Health and Mental Retardation, 1983-84; cons. Ministry Edn., Manitoba, Can., 1980-82; pres. Tchr. Edn. Coun. State Colls. and Univs., 1993-94. Author: Families of Children with Special Needs, 1983; co-author: Teaching the Severely Retarded, 1980, Handbook of Preschool, Special Education, 1980, Adapted Physical Education, 1983, A Vocational Training Continuum for the Mentally and Physically Disabled, 1985, Teaching Secondary Students with Mild Learning and Behavior Problems, 1986, 93, 99; author numerous articles, book revs. and monographs. Bd. dirs. Assn. Retarded Citizens San Gabriel Valley, ElMonte, 1989—94. Recipient grants U.S. Dept. Edn., 1976-91, Nev. Dept. Edn., W.Va. Dept. Edn., Calif. State U. Chancellor's Office. Mem. Assn. Tchr. Educators, Coun. for Exceptional Children (div. on Career Devel. exec. com. 1981-83), Nat. Soc. for Study of Edn., Phi Beta Delta, Phi Delta Kappa, Pi Lambda Theta, Phi Kappa Phi. Avocations: wine collecting, travel. Office: Calif State U Dominguez Hills 1000 E Victoria Carson CA 90747 Office Phone: 310-243-3307. Business E-Mail: amori@csudh.edu.

MORI, YOSHIKO, language educator; b. Tokyo; children: Misa, Mina. AA, Nanzan Jr. Coll., Japan, 1980; BA, Nanzan U., Japan, 0198; MA, Ohio U., Athens, 1991; PhD, U. Ill., Urbana-Champaign, 1996. Cert. second language acquistion, tchr. edn. U. Ill. at Urbana-Champaign, 1996. Tchr. Hikarigaoka Girls' HS, Okazaki, Japan, 1983—84, Tokyo Met. Edn. Bd., 1984—89; tchg. asst. Ohio U., Athens, 1989—91; tchg., rsch. asst. U. Ill., Urbana-Champaign, 1991—96; assoc. prof. Georgetown U., Washington, dir. Japanese lang. program; vis. prof., Japanese pedagogy Columbia U., NYC. Bd. mem. Assn. for Tchrs. of Japanese, 2005—; editl. bd. mem. Japanese Assn. Second Lang. Acquisition (JASLA), Tokyo, 2006—. Contbr. articles various profl. jours. Recipient Acknowledged Academic Excellence by the Internat. Student Union award, Ohio U., 1990; grantee, Georgetown U., 2003-2004, Fund for Improvement of Post Secondary Edn., 1999, Japanese Tchg. Material Donation Program, Japan Found., 2000; Competitive grants-in-Aid, Georgetown U., 1997, Summer Academic grant, Grad. Sch. of Arts and Sci., 1999, Nanzan U. Exch. Student fellowship, DePauw U., Nanzan U., 1981-1982, Faculty of Lang. and Linguistics (FLL) Summer Rsch. grant, Georgetown U., 1997, 2002, Workshops Conf. grant, Japan Found., 1999, Jr. Faculty Rsch. fellowship, Georgetown U., 2000. Mem.: Internat. Reading Assn., Assn. Tchrs. of Japanese, Am. Coun. on Tchg. of Fgn. Lang., Am. Ednl. Rsch. Assn. Office: Georgetown U ICC 306 O & 37 St Washington DC 20057-1052 Office Phone: 202-687-5098. Office Fax: 202-687-2408. Business E-Mail: moriy@georgetown.edu.

MORIAL, MARC HAYDEL, association executive, former mayor; b. New Orleans, Jan. 3, 1958; s. Ernest and Sybil M.; m. Michelle Miller; 2 children, Mason and Margeaux; 1 child from previous marriage, Kemah. Bar: La. Legis. intern U.S. Sen. Russell Long, Washington, 1979; dir. U. Pa. Office of Supportive Svcs., Phila., 1979-80; summer assoc. U.S. Atty. U.S. Dist. Ct. (so. dist.) N.Y., 1982; legis. asst. U.S. Rep. George T. Leland, Washington, 1983; atty. Barham & Churchill, New Orleans, 1983-85; pvt. practice New Orleans, 1985—; mem. La. Senate, Baton Rouge, 1991-93, mem. revenue and fiscal affairs com., commerce com., labor and indsl. rels. com., select com. crime & drugs, intergovtl. rels. com., Pres. Clinton's action com. on crime & drugs, senate select com. on econ. devel.; mayor City of New Orleans, 1993—2002; ptnr. Adams & Reese, 2002—03; pres. Nat. Urban League, NYC, 2003—. Adj. prof. law, polit. sci. Xavier U. La., New Orleans, 1988-90. Del. Nat. Rainbow Coalition Conv., 1986, La. State Dem. Conv., 1986, Dem. Nat. Conv., Atlanta, 1988; cooperating atty. NAACP Legal Def. Fund, mem. nat., New Orleans br.; gen. counsel La. Assn. Minority and Women Owned Businesses, Inc., La. Voter Registration/Edn. Crusade; cooperating atty. Minority Bus. Enterprise Legal Def. and Edn. Fund; divestment coord., legal advisor New Orleans Anti-Apartheid Coalition, 1983—; bd. dirs. La. ACLU, La. Spl. Olympics, Milne Boys Home; mem. project steering com. Voting Rights Law Reporter; mem. Young Leadership Coun., Friend of New Orleans Ctr. for Creative Arts. Recipient Chmns. award Congl. Black Caucus, 1989, Outstanding Svc. award Lutcher H.S., 1990, La. NAACP Cmty. Svc. award, 1988; named Legis. Rookie of Yr. Baton Rouge Bus. Report, 1992, All Rookie Team by polit. columnist John Maginnis, 1993, Legis. Newcome of Yr., 1992; named one of Most Influential Black Americans, Ebony mag., 2006 Mem. ABA (standing com. on world order under law 1982-83), Nat. Bar Assn., La. State Bar Assn. (Pro Bono Pub. award 1988), La. Assn. Criminal Def. Attys., Nat. Conf. Black Lawyers, Amnesty Internat. USA, Transafrica, Louis A. Martinet Legal Soc. New Orleans, La. Trial Lawyers Assn. (pres. adv. coun.), Nat. Black Law Students Assn. (nat. bd. dirs. 1981-83), US Conf. Mayors (pres. 2001-02), Alpha Phi Alpha. Office: Nat Urban League 120 Wall St 8th Fl New York NY 10005 *

MORIARTY, DONALD WILLIAM, JR., bank executive; b. Amarillo, Tex., Sept. 15, 1939; s. Donald William and Lorraine Julia (Walck) Moriarty; m. Rita Ann Giller, Nov. 28, 1964; children: Mary Kathleen, Jennifer Ann, Anne Marie, Kerry Lee, Erin Teresa. Student, St. Benedict's Coll., 1957-59, 60-61; BSc, Washington U., 1962; MSc, St. Louis U., 1965, PhD, 1970. Cost acct. Emerson Electric, St. Louis, 1959-63; grad. fellow in econs. St. Louis U., 1963-65, instr., 1965-68; asst. prof. U. Mo., St. Louis, 1968-70; with Fed. Res. Bank of St. Louis, 1968-83, v.p., 1971-74, sr. v.p., controller, 1974-77, 1st v.p., 1977-83; sr. v.p. Gen. Bancshares Corp., 1983-86; exec. v.p. Commerce Bancshares, Inc., 1986-87; bank cons., 1987-89; pres., CEO, bd. dirs. Duchesne Bank, St. Peters, Mo., 1989-95; sr. cons. Universal Fin. Group, Inc., 1996—2003; assoc. prof. bus. Fontbonne U., St. Louis, 1998—2005; bus. cons., 2005—. Vis. instr. Webster Coll., 1975—82; adviser City of Des Peres, Mo., chmn. fin. com., 1976—78, chmn. mgmt. com., 1978—81, mem. pers. commn., 1978—81, mem. planning and zoning com., 1981—83; bd. dirs. Mid-Am. Payments Exch., Duchesne Bank; arbitrator N.Y. Stock Exch., 2006—. Mem. parent's coun. Creighton U., Omaha, 1995—97; mem. adv. bd. St. Joseph Acad., 1982—86; mem. pres.'s coun. St. Louis U., 1983—; dist. chmn. Boy Scouts Am., 1991—93, vice chmn., 1994—2001; trustee, chmn. St. Joseph Hosp., 1982—93; bd. dirs. ea. Mo. region NCCJ, 1987—93. Recipient Alumni Merit award, St. Louis U., 1979. Mem.: Nat. Assn. Securities Dealers (arbitrator 2006—), Alpha Kappa Psi, Beta Gamma Sigma.

MORIARTY, GEORGE MARSHALL, lawyer; b. Youngstown, Ohio, Sept. 16, 1942; s. George Albert Moriarty and Caroline (Jones) Bass; m. Elizabeth Bradley Moore, Sept. 11, 1965 (div. 1986); children: Bradley Marshall, Caroline Walden, Sarah Cameron; m. Phyllis A.N. Thompson, May 2, 1998. BA magna cum laude, Harvard U., 1964, LLB magna cum laude, 1968. Bar: Mass. 1969, U.S. Dist. Ct. Mass. 1973, U.S. Ct. Appeals (1st cir.) 1976, U.S. Ct. Appeals (D.C. cir.) 1984, U.S. Claims Ct. 1983, U.S. Supreme Ct. 1976, U.S. Ct. Appeals (2d cir.) 1997. Law clk. to Hon. Bailey Aldrich U.S. Ct. Appeals (1st cir.), Boston, 1968-69; law clk. to Hon. Warren Burger, Hon. Hugo Black, Hon. Potter Stewart, Hon. Byron White U.S. Supreme Ct., Washington, 1969-70; spl. asst. to Hon. Elliot L. Richardson, Dept. Health, Edn. & Welfare, Washington, 1970-71, exec. asst., 1971-72; assoc. Ropes & Gray, Boston, 1972-77, ptnr., 1977—. Bd. dirs. Ptnrs. Healthcare Sys. Pres. Boston Athenaeum; chmn. Brigham and Women's Hosp. Mem. ABA, Am. Law Inst., Boston Bar Assn., Somerset Club, Tavern Club, Met. Club. Office: Ropes & Gray 1 Internat Pl Boston MA 02110

MORIARTY, JOHN, opera administrator, artistic director; b. Fall River, Mass., Sept. 30, 1930; s. John J. and Fabiola Marie (Ripeau) M. MusB summa cum laude, New Eng. Conservatory, 1952, DM, 1992. Artistic adminstr. Opera Soc. of Washington, 1960-62, Santa Fe Opera, 1962-65; dir. Wolf Trap Co., Vienna, Va., 1972-77; chmn. opera dept. Boston

Conservatory, 1973-89, New Eng. Conservatory, 1989—. Prin. condr. Central City Opera, Denver, 1978—, artistic dir., 1982-98, artistic dir. emeritus, 1998—; panelist Nat. Inst. Music Theater, 1985, 86, 87, Conn. Arts Coun., 1982, 84; adjudicator various contests including Met. Opera auditions, 1965—. Author: Diction, 1975. Bd. dirs. Wm. Matheus Sullivan Found., Fall River Hist. Preservation Soc.; trustee Boston Concert Opera; recs. on Cambridge Records, Newport Classics, Parnassus Records; mem. adv. bd. Shoshana Found. Recipient Frank Huntington Beebe award, Boston, 1954, Disting. Alumni award New Eng. Conservatory Alumni Assn., 1982, Gold Chair award Central City Opera House Assn., 1988, Disting. Alumni award, River H.S. Alumni Assn. Mem. Nat. Opera Assn., Sigma Alpha Iota, Delta Omicron, Pi Kappa Lambda. Office: New Eng Conservatory 290 Huntington Ave Boston MA 02115-5018 also: Central City Opera House Assn 400 S Colorado Blvd Ste 530 Denver CO 80246-1255 Office Phone: 617-585-1100.

MORIARTY, JOHN KLINGE, electrical engineer, consultant; b. Washington, Feb. 6, 1956; s. John Klinge and Mary (Cozart) M.; m. Elizabeth Rouse, Dec. 31, 1987; children: Maire Elizabeth, John Lank, Harris James. BS in Physics, Va. Tech., Blacksburg, 1981; M of Engring. in Elec. Engring., Clemson U., SC, 1996. Project engr. Delco Electronics divsn. G.M.C., Kokomo, Ind., 1981-84; staff engr. Hekimian Labs., Gaithersburg, Md., 1984-85; sr. LSI design engr. Case Comms., Inc., Columbia, Md., 1985-86; ind. electronics cons. Gaithersburg, 1986-88; mem. tech. staff Bell Labs., Reading, Pa., 1988-97; ind. electronics cons. Reading, 1997—. Cons. Squire Comms., Miami, Fla., 1986, Delco Electronics Corp., Kokomo, 1986—88, Mfg. Networks Inc., San Francisco, CPClare Corp., Beverly, Mass., Wireless Sys. Techs., Inc., San Jose, Calif.; mem. tech. adv. bd. SOMA Networks, Inc., San Francisco; tutorial presenter West Med. Design and Mfg. Conf., Anaheim, Calif., 1991, East Med. Design and Mfg. Conf., NYC, 1991; sen. mem Tech. Staff Legerity, 2003—. Contbr. articles to profl. jours. including IEEE Jour. Solid State Cirs., Procs. IEEE Custom Integrated Cirs., Cons. Record of IEEE Indsl. Applications Soc., Cancer Treatment Reports. Recipient Supplier Recognition award Hughes Aircraft Corp., 1992. Mem. IEEE, IEEE Electron Device Soc., IEEE Solid State Cirs. Soc., IEEE Cirs. and Sys. Soc. Achievements include patents in field. Home: 2557 River Rd Reading PA 19605-2840 Office Phone: 610-929-7223. Personal E-mail: jmoriarty@ieee.org.

MORIARTY, JOHN TIMOTHY, transportation consultant, writer; b. Cleve., Jan. 23, 1939; s. James Joseph and Margaret (Healy) Moriarty; m. Angela Marie Veneziano, June 29, 1968; children: Patrick J., Sean Gerald. Student, John Carroll U., 1957, Cleve. State U., 1964—67. Traffic analyst, Cleve., 1957—82; transp. cons. Norfolk So. R.R., Cleve., 1982—. Author: One Square Mile of Mayhem, 1998, Honest John, 1998, The Phantom Employee, 1998, Sister Mommy, 1999, Thin Ice, 2001, Streets of Gold, 2001, Angela's Valor, 2006, United By God's Hand. With US Army, 1961—63. Mem.: Ill. Internat. Freight Coun. Roman Catholic. Avocations: basketball, billiards, reading. Home: Apt 2615 1111 Independence Ave Akron OH 44310-1896 Personal E-mail: nwpm2006@yahoo.com.

MORIE, G. GLEN, lawyer, manufacturing executive; BA, Bowdoin Coll., 1964; LLB, U. Pa., 1967. Bar: Wash. 1968. Pvt. practice law, Wash., 1970-73; asst. counsel PACCAR, Inc., Bellevue, Wash., 1973-79, asst. gen. counsel, 1979-82, gen. counsel, 1983-85, v.p., gen. counsel, 1985—2004. Sec. bd. dirs. Seattle Virtuosi Found. Mailing: PO Box 1518 Bellevue WA 98009-1518 Office Phone: 425-468-7676.

MORIKIS, JOHN G., manufacturing executive; BBA, St. Joseph's Coll.; MBA. Mgmt. trainee Sherwin-Williams Co., Cleve., 1984, sr. v.p., dir. mktg. Paint Stores Group, 1997—98, pres., gen. mgr. Ea. Divsn. Paint Stores Group, 1998—99, pres. Paint Stores Group, 1999—2006, pres., COO, 2006—. Bd. dirs. ARC Greater Cleve. chpt. Office: Sherwin Williams Co 101 Prospect Ave NW Cleveland OH 44115 Office Phone: 216-566-2000. *

MORILLO, JUAN P., lawyer; b. 1969; BA, U. Miami, 1992; JD, Georgetown U. Law Ctr., 1995. Bar: Fla. 1998, DC 2001, admitted to: US Dist. Ct., Southern Dist. Tex., US Dist. Ct., Northern Dist. Ga., US Dist. Ct., DC 2004, US Dist. Ct., Ctrl. Dist. Calif., US Dist. Ct. of Appeals, 11th Cir. 2004, US Ct. of Appeals, 9th Cir. 2006, US Supreme Ct. 2006. Clerk US Dist. Ct., DC; ptnr. Sidley Austin LLP, Washington. Named one of Litigation's Rising Stars, The Am. Lawyer, 2007. Mem.: ABA. Office: Sidley Austin LLP 1501 K St NW Washington DC 20005 Office Phone: 202-736-8063. Office Fax: 202-736-8711. *

MORIMOTO, MASAHARU, chef, television personality; b. Hiroshima, Japan, May 26, 1955; Trained in Sushi and traditional Kaiseki cuisine, Hiroshima. Exec. chef Sony Club, NYC, 1993—98, Nobu Restaurant, NYC, 1998—2001; chef, owner Morimoto Restaurant, Phila., 2001—, NYC, 2004—, Wasabi, Mumbai, India. Iron chef Japan Iron Chef (Food Network), 1995—99, Iron Chef America, 2005—. Office: Morimoto Restaurant 723 Chestnut St Philadelphia PA 19102

MORIN, CHRISTOPHER JOSEPH, vascular surgeon; s. Louis Peter and Rosamond Agatha Morin; m. Christine Sotorp, Feb. 17, 1996; children: Colleen Campbell, Kelly Anne, Chrisotpher Jr. BA, Coll. the Holy Cross, Worcester, Mass.; MD, Brown U., Providence, RI; MBA, U.RI, Kingston. Lic. Vascular Surgery Am. Bd. Surgery, Clincial Instr. Surgery Harvard Med. Sch. Chmn. dept. surgery St. Luke's Hosp. and Health Network, Bethlehem, Pa., 1997—2002; clin. asst. prof. surgery Brown U., 1982—97, U. Pa., 1998—2005; chmn. cardiovasc. ops. St. Francis Cardiac and Vascular Care Ctr., Indpls., 2002—06; vascular surgeon Brantigan and Morin, Denver, 2006—; cons. Heart Works Advisors, Indpls., 2006—; endovascular surgery cons. Internat. Hosp., Cairo, 2006—; clin. prof. DeSales U., 1998—. Cons. DeSales U. Ctr. for Faith and Culture, Center Valley, Pa.; dir. Brown U. Med. Alumni Assn., Providence, 1980—97, pres., 1986—88. Comdr. USNR, 1984—91. Named one of Top Surgeon in the US, Consumer Rsch. Concil. Fellow: ACS; mem.: Am. Coll. Physician Execs., Internat. Soc. for Vascular Surgery, European Soc. for Vascular Surgery, Soc. for Vascular Surgery. Office: Brantigan & Morin 2253 Downing St Denver CO 80205 Office Phone: 303-830-8822. Business E-Mail: vascsurg@aol.com.

MORIN, JOYANN HAUGE, education educator; d. Harry Adrian and Anna (Barnec) Hauge; m. Dale Arthur Morin, May 21, 1954; children: David Dale, Angelique Marie, Debra Kay(dec.). AA, ElCamino Coll., 1967; BA in History, Calif. State U., Dominguez Hills, 1969, MA, 1977; EdD in Curriculum and Instrn., U. So. Calif., 1986. Elem. tchg. credential Commn. on Tchr. Credentialing, Calif. Elem. tchr. St. Catherine Laboure Sch., Torrance, Calif., 1969—71, L.A. Unified Sch. Dist., 1971—77; curriculum coord. L.A. Sch. Dist., 1977—84; prof. Calif. State U., Northridge, 1984—93, LA, 1993—, prof. emeritus, 2002. Presenter in field. Author: Social Education Instruction, 2003; contbr. articles to profl. jours. Recipient Spl. Merit award, Edn. Jour., 1996; Innovative Tchg. grant, Calif. State U., L.A., 1994. Mem.: AAUP, Calif. Coun.on the Edn. Tchrs., Nat. Coun. for the Social Studies. Avocations: creative writing, researching. Home: PO Box 875 Wolf Point MT 59201 Office: Calif State Univ PO Box 875 6309 Rodeo Rd Wolf Point MT 59201

MORIN, LOUIS, lawyer; b. Que., Can., Sept. 29, 1941; s. Paul-Emile and Jeanne Dechene) M.; m. Marthe Champoux, Sept. 12, 1970; children: Francois, Antoine, Brigitte. BA, Coll. Jesuites, 1962; LLL, U. Laval, 1965. Atty. Grondin LeBel Morin, Que., Canada, 1966—77; judge Que. Labor Ct., 1977—2002, chief judge, 1990—98; pres. Que. Labour Rels. Bd., 2002—04; atty. Grondin Poudrier Bernier, Québec, Canada, 2004—. Mem. Que. Jud. Coun., Montreal, 1992-96; tchr. labor law U. Laval, Que., 1989. Mem. Can. Bar Assn., Que. Bar Assn., Que. Young Bar Assn. (pres. 1975-76), Que. Judge's Assn. (pres. 1989-90). Avocations: skiing, bicycling. Office: Grondin Poudrier Bernier 500 Grande Allée Est Bur 900 Quebec City PQ Canada G1R 2J7 Office Phone: 418-683-3000. Business E-Mail: lmorin@grondinpoudrier.com.

MORIN, LYNN P., music educator, director, secondary school educator; d. Marjorie Huber. BA in Voice and Theatre Performance, Rocky Mountain Coll., 1995; BA in Music Edn., U. Mont., 1996. Dir. band and choir St. Regis (Mont.) Sch., 1996—2001; dir. choral Richland (Wash.) H.S., 2001—04; choral dir. Torrington (Conn.) H.S., 2004—. Dir. Mineral County Choir, St. Regis, Mont., 1999—2001; soprano Mont. Chorale, Great Falls, Mont., 1998—2001, Hartford (Conn.) Chorale, 2004—05; vocal dir. Richland (Wash.) Light Opera Co., 2003—04. Actor: (plays) Praise team Southside Ch., Richland, 2001—04; bd. dirs. Richland (Wash.) Cmty. Concerts, 2002—03. Schieffelin scholar, Rocky Mountain Coll., 1992—95. Mem.: NEA, Music Educator's Nat. Conf., Am. Choral Dirs. Assn. (assoc.). Republican. Avocations: travel, acting, theater, scrapbooks. Home Phone: 860-844-0299.

MORIN, PIERRE JEAN, retired management consultant, social services administrator; b. Quebec City, Que., Can., Aug. 5, 1931; s. Augustin Norbert and Yvonne (Gaudry) M.; m. Colette Poulin, Apr. 3, 1954; children: Anne, Gilles, Louis. BS, Concordia U., Montreal, 1964; MS, Laval U., Que., 1970, D.Sc., 1973. Quality control technician Dow Brevery, Montreal, Que., 1952-56; research assoc. Royal Victoria Hosp., Montreal, 1957-67; coordinator of research Que. Heart Inst., 1967-73; dir. research labs. Laval Hosp., Que., 1973-80, lectr. dept. medicine Que., 1973-77; dir. gen. Community Service Ctr., 1980-88; mgmt. cons., 1988-91; ret., 1991. Cons. Que. Minister of Environ., 1975-84. Co-author: La Fluoration-Autopsie d'une Erreur Scientifique A Classic on Fluorides; contbr. articles to profl. jours. Schering Travelling fellow, 1971 Mem. AAAS Roman Catholic. Home: 336 Rg Castor Leclercville PQ Canada G0S 2K0 *Well assumed failure may be a must towards later success.*

MORING, JOHN FREDERICK, lawyer; b. Farmville, Va., Oct. 30, 1935; s. Scott O'Ferrall and Margaret Macon (Mitchell) M.; m. Margaret Ann Clarke, Mar. 30, 1959; children: Martha, Elizabeth, Scott, Lee. BS, Va. Poly. Inst., 1957; JD, George Washington U., 1961. Bar: Va. 1961, DC 1962, US Supreme Ct. 1964; cert. mediator civil disputes Supreme Ct. Va. 2004, US Dist. Ct. Va., 2004, US Cir. Ct., 2004. Assoc. Morgan, Lewis & Bockius, Washington, 1961-68, ptnr., 1969-78, Jones, Day, Reavis & Pogue, Washington, 1978-79; founding ptnr. Crowell & Moring, Washington, Irvine, NY, London, Brussels, 1979—2000. Sec. Associated Gas Distbrs., Inc., 1977-2000. Local gas utility columnist: Nat. Gas Jour., 1989—2000; mem. editl. bd. Natural Gas Contracts, 1994—2001. Mem. nat. panel neutrals Am. Arbitration Assn., 2003—; chmn. bd. dirs. Washington Legal Counsel for Elderly, 2000—01; Rep. candidate 23d Dist./Va. Gen. Assembly, Alexandria, 1973; mem. bd. govs. St. Stephen's and St. Agnes Sch., Alexandria, 1989—95; pres. St. Stephen's Found., Inc., 1990—93; sr. warden Immanuel Ch. on the Hill, Alexandria, 1988, 1989; trustee Ch. Schs. of Diocese of Va., 1996—; mem. found. bd. Shrine Mont Conf. Ctr. Episc. Diocese Va., Orkney Springs, Va., 2001—; mem. bd. govs. St. Margaret's Sch., Tappahannock, Va., 2002—. 2d lt. US Army, 1958. Mem.: ABA (natural resources law sect. 1982—86, coun.), Am. Arbitration Assn., Fed. Energy Bar Assn. (sec. 1963—66, pres. 1982—83), Indian Creek Yacht and Country Club (Kilmarnock, Va.). Episcopalian. Avocations: golf, fishing, canoeing. Home: PO Box 224 White Stone VA 22578 Office: Crowell & Moring 1001 Pennsylvania Ave NW Fl 10 Washington DC 20004-2595 also: 3 Park Plaza 20th Fl Irvine CA 92614-8505 also: 11 Pilgrim St London EC4V 6RN England also: 71 Rue Royale B 1000 Brussels Belgium also: 153 E 53rd St 31st Fl New York NY 10022-4611 Business E-Mail: fredmoring@rivnet.net.

MORIS, LAMBERTO GIULIANO, architect; b. Siena, Tuscany, Italy, Mar. 29, 1944; arrived in US, 1972; s. Gualtiero Luigi and Giovanna (Avanzati) M.; m. Tracy P. Schilling, 1970 (div. 1985); children: Giacomo, Stefano; m. Beverly Chiang, Mar. 28, 1986; 1 child, Christopher. MA in Arch., U. Florence, Italy, 1970. Assoc. Marquis Assocs., San Francisco, 1972-78, prin., 1978-85, Simon Martin-Vegue Winkelstein Moris, San Francisco, 1985—2005, Moris/Marino and Assoc., San Francisco, 2005—. Tchr. San Francisco City Coll., 1982—84; juror DuPont Antron Design Awards, 1989, AIA Hon. Awards, 1995, AIA Interior Architecture Awards, Chgo. chpt., 1997; mem. interior design adv. coun. Acad. Art Coll., San Francisco, 1992—2001; lectr. AIA Nat. Conf., 1996, Aircraft Interiors Expo, Canne, France, 2000, Aircraft Interiors Conf. and Exhbn., Long Beach, Calif., 2001, AIA- Italy Summit, San Francisco, 2003. Mem. design com. Clairmont Pines Task Force, 1991; charter mem. Forecast 21 Principals Roundtable, 1993; mem. Bldg. Industry Conf. Bd. (BICB), 2001—; mem. bd. dirs. ItaLingua Inst., 1984—. Mem.: FAIA (mem. selection com. 2003), AIA (mem. internat. com. 2003), Interior Architecture, No. Calif. chpt., Am. Inst. Architects, Coll. Fellows, Am. Inst. Architects (corp. mem. 1979—), Am. C. of C. in Italy, Oakland Met. C. of C., Accademia Italiane della Cucina, Cath. Prof. Bus. Club, San Francisco Opera Assn., Il Cenacolo (bd. dirs. 1991), San Francisco Heritage Assn., Engr. Club. Roman Catholic. Avocations: coin collecting/numismatics, skiing, travel. Office: Page and Moris 48 2d St San Francisco CA 94105 Home Phone: 510-654-7581; Office Phone: 510-381-5083. Personal E-mail: lgmoris@mindspring.com.

MORISATO, SUSAN CAY, actuary; b. Chgo., Feb. 11, 1955; d. George and Jessie (Fujita) M.; m. Thomas Michael Remec, Mar. 6, 1981. BS, U. Ill., 1975, MS, 1977. Actuarial student Aetna Life & Casualty, Hartford, Conn., 1977-79; actuarial asst. Bankers Life & Casualty Co., Chgo., 1979-80, asst. actuary, 1980-83, assoc. actuary, 1983-85, health product actuary, 1985-86, v.p., 1986-95, sr. v.p., 1996—2004, also bd. dirs., 2000—04; chief operating officer, sr. and retiree svcs. Ovations (a UnitedHealth Group co.), 2005—. Participant individual forum Am.'s Health Ins. Plans, 1983; spkr. in field. Adv. panel on long term care financing Brookings' Inst.; trustee Minn. Zoo Found., 2005—. Fellow Soc. Actuaries (workshop leader 1990, 93, news editor health sect. news 1988-90, conf. spkr. 2001, 02); mem. Am. Acad. Actuaries, Am.'s Health Ins. Plans (long term care task force 1988-04, chair 1993-95, tech. adv. com. 1991-93, legis. policy com. 1996-99, nominating com. 1996-98, other coms., policy coord. coun. 1999-03, sr. mktg. task force chair 2000-01, chmn. task force on Medicare modernization 2002-04, exec. com. 2004, bd. dirs. 2004, policy com. 2004, medicare com. 2005—. Founders award 1996), Health Ins. Assn. Am. (conf. spkr. 2000), LIMRA Internat. (strategic mktg. ins. com. 2001-06, bd. dirs. 2003—, chmn. compensation and benefits com. 2004-05, vice-chair bd. dirs. 2005-06, chair bd. 2006), Nat. Assn. Ins. Commrs. (ad hoc actuarial working group for long term care nonforfeiture benefits 1992), Am. Coun. Life Ins. (accelerated benefits/long term care com. 1997-01), Chgo. Actuarial Assn. (sec. 1983-85, program com. 1987-89), Phi Beta Kappa, Kappa Delta Pi, Phi Kappa Phi. Office: Ovations UnitedHealth Group MN008-T440 9900 Bren Rd E Minnetonka MN 55343 Home Phone: 847-299-0560; Office Phone: 952-945-7555. Business E-Mail: susan_c_morisato@uhc.com.

MORISHITA, AKIHIKO, trading company executive; b. Osaka, Japan, Oct. 14, 1941; came to U.S., 1981; s. Sueyoshi and Toshiko Morishita; m. Fumiko Okamura; children: Shizuko, Kumiko, Okamura. BA in Econs., Wakayama U., Wakayama, Japan, 1965. Mgr. Hanwa & Co. Ltd., Osaka, 1965-80; cons. oil dept. Pacific Southwest Trading Co., San Diego, 1981-82; exec. Pacific Marine Bunkering, Inc., LA, 1982—. Mem.: Club Leconte. Home: 4610 Don Pio Dr Woodland Hills CA 91364-4205

MORISUE, GLENN T., graphics designer; b. San Francisco, Nov. 22, 1940; BA, Art Inst. Pitts., 1962; BFA, Cleve. Inst. Art, 1964. Greeting card designer Am. Greetings Corp., Cleve., 1965—69; art dir. Schuckert Studio, Cleve., 1970—73; creative dir. Hauser King Marford Co., Cleve., 1974—76; v.p., design dir. Copper K Industries, Cleve., 1977—79; dean edn. Cooper Sch. Art, Cleve., 1980—82; free-lance illustrator, 1983—93. Recipient numerous Best of Show awards, Nat. Drawing Competition award winner, Am. Artist Drawing Mag., 2004. Mem.: Pastel Soc. Am., Am. Soc. Portrait Artists, Meadville Coun. on the Arts. Home: 6201 1/2 Lake Rd W Ashtabula OH 44004-9757

MORITA, RICHARD YUKIO, microbiology and oceanography educator; b. Pasadena, Calif., Mar. 27, 1923; s. Jiro and Reiko (Yamamoto) M.; m. Toshiko Nishihara, May 29, 1926; children— Sally Jean, Ellen Jane, Peter Wayne BS, U. Nebr., 1947; MS, U. So. Calif., 1949; PhD, U. Calif., 1954. Microbiologist Mid-Pacific Expdn., 1950, Danish Galathea Deep-Sea Expdn., 1952, Trans-Pacific Expdn.; Postdoctoral fellow U. Calif., Scripps Inst. Oceanography, 1954-55; asst. prof. U. Houston, 1955-58; asst. prof., assoc. prof. U. Neb., 1958-62; prof. microbiology and oceanography Oreg. State U., Corvallis, 1962-89, prof. emeritus microbiology and oceanography, 1989—. Prog. dir. biochemistry NSF, 1968-69; Disting. vis. prof. Kyoto Univ.; cons. NIH, 1968-70; rschr. in field. Contbr. articles to sci. lit. Patentee in field. Served with U.S. Army, 1944-46 Grantee NSF, 1962—, NIH, 1960-68, NASA, 1967-72, Office Naval Research, 1966-70, Dept. Interior, 1968-72, NOAA, 1975-82, Bur. Land Mgmt., 1982, EPA, 1986—; recipient awards including King Fredericus IX Medal and Ribbon, 1954, Sr. Queen Elizabeth II Fellowship, 1973-74, Hotpack lectr. and award Can. Soc. Fellow Japan Soc. for Promotion Sci.; mem. Am. Soc. Microbiology (Fisher award). Home: 1515 NW 14th St Corvallis OR 97330 Personal E-mail: dickmorita@aol.com.

MORITSUGU, KENNETH PAUL, federal official, career military officer; b. Honolulu, Mar. 5, 1945; s. Richard Yutaka and Hisayo Joan (Nishikawa) M.; m. Donna Lee Jones (dec. 1992); children: Erika Lizabeth, Vikki Lianne (deceased), Emily Renee; m. Lisa Kory. Student, Chaminade Coll. Honolulu, 1963-65; BA in Classical Langs. with honors, U. Hawaii, 1967; MD, George Washington U. Sch. Medicine, 1971; MPH in Health Adminstrn. and Planning, U. Calif., Berkeley, 1975; DSc (hon.), Coll. Osteopathic Medicine, U. New Eng., 1988; DSc, U. New England; DSc (hon.), Midwestern U. Chgo., 1993, Des Moines U., Iowa, 2005; DSC (hon.), Still U., 2005; D Pub. Svc. (hon.), U. North Tex., 1994; DHL (hon.), Western U. Health Scis., 2002, Alliant Internat. U., 2002; DDL (hon.), Phila. Coll. Osteo. Medicine; DHL (hon.), Campbell U., 2003, Nova Southeastern U., 2004. Diplomate Am. Bd. Preventive Medicine (fellow); cert. correctional health profl. Intern USPHS Hosp., San Francisco, 1971-72, resident, 1972-75; commd. USPHS, 1968, advanced through grades to med. dir., 1979; promoted to rank of rear adm., asst. surgeon gen., 1988; staff med. officer USPHS Hosp., San Francisco, 1972-73; regional cons. med. manpower planning and devel. US Dept. Health, Edn. & Welfare, San Francisco, 1976-78, chief internat. edn. programs br. Washington, 1978, dep. dir. divsn. medicine, 1978; dir. Bur. Health Professions, div. medicine US Dept. Health & Human Services, Rockville, Md., 1978-83, dir. Nat. Health Service Corps, 1983-87, dep. dir. Bur. Health Professions, 1987; asst. bur. dir., med. dir. Fed. Bur. Prisons US Dept. Justice, Washington, 1987-98; dep. surgeon gen. US Dept. Health & Human Services, Rockville, Md., 1998—, acting surgeon gen., 2002, 2006—. Adj. assoc. prof. pub. health Uniformed Svcs. U. Health Scis.; invited spkr. in field. Bd. dir. United Network for Organ Sharing; founding chair bd. trustees Certified Correctional Health Professions Program; chair Am. Correctional Assn. Com. on Health Care in Corrections; dedicated advocate for tissue and organ donation; active participant Donor Family Recognition Programs, Washington; sec., treas., bd. dir. Washington Regional Transplant Consortium; mem. nat. adv. bd. Minority Organ and Tissue Transplant Edn. Program; active vol. Transplant Recipients Internat. Orgn.; former bd. trustee Nat. Kidney Found.; former mem. exec. com. Nat. Donor Family Coun.; former past mem. pub. affairs com. and minority affairs com. Washington Regional Transport Consortium Donor Family Coun.; trustee, treas. Physician Assistants Found., Am. Acad. Physician Assistants; chmn. bd. Anchor and Caduceus Soc. U.S. Pub. Health Svc.; bd. dir. Royal Soc. Medicine Found.; immediate past chair U.S. Chpt. Royal Soc. Health. Decorated D.S.M., knight grand cross Mil. and Hospitaller Order St. Lazarus of Jerusalem; named Disting. Alumnus, George Washington U., 2002; recipient Commendation medal, U.S. Pub. Health Svc., Meritorious Svc. medal, Outstanding Svc. medal, Disting. Svc., Surgeon Gen.'s medallion, Surgeon Gen.'s medal for Exemplary Svc., Army Achievement medal, Coast Guard Arctic Svc. medal, Dirs. Spl. Achievement award, U.S. Marshal's Svcs., John D. Chase award, Assn. Mil. Surgeons US, Nathan Davis award, AMA, Disting. Svc. award, Am. Correctional Health Svcs. Assn., Disting. Svc. medal, U.S. Dept. Justice, Fed. Bur. Prisons, Meritorious Svc. medal, Health Leader of Yr., Commd. Officers Assn., William B. Miller award, Assn. Colls. Osteopathic Medicine, Spl. Achievement award, Nat. Comm. on Correctional Health Care, Phillips medal Pub. Svc., Ohio U. Fellow Am. Coll. Preventive Medicine, Royal Soc. Health, Royal Soc. Medicine; mem. APHA, Assn. Tchrs. Preventive Medicine, Assn. Mil. Surgeons U.S., Res. Officers Assn., Mensa, Am. Guild Organists, Am. Acad. Physicians Assts. (hon.)(President's award), Delta Omega, Omicron Delta Kappa. Office: US Dept Health & Human Svcs Office of Surgeon Gen 200 Independent Ave SW Washington DC 20201 Personal E-mail: 1samurai@cox.net. *

MORITZ, CHAD HENRY, research scientist; Grad. magna cum laude, U. Wis., 1977. Diagnostic radiographer Aurora Health Care, Milw., 1991—93, Covenant Health Care, Milw., 1993—94; MRI rsch. technologist Med. Coll. Wis., Milw., 1994—96; rsch. assoc. Dartmouth Coll., Hanover, NH, 1996—98; rsch. program mgr. radiology dept. U. Wis. Med. Sch., Madison, 1999—. Presenter in field. Contbr. chapters to books, articles to profl. jours. Recipient award for Excellence, St. Luke's Sch. Radiol. Tech., 1993; Profl. devel. grantee, U. Wis., 2003. Mem.: Am. Soc. Functional Neuroradiology, Soc. for Magnetic Resonance Technologists, Am. Soc. Radiol. Technologists (cert. radiologic technologist), Orgn. for Human Brain Mapping, Internat. Soc. for Magnetic Resonance in Medicine. Avocations: bicycling, accordion. Business E-Mail: cmoritz@uwhealth.org.

MORITZ, DANA DEE, language educator; b. Moravia, Iowa, June 16, 1939; d. Fern William and Vivien Agnes (Wilson) Wright; m. Glenn Garnett Moritz, June 3, 1961; children: Henry Warren, Andrew William. BS in English Edn., Truman State U., 1960, MA in English Edn., 1970; AAS in Computer Programming, Indian Hills C.C., 2004. Cert. choice theory, reality therapy and lead mgmt. William Glasser Inst. Tchr. secondary English, Sanborn Cmty. Schs., Iowa, 1960—64, Centerville Cmty. Schs., Iowa, 1978—2002, dir. drama, 1980—89. Negotiator Centerville Edn. Assn., Iowa, 1980—2002, pres., 1992—93. Dir. Cmty. Theater, Centerville, Iowa, 1983, 1985, 1996; mem. Mcpl. Housing Authority, Centerville, Iowa, 2005—, chair, 2006. Recipient Ctrs. of Excellence award, Nt. Coun. Tchrs. of English, 1987. Mem.: NEA, PEO, DAR. Democrat. United Methodist. Avocations: reading, sewing, walking, computer programming. Home: 511 W Grand St Centerville IA 52544 E-mail: dmoritz@mchsi.com.

MORITZ, DONALD BROOKS, mechanical engineer, consultant; b. Mpls., June 17, 1927; s. Donald B. and Frances W. (Whalen) M.; m. Joan Claire Betzenderfer, June 17, 1950 (dec. Dec. 21, 2004); children: Craig,

Pamela, Brian. BS in Mech. Engring., U. Minn., 1950; postgrad., Western Res. U., 1956-58. Registered profl. engr., Ill. Minn., Ohio. V.p., gen. mgr. Waco Scaffold Shoring Co., Addison, Ill., 1950-72; group v.p. Bliss and Laughlin Industries, Oak Brook, Ill., 1972-83; sr. v.p. AXIA Inc. (formerly Bliss and Laughlin Industries, Oak Brook, 1983-84, exec. v.p., chief operating officer, 1984-88; cons. Exec. Svc. Corps Chgo., 1988—; pres. Image-A-Nation, Unltd., 1988—. Bd. dirs. Am. Photographic Acad. Patentee in field. Served with USN, 1945-46. Mem. ASME, Scaffold and Shoring Inst. (founder, past pres.), Mensa, Five Seasons Country Club. Office: Moritz and Assocs PO Box 305 Clarendon Hills IL 60514-0305

MORITZ, MARK WILLIAM, vascular surgeon; BS in Engring., Brown U., Providence, 1973; MD, Johns Hopkins U., Balt., 1977. Resident in gen. surgery Washington U., St. Louis, 1977—84; fellow in vascular surgery Emory U., Atlanta, 1984—85; asst. prof. surgery Wayne State U., Detroit, 1985—89; pvt. practice vascular surgery Morristown, NJ, 1989—; clin. assoc. prof. vascular surgery U. Medicine and Dentistry NJ, Newark, 1989—. Contbr. numerous articles to med. and sci. jours. Pres. bd. dirs., various offices Hebrew Acad. Morris County, NJ, 1990—2005. Mem.: ACS (pres.-elect NJ chpt. 2006—), Vascular Soc. NJ (pres. 1999—2000). Office: Vain Inst NJ 95 Madison Ave Morristown NJ 07960

MORITZ, MICHAEL J., venture capitalist; b. Cardiff, Wales, 1952; married; 2 children. MA in Hist., U. Oxford, 1976; MBA, The Wharton Sch., U. Pa., 1978. Corr. TIME mag., 1979; with Time Warner; founder Technologic Partners; gen. ptnr., mng. dir. Sequoia Cap., 1986—. Mem. bd. dirs. Flextronics, 1993—2005, Yahoo!, 1995—2003, Google, Inc., 1999—2007. Author: The Little Kingdom: The Private Story of Apple Computer, 1986. Named one of The World's Most Influential People, TIME mag., 2007, 50 Who Matter Now, Business 2.0, 2007. Office: Sequoia Capital Bldg 4 Ste 180 3000 Sand Hill Rd Menlo Park CA 94025 Office Phone: 650-854-3927. Office Fax: 650-854-2977. Business E-Mail: moritz@sequoiacap.com. *

MORITZ, MILTON EDWARD, security consultant; b. Reading, Pa., Sept. 5, 1931; s. Edward Raymond and Anna May M.; m. Elizabeth Ann Walls, June 6, 1952; children: Betsy Ann Moritz Koppenhaver, Stephen Edward, Sandra E. Student, U. Md., 1950-51, Fla. State U., 1959-60. Enlisted U.S. Army, 1949, chief warrant officer 3, 1968, spl. agt. M.I.; ret., 1970; safety and security dir. Harrisburg Hosp., Pa., 1970-72; security mgr. Sprint, Carlisle, Pa., 1972-94; prin. Moritz Assocs., Harrisburg, 1994—. Lectr., instr. Harrisburg Area Community Coll.; mem. Indsl. Security Adv. Coun. Assoc. editor: Protection of Assets Manual. Pres. Greater Harrisburg Crime Clinic, 1974. Decorated Bronze Star with oak leaf cluster. Mem. Am. Soc. Indsl. Security (past pres., chmn. bd. dirs.), Assn. Former Intelligence Officers, Internat. Narcotic Enforcement Officers Assn., Pa. Crime Prevention Assn. (bd. dirs). Republican. Lutheran. Home and Office: 215 Brookridge Ct Harrisburg PA 17112-9665

MORITZ, TIMOTHY BOVIE, psychiatrist; b. Portsmouth, Ohio, July 26, 1936; s. Charles Raymond and Elisabeth Bovie (Morgan) M.; m. Joyce Elizabeth Rasmussen, Oct. 13, 1962 (div. Sept. 1969); children: Elizabeth Wynne, Laura Morgan; m. Antoinette Tanasichuk, Oct. 31, 1981; children: David Michael, Stephanie Lysbeth. *Wife Antoinette, a teacher, with a master's degree from Ohio State and graduate work at University of Georgia, has devoted herself to raising her children. Son David has a B.S. in Psychology from Arizona State University. Daughter Stephanie is a student at Wilson College. Daughter Laura Tresca, a teacher with a master's degree from Boston College, is mother of Thomas John, Katherine Elizabeth, and Phillip Timothy Tresca. Daughter Elizabeth Moss was Business and Scientific Administrator, MRC Centre for Developmental Neurobiology, King's College London, and is mother of James Frederick and Lucy Amelia Moss. She has an MBA from Loyola Coll., Md.* BA, Ohio State U., 1959; MD, Cornell U., 1963. Diplomate Am. Bd. Psychiatry and Neurology. Intern in medicine N.Y. Hosp., NYC, 1963-64, resident in psychiatry, 1964-67; spl. asst. to dir. NIMH, Bethesda, Md., 1967-69; dir. Community Mental Health Ctr., Rockland County, NY, 1970-74, Ohio Dept. Mental Health, Columbus, Ohio, 1975-81; med. dir. psychiatry Miami Valley Hosp., Dayton, Ohio, 1981-82; med. dir. N.E. Ga. Community Mental Health Ctr., Athens, Ga., 1982-83, Charter Vista Hosp., Fayetteville, Ark., 1983-87; clin. dir. adult psychiatry Charter Hosp., Las Vegas, Nev., 1987-94; pvt. practice psychiatry Las Vegas, 1987—; med. dir. Problem Gambling Cons., Las Vegas, 2000—. Prof. Wright State U., Dayton, Ohio, 1981-82; asst. prof. Cornell U., N.Y.C., 1970-73; mem. human subjects biomed. scis. rev. com. U. Nev., Las Vegas, 2000-2001; cons. NIMH, Rockville, Md., 1973-83. *After he provided 6 years of leadership improving its state and community mental health, mental retardation, and drug abuse services, the State of Ohio renamed its Central Ohio Forensic Psychiatric Hospital as "The Timothy B. Moritz Forensic Psychiatric Hospital". During his 16 years of fulltime public service as a psychiatrist at the federal, state, and community levels, he received recognition for leadership in developing comprehensive community services and improved state services. Since 1983 he has been fulltime in the private practice of psychiatry devoted to providing the best possible quality treatment to individual patients.* Author: (chpt.) Rehabilitation Medicine and Psychiatry, 1976; mem. editorial bd. Directions in Psychiatry, 1981-1993. Dir. dept. mental health and mental retardation Gov.'s Cabinet, State of Ohio, Columbus, 1975-81. Recipient Svc. award Ohio Senate, 1981, Svc. Achievement award Ohio Gov., 1981. Fellow Am. Psychiat. Assn. (disting. life, Disting. Svc. award 1981); mem. AMA, Nev. Assn. Psychiat. Physicians, Nev. State Med. Assn., Am. Assn. Chronic Fatigue Syndrome, Clark County Med. Soc., Cornell U. Med. Coll. Alumni Assn., Ohio State U. Alumni Assn. (life). Office: 2330 Paseo del Prado Ste C-109 Las Vegas NV 89102-4336 Office Phone: 702-363-3633.

MORIUCHI, K. DEREK, secondary school educator; b. LA, 1958; BA, UCLA, 1981; MA, Calif. State U., 1982; MA in Ednl. Adminstrn., Calif. State U., LA, 2005. Cert. single subject tchg. credential in math., cross cultural lang. acquisition devel., nat. bd. cert. tchr., lic. in adminstrv. svcs. Tchr. math. Marshall Mid. Sch., 1986—90, Ganesha H.S., 1991—93; tchr. history Stevenson Middle Sch., LA, 1993—2003, chairdept. math.; secondary math. expert L.A. Unified Sch. Dist., LA, 2003—. Spkr. in field. Mem.: Calif. Math. Coun. (spkr. 2000—03), Nat. Bd. for Profl. Tchg. Stds. (bd. mem. 2001—), Pi Lambda Theta. Office: Local Dist 5 LA Unified Sch Dist 2151 N Soto St Los Angeles CA 90032 Office Phone: 323-224-3132. Personal E-mail: k12536@aol.com. E-mail: derek.moriuchi@lausd.net.

MORK, GORDON ROBERT, historian, educator; b. St. Cloud, Minn., May 6, 1938; s. Gordon Matthew and Agnes (Gibb) Mork; m. Dianne Jeannette Muetzel, Aug. 11, 1963; children: Robert, Kristiana, Elizabeth. BA, Yale U., 1960; MA, U. Minn., 1963, PhD, 1966. Instr. history U. Minn., Mpls., 1966; lectr., asst. prof. U. Calif., Davis, 1966-70; mem. faculty Purdue U., West Lafayette, Ind., 1970—, assoc. prof., 1973-94, prof. history, 1994—, dir. honors program humanities, 1985-87, dir grad. studies history, Am. studies, 1987-93, mem. Jewish studies com., 1980—, head dept. history, 1998—2003; resident dir. Purdue U.-Ind. U. Program, Hamburg, Germany, 1975-76. Rsch. fellow in humanities U. Wis., Madison, 1969—70; mem. test devel. com. advanced placement European history Ednl. Testing Svc., 1993—99, chair, 1995—99; cons. Coll. Bd. and Ednl. Testing Svc., 1999—. Author: Modern Western Civilization: A Concise History, 3d edit., 1994, AP Instructor's Manual, 2007; editor: The Homes of Ober-Ammergau, 2000; mem. adv. bd. Teaching History, 1983—, History Teacher, 1986—2002. Mem. citizens task force Lafayette Sch. Corp., 1978—79; bd. dirs. Ind. Humanities Coun., 1986—89; elder Ctrl. Presbyn. Ch., Lafayette, 1973—75, deacon, 1996—99, trustee, 2001—04; bd. dirs., sec. Murdock-Sunnyside Bldg. Corp., 1980—2000. Mem.: Soc. History Edn., German Studies Assn., Am. Hist. Assn., Internat. Soc. History Didactics (v.p. 1991—95, 1996—2000), Mortar Bd., Phi Beta Kappa. Home: 1521 Cason St Lafayette IN 47904-2642 Office: Purdue U Dept History 672 Oval Dr West Lafayette IN 47907-2087 Office Phone: 765-494-4138. Business E-Mail: gmork@purdue.edu.

MORKOÇ, HADIS, electrical engineer, educator; b. Senkaya, Erzurum, Turkey, Oct. 2, 1947; came to U.S., 1971; s. Mustafa and Saadet (Metin) M.; m. Amy C. Ahlberg, Sept. 5, 1975; 1 child, Erol Taner. MS, Tech. U., Istanbul, 1969; PhD, Cornell U., 1975. Postdoctoral fellow Cornell U., Ithaca, NY, 1975-76; mem. tech. staff Varian Assocs., Palo Alto, Calif., 1976-78; prof. elec. engring. U. Ill., Urbana, 1978-97, Va. Commonwealth U., 1997—. Disting. vis. scientist Calif. Inst. Tech., Pasadena, 1987-88; cons., Motorola, IBM, AT&T, others. Author: Principles and Technology of ModFETs, 1991, Nitride Semiconductors and Devices, 1999, 2d edit., 2006, Advanced Semiconductor and Organic Nano-techniques, 2004; contbr. chpts. to books, articles to profl. jours. Scholar, Va. Commonwealth U., 2002. Fellow IEEE, AAAS, Am. Phys. Soc.; mem. Math. Rsch. Soc., Optical Soc. Am., Sigma Xi, Eta Kappa Nu, Sigma Phi Sigma. Achievements include invention of fastest transistor in world. Home: 2403 Lake Loreine Ln Richmond VA 23233-2523 Office: Va Commonwealth U PO Box 843072 601 W Main St Richmond VA 23284-9052 Office Phone: 804-827-3765. Business E-Mail: hmorkoc@vcu.edu.

MORLAN, MERWYN EUGENE, retired music educator; b. Indpls., Oct. 25, 1917; s. Willard Merwyn Morlan and Edna Eugenia Collins; m. Betty B. James, June 8, 1940; children: Richard Eugene, Ann Christine Bayba, Steven Collins, Mary Eugenia Howell, John Allan, Beth Ann Schill, Michelle Mary St. Clair. BA, Ind. State U., Terre Haute, 1939; Masters, George Peabody Coll., Nashville, 1945, EdD, 1966. Music and social studies tchr. Westfield (Ill.) Twp. HS, 1939—41; supr. music Shenandoah County Va. Pub. Schs., Woodstock, 1941—54; dir. profl. programs Music Educators Nat. Conf., Washington, 1955—85. Pres. Lions Internat., Westfield, Ill., 1939—40, Woodstock, Va., 1948—49, Shenandoah Co. Chpt. for Crippled Children, Woodstock, Va., 1946—48; condr. Woodstock (Va.) Cmty. Chorus, 1946—52, McLean (Va.) Choral Soc., 1992—94; min. of music Luth. Ch. of the Redeemer, McLean, Va., 1958—71; condr. McLean (Va.) Ward I Choir, 1971—2001; condr., musical dir. The Mormon Choir of Wash. (DC), 1980—2000; chmn., condr. Interfaith Conf. of Met. Wash. (DC), Washington, 1987—97; condr. emeritus Mormon Choir of Wash. (DC), 2000; condr. McLean (Va.) Handbell Choir, 1971. Sgt. US Army, 1945—46. Recipient Disting. Music Alumni Achievement award, Ind. State U., 1995. Mem. Ch. Of Jesus Christ Of Lds. Avocations: music, ornithology. Home: 6933 Espey Ln Mc Lean VA 22101-5456 Home Phone: 703-821-2989. Personal E-mail: satb@cox.net.

MORLEY, HARRY THOMAS, JR., real estate executive; b. St. Louis, Aug. 13, 1930; s. Harry Thomas and Celeste Elizabeth (Davies) M.; m. Nelda Lee Mulholland, Sept. 3, 1960; children: Lisa, Mark, Marci. BA, U. Mo., 1955; MA, U. Denver, 1959. Dir. men's student activities Iowa State Tchrs. Coll., 1955-57; dir. student housing U. Denver, 1957-60; pvt. practice psychol. consulting St. Louis, 1960-63; dir. adminstrn. County of St. Louis, Mo., 1963-70; regional dir. HUD, Kansas City, Mo., 1970-71, asst. sec. adminstrn., 1971-73; pres. St. Louis Regional Commerce and Growth Assn., 1973-78, Taylor, Morley, Inc., St. Louis, 1978—2005, Morley Investments, Inc., 2005—. Teaching cons., lectr. Washington U., St. Louis, 1962-70; bd. dirs. Mid-Am. Alliance Corp., Life Ins. Co. Bd. dirs., exec. com. St. Louis Coll. Pharmacy; past chmn. Better Bus. Bur.; chmn. Mo. Indsl. Devel. Bd., Mo. State Hwy. Commn.; bd. dirs. St. Luke's Hosps., St. Johns Hosp., Downtown St. Louis, Inc., Laclede's Landing Redevel. Corp. With USN, 1951-53. Mem. Am. Nat. Assn. Homebuilders, St. Louis Homebuilders Assn. (pres.), St. Louis Advt. Club, Mo. Athletic Club, St. Louis Club, Noonday Club, Castle Oak Country Club, Round Table Club, Sunset Country Club. Republican. Methodist. Home: 14238 Forest Crest Dr Chesterfield MO 63017-2818 E-mail: morleyh@charter.net.

MORLEY, JAMES EVERITT, JR., (JAY MORLEY JR.), retired academic and educational association administrator; b. Middletown, NY, Dec. 23, 1940; s. James Everitt and Helen Scott (Fiero) Morley; m. Elizabeth Chadwell Wyman, Dec. 8, 1962; children: Margaret, Scott, Sarah, Sarah, James Everitt III. BME, Rensselaer Poly. Inst., 1962; MS in Acctg., Syracuse U., 1969. Mgmt. cons. Ernst & Ernst, NYC, 1969—72; comptroller Syracuse U., 1972—76; v.p. Rider Coll., Lawrenceville, NJ, 1976—78, Rensselaer Poly. Inst., Troy, NY, 1978—85; v.p., treas. Cornell U., Ithaca, NY, 1985—87, sr. v.p., 1987. Contbr. Mem. Troy Indsl. Devel. Authority, 1979—85; bd. dir. Capital Regional Tech. Devel. Coun., Albany, NY, 1983—85, Tompkins County Area Devel., NY, 1985—. Served to col USMC, 1962—. Mem.: Eastern Assn. Coll. and U. Bus. Officers, Nat. Assn. Coll. and U. Bus. Officers (bd. dir. 1984—, pres., CEO). Office Phone: 202-861-2510. Office Fax: 202-861-2583. E-mail: james.morley@nacubo.orr.

MORLEY, JOHN EDWARD, physician; b. Eshowe, Zululand, South Africa, June 13, 1946; came to U.S., 1977; s. Peter and Vera Rose (Phipson) M.; m. Patricia Morley, Apr. 4, 1970; children: Robert, Susan, Jacqueline. MB, BCh, U. Witwatersrand, Johannesburg, South Africa, 1972. Diplomate Am. Bd. Internal Medicine, subspecialty cert. endocrinology and geriatrics. Asst. prof. Mpls. VA Med. Ctr. and U. Minn., 1979-81; assoc. prof. U. Minn., Mpls., 1981-84; prof. UCLA San Fernando Valley, 1985-89; dir. GRECC Sepulveda (Calif.) VA Med. Ctr., 1985-89; Dammert prof. gerontology, dir. div. geriatric medicine St. Louis U. Med. Ctr., 1989—; dir. geriatric rsch., edn. and clin. ctr. St. Louis VA Med. Ctr., 1989—. Author: (with others) Nutritional Modulation of Neuronal Function, 1988, Neuropeptides and Stress, 1988, Geriatric Nutrition, 1990, 2d edit., 1995, Medical Care in the Nursing Home, 1991, 2d edit., 1997, Endocrinology and Metabolism in the Elderly, 1992, Memory Function and Aging Related Disorders, 1992, Aging and Musculoskeletal Disorders, 1993, Aging, Immunity and Infection, 1994, Sleep Disorders and Insomnia in the Elderly, 1993, Quality Improvement in Geriatric Care, 1995, Focus on Nutrition, 1995, Applying Health Services Research to Long-Term Care, 1996, Cardiovascular Disease in Older People, 1997, Hydration and Aging, 1997, Advances in Care of Older People with Diabetes, 1999, Endocrinology of Aging, 1999, Science of Geriatrics, 2000, Subacute Care, 2000, Anti-Aging, 2004, Principles and Practices of Geriatric Medicine, 4th edit., 2006; mem. editl. bd. Peptides, 1983—, Internat. Jour. Obesity, 1986-89, Jour. Nutritional Medicine, 1990—, Clinics in Applied Nutrition, 1990-92; editor geriatrics sect. Yearbook of Endocrinology, 1987-2001, Nursing Home Medicine, 1992-97, Clin. Geriatrics, 1992-97, Sandwich Generation, 1997, others; editor Jour. Gerontology: Med. Scis., 2000-06, Jour. Am. Med. Dirs. Assn., 2006—. Mem. adv. bd. Alzheimer's Assn., St. Louis, 1990-92; mem. adv. com. for physicians Mo. Divsn. Aging, Jefferson City, 1990-2001; bd. dirs. Mo. Assn. Long Term Care Physicians, 1991—, Long Term Care Ombudsman Program, St. Louis, 1992, Fund for Psychoneuroimmunology, 1990-2001, Hamilton Hts. Health Resource Ctr., 1992—. Recipient Mead Johnson award, Am. Inst. Nutrition, 1985, Cmty. Svc. award, BREM, 1997, Robert H. Bollinger Disting. Acad. award, U. Kans., 1997, Longevity prize, Ispen Found., 1999, Circle award, Am. Dietetics Assn., 2001, Marsha Goodwin-Beck Interdisciplinary award for excellence in geriatric leadership, Dept. Vets. Affairs, 2005. Mem. ACP (geriatrics subcom. 1991-92), Am. Geriatric Soc. (Nasher/Manning award 2002), Internat. Soc. Study-Aging Male, Am. Soc. Clin. Investigation, Endocrine Soc., Am. Fedn. Clin. Rsch., Am. Acad. Behavioral Sci., Gerontology Soc. Am. (Freeman award, 2004), Am. Diabetes Assn., Am. Soc. Pharmacy and Therapeutics, Soc. for Neurosci., La Asociacion de Gerontologica y Geriatrica, A.C. (hon.), Assn. Dirs. Geriatric Acad. Programs, Internat. Soc. Study Male Aging, Phi Beta Kappa. Office: Saint Louis U Sch Medicine 1402 S Grand Blvd Rm M238 Saint Louis MO 63104-1004 Office Phone: 314-977-8462. E-mail: morley@slu.edu.

MORLEY, LAWRENCE WHITAKER, geophysicist, consultant; b. Toronto, Feb. 19, 1920; s. George Whitaker and Mary Olive (Boyd) M.; divorced; children; Lawrence, Patricia, Chris, David (dec.); m. Beverly Anne Beckworth; step-children: Sandra Wellman, Stephen Burdett, Richard Burdett. BA, U. Toronto, 1946, MA, 1949, PhD, 1952; DSc (hon.) (hon.), York U., Toronto, 1974; Dr Environ. Studies (hon.), U. Waterloo, 2001. Dir. geophysics div. Geol. Survey Can., Ottawa, 1952-71; founding dir. gen. Can. Centre for Remote Sensing, Ottawa, 1971-80; founding exec. dir. Inst. for Space and Terrestrial Sci., Toronto, 1987-91; pres. Teledetection Internat., 1991—. Sci. counselor Can. High Commn., London. Lt. Can. Navy, 1941-45. Decorated Order of Can. Fellow Royal Soc. Can., Can. Aeronautics and Space Inst., Royal Can. Geog. Soc.; mem. Can. Soc. Remote Sensing (founding pres. 1971-74), Am. Geophys. Union, Am. Soc. Photogrammetry and Remote Sensing, Soc. Exploration Geophysicists, Can. Geophys. Union, Can. Geomatics Inst. Home and Office: 359340 Grey Rd 15 RR1 Owen Sound ON N4K 5N3 Canada

MORLEY, LLOYD ALBERT, electrical engineering educator; b. Provo, Utah, Oct. 28, 1940; s. John Jr. and Dorothea (Nielsen) M.; m. Jo Ann Bryant, Feb. 22, 1975; 1 child, Paul Loring. BS in Mining Engring., U. Utah, 1968, PhD in Mining Engring., 1972. Tchg. asst., rsch. assoc. U. Utah, Salt Lake City, 1968-71; asst. prof. mining engring. Pa. State U., University Park, 1971-75, assoc. prof., 1975-80, prof., 1980-85; prof., head dept. mineral engring. U. Ala., Tuscaloosa, 1985-93, endowed chair mining engring., 1993-99, prof. elec. engring., 1996—2006, assoc. dept. head elec. and computer engring., 1997-99, interim head, 1999-2000, head, 2000—04, prof. emeritus, 2007—. Cons. Jim Walter Resources, Inc., Brookwood, Ala., 1987-98, Pitts. and Midway Coal Mining Co., Englewood, Colo., 1990-98, Drummond Co., Inc., Birmingham, Ala., 1991-98. Author: Mine Power Systems, 1990; contbr. articles to profl. jours. Staff sgt. USNG, 1958-66. Recipient Wilson Outstanding Tchg. award Pa. State U., 1980; Outstanding Rsch. Report awards U.S. Bur. Mines, 1983-84, Hackney Faculty Leadership award, U. Ala., 2000, HKN Outstanding Tchg. award, U. Ala., 2004. Fellow IEEE (bd. dirs. 1991-92, 94, 97-99, v.p. publs. 1994, 99, v.p. tech. activities 1997, 98, corp. integrity office 2006—, Richard M. Emberson award 2005); mem. Industry Applications Soc. IEEE (Mining Best Paper awards 1984, 88, 90, pres. 1988, Disting. lectr. 1991, Disting. Svc. award 1995), Power Engr. Soc., Computer Soc., Phi Kappa Phi, Eta Kappa Nu. Avocations: high-fidelity systems, classic sports cars, rose growing, music. Office Phone: 205-348-0672. Business E-Mail: lmorley@eng.ua.edu.

MORLOK, EDWARD KARL, engineering educator, consultant; b. Phila., Nov. 3, 1940; s. Edward Karl and Anna Marie (Kurtz) M.; m. Ottilia Angela Husz, Dec. 14, 1968 (div. July 1983); 1 child, Jessica Angela; m. Patricia Campbell Conboy, Mar. 23, 1991. BE, Yale U., 1962; PhD, Northwestern U., 1967; MA (hon.), U. Pa., 1973. Civil engr., transp. U.S. Dept. Commerce, Washington, 1966-67; from asst. prof. civil engring. to assoc. prof. Northwestern U., Evanston, Ill., 1967-73, asst. dir. rsch., transp. ctr., 1969-73; 1907 Found. assoc. prof. U. Pa., Phila., 1973-75, chmn., transp. grad. group, 1983-86, 91-95, UPS found. prof. transp., 1975—, prof. systems engring., 1986—, chair systems grad. program, 1988-91, emeritus, 2004—. Cons. nat. transp. policy study commn., Washington, 1978-79. Author: Analysis Transportation Technology and Network Structure, 1969, Introduction to Transportation Engineering and Planning, 1978; assoc. editor Transp. Rsch. Jour., 1975-2004; consulting editor series in transp. for McGraw-Hill Publ. Co., 1980-98; contbr. more than 80 articles to profl. jours. Mem. Nat. Assembly Engring. panel on innovation in transp., Washington, 1979-80, panel on hazardous material transp., Washington, 1980-81. Recipient U.S. Sr. Scientist award Alexander von Humboldt Found., 1980-81; Rsch. grantee Commonwealth of Pa., Consol. Rail Corp., K-Line Am., U.S. Dept. Transp., NASA, NSF. Mem. ASCE, Transp. Rsch. Forum (v.p. 1974-75, pres. 1975-76, bd. disting. mems. 1983—, Disting. Transp. Rsch. award 1998), Transp. Rsch. Bd. (rev. com. of coun. of univ. transp. ctrs. 1985-88, coun. mem. 1988-90, chair freight transp. planning and logistics com. 1994-99, chair com. on policy options for intermodal freight trans. 1996-98). Lutheran. Office: U Pa Dept Elec and Systems Engring 220 S 33rd St Philadelphia PA 19104-6315 Business E-Mail: morlok@seas.upenn.edu.

MORMAN, DEAN SMITH, accountant, consultant; b. Owosso, Mich., Jan. 4, 1936; s. Corneilius Frank and Alliene Delight Morman; m. Christine Marie Paletta, Oct. 26, 1985; m. Betty Ann Branham, Aug. 7, 1954 (div. Oct. 21, 1985); 1 child, Dawn Denise Bogert. BBA, Kettering U. (GMI), Flint, Mich., 1959. Acctg. mgr. Ctrl. Foundry Divsn., GMC, Saginaw, Mich., 1954—63; mgr. of material control Midland-Ross Corp., Cleveland, Ohio, 1963—66; various mgmt. and exec. positions IBM Corp., Armonk, NY, 1966—88; pres. Self Funded Svcs., Ocean City, NJ, 1989—2009; bus. controls mgr. Atlantic City Coin and Slot Svc. Co., Pleasantvile, NJ, 1999—2002. Author: (poem) The Living Sea, 2003, (essay) Pets, 2003. Treas. South Jersey Cancer Fund, Brigantine, NJ, 1991—2000, St. Andrew by-the-Sea Luth. Ch., Atlantic City, 1988—99. R-Conservative. Lutheran. Avocations: travel, reading, creative writing. Personal E-mail: dmor136@aol.com.

MORNEAU, JUSTIN ERNEST GEORGE, professional baseball player; b. New Westminster, BC, May 15, 1981; Draft pick Minn.Twins, 1999, player, 2003—. Mem. Can. World Jr. Team, 1999; mem. Can. Nat. Team World Baseball Championship, 2001. Named Am. League MVP, Baseball Writers' Assn. of Am., 2006; named to Am. League All-Star Team, 2007; recipient Am. League Silver Slugger award, 2006. Office: Minn Twins 34 Kirby Puckett Plc Minneapolis MN 55415 *

MORNEAU, WILLIAM, pension and benefits company executive; BA, U. Western Ontario; MSc, London Sch. Econs.; MBA, INSEAD, France. Pres., CEO Morneau Sobeco, Toronto. Apptd. bd. dirs. AGF Mgmt. Ltd., 2000. Involved with numerous charitable and community organizations. Named one of Canada's Top 40 under 40, 2001. Office: Morneau Sobeco 895 Don Mills Rd Ste 700 Toronto ON Canada M3C 1W3

MORNINGSTAR, COLIN JON, physicist, researcher; b. Fort Erie, Canada, Mar. 7, 1962; arrived in U.S., 2005, permanent resident; s. Robert Baker and Katherine Caroline Morningstar; m. Mary Louise Linton; children: Amberly Joyce, Solana Bree, Jocelyn Paige. BS, U. Toronto, 1985, PhD, 1991. Postdoctoral rsch. assoc. Stanford (Calif.) Accelerator Ctr., 1991—93; postdoctoral rsch. fellow U. Edinburgh, Scotland, 1993—95; postdoctoral rsch. assoc. U. Calif., San Diego, 1995—99; asst. prof. physics Fla. Internat. U., Miami, Fla., 1999—2000, Carnegie Mellon U., Pitts., 2000—. Grantee, NSF, 1999—2006. Mem.: Am. Physics Soc. Achievements include research in comprehensive determination of the mass spectrum of glueballs using Monte Carlo computations in lattice gauge theory. Office: Carnegie Mellon University 5000 Forbes Avenue Pittsburgh PA 15213 Office Phone: 412-268-2728. Office Fax: 412-681-0648. Business E-Mail: colin_morningstar@cmu.edu.

MOROF, JEFFREY W., lawyer; AB, U. Mich, 1976; JD, Washington U., St. Louis, 1979. Bar: Calif., Mo., US Dist. Ct. (Ctrl. & No. dists.) Calif., US Dist. Ct. Colo., US Dist. Ct. (So. dist.) Fla., US Dist. Ct. NJ. With Bryan Cave LLP, Chgo., 1979—, ptnr., 1988—, mng. ptnr., mem. exec.

com.; settlement conference atty. US Dist. Ct. (Ctrl. dist.) Calif., 1998—2000, 2001—03. Office Phone: 312-602-5045. Office Fax: 312-602-5045. E-mail: jwmorof@bryancave.com.

MORONEY, JAMES M., III, publishing executive; b. 1957; m. Barbara Moroney; 5 children. BA in Am. Studies, Stanford U., 1978; MBA, U. Tex., 1983. Acct. exec. WFAA-TV, KFDM-TV, Beaumont, Tex., 1978—84; local sales mgr. WFAA-TV, Dallas-Ft. Worth, 1985; gen. sales mgr. KOTV, Tulsa, Okla., 1985—89, v.p., gen. mgr., 1992—93, pres., gen. mgr., 1993; with Belo Corp., Dallas, 1978—86, controller, 1989, asst. to pres. broadcast divsn., 1990—92, v.p. broadcast divsn., 1993—95, exec. v.p. TV Group, 1995—97, pres. TV Group, 1997—98, exec. v.p., 1998—99; founding pres. Belo Interactive, Inc., Dallas, 1999—2001; pub. & CEO Dallas Morning News, 2001—. Mem. Dallas Citizens Coun.; mem. bd. dirs. TV Bur. Adv., Goodwill Industries, Dallas, Tulsa, United Way Tulsa, Cath. Charities Tulsa, Jr. Achievement Tulsa, Gilcrease Mus. Tulsa, Cistercian Perp. Sch. Dallas, Greater Dallas Chamber, State Fair Tex.; mem. bd. dirs. Coll. Comm. U. Tex. Austin; mem. bd. State Fair of Tex., Cistercian Prep. Sch., Dallas. Named Pub. of Yr., Editor & Pub. mag., 2004. Office: Dallas Morning News 508 Young St Dallas TX 75202 also: Belo Corp PO Box 655237 Dallas TX 75265-7526 Business E-Mail: jmoroney@dallasnews.com. *

MORONEY, JOHN RODGERS, economist, educator; b. Dallas, Jan. 29, 1939; s. John Rodgers and Irene (Lewis) M.; m. Margaret Cecil Kearny, May 30, 1959; children: John Rodgers, Stephen Kearny, Helen, Michael Edward; m. Carmen Lambert, May 22, 1993 BA, So. Meth. U., Dallas, 1960; PhD, Duke U., Durham, NC, 1964. Asst. prof. econs. Fla. State U., 1964—66; assoc. prof. econs. Mich. State U., 1966—69; mem. exec. com. Inst. Pub. Utilities, 1968—69; prof. econs., chmn. dept. Tulane U., New Orleans, 1969—81; prof., head dept. econs. Tex. A&M U., College Station, 1981—. Vis. prof. econs. MIT, 1975-76; Schmidt internat. prof. A.B. Freeman Sch. Bus., Tulane U., New Orleans, 1998—; pres. Moroney Econ. Rsch. Assocs., 1992— Author: The Structure of Production in American Manufacturing, 1972, Exploration, Development, and Production: Texas Oil and Gas, 1997, Energy and Sustainable Development in Mexico, 2005; editor, contbr.: Income Inequality: Trends and Internat. Comparisons, 1979, Economic Aspects of New Technology, 1980, Formal Energy and Resource Models, 1982; editor: Econometric Models of the Demand for Energy, 1984; editor, contbr.: Energy, Capital, and Technological Change, 1987, Energy, Growth, and the Environment, 1992, Energy Prices and Production, 1994, Sustainable Economic Growth, 1995, Energy Supply and Demand, 1997, Fuels for the Future, 1999; mem. editl. bd. Bus. Topics, 1968-69, So. Econ. Jour, 1975— Social Sci. Rsch. Coun. faculty rsch. fellow, 1969; NSF rsch. fellow, 1975-76, 77-79 Mem. Am. Econ. Assn., So. Econ. Assn. (exec. com. 1975—, v.p. 1980), Royal Econ. Assn., Econometric Soc., Phi Beta Kappa Home: 210 Fireside Cir College Station TX 77840-1877 Office: Dept Econs Tex A&M U College Station TX 77843-4228 Office Phone: 979-845-1363. Business E-Mail: jmoroney@econmail.tamu.edu.

MORONEY, LINDA L.S. (MUFFIE), lawyer, educator; b. Washington, May 27, 1943; d. Robert Emmet and Jessie (Robinson) M.; m. Clarence Renshaw II, Mar. 28, 1967 (div. 1977); children: Robert Milnor, Justin W.R. BA, Randolph-Macon Woman's Coll., 1965; JD cum laude, U. Houston, 1982. Bar: Tex. 1982, U.S. Ct. Appeals (5th cir.) 1982, U.S. Dist. Ct. (so. dist.) Tex. 1982, U.S. Supreme Ct. 1988. Law clk. to assoc. justice 14th Ct. Appeals, Houston, 1982-83; assoc. Pannill and Reynolds, Houston, 1983-85, Gilpin, Pohl & Bennett, Houston, 1985-89, Vinson & Elkins, Houston, 1989-92. Adj. prof. law U. Houston, 1986—91, dir. legal rsch. and writing, 1992—96, civil trial and appellate litigation and mediation, 1996—. Bd. dirs. Episcopal Ch. Pub. Co.; mem. exec. com. River Oaks Area Dem. Women (Roadwomen), 1994—; bd. dirs. Planned Parenthood of Houston and S.E. Tex., 1996—. Mem. ABA, State Bar Tex., Houston Bar Assn., Assn. Women Attys., Tex. Women Lawyers, Randolph-Macon Women's Coll. Alumnae Assn. (bd. dirs. 2006—), Order of Barons, Phi Delta Phi. Episcopalian. Home and Office: 4010 Whitman St Houston TX 77027-6334 Office Phone: 713-542-5073. Business E-Mail: mmoroney@hal-pc.org.

MOROOKA, HIROSHI, neurosurgeon; b. Kurashiki, Okayama, Japan, Aug. 28, 1946; s. Shigeru and Akiko (Kobayashi) M.; m. Michiko Ninomiya, June 6, 1976; children: Takatoshi, Hanako, Teruko. MD, U. Okayama, 1971, PhD, 1978. Diplomate Japanese Bd. Neurol. Surgery. Clin. asst. neurosurgery U. Okayama Med. Sch., 1972-77, instr. neurosurgery, 1980-83, asst. prof. neurosurgery, 1984-86; rsch. assoc. neurology U. Miami Med. Sch., Fla., 1977-79; chief neurosurgery Okayama Rousai Hosp., 1987-92, Bizen City Hosp., 1993-95, Okayama Saidaiji Hosp., 1996—. Author: Cytoprotection & Cytobiology, 1995-97, Medical Biochemical & Chemical Aspects of Free Radicals, 1989, Intracranial Pressure VII, 1989, Brain Edema IX, 1993. Recipient Disting. Prof. award, BWW Soc., Inst. Advancement of Positive Global Solutions, Calif., 2003, Legion of Honor award, United Cultural Conv., NC, 2005, Leading Health Profls. of World award, IBC, Cambridge, Eng., 2005; Nat. Rsch. grantee, 1981. Mem. AAAS, Japan Neurol. Soc., Societas Neurologica Japonica, NY Acad. Scis., Am. Heart Assn., Am. Chem. Soc. Liberal Dem. Christian. Avocation: golf. Home: 880-165 Minato 703 8266 Okayama Japan Office: Okayama Saidaiji Hosp 8-41 Saidaiji Nakano Honmachi Okayama 704-8192 Japan Business E-Mail: morooka@okym.enjoy.ne.jp.

MOROSAN, RONALD, artist, educator; b. Detroit, Mar. 25, 1947; s. George and Dolores Morosan. BFA, Wayne State U., Detroit, 1971; MFA, U. Iowa, Iowa City, 1974. Asst. prof. Worcester Mus. Sch., Mass., 1980—81; vis. artist North Tex. State U., Denton, 1983—84; adj. prof. Molloy Coll., Rockville Ctr., NY, 2003—. Grantee Tiffany Found., 1980. Mem.: Coll. Art Assn., Am. Assn. Museums. Home: 315 8th Ave New York NY 10001

MOROWITZ, HAROLD JOSEPH, biophysicist, educator; b. Poughkeepsie, NY, Dec. 4, 1927; s. Philip Frank and Anna (Levine) M.; m. Lucille Rita Stein, Jan. 30, 1949; children: Joanna Lynn, Eli David, Joshua Alan, Zachary Adam, Noah Daniel. BS, Yale U., 1947, MS, 1950, PhD, 1951. Physicist Nat. Bur. Stds., 1951-53, Nat. Heart Inst., Bethesda, Md., 1953-55; mem. faculty Yale U., 1955-88, assoc. prof. biophysics, 1960-68, prof. molecular biophysics and biochemistry, 1968-88, master Pierson Coll., 1981-86; mem. faculty George Mason U., Fairfax, Va., 1988—, Robinson prof. biology and natural philosophy, 1988—; dir. Krasnow Inst. for Advanced Study, 1993-98. Chmn. com. on models for biomed. rsch. NRC, 1983-85, mem. bd. on basic biology, 1986-92. Author: Life and the Physical Sciences, 1964, (with Waterman) Theoretical and Mathematical Biology, 1965, Energy Flow in Biology, 1968, Entropy for Biologists, 1970, (with Lucille Morowitz) Life On The Planet Earth, 1974, Ego Niches, 1977, Foundations of Bioenergetics, 1978, The Wine of Life, 1979, Mayonnaise and the Origin of Life, 1985, Cosmic Joy and Local Pain, 1987, The Thermodynamics of Pizza, 1991, Beginnings of Cellular Life, 1992, (with James Trefil) The Facts of Life, 1992, Entropy and the Magic Flute, 1993, The Kindly Dr. Guillotin, 1997, The Emergence of Everything, 2002; editor Complexity, 1994-2002; contbr. articles to profl. jours. Mem. sci. adv. bd. Santa Fe Inst., 1991-97, co-chmn. sci. adv. bd., 2000—06. Recipient Biol. Scis. award, Washington Acad. Scis., 2004. Mem. Biophys. Soc. (exec. com. 1965), Nat. Ctr. for Rsch. Resources (coun. 1987-92). Office: George Mason U Mail Stop 2A1 Krasnow Inst Advanced Study Fairfax VA 22030 Office Phone: 703-993-4334.

MOROZ, PAVEL EMANUEL, retired research scientist; b. Leningrad, Russia, 1928; came to U.S., 1976. Degree in Medicine, Pavlov Med. Inst., Leningrad, 1952, MD in Cytology and Biophysics, 1960. Rsch. scientist various insts., Leningrad, 1952-75, ret., 1975. Author: (in Russian) A Book of Aphorisms, 2002, Balding in the Spheromobile, 2005, The Fever, 2006; contbr. articles articles to profl. jours. Mem. N.Y. Acad. Scis. Achievements include development of centrifuge microscope; analysis of the physical limits of biological evolution, particularly of the vertical posture in man; research in the effects of the force of gravity and centrifugal force on the cell.

MORPHY, JAMES CALVIN, lawyer; b. Pitts., Jan. 16, 1954; s. Robert Samson and Autumn (Phillips) M.; m. Priscilla Winslow Plimpton, July 11, 1981; children: Calvin, Katherine, Victoria. BA, Harvard U., Cambridge, Mass., 1976, JD, 1979. Bar: NY 1980. Assoc. Sullivan & Cromwell LLP, NYC, 1979-86, ptnr., 1986—, mng. ptnr. com., 1992—95, mng. ptnr. M&A group, 1995—2007, firm mng. ptnr., 2007—. Co-chmn. Tulane M&A Law Inst.; guest lectr. Harvard Law Sch.; mem. adv. bd. govs. Harvard Corp. Governance Program. Contbg. author: treatise New York and Delaware Business Entities: Choice Formation, Operation, Financing, and Acquisition, 1997, Transactional Lawyer's Deskbook, 2001. Trustee Greenwich Acad. Mem. ABA (com. on fed. securities law 1992—), Assn. Bar of City of NY, Wianno Club (bd. govs.), Greenwich Country Club, Harvard Club NY, Wianno Yacht Club, Phi Beta Kappa. Office: Sullivan & Cromwell LLP 125 Broad St New York NY 10004-2489 Office Phone: 212-558-4000. Office Fax: 212-558-3588. Business E-Mail: morphyj@sullcrom.com.

MORPHY, MARTHA A., archivist; b. 1954; BS in Edn., SUNY, Oswego, NY; MS in Computer Systems Mgmt., Rochester Inst. Tech. With systems engrng. staff Nat. Oceanic & Atmospheric Adminstrn. (NOAA), US Dept. Commerce; served in various position including software architect, dir. info. tech. policy, dep. chief info. officer The Nat. Archives & Records Adminstrn., 1998—, chief info. officer, asst. archivist for info. svcs., 2005—. Office: The Nat Archives & Records Adminstrn 8601 Adelphi Rd College Park MD 20740 E-mail: martha.morphy@nara.gov. *

MORREALE, JOSEPH CONSTANTINO, academic administrator, educator, economist, consultant; b. Bronx, NY, Oct. 26, 1944; s. Joseph Vincent Morreale and Grace (Soricelli); m. Barbara McAdorey; children: Gwenn F., Margaret I., Adam J.; stepchildren: Neil J., Michael D., John D. BA, Queens Coll. CUNY, 1967; MA, SUNY, Buffalo, 1969, PhD in Econs., 1972; MS in Higher Ednl. Adminstrn., SUNY, Albany, 1989. Asst. prof. econs. Western Mich. U., Kalamazoo, 1970-74; rsch. assoc. U. Wis., Madison, 1974-75; asst. to assoc. prof. health svcs. adminstrn., econs. Grad. Sch. Pub. Health U. Pitts., 1975-79; assoc. to prof. econs., environ. studies Bard Coll., Annandale-On-Hudson, NY, 1979-88; vis. rsch. fellow Grad. Sch. Edn., H.E. Adminstrn. SUNY, Albany, 1988-89; prof., chmn. dept. pub. adminstrn. Grad. Sch. Pace U., White Plains, NY, 1989-96; vice provost for planning assessment and instnl. rsch. Pace U., NYC, Westchester, 1996-98, v.p. planning, assessment, rsch. and acad. support, 1998—2003, provost, 2003—. Health care and govt. fin. cons. to fed. agencies, state and local govts., pvt. firms, 1979—; adj. prof. law Pace U., 1990-96; adj. prof. pub. adminstrn. Grad. Sch. Pub. Affairs, SUNY-Albany, 1990-96; vis. prof. U. Lancaster, Eng., 1984-85; rsch. assoc., bd. dirs. Hudsonia Environ. Rsch., Annandale, 1985-95; fin. planner Prudential Fin. Svcs., Newburgh, N.Y., 1987-89. Author: Health Care Economics, 1977, Post Tenure Review and Renewal: Experienced Voices, 2002; editor: The U.S. Medical Care Industry, 1974, Post-tenure Review: Policies, Practices, Precautions, 1997; contbr. articles to profl. jours. Appoint pub. rep. Westchester County Deferred Compensation Bd., Mt. Kisco Planning Bd. Recipient NDEA fellowship, 1967-70, Pharm. Mfg. Assn. fellowship, 1969-70, post-doctoral fellowship Health Econ. Rsch. Ctr. U. Wis., 1974-75, rsch. fellowship Grad. Sch. Edn. SUNY-Albany, 1988-89, ACE fellowship UNC, Charlotte, 1995-96, sr. rsch. fellow Harvard IEM Inst., 2000. Mem. Am. Soc. for Pub. Adminstrn., Am. Econ. Assn., Am. Ednl. Fin. Assn., Assn. Instl. Rsch., Am. Assn. Higher Edn., Am. Coun. Edn. (fellow 1995-96). Mem. Soc. Of Friends. Avocations: photography, tennis, music. Office: Pace U VP 1 Pace Plz New York NY 10038-1598 Business E-Mail: jmorreale@pace.edu.

MORREIM, E. HAAVI, medical ethics educator; b. July 21, 1950; d. Paul and Florence Morreim. BA in Philosophy, St. Olaf Coll., 1972; MA in Philosophy, U. Va., 1976, PhD, 1980. Med. philosopher program in human biology and soc. U. Va. Sch. Medicine, Charlottesville, 1980-82, asst. prof. philosophy in medicine, 1982-84; from asst. to assoc. prof. dept. human values and ethics U. Tenn. Coll. Medicine, Memphis, 1988—93, prof. dept. human values and ethics, 1993—. Adj. prof. philosophy Va. Commonwealth U., Richmond, 1980; vis. prof. philosophy St. Olaf Coll., Northfield, Minn., 1982; Andrew Mellon vis. asst. prof. humanities and medicine Georgetown U. Sch. Medicine, Washington, 1983; sr. vis. rsch. scholar Kennedy Inst. Ethics, Georgetown U., 1983; manuscript reviewer; presenter and lectr. in field. Author: Balancing Act: The New Medical Ethics of Medicine's New Economics, 1991, Holding Health Care Accountable: Law and the New Medical Marketplace, 2001; mem. editl. adv. bd. Jour. Medicine and Philosophy; bd. editors: Jour. Law, Medicine and Ethics, IRB: Ethics and Human Research; contbr. articles to profl. jours. Active Hastings Ctr. Mem. Am. Health Lawyers Assn., Am. Soc. Law, Medicine, and Ethics, Am. Soc. for Bioethics and Humanities, Phi Beta Kappa. Avocations: running, high-performance automobile driving, photography, skiing. Office: Univ Tenn Coll Medicine 910 Madison #314 Memphis TN 38163-2814 Office Phone: 901-448-5725. Business E-Mail: hmorreim@utmem.edu.

MORRELL, ERNEST DAVIS, literature and language professor; b. Alameda, Calif., Apr. 27, 1971; s. Ernest Davis and Katherine Yvonne Morrell; m. Jodene Michele Kersten, July 23, 1994; children: Amani Kisho, Antonio Kiyoshi. BA, U. Calif., Santa Barbara, 1993; MA, U. Calif., Berkeley, 1997, PhD, 2001. Cert. tchr. Calif., 1994. Asst. prof. Mich. State U., East Lansing, 2001—05, UCLA, 2005—. Co-dir. summer seminar Inst. Democracy Edn. and Access, LA, 1999—2006. Author: Becoming Critical Researchers: Literacy and Empowerment for Urban Youth, Linking Literacy and Popular Culture: Finding Connections for Lifelong Learning; contbr. articles to profl. jours. Co-dir. R.O.O.T., Music Found., LA, 2006. Mem.: Nat. Coun. Tchrs. English (exec. com. 2003—), Am. Ednl. Rsch. Assn. Democrat. Avocations: poetry, screenwriting. Home: 28915 Thousand Oaks Blvd #2003 Agoura Hills CA 91301 Office: UCLA Grad Sch Edn 2022A Moore Hall Box 951521 Los Angeles CA 90095 Home Phone: 310-966-0538; Office Phone: 310-825-7548. Office Fax: 310-206-6293; Home Fax: 818-879-1538. Business E-Mail: morrell@gseis.ucla.edu.

MORRELL, GENE PAUL, gas industry executive, consultant; b. Ardmore, Okla., Oct. 4, 1932; s. Paul T. and Etta L. (Weaver) M.; m. Jan A. Foster, Aug. 20, 1954; children: Jeffrey T., Kelly Ann, Rob Redman. BS in Geology, U. Okla., 1954, LLB, 1962. Bar: D.C. 1973. Geologist Gilmer Oil Co., Ardmore, Okla., 1957-59, atty.-geologist, 1962-63; pvt. practice Ardmore, 1963-69; ofcl. Dept. Interior, Washington, 1969-72; v.p. Lone Star Gas Co., Washington, 1972-76; sr. v.p. United Energy Resources, Inc., Houston, 1976-86; vice chmn. Petro United Terminals, Inc., Houston, 1986-98; cons. on investments, 1998—. Contbr. articles to profl. jours. Commr. City of Ardmore, 1967-69, vice-mayor, 1968. Mem. D.C. Bar Assn., Am. Assn. Petroleum Geologists, River Oaks Country Club (Houston), Phi Alpha Delta, Sigma Alpha Epsilon. Episcopalian. Personal E-mail: jfmorrell@aol.com.

MORRICAL, GLENN EDWIN, lawyer; b. Columbus, Ohio, Mar. 19, 1952; s. Herman E. and Mary Esther (Burgett) M.; m. Mae F. Cohen, Sept. 8, 1979; children: Michael, Stephen, David. BA summa cum laude, Ohio State U., 1974; JD cum laude, Harvard U., 1977; MBA, Cleve. State U., 1983. Bar: Ohio 1977, U.S. Dist. Ct. (no. dist.) Ohio 1977, U.S. Tax Ct. 1977. Assoc. Arter & Hadden, Cleve., 1977-85, ptnr., 1986—, Tucker, Ellis & West. Trustee Fairmont Presbyn. Ch., Cleve., scout leader (past ten years) Boy Scouts Am. Mem. Ohio Bar Assn. (chmn. partnership law subcom.), Cleve. Bar Assn. (securities sect., former chair) 1990-91, assoc. mem. Assn. Investment Mgmt. & Rsch. Office: Tucker Ellis West 925 Euclid Ave Ste 1150 Cleveland OH 44115 Office Phone: 216-696-3431. Office Fax: 216-592-5009. Business E-Mail: glenn.morrical@tuckerellis.com.

MORRILL, PENNY CHITTIM, art historian; b. San Antonio, Feb. 4, 1947; d. Jack Robert and Dorothy Born (Sutherland) Chittim; m. James Agrippa Morrill, July 12, 1969; children: Jackson Forrest, Julia Chiltipin. BA with honors, Tulane U., New Orleans, 1969; MA, U. Pa., Phila., 1971; PhD, U. Md., 2001. Program coord. Cancer Rsch. Found. Am., Alexandria, Va., 1990—95; adj. prof. Md. Inst. Coll. Art, Balt., 2000, Corcoran Coll. Art, Washington, 2003, Georgetown U., 2004—05, Hood Coll., Md., 2006—. Author: Silver Masters of Mexico, 1996, Mexican Silver, 1994; curator Carlyle Ho. Mus., Alexandria, 1980; curator, catalogue author traveling exhbn. Maestros de Plata: William Spratling and the Mex. Silver Renaissance, San Antonio Mus. Art, 1998-2004; contbr. articles to profl. jours. Vol. teen pregnancy prevention Nat. ARC, Washington, 1986-98; participant Coro Women in Leadership, Washington, 1988; adv. com. Betty Ford Breast Health Ctr., Washington, 1997-98, adv. bd.; bd. dirs. Nat. Rehab. Hosp., Washington, 1991-2006, pres., 2005-06; alumnae bd. Newcomb Coll./Tulane U., 1990-94, v.p., 1994; bd. dirs., v.p., pres. Lyceum Mus., Alexandria, 1992-97; bd. dirs., editor, pres. Hist. Alexandria Found., 1980-89. Recipient Achievement award Jr. League Phila., 1985, RAP and AMAZE award, Nat. ARC, 1988, Spirit Volunteerism award Jr. League Washington, 1992, Recognition award Nat. Rehab. Hosp., 1997, Bd. Dirs. award, 2005. Mem. Coll. Art Assn., Am. Soc. Jewelry Historians Episcopalian. Avocations: knitting, gardening.

MORRIN, PETER PATRICK, museum director; b. St. Louis, Oct. 31, 1945; s. Kevin Charles and Helen Louise (Clanton) M.; m. Carolyn Brooks, Oct. 5, 1974; children: Matthew, Rebecca. AB, Harvard U., 1968; MFA, Princeton U., 1972. Asst. prof., dir. art gallery Vassar Coll., Poughkeepsie, NY, 1974-78; curator 20th century art High Mus. Art, Atlanta, 1979-86; dir. Speed Art Mus., Louisville, 1986—. Panelist Nat. Endowment Arts. Contbr. articles to profl. publs. Served with USAR, 1968-74. Mem.: Assn. Art Mus. Dirs. (pres. 2003—04). Office: Speed Art Mus 2035 S 3rd St Louisville KY 40208-1812 Office Phone: 502-634-2700. Business E-Mail: pmorrin@speedmuseum.org.

MORRIS, ALVIN LEONARD, retired dentist, academic administrator; b. Detroit, July 2, 1927; s. Frank and Lulu (Cornett) M.; m. Arlene Teschler, Feb. 1, 1947 (dec. Apr. 1974); children: Jeffry, Gregg, Beth; m. Beverly Hackman, 1975. Student, U. Ill., 1944-45; D.D.S., U. Mich., 1951; PhD, U. Rochester, 1957; D.Sc. (hon.), U. Md., 1983. Intern Letterman Army Hosp., San Francisco, 1951-52; postdoctoral research fellow NIH, 1954-57; head dept. oral diagnosis U. Pa. Sch. Dentistry, 1957-61; dean U. Ky. Coll. Dentistry, Lexington, 1961-68; asst. v.p. U. Ky. Coll. Dentistry (Med. Center), 1968-69, v.p. adminstrn. univ., 1970-75; exec. dir. Assn. for Acad. Health Centers, Washington, 1975-79; prof. dental care systems Sch. Dental Medicine, asso. v.p. health affairs U. Pa., 1979-87, sr. assoc. Leonard Davis Inst. Health Econs., Wharton Grad. Sch., 1980-87, prof. emeritus, 1987-89; research prof. Health Services Research Ctr./Sch. of Dentistry, U. N.C., Chapel Hill, 1987-89. Cons. Dental Corps, U.S. Army, 1960-70, VA, 1962-75, U.S. Dept. Def., 1969-72; pub. health service cons. dental study sect. USPHS, 1963-67; also chmn.; cons., lectr. USN Dental Sch.; cons. Army Med. Service Adv. Com. Preventive Dentistry, 1967-71; mem. Nat. Adv. Council Edn. Health Professions, 1968-72; bd. dirs. Nat. Center Health Edn., 1977-84; adv. com. Ednl. Testing Service, 1977-82; chmn. adv. com. Nat. Preventive Dental Demonstration Program, 1976-83 Served with inf. AUS, 1944-46; to 1st lt. Dental Corps 1951-54. Recipient Pierre Fauchard medal, 1974, Henry Spenadel medal, 1982, Callahan medal, 1991. Fellow Internat., Am. colls. dentists; mem. ADA (Disting. Svc. award 1985), Inst. Medicine of NAS, AAAS, Internat. Assn. Dental Rsch., So. Conf. Dental Deans and Examiners (pres. 1964-65), Sigma Xi. Presbyterian (deacon, trustee). Home: 302 Briarcliff Ln Danville KY 40422

MORRIS, BETTY ANN, artist; b. New Bedford, Mass., Nov. 21, 1948; d. George Morris and Deolinda Perry, Veriot Perry (Stepfather). Leather crafts woman Moods, Wilkes Barre, Pa., 1972—85; purveyor of antiques Olde Friends, Beaumont, Pa., 1985—92, Harbor Antiques, Newport, RI, 1995—2006; artist Betty Ann Morris Gallery, Newport, 2003—. With USMC, 1967—70. Home: 60 Church St Newport RI 02840 Office: Betty Ann Morris Studio 60 Church St Newport RI 02840 Home Phone: 401-338-4462; Office Phone: 401-338-4462. Home Fax: 401-848-9711. Business E-Mail: bettyannmorris@cox.net.

MORRIS, BRENDA DENISE, music educator, director; b. Kansas City, Mo., Mar. 27, 1952; d. Clyde Edward and Irene Perdue; m. Casey Thomas Morris, June 1, 1991; m. Walter Edward Freeman (dec.); children: Kerri, Michelle, Derek, Jamie. At, U. Mo. Music Conservatory, Kansas City. Pvt. music tchr., 1967—2006; prin. tchr. Prodigy Sch. MusicArts, 2006—. Ch. musician First Assembly of God Ch., 1961—70; condr. 12th grade Lee's Summit H.S., 1969—70; music dir. Longview Christian Ch., 1989—99, Longview Bapt. Ch., 2000—02, One Spirit Meth. Ch., Kansas City, 2004—, Aldersgate Meth. Ch., Olathe, Kans.

MORRIS, BRIAN, advertising executive; m. Cindy Morris; 2 children. Graduate, So. Meth. Univ., Dallas; M in Personnel Svcs., Miami Univ., Ohio. Pres. Dailey & Assoc., LA, CEO. Named Leader of Yr., LA Advt. Agencies Assn.; recipient Silver Medal award, Am. Advt. Fedn. Office: Dailey & Assoc 8687 Melrose Ave Ste G300 West Hollywood CA 90069-5725

MORRIS, BRIAN, state supreme court justice; b. Butte, Mont., Sept. 5, 1963; m. Cherche Prezeau; 3 children. BA in Economics, Stanford U., 1986, MA in Economics, 1987; JD, Stanford Law Sch., 1992. Law clerk for Judge John T. Noonan, Jr. U.S. Ct. of Appeals for Ninth Circuit, 1992—93; law clerk for Justice William H. Rehnquist U.S. Supreme Ct., 1993—94; legal asst. Iran-U.S. Claims Tribunal, The Hague, 1994—95; prtnr. Goetz, Gallik, Baldwin & Dolan, 1995—99; sr. legal officer UN Compensation Commn., 2000—01; state solicitor Mont. Dept. of Justice, 2001—04; justice Mont. Supreme Ct., 2005—. Author several law review and professional jour. articles. Office: Mont Supreme Ct PO Box 203003 Helena MT 59620-3003 *

MORRIS, DANIEL S., computer scientist, researcher; b. NYC, Feb. 5, 1978; s. Robert and Fran Morris; m. Morris June Ringel, Dec. 19, 2004. BS in Neurosci., Brown U., Providence, 2000; PhD in Computer Sci., Stanford U., Calif., 2006. Rschr. Microsoft Rsch., Redmond, Wash., 2006—. Computer engrng. cons. CyberKinetics, Inc., Foxboro, Mass., 2000—06. Musician: (albums) Careless Hearts. Nat. Def. Sci. and Engrng. Grad. fellow, ASEE, 2000—03. Democrat. Achievements include five patents pending in neurotechnology. Avocations: guitar, bass.

MORRIS, DAVID MICHAEL, insurance executive, lawyer; b. San Juan, Dec. 8, 1948; s. Edwin Thaddeus and Winifred Isabel (Walsh) M.; m. Carol Anderson Worden, Aug. 7, 1971; children: Laura H., John C. BA, U. Md., 1971; JD, U. Balt., 1975. Bar: Md. 1976, U.S. Dist. Ct. Md. 1976; CLU. Owner Franklin/Morris Assocs., LLC, Balt., 1976—. Columnist legal newspaper Daily Record, 1985-87. Pres., trustee 2d Presbyn. Ch., Balt., 1980-86, elder, 1988-98; vice chmn. Balt. div. United Way, 1981-84; fund raiser Johns Hopkins Children's Ctr., Balt., 1984-88; trustee Roland Park Country Sch., 1988-89, 90-98; mem. exec. com. Gilman Sch. Parents Assn., 1989-91; grad. Leadership Md., 1998. Mem. ABA, Md. Bar Assn., Balt. Bar Assn., Assn. Advanced Life Underwriting, Balt. Life Underwriters Assn. (chmn. ethics 1977-80, bd. dirs. 1982-85, bd. dirs. Charitable Found.), Balt. Soc. CLU and Chartered Fin. Cons. (chmn. ethical guidance com., bd. dirs.), Million Dollar Round Table and Top of the Table (life), Md. Club, Balt. Country Club, Ctr. Club, Balt. Wine and Food Soc. (bd. dirs., treas. 2006—), Leadership Md. (exec. com., sec. adv. bd.) Avocations: golf, wine. Home: 205 Paddington Rd Baltimore MD 21212-3438 Office: Franklin/Morris Assocs LLC One N Charles St Ste 2400 Baltimore MD 21201

MORRIS, DAVID S., publishing executive; Grad., St. Anselm Coll. From NY adv. mgr. Entertainment Weekly to assoc. pub. Time Inc., NYC, 1991—2000, pres., pub., Entertainment Weekly, 2000—03, 2005—, pres., pub., Sports Illustrated, 2003—05. Office: Time Inc Entertainment Weekly 1675 Broadway 30th Fl New York NY 10019 *

MORRIS, DESMOND (JOHN) (DESMOND JOHN MORRIS), zoologist, writer, artist; s. Harry Howe Morris and Dorothy Marjorie (Hunt) Fuller; m. Ramona Joy Baulch, July 30, 1952; 1 son, Jason. BSc, Birmingham U., Eng.; DPhil, Oxford U., Eng.; DSc (hon.), Reading U., Eng., 1998. Rsch. worker zoology U. Oxford, Eng., 1954-56; head Granada T.V. and Film Unit, Zool. Soc. London, 1956-59, curator mammals, 1959-67; dir. Inst. Contemporary Arts, London, 1967-68; rsch. fellow Wolfson Coll., Oxford, 1973-81. Author: Biology of Art, 1962, Apes and Monkeys, 1965, Big Cats, 1965, Mammals: A Guide to the Living Species, 1966, The Naked Ape, 1968, The Human Zoo, 1969, Intimate Behavior, 1971, Manwatching: A Field Guide to Human Behavior, 1977, The Soccer Tribe, 1981, The Book of Ages, 1983, The Art of Ancient Cyprus, 1985, Bodywatching: A Field Guide to the Human Species, 1985, The Illustrated Naked Ape, 1986, Catwatching, 1986, Dogwatching, 1986, The Secret Surrealist, 1987, Catlore, 1987, The Animals Roadshow, 1988, The Human Nestbuilders, 1988, Horsewatching, 1988, The Animal Contract, 1990, Animalwatching, 1990, Babywatching, 1991; Christmas Watching, 1992, The World of Animals, 1993, The Human Animal, 1994, Body Talk, A World Guide to Gestures, 1994, The Naked Ape Trilogy, 1994, Illustrated Cat Watching, 1994, Illustrated Babywatching, 1995, Illustrated Dogwatching, 1996, Catworld: A Feline Encyclopedia, 1996, The Human Sexes, 1997, Illustrated Horsewatching, 1998, Cool Cats: The 100 Cat Breeds of the World, 1999, Body Guards, 1999, Dogs: A Dictionary of Dog Breeds, 2001, Peoplewatching, 2002, The Nature of Happiness, 2004, The Naked Woman, 2004, Watching: Encounters With Humans and Other Animals, 2006, others; co-author: (with Ramona Morris) Men and Snakes, 1965, Men and Apes, 1966, Men and Pandas, 1966, The Giant Panda, 1981, Gestures: Their Origins and Distribution, 1979; autobiography Animal Days, 1979, The Naked Eye, 2000; editor: Primate Ethology, 1969, (fiction) Inrock, 1983; contbr. numerous articles to zool. jours.; one-man shows include Mayor Gallery, London, 1997, Pub. Art Gallery, Buxton, 1997, Keitelman Gallery, Brussels, 1998, Rossaert Gallery, Antwerp, 1998, Witteveen Gallery, Amsterdam, 1999, Mus. Modern Art, Ostend, 2002, others. Address: care Jonathan Cape RandomCH 20 Vauxhall Bridge Rd London SWIV 2SA England

MORRIS, DICK, columnist, political consultant; b. NY, Nov. 28, 1948; s. Eugene Morris; m. Eileen McGann. BA in Govt., Columbia U., 1967. Polit. cons. Bill Clinton's Campaign for Gov., Ark., 1977, Ark., 1982, Bill Clinton's Re-Election Campaign for Gov., Ark., 1984, Ark., 1986, Ark., 1990; chief strategist for Argentina Pres. Fernando de la Rua Campaign for Pres., 1999, for Uruguay Pres. Jorge Battle Campaign for Pres., 1999, for Mexican Reformer Vicente Fox's Campaign, 2000; commentator FOX News Channel; weekly columnist New York Post, The Hill Mag., Nat. Post, Canada. Founder Vote.com, 1999; co-founder (with Eileen McGann) Legalvote.com, 2000. Author: Bum Rap on Am. Cities - The Real Causes of Urban Decay, 1977, Behind the Oval Office: Getting Re-Elected Against All Odds, 1998, The New Prince: Machiavelli Updated for the 21st Century, 1999, Vote.com - A Guide to the Internet basted politics of the future, 2000, Power Plays: Win or Lose - How History's Great Polit. Leaders Play the Game, 2003, Off With Their Heads: Traitors, Crooks & Obstructionists in Am. Politics, Media & Bus., 2003; co-author (with Eileen McGann): Because He Could, 2004, Rewriting History, 2004, Condi vs. Hillary: The Next Great Presidential Race, 2005, Outrage, 2007. Achievements include working as polit. cons. for winning campaigns of more than 30 senators or governors. Office: NY Post 1211 Avenue Of The Americas New York NY 10036 *

MORRIS, DONALD, tax specialist; b. Chgo., Oct. 13, 1945; s. Donald Charles and Cathleen (Lautner) M.; children: Keith, Sarah. BA, Calif. State U., LA, 1968; MA, De Paul U., 1972, MS in Taxation, 1987; PhD, So. Ill. U., 1978. CPA Ill., N.Mex.; CFP, cert. fraud examiner. Prof. philosophy John A. Logan Coll., Carterville, Ill., 1972-79; tax mgr. Evans-Gries & Co. CPAs, Addison, Ill., 1980-83; sr. tax advisor Alexander Grant, CPA, Chgo., 1983-84; tax mgr. Evans & Co., Itasca, Ill., 1984-87; pvt. practice Addison, 1987—88, Bloomingdale, 1988—93, Roselle, Ill., 1993—97; prof. acctg. E. N.Mex. U., Portales, 1997—2006, chmn. Dept. Acctg., Fin. and CIS; prof. acctg. U. Ill., Springfield, 2006—. Author: Dewey and the Behavioristic Context of Ethics, 1995, Opportunity: Optimizing Life's Chances, 2006; co-author: Accounting Desk Book, 2006, 2d edit., 2007. Libertarian candidate for comptroller State of Ill., 1986. Mem. AICPA, N.Mex. Soc. CPAs, Ill. CPA Soc., Am. Philos. Assn., Am. Acctg. Assn., Assn. Cert. Fraud Examiners, Soc. for Bus. Ethics, Assn. Informal Logic and Critical Thinking, Delta Mu Delta. Avocations: distance running (4 marathons), tennis, woodworking. Home: 1516 Saltcedar Ct Springfield IL 62712 Office: U Ill at Springfield Dept Accountancy UHB 4088 4900 Shephard Rd Springfield IL 62703 Business E-Mail: dmorr2@uis.edu.

MORRIS, DONALD GEORGE, engineering company executive; s. Donald and Betty (Lewis) Morris; m. Anita M. Janicek; children: Suzanne, Mary Ellen, Catherine, Donald III. BSBA, North Ga. Coll. and State U., 2000, MS in Pub. Adminstrn., 2001. Various to mgr. engr. Goetze Corp. of Am., LaGrange, Ga., 1986—89; plant mgr. Jakes Mfg., Greenwood, Miss., 1989—92; CEO Morris & Assocs., Gainesville, Ga., 1992—. Contbr. articles to profl. jours. Recipient Leadership award, Wall Street Jour., 2000. Mem.: Fabricators and Mfrs. Assn., Soc. Die Cast Engrs. Business E-Mail: dgmorr@consultant.com.

MORRIS, DONNA, library director; m. Kenny Morris; children: Jeff, Matt. BS in Edn., U. Ctrl. Okla., Edmond, 1971; MLS, U. Okla., Norman, 1977. Positions including clk. Belle Isle libr., dep. dir. pub. svcs., asst. chief ext. svcs., regional br. mgr., br. mgr., reference and children's libr. Met. Libr. Sys., Okla., 1969—2000, dep. dir. support svcs., 2000—02, interim exec. dir., 2000, 2002, exec. dir., 2002—. Pres. Okla. Libr. Assn., ALA councilor, legis. chair, prog. chair, local arrangements co-chair, awards chair, nominating com. chair; non-voting sec. Met. Libr. Sys. Commn. Mem. Leadership Okla. City, Greater Okla. C. of C., Okla. C. of C., McFarlin Meth. Ch. Mem.: ALA, Okla. Libr. Assn. (legis. com. co-chair 1988—89, prog. com. chair 1988—89, awards com. chair 1995—96, legis. com. co-chair 1996—98, v.p./pres.-elect 1998—99, pres. 1999—2000, ALA chpt. councilor 2004—06, chair pub. libr. divsn., local arrangements com. co-chair), Urban Librs. Coun., Pub. Libr. Assn. (mem. bylaws and constn. com., mem. workload measures com., mem. met. librs. com.), Downtown Okla. City Rotary Club (chair roster com. 2004—05). Avocations: scuba diving, swimming, boating, skiing, puzzles. Office: Met Libr Sys 10 S Boulevard Edmond OK 73034 Office Phone: 405-606-3720. E-mail: dmorris@metrolibrary.org.

MORRIS, DONNA JONES, library director; Dir. Ark. Valley Regional Libr. Svc. Sys., Pueblo, Colo., 1985—2004; state libr., dir. Utah State Libr., Salt Lake City, 2004—. Former pres. Colo. Assn. Librs. Named Colo. Libr. of Yr., 1992; recipient Francis Keppel award, 2005. Mem.: ALA (Nat. Advocacy Honor Roll 2000), Utah Libr. Assn., Chief Officers of State Libr. Agencies, Western Coun. State Librs., Utah Academic Libr. Consortium, Mountain Plains Libr. Assn. (Disting. award 2005). Office: Utah State Libr 250 N 1950 W Ste A Salt Lake City UT 84116-7901 Office Phone: 801-715-6770. Office Fax: 801-715-6767. E-mail: dmorris@utah.gov. *

MORRIS, DOUG (DOUGLAS PETER MORRIS), recording industry executive; b. Far Rockaway, NY, Nov. 23, 1938; s. Walter and Mary (Lerner) Morris; m. Monique Jequel, Mar. 20, 1964; children: Walter, Peter. BA, Columbia Coll., 1960. Gen. mgr. Robert Mellin, Inc., NYC, 1964—65; writer. producer Laurie Records, Inc., NYC, 1965—69, v.p., gen. mgr.; owner Big Tree Records (acquired by Atlantic Records), NYC, 1970—78; pres. ATCO Records, Swan Song and Rolling Stones Records (subs. of Warner Music), 1978, Atlantic Records, NYC, 1980—90; co-chmn., co-CEO Atlantic Recording Group, NYC, 1990—94; chmn., COO, pres. Warner Music-U.S., 1994—95; chmn., CEO Universal Music Group (formerly MCA Music Ent.), NYC, 1995—. Cons. Ampex Records, 1968; bd. dirs. CBS Corp., 2007—. Composer: (songs) Sweet Talkin Guys, 1968, Smoking in the Boys' Room, 1970; prodr.: (song) Wave on Wave, 2003. Served in US Army, 1962—64. Named Man of Yr. in Record Industry, United Jewish Appeal, 1981; named one of 25 Most Influential People in Web Music, Powergeek 25, 2007; scholar, Paragon Oil, 1954, Columbia Coll., 1960. Mem.: ASCAP. Office: Universal Music Group 1755 Broadway Fl 7 New York NY 10019-3743 *

MORRIS, EDWARD WILLIAM, JR., lawyer; b. Medford, Oreg., Apr. 12, 1943; s. Edward William and Julia Loretta (Sullivan) M.; m. Margaret Ellen McKenna, 1976; children: John McKenna, Elizabeth Anne. BS, Fordham Coll., 1965, JD, 1971. Bar: NY 1973. Dir. Drug Products Co., Inc., Union City, N.J., 1968-71; asst. arbitration dir. N.Y. Stock Exch., NYC, 1971-73, arbitration dir., 1973-74, asst. sec., arbitration dir., 1974-89, v.p. arbitration, 1989-91, chief hearing officer, 1991—2003, alt. hearing officer, 2006. Served to sgt. U.S. Army, 1965-68, Vietnam. Mem. ABA (alternate hearing officer 2006—), Am. Arbitration Assn. (comml. law com. 1983—), N.Y. County Lawyers Assn. (sec. com. on arbitration 1983—), High Mountain Golf Club. Home: 67 Arlton Ave Allendale NJ 07401-1331 Personal E-mail: emorrisesq@yahoo.com.

MORRIS, ERROL M., filmmaker; b. Hewlett, NY, Feb. 5, 1948; s. Abner and Cinnabelle (Burzinsky) M.; m. Julia Bynum Sheehan; 1 child, Nathaniel Hamilton. BA, U. Wis., 1969; postgrad., Princeton U., 1970-71, U. Calif., Berkeley, 1972-76. Pres. Fourth Floor Prodns., Inc., Cambridge, Mass. Dir., prodr.: Gates of Heaven, 1978, A Brief History of Time, 1992, Fast, Cheap and Out of Control, 1997, Mr. Death: The Rise and Fall of Fred Leuchter, Jr., 1999, First Person (TV series), 2000, The Fog of War: Eleven Lessons from the Life of Robert S. McNamara, 2003; dir. only: The Thin Blue Line, 1988, The Dark Wind, 1991; actor: Hotel New York, 1984. Guggenheim fellow, 1990, MacArthur fellow, 1990-94. Fellow Am. Acad. Arts & Scis. Office: Fourth Floor Prodns 678 Massachusetts Ave Cambridge MA 02139-3355 *

MORRIS, G. MICHAEL, science educator; BS in Engring. Physics with spl. distinction, U. Okla., 1975; MS in Elec. Engring., Calif. Inst. Tech., 1976, PhD, 1979. Scientist U. Rochester, Inst. of Optics, 1979—82; prof. of optics U. Roch., Inst. of Optics, 1982—2001; adj. prof. of optics U. Rochester, Inst. of Optics, 2001—; co-founder Rochester Photonics Corp. (RPC), 1989—. CEO Apollo Optical Systems LLC, Rochester Photonics Corp., 1989—. Recipient Rochester C. of C. Civic award for sci. and tech., 1997. Fellow: Optical Soc. of Am. (pres. 2003); mem.: Optical Soc. of Am., Rochester Sect. (hon.). Office: Optical Society of America 8SCR Lane Victor NY 14564

MORRIS, G. RONALD, automotive executive; b. East St. Louis, Ill., Aug. 30, 1936; s. George H. and Mildred C. M.; m. Margaret Heino, June 20, 1959; children: David, Michele, James. BS in Metall. Engring, U. Ill., 1959. Metall. engr. Delco-Remy divsn. Gen. Motors Corp., 1959-60; factory metallurgist Dubuque Tractor Works, John Deere Co., Iowa, 1960-66; with Fed.-Mogul Corp., 1966-79, v.p., group mgr. ball and roller bearing group, 1979; pres. Tenneco Automotive divsn. Tenneco, Inc., Deerfield, Ill., 1979-82; pres., CEO PT Components, Inc., Indpls., 1982-88; vice-chmn. Rexnord Corp., Indpls., 1988-89; chmn., pres., CEO CTP Holdings Inc., 1986-88; chmn. Integrated Technologies, Inc., Indpls., 1990-92, also bd. dirs.; pres., CEO Western Industries, Inc., Milw., 1991-99. Bd. dirs. NN, Inc., Erwin, Tenn., Prism Capital Inc. Mem. Pres.'s Coun., U. Ill., mem. sr. adv. bd. Sch. Materials Sci. and Engring, U. Ill.; mem. U. Ill. Found. Mem. ASM, SAE, U. Ill. Alumni Assn. (bd. dirs.), The Landings Club (Savannah, Ga.), Masons, Scottish Rite, Kiwanis Internat. Republican. Presbyterian. E-mail: savannahronm@yahoo.com.

MORRIS, GERALD MICHAEL, lawyer, educator; b. Endicott, NY, July 17, 1951; s. John Philip and Rita Cathrine Morris; m. Lynn Carol (Baker), Apr. 12, 1980; children: David, Kathrine, Mary. BA in History, LeMoyne Coll., 1973; JD with honors, Nova So. Ea. U. Law Ctr., 1977; LLM, U. Houston Law Ctr., 2002. Cert.: Fla. Bar (health law) 1995, bar: Fla. 1977, US Dist. Ct. (so. dist.) Fla. 1977, US Dist. Ct. (mid. dist.) Fla. 1983, US Ct. Appeals (5th cir.) Fla. 1981, US Ct. Appeals (11th cir.) Fla. 1981, US Supreme Ct. 1981. Law clk. Saunders, Curtis, Ginestra & Gore, Ft. Lauderdale, Fla., 1975—77, assoc., 1977—82, ptnr., 1982—86; sr. assoc. Finley, Kumble, Wagner, Heine, Underberg, Manley, Myerson & Casey and successor firm Tew, Jordon & Schulte, 1986—88, Heinrich, Gordon, Batchelder, Hargrove, Weihe & James, 1989, ptnr., 1990—92; gen. coun. Holy Cross Hosp., Inc., 1992—. Mem. Fla. Bar Young Lawyers, 1977—88, bd. governors rep., 1984—87; mem. Fla. Bar Health Law Com., 1983—87, Fla. Bar Health Law Sect., 1989—; grievance com. mem. Fla. Bar 17th cir., 1987—90, grievance chmn., 1990; mem. bd. govenors Shepard Broad Law Ctr. Nova So. Ea. U., 1990—, adj. prof., 1992—; spkr. various seminars, 1989—. Bd. dirs. Boys and Girls Club Broward County, 1987—2001; mem. FDA Instl. Review Bd., Holy Cross Hosp., Fla., 1986—92; profit magazine editl. bd. mem. Greater Ft. Lauderdale C. of C., Fla., 1987—88, selection com. mem. Youth Leadership Broward, 1988—90, mem., 1988—92, chmn. legis. action sub-com., 1989—91, co-chmn. A1A Beach Redevel. Task Force, 1990, chmn., 1991, vice-chair com. affairs, 1992, exec. com. mem., 1992—93, chmn. Health Care Com., 1992—94, bd. govs., 1992—94; lector, extraordinary min. St. David Catholic Ch., Davie, Fla., 1974—2001. Nominee Alumus of Yr., NSU, 2006; recipient Vision Broward award, Greater Ft. Lauderdale C. of C., 1990. Mem.: Bioethics & Health Law Consortium of South Fla., Am. Soc. Law Medicine and Ethics, Am. Health Lawyers Assn., Broward County Bar Assn. (Young Lawyers Sect.) (exec. com. 1983—88, sec., treas. 1985—86, pres.-elect 1986—87, pres. 1987—88), Broward County Bar Assn. (law day com. 1985—88, chmn. 1986—87, exec. com. 1986—88, legal/medical com. 1997—99, President's award 1987), Phi Alpha Delta (legal frat.) (chpt. vice justice 1976—77). Office: Holy Cross Hosp Inc Legal Affairs Dept 4725 N Fed Hwy Fort Lauderdale FL 33308 Office Phone: 954-229-8500. Office Fax: 954-351-4730. Business E-Mail: gerald.morris@holy-cross.com.

MORRIS, GORDON JAMES, financial company executive, consultant; b. Mt. Vernon, Ohio, Oct. 6, 1942; s. R. Hugh and Betty Jane (Roberts) M.; m. Janet Ann Swanson, Aug. 28, 1965 (div. 1971); m. Nancy Joan Meyfarth, July 26, 1975 (div. Oct. 1998); 1 child, Lawrence Hugh; m. Phyllis J. Hersha, Jan. 1, 2000. Student, Ohio State U., 1960-61; BA, Otterbein Coll., 1966; postgrad. in law, Capital U., Bexley, Ohio, 1967-68; postgrad., Coll. Fin. Planning, Denver, 1983-90, Inst. Cert. Fund Specialists, 1991. Registered investment advisor; cert. fin. planner; cert. fund specialist; lic. loving trust advisor; cert. divorce planner; life lic., Fla., 1974—; security lic. NASD, 1976—; real estate lic., Fla., 1986—. Asst. to pres. Jaeger Machine Co., Columbus, Ohio, 1968-73; rep. Equitable Fin. Svcs., Sarasota, Fla., 1974-81; pres. Beacon Wealth Mgmt. (formerly Morris & Assocs., P.A.), Sarasota, 1981—; co-gen. ptnr. Beacon Bridge Loan Pool, Ltd., 1994-97. Chmn. bd. dirs. MAP Fin. Group, Inc., Sarasota, 1985-89; co-owner U.S.I.S.L. West Fla. Fury Soccer Team, 1996-98; bd. dirs., v.p. Soccer Resource Group, Sarasota, 1997-99, Radyx Capital Ptnr., Tampa, 1999-2003, seminar lectr. High Mark Ins. Svcs., Inc., Beacon Wealth Mgmt., 2003—. Past columnist The Creative News. Past chmn. West Coast chpt. March of Dimes, Bradenton, Fla., bd. dirs., 1986-88; v.p. All Sch. Kids, Inc., 1998-99; pres. Epilepsy Found. S.W. Fla., Inc., 1986-87. Mem. Inst. Cert. Fin. Planners, Million Dollar Roundtable, Sertoma (pres. local club 1979-80). Republican. Methodist. Home and Office: 3822 Countryside Ln Sarasota FL 34233-2122 Personal E-mail: striker.five@comcast.net. Business E-Mail: beaconl@sigmarep.com.

MORRIS, GRANT HAROLD, law educator; b. Syracuse, NY, Dec. 10, 1940; s. Benjamin and Caroline Grace (Judelson) Morris; m. Phyllis Silberstein, July 4, 1967; children: Joshua, Sara. AB, Syracuse U., 1962, JD, 1964; LLM, Harvard U., 1971. Bar: N.Y. 1964. Atty. NY Mental Hygiene Law Recodification Project, Inst. Public Adminstrn., NYC, 1964-66; from asst. prof. to assoc. prof. Wayne State U. Law Sch., 1967—70, prof., 1970-73, dean acad. affairs, 1971-73; prof. U. San Diego Law Sch., 1973—, univ. prof., 1996-97, 2007—, acting dean, 1977-78, 88-89, assoc. dean grad. legal edn., 1978-81, interim dean, 1997-98; prof. law in psychiatry Wayne State U. Med. Sch., 1970-73; adj. prof. U. Calif. -San Diego Med. Sch., 1974-84; clin. prof. dept. psychiatry U. Calif. Med. Sch., San Diego, 1984—. Legal counsel Mich. Legis. Com. to Revise Mental Health Statutes, 1970-73; organizer law and psychiatry sect. Assn. Am. Law Schs., 1973, chmn., 1973-74; patients advocate, San Diego County, 1977-78; cons. Criminal Code Commn., Ariz. Legis., 1974; reporter task force on guidelines governing roles of mental health profls. in criminal process Am. Bar Assn. standing com. on assn. standards for criminal justice, 1981-84; cert. rev. hearing officer San Diego Superior Ct., 1984-90, ct. commr./judge pro tem, 1990-92, mental health hearing officer, 1992-97; hearing officer San Diego Housing Commn., 1988-92; mem. exec. com. sect. law and mental disability Assn. Am. Law Schs., 1990-97. Author: The Insanity Defense: A Blueprint for Legislative Reform, 1975, Refusing the Right to Refuse: Coerced Treatment of Mentally Disordered Persons, 2006; co-author: Mental Disorder in the Criminal Process: Stan Stress and the Vietnam/Sports Conspiracy, 1993; editor, contbr.: The Mentally Ill and the Right to Treatment, 1970. Mem. Atascadero State Hosp. adv. bd., 2000-07, chair, 2003-07. Mem. Phi Alpha Delta (faculty adv. 1970-73, 75-92). Office: U San Diego Law Sch 5998 Alcala Park San Diego CA 92110-2492 Office Phone: 619-260-2321. Business E-Mail: gmorris@sandiego.edu.

MORRIS, HENRY MADISON, III, minister, writer, speech professional, consultant; b. El Paso, Tex., May 15, 1942; s. Henry Madison and Mry Louis (Beach) M.; m. Janet Deckman, July 25, 1965; children: Henry M., Scotta Marie. BA summa cum laude, Christian Heritage Coll., 1976; MDiv, Luther Rice Sem., 1977; DMin, 1978; MBA, Pepperdine U., 1989. Ordained to ministry Bapt. Ch., 1968. Regional mgr. Integon Ins. Co., Greenville, SC, 1969-75; pastor Hallmark Bapt. Ch., Greenville, SC, 1969-75; assoc. prof. Bible Christian Heritage Coll., El Cajon, Calif., 1977-78; adminstrv. v.p., 1978-80; pastor First Bapt. Ch., Canoga Park, Calif., 1980-86; chief adminstrv. officer, CFO SunGard Fin. Sys. Inc., Canoga Park, 1986-94; v.p. sales and mktg., 1994-96; adminstrv. pastor Ch. at Rocky Peak, Chatsworth, Calif., 1996-99; regional sales mgr. SunGard Ins. Sys., 2000—06; exec. v.p. Inst. for Creation Rsch., Santee, Calif., 2002—07, CEO, 2007—. Cons. World Pubs., 1995; commr. Transitional Assn. Christian Colls. and Schs., 2003—; lectr. in field. Author: Baptism: What is It?, 1977, Explore the Word, 1978, Churches: History and Doctrine, 1980, After Eden, 2003; co-author: Many Infallible Proofs, 1996, Sampling the Psalms, 1999; contbg. editor: The Defenders Bible, 1995. Served with U.S. Army, 1959-66. Republican. Office: Inst for Creation Rsch 10996 Woodside Ave N Santee CA 92091 Office Phone: 214-615-8300. Business E-Mail: hmorrisiii@icr.org.

MORRIS, JACK AUSTIN, JR., art gallery executive; b. Macon, Ga., Sept. 29, 1939; s. Jack Austin and Mattie Wise (Elliott) M. AB in Fine Arts, U. S.C., 1962; cert. in arts adminstrn., Harvard U., 1970. Trainee Columbia (S.C.) Mus. Art, 1962-63, lectr., 1963-64, asst. to dir., 1964-65; exec. dir. Greenville County (S.C.) Mus. Art, 1965-80, Period Gallery West, Scottsdale, Ariz., 1980-81; pres. Morris Fine Arts, 1981-83; dir. Connally/Altermann Art Gallery, Houston, 1983—. Art cons., 1975—; pres. Concept II, Inc., Greenville, S.C., 1969-77; instr. art Richland Art Sch., Columbia, 1962-65; lectr. Mus. Sch. Art, Greenville, 1965-80; pres. Ind. So. Films, Inc., 1976-80; v.p. Synectics Corp., 1977-80; organizer numerous major exhbns. Chmn. Liberty Life scholastic art award, 1967; chmn. S.C. Arts Commn.; mem. S.C. Com. for Humanities; pres. Met. Arts Council. Author: Contemporary Artists of South Carolina, 1970, William M. Halsey: Retrospective, 1972. Bd. dirs. Greenville Symphony, Greenville Civic Choral. Named Young Man of Yr. Greenville 1973. Mem. S.E. Mus. Conf., Am. Assn. Mus., S.C. Craftsman's Council (exec. bd. 1965—), Guild S.C. Artists (pres. 1968), S.C. Fedn. Mus. (founder 1970, pres. 1973) Clubs: Poinsett (dir.). Lodges: Rotary.

MORRIS, JAMES CARL, architect; b. Richmond, Va., Sept. 2, 1930; s. James Carl and Florence Virginia (Hey) M.; m. Frances Parrott Wooten, June 9, 1952; children: James Carl Jr., David Palmer. Student, N.C. State U., 1948—50; BS in Bldg. Constrn., Va. Polytechnic Inst., Blacksburg, 1952. Cert. Nat. Coun. Archtl. Registration Bds. Archtl. draftsman Va. Electric & Power Co., Richmond, Va., 1955-56, Marcellus, Wright & Son, Richmond, 1956-57; architect C.W. Huff, Jr., Richmond, 1957; ptnr. to prin./owner Huff-Morris Architects, Richmond, 1966—2006, cons., 2006—. Ptnr. JCM Partnership, Chesterfield, 1988—; cons. to Huff-Morris Arch. PC, 2006-. Contbr. articles to profl. jours. Bd. dirs. Chesterfield Preservation Commn.; deacon Branch's Ch., Richmond, 1986-90; chmn. Va. Bapt. Extension Bd., Richmond, 1991-2001, 2004-; mem. 250th anniversary com. Chesterfield County, 1999. With U.S. Army, 1953-54. Recipient award of Merit S.S. Bd. of So. Bapt., Nashville, Excellence in Masonry Design award Va. Masonry Coun., Richmond. Mem. AIA (past pres. Richmond chpt.), Commonwealth Club of Va. Avocations: woodworking, fishing, hunting. Office: Huff-Morris Arch PC 400 E Grace St Richmond VA 23219-2102 Home: 5907 Village Lake Ct Richmond VA 23234-6945 Office Phone: 804-343-1505. Business E-Mail: architecture@huffmorris.com.

MORRIS, JAMES MALACHY, lawyer; b. Champaign, Ill., June 5, 1952; s. Walter Michael and Ellen Frances (Solon) M.; m. Mary Delilah Baker, Oct. 17, 1987; children: James Malachy Jr., Elliot Rice Baker, Walter Michael, Nicholas Aidan. Student, Oxford U., Eng., 1972; BA, Brown U., 1974; JD, U. Pa., 1977. Bar: NY 1978, US Dist. Ct. (so. and ea. dists.) NY 1978, Ill. 1980, US Tax Ct. 1982, US Supreme Ct. 1983; admitted to Barristers Chambers, Manchester, Eng., 1987. Assoc. Reid & Priest, NYC, 1977-80; sr. law clk. Supreme Ct. Ill., Springfield, 1980-81;

assoc. Carter, Ledyard & Milburn, NYC, 1981-83; sole practice NYC, 1983-87; counsel FCA, Washington, 1987—; acting sec., gen. counsel FCS Ins. Corp., McLean, Va., 1990-98, exec. asst., bd. chmn., 2005—06, gen counsel, 2006—. Cons. Internat. Awards Found., Zurich, 1981—2002, Pritzker Architecture Prize Found., NYC, 1981—2002, Herbert Oppenheimer, Nathan & VanDyck, London, 1985—2004. Contbr. articles to profl. jours. Mem. ABA, Ill. Bar Assn., NY State Bar Assn., NY County Lawyers Assn., Assn. Bar City NY, Brit. Inst. Internat. and Comparative Law, Am. Inst. Parliamentarians, Lansdowne Club (London), Penn Club (NYC), Casanova (Va.) Hunt Club. Office: PO Box 1407 Mc Lean VA 22101-1407

MORRIS, JAMES T., insurance company executive; BA, UCLA, 1982. Asst. actuary, spl. mktg. Pacific Life Ins. Co., Newport Beach, Calif., 1982—86, asst. v.p. product rsch. & develop., 1986—87, 2d v.p. product design & develop., 1987—90, v.p. product design, 1990—93, v.p. m-ops., 1993—96, sr. v.p. m-ops., 1996—2002, exec. v.p. life ins. div., 2002—05, exec. v.p. chief ins. officer, 2005—06, COO, 2006—07, pres., CEO, 2007—. Fellow: Soc. Actuaries; mem.: Am. Acad. Actuaries, LA Actuarial Club. Office: Pacific Life Ins Co 700 Newport Ctr Dr Newport Beach CA 92658-9030 *

MORRIS, JAMES THOMAS, former international organization official; b. Terre Haute, Ind., Apr. 18, 1943; s. Howard James and Kathlyne (Eastes) M.; m. Jacqueline Harrell, Apr. 2, 1965; children: John Timothy, Jeffrey Todd, Jennifer Lynn. BA in Polit. sci., Ind. U., 1965; MBA, Butler U., 1970; DBA (hon.), Vincennes U., 1978, Butler U., 1982, Ind. State U., 1985, U. So. Ind., 1987, Franklin Coll., 1987, Rose-Hulman Inst. Tech., 1990, Martin U., 1992. Trainee Am. Fletcher Nat. Bank, Indpls., 1966-67; adminstrv. asst., chief of staff Mayor Richard G. Lugar, Indpls., 1967-73; v.p. Lilly Endowment, Inc., Indpls., 1973-84, pres., 1984-89, Indpls. Water Co. and IWC Resources, 1989—2002; exec. dir. World Food Programme UN, Rome, 2002—06. Mem. U.S. del. NATO Com. on Challenges of Modern Soc., 1970-71; bd. dir., Am. Red Cross (treas. and chmn. audit and ethics com.); mem., US Olympics Com. Chmn. bd. trustees Marion County Health and Hosp. Corp., 1976-83; chmn., trustee Ind. State U., 1971-79; bd. dirs. Indpls. Conv. and Visitors Assn., United Way of Greater Indpls., 1980—, Goodwill Industries Ind., Greater Indpls. Progress com., YMCA of Greater Indpls., Boy Scouts Am.; mem. exec. bd. U.S. Olympic Com., 1985-92; trustee, vice chmn. U.S. Olympic Found., 1987-93, Butler U., Christian Theol. Sem.; mem. U.S. Olympic Oversight Commn., 1988; elder Second Presbyn. Ch.; trustee NCAA Found., 1990, Freedoms Found., 1990; apptd. dir. by Pres. Bush Environ. of The Americas Bd., 1991. Named Outstanding Young Man in Indpls., 1972, one of five Outstanding Young Hoosiers, 1973; recipient Disting. Eagle Scout award, 1985, Disting. Alumni award Butler U., 1986, Disting. Service award Ind. U., 1987, Disting. Alumni Svc. award Ind. U., 1991, Horatio Alger award 1992, Whitney Young award Indpls. Urban League. Mem. Indpls. C. of C. (bd. dirs. 1985-89), Meridian Clubs. Republican.

MORRIS, JAMES WATSON, III, lawyer; s. James Watson Morris Jr. and Annie Florence Browder; m. Jane Carolyn Mallory; children: James Watson IV, Carolyn Morris O'Connor. Student, Va. Mil. Inst., 1951-52, Randolph Macon Coll., 1952-54; LLB, T.C. Williams Sch. of Law, 1957. Bar: Va. 1958, U.S. Dist. Ct. (ea. dist.) Va. 1958, U.S. Dist. Ct. (we. dist.) Va. 1959, U.S. Ct. Appeals (4th cir.) 1959. Assoc. Lehman, Browder & Russell, Richmond, 1958-61; ptnr. Browder, Russell & Morris, Richmond, 1961-63; ptnr., mem. exec. com. Browder, Russell, Little, Morris & Butcher, Richmond, 1964-76; ptnr., mem. exec. com., chmn. Browder, Russell, Morris & Butcher, Richmond, 1977-89; ptnr., chmn. Morris and Morris, P.C., Richmond, 1989—. Spkr. in field. Contbr. articles to profl. publs. Pres., founder Va. Assn. Def. Attys., 1973-76; bd. dirs. Product Liability Adv. Coun., Detroit, 1989-92, Lawyer for Civil Justice, 1989-92, Oliver White Hill Found; trustee Supreme Ct. Hist. Soc., exec. com., 2005—; bd. dirs., v.p. John Marshall Found. 1st lt. JAG USAR, 1957—63. Recipient Excellence in Civil Litigation award Va. Assn. Def. Attys., Hunter W. Martin Professionalism award, 2005; named a Va. Legal Elite; named one of Top 30 Ind. Def. Lawyers in USA, Nat. Law Jour., 1991, Top 10 Super Lawyers Va., 2006, 07, Chambers Leading Lawyers, Best Lawyers in Am. Fellow Am. Coll. Trial Lawyers (regent 1997-01, treas. 2001-03, pres.-elect 2003-04, pres. 2004-05), Am. Bar Found., Trial Attys. Am., Internat. Acad. Trial Lawyers, Va. Law Found.; mem. ABA, Va. State Bar Assn., Va. Bar Assn., Richmond Bar Assn. (pres. 1998-99, Professionalism award), Internat. Assn. Def. Counsel (chmn. civil rights com.), 4th U.S. Cir. Ct. Jud. Conf., Va. Assn. Def. Attys. (pres. 1973-76), Def. Rsch. Inst. (pres. 1988-89, chmn. bd. 1989-90) Democrat. Episcopalian. Avocations: reading, contract bridge. Home: 6130 St Andrews Cir Richmond VA 23226-3209 Office: Morris and Morris PC 1200 Wytestone Plaza PO Box 30 801 E Main St 12th Fl 23219 Richmond VA 23218-0030 Home Phone: 804-285-0473; Office Phone: 804-344-8200. Office Fax: 804-344-8359. Business E-Mail: jmorris@morrismorris.com.

MORRIS, JEFFREY BRANDON, law educator; b. NYC, Jan. 8, 1941; s. Richard B. and Berenice (Robinson) M.; m. Dona Gene Baron, July 9, 1972; children: David Brandon, Deborah Helaine. AB, Princeton U., 1962; JD, Columbia U., 1965, PhD in Polit. Sci., 1972. Bar: N.Y. 1967, U.S. Supreme Ct. 1970, D.C. 1978, U.S. Dist. Ct. D.C. 1978. Lectr., instr., asst. prof. CUNY, NYC, 1968-74; spl. asst. to provost Columbia U., NYC, 1974-76; jud. fellow U.S. Supreme Ct., Washington, 1976-77, rsch. assoc. adminstrv. asst. chief justice, 1977-81; asst. prof. polit. sci. U. Pa., Phila., 1981-88; vis. assoc. prof. Bklyn. Law Sch., NYC, 1988-90; from assoc. prof. to prof. law Touro Law Sch., Huntington, NY, 1990—. Rapporteur Nat. Conf. on Causes Population Dissatisfaction, with Popular Dissatisfaction Adminstrn. of Justice, St. Paul, 1976; cons. bicentennial exhibitions Independence Nat. Hist. Park, 1986. Author: Federal Justice in the Second Circuit, 1988, U.S. District Court Eastern District N.Y., 1965-90, 1992, Making Sure We are True to Our Founders, 1997, Brooklyn Law School: The First Hundred Years, 2001, Calmly to Poise the Scales of Justice, 2001; co-author: A Pocket History of the United States, 9th rev. edit., 1992; editor: Encyclopedia of American History, 1982, 7th edit., 1996; assoc. editor Yearbook, Supreme Ct. Hist. Soc., 1979-83. Mem. Brookings Conf. on Interbr. Rels., Williamsburg, Va., 1980, 81. Jewish. Avocations: opera, dance, theater. Home: 234 Forest Rd Flushing NY 11363-1303 Office: Touro Law Sch 225 Eastview Dr Central Islip NY 11722 Business E-Mail: jeffreym@tourolaw.edu.

MORRIS, JOHN SELWYN, philosopher, educator, retired academic administrator; b. Tonypandy, Wales, July 2, 1925; came to U.S., 1954, naturalized, 1993; s. Jenkin and Hannah M. (Williams) M.; m. Enid Elry Walters, Apr. 10, 1954; 1 child, Paul John. BA, Univ. Coll. South Wales and Monmouthshire, 1951; MA, Cambridge U., Eng., 1953; student, Union Theol. Sem., 1957-60; MA, Colgate U., 1961; PhD, Columbia U., 1961; LL.D. (hon.), Hartwick Coll., 1979; LHD (hon.), Elmyra Coll., 1990; DLitt, Skidmore Coll., 1991. Ordained to ministry Presbyterian Ch., 1954; minister Vernon (N.Y.) and Vernon Center Presbyn. chs., 1954-57; instr. Colgate U., Hamilton, NY, 1960-63, asst. prof., 1963-66, asso. prof., 1966-70, prof. philosophy and religion, 1970-79, dir. div. humanities, 1970-72, dir. div. univ. studies, 1972-73, provost, dean of faculty, 1973-79, acting pres., 1977; prof. philosophy Union Coll., Schenectady, 1979-90, pres., 1979-90; chancellor Union U., 1979—90; pres. emeritus, rsch. prof. philosophy Union Coll., Schenectady, 1990—. Leverhulme vis. fellow U. Exeter, Eng., 1968-69; chmn. Commn. Ind. Colls. and Univs., 1984-86; trustee Cazenovia Coll., N.Y. Trustee Skidmore Coll. With RAF, 1943-47. Recipient Disting. Svc. award Colgate U. Alumni Corp., 1978, Schenectady Patroon award, 1989, Union Coll. Founders Medal, 1990; fellow Cardiff U. Mem. AAUP, Am. Philos. Assn., Am. Acad. Religion, Royal Inst. Philosophy, Soc. for Study Theology, Nat. Welsh Am. Found. (bd. advisors). Office: Union Coll Humanities Ctr Schenectady NY 12308

MORRIS, JOHN WILLIAM, JR., metallurgy educator; b. Birmingham, Ala., June 7, 1943; s. John William and Lillian Lucille (Burnette) M.; m. Pamela Mary Dryer, Dec. 30, 1966 (div. 1978); 1 child, McKinley Lee. BS in Metall. Engring., MIT, 1964, ScD in Materials Sci., 1969. Rsch. scientist Bell Aerospace Co., Buffalo, 1968-70, mgr. materials sci., 1970-71; sr. sci. faculty mem. Lawrence Berkeley Nat. Lab., 1971—; asst. prof. dept. materials sci. and mineral engring. U. Calif., Berkeley, 1971-74, assoc. prof., 1974-77, Miller rsch. prof., 1976-77, prof. metallurgy, materials sci. and mineral engring., 1977—. Prog. leader structural materials Ctr. Advanced Materials Lawrence Berkeley Lab., 1985—; lectr., chmn. various tech. confs. Author: The Structure and Propeties of Dual Phase Steels, 1979; patentee various steels and alloys; contbr. articles to profl. jours. Disting. exch. scholar Peoples Republic of China, 1985; recipient Materials Rsch. award US Dept. Energy, 1981, Tech. 100 Citation for advancement of tech. in US Tech. Mag., 1981, Disting. Tchg. award U. Calif. Berkeley, 1988. Fellow Am. Soc. Metals (chmn. Golden Gate chpt. 1979-80, edn. com., Bradley Stoughton Tchg. award 1975); mem. NAE, Metall. Soc.- AIME (chmn. chemistry and physics of metals com. 1978-80, chmn. publs. com. 1978-79, heat treatment com., Robert Lansing Hardy gold medal 1972), Am. Phys. Soc., Am. Soc. Engring. Edn. (AT&T Found. award 1989), Internat. Cryogenic Materials Conf. (bd. dirs.), Phi Delta Theta. Republican. Avocation: golf. Office: Dept Materials Sci and Engring U Calif Berkeley 210 Hearst Meml Mining Bldg Rm 228 Berkeley CA 94720 Office Phone: 510-486-6482. Office Fax: 510-643-5792. E-mail: jwmorris@berkeley.edu. *

MORRIS, JOHN WOODLAND, II, retired engineering consultant, military officer; b. Princess Anne, Md., Sept. 10, 1921; s. John Earl and Allice (Cropper) M.; m. Geraldine Moore King, May 12, 1947; children: Susan K., John Woodland III. BS, U.S. Mil. Acad., 1943; MS, U. Iowa, 1948; postgrad., Army War Coll., 1961—62, U. Pitts., 1966. Commd. 2d lt. U.S. Army, 1943, advanced through grades to lt. gen., 1976; dep. dist. engr. Savannah, Ga., 1952-54; resident engr. Goose Bay, Labrador, 1955-57; staff officer Office Chief Engrs., 1957-60; comdg. officer 8th Engr. Bn., Korea, 1960-61; dist. engr. Tulsa, 1962-65; dep. comdt. U.S. Mil. Acad., 1965-67; dep. chief legis. liaison Office Sec. Army, Washington, 1967-69; comdg. gen. 18th Engr. Brigade, Vietnam, 1969-70; div. engr. Missouri River Div., Omaha, 1970-72; dir. civil works Office C.E., Washington, 1972-75; dep. chief engr. U.S. Army, 1975-76, chief engr., 1976-80; ret., 1980; exec. dir. Royal Volker Stevin, 1980-84; pres. J.W. Morris Ltd., 1981—2006; ret., 2006; prof. U. Md., 1983-86; chmn. bd., CEO PRC Engring., 1986-88. Engr. advisor, cons. Zorc, Rissetto, Weaver & Rosen, 1988-92; engr. advisor Seltzer & Rosen, 1992-98; bd. dirs. Air Water Tech., Morganti Constrn. Co., Search Techs. Inc., Thaco Rsch. Inc., Dutra Corp.; mem. adv. bd. AMEC Ltd. Mem. Indian Nations coun. Boy Scouts Am., 1962-65; chmn. Water Resources Congress, 1988-90; trustee U.S. Mil. Acad. Assn. Grads, 1986—; advisor dean engring. and math. U. Vt., 1990-96. Decorated Legion of Merit with three oak leaf clusters, Army D.S.M., Def. D.S.M.; recipient Merit award Am. Cons. Engrs. Council; Palladium medal Audubon Soc.; Excellence award, Constrn. Industry Inst., 1997. Fellow ASCE (Disting. Constructor award 2000); mem. AIA (hon.), Internat. Navigation Congress (v.p.), U.S. Soc. Mil. Engrs. (pres.), Nat. Acad. Engrs. (Founders award 1996), U.S. Com. on Large Dams (past chmn. environ. effect com., named Constrn. Man of Yr. 1977, Navigation Hall of Fame 1990, Golden Beaver award for engring. 1995, Golden Eagle award, 1998, Acad. of Dist. Eng. U. Iowa, 1998, Dist. Grad. of U.S. Mil. Acad., 1998). Episcopalian. E-mail: morrisJ@aol.com.

MORRIS, JUSTIN ROY, food scientist, consultant; b. Nashville, Ark., Feb. 20, 1937; s. Roy Morris; m. Ruby Lee Blackwood, Sept. 5, 1956; children: Linda Lee, Michael Justin. BS, U. Ark., 1957, MS, 1961; PhD, Rutgers U., 1964. Instr. Rutgers U., New Brunswick, NJ, 1964-67; ext. horticulturist U. Ark., Fayetteville, 1964-67, from asst. to assoc. prof., 1967-75, prof., 1975-85, univ. prof., 1985-97, disting. prof., 1997—, dir. Inst. Food Sci. and Engring., Ctr. Food Processing and Engring., 1995—. Cons. viticulture sci. program Fla. A&M U., Tallahassee, 1979—81; cons. viticulture and enology program Grayson City Coll., Denison, Tex., 1987—97; cons. J. M. Smucker Co., 1982—91. Co-author: Small Fruit Crop Management, 1990, Quality and Preservation of Fruits, 1991, Modern Fruit Science Text Book, 1995; contbr. over 400 rsch. articles to sci. jours., chapters to books; assoc. editor: Am. Jour. Enology and Viticulture, 1985. Apptd. by gov. Ark. Wine Prodrs. Coun., 2002—. Named to Ark. Hort. Hall of Fame, 2005; recipient Rsch. award, Nat. Food Processors Assn., 1982, Food Processors 49er Leadership award, 1998, Food Sci. Rsch. award, 1998, award of merit, Am. Wine Soc., 1999, John White Outstanding Team award, 2002, So. Region Grape Rsch. award, 2003, Outstanding Alumnus award, U. Ark. Horticulture Dept., 2003, Disting. Alumni award, U. So. Ark., 2004; Spitze Land grantee, 1997. Fellow: Inst. Food Technologists (co-organizer fruit and vegetable divsn. 1987—), Am. Soc. Hort. Sci. (assoc. editor 1985, Gourley award 1979, Outstanding Rsch. award 1983); mem.: Am. Soc. Enology and Viticultures (chairperson 1996—97, Disting. Achievement award ea. sect. 1995, Nat. Merit award 1996), Food Processors Guard Soc. (life Grape Team Rsch. award 2002, Outstanding Grape and Wine Rsch. award So. Region 2003, Ark. Hort. Hall of Fame 2005), Coun. Agrl. Sci. and Tech. (chmn. nat. concerns 1987—91, bd. dirs. 1987—93, pres.-elect 1993, pres. 1994, 1995), Ozark Food Processers Assn. (exec. v.p. 1988—), Gamma Sigma Delta (pres. 1990—91). Achievements include development of mechanical cane fruit harvester; mechanical strawberry harvester; modified grape harvester for wine grapes; mechanical shoot positioner for grapes; patents for mechanized systems for the production, harvesting, handling and utilization of grapes. Office: U Ark Inst Food Sci and Engring 2650 N Young Ave Fayetteville AR 72704-5690 Office Phone: 479-575-4040. Business E-Mail: jumorris@uark.edu.

MORRIS, LEIGH EDWARD, mayor, retired health facility administrator; b. Hartford City, Ind., Dec. 26, 1934; s. Fredus Orlando and Martha (Malott) M.; m. Marcia Renee Meredith, Oct. 7, 1967; children: Meredith Anne, Curtis Paul. BS in Commerce, Internat. Coll., 1954; BSBA, Ball State U., 1958; M in Health Adminstrn., U. Minn., 1972. Mem. labor relations staff Borg-Warner Corp., Muncie, Ind., 1961-64; various positions then personnel mgr. Internat. Harvester Co., Ft. Wayne, Ind., 1964-70; pres. Huntington (Ind.) Meml. Hosp., 1972-78, La Porte (Ind.) Hosp., 1978-2000; ret.; mayor City of LaPorte. Bd. dirs First of Am. Bank of Ind., Am. Hosp. Svcs., Inc., Health Forum, Inc.; chmn., bd. dirs. Am. Hosp. Pub. Co.; chmn. La Porte Devel. Corp., 1980-81. Chmn. LaPorte chpt. ARC, 1984-86; bd. dirs. John G. Blank Ctr. for the Arts, Lubeznik Ctr. for the Arts, LaPorte County Symphony Orch. With U.S. Army, 1958-60. Recipient Disting. Alumni award Ball State U., Muncie, Ind., 1968, James A. Hamilton award U. Minn., Mpls., 1972, Trustees award Am. Hosp. Assn., 1996. Fellow Am. Coll. Healthcare Adminstrn. (life), Health Care Fin. Mgmt. Assn.; mem. APHA, Am. Hosp. Assn. (trustee, regional chmn. 1985-89), Soc. for Healthcare Planning and Mktg. (bd. dirs.), Soc. Ind. Pioneers (bd. dirs., pres.), Ind. Hosp. Assn. (chmn. 1980-81), La Porte C. of C. (chmn. 1981-82). Republican. Presbyterian. Avocations: classic cars, civic affairs. Home: 424 Lake Shore Dr La Porte IN 46350-2917 Home Phone: 219-362-4998; Office Phone: 219-362-8220. Personal E-mail: lmorris@csinet.net. Business E-Mail: leighmorris@cityoflaporte.com.

MORRIS, LOIS LAWSON, retired education educator; b. Antoine, Ark., Nov. 27, 1914; d. Oscar Moran and Dona Alice (Ward) Lawson; m. William D. Morris, July 2, 1932 (dec.); 1 child, Lavonne Morris Howell (dec.). BA, Henderson U., 1948; specialist degree, U. Ark., 1956, MS, 1951, MA, 1966; postgrad., U. Colo., 1954, Am. U., 1958, U. N.C., 1968. History tchr. Delight H.S., Ark., 1942-47; counselor Huntsville Vocat. Sch., 1947-48; guidance dir. Russellville Pub. Sch. Sys., Ark., 1948-55; asst. prof. edn. U. Ark., Fayetteville, 1955-82; prof. emeritus, 1982—. Ednl. cons. Ark. Pub. Schs., 1965—78. Author: Biographical Essays, 2000; contbr. book reviews and articles to mags. and profl. jours. including Ga. Hist. Quar., 1998, Ark. Biography, 2000. Mem. Hist. Preservation Alliance Ark.; pres. Washington County Hist. Soc., 1983-85, Pope County Hist. Assn.; mem. Ark. Symphony Guild; charter mem. Nat. Mus. in Arts; bd. dirs. Potts Inn Mus. Found. Named Ark. Coll. Tchr. of Yr., 1972; recipient Plaque for Outstanding Svcs. to Washington County Hist. Soc., 1984. Mem. LWV, AAUW, NEA, Washington County Hist., Soc. (exec. bd. 1977-80), Ark. Edn. Assn., Ark. Hist. Assn., Pope County Hist. Assn. (pres. 1991-92), The Ga. Hist. Soc., U. Ark. Alumni Assn., Sierra Club, Nature Conservancy, Ark. River Valley Arts Assn., Phi Delta Kappa, Kappa Delta Pi, Phi Alpha Theta. Democrat. Episcopalian. Address: 1601 W 3d St Russellville AR 72801-4725

MORRIS, M. CATHERINE, electronics executive; B in Fin., Colo. State U., Ft. Collins; grad. Gen. Mgmt. Prog., Harvard Bus. Sch. V.p. fin., corp. contr. Anthem Electronics; with Arrow Electronics, Inc., Melville, NY, 1994, v.p. corp. devel., v.p. fin. and support svcs. Enterprise Computing Solutions, v.p. support svcs. N.Am., sr. v.p., pres. Enterprise Computing Solutions. Office: Arrow Electronics Inc 50 Marcus Dr Melville NY 11747-4210 Office Phone: 631-847-2000. *

MORRIS, MAC GLENN, advertising executive; b. Bessemer City, NC, Jan. 24, 1922; s. Manly T. and Erin C. (Cline) M.; m. Janelle Connevey, July 27, 1946; children— Robert S., Janelle C., Patricia A., John Logan. AB, Davidson Coll., 1942. Space salesman Progressive Farmer mag., NYC, 1946-52; exec. v.p., advt. dir. This Week mag., 1952-68; pres. Newspaper One, NYC, 1968-71; sr. v.p. nat. sales Newspaper Advt. Bur., NYC, 1972-87; proprietor MGM Assocs., Princeton, NJ, 1987—. Bd. dirs. Princeton Bank & Trust Co. divsn. Chem. Bank N.J., N.A., now owned by P.N.C. Bank, N.Y.C. Served to 1st lt., pilot USMCR, World War II. Decorated D.F.C. (2), Air medal (7). Mem. Newcomen Soc. in N. Am., Pi Kappa Phi. Presbyn. (deacon). Club: Springdale Golf (Princeton, N.J.) (bd. govs.). Home and Office: 383 Herrontown Rd Princeton NJ 08540 *I am always an optimist at my work, with friends, and with my family.*

MORRIS, MALCOLM STEWART, title company executive, lawyer; b. Houston, May 8, 1946; s. Carloss M.; m. Rebecca Ann Simmons, June 14, 1969; children: Matthew William, Andrew James. BBA, So. Meth. U., 1968; JD, U. Tex., 1970, MBA, 1972. Bar: Tex. 1970. Legis. aid State of Tex., Sen. Charles Wilson, Austin, 1969-70; examiner Stewart Title Austin Inc., 1970-71; analyst Bank of the S.W., Houston, 1973-74; bus. mgr. Richard Hogue Evangelism, Inc., Houston, 1974-75; cons. Morris, Lendais, Hollrah & Snowden, Houston; v.p. ops. Stewart Title Guaranty Co., Houston, 1975-87, sr. exec. v.p., asst. chmn., 1987-91, pres., CEO, 1991—; chmn. Stewart Title Co.; chmn., co-CEO Stewart Info. Services Corp., Houston, 2000—. Mem. bd. Stewart Title Ins. Co., N.Y.C., Stewart Title Ins. Co. U.K.; past pres. Tex. Land Title Assn., Am. Land Title Assn. Past chmn. Deacons, 1st Bapt. Ch., Houston; past chmn. Living Water Internat.; chmn. Millennium Water Alliance. Fellow Am. Bar Found., Houston Bar Assn.; mem. ABA, State Bar Tex., Houston Bar Assn., Phi Delta Phi. Baptist. Office: 1980 Post Oak Blvd Ste 800 Houston TX 77056-3826 also: Stewart Info Services Corp 1980 Post Oak Blvd Houston TX 77056 *

MORRIS, MARK WILLIAM, choreographer; b. Seattle, Aug. 29, 1956; s. William and Maxine (Crittenden) Morris. Studied with, Verla Flowers and Perry Brunson; D (hon.), Boston Conservatory of Music, Juilliard Sch., L.I. U., Pratt Inst., Bowdoin Coll. Artistic dir. Mark Morris Dance Group, NYC, 1980—, Théâtre Royal de la Monnaie, Brussels, 1988—91; co-founder White Oak Dance Project, 1990; owner Mark Morris Dance Ctr., Bklyn., 2001—. Performed with Lar Lubovitch Dance Co., Hannah Kahn Dance Co., Laura Dean Dancers and Musicians, Eliot Feld Ballet, Koleda Balkan Dance Ensemble. Choreographer Esteemed Guests, Joffrey Ballet, 1986, Nixon in China, Houston Grand Opera, 1987, L'Allegro, il Penseroso ed il Moderato, 1988, Drink to Me Only With Thine Eyes, Am. Ballet Theatre, 1988, Orféo et Euridice, Seattle Opera, 1988, Dido and Aeneas, 1989, Ein Herz, Paris Opera Ballet, 1990, The Death of Klinghoffer, Théâtre de la Monnaie, 1991, The Hard Nut, 1991, Great Performances/Dance in Am. The Hard Nut, 1992, Maelstrom, San Francisco Ballet, 1994, The Office, 1994, Lucky Charms, 1994, Pacific, San Francisco Ballet, 1995, Platée, Royal Opera Covent Garden, 1997, Sandpaper Ballet, San Francisco Ballet, 1999, Four Saints in Three Acts, 2000, Sang-Froid, 2000, A Garden, San Francisco Ballet, 2001, Gong, Am. Ballet Theatre, 2001; dir.: Die Fledermaus, 1988, Falling Down Stairs, 1997 (Emmy award, 1997), The Capeman, Kolam, 2002. Recipient Dance and Performance award, 1984, 1990; fellow, Guggenheim Found., 1986, MacArthur Found., 1991. Office: Mark Morris Dance Group 3 Lafayette Ave Brooklyn NY 11217 Office Phone: 718-624-8400. E-mail: info@mmdg.org, barbie@mmdg.org. *

MORRIS, MARY ELIZABETH, pastor; b. Schenectady, NY; d. William and Kathryn Dilkes (Wilkins) Simpson; m. David John Stevens, Sept. 10, 1966 (dec. Dec. 1975); children: Jeffrey David, Wendy Elizabeth; m. Gerald Douglas Morris, Apr. 15, 1977; stepchildren: Laura Louise, Douglas Owen. BS with cert. in phys. therapy, Simmons Coll., 1966; MDiv, Boston U. Theology, 1988. Ordained min. 1993. Pvt. phys. therapist Muscular Dystrophy Assn., Dedham, Mass., 1971—93; vicar Holy Trinity Luth. Ch., North Easton, Mass., 1988—89; interim pastoral asst. Zion Luth. Ch., Plymouth, Mass., 1989—91; interim chaplain Symmes Hosp., Arlington, Mass., 1990—91; phys. therapist South Shore Vis. Nurse Assn, Braintree, Mass., 1991—93; pastor Bethany Luth. Ch., Orange, Mass., 1993—98, St. Mark Evangelical Luth. Ch., Woonsocket, RI, 1999—2007; ret., 2007. Dean R.I. Conf. of New Eng. Synod of Evangelical Luth. Ch. in Am., 2002—05; ecumenical rep. R.I. State Coun. Chs., 2001—07. Mem. Evangelical Luth. Ch. In Am. Home Phone: 401-762-2959; Office Phone: 401-769-8320.

MORRIS, MATTHEW CHRISTIAN, professional baseball player; b. Middletown, NY, Aug. 9, 1974; Attended, Seton Hall Univ. Played Team USA, 1994; pitcher St. Louis Cardinals, 1997—. Named All-Am. Office: St Louis Cardinals 250 Stadium Plz Saint Louis MO 63102

MORRIS, MICHAEL DAVID, chemistry professor; b. NYC, Mar. 27, 1939; s. Melvin M. and Rose (Pollock) M.; m. Leslie Tuttle, June 5, 1961; children: Susannah, David, Rebecca, Ari. BA in Chemistry, Reed Coll., 1960; PhD in Chemistry, Harvard U., 1964. Asst. prof. Pa. State U., University Park, Pa., 1969; assoc. prof. U. Mich., Ann Arbor, 1969-82, prof., 1982—. Assoc. chmn. U. Mich., Ann Arbor, 1992-97. Editor: Spectroscopic and Microscopic Imaging of the Chemical State, 1993; mem. editorial bd. Applied Spectroscopy, 1994— (Gold medal N.Y. sect. 1993), Spectrochim Acta Rev., 1987-92, editor, 1993. Recipient Anachem award Assn. Analytical Chemists, 1997. Mem. Am. Chem. Soc. (award in Spectrochemical Analysis Divsn. Analytical Chemistry 1995), Soc. Applied Spectroscopy (Strock award 1995), Microbeam Analysis Soc. Office: Univ Mich Dept Chemistry Ann Arbor MI 48109 E-mail: mdmorris@umich.edu.

MORRIS, MICHAEL G., electric power industry executive; b. Fremont, Ohio, Nov. 11, 1946; married, Linda Lindstrom, 1970; two children. BS, Ea. Mich. U., MS, 1973; JD cum laude, Detroit Coll. Law, 1981. With environ. dept. Commonwealth Assocs., Jackson, Mich., 1973—76; pres.

ANR Gathering Co.; exec. v.p. mktg., transp. and gas supply ANR Pipeline Co., 1982—87; pres. Colo. Interstate Gas Co., 1987—88; exec. v.p., natural gas & mktg. Consumers Energy subsidiary of CMS Energy Corp., 1988—92, COO, 1992—94, pres., CEO, 1994—97; chmn., pres., CEO Northeast Utilities, Berlin, Conn., 1997—2003; pres., CEO Am. Electric Power Co., Springfield, Mass., 2004—, chmn., 2004—. Past chmn. Conn. Bus. & Industry Assn.; chmn. Edison Electric Inst.; bd. dir. Nuclear Electric Ins. Ltd., Flint Ink Corp., Cincinnati Bell, Hartford Fin. Svc. Group Inc. Exec. com., trustee Inst. Gas Tech.; trustee Ea. Mich. U. Found.; trustee Detroit Coll. Law, Delta Sigma Phi Found.; mem. Olivet Coll. Leadership Adv. Coun.; US Dept. Energy, Electricity Adv. Bd.; Task Force Electricity Infrastructure, Nat. Gov. Assn.; Inst. Nuclear Power Ops.; Bus. Roundtable; Columbus Downtown Devel. Corp.; bd. dirs. Libr. Mich. Found.; bd. regents Ea. Mich. U., 1997—. Recipient Disting. Alumnus award Ea. Mich. U., 1995. Mem. Mich. Bar Assn., Delta Sigma Phi (pres.). Office: Am Electric Power Co 1 Riverside Plz Columbus OH 43215-2372 *

MORRIS, OWEN GLENN, engineering corporation executive; b. Shawnee, Okla., Feb. 3, 1927; s. Vestus and Myrtle (Lindsey) M.; m. Joyce Gast; children: Deborah Moree, Janine Inez. BS in Mech. Engring, U. Okla., 1947, M.Aero. Engring., 1948; postgrad., U. Va., 1952-53, Va. Poly. Inst., 1955-56, Coll. William and Mary, 1957-58. Aero., research scientist NASA, Langley Field, Va., 1948-61, mgr. mission engring. Apollo to mgr. sys. integration space shuttle Houston, 1961—74, mgr. sys. integration space shuttle, 1974—80; pres. Eagle Engring., 1980-86; pres., chief exec. officer Eagle Aerospace, Houston, 1987-90, chmn., chief exec. officer, 1990-93, chmn. bd., 1992—. Served with USNR, 1943-46. Recipient U.S. Medal of Freedom, 1972, NASA Distinguished Service medal, 1973, NASA Exceptional Service medal, 1969, Outstanding Leadership medal NASA, 1979. Asso. fellow Am. Inst. Aeros. and Astronautics; mem. Am. Astronautical Soc., Acad. Model Aeros., Tau Beta Pi, Tau Omega. Presbyterian (elder 1964—). Club: Rotary. Home: 14914 Timberland Ct Houston TX 77062-2922

MORRIS, RICHARD GILBERT, retired medical transcriber; b. San Mateo, Calif., Oct. 28, 1918; s. Thomas Jefferson and Clara (Adams) Morris; m. Nikki Jean Wilson, Jan. 19, 2006. Diploma with honors, San Mateo HS, Calif., 1937; degree in landscape gardening and constrn., San Mateo Coll., Calif., 1990. Chief purser US Mcht. Marine, San Francisco, 1941—53; teller Bank of Am., San Francisco, 1953—56; med. transcriber typist coroner's office City and County San Francisco, 1956—86, ret., 1986. Musician: Recreational Orch., 1987—. Mem. Dem. Nat. Com., Washington, 1941—2007. Mem.: Peace Action, Citizens Against Govt. Waste, Paralyzed Vets. Am. (hon.), DeYoung Legion Honor Mus. (life), Seniors In Retirement (life), Crestmont Acad. Music (life), ProLiteracy Worldwide (life), The So. Poverty Law Ctr. (life), Planned Parenthood Fedn. Am. (life), Am. Mcht. Marine Vets. (life), Disabled Am. Vets. (life), Nat. Parks Conservation Assn. (life). Democrat. Avocations: music, literature, travel, gardening, bowling. Home: 1305 Maple St San Mateo CA 94402-2918

MORRIS, ROBERT, education educator; b. Akron, Ohio, Nov. 21, 1910; s. Joseph and Katherine (Spielberger) Schmaltz; m. Sara Goldman, Dec. 20, 1940. AB, U. Akron, 1931; MSc, Western Res. U., 1935; DSW, Columbia U. Sch. Social Work, 1959; D of Humane Letters (hon.), Brandeis U., 1984. Prin. welfare officer UNRRA, 1945; regional dir. social services VA, Chgo., 1946-48; social planning cons. Council Jewish Fedns. and Welfare Funds, NYC, 1948-58; prof. social planning Brandeis U., Waltham, Mass., 1959-68, Kirstein prof. social planning, 1968-83, Kirstein prof. social planning emeritus, 1983—. Cardinal Medeiros lectr. U. Mass., Boston, 1983—, lectr. Harvard U. Sch. Pub Health, 1974-88; prof. Inst. Health Professions, Mass. Gen. Hosp., 1980-83, U. Md. cons. adj. prof., 1999—; mem. adv. com. Aging Rsch., U.S. Dept. Health, Edn. and Welfare, 1971, Helen Keller Internat. Found. on the Overseas Blind, 1971-74; mem. spl. med. adv. group VA, Washington, 1969-71; cons. on Geriatric Rsch., Nat. VA, 1974-78, U.S. Office of Human Devel. Svcs., 1978-79; v.p. Vis. Nurses Assn., Boston, 1979-92; mem. Fed. Adv. Coun. on Aging Rsch., Mass. State Health Coord. Coun., 1984-85; vice chmn. Mass. Health Data Consortium, 1979-89; chmn. Internat. Rev. Com. Brookdale Inst. for Gerontology and Adult Human Devel., Israel, 1982-83, cons., 1984-85; chmn. Am. Found. for the Blind Com. on Geriatric Blindness, 1969-74; adv. com. Md. Dept. Health and Mental Health, 1993-95; pub. policy com. Nat. Coun. on the Aging, 1993-95, Ctr. for Health Planning, Program and Devel., U. Md. Baltimore County, 2000-03. Author: Feasible Planning for Social Change, 1966, Urban Planning and Social Policy, 1968, Centrally Planned Change, 1964, Trends and Issues in Jewish Social Welfare in the U.S., 1966, Encyclopedia Social Work and Social Welfare, 1971, Toward a Caring Society, 1974, Centrally Planned Change: A Re-Examination of Theories and Concepts, 1974, Social Policy of the American Welfare State, 1979, 2d edit., 1985, Allocating Resources for the Aged and Disabled, 1981, Rethinking Social Welfare: Why Care for the Stranger, 1986, Retirement Reconsidered, 1988, Economic Roles for the Elderly, 1987, 88, Testing the Limits of Social Welfare; International Perspectives on Policy Changes in Nine Countries, 1988, International Perspectives on State and Family Support for the Elderly, 1993, The National Government and Social Welfare, 1997, Personal Assistance: The Future of Home Care, 1998, Welfare Reform 1996-2000: Is There a Safety Net, 1999, Social Work at the Millenum, 2000; editor Jour. of Social Work, 1960-72, Jour. Aging and Social Policy, 1983—. Cons. NIMH, 1964-70; chmn. adv. bd. Mass. Dept. Welfare, 1968-69; profl. adv. com. Easter Seal Soc., 1971-80; mem. Mass. Gov.'s Commn. on Nursing Homes, 1962-67, on Aging, 1962-67, on Hosp. Costs, 1967, Mass. Soc. Prevention Blindness, 1971-75; organizer Odyssey Forum on Federal Social Policy, 1995—. With AUS, 1943-44. Fulbright award, Italy, 1965-66, 68, Ford Found. fellow U.K., 1969-70; recipient rsch. awards Ford Found., 1960-65, Treuhaft Found., 1964, 72, Max and Anna Levinson Fund, 1970, 72, U.S. Pub. Health Svcs., 1957, 59, 65, NSF, 1975-78, W.K. Kellog Found., 1997, Retirement Rsch. Found., 1998, Louis Lowy award Mass. Gerontology Soc., 1994. Fellow AAAS, APHA, Gerontol. Soc. Am. (Kent award 1988, Maxwell Pollack award 1992, pres. 1966-67), Mass. Pub. Health Assn. (Lemuel Shattuck medal 1976), Ctr. for Applied Gerontology (Heritage award 1987), Commonwealth of Mass. and Assn. for Gerontology in Higher Edn. (Spl. Recognition award 1987), Columbia U. Sch. Social Wor (centennial award for leadership in edn.). Office: Univ Mass Boston MA 02125 Home: 215 Saint Dunstans Rd Baltimore MD 21212-3410 Office Phone: 410-243-5990.

MORRIS, COLONEL ROBERT, songwriter, musician, music educator; b. Memphis, Dec. 12, 1951; s. Ray and Mable Morris; m. Irene Morris, June 11, 1990; 4 stepchildren. Cameo appearance: (Finnish movie) Leningrad Cowboys Go America, 1989; songwriter: (gold) Trucker's Last Ride, 1995, Trucker's Last Ride (German transl.), songwriter: over 600 songs, co-writer with: Rick Christian, Irene Morris, Cliff Hutchison, Joe Berry, Cordell (Rockin' Grandma) Jackson, Eva Jo Hensley, Charlie Louvin, performer with: Charlie Feathers, John The Baptist, Capt'n Blue, Ma Rainey, Little Laura Dukes, Cordell Jackson; musician: (shared show billings with) Billie Jo Spears, Justin Timberlake, David Frizzell, Dale Street, Mike Crews, Nika Vann, (album) Robert Morris Greatest Hits, Trucker's Last Ride And Other Trucking Songs. Named a Col., State of Tenn., 2000; named to, Rockabilly Hall of Fame, 2000, Traditional Country Music Hall of Fame, 2002; recipient Pioneer Lifetime Achievement award, United Music Heritage Inc., 1999, Gov.'s award, Tenn. Gov. Don Sundquist, 1999, Miss. Gov. Don Musgrove, 2000, Key to City of Memphis, Promoter of Large Events award, Tex. River Best of Country Award Show, 2004. Personal E-mail: goldenpen@bellsouth.net.

MORRIS, ROBERT GEMMILL, retired foreign service officer; b. Des Moines, July 20, 1929; s. Robert William and Iva May (Gemmill) M.; m. Beverly Schupfer, July 3, 1955; children: Robert William II, John Schupfer, Richard Edward. BS, Iowa State U., 1951; postgrad., Charles Francis U., Graz, 1951—52; MS, Calif. Inst. Tech., 1954; PhD, Iowa State U., 1957. Asst. prof. S.D. Sch. Mines and Tech., Rapid City, 1958-59, assoc. prof., 1959-62, prof., head dept. physics, 1962-68; phys. sci. officer Office of Naval Research, Washington, 1968-73, dir. electronics program, 1973-74; U.S. fgn. service officer U.S. Dept. State, Washington, 1974-78; counselor for sci. and technol. affairs U.S. Mission to OECD, Paris, 1978-82, U.S. Embassy, Bonn, Fed. Republic Germany, 1982-85; dep. asst. sec. of state for sci. and tech. affairs Washington, 1985-87; fgn. svc. officer U.S. Embassy, Buenos Aires, 1987-90, Madrid, 1990-92. Contbr. articles to profl. jours. Fulbright scholar, Austria, 1951; Swiss govt. fellow, Zurich, 1957. Mem. APS. Personal E-mail: morrash@mind.net.

MORRIS, ROBERT LEE, gallery administrator, jewelry designer; b. Nurnberg, Federal Republic Germany, July 7, 1947; came to US, 1947; s. Jack Bret and Sara Ellen (Holloway) M. BA, Beloit Coll., 1969. Owner, pres. Robert Lee Morris, NYC, 1977—, Artwear, 1977-94. Trustee Beloit (Wis.) Coll., 1989—. Recipient Coty award NYC, 1981, Coun. Fashion Designers Am. award, 1985, M Spl. award Internat. Gold, NYC, 1986, Disting. Svc. award Beloit Coll. Alumni Assn., 1988, Woodmark award, 1992, FAAB award, 1992, Coun. Fashion Designers Am. award, 1994, Geoffrey Beene Lifetime Achievement award, 2007. Office: Robert Lee Morris Co 161 6th Ave Fl 14 New York NY 10013-1205 *

MORRIS, ROBERT LOUIS, management consultant; b. Phila., Aug. 24, 1932; s. Joseph Aloysius and Philomena Mary Ellen (Clauser) M.; m. Elizabeth Marie Smyth, Sept. 10, 1955; children: Robert L., Thomas J., Lawrence F., Elizabeth M., Mary Ellen, Richard B. BS, Drexel U., Phila., 1955; MS, U. Pa., Phila., 1957; postgrad., U. Cin., 1965-66, U. Chgo., 1969-71. Group leader Procter & Gamble Co., Miami Valley Labs., 1958-68; dir. computing svcs. rsch. & devel. divsn. Kraft, Inc., Glenview, Ill., 1968-71; dir. rsch. and process devel. Continental Baking Co., St. Louis and Rye, NY, 1971-77, v.p. tech. affairs, 1978-92; tech. dir. food and chem. products ITT, Inc., NYC, 1977-78; pres. Mng. Tech., Inc., Williamsburg, Va., 1992—, Regu-Tech. Assocs., Inc., Lightfoot, Va., 1997—. Patentee in field. Bd. dirs. Fundacion Chile, Santiago, 1978-79, 83-85; mem. Greenwich Rep. Town Meeting, 1977; bd. dirs. Olde Towne Med. Ctr., Williamsburg, 2000-05, vice chair, 2003-05. With US Army, 1957 NSF fellow, 1955-56, Wilson S. Yerger fellow, 1956-57. Fellow AIChE.; mem. Assn. Rsch. Dirs., Indsl. Rsch. Inst. (bd. dirs. 1988-91), Am. Assn. Cereal Chemists, Ford's Colony Golf Club. Roman Catholic. Office: MTI Group PO Box 6506 Williamsburg VA 23188-6506 Home Phone: 757-258-3845; Office Phone: 757-345-2425. Personal E-mail: rlmatmti@cox.net.

MORRIS, ROY LESLIE, lawyer, electrical engineer, venture capitalist; b. NYC; BE, SUNY, Stony Brook, 1975; EE, SM, MIT, 1978; JD, George Washington U., 1984; MBA, Wharton U., 1995. Bar: D.C. 1984, U.S. Patent Office. Mem. tech. staff Bell Telephone Labs., Holmdel, NJ, 1978-80; sr. staff engr. FCC, Washington, 1981-83; assoc. regulatory counsel MCI Communications, Washington, 1983-87; dep. gen. counsel Allnet Comms., Washington, 1988-95; dir. pub. policy and regulatory affairs Allnet/Frontier Comms., Washington, 1989-96; mng. ptnr. RoyLyn L.L.C., Arlington, Va., 1996—; v.p. govt. affairs and revenue devel. US ONE Comms., McLean, Va., 1996-97; mng. ptnr. Strategic Tech. Investors LLC, Arlington, Va., 1998—; pres. MIT Enterprise Forum, Washington/Balt., 1998—2004. Ednl. counselor MIT; adj. prof. Capitol Coll., Laurel, Md., 1998—; advisor VC, 2002; bd. dirs. MIT Enterprise Forum, Inc. Contbr. Author: Internet Encyclopedia, 2003; contbr. articles to profl. jours. Mem. ABA, IEEE, MIT Enterprise Forum, Sigma Xi, Tau Beta Pi.

MORRIS, SANDRA K., computer company executive; b. Paxtang, Pa., 1954; BS with honors and distinction, U. Del., 1976, MS, 1981; postgrad., U. Pa. Faculty mem. U. Del.; with RCA Corp. David Sarnoff Rsch. Ctr.; product mgr. Intel Corp., 1985, v.p. e-bus. group, 1999—2002; CIO, and V.P. Intel Corp, 2002—. Co-author: Multimedia Application Development Using Indeo video and DVI Technology, 1982. Office: Intel Corp PO Box 58119 2200 Mission College Blvd Santa Clara CA 95052-8119

MORRIS, SARAH, literature and language educator; BA, MA, W.Va. Univ. Substitute tchr. Preston County Schs., W.Va., 2000—01; English tchr. Berkeley Springs (W.Va.) H.S., 2001—. Author: Burying Opal, Nantahala Rev., 2002, My Father Teaches Me to Fish, Gray's Sporting Jour., 2005. Named W.Va. Tchr. of Yr., 2007; recipient Mary Linn Fox First Year Tchr. award, 2002; grantee Japan Fulbright Meml. Fund Tchr. Program, 2006. Office: Berkeley Springs High Sch 149 Concord Ave Berkeley Springs WV 25411 Business E-Mail: srmorris@access.k12.wv.us. *

MORRIS, SHARON, librarian; BA in Mass Communications, Fla. St. U., 1982. Former exhibits and program mgr. Broward Co. Libr., Ft. Lauderdale, Fla., customer svc. coord. Named one of the Movers & Shakers, Libr. Jour., 2007; recipient Nat. Assn. Black Journalists award, Assn. TV Prodr., Execs. award, Applause award for Outstanding Libr. Svcs., Broward Co., 1998. Achievements include being first woman to produce and co-host TV series on WFSU-TV, first to produce and co-host live woman's talkshow for WFSU-TV. Office: Broward Co Library 115 S Andrews Ave Fort Lauderdale FL 33312

MORRIS, STEPHEN BURRITT, marketing information company executive; b. Morristown, NJ, Aug. 13, 1943; s. Grinnell and Cornelia (Kellogg) M.; m. Victoria Ann French, Feb. 18, 1967; children: Christopher Jackson, Robin Taylor BA, Yale U., 1965; MBA, Harvard U., 1969. With product mgmt. Gen. Foods Corp., White Plains, NY, 1969—83, gen. mgr. Maxwell House Coffee div., 1983-85, v.p., 1983-87, pres. Maxwell House div., 1986-87; founder, dir. Spectra Mktg. Systems Inc., Chgo., 1987-90; pres., CEO Vid Code Inc., Waltham, Mass., 1990-92; chmn., pres., CEO Arbitron Inc., NYC, 1992—. Bd. dirs. John B. Stetson Co. Trustee David Parsons Dance Co., 2003. Served to 2d lt. USMCR, 1965-66. Avocations: travel, gardening. Home: 300 Mt Holly Rd Katonah NY 10536-3546 Office: Arbitron Inc 142 W 57th St Fl 12 New York NY 10019-3397

MORRIS, STEPHEN JAY, music educator; b. Angola, Ind., Aug. 23, 1956; s. Jay Allen and Marilyn Jean Morris; m. Lyn Adams, June 19, 1982. MusB, DePauw U., Greencastle, Ind., 1978; MusM, Baylor U., Waco, Tex., 2001. Chmn. dept music St. Francis de Sales H.S., Chgo., 1978—84; organist, choirmaster Spring Woods United Meth. Ch., Houston, 1987—92, Bethany United Meth. Ch., Houston, 1992—94; accompanist, vocal coach Houston Bapt. U., 1994—98, Baylor U., Waco, Tex., 1998—; dir. music ministries Episcopal Ch. of Holy Spirit, Houston, 1999—; vocal instr. Clear Creek Ind. Sch. Dist., Houston, 2000—; lectr. music Baylor U., Waco, Tex., 2004—; pvt. instr. voice, organ Houston. Composer: (hymn tunes) Spring Woods, God's Home, Compassion, and others (Best New Hymn, Hon. Mention, Best New Hymn, Hymn Soc. of U.S. and Can., 1988), works for voice, choir, organ, piano, musician (recitalist) organ recitals in US and Europe (7 tours). Mem.: Nat. Assn. Tchrs. of Singing, Am. Choral Dirs. Assn., Hymn Soc. of US and Can., Organ Hist. Soc., Am. Guild Organists (mem.-at-large, chpt. dean 1985—87), Pi Kappa Lambda. Independent. Episcopalian. Achievements include research in early adolescent female singing voice; performance of complete organ works of Dietrich Buxtehude in 2007. Home: 1422 Big Horn Dr Houston TX 77090-1859 Office: Episcopal Ch of Holy Spirit 12535 Perthshire Rd Houston TX 77024 Home Phone: 713-591-1499; Office Phone: 713-468-7796. Personal E-mail: sjaymorris@yahoo.com.

MORRIS, STEVEN LYNN, engineering consultant, retired military officer; b. Dallas, Dec. 7, 1952; s. William Ira and Alta Faye (McCarley) M.; m. Jacqueline Ann Fenter, July 30, 1977; children: Steven Sean, Michael Wayne. BS in Engring. Scis., USAF Acad., Colorado Springs, Colo., 1975; MS in Aero. Engring, Air Force Inst. Tech., Dayton, Ohio, 1980; PhD in Aerospace Engring., Tex. A&M U., College Station, 1989. Registered profl. engr., Tex., Colo. Commd. 2d lt. USAF, 1975, advanced through grades to lt. col., 1991, ret., 1999; assoc. prof., dep. head dept. aeronautics USAF Acad., Colo., 1989-99; engring. specialist SRS Techs., Colorado Springs, Colo., 1999-2000; sr. cons. Engring. Systems, Inc., 2000—. Named to Outstanding Young Men in Am., 1981. Fellow AIAA (assoc., flight mechanics tech. com. 1991-94, 98-01, mem. applied aerodynamics tech. com. 2003-06, dep. dir. for edn. region V 1992-94, dep. dir. for precoll. outreach region V 1998-02 Sustained Svc. award 2005, Summerfield Book award 2006); mem. USAF Acad. Assn. Grads., Soc. Automotive Engrs. (mem. aircraft icing subcom.), Air Force Assn., Tex. A&M U. Assn. Former Students, Tau Beta Pi, Sigma Gamma Tau. Baptist. Avocations: running, photography, hiking. Home: 5331 Wells Fargo Dr Colorado Springs CO 80918 Office: Engring Systems Inc Ste 106 4775 Centennial Blvd Colorado Springs CO 80919 Office Phone: 719-535-0400. Business E-Mail: slmorris@esi-co.com.

MORRIS, STEVLAND See WONDER, STEVIE

MORRIS, STEWART, JR., title insurance company executive; b. Houston, Oct. 14, 1948; s. Stewart Sr. and Joella (Mitchel) M. BA, Rice U., 1971; MBA, U. Tex., 1973. With Stewart Title Co., 1973—, v.p. Houston, 1975-87, sr. exec. v.p., asst. to pres., 1987-91, chmn., pres., 1991—; advisory dir. Stewart Information Services Corp., 1997—2000, bd. dir., pres., co-CEO, 2000—. Bd. dirs. Southern Nat. Bank, Houston. Bd. dirs. Houston chpt. Cystic Fibrosis Found., 1985—. Mem. Am. Land Title Assn., Am. Driving Soc. (bd. dirs. 1984—), Houston Area Carriage Assn. (pres. 1995—), Carriage Assn. Am. (pres. 1995—). Office: 1980 Post Oak Blvd Ste 800 Houston TX 77056-3826 *

MORRIS, STUART R., lawyer; b. Bklyn. married; 3 children. BA with honors, U. Fla., Gainesville, 1986, MA with honors in Acctg., JD with honors, 1989. CPA Fla., 1989; bar: Fla. 1989, cert.: Fla. Bar Bd. Legal Specialization and Edn. (wills, trusts and estates and elder law). Founding ptnr. Morris Law Grp., Boca Raton, Fla., 1991—. Mem. adv. bd. First United Bank. Mem. profl. adv. com. Am. Friends of Hebrew U.; bd. dirs. SOS Children's Village Fla., Inc., Coconut Creek; bd. dirs., gen. counsel, chmn. endowment com. Temple Beth Am, Margate, Fla. Named Fla. Super Lawyer, Law & Politics, 2007; named one of Top 100 Attys., Worth mag., 2006. Mem.: ABA, Fla. Inst. CPA, Alzheimer's Assn. (S.E. Fla. chpt.). Office: Morris Law Group 7000 W Palmetto Park Rd Ste 205 Boca Raton FL 33433 Office Phone: 561-750-3850. Office Fax: 561-750-4069.

MORRIS, SYLVIA JUNE BURBANK, retired physician; b. Le Roy, Iowa, June 18, 1921; d. Dean Stanley and Myra G. (Douglas) Burbank; m. John Thomas Morris, Jan. 1, 1948 (div.); children: Thomas Dean, Richard Lee, John Douglas. BA in Chemistry, Grinnell Coll., 1942; MD, U. Iowa, 1945; MPH, U. Ala., 1981. Intern Balt. City Hosp., 1945—46; pediat. intern. Johns Hopkins Hosp., 1946—47; pvt. practice Pleasantville, Iowa, 1947—48, Hanceville, Ala., 1949—53; asst. med. dir. Tri-County Health Dept., Decatur, 1972—88, epidemiologist, 1981—88; ret., 1988. Instr. pediat. U. Ala. Sch. Medicine, Birmingham, 1948—49; asst. prof. health policy U. Ala. Sch. Pub. Health, Birmingham, 1983—88; mem. children's policy coun. Juvenile Ct., Cullman, Ala., 1994—. Editor: Jerome-Civil War Letters, 1994; author: Jennifer, 1999, Jennifer Again, 2003, Piggy Flu & Lil' Sam Too: Medical Adventures in Appalacia, 2003, Beth's Song, 2005; editor: Doctoring in Cullman County Before 1900, 1996, Jennifer-A Cat Tale, 2003; contbr. articles to profl. publs. Mem. Cullman County Hist. Soc., Ala. Hist. Assn. Mem.: AMA, Med. Assn. State of Ala. (dist. counselor 1999—2006), Ala. Writer's Conclave, Ala. Hist. Assn., Cullman County Hist. Soc., Symphony Club. Home: PO Box 305 Cullman AL 35056-0305

MORRIS, TAMMY KAY, bank executive; d. George Allan and Harriet Nadine Zumwalt; m. Vincent Carl Morris, Sept. 14, 1985; children: Vincent Keath, Kerry Lashell. Mortgage banker Wells Fargo Home Mortgage, Show Low, Ariz., 1999—2004; banking ctr. mgr. Bank Am., 2004—. Pres., charter mem. Kiwanis Internat., Show Low, 2005—. Recipient Sales & Svc. Excellence award, Bank Am. Pacific SW Divsn., 2005—. Conservative. Evangelical. Avocation: reading. Home Phone: 928-537-4856.

MORRIS, THOMAS BATEMAN, JR., lawyer; b. Columbus, Ohio, Aug. 11, 1936; s. Thomas Bateman and Margaret (O'Shaughnessy) M.; m. Ann Peirce, Feb. 23, 1963; children: Lauren, Thomas III, Richard. AB, Princeton U., 1958; JD, Harvard U., 1962. Bar: Pa. 1962. Sr. ptnr. Dechert LLP, Phila., 1962—2001, chmn., 1990-96. Bd. dirs. Berwind Corp., Phila., AstenJohnson, Inc., Charleston, S.C., Envirite Corp., Plymouth Meeting, Pa., Peirce-Phelps, Inc., Phila., The Contributionship Cos. Co-chmn. Greater Phila. First, 1996-2000; trustee Princeton U., 1975-80; bd. trustees Thomas Jefferson U., 1989—. Hon. Consul King of Belgium, Phila., 1974-89. Mem. ABA, Pa. Bar Assn., Phila. Bar Assn. (chmn. city tax policy com.), Internat. Bar Assn. (chmn. com. on structure and ethics of law practice), Phila. Club, Princeton Club, Sunnybrook Golf Club, Pine Valley Golf Club, NY Athletic Club. E-mail: tmorris@dechert.com.

MORRIS, VICTOR FRANKLIN, JR., retired meteorology educator; b. Hyannis, Mass., Mar. 1, 1947; s. Victor Franklin and Florence Muriel (Rund) M. Student, MIT, 1965-66; BS in Atmospheric Scis., U. Wash., 1969; MS in Meteorology, U. Hawaii, 1975; MA in Environ. Geography, San Diego State U., 1979. Cert. community coll. instr. earth scis., Calif.; cert. advanced and instrument ground instr. FAA. Rsch. asst. U. Hawaii, Honolulu, 1973-75; teaching asst., lectr. San Diego State U., 1976-80; instr. San Diego Community Colls., 1976-80; prof. aero. sci. in meteorology Embry-Riddle Aero. U., Daytona Beach, Fla., 1981-94; pres. Caribbean Weather Svc., Rincon, PR, 1994—2001, ret., 2001. Cons. meteorologist Surfer Publs., Dana Point, Calif., 1980—2001; chief East Coast meteorologist Surf Line, Huntington Beach, Calif., 1987—2001. Author: The Weather Surfer, 1977, Meteorology: A Study Guide, 1985; writer monthly newsletter Sea Watch, 1980—2001; contbr. articles to profl. jours. and mags. Lt. USN, 1970-72. Mem. Am. Meteorol. Soc., Phi Kappa Phi. Avocations: surfing, distance running, gardening, beachcombing, amateur radio. Home: PO Box 384874 Waikoloa HI 96738-4874

MORRIS, WILLIAM CHARLES, investor; b. St. Louis, Apr. 15, 1938; s. Barney Lockhart and Kathryn (Evers) M.; m. Susan VanAvery Follett, Aug. 26, 1961; children: Edward F., David L., Kenneth V. SB in Chem. Engring., MIT, 1960; MBA, Harvard U., 1963. Assoc. Mobil Chem. Co., NYC, 1963-66; with Lehman Bros., NYC, 1967—84; chmn. Carbo Ceramics Inc., Dallas, 1987—, J&W Seligman & Co., Inc., NYC, 1988—. Chmn. Tri-Continental Corp., NYC, 1988—, Seligman Group of Investment Cos., NYC, 1988—. Mng. dir. Met. Opera Assn., NY, 1995—, pres., CEO NY, 2003—; trustee Woods Hole (Mass.) Oceanog. Instn., 2001—. Ensign USCGR, 1961. Office: J & W Seligman & Co Inc 100 Park Ave New York NY 10017-5598 Office Phone: 212-850-1864.

MORRIS, WILLIAM OTIS, JR., lawyer, educator; b. Fairmont, W.Va., Dec. 2, 1922; s. William Otis and Flora Helois (Preston) M.; m. Hazel Irene Kolbus, May 28, 1948; children: Barbara Ann, Melinda Lou. Student, Fairmont State Coll., W.Va., 1940—41; AB, Coll. William and Mary, Williamsburg, Va., 1944; LLB, U. Ill., Champaign/Urbana, 1946; JD, U. Ill., Champaign, 1968; HDC, Nicholas Copernicus U., Torun, Poland, 1992; LLD, Fairmont State U., W.Va., 2003. Bar: Va. 1945, Ill. 1946, U.S. Supreme Ct. 1949. Prof. bus. law U. Ill., 1947-55; assoc. prof. law Stetson U., 1955-58; prof. law W.Va. U., Morgantown, 1958-94, prof. emeritus law, 1994—. Vis. U. Vienna, Austria, Nat. U., Singapore, Nat. U., Seoul, Korea, U. Sydney, Australia, East China Inst. Law and Politics, U. Thessaloniki, Greece; vis. prof. U. Tex., U. Miss., Baylor U., U. San Diego, Samford U., Stetson U., George Washington U., others. Author: Dental Litigation, 1972, 2d edit., 1977, The Law of Domestic Relations in West Virginia, 1975, Veterinarian in Litigation, 1976, Revocation of Professional License, 1985, Handbook of Dental Law, 1994, The Dentist's Legal Advisor, 1994; mem. bd. editors Jour. Law and Ethics in Dentistry, Med. Malpractice Prevention, Clin. Jour.; contbr. articles to profl. jours. With USAR, 1942—43. Decorated Merit medal (Poland); recipient Spl. award Nat. U. Seoul, Old Guard Medallion Coll. William and Mary, 1994, Lifetime Achievement Award Dentistry, 1994. Fellow Cleve. Clinic Med. Inst.; mem. ATLA, Va. Bar, Ill. Bar, W.Va. Trial Lawyers Assn., Order of Coif, Order of White Jackets, Sir Robert Boyle Soc. Republican. Lutheran. Home: 644 Bellaire Dr Morgantown WV 26505-2421 Home Phone: 304-599-2664; Office Phone: 304-599-2664. Personal E-mail: bajrmig@webtv.net, wmillini@aol.com.

MORRIS-BRYANT, EDYE DARLENE, principal; d. W. J. and Carole Morris; m. Chris Bryant; children: Christopher, Daniel, Sydney. BS, NC State U., Raleigh, 1993, MEd, 1999, MS in Adminstrn., 2006. Cert. tchr. Nat. Bd. Tchg. Cert., 2000, lic. prin. 2003. Tchr. West Millbrook Mid. Sch., Raleigh, 1994—99; lead tchr. Wake County Pub. Schs., Raleigh, 1999—2001; instrnl. specialist NC Dept. Pub. Instrn., Raleigh, 2000—01; asst. prin. Carroll Mid. Sch., Raleigh, 2001—06; prin. Centennial Campus Mid. Sch., Raleigh, 2006—. Deaconess Rock Spring United Ch. Christ, Creedmoor, NC, 2006. Recipient Nat. Geog. Literacy award, Nat. Coun. Spl. Studies, 2001. Mem.: ASCD, Nat. Assn. Secondary Prins., NC Coun. Social Studies (pres.-elect 2005—). Office: Centennial Campus Mid Sch 1900 Main Campus Dr Raleigh NC 27606

MORRISEY, MARENA GRANT, art museum administrator; b. Newport News, Va., May 28, 1945; BFA in Interior Design, Va. Commonwealth U., 1967, MA in Art History, 1970. With Orlando (Fla.) Mus. Art, 1970—, exec. dir., 1976—. Former v.p., chmn. mus. svcs. com., mem. ad hoc com. on collections sharing and long range planning com., past chmn. exhbns. and edn. com. Am. Fedn. Arts; former mem. nat. adv. coun. George Washington U. Clearinghouse on Mus. Edn.; former mem. accreditation com. Nat. Found. for Interior Design Edn. Rsch. Former mem. strategic planning adv. coun. Orange County Sch. Dist.; former mem. advt. rev. bd. BBB; former mem. Orlando Pub. Art Adv. Bd., Orlando Leadership Coun., Orlando Hist. Bldg. Commn.; mem. art selection com. Orlando Internat. Airport, former chmn.; former mem. bd. dirs. Sta. WMFE-TV; bd. dirs. New World Sch. of Arts; vol. Sister Cities of Orlando; mem. internat. arts and culture com. Metro Orlando Internat. Affairs Commn.; pub. art review com. Orange County; exec. com. Uptown Dist. Named Orlando's Outstanding Woman of Yr. in Field of Art; recipient Fla. State of Arts award. Mem. Am. Assn. Mus. (former mem. governing bd., accreditation commn., profl. stds. and practices com., internat. coun. of mus.), Assn. Art Mus. Dirs. (comm. and publs. com.), Southeastern Mus. Conf. (past pres.), Fla. Art Mus. Dirs. Assn. (past pres.), Fla. Assn. Mus. (former bd. dirs.), Greater Orlando C. of C. (past mem. steering com. Leadership Orlando), Jr. League Orlando-Winter Park, Rotary Club Orlando (Paul Harris fellow). Office: Orlando Museum of Art 2416 N Mills Ave Orlando FL 32803-1483 Office Phone: 407-896-4231. Business E-Mail: mgmorrisey@omart.org.

MORRISEY, MICHAEL A., health economics educator; b. Crookston, Minn., Mar. 20, 1952; s. Charles Arthur and Eleanor E. (LaFleur) M.; m. Elaine M. Mardian, Aug. 26, 1972; children: Michelle Ann, David Michael. BA, No. State U., Aberdeen, SD, 1974; MA in Econs., U. Wash., 1975, PhD in Econs., 1979. Rsch. asst., specialist Battelle HARC, Seattle, 1976—79; sr. economist Am. Hosp. Assn., Chgo., 1979-85; sr. economist, asst. dir. Hosp. Rsch. & Ednl. Trust, Chgo., 1983-85; vis. scholar Northwestern U., Evanston, Ill., 1984-85; assoc. prof. U. Ala., Birmingham, 1985-88, prof., 1988—, disting. faculty investigator, 1999-2000; dir. Lister Hill Ctr. for Health Policy, Birmingham, 1990—. Dep. editor Med. Care, Cleve., 1987—96; mem. Pa. Mandates Benefits Rev. Panel, Harrisburg, 1987—, Ala. Task Force on Rural Health Care Crisis, 1989; mem. health svcs. devel. grants rev. com. Agy. for Health Care Rsch. and Quality, Rockville, Md., 1992—96; cons. in field. Author: Price Sensitivity in Health Care, 1992, 2d edit., 2005, Cost Shifting in Health Care, 1994, Managed Care and Changing Health Care Markets, 1998; mem. editl. bd. Health Svcs. Rsch., 1985-94, Health Affairs, 1998—, Jour. Gerontology, 1998-2001, Health Svcs. and Outcomes Rsch. Methodology, 1999—, Health Adminstrn. Press, 1999-2002, 2005—, Med. Care Rsch. and Rev., 2000—; contbr. more than 140 articles to profl. jours. Recipient John D. Thompson prize in health svc. rsch., Assn. Univ. Programs in Health Adminstrn., 1991, UAB Pres. award for excellence in tchg., 2000—01; fellow, Employee Benefits Rsch. Inst.; grantee, Nat. Ctr. Health Svcs. Rsch., NIH, Agy. for Health Care Rsch. and Quality, Robert Wood Johnson Found.; Adj. scholar, Am. Enterprise Inst., 2002—06. Mem.: Am. Soc. Health Economists (adv. bd. 2004—), Internat. Health Econs. Assn. (treas. 1994—2000, sec.-treas. 2000—04), Acad. Health (chmn. com. 2000), Am. Econ. Assn. Republican. Roman Catholic. Office: UAB Sch Pub Health Birmingham AL 35294-0022 Office Phone: 205-975-8966. Business E-Mail: morrisey@uab.edu.

MORRISH, THOMAS JAY, golf course architect; b. Grand Junction, Colo., July 6, 1936; s. Wilbur Merle and Margaret Beula (Cronk) M.; m. Louise Ann Dunn, Apr. 2, 1965; children: Carter J., Kimberly L. Coder. AA, Mesa Coll., Grand Junction, 1956; BS in Landscape and Nursery Mgmt., Colo. State U., 1964. Golf course arch. Robert Trent Jones, Montclaire, N.J., 1964-67, George Fazio, Jupiter, Fla., 1967-69, Desmond Muirhead, Newport Beach, Calif., 1969-72, Jack Nicklaus, North Palm Beach, Fla., 1972-83; prin. Jay Morrish & Assocs. Ltd., Flower Mound, Tex., 1983—. Prin. golf course designs include: Troon Golf & Country Club, Scottsdale, Ariz., Las Colinas Sports Club, Irving, Tex., Mira Vista, Ft. Worth, Foothills Golf Course, Phoenix, Forest Highlands, Flagstaff, Ariz. (One of 100 Top Golf Courses in World, Golf mag., Golf Digest), Bentwater on Lake Conroe, Houston, Shadow Glen Golf Club, Olathe, Kans. (Best New Private Course, Golf Digest 1989), Troon North Golf & Country Club, Scottsdale (One of 100 Top Courses in U.S., Golf mag.), Harbor Club on Lake Oconee, Greensboro, Ga., Loch Lomond, Scotland, The Country Club of St. Albans, Mo., Broken Top, Bend, Oreg., Dauble Eagle Club, Galena, Ohio (one of Top 100 Courses in World, Golf Mag.), Buffalo Creek Golf Course, Rockwall, Tex., La Cantera, San Antonio (Best New Pub. Course of 1995, Golf Digest Mag.), numerous others. Edn. grantee State of Colo., 1961-64; Trans-Miss. golf scholar, 1962-64; named Architect of Yr. Golf World Mag., 1996. Mem. Am. Soc. Golf Course Archs. (pres. 2002), Dallas Safari Club. Republican. Avocation: hunting.

MORRISON, ANN M., not-for-profit fundraiser; b. Washington, Apr. 10, 1964; d. William E. B. and Betty A. Graves; m. John B. Morrison, Jr., Dec. 14, 1985; children: Christine A., Katherine E., Colleen M., Kelly V. BBA, James Madison U., Harrisonburg, Va., 1986. Cmty. svc. mgr. Greater Carolinas chpt. Nat. MS Soc., Charlotte, NC, 1992—95; devel. assoc. Med. Washington chpt. Arthritis Found., 1995—97; exec. dir. Fairfax Choral Soc., Va., 2001—03; dir. devel. Vive Les Arts Theatre, Killeen, Tex., 2003—05, Fairfax Symphony Orch., Va., 2005—. Chmn. parade Fayetteville Dogwood Festival, NC, 1993—95; 1st v.p. Fort Hood Officers Wives Club, Tex., 1999—2001. Recipient Dr. Mary E. Walker award, US Forces Command, US Army, 2001, Yellow Rose of Tex., State of Tex., 2006. Mem.: Assn. Fundraising Profls., Am. Symphony Orch. League. Office: Fairfax Symphony Orch 3905 Railroad Ave Ste 202N Fairfax VA 22030 Home Phone: 703-740-6915; Office Phone: 703-563-1990. Office Fax: 703-293-9349. Personal E-mail: ann.morrison1@us.army.mil.

MORRISON, BRUCE ANDREW, federal official, public information officer; b. NYC, Oct. 8, 1944; s. George and Dorothea A. (Meyer) M.; m. Nancy A. Wanat, Sept. 22, 1991; 1 child, Drew. S.B., MIT, 1965; MS, U. Ill., 1970; JD, Yale U., 1973; LittD (hon.), Quinnipac Coll.; LLD (hon.), U. Coll. Dublin. Staff atty. New Haven Legal Assistance Assn., 1973-74, mng. atty., 1974-76, exec. dir., 1976-82; mem. 98th-101st Congresses from 3d Conn. dist., 1983-91; chmn. LI Sound Caucus, chmn. Third World Debt Caucus. Chmn. judiciary subcom. on immigration, refugees, and internat. law U.S. Ho. of Reps.; chmn. Fed. Housing Fin. Bd., 1995-2000; co-chmn. ad hoc com. on Irish affairs; mem. U.S. commn. on immigration reform, 1991-97; chair Irish Ams. for Clinton-Gore, 1992, 96; chair Ams. for a New Irish Agenda, 1993-95; vice chmn. GPC Internat., 2000-2001; chmn. Morrison Pub. Affairs Group, 2001-. Mem. Nat. Dem. Ethnic Coordinating Com., Nat. Dem. Ethnic Leadership Coun.; bd. dirs. Alliance for Responsible Cuba Policy; bd. dirs. USA br. Internat. Social Svcs. Mem. ABA, Conn. Bar Assn., Am. Immigration Lawyers Assn. Democrat. Lutheran. Office: 6004 Onondaga Rd Bethesda MD 20816 Home Phone: 301-263-1140; Office Phone: 301-263-1142. Personal E-mail: b.a.m@att.net.

MORRISON, CHARLES EDWARD, think-tank executive; b. Billings, Mont., 1944; m. Chieko Hayashi; children: Karen, Erica, Kenneth, Douglas. BA in Internat. Studies, Johns Hopkins U., MA, PhD, Johns Hopkins U. Legis. asst. U.S. Senate, 1972-80; part-time sr. rsch. assoc. Japan Ctr. for Internat. Exch., 1980-92; asst. to pres. East-West Ctr., 1986-92, dir. program on internat. econs. and politics, 1992-95, pres., 1998—; chair U.S. Consortium of APEC Study Ctrs., 1996-98; internat. chair Pacific Econ. Cooperation Coun., 2006—. Author: wide range of books, papers and analyses; widely quoted by major news media on issues of regional cooperation, internat. rels., U.S. Asia policy and trade policies. Mem.: U.S. Asia Pacific Coun. (founding mem. 2003). Office: East West Ctr 1601 E West Rd Honolulu HI 96848-1601 Office Phone: 808-944-7111.

MORRISON, CLARENCE CLAPP, retired economics professor; b. Greensboro, NC, June 19, 1932; s. Clarence Nickolson and Ava Clapp Morrison; m. Geraldine Whitesides Morrison, Sept. 11, 1955; children: Robert Hall, Frederick Clapp. BS, Davidson Coll., NC, 1954; MA, U. NC, Chapel Hill, 1956, PhD, 1964. Instr. Norfolk Coll. of William & Mary, Va., 1959—60; asst. prof. U. Va., Charlottesville, 1964—67; assoc. prof. U. Ga., Athens, 1967—70; prof. Ind. U., Bloomington, 1970—96, prof. emeritus, 1996—. Vis. prof. U. NC, Chapel Hill, 1976. Bd. editors Atlantic Econ. Jour., St. Louis, 1977—; contbr. articles to profl. jours. Unit leader United Way Ind. U. Dept. Econs., 1995—2005. Lt. j.g. USN, 1956—59. Recipient A.K. Pfifer award in econs., Davidson Coll., 1953—54; tchg. fellow, U. NC, 1955—56, Wachovia fellow, 1962—63. Mem.: So. Econ. Assn., Am. Econ. Assn., Internat. Atlantic Econ. Soc. (v.p. 1979—80, pres. 1995—96). Avocations: travel, genealogy. Home: 4587 E Heritage Woods Rd Bloomington IN 47401 Office: Econs Dept Ind U Wylie Hall Bloomington IN 47405 Office Phone: 812-856-1382. Office Fax: 812-855-3736. Business E-Mail: morrison@indiana.edu.

MORRISON, CRAIG O., chemicals executive; Grad., Ea. Ky. Univ.; MBA, Harvard Univ., 1987. Cons. Bain & Co., 1987—90; sr. operational and bus. mgmt. pos. GE Co., 1990—93; pres., gen. mgr. Van Leer, Inc., 1993—98, Alcan Pharm. and Cosmetic Packaging, divsn. Alcan, Inc., Millville, NJ, 1998—2002; pres., CEO Hexion Specialty Chemicals Inc., Columbus, Ohio, 2002—, chmn., 2005—. Office: Hexion 180 E Broad St Columbus OH 43215 *

MORRISON, DENISE M., sales executive; b. Neptune, NJ, Jan. 13, 1954; d. Dennis J. and Constance R. (Shields) Sullivan; m. Barry J. Mullen, June 21, 1975, (div. Apr. 1984); 1 child, Michelle; m. Thomas C. Morrison, Oct. 26, 1985; 1 child, Kelly. BS in Econs. & Psychology, Boston Coll., 1975. Unit sales mgr. Procter & Gamble, Boston, 1975-82; trade developer mgr. Pepsi, U.S.A., Purchase, NY, 1982-84; dir. conjections mktg. Nestle USA, Purchase, NY, 1984-89, west zone v.p. Bakersfield, Calif., 1991-95, v.p. impulse sales, 1995; area v.p. sales & logistics Nabisco, Pleasanton, Calif., 1995, sr. v.p., gen. mgr. Down the Street divsn.; exec. v.p., gen. mgr. Snacks and Confections divsn. Kraft Foods; pres. global sales, chief customer services Campbell USA, 2003, pres. US soup, sauces and beverages, 2005—. Named a Woman of Influence, NJBiz mag., 2003; named Exec. of the Year, Snack Food & Bakery mag., 2003; named one of Most Powerful Women in Bus., Fortune mag., 1999—; named to NY YWCA Academy of Women Achievers, 2001; recipient Althea Gibson Beacon award for Business Leadership, 2003, Salute to Policy Makers, Exec. Women NJ, 2006. Mem. Republican Womens Club. Roman Catholic. Avocations: hiking, reading, boating, skiing, music. *

MORRISON, DONALD FRANKLIN, statistician, educator; b. Stoneham, Mass., Feb. 10, 1931; s. Daniel Norman and Agnes Beatrice (Packard) M.; m. Phyllis Ann Hazen, Aug. 19, 1967; children: Norman Hazen, Stephen Donald. BS in Bus. Adminstrn, Boston U., 1953, AM, 1954; MS, U. N.C., 1957; PhD, Va. Poly. Inst. and State U., 1960; MA (hon.), U. Pa., 1971. Mem. staff Lincoln Lab., M.I.T., 1956; cons. math. statistician NIMH, Bethesda, Md., 1956-63; mem. tech. staff Bell Labs., Holmdel, NJ, 1967; mem. faculty, dept. stats. Wharton Sch., U. Pa., 1963-99, prof. stats., 1973-99, chmn. dept., 1978-85, prof. emeritus, 2000—. Author: Multivariate Statistical Methods, 4th edit., 2005, Applied Linear Statistical Methods, 1983; editor The Am. Statistician, 1972-75; assoc. editor Biometrics, 1972-74; contbr. articles to profl. jours. Served with USPHS, 1956-58. NSF grantee, 1966 Fellow Am. Statis. Assn., Inst. Math. Stats.; mem. Internat. Statis. Inst., B&M R.R. Hist. Soc., Nat. R.R. Hist. Soc., R.R. and Locomotive Hist. Soc., N&W Hist. Soc., Bridge Line Hist. Soc., N.E. Elec. Rwy. Hist. Soc. Democrat. Lutheran. Home: 118 E Brookhaven Rd Wallingford PA 19086-6327 E-mail: donaldm@wharton.upenn.edu.

MORRISON, DONALD WILLIAM, lawyer; b. Portland, Oreg., Mar. 31, 1926; s. Robert Angus and Laura Calista (Hodgson) M.; m. Elizabeth Margaret Perry, July 25, 1953; children: Elizabeth Laura, Carol Margaret. BSE.E., U. Wash., 1946; LL.B., Stanford U., 1950. Bar: Oreg. 1950, Calif. 1950, N.Y. 1967, Ill. 1968, Ohio 1974. Assoc. Pendergrass, Spackman, Bullivant & Wright, Portland, 1950-57, ptnr., 1957-60; gen. atty. Pacific N.W. Bell, Portland, 1960-66; atty. AT&T, NYC, 1966-68; counsel Ill. Bell Telephone Co., Chgo., 1968-74; v.p., gen. counsel Ohio Bell Telephone Co., Cleve., 1974-91; of counsel Arter & Hadden, Cleve., 1992—2003. Trustee Archael. Inst. Am., Cleve. Archaeol. Soc., Cleve. Chamber Music Soc., Cleve. Coun. on World Affairs; mem. adv. com. Cleve. Play House, Cleve. Bot. Garden; mem. Ohio adv. bd. Trust for Pub. Land. With USN, 1943—50. Recipient various bar and civic appreciation awards. Mem. ABA, Ohio State Bar Assn., Oreg. State Bar Assn., Calif. Bar Assn., Rowfant Club.

MORRISON, FRED LAMONT, law educator, dean; b. Salina, Kans., Dec. 12, 1939; s. Earl F. and Madge Louise (Glass) M.; m. Charlotte Foot, Dec. 27, 1971; children: Charles, Theodore, George, David. AB, U. Kans., 1961; BA, Oxford U., Eng., 1963, MA, 1968; PhD, Princeton U., 1966; JD, U. Chgo., 1967. Bar: Minn. 1973. Asst. prof. law U. Iowa, Iowa City, 1967-69; counselor on internat. law U.S. State Dept., Washington, 1982-83; assoc. prof. law U. Minn., Mpls., 1969-73, prof. law, 1973-90, Oppenheimer Wolff and Donnelly prof., 1990-97, acting dean, 1994-95, Popham Haik/Lindquist & Vennum prof., 1998—, interim co-dean, 2006—. Of counsel Popham, Haik, Schnobrich & Kaufman, Mpls., 1983-97. Dir. Am. Soc. for Comparative Study of Law; mem. adv. com. on internat. law U.S. Dept. State, Washington, 1987-89; mem. internat. adv. bd. Inst. on Internat. Law, Kiel, Germany, 1989—; mem. Am. Law Inst., bd. editors for Am. Jour. Comparative Law. Recipient President's Award for Outstanding Svc., U. Minn., 1997. Home: 1412 W 47th St Minneapolis MN 55419-5204 Office: U Minn Law Sch 229 19th Ave S Minneapolis MN 55455-0400 Office Phone: 612-625-0321. Business E-Mail: morrison@umn.edu. *

MORRISON, GAIL, internist, nephrologist, educator; BA in Biology, Chemistry magna cum laude, Boston U., 1967; MD, U. Pa., 1971. Diplomate Am. Bd. Med. Examiners, Am. Bd. Internal Medicine, Am. Bd. Nephrology. Instr. dept. continuing edn. Boston U., 1966-67; clin. fellow Harvard U., Boston, 1971-72; intern Beth Israel Hosp., Boston, 1971-72; jr. asst. resident Georgetown U. Hosp., Washington, 1972-73; staff physician clin. ctr. NIH, Bethesda, Md., 1973-74, staff assoc. Nat. Heart & Lung Inst., 1973-74; fellow in nephrology renal electrolyte sect. U. Pa. Hosp., Phila., 1974-76, rsch. fellow in nephrology renal electrolyte sect. NIH, 1975-76, asst. prof. medicine, 1982-83; from asst. prof. to assoc. prof. medicine U. Pa. Sch. Medicine, Phila., 1976-94, prof. medicine, 1994—, vice dean edn., 1995—, dir. acad. programs, 1995—; attending Phila. Vets. Adminstrn. Med. Ctr., 1976-77, U. Pa. Health Sys., 1996—. Asst. dir. dialysis unit U. Pa. Hosp., Phila., 1976-77, assoc. dir., 1977-82, dir. renal outpatient prog., 1976-82, dir. outpatient dialysis unit, 1979-84, acting dir. dialysis prog. for inpatient and outpatient dialysis units, 1981-82, dir., 1982-86; acad. coord. dept. medicine U. Pa. Hosp., Phila., 1985-96; assoc. chmn. dept. medicine for student edn. U. Pa. Sch. Medicine, Phila., 1986-96, acting assoc. dean for clin. curriculum, 1991, assoc. dean for clin. curriculum, 1991-95, vice dean for edn., dir. acad. progs., 1995—, mem. numerous acad., search, planning, steering, alumni, budget, nutrition coms., others; cons., advisor in field; presenter, co-dir., tchr., leader workshops, symposiums, confs. Author: (with A. Goroll) Core Medicine Clerkship: A Curriculum Guide, Manual for Curriculum 2000, 1996; editor: (with others) Introduction to Clinical Medicine, 2d rev. edit., 1995, Concepts in Basic Science, 1995, Essentials of Nutrition: A Case-Based Approach, 1995; mem. editorial bd. Am. Jour. Medicine, 1996-99; author papers, reviews, abstracts, chpts. to books; contbr. articles to profl. jours. Recipient Daniel C. Tosteson award for leadership in med. edn., Disting. Aumni Svc. award U. Pa.; grantee Pa. Sch. Nursing, 1989-90, Heinz Endowment Fund, 1990-95, U. Pa. Sch. Medicine, 1993-95, 93-96, 97-98. Fellow ACP, Coll. Physicians of Pa. (mem. sect. on pub. health and preventive medicine 1995—); mem. AAAS, Internat. Soc. Nephrology, Am. Soc. Nephrology, Am. Fedn. for Clin. Rsch., Am. Assn. Med. Colls. Women's Liaison Officer, Pa. Soc. Nephrology (coun. mem. network #24 federally funded end-stage renal disease orgn. 1978-83, mem. facility planning bd. 1979-80, chmn. 1980-82, mem. exec. com. 1980-82, ad-hoc mem. med. review bd. 1980-82, mem. nomination and credential com. 1982-83), Southeastern Nat. Kidney Found. (bd. dirs. 1984-88), Phi Beta Kappa, Sigma Xi, Alpha Omega Alpha. Home: 1040 Stony Ln Gladwyne PA 19035-1136 Office Phone: 215-898-8034. Fax: 215-573-4289. Business E-Mail: morrisog@mailmed.upenn.edu.

MORRISON, GLENN LESLIE, minister; b. Cortez, Colo., Feb. 26, 1929; s. Ward Carl Morrison and Alma Irene (Butler) Anderson; m. Beverely Joanne Buck, Aug. 26, 1949; children: David Mark, Betty Jo Morrison Mullen, Gary Alan, Judith Lynn Morrison Oltmann, Stephen Scott. Student, San Diego State U., 1948-49, Chabot Coll., 1968-69. Ordained ministry Evang. Ch. Alliance, 1961. Dir. counseling follow-up Oakland (Calif.) Youth Christ, 1954-56; pres. Follow Up Ministries, Inc., Castro Valley, Calif., 1956—. Assoc. pastor 1st Covenant Ch., Oakland, 1956-58; exec. dir. East Bay Youth Christ, Oakland, 1960-66; supervising chaplain Alameda County (Calif.) Probation Dept., 1971-90; vol. chaplain Alameda County Sheriff's Dept., 1971—; founder, dir. God Squad Vol. Program Prison Workers, 1972—; seminar leader Calif. Dept. Corrections, Sacramento, 1978—, mem. chaplains coordinating com., 1988—. Author: Scripture Investigation Course, 1956, Tired of the Same Ol' Same Ol'? There is a Better Way, 1978. Mem. Am. Correctional Assn., Am. Protestant Correctional Chaplains Assn. (regional pres., sec. 1980-86, nat. sec. 1986-88, nat. 2nd v.p. 1996-98). Office: Follow Up Ministries Inc PO Box 2514 Castro Valley CA 94546-2514 Personal E-mail: fumi2000@msn.com.

MORRISON, GORDON MACKAY, JR., retired investment company executive; b. Boston, Jan. 18, 1930; s. Gordon Mackay and Alice (Blodgett) M.; m. Barbara J. Lee, June 15, 1954; children: Lee (dec.), Leighton, Faith. AB, Harvard U., 1952, MBA, 1954. Regional mgr. Bankers Leasing Corp., Boston, 1965-68; portfolio mgr. Loomis, Sayles and Co., Boston, 1969-71; sr. v.p. Ft. Hill Investors Mgmt., Boston, 1972-75; chmn. bd. Bradford Gordon Inc., Boston, 1977—2001; gen. ptnr. Bradford Gordon Ptnrs., Boston, 1977—; ret. Trustee East Boston Savs. Bank, 1962-91; trustee Meridian Fin. Svcs., Inc., 1991-2002, hon. trustee, 2002--. Bd. dirs. The New Eng. Hosp., 1961-96, emeritus, 1996—. Republican. Congl. Club: Harvard. Lodge: Masons. Home: 3 Mountain Gate Rd Ashland MA 01721

MORRISON, H. ROBERT, small business owner, photographer, retired municipal official; b. Pitts., Apr. 7, 1938; s. Hugh and Gertrude Mary (Gehenio) Morrison; m. Meredith Wollenberg, Dec. 8, 1979; children: Justin William, Elizabeth Jeanne. BA in English, Howard U., 1969. Writer Nat. Geog. Soc., Washington, 1969-73, editor ednl. filmstrips, 1973-77, sr. writer, 1977-88, mng. editor nat. geography bee, 1988-89; elected treas. City of Falls Ch., Va., 1993—2006; ret., 2006. Exec. bd. dirs. Tapestry Theatre, Alexandria, Va.; bd. dirs. Falls Ch. Cable Access Corp., pres., 1990—93, Bonnie Briar Prodns., LLC, 2003—. Contbg. author: book As We Live and Breathe, 1971, The Ocean Realm, 1978, America's Majestic Canyons, 1979, Mysteries of the Ancient World, 1979, America's Magnificent Mountains, 1980, America's Hidden Corners, 1983, Exploring America's Valleys, 1984, America's Seashore Wonderlands, 1985; co-author: America's Atlantic Isles, 1981. Vice chmn. Falls Church Dem. Com., 1988—89, 1998—99. With US Army, 1961—64. Mem.: NAACP, Treas. Assn. Va. (bd. dirs. 1996—97), Clan Morrison N.Am. (life), St. Andrew's Soc. Washington. Avocations: reading, TV production, historic preservation. Home: Bonnie Briar 502 Walden Ct Falls Church VA 22046-2628 Office: City Hall 300 Park Ave Falls Church VA 22046-3332 Office Phone: 703-929-3376. Personal E-mail: bbppix@aol.com.

MORRISON, HARRY, chemistry professor; b. Bklyn., Apr. 25, 1937; s. Edward and Pauline (Sommers) M.; m. Harriet Thurman, Aug. 23, 1958; children: Howard, David, Daniel. BA, Brandeis U., 1957; PhD, Harvard U., 1961. NATO-NSF postdoctoral fellow Swiss Fed. Inst., Zurich, 1961-62; rsch. assoc. U. Wis., Madison, 1962-63; asst. prof. chemistry Purdue U., West Lafayette, Ind., 1963-69, assoc. prof., 1969-76, prof., 1976—, dept. head, 1987-92, dean Sch. Sci., 1992—2002. Mem. acad. adv. com. Indsl. Rsch. Inst., 1993-96. Contbr. numerous articles to profl. jours. Bd. fellows Brandeis U. Mem. Am. Chem. Soc., Am. Soc. Photobiology, Inter-Am. Photochem. Soc., Coun. for Chem. Rsch. (chmn. 1995), Phi Beta Kappa Office: Purdue Univ Dept Chemistry Brown Bldg West Lafayette IN 47907-2084 Office Phone: 765-494-5246. Business E-Mail: hmorrison@purdue.edu.

MORRISON, JAMES FRANK, optometrist, state legislator; b. Colby, Kans., Apr. 11, 1942; s. Lloyd Wayne and Catherine Louise (Beckner) M.; m. Karen Jean Carr, Aug. 25, 1963; children: Mike, Jeff, Scott. Student, U. Kans., 1960-64; BS, OD, So. Coll. Optometry, 1967. Pvt. practice, 1969-75; founder, chief staff N.W. Kans. Ednl. Diagnostic and Referral Ctr. Children, Inc., Colby; asst. chief engr. Sta. KXXX-FM, 1977-80, chief engr., 1980-82; prof. vision dept. Colby Community Coll., 1979-84; mem. Kans. Ho. Reps., Topeka, 1992—. Cubmaster pack 140 Cub Scouts Am., 1970-80, dist. chmn., 1977-79. Fellow Am. Acad. Optometry, Coll. Optometrists in Vision Devel.; mem. Am. Optometric Assn., Am. Soc. Broadcast Engrs., Kans. Soc. Broadcast Engrs. (founder, pres. 1970-71), Kans. Optometric Assn., Kans. Assn. Children with Learning Disabilities, Mo. Optometric Assn., Thomas County Assn. Retarded Children, Rotary, Lions, Kiwanies (pres. 1971-72), Masons, Shriners. Rotary. Mem. Assemblies of God. Ch. Avocations: amateur radio, photography, astronomy. Home: 3 Cottonwood Dr Colby KS 67701-3902 Office: Morrison Optometric Assocs 180 W 6th St Colby KS 67701-2315

MORRISON, JAMES V., biology professor; s. James V. and Mary E. Morrison; m. Louise V. Mottashed, Aug. 5, 1968; children: Jennifer Forte, James. BA in Biology, Kans. State U., Manhattan, 1968, MS in Zoology, 1971; MPH in Epidemiology, Loma Linda U., Calif., 1978. Assoc. prof. biology Riverside CC, Calif., 1971—. Mem.: Phi Kappa Phi, Delta Omega (life). Avocations: sailing, scuba diving, travel. Office: Riverside CC 2001 Third St Norco CA 92860-2600 Home Phone: 951-372-7169; Office Phone: 951-372-7169. Office Fax: 951-372-7050; Home Fax: 951-372-7050.

MORRISON, JOHN HENRY, neuroscientist, educator, lab administrator; b. Cleve., July 17, 1952; s. Malcolm Gray and Leonie Johnson Morrison; m. Abbie Ruth Pollack, Dec. 4, 1954; children: Kelsey Ilana, Alexander Malcolm. BA, Johns Hopkins U., Balt., 1974, PhD, 1979. Postdoctoral fellow Salk Inst., La Jolla, Calif., 1980—83; asst. prof. to assoc. prof. Scripps Rsch. Inst., La Jolla, Calif., 1983—89; Johnson Prof. Geriat. and Adult Devel. Mt. Sinai Sch. Medicine, NYC, 1989—, prof., co-dir. neurobiology, 1991—2002, prof., dir. neurobiology, 2002—04, prof., chmn. dept. neuroscience, 2004—06, dean basic scis. and Grad. Sch. Biol. Scis., 2006—. Dir. Am. Fedn. Aging Rsch., NYC, 1990—2002; mem. Dana Alliance for Brain Initiatives Dana Found., NYC, 1993—; sci. adv. bd. Bachman-Strauss Dystonia and Parkinson Found., NYC, 1996—; co-founder, dir. Neurome, Inc., La Jolla, Calif., 2000—. Editor (sect. editor): (sci. jour.) Neuroscience, Exptl. Neurology; contbr. articles to profl. jours. Recipient Faculty/Scholar award, Alzheimer's Assn., 1984—87, Method to Extend Rsch. in Time (MERIT) award, NIH, 2007; grantee, 1991—. Mem.: NY Acad. Sci. (co-chair sect. neuroscience 2000—02), Soc. Neuroscience (com. chair 2003—05), Shenorock Shore Club, Cajal Club (pres. 2002—04). Achievements include elucidating key elements of neuropathology in Alzheimer's disease and their relationship to dementia. In addition, discovered several key characteristics of normal brain aging. Avocations: cycling, enology, fishing. Office: Mt Sinai Sch Medicine Box 1065 One Gustave L Levy Pl New York NY 10029-6574 Office Phone: 212-659-5985. Office Fax: 212-849-2510. E-mail: john.morrison@mssm.edu. *

MORRISON, JOHN HORTON, lawyer, arbitrator; b. Sept. 15, 1933; BBA, U. N.Mex., Albuquerque, 1955; BA, U. Oxford, 1957; JD, Harvard U., Cambridge, Mass., 1962. Bar: Ill. 1962, US Supreme Ct. 1966. Assoc. Kirkland & Ellis, Chgo., 1962-67, ptnr., 1968-99. Named Hon. Officer Most Excellent Order Brit. Empire, 1994; Rhodes scholar. Mem. ABA, Internat. Bar Assn., Assn. Am. Rhodes Scholars (pres. 1998-2006), Chgo. Internat. Dispute Resolution Assn. (dir.). Home: 2550 Princeton Ave Evanston IL 60201-4941 Personal E-mail: johnhmorrison@post.harvard.edu. Business E-Mail: jmorrison@kirkland.com.

MORRISON, JOHN M., bank executive; Owner, CEO Ctrl. Bank Group, Golden Valley, Minn.; interim chmn., CEO Allina Health Sys., 2001—02, bd. chmn., 2004—. Mem. Fairview U. Med. Ctr. Bd., Fairview Health Sys. Corp. Bd.; chmn. exec. com. bd. trustees U. St. Thomas; former mem. bd. govs., chmn. bd.'s fin. com. U. Minn. Acad. Health Ctr.; former mem. Johns Hopkins Medicine bd. visitors Johns Hopkins U. Mem.: U. St. Thomas Sch. Law (mem. bd. govs., founder John. M. Morrison Ctr. Entrepreneurship).

MORRISON, JOHN MARTIN, lawyer; b. McCook, Nebr., June 18, 1961; s. Frank Brennor and Sharon Romain (McDonald) M.; m. Catherine Helen Wright, Aug. 17, 1991; children: Allison Kay, Amanda Grace. BA, Whitman Coll., 1983; JD, U. Denver, 1986. Bar: Mont. 1987, U.S. Dist. Ct. Mont. 1988, U.S. Ct. Appeals (9th cir.) 1989, U.S. Supreme Ct. 1996. Legis. asst., legal counsel U.S. Senate, Washington, 1987-88; ptnr. Morrison Law Offices, Helena, Mont., 1988-93, Meloy & Morrison, Helena, 1994-2000; auditor State of Mont., 2000—, ins. and securities commr. Author: Mavericks: The Lives and Battles of Montana's Political Legends, 1997; contbr. articles to profl. jours. Del. Dem. Nat. Platform Com., 1992; Dem. candidate for U.S. Senate, 2006. Mem. Mont. Trial Lawyers Assn. (past pres., bd. dirs. 1991-2000), Western Trial Lawyers Assn. (bd. govs. 1990-95), Trial Lawyers Pub. Justice (chair 1989-90), Nat. Assn. Ins. Commn., N.Am. Assn. Securities Adminstrs. Avocations: skiing, fly fishing, mountain climbing, river rafting, running. Office: Office of the Mont State Auditor PO Box 4009 840 Helena Ave Helena MT 59604 Office Phone: 406-444-2040. Business E-Mail: jmorrison@mt.gov.

MORRISON, JOSEPH YOUNG, transportation executive, consultant; b. Flushing, NY, Jan. 4, 1951; s. William Barrier and Barbara Helen (Lowe) Morrison; children: Susan Parker, Travis Barrier. AS, Montreat Anderson Coll., NC, 1971; BA, Oglethorpe U., 1989. Dept. head J.C. Penny & Co., Atlanta, 1971-74; uniform patrol officer City of Atlanta, 1974-80; spl. agt. U.S. Dept. Transp., Atlanta, 1980-82; group dir. safety and ins. Western Express, Atlanta, 1982-85; dir. safety Taylor Maid Transp., Albany, Ga., 1985-86; v.p. risk mgmt. Burlington Motor Carriers, Inc., Daleville, Ind., 1986-96; pres. Motor Carrier Safety Cons. Inc., Noblesville, Ind., 1996-97, Nat. Transp. Cons., Inc., Noblesville, Ind., 1997—. Co-author: Guide to Handling Hazardous Material, 1986. Mem.: Am. Soc. Safety Engrs., Am. Trucking Assn. (mem. hazardous materials com. 1982—86, mem. safety mgmt. coun. 1982—, chmn. injury control com. 1984—88, mem. interstate carrier conf. 1985—, mem. nat. freight claims and security coun. 1985—, Safety Improvement award, Accident Reduction award, Injury Reduction award), Sertoma Club, Kenilworth Civic Club (treas. Stone Mountain Ga. chpt. 1981—83, pres. 1983—84), Sigma Alpha Epsilon. Methodist. Avocations: home remodeling, restoring old cars. Home: 7111 Oakview Cir Noblesville IN 46062-9419 Office: Nat Transp Cons 1109 S 10th St Noblesville IN 46060 Office Phone: 317-770-0953. E-mail: jmorrison@ntconsult.com.

MORRISON, KENDRA ANN, environmental scientist; b. Hugo, Colo., June 8, 1970; d. Kenneth Patrick and Judy Ann Morrison. BS in Environ. Health, Colo. State U., Ft. Collins, 1993; MS in Environ. Scis., U. Colo., 1999. Specialist consumer health and protection Colo. Dept. Pub. Health and Environ., Denver, 1993; specialist environ. health Tri-County Health Dept., Commerce City, Colo., 1993—98; scientist U.S. Environ. Protection Agy., Denver, 1998—. Rsch. asst. U. Colo., Denver, 2001; mem. adv. bd. Engrs. Without Borders, Longmont, Colo., 2003—05; intern, lab. and rsch. asst. MIT, Honolulu, 1994. Named Environ. Pub. Health Emerging Leader, U.S. Dept. Health and Human Svcs. Ctrs. Disease Control and Prevention, 2003. Mem.: Colo. Hazardous Waste Mgmt. Soc., Air and Waste Mgmt. Assn., Nat. Environ. Health Assn. (registered environ. health specialist 2000, registered sanitarian 2000, Merit award 2004, scholar 1998). Avocations: tropical plants, travel. Home: 180 Poplar St Unit G Denver CO 80220 Office: US EPA Region 8 1595 Wynkoop St Denver CO 80202

MORRISON, KENNETH DOUGLAS, writer, columnist; b. Mpls., Apr. 1, 1918; s. Kenneth Mortimore and Florence Myrtle (Sutton) M.; m. Helen Curtis, Feb. 25, 1943; children: Kenneth D., Sally, Steven C., Mary. AB, Carleton Coll., 1940; postgrad., U. Miami, 1940—41, U. Minn., 1941. Free lance writer, Mpls., 1941; editor publs. Minn. Dept. Conservation, 1942-47; Minn. rep. to Nat. Audubon Soc., 1947-49, dir. pub relations, editor Audubon mag., 1949-56, v.p., 1955-56; dir. Mountain Lake Sanctuary and Singing Tower Am. Found., 1956-80, dir. environ. concerns, 1980-82, fellow, 1982-83; syndicated nature-conservation newspaper columnist 4 papers, 1985—95. Audubon tour lectr., 1958-63; interviewer naturalists Wildlife Unltd., TV sta. WOR-TV, N.Y.C., 1951- 52; Mem. Minn. Bird Commn., 1951-54; trustee emeritus Fla. Nature Conservancy; trustee Fla. Conservation Found.; v.p., trustee Conservation 70's; mem. Gov. Fla. Natural Resources Com., State Parks Adv. Council, 1971-79. Author: Favorite Birds of America, 1951, Favorite Animals of America, 1951, Mountain Lake Almanac, 1984, Tonic of Wildness, 2006; Compiler: (with Mrs. M. E. Herz) Where to Find Birds In Minnesota, 1950. Bd. dirs. Defenders Wildlife. Recipient Gov. Fla. Wildlife Conservation award, 1960, Gulf Oil Conservation award, 1982, Feinstone Environ. award SUNY, 1987, Carleton Coll. Disting. Achievement award, 1990, Grassroots Leadership award Fla. Nature Conservancy, 1996. Mem. Wilson Ornithol. Soc., Wilderness Soc., Greenpeace, Native Plant Soc., Fla. Audubon Soc. (pres., Award of Merit 1964, Cruickshank Conservation award 1993), Hawk Mountain Sanctuary Assn. (bd. sponsors), Nature Conservancy (lifetime Conservation award, 2006, Sierra Club, Friends of Earth, Green Horizon Land Trust (bd. dirs. 1999-2007), Pi Delta Epsilon. Methodist. Home: 1351 Hollister Rd Babson Park FL 33827-9684 *We ought to keep in mind that we are mammals and that we need to renew regularly our contact with the basic, simple life of soil, sun, water, animals and trees.*

MORRISON, MALCOLM CAMERON, engineering management professional; b. Pitts., Apr. 12, 1942; s. Malcolm Smith and Floy Alphine (Sample) M.; m. Julia Gertrude Collette, Dec. 30, 1960 (div. oct. 1972); 1 child, Malcolm Paul; m. Lois Roxane Florian, July 27, 1974; 1 child, Rachel Floy. BS, Caltech, Pasadena, Calif., 1964, PhD, 1969. Sr. scientist Havens Internat., San Diego, 1969-71; group leader Calgon Corp., San Diego, 1971-72; v.p. Chem. Systems, Irvine, Calif., 1972-79, Purolator Puropore, Tustin, Calif., 1979-82, Puropore, Inc., Tustin, 1982-85; dir. Microgon, Laguna Hills, Calif., 1985-95, Spectrum Cos., Laguna Hills, 1995-98; v.p. Spectrum Labs., Rancho Dominquez, Calif., 1998—2002; sr. process engr. Santa Fe Sci. and Tech., 2004—. Cons. in field, 1985—; v.p./owner OMMS Engrs., Inc., Santa Ana, Calif., 1982-2005. Contbr. articles to profl. jours. Dir. Santiago Sanitation Dist., Silverado, Calif., 1978-80. Mem. Am. Inst. Chem. Engrs., Orange County CAER (sec./treas. 1990-2005), Am. Filtration Soc. (pres. Golden State chpt. 1985-91), The Nature Conservancy. Republican. Roman Catholic. Avocations: horseback riding, gardening, birding, church activities. Home: Box 810 El Rito NM 87530-0810 Office: Santa Fe Sci and Tech 3216 Richards Ln Santa Fe NM 87507 Home Phone: 505-581-9115; Office Phone: 505-474-3500 ext. 22. Business E-Mail: morrison@sfst.net.

MORRISON, MARGARET ANNE, literature educator; b. Lakenheath AFB, Suffix, England, May 2, 1967; d. Lewis Eugene Robinson and Sarah E. Spear; m. Kenneth William Morrison, Aug. 30, 1966; children: Elora Danielle, Kenneth Joshua. BA in English, Psychology, U. North Fla., Jacksonville, 1999. Cert. mid. grades English edn. Fla. Dept Edn., gifted edn. Fla. Dept. Edn., Wilson lang. sys. level 1 WIlson Lang. Tng. English tchr. Seacoast Christian Acad., Jacksonville, Fla., 1999—2000; gifted lang. arts tchr. Duval County Pub. Sch., Jacksonville, 2000—03; educator Inspired Ednl. Svcs., Jacksonville, 2003—. Homecoming chair USS Spruance Captain's Steering Com., Jacksonville, 1997. Recipient Nat. Dean's List, Ednl. Comm., 1996—97, Ednl. Comm. Scholarship Found., 1997—98, Lifetime Psi Chi Mem., Nat. Honor Soc. in Psychology. Mem.: The Assn. for the Gifted, Acad. of Orton-Gillingham Practitioners and Educators, Coun. for Exceptional Children, Learning Disabilities Assocation, Internat. Dyslexia Assn., Golden Key Honor Soc. Home Phone: 904-744-1034. Personal E-mail: inspirededucation@comcast.net.

MORRISON, MARTIN, writer; b. Oakland, Calif., Mar. 28, 1947; s. Raymond Earl and June (Cabral) M. AB with distinction, U. Calif., Berkeley, 1967, MA, 1969, postgrad., 1969-73. Certified (life) nat. tournament dir.; cert. jr./community coll. tchr. (life), Calif. Instr. classics and English composition U. Calif. at Berkeley, 1967-73; instr. legal argument Boalt Hall Law Sch., 1972; with exec. office CF Air Freight, Inc., 1979-83, asst. to traffic mgr. for spl. projects, 1982-83, computer systems mgr., 1982-83; computer systems analyst Qantel Bus. Computers, 1983-86, sr. computer systems analyst, 1986-92; sr. tech. writer Shared Med. Systems, 1992-96, supr. tech. writing, 1996-98, mgr. tech. writing, 1998—2000; lead tech. writer Kaiser Permanent, 2001—. Mem. Amateur Chamber Music Players, 1978—. Author: Writing Argument, 1972, USCF Yearbooks, 1974-76, Official Rules of Chess, 1975, 77, Chess Competitor's Handbook, 1980, Latin Works for Transparent Language Computer Program, 1992-93; editor: Chess Voice, 1968-73, Keeping Ancient Rome Alive, 1987-89; contbg. author: Fundamentals of Management, 3d edit., 2000; chess editor: Oakland Tribune, 1965-66; columnist Via Lorenzo, 1987-88, Metric Today, 1985—; pub., bus. mgr. Chess Life & Rev., 1977-78, Bancroft Music Sch., 1958-60. Asst. concertmaster Berkeley Chamber Chorus and Orch., 1980-83; concertmaster Oakland Philharm., 1987-90, bd. dirs., corp. sec., 1988-90; 1st violin Albany Trio, 1987-91, Mostly Baroque Ensemble, 1999-2000; vol. staff Chabot Sci. Ctr., 1981-84, chmn. computer system mgmt. staff; sec., treas. AstroSoft, 1983-87. Schola Gregoriana San Francisco, 1989-92, Schola Cantemus, 1992-95; dir. St. John Schola, 1995—. Fellow U.S. Metric Assn. (life, chmn. consumer edn. com. 1984—, Spl. Citation 1986, cert. advanced metrication specialist 1987); mem. Am. Philol. Assn., Am. Classical League, Eastbay Astron. Soc. (bd. dirs. 1981-84, v.p. 1983-84), Internat. Assn. Chess Press (v.p. 1973-77), Soc. for Tech. Comm. (sr.), Chess Journalists Assn. (pres. 1972-75), World Chess Fedn. (internat. life arbiter, mem. rules com. 1973-78, chmn. 1976-78), U.S. Chess Fedn. (bd. dels. 1968-78, 1st v.p. Pacific Region 1972-73, nat. sec. 1972-75, tech. dir. 1973-76, exec. dir. 1976-78, Disting. Vol. award, 1982, Spl. citation, 1984, Disting. Svc. award 1995), Calif. Alumni Assn. (life, scholarship com., chmn. 1987-93, Disting. Chmn. award 1990), San Lorenzo Garden Homes Assn. (v.p./sec. 1985-86, pres. 1986-92), Mensa, Friends of the Alameda Free Library, Phi Beta Kappa.

MORRISON, MICHAEL DEAN, lawyer, law educator; BA with high honors, Okla. U., 1971, JD, 1974. Bar: Okla. 1975, Kans. 1975, Tex. 1981, US Ct. Appeals (5th cir.) 1980, US Dist. Ct. (ea., no. and so. dists.) Tex. 1983, US Dist. Ct. (we. dist.) Tex. 1980, US Dist. Ct. (we. dist.) Okla. 1975, US Supreme Ct. 1979. Pvt. practice, Wichita, Kans., 1974-75; asst. dir. Law Ctr. Okla. U., 1975-77, asst. prof., 1977-80, assoc. prof., 1980-82, prof. law, 1982-90, William J. Boswell chair of law, 1990—2005; chief of staff to pres. Baylor U., 2005—06, Jo Murphy chair & dir. internat. edn., 2007—. Mayor City of Waco, 1996—2000; ordained elder 1st Presbyn. Ch. Waco, stated clk. of session, 1996—98. Mem. Order of Coif, Phi Beta Kappa. Office: PO Box 97288 Waco TX 76798-7288

MORRISON, MURRAY ALLAN, orthopaedic surgeon; b. Columbus, Ohio, Dec. 6, 1939; s. Benjamin Gerald and Mildred (Jacobs) M.; m. Susan Gail Kobren, July 30, 1967; children: Jennifer Anne, Sarah Elise. AB, Harvard U., 1961; MD, NYU, 1965. Diplomate Am. Bd. Orthopaedic Surgery. Surg. intern U. Mich. Med. Ctr., Ann Arbor, 1965-66, asst. resident surgery, 1966-67; orthodaedic resident Hosp. of U. of Pa., Phila., 1967-70; orthopedist; attending surgeon Bridgeport (Conn.) Hosp., 1970—80; sr. attending surgeon Bridgeport Hosp., 1980—, chief sect. of orthopedic surgery, 1992—2002; clin. instr., orthopaedics, rehabilitation Yale Univ. Med. Sch. Clin. instr. Yale U. Sch. Medicine, New Haven, 1985—; dir. Ralston Orthopedic Libr., U. Pa. Dept. Ortho-surgery, Phila., 1984—98. Fellow ACS, Am. Acad. Orthop. Surgeons, Am. Assn. Hip and Knee Surgeons, Ea. Orthop. Assn., Conn. State Med. Soc. Office: Orthopedic Specialty Group 75 Kings Highway Cutoff Fairfield CT 06430-5358 Office Phone: 203-337-2600, 203-785-2579. *

MORRISON, PATRICE BURGERT, lawyer; b. St. Louis, July 8, 1948; d. Frank J. and Loretta S. Burgert; m. William Brian Morrison; 1 child, W. Brett. AB, U. Miami, 1971, MA, 1972; JD, Am. U., 1975; LLM in Taxation, Georgetown U., 1978. Bar: Fla. 1975, DC 1977, NY 1983. Atty. US Dept. Treas., Washington, 1975-79; atty., ptnr. Nixon Hargrave Devans & Doyle, LLP, Palm Beach County, Fla., 1980-89, Nixon Peabody LLP (formerly Nixon, Hargrave, Devans & Doyle), Rochester, NY, 1989—. Bd. dirs. Rochester Friendly Sr. Svcs., Inc., 1996—. Bd. dirs. Alzheimer's Assn., Rochester, 1996—, Nat. Women's Hall of Fame, 1990—92; mem. exec. com. Estate Planning Coun. Rochester, 1992—95; dir. Cloverwood Sr. Living, Inc., 2000—. Mem.: Am. Immigration Lawyers Assn. Office: Nixon Peabody LLP 1100 Clinton Sq Rochester NY 14604

MORRISON, PATRICIA B., information technology executive; BA in Math. & Stats. summa cum laude, Miami Univ., BS in Secondary Edn. Sys. mgmt., IT positions Procter & Gamble; CIO GE Indsl. Sys. Gen. Electric, 1997—2000; CIO Quaker Oats Co., Chgo., 2000—02, Office Depot, Inc., Delray Beach, Fla., 2002—05; sr. v.p., chief info. officer Motorola Inc., 2005—. Bd. dir. Jo-Ann Stores, Inc. Office: Motorola Inc 1303 E Algonquin Rd Schaumburg IL 60196

MORRISON, PAUL J., state attorney general, former prosecutor; b. Dodge City, Kans., June 1, 1954; m. Joyce Morrison; 3 children. Student, Kans. State U.; BA in Criminal Justice, Washburn U., Topeka; JD, Washburn U. Sch. Law, Topeka, 1980. Asst. dist. atty. Johnson County, Kans., 1980—89, dist. atty. Kans., 1989—2005; atty. gen. State of Kans., Topeka, 2007—. Vice chair Kans. Sentencing Commn. Chmn. fundraising effort Johnson County United Way, 2004; mem. Good Shepherd Cath. Ch.; pres., bd. mem. Sunflower House, SafeHome, Inc. Named Prosecutor of the Yr., Kans. County & Dist. Attorney's Assn., 2001; recipient Clarence M. Kelley award for Excellence in Criminal Justice Adminstrn. Mem.: Johnson County Bar Found. (former pres.), Kans. County and Dist. Attys. Assn. (former pres.). Democrat. Office: Office of Atty Gen 120 SW 10th Ave 2nd Fl Topeka KS 66612-1597 Office Phone: 785-296-2215. *

MORRISON, PORTIA OWEN, lawyer; b. Charlotte, NC, Apr. 1, 1944; d. Robert Hall Jr. and Josephine Currier (Hutchison) M.; m. Alan Peter Richmond, June 19, 1976; 1 child, Anne Morrison. BA in English, Agnes Scott Coll., 1966; MA, U. Wis., 1967; JD, U. Chgo., 1978. Bar: Ill. 1978. Sr. counsel DLA Piper U.S. LLP, Chgo., 1978—. Lectr. in field. Past pres. Girl Scouts of Chgo. Mem.: ABA, CREW Chgo., Chgo. Fin. Exch., Pension Real Estate Assn., Chgo. Bar Assn. (real property com., subcom. real property fin., alliance for women), Am. Coll. Real Estate Lawyers (past pres. bd. govs., bd. govs.). Office: DLA Piper US LLP 203 N La Salle St Chicago IL 60601-1210 Office Phone: 312-368-4013. Business E-Mail: portia.morrison@dlapiper.com.

MORRISON, RAY LEON, library director, education educator; b. Boise, Idaho, Sept. 17, 1952; s. Duane Alton and Wilma Lucille (Bybee) M.; m. Barbara Ann Derrenbacher, Apr. 2, 1977; children: Eric, Shawn. BJ, San Jose State U., Calif., 1974, MA in Library Sci., 1975; CAS in Library Sci., U. Ill., Champaign-Urbana, 1984; EdD, U. Ark., Fayetteville, 1992. Reference librarian Olivet Nazarene Coll., Kankakee, Ill., 1975-80; Bibl. Inst. librarian Pittsburg State U., Kans., 1980-85; library dir. Mid-Am. Nazarene U., Olathe, Kans., 1986—. Adj. prof. edn. Mid Am. Nazarene U. Author: Library Skills Workbook, 1981, 2d rev. edit., 1983; contbr. articles to profl. jours., book revs. to pubs. Pres. bd. dirs. Olathe Libr.; dist. commr. Boy Scouts Am. Mem. ALA, Kans. Libr. Assn., Christian Librarians Fellowship, Nazarene Librarians Fellowship, Kans. Libr. Network Bd., Kansas City Met. Libr. Network. Republican. Mem. Ch. of Nazarene. Avocations: cross country skiing, NASCAR, olympic games, track and field, reading. Home: 1904 S Parkwood Dr Olathe KS 66062-2806 Office: Mid-Am Nazarene U PO Box 1776 Olathe KS 66051-1776 Office Phone: 913-971-3561. Business E-Mail: rmorriso@mnu.edu.

MORRISON, REY EILEEN, history educator, writer; b. Grand Rapids, Mich., May 14, 1980; d. Henry Scott and Loretta Gene (Richmond) Davis; m. David Michael Morrison, Apr. 4, 2004; 1 child, Leah Rose. BA in History, Mich. State. U., East Lansing, 2002; M in Edn., Western Mich. U., Kalamazoo, 2003. Cert. tchr. Mich., 2003. Tchr. history Kalamazoo HS, 2002—05, Meriks Meml. HS, Paducah, Ky., 2005—. Co-author: (book) A View from the Top: American History 1900 to Present, 2006; contbr. articles to profl. jours., chapters to books. Mem.: Am. Hist. Assn. (jour. editor 2004—). Democrat. Presbyterian. Avocations: reading, history, genealogy, travel.

MORRISON, RICHARD DRURY, health policy consultant, medical educator; b. Logan, W.Va., Nov. 14, 1935; s. William Cline Morrison and Gladys Leone Rogers-Morrison-Taylor; m. Carolee Benefico, Oct. 15, 1971 (div.). PhD, Va. Commonwealth U., Richmond, 1988; MA, Coll. of William and Mary in Va., Williamsburg, 1985; BA, Christopher Newport Coll., Newport News, Va., 1976. Adj. asst. prof. Old Dominion U., Norfolk, Va., 1999—2003; cons. in evidence based medicine Ea. Va. Med. Sch., Norfolk, 1999—2003. Cons. and fellow Am. Internat. Health Alliance, Washington, 1996—98, UCSF Ctr. for the Health Professions, Pew Charitable Trusts, San Francisco, 1994—96; dep. dir. Va. Dept. of Health Professions, Richmond, 1984—94; dir. of membership svcs. AVMA, Chgo., 1963—65; asst. dir. Am. Assn. of Dental Schools, Chgo., 1965—69; bd. dirs. Bd. of Certification for Emergency Nurses; standards com. commn. grad. Foreign Nursing Sch.; bd. dirs. Va. Health Quality Ctr.; exec. council health policy AARP/Va. Author (more than 50): (published health policy reviews) On Request. Specialist 5 US Army, 1956—59, Fort Lee, Virginia. Johnataan Duncan McGregor scholar, U. Chgo., 1952—55. Achievements include serving on bd. of dir. Coun. on Licensure, Enforcement and Regulation; The Center for Public Affairs, Virginia Commonwealth University; consulting, Bur. of Health Professions, US Department of Health & Human Services; bd. of dr., v.p., Citizen Advocacy Ctr; cons., Inst. of Medicine, Nat. Acad. of Sciences; cons., The Pew Charitable Trusts; cons., Robert Wood Johnson Found; intern, Va. Joint Legis. Audit and Review Cmmn; intern, The Va. Crime Cmmn; cons. and sr. rsch. fellow, The Williamson Institue, Medical Coll. of Va; mem., Task Force of Pres. Carter's Cmmn.on Mental Health. Avocations: international travel, creative writing. Personal E-mail: richmorr10@hotmail.com, richmorr10@yahoo.ie. E-mail: riehmorr10@yahoo.ie.

MORRISON, ROBERT LEE, physical scientist; b. Omaha, Nov. 22, 1932; s. Robert Alton and Lulu Irene (Ross) M.; m. Sharon Faith Galliher, Feb. 19, 1966; children: Dennis, Karyn, Cheryl, Tamara, Traci. BA, U. Pacific, Stockton, Calif., 1957, MS, 1960. Chief chemist Gallo Winery, Modesto, Calif., 1957-66; rsch. scientist Lawrence Livermore Nat. Lab., Livermore, Calif., 1966-69, sr. rsch. scientist, 1973-93; pres. Poolinator, Inc., Gardena, Calif., 1970-72; owner R.L. Morrison Techs., Modesto, 1993—. Cons., speaker, presenter in field. Contbr. numerous articles to profl. jours.; patentee in field. Recipinet Excellence in Nuclear Weapons award U.S. Dept. Energy, 1990, others. Mem. Am. Chem. Soc. Avocations: flying, skiing, scuba diving, photography. Home: 1117 Springcreek Dr Modesto CA 95355-4820

MORRISON, ROBERT SCHECK, former manufacturing, food marketing processing company executive; b. NYC, Apr. 4, 1942; s. Forrest John and Grayce Scheck (Hopkins) Morrison; m. Susan E. Brennan, Oct. 8, 1988; children: R. Scott, Stephen L., James F., Emily E., Catherine A. BS in English, Coll. Holy Cross, 1963; MBA, U. Pa., 1969. With Procter & Gamble, Cin., 1969—83; chmn., CEO Kraft Inc., Northfield, Ill., 1983—97; chmn., pres. CEO Quaker Oats Co., Chgo., 1997—2001; vice chmn. PepsiCo., Inc., Purchase, NY, 2001—03; interim chmn., CEO 3M Co., St. Paul, 2005. Bd. dirs. Aon Corp., 2000—, Tribune Co., 2001—, 3M Corp., 2002—, Ill. Tool Works Inc., 2003—, Grocery Mfrs. Am. Bd. trustees Lyric Opera Chgo., Mus. Sci. and Industry, Chgo., Rush Med. Ctr., Chgo. Capt. USMC, 1963—67. Decorated Silver Star, Purple Heart. Mem.: Onwentsia Club, Old Elm Club, Luianno Club, Red Stick Golf Club. Avocations: golf, tennis, skiing.

MORRISON, SARAH LYDDON, author; b. Rochester, NY, May 19, 1939; d. Paul William and Winifred (Cowles) Lyddon. BA, U. Vt., 1961. Sec. asst. Glamour mag., NYC, 1961-63, Vogue mag., NYC, 1963-65; asst. editor Venture mag., NYC, 1966-71; dir. pub. rels. for tourism Commonwealth of P.R., NYC, 1971-75; asst. Am. Legion, Washington, 1988-98; owner Sarah Lyddon Morrison Pub. Rels., Washington, 1999—2003. Author: The Modern Witch's Spellbook, 1971, Book II, 1983, The Modern Witch's Dream Book, 1985, The Modern Witch's Book of Home Remedies, 1988, The Modern Witch's Book of Symbols, 1997, Modern Witch's Guide to Magic and Spells, 1998. Advisor to nat. security coord. John Kerry Presdl. Campaign, 2003—04. Mem. DAR (Emily Nelson chpt.), Women's Nat. Dem. Club, Colonial Dames XVII Century (nat. def. chmn.), Am. News Women's Club. Avocations: travel, reading, swimming, rock music, cooking. Office Phone: 202-966-2981. Personal E-mail: sarahlyd@verizon.net.

MORRISON, SCOTT DAVID, management consultant, small business owner; b. Duluth, Minn., May 8, 1952; s. Robert Henry and Shirley Elaine (Tester) M. (dec. 1990); m. Jana Louise Bergeron, May 29, 1976; chilren: Robert Scott (dec. 1999), Matthew John. Cert. in welding, Duluth Area Inst. Tech., 1971; student, U. Wis.-Superior, 1976-77; A in Mfg. Mgmt., N. Hennepin C.C., 1985; BA, Concordia Coll., St. Paul, 1988; MBA, St. Thomas U., St. Paul, 1991. Cert. in quality tech., Am. Soc. Quality, 1985, Dell Computer, Inc. instr. Six Sigma; lic. vocat. instr., Minn. Cert. welder Litton Ship Systems, Pascagoula, Miss., 1971-72, Barko Hydraulics, Superior, Wis., 1972-76, Am. Hoist and Derrick Co., Mpls., 1977-79, cert. level II non-destructive exam. insp., 1979-80; quality supr. Colight Inc., Mpls., 1980, Tol-O-Matic, Inc., Mpls., 1980-82; quality assurance engr. ADC Telecomm., Mpls., 1982-84, design assurance engr., 1985-86, product assurance engr., 1986-87, sr. product assurance engr., quality improvement facilitator, 1987-88, product engr. supr., 1988-90, mgr. design assurance, quality assurance, component engring., 1990-92; dir. quality and reg. affairs Waters Instruments, Inc., 1992-96, sr. quality engr., 1996, corp. quality sys. mgr., 1996-98; corp. mfg. and quality Compaq Computer Corp., Houston, 1996-98; sys. engr., sr. cons. Dimension Product Group, 1998—2001, Dell Computer Corp., Austin, Tex., 1998—, quality engr., sr. cons. Transactional Line of Bus., 1999—2000, mgr. quality sys. application team project, 2000, supplier quality engr., sr. cons., 2000—01; sr. cons. ABS Cons. Mgmt. Sys. divsns., Houston, 2001—03; mgr. Mgmt. Sys. Cons., 2002—03; owner Dimensions in Quality, LLC, 2003—; contract mgmt. sys. auditor Moody Internat., 2004—, auditor quality, environ. and health and safety mgmt. sys., 2006—. Judge U.S. Amateur Boxing Fedn., Mpls., 1978-87, 95-97; examiner Minn. Quality Award Minn. Coun. for Quality, 1993, 95, Tex. Quality Award, 1997; mem. quality coun. Am. Electronics Assn., 1994-95; mem. bd. dirs. Rochester Quality Coun., 1994-95; examiner Malcolm Baldridge Nat. Quality award Nat. Inst. Standards and Technology, 1994-95, sr. examiner, 1996-97, alumni examiner, 1999-2000; reviewer fellowship grant applications ASQ, 1996; adj. instr. Riverland Tech. Coll., Rochester, Minn., 1995; lic. profl. boxing judge Tex. Dept. Licensing and Regulation, 1996—; cert. lead quality auditor Brit. Standards Internat., 1996, cert. lead environ. sys. auditor, 2001; facilitator Malcolm Bridge Nat. Quality Award Regional Conf., 1997; cons. in field. Recipient Tech. Excellence award ADC Telecoms., 1987, 88. Mem. ASTM, Am. Soc. Quality (cert. quality engr. cert. quality auditor, cert. quality mgr., cert. six sigma black belt, chmn. host and attendance subcom. 1986-87), Am. Welding Soc., Soc. Mfg. Engrs., Internat. Platform Assn. Roman Catholic. Home and Office: 18 Seneca Pl The Woodlands TX 77382-5353 Office Phone: 281-419-1253.

MORRISON, SHELLEY, actress; b. NYC, Oct. 26, 1936; d. Maurice Nissim and Hortense Mitrani; m. Walter R. Dominguez, Aug. 11, 1973. Student, L.A. City Coll., 1954—56. Presenter Alma awards, 2001—02, Imagan Awards, 2001, Nosotros Golden Eagle awards, 2002. Actress: (films) Interns, 1962, The Greatest Story Ever Told, 1964, Castle of Evil, 1965, Divorce, American Style, 1965, How to Save a Marriage, 1966, Funny Girl, 1967, Three Guns for Texas, 1969, Man and Boy, 1971, Blume in Love, 1972, McKenna's Gold, 1967, Breezy, 1973, People Toys, 1973, Rabbit Test, 1975, Max Dugan Returns, 1982, Troop Beverly Hills, 1988, Fools Rush In, 1996, Shark Tale, 2004, Food Fight, 2007, others, (TV movies) The Girl Who Came Giftwrapped, Three's a Crowd, 1969, Once an Eagle, 1974, The Night That Panicked America, 1975, Kids Don't Tell, 1984, Cries From the Heart, 1994, Columbo: It's All In the Game, Lassie: A New Beginning, others, (TV series) Laredo, 1965-67, The Flying Nun, 1966-70, First and Ten, 1987, I'm Home, 1990, The Fanelli Boys, 1990, Love, Lies and Murder, 1990, Playhouse 90, Dr. Kildare, The Fugitive, Gunsmoke, Marcus Welby, General Hospital, and many others, 1960-70, Man of the People, Sisters, 1991, 92, Murder She Wrote, 1992, Johnny Bago, 1993, Columbo, 1993, L.A. Law, 1994, Live Shot, 1995, Courthouse, Home Improvement, 1997, Nothing Sacred, 1997, Prey, 1997, Nearly Yours, 1998; recurring role in Will & Grace, 1998-, series regular 1999-06 (Diversity award 2004, People's Choice award 2005, nominee Golden Globe award 2005, nominee SAG award 2005); TV guest appearances include Prey, Nothing Sacred, L.A. Law, Busting Loose, Marcus Welby, M.D., Occasional Wife, Between the Lines, Home Improvement, Murder, She Wrote, The Bold Ones, Divorce Court, Soap, The Streets of San Francisco, Dr. Kildare, Man of the People, The Partridge Family, My Favorite Martian, The Outer Limits, The Robert Taylor Show, My Name is Earl, The Megan Mullally Show, numerous others; (voice over animated cartoon comml.) Handy Manny, 2006, 07 (voice animated cartoon series), (A&E) Letters, 2003, numerous others, (stage prodns.) Pal Joey, 1956, Bus Stop, 1956, Only in America, 1960, Orpheus Descending, 1960, Spring's Awakening, 1962, over 65 other prodns., 1956-1970, also appeared in The Mikado, Pal Joey, Anastasia, Orpheus Descending, A Streetcar Named Desire, Sweet Bird of Youth, The Crucible, Zoo Story, Rashomon, Desk Set, Pygmalion, The Would-Be Gentleman, Comedy of Errors, Tiger at the Gates, The Rose Tattoo, Orpheus Descending, Come Back Little Sheba, The Odd Couple, Only in America, El Camino Real, Hamlet, Country Girl, Romeo and Juliet, Cotton Candy, Point of View, Coney Island of the Mind, Last of the Aztecs, numerous others; prodr., writer, 1975—; prodr. (with husband Walter Dominguez) documentary Mexican culture, 2003. Condr. seminars (with husband Walter Dominquez) about Native Americans to keep traditions and ceremonies flourishing. Honored (with husband Walter Dominguez) for work with homeless City of LA, 1985, for work during LA riots, 1992, Bronx Walk of Fame, 2004, Eternity award Women's Theater Group, 2004; nominated for Alma awards SAG, 2000, 01, 02, 06; recipient Emmy award Best Comedy for Will and Grace, 2000, SAG award for Will and Grace, 2002, Halo award, 2003, People's Choice award for Will and Grace ensemble, 2004, Gladd award for Will and Grace ensemble, 2004, Diversity award for Will and Grace ensemble, 2004. Mem. SAG, AFTRA, Actors Equity Assn. Democrat.

MORRISON, STACY LYNNE, editor; b. Jenkintown, Pa., Jan. 17, 1969; d. Robert Isaac and Sharon Lee (Wiley) Morrison; m. Christopher Cole Shannon, Oct. 1, 1994. BA, Washington & Lee U., 1990. Editl. asst. Mirabella mag., NYC, 1991-92, asst. editor, 1992-93, assoc. features editor, 1993-95; mng. editor J. Crew Group Inc., NYC, 1995, Time Out New York, NYC, Conde Nast Sports for Women; editor-in-chief Modern Bride, 1998—2000, ONE, 2000—01; exec. editor Marie Claire, NYC, 2001—04; editor-in-chief Redbook, NYC, 2004—. Office: Redbook 224 W 57th St New York NY 10019 *

MORRISON, TONI (CHLOE ANTHONY WOFFORD), writer, educator, editor; b. Lorain, Ohio, Feb. 18, 1931; d. George and Ella Ramah (Willis) Wofford; m. Harold Morrison, 1958 (div. 1964); children: Harold Ford, Slade Kevin. BA in English, Howard U., 1953; MA in Am. Lit., Cornell U., 1955; degree (hon.), Harvard U., U. Pa., Sarah Lawrence, Oberlin, Dartmouth, Yale, Georgetown, Columbia U., Brown U., U. Mich., Universite Paris 7-Denis Diderot. Instr. English Tex. So. U., 1955-57, Howard U., 1957-64; assoc. editor Random House, Syracuse, NY, 1965—67, sr. editor NYC, 1967—83; assoc. prof. English SUNY, Purchase, 1971-72, Albert Schweitzer Prof. in the Humanities Albany, NY, 1984-89; Robert F. Goheen Prof. in the Humanities Princeton U., Princeton, NJ, 1989—, dir. Princeton Atelier, 1994—. Vis. lectr. Yale Univ., 1976-77, Bard Coll., 1986-88, Obert C. Tanner Lectr. U. Mich., Ann Arbor, 1988, Jeannette K. Watson Disting. Prof., Syracuse U., 1988; delivered the Clark lectures, Trinity Coll., Cambridge, 1990, Massey Lectures, Harvard U., 1990; Internat. Cordorcet Chair, Ecole Normale Superieure and College de France, 1994. Author: (novels) The Bluest Eye, 1969, Sula, 1973 (Nat. Book award nomination 1975, Ohioana Book Award 1975), Song of Solomon, 1977 (Nat. Book Critics Circle award 1977, American Acad. and Inst. of Arts and Letters award 1977), Tar Baby, 1981, Beloved, 1987 (Pulitzer Prize for fiction 1988, Robert F. Kennedy Meml. Book award 1988, Melcher Book award Unitarian Universalist Assn. 1988, Nat. Book award nomination 1987, Nat. Book Critics Circle award nomination 1987, Best Ama Fiction of Past 25 Years, NY Times, 2006), Jazz, 1992, Paradise, 1998, Love, 2003, (children's book) Remember: The Journey to School Integration, 2004 (Coretta Scott King award ALA, 2005), (play) Dreaming Emmett, 1986, (non-fiction) Playing in the Dark: Whiteness and the Literary Imagination, 1992, (speech) The Dancing Mind, 1996; co-author (with son Slade Kevin) (children's books) The Big Box, 1999, The Book of Mean People, 2002, The Lion or the Mouse?, 2003, The Ant or the Grashopper?, 2003, The Poppy or the Snake?, 2003; editor: The Black Book, 1974, Race-ing Justice, En-Gendering Power: Essays on Anita Hill, Clarence Thomas, and the Construction of Social Reality, 1992, To Die for the People: The Writings of Huey P. Newton, 1995; co-editor Birth of a Nation'Hood: Gaze, Script, Spectacle in the O.J. Simpson Case, 1997; lyricist: Honey and Rue, 1992. Recipient NY State Governor's Art award, 1986, Elizabeth Cady Stanton award National Orgn. Women, Nobel Prize in Lit., 1993, Nat. Book Found. Medal for Disting. Contbn. to Am. Letters, 1996, Nat. Humanities Medal, 2000, Golden Plate award, Acad. Achievement, 2005. Mem. Am. Acad. Arts and Letters, Author's Guild (coun.), Nat. Coun. Arts. Achievements include being first African American woman to win the Nobel Prize in Literature. *

MORRISON, WILLIAM FOSDICK, business educator, retired electrical company executive; b. Bridgeport, Conn., Mar. 14, 1935; s. Robert Louis and Helen Fosdick (Mulroney) M.; m. E. Drake Miller, Dec. 14, 1957 (div. Sept. 1972); children: Donna Drake, Deanne Fosdick, William Fosdick; m. Carol Ann Stover, Nov. 20, 1972. BA in Econs., Trinity Coll., 1957. Mgr. purchasing dept. Westinghouse Electric Co., Lima, Ohio, 1960—68, mgr. mfg. Upper Sandusky, Ohio, 1969, gen. mgr. Gurabo, Puerto Rico, 1970—71, mgr. tng. Pitts., 1972—84, program mgr. Sunnyvale, Calif., 1984—89, procurement project dir., 1990—94; prof. San Jose State U., Calif., 1993—, Golden Gate U., San Francisco, 1995—; lead negotiator Advanced Micro Devices, Santa Clara, Calif., 1995—97; prof. U. Calif., Berkeley, 1996—2002, Menlo Coll., 1998—2001; faculty adv. Beta Gamma Sigma, 2002—. Negotiation cons. and trainer, 1969—; lead negotiator ReSound Corp., 1998-99; mgr. renovation project San Jose State U., 1999-2000. Author: The Pre-Negotiation Planning Book, 1985, The Human Side of Negotiations, 1994, The Savvy Negotiator, 2006; contbr. articles to profl. jours. Bd. dirs. Valley Inst. of the Theatre Arts, Saratoga, Calif., 1986-90, Manhattan Playhouse, 1989-94; chmn. Sensory Access Found. Golf Tournament, 1995-96; dir. protocol office World Cup USA, 1994. Served to capt. USAFR, 1958-64. Named Man of the Yr. Midwest Lacrosse Coaches Assn., 1983, recipient Service award U.S. Lacrosse Assn., 1982. Mem.: Nat. Assn. Purchasing Mgmt. (pres. Lima chpt. 1966—67, dir. nat. affairs 1967—68, dist. treas. 1968—70), The Propeller Club (sec., San Francisco port 2002—), Circumnaviagators Club (founder, pres. San Francisco chpt. 2001—), Sunnyvale Golf Assn. (vice-chmn. 1985, chmn. 1986, handicap scorer 1992—93, chmn. 1993), Elks. Avocation: golf. Home: 3902 Duncan Pl Palo Alto CA 94306-4550 Office Phone: 650-815-1299. E-mail: wfmorrison@earthlink.net.

MORRIS-ROGERS, CHERYL-ANN, daycare provider, director, educator; b. Chgo., Feb. 26, 1958; d. Richard Lee and Ruth Hortence (Davis) M. AA, Cen. YMCA Coll., 1979; BA, DePaul U., 1982. Cert. in child devel. Supr. C.E.T.A. Program, Chgo., 1979; asst. dir. WLS AM/FM Radio Pub. Affairs, Chgo., 1981-82; educator Auburn Pk. Day Care, Kindergarten, Chgo., 1982-83, pres., dir., 1983—; educator, pres., dir. Lakefront Children's Acad., Chgo., 1999—. Cons. in field. Mem. NAACP, Chgo., 1988—, United Negro Coll. Fund, Chgo., 1988—; com. mem. Election Judge Loretta Hall Morgan, Chgo., 1989; vol. Election Mayor Harold Washington, Chgo., 1987. Recipient Child Devel. award Love Drops Mag., 1987; named to Dean's List, 1980. Mem. Nat. Assn. Women-Bus. Owners, League Black Women, Preschool Owners Assn., Nat. Assn. for Edn. Young Children, Chgo. Assn. for Edn. Young Children. Avocations: reading, writing, swimming, camping, travel. Office: Auburn Pk Day Care 741 W 79th St Chicago IL 60620-2423 also: Lakefront Childrens Acad 400 E Randolph St Chicago IL 60601-7329

MORRISS, FRANK, writer, educator; b. Pasadena, Calif., Mar. 28, 1923; s. B. Gerard Morriss and Regina Spann; m. Mary Rita Moynihan, Feb. 11, 1950 (dec. Oct. 23, 1996); children: Patricia, Mary Ellen Hill, Regina Sister M John, OSF(dec.), Gerard. BS in Philosophy magna cum laude, Regis Coll., Denver, 1943; JD, Georgetown U., 1948. Editor Register Newspapers, Denver, 1949—61, 1963—67; assoc. editor Vt. Cath. Tribune, Burlington, 1961—63; contbg. editor The Wanderer, St. Paul, 1967—; educator Colorado Cath. Acad., Wheat Ridge, Colo., 1973—. Bd. dirs. Wanderer Forum Found., St. Paul, 1969—; policy expert Heritage Found., 1995—. Author: Saints In Verse, Two Chapels, The Divine Epic, The Catholic as Citizen, The Conservative Imperative, Boy of Philadelphia, Alfred of Wessex, The Adventures of Broken Hand, Submarine Pioneer, (lectrs. on CD) Saints Speak to Modern World. Founder Colo. Cath. Acad., Wheat Ridge, 1970—2002. Sgt. US Army, 1943—45, PTO. Recipient Frederic Ozanam award, Soc. Cath. Social Scientists, 2003. Mem.: Fellowship of Cath. Scholars, VFW. Republican. Roman Catholic. Home: 3505 Owens Street Wheat Ridge CO 80033 Office Fax: 303-422-1475.

MORRISS, FRANK HOWARD, JR., pediatrics educator; b. Birmingham, Ala., Apr. 20, 1940; s. Frank Howard Sr. and Rochelle (Snow) M.; m. Mary J. Hagan, June 29, 1968; children: John Hagan, Matthew Snow. BA, U. Va., 1962; MD, Duke U., 1966. Diplomate Am. Bd. Pediatrics, Am. Bd. Perinatal and Neonatal Medicine. Intern Duke U. Med. Ctr., Durham, NC, 1966-67, resident in pediatrics, 1967-68, fellow in neonatology, 1970-71, U. Colo., Denver, 1971-73; asst. prof. to prof. U. Tex. Med. Sch., Houston, 1973-86; prof. U. Iowa Coll. Medicine, Iowa City, 1987—, chmn. dept., 1987—2004. Editor: Role of Human Milk in Infant Nutrition and Health, 1986; contbr. numerous articles to profl. jours, chpts. to books. Lt. comdr. USN, 1968-70. Grantee, NIH, 1977—87, 1990—2004. Mem. Am. Pediatric Soc., Soc. Pediatric Rsch., Am. Acad. Pediatrics, Soc. Gynecol. Investigation, Midwest Soc. Pediatric Rsch. Office: U Iowa Hosps & Clinics Dept Pediatrics Iowa City IA 52242 Office Phone: 319-384-6530.

MORRISSETTE, JENNIFER J. D., geneticist; b. NY; PhD, U. Buffalo, NY, 1992. Cert. clin. cytogenetics and molecular genetics ABMG, 2002. Dir. clin. cytogenetics St. Christopher's Hosp. for Children, Phila., 2004; asst. prof. Drexel Coll. Medicine, Phila., 2004—. Office: St Christophers Hospital for Children 3601 A St Philadelphia PA 19134 Office Phone: 215-427-5290.

MORRISSEY, CHARLES RICHARD, SR., retired elementary school educator; b. New Haven, Conn., Feb. 19, 1943; s. Charles Joseph and Anne Morrissey; m. Janice Morrissey; children: Charles Jr., Amy Ann, Melissa Mary, Jennifer Ann, Heather Kathleen. BA, Providence Coll., 1964; MS, So. Conn. State Coll., New Haven, 1968, cert., 1973. Tchr. grades 8 and 9 New Haven Bd. Edn., 1964—65, tchr. grade 5 and 6, 1968—2001; substitute tchr. Wallingford Bd. Edn., Conn., 2005. Tchr. algebra, elem. math. and computers Hopkins Grammar Sch., New Haven, 1982—. Mem.: Am. Legion (mem. exec. com. 2005—07), Phi Delta Kappa (mem. exec. bd., pres.). Avocations: photography, music. Home: 106 Shawmut Ave North Haven CT 06473

MORRISSEY, EDMOND JOSEPH, philologist; b. NYC, June 5, 1943; s. William J. and Anne K. (Gaffney) M.; m. Patricia M. Hanlon, Oct. 11, 1987; children: William, Edmond, Kathleen, Patrick, Jennifer, Lisa, Paula. AB summa cum laude, Boston Coll., 1965; BA, U. Oxford, 1967, MA, 1971, Harvard U., 1969, PhD, 1974. Seminarian Pope John XXIII Nat. Sem., Weston, Mass., 1974-77; collaborator prof. Sterling Dow Harvard U., Cambridge, Mass., 1977-95. Cons. in pub. and photoreprodn. Author: Studies in Inscriptions Listing the Agonistic Festivals, 1974, A Quinquagesimal History of the Church of St. Bernadette, 1987; contbr. articles to profl. jours. Pres., chmn. adminstrn. fin., St. Bernadette's Ch., Archdiocese of Boston, 1980—; founding dir. Theol. Lectures Series, Randolph, Mass., 1978—, Randolph Hist. Commn., 1988—; staff vol. Cardinal Medeiros Program for Handicapped, 1980-82; treas., bd. dirs. Randolph Community Food Pantry, 1994—. Marshall scholar, 1965—67, Wilson scholar, 1965—, Gen. Motors scholar, 1962—65, Ford Found. fellow, 1967—69, Harvard U. fellow, 1969—71. Mem. Am. Inst. Archaeology, Am. Philol. Assn., Alumni Assn. Harvard, Oxford U. Alumni Assn., Boston Coll. Alumni Assn. Democrat. Roman Catholic. Home: 4 Bennington St Randolph MA 02368-2106 Personal E-mail: EdmondusM@msn.com.

MORRISSEY, EDWARD T., II, conservative political blogger, nationally-syndicated radio co-host, columnist; b. Apr. 1963; m. Marcia A. Morrissey; 1 child, David. Polit. blog writer Captainsquarters.blog.com, 2003—; polit. dir. Blog Talk Radio. Invited spkr. Contbr. essays to NY Sun, NY Post, and the Daily Standard; co-host (weekly talk-radio show), Mpls., 2004—, guest appearances TV and radio shows in the US and Canada, regular contbr. (online, Daily Standard). Mem. Northern Alliance, Minn. Named Blogger of Yr., The Week mag., 2006. Conservative. E-mail: captain@captainsquartersblog.com. *

MORRISSEY, J. RICHARD, lawyer; b. LA, Jan. 8, 1941; BA, Santa Clara Univ., 1963; JD, Univ. Calif., Berkeley, 1966. Bar: Calif. 1966, US Ct. Mil. Appeals 1967, US Supreme Ct. 1980. Ptnr., co-leader Product Liability practice, head LA Litigation sect. Pillsbury Winthrop Shaw Pittman, LA. Mem.: ABA, LA County Bar Assn. Office: Pillsbury Winthrop Shaw Pittman Suite 2800 725 S Figueroa St Los Angeles CA 90017 Office Phone: 213-488-7525. Office Fax: 213-629-1033. Business E-Mail: richard.morrissey@pillsburylaw.com.

MORRISSEY, JOHN CARROLL, SR., lawyer; b. NYC, Sept. 2, 1914; s. Edward Joseph and Estelle (Caine) M.; m. Eileen Colligan, Oct. 14, 1950; children: Jonathan Edward, Ellen (Mrs. James A. Jenkins), Katherine, John, Patricia, Richard, Brian, Peter. BA magna cum laude, Yale U., 1937, LLB, 1940; JSD, N.Y. U., 1951; grad., Command and Gen. Staff Sch., 1944. Bar: N.Y. State 1940, D.C. 1953, Calif. 1954, U.S. Supreme Ct. 1944. Asso. firm Dorsey and Adams, 1940-41, Dorsey, Adams and Walker, 1946-50; counsel Office of Sec. of Def., Dept. Def., Washington, 1950-52; acting gen. counsel def. Electric Power Adminstrn., 1952-53; atty. Pacific Gas and Electric Co., San Francisco, 1953-70, assoc. gen. counsel, 1970-74, v.p., gen. counsel, 1975-80; individual practice law San Francisco, 1980-2000. Dir. Gas Lines, Inc. Bd. dirs. Legal Aid Soc., San Francisco; chmn. Golden Gate dist. Boy Scouts Am., 1973-75; commr. Human Rights Commn. of San Francisco, 1976-89, chmn., 1980-82; chmn. Cath. Social Svc. of San Francisco, 1966-68; adv. com. Archdiocesean Legal Affairs, 1981—; regent Archdiocesan Sch. of Theology, St. Patrick's Sem., 1994-99; dir. Presidio Preservation Assn., 1995-99. Served to col. F.A. U.S. Army, ETO, 1941-46. Decorated Bronze star, Army Commendation medal. Mem. NAS, AAAS, ABA, Calif. State Bar Assn., Fed. Power Bar Assn., N.Y. Acad. Scis., Calif. Conf. Pub. Utility Counsel, Pacific Coast Electric Assn., Pacific Coast Gas Assn., Econ. Round Table of San Francisco, World Affairs Council, San Francisco C. of C., Calif. State C. of C., Harold Brunn Soc. Med. Rsch., Electric Club, Serra Club, Commonwealth Club, Yale Club of San Francisco (pres. 1989-90), Pacific-Union Club, Sometimes Tuesday Club, Sovereign Mil. Order Malta, Phi Beta Kappa. Roman Catholic. Office: 1661 Pine St # 1135 San Francisco CA 94109-0426 Personal E-mail: dadjcm@aol.com.

MORRISSEY, MICHAEL JOSEPH, investment banker; b. Mount Holly, NJ, June 26, 1947; s. Edward Francis and Winifred (Monahan) M.; m. Joanne Stone, June 5, 1982; children: Scott Christopher, Nathanial Joseph Cake. AB, Boston Coll., 1969; MBA, Dartmouth Coll., 1971; grad. Corp. Fin. Mgmt. Program, Harvard U., 1979. Security analyst Philo Smith & Co., Inc., Stamford, Conn., 1971-73, Kidder Peabody & Co., Inc., NYC, 1973-74, asst. v.p., 1974-76, v.p., 1976-77, Dean Witter Reynolds, Inc., NYC, 1977-78, Crum and Forster, Morristown, NJ, 1978-80, sr. v.p., 1980-83; pres. Firemark Investments, Morristown, NJ, 1983-85, chmn. bd., 1985—; exec. v.p. Manhattan Nat. Corp., NYC, 1985, pres., chief operating officer, 1985-86; mng. ptnr. Firemark Tiger Fund, 2005. Bd. dir. Fin. Pacific Ins. Group, Calif., CGA Group Ltd., Bermuda. Vice chmn. Rep. Party Santa Fe County; bd. dirs. Boys & Girls Club, Santa Fe. Recipient CFA award, 1977. Mem. Internat. Ins. Soc., Young Pres.' Orgn., Dartmouth Club (N.Y.C.), Spring Brook Country Club. Republican. Episcopalian. Office: FireMark Investments 200 W De Vargas St Santa Fe NM 87501 Home Phone: 505-995-9981. E-mail: mjm@firemarkinv.com.

MORRISSEY, PATRICIA A., federal agency administrator; AA in Liberal Arts, Hartford CC, 1964; BA in Psychology, Stetson U., 1966; M.Ed. in Spl. Edn., Pa. State U., 1971, PhD in Spl. Edn., 1974. Positions with US Ho. of Reps. Com. on Edn. and Labor, Senate Com. on Health, Edn., Labor, and Pensions; sr. assoc. Booz Allen Hamilton, McLean, Va.; commr. Adminstrn. Devel. Disabilities Adminstrn. Children and Families, HHS, 2001—. Republican. Office: Adminstrn Children and Families Adminstrn Devel Disabilities 370 L'Enfant Promenade SW Washington DC 20447 Office Phone: 202-690-6590. Business E-Mail: pmorrissey@acf.hhs.gov.

MORRISSEY, THOMAS A., publishing executive; Pub. Entertainment Weekly. Office: Entertainment Weekly 1675 Broadway New York NY 10019 Office Phone: 212-522-5600. Office Fax: 212-522-6104.

MORRISSEY, THOMAS F., art educator; MFA, Ariz. State U., Tempe, 1978; PhD, Mellon U., 1992; MPA, U. RI, Providence, 2000. Prof. C.C. RI, Lincoln, MIT, Boston, Providence Coll. Exec. dir. Texarkana Artworks, Ark., 2002—, Warwick Mus., RI, 2006. Author: Between the Lines, 2000. Chair RI Vietnam Monument Com., 1984—. With US Army, 1969—71, Vietnam. Fellow, Kellogg Found., 1987—89; scholar, Fulbright Found., 2003. Mem.: Coll. Art Assn. Office: CC RI 1762 Louis Pike Lincoln RI 02865

MORRISSEY, THOMAS PAUL, medical educator, physician; b. Hudson, NY, May 1, 1969; s. Thomas Edward and Barbara Ann Morrissey; m. Lynn Claudine Berger, May 5, 1996; children: Julia, Caroline, Olivia. BA in Biochemistry, Columbia U., NYC, 1991; MA cum laude, SUNY, Syracuse, 1995. Lic. Ob-gyn Pa., 1997, NC, 1999, NY, 2002, diplomate Am. Bd. Obstetrics and Gynecology, 2003, gynecologic oncology 2005. Resident ob-gyn and reproductive scis. Magee-Womens Hosp., U. Pitts. Med. Ctr., 1995—99; attending gynecologic oncologist North Shore U. Hosp., Manhasset, NY, 2002—; asst. prof. dept. ob-gyn NYU, 2002—. Dir. gynecologic oncology lectr. series dept. ob-gyn North Shore U. Hosp.; co-prin. investigator Gynecologic Oncology Group. Fellow: ACS, Soc. Gynecologic Oncologists, Am. Coll. Ob-gyn (3M Pharm. Rsch. award 2000—01); mem.: AMA, Columbia Coll. Alumni Assn., Syracuse Med. Alumni Assn., Metro. Gynecol. Cancer Soc., Nassau Obstet. and Gynecol. Soc., Alpha Omega Alpha. Avocations: basketball, running.

MORRONE, FRANK, electronics executive; b. Marano Marchesato, Cosenza, Italy, May 13, 1949; s. Luigi and Emma (Molinaro) M.; m. Katherine Ann Kuehn, Feb. 1, 1975; children: Louis H., Cecilia E., Joseph V. BSEE, U. Wis., 1972; MBA, Northwestern U., 1993. Project engr. 3M Co., St. Paul, 1972—73; product engr., mgr. Eaton Corp., Kenosha, Wis., 1973—79; chief elec. engr. Tree Machine Tool, Racine, Wis., 1979—80; v.p. engring. MacPower divsn. Manu-Tronics, Inc., Kenosha, 1980—84, exec. v.p., 1984—99, bd. dirs., sec., 1988—99; v.p. ops. Sanmina Corp., 1999—2001, sr. v.p., 2001—. Exec. bd. Southeast coun. Boy Scouts Am., Racine, 1987—; bd. dirs. Kenosha Libr., 1987-98, U. Wis.-Parkside Benevolent Found., 2000—; mgmt. coun. Lakeview Tech. Acad., 1997-99. Mem. IEEE, Kenosha County Club (bd. dirs.). Office: Sanmina-SCI Corp 8701 100th St Pleasant Prairie WI 53158-2202 Office Phone: 262-947-7700.

MORROW, BARRY NELSON, screenwriter, producer; b. Austin, Minn., June 12, 1948; s. Robert Clayton and Rose Nell (Nelson) M.; m. Beverly Lee McKenzie, Mar. 3, 1969; children: Clayton McKenzie, ZoeAnna Rachel. BA, St. Olaf Coll., 1970; DHL (hon.), U. La Verne, Calif., 1990. Media specialist U. Iowa, Iowa City, 1974-81; freelance screenwriter Los Angeles, 1981-90; pres. Morrow-Heus Prodns., 1990-00. Storywriter (TV film) Bill, 1981 (Emmy award 1982); screenwriter: (TV films) Bill: On His Own, 1983, Conspiracy of Love, 1987, Silent Victory, 1988, The Karen Carpenter Story, 1989, (feature film) Rain Man, 1988 (co-recipient Acad. award Best Original Screenplay 1989); screenwriter, exec. prodr.: Christmas on Division Street, 1991; exec. prodr.: Switched at Birth, 1991 (Emmy nomination), Gospa, 1995, The Fifties, 1997, Behind the Mask, 1999; screenwriter, prodr. Race the Sun, 1996; monologist: Bill for Short, 1992. Recipient Pres.'s award Am. Acad. for Devel. Medicine, 1978, Outstanding Contbn. award Mid-Am. Congress on Aging, 1983, SI award NASW, 1991, Pope John XXIII award Viterbo Coll., 1992. Mem. Writers Guild Am. West, Acad. TV Arts and Scis., Acad. Motion Picture Arts and Scis., Motion Picture Screen Cartoonists Guild.

MORROW, BRUCE WILLIAM, academic administrator, management consultant; b. Rochester, Minn., May 20, 1946; s. J. Robert and Frances P. Morrow; m. Jenny Lea Morrow. BA, U. Notre Dame, 1968, MBA in Mgmt. with honors, 1974, MA in Comparative Lit., 1975; grad., U.S. Army Command and Gen. Staff Coll., 1978. Cert. project mgmt. profl. Project Mgmt. Inst., 2003. Chmn. elem. German U. Notre Dame, 1973—75; co-mgr. Wendy's Old Fashioned Hamburgers, South Bend, Ind., 1976—77; adminstrn. mgr. Ea. States Devel. Corp., Richmond, Va., 1977; v.p. JDB Assocs., Inc., Alexandria, Va., 1976—78; sr. cons. Data Base Mgmt., Inc., Springfield, Va., 1979—80; owner Aardvark Prodns., Alexandria, Va., 1980—82; sys. analyst, staff officer Hdqrs., Dept. Army, Washington, 1980—84; chmn. bd. Commonwealth Dominion Corp., Sierra Vista, Ariz., 1982—. Strategic planner, dep. comdr. Fort Pickett, Blackstone, Va., 1986—89; dir. continuing edn. Southside Va. C.C., Alberta, 1989—91; co-founder S.W. Bus. Group, Tucson, 1995—99; pres. Sierra Vista Golf, Inc., Ariz., 1994—95; Cochise County team leader Ariz. Coun. Econ. Conversion, 1994—95; mem. com. Ariz. Small Bus. Initiative, 1994—99; internet webmaster, 1996—; exec. dir. Southea. Ariz. Contrs. Assn., 1997—98; corp. adminstr. Garcia Cos., Sierra Vista, Tucson, Phoenix, 1997—99; property adminstr. Brown & Root Svcs., Ft. Huachuca, Ariz., Land Between the Lakes, Ky., 1999—2000, logistics coord., 2000—02; dir. assessment ctr. Transport. Security Agy. NCS Pearson, Nashville and Fresno, 2002; project advisor Dyncorp Internat., Irving, Tex., 2004. Author: (radio series) Survival in the Computer Jungle, 1986, (classroom text) Introduction to Computers, 1988, 2d edit., 1993, Defense Conversion Handbook, 1995, Business Assessment Manual, 1996, Employee Manual Guide, 1996, Business Plan Guide, 1996, Marketing Plan Guide, 1996, (screenplay) Gray Rock, 2000; contbg. columnist Notre Dame mag., 1974—86; exec. prodr.: (motion picture) Beneath the Law, 1995—96; composer songs. Active Boy Scouts Am., 1960—69; firefighter Roanoke Wildwood Vol. Fire Dept., 1991—93. Lt. col. USAR, ret. Decorated Bronze Stars, Army commendation medals, Army Achievement medal, Meritorious Svc. medals, Parachutist's badge, Army Gen. Staff badge. Mem. VFW (life), Nat. Eagle Scout Assn., Lake Gaston C. of C. (bd. dirs.), Am. Legion, Sierra Vista Area C. of C., Lions (v.p. local club), Friends Internat. (Am. v.p. 1969-71, Boeblingen, Germany), Order of DeMolay, Beta Gamma Sigma, Delta Phi Alpha. Office: Commonwealth Dominion Corp 334 Landing Strip Rd Hardin KY 42048-9413 E-mail: cdc@theriver.com.

MORROW, CAROLINE DONOVAN, retired social worker; b. Houston, Tex., Dec. 11, 1937; d. Ira and Verda Ree Donovan; m. Leonard Emery Morrow, June 17, 1967; children: Emery Donovan, April Antionette. BS, Wiley Coll., 1960; MSW, Atlanta U., 1962. LCSW Colo. Counselor Ansel Rd. Golden Age Ctr., Cleve., 1962—67; vol. counselor Rhein Main AFB, Frankfurt, Germany, 1967—69; adminstr. Job Corp. YWCA, Denver, 1970—75; med. social worker Rose Med. Ctr., Denver, 1976—2003, ret., 2003. Cons. in field. Vol. Village East Elem. Sch., Aurora, Colo., 2002—04; vol. presdl. election Dem Com., Denver, 2004; vol. food bank Mt. Glilead Bapt. Ch., Denver, sec., 1999. Recipient Appreciation cert., USAF, 1978, Wall Tolerance, 2004, Recognition cert., NAACP, 2004. Mem.: Order Ea. Star, Alpha Kappa Alpha. Democrat. Avocations: reading, writing, puzzles, collecting recipes, decorating. Home: 1358 So Oswego Ct Aurora CO 80012

MORROW, DONALD L., lawyer; b. Inglewood, Calif., Apr. 14, 1951; BA cum laude, U. So. Calif., 1972, JD, 1975. Bar: Calif. 1975. Ptnr. Paul, Hastings, Janofsky & Walker, Costa Mesa, Calif., mem. policy com., chmn. profl. devel. com. Lawyer rep. 9th Cir. Jud. Conf., 1989, 91-92. Dir. Pacific Symphony Orch., 1990-91. Fellow Am. Coll. Trial Lawyers; mem. Orange County Bar Assn. (dir. 1992—), Orange County Bar Found. (pres. 1993, dir. 1990—), Robert A. Banyard Am. Inn of Ct. (master bencher 1987-92). Office: Paul Hastings Janofsky & Walker 17th flr 695 Town Center Dr Costa Mesa CA 92626-1924 Office Phone: 714-668-6291. Office Fax: 714-668-6391. Business E-Mail: donaldmorrow@paulhastings.com.

MORROW, GEORGE J., medical products executive; m. Katherine Morrow; 3 children. BA, Southampton Coll.; MA in Biochemistry, Bryn Mawr Coll., Pa.; MBA, Duke U., Durham, NC. V.p., gen. mgr. sales and mktg. divsn. Glaxo, Inc., 1992, group v.p. comml. ops., 1993—96; mng. dir. Glaxo Wellcome UK, 1997—98; pres., CEO Glaxo Wellcome Inc., Research Park Triangle, NC, 1999—2001; exec. v.p., worldwide sales and mktg. Amgen, Inc., Thousand Oaks, Calif., 2001—03, exec. v.p. global comml. ops., 2003—. Mem. adv. bd. Duke U. Fuqua Sch. Bus.; bd. visitors Duke U. Med. Ctr. Office: Amgen Inc 1 Amgen Ctr Dr Thousand Oaks CA 91320-1799 Office Phone: 805-447-1000. Office Fax: 805-447-1010. *

MORROW, GRANT, III, medical research director, pediatrician; b. Pitts., Mar. 18, 1933; married, 1960; 2 children. BA, Haverford Coll., 1955; MD, U. Pa., 1959. Intern U. Colo., 1959-60; resident in pediat. U. Pa., 1960-62, fellow neonatology, asst. instr., 1962-63, instr., 1963-66, assoc., 1966-68, asst. prof., 1968-70, assoc. prof., 1970-72, U. Ariz., 1972—78, prof., 1974-78, assoc. chmn. dept., 1976-78; med. dir. Columbus (Ohio) Children's Hosp., 1978-94; prof. neonatology and metabolism, chmn. dept. Ohio State U., 1978-94; med. dir. divsn. molecular and human genetics Children's Hosp. Rsch. Found., Columbus, 1994-98. Med. dir. Children's Rsch. Inst., Columbus, Ohio, 1978—. Mem. Am. Pediat. Soc., Am. Soc. Clin. Nutrition, Soc. Pediat. Rsch. Achievements include research on children suffering inborn errors of metabolism, mainly amino and organic acids. Office: Children's Rsch Inst 700 Childrens Dr Columbus OH 43205-2696 Home Phone: 614-253-5693; Office Phone: 614-722-2708. Office Fax: 614-722-2716. Business E-Mail: morrowg@ccri.net.

MORROW, JAMES FRANKLIN, lawyer; b. Shenandoah, Iowa, Oct. 23, 1944; s. Warren Ralph and Margaret Glee (Palm) M. BS, Kans. State U., 1967; JD, U. Ariz., 1973. Bar: Ariz. 1973, U.S. Dist. Ct. Ariz. 1973. Ptnr. Bilby, Shoenhair, Warnock & Dolph, Tucson, 1973-83, Quarles & Brady Streich Lang LLP, Tucson, 1984—. Mng. editor U. Ariz. Law Rev., 1972-73. Past chmn. bd. trustees Palo Verde Mental Health Svcs.; past pres. U. Ariz. Alumni Assn.; past chmn. bd. Palo Verde Hosp., Ariz. Tech. Devel. Corp.; past pres. bd. Cath. Cmty. Svcs.; past chmn. bd. dirs. U. Ariz. Found. Capt. U.S. Army, 1967-70. Mem. Am. Coll. Real Estate Lawyers, Am. Coll. Mortgage Attys., State Bar Ariz. (cert. real estate specialist, adv. com. real estate specialists, past chmn. real estate property sect.), Pima County Bar Assn., Calif. Bar Assn. Democrat. Roman Catholic. Avocation: golf. Office: Quarles & Brady Streich Lang LLP Ste 1700 One South Church Ave Tucson AZ 85701

MORROW, JAMES THOMAS, energy executive; b. Seattle, Apr. 24, 1941; s. James Elroy and Helen Margaret (Helzer) M.; 1 child, Shannon F. BSEE, BS Gen. Sci., Oreg. State U., 1964; MBA, U. Santa Clara, 1966, PhD, 1973. Registered investment advisor, SEC; profl. engr., Calif. Engr. GE Co., San Jose, Calif., 1964—66; mgr. engring. Beckman Instruments, Inc., Palo Alto, Calif., 1966—69; pres. MSA Cons., Inc., Portland, Oreg., 1969—75; mgr. A.T. Kearney, Inc., San Francisco, 1975—78; v.p. mktg. Pierce Pacific Mfg., Portland, 1978—79; chmn., CEO Lanco Internat., Inc., Clackamas, Oreg., 1979—81; regional mgr., v.p. Case & Co., Portland, 1981—82; chmn. bd., exec. v.p. Morley Fin. Svcs. Inc., 1982—94; chmn., pres., CEO Capital Devel. Group, Inc., Portland, 1994—96; chmn., CEO Apollo Fin. Group, NYC, 1996—98, Olympic Healthcare Tech., Inc., Portland, NYC, 1998—2002; sr. v.p. El Rincon Resort, Cabo San Lucas, Mexico, 2002—03; pres., CEO, dir. Naanovo Energy, Inc., Calgary, Alta., Canada, 2003—; pres., CEO Naanovo Energy USA, Inc., Lincoln City, Oreg., 2003—, Naanovo Internat. Free Zone N.V., Oranjestad, Aruba, 2005—, Naanovo Internat. FZC, Dubai, United Arab Emirates, 2005; mgr. T Squared LLC, Newport, Oreg., 2005—. Chmn. bd. dirs. Ship Harbor Resort and Marina, Inc., 1998-2004, Turtle Cove Resort, Inc., 1998, Olympic Capital, Inc., 1998-2003; bd. dirs. Naanove Energy, Accucom Data Network, Inc., Pierce Pacific Mfg., Lanco Internat., Energy Guard, Inc., G&R Devel. Co., Inc., MSA Cons., Inc.; sec.-treas. Everybody's Record Co., Inc. Contbr. articles to profl. jours., chpts. to textbooks Bd. dirs. Found. for Oreg. Rsch. and Edn., Jr. Achievement, First August Fin., Inc., Met. Youth Symphony; chmn. steering com. R.S. Dow Neurol. Scis. Inst.; mem. Russian ANT-25 Aviation Com. Mem. Oreg. Pilots Assn. (pres. Beaverton chpt.). Republican. Congregationalist. Achievements include patents for waste to energy technology; solar energy to electricity; biojector needleless syringe. Home: 3575 NE Reef Dr Lincoln City OR 97367 Office Phone: 971-223-0628. Business E-Mail: tmorrow@naanovo.com.

MORROW, JASON DREW, pharmacologist, medical researcher; b. St. Louis, Mar. 30, 1957; s. Ralph Ernest and Vera Rowena (Cummings) M.; m. Lisa Lee Hyman, Mar. 26, 1983; children: Jeremy Nash, Stephanie Rose. BA magna cum laude, Vanderbilt U., 1979; MD, Washington U., St. Louis, 1983. Diplomate Am. Bd. Internal Medicine, Am. Bd. Infectious Diseases. Med. intern, resident Vanderbilt U. Hosp., Nashville, 1983-86, Hugh J. Morgan chief med. resident, 1987-88, rsch. fellow in clin. pharmacology, 1988-91; sr. rsch. fellow dept. pharmacology Vanderbilt U., Sch. Medicine, Nashville, 1991-94, asst. prof. pharmacology and medicine, 1994-95; assoc. prof. Vanderbilt U., Nashville, 1995-99, F. Tremaine Billings prof. medicine, 1999—, dir. Eicosanoid Core Lab. dept. pharmacology, 1992—; clin. fellow in infectious diseases Barnes Hosp./Washington U., 1986-87; staff physician in medicine and infectious diseases VA Med. Ctr., Nashville, 1991—; dir. rsch. ctr. pharmacology drug toxicology Vanderbilt Med. Sch., 1999—, assoc. dean, 2003—06, chief divsn. clin. pharm., 2004—. Mem. internat. adv. com. 9th Internat. Conf. on Prostglandins and Related Compounds, Florence, Italy, 1994, 10th Conf., Vienna, Austria, 1996, Intl. Conf. on Prostaglandins, Montreal, Canada, 2007. Contbr. over 450 articles, revs. and papers to sci. jours., chpts. to books; mem. editl. bd. numerous sci. and med. jours. Physician Nashville Union Rescue Mission, 1988-00. Recipient Physician-Scientist award NIH, 1990-91, grantee; recipient Rsch. Found. Devel. award Internat. Life Scis. Inst., 1992-96, Burroughs Wellcome Fund award in Transitional Rsch., 1999-2004; Centennial Clin. Pharmacology fellow Boehringer-Ingelheim, 1990-91, Howard Hughes Med. Inst. Physician rsch. fellow, 1991-94; grantee Liddle Med. Rsch., 1996, Stanley Cohen Rsch. award, 2006. Mem. AMA, ACP, AAAS, Am. Fedn. Clin. Rsch., Am. Soc. Clin. Investigation, Assn. Am. Physicians, So. Soc. Clin. Investigation, Soc. Free Radiol. Biol. Medicine (bd. dirs., Discovery award 2006), Infectious Diseases Soc. Am., Am. Fed. Med. Rsch., Am. Soc. Pharmacology Exptl. Therapeutics, Am. Soc. Biochemistry and Molecular Biology, Am. Soc. Clinical Pharmacology and Therapeutics (bd. dirs. 2007-), Phi Beta Kappa. Avocations: running, fishing, outdoors. Home: 6408 Eastbourne Dr Brentwood TN 37027-4802 Office: Vanderbilt U Divsn Clin Pharmacology 23d and Pierce Nashville TN 37232-6602 Home Phone: 615-221-8869; Office Phone: 615-322-4785. Business E-Mail: jason.morrow@vanderbilt.edu.

MORROW, JENNIFER LEIGH See LEIGH, JENNIFER

MORROW, JOHN E., lawyer; b. LA, Mar. 17, 1943; s. Charles Henry and Lillian (Harmon) M.; m. Sue C. Taylor, June 28, 1989. BS, U. Southern Calif., 1965; JD, U. Chgo., 1968; postgrad., U. Munich, 1969. Bar: Calif. 1969, Ill. 1971. Law clk. to judge U.S. Dist. Ct. (cen. dist.) Calif., 1969-70; ptnr. Baker & McKenzie, Chgo., 1970-73, 75-76, 83—, Zurich, Switzerland, 1974-75, Hong Kong, 1976-82. Mem. ABA (subcom. on internat. bus. law com. corp. sect.). Office: Baker & McKenzie One Prudential Plz 130 E Randolph St Fl 32 Chicago IL 60601-6207 E-mail: john.e.morrow@bakernet.com.

MORROW, MARGARET M., lawyer, judge; b. Columbus, Nebr., Oct. 29, 1950; BA magna cum laude, Bryn Mawr Coll., 1971; JD cum laude, Harvard U., 1974. Bar: Calif. 1974. Ptnr. Quinn, Kully & Morrow, PLC, LA; pvt. practice, 1974—98; judge US Dist. Ct., Ctrl. Dist. of Calif., LA, 1998—. Fellow Am. Bar Found; mem. ABA (bd. dirs. young lawyers div. 1984-85), L.A. County Bar Assn. (bd. trustee 1981-83, 84-89, pres. barristers 1982-83, pres. 1988-89), State Bar of Calif. (conf. of dels. exec. com. 1985-88), Assn. Bus., Trial Trial Lawyers (bd. govs. 1982-83), U. So. Calif. Law Sch. Bd. Councillers. Office: US Dist Ct Ctrl Dist of Calif 255 E Temple St Los Angeles CA 90012 Office Phone: 213-894-7857.

MORROW, MONICA, medical educator; b. Abington, Pa., Sept. 16, 1953; d. James Robert and Maxine Cooper Morrow; m. Virgil Craig Jordan, OBE, PhD, DSc. BS magna cum laude, Pa. State U., 1974; MD, Jefferson Med. Coll., 1976. Diplomate Am. Bd. of Surgery. Fellow in surg. oncology Meml. Sloan Kettering Cancer Ctr., New York, NY, 1981—83; asst. prof. of surgery SUNY Health Sci. Ctr. at Bklyn, Brooklyn, NY, 1983—88; assoc. prof. of surgery U. of Chgo., Chicago, Ill., 1988—93, Northwestern U., Chicago, Ill., 1993—97, prof. of surgery, 1997—2004; chmn. dept. surgical oncology and G. Willing Pepper chair cancer rsch. Fox Chase Cancer Ctr., Phila., 2004—. Dir., cancer dept. ACS, Chgo., 1999—2001; exec. dir. Am. Joint Com. on Cancer, Chgo., 1999—2001; mem. Nat. Cancer Policy Bd., Inst. of Medicine, Washington, 1999—2002; co-chair Joint Com. of the ACS, Am. Coll. of Radiology, and Coll. of Am. Pathologists on Standards for Breast Conservation, 2000—02, 2005. Editor: (book) Managing Breast Cancer Risk, American Joint Committee on Cancer Staging Manual, sixth edition, Diseases of the Breast, Breast Diseases: A Problem Based Approach. Named Distinguished Alumni, Pa. State U., 2002; recipient Alumni Achievement award, Jefferson Med. Coll., 2006; Co-Principal Investigator, Specialized Program Rsch. Excellence in Breast Cancer grantee, Nat. Cancer Inst., 2000—05, Avon Found. Ctr. Excellence grantee prin. investigator, 2000—06. Fellow: Am. Coll. Surgeons, Royal Coll. Physicians and Surgeons Glasgow (hon.); mem.: Am. Surg. Assn., Am. Soc. Clin. Oncology (bd. dirs. 1998—2001), Soc. Surg. Oncology (exec. com. 1993—96, 2003—06, sec. 2007—). Avocations: travel, history, wine. Office: Fox Chase Cancer Ctr 333 Cottman Ave Philadelphia PA 19111-2497 Office Phone: 215-728-3096.

MORROW, NANA KWASI SCOTT DOUGLAS, choreographer, director, writer, filmmaker, educator; b. NYC, Jan. 29, 1954; s. Alfredo and Lorraine (Lopez) Morro. BFA in Dance, SUNY, Purchase, 1976; MA in Choreography, UCLA, 1986. Ordained interfaith min. 2004. Prin. instr. Phil Black Dance Studio, NYC, 1969—77; dir. dance divsn. No. Ill. U., DeKalb, 1976—78; artistic dir., resident choreographer No. Ill. Repertory Dance Co., 1976—78; artistic dir. Scott Morrow Dance Theatre Co. and Sch., LA, 1978—85; prin. instr. Mary Tyler Moore Los Angeles Dance Ctr., 1979—80; resident dance master South Coast Repertory Acting Conservatory, Calif., 1979—82; vis. prof. Wright State U., Ohio, 1981; ballet master, resident choreographer Empire State Ballet, Buffalo, 1984—85; asst. prof. U. Kans., Lawrence, 1985—89. Choreographer Morrow Dance Theatre-in-Residence, U. Kans., 1985-88, 92d St. Dancer Ctr., YMHA and YWHA, NYC, 1989, Morrow Dance Theater Co., Sch. and Summer Inst., NYC, 1990-2002; founder, dir. Jazz Dance Ministry for Racial Reconciliation, Peace and Healing, NYC, 1988—; assoc. dir., dir. edn. pub. sch. dance programs K-12, Bronx Dance Theatre Performing Arts Ctr., NYC, 1990-93; faculty Internat. Summer Sch. Royal Acad. Dancing, NYC, 1991-92, Calif. State U. Sys. Summer Inst. for Tchg. and Learning, 1994; sr. faculty Lilly Conf. on Coll. Tchg., Miami U., Ohio, 1991-2001; founder, dir. in chief Inst. Advancement Edn. Dance, NYC, 1992-02; adv. bd. Internat. Found. for Performing Arts Medicine, 1992—; adv. Performing Arts Medicine Ctr., Kessler Inst. Rehab., NJ, 1995—; Walter H. Annenberg disting. vis. artist-scholar The Renaissance Sch., NYC, 1995-96; cons. presenting and commissioning program Nat. Endowment for Arts, 1993-95; peer rev. panel Fund for Innovation in Edn. US. Edn. Dept., 1993-94; co-chmn. dance edn. com. World Dance Allliance: Americas Ctr., 1993-97; internat. artistic advisor Noyam Exptl. Dance Co. and Rsch. Project, Ghana, 1998—; founder, min. in chief Embassy of Sekyere Kwamang Traditional Area, Asante Nation, Ghana to USA, 1998—; internat. adv. bd. Ctr. for Nat. Culture, Kumasi, Astante Nation, Ghana, 2001—; co-founder and co-pastor Of One Blood Ministries, NYC, 2004—. Choreographer: (mus. theater) Broadway Musical Classics on International Tour, (musical stage rev) Bebop Hot! Celebrating the Music of Dizzy Gillespie & Charlie Parker, (vaudeville revue) Horn & Hardart Theater District Cafeteria, NYC; (film musical) Chestnuts, Rainbows Edn.; (documentary film) Broadway Babies: Long Forgotten Performers of the Vaudeville Era, (teleseries) Adventures of Hans Christian Andersen, (telespecial) Rapsodia Afrikiko: A Celebration in Dance, (indsl. show) Le Parfum Salvador Dali, (nightclub) The African Room, NYC; (fashion show) Abraham & Straus, NYC; choreographic asst. (Broadway musical) Safari 300: A Musical Experience of 300 Years of Black Culture, Song & Dance, NYC; film dir., editor Of One Blood: Returning Home to Africa, 1999 (Best Documentary Film award Black Internat. Cinema Festival); co-author, dir., choreographer, co-star (nat. stage prodn.) Realizing the Dream: Celebrating the Enduring Spirit of Rev. Dr. Martin Luther King Jr.; world premieres presented at festivals including Morningside Dance Festival, NYC, Mid Am. Dance Festival, L.A. Dance Kaleidoscope Festival, Middfest Internat., Ohio, Smithsonian Instn.'s Duke Ellington Festival, Washington, Marche Internat. de Disque et de l'Edition Musicale, Cannes, France, Anokyekrome Festival, Kumasi, Asante Nation, Ghana, Royal Performance King Nana Barimah Abeyie Ntori Nimpah II, Sekyere Kwamang, Asante Nation, Ghana, Black Internat. Cinema Festival, Berlin; creator over 40 ballets; contbr. to profl. publs. including African Profiles USA Mag., African Personality Mag., African Press. Nat. Festival for the Performing Arts Choreographers fellow, 1989; Josephine & Randolph Stewart African Heritage Fund Edn. and Rsch. grantee, 1997; named Master Educator and Disting. Fellow, Am. Bd. Master Educators, 1987; Alvin Ailey scholar, Sch. Am. Ballet scholar, Harkness House for Ballet Arts scholar; recipient Grand Prize for Choreography, Ann. Internat. Artistic Impression Competition, 1991, citation U.S. Edn. Dept., 1993, Contbns. to Growth and Advancement of Performing Arts award U.S. Arts Coun. Co-op, 1993; named Traditional Chief and Spl. Advisor in Edn. and Human Devel. to King, Sekyere Kwamang, Asante Nation, Ghana, 1997, Pan-African and Humanitarian Vision award African Profiles USA mag., 2001. Personal E-mail: nanasmorrow@hotmail.com.

MORROW, RICHARD MARTIN, retired oil company executive; b. Wheeling, W.Va., Feb. 27, 1926; B.M.E., Ohio State U., 1948. With Amoco Corp., 1948-91; v.p. Amoco Prodn. Co., 1964-66; exec. v.p. Amoco Internat. Oil Co., 1966-70, Amoco Chem. Corp., 1970-74, pres., 1974-78, Amoco Corp., 1978-83, chmn. chief exec. officer, 1983-91; ret., 1991. Trustee U. Chgo. and Rush U. Med. Ctr. Office: 200 E Randolph Dr Ste 6952 Chicago IL 60601-7704

MORROW, WALTER EDWIN, JR., electrical engineer, lab administrator; b. Springfield, Mass., July 24, 1928; s. Walter Edwin and Mary Elizabeth (Ganley) M.; m. Janice Lila Lombard, Feb. 25, 1951; children: Clifford E., Gregory A., Carolyn F. S.B., M.I.T., 1949, S.M., 1951. Mem. staff Lincoln Lab., MIT, Lexington, Mass., 1951-55, group leader, 1956-65; head div. communications MIT Lincoln Lab., 1966-68, asst. dir., 1968-71, asso. dir., 1972-77, dir., 1977-98, dir. emeritus, 1998—. Contbr. articles to profl. publs. Recipient award for outstanding achievement Pres. M.I.T., 1963, Edwin Howard Armstrong Achievement award IEEE Communications Soc., 1976 Fellow IEEE, Nat. Acad. Engring. Achievements include patent for synchronous satellite, electric power plant using electrolytic cell-fuel cell combination. Office: MIT Lincoln Lab PO Box 73 Lexington MA 02420-9108

MORROW, WILLIAM CLARENCE, judge, lawyer, arbitrator; b. Austin, Tex., Aug. 9, 1935; s. Theodore Faulkner and Gladys Lee (Ames) M.; m. Sheila Beth Pfost, June 29, 1973; children: Scott Fitzgerald Morrow, Elizabeth Ann Rettig, Shana Lynn Peterson. BA, Baylor U., 1957; JD, So. Meth. U., 1962. Bar: Tex. 1962. Trial atty. SEC, Ft. Worth, 1963-65; former ptnr. Cotton, Bledsoe, Tighe, Morrow & Dawson, Lynch, Chappell and Alsup; v.p. Magnatex Corp., Midland, 1980-86; v.p., gen. cousnel, sec. Elcor Corp., Midland, 1986-88; county judge Midland County, Tex., 1999—. Mem. Tex. Jail Standards Commn., Austin, Tex., 2002—. Mem. Midland City Coun., 1992-95, Tex. Jail Commn., 2002-, mayor pro tem, 1994-95; former vice chmn. Tex. Rehab. Commn.; pres. Found. Mental Health and Mental Retardation Permian Basin; pres. United Way of Midland, 1985, Indsl. Found. Midland, 1987; trustee Midland Cmty. Theatre, 1980—, chmn., 1995-96; elder First Presbyn. Ch., Midland. Mem. Coll. of State Bar Tex., Tex. Bar Assn., Midland County Bar Assn., Tex. Coll. of Probate Judges, Phi Delta Phi. Home: 3110 Gulf Ave Midland TX 79705-8205 Office: 200 W Wall Ste 006 Midland TX 79701-4512

MORROW, WILLIAM EARL, retired government official, retired law educator; b. Perryopolis, Pa., Oct. 22, 1923; s. Robert Ferguson and Daisy (Johnson) M.; m. Danna Katunaric, Apr. 26, 1958; children: Jamie Johnson, Tammara Marie, Kim Ina, William Joseph, Geoffrey Sean. BS in Psychology and Edn., Waynesburg Coll., 1948; MA in Human Resource Mgmt. and Industry, U. Pitts., 1953; LLD (hon.), U. Zagreb, 1958; postgrad., U. Md., 1969, Indsl. Coll. Armed Forces, 1969-70. With Survey Rsch. Ct. U. Mich., 1947; auditor, employment interviewer, then asst. dir. pers. Jones & Laughlin Steel Corp., 1948—54; exec. coord. Peoples Cab Co., 1954; labor-mgmt. adviser, policy coord. Arabian Am. Oil Co., Saudi Arabia, 1954—57; pers. expert UN/ILO, Geneva, Zagreb, Yugoslavia, 1957—58; cons., 1958—59; tng./program officer AID U.S. Dept. State, 1959—65; adminstrv. officer Bur. Internat. Labor Affairs U.S. Labor Dept., 1965—68; dep. divsn. chief Bur. Internat. Labor Affairs Labor Dept., 1968—72, projects dir. L.Am., Caribbean, 1973—80; asst. dir. Office Fgn. Rels., 1980—86; exec. sec. Employee Retirement Income Security Act Office of Sec. Labor U.S. Dept. Labor, 1986—95; ret., 1995. Guest prof. U. Coll. W.I., 1960-64; lectr. Prince George's Community Coll., 1965-97; lectr. U. Md., 1967-97; adj. prof. U. Md., 1997-2003. Mem. Tantallon (Md.) Citizens Assn. With USAF, 1942-44. Mem. Indsl. Rels. Rsch. Assn., Prince George's County Bd. Realtors, Am. Fedn. Govt. Employees, Am. Soc. Tng. Dirs., Am. Legion, D.A.V., Masons, Scottish Rite, Shriners, U. Md. Faculty Club, Dominion Valley Golf and Country Club, Tantallon-On-The-Potomac Golf and Country Club, Psi Chi Iota, Phi Alpha Theta, Delta Sigma Phi. Methodist. Home (Winter): Village Walk on Palmer Ranch 8308 Jesolo Ln Sarasota FL 34238 Home (Summer): Dominion Valley Golf and Country Club 5726 Wheelwright Way Haymarket VA 20169 Personal E-mail: willmorrow@aol.com.

MORROW, WINSTON VAUGHAN, financial executive; b. Grand Rapids, Mich., Mar. 22, 1924; s. Winston V. and Selma (von Egloffstein) M.; m. Margaret Ellen Staples, June 25, 1948 (div.); children: Thomas Christopher, Mark Staples; m. Edith Burrows Ulrich, Mar. 2, 1990. AB cum laude, Williams Coll., 1947; JD, Harvard U., 1950. Bar: RI 1950, US Dist. Ct., US Supreme Ct. Assoc. atty. Edwards & Angell, Providence, 1950-57; exec. v.p., asst. treas., gen. counsel, bd. dirs. Avis, Inc. and subs., 1957-61; v.p., gen. mgr. Rent A Car div. Avis, Inc., 1962-64, pres., bd. dirs., 1964-75; chmn., chief exec. officer, bd. dirs. Avis, Inc. and Avis Rent A Car System, Inc., 1965-77; chmn., pres., bd. dirs. Teleflorists Inc. and subs., 1978-80; pres. Westwood Equities Corp., LA, 1981-95, CEO, 1984-95, also bd. dirs.; chmn., pres., chief exec. officer Ticor Title Ins. Co., 1982-91, also bd. dirs.; chmn. TRTS Data Svcs. Inc., 1985-91; bd. dirs. AECOM Tech. Corp., LA, 1990-99. Mem. Pres.'s Industry and Govt. Spl. Travel Task Force, 1968, travel adv. bd. US Travel Svcs., 1968-76, LA City-wide Airport Adv. Com., 1983-85; co-chmn. LA Transp. Coalition, 1985-91. Mem. juvenile delinquency task force Nat. Coun. Crime and Delinquency, 1985-86, LA Mayor's Bus. Coun., 1983-86, Housing Roundtable, Washington, 1983-85, Calif. Bus. Roundtable, 1985-90; chmn., pres. Spring St. Found., 1991-2006; bd. dir. Police Found., Washington, 1983-91; trustee Com. Econ. Devel., Washington, 1987-91; trustee Adelphi U., 1970-75. Decorated Stella Della Solidarieta Italy, Gold Tourism medal Austria. Fellow The Huntington; mem. Car and Truck Rental Leasing Assn. (nat. pres. 1961-63), Am. Land Title Assn. (bd. govs. 1989-90), LA Area C. of C. (bd. dirs. 1983-90), Calif. Club, Williams Club, LA Tennis Club, Phi Beta Kappa, Kappa Alpha. Home: 4056 Farmouth Dr Los Angeles CA 90027-1314 also: Meadowview Farm 286 Cushing Corner Rd Freedom NH 03836 Personal E-mail: wvm4291@aol.com.

MORSCH, THOMAS HARVEY, lawyer, educator; b. Oak Park, Ill., Sept. 5, 1931; s. Harvey William and Gwenodyne (Maun) M.; m. Jacquelyn Casey, Dec. 27, 1954; children: Thomas H. Jr., Margaret, Mary Susan, James, Kathryn, Julia. BA, Notre Dame U., 1953; BSL., Northwestern U., 1953, JD, 1955. Bar: Ill. 1955, D.C. 1955. Assoc. Crowell & Leibman, Chgo., 1955-62; ptnr. Leibman, Williams, Bennett, Baird & Minow, Chgo., 1962-72, Sidley & Austin, Chgo., 1972-97, counsel, 1998-2000. Bd. dirs. Chgo. Lawyers Com. for Civil Rights Under Law, chmn., 1982-83; bd. dirs. Pub. Interest Law Initiative, pres., 1993-95; No. Dist. Ill. Civil Justice Reform Com., 1991-95, Ill. Equal Justice Commn., 1999—2003; mem. vis. com. Law Sch. Northwestern U., 1989-90, dir. Small Bus. Opportunity Ctr., 1998—, assoc. clin. prof., 1998-2003, clin. prof., 2003—; mem. adv. bd. Kellogg Ctr. for Nonprofit Mgmt., 2001-06. Pres. Republican Workshops of Ill., 1970; gen. counsel Ill. Com. to Re-elect the Pres., 1972; mem. LaGrange Plan Commn., Ill., 1972-80, LaGrange Fire and Police Commn., 1968-72; trustee LaGrange Meml. Hosp., 1983-89; mem. adv. bd. Cath. Charities of Chgo., 1985-2006; mem. bd. dir. Cath. Charities of Chgo., 2007-. Fellow Am. Coll. Trial Lawyers; mem. ABA, Ill. State Bar Assn., Chgo. Bar Assn. (bd. mgrs. 1979-81), DC Bar, 7th Cir. Bar Assn., Northwestern Law Sch. Alumni Assn. (pres. 1988-89), Chgo. Bar Found. (bd. dirs., pres. 1995-97), Univ. Club (Chgo.), LaGrange Country Club, Palisades Park Country Club (Mich.), Point O'Woods Country Club (Mich.). Roman Catholic. Home: 301 S Edgewood Ave La Grange IL 60525-2153 Office: Northwestern U Sch Law 357 E Chicago Ave Chicago IL 60611 Business E-Mail: tmorsch@law.northwestern.edu.

MORSE, BARBARA, mathematics educator; BA, Univ. RI; Master's student in Tchg. Secondary Math, Providence Coll. Math tchr. Davisville Mid. Sch., N. Kingstown, RI, 1996—99, N. Kingstown (RI) H.S., 1999—, and math. dept. chair, 2003—. Named N. Kingstown Tchr. of Yr., 2005, RI Tchr. of Yr., 2006. Office: N Kingstown Sr High Sch 150 Fairway Dr North Kingstown RI 02852 Business E-Mail: Barbara_Morse@nksd.net. *

MORSE, EDWARD LEWIS, energy economist, director; b. NYC, Jan. 5, 1942; s. Jonah Benjamin and Rebecca (Freiberg) M.; m. Linda Kasle Jones, Aug. 15, 1965; children: Michael Ari, Molly Rachel. BA, Johns Hopkins U., Balt., 1963; MA, Johns Hopkins U., Washington, 1966; PhD, Princeton U., 1969. Asst. prof. internat. politics Woodrow Wilson Sch. Princeton (N.J.) U., 1969-75; sr. rsch. fellow Coun. on Fgn. Rels., NYC, 1975-78; exec. asst. to undersec. econ. affairs U.S. Dept. State, Washington, 1978-79, dep. asst. sec. for internat. energy policy, 1979-81; dir. internat. affairs Phillips Petroleum Co., Bartlesville, Okla., 1981-84; mng. dir. Petroleum Fin. Co., Ltd., Washington, 1984-96; pres., publisher Petroleum Intelligence Weekly, NYC, 1988-99, The Oil Daily Co., NYC, 1996-99; exec. Hess Energy Trading Co., NYC, 1999—2006; mng. dir., chief energy economist Lehman Bros., NYC, 2006—. Author: Foreign Policy and Interdependence in Gaullist France, 1973, Modernization and the Transformation of International Relations, 1976; contbr. articles to various publs. Office: Lehman 735 7th Ave New York NY 10019 Office Phone: 212-526-3767. E-mail: emorse@lehman.com, edmorse@aol.com.

MORSE, ELIZABETH, conservator; b. Hartford, Conn., Apr. 4, 1957; d. Robert Francis and Elinor Lois (Marshall) Morse; m. Richard Harold Wendorf, Oct. 12, 1997. BA, Defiance Coll., Ohio, 1979; MS, Columbia U., NYC, 1986, cert. in libr. and archive conservation, 1986; MA, Syracuse U., NY, 1996. Paper conservator Strong Mus., Rochester, NY, 1987—92, Harvard U., Cambridge, Mass., 1992—2001; instr. Harvard U. Ext. Sch., Cambridge, 1999—2003; paper conservator Cohasset, Mass., 2001—. Mem.: New Eng. Conservation Assn., Inst. Paper Conservation, Am. Inst. Conservation of Hist. and Artistic Works (sec./treas. book and paper group 1995—97, Profl. Devel. award 2003, Carolyn Horton award 1995). Home and Office: 24 Cedar St Cohasset MA 02025 Home Phone: 781-383-2644; Office Phone: 781-383-2011. Personal E-mail: papercons@comcast.net.

MORSE, GAYLE SKAWENNIO, psychologist, consultant; d. Arthur T. Lamendola and Karonhiosta Thomas; children: Mark T., Catherine Ann, Alexander Granville(dec.). BA, Kennesaw U., Ga., 1992; PhD, SUNY, Albany, 2000. Lic. psychologist N.Y. State Bd. of Edn. Program dir. Crossroads/CDPC/NYS-OMH, Castleton, NY, 2004—06; psychologist, cons. mobil team, office of child and family svcs. Capital Dist. Psychiat. Ctr., Albany, NY, 2000—04; asst. prof. The Sage Colls., Albany, NY, 2005—. Cons. NY State Police, Albany, 2000—06; adj. faculty SUNY, Albany, 2000—. Contbr. articles to rsch. jours. and numerous nat. publs. and presentations. Mem. Foster Children Program Women's Club of Albany, 2005—. Mem.: ACA (mem. Native Am. concerns com. 1997—98, jour. reviewer Jour. Counseling and Devel. 2003—06, interim v.p. Assn. for Multicultural Counseling and Devel.), APA (mem. partnership com. 1999—2002, mem. working group Assn. Grad. Students and Bd. Ednl. Affairs 1999—2002). Achievements include research in relationships among culture, mental health and quality of life; impact of environmental toxins on health. Home Phone: 518-459-9285; Office Phone: 518-956-3098.

MORSE, JACK CRAIG, lawyer, arbitrator; b. Evanston, Aug. 11, 1936; s. Leland Robert and Pauline (Pettibone) Morse; children from previous marriage: David Leland, Katherine Malia. BA, Beloit Coll., 1958; JD, Northwestern U., Evanston, Ill., 1965. Bar: Hawaii 1967, U.S. Dist. Ct. Hawaii 1969, U.S. Ct. Appeals (9th cir.) 1977. Legal staff Bishop Estate, Honolulu, 1966—68; dep. atty. gen. State of Hawaii, 1968—71; ptnr. Saunders & Morse, 1971—73; assoc. Chuck & Wong, 1974—75; officer and dir. Morse, Nelson & Ross, 1976—85; mem. Hawaii Med. Claim Conciliation Panel, 1977—, chmn., 1980—; mem. panel of arbitrators First Judicial Cir., 1986—. Lt. USN, 1959—62. Hardy scholar, Northwestern U., 1962. Mem.: Assn. Trial Lawyers Am., Am. Judicature Soc., Omicron Delta Kappa. Office: 700 Richards St Ste 1706 Honolulu HI 96813-4619 Office Phone: 808-531-7511. E-mail: jmorseesq@hawaii.rr.com.

MORSE, JEAN AVNET, educational association administrator, lawyer; b. NYC, Jan. 2, 1947; d. Samuel and Helen Avnet; m. Stephen John Morse, Dec. 26, 1966; 1 child, Elisabeth Avnet Morse. BA with high honors in Hist., Wellesley Coll., 1968; JD cum laude, Harvard U., 1971. Bar: Mass. 1971, Calif. 1974. Law clk. Superior Ct. Commonwealth of Mass., Boston, 1971—72; atty. Palmer & Dodge, Boston, 1972—74; assoc. to ptnr. Kaplan, Livingston, Goodwin, Berkowitz & Selvin, Beverly Hills, Calif., 1974—81; ptnr. Hufstedler & Kaus, LA, 1981—87, of counsel, 1988; dep. assoc. dean, dir. coll. office, Sch. Arts and Sci. U. Pa., Phila., 1989—93; lectr. sociology U. Pa. Sch. Arts and Sci., Phila., 1991; acting asst. provost U. Pa., Phila., 1991—92, dean's acad. planning cons., 1992—93; assoc. dean for adminstrn. NYU Sch. Law, NYC, 1993—94; dep. to pres. U. Pa., 1994—95; exec. dir. Commn. on Higher Edn. Mid. States Assn. of Coll. and Sch., Phila., 1996; pres. Mid. State Commn. Higher Edn., Phila. Bd. dir. Women in Bus., 1985-88, The Women's Bldg., 1985-86; chair individual rights sect. LA County Bar Assn., 1985-86. Office: Mid State Commn Higher Edn 3624 Market St Philadelphia PA 19104 Office Phone: 215-382-7827, 267-284-5025. E-mail: jmorse@msche.org. *

MORSE, JONATHAN KENT, religious organization administrator; b. Teaneck, NJ, Dec. 10, 1951; s. Alfred George and Agnes Marie (Lagatol) M.; m. Kathleen Zylinsky, May 10, 1980; children: Charlanne Marie, Justin George. BA, Cath. U., 1973, MRE, 1976; MA, Maryknoll Sem., 1978; PhD, Greenwich Sch. Theology, 1996. Ordained priest Ukrainian Cath. Ch., 1988. Instr. Manor Jr. Coll., Jenkintown, Pa., 1977-84; dir. religious edn. Maternity, Phila., 1984-89; adminstr. Sts. Peter and Paul, Spring Valley, NY, 1988-93; pres. Ukrainian Cath. Relief, Stamford, Conn., 1989—. Dir. religious edn. Diocese of Stamford, 1990—, dir. youth ministry, 1989—, dir. family life, 1991—; asst. dir. religious edn. Archdiocese of Phila., 1982-88; adminstr. Sacred Heart Ch., Phila., 1982-88; bd. dirs. Ea. Christian Publs., Fairfax, Va., Hallel Missionaries, Sparkill, N.Y., Nat. Conf. Catechetical Leadership. Author: Ukrainian Catholics, 1987, Through the Son, vol. 1 and vol. 2, 1997; author, editor: Rich in Compassion, 1986; columnist: The Subtle Sense in The Way, 1982-88. Chaplain K.C., Pearl River, N.Y., 1989—, Columbiettes, Stamford, 1993—; presentor UN, N.Y.C., 1992. Mem. NAFSA, Serra Internat. (chaplain 1982-91), Ancient Order Hibernians, Pi Gamma Mu. Republican. Ukrainian Cath. Avocations: science fiction reading, travel. Home: 24 Hope St Stamford CT 06906-2603 Office: Ukrainian Cath Relief 14 Peveril Rd Stamford CT 06902-3019

MORSE, JOSEPH GRANT, chemistry educator; b. Colorado Springs, Colo., Oct. 16, 1939; s. Grant Addison and Faris Ellen (Winninger) M.; m. Karen Dale Williams, Apr. 6, 1963; children: Robert Grant, Geoffrey Easton. BS, S.D. State Coll., 1961; MS in Chemistry, U. Mich., 1963, PhD, 1966. Instr. U. Mich., Ann Arbor, 1965-66; asst. prof. Utah State U., Logan, 1968-74, assoc. prof., 1974-93; prof. Western Wash. U., Bellingham, 1993-2000, dir. sci. edn., 1996-2000. Councilman Cache County, Utah. Capt. U.S. Army, 1966-68. Fellow AAAS; mem. Am. Chem. Soc.

MORSE, KAREN WILLIAMS, academic administrator; b. Monroe, Mich., May 8, 1940; m. Joseph G. Morse; children: Robert G., Geoffrey E. BS, Denison U., 1962; MS, U. Mich., 1964, PhD, 1967; DSc (hon.), Denison U., 1990. Rsch. chemist Ballistic Rsch. Lab., Aberdeen Proving Ground, Md., 1966-68; lectr. chemistry dept. Utah State U., Logan, 1968-69, from asst. to assoc. prof. chemistry, 1969-83, prof. chemistry dept., 1983-93, dept. head Coll. Sci., 1981-88, dean Coll. Sci., 1988-89, univ. provost, 1989-93; pres. Western Wash. U., Bellingham, 1993—. Mem., chair Grad. Record Exam in chemistry com., Princeton, N.J., 1980-89, Gov.'s Sci. Coun., Salt Lake City, 1986-93, Gov.'s Coun. on Fusion, 1989-91, ACS Com. on Profl. Tng., 1984-92; cons. 1993; nat. ChemLinks adv. com. NSF, 1995; bd. advisor's orgn. com. 2008 summer Olympic Games, Seattle, 1995; faculty Am. Assn. State Colls. and Univs. Pres.'s Acad., 1995, 96; chair Wash. Coun. of Pres., 1995-96; bd. dirs. Whatcom State Bank; NCAA Divsn. II Pres.'s Coun., 1999—, CHEA bd., 2000—; Nat. Rsch. Coun. Chem. Svcs. Roundtable, 1999—. Contbr. articles to profl. jours. Mem. Cache County Sch. Dist. Found., Cache Valley, Logan, 1988-93; swim coach, soccer coach; trustee First United Presbyn. Ch., Logan, 1979-81, 82-85; adv. bd. Sci. Discovery Ctr., Logan, 1993, KCTS-TV, Bellingham, 1996—, Seattle Opera Bd., 1999—; mem. bd. dirs. United Way, Whatcom County, 1993—; exec. com. Bellingham-Whatcom Econ. Devel. Com., 1993—. Recipient Disting. Alumni in Residence award U. Mich., 1989, Francis P. Garvan and John M. Olin medal, 1997. Fellow AAAS; mem. Am. Chem. Soc. (Utah award Salt Lake City and Cen. dists. 1988, Garvan-Olin medal 1997), Am. Assn. State Colls. and Univs. (mem. policy and purposes com. 1995, chair 1996), Bus. and Profl. Women Club (pres. 1984-85), Philanthropic Edn. Orgn., Phi Beta Kappa, Sigma Xi, Phi Beta Kappa Assocs., Phi Kappa Phi, Beta Gamma Sigma. Avocations: skiing, bicycling, photography. Office: Office of the Pres Western Washington U 516 High St Old Main 450 MS 9000 Bellingham WA 98225-5946

MORSE, LARRY EUGENE, botanist, conservationist; b. Dayton, Ohio, Nov. 15, 1947; s. Carson Clark and Dorothy Virginia (Clum) Morse. BS, Mich. State U., East Lansing, 1970; AM, Harvard U., Cambridge, Mass., 1971, PhD, 1979. Staff botanist Dayton Mus. of Natural History, Ohio, 1966, 1969; rsch. asst. Smithsonian Instn., Washington, 1971—72, N.Y. Bot. Garden, Bronx, 1976—78; chief botanist The Nature Conservancy, Arlington, Va., 1979—2000; N.Am. botanist NatureServe, Arlington, Va., 2001—06; ind. cons. L.E.M. Natural Diversity, 2006—. Founder, convener Plant Conservation Roundtable, Washington, 1981—88. Author: Computer Programs for Specimen Identification; co-editor: Rare Plant Conservation: Geographical Data Organization; contbr. chapters to books, articles to profl. jours. Fellow, NSF, 1970, Woodrow Wilson Fellowship Found., 1970. Mem.: New Eng. Bot. Club, Mich. Bot. Club, Bot. Soc. Washington (pres. 1985—86, mem. centennial symposium com. 2001, chair field trip com. 2006—), Ottawa Field-Naturalists' Club (life), So. Appalachian Bot. Soc. (life), Internat. Assn. for Plant Taxonomy (life). Achievements include development of a methodology for plant specimen identification with computers, a methodology for conservation status ranking, guidelines for conservation status reports, a methodology for invasiveness assessment of non-native plants; discovery of fern species Gymnocarpium appalachianum; design of central scientific databases; recognition that Appalachian shale barrens can occur on Silurian bedrock. Avocations: nature photography, paleontology, stamp collecting/philately, contra dancing. Home: 1306 Corbin Pl NE Washington DC 20002 Office: LEM Natral Diversity PO Box 77157 Washington DC 20013 Business E-Mail: larry.e.morse@lem-natural-diversity.com.

MORSE, LEONARD J., epidemiologist, public health service officer; MD, U. Md., 1955. Internand resident in internal medicine, fellow in infectious diseases U. Md. Med. Sys.; resident in internal medicine New Eng. Med. Care Hosp.; pvt. practice Worcester, Mass.; ret., 1996; med. dir. New Bedford Cmty. Health Ctr., 1996—2001; prof. clin. medicine, family medicine, cmty. health U. Mass. Med. Sch., Worcester; pub. health commr. Worcester, 2001—. Mem.: AMA (past chair coun. ethical and jud. affairs, Pride in Profession award 2004), Am. Soc. History Medicine, Am. Soc. Microbiology, Infectious Diseases Soc. Am., Mass. Med. Soc. (pres. 1993—94, past chmn. com. ethics and discipline, Lifetime Achievement award 1997, Grant V. Rodkey award 1997), Am. Coll. Physicians (Named Internist of Yr. Mass. chpt. 1998). Office: Worcester Pub Health 25 Meade St Worcester MA 01610 Office Phone: 508-799-8531. Business E-Mail: morsel@ci.worcester.ma.us.

MORSE, M. HOWARD, lawyer; b. Louisville, May 30, 1959; s. Marvin Henry and Betty Anne (Hess) M.; m. Laura E. Loeb, Apr. 17, 1988; children: Elizabeth L., Marni L. AB summa cum laude, Dartmouth Coll., 1981; JD cum laude, Harvard U., 1984. Bar: D.C. 1984, U.S. Ct. of Internat. Trade 1985, U.S. Ct. Appeals (fed. cir.) 1985, U.S. Dist. Ct. D.C. 1986, U.S. Ct. Appeals (D.C. cir.) 1986, U.S. Ct. Appeals (4th cir.) 1987. Assoc. Arnold & Porter, Washington, 1984-88; atty. FTC Bur. Competition, Washington, 1988-91, dep. asst. dir. for policy, 1991-93, asst. dir., 1993-97; ptnr., co-chair, antitrust group Drinker, Biddle & Reath LLP, Washington, 1998—. Adj. prof. law Georgetown Law Ctr., Washington, 1995—2000. Dist. enrollment dir. Dartmouth Coll., 2004—. Mem.: ABA (chair computer industry com. 1996—99, chair intellectual property com. 1999—2002, coun. 2002—05, chair exemptions and immunities com. 2006—, mem. antitrust sect.), D.C. Bar Assn., Intellectual Property Owners Assn. (vice chair antitrust and competition law com.), Phi Beta Kappa. Office: Drinker Biddle & Reath LLP 1500 K St NW Ste 1100 Washington DC 20005-1209 Office Phone: 202-842-8883. Office Fax: 202-842-8465. E-mail: howard.morse@dbr.com.

MORSE, MARVIN HENRY, retired judge; b. Mt. Vernon, NY, July 19, 1929; s. Frank Irving and Lillian (Seeger) M.; m. Betty Anne Hess, Dec. 27, 1953; children: Martin Albert, Michael Howard, Lee Anne. AB, Colgate U., 1949; LLB, Yale U., 1952. Bar: N.Y. 1952, Ky. 1956, Md. 1964, U.S. Supreme Ct. 1960, U.S. Ct. Appeals (6th cir.), U.S. Dist. Ct. (we. dist.) Ky., U.S. Ct. Mil. Appeals, U.S. Ct. Claims, U.S. Ct. Appeals (D.C. cir.), U.S. Ct. Appeals (fed. cir.), U.S. Dist. Ct. (no. dist.) Tex., U.S. Dist. Ct. Hawaii. Pvt. practice, Louisville, 1956-62; asst. counsel Office of Gen. Counsel Dept. Navy, Washington, 1962-65, Office of Gen. Counsel Office Sec. Def., Washington, 1965-68; asst. gen. counsel GSA, Washington, 1968-70, U.S. Postal Svc., Washington, 1970-73; adminstrv. law judge Fed. Energy Regulatory Commn., Washington, 1973-75, Postal Rate Commn., Washington, 1975-77, CAB, Washington, 1977-80; dir. adminstrv. law judges Office Pers. Mgmt., Washington, 1980-82; chief adminstrv. law judge SBA, Washington, 1982-87, asst. adminstr. hearings and appeals, 1985-87; adminstrv. law judge Exec. Office of Immigration Rev. Dept. Justice, Washington, 1987—2002; temp. mem. Bd. of Immigration Appeals, 1998—2002; ret., 2002. Mem. Adminstrv. Conf. of U.S., 1980-84, govt. mem., 1985-86, 87-95, liaison mem.; faculty and faculty coord. The Nat. Jud. Coll., 1977, 79-80. Author: (with S. Groner) ABA Handbook chpt. on adminstrv. law, 1981, (with Lucy Moran) Troubling the Waters: Human Cargos, 2002. Trustee Washington area chpt. Am. Digestive Disease Soc., 1976-87. With JAGC, USAF, 1952-56, to col. USAFR, ret. 1979. Decorated USAF Legion of Merit; recipient Disting. Svc. award Am. Digestive Disease Soc., 1980. Mem. ABA (exec. com. 1977-82, 84-87, chmn. 1980-81, conf. adminstrv. law judges, del. ho. of dels. 1984-87, lawyers in govt. com. 1985-86, jud. selection, tenure and compensation com. 1987-93, govt. pub. sect. lawyers divsn., coun. 1996-02), Fed. Bar Assn. (nat. coun. 1976—, chmn. career svc. sect. 1983-86, chmn. judiciary sect. 1986-88, sect. coord. 1988-90, sec. 1991-92, del. to ABA ho. of dels. 1992-93, 97-99, v.p. 1993-94, pres.-elect 1994-95, pres. 1995-96), Am. Law Inst., Fed. Adminstrv. Law Judges Conf. (exec. com. 1975-77, 82-96, 2000-01), Nat. Assn. Adminstrv. Law Judges (hon.), Fed. Am. Inn of Ct. (coun. 1990-92, pres. 1992-94).: 2425 Gulf of Mexico Dr Apt 6A Longboat Key FL 34228-3287 Home Phone: 941-383-4701. Personal E-mail: bhmmhm@comcast.net.

MORSE, RICHARD JAY, human resources specialist, consultant; b. Detroit, Mich., Aug. 2, 1933; s. Maurice and Belle Rosalyn (Jacobson) M. BA, U. Va., 1955; MA in Clin. Psychology, Calif. State U., LA, 1967. Area pers. adminstr. Gen. Tel. Co. of Calif., Santa Monica, 1957-67; sr. v.p. human resources The Bekins Co., Glendale, Calif., 1967-83; pvt. cons. human resources and orgn. devel. Cambria, 1983—. Contbr. articles to profl. jours. Fund raiser various orgns., So. Calif., 1970—. Mem. Internat. Soc. Performance Improvement (founding mem. 1958—). Republican. Jewish. Avocations: travel, tennis, walking, swimming. Home and Office: 6410 Cambria Pines Rd Cambria CA 93428-2009 Office Phone: 805-927-3457. Personal E-mail: dickmorse@earthlink.net.

MORSE, ROBERT HARRY, lawyer; b. Bklyn., May 25, 1941; s. Soll and Rachel Morse; m. Sandra Goldstein, July 22, 1967; children: Lisa Jennifer, Eric Jeffrey. BSEE with honors, MIT, 1963, MSEE with honors, 1964; JD, Harvard U., 1967. Bar: N.Y. 1968, D.C. 1978, Md. 1985. Assoc. Kenyon & Kenyon, Reilly, Carr & Chapin, NYC, 1967-71; trial atty. antitrust divsn. Dept. Justice, Washington, 1971-74, sr. trial atty., 1974-78; ptnr. Peabody, Lambert & Meyers, Washington, 1978-82, Galland, Kharasch, Morse & Garfinkle, Washington, 1982-96, Ropes and Gray, Washington, 1997-2000; pres., CEO Esrom Consulting LLC, Rockville, Md., 2000—; ptnr. Farkas & Morse LLC, Washington, 2003—05. Dir. Earle Palmer Brown Cos., 1984-98. Mem. nat. capital area coun. Boy Scouts

Am., gen. counsel, 1991-94, exec. bd. dirs., 1990—, pres. 2001-02, chmn., 2002-2003. Recipient Spl. Achievement award Dept. Justice, 1973, Meritorious award Dept. Justice, 1976, Silver Beaver award Boy Scouts Am., 1999. Mem.: ABA, Patent Bar, D.C. Bar Assn., Nat. Alumni Assn. MIT (bd. dirs. 1986—88), MIT Club Washington (sec. 1981—82, pres. 1983—84), Eta Kappa Nu, Tau Beta Pi, Sigma Xi. Avocation: tennis. Office Phone: 301-929-1010. Business E-Mail: courtmaven@alum.mit.edu.

MORSE, ROBERT PARKER, investment company executive; b. Nyack, NY, May 8, 1945; s. Robert Willard Parker and Julia (Larson) M.; m. Sarah Morgan Cumings, Sept. 23, 1978; children: Robert Bradley St. Clair, Parker Morgan, Sarah Spencer. BS in Econs., U. Pa., 1967; student in advanced currency theory, Adelphi Suffolk U., 1970-71. V.p. Am. Express/W.H. Morton Divsn., NYC, 1970-74; sr. v.p., ptnr. William G. Campbell & Co., Inc., NYC, 1975-80; chmn., CEO Morse, Williams & Co., Inc., NYC, 1981—. Bd. dirs. Dialog Comm., 2005—06, eLottery, Inc., 860 UN Plaza, Inc., Stowe, Vt., 2007—. Gov. emeritus Soc. Mayflower Descs., N.Y., 1993-98; trustee Plimoth Plantation, Mass., 1994-2000, Bermuda Biol. Sta. Rsch., 1983-2000, Gen. Svc. Bd., N.Y., 1981-93, trustee, chmn. fin. English Spkg. Union, 1998—, U.S. del. internat. coun., English Spkg. Union, London, 2002; bd. assocs. The Whitehead Inst., MIT, 1996—; bd. dirs. Arlington Inst., 1995-2001; chmn. bd. The Wall Street Fund, 1984—. Lt. USNR, 1967-78. Mem. Am. Def. Preparedness Assn., Pilgrims of U.S., River Club, Bond Club N.Y., U.S. Naval Inst., Union Club, N.Y. Yacht Club, Links Club, River Club. Episcopalian. Avocations: sailing, skiing, reading, golf, tennis. Office: Morse Williams & Co Inc 230 Park Ave Rm 1635 New York NY 10169-1602 Office Phone: 212-856-8200. Business E-Mail: rpm@morsewilliams.com.

MORSE, SAUL JULIAN, lawyer; b. Jan. 17, 1948; s. Leon William and Goldie (Kohn) M.; m. Anne Bruce Morgan, Aug. 21, 1982; children: John Samuel, Elizabeth Miriam. BA, U. Ill., 1969, JD, 1972. Bar: Ill. 1973, U.S. Dist. Ct. (so. dist.) Ill. 1976, U.S. Ct. Appeals (7th cir.) 1983, U.S. Supreme Ct. 1979, U.S. Tax Ct. 1982. Law clk. State of Ill. EPA, 1971-72, Ill. Commerce Commn., 1972, hearing examiner, 1972-73, trial atty., 1973-75; asst. minority legal counsel Ill. Senate, 1975, minority legal counsel, 1975-77; mem. Ill. Human Rights Commn., 1985-91; dir., treas., chair grievance com. Ill. Comprehensive Health Ins. Plan, 1987—2002; gen. counsel Ill. Legis. Space Needs Commn., 1978-92; pvt. practice Springfield, Ill., 1977-79; ptnr. Gramlich & Morse, Springfield, 1980-85; prin. Saul J. Morse and Assocs., 1985-87; ptnr. Morse, Giganti and Appleton, 1987-92; v.p., gen. counsel Ill. State Med. Soc., 1992—2004; of counsel Brown, Hay & Stephens, LLP, Springfield, Ill., 2004—. Lectr. in continuing med. edn, 1986—90; counsel symposia; adj. asst. prof. med. humanities So. Ill. Univ. Sch. Medicine; adj. lectr. legal studies U. Ill., Springfield, 2004; pres. Springfield Profl. Baseball, LLC. Bd. dirs. Springfield Ctr. for Ind. Living, 1984-89, Ill. Comprehensive Health Ins. Plan Bd., 1987-02, United Way Ctrl. Ill., Inc., 1991-97, G.I.N.I. Inst., 2002, Hope Sch., Springfield, 1996-03, Springfield Jewish Fedn., 1992-95; mem. task force on transp. Rep. Nat. Com., 1979-80; mem. Springfield Jewish Cmty. Rels. Coun., 1976-79, 97-2002; bd. dirs. internat. Post Polio Health Internat., 2002—, asst. treas.; bd. dirs. Springfield Jewish Fedn. Endowment; mem. spl. com. on zoning and land use planning Sangamon County Bd., 1978; treas. City of Leland Grove, 1999—; exec. com. AMA and State Med. Socs. Litig. Ctr., 1999-04, chmn. 2003-04; commr. Ill. Guardianship and Advocacy Commn., 2002, chmn., 2005-07; mem. chancellor's cmty. adv. coun. U. Ill., Springfield, 2002—; bd. dirs. Vis. Nurse Assn. Ctrl. Ill., 2004-07; vice chmn. United Cerebral Palsy Land of Lincoln, 2002-07, pres., 2006—. Named Disabled Adv. of Yr., Ill. Dept. Rehab. Svcs., 1985; recipient Chmn.'s Spl. award Ill. State Med. Soc., 1987, Susan S. Suter award as outstanding disabled citizen of Ill. Peers Leading Lawyers Network, 1990, 06. Mem. ABA (vice-chmn. medicine and law com. 1988-90, tort and ins. practice sect., forum com. on health law), Am. Assn. Health Lawyers, Am. Soc. Law and Medicine, Ill. State Bar Assn. (spl. com. on reform of legis. process 1976-82, spl. com. on the disabled lawyer 1978-82, young lawyers sect. com. on role of govt. atty. 1977-80, chmn. 1982, sect. coun. adminstrv. law, vice-chmn. 1981-82), Sangamon County Bar Assn., Am. Soc. Med. Assn. Counsel, Phi Delta Phi. Home: 1701 S Illini Rd Springfield IL 62704-3301 Office: Brown Hay Stephens LLP PO Box 2459 205 S Fifth St Ste 700 Springfield IL 62705 Office Phone: 217-241-5053. Personal E-mail: saulmorse@sbcglobal.net. Business E-Mail: smorse@bhslaw.com.

MORSE, STEPHEN SCOTT, virologist, epidemiologist, immunologist, educator; b. NYC, Nov. 22, 1951; s. Murray H. and Phyllis Morse; m. Marilyn Gewirtz, Feb. 1991. BS, CCNY, 1971; MS, U. Wis., 1974, PhD, 1977. NSF trainee dept. bacteriology U. Wis., Madison, 1971-72, rsch. asst., 1972-77; Nat. Cancer Inst. rsch. fellow Med. Coll. Va./Va. Commonwealth U., Richmond, 1977-80, instr. microbiology, 1980-81; asst. prof. microbiology Rutgers U., New Brunswick, NJ, 1981-85; rsch. assoc. Rockefeller U., NYC, 1985-88, asst. prof., 1988-96, adj. faculty, 1996—; program mgr. Def. Advanced Rsch. Projects Agy., 1996-2000; asst. prof. to assoc. prof. epidemiology, Mailman Sch. Pub. Health, Columbia U., 1996—, dir. Ctr. Pub. Health Preparedness, Mailman Sch. Pub. Health, 2000—05. Cons. US Congress Office Tech. Assessment, Washington, 1989; chair conf. on emerging viruses NIH, 1989; mem. com. microbial threats to health, chair subcom. on viruses Inst. Medicine-NAS, 1990—92, steering com. forum on emerging infections, 1996—, com. future biothreats, 2003—05; chair program for monitoring emerging diseases (ProMED) Fedn. Am. Scientists, 1993—99; mem. com. on biodef. analysis and countermeasures NAS-NRC, 2005—. Author: Emerging Viruses, 1993, Evolutionary Biology of Viruses, 1994; editor-in-chief Pasteur Inst. Jour., 1996—99; sect. editor: Ctr. for Disease Control and Prevention Jour., Emerging Infectious Diseases, 1995—2002, mem. editl. bd.: Emerging Infectious Diseases, 2003—06, Biosecurity and Bioterrorism, 2003—. Fellow: NY Acad. Medicine, Am. Coll. Epidemiology, NY Acad. Scis. (vice chair microbiology sect. 1994—96, chair 1996—98), Am. Acad. Microbiology; mem.: Marine Biology Lab., Am. Assn. Immunologists, Am. Soc. Microbiology, Coun. on Fgn. Rels., Sigma Xi. Office: Columbia U Mailman Sch Pub Health 722 W 168th St New York NY 10032-3722 Business E-Mail: ssm20@columbia.edu.

MORSE-MCNEELY, PATRICIA, poet, writer, retired secondary school educator; b. Galveston, Tex., Apr. 2, 1923; d. Bleecker Lansing Sr. and Annie Maud (Pillow) Morse; m. Chalmers Rankin McNeely, Mar. 22, 1949 (div. Aug. 1959); children: David Lansing McNeely, Timothy Ann McNeely Caldwell, Patricia Grace McNeely Dragon, Abigail Rankin McNeely. BS in Edn., U. Tex., 1972; MA in Ednl. Psychology/Spl. Edn., U. Tex., San Antonio, 1976, MA in Ednl. Psychology/Counseling, 1981. Cert. tchr. Tex., profl. counselor. Sec./adminstrv. sec. various cos., Galveston & Austin, Tex., 1945-49, 60-70; dep. clk. Ct. of Civil Appeals, Galveston, 1947-48; police stenographer Austin Police Dept., 1970-74; history and spl. edn. tchr. N.E. Ind. Sch. Dist., San Antonio, 1974-76; spl. edn. tchr. S.W. Ind. Sch. Dist., San Antonio, 1978-81; vocat. adjustment coord. East Ctrl. Ind. Sch. Dist., San Antonio, 1981-82; counselor, tchr. Stockdale Ind. Sch. Dist., Tex., 1982-84; clinic sec. Humana Hosp., Dallas, 1985-87; tchr. history, spl. edn. and lang. arts Dallas Ind. Sch. Dist., 1987-2000; ret., 2000. TSTA/NEA assn. rep. Hill Mid. Sch., Dallas, 1990—91, E.B. Comstock Mid. Sch., Dallas, 1991—2000. Author: (poetry) Texas City, 1947, A Gift of Love, 1978, The Key, 1991, The House Part I, 1995, The Gull's Quill, 2001, 2d edit., 2005, Pat's Portfolio, 2002, The House Parts I and II, 2002, From Mother's Writings, 2005, numerous poems in lit. publs. and anthologies; contbr. articles to newsletters and profl. jours. V.p. zone, corr. sec., libr., various coms. Parents Without Ptnrs., Inc., Austin, 1965—74, 1976—78, internat. chmn. ad hoc com. for writing leadership tng. program, 1968, newsletter editor, 1967—72. Recipient awards for poetry. Mem.: AARP, NEA (life), San Gabriel Writers League, Soc. Children's Book Writers and Illustrators, Nat. Trust for Edn. (trustee), U. Tex. Austin Alumni Assn. (First Bernice Milburn Moore scholarship award 1972), Internat. Libr. Poetry (Hall of Fame 1997), Assn. Am. Poets, Nat. Edn. Assn. (life), Tex. Ret. Tchrs. (life), Tex. State Tchrs. Assn. (life; del. to Tex. State Tchrs. Assn. Conf. 1978—81, 1991—97), Internat. Soc. Poets (life). Episcopalian. Avocations: reading, music, sewing/handcrafts, book collecting.

MORTENSEN, CHRIS, sports analyst, reporter; b. Nov. 7, 1952; Student, El Camino Coll. Reporter South Bay (Calif.) Daily Breeze, 1969-83; reporter Atlanta Braves Atlanta-Jour. Constn., 1983-85, reporter Atlanta Falcons, 1985-86, reporter NFL, 1987-89, The Nat., 1989-90; analyst NFL draft ESPN, 1991, 92, reporter NFL Game Day, NFL Prime Monday, SportsCenter, 1991—, reporter Outside the Lines series, 1991—. Author: Playing for Keeps: A True Story about Football, Playoffs and the Mob; NFL columnist The Sporting News; contbg. writer Sport mag. Served with U.S. Army. Recipient George Polk award for reporting, 1987, 18 awards in journalism, Nat. Headliner award for investigative reporting, 1978; nominated for two Pulitzer Prizes. Office: c/o ESPN ESPN Pla Bristol CT 06010

MORTENSEN, GORDON LOUIS, artist, printmaker; b. Arnegard, ND, Apr. 27, 1938; s. Gunner and Otillia Ernestine (Reiner) M.; m. Phoebe Hollis Hansen, Apr. 10, 1965 (div. 1968); m. Linda Johanna Sisson, Dec. 7, 1969. BFA, Mpls. Coll. Art and Design, 1964; postgrad., U. Minn., 1969—72. One-man shows include Minn. Mus., St. Paul, 1967, Concept Art Gallery, Pitts., 1981, 1983, 1985, 1987, 1989, 1991, 1993, C.G. Rein Galleries, Mpls., 1978, 1980, 1985, 1989, 1991, 1993, others, exhibited in group shows at Miami U., Oxford, Ohio (1st pl. award, 1977), Phila. Print Club (George Bunker award, 1977), 12th Nat. Silvermine Guild Print Exhbn., New Canaan, Conn., 1976, 1978, 1980, 1983, 1986, 1994, 1996 (Hearsch Mag. award, 1978, Purchase award, 1983, 1986), 4th Miami Internat. Print Biennial (4th pl. award, 1980), Rockford Internat., 1981, 1985 (Juror's award, 1981), Boston Printmakers Nat. Exhbn., 1977, 1979—81, 1983, 1997, 2003 (Purchase award, 1977, 1979, 1983, Juror's Accomodation), 2007, others, Represented in permanent collections Achenbach Found. Graphic Arts at Palace Legion of Honor, San Francisco, Bklyn. Mus., Phila. Mus. Art, Libr. of Congress, Minn. Mus. Art, Met. Mus. and Art Ctr., Miami, Fla., Mus. Am. Art, Washington, Art Inst. Chgo., Mus. Art at Carnegie-Mellon Inst., Pitts., Walker Art Ctr., Mpls., Dulin Gallery Art, Knoxville, Tenn., Phila. Mus. Art, Tokyo Fuji Art Mus., numerous corp. collections; profiled in numerous art jours. Served with USMC, 1957-60. Mem. Boston Printmakers, Phila. Print Club, L.A. Printmaking Soc., Albany Print Club, Am. Print Alliance. Home and Office: 4153 Crest Rd Pebble Beach CA 93953-3052 Office Phone: 831-625-0960.

MORTENSEN, ROBERT HENRY, landscape and golf course architect; b. Jackson, Mich., June 9, 1939; s. Henry and Charlotte Marie (Brown) Mortensen; m. Linda McGinnis, 2005; children: Phillip, Paul, Susan, Julia. B in Landscape Architecture, Ohio State U., 1961; M in Landscape Architecture, U. Mich., 1965. Registered landscape arch., Va., Md. Landscape arch. various firms, Louisville, 1960, 61-63; with Ohio Divsn. Pks., Columbus, 1960-61; landscape arch. various firms, Toledo, 1963, 65-67; pvt. practice Ann Arbor, Mich., 1963-65; ptnr. firms Toledo, 1967-78; pres. Harvey Jones and Assocs., Clearwater, Fla., 1979-81; owner Mortensen Assocs., Toledo and Falls Church, Va., 1979-85; prin. Mortensen, Lewis & Scully, Inc., Vienna, Va., 1985-93; owner Mortensen Assocs., McLean, Va., 1993—. Assoc. prof. U. Mich. Grad. Sch., 1973; vis. lectr. Ohio State U., 1965—, Bowling Green State U., Ohio, 1969—, U. Mich., 1971, Purdue U., 1971, Mich. State U., 1973—, U. Mass., 1986—, U. Cath., Cordoba, Argentina, 2007, U. Buenus Aires, 2007; archtl. environ. rev. com. Ohio Arts Coun., 1974-78; adj. prof. Dept. Landscape Architecture, U. Md., 1992—; chmn. Merrifield Master Plan Task Force, 1998-2001. Editor: Handbook of Professional Practice, 1972, Marketing Landscape Architectural Services to the Federal Government, 1974. Mem. Ohio Bd. Unreclaimed Strip Mined Lands, 1973-76; mem. Lucas County facilities rev. com. Health Planning Assn. N.W. Ohio, 1972-76, chmn. maternal and child health subcom., 1972-74; bd. dirs. No. Va. Cmty. Appearance Alliance, 1988—2002, chair, 1991, pres., 1994. Recipient Disting. Svc. award Health Planning Assn. N.W. Ohio, 1973, Disting. Alumni award U. Mich. Sch. Natural Resources, 1985, Disting. Alumnus award Ohio State U. Coll. Engring., 1985. Fellow Am. Soc. Landscape Architects (trustee 1977-82, v.p. 1982-83, pres.-elect 1983-84, nat. pres. 1984-85, del. to Internat. Fedn. Landscape Architects 1987-92, del. Internat. Landscape Alliance 1994-2000); mem. Ohio Soc. Landscape Architects (pres. 1969-74), Landscape Inst. U.K. (hon. corr.), Toledo C. of C. (chmn. sts. and hwys. transit com. 1972-73), Greater Merrifield Bus. and Profl. Assn. (bd. dirs. 1993-2002, chmn. bd. dirs. 1998, pres. 1997), Nat. Bldg. Stone Inst. (mem. adv. bd.), Washington Golf and Country Club (officer, bd. dirs. 1999-2003, pres. 2002-03), Sigma Phi Epsilon. Home: 6843 Churchill Rd Mc Lean VA 22101-2822 Office: Mortensen Assocs 6843 Churchill Rd Mc Lean VA 22101 Home Phone: 703-827-0995; Office Phone: 703-917-1515. Personal E-mail: rhmort@aol.com. *One of the best continuing educational experiences for a practising professional is to teach students what you have learned. They respond in a critical and ever-so-fresh "so what" atmosphere, and demand more of you sometimes than you demand of yourself. Thus, there is learning on both sides of the lectern.*

MORTENSEN, VIGGO, actor, writer; b. NYC, Oct. 20, 1958; s. Viggo P. and Grace Mortensen; m. Christine Cervenka, July 8, 1987 (div. Mar. 13, 1998); 1 child, Henry. BA in Govt. and Spanish, St. Lawrence U., 1980, ArtsD (hon.), 2006. Owner Perceval Press, 2002—. Actor: (films) Witness, 1985, Salvation!, 1987, Fresh Horses, 1988, Prison, 1988, Leatherface: Texas Chainsaw Massacre III, 1990, Young Guns II, 1990, Reflecting Skin, The, 1990, Tripwire, 1990, Indian Runner, The, 1991, Boiling Point, 1993, Ruby Cairo, 1993, Carlito's Way, 1993, Young Americans, The, 1993, Ewangelia wedlug Harry'ego, 1993, Desert Lunch, 1994, Floundering, 1994, Crew, The, 1994, American Yakuza, 1994, Crimson Tide, 1995, Black Velvet Pantsuit, 1995, Prophecy, The, 1995, Gimlet, 1995, Albino Alligator, 1996, Portrait of a Lady, The, 1996, Daylight, 1996, G.I. Jane, 1997, Pistola de mi hermano, La, 1997, Perfect Murder, A, 1998, Psycho, 1998, Walk on the Moon, A, 1999, 28 Days, 2000, Lord of the Rings: The Fellowship of the Ring, 2001, Lord of the Rings: The Two Towers, 2002, Lord of the Rings: The Return of the King, 2003, Hidalgo, 2004, A History of Violence, 2005, Alatriste, 2006; (TV films) Once In a Blue Moon, 1990; (TV miniseries) George Washington, 1984; author: (poetry) Ten Last Night, 1993, (essays) I Forget You Forever, 2006. Office: Creative Artists Agy 9830 Wilshire Blvd Beverly Hills CA 90212-1825

MORTENSEN-SAY, MARLYS, retired school system administrator; b. Yankton, SD, Mar. 11, 1924; d. Melvin A. and Edith L. (Fargo) Mortensen; m. John Theodore Say, June 21, 1951; children: Mary Louise, James Kenneth, John Melvin, Margaret Ann. BA, U. Colo., 1949, MEd, 1953; Adminstrv. Specialist, U. Nebr., 1973. Tchr. Huron (S.D.) Jr. H.S., 1944-48, Lamar (Colo.) Jr. H.S., 1950-52, Norfolk Pub. Sch., 1962-63; sch. supr. Madison County, Madison, Nebr., 1963-79; ret., 1979. Mem. ASCD, NEA (life) AAUW, Am. Assn. Sch. Adminstrs., Dept. Rural Edn., Nebr. Assn. County Supts., N.E. Nebr. County Supts. Assn. Assn. Sch. Bus. Ofcls., Nat. Orgn. Legal Problems in Edn., Nebr. Edn. Assn., Nebr. Sch. Adminstrs. Assn. Republican. Methodist.

MORTENSON, KRISTIN OPPENHEIM, musician; b. San Antonio, July 14, 1964; d. Russell E. and Martha Kunkel Oppenheim; m. Gary Curtiss Mortenson; children: Leah Marie, Sarah Grace. Attended, U. Tex., 1984; MusB, La. State U., 1987, MusM, 1988. Violinist Austin Symphony Orch., Austin, Tex., 1981—84, Baton Rouge Symphony, Baton Rouge, 1985—89, Wichita Symphony Orch., Wichita, Kans., 1991—93, Des Moines Symphony, Des Moines, 1993—2001; assoc. concertmaster Topeka Symphony Orch., Topeka, 2001—; instr. music Kans. State U., 2004—. Assistant editor The International Trumpet Guild Jour., 2001—, violinist (live performances with) Ray Charles, Dionne Warwick, Bob Hope, Shirley Jones, Marvin Hamlisch, Rich Little. Mem. Lee Sch. Site Coun., Manhattan, Kans., 2000—02; pres. Lee Sch. PTO, Manhattan, Kans., 2000—01, 2005—06, treas., 2004—05. Mem.: Am. String Tchrs. Assn. (state pres. La. 1988—89), Sigma Alpha Iota (life; pres. U. Tex. 1983—84, Coll. Honor award, Sword of Honor 1984). Home: 522 Westview Dr Manhattan KS 66502

MORTENSON, THOMAS THEODORE, health products executive, management consultant; b. Hallock, Minn., Dec. 18, 1934; s. Theodore William and Esther (Hanson) M.; m. Alice L. Girdvain, June 27, 1958; children: Kim M., Laura Dee Mortenson Pavlides. BSBA, U. ND, 1956, postgrad., 1957—58. Sales rep. Johnson & Johnson, Detroit, 1960-66, tng. and product dir. New Brunswick, NJ, 1967-72; dir. market devel. C.R. Bard, Murray Hill, NJ, 1973-75; gen. mgr. MacBick, Murray Hill, 1976-78; dir. mktg. Bard Med. Systems, Murray Hill, 1979-81, dir. sales, 1982; dir. sales/mktg., bd. dirs. Bac-Data Med. Info. Systems, Totowa, NJ, 1983-84; v.p. mktg. and sales United Med. Corp., Haddonfield, NJ, 1985—86; exec. v.p. Daltex Med. Scis., West Orange, NJ, 1987-92; dir. ConMed Corp., Utica, NY, 1993—2005; ret., 2005. Guest lectr. Am. Mgmt. Assn., 1971, Mktg. Scis. Inc., NYC, 1978, Internat. Novel Drug Delivery Techs., Tustin, Calif., 1987. With U.S. Army, USMC reserves, 1953—58. Mem. Am. Mgmt. Assn. (instr. 1971), Berkeley Swim Club (Berkeley Heights, NJ, pres. 1979-82, bd. dirs. 1974-84). Avocations: auto model collecting, woodworking, gardening, WWII history. Home: 29169 Irons Lane Dagsboro DE 19939 E-mail: viking252@mchsi.com.

MORTHAM, SANDRA BARRINGER, former state official, medical association administrator; b. Erie, Pa., Jan. 4, 1951; d. Norman Lyell and Ruth (Harer) Barringer; m. Allen Mortham, Aug. 21, 1950; children: Allen Jr., Jeffrey. AS, St. Petersburg Jr. Coll., 1971; BA, Eckerd Coll. Cons. Capital Formation Counselors, Inc., Bellair Bluffs, Fla., 1972-74; commr. City of Largo, Fla., 1982-86, vice mayor Fla., 1985-86; mem. Fla. Ho. of Reps., 1986-94, Rep. leader pro tempore, 1990-92, Rep. leader, 1992-94; Sec. of State State of Fla., 1995-98; pub. affairs dir., CEO, exec. v.p. Fla. Med. Assn., 1999—. Bd. dirs. Performing Arts Ctr. & Theatre, Clearwater, Fla.; exec. com. Pinellas County Rep. Com., Rep. Nat. Com. Named Citizen of Yr., 1990; recipient Tax Watch Competitive Govt. award, 1994, Bus. and Profl. Women "Break the Glass Ceiling" award, 1995, Fla. League of Cities Quality Floridian award, 1995, Med. Exec. Meritorious Achievement award, AMA, 2006, also numerous outstanding legislator awards, achievement among women awards from civic and profl. orgns. Mem. Am. Legis. Exch. Coun., Nat. Rep. Legislators Assn., Largo C. of C. (bd. dirs. 1987—, pres.), Largo Jr. Woman's Club (pres., Woman of Yr. award 1979), Suncoast Community Woman's Club (pres., Outstanding Svc. award 1981, Woman of Yr. award 1986), Suncoast Tiger Bay, Greater Largo Rep., Belleair Rep. Woman's, Clearwater Rep. Woman's, Tallahassee Rep. Woman's Club (pres. 1999-2000), Fla. Fedn. Rep. Women (2d v.p.). Republican. Presbyterian. Office: Fla Medical Assn 123 Adams St Tallahassee FL 32301 Office Phone: 850-224-6496. Business E-Mail: smortham@medone.org. *

MORTIER, GERARD, opera director; b. Ghent, Belgium, Nov. 25, 1943. Student law U. Ghent, 1961-66, journalism and communications, 1966-67; hon. doctorate, U. Antwerp, Belgium. Adminstrv. asst. Flanders Festival, 1968-72; artistic planner Deutsche Oper am Rhein, Düsseldorf, 1972-73; asst. adminstr. Oper der Stadt Frankfurt am Main, 1973-77; dir. artistic prodn. Hamburg Staatsoper, 1977-79; tech. program cons. Théâtre National de l'Opéra de Paris, 1979-81; dir. gen. Opéra National, Brussels, 1981-91; counselor Bastille Opera, 1986-87; dir. Intendant Salzburger Festspiele, 1992-2001; dir. Ruhr Triennial & Festivals, Germany, 2001-04; dir. Paris National Opera, 2004-; gen. mgr. designate New York City Opera, 2007-. Office: Opera National de Paris 8 rue Scribe 75 009 Paris France also: New York City Opera NY State Theater at Lincoln Ctr New York NY 10023 Office Phone: 0140011789.

MORTIMER, JAMES WINSLOW, chemist; b. Mt. Kisco, NY, Mar. 11, 1955; s. James Winslow and Eileen Ruth (Cutting) M.; m. Dawn Romay Kania, Apr. 30, 1977. BA, Washington and Jefferson U., 1976. Tech. sales rep. Waters Assocs., Milford, Mass., 1978-82; dir. nat. accounts Zymark Corp., Hopkinton, Mass., 1982-89; v.p. Microflex Tech., Triadelphia, W.Va., 1989-90; mgr. mktg. Berthold Systems, Inc., Aliquippa, Pa., 1990-95; dir. life sci. and chems. Fisher Sci., Pitts., 1995—2002; v.p. sales Integra-Bioscis., 2002—03; pres. Micronic N.Am., 2003—. Spkr. at profl. confs. Author: Laboratory Robotics, 1987; cons. editor Lab. Robotics Jour., Hershey, Pa., 1990—; assoc. editor Lab. Robotics and Automation, 1988, 90; contbr. articles to tech. publs. Mem. TAPPI, Soc. Analytical Chemists (speaker 1978, 87), Masons. Achievements include development of a cleavastat surgical instrument, a beaker that will not cause vortexing action. Home: 113 Little John Dr Mc Murray PA 15317-2542 Office Phone: 724-941-6411. E-mail: mortek@aol.com, micronicna@cs.com.

MORTIMER, NORMA SUE, music educator; d. Elroy and Mildred Louise Buth; m. William Martz; m. Gerald G. Mortimer; 1 child, Louise. BA, diploma in performance, Carthage Coll., Kenosha, Wis., 1970; M Music Edn., VanderCook Coll. Music, Chgo., 1972. Cert. gifted and talented edn. tchr., English lang. arts tchr. Music dir. Richmond-Burton HS, Richmond, Ill., 1971—76, Sun Prairie Schs., Wis., 1976—81, Sioux Empire Youth Symphony, Sioux Falls, SD, 1984—90, Milw. Pub. Schs., 1990—; chess organizer Wis. Chess, 1981—83. Asst. dir., dir., actor Bristol Renaissance Faire, Kenosha, 2000—06; cons. edn. dept. Milw. Symphony Orch., 1990—99; presenter in field. Contbr. articles to profl. jours. Named Outstanding Educator, Milw. Bus. Times; recipient Tchr. Recognition award, Ameritech, Milw., 1992. Mem.: Wis. Sch. Music Assn. (strategic planner 1999). Avocations: theater, writing, reading. Office: Samuel Morse Mid Sch 4601 N 84th St Milwaukee WI 53225

MORTIMER, RICHARD WALTER, mechanical engineer, educator; b. Phila., Dec. 7, 1936; s. Horace and Almira Duffield (Matthews) M.; m. Doris Claire Ridler, June 29, 1957; children: Patrick Lee, David Walter, James Matthew, Daniel Scott. BSME, Drexel U., 1962, MSME, 1964, PhD, 1967. Prof. Drexel U., Phila., 1967—2002, assoc. dean grad. sch., 1974-76, head dept. mech. engring., 1976-85, assoc. v.p. acad. affairs, 1985-89. Mem. exec. com. Engring. Accreditation Com., N.Y.C., 1986-91. Contbr. over 40 articles to profl. jours. Pres. Haverford (Pa.) Twp. Sch. Dist., 1980-83. With US Army, 1958—60. Recipient Achievement award Am. Soc. Nondestructive Testing, 1973, Best Tech. Paper award, 1973; fellow NASA, 1967, 68; grantee numerous orgns. including NASA, USAF, NSF, 1967-87; Fellow Members awd., Am. Soc. for Engineering Education, 1992. Fellow Am. Soc. Engring. Educators; mem. ASME (mem. numerous coms., bds. and chairs 1976-92). Republican. Episcopalian. Achievements include research in fields of structural dynamics and composite materials. Personal E-mail: dickmortimer@earthlink.net.

MORTIMER, WENDELL REED, JR., judge; b. Alhambra, Calif., Apr. 7, 1937; s. Wendell Reed and Blanche (Wilson) M.; m. Cecilia Vick, Aug. 11, 1962; children: Michelle Dawn, Kimberly Grace. AB, Occidental Coll., 1958; JD, U. So. Calif., LA, 1965. Bar: Calif. 1966. Trial atty. Legal div. State of Calif., LA, 1965-73; assoc. Thelen, Marrin, Johnson & Bridges, LA, 1973-76, ptnr., 1976-93; pvt. practice San Marino, Calif., 1994-95; judge L.A. Superior Ct., 1995—, mem. complex litigation panel, 2000—. With U.S. Army, 1960-62. Mem. ABA, Internat. Acad. Trial Judges, Los

Angeles County Bar Assn., Calif. Judges Assn., Am. Judicature Soc., Am. Judges Assn., Legion Lex., Irish-Am. Bar Assn., Am. Bd. Trial Advocacy (nat. bd. dirs., exec. com. L.A. chpt.), San Marino City Club (bd. dirs., pres.), Pasadena Bar Assn., Balboa Yacht Club Home: 1420 San Marino Ave San Marino CA 91108-2042

MORTLOCK, ROBERT PAUL, microbiologist, educator; b. Bronxville, NY, May 12, 1931; s. Donald Robert and Florance Mary (Bellaby) M.; m. Florita Mary Welling, Sept., 1954; children: Florita M., Jeffrey R., Douglas P. BS, Rensselaer Poly. Inst., NYC, 1953; PhD, U. Ill., Urbana, 1958. Asst. prof. microbiology U. Mass., Amherst, 1963-68, assoc. prof. microbiology, 1968-73, prof. microbiology, 1973-78, Cornell U., Ithaca, NY, 1978-99, prof. emeritus, 2000. Editor: Microorganisms as Model Systems for Studying Evolution, 1984, The Evolution of Metabolic Function, 1992. Served to 1st lt. U.S. Army, 1959-61 Fellow Am. Acad. Microbiology; mem. AAAS, Am. Soc. Microbiology, Northeastern Microbiologists, Physiology, Ecology and Taxonomy (pres. 1984-91). Office: Cornell U Dept Microbiology Wing Hall Ithaca NY 14852 Home Phone: 607-533-7806. Business E-Mail: rpm2@cornell.edu.

MORTON, CRAIG RICHARD, real estate investor; b. Mpls., Dec. 8, 1942; s. William Charles and Patricia Louise (Hare) M.; m. Barbara Jean Larsen, 1998; children: Kelly McCall, Bradley Winslow; step-son Thomas Paul Caspers. Student, U. Philippines, Quezon City, 1961-62; BA in Geography of Southeast Asia, U. Minn., 1966; postgrad., St. John's Coll., Annapolis, 1966. Vol. U.S. Peace Corps, Philippines, 1966-68; v.p. Rent Mgmt., Inc., Mpls., 1970-80; pres. Diversified Hawaiian Investments, Inc., Mpls., 1981-99, Craig R. Morton & Assoc., Inc., Mpls., 1980-2000, No. Am. Land Corp., 1992—. Founder 49 real estate ltd. partnerships, Minn., N.Mex., Hawaii, Tex.; real estate developer Enchanted Lakes, Minn., 1990; pres. Am. Forex Corp., 1995—98, Sweet Magnolia HOA, 2001—, Royal Palms HOA, 2002—, Ashby Cove HOA, 2003—, Space Coast Barter, 2003—, Am. Eagle Trade Exch., 2006—. Am. Field Svc. scholar to Pakistan, 1960. Mem. Soc. Mayflower Descs., Jaguar Club Minn., Country Classics Car Club, Rotary (Paul Harris fellow), Order of DeMolay, Boy Scouts Order of Arrow, Loyal Order of Moose, Internat. Arabian Horse Assn., U.S. Space Walk of Fame Found. (life). Republican. Avocations: Jaguar automobiles, reading, stamp collecting/philately, woodsmanship, raising arabian horses. Home: 3569 Muirfield Dr Titusville FL 32780 Office Phone: 321-264-1615. E-mail: craig@spirithollow.us.

MORTON, D. HOLMES, physician; m. Caroline Smith; children: Mary Caperton, Sarah McRae, Paul Holmes. Grad., Trinity Coll., 1979; MD, Harvard Med. Sch., 1983. Resident Children's Hosp. Boston; conducted biochemical genetics rsch. John Hopkins U., Children's Hosp. Phila.; country doctor, rsch. physician, clinic dir., co-founder Clinic for Spl. Children, Strasburg, Pa., 1989—. Contbr. articles to Nature Genetics, American Journal of Medical Genetics, Pediatrics and others. Recipient Albert Schweitzer prize for humanitarianism, 1993; MacArthur fellow, John D. and Catherine T. MacArthur Found., 2006. being co-founder with wife of a non-profit medical and diagnostic service for children with inherited metabolic disorders in Lancaster County, Pennsylvania. The clinic was established to provide comprehensive medical care for children with chronic, complex medical problems due to inherited disorders. Office: Clinic for Special Children 535 Bunker Hill Rd Strasburg PA 17579

MORTON, DAVID RAY, sales and marketing executive; b. Rockford, Ill., Dec. 7, 1948; s. Raymond Thomas and Nathalie Ilene (Hendricks) Morton; m. Carol Lynn Pott, Apr. 1, 1972; children: Rebecca Lynn, Eric David. BS in Forestry and Wood Scis., U. Ill., Champaign/Urbana, 1971; MBA, Ohio State U., Columbus, 1983. Field svc. rep. So. Forest Products Assn., New Orleans, 1972-73; sales rep. chem. divsn. Ga. Pacific Corp., Columbus, Ohio, 1973-76; lumber broker Fireside Forest Industries, Columbus, 1976-77; sr. tech. sales & svc. rep. chem. divsn. Ga. Pacific Corp., Columbus, 1977-84; dir. mktg. Monitronix Corp., Columbus, 1984-85; dir. mktg. & sales Freeman Mfg. & Supply Co., Cleve., 1985-88; nat. sales and mktg. mgr. Hexcel Corp.-Resins Group, LA, 1988-95; sales mgr. Hapco, Inc., Hanover, Mass., 1995-96; nat. sales mgr. Conap, Olean, NY, 1996-99; sr. market devel. mgr. H.B. Fuller Co., N.Am. ASC Group, Assembly Group, St. Paul, 1999—2003; owner Rezolin, LLC, Ormond Beach, Fla., 2003—05; owner, pres. Polaris Polymers LLC, Avon Lake, 2006—. Del.-at-large Rep. Platform Planning Com., Avon Lake, Ohio, 1992. Command sgt. maj. N.G. US Army, 1971—99. Mem.: Polyurethane Mfr. Assn. (del. 1990—95), Am. Foundrymen's Soc. (publ. chmn. 1992—99), Soc. Mfg. Engr. (treas. 1982—84), Enlisted Assn. N.G. US, Ohio State Alumni Assn., U. Ill. Alumni Assn., Ohio N.G. Enlisted Assn., Phi Kappa Sigma. Avocations: sailing, handball, tennis, woodworking. Home: 296 Chestnut Ct Avon Lake OH 44012-2141 Office Phone: 440-933-7196. Office Fax: 440-930-8685. Business E-Mail: dave.morton@polorispolymers.com.

MORTON, DONALD CHARLES, astronomer; b. Kapuskasing, Ont., Can., June 12, 1933; s. Charles Orr and Irene Mary (Wightman) M.; m. Winifred May Austin, Dec. 12, 1970; children: Keith James, Christine Elizabeth. BA, U. Toronto, 1956; PhD, Princeton U., 1959. Astronomer U.S. Naval Rsch. Lab., Washington, 1959-61; from rsch. assoc. to sr. rsch. astronomer with rank of prof. Princeton (N.J.) U., 1961-76; dir. Anglo-Australian Obs., Epping and Coonabarabran, Australia, 1976-86; dir. gen. Herzberg Inst. Astrophysics, NRC of Can., Ottawa and Victoria, 1986—2000; rsch. emeritus NRC of Can., 2001—. Contbr. numerous articles to profl. jours. Fellow Australian Acad. Sci.; mem. Internat. Astron. Union, Royal Astron. Soc. (assoc. 1980), Astron. Soc. Australia (pres. 1981-83, hon. mem. 1986), Royal Astron. Soc. Can., Am. Astron. Soc. (councilor 1970-73), Can. Astron. Soc., Can. Assn. Physicists, U.K. Alpine Club, Am. Alpine Club, Alpine Club Can. Avocations: mountain climbing, rock climbing, ice climbing, marathon running. Office: Herzberg Inst Astrophysics NRC Can 5071 W Saanich Rd Victoria BC Canada V9E 2E7 Home Phone: 250-721-4942.

MORTON, DONALD JOHN, librarian; b. Bklyn., Jan. 11, 1931; s. Ellwood Stokes and Gladys (Hassler) M.; m. Ann Mayo Tilden, Aug. 16, 1958; children— Saundra Kay, Donald John, Mary Ann. BS, U. Del., 1952; MS, La. State U., 1954; PhD, U. Calif., Berkeley, 1958; MS in Libr. Sci., Simmons Coll., 1969, Dr. in Libr. Sci., 1976. Asst. prof. botany N.M. State U., Las Cruces, 1957-58; asst. prof. plant pathology N.D. State U., Fargo, 1959-61; plant pathologist Agr. Dept., Tifton, Ga., 1961-65; asso. prof. plant pathology U. Del., Newark, 1965-68; librarian Northeastern U., Boston, 1968-70; head librarian, asst. prof. history of medicine U. Mass. Med. Sch., Worcester, 1970-74, dir. libr., assoc. prof. libr. sci., 1974-94, libr. cons., 1994—; tchr. med. librarianship Worcester State Coll., 1974-94; libr. cons., 1994—; computer cons. Hampton Hist. Soc., 1995—2006; libr. advisor Exeter Hosp., NH, 1996—2006; libr. vol. Maine Med. Ctr., 2006—. Cons. in field; mem. adv. com. med. librarianship Simmons Coll., 1972-94; mem. task force com. New Eng. Regional Libr. Svc., 1971-94; mem. cooperating staff Worcester Found. Exptl. Biology, 1972-94; chmn. Coun. Developing Med. Librs., 1974; pres. North Atlantic Health Scis. Librs., 1974-75, Worcester Area Coop. Librs., 1974-75. Contbr. articles to profl. jours. Mem. Oliver Wendell Holmes endowment com. Boston Med. Libr., 1973-74, U. Mass. Bicentennial Com., 1973-75. Mem. Am. Assn. Univ. Adminstrs., Simmons Coll. Libr. Sch. Alumni Assn. (pres. 1975-76), Worcester Art Mus., Worcester Hist. Soc., Northboro Hist. Soc., Hampton Hist. Soc., N.H. Hist. Soc., Am. Soc. Info. Sci., ALA, Mass. Libr. Assn., Med. Libr. Assn. (chmn. New Eng. group 1974-75), Mycol. Soc. Am., Spl. Librs. Assn., New Eng. Coll. Librarians, Piscataqua Pioneers Hereditary Soc., Sigma Xi, Phi Kappa Phi, Phi Sigma, Delta Tau Delta, Alpha Zeta. Personal E-mail: atmdjm@maine.rr.com.

MORTON, EDWARD JAMES, insurance company executive; b. Ft. Wayne, Ind., Nov. 8, 1926; s. Clifford Leroy and Clara Marie (Merklein) M.; m. Jean Ann McClernon, Apr. 30, 1949; children: Marcia Lynn, Anne; m. Matthild Schneider, Sept. 19, 1986; 1 child, Katherine. BA, Yale U., 1949. With John Hancock Mut. Life Ins. Co., Boston, 1949—, v.p., then sr. v.p., 1967-74, exec. v.p., 1974-82, pres., chief operating officer, 1982-86, chmn., chief exec. officer, 1987-92, also bd. dirs. Trustee Gettysburg Coll. 1990-2002, trustee emeritus, 2002—; hon. life overseer Children's Hosp. Fellow Soc. Actuaries; mem. Actuaries Club Boston, Comml. Club Boston, Phi Beta Kappa. Office: John Hancock Life Ins Co PO Box 111 C-01-03 Boston MA 02117-0111 Personal E-mail: ejmorton@potomacnet.com.

MORTON, ELIZABETH GRON, art historian, educator; m. Barry Morton, July 17, 2000; children: Samuel B., Sarah K,. MA in History, U. Botswana, 1996; MA in Art History, Emory U., Atlanta, 2003, PhD, 2003; BA Art History, Ind. U., Bloomington, 1986—92. Curator Nat. Mus., Monuments and Art Gallery, Gaborone, Botswana, 1992—97; visual arts specialist Lakewood Cultural Ctr., Colo., 2001—02; asst. prof., art history U. West Ga., Carrollton, 2003—, dir. summer art program in Europe, 2003. Author: (exhibition catalogue) Botswana Live, Crafts of Botswana; curator (exhibition) Weaving the Fruits of the Earth: Textiles from Southern and West Africa, Robert Maine Coultas: A Retrospective. Grad. Sch. Arts and Scis. fellow, Emory U., 1997—2001, rsch. grantee, U. West Ga., 2006—07, Fund Internationalization Dissertation grantee, Office Internat. Affairs, Emory U., 1999, 2002. Mem.: Coll. Art Assn., Art Coun. African Studies Assn., Kappa Delta. Avocations: travel, snowboarding. Office: U West Ga Art Dept Carrollton GA 30118 Home Phone: 770-838-0538; Office Phone: 678-839-4951. Office Fax: 678-839-4961. Business E-Mail: emorton@westga.edu.

MORTON, ERIC, liberal arts educator; b. Detroit, Feb. 24, 1934; s. Lee Jack and Theresa Magdalen (Leonard) M.; children: Tracey Lynn, Theresa Dallas; m. Virgie Tillman, Sept. 27, 1997. AA, Merritt Coll., 1992; BA, U. Calif., Berkeley, 1992; M of Profl. Studies, Cornell U., 1994; MA, SUNY, Binghamton, 1998, PhD, 1999. Internat. organizer Am. Fedn. of State, County, Mcpl. Employees, Calif., 1970-73; field rep. State Senator Nicholas Petris, Oakland, Calif., 1973-75; mktg. adminstr. Safegate Aviation Systems, Oakland, 1975-80; asst. to dir. recreational sports U. Calif., 1980-92; grad. tchg. asst. Africana Studies and Rsch. Ctr., Cornell U., 1992-94; adj. lectr., rschr., tchr. SUNY, Binghamton, 1994-2000; assoc. prof. philosophy Fort Valley (Ga.) State U., 2000—. Mem., multicultural core group Cornell U., 1992-94; lectr., rschr., tchr. SUNY Binghamton, 1994-2000; assoc. prof. philosophy Fort Valley State U., Ga., 2000—. Compiler (book) Mississippi Black Paper, 1965; contbr. articles to profl. jours. Active polit. campaigns; project mgr. Ctr. for Ind. Living, Berkeley, 1975-77. With U.S. Army, 1951-54. Recipient Award Met. Trans. Commn., 1973. Avocations: photography, reading. Home: 108 Red Oak Ct Byron GA 31008 Office Phone: 478-825-6686. Business E-Mail: be83464@binghamton.edu. E-mail: mortone@mail.fvsu.edu.

MORTON, FRED J., lawyer; b. El Paso, Tex., Nov. 13, 1935; s. R.A.D. and Julianne (More) M.; m. Anne Adele Reynolds, July 19, 1960; children: Chris, Anne, John, Robert, Peter, Mary Virginia, Thomas, Mary Katherine. BA, U. Tex., El Paso, 1957; LLB, U. Tex., Austin, 1958. Bar: Tex. 1958. Asst. U.S. atty., El Paso, 1961-65; U.S. commr. cts., 1966-71. Trustee, Southwestern Children's Home Trust, El Paso, 1983—; pres. El Paso County Hist. Soc., 1967. Fellow U. Tex. Law Sch. Ctr. for Pub. Policy Dispute Resolution, 1996. Mem. Tex. Bar Assn., El Paso Trial Lawyers Assn. (pres. 1972), El Paso Bar Assn. (pres. 1985), Sigma Alpha Epsilon, Phi Delta Phi. Democrat. Roman Catholic. Home: 1101 Montana Ave El Paso TX 79902-5509 Home Phone: 915-532-6810; Office Phone: 915-542-1142. Personal E-mail: fredmorton713@msn.com.

MORTON, FREDERIC, author; b. Vienna, Oct. 5, 1924; s. Frank and Rose (Ungvary) M.; m. Marcia Colman, Mar. 28, 1957; 1 dau., Rebecca. BS, Coll. City N.Y., 1947; MA, New Sch. Social Research, 1949. Author: The Hound, 1947, The Darkness Below, 1949, Asphalt and Desire, 1952, The Witching Ship, 1960, The Schatten Affair, 1965, Snow Gods, 1969, An Unknown Woman, 1976, The Forever Street, 1984, Crosstown Sabbath, 1987, (biography) The Rothschilds, 1962, A Nervous Splendor-Vienna 1888/9, 1979, Thunder at Twilight-Vienna 1913/14, 1989, Runaway Waltz--A Memoir From Vienna To New York, 2005; books translated into 14 langs.; actor (documentary) Crosstown Sabbath, 1995; contbg. editor: Vanity Fair; contbr. to publs. including Best Am. Short Stories, 1965, Best Am. Essays of 2003, and other anthologies, N.Y. Times, Harper's mag., Atlantic mag., Nation, Playboy, Esquire, N.Y. Mag., Hudson Rev., Wall Street Jour., Vanity Fair, L.A. Times, others; columnist Village Voice, Conde-Nast Traveler, Wall Street Jour.3.2 Recipient Author of Year award Nat. Anti-Defamation League, B'nai B'rith; Hon. Professorship award Republic of Austria, 1980, Tom Osborne Disting. lectureship U. Nebr., 1989; Dodd, Mead Intercollegiate Lit. fellow, 1947; Yaddo residence fellow, 1948, 50; Breadloaf Writers' Conf. fellow, 1947; Columbia U. fellow, 1953; recipient Golden Merit award City of Vienna, 1986, City of Vienna medal of honor in gold, 2001, Cross of Honor for Achievements in Arts, Republic of Austria, 2003. Mem. Author's Guild (exec. coun.), P.E.N. Home: 110 Riverside Dr New York NY 10024-3715 Office: Sandra Diskstra Agy PMB 515 1155 Camino Del Mar Del Mar CA 92014 Home Phone: 212-721-6938. *As a writer I'm trying to tell the truth interestingly.*

MORTON, HARVEY LEON, lawyer; b. Sweetwater, Tex., May 9, 1941; s. William Allen and Lenora Elizabeth Morton; m. Betty Catherine Morton, Jan. 30, 1965; children: Allison Pritchard, Kimberly Hendrix, Craig. BA, McMurry Coll., Abilene, Tex., 1964; JD, U. Tex., Austin, 1967. Bar: Tex. 1967. Pvt. practice, Lubbock, 1970—; ptnr. Brock, Morton & Pigg, Lubbock, Tex., 1978—88. Atty. City of Slaton, Tex., 1970—; panel trustee US Trustee Program, Dallas, 1982—; pres. West Tex. Bankruptcy Bar, Lubbock, 1999; pres., chmn. bd. dirs. Dreyer Music Co., San Angelo, Tex., 1990—95, InstaChek San Angelo, 1998—2000, Queen City Land Devel. Co. San Angelo, 1999—2000. Chmn. bd. dirs. Lubbock Regional Mental Health Bd., 1995—97; dist. dir. McMurry Coll. Alumni, 1973—74; mem. criminal justice planning coun. South Plains Assn. Govts., 1973—74; county chmn. State Dem. Party, Lubbock County, 1982—88, mem. exec. com. Tex., 1978—82; long range planning chmn. St. Luke's United Meth. Ch., 1988—95, former charge lay leader, youth sponsor, chmn. adminstrv. bd., Sunday sch. tchr.; bd. dirs. Meth. Home, Waco, Tex., 1988—92, Tex. Coun. Risk Mgmt. Fund, Lubbock, 1991—, chmn. bd. dirs., 1995—97; bd. dirs. Wesley Found., Tex. Tech U., 1974, Marion Moss Found., 1986. Named Man of Yr., Slaton C. of C., 1991; recipient Scrappy award for vol. svc., Lubbock Regional Mental Health Bd., 1995. Mem.: Lubbock County Bar Assn. (treas. 1997—98), West Tex. Bankruptcy Bar Assn. (pres.-elect 1998—99, pres. 1999—2000), State Bar Tex., Rotary (pres. Slaton chpt. 1995—2000). Office: PO Box 10305 Lubbock TX 79408

MORTON, JAMES CARNES, JR., automotive executive; b. Duncan, Okla., May 8, 1945; s. James Carnes and Syble Lyda (Looney) Morton; m. Susan Phillips, May 25, 1968; children: James III, Terrissa Anne, Scott Thomas. BA, Westminster Coll., 1967; JD, U. Mo., 1972. Bar: Mo. 1972. Tax acct. Arthur Andersen Co., St. Louis, 1972—74; tax atty. Gen. Dynamics Corp., St. Louis, 1974—76; asst. gen. counsel Michelin Tire Corp., Greenville, SC, 1976—86; gen. counsel Michelin Tire Corp. and Michelin Tires (Can.) Ltd., Greenville, 1990—92; dir. pub. rels. and govt. affairs Michelin Tire Corp., Greenville, 1986—92; exec. dir. external rels. Michelin N.Am., Inc., Greenville, 1992—96, v.p. pub. rels. and govt. rels., 1996—2000; sr. v.p. fin. and adminstrn., bd. dirs., mem. mgmt. com. Nissan N.Am., Inc., Franklin, Tenn., 2000—06, vice chmn. Nashville, 2006—07, asst. to CEO, sr. advisor govt. affairs, 2007—. Adv. bd. Hollings Cancer Ctr. Med. U. SC, 2005—, Trent Lott Leadership Inst., U. Miss., 2006—. Bd. dirs. Greenville Symphony Orch., 1986—89, United Way Greenville, 1987—88, Greenville YMCA, 1988—89, Greenville Tech Found., 2007—; mem. S.C. Reorganization Commn., 1985—98; trustee S.C. Gov.'s Sch. Sci. and Math., 1996—99; mem. sch. bd. Christ Ch. Episcopal Sch., Greenville, 1997—2000; vice chmn. S.C. Ports Authority, 1999—2000; pres. Nissan Found., 2003—07. Lt. US Army, 1967—70, capt. Mo. Army N.G., 1970—72. Recipient Alumni Achievement award, Westminster Coll., 2003. Mem.: ABA, Mo. Bar Assn. (non-resident), Alliance Automobile Mfrs. (bd. dirs. 2000—03), Rubber Mfrs. Assn. (bd. dirs. 1995—2000, govt. affairs com., tire mgmt. com.), Assn. Internat. Automobile Mfrs. (exec. com. 2000—07, chmn. bd. dirs. 2005—07), Nat. Urban League (trustee 2004—07), S.C. C. of C. (exec. com. 1981—84, 1986—95, pres. 1993—94, chmn. 1994—95, bd. dirs.), Greater Greenville C. of C. (bd. dirs. 1990—93, chmn. legis. affairs com. 1996—98), L.A. Urban League (bd. dirs. 2001—05), Calif. C. of C. (bd. dirs. 2001—04), Kiawah Island Club, Greenville Country Club. Presbyterian. Avocation: golf. Home Phone: 864-232-5841; Office Phone: 615-727-2677. Business E-Mail: jim.morton@nissan-usa.com.

MORTON, JOE, actor; b. NYC, Oct. 18, 1947; m. Nora Chavooshian, Oct. 1984; children: Ara, Seta. Student, Hofstra U. Actor Actors Theatre of Louisville, 1984-85. Dir. play: Heliotrope Bouquet; film appearances include Between the Lines, 1977, ...And Justice for All, 1979, The Killing Hour, 1981, The Brother From Another Planet, 1984, Crossroads, 1985, Trouble n Mind, 1985, Zelly and Me, 1988, The Good Mother, 1988, Tap, 1989, City of Hope, 1991, Judgment Day, 1991, Of Mice and Men, 1992, Forever Young, 1992, The Walking Dead, 1994, The Inkwell, 1994, In the Hands of the Enemy, 1994, Speed, 1994, Executive Decision, 1996, Lone Star, 1996, Toubles on the Corner, 1997, The Pest, 1997, Speed 2: Cruise Control, The Astronaut's Wife, 1998, Blues Brother's 2000, 1998, APT Pupil, 1998, What Lies Beneath, 2000, Ali, 2001, Dragonfly, 2002, Crossing, 2003, Thoughtcrimes, 2003, Paycheck, 2003, Lenny the Wonder Dog, 2004, Breaking Dawn, 2004, Back in the Day, 2005, Stealth, 2005, The Night Listener, 2006; TV appearances include Feeling Good, 1974-75, Grady, 1975-76, Watch Your Mouth, 1978, Equal Justice, 1990, A Different World, 1991-92, Tribeca, 1993, The Great Depression, 1993, Under One Roof, 1995, New York News, 1995, Mercy Point, 1998, also on daytime series Search for Tomorrow, 1973-74, Prince Street, 1997, Another World, 1983-84, All My Children, 2002, on TV movies, This Man Stands Aline, 1979, Death Penalty, 1980, A Good Sport, 1984, Alone in the Neon Jungle, 1988, burnout, 1988, Terrorist on Trial: The United States versus Salim Ajami, 1988, Howard Beach: Making the Case for Murder, 1989, Legacy of Lies, 1992, In the Shadow of Evil, 1995, Miss Ever's Boys, 1997, Mutiny, 1999, Y2K, 1999, Ali: An American Hero, 2000, Jasper, Texas, 2003, Gone But Not Forgotten, 2004; also episodes and spls.; numerous stage appearances including, Raisin, Honky Tonk Nights, 1986, King John, 1988, Elektra, 1988, Crumbs from the Table, 1995, Hair, A Midsummer Night's Dream, Crazy Horse, Electra, Julius Caesar, The Tempest; recordings include Days of Grace, 1993, God's Trombones: Seven Negro Sermons in Verse, 1993, Possessing the Secret of Joy, 1993, The Autobiography of Malcolm X, 1993. Avocation: magic. Office: Judy Schoen and Assocs 606 N Larchmont Blvd Ste 309 Los Angeles CA 90004-1309

MORTON, JOHN DOUGLAS, retail executive; b. 1951; With Wolfe's Sporting Goods, 1972-80; dist. mgr. sporting goods divsn. Malone and Hyde, 1980-86; divsn. mgr. Utah region Gart Sports Co., Denver, 1986-88, divsn. v.p. Utah region, 1988-90, v.p. ops., 1990-94, exec. v.p., 1994-95, pres., CEO, chmn. bd., 1995—2003; vice chmn., CEO The Sports Authority, Englewood, Colo., 2003—04, chmn., pres., CEO, 2004—. Office: The Sports Authority 1050 W Hampden Ave Englewood CO 80110 Fax: 303-829-1511.

MORTON, JOSEPH, school system administrator; BS, Auburn U.; MS, U. Ala., PhD in Ednl. Adminstrn. Supt. of edn. Sumter County Schs., Ala., Sylacauga City Schs., Ala.; dep. state supt. edn. Ala. Dept. Edn., 1996—2004, interim state supt. edn., 2004, state supt. edn., 2004—. Founder Sylacauga City Schools Found. Founder Sylacauga City Schs. Found. Named one of Top 100 Sch. Executives in N.Am., Exec. Educator Mag. Office: Ala Dept Edn 50 N Ripley St PO Box 302101 Montgomery AL 36104 Office Phone: 334-242-9700. E-mail: jmorton@alsde.edu. *

MORTON, LINDA JUNE, academic administrator; b. Nashville, Jan. 21, 1943; d. William Taylor Morton and Ruby Grayson (Maiden name-Page) Morton. BA, George Peabody Coll., 1964, MS, 1976; PhD, Vanderbilt U., 1981. Cert. ednl. adminstr. Tenn., 1981, tchr. English 7-12 Tenn., 1964, tchr. music K-12 Tenn., 1964, career ladder III tchr. Tenn., 1985. Tchr. high sch. English, music Metro Nashville Pub. Schs., 1964—67, tchr. mid. sch. tchr. music, 1967—89, asst. prin., 1989—2000. Chair, McGavock cluster prins. Metro Nashville Pub. Schools, 1990—91, spl. edn. prins. adv. com. mem., 1992—94; chair curriculum com. 10 yr. sacs evaluation McGavock H.S., 1992—92. Wrote and compiled (7th grade music curriculum outline) 7th Grade Music Curriculum Outline. Dir. Jr. Dept. Woman's Club Nashville, 1972—74; vice-moderator, bd. trustees Memphis Theol. Sem., 1998—2003; mem. bd. dirs. Kidney Found. Mid. Tenn., 1981—83. Mem.: Fla. Oceanographic Soc., Aerospace Edn., Internat. Soc. Music Edn., U. Club Nashville, Woman's Club Nashville (life), Phi Delta Kappa, Alpha Delta Kappa. Avocations: photography, swimming, travel, music, scuba diving. Home: 6740 Currywood Dr Nashville TN 37205 Home Phone: 615-356-0407; Office Phone: 772-225-1599. Personal E-mail: laquarius@aol.com.

MORTON, M. JUANITA, writer, accountant; b. Balt., Mar. 22, 1951; d. Ethel R. Brown; m. William L. Morton, July 1, 1972 (div. Nov. 19, 2002); 1 child, William L. II. Student, U. Philippines, Quezon City, 1977, CC Balt., 1979; BBA in Acctg., Loyola Coll., Balt., 1984; MBA in Fin., U. Balt., 1990. Cert. diversified cash flow specialist, Am. Cash Flow Assn., 1999. Sr. fin. analyst US Fidelity & Guaranty Co., Balt., 1978—96; mgr. customer svc. Hecht's, Balt., 1996—97; asst. contr. Marcorp, Ltd., Balt., 1998—99; acctg. mgr. The Walter's Art Mus., Balt., 1999—2001; sr. reins. acct. Aegon Direct Mktg. Svcs., Balt., 2001—04; corp. fin. mgr. World Relief Corp., Balt., 2005. Mentor USF&G/Mevro Partnership Program, Balt., 1980—85, Abell Found./New Shiloh Bapt. Ch., Balt., 1983—88; youth coun. advisor NAACP, Balt., 1988—97; NAACP youth coun. advisor New Shiloh Bapt. Ch., Balt., 1988—97. Named Nat. Best Youth Coun. Co-Advisor, NAACP, 1992; recipient Pastor's citation, New Shiloh Bapt. Ch., 1993, Civic Recognition & Svc. award, New Shiloh NAACP Youth Coun., 1997. Mem.: Md. Writers Assocs. (assoc.), Les Gemmes, Inc. (assoc.). Avocations: reading, investing, cultural/spa activities, gardening, travel. Home Phone: 443-919-5869.

MORTON, R. STEVEN, lawyer; b. Atlanta, Dec. 3, 1958; BS in Environ. Studies, Allegheny Coll., 1980; grad. studies in Hydrogeology, U. Tex.; JD, Vanderbilt U., 1984. Bar: Tenn. 1985, Tex. 1986. Ptnr. Brown McCarroll & Oaks Hartline, Austin, Tex.; shareholder Jenkens & Gilchrist, P.C., Austin, 1995—2007; ptnr. Moltz Morton O'Toole LLC, Austin, 2007—. Office: Moltz Morton OToole The Littlefield Bldg 106 E 6th St Ste 700 Austin TX 78701 Office Phone: 512-499-3856. Office Fax: 512-499-3810. Business E-Mail: smorton@jenkens.com.

MORTON, ROGER LARKIN, finance educator; b. Wash., Nov. 14, 1970; s. Jim and Leona Gail Irwin Morton; m. Regina Khong, Nov. 28, 1998; 1 child, Jarrett Ruslan Khong. BA, Claremont McKenna Coll., Calif., 1992; MPA, Calif. State U., Fullerton, 1998; PhD, U. Calif., Irvine, 2003. Cert. fin. planner Am. Planning Assn., 2004. Ptnr. Morton & Henderson Pub. Rels. Svcs., Claremont, Calif., 1993—94; adminstr. Cmty. Wellness

Partnership, Pomona, Calif., 1995—97; coord. Pomona Valley Youth Employment Svcs., 1997—98; rsch. cons. Orange County Bus. Coun., Irvine, Calif., 1998—; prof. Calif. State U., Fullerton, 2002—05; rschr. Gianneschi Ctr. for Nonprofit Rsch., Fullerton, 2001—03; prof. Calif. State U., Long Beach, 2005—. Commr. Cmty. Life Commn., Pomona, Calif., 1993—97; dir. First Presbyn. Ch. of Pomona, 1995—95. Recipient Eagle Scout, Boy Scouts of Am., 1985; fellow, Calif. State U., 2000—03; scholar, Coll. Bd., 1988; McKenna scholar, Claremont McKenna Coll., 1988, Eugene Cota Robles fellow, U. Calif., 1998. Mem.: Mensa. Roman Catholic. Office: Orange County Bus Coun 2 Park Plaza Ste 100 Irvine CA 92614 Office Phone: 949-794-7209. Personal E-mail: zebrazebra1970@yahoo.com.

MORTON, SALLIE W., music educator; b. Columbus, Ohio, Nov. 5, 1947; d. William Waldo Waters and Lillianne Stewart Rudisill; m. Charles Ward Morton, July 1, 1989; children: Ari Shawn Williams, Tara Donielle Sutter, Christy Lyn Winkler. B in Music Edn., Denison U., Granville, Ohio, 1968; MA in Christian Edn., Scarritt Coll., Nashville, 1970. Cert. elem./intermediate, advanced piano tchr. Ohio, Orff level I and II. Dir. Scarritt Coll. Singers Scarritt Coll., Nashville, 1969—70; dir. music Brentwood United Meth. Ch., Nashville, 1971—76; dir. Christian Edn., music and youth Brooksville United Meth. Ch., Fla., 1976—80; band dir. Rittman H.S., Ohio, 1980—81; tchr. music Chippewa Local Schs., Doylestown, Ohio, 1981—. Pvt. piano, flute tchr., 1963—. Vocal judge MacDowell Club of Wooster, Ohio, 2002—07; tone chime dir. Dalton Presbyn. Ch., 2004—07. Recipient Sallie Williams Day, Brooksville United Meth. Ch., 1978. Mem.: Nat. Guild Piano Tchrs., Ohio Music Educators Assn., MacDowell Music Club Wooster. Republican. Methodist. Avocations: camping, swimming, crafts. Home: 3472 Tamarack Ln Wooster OH 44691 Office: Hazel Harvey Elementary Sch 165 Brooklyn Ave Doylestown OH 44230

MORTON, SAMANTHA, actress; b. Nottingham, Eng., May 13, 1977; d. Peter and Pamela; 1 child, Esme. Actor: (TV miniseries) Band of Gold, 1995, The History of Tom Jones, a Foundling, 1997; (TV series) Soldier Soldier, 1991, Max and Ruby, 2002; (TV films) The Token King, 1993, Emma, 1996, Jane Eyre, 1997; (films) The Future Lasts a Long Time, 1996, Under the Skin, 1997, This is the Sea, 1998, Sweet and Lowdown, 1999 (Acad. award nomination for best supporting actress, 2000), Jesus' Son, 1999, The Last Yellow, 1999, Eden, 2001, Morvern Callar, 2002, Minority Report, 2002, In America, 2002 (Acad. award nomination for best actress, 2004), Code 46, 2003, The Libertine, 2004, River Queen, 2005, Lassie, 2005. Mailing: c/o Creative Artists Agy 9830 Wilshire Blvd Beverly Hills CA 90212

MORTON, STEPHEN DANA, chemist, consultant; b. Madison, Wis., Sept. 7, 1932; s. Walter Albert and Rosalie (Amlie) M. BS, U. Wis., 1954, PhD, 1962. Asst. prof. chemistry Otterbein Coll., Westerville, Ohio, 1962-66; postdoctoral fellow water chemistry, pollution control U. Wis., Madison, 1966-67; water pollution rsch. chemist WARF Inst., Madison, 1967-73, head environ. quality dept., 1973-76; mgr. quality assurance Raltech Sci. Svcs., 1977-82; pres. SDM Cons., 1982—. Author: Water Pollution-Causes and Cures, 1976. 1st lt. Chem. Corps, AUS, 1954-56. Mem. AAAS, Am. Chem. Soc. Home and Office: 1126 Sherman Ave Madison WI 53703-1620

MORTON-YOUNG, TOMMIE, psychology professor, writer; b. Nashville; BA cum laude, Tenn. State U., Nashville, 1951; MA, Peabody Vanderbilt U., 1955; PhD, Duke U., Durham, NC, 1977; postgrad., U. Okla., Norman, 1967, U. Nebr., 1968. Coord. Young Adult Program Lucy Thurman br. YWCA, 1951-52; instr. edn. Tenn. State U., Nashville, 1956-59; instr. coord. media program Prairie View Coll., Tex., 1959-61; asst. prof. edn., assoc. prof. English, dir. IMC Ctr. U. Ark., Pine Bluff, 1965-69; asst. prof. English and edn., dir. learning lab NC Ctrl. U., Durham, 1969-74; prof., dir./chairperson libr. /dir. Afro-Am. Family Project, prof. philosophy sociol. found. NC Agrl. and Tech. State U., Greensboro, 1975—92; adj. prof. langs., lit. and philosophy, dir. schs. history project Tenn. State U., Nashville, 1994—. Dir. workshops, grants; pres., dir. Ednl. Cons. Svcs.; owner Historic Black Nashville Tours. Author: Afro-Am. Genealogy Sourcebook, 1987, Oral Histories of Former All-Black Public Schs., 1991, After School Program for At-Risk Youth and Their Families, 1997, Sable Scenes, 1996, Genealogist's Guide to Discovering Your African Ancestors, 1997, A Sister Speaks, 1998, Nashville, Tennessee, 2000, Fabulous You: Women Celebrating the Fabulous Self, 2005, Ride a Dark Horse, 2007; contbr. poem to Poetry: American Heritage; contbr. rsch. papers, articles to profl. jours. Nat. chmn. Com. to Re-Elect the Pres.; past sec. Fedn. Colored Women's Clubs; bd. dirs. Southwestern div. ARC, Nashville area, 1994-, dir. Volun-Teens; chairperson schs. div. Durham County Unit Am. Cancer Soc.; past adv. bd., bd. dirs. YMCA, Atlanta; chair Guilford County Commn. on Needs of Children; bd. advisors NIH, NC Coun. of the Arts; mem. Guilford County Involvement Coun.; chmn. NC adv. com. US Civil Rights Com.; exec. planning com. Greensboro; hon. staff 54th Legis. Dist., Nashville, 1996; pres. Davidson County Dem. Women, 2003-04; rep. dist. I exec. com. Davidson County Dem. Party; chair resolutions com. Nat. Fedn. Dem. Women. Recipient awards ARC, 1968, 73, NAACP, 1973, HEW, 1978, US Commn. on Civil Rights, 1982, cert. of Accomplishement Contributing to Youth Devel. Bus. and Profl. Women, 2000, Extraordinary Cmty. Svc. award Tenn. Coun. Women, 2005, Civic and Bus. Leaders Enterprising award, 2006, Civil Rights Leadership award Tenn. Dem. Party, 2006, Athena award Athena Powerlink, Nashville, 2006, others; named Disting. Alumni Tenn. State U., 1994, Peabody Colls. Gift to the World. Mem. AAUW (honor award 1983, pres. Greensboro br., chairperson internat. rels. com.), ALA (divsn. coll. and rsch. librs., past chair), NAACP (life, 1st v.p. Durham br., exec. bd. Greensboro br. dir. parent edn./child advocacy program, chair exec. com. Nashville, Woman of Yr. 1992, Dedicated Svc. to Civil Rights, 2005, President's award Nashville br. 2006), NEA, LWV (bd. dirs. Nashville), Assn. Childhood Ednl. Internat., Competative and Internat. Edn. Assn., Archives Assoc., Internat. Platform Assn., Nat. Hist. Soc., Greenboro Jr. League (community adv. bd. 1991—), African Am. Gen. Soc. Tenn. (founder 1994), Zeta Phi Beta (chairperson polit. action com. eastern region, nat. grammateus, Polit. and Civic Svc. award 1974, Outstanding Social-Polit. Svc. award 1982, Woman of Yr. 1977), Comm. on Status of Women (Woman of Achievement 1991), Phi Kappa Phi (Disting. Alumni award Tenn. State U. 1994, Disting. Alumni NAFEO award, 1995, Carl Rowan-Oprah Winfrey lectr. Tenn. State U., 1995, Excellence in Journlism award SPJ, 1995, Tenn. Outstanding Achievement award, 1997), 100 Black Women, Steering Com., Tenn. Trust for Historic Preservation, 1999 (named Woman of Distinction Top Ladies, 2001, named Peabody/Vanderbilt Jnin Great, 2005, nominee Athena award 2005). Achievements include being the first African American to graduate from Peabody College (Vanderbilt University) 2006; having a community Service award named in her honor by Vanderbilt University, 2006. Home: PO Box 281613 Nashville TN 37228-8506

MORTVEDT, JOHN JACOB, soil scientist, researcher; b. Dell Rapids, SD, Jan. 25, 1932; s. Ernest R. and Clara (Halvorson) M.; m. Marlene L. Fodness, Jan. 23, 1955; children: Sheryl Mortvedt Jarratt, Lori Mortvedt Klopf, Julie Mortvedt Stride. BS, SD State U., 1953, MS, 1959; PhD, U. Wis., 1962. Soil chemist TVA, Muscle Shoals, Ala., 1962-87, sr. scientist, 1987-92, regional mgr. field programs dept., 1992-93; ext. soils specialist Colo. State U., Ft. Collins, 1994-95, ext. environ. and pesticide edn. specialist, 1996. Agr. cons. U.S. Borax, 1997—. Co-author: Fertilizer Technology and Application, 1999; editor: Micronutrients in Agriculture, 1972, 2d edit., 1991; contbr. articles to profl. jours. 1st lt. U.S. Army, 1953-57. Fellow AAAS, Soil Sci. Soc. Am. (pres. 1988-89, editor-in-chief 1982-87, Profl. Svc. award 1991, Disting. Svc. award 1996), Am. Soc. Agronomy (exec. com. 1987-90, Agronomic Svc. award 2003); mem. Internat. Union Soil Sci., Colombian Soil Sci. Soc. (hon.), Exch. Club (pres. Florence, Ala. chpt. 1987-88), Toastmasters (pres. Florence chpt. 1964-65), Phi Kappa Phi. Avocations: photography, golf. Office: Colo State U Dept Soil And Crop Scis Fort Collins CO 80523-1170

MORVILLO, ROBERT GUY, lawyer; b. NYC, Jan. 22, 1938; s. M. Victor and Marie (Santeramo) M.; m. Catherine A. Shields, Apr. 20, 1963; children: Christopher, Gregory, Edward, Robert. AB, Colgate U., 1960; JD, Columbia U., 1963. Bar: N.Y. 1964, U.S. Dist. Ct. (so. dist.) 1966, U.S. Ct. Appeals (2nd cir.) 1964, U.S. Ct. Appeals (3rd cir.) 1979, U.S. Ct. Appeals (10th cir.) 1983, U.S. Supreme Ct. 1982. Law clk. to Hon. William B. Herlands U.S. Dist. Ct. (so. dist.), NYC, 1963-64, asst. U.S. atty., 1964-68, chief trial counsel fraud unit, 1970-71, chief criminal div., 1971-73; assoc. Reavis & McGrath, NYC, 1968-70; prin. Morvillo, Abramowitz & Grand, P.C. and predecessors, NYC, 1973—. Lectr. Columbia Law Sch., N.Y.C., 1973-85. Columnist, N.Y. Law Jour., N.Y.C., 1982—; editor, White Collar Crime: Business and Regulatory Offenses, 1990. Bd. dirs. South Nassau Cmty. Hosp., 2005—. Fellow Am. Coll. Trial Lawyers; mem. ABA, Assn. of Bar of City of N.Y., N.Y. State Bar Assn., N.Y. Coun. of Def. Lawyers (bd. dirs. 1987—91). Office: Morvillo Abramowitz Grand Iason Anello & Bohrer PC 565 Fifth Ave New York NY 10017 Home Phone: 516-766-3728; Office Phone: 212-880-9400. E-mail: rmorvillo@magislaw.com.

MORWAY, DAVID S., professional sports team executive; b. Bklyn., Nov. 9, 1959; s. Richard S. and Carol Morway; m. Karen E. Chellis, Oct. 10, 1996; children: Robbie, Michael. BS in Bus., U. Ariz., 1982; JD, U. San Diego, 1985. Bar: Calif. 1987. Asst. to pres. San Diego Padres, 1985—88; pres. Profl. Excellence in Sports, Inc., San Diego, 1989—95, DSM Inc., Salt Lake City, 1996—98; sr. v.p. basketball ops. Ind. Pacers, Indpls., 1999—. Mem.: Calif. Bar Assn. Avocations: tennis, golf. Office: Ind Pacers 125 S Pennsylvania St Indianapolis IN 46204-3610 *

MOSALLAEI, HOSSEIN, science educator; s. Keramatollah Mosallaei and Sedigheh Moradi; m. Afsaneh Ghanavati, Apr. 20, 1995; 1 child, Ali. PhD, UCLA, 1997—2001. Postdoctoral rsch. fellow UCLA, 2001—02; asst. rsch. scientist U. of Mich., 2002—05; asst. prof. Northeastern U., Boston, 2005—. Recipient Young Scientist award, URSI, 2001, Raj Mittra Travel grant, AP-S and URSI, 2002; Grad. fellowship, UCLA, 1997—98. Mem.: IEEE, URSI. Achievements include first to advanced meta-materials for RF/wireless and micro-nano-scale front-ends. Home Phone: 617-469-5461.

MOSBACHER, GEORGETTE PAULSIN, cosmetics executive; b. Hammond, Ind., Jan. 16, 1947; d. George Michael and Dorothy (Bell) Paulsin; m. Robert Mosbacher Sr., Mar. 1, 1985. BS, Ind. U., 1969; DFA (hon.), Internat. Fine Arts Coll., 1990; DBA (hon.), Bryant U., 1992. V.p. lic. Faberge, Inc.; CEO La Prairie, Inc., NYC, 1987—95; pres., CEO Borghese, NYC; chair, CEO Georgette Mosbacher Enterprises. Author: Feminine Force, It Takes Money Honey. Bd. dirs. Houston Gran Opera Exec. Com., Am. Hosp. in Paris, Ind. U. Found., Statute of Liberty/Ellis Island Commn., Am. Art Alliance, M.D. Anderson Hosp., United Negro Coll. Fund, Child Help U.S.A., Hudson River Park Trust; mem. adv. bd. Ctr. Strategic Internat. Studies; presdl. appointment Advocate Com. for Trade and Internat. Negotiations; Republican Nat. Committeewomen, State NY. Mem. Women's Econ. Alliance. Avocations: scuba diving, sailing. Office: Borghese 10 E 34th St New York NY 10016

MOSBACHER, ROBERT A., investment company executive; BA, Georgetown U., 1973; JD, So. Methodist U., 1977. Chmn. Tex. Welfare Reform Task Force, 1998; chmn. bd. Tex. Dept. Human Svcs., 1989—91; pres., CEO Mosbacher Energy Co., Houston, 1986—2005, Overseas Pvt. Investment Corp. (OPIC), 2005—. Immedicate past-chmn. Greater Houston Partnership, chmn. health care advisory com., mem. edn. and workforce advisory com.; founder, co-chmn. Rebuidling Together Houston; bd. dirs. South Tex. Coll. Law, Soc. Performing Arts. Office: Overseas Pvt Investment Corp 1100 NY Ave NW Washington DC 20527 Office Phone: 202-336-8400. Office Fax: 202-408-9859.

MOSBY, NORA JANE, music educator; b. El Paso, Tex., June 9, 1970; d. Knox Wesley and Bettie Mae Mosby. BS, U. Tex., Tyler, 1995, MA, 1997; MEd, No. Ariz. U., Flagstaff, 2005. Chair dept. fine arts Higley HS, Gilbert, Ariz., 2000—05; band dir. Florence Unified Sch. Dist., Ariz., 2005—07, Manor Intermediate Sch. Dist., 2007—. Recipient Reacher of Month, Higley Unified Sch. Dist., 2005. Mem.: Ariz. Music Educator's Assn., Soc. for Ethnomusicology, Internat. Clarinet Assn., Ariz. Band and Orch. Dirs. Assn., Phi Kappa Phi. Home: 2110 E Spruce Dr Chandler AZ 85249 Office: Florence Unified Sch Dist 250 S Main St Florence AZ 85232 Personal E-mail: muzik77@cox.net.

MOSCATO, JOSEPH LOUIS, JR., health facility administrator, military officer; b. Erie, Pa., Feb. 25, 1948; s. Joseph Louis and Anna Mae Moscato; m. Kimberly Lynn Williams, July 5, 1991; children: Jack McKinney, Joseph III, Rachel, Kelly. BA, BS in Biology, Oglethorpe U., 1971; BBA, Kennesaw State U., 1982; MBA, Brenau U., 1984; Masters in Healthcare Adminstrn., Mercer U., 1996. Commd. 2d lt. USAF, 1972—, advanced through grades to maj., 2002; v.p. bus. devel. Am. Outpatient, Ft. Lauderdale, Fla., 1996; v.p. sales and mktg. Med Lab Specialist, Atlanta, 1998; ea. mgr. Gambro Lab, Ft. Lauderdale, 2003—04; ea. regional mgr. DVA Lab. Inc., Ft. Lauderdale, 2004—. Mem. adv. bd. Atlanta Dialysis Ctr. Mem.: Am. Acad. Med. Adminstrs., Med. Svc. Choir, Res. Officers Assn. (jr. v.p. USAF 2001, pres.). Republican. Roman Catholic. Avocations: golf, tennis, basketball, theater, hiking. Home: 1321 Indian Rocks Rd Largo FL 33770 Office Phone: 770-713-9414. Personal E-mail: jlmoscato@aol.com.

MOSCHELLA, SAMUEL L., dermatology educator; b. East Boston, Mass., Apr. 22, 1921; BS, Tufts U., 1943, MD cum laude, 1946. Diplomate Am. Bd. Dermatology. Intern in medicine Boston City Hosp., 1946-47; resident in dermatology U.S. Naval Hosp., Phila., 1948, St. Albans, 1951; postgrad. in skin and cancer Bellevue Hosp., NYC, 1952-53; chief dermatology U.S. Naval Hosp., Phila., 1953-54, chief dermatology, asst. chief medicine, Guantanamo Bay, Cuba, 1948-51, chief dermatology, Chelsea, Mass., 1956-62, chmn. dept. dermatology, Phila., 1962-67; chmn. dept. dermatology Lahey Clinic Med. Ctr., Burlington, Mass., 1969-82; clin. prof. dermatology Harvard U. Med. Sch., Boston, 1980-91, prof. emeritus, 1991—. Cons. U.S. Naval Hosp., Phila., 1967-72, U. Pa. Grad. Sch., 1962-67, Harvard Sch. Tropical Medicine, 1975-2002, Nat. Hansen's Disease Ctr., Baton Rouge, 2002—. Author/editor: (with otherw) Dermatology, 3d edit., 1992; contbr. articles to profl. jours.; also papers, book chpts. Fellow ACP; mem. Am. Acad. Dermatology, Am. Dermatol. Assn., Am. Soc. Dermapathology, Internat. Soc. Dermatology, New Eng. Dermatologic Soc., Soc. Investigative Dermatology. Home: 887 Commonwealth Ave Newton MA 02459-1036 Office: Lahey Clinic Med Ctr 41 Mall Rd Burlington MA 01805-0002 E-mail: samuel.l.moschella@lahey.org.

MOSCHELLA, WILLIAM EMIL, federal agency administrator; b. 1968; BA, U. Va.; JD, George Mason Univ. Sch. of Law. Gen. coun. House Commn. on Rules, 1999, chief investment coun., 1999—2001; chief legis. counsel, parliamentarian House Com. on the Judiciary, 2001—03; asst. atty. gen. Office Legis. Affairs US Dept. of Justice, Washington, DC, 2003—06, prin. assoc. dep. atty. gen., 2006—. Office: US Dept Justice 950 Pennsylvania Ave NW Washington DC 20530 Office Phone: 202-514-2141. *

MOSCHOS, DEMITRIOS MINA, lawyer; s. Constantine Mina and Vasiliky (Strates) Moschos; m. Celeste Thomaris, Sept. 28, 1975; children: Kristin M, Thomas W. BA magna cum laude, U. Mass., 1962; JD magna cum laude, Boston U., 1965; grad., U.S. Army JAG Sch., 1966. Bar: Mass 1965, US Dist Ct Mass 1975, US Ct Mil Appeals 1966. Exec. asst. to city mgr., spl. legal counsel City of Worcester, 1968-75, asst. city mgr., spl. legal counsel, 1975-80; assoc. Mirick, O'Connell, Worcester, 1980-81, ptnr., 1982—. Lectr labor relations Worcester State Col, 1975—88, Clark Univ, 1978—; chmn Worcester Housing Comt, 1968—78, Worcester Energy Comt, 1978—80; mem Mass Joint Labor Mgt Comt, 1978—80. Drafter admin codes:; contbr. articles to profl jours. Clk. Worcester Regional Rsch. Bur., bd. dirs., Worcester Regional C. of C., vice chmn.; past pres. archiocesan coun. Greek Orthodox Archdiocese Am. Capt JAGC US Army, 1966—68. Decorated Army Commendation medal; named Outstanding Young Man of Worcester County, Worcester County Jaycees, 1969; recipient Alumni Acad Achievement award, Boston Univ Law Sch, 1965, Resolution of Commendation award, Worcester City Coun., 1980. Fellow: Coll. Labor and Employment Lawyers; mem.: ABA, Worcester County Bar Assn. (former chmn labor sect), Mass. Bar Assn. (Comty Serv Award 1987), Tatnuck Country Club. Office: Mirick O'Connell 100 Front St Ste 1700 Worcester MA 01608-1426 Office Phone: 508-791-8500. Business E-Mail: dmmoschos@modl.com.

MOSCOWITZ, TODD, music company executive; b. 1970; Various positions Rush Comm., 1991—2000, pres. Def Jam Music Publishing, Def Jam Interactive Gaming; ptnr. Violator Mgmt., 2000—04; pres. Asylum Records Warner Music Group, 2004—, pres. Independent Label Group, 2006—. Office: Warner Music Group Corp 75 Rockefeller Plz New York NY 10019 Office Phone: 212-275-2000. Office Fax: 212-757-3985.

MOSELEY, CHRIS ROSSER, marketing executive; b. Balt., Apr. 13, 1950; d. Thomas Earl and Fern Elaine (Coleman) Rosser; m. Thomas Kenneth Moseley. BA with honors, The Coll. of Wooster, 1972. Asst. dir. advt. and promotion Sta. WBAL-TV, Balt., 1972-74; dir. pub. rels. Mintz & Hoke Advt. Inc., Hartford, Conn., 1974-75; promotion mgr. Sta. WFSB-TV, Hartford, 1975-77; audience promotion mgr. Sta. WTVJ-TV, Miami, Fla., 1977-78; pres. CMA Mktg. Cons., Hyde Park, NY, 1979-82; promotion mgr. Ind. Network News-Sta. WPIX-TV, NYC, 1982-84; sr. v.p., mgmt. supr. Christopher Thomas Muller Jordan Weiss, NYC, 1984-89, Earle Palmer Brown/N.Y., NYC, 1989-90; sr. v.p. advt., promotion Discovery Networks, U.S., Bethesda, Md., 1990-99; exec. v.p. mktg. ABC, Inc., NYC, 1999—2000; exec. v.p., chief mktg. officer Hallmark Channel, Studio City, Calif., 2000—. Bd. dirs. Promax/BDA, Cable Positive, WICT, CTAM. Recipient Best Bus.-to-Bus. award Art Direction mag., 1984, achievement award in media rels. and edn. Nat. Resources Coun. Am., 1991, Best Editorial Excellence award Mag. Age, 1992, Best Overall Mktg. Campaign award MIP/MIPCOM, 1994, 1st Place Print award: Media Promotion, London Internat. Advt. awards, 1993, Gold award Broadcast Designers, 1993, Mktg. 100 award Ad Age, 1995, Cable Marketer of Yr. award Ad Age, 1995. Mem.: Advt. Women N.Y., Nat. Cable TV Assn. (conv. com. 1995, 1996, named one of Multichannel News' Wonderwomen of Yr. 2002, Vanguard award 1996), Cable and Telecom. Assn. Mktg. (chair Mark award 1995, bd. dir. 1996, co-chair 1997, bd. dir. 1997). Avocations: horticulture, travel. Home: 5224 Los Encantos Way Los Angeles CA 90027 Office: Hallmark Channel 12700 Ventura Blvd Ste 100 Studio City CA 91604-6201 Office Phone: 818-755-2587. E-mail: chrismoseley@hallmarkchannel.com.

MOSELEY, JAMES FRANCIS, lawyer; b. Charleston, SC, Dec. 6, 1936; s. John Olin and Kathryn (Moran) M.; m. Anne McGehee, June 10, 1961; children: James Francis Jr., John McGehee. AB, The Citadel, 1958; JD, U. Fla., 1961. Bar: Fla. 1961, U.S. Supreme Ct. 1970. Pres. Moseley, Prichard, Parrish, Knight & Jones, Jacksonville, Fla., 1963—. Chmn. jud. nominating com. 4th Jud. Cir., 1978-80 Assoc. editor: American Maritime Cases; contbr. articles on admiralty, transp. and ins. law to legal jours. Pres. Jacksonville United Way, 1979; chmn. bd. dirs. United Way Fla., 1992-93, S.E. regional coun. United Way, 1992-96; trustee Jacksonville Cmty. Found.; chmn. bd. trustees Jacksonville Pub. Libr.; trustee Libr. Found., sec., 1987-91; trustee CMI Am. Found.; chmn. Jacksonville Human Svcs. Coun., 1989-91; chmn. bd. trustees United Way N.E. Fla., 1995-97; bd. govs. United Way Am., 1996-2002. Recipient Meritorious Pub. Svc. award/medal U.S. Dept. Transp./USCG, 1998. Fellow Am. Coll. Trial Lawyers, Am. Bar Found.; mem. ABA (ho. of del. 2002—), Jacksonville Bar Assn. (pres. 1975), Fla. Coun. Bar Pres. (chmn. 1979), Maritime Law Assn. U.S. (exec. com. 1978-81, chmn. navigation com. 1981-88, v.p. 1992-96, pres. 1996-98), Comm. Maritime Internat. (titulary), Com. on Collision (Lisbon Rules), Fed. Ins. Corp. Counsel (chmn. maritime law sect.), Internat. Assn. Def. Counsel (chmn. maritime com. 1989-91), Am. Inns of Ct. (master of bench), Assn. of Citadel Men (bd. dir. 1989-93, exec. com. 1994, Man of Yr. award 1992, S.C. Palmetto medal and award 2001, Citadel Inn of Ct. sr. bencher), Deerwood Club, River Club, India House (N.Y.C.), Army Navy Club (Washington), St. John's Dinner Club (pres. 1988). Office: Moseley Prichard Parrish Knight & Jones 1887 West Rd Bay St Jacksonville FL 32202 Office Phone: 904-356-1306. Office Fax: 904-354-0194. Business E-Mail: jfmoseley@mppjk.com.

MOSELEY, JAMES R., former federal agency administrator, farmer; b. Peru, Ind., June 2, 1948; s. Donald and Violet (Love) Moseley; m. Kathryn Lynn Maple, 1969; children: Jeff, Jennifer, Bethany, Amanda, Neil, Brandon, Kyle. BS in horticulture, Purdue U., 1980. Owner Ag Ridge Farms, Clarks Hill, Ind.; mng. ptnr. Infinity Pork LLC, Clarks Hill; asst. sec. agr. natural resources and environ. USDA, 1990—92; dir. agrl. svcs. and regulations. State of Ind., Purdue U., West Lafayette, 1992—95; dep. sec. USDA, Washington, 2001—05. Agrl. advisor to adminstr. U.S. Environ. Protection Agy., 1989—90; chmn. industry negotiating team Am. Clean Water Found. Nat. Environ. Dialogue on Pork Prodn., 1997; cons. Nat. Assn. State Depts. Agr., 1995. Past. mem. editl. bd. Farm Jour. Pub., past polit. analyst.

MOSELEY, JOHN TRAVIS, academic administrator, physicist, researcher; b. New Orleans, Feb. 26, 1942; s. Fred Baker and Lily Gay (Lord) M.; m. Belva McCall Hudson, Aug. 11 1964 (div. June 1979); m. Susan Diane Callow, Aug. 6, 1979; children: Melanie Lord, John Mark, Stephanie Marie, Shannon Eleanor. BS in Physics, Ga. Inst. Tech., 1964, MS in Physics, 1966, PhD in Physics, 1969. Asst. prof. physics U. West Fla., Pensacola, 1968-69; sr. physicist SRI Internat., Menlo Park, Calif., 1969-75, program mgr., 1976-79; vis. prof. U. Paris, 1975-76; assoc. prof. U. Oreg., Eugene, 1979-81, dir. chem. physics inst., 1980-84, prof. physics, 1984—, head physics dept., 1984-85, v.p. rsch., 1985-94, v.p. acad. affairs, provost, 1994-2001, sr. v.p., provost, 2001—06, spl. asst. to pres. and provost, 2006—. Mem. exec. com., coun. on acad. affairs NASULGC, 1994-2000, chair, 1996-97; bd. dirs. Oreg. Resource and Tech., Portland; mem. com. on Atomic and Molecular Sci., 1983-85. Contbr. numerous articles to profl. jours. Mem. So. Willamette Rsch. Corridor, Eugene, 1985-00, Lane Econ. Devel. Com., Eugene, 1988-94; bd. dirs. Eugene/Springfield Metro Partnership, 1985-01, Oreg. Bach Festival, Eugene, 1987-94, Eugene Arts Found., 1995-97. Recipient Doctoral Thesis award Sigma Xi, 1969; Fulbright fellow, 1975; numerous rsch. grants, 1969—. Fellow AAAS, Am. Physical Soc.; mem. AAUP, Am. Chem. Soc. Avocations: skiing, backpacking. Home: 2140 Essex Ln Eugene OR 97403-1851 Office: U Oreg Office of Sr VP and Provost Eugene OR 97403-1258 Business E-Mail: jtm@uoregon.edu.

MOSELEY, MARC ROBARDS, sales executive; b. LA, July 14, 1954; s. Thomas Robards and Doris Cecile (Tye) M.; m. Laura Hoon Hamilton, 1999. Student, U. Ky., Lexington, 1972-74, U. Ga., Athens, 1977-78; BA,

La. Tech. U., Ruston, 1985; postgrad., Western Mich. U., Kalamazoo, 1986. Svc. rep. Ky. Mortgage Co., Lexington, 1973; loan rep. Termplan Fin. Co., Atlanta, 1975-77; sr. cons. Co-Ordinated Planning Assocs., Atlanta, 1979-80; sales rep. Nat. Starch & Chem. Corp., Monroe, La., 1980-84; v.p. sales Ednl. Funding Svc., Monroe, 1984-85; tech. sales rep. polymer divsn. Ralston Purina, St. Louis, 1985-87; account mgr. Protein Techs. Internat. Polymer Group subs. Ralston Purina, St. Louis, 1988-90, sr. account mgr., 1990-92, area dir. market ops., 1992-96; dir. industry mgmt. and bus. devel. Polymer Group subs. Dupont Ag Enterprise, 1996-98; dir. strategic accounts Polymer Group Dupont Soy Polymers, 1999—2002; reg. sales mgr. Phila. Mixing Solutions, Palmyra, Pa., 2004—06; mgr. N.Am. Pulp and Paper Divsn., 2006—. V.p. sales and mktg. RANA Enterprises, Inc., Atlanta, 1991-98; dir. Radiant Chem., Atlanta, 1992-2001; v.p., dir. Bishop Pharm. Co., Inc., West Monroe, La., 1994-96. Mem. TAPPI, U. Ky. Alumni Assn. (bd. dirs. 1991-97, exec. v.p. Ga. sect. 1992-94). Avocations: water and snow skiing, basketball, music, golf. Home: 12220 Brookfield Club Dr Roswell GA 30075-1265 Personal E-mail: mrmosley@mindspring.com.

MOSELEY, PATRICIA ANN, lawyer; d. Percy and Virginia Elizabeth (Gregg) M.; m. Norman L. Williamson, Oct. 15, 1981; children: Norma Williamson Nash, W. Scott Williamson. BS in Secondary Edn., Tex. A&I, 1968; MA, U. Tex., 1972; JD, Tex. Tech U., 1978. Bar: Tex. 1978, U.S. Dist. Ct. (no. dist.) Tex. 1979, U.S. Ct. Appeals (5th cir.) 1981. Tchr. Galena Park Ind. Sch. Dist., Houston, 1968-70; teaching asst. journalism dept. U. Tex., Austin, 1970-71; tchr. Corsicana (Tex.) Ind. Sch. Dist., 1972-75; atty. West Tex. Legal Svcs., Lubbock, 1978-83; pvt. practice Lubbock, 1983-92. Apptd. 1V-D assoc. judge 9th Region Tex., 1989. Mem. Tex. Bar Assn. (family law sect. 1989—), Lubbock County Bar Assn. (family law sect.), Lubbock Criminal Def. Lawyers Assn., Lubbock Women Lawyers Assn., Lubbock LWV (bd. dirs. 1981-84, v.p. 1986-87, bd. 1988), WIN Club (Lubbock). Home: PO Box 466 Lubbock TX 79408-0466 Office: 904 Broadway Ste 116 Lubbock TX 79401-3421 Business E-Mail: pmoseley@co.lubbock.tx.us.

MOSELEY, T. MICHAEL (TEED MICHAEL MOSELEY), military officer; BA in Polit. Sci., Tex. A&M U., 1971, MA in Polit. Sci., 1972; grad., Squadron Officer Sch., Maxwell AFB, Ala., 1977, U.S. Navy Fighter Weapons Sch., 1979, Fighters Weapons Instr. Course, 1981, Air Command, Staff Coll, 1984, USAF Jt. Sr. Battle comdr. Cos, Hurlbut Field, Fla., 1988, Nat. War Coll., Ft. Lesley J. McNair, 1990; grad, Combined Forces Air Component Comdr. Course, Maxwell AFB, Ala. & Hurlbert Field, Fla., 2000. Commd. 2d. lt. USAF, 1971, advanced through grades to gen., 2003—; undergrad. pilot tng. Webb AFB, Tex., 1972-73; T-37 instr. pilot, spin flight test pilot, flight test pilot, standardization and evaluation flight examiner 3389th Flying Tng. Squadron, 78th Flying Tng. Wing, Webb AFB, Tex., 1973-77; F-15 instr. pilot, flight lead mission comdr. 7th Tactical Fighter Squadron, Holloman AFB, N.M., 1977-79; F-15 weapons tactics officer, instr. pilot, flight lead and mission comdr., standardization and evaluation and flight examiner 44th Tactical Fighter Squadron, 12th Tactical Fighter Squadron, Kadena Air Base, Japan, 1979-83; course officer Air Command & Staff Coll., Maxwell AFB, Ala., 1983—84; chief, Tactical Fighter Branch, Tactical Forces Divsn., Directorate of Plans, Dep. Chief of Staff for Plans & Ops. USAF, Washington, 1984—87; comdr. F-15 divsn. & instr. pilot, fighter weapons instr. course USAF Fighter Weapons Sch., Nellis AFB, Nev., 1987—89; course officer Nat. War Coll., Washington, 1989-90, chief staff, 1990-92; comdr. 33rd Ops. Group, Englin AFB, Fla., 1992-94; chief Hdqs. USAF, Washington, 1994-96; comdr. 57th Wing, Nellis AFB, Nev., 1996-97; dep. dir. polit.-mil. affairs Joint Chiefs Staff, Washington, 1997-99; dir. legis. liaison, Office Sec. Air Force USAF, Washington, 1999—2001; comdr. 9th Air Force & US Ctrl. Command Air Force, Shaw AFB, SC, 2001—03; vice chief of staff USAF, Washington, 2003—05, chief of staff, 2005—. Decorated Def. Disting. Svc. Medal, DSM, Def. Superior Svc. medal with oak leaf cluster, Legion of Merit award with oak leaf cluster, Meritorious Svc. medal with three oak leaf clusters, Air medal, Joint Svc. Commendation medal, Air Force Commendation medal, Air Force Achievement medal, Global War on Terrorism Expeditionary medal, French Nat. Order of Merit, United Arab Emirates Military medal, 1st Class; recipient H.H. Arnold award, Air Force Assn., 2003. Office: USAF 1670 Air Force Pentagon Washington DC 20330

MOSEMANN, LLOYD KENNETH, II, retired research and development company executive; b. Lancaster, Pa., May 16, 1936; s. Lloyd Kreider and Beatrice Elizabeth (Frey) M.; m. Arlene K. White, Sept. 6, 1957; children— Gigi Renee Mosemann Falke, Lloyd Kenneth III, Douglas Lamar, Holly Joy AB in Social Sci., U. Chgo., 1957, AM in Internat. Rels., 1959. Gen. supply officer Navy Electronics Supply Office, Great Lakes, Ill., 1958-62; inventory mgmt. specialist Def. Electronics Supply Ctr., Dayton, Ohio, 1962-63; head integrated-retail supply and support br. Naval Supply Systems Command, Washington, 1963-69; dep. chief logistics support analysis office Def. Logistics Agy., Alexandria, Va., 1969-71; dep. for supply and maintenance Office Sec. of Air Force, Washington, 1971-74; dep. asst. sec. for logistics and communications Dept. Air Force, Washington, 1974-91, dep. asst. sec. for comm., computers and logistics, 1991-93, dep. asst. sec. for comm., computers and support systems, 1993-96; software and acquisition cons., 1996-97; sr. v.p. corp. devel. Sci. Applications Internat. Corp., McLean, Va., 1997—2007; ret., 2007. Mem. Air Force Exec. Resources Bd., 1981—95. Author: AntiChirst in the Midst, 2006. Decorated DSM; recipient Meritorious Svc. medal Sec. Air Force, 1977, Exceptional Civilian Svc. medal sec. Air Force, 1979, 81, 82, 87, 96, Meritorious Sr. Exec. award Pres. of US, 1982, 87, Def. Meritorious Civilian Svc. medal, 1985. Mem. Soc. Logistics Engrs. (bd. advisers 1983—, Founders medal 1983, H. Mark Grove award for excellence in software mgmt. 1996, Govt. Computer News Hall of Fame 1996, Fed. Computer Week "100" award 1996), Am. Def. Preparedness Assn. (bd. dirs. 1974-83), Nat. Inst. for Urban Search and Rescue (exec. bd. dirs. 1990-2005).

MOSENA, DAVID R., museum administrator; M in City Planning, U. Tenn. Dir. rsch. Am. Planning Assn., Chgo.; mem. staff City of Chgo., 1984-89, planning commr., 1989-91, chief of staff, 1991-92, aviation commr., 1992-96; pres. CTA, 1996—97; pres., CEO Museum of Science and Industry, Chicago, 1997—. Chmn. bd. dirs. U. Chgo. Lab. Schs. Office: Museum of Science and Industry 5700 S Lake Shore Dr Chicago IL 60637

MOSENSON, STEVEN HARRIS, lawyer; b. Phila., Dec. 3, 1956; BS, NYU, 1978, M of Pub. Adminstrn., 1979; JD, Yeshiva U., 1982. Bar: N.Y. 1983, U.S. Ct. Appeals (2d cir.) 1983, U.S. Dist. Ct. (so., ea., no. and we. dists.) N.Y. 1983, U.S. Ct. Internat. Trade 1985, U.S. Supreme Ct. 1986. Assoc. Baden Kramer Huffman & Brodsky, NYC, 1982-85; asst. corp. counsel N.Y.C. Law Dept., 1985-89; gen. counsel United Cerebral Palsy Assns. of N.Y. State, Inc., NYC, 1989—. Adj. instr. NYU, 1998—. Pres. bd. dirs. Bklyn. Heights Ctr. for Counseling, Inc., 1992-2000; bd. dirs. Walden, N.Y. Local Devel. Corp., 1998-2000; mem. Walden Cmty. Coun., 1998—. Mem. N.Y. State Bar Assn. (former chmn. com. on issues affecting people 1997—, vice chair treas. corp. counsel sect.), Guardianship Assn. of N.Y. State, Inc. (v.p. 1995-2004). Office: United Cerebral Palsy Assns of NY 330 W 34th St 15th Fl New York NY 10001-2488 Office Phone: 212-356-1224. Office Fax: 212-356-0746. Business E-Mail: steven.mosenson@nyu.edu.

MOSER, BARRY, artist; b. Chattanooga, Oct. 15, 1940; Student, Auburn U., U. Tenn., Chattanooga; postgrad., U. Mass. Owner, pub. Pennyroyal Press, 1970—; faculty RI Sch. Design, 1991—98; prof. in residence, printer to the coll. Smith Coll., 2001—. Illustrator: The Divine Comedy, 1980, Alice in Wonderland, 1983 (Nat. Book award for Design and illustration), Scarlet Letter, 1984, A River Runs Through It, 1989, Appalachia, the Voices of Sleeping Birds, 1991 (Boston Globe-Horn Book award), And Still the Turtle Watched, 1991, Tales of Edgar Allan Poe, 1991, Ariadne, Awake!, 1994, Call of the Wild, 1994, Cloud Eyes, 1994, Farm Summer 1942, 1994, Pilgrim's Progress, 1994, What You Know First, 1995, When Birds Could Talk and Bats Could Sing, 1996, Pennyroyal-Caxton Bible, 1999, Earthquack!, 2002, Voices of Egypt, 2003; represented in permanent collections: Met. Mus., British Mus., Harvard U., Princeton U., Libr. of Congress, Victoria & Albert, Vatican Libr. Mem.: NAD (academician 1994—). Business E-Mail: sales@moser-pennyroyal.com.

MOSER, GLENDA FAYE, media specialist; b. Fairview, Okla., May 27, 1944; d. Leon Lyle Hunt and Faye Gladys Hunt (Gooch); m. James Calvin Moser; children: Bruce Wayne Brinson, Bret Orin Brinson, James Lee Huckaby, Darla Durree Brinson, Dianna Leigh Fisher. B in Edn., Brinson U., 1978; M in Libr. Edn. (hon.), SW Okla. State U., 1982. 3rd gr. tchr., libr. Verden (Okla.) Pub. Sch., 1990—91; humanities 8th gr. tchr., k-12 libr. media specialist Davenport (Okla.) Pub. Sch., 1992—98; libr. media specialist Tecumseh (Okla.) Mid. Sch., 1998—. Author (illustrator): (children's book) Mancestor (Writer's award at NWOSU, 1980). Writer marionette play Lincoln County Children's Mus., Chandler, Okla., 1994—2006. Recipient Overall Best Show for History Day, S.W. Okla. State U., 1982—84. Mem.: NEA, ALA (assoc. Pres. 1985). Independent. Achievements include research in teach the 8 parts of speech for middle School, I called it NAPVAPIC' IT'S MAGIC!. Avocations: cake decorating, sewing, farm animals, reading, writing. Home: RR #1 Box 27 Sparks OK 74869 Office: Tecumseh Mid Sch 315 W Park St Tecumseh OK 74873 Home Phone: 918-866-2439; Office Phone: 405-598-2067. Office Fax: 405-598-1948. Personal E-mail: jgmosaic@yahoo.com. Business E-Mail: moserg@tecumseh.k12.ok.us.

MOSER, JEFFERY RICHARD, real estate manager; b. Miller, SD, Feb. 8, 1961; s. Richard and Ardessa Joan (Yost) M. Student, U. Minn., 1979—84, Duke U., 1995, Northwestern U., 1997, U. Denver, 2005—. Cert. lay minister; cert. in pub. policy and pub. fin.; cert. CPR, Am. Red Cross. Lab asst., intern U. Minn. Dept. Limnology, Mpls., 1980-81; exec. intern pub. affairs dept. Target Corp., Mpls., 1982, Nat. Farmers Union, Nat. Youth Adv. Coun., Denver, 1980-81; intern/asst. for legis. and policy Minn. Agri-Growth Coun., Bloomington, 1984-85; field office asst. US Congressman Thomas A. Daschle, Aberdeen, SD, 1986; pvt. cons. to non-profit orgns. Huron, SD, 1986—89; notary pub. State of SD, 1986-99; acting camp dir. SD Farmers Union Edn. Program, 1987-88; small bus. owner Wessington, SD, 1986—2002; exec. dir. SD Assn. Towns and Twps., 1990-95; dep. state treas. to treas. Richard D. Butler State of SD, Pierre, 1995-99; dir. econ. and coop. devel. Nat. Farmer's Union, Greenwood Village, Colo., 1999—. Participant 4-H/UN/USAID Presdl. young adult exch. program to Kenya and Botswana, Africa, summer 1985. Vol. U. Minn. Hosps., 1979-83, U. Minn. Dept. Minn. Unions, Mpls., 1983-84; gen. election poll watcher Hand County Rural precincts, 1988; past mem. Beadle County Dems., Hand County Dems., Brown County Dems., Hughes County Dems., v.p., 1997-98, Arapahoe County Dems., 1999—; del. State Dem. Conv., 1990, 92, 94; alt. del. Nat. Dem. Conv., Chgo., 1996, Clinton for Pres., 1992; nom. Dem. candidate State Auditor, 1994, US House, 1998; donor SD Dems., Dem. Nat. Com.; Dem. Nat. Senate Task Force; Dem. Congl. Campaign Com.; chair, del. Selection/Affirmative Action Com., 1996; Clinton-Gore, mem. State Adv. Com., 1996; at. del. Dem. Nat. Conv., 1996; mem. Hughes County Steering Com. to Re-Elect Senator Tom Daschle, 1997-98; dem. candidate SD at-large dist. US Ho. of Rep., 1998; vol. leader, advisor, and state fair judge SD 4-H Program, 1981-94; bd. dirs. SD Rural Devel. Coun., 1993-95, SD State Adv. Com. for Green Thumb, Inc., 1993-95; mem. task force Nat. Urban Comparative Risk Environ., 1994, Common Cause SD, 1991-94; dist. edn. dir. SD Farmers Union, 1988-93; dir. Minn. Union Coordinating Bd., U. Minn., 1982-84; bd. dirs. Golden Razor Hair Salon, Inc., Mpls., 1983-84, bd. dirs. Internat. Study & Travel Assn., Mpls., 1982-83; mem. Rose Hill Presbyn. Ch., Clan Campbell Soc. (N.Am.), E. River Sierra Club, Rocky Mountains/Hi Plains Group Sierra Club, SD AG Heritage Mus., SD Com. for World Food Day, SD Bread for the World, Dakota Rural Action, SD Project Prosperity Coalition, SD Farmers Union, SD Horticulture Soc., Dakota Rural Action, South Dakotans For the Arts, Wilson Ctr., Am. Mus. Nat. Hist., Smithsonian Assocs., Lib. Congress, Oscar Howe Art Ctr., Siouxland chpt. Alzheimer's Assn., SD Health Care Reform Coalition, S.D. Artists Network, SD Hist. Soc., Colo. Pub. Radio/TV (donor), Nat. Farmers Union Found. (donor), Cmty. Shares of Colo. (donor), 9th Jud. Circuit Ct. Soc., Nat. Resource Defense Coun., Nat. Audubon Soc., Internat. 4-H Programs; host family Botswana Agr. Exch. Program, 1992; Presbytery of S.D., sec. Congl. Devel. Ministry, 1988-91, Advocacy Devel. Ministry unit, 1992-93, ch. camp dean, moderator Soc. Witness and Action Com., 1995-99, mem. com. representation, 1995-99, mem. com. Self-Devel. People, 1995-99; exec. Presbytery Search com., 1995-96, active Am. Heart Assn. Pierre Area Heart Walk, 1995, 97; vol. coord. Bread for the World Hunger Awareness event, Huron, 1993; mem. planning com. 1993 Regional 4-H Leaders Forum, Sioux Falls; past del. rep. SD Nat. 4-H Congress, 1981; past del. rep. Nat. Farmers Union Nat. conf., Presbyn. Ch. USA Gen. Assembly, 1990, Presbyn. Ch. USA Consultation on Sustainable Devel., 1995, Nat. 4-H Coun. Master Communicators Conf., Albuquerque, Presbyn. Ch. USA Synod Lakes and Prairies Workshop on Representation and Nominations, Rochester, Minn., 1997, Common Cause Nat. Leadership conf., Washington, 1993, Sharing Global Harvests Nat. Tng., Nat. Assn. Towns and Twps. Am.'s Town Meeting, Washington, 1992, strategic leadership for state execs. course Duke U., 1995, Inst. Pub. Fin. Northwestern U., 1997; bd. co-chair Huron Postal Customer Adv. Bd., 1993-95; bd. dirs. SD Peace and Justice Ctr., sec.-treas., 1994, v.p., 1995, dir. 1994-97; copywriter Minn. Ag. Manual, 1985; active Farmers Union Fed. Credit Union, bd. dirs, 2007-; vol. comty. data reporter US Census Bur., 2000-2002; participant Future Coop Leaders program N.C.B.A., Washington, 2002; mem. Nat. Grants Rev. panel USDA, CSREES, 2001-03, 05; vol. Population, Employment and Labor Survey Reporting, US Census Bur., 2001-02; mem. Nat. Trust for Hist. Preservation; sec. Mich. Farmers Union Found., 1999—; mem. Colo. Criminal Justice Reform Coalition, Bread for the World, Cmty. Alliance with Family Farmers 2003—. Mem. Nat. Audubon Soc., Assn. of Coop. Educators, Nat. Farmers Union, Phi Beta Kappa, Omicron Delta Kappa, Mortar Bd., Golden Key, Sierra Club. Democrat. Avocations: piano, painting, poetry, writing. E-mail: jeff.moser@nfu.org.

MOSER, KENNETH ALLEN, lawyer; b. Rowan County, NC, Sept. 8, 1942; BA, Wake Forest U., 1965, JD cum laude, 1968. Bar: NC 1968. Mng. mem. Winston-Salem office Womble Carlyle Sandridge & Rice PLLC. Mem. faculty Grad. Sch. Banking of South, Baton Rouge, La., 1987-89; pres. Wake Forest U. Law Alumni Coun., 1998, mem. bd. vis. Wake Forest U. Sch. Law. Assoc. editor: Wake Forest Law Rev., 1967-68. Mem.: ABA (chair loan practices and lender liability com. 1988—93, mem. books and media com. 1995—99, real estate, probate and trust law sect.), Am. Counsel Assn., Forsyth County Bar Assn., NC Bar Assn., Am. Coll. Mortgage Attorneys, Am. Coll. Real Estate Lawyers. Office: Womble Carlyle Sandridge & Rice PLLC One West Fourth St Winston Salem NC 27101 Home Phone: 336-761-0127; Office Phone: 336-721-3504. Business E-Mail: kmoser@wcsr.com.

MOSER, M(ARTIN) PETER, lawyer; b. Balt., Jan. 16, 1928; s. Herman and Henrietta (Lehmayer) M.; m. Elizabeth Kohn, June 14, 1949; children— Mike, Moriah, Jeremy AB, The Citadel, Charleston, SC, 1947; LLB, Harvard U., 1950. Bar: Md. 1950, U.S. Supreme Ct., U.S. Ct. Appeals (4th cir.). Asst. states atty. City of Balt., 1951, 53-54; assoc. Blades Rosenfeld, Balt., 1950, 53-54; ptnr. Frank, Bernstein, Conaway & Goldman and predecessor firms, Balt., 1955-90, co-chmn. firm, 1983-86; counsel, 1991-92; of counsel DLA Piper US LLP, 1992—. Instr. U. Balt. Law Sch., 1954-56, 86, U. Md. Law Sch., 1986-87. Contbr. articles to profl. jours. Del., chmn. local govt. com. Md. Constl. Conv., 1967-68; mem. Balt. City Planning Commn., 1961-66, Balt. Regional Planning Council, 1963-66, Md. Commn. to Study Narcotics Laws, 1965-67, Mayor's Task Force on EEO, 1966-67, Met. Transit Authority Adv. Council, 1962, Com. to Revise Balt. City Planning Laws, 1962, Com. to Revise Balt. City Charter Provision on Conflicts of Interest, 1969-70; mem. Citizens Adv. Com. on Dist. Ct., chmn., 1971, Dist. Adv. Bd. for Pub. Defender System for Dist. 1, 1973-85; mem. Atty. Grievance Commn. of Md., 1975-78, chmn. 82-86; chmn. Md. State Ethics Commn., 1987-89; bd. dirs. Sinai Hosp., 1983-2004, Lifebridge Health Sys., 1998—, Ct. of Appeals Comm. to Study the Model Rules, 1983-86, 2002-05. With JAGC, U.S. Army, 1951-53. Fellow: Balt. Bar Found., Md. Bar Found., Am. Bar Found. (pres. 2002—04); mem.: ABA (ho. of dels. 1978—2002, bd. govs. 1984—87, 1992—96, treas. 1993—96), Balt. Bar Assn. (pres. 1970—71), Md. State Bar Assn. (pres. 1979—80), Wednesday Law Club, Lawyers' Roundtable. Democrat. Jewish. Office: DLA Piper 6225 Smith Ave Baltimore MD 21209-3600 Office Phone: 410-580-4218. Business E-Mail: peter.moser@dlapiper.com.

MOSER, MARVIN, physician, educator, author; b. Newark, Jan. 24, 1924; s. Sol and Sophia (Markowitz) M.; m. Joy Diane Lipez, July 1, 1954; children: Jill, Stephen, John. AB, Cornell U., 1943; MD, Downstate Coll. Medicine, NYC, 1947. Diplomate in internal medicine and cardiovasc. disease Am. Bd. Internal Medicine; cert. specialist in hypertension Am. Soc. Hypertension. Intern univ. div. Kings County Hosp., NYC, 1947-48, resident in medicine, 1948-49, Montefiore Hosp., NYC, 1949-50; Nat. Heart Assn. fellow Mt. Sinai Hosp., NYC, 1950-51; charge vascular service Walter Reed Army Hosp. Med. Centre, Washington, 1951-53; practice medicine specializing in cardiology White Plains, NY, 1953-95; assoc. physician cardiology Montefiore Hosp., 1953-75, in charge hypertension sect., 1960—74. Attending physician cardiology White Plains Hosp., 1968-95, chief cardiology, 1969-78; adj. physician in cardiology Grasslands Hosp., Valhalla, NY, 1953-60; attending physician in medicine in charge Hypertension Clinic, Westchester County Med. Center, Valhalla, 1974-84; asst. clin. prof. medicine Albert Einstein Coll. Medicine, 1965-75; clin. prof. medicine NY Med. Coll., 1974-84, Yale U. Sch. Medicine, 1984—; sr. med. cons. nat. high blood pressure program NIH, 1975-2002, mem. nat. high blood pressure coordinating com., 1976-2005; chmn. Joint Nat. Com. Hypertension, 1977, vice-chmn., 1979, mem., 1984-88, 92, 96, 2003; exec. com. Nat. Citizens for Treatment High Blood Pressure, 1976-78, vice-chmn., 1978-88; mem. NY State Adv. Com. on Hypertension, 1977-84; chmn. Nat. Conf. on High Blood Pressure Control, 1979; mem. select panel on hypertension in Am. Congl. Subcom. on Aging, 1978-79; cons. cardiology NY State Dept. Health, Gen. Hosp., Saranac Lake, NY, 1980-90; med. dir. Westchester County Hypertension Program, NY, 1979-88. Author: (with A.M. Master, M. Moser. H. Jaffee) Cardiac Emergencies and Heart Failure, 2d edit., 1955; (with A. Goldman) Hypertensive Vascular Disease, 1967, Hypertension, A Practical Approach, 1975, Lower Your Blood Pressure and Live Longer, 1988; co-editor, contbr. Yale University School of Medicine Heart Book, 1992, Week by Week to a Strong Heart, 1992, Heart Healthy Cooking for all Seasons, 1996, Clinical Management of Hypertension, 1996, 7th edit., 2004, 8th edit., 2007, Myths, Misconceptions and Heroics, the Story of the Treatment of Hypertension, 1997, 2002, (with J. Sowers) Management of Cardiovascular Risk Factors in Diabetes, 2001, 2d edit., 2005, 3rd edit., 2007; mem. editl. bd. Preventive Cardiology, 1998—, Jour. Medicine and Sports, 1999-2004; assoc. editor Angiology, 1976-85; bd. editors Primary Cardiology, 1975-78, assoc. editor-in-chief, 1978-96; editor-in-chief Jour. Clin. Hypertension, 1999—; sr. editor Jour. of Cardio Metabolic Syndrome, 2006—; contbr. 500 scientific papers. Chmn. Narcotics Guidance Coun., Scarsdale, 1968-72; trustee Scarsdale Bd. Edn., 1970-73, Trudeau Inst., 1990-2004, Nat. Hypertension Found., 1992-2001, Nutrition 21, 1997—, Comprehensive Neuroscience; bd. dirs. Third Ave. Value and Small Cap Funds, 1994—; pres. Hypertension Edn. Found., 1977—. Served U.S. Army, 1941-46; capt. M.C. USAF, 1951-53. Recipient Achievement awards Nat. High Blood Pressure Edn. Program, 1985, 97, award Internat. Soc. Hypertension, 2004, 06, award Am. Soc. Hypertension, 2006, award Down State Coll. Medicine, 2007; grantee NIH, 1958-62. Fellow: ACP, Am. Soc. Hypertension, Am. Heart Assn. ((various offices: pres. coun. geriatric cardiology 1996-97, others)), Am. Coll. Cardiology, Royal Coll. Physicians and Surgeons (hon.); mem.: Century Country Club. Home and Office: 13 Murray Hill Rd Scarsdale NY 10583 Personal E-mail: moserbp@aol.com.

MOSER, ROBERT HARLAN, internist, educator, writer; b. Trenton, NJ, June 16, 1923; s. Simon and Helena (Silvers) Moser; m. Linda Mae Salsinger, Mar. 18, 1989; children from previous marriage: Steven Michael, Jonathan Evan. BS, Loyola U., Balt., 1944; MD, Georgetown U., Washington, DC, 1948. Diplomate Am. Bd. Internal Medicine. Commd. 1st lt. U.S. Army, 1948, advanced through grades to col., 1966, intern D.C. Gen. Hosp., 1948—49, fellow pulmonary disease D.C. Gen. Hosp., 1949—50, bn. surgeon Republic of Korea, 1950—51; asst. resident Georgetown U. Hosp., 1951—52; chief resident Georgetown U. Hosp. U.S. Army, 1952—53, chief med. service U.S. Army Hosp. Salzburg, Austria, 1953—55, Wurzburg, Germany, 1955—56, resident in cardiology Brooke Gen. Hosp., 1956—57, asst. chief dept. medicine Brooke Gen. Hosp., 1957—59, chief Brooke Gen. Hosp., 1967—68, fellow hematology U. Utah Coll. Medicine, 1959—60, asst. chief U.S. Army Tripler Gen. Hosp., 1960—64, chief William Beaumont Gen. Hosp., 1965—67, chief Walter Reed Gen. Hosp., 1968—69, ret., 1969; chief of staff Maui (Hawaii) Meml. Hosp., 1969—73, chief dept. medicine, 1975—77; exec. v.p. Am. Coll. Physicians, Phila., 1976—86; v.p. med. affairs The NutraSweet Co., Deerfield, Ill., 1986—91. Assoc. prof. medicine Baylor U., 1958—59; clin. prof. medicine Hawaii U., 1969—77, Washington U., 1970—77, Abraham Lincoln Sch. Medicine, 1974—75; adj. prof. medicine U. Pa., 1977—86, Northwestern U., 1987—91; adj. prof. Uniformed Svcs. U. Health Scis., 1979—97; clin. prof. medicine U. N.Mex. Coll. Medicine, 1992—96, emeritus, 1996—; flight contr. Project Mercury, 1959—62; cons. mem. med. evaluation team Project Gemini, 1962—66; cons. Project Apollo, 1967—73, Tripler Gen. Hosp., 1970—77, Walter Reed Army Med. Ctr., 1974—86; sr. med. cons. Canyon Cons. Corp., 1991—2004; mem. cardiovascular and renal adv. com. FDA, 1978—82; chmn. life scis. adv. com. NASA, 1984—87, mem. adv. coun., 1983—88; chmn. gen. med. panel Hosp. Satellite Network, 1984—86; mem. adv. com. NASA Space Sta., 1988—93; mem. Dept. Def. Com. on Grad. Med. Edn., 1986—87, Life Scis. Strategic Planning Study Group, 1986—88; mem. space studies bd. NRC, 1988—93, space exploration initiation study, 1990; mem. NASA Space Sta. Commn., 1992—93, mem. com. adv. tech. human supp. space, 1996—97; mem. med. adv. bd. the patient channel GE Healthcare, 2001—. Editor, chief divsn. sci. publs. Jour. AMA, Chgo., 1973—75, contbg. editor Med. Opinion and Rev., 1966—75, chmn. editorial bd. Diagnosis mag., 1986—89, mem. editorial bd. Hawaii Med. Jour., Family Physicians, Archives of Internal Medicine, 1967—73, Western Jour. Medicine, 1975—87, Chest, 1975—80, Med. Times, 1977—84, Quality Rev. Bull., 1979—91, The Pharos, 1991—, book rev. editor, 2000—05, mem. editorial bd. Travel Medicine, 1994—96; contbr. over 200 articles to med. sci. jours. and med. books; author: Diseases of Medical Progress, 1955, 1969, House Officer Training, 1970, Decade of Decision, 1992, Past Imperfect A Personal History of Life In and Around Medicine, 2003; co-author Adventures in Medical Writing, 1970, editor chief divsn. sci. publs. Jour. AMA, Chgo., 1973—75, contbg. editor Med. Opinion and Rev., 1966—75, chmn. editl. bd. Diagnosis mag., 1986—89; contbr. articles to med. sci. jours. and med. books. Master: ACP (exec. v.p. 1977—86); fellow: Am.

Clin. and Climatol. Assn., Am. Coll. Cardiology, Royal Coll. Physicians and Surgeons Can. (hon.); mem.: AMA (adv. panel registry of adverse drug reactions 1960—67, coun. on drugs 1967—73), Soc. Med. Cons. to Armed Forces, Coll. Physicians Phila., Chgo. Soc. Internal Medicine, Nat. Assn. Physician Broadcasters, Inst. Medicine-NAS, Am. Osler Soc., Am. Therapeutic Soc., Am. Med. Writers Assn., Alpha Omega Alpha, Alpha Sigma Nu. Democrat. Jewish. Avocations: hiking, travel, writing. Home and Office: 943 E Sawmill Canyon Pl Green Valley AZ 85614 Office Phone: 520-399-2526. Personal E-mail: rhmoser@earthlink.net.

MOSER, ROBERT LAWRENCE, pathologist, health facility administrator; b. Passaic, NJ, Mar. 22, 1952; s. Robert George and Marjorie Ann (Frankenberger) M.; m. Rosemarie Scolaro, June 16, 1978; children: Rachel Ann, Alexander Robert. BA in Biology magna cum laude, Lafayette Coll., 1974; MD Microbiology/Internal Med. with honors, Hahnemann Med. Coll., 1978. Diplomate Am. Bd. Pathology, Am. Bd. Anatomic Pathology, Am. Bd. Clin. Pathology, Am. Bd. Forensic Medicine. Intern, fellow dept. pathology The Johns Hopkins Hosp., Balt., 1978-79, resident, fellow dept. pathology, 1979-81, chief resident, fellow dept. pathology, 1981-82, resident, fellow dept. lab. medicine, 1982-84; cons. pathologist Perry Point (Md.) VA Med. Ctr., 1983-84; pathologist Helene Fuld Med. Ctr., Trenton, N.J., 1984-88; med. dir. St. Francis Med. Ctr., Trenton, 1988—, dir. clin. info. sys., 1995—, Franciscan Health Sys., 1995-96, Cath. Health Initiatives, 1996—2000. Pres. Pathology Assocs., Lawrenceville, N.J., 1981—. Contbr. articles to profl. jours. Fellow Coll. Am. Pathologists, Coll. Physicians of Phila.; mem. Am. Med. Informatics Assn., Med. Soc. N.J., Mercer County Med. Soc., Ctrl. Jersey Ind. Physician Assn. (v.p. 1994-95, sec.-treas. 1995-96, exec. v.p. 1997—), Ea. Pathology Assn. (v.p. 1996-2003), Phi Beta Kappa. Avocations: golf, gardening, skiing.

MOSER, ROYCE, JR., preventive medicine physician, educator; b. Versailles, Mo., Aug. 21, 1935; s. Royce and Russie Frances (Stringer) M.; m. Lois Anne Hunter, June 14, 1958; children: Beth Anne Moser McLean, Donald Royce. BA, Harvard U., Cambridge, Mass., 1957, MD, 1961; MPH, Harvard Sch. Pub. Health, Boston, 1965. Diplomate Am. Bd. Preventive Medicine (trustee 1989-98). Commd. officer USAF, 1962, advanced through grades to col., 1974; resident in aerospace medicine USAF Sch. Aerospace Medicine, Brooks AFB, Tex., 1965-67; chief aerospace medicine Aerospace Def. Command, Colorado Springs, Colo., 1967-70; comdr. 35th USAF Dispensary Phan Rang, Vietnam, 1970-71; chief aerospace medicine br. USAF Sch. Aerospace Medicine, Brooks AFB, 1971-77; comdr. USAF Hosp., Tyndall AFB, Fla., 1977-79; chief clin. scis. divsn. USAF Sch. Aerospace Medicine, Brooks AFB, 1979-81, chief edn. divsn., 1981-83, sch. comdr., 1983-85, ret., 1985; prof. dept. family and preventive medicine U. Utah Sch. Medicine, Salt Lake City, 1985—, vice chmn. dept., 1985-95; dir. Rocky Mountain Ctr. for Occupl. and Environ. Health, Salt Lake City, 1987—2003. Cons. in occupl., environ. and aerospace medicine, Salt Lake City, 1985—; presenter in field. Author: Effective Management of Occupational and Environmental Health and Safety Programs, 1992, 2d edit. 1999; contbr. book chpts. and articles to profl. jours. Past pres. 1st Bapt. Ch. Found., Salt Lake City, 1987-89, moderator, 2006; chmn. numerous univ. coms., Salt Lake City, 1985—; bd. dirs. Hanford Environ. Health Found., 1990-92; preventive medicine residency rev. com. Accreditation Coun. Grad. Med. Edn., 1991-97; ednl. adv. bd. USAF Human Sys. Ctr., 1991-96; chmn. long-range planning com. Am. Bd. Preventive Medicine, 1992-95; mem. alumni coun. Harvard Sch. Pub. Health, 2003-06, chair alumni award of merit com., 2005—. Decorated Legion of Merit (2); recipient Harriet Hardy award New Eng. Coll. Occupl. and Environ. Medicine, 1998, Rutherford T. Johnstone award Western Occupl. and Environ. Med. Assn., 2002. Fellow Aerospace Med. Assn. (pres. 1989-90, chair fellows group 1994-97, Harry G. Mosely award 1981, Theodore C. Lyster award 1988, Eric Liljencrantz award 2001, Pres.'s citation, 2006), Am. Coll. Preventive Medicine (regent 1981-82), Am. Coll. Occupl. and Environ. Medicine (v.p. med. affairs 1995-97, Robert A. Kehoe award 1996); mem. Internat. Acad. Aviation and Space Medicine (selector 1989-94, chancellor 1994-98), Soc. of USAF Flight Surgeons (pres. 1978-79, George E. Schafer award 1982), Phi Beta Kappa. Avocations: photography, fishing. Home: 664 Aloha Rd Salt Lake City UT 84103-3329 Office: Rocky Mountain Ctr Occupl & Environ Health 391 Chipeta Way Ste C Salt Lake City UT 84108 Office Phone: 801-581-8719. Business E-Mail: Royce.Moser@hsc.utah.edu.

MOSER, SANDRA KAY, secondary school educator; b. LaPorte, Ind., Aug. 16, 1940; d. Richard Wayne and Elizabeth Frances Prentiss; divorced; children: Stacy Karen, Shae Kimberly, Jae Emmert. BS, Ball State U., 1958—62; MA, Purdue U., 1977—80; postgrad., Ind. U., 1990—95. Tchr. Barker Jr. H.S., Michigan City, Ind., 1962—69, Wanatah (Ind.) Pub. Sch., 1977—, tech. dir., 1996—. Author poetry. Mem.: NEA, Ind. State Tchr. Assn. Roman Catholic. Avocation: travel. Home: 2 Ave B Westville IN 46391 Office: Wanatah Pub Sch 309 School Dr Wanatah IN 46390

MOSER, SARAH GUNNING, manufacturing engineer, small business owner; b. Seattle, Sept. 17, 1953; d. Harvey Dade and Grace Wills (Bell) Gunning; m. Lawrence Herman Moser, May 18, 1985; children: Grace Elizabeth, Gregory Edward. BA in Archtl. Planning, Evergreen State Coll., Olympia, Wash., 1975; mfg. engring. cert., Boeing Mfg. Engring. Sch., Everett, Wash., 1980. Asst. variety dept. mgr., clk. The Safeway Corp., Seattle, 1977-79; mfg. engr. Boeing Co., 747/767 div., Everett, 1980-82; mfg. engr., sr. mfg. engr. McDonnell Douglas Helicopter Co., Mesa, Ariz., 1982-87; co-owner Moser Design Assocs., Vashon, Wash., 1988—, Moser Design Svcs., Vashon, Wash., 1989-90; bus. mgr. for opera singer Patricia S. Lott, Vashon, 1989-90. Engring. trainer McDonnell Douglas Helicopter Co., Mesa, 1986-87, procedure writer, 1986-87; procedure writer The Boeing Co., Everett, 1981. Cmty. outreach speaker Alcohol Pub. Info. Com., Wash., 1976-80, 88-89; coord. Women's Ctr., Evergreen State Coll., 1973-74; trainer, bd. dirs. Sta. KAOS-FM, Olympia, 1972-74; soloist Unity Ch. of Truth, Seattle, Everett, 1978-82; guest soloist various chs.; co-chmn. Vashon-Maury Island Babysitting Coop., 1988-89, chmn., 1989; coord. Island Home Educators, 1991-92, publicist, 1992-94; sec. Vashon Island Cmty. Ch., 1995—. Recipient Cost Savs. awards Boeing Co., 1980-82. Avocations: classical singing, performing, world war ii history, international penfriends, walking. Office: Moser Design Assocs PO Box 1406 Vashon WA 98070-1406

MOSER, WILLIAM OSCAR JULES, mathematics professor; b. Winnipeg, Can., Sept. 5, 1927; s. Robert and Laura (Fenson) M.; m. Beryl Rita Pearlman, Sept. 2, 1953; children— Marla, Lionel, Paula. B.Sc., U. Man., 1949; MA, U. Minn., 1951; PhD, U. Toronto, 1957. Lectr. U. Sask., 1955-57, asst. prof., 1957-59; asso. prof. U. Man., 1959-64, McGill U., 1964-66, prof., 1966-97, prof. emeritus, 1997—. Author: (with H.S.M. Coxeter) Generators and Relations for Discrete Groups, 1957, 4th edit., 1980, (with E. Barbeau, M. Klamkin) 500 Mathematical Challenges, 1995, (with P. Brass and J. Pach) Research Problems in Discrete Geometry, 2005, also rsch. papers; editor: Can. Math. Bull, 1962-70, Can. Jour. Math., 1982-85. NRC fellow, 1951-53; Can. Coun. leave fellow, 1971. Mem.: Am. Math. Soc., Can. Math. Soc. (pres. 1975—77), Math. Assn. Am. Office: McGill U Dept Math 805 Sherbrooke St W Montreal PQ Canada H3A 2K6 Office Phone: 514-398-3820. E-mail: moser@math.mcgill.ca.

MOSES, ABE JOSEPH, financial planner, consultant; b. Springfield, Mass., July 15, 1931; s. Mohammed Mustapha and Fatima (Merriam) M.; m. Donna C. Moses (dec. 1987); children: James Douglas, John C., Peter J.; m. Mary Jo Morris, Aug. 25, 2001. BA, Amherst Coll., 1955; MA in Internat. Affairs, Johns Hopkins U., 1957. Legis. aide Sen. J.F. Kennedy, 1955-57; Goodwill Amb. to Middle East and South Asia, 1957; fgn. service officer Dept. State, 1960-65; v.p., gen. mgr. Libyan Desert Oil Co., Texfel Petroleum Corp., Tripoli, Libya, 1965-67; v.p. adminstrn., fin. Occidental Petroleum Corp., Libya, 1967-70; v.p. fin., dir. Northrop Corp., 1970-74; chmn. Transworld Trade Ltd., Washington, 1971—; v.p., mng. dir. world adv. group Chase Manhattan Bank, 1974-80; pres. Berkshire Properties, 1976-95; pres., COO, Grolier Internat., Inc., Danbury, Conn., 1980-82; CEO, dir. Galadari Bros., Dubai, United Arab Emirates, 1982-86; internat. bus. and fin. cons. Traxol, Dubai, 1986—; fin. cons. Govt. Costa Rica, 1986-89. Chmn. Aviation Sys. Corp., Northampton, Mass., 1974, Dillon Internat., Akron, Ohio, 1986—; mem. bd. dirs. Near East Found. NYC, 1977—; mng. dir. Sheraton Suites Akron, Cuyahoga Falls, Ohio, 1990—; owner's rep. Monarch Sheraton Hotel, Springfield, Mass., 1993-95; bd. dirs., v.p. Morgan Freeport Co., Hudson, Ohio; bd. dirs. Seeds of Peace, Washington; gen. ptnr. BPM Ltd. Partnership, 1995—; bd. dirs. owners adv. bd. Starwood Hotels and Resorts, 2005-; bd. dir. ETRA Corp., Cuyahoga Falls, Ohio, 2005-. Pres., bd. dirs. Riverside Cmty. Urban Redevel. Corp.; mem. exec. com., bd. dirs. Near East Found., NYC, 1975-; pres. Riverfront Ctr. Assn., Cuyahoga Falls, 1992-95; bd. dirs. Gulfcoast Radio Ptnrs., 1997-99, Capitol City Radio Ptnrs., 1998-2000, Ind. Radio Ptnrs., Monroe (La.) Radio mems., LLC, Commonwealth Opera Co., Northampton, Mass., 2002—; bd. dir. N. Am. Owners Adv. Bd., 2005-07. From 1st lt. to capt. USAF, 1956—60. Ford Found. fellow Johns Hopkins U., 1955, Barr Found. fellow, 1955-57, Amherst Coll. fellow in Internat. Relations, 1955-57, Barr Found. fellow, Springfield, Mass., 1955-57; Obed Finch Slingerland award, Amherst Coll., Mass. Mem.: Assn. Starwood Franchise Owners N.Am. (bd. dirs. 2006—), Assn. Sheraton Franchise Owners N.Am. (bd. dirs. 2004—06). Democrat. Avocations: art, oriental carpet, flying. Home: 16 Highmeadow Rd Northampton MA 01062-2625 Office: Riverside CURC 1989 Front St Cuyahoga Falls OH 44221-3811 Office Phone: 330-920-7502. Personal E-mail: abejmoses@comcast.net.

MOSES, ALFRED HENRY, lawyer, writer, diplomat; b. Balt., July 24, 1929; s. Leslie William and Helene Amelia (Lobe) Moses; m. Carol Whitehill, Nov. 24, 1955 (dec.); children: Barbara, Jennifer, David, Amalie; m. Fern Magonet Schad, Aug. 28, 2005. BA, Dartmouth, 1951; postgrad., Woodrow Wilson Sch., Princeton U., 1951-52; JD, Georgetown U., 1956. Bar: D.C. 1956. Assoc. Covington & Burling, Washington, 1956-65, ptnr., 1965—94, 1997—99, sr. counsel, 1999—. Co-founder, sr. ptnr., COO Promontory Fin. Group LLC and affiliates, Washington, 2001—; legal advisor minority rights Dem. Nat. Com., Washington, DC Commn. Urban Renewal; commr. Pub. Housing Fairfax County, Va., 1971—72; spl. advisor, spl. counsel Pres. Jimmy Carter, Washington, 1980—81; amb. U.S. Dept. State, Romania, 1994—97; spl. Presdl. emissary Cyprus conflict Pres. William J. Clinton, 1999—2001; chmn. UN Watch, Geneva, 2001—; chmn. nat. bd. Hebrew Coll., Newton Ctr., Mass., 2002—; bd. chair Project on Ethnic Rels., Inc., Princeton, NJ, 2006—; lectr. in field. Contbr. articles to profl. jours. Pres. Am. Jewish Com., 1991—94, chmn. centennial com., 2004—, chmn. adv. coun., 1997—; bd. dirs. Paralysis Cure Rsch. Found., 1978—81; trustee Phelps Stokes Fund, NYC, 1978—84, Jewish Publ. Soc., 1989—94, Haifa U., 1988—90; co-chmn. legal divsn. United Givers Fund, Washington, 1975—76; active Coun. Fgn. Rels., NYC, 1977—; pres. Nat. Children's Island, Washington, 1975—76, Golda Meir Assn., 1986—88, nat. chmn., 1988—93; bd. regents Georgetown U., 1986—92. Recipient Pentru Merit award, Govt. of Romania, Frizis award, Nat. Coordinated Effort of Helenes. Mem.: ABA, D.C. Bar Assn., Econ. Club Washington, Met. Club. Democrat. Jewish. Home: 7710 Georgetown Pike Mc Lean VA 22102-1431 Office: 1201 Pennsylvania Ave NW Washington DC 20004-2401

MOSES, GREGORY H., JR., health services administrator; m. Johnella Moses. Lead engagement ptnr. Sister Mercy Health Corp.; ptnr.-in-charge Healthcare Consulting Group, N.Y., N.J.; ptnr. Coopers & Lybrand; pres., COO United Am. Healthcare Corp., Detroit, 1998—. Office: United American Health Care 300 River Place Dr Ste 4700 Detroit MI 48207-5069 Fax: 313-393-7944.

MOSES, HAMILTON, III, neurologist, hospital administrator, author; s. Hamilton Jr. and Betty Anne Moses; m. Elizabeth Hormel, 1977 (dec. 1988); m. Alexandra McCullough Gibson, 1992. BA in Psychology, U. Pa., 1972; MD, Rush Med. Coll., Chgo., 1975. Clk. Nat. Hosp. for Nervous Diseases, London, 1974; intern in medicine Johns Hopkins Hosp., Balt., 1976-77, resident in neurology, 1977-79, chief resident, 1979-80, assoc. prof. neurology, 1986-94, vice chmn. neurology and neurosurgery, 1980-88, v.p., 1988-94, dir. Parkinson's Ctr., 1984-94; dir. neurol. inst., prof. neurology and neurosurgery and mgmt. U. Va., Charlottesville, 1994-97; sr. advisor Boston Cons. Group, 1995—; prof. Darden Sch. Bus. U. Va., Charlottesville, 1994-98; cons. neurologist Mass. Gen. Hosp., Boston, 1997—; vis. prof. neurology and psychiatry Harvard U. Sch. Medicine, Boston, 1997-99; chmn. The Alerion Inst., 2002—. Sr. advisor Ptnrs. Healthcare, Boston; spl. advisor Nat. Health Svc., Eng., 1988-91; dir. various tech. companies. Co- editor, major author: Hopkins' Principles and Practice of Medicine, 1985-96; editor newsletter Johns Hopkins Health, 1988-94; contbr. articles to profl. jours. Com. on med. ministries Episcopal Diocese Md., Balt., 1987; bd. dirs. Valleys Planning Ct.; trustee McLean Hosp., Belmont, Mass., 1997—. Fellow Am. Acad. Neurology (sec. 1989-91), Royal Soc. Medicine (UK); mem. Am. Neurol. Assn., Md. Neurol. Soc. (pres. 1984-86), Movement Disorders Soc. Avocations: photography, sailing. Office: PO Box 150 North Garden VA 22959-0150 Business E-Mail: hm3@alerion.us.

MOSES, HAROLD L., oncologist; MD, Vanderbilt U., 1962. Rschr. NIH, 1965—68; faculty Vanderbilt U., Nashville, 1985—, prof. cancer biology, the Benjamin F. Byrd Jr. prof. of clin. oncology, prof. pathology and prof. medicine, 1993—, dir. Vanderbilt-Ingram Cancer Ctr., 1999—, chair dept. cell biology, 1985—98. Dir. Frances Williams Preston Rsch. Labs. T.J. Martell Found., 1993—; clin. oncologist Mayo Clinic, Rochester, Minn., 1973—85; mem. nat. dialogue on cancer, vice chair cancer rsch. team, chair parent com. Nat. Cancer Inst., mem. bd. sci. counselors, co-chair breast cancer progress rev. group. Recipient Outstanding Investigator award, Nat. Cancer Inst., 1986, 1993. Mem.: Am. Assn. for Cancer Rsch. (past pres.), Assn. of Am. Cancer Insts. (pres.), Inst. Medicine. Office: Vanderbilt-Ingram Cancer Ctr 691 Preston Bldg Nashville TN 37232 Office Phone: 615-936-1782.

MOSES, JEFFREY WARREN, cardiologist, educator; b. Bklyn., May 12, 1948; s. Julian and Mildred Moses; m. Laurie Levinberg, Nov. 4, 1983; children: Ariel, Jarret, Chandler, Harrison. BA, Yale U., New Haven, Conn., 1970; MD, U. Pa., Phila., 1974. Intern Presbyn.-U. Pa., Phila., 1974—75, resident in medicine, 1975—77, fellow in cardiology, 1978—80; asst. instr. U. Pa., Phila., 1975—77; med. adv. staff Blue Cross/Blue Shield Greater N.Y., 1977—78; asst. med. dir. Equitable Life Soc., NYC, 1977—78; asst. attending physician NY Hosp., NYC, 1980—87, asst. dir. Adult Cardiac Catheterization Lab., 1980—83, dir. clin. electrophysiology, 1981—87, assoc. dir. Adult Cardiac Catheterization Lab., 1983—87, assoc. attending physician, 1987; instr. medicine Cornell U. Med. Coll., NYC, 1980—81, asst. prof., 1981—87, assoc. prof. clin. medicine, 1987; chief interventional cardiology Lenox Hill Hosp., NYC, 1987—2005, assoc. attending physician, 1987—88, sr. attending physician, 1988—2005; clin. assoc. prof. medicine NYU Sch. Medicine, NYC, 1993—96, clin. prof. medicine, 1996—2004; prof. medicine, dir. Ctr. Interventional Vascular Therapy, dir. Cardiac Catheterization Lab. NY Presbyn. Hosp./Columbia U. Med. Ctr., NYC, 2004—, interventional cardiologist, 2005—. Fellow: ACP, Soc. Cardiac Angiography and Intervention, Am. Coll. Cardiology. Office Phone: 212-305-7060. Office Fax: 212-305-4825, 212-342-3660. Business E-Mail: jm2456@columbia.edu.

MOSES, JOEL, computer scientist, educator; b. Petach Tikvah, Israel, Nov. 25, 1941; came to U.S., 1954, naturalized, 1960; s. Bernhard and Golda (Losner) M.; m. Margaret A. Garvey, Dec. 27, 1970; children: Jesse, David. BA, Columbia U., 1962, MA, 1963; PhD, MIT, 1967. Asst. prof. dept. elec. engring. and computer sci. MIT, Cambridge, 1967-71, assoc. prof., 1971-77, prof., 1977—, assoc. dir. Lab for Computer Sci., 1974-78, assoc. head computer sci. and engring., dept. elec. engring. and computer sci., 1978-81, head dept., 1981-89, D.C. Jackson prof., 1989-99, dean Sch. Engring., 1991-95, provost, 1995-98, prof. engring. sys. divsn., 1999—, Inst. prof., 1999—, acting dir. engring. sys. divsn., 2006—, acting. dir. Ctr. Tech., Policy and Indsl. Devel., 2006—. Vis. prof. Harvard Grad. Sch. Bus. Adminstrn., 1989-90; vis. adj. sr. rsch. scientist Columbia U. FU Found. Sch. Engring. and Applied Sci., 1998. Editor: The Computer Age: A Twenty Year View, 1979; co-originator Knowledge Based System Concept; developer MACSYMA system for formula manipulation, complexity and flexibility of large scale systems. Recipient Achievement award MIT Lab. for Computer Sci., 1985. Fellow IEEE, AAAS, Am. Acad. Arts and Scis.; mem. NAE, Assn. for Computing Machinery, Am. Soc. Engring. Edn. (Centennial cert.). Office: MIT Computer Sci Artificial Intelligence Lab 32-249 Cambridge MA 02139 Office Phone: 617-253-8592. E-mail: moses@mit.edu.

MOSES, JUDY, real estate company executive; m. Charlie Capace. Ed., Simmons Coll. Owner, broker Pathway Home Realty Group Inc. Volunteer Big Sister Assn. of Greater Boston; pres. Alumnae Club Simmons Coll., Boston. Mem.: Mass. Assn. Realtors (dir.), Women's Coun. of Realtors (local chpt. pres. 1997, state chpt. pres. 1999, gov. 2000, pres. 2007, chair, leadership development com., chair, bus. value com., exec. com., strategic planning com., fin. adn budget com., products and services com.). Office: Pathway Home Realty Group 123 Wolcott Rd Chestnut Hill MA 02467 Office Phone: 617-734-6188. Office Fax: 617-734-1677. E-mail: judymoses@judymoses.com. *

MOSES, MICHAEL JAMES, insurance company executive, small business owner; b. Roaring Spring, Pa., Apr. 13, 1956; s. William E. and Carol J. (Berkey) M.; m. Laura L. Bishop, June 7, 1980 (div. 1990); children: J'aime Lee, Justin Michael. AS, Williamson Trade Sch. Salesman 84 Lumber, Cresson, Pa., 1977-78; area mgr. Nat. Home Life Ins. Co., Valley Forge, Pa., 1978-80; regional v.p. A.L. Williams Agy. (name changed to Primerica), Duluth, Ga., 1981—; owner Luigetta's Restaurant, Altoona, Pa., 2003—. Republican. Mem. Pentecostal Ch. Avocations: basketball, golf, tennis, guitar, drums. Office Phone: 814-942-6167.

MOSES, SAMUEL B., accountant, consultant; s. Alfred J. and Alice R. Moses. BA, Calif. State U., Fullerton, 1985. CPA Calif., 1990. Auditor Arthur Andersen & Co., Costa Mesa, Calif., 1985—86; tax sr. cpa BDO Seidman, Orange, Calif., 1987—90; owner Samuel B. Moses, Santa Monica, Calif., 1991—. Western dir. Intertel (Top 1% IQs), LA, 2002—03. Recipient Peat Marwick award, Beta Alpha Psi Chpt., 1985. Mem.: Mensa (licentiate; chmn. Greater L.A. area chpt. 1996—2000). Office: Samuel B Moses CPA Ste 1800 100 Wilshire Blvd Santa Monica CA 90401 Home Phone: 310-505-8515; Office Phone: 310-395-9922. Business E-Mail: smosescpa@aol.com.

MOSES, SHELIA P., writer, poet, playwright, producer; b. Rich Square, NC, 1961; Author: So They Burned the Black Churches, 1996, One More River to Cross, The Legend of Buddy Bush, 2004 (Nat. Book Award finalist, 2004), I, Dred Scott, 2005; co-author (with Dick Gregory): Callus on My Soul: A Memoir, 2000; co-author: (plays) Ain't No God in Hollywood. Recipient Coretta Scott King Honor Book award, 2005.

MOSESSO, VINCENT NICHOLAS, JR., emergency physician, health facility administrator; b. Pitts., Pa., Sept. 28, 1957; s. Vincent Nicholas and Jean Lois Mosesso; m. Janet L. Mosesso, June 17, 1983; children: Jennifer Moss, Chadwick. BA, Duquesne U., Pitts., 1979; MD, U. of Pitts., 1988. Lic. emergency medicine Am. Bd. of Emergency Medicine. Assoc. prof. of emergency medicine U. of Pitts. Sch. of Medicine, 1991—. Asst. med. dir. dept. of pub. safety City of Pitts., 1993—; med. dir. prehospital care U. of Pitts. Med. Ctr., 1996—; mem. nat. BLS subcom. Am. Heart Assn., Emergency Cardiac Care Com., Dallas, 2001—; med. dir. advanced med. life support Nat. Assn. of Emergency Med. Technicians, Clinton, Miss., 2002—. Mem. editl. bd.: med. jours. Prehospital Emergency Care. Mem. Allegheny divsn. Am. Heart Assn., Pitts., 1998—; bd. dirs., med. dir. Sudden Cardiac Arrest Assn., Washington, 2005—06. Named Emergency Physician of the Yr., Pa. Emergency Health Svcs. Coun., 1998; grantee, Medtrionic Found., 2000—02. Fellow: Am. Coll. of Emergency Medicine; mem.: Nat. Assn. of EMS Physicians (bd. dirs. 2003—05). Avocations: golf, travel, sports, exercise. Office: U Pitt Ste 911 230 McKee Pl Pittsburgh PA 15213 Office Phone: 412-647-1103. E-mail: mosessovn@upmc.edu.

MOSHER, KENNETH VESTER, II, property tax appraiser; b. Rushville, Ill., Aug. 25, 1962; s. Kenneth Vester and Elsie Nona (Weaver) Mosher; m. Kris Fultz, Mar. 21, 1985 (div. 1988); children: Shannan Only Hauser, Kenneth Vester Mosher, III; m. Patricia Lee Allen, Feb. 29, 2004. Honor Grad. Diploma, US Army Q.M. Sch., Fort Lee, Va., 1985—85; AA, Carl Sandburg Coll., Galesburg, Ill., 1990—92; BA in Liberal Arts & Polit. Sci., Regents Coll. USNY, Albany, 1991—94; BA in Sociology & Edn. cum laude, Western Ill. U., Macomb, 1992—94. Lic. pre-need funeral insurance agent Tex. Dept. Ins., 2005; cert. tchr. grades 6-12 State Tchr. Cert. Bd., Ill., 1995, lic. appraiser II Tex. Bd. Profl. Tax Examiners, 2006. Material handling dept. Iowa Beef Processors, Columbus Junction, Iowa, 1989—92; tchr. Gonzales Ind. Sch. Dist., Tex., 1995—96; office mgr. Tex. Surveying Co., Inc., Gonzales, 1996—2005; family svc. counselor Buffington Funeral Home, Gonzales, 2005—06; sr. pre-need counselor Harris Family Mortuary, Gonzales, 2005—06; appraiser Gonzales County Appraisal Dist., 2006—. Organizing com. Teamsters Union Local 238, Columbus Junction, Iowa, 1991—92; NASA tchrs. workshop participant Edn. Region Svc. Ctr. XIII, Houston, 1996. Cartographer, rschr. (map) Satellite Map of Gonzales Cemeteries; editor (webmaster): (website) Gonzales Lions Website (MD-2 award for pub. rels. excellence, 2002), Lions District 2-S5 (Internat. Pres. Cert. Appreciation award, 2003), Gonzales County Democrats. Bd. mem. Gonzales County Hist. Commn., 2000—06; county chmn. Gonzales Dem. Party, 2006; mem. Gonzales Christian Assistance Min., 2004—06, Gonzales Main St. Bd., 2004—04. Sgt. e5 US Army, 1985—88, Mannheim, Germany. Decorated Driver's Badge/Wheel US Army, Army Svc. Ribbon, Expert Grenadier, Sharpshooter award, Army Commendation medal, NATO Svc. Ribbon NATO, 97th Signal Bn. Superior Unit award US Army, Overseas Svc. Ribbon, Good Conduct medal; recipient Cert. Achievement award, 1985, Dist. Govs. Cert. Appreciation award, Lions Dist. 2-S5, 2002—03, Patriotic Citizen award, VFW, 2004. Fellow: Gonzales Christian Assistance Ministry (assoc.); mem.: Gonzales County Hist. Commn. (commn. mem. 2000—06), Tex. Assn. Assessing Officers (mem. appraiser 2006—), AMVETS (vice-comdr. 1992—93), United Svc. Orgn. (assoc.), Gonzales County Dems. (chmn. 2006), Cold War Vets. Assn. (silver mem. 2005—06), Lions Club Internat. (dist. 2-s5 zone 1-b chair 2002—03, Internat. Pres. Cert. Appreciation award 2003), Gonzales Evening Lions Club (pres. 2000—05), Tex. Lions Camp (life), Gonzales Noon Lions Club (sec. 2006—, Lion of the Month 2006, Lion of Month award 2005), Phi Kappa Phi, Mensa. D-Liberal. Avocations: history, genealogy. Home: 1207 Water St Gonzales TX 78629 Home Phone: 830-672-4557.

MOSHER, SALLY EKENBERG, lawyer, musician; b. NYC, July 26, 1934; d. Leslie Joseph and Frances Josephine (McArdle) Ekenberg; m. James Kimberly Mosher, Aug. 13, 1960 (dec. Aug. 1982). MusB, Manhattanville Coll., 1956; postgrad., Hofstra U., 1958-60, U. So. Calif., 1971-73, JD, 1981. Bar: Calif., 1982. Musician, pianist, tchr., 1957-74; music critic Pasadena Star-News, 1967-72; mgr. Contrasts Concerts, Pasadena Art Mus., 1971-72; rep. Occidental Life Ins. Co., Pasadena, 1975-78; v.p. James K. Mosher Co., Pasadena, 1961-82, pres., 1982—, Oakhill Enterprises, Pasadena, 1984—; assoc. White-Howell, Inc., Pasadena, 1984-94; real estate broker, 1984-96. Harpsichordist, lectr., composer, 1994—; pub. Silver Wheels Pub., ASCAP. Musician (CD recs.) William Byrd: Songs, Dances, Battles, Games, 1995, From Now On: New Directions For Harpsichord, 1998, Sally Mosher Plays English Renaissance Harpsichord Music, Images and Moods, (with Patrick Lindley, Scott Frasier, Justin Weaver) Towards the Light; author: People and Their Contexts: A Chronology of the 16th Century World; contbr. articles to various publs. Bd. dirs. Jr. League Pasadena, 1966-67, Encounters Concerts, Pasadena, 1966-72, U. So. Calif. Friends of Music, L.A., 1973-76, Calif. Music Theatre, 1988-90, Pasadena Hist. Soc., 1989-91, I Cantori, 1989-91; bd. dirs. Pasadena Arts Coun., 1986-92, pres., 1989-92, chair adv. bd., 1992-93; v.p., bd. dirs. Pasadena Chamber Orch., 1986-88, pres., 1987-88; mem. Calif. 200 Coun. for Bicentennial of U.S. Constn., 1987-90; mem. Endowment Adv. Commn., Pasadena, 1988-90; bd. dirs. Foothill Area Cmty. Svcs., 1990-95, treas., 1991, vice chair, 1992-94, chair, 1994-95; sec., bd. dirs. Piano Spheres, 2001-02, pres., 2002—. Manhattanville Coll. hon. scholar, 1952-56. Mem. ABA, Calif. Bar Assn., Assocs. of Calif. Inst. Tech., So. Calif. Baroque Assn. (bd. dirs., 2004—), Athenaeum, Kappa Gamma Pi, Mu Phi Epsilon, Phi Alpha Delta. Home: 1260 Rancheros Rd Pasadena CA 91103-2759 Fax: 626-795-3146. E-mail: sally@cyberverse.com.

MOSHIER, DAVID IRWIN, church administrator; b. Roanoke, Va., Sept. 14, 1954; s. Emery Irwin (dec.) and Evelyn Mae (Kunkel) M.; m. Bonnie Sharon Dailey, Feb. 13, 1982. STD, Am. Bible Inst., 1991; DD, World Christianship Mins., 1997; ThB, Sch. Christian Min., 1998; ThM, Greensburg Bible Coll. & Sem., Ind., 1998. Ordained to ministry Am. Evang. Christian Chs., 1992, Reformed Presbyn. Ch., 1995, World Christianship Ministries, 1997, St. Thomas-A-Becket Mins., 1998, Gen. Conf. Evang. Protestant Chs., 2000. Rsch. asst. mktg. dept. Clarendon Bank & Trust, Arlington, 1974, collection agt., installment loan dept., 1974-75; loan collection officer George Washington U., Washington, 1975-77, sr. loan collection officer, 1977-79; student loan collection coord. Hahnemann Med. Coll. and Hosp., Phila., 1979-80; prin. account clk. George Washington U., Washington, 1980-83; pastor The Wesleyan Ch., Waldorf, Md., 1983-86; asst. pastor Floor Meml. Wesleyan Ch., Arlington, 1986-89; pastor First Wesleyan Ch., Alexandria, Va., 1989-91; dir. govt. rels. Am. Evang. Christian Chs., Alexandria, 1992-93, moderator Mid-Atlantic region, 1992-95, nat. exec. dir., 1993; pastor Fredericksburg Area Reformed Presbyn. Mission, Va., 1995; stated clk. Reformed Presbyn. Ch., Hanover, 1996-99, 2000—02; v.p., prof. homiletics Greensburg Bible Coll. and Theol. Sems., Ind., 1998-99; special counsel to pres. Sch. Christian Ministry and Theological Seminary, 1999—. Coord. Conf. Confessing Presbyn. Chs., 1996-98; bishop Va., USA Fountain Revival Missions Worldwide Internat., 1999-; bd. dirs. Rate Wave Tariff Svcs., Falls Church, Va., ops. mgr., 1999; sec. ext. and evangelism Capital Dist. Wesleyan Ch., Great Falls, Va., 1986-88; spl. asst. Office Army Chief of Chaplains, Arlington, 1987-90, cemetery rep. Arlington Nat. Cemetery, 1996-97, 2004-05; supt. US Soldiers' and Airmen's Home Nat. Cemetery, 2005-; chaplain (2d lt.) Va. Defense Force, 1999-2004; alumni coun. Flint Hill Sch., Oakton, Va., 1991-98; supply pastor Cmty. Ch./Am. Rescue Workers, Capitol Heights, Md., 1992; ch. resls. cons. WABS Radio, Arlington, 1992-94; mem. adv. bd. Covered Bridge Ministries, St. Paul, Ind., 1993—, others. Contbr. articles to profl. jours. Officer of election Electoral Bd., Alexandria, 1991-92, Arlington, 1992-93. Recipient Cert. of Commendation, Army Chief of Chaplains, Washington, 1988, 89, 90, Cert. of Civil Svc., Desert Shield-Storm/Hqrs. U.S. Army, Washington, 1992, Knight Grad Collar, Order of St. Oswald, 1995; fellow in philosophy of religion St. Aidan's Acad., 1995; created Baron of Mesta, Byzantine Dynastic House of Polanie-Patrikios, 1998. Mem. George Washington U. Gen. Alumni Assn., Sons of the Am. Legion, State Guard Assn. US. Republican. Home: 21 Harewood Rd NW Washington DC 20011-4902 Home Phone: 202-726-1944; Office Phone: 202-829-1829. Personal E-mail: moshiel109@yahoo.com.

MOSHMAN, JACK, statistical consultant; b. Richmond Hill, N.Y., Aug. 12, 1924; s. Morris and Sadye (Posner) M.; m. Annette Gordon, Aug. 10, 1947; children: Gordon, Marc, Sherri, Ira. BA, NYU, 1946; MA, Columbia U., NYC, 1947; PhD, U. Tenn., Knoxville, 1953. Instr. Queens Coll., Flushing, NY, 1946-47, U. Tenn., Knoxville, 1947-53; statistician AEC, Oak Ridge, Tenn., 1948-50; sr. statistician Oak Ridge Nat. Labs., Tenn., 1950-54; mem. tech. staff Bell Tel. Labs., Murray Hill, NJ, 1954-57; v.p. C-E-I-R Inc., Washington, 1957-66; mng. dir. EBS Mgmt. Cons., Washington, 1966-68; sr. v.p. Leasco Systems & Rsch., Bethesda, Md., 1968-69; pres. Moshman Assocs. Inc., Bethesda, Md., 1970—. Adj. prof. Rutgers U., 1963-66; professorial lectr. George Washington U., 1959-62; chmn. Inst. for Safety Analysis, Rockville, Md., 1975-89, mem. office of mgmt. and budget adv. com. on statistical policy. Editor: Faith, Hope & Parity, 1967; author Ency. sect. Computers & Politics, 1985, 90, 93; contbr. articles to profl. jours. Trustee Babbage Found., St. Paul, 1983-87; pres. Moshman Charitable Found., Bethesda, 1996—; v.p. Eleanor & George Kokiko Sr. Found., Bethesda, 1997—. With U.S. Army, 1943-46, ETO. Fellow Am. Statis. Assn. (coun. 1956, 58); mem. Am. Fedn. Info. Processing Soc. Am. (bd. dirs., pres. 1986-87), Assn. for Computing Machinery (sec. 1956-64, v.p 1965), Inst. for Math. Stats., Inst. for Mgmt. Scis., Ops. Rsch. Soc. Am., Biometrics Soc. Avocation: psephology. Office: Moshman Assocs Inc 4340 East West Hwy Bethesda MD 20814-4411 Home Phone: 301-229-4040; Office Phone: 301-229-3000. Personal E-mail: jmoshman@aol.com.

MOSHOLDER, ANDREW DONALD, psychiatrist; b. Washington, Sept. 25, 1957; s. Donald and Mary Mosholder; m. Janet Marie Rauch, Aug. 5, 1989; 1 stepchild, Erik Harrison. BA, Haverford Coll., Pa., 1979; MD, U. Va., 1983; MPH, Johns Hopkins U., 2001. Diplomate Am. Bd. Psychiatry and Neurology, 1988, lic. in child and adolescent psychiatry Am. Bd. Psychiatry and Neurology, 1991, psychiatrist Va., 1985. Resident psychiatry Med. Coll. Va., Richmond, 1983—87; resident child and adolescent psychiatry U. Va., Charlottesville, 1987—89; psychiatrist Ctrl. Va. Cmty. Svcs., Lynchburg, Va., 1989—92; med. officer FDA, Rockville, Md., 1992—. Recipient Frances Kelsey Drug Safety Excellence award, FDA Ctr. for Drug Evaluation and Rsch., 2005. Mem.: APHA, Am. Acad. Child and Adolescent Psychiatry. Mem. Soc. Of Friends. Avocation: bass guitar. Office: FDA 10903 New Hampshire Ave Mail Stop 3411 Silver Spring MD 20993-0002 Office Phone: 301-796-0508. Business E-Mail: andrew.mosholder@fda.hhs.gov.

MOSICH, ANELIS NICK, accountant, writer, educator, consultant; b. Croatia, Aug. 30, 1928; came to U.S., 1939, naturalized, 1951; s. Dinko and Josephine (Ursich) M.; m. Dorothy V. Rasich, June 15, 1958; children: Lori, Lisa, Jeffrey. BS, UCLA, 1951, MBA, 1953, PhD, 1963. CPA, Calif. Mem. faculty UCLA, 1955-63, Calif. State U., Northridge, 1963-64; examiner for Calif. State Bd. Accountancy, 1964-70; prof. acctg. U. So. Calif., LA, 1964-74, William C. Hallett prof. acctg., 1974-81, Ernst & Young prof., 1981-90, chmn. acctg. dept., 1970-74, 77-78, prof. emeritus, 1993. Cons. various bus. orgns., 1953—; expert witness; guest spkr. various profl. and bus. groups in Calif., Oreg., NY, Tex., Fla., Hawaii, Mex., 1963—95; bd. dirs. Metro-Goldwyn-Mayer, Inc., 2003—05. Author: Intermediate Accounting, rev. 6th edit., 1989, Financial Accounting, 1970, 75, Accounting: A Basis for Business Decision, 1972, Modern Advanced Accounting, 4th edit., 1988, The CPA Examination: Text, Problems and Solutions, 1978; editor: Education column Calif. CPA Quar., 1965-66; contbg. editor: Education and Professional Training column Jour. Accountancy, 1971-77; contbr. numerous articles to jours. and acctg. Mem. productivity commn. City of L.A., 1993—94; bd. dirs. Bill Hannon Found. With US Army, 1953—55. Fellow UCLA, 1963; recipient Dean's award Sch. Bus. Adminstrn., U. So. Calif., 1973, 78, Fred B. Olds Support Group award U. So. Calif., 1994, Disting. Svc. award for Leventhal Sch. Acctg., 1999, Mosich Endowment Chair award, U. So. Calif., 2006 Office: U So Calif Leventhal Sch Acctg University Park Los Angeles CA 90089-1425

MOSICH, NICHOLAS JOSEPH, lawyer; b. San Pedro, Calif., July 2, 1951; s. Nicholas Andrew and Barbara Yvonne (Chutuk) M.; m. Susanne Melinda Wolf, Dec. 18, 1976 (dec. Jan. 1998); m. Jessica V. Schutte, Dec. 22, 2002; children: Nicholas Daniel, Andrea Michelle. BA, Santa Clara U., 1974; JD, Pepperdine U., 1977. Bar: Calif. 1977, U.S. Dist. Ct. (so. dist.) Calif. 1979, U.S. Dist. Ct. (ctrl. dist.) Calif. 1980. Assoc. Forgy & Inadomi, Santa Ana, Calif., 1978-83, ptnr., 1983-92, Mosich & Fatone, 2002—04, Mosich & Assocs., 2004—. Bd. dirs. Young Men's Christian Assn., Santa Ana, 1980-87. Mem. ABA, Orange County Bar Assn., Assn. Trial Lawyers Am. Republican. Roman Catholic. Office: 2204 E 4th St Ste 100 Santa Ana CA 92705-4071 Office Phone: 714-560-0944. E-mail: nick@mosichlaw.com.

MOSIER, ARVIN RAY, chemist, researcher; b. Olney Springs, Colo., June 11, 1945; s. Isaac James Ellen Rena (Ross) M.; m. Susan Minnick, Dec. 30, 1965; children: Andrew, Katherine. BS, Colo. State U., 1967, MS, 1967-68, PhD, 1974. Chemist agr. rsch. svcs. USDA, Ft. Collins, 1967—2004, with global environ. change and food sys. program Gainesville, Fla., 2005—. Contbr. papers and book chpt. to profl. publ. Mem. AAAS, Am. Soc. Agronomy, Soil Sci. Soc. Am., Internat. Soil Sci. Sco., Council Agrl. Sci. Tech., Phi Kappa Phi, Sigma XI, Gamma Sigma Delta. Republican. Methodist. Avocations: tennis, soccer. Home: 7555 NW 47th Way Gainesville FL 32653 Office: Agrl and Biol Engring Dept U Fla 281 Frazier Rogers Bldg Gainesville FL 32611 Home Phone: 352-381-3562; Office Phone: 352-392-1864 281. E-mail: armosier@ufl.edu.

MOSIER, WILLIAM ARTHUR, psychiatrist, psychotherapist, director, medical educator, researcher; b. Richmond, Calif., Oct. 21, 1946; s. William Nathaniel and Violet Olga (Luzum) M.; m. Virginia Rondero (div. Apr. 1992); children: Robert Carlos, Cristina Dominique; m. Gloria Sifuentes (div. 1998); 1 child, William Nathaniel; m. Gabriela Pickett; children: Gabriela, Diana. BA, Webster U., 1971, MA in Tchg., 1973; MD, U. Ctrl. del Este, Dominican Republic, 1986; EdD, U. So. Calif., 1987; BS with distinction, U. Okla., 1991; MPAS in Psychiatry, U. Nebr., 1997. Diplomate Am. Bd. Forensic Medicine, Am. Bd. Med. Psychotherapists, Am. Bd. Psychol. Specialties, lic. physician asst. Tex., Fla., N.Y., Va.; marraige and family therapist, chem. dependency counselor Tex.; marriage and family therapist Ohio. Tchr. St. Louis Pub. Schs., 1971—74; tchr., ctr. dir. Project Head Start, Vallejo, Calif., 1975—77; dir. rsch. Ctr. for Study of Child Devel., Sacramento, 1977—95; physician asst. U.S. Army, Ft. Hood/Ft. Sam Houston, Tex., 1989—91; assoc. prof. U. Mary Hardin-Baylor, Belton, Tex., 1991—92; psychotherapist pvt. practice, Tex., 1993—95; mem. adj. faculty dept. psychiatry Barry U., Miami Shores, Fla., 1997—2000; med. dir. Fla. Inst. Neuro Devel., Vero Beach, Fla., 1995—2000; clin. assoc. prof. psychiatry Nova Southeastern U., Ft. Lauderdale, Fla., 1997—99; asst. prof. medicine, assoc. dir. acad. curriculum George Washington U., 2000—01; assoc. prof. psychiatry Kettering Coll. med. Arts Kettering (Ohio) Med. Ctr., 2001—02, dir. physicians asst. program; child devel. cons., marriage and family therapist, 2001—; asst. prof., child devel. Wright State U., Dayton, Ohio, 2002—. Mem. test writing com. Nat. Assn. Cert. Physicians Assts., 1995—, Nat. Bd. Med. Examiners; bd. dir. Ohio State Counselor, Social Worker and Marriage and Family Therapist Regulatory Bd. Newspaper columnist:, mem. editl. adv. bd.: Advance for PAs; contbr. articles to profl. jours., chapters to books. Lt. col. USAF, 1967-68, Vietnam, maj. USAFR, 1987—. Decorated Bronze Star, Air medal. Fellow: APA (mem. adv. bd. 1997—, editl. adv. bd. Annals of Am. Psychotherapy Assn.), Am. Assn. Surg. PAS, Am. Acad. Physician Assts., Assn. Mil. Surgeons U.S. (life), Aerospace Med. Assn. (life), Am. Coll. Forensic Examners (life); mem.: Ohio Assn. Marriage and Family Therapy (bd. dir.), Am. Assn. Marriage and Family Therapy (del. regulatory bd. Ohio), Assn. of Psychiat. PAs (founding mem., pres.), Soc. PAs in the Addiction Medicine (exec. bd., pres.). Democrat. Mem. Soc. Of Friends. Avocations: musical composition, piano, guitar, swimming, yoga. Office: 649 Greenlawn Ave Dayton OH 45403-3356 E-mail: drwillmosier@yahoo.com.

MOSIMAN, RITA ESTHER, music educator, performing artist; children: Theresa, Mark, Brian. B in Music (hon.), U. Ariz., 1963. Lic. secondary tchg. Ariz., 1963. Solo artist Ariz. Symphony, 1962; English, speech tchr. Dreux Am. HS, France, 1964—65; adminstrv. asst. US Dept. Def., Supt. Sch. Office, Orleans, France, 1965—66; choral dir. Los Lunas Consol. Sch., N.Mex., 1980; pvt. voice and piano tchr. Albuquerque, 1980—. Guest conductor, choral clinician Am. All Spain HS Music Festival, Zaragoza, Spain, 1979. Singer (soloist): Northern Ariz. Symphony, 1962, U. N.Mex., 1982, U. Ariz., 1985; Whitworth Coll., 1988; prodr.(vocalist, pianist): America's Best Kept Secret-Rita M., 2004; dir.(soloist): La Gran Via, 1988, Santa Fe Spirit, 1989. Vol. Concert for Humanity, Albuquerque, 1984; dir., pianist benefit concert Pennies for the Homeless, Albuquerque, 1998. Named Outstanding Ind. Woman, U. Ariz., 1963; recipient Leadership award, Sigma Alpha Iota, we. dist., 1963. Mem.: Nat. Assn. Tchrs. Singing. Avocations: hiking, photography, travel, birdwatching. Office Phone: 505-294-6018. Personal E-mail: ritaem@gmail.com.

MOSJIDIS, JORGE, agricultural studies educator, researcher; b. Santiago, Chile; arrived in U.S., 1976; d. Georgios and Aliky Mosjidis; m. Cecilia O'Hara Mosjidis, Mar. 23, 1986; children: Christina Zoe Wood, Alexis Georgios. B in Agronomy, U. Chile, Santiago, 1970; PhD, U. Calif., Riverside, 1981. Asst. prof. Auburn (Ala.) U., assoc. prof., 1986—96, prof., 1996—. Chair clover crop germplasm com. USDA, 2005—, sec., 2002—05; assoc. editor Crop Sci., 1995—2000. Contbr. articles to profl. jours. Recipient Dir.'s Rsch. award, Ala. Agr. Exptl. Sta., 2005; grantee, USDA-CSREES-NRI, 2003—06, CSREES, Integrated Organic Program, 2005—, So. Region SARE, 2005—, 2005—. Mem.: Am. Forage and Grassland Coun., Am. Genetic Assn., Am. Soc. Agronomy, Crop Sci. Soc. Am. (assoc. editor 2000), Gamma Sigma Delta, Sigma Xi. Greek Orthodox. Achievements include patents pending for utilization of a plant to control gastrointestinal parasites in ruminants; obtained a certificate of plant variety protection for 18 years for a sericea lespedeza cultivar. Avocations: yoga, flower and vegetable gardening, tai chi, qi kung. Office: Auburn Univ 202 Funchess Hall Auburn University AL 36849-5412

MOSK, RICHARD MITCHELL, judge; b. LA, May 18, 1939; s. Stanley and Edna M.; m. Sandra Lee Budnitz, Mar. 21, 1964; children: Julie, Matthew. AB with great distinction, Stanford U., 1960; JD cum laude, Harvard U., 1963. Bar: Calif. 1964, U.S. Supreme Ct. 1970, U.S. Ct. Mil. Appeals 1970, U.S. Dist. Ct. (no., so., ea., and cen. dists.) Calif 1964, U.S. Ct. Appeals (9th dist.) 1964. Staff Pres.'s Commn. on Assassination Pres. Kennedy, 1964; rsch. clk. Calif. Supreme Ct., 1964-65; ptnr. Mitchell, Silberberg & Knupp, LA, 1965-87; prin. Sanders, Barnet, Goldman, Simons & Mosk, PC, LA, 1987-2000; justice Calif. Ct. Appeal, 2nd Dist., 2001—. Spl. dep. Fed. Pub. Defender, LA, 1975—76; instr. U. So. Calif. Law Sch., 1978; judge Iran-U.S. Claims Tribunal, 1981—84, 1997—2001, substitute arbitrator, 1984—97; mem. L.A. County Jud. Procedures Commn., 1973—82, chmn., 1978; chmn., co-chmn. Motion Picture Assn. Classification and Rating Adminstrn., 1994—2000; mem. panel Ct. Arbitration for Sport-Geneva, 1998—2001; lectr. internat. law Hague Acad., 2003. Contbr. articles to profl. jours. Mem. L.A. City-County Inquiry on Brush Fires, 1970; bd. dirs. Calif. Mus. Sci. and Industry, 1979-82, Vista Del Mar Child Ctr., 1979-82; trustee L.A. County Law Libr., 1985-86; bd. govs. Town Hall Calif., 1986-91; mem. Christopher Commn. on L.A. Police Dept., 1991; mem. Stanford U. Athletic Bd., 1991-95. With USNR, 1964-75. Hon. Woodrow Wilson fellow, 1960; recipient Roscoe Pound prize, 1961. Mem.: ABA (coun. internat. law sect. 1986—90), Am. Law Inst., L.A. County Bar Assn., Beverly Hills Bar Assn., Am. Bar Found., Phi Beta Kappa. Office: Ct Appeal 300 S Spring St Los Angeles CA 90013

MOSKAL, ANTHONY JOHN, retired dean, management consultant, educator; b. South Amboy, NJ, May 31, 1946; s. Anthony Joseph and Jennie (Salamon) M.; m. Kathryn Jean Coakley, July 8, 1978; 1 child, Nicole Elizabeth. AB, Villanova U., Pa., 1968, MA, 1972; MEd, Ga. State U., 1974; PhD, Columbia Pacific U., San Rafael, Calif., 1987. Prin. instr. U.S. Army, Ft. Benning, Ga., 1969-71; research mgr. Blue Cross and Blue Shield, Columbus, Ga., 1972-74; sales rep. J.C. Penney Co., Parlin, N.J., 1974-76; dean of students Alliance Coll., Cambridge Springs, Pa., 1976-77; tchr. Sayreville (N.J.) pub. schs., 1977-79; county 4-H agt. Rutgers U., New Brunswick, 1979-86; pres. Eagle Assocs., South Amboy, N.J., 1985—; dir. Burming Bush Prodns., 1986—. Adj. faculty Georgian Ct. Coll., Lakewood, NJ, 1987—, U.S. Army Command and Gen. Staff Coll., Ft. Leavenworth, Kans., 1989—2000, Nat. Def. U., Washington, 1991—2000; cons. dir. Union County Ednl. Svcs. Commn., 2000—; spl. liaison to Mcpl. Bd. Edn., Sayreville, 1991—95, Sayreville, 2000—06; area admissions rep. U.S. Mil. Acad., 1984—91; bd. dirs. Burning Bush Prodn.; mem. Environ. Commn., Sayreville, 2004—06; cons. in field. Contbr. articles pub. to profl. jours. Active Boy Scouts Am.; counselor, mem. dist. com. Ctrl. N.J. Coun. Boy Scouts Am., 1982—; pres., bd. dirs. Vol. Action Ctr., Middlesex County, NJ, 1979—87; pres. Sayreville War Meml. H.S. Band Parents Assn., 1994—96, NJ 4-H Agts. Assn., 1985—86; commr. Environ. Commn., Sayreville, 2004—06; county committeeman Middlesex County, 1990—94, 2000—06; dir. religious edn. Sacred Heart Parish, South Amboy, NJ, 1988—91. With U.S. Army, 1969—71, with US Army, 1990—92, lt. col. USAR. Decorated Meritorious Svc. medal, Army Commendation medal (2), Mil. Outstanding Vol. Svc. medal; recipient Order of the Arrow award Boy Scouts Am., 1960, 20th Century award of Achievement, Nat. Assn. Chiefs of Police, Desert Shield/Desert Storm medal State of N.J., Disting. Svc. medal State of N.J.; United Way of Ctrl. Jersey grantee, 1984, others. Mem.: ASCD, Holy Name Soc., U.S. Army Officer Candidate Alumni Assn., Am. Fedn. Police (award of merit 1989, legion of honor 1990, J Edgar Hoover Meml. medal 1991, St. Michael the Archangel award 1992, patriotism award 1993), Nat. Assn. Ext. 4-H Agts. (regional contact 1981—83, profl. devel. chmn. 1984—86, cert. appreciation 1983), Res. Officers Assn., Mil. Police Regtl. Assn., N.J. Assn. 4-H Agts. (pres. 1985—86, outstanding svc. citation 1981, 1987), Vietnam Vets. of Am. (life; rec. sec., honor guard), Nat. Infantry Assn. (life), Nat. Eagle Scout Assn., Am. Legion, KC (3d degree past Grand Knight, program dir., degree team capt., vol. coord. fife and drum corps, diocesan degree team, color corps commdr., dist. degree team, 3d degree Dist. Warden, 4th degree Past Faithful Navigator, 4th degree aide to Dist. Master, family of mo., Assembly Color Corps man of yr.(2), 3d degree family of yr., Assembly Color Corps man of yr., Dist. Color Corps man of yr., 4th degree family of yr., Knight of mo. (3), 4th degree knight of yr.), Kiwanis, Pi Gamma Mu, Epsilon Sigma Phi, Alpha Phi Omega. Republican. Roman Catholic. Avocations: reading, music, recreational camping, travel, woodworking. Office: Eagle Assocs 166 Luke St South Amboy NJ 08879-2231 Personal E-mail: ajmoskal@verizon.net.

MOSKALENKO, IGOR VLADIMIROVICH, physicist, astrophysicist; b. Moscow, May 4, 1962; s. Vladimir Anatolievich and Galina Petrovna (Kuznetsova) M.; m. Irina Viktorovna Surikova, July 12, 1984 (div. May 1992); 1 child, Maria; m. Irina Vladimirovna Malkova, June 10, 1994. MS, M.V. Lomonosov Moscow State U., 1985, PhD in Physics, 1990. Rschr. Moscow State U. Inst. Nuc. Physics, 1985-93, sr. scientist, 1993—2002; sr. rsch. assoc. Lab. for High Energy Astrophysics NASA/Goddard Space Flight Ctr., Greenbelt, Md., 1999—2001; assoc. rsch. scientist NASA/Goddard Space Flight Ctr. and Joint Ctr. for Astrophysics/U. Md. Baltimore County, 2002—05; sr. rsch. scientist Hansen Experimental Physics Lab. and Kavli Inst. for Particle and Astrophysics and Cosmology, Stanford U., 2005—. Guest scientist Lodz (Poland) Inst. Physics, 1990-91, Ctr. d'Etude Spatiale des Rayonnements, CNRS, Toulouse, France, 1994-95, Internat. Ctr. for Theoretical Physics, Trieste, Italy, 1995, Max-Planck-Inst. für Extraterrestrische Physik, Garching, Germany, 1996-99; prin. investigator astrophysics theory program NASA, 2002-04; prin. investigator NASA Astronomy and Physics Rsch. and Analysis Program, 2005-. Contbr. numerous articles to profl. jours., chpts. to books, and conf. procs; referee profl. jours. and book series. Grantee Am. Astron. Soc., 1992, Am. Phys. Soc., 1992, Soros Found., Moscow, 1993; Max Planck fellowship Max Planck Soc., 1996-99; sr. associateship NRC-NASA/GSFC, 1999-2001. Russian Orthodox. Avocations: tennis, skiing, swimming, travel. Home: 106 Charles Marx Way Palo Alto CA 94304-2412 Office: HEPL/Stanford Univ Stanford CA 94305-4085 Business E-Mail: imos@stanford.edu.

MOSKIN, JOHN ROBERT, editor, writer; b. NYC, May 9, 1923; s. Morris and Irma (Rosenfeld) M.; m. Doris Marianne Bloch, Oct. 7, 1948 (div. 1978); children: Mark Douglas, David Scott, Nancy Irma; m. Lynn Carole Goldberg, Apr. 10, 1986. Grad., Horace Mann Sch., 1940; BS, Harvard U., 1944; MA, Columbia U., 1947. Reporter Boston Post, 1941-42, Newark News, 1947-48; asst. to gen. mgr. N.Y. Star, 1948-49; editor Westport (Conn.) Town Crier, 1949; med. editor Look mag., NYC, 1950-51, articles editor, 1951-53, sr. editor, 1956-66, fgn. editor, 1966-71; mng. editor Woman's Home Companion, 1953-56; sr. editor Collier's, 1956; editor at large Saturday Rev., 1972-75; sr. editor World Press Rev., 1976-87, contbg. editor, 1987-93; editl. dir. Aspen Inst., 1977-83. Editl. dir. Commonwealth Fund, 1984-87, sr. editl. advisor, 1987-93. Author: (with others) The Decline of the American Male, 1958, Morality in America, 1966, Turncoat, 1968, The U.S. Marine Corps Story, 1977, 82, 87, 92, Among Lions, 1982, (with Julia Vitullo-Martin) The Executive's Book of Quotations, 1994, Mr. Truman's War, 1996, 2002; editor: The Marines, 1998; mem. editl. adv. com. Dimensions mag, 1970-71, Present Tense, 1973-90. Trustee Scarsdale Adult Sch., 1965—72, chmn., 1969—70; mem. comm. screening com. Coun. Internat. Exch. Scholars, 1974—77, Pres.'s Coun. Heritage U., 1995—; bd. dirs. SIECUS, 1972—80, Jerusalem Found., 1977—2003, Marine Corps Hist. Found., 1979—82, 1989—95, Faculty for Continuing Med. Edn., 1983—86, Authors Guild Found., 2000—; bd. dirs., sec. Lotos Club Found., 2000—; mem. Dana Reed Prize com. Harvard U., 1947—2000, mem. com. Class of 1944, 1943—. With AUS, 1943—46. Recipient Benjamin Franklin Gold medal for pub. svc. Woman's Home Companion, 1955, Page One award Newspaper Guild N.Y., 1965, Sidney Hillman Found. award, 1965, National Headliners award, 1967, Overseas Press Club award, 1969, citation for excellence, 1971, Disting. Svc. award Marine Corps Combat Corrs. Assn., 1978, 99, Nat. Jewish Book award, 1983, Disting. Svc. award Marine Corps Hist. Found., 1996, Gen. O.P. Smith award Marine Corps Heritage Found., 1999. Mem.: PEN, Nat. Press Club (Washington), Fgn. Editors Group (chmn. 1970—71), Am. Hist. Assn., Soc. Mil. History, Authors Guild, Lotos Club (bd. dirs. 1988—90, pres. 1991—94, bd. dirs. 1994—2002, historian), Harvard Club (N.Y.C.), The Century Assn., Overseas Press Club (gov. 1975—79), Sigma Delta Chi (nat. freedom of info. com. 1964, 1971). Home: 945 5th Ave New York NY 10021-2666 also: 157 Jerusalem Rd Tyringham MA 01264 E-mail: jrmedit@att.net.

MOSKIN, MORTON, lawyer, director; b. NYC, Mar. 28, 1927; s. Barnett and Sonia (Burr) M.; m. Rita Lee Goldberg, June 15, 1952; children: Tina, Ilene, Jonathan. BA, Pa. State Coll., 1947; LLB, Cornell U., 1950. Assoc.

White & Case, NYC, 1950—61, ptnr., 1962—94, cons., 1995—. Chmn. exec. com. Mallinckrodt, Inc. (formerly IMCERA, previously Internat. Minerals and Chem. Corp.), St. Louis, 1988-91, chmn. corp. governance com., 1993-97; sec. BT Mortgage Investors, Garden City, NY, 1975-82; bd. dirs. NY County Lawyers' Assn. Found., Inc., 2004, 05, 06. Author (with E. Carolan Berkley): Third Party Legal Opinions, 2005; editor (with Field): New York and Delaware Business Entities: Choice, Formation, Operation, Financing, Acquisitions, 1997, Transactional Lawyer's Deskbook: Advising Business Entities, 2001; editor: Commercial Contracts: Strategies for Drafting and Negotiating, 2002. Bd. dirs. Fedn. Employment and Guidance Svcs.; bd. dirs., pres. Henry M. Blackmer Found., N.Y.C.; bd. dirs. Achievement Found., Stamford, Conn., pres., 1988-94; bd. dirs. Jewish Cmty. Svcs. L.I., 1974-93, pres., 1984-87. Fellow Am. Bar Found.; mem. ABA, NY County Lawyers Assn. (bd. dirs. 1981-86, 99-02, 04, 05, 06), N.Y. County Lawyers Assn. Found. Inc. (bd. dirs. 2004-06), Norfolk (Conn.) Country Club, Cornell Club. Home: 1160 Park Ave Apt 15B New York NY 10128-1212 Office: White & Case 1155 Ave of Americas New York NY 10036-2711 Business E-Mail: mmoskin@whitecase.com.

MOSKOS, CHARLES C., social studies educator; b. Chgo., May 20, 1934; s. Charles and Rita (Shukas) M.; m. Ilca Hohn, July 3, 1966; children— Andrew, Peter. BA cum laude, Princeton U., NJ, 1956; MA, UCLA, 1961, PhD, 1963; LHD (hon.), Norwich U., Northfield, Vt., 1992, Towson U., Md., 2002. Asst. prof. U. Mich., Ann Arbor, 1964-66; assoc. prof. sociology Northwestern U., Evanston, Ill., 1966-70, prof., 1970—. Fellow Progressive Policy Inst., 1992—; mem. Presdl. Commn. on Women in the Mil., 1992. Author: The Sociology of Political Independence, 1967, The American Enlisted Man, 1970, Public Opinion and the Military Establishment, 1971, Peace Soldiers, 1976, Fuerzas Armadas y Societdad, 1984, The Military--More Than Just A Job?, 1988, A Call to Civic Service, 1988, Greek Americans, 1989, Soldiers and Sociology, 1989, New Directions in Greek American Studies, 1991, The New Conscientious Objection, 1993, All That We Can Be, 1996, Reporting War When There Is No War, 1996, The Media and the Military, 2000, The Postmodern Military, 2000. Chmn. Theodore Saloutos Meml. Fund; mem. Archdiocesean Commn. Third Millenium, 1982-88; mem adv. bd. Vets. for Am., 1997—; mem. Congl. Commn. on Mil. Tng. and Gender-Related Issues, 1998-99, Nat. Security Study Group, 1998-2001. Served with AUS, 1956-58. Decorated D.S.M., Fondation pour les Etudes de Def. Nat. (France), S.M.K. (The Netherlands); named to Marshall rsch. chair ARI, 1987-88, 95-96, 03; Ford. Found. faculty fellow, 1969-70; fellow Wilson Ctr., 1980-81, guest scholar, 1991; fellow Rockefeller Found. Humanities, 1983-84, Guggenheim fellow, 1992-93, fellow Annenberg Washington Program, 1995; grantee 20th Century Fund, 1983-87, 92-94, Ford Found., 1989-90; recipient Nat. Educator Leadership award Todd Found., 1997, Book award Washington Monthly, 1997, Honored Patriot award Selective Svc. Sys., 1998; Pub. Policy fellow Wilson Ctr., 2002; Eisenhower chair Royal Mil. Acad. Netherlands, 2002. Mem. Am. Sociol. Assn., Internat. Sociol. Assn. (pres. rsch. com. on armed forces and conflict resolution 1982-86), Inter-Univ. Seminar on Armed Forces and Soc. (chmn. 1987-99), Am. Acad. Arts and Scis. Greek Orthodox. Address: 1040 4th St #309 Santa Monica CA 90403 Office Phone: 847-491-2705. Business E-Mail: c-moskos@northwestern.edu.

MOSKOS, HARRY, columnist, editor; b. Chgo., Oct. 8, 1936; m. Victoria Marie Poulos; 3 children. BA, U. N.Mex., Albuquerque, 1958. With Albuquerque Tribune, 1953-59; editor Grants (N.Mex.) Daily Beacon, 1959-60; newsman AP, Albuquerque, 1960, state editor, 1961-63, chief of bur. Honolulu, 1963-69; city editor Albuquerque Tribune, 1969-73, mng. editor, 1973—80; editor El Paso Herald-Post, 1980—84, Knoxville News-Sentinel, 1984—2001; columnist, letters editor Albuquerque Jour., 2001—. Office: 7777 Jefferson St NE Albuquerque NM 87109 Office Phone: 505-823-3837. Business E-Mail: hmoskos@abqjournal.com.

MOSKOVITZ, JACKOB, biology professor; arrived in U.S., 1992; s. Raphael and Zipora Moskovitz. BA in Biology, Technion, 1985, MS in Biology, 1988, DS in Medicine, 1992. Asst. prof. U. Kans., Lawrence, 2004—. Cons. Amgen, Thousand Oaks, Calif., 2000, UBI, Lake Placid, NY, 2004—. Contbr. articles to profl. jours. Fellow, Roch Inst. Molecular Biuology, Nutley, NJ, 1992—95, NIH, Bethesda, Md., 1996—2004. Mem.: Neurosci. Assn. Avocations: piano, painting, sports, travel. Business E-Mail: moskovij@ku.edu.

MOSKOW, MICHAEL H., retired bank executive; b. Paterson, NJ, Jan. 7, 1938; s. Jacob and Sylvia (Edelstein) M.; m. Constance Bain, Dec. 18, 1966; children: Robert Bain, Eliot Marc, Lisa Danielle. AB, Lafayette Coll., Easton, Pa., 1959; MA in Econs., U. Pa., 1962, PhD, 1965. Instr. econs. Lafayette Coll., 1964—65; asst. prof. mgmt. Drexel Inst. Tech., Phila., 1963-64, 65-67; assoc. prof. econs., dir. Bus. Econ. and Bus. Research, Temple U., Phila., 1967-69; sr. staff economist Coun. Econ. Advisers The White House, Washington, 1969-70; exec. dir. Constrn. Industry Collective Bargaining Commn., 1970-71; dep. under sec. U.S. Dept. Labor, 1971-72, asst. sec. for policy, evaluation and research, 1972-73, under-sec., 1976-77; asst. sec. for policy devel. and research US Dept. Housing & Urban Devel., 1973-75; dir. Council on Wage and Price Stability, 1975-76; cons. Com. for Econ. Devel., 1977; dir. corp. devel. and planning Esmark, Inc., 1977-78, v.p. corp. devel. and planning, 1978-80; exec. v.p. Estronics, Inc. div. Esmark, Inc., 1980-82; pres. Velsicol Chem. Corp. div. N.W. Industries, Inc., Chgo., 1982-84; v.p. corp. devel. Dart & Kraft, Inc., Northbrook, Ill., 1985-86; v.p. strategy and bus. devel. Premark Internat. Inc. (spinoff from Dart & Kraft), Deerfield, 1986-90; dep. U.S. Trade Rep. Exec. Office of the Pres., Washington, 1991-93; prof. strategy and internat mgmt. Northwestern U. Kellogg Grad. Sch. Mgmt., Evanston, Ill., 1993-94; pres. Fed. Res. Bank Chgo., 1994—2007. Bd. dirs. Conrail, Inc., 1994. Author: Teachers and Unions, 1966, Labor Relations in the Performing Arts: An Introductory Survey, 1970; co-author: Collective Negotiations for Teachers, 1966, Collective Bargaining in Public Employment, 1970, Strategic Planning in Business and Government, 1978; co-editor: Readings on Collective Negotiations in Public Education, 1967, Employment Relations in Higher Education, 1969, Women and Work, 1987; contbr. articles to profl. jours. Bd. trustees Lafayette Coll; mem. Coun. Foreign Location; dir. Chgo. Coun. Foreign Rels., Coun. Fgn. Rels. NYC, Northwestern Meml. Found., World Bus. Chgo., Chicagoland C. of C.; mem. governing bd. Ill. Coun. Econ. Edn.; 1st lt. AUS, 1959-60. Fellow Nat. Acad. Pub. Adnminstrn.; mem. Indsl. Rels. Rsch. Assn. (pres. 1987), Nat. Bur. Econ. Rsch. (chmn. 2002-05), Comml. Club Chgo. (civic com.), Econs. Club Chgo. (chmn. 2001-03). *

MOSKOWITZ, ANITA FIDERER, art historian, educator; arrived in US, 1941; d. Chayim Fiderer-Margolis and Sarah Just Fiderer; m. Martin Allen Moskowitz, Dec. 31, 1958; children: Andre Joseph Moskwitz, Eva Sarah. Cert., Cooper Union, NY, 1957; MA in Fine Arts, PhD in Fine Arts, NYU, NYC, 1978. Adj. instr. Bklyn Coll., 1971—73; adj. asst. prof. Cooper Union, 1981; from asst. prof. to prof. U. Stony Brook, NY, 1981—93, prof., 1993—, chairperson art dept., 2003—. Author: (book) The Sculpture of Andrea and Nino Pisano, 1986, Nicola Pisano's Arca di San Domenico and its Legacy, 1994, Italian Gothic Sculpture c. 1250-c. 1400, 2001, Nicola and Giovanni Pisano Pulpits: Pious Devotion, Pious Diversion, 2005; contbr. numerous articles to profl. jours. Fellow, NEH, 1988—89, 1994—95, Ctr. Advanced Study in Visual Arts, 2003; Villa I Tatti fellowship, Harvard U., 1979—80, Lila Acheson Wallace Reader's Digest grantee, 1996—99. Mem.: Verein zur Foerderung des Kunsthistorischen Inst., Renaissance Soc. Am., Internat. Ctr. Medieval Art, Italian Art Soc. (pres. 1995—97, v.p. 1993—95). Office: Art Dept Univ Stony Brook Stony Brook NY 11794-5400 Office Phone: 631-632-7260. Office Fax: 631-632-7261.

MOSKOWITZ, DAVID K., lawyer; b. Glen Burnie, Md., Apr. 24, 1958; m. Hallie A. Moskowitz. BA summa cum laude, Western Md. College, 1980; JD with honors, George Washington U., 1983. Corp. counsel MDC Holdings Inc., 1986—90; with Echostar Communications, Englewood, Colo., 1990, exec. v.p., gen. counsel, sec., dir. Mem.: Am. Corp. Counsel Assn., Denver Bar Assn., Colo. Bar Assn., ABA. Office: Echostar Communications 9601 S Meridan Blvd Englewood CO 80112 Home: 7 Waterside Ter Englewood CO 80113-4141 Office Phone: 303-723-1040. Office Fax: 303-723-1699. Business E-Mail: david.moskowitz@echostar.com. *

MOSKOWITZ, HAROLD J., lawyer; b. NYC, Oct. 8, 1940; BS, CUNY, 1962; JD, St. John's U., 1965. Bar: NY 1966, DC 1972, US Dist. Ct. Ea. Dist. NY, US Dist. Ct. So. Dist. NY. Founding ptnr. Wilson, Elser, Moskowitz, Edelman & Dicker LLP, NYC, vice chmn. exec. com. Mem.: ABA, Profl. Liability Underwriting Soc., DC Bar Assn., Internat. Bar Assn., NY State Bar Assn., Def. Rsch. Inst., Assn. of the Bar of the City of NY. Office: Wilson Elser Moskowitz Edelman & Dicker LLP 23rd Fl 150 E 42nd St New York NY 10017-5639 Office Phone: 212-490-3000 ext. 2230. Office Fax: 212-490-3038. Business E-Mail: moskowitzh@wemed.com.

MOSKOWITZ, HERBERT, management educator; b. Paterson, NJ, May 26, 1935; s. David and Ruth (Abrams) Moskowitz; m. Heather Mary Lesgnier, Feb. 25, 1968; children: Tobias, Rebecca, Jonas. BS in Mech. Engring., Newark Coll. Engring., 1956; MBA, U.S. Internat. U., 1964; PhD, UCLA, 1970. Rsch. engr. GE, 1956-60; systems design engr. Gen. Dynamics Convair, San Diego, 1960-65; asst. prof. Purdue U., West Lafayette, Ind., 1970-75, assoc. prof., 1975-79, prof., 1979-85, Disting. prof. mfg. mgmt., 1985-87, James B. Henderson Disting. prof., 1987-91, dir. Dauch Ctr. Mgmt. Mfg. Enterprises, 1991—2005, Lewis B. Cullman Disting. prof. mfg. mgmt., 1991—. Cons. AT&T, Inland Steel Co.; adv. panelist NSF, 1990—. Author: Management Science and Statistics Texts, 1975—90; assoc. editor Decision Scis. Jour., 1984—90, Jour. Behavioral Decision Making, 1986—90; contbr. articles to jours. in field. Bd. dirs. Sons of Abraham Synagogue, Lafayette; mem. Lafayette Klezmorem, 1973—. Capt. USAF, 1956—60. Recipient Disting. Doctoral Student award, UCLA Alumni Assn., 1969—70; Fulbright Rsch. scholar, 1985—86. Fellow: Decision Scis. Inst. (sec. 1985—87, v.p. 1978—80); mem.: Ops. Rsch. Soc. Am./Inst. Mgmt. Sci. (liaison officer 1977—, panelist, advisor NSF and Fulbright Scholar program 1993—), Pi Tau Sigma, Tau Beta Pi. Jewish. Avocations: jewish music, tennis. Home: 1430 N Salisbury St West Lafayette IN 47906-2420 Office: Purdue Univ Krannert Sch Mgmt 100 S Grant St West Lafayette IN 47907-2076 Home Phone: 765-497-1483.

MOSKOWITZ, JAY, health science association administrator, educator, dean; b. NYC, Jan. 9, 1943; s. Murray and Helene Moskowitz; m. Joanne Cathy Schindelheim, Dec. 27, 1970; children: Michael Bradley, Andrew Cory. BS, Queens Coll., 1964; postgrad., CUNY, 1965; PhD, Brown U., 1969. From research assoc. in pharmacology to dep. dir. NIH, Bethesda, Md., 1969—93, dep. dir. sci. policy and tech. transfer, prin. dep. dir., 1993; with Nat. Heart, Lung and Blood Inst., Bethesda, 1976—86; acting dir. Nat. Inst. Deafness and Other Comm. Disorders, Bethesda, 1988—90, dep. dir., 1993—95; sr. assoc. dean rsch. devel., prof. pub. health scis. Wake Forest U. Sch. Medicine, Winston-Salem, NC, 1995—2001, sr. assoc. dean, 1997—2001; assoc. v.p. health sci. rsch. Pa. State U., University Park, 2002—, vice dean rsch. coll. medicine, 2002—07, prof. medicine, 2002—07; chief sci. officer Milton Hershey Med. Ctr., Pa., 2004—07; pres. Health Scis. SC, Columbia, 2007—. Contbr. articles to profl. jours. Served to lt. comdr. USPHS. Recipient Meritorious award William A. Jump Meml. Found., 1977, Dir.'s award NIH, 1978, Superior Svc. award USPHS, 1980, performance awards Sr. Exec. Svc., Presdl. Meritorious Exch. Rank award 1989, Disting. Svc. award HHS, 1991, Disting. Svc. award Nat. Inst. on Deafness and Other Comm. Disorders, 1994. Mem. AAAS, Soc. Exptl. Biology and Medicine, N.C. Inst. Medicine. Jewish. Home: 1760 Adeline Dr Mechanicsburg PA 17050 Office: Penn State College Medicine 500 University Hershey PA 00033 Home Phone: 717-732-1874; Office Phone: 717-531-7199. Business E-Mail: jmoskowitz@psu.edu.

MOSKOWITZ, JOEL STEVEN, lawyer; b. NYC, Jan. 14, 1947; s. Jack I. and Myra (Shor) M.; m. Anna Boucher; children: David, Michael, Ellen. BA, UCLA, 1967, JD, 1970. Bar: Calif. 1971, U.S. Ct. Appeals (9th cir.) 1971, U.S. Ct. Appeals (D.C. cir.) 1975, U.S. Supreme Ct. 1975, U.S. Ct. Appeals (2d cir.) 1979. Dep. atty. gen. Calif. Dept. Justice, Sacramento, 1970-83; dep. dir. Calif. Dept. Health Svcs., Sacramento, 1983-85; of counsel Gibson, Dunn & Crutcher, LA, 1985-88, ptnr., 1988-96, Moskowitz, Brestoff, Winston & Blinderman LLP, 1996—. Author: Environmental Liability in Real Property Transactions, 1995; contbr. articles to legal publs. Mem. Phi Beta Kappa. Office: 1880 Century Park E Ste 300 Los Angeles CA 90067-1631 Home Phone: 310-373-9790; Office Phone: 310-373-9790. Personal E-mail: joel_s_moskowitz@yahoo.com. Business E-Mail: joel@moskowitzhq.com.

MOSKOWITZ, MICHAEL ARTHUR, neuroscientist; b. NYC, May 26, 1942; s. Irving Lawrence and Clara (Dranoff) M.; m. Mary Henderson, May 18, 1991; 1 child, Jenna Rachel. AB, Johns Hopkins U., 1964; MD, Tufts U., 1968; MSc (hon.), Harvard U., 1992. Diplomate Am. Bd. Psychiaty and Neurology, Am. Bd. Internal Medicine. Intern Yale U. Dept. Medicine, 1968-69, resident, 1969-71; resident in neurology Peter Bent Brigham Children Hosp., 1971-74; asst. prof. Med. Sch., Harvard U., Boston, 1975-79, assoc. prof., 1979-92; prof. divsn. health sci. and tech. Harvard-MIT, Boston, 1992—. Established investigator Am. Heart Assn., 1980-85; neurophysiologist and assoc. neurologist Mass. Gen. Hosp., Boston, 1981—; H.J. Barnett lectr. Canadian Heart Assn., Queens U., Kingston, Ont., 1993—, Witter lectr. U. Calif., San Francisco, 1994—, Barraquer-LaFora lectr. Spanish Neurol. Soc., Barcelona, Spain, 1994—, Decade of the Brain lectr. Am. Acad. Neurology, 1995, Briggs lecture dept. pharmacology U. Tex., San Antonio, 1995, Richardson lectr. Canadian Neurol. Assn., 1998, John Graham lectr. Am. Assn. Study Headache, Merck Sharpe Dohme Neurosci. lectr. Birmingham, Eng., 2000, Soriano lectr. Am. Neurol. Assn., 2003, Dr. Chaim Mayman lectr. Beth Israel Hosp., Boston, 2003, Kenneth Carey lectr. U. Mich., 2006, Seymour Diamond lectr., 2007, others; chmn. sci. adv. bd. Max Plank Inst., Köln; program project dir. stroke and migraine NIH program projects, NIH rev. study sect. mem. 1982-85, 88-91, 97—; 2nd internat. hon. lectr. European Stroke Conf., 1997; cons. pharm. industry; chmn. sci. adv. bd. Max Planck Inst., U. of Ottawa, Can., Queen's Neurosc. Inst.; mem. sic. adv. bd. Queen's Med. Ctr., Honolulu, U. Ottawa. Editl. bd. Stroke, Acta Neurol. Scandinavica Cephalalgia, Jour. Cerebral Blood Flow & Metabolism, Cerebrovascular Disease; editor: Animal Models of Headache, 1996; basic sci. editor Stroke (AHA jour.); contbr. numerous articles to profl. jours; patentee in field. MIT postdoctoral fellow, 1974-76, Alfred Sloan Found. fellow, 1978-80; recipient Enrico Greppi award Italian Neurology Soc., 1986, 88, Tchr.-Investigator award Nat. Inst. Neurol. Disease and Stroke, 1975-80, Zülch prize Max-Planck Soc./Inst., 1996, John Graham award AASH, 1998, Arnold Friedman award Am. Headache Soc., Thomas Willis award Am. Stroke Assn., 2006, C. Miller Fisher award Am. Stroke Assn. N.E. affiliate, 2005, Top 200 Most Highly Cited in Neurosci., Info. Svcs. Inst.; rsch. grantee Bristol-Myers Squibb, 1993—, MGH Interdepartmental Stroke Ctr. Mem. Am. Heart Assn. (nat. rsch. com. 1991-96, exec. com. stroke coun. 1991-96), Am. Neurol. Assn. (Soriano lectr., 2003, 04), Am. Heart and Stroke Assn. (co-chair program com. 2001—), Am. Acad. Neurology, Am. Pain Soc., Soc. Neurosci., Internat. Soc. for Cerebral Blood Flow and Metabolism (bd. dirs., pres. 2001—), Internat. Symposium Pharm. of Cerebral Ischemia, Can. Neurol. Soc. (hon.). Achievements include research in neuroscientific, neurology literature including stroke and migraine. Office: Mass Gen Hosp Charleston Navy Yard 149 13th St Charlestown MA 02129-2020 Home Phone: 617-489-0343; Office Phone: 617-726-8442.

MOSKOWITZ, RANDI ZUCKER, nurse; b. NYC, Oct. 19, 1948; d. Seymour and Gertrude (Levy) Zucker; m. Marc N. Moskowitz, July 11, 1976. RN, Jewish Hosp. and Med. Ctr., 1969; BA, Marymount Manhattan Coll., 1975; MS, Hunter Coll., 1979; MBA, Columbia U., 1990. Gen. staff nurse neurosurgery unit N.Y. Hosp., NYC, 1969—71, sr. staff nurse recovery rm., 1971—76, nurse coord. utilization rev., 1976—79; health educator Office of Cancer Commn. Meml. Sloan-Kettering Cancer Ctr., NYC, 1979—81, adminstr. Surg. Day Hosp., 1990—98; adminstrv. nurse oncologist Bklyn. Cmty. Hosp. and Meth. Hosp., 1981—83, grants coord. radiotherapy dept., 1983—86; adminstr. Ambulatory Oncology Ctr. Columbia-Presbyn. Med. Ctr., NYC, 1986—89; mgr. Oncology Svcs., St. Vincent Cath. Med. Ctrs., Jamaica, NY, 1999—2006; adminstr. pediat. oncology Columbia U. Med. Ctr., NYC, 2006—. Masters prof. oncology Columbia U. Sch. Nursing. Co-editor Oncology Nursing: Advances, Treatments and Trends into the Twenty-first Century; contbr. articles to profl. jours. Mem. N.Y. Assn. Ambulatory Care, Oncology Nursing Soc. (sec. N.Y.C. chpt. 1983-87, pres. 1988-89). Home: 446 E 86th St Apt 5F New York NY 10028-6474 Office: Columbia Univ Med Ctr 161 Ft Washington Ave New York NY 10032 Office Phone: 212-342-3455. Personal E-mail: rm2505@columbia.edu.

MOSKOWITZ, ROLAND WALLACE, internist; b. Shamokin, Pa., Nov. 3, 1929; MD, Temple U., 1953. Intern Temple U. Hosp., Phila., 1953-54; fellow in internal medicine Mayo Clinic, Rochester, Minn., 1954-55, 57-60; mem. staff U. Hosps. Cleve.; prof. medicine Case Western Res. U. Sch. Medicine, Cleve. Mem.: ACR, Alpha Omega Alpha. Office: Parkway Med Ctr 3609 Park East Dr STe 307N Beachwood OH 44122

MOSKOWITZ, ROSS F., lawyer; b. NYC, Feb. 8, 1959; BA, George Washington Univ., 1981; JD, NY Law Sch., 1984. Bar: NY 1985. Exec. dir. NYC Indsl. Devel. Agy., 1994—98; exec. v.p. NYC Econ. Devel. Corp., 1994—98; with real estate practice group Stroock & Stroock & Lavan LLP, NYC, 1998—, now also hiring ptnr. Bd. dir. Lawyers Alliance for NY, 1991—95; mem., econ. devel. com and zoning and esign com. Real Estate Bd., NYC, 1999—; tech. adv. com. mem. Group of 35, Schumer task force on NYC comml. space, 2000—01; bd. dir. Bklyn. Navy Yard Devel. Corp., 2002—. Office: Stroock & Stroock & Lavan LLP 1809 Maiden Ln New York NY 10038-4982 Office Phone: 212-806-5550. Office Fax: 212-806-6006. Business E-Mail: rmoskowitz@stroock.com.

MOSKOWITZ, STANLEY ADAM, finance company executive; b. NYC, June 8, 1956; s. Sol and Kate (Mermelstein) M.; m. Eve Kronenberger, Sept. 20, 1981 (div Apr. 2003); children: Alana, Kate. BA, Queens Coll., 1978; MBA in Fin., St. John's U., 1980. Sr. credit analyst Mfrs. Hanover Leasing Corp., NYC, 1979-81; gen. ptnr. Exec. Leasing Co., NYC, 1981-83; pres. Execulease Corp., Elmont, NY, 1983-97; pres., CEO QuesTech Fin. LLC, Danbury, Conn., 1998—2007, Petroleum & Franchise Capital LLC, Danbury, 2007—. Treas. UFA/Fedn. of Greenwich, Conn., 1997-2003. Named finalist, Ernst & Young Entrepreneur of Yr., 2001. Mem. Ea. Assn. Equipment Lessors (chmn. pub. rels. 1985-90, bd. dirs. 1988-92, Meretorious Svc. award 1986-87, chmn. ethics com. 1991-92), Omicron Delta Epsilon. Republican. Jewish. Avocations: reading, bicycling. Office: QuesTech Fin LLC 33 Mill Plain Rd Danbury CT 06811-6101 Office Phone: 203-778-1000. E-mail: sammy@qtfc.com.

MOSKOWITZ, WILLIAM B., cardiologist; b. Bronx, NY, Feb. 23, 1954; s. Arthur and Helen R. Moskowitz; m. Gail Shookoff, May 30, 1993; children: Michael J., Holly M., Andrea D., Juliana R. BS, U. Ctrl. Fla., 1975; MD, U. South Fla., Tampa, 1978. Diplomate Am. Bd. Pediat., 1985, Am. Bd. Pediatric Cardiology. Prof. pediat. and internal medicine, dir. pediatric cardiology fellowship program, dir. pediatric catheterization lab. Va. Commonwealth U. Health Scis., Richmond, Va., 1984—. Fellow: Soc. Cardiac Angiography and Intervention, Am. Acad. Pediat. (sec.-treas. Va. chpt.); mem.: Am. Coll. Cardiology. Office: Virginia Commonwealth U Health Scis PO Box 980543 Richmond VA 23298-0543 Office Phone: 804-828-9143. Office Fax: 804-828-8517. E-mail: wmoskowitz@mcvh-vcu.edu.

MOSKUS, JERRY RAY, retired academic administrator; b. Springfield, Ill., Dec. 10, 1942; s. Raymond Charles and Jean (Riley) M.; children: Elizabeth, Jane. BS in English, Ill. State U., 1965, MS in English, 1968, PhD in Edn. Adminstrn., 1983. Tchr. English Saybrook (Ill.) Arrowsmith High Sch., 1966-69; instr. Lincoln Land CC, Springfield, 1969-71, asst. to pres., 1971-73, dir. rsch., 1973-75, dean, 1975-84, v.p. acad. svcs., 1984-85; exec. v.p. Des Moines Area CC, Ankeny, Iowa, 1985-90; pres. Lane CC, Eugene, Oreg., 1990—2001, Metro. CC, Omaha, 2001—05; ret. Mem. Am. Assn. C.C.s (bd. dir. 1999-2001), League for Innovation, Phi Delta Kappa, Sigma Tau Delta. Home: 1100 County Rd P15 Arlington NE 68002-5621 Business E-Mail: jmoskus@gmail.com.

MOSLER, BRUCE E., real estate company executive; b. NYC; s. John and Sheila Sanders Mosler; m. Wendy Beth Fass, Aug. 15, 1981. Grad., Duke U., 1980. Salesman comml. leasing divsn. Newmark & Co.; exec. v.p. Cushman & Wakefield, Inc., NYC, pres. U.S. ops., 2000—, CEO, 2005—, also bd. dirs. Bd. mem. Modell Found., Urban Tech.; mem. bd. govs., exec. com. Real Estate Bd. N.Y.; mem. profl. svcs. adv. coun. Lower Manhattan Devel. Corp. Bd. mem. Fisher Ctr. Alzheimer's Rsch. Found., Fuqua Bus. Sch. Duke U.; capital campaign com. Am. Cancer Soc.; bd. mem. Bowery Residents Com., Intrepid Mus. Found., Achilles Track Club, Kingsbrook Hosp. Named Property Svcs. Exec. of Yr., Comml. Property News, 2002, Brokerage Exec. of Yr., 2004; named one of 40 Under 40, Crain's N.Y. Bus., 1994; recipient Deal of the Yr. award, Real Estate Bd. NY, 1999, 2000, Kenneth R. Gerrety Humanitarian award, 2003. Office: Cushman & Wakefield Inc 51 W 52nd St New York NY 10019-6178 Office Phone: 212-841-7500. Office Fax: 212-841-7767. *

MOSLEY, DANIEL LYNN, lawyer; b. Birmingham, Ala., Nov. 2, 1956; s. Lynn Houston and Phyllis (Stanley) M.; m. Heather Stanton, Jan. 26, 1991. BA, U. Ala., 1977, JD, 1980; LLM, NYU, 1981. Assoc. Sullivan & Cromwell, NYC, 1981-84, Cravath, Swaine & Moore, NYC, 1984-87, ptnr., 1987—. Bd. dirs. Greenwich Hosp., Pinkerton Found., William S. Paley Found., William E. Simon Found., Edward J. Noble Found., Thomas J. Watson Found. Mem. Ala. Bar Assn., N.Y. State Bar Assn., Assn. of Bar of City of N.Y. Office: Cravath Swaine & Moore 825 8th Ave Fl 38 New York NY 10019-7475 Office Phone: 212-474-1696. Office Fax: 212-474-3700. Business E-Mail: dmosley@cravath.com.

MOSLEY, MARY MAC, retired librarian; b. Rome, Ga., Nov. 11, 1926; d. William McKinley and Mary (Caldwell) H.; m. Samuel A. Mosley, June 12, 1946 (div. 1964); children: Samuel A. Jr., Pamela Ann, James Irwin. Student, Ga. State Coll. for Women, 1943-45; BS, Auburn U., 1947; cert. in teaching, Athens Coll., 1963; M in Library, Emory U., 1968. Tchr. sci. Rome City Schs., 1964-66; extension libr. Tri-County Regional Libr., 1966-67; libr. Shorter Coll., 1967-68, assoc. prof. libr. sci., 1968-76, dir. libr. svcs., 1968-93. Ch. linr., Decaon, historian Christian Women's Fellowship, 1st Christian Ch., 1998—; corr. sec. Rome Symphony Women's Assn., v.p., 1996-99, pres., 1999-2001; vol. Good Neighbor Ministry, Rome Floyd County Libr. Mem. ALA, AAUW (pres. Rome br. 1974-1976, v.p. 2002-2004, 2006), Delta Kappa Gamma. Democrat. Mem. Christian Ch. Avocations: piano, reading, gardening, bridge. Home: 205 Benton Dr Rome GA 30165-1703 E-mail: marymacmo@bellsouth.net.

MOSLEY, MARY NELL H., retired elementary school educator; b. Bowdon, Ga., June 27, 1927; d. Lee Alexander and Lizzie Annie (Kight) Hunt; m. Loye Edmon Harrell (dec.); children: Dennis Calvin Harrell, Joel Vincent Harrell; m. John Wesley Mosley, July 14, 1967. BS, Rust Coll., Holly Springs, Miss., 1953, HHD (hon.), 2005; MEd, Miss. State U., Starkville, 1978. Tchr. Oktibbeha County Sch., Sturgis, Miss., 1950—52, Starkville, 1955—62, prin., 1952—55; tchr. Starkville Pub. Sch., 1962—70, 1975—84, Winona Pub. Sch., Miss., 1970—75; ret., 1984. Chairperson UNICEF, Starkville. Named Honoree of the Yr., NAACP, Alumni of the Yr., Rust Coll., 1972, Tchr. of the Yr., Starkville Pub. Sch., 1984; recipient Emma Elzy award, United Meth. Ch., 2001. Mem.: Min. Wives Oktibbeha County (sec. S.E. NC), Zeta Phi Beta. Methodist. Avocations: travel, reading, gardening, cooking. Home: 72 Chickasaw Dr Starkville MS 39759

MOSLEY, RAYMOND A., archivist; b. Greenville, Miss., July 27, 1947; s. Raymond Clay and Grace Elizabeth (Correro) M.; m. Julia A. Fisk. BA, Miss. State U., 1969; postgrad., Georgetown U. Dir. Records Appraisal Disposition Divsn., Nat. Archives, 1981-84; dep. asst. archivist Fed. Records Ctrs., 1984-89, chief of staff, 1989-94; asst. archivist Spl. & Regional Archives The Nat. Archives & Records Adminstrn., 1994-96, dir. Office Fed. Register, 1996—. Office: The Nat Archives & Records Adminstrn 8601 Adelphi Rd College Park MD 20740 E-mail: raymondamosley@hotmail.com, ray.mosley@fedreg.nara.gov. *

MOSLEY, TIMOTHY Z. See TIMBALAND

MOSLEY, WALTER, writer; b. LA, Jan. 12, 1952; s. LeRoy and Ella Mosley; m. Joy Kellman (div.), 1987. Student, Goddard Coll., 1971; BA, Johnson State Coll., 1977; PhD (hon.), City Coll., CUNY. Artist in residence Africana Studies Inst., NYU, NYC, 1996—. Bd. dir. Full Frame Documentary Film Festival. Author: (fiction) Devil in a Blue Dress, 1990 (Shamus award Private Eye Writers Am. 1990, Edgar award nomination Mystery Writers Am. 1990), A Red Death, 1991, White Butterfly, 1992, Black Betty, 1994, RL's Dream, 1995, A Little Yellow Dog, 1996, Gone Fishin', 1997, Always Outnumbered, Always Outgunned: The Socrates Fortlow Stories, 1998, Blue Light, 1998, Walkin' the Dog, 1999, Fearless Jones: A Novel, 2001, Futureland: Nine Stories of an Imminent Future, 2001, Bad Boy Brawley Brown, 2002, Six Easy Pieces, 2003, Fear Itself: A Mystery, 2003, The Man in My Basement, 2004, Little Scarlet, 2004, Cinnamon Kiss, 2005, The Wave, 2005, Fortunate Son, 2006, Fear of the Dark, 2006, Killing Johnny Fry: A Sexistential Novel, 2006; (non-fiction) Workin' on the Chain Gang: Shaking Off the Dead Hand of History, 2000, What Next: An African American Initiative Toward World Peace, 2003, Life Out of Context: Which Includes a Proposal for the Non-violent Takeover of the House of Representatives, 2006, This Year You Write Your Novel, 2007; (children's books) 47, 2005; writer, prodr. (films) Devil in a Blue Dress, 1995. Recipient John Creasey Meml. award, Black Caucus of the Am. Library Assn. Literary award, O. Henry award, 1996, Anisfield-Wolf Book award, 1996, TransAfrican Internat. Literary prize, 1998, Risktaker award Sundance Inst., 2004, Carl Brandon Soc. Parallax award, 2006. Mem.: Mystery Writers Am. (past pres.), Manhattan Theater Club, Poetry Soc. Am. (bd. dir.), Nat. Book Found., TransAfrica (bd. dir.). Mailing: c/o Nation Books 8th fl 33 Irving Place New York NY 10003 *

MOSMAN, MICHAEL W., federal judge, former prosecutor; b. Eugene, Ore. BA, Utah State U., 1981; JD, Brigham Young U., 1984. Law clk. U.S. Ct. Appeals, 1984—85, U.S. Supreme Ct., 1985—86; assoc. Miller, Nash, Portland, Oreg., 1986—88; asst. U.S. atty. Dist. Oreg. U.S. Dept. Justice, 1988—2001, U.S. atty. Dist. Oreg., 2001—03; judge U.S. Dist. Ct., Oreg., 2003—. Office: 1000 SW 3rd Ave Portland OR 97204-2902

MOSNER, LAWRENCE J., retired financial administration company executive; BA, Midland Coll., Fremont, Nebr.; MBA, Roosevelt Univ. With Sears Roebuck & Co.; exec. v.p., COO Hanover Direct; pres. Deluxe Direct, Shoreview, Minn., 1995—97, Deluxe Fin. Svcs., Shoreview, Minn., 1997; exec. v.p. Deluxe Corp., Shoreview, Minn., 1997—2001, vice chmn., 1999—2001, chmn., CEO, 2001—05. Office Phone: 651-483-7111.

MOSORA-STAN, FLORENTINA IOANA, physics professor; b. Cluj, Romania, Jan. 7, 1940; arrived in Belgium, 1968; d. Oprea and Cornelia (Stanescu) M.; m. Stephan Stan, Jan. 22, 1977; 1 child, Guy Bart. B in Biol. Sci. with highest distinction, U. Bucharest, Romania, 1961, B in Phys. Sci. with highest distinction, 1967, PhD in Biophysics cum laude, 1971. Cert. biologist and physicist. Rsch. fellow U. Bucharest, 1967-71, U. Liege, Belgium, 1971-74, maitre de conferences, 1974-75; head rsch. fellow Inst. Physics, U. Liege, Belgium, 1975-79, lectr., 1979-88, prof., 1988—. Author: Elements of General Physics and Biophysics, vol. 1, 1974, vol. 2, 1975, Introduction to the Mechanics of Physiologic Fluids, 1984-85, Mechanics of Microcirculation, 1990; Editor: Biomechanical Transport Processes, 1991. Mem. European Med. Rsch. Coun. Devel. of Resch. in Nutrition and Stable Isotopes, 1991—. Decorated officer Ordre of Leopold II, (Belgium), 1981, comdr. Ordre de la Couronne (Belgium, 1992; recipient Agathon de Potter prize Royal Acad. Belgium, 1982. Mem. Stareso Oceanographic Rsch. Calvi (sci. coun. 1987—), Isotopes Stables (v.p. 1987—), Inst. Recherches Marines et Interactions Air-Mer (pres. 1989—), Hemo Liege (founder), Belgian Soc. Biophysics, Internat. Soc. Rsch. Circulation and Environ. Diseases, N.Y. Acad. Scis. Roman Catholic. Avocations: swimming, gymnastics. Home: Residence Verdi Av Blonden 7 4000 Liège Belgium Office: U Liege Inst Physics B5 4000 Liège Belgium

MOSPAW, KATHAN J., retired social studies educator; b. Woonsocket, RI, Dec. 29, 1945; d. George Harold and Dorothy Wilson Moroney; m. Jeffrey G. Mospaw (div.); children: Jennifer Mospaw Wilson, Elizabeth Mospaw Schaafsma. AB, Syracuse U., NY, 1967; MEd, R.I. Coll., Providence, 1977; JD, So. New Eng. Sch. Law, New Bedford, Mass., 1994. Bar: Mass. 1994; cert. tchr. R.I. Tchr. social studies Burrillville Sch. Dept., Harrisville, RI, 1969—2004; ret., 2004. Exec. bd. NEA R.I., Cranston, 1990—2000; pres. Burrillville Tchrs. Assn., Harrisville, 1990—2000. Chmn. No. R.I. Coun. Arts, Woonsocket, 1986—90, Burrillville Orgn. Substance Abuse Prevention, Pascoag, RI, 1990—2005; vol. local schs.; sec. Burrillville Dem. Town Com., Harrisville, 2005—07, chmn., 2007—; bd. dir. R.I. Legal - Ednl. Partnership, Providence, 1992—2000. Named R.I. Law Related Tchr. of Yr., R.I. Legal - Ednl. Partnership, 1992. Mem.: Sr. Citizens Assn. (sec. 2004—).

MOSS, ADAM, editor; b. Bklyn., May 6, 1957; s. Paul and Abigail (Wender) M. BA, Oberlin Coll., 1979. Assoc. editor Rolling Stone Collected Papers, NYC, 1979-81; asst. editor, assoc. editor, sr. editor, mng. editor, dep. editor Esquire mag., NYC, 1981-87; editor in chief 7 Days, NYC, 1987-90; cons. editor NY Times, NYC, 1991—93; editl. dir. NY Times Mag., NYC, 1993—98, editor, 1998—2003; assoc. mng. editor NY Times, 2002—03, asst. mng. editor, features NYC, 2003—04; editor NY Mag., NYC, 2004—. Named Editor of the Yr., Advt. Age, 2001; recipient 5 Nat. Mag. awards for Gen. Excellence 250,000-500,000 circulation, for Profile Writing, for Mag. Sect, for Design, and for Interactive Feature, Am. Soc. Mag. Editors, 2007. Mem.: Am. Soc. Mag. Editors (sec. 2007—08). Office: NY Mag 444 Madison Ave New York NY 10022 *

MOSS, ALAN C., physician, researcher; MB, BCh, BAO, Royal Coll. Surgeons Ireland, Dublin, 1997. Dir. translational rsch. Beth Israel Deaconess Med. Ctr., Boston, 2007—. Contbr. articles to profl. jours. Mem.: Royal Coll. Physicians Ireland, Am. Gastroenterolgy Assn. Office: Beth Israel Deaconess Med Ctr 330 Brookline Ave Boston MA 02446 Office Phone: 617-667-2136.

MOSS, AMBLER HOLMES, JR., lawyer, educator, former ambassador; b. Balt., Sept. 1, 1937; s. Ambler Holmes and Dorothea Dandridge (Williams) M.; m. Serena Welles, May 6, 1972; children: Ambler H., Benjamin Sumner, Serena Montserrat, Nicholas George Oliver. BA, Yale U., 1960; JD, George Washington U., 1970. Bar: D.C., Fla. Joined Fgn. Svc., Dept. State, 1964; vice consul Barcelona, 1964—66; adviser U.S. del. to OAS, 1966—69; Spanish desk officer Dept. State, Washington, 1968—70; assoc. Coudert Bros., Washington, 1971—73, resident atty. Brussels, 1973—76; mem. U.S. Negotiating Team for Panama Canal treaties, 1977; dep. asst. Sec. of State, Washington, 1977—78; amb. to Panama Am. Embassy, Panama City, 1978—82; of counsel Greenberg, Traurig, LLP, Miami, 1982—87, 1995—; prof. U. Miami, Fla., 1984—, dean Grad. Sch. Internat. Studies, 1984—94. Bd. dirs. Espirito Santo Bank of Fla., Caucedo Investments Inc. Mem. Panama Canal Consultative Com., 1995-2000. With USN, 1960-64. Mem. ABA, Am. Soc. Internat. Law, Am. Fgn. Svc. Assn., Coun. Fgn. Rels., Am. Legion, Inter-Am. Dialogue (Washington), Navy League, Greater Miami C. of C. (gov. 1983-86), Royal Inst. Internat. Affairs (London), Internat. Inst. Strategic Studies (London), Army and Navy Club, Order of the Coif. Home: 5711 San Vicente St Coral Gables FL 33146-2724 Business E-Mail: ahmoss@miami.edu, mossa@gtlaw.com.

MOSS, ARTHUR HENSHEY, lawyer; b. Reading, Pa., July 26, 1930; s. John Arthur and Christine Bracken (Henshey) M.; m. E. Leslie Fritz, Feb. 1982; 1 child by previous marriage, John Arthur. AB, Williams Coll., 1952; JD, U. Pa., 1955. Bar: Pa. 1956. Assoc. Montgomery, McCracken, Walker & Rhoads, Phila., 1960-69, ptnr., 1969-2000, of counsel, 2000—. Editor U. Pa. Law Rev., 1953-55; contbr. articles to profl. jours. Pres. Wayne Civic Assn., 1964—65; commr. gen. assembly Presbyn. Ch. (U.S.A.), 1983; steward, deacon Wayne Presbyn. Ch., 1966—72, 1979—84, 1989—95, ruling elder, 1966—72, 1979—84, 1989—95, clk. of session, 1973—74, 1978—89, trustee, 1987—93, Presbytery of Phila., 1984, 1994—2001, treas., 1996—2001; chmn. Radnor-Haverford-Marple Sewer Authority, 1968—83; bd. dir. John Bartram Assn., 1987—2002, treas., 1989—2002, emeritus dir., 2002—; trustee Radnor Twp. Meml. Libr., 2001—. Lt. JAGC USN, 1956—60. Mem. Radnor Hist. Soc. (dir., sec. 1978-90), Broadacres Trouting Assn., Athenaeum of Phila., Merion Golf Club, Edgemere Club. Home: 200 Walnut Ave Wayne PA 19087-3423 Office: Montgomery McCracken Walker & Rhoads 123 S Broad St Philadelphia PA 19109-1030 Office Phone: 215-772-1500.

MOSS, ARTHUR JAY, physician; b. White Plains, NY, June 21, 1931; s. Abraham Loeb and Ida (Bank) M.; m. Joy Folkman, June 23, 1957; children: Katherine, Deborah, David. BA, Yale U., 1953; MD, Harvard U., 1957. Resident Mass. Gen. Hosp., 1957-58, 60-61; fellow in cardiology med. ctr. U. Rochester, NY, 1961-65, from asst. to assoc. prof. sch. medicine and dentistry, 1966-71, clin. assoc. prof., 1971-82, clin. prof., 1982-91, prof. medicine, 1991—, dir. heart rsch. follow-up program med. ctr., 1971—. Mem. cardiology adv. com. Nat. Heart, Lung, and Blood Inst., NIH, 1980-82, chmn., 1982-84, mem. epidemiology and disease control study sect., 1998—. Author: Antiarrhythmic Agents, 1973; editor: Clinical Aspects of Life-threatening Arrhythmias, 1984, QT Prolongation and Ventricular Arrhythmias, 1992, Noninvasive Electrocardiology, 1995; editor-in-chief Ann. Noninvasive Electrocardiology, 1996—; mem. editl. bd. Am. Jour. Cardiology, 1988—, Jour. Am. Coll. Cardiology, 1997-2001, 2005—. Lt. USNR, 1958—60. Mem.: Assn. Am. Physicians, Alpha Omega Alpha. Home: 581 Claybourne Rd Rochester NY 14618-1224 Office: Univ Rochester Med Ctr PO Box 653 Rochester NY 14642-8653 Home Phone: 585-244-3809; Office Phone: 585-275-5391. Business E-Mail: heartajm@heart.rochester.edu.

MOSS, BERNARD, virologist, researcher; b. NYC, July 26, 1937; s. Jack and Goldie (Altman) M.; m. Toby Frima Lieberman, Dec. 25, 1960; children: Robert, Jennifer, David. BA, NYU, 1957, MD, 1961; PhD, MIT, 1967. Diplomate Am. Bd. Med. Examiners. Intern Children's Hosp., Boston, 1961-62; investigator, sect. head NIH, Bethesda, Md., 1966—, lab. chief, 1984—. Mem. adv. bd. Virus Res., 1984—, Current Opinion Biotech., 1989—. Assoc. editor Virology Jour., 1976-92, editor., 1992—; mem. editorial bd. Jour. of Virology, 1972—, Antimicrobial Agts. and Chemotherapy, 1973-79, Jour. Biol. Chemistry, 1982-87; AIDS rsch. Human Retroviruses, 1989—; contbr. more than 600 articles to profl. jours. Mem. adv. com. Am. Cancer Soc., N.Y.C., 1983-86; bd. dirs. Found. Advanced Edn. in Scis., Bethesda, 1985-91; mem. NIH AIDS vaccine selection com., 1989—. Served as med. dir. USPHS, 1966-98. Named one of 100 Most Innovative Scientists of 1986, Sci. Digest; recipient Solomon A. Berson Alumni Achievement award Sch. Medicine, NYU, Meritorious Svc. medal USPHS, Disting. Svc. medal USPHS, Dickson prize in medicine, Invitrogen award for eukaryotic gene expression, ICN Internat. prize in Virology, Taylor Internat. prize in medicine., Bristol-Myers Squibb Award, Distinguished Achievement in Infectious Disease Research, 2000. Fellow AAAS; mem. Am. Soc. for Biochemistry and Molecular Biology, Am. Acad. Microbiology, Am. Soc. Microbiology, Am. Soc. Virology (pres. 1995), Nat. Acad. Sci., Phi Beta Kappa, Sigma Xi, Alpha Omega Alpha. Office: NIH 4 Center Dr Bethesda MD 20892-0445 E-mail: bmoss@nih.gov.

MOSS, BILL RALPH, lawyer; b. Amarillo, Tex., Sept. 27, 1950; s. Ralph Voniver and Virginia May (Atkins) M.; 1 child, Brandon Price. BS with honors, West Tex. A&M U., 1972, MA, 1974; JD, Baylor U., 1976; cert. regulatory studies program, Mich. State U., 1981. Bar: Tex. 1976, U.S. Dist. Ct. (no. dist.) Tex. 1976, U.S. Dist. Ct. (we. dist.) Tex. 2005, U.S. Tax Ct. 1979, U.S. Ct. Appeals (5th cir.) 1983. Briefing atty. Ct. Appeals 7th Supreme Jud. Dist. Tex., Amarillo, 1976-77; assoc. Culton, Morgan, Britain & White, Amarillo, 1977-80; hearings examiner Pub. Utility Commn. Tex., Austin, 1981-83; asst. gen. counsel State Bar Tex., Austin, 1983-87; founder, owner Price & Co. Publs., Austin, 1987-97; asst. gen. counsel Tex. Ethics Commn., Austin, 1997—2004; asst. atty. gen. antitrust and civil medicaid fraud div. Office Atty. Gen., Tex., 2004—. Instr., lectr. West Tex. State U., Canyon, Ea. N.Mex. U., Portales, 1977-80; spkr. in field. Active St. Matthew's Episcopal Ch.; election inspector State of Tex., 1998—. Mem. ABA, Tex. Bar Assn., Nat. Orgn. Bar Counsel, Internat. Platform Assn., Capitol of Tex. Rotary Club, Alpha Chi, Lambda Chi Alpha, Omicron Delta Epsilon, Phi Alpha Delta, Sigma Tau Delta, Pi Gamma Mu. Home: 506 Explorer St Lakeway TX 78734-3447 Office: Office of Atty Gen William P Clements Bldg 300 W 15th St 9th Fl Austin TX 78701 Business E-Mail: bill.moss@oag.state.tx.us.

MOSS, CARRIE-ANNE, actress; b. Vancouver, British Columbia, Can., Aug. 21, 1967; m. Steven Roy, Nov. 1999; 2 children. Actor: (films) Flashfire, 1993, The Soft Kill, 1994, Terrified, 1995, Sabotage, 1996, Secret Life of Algernon, 1997, Lethal Tender, 1997, New Blood, 1999, The Matrix, 1999, Memento, 2000, The Crew, 2000, Red Planet, 2000, Chocolat, 2000, The Matrix Reloaded, 2003, (voice) Kid's Story, 2003, The Matrix Revolutions, 2003, Suspect Zero, 2004, Sledge: The Untold Story, 2005, The Chumscrubber, 2005, Mini's First Time, 2006, Fido, 2006, Disturbia, 2007, (TV films) Doorways, 1993; television appearances: L.A. Law, 1986, Baywatch, 1989, Dark Justice, 1991, Silk Stalkings, 1991, Street Justice, 1992, Nightmare Cafe, 1992, Forever Knight, 1992, Matrix, 1993, Models Inc., 1994, Nowhere Man, 1995, Nowhere Man, 1996, F/X: The Series, 1996, Viper, 1997. *

MOSS, DAVID, music company executive; Cert., Musician's Inst. in Hollywood, 1985; B of commerce in mktg and fin., Concordia U., 1989. Dir., sch. of fine arts Saidye Bronfman Ctr. for the Arts, 1994—96, exec. dir., 1996—2003; gen. dir. Montreal Opera, 2003—. Founding mem., mem. exec. com. Culture Montreal; apptd. to Groupe Conseil pour la Politique Culturelle de Montreal, 2002; appt. to bd. La Vitrine Culturelle de Montreal, 2003. Office: L'Opera de Montreal 260 Maisonneuve Blvd W Montreal PQ H2X 1Y9 Canada Office Phone: 514-985-2222.

MOSS, ERIC OWEN, architect; b. LA, July 25, 1943; BA, UCLA, 1965; MArch with honors, U. Calif., Berkeley, 1968, Harvard U., 1972. Prof. design So. Calif. Inst. Architecture, 1974—, dir., 2002—; prin. Eric Owen Moss Archs., Culver City, Calif., 1973—; Eliot Noyes chair Harvard U., Cambridge, Mass., 1990; Eero Saarinen chair Yale U., New Haven, 1991. Lectr. Hirshhorn Mus. Symposium, Washington, 1990, Nat. AIA Conv., 1990, Mus. Contemporary Art, LA, 1991, NY Archtl. League, 1991, Archtl. Assn. Ireland, Dublin, Archtl. Assn., London, 1991, Royal Coll. Art, London, 1991, Smithsonian Instn., Washington, 1992, U. Calif., Berkeley, 1992, Osterreichiaches Mus. fur Angewandte Kunst, Vienna, 1992, UCLA, 1992, Royal Danish Acad. Fine Arts, Copenhagen, 1993, U. Lund, Sweden, 1993, Mus. Finnish Architecture, Helsinki, 1993, Royal Acad. Arts, London, 1993, U. Pa., Phila., 1994, others; tchr. U. Tex., Austin, 1983, Wash. U., St. Louis, 1984, U. Ill., Chgo., 1985, Tulane U., New Orleans, 1985, U. Minn., Mpls., 1985, Columbia U., NYC, 1986, Rice U., Houston, 1988; participant various confs. Exhbns. of work include World Biennial of Architecture, Sofia, Bulgaria, 1989, Salle des Tirages du Credit Foncier de France, Paris, 1990, Bartlett Sch. Architecture and Urban Design, London, 1991, Gallery of Functional Art, Santa Monica, Calif., 1992, GA Gallery, Tokyo, 1992, Mus. fur Gestaltung Zurich, Switzerland, 1993, Santa Monica Mus. Art, 1993, Fonds Regional D'Art Contemporain du Centre, 1993, Aspen Art Mus., Colo., 1993, Centro de Arte y Comunicacion, Buenos Aires, 1993, Contemporary Arts Ctr., Cin., 1993, Philippe Uzzan Galerie, Paris, 1993, Contemporary Arts Ctr., Tours, France, 1993, Internat. Exhbn. Contemporary Architecture, Havana, Cuba, 1994, others. Recipient Progressive Architecture Design award, 1978, 92, Winning Interior Archtl. Record award, 1984, Interiors Design award, 1991, Award in Architecture, AAAL, 1999, Andrew W. Brunner Meml. prize, Architecture, 2007. Fellow AIA (LA awards 1977, 79, 83, 88, 90, Calif. Coun. awards 1981, 86, 88, LA Honor awards 1991, Nat. Honor awards 88, 89, Calif. Coun. Urban Design/Adaptive Re-Use awards 1991, Nat. Interior Design awards 1992, 94, LA Design awards 1992, 93, LA Gold Medal award 2001, Educator of Yr., 2006). Achievements include being subject of monographs and numerous articles in mags. and jours. Office: Eric Owen Moss Archs 8557 Higuera St Culver City CA 90232-2535 Office Phone: 310-839-1199. Office Fax: 310-839-7922. E-mail: mail@ericowenmoss.com. *

MOSS, GARY CURTIS, lawyer; b. Taylorville, Ill., Feb. 17, 1944; s. William Clary and Sophronia Irene (McClellan) M.; m. Judith K. Jones, April 14, 1945; children— Gary Curtis, Kristin Suzanne. B.A., U. Ill.-Champaign, 1966; J.D., U. Iowa-Iowa City, 1969. Bar: Iowa 1969, Calif. 1970, U.S. Dist. Ct. (cen. dist.) Calif. 1972, Nev. 1991, U.S. Ct. Appeals (9th cir.) 1974, U.S. Dist. Ct. (so. and no. dists.) Calif. 1981, U.S. Dist Ct. Nev. 1991. Assoc., O'Melveny & Myers, Los Angeles, 1969-75; assoc. Seyfarth, Shaw, Fairweather & Geraldson, Los Angeles, 1975-78, ptnr., 1978-87; judge pro tem West Los Angeles Mcpl. Ct., 1981-83, Pasadena Mcpl. Ct., 1983—; ptnr.-in-charge Las Vegas off., DLA Piper Rudnick Gray Cary, Las Vegas. Mem. ABA, State Bar Calif. (hearing referee, arbitrator mandatory fee arbitrations), State Bar Iowa, Los Angeles County Bar Assn. Republican. Club: Athletic (Los Angeles). Office: DLA Piper Rudnick Gray Cary Ste 400 3960 Howard Hughes Pkwy Las Vegas NV 89109-0993 Office Phone: 702-737-3433, 702-737-1612. Business E-Mail: gary.moss@piperrudnick.com.

MOSS, JEROME (JERRY) S., recording industry executive; b. Bronx, NY, May 8, 1935; s. Irving and Rose Moss; m. Ann Moss. BA, Brooklyn Coll. Record promoter, NYC, LA; co-founder Carnival Records, 1961; owner, co-founder A&M Records, 1962—94; co-founder Almo Sounds, 1994—2002; co-founder, chmn. Rondor Music Inc., 1994—. Founding mem. UCLArts Bd. of Visitors; bd. mem. Calif. Horse Racing Bd., 2004—. With US Army. Recipient Lifetime Achievement award, Rock and Roll Hall of Fame, 2006. Avocation: owns racehorse Giacomo, winner of the 131st Kentucky Derby, 2005. Office: 2440 Sepulveda Blvd Los Angeles CA 90064 also: 1010 Hurley Way Ste 300 Sacramento CA 95825

MOSS, KATE, model; b. Croydon, England, Jan. 16, 1974; 1 child, Lila Grace. With Storm Agy., England, Women Model Mgmt., NYC; model Calvin Klein Jeans, Yves Saint Laurent, Prada, Versace, Burberry, Celine, Gucci, Louis Vuitton, Chanel, Dior, Virgin Mobile, Rimmel, Nokion; clothing designer Topshop, 2007—. Appeared in films Unzipped, 1995, Catwalk, 1995, Beautopia, 1998, Blackadder Back and Forth, 1999, Original Copies, 1999, (TV films) Inferno, 1992, Naomi Conquers Africa, 1998, Astley's Way, 2001, We Know Where You Live, 2001, Terry & Liz, 2004, (TV series) French and Saunders, 1987; appeared in multiple music videos including "Kowalski" by Primal Scream, "I Just Don't Know What to do with Myself" by the White Stripes, "Something About The Way You Look Tonight" by Elton John, "Sex with strangers" by Marianne Faithfull and "Delia's Gone", "God's Gonna Cut You Down" by Johnny Cash Named Model of the Year, British Fashion Awards, 2006; named one of the World's Most Influential People, Time Magazine, 2007, World's Richest Model (#2), Forbes, 2007; recipient Lifetime Achievement award, Coun. Fashion Designers Am., 2005. Achievements include being the second highest paid model in the world, 99th richest woman in Britain. Office: Storm Model Mgmt 5 Jubilee Pl 1st Fl London SW3 3TD England *

MOSS, LESLIE OTHA, homeland security specialist; b. Detroit, Mar. 8, 1952; s. Lonnie and Emma (Robinson) M. BA, U. Mich., 1982, postgrad., 1990—. Cert. protection officer, security supr. Dept. Homeland Security, protection profl., security specialist 2005. Technician oper. rm. Sinai Hosp., Detroit, 1972-75; nurses' technician Detroit Osteo. Hosp., 1976-83; supr. Southfield Placement Ctr., Mich., 1983-85; rsch. asst. Wayne County Commr.'s Office, Detroit, 1985-86; fin. aid counselor Wayne State U., 1986-87; probation officer Dept. Corrections State of Mich., 1988—; exec. asst. Human Rights Dept., City of Detroit; rsch. asst. Law Dept. City of Detroit, 1990; asst. pers. mgr. Detroit Osteo. Hosp., 1991-93, Highland Pk. C.C., 1991-93; mental health worker Mich. Health Ctr.-Adult Mental Health and New Ctr. Hosp., Detroit, 1992-94; legal technician Ptnrs. Against Crime, Detroit, 1994; social work technician, 1994. Sgt. of arms Detroit Police Res., 1987—; intern, assoc. prodr. local TV sta., Detroit, 1993; mem. bd. advisors, mem. bd. govs. Am. Biog. Rsch. Inst., dep. gov., 1994; exec. cons. in field., 1993—; asst. pers. mgr., 1993—. Mem. re-election com. Mayor Coleman A. Young, Detroit, 1989-93; patient care counselor; adv. various causes, including industrialized Am., higher edn., automotive quality. Recipient Twentieth Century Achievement award Biog. Centre, 1994, Spl. Recognition award Detroit Pub. Sch. Sys., 1992, Internat. Man of Yr. award, 1992-93; award for mass media svc. participation Barden Cable Vision, Detroit, 1991, Man of the Yr. award, 1996, Disting. Alumni Award Mumford H.S. Detroit, 1996, Most Outstanding Men of the Twentieth Century award, 1999; named Most Admired Man of Decade, 1994, Disting. Alumnus, Detroit Pub. Schs. Mich., 1995, Most Admired Man of the Yr., State of Mich., 1995; named to Internat. Honors Hall of Fame, 1998, Millenium Hall of Fame, 1998; inducted 500 Leaders of Influence Pub., 2000. Mem. NAFE, NAACP (advisor 1989), Internat. Order of Merit, Assn. Pre-Med Students (cons. 1988—), Assn. Psychologists, Am. Biog. Rsch. Inst. Assn. (mem. bd. govs. 1993, dep. gov.), Internat. Platform Assn., U. Mich. Alumni Assn., Golden Key Internat. Honor Soc. (life), Kappa Alpha Psi, Phi Theta Kappa. Home and Office: 1190 Seward St Apt 306 Detroit MI 48202-2336

MOSS, LINDA ELAINE, science educator; d. Howard Adkins and Reva Helen Barnes Tribble; m. Leonard Joe Moss, July 25, 1980; children: Gayle Lynne Nichols, Cheryl Diane Zeiss. BS Agr., U. of Mo., 1972; BS in Chemistry Edn., Ark. State U., 1991, MS in Chemistry Edn., 1991, Specialist in C.C. Tchg., Biology, 1993, D of Ednl. Leadership, 2000. Lic. tchr. Ark. Acctg. clk. Empire Gas, Lebanon, Mo., 1972—73; sci. and fgn. lang. tchr. Poughkeepsie H.S., Ark., 1987—89, Evening Shade H.S., Ark., 1987—95; sci. instr. Ozarka Tech. Coll., Melbourne, Ark., 1993—95, Black River Tech. Coll., Pocahontas, Ark., 1995—. Beta delta phi chpt. adv. Phi Theta Kappa Internat. Honor Soc., Pocahontas, Ark., 2000—; sci. club adv. Black River Tech. Coll., Pocahontas, Ark., 1995—, north ctrl. accreditation steering com., 1998—2003, north ctrl. accreditation instl. integrity com. chair, 1998—2003; pres. black river coll. edn. assn. Ark. Edn. Assn., 1995—; chair, hazards identification com. Black River Tech. Coll., Pocahontas, 2003—. Mem. Keep Randolph County Beautiful, Pocahontas, Ark., 1998—2006. Recipient Ark. Acad. of Sci. Best Grad. Student Presentation, Ark. Acad. of Sci., 1995, Student Body Choice Tchr., Black River Tech. Coll. Student Coun., 1997, Phi Theta Kappa Faculty Scholar, Phi Theta Kappa Internat. Honor Soc., 2002, Most Disting. Faculty Advisor, Okla./Ark. Region Phi Theta Kappa Internat. Honor Soc., 2006, Empire Who's Who Registry of Executives and Professionals, 2005, Appreciation of Outstanding Svc., Okla./Ark. Region Phi Theta Kappa Internat. Honor Soc., 2006. Mem.: NEA, Ark. Edn. Assn. (assoc.; pres. local chpt. 1995—2006), Okla./Ark. Region Assn. of Chpt. Advisors Phi Theta Kappa Internat. Honor Soc., Phi Theta Kappa Internat. Honor Soc., Kappa Delta Phi Internat. Edn. Honor Soc. Home: 314 Elmont Road Maynard AR 72444 Office: Black River Tech Coll Highway 304 East Pocahontas AR 72455 Home Phone: 870-647-8416; 8708101746; Office Phone: 870-248-4000 4136. Office Fax: 870-248-4100. E-mail: lindam@blackrivertech.org.

MOSS, LOGAN VANSEN, lawyer; b. Atlanta, Apr. 17, 1957; s. Joseph Henry and Elise Louise (McCown); m. Janet Moss; children: Logan Jr., Hannah, Abigail. BA, Bates Coll., Lewiston, Maine, 1979; JD, U. Tulsa, Okla., 1982; MTS, Ave Maria U., Orchard Lake, Mich., 2003; cert. of Advanced Study in Bioethics and Health Policy, Loyola U., 2006. Bar: Okla. 1982, U.S. Dist. Ct. Okla. 1982, Maine 1984, U.S. Dist. Ct. Maine 1984, U.S. Supreme Ct. 1986, Tex. 1991. Law clk. to presiding justice Okla. Ct. Appeals, Tulsa, 1982—84; assoc. Strout, Payson et al, Rockland, Maine, 1984—87, Joseph M. Cloutier & Assocs., Camden, Maine, 1987—88, Armstrong & Assoc., Tulsa, 1988—91; asst. gen. counsel Temple-Inland Forest Products Corp., Diboll, Tex., 1991—2002; gen. counsel litig. Temple-Inland, Austin, 2003—. Named Best Bus. Atty. Large Staff Dept., Austin Bus. Jour., 2007. Republican. Roman Catholic. Avocation: catholic studies. Office: Temple Inland 1300 S Mopac Expy Austin TX 78746 Home Phone: 512-402-1688; Office Phone: 512-434-8050. Business E-Mail: loganmoss@templeinland.com.

MOSS, MADISON SCOTT, editor; b. Charlotte, NC, May 23, 1948; s. James Madison and Nellie Lee (Jenkins) M. BA in English, U. N.C., 1970. Editl. aide NASW, Inc., Washington, 1974, promotions specialist, 1974-79, assoc. editor, 1979-80, editor, 1980-90, mng. editor, 1990—. Campaign coord. Eugene McCarthy for Pres., Rutherford County, N.C., 1968. Recipient award for Pub. Excellence Comms. Concepts, 1993, 94, 95, 96, 97, 98, Bronze award newspaper gen. excellence Soc. Nat. Assn. Publs., 1996, Silver award, 1997, Bronze awards, 2005, 06. Mem. Am. Assn. Ret. Persons, U. N.C. Gen. Alumni Assn. Democrat. Office: NASW Inc 750 1st St NE Ste 700 Washington DC 20002-4241 Business E-Mail: naswnews@naswdc.org.

MOSS, MYRA ELLEN (MYRA MOSS ROLLE), philosophy educator; b. LA, Mar. 22, 1937; m. Andrew Rolle, Nov. 5, 1983. BA, U. Rome, Italy, 1958; PhD, Johns Hopkins U., Balt., 1965. Asst. prof. Santa Clara (Calif.) U., 1968-74; prof. Claremont McKenna Coll., 1975—, chmn. dept. philosophy, 1992-95. Assoc. dir. Gould Ctr. for Humanities, Claremont, Calif., 1993-94; adv. coun. Milton S. Eisenhower Libr./Johns Hopkins U., 1994-96, 2001—; vis. scholar Am. Acad. Rome, 2005. Author: Benedetto Croce Reconsidered, 1987, Mussolini's Fascist Philosopher: Giovanni Gentile Reconsidered, 2004, Italian edit., Armando, 2007; translator: Benedetto Croce's Essays on Literature & Literary Criticism, 1990; co-author: Values and Education, 1998; assoc. editor Special Issues; Journal of Value Inquiry, 1990-95 (Honorable Mention, Phoenix award); cons. editor Jour. Social Philosophy, 1988—; assoc. editor: Value Enquiry Book Series, 1990-95; editor: The Philosophy of José Gaos, by Pio Colonnello, Value Inquiry Book Series, 1997. Bogliasco fellow, Liguria, Italy, 2000; vis. scholar Am. Acad. Rome, 2005. Mem. Am. Philos. Assn., Am. and Internat. Soc. for Value Inquiry, Soc. for Aesthetics, Internat. Ctr. for the Arts, Humanities and Value Inquiry (assoc.), Collingwood Soc. (life), Phi Beta Kappa. Avocations: gardening, horseback riding. Office: Claremont McKenna Coll 850 Columbia Ave Claremont CA 91711-3901

MOSS, PATRICIA L., bank executive; m. Greg Moss; children: Jennifer, Jeffrey. BS in bus. adminstrn., Linfield Coll., Oreg.; masters studies Portland State U.; certification ABA Comml. Banking Sch., U. Okla. From mem. staff to pres., CEO Cascade Bancorp, Bend, Oreg., 1977—99, pres., CEO, 1998—; CEO Bank of the Cascades, Bend, Oreg., 1998—. Bd. dirs. Cascade Bancorp, Bank of the Cascades, Aquilla Tax-Free Trust of Oreg., Ctrl. Oreg. Ind. Health Svcs., MDU Resources Group Inc., 2003—. Adv. bd. Oreg. State U. Cascade Campus. Named Disting. Citizen of Yr., Bend C. of C., Ctrl. Oreg. Bus. Woman of Yr.; named one of 25 Most Powerful Women in Banking, US Banker, 2006. Mem.: Ind. Cmty. Bankers Assn. Am., Oreg. Bankers Assn. (bd. dir.), Oreg. Women's Forum. Office: Cascade Bancorp 1100 NW Wall St Bend OR 97701 *

MOSS, RANDY GENE, professional football player; b. Rand, W.Va., Feb. 13, 1977; s. Randy Pratt and Maxine Moss; children: Sidney, Senali, Thaddeus, Montigo. Attended, Fla. State U., 1996, Marshall U., 1996—98. Wide receiver Minn. Vikings, 1998—2005, Oakland Raiders, 2005—07, New England Patriots, 2007—. Named NFL Offensive Rookie of Yr., 1998, NFL Pro Bowl MVP, 2000; named to Nat. Football Conf. (NFC) Pro-Bowl Team, 1998—2000, 2002—03; recipient Fred Biletnikoff award, 1997, Espy Award for Breakthrough Athlete of the Yr., 1999. Achievements include leading NFL in recieving touchdowns, 1998, 2000, 2003; holds NFL record for most receptions in first five seasons (414), 2002; holds NFL record for fewest games to reach 5,000 career receiving yards (59 games); holds every receiving record at Marshall U. Office: New England Patriots One Patriot Pl Foxboro MA 02035-1388 *

MOSS, RICHARD B., pediatrician; b. NYC, Oct. 30, 1949; MD, SUNY, Downstate Medical Ctr., Brooklyn, 1975. Cert. Am. Bd. Allergy/Immunology, Am. Bd. Pediatrics. Intern Children's Meml. Hosp., Chgo., 1975-76, resident, 1976-77; fellow Stanford (Calif.) U. Med. Sch., 1977-79, 80-81; now pediatrician Lucile Salter Packard Children's Hosp., Palo Alto, Calif. Prof. pediats. Stanford U. Med. Sch. Office: Ctr Excellence Pulmonary Biology Lucile Packard Children's Hospital 770 Welch Rd Ste 350 Palo Alto CA 94304 Office Phone: 650-723-5191.

MOSS, ROGER WILLIAM, historian, writer, administrator; b. Zanesville, Ohio, Jan. 31, 1940; s. Roger William and Dorothy Elizabeth Moss; m. Gail Caskey Winkler, 1981; children: Elizabeth Moss McQuiston, Victoria Stiles. BS in Edn., Ohio U., 1963, MA, 1964; postgrad., Attingham, Eng., 1966; PhD, U. Del., 1972. Staff Peace Corps, Cameroon, 1962-63; curator of rare books Ohio U., 1962-64; lectr., dept. history U. Del., 1966-68, U. Md., 1967-68; exec. dir. Athenaeum of Phila., 1968—. Lectr. to adj. prof. architecture U. Pa., Phila., 1981—2004. Publs. include Master Builders, 1972, Century of Color, 1981, Biographical Dictionary of Philadelphia Architects, 1985, Victorian Interior Decoration, 1986, Victorian Exterior Decoration, 1987, Lighting for Historic Buildings, 1988 (Joel Polsky prize 1989), The American Country House, 1990, Philadelphia Victorian, 1998, Historic Houses of Philadelphia, 1998, Historic Sacred Places of Philadelphia, 2004; editor: Paint in America, 1994; contbr. articles to profl. jours. Assoc. mem. Nat. Preservation Inst., 1982—93; sec. Christopher Ludwick Found., 1969—, bd. dirs., 1969—; sec.-treas. Brit. Cathedrals and Hist. Chs. Found., 1996—2001, pres., 2002—04, bd. dirs.; sec. Victorian Soc. in Am., 1969—88, treas., 1969—88, bd. dirs., 1969—88; treas. Phila. Area Cultural Consortium, 1977—82, bd. dirs., 1977—82; sec. Hopkinson House Coun., 1982—93, Cliveden Coun., Nat. Trust Hist. Preservation, 1974—81, 1984—86; exec. com. Phila. Area Consortium Spl. Coll., 1988—93, Friends of Laurel Hill, 1978—83; bd. dirs. Conservation Ctr. for Art and Hist. Artifacts, 1984—96, chmn., 1993—95; sec. Harriton House, 1969—81, bd. dirs., 1969—81, Hist. House Assn. Am., 1978—83, Com. Preservation of Archtl. Records, 1978—80, Mus. Coun. Phila., 1976—78, Woodlands Cemetery Co., 1990—99, Rsch. Librs. Group, 1993—96, Abraham Lincoln Found., 1996—2005, Am. Friends Attingham Summer Schs., 2006—. NEH grantee, 1983-85; recipient Biddle award Preservation Alliance, 2004, Athenaeum Lit. award, 2005. Mem. Carpenters' Co. (hon.), Soc. Archtl. Historians, Hist. New Eng., Castine Yacht Club, Phila. Club. Office: 604 S Washington Sq Philadelphia PA 19106 Office Phone: 215-925-2688. E-mail: rwmoss@athenaonline.org.

MOSS, SANTANA, professional football player; b. Miami, Fla., June 1, 1979; s. Lloyd, Natalie; children: Santana Jr., Saniya. BA in Liberal Arts, Univ. Miami, 2000. Wide receiver NY Jets, 2000—04, Wash. Redskins, 2005—. Named to NFC ProBowl Team, 2005; recipient BIG East Offensive and Special Teams Player Yr. awards, 2000. Achievements include holding all-time receiving yards record at the University of Miami. Office: Washington Redskins 21300 Redskin Park Dr Ashburn VA 20147

MOSS, SARA E., lawyer, cosmetics executive; b. NYC, Nov. 13, 1946; 4 children. BA magna cum laude, U. Mass., 1968; JD, NYU, 1974. Bar: NY 1975, US Dist. Ct. (so. dist. NY) 1976, US Ct. Appeals (2nd cir.) 1975, US Tax Ct. 1983, US Supreme Ct. 1983. Law clk. to Hon. Constance Baker Motley US Dist. Ct. (so. dist. NY), 1974-75, asst. US atty., 1978-81; law clk. Davis, Polk & Wardell, 1975-78, 80-84; ptnr. Howard, Smith & Levin, 1984-96; v.p., gen. counsel Pitney Bowes, Inc., Stamford, Conn., 1996—2003; sr. v.p., gen. counsel, sec. Estée Lauder, NYC, 2003—. Instr. Nat. Inst. Trial Advocacy. Contbr. articles to profl. jours. Mem. ABA, Fed. Bar Coun. (trustee 1996—), Am. Arbitration Assn. (bd. dirs.), NY Coun. Def. Lawyers (bd. dirs. 1994-96), Assn. Bar City of NY (mem. fed. cts. com., mem. litig. com.), Phi Beta Kappa. Office: Estee Lauder 767 Fifth Ave New York NY 10153 Office Phone: 212-572-4200. E-mail: emoss@estee.com. *

MOSS, SHAD GREGORY (BOW WOW, LIL' BOW WOW), rap artist; b. Columbus, Ohio, Mar. 9, 1987; s. Teresa and Alfonso Moss, Rodney Caldwell (Stepfather). Singer: (albums) Beware of Dog, 2000, Doggy Bag, 2001, Unleashed, 2003, Wanted, 2005, Signal Fire, 2006, The Price of Fame, 2006, (songs) Bounce With Me, 2000, Let Me Hold You, 2005, Fresh Azimiz, 2005, Like You, 2006, (featured on film soundtracks) Hardball, 2001, Like Mike, 2002; actor: (TV films) Carmen: A Hip Hopera, 2001; (films) All About the Benjamins, 2002, Like Mike, 2002, Johnson Family Vacation, 2004, Roll Bounce, 2005, The Fast & the Furious: Tokyo Drift, 2006. Achievements include youngest solo rapper to ever hit number one. Office: Bow Wow Found Ste 307 6555 Sugarloaf Pkwy PMB 223 Duluth GA 30097 Office Fax: 678-376-5911. *

MOSS, STEPHEN BRUCE, lawyer; b. Jacksonville, Fla., July 14, 1943; s. Rudy and Betty (Sobel) M.; m. Rhoda Goodman, Nov. 24, 1984; children: Kurt, Shannon. BA, Tulane U., 1964; JD, Cumberland Sch. Law, 1968. Bar: Fla. 1968, U.S. Dist. Ct. (So. Dist.) Fla., U.S. Tax Ct. 1971. From assoc. to ptnr. Heiman & Crary, Miami, Fla., 1971-74; pvt. practice law So. Miami, Fla., 1974-75; ptnr. Glass, Schultz, Weinstein & Moss P.A., Coral Gables, Fla., 1975-78, Ft. Lauderdale, Fla., 1978-80, Holland & Knight, LLP, Ft. Lauderdale, 1980—, mem. dir. com. Lectr. in the field. Mem. pro bono com. 17th Jud. Cir., 2000; co-founder, co-chair Broward County Child Welfare Initiative, 2001. Capt. U.S. Army, 1968-70, Vietnam. Named Outstanding Kiwanian, Miami, Fla., 1974, Child Advocate of the Yr., Broward County, Fla., 2003, Role Model, 2004, Legal Elite, Fla. Trend Mag., 2004; named an Olympic torchbearer, 1996; named one of Best Lawyers in Am., 2007. Fellow: Am. Bar Found., Fla. Bar Found.; mem.: ABA (mem. real property, probate and trust sect.), Internat. Law Moot Ct., Broward County Bar Assn., Legal Aid Svc. of Broward County (bd. dirs. 2000), Fla. Bar Assn. (real property, probate and trust law sect.), Greater Ft. Lauderdale C. of C. (gen. counsel 1991—92, chmn. bd. dirs., bd. govs. 1995, trustee rep. 2005, past chair, Chmn.'s award 1991, 2000, Sr. Exec. Alumni of Year 2003), Tower Forum (pres. 1993—94, bd. dirs. 1995—2005), Tower Club, Phi Alpha Delta. Democrat. Jewish. Avocations: baseball, travel, child welfare. Office: Holland & Knight LLP 1 E Broward Blvd Ste 1300 Fort Lauderdale FL 33301-1845 Office Phone: 954-468-7857. Business E-Mail: stephen.moss@hklaw.com.

MOSS, THOMAS E., prosecutor; b. 1937; BA, U. Idaho; JD, U. Idaho Coll. Law, 1965. Prosecuting atty. Bingham County Dist. Ct., 1967—71, 1979—99; ptnr. Moss, Cannon and Romrell, Blackfoot, Idaho; mem. Idaho Ho. Reps., 2001; US atty. dist. Idaho US Dept. Justice, Boise, 2001—. Faculty mem. Nat. Advocacy Ctr., Columbia, SC; adv. coun. U. Idaho Coll. of Law; mem. Attn. Gen. Adv. Com., 2005—, Atty. Gen. Exec. Working Grp. Pres. Blackfoot Chamber of Commerce, Blackfoot Rotary Club; mem. Governor's Coordinating Coun. for Families and Children. Fellow: Am. Coll. Trial Lawyers; mem.: Idaho Prosecuting Attorneys' Assn. (pres.), Seventh Jud. Dist. Bar Assn. (pres.), Idaho State Bar Assn. (pres.), Idaho Ho. of Reps. Office: US Attys Office MK Plaza IV Ste 600 800 Park Blvd Boise ID 83712-9903 *

MOSS, THOMAS HENRY, science foundation director, physicist; b. Cleve., June 27, 1939; s. Joseph Harold and Elsa Margaret (Lemkau) M.; m. Kathleen Goddard, May 31, 1966; children: Ellen, Joseph, Cheryl, David. AB, Harvard U., 1961; PhD, Cornell U., 1965. Cons. analyst govtl. sci. policy U.S. Govt. Office Mgmt. and Budget, Washington, 1963-67; research physicist IBM Corp., Yorktown, NY, 1967-74, 75-76; staff dir., sci. advisor Office of Congressman George E. Brown, Washington, 1976-79; staff dir. subcom. sci., research and tech. Ho. of Reps., Washington, 1979-82; prof. physics, dean grad. studies and research Case Western Res. U., Cleve., 1982-96; exec. dir. Govt.-U.-Industry Roundtable, 1996—2001; with Nat. Acad. Scis, Washington; dir. U. relations Ohio Aerospace Inst., 2001—03. Adj. prof. physics Columbia U., NYC, 1966-76; mem. nat rev. com. Office of Nuclear Waste Isolation, Columbus, 1983-87; bd. dirs. U. Tech. Inc., Cleve., G. Mason U. Intellectual Properties, Inc., 2004—; bd. dirs. Ctr. Great Lakes, Chgo., 1985-89; v.p. Edison Poymer Innovation Corp., Independence, Ohio, 1986-90. Editor: The Three Mile Island Nuclear Accident-Lessons, 1981; asst. editor Environ. Profl. mag.; cons. editor Sci, Tech. and Human Values Environ. mag.; contbr. articles to profl. jours. Treas. Lake Bancroft Cmty. Assn., Falls Church, Va., 1980; mem. adv. bd. Small Bus. SBIR Program, Cleve., 1983-85; mem., v.p. Shaker Heights Bd. Edn., Ohio, 1989-96; chmn. NE Region Ohio Systemic Statewide Initiative in Sci. and Math. Edn., 1992-95. ASME fellow, 1995-96, NSF fellow Nobel Instn., 1966-67. Fellow Am. Phys. Soc. (chmn. forum on physics and soc. 1990-91), Nat. Coun. U. Rsch. Adminstrs. (Nat. Innovation Program award 1987), Scientists Inst. Pub. Info. (Disting. Svc. award Harlem Prep. Sch. 1971), AAAS (chmn. com. on sci., engrng. and pub. policy 1989-91, chmn. sect. X 1998-99, exec. com. sect. P 2004—). Avocations: gardening, camping. Office Phone: 703-914-2854. Personal E-mail: tomhmoss@verizon.net.

MOSSAWIR, HARVE H., JR., retired lawyer; b. Morton, Miss., Aug. 9, 1942; s. Harve H. and Madeline (Price) M.; children: Anna Christine, Karen Elyse; m. Judy S. Bardugo, Aug. 5, 1985; 1 child, Leigh Sarah. BA with honors, U. Ala., 1964; MA in Econs., U. Manchester, 1965; JD with honors, U. Chgo., 1968. Bar: Calif. 1970. Asst. prof. U. Ala. Law Sch., Tuscaloosa, 1968-69; assoc. Irell & Manella, LA, 1969-74, ptnr., 1974-94, of counsel, 1994-96. Mem. bd. editors U. Chgo. Law Rev., 1966-68; contbr. articles to profl. jours. Fulbright scholar, 1964-65, Floyd Russell Mecham scholar, 1965-68. Republican. Presbyterian. E-mail: labard1@yahoo.com.

MOSSE, PETER JOHN CHARLES, financial services executive; b. Mtarfa, Malta, Sept. 8, 1947; arrived in US, 1977; s. John Herbert Charles and Barbara Haworth (Holden) M.; m. Christine Marielle St. Preux, Oct. 17, 1994. BA, Oxford U., Eng., 1969, MA, 1989; MBA, U. Pa., Phila., 1971. Bank officer N.M. Rothschild & Sons Ltd., London, 1971-76; spl. projects officer banking Bumiputra Mcht. Bankers Berhad, Kuala Lumpur, Malaysia, 1976-77; v.p., treas., sec. NMR Metals Incorp., NYC, 1977-79, exec. v.p., 1979-83; sr. v.p. Rothschild, Inc., NYC, 1983-90; v.p., CFO, The Arista Group Inc., NYC, 1991-93; U.S. rep. Travelex Fin. Svcs. Ltd., London, 1994-95; ptnr. Creelman Fine Arts, NYC, 1995—2003; chmn. 2nd Ave. Physician Practice, 2005—. Treas. Circumnavigators Found., 2004—05. Fellow Royal Soc. Arts.; mem. NY Acad. Scis., Pilgrims of the U.S. (life), St. George's Soc. NY (life, bd. dirs. 2006—), Oxford U. Alumni Soc. (exec. com. 1994-96), Gold Inst. (co. rep., bd. dirs. 1985-90), Silver Inst. (co. rep., bd. dirs. 1989-90), NY Acad. Scis., Copper Club, Commodity Exch., Inc. (co. rep. 1979-90), Circumnavigators Club (bd. govs. 2006—), Travelers Century Club. Episcopalian. Avocations: travel, trains, railroad art. Home and Office: 353 E 72nd St Apt 33D New York NY 10021-4622

MOSSELMANS, CAREL MAURITS, investment banker; b. East Knoyle, Wiltshire, Eng., Mar. 9, 1929; s. Adriaan Willem and Nancy Henriette (Van der Wyck) M.; m. Prudence Fiona McCorquodale, Jan. 4, 1962; children: Michael Lodowick Stewart, Julian Frederick Willem. MA, Trinity Coll., Cambridge, Eng., 1952. With Sedgwick Collins & Co., 1952-63; dir. Sedgwick Collins & Co. Ltd., 1963-71; dir., mng. dir. Sedgwick Collins (Underwriting) Ltd., 1971, 72-73; chmn. Sedgwick Lloyd's Underwriting Agts., 1974-89, Sedgwick Forbes Marine Ltd., 1974-78, Sedgwick Forbes Svcs. Ltd., 1978-81, Sedgwick Ltd., 1981-84, Sedgwick Group Plc., 1984-89, The Sumitomo Marine & Fire Ins. Co. (Europe) Ltd., 1981-90; Coutts & Co., 1981-95; chmn. Rothschild Asset Mgmt. Ltd., 1989-99, Rothschild Int. Asset Mgmt., 1989-96. Chmn. Exco Plc, 1991-96, Janson Green Holdings Spl. Trust Ltd., 1993-96, Rothschild Fund Mgmt. Ltd., 1990-96; chmn. Janson Green Ltd., 1993-96, non-exec. dir., 1997-98. Avocations: shooting, fishing, music, golf. Home: 15 Chelsea Sq London SW3 6LF England

MOSSINGHOFF, GERALD JOSEPH, lawyer, educator; b. St. Louis, Sept. 30, 1935; m. Jeanne Carole Jack, Dec. 29, 1958; children: Pamela Ann Jennings, Gregory Joseph, Melissa M. Ronayne. BSEE, St. Louis U., 1957; JD with honors, George Washington U., 1961. Bar: Mo. 1961, DC 1965, Va. 1981. Project engr. Sachs Electric Corp., 1954-57; dir. congl. liaison NASA, Washington, 1967-73, dep. gen. counsel, 1976-81; asst. Sec. Commerce, commr. patents and trademarks U.S. Patent Office, 1981-85; pres. Pharm. Rsch. and Mfrs. Am., Washington, 1985-96; Cifelli prof. intellectual property law George Washington U., Washington, 1996—; sr. counsel Oblon, Spivak, McClelland, Maier & Neustadt, Arlington, Va., 1997—. Amb. Paris Conv. Diplomatic Conf.; adj. prof. George Mason U. Law Sch. Named Disting. Alumnus, George Washington U., 1996, presdl. rank of meritorious exec., 1980; recipient Exceptional Svc. medal, NASA, 1971, DSM, 1980, Outstanding Leadership medal, 1981, Jefferson medal, 2000, Disting. Pub. Svc. award, Sec. of Commerce, 1983. Fellow: Am. Acad. Pub. Adminstrn.; mem.: Reagan Alumni Assn. (bd. dirs.), Cosmos Club, Knights of Malta, Order of Coif, Pi Mu Epsilon, Eta Kappa Nu. Home: 1530 Key Blvd Penthouse 28 Arlington VA 22209-1532 Office: Oblon Spivak McClelland Maier and Neustadt 1940 Duke St Alexandria VA 22314 Personal E-mail: gmossing@aol.com.

MOSSO, LYLE DAVID, finance company executive; b. Pasadena, Calif., Aug. 13, 1926; s. Joseph Ernest and Marian (Ure) M.; m. Lee McVoy Pierce, June 11, 1955; children: Janet, Andrew, Jocelyn. BBA magna cum laude, Washburn U., 1950, D in Commerce (hon.), 1982; MA in Econs, U. Minn., 1951. CPA, Va. With Santa Fe Ry., 1942-44; instr. econs. and acctg. Washburn U., 1954-55; with U.S. Treasury Dept., 1955-77, commr. accounts, 1971-73, dep. asst. sec. treasury, 1973-75, asst. sec., 1975-77; with Fin. Acctg. Stds. Bd., 1978-96; vice chmn. Fin. Acctg. Standards Bd., 1986-87; adj. prof. acctg. Fordham U., 1996—; chmn. Fed. Acctg. Stds. Adv. Bd., 1997—. Arbitrator Am. Arbitration Assn., 1997—. Contbr. articles to profl. jours. Mem. Comptr. Gen.'s Acctg. Stds. Adv. Coun., 1987-90; mem. charter revision commn. City of Stamford, 1986-87, Can.-U.S. Adv. Group on Fed. Reporting, 1984-86; alt. trustee Nat. Gallery Art, 1975-77; dir. Stamford Emergency Med. Svc., 1993-94. 1st lt. AUS, 1944-46, 51-53. Recipient Alexander Hamilton award Treasury Dept., 1977, Braden award Case Western Res. U., 2002. Mem. AICPA (Elijah Watt Sells award 1962), Va. Soc. CPAs (Gold medal 1962), Am. Acctg. Assn., Assn. Govt Accts. (dir. Washington chpt. 1972-73, Disting. Leadership award 1977, Elmer Staats award 1990), Treasury Hist. Assn. (pres. 1978), Tau Delta Pi, Pi Gamma Mu, Phi Kappa Phi. Home: 111 Saddle Hill Rd Stamford CT 06903-2307 Office: 441 G St NW Ste 6814 Washington DC 20548-0001 Personal E-mail: ossomd@hotmail.com.

MOSS-SALENTIJN, LETTY (ALEIDA), anatomist, educator; b. Amsterdam, The Netherlands, Apr. 14, 1943; arrived in U.S., 1968; d. Ewoud and Johanna Maria (Schoonhoven) Salentijn; m. Melvin Lionel Moss, Apr. 17, 1970. DDS, State U. Utrecht, Netherlands, 1967, PhD, 1976. Asst. prof. histology State U. Utrecht, 1967-68; asst. prof. Columbia U., NYC, 1968-74, assoc. prof., 1974-86, prof., 1986—, Edwin S. Robinson prof., 1999—, dir. dental radiology, 1980-86, dir. grad. program dental sci., 1986—, dir. postdoctoral affairs, 1987-90, asst. dean postdoctoral programs, 1990-94, assoc. dean acad. affairs, 1994—2005, sr. assoc. dean acad. affairs, 2005—. Author: Orofacial Histology & Embryology, 1972; Dental and Oral Tissues, 1980, 2d edit., 1984, 3d edit., 1990; contbr. chpts. to books, articles to profl. jours. Fellow Royal Microscopical Soc., Am. Coll. Dentists, NY Acad. Dentistry; mem. Am. Assn. Anatomists, Internat. Assn. Dental Rsch., Am. Soc. Biomechs., Sigma Xi (chpt. sec. 1980-87, pres. 1987-89, 98-99), Omicron Kappa Upsilon (pres. local chpt. 1987). Avocation: stained glass art. Home: 560 Riverside Dr Apt 20K New York NY 10027-3239 Office: Columbia Univ Coll Dental Medicine Sr Assoc Dean Acad Affairs 630 W 168th St New York NY 10032-3702 Office Phone: 212-305-8334. Business E-Mail: lm23@columbia.edu.

MOSTAGHIMI, MEHDI, economist, educator; arrived in U.S., 1975; s. Abolfazle Mostaghimi and Toba Rashidzadeh; m. Du D Cheng, Aug. 28, 1991; children: Darius, Alexander. BA in Econs., Nat. U. Iran, 1975; PhD in Info. and Sys. Engring., U. Va., 1987; MS in Ops. Rsch., We. Mich. U., 1999. Sr. mgr. portfolio and decision analysis group Pfizer Pharm., NYC, 1997—99; prof. economics and decision analysis scis. Sch. of Bus. So. Conn. State U., New Haven, 1984—. Chmn. internat. chapts. subcom. Inst. of Ops. Rsch. and Mgmt. Scis., 2001—03; Grad. Rsch. Fellowship panel NSF, 2006. Co-author: Analysis of Bus. Cycles, 2004; contbr. articles to profl. jours. Fellow: Inst. of Ops. Rsch. and the Mgmt. Scis. (chmn. internat. chapts. subcommittee 2001—02); mem.: Am. Statis. Assn. (pres. Conn. chpt. 1994—97, com. on internat. rels. 1994—98). Achievements include research in modeling combining information and forecasts; predicting a turning point in economy; strategic and policy decision making. Home: PO Box 569 Madison CT 06443 Office: Southern Connecticut State Univ 501 Crescent Street New Haven CT 06515 Home Phone: 203-245-4865; Office Phone: 203-392-5625. Personal E-mail: mostaghimi@yahoo.com.

MOSTELLER, DARLA BROOKS, singer; d. Thomas Jefferson and Sue Osborne Brooks; m. Paul Mosteller, July 5, 2000. MusB, Birmingham-Southern Coll., Ala., 1977. Young artist Lyric Opera Chgo., 1980—81; leading soprano Lucerne (Switzerland) Opera, 1984—85, Würzburg (Germany) Opera, 1985—86, Cologne (Germany) Opera, 1987—96; pvt. voice tchr. Birmingham, Ala., 2000—. Guest artist Dortmund (Germany) Opera, 1990—96; guest soloist Vienna (Austria) State Opera, 1991—96; artist Schwetzingen (Germany) Festival, 1993—95; soloist Trondheim (Norway) Symphony, 1993—95, Bergen (Norway) Symphony, 1995; guest artist Opera Bonn, Bonn, Germany, 1986—87, Mannheim (Germany) Opera, 1986—95, German Opera on the Rhine, Düsseldorf, Germany, 1989—96, Gran Teatre del Liceu, Barcelona, 1991—96, Mozart Festival, Prague, Czech Republic, 1991, Bavarian State Opera, Munich, 1993—94, Deutsche Oper, Berlin, 1993—95, Min-On Concert Assn., Tokyo, 1993, Salzburg (Austria) Festival, 1995—96; tchr. voice Birmingham (Ala.) So. Coll., 1997—2000. Singer (actor): (TV films) LIncoronazione di Poppea, 1991, (films) Falstaff (Salieri), 1993. Finalist, Met. Opera Nat. Coun., 1976, 1977, 1978, 1980, 1983, 1984; scholar, Am. Inst. Musical Studies, 1981; Singer's scholar, Norman Treigle Scholarship Fund, 1980. Mem.: Coll. Music Soc., Coll. Music Soc., Nat. Assn. Tchrs. Singing. Home Phone: 205-824-3476. Personal E-mail: pmosteller3476@charter.net.

MOSTER, MARY CLARE, public relations executive; b. Morristown, NJ, Apr. 7, 1950; d. Clarence R. and Ruth M. Moster; m. Louis C. Williams, Jr., Oct. 4, 1987. BA in English with honors, Douglass Coll., 1972; MA in English Lit., Univ. Chgo., 1973. Accredited pub. rels. counselor. Editor No. Trust Bank, Chgo., 1973-75, advt. supr., 1975-77, communications officer, 1977-78; account exec. Hill & Knowlton, Inc., Chgo., 1978-80, v.p., 1980-83, sr. v.p., 1983-87, sr. v.p., mng. dir., 1987-88; staff v.p. comms. Navistar Internat. Corp., Chgo., 1988-93; v.p. corp. comms. Comdisco, Inc., Rosemont, Ill., 1993—2002; sr. v.p. L.C. Williams and Assocs., Chgo., 2002—. Adj. prof. Integrated Mktg. Comm. Medill Sch., Northwestern U., 2000-05 Author poetry, poetry translation. Bd. govs. Met. Planning Coun., Chgo., 1988-94; fellow Leadership Greater Chgo., 1989-90; bd. dirs. New City YMCA, Chgo., 1986-92; corp. devel. bd. Steppenwolf Theatre Co., Chgo., 1988-90; active Chgo. Network, 1994—, bd. dirs., 1996-99. Mem. Nat. Investor Rels. Inst. (bd. dirs. 1988-89, 90-99, pres. Chgo. chpt. 1998-99), Arthur W. Page Soc., Pub. Rels. Soc. Am. Avocations: sailing, cross country skiing, book groups, biking. Office: L C Williams & Assocs 150 N Michigan Ave Ste 3800 Chicago IL 60601

MOSTERT, PAUL STALLINGS, retired mathematician; b. Morrilton, Ark., Nov. 27, 1927; s. Johannes F. T. and Lucy (Stallings) Mostert; m. Barbara Bond; children: Paul Theodore, Richard Stallings, Kathleen, Kristina. AB, Rhodes Coll., 1950; MS, U. Chgo., 1951; PhD, Purdue U., 1953. Mem. faculty Tulane U., 1953-70, prof. math., 1962-70, chmn. dept., 1968-70; prof. U. Kans., 1970-91, prof. emeritus math., 1991—, chmn. dept., 1970-73. Vis. prof. U. Tubingen, Germany, 1962—63; mem. Inst. Advanced Study, Princeton, 1967—68; vis. prof. math. U. Ky., 1984—85; chmn. Rhodes Coll. Sci. Initiaitve Task Force, 1989—90; pres. Equix, Inc., 1984—85, Pennfield Biomechanics Corp., Inc., 1985—89, Equix Biomechanics, 1989—97, Equix Rsch. Corp., 1989—2005; proprietor Mostert Group, 1997—2003; dir. rsch. Mostert-Group LLC-Equix Biomechanics, 2004—06; mgr. MSRCO, LLC, 2004—. Co-author: Splitting in Topological Groups, 1963, 3d edit., 1993, Elements of Compact Semigroups, 1966, The Cohomology Ring of Finite and Compact Abelian Groups, 1974; editor: Proc. Conf. Transformation Groups at New Orleans, 1969, Questiones Mathematicae, 1973—95; co-founder, editor: Semigroup Forum, 1970—85, mng. editor:, 1967—85; editor, 1985—88; creator 9 software programs. Mem. Ky. Statewide Exptl. Program Stimulate Competitive Rsch. Com., 1994—96. With USN, 1945—46. Recipient Rsch. award, Small Bus. Innovative Rsch., 2000—05; Sr. postdoctoral fellow, NSF, 1987—88. Mem.: AAAS, Assn. Computing Machinery, Assn. Mems. Inst. Advanced Studies, Am. Math. Soc. (mem. at large coun. 1972—75, chmn. com. acad. freedom, tenure and employment security 1973—76), Thoroughbred Owners and Breeders Assn. Achievements include patents for methods and computer-readable medium for tracking motion and for navigating between a plurality of discrete images. Office: 3298 Roxburg Dr Lexington KY 40503-3432 Office Phone: 859-223-1490. E-mail: pmostert@windstream.net.

MOSTILLO, RALPH, medical association administrator; s. Joseph and Antoinette Mostillo. BA in Chemistry magna cum laude, Rutgers U., Newark, 1972; MA in Biochemistry, Princeton U., NJ, 1974, PhD in Biochemistry, 1978. Rsch. fellow Princeton U., 1972-78; sr. scientist drug regulatory affairs Hoffmann-La Roche, Inc., Nutley, NJ, 1979-85; founder, chmn., CEO Am. Cancer Assn., Nutley, 1986—. With USN, 1962—66, Vietnam. Fellow, NIH, 1972—78. Mem.: NY Acad. Scis., Am. Mktg. Assn., Am. Mgmt. Assn., Am. Chem. Soc., Vietnam Vets. Am., Am. Legion, Phi Beta Kappa, Sigma Xi. Achievements include research in molecular transport systems in E. coli as general models for drug delivery into cells. Home: PO Box 505 Nutley NJ 07110-0505 Office: Am Cancer Assn PO Box 87 Nutley NJ 07110-0087

MOSTOFF, ALLAN SAMUEL, lawyer, consultant; b. NYC, Oct. 19, 1932; s. Morris and Ida (Goldman) M.; m. Alice Tamara Popelowsky, July 31, 1955; children: Peter Alexander, Nina Valerie. BS, Cornell U., 1953; MBA, NYU, 1954; LLB, NY Law Sch., 1957. Bar: NY 1958, DC 1964. Assoc. Olwine Connelly Chase O'Donnell & Weyher, NYC, 1958-61; atty. SEC, Washington, 1962-66, asst. dir., 1966-69, assoc. dir., 1969-72, dir. divsn. investment mgmt. regulation, 1972-76; ptnr. Dechert Price & Rhoads, Washington, 1976—2002, Dechert, Washington, 2000—03; ptnr. emeritus, sr. counsel Dechert LLP, Washington, 2002—03, of counsel, 2004—; pres. Mut. Fund Dirs. Forum, 2002—. Adj. prof. Georgetown U. Law Ctr., 1972-82; mem. Fin. Acctg. Standards Adv. Bd., 1982-86; mem. adv. bd. Investment Lawyer, 2000—, BNA Securities Regulation and Law Report, 1977-87. Recipient Lifetime Achievement award, Fund Directions, 2007. Mem. ABA, Assn. of Bar of City of NY, Fed. Bar Assn. (past chmn. exec. coun. securities regulation com. 1990-92), Am. Law Inst. Home: 6417 Waterway Dr Falls Church VA 22044-1325 Office: 1255 23rd St NW Ste 200 Washington DC 20037 Business E-Mail: allan.mostoff@mfdf.com.

MOSTOW, GEORGE DANIEL, mathematics professor; b. Boston, July 4, 1923; s. Isaac J. and Ida (Rotman) M.; m. Evelyn Davidoff, Sept. 1, 1947; children: Mark Alan, David Jechiel, Carol Held, Jonathan Carl. BA, Harvard U., 1943, MA, 1946, PhD, 1948; DSc (hon.), U. Ill., Chgo., 1989. Instr. math. Princeton U., 1947-48; mem. Inst. Advanced Study, 1947-49, 56-57, 75, mem. bd. of trustees, 1982-92; asst. prof. Syracuse U., 1949-52; asst. prof. math. Johns Hopkins U., 1952-53, assoc. prof., 1954-56, prof., 1957-61; prof. math. Yale U., 1961-66, James E. English prof. math., 1966-81, Henry Ford II prof. math., 1981-98, chmn., 1971-74, prof. emeritus, 1998—. Vis. prof. Conselho Nat. des Pesquisas, Inst. de Matematica, Rio de Janiero, Brazil, 1953-54, 91, U. Paris, 1966-67, Hebrew U., Jerusalem, 1967, Tata Inst. Fundamental Rsch., Bombay, 1970, Inst. des Hautes Etudes Scientifiques, Bures-Sur-Yvette, 1966, 71, 75, Japan Soc. for Promotion of Sci., 1985, Eidgenossische Technische Hochschule, Switzerland, 1986; chmn. U.S. Nat. Com. for Math, 1971-73, 83-85, Office Math. Scis., NRC, 1975-78; mem. sci. adv. coun. Math. Scis. Rsch. Inst., Berkeley, Calif., 1988-91; mem. sci. adv. com., bd. govs. Weizmann Inst., Israel, 1987—2003; bd. govs. Tel Aviv U., 1990-2000; mem. Harvard Grad. Coun., 1988-91; mem. vis. com. dept. math. Harvard U., 1975-81, MIT, 1981-94; Ritt lectr. Columbia U., 1982, Bergman lectr. Stanford U., 1983, Sachar lectr. Tel Aviv U., 1985, Karcher lectr. U. Okla., 1986, Markert lectr. Pa. State U., 1993. Assoc. editor Annals of Math., 1957—64, Trans. Am. Math. Soc., 1958—65, Am. Scientist, 1970—82, Geometriae Dedicata, 1985—90, bd. cons. Jour. D'Analyse Mathématique, 1994—; editor: Am. Jour. Math., 1965—69; assoc. editor Am. Jour. Math., 1969—79; author rsch. articles:. Fulbright rsch. scholar, Utrecht U., The Netherlands; Guggenheim fellow, 1957-58 Mem. AAAS, NAS (chmn. sect. math. 1982-84), Am. Math. Soc. (pres. 1987-88, Steele prize for Paper of Lasting Importance 1993), Internat. Math. Union (chmn. U.S. del. to Gen. Assembly Warsaw 1982, exec. com. 1983-86), Phi Beta Kappa, Sigma Xi. Home: 25 Beechwood Rd Woodbridge CT 06525-1309 Office: Yale Univ Dept Mathematics New Haven CT 06520 Business E-Mail: george.mostow@yale.edu.

MOSZKOWSKI, NEAL, health products executive; Degree, Amherst Coll.; MBA, Stanford Univ. Grad. Sch. Bus. Vice-pres., exec. dir. principal investment area Goldman, Sachs & Co.; co-head, ptnr. Soros Private Equity Partners, LLC, 1998, chmn. bd. dir., 2002—. Dir. Bluefly, Inc., Day Internat Group, Inc., Jet Blue Airways Corp., Integra LifeSciences Holding Corp. Office: WellCare Health Plans Renaissance 1 8725 Henderson Rd Tampa FL 33634 Office Phone: 813-290-6200. Office Fax: 813-262-2802.

MOTAMED, THOMAS FIROUZ, insurance company executive; BA in Biology, Adelphi U., Garden City, NY, 1971; JD, Widener U., 1975. Sci. faculty Malvern Prep. Sch., Pa., 1975-76; field underwriter NY Life, Carle Place, NY, 1976-77; claims trainee The Chubb Corp., LI, 1977—78, claims unit mgr., 1978—80, NY br. office mgr., 1980—81, litig. mgr. claims dept. Short Hills, NJ, 1981—83, nat. claim audit mgr. Warren, NJ, 1983—84, nat. claim adminstr., 1984—86, claim mgr. NYC, 1986—88, adminstrv. mgr., 1988—89, LI mktg. mgr., 1989—90, br. mgr. Westchester, NY, 1990—93, midtown NY br. mgr., 1993—96, western zone officer, 1996—97, exec. v.p., COO Warren, NJ, 1997—2002, vice chmn., COO, 2002—; pres., COO, mng. dir. Chubb & Son Inc. divsn. of Fed. Ins. Co., Warren, NJ. Office: The Chubb Corp 15 Mountain View Rd Warren NJ 07059 Office Phone: 908-903-3700. E-mail: tmotamed@chubb.com. *

MOTAWI, KARIM, textiles executive; b. 1970; s. Kamal and Karen. Grad., U. Mich. V.p., co-owner Motawi Tileworks Inc., Ann Arbor, Mich., 1992—. Sec. Ann Arbor Art Ctr. Named one of 40 Under 40, Crain's Detroit Bus., 2006. Office: Motawi Tileworks Inc 170 Enterprise Dr Ann Arbor MI 48103 Office Phone: 734-213-0017. Office Fax: 734-213-2569.

MOTCH, MARJORIE MCCULLOUGH, service organization executive; b. Cin., July 12, 1923; d. Robert Stedman and Mildred (Rogers) McCullough; m. Homer E. Lunken, Apr. 15, 1944 (dec. 1970); children: Karen Lunken(dec.), Kathryn Lunken Summers, Margo Lunken Yesner; m. William McLeod Ittmann, Mar. 17, 1972 (dec. 1982); m. Harold Hiatt, Apr. 14, 1984 (dec. 1999); m. Graham E. Marx, Jan. 4, 2003 (dec. 2003); m. Arthur E. Motch Jr., Sept. 18, 2004 (dec. 2005). Student, U. Cin., 1941—43, DFA (hon.), 2003. Active Girl Scouts US, 1962—, chmn. conv. com., 1972, del. world convs., 1969, 72, 75, 78, 81, 84, 87, 93, chmn. pub. relations com., 1963-66, mem. nat. exec. com., 1963-75, mem. nat. bd., 1962—, 4th v.p., 1966-69, 1st v.p., 1969-72, nat. pres., 1972-75, chmn. nat. adv. coun., 1975-82, mem. birthplace adv. com., 1980-97. Vice chmn. world conf., Orleans, France, 1981; world com. World Assn. Girl Guides and Girl Scouts, 1978-87, vice chmn., 1984-87; trustee emeritus U. Cin. Found. Regional dir. Assn. Jr. Leagues Am., 1958—60, nat. pres., 1960—62; mem. br. Nat. Assembly for Social Policy and Devel., 1968—71; mem. exec. com. Coun. Nat. Orgns. for Children and Youth, 1960—62, 1968—72; mem. br. Jr. League Cin., 1944—58, Nat. Tng. Labs., 1963—66; mem. policy com. Ctr. Vol. Soc., 1971—72; mem. Ohio Citizens Coun., 1956—58; mem. bd. advisors U. Cin. Coll. Nursing, 2000—; bd. dirs. 7th Presbyn. Ch., 1967—74, 1985—, ruling elder, 1976—78, 2000—, chmn. bd. trustees, 1992—94; sr. warden St. Martin's in the Field, Biddeford Pool, Maine; bd. dirs. United Way Am., 1962—67, sec., 1965—66, v.p., 1966—67, 1989—; bd. dirs. Fine Arts Fund, 2002—, Coll. Prep. Sch., Cin., 1962—69, pres., 1964—69; bd. dirs. Cin. Speech and Hearing Ctr., 1955—66, v.p., 1958—62, pres., 1963—66, trustee emeritus, 1966—; mem. bd. Children's Theatre, Cin., 1948—58, pres., 1948—50; bd. dirs. Cmty. Health and Welfare Coun. Cin., 1957—63, Hamilton County Rsch. Found., Ohio, 1963—65, Cancer Family Care, Cin., 1971—72, Boys Clubs Greater Cin., Marjorie P. Lee Home for the Aged, Ctrl. Psychiat. Clinic, Music Hall Assn., Cin. Symphony Orch., Beechwood Home for Incurables, 1975—87, St. Margaret Hall, 1991—, Cin. Civic Garden Ctr., 1992—95, Greater Cin. Found., 1979—87, Ctrl. Clinic, 2000—, YWCA, 1998—, Fine Arts Fund, 2002—. Recipient Mary Herriman award, 2000, Mardee Wachs Vol. Svc. award, Hearing, Speech, and Deaf Ctrs., 2006. Mem. Olave Baden-Powell Soc. (v.p. 1991-93, pres. 1993-97), World Found. for Girl Guides and Girl Scouts (v.p. 1989—), Garden Club Am. (vice chmn. founder's fund 1991-92), Am. Psychiat. Assn. Aux. (bd. dirs., rec. sec. 1991-92). Home: 2353 Bedford Ave Cincinnati OH 45208-2656

MOTCHAN, DENNIS GLENN, physician; b. St. Louis, Apr. 6, 1950; s. Harold Lloyd and Radine (Goldman) Motchan; m. Nancy Helene Shulman, Jan. 26, 1975; children: Randall Kenneth, Katherine Rae. BS, Northwestern U., Evanston, Ill., 1972, MD, 1974. Diplomate Am. Bd. Internal Medicine. Intern St. John's Mercy Med. Ctr., Creve Coeur, Mo., 1974-75, resident in internal medicine, 1975-77, chief resident in internal medicine, 1977-78, attending physician, instr. internal medicine, 1978—; practice medicine specializing in internal medicine Northway Internists, Inc., Bridgeton, Mo., 1978—2005; pvt. practice specializing in occupl. medicine Maryland Heights, Mo., 2006—. Mem. AMA (Physician's Recognition award in continuing med. edn. 2000), St. Louis County Met. Med. Soc. Office: Concentra Med Ctr 83 Progress Pkwy Maryland Heights MO 63043 Office Phone: 314-434-8174.

MOTE, CLAYTON DANIEL, JR., academic administrator, mechanical engineer, educator; b. San Francisco, Feb. 5, 1937; s. Clayton Daniel and Eugenia (Isnardi) M.; m. Patricia Jane Lewis, Aug. 18, 1962; children: Melissa Michelle, Adam Jonathan. BSc, U. Calif., Berkeley, 1959, MS, 1960, PhD, 1963; Doctorate (hon.), Tashkent State Tech. U., 2001; DSc, Ohio State U., 2001; Dr Sci. and Tech. (hon.), Carnegie Mellon U., 2004. Registered profl. engr., Calif. Asst. specialist U. Calif. Forest Products Labs., 1961-62, asst. mech. engr., 1962-63; lectr. mech. engring. U. Calif., Berkeley, 1962-63, asst. prof., 1967-69, asst. research engr., 1968-69, assoc. prof., assoc. research engr., 1969-73, prof., 1973-98, vice chmn. mech. engring. dept., 1976-80, 83-86, chmn. mech. engring. dept., 1987-91, vice chancellor univ. rels., FANUC chair mech. systems, 1991-98; research fellow U. Birmingham, Eng., 1963-64; asst. prof. Carnegie Inst. Tech., 1964-67; Glen L. Martin Inst. prof. engring. U. Md., College Park, 1998—, pres., 1998—. Vis. prof. Norwegian Inst. Wood Tech., 1972—73, vis. sr. scientist, 1976, 78, 80, 84, 85; cons. in engring., design and analysis; cons. in engring. NAE, 1988, Nat. Acad. Arts and Sci., 2004; sr. scientist Alexander Von Humboldt Found., Germany, 1988, Japan Soc. for Promotion of Sci., Japan, 1991. Mem. editl. bd. Soma Jour. Sound and Vibration, Machine Vibration; contbr. articles to profl. jours.; patentee in field. NSF fellow, 1963-64, Sr. Scientist fellow Japan Soc. Promotion Sci., 1991, Berkeley fellow, 2001; recipient Disting. Tchg. award U. Calif., 1971, Pi Tau Sigma Excellence in Tchg. award U. Calif., 1975, Humboldt prize, Fed. Republic Germany, 1988, Disting. Engring. Alumnus award U. Calif., 2001, Frederick W. Taylor Rsch. medal. Soc. Mfg. Engrs., 1991, Hetenyi award Soc. Exptl. Mechanics, 1992, Eagle award Met. Washington chpt. ARCS, 2000, Excellence in Achievement award Calif. Alumni Assn., 2007. Fellow: Am. Acad. Arts and Sci. (coun. del. Sect M 2003—), NAE (coun. 2002—, former program com., peer com., Founder's award 2005), ASME (hon.; chmn. San Francisco sect. 1978—79, nat. chmn. noise control and acoustics 1980—84, v.p. environ. and transp. 1986—90, Blackall award 1975, Disting. Svc. award 1991, Charles Russ Richards award 1994, Rayleigh lectr. 1994, Applied Mechanics award 2001, Den Hertog award 2005), Acoustical Soc. Am., Internat. Acad. Wood Sci.; mem.: NRC (vice chair com. on dept. basic rsch. 2004, nat. acad. press 2005, com. on prospering in global economy of the 21st century, com. on sci., engring. and pub. policy 2005, governing bd. 2007—), AAAS, ASTM (com. on snow skiing F-27 1984—87), Orthopaedic Rsch. Soc., Am. Soc. Biomechanics, Am. Acad. Mechanics, Am. Soc. Engring. Edn. (Ralph Coast Roe award 1997), Internat. Soc. Skiing Safety (hon.; sec. 1977—85, bd.dirs. 1977—, chmn. sci. com. 1985—, v.p.), Tau Beta Pi, Sigma Xi, Nat. Soc. Collegiate Scholars, Golden Key Nat. Honor Soc., Phi Kappa Phi, Omicron Delta Kappa, Pi Tau Sigma. Office: Office of Pres U Md Main Adminstrn Bldg College Park MD 20742-5025 Office Phone: 301-405-5803. Business E-Mail: president@umd.edu.

MOTE, CLYDE A, retired lawyer; b. Vernon, Tex., Feb. 12, 1926; s. Neven and Lona (May) M.; m. Jean Henderson, Apr. 26, 1952 (dec. May 1998); children— Terron, Bruce, Douglas; m. Roxann Evans, Jan. 21, 1999. J.D., Baylor U., 1950. Bar: Tex. 1950, Okla. 1960. Ptnr. Cummings & Mote, Abilene, Tex., 1950-52; asst. city atty. City of Lubbock, Tex., 1952-54; ptnr. Napier & Mote, Lubbock, 1954-59; atty. Amoco Prodn. Co., Houston, 1959-86, regional atty., New Orleans Region, 1986—89. Served to sgt. U.S. Army, 1943-46, ETO. Mem. Am. Petroleum Inst. (subcom. on exploration and prodn. law), Interstate Oil Compact Commn., Phi Alpha Delta. Republican. Baptist. Home: 244 N Bay Dr Bullard TX 75757-8917

MOTEJUNAS, GERALD WILLIAM, lawyer; b. Boston, Jan. 18, 1950; s. Peter and Eva C. (Jankus) M.; m. Patricia A. McKeon, June 23, 1984; children: Scott Peterson, Mark Whitney. BA, Northeastern U., 1972; JD, Suffolk U., 1976. Bar: Mass. 1976, U.S. Dist. Ct. Mass., 1977, U.S. Supreme Ct. 1983. Assoc. Lecomte, Emanuelson, Motejunas & Doyle, Boston, 1976-85, ptnr., 1985—2002; shareholder Smith & Brink, 2002—. Author: Suffolk U. Law Rev., 1975; editor, 1976. Mem. ABA (chmn., editor, vice chmn. property ins. law com.), ATLA, Def. Rsch. Inst., Mass. Bar Assn., Boston Bar Assn., Loss Execs. Assn., Boston Athenaeum, Appalachian Mountain Club (exec. com. 1980-81). Avocations: skiing, golf. Office: Smith & Brink 122 Quincy Shore Dr Quincy MA 02171

MOTEN, DARLENE, elementary school educator; d. Spencer and Arlishie Moten; children: Nichole Antoinette, Ana Lisa, Candy Sue, Sandy Darlene, Micah Jeremiah, Ann Marie, Taheerah Janiece, Donald Vance, Ebonee Lashey, Aleizah Janae. BS in Bus. Edn., U. Ariz., Tucson, 1975; MEd, U. Ariz., 1981. Sec. U. Ariz., Tucson, 1972—76; tchr. bus. edn. Amphitheater Pub. Schs., Tucson, 1977—. Libr. rev. com. Amphitheater Pub. Schs., Tucson, 1995—99; poetry contest judge Amphitheater Mid. Sch., Tucson, 2004—. Dir. of children's ministry Mt. Olive Ch. Of God In Christ, Tucson, 1975; state children's dir. Ch. Of God In Christ, Phoenix, 1986. Recipient Cmty. Svc. award, Mayor City of Tucson, 2000, Pima County Supr. Dan Eckstrom, 2000. Mem.: NEA (assoc.), Amphitheater Edn. Assn. (assoc.). Penecostal. Avocations: reading, travel, writing, home remodeling. Office: Amphitheater Public Schools 315 E Prince Rd Tucson AZ 85705 Home Phone: 520-882-5938; Office Phone: 520-696-6305. E-mail: dmoten@amphi.com.

MOTEN, SARAH ELIZABETH, federal agency administrator, educator; b. Norfolk, Va., Dec. 9, 1941; d. Woodrow Wilson and Mary Elizabeth (Peelich) Price; 1 child, Michele Denise Moten. B.S., Hampton U., 1964; M.A., George Washington U., 1970; Ed.D., Atlanta U., 1979. Tchr. D.C. Pub. Schs., Washington, 1964-67, tchr. reading, 1967-70, counselor, 1970-74, asst. prin., 1974-80; adminstr. research Howard U., Washington, 1980-82; country dir. U.S. Peace Corps, Swaziland, 1982; deputy asst. sec. refugee programs, Dept. State; coord, Edn. Devel. Democracy Initiative; edn. div. chief, Office Sustainable Devel., US Agency Internat. Develop.; lectr. Spelman Coll., Atlanta, 1977-78; asst. to pres. Morehouse Coll., Atlanta, 1978-79; chairperson Nat. Council for Accreditation Tchr. Edn., Washington, 1970-82. Speaker Nat. Black Republicans, San Francisco, 1980; mem. Coalition for Social and Econ. Change, San Francisco, 1980; mem. U.S. del. UN Conf. for Women, Nairobi, Kenya, 1985. Rockefeller Found. fellow, 1977. Episcopalian. Avocations: reading; bowling; playing cards. Office: Ronald Reagan Bldg 1300 Pennsylvania Ave NW Romm 4 07 105 Washington DC 20523-4600

MOTENKO, NEIL PHILIP, lawyer; b. Chgo., July 27, 1951; s. Max Narad Motenko and Carolyn (Friedman) Rose; m. Aluma Kopito; children: Adam, Joshua, Micah. AB magna cum laude (hon.), Harvard U., 1973, JD, 1976. Bar: Mass. 1977, US Dist. Ct. Mass. 1978. Assoc. Nutter, McClennen & Fish, Boston, 1976-81, jr. ptnr., 1981-85, ptnr., 1985—. Co-chmn. New Eng. Antitrust Conf., Boston, 1987—, taught Harvard Sch. of Pub. Health, Boston U Sch. of Law, Tufts Sch of Medicine, spkr. in field. Contbr. articles to profl. jour. Named The Best Lawyers in Am., Leading US Antitrust Atty., Chambers and Ptnr., 2003—06, Mass. Super Lawyer, Boston mag., 2004—06, Am. Leading Bus. Lawyers, Chambers USA. Mem. ABA (antitrust sect.,litigation sect chmn. health care com., co-chair ops. com.), Boston Bar Assn. (past chmn. antitrust com.). Office: Nutter McClennen & Fish 155 Seaport Blvd World Trade Center W Boston MA 02210 Office Phone: 617-439-2216. Office Fax: 617-310-9216. Business E-Mail: nmotenko@nutter.com.

MOTHERAL, BRENDA R., health products executive; Grad., MBA, U. Ky.; PhD, U. SC. Dir. Ctr. Pharm. Policy; mem. faculty U. Ariz. Coll. Pharmacy; sr. dir. rsch. Express Scripts, Inc., Md. Heights, Mo., 2000—03, v.p. rsch., 2003, v.p. rsch. and trend mgmt., 2003—04, v.p. product devel., 2005—06, sr. v.p. product mgmt., 2006, sr. v.p. rsch. and product mgmt., 2006—. Contbr. articles to profl. jours. Office: Express Scripts Inc 13900 Riverport Dr Maryland Heights MO 63043 Office Phone: 314-770-1666. *

MOTHERWAY, NICHOLAS J., lawyer; b. Chgo., Jan. 21, 1940; s. Daniel Lawrence and Margaret Ann Motherway; m. Kathleen Elizabeth Butler, Dec. 23, 1967; children: Daniel, Nicholas, Carolyn, Brian. BSc, Loyola U., 1961; JD, DePaul U., 1965. Bar: Ill. 1965, U.S. Dist. Ct. (no. dist.) Ill. 1965, U.S. Ct. Appeals (7th cir.) 1996. Asst. states atty. Cook County States Atty., Chgo., 1966—73; assoc. Philip H. Corboy, Chgo., 1973—82; prin. Motherway and Napleton, Chgo., 1982—. Mem. Ill. Supreme Ct. Rules Com., 2007—. Lt. USAR, 1961—67. Fellow: Am. Coll. Trial Lawyers; mem.: ATLA (bd. govs. 1990—95), Am. Bd. Trial Adv. (pres. Ill. chpt. 1995—96, nat. bd. dirs. 1996—). Office: Motherway and Napleton 100 W Monroe St Chicago IL 60603 Office Phone: 312-726-2699. Business E-Mail: nmotherway@mnlawoffice.com.

MOTHKUR, SRIDHAR RAO, radiologist; b. Mothkur, India, Oct. 5, 1950; arrived in U.S., 1975, naturalized; s. Venkat Rao and Laxmi Bai (Gundepally) Mothkur; m. Sheila Rama Rao Paga, Nov. 30, 1973; children: Swathi, Preethi, Venkat Krishna. Student, Coll. Arts and Sci. Osmania U., Hyderabad, India, 1966; MB, BS, Osmania U., Hyderabad, India, 1972, DPH, 1974; MPA, Ind. U. N.W., 2000. Diplomate Am. Bd. Radiology. Rotating intern Osmania Gen. Hosp., Hyderabad, 1972-73, internal medicine intern, 1973, resident in surgery, 1974-75; resident Resurrection Hosp., Chgo., 1975-76; resident in radiology Luth. Gen. Hosp., Park Ridge, Ill., 1976-79, chief resident radiology, 1978-79; with rotations in nuclear medicine, angiography and neuroradiology Rush-Presbyn. St. Luke's Med. Ctr., Chgo., 1978; chmn. and med. dir. dept. radiology Louise Burg Hosp., Chgo., 1979-85, Shriner's Hosp., Chgo., 1986-88; fellow in ultrasound and computered tomography U. Ill., Chgo., 1988-89, fellow in magnetic resonance imaging, 1988-89; staff radiologist St. Anthony Hosp., Michigan City, Ind., 1989—, med. dir. MRI Ctr., 1989—; pvt. practice, Michigan City, 1989—; staff radiologist Kingwood Hosp., Michigan City, 1989-94, Charter Hosp., Behavioral Health Sys. Ind., Michigan City, 1994-96; pres. Michigan City Radiologists, Inc., Michigan City, 1998—2003; med. dir. dept. diagnostic imaging St. Anthony Meml. Med. Ctr., Michigan City, 2004—. Cons., radiologist Med. Group Michigan City, 1989—98, Franklin Clin. and Med. Watch, Michigan City, 1989—; spl. staff radiologist Christ hosp. Med. Ctr., Oak Lawn, Ill., 1988—89, Jasper County Meml. Hosp., Rensselaer, Ind., 1994—, United Diagnostic Svcs., Westchester, Ill., 1979—2000; dir. MRI Ctr. Meml. Hosp., 1989—97; med. dir. interventional radiology St. Anthony and Meml. Hosp., Michigan City, 1989—93; clin. asst. prof. radiology U. Ill., Chgo., 1990—2004; cons. radiologist Health Partners Medical Group, St. Francis, 2004—; others in field. Mem. Chinmaya Mission, Vishva Hindu Parishad. Fellow: Internat. Coll. Angiology, Am. Coll. Angiology, Am. Coll. Internat. Physicians; mem.: AMA, AmAm. Assn. Therapeutic and Interventional Neuroradiology, La Porte County Med. Soc., Telugu Assn. Greater Chgo., Chgo. Med. Soc., Ind. Med. Soc., Ill. Med. Soc., Ind. Assn. Physicians Indian Origin, India Med. Assn. N.W. Ind. (bd. dirs. 1999—2001), Am. Assn. Radiologists Indian Origins, Ind. Interventional Radiol. Assn., Tristate Telugu Assn., Indian Radiol. and Imaging Assn., Ind. Assn. Physicians from India, Soc. Magnetic Resonance in Medicine, Soc. Cardiovascular and Interventional Radiology, Soc. Magnetic Resonance Imaging, Am. Coll. Healthcare Execs., Am. Telugu Assn., Am. Soc. Head and Neck Radiology, Am. Coll. Emergency Physicians, Am. Diabetes Assn., Am. Assn. Physicians of Indian Origin, Am. Roentgen Ray Soc., Telugu Assn., Radiol. Soc. N.Am., Am. Assn. Andhra Brahmins, Internat. Soc. Krishna Consciousness, Pi Alpha Alpha. Republican. Home: 1481 Nelson Dr Chesterton IN 46304-3393 Office: Michigan City Radiologists Inc 8865 W 400 N Ste 115 Michigan City IN 46360-9223 Office Phone: 219-872-7268.

MOTIKA, LIDIA See BASTIANICH, LIDIA

MOTLEY, JOHN PAUL, retired psychiatrist; b. Carbondale, Pa., July 5, 1927; s. Joseph Adrian and Lillian (McCormick) Motley; children: Marianne, Patricia, Kathleen, John Paul, Elizabeth, Joseph A. III, Grace, Michael. BS, Georgetown U., Washington, 1951; MD, Hahnemann Med. Coll., Phila., 1955. Diplomate Am. Bd. Psychiatry and Neurology. Intern Hahnemann Med. Coll. Hosp., Phila., 1955—56; resident in psychiatry Inst. of Living, Hartford, Conn., 1956—59; practice medicine specializing in psychiatry Point Pleasant, NJ, 1961—2005; ret. Mem. staff Jersey Shore Med. Ctr., 1961—72, chief of psychiatry, 1970—72; mem. staff Point Pleasant Hosp., 1961—, chief psychiatry, 1961—; cons. in forensic psychiatry to various cts. and agys. With US Army, 1944—47. Fellow: Am. Psychiat. Assn. (disting. life); mem.: AMA, Springlake Golf Club. Republican. Roman Catholic. Address: 1738 Hwy 35 D-61 Wall NJ 07719 Personal E-mail: kacjyel@aol.com.

MOTOC, MIHNEA IOAN, international organization official; b. Bucharest, Nov. 11, 1966; married; 1 child. JD, U. Bucharest Sch. of Law; LLM in Pub. Internat. and Comparative Law, George Washington U., Washington, DC; post-graduate studies in Pub. and Private Internat. Law, Nice U., France. Worked as magistrate; dir.-gen. of the Directorate General European and Euro-Atlantic Orgns.; joined Ministry Foreign Affairs, 1991, dep. dir., human rights dept., 1994, dir., European Union dept., 1996; appointed amb. Romania to the Netherlands and permanent rep. to the Organization for Prohibition of Chemical Weapons, 1999; state sec. European Integration and Multilateral Affairs, 2001—03; permanent rep. of Romania UN, NY, 2003—. Participated in political treaty talks with neighbouring countries, 1992—96; permanent secretariat Inter-ministerial Committee for European Integration, 1996—98; mem. Internat. Humanitarian Fact Finding Commn., 1996—2000; vice-chmn. Exec. Coun. of the Orgn. for Prohibition of Chemical Weapons, 2000; pres. of the Inter-departmental Commn. for Romania's Accession to NATO, 01; nat. coordinator South-East Europe Stability Pact, 2001; pres. Nat. Security Authority, 2001, 02; head of the Romanian Delegation for Accession Talks to NATO, 03; headed Romanian delegations to international meetings of the United Nations, Council of Europe, OSCE and the European Union. Office: UN Hdqs First Ave at 46th St New York NY 10017

MOTRONI, HECTOR JOHN, printing company executive; b. Havana, Cuba, Dec. 2, 1943; came to US, 1956; s. Marco Antonio and Lilia Ines (Suarez) M.; m. Myra Helene Egan, Aug. 9, 1969; children: Marcus Alan, Melissa Aimee. BA, Dartmouth Coll., 1966, BE, 1967, ME, 1968. Engr. USPHS, Bethesda, Md., 1969-71, Xerox Corp., 1971—73, various positions Stamford, Conn., 1971-99, with Xerox Latin Am. Group, 1973, group v.p. quality, customer satisfaction and orgnl. effectiveness, 1991, v.p. human resources and quality, corp. sr. v.p., chief staff officer Stamford, 1999—2002, corp. sr. v.p., chief staff and ethics officer, 2003—. Bd. dirs. Prep for Prep. Trustee Temple Israel, Westport, Conn., 1981-84; bd. adv. Outward Bound USA, 1998; bd. dirs. Nat. Action Coun. Minorities in Engring., Horizons at Greens Farms Acad., 2005; chmn. bd. trustees Xerox Polit. Action Com., 2001—. Named Hispanic Achiever of Yr., Hispanic Corp. Achievers, 1997; named one of 50 Most Important Hispanics in Bus. and Tech., Hispanic Engrs. and Info. Tech. Mag., 2003, 2004, 2005, 2006, 25 Top Hispanic Execs., Hispanic Trends Mag., 2005, 100 Most Important Hispanics of 2005, Hispanic Bus. Mag.; recipient Eagle award, Nat. Eagle Inst., 1997. Mem. Nat. Policy Assn. (bd. dirs., chmn. com. new Am. realities 1996-2002), Dartmouth Soc. Engrs. (pres. 1977-85), Dartmouth Coll. Alumni Coun. (chmn. comm. 1983-88, Dartmouth Alumni award 2006), Coun. of the Ams. (adv. bd. 1983-89), Forum for World Affairs (bd. dirs. 1996-2001). Avocation: running. Office: Xerox Corp 800 Long Ridge Rd Stamford CT 06904 Office Phone: 203-968-3000.

MOTSENBOCKER, REX ALAN, construction company executive; b. Norman, Okla., Dec. 14, 1962; s. Rex Albert and Nondace Nadine (Bonner) M.; m. Karla Doreen Miller, Nov. 14, 1992. BS in BA, Calif. State U., Sacramento, 1984; BS in Constrn. Engring., Ariz. State U., 1986; MBA in Fin. magna cum laude, Western Internat. U., Phoenix, 1994; postgrad., So. Calif. U., Newport, 1994—. Cert. fin. cons. Project coord. Tibshraeny Bros., Mesa, Ariz., 1986; project mgr. Joe E. Woods, Tempe, Ariz., 1986-87; project engr. Sundt Corp., Phoenix, 1987—; pres. Master Investments, Phoenix, 1994—; CFO Master Builders Devel., LLC, Las Vegas, Nev., 1994—; mgr., CFO Remington Estates Devel., L.L.C., Phoenix, 1995—. Bd. dirs. bullion Recovery Sys., Inc., Phoenix. Author: Financial Aspects of Investing in Mexico, 1994. Team leader Senator McCain Re-election Campaign, Phoenix, 1992-94; project dir. Christmas in April, Phoenix, 1989-93. Mem. Project Mgrs. Inst. (v.p. membership 1990—), Am. Mgrs. Assn., Constrn. Mgmt. Assn., Phoenix C. of C., Nat. Asbestoc Council, Ariz. State U. Alumni Assn. (v.p. bd. 1994—), Delta Mu Delta (v.p. 1993—). Republican. Avocations: triathlons, singing.

MOTSETT, CHARLES BOURKE, retired sales, marketing and leadership executive; b. Peoria, Ill., Jan. 13, 1949; s. William James and Matilda (Robb) M.; m. Mary T. Werner, Aug. 26, 1972; children: Jon Bourke, Jill Suzanne, Brian Werner. BA in Polit. Sci., Econs. and Mktg., U. South Fla., Tampa, 1974. Product support mktg. analyst Caterpillar Tractor Co., 1974-75; parts and svc. sales rep. Caterpillar Ams. Co., Mexico City, 1976-79; product support rep. Caterpillar Tractor Co., Vancouver, B.C., Can., 1979-80, group prodr. mgr. remanufactured products Peoria, 1981-84, dist. mgr. parts and svc. sales Jacksonville, Fla., 1984-85; v.p. sales, customer svc. and mktg. Multi Media Productions of Am., Inc., Jacksonville, 1985-86; v.p. sales and mktg. Consol. Indsl. Skills Corp., Jacksonville, 1987—, corp. officer, 1988-92; v.p. and gen. mgr. Ogden CISCO Inc., Jacksonville, 1992—94; v.p. sales and mktg. CompuTower Technologies Corp., Miami, 1994—95, Shred All, 1995—96; pres. and CEO Bus. Devel. Specialists, Inc. and the Alternative Bd., Jacksonville, 1996—2005; ret., 2005. Participant Exec. Coach Summit, 2001, 02, 03, 04, 05; edtl. bd. Internat. Jour. Coaching Orgns. Author: If It Wasn't for the People...This Job Would Be Fun (Coaching for Buy-in and Results, 1998; co-author: How To Find a Qualified Corporate or Executive Coach, 2001; contbr. articles to profl. jours.; mem. editl. bd.: Internat. Jour. Coaching in Orgns. V.p. PTO, Dunlap, Ill., 1981—82; mem. adv. coun. Sch. Bd. Vocat. Edn., 1991—92; pres. bd. dirs. N.E. Fla. Jr. Achievement, Jr. Achievement Fla. First Coast, Inc.; vice chmn. St. Anthony's Ch., Vancouver, 1979—80; chmn. St. Jude Ch., Dunlap, 1982—83, Bishop Kenny H.S. PTO Polit. Action Com., 1989; pres. bd. dirs. Cath. Charities Housing Assn. Capt. US Army, 1967—70. Decorated Silver Star, Air medal with V device, Bronze Star with V device and oak leaf cluster, Purple Heart with 2 oak leaf clusters, Army Commendation medal with V device, Good Conduct medal, Combat Infantryman's badge. Mem. ASTD, Internat. Coach Fedn., Internat. Consortium Coaching in Orgns. (founding mem.), Assn. Facilities Engring., Soc. Automotive Engrs., Am. Soc. Naval Engrs., Soc. Naval Architects and Marine Engrs., Am. Nuclear Soc., Assn. Plant Engrs., U.S. Army Spl. Forces Assn., Worldwide Assn. Bus. Coaches (bd. dir., chmn. credentialing com., exec. coach summit 2002-03), Spl. Ops. Assn., Internat. Coach Fedn., Propellor Club. Republican. Roman Catholic. Avocations: scuba diving, sailing, reading, golf. Home: 4457 Barrington Oaks Dr Jacksonville FL 32257-5092 Personal E-mail: cork130@comcast.net.

MOTT, EARL, artist, poet, writer; b. San Augustine, Tex., May 9, 1949; s. J.B. and Lillie Mae M.; m. Frances Katherene Mott, Oct. 30, 1975 (dec. Apr. 1993); children: Amber Katherene Fanning; stepchildren: Ricky Lynn Plunk, Gary Lee Plunk, Jamey Leon Plunk. Student, Art Instrn. Schs., 1968—71, Virginia Blackmon, 1973—74, Foster Caddell's Art Sch., 1977. Author, artist: Secrets From an Oil Painting Diary, 1988; artist: The Best of Portrait Painting, 1998; artist, poet: The Unseen Hand, 2003, Cherished Moments, 2006, Best of America, 2007; contbr. articles to profl. publ.; one man shows at Angelina Coll., 1975, 82, 83, 87, Kurth Meml. Libr., 2001; group shows at Mus. East Tex., 1995, others. With USN, 1968—70. Recipient numerous awards for paintings. Mem.: Oil Painters of Am. Baptist. Avocations: poetry, reading, hiking, writing, photography. Home and Office: 304 Paul Ave Lufkin TX 75901 E-mail: art_tailored@yahoo.com.

MOTT, RANDY (RANDALL D. MOTT), computer company executive; b. 1956; BS in Math., U. Ark., Fayetteville, 1978. Various positions Wal-Mart Stores, Inc., 1978—94, sr. v.p., chief info. officer, 1994—97, mem. exec. com., 1997; sr. v.p., chief info. officer Dell, Inc., Round Rock, Tex., 2000—05; exec. v.p., chief info. officer Hewlett-Packard Co., Palo Alto, Calif., 2005—. Mem. Pres. Info. Tech. Adv. Com., 2003—. Named Chief Info. Officer of Yr., Info. Week mag., 1997, Disting. Alumni, Fulbright Coll. Alumni Acad., 2005. Office: Hewlett-Packard Co 3000 Hanover St Palo Alto CA 94304-1185 Office Phone: 650-857-1501. Office Fax: 650-857-5518. *

MOTT, RODNEY B., metal products executive; BS in Indsl. Engring., Northeastern U., 1974; MSc in Mgmt., Trenton State Coll., 1978. Various mgmt. positions US Steel, Fairless Hills, Pa., 1974—86; supt. ops. Lone Star Steel, 1986—88; v.p., gen. mgr. South Carolina plant, Arkasnas plant, Crawfordsville plant Nucor Steel, 1988—2000; pres., CEO Pechiney Rolled Products, 2000—01, Internat. Steel Group, Richfield, Ohio, 2002—05; cons. Tricap Mgmt. Ltd.; pres, CEO Stelco Inc., Hamilton, Ont., 2006—. Named Mgr. of Yr., New Steel Mag., 1995. Mem.: Am. Iron and Steel Engrs. (pres. 1998). Office: Stelco Inc PO Box 2030 Hamilton ON L8N 3T1 Canada

MOTT, STEWART RAWLINGS, food products executive, political organization worker; b. Flint, Mich., Dec. 4, 1937; s. Charles Stewart and Ruth (Rawlings) M.; m. Kappy Wells, Oct. 13, 1979 (div. Mar. 1999); 1 child, Samuel Apple Axle. BS in Bus. Adminstrn, Columbia, 1961, BA in Comparative Lit, 1961, postgrad. English lit., 1961-62. Exec. trainee various cos., 1956-63; English instr. Eastern Mich. U., 1963-64; corp. dir. U.S. Sugar Corp., Clewiston, Fla., 1965—98. Investor various diversified cos., 1968—. Founder Flint Cmty. Planned Parenthood, 1963; pres. S.R. Mott Charitable Trust, 1968—; pres., founder Spectemur Agendo, N.Y.C. and Flint, 1965—; bd. dirs. Fund For Peace, N.Y.C., 1967-90, Nat. Com. for Effective Congress, N.Y.C., 1968-, Planned Parenthood Fedn. Am., 1964-81, Am. Commn. on U.S.-Soviet Rels., 1977-92, Citizens Research Found., 1977-91, Ams. for Dem. Action, 1978-90, Friends of Family Planning, 1979-84, Voters for Choice, 1979-89; bd. dirs., founder Fund Constl. Govt., 1974-; bd. dirs. Population Action Council, 1978-82; maj. donor McCarthy, McGovern, Anderson campaigns. Mem. Phi Beta Kappa. *At age 18 I realized that two problems confront planet earth that dwarf and aggravate all conventional problems: namely the threat of nuclear war and the continuing worldwide population explosion. Coming to grips with these realities, I decided to dedicate my life to help find solutions to these two problems through public service in philanthropy and politics.*

MOTTELSON, BEN ROY, physicist; b. Chgo., July 9, 1926; naturalized Danish citizen, 1971. s. Goodman and Georgia (Blum) M.; m. Nancy Jane Reno, 1948 (dec. 1975); 3 children; m. Britta Marger Siegumfeldt, 1983. BSc, Purdue U., 1947; PhD, Harvard U., 1950; degree (hon.), Purdue U., U. Heidelberg, Fed. Republic Germany, Lund U., Sweden, Liverpool U., Eng. Sheldon traveling fellow Inst. Theoretical Physics, Copenhagen, 1950—51, U.S. AEC fellow, 1951—53; with theoretical study group CERN, Copenhagen, 1953—57; prof. Nordic Inst. for Theoretical Atomic Physics, Copenhagen, 1957—; dir. European ctr. Theoretical Studies in Nuc. Physics and Related Areas, Trento, Italy, 1980—97. Physicist Neils Bohr Inst., Copenhagen; bd. dir. Nordita; vis. prof. U. Calif., Berkeley, 1959, Berkeley, 84; adj. prof. Niels Bohr Inst., Copenhagen, 1994; Feshbach lectureship, 96. Author: Nuclear Structure, vol. 1, 1969, vol. 2 (with A. Bohr), 1975; numerous other publications in field. Recipient Nobel prize for physics, 1975. Mem.: Norwegian Acad. of Sci. and Letters, Polish Acad. of Sci., Kroatian Acad. Sci. (fgn. assoc.), Finnish Soc. Sci. and Letters, European Acad. of Arts, Sci., and Letters, Kgl. Fys. Graf, Lund, Sweden, Am. Acad. Arts and Letters, Royal Dan. Acad. Sci. and Letters, Nat. Acad. Sci. (fgn. assoc.). Address: NORDITA and The Niels Bohr Inst Blegdamsvej 17 DK-2100 Copenhagen Denmark Business E-Mail: mottelson@nordita.dk.

MOTTO, JEROME ARTHUR, psychiatrist, educator; b. Kansas City, Mo., Oct. 16, 1921; MD, U. Calif., San Francisco, 1951. Diplomate Am. Bd. Neurology and Psychiatry. Intern San Francisco Gen. Hosp., 1951-52; resident Johns Hopkins Hosp., Balt., 1952-55; sr. resident U. Calif., San Francisco, 1955-56; from instr. to prof. U. Calif. Sch. Medicine, San Francisco, 1956—91, prof. emeritus, 1991—. Pres. Am. Assn. Suicidology, 1972—73; sec. gen. Internat. Assn. Suicide Prevention, 1973—77. Contbr. articles to profl. jours. With AUS, 1942-46, ETO. Fellow: Am. Psychiatric Assn. (life; disting. fellow).

MOTTOLA, TOMMY (THOMAS D. MOTTOLA), recording industry executive; b. Bronx, NY, July 14, 1949; m. Lisa Clark, 1971 (div. 1990); 2 children; m. Mariah Carey, June 5, 1993 (div. Mar. 5, 1998); m. Thalía Sodi, Dec. 2, 2000. Attended, Hofstra U. Pres., CEO Sony Music Entertainment Inc, NYC, chmn., CEO, 1998—2003; pres. Casablanca Records, 2004—.

MOTTRAM, LISA MARIE, pediatric psychologist; b. Schenectady, NY, Feb. 15, 1975; d. Craig R. and Mary Mottram. BA, Bellarmine Coll., 1997; MA, St. John's U., NY, 2001, PhD, 2002. Lic. clin. psychologist Ill., 2006. Pediatric neuropsychologist Delnor-Cmty. Hosp., Geneva, Ill., 2005—06, Rockford Health Sys., Ill., 2006—. Musician: Rock Valley Chamber Orch., 2006—; contbr. articles to profl. jours. Mem.: APA. Roman Catholic. Avocations: viola, mezzo-soprano. Home: 2795 Stowmarket Ave 10 Rockford IL 61109 Office: Rockford Health Sys 2300 North Rockton Ave Rockford IL 61103 Office Phone: 815-971-4920. Personal E-mail: neuro215@juno.com. Business E-Mail: lmottram@rhsnet.org.

MOTTS, WARREN EARL, museum director; b. Brice, Ohio, Nov. 10, 1940; s. Wilbur Ernest and Mabel Marie Motts; m. Daisy Nell Blair, July 1, 1966; children: Wayne Earl, Lori Lynn. M in photography, Profl. Photographers of Am., 1977; MS in photography, Brooks Inst. Sch. of Profl. Photography, 1990; M, China, 1990, Mexico, 1990. Photo lab tech. Battelle Meml. Inst., Columbus, Ohio, 1960—62; med. photographer Ohio State Hosp., Columbus, 1962—64; photographer Columbus and Southern Electric, Columbus, 1964—67; commercial photographer Columbus Art, Columbus, 1967—69; v.p. Moor Photography, Columbus, 1969—72; pres., owner Motts Photographic Ctr., Columbus, 1972—97; founder, dir. Motts Mil. Mus., Groveport, Ohio, 1988—. Pres. Profl. Photo of Am., Atlanta, 1990—91, Mil. Vets Edn., Columbus, Ohio, 1999—2000; bd. dirs. Veterans Meml., Columbus, 2001—; lectr. Mathew Brady: Civil War Photographer, 1994. Creator: (films) American Freedom Train, 1976; Gettysburg: A Portrait in Red, Gray, and Blue; contbr. articles various profl. jours. Pres. Groveport Lions Club, Groveport, Ohio, 1999—2000, Columbus Civil War, Columbus, Ohio, 1967; chmn. of bd. Brice United Meth. Ch., Brice, Ohio, 1981—; 32nd Mason Masonic Order, Columbus, Ohio, 1981. With Ohio Nat. Guard, 1959—68. Named Communicator of Yr., Communicatings Arts, 1991; recipient Patriotic, Daughters of Am. Revolution, 1982, Dist. Svc. award, PP of Am., 1991. Mem.: Ohio Hist. Mus., Am. Mus. Assoc., Airforce Assn. (life). Republican. Meth. Avocation: antiques. Office: Motts Mil Mus 5075 S Hamilton Rd Groveport OH 43125 Office Phone: 614-836-1500. Office Fax: 614-836-5110.

MOTULSKY, ARNO GUNTHER, internist, geneticist, educator; b. Fischhausen, Germany, July 5, 1923; arrived in U.S., 1941; s. Herman and Rena (Sass) Molton; m. Gretel C. Stern, Mar. 22, 1945; children: Judy, Harvey, Arlene. Student, Cen. YMCA Coll., Chgo., 1941—43, Yale U., 1943—44; BS, U. Ill., 1945, MD, 1947, DSc (hon.), 1982, MD (hon.), 1991. Diplomate Am. Bd. Internal Medicine, Am. Bd. Med. Genetics. Intern, fellow, resident Michael Reese Hosp., Chgo., 1947—51; staff mem. charge clin. investigation dept. hematology Army Med. Service Grad. Sch., Walter Reed Army Med. Ctr., Washington, 1952—53; research assoc. internal medicine George Washington U. Sch. Medicine, 1952—53; from instr. to assoc. prof. dept. medicine U. Wash. Sch. Medicine, Seattle, 1953—61, prof. medicine, prof. genetics, 1961—; head div. med. genetics, dir. genetics clinic Univ. Hosp., Seattle, 1959—89; dir. Ctr. for Inherited Diseases, Seattle, 1972—90. Attending physician Univ. Hosp., Seattle; cons. Pres.'s Commn. for Study of Ethical Problems in Medicine and Biomed. and Behavioral Rsch., 1979—83; cons. various coms. NRC, NIH, WHO, and others. Editor: Am. Jour. Human Genetics, 1969—75, Human Genetics, 1969—97. Fellow Commonwealth Fund in human genetics, Univ. Coll., London, 1957—58, Ctr. Advanced Study in Behavorial Scis., Stanford U., 1976—77, Inst. Advanced Study, Berlin, 1984; scholar John and Mary Markle in med. sci., 1957—62. Fellow: AAAS, ACP; mem.: NAS, Am. Philos. Soc., Am. Acad. Arts and Scis., Inst. of Medicine, Am. Assn. Physicians, Am. Soc. Clin. Investigation, Am. Soc. Human Genetics, Western Soc. Clin. Rsch., Genetics Soc. Am., Am. Fedn. Clin. Rsch., Internat. Soc. Hematology. Home: 4347 53rd Ave NE Seattle WA 98105-4938 Office: Univ Wash Medicine and Genome Scis PO Box 355065 Seattle WA 98195-5065 Business E-Mail: agmot@u.washington.edu.

MOTURI, SRICHARAN, psychiatrist; b. Mahallat, Iran, Nov. 2, 1976; s. Bose Subhaschandra and Usha Moturi; m. Anuradha Chinta, Dec. 25, 2004. MBBS, Kasturba Med. Coll., Manipal, India, 2001; MPH, U. Ala., Birmingham, 2003, MD, 2007. Cert. Ednl. Commn. for Fgn. Med. Grads., 2003, BLS Am. Heart Assn., 2006, ACLS Am. Heart Assn., 2006. Basic sci. anesthesiology rschr. U. Ala., Birmingham, 2001—04, mem. ho. staff dept. psychiatry and behavioral neurobiology, 2004—06, chief of ho. staff, 2006—. V.p. Psychiatry Residents' Assn., dept. psychiatry and behavioral neurobiology U. Ala., 2005—06. Lead singer Best of Kishore Kumar (Best Male Vocalist, 2000). Recipient Most Helpful Resident award, Dept. Psychiatry and Behavioral Neurobiology, U. Ala., Birmingham, 2004, Argus award, U. Ala. Sch. Medicine, 2004, 2005; fellow, APA/GlaxoSmithKline, 2006, Lasdon Found./ Am. Acad. Child and Adolescent Psychiatry, 2006, Assn. Academic Psychiatry, 2007; Shire Child and Adolescent Psychiatry fellow, APA, 2004, 2005, PRITE fellow, Am. Coll. Psychiatrists, 2005, Laughlin fellow, 2006. Mem.: APHA, Am. Acad. Child and Adolescent Psychiatry (travel grantee 2004), Am. Psychiat. Assn., Rotaract Club (gen. sec., dir. program implementation 1998—2000). Hindu. Achievements include research in prodromal schizophrenia, ongoing clinical trials in treatment of mental illness. Avocation: sports. Home: 274 Woodmere Creek Ln Birmingham AL 35226 Home Phone: 205-934-8619; Office Phone: 205-934-8619. Office Fax: 205-975-7248. Personal E-mail: charan@uab.edu.

MOTYKIE, GARY, plastic surgeon; Attended night sch., Kellogg Grad. Sch. Mgmt., 1997—99; BS in Bio-Med. Engring. (summa cum laude), Univ. Ill., Chgo., 1993; MD, Northwestern Univ. Med. Sch., Chgo., 1999. Clin. rsch. fellow, dept. surgery Northwestern U. Med. Sch., 1997—99; resident, plastic surgery U. Tex. Med. Branch, Galveston, Tex., 1999—2004; externship, Aesthetic Surgery James M. Stuzin, Thomas & Tracy Baker, Miami, Fla., 2003; externship, Microsurgery & Cancer Reconstruction M.D. Anderson Cancer Ctr., Houston, 2003; fellow in advanced cosmetic surgery Beverly Hills, Calif., 2004; with Beverly Hills Body, Calif. Spkr. in field. Contbr. articles to profl. jours., chapters to books; featured in The Smart Surgeon, plasticsurgeryproductsonline.com, 2007. Mem.: ACS (cand. and assoc. soc. 2000—, mem.-elect, issues com. 2002—, mem. adv. coun. for plastic and maxillofacial surgery cand. 2002—, assoc. soc. respresentative 2002—), Am. Soc. Plastic Surgeons (mem., resident affiliate group 2000—, mem. com. edn., ASMS 2002—), Plastic Surgery Rsch. Coun., Tex. Med. Assn. (resident and fellow sect. 1999—2004, representative, com. continuing edn. 1999—2004), AMA (mem. polit. action com. 2002—), Tau Beta Pi. Office: Beverly Hills Body 9201 Sunset Blvd Ste 202 Los Angeles CA 90069 Office Phone: 310-276-3183. *

MOTZ, DIANA GRIBBON, federal judge; b. Washington, July 15, 1943; d. Daniel McNamara and Jane (Retzler) Gribbon; m. John Frederick Motz, Sept. 20, 1968; children: Catherine Jane, Daniel Gribbon. BA, Vassar Coll., 1965; LLB, U. Va., 1968. Bar: US Dist. Ct. Md. 1969, US Ct. Appeals (4th cir.) 1969, US Supreme Ct. 1980. Assoc. Piper & Marbury, Balt.,

1968—71; asst. atty. gen. State of Md., Balt., 1972—81, chief of litigation, 1981—86; ptnr. Frank, Bernstein, Conaway & Goldman, Balt., 1986—91; judge Md. Ct. of Special Appeals, 1991—94, US Ct. Appeals (4th cir.), 1994—. Mem.: ABA, Fed. Cts. Study Com., Lawyers Round Table, Md. Bar Found., Am. Bar Found., Am. Law Inst., Balt. City Bar Assn. (exec. com. 1988), Md. Bar Assn., Wranglers Law Club. Roman Catholic. Office: 920 US Courthouse 101 W Lombard St Ste 920 Baltimore MD 21201-2611 *

MOTZ, JOHN FREDERICK, federal judge; b. Balt., Dec. 30, 1942; s. John Eldred and Catherine (Grauel) M.; m. Diana Jane Gribbon, Sept. 20, 1968; children: Catherine Jane, Daniel Gribbon AB, Wesleyan U., Conn., 1964; LLB, U. Va., 1967. Bar: Md. 1967, U.S. Ct. Appeals (4th cir.) 1968, U.S. Dist. Ct. Md. 1968. Law clk. to Hon. Harrison L. Winter US Ct. Appeals (4th cir.), 1967-68; assoc. Venable, Baetjer & Howard LLP, Balt., 1968-69; asst. U.S. atty. US Dept. Justice, Balt., 1969-71; assoc. Venable, Baetjer & Howard, Balt., 1971-75; ptnr. Venable, Baetjer & Howard LLP, Balt., 1976-81; US atty. US Dept. Justice, Balt., 1981-85; judge US Dist. Ct. Md., Balt., 1985—, chief judge, 1994—2001. Mem. US Jud. Panel on Multidistrict Litig., 2001—. Trustees Friends Sch., Balt., 1970-77, 1981-88, Sheppard Pratt Hosp., 1987-97, 99—. Mem.: ABA, Am. Coll. Trial Lawyers (mem. bd. editors. Manual of Complex Litigation (4th)), Am. Law Inst., Am. Bar Found., Md. State Bar Assn. Republican. Mem. Soc. Of Friends. Office: US Dist Ct 101 W Lombard St Rm 510 Baltimore MD 21201-2605

MOU, THOMAS WILLIAM, retired physician, medical educator, consultant; b. Phila., May 17, 1920; s. Thomas Simonsen and Ellen Marie (Mathiesen) Mou; m. Marie Elizabeth Hartmann, Dec. 29, 1945 (div. Oct. 1976); m. Delma Jane Schreiber, Nov. 11, 1976. BSc in Bacteriology, Phila. Coll. Pharm & Sci., 1941; MD, U. Rochester, 1950. Diplomate Nat. Bd. Med. Examiners. Instr. medicine and bacteriology Sch. Medicine U. Rochester, NY, 1954-56; from asst. prof. preventive medicine to prof. cmty. medicine SUNY, Syracuse, 1956-70, from exec. dean to assoc chancellor health sci. Ctrl. Adminstrn. Albany, 1970-77; dean clin. campus W. Va. U., Charleston, 1977-85, dean emeritus Med. Ctr. Morgantown, 1986—; pres. Ednl. Commn. Fgn. Med. Grads., Phila., 1986-88; geriatric practice Adult Medicine Specialists, Pueblo, Colo., 1990-2000, ret. Cons. Carnegie Commn. Advancement Tchg., Princeton, NJ, 1987—88, Charles A. Dana Found., NYC, 1988, Geriatric Pharmacy Inst., Phila. Coll. Pharmacy and Sci., 1988. Contbr. articles to profl. jours. Trustee Phila. Coll. Pharmacy and Sci., 1972—81. Capt. Sanitary Corps US Army, 1941—45. Named T. W. Mou Endowment Lectureship in his honor, W.Va. U., 1985—; recipient Alumnus award, Phila. Coll. Pharmacy and Sci., 1975, award of distinction and honor, Ben Franklin Soc. SUNY, 1975, Koch medal, Am. Optometric Soc., 1976. Fellow: ACP, Infectious Diseases Soc. Am. (founding fellow), Phila. Coll. Physicians, Am. Coll. Preventive Medicine. Avocations: violin, travel. Home: 3050 Valleybrook Ln Colorado Springs CO 80904-1154 Personal E-mail: moutw@comcast.net.

MOUL, BRIAN E., music educator; b. Gettysburg, Pa., July 10, 1958; s. Henry Edgar and Betty Jane Moul; m. Anne Denney. BS in Music Edn., West Chester U., Pa., 1980. Instrumental music tchr. Easton (Md.) HS, 1980—81, Penn Wood HS, Lansdowne, Pa., 1981—84, Dover (Pa.) HS, 1984—92, Dover Sch. Dist., 1992—. Brass instr. Lancers Drum and Bugle Corps, Hanover, Pa., 1989—; pvt. trombone instr.; arranger band music and drum and bugle corps music. Treas. Emmanuel United Ch. of Christ, 1992—; mem. Phoenix Vocal Ensemble, York, Pa., 1991—2005, Wheatland Chorale, Lancaster, Pa., 2005—. Mem.: Internat. Trombone Assn., Pa. State Edn. Assn., Pa. Music Educators Assn., Music Educators Nat. Conf. Republican. Avocations: golf, singing, drum and bugle corps. Home: 3045 Brookfield Dr York PA 17404 Office: North Salem Elem Sch 5161 N Salem Church Rd Dover PA 17315 Office Phone: 717-292-3671 ext 346. Fax: 717-292-4388. E-mail: golfnband@comcast.net.

MOUL, WILLIAM CHARLES, lawyer; b. Columbus, Ohio, Jan. 12, 1940; s. Charles Emerson and Lillian Ann (Mackenbach) M.; m. Margine Ann Tessendorf, June 10, 1962; children: Gregory, Geoffrey. BA, Miami U., Oxford, Ohio, 1961; JD, Ohio State U., 1964. Bar: Ohio 1964, U.S. Dist. Ct. (so. dist.) Ohio 1965, U.S. Ct. Appeals (2d cir.) 1982, U.S. Ct. Appeals (6th cir.) 1984, U.S. Ct. Appeals (3d cir.) 1985. Assoc., ptnr. George, Greek, King, McMahon & McConnaughey, Columbus, 1964-79; ptnr. McConnaughey, Stradley, Mone & Moul, Columbus, 1979-81; ptnr.-in-charge Thompson, Hine & Flory, Columbus, 1981-89, exec. com., 1989-98. Chmn. Upper Arlington Civil Svc. Commn., Ohio, 1981-86. Mem. ABA, Ohio State Bar Assn. (labor sect. bd. dirs. 1983—), Columbus Bar Assn. (chmn. ethics com. 1980-82), Lawyers Club Columbus (pres. 1976-77), Athletic Club, Scioto Country Club, Wedgewood Country Club, Masons. Lutheran. Home: 2512 Danvers Ct Columbus OH 43220-2822 Office: Thompson Hine LLP 10 W Broad St Ste 700 Columbus OH 43215-3435 Office Phone: 614-469-3220. Business E-mail: william.moul@thompsonhine.com.

MOULD, JEREMY RICHARD, astronomer; b. Bristol, Eng., July 31, 1949; s. Michael Thomas and Sheila Patricia (Pickering Clarke) Mould; m. Joan Mary Milesi, Dec. 11, 1971; children: Helen, Kate. BSc with honors, U. Melbourne, Australia, 1971; PhD, Australian Nat. U., 1975. Rsch. fellow Royal Greenwich (Eng.) Obs., 1976; postdoctoral fellow Kitt Peak Nat. Obs., Tucson, 1976—78, asst. astronomer, 1980—82; Carnegie fellow Hale Obs., 1978—79; prof. Calif. Inst. Tech., Pasadena, 1982—93, exec. officer for astronomy, 1987—90; prof. Australian Nat. U., Canberra, 1993—2001; dir. Mt. Stromlo & Siding Obs., Weston, Australia, 1993—2001, Nat. Optical Astronomy Obs., Tucson, 2001—. Mem. Anglo Australian Telescope Bd., 1993—2001, chair, 1999; mem. Australia Telescope Steering Com., 1995—2000; mem. space sci. adv. com. NASA. Mem.: Australian Acad. Sci., Assn. Univ. Rsch. Astronomy (bd. dirs. 1997—2001), Astron. Soc. Pacific, Astron. Soc. Australia, Am. Astron. Soc. Office: NOAO Mail Stop DODP 950 N Cherry Ave Tucson AZ 85726-6732 Business E-Mail: jmould@noao.edu.

MOULDER, T. EARLINE, musician; b. Buffalo, Mo., Oct. 11; d. Earl Young and Ruby M. (Phillipot); m. R. David Plank, Dec. 21, 1980; children: Jeannine Stanton, Jon Stanton, Timothy Stanton. AB in Biology and French, Drury Univ., 1973; studied piano with Soulima Stravinsky, 1961; M in Music, Ind. U., 0000; D in Musical Arts, U. Kansas, 1991; pvt. organ study, Andre Marchal, Paris, France, 1971. Concert organist, 1964—; chair organ dept. Drury U., Springfield, Mo., 1968—; exec. editor Drury Coll. Mirror, Springfield, Mo., 1971-73; rschr. Am. U., Beirut, 1973; journalist US Naval Res., Springfield and Treasure Island, Calif., 1975-77; u. organist Drury U., Springfield, Mo., 1991—. Translator, Profl. documents, 1990—; guest artist Liszt Acad. Music, Budapest, Hungary, 2006; lectr. in field. Author: Organ Works of Elsa Barraine, 1995, Music of Alice Jordan, 1998; composer organ composition The Crucifixion, 1995; musician (organ recital series) Queen's Golden Jubilee, London, Eng., 2002; contbr. articles to profl. jours. Charter mem. Nat. Mus. Am. Indian, 1994—. Recipient Teaching fellow U. Kans., Drury Mirror award Rank I Mo. Coll. Newspaper Assn. Mem. Mortar Bd., Sigma Alpha Iota, Alpha Lambda Delta, Pi Delta Phi, Beta Beta Beta, Pi Kappa Lambda, Organ Hist. Soc., Am. Guild Organist. Office: Drury Univ 900 N Benton Ave Springfield MO 65802-3712 Address: 95 rue de Seine 75006 Paris France Mailing: 3563 E Linwood Dr Springfield MO 65809 Office Phone: 417-873-7376. Personal E-mail: dplank@msn.com. Business E-mail: emoulder@drury.edu.

MOULDS, ERIC SHANNON, professional football player; b. Lucedale, Miss., July 17, 1973; BS in Edn. Psychology, Miss. State U. Wide receiver, kickoff return Buffalo Bills, 1996—2006, Houston Texans, 2006—. Named to Pro-Bowl, 1998, 2000, 2002. Achievements include first round draft pick NFL, 1996. Office: Houston Texans Two Reliant Park Houston TX 77054

MOULDS, JOHN F., judge; m. Elizabeth Fry, Aug. 29, 1964; children: Donald B., Gerald B. Student, Stanford U., 1955-58; BA with honors, Calif. State U., Sacramento, 1960; JD, U. Calif, Berkeley, 1963. Bar: U.S. Supreme Ct., U.S. Dist. Ct. (no. dist.) Calif., U.S. Dist. Ct. (ea. dist.) Calif. 1968, U.S. Ct. Claims 1982, U.S. Ct. Appeals (9th cir.) 1967, Calif. Rsch. analyst Calif. State Senate Fact-Finding Com. on Edn., 1960-61; adminstrv. asst. Senator Albert S. Rodda, Calif., 1961-63; staff atty. Calif. Rural Legal Assistance, Marysville, 1966-68, dir. atty. Marysville field office and Sacramento legis. adv. office, 1968-69; staff atty. Sacramento Legal Aid, 1968-69; ptnr. Blackmon, Isenberg & Moulds, 1969-85, Isenberg, Moulds & Hemmer, 1985; magistrate judge U.S. Dist. Ct. (ea. dist.) Calif., 1985—, chief magistrate jduge, 1988-97. Moot ct. and trial practice judge U. Calif. Davis Law Sch., 1975—, U. of Pacific McGeorge Coll. Law, 1985—; part-time U.S. magistrate judge U.S. Dist. Ct. (ea. dist.) Calif., 1983-85; mem. 9th Cir. Capital Case Com., 1992—, U.S. Jud. Conf. Com. on the Magistrate Judge Sys., 1992—, Adv. Com. to the Magistrate Judges' Divsn. Adminstv. Office of U.S. Jud. Conf., 1989—. Author: (with others) Review of California Code Legislation, 1965, Welfare Recipients' Handbook, 1967; editor: Ninth Circuit Capital Punishment Handbook, 1991. Atty. Sacramento Singlemen's Self-Help Ctr., 1969-74; active Sacramento Human Relations Commn., 1969-75, chair, 1974-75; active community support orgn. U. Calif. at Davis Law Sch., 1971—; mem., atty. Sacramento Community Coalition for Media Change, 1972-75; bd. dirs. Sacramento Country Day Sch., 1982-90, Sacramento Pub. Libr. Found., 1985-87; active various polit. orgns. and campaigns, 1960-82. Mem. ABA, Fed. Bar Assn., Nat. Coun. Magistrates (cir. dir. 1986-88, treas. 1988-89, 2d v.p. 1989-90, 1st v.p. 1990-91), Fed. Magistrate Judges Assn. (pres.-elect 1991, pres. 1992-93), Calif. State-Fed. Jud. Coun. Conf. (panelist capital habeas corpus litigation 1992), Fed. Jud. Ctr. Training Conf. for U.S. Magistrate Judges (panel leader 1993), Milton L. Schwartz Inns of Ct. Office: 16-400 US Courthouse 501 I St 16th Fl Ste 1640 Sacramento CA 95814-7300

MOULITSAS ZÚNIGA, MARKOS, former military officer, blog writer; b. Chgo., Sept. 11, 1971; married; 2 children. B in Philosophy, Polit. Sci. and Journalism, Northern Ill. U.; JD, Boston U. Sch. Law. Founder, writer dailykos.com, Kos Media LLC, 2002—. Former cons., 2003; writer The Guardian, 2005; co-founder SB Nation (Sport Blog Nation), SportsBlogs, Inc.; fellow New Politics Inst. Writer, performer (several piano compositions); co-author: Crashing the Gate: Netroots, Grassroots, and the Rise of People Powered Politics, 2006. MLRS/Lance Fire Direction Specialist (artillery) US Army, 1989—92. Named No. 3 of Top 25 Web Celebs, Forbes mag., 2007. Achievements include having what is considered the highest-traffic weblog. Avocations: music, piano. *

MOULTHROP, REBECCA LEE STILPHEN, retired elementary school educator; b. Lubbock, Tex., Mar. 5, 1944; d. Lee Edward and Geraldine (Lansford) Stilphen; m. John Stephen Martin Moulthrop, June 1967 (div. 1968); 1 child, Paul Martin. BS in edn., U. New Mex., 1966; MS in reading edn., Calif. State U., Fullerton, 1971; postgrad., U. LaVerne. Elem. tchr. Arnold Heights Elem. Sch., Moreno Valley, Calif., 1966-67, Hawthorn Elem. Sch., El Monte, Calif., 1968-69; chap. 1 reading specialist Posey Elem. Sch., Lubbock, 1971-72; elem. tchr. Arnold Heights Elem. Sch., Moreno Valley, 1972-74, Sunnymead Elem. Sch., Moreno Valley, 1974-80, Moreno Elem. Sch., Moreno Valley, 1980-88; chap. 1 program coord. Edgemont Elem. Sch., Moreno Valley, 1988-91; elem. tchr. Sunnymeadows Elem. Sch., Moreno Valley, 1991—2005, ret., 2005. Assertive discipline cons. Moreno Valley (Calif.) Unified Sch. Dist., 1979-85, mentor/tchr., 1985-89, adminstrn. designee/trainee, 1988-95; effective tchg./supervision coach Riverside (Calif.) County Sch. Office, 1984-87. Recipient Tchr. of Yr., Moreno Valley Unified Sch. Dist., 2005. Mem. NEA, Calif. Reading Assn., Internat. Reading Assn., Reading Edn. Guild, Delta Kappa Gamma, Phi Delta Kappa. Avocations: travel, dance, painting.

MOULTON, EDWARD QUENTIN, civil engineer, educator; b. Kalamazoo, Mich., Nov. 16, 1926; s. Burt Frederick and Esther (Fairchild) M.; m. Joy Wade, Jan. 2, 1954; children: Jennifer Fairchild, Charles Wade, David Frederick II, Alison Joy. BS, Mich. State U., East Lansing, 1947; MS, La. State U., 1948; PhD, U. Calif., Berkeley, 1956; DSc (hon.), Wittenberg U., Springfield, Ohio, 1980; LLD (hon.), Xavier U., Cin., 1983, Wilmington Coll., Ohio, 1983. Registered profl. engr., Ohio. Instr. civil engring Mich. State U., 1947; hydraulic engring. fellow La. State U., 1947-48; engr. US Waterways Expt. Sta., Vicksburg, Miss., 1948; rsch. fellow U. Wis., 1948-49; asst. prof. civil engring. Auburn U., 1949-50; lectr. civil engring. U. Calif., Berkeley, 1950-54; asst. prof. civil engring. Ohio State U., 1954-58, assoc. prof., 1958-64; asst. dean Ohio State U. (Grad. Sch.), 1958-62, assoc. dean Grad. Sch., Coll. Arts and Scis., chmn. geodetic sci., 1962-64; dean off-campus edn., asso. dean faculties for personnel budget, prof. engring. mechanics Ohio State U. Grad. Sch., Columbus, 1964-66; dir. Coll. Sci. and Engring. Dayton campus Miami U.-Ohio State U., 1963-66; pres. U. SD, 1966-68; exec. asst. to pres. Ohio State U., 1968-69, sec. bd. trustees, 1968-79, prof. civil engring., 1968-79, v.p. adminstrv. ops., 1969-70, exec. v.p. adminstrv. ops., 1970-71, exec. v.p., 1971-73, v.p. bus. and adminstrn., 1973-79, v.p., sec. emeritus, 1984—; chancellor Ohio Bd. Regents, 1979-84, chancellor emeritus, 1984—; exec. v.p. Cranston Securities Co., 1984; pres. Lake Erie Coll., 1985-86; pres., gen. mgr. Columbus Symphony Orch., 1986-88, mem. trustees cir., 2000—. Cons. civil engring. 1954—. Author articles, reports, bulls. on environ. engring. and edn. Trustee Blue Cross Ctrl. Ohio, 1971-77, 80-82, Columbus Symphony Orch., 1980-85, Riverside Meth. Hosp., 1979-95, chmn. fin. and assets com., 1983-94, treas., 1988-94, vice-chmn., 1994-95, chmn., 1995-96; nat. adv. coun. for small bus. to US Sec. Treasury, 1975-76; steering com. Devel. Com. Greater Columbus, 1970-1980, chmn., 1978-79; nat. adv. coun. SBA, 1973-76; bd. dirs. Columbus Safety Coun., 1970-79; bd. mem. Greater Columbus Arts Coun., 1970-78, Mid-Ohio Health Planning Commn., 1973-74, Am. Univs. for Rsch. in Astronomy, 1972-79, Ohio Transp. Rsch. Ctr., 1979-83, US Health Corp. (now Ohio Health), 1995-97; chmn. Grant/Riverside Meth. Hosps., 1995-97, mem. trustees' coun., 1998—, trustee emeritus, 1999—; vice-chmn. Ohio Higher Edn. facilities Commn., 1979-83; mem. Ohio Sch. and Coll. Bd. Registration, 1979-83, Ohio Ednl. TV Commn., 1979-83, Midwest Edn. Commn., 1979-85; chmn. Columbus Symphony Grand Ball, 1983; chmn. judging Internat. Sci. and Engring. Fair, 1984. With USN, 1945-46, PTO. Fellow ASCE; mem. Ohio Hist. Soc. (bd. dirs. 1979-83), State Higher Edn. Exec. Officers (exec. com. 1981-83), Meml. Soc. Columbus Area (pres. 1999-2000, bd. mem.), Ohio Commodore, Scioto Country Club, Faculty Club (Columbus), Athletic Club Columbus, Sigma Xi, Tau Beta Pi, Pi Mu Epsilon, Chi Epsilon, Delta Omega, Romophos, Sigma Alpha Epsilon. Congregationalist. Home: 1303 London Dr Columbus OH 43221-1541

MOULTON, GRACE CHARBONNET, retired physicist; b. New Orleans, Nov. 1, 1923; d. Wilfred J. and Louise A. (Hellmers) Charbonnet; m. William Gates Moulton, June 1, 1947; children: Paul Charbonnet Moulton, Nancy Gates Moulton. BA, Tulane U., 1944; MS, U. Ill., 1948; PhD, U. Ala., 1962. Asst. prof. physics U. Ala., Tuscaloosa, 1962-65, Fla. State U., Tallahassee, 1965-74, assoc. prof. physics, 1974-80, prof. physics, 1980-91, prof. emerita, 1991. Cons. State Bd. Regents, Fla., 1985-90, Fla. Univ. System, 1985, 90. Referee jour. articles Jour. Chem. Physics, Radiation Rsch.; contbr. many sci. rsch. articles to profl. jours. Scholar, U. Ill.; Four Yr. Undergrad. scholar, Tulane U., rsch. grantee, NIH. Mem. Am. Phys. Soc., (mem. coun. southeastern sect. 1988-92). Avocations: gardening, music (classical and folk), birding. Personal E-mail: gmoulton@phy.fsu.edu.

MOULTON, SARA, chef, magazine editor; m. Bill Moulton; children: Ruth, Sam. Grad., U. Mich., 1974, Culinary Inst. Am., 1977; postgrad. stagaire with a master chef, Chartres, France, 1979. With Julia Child and More Co., 1979; mem. test kitchen Gourmet mag., 1984—88, exec. chef, 1988—, Good Morning Am., food corr., 1997, food editor; sous chef La Tulipe, NY; instr. Peter Kump's NY Cooking Sch. Co-founder NY Women's Culinary Alliance. Host Cooking Live, Food Network, 1996—2002, Sara's Secrets, 2002—; co-author (with Jean Anderson): (cookbooks) Good Morning America Cut the Calories Cookbook, 2000; author: Sara Moulton Cooks at Home, 2002, Sara's Secrets for Weeknight Meals, 2005. Office: Sara Moulton Enterprises Inc 130 W 24th St 3B New York NY 10011 Business E-Mail: sara@saramoulton.com. *

MOULTRIE, FRED, geneticist, researcher; b. Albertville, Ala., Apr. 18, 1923; s. Walter Louis and Minnie Alma (Bodine) M.; m. Frances Grace Aldridge, May 28, 1947; children: Marilyn R. Moultrie Phillips, Elizabeth Anne Moultrie Becker, Janet Carol Moultrie Gauger. BS, Auburn U., 1948, MS, 1949; PhD in Genetics, Kan State U., 1953. Asso. prof. Auburn U., 1951-55, prof., 1955-56; geneticist Arbor Acres Farm, Inc., Glastonbury, Conn., 1956-59, research coordinator, 1959-62, v.p., dir. research, 1962-64, exec. v.p., 1964-72, pres. domestic div., 1972-73; pres. Corbett Breeders, Westover, Md., 1973-81; v.p., dir. research Corbett Enterprises, Inc., 1973-81, Kennebec Internat., 1981-84; geneticist Perdue Farms, Salisbury, Md., 1984-88; genetics cons., 1988—. Served with USCGR, 1942-46. Mem. World's Poultry Sci. Assn., Am. Poultry Sci. Assn., Poultry Breeders Am. (pres. 1967-68), Sigma Xi, Phi Kappa Phi, Alpha Zeta, Gamma Sigma Delta. Clubs: Masons. Home and Office: 918 Winding Way Salisbury MD 21804

MOUNCE, CAROLYN P., retired school librarian; b. Ecru, Miss., Dec. 18, 1938; d. Walter Gerald and Mary Ozelle Mounce. BA, Blue Mountain Coll., 1960; MA in Libr. Sci., George Peabody Coll., 1963. Asst. libr. Guyton Libr, Blue Mountain Coll., Miss., 1960—70, head libr., 1971—2004; ret., 2004. Libr. sci. instr. Blue Mountain Coll., 1967—87. Mem.: AAUW (officer, Branch Woman Achievement award 1990), Blue Mountain Coll. Alumnae Assn., Pontotoc Fed. Womans CLub (officer), Woodmen of World Lodge (officer, Fraternal Spirit award 2005). Democrat. Baptist. Avocation: sports. Home: 785 North Rd Ecru MS 38841

MOUNT, THOMAS H(ENDERSON), motion picture and stage producer; b. Durham, NC, May 26, 1948; s. Lillard H. and Bonnie M.; m. Katrina Woodard. Student, Bard Coll., 1968-70; MFA, Calif. Inst. Arts, 1973. Prodn. exec. Universal Studios, Universal City, Calif., 1974-79, pres. for prodn., 1976-84, ind. film prodr., 1984—; mng. ptnr. L.A. Film Sch. and Hollywood Broadcasting.com. Adj. prof. Columbia U. Grad. Sch. Film, 1995-96. Prodr.: (films) My Man Adam, 1985, Roman Polanski's Pirates, 1985, Can't Buy Me Love, 1987, Frantic, 1987, Bull Durham, 1988, Stealing Home, 1988, Tequila Sunrise, 1988, Frankenstein Unbound, 1989, The Indian Runner, 1990, Death and the Maiden, 1994, Night Falls on Manhattan, 1997, Are We Done Yet?, 2007; (TV) Open Admissions, 1986, Cinemax Comedy Experiment (series) 1987, Son of the Morning Star, 1987; (stage) Death and the Maiden, 1993. Trustee Prodrs. Guild Am., 1995—, Calif. Inst. Arts, 1971-72, Bard Coll., 1980-93. NEH artist in residence Duke U., Durham, N.C., 1990. Mem. Prodrs. Guild Am. (pres. 1998—). *

MOUNT, WILLIE LANDRY, state legislator; b. Lake Charles, La., Aug. 25, 1949; d. Lee Robert and Willie Veatrice (McCullor) Landry; m. Benjamin Wakefield Mount, Aug. 19, 1976. BS, McNeese State U., 1971. Geophys. asst. La. Land and Exploration, Lake Charles, La., 1971-76; pharm. rep. Lederle, Lake Charles, 1976-80; realtor Mary Kay Hopkins, Lake Charles, 1976-87; co-owner Paper Place, Lake Charles, 1991-95; mayor City of Lake Charles, 1993—2000; mem. La. State Senate, 2000—, mem. select com. on consumer protection, mem. jud. C, health and welfare, legis. audit adv. commn., bond commn., mem. state tech. adv. commn., joint juvenile justice commn., millennium port com., sch. fin. rev. commn., mem. edn. com., vice chair joint legis. com. on capital outlay, chmn. revenue and fiscal affairs com. Gov. Violent Crime & Homicide Task Force, Baton Rouge, 1993—95; mem. steering com. La. conf. Mayors bd. pres. La. Asset Mgmt. Pool Bd., 1997. Guest condr. Lake Charles Symphony, 1992; active La. Mcpl. Assn., Baton Rouge, 1995-98; pres. Jr. League of Lake Charles; mem. state interagy. coordinating coun. Dyslexia Study Com.; mem. adv. bd. S.W. La. Literacy Coalition; mem. adv. coun. Pet Overpopulation; active First United Meth. Ch., La. Meth. Conf., McNeese State U. Found., Prevent Child Abuse bd. Micro-Enterprise Devel. Alliance of La. Bd., McNeese State U. Found. Bd., St. Patrick Hosp. Bd. Councillors, Coastal Plain Conservancy Bd., United Way, Children's Miracle Network; exec. com. Coun. for a Better La. Recipient Spiritual Aims award Kiwanis Club, 1991, Cmty. Svc. award, 1995, Citizen of Yr. 1996-97, Dorthea Combre award NAACP, 1994, La. Mcpl. Assn. Cmty. Achievement award, 1995-97, Disting. Citizen award Boy Scouts Am., 1999, Patron Architecture, 2000, Disting. Alumni award McNeese State U., 2000, Golden Apple award Delta Kappa Gamma, 2002, Disting. Svc. award La. Restaurant Assn., 2002, Spl. Friend of La. Mcpl. Assn. award, 2003, Wilton Bellard Jr. award S.W. La. Ctr. for Health Svcs., Ron Schroeder award MEDAL; named Woman of Yr., Quota Club, 1991, Citizen of Yr., Women's com. S.W. La., 1992, Woman of Yr., Pub. Ofcl. of Yr. Msgr. Cramers KC, Pub. Ofcl. of Yr., NASW, 1997, Legislator of Yr., La. Orthopaedic Assn., Champion for Children, Prevent Child Abuse. Mem.: LWV, S.W. La. Mayor's Assn. (chmn. 1993—94). Home: 205 Shell Beach Dr Lake Charles LA 70601-5933 Office: PO Box 3004 Lake Charles LA 70602-3004 Business E-mail: lasen27@legis.state.la.us.

MOUNTAIN, JANET M., foundation administrator, former computer company executive; b. Oct. 19, 1967; BBA, U. Tex., Austin; MBA, Harvard Bus. Sch. Former sr. consultant Andersen Consulting, Houston; v.p., gen. mgr., US consumer divsn. Dell Inc., Round Rock, Tex., 1993—2003; exec. dir. The Michael & Susan Dell Found., Austin, Tex., 2003—. Named a Young Global Leader, Forum of Young Global Leaders, 2006. Office: The Michael & Susan Dell Found PO Box 163867 Austin TX 78716 *

MOUNTCASTLE, VERNON BENJAMIN, retired neuroscientist; b. Shelbyville, Ky., July 15, 1918; s. Vernon and Anne-Francis Marguerite (Waugh) Mountcastle; m. Nancy Clayton Pierpont, Sept. 6, 1945; children: Vernon Benjamin III, Anne Clayton, George Earle Pierpont. BS in Chemistry, Roanoke Coll., Salem, Va., 1938, DSc (hon.), 1968; MD, Johns Hopkins U., 1942; DSc (hon.), U. Pa., 1976, Northwestern U., 1985, U. Minn., 1995; MD (hon.), U. Zurich, 1983, U. Siena, 1984, U. Santiago, Spain, 1990. House officer surgery Johns Hopkins Hosp., 1942—43; mem. faculty Johns Hopkins Sch. Medicine, 1946—, prof. physiology, 1959, dir. dept., 1964—80, prof. neurosci., 1980—92, prof. emeritus, 1992—; dir. Bard Labs. Neurophysiology Johns Hopkins U., Balt., 1981—91. Spl. rsch. physiology brain; chmn. physiology study sect., mem. physiology tng. com. NIH, 1958—61; adv. coun. Nat. Eye Inst., 1971—74; vis. prof. Coll. de France, Paris, 1980. Author: Perciptual Neuroscience: The Cerebrel Cortex, 1996, The Sensory Hand: Neural Mechanisms in Somatic Sensation, 2005; editor-in-chief: Jour. Neurophysiology, 1961—64, editor, contbr.: Med. Physiology, 12th edit., 1968, Med. Physiology, 13th edit., 1974, Med. Physiology, 14th edit., 1980; contbr. articles to profl. jours. Lt. (s.g.) M.C. USNR, 1943—46. Recipient Lashley prize, Am. Philos. Soc., 1974, F.O. Schmitt prize and medal, MIT, 1975, Sherrington prize and Gold medal, Royal Acad. Medicine, London, 1977, Horowitz prize, Columbia U., 1978, Helmholtz prize, 1982, Fyssen Internat. prize, Paris, 1983, Lasker award, 1983, Nat. Medal Sci., 1986, Zotterman prize and medal, Swedish Physiol. Soc., 1989, award in neurosci., Fidia Fedn., 1990,

Australia prize, 1993. Mem.: AAAS (McGovern prize and medal 1990), NAS (chmn. sect. on physiology 1971—74, award in neurosci. 1998), Acad. Sci. (Finland, fgn.), Royal Soc. London (fgn.), Acad. Scis. (France, fgn.), Nat. Inst. Medicine, Am. Philos. Soc. (councillor 1979—82), Soc. Neurosci. (pres. 1970—72, Gerard prize 1980), Harvey Cushing Soc., Am. Acad. Arts and Scis., Am. Physiol. Soc., Physiol. Soc. London (hon.), Am. Neurol. Assn. (hon. Bennett lectr. 1978), Sigma Xi, Phi Chi, Alpha Omega Alpha, Phi Beta Kappa. Home: 6605 Walnutwood Cir Baltimore MD 21212 Business E-Mail: mountcastle@mbi.mb.jhu.edu.

MOUNTCASTLE, WILLIAM WALLACE, JR., retired philosophy and religion educator; b. Hanover, NH, July 10, 1925; s. William Wallace and Grace Elizabeth (Zottarelli) M.; m. Ila M. Warner (div.); children: Christine, Susan, Gregory, Eric; m. Barbara Kaye Teelin, Oct. 19, 1979; 1 child, Cathleena; stepdaughter, Dasha Teelin. BA, Whittier Coll., 1951; STB, Boston U., 1954, PhD, 1958. Ordained to ministry United Meth. Ch. Asst. prof. philosophy and religion High Point Coll., NC, 1958—60; mem. So. Calif. Ann. Conf. United Meth. Ch., 1954—60; assoc. prof., head dept. philosophy Nebr. Wesleyan U., Lincoln, 1960—63, prof., head dept. philosophy, 1963—67; mem. Nebr. Ann. Conf. United Meth. Ch., 1960—95; prof. philosophy Fla. So. Coll., Lakeland, 1967—68; assoc. prof. philosophy and religion U. West Fla., Pensacola, 1968—79, prof. philosophy and religion, 1979—, M.L. Tipton prof. philosophy and religion, 1980—2003, emeritus M.L. Tipton prof., 2003. Author: Religion in Planetary Perspective, 1979, Science Fantasy Voices and Visions of Cosmic Religion, 1996, The Secret Ministry of Jesus, 2007; contbr. articles to profl. jours. Fighter pilot USAAF, 1942-48, PTO. Mem. NEA/United Faculty Fla., Am. Assn. Religion, Am. Philos. Assn., Democrat. Office: U West Fla Dept Phil-Religious Studies Pensacola FL 32514 Office Phone: 850-474-2678.

MOUNTS, L. DAVID, food products executive; married; 3 children. BSBA in Fin. and Mgmt. Info., U. Nev.; MBA, U. Pa. Wharton Sch. Bus. Joined UPS Inc., 1983, v.p. mergers and aquisitions, 1999—2002, CFO Supply Chain Solutions Group, 2002—05; exec. v.p., CFO Domino's Pizza Inc., 2005—, also bd. dirs. Bd. dirs. The Genesis Shelter. Office: Dominos Pizza 30 Frank Lloyd Wright Dr Ann Arbor MI 48106

MOUNTS, NANCY, secondary school educator; Tchr. home econs. North High Sch., Sioux City, Iowa; tech. prep. specialist Cen. Campus, Sioux City, 1995—; dir. Northwest Iowa Ctr. Teaching and Learning Morningside Coll. Recipient State Tchr. of Yr. Home Econs. award Iowa, 1992. Office: Cen Campus 1121 Jackson St Sioux City IA 51105-1434

MOUNTZ, WADE, retired healthcare executive; b. Winona, Ohio, Nov. 19, 1924; s. Lowell J. and Ethel M. (Coppock) M.; m. Betty G. Wilson, June 3, 1946; children: David John, Timothy Wilson. BA, Baldwin-Wallace Coll., Berea, Ohio, 1948; MHA, U. Minn., Mpls., 1951; LHD (hon.), Ky. Wesleyan Coll., Owensboro, 1991. With Norton Meml. Infirmary, Louisville, 1951-69, adminstr., 1958-69; pres. Norton-Children's Hosps., Inc., Louisville, 1969-81, NKC, Inc., Louisville, 1981-85, vice chmn., 1985-87; pres. emeritus Norton Healthcare, 1987—. Vice chmn. Comprehensive Health Planning Council Ky., 1968-73, chmn., 1973-79; bd. dirs. Louisville chpt. ARC, 1961-74; trustee Blue Cross Hosp. Plan, 1959-72; trustee Am. Hosp. Assn., 1971-76, chmn. bd., 1975. Served with A.C., USNR, 1943-45. Recipient Disting. Service award Ky. Hosp. Assn.; Disting. Layman award Ky. Med. Assn. Fellow Am. Coll. Hosp. Healthcare Execs. (life, gold medal), Masons. Home and Office: 9 Muirfield Pl Louisville KY 40222-5074 Office Phone: 502-412-9210. Personal E-mail: wmountz@insightbb.com.

MOURDOCK, RICHARD E., state official; BS, Defiance Coll.; MS in Geology, Ball State Univ. Lic. Profl. Geologist. Exec. Koester Companies, Inc.; cons., environ., energy bus.; state treas. State of Ind., 2006—; and chmn. Ind. Bond Bank. County commr. Vanderburgh County, 1995—2002. Office: State Treas 242 State House Indianapolis IN 46204 Office Phone: 317-232-6386. Office Fax: 317-233-1780. *

MOURNING, PAUL W., lawyer; b. Hattiesburg, Miss., Dec. 21, 1957; BA magna cum laude, Dartmouth Coll., 1980; JD, Univ. Va., 1983. Bar: N.Y. 1984. Ptnr. Health Corp. dept., recruiting ptnr. Cadwalader Wickersham & Taft, NYC. Editor (in chief): Va. Jour. Internat. Law. Mem.: ABA, N.Y. State Bar Assn., Phi Beta Kappa. Office: Cadwalader Wickersham & Taft LLP 1 World Fin Ctr New York NY 10281 Office Phone: 212-504-6216. Office Fax: 212-504-6666. Business E-Mail: paul.mourning@cwt.com.

MOUSER, LES (LYMAN MOUSER), advertising executive; Pres., COO Campbell Mithun Esty, Mpls., 1999—; CEO Campbell Mithun, Mpls., 2001—04, chmn. Office: Campbell Mithun Esty 222 S 9th St Minneapolis MN 55402-3389 Office Phone: 612-347-1000. Office Fax: 612-347-1515.

MOUSSEUX, RENATE, language educator; b. Stuttgart, Germany, Oct. 27, 1942; came to U.S., 1964; d. Emile and Gertrud Muller; m. Patrick Mousseux, Dec. 12, 1974; 1 child, Marc. BA, Padagogische Hochschule, Germany; MA, Grand Canyon U.; BL French, German, ESL, Phoenix U. Cert. French, German, psychology, bilingual French, ESL, secondary grades 7-12, Ariz., Calif. Prof. German Berlitz Sch. Lang., Sherman Oaks, Calif., 1966-67, Thunderbird Grad. Sch. Internat. Mgmt., Glendale, Ariz., 1968-72; prof. German and French Scottsdale Dist. H.S., 1980—; prof. French and German Rio Salado C.C., 1976-86; prof. French Scottsdale C.C., 1990-96, U. Phoenix, 1991—95; lit. and talent agt., co-prodr. for film and lit., 1991—99; editor, pub. poetry books, 1991—. Distbr. Native Am. Music; bus. lang. trainer, course developer various corps.; trainer student tchrs. Ariz. State U., Ottawa U. Author: Accellerated French (Vive le Francais), 1989, Accellerated German (Willkommen Deutsch), 1990, Accellerated Spanish (Viva el Espanol), 1991, Accellerated Japanese (Moshi Moshi), 1991, Accellerated English (Hello English), 1992. With Essential Skills Com. Ariz. State Bd. Edn. Recipient Ariz. Fgn. Lang. Tchr. of Yr. award Ariz. Assn. Fgn. Lang. Tchrs., 1986, Exceptional Mentorship Skills award Ariz. State U., 1994, Excellence in Mentorship cert. Ariz. State U., 1995; named Tchr. of Yr., U.S. West Outstanding Tchr. Program, 1989, Nat. Day of Excellence award 1996, award in leadership and quality in edn. ASCD, 1990. Mem. NEA, Nat. Geographic Soc., Am. Assn. Tchrs. German, Alliance Francaise, French Tchrs. Assn., Cultural Heritage Alliance, Ariz. Fgn. Lang. Assn., Scottsdale Edn. Assn. Avocations: reading, writing, psychology, anthropology. Home: 15611 N Boulder Dr Fountain Hills AZ 85268-1814 Home Phone: 602-910-3450. Personal E-mail: rmousseux@yahoo.com. Business E-Mail: rmousseux@fhusd.org.

MOW, ROBERT HENRY, JR., lawyer; b. Cape Girardeau, Mo., Dec. 10, 1938; s. Robert H. Sr. and Ann Elise (Beck) M.; m. Jody K. Boggs, Aug. 29, 1987; children: Robert M., Brynn A., W. Brett, Rebecca M., W. Kirk, Allison M. Student, Westminster Coll., 1956-57; AB with distinction, U. Mo., 1960; LLB magna cum laude, So. Meth. U., 1963. Bar: Tex. 1963, US Dist. Ct. (no. dist. Tex.) 1965, US Dist. Ct. (so. dist. Tex.) 1969, US Dist. Ct. (ea. and we. dists. Tex.) 1976, US Ct. Appeals (5th cir.) 1972, US Ct. Appeals (11th cir.) 1981, US Ct. Appeals (fed. cir.) 1994, US Supreme Ct. 1978. Assoc. Carrington, Johnson & Stephens, Dallas, 1963-69; ptnr. Carrington, Coleman, Sloman & Blumenthal, Dallas, 1970-85, Hughes & Luce, LLP, Dallas, 1985—, mng. ptnr., 2003—07. Editor-in-chief Southwestern Law Jour., 1962-63. Trustee First Bapt. Acad., chair, 1999-2002. Served to 1st lt. US Army, 1963-65. Fellow: Am. Coll. Trial Lawyers; mem.: Dallas Bar Assn. (Dallas Bar Trial Lawyer of Yr. 2003), ABA (first chair intellectual property com. litig. sect.), State Bar Tex., Dallas Bar Fellows (chmn. com. qualified judiciary 2003—04), Am. Bd. Trial Advs. (pres. Dallas chpt. 1983—84), Tex. Assn. Def. Counsel (v.p. and dir. 1981—82), Dallas Assn. Def. Counsel. Republican. Baptist. Office: Hughes & Luce LLP 1717 Main St Ste 2800 Dallas TX 75201 Office Phone: 214-939-5448. Office Fax: 214-939-5849. Business E-Mail: bob.mow@hughesluce.com.

MOW, VAN C., engineering educator, researcher; b. Chengdu, China, Jan. 10, 1939; B. Aero. Engrng., Rensselaer Poly. Inst., 1962, PhD, 1966. Mem. tech. staff Bell Telephone Labs., Whippany, NJ, 1968-69; assoc. prof. mechanics Rensselaer Poly. Inst., Troy, NY, 1969-76, prof. mechanics and biomed. engrng., 1976-82, John A. Clark and Edward T. Crossan prof. engrng., 1982-86; prof. mech. engrng. and orthopedic bioengrng. Columbia U., NYC, 1986—98, chmn. dept. biomed. engrng. Fu Found. Sch. Engrng. and Applied Sci., 1998—; dir. Orthopedic Rsch. Lab., Columbia-Presbyn. Med. Ctr., NYC, 1986—, Stanley Dicker prof. biomed. engrng., 1998—. Vis. mem. Courant Inst. Math. Sci., NYU, 1967-68; vis. prof. Harvard U., Boston, 1976-77; chmn. orthopaedics and musculoskeletal study sect. NIH, Bethesda, Md., 1982-84; hon. prof. Sichuan U., 1981, Shanghai Jiao Tong U., 1987, Shanghai U., 1983, Hong Kong Poly. U., 2003, Zhejiang U., 2004, Beihang U., 2004; chmn. grants rev. bd. Orthopaedic Rsch. Edn. Found., 1992-96; bd. dirs. Hoar Rsch. Found., 1993—; chmn. adv. com. divsn. Med. Engring. Rsch. Nat. Health Rsch. Inst., Taiwan, 1999—; cons. in field. Assoc. editor Jour. Biomechanics, 1981—, Jour. Biomech. Engrng., 1979-86; chmn. editorial adv. bd. Jour. Orthopedic Rsch., 1983-90; adv. editor Clin. Orthopedic Rel. Rsch., 1993—; assoc./co-editor Osteo-arthritis & Cartilage; contbr. numerous articles to profl. jours. Founder Gordon Research Conf. on Bioengring. and Orthopedic Sci., 1980. NATO sr. fellow, 1978; recipient William H. Wiley Disting. Faculty award Rensselaer Poly. Inst., 1981, ASME Van C. Mow medal for bioengrng., 2004; Japan Soc. for Promotion Sci. Fellow, 1986, Fogarty Sr. Internat. fellow, 1987; Alza disting. lectr. Biomed. Engring. Soc., 1987; H.R. Lissner award ASME, 1987, Kappa Delta award AAOS, 1980, Giovani Borelli award, 1991. Fellow ASME (chmn. biomechanics divsn. 1984-85, Melville medal 1982, R.H. Thurston lectr., Van C. Mow medal for bioengring. 2004), Am. Inst. Med. Biol. Engring.; mem. Orthopaedic Rsch. Soc. (pres. 1982-83), Am. Soc. Biomechanics (founding), Internat. Soc. Biorheology, U.S. Nat. Com. on Biomechanics (sec.-treas. 1985-90, chmn. 1991-94), Nat. Acad. Engring., Inst. of Medicine, Nat. Acad. Sci., Academia Sinica. Business E-Mail: vcm1@columbia.edu.

MOWBRAY, KEVIN D., publishing executive; b. 1962; m. Linda Mowbray; 4 children. BA, Western Ill. U. Advt. sales rep. Lee Enterprises, Inc., Kewanee, Ill., 1986, nat. sales mgr. corp. sales & mktg. Chgo.; advt. mgr. Lincoln (Nebr.) Journal Star, 1995—98; gen. mgr. Missoulian, Missoula, Mont., 1998—2000; pub. Bismarck (ND) Tribune, 2000—02, v.p. sales & mktg., 2002—04; v.p. pub., pub. Times of Northwest Ind., Munster, Ind., 2004—05; pres. & pub. St. Louis Post-Dispatch, 2006—. Office: St Louis Post-Dispatch 900 N Tucker Blvd Saint Louis MO 63101 Office Phone: 314-340-8970. E-mail: kmowbray@post-dispatch.com. *

MOWE, GREGORY ROBERT, lawyer; b. Aberdeen, Wash., Feb. 23, 1946; s. Robert Eden and Jeannette Effie (Deyoung) M.; m. Rebecca Louise Nobles, June 14, 1969; children: Emily, Tom. BA, U. Oreg., 1968, MA, 1969; JD magna cum laude, Harvard Law Sch., 1974. Bar: Oreg. 1974, U.S. Dist. Ct. Oreg. 1974, U.S. Ct. Appeals (9th cir.) 1974. Assoc. atty. Stoel Rives Boley Jones & Grey, Portland, Oreg., 1974-79, ptnr., 1979—. Pres. bd. dirs. Planned Parenthood of Columbia/Willamette, Portland, 1989-90. 1st lt. U.S. Army, 1969-71, Vietnam. Mem. ABA, Phi Beta Kappa. Office: Stoel Rives Boley Jones & Grey 900 SW 5th Ave Ste 2300 Portland OR 97204-1229 Home Phone: 503-294-9458; Office Phone: 503-294-9458. Business E-Mail: grmowe@stoel.com.

MOWELL, GEORGE MITCHELL, lawyer; b. Balt., July 31, 1951; s. George Robert and Polly (Sattler) M.; m. Patricia Edith Forbes, Sept. 23, 1978; children: Rachel Elizabeth, George Robert. BA, Washington Coll., Chestertown, Md., 1973; JD, U. Balt., 1977. Bar: Md. 1978, U.S. Dist. Ct. Md. 1981, U.S. Bankruptcy Ct. 1982. Claims authorizer Social Security Adminstrn., Balt., 1973-79; law clk. to presiding justice Kent County Cir. Ct., Chestertown, 1979-81; ptnr. Boyer & Mowell, Chestertown, 1981-87, Mowell, Nunn & Wadkorsky, Chestertown, 1987-98, Wadkovsky & Mowell, Chestertown, 1998—. Atty. Kent County Planning Commn., Chestertown, 1982—, Betterton Planning Commn., 1987—, Town of Rock Hall, 1987—; panel atty. Md. Vol. Lawyers, 1981—; mem. adv. bd. Farmers Bank of Md., 1994-99. Bd. dirs. Kent County Heart Assn., Chestertown, 1983-84; atty. Galena Planning Commn., 1997—. Mem. Kent County Bar Assn. (sec. 1985-86, treas. 1987-88, v.p. 1988-89, pres. 1990-93). Democrat. Episcopalian. Home: 140 Deer Field Dr Chestertown MD 21620-2482 Office: Wadkovsky & Mowell 107 Court St Chestertown MD 21620-1507 Home Phone: 410-778-0779; Office Phone: 410-778-1630. Fax: 410-778-9325.

MOWERY, GERALD EUGENE, publishing executive, writer; b. Buena, Wash., Mar. 7, 1927; s. Jennings Bryan and Opal Mae Mowery; children: Colleen, Theresa, Rhonda, Laura, Victoria, Charles, Peggy. Degree in bus., Kinmen's U. Lic. pub. acct., Wash. Supr. Boeing Airplane Co., Seattle, 1968-78; owner Jerry's Coin, Book and Frame Shops, Puyallup, Wash., 1978-85, Rudolph Maurer Pub., Puyallup, Wash., Tampa, Fla., 1985—. Author and pub. more than 152 books including All Matter Originates from Electrons, Positrons and Neutrinos, 1981, E=GM Squared, 1994, The Revised Periodic Table of Elements, The Four Unacknowledged Elements, 1999; co-author with Gene Buck: The Entrepreneurs Favorite Short Stories, Favorite Poems, Favorite Facts and Stuff; author, publ. Adjusted Periodic Table of Elements, 1982, 93, 97, 98, 2001; author children's books The Adventures of Alexander Smiriotes series including Alexander Simiriotes Rides his Alligator Through Tampa, Alexander Visits Athens, Greece, Chelsea Thompson Visits Seattle. Achievements include defining the atomic mass make up of sub atomic particles and their relationship to carbon 12; prepared (atomic mass) sub atomic particle table from the equation atomic mass squared x 938.27231 equals measured MeV Values; illustrated that elements are periodic, paired functions of Electrons, Protons, Neutrinos and .000249089 atomic mass particles; developed periodic table of elements progression law of 1+2+2+2+2; confirming the existence of six additional elements within the table and predicting their measurements, configuration, composition, charge, isotopes, and other values; established that isotopes have a periodic progression and are not randomly added; established the theory and concept of compact neutrons as the basis for the periodic table; illustrated that the configuration and measurements of elements are paired with themselves, that all atoms are paired in a solid state, singular in a gas state, and both paired and unpaired in a liquid state; confirmed and illustrated how matter has a periodic atomic mass progression from the subatomic particles through the elements; put on a firm basis the theory that subatomic particles are the result of Proton Fractures at certain points in the 27 electron/proton chain and releasing energy (MeV) in the process; illustrated that the atomic number of an element should be two times its configuration plus one. Address: 203 South G St #217 Tacoma WA 98405 Personal E-mail: gemowery@msn.com.

MOWL, LINDA, special education educator; m. Gary Mowl, Aug. 24, 1991. BS in Edn., Truman State U., Kirksville, Mo., 1975. Tchr. assoc., athletic coach Davenport Cmty. Schs., Walcott, Iowa, 1975—83; devel. edn. instr. Muscatine CC, Iowa, 1983—. Recipient Chancellor's award, Eastern Iowa C.C., 2000, Excellence award, Nat. Inst. for Staff and Orgnl. Devel., 2000, Outstanding Employee award, Muscatine C.C., 1998. Avocations: gardening, floral design, reading, travel. Office: Muscatine CC 152 Colorado St Muscatine IA 52761

MOWREY, ROBERT D., lawyer; b. Cin., Sept. 27, 1963; BA summa cum laude, Wittenberg Univ., Springfield, Ohio, 1985; JD cum laude, Univ. Chgo., 1988. Bar: Ga. 1988. Ptnr., chmn., environ. and land use group Alston & Bird LLP, Atlanta. Adj. prof., environ law Emory Univ., Atlanta. Mem. Chgo. Law Rev. Office: Alston & Bird LLP One Atlantic Plz 1201 W Peachtree St NW Atlanta GA 30309-3424 Office Phone: 404-881-7242. Office Fax: 404-881-7777. Business E-Mail: bmowrey@alston.com.

MOWRIS, GERALD WILLIAM, lawyer; b. Grand Forks, ND, Oct. 2, 1948; s. Robert Earl and Lillian Vivian Mowris; m. Susan Leah Sachtjen; children: Danae E., Jeffrey W. Student, Mich. State U., East Lansing, 1966-67; JD, U. Wis., 1973. Bar: Wis. 1973, US Dist. Ct. (we. dist.) Wis. 1973, US Ct. Appeals (7th cir.) 1984, US Ct. Mil. Appeals 1984. Asst. dist. atty. Dane County Dist. Atty.'s Office, Madison, 1973-79; ptnr. Pellino, Rosen, Mowris & Kirkhuff, Madison, 1979—. Co-founder, mem. steering com. Wis. Criminal Justice Study Commn. Bd. dirs. YMCA of Met. Madison, 1991-94; mem. ARC Cmty. Svcs., Madison, 1980—, past pres., apptd. by gov. Wis. Sentencing Commn., 2003-. Major JAG Corp. USAR, 1970—92. Mem. State Bar Wis. (co-chmn. com. for local bar leaders 1995-97, bd. govs. 1999-2003, pres. 2001-02), Dane County Bar Assn. (pres. 1994-95), Wis. Assn. Criminal Def. Lawyers (pres. 1995-96), Nat. Assn. Criminal Def. Lawyers, Wis. Acad. Trial Lawyers, Nat. Ski Patrol (patroller 1967—). Avocations: skiing, fishing, hiking, canoeing, golf. Office: Pellino Rosen Mowris & Kirkhuff SC 131 W Wilson St Ste 1201 Madison WI 53703-3243 Office Phone: 608-255-4501. Office Fax: 608-255-4345. Business E-Mail: gmowris@prmk.com.

MOWRY, MAXWELL REED, language educator; b. Chelsea, Mass., Feb. 3, 1944; s. Maxwell Reed Mowry and Susan Lewis Byrd Thompson. BA with honors, U. NC, Chapel Hill, 1965; MA, U. Ill., Champaign-Urbana, 1967, PhD, 1974; MEd, The Citadel, Charleston, 1982. Spanish educator Valparaiso U., Ind., 1974—76, Porter-Gaud Sch., Charleston, 1976—, coll. advisor, 1979—; docent Hist. Charleston Found., Charleston, 1981—. Grant, Rockefeller Found., 1991. Mem.: Am. Assn. Tchrs. Spanish and Portuguese (SC chpt.), English Speaking Union (Charleston chpt.), Footlight Players, SAR (Gen. William Moultrie chpt.), Huguenot Soc. SC (life), Soc. Colonial Wars in the State SC, Am. Mensa Ltd. (Coastal Carolina chpt.) (treas. 1983—86), Lowcountry Phi Beta Kappa. Home: 34 N Adger's Wharf Charleston SC 29401 Office: Porter-Gaud Sch 300 Albemarle Rd Charleston SC 29407 Home Phone: 843-577-0594; Office Phone: 843-402-4716.

MOWRY, ROBERT WILBUR, pathologist, educator; b. Griffin, Ga., Jan. 10, 1923; s. Roy Burnell and Mary Frances (Swilling) Mowry; m. Margaret Neilson Black, June 11, 1949; children: Janet Lee, Robert Gordon, Barbara Ann. BS, Birmingham So. Coll., 1944; MD, Johns Hopkins U., 1946. Rotating intern U. Ala. Med. Coll., 1946-47, resident pathology, 1947-48; sr. asst. surgeon USPHS-NIH, Bethesda, Md., 1948-52; fellow pathology Boston City Hosp., 1949-50; asst. prof. pathology Washington U., St. Louis, 1952-53; from asst. prof. pathology to prof. emeritus U. Ala. Med. Ctr., Birmingham, 1953—89; prof. emeritus U. Ala. Med. Center, 1989—2003. Sr. scientist U. Ala. Inst. Dental Rsch., 1967—72, dir. autopsy svcs., 1975—79; vis. scholar dept. pathology U. Cambridge, England, 1972—73; cons. FDA, 1975—81. Author (with J. F. A. McManus): Stainging Methods: Histologic and Histochemical, 1960; mem. editl. bd. Jour. Histochemistry and Cytochemistry, 1960—75, Stain Tech., 1965—90, AMA Archives Pathology, 1967—76, Biotechnics and Histochemistry, 1991—. With USPHS, 1948—52. Mem.: Am. Assn. Univ. Profs. Pathology, Biol. Stain Commn. (v.p. 1974—76, pres. 1976—81, trustee 1966—), Internat. Acad. Pathology, Am. Soc. Investigative Pathology, Sigma Xi, Phi Beta Kappa, Alpha Kappa Kappa, Delta Sigma Phi. Presbyterian. Achievements include research in perfection of staining methods for complex carbohydrates (Alcian blue and colloidal iron) and insulin (Alcian blue-aldehyde fuchsin) and utility of these in diagnostic histopathology. Home: 9293 Poplar Ave Apt 218 Germantown TN 38138

MOXLEY, JOHN HOWARD, III, internist; b. Elizabeth, NJ, Jan. 10, 1935; s. John Howard Jr. and Cleopatra (Mundy) Moxley; m. Doris Banchik; children: John Howard IV, Brook, Mark. BA, Williams Coll., 1957; MD, U. Colo., 1961; DSc (hon.), Sch. Medicine Hannemann U. Diplomate Am. Bd. Internal Medicine. Intern Peter Bent Brigham Hosp., Boston, 1961—62, resident in internal medicine, 1962—66; with Nat. Cancer Inst., USPHS, 1963—65; asst. to dean, instr. medicine Harvard Med. Sch., Boston, 1966—69; dean Sch. Medicine, U. Md., 1969—73; vice chancellor health scis., dean Med. Sch., U. Calif.-San Diego, 1973—79; asst. sec. for health affairs Dept. Def., Washington, 1979—81; sr. v.p. Am. Med. Internat., Beverly Hills, Calif., 1981—87; pres. MetaMed. Inc., Playa Del Rey, Calif., 1987—89; mgr. dir. Korn/Ferry Internat., LA, 1989—. Cons. FDA, NIH; dir. Nat. Fund for Med. Edn., 1986—94, chmn., 1993—94; dir. Henry M. Jackson Found. for Adv. Mil. Medicine. Contbr. articles to profl. jours. Dir. Polyclinic Health Svcs. Games of XXIII Olympiad. Recipient Gold and Silver award, U. Colo. Med. Sch., 1974, commr.'s citation for outstanding svc. to over-the-counter drug study, FDA, 1977, spl. achievement citation, Am. Hosp. Assn., 1983, Sec. of Def. medal for disting. pub. svc., 1981. Fellow: ACP, Am. Coll. Physician Execs. (disting.); mem.: AMA (chmn. coun. sci. affairs 1985), Am. Hosp. Assn. (trustee 1979—81), Soc. Med. Adminstrs., Calif. Med. Assn. (chmn. sci. bd. 1978—83, councilor), Inst. Medicine NAS, San Diego C. of C., Rotary, Alpha Omega Alpha. Office: Korn Ferry Internat 1900 Ave of the Stars Ste 2600 Los Angeles CA 90067-1512 Office Phone: 310-200-1296. E-mail: moxleyj@kornferry.com.

MOXLEY, ROY ANTHONY, early childhood educator; b. Grosse Pointe Farms, Mich., Jan. 30, 1934; s. Roy Anthony and Anetta May (Van Alstyne) M. B.S. in Sci., U. Detroit, 1958; M.A. in English, Wayne State U., 1962; Ph.D. in Edn., U. Mich., 1972. Instr. U. Mich., Ann Arbor, 1970-71; asst. prof. edn. Ind. U., 1971-72; prof. edn. W.Va. U., Morgantown, 1972-2005, prof. emeritus 2005—. Mem. Am. Assn. Behavior Analysis. Author: (with Mary Fitch) Changing Patient Behavior: A Behavior Modification Manual for Dental Professionals, 1978, 2d edit., 1984; Writing and Reading in Early Childhood, 1982; contbr. articles to profl. jours. Home: 884 E Everly St Apt 15 Morgantown WV 26505-3454

MOY, EDMUND C., federal agency administrator; b. 1957; m. Karen Moy; 1 child, Nora. Grad., U. Wis., 1979. Sales and mktg. exec. Blue Cross Blue Shield United, Wis., 1979—89; polit. appointee Health Care Financing Adminstrn. HHS, 1989—93; with Welsh, Carson, Anderson & Stowe; various positions with venture capital firms; spl. asst. to Pres. for presdl. personnel The White House, Washington; dir., US Mint US Dept. Treasury, Washington, 2006—. Bd. dirs. Christianity Today, Christianity Today Found. Office: US Mint 801 9th St NW Washington DC 20220

MOY, RICHARD L., research scientist; BA in Biochemistry, Columbia U., 1996—2000; MPhil in Microbiology, Mt. Sinai Sch. of Medicine, NYC, 2006; student, Mt. Sinai Sch. Medicine, NYC, 2001—06. Lab. technician Aaron Diamond AIDS Rsch. Ctr., Rockefeller U., NYC, 2000—01; rsch. technician Weill Med. Coll., Cornell U., 2006—. Recipient Semifinalist, 55th Ann. Westinghouse Sci. Talent Search, Sci. Svcs., 1996; fellow (T32) Tng. Program in Mechanisms of Virus-Host Interactions, NIH (NIH), 2001-2, Student Internship (awarded twice), Elizabeth Glaser Pediatric AIDS Found., 1999, 2001. Mem.: Am. Soc. Virology (student travel grant 2005), Am. Soc. Microbiology, AAAS, Am. Soc. for Biochemistry and Molecular Biology (assoc.). Office: Mt Sinai Sch of Medicine One Gustave L Levy Pl Box 1124 New York NY 10029

MOY, RONALD LEONARD, dermasurgeon; b. Stuttgart, Germany, June 10, 1957; s. Howard Leonard Stephen and Jenny (Yee) M.; m. Lisa Wing Lan Lin, Aug. 10, 1986; children: Lauren, Erin. Grad., Rensselaer Poly. Inst., 1977, Albany Med. Coll., 1981. Dir. Mohs micrographic surgery div. dermatology UCLA, 1988-93, dir. dermatologic surgery div. dermatology, 1988-93, co-chief div. dermatology, 1992-93, clin. prof. David Geffen Sch. Medicine, 2005—; chief dermatologic surgery VA-West Los Angeles Med. Ctr., 1988—. Mem. med. Bd. Calif., 2000-07, pres. divsn. med. quality, 2005—. Author: Atlas of Cutaneous Flaps and Grafts, 1990, Facial Rejuvenation, 1999; editor: Principle and Practice of Dermatologic Surgery, 1993, Facial Rejuenation, 2000, Advanced Facelift, 2006, Blepharoplasty, 2006; editor-in-chief: Dermatologic Surgery, 1997—2001; mem. editl. bd. Archives Facial Plastic Surgery, Archives of Dermatology, Jour. Am. Acad. Cosmetic Surgery; contbr. articles to profl. jours. Bd. dirs. L.A. Costal unit Am. Cancer Soc., 1988. Recipient J. Lewis Pipkin award in dermatology Nat. Student Rsch. Forum, 1981, Henry Christian award Am. Fedn. Clin. Rsch., T-cell and Cytokine Patterns in Skin Cancer award NIH, 1992. Fellow: Am. Acad. Cosmetic Surgery (bd. dirs. 2004—), Am. Acad. Dermatology (bd. dirs., Gold award 1986); mem.: Pacific Dermatol. Assn. (pres. 2006—07), Am. Acad. Facial Plastic Surgery, L.A. County Med. Assn. (pres. Bay dist. 1997—98), Assn. Acad. Dermatol. Surgeons (bd. dirs. 1992—95), Am. Coll. Mohs Micrographic Surgery and Cutaneous Oncology (bd. dirs. 1992—95), Am. Soc. Dermatol. Surgery (bd. dirs. 1993—96, v.p. 2001—02, pres. 2003—04). Presbyterian. Office: 100 UCLA Med Plz Ste 590 Los Angeles CA 90024-6992 Office Phone: 310-794-7422.

MOYA, CARLOS, professional tennis player; b. Palma de Mallorca, Spain, Aug. 27, 1976; s. Andres and Pilar Moya. Profl. tennis player ATP, 1995—. Owner cologne product line, 2000—. Actor: (films) Torrente II, 2001. Named Arthur Ashe Humanitarian of Yr., 2005. Achievements include winning 20 career singles titles, ATP; winning Buenos Aires, 1995, 2003, 2006, Umag, 1996, 2001-03, 2007, LI, 1997, Monte Carlo, 1998, Roland Garros, 1998, Estoril, 2000, Acapulco, 2002, 2004, Chennai, 2004-05; winning 18 European singles and doubles titles. Avocations: video games, music, soccer. Office: c/o ATP Tour Internat Hdqrs 201 Atp Tour Blvd Ponte Vedra Beach FL 32082 *

MOYA, CYNTHIA ANN, small business owner, librarian; b. LA, Calif., Oct. 30, 1962; d. Ephraim F. and Mary A. Moya; life ptnr. Ivan Stormgart. BA, U. Calif., LA, Calif., 1987; M of Libr. Info. Scis., U. Wash., 2001; PhD in Sexology, Inst. for Advanced Study of Human Sexuality, San Francisco, 2006. Archives cataloguer Vulcan Inc, Seattle, 2001—04; prin., owner Moya Svcs., Seattle, 2004—; pres. Alta-Glamour, Inc., 2006—. Dir. libr. Seattle (Wash.) Sex-Positive Cmty. Ctr., 2001—04. Mem.: ALA, Am. Assn. Mus., Am. Assn. Sex Educators, Counselors and Therapists, Soc. Sci. Study of Sexuality. Office: Alta-Glamour Inc PO Box 4632 Seattle WA 98194 Office Phone: 206-328-7282. Business E-Mail: alta-glamour@earthlink.net.

MOYA, EVA M., health services executive; b. El Paso Ciudad Juarez; BA, MS, U. Tex. Exec. dir. U.S.-Mex. Border Health Commn. Sr. program coord. U.S.-Mex. Border health collaborative outreach project U. Ariz., 1995—2001, assoc. dir. health career occupation program; project dir. Cmty. Health Worker's Evaluation Tool Kit Project, 1998—2001; co-dir. Cmty. Access Program for Ariz.; pres. U.S.-Mex. Border Health Assn., 1999—2000. Contbr. articles to profl. jours. Named one of Top 10 Latinos in Healthcare, LatinoLeaders mag., 2004; recipient Adelante Mujer Hispana: Cmty. Involvement award, Tex. Cmty. Health Program award, 1990, Award for Excellence, U.S. Dept. Health & Human Services, Human Svcs. Nat. Health Program award. Office: US Mex Border Health Commn 201 E Main Ste 1616 El Paso TX 79901 E-mail: emoya@borderhealth.net.

MOYA, OLGA LYDIA, law educator; b. Weslaco, Tex., Dec. 27, 1959; d. Leonel V. and Genoveva (Tamez) M.; children: Leanessa Geneva Byrd, Taylor Moya Byrd. BA, U. Tex., 1981, JD, 1984. Bar: Tex. 1984. Legis. atty. Tex. Ho. of Reps., Austin, 1985; atty. Tex. Dept. Agr., Austin, 1985-90; asst. regional counsel U.S. EPA, Dallas, 1990-91; from asst. prof. to assoc. prof. South Tex. Coll. of Law, Houston, 1992-97; prof. law South Tex. Coll. Law, Houston, 1997—, dir. continuing legal edn., 2003—06. Author: (with Andrew L. Fono) Federal Environmental Law: The User's Guide, 1997, 2d edit., 2001. Bd. dirs. Hermann Children's Hosp., Houston, 1993-97; mem. Leadership Tex., Austin, 1991—; bd. trustees Meml. Hermann Healthcare Sys. Found., 1997-99; bd. dirs. Tex. Clean Water Coun., Austin, 199-2003, Met. Transit Authority of Harris County, 1999—; U.S. del. to UN Conf. on the Environ. for Latin Am. and the Caribbean, San Juan, P.R., 1995; v.p. pub. policy and bd. dirs. Scenic Houston, 2004—. Recipient Nat. Top 12 Hispanics in Law, Miller Brewing Co., 1996; Vol. of Yr. award George H. Hermann Soc., 1995, Hispanic Law Prof. of Yr. Hispanic Nat. Bar Assn., 1995. Mem. ABA (environ. law sect.), Hispanic Bar Assn. (bd. dirs. 1992—, Excellence award 1995, 96), Mex.-Am. Bar Assn. Office: South Tex Coll of Law 1303 San Jacinto St Houston TX 77002-7013 Office Phone: 713-646-1847. Business E-Mail: omoya@stcl.edu.

MOYA, PATRICK ROBERT, lawyer; b. Belen, N.Mex., Nov. 7, 1944; s. Adelicio E. and Eva (Sanchez) Moya; m. Sara Dreier, May 30, 1966; children: Jeremy Brill, Joshua Dreier. AB, Princeton U., 1966; JD, Stanford U., 1969. Bar: Calif. 1970, Ariz. 1970, DC 1970, U.S. Dist. Ct. (no. dist.) Calif. 1970, U.S. Ct. Claims 1970, U.S. Tax Ct. 1970, U.S. Ct. Appeals (DC cir.) 1970, U.S. Supreme Ct. 1973. Assoc. Lewis and Roca, Phoenix, 1969—73, ptnr., 1973—83; sr. ptnr. Moya, Bailey, Bowers & Jones, P.C., Phoenix, 1983—84; ptnr., mem. nat. exec. com. Gaston & Snow, Phoenix, 1985—91; ptnr. Quarles & Brady LLP, Phoenix, 1991—2003, mem. nat. exec. com., 2000—02, of counsel, 2005—; exec. v.p. Insight Enterprises, Inc., Tempe, Ariz., 2002—05, chief adminstrv. officer, 2003—05, sec., 2002—05, gen. counsel, 2002—05. Instr. Sch. of Law, Ariz. State U., 1972; bd. dirs. Plusnet, plc, InPlay Techs., Inc. Mem. Paradise Valley Bd. Adjustment, 1976-80, chmn., 1978-80; mem. Paradise Valley Town Coun., 1980-82; bd. dirs. Phoenix Men's Arts Coun., 1973-81, pres., 1979-80; bd. dirs. The Silent Witness, Inc., 1979-84, pres., 1981-83; bd. dirs. Enterprise Network, Inc., 1989-94, pres., 1991-92; bd. dirs. Phoenix Little Theatre, 1973-75, Interfaith Counseling Svc., 1973-75; precinct committeeman Phoenix Rep. Com., 1975-77; dep. voter registrar Maricopa County, 1975-76; mem. exec. bd. dirs. Gov.'s Strategic Partnership for Econ. Devel.; pres. GSPED, Inc.; mem. of Steering Com. for Sonora-Ariz. Joint Econ. Plan; mem. Gov.'s Adv. Com., Ariz. and Mex., Ariz. Corp. Commn. Stock Exch. Adv. Coun., Ariz. Town Hall. Mem. ABA, Nat. Hispanic Bar Assn., Los Abogados Hispanic Lawyers Assn., Nat. Assn. Bond Lawyers, Ariz. Bar Assn., Maricopa County Bar Assn., Paradise Valley Country Club, Univ. Club. Office Phone: 602-230-5580.

MOYA, STEVE, health products executive; BA in Urban Affairs, U. So. Calif.; postgrad., Va. Poly. Inst. and State U. Formerly sr. v.p. Manning, Selvage and Lee, NYC; founder Moya Villanueva & Assocs.; former v.p. strategic planning and comm. LatinWorks Mktg., Austin, Tex.; former prin. Growth Strategies Consulting; sr. v.p., chief mktg. officer Humana, Inc., Louisville. Office: Humana Inc 500 W Main St Louisville KY 40202

MOYARS-JOHNSON, MARY ANNIS, retired academic administrator; b. Lafayette, Ind., July 19, 1938; d. Edward Raymond and Veronica Marie (Quigg) Moyars; m. Raymond Leon Molter, Aug. 1, 1959 (div. 1970); children: Marilyn Eileen Molter Davis, William Raymond Molter Johnson, Ann Marie Molter Guentert; m. Thomas Elmer Johnson, May 25, 1973 (div. 1989); children: Thomas Edward, John Alan, Barbara Suzanne. BS, Purdue U., 1960; MA, Purdue U., West Lafayette, Ind., 1991, postgrad., 1985—. Grader great issues Purdue U., West Lafayette, 1960-63, writer ednl. films, 1962-65, publicity dir. convocations and lectures, 1969-74, devel. officer Sch. Humanities, 1979-88, asst. to dir. Optoelectronics Rsch. Ctr., 1989-90, mgr. indsl. rels. Sch. Elec. and Computer Engrng., 1990—2002, assoc. v.p. for info. tech., for comm., 2002—04; tchr. English and math. Benton Cmty. Schs., Fowler, Ind., 1966-69, ret., 1969; pub. rels. dir. Sycamore Girl Scout Coun., Lafayette, Ind., 1974-78; dir. pub. info. Ind. Senate, Majority Caucus, Indpls., 1977-78; sr. script writer Walters & Steinberg, Lafayette, 1988-89; ret., 2004. Adj. faculty Ivy Tech State Univ., 2005. Author: Colonial Potpourri, 1975, Ouiatanon--The French Post Among the Ouia, 2000; co-author: Historic Colonial French Dress, 1982, 2nd edit., 1998; contbr. articles to profl. jours. Bd. govs. Tippecanoe County Hist. Assn., Lafayette, 1981-97. Mem. Women in Comms., Inc. (Pres. award 1983, pres. Lafayette chpt. 2004-05), Ctr. for French Colonial Rsch. (dir. 1986-89, 2006-, editor 1988-89), Palatines to Am., Ind. History Assn., Ind. Hist. Soc., French Colonial Hist. Soc. Roman Catholic. Avocations: history, genealogy, embroidery. Home: 924 Elm Dr West Lafayette IN 47906-2246 Personal E-mail: mamoyars@indy.net.

MOYER, ALAN DEAN, retired newspaper editor; b. Galva, Iowa, Sept. 4, 1928; s. Clifford Lee and Harriet (Jacques) M.; m. Patricia Helen Krecker, July 15, 1950; children: Virginia, Stanley, Glenn. BS in Journalism, U. Iowa, 1950. Reporter, copy editor Wis. State Jour., Madison, 1950-53; reporter, photographer Bartlesville (Okla.) Examiner-Enterprise, 1953; telegraph editor Abilene (Tex.) Reporter-News, 1954-55; makeup editor Cleve. Plain Dealer, 1955-63; mng. editor Wichita (Kans.) Eagle, 1963-70; exec. editor Wichita Eagle and Beacon, 1970-73; mng. editor Phoenix Gazette, 1973-82, Ariz. Republic, 1982-89; ret., 1989. Pres., dir. Wichita Profl. Baseball, Inc., 1969-75; mem. jury Pulitzer Prizes, 1973-74, 85, 86, 88. Mem. AP Mng. Editors Assn. (dir. 1973-78), Am. Soc. Newspaper Editors, Wichita Area C. of C. (dir. 1970-72), Sigma Delta Chi. Office: Phoenix Newspapers Inc 200 E Van Buren St Phoenix AZ 85004-2238 Personal E-mail: moyeralan@cox.net.

MOYER, CRAIG ALAN, lawyer; b. Bethlehem, Pa., Oct. 17, 1955; s. Charles Alvin and Doris Mae (Schantz) M.; 1 stepchild, Jason; 1 child, Chelsea A. BA, U. So. Calif., 1977; JD, U. Calif., LA, 1980. Bar: Calif. 1980, US Dist. Ct. (cen. dist.) Calif. 1980. Assoc. Nossaman, Krueger et al, LA, 1980-83, Finley, Kumble et al, Beverly Hills, Calif., 1983-85; ptnr. Demetriou, Del Guercio, Springer & Moyer, LA, 1985—2000, Manatt, Phelps, & Phillips, LLP, LA, 2000—. Instr. Air Resources Bd. Symposium, Sacramento, 1985—, U. Calif., Santa Barbara, 1989—; lectr. Hazmat Conf., Long Beach, Calif., 1986—, Pacific Automotive Show, Reno, Nev., 1989—; lectr. hazardous materials, environ. law UCLA; lectr. environ. law U. Calif., Santa Barbara; lectr. hazardous materials regulatory framework U. Calif., Santa Barbara. Co-author: Hazard Communication Handbook: A Right to Know Compliance Guide, 1990, Clean Air Act Handbook, 1991, Brownfields: A Practical Guide to the Cleanup, Transfer and Redevelopment of Contaminated Property, 1997; contbr. articles to profl. jours. Pres. Calif. Pub. Interest Rsch. Group, LA, 1978-80. Mem. ABA (natural resources sect.), Calif. Bar Assn., LA County Bar Assn. (environ. law sect., chmn. legis. rev. com., mem. exec. com.), Tau Kappa Epsilon (pres. LA chpt. 1975-76, Outstanding Alumnus 1983). Republican. Avocation: bicycling. Home Phone: 310-568-1107; Office Phone: 310-312-4353. Fax: 310-312-4224. Business E-Mail: cmoyer@manatt.com.

MOYER, DAVID S., executive search consultant; BA in History, SUNY, Purchase, 1975. Spl. asst. for pub. affairs Grumman Corp., Bethpage, NY, 1975-76; instr. R.T.Y., Inc., NYC and Miami, Fla., 1976-77; exec. v.p. Wesley-Brown, Ltd., NYC and L.A., 1977-83; v.p. Paul Stafford Assocs. Ltd., NYC, 1983-90, Fenwick Ptnrs., Inc., NYC, 1990-91, Moyer, Sherwood Assocs., Inc., Stamford, Conn., 1991-97, NYC, 1997—. Contbr. articles to profl. publs. Bd. dirs. The Helicon Found., N.Y.C., 1999—. Mem. Assn. Exec. Search Cons. (bd. dirs. 2003-05, mem. Ams. coun. 2005—), Stamford Yacht Club (chmn. membership com. 1993-97). Office: 1285 Ave Americas 35th Fl New York NY 10019

MOYER, F. STANTON, financial executive; b. Phila., June 7, 1929; s. Edward T. and Beatrice (Stanton) M.; m. Ann P. Stovell, May 16, 1953; 1 child, Alice E. BS in Econs., U. Pa., 1951. Registered rep. Smith, Barney & Co., Phila., 1951-54, Kidder, Peabody & Co., Phila., 1954-60; mgr. corp. dept. Blyth Eastman Dillon & Co., Inc. (formerly Eastman Dillon, Union Securities & Co.), Phila., 1960-65, instl. sales mgr., 1965-67, gen. partner, 1967-71, 1st v.p., 1971-74, sr. v.p., 1974-80; v.p., resident officer Kidder, Peabody & Co. Inc., Phila., 1980-86; chmn. Pa. Mcht. Group Ltd., Radnor, 1987-88; exec. v.p. Rorer Asset Mgmt., Phila., 1990-92; chmn. Mercer Capital Mgmt., 1992-93, Global Mgmt. Group, Inc., 1993-95; mng. dir. Avonwood Capital Corp., 1995-97; chmn. Main Line Capital Ptnrs. Inc., 1997—. Trustee U. Pa., 1978-83, Hosp. of U. Pa., 1978-87; bd. dirs. Atwater Kent Mus., Phila., 1983—. Mem. Racquet Club (Phila.), St. Anthony Club (Phila.), Merion Cricket Club (Haverford, Pa.), Gulph Mills Golf Club (King of Prussia, Pa.), Gulf Stream Golf Club (Fla.), Gulf Stream Bath and Tennis Club, Delta Psi. Republican. Episcopalian. Home (Summer): 445 Caversham Rd Bryn Mawr PA 19010 Home (Winter): 3 Little Club Rd Gulf Stream FL 33483 Office Phone: 561-274-8378, 610-527-5015. E-mail: growthguy@aol.com.

MOYER, GENEVIEVE J., counselor; b. Toledo, Ohio, Mar. 19, 1949; d. John Thomas and Genevieve Mary Bork; m. Thomas Eugene Moyer (dec.); 1 child, Eugene Thomas. BA, U. Toledo, 1977, MEd in Counseling, 1983, EdS in Counseling, 1986. Lic. counselor Mich., 1990, registered technologist Am. Registry Radiol. Tech., 1969. Student radiol. tech. St. Vincent Med. Ctr., Toledo, 1967—69; radiol. tech. Toledo (Ohio) Hosp., 1969—70, Flower Meml. Hosp., Sylvania, Ohio, 1970—88; vocat. counselor State of Mich., Adrian, 1988—95, Saginaw, 1995—. Adj. tchr. Monroe (Mich.) C.C., 1989—95; breeder Alpaca Registry Inc., Midland, Mich., 2003—05. Represented in permanent collections Toledo (Ohio) Art Mus. Bd. dirs. Cath. Social Svcs., Monroe, Mich. Mem.: Lions Club (bd. dirs. 1998—2005, officer, 3d v.p. 2004, 2d v.p. 2005). Republican. Roman Cath. Avocations: sewing, hand spinning fleece, needlecrafts, painting, drawing. Home: 4114 N Ehlers Rd Midland MI 48642 Office: Michigan Rehabilitation Svcs 3875 Bay Rd Ste 7 Saginaw MI 48603

MOYER, J. KEITH, former publishing executive; b. Louisville, Ky. s. Billye Pearl (Watkins) Moyer; m. Marilyn Moyer; children: Austin, Alexis, Samantha. B in journalism, U. Fla., 1977. City hall reporter Tampa Times, Fla.; with Lakeland Ledger, Fla.; exec. editor News-Press, Fort Myers, Fla., 1986—90; named v.p., editor Ark. Gazette, Little Rock, 1990; v.p., editor Times-Union, Rochester, NY, Democrat & Chronicle, Rochester, NY; exec. editor The Fresno Bee, Calif., 1994—97, pub. Calif., 1997—2001; pub., pres. Star Tribune, Mpls., 2001—07. Mem. Itasca Project; bd. mem. Capital Cities Partnership, Minn. Bus. Partnership. Bd. mem. Walker Art Mus., Mpls.; mem. nat. adv. com. Sch. Journalism and Mass Communication, U. Minn. Named Editor of Yr., Gannett Co., 1989, Alumnus of Distinction, Coll. Journalism and Comm., U. Fla., 2003. *

MOYER, R. CHARLES, finance company executive, educator, retired dean; b. Reading, Pa., July 11, 1945; s. Ralph Charles and Jane Anne (Huls) M.; m. Sally Louise Prizer, May 19, 1973; children: Laura Prizer, Craig Prizer. BA in Econs., Howard U., 1967; MBA, U. Pitts., 1968, PhD in Fin., 1971. Asst. prof. fin. U. Houston, 1971-76; fin. economist U.S. Maritime Adminstrn., Washington, 1973-74; assoc. prof. Lehigh U., Bethlehem, Pa., 1976-77; from assoc. prof. to prof. U. N.Mex., Albuquerque, 1977-80; prof., chmn. fin. dept. Tex. Tech U., Lubbock, 1980-87; GMAC ins. chair in fin., Babcock Grad. Sch. Wake Forest U., Winston-Salem, NC, 1988—2004, dean Babcock Grad. Sch. of Mgmt., 1996—2003, dean emeritus, 2003—; dir. King Pharm., Inc., Bristol, Tenn., 2000—; dean Coll. Bus. U. Louisville, 2005—. Pres., founder R.O.E. Cons. Group, Lubbock, 1978; cons. Pub. Svc. Co. N.Mex., 1978—, KN Energy, Denver, 1979—, Gas Co. N.Mex., 1985—, San Diego Gas Electric Co., 1986—; mem. adv. bd. Amarr Garage Door Co., Winston-Salem, 2001-05; bd. dirs. Metacyte, Ky. Seed Capital Fund. Author: Financial Management with Lotus 1-2-3, 1986, Contemporary Financial Management, 10th edit., 2006, Contemporary Financial Management Fundamentals, 2d edit., 2006, Managerial Economics, 11th edit., 2007; contbr. numerous articles to profl. jours. Vice-chmn. Lubbock Gen. Hosp. Found., 1985-88. Capt. US Army, 1972-74. Fed. Res. Bank Cleve. fellow, 1970-71. Mem.: We. Fin. Assn., Ea. Fin. Assn., So. Fin. Assn. (v.p. 1990—93, pres. 1993), Am. Econs. Assn., Am. Fin. Assn., Fin. Mgmt. Assn. (bd. dir. ombudsman 1985—87, v.p. 1988—, sec.-treas. 1994—2002), Cardinal Golf Club, Louisville Boat Club, Old Town Club, Beta Gamma Sigma, Phi Beta Kappa. Avocations: tennis, golf, bicycling.

MOYER, TERRY T., lawyer; b. Danville, Pa., Feb. 27, 1947; s. Thomas A. and Zereta (Bogart) M.; m. Terrie Lynn Crews, Jul. 10, 1987; children: Erin, Lauren, Jessie. BA, Rutgers U., 1969; JD with honors, George Washington U., 1974. Bar: Va. 1974, D.C. 1976, SC 1991, US Ct. Appeals (DC cir.) 1976, US Patent & Trademark Office. Patent trainee Am. Cyanamid Co., Arlington, Va., 1969-74; law clerk and tech. adv. Ct. Customs & Patent Appeals, Washington, 1974-76; assoc. Finnegan, Henderson, Washington, 1966-77, Bernard & Brown, Washington, 1977-79; patent atty. Milliken & Co., Spartanburg, S.C., 1979-83, chief patent coun., 1984-92, v.p., gen. coun., 1992—. Mem. ABA, Assn. Corp. Patent Counsel, Am. Intellectual Property Law Assn., Carolina Patent Trademark & Copyright Law Assn., Order of the Coif. Protestant. Office: Milliken & Co 920 Milliken Rd PO Box 1927 M-495 Spartanburg SC 29303

MOYER, THOMAS J., state supreme court chief justice; b. Sandusky, Ohio, Apr. 18, 1939; s. Clarence and Idamae (Hessler) M.; m. Mary Francis Moyer, Dec. 15, 1984; 1 child, Drew; stepchildren: Anne, Jack, Alaine, Elizabeth. BA, Ohio State U., 1961, JD, 1964. Asst. atty. gen. State of Ohio, Columbus, 1964-66; pvt. practice law Columbus, 1966-69; dep. asst. Office Gov. State of Ohio, Columbus, 1969-71, exec. asst., 1975-79; assoc. Crabbe, Brown, Jones, Potts & Schmidt, Columbus, 1972-75; judge U.S. Ct. Appeals (10th cir.), Columbus, 1979-86; chief justice Ohio Supreme Ct., Columbus, 1987—. Chair Conference of Chief Justices, 1995—96, Nat. Conf. on Ct. Security, 2005. Sec. bd. trustees Franklin U., Columbus, 1986-87; trustee Univ. Club, Columbus, 1986; mem. nat. council adv. com. Ohio State U. Coll. Law, Columbus. Recipient Award of Merit, Ohio Legal Ctr. Inst., Am. Judicature Soc. award, Disting. Service award Nat. Ctr. for State Cts., 1997, Innovative Program award Assn. Family & Conciliation Cts., 1998, Better World award Ohio Mediation Assn., 1999, Whitney North Seymour medal Am. Arbitration Assn., 2000, James F. Henry award, 2003; named Outstanding Young Man of Columbus, Columbus Jaycees, 1969. Mem. Ohio State Bar Assn. (exec. com., council dels., Ohio Bar medal 1991), Columbus Bar Assn. (pres. 1980-81, Liberty Bell award), Critchon Club, Columbus Maennerchor Club; fellow Ohio State Bar Found. (Ritter award 1996). Republican. Avocations: sailing, tennis. Office: Ohio Supreme Ct 65 S Front St Columbus OH 43215 *

MOYERS, SYLVIA DEAN, retired medical librarian; b. Independence, W.Va., Oct. 22, 1936; d. Wilkie Russell and Ina Laura (Watkins) Collins; m. Paul Franklin Moyers, June 29, 1957; children: Tammy Jeanne, Thomas Paul, Tara Sue. Student, Am. Med. Record Assn., 1977—79. Sec. Teets Lumber Co., Terra Alta, W.Va., 1954-58, Preston County News, 1958-60; med. record clk. med. record dept. Hopemont (W.Va.) Hosp., W.Va., 1960-75, dir., 1975-88; sec. The Terra Alta Bank, 1990-95; ret., 1995. Charter mem., past mother advisor Order of Rainbow Girls (Terra Alta Assembly No. 26), past grand editor Mountain Echoes; vol. Preston Meml. Hosp., ARC, Salvation Army, Am. Cancer Soc., Boy Scouts Am., Muscular Dystrophy Assn.; active Kingwood Fire Dept. Aux. Mem.: Preston County Hist. Soc., Kingwood Red Hat Mamas (charter), Preston Meml. Hosp. Aux., Kingwood Women's Civic Club. Republican. Methodist. Home: 120 Miller Rd Kingwood WV 26537-1321

MOYES, JERRY C., transportation executive; b. Plain City, Utah; m. Vickie Moyes; 10 children. Grad., Weber State Coll. Co-founder Swift Transp. Co., Inc., 1966—, v.p., 1966—84, chmn., pres., CEO Phoenix, 1984—2005, 2007—; owner SME Steel. Limited ptnr. Ariz. Diamondbacks, Phoenix Suns; co-owner Phoenix Coyotes, 2001—. Mem.: Am. Trucking Assn. (v.p.), Ariz. Motor Transportation Assn. (pres. 1987—88). Office: Swift Transp Co 2200 S 75th Ave Phoenix AZ 85043-7410 also: PO Box 29243 Phoenix AZ 85038-9243 Fax: 623-907-7380. *

MOYLAN, JAMES JOSEPH, lawyer; b. Forest Hills, NY, Feb. 3, 1948; s. James Gerard and Jessie Cora (Geary) M.; m. Barbara Chesrow, Aug. 29, 1970; children: James, C., Joseph O., Alicia G. BSBA, U. Denver, 1969, JD, 1971. Bar: Colo. 1972, D.C. 1972, Ill. 1975, U.S. Dist. Ct. Colo. 1972, U.S. Supreme Ct. 1975. Trial atty. SEC, Washington, 1972-75; assoc. gen. counsel Chgo. Bd. Options Exch., Ill., 1975-77; assoc. Abramson & Fox, Chgo., 1977-80; ptnr. Bowen, Knepper & Moylan Ltd., Chgo., 1980-82, Moylan & Early, Ltd., Chgo., 1983-84; prin. James J. Moylan and Assocs., Ltd., Chgo., 1984-95, 2003—; ptnr. Arnstein & Lehr, Chgo., 1995-2000, Tressler, Soderstrom, Maloney & Priess, Chgo., 2000—03, James J. Moylan and Assocs. PC, 2003—. Adj. prof. law IIT Chgo. Kent Coll. Law, 1976-2002, U. Denver Coll. Law, 2005—; former pub. dir. MidAm. Commodity Exch. divsn. Chgo. Bd. Trade, Chgo. Contbr. articles to profl. jours. Mem.: ABA (sect. corp., banking and bus. law, sect. litigation), Colo. Bar Assn., D.C. Bar Assn., Chgo. Bar Assn., Ill. State Bar Assn. (sect. coun. mem.), Theta Chi (grand chpt. 1993—2000, funds bd. 2000—03, found. chpt. 2003—). Republican. Roman Catholic. Office: PO Box 775965 31685 Inca Way Steamboat Springs CO 80477-5965 Office Phone: 970-870-0730. Business E-Mail: jjmoylanlaw@aol.com.

MOYLE, MICHAEL R., lawyer; b. Pepeekeo, Hawaii, 1948; AB, Harvard U., 1971, JD, 1976; student, Kyoto U., Japan. Bar: Calif. 1977. Atty. Graham & James, San Francisco; ptnr. Squire Sanders & Dempsey LLP, San Francisco. Past pres. & dir. emeritus Japan Soc. No. Calif., dir. & auditor Japanese C. of C. No. Calif., mem. bd. adv. US-Japan Bus. Incubation Ctr. San Jose Calif. Recipient JETRO, 2003. Mem. ABA (mem. sci. & tech. sects., mem. patent, trademark & copyright law sects., mem. internat. law sect.), State Bar Calif. (mem. bus. law sect.), Licensing Execs. Soc. Office: Squire Sanders & Dempsey LLP One Maritime Plz Ste 300 San Francisco CA 94111-3492 Business E-Mail: mmoyle@ssd.com.

MOYLE, PETER BRIGGS, marine biologist, educator; b. May 29, 1942; s. John Briggs and Evelyn (Wood) M.; m. Marilyn Arneson, June 11, 1966; children: Petrea Ruth, John Noah. BA, U. Minn., 1964, PhD, 1969; MS, Cornell U., 1966. Asst. prof. Calif. State U., Fresno, 1969-72; from asst. prof. to prof. U. Calif., Davis, 1972—, chmn. dept. wildlife and fisheries, 1982-87, Pres.'s chair in undergrad. edn., 2003—. Head, Delta Native Fishes Recovery Team, 1993-95. Author: Inland Fishes of California, 1976, 2d edit., 2002, Fishes: An Introduction to Ichthyology, 5th edit., 2003, Fish: An Enthusiast's Guide, 1993. Fellow Calif. Acad. Sci.; mem. Am. Fisheries Soc. (life, award of excellence West divsn. 1991, Outstanding Educator award 1995), Ecol. Soc. Am., Am. Soc. Ichthyologists and Herpetologists, Soc. Conservation Biology, Natural Heritage Inst. (v.p. 1994—). Home: 612 Eisenhower St Davis CA 95616-3031 Office: U Calif Dept Wildlife Fish & Conservation Biolog 1 Shields Ave Davis CA 95616 E-mail: pbmoyle@ucdavis.edu.

MOYLES, PHILIP VINCENT, JR., financial services company executive; b. NYC, July 14, 1964; s. Philip Vincent and Anne Kane Moyles; m. Beth O'Connor. BA in History, Kenyon Coll., 1986; postgrad., Dartmouth Coll., 2000. Mgmt. trainee Rollins Burdick Hunter Co., Chgo., 1986-87; assoc. Johnson & Higgins, NYC, 1987-90; sr. acct. rep. Marsh & McLennan Inc., NYC, 1990-91, asst. v.p., 1991-93, v.p., 1993-95, sr. v.p., 1995-96; from mng. dir., practice leader mergers and acquisitions to exec. v.p. Marsh Inc., NYC, 1996—2004, exec. v.p., 2004—. Mem. Union League Club N.Y., Allegheny Country Club, Apavaounis Clubn Hudson Nat. Golf Club Republican. Roman Catholic. Office: Marsh Inc 1166 Ave of Americas 44th Floor New York NY 10036

MOYNA, JOHN LAWRENCE, priest; b. NYC, Aug. 20, 1945; s. John Lawrence and Margaret Mary (Healy) Moyna. BA, St. Joseph's Sem. Coll., 1969; MDiv, Christ the King Sem., 1975. Ordained Roman Catholic Priest Diocese of Albany, 1973. Assoc. pastor St. Clare's Ch., Colonie, NY, 1973—75, St. Mary's Ch., Clinton Heights, NY, 1975—79, St. Pius X Ch., Londonville, NY, 1979—83, St. John the Evangelist Ch., Schenectady, NY, 1983—86; pastor St. Mary's Ch., Coxsackie, NY, 1986—; chaplain N.Y. State Dept. of Corrections, 1996—. Dean Suburban Albany, NY, 1982—83, dean Greene County, NY, 2006—. Mem. Ministerial Assoc., Coxsackie, 1986—, Presbyterial Coun., Albany, 1975—79, 1988—93, chmn., 1991—93; mem. strategic pastoral planning com. Diocese of Albany, 1990—91; mem. NY State Cath. Conf. Com. On Apostolate, 2006—. Mem.: Am. Correctional Assn., Acad. Correctional Health Profls. Roman Catholic. Achievements include development of hospice tng. for prison inmates. Home and Office: St Mary's Ch 80 Mansion St Coxsackie NY 12051 Office Phone: 518-731-8800.

MOYNAHAN, BRIDGET (KATHRYN BRIDGET MOYNAHAN), actress; b. Binghamton, NY, USA, Sept. 21, 1970; d. Brad Moynahan; 1 child, John Edward. Trained as actress, Caymichael Patten Studio, NYC. Actor: (TV series) Sex and the City, 1999—2001, Going to California, 2001, The Late Show with Craig Kilborn, 2004, Six Degrees, 2006; (films) Row Your Boat, 2000, In the Weeds, 2000, Trifling with Fate, 2000, Coyote Ugly, 2000, Whipped, 2000, Serendipity, 2001, The Sum of All Fears, 2002, The Recruit, 2003, I, Robot, 2004, Gray Matters, 2005, Lord of War, 2005. Office: c/o Endeavor Talent Agy 9601 Wilshire Blvd 10th Fl Beverly Hills CA 90212 *

MOYNAHAN, JOHN DANIEL, JR., retired insurance executive; b. Chgo., Dec. 10, 1935; s. John Daniel and Helen (Hurley) M.; m. Virginia Thomas, Oct. 10, 1959; children: Laura, Mark, Tricia, Kate. BA cum laude, U. Notre Dame, 1957. With Met. Life Ins. Co., NYC, 1957—, regional v.p., from 1971, with nat. div. group nat. accounts, 1979-80, sr. v.p. group life and health ops., 1980-86, exec. v.p., 1986-97; ret., 1997.

MOYNAHAN, JULIAN LANE, retired literature educator, writer; b. Cambridge, Mass., May 21, 1925; s. Joseph Leo and Mary (Shea) M.; m. Elizabeth Rose Reilly, Aug. 6, 1945; children: Catherine (dec.), Brigid, Mary Ellen. AB, Harvard U., 1946, A.M., 1951, PhD, 1957. Cataloguer, rare books asst. Boston Pub. Library, 1948-49, 51; tchg. fellow Harvard U., 1951-53; instr. English Amherst Coll., 1953-55; instr., asst. prof. English Princeton, 1955-63; Fulbright lectr. Am. and English lit. Univ. Coll., Dublin, 1963-64; assoc. prof. English Rutgers U., 1964-66, prof., 1966-93, disting. prof., 1976-93, prof. emeritus, 1993—. Vis. prof. U. Wyo., summer 1965, Harvard U., summer 1967, Bread Loaf Sch., 1969, NYU, 1997; NEH vis. prof. Manhattanville Coll., 1972; Gauss lectr. Princeton U., 1975; vis. scholar English dept. U. Utah, spring 1980; lectr. N.J. Coun. for Humanities, 1998, 99. Author: Sisters and Brothers, 1960, The Deed of Life, A Critical Study of D.H. Lawrence, 1963, Pairing Off, 1969, Vladimir Nabokov, 1971, Garden State, 1973, Where the Land and Water Meet, 1979, Anglo-Irish: The Literary Imagination in a Hyphenated Culture, 1995; editor: (D.H. Lawrence) Sons and Lovers: Text, Criticism, Backgrounds, 1968, 77, The Viking Portable Thomas Hardy, 1977; contbr. revs. and criticism to N.Y. Times Book Rev., T.L.S., Washington Post Book World, N.Y. Rev. Books; contbr., mem. editl. bd. The Recorder, Jour. Am. Irish Hist. Soc., 1994—; contbr. poetry to jours. Bicentennial preceptorship Princeton, 1960-63, grants-in-aid Am. Coun. Learned Socs., Am. Philos. Soc.; mem. Pulitzer Prize Fiction Jury, 1981, chmn., 1987; mem. Friends of Princeton U. Libr., 2002—. Served with AUS, 1943-44. 7500 creative writing award Nat. Found. Arts, 1966; Ingram-Merrill award, 1967; NEH fellow, 1975; Guggenheim fellow, 1983-84. Mem. MLA, PEN, Harvard Club of Princeton. Democrat. Home: 136 Bayard Ln Princeton NJ 08540-3041 Address: Apt 9B London Ter 405 W 23d St New York NY 10011 E-mail: moy@patmedia.net.

MOYNE, JOHN ABEL, computer scientist, linguist, educator; b. Yezd, Iran, July 6, 1920; came to U.S., 1956, naturalized, 1965; s. Abul Kasim and Sogra (Afshar) M.; m. Claudia Wienert, July 4, 1963; children: David, Nicholas, Parvin. BA, Georgetown U., DC, 1959, MA, 1960; PhD, Harvard U., Cambridge, Mass., 1970. With Brit. Govt., Iran and India, 1943-52, market rsch. officer Tehran, 1952; linguist U.S. Govt., Cyprus, 1953-56; rsch. assoc. Georgetown U., Washington, 1960-63; mgr. applied linguistics dept. IBM Corp., Cambridge, Mass., 1963-71; prof., chmn. computer sci. dept. Queens Coll. CUNY, Flushing, 1971-81, chmn. divsn. math. and natural scis., 1978-81, chmn. univ. faculty for PhD in Computer Sci., 1978-82, exec. officer Grad. Sch. PhD Program in Linguistics, 1983-88, prof. linguistics and computer sci., 1971—91, prof. emeritus linguistics and computer sci., 1991—. Author, co-author: Hafiz of Shiraz, 1946, Life in India, 1949, Open Secret, 1984, Understanding Language: Man or Machine, 1985, Unseen Rain, 1986, Rumi: These Branching Moments, 1988, This Longing Poetry, Teaching Stories, and Letters of Rumi, 1988, LISP: A First Language for Computing, 1991, Say I Am You, 1994, The Essential Rumi, 1995, Rumi and the Sufic Tradition: Essays on the Mowlavi Order and Mysticism, 1998, The Drowned Book, 2004, The Structures of Verbal Constructions in Persian, 2007, A Bird in the Garden of Angel; contbr. articles to profl. jours., chpts. to books. Grantee EURATOM, AEC, NSF, CUNY. Mem. Linguistics Soc. Am., Brit. Inst. Engring. Tech., The Acad. Am. Poets. Democrat. Home: 40 Prospect Ave Sea Cliff NY 11579-1029 Office: CUNY PhD Program Linguistics Grad Ctr 365 5th Ave New York NY 10016-4334 Personal E-mail: jmoyne@post.harvard.edu, jmoyne@verizon.net. Business E-Mail: jmoyne@gc.cuny.edu.

MOYNIHAN, BRIAN T., finance company executive; b. 1960; m. Susan Berry; 3 children. Grad., Brown U., U. Notre Dame Law Sch. Dep. gen. coun. FleetBoston Fin. Corp., 1993—94, mng. dir. corp. strategy and devel., 1994—2000, sr. v.p., 1998—99, exec. v.p., 1999, exec. v.p. brokerage and wealth mgmt., 2000—04; pres. global wealth & investment mgmt. Bank Am. Corp., 2004—. Bd. dirs. YouthBuild Boston; chmn. Providence Haitian Project, Inc. Office: Bank Am Corp Ctr 100 N Tryon St Fl 58 Charlotte NC 28255-0001 *

MOYNIHAN, GARY PETER, industrial engineering educator; b. Little Falls, NY, Mar. 5, 1956; s. Peter H. and Frances S. (Ferjanec) M.; m. Eleanor T. McCusker, Mar. 10, 1984; children: Andrew Ross, Keith Patrick. BS in Chemistry, Rensselaer Polytech. Inst., 1978, MBA in Opsl. Mgmt., 1980; PhD in Indsl. Engring., U. Ctrl. Fla., 1990. Prodn. supr. Am. Cyanamid, Bound Brook, N.J., 1978-79, Nat. Micronetics, Kingston, N.Y., 1980-81; assoc. mfg. engr. Martin Marietta Aerospace, Orlando, Fla., 1981-82, indsl. engr., 1982-85, sr. indsl. engr., 1985-87, group indsl. engr., 1987-90; asst. prof. indsl. engring. U. Ala., Tuscaloosa, 1990-96, assoc. prof., 1996—2001, prof., 2001—. Cons. in field. Contbr. articles to profl. jours. Regents scholar N.Y. State Bd. Regents, 1974-78; rsch. fellow NASA, 1992-93, 98-99; rsch. grant BellSouth Telecomm., 1994-96; recipient Outstanding Tchg. award AMOCO Found., 1993-94, Ralph R. Teetor Engring. Educator award Soc. Automotive Engrs, 2000. Mem.: IEEE (sr.), Aerospace and Def. Soc. (v.p. fin. and adminstrn. 1994—97), Inst. Indsl. Engrs. (sr.; chpt. dir. 1991—95, chpt. pres. 1996—97, regional v.p. 2004—06, Outstanding Faculty Adv. SE Region award 2004, 2006). Achievements include design and development of information systems applications for the aerospace and foundry industries; 4 software copyrights. Office: U Ala Dept Indsl Engring Tuscaloosa AL 35487-0001

MOYNIHAN, JAMES M., bishop; b. Rochester, NY, July 16, 1932; Student, St. Bernard's Sem., Rochester, N.Am. Coll., Rome, Gregorian U. Ordained priest Roman Cath. Ch. 1957. Bishop Diocese of Syracuse, Syracuse, NY, 1995—. Office: 240 E Onondaga St Syracuse NY 13202-2608

MOYNIHAN, JOHN BIGNELL, retired lawyer; b. NYC, July 25, 1933; s. Jerome J. and Stephanie (Bignell) M.; m. Odilia Marie Jacques, Nov. 13, 1965; children: Blair, Dana. BS, Fordham U., 1955; JD, St. John's U., NYC, 1958. Bar: Tex. 1961, U.S. Supreme Ct. 1965, U.S. Dist. Ct. (we. dist.) Tex. 1968, U.S. Ct. Appeals (5th cir.) 1973. Sole practice, Brownsville, Tex., 1961-62; asst. city atty. City of San Antonio, 1962-63; sole practice San Antonio, 1963-65; estate tax atty. IRS, San Antonio, 1965-73; dist. counsel EEOC, San Antonio, 1974-79; asst. U.S. atty. Office U.S. Atty., San Antonio, 1980-87, sr. litigation counsel, 1987-94; sole practice San Antonio, 1995-98; ret., 1998. Chmn. reform and renewal com., San Antonio Roman Cath. Archdiocese, 1968. Served with U.S. Army, 1958-60; lt. col. USAFR (ret.), 1986. Mem. San Antonio Bar Assn. (chmn. state and nat. legis. com. 1972-73, Meritorious Svc. award 1968), Fed. Bar Assn. (bd. dirs. San Antonio chpt. 1983—, pres. elect 1986, pres. 1987), KC (pres. 1967). Home: 11011 Whispering Wind St San Antonio TX 78230-3746 E-mail: jmoynihan@satx.rr.com.

MOYNIHAN, WILLIAM J., museum executive; b. Little Falls, NY, Apr. 8, 1942; s. Bernard J. and Mary A. (Flynn) M.; m. Irene A. Sheilds, July 2, 1966; children: Patricia, Erin, Sean. BA, SUNY, Binghamton, 1964; MA, Colgate U., 1966; PhD, Syracuse U., 1973. From asst. to assoc. prof. Colgate U., Hamilton, NY, 1973—77, from asst. to assoc. dean faculty, 1977—80, dean students, 1980—83, dean coll., 1983—88; v.p.m. dir. Am. Mus. Natural History, NYC, 1988—95; pres., CEO Milw. Pub. Mus., 1995—2002; ret., 2002. Bd. dirs. N.Y. State Mus.; adv. com. arts and culture Congressman J. Nadler, N.Y.C., 1993-95. Adv. editor Curator jour., 1991-95. Mem. Am. Mus. Assn., Am. Assn. Museums (mem. ethics com., bd. dirs.), Wis. Acad. of Scis., Arts and Letters (councillor-at-large 1995-02), Univ. Club. Home: 84 Eaton St Hamilton NY 13346

MOYO, KIMYA MAUNDA, elementary school educator; b. Dayton, Ohio, Jan. 23, 1948; d. George William and Ruby Mae (Wills) Malone; m. Karega Kofi Moyo, Oct. 21, 1973 (div. 1988); children: Kweli, Ki-afi, Kilolo, Kevani, Kush. BS, Northwestern U., 1969; MA, U. Cin., 1988. Tchr. Chgo. Pub. Schs., 1969-73, New Concept Devel. Ctr., Chgo., 1972-75, 77-79; dir., tchr. Inst. Divine Edn., Monrovia, Liberia, 1979-84; tchr. Cin. Pub. Schs., 1987—. Founder, dir. Sankofa, 1993—. Mem. Cin. Youth Cooperation, 1989—. Recipient Excellence in Teaching award Nat. Coun. Negro Women and Shell Oil Co., 1992. Mem. Nat. Coun. Tchrs. Math., Assn. Supervision Curriculum Devel., Ohio Coun. Tchrs. Math., Coun. Ind. Black Instns., Black Achievers. Avocations: working puzzles, solving logic problems, swimming, aerobics. Office: Sch for Creative and Performing Arts 1310 Sycamore St Cincinnati OH 45210-2022

MOYSE, HERMANN, III, banker; b. Baton Rouge, Dec. 28, 1948; s. Hermann Jr. and Marie Louise (Levy) M.; m. Janet Lee Doise; children: Allison Leze, David Hermann, Aaron Lewis. BA, Coll. of Emporia, 1970; MSW, La. State U., 1973. Asst. dir. Capital Area Health Planning Agy., 1973-74; research assoc. La. State U., Baton Rouge, 1974-78; trainee to v.p. City Nat. Bank, Baton Rouge, 1978—, sr. v.p., 1985-94, also bd. dirs., chmn., 1994-98; owner, pres. HM3 Corp., 1999—. Sec.-treas. Melrose Devel. Corp., Baton Rouge, 1986-87; bd. dirs. La. Cos., Charter Chambers, LLC, First NBC Bank, New Orleans, Bizzuka, Inc.; CEO Health Net One, 1999; adv. bd. Iberra Bank, 2004-05; pres. WRKF Radio, 2003-04. Active Capital Area United Way Agy. Svcs. Div., Baton Rouge, 1979-86, 88-91, vice chmn. 1981, bd. dirs., 1987—, chmn., 1989-90; v.p. Arts Coun. Greater Baton Rouge, 1990—; 1st v.p. La. Arts & Sci. Ctr., Baton Rouge, 1985—, pres., 1988; mem. Community Funds for Arts, 1989-90; mem. Arts & Humanities Coun., 1990—, v.p., 1991—, treas., 1992; mem. Cmty. Funds for the Arts, 1989—, vice-chmn., 1992; pres. Cath. Cmty. Life Office, Baton Rouge, 1981, Baton Rouge Speech and Hearing Found., 1986, pres. 1983, treas., 1981; v.p. St. Joseph's Acad. Adv. Bd., 1986-88, pres., 1987-88; bd. dirs. St. James Place; treas. Baton Rouge Crisis Intervention Ctr., 1984-85, v.p., 1987, pres., 1987; sec. St. Joseph's Children's Home, 1980; bd. dirs. Crime Stoppers, Inc., 1986—, v.p., 1989, pres. 1991—; pres. Mid City Devel. Alliance, 1991-93, 97—; adv. bd. Tau Ctr., 1990-93; trustee Episc. HS, 1990-92; treas. La. Delta Svc. Corps. Inc., 1995—; bd. trustees Gen. Health Sys., Inc, 1994-98, La. Nature Conservancy, 2001—, Our Lady of Lake Coll., 2001—, sec., 2003-05; chmn. fin. com. Baton Rouge Crimestoppers, 1997—; chmn. First Commerce Cmty. Devel. Corp., 1993-99, La. State U. Health Care Svcs. Found., 2002—. Mem. La. Bankers Assn. (fed. affairs com. 1990—), La. Coun. Econ. Edn. (trustee 1987, regional v.p. 1990—, Community Vol. Activist award 1988), NCCJ (chpt. bd. dirs. 1988, treas. 1995), City Club, Baton Rouge Country Club. Democrat. Jewish. Personal E-mail: hmoyse3@yahoo.com.

MOZELL, HERBERT LEE, mental health services professional; b. Miami, Fla., Feb. 16, 1963; s. Alfonzo and Ethel Mae Mozell. BA in Psychology, A&T State U., 1988, MS in Adult Edn., 1997; postgrad., Nova Southeastern U. Habilitation tech, Greensboro, NC, 1990—96; exec. dir. Visions of N.C. Inc., Greensboro, 1997—. Mental health tech., Greensboro, 1988—97; tchr. Allen Jay Mid. Sch., Archdale, 1999—2001; cons., Greensboro, 2004—, Little Seedlings, Greensboro, 2004—, Faith House, Lexington, 2004—, Sensational Living, Raleigh, 2004—. Recipient Humanitarian award, Nova S.E. U., 2004. Mem.: Am. Mental Health Counselor Assn., Kappa Delta Pi. Democrat. Baptist. Avocations: Karate, weightlifting. Office: Visions of NC Inc 7607-A Alcorn Rd Greensboro NC 27409 Office Phone: 336-931-0432.

MOZILO, ANGELO R., diversified financial services company executive; b. NYC, 1938; m. Phyllis Mozilo; 5 children. BS, Fordham U., 1960; LLD (hon.), Pepperdine U. Co-founder, vice chmn. Countrywide Fin. Corp., Calabasas, Calif., 1969—99, pres., 2000—03, CEO, 1998—99, chmn., CEO, 1999—. Bd. dirs. The Home Depot, Inc., 2006—. Bd. mem. Nat. Housing Endowment, Joint Ctr. for Housing Studies, Harvard U., Homes for Working Families; trustee Gonzaga U. Named one of 30 most respected CEOs, Barron's mag., 2005; named to Nat. Assn. of Home Builders' Hall of Fame; recipient Boy Scouts of Am. James E. West Fellowship award, Ellis Island Medal of Honor, Albert Schweitzer award, Special Achiev. award, Nat. Italian Am. Found., Horatio Alger Assn. of Disting. Am. award. Mem.: Mortgage Bankers Assn. of Am. (pres. 1991—92). Office: Countrywide Fin Corp 4500 Park Granada Calabasas CA 91302-1613 *

MOZLEY, ANITA VENTURA, retired curator, retired art historian; b. Wash., DC, Aug. 29, 1928; d. Mario Fiorino Ventura and Juanita Magruder Lewis; m. Robert Fred Mozley, May 29, 1967 (dec. 1999); 1 stepchild, Peter Snow. BA in Liberal Arts with honors, Northwestern U., Evanston, Ill., 1950. Mng. editor Arts Mag., NYC; sea letter St. Maritime Mus., San Francisco; registrar Stanford Mus., Calif., curator. Reviewer Arts Mag., NYC, 1950; co-author (with Sydney Geist): (art review) Scrap, 1963; author: (exhibition catalogue) Edwsard Muybridge: The Stanford Years, 1972, Mrs. Cameron's Photographs from the Life, 1974. Recipient 1st prize award, Pacific Art League, Figurative Art Exhibition, 1972. Democrat. Avocation: painting. Home: 601 Laurel Ave Menlo Park CA 94025

MOZLEY, PAUL DAVID, retired obstetrics and gynecology educator; b. Decatur, Ala., Oct. 27, 1928; s. James Howard and Ruth Dianne (Brindley) Mozley; m. Mary Dale Goss, Aug. 30, 1983; children from previous marriage: Susan Ruth, Paul David Jr., Sally Robin. BA, U. Ala., 1950; MD, Med. Coll. Ala., 1955. Diplomate Am. Bd. Ob-Gyn, Am. Bd. Psychiatry and Neurology. Commd. lt. USN, 1955, advanced through grades to capt., 1970; resident ob-gyn Corona (Calif.) and San Diego Naval Hosp., 1956-59; resident in psychiatry Bethesda, Md., 1964-66, Phila. Naval Hosp., 1969-70; staff gynecologist U.S. Naval Hosp., Yokosuku, Japan, 1959-62, chief gynecologist Memphis, 1962-64, dir. med. services Naples, Italy, 1966-68, comdg. officer, 1969; chmn. neuropsychiatry Naval Regional Med. Ctr., Portsmouth, Va., 1970-75; ret., 1975; assoc. prof. psychiatry Eastern Va. Med. Sch., Norfolk, 1975-77, prof., interim chmn. dept., 1977-78, vice chmn. psychiatry, 1978-79; prof., dir. undergrad. edn. Dept. Ob-Gyn Sch. Medicine, East Carolina U., Greenville, 1979-84; prof. ob-gyn, chmn. dept., Coll. Community Health Scis. U. Ala., Tuscaloosa, 1984-99, prof. ob-gyn, assoc. chmn. dept. Sch. Medicine, 1984-99, prof., chmn. emeritus Sch. Medicine, prof. emeritus obstetrics, 1999—; ret., 2002. Dir. psychiat. svcs. Norfolk Gen. Hosp., 1975—79; chmn. dept. ob-gyn DCH Regional Med. Ctr., Tuscaloosa, 1986—; obstetrician BAldwin Clinic; cons. med. liability law legal firms, Ala., Tenn., 1980—. Contbr. articles to profl. jours. Mem. Regional Parental Adv. Coun., Montgomery, Ala., 1986—87; sponsor Tuscaloosa Symphony Assn. Named one of Outstanding Young Men in Am., Jaycees, 1964; recipient Meritorious Svc. medal, US Pres., 1975, Surgeon Gen.'s Merit award, 1975, Attending of the Yr. award, Resident's in Psychiatry, 1979, Clin. Sci. Course award, Dept. Ob-Gyn grad. class 1982, Eastern Va. Sch. Medicine. Fellow: ACS, ACOG (life; chmn. various programs 1974, 1976, 1977, Chmn.'s award clin. rsch. 1969), Am. Psychiat. Assn. (life Continuing Med. Edn. Stds. award 1977); mem.: LWV, AMA (Physician's Recognition award 1986), Ala. Psychiat. Assn., Med. Assn. Ala., Pitt County Med. Soc., NC Neuropsychiatric Assn., Va. Med. Soc., Assn. Acad. Psychiatry, Va. Ob-Gyn. Soc., Am. Soc. Psychosomatic Ob-Gyn (founding mem., pres. 1979—80, chmn. nominating com. 1981, mem. permanent steering com. 1982), Torch Club (Portsmouth), Alpha Epsilon Delta. Mem. Ch. Of Christ. Avocations: cabinetry, goldsmithing. Home: 563 N Mobile St Fairhope AL 36532-2609 Personal E-mail: pm02@bellsouth.net.

MRACHEK, LORIN LOUIS, lawyer; b. Fairmont, Minn., Jan. 5, 1946; s. Louis L. and Kathleen (Loring) M.; m. Elizabeth Moss, Aug. 31, 1968; children: Kathleen Elizabeth, Louis Moss. BA with honors, Fla. State U., 1968; MBA, JD, Columbia U., 1974. Bar: Fla. 1974, Va. 1977, U.S. Ct. Mil. Appeals 1977, U.S. Dist. Ct., U.S. Ct. Appeals (5th cir.), U.S. Ct. Appeals (7th cir.), U.S. Ct. (11th cir.), U.S. Supreme Ct. 1978, U.S. Bankruptcy Ct. (so. dist.) Fla., U.S. Bankruptcy Ct. (mid. dist.) Fla., U.S. Bankruptcy Ct. (no. dist.) Fla.; cert. in civil trial law, 1985, bus. litigation, 1997, Fla. Bar Bd. Certification; cert. in bus. bankruptcy law Am. Bd. Bankruptcy Certification, 1992; cert. in civil trial advocacy Nat. Bd. Trial Advocacy, 1995. Commd. 2d lt. USMC, 1969, advanced through grades to capt., 1974, chief def. counsel Marine Corps. Recruit Depoit, Paris Island, 1975-77, resigned, 1977; spl. asst. to gen. counsel U.S. Ry. Assn., Washington, 1977-78; shareholder Gunster, Yoakley, Valdes-Fauli & Stewart, P.A., West Palm Beach, Fla., 1978-2000; founding shareholder Page, Mrachek, Fitzgerald & Rose, West Palm Beach, Fla., 2000—. Editor-in-chief Columbia Jour. Law and Social Problems, 1973-74; contbr. articles to profl. jours. Named one of Best Lawyers in Am.; Harlan Fiske Stone scholar. Fellow Am. Coll. Trial Attys.; mem. ABA, Am. Bankruptcy Inst., So. Fla. Bankruptcy Bar Assn. Avocations: travel, golf. Office: 505 S Flagler Dr Ste 600 West Palm Beach FL 33401-5941 Office Phone: 561-655-2250. Business E-Mail: lmrachek@pm-law.com.

MRACKY, RONALD SYDNEY, marketing executive, tourism consultant, media specialist; b. Sydney, Oct. 22, 1932; came to US, 1947, naturalized, 1957; s. Joseph and Anna (Janousek) M.; m. Sylvia Frommer, Jan. 1, 1960; children: Enid Hillevi, Jason Adam. Student, English Inst., Prague, Czech Republic, 1943—47; grad., Parsons Sch. Design, NYC, 1953—2001; postgrad., NYU, 1953—54. Designer D. Deskey Assocs., NYC, 1952-53; art dir., designer ABC-TV, Hollywood, Calif., 1956-57; creative dir. Neal Advt. Assocs., LA, 1957-59; pres. Richter & Mracky Design Assocs., LA, 1959-68; pres., CEO Richter & Mracky-Bates divsn. Ted Bates & Co., LA, 1968-73, Regency Fin., Internat. Fin. Svcs., Beverly Hills, Calif., 1974-76; sr. ptnr. Sylron Internat., LA, 1973—, mgmt. dir. for N.Am. Standard Advt.-Tokyo, 1978-91. CEO, Std./Worldwide Cons. Group, LA, Tokyo, 1981-87; officer, bd. dirs. Theme Resorts, Inc., Denver, 1979—; prin., officer Prodn. Travel & Tours, Universal City, 1981—, Eques Ltd., LA, 1988-93; mng. ptnr. GO! Pubs., 1993—; cons. in field; exec. dir. Inst. for Internat. Studies and Devel. LA, 1976-77; mng. ptnr. Africa Consult Group, 1998—. Dir. MedicusTravel.com, 2003—; mem. editl. bd., mktg. dir. The African Times and Africa Quar., 1990—; contbr. articles to profl. jours With US Army, 1954-56. Recipient nat. and internat. awards design and mktg. Mem. Am. Mktg. Assn., Africa Travel Assn. (amb.-at-large, internat. secretariat, bd. dirs.), LA Publicity Club, Pacific Asia Travel Assn., S.Am. Travel Assn., Am. Soc. Travel Agts. Personal E-mail: medicustravel@earthlink.net, africaconsult@mindspring.com.

MRAK, ROBERT EMIL, neuropathologist, educator; b. Oakland, Calif., Dec. 18, 1948; s. Emil Marcel and Vera Dudley (Greaves) M.; m. Paula Elizabeth North, Oct. 18, 1980; children: Lara North, Eric North, Ian North. BS in Math., U. Calif., Davis, 1970, MD, 1975, PhD in Zoology, 1976. Diplomate Am. Bd. Pathology, Am. Bd. Neuropathology. Resident in pathology Vanderbilt U. Hosp., Nashville, 1976-78, fellow in molecular biology, 1978-80; asst. prof. pathology Vanderbilt U., 1980-84; assoc. prof. U. Ark. for Med. Scis., Little Rock, 1984—87, prof., 1993—98, chief neuropathology, 1999—2007, dir. neuropathology core, Alzheimer Disease Core Ctr., 2001—07, prof. pathology, neurobiology and devel. scis., 1998—2007, chief autopsy, 2003—07; prof., chmn. of pathology U. Toledo Health Sci. Campus, 2007—. Chief electron microscopy VA Hosp., Little Rock, 1984-98; cons. in neuropathology Ark. Children's Hosp., Little Rock, 1984—. Editl. bd. mem. Jour. Neuropathy & Explt. Neurology, 1996-99, Human Pathology, 1996-2004; editor-in-chief Jour. Neurinflammation, 2003—; contbr. articles and abstracts to profl. jours Rsch. grantee VA, 1980-83, 86-89, Muscular Dystrophy Assn., 1981-85, NIH, 1986-90, 95—. Mem. Am. Assn. Neuropathologists, Soc. for Neurosci., U.S. and Can. Acad. Pathology. Avocations: running, skiing. Office: Dept Pathology Univ Toledo Health Sci Campus 3000 Arlington Ave Toledo OH 43614

MRAMOR, MARTI, engineer, linguist; b. Indpls., Apr. 17, 1971; d. Joseph Thomas Mramor and Nancy Ann Clark Mramor. BA in Biology and Chemistry, Spring Arbor U., Mich., 1994; Paralegal Cert. in Gen. Law with highest honors, Nat. Ctr. for Paralegal Tng., Ga., 1995; AA in Russian, Def. Lang. Inst., Calif., 1998; AAS in Comm. Tech., C.C. of the Air Force, Ala., 2001; MS in Geosciences, Miss. State U., 2005. Engr. L-3 Comm., Bellevue, Nebr., 2004—. Vol. Fontenelle Nature Assn., Bellevue, 2002—06, Katherine and Fred Buffett Forest Learning Ctr., Bellevue, 2002—06, Neale Woods Nature Ctr./Obs., Omaha, 2002—06, Creighton U. Med. Ctr., Omaha, 2006—06; vol. tutor and transl. Staff sgt. USAF, 1997—2001, Okinawa, Japan, master sgt. USAFR, 2001—. Decorated Good Conduct medal USAF, Longevity Svc. medal, Overseas Long Tour ribbon, Aerial Achievement medals, Achievement medals, Noncommissioned Officer Grad. ribbon, Armed Forces Expeditionary medal, Global War on Terrorism Expeditionary medal, Iraq Campaign medal, Afghanistan

Campaign medal, Air Force Expeditionary Svc. medal, Air medals, Meritorious Unit award, Commendation medal; named Airman of the Yr., 1999; recipient Martin J. Kellogg award for Excellence, Def. Lang. Inst., 1998; Academic Athlete scholar, Spring Arbor U., 1990—94. Mem.: VFW (life), Air Force Sgts. Assn., Nat. Weather Assn., Am. Meteorol. Soc., Am. Math. Soc., Am. Phys. Soc., Am. Mensa Soc. Avocations: swimming, running, writing, art, astronomy. Home Phone: 402-614-8982.

MRAZEK, DAVID ALLEN, child and adolescent psychiatrist; b. Ft. Riley, Kans., Oct. 1, 1947; s. Rudolph George and Hazel Ruth (Schayes) M.; m. Patricia Jean, Sept. 2, 1978; children: Nicola, Matthew, Michael, Alissa. AB in Genetics, Cornell U., 1969; MD, Wake Forest U., 1973. Lic. psychiatrist, child psychiatrist, N.C., Ohio, Colo., D.C., Va., Md., Minn., Ariz., Fla. Lectr. child psychiatry Inst. of Psychiatry, London, 1977-79; dir. pediatric psychiatry Nat. Jewish Ctr. for Immunology and Respiratory Medicine, Denver, 1979-91; chmn. psychiatry Children's Nat. Med. Ctr., Washington, 1991-98; chair psychiatry and behavioral scis. George Washington U. Sch. Medicine, 1996-2000; dir. Children's Rsch. Inst. Neurosci., 1995-98; chair psychiatry and psychology Mayo Clinic, Rochester, Minn., 2000—; prof. psychiatry and pediatrics Mayo Sch. Medicine, Rochester, 2000—; dir. Mayo Clinic S.C. Johnson Genomics of Addictions Program, 2004—. Asst. prof. psychiatry U. Colo. Sch. Medicine, 1979-83, assoc. prof. psychiatry and pediatrics, 1984-89, prof., 1990-91; prof. psychiatry and pediatrics George Washington U. Sch. Medicine, 1991-2000, Leon Yochelson prof. psychiatry and behavioral scis.; dir. Am. Bd. Psychiatry and Neurology, 2003-. Contbr. chapters to books, articles to profl. jours. Recipient Rsch. Scientist Devel. awards NIMH, 1983-88, 88-91, Irving Phillips Meml. award for outstanding rsch. in prevention Acad. Child and Adolescent Psychiatry, 2000, Simon Wile award Am. Acad. Child and Adolescent Psychiatry, 2005 Fellow Am. Acad. Child and Adolescent Psychiatry (Simon Wile award 2005), Royal Soc. Medicine, Am. Psychiat. Assn. (chmn. coun. children, adolescents and families 2006—, Blanche F. Ittleson award 1996, Agnes Purcell McGavin award 1999), Royal Coll. Psychiatrists, Am. Coll. Psychiatrists; mem. Group for the Advancement of Psychiatry, Colo. Child and Adolescent Psychiatry Soc. (pres. 1984), Benjamin Rush Soc., Am. Bd. Psychiatry Neurology (bd. dirs. 2003—). Office: Mayo Clinic Dept Psychiatry/Pschology 200 1st St SW Rochester MN 55905 Home Phone: 507-285-5656; Office Phone: 507-284-8891. Office Fax: 507-266-3319. Business E-Mail: mrazek.david@mayo.edu.

MRKVICKA, EDWARD FRANCIS, JR., writer, finance company executive; b. Aurora, Ill., Oct. 17, 1944; s. Edward Francis Sr. and Ruth Caroline (Phillips) M.; children: Edward Francis III, Kelly Helen. Cert. comml. pilot, U. Ill., 1965; diploma, Dept. Def., 1967, Bank Mktg. Assn., 1972, grad. cert., 1973. Mktg. officer Downers Grove (Ill.) Nat. Bank, 1964-72; asst. v.p., mktg. officer Bank of Westmont, Ill., 1972-73; v.p., cashier 1st State Bank Hanover Park, Ill., 1973-76; pres. 1st Nat. Bank Marengo, Ill., 1976-81, Reliance Enterprises, Inc., Fin. News Syndicate, Omni, Fin. Group, Eagle Publishing, Marengo, 1981—. Adv. coun. Am. Monetary Found., Fullerton, Calif., 1987; mem. panel of experts Boardroom Reports, 1990—. Pub.: (newletter) Money Insider; author: Battle Your Bank-And Win!, 1984, Moving Up, 1985; (with others) The Complete Book of Personal Finance, 1987, The Bank Book, 1989, 91, 94, 1,037 Ways to Make or Save Up to $100,000 This Year Alone, 1991, The Rational Investor, 1992, Your Bank is Ripping You Off, 1997, 99, J.K. Lasser's Pick Winning Stocks, 2000, Be Not Deceived, 2006; contbr. articles to profl. jours. and newspapers; fin. columnist Nat. Enquirer, 1996—. Bd. dirs. DuPage County Lung Assn., Downers Grove, 1970, Western Suburbs Combined Com. Appeal, Downers Grove, 1971, McHenry County Easter Seals Clinic, Woodstock, Ill., 1979; v.p., treas. Marengo/Union Chamber, 1980; Am. rep. Cans. for Constitutional Money, 1990—. Sgt. USAF, 1965-69. Mem. Nat. Writers Union. Republican. Avocations: bowling, fishing. Office: Reliance Enterprises Inc PO Box 413 Marengo IL 60152-0413 Office Phone: 815-568-8267. Business E-Mail: reliance@cin.net.

MROCZKOWSKI, MATTHEW, biomedical engineer; MS, Syracuse U., NYC, 2003. Rsch. engr. Zimmer, Inc., Warsaw, Ind., 2003—05. Contbr. articles to profl. jours. Recipient Bioengineering Founder's award, Syracuse U., Dept. Bioengring., 2001. Mem.: Orthop. Rsch. Soc. Office: Zimmer 1800 W Center St Warsaw IN 46580 Office Phone: 574-267-6131. Office Fax: 574-372-4922. E-mail: matt.mroczkowski@zimmer.com.

MROSKO, MATTHEW L., music educator; b. Warren, Mich., Oct. 10, 1979; s. Richard John and Marie Christina Mrosko. BA in Music Edn., Shenandoah U., 2003. Cert. tchr. Va. Band tchr. Shenandoah County Pub. Schs., Woodstock, Va., 2004—. Mem.: Sons of Am. Legion Squadron, SCEA, VEA, NEA, Music Educators Nat. Conf. Avocations: travel, hiking. Office: Peter Muhlenberg Mid Sch 1251 Susan Ave Woodstock VA 22664 Home Phone: 540-459-7895; Office Phone: 540-459-2941. Personal E-mail: morosoko@yahoo.com. Business E-Mail: mlmrosko@shenandoah.k12.va.us.

MROWKA, TOMASZ, mathematics professor; BS in Math., MIT, 1983; PhD, Univ. Calif., Berkeley, 1988. Faculty Stanford Univ., Calif. Inst. Tech., Harvard Univ.; prof., math. MIT, 1996—. Co-recipient AMS Oswald Veblen Prize in Geometry, 2007; recipient Nat. Young Investigator award, 1983; grantee Alfred P. Sloan Rsch. Fellowship, 1983. Fellow: Am. Acad. Arts & Scis. Office: Dept Math MIT Rm 2-367 77 Massachusetts Ave Cambridge MA 02139-4307 *

MROZ, JOHN EDWIN, political scientist; b. Lowell, Mass., May 1, 1948; s. Edwin T. and Margaret Mary (Little) M.; m. Karen Linehan, June 17, 1972; children: Jonathan E.R., Jessica, Jeffrey. BA, cert. Soviet and East European studies, U. Notre Dame, 1970; AM, Northeastern U., 1972; MA, MALD, Tufts U., 1974. Exec. sec. UN Assn. Greater Boston, 1971-73; exec. v.p., dir. Middle East Studies, Internat. Peace Acad., Inc., N.Y.C., 1976-81; pres. Inst. East West Studies, N.Y.C., 1981—; cons., U.S. Govt. intermediary in Middle East, U.S. Dept. State, 1981-82; cons. Fgn. Svc. Inst., Dept. State, 1977-81; cons. Coun. of Europe, Strasbourg, Fed. Republic Germany, 1989—, East European govts., 1990—. Author: Beyond Security: Private Perceptions Among Arabs and Israelis, 1980. Contbr. articles to profl. jours. Teaching fellow NSF, 1971-72. Decorated Officer's Cross of Order of Merit Fed. Republic of Germany, 1991. Mem. Coun. on Fgn. Rels., Internat. Inst. Strategic Studies. Republican. Avocations: travel, falconry. Office: Inst East West Studies 700 Broadway New York NY 10003-9536

MROZEK, ERNEST J., customer service administrator; married; 2 children. Grad. in Acctg., U. Ill., 1976. CPA Ill. V.p. acctg. The ServiceMaster Co., Downers Grove, Ill., 1987, pres., COO, Consumer Svcs., 1997—98, group pres. consumer and comml. svcs., 1998—2002, pres., COO, 2002—04, pres., CFO, 2004—06, vice-chmn., 2006—. Bd. dir. G&K Services Inc., U.S. C. of C. Mem.: AICPAs, Ill. CPA Soc. Office: ServiceMaster 3250 Lacey Rd Downers Grove IL 60515 *

MROZEK, LAWRENCE JAMES, director; s. Mary Anna and Albin Bruno Mrozek. BS in Psychology, Mich. State U., 1984, MA in Phys. Exercise and Exercise Sci., 1989; Cert. - Alcohol and Other Drug Specialist, Calif. State Univeristy, LA, Los Angeles, CA, 1992—93; Cert. - Family Violence and Child Maltreatment, Calif. State U., LA, Los Angeles, CA, 1993—2003; PhD in Edn., Ohio State U., 2003—. Cert. alcohol and other drug specialist Calif. State U., 1993, family violence and child maltreatment specialist Calif. State U., 2003. Area coord. Whittier Coll., Calif., 1986—87; resident dir. Calif. State U., LA, 1987—89; from asst. to dir. to asst. dir. for programs U. Student Union, LA, 1989—92, from asst. dir. for ops. to ops. mgr. Northridge, Calif., 1992—2002. Directorate - commn. for alcohol and other drug issues Am. Coll. Pers. Assn., Washington, 1990—92, directorate - commn. on assessment for student devel., 2002—03; conf. planning com. Assn. of Coll. Unions Internat. - Region 15, LA, 1995—95, San Bernardino, Calif., 1997—97. Del. Coun. of Grad. Students, Columbus, Ohio, 2005. Recipient Employee of Yr. award, U. Student Union - Calif. State U., Northridge, 1994-1995, Aida C. Salazar award, 1995-1996. Mem.: NEA, Am. Ednl. Rsch. Assn., Assn. for Study of Higher Edn., Nat. Assn. of Student Pers. Administrs., Am. Coll. Pers. Assn., Phi Kappa Phi, Pi Lambda Theta. Office: Ohio State Univ 47 Curl Dr Columbus OH 43210-1111 Home Phone: 614-262-1641; Office Phone: 614-247-6220.

MRUK, EUGENE ROBERT, retired marketing professional, urban planner; b. Buffalo, Sept. 12, 1927; s. Stanley and Lucy Ann (Wolanski) M.; m. Florence Helen Guzy, Apr. 15, 1950; children: Linda, Lawrence, Edith, Ginny. AA in Engring., U. Buffalo, 1966, BA in Sociology, 1970; cert. sys. analysis & application admin., U. Wis., 1971; MA in Econs., U. Buffalo, 1974. Asst. dir. planning City of Buffalo, 1958-70; commr. planning Erie County, N.Y., Buffalo, 1970-74; dir. socioecon. studies Ecology and Environment, Inc., Buffalo, 1974-79, dir. transp. system studies, 1979-81, dir. bus. devel., 1981-86, v.p. sales and mktg., 1986-90, sr. v.p. sales and mktg. nat. and internat., 1990-94, cons., 1994-96; ret., 1996. Pvt. practice planning cons. Buffalo area, 1950-64; v.p. rsch. and planning coun. WNY, 1971-74; mem. indsl. adv. bd. dept. chem. engring. SUNY, Buffalo. Author various mcpl. govt. plans. Coord. Econ. Devel. program, Buffalo, 1966; exam. cons. Civil Svc. Commn. City of Buffalo, 1974; grand marshal Gen. Pulaski Parade com., Buffalo, 1972; trustee Villa Maria Coll. Buffalo, 1992-93. Named Man of Yr. in Govt. Am-Pole Eagle newspaper, 1970; gold medal Sr. Olympics, N.H., N.Y., 2003, 04, 05, 06, Bronze medal Nat. Sr. Games 80+ divsn., 2007. Mem. Am. Assn. Cert. Planners, Am. Planning Assn. (Disting. Leadership award N.Y. upstate chpt. 1992, dir.), Profl. Businessmen's Assn., Fr. Kolbe Soc./Polish Union of Am. (pres. 1995-2000). Democrat. Roman Catholic. Avocations: tennis, senior olympic basketball, photography, oil and acrylic painting. Home: 3 Dennis Ln Cheektowaga NY 14227-1301

MRUTHINTI, SHYAMALA, pharmacologist, educator; b. Hyderabad, Andhra Pradesh, India, July 4, 1951; arrived in US, 1986; m. Swamy S. Mruthinti, May 2, 1980; children: Harshita K, Navyata, Namrata. BSc, RBVRR Womens Coll., Hyderabad, 1972; MPhil, Osmania U., Hyderabad, 1974; MSc, U. Baroda, India, 1977, PhD, 1982. Rsch. pharmacologist Vets. Med. Adminstrn., Augusta, Ga., 1996—, prin. investigator, 2006—. Adj. faculty dept. pharmacology/toxicology Med. Coll. Ga., Augusta, Ga. Author: Neuroscience. Merit Rev. grantee, VA Med. Ctr., 2006—. Achievements include patents pending for generation of monoclonal antibody specific to RAGE (receptor for advanced glycation end prducts); research in Beta amyloid and RAGE auto-antibodies are elevated in Alzheimer's patients compared to age-match controls; first to RAGE-Beta amyloid complex as a novel vaccine therapy for Alzheimers. Home Phone: 706-869-8791; Office Phone: 706-733-0188 2057. Business E-Mail: smruthinti@mail.mcg.edu.

MUBARAK, KAMAL K., pulmonologist, intensivist; arrived in US, 1989; s. Ali Khan and Azra Mubarak; m. Tabinda Khan Mubarak, Dec. 20, 1995; children: Eman Azra, Izan Ali. MD, Aga Khan U., Karachi, 1988. Cert. in pulmonary medicine and critical care medicine, diplomate Am. Bd. Internal Medicine. Asst. prof. internal medicine Wayne State U., Detroit, 2000—07; dir. Pulmonary Hypertension Clinic, Detroit, 2001—07; dir. pulmonary vascular disease program U. Fla., Gainesville, 2007—. Fellow: Am. Coll. Chest Physicians; mem.: Am. Thoracic Soc., Internat. Soc. Philos. Enquiry. Office: 1600 SW Archer Rd M452 Gainesville FL 32610 Office Phone: 352-392-2666. Office Fax: 352-239-0821. Business E-Mail: mubarak@ufl.edu.

MUCCI, GARY LOUIS, lawyer; b. Buffalo, Nov. 12, 1946; s. Guy Charles and Sally Rose (Battaglia) M.; m. Carolyn Belle Taylor, May 4, 1991. BA cum laude, St. John Fisher Coll., 1968; JD, Cath. U., 1972. Bar: N.Y. 1972. Law clk. to Hon. John T. Curtin U.S. Dist. Ct., Buffalo, 1972-74; assoc. atty. Donovan Leisure Newton & Irvine, NYC, 1974-75, Saperston & Day P.C., Buffalo, 1975-80, sr. ptnr., 1980—2001; ptnr. Hiscock Barclay, 2001—. Chmn. bd. Buffalo Philharm. Orch., 1985-86; pres. Hospice Buffalo, 1986-87; mem. N.Y. State Coun. on the Arts, 1987-2000; chmn. Citizens Com. on Cultural Aid, Buffalo, 1992-98; trustee St. John Fisher Coll.; chmn. bd. trustees Nardin Acad., 2005—. Recipient Brotherhood award NCCJ, Buffalo, 1983; named Man of Yr. William Paca Soc., 1984. Mem. Erie County Bar Assn., N.Y. State Bar Assn. Home: 27 Tudor Pl Buffalo NY 14222-1615 Office: Hiscock Barclay 3 Fountain Plz Ste 1100 Buffalo NY 14203-1486 Home Phone: 716-885-5175; Office Phone: 716-566-1520. Business E-Mail: gmucci@hiscockbarclay.com.

MUCCI, PATRICK JOHN, financial consultant, realtor, commercial loan broker; b. Albany, NY, July 5, 1947; s. Philip and Angelina (Patrella) M.; m. Beverly Ann Scully, June 8, 1968; children: Philip Michael, Angelina Maria. AAS, Hudson Valley Community Coll., Troy, NY, 1967; BS, SUNY, Albany, 1977; MBA, Fairleigh Dickinson U., 1979, Cert. review appraiser, comml. investment mgr., real estate broker, internat. financier; registered mortgage underwriter; lic. ins. broker for life and accident ins. Adminstrv. asst. Nat. Savs. Bank, Albany, 1973-76; asst. v.p. Heritage Savs. Bank, Kingston, N.Y., 1976-78, Home Savs. Bank, Albany, 1978-81, v.p., 1981, Home & City Savs. Bank, Albany, 1981-83, sr. v.p. lending, 1983-90; pres., chmn. bd., founder Greenbush Assocs., Inc., East Greenbush, 1990—2003. Chmn. bd., founder, pres. Patrician Funding, Inc., 1997—, East Greenbush; bd. dirs. Vec Tech., Inc., Philangie Corp.; v.p., sr. comml. loan officer Provantage Funding Corp., 2000-02; v.p. govt. guaranteed lending, Key Bank, 2003-. Active Nat. Assn. Govt. Guarenteed Lenders; treas., bd. dirs. Theater Voices, 1990; bd. dirs. Albany League Arts, Discovery Ctr. Capital Region, 1990, N.Y. State Mus. Inst., Capital Affordable Housing Funding Com., Albany County Affordable Housing Corp., Grand St. Cmty. Arts; mem. Rensselaer County Com. Sewer & Water Authority, 1993-94. Staff sgt. USAF, 1969-72. Mem. NY State Assn. Bus. Brokers (bd. dirs., treas., sec. 2006—), Internat. Bus. Brokers Assn., NY State Comml. Assn. Realtors. Avocations: travel, reading, photography, computers. Home: 296 Luther Rd East Greenbush NY 12061-4312 Office Phone: 518-257-9405. Business E-Mail: patrick_mucci@keybank.com.

MUCCIA, JOSEPH WILLIAM, lawyer; b. NYC, May 31, 1948; s. Joseph Anthony and Charlotte (Mohring) M.; m. Margaret M. Reynolds, June 29, 1985. BA magna cum laude, Fordham U., 1970, JD, 1973. Bar: N.Y. 1974, U.S. Dist. Ct. (so. dist.) N.Y. 1974, U.S. Dist. Ct. (ea. dist.) N.Y. 1980, U.S. Ct. Appeals (2d cir.) 1974, U.S. Ct. Appeals (D.C. cir.) 1980, U.S. Supreme Ct. 1980. Assoc. Cahill Gordon & Reindel, NYC, 1973-82; ptnr. Corbin Silverman & Sanseverino, NYC, 1983—2001, Thelen Reid Brown Raysman & Steiner LLP, NYC, 2002—. Assoc. editor Fordham Law Rev., 1972-73. Mem. ABA (litigation sect.), N.Y. County Lawyers Assn., Fed. Bar Coun., N.Y. State Bar Assn. (com. litigation sect.), Phi Beta Kappa, Pi Sigma Alpha. Office: Thelen Reid Brown Raysman & Steiner LLP 875 3d Ave New York NY 10022 Office Phone: 212-603-2436. Business E-Mail: jmuccia@thelen.com.

MUCCIE, MARY ROSE, publishing executive; BA, U. Pa. Editl., prod. positions Phila. Bar Assn., 1986, J.B. Lippencott Co., 1986—93; mng. editor Soc. Indsl. & Applied Math., Phila., 1993—97, pub., 1997—2006; dir. project MUSE Johns Hopkins U. Press, Balt., 2006—. Mem.: No. Am. Serials Interest Group, Spl. Libraries Assn., Soc. Scholarly Publishing. Office: Project MUSE Johns Hopkins Univ Press 2715 N Charles St Baltimore MD 21218 Office Phone: 410-516-6900. Business E-Mail: mrm@press.jhu.edu.

MUCHIN, ARDEN ARCHIE, lawyer, director; b. Manitowoc, Wis., Dec. 9, 1920; s. Alfred and Ida (Golden) M.; m. Bettie Lou Barenbaum, Dec. 19, 1948; children: Ann L., Efrem B., Jay Z. BA, U. Wis., 1942, JD, 1947; IA, Harvard U. Grad. Sch. Bus. Adminstrn., 1943. Bar: Wis. 1947, U.S. Dist. Ct. (ea. dist.) Wis. 1948, U.S. Tax Ct. 1965. Pres. Muchin, Muchin & Bruce, S.C. and predecessors, Manitowoc, 1947-92; ptnr. Nash, Spindler, Dean & Grimstad, 1993-99, Michael Best & Friedrich, 1991-2001; sec. and/or dir. Foster Needle Co., Inc., Manitowoc, Foster Needle Ltd. (Eng.), Sorenson Industries, Inc., Manitowoc; sec., dir. WaterCare Corp., Water Svcs. Corp.; sec. Schwartz Mfg. Co., Heresite Protective Coatings, Inc.; sec., v.p. CUB Radio, Inc., Manitowoc; gov. State Bar Wis., 1976-80. Bd. dirs. Manitowoc United Way Inc., 1968-92; mem. Wis. adv. com. U.S. Commn. Civil Rights, 1985-89. Mem. ABA, Manitowoc County Bar Assn. (pres. 1972-73), B'nai Brith (nat. commn. anti-defamation league). Home and Office: 1426 Arden Ln Manitowoc WI 54220-2517 Office Phone: 920-684-9150.

MUCHMORE, DON MONCRIEF, retired cultural organization administrator, retired museum director, foundation administrator; b. Wichita, Kans., Dec. 26, 1922; s. Floyd Stephen and Ivy Fay (Campbell) Muchmore; m. Virginia Gunn, June 18, 1949 (div. Dec. 1978); children: Melinda, Marcia. BA, Occidental Coll., Los Angeles, 1945; postgrad., U. So. Calif. Law Sch., 1945, UCLA. Intern Nat. Inst. Pub. Affairs, Washington, 1944; exec. asst. to congressman Washington, 1946-48; teaching asst. UCLA, 1949-50; mem. faculty San Diego State U., 1950-51; asst. prof., adminstr. Calif. State U., Long Beach, 1951-56; pres., CEO The Campbell Found., LA, 1956—2002; spl. asst. to supt. pub. instrn. Calif. Dept. Edn., Sacramento, 1956-57; exec. mus. dir. Calif. Mus. Sci. and Industry, LA, 1957-62, 82-89; exec. v.p., chief exec. officer Calif. Mus. Found., LA, 1957-62, 82-89; dep. dir. (on loan from mus.) Calif. Dept. Fin., Sacramento, 1960; exec. vice chancellor Calif. State Colls. and Univs. System, Long Beach, 1962-64; first exec. asst. to chmn. and chief exec. officer Calif. Fed. Savs. and Loan Assn., LA, 1964-66; sr. v.p. Calif. Fed. Savs. and Loan Assn, LA, 1966-82; pres., CEO PE Conservation Svcs., Inc., 1990-94; ret., 2002. Chmn. bd. dirs., CEO Opinion Rsch. of Calif. Opinion Surveyors, The State Poll and Mktg. Surveys, Inc., Long Beach, 1948—71; syndicated by L.A. Times, 1961—70; also M-R Assocs. Campaigns; cons. in pub. opinion mus. mgmt. and fund raising, 1948—71; chmn., CEO, cons. DMM & Assocs., Long Beach, 1961—2002; sec., treas. EVENUP for the Homeless, 1994—97; mem. Inst. Mus. Svcs., 1983—88. Contbr. chapters to books. Participant in pub. opinion work Dem. and Rep. Campaigns, 1954—72; mem., chmn. 4 presdl. commns., 1970—82, Just Say No Internat., 1989—91, Reading is Fundamental, 1989—, The Buckley Sch., 1989—90; cons. overseas traveling sci. exhibit, planning mus., 1984—96; sr. adminstr., advisor, cons. PCS (South Ctrl. L.A.) Sr. Citizens, 1995—96; cons. Long Beach com. Improvement League, 1995—96; lead cons. New Solution to Homeless, 1993—98; prin. officer Peruvians Cultural Exhibit, 1988—96; prin. cons. cultural exhibit Wonders of World, 1992—95, Queensway Bay, Long Beach, 1992—98; bd. dirs. Bus. Tele Network, 1995—97; active Even up for the Homeless, 1996—98; cons. Christian Outreach Agy., 1998—99; pres. Harborplace Tower Home Owners Assn., 1999—; pres. bd. trustees East Village Cmty. Ch., 1998—, pres., 1998—2001. Named Chpt. Advisor of Yr., Sigma Alpha Epsilon, 1999, Pollster of Yr., Newsweek, 1968; recipient Highest Mus. Edn. award, Sigma Alpha Epsilon, 1992, Citizen of Yr. award and numerous other awards from nat., state and local groups; scholar Elks Nat. scholar. Mem.: AAAS, Calif. Mus. Assn. (pres. 1960, bd. dirs. 1982—88), Am. Polit. Sci. Assn., Am. Assn. Pub. Opinion Rsch., Assn. Sci. and Tech. Ctrs. (bd. dirs. 1982—88), Am. Assn. Mus.

MUCHMORE, ROBERT BOYER, engineering executive, consultant; b. Augusta, Kans., July 8, 1917; s. Ray Boyer and Charlotte (McPherron) M.; m. Betty Vaughan, Jan. 29, 1944; children: Andrew Vaughan, Douglas Boyer. BS, U. Calif., Berkeley, 1939; degree in Elec. Engring., Stanford U., 1942. Project engr. Sperry Gyroscope Co., Garden City, NY, 1942-46; sr. mem. tech. staff Hughes Aircraft, Culver City, Calif., 1946-54; v.p., chief scientist TRW Systems, Redondo Beach, Calif., 1954-73, cons. Sonoma, Calif., 1973—. Lectr. in engring. UCLA, 1954-58. Author: Essentials of Microwaves, 1952. Fellow IEEE; mem. AAAS, Assn. Computing Machinery, Sierra Club. Home: 4311 Grove St Sonoma CA 95476-6046 E-mail: rbm@sonic.net.

MUCHNICK, RICHARD STUART, ophthalmologist, educator; b. Bklyn., June 21, 1942; s. Max and Rae (Kozinsky) Muchnick; m. Felice Dee Greenberg, Oct. 29, 1978; 1 child, Amanda Michelle. BA with honors, Cornell U., 1963, MD, 1967. Diplomate Am. Bd. Ophthalmology, Nat. Bd. Med. Examiners. Intern in medicine N.Y. Hosp., NYC, 1967—68, now assoc. attending ophthalmologist, chief Pediatric Ophthalmology Clinic, resident in ophthalmology, 1970—73, practice medicine, specializing in ophthalmology, notably strabismus and ophthalmic plastic surgery, 1974—. Attending surgeon, chief Ocular Motility Clinic Manhattan Eye, Ear and Throat Hosp., NYC; clin. assoc. prof. ophthalmology Cornell U., NYC, 1984—; clin. rschr. strabismus, ophthalmic plastic surgery, 1973—. With USPHS, 1968—70. Recipient Coryell Prize Surgery, Cornell U. Med. Coll., 1967, McLean Medal in Ophthalmology, Weill Med. Coll. of Cornell U., 2006. Fellow: ACS, Am. Acad. Ophthalmology; mem.: AMA, Manhattan Ophthal. Soc., Greater N.Y. Soc. Pediat. Ophthalmology and Strabismus (pres.), N.Y. Acad. Medicine, N.Y. Soc. Clin. Ophthalmology, Internat. Strabismological Assn., Am. Assn. Pediatric Ophthalmology and Strabismus, Am. Soc. Ophthalmic Plastic and Reconstructive Surgery, 7th Regt. Tennis, Lotos, Alpha Epsilon Delta, Alpha Omega Alpha. Office: 69 E 71st St New York NY 10021-4213 Office Phone: 212-744-1726.

MUCKENFUSS, CANTWELL FAULKNER, III, lawyer; b. Montgomery, Ala., Apr. 25, 1945; s. Cantwell F. and Dorothy (Dauphine) M.; m. A. Angela Lancaster, June 25, 1978; children: Alice Paran Lancaster, Cantwell F. IV. BA, Vanderbilt U., 1967; JD, Yale U., 1971. Bar: N.Y. 1973, D.C. 1976. Law clk. to Hon. William E. Miller U.S. Ct. Appeals (6th Cir.), 1971-72; atty., project developer Bedford Stuyvesant D and S Corp., Bklyn., 1972-73; spl. asst. to the dir. FDIC, Washington, 1974-77, counsel to the chmn., 1977-78; sr. dep. comptroller for policy Office of the Comptroller of the Currency, Washington, 1978-81; ptnr. Gibson, Dunn & Crutcher LLP, Washington, 1981—. Mem. editorial adv. bd. Issues in Bank Regulation, Rolling Meadows, Ill., 1977-91, Electronic Banking Law and Commerce Report, 1996—; mem. bd. advisors Rev. Banking and Fin. Svcs., N.Y.C., 1985—; bd. dis. Fair Tax Edn. Fund, Washington, 1987-90. Served with USNG, 1968-70, USAR, 1970-74. Recipient Spl. Achievement award U.S. Dept. Treasury, 1979, Presdl. Rank award U.S. Govt., 1980. Mem. ABA, Fed. Bar Assn. Clubs: Kenwood Country (Bethesda, Md.); Yale (N.Y.C.). Democrat. Episcopalian. Office: Gibson Dunn & Crutcher LLP 1050 Connecticut Ave NW Ste 900 Washington DC 20036-5306

MUCKENHOUPT, BENJAMIN, retired mathematics professor; b. Newton, Mass., Dec. 22, 1933; s. Carl Frederick and Sarah Joanna (Boell) M.; m. Mary Kathryn Heath, Aug. 29, 1964; children: Margaret, Carl Edward. AB, Harvard U., 1954; MS, U. Chgo., 1955, PhD, 1958. Instr. DePaul U., Chgo., 1958-59, asst. prof. math., 1959-60; faculty Rutgers U., New Brunswick, NJ, 1960-91, prof. math., 1970-91. Vis. assoc. prof. Mt. Holyoke Coll., 1963-65; visitor Inst. Advanced Study, Princeton, N.J., 1968-69, 75-76; vis. prof. SUNY-Albany, 1970-71 Contbr. articles to profl.

jours. NSF rsch. grantee, 1965-88; Rutgers Rsch. Coun. fellow, 1968-69. Mem. Am. Math. Soc., Math. Assn. Am., Phi Beta Kappa, Sigma Xi. Home: 196 Woodfern Rd Neshanic Station NJ 08853-4054 E-mail: muckenho@post.harvard.edu.

MUCKERMAN, NORMAN JAMES, priest, writer; b. Webster Groves, Mo., Feb. 1, 1917; s. Oliver Christopher and Edna Gertrude (Hartman) M. BA, Immaculate Conception Coll., 1940, M. in Religious Edn., 1942. Ordained priest Roman Catholic Ch., 1942. Missionary Redemptorist Missions, Amazonas, Para, Brazil, 1943-53, procurator missions St. Louis, 1953-58; pastor, adminstr. St. Alphonsus Ch., Chgo., 1958-67, St. Gerard, Kirkwood, Mo., 1967-71; mktg. mgr. circulation Liguori Pubs., Liguori, Mo., 1971-76; editor Liguorian Mag., Liguori, Mo., 1977-89. Author: How to Face Death Without Fear, 1976, Redemptorists on the Amazon, 1992, Preparation for Death, 1998, Into Your Hands, 2001, From the Heart of St. Alphonsus, 2002; contbg. editor: Liguorian, 1989—95. Recipient Nota Dez award Caixa Fed. Do Para, Brazil, 1958 Mem. Cath. Press Assn. (cons. 1971-95, bd. dirs. 1976-85, pres. 1981-84, St. Francis De Sales award 1985). Avocations: reading, writing. Home Phone: 636-464-3666. Personal E-mail: nmuckerman@liguori.org.

MUCKLER, JOHN E., former professional sports team executive, former professional hockey coach; b. Midland, Ont., Can., Apr. 3, 1934; m. Audrey C. Muckler; children: Karen, John, Tracy, Jenny. Coach, gen. mgr. Long Island Ducks; 1st pres. NY Jr. Met. League; coach, gen. dir. player pers., mgr. NY Rangers affiliate team, Am. Hockey League, Providence; head coach Minn. North Stars, 1968—69; asst. coach Edmonton Oilers, 1984—85, co-coach, 1987—88, head coach, 1989—91, Buffalo Sabres, 1991-94, gen. mgr., 1994-98; head coach NY Rangers, NYC, 1997—98, 1999—2000; gen. mgr. Ottawa Senators, 2002—07. *

MUDAVANHU, BLESSING, research scientist; b. Harare, Mashonaland, Zimbabwe, May 26, 1971; s. Jackson and Gladys Mudavanhu; m. Mutsa Tongoona, July 22, 1996; children: Mandisa, Thandeka, Baraka. BS in Gen. Math. and Stats., U. Zimbabwe, Harare, 1993, BS in Math., 1995; M in Fin. Engring., U. Calif., Berkeley, 2002; MS, U. Wash., Seattle, 1998, PhD, 2002. Rsch. asst. U. Wash., Seattle, 1996—2001; derivatives quantitative analyst Am. Internat. Group, NYC, 2002—05, v.p., 2002—05; v.p. corp. risk mgmt. Merrill Lynch & Co., NYC, 2005—. Book reviewer: Soc. Indsl. and Applied Math., 2003—; contbr. articles to profl. jours. Fellow U. of Zimbabwe Math. fellow, 1995; scholar Fulbright scholar, U.S. Govt., 1996—98. Mem.: Internat. Assn. for Fin. Engrs., Soc. for Indsl. and Applied Math., Am. Math. Soc., Fulbright Assn. (bd. dirs. Puget Sound chpt. 2000—02). Office Phone: 212-449-4464. Personal E-mail: blessing_mudavanhu@yahoo.com.

MUDD, ANNE CHESTNEY, mediator, law educator, real estate broker; b. Macon, Ga., June 30, 1944; d. Bard Sherman Chestney and Betty (Bartow) Houston; children: Charles Lee Jr., Richard Chestney, Robert Jason. BA, U. Louisville, 1966, MA, 1976; JD cum laude, John Marshall Law Sch., 1998. Math statistician U.S. Bur. Census, Jeffersonville, Ind., 1966-70; instr. math. U. Louisville, 1975-77, Coll. DuPage, Glen Ellyn, Ill., 1978-85, 92; tchr. math and substitute tchr. Lyons Twp. High Sch., La Grange, Ill., 1986-91; realtor First United Realtors, Western Springs, Ill., 1989-92; owner, mgr. retail bus., 1992—2000; lawyer Mudd Law Offices, 1998—. Adj. prof. law. Editor: Mathematics Textbook, 1991-92. Steering com. Village Western Springs, 1986-87; bd. dirs. Children's Theater, 1987-91; sec. Collaborative Law Inst. of Ill., Leave a Legacy N.E. Ill. Outreach Com.; major gift task force Am. Cancer Soc. DuPage County. Mem.: LWV (pres. 1983—85, bd. dirs.), DuPage Assn. Women Lawyers, DuPage County Bar Assn., West Suburban Bar Assn., Ill. State Bar Assn., ABA, Collaborative Law Inst. Ill. (sec. bd. dir.), Suburban Chgo. Planned Giving Assn., Nat. Assn. Women Bus. Owners, Nat. Assn. Women Entrepreneurs (pres.), Assn. for Conflict Resolution, Mediation Coun. Ill. Avocations: gardening, politics, local govt. Office: Mudd Law Offices 3344 North Albany Ave Chicago IL 60618 Office Phone: 773-588-5410. Office Fax: 773-588-5440. E-mail: amudd@muddlawoffices.com.

MUDD, DANIEL H., finance company executive; married; 4 children. BA in History, U. Va.; MPA in Econs. and Internat. Affairs, Harvard U., 1986. V.p. bus. devel. GE Capital, 1991—93, mng. dir. internat. financing, 1993—95, pres., CEO, European Fleet Services Brussels, 1995—96, pres. Asia Pacific, 1996-99, pres., CEO Japan, 1999—2000; vice chmn., COO Fannie Mae, Washington, 2000—04, interim CEO, 2004—05, pres., CEO, 2005—. Mem. Coun. Fgn. Relations; bd. dirs. Fannie Mae, 2000—, Oriental & Gen. Fund Ltd., Fannie Mae Found., Ryder System Inc., Local Initiative Support Corp., Nat. Bldg. Museum, Hampton U., St. Patrick Sch. Officer USMC. Robert Bosch Found. fellow, 1989. Office: Fannie Mae 3900 Wisconsin Ave NW Washington DC 20016-2892

MUDD, JOHN O., lawyer; b. 1943; BA, Cath. U., 1965, MA, 1966; JD, U. Mont., 1973; LLM, Columbia U., 1986; JSD of Law, 1994. Bar: Mont. 1973. Pntr. Mulroney, Delaney, Dalby & Mudd, Missoula, Mont., 1973-79; lectr. U. Mont., Missoula, 1973-74, 75-76, prof. law, dean, 1979-88; ptnr. Garlington, Lohn & Robinson, Missoula, 1988—99; sr. v.p. Providence Svcs., 2000—05, also bd. dir.; sr. v.p. Providence Health & Svcs., 2006—. Pres. Mid-Continent Assn. Law Schs., 1982—83; chmn. bd. dir. Ascension Health, 2004—. Editor: Mont. Law Rev., 1972—73. Chmn. Mont. Commn. Future of Higher Edn.; Dem. candidate U.S. Senate, 1994; bd. dir. St. Patrick Hosp., 1985—90. With US Army, 1967—73. Mem.: State Bar Mont., Am. Judicature Soc. (bd. dirs. 1985—89).

MUDD, MARY, historian; b. Oak Park, Ill., July 24, 1948; d. Edward Lee and Audrey Sack Michaels; m. John Edward Mudd, Sept. 4, 1976 (dec.); 1 child, Andrew. BA in English cum laude, U. Houston, 1969, BS in Math., 1969; MA in History, Rutgers U., New Brunswick, NJ, 1974, PhD in History, 1984. Ind. scholar Roman and Byzantine History, Wall, NJ, 1984—; med. sec., 1997—; physician credentials coord., interpreter French Meridian Health, Wall, 2004—. Freelance lectr. archaeology and Roman history, 1978—95. Author: I, Livia: The Counterfeit Criminal, 2005, Studies in Reign of Constantius II, 1989; contbr. articles to scholarly publs. Recording sec. Freedom Theatre Parents Group, Phila., 1993—95; environ. activist Clean Ocean Action, Highlands, NJ, 1984—. Mem.: Nat. Assn. Med. Staff Svcs., Am. Hist. Assn., NJ Environ. Fedn., Earthjustice. Democrat. Avocations: bicycling, swimming, theater, ballet, cooking. Home and Office: PO Box 1275 Wall NJ 07719 Office Phone: 732-299-8608.

MUDD, ROGER HARRISON, newscaster, educator; b. Washington, Feb. 9, 1928; s. Kostka and Irma Iris (Harrison) M.; m. Emma Jeanne Spears, Oct. 26, 1957; children: Daniel H., Maria M., Jonathan, Matthew M. AB, Washington and Lee U., 1950; MA, U. N.C., 1953. Tchr. Darlington Sch., Rome, Ga., 1951—52; reporter Richmond News Leader, Va., 1953; news dir. Sta. WRNL, Richmond, 1953—56; reporter radio and TV Sta. WTOP, Washington, 1956—61; corr. CBS, 1961—80; chief Washington corr. NBC, 1980—87; Congl. corr. MacNeil/Lehrer News Hour, 1987—92; prof. journalism Princeton U., 1992—94, Washington & Lee U., 1995—96. Host The History Channel, 1995-2005. Trustee Randolph-Macon Women's Coll., Lynchburg, Va., 1971-78, Robert F. Kennedy Journalism Awards Com., 1971-78, Blue Ridge Sch., Dyke, Va., 1978-84; bd. dirs. Fund for Investigative Journalism, PEN/Faulkner, 1985-92, Va. Found. for Humanities, Va. Hist. Soc., 1988-94, RIAS Berlin Commn., 1996-99, Va. Found. for Ind. Colls., Nat. Portrait Gallery Commn., Civil War Trust, 1999-01; chmn. adv. com. Mt. Vernon Ladies Assn., 2000-06, Eudora Welty Found., 2002—; bd. dirs. Media Gen., 1998-01. With AUS, 1945-47. Mem. Radio-TV Corr. Assn. (chmn. exec. com. 1969-70), Am. Antiquarian Soc.

MUDER, ROBERT RICHARD, physician, epidemiologist; b. Pitts., June 11, 1951; s. Richard Edward and Gemma (Lombardi) M.; m. Janet D. Vlha, June 4, 1977 (div. 1993); children: Jane Elizabeth, Michael Richard. BA, Oberlin Coll., Ohio, 1973; MD, U. Pitts. Sch. Medicine, 1977. Diplomate Am. Bd. Internal Medicine; subspecialty of infectious diseases. Intern then resident internal medicine Mercy Hosp., Pitts., 1977—80, chief med. resident, 1980—81, asst. coord. med. edn., 1983-84, coord. med. edn., 1984-86, assoc. program dir., 1986-89, fellow in infectious disease, 1981-83; asst. prof. medicine U. Pitts., 1989-94, assoc. prof., 1994—2001, prof. medicine, divsn. infectious diseases; chief infection control VA Pitts. Healthcare Sys., 1986—2006, chief infectious disease sect., 2007—. Sect. editor Infectious Disease Alert; contbr. articles to profl. jours. Mem. Infectious Diseases Soc. Am., Soc. for Healthcare Epidemiology Am. Office: VA Pitts Healthcare Sys 2A135 Veterans Affairs Med Ctr University Dr C ID Section Pittsburgh PA 15240 Office Phone: 412-688-6179. Office Fax: 412-688-6950. Business E-Mail: robert.muder@va.gov.

MUDRY, MICHAEL, pension and benefit consultant; b. Lucina, Czechoslovakia, Dec. 5, 1926; (parents Am. citizens); s. John Zaleta and Helen (Molchan) M.; m. Kendall Archer, June 17, 1960; children: F. Goodrich Archer, Benjamin Kendall. BA, U. Conn., 1951. Sr. v.p. Hay/Huggins Co. Inc., Phila., 1956-93; self-employed pension and benefit cons. Wayne, Pa., 1994—. Former actuary Ch. Pensions Conf. Contbr. articles to profl. jours. Bd. dirs., actuary Am. Coun. on Gift Annuities, Indpls., 1978—; mem. exec. bd., treas. St. Davids Park Condominium Assn., 2005-. With US Army, 1945—46. Fellow: Conf. Cons. Actuaries, Soc. Actuaries; mem.: Internat. Assn. Cons. Actuaries, Internat. Actuarial Assn., Am. Acad. Actuaries, Tri-State Jazz Soc. (bd. dirs. 2001—, treas. 2001—).

MUEGGE, UWE, terminology professor; m. Christine Carola Muegge; children: Jule Maren, Mia Maria, Hanna Margareta. BA, U. Tuebingen, Germany, 1986; MA, U. Oreg., 1990, Monterey Inst. Internat. Studies, 1998. Corp. terminologist Medtronic, Inc., Mpls., 2004—; adj. prof. Monterey Inst. Internat. Studies, Calif., 2005—. Owner Muegge.cc - Computer-driven Transl. Solutions, Tuebingen, Germany, 1991—2002; terminologist Sun Microsystems, Cupertino, Calif., 1998, cons., Dublin, 99, SAP, Walldorf, Germany, 2001, DaimlerChrysler, Stuttgart, Germany, 2002; translator J.D. Edwards, Denver, 2002—04; mem. terminology sig Localization Industry Standards Assn., Romainmôtier, Switzerland, 2004—; cons. Merrill Corp., St. Paul, 2006—, U. Minn., Mpls., 2006—. Author: Translation contract: a standards-based model solution, 2005; co-author: Lokalisierung von Technischer Dokumentation, 2002. Mem.: Internat. Orgn. Standardization (TC37/SC3), Localization Industry Stds. Assn., Inst. Localization Profls. (assoc.). Achievements include development of a High-Performance Solution For Automatic Terminology Extration; the CLOUT rule set, a controlled language for authoring translation-friendly source texts; a website (muegge.cc) that enables on-the-fly automatic translation using the Google machine translation system; processes that result in the availability of project-specific multilingual terminology before source texts for translation are written; implementation of a machine translation program at Medtronic, the world's leading medical technology vendor. Avocation: distance running; modern art. Home Phone: 952-931-9209; Office Phone: 763-514-7792.

MUEHLBAUER, JAMES HERMAN, manufacturing and distribution executive; b. Evansville, Ind., Nov. 13, 1940; s. Herman Joseph and Anna Louise (Overfield) M.; m. Mary Kay Koch, June 26, 1965; children: Stacey, Brad, Glen, Beth, Katy. BSME, Purdue U., West Lafayette, Ind., 1963, MS in Indsl. Adminstrn., 1964. Registered profl. engr., Ind., 1970. Engr. George Koch Sons, Inc., Evansville, 1966-67, chief estimator, 1968-72, chief engr., 1973-74, v.p., 1975-81, dir., 1978—98, exec. v.p., 1982-98; pres. George Koch Sons LLC, Evansville, 1999—2003, chmn., 2003—04; exec. v.p., bd. dirs. Koch Enterprises, Inc., 1999—; pres. Koch Air LLC, 2003—. V.p., bd. dirs. Brake Supply Co., Evansville, Gibbs Die Casting Corp., Henderson, Ky., Uniseal, Inc., Evansville, George Koch Sons LLC, Evansville, Southwestern Comm., Inc., Evansville, Comfort Fin. Svcs. LLC, Evansville; bd. dirs. Fifth Third Bank Indiana, George Koch Sons Ltd., Lichfield, Eng., Red Spot Paint & Varnish Co., Inc., Evansville, George Koch Sons de Mex., Monterrey, Koch Air LLC, Evansville. Co-author: Tool & Manufacturing Engineering Handbook, 1976; patentee in paint finishing equipment. Bd. dirs., past pres. Evansville Indsl. Found., 1980—; bd. dirs., past pres., past campaign chmn. United Way S.W. Ind., Evansville, 1983—; bd. dirs., past vice-chmn. Univ. So. Ind. Found., Evansville, 1988-2001; bd. dirs. Deaconess Hosp., Evansville, 1986-2007, treas., 1991-96, vice-chmn., 1999-2003, chmn., 2003-07; bd. dirs. Cath. Found. Southwestern Ind., 1998-2004; dir. bd. advisors U. So. Ind. Sch. Bus., 1997—, chmn., 2001-02; bd. dirs. Ind. Assn. United Ways, 2000-06, Alliance Indpls., 1993-2004, pres. 1999; mem. Brute Soc., Cath. Diocese Evansville, 1997, Equestrian Order of the Holy Sepulchre of Jerusalem, 1996—. Named Engr. of Yr. S.W. chpt. Ind. Soc. Profl. Engrs., 1983; recipient Tech. Achievement award Tri-State Coun. for Sci. and Engring., Evansville, 1984, Purdue U. Alumni Citizenship award, 1991. Mem. Soc. Mfg. Engrs. (past nat. chmn. finishing and coating tech. divsn.), ASME, NSPE, Evansville Country Club, Evansville Kennel Club (bd. dirs. 1997-2001). Republican. Roman Catholic. Home: 2300 E Gum St Evansville IN 47714-2338 Office: Koch Enterprises 14 S 11th Ave Evansville IN 47744-0001 Home Phone: 812-477-8495; Office Phone: 812-962-5260. Business E-Mail: jmuehlbauer@kochair.com.

MUEHLNER, SUANNE WILSON, library director; b. Rochester, Minn., June 29, 1943; d. George T. and Rhoda (Westin) Wilson. Student Smith Coll., 1961-63; A.B., U. Calif.-Berkeley, 1965; M.L.S., Simmons Coll., 1968; M.B.A., Northeastern U., Boston, 1979. Librarian, Technische Univ. Berlin, Germany, 1970-71; earth and planetary scis. librarian MIT Libraries, Cambridge, 1968-70, 1971-73; personnel librarian, 1973-74, asst. dir. personnel services, 1974-76, asst. dir. pub. services, 1976-81; dir. libraries Colby Coll., Waterville, Maine, 1981—. Mem. ALA, New Eng. Assn. Coll. and Research Librarians (sec.-treas. 1983-85, pres. 1986-87), Maine Libr. Assn. (chmn. intellectual freedom com. 1984-88, OCLC Users Coun., 1988-95), Nelinet (bd. dirs. 1985-91, chair 1989-91). Office: Colby Coll Miller Libr Waterville ME 04901

MUELLER, BETTY JEANNE, social work educator; b. Wichita, Kans., July 7, 1925; d. Bert C. and Clara A. (Pelton) Judkins; children— Michael J., Madelynn J. MSSW, U. Wis., Madison, 1964, PhD, 1969. Asst. prof. U. Wis., Madison, 1969-72; vis. asso. prof. Bryn Mawr (Pa.) Coll., 1971-72; asso. prof., dir. social work Cornell U., Ithaca, NY, 1972-78, prof. human svcs. studies, 1979-96, prof. policy and mgmt., 1996-98, prof. emeritus, 1998—. Nat. cons. Head Start, Follow Through, Appalachian Regional Commn., N.Y. State Office Planning Svcs., N.Y. State Dept. Social Svcs., N.Y. State Divsn. Mental Hygiene, Nat. Congress PTA, ILO; mem. internat. adv. com. Family Resources Tng. Ctr., Singapore, 1999—. Author: (with H. Morgan) Social Services in Early Education, 1974, (with R. Reinoehl) Computers in Human Service Education, 1989, Determinants of Human Behavior, 1995; contbr. articles to profl. jours. Recipient Fulbright Rsch. award, 1990; grantee, HEW, 1974—76, 1979—80, State of N.Y., 1975—95, Israeli Jewish Agy., 1985—87. Mem. Leadership Am., Chi Omega. Democrat. Unitarian Universalist. Home: 412 Highland Rd Ithaca NY 14850-2216 Office: Cornell U Policy and Mgmt 108 MVR Hall Ithaca NY 14853 Personal E-mail: bjm5@cornell.edu.

MUELLER, CARL RICHARD, theater arts educator, author; b. St. Louis, Oct. 7, 1931; s. Anton John and Bonita Blanche (Lacy) M. BS, Northwestern U., 1954; MA, UCLA, 1960, PhD, 1967; cert., Freie U., Berlin, 1961. Prof. theater dept. Sch. Theater, Film and Television UCLA, 1967—; dramaturg New Theatre, Inc., LA, 1975-2000. Cons. U. Calif. Press, 1972—2005. Translator plays published include Buechner: Complete Plays and Prose, 1963, Brecht: The Visions of Simone Machard, 1965, Brecht: The Measures Taken, 1977, Hauptmann: The Weavers, 1965, Hebbel: Maria Magdalena, 1962, Strindberg: A Dream Play and The Ghost Sonata, 1966, Strindberg: Five Major Plays, 2000, Schnitzler: La Ronde and Game of Love, 1964, Hofmannsthal: Electra, 1964, Wedekind: The Marquis of Keith, 1964, Wedekind: The Lulu Plays, 1967, Wedekind: Four Major Plays, 2000, Zuckmayer: The Captain of Koepenick, 1972, Horváth: Tales from the Vienna Woods, 1998, Schnitzler: Four Major Plays, 1999, Sophocles: The Complete Plays, 2000, Pirandello: Three Major Plays, 2000, Kleist: Three Major Plays, 2000, Wedekind: Four Plays, vol. 2, 2002, Strindberg: Five Major Plays, vol. 2, 2002, Aeschylus: The Complete Plays, vol. 1, Oresteia, 2002, Aeschylus: The Complete Plays, vol. 2, Four Plays, 2002, Goethe: Faust, 2004, Euripides: The Complete Plays, vols. 1-4, 2005, Schnitzler: LaRonde, 2006, Wedekind: Spring's Awakening, 2006; translator plays produced include Anon: The Puppet Play of Dr. Johannes Faustus, Hauptmann: The Beaver Coat, Schnitzler: Dr. Bernhardi, Schnitzler: Anatol, Sternheim: The Underpants, Brecht: Mother Courage, Brecht: Caucasian Chalk Circle, Brecht: The Trial of Joan of Arc, Brecht: In the Jungle of Cities, Brecht: Man is Man, Brecht: He Who Says Yes, Brecht: He Who Says No, Brecht: The Exception and the Rule, Brecht: Round Heads, Peaked Heads, Brecht: Schweyk in the Second World War, Kleist: The Broken Jug, 1992, Lessing: Nathan the Wise, 1993, Toller, The Blind Goddess, 1993, Sophokles, Elektra, 1994, Zweig, Volpone, 1995, Sternheim, The Snob, 1996; gen. editor Visual Resources, Inc., 1976-2000; theater editor Mankind mag., 1975-82; editor New Theater/Teatro Nuevo, 1985-87; author catalogue and slides A Visual History of European Theater Arts, 1978, A Visual History of European Experimental Theater, 1983, Greek and Roman Classical Theatre Structures and Performance Iconography, 1991, Medieval Theater and Performance Iconography, 1991, The Theater of Meyerhold, 1992, Stanislavsky and the Moscow Art Theater, 1992, The Commedia dell'Arte, 1992, Russian Scene and Costume Design, vols. 1 and 2, 1993, The Baroque Stage, 1993, 18th and 19th Cen. European Theater Structures, Performance Iconography and Costume Designs, 1994, Renaissance Theater Structures, Performance Iconography and Costume Designs, 1994, The Genius of the Russian Theatre 1900-1990, 1995, 20th Century World Theater, From Appia to Dali, 1900-50, vol. 1, 1996, 20th Century World Theater, From Mother Courage to Hair, 1951-68, vol. 2, 1996, 20th Century World Theater, From Svoboda to Hockney, 1968-91, vol. 3, 1996, The Genius of the Russian Theater, From Meyerhold to the Present, 1996, Contemporary European Experimental Theater, vol. 1, Italy and Germany, 1996, The Classical Experience: The Greek Theater and Its World, 1996, The Classical Experience: The Roman Theater and Its World, 1996; dir.: (plays) Spring's Awakening, Endangered Species, Hedda Gabler, My Body, Frankly Yours, Hamlet, Macbeth, Dionysos. Served with U.S. Army, 1954-56. Recipient Samuel Goldwyn Creative Writing award Goldwyn Found., 1959; Fulbright exchange grantee Berlin, 1960-61 Mem. Internat. Arthur Schnitzler Research Assn., UCLA Center for Medieval and Renaissance Studies (mem. adv. com. 1980-83) Democrat. Office: UCLA Dept Theater Sch Theater Film TV 102 E Melnitz Box 951622 Los Angeles CA 90095-1622 Home Phone: 310-446-9706; Office Phone: 310-825-2707. Business E-Mail: cmueller@tft.ucla.edu. *Communication has always been the primary goal of my life. The challenge of passing on to generations of new students the life sustaining ideas of human culture is formidable; the joy of searching out new ideas and methods of thought and action is a privilege of which far too few of us take proper advantage.*

MUELLER, CHARLES FREDERICK, radiologist, educator; b. Dayton, Ohio, May 26, 1936; s. Susan Elizabeth (Wine) W.; m. Kathe Louise Lutterbei, May 28, 1966; children: Charles Jeffrey, Theodore Martin, Kathryn Suzanne. BA in English, U. Cin., 1958, MD, 1962. Diplomate Am. Bd. Radiology, Am. Bd. Nuclear Medicine. Asst. prof. radiology U. N.Mex., Albuquerque, 1968-72, assoc. prof. radiology, 1972-74, Ohio State U., Columbus, 1974-79, acting chmn. dept. radiology, 1975, prof. radiology, 1979—2002, prof. radiology, dir. post grad. program radiology, 1980-2000, acting chmn. dept. radiology, 1990—93, prof. emeritus, 2002—. Bd. dirs. Univ. Radiologists, Inc., Columbus, v.p., 1980—86; pres., founder Ambulatory Imaging, Inc., Columbus, 1985—2002. Author: Emergency Radiology, 1982; contbr. numerous articles to profl. jours.; editl. bd. Emergency radiology, 1995-2002; editor Internat. Trauma, Am. Jour. Roentgenology, 1997-2004. Com. chmn. Boy Scouts Am., Columbus, 1980—84; vol. Columbus Free Clinic, 2003—, Franklin Park Conservatory, 2003—. Capt. USAF, 1966—68. Research grantee Ohio State U. 1975, Gen. Electric Co., 1986-88; Gold medalist ASER, 2001. Fellow Am. Coll. Radiologists; mem. AMA, Assn. Univ. Radiologists, Am. Roentgen Ray Soc., Am. Soc. Emergency Radiology (founder 1988, pres. 1993-94, Gold medal 2001), Radiol. Soc. N.Am., N.Mex. Soc. Radiologists (pres. 1973-74), Ohio State Radiol. Soc. (pres. 1986-87). Republican. Presbyterian. Avocations: fly fishing, hiking, model railroading. Office: Ohio State Univ Hosps Dept Radiology 410 W 10th Ave Columbus OH 43210-1240 E-mail: cmueller@columbus.rr.com.

MUELLER, CHERONE, religious organization administrator, writer, minister; b. The Dalles, Oreg. Diploma in Acctg., Chemeketa Coll., Oreg., 1984, diploma in Bus. Mgmt., 1984; DD (hon.), World Christianship Ministries, Calif., 2002. Ordained minister World Christianship Ministries, 2002, cert. counselor World Christianship Ministries, 2002. Founder Cherone Faith Ministry, Jacksonville, 1999—, pres., CEO, 2000—. Ordained min. A Call to Worship Ch., Jacksonville, 2001—. Author: (book) At San Jose Make a Left, Dancing Around the Throne, of numerous poems. V.p. singles group Salem UPC, 1983—91, choir Salem, 1982—91, treas. ladies aux., 1984—90, v.p. Singles Group, 1983—91; nursery caregiver First UPC, Jacksonville, 1995—97; Sunday sch. tchr. Christ Ch. Jacksonville, 1997—98, praise singer, fellowship coord., 1997—2001; dir. Daughters of Zion (praying for our children) UPC Internat., Jacksonville, 1999—2001. Named Pastor of the Month, Radio WAYR, Jacksonville, Fla. June, 2003; recipient Editor's Choice award, Internat. Libr. Poetry, 2001, 2002, 2003, 2004, 2005, 2006. Master: World Christianship Ministries (licentiate; rev. 2002). Avocations: sewing, cooking, crocheting, sign language, designing clothes. Office: Cherone Faith Ministry PO Box 47077 Jacksonville FL 32247-7077 Personal E-mail: cheronefaith@mail.com.

MUELLER, CHRISTA, radiologist; b. Sonthofen, Germany, June 5, 1962; d. Joachim Friedrich and Waltraud Mueller. MD, Ludwig-Maximilians U., Munich, Germany, 1994; PhD, Ludwig-Maximilians U., 1995. Physician Technic U., Munich, 1992—93, Ludwig-Maximilians U., Munich, 1994—96, Katharinen Hosp., Stuttgart, Germany, 1996—98; physician, rschr. Georg-August U., Goettingen, Germany, 1998—2002, sr. radiologist, rschr., 2002—04; radiologist Paracelsus U., Salzburg, Austria, 2004—. Contbr. articles to profl. jours. Mem.: German Roentgen Soc. Office: Paracelsus Univ Hinterreit 478 A 5084 Grossgmain Austria Home Phone: 0043-6247-7369; Office Phone: 0043-662-4482-57769. Personal E-mail: christamueller@yahoo.de. Business E-Mail: ch.mueller@salk.at.

MUELLER, DIANE MAYNE, lawyer; b. Milw., Aug. 8, 1934; d. George and Ann (Matuszewski) Markussen; widowed; 1 child, Paul Wilhite; m. Milton W. Mueller, Jan. 1, 1990. AB, Valparaiso U., 1956; MSW, Fla. State U., 1963; JD summa cum laude, DePaul U., 1974. Bar: Ill. 1974, U.S. Dist. Ct. (no. dist.) Ill. 1974, U.S. Dist. Ct. (ea. dist.) Wis. 1977, N. Mex., 1996. Assoc. Seyfarth, Shaw, Fairweather & Geraldson, Chgo., 1974-82, ptnr.,

1982-86; asst. group counsel LTV Steel Co., Cleve., 1986-93, sr. atty., 1993-95. Adj. prof. Northwestern U. Sch. Law, 1984-86. Mem. Exec. Club Chgo. (chmn. bd. 1984-85, mem. adv. bd. 1986-96). Home: 1216 Rock Rose Rd Albuquerque NM 87122-1115

MUELLER, EDWARD A., telecommunications industry executive; b. St. Louis, Mo. BCE, U. Mo.; MBA, Wash. U. Pres., CEO Southwestern Bell Telephone, Pacific Bell, 1997—99; pres. SBC Internat. Ops., 1999—2000; pres., CEO SBC Ameritech, San Antonio, 2000—02; CEO Williams-Sonoma, Inc., 2003—06; chmn. VeriSign, Inc., 2007—; chmn., CEO Qwest Communications Internat. Inc., Denver, 2007—. Bd. dirs. VeriSign, Inc., 2005—, Clorox Co., GSC Acquisition Co. Office: Qwest Communications International Inc 1801 California St Denver CO 80202 *

MUELLER, EDWARD ALBERT, retired transportation engineer; b. Madison, Wis., May 12, 1923; s. Edward F. and Lulu (Wittl) M.; m. Margaret Wetzel, Sept. 12, 1953; children: Lynn, Karen. Student, U. Wis., 1941-43; BCE, Notre Dame U., 1947; cert. in traffic, Yale U., 1953, postgrad., 1952—53, Fla. State U., 1955-62; MCE, Catholic U. Am., 1967. Registered profl. engr., Fla. Project engr. Carl C. Crane, Inc., 1947-50; engr. Ammann & Whitney, Inc., Milw., 1950-52; rsch. asst. Yale U., 1953-55; asst. dir., dir. traffic and planning div. Fla. State Rd. Dept., Tallahassee, 1955-63; engr. traffic and ops. Transp. Rsch. Bd., Washington, 1963-70; sec. Fla. Dept. Transp., Tallahassee, 1970-72; exec. dir. Jacksonville (Fla.) Transp. Authority, 1972-80; mgr. transp. div. Reynolds, Smith & Hills, 1980-83; v.p. Morales and Shumer Engrs., Inc., 1983-95. Occasional lectr. U. Fla., 1971-76, U. N.Fla., 1974-76 Author: Steamboating on the St. Johns, 1979, Ocklawaha River Steamboats, 1983, St. Johns River Steamboats, 1986, Perilous Journeys, 1990, Upper Mississippi River Ratting Steamboats, 1995, Steamships of the Two Henrys, 1996, Along the St. Johns and Ocklawaha River, 1999, Queen of Sea Routes, 2000, The Savannah Line, 2001, First Coast Steamboat Days, 2005, (DVD) St. Johns Steamboat Days, 2006; contbr. engring. articles to profl. jours. Mem. Fla. Com. of 100, 1970-72; bd. dirs. Luth. Social Svcs., Jacksonville, 1982-94, v.p., 1981-91; regional v.p. Fla.-Ga. dist. Luth. Laymen's League, 1982-92; curator Jacksonville Maritime Mus., 1990-99, mem. exec. com., 1989-95, pres., 1993-95, exec. dir., 1995-99. Recipient Disting. Svc. award Coll. Engring., U. Fla., 1975, Samuel Ward Stanton award for life achievement Steamship Hist. Soc. Am., 2001; named one of top 10 pub. works ofcls. in U.S., 1978. Mem. Southeastern Assn. State Hwy. Ofcls. (pres., v.p. 1971-72), Engrs. in Govt. (chmn., vice-chmn. sec.), Fla. Engring. Soc. (pres. Northeast chpt. 1982-83, Engr. of Yr. Tallahassee chpt. 1972, Jacksonville chpt. 1974, award for outstanding tech. achievement 1976, outstanding svc. to engring. profession 1989, James Shivler award 1993), Inst. Transp. Engrs. (pres. 1977, disting. svc. award Fla. sect. 1976), Fla. Transit Assn. (pres. 1974-75), Fla. Engring. Found. (sec. 1986-95). Lutheran. Home: 4734 Empire Ave Jacksonville FL 32207-2136

MUELLER, GARY ALFRED, software engineer; b. Denver, Oct. 6, 1950; s. Alfred Henry and Verna Mae (Ashmore) M. BS in Mineral Engring. Physics, Colo. Sch. Mines, 1972, BS in Mineral Engring. Math., 1973; BSEE and Computer Sci. with honors, U. Colo., Denver, 1975; MSEE, U. Colo., Boulder, 1995. Registered profl. engr., Colo. Computer programmer, mathematician U.S. Geol. Survey, Denver, 1977-81; mem. tech. staff AT&T Bell Labs., Denver, 1982-84; adv. software engr. Storage Tech. Corp., Louisville, Colo., 1985—2001; cons., 2002—. Adj. prof. U. Phoenix, 2002—. Mem.: Assn. for Computing Machinery, IEEE (sr.), Tau Beta Pi, Kappa Mu Epsilon, Eta Kappa Nu.

MUELLER, GERARD, realtor, investor, former Internet executive; b. NYC, Mar. 17, 1944; s. John and Mary (Choisy) M.; m. Debra Pritt, Sept. 17, 2000. BA, St. Johns U., 1965; MBA, Adelphi U., 1970. Mktg. exec. IBM, White Plains, NY, 1967-84; pres., gen. mgr. Prodigy Network, White Plains, 1985-97; now realtor and investor. Avocations: wine collecting, golf. Home: 6738 N Ocean Blvd Ocean Ridge FL 33435 Office Phone: 561-573-2363. E-mail: muellerg@bellsouth.net.

MUELLER, GERHARD GOTTLOB, retired financial accounting executive, educator; b. Eineborn, Germany, Dec. 4, 1930; arrived in US, 1952, naturalized, 1957; s. Gottlob Karl and Elisabeth Charlotte (Hossack) M.; m. Coralie George, June 7, 1958; children: Kent, Elisabeth, Jeffrey. AA, Coll. of Sequoias, 1954; BS with honors, U. Calif.-Berkeley, 1956, MBA, 1957, PhD, 1962; D Econs. (hon.), Swedish Sch. Econs. and Bus. Adminstrn., 1994; D Laws (hon.), Kwansei Gakuin U., 2000. CPA (ret.), Wash. Staff acct. FMC Corp., San Jose, Calif., 1957-58; faculty dept. acctg. U. Wash., Seattle, 1960-96, assoc. prof., 1963-67, prof., 1967-96, chmn. dept., 1969-78, dir. grad. profl. acctg. program, 1979-90, sr. assoc. dean, 1990-95, acting dean, 1994, Hughes M. Blake prof. internat. bus. mgmt., 1992-95, Julius A. Roller prof. acctg., 1995-96, mem. fin. acctg. stds. bd., 1996—2001; ret., 2001. Dir. U. Wash. Acctg. Devel. Fund, Overlake Hosp. Med. Ctr., Bellevue, 1984-96, chmn. bd. trustees, 1991-93; cons. internat. tax matters U.S. Treasury Dept., 1963-68; cons. Internat. Acctg. Rsch., 1964-96; vis. prof. Cranfield Sch. Mgmt., Eng., 1973-74, U. Zurich, Switzerland, 1973-74; lectr. San Diego State U., 2006—; lectr. in field. Author: International Accounting, 1967; co-author: Introductory Financial Accounting, 3d edit., 1991, A Brief Introduction to Managerial and Social Uses of Accounting, 1975, International Accounting, 1978, 2nd edit., 1992, Accounting: An International Perspective, 1987, 4th edit., 1997; editor: Readings in International Accounting, 1969, Accounting-A Book of Readings, 2d edit., 1976, A New Introduction to Accounting, 1971, A Bibliography of Internat. Accounting, 3d edit., 1973, Essentials of Multinational Accounting— An Anthology, 1979, Frontiers of International Accounting, 1986, AACSB Curriculum Internationalization Resource Guide, 1988; contbr. chpts. to books, numerous articles to profl. jours. Recipient U. Wash. Disting. Tchg. award, 1983, Disting. Svc. award, U. Wash., 1984; Ford Found. fellow, 1958—59, Price Waterhouse Internat. Acctg. Rsch. fellow, 1962—64. Fellow Acad. Internat. Bus.; mem. AICPA (internat. practice exec. com. 1972-75, exec. coun. 1987-89, Disting. Achievement in Acctg. Edn. award 2000), Am. Acctg. Assn. (pres. 1988-89, acad. v.p. 1970-71, chmn. adv. bd. internat. acctg. sect. 1977-79, Wildman medal 1986, Nat. Outstanding Educator 1981, Disting. Internat. Lectr. in Black Africa 1987, Outstanding Internat. Acctg. Educator 1991), Wash. Soc. CPAs (pres. 1988-89, Outstanding Educator award 1985, Pub. Svc. award 1995), Acctg. Edn. Change Commn. (chmn. 1994-96), Beta Alpha Psi (Acad. Acct. of Yr. 1987), Beta Gamma Sigma (Disting. scholar 1978-79), Alpha Gamma Sigma. Home: 15794 Dovewood Ct Poway CA 92064-2282 Home Phone: 858-748-0872. Business E-Mail: gmueller@u.washington.edu. *It has always been important to me to associate with people and tangible and intangible things of the highest quality. I make it a practice to set clear goals and then pursue them actively. A broad world view on all aspects of life engenders more success and happiness than special interest perspectives. I welcome change in professional matters, but seek constancy in personal and family affairs. Fate has played a role in my successes. I believe in God, Protestant ethics, and the merits of classical academic scholarship.*

MUELLER, HOLGER, physicist; b. Munich, Jan. 20, 1974; arrived in U.S., 2004; s. Claus Erich Mueller and Maren Mueller-Rasmussen; m. Cornelia Sabine Becker-Weimann, Feb. 27, 2004; children: Felix Maximilian children: Amelie Felicitas. PhD, Humboldt-U., Berlin, Germany, 2004; physics diploma, U. Konstanz, Germany, 2000. Rsch. asst. U. Konstanz, Germany, 2000—02, Humboldt-U., Berlin, 2002—04; postdoctoral rschr. Stanford U., Calif., 2004—. Cons. GW-Elektronik, Munich, 1990—; cons. (electronic design) Fritz-Haber-Institut der Max-Planck Gesellschaft, Munich, 2006—. Contbr. rsch. (Joung Rschr.'s award Conf. on Precision Electromagnetic Measurement, 2002). Fellow: Alexander von Humboldt Found. (Feodor Lynen fellowship 2004—06); mem.: AAAS. Achievements include patents for TV and Microwave technology; research in Atom Interferometry and Tests of Special Relativity. Office: Stanford Univ 382 Via Pueblo Mall Stanford CA 94305 Home: 770 Coleman Ave Menlo Park CA 94025 Home Phone: 650-492-0952; Office Phone: 650-725-2354. Business E-Mail: holgerm@stanford.edu.

MUELLER, I. LYNN, strategic planning and communications consultant; b. Cin., Feb. 2, 1941; s. Irwin Ludwig and Helen Marie (Bloomfield) Mueller; m. Maria Rose Cavallino; children: Shallah Whitney, Geoffrey Koskinen. BBA, U. Cin., 1964, MBA, 1966; postgrad., George Washington U., 1966-68. V.p., founder Robert-Lynn Assoc., Ltd., Washington, 1968-72; spl. asst. N.Y. State Assembly Spkr., Albany, 1971-74; v.p. adminstrn. and fin. Epsilon Data Mgmt., Boston, 1974-75; founder, sr. v.p. First Tuesday Comms., Buffalo, 1974-78; v.p. cmty. affairs Gardenway Mgmt., Troy, NY, 1976; pres. ILM Enterprises, Old Chatham, NY, 1977-91; exec. dir. Minority Leader, N.Y. State Assembly, Albany, 1983-91; founder Decision Strategies Group, Albany, 1991—. Contbr. chpt. to book. Trustee Chatham (N.Y.) Meth. Ch., 1992-94; mem. Chatham Sch. Bd., 1990-93; Cons. to Gov. George Pataki Transition Com., 1994; advisor Morris Meml. Bd., Chatham, 1984-98; alumni rep. George Washington U., Albany, 1993—. Mem. Nat. Space Soc., Planetary Soc., Cin. Soc. (pres. 1961-62), Mc-Micken Soc., Sigma Sigma, Omicron Delta Kappa, Alpha Kappa Psi, Beta Alpha Psi. Republican. Presbyterian. Avocations: basketball, tennis, sailing, bridge, reading. Office: Decision Strategies Group 111 Washington Ave # 409 Albany NY 12210 Business E-Mail: lynnmueller@dsgny.com.

MUELLER, JOHN ERNEST, political science professor, dance critic; b. St. Paul, June 21, 1937; s. Ernst A. and Elsie E. (Schleh) M.; m. Judy A. Reader, Sept. 6, 1960; children: Karl, Karen, Susan AB, U. Chgo., 1960; MA, UCLA, 1963, PhD, 1965. Asst. prof. polit. sci. U. Rochester, NY, 1965-69, assoc. prof., 1969-72, prof., 1972-2000, prof. film studies, 1983-2000, founder, dir. Dance Film Archive, 1973—; prof. polit. sci., Woody Hayes chair nat. security studies Ohio State U., 2000—. Lectr. on dance in U.S., Europe, Australia, 1973—; OP-ED columnist Wall St. Jour., 1984—, L.A. Times, 1988—, N.Y. Times, 1990—; mem. dance panel NEA, 1983-85; columnist Dance Mag., 1974-82; dance critic Rochester Dem. and Chronicle, 1974-82; mem. adv. bd. Dance in Am., PBS, 1975; mem. editl. bd. Ohio State U. Press, 2000—04. Author: War, Presidents and Public Opinion, 1973 (one of Fifty Books That Significantly Shaped Public Opinion Rsch. 1946-95 Am. Assn. Pub. Opinion Rsch. 1995), Dance Film Directory, 1979, Astaire Dancing: The Musical Films, 1985 (de la Torre Bueno prize 1983), Retreat From Doomsday: The Obsolescence of Major War, 1989, Policy and Opinion in the Gulf War, 1994, Quiet Cataclysm: Reflections on the Recent Transformation of World Politics, 1995, Capitalism, Democracy, and Ralph's Pretty Good Grocery, 1999, The Remnants of War, 2004 (Lepgold prize 2004), Overblown, 2006; co-author: Trends in Public Opinion: A Compendium of Survey Data, 1989; editor: Approaches to Measurement, 1969, Peace, Prosperity, and Politics, 2000; co-editor Jour. Policy Analysis and Mgmt., 1985-89; mem. editl. bd. Pub. Opinion Quar., 1988-91, Jour. Cold War Studies, 1999—, Internat. Polit. Sociology, 2005—; prodr. 12 dance films, 2 dance DVDs; commentator on 2nd soundtrack of laser disc edit. Swing Time, 1986, DVD edit., 2005; co-adapter (musical) A Foggy Day, 1998; prodr. Shaw Festival Niagara-on-the-Lake, Ont., 1998, 99. Grantee NSF, 1967-70, 74-75, NEH, 1972-73, 74-75, 77-78, 79-81; Guggenheim fellow, 1988. Mem. Am. Acad. Arts and Scis., Am. Polit. Sci. Assn., Dance Critics Assn. (bd. dirs. 1983-85). Home: 420 W 5th Ave Columbus OH 43201-3159 Office: Ohio State U Polit Sci Dept Columbus OH 43210-1373 Home Phone: 614-421-2448; Office Phone: 614-247-6007. Business E-Mail: bbbb@osu.edu.

MUELLER, KATHRYN LUCILE, medical educator; b. Lincoln, Nebr., Feb. 14, 1951; m. Rex A. Logemann, Apr. 27, 1978. BA, U. Nebr., 1973, MD, 1977; MPH, Med. Coll. Wis., 1994. Diplomate Am. Bd. Preventive Medicine, Am. Bd. Occupl. Medicine. Instr. Rush Med. Sch., Chgo., 1981-87; asst. prof. U. Colo. Health Scis. Ctr., Denver, 1987-98, dir. student and occupational health svcs., 1989-96, assoc. prof. surgery and preventive medicine, 1998—2004; med. dir. Colo. Divsn. Worker's Compensation, Denver, 1991—; prof. surgery and preventive medicine U. Colo. Health Scis. Ctr., Denver, 2005—. Project med. dir. Christ Hosp. EMS Program, Chgo., 1983—87; physician advisor Emergency Med. Svcs. State of Colo., Denver, 1991—92; peer reviewer Tomes Plus, 1991—2001; oral bd. examiner Am. Bd. Emergency Medicine, Ill., 1992—95; chair first test com. Am. Bd. Med. Ind. Med. Examiners, 1994—95. Mem. editl. bd.: Guides Newsletter AMA, 1996—; mem. editl. bd. AMA Guides to Permanent Impairment, 2005—. Am. Coll. Emergency Medicine fellow, 1983—2002, Robert Wood Johnson grantee, 1998—2000. Fellow: Am. Coll. Occupl. and Environ. Medicine (chair com. state legis. affairs 1996—2002, bd. dirs. 2000—04, co-chair coun. on govtl. affairs 2002—03, sec.-treas. 2004—06); mem.: Rocky Mountain Acad. Occupl. and Environ. Medicine (bd. dirs. 1992—94, pres. 1997). Avocations: cross country skiing, travel, reading. Office: U Colo Health Scis Ctr 4200 E 9th Ave B 211 Denver CO 80262-0001 Business E-Mail: kathryn.mueller@uchsc.edu.

MUELLER, LISEL, writer, poet; b. Hamburg, Germany, Feb. 8, 1924; BA in Sociology, U. Evansville; postgrad., Ind. U. Vis. faculty Goddard Coll., 1977-80, Warren Wilson Coll., 1983, 85-86; vis. lectr. U. Chgo., 1984; disting. writer-in-residence Wichita State U., 1981. Author: Dependencies, 1965, 2d edit. 1998, Life of a Queen, 1970, The Private Life, 1976, Voices from the Forest, 1977, The Need to Hold Still, 1980, Waving from Shore, 1989, Second Language, 1986, Learning to Play by Ear, 1990, Alive Together: New & Selected Poems, 1996 (Pulitzer prize). Recipient Pulitzer prize for poetry, Nat. Book award for poetry, Carl Sandburg award, Ruth Lilly Poetry prize, 2002, Jacob Glatstein Meml. prize, Eunice Tietjens Meml. prize; NEA fellow. Mem.: Poetry Ctr. Chgo. (founding mem.). Office: La State U Press PO Box 25053 Baton Rouge LA 10894-5053

MUELLER, MARGARET S., musician, educator; b. Creston, Iowa, Dec. 3, 1924; d. Homer Cowan and Pearl Callahan Snodgrass; m. John Storm Mueller, June 10, 1958; 1 child, Laura Marjorie Mueller Woods. Student, Kans. U., 1943-46; MusB, Oberlin Conservatory, 1950, MusM, 1958. Instr. piano N.D. State Tchrs. Coll., Minot, 1950-51; instr. piano and organ Iowa State U., Ames, 1951-55, Randolph-Macon Woman's Coll., Lynchburg, Va., 1957-58; prof. organ and theory Salem Coll., Winston-Salem, N.C., 1958-95, prof. emerita, 1995—. Performing artist organ various concerts throughout the U.S. and Europe, 1953—; organist St. Paul's Episcopal Ch., Winston-Salem, 1963—2001; judge André Marchal Internat. Competition, Biarritz, France, 2001. Grantee Fulbright Assn., Frankfurt, Germany, 1955-56, Aeolian grantee, Paris, 1956-57. Mem.: Nat. Guild Piano Tchrs. (judge piano and organ), Winston-Salem Profl. Piano Tchrs. Assn., Music Tchrs. Nat. Assn. (judge piano and organ), Organ Hist. Soc., Am. Guild Organists (judge state, regional and nat. competitions 1965—, performing artist organ nat. and regional convs. 1973, 1976, 1987, 1993), Pi Kappa Lambda, Mu Phi Epsilon. Democrat. Episcopalian. Home: 1524 Sharon Rd Winston Salem NC 27103-4816 Office: Salem Coll Salem Square Winston Salem NC 27108

MUELLER, MARK CHRISTOPHER, lawyer; b. Dallas, June 19, 1945; s. Herman August and Hazel Deane (Hatzenbuehler) M.; m. Linda Jane Reed. BA in Econs., So. Meth. U., Dallas, 1967; MBA in Acctg., 1969, JD, 1971. Bar: Tex. 1971, US Dist. Ct. (no. dist.) Tex. 1974, US Tax Ct. 1974; CPA, Tex. Acct. Arthur Young & Co., Dallas, 1967-68, A.E. Krutilek, Dallas, 1968-71; pvt. practice law Dallas, 1971—; assoc. L. Vance Stanton, Dallas, 1971-72. Instr. legal writing and rsch. So. Meth. U., Dallas, 1970-71, instr. legal acctg., 1975; unauthorized practice of law com. Supreme Ct. Tex. Leading articles editor Southwestern Law Jour., 1970-71. Mem. NRA (patron mem.), Tex. Bar Assn., Tex. State Rifle Assn. (life), Dallas Arms Coll. (life), Tex. Soc. CPA's, Dallas Bar Assn., SAR, Sons Republic Tex., Sons of Union Vets. of Civil War, Sons Confederate Vets., Mil. Order Stars and Bars, Dallas Arms Coll., Order of Coif, Dallas Hist. Soc., Dallas County Pioneer Assn., Rock Creek Barbeque Club, Masons (Hillcrest Lodge #1318, Tannehill Lodge #52), Shriners, York Rite, Grotto, Scottish Rite (32 degree knight comdr. Ct. of Honor), Beta Alpha Psi, Phi Delta Phi, Sigma Chi (life). Home: 7310 Brennans Dr Dallas TX 75214-2804 Office: 6510 Abrams Rd Ste 565 Dallas TX 75231-7292 Office Phone: 214-221-6888.

MUELLER, NANCY SCHNEIDER, retired biology professor; b. Wooster, Ohio, Mar. 8, 1933; d. Gilbert Daniel and Winifred (Porter) Schneider; m. Helmut Charles Mueller, Jan. 27, 1959; 1 child, Karl Gilbert. AB in Biology, Coll. of Wooster, Ohio, 1955; MS in Zoology, U. Wis., Madison, 1957, PhD in Zoology, 1962. Instr. zoology U. Wis., Madison, 1966; asst. prof. poultry sci. and zoology N.C. State U., Raleigh, 1968-71; vis. prof. biology N.C. Ctrl. U., Durham, 1971-73, assoc. prof., 1973-79, prof., 1979-93; ret., 1993. Vis. scientist U. Vienna, Austria, 1975. Contbr. articles, abstracts to profl. publs. Mem. Soc. for Integrative and Comparative Biology, Wis. Acad. Sci., Arts and Letters, N.C. Acad. Sci., LWV, Sigma Xi. Avocations: bird migration, conservation and environmental issues. Home: 409 Moonridge Rd Chapel Hill NC 27516-5576 E-mail: hmuelle@earthlink.net.

MUELLER, O. THOMAS, molecular geneticist, pediatrics educator; b. Berlin, Aug. 17, 1950; arrived in U.S., 1955; s. Heinz Carl and Gertrud (Jung) M.; m. Mary Gail Craig, April 24, 1976; children: Cara Lynne, Kyle Thomas, Eric Andreas. BA, Lehigh U., 1972; PhD in biol. chemistry, Pa. State U., 1978. Diplomate: Am. Bd. Med. Genetics in Molecular and Biochemical Genetics. Postdoctoral fellow U. Colo. Med. Ctr., Denver, 1978-80; rsch. asst. Roswell Park Meml. Inst., Buffalo, 1980-84, rsch. affiliate, 1984-87; assoc. prof. pediats. U. So. Fla., Tampa, 1987—; dir. molecular genetics All Children's Hosp., St. Petersburg, Fla., 1994—. Contbr. numerous articles to scientific jours. including Human Genetics, Am. Jour. Med. Genetics, Am. Jour. Human Genetics, Jour. Biol. Chemistry, and others. Avocations: triathlons, sailing. Home: 2001 Point Overlook Dr NE Saint Petersburg FL 33703-3435 Office: Dept Pathology All Children's Hosp 801 6th St S Saint Petersburg FL 33701-4816 Office Phone: 727-767-8985. Business E-Mail: muellert@allkids.org.

MUELLER, PAUL HENRY, retired bank executive; b. NYC, June 24, 1917; s. Paul Herbert and Helen (Cantwell) M.; m. Jean Bonnel Vreeland, Sept. 10, 1949; 1 child, Donald Vreeland. BS, NYU, 1940; AB, Princeton U., 1941; LittD (hon.), Heriot-Watt U., Edinburgh, Scotland, 1981; LHD (hon.), Bloomfield Coll., 1991. From page to sr. v.p. Citibank N.A., 1934—65, sr. v.p., 1965—74, chmn. credit policy com., 1974—82; chmn. Saab-Scania Am. Inc., 1982—90; ret., 1990. Joined U.S. Fgn. Svc., served in Panama, Cairo, Washington, 1941-43; asst. adminstrv. sec. UN Montary and Fin. Conf., Bretton Woods, N.H., 1944; divisional asst. Dept. State, 1946; sec. West Indian Conf., 2d session, St. Thomas, V.I., 1946; vis. lectr. U. Va., 1980-2001; founding chmn., sr. fellow Ctr. Internat. Banking Studies, 1977-91. Author (contbg.): Offshore Lending by U.S. Commercial Banks, 1975, 2d edit., 1981, Bank Credit, 1981, Classics in Commercial Bank Lending, 1981, Vol. II, 1985, Loan Portfolio Management, 1988, Credit Culture, 1994, Credit Risk Management, 1995; author: (with Leif H. Olsen) Credit and the Business Cycle, 1979; author: Learning from Lending, 1979, Credit Doctrine for Lending Officers, 1976, 1981, 2d edit., 1997, Credit Endpapers, 1982, Perspective on Credit Risk, 1988, In a Nutshell, 2002; contbr. articles to profl. jours. Trustee Bloomfield Coll., N.J., 1983-91, vice chmn., 1987-88, chmn., 1988-91, trustee emeritus; treas. Marcus Wallenberg Found. (U.S.), 1984—. Served from 2d lt. to capt. USMCR, 1944-59. Decorated Order Polar Star, Sweden; recipient Alumni award Grad. Sch. Credit and Fin. Mgmt., Dartmouth Coll., 1958, Disting. Svc. award Robert Morris Assocs., 1981. Mem. Bankers Assn. Fgn. Trade (hon., v.p. 1976), Pilgrims, SAR, Swedish-Am. C. of C. USA (chmn. 1989-90, hon. dir.), Royal Econ. Soc. (U.K.), Univ. Club (N.Y.C.), Beta Gamma Sigma. Republican. Presbyterian. Home: 75 Rotary Dr Summit NJ 07901-3131

MUELLER, PEGGY JEAN, dance educator, choreographer, rancher; b. Austin, Tex., June 14, 1952; d. Rudolph George Jr. and Margaret Jean (Locke) M.; m. John Yerby Tarlton, June 24, 1972 (div. June 1983). BS in Home Econs., Child Devel., U. Tex., Austin, 1974. Dance tchr. Shirley McPhail Sch. Dance, Austin, 1972-75, Jean Tarlton Sch. Dance, Alpine, Tex., 1975-77, College Station, Tex., 1977-80, Sul Ross State U., Alpine, 1975-77, Tex. A&M U., College Station, 1977-80, A&M Consol. Community Edn., Coll. Station, 1977-78, Jean Mueller Sch. Dance, Austin, 1980—, U. Tex., Austin, 1980—. Dancer, contest judge Gt. Tex. Dance-Off, Austin, 1985—86; mem. equestrian com. Austin Travis County Livestock Show and Rodeo, 1980—92, chmn. trail ride, 1986—, Star Tex. Fair and PRCA Rodeo, 2000—; trial boss, pres. Austin Founders Trail Ride, 1986—; trail boss Bandera Longhorn Cattle Dr. and Trail Ride, 1990, 91; choreographer, head cheerleader Austin Texans Pro Football Team, 1981; dance tchr. Austin Ballroom Dancers, 1988, the Austin Club, 1997, 98; dancer, agt. George Strait/Bud Light Comml. Auditions, 1990; head contest judge Am.'s Ultimate Dance Contest, Austin, 1994; contest judge Two-Stepping Across Am., Austin, 1994; hon. trial boss Dream Catcher Ranch Trail Ride, Franklin, Tex., 1995, 96, Grapevine/Housgon Country Donkey, Mule and Horse Trail Ride, 1997, 2000. Dancer Oklahoma, Austin, 1969, Kiss Me Kate, Austin, 1970; choreographer, lead role Cabaret, Alpine, 1976, (mini-series) True Women, 1997. Active Women's Symphony League Austin, 1972—, Settlement Club, Austin, 1987—; recreation chmn. St. Martin's Evang. Luth. Ch., Austin, 1972—; hon. trail boss St. Jude Children's Rsch. Hosp. Trail Ride, Austin and Kyle, Tex., 1991. Recipient Outstanding Trail Rider of Yr. award Wild Horse Trail Ride, Okla., 1984; named Tex. First Lady Trail Boss, Gov. Mark White, Mayor Frank Cooksey, Austin City Coun., 1986, Judge Bill Aleshire, Travis County Commrs., 1989, Outstanding Intramural Sports Team Mgr.-Player, Tex. A&M U., 1978-79. Mem. Tex Assn. Tchrs. of Dancing, Inc., U.S. Twirling and Gymnastics Assn., Univ. Tex. Ex-Students Assn., Tex. Execs. in Home Econs., Am. Vet. Med. Assn. Aux. (v.p. 1978-79, pres. 1979-80), Am. Horse Shows Assn., Internat. Arabian Horse Assn., Austin Women's Tennis Assn. (v.p. 1985-86, pres. 1986-90, spl. events chmn. 1990-92, advisor 1990—, winner 2d ann. Harriet Crosson Outstanding Player & Community Svc. award), Women's Team Tennis of Austin Assn. (pres.-elect 1992-93, pres. 1993-94), Capital Area Tennis Assn. (membership com. 1991, 92), Houston Salt Grass Trail Ride Assn., San Antonio Alamo Trail Ride Assn., Ft. Worth Chisholm Trail Ride Assn., U. Tex. Longhorn Alumni Band, Austin C. of C., Am. Bus. Women's Assn., Austin Alumnae Panhellenic Assn. (1st v.p. 1989-90, rush forum chmn. 1990, pres. 1990-91, parliamentarian 1991-92), Lone Grove Cmty. Club (treas. 199697, v.p. 1997-99, pres. 1999—, exec. trustee 1997-99, exec. dir. 1999-2000), Omicron Nu (v.p. 1973-74), Jr. Austin Woman's Club (historian 1990-91), Austin Country Club (team tennis captain 1994-95, player 1994—, dance tchr. 1993-96), Zeta Tau Alpha (Austin Alumnae Chpt., alumnae photographer, social advisor 1982-87, treas. 1987-89, publicity chmn. 1989, Easter Seals fundraiser, Honor Cup winner 1990, pres. 1991-92, internat. convention official del. 1988, 92, nominating chmn. 1992-93, mem. yearbook com. 1992-94, 2d v.p. 1993-94). Clubs: Cen. Tex. Arabian Horse, Capitol Area Quarter Horse Assn., Jr. Austin Woman's, Austin Country. Republican. Avocations: theater, piano, drums, sports, travel. Home and Office: PO Box 5868 Austin TX 78763-5868 E-mail: aftr@USATrailRides.com.

MUELLER, PETER STERLING, psychiatrist, educator; b. NYC, Dec. 28, 1930; s. Reginald Sterling and Edith Louise (Welleck) M.; m. Ruth Antonia Shipman, Aug. 9, 1958; children: Anne Louise, Peter Sterling, Paul Shipman, Elizabeth Ruth. AB, Princeton U., 1952; MD, U. Rochester, 1956. Am. Cancer Soc. student fellow Francis Delafield Hosp., NYC, summer 1955; intern Bellevue Hosp., Columbia U., NYC, 1956-57; asst. resident in psychiatry Henry Phipps Psychiat. Clinic, Johns Hopkins Hosp., Balt., 1963-66; asst. prof. psychiatry Sch. Medicine, Yale U., New Haven, 1966-72; asso. prof. psychiatry Coll. Medicine and Dentistry of N.J., Rutgers Med. Sch., Piscataway, 1972-76, clin. prof. psychiatry, 1976-82; cons. for Rehab. Unit and Center for Indsl. Human Resources, Community Mental Health Center, 1973—; mem. courtesy staff dept. psychiatry Princeton Med. Center, 1976—. Cons. in psychotherapy Conn. Valley Hosp., Middletown, 1966-72; cons. in psychiatry Carrier Clinic, Belle Mead, N.J., 1973-82, VA Hosp., Lyons, N.J., 1975-78 Contbr. writings in field to profl. publs. U.S. and Brit., papers to profl. confs. on the use patents in U.S. and fgn. countries for direct dopamine agonists in the treatment of tobacco addiction. Served with USPHS, 1957-63. Recipient Exemplary Psychiatrist award Nat. Alliance for the Mentally Ill, 1994. Mem. Am. Psychosomatic Soc., Am. Psychiat. Assn., AAAS, Amyotrophic Lateral Sclerosis Found. (adv. bd.), Sigma Xi. Episcopalian. Achievements include patents for treatment of disorders secondary to organic impairment with sibutramine; method of treatment of Irritable Bowel Syndrome with a fibric acid. Home: 182 Snowden Ln Princeton NJ 08540-3915 Office: 601 Ewing St Ste B-3 Princeton NJ 08540-2757 Office Phone: 609-924-4061. *For some, a hyperactive learning disorder is a curse that hobbles them throughout life; but for others, including myself, this disorder has become a somewhat uncomfortable and bewildering spur for lifelong compulsive puzzle-solving. This bittersweet mandate has produced the original, serendipitous, and occasionally disconcerting ideas which have marked my life.*

MUELLER, PHILIP KEARNS, retired minister; b. Tabriz, Iran, Oct. 24, 1929; s. Henry Albert and Margaret Elinore Mueller; m. Regina May Welsch, Aug. 27, 1954; children: Michal, Marc, David, Deborah, Keren, Nathan. BA, Wartburg Coll., Waverly, Iowa, 1952; BD, Wartburg Theol. Sem., Duberque, Iowa, 1955, MDiv, 1989; AS in Nursing, Hibbing State U., Minn., 1972. RN Minn., 1972, Wis., 72. Missionary Luth. Orient Mission, Mosul and Aril, Iraq, 1955—58; pastor Grace Luth. Ch., Cashton, Wis., 1959—64; missionary Mekane Jesu, Ethiopia, East Africa, 1964—69; pastor Bethel and Immanuel Luth. Ch., Cherry, Minn., 1969—71, serveral Luth. congregations, Cashton, Wis., 1971—78; missionary Eglise Evang. du Senegal, West Africa, 1978—88; pastor Bethlehem and St. John Luth. Ch., Marion, Wis., 1989—99; visitation pastor Bethany Luth. Ch., Rice Lake, Wis., 1999—2007. Justice of peace Village of Nasonville, Wis., 1957—58; bd. dirs. Village of Cashton, Wis., 1977—78. Avocations: reading, birdwatching, fishing. Home: 2039 22 1/4 Ave Rice Lake WI 54868

MUELLER, ROBERT LOUIS, manufacturing executive; b. Denver, Aug. 25, 1927; s. George Winchester and Ruth Mabel (Cole) M.; m. Sue McCoy, July 3, 1949; children: Robert, Richard, Edward, Mark; m. Susan Galbraith, June 23, 1985. BSMechE, Yale U., 1948. Chief computer Western Geophys. Co., Mont., Wyo., Colo., Tex., 1949-50; dist. mgr. Armco Steel Corp., Colo., Ohio, N.Y., 1950-63, L.B. Foster Co., NYC, 1963-66; v.p. Wheeeling Pitts. Steel Co., W.Va. and Pa., 1966-75; chmn., pres., chief exec. officer Connors Steel Co., Ala., 1975-82; pres., chief exec. officer Judson Steel Co., Calif., 1982-87; pres., COO Proler Internat., Houston, 1987-94, also bd. dirs., 1987-94, cons., 1994—; dir. Employee Solutions, Inc., 1995—; pres. Mueller Resources, Inc., Sedona, Ariz., 1993—. Co-author: Handbook of Drainage and Construction Products, 1954. With USN, 1945-46. Mem. ASCE, Assn. Iron and Steel Engrs., Duquesne Club (Pitts.), Houston City Club, Sedona Racquet Club, The Sedona 30.

MUELLER, ROBERT SWAN, III, FBI director; b. NYC, Aug. 7, 1944; s. Robert Swan Jr. and Alice (Truesdale) Mueller; m. Ann Standish, Sept. 3, 1966; children: Cynthia, Melissa. BA, Princeton U., 1966; MA, NYU, 1967; JD, U. Va., 1973. Bar: Mass., U.S. Dist. Ct. Mass., U.S. Ct. Appeals (1st cir.), Calif., U.S. Dist. Ct. (no. dist.) Calif., U.S. Ct Appeals (9th cir.). Assoc. Pillsbury, Madison & Sutro, San Francisco, 1973-76; asst. U.S. atty. (No. dist.) Calif. US Dept. Justice, San Francisco, 1976-80, chief unit spl. prosecutions, 1980-81, chief criminal divsn., 1981-82, chief criminal divsn. Mass. dist. Boston, 1982-85, 1st asst. U.S. atty., 1985, U.S. atty., 1986-87, dep. U.S. atty., 1987-88; ptnr. Hill & Barlow, Boston, 1988-89; asst. to atty. gen. for criminal matters U.S. Dept. Justice, Washington, 1989-90, asst. atty. gen. criminal divsn., 1990-93; lawyer Hale & Dorr, Washington, 1993—95; sr. litigator, homicide sect., DC US Atty's Office US Dept. Justice, Washington, 1995—98; US atty. (No. dist) Calif. U.S. Dept. Justice, 1998—2001, acting dep. atty. gen., 2001, dir. FBI, 2001—. Capt. USMC, 1967-70; Vietnam. Decorated Bronze Star, Purple Heart, Vietnamese Cross of Gallantry. Office: FBI J Edgar Hoover Bldg 935 Pennsylvania Ave NW Washington DC 20535-3404 *

MUELLER, SHARON LEE (SHERRY MUELLER), educational organization executive; b. Chgo., Aug. 17, 1943; d. LeRoy Elmer Arthur and Lucille Viola (Armborst) M. BA, Am. U., DC, 1965; MA in Law and Diplomacy, Tufts U., Medford, Mass., 1966, PhD, 1977. Group leader Experiment in Internat. Living, 1969; cross-cultural trainer Nat. 4-H Found., 1970-71; cons. U.S. Dept. State, 1972, contract escort officer, 1970-77; cons. Fletcher Sch. Law and Diplomacy, 1976-81; lectr. dept. polit. sci. U. R.I., Kingston, 1975-77; adj. prof. Sch. Internat. Svc. Am. U., Washington, 1981-87; program officer Inst. Internat. Edn., Washington, 1978-82, dir. prof. exch. programs, 1982-96; exec. dir. Nat. Coun. for Internat. Visitors, Washington, 1996—2001, pres., 2001—. Mem. editl. adv. bd. Internat. Educator, 1991-2005; bd. dir. Nat. Coun. for Internat. Visitors, 1983-88; bd. dir., trustee World Learning, 1999-, bd. mem. PUb. Diplomacy Coun.; vice chair Coalition for Am. Leadership Abroad. Author: Careers in International Education, Exchange, and Development, 1998; contbr. chpts. to books; guest editor, contbr. Internat. Educator, 1992. Mem. exec. com. Internat. Student House, Washington, 1992-95; usher Foundry Meth. Ch., Washington, 1990-2004; mem. The Pres.'s Cir. Coun., Am. U., Washington, 1988-98, chair, 1996-98; mem. bd. Friendship Force Internat. Recipient Alumni Recognition award Am. U., 1990, award of appreciation Nat. Coun. for Internat. Visitors, 1988, award of appreciation World Ctr. for Tng. and Devel., 1988, Disting. Alumni award Lake Park High Sch., 1995, Outstanding Svc. award U.S.I.A., 1996. Mem. Nat. Press Club (assoc.), Sch. Internat. Svc. Alumni Assn. The Am. U. (founding pres. 1981-83, Alumna of Yr. 2007), Sigma Iota Rho (hon.), Cosmos Club. Home: 1317 N Lynnbrook Dr Arlington VA 22201-4918 Office: NCIV 1420 K St NW Ste 800 Washington DC 20005-2500 Office Phone: 202-842-1414.

MUELLER, WILLARD FRITZ, economics professor; b. Ortonville, Minn., Jan. 23, 1925; s. Fritz and Adele C. (Thrmaehlen) Mueller; m. Shirley I. Liesch, June 26, 1948; children: Keith, Scott, Kay. BS, U. Wis., 1950, MS, 1951; PhD, Vanderbilt U., 1955. Asst. prof. U. Calif., Davis, 1954-57; prof. U. Wis., 1957-61, prof. agrl. and applied econs. dept. econ. Sch. Law Madison, 1969—; chief economist small bus. com. U.S. Ho. of Reps., 1961; chief economist, dir. bur. econs. FTC, 1961-68; exec. dir. Pres.'s Cabinet Com. Price Stability, 1968-69. Expert House and Senate Com., 1960—96; cons. in indsl. orgn. and pub. policy. Past bd. editors Rev. Ind. Orgn., Antitrust Law and Econ. Rev., Antitrust Bull., Jour. Reprints for Antitrust Law and Econs. Mem. Econ. Policy Inst., 1987—90. With USN, 1943—46. Recipient Disting. Svc. award, FTC, 1978. Fellow: Am. Agrl. Econs. Assn. (profl. excellence awards in policy contbn. 1980, in comm. 1985, in rsch. discovery 1988); mem.: Argus Econ. Svcs. (pres. 1985—), Indsl. Orgn. Soc. (pres. 1989—90), Assn. Evolutionary Econs. (pres. 1974—75), Am. Econ. Assn. Unitarian Universalist. Office: U Wis 427 Lorch St Madison WI 53706-1513 Home: 8625 Wood Violet Way Madison WI 53717 Personal E-mail: wfritzmueller@aol.com.

MUELLER-HEUBACH, EBERHARD, medical educator; b. Berlin, Feb. 24, 1942; came to U.S., 1968; s. Heinrich Gustav and Elisabeth (Heubach) M.; m. Cornelia Rosemarie Uffmann, Sept. 6, 1941; 1 child, Oliver Maximilian. MD, U. Koeln, 1966. Intern U. Koeln (Germany) Women's Hosp., 1967-68, Middlesex Gen. Hosp., New Brunswick, NJ, 1968-69; rsch. fellow Columbia U., 1969-71; resident Columbia-Presbyn. Med. Ctr., NYC, 1971-74, chief resident, 1974-75; asst. prof. Magee-Women's Hosp. U. Pitts., 1975-81, assoc. prof. Magee-Women's Hosp., 1981-89; prof., chmn. ob-gyn. Sch. Medicine Wake Forest U., Winston-Salem, 1989—2002, prof. ob-gyn., 2002—07, prof. emeritus, 2007—. Mem. editl. bd.: Ob-Gyn, 1999—2002. Mem. Am. Gyn.-Ob. Soc. (asst. sec. 1999-2001, sec. 2002-04, pres.-elect 2004-05, pres. 2005-06), Soc. Gynecol. Investigation, The Perinatal Rsch. Soc., Coun. Univ. Chairs Ob-Gyn. (pres. 1998-2000). Avocations: horses, travel, arts. E-mail: emueller@wfubmc.edu.

MUENCH, KARL HUGO, clinical geneticist; b. St. Louis, May 3, 1934; MD, Washington U., St. Louis, 1960. Diplomate Am. Bd. Med. Genetics. Intern Barnes Hosp., St. Louis, 1960-61; fellow in biological chemistry Stanford U. Sch. Medicine, 1961-65; staff mem. Jackson Meml. Hosp., Miami, Fla.; prof. medicine U. Miami Sch. Medicine. Mem. AMA, ACP, Am. Coll. Med. Genetics. Office: U Miami Sch Med Div Genetic Med PO Box 16960 Miami FL 33101-6960 Office Phone: 305-243-6653. Business E-Mail: kmuench@med.miami.edu.

MUES, ROBERT LEIGHTON, lawyer; b. Summit, NJ, Apr. 14, 1954; s. Edward Frederick Jr. and Evelyn (Moulton) M.; m. Elizabeth Ann Beard, Aug. 26, 1978; children: Jeffrey Scott, Robert Colin. BA, Wittenberg U., Springfield, Ohio, 1975; JD, U. Dayton, 1978. Bar: Ohio 1978, U.S. Dist. Ct. (so. dist.) Ohio 1978, U.S. Ct. Appeals (6th cir.) 1995. With firm Meily & Mues Attys., Dayton, Ohio, 1981-91, Holzfaster, Cecil, McKnight & Mues, Dayton, 1991—. Impartial due process hearing officer Ohio Dept. Edn., 1981-96, State of Ohio hearing rev. officer, 1997. Author brochure: Divorce in Ohio, 1994. Bd. dirs. For Love of Children, Inc., Dayton, 1983-91, Montgomery County Children Svcs. Bd., Dayton, 1988-91; state legal rev. officer State of Ohio Dept. Edn., 1997-; treas. Dayton Children's Med. Ctr. Found. Bd., 2004-. Mem. ABA, Assn. Trial Lawyers Am., Ohio State Bar Assn., Ohio Acad. Trial Lawyers, Dayton Bar Assn. (com. on profl. ethics 1982—), Miami Valley Trial Lawyers Assn. Office: Holzfaster Cecil McKnight & Mues 1105 Wilmington Ave Ste 1 Dayton OH 45420-4108 Office Phone: 937-293-2141. Business E-Mail: mues@hcmmlaw.com.

MUETH, JOSEPH EDWARD, lawyer; b. St. Louis, Aug. 8, 1935; s. Joseph and Marie Clare (Reher) M.; m. Ellen Agnes O'Heron, Dec. 24, 1973; children: Erin R., Patricia A. B.Chem. Engring., U. Dayton, 1957; LL.B., Georgetown U., 1960, LL.M., 1961. Bar: Calif. 1964. Practice law, LA; ptnr. Wills, Green & Mueth, LA, 1974-83; pvt. practice law Calif., 1983-94; of counsel Sheldon & Mak, Pasadena, Calif., 1994—. Adj. prof. law U. Calif. Hastings Coll. Law, San Francisco, 1972-75; lectr. Claremont Grad. Sch., 1982—. Author: Copyrights Patents and Trademarks, 1974. Chmn. bd. Rio Hondo council Camp Fire Girls Inc., 1967-72. Mem. AAAS, Am., Los Angeles County bar assns., State Bar Calif., N.Y. Acad. Scis., L.A. Athletic Club. Home: PO Box 3369 1217 Seal Way Seal Beach CA 90740-6419 Office: 100 E Corson St Pasadena CA 91103

MUFSON, MAURICE ALBERT, infectious diseases physician, educator; b. NYC, July 7, 1932; s. Max and Faye M.; m. Diane Cecile Weiss, Apr. 1, 1962; children: Michael Jeffrey, Karen Andrea, Pamela Beth. AB, Bucknell U., 1953; MD, NYU, 1957. Intern Bellevue Hosp., NYC, 1957-58, resident, 1958-59; chief resident Cook County Hosp., Chgo., 1965-66; sr. surgeon USPHS Lab. Infectious Diseases, NIH, 1961-65; from asst. prof. medicine to prof. U. Ill., 1965-76; prof. Marshall U., 1976—2002, prof. emeritus, 2002—, chmn. dept. medicine, 1976—2000, chmn. emeritus, 2000—. Vis. scientist Karolinska Inst., 1984-85. Contbr. articles to profl. jours. Served with U.S. Navy, 1959-61. WHO grantee, 1967; recipient Meet-the-Scholar award Marshall U., 1986, Rschr. of Yr. award Sigma Xi, Marshall U., 1989, Solomon A. Berson Alumni Achievement award in health sci. NYU Sch Medicine, 1997; co-recipient Louis Weinstein award Jour. Clin. Infectious Diseases, 1994; named to Greater Huntington Wall of Fame, 2002. Master ACP (traveling scholar 1987, Laureate award W.Va. chpt.), Infectious Diseases Soc. Am.; mem. AMA, Soc. Exptl. Biology and Medicine, Ctrl. Soc. Clin. Rsch., So. Soc. Clin. Investigation, W.Va. State Med. Assn., Assn. Profs. Medicine (counselor 1992-95, pres.-elect 1995-96, pres. 1996-97, past pres. 1997-98), Marshall U. Joan C. Edwards Sch. Medicine Alumni Assn. (hon.), Alpha Omega Alpha. Office: Marshall U Sch Medicine 1249 15th St 2nd Fl Huntington WV 25701 Home Phone: 304-522-9357. Personal E-mail: mmufson@adelphia.net. Business E-Mail: mufson@marshall.edu.

MUFTI, AFTAB A., civil engineering educator; b. Sukkur, Sind, Pakistan, Apr. 24, 1940; arrived in Can., 1963; s. Abdul Wahid D. and Shah Jahan M.; children: Javed, Alex; m. Zehra Mehdi, Sept. 22, 2000. BCE, NED Engring. U., Karachi, 1962; MCE, McGill U., Montreal, 1965, PhD, 1969. Registered profl. engr., Man., B.C. Asst. prof. McGill U., 1969-72; assoc. prof., head dept. comp. sci. Acadia U., Wolfville, N.S., 1972-76, prof., dir. Sch. Comp. Sci., 1976-80; prof. civil engring. Dalhousie U., Halifax, 1980-2000; pres. Intelligent Sensing for Innovative Structures Can. Network of Ctrs. of Excellence U. Man., Winnipeg, Canada, 2000—, prof. structural engring., 2000—, pres. Internat. Soc. Structural Health Monitoring Intelligent Infrastructure, 2002—. Pres. Advanced Composite Materials in Bridges and Structures Network of Can., 1992-98; judge Can. Cons. Engring. Awards, 1987; earthquake cons. Lepereau Nuclear Power Plant and Confedn. Bridge. Author: Elementary Computer Graphics, 1982, Bridge Engineering, 1994; editor: Advanced Composite Materials in Bridges and Structures, 1972, Finite Element Method in Civil Engineering, 1993, Developments in Short and Medium Span Bridge Engineering, 1994, Bridge Superstructures New Developments, 1996; contbr. numerous articles to refereed jours., also conf. papers. Vol. fireman Wolfville Fire Dept., 1976-77. Recipient award for Distinction in Engring., Assn. Profl. Engrs. of N.S., 1996, award of merit Consulting Engrs. Man., 2003, award of excellence Consulting Engrs. Man., 2003, award of recognition Natural Scis. and Engring. Rsch. Coun., 2004, award of appreciation ISIS Can. Rsch. Network, 2004, Mirko-Ros Gold medal outstanding life's work rsch. and edn. Swiss Fed. Labs. Materials, Testing and Rsch., Dubendorf, Switzerland, 2005, Merit award Assn. Profl. Engrs. and Geoscientists Man., 2005, Nat. Sci. and Rsch Found. Synergy award, 2005. Fellow Can. Acad. Engring., Engring. Inst. Can. (Phelp Johnson prize 1969), Can. Soc. Civil Engring. (Whitman Wright award 1990, Pratley award 1993, A.B. Sanderson award 2006), ASCE (Lt. Govs. award Engring. Excellence in Nova Scotia 1996, IRF award 1997, ACI design award 1998, Nova award 2000). Achievements include patents for Bridge Deck and Steel Free Bridge Deck. Office: ISIS Can Admin Ctr U Man A250-96 Dafoe Rd Winnipeg MB Canada R3T 2N2 Office Phone: 204-474-7476. Office Fax: 204-474-7519. Business E-Mail: muftia@cc.umanitoba.ca.

MUGGERIDGE, DEREK BRIAN, engineering executive, consultant; b. Godalming, Surrey, U.K., Oct. 10, 1943; arrived in Can., 1956; s. Donald William and Vera Elvina (Jackson) M.; m. Hanny Meta Buurman, Dec. 4, 1965; children: Karen Julie, Michael Brent. BS in Aero. Engring., Calif. State Polytech. U., 1965; MASc in Aerospace Engring., U. Toronto, 1966, PhD in Aerospace Engring., 1970. Grad. fellow U. Toronto, 1965—66, NRC, Canada, 1967—70, indsl. post-doctoral fellow, 1971—72, Fleet Mfg. Co., Fort Erie, Ont., 1970-72; spl. lectr. U. Toronto, Ont., Canada, 1971; from asst. prof. to prof. Meml. U. of Nfld., St. John's, 1972-93, univ. rsch. prof., 1990-93; dir. Ocean Engring. Rsch. Ctr., 1982-93; dean Okanagan U. Coll., Kelowna, B.C., Canada, 1993—2003, assoc. v.p. rsch., 1998—2003; pvt. practice Lake County, B.C., Canada, 2003—. Pres. Offshore Design Assocs. Ltd., St. John's, Nfld., 1980—; sec., ptnr. Nfld. Ocean Cons., St. John's, 1981-93; ptnr. LNF Joint Venture Ltd., St. John's, 1984-90; vis. prof. Norwegian Inst. Tech., Trondheim, Norway, 1976, NRC, Ottawa, Can., 1976, U. Victoria, B.C., 1988-89. Co-author: Ice Interaction with Offshore Structures, 1988; contbr. articles to profl. jours.; contbr. conf. articles, reports. Mem. Assn. Profl. Engrs. and Geoscientists of Province of B.C. Marine and Naval. Avocations: windsurfing, sailing, rock collecting. Home and Office: 16438 Carr's Landing Rd Lake Country BC Canada V4V 1C3 Office Phone: 250-766-1023. Business E-Mail: dmuggeridge@cablelan.net.

MUGNAINI, ENRICO, neuroscience educator; b. Colle Val d'Elsa, Italy, Dec. 10, 1937; came to U.S., 1969. children: Karin E., Emiliano N.G. MD cum laude, U. Pisa, Italy, 1962; degree (hon.), U. Torino, 2005, U. Pisa, 2005, U. Salamanca, 2006. Microscopy lab. rsch. fellow dept. anatomy U. Oslo Med. Sch., 1963, asst. prof., head of electron microscopy lab., 1964-66, assoc. prof., 1967-69; prof. biobehavioral scis. and psychology, head lab. of neuromorphology U. Conn., Storrs, 1969-95; E.C. Stuntz prof. cell biology, dir. Inst. for Neurosci., Northwestern U., Chgo., 1995—2006. Vis. prof. dept. anatomy Harvard U., Boston, 1969-70; traveling lectr. Grass Found., 1986, 1990. Mng. editor USA Anatomy and Embryology Jour., 1989—; contbr. more than 200 articles to books and jours. Recipient Decennial Camillo Golgi award Acad. Nat. dei Lincei, 1981, Campano d'Oro award, 2005; Sen. Javits Neurosci. Rsch. Investigator grantee NIH, 1985-92, Fernandez-Lindsay Lectureship grantee U. Chgo., 2003. Mem. AAAS, Am. Assn. Anatomists, Am. Soc. Cell Biology, Internat. Brain Rsch. Orgn., Internat. Soc. Developmental Neurosci., Norwegian Nat. Acad. Scis. and Letters, Soc. Neurosci., Inst. Lombardo, Acad. Sci. Lettere (corr. 2005-), Cajal Club (pres. 1987-88). Office: U Northwestern Feinberg Sch Medicine 5-474 Searle Bldg 320 E Superior St Chicago IL 60611-3010 Home Phone: 312-915-0922; Office Phone: 312-503-4333. Business E-Mail: e-mugnaini@northwestern.edu.

MUGRIDGE, DAVID RAYMOND, lawyer, educator, writer; b. Detroit, Aug. 6, 1949; s. Harry Raymond and Elizabeth Lou (Aldrich) M.; m. Sandra Lee Jackson, June 25, 1988; children: James Raymond, Sarah Lorraine. BA, U. of Ams., Puebla, Mex., 1970; MA, Santa Clara U., 1973; JD, San Joaquin Coll. of Law, 1985. Bar: Calif. 1986, U.S. Dist. Ct. (ea. dist.) Calif. 1986, U.S. Ct. Appeals (9th cir.) 1987, U.S. Supreme Ct. 1996; cert. specialist in criminal law. Staff atty. to presiding justice 5th Dist. Ct. Appeals, Fresno, Calif., 1985-87; assoc. Law Office of Nuttall, Berman, Magill, Fresno, 1987-88; pvt. practice Fresno, 1988—. Tchr. Fresno City Coll., 1988-96; tchr. Spanish for legal profession, Fresno, 1994; tchr. Fresno Pacific U., 1997—, San Joaquin Coll. Law, 2006-; arbitrator Fresno County Bar Assn., 1988-2002; judge pro-tem juvenile, traffic and small claims Fresno County Superior Ct., 1988-05. Contbg. author: Practical Real Estate Law, 1995,99, 2003. Mem. Calif. Attys. for Criminal Justice, Calif. State Bar Assn. (cert. specialist in criminal law). Republican. Roman Catholic. Avocations: fishing, travel, photography, hiking. Office Phone: 559-264-2688. Business E-Mail: mugridgelaw@sbcglobal.net.

MUHAMMAD, CLAUDETTE MARIE, religious organization administrator; d. Travis and Ernestine Johnson; 1 child, Anthony L. Pinkins. Student, U. Abidjan, 1978—79; BA, Am. U., 1982; postgrad., UN, Geneva, 1982, U. Geneva, 1982, Johns Hopkins Sch. Advanced Internat. Studies, 1982. Tech. libr. Gen. Dynamics Astronautics, 1960—62; sec. to Congressman Lionel Van Deerlin U.S. Congress, Washington, 1963—68; spl. asst. to commrs. Pres.'s Commn. on Civil Disorders, Washington, 1968—69; dir. cmty. affairs Fed. City Coll., Washington, 1973—75; dir. of mayor's call program Dep. Mayor Econ. Devel., Washington; dir. mktg. Manara Travel Agy., Washington, 1987—88; enrollment mgmt./recruitment counselor U. D.C., Washington, 1988; chief protocol to Hon. Min. Louis Farrakhan Nation of Islam, 1989—2005; commr. commn. discrimination and hate crimes Gov. Ill., 2005—. Contbr. articles to profl. jours. Model Ebony Fashion Model, 1963; pres. Jimmy Carter's Inauguration Com. Protocol; mem. exec. bd. Millions More Movement, Inc., 2005; nat. dep. dir. Million Man March, Washington, 1995, Million Family March, Washington, 2000. Finalist 3d runner-up Miss Bronze California, 1958; recipient Women in History award, Urban League, 2002, Jerusalem 2000 Unity Day Conf. award, 2000, Jr. Achievement award, 1961—62.

MÜHLANGER, ERICH, ski manufacturing company executive; b. Aug. 26, 1941; arrived in U.S., 1971, naturalized, 1975; s. Alois Mühlnager and Maria (Stückelschweiger) Mühlanger; m. Gilda V. Oliver, July 13, 1973; 1 child, Erich. A in Engring., Murau Berufsschule Spl. Trade, Austria, 1959; student, Inst. Tech. and Engring., Weiler Im Allgau, Germany, 1963—65. Salesman Olin Ski Co. (Olin-Authier), Switzerland, 1965—67, mem. mktg. dept., 1967—67, svc. and mfg., 1969—71, quality control insp. Middletown, Conn., 1971—77, supr., 1977—78, gen. foreman, 1978—83, process control mgr., 1983—88; dir. mfg. Entech Corp., 1988—89; prodn. mgr. metallizing divsn. Risden Corp., Thomaston, Conn., 1989—94, quality process engr., 1994—. Pres. Bus. Consolidating Svcs. Internat., Rocky Hill, Conn., 1989—, quality control technician, 1990—, quality process request divsn., fragrance divsn., 1993—; pres. Bus. Cons. Svcs. Internat., 2004—. Chartered mem. Presdl. Task Force, trustee; preferred mem. U.S. Senatorial Club. Served to cpl. Austrian Air Force, 1959—60. Mem.: Mgmt. Club, Am. Soc. Quality Control, Am. Mgmt. Assn., Screenprinting Assn. Am. Roman Catholic. Home: 13 Clemens Ct Rocky Hill CT 06067-3218 Office: 60 Electric Ave Thomaston CT 06787-1617 also: Bus Consolidating Svcs Internat Rocky Hill CT 06067 Office Phone: 860-416-5849. E-mail: erich.muhlanger@cox.net.

MUHLBACH, ROBERT ARTHUR, lawyer; b. LA, Apr. 13, 1946; s. Richard and Jeanette (Marcus) M.; m. Kerry Eldene Mahoney, July 26, 1986. BSME, U. Calif., Berkeley, 1967; JD, U. Calif., San Francisco, 1976; MME, Calif. State U., 1969; M in Pub. Adminstrn., U. So. Calif., 1978. Bar: Calif. 1976. Pub. defender County of Los Angeles, 1977-79; assoc. Kirtland & Packard LLP, Los Angeles, 1979—85, ptnr., 1986—2001, sr. ptnr., 2001—. Chmn. Santa Monica Airport Commn., Calif., 1984-87, chmn., bd. dirs. Hawthorne Airport Cmty. Assn. Inc. Served to capt. USAF, 1969-73. Mem. AIAA, Internat. Assn. Def. Counsel, Am. Bd. Trial Advs. Office: Kirtland & Packard LLP 2361 Rosecrans Ave 4th Fl El Segundo CA 90245 Office Phone: 310-536-1000. Business E-Mail: ram@kirtland-packard.com.

MUHLBERGER, RICHARD CHARLES, museum director, writer, educator; b. Englewood, NJ, Jan. 20, 1938; s. George Albert and Margaret Bertha (Heins) M. AA, Calif. Concordia Coll., 1958; BA, Wayne State U., 1964; MA in Art History, Johns Hopkins U., 1967. Curator mus. edn. Worcester Art Mus., Mass., 1966-72; chmn. edn. Detroit Inst. Arts, 1972-75; dir. Mus. Fine Arts and George Walter Vincent Smith Art Mus., Springfield, Mass., 1976-87; vice dir. for edn. Met. Mus. Art, NYC, 1987-89; dir. Knoxville (Tenn.) Mus. Art, 1990-91; adj. prof. art history Western New England Coll., Springfield, Mass., 1991—. Guest curator Mus. Am. Folk Art, 1997-98; mem. adv. panel NEH, 1976-78, Mass. Coun. on Arts and Humanities, 1979-81; mem. policy panel, mus. program Nat. Endowment Arts, 1981-83. Author: The Bible in Art, The New Testament, 1990, The Bible in Art, The Old Testament, 1990, The Christmas Story,

1990, What Makes a Raphael a Raphael, 1993, What Make a Bruegel a Bruegel, 1993, What Makes a Rembrandt a Rembrandt, 1993, What Makes a Monet a Monet, 1993, What Makes a Degas a Degas, 1993, What Make a Van Gogh a Van Gogh, 1993, What Makes a Leonardo a Leonardo, 1994, What Makes a Goya a Goya, 1994, What Makes a Cassatt a Cassatt, 1994, What Makes a Picasso a Picasso, 1994, The Unseen Van Gogh, 1998, American Folk Marquetry, 1998, Charles Webster Hawthorne: Paintings and Watercolors, 1999; contbr. chpts to books. Woodrow Wilson fellow, 1965-66; recipient Outstanding Young Man award Greater Worcester Jaycees, 1970 Mem. Am. Assn. Museums (chmn. com. on edn. 1974-76, councilor 1988-91), New England Mus. Assn. (pres. 1985-87), Phi Beta Kappa. Home: 41 Smithfield Ct Springfield MA 01108-3129 Office Phone: 413-737-9660.

MUHLENBRUCK-FLEISCHER, DEBORAH LYNN, music educator; b. Mason City, Iowa, Oct. 28, 1969; d. Robert Floyd and Jeannette Jeraldine Muhlenbruck; m. Eric Matthew Fleischer, May 22, 1999; 1 child, Julia Lynn Fleischer. MusB in Vocal Performance, No. Ariz. U., 1993; MusM in Vocal Performance, U. Nev., 1997. Pvt. voice prof. U. Nev., Las Vegas, 1997—2002, C.C. So. Nev., 1998—2001. Prodr.: (vocal instruction cd) Sing Like the Pros. Recipient Rave Rev. award, Clark County Sch. Dist., 2001—02. Mem.: Music Educators Nat. Conf., Am. Choral Dirs. Assn. (assoc.), Nat. Assn.Tchrs. Singing (life; Las Vegas chpt. v.p. 2000—01, Las Vegas chpt. pres. 2001—03), U. Nev. Alumni Assn. (life). Conservative. Presbyterian. Office: Schofield Mid Sch Choirs 8625 Spencer St Las Vegas NV 89123 Home Phone: 702-896-2036; Office Phone: 702-799-2290.

MUHLENFELD, ELISABETH SHOWALTER, academic administrator, literature educator, writer; b. Washington, Nov. 12, 1944; d. Merle Roberts and Cornelia Elizabeth (Herring) Showalter; m. Edward F. Muhlenfeld, Sept. 10, 1966 (div. 1975); children: Allison Elisabeth Finch, David Edward; m. Laurin A. Wollan, Jr., June 5, 1982; stepchildren: Ann Louise Wollan Westberg, Laurin A. Wollan III. BA in Philosophy, Goucher Coll., 1966; MA in English, U. Tex., Arlington, 1973; PhD, U. S.C., 1978. With U. SC, Columbia, 1975-78; asst. prof. English Fla. State U., Tallahassee, 1978-82, assoc. prof., 1982-87, prof. English, 1987-96, dean undergrad. studies, 1984—96; pres. Sweet Briar Coll., Va., 1996—. Mem. ABA Commn. on Coll. and Univ. Legal Studies, 1991—94; mem. adv. com. US Com. UN Devel. Fund for Women; bd. dirs. United Way Ctrl. Va., chair, 2003. Author: Mary Boykin Chesnut: A Biography, 1981; editor: William Faulkner's Absolom, Absolom: A Critical Casebook, 1984, The Private Mary Chesnut: The Unpublished Civil War Diaries, 1984, Two Novels By Mary Chesnut, 2002; contbr. chpts. to books and articles to publs. Chair Coun. Ind. Colls. in Va., 2001—02; mem. exec. com. Va. Found. Ind. Colls.; mem. commn. on colls. So. Assn. Colls. and Schs., 2001—06, mem. exec. com., 2003—05, vice chair, 2005—06; bd. dirs. Am. Civil War Ctr. at Tredegar, Coun. Ind. Colls., 2005—, Women's Coll. Coalition, 2004—, chair, 2007—. NEH Dir.'s grantee, 1983-84. Mem. MLA, St. George Tucker Soc. (charter fellow), So. Assn. Women Historians, William Faulkner Soc. (charter mem; sec.-treas. 1991-94), Phi Kappa Phi (exec. bd., pres. 1992-93). Office: Sweet Briar Coll Pres's Office Box C Sweet Briar VA 24595 Home Phone: 434-381-6261; Office Phone: 434-381-6210. Business E-Mail: muhlenfeld@sbc.edu.

MUHLERT, JAN KEENE, art museum director; b. Oak Park, Ill., Oct. 4, 1942; d. William Henry and Isabel Janette (Cole) Keene; m. Christopher Layton Muhlert, Jan. 1, 1966; 1 son, Michael Keene. BA in Art and French, Albion Coll., Mich., 1964; MA in Art History, Oberlin Coll., Ohio, 1967; student, Neuchatel U., Switzerland, Inst. European Studies, Paris, Inst. de Phonetique, Acad. Grande Chaumiere. Asst. curator Allen Meml. Art Mus., Oberlin, 1967-68; asst. curator 20th Century painting and sculpture Nat. Collection Fine Arts, Smithsonian Instn., Washington, 1968-73, assoc. curator, 1974-75; dir. U. Iowa Mus. Art, 1975-79, Amon Carter Mus., Ft. Worth, 1980-95, Palmer Museum of Art, University Park, Pa., 1996—. Author museum brochures, catalogues. Mem. Nat. Mus. Act. Adv. Coun., 1980—83; vis. com. Allen Meml. Art Mus. Oberlin Coll., Ohio, 1992—2003; chair adv. com. North Tex. Inst. Educators on the Visual Arts, U. North Tex., 1992—95. Grantee Nat. Endowment Arts-Donner Found., 1979; recipient Friend of Art Edn. award Tex. Art Edn. Assn., 1994. Mem. Assn. Art Mus. Dirs. (trustee 1981-82, 84-86, 92-93, chmn. govt. and art com. 1982-84, chmn. profl. practices com. 1990-92), Western Assn. Art Mus. (regional rep. 1978-79), Am. Assn. Mus. (commn. for new century 1981-84, gen. co-chair 1993 ann. meeting), Am. Arts Alliance (dir. 1980-86, vice-chmn. 1982-84). Office: Palmer Museum of Art Pa State U Curtin Rd University Park PA 16802-2507 Office Phone: 814-865-7673.

MUHN, JUDY ANN, psychologist, genealogist, trainer; b. Detroit, Dec. 29, 1952; d. Wilbur William and Dolores Eleanor (Sutinen) Nimer; m. Dennis James Muhn, June 6, 1975. BS, Mich. State U., East Lansing, 1975; MEd, Boston U., Mass., 1992; MA in Counseling, U. San Francisco, Calif., 1997. Lic. psychologist Mich. Legis. aide press sec. to Calif. state senator, 1982—84; dir. pub. rels. Tierra del Oro coun. Girl Scouts U.S., 1984—86, mgr. mem. devel. San Antonio area coun., 1986—90; adj. faculty U. Md. Germany, 1992—94; ind. cons. Capital Enquiry, Sacramento, 1994—96; counselor Yuba City Indian Health Ctr., 1997; intervention counselor Sutter-Yuba Mental Health, 1997—98; counselor, intern White Ho. Cmty. Counseling Ctr., 1998; pvt. practice Wixom, Mich., 1998—; dep. exec. dir. U. Santo Tomas Alumni Assn., 1998—2000; therapist Brighton Hosp., 2000—01; dir. adult devel. and vol. svcs. Girl Scouts Metro Detroit, 2002—. Adj. faculty Henry Ford CC, 1998—2001, Oakland CC, 1998—2001; therapist Brighton Hosp., 2000—01, Advanced Counseling Svcs., Brighton, 2001—03; spkr. in field. Columnist: Press-Republican, 1995—98. Bd. dirs., chmn. pub. affairs com. Planned Parenthood Clinton County, NY, 1980—81; bd. dirs. Family Planning Advs., Albany, 1981, Planned Parenthood San Antonio, 1987—89; founder Women's Roundtable, Plattsburgh, 1981; pres. Planned Parenthood Assn. Sacramento Valley, 1982—84; sec. San Antonio Coun. Native Ams., 1986—89; co-founder Womanspirit Rising, 1987—89; mem. Metis Cmty. Ea. Can. Named Bd. Mem. of Yr., Planned Parenthood Sacramento Valley, 1982; recipient Human Rights award, Sacramento Fair Housing Commn., 1983, Woman of Yr. award-Nonprofit, YWCA, Sacramento, 1984. Mem.: ASTD, Nat. Geneal. Soc., Assn. Prof. Genealogists, Metis Cmty. Ea. Can., Assn. Vol. Adminstrs., Met. Detroit Vol. Adminstrs., Assn. Univ. Women, Amnesty Internat., Greenpeace, San Antonio Women's C. of C. (bd. dirs. 1989), Assn. Girl Scout Exec. Staff. Personal E-mail: jmuhn@aol.com. Business E-Mail: jmuhn@gsofmd.org.

MUIR, DOUGLAS R., food service executive; BS in Bus. Adminstrn., Washington & Lee U. CPA. Various positions to audit ptnr. Price Waterhouse, Charlotte, NC, 1976—93; various sr. mgmt. roles to exec. v.p. and CFO Oakwood Homes, 1993—2004; cons. Krispy Kreme, 2004—05, chief acctg. officer, 2005—07, CFO, 2007—. Office: Krispy Kreme Doughnut Corp PO Box 83 Winston Salem NC 27102 *

MUIR, J. DAPRAY, lawyer; b. Washington, Nov. 9, 1936; s. Brockett and Helen Cassin (Dapray) M.; m. Louise Rutherfurd Pierrepont, July 16, 1966. AB, Williams Coll., 1958; JD, U. Va., 1964. Bar: Md., Va., D.C. 1964, U.S. Supreme Ct. 1967. Asst. legal advisor for econ. and bus. affairs U.S. Dept. State, 1971-73; pvt. practice Washington, 1973—. Mem. U.S. del. to Joint U.S./USSR Comml. Commn., 1972; chmn. D.C. Securities Adv. Com., 1981-84, mem. 1985-88. Bd. editors Va. Law Rev, 1963-64; contbr. articles to profl. jours. Bd. dirs. Trust Mus. Exhbns., 1997—2005, Internat. Fedn. Insts. Advanced Study, 1992—97. Lt. (j.g.) USNR, 1958—61. Mem. Am. Arbitration Assn. (panel of comml. arbitrators, 1997—), DC Bar (chmn. internat. law div. 1977-78, chmn. environ., energy and natural resources div. 1982-83), Met. Club, Washington, Chevy Chase Club, Md. Office: 1629 K St NW Ste 300 Washington DC 20006 Office Phone: 202-337-1724. Business E-Mail: jdmuir@muirlaw.net.

MUIR, MALCOLM, federal judge; b. Englewood, NJ, Oct. 20, 1914; s. John Merton and Sarah Elizabeth Muir; m. Alma M. Brohard, Sept. 6, 1940 (dec. 1985); children: Malcolm, Thomas, Ann Muir, Barbara (dec.), David Clay. BA, Lehigh U., 1935; LL.B., Harvard U., 1938. Sole practice, Williamsport, Pa., 1938-42, 45-49, 68-70; mem. firm, 1949-68; judge U.S. Dist. Ct. (mid. dist.) Pa., 1970—. Active charitable orgns., Williamsport, 1939-70 Mem. ABA, Pa. Bar Assn. (pres.-elect 1970) Avocation: reading. Office: US Dist Ct Ste 401 240 W 3rd St Williamsport PA 17701-6461 Office Phone: 570-322-0287.

MUIR, PATRICIA ALLEN, professional association administrator; b. Dallas, Nov. 4, 1929; d. Jack Charleton Allen and Anna Patricia (Hovis) Allen Atchison; m. Lester Doyle Rader, Jr., Aug. 4, 1950 (dec. Sept. 1950); 1 child, Lester Doyle III; m. Perren James Muir, June 2, 1956 (div.); children: Edward John, Patricia Jane. Grad., Our Lady of Victory Coll., 1948; student, George Washington U., 1948-49, Washington Sch. for Sec., 1949-50. Traffic mgr. Am. Storage Co., Washington, 1960-69; asst. sec. Ind. Tele. Pioneer Assn., Washington, 1969-76; adminstrv. asst. ALA, Washington, 1977-98, staff liaison to Fed. Libr. Round Table, 1991-98, staff liaison to Armed Forces Libr. Round Table, 1991-98, staff liaison to Govt. Documents Round Table, 1991-98; office mgr. Fed. Documents Clearing House, Washington, 1998-2000; cons., 2000—. Columnist, contbr. The Ind. Pioneer, 1969-76. V.p. Friendship House Child Devel. Ctr. Parents, Washington, 1978, pres., 1979—83; mem. parish coun. St. Peter's Cath. Ch., 1987—91, mem. edn. and spiritual devel. com., 1986—, chair, 1988—91, coord. Bible study, 1999—2003; vol. St. Peter's Interparish Sch. Reading Program, 2001—02. Mem. Ladies Ancient Order of Hibernians (state pres. 1991-97, nat. budget com. 1996-98, nat. elections com. 1998—, nat. constn. com. 1998-02, nat. rules of order com. 2000-02). Avocations: travel, genealogy, reading, writing.

MUIR, RUTH BROOKS, alcohol/drug abuse services professional, consultant; b. Washington, Nov. 27, 1924; d. Charles and Adelaide Chenery (Masters) B.; m. Robert Mathew Muir, Nov. 26, 1947 (dec. Feb. 20, 1996); children: Robert Brooks, Martha Louise, Heather Sue. BA in Art, Rollins Coll., Winter Park, Fla., 1947; MA in Rehab. Counseling, U. Iowa, 1979. Cert. substance abuse counselor, Iowa. Program advisor Iowa Meml. Union, Iowa City, 1959-66; counselor, coord. Mid Eastern Coun. on Chem. Abuse, Iowa City, 1976-81; patient rep. Univ. Hosp., Iowa City, 1982-85; rsch. project interviewer dept. psychiatry U. Iowa Coll. Medicine, 1985-88; pvt. practice family counselor, 1984—. Docent U. Iowa Mus. of Art, 1999—. Artist: exhibitions include Iowa City Sr. Ctr., 1987, 92, Iowa City Art Ctr., 1989, U. Iowa Hosp., 1991, Great Midwestern Ice Cream Co., 1991, Summit St. Gallery, 1995, Iowa City C. of C., 2001, Iowa City's First Art Walk March, 2003; creator, coord. therapeutic series Taking Control, Iowa City Sr. Ctr., 1986-87, Art Walk Lorenz Boot Shop, 2003; one woman shows include Eng. Theatre, Iowa City, 2006. Vol. coord. art exhibits Sr. Ctr., Iowa City, 1992-94, Iowa City Arts Exhbn. Com., 1996, Arrowmont Sch. Art, 1996—, Arrowmont Amb., 1996-98; treas. bd. dirs. Crisis Ctr., Iowa City, 1976-77; sec. coun. elders Sr. Citizens Ctr., Iowa City, 1976-78; pres. Unitarian-Universalist Iowa City Women's Fedn., 1985, mem. pastoral com., 2006; friend U. Iowa Mus. Art, docent, 1999—; active Opera Supers, Iowa City Unitarian U.N. Envoy; fgn. rels. coun., bd. dirs. annual changing family conf. U. Iowa, 1986-92; non-govtl. rep. Earth Summit Global Forum, 1992; care review bd. Mental Health Homes, 1997-99; bd. dirs., exhbn. chair Arts Iowa City, 2002—. Mem.: AAUW (state cultural rep. 1990—92, Iowa City chpt. co-chair for programs 1998—99), Health Care: Health Svcs., Nat. League Am. PEN Women (membership chair 2002—04, v.p. 2004—), Iowa City Unitarian Soc. (adult program com. 1993—94, unitarian care com. 1993—, membership com.), Nat. Soc. Colonial Dames, U. Iowa Retirees Assn. (bd. mem. 2004—, chair membership 2005—, membership chair), U. Iowa Print and Drawing Study Club (bd. dirs. 2003—04, pres. elect 2005), Pi Beta Phi (pres. alumnae club 1995—97). Home and Office: 6 Glendale Ct Iowa City IA 52245-4430 Office Phone: 319-337-7287. Business E-Mail: ruthmuir2989@inavia.net.

MUIR, WARREN ROGER, chemist, educator; b. NY, 1945; s. Ernest Roger and Phyllis (Stirn) M.; m. Jo-Ann McNally; children: Amy, Douglas, Michael, Gregory, Daniel. AB in Chemistry cum laude, Amherst Coll., 1967; MS in Chemistry, Northwestern U., Evanston, Ill., 1968, PhD in Chemistry, 1971; postgrad. in epidemiology, Johns Hopkins U., 1975-77. Sr. staff mem. environ. health Council on Environ. Quality, EPA, Washington, 1971-78; dir. Office of Toxic Substances, EPA, 1978-81; pres. Hampshire Rsch. Assocs., Inc., 1981-99, Hampshire Rsch. Inst., 1987-99; exec. dir. divsn. earth and life studies NRC/Nat. Acad. Scis., 1999—. Assoc. environ. health scis. Johns Hopkins U., 1981-99; rsch. prof. biology Am. U., 1985; sr. fellow INFORM, 1982-95; mem. Nat. Conf. Lawyers and Scientists, 1987-89; bd. environ. scis. and toxicology NRC, 1997-99. Contbr. articles on environ. quality to profl. jours. Mem., chair several Nat. Rsch. Coun. coms.; pres. Children's Friendship Project for No. Ireland, 1997-99, bd. dirs. 1995—, chair 1997-2002, bd. dirs. HasNa, Inc., chair, 2007—. Recipient NSF Acad. award, 1966, Howard Waters Doughty prize Amherst Coll., 1967, Forris Jewett Moore fellow, 1967; comdr., 1996, officer brother Most Venerable Order of St. John, 1992; co-recipient Adminstrs. award U.S. EPA, 1992, Cmty. Svc. award Nat. Acads., 2003. Mem.: AAAS, Am. Chem. Soc. Home: 9426 Forest Haven Dr Alexandria VA 22309-3151

MUIR, WILLIAM KER, JR., political science professor; b. Detroit, Oct. 30, 1931; s. William Ker and Florence Taylor (Bodman) M.; m. Paulette Irene Wauters, Jan. 16, 1960; children: Kerry Macaire, Harriet Bodman. BA, Yale U., 1954, PhD, 1965; JD, U. Mich., 1958. Bar: N.Y. 1960, Conn. 1965. Instr. U. Mich. Law Sch., 1958-59; assoc. firm Davis Polk & Wardwell, NYC, 1959-60; lectr. in polit. sci. Yale U., 1960-64, 65-67; from assoc. to ptnr. Tyler Cooper Grant Bowerman & Keefe, New Haven, 1964-68; prof. emeritus polit. sci. U. Calif., Berkeley, 1968-98, dept. chmn., 1980-83; speechwriter v.p. U.S., 1983-85; columnist Oakland (Calif.) Tribune, 1992-93; writer Gov. of Calif., Sacramento, 1994. Sr. cons. Calif. State Assembly, Sacramento, 1975-76; cons. Oakland Police Dept., 1969-74; vis. prof. polit. sci. Harvard U., summers 1976, 79; vis. prof. Hawaii Pacific U., 2000, U. Ariz., 2002. Author: Prayer in the Public School, 1967, later republished as Law and Attitude Change, 1974, Police: Streetcorner Politicians, 1977, Legislature: California's School for Politics, 1982, The Bully Pulpit: The Presidential Leadership of Ronald Reagan, 1993, An Understanding of Democracy, 2003, Power and American Democracy, 2003, memoirs, 2003. Mem. Berkeley Police Rev. Commn., 1981-83; chmn. New Haven Civil Liberties Coun., 1965-68; Rep. candidate Calif. State Assembly, 1996. Recipient Hadley B. Cantril Meml. award, 1979, Disting. Tchg. award U. Calif., Berkeley, 1974, Phi Beta Kappa No. Calif. Assoc. Excellence in Tchg. award, 1994. Mem. Am. Polit. Sci. Assn. (Edward S. Corwin award 1966). Republican. Presbyterian. Office: U Calif Dept Polit Sci Berkeley CA 94720-1950 Personal E-mail: sandymuir@aol.com.

MUIR, WILLIAM LLOYD, III, academic administrator; b. Norton, Kans., Mar. 20, 1948; s. John Thomas and Rosalie June (Benton) M. BBA, Kans. State U., 1977. Asst. sec. of state State of Kans., Topeka, 1971—72, fin. adminstr. atty. gen. office, 1972—79, comptr. Office of Gov., 1979—87, sec. of cabinet, 1979—87, asst. sec. adminstrn., 1986—87; dir. econ. devel. Kans. State U., Manhattan, 1987—91, asst. to v.p. for cmty. rels., 1991—2002, asst. v.p. for cmty. rels., 2002—, faculty rep., senator Student Governing Assn., 1992—, mem. union governing bd., 1997—, mem. coun. on parking ops., 2001—. Chmn. housing appeals bd. City of Manhattan, 1996—; trustee Kans. State U. Found., 1993—; mem. Leadership Kans., 1989; state officer Native Sons and Daus., 1997—2002, pres., 2001; mem. Kans. Territorial Sesquicentennial Commn., 2003—, Kans. Capitol Area Plaza Authority, 2004—; bd. dirs. United Way Riley County, 1989—99, chmn., 1992; treas. Flint Hills Regional Leadership Program, 2002—. Mem.: Nat. Geog. Soc., Friends of Cedar Crest Assn., Sierra Club, Blue Key, Masons (Scottish Rite), Alpha Kappa Psi, Alpha Tau Omega (nat. officer, bd. govs. Alpha Tau Omega Found.). Episcopalian. Avocation: travel. Home: 2040 Shirley Ln Manhattan KS 66502-2059 Office: Kansas State U 122 Anderson Hall Manhattan KS 66506-0100 Office Phone: 785-532-6269. Business E-Mail: billmuir@ksu.edu.

MUIRHEAD, VINCENT URIEL, retired aerospace engineer; b. Dresden, Kans., Feb. 6, 1919; s. John Hadsell and Lily Irene (McKinney) M.; m. Bobby Jo Thompson, Nov. 5, 1943; children: Rosalind, Jean, Juleigh. BS, U.S. Naval Acad., 1941; BS in Aero. Engring, U.S. Naval Postgrad. Sch., 1948; Aero. Engr., Calif. Inst. Tech., 1949; postgrad., U. Ariz., 1962-64, Okla. State U., 1963. Midshipman U.S. Navy, 1937, commd. ensign, 1941, advanced through grades to comdr., 1951; nav. officer U.S.S. White Plains, 1945-46; comdr. Fleet Aircraft Service Squad, 1951-52; with Bur. Aeros., Ft. Worth, 1953-54; comdr. Helicopter Utility Squadron I, Pacific Fleet, 1955-56; chief staff officer Comdr. Fleet Air, Philippines, 1956-58; exec. officer Naval Air Tng. Center, Memphis, 1958-61; ret., 1961; asst. prof. U. Kans., Lawrence, 1961-63, assoc. prof. aerospace engring., 1964-76, prof., 1976-89, prof. emeritus, 1989—, chmn. dept., 1976-88. Cons. Black & Veatch (cons. engrs.), Kansas City, Mo., 1964—. Author: Introduction to Aerospace, 1972, 6th edit., 2004, Thunderstorms, Tornadoes and Building Damage, 1975. Decorated Air medal. Fellow AIAA (assoc.); mem. Am. Acad. Mechanics, Am. Soc. Engring. Edn., Tau Beta Pi, Sigma Gamma Tau. Mem. Ch. of Christ (elder 1972-96). Achievements include research on aircraft, tornado vortices, shock tubes and waves. Home: 503 Park Hill Ter Lawrence KS 66046-4841 Office: Dept Aerospace Engring Univ Kans Lawrence KS 66045-0001 Personal E-mail: vmuirhead@sunflower.com.

MUIR-TAYLOR, DOUGLAS JAMES, ophthalmologist; b. Edinburgh, May 4, 1932; s. Thomas William and Jane Craig Muir-Taylor; m. Lesley Elizabeth Muir-Taylor; children: Victoria Grace, Elizabeth Laura. Grad., Heriot-Watt U., Edinburgh, 1954; MB BChir, U. London, 1960. House surgeon ophthalmology Kings Coll. Hosp., London, 1960—60, house physician medicine, 1960—61; sr. house surgeon A&E Lewisham Hosp., London, 1961—62; gen. practice prin. London Redbridge, 1962; clin. assoc. ophthalmology Moorfields Hosp., London, 1962—66, Royal London Hosp., 1978—85, assoc. specialist ophthalmology, 1978—85, clin. dir. contact lens and prosthetic dept., 1991—. Clin. dir. Telephone Cables GEC, London, 1963—90, Electric Windings Ltd., London, 1970—94, F.J. Cipa Panel Craft PT Ltd., London, 1996—. Fellow: Rpyal Soc. Medicine, Brit. Optical Assn., Brit. Coll. Optometry; mem.: Contact Lens Assn. Ophthalmologists, Royal Coll. Physicians (licentiate), Am. Soc. Cataract and Refractive Surgery, Royal Coll. Ophthalmologists, Royal Coll. Surgeons. Achievements include research in photorefractive keratectomy in high myopia; photorefractive keratectomy after corneal surgery; photorefractive keratectomy in pregnancy and menopause; correction of aphakia with extended wear gas permeable contact lenses, serum markers in germ cell tumours. Avocations: fishing, winter sports, shooting, fine wines, golf. Home: 63 Plover Way London SE16 7TS England Office: Blackheath Eyecare Ctr 16 Old Dover Rd London SE16 7TS England Office Fax: 020 8858 5627. E-mail: muirtaylor@aol.com.

MUJICA, BARBARA LOUISE, language educator, writer; d. Louis and Frieda (Kline) Kaminar; m. Mauro E. Mujica, Dec. 26, 1966; children: Lillian Louise, Mariana Ximena, Mauro Eduardo Ignacio. AB, UCLA, 1964; MA, Middlebury Coll., 1965; PhD, NYU, 1974. Instr. French UCLA, 1963-64; assoc. editor modern langs. Harcourt Brace Jovanovich, NYC, 1966-73; instr., asst. prof. Romance langs. CUNY, 1973-74; prof. Spanish Georgetown U., Washington, 1974—. Mem. faculty NEH Summer Inst., 1980. Author: (book) A-LM Spanish, Levels I-IV, 1969—74, Readings in Spanish Literature, 1975, Calderon's Characters: An Existential Point of View, 1980, Pasaporte, 1980, rev. edit., 1984, Aqui y ahora, 1979, Entrevista, 1982, Iberian Pastoral Characters, 1986, Texto y Espectáculo, 1987, Et in Arcadia Ego, 1990, Texto y Vida: Introduccion a la Literature Española, 1990, Antología de la Literatura Española: La Edad Media, 1991, Renacimiento y Siglo de Oro, 1991, Siglos XVII y XIX, 1999, Texto y Vida: Introduccion a la Literature Hispano-Americana, 1992, Looking at the Comedia in the Year of the Quincentennial, 1993, Premio Nobel, 1997, Books of the Americas, 1997, El Texto Puesto en Escena, 2000, (novels) Sanchez Across the Street, 1997, The Deaths of Don Bernardo, 1990, Far From My Mother's Home, 1999, Frida: A Novel, 2001, (book) Teresa de Jesus: Espiritualidad y feminismo, Milenio, 2002, Sister Teresa, 2006; editor: Comedia Performance Jour.; editor, pub. Verbena: Bilingual Rev. of Arts, 1979—85, sr. assoc. editor, bd. dirs. Washington Rev., mem. editl. bd. Bull. of Comediantes Hispana; editor: (book) Women Writers of Early Modern Spain: Sophia's Daughters, 2004, (jour.) Comedia Performance. Named winner, E.L. Doctorow Internat. Fiction Competition, 1992; named one of 50 Best Op Eds of Decade, N.Y. Times, 1990; recipient Pangolin prize best short story, 1998, Hoepner award for fiction, 2002, Trailblazers award, 2004; grantee, Spanish Govt., 1987, Poets and Writers of N.Y., Georgetown U., 2005—06; Penfield fellow, 1971. Mem.: MLA (pres. Golden Age sect.), Assn. Hispanic Classical Theater (pres.). Office: Georgetown U Dept Spanish Washington DC 20057-1039 Home Phone: 301-365-7733; Office Phone: 202-687-5778. Business E-Mail: mujica@georgetown.edu.

MUJICA, MAURO E., architect; b. Antofagasta, Chile, Apr. 20, 1941; came to U.S., 1965, naturalized, 1970; s. Mauro Raul and Graciela (Parodi-Blayfus) M.; m. Barbara Louise Kaminar, Dec. 26, 1966; children: Lillian Louise, Mariana Ximena, Mauro Eduardo Ignacio III. BArch, MArch, Columbia U., 1971. Head designer Columbia U. Office Archtl. Planning, NYC, 1966-71; project mgr. Walker, Sander, Ford & Kerr, Architects, Princeton, NJ, 1971-72; prin. Mauro E. Mujica, Architect, NYC, 1972-74; dir. internat. divsn. Greenhorne & O'Mara, Inc., Riverdale, Md., 1974-78; ptnr. Mujica & Reddy Architects, Washington, 1978-80; prin. Mauro E. Mujica, Architect, Washington, 1980-81; ptnr. Mujica & Berlin Investment Bankers, Washington, 1982-85, Mujica Keppie Henderson Internat., Washington and Glasgow, Scotland, 1981-83, Mujica-Seifert Architects, Washington and London, 1983-87; pres.,CDEO, The Pace Group, Washington, 1987-91; ptnr. Pace/Walsh Internat., London and Washington. Chmn. bd., CEO, U.S. English Found., Washington, 1993—; hon. mem. Emmanuel Coll. Cambridge (Eng.) U., 1995; mem. adv. bd. U.S.-U.K. Fulbright Commn., 1995-2000.

MUJUMDAR, VILAS SITARAM, structural engineer, researcher; b. Indore, India, June 26, 1941; arrived in U.S., 1968; s. Sitaram and Kamala (Kulkarni) Mujumdar; m. Ingrid M. Dietrich, Mar. 1, 1969. BSCE, Vikram U., India, 1961; MS, U. Roorkee, India, 1962; MBA, U. Santa Clara, Calif., 1980; D in Pub. Adminstrn., U. So. Calif., 2000. Registered profl. engr., U.S., Can., Eng., structural engr., Calif. Design engr. U.S.D. & Co., India, 1962-65, Donovan H. Lee & Ptnrs., London, 1965-66; asst. chief engr. Francon & Spancrete Ltd., Montreal, Canada, 1966-68; gen. mgr., dir. engring. Modular Constructors, Woburn, Mass., 1968-70; sr. project engr., tech. mgr. LeMessurier Assocs., Cambridge, Mass., 1970-74; v.p. Precast Sys. Cons., Woburn, 1974-77; prin. structural engr. Ecodyne Corp., Santa Rosa, Calif., 1977-79; v.p. Foster Engring., Inc., San Francisco, 1979-81, 3D/Internat. Inc., Houston, 1981-85; pres. VSM Assocs., Santa Rosa,

1985-88; v.p. BSHA, Inc., San Diego, 1988-90; pres. McNamara, Salvia, Mujumdar, Inc., San Diego, 1990-92; chief ops. Divsn. State Arch. Dept. Gen. Svcs., Calif., 1992-2000; exec. dir. Concrete Masonry Assn. Calif., Nev., 2000—02; program dir. NSF, 2002—. Chmn. several earthquake engring. coms. Author: (book) Concrete Design Manual, Structural Engineer Review Course, Reinforced Concrete Masonry Design; contbr. more than 50 to profl. jours. Recipient numerous awards; Merit scholar, Govt. India, 1957—62. Fellow: ASCE, Prestressed Concrete Inst., Am. Concrete Inst., Inst. Structural Engrs. U.K.; mem.: Soc. Risk Analysis, Masonry Soc., Structural Engrs. Assn. Calif. (chmn. seismology com. 1992—93), Beta Gamma Sigma (hon. bus. soc.). Achievements include invention of pre-cast concrete buidling system. Home: 9905 Trosby Ct Vienna VA 22181 Office Phone: 703-292-7262. Personal E-mail: vilas.mujumdar@earthlink.net. Business E-Mail: vmujumda@nsf.gov.

MUKAI, AI, physiatrist; b. Tokyo, Oct. 13, 1977; arrived in U.S., 1989; d. Kazuko Mukai. Studied piano, Manhattan Sch. of Music, 1993—95; BA in Psychology, Columbia U., NYC, 1999; MD, Pa. State U., 2004. Lic. Ill., 2005, cert. in advanced cardiac life support 2004, in pediat. advanced life support 2004. Intern Pa. State U. Coll. Medicine, Hershey Med. Ctr., 2004—05; resident phys. medicine and rehab. Northwestern U., Rehab. Inst. Chgo., 2005—. Preceptor phys. diagnosis curriculum Pa. State Coll. Medicine, 2004—05; co-moderator Phys. Medicine and Rehab. Forum, Studentdoctor.net, 2005—; mem. various coms. Rehab. Inst. Chgo., 2005—, mem. ethics com., 2005—06, mem. continuous quality improvement, 2005—, mem. labs. and x-rays com., 2006—, super-user, Cerner Project Mercury, 2006—; presenter, lectr., rschr. in field. Contbg. editor, coord.: Rehab in Review, 2006—, book reviewer: Lippincott Williams and Wilkins, 2001—; contbr. articles to profl. jours., chapters to books; jour. reviewer: Archives of Phys. Medicine and Rehab., 2005—, Jour. Gen. Internal Medicine, 2005. Named Intern of Yr., Hershey Med. Ctr., Dept. Gastroenterology and Hepatology, 2005, Hershey Med. Ctr., Dept. Hematology and Oncology, 2005; recipient 1st pl., NYC Dept. Health, Health Rsch. Tng. Program Competition, 1998, Med. Student Rsch. award, Pa. State Coll. Medicine, 2004, 2nd pl., Pa. Med. Soc. Poster Competition, 2004; grantee, William Randolph Hearst Found., 2006—07; scholar, Internat. Starr Found., 1995, Japanese-Am. Assn., 1995; Roslyn S. Silver '27 scholar, 1999, Gen. Clin. Rsch. Ctr. scholar, Pa. State Coll. Medicine, 2000, Mohler scholar, 2000, Hammersla scholar, 2001, 2002, Hershey Foods scholar, 2003. Mem.: AMA, Asian and Pacific Islander Am. Health Forum, Student Nat. Med. Assn. (chpt. co-pres. Penn State Coll. Medicine 2000—01, nat. liaison to Am. Med. Student Assn. 2001—02), Asian and Pacific Am. Med. Student Assn., Am. Med. Student Assn. (chpt. co-pres. Penn State Coll. Medicine 2000—01, assoc. trustee region III 2001—02), Am. Acad. Phys. Medicine and Rehab. (chair bylaws/ops. and strategic planning com. resident physician coun. 2004—05, sec. 2005—06, mentor med. student mentoring program 2005—, pres. resident physician coun. 2006—07), Am. Congress Rehab. Medicine (mem. membership com. and info. tech. com. 2005—06, 2005—), Physiatric Assn. for Spine Sports and Occupl. Rehab., Assn. Acad. Physiatrists, Ill. State Phys. Medicine and Rehab. Soc. Avocations: piano, drawing, photography, languages. Office: Rehab Inst Chgo 345 E Superior St Chicago IL 60611 Personal E-mail: amukai355@gmail.com.

MUKAIYAMA, TERUAKI, chemist, educator; b. Ina, Japan, Jan. 5, 1927; s. Mikio and Akiko (Osada) M.; m. Hiroko Hoshino, Mar. 30, 1953; 1 child, Taketo. BSc, Tokyo Inst. Tech., 1948; PhD, Tokyo U., 1957; degree (hon.), Tech. U. Munich, 1976. Asst. prof. Gakushuin U., Tokyo, 1953-58; from asst. prof. to prof. Tokyo Inst. Tech., 1958-73; prof. U. Tokyo, 1973-87, prof. emeritus chemistry; prof. Sci. U. Tokyo, 1987—2002; prof. Ctr. Basic Rsch. Kitasato Inst., Tokyo, 2002—. Disting. prof. Sci. U. Tokyo, 1992—; pres. Rsch. Inst. Sci. & Tech., Noda, Japan, 1991-02; advisor basic rsch. ctr. Mitsui Petrochem. Industries, Ltd., Chiba, Japan, 1987-90; cons. Syntex, Palo Alto, Calif., 1976-94. Author: Challenges in Synthetic Organic Chemistry, 1990. Decorated Chevalier de l'ordre Nat. du Mérite, France, Order of Culture, Japan, 1997; recipient Imperial and Acad. prize, Japan, 1983, Copernicus medal, Poland, 1985, Sir Derek Barton Gold medal, Eng., 2006; named Person of Cultural Merit, Japan, 1992. Mem. Polish Acad. Scis., French Acad. Scis., Pharm. Soc. Japan, Chem. Soc. Japan, NAS (fgn. assoc.). Office: Kitasato Inst Ctr for Basic Rsch TCI 6-15-5 Toshima Tokyo 114-0003 Japan Office Phone: 81-3-3911-3111. E-mail: mukaiyam@abeam.ocn.ne.jp.

MUKAMAL, DAVID SAMIER, sign manufacturing company executive; b. Baghdad, Iraq, Oct. 6, 1944; arrived in US, 1950; s. Abraham Sassoon and Mary (Murad) M.; m. Anitamarie Costa, July 31, 1970; children: Adam Scott, Rebecca Kate. BBA in Econs. with honors, Bryant Coll., 1970; MBA in Fin. Mgmt., Iona Coll., 1975. Budget analyst USV Pharm./Revlon, Inc., Tuckahoe, NY, 1970-72; sr. budget officer Met. Transp. Authority, NYC, 1972-74; sr. fin. analyst Am. Airlines, Inc., Dallas, 1974-82; chmn. DSM Industries Inc.; pres. All State Signs, Richardson, Tex., 1982—, Framed Enterprises, Inc., Irving, Tex., 1995-99. With USN, 1965-66. Recipient Jerremiah Clarke Barber award Bryant Coll., 1970. Mem. Dallas Apt. Assn., Tex. Sign Mfrs. Assn., Internat. Sign Assn., La Cima Club (bd. dirs.), Omicron Delta Epsilon. Republican. Jewish. Home Phone: 972-791-1124; Office Phone: 972-238-7049. E-mail: dmukamal5@comcast.net, dmukamal5@birch.net.

MUKASEY, MICHAEL B., lawyer, former federal judge; b. Bronx, NY, 1941; AB, Columbia U., 1963; LLB, Yale U., 1967. Assoc. Webster Sheffield Fleishchmann Hitchcock & Brookfield, 1967-72, Patterson, Belknap, Webb & Tyler, 1976-88; asst. U.S. atty. criminal divsn. (so. dist.) NY US Dept. Justice, 1972-76; judge US Dist. Ct. (so. dist.) NY, 1988—2006, chief judge, 2000—06; ptnr. Patterson Belknap Webb & Tyler LLP, NYC, 2006—. Lectr. in law Columbia Law Sch. Contbr. articles to profl. jour. Office: Patterson Belknap Webb & Tyler LLP 1133 Ave Americas New York NY 10036 Office Phone: 212-336-2900. E-mail: mbmukasey@pbwt.com.

MUKERJEE, PASUPATI, chemistry professor; b. Calcutta, India, Feb. 13, 1932; s. Nani Gopal and Probhabati (Ghosal) M.; m. Lalita Sarkar, Feb. 29, 1964 (dec.); m. Mina Maitra, Nov. 14, 1998. B.Sc., Calcutta U., 1949, M.Sc., 1951; PhD, U. So. Calif., 1957. Lectr., vis. asst. prof. U. So. Calif., 1956-57; rsch. assoc. Brookhaven Nat. Lab., LI, 1957-59; reader in phys. chemistry Indian Assn. Cultivation of Sci., Calcutta, 1959-64; guest scientist U. Utrecht, Holland, 1964; sr. scientist chemistry dept. U. So. Calif., 1964-66; vis. assoc. prof. U. Wis., Madison, 1966-67, prof. Sch. Pharmacy, 1967-94, emeritus prof., 1994—. Vis. prof. Indian Inst. Tech., Kharagpur, 1971-72; mem. commn. on colloid and surface chemistry Internat. Union Pure and Applied Chemistry Contbr. articles to profl. jours.; mem. editl. bd. Jour. Colloid and Interface Sci., 1978-80, Asian Jour. Pharm. Scis., 1978-85, Colloids and Surfaces, 1980-86. Grantee USPHS, NSF, Nat. Bur. Stds., Petroleum Rsch. Fund. Fellow AAAS, Acad. Pharm. Scis., Am. Inst. Chemistry; mem. Am. Chem. Soc. (editorial bd. Langmuir 1985-86), Am. Pharm. Assn., Acad. Pharm. Scis., Rho Chi. Home: 5526 Varsity Hl Madison WI 53705-4652 Office: 777 Highland Ave Madison WI 53705-2222 Office Phone: 608-262-7289.

MUKHERJEE, ABHIJIT, mechanical engineer, educator; b. Kolkata, India, Feb. 28, 1971; s. Pranab Kumar and Chandralekha Mukherjee; m. Mahuya Banerjee, Jan. 20, 2002; 1 child, Aniket. B, Jadavpur U., Kolkata, India, 1993; MME, Villanova U., Pa., 1998; MS, U. Calif., LA, 2000, PhD, 2003. Design engr. Devel. Consultants Ltd., Kolkata, India, 1993—95; engr. mech. auxiliaries and offsites Lurgi, India, New Delhi, 1995—96; post doctoral fellow Rochester Inst. Tech., NY, 2003—05, vis. asst. prof., 2005—06; asst. prof. Mich. Technol. U., Houghton, Mich., 2006—. Vis. instr. Jadavpur U., Kolkata, India, 1995. Vol. ASHA for Edn., India, 2000—07. Recipient U. medal, Jadavpur U., 1993; James R. Birle Rsch. fellow, Villanova U., 1996—98. Mem.: ASME (Jour. Heat Transfer Best Paper award 2006). Achievements include research in complete 3D numerical simulation of nucleate boiling. Office: Michigan Technol Univ 1400 Townsend Dr Houghton MI 49931 Office Phone: 906-487-1174.

MUKHERJEE, AMIYA K., metallurgy and materials science educator; PhD, Oxford U., Eng., 1962. Prof. U. Calif., Davis. Recipient Alexander von Humboldt award Fed. Republic Germany, 1988, Albert Easton White Disting. Tchr. award Am. Soc. Materials, 1992, Pfeil medal and prize Inst. Materials, 1993, U. Calif. prize and citation, 1993, Anatoly Bochvar medal U. Moscow, 1996, Inst. medal Max Planck Inst. for Metallforschung, 1997. Office: U Calif Davis Dept Chem Engring & Material Sci Davis CA 95616 E-mail: akmukherjee@ucdavis.edu.

MUKHERJEE, ANN (ANINDITA MUKHERJEE), advertising executive; b. Kolkata, India, Oct. 26, 1965; married; 2 children. BA, U. Chgo., 1987, MBA, 1994. Product devel. Citibank Diners Club; joined mktg. team Kraft; v.p. mktg. Frito-Lay divsn. PepsiCo, 2006—. Named a Woman to Watch, Advt. Age, 2007. Office: Frito-Lay PO Box 660634 Dallas TX 75266-0634 Office Phone: 972-334-7000. *

MUKHERJEE, ASIT BARAN, geneticist, educator; b. Suri, India; arrived in U.S., 1963; s. Shyama Pada and Sabasana (Chatterjee) M.; m. Tapani Ghoshal; 1 child, Deepro. BS, U. Utah, 1965, MS, 1966, PhD, 1968. Rsch. assoc. Upstate Med. Ctr., Syracuse, NY, 1968-69, Columbia U. Med. Ctr., NYC, 1969-70; instr. Albert Einstein Coll. Medicine, NYC, 1970-72; from asst. prof. to prof. Fordham U., NYC, 1972-83, prof., 1983—. Author, co-author monographs, book chpts.; contbr. over 50 articles to profl. jours. Tchg. fellow U. Utah, 1965-67, Presl. fellow, 1967-68, NIH fellow, 1969-70; grantee W. Alton Jones Found., 1973-83, Whitehall Found., 1977-83, NIH, Minority Access to Rsch. Career, 1984-89. Mem. Gerentol. Soc. Am., Am. Soc. Human Genetics. Office: Fordham U 441 E Fordham Rd Bronx NY 10458-9993 Home Phone: 718-653-1396. Business E-Mail: mukherjee@fordham.edu.

MUKHERJEE, AVINANDAN, business educator; b. Calcutta, West Bengal, India, Apr. 16, 1968; s. Ashok and Puspa Mukherjee. BEE, Jadavpur U., Calcutta, 1990; PhD in Mgmt., Indian Inst. Mgmt., Ahmedabad, 1998. Asst. prof. Nanyang Technol. U., Singapore, 1998—2001, U. Bradford, West Yorkshire, England, 2002—03, Pa. State U., Erie, 2003—04; assoc. prof. Montclair State U., NJ, 2004—. Named One of Best Citizens India award, Internat. Pub. Ho., 1999. Mem.: Acad. Mktg., Am. Mktg. Assn. Achievements include research in marketing in emerging countries; quantitative applications in marketing. Office: Montclair State U 1 Normal Ave Montclair NJ 07043 Home Phone: 973-857-0604; Office Phone: 973-655-5126. Office Fax: 973-655-7673. Personal E-mail: avinandan@hotmail.com. Business E-Mail: mukherjeeav@mail.montclair.edu.

MUKHERJEE, DEBABRATA, cardiologist, researcher; naturalized, USA; s. Prabodh Chandra Mukherjee. MD, Govt. Med. Coll., Nagpur, India, 1988; M in Clin. Rsch., U. Mich., Ann Arbor, 2003. Med. lic. Ohio, Mich., Ky., bd. cert. in internal medicine 1996, bd. cert. in cardiovascular diseases 1999, bd. cert. in interventional cardiology 2000. Fellow in molecular cardiology Cleveland Clinic Found., 1989—92, resident in internal medicine, 1993—96, fellow in clin. cardiology, 1996—99, fellow in interventional cardiology and peripheral vascular interventions, 1999—2000, chief interventional cardiology fellow, 2000—01; dir. peripheral vascular interventions for cardiology, asst. prof. divsn. cardiology U. Mich., 2001—04; Gill Foundation prof. interventional cardiology, dir. peripheral vascular interventions, dir. cardiac catheterization lab U. Ky., Ky., 2006—. Mem. spl. emphasis panel Nat. Heart Lung and Blood Inst., 2003; external reviewer Can. Inst. Health Rsch., 2003. Asst. editor ACC Current Jour. Review, 2002—, internat. editor The Reviews, 2004—, mem. editl. bd. Vascular Disease Prevention, 2003—, Internat. Jour. Angiology, 2005—, Am. Heart Jour., 2005—;, author manual of vascular diseases; reviewer (various manuscripts); contbr. chapters to books. Finalist Astra-Zeneca Young Investigator, 1999, 2000; recipient Recognition award, Indian Coun. Med. Rsch., 1986, LN Jaiswal Gold Medal, 1988, Sadiq Vali Gold Medal, 1988, DB Jaiswal Gold Medal, 1988, Robert C. Tarazi Fellowship award for Excellence in Cardiovascular Rsch., 1990, Joseph Cash Meml. award for excellence in health outcome rsch., 2001; McKay Rsch. grant for peripheral arterial disease, U. Mich. Cardiovascular Ctr., 2003—04. Fellow: Am. Coll. Cardiology, Soc. Vascular Medicine and Biology; mem.: AAAS, AMA, ACP, Am. Heart Assn. (Rsch. fellowship 1990, 1991, Bristol-Myers Squibb Travel award 1997, Grant-in-Aid 1999—2001), Internat. Fedn. Advancement Genetic Engring. and Biotechnology, Am. Coll. Cardiology (mem. cardiac catheterization and intervention com. 2005—08, summit adv. work group 2006—09, Affiliate Travel award 1998, finalist Young Investigator award 1999, First prize for abstract 1999, Career Devel. Award 2002—03, First prize for abstract 2000, William F. Keating Career Devel. award for hypertension and peripheral vascular disease 2002—03). Achievements include research in Impact of combination evidence-based med. therapy on mortality in patients with acute coronary syndromes; Missed opportunities to treat atherosclerosis in patients undergoing peripheral vascular interventions; Risk of cardiovascular events associated with selective COX-2 inhibitors. Office: Univ Ky 326B Wethington Bldg 900 S Limestone St Lexington KY 40536-0200 Office Phone: 859-323-5630. Office Fax: 859-323-6475.

MUKHERJEE, DIPANKAR, surgeon; b. New Delhi, Feb. 9, 1953; BS, U. New Delhi, 1970; MD, All-India Inst. Med. Sci., New Delhi, 1975. Cert. Am. Bd. Surgery, Am. Registry Diagnostic Med. Sonographers. Sr. house officer surgery Auckland Hosp. Bd., New Zealand, 1976—77; intern gen. surgery St. Mary's Hosp., Rochester, NY, 1977—78; resident gen. surgery Genesee, Highland and Rochester Gen. Hosps., 1978—79, 1981—82, Genesee, Rochester Gen. and Strong Meml. Hosps., 1979—82, Rochester Gen. and Strong Meml. Hosps., 1980—81; fellow peripheral vascular surgery St. Vincent Hosp., Portland, Oreg., 1982—83; pvt. practice, 1983—87; chief divsn. vascular surgery Madigan Army Med. Ctr., Tacoma, 1988—90, surg. dir. ICU, 1988—90; active staff Inova Fairfax Hosp., Falls Church, Va., 1990—, Va. Hosp. Ctr., Arlington, 1990—, Columbia Reston Hosp., Va., 1990—, chief dept. surgery, 1998—99; clin. asst. prof. surgery Uniformed Svs. U. Health Scis., F. Edward Herbert Sch. Medicine, Bethesda, Md., 1990—, Georgetown U. Hosp., Washington, 1998—; pvt. practice Cardiac, Vascular and Thoracic Surgery Assocs., P.C., Annandale, Va., 2003—; clin. assoc. prof. surgery and neurol. surgery George Washington U. Sch. Medicine and Health Scis., 2006—. Clin. asst. prof. surgery divsn. vascular surgery Oreg. Health Scis. U. Sch. Medicine, Portland, 1983—88; program co-chmn. Pacific NW Vascular Soc., 1988; pres. India Physicians No. Va., 1995—96; spkr. in field. Contbr. articles to profl. jours. Decorated Army Commendation medal Dept. of the Army; named Outstanding Tchr. of Yr., Georgetown U. Med. Ctr., 1999; named one of Top Doctors, Washingtonian Mag., 1993, 1995, 1999, Area's Outstanding Physician Specialists, Washington Consumers Checkbook, 1996, 1998, Best Doctors in Am., 1998. Fellow: ACS, Soc. for Vascular Surgery (disting.); mem.: Faifax County Med. Soc., Portland Surg. Soc. (program chmn. 1986), Portland Vascular Soc. (program chmn. 1985), NW Vascular Soc., North Pacific Surg. Assn., Internat. Soc. for Endovascular Surgery, Internat. Soc. for Cardiovasc. Surgery, Chesapeake Vascular Soc. (pres.-elect 2004—05). Achievements include patents for catheter introducer for antegrade and retrograde medical procedures. Office: Cardiac Vascular and Thoracic Surgery Assocs 2921 Telestar Ct Ste 140 Falls Church VA 22042

MUKHERJEE, PARTHA S., research scientist; s. Debadi P and Ila Mukherjee; m. Suparna Mukherjee. PhD, Va. Commonwealth U., Richmond, 1996. Study dir. Battelle, Columbus, Ohio, 1996—2000; sr. prin. scientist Pfizer, Ann Arbor, Mich., 2000—05; assoc. prin. scientist Astra-Zeneca, Wilmington, Del., 2005—. Paper screening com. chair AAPS, Arlington, Va., 2001—03. Contbr. scientific papers. Office: Astrazeneca 1800 Concord Pike Wilmington DE 19850 Home Phone: 610-485-1960; Office Phone: 302-885-6992. Business E-Mail: partha.mukherjee@astrazeneca.com.

MUKHERJEE, SANDIP KUMAR, cardiologist; b. India, Oct. 28, 1961; came to U.S, 1965; s. Tridib and Debdasi (Chatterjee) M.; m. Sholeh Moghaddam, Dec. 21, 1985; children: Mina, Alexander. BS, Tex. A&M U., 1982; MD, Tex. Tech U., 1988. Diplomate Am. Bd. Internal Medicine, Am. Bd. Cardiovascular Disease. Intern and resident in internal medicine Yale U. Sch. Medicine, New Haven, 1988-91, chief med. resident, 1991-92, fellow in cardiovascular medicine, 1992-95, asst. clin. prof. medicine, 1996—; ptnr. pvt. practice Cardiology Assocs. of New Haven, P.C. Co-dir. NIH/NHLBI study, 1996—; dir. cardiovascular workshop Yale Med. Sch.; presenter in field. Editl. fellow Med. Letter, 1997—; contbr. articles to profl. jours. Fellow Am. Coll. Cardiology; mem. AMA, ACP, Am. Heart Assn. Clin. Cardiology Coun., Beta Beta Beta. Office: Cardiology Assn New Haven 40 Temple St Ste 6A New Haven CT 06510-2715

MUKHERJEE, SAYANDEV, electrical engineer, researcher; s. Ashok Kumar and Manisha Mukherjee; m. Chandreyee Purkayastha, Jan. 16, 2000; 1 child, Rik Dev. BTech, Indian Inst. Tech., Kanpur, 1991; MS, Cornell U., Ithaca, NY, 1994, PhD, 1997. Mem. tech. staff Bell Lab. Lucent Technologies, Murray Hill, NJ, 1996—2006; sr. staff design engr. Marvell Semiconductor, Santa Clara, Calif., 2006—. Mem.editl. bd. EURASIP Jour. Wireless Comm. and Networking, NYC, 2004—. Mem.: IEEE. Achievements include patents for distributed channel assignment method for the fixed wireless local loop; method to mute a cell phone user in a conference call. Office: Marvell Semiconductor 5488 Marvell Lane Santa Clara CA 95054 Home Phone: 408-553-9957. Personal E-mail: sayandev@hotmail.com. Business E-Mail: sayandev@marvell.com.

MUKHOPADHYAY, SHARMILA MITRA, materials engineer, educator; d. Arun Kumar and Bani Mitra; m. Bhaskar Mukhopadhyay, June 29, 1985; 1 child, Amrita. BS, MS, Indian Inst. Tech.; PhD, Cornell U., 1989. Assoc./asst. prof. Wright Sate U., Dayton, Ohio, 1997—2003, prof. materials sci. and engring., 2003—, dir. Ctr. for Nanoscale Materials, 2007—. Reviewer NSF, 1994—. Editor: MPMD Fifth Global Innovations Procs: Surfaces and Interfacesin Nanostructured Materials; contbr. articles to profl. jours. Recipient cert. for nat. ranking (top 10), Indian Sch. Cert. Orgn., 1977, several scholarship awards, including Nat. Merit scholarship, Indian Inst. Tech. and W.B. Govt., 1981, rsch. awards, NSF, DOE, NASA, AFOSR, EPA, several rsch. grants, Procter & Gamble; Summer Faculty Rsch. fellow, Air Force Rsch. Lab., Propulsion Directorate. Fellow: Am. Ceramic Soc. (exec. com. electronics divsn. 2005—); mem.: Materials Rsch. Soc., Am. Soc. Engring. Edn., TMS (symposium organizer 2003—06), ASM Internat. (exec. com. Dayton chpt. 1998—). Achievements include development of thin film techniques, including fabrication of superconducting oxides from nanoparticles; research in modification of interfaces using plasma; surface activity measurements using XPS; modification of nanostructural materials. Avocations: travel, painting, poetry. Office: Wright State U Mech and Materials Engring Dept Dayton OH 45435 Home Phone: 937-426-1105; Office Phone: 937-775-5092. Business E-Mail: sharmila.mukhopadhyay@wright.edu.

MUKHOTI, BELA BANERJEE, economics professor; b. Vikrampur, Bengal, India, Mar. 1, 1932; came to U.S., 1965; d. Priyanath and Labanya (Ganguli) B.; m. Santi Ranjan Mukhoti, Dec. 14, 1957 (dec. 1988); children: Jayati, Mona. BA in Econs. with honors, Calcutta U., 1950, MA in Econs., 1953; PhD in Econs., London Sch. Econs., 1964. Rsch. specialist U. Ky., Lexington, 1965-66; assoc. prof. Memphis State U., 1966-68, U. No. Iowa, Cedar Falls, 1972-74; asst. prof. Lakehead U., Ont., Canada, 1968-69; rsch. officer Planning Commn. Govt. of India, New Delhi, 1969-71; agrl. economist Econ. Rsch. Svc., USDA, Washington, 1979-86; prof. econs. Rowan U., Glassboro, NJ, 1987—. Author: Agriculture and Employment in Developing Countries--Strategy for Effective Rural Development, 1985; Measures of Development, 1986, International Monetary Fund and Low-Income Countries, 1986, Impact of Agricultural Growth Patterns on Import Demand for Food and Agricultural Commodities, 1983; contbr. articles to profl. jours. Recipient Rhoda Freeman recognition award N.J. Coll. and Univ. Coalition for Women's Edn., 1988, merit award Rowan U., 1989; Sr. Ernest Cassels Trust grantee, 1962-63, Brit. Univ. and Coll. Tchr.'s Assn. grantee, 1964. Mem. Assn. Indian Econ. Studies, Congress Econ. and Polit. Democracy Internat., Am. Friends London Sch. Econs. Hindu. Avocations: horticulture, cooking, photography, travel. Home: 49 E Holly Ave Sewell NJ 08080-2603 Office: Rowan U Dept Econs Bunce Hall Glassboro NJ 08028 E-mail: mukhoti@rowan.edu.

MUKHTAR, MOHAMED HAJI, social sciences educator; b. Huddur, Bakool, Somalia, June 13, 1947; s. Keera Alyow Haydar and Malak Mukhtar Malak Hassan Mursal, Shamsa Sheikh Emet Moallim (Stepmother); children: Saida Mohamed, Salah Mohamed, Subeida Mohamed. MA, Al-Azhar U., Cairo, 1973, PhD, 1983. Cert. translator and interpreter English-Arabic and Arabic-English Polytecnic Ctrl. London, U.K., 1986. Prof. Somali, African and Mid. Ea. history Somali Nat. U., Lafoole Coll., Somalia, 1975—85; assoc. prof. U. Kebangsaan Malaysia, Kuala Lumpur, 1986—90; prof. African and Mid. Ea. history Savannah State U., Ga., 1991—. Chmn. Ergada, Harrisburg, Pa., 1996; pres. Ctr. for Peace Bldg. Initiative, Savannah, 2006; vis. prof. U. SC, Columbia, 1984—85. Author: Methodology of Writing History, 1978, Historical Dictionary of Somalia, 2003, English-Maay Dictionary, 2007; prodr.(and correspondent): BBC programs concerning African history and politics, 1986—; mem. editl. bd.: Islamiyyat, Annual Jour. for U. Kebangsaan Malaysia, 1987—90; editor (with others): Somalia World Bibliographical Series, 1989; mem. internat. adv. bd.: Bildhan, Internat. Quarterly Jour. for Somali Studies, 2001—; contbr. chapters to books, articles to profl. pubs. Advisor Guardians of the Culture, Savannah; mem. global adv. bd. Human Dignity and Humiliation Studies, 2003—; founding mem., mem. exec. bd. Somali Profl. Trust, London, 1997—; advisor Somalia Internat. Rehab. Ctr., Lund, Sweden; mem. internat. com. Red Cross, pres. Savannah chpt., 2004—. Fellow, Istituto Italiano per L'Africa, 1979—80, NEH, 2002; grantee, Swedish Life and Peace Inst., 1993—94; scholar, Arab League Edn. Culture and Sci. Orgn., 1980—82, Fulbright, 1983, 1984—85. Mem.: Royal Inst. Internat. Affairs, UK, Egyptian Hist. Soc., Assn. Muslim Social Scientists, Mid. Ea. Studies Assn., Somali Internat. Studies Assn. (founding mem.), Interriverine Studies Assn. (chmn. 1996—, Chief editor Demenedung 1996—2001), African Studies Assn. Muslim. Home: 1916 E 64th St Savannah GA 31404 Office: Savannah State Univ 3219 College St Savannah GA 31404 Home Phone: 912-354-7270; Office Phone: 912-356-2351. Office Fax: 912-692-4558. Personal E-mail: demenedung@comcast.net. Business E-Mail: mukhtarm@savstate.edu.

MUKOYAMA, JAMES HIDEFUMI, JR., security firm executive; b. Chgo., Aug. 3, 1944; s. Hidefumi James and Miye (Maruyama) M.; m. Kyung Ja Woo, June 20, 1971; children: Sumi Martha, Jae Thomas. BA in English, U. Ill., 1965, MA in Social Studies, 1966; grad. (hon.), US Army Inf. Sch., 1966; grad., US Army Command Gen. Staff Coll., 1979, US Army War Coll., 1984. Registered prin., sr. registered options prin. Nat. Assn. Securities Dealers. Commd. 2d lt. U.S. Army, 1965; advanced through grades to maj. gen. USAR, 1990, ret., 2004; asst. dept. mgr. Mitsui & Co. (USA), Inc., Chgo., 1971-74; mem. Chgo. Bd. Options Exch.,

1974—75; allied mem. N.Y. Stock Exch., 1982-84; v.p. Heartland Securities Inc. & Lefta Advt., Chgo., 1976-90, Fleet Brokerage, Chgo., 1990-95; exec. v.p., COO, Regal Discount Securities, 1995—. Mem. exec. bd. Hillside Free Meth. Ch., Evanston, Ill., 1982-93, participating mem. Willow Creek Ch., 2003-; dir. Chgo. coun. Boy Scouts Am., 1993-95; bd. dirs. Nat. Japanese Am. Meml. Found., 1995-2004; patient vol. Rainbow Hospice, 2003-; vice chair adv. com. minority vets. Dept. VA, 2003-; pres. bd. dirs. Japanese Assn. Svc. Corr. Housing Corp., 2005-. Decorated Silver Star, Legion of Merit, Purple Heart, 3 Bronze Stars, Disting. Svc. medal; Vietnamese Army Cross of Gallantry; Japanese Army Parachutist badge; recipient cert. of merit Korean Army, others. Mem. VFW (life), U. Ill. Alumni Assn. (life), Assn. U.S. Army (life), U.S. Army Warr Coll. Alumni Assn. (life), Army Res. Assn. (pres., founder 1992—), Mil. Order Purple Heart (life), Am. Legion (life), Res. Officers Assn. (life), Sr. Army Res. Comdrs. Assn. (life), Nat. Infantryman's Assn. (life). Home: 4009 Tracey Ct Glenview IL 60025-2468 Office: Regal Securities 950 Milwaukee Ave Ste 101 Glenview IL 60025-3766 Personal E-mail: jhmukoyama@yahoo.com.

MULALLY, ALAN R., automotive company executive, former aerospace company executive; b. Oakland, Calif., Aug. 4, 1945; m. Nicki Mulally; 5 children. BS in Aerospace Engring., U. Kans., 1968, MS in Aerospace Engring., 1969; MA in Mgmt., MIT, 1982. With Boeing Def. and Space Group, Seattle, 1969—2006, v.p. 777 engring., v.p., gen. mgr. 777 divsn., sr. v.p. airplane devel., 1994—97, pres., 1997-99; exec. v.p Boeing Co., 1997—2006; pres. Boeing Comml. Air Group, 1998—2006; pres., CEO Ford Motor Co., Dearborn, Mich., 2006—. Mem. adv. bd. NASA, U. Wash., U. Kans.; mem. sci. adv. bd. USAF. Alfred P. Sloan fellow, 1982; recipient Leadership Tomorrow Program award, Seattle C. of C., 1984, One of 25 Bus. Leaders award, Puget Sound Bus. Jour., 1985, Disting. Engring. Svc. award, U. Kans. Engring. Sch., 1994, Laurels award, Aviation Week and Space Tech. mag., 1996, Engr. of Yr. award, Design News, 1996, Robert J. Collier Trophy (on behalf of 777 team), Nat. Aero. Assn., 1996. Fellow Royal Aero. Soc. (Eng.), AIAA (Tech. Mgmt. award 1986, Reed Aeronautics award 1996); mem. NSPE (Industry Engr. of Yr. 1978), NAE. Avocations: private pilot, reading, tennis, golf. Office: Ford Motor Co 1 American Rd Dearborn MI 48126 *

MULARKEY, MIKE, professional football coach; b. Ft. Lauderdale, Fl, Nov. 19, 1961; m. Betsy Mularkey. Degree in Kinesiology and Sociology, U. Minn. Player Minn. Vikings, 1983—88, Pitts. Steelers, 1989—91; offensive line coach Concordia Coll., 1993; quality control coach Tampa Bay Buccaneers, 1994; tight ends coach Pitts. Steelers, 1996—2000, offensive coord., 2001—03; head coach Buffalo Bills, 2004—05; offensive coord. Miami Dolphins, 2006—.

MULARZ, THEODORE LEONARD, architect; b. Chgo., Nov. 6, 1933; s. Stanley A. and Frances (Baycar) Mularz; m. Ruth L. Larson, Nov. 9, 1963; children: Anne Catherine, Mark Andrew. BArch, U. Ill., 1959. Registered arch., Colo., Oreg. Prin. Theodore L. Mularz, AIA Architects, Aspen, Colo., 1981-90; v.p. Benedict-Mularz Assocs., Inc., 1978-81; pvt. practice Ashland, Oreg., 1990—. Prin. works include numerous archtl. projects, including comml., indsl., religious, recreational, residential and hist. restoration. Vice-chmn. Pitkin County Bd. Appeals, 1972—90; mem. Colo. Bd. Examiners Archs., 1975—85, pres., 1976—80, v.p., 1978; vice-chmn. City of Aspen Bd. Appeals, 1985—90; mem. adv. com. City of Aspen Planning/Bldg. Dept., 1989; bd. dirs. Rogue Valley Symphony, Ashland, 1990—92, treas., 1991—92, chmn. fin. com., 1991—92; mem. Oreg. Bd. Examiners Archs., 1996—2000. With USCGR, 1953—55. Fellow: AIA; mem.: Colo. Soc. Archs. (Cmty. Svc. award 1975), Nat. Coun. Archtl. Registration Bds. (profl. conduct com. 1977—78, procedures/docs. com. 1978—82, chmn. edn. com. 1982—83, bd. dirs. 1982—87, chmn. 1983—84, mem. interprofessional coun. registration 1984—85, exec. com. 1984—87, internat. rels. com. 1984—89, interant. oral exam. com. 1984—89, v.p. 1985, pres. 1985, 1986, broadly experienced arch. interview com. 1987—2001), Aspen Hist. Soc. (com. chmn. 1963—64), Aspen C. of C. (past dir., pres., v.p.), Rotary (dir. Ashland Found. 2001—03, pres. 2001—02). Roman Catholic. Studio: 793 Elkader St Ashland OR 97520-3307 Personal E-mail: tmularz@aol.com.

MULCAHY, ANNE MARIE, printing company executive; b. Rockville Centre, NY, Oct. 21, 1952; d. Thomas and Anne Dolan; m. Joe Mulcahy; 2 children. BA in English & Journalism, Marymount Coll., Tarrytown, NY, 1974. With Chase Manhattan Bank, 1974—76; various mgmt. positions Xerox Corp., 1976—88, v.p. regional gen. mgr., 1988—91, v.p. worldwide mktg. ops. planning, 1991, dir. corp. human resources, 1991—92, v.p. human resources, 1992-95, v.p., staff officer customer ops., 1996-97, sr. v.p., chief staff officer, 1998, pres. gen. markets ops. Stamford, Conn., 1999—2000, COO, 2000—01, pres., 2000—02, CEO, 2001—, chmn., 2002—. Bd. dirs. Xerox Corp., 2000—, Fannie Mae, 2000—, Catalyst, Citigroup Inc., 2004—, Fuji-Xerox Co. Ltd., Target Corp. Named one of Most Powerful Women, Forbes mag., 2005, World's Best CEO, Barron's Mag., 2006, The TIME 100-The People Who Shape Our World, 2006, 100 Most Powerful Women, Forbes Mag., 2006, 50 Most Powerful Women in Bus., Fortune mag., 2006, 50 Women to Watch, Wall St. Jour., 2006. Mem.: Bus. Coun. Office: Xerox Corp 800 Long Ridge Rd Stamford CT 06904-1227 Office Phone: 203-968-3000. Office Fax: 203-968-3218. *

MULCAHY, GABRIEL M., pathologist; b. Jersey City, Feb. 16, 1929; s. Joseph Alphonsus and Anna Elizabeth Mulcahy; m. Vesna Maria Mulcahy, May 24, 1958; children: Mary, Michael, Robert, Richard, Thomas, John, Gabriel Jr. AB, St. Peter's Coll., Jersey City, 1950; MD, Georgetown U., 1954. Diplomate Nat. Bd. Med. Examiners, Am. Bd. Pathology. Intern St. Michaels Hosp., Newark, 1954-55; med. officer U.S. Pub. Health Svc., Crownpoint, N.Mex., 1955-57, resident in pathology Seattle, 1957-59, Staten Island, NY, 1959-61, chief pathology svc. Detroit, 1961-62; with pathology faculty Creighton U., Omaha, 1962-69; dir. pathology Jersey City Med. Ctr., 1969-78; mem. pathology faculty Univ. Medicine and Dentistry N.J., Newark, 1978-2001; chief lab. med. Univ. Hosp., Newark, 1978-2001. Mem. editl bd.: Annals of Clin. and Lab. Sci., 2000—; contbr. articles to profl. jours. Mem. adv. bd. St. Ann's Home for the Aged, Jersey City, 1973-89, sec., 1973-83; pres. bd. edn. St. Paul's Parish Sch., Jersey City, 1973-78. Mem. AAAS, Am. Soc. Human Genetics, Am. Assn. Blood Banks, Assn. Clin. Scientists (sci. coun. 1999—), Coll. Am. Pathologists, Soc. Med. Decision Making. Roman Catholic. Avocations: history, philosophy, philology, photography. Home Phone: 201-434-1897. E-mail: mulcahy@comapp.org, mulcahy21@comcast.net.

MULCAHY, ROBERT EDWARD, management consultant; b. Cambridge, Mass., Mar. 2, 1932; s. George Frances and Hazel (Douglas) M.; m. Ethel Walworth, Nov. 14, 1953; children: Linda, Scott, Steven, Susan. BS, Lowell Textile Inst., 1953. With Allied Chem. Corp., Morristown, NJ, 1953—; from engr. to mktg. mgr. Nat. Aniline div. Allied Corp., 1953-63, from dir. indsl. mktg. to v.p.-mktg. Fibers div., 1963-69, asst. to group v.p., corporate office, 1969, v.p. and gen. mgr.-consumer group Fabricated Products div., 1969-71, pres. Fibers div., 1971-74, group v.p., 1974-75, pres., dir., 1975-79, asst. to chmn. and dir., 1979-80; sr. assoc. The Corp. Dir., Inc., NYC, 1981-83; pres. Counselors to Mgmt. Inc., 1984—.

MULCAHY, ROBERT WILLIAM, lawyer; b. Milw., Jan. 11, 1951; s. T. Larry and Mary Margaret (Chambers) M.; m. Mary M. Andrews, Aug. 3, 1974; children: Molly, Kathleen, Margaret, Michael. BS, Marquette U., 1973, JD, 1976. Staff atty. NLRB, Milw., 1976-79; ptnr. Mulcahy & Wherry, S.C., Milw., 1979-90, Michael, Best & Friedrich, Milw., 1990—. Co-author: Strike Prevention and Control Handbook, 1983, 2d edit., 2006, Comparable Worth: A Negotiator's Guide, 1985, Public Sector Labor Relations in Wisconsin, 1994. Bd. dirs. Milw. Repertory Theater, 1993-97, Gateway Tech. Coll. Found., 2004—; chmn. St. Monica Parish Coun., 1988-96, Charles Allis/Villa Terrace, 1991-, Whitefish Bay Police Commn.; divsn. chmn. United Performing Arts Fund, 1993-94; co-chmn. Villa Terrace Garden Renaissance Project, 2000-04, co-chair, Am. Diabetes Assn., Gala. Mem. ABA, State Bar Wis. (chair labor sect. 1986-87), Milw. Bar Assn. (co-chair labor sect. 1988-95), Nat. Assn. Counties, Nat. Pub. Employers Labor Rels. Assn., Nat. Assn. Coll. & Univ. Attys., Wis. Counties Assn., Indsl. Rels. Rsch. Assn., Mgmt. Resources Assn., Wis. Sch. Attys. Assn., Milw. Area Mcpl. Employers Assn. Office: Michael Best & Friedrich 100 E Wisconsin Ave Ste 3300 Milwaukee WI 53202-4108 E-mail: rwmulcahy@mbf-law.com, rwmulcahy@michaelbest.com.

MULCH, ROBERT F., JR., physician; b. Quincy, Ill., June 21, 1951; s. Robert Franklin and Martha Jo (Nisi) M.; m. Barbara Ann Best, Apr. 5, 1975; children: Matthew, Luke. BS, U. Ill., 1973; MD, Rush Med. Coll., Chgo., 1977. Diplomate Am. Bd. Family Practice; cert. in geriatrics. Intern Riverside Meth. Hosp., Columbus, Ohio, 1977-78, resident in family practice, 1978-80; family physician Hillsboro (Ill.) Med. Ctr., 1980—; ptnr., assoc. med. dir. Springfield Clin., 1998—; pres. med. staff Hillsboro Area Hosp. Asst. clin. prof. family medicine So. Ill. U., Springfield, 1981—90; reviewer Ctrl. Ill. Peer Rev. Orgn.; pres. med. staff Hillsboro Area Hosp. Fellow Am. Acad. Family Practice; mem. Am. Coll. Physician Execs. Lutheran. Avocations: computers, swimming. Office: Hillsboro Med Ctr SC 1250 E Tremont St Hillsboro IL 62049-1912 Office Phone: 217-532-6911. E-mail: rmulch@consolidated.net, rmulch@springfieldclinic.com.

MULCONREY, BRIAN GEORGE, management consultant, futurist; b. Chgo., Ill., Oct. 19, 1953; s. George Thomas and Mary Mulconrey; m. Linda Marie Szopa, Apr. 20, 1974; children: Hailey Kathryn, Matthew George. MS in Fin. Svcs., Am. Coll., Bryn Mawr, Pa., 1985. Chartered fin. cons. Am. Coll.; cert. project mgmt. profl. Project Mgmt. Inst. Consulting prin., dir. mktg. Continuum, Inc. (now CSC, Inc., fin. svcs. divsn.), Austin, Tex., 1983—90; mgmt. cons., futurist BG Mulconrey, Inc., Austin, 1990—. Web log host Global Bus. Network, Emeryville, Calif., 1998—2006; scenario strategist Keystone Equities Group, Oaks, Pa. Author: (study) Role of Brands in the Digital Economy; contbr. articles to nat. and profl. jours. Fellow: Life Office Mgmt. Assn. Achievements include development of literary format for imagining the enterprises of tomorrow called enterprise poetry; detailed business model for launching the personal information management services industry; research in operational blueprints to advance organizational learning called Organizational Learning Laboratories; founded Enterprise Poets prize in Imagining the Future at MIT. Office: BG Mulconrey Inc 6315 Big Cat Cove Austin TX 78750 Office Phone: 512-338-9557. Personal E-mail: brian@mulconrey.com.

MULDAUR, DIANA CHARLTON, actress; b. NYC, Aug. 19, 1938; d. Charles Edward Arrowsmith and Alice Patricia (Jones) M.; m. James Mitchell Vickery, July 26, 1969 (dec. 1979); m. Robert J. Dozier, Oct. 11, 1981. BA, Sweet Briar Coll., 1960. Actress appearing in: Off-Broadway theatrical prodns., summer stock, Broadway plays including A Very Rich Woman, 1963-68; guest appearances on TV in maj. dramatic shows; appeared on: TV series Survivors, 1970-71, McCloud, 1971-73, Tony Randall Show, 1976, Black Beauty, 1978; star: TV series Born Free, 1974, Hizzoner, 1979, Fitz & Bones, 1980, Star Trek: The Next Generation, 1988-89; NBC miniseries and TV series A Year in the Life, 1986; TV movie Murder in Three Acts, The Return of Sam McCloud, 1989; TV series L.A. Law, 1989-91; motion picture credits include McQ, The Lawyer, The Other, One More Train to Rob, Mati, etc. Bd. dirs. Los Angeles chpt. Asthma and Allergy Found. Am.; bd. advisors Nat. Ctr. Film and Video Preservation, John F. Kennedy Ctr. Performing Arts, 1986. Recipient 13th Ann. Commendation award Am. Women in Radio and TV, 1988, Disting. Alumnae award Sweet Briar Coll., 1988. Mem. Acad. Motion Picture Arts and Scis., Screen Actors Guild (dir. 1978), Acad. TV Arts and Scis. (exec. bd., dir., pres. 1983-85), Conservation Soc. Martha's Vineyard Island. Office: Bauman Bedanty & Shaul 5757 Wilshire Blvd Ste 473 Los Angeles CA 90036 Home Phone: 508-627-5070; Office Phone: 310-454-2241.

MULDER, DAVID S., cardiovascular surgeon; b. Eston, Sask., Can., July 28, 1938; s. Peter and Laura (Lovie) M.; m. Norma D. Johnston, Aug. 19, 1961; children— Scott D., Lizabeth J., John C. MD, U. Sask., 1962; M.Sc., McGill U., 1964. Intern, resident in surgery Montreal Gen. Hosp., McGill U., 1963-67; resident in cardiac surgery U. Iowa, 1967-69; surgeon-in-chief Montreal Gen. Hosp., 1977-98; prof. surgery McGill U., 1979—; chmn. dept. surgery, 1993-98. Contbr. articles to med. jours. Fellow: ACS, Royal Coll. Surgeons Can.; mem.: Soc. Thoracic Surgeons (named Order Can. 1997), Am. Assn Thoracic Surgery, Am. Assn. Trauma, Nat. Hockey League Team Physicians Assn., Soc..Univ. Surgeons. Conservative. Home: 76 Sunnyside Ave Westmount PQ Canada H3Y 1C2 Office: Montreal Gen Hosp Room L-512 Montreal PQ Canada H3G 1A4 Home Phone: 514-482-4620; Office Phone: 514-935-4888. Personal E-mail: dsmulder@sympatico.ca. Business E-Mail: david.mulder@muhc.mcgill.ca.

MULDOON, PAUL, poet, educator; b. Portadown, No. Ireland, 1951; came to U.S., 1987; m. Jean Hanff Korelitz; 2 children. BA in English Lang. and Lit., Queen's U., Belfast, No. Ireland, 1973. Prodr. arts programs radio BBC No. Ireland, 1973-78, sr. prodr. arts programs radio, 1978-85, TV prodr., 1985-86; Judith E. Wilson vis. fellow Cambridge U., 1986-87; creative writing fellow U. East Anglia, 1987; Roberta Holloway lectr. U. Calif., Berkeley, 1989; lectr. Princeton U., NJ, 1990—, prof., 1995, dir. creative writing program, 1993—2002, Howard G.B. Clark '21 Univ. Prof. humanities and creative writing, 1998—, founding chair Ctr. for Creative and Performing Arts, 2006—; prof. poetry U. Oxford, 1999—2004. Part-time tchr. writing divsn. Sch. of Arts, Columbia U., 1987-88; part-time tchr. creative writing program Princeton U., 1987-88; vis. prof. U. Mass., Amherst, 1989-90. Author: (poetry) Knowing My Place, 1971, New Weather, 1973, Spirit of Dawn, 1975, Mules, 1977, Immram, 1980, Why Brownlee Left, 1980, Out of Siberia, 1982, Quoof, 1983, Selected Poems 1968-83, 1986, Meeting the British, 1987, Madoc: A Mystery, 1990, Incantata, 1994, The Prince of the Quotidian, 1994, The Annals of Chile, 1994, Hay, 1998, Moy Sand and Gravel, 2002, Reverse Flannery: Magical Tales of Ireland, 2003, Medley for Morin Khur, 2005, Sixty Instant Messages to Tom Moore, 2005, Horse Latitudes, 2006, others, (criticism) To Ireland, I, 2000, The End of the Poem, 2006, (opera libretto) Shining Brow, 1993, Bandanna, 1999, (TV play) Monkeys, 1989, (translation from Irish) The Astrakhan Cloak, 1993, (children's book) The O-O's Party, 1981, The Noctuary of Narcissus Batt, 1997; editor: (poetry) The Scrake of Dawn, 1979, The Faber Book of Contemporary Irish Poetry, 1986, The Essential Byron, 1989, The Faber Book of Beasts, 1997; contbr. to anthologies. Recipient Eric Gregory award, 1972, Sir Geoffrey Faber Meml. award, 1980, 91, T.S. Eliot prize, 1994, Acad. award in lit. Am. Acad. Arts and Letters, 1996, Irish Times prize for poetry, 1997, Pulitzer Prize for poetry, 2003, Griffin Internat. prize excellence in poetry, 2003, Shakespeare prize, 2004, Aspen prize for poetry, 2005, Am. Ireland Fund Lit. award, 2004; John Simon Guggenheim Meml. fellow, 1990. Fellow Royal Soc. Lit.; mem. Am. Acad. Arts and Scis., Aosdana. Office: Princeton Univ Rm 122 185 Nassau St Princeton NJ 08544-0001 Office Phone: 609-258-4708. E-mail: muldoon@princeton.edu.

MULDOON, ROBERT JOSEPH, JR., lawyer; b. Somerville, Mass., Nov. 16, 1936; s. Robert Joseph and Catherine Eileen (Hurley) M.; m. Barbara Joyce Mooney, Aug. 24, 1968; children: Andrew Robert, Catherine Lane, Timothy John. AB, Boston Coll., 1960, MA, 1961, LLB, 1965. Bar: Mass. 1965, U.S. Tax Ct. 1966, U.S. Supreme Ct. 1970. Law clk. Supreme Jud. Ct. Mass., 1965-66; assoc. Withington, Cross, Park & Groden, Boston, 1966-71, ptnr., 1972-82, Sherin and Lodgen, LLP, Boston, 1982—. Mem. Bd. Bar Examiners Mass., 1974-2006, chmn., 2005-06; chmn. Nat. Conf. Bar Examiners, 1985-86; pres. Mass. Continuing Legal Edn., Inc., 1992-94. Trustee Boston Coll. H.S., 1990-96, chmn. bd. trustees, 1995-96. Fellow Am. Coll. Trial Lawyers; mem. Am. Law Inst., Boston Bar Assn., Curtis Club, Nisi Prius Club, Tavern Club. Office: Sherin and Lodgen LLP 101 Federal St Boston MA 02110 Office Phone: 617-646-2225. Business E-Mail: rjmuldoon@sherin.com.

MULÉ, ANN C., oil industry executive; b. Phila., Oct. 22, 1956; BA magna cum laude, St. Joseph's U., 1978; JD cum laude, Villanova U., 1981. Bar: Pa. 1981, U.S. Supreme Ct. 1988. From atty. to chief governance officer Sunoco Inc., Phila., 1980—2002, chief governance officer, 2002—. Bd. dirs. Phila. Zoo; mem. adv. bd. Ctr. Corp. Governance, U. Del. Mem.: ABA, Am. Corp. Counsel Assn. (vice chmn. exec. counsel, mem. corp. and securities law com.), Phila. Bar Assn., Pa. Bar Assn. (chmn. bus. law sect., mem. bd. govs., chmn. com. securities regulation, mem. title 15 task force), Am. Soc. Corp. Secs. (bd. dir., mem. exec. steering com., mem. nat. conf. com., mem. corp. practices com.). Office: Sunoco Inc Mellon Bank Ctr 1735 Market St Ste LL Philadelphia PA 19103

MULETA, JOHN B., lawyer; b. Addis Ababa, Ethiopia, Dec. 13, 1964; BS in Sys. Engring., Univ. Va., 1986, MBA, JD, Univ. Va., 1993. Bar: Va. 1993. With GTE Corp; co-founder OI Systems Inc; pres., CEO Source 1 Technologies LLC; pres. PSINet India, Middle East and Africa Divsn., PSINet's Global Facilities Divsn., PSINet Ventures, Inc., Washington, 1998—2000; with Coopers & Lybrand Consulting, LLC; dep. bur. chief, Common Carrier Bur. to chief, Enforcement Divsn. FCC, 1994—98; chief FCC Wireless Telecom. Bur.; ptnr., co-chair comm. group Venable LLP, Washington. Office: Venable LLP 575 Seventh St NW Washington DC 20004 Office Phone: 202-344-4281. Office Fax: 202-344-8300. Business E-Mail: jmuleta@venable.com.

MULEY, ARUN, aerospace engineer; s. Hari Mahadev and Sudha Muley; m. Tejashree Chawla, Mar. 1, 2002. B of Tech., U. Calicut, India, 1988; MS, U. Cin., 1992, PhD, 1997. Sr. staff engr. Honeywell Aerospace, Torrance, Calif., 2001—03, prin. engr., 2003—. Mem. editl. bd. Internat. Jour. Heat Exchangers, 2003—. Recipient Site Vision award, Honeywell Aerospace, 2001. Mem.: ASME (vice chair exec. com. process industries divsn. 2003—, chair K-10 heat transfer equipment com. heat transfer divsn. 2004—, Outstanding Svc. award 2003). Avocations: tennis, running, travel. Office: Honeywell Aerospace 2525 W 190 St ML 36-1-93055 Torrance CA 90504 Home Phone: 310-377-0792; Office Phone: 310-512-1827. Office Fax: 310-512-3320. Personal E-mail: arun.muley@gmail.com. Business E-Mail: arun.muley@honeywell.com.

MULFORD, DAVID CAMPBELL, ambassador, former finance company executive; b. Rockford, Ill., June 27, 1937; s. Robert Lewis Mulford and Theodora Henie Countryman; m. Jeannie Louise Simmons, Oct. 19, 1985; children: Robert Ian, Edward Maitland. BA cum laude in Econs., Lawrence U., 1959; postgraduate student, U. Cape Town, South Africa, 1960; MA in Polit. Sci., Boston U., 1962; PhD, Oxford U., 1966; LLD (hon.), Lawrence U., 1984. White House fellow US Dept. Treasury, Washington, 1965-66, under asst. sec. internat. affairs, 1984-89; dir. White Weld & Co., NYC and London, 1966-74; sr. investment adv. Saudi Arabian Monetary Agy., Riyadh, 1974-84; asst. sec. internat. affairs US Dept. Treasury, 1984-89, under sec. treasury internat. affairs Washington, 1989-92; vice chmn. CS First Boston, NYC, 1992—93; chmn. Credit Suisse First Boston, London, 1993-98, internat. chmn., 1998—2003; US amb. to India US Dept. State, New Delhi, 2004—. Author: Northern Rhodesia General Election, 1962, Zambia: The Politics of Independence, 1967. Trustee Lawrence U., 1986—. Decorated Legion d'Honneur, 1990; recipient Order of May Merit Pres. Argentina, 1993, Officers Cross of the Medal of Merit Pres. Poland, 1995; Rotary Internat. fellow Oxford U., U. Cape Town, 1961-62, Woodrow Wilson fellow Boston U., Oxford U., 1962, Ford Found. fellow St. Anthony's Coll., Oxford, 1963-65; named Disting. Alumni Boston U., 1992; Disting. scholar Ctr. Strategic and Internat. Studies, Washington, 1993—. Mem. Coun. Fgn. Rels., White House Fellows Assn., Met. Club, Washington. Republican. Office: US Dept State 9000 New Delhi Pl Washington DC 20521-9000 *

MULFORD, RICHARD ALBERT, mechanical engineer, professional society administrator; b. Phila., Dec. 13, 1930; s. William Abernathy and Jeanne Ann (Roy) Mulford. BSME, U. Pa., 1952, MS in Mech. Engring., 1957; Diploma in Bus., Dartmouth Coll., 1985. Registered profl. engr., Pa. Engr. Phila. Elec. Co., 1952-64, sr. engr., 1964-67, project mgr., 1967-85, staff engr., 1985-91; exec. dir. Engrs. Club of Phila., 1991—. Vol. Paoli Meml. Hosp., Pa., 1991—; donor Phila. Orch. Assn., 1980—; treas., donor Phila. Engring. Found., 1991—. Recipient Disting. Svc. award, Pa. Soc. Profl. Engrs., 1991, 1998, D. Robert Yarnall award (Outstanding Engring. Alumnus), U. Pa., 1981, Alumni award of merit, 1993, Presdl. award, Phila. sect. ASCE, 2002, Outstanding Svc. award, Del. Valley Engrs. Week Coun., 2003. Fellow: Engrs. Club Phila. (sec.-treas. 1953—, George Washington medal 1988); mem.: NSPE, Union League Phila. (scholarship trustee 1963—), Racquet Club Phila. Republican. Achievements include patents in field. Avocations: classical music, antique cars, home and lawn maintenance. Home: 1231 Wisteria Dr Malvern PA 19355-9736 Office: Engrs Club of Phila 215 S 16th St Ste 36 Philadelphia PA 19102-3349 Home Phone: 610-644-1983; Office Phone: 215-985-5701. Business E-Mail: info@engrclub.org.

MULHERN, EDWIN JOSEPH, lawyer; b. Bklyn., Mar. 8, 1927; s. Edward Thomas and Jennie (Keenan) M.; m. Maureen P. Purcell, Oct. 2, 1964; children: Edwin T., Deborah J., Kevin T. BBA, St. John's U., 1950, LLB, 1954. Bar: N.Y. 1954, U.S. Dist. Ct. (ea. and so. dists.) N.Y. 1954, U.S. Supreme Ct. 1960. Sr. acct. Susquehanna Mills Inc., N.Y.C., 1947-53; chief acct. Rockwood Chocolate Co., Bklyn., 1953-54; trial atty. Allstate Ins. Co., Freeport, N.Y., 1954-57; claims rep. State Farm Ins. Co., Hempstead, N.Y., 1957-58; sole practice, Bellmore, N.Y., 1958-70, Mineola, N.Y., Carle Place, N.Y., 1970—; mem. joint grievance com. for 10th jud. dist. (N.Y.), 1981-89. Pres. Christian Bros. Boys' Assn., 1975-82; bd. dirs. Legal Aid Soc. of Nassau County, 1980—. Served with USAAF, 1945-46. Mem. ABA, N.Y. State Bar Assn., Nassau Bar Assn. (bd. dirs. 1981-83, chmn. admissions com. 1979, chmn. grievance com. 1980-82), Suffolk County Bar Assn., Nassau Lawyers Assn. (pres. 1975, exec. dir. 1993—, Man of Yr. 1981), Criminal Cts. Bar Assn. of Nassau County (pres. 1976), Criminal Cts. Bar Assn. of Suffolk County, Am. Assn. Trial Lawyers. Clubs: University of L.I. (Hempstead), K.C. (new Hyde Park, N.Y.). Office: 1 Old Country Rd Ste 145 Carle Place NY 11514-1801 Office Phone: 516-294-8000.

MULHERN, MARTIN ROBERT, engineer; b. New Brunswick, NJ, June 12, 1946; s. Thomas Desmond and Helen Casserly M. BS in Civil Engring., U. Calif., Berkeley, 1968; MS in Civil Engring., U. Wash., 1982. Cert. inshore/offshore hydographer Am. Congress of Surveying and Mapping; unltd. master merchant marine lic. USCG. Structures weights engr. The Boeing Co., Everett, Wash., 1968; capt. NOAA Corps., Silver Spring, Md., 1969-98; cons. Boulder, Colo., 1998-2001. NOAA rep. U. Nat. Oceanographic Lab. System, Silver Spring, 1992-96; comdg. officer NOAA ship Whiting. Recipient H. Arnold Karo award Soc. of Am. Mil. Engrs., 1980, 88. Mem. The Oceanography Soc. (charter, life mem.), Soc. Am. Mil. Engrs. (life), Am. Geophys. Union (life), The Hydrographic Soc. Achievements include conducting geodetic and hydrographic surveys with the Nat.

Ocean Survey, extensive duty with labs. and hdqtrs. of the Office of Atmospheric and Oceanographic Rsch. Office: PO Box 19545 Boulder CO 80308-2545 E-mail: mmulhern@attglobal.net.

MULHOLLAN, DANIEL PATRICK, research director; b. Louisville, July 12, 1944; s. Daniel Paul and Martha Nell (McClain) M.; m. Julianne Finlayson, June 3, 1967; children: Willa Joanna Mulhollan Neale, Erin Finlayson, Julianne Gertrude. BA with honors, Coll. St. Thomas, St. Paul, 1966; PhD, Georgetown U., 1969. Analyst Am. nat. govt., Govt. and Gen. Rsch. Div., Legis. Reference Svc. Libr. of Congress, Washington, 1969, mem. Mgmt. and Planning Com., 1987, sec. divsn. head Congl. Rsch. Svc., 1973—81, asst. chief govt. divsn. Congl. Rsch. Svc., 1981, chief govt. divsn. Congl. Rsch. Svc., 1991—94, dir. Congl. Rsch. Svc., 1994—, acting dep. libr., 1992-94. Cons. Georgetown U., Washington, 1990-92; bd. visitors Sch. Info. Scis., U. Pitts., 1995; mem. adv. bd. Ind. U. Libr. Contbr. essays to book and articles to profl. jours. GE scholar, 1962; NDEA fellow, 1966. Mem. ALA, Am. Polit. Sci. Assn. (mem. centennial exec. com.), Midwest Polit. Sci. Assn. Roman Catholic. Office: Library of Congress Congressional Rsch Svc 101 Independence Ave, SE Washington DC 20540-0001 *

MULHOLLAND, JANET LYNN HEALY, retired language educator, writer; b. Mishawaka, Ind., Oct. 30, 1950; m. Thomas J. Mulholland Sr., July 3, 1993. BA, Ind. U., South Bend, 1974, MEd, 1980; postgrad., No. Ill. U., DeKalb, Ill. Renewal Inst. Spanish tchr. Concord Jr. HS, Concord HS, Elkhart, Ill., 1974—77, Schaumburg Sch. Dist., Ill., 1977—2005; ret., 2005. Presenter in field. Author, illustrator: Chico Chile books and games. Home: 215 River Park Dr Middlebury IN 46540-8782

MULHOLLAND, JULIE A., marketing executive; b. Aug. 21, 1967; Student, NYU. With McCann Erickson Worldwide, 1989—95, Wells, Rich, Greene; account mgr. Publicis USA; founder, pres., CEO Mulholland Drive Entertainment, Ltd., L.A., NYC, 2003—. Named a Woman to Watch, Advt. Age, 2007; recipient Co-Branded Audiovisual, Key Art Award, 2004. Office: Mulholland Drive Entertainment Ltd 1023 N Orlando Ave West Hollywood CA 90069 E-mail: jmulholland@mulholland.com. *

MULHOLLAND, MICHAEL WILLIAM, surgeon, researcher; b. Decatur, Ill., Nov. 2, 1953; s. Roger Lloyd and Shirley Marie (Witt) M.; m. Patricia Mary Heyhoer. BA, Northwestern U., 1975, MD, 1978; PhD, U. Minn., 1985. Diplomate Am. Bd. Surgery. Prof. surgery U. Wash., Seattle, 1985-88; asst. prof. surgery U. Mich., Ann Arbor, 1988-91, assoc. prof. surgery, 1991-95, prof. surgery, 1995—, chmn. dept. surgery, 2002—, Frederick A. Coller disting. prof. surgery. Cons. NIH, Bethesda, Md., 1994—. Author, editor: Reoperative Surgery, 1988, Review for Surgery: Scientific Principles, 1992, 2d edit., 1997; editor: Surgery: Scientific Principles, 1991, 3d edit., 2001, Digestive Tract Surgery, 1995. Mem. AMA, Assn. for Acad. Surgery, Soc. Univ. Surgeons, Ctrl. Surg. Soc., Western Surg. Soc., Assn. Am. Coll. Surgeons, Midwest Surg. Assn., Am. Surg. Assn., Am. Physiol. Soc., Am. Gastroenterol. Assn., Soc. for Surgery of the Alimentary Tract, Inst. Medicine. Achievements include studies of neural control of pancreatic function; investigations of enteric nervous system. Office: Univ Mich Health Sys 2101 Taubman Ctr 0346 1500 E Medical Center Dr Ann Arbor MI 48109 Office Phone: 313-936-3236. E-mail: micham@umich.edu.

MULHOLLAND, PAUL A., gas industry executive; BS, Drexel U., 1975, MBA, 1978. Mgr. fin., mergers and acquisitions Sunoco Inc., Phila., 1993—97, dir. corp. fin., 1997—2000, treas., 2000—, Sunoco Logistics Ptnrs., 2002—. Office: Sunoco Inc Ten Penn Ctr 1801 Market St Philadelphia PA 19103-1699

MULHOLLAND, WILLIAM DAVID, JR., retired bank executive; b. Albany, NY, June 16, 1926; s. William David and Helen E. (Flack) M.; m. Nancy Louise Booth, June 22, 1957; children: William David III, Charles Douglass, James Andrew, John Alexander, Elizabeth Helen, Madeline Louise, Sarah Alexandra, Caroline Marie, Bruce Henry. AB cum laude, Harvard U., 1950, MBA, 1952; LLD, Meml. U., 1972, Queens U., 1988. Mem. staff Morgan Stanley & Co., NYC, 1952-61, gen. ptnr., 1962-69; pres., chief exec. officer Brinco Ltd., Montreal, Que., Can., 1970-74, Churchill Falls (Labrador) Corp. Ltd., 1970-74; pres. Bank of Montreal, 1975-81, chief exec. officer, 1979-89, chmn. bd., 1981-90. Bd. dirs., mem. exec. com. Bank of Montreal, Can. Pacific Ltd., Upjohn Co.; bd. dirs. Brooks Fashion Stores, Kimberly-Clark Corp., Harris Bank Corp., Chgo., Rio Tinto-Zinc Corp., London, Standard Life Assurance Corp., Edinburgh, Consol. Bathhurst Corp.; chmn. exec. com. Bank of Montreal, Upjohn. Life gov. Douglas Hosp., Montreal; hon. v.p. Quebec provincial coun. Boy Scouts Can.; mem. adv. com. Ecole des Hautes Etudes Commerciales, Montreal; mem. adv. coun. Ctr. Can. Studies Sch. Advanced Internat. Studies Johns Hopkins U.; bd. dirs. Atlantic Salmon Fedn., St. Michael's Coll. Found., Mounted Police Found., Conf. Bd. Can., Monreal Symphony Orch.; trustee Hudson Inst., Queen's U., Kingston, Can. Olympic Trust; fin. com. Queen's U.; nat. co-chmn. Can. Coun. Christians and Jews. Served as officer, inf. U.S. Army, 1944-46, PTO. Decorated Knight Comdr.'s Cross (Badge and Star) Order of Merit, Fed. Republic of Germany, 1989, Prime Minister's medal State of Israel, 1987; recipient Human Rels. award, Good Servant's medal Can. Coun. Christians and Jews, 1985. Mem. Mount Royal Club (Montreal), Caledon Riding and Hunt Club, Toronto Club. Roman Catholic. Office: Bank of Montreal 302 Bay St Ste 400 Toronto ON Canada M5X 1A1 Office Phone: 416-867-7611.

MULHOLLEM, PAUL B., agricultural products executive; m. Valerie Mulhollem; 1 child, Claire Jean. Grad., U. Minn., 1971. Mng. dir. Archer Daniels Midland Internat. Ltd., London, 1992—96; v.p. Archer Daniels Midland Co., 1996—97, group v.p., 1997—99, sr. v.p. Global Oilseeds & Cocoa Decatur, Ill., 1999—2001, sr. v.p., Global Grain Ops., 2001, pres. & CEO, 2001—. Mem. Alfred C. Toepfer Internat. Bd., Agricore United Bd., Carle Found., Champaign, Ill. Office: Archer Daniels Midland Co 4666 Faries Pkwy Decatur IL 62526

MULKERN-KOLOSEY, SANDY KATHLEEN, college counselor, educator, realtor; d. Thomas Joseph and Elizabeth (Bjornson) Mulkern; m. Michael George Kolosey, July 15, 1972; 1 child, Michael Thomas Kolosey. AA, Coll. Marin, Kentfield, Calif., 1989, AS in Dental Assisting with honors, 1989; BA in Clin. Psychology summa cum laude, San Francisco State U., 1991; MA in Counseling, Psychology, Edn., U. San Francisco, 1993, EdD in Orgn. and Leadership, 2006. Cert. in pupil pers. svcs., psychol. svcs. Acad. advisor, counselor Santa Rosa (Calif.) Jr. Coll., 1992—. Ednl. cons., San Francisco Bay area, 1994; career coach and workshop facilitator, Sonoma County. Mem. AAUW, APA, Alumni Assn. U. San Francisco and San Francisco State U., Golden Key Nat. Honor Soc., N. Bay Assn. Realtors and Bay Area Real Estate Info. Sys., Psi Chi, Alpha Gamma Sigma, Phi Delta Kappa. Avocations: bicycling, reading, computers, travel, real estate investing. Home: PO Box 543 Valley Ford CA 94972

MULKEY, JACK CLARENDON, retired library director; b. Shreveport, La., Oct. 31, 1939; s. Jack Youmans and Hilda Lillian (Beatty) Mulkey; m. Mary Lynn Shepherd, Jan. 30, 1971; 1 child, Mary Clarendon. BA, Centenary Coll., 1961; postgrad. (Rotary scholar), U. Dijon, France, 1961-62, Duke U. Law Sch., 1962-63; MS, La. State U., 1969. Jr. exec. Lykes Bros. S.S. Co., 1964-66; asst. dir. admissions Centenary Coll. of La., 1966-67; head reference services and acquisitions Shreveport Pub. Library, 1968-71; dir. Green Gold Library System of N.W. La., 1971-73; mgmt. cons. Miss. Library Commn., 1973-74, asst. dir., 1974-76, dir., 1976-78, Jackson Met. Library System, 1978-85; assoc. dir. Ark. State Library, 1986-2000; State Librarian of Ark., 2000—05; ret., 2005. Adj. prof. U. So. Miss. Grad. Sch. Libr. Sci., 1979—; treas., bd. dirs. Southeastern Library Network (SOLINET), 1985-86; cons. in field; mem. White House Conf. Taskforce on Libraries and Info. Services, 1980—. Chmn. Miss. Govs. Conf. on Libraries, 1979; chmn. Miss. delegation White House Conf. on Libraries, 1979; hon. del. White House Conf. on Librs., 1991. Served with USAF, 1963-64. Mem. ALA (chmn. state libr. agy. sect. 1995-97), Southeastern Libr. Assn. (bd. dirs. 1994—), Miss. Libr. Assn. (pres. 1981-82), Ark. Libr. Assn. (exec. bd. dirs. 1994—), Chief Officers of State Libr. Agys., Phi Alpha Delta, Beta Phi Mu, Omicron Delta Kappa, Phi Kappa Phi. Episcopalian. Home: 1805 Martha Dr Little Rock AR 72212-3840 Office: 1 Capitol Mall Little Rock AR 72201-1049 Personal E-mail: jmulkey@webtv.net.

MULL, GALE W., lawyer; b. Hillsdale, Mich., Sept. 8, 1945; s. Wayne E. and Vivian M. (Bavin) M.; m. Holly Ann Allen, Aug. 2, 1969 (div. Nov. 1983); 1 child, Carter B.; m. Jeanne Anne Haughey, Aug. 18, 1985. BA, Mich. State U., 1967; MA in Sociology, Ind. U., 1969; JD, Emory U., 1972. Bar: Ga. 1972, U.S. Dist. Ct. (no. dist.) Ga. 1972, U.S. Ct. Appeals (5th cir.) 1973, U.S. Ct. Appeals (11th cir.) 1981. Instr. sociology Clemson (S.C.) U., 1968-69, Spelman Coll., Atlanta, 1969-70; pvt. practice, Atlanta, 1972-75; ptnr. Mull & Sweet, Atlanta, 1975-81; pres. Gale W. Mull, P.C., Atlanta, 1981—. Bd. dirs. BOND Community Fed. Credit Union, Atlanta, 1975-81; directing atty. Emory Student Legal Services, Atlanta, 1975-91; Sociology instr. Clemson U., Clemson, S.C., 1968-69, Spelman Coll., Atlanta, Ga., 1969-70. Pres. Inman Park Restoration, Inc., Atlanta, 1972—74, BASS Orgn. for Neighborhood Devel., Inc., 1974—78; mem. Housing Appeals Bd., Atlanta, 1982—88, Mayor's Task Force on Prostitution, 1984—86; bd. dirs. Trinity Towers, Inc., 1999—2000; vestry St. John's Episc. Ch., 1992—99, 2003—05, sr. warden, 1998—99, 2005—06; bd. dirs. St. John's Episcopal Day Sch., 1992—97, Bethlehem Ministries, 1997—, ACLU Ga., 1981—92, sec. bd. dirs., 1983—85, cooperating atty., 1972—. Mem. ABA, Ga. Bar Assn., Atlanta Bar Assn., Lawyers Club Atlanta. Clubs: Quail Unltd. (bd. dirs., sec. 1984-86). Office: 2149 Rugby Ave Atlanta GA 30337 Office Phone: 404-761-6600. Personal E-mail: g_mull@bellsouth.net.

MULL, STEPHEN D., federal agency administrator, former ambassador; b. Reading, Pa., Apr. 30, 1958; m. Cheryl Stephan; 1 child, Ryan. BS, Georgetown U., 1980. Joined Fgn. Svc. US Dept. State, 1982, dep. exec. sec., dir. So. Europe, dep. dir. Ops. Ctr., US Ambassador to Lithuania, 2003—06, prin. dep. asst. sec. Bur. Polit.-Mil. Affairs Washington, 2006, acting asst. sec., 2007—; dep. chief of mission US Embassy, South Africa, Jakarta, Indonesia, counselor polit. & polit.-military affairs Poland. Decorated Knight's Order of Merit Poland; recipient Baker-Wilkins Award, Presdl. Meritorious Svc. Award, 2002. Office: US Dept State 2201 C St NW Washington DC 20520 *

MULLALLY, MEGAN, actress; b. LA, Nov. 12, 1958; d. Carter and Martha Mullally; m. Michael A. Katcher, 1992 (div. 1996); m. Nick Offerman, Sept. 20, 2003. Student, Northwestern U. Actor: (TV films) Rainbow Drive, 1990, Winchell, 1998, Everything Put Together, 2000, Lifetime, The Pact, 2002; (TV series) My Life and Times, 1991, Ellen Burstyn Show, 1986, Fish Police, 1992, Rachel Gunn, RN, 1992, Will and Grace, 1998—2006 (Emmy Award Supporting Actress in a Comedy, 2000, Outstanding Comedy Series award, 2000, Am. Comedy Award, 2001, Outstanding Female Actor Award, 2001, Screen Actors Guild award Oustanding Actress in a Comedy Series, 2001, 2002, 2003, Emmy award for Outstanding Supporting Actress in a Comedy Series, 2006); (Broadway plays) Grease, 1994, How to Succeed in Business Without Really Trying, 1995—96; host (talk show) Megan Mullally Show, 2006—07; actor: (films) Once Bitten, 1985, Last Resort, 1986, About Last Night, 1986, Anywhere But Here, 1999, Best Man in Grass Creek, 1999, Everything Put Together, 2000, Monkey Bone, 2001, Stealing Harvard, 2002; actor, actor: (films) Speaking of Sex, 2001, (voice) Teacher's Pet, 2004, Rebound, 2005, (guest appearance): (TV series) Murder, She Wrote, 1988, China Beach, 1989, Wings, 1990, Herman's Head, 1991, Seinfeld, 1993, Frasier, 1997, Mad About You, 1997, Caroline in the City, 1997, Just Shoot Me!, 1998, 3rd Rock from the Sun, 2000; (TV series, voice) King of the Hill, 2002. Office: The Gersh Agency PO Box 5617 Beverly Hills CA 90210

MULLAN, BRIAN, medical educator; b. Chgo., Apr. 21, 1963; s. Sean F. and Vivian C. Mullan; m. Karyn Shanks; children: Sean, Aidan. BA, Johns Hopkins U., Balt., 1985; MS, Northwestern U., Evanston, Ill., 1986; MD, U. Chgo. Med. Sch., 1991. Diplomate Am. Bd. Radiology, 1996. Assoc. prof and vice-chair dept. radiology U. Iowa, Iowa City, 2003—, chair, med. edn. com. Carver Coll. Medicine, 2004—06. Author: jour. articles in field. Recipient Collegiate Tchg. Award, U. Iowa, 2004, Louis D. Holloway award for Rsch. in Health Scis. Edn., 2004, Tchr. of Yr. for Med. Student Tchg., Dept. Radiology, Carver Coll. Medicine, U. Iowa, 1997, 1998, 1999, 2005. Office: Univ Iowa Dept Radiology 200 Hawkins Dr Iowa City IA 52245 Office Phone: 319-356-3562. Business E-Mail: brian-mullan@uiowa.edu.

MULLAN, FITZHUGH, public health physician; b. Tampa, Fla., July 22, 1942; s. Hugh and Mariquita (MacManus) Mullan; children: Meghan Elizabeth, Jason Michael, Caitlin Patricia. BA, Harvard U., 1964; MD, U. Chgo., 1968; DSc, U. Osteo. Medicine, 1993; LHD, Coll. Osteo. Medicine Pacific, 1993. Intern Jacobi Hosp., Bronx, 1968—70; resident Lincoln Hosp., Bronx, 1970—72; physician Nat. Health Svc. Corps., Santa Fe, 1972—75; dir. Nat. Health Svc. Corps, Rockville, Md., 1977—81; scholar-in-residence Inst. Medicine, Washington, 1981—82; dir. pub. health history project Office of Surgeon Gen., Rockville, 1988—90; sr. med. officer NIH, Bethesda, Md., 1982—84; sec. for health and environment State of N.Mex., Santa Fe, 1984—85; assoc. prof. Johns Hopkins Sch. Hygiene and Pub. Health, Balt., 1986—88; dir. bur. health professions USPHS, Rockville, 1990—96; contbr. editor Health Affairs, Bethesda, 1996—; clin. prof. pediats. and pub. health George Washington U., 1996—; staff physician Upper Cardozo Cmty. Health Ctr., 1996—; Asst. Atty. Gen. US Pub. Health Svc. Author: White Coat, Clenched Fist: The Political Education of an American Physician, 1976, Vital Signs: A Young Doctor's Struggle With Cancer, 1983, Plagues and Politics: The Story of the United States Public Health Service, 1989; contbr. articles to profl. jours.; contbg. editor: Health Affairs, narrative matters section. Fellow: Am. Acad. Pediats.; mem.: Inst. of Medicine of NAS, Am. Assn. for History of Medicine, APHA, AMA. Office: Health Affairs 7500 Old Georgetown Rd Ste 600 Bethesda MD 20814-6133

MULLANE, DENIS FRANCIS, insurance company executive; b. Astoria, NY, Aug. 28, 1930; s. Patrick F. and Margaret (O'Neill) M.; m. Kathryn Mullman, June 28, 1952; children: Gerard, Kevin, Denise. BS in Mil. Engring, U.S. Mil. Acad., 1952; LHD (hon.), U. Conn., 1988, St. Joseph's Coll., 1990; LLD (hon.), U. Hartford, 1993, Trinity Coll., Hartford, Conn., 1995; MS in Fin. Svcs., The Am. Coll., Bryn Mawr, Pa., 1995. CLU. With Conn. Mut. Life Ins. Co., Hartford, 1956—, v.p., 1969-72, sr. v.p., 1972-74, exec. v.p., 1974-76, pres., 1977—, chief exec. officer, 1983-85, chmn., chief exec. officer, 1985-90, chief exec. officer, pres., 1990-93; chmn. Mulane Enterprises, Inc., Hartford, Conn., 1994—; with Mullane Enterprises, West Hartford, Conn., 1994—. Bd. dirs. Conn. Natural Gas Co.; chmn. The Am. Coll., Bryn Mawr, Pa., 1993-96; chmn. joint planning com. Am. Coll. and Soc. Fin. Svcs. Profls., 1996-99. Dir. U.S. Chamber, 1991-95. 1st lt. C.E., U.S. Army, 1952-56. Recipient John Newton Russell award, 1987, Knight of St. Gregory award, Disting. Grad. award USMA, 2004. Mem.: Assn. Grads. U.S. Mil. Acad. (pres. 1989—93), Nat. Assn. Ins. and Fin. Advisors, Am. Soc. Corp. Execs. Republican. Roman Catholic. Office: Mullane Enterprises Inc 29 S Main St Hartford CT 06107-2449 Home Phone: 860-561-1692, 561-735-7886; Office Phone: 860-561-7650. E-mail: dmullane52@juno.com.

MULLANE, JOHN FRANCIS, pharmaceutical executive; b. NYC, Mar. 10, 1937; s. John Gerald and Rita Ann (Hoben) Mullane; m. Ruth Ann Cecka, Nov. 17, 1962; children: Rosemarie, Michael, Kathleen, Therese, Thomas. MD, SUNY Med. Ctr., 1963; PhD, SUNY, 1968; JD, Fordham U., 1977. Bar: NY 1978, DC 1979. Assoc. med. dir. Ayerst Labs. div. Am. Home Products Corp., NYC, 1973-75, dir. clin. research, 1975-76, v.p. clin., 1977, v.p. sci., 1978-82, sr. v.p., 1982, exec. v.p., 1983-88; pres. Mullane Health Care Cons., NYC and Sarasota, Fla., 1989—; dir. drug devel. DuPont Med. Products, Wilmington, Del., 1990; sr. v.p. DuPont-Merck, Wilmington, 1991-94; exec. v.p. Amylin Pharms., 1994-96. Contbr. articles to profl. jours. Served to lt. col. US Army, 1970-73 Recipient Upjohn Achievement award, 1970; NY Heart Assn. Crawford-Maynard fellow, 1966-68 Fellow Am. Coll. Clin. Pharmacology; mem. ABA, Am. Soc. Clin. Pharmacology and Therapeutics, Am. Assn. Study of Liver Diseases, Misty Creek Country Club (pres. 2004-2005). Roman Catholic. Achievements include development of major drugs including Inderal, Premarin, Lodine, Coumadin, Cozaar. Avocation: golf. Home and Office: 9047 Misty Creek Dr Sarasota FL 34241-9542 E-mail: johnmullane9047@comcast.net.

MULLANEY, THOMAS JOSEPH, lawyer; b. NYC, Feb. 9, 1946; s. James Joseph and Dorothy Mary (Fulling) M.; m. Christine E. Hampton, Aug. 16, 1969; children: Richard, Jennette. BA, Fordham U., 1967; JD, U. Va., 1970; LLM, NYU, 1977. Bar: Va. 1970, N.Y. 1971, U.S. Dist. Ct. (so. and ea. dists.) N.Y. 1972, U.S. Ct. Appeals (2d cir.) 1972, U.S. Supreme Ct. 1975. Assoc. Brown, Wood, Ivey, Mitchell & Petty, NYC, 1970-79, Law Offices of John M. Kenney, Garden City, N.Y., 1979-84; ptnr. Abrams, Thaw & Mullaney, NYC, Farmingdale, N.Y., 1985-91; dir., sr. counsel law dept. Merrill Lynch & Co., Inc., NYC, 1991—. Capt. JAGC, U.S. Army, 1971-74. Mem. Va. State Bar Assn., N.Y. State Bar Assn. Republican. Roman Catholic. Home: 104 Huntington Rd Garden City NY 11530-3122 Office: 222 Broadway Fl 14 New York NY 10038-2510 Office Phone: 212-670-0335. Business E-Mail: thomas_mullaney@ml.com.

MULLANEY, WILLIAM J., insurance company executive; BA, Univ. Pitts.; MBA, Pace Univ. CLU Am. Coll. Mgmt. positions Met Life Inc., 1982—90, v.p., 1990—2002, v.p. group nat. accounts. claim ops., 1992—94, v.p. nat. accounts, 1994—96, v.p. Gen. Motors account, 1996—98, v.p. voluntary benefits, 1998—2002, sr. v.p. claims & customer svc., auto & home, 2002—04, pres. auto & home, 2004—07, pres. inst. bus. segment, 2007—. Bd. dir. Hyatt Legal Plans, Ins. Info. Inst., Ins. Inst. Highway Safety. Bd. dir. Greater Providence C.of C. Office: Met Life Inc 200 Park Ave New York NY 10166 *

MULLANGI, SIVAPRASAD, surgeon; b. Punganuru, India, Nov. 6, 1959; s. Satyanarayana Gupta and Santha Kumari Mullangi; m. Anitha Lakshmi Garlapati, May 29, 1987; children: Samyukta, Praneetha. MB, BChir, Sri Venkateswara U., India, 1984; CM, Postgraduate Inst. Med. Edn. and Rsch., Chandigarh, India, 1988; CM in Cardiothoracic and Vascular Surgery, All India Inst. Med. Scis., New Delhi, 1993. Diplomate Nat. Bd. Examinations, 1993. Fellow adult cardiac surgery Mayo Grad. Sch. Medicine, Rochester, Minn., 1994; fellow cardiothoracic surgery U. Ariz. Health Scis. Ctr., Tucson, 1997; cardiothoracic vascular surgeon Srinivasa Nursing Home (Hosp.), Guntur, India, 1997—2003; chief house-staff Bronx-Lebanon Hosp. Ctr., NY, 2003—. Presenter in field. Recipient First Rank in Biochemistry, Sri Venkateswara U., Tirupati, India, 1980, Second Rank in ENT and Ophthalmology, 1982, First Class in MBBS, 1983, First Rank in Ob-gyn., 1983. Mem.: ACS (candidate mem. 2003—07), AMA, Southeastern Surg. Congress, Soc. Gastrointestional Endoscopic Surgeons, Indian Med. Assn. (life). Achievements include research in surgery in HIV positive. Office: Bronx-Lebanon Hospital Center 1650 Selwyn Ave Ste 4A Bronx NY 10457 Home Phone: 914-713-4056; Office Phone: 718-960-1216. Personal E-mail: sivamullangi@yahoo.com.

MULLANY, GERRY, editor; married. BA, Binghampton U., 1984. Dep. met. editor NY Times, asst. met. editor, politics. Office: NY Times Metropolitan Desk 229 West 43rd St New York NY 10036 Office Phone: 212-556-1533. Office Fax: 212-556-3690. E-mail: gemull@nytimes.com.

MULLANY, KEVIN FERGUS, music educator, director; b. NYC, June 7, 1968; s. Fergus and Elaine (Sigle) M.; m. Cristina; 1 child, Meghan L. BA in English, Queens Coll., 1997; MA in Music Edn., CUNY, 2004. Cert. music, English tchr. N.Y. Tchr. Forest Hills (N.Y.) Montessori Sch., 1992-97, Harbor Conservatory, NYC, 1994-96; music dir. Garden Sch., Jackson Heights, NY, 1997—98; choral dir. Flushing HS, Queens, NY, 1999—. Author: (novel) La Telaraña, 1997, Collection of Short Stories, 1997, I Like to Hop; composer: Complete Literary Works, 2004, Complete Musical Works, 2005. Choir dir. St. Lucy-St. Patrick Ch., Bklyn., 1995—, organist, 1995—; children's choir dir. St. John Evangelist Ch., Bklyn., 1996-98. Writing award Queens Coll., 1994, 96, Silver award level IV work with chorus NY State Sch. Music Assn., 2006; hon. mention Composer's Guild Music Composition Comp., 2006. Mem. Tri-M Music Honor Soc., Music Educators Nat. Conf., Composers Guild, Am. Choral Dirs. Assn., Nat. Assn. Composers (life). Home: 210-50 41 Ave Apt 4H Bayside NY 11361 Office Phone: 718-888-7500 ext. 155. Personal E-mail: mullanykevin@aol.com. Business E-Mail: kmullan@nycboe.net.

MULLARKEY, MARY J., state supreme court chief justice; b. New London, Wis., Sept. 28, 1943; d. John Clifford and Isabelle A. (Steffes) M.; m. Thomas E. Korson, July 24, 1971; 1 child, Andrew Steffes Korson. BA, St. Norbert Coll., 1965, LLD (hon.), 1989; LLB, Harvard U., 1968. Bar: Wis. 1968, Colo. 1974. Atty.-advisor U.S. Dept. Interior, Washington, 1968-73; asst. regional atty. EEOC, Denver, 1973-75; 1st atty. gen. Colo. Dept. Law, Denver, 1975-79, solicitor gen., 1979-82; legal advisor to Gov. Lamm State of Colo., Denver, 1982-85; ptnr. Mullarkey & Seymour, Denver, 1985-87; justice Colo. Supreme Ct., Denver, 1987—, chief justice, 1998—. Fellow: Colo. Bar Found., ABA Found.; mem.: ABA, Denver Bar Assn. (Jud. Excellence award 2003), Colo. Women's Bar Assn. (Mary Lathrop award 2002), Colo. Bar Assn., Thompson G. Marsh Inn of Ct. (pres. 1993—94). Office: Supreme Ct Colo Jud Bldg 2 E 14th Ave Denver CO 80203-2115 *

MULLEN, DANIEL ROBERT, finance company executive; b. Swedesboro, NJ, Apr. 17, 1941; s. Harold Legrand and Gladys (DeVault) M.; m. Elizabeth A. Willers, Dec. 17, 1977; children: William H., Jonathan O. BS in Fin., Ariz. State U., 1966, postgrad., 1966-67. Appraiser Ariz. Dept. Revenue, 1966—68; financial analyst Amerco, 1968—70, treas., 1970—82; pres., dir. Continental Leasing Co., 1980—; v.p. Southwest Pipe and Supply Co., 1982; treas. Talley Industries, Inc., 1982—93, v.p., 1993—98; COO Friendship Publs., 1998—99. Bd. dirs. C. Myers Corp., Amerco, U-Haul Internat. Oxford Life Ins. Co. Del. Ariz. Presdl. Dem. Conv., 1972; bd. dirs. Big Sisters of Ariz., 1975, Found. for Blind Children, 1984-90, Phoenix Little Theatre, 1985-91, Kachina Country Day Sch., 1988-94, New Way Sch., 1994-2000, Interfaith Coop. Ministries, 2003-, With U.S. Army, 1959-62. Ariz. Soc. CPAs grantee, 1964-65 Mem. Fin. Execs. Internat. Home: 3627 E Medlock Dr Phoenix AZ 85018-1505 Office Phone: 602-263-6123.

MULLEN, EDWARD JOHN, JR., Spanish language educator; b. Hackensack, NJ, July 12, 1942; s. Edward J. and Elsie (Powell) Mullen; m. Helen Cloe Braley, Apr. 2, 1971; children: Kathleen, Julie Ann. BA, W.Va. Wesleyan Coll., 1964; MA, Northwestern U., 1965, PhD, 1968. Asst. prof. modern langs. Purdue U., West Lafayette, Ind., 1967-71; assoc. prof. Spanish U. Mo., Columbia, 1971-78, prof. Spanish, 1978—. Author: La Revista Contemporaneos, 1972, Carlos Pellicer, 1977, Langston Hughes in the Hispanic World and Haiti, 1977, The Life and Poems of Cuban Slave: Juan Francisco Manzano 1797-1854, 1981, Critical Essays on Langston Hughes, 1986, Sendas Literarias: Hispanoamerica, 1988, El Cuento Hispanico, 1980, 2007, Afro-Cuban Literature: Critical Junctures, 1998; editor: The Harlem Group of Negro Writers (Melvin B. Tolson), 2001; co-editor: Afro-Hispanic Rev., 1987—. Recipient diploma de honor, Inst. de Cultura Hispanica, 1964; fellow, Northwestern U., 1965—67; grantee, Am. Coun. Learned Socs., 1979; Woodrow Wilson fellow, 1964—65, Rsch. grantee, U. Mo., 1972, 1976. Mem.: MLA, Assn. Depts. Fgn. Langs. (pres. 1989—91), Am. Tchrs. Spanish and Protuguese. Home: 207 Edgewood Ave Columbia MO 65203-3413 Office: U Mo Dept Romance Langs 143 Arts And Sci Bldg Columbia MO 65211-0001 Home Phone: 573-443-8340; Office Phone: 573-882-5041. Business E-Mail: mullene@missouri.edu.

MULLEN, EILEEN ANNE, human resources executive; b. Phila., Feb. 14, 1943; d. Joseph Gregory and Helen Rita (Kane) M.; m. William John Raschiatore (dec.). BS in English, St. Joseph's U., 1967; MA in English, Villanova U., 1978. Cert. tchr., Pa. Tchr. St. Anastasia Sch., Newtown Square, 1960-67, West Cath. Girls H.S., 1967-74; mgr. staff tng. and devel. ASTM, Phila., 1974-96, dir. human resources, 1996—. Instr. lit., speech and communications Widener U., Chester, Pa. and Wilmington, Del. Contbg. author articles on comms. tng. programs; contbr. articles to profl. jours. Mem. ASTD (pres. Phila./Del. Valley chpt. 1980-81, Outstanding Leadership as Pres. award 1981), Soc. for Human Resource Mgmt. Democrat. Roman Catholic. Office: ASTM 100 Barr Harbor Dr West Conshohocken PA 19428-0700 Home Phone: 610-240-9090; Office Phone: 610-832-9766. Business E-Mail: emullen@astm.org.

MULLEN, GRAHAM C., judge; b. 1940; BA, Duke U., 1962, JD, 1969. Bar: NC 1969. Ptnr. Mullen, Holland, Cooper, Morrow, Wilder & Sumner, 1969-90; judge US Dist. Ct. (We. Dist.) NC, Charlotte, 1990—98, chief judge, 1998—2005, sr. judge, 2005—. Lt. USN, 1962—66. Mem.: Mecklenburg County Bar Assn., NC Bar Assn. (bd. gov. 1983—88). Office: US Courthouse 401 W Trade St Rm 230 Charlotte NC 28202-1619 Office Phone: 704-350-7450. Business E-Mail: graham_mullen@ncwd.uscourts.gov.

MULLEN, J. THOMAS, lawyer; b. Evanston, Ill., Aug. 27, 1940; BSE, Princeton U., 1963; JD cum laude, U. Mich., 1967. Bar: Ill. 1967. Atty. Mayer, Brown, Rowe & Maw LLP, Chgo., 1967—74, ptnr., 1974—, ptnr.-in-charge London office London, 1974-78, ptnr. Chgo., 1978—. Chmn., recruiting com. Mayer, Brown, Rowe & Maw LLP. Bd. dirs. Legal Assistance Found. Chgo., 1979-85. Mem. ABA, Chgo. Bar Assn., Chgo. Coun. Lawyers, Ill. State Bar Assn., Law Club of Chgo. Office: Mayer Brown Rowe & Maw 71 S Wacker Dr Chicago IL 60606-4637 E-mail: tmullen@mayerbrownrowe.com.

MULLEN, JAMES C., biotechnology company executive; b. 1959; m. Justine Mullen; 4 children. BS in Chem. Engring., Rensselaer Polytech. Inst., 1980; MBA, Villanova U., 1984. Various positions SmithKline Beckman Corp. (now GlaxoSmithKline plc), 1984—88; dir. facilities engring. Biogen, Inc., 1989—92, v.p. ops., 1992—96, v.p. internat., 1996—99, CEO, pres., 2000—03, chmn. bd., 2002—03; pres., CEO Biogen Idec Inc., 2003—. Bd. trustees Rensselaer Polytech. Inst.; bd. dirs. Biotech. Industry Orgn., Biomed. Scis. Careers Program, Pharmaceuticals Rsch. and Manufacturers Am., PerkinElmer, Inc., 2004—. Co-chair capital campaign steering com. Cambridge Family and Children's Svc. Responsible for the manufacturing and successful launch of AVONEX (Interferon beta-la), a world leading therapy for relapsing forms of multiple sclerosis. Office: Biogen Idec Inc 14 Cambridge Ctr Cambridge MA 02142 *

MULLEN, JAMES JOSEPH, III, lawyer; s. James Joseph and Maria Isabel Mullen; m. Nancy Ellen Ross, July 27, 1996; children: Isabella Zenovia, Olivia Rasha, Samantha Maria. BA, U. Calif., San Diego, 1988; JD, U. Calif. Hastings Coll. Law, San Francisco, California, 1997; PhD, U.Tex. Grad. Sch. of Biomedical Scis., 1994. Bar: United State Patent and Trademark Office 1999, Calif. 1998. Assoc. Knobbe, Martens, Olson and Bear, LLP, San Diego, 1997—2003, Morrison & Foerster, LLP, San Diego, 2003—06, of counsel, 2006—. Office: Morrison Foerster Llp 12531 High Bluff Dr San Diego CA 92130-3014 Home Phone: 858-536-7737; Office Phone: 858-720-7940. Business E-Mail: jmullen@mofo.com.

MULLEN, JOHN E., orthopedist, surgeon; m. Karen Mullen. BS, Providence Coll., 1989; MD, NY Med. Coll., 1993. Cert. Am. Bd. Orthop. Surgeons. Intern St. Vincent's Med. Ctr., Bridgeport, Conn.; intern gen. surgery Mt. Sinai Med. Ctr., Cleve., 1998; resident orthop. surgery Hosp. for Spl. Surgery, NYC, 2002; orthopaedic surgeon New Milford Orthop. Assocs. PC, Conn., 2002—. House physician Madison Square Garden. Battalion surgeon USN, 1994—97. Mem.: Am. Acad. Orthopaedic Surgeons. Office: New Milford Orthop Assocs 131 Kent Rd New Milford CT 06776 Office Phone: 860-355-8000. Office Fax: 860-350-6291. *

MULLEN, JOHN P., retired government executive; b. Oct. 10, 1942; BS, Wright-State U., Dayton, Ohio, 1973. Dir. pers. USAF, Warner Robins, Ga., 1986—99; ret., 1999. Author: Chasm Leap, 1999, Sound of Death, 2005, My Name Is Smith, 2006. Recipient Ky. Col. award, Aide-De-Camp Gov. Ga., Bill Clinton award, Mem. City Coun., 1999. Mem.: Mensa. Home: PO Box 14284 Mexico Beach FL 32410-4284

MULLEN, MAUREEN ANN, social worker; b. Chgo., Mar. 22, 1949; d. Robert Vincent and Mary Geraldine M. BA, U. Ill., 1971; MEd, Coll. of William and Mary, 1974; MSW, Univ. Ill., 1990; postgrad., U. Chgo., 1985-86. Programmer Computer Task Group, NYC, 1980-81; analyst, programmer Guy Carpenter, NYC, 1981-82; analyst C.N.A. Ins., Chgo., 1982-84; analyst, programmer Lakeshore Nat. Bank, Chgo., 1984-85; sales support Sterling Software, Chgo., 1986; owner Mullen Designs, Chgo., 1987; dir. of social svcs. Vista Health, Fayetteville, Ark., 2002—03; employee assistance counselor Ark. Employee Assistance Program, Fayetteville, 2003—06. Prodr., host (TV show) Ozarks Live!, 2003—06. Vol. Samaritans Hotline, Chgo., 1986; adv. bd. Lakeview Mental Health Ctr., Chgo., 1986; active Chgo. Coun. on Fgn. Rels., 1986—87; chmn. fundraiser Habitat for Humanity, 1987; vol. Manic Depressive and Depressive Assn. and Nat. Alliance for Rsch. into Schizophrenia and Depression, 1988, Wilmette Sch. Bd. Caucus, 1997, endowment fund com., 1996—97; vol. Chgo. Bot. Garden, 1999; spkrs. chmn. Fayetteville Freedom Festival, 2003; nominating com. ACLU, 2005—06; vol. Thomas Hynes campaign, Chgo., 1987, New Trier Dem. Orgn., 2000; alderman candidate, 2004; bd. dirs. ACLU N.W. Ark., 2005—06, N.W. Ark. Mental Health Assn., 2002—04, chmn. sch. libr. book project, 2002, 2003; bd. dirs. Cmty. Access TV, Fayetteville, 2003—. Recipient Fat Cat award, Cmty. Access TV, Fayetteville, 2003—05; Ill. State scholar, 1971. Mem.: ACLU (bd. dirs. NW Ark. chpt. 2005—06), NOW, Nature Conservancy, Sierra Club, Dem. Nat. Com., So. Poverty Law Ctr. Avocations: painting, poetry, backpacking, photography, acting. Home: 51 Grove Hill Ave Newton MA 02460 Office Phone: 617-678-3773. Personal E-mail: momoses2002@yahoo.com.

MULLEN, MICHAEL G., career military officer; b. LA, Oct. 4, 1946; m. Deborah Morgan; children: John, Michael. Graduate, U.S. Naval Acad., 1968; MSc in Ops. Rsch., Naval Postgraduate Sch., 1985. Enlisted USN, 1968, advanced through grades to adm., 2003; stationed on USS Collett, USS Blandy; comdr. USS Noxubee, 1973-75; company officer, exec. asst. U.S. Naval Acad., 1975-78; chief engr. USS Fox, 1978-80; exec. officer USS Sterett, 1981-83; comdr. USS Goldsborough, 1985-87; dir. divsn. officer course Surface Warfare Officer's Sch., 1987-89; staff asst. for navy programs Office of the Sec. Defense, 1989-91; comdr. USS Yorktown, 1992-94; from dir. surface officer distribution divsn. to dep. dir. Bureau of Naval Personnel, 1994-96; comdr. Cruiser-Destroyer Group 2, 1996-98; dir. surface warfare divsn. Office of Chief of Naval Ops., 1998—2000; comdr. SECOND fleet/ Striking Fleet Atlantic, 2000—01; dep. chief naval ops., resources, requirements & assessments USN, 2001—03, vice chief naval ops., 2003—04, chief of naval ops. Washington, 2005—; comdr. US Naval Forces Europe, 2004—05, Regional Command South, Naples, Italy, 2004—05. Office: Office Chief Naval Oper 1200 Navy Pentagon Washington DC 20350 *

MULLEN, MICHAEL T., lawyer; b. Evanston, Ill., Apr. 15, 1956; s. George Martin and Marguerite (Tully) M.; m. Patricia Reilly, Apr. 24, 1987; children: Claire, Catherine, Michael, Conor. BA, Marquette U., 1978; JD, Loyola U., 1981. Bar: Ill. 1981, U.S. Dist. Ct. (no. dist.) Ill. 1981, U.S. Ct. Appeals (7th cir.) 1981, U.S. Supreme Ct., 2000. Asst. atty. gen. Ill. Atty. Gen., Chgo., 1981—85; asst. U.S. atty. U.S. Atty., Chgo., 1985—90, 1990—92, dep. chief, 1990—92; ptnr. Mullen & Minella, Chgo., 1992—98, Paul B. Episcope, Ltd., Chgo., 1998—. Contbr. articles to profl. jours. Trustee Village of Western Springs (Ill.), 1995—. Recipient Spl. Achievement award for sustained superior U.S. Dept. Justice, 1988, performance award 1990; named to Loyola Acad. Athletic Hall of Fame. Mem. Ill. State Bar Assn., Ill. Trial Lawyers Assn., West Suburban Bar Assn. lawyer for multiple cases with multimillion dollar jury verdicts and settlements. Office: Paul B Episcope Ltd 77 W Washington St Ste 300 Chicago IL 60602-2896 Office Phone: 312-782-6636. Business E-Mail: mtm@episcopeltd.com.

MULLEN, PETER P., lawyer; b. NYC, Apr. 8, 1928; m. Cecilia Kirby; 5 children. AB cum laude, Georgetown U., 1948; LLB, Columbia U., 1951. Bar: N.Y. 1951. Ptnr. Skadden, Arps, Slate, Meagher & Flom LLP, NYC, 1961—98, exec. ptnr., 1981—94, of counsel, 1998—. Co-chmn. Cardinal's Com. Laity Archdiocese N.Y., 1989-2003; bd. dirs., sec., treas., Eye Surgery, Inc. Formerly mem., pres. Bd. Edn. Pub. Schs., Bronxville, N.Y., 1979-81; chmn. Skadden Fellowship Found., 1988—; bd. dirs., vice-chmn. Lawrence Hosp., Bronxville, 1984-89; bd. dirs., sec. Project Orbis Internat., 1985—, Georgetown U., Washington, 1982-99, chmn., 1985-92; bd. dirs. Legal Aid Soc., 1987-93, Vols. Legal Svcs., Inc., 1988-99, United Way Bronxville, 1985-93, New Milford Hosp. Found., 1997-, Practicing Attys. Law Students, 1988-99; trustee Lawyer's Commn. Civil Rights Under Law, 1984-99; chmn. Gregorian U. Found., 1989—; bd. dirs., exec. com. Vatican Obs. Found., 1993-2006. Named Man of Yr. Cath. Big Bros., 1987; recipient John Carroll award Georgetown U., 1984, John Carroll Medal Merit, 1988, Thomas More award Lawyers Com. Cardinal's Com. of the Laity, 1996, Elizabeth Ann Seton award Nat. Cath. Edn. Assn., 1998; named Stone scholar Columbia U., 1951. Mem. ABA, Assn. Bar City N.Y., Soc. Friendly Sons St. Patrick (N.Y., pres. 1989-90), Knight Malta. Office: Skadden Arps Slate et al LLP 4 Times Sq New York NY 10036-6522

MULLEN, ROBERT W., construction executive; BS, MS, NJ Inst. Tech., Newark. Pres., CEO Sordoni Skanska Constrn. Co.; various positions including corp. exec. v.p., pres. Skanska Sci. and Tech. divsn. and COO NE, mid-Atlantic and PR ops. Skanska USA Bldg. (formerly Sordoni Skanska Constrn. Co.); CEO Structure Tone, NYC, 2005—. Office: Structure Tone 770 Broadway New York NY 10003 Office Phone: 212-481-6100. E-mail: NYInfo@structuretone.com. *

MULLEN, ROD, nonprofit organization executive; b. Puyallup, Wash., Aug. 2, 1943; s. Charles Rodney and Grace Violet (Fritsch) M.; m. Lois Fern Tobiska, May 3, 1963 (div. Jan. 1977); children: Cristina, Charles, Moneka; m. Naya Arbiter, Oct. 17, 1977; 1 child: Angelo. Student, U. Idaho, Moscow, 1961—63; AB in Polit. Sci., U. Calif., Berkeley, 1966; postgrad., San Francisco Art Inst., 1968. Dir. Oakland (Calif.) facility Synanon Found., Inc., 1971-72, dir. San Francisco facility, 1972-73, dir. Tomales Bay (Calif.) facility, 1976-78, dir. Synanon edn. programs, 1973-76; treatment dir. nat. programs Vision Quest, Inc., Tucson, 1981-82; dir. resources and devel. Amity, Inc., Tucson, 1982-84, exec. dir., 1984-95; founder, pres., CEO, Amity Found., Porterville, Calif., 1995—. Mem. Nat. Adv. Com. Substance Abuse Prevention, 1990-96; adv. bd. Ctr. Therapeutic Cmty. Rsch., Nat. Devel. and Rsch. Insts., NYC, 1991-2002; cons. Calif. Office Criminal Justice Planning, Sacramento, 1993; prin. investigator program Nat. Inst. on Drug Abuse, 1990-93; pres. Calif. Therapeutic Com., 2004-06; editl. adv. bd. Offender Substance Abuse Report, 2000-2004; bd. dirs. Amity Found., Calif., 1995-, Amity Works Found., Ariz., 2006-. Dir.: (documentaries) Prodigal Daughters, 2002, TC Pioneers, 2003, Essential Elements of the Therapeutic Community, 2005, Improving TC Encounter Groups, 2006, History of Therapeutic Communities in Corrections, 2006; contbr. chapters to books, articles to profl. jours. Mem.: Calif. Therapeutic C. (pres. 2004—06), Therapeutic Coms. of Am. (treas. 2006—), Am. Correctional Assn. Achievements include development of in-prison therapeutic community programs for addicted offenders and violent offenders which demonstrated significant reductions in recidivism to drug abuse, violence and other criminal activities; collaborated with Naya Arbiter in the development and implementation of a comprehensive holistic curriculum for therapeutic communities; participated in numerous research studies to advance knowledge in the field of holistic addiction treatment. Avocations: hiking, photography, videography. Office: Amity Found 120 S Houghton Rd Ste 138-321 Tucson AZ 85748-2155 Office Phone: 520-749-7178. Business E-Mail: rmullen@amityfdn.org.

MULLEN, RON, insurance company executive; b. Tex., Aug. 8, 1939; s. Durward Lacy and Blanche V. (Coulson) M.; m. Carole King, Dec. 29, 1959; children: Lacy Lynne Holcomb, Misty Kay. Student, Abilene Christian Coll., 1957-58, San Antonio Coll., 1958-59; BBA, S.W. Tex. State U., 1965. C.L.U., Chartered Fin. Cons. City council mem. City of Austin, 1977-83, mayor, 1983-85; mgr. Prin. Fin. Group, Austin, 1965-98, Ron Mullen & Assocs. Inc., Austin, 1966—, InNet Fin. Group; prin. Small Employer Benefits L.P. Chmn. TML Ins. Trust Fund Com., 1983—; mem. Gov.'s Task Force on State Employees Health Ins. Benefits, Austin, 1984 Chmn. Austin Transp. Study Com., Austin, 1983—, Greater Austin-San Antonio Corridor Coun., 1984—, Social Policy Adv. Com., Austin, 1979-80, March of Dimes campaign, Austin, 1974-75; co-chmn. Consumers United for Rail Equity, Austin, 1983—; v.p. Austin Symphony Orch., 1974-75; mem. exec. com. Capital Area Planning Coun., Austin, 1976—, exec. bd. Tex. Mcpl. League, Austin, 1983—, Gov.'s Task Force on Indigent Health Care, Austin, 1984, Tex. Adv. Commn. on Intergovtl. Rels., Austin, 1981—; chmn. Infant Parent Tng. Ctr., 1985-98; bd. dirs., chmn. South MoPac Transp. Com., 1986-87; life mem. Austin Jaycees, bd. dirs., 1974-75; vice-chmn. Mental Health Mental Retardation Bd.; vice chmn. South Tex. Audio Reader Svc.; bd. dirs. BBB, Inc., Hyde Park Bapt. Sch., 1999—. Recipient Road Hand award Tex. Dept. Hwys. and Transp., 1985, award for regional statesmanship Greater Austin-San Antonio Corridor Commn.; named Boss of Yr., Treaty Oaks chpt. Am. Bus. Women's Assn., 1978, Nat. Mgr. of Yr., Bankers Life Ins. Co., 1977, 82, 84-85, Alumnus of Yr. Austin Jaycees, 1988-90. Mem. Am. Coll. Life Underwriters (pres.), Tex. Assn. Life Underwriters (pres. 1997-98), Austin Assn. Life Underwriters (pres. 1974-75), Austin Gen. Agts. and Mgrs. Assn. (pres. 1978-80), Sales and Mktg. Execs. of Austin (pres. 1972-73), Downtown Rotary (pres. 1996-97), Tex. Assn. Ins. and fin. Advisors (nat. committeeman). Baptist. Home: 6902 Mesa Dr Austin TX 78731-2822 Office Phone: 512-973-9993. Personal E-mail: ron9991@msn.com.

MULLEN, TERRI ANN, retired special education educator; b. St. Louis, Apr. 01; d. William Earl and Sophia Kinniff; m. Thomas Patrick Mullen; children: David, Mark, Debi. BS in Edn., S.E. Mo. State U.; M in Sch. Adminstrn., Calif. State U., 1978, M in Spl. Edn., 1981; EdD in Institutional Mgmt., Pepperdine U., 1985. Cert. spl. edn., std. sec., std. elem., adminstrv. svc. K-12, cmty. coll. instr. Tchr. Irvine (Calif.) Unified Sch. Dist., 1972-84; lectr., spl. edn. Calif. State U., Fullerton, 1989-90; asst. prin. Moreno Valley (Calif.) Unified Sch. Dist., 1984-85; adminstr. of spl. svcs. Centralia Sch. Dist., Buena Park, Calif., 1984-89; elem. prin. Capistrano Unified Sch. Dist., San Juan Capistrano, 1989-93; spl. edn. tchr., dept. chair Moreno Valley (Calif.) Unified Sch. Dist., 1993—. Chair, cmty. staff ednl. planning com. Santiago Elem. Sch., Irvine Unified Sch. Dist., 1981; dir., staff devel. for spl. programs pers. Centralia Sch. Dist., Buena Park, 1984-89; workshop presenter Assn. of Calif. Sch. Adminstrs. Conf., San Francisco, 1983. Author: Resource Book of Classroom Interventions for the Collaborative Teaching Model, 1994, Tips of the Trade for the Classroom Aide, 1984; contbr. articles to profl. jours. Adv. bd. for sp. edn. Calif. State U. Fullerton, 1988-89. Recipient Cmty. Svc. award Disneyland, 1992, 93; named Outstanding Educator of Yr. Rotary Club, 1983. Mem. Coun. for Exceptional Children, Kappa Delta Pi, Phi Kappa Phi. Avocations: roller skating, fashion design, interior design, computer applications, writing. E-mail: tmullen@pacbell.net.

MULLEN, THOMAS EDGAR, real estate consultant; b. Hackensack, NJ, Feb. 10, 1936; s. Luke B. and Jean (Edgar) M.; m. Sarah Lee Huff, Aug. 17, 1984. BS in Engring., Va. Poly. Tech., 1954; grad mgmt. program, Harvard U., 1964. Cons. in field. Mgr. mktg. Eastern Airlines, NYC, 1955—69; pres. Profl. Sprits Mktg., NYC, 1969—72, Shelter Devel. Corp. Am., NYC, 1972—79; supr. ops. Gen. Mills, Orlando, Fla., 1980—86; cons., exec., realtor A.H.M. Graves Co. Inc., Indpls., 1986—92; pres. Pegasus Assocs. Ltd., 1992—. Inventor TV Guider Holder, patent, 1971. Fundraiser Am. Cancer Soc., Miami, 1967-70, Westchester Hosp., N.Y.C., 1967-70; pres. Brighton Found. Mem. Met. Bd. Realtors, Builders Assn. Greater Indpls. (bd. dirs.), Ind. Builders Assn. (bd. dirs.), Nat. Assn. Realtors, Inst. Residential Mktg. (pres. sales & mktg. coun., bd. dirs.). Republican. Roman Catholic. Avocations: tennis, recreational pilot. Home: 6251 Behner Way Indianapolis IN 46250-1494 Office Phone: 317-845-8467. Personal E-mail: tom.mullen@att.net. E-mail: t.mullen@mindspring.com.

MULLEN, WILLIAM JOSEPH, III, military analyst, retired army career officer; b. Plattsburg, NY, Dec. 26, 1937; s. William Joseph Jr. and Georgia (Cook) M.; m. Norma Sturgeon, Aug. 6, 1962; 1 child, William Joseph IV. BS, U.S. Mil. Acad., West Point, NY, 1959; MS in Internat. Affairs, George Washington U., Washington, 1971. Commd. 2d lt. U.S. Army, 1959, advanced through grades to brig. gen., 1987; various assignments in U.S., Vietnam, Korea, Panama, Germany, Saudi Arabia, 1959-92; mem. staff, faculty U.S. Mil. Acad., West Point, 1967-70; comdr. 1st Brigade, 1st Inf. Div., Ft. Riley, Kans., 1983-86; asst. div. comdr. 5th Inf. Div., Ft. Polk, La., 1986-87; comdg. gen. U.S. Army Combined Arms Tng. Activity, Ft. Leavenworth, Kans., 1987-89, 1st Inf. Div. (Forward), Germany, 1989-91; dep. dir. ops. J3 Forces Command, Ft. McPherson, Ga., 1991-92; sr. mgr. mil. tng. and analysis sys. BDM Fed., Inc., Monterey, Calif., 1992-98; sr. program mgr. tng. mgmt. sys. Northrop Grumman Mission Sys., Monterey, 1998—2004; ret., 2004; cons. Army Operations and Tng., 2004—. Co-author: Changing an Army, An Oral History of Gen. W.E. DePuy, 1979; contbr. articles, book revs. to Mil. Rev. Decorated D.S.C., D.S.M. Mem. Assn. U.S. Army, Assn. Grads. U.S. Mil. Acad. (bd. dir. West Point Soc. of Monterey Peninsula 2005-), Soc. 1st Div. (chpt. officer 1968, assoc. 1989-93, trustee found. 1989-93, bd. dir.), Legion of Valor (bd. dir. 2005-), Nat. Infantry Assn. (Order of St. Maurice). Avocations: sports, reading. *When in doubt, I have always found direction from the guidance explicit in the 1st Infantry Division's motto, "Duty First!".*

MULLENBACH, LINDA HERMAN, lawyer; b. Sioux City, Iowa, Dec. 25, 1948; d. Verner Wilhelm and Margaretta Victoria (Grant) Herman; m. Hugh James Mullenbach, Aug. 22, 1970; children: Erika Lynn, Linnea Britt. BS in Speech, Northwestern U., 1971, MS in Speech, 1972, JD, 1979. Bar: Ill. 1979, U.S. Dist. Ct. (no. dist.) Ill. 1979, DC 1983, U.S. Dist. Ct. DC 1983, U.S. Ct. Appeals (7th, DC and fed. cirs.) 1983, U.S. Supreme Ct. 1984. Assoc. Jenner & Block, Chgo., 1979-83, Dickstein, Shapiro & Morin, Washington, 1983-85, prin., 1985-87, ptnr., 1988-93; v.p., assoc. gen. counsel Zurich Small Bus. and Zurich Comml. Legal Divsn., Balt., 1994-99; asst. gen. counsel, v.p. Corp. Law Divsn. Zurich U.S., Balt., 1999-2001; asst. gen. counsel, v.p. corp. law divsn. Zurich N.Am., Balt., 2001—02, sr. v.p., assoc. gen. counsel corp. law divsn., 2002—. Mem.: ABA, DC Bar Assn., Mortar Bd., Zeta Phi Eta. Home: 8201 Killean Way Potomac MD 20854-2728 Office Phone: 410-554-1346. E-mail: linda.mullenbach@zurichna.com.

MULLENDORE, JAMES MYERS, lawyer; b. Charlottesville, Va., Mar. 21, 1946; s. James M. and Elaine (Gregg) M.; m. Kristine B. Mullendore; children: Margaret E., Sean T. BS, W.Va. U., 1968; JD, U. Va., 1975. Bar: Mich. 1975, U.S. Dist. Ct. (we. dist.) Mich. Ptnr. Mullendore & Thrall, Greenville, Mich., 1975—. Pres., v.p. Greenville Bd. Edn., 1976-82; ofcl. Mid-Am. Football Conf., 1985-86, Big Ten Football Ofcls., 1987-2001,—; bd. dirs. United Way Greenville, 1978-83; chmn. controlled substances adv.com. State Mich., 1994-2001; bd. dirs. Danish Festival Inc, 1997-2000; bd. advisors W.Va. U. Sch. Bus. and Econs., 1996—. Mem. ABA, Assn. Trial Lawyers Am., Mich. Trial Lawyers Assn., U.S. Football League (ofcl. 1983), Greenville Area C. of C. (chmn. bd. dirs.), Rotary (v.p. 1983-84). Congregationalist. Home: 7678 Greenbrier NE Rockford MI 49341 Office: PO Box 40 Greenville MI 48838 Home Phone: 616-874-1467; Office Phone: 616-754-4611. Personal E-mail: mullendore_jim@yahoo.com.

MULLENDORE, WALTER EDWARD, retired economist; b. Harrah, Okla., Apr. 22, 1940; s. Newton and Ida Minnie (Lohmann) M.; m. Edra Janell Havenstrite, July 4, 1963; children: Matthew Edward, Karen Kay, Mark Andrew. BS, Okla. State U., 1961, MS, 1963; PhD in Econs., Iowa State U., 1968. Grad. asst. Okla. State U., 1961-63; instr. Iowa State U., 1965-67; mem. faculty dept. econs. U. Tex., Arlington, 1968—2002, prof., 1975—2002, dean Coll. of Bus., 1980—93; ret., 2002. Contbr. articles to profl. jours. Served with U.S. Army, 1963-65. Mem. Mo. Valley Econ. Assn. (v.p. 1980-81, pres. 1982-83), Gt. S.W. Rotary (pres. 1989-90), Omicron Delta Epsilon. Methodist. Home: 8003 John T White Rd Fort Worth TX 76120-3611

MULLENIX, LINDA SUSAN, law educator; b. NYC, Oct. 16, 1950; d. Andrew Michael and Roslyn Marasco; children: Robert Bartholomew, John Theodore, William Joseph. BA, CCNY, 1971; M Philosophy, Columbia U., 1974; PhD Pres.'s fellow, 1977; JD, Georgetown U., 1980. Bar: D.C. 1981, U.S. Dist. Ct. D.C. 1981, U.S. Ct. Appeals (D.C. cir.) 1981, U.S. Supreme Ct. 1986, Tex. 1991, U.S. Ct. Appeals (5th cir.) 1995. U. Md. European divsn.; Ramstein, Germany, 1974; adj. instr. Fordham U., NYC, 1975—76, adj. asst. prof., 1977; instr. N.Y. Inst. Tech., NYC, 1976; assoc. prof., lectr. George Washington U., Washington, 1977-80; asst. prof. Am. U., Washington, 1979; assoc. Pierson, Ball & Dowd, Washington, 1980-81; clin. prof. Loyola U. Law Sch., LA, 1981-82; asst. prof. Cath. U. Law Sch., Washington, 1984-86; assoc. prof., 1986-90; prof., 1990; Reuschlein disting. vis. chair Villanova Law Sch., 2000. Vis. asst. prof. CCNY, 1977, Cooper Union Advancement Sci., Art, N.Y.C., 1977, Loyola U. Law Sch.,

L.A., 1982-83, Cath. U. Law Sch., Washington, 1983-84; jud. fellow U.S. Supreme ct. and fed. Jud. Ctr., 1989-90; Bernard J. Ward Centennial prof. U. Tex., 1991-2001, Morris and Rita Atlas chair in advocacy, 2001—; vis. prof. Harvard Law Sch., 1994-95, Mich. Law Sch., 1996; resident scholar Rockefeller Found. Bellagio (Italy) Study Ctr., 2002; Fulbright scholar Disting. Chair in Law, Trento, Italy, 2007. Author: Mass Tort Litigation: Cases and Materials, 1996, Civil Procedure Roadmap, 1997, Casenotes: Federal Courts, 1997, ExamPro: Civil Procedure, 1998, State Class Actions: Practice and Procedure, 2000, Civil Procedure, 2004; co-author: Understanding Federal Courts, 1998, Federal Courts in the Twenty-First Century, 1996, 3d edit., 2007; Moore's Federal Practice and Procedure, 1991, 97, and annual updates; editor bibliographies Polit. Theory, A. Jour. Polit. Philosophy, 1972-74, The Tax Lawyer Jour., 1978-80; columnist The National Law Jour., 1998—; contbr. editor preview of U.S. Supreme Ct. Cases; co-reporter Report and Plan of Civil Justice Reform Act Adv. Group, S.d., Tex., 1991; assoc. reporter ALI, Restatement of the Law Governing Lawyers; contbr. articles to profl. jours. Alt. del. Dem. State Conv., 1980. Fellow NDEA, 1971-74; N.Y. State Regents Scholar, 1967-71. Fellow Tex. Bar Found.; mem. ABA (reporter task force on class actions 1995-97), Internat. Assn. Procedural Law, Am. Law Inst., DC Bar Assn. (com. on ethics, CLE and the Model Rules 1987), Am. Assn. Law Schs. (exec. com. sect. on civil proc. 1987-88, exec. com. sec. on conflicts of law 1991-92, chair prof. devel. com. 1991-93), Jour. Legal Edn. (editl. bd. 1997-1999), Phi Beta Kappa. Home: 722 Crystal Creek Dr Austin TX 78746-4730 Office: U Tex Sch Law 727 E Dean Keeton St Austin TX 78705-3224 Office Phone: 512-232-1375. Business E-Mail: lmullenix@law.utexas.edu.

MULLENS, WILLIAM REESE, retired insurance company executive; b. Franklin, Tenn., Sept. 12, 1921; s. William Pope and Elizabeth (Reese) M.; m. Katherine Ann Jones, Nov. 24, 1945; children: Jo Ann Mullens Sanditz, Carol Ann Mullens Slegers. BA, Vanderbilt U., 1942. With Bus. Men's Assurance Co., Kansas City, Mo., 1947-75, exec. v.p., dir., 1969-75; pres., dir. J.C. Penney Life Ins. Co., 1975-82; pres. Gt. Am. Res. Ins. Co., 1975-84, dir., 1975-89. Dir. Nat. Fidelity Life Ins. Co., 1986-89 Served to lt. comdr. USNR, 1943-46. Fellow Soc. Actuaries; mem. Phi Beta Kappa, Alpha Tau Omega. Presbyterian. Home: One McKnight Pl Apt 118 Saint Louis MO 63124

MULLER, CAROLYN BUE, physical therapist, volunteer; b. Crosby, ND, Feb. 24; d. Sigurd Christian and Eleanor (Rushfeldt) Bue; m. Willard Chester Muller, Jan. 27, 1945; children: Marolyn Jean, Barbara Anne, Nancy Eleanor. BA, St. Olaf Coll., 1940; cert. in phys. therapy, Harvard U., 1944. Assoc. dir. younger girls and phys. edn. sect. YWCA, Syracuse, N.Y., 1940-43; phys. therapist Valley Forge Hosp., Phoenixville, Pa., 1944-45; med. records libr. Trust Territory of Pacific Islands, Truk, Caroline Islands, 1951-52. Founder, prin. organizer Am. Cmty. Sch., Truk, 1952, Lincoln Sch., Katmandu, Nepal, 1956, Am. Cmty. Sch., Mogadiscio, Somali Republic, 1958, Kampala, Uganda, 1966; panelist workshop Wash. Commn. for Humanities, Yakima, 1996. Author: Living in Uganda, 1967; cartographer: Maudie - An Oregon Trail Childhood, 1993. Charter registrar Clallam County Mus. and Hist. Soc., Port Angeles, Wash., 1977-87; vol. reading tutor Port Angeles Sch. Dist., 1980—; cmty. coord. UNICEF, Port Angeles, 1982-85; rep. Target Wash. Seminar, Seattle, 1984; rep. Asia-Can. Women in Mgmt. Conf., Victoria, B.C., Can., 1985; regional judge Wash. State Nat. History Day Contest, Port Angeles, 1985-2002; selection judge Wash. State Inquiring Mind Lecture Series, Seattle, 1989, 90, 96, organizer/coord., Inquiring Mind Lecture Series 1983-2002; Wash. state judge Nat. History Day Contest, Ellensburg, Wash., 1993-2003; bd. dirs. Wash. State Friends of the Humanities, 1991-94; trustee Wash. Commn. for the Humanities, 1995-97; pres. Am. Women's Club, Katmandu, 1957-58, Mogadiscio, 1959-60; v.p. Internat. Women's Club, Saigon, South Vietnam, 1971; selection com. Evergreen State Soc. Awards, 1998-99. Recipient Women Making a Difference award Soropimist Internat., 1984, Outstanding Vol. award Citizens' Ednl. Ctr. N.W., 1988, Evergreen award Evergreen State Soc., 1992. Mem. AAUW (br. pres. 1980-84, Edn. Found. scholarship in her name 1996). PEO (rec. sec. 1984-85, v.p. 1985-86, pres. 1987-89, chaplain 1994, Internat. Peace scholarship in her name 1990, state chmn. Internat. Peace scholarship 1989-90), Washington Athletic Club. Avocations: growing flowers, cross-country walking, painting, reading, travel. Home: 3624 S Mount Angeles Rd Port Angeles WA 98362-8910 E-mail: muller@tenforward.com.

MULLER, CHARLOTTE FELDMAN, economist, educator; b. NYC, Feb. 19, 1921; d. Louis and Lillian (Drogin) Feldman; m. Jonas N. Muller, 1942 (dec.); m. Carl Schoenberg, 1970; children: Jeremy Lewis Muller, Sara Linda Muller. AB, Vassar Coll., 1941; A.M., Columbia U., 1942, PhD in Econs., 1946. Instr. econs. Bklyn. Coll., 1943; lectr. Barnard Coll., 1943-46; asst. prof. Occidental Coll., 1947; asst. study dir. Survey Rsch. Ctr., U. Mich., 1948; rsch. assoc. U. Calif., Berkeley, 1948-50; lectr. Yale U. Sch. Pub. Health, 1952-53; asst. prof. Columbia U. Sch. Pub. Health, 1957-67; assoc. dir. Ctr. for Social Rsch. CUNY, 1967-86, prof. econs., 1978-91, prof. emerita, 1991—, prof. sociology, 1982-91, prof. urban studies Ctr. for Social Rsch., 1967-78; v.p. CUNY Acad. for Humanities and Scis., 1985-88; prof. health econs. Mt. Sinai Sch. Medicine, 1986-91, prof. emerita, 1991—, dir. div. health econs., 1988-91, prof. dept. geriatrics, 1990-91, assoc. dir. Internat. Longevity Ctr.-USA, Ltd., 1991-97, sr. economist Internat. Longevity Ctr.-USA, Ltd., 1998—, co-dir. rsch. program Internat. Longevity Ctr.-USA, Ltd., 1999—2004, dir. longevity rsch. Internat. Longevity Ctr.-USA, Ltd., 2005—; sr. investigator health indicators, productive engagement Alliance for Health and the Future, 2003—04. Cons. Health Care Financing Adminstrn., U.S. VA; disting. alumna speaker Vassar Centennial, 1971. Author: Health Care and Gender, 1990; mem. editorial bd. Am. Jour. Pub. Health, 1980-84, Women and Health, Rsch. on Aging; contbr. numerous articles on health econs. to profl. publs. Mem. N.Y.C. Mayor's Com. on Prescription Drug Abuse, 1970-73; bd. dirs. Alan Guttmacher Inst., 1972-81, CUNY Rsch. Found., 1985-91; vice chmn. Med. and Health Rsch. Assn., N.Y.C.; mem. health care tech. study sect. Nat. Ctr. Health Svcs. Rsch., 1976-79; mem. commn. on nat. policy Am. Jewish Congress, 1980-91. Grantee Ford/Rockefeller Founds., 1972-73, 75-76, Russell Sage Found., 1985-90. Mem.: APHA, Am. Econ. Assn. Jewish. Achievements include presenting report on Economic Status of Older Women to UN 2nd World Assembly on Aging., Madrid, 2002; sr. investigator Indicators of Health and Productive Engagement, Occupations of Older Workers. Office: Internat Longevity Ctr-USA Ltd 60 E 86th St New York NY 10028-1009 Business E-Mail: charlottem@ilcusa.org.

MULLER, DAVID EUGENE, retired mathematics professor, computer scientist, educator; b. Austin, Tex., Nov. 2, 1924; s. Hermann Joseph Muller and Jessie Marie Jacobs; m. Denise Josee Impens, Mar. 3, 1990; m. Alice Mimi Held (dec.); children: Kenneth, Chandra. BS, Caltech, Pasadena, 1947, PhD, 1951; PhD (hon.), U. Paris, 1989. Prof. U. Ill., Urbana, 1952—92, prof. emeritus, 1992—. Adj. prof. N.Mex. State U., N.Mex., 1995—. With USN, 1944—46. Fellow: AAAS. Home: 4200 Sotol Dr Las Cruces NM 88011 Personal E-mail: dmuller@cybermesa.com.

MULLER, EDWARD ROBERT, energy executive, lawyer; b. Phila., Mar. 26, 1952; s. Rudolph E. and Elizabeth (Steiner) M.; m. Patricia Eileen Bauer, Sept. 27, 1980; children: Margaret Anne, John Frederick. AB summa cum laude, Dartmouth Coll., 1973; JD, Yale U., 1976. Assoc. Leva, Hawes, Symington, Martin & Oppenheimer, Washington, 1977-83; dir. legal affairs Life Scis. group Whittaker Corp., Arlington, Va., 1983-84; v.p. Whittaker Health Svcs., Arlington, Va., 1984-85; v.p., gen. counsel, sec. Whittaker Corp., LA, 1985-93, chief adminstrv. officer, 1988-92, CFO, 1992-93, bd. dirs., 1993-99; v.p., gen. counsel, sec. BioWhittaker, Inc., Walkersville, Md., 1991-93; pres., CEO, bd. dirs. Edison Mission Energy, Irvine, Calif., 1993-2000; chmn., pres., CEO Mirant Corp., Atlanta, 2005—. Bd. dirs. Oasis Residential, Inc., Las Vegas, 1995—98, GlobalSantaFe Corp., Houston, 1997—, Interval, Inc., Marina del Rey, Calif., 2000—05, Strategic Data Corp., Santa Monica, Calif., 2001—05, The Keith Cos., Inc., Irvine, Calif., 2001—05, RigNet, Inc., Houston, 2002—05, RealEnergy, Inc., Woodland Hills, Calif., 2003—05, Ormat Tech., Inc., Sparks, Nev., 2004—05; mem. Brookings Task Force on Civil Justice Reform, 1988—89; chmn. U.S.-Philippines Bus. Com., 1998—2000; adv. bd. Tennenbaum Capital Ptnrs., LLC, LA, 1997—2003; mem. Coun. on Fgn. Rels., 1998—, Pacific Coun. on Internat. Policy, 1998—; dep. chmn. Contact Energy Ltd., Wellington, New Zealand, 1999—2000. Trustee Exceptional Children's Found., L.A., 1988-94, treas., 1988-93; co-chair Internat. Energy Devel. Coun., Washington, 1993-00; bd. govs. Jr. Achievement of Orange County and the Inland Empire, 1995-96; mem. Pres. Leadership Coun., Dartmouth Coll., 2003—; trustee Riverview Sch., East Sandwich, Mass, 2004—; bd. advisors The Pathway Program UCLA Ext., LA, 2004—. Office: Mirant Corp 1155 Perimeter Ctr W Atlanta GA 30338

MÜLLER, GENE ALAN, historian, consultant; b. Grand Island, Nebr., Jan. 10, 1943; s. Ludwig Frederick Alex and Erma Gertrude (Gorin) M.; m. Diana June Currey; children: Michelle Nicole Müller-Mehta, Alyssa Katherine, Alexandra Mariel, Nicholas Christian. B.A. cum laude, Midland Lutheran Coll., Fremont, Nebr., 1965; NYU in Spain scholar, U. Madrid, 1963-64; Fulbright-Hays scholar, U. Nacional Tucuman, Argentina, 1965-66; M.A., U. Kans., Lawrence, 1969, Ph.D., 1982. Asst. instr. U. Kans., 1967-73; asst. prof. history Ft. Hays State U., Kans., 1973-74; bilingual prof. history, El Paso Community Coll., Tex., 1974—; project reviewer Nat. Endowment Humanities, 1978—. Author: The Church in Poverty: Bishops, Bourbons, and Tithes in Spanish Honduras, 1700-1821; A Select Bibliography on the Catholic Church in Latin America, The Status of the Clergy and the Condition of the Church Wealth in Mexico: 1800-1850, Dr. Tomas Ruiz: Founder of Univ. of Nicaragua and Precursor of C.Am. Independence, 1777-1819, John Gorin of Fairfax County, Virginia: Defender of Mt. Vernon in 1781; also articles, book revs., chpts. in books. Mem., v.p. El Paso Council Internat. Visitors, 1982-83, pres., 1983-85; pres. So. N.Mex./El Paso br. Lutheran Brotherhood, v.p. Thrivent fraternal chpt., 2003-05; bd. dirs. Nat. Council for Internat. Visitors, Leadership El Paso, Class VIII; pres. El Paso chpt. Am. Field Service; mem. El Paso County Coun. for the Social Studies, regional chairperson, Regional Fulbright Tchr. Exchg. Interview Com.; pres., bd. dirs. El Paso Mission Trails Assn.; moderator Nat. Issues Forums, 1985—; coordinator NCIV/USAID Midwinter Seminar, El Paso, 1983-86, NEH Summer Seminar U. Tex., El Paso, 1986; lay asst. Luth. Quad Parish of Western, Kans. Am. Field Service scholar, New Zealand, 1960; NDFL Title VI fellow U. Kans., 1969; Ford Found. grantee, Nicaragua, 1969, Central Am., 1970; OAS fellow to Guatemala, 1973; Fulbright summer grantee, Brazil, 1982, Netherlands, 1983; sr. Fulbright lectr., U. Costa Rica, 1987, Fulbright-Alfonso Gercia Robles sr. lectr., UACJ, Mex., 1992-93, Fulbright-Hays, Nepal and India, 2003; recipient Burlington No. Teaching award, 1988, Outstanding Alumni award Midland Luth. Coll., 1988, El Paso Energy Found. award, 1993-94, EPCC Faculty Achievement award, 2004, NISOD Master Tchr. Award, 2004, NCIV award, 2005. Mem. Am. Hist. Assn., Am. Cath. Hist. Assn., Latin Am. Studies Assn., Conf. Latin Am. Studies, Tex. Cath. Hist. Assn., Rocky Mountain Council Latin Am. Studies, Midwest Assn. Latin Am. Studies., Fulbright Assn. (pres. del Norte chpt. 1989—). Democrat. Home: 10708 Vista Lomas Dr El Paso TX 79935-3611 Office: El Paso Community Coll PO Box 20500 El Paso TX 79998-0500 Office Phone: 915-831-2483. Business E-Mail: genem@epcc.edu.

MULLER, HENRY NICHOLAS, III, retired foundation administrator; b. Pitts., Nov. 18, 1938; s. Henry N., Jr. and Harriet (Kerschner) Muller; m. Nancy Clagett, June 20, 1959 (div. 1985); children: Charles T., Brook W.; m. Carol A. Cook, Jan. 4, 1986. BA, Dartmouth Coll., 1960; PhD, U. Rochester, 1968. Instr. Dartmouth Coll., Hanover, NH, 1964; lectr. Mt. Allison U., Sackville, Canada, 1964—66; asst. prof., prof. history U. Vt., Burlington, 1966—78, asst. dean Coll. Arts, Scis., 1969—70, assoc. dean Coll. Arts, Scis., 1970—73, dir. Living, Learning Ctr., 1973—78; pres. Colby-Sawyer Coll., New London, NH, 1978—85; dir. State Hist. Soc. Wis., Madison, 1985—96; pres., CEO Frank Lloyd Wright Found., Scotsdale, Ariz., 1996—2002; ret., 2002. Chair corp. governance and nom. com. Standex Internat. Corp., mem. pension plan investment and compensation com., also bd. dirs.; mem. Wis. State Hist. Records Adv. Bd., 1985—96, Gov. Coun. Tourism, 1987—96; chmn. Wis. Burial Sites Bd., 1988—96; trustee Nat. Trust Hist. Preservation, 1989—98; chair Wis. Submerged Cultural Resources, 1993—96; bd. dirs. Nat. Trust CDFI Corp., Willsboro Devel. Corp. Co-author: An Anxious Democracy, 1982; coeditor: Science, Technology and Culture, 1974, In a state of Nature, 1982, The Quotable Ethan Allen, 2005; sr. editor: Vt. Life mag., 1975—87; editor: Vt. History, 1977—85. Fin. chmn. Vt. Bicentennial Commn., 1970—77; trustee Vt. Hist. Soc., 1972—85, 2003—, v.p., 1975—82; chmn. Vt. Coun. Hist. Preservation, 1977—78, Bicentennial Com., Burlington, 1976; active NH Postsecondary Edn. Commn., 1983—85, Wis. Sesquicentennial Commn., 1995—99; trustee, pres. Taliesin Preservation, Inc., 1991—2001; trustee Frank Lloyd Wright Found., 1996—2004; v.p. Ind. Coll. Univ. Coun. Ariz., 1998—2000, bd. dirs., 1998—2002; interim chmn. Taliesin Archs., 2000—01; counselor Essex Cmty. Fund, NY, 2002—, sec.-treas., 2007—; counselor Adirondack Archtl. Heritage Ctr., 2005—; bd. dirs. Wis. Preservation Fund Inc., 1989—2006, USS Wis., 1989—93; trustee Ethan Allen Homestead Trust, 2002—, treas., 2003—05; v.p., 2005—; dir., vice chmn. Essex Cmty. Heritage Orgn., NY, 2003—04; bd. dirs., vice chmn., chmn. Smith House Health Care Ctr., Willsboro, NY, 2004—, chmn., 2006—; active Essex Bicentennial Com., 2004—05, Essex Planning Bd., 2005—; dir. Nat. Trust CDFI, Inc., 2006—. Fellow: Ctr. Rsch. Vt.; mem.: Am. Assn. State and Local History (councillor 1988—91), Vt. Archeol. Soc. (pres. 1971—74), Nat. Coun. Pub. History (bd. dirs. 1988—90), Madison Club.

MULLER, JANICE ELAINE, secondary school educator; b. Littlefield, Tex., Oct. 23, 1955; d. Calvin Roy and Hazel Louise Stevens; m. Mark C. Muller, Aug. 24, 1973; 1 child, Amanda Marie Thompson. BS, Tex. Tech U., Lubbock, 1977, MEd, 1995. Cert. tchr. Tex., 1977, mid mgmt./ednl. adminstrn. Tex., 1995. Tchr. Littlefield H.S., Tex., 1984—. Mem. reading com. ETS/TEA, Austin, 1996—99; mem. site based com. on edn. Littlefield H.S., 1998—, TAKS com. chmn., 2000—04; academic coord. U. Interscholastic League, Littlefield, 1999—. Founder Friends of the Libr., Littlefield, 1978—84; mem. adminstrv. bd. First United Meth. Ch., Littlefield, 2003—06; bd. dirs. Meals on Wheels, Littlefield, 1978—90. Named Outstanding Tex. H.S. Tchr., U. Tex., 1992, Tchr. of Yr., Tex. Assn. of Future Educators, 1997, 2005; fellow Caprock Area Writing Project, Tex. Tech. U., 1992. Mem.: Tex. Classroom Tchrs. Assn. (assoc.), Golden Key Nat. Honor Soc. (assoc.), Delta Kappa Gamma (assoc.; sec. 2000—02, Achievement award 2003). Democrat. Methodist. Avocations: golf, travel, writing. Home: 136 E 23rd St Littlefield TX 79339 Office: Littlefield HS 1100 Waylon Jennings Blvd Littlefield TX 79339 Home Phone: 806-385-0535; Office Phone: 806-385-5683. Personal E-mail: jmu1952672@aol.com.

MULLER, JENNIFER, choreographer, dancer; b. Yonkers, NY, Oct. 16, 1944; d. Don Medford and Lynette (Heldman) Muller. BS, Juilliard Sch. Music, 1967. Instr. in dance H.S. Performing Arts, 1967-72, Sarah Lawrence Coll., 1968-72, The Juilliard Sch., 1969-70, Nederlands Dans Theater, 1971-76, Utah rep., 1973-74, Centre Nat. de la Dance, Paris, 1998, Acad. Isola Danzo, Venice, 1999-2001, Atelier de Paris, 1999, Institut del Teatre de Barcelona, 2001, Centro Andaluz de Danza-Seville, 2003-05; commns.: Alvin Ailey Am. Dance Theatre, N.Y.C., 1977, 85, 2005, Festival d'Avignon, France, 1980, Lyon Opera Ballet, France, 1984, Aterballetto, 1988, Ballet Stagium, 1991, Dansgroep Krisztina de Chatel, 1992, Tanz-Forum Staatsoper Koln, Sachsische Staatsopera-Dresden, ARTSCAPE-Balt., 1991, 95, Aterballetto, Italy, 1993, Les Ballet Jazz de Montreal, 1994, Ballet du Nord, France, 1995, White Wave Rising, 1996, Bat Dor Dance Co., Israel, Nederlands Dans Theatre 3, Ballet Contemporaneo, Argentina, Ohio Ballet, 2000, Dance Inst. U. Akron, 2003; cons. Met. Mus. Art, 1971-72. Mem. Pearl Lang Dance Co., NYC, 1959-63; prin. dancer: Jose Limon Dance Co., NYC, 1963-71; assoc. dir., choreographer, prin. dancer: Louis Falco Dance Co., NYC, 1968-74; founder, dir., choreographer: Jennifer Muller/The Works, NYC, 1974-; choreographic works include: Nostalgia, 1971, Rust, 1971, Cantata, 1972, Tub, 1973, An American Beauty Rose, 1974, Biography, 1974, Speeds, 1974, Winter Pieces, 1974, Clown, 1974, Four Chairs, 1974, Wyeth, 1974, White, 1975, Strangers, 1975, Beach, 1976, Crossword, 1977, Predicaments for Five, 1977, Mondriaan, 1977, Lovers, 1978, Solo, 1979, Conversations, 1979, Chant, 1980, Terrain, 1981, Shed, 1982, Kite, 1983, Souls, 1984, The Enigma, 1986, Fields, 1986, Couches, 1986, Life/Times, 1986, Darkness and Light, 1986, Interrupted River, 1987, Occasional Encounters, 1988, City, 1988, The Flight of a Predatory Bird, 1989, Refracted Light, 1990, RIGHTeous About Passing (on the LEFT), 1990, Woman with Visitors at 3am, 1991, Regards, 1991, arm in arm in arm..., 1991, Thesaurus, 1991, Glass Houses, 1991, 2-1-1/Attic, 1992, Momentary Gathering, 1992, The Waiting Room, 1993, The Politician/Peeling the Onion, 1993, Orbs, Spheres and Other Circular Bodies, 1993, HUMAN/NATURE-A Response to the Longhouse Gardens, 1993, Pierrot, 1993, Desire-That DNA Urge, 1994, Point of View (A Case of Persimmons and Picasso), 1994, The Spotted Owl, 1995, Some Days are Like That, 1995, Promontory, 1996, Fruit, 1996, The Dinner Party, 1996, A Broken Wing, 1996, Ricochet, 1997, Degas Revisited, 1998, Dialectics Part I, 1998, Spores, Solitude & Summer Humming, 1999, Beethoven-Not Four Naught, 2000, aSOlo, 2000, Hymn for Her, 2000, Time Treading, 2000, China Project: Sagone; Suk Road; Dancing Waves, 2001, The Door, 2001, Never in The Same Room, 2002, To Live Alone..., 2002, Moon, 2002, It's a c#!* City, 2002, Prayer, 2003, Bounce, 2003, Footprints, 2003, Flowers, 2004, Ecstatic Poems, 2004, A Candle at Both Ends, 2004, Island, 2005, Sunlight and Shadow, 2005, Momentum, 2005, Metamorphosis, 2006, Passion Fruit, 2006, Edge, 2007; choreographer (theatre) Frimbo, 1980, The Death of von Richthofen..., 1982, Fame, The Musical, 1988, Up Against It, 1989, The Seven Deadly Sins, 1990, Signature, 1990, Esther, 1993, Once Around the City, 1998, 2001; dir.: Le Jongleur, 2000. Recipient Best Performance award Berlin Festival, 1977, Acad. award Juilliard Sch. Music, 1967, Carbonell award, 1989; grantee Nat. Endowment for Arts, 1971-77, 80-85, 86-87, 87-88, Creative Artists Pub. Svc., 1976-77, NY State Coun. on Arts, 1976-77, 78-79, 85-93, NYC Dept. Cultural Affairs, 1978-79, 94-2007, NYC Dept. Youth and Cmty. Devel., 2001-05. Mem. Am. Guild Mus. Artists, Soc. Stage Drs. and Choreographers, World Arts Coun. (founding mem.). Home and Office: The Muller Works Found Inc 131 W 24th St New York NY 10011-1942 Office Phone: 212-691-3803. Business E-Mail: jmuller@jmtw.org, twinfo@jmtw.org.

MULLER, JENNY HELEN, physician, psychiatrist; b. Johannesburg, Dec. 21, 1953; d. Eric and Lily Muller; 1 child, Jonathan Meshekow. MD, U. Witwatersrand, South Africa, 1977. Diplomate Am. Bd. Psychiatry and Neurology. Intern in internal medicine, surgery, orthop., Johannesburg, 1978; intern in internal medicine and psychiatry Va. Med. Ctr., Sepulveda, Calif., 1986—87, resident in psychiatry, 1987—90, VA and Olive View Hosp. Child and Adolescent Rotation UCLA, 1987—90; pvt. practice LA, 1990—. Mem.: APA, So. Calif. Psychiat. Assn. Avocation: horseback riding. Office: 9808 Venice Blvd Ste 505 Culver City CA 90232-6818 Office Phone: 310-204-1057. Office Fax: 310-204-1006. Personal E-mail: phy1@sbcglobal.net.

MULLER, JEROME KENNETH, photographer, art director, editor; b. Amityville, NY, July 18, 1934; s. Alphons and Helen (Haberl) M.; m. Nora Marie (Nestor), Dec. 21, 1974. BS, Marquette U., Milw., 1961; post grad., Calif. State U., Fullerton, 1985—86; MA, Nat. U., San Diego, 1988; post grad., Newport Psychoanalytic Inst., 1988—90. Comml. and editorial photographer, NYC, 1952-55; mng. editor Country Beautiful mag., Milw., 1961-62, Reproductions Rev. mag., NYC, 1967-68; editor, art dir. Orange County Illustrated, Newport Beach, Calif., 1962-67, art editor, 1970-79, exec. editor, art dir., 1968-69; owner, CEO Creative Svcs. Advt. Agy., Newport Beach, Calif., 1969-79. Founder, CEO, Mus. Graphics, Costa Mesa, Calif., 1978—; tchr. photography Lindenhurst H.S., NY, 1952-54, comic art U. Calif., Irvine, 1979, publ. design Orange Coast Coll., Costa Mesa, Calif., 1997-2002; guest curator Fiftieth Anniversary Exhbn. Mickey Mouse, 1928-78, The Bower's Mus., Santa Ana, Calif., 1978. One-man shows include Souk Gallery, Newport Beach, 1970, Gallery Two, Santa Ana, Calif., 1972, Cannery Gallery, Newport Beach, 1974, Mus. Graphics Gallery, 1993, White Gallery Portland State U., 1996, U. Calif., Irvine, 1997, Nat. Telephone and Comm., Irvine, Calif., 1998, Robert Mondavi Wine and Food Center, Costa Mesa, 2000; author: Rex Brandt, 1972, Publication Design and Production, 2000, Other Worlds: The Photography of Mike Glade, 2007; contbr. photographs and articles to mag. Mem. Cultural Arts Com., City of Costa Mesa, CA., 2000-2002. With USAF, 1956-57. Recipient, two silver medals Twentieth Ann. Exhbn. Advt. and Editorial Art in West, 1965, Inkpot award, San Diego Comic Conv., 1980. Mem.: Laguna Beach Art Mus., Met. Mus. Art, Mus. Modern Art (NYC), Orange County Mus. Art, Alpha Sigma Nu. Office: PO Box 11155 Costa Mesa CA 92627 Office Phone: 949-644-0808.

MULLER, JOHN BARTLETT, university president; b. Port Jefferson, NY, Nov. 8, 1940; s. Frederick Henry and Estelle May (Reeve) M.; m. Barbara Ann Schmidt, May 30, 1964 (dec. 1972); m. Lynn Anne Spongberg, Oct. 10, 1987. AB in Polit. Sci., U. Rochester, 1962; postgrad. in apologetics, Westminster Sem., Phila., 1962-63; MS in Psychology, Purdue U., 1968, PhD in Psychology, 1975. Asst. prof. psychology Roberts Wesleyan Coll., Rochester, NY, 1964-66, acting chmn. div. behavioral sci., dir. instl. research, 1967-70; vis. asst. prof. psychology Wabash Coll., Crawfordsville, Ind., 1970-71; research assoc. Ind. U.-Purdue U., Indpls., 1971-72; prof. psychology, v.p. for acad. affairs Hillsdale (Mich.) Coll., 1972-85; pres. BMW Assocs., Osseo, Mich., 1984-85, Bellevue (Nebr.) U., 1985—. Bd. dir. Nebr. Ind. Coll. Found., Omaha, Assn. Ind. Colls. Nebr., Lincoln; bd. advisors Applied Info. Mgmt. Inst., Gt. Western Bank. Contbr. articles to profl. jours. and textbooks. Bd. dir. Mid-American Coun. Boy Scouts Mental Health fellowship Purdue U., 1963, Nat. Tchg. fellowship Fed. Govt., 1967, Townsend fellowship U. Rochester, 1962. Mem. APA, Bellevue C. of C. (bd. dir. 1989-95), Phi Beta Kappa, Phi Kappa Phi. Republican. Home: 13303 Lochmoor Cir Bellevue NE 68123-3770 Office: Bellevue U Office of the Pres 1000 Galvin Rd S Bellevue NE 68005-3098 Office Phone: 402-557-7001. Business E-Mail: jmuller@bellevue.edu.

MULLER, KATHERINE LYNN, clinical psychologist; b. Point Pleasant, NJ, Nov. 22, 1973; d. Barbara Jean (Mahlschnee) Morey Hahn and Charles Muller; m. Simon Alexander Rego, May 18, 2003. BA, Douglass Coll., 1992—96; M in Psychology, Rutgers U., 1999, D in Psychology, 2001. Lic. psychologist State of NY, 2003, State of Pa., 2004. Rsch. asst. Rutgers U., New Brunswick, NY, 1996—2000; psychology intern Montefiore Med. Ctr., Bronx, NY, 2000—01; clinician/rschr. U. of Pa., Ctr. for the Treatment and Study of Anxiety, 2001—03; assoc. dir. of psychology tng./dir., cognitive behavior therapy program Montefiore Med. Ctr., Bronx, 2003—; asst. prof. of psychiatry and behavioral sciences Albert Einstein Coll. of Medicine, Bronx, 2003—. Curriculum dir., cognitive behavior therapy program Montefiore Med. Ctr., Bronx, 2003—; cons. Healthcare Coun., NY, 2004—. Contbg. editor: Einstein Journal of Biology and Medicine.

V.p. Fairmount Tenants Assn., Phila., 2002—03; mental health provider NY Project Liberty 9-11 Program, Bronx, 2003—04. Grad. Excellence fellowship, Rutgers U. Grad. Sch. of Applied and Profl. Psychology, 1996—2000, Agnes McDede Murray fellowship, Douglass Coll., 1996, Ocean County C. of C. scholarship, Toms River, NJ, 1996. Mem.: Assn. for Advancement of Behavior Therapy, Nat. Assn. of Cognitive Behavioral Therapists, Am. Psychol. Assn., Phi Beta Kappa. Avocations: music, theater. Office: Montefiore Med Ctr 111 East 210th St Bronx NY 10467 Home Phone: 914-965-8368; Office Phone: 718-920-5024. Office Fax: 718-920-6538. Business E-Mail: kmuller@montefiore.org.

MULLER, KURT ALEXANDER, lawyer; b. Chgo., June 21, 1955; s. Jack and Janet (Kasten) M.; m. Sylvia Saltoon, Apr. 6, 1986; 1 child, Marissa Grace. BS, U. Wis., Parkside, 1977; JD, John Marshall Law Sch., 1986. Bar: Ill. 1986, U.S. Dist. Ct. (no. dist.) Ill. 1986, Ariz. 1987, U.S. Dist. Ct. (ea. dist.) Wis. 1989; approved child rep. Cook County Ct. Creative dir. Brand Advt., Chgo., 1977-80; dep. sheriff Cook County, Chgo., 1978-86; broker Gerstenberg Commodities, Chgo., 1980-83; assoc. Gordon & Glickson, P.C., Chgo., 1986-87, Michael Harry Minton, P.C., Chgo., 1987-90; pvt. practice Chgo., 1990-92; ptnr. Law Offices of Richter-Muller, P.C., Chgo., 1992-95; lawyer, CEO The Muller Firm, Ltd., Chgo., 1995—. Lectr. Nat. Bus. Inst. Author: In Consideration of Divorce: Giving Credit (and Debits) to Dissolution, 1991, 3d edit., 1998; contbr. The Jewish American Prince Handbook, 1986; contbr. articles to profl. jours. and newspapers; host (Air Am. radio show) Kurt Muller's Uncommon Law; monthly columnist for Chgo. Social: Ask Muller, information source for FOX news. Mem. ABA, ACLU, Nat. Smoker's Alliance, Chgo. Bar Assn., Masons. Avocations: interior decorating, films, theater, writing. Office: The Muller Bldg 110 W Grand Ave Chicago IL 60610-4269 Office Phone: 312-467-6700. Business E-Mail: kmuller@mullaw.com.

MULLER, LEON, writer; b. Chgo., Mar. 16, 1918; Author of poems. With U.S. Army, 1942-45. Avocations: art, writing. Home: 69 W Washington St Ste 1800 Chicago IL 60602-3018

MULLER, MERVIN EDGAR, computer scientist, consultant, statistician, educator; b. Hollywood, Calif., June 1, 1928; s. Emanuel and Bertha (Zimmerman) Muller; m. Barbara McAdam, July 13, 1963; children: Jeffrey McAdam, Stephen McAdam, Todd McAdam. AB, UCLA, 1949, MA, 1951, PhD, 1954. Instr. in math. Cornell U., 1954-56; rsch. assoc. in math. Princeton (NJ) U., 1956-59, sr. scientist statis. and elec. engring., 1968-69; sr. statistician, dept. mgr. IBM, NYC, White Plains, 1956-64; prof. computer sci. and stats. U. Wis., 1964-71; prof. computer sci. George Mason U., 1985; dept. dir. World Bank, Washington, 1971-81, sr. advisor, 1981-85; Robert M. Critchfield prof. computer info. sci. Ohio State U., 1985-98, prof. emeritus, 1994-98, dept. chair, 1985-94. Chair sci. and tech. info. bd. NRC, NAS; bd. dirs. Advanced Info. Tech. Ctr., Columbus, Ohio. Mem. editl. bd. Computation and Stats., 1990, Jour. Computational and Graphical Stats., 1990; contbr. articles to profl. jours. Trustee First Unitarian Ch., Bethesda, Md., 1975—79; bd. mem. Chamber Music Columbus, 2006. Rsch. grantee, AT&T, Columbus, 1987. Fellow: World Acad. Productivity Sci., Am. Statis. Assn.; mem.: Internat. Assn. Statis. Computing (sci. sec. 1979—83, pres. 1977—79), Internat. Statis. Inst. (mem. steering com. Internat. Rsch. Ctr. 1987—89). Avocations: reading, exercise, walking, bridge. Home: 4171 Clairmont Rd Upper Arlington OH 43220-4501 Office: Ohio State U Dept Computer Info Sci Rm 395 2015 Neil Ave Columbus OH 43210-1210 Office Phone: 614-292-4281. E-mail: mmuller@columbus.rr.com, muller.m@cse-ohio-state.edu.

MULLER, PATRICIA ANN, nursing administrator, educator; b. NYC, July 22, 1943; d. Joseph H. and Rosanne (Bautz) Felter; m. David G. Smith, Mar. 19, 1988; children: Frank M. Muller III, Kimberly M. Muller. BSN, Georgetown U., 1965; MA, U. Tulsa, 1978, EdD, 1983. RN. Coord. staff devel. St. Francis Hosp., Tulsa, 1978—79, asst. dir. for nursing svc., nursing edn., 1979—82, dir. dept. edn., 1982—98, St. Francis Health Sys., 1998—2002, cons., 2002—; CEO, Smith Assocs. LLC, 2002. Mem. faculty Okla. U., Northeastern U., Tulsa U.; presenter at confs. and convs. Contbg. editor JOPAN, 1992-2001; contbr. articles to profl. jours. Mem. Leadership Tulsa, 1991; bd. dirs. Am. Heart Assn., Ronald McDonald House. Mem. ANA, Nat. League for Nursing, Am. Soc. for Nursing Svc. Adminstrs., Am. Soc. for Health Manpower Edn. and Tng., Okla. Nurses Assn., Okla. Orgn. of Nurse Execs. (pres. 1992-93), Sigma Theta Tau. Home and Office: 6203 W Utica Ct Broken Arrow OK 74011 Office Phone: 918-671-7767. E-mail: mullsmi@aol.com.

MULLER, PETER, lawyer, film company and retail executive; b. Teplitz-Sanov, Czechoslovakia, Mar. 4, 1947; came to US, 1949; s. Alexander and Elizabeth Rudolpha (Weingarten) M.; m. Irene Smolarski, Nov. 18, 1971 (div. 1973); children: Chloe, Aurisha; m. Esther Unterman Meisler, Jan. 4, 1987 (div. 1995). BA, NYU, 1968, JD cum laude. Entertainment editor Ambience mag., NYC, 1978-79, Women's Life mag., NYC, 1980-81; sole practice NYC, 1984—; entertainment writer Jewish Press; CEO Producers Releasing Corp., NY, 1987-88, Nev., 1987—88, pres. entertainment div. NY, 1987-88, Nev., 1987—88; pres., founder Muller Entertainment Group, NYC, 1988—, Calif., 1988—; pres., chief oper. officer ACA Joe, Inc., San Francisco and NYC, also bd. dirs. Expert tech. adv. svc. for attys., Pa., 1987—; adj. prof. NYU, UCLA, LaGuardia CUNY, Zicklin Sch. Bus. Baruch Coll. CUNY; arbitrator ICC Internat. Ct. Arbitration, 2007; lectr. entertainment and comm. bus. to various orgns. Author: Show Business Law, 1991, The Music Business: A Legal Perspective, 1994. Bd. dirs. NYU Coll. Arts and Sci.; vol. Lawyers for the Arts, NYC, 1987—. Mem. ABA (forum on entertainment and sports industries, forum on copyright, trademark and patent law), NY State Bar Assn., NYU Alumni Assn. (bd. dirs. 1987—, v.p. bd. dirs., coun.), Assn. of Am. Mgmt. Assn. (pres.). Avocations: sports, history, writing, travel, hiking. Home Phone: 212-358-3406; Office Phone: 212-358-3406.

MULLER, RALPH W., hospital administrator; b. Oct. 26, 1945; married. BA in economics, Syracuse U., NY, 1966; MA in govt., Harvard U., Cambridge, Mass., 1968. Asst. to commr. Nicholas Johnson FCC, Washington, 1967; assoc., health care consulting Orgn. for Social and Tech. Innovation, Cambridge, Mass., 1969-70; rsch. asst. to Prof. Samuel H. Beer Harvard U., 1967—68, teaching fellow, govt., and resident tutor, 1969—72; govt. instr. Suffolk U., Boston, 1972—74; budget dir., dept. of public welfare Commonwealth of Mass., Boston, 1975—78, dep. commr., dept. public welfare, 1978—80; dir. fin. planning and budget U. Chgo., 1980—83, assoc. v.p. budget, computing and info. sys., 1984, v.p., hospitals and clinics and dep. dean, divsn. biological sciences, 1985—86; pres., CEO U. Chgo. Hospitals and Health Sys., 1986—2003; CEO U. Pa. Health Sys., 2003—. Fellow: AAAS; mem.: Coun. of Tchg. Hospitals (chmn. 1997—98), Am. Assoc. of Med. Colleges (AAMC) (chmn. 1999—2000). Office: U Pa Health Sys 3400 Spruce St Philadelphia PA 19104

MULLER, RIANA RICCI, musician, educator; b. Orange, Calif., July 14, 1943; d. Ruggerio Ricci and Ruth (Ricci) (Rink) Mairs; m. William Paul Muller, Aug. 17, 1968; 1 child, Christine Rae. BM with distinction, Eastman Sch. Music, Rochester, NY, 1965, MM in Performance, Music Lit., 1969. Instr. Amarillo Coll, Tex., 1973—76; asst. prof. Coll. St. Benedict, St. Joseph, Minn., 1976—78; violinist Puerto Rico Symphony, San Juan, 1978—79; music tchr. (orch.) Hendrick Hudson Pub. Sch., Montrose, NY, 1984—2004; violinist freelance, Greater NY Area, 1984—2004, Pa., 2004—, Muller Duo, Lewisburg, Pa., 1979—; instr. Lycoming Coll., Williamsport, Pa. Violin study with Carrol Glenn, Joseph Knitzer, Louis Persinger and Ruggerio Ricci (my father). Author (and violinist): (DVD) Classical Music in the Foreign Language Classes, 2005; author: Ear Training Exercises for Violin Students, 2006. Decorated with medal and Diplome d'Honneur Eugene Ysaÿe Found., Brussels; recipient Cert. of Commendation for Chamber Music Tchg., Chamber Music Am., 1993. Mem.: Sigma Alpha Iota. Achievements include world premiere performance of Ysaÿe Violin Concerto No.8 (1977). Home: 1119 W Market St Lewisburg PA 17837 Personal E-mail: wpmuller@ptd.net.

MULLER, RICHARD STEPHEN, electrical engineer, educator; b. Weehawken, NJ, May 5, 1933; s. Irving Ernest and Marie Victoria Muller; m. Joyce E. Regal, June 29, 1957; children: Paul Stephen, Thomas Richard. ME, Stevens Inst. Tech., Hoboken, NJ, 1955; MSEE, Calif. Inst. Tech., Pasadena, 1957, PhD in Elec. Engring. and Physics, 1962. Test engr. Wright Aero/Curtiss Wright, Woodridge, NJ, 1953-54; mem. tech. staff Hughes Aircraft Co., Culver City, Calif., 1955-61; instr. U. So. Calif., LA, 1960-61; asst. prof., then assoc. prof. U. Calif., Berkeley, 1962-72, prof., 1973—. Guest prof. Swiss Fed. Inst. Tech., 1993; founder, dir. Berkeley Sensor & Actuator Ctr., 1985—; chmn. sensors electron devices NRC Army Rsch. Lab., 2003-04, chmn. microtech. adv. com. Helmholtz Assn., Germany, 2003—; chmn. steering com. Internat. Sensor and Actuator Meeting. Co-author: Device Electronics for Integrated Circuits, 1977, 3d, rev. edit., 2002, Microsensors, 1990; editor-in-chief IEEE/ASME Jour. Microelectromech. Sys., 1998—; contbr. over 200 articles to profl. jours. Pres. Kensington Mcpl. Adv. Coun., Calif., 1992-98; trustee Stevens Inst. Tech., 1996-2005. Fellow Hughes Aircraft Co., 1955-57, NSF, 1959-62, NATO postdoctoral fellow, 1968-69, Fulbright fellow, 1982-83, Alexander von Humboldt prize, 1993, Tech. U. Berlin, 1994; Berkeley citation, 1994, Stevens Renaissance award, 1995, Career Achievement award Internat. Conf. on Sensors and Actuators, 1997. Fellow IEEE (life, Cledo Brunetti award 1998, Millennium prize 2000); mem. IEEE Press Bd., NAE, NRC (chmn. sensors adv. bd. U.S. Army Rsch. Lab. 2003-04, liaison between NAE and NRC 2003—), Nat. Acad. Engring., Nat. Materials (adv. bd. 1994-98), Electron Devices Soc. (adv. com. 1984-98). Achievements include patents in field; development of operating micromotor and introduction of silicon surface micromachining. Office: U Calif Dept EECS # 1770 401 Cory Hall Berkeley CA 94720-1770 Office Phone: 510-642-0614.

MULLER, ROBERT JOSEPH, gynecologist; b. New Orleans, Dec. 5, 1946; s. Robert Harry and Camille (Eckert) Muller; m. Susan Philipsen, Aug. 22, 1974; children: Ryan, Matt. BS, St. Louis U., 1968; BS, MSc, Emory U., 1976; MD, La. State U., New Orleans, 1981; cert. in emergency mgmt., FEMA, 1998; cert. in Mgmt., Auburn U., 2001, MBA/MHA, 2003. Intern Charity Hosp., New Orleans, 1981-82; resident La. State U. Affiliate Hosp., 1982-85; resident staff physician La. State U. Med. Ctr., New Orleans, 1981-85; pvt. practice Camellia Women's Ctr., Slidell, La., 1985—; staff physician Tulane Med. Ctr., New Orleans, 1986—. Med. dir. Northshore Regional Med. Ctr., Slidell, 1987—, chief staff, 1998, vice chair governing bd., 2004—; mem. adv. bd. Auburn U., 2004—; med. dir. New Orleans Police Dept., 1981—95, S.W. La. Search and Rescue, Covington, La., 1986—, St. Tammany Parish Sheriff Dept., Covington, 1989—, comdr., 1990—, Camellia City Classic, Slidell, 1989—, Crawfishman Triathalon, Mandeville, La., 1988—, Res-Q-Med Laser Team, 1984—. Contbr. articles to profl. jours. Named one of Outstanding Young Men of Am., 1984, Am.'s Top Gynecologists, 2005—06; recipient Commendation medal, New Orleans Police Dept., 1986—87, 1989, medal of Valor, St. Tammany Parish Sheriff Office, 1990, cert. of Valor, S.E. La. Search and Rescue, 1990, Hurricane Katrina award, St. Tammany Parish, 2006, State of La. Dept. Health Hosp., 2007. Mem.: Am. Power Boat Assn. (med. staff 1984—89), Offshore Profl. Racing Tour (med. dir. staff 1990—95), So. Offshore Racing Assn. (med. dir. 1982—95), Profl. Assn. Diving Instrs. (divemaster 1991, asst. instr. 1995), La. State Med. Soc. Roman Catholic. Avocations: scuba diving, boating, shooting. Home: 1181 Yorktown Dr Slidell LA 70461-3023 Office: Camellia Womens Ctr 105 Smart Pl Slidell LA 70458-2039 Home Phone: 985-641-2152; Office Phone: 985-641-2100. Personal E-mail: rmullermd@aol.com.

MULLER, SCOTT WILLIAM, lawyer; b. Stamford, Conn., Feb. 15, 1950; s. Robert Sielke and Patricia (Harris) M.; m. Caroline Severance Adams, June 24, 1972; children: Christopher Adams, Robin McPherson, Peter Severance. BA cum laude, Princeton U., 1971; JD, Georgetown U. Law Ctr., 1975. Bar: NY 1976, US Dist. Ct. (so. dist.) NY 1977, US Ct. Appeals (2d. cir.) 1978, US Supreme Ct. 1978, US Tax Ct. 1984, DC 1986. Law clk. to presiding justice US Ct. Appeals (3d cir.), Phila., 1975-76; asst. atty. criminal div. US Atty.'s Office, NYC, 1978-82; assoc., litigator Davis, Polk & Wardwell, Washington, 1976-78, 82-84, mng. ptnr., 1985—2002; gen. counsel CIA, Washington, 2002—04. Adj. prof. in fed. law enforcement Georgetown U. Law Ctr. Nat. trustee Boys and Girls Clubs of Am.; mem. governing bd. St. Albans Sch.; mem. audit com. Protestant Episcopal Cathedral Found. (the Nat. Cathedral); bd. and former chmn. Ctr. for the Community Interest. Served N.G., 1971—72. Mem. ABA (vice-chmn, white collar crime com.), NY State Bar Assn., Fed. Bar Assn., Assn. of Bar of City of NY, Am. Law Inst. Republican. Episcopalian.

MULLER, STEVEN, international studies educator, academic administrator; b. Hamburg, Germany, Nov. 22, 1927; came to U.S., 1940, naturalized, 1949; 0. Werner Adolph and Marianne (Hartstein) M.; m. Margie Hellman, June 19, 1951 (dec. July 1999); children: Julie, Elizabeth; m. Jill E. McGovern, Feb. 5, 2000. BA, UCLA, 1948; BLitt (Rhodes scholar), Oxford U., Eng., 1951; PhD, Cornell U., 1958. Asst. prof. Haverford (Pa.) Coll., 1956-58; mem. faculty and adminstrn. Cornell U., 1958-71, dir. Ctr. Internat. Studies, 1961-66, v.p. pub. affairs, 1966-71; provost Johns Hopkins U., 1971-72, pres., 1972-90, pres. emeritus, 1990—, fellow Fgn. Policy Inst., disting. lectr., 1993—. Cons. Dept. Def., 1962-67, ACDA, 1967-77; bd. dirs. Orgn. Resources Counselors, Inc., Atlantic Coun. of the U.S. Author: Documents on European Government, 1963; co-editor: From Occupation to Cooperation, 1992, In Search of Germany, 1996; editor: Universities in the Twenty First Century, 1996. Trustee, chmn. St. Mary's Coll., 1991—2003; trustee German Marshall Fund of the US. Decorated comdr. Order of Merit (Fed. Republic of Germany), commendatore Republic of Italy. Mem. Am. Inst. Contemporary German Studies (co-chmn. emeritus), Coun. Fgn. Rels., Am. Polit. Sci. Assn., Internat. Inst. Strategic Studies, Am. Assn. Rhodes Scholars, Phi Beta Kappa, Cosmos Club (Washington). Office: Johns Hopkins U Sch Advanced Internat Studies 1619 Massachusetts Ave NW Washington DC 20036-2213 Office Phone: 202-663-5821. Business E-Mail: smuller1@jhu.edu.

MULLER, WILLARD C(HESTER), writer; b. Havre, Mont., May 7, 1916; s. Chester Rudolph and Clara (Hansen) M.; m. Carolyn Elfrid Bue, Jan. 27, 1945; children: Marolyn Jean, Barbara Anne, Nancy Eleanor. BA, Stanford U., 1941; MPA, Maxwell Grad. Sch. Govt. Adminstrn., 1943; student, Nat. War Coll., 1961-62. Newspaper reporter, short story writer Bremerton (Wash.) Daily Searchlight, 1934-36; White House corr. Bremerton Daily Searchlight and Port Angeles Evening News, 1941; mgmt. analyst USDA, 1942, 46-47; mem. staff for food, agr. and forestry U.S. Dept. Army and U.S. High Commr. for Germany, Munich and Frankfurt, Fed. Republic Germany, 1948-50; dist. adminstr., Am. consul U.S. Trust Territory of Pacific Islands, Truk, Caroline Islands, 1951-55; dep. dir. ICA, U.S. Ops. Mission to Nepal, Kathmandu, 1956-58; dir. U.S. Ops. to Somali Republic, 1958-61, Office East and Southern African Affairs, AID, Dept. State, Washington, 1962-65, AID, Kampala, Uganda, 1965-70, assoc. dir. mission, rep. for land reform Saigon, Vietnam, 1970—73, ret., 1973, cons., 1974-81; free lance writer, 1973—. Author various short stories; contbr. articles to profl. jours. Chmn. steering com. 4-state program dialogue on peace Pacific NW dist. Am. Luth. Ch., Tacoma, 1983-85; mem. Clallam br. Wash. State Centennial Commn., 1986-89; mem. Food Bank Bd., Port Angeles, Wash., 1986-90. Lt. USNR, 1943-45, PTO. Mem.: Am. Fgn. Svc. Assn., Am. Soc. Pub. Adminstrn., Kiwanis. Avocation: travel. Home and Office: 3624 S Mount Angeles Rd Port Angeles WA 98362-8910 Home Phone: 360-457-5315. Personal E-mail: muller@tenforward.com.

MULLER, WILLIAM ALBERT, III, retired library director; b. Savannah, Ga., Jan. 1, 1943; s. William Albert Jr. and Julia Anne (Cleary) M.; m. Claudya Barbara Burkett, Dec. 12, 1965 (div. 1986); 1 child, Martha Genevieve; m. Pamala Qualls, Apr. 9, 1988; 1 child, Tabitha Wade. BS, Ga. So. Coll., 1966; MLS, Emory U., 1969. Dir. War Woman Regional Libr., Elberton, Ga., 1969-73; rsch. libr. City of Savannah, 1973-75; dir. Mason County Pub. Libr., Point Pleasant, W.Va., 1976-78; pub. rels. cons. Eastern Shore Regional Libr., Salisbury, Md., 1978-81; dir. Brooke County Pub. Libr., Wellsburg, W.Va., 1982-84, McDowell Pub. Libr., Welch, W.Va., 1984-88, Bristol (Va.) Pub. Libr., 1988—2000; ret., 2000. Dir. Albermarle Regl. Libr., Winton, N.C., 2003-; sec. So. W.Va. Libr. Automation Corp., Beckley, 1984-87, pres. 1987-88, S.W. Info. Network Group, Abindgdon, Va., 1990-91, treas. (swing) 1993—; bd. dir. Albermarle Regional Libr., Winton, NC. Fundraiser Paramount Fund, Bristol, 1989; acct. exec. United Way Fund of Bristol, 1991; vol. Murfreesboro Pub. Libr., 2004—07; Sunday Sch. tchr. St. Thomas Episcopal Ch., Ahoskie, NC, 2004—07; choir St. Stephens Episcopal Ch., Oxford, NC; bd. dirs. Mid-Atlantic Chamber Orch., Bristol, 1988—92, treas., 1992; bd. dirs. Bristol Preservation Soc., 1988—98, Nat. Ctr. for Quality, 1992—98, Main St. Bristol, 1991—95, treas., 1994; bd. dirs. Jr. Achievement, 1992—99, pres., 1997—99; bd. dirs. Vol. Bristol, 1998; bd. dirs., vol. chair Racefest, 1998—99. Mem.: N.Y.C. Ballet Guild, Smithsonian Assocs., N.C. Mus. Art. Democrat. Avocations: gardening, cabinetry, photography, travel, model railroads. Home: 2769 Garland Ct Creedmoor NC 27522 Office Phone: 252-287-9753. Personal E-mail: unclebillm@yahoo.com.

MULLER, WILLIAM HENRY, JR., retired surgeon, educator; b. Dillon, SC, Aug. 19, 1919; s. William Henry and Octavia Elizabeth (Bethea) M.; m. Hildwin Clare Headly, Mar. 23, 1946; children: William Henry III, Marietta John Lewis. BS, The Citadel, 1940, DS (hon.), 1972; MD, Duke U., 1943; DHL (hon.), Med. U. S.C., 1977. Diplomate Am. Bd. Thoracic Surgery, Am. Bd. Surgery (rep. conf. com. grad. tng. in surgery). Intern Johns Hopkins Hosp., Balt., 1944, asst. surgery, asst. resident, 1944-46, resident gen. surgery, instr. surgery, 1948-49, resident cardiovascular surgery, 1949; practice gen. surgery Dillon, 1947-48; asst. prof. surgery UCLA, 1949-53, assoc. prof. Sch. Medicine, 1953-54; attending specialist thoracic surgery Wadsworth VA Hosp., Los Angeles; chief sect. cardiovascular surgery Los Angeles County-Harbor Gen. Hosp., Torrance, Calif.; cons. surgery St. Johns's, Santa Monica Hosps., 1949-54; cons. cardiovascular surgery U.S. Naval Hosp., San Diego, 1953-54; Stephen H. Watts prof. surgery, chmn. dept. U. Va. Sch. Medicine, 1954-82, v.p. health affairs, 1976-88, univ. prof. surgery and health policy, 1988-90, S. Hurt Watts prof. surgery emeritus, 1990—, v.p. for health affairs emeritus; surgeon-in-chief U. Va. Hosp., 1954-82; chmn. S.E. Surg. Congress; mem. panel heart disease Pres.'s, 1972; past chmn. surgery study sect. NIH; mem. exec. com., div. med. scis. NRC. Mem. editorial bd.: Am. Jour Surgery, Annals of Surgery, Am. Surgeon; contbr. articles to med jours. Trustee, mem. exec. com. Duke U. Served as capt. M.C. AUS, 1946-47. Named One of 10 Outstanding Young Men of Yr. U.S. Jr. C. of C., Calif. Jr. C. of C., 1952; recipient Disting. Alumni award (1st award) Duke U. Med. Ctr., 1969; Thomas Jefferson award U. Va., 1982; McCallie Sch. Alumni Achievement award, 1986; Paul Harris fellow Nat. Rotary Found., 1988. Fellow ACS (past chmn., forum com. fundamental surg. problems, regent 1971—, chmn. bd. regents 1976-78, pres.-elect 1979); mem. Internat. Soc. Surgery, Internat. Cardiovascular Soc. (past v.p.), AMA, Am. Surg. Assn. (pres. 1974-75), So. Surg. Assn. (pres. 1975), Pacific Coast Surg. Assn., Am. Assn. Thoracic Surgery, Soc. Univ. Surgeons (past pres.), Soc. Surgery Alimentary Tract, Assn. Acad. Surgeons, James IV Assn. Surgeons (v.p. U.S.), Med. Soc. Va., Albemarle County Med. Soc., Soc. Vascular Surgery (past pres.), Am. Heart Assn. (chmn. surgery research study com., mem. central research com.), Va. Surg. Soc, Halsted Soc., Johns Hopkins Soc. Scholars, Raven Soc., Sigma Xi, Alpha Omega Alpha, Phi Chi Home: 900 Flordon Dr Charlottesville VA 22901-7844

MULLET, ROBIN M., retired accountant; b. Oregon, Ohio, Mar. 24, 1950; d. Verne J. and Hedwig T. Hofbauer, Bonnie Hofbauer (Stepmother); m. Richard A. Mullet, June 10, 1989; children: Chad J., Miranda J., Kristin L. Schwartz. BA in Liberal Arts, SUNY, Albany, 1990. CPA Ohio, 1993. Sr. staff acct. J. M. Green & Associates, Inc., Wapakoneta, Ohio, 1987—98; pvt. practice Belle Center, Ohio, 1998—2000; ret., 2000. Guest instr. Wright State U., Celina, Ohio, 1987—98; adj. prof. Lima Tech. Coll., Ohio, 1998—99. Pres., bd. dirs. Wolf Recovery Found., Inc., Boise, Idaho, 1997—2003; bd. dirs. Audubon Ohio, Columbus, 2006—. Mem.: Write-On Writers' Group, Nat. Honor Soc. (gt. lakes guardian). Avocations: writing, conservation, weaving.

MULLICK, FLORABEL GARCIA, pathologist, director; b. Spain; MD, U. PR, 1964; DSc (hon.), Met. U., PR. Diplomate Am. Bd. Pathology, lic. Md., Washington, PR. Internship pediatric pathology U. Hosp. PR, Rio Piedras, 1964—65, residency, 1965—66, Children's Hosp. DC, 1966—67, fellow, 1967—68; residency Georgetown U. Hosp., Washington, 1968—69; assoc. dir. Armed Forced Inst. Pathology, Washington, prin. dep. dir., 1999—2007, dir., 2007—. Dir. Ctr. for Advanced Pathology Armed Forces Inst. Pathology, 1994—, chair dept. environ. and infectious disease scis., 1996—; prof. pathology U. PR, Uniformed Svcs. U. of Health Scis., Bethesda, Md.; adj. prof. pathology Georgetown U. Hosp. Med. Sch.; disting. physician exec. med. adv. bd. FindCancerExperts.com; bd. dirs. Ana G. Mendez U. Sys.; cons. in field. Cons. editor: Annals of Diagnostic Pathology, mem. editl. bd.: Modern Pathology, Toxicology Pathology, Electronic Jour. Pathology and Histology; contbr. chapters to books, scientific papers to profl. jours. Recipient Disting. Exec. Svc. award, Sr. Execs. Assn. Profl. Devel. League, 1994, Excellence in Edn. award, Ana G. Mendez U. Sys. Fellow: Coll. Am. Pathologists; mem.: History of Pathology Soc. (founding trustee), US Fed. Sr. Exec. Svc. (Meritorious Exec. 1992, Disting. Exec. 1993), Spanish Soc. Pathology (hon.), Internat. Acad. Pathology (sec. 1995—2006, mem. fin. com. 2006—, pres.-elect 2006—). Achievements include development of the International Database on Toxic Lesions in Animals and Humans (INTOX); research in human health effects of toxic drugs and toxic trace metals with emphasis on liver diseases and pediatric pathology cases. Office: Armed Forces Inst Pathology 6825 16th St NW Washington DC 20306-6000 Business E-Mail: mullick@afip.osd.mil. *

MULLIGAN, BRIAN C., film company executive; BBA, U. So. Calif.; MBA, UCLA. Sr. v.p. bus. develop. & strategic planning Universal Studios, 1995—98, exec. v.p. ops. & fin., 1998—99; co-chmn. Universal Pictures, Universal City, Calif., 1999; exec. v.p., CFO Seagram Co., Ltd., 1999—2001; chmn. Fox TV Stations, Inc., 2001—02; venture capitalist, advisor to Marvin Davis, 2001; exec. adv. The Boston Consulting Group, Inc., 2002; founder, principal Universal Partners, 2002—04; sr. exec. adv. media & entertainment Cerberus Capital Mgmt. LP. Bd. mem. Roxio, 2003—. Bd. dir. Napster, 2003—.

MULLIGAN, DAVID KEITH, consulting company executive, securities arbitrator; s. Robert Keith and Yvonne Bette Mulligan. BA in Bus. Adminstrn., Oakland Coll., 1979. Cert. data processor, quality technician, quality auditor, software quality engr.; NASD gen. securities registered rep. Pres. Atlas Prodns., NYC, 1973—. Cons. info. systems, human factors, tech. and mktg. comm. Author: Human Factors in Document Design, 1982, Computer Aids to Software Engineering, 1984, Document Design and Production for the '90s, 1989, Documentation and System Maintenance,

1989, Avoiding Outsourcing and Its Demoralizing Consequences, 1990, Programmer-Analyst: Dinosaur of the '90s, 1990, Information Management: New Thinking for the '90s, 1991, Product Documentation: Key to Internat. Marketing Success, 1993, Joint Application Design Critical Success Factors, 1994, Successful Worldwide Interactive Marketing, 1995, Management Information: Lifeblood of Business, 1996, Executive Ego: Most Powerful Force in Business, 1997, Investigation Techniques in the Healthcare Industry, 1997, Oracle Data Base Adminstration: A Structured Approach, 1999, Information Management in the Entertainment Industry, 1999, Database Application Implementation in the New Millennium, 1999, Sixty Minute Methodology for Desktop Development, 2000, Broad Band Communications: A Business Blueprint, 2000, Data Design: Key To Effective Telecom Provisioning, 2001, Data Management in the Mortgage Banking Industry, 2002, Data Design: Key to Effective Mortgage Banking, 2002, Dysfunction in Corporate America, 2002, Corporate Politics: The Greatest Menace to Productivity, 2003, Automotive Information Management: Engine of Success, 2004, Accounting Controls: Key to Coherence in the Entertainment Industry, 2005, Creative Accounting Processes for the Entertainment Industry, 2005, A New Paradigm for Ocean Shipping and International Logistics, 2006, 21st Century Logistics for the Entertainment Industry, 2006; co-author: Structured Analysis and Design for the Case User, 1993. Mem. ASCAP, NARAS, Am. Soc. Quality, Am. Fedn. of Musicians, NY Friars Club, The Authors Guild, Am. Mensa, NASD (bd. arbitrators). Avocations: musical composition, music performance, photography.

MULLIGAN, DONAL L., consumer products company executive; Fin. mgmt. positions PepsiCo Inc. & YUM! Brands, 1987—98, Pillsbury Co., 1998—2001; v.p. fin. ops. internat. div. Gen. Mills, Mpls., 2001—04, v.p. fin. ops., 2004—06, v.p., treas., 2006—07, sr. v.p. fin. ops., 2007, exec. v.p., CFO, 2007—. Office: General Mills 1 General Mills Blvd Minneapolis MN 55426 *

MULLIGAN, ELINOR PATTERSON, lawyer; d. Frank Clark and Agnes (Murphy) Patterson; m. John C. O'Connor; children: Christine Fulena, Valerie Clark, Amy O'Connor, Christopher Criffan O'Connor; m. William G. Mulligan, Dec. 6, 1975. BA, U. Mich.; JD, Seton Hall U., 1970. Bar: N.J. 1970. Assoc., Springfield and Newark, 1970—72; pvt. practice Hackettstown, NJ, 1972; ptnr. Mulligan & Jacobson, NYC, 1973—91, Mulligan & Mulligan, Hackettstown, 1976—. Atty. Hackettstown Planning Bd., 1973-86, Blairstown Bd. Adjustment, 1973-95; sec. Warren County Ethics Com., 1976-78, sec. Dist. X and XIII Fee Arbitration Com., 1979-87, mem. and chair, 1987-91, mem. dist. ethics com. XIII, 1992—; mem. spl. com. on atty. disciplinary structure N.J. Supreme Ct., 1981—; lectr. Nat. Assn. Women Judges, 1979, N.J. Inst. Continuing Legal Edn., 1988—. Contbr. articles to profl. jours. Named Vol. of Yr., Attys. Vols. in Parole Program, 1978. Fellow Am. Acad. Matrimonial Lawyers (1st woman pres. N.J. chpt. 1995-96); mem. ABA, Warren County Bar Assn. (1st woman pres. 1987-88), N.J. State Bar ASsn., N.J. Women Lawyers Assn. (v.p. 1985—), Am. Mensa Soc., Union League Club (N.Y.C.), Baltusrol Golf Club (Springfield, N.J.), Panther Valley Golf and Country Club (Allamuchy, N.J.), Kappa Alpha Theta. Republican. Home: 12 Goldfinch Way Hackettstown NJ 07840-3007 Office: 933 County Road 517 Hackettstown NJ 07840-4654 Office Phone: 908-852-0202. Personal E-mail: llp-nj@mindspring.com. Business E-Mail: elinormulligan@mulliganmulligan.com.

MULLIGAN, JEREMIAH T., lawyer; b. Rochester, NY, 1944; BA, St. Bernard's Seminary and Coll., 1966; JD, Fordham U., 1970. Mem. Curtis, Mallet-Prevost, Colt & Mosle, NYC. Office: Curtis Mallet-Prevost Colt & Mosle 101 Park Ave Fl 34 New York NY 10178-0061 Office Phone: 212-696-6040. Business E-Mail: jmulligan@cm-p.com.

MULLIGAN, JOHN J., corporate financial executive; Student, Holy Cross Coll.; BA in Liberal Arts, St. John's U., NYC, 1976; M in Bus. and Acctg., Fordham U., NYC, 1981. With Mfrs. Hanover Leasing Corp., 1979—86; mgr. lease financing Philip Morris Capital Corp., 1986—87, dir. structured fin., 1987—94, v.p. lease/structured fin., 1994—2001, pres., CEO, 2001—. Office: Altria Grp Inc 120 Park Ave New York NY 10017

MULLIGAN, MICHAEL DENNIS, lawyer; b. St. Louis, Mar. 9, 1947; s. Leo Virgil and Elizabeth (Leyse) M.; m. Theresa Baker, Aug. 7, 1971; children: Brennan, Colin. BA in Biology, Amherst Coll., 1968; JD, Columbia U., 1971. Bar: Mo. 1971, U.S. Dist. Ct. (ea. dist.) Mo. 1972, U.S. Ct. Appeals (8th cir.) 1982, U.S. Tax Ct. 1985. Law clk. to judge U.S. Dist. Ct. (ea. dist.) Mo., 1971-72; assoc. Lewis, Rice & Fingersh, L.C., St. Louis, 1972-80, ptnr., 1980—. Mem. editl. bd. Estate Planning Mag., 1985—, Jour. of Taxation, BNA Estates, Gifts and Trusts Jour. Served as cpl. USMC, 1968-70. Fellow Am. Coll. Trust and Estate Counsel; mem. ABA (mem. real property, probate and trust, and taxation sects.), Mo. Bar Assn. (mem. probate and trust, taxation sects.). Office: Lewis Rice & Fingersh LC 500 N Broadway Ste 2000 Saint Louis MO 63102-2147 Home Phone: 317-726-0139; Office Phone: 314-444-7757. Business E-Mail: mmulligan@lewisrice.com.

MULLIGAN, MICHAEL K., headmaster; m. Joy Mulligan; 1 child. BA, Middlebury Coll.; EdM, Harvard U.; MA in English, Middlebury Coll. History and English teacher & soccer, lacrosse, and wrestling coach Gov. Dummer Acad., 1977—82, dir., coll. placement, 1982—86; dean of administration, teacher, and coach The Thacher Sch., Ojai, Calif., 1986—93, head of sch., 1993—. Mem.: Assn. of Boarding Schools. Office: Thacher Sch 5025 Thacher Rd Ojai CA 93023 E-mail: mmulligan@thacher.org. *

MULLIGAN, ROBERT, film director, producer; b. NYC, Aug. 23, 1925; s. Robert Edward and Elizabeth (Gingell) M. Grad., Fordham U. Dir. Goodyear TV Playhouse, 1951, Suspense, 1953-54, Philco TV Playhouse, 1955, The Alcoa Hour (1 episode), 1955, Rendezvous, 1957, Studio One (3 episodes), 1957, The DuPont Show of the Month (3 episodes), 1958; dir. (TV films) The Moon and Sixpence, 1959; dir. (films) Fear Strikes Out, 1957, The Rat Race, 1960, THe Great Impostor, 1961, Come September, 1961, The Spiral Road, 1962, To Kill a Mockingbird, 1962, Love with the Proper Stranger, 1963, Baby the Rain Must Fall, 1965, Inside Daisy Clover, 1965, Up the Down Staircase, 1967, Stalking Moon, 1968, Pursuit of Happiness, 1971, Summer of '42, 1971, Bloodbrothers, 1978, Same Time Next Year, 1978, Clara's Heart, 1988, The Man in the Moon, 1991; prodr., dir. The Other, 1972, Nickel Ride, 1974, Kiss Me Goodbye, 1982. Recipient Career Achievement award, LA Film Critics Assn., 2006. *

MULLIKIN, THOMAS WILSON, mathematics professor; b. Flintville, Tenn., Jan. 9, 1928; s. Houston Yost and Daisy (Copeland) M.; m. Mildred Virginia Sugg, June 14, 1952; children: Sarah Virginia, Thomas Wilson, James Copeland. Student, U. South, 1946-47; AB, U. Tenn., 1950; postgrad., Iowa State U., 1952-53; A.M., Harvard, 1954, PhD, 1958. Mathematician Rand Corp., Santa Monica, Calif., 1957-64; prof. math. Purdue U., 1964-93, interim v.p., dean grad. sch., 1991-93, dean grad. sch., prof. math emeritus, 1993—. Served with USNR, 1950-52. Mem.: AAAS, Am. Math. Soc. Home: 104 Club Ct Cape Carteret NC 28584-9736

MULLIN, BERNARD JAMES, professional sports team executive; b. Liverpool, Eng., May 3, 1949; came to US, 1973; s. Bernard F. and Mary A. Mullin; m. Valerie Mullin; children: Julie, Lara, Steven 1 stepchild, Chad. BA in Bus. Studies, Coventry U., Eng., 1972; MS in Mktg., U. Kans., 1974, MBA, 1976, PhD in Bus., 1978. Mgr. mktg. rsch. Brit. Leyland Motor Corp., Oxford, England, 1970—73; mktg. devel. mgr. Serck Tubes Ltd., Birmingham, England, 1973; instr. U. Kans., Lawrence, 1974-77; prof. sport mgmt. U. Mass., Amherst, 1977-86; pres. NSM Mgmt. Cons., Amherst, 1979-86; sr. v.p. bus. Maj. League Baseball Pitts. Pirates, 1986—91; sr. v.p. bus. ops. Maj. League Baseball Colo. Rockies, 1991—93; pres., gen. mgr. Internat. Hockey League Denver Grizzlies, 1993; vice chancellor athletics U. Denver; sr. v.p. mktg. and team bus. ops. NBA, 2000—04; pres., CEO Atlanta Spirit, LLC (parent co. of NBA Atlanta Hawks, NHL Atlanta Thrashers and Philips Arena), 2004—. Author: Sport Marketing. Chmn. bd. mgmt. YMCA Pitts., 1988; bd. mem. Ctrl. Atlanta Progress, Atlanta Sports Coun., Metro Atlanta C. of C. Mem. Rotary Internat. (substance abuse com. 1988), Beta Gamma Sigma. Roman Catholic. Avocations: golf, tennis, soccer, reading. Office: Atlanta Spirit LLC 101 Marietta St NW Ste 1900 Atlanta GA 30303 *

MULLIN, CHRISTOPHER PAUL, professional sports team executive, retired professional basketball player; b. NYC, July 30, 1963; m. Liz Mullin; children: Sean, Christopher, Liam. Student, St. John's U., 1981—85. Player Golden State Warriors, 1985—97, 2000, exec. v.p. basketball ops., 2004—; player Ind. Pacers, 1997—2000. Mem. US Olympic Team (gold medal), 1984, 92. Recipient Wooden award, 1985; named to Sporting News All-Am. First Team, 1985; NBA All-Star team, 1989-93, All-NBA First Team, 1992. Office: Golden State Warriors 1011 Broadway Oakland CA 94607 *

MULLIN, DANIEL KARL, emergency physician, educator; b. NYC, Apr. 9, 1972; s. Neil Marc Mullin and Audrey Joan Bomse, Nancy Erika Smith (Stepmother); m. Margot Nicole Thien, Apr. 6, 1997; children: Kacie Michaela, Sydney Allison. BA, U. Calif., Berkeley, 1994; MD summa cum laude, Keck Sch. Medicine, UCLA, 2002. Cert. Am. Bd. Emergency Medicine, 2007, lic. med. physician Commonwealth of Pa., cert. ACLS Am. Heart Assn., PALS Am. Heart Assn., ATLS Am. Coll. Surgeons, diplomate Nat. Bd. Med. Examiners. Intern Hosp. U. Pa., Phila., 2002; resident Drexel U. Coll. Medicine, Phila., 2003—06, asst. prof. emergency medicine, 2006—. Continuing med. edn. dir. Drexel U. Coll. Medicine, 2006—. Contbr. monthly columns. Fellow: Am. Acad. Emergency Medicine; mem.: AMA (Physician's Recognition award), Pa. Med. Soc., Am. Coll. Emergency Physicians, Soc. for Academic Emergency Medicine. Democrat. Jewish. Avocations: triathalons, mountain biking, tennis, ping pong/table tennis. Office: Drexel Univ Coll Medicine 245 N 15th St Mail Stop 1011 Philadelphia PA 19102 Home Phone: 856-428-9301; Office Phone: 215-762-2365. Office Fax: 215-762-1307.

MULLIN, GENE, state legislator; b. San Francisco, Apr. 21, 1937; m. Terri Mullin; children: Jennifer, Kevin. BA in Polit. Sci., U. San Francisco, 1960. Lifetime secondary tchg. credential U. San Francisco, 1967. Tchr. govt. South San Francisco High Sch., 1967—99; mem. planning commn. City of South San Francisco, 1972—80, mem. city council, 1995—, mayor, 1998, 2001—02; mem. Calif. State Assembly from 19th dist., 2002—. Chair negotiations com. South San Francisco CTA, 1986—90; lectr., cons. Inst. Local Self Govt., 1989—97, Ctr. Youth Citizenship, 1999—; vice chair Labor and Employment Com.; mem. Edn. Com., Housing and Cmty. Devel. Com., Human Svcs. Com., Local Govt. Com., Vets. Affairs Com.; pres. Soutn San Francisco Classroom Tchr.'s Assn., 1992—95. Author: 2 books on local govt. JAG gen. corps US Army, 1959—60. Mem.: Assn. Bay Area Govts. (mem. exec. com. 1999—), San Mateo County Retired Tchrs. Assn., Young Men's Inst. Democrat. Roman Catholic. Mailing: Capitol Office PO Box 942849 Sacramento CA 94294 Office: Dist Office Ste 302 1528 S El Camino Real San Mateo CA 94402

MULLIN, LEO FRANCIS, airline executive; b. Concord, Mass., Jan. 26, 1943; s. Leo F. and Alice L. (Fearns) M.; m. Leah J. Malmberg, Sept. 10, 1966; children: Jessica, Matthew. AB, Harvard U., 1964, MS, 1965, MBA, 1967. Assoc. McKinsey & Co., Washington, 1967-73, prin., 1973-76; sr. v.p. strategic planning Consol. Rail Corp., Phila., 1976-78; sr. v.p. 1st Chgo. Corp., Chgo., 1981-84, exec. v.p., 1984-91, chmn. Am. Nat. Bank and Trust Co., 1991-93, pres., COO, 1993-95; vice chmn. Unicom/Commonwealth Edison, Chgo., 1995—97; CEO Delta Airlines, Atlanta, 1997—2003, chmn. bd. dirs., 1999—2004; sr. advisor pvt. equity group Goldman Sachs, NYC, 2004—. Bd. dirs. Johnson & Johnson, BellSouth, 1998—. Vice chmn. Chgo. Urban League, 1993—; chmn. bd. trustees Field Mus. Natural History, 1994—; bd. dirs. Chgo. chpt. Juvenile Diabetes Found., 1985—, Met. Planning Coun., 1983—, Children's Meml. Hosp., Chgo., 1989—, Chgo. Coun. Fgn. Rels., 1994—; mem. Chgo. Econ. Devel. Commn., 1992-95; trustee Northwestern U., 1992—. Mem. Chgo. Club, Harvard Club of Chgo., Econ. Club of Chgo.

MULLIN, PATRICK ALLEN, lawyer; b. Newark, Jan. 13, 1950; s. Gerard Vincent and Frances Regina (Magnanti) M. BA, William Paterson U., 1972, MEd, 1974; JD with honors, NY Law Sch., 1979, LLM in Taxation, 1990; postgrad., Harvard Law Sch., 1979. Bar: NJ 1979, DC 1980, NY 1990; cert. criminal trial atty. NJ Supreme Ct. Law clk. to Hon. Dickinson R. DeBevoise, US Dist. Ct. NJ, Trenton, 1979-80; assoc. Charles Morgan Assocs., Washington, 1980-81; pvt. practice, Hackensack, NJ, 1988—; instr., 1985—. Mem. Practitioners Adv. Group US Sentencing Commn., 1995—; lectr. Seton Hall Law Sch., 2001, 02, 04, 06, 07, ATLA, 2003; instr. Gerry Spence's Trial Lawyers Coll., 2001-06; moderator ICLE program Upheaval in Fed. and State Sentencing, 2005, with criminal trial practice, 1999-2007; lectr. criminal trial practice Seton Hall Law Sch., 2005. Contbr. articles to profl. jours. Mem. ABA. Roman Catholic. Avocations: jogging, martial arts. Address: 25 Main St # 200 Hackensack NJ 07601-7015 also: 305 Madison Ave Ste 449 New York NY 10165-0006 Office Phone: 201-488-5500. Home Fax: 201-487-2840.

MULLIN, STAN, real estate company executive; BS, U. Southern Calif., 1980. Cert. Comml. Investment Member, 1988. Joined Grubb & Ellis, 1982—, sr. v.p. Named Broker of Yr., 1984, 1991, 1997, 1999, 2000, 2001. Mem.: Counselors of Real Estate, Soc. Industrial and Office Realtors (chpt. pres. 1997, chmn. rsch. and publications com. 2001, com. restructure task force 2001, chmn. comm. com. 2002, mem. bd. dirs. 2002, chmn. edn. com. 2003, leadership develop. com. 2003, v.p. 2004, pres.-elect 2005, Roy Seeley award 2002), Am. Industrial Real Estate Assn. (pres. 2006). Office: Grubb & Ellis 4675 MacArthur Court Ste 1600 Newport Beach CA 92660 Office Phone: 949-608-2027. Office Fax: 949-608-2003. E-mail: stan@stanmullin.com. *

MULLIN, THOMAS J., lawyer, food products executive; b. 1951; BA, NYU; JD, Albany Law Sch. Bar: NY 1977. Prtnr. Phillips, Lytle, Hitchcock, Blaine & Huber, 1982—85; vice chmn., sr. exec. v.p. First Federal Savings and Loan Assn., Rochester, 1985—97; exec. v.p. bus. devel. & corp. strategy C.T. Financial Services, Inc., 1997—2000; pres., CEO TD Waterhouse Bank, 2000; exec. v.p., gen. counsel Constellation Brands, Inc. (formerly Canandaigua Brands, Inc.), 2000—. Office: Constellation Brands Inc 370 Woodcliff Dr Ste 300 Fairport NY 14450 Office Phone: 585-218-3600.

MULLIN, WILLIAM JESSE, physics professor; b. St. Louis, Dec. 8, 1934; s. Charles Francis and Mae Ella (Saindon) M.; m. Sandra Carole Willmering, Feb. 11, 1961; children: Paul Andrew, Christopher Michael, Carole Elizabeth. BS summa cum laude, St. Louis U., 1956; PhD, Washington U., St. Louis, 1965. Rsch. assoc. U. Minn., Mpls., 1965-67; asst. prof. U. Mass., Amherst, 1967-71, assoc. prof., 1971-79, prof., 1979—2000; sr. vis. fellow U. Sussex, Brighton, Eng., 1973, 81, 88, Ecole Normale Superieure, Paris, 1988; prof. emeritus U. Mass., Amherst, 2000. Co-author: Introduction to the Structure of Matter, 1989, Fundamentals of Sound with Applications to Speech and Hearing, 2002; cons. editor Am. Jour. Physics; contbr. articles to profl. jours. 1st lt. USAF, 1961-64. Fellow NSF, Wash. U., 1959-60; grantee ONR, NSF. Mem. Am. Phys. Soc. Home: 10 Forestedge Rd Amherst MA 01002-1534 Office: Dept Physics/Astronomy Hasbrouck Lab U Mass Amherst MA 01003 Home Phone: 413-549-0058. Business E-Mail: mullin@physics.umass.edu.

MULLINAX, PERRY FRANKLIN, rheumatologist, immunologist, allergist; b. Quebec City, Que., Can., June 7, 1931; MD, Med. Coll. Va., 1955. Diplomate Am. Bd. Allergy and Immunology, Am. Bd. Diagnostic Lab. Immunology, Am. Bd. Internal Medicine, Am. Bd. Rheumatology. Intern Yale Med. Ctr., New Haven, 1955-56, resident in medicine, 1958-59; fellow in medicine Mass. Gen. Hosp., Boston, 1959-61; fellow in microbiology immunology Washington U., St. Louis; fellow in biology MIT, Boston, 1962-63; mem. faculty dept. internal medicine Med. Coll. Va./Va. Commonwealth U., 1963—, prof. internal medicine, 1977-2000, emeritus prof. internal medicine, 2000—. Mem. AAAS, Am. Coll. Rheumatology. Office: Med Coll Va VA Commonwealth U PO Box 980263 Richmond VA 23298-0263 Office Phone: 804-828-9685. Business E-Mail: pfmullin@vcu.edu.

MULLINEAUX, DONAL RAY, geologist; b. Weed, Calif., Feb. 16, 1925; s. Lester Ray and Mary Lorene (Drew) M.; m. Diana Suzanne Charais, Nov. 21, 1951; children: Peter, Lauren, Keith. Student, U. Wash., 1942, BS in Math., 1947, BS in Geology, 1949, MS in Geology, 1950, PhD in Geology, 1961. Drilling insp. U.S. Army C.E., 1948; geologist U.S. Geol. Survey, 1950-86; contracting geologist, 1987-90; scientist emeritus U.S. Geol. Survey, 1990—2005. Author articles on volcanic activity and hazards, Mt. St. Helens, other Cascade Range volcanoes, stratigraphy and engrng. geology of Puget Sound Lowland, Wash. With USNR, 1943-54, active duty, 1943-46, 51-53. Rsch. fellow Engrng. Expt. Sta. U. Wash., 1949-50. Fellow Geol. Soc. Am. (E.B. Burwell Jr. award 1983); mem. Colo. Sci. Soc. Home: 14155 W 54th Ave Arvada CO 80002-1513 Home Phone: 303-278-7245. Personal E-mail: dondiana@mullineaux.us.

MULLINIX, KATHLEEN PATRICIA, food products executive, biochemist; b. Boston, Mar. 19, 1944; d. John Anthony and Agnes Kathryn (Birmingham) Mullin; m. Joseph P. Mullinix, June 18, 1966; children: Jonathan Thomas, David Joseph, Brendan Philip. BA in Chemistry, Trinity Coll., Hartford, Conn., 1965; PhD in Chem. Biology, Columbia U., NYC, 1969. NIH postdoctoral fellow Harvard U., Cambridge, Mass., 1969-72; staff fellow to deputy dir. NIH, Bethesda, Md., 1972-81; vice-provost Columbia U., NYC, 1981-87; founder, chmn., pres., CEO Synaptic Pharm. Corp. (formerly Neurogenetic Corp.), Paramus, NJ, 1987—2002; founder Kathleen P. Mullinix & Assocs., 2002—06; pres., CEO WellGen, Inc., New Brunswick, NJ, 2006—. Bd. dirs. Jackson Lab., Cylex, Intellect Neurosciences, Inc. Avocations: tennis, cooking, travel. Office: WellGen Inc c/o Rutgers U Ctr Advanced Food Tech 63 Dudley Rd New Brunswick NJ 08901-8520 Office Phone: 732-214-8834. E-mail: kpmullinix@wellgen.com. *

MULLINS, CHARLES BROWN, physician, academic administrator; b. Rochester, Ind., July 29, 1934; s. Charles E. and Mary Ruth B. (Bamberger) M.; BA, N. Tex. State U., 1954; MD, U. Tex., 1958; m. Stella Churchill, Dec. 27, 1955; children: Holly, David. Diplomate Am. Bd. Internal Medicine. Intern, U. Colo. Med. Ctr., Denver, 1958-59; resident in internal medicine Parkland Meml. Hosp., Dallas, 1962-64; USPHS rsch. fellow U. Tex. Southwestern Med. Sch., Dallas, 1964-65; chief resident medicine Parkland Meml. Hosp., 1965-66; USPHS spl. rsch. fellow cardiology br. Nat. Heart Inst., Bethesda, Md., 1967-68; practice medicine specializing in cardiology, Dallas, 1966-81; sr. attending staff Parkland Meml. Hosp., dir. med. affairs, 1977-79; asst. prof. medicine U. Tex. Southwestern Med. Sch., Dallas, 1968-71, assoc. prof., 1971-75, dir. clin. cardiology, 1971-77, prof., 1975-79, clin. prof. medicine, 1979-81; prof. medicine U. Tex. Health Sci. Ctr., Dallas, 1981-; exec. vice-chancellor health affairs U. Tex. System, 1981-2001, spl. projects dir., 2001-02; CEO Dallas County Hosp. Dist., 1979-81. Contbr. articles to profl. jours. With M.C., USAF, 1959-62. Fellow ACP, Am. Coll. Cardiology (Tex. gov. 1974-77, chmn. bd. govs. 1976), Am. Heart Assn. Coun. on Clin. Cardiology; mem. AMA, Am. Fedn. Clin. Rsch., Assn. Acad. Health Ctrs., Assn. Univ. Cardiologists, Laennec Soc., Alpha Omega Alpha.

MULLINS, EUSTACE CLARENCE, writer; b. Roanoke, Va., Mar. 9, 1923; s. Eustace Clarence and Jane Katherine (Muse) Mullins. BA, Wahington & Lee U., Lexington, Va., 1947; MFA, Inst. Contemporary Art, 1999. Author: (books) Secrets of the Fed., 1953, This Difficult Individual, Ezra Pound, 1959. Mem.: Nat. Com. for Med. Rsch., Nat. Commn. for Judicial Reform. Avocations: painting, photography, lecturing.

MULLINS, JACK ALLEN, cardiologist, educator; b. Oklahoma City, 1952; MD, U. Okla., 1982. Diplomate in internal medicine, cardiovasc. disease, interventional cardiology Am. Bd. Internal Medicine. Intern U. Tex., Houston, 1982-83, resident in internal medicine, 1983-85; fellow in cardiology U. Okla., Oklahoma City, 1985-88; dir. cardiac cath. lab. Columbia Bayshore Med. Ctr., Pasadena, Tex.; clin. instr. cardiology Baylor Coll. Medicine, 1988—, U. Tex. Med. Sch., Houston, 1988—. Mem. ACP, Am. Coll. Cardiology. Office: Cardiovasc Ctr PA 3337 Plainview St Ste 8 Pasadena TX 77504-1924 Office Phone: 713-941-6083.

MULLINS, JAMES LEE, librarian, dean; b. Perry, Iowa, Nov. 29, 1949; s. Kenneth Wiley and Lorene (Gift) M.; m. Kathleen Stiso, May 10, 1986; 1 stepchild, Michael Stiso. BA, U. Iowa, 1972, MA, 1973; PhD, Ind. U., 1984. Instr. Ga. So. U., Statesboro, 1973-74; assoc. law librarian Ind. U., Bloomington, 1974-78; dir. Ind. U. Libr., South Bend, 1978-96, Falvey Meml. Libr., Villanova U., 1996-2000; assoc. dir. adminstrn. MIT, Cambridge, 2000—04; dean libraries Purdue U., West Lafayette, Ind., 2004—. Contbr. articles to profl. publs. Mem. exec. com. South Bend Art Ctr., 1984—89; mem. Mayor's Task Force Re-devel., South Bend, 1986; pres. Fischoff Nat. Chamber Music Assn., 1989—91, Gov. Conf. Libr. Planning Com., 1989—91, Mich. Freenet bd., 1993—96, Ind. Coop. Libr. Svcs. Authority, 1993—94; mem. Hugh Atkinson Award Com., 2001—; mem. planning com. Libr. Adminstrn. & Mgmt. Assn. Inst., 2001—02, IFLA mktg. & mgmgt. sect. standing com., 2003—07. Mem. ALA, LAMA (program com. 1997-2001, exec. com. 1998-2000), Ind. Libr. Assn., Assn. Coll. and Rsch. Librs. (stds. com. 1994-2000, stds. & accreditation com, 2000-02), Ind. Libr. Endowment Bd. (pres. 1988-91), Rotary. Avocations: reading, gardening, cross country skiing, historic preservation. Office: Purdue Univ 504 W State St West Lafayette IN 47907 Business E-Mail: jmullins@purdue.edu.

MULLINS, PATTY, artist; MFA, Ctr. for Emerging Visual Artists, 2001. Exhibitions include New Arts Gallery, Litchfield Hills, Ct., Main. St. Art Festival, 2005, Whitney Mus. Invitational, Whitney Mus. Am. Arts, 2006; author: (book) The Best Work of Your Life. Office: New Arts Gallery 513 Maple St Litchfield CT 06759

MULLINS, ROBERT F., cell biologist; b. St. Louis, May 22, 1967; s. John Edward and Cora Mayo Mullins; m. Rebecca L. Wang, June 10, 1989; children: Jenna M., Natalie C. BS in Biology, Wheaton Coll., Ill., 1989; MS in Biology, St. Louis U., 1991, PhD in Cell and Molecular Biology, 1998. Postdoctoral fellow U. Iowa, Iowa City, 1998—2001, asst. prof., 2001—. Grantee, Nat. Eye Inst., 2004—06. Mem.: Am. Sci. Affiliation, Assn. Rsch. Vision Ophthalmology. Office: Univ Iowa 375 Newton Rd Iowa City IA 52242 Office Phone: 319-335-8222. Personal E-mail: robert-mullins@uiowa.edu.

MULLINS BERG, RUTH GLADYS, nurse; b. Westville, NS, Can., Aug. 25, 1943; came to U.S., 1949, naturalized, 1955; d. William G. and Gladys H.; m. Leonard E. Mullins, Aug. 27, 1963 (dec.); children: Deborah R. Jenkins, Catherine M., Leonard III; m. Berknard J. Berg, June 19, 2004 BS in Nursing, Calif. State U., Long Beach, 1966; MSN, UCLA, 1973; PhD, Columbia Pacific U. Cert. pediatric nurse practitioner. Pub. health nurse Los Angeles County Health Dept., 1967-68; nure Meml. Hosp. Med. Ctr., Long Beach, 1968-72; dir. pediatric nurse practitioner program Calif. State U., Long Beach, 1973-97, asst. prof., 1975-80, assoc. prof., 1980-85, prof., 1985—, coord. accelerated BSN program, 2003—04. Health svc. credential coord. Sch. Nursing Calif. State U., Long Beach, chmn., 1979-81, coord. grad. programs, 1985-92; mem. Calif. Maternal, Child and Adolescent Health Bd., 1977-84; vice chair Long Beach/Orange County Health Consortium, 1984-85, chair 1985-86. Author: (with B. Nelms) Growth and Development: A Primary Health Care Approach; contbg. author: Quick Reference to Pediatric Nursing, 1984; assoc. editor Jour. Pediatric Health Care, 1985—. Tng. grantee HHS, Divsn. Nursing Calif. Dept. Health. Fellow Nat. Assn. Pediatric Nurse Assocs. and Practitioners (exec. bd., pres. 1990-91), Nat. Fedn. Nursing Splty. Orgns. (sec. 1991-93); mem. APHA, Nat. Alliance Nurse Practitioners (governing body 1990-92), Assn. Faculties Pediatric Nurse Practitioner Programs. L.A. and Orange County Assn. Pediatric Nurse Practitioners and Assocs. (treas. 1998—05), Am. Assn. Univ. Faculty. Democrat. Methodist. Office: Calif State U Dept Nursing 1250 N Bellflower Blvd Long Beach CA 90840-0001 Office Phone: 562-985-4476. Personal E-mail: rgmullins@sprintmail.com. Business E-Mail: rmullins@csulb.edu.

MULLIS, KARY BANKS, biochemist; b. Lenoir, NC, Dec. 28, 1944; s. Cecil Banks Mullis and Bernice Alberta (Barker) Fredericks; m. Richards Mullis (div.); 1 child, Louise; m. Cynthia Mullis (div.); children: Christopher, Jeremy; m. Nancy Lier Cosgrove, 1998. BS in Chemistry, Ga. Inst. Tech, 1966; PhD in Biochemistry, U. Calif., Berkeley, 1973; DSc (hon.), U. S.C., 1994. Lectr. biochemistry U. Calif., Berkeley, 1972, postdoctoral fellow San Francisco, 1977—79, U. Kans. Med. Sch., Kansas City, 1973—76; scientist Cetus Corp., Emeryville, Calif., 1979—86; dir. molecular biology Xytronyx, Inc., San Diego, 1986—88; cons. Specialty Labs, Inc., Amersham, Inc., Chiron Inc. and various others, Calif., 1988—96; chmn. StarGene, Inc., San Rafael, Calif.; v.p. Histotec, Inc., Cedar Rapids, Iowa; v.p. molecular biology chemistry Vyrex Inc., La Jolla, Calif.; disting. rschr. Children's Hosp., Rsch. Inst., Oakland, Calif. Disting. vis. prof. U. S.C. Coll. of Sci. and Math. Author: (autobiography) Dancing Naked in the Mind Field, 1998; contbr. articles to profl. jours.; patentee in field. Bd. dir. Nat. Orgn. Reform of Marijuana Laws, 2000—. Named Scientist of Yr., R&D Mag., 1991, Calif. Scientist of Yr., 1992; named to National Inventors Hall of Fame, 1998; recipient Preis Biochemische Analytik award, German Soc. Clin. Chem., 1990, Allan award, 1990, award, Gairdner Found. Internat., 1991, Nat. Biotech. award, 1991, Robert Koch award, 1992, Chiron Corp. Biotechnology Rsch. award, Am. Soc. Microbiology, 1992, Japan prize, Sci. and Tech. Found. Japan, 1993, Nobel Prize in Chemistry, Nobel Foundation, 1993. Mem.: Inst. Further Study (dir. 1983—), Am. Acad. Achievement, Am. Chem. Soc. Achievements include invention of invention of Polymerase Chain Reaction (PCR). Avocations: astrology, surfing.

MULLOOLY, MICHAEL SEAN, pilot; b. San Francisco, Calif., Apr. 22, 1969; s. Thomas Leo and Catherine Urquhart Mullooly; m. Tiffany Doelger, Aug. 23, 1997. AA in Anthropology, Can. Coll., Redwood City, Calif., 1990; BA in Anthropology, U. Calif., Berkeley, 1993. Lic. air transport pilot FAA, 2000. Airport ops. specialist San Mateo County Airports, San Carlos, Calif., 1990—97; owner / pilot Diamond Aviation, San Carlos, 1994—96; capt., check airman ExpressJet Airlines, Houston, 1996—2004; capt. Hawker 800xp Exec. Jet Mgmt., Oakland, Calif., 2004—. Pilot SMC Sheriff's Air Squadron, San Carlos, 1994—. Mem.: Mensa. Republican. Avocations: bicycling, travel, guitar. Home: 445 Cork Harbour Cir Unit H Redwood City CA 94065 Home Phone: 650-631-7494. Personal E-mail: mikemullooly@hotmail.com.

MULLOY, PATRICK ALOYSIUS, lawyer; b. Wilkes-Barre, Pa., Sept. 14, 1941; s. Hugh Patrick and Ellen Mary (Meagher) M.; m. Marjorie Baumer; children: Maura Alice, Daniel Patrick, Claire Ellen. BA magna cum laude, King's Coll., 1963; MA, U. Notre Dame, 1965; JD with honors, George Washington U., 1971; LLM, Harvard U., 1978. Bar: D.C. 1972, Pa. 1972, U.S. Ct. Appeals (D.C., 2d, and 9th cirs.) 1975, U.S. Supreme Ct. 1975, U.S. Ct. Appeals (5th and 9th cirs.) 1976. Fgn. service officer U.S. Dept. State, Washington, 1965-72; trial lawyer Dept. Justice, Washington, 1973-77, sr. lawyer antitrust div., 1978-82; Congl. fellow U.S. Congress, 1983; minority gen. counsel U.S. Senate Banking Com., 1984-86, gen. counsel, 1987-89, sr. counsel, internat. affairs advisor, 1989-92, chief internat. counsel, 1993-94, chief internat. coun. (minority) Washington, 1995-98; asst. sec. market access and compliance Internat. Trade Adminstrn., U.S. Dept. Commerce, Washington, 1998-2001. Apptd. asst. sec., exec. br. commn. on security and coop. in Europe by Pres. Clinton, 1999-2001; apptd. commr. Joint House Senate U.S.-China Econ. and Security Rev. Commn., Washington, 2001—06; adj. prof. internat. trade law Cath. U. Law Sch., Washington, 2002-, George Mason Law Sch., Arlington, Va., 2003—; rep. Alfred P. Sloan Found., Washington, 2006-07. Home: 304 W Masonic View Ave Alexandria VA 22301-2419 Office: Hall of States Ste 373 444 N Capitol St NW Washington DC 20001 Office Phone: 202-220-1327. Business E-Mail: pmulloy@sso.org. E-mail: pamulloy@aol.com.

MULRONEY, BRIAN (MARTIN BRIAN MULRONEY), former Prime Minister of Canada; b. Baie Comeau, Que., Can., Mar. 20, 1939; s. Benedict and Irene (O'Shea) M.; m. Mila Pivnicki, 1973; children: Caroline, Benedict, Mark, Nicolas. BA, St. Francis Xavier U., LLD, 1979; LLL, U. Laval, Que.; LLD (hon.), Meml. U. Nfld., Nfld., 1980, U. W.I., 1993, Tel Aviv U., 1994, Ctrl. Conn. State U., 1994, Barry U., 1995. Ptnr. Ogilvy Renault, Montreal, Canada, 1965-76; exec. v.p. Iron Ore Co. Can., Montreal, 1977-83, 1976-77, pres., 1977-83; mem. Parliament Can. from Ctrl. N.S., Ottawa, Ont., 1983-84; mem. Parliament Can. from Manicouagan, 1984-88; mem. Parliament Can. from Charlevoix, 1988-93; leader of Her Majesty's Loyal Opposition, 1983-84; prime min., 1984-93; royal commr. Cliche Commn. investigating violence in Que. constrn. industry, 1974; sr. ptnr. Ogilvy Renault, Montreal, 1993—. Chmn. internat. adv. bd. Barrick Gold Corp., The J.P. Morgan Chase Corp.; mem. internat. adv. coun. Power Corp. Can.; mem. adv. bd. The China Internat. Trust and Investment Corp.; mem. Hicks Muse Capital Ptnrs. Ind. News and Media, PLC; mem. internat. adv. coun. Inst. Internat. Studies; bd. dirs. Archer Daniels Midland Co., Barrick Gold Corp., The Trizec Properties Inc., Power Corp., Quebecor World Inc.; chmn. Forbes, NYC. Author: Where I Stand, 1983. Trustee Montreal Heart Inst.; mem. internat. adv. coun. Les Hautes Etudes Commerciales l'Université de Montréal. Named Grand Officer, Ordre Nat. du Que.; recipient Companion of the Order of Can. Office: Ogilvy Renault 1981 McGill College Ave Ste 1100 Montreal PQ Canada H3A 3C1 Business E-Mail: bmulroney@ogilvyrenault.com.

MULRONEY, DERMOT, actor; b. Alexandria, Va., Oct. 31, 1963; m. Catherine Keener, Nov. 1990 (separated May 2005); 1 child, Clyde. Grad., Northeastern U., 1985; BS, Northwestern U., 1985. Actor: (films) Sunset, 1988, Young Guns, 1988, Staying Together, 1989, Longtime Companion, 1989, Survival Quest, 1990, Bright Angel, 1991, Career Opportunities, 1991, Where the Day Takes You, 1992, Point of No Return, 1993, Samantha, 1993, The Thing Called Love, 1993, Silent Tongue, 1993, Bad Girls, 1994, There Goes My Baby, 1994, Angels in the Outfield, 1994, Box of Moonlight, 1996, Bastard Out of Carolina, 1996, Kansas City, 1996, The Trigger Effect, 1996, My Best Friend's Wedding, 1997, Where the Money Is, 1999, Goodbye Lover, 1999, Trixie, 2000, The Safety of Objects, 2001, Lovely & Amazing, 2001, Investigating Sex, 2001, About Schmidt, 2002, Undertow, 2004, Something Borrowed, 2004, Wedding Date, 2005, Must Love Dogs, 2005, The Family Stone, 2005, Griffin & Phoenix, 2006, Zodiac, 2007, Gracie, 2007, Georgia Rule, 2007; (TV appearances) Fame, 1982, Sin of Innocence, 1986, Daddy, 1987, Long Gone, 1987, Unconquered, 1989, The Heart of Justice, 1993, The Last Outlaw, 1993, Friends, 2003, (mini-series) Family Pictures, 1993, (spls.) The Drug Knot, 1986; prodr.: (films) Living in Oblivion, 1995. Office: Internat Creative Mgmt 8942 Wilshire Blvd Beverly Hills CA 90211 Address: PMK/KBH Ste 700 8500 Wilshire Blvd Beverly Hills CA 90211 *

MULROW, PATRICK JOSEPH, medical educator; s. Patrick J. and Delia M.; m. Jacquelyn Pinover, Aug. 8, 1953; children: Deborah, Nancy, Robert, Catherine. AB, Colgate U., 1947; MD, Cornell U., 1951; MSc (hon.), Yale U., 1969; DSc (hon.), Med. Coll. Ohio, 2005. Intern N.Y. Hosp., 1951-52, resident, 1952-54; instr. physiology Med. Coll. Cornell U., 1954-55; research fellow Stanford U., 1955-57; instr. medicine Yale U., 1957-60, asst. prof., 1960-66, assoc. prof., 1966-69, prof. medicine, 1969-75; chmn. dept. medicine Med. Coll. Ohio, Toledo, 1975—95, prof. medicine, 1975—97, prof. emeritus, 1997—. Chmn. ednl. com. Council for high blood pressure rsch. Am. Heart Assn., 1968-70, mem. exec. com., 1986-96, vice-chmn. of coun., 1990-92, chmn. 1992-94, past chmn., 1995-96; mem. study sect. NIH, 1970-74. Editorial bd. Jour. Clin. Endocrinology and Metabolism, 1966-70, 75-79, Endocrine Rsch., 1974—, Jour. Exptl. Biology and Medicine, Hypertension, 1994-98; contbr. articles to profl. jours. With USNR, 1944-46. Mem. ACP, Am. Soc. Clin. Investigation, Assn. Am. Physicians, Am. Physiol. Soc., Endocrine Soc., Am. Fedn. Clin. Rsch., Am. Clin. and Climatol. Assn., Am. Heart Assn. (nat. rsch. com., chmn. cardiovasc. regulation rsch. study com. 1986-91), Assn. Profs. Medicine, Assn. Program Dirs. in Internal Medicine, Cen. Soc. Clin. Rsch. (pres. 1988-89), Internat. Soc. Hypertension, World Hypertension League (sec.-gen. 1995-2005), Inter-Am. Soc. Hypertension, Sigma Xi (pres. Yale chpt. 1965-66), Alpha Omega Alpha. Home: 9526 Carnoustie Rd Perrysburg OH 43551-3501 Office: Med Coll Ohio Dept Medicine 3120 Glendale Ave Toledo OH 43614-5809 Business E-Mail: pmulrow@meduohio.edu.

MULRYAN, HENRY TRIST, mining executive, consultant; b. Palo Alto, Calif., Jan. 6, 1927; s. Henry and Marian Abigail (Trist) M.; m. Lenore Hoag, Aug. 25, 1948; children: James W., Carol. Student, Yale U., 1945-46; AB in Econs., Stanford U., 1948; postgrad., Am. Grad. Sch. Internat. Bus., 1949, Columbia U., 1983. V.p. mktg. Sierra Talc Co., South Pasadena, Calif., 1955-65, United Sierra, Trenton, NJ, 1965-67, v.p., gen. mgr., 1967-70, pres., 1970-77; v.p. Cyprus Mines Corp., Los Angeles, 1978-80; sr. v.p. ops. Cyprus indsl. minerals div. Amoco Minerals Co., Englewood, Colo., 1980-85; pres. Cyprus Indls. Minerals Co., Englewood, 1985-87; v.p. Cyprus Minerals Co., Englewood, 1985-87, sr. v.p. mktg., corp. adminstr., 1987-89; pres. Mineral Econs. Internat., 1989—. Vol. exec. Internat. Exec. Svc. Corps., Zimbabwe, 1998, Romania, 98, Jordan, 2000, Jordan, 01, Jordan, 02, Jordan, 04, Armenia, 03; pres. Jonathan Art Found., 2004—05. Served with U.S. Army, 1944-46. Mem.: Rotary (pres. South Pasadena club 1964—65, bd. dir. Princeton, N.J. club 1969—75), Jonathan Club. Office: 539 Muskingum Ave Pacific Palisades CA 90272-4252 E-mail: htmulryan@verizon.net.

MULSANT, BENOIT HENRI, psychiatrist, educator, medical researcher; b. Paris, Feb. 28, 1960; arrived in U.S., 1985; s. Henri Edmond and Francoise Emilie Mulsant; m. Sharon Jane Laufenberg, Feb. 17, 1995; children: Louise Sharon, Sophie Sharon, Xavier Benoit. MD, U. Laval, Que., Can., 1983—84; MS, Carnegie Mellon U., 1989. Lic. Am. Bd. of Psychiatry and Neurology. Assoc. prof. psychiatry U. Pitts., 1996—2004, prof. psychiatry, 2004—; med. dir. ECT svc. U. Pitts. Med. Ctr., 1994—2005. Prin. investigator federally-funded and industry-sponsored clin. rsch. trials on psychiat. disorders in geriatric patients. Contbr. articles to profl. jours., chpts. to books. Recipient Jr. Investigator award, Am. Assn. for Geriatric Psychiatry, 1994, Ann. Award for Merit, Nat. Psychiat. Endowment Fund, 1990, Laughlin fellowship, Am. Coll. of Psychiatrists, 1990, NIH Career Development award. Mem.: Internat. Coll. Geriatric Neuropsychopharmacology (founding mem. 2001), Am. Psychiat. Assn. Office: U Pitts - WPIC 3811 O'Hara St Pittsburgh PA 15213

MULTHAUP, MERREL KEYES, artist; b. Cedar Rapids, Iowa, Sept. 27, 1922; d. Stephen Dows and Edna Gertrude (Gard) Keyes; m. Robert Hansen Multhaup, Apr. 7, 1944; children: Eric Stephen, Robert Bruce. Student, State U. Iowa, 1942—43, Rice U., 1971. Tchg. faculty Summit (NJ) Art Assn., 1956—60; art instr. studio classes Springfield, NJ, 1954—55, Bloomfield (NJ) Art Group, 1955—56, Westport, Conn., 1962—63; tchg. faculty Hunterdon Art Ctr., Clinton, NJ, 1985—92. Numerous one-woman shows including Summit Art Assn., 1955, Papermill Playhouse, NJ, 1957, 1959, 1960, 1978, 1979, Benedict Gallery, NJ, 1976, Coriell Gallery, 1995; exhibited in group shows at Nat. Assn. Women Artists, NYC, 1957-2001 (awards in figure painting), Hartford (Conn.) Athanaeum Mus., 1961 (1st prize), Highgate Gallery, NYC, Waverly Gallery, NYC, Leicester Gallery, London, Silvermine Gallery, Conn., Leicester Gallery, London, Pendut Gallery, Tex., Benedict Gallery, Sidney Rothman Gallery, NJ, Stamford (Conn.) Mus., Bridgeport (Conn.) Mus., Montclair (NJ) Mus., Newark Mus., Coriell Gallery, Albuquerque, Leicester Gallery, London; (traveling exhibit) Nat. Assn. Women Artists, 1996—, Travel USA, 1999, New World Art Ctr., NYC, 1998-99, Gallery Art 54, NYC, 1997, Atelier 14 Gallery, NYC, 2000-02; more than 30 commd. portraits, 1960—. Bd. dirs., exhbn. chmn. Summit Art Assn., 1950-60, Silvermine Guild of Art, New Canaan, Conn., 1960-64; bd. dirs. Artist's Equity of NJ, 1977-84, chmn. state-wide event, 1983, 86; artist's adv. coun. Hunterdon Art Ctr., Clinton, 1988-92; pres. Four Hills Neighbors, 1998-2000. Recipient awards in juried exhbns. in Iowa, Pa., NJ, Conn., NYC. Mem. Nat. Mus. for Women in Arts (charter mem.), Nat. Assn. Women Artists Inc. (awards for figure painting 1957, 80-89), Silvermine Nat. Portrait Group of Artists. Avocations: entertaining, singing, dance, playing the piano, reading. Home: 1321 Stagecoach Rd SE Albuquerque NM 87123-4320

MULUK, SATISH CHANDRA, vascular surgeon; b. Tenali, A.P., India, Nov. 26, 1962; came to U.S., 1965; MD, Boston U., 1985. Diplomate Am. Bd. Surgery, Am. Bd. Gen. Vascular Surgery, Am. Bd. Surg. Critical Care. Intern Mass. Gen. Hosp., Boston, 1985-86, resident in surgery, 1986-88, 90-92, chief e. svcs. surgery, 1992-93, fellow vascular surgery, 1993-94; rsch. fellow NIH, Bethesda, Md., 1988-90; asst. prof. surgery U. Pitts., 1994—. Office: A-1011 PUH 200 Lothrop St Pittsburgh PA 15213

MULVA, JAMES JOSEPH, oil industry executive; b. Oshkosh, Wis., June 19, 1946; m. Miriam Mulva; 2 children. BBA in Fin., U. Tex., 1968, MBA in Fin., 1969. Mgmt. trainee, treas. Phillips Petroleum Co., Bartlesville, Okla., 1973, asst. treas. London, 1974, mgr. fgn. exch. and investment Bartlesville, Okla., 1976, v.p., treas. Europe/Africa div. London, 1980, mgr. corp. and planning Bartlesville, Okla., 1984, asst. treas., 1985, treas., 1986, v.p., treas., 1988—90, chief fin. officer, 1990—99, pres., COO, 1994—99, vice-chmn., pres. & CEO, 1999, chmn., CEO, 1999—2002; pres., CEO ConocoPhillips, Houston, 2002—04, chmn., pres., CEO, 2004—. Officer Navy, 1969—73. Roman Catholic. Office: ConocoPhillips PO Box 2197 Houston TX 77252-2197 *

MULVA, PATRICK T., oil industry executive; b. Green Bay; BBA, Notre Dame U.; MBA, U. Tex. Fin. analyst ExxonMobil Corp., Baton Rouge, 1976, exec. asst. to pres. U.S. affiliate, 1987, asst. contr. internat. affiliate, fin. dir. Malaysia, 1991, upstream to asst. contr., 1993; contr. Imperial Oil Ltd., 1996, sr. v.p. fin. and adminstrn., 1998—2002, contr., 2000—02; v.p. investor rels. and sec. ExxonMobil Corp., 2002, v.p., contr. With USAF, 1972—75. Office: ExxonMobil Corp 5959 Las Colinas Blvd Irving TX 75039-2298 *

MULVANEY, JAMES FRANCIS, lawyer; b. Chgo., Nov. 2, 1922; m. Mary Ruth Rinderer, 1945; 7 children. BS, Loyola U., Chgo., 1942, JD, 1948. Atty., Chgo., 1948-55, San Diego, Calif., 1956-62; exec. v.p. U.S. Nat. Bank, 1963-72, pres., CEO, 1972-73; pres. San Diego Baseball Co., 1955-68; v.p., gen. counsel San Diego Padres Nat. League, 1968-73; sr. ptnr. Mulvaney, Kahan & Barry, San Diego, 1974—. Chmn., CEO Chela Fin., San Francisco, 1983—. Bd. vis. U. San Diego Sch. Law, 1971-88; chmn. United Way Internat., 1991-94, mem. exec. com., United Way Am., 1987-93, various officers; co-chmn. San Diego Organizing Project, 1983—; bd. dirs. World SHARE, Inc., 1986-92, Old Globe Theatre London, Del Mar Charities, 1985-95; numerous other civic activities. Officer USN, WWII; lt. comdr. USNR, Korea. Recipient Mr. San Diego award, 1991, First Annual Spirit of Charity award Cath. Community Svcs., 1984, Brotherhood award Nat. Conf. Christians and Jews, Inc., 1983, Citizen of Yr. award Jr. C. of C. and The City Club, 1983, numerous others. Mem. San Diego County Bar Found. (treas., Outstanding Svc. award 1988), ABA, Calif. State Bar Assn., Ill. State Bar Assn., San Diego C. of C., San Diego Coun. on World Affairs, The City Club of San Diego, Navy League. Office: Mulvaney Kahan & Barry 401 W A St Fl 17 San Diego CA 92101-7901

MULVANEY, MARY FREDERICA, systems analyst; b. NY, Nov. 27, 1945; d. Michael Joseph and Mary Catherine (Clapper) Mulvaney. BA, Marymount Coll., 1967; MA, U. Va., 1968; MS in Computer Sci., Marymount U., 1999. Cert. data processor Inst. Cert. Computer Profls. Computer systems analyst Dept. of Def., Ft. Meade, Md., 1968-74; sr. programmer analyst Planning Rsch. Corp., McLean, Va., 1974-83; mem. tech. staff Fed. Systems Group TRW, Inc., Fairfax, Va., 1983-90, engr., scientist, 1994—2002; sr. mem. tech. staff GTE Govt. Sys. Corp., Rockville, Md., 1990-94; software engr. Northrop Grumman, Fairfax, 2003—. Mem.: IEEE, Cath. Assn. Scientists and Engrs., Computer Measurement Group, Data Processing Mgmt. Assn. Roman Catholic. Office: Northrop Grumman Mission Sys 12900 Federal Sys Park Dr Fairfax VA 22033

MULVANEY, MARY JEAN, retired physical education educator; b. Omaha, Jan. 6, 1927; d. Marion Fowler and Blanche Gibons (McKee) M. BS, U. Nebr., 1948; MS, Wellesley Coll., 1951; LHD (hon.), U. Nebr., 1986. Instr. Kans. State U., Manhattan, 1948-50, U. Nebr., Lincoln, 1951-57, asst. prof., 1957-62, U. Kans., Lawrence, 1962-66; assoc. prof. U. Chgo., 1966-76, prof., 1976-90, prof. emeritus, 1990—, chmn. women's divsn., 1966-76, chmn. dept. phys. edn. and athletics, 1976-90; mem. vis. com. on athletics MIT, 1978-81, Wellesley Coll., 1978-79. Dir. athletics U. Chgo., 1980—90; mem. selection com. U. Chgo. Athletic Hall of Fame, 2004—07. Recipient Honor award Nebr. Assn. Health, Phys. Edn. and Recreation, 1962, U. Nebr. Alumni Achievement award, 1998; named to U. Chgo. Athletic Hall of Fame, 2003; Office of Dir. Athletics, U. Chgo., named in honor, 2003. Mem.: AAHPERD, Univ. Athletic Assn. (chmn. athletic adminstrs. com. 1986—88, sec. 1986—90, exec. com. 1986—90, dels. com. 1986—90), Ill. Assn. Intercollegiate Athletics for Women (chmn. 1978—80), Nat. Assn. Collegiate Dirs. of Athletics (exec. com. 1976—80, Hall of Fame 1990), Midwest Assn. Intercollegiate Athletics for Women (chmn. 1979—81), Nat. Collegiate Assn. Women Athletic Adminstrs. (Lifetime Achievement award 2006), Nat. Collegiate Athletic Assn. (coun. 1983—87, com. mem.), Alpha Chi Omega, Mortar Bd. Home: 5821 Kennelley Ct Lincoln NE 68516-3799 Personal E-mail: maryjeanmulvany@aol.com.

MULVEE, ROBERT EDWARD, bishop; b. Boston, Feb. 15, 1930; s. John F. and Jennie T. Mulvee. BA, PhB, U. Sem. Ottawa, 1953; MRE, Am. Coll., Louvain, Belgium, 1957; D Canon Law, Lateran U., Rome, 1964; DD (hon.), Rivier Coll., Nashua, NH, 1979. Ordained priest Diocese of Manchester, NH, 1957; asst. chancellor of diocese, 1964—72; named monsignor, 1966; elevated to domestic prelate, 1970; named chancellor, 1972; Aux. Bishop of Manchester NH, 1977—85; Bishop of Wilmington Del., 1985—95; Coadjutor Bishop of Providence RI, 1995—97; Bishop of Providence RI, 1997—2005; ret., 2005. Trustee Nat. Shrine Imaculate Conception, Washington, 1987. Mem.: Nat. Conf. Cath. Bishops. Roman Catholic.

MULVEY, GERALD JOHN, meteorologist; b. Cambria Heights, NY, Dec. 20, 1949; s. George Patrick and Estelle Florence M.; m. Katherine Louise Strick, July 7, 1973. BS in Physics, York Coll., Jamaica, NY, 1971; MS in Atmospheric Sci., SUNY, Albany, 1973; PhD in Atmospheric Sci., Colo. State U., 1977. Rsch. assoc. dept. atmospheric sci. Colo. State U., 1977—78; mgr. dept. atmospheric physics Meteorology Rsch., Inc., Altadena, Calif., 1978—80; sr. rsch. engr. Lockheed Martin Missiles and Space, Sunnyvale, Calif., 1980—97; advanced programs mgr. Lockheed Martin Western Devel. Labs., 1997—98; lectr. dept. geoscis. San Francisco State U., 1995—98; advanced programs mgr. Lockheed Martin Global Telecomm., Sunnyvale, Calif., 1998—99; prin. sys. engr. DIVA Sys. Corp., Redwood City, Calif., 1999—2002; sr. mgr., sr. sys. engr. NPOESS Northrop Grumman, 2002—. Co-author: Environmental Impacts of Artificial Ice Nucleating Agents, 1978; contbr. articles to profl. jours. including Analytical Chemistry and Jour. Applied Meteorology. Mem. Cupertino (Calif.) Libr. Commn., 1989—93; v.p. bd. dirs. Cupertino Libr. Found., 2000—01. Mem.: AAAS, Cert. Consulting Meteorologists, Internat. Soc. Measurement and Control (v.p. Santa Clara Valley 1996—97), Am. Meterol. Soc. (bd. cert. cons. meteorologist 1997—, Bd. Cert. 1997—), Sigma Xi. Roman Catholic. Achievements include verifying/documenting of long range transport of active artificial cloud nucleating agents. Office: Nothrop Grumman R10/1791 Mission One Space Pk Redondo Beach CA 90278 Home Phone: 310-377-6674; Office Phone: 310-812-5196. Business E-Mail: gerry.mulvey@ngc.com.

MULVIHILL, JAMES EDWARD, periodontist, educator; b. Cleve., Sept. 24, 1940; s. John F. and Teresa J. (Carlos) M.; m. May Jane Forino, 1963; children— Karen, Kristen, Jason BA, Coll. of Holy Cross, 1962; DMD, Harvard U., 1966. Asst. dean for student affairs, coordinator Harvard-VA continuing edn. program Harvard Sch. Dental Medicine, Boston, 1970-71; dean clin. campus L.I. Jewish-Hillside Med. Ctr., Queens Hosp. Ctr. Affiliation, Jewish Inst. for Geriatric Care, Health Scis. Ctr. SUNY-Stony Brook, 1971-80; v.p. for edn. and research L.I. Jewish-Hillside Med. Ctr., New Hyde Park, NY, 1975-80; v.p., provost for health affairs, exec. dir. Health Ctr., prof. periodontics U. Conn., Farmington, 1980-92; attending periodontist John Dempsey Hosp., U. Conn. Health Ctr., Farmington, 1982-92; pres. John Dempsey Fin. Corp., Farmington, 1988-92; sr. v.p. for health policy The Travelers Corp., Hartford, Conn., 1992-94; chmn. bd. The Travelers Health Co., Hartford, 1992-93; sr. fellow in health policy Assn. of Acad. Health Ctrs., 1994; pres. CEO Managed Health, Inc., 1994, Comty. Health Plan of Queens/Nassau, New Hyde Park, NY, 1994-95, Forsyth Dental Ctr., Boston, 1995-96, Juvenile Diabetes Found. Internat., 1996-99; dir. instnl. advancement and corp. rels. Am. Dental Edn. Assn., 2000—; asst. to pres. So. Maine Med. Ctr., 2000—01; chief dept. dentistry Harvard U. Health Svcs., 2003—07. Cons. in field Author: (with others) Guide to Foreign Medical Schools, 1975, Editorial Instructions for Dental Authors, 1979-80, 1979, Human Subjects Research: The Operational Handbook for IRB's, 1982, 2d edit., 1984, Japanese edit., 1987; also articles, chpt. in book Bd. dirs. Nat. Dentex Corp., Nat. Fund for Med. Edn.; overseer Joslin Diabetes Ctr. Recipient Disting. Alumnus award Harvard Sch. Dental Medicine, 1982, Disting. alumnus award Holy Cross Coll., 1991. Fellow AAAS, Am. Coll. Dentistry, Internat. Coll. Dentistry;

mem. ADA, Am. Acad. Periodontology, Conn. State Dental Assn. (Fones award 2004), Harvard Dental Alumni Assn., Alpha Sigma Nu, Sigma Psi. Avocations: golf, gardening, photography. Address: 117 Kings Hwy Kennebunkport ME 04046-5606 Home Phone: 207-967-8838. Personal E-mail: mulvi@adelphia.net.

MUMFORD, CHRISTOPHER GREENE, corporate financial executive; b. Washington, Oct. 21, 1945; s. Milton C. and Dorothea L. (Greene) Mumford. BA, Stanford U., 1968, MBA, 1975. Cons. Internat. Tech. Resources Inc., 1974; asst. v.p. Wells Fargo Bank, San Francisco, 1975-78; asst. treas. Arcata Corp., San Francisco, 1978-82, v.p. fin., 1982-87, exec. v.p. fin., 1987-94. Gen. ptnr. Scarff, Sears & Assocs., San Francisco, 1986—95; mng. dir. Questor Ptnrs. Fund, L.P., San Francisco, 1995—98; v.p. bd. dirs. Triangle Pacific Corp., Dallas, 1986—88, Norton Enterprises Inc., Salt Lake City, 1988—90, Crown Pacific Ptnrs., Portland, Oreg., 1991—2004, Ryder TRS, Inc., Miami, Fla., 1996—98, Ockham PLC, London, 1996—98, Impco Technologies, Inc., Cerritos, Calif., 1998—2000. Office: PO Box 1340 Mill Valley CA 94942-1340 Office Phone: 415-601-6800. Personal E-mail: cgmumford@aol.com.

MUMFORD, DAVID BRYANT, mathematics professor; b. Worth, Sussex, Eng., June 11, 1937; came to U.S., 1940; s. William Bryant and Grace (Schiott) M.; m. Erika Jentsch, June 27, 1959 (dec. July 30, 1988); children: Stephen, Peter, Jeremy, Suchitra; m. Jenifer Moore, Dec. 29, 1989. BA, Harvard U., 1957, PhD, 1961; DSc (hon.), U. Warwick, 1983, Norwegian U. Sci. Tech., 2000, Rockefeller U., 2001. Jr. fellow Harvard U., 1958-61, assoc. prof., 1962—67, prof. math., 1967—77, Higgins prof., 1977-97, chmn. dept. math., 1981-84, prof., divsn. applied math., 1995—96, Brown U., 1996—. V.p. Internat. Math. Union, 1991-94, pres., 1995-99. Author: Geometric Invariant Theory, 1965, Abelian Varieties, 1970, Introduction to Algebraic Geometry, 1976, 2 and 3 Dimensional Patterns of the Face, 1999, Indra's Pearls, 2002. Recipient Fields medal Internat. Congress Mathematicians, 1974, Longuet-Higgins prize, 2005, Shaw prize in Math. Sciences, Shaw Found., Hong Kong, 2006, Leroy P. Steele prize for Math. Exposition, Am. Math. Soc., 2007; MacArthur Found. fellow, 1987-92. Fellow Tata Inst. (hon.); mem. Acad. Nazionale dei Lincei, Nat. Acad. Scis., Am. Acad. Arts and Scis., Am. Philos. Soc., Norwegian Acad. Sci. and Letters. Office: Brown U 182 George St Providence RI 02912-9056 Home: 15 Sleeper St Boston MA 02210 Office Phone: 401-863-3441. E-mail: david_mumford@brown.edu.

MUMFORD, JEFFREY, composer, educator; b. Washington, 1955; BA in Painting, U. Calif.-Irvine, 1977; student in composition, Aspen Music Sch., 1977—81; MA in Musical Composition, U. Calif.-San Diego, 1981. Pvt. studies in composition with Lawrence Moss, 1977—78; pvt. studies in composition with Elliott Carter, 1980—83; theory and composition instr. Settlement Music Sch., Phila., 1985—89; theory instr. Westchester Conservatory of Music, White Plains, NY, 1986—89; theory and composition instr./spl. projects coord. Washington Conservatory of Music, Washington, 1989—99; artist in residence, composition Bowling Green State U., Ohio, 1999—2000; asst. prof. composition Oberlin Conservatory of Music, 2000—04, composer-in-residence, 2004—06. Co-coord., Washington/Balt. chpt. Am. Composers Forum, 1977; asst. dir., prodn./media liaison Washington Bach Consort, 1989—90; seminar coord., grant writing and prodn., contemporary music specialist, program note annotator, prodn. supr. The Concert Soc. at Md., U. Md., College Park, 1990—95; mem. Pa. State Arts Coun. Music Panel (Composition), 1990, Md. State Arts Coun. Music Panel (Composition), 1991, N.C. State Arts Coun. Music Panel (Composition), 1992, NEA Composer Fellowship Panels, 1990, 94; juror Mayor's Arts Awards, Washington, 1994; mem. NEA Chamber Music Panel, 1994; cons. Mary Flagler Cary Charitable Trust Recording Program, 1996; mem. Mass. Cultural Coun. Panel (Organizations), 1999, 2000, 05, Ill. State Arts Coun. Panel, 2001, NEA Presenters Panel, 2004, NEA Access to Artistic Excellence Panel, 2006; lectr. in field. Composer: (for piano) barbaglio dal manca, 1981, rev., 1992, 2000, for Elliott, 1983, tango variations, 1984, fragments from the surrounding evening, 1984, a flower in folding shadows, 1986, a landscape of interior resonances, 2001, four dances for Boris, 2004, (solo instrumental) linear cycles VII (cambiamenti II), 1979, rev., 1993, variazioni elegiaci, 1979, rev., 1997, morning thunder for solo flute, 1979—80, a window's gathering of clouds, 1981, variazioni elegiaci II, 1983, amid fleeting pockets of billowing radiance, 1990, the clarity of remembered springs, 1992—93, revisiting variazioni elegiaci, 2001, wending, 2001, the milliner's fancy, 2003, eight musings...revisiting memories, 2005, an expanding distance of multiple voices, 2005, (chamber) linear cycles II, 1978, string quartet no. 1 (formerly quartet no. 3), 1978, rev., 1980, the promise of the far horizon, 2000, toward the deepening stillness beyond visible light, 2004, recordings, Bang on a Can Live, the focus of blue light, Dark Fires, Telling Tales, the promise of the far horizon, linear cylces II, quartet no. 3 (string quartet no. I); composer/performer: WCLV radio sta., Cleve.; composer: (interview programs) Around Noon, WCPN-FM, Cleve., Artsbeat, WPFW-FM, Washington, Desert Island Discs, WETA-FM, Washington, The Diane Rehm Show, (vocal) two haiku settings: of place and love, 2006. Recipient Meet the Composer, 2003, 2006; grantee, U. Calif., 1977, ASCAP Found., 1979, Martha Baird Rockefeller Fund for Music, Inc., 1979, 1981, Meet the Composer, 1980, 1981—82, 1983, 1985, 1987, 1989, 1991, Meet the Composer/Arts Endowment Commissioning Music U.S.A., 1996, Alice M. Ditson Fund of Columbia U., 1980, Aaron Copland scholarship, Am. Soc. Composers, Authors and Publishers, 1981, fellowship, Composers' Conf., Johnson, Vt., 1982, Am. Music Ctr., 1982, 1994, Minn. Composers' Forum, 1985—86, D.C. Commn. Arts & Humanities, 1994, small projects grant, 1997, Guggenheim fellowship, 1995—96, Recording grant, Oberlin Coll., 2001, Individual Artist fellowship, Ohio Arts Coun., 2002, Individual Excellence award, 2006, Academy Award in Music, Am. Acad. Arts & Letters, 2003. Mem.: Am. Soc. Composers, Authors, and Pubs., Am. Composers Forum, League of Composers (U.S. sect., N.Y.C., bd. dirs.), Bascom Little Fund (adv. bd.). Home: 22 King Street Oberlin OH 44074-1321 Business E-Mail: jeffrey.mumford@oberlin.edu. E-mail: jmdc@oberlin.net.

MUMFORD, LAWRENCE R., composer, educator; s. Richard W. and Mary Margaret Mumford; m. Donna L. Mumford, Mar. 9, 1996. BA in Music, George Washington U., 1975; MMus, Peabody Conservatory, Balt., 1976; DMus, U. So. Calif., LA, 1989. Cert. tchr. Ind. U., Bloomington, 1977. Music accompanist Glendale Coll., 1990—91; music prof. The Master's Coll., Santa Clarita, Calif., 1992—2004; adj. music prof. Calif. State U., Northridge, 1993—94, Concordia U., Irvine, Calif., 2001—04; prof. music Vanguard U., Costa Mesa, 2004—. Compositions and arrangements published by 7 different cos. Recipient Composition Prize, Culver Chamber Soc., 1999. Mem.: Soc. for Music Theory, Soc. of Composers, Inc., Music Tchrs. Assn. of Calif. (branch pres. 1989—90, pres. emeritus), Pi Kappa Lambda, Phi Beta Kappa. Home: 15 Cortona Irvine CA 92614 Office: Vanguard U 55 Fair Dr Costa Mesa CA 92626 Office Phone: 714-556-3610 ext. 3012. Business E-Mail: lmumford@vanguard.edu.

MUMFORD, STEPHEN DOUGLAS, research scientist; b. Louisville, Aug. 28, 1942; s. Adrian Leroy and Mildred Margaret (Cardwell) M.; m. Judy Sheng-Ju Lee, Dec. 26, 1966; children: Christopher Lee, Sonia Lea BS in Agr., U. Ky., 1966; MPH Internat. Health/Population Study, U. Tex., Houston, 1971, DrPH Health Svcs. Adminstrn., 1975. Indsl. hygienist Ky. State Dept. Health, Frankfort, 1966—67; rsch. asst. dept. ob.-gyn. Baylor Coll. Medicine, Houston, 1973—75; rsch. statis. aide population studies U. Tex., Houston, 1971—75, rsch. asst. dept. reproductive biology/endocrinology, 1974—76; dir. rsch., sr. vasectomy counselor Planned Parenthood Houston, 1975—76; adminstr. Nat. Swine Flu Immunization Program/Houston/Harris County, Tex., 1976—77; from sect. leader design/analysis divsn. to scientist Internat. Fertility Rsch. Program, Research Triangle Park, NC, 1977—83; pres. Ctr. for Rsch. on Population and Security, Research Triangle Park, 1984—; CEO ISAF, Research Triangle Park, 2005—. Author: The Pope and the New Apocalypse: The Holy War Against Family Planning, 1986, American Democracy and the Vatican: Population Growth and National Security, 1984, Population Growth Control: The Next Move is America's, 1977, The Decision-Making Process that Leads to Vasectomy: A Guide for Promoters, 1977, Vasectomy Counseling, 1977, The Life and Death of NSSM 200: How the Destruction of Political Will Doomed a U.S. Population Policy, 1996; contbr. numerous articles to profl. jours., chpts. to books; contbr. editor The Churchman, 1991-98 Mem. Alan Guttmacher Inst., Assn. for Vol. Sterilization, Environ. Def. Fund, Fund for Feminist Majority, Nat. Abortion Rights Action League, Population Inst., Population Ref. Bur., Ams. United for Separation of Ch. and State, Religious Coalition for Abortion Rights. Capt. U.S. Army, 1966-70 Recipient Cert. of Appreciation for Outstanding Contbns. to Advancing the Cause of Reproductive Rights, Feminist Caucus of Am. Humanist Assn., 1986, Humanist Disting. Svc. award, 1981, Margaret Mead Leadership prize in population and ecology, 1981, Award for Outstanding Single Project in Area of Human Rels., U.S. Jaycees, 1974-75, Award for Outstanding Chmn. of a Single Project in Area of Human Rels., 1974-75 Mem. AAAS, Am. Humanist Assn., APHA (population sect.), Ams. for Immigration Control, Ams. for Religious Liberty, Fedn. for Am. Immigration Reform, Internat. Epidemiol. Assn., Negative Population Growth, Carrying Capacity Network, Soc. for Epidemiologic Rsch., Zero Population Growth, NOW Avocations: gardening, fruit growing, woodworking, fishing, running. Office: ISAF 99 TW Alexander Dr PO Box 13067 Research Triangle Park NC 27709 Home: 18 White Pine Way Chapel Hill NC 27516-0815 Office Phone: 919-990-9099. Personal E-mail: smumford@mindspring.com.

MUMMA, ALBERT GIRARD, JR., architect; b. Long Beach, Calif., July 2, 1928; s. Albert Girard and Carmen (Braley) M.; m. Janeal Thomas Woolf, Dec. 24, 1973; children: Eugenia M. Villagra, Albert Girard III, Peter Brenaman. B.Arch., U. Va., 1951. Designer McLeod & Ferrara, Architects, Washington, 1951-56; assoc. Deigert & Yerkes, Architects, 1956-62; prin. Mumma & Assocs., Washington, 1962—. Archtl. designer hotel div. Marriott Corp., 1980-82 Prin. archtl. works include Nat. Arboretum Hdqrs. Bldg, 1961, Finnmark Sq., Silver Spring, Md., 1964, Inverness townhouses, Potomac, Md., 1971, Post Office and Fed. Bldg., Elkins, W.Va., 1971, U.S. Trade Fairs in Spain, Finland, Japan, El Salvador, Poland 1963-72, Fallswood housing project, Falls Church, Va., 1972, Bristow Village townhouses, Annandale, Va., 1972-73, Marriott Hotel, Dayton, Ohio, 1982, Plaza Venetia, Biscayne Bay, Miami, Fla., 1983, Houston Med. Ctr. Hotel, Newark Airport Hotel, 1984, pvt. residences, No. Neck, Rappahanock River, Lancaster County, Va., 1993-2004, subdivision and townhouse projects, Washington, Md., Va., Pa., 1962—. Served with USMC, 1945-47. Recipient Design award Washington Bd. Trade, 1964; winner Newark Airport Hotel Competition, 1981. Mem. AIA (medal 1951), Rappahannock River Yacht Club, Indian Creek Yacht and Country Club, Moran Creek Yacht Club.

MUMMA, MICHAEL JON, research scientist; b. Lancaster, Pa., Dec. 3, 1941; s. John Henry and Violet Lyndell (Baxter) M.; m. Sage Bailey Tower, Aug. 20, 1966; children: Peter Robb, Amy Elizabeth. AB in Physics with honors, Franklin and Marshall Coll., 1963; PhD in Physics, U. Pitts., 1970. Grad. research asst. U. Pitts., 1963-70; astrophysicist NASA Goddard Space Flight Center, Greenbelt, Md., 1970-76, head br. Infrared and Radio Astronomy, 1976-84, assoc. chief Lab. Extraterrestrial Physics, 1984-85, head Planetary Systems br., 1985-90, chief scientist Lab. Extraterrestrial Physics, 1990—, dir. Goddard Ctr. Astrobiology, 2003—; adj. rsch. assoc. in physics Pa. State U., 1978—81, prof. physics, 1981-88; sr. scientist Solar Sys. Exploration Divsn., 2005—. Mem. numerous working groups and adv. coms. NASA, Nat. Bur. Standards, NSF, Nat. Acad. Scis., 1973—; adj. prof. physics U. Toledo, 2002-05; lectr. in field. Contbr. numerous articles to profl. publs., 1970—; editor: The Study of Comets, Vols. 1, 2, 1976, Vibrational-Rotational Spectroscopy for Planetary Atmospheres, vols. 1, 2, 1982, Astrophysics from the Moon, 1990. Recipient NASA medal for Exceptional Sci. Achievement, 1988, 97; Kershner award for physics, 1962; Coll. Trustee's scholar Franklin and Marshall Coll., 1963., Asteroid 8340 named "Michael J. Mumma" by Internat. Astron. Union, 1999. Fellow Am. Phys. Soc., Washington Acad. Sci.; mem. AAAS, Am. Astron. Soc., Am. Geophys. Union, Internat. Astron. Union, Sigma Pi Sigma. Achievements include discovery of natural lasers in atmospheres of Mars, Venus, and Jupiter; first detection of water vapor in comets, discovery of formaldehyde, methanol, methane, and ethane in comets; discovery of x-rays in comets; first definitive measurements of deuterium and hydrogen on Mars and Venus; first absolute wind measurements on Venus and Mars; invention of tunable diode laser heterodyne spectrometer and other advanced instruments; development of Doppler-limited infrared spectroscopy for laboratory and astrophysical applications, of absolute calibration procedures in vacuum ultraviolet, of molecular branching ratio technique for intensity calibration in vacuum ultraviolet; measurement of many absolute cross sections in vacuum ultraviolet; research on atomic and molecular physics and chemistry, on comets, on planetary atmospheres, on infrared astronomy, on high-resolution spectroscopy, and in the field of dissociative excitation of molecules. Office: Code 690.3 Goddard Space Flight Ctr Greenbelt MD 20771-0001

MUMMANENI, PADMAJA, research scientist, educator; d. Ram Mohan Rao and Lakshmiswaramma Mummaneni. BSc in Life Scis., Delhi U., India, 1980, MSc, 1982, PhD, 1989. Postdoctoral rsch. fellow U. Ky., Lexington, 1989—96; staff fellow NIH, Bethesda, Md., 1996—2000; scientist Neuralstem Inc., Gaithersburg, Md., 2000—03; vol. consult dir. Neuronascent Inc., Md., 2004; contract RSR fellow CDER, FDA, Rockville, Md., 2004—05; adj. prof. microbiology Marymount U., Va., 2005. Guest lectr. Found. for Advanced Edn. in the Scis. NIH, Bethesda, Md., 1998—2000, juror, 1998—2000. Contbr. articles to profl./peer-reviewed jours. Fellow: AAAS, Am. Soc. of Cellular and Molecular Biology, N.Y. Acad. Scis.; mem.: Am. Women In Sci. Hindu. Avocations: painting, art. Home: 10513 Montrose Ave Bethesda MD 20814 Office: FDA 1451 Rockville Pike Rockville MD 20852 Personal E-mail: pmummaneni@aol.com.

MUMMERY, DANIEL R., lawyer; b. Miami, Fla., Mar. 4, 1959; s. Charles R. Mummery and Kathleen M. Osborne; m. Frances D. Nuelle, Oct. 11, 1997; children: Amanda F., William G., Alexander G. AB, Bowdoin Coll., 1977—81; JD, Fordham U. Sch. Law, 1985—88. Bar: Mass. 1989, NY 1989, Calif. 2002. Assoc. Milbank, Tweed, Hadley & McCloy, New York, NY, 1988—96, ptnr., 1996—2001, Cooley Godward LLP, Palo Alto, Calif., 2001—04, Latham & Watkins LLP, Menlo Park, Calif., 2004—. Editor-in-chief Fordham Urban Law Jour., 1987. Recipient Chambers and Ptnrs., 2000—05. Mem.: ABA (assoc.), NYC Bar. Assn. (assoc.). Avocations: tennis, wine, films. Office: Latham & Watkins LLP 140 Scott Dr Menlo Park CA 94025-1008 Office Phone: 650-463-3069. Office Fax: 650-463-2600. Business E-Mail: daniel.mummery@lw.com.

MUMPOWER, JERYL L., academic administrator; m. Edwina Dorch; 1 child, Sarah. BA, Coll. William and Mary; PhD in Social and Quantitative Psychology, U. Colo. Dir., policy analyst NSF; assoc. dir. Rockfeller Inst. Govt.; prof. pub. adminstrn., pub. policy and info. sci. U. Albany, SUNY, 1984—, dir. Ctr. for Policy Rsch., assoc. provost, dean grad. studies, interim provost, v.p. for acad. affairs, 2004—. Contbr. chapters to books, articles to profl. jours. Office: Univ Albany SUNY UAB 400 1400 Washington Ave Albany NY 12222 *

MUNAS, FALIES A., psychiatric physician; b. Colombo, Sri Lanka, Aug. 30, 1946; came to U.S., 1972; s. M.H.M. and C.P. M. MBBS, MD, Christian Med. Coll., Vellore, India, 1971. Diplomate Am. Bd. Psychiatry and Neurology. Dir. geropsychiatry Trinity Meml. Hosp., Cudahy, Wis., 1991-95; dir. clin. svcs./chief of staff De Paul Hosp., Milw., 1996-97; dir. behavioral medicine VA Med. Ctr., Marion, Ill., 1998-2000; assoc. clinical prof. psychiatry S.I.U. Sch. Medicine, Springfield, Ill., 1999—2004. Pres. Extended Family Svc, Pitts., 1989—; assoc. clin. prof. psychiatry So. Ill. U. Sch. Medicine, Springfield, 1999—2004. Home: 23107 Galatia Post Rd Pittsburg IL 62974-1832 Office: Extended Family Svc PO Box 753 Marion IL 62959 Business E-Mail: famunasmd@gmail.com.

MUNCIE, RONALD JAMES, environmental services administrator, minister; b. Lansing, Mich., Apr. 24, 1952; s. Robert Amos and Glennis Leone Muncie; m. Sandra Kay Robbins, Sept. 16, 1978; children: Andrea K. Cook, Patrick R. BS in Bus. Personnel and Indsl. Rels., Ind. U., Bloomington, 1974. Ins. investigator Comml. Svcs. Inc., Indpls., 1976—79; environ. health inspector Marion Counth Health Dept., Indpls., 1979—. Min. Jehovah's Witnesses. Recipient Outstanding Svc. award, Marion County Soil and Water Conservation Dist., 1989. Mem.: Nat. Environ. Health Assn., Ind. Environ. Health Assn. Avocations: walking, jogging, carpentry, swimming, boating. Home: 3120 Carlsbad Dr Indianapolis IN 46241

MUNCK, ALLAN ULF, physiologist, educator; b. Buenos Aires, July 4, 1925; came to U.S., 1945, naturalized, 1959; s. Carl and Elisabeth (Schmidt) M.; m. Claire Brosi, Oct. 5, 1957; children— Alexander Charles, Ingrid Claire, Kirsten Tanya. BS in Chem. Engring, MIT, 1948, MS, 1949, PhD in Biophysics, 1956. Chem. engr., Ducilo, Buenos Aires, 1949-50; mem. staff Huntington Lab. Mass. Gen. Hosp., Boston, 1956-57, Worcester Found. Exptl. Biology, Shrewsbury, Mass., 1957-59; mem. med. sch. faculty Dartmouth Coll., 1959—; prof. physiology Dartmouth Med. Sch., 1967—2001, prof. physiology emeritus, 2001—. Marius Tausk prof. Leiden U., The Netherlands, 1998. Served with Argentine Army, 1949. Home: PO Box 114 Norwich VT 05055-0114 Office: Dartmouth Med Sch Dept Physiology Lebanon NH 03756 Home Phone: 802-649-1456. Business E-Mail: allan.u.munck@dartmouth.edu.

MÜNCK, ECKARD, chemistry professor; PhD in Nuclear Physics, Technical Univ. Darmstadt, Germany, 1967. Rsch. assoc., dept. physics U. Ill., 1967—69, rsch. asst. prof., dept. physics, 1969—73; assoc. prof., biochemistry, Gray Freshwater Biol. Inst. U. Minn., 1974—78, prof. biochemistry, Gray Freshwater Biol. Inst., 1978—90; acting dir. Gray Freshwater Biol. Inst., 1979—81; prof. chemistry Carnegie Mellon U., 1990—. Recipient Alfred Bader award in Bioinorganic and Bioorganic Chemistry, Am. Chem. Soc., 2007. Fellow: AAAS. Office: Carnegie Mellon U Mellon Inst Rm 546 4400 Fifth Ave Pittsburgh PA 15213 Office Phone: 412-268-5058. Office Fax: 412-268-1061. Business E-Mail: emunck@cmu.edu. *

MUNCY, ESTLE PERSHING, physician; b. Tazewell, Tenn., Apr. 9, 1918; s. William Loyd and Flora Media (Monday) M.; m. Dorothy Davis, Dec. 31, 1946 (div. Apr. 1980); children: Robert H., Teresa A., Dorothy J., Estle II,James; m. Jean Marie Hayter, Mar. 19, 1985. AB, Lincoln Meml. U., 1939; MD, U. Tenn., 1943. Resident Dallas Meth. Hosp., 1948; tchg. resident Tufts Med. Sch., Boston, 1949-50; physician Jefferson City, Tenn., 1950-96. Author: The Muncys in the New World, 1988, People and Places in Jefferson County, Tennessee, 1994. Alderman Jefferson City, 1974-77; chmn. Jefferson City Planning Commn., 1976-79. Capt. M.C., U.S. Army, 1944-46. Recipient Commendation for work on Tenn. history Gov. Don Sundquist, Jefferson award Am. Inst. Pub. Svc., 1995, Covenant Health Platinum award, 2000; named to Lincoln Meml. U. Lit. and Profl. Halls of Fame, 1997. Mem. Tenn. Heart Assn. (pres. 1966-67), Hamblen County Med. Soc. (pres. 1960-61), Jefferson County Hist. Soc. (pres. 1993-94, historian 1995—). Republican. Baptist. Avocations: photography, gardening. Home: 1428 Russell Ave Jefferson City TN 37760-2216 Office Phone: 865-475-3377.

MUND, GERALDINE, judge; b. LA, July 7, 1943; d. Charles J. and Pearl M. BA, Brandeis U., 1965; MS, Smith Coll., 1967; JD, Loyola U., 1977; MA, Calif. State U., Northridge, 2007. Bar: Calif. 1977. Bankruptcy judge U.S. Ctrl. Dist. Calif., 1984—, bankruptcy chief judge, 1997—2002. Past pres. Temple Israel, Hollywood, Calif.; past mem. Bd. Jewish Fedn. Coun. of Greater L.A. Mem. ABA, L.A. County Bar Assn. Office: 21041 Burbank Blvd Woodland Hills CA 91367-6606 Office Phone: 818-587-2840.

MUNDAY, STEPHEN DALE, writer, artist; b. Haskell, Tex., Mar. 10, 1949; s. Edna Mae Moody; m. Joyce Lavern Stuteville, June 19, 1981. BA, West Tex. State U., 1970. Farm and ranch editor Abilene Reporter-News, Tex., 1971—72; field editor The Cattleman Mag. Tex. and Southwestern Cattle Raisers Assn., Fort Worth, 1972—74, editl. dir., 1976—78; info. dir. Tex. Cattle Feeders Assn., Amarillo, 1974; freelance writer Arlington, 1974—76; dir. field svcs. Simmental Shield Mag. Am. Simmental Assn., 1975; news dir. Tex. and Southwestern Cattle Raisers Assn., Fort Worth, 1978—81, adminstrv. asst. media and govt. rels., 1981—95, exec. v.p., 1995—2001. Asst. sec. Tex. and Southwestern Cattle Raisers Found., Fort Worth, 1995-2001; sec.-treas. Tex. and Southwestern Cattle Raisers Assn. Ins. Svcs., Inc., Ft. Worth, 1995-2001, Tex. and Southwestern Cattle Raisers Assn. Legal Def. Fund, 1995-2001. Editor: TSCRA News Update, 1979-1995 (1st pl. gen. excellence Livestock Pubs. Coun. 1986, 88, 90-91, 2d pl., 1989). Bd. dir. Hist. Camp Bowie, Inc., Fort Worth, 2001. Capt. U.S. Army, 1971-79. Avocations: reading, painting, cartooning, collectibles. Home: 3415 Bristol Rd Fort Worth TX 76107 Office Phone: 817-878-2440. E-mail: stevemunday@sbcglobal.net.

MUNDELL, ROBERT ALEXANDER, economist, educator; b. Kingston, Ont., Can., Oct. 24, 1932; s. William C. and Lila (Knifton) Mundell; m. Barbara Sheff, Oct. 14, 1957 (div. 1972); children: Paul Alexander, William Andrew, Robyn Leslie; m. Valerie Sophia Natsios, Nov. 10, 1998; 1 child, Nicholas Robert. BA, U. B.C., Can., 1953; postgrad., U. Wash., 1953—54, London Sch. Econs. and Polit. Sci., 1955—56; PhD, MIT, 1956; postdoc., U. Chgo., 1956—57; PhD (hon.), Renmin U. China, 1985, U. Paris, 1992. Instr. econs. U. B.C., Vancouver, Canada, 1957—58; acting asst. prof. econs. Stanford U., Calif., 1958—59; vis. prof. econs. Sch. Advanced Internat. Studies, Johns Hopkins U. Ctr., Bologna, Italy, 1959—61; sr. economist research dept. IMF, Washington, 1961—63; vis. prof. econs. McGill U., Montreal, Que., Canada, 1963—64; Rockefeller vis. research prof. internat. econs. Brookings Instn., Washington, 1964—65; prof. Grad. Inst. Internat. Studies, Geneva, 1965—75; Ford Found. vis. research prof. econs. U. Chgo., 1965—66, prof., 1966—71; prof. econs., chmn. dept. U. Waterloo, Ont., Canada, 1972—74; prof. econs. Columbia U., NYC, 1974—. Marshall lectr. Cambridge U.,, 1974; economist Can. Royal Commnl on Price Spreads on Food Products, 1957; mem. joint fiscal mission to Peru OAS and Inter-am. Devel. Bank, 1964; cons. FRS, IBRD, 1966—, U.S. Treasury Dept., 1969—74, EEC, 1970—73, UN, Govt. Panama; organizer, participant internat. confs.; lectr. numerous univs. and profl. orgn. meetings; hon. prof. Renmin U. China, Beijing. Author: The Internat. Monetary System- Conflict and Reform, 1965, Man and Economics, 1968, International Economics, 1968, Monetary Theory-Interest, Inflation and Growth in the World Economy, 1971; contbr. articles to profl. jours.; co-editor: Monetary Problems of the International Economy, 1969, Trade Blaance of Payments and Growth, 1971, The International Monetary System, 1977; editor: Jour. Polit. Economy, 1966—70, Global Disequilibrium in the World Economy, 1989, 1992, Building the New Europe, 1991, Debt, Deficit and Economic Importance, 1990, Inflation and Growth in China, 1996. Named Companion of Order of Can., 2003; recipient James Rueff medal, French Senate, 1983, Nobel prize in Econs., 1999; fellow, Guggenheim, 1970—71; grantee, NSF, 1967—70. Fellow: AAAS, 1998; mem.: Am. Econ. Assn. (Disting. fellow 1997). Office: Dept Econs Columbia U 1031 Internat Affairs 420 W 118th St # Mc3308 New York NY 10027-7213 *

MUNDHEIM, ROBERT HARRY, law educator; b. Hamburg, Germany, Feb. 24, 1933; m. Guna Smitchens; children: Susan, Peter. BA, Harvard U., 1954, LLB, 1957; MA (hon.), U. Pa., 1971. Bar: NY 1958, Pa. 1979. Assoc. Shearman & Sterling, NYC, 1958-61; spl. counsel to SEC Washington, 1962-63; vis. prof. Duke Law Sch., Durham, NC, 1964; prof. law U. Pa., Phila., 1965—. Univ. prof. law and fin., 1980-93, dean, 1982-89, Bernard G. Segal prof. law, 1987-89; co-chmn. Fried, Frank, Harris, Shriver & Jacobson, NYC, 1990-92; exec. v.p., gen. counsel Salomon Inc., 1992-97; sr. exec. v.p., gen. counsel Salomon Smith Barney Holdings, Inc., 1997-98; of counsel Shearman & Sterling, 1999—; gen. counsel U.S. Dept. Treasury, Washington, 1977-80, trustee, pres., 2000-06, Am. Acad. in Berlin; chmn. legal adv. bd. NASDAQ, chmn. legal adv. bd. NASD; dir. Appleseed Found., 1996-06; trustee New Sch. U.; coun. Am. Law Inst.; bd. dirs. eCollege, 2001-2007, Arnhold & S. Bleichroder, 2004—, Quadra Real Estate Investment Trust, chair 2007—; gen. counsel Chrysler Loan Guarantee Bd., 1980; mng. dir., mgmt. bd. Salomon Bros. Inc., NYC, 1992-97; trustee Curtis Inst., 2000—; mem. supervisory bd. Hypo Real Estate Holdings AG, 2004-07. Author: Outside Director of the Publicity Held Corporation, 1976; American Attitudes Toward Foreign Direct Investment in the United States, 1979; Conflict of Interest and the Former Government Employee: Re-thinking the Revolving Door, 1981; chmn. adv. bd. Jour. Internat. Econ. Law, 1996-97. Trustee SEC Hist. Soc. With USAF, 1961-62. Recipient Alexander Hamilton award U.S. Dept. Treasury, 1980, Harold P. Seligson award Practicing Law Inst., 1988, Francis J. Rawle award, ABA-ALI, 1992, Anti-Defamation League Human Rels. award, 1999, Officer's Cross of Order Merit, Republic of Germany, 2007. Mem. ABA (task force on corp. responsiblity), Am. Law Inst., San Diego Securities Regulation Inst. (exec. com.). Office: Shearman & Sterling 599 Lexington Ave Fl 16 New York NY 10022-6069 Office Phone: 212-848-7738.

MUNDIE, CRAIG JAMES, computers software company executive; b. 1949; BEE, Ga. Inst. Tech., M in Info. Theory and Computer Sci. Software developer Data Gen. Corp., 1972; co-founder, CEO Alliant Computer Systems Corp., 1982—92; with Microsoft Corp., Redmond, Wash., 1992—, gen, mgr., advanced consumer tech., 1992—93, v.p., advanced consumer tech. group, 1993—96, sr. v.p., consumer platforms divsn., 1996—2001, sr. v.p. advanced strategies and policy, 2001—02, chief tech. officer, advanced strategies & policy, 2001—06, sr. v.p., advanced strategies & policy, 2001—06, chief rsch. & strategy officer, 2006—. Presdl. appointee Nat. Security Telecom. Adv. Com., 2000; mem. Coun. on Fgn. Rels., 2002—, Task Force on Nat. Security in the Info. Age, 2002—; trustee Fred Hutchinson Cancer Rsch. Ctr., Seattle; adv. bd. mem. Coll. of Computing Ga. Inst. Tech., Atlanta; mem. adv. bd., Live Labs (Rsch. partnership between MSN and Microsoft Rsch.) Microsoft Corp., 2006—. Office: Microsoft Corp One Microsoft Way Redmond WA 98052-6399 *

MUNDINGER, DONALD CHARLES, retired college president; b. Chgo., Sept. 2, 1929; s. George Edward and Bertha (Trelkenberg) M.; m. June Myrtle Grubbe, June 17, 1951; children: Debra Sue, Donald William, Mary Ruth (dec.). Student, U. Ill., 1947-48; BA, Concordia Coll., River Forest, Ill., 1951, LLD (hon.), 1982; MA, Northwestern U., 1952; PhD, Washington U., St. Louis, 1956; DH (hon.), MacMurray Coll., Jacksonville, Ill., 1984, Ritsumeikan U., Kyoto, Japan, 1992; LLD (hon.), Ill. Coll., Jacksonville, 1993; postdoctoral study, Cambridge U.Eng., 1967-68. Asst. prof. polit. sci., chmn. dept. Augustana Coll., Sioux Falls, S.D., 1956-58; asst. prof. govt. Valparaiso (Ind.) U., 1958-61, assoc. prof., 1961-65, prof., 1965-73; dean Valparaiso (Ind.) U. (Coll. Arts and Scis.), 1965-67; dir. Overseas Center, Cambridge, Eng., 1967-68, v.p. acad. affairs, 1968-73; pres. Ill. Coll., Jacksonville, 1973-93; chmn. Fedn. Ind. Ill. Colls. and Univs., 1975-78; chmn. non-public adv. com. Ill. Bd. Higher Edn., 1988-91. Postdoctoral fellow Center Study Higher Edn., U. Mich., 1964-65; chmn. bd. Council Ind. Colls., 1988-90. Contbr. articles to profl. jours. Mem. Ill. State Bar Assn. (com. on fed. judicial and related appointments 1983-89), Nat. Assn. Ind. Colls. and Univs. (commn. on new initiatives, 1988-90), Pi Sigma Alpha, Phi Eta Sigma. Home: 3803 Pheasant Walk Dr Valparaiso IN 46383-2205

MUNDINGER, MARY O'NEIL, nursing educator; b. Fredonia, NY, Apr. 27, 1937; d. Thomas Lewis and Dorothy (Hanselman) O'Neil; m. Paul C. Mundinger, Aug. 23, 1958; children: Paul Jr., Ann Mundinger Schimenti, Thomas, Elizabeth. BS, U. Mich., 1959; MA, Columbia U., 1974, PhD, 1981; LHD (hon.), Hamilton Coll., 1996. Adminstr., instr. Tchrs. Coll. Columbia U., NYC, 1975; adj. instr. Pace U., NYC, 1975-77, asst. prof., 1977-82; asst. prof. nursing, dir. grad. program Columbia U. Sch. Nursing, NYC, 1982-83, assoc. prof. nursing, dir. grad. program, 1983-84, assoc. prof., assoc. dean adminstrv. affairs, 1984-85, assoc. prof., asst. dean faculty of medicine, 1986, dean, Centennial prof. health policy, 1986—. Bd. dirs. Conn. Hospice, Branford, UnitedHealth Group, 1997-, Cell Therapeutics, Inc., 1997-, Gentiva Health Services, 2002-, Welch Allyn Inc., 2002-; adv. group steering com. N.Y. Acad. Medicine, N.Y.C., 1992—; regional adv. com. Nat. Network Librs. of Medicine, N.Y.C., 1992—; Robert Wood Johnson health policy fellows bd. Inst. Medicine, Washington, 1990—, Health Svcs. Improvement Fund, NYC, 1992—, health policy adv. com. Sen. Edward Kennedy, Washington, 1985—, med. adv. bd. Walt Disney Imagineering (Wonders of Life), Orlando, Fla., 1988-89; charter mem. health care tech., Inst. Medicine, NAS, 1985-. Author: Home Care Controversy: Too Little, Too Late, Too Costly, 1983 (Book of Yr. 1984), Autonomy in Nursing, 1980 (Book of Yr. 1981). Recipient grant W.K. Kellogg Found., 1989, grant Katzenbach Found., 1986; Nurse Practitioner Year award, The Nurse Practitioner Journal, 1998. Fellow: Am. Acad. Nursing, NY Acad. Medicine; mem.: Inst. Medicine. Avocations: skiing, reading. Office: Office of Dean of Nursing 630 W 168th St Box 6 New York NY 10032-3702 Fax: (212) 305-1116.

MUNDT, BARRY MAYNARD, management consultant; b. San Francisco, June 28, 1936; s. Kenneth Francis and Janet (Doughty) M.; m. Sally Hanscom, June 13, 1960; children: Kevin Warren, Trevor Stevens, Stacey Corbin BS in Indsl. Engring., Stanford U., 1959; MBA, Santa Clara U., 1964. Registered indsl. engr., Calif. Statistician Aerojet-Gen., Sacramento, 1957-58; reliability engr. Lockheed Missiles, Sunnyvale, Calif., 1959-61; mgmt. engr. C-E-I-R, Inc., Los Altos, Calif., 1961-65; sr. cons. Peat, Marwick, Livingston & Co., Los Angeles, 1965-68; mgr., prin. Peat, Marwick, Mitchell & Co., Atlanta, 1968-84; ptnr.-in-charge, ops. mgmt. cons. KPMG Peat Marwick Main & Co., NYC, 1984-88; internat. mgmt. cons. ptnr. KPMG Internat., NYC and Amsterdam, The Netherlands, 1988-92; mgmt. cons., ptnr. KPMG Peat Marwick U.S., Montvale, NJ, 1992-95; prin. The Strategy Facilitation Group, Asheville, NC, 1995—. Bd. dirs. Adjusters Internat., Inc., 2005—; Mosaic Acctg., Inc., 2005—. Author-editor: Managing Public Resources, 1982; co-author Il Manager Pubblico (Italy), 1986; mem. editl. bd., contbg. author Handbook of Industrial Engineering, 3rd edit., 2001; contbr. articles to profl. jours. Mem. ann. campaign Atlanta Symphony Orch., 1974-82, Atlanta Arts Alliance, 1976-81; del. to assembly United Way of Met. Atlanta, 1974-84; bd. chmn., mem. Brandon Hall Sch., Atlanta, 1980—2002; vice chmn. steering coun., NC Ctr. Creative Retirement, 2007—. Fellow Inst. Indsl. Engrs. (treas. 1976-81, pres. 1982-83, asst. treas. 1985-92); mem. Asheville Country Club. Episcopalian. Avocations: golf, boating. Home and Office: 32 Dover St Asheville NC 28804 Office Phone: 828-254-2769. Personal E-mail: bmundt@charter.net.

MUNDT, MARVIN GLEN, retired mathematics professor; b. Ossian, Iowa, Apr. 5, 1933; s. Glen Charles and Edna Marie (Gipp) M.; m. Margaret Rose Fuchs, Mar. 20, 1958; children: Mark Osroe, Marlon Paul, Martin David, Marshall Jared, Marston Charles. BA magna cum laude, Luther Coll., 1955; MS, Iowa State U., 1958, PhD, 1961. Tchg. asst. Iowa State U., Ames, 1955—60; mathematician White Sands Missile Range, N.Mex., 1956—59; assoc. prof. math. Tex. Luth. Coll., Seguin, 1966—68; asst. prof. math. Valparaiso (Ind.) U., 1961—66, prof. math., 1964—95; ret., 1995. Tchr. NSF Inst., Valparaiso, 1962—69; tchg. chair in math. Tex. Luth.; faculty adviser Sigma Tau Gamma; chmn. math. dept. Valparaiso U., 1976—80. Contbr. articles to profl. jours. Vol. St. Agnes Ctr. for Srs., Valparaiso, 1999—, Meals on Wheels, Valparaiso, 1998—; communion asst., mem. choir Immanuel Luth. Ch., Valparaiso, 1982—; treas. Family House Bd., Valparaiso, 1986—. Mem.: Am. Math. Soc., Math. Assn. Am. (chmn. Ind. sect. 1982), Nat. Exch. Club (pres. No. Ind. dist. 1999), Pi Mu Epsilon. Avocations: golf, racquetball, softball, travel. Home: 555 Meadlow Ln Valparaiso IN 46385

MUNDY, B. JO ANN, minister; b. Phila., Mar. 5, 1960; d. William John and V. Dolores Mundy. BA in Bibl. Studies, San Diego Christian Coll., El Cajon, 1991; MA in Bibl. Studies, Dallas Theol. Sem., 1996; MDiv, No. Sem., Lombard, Ill., 2004; Dr. in Worship Studies, Robert E. Webber Inst. Worship Studies, Oragne Park, Fla., 2007. Assoc. worship pastor Irving Bible Ch., Tex., 1997—99; worship pastor N. Farmington Cmty. Ch., Farmington Hills, Mich., 1999—2004; sr. pastor First Bapt. Ch., Three Rivers, Mich., 2005—. Assoc. worship pastor Irving Bible Ch., Irving, Tex., 1997—99. Founding mem. Nia Project, Three Rivers, TRAFC, Three Rivers, 2005; mem. Three Rivers Health Found., 2005; co-chair ERAC/CE, Kalamazoo, 2006. Po3 USN, 1980—86, Guam, San Diego. Mem.: NAACP (local pres. 2006—07). Office: First Baptist Ch 1020 Portage Ave Three Rivers MI 49093 Office Fax: 269-278-4565.

MUNDY, GARDNER MARSHALL, lawyer; b. Roanoke, Va., July 19, 1934; s. Gardner Adams and Betty (Marshall) M.; m. Jean Stephens, Nov. 13, 1956 (div. 1979); children: Stephens M., Liza I.; m. Jenice Hamrick, June 21, 1980 (div. 1998); children: G. Marshall Jr., Natalie J.; m. Monika Ferguson, Aug. 28, 1999. BA, Va. Mil. Inst., 1956; LLB, U. Va., 1962. Bar: Va. 1962, U.S. Dist. Ct. (we. dist.) Va. 1962, U.S. Ct. Appeals (4th cir.) 1962. Ptnr. Woods, Rogers & Hazlegrove, Roanoke, 1962-71, Mundy & Garrison, Roanoke, 1973-76, Mundy & Strickland, Roanoke, 1976-82; pvt. practice Roanoke, 1982-86; ptnr. Mundy, Rogers & Frith, Roanoke, 1986—2003, Mundy Rogers & Assocs., Roanoke, 2003—. Bd. visitors Va. Mil. Inst., 2005—. 1st lt. U.S. Army, 1957-59. Fellow Am. Coll. Trial Lawyers, Am. Bd. Trial Advocates (pres. Western Va. chpt. 1990-91), Am. Bar Found., Va. Bar Found.; mem. ABA, Va. State Bar (chmn. bd. govs. litig. sect. 1985-86, bd. govs. sr. law sect. 2000-04), Roanoke Bar Assn. (bd. dirs. 1986-90, pres. 1990-91), Shenandoah Club, Roanoke Country Club, Coral Beach and Tennis Club (Bermuda). Presbyterian. Avocations: golf, skiing, cooking, growing roses. Home: 1542 Electric Rd Roanoke VA 24018-1106 Office: Mundy Rogers & Assocs 1328 3rd St SW Roanoke VA 24016-5219 Office Phone: 540-982-2900. Office Fax: 540-982-1362. Business E-Mail: gmundy@mundyrogers.com.

MUNERA, GERARD EMMANUEL, manufacturing executive; b. Algiers, Algeria, Dec. 2, 1935; s. Gabriel and Laure (Labrousse) M.; m. Paule A. Ramos, July 28, 1959; children: Catherine, Philippe, Emmanuelle, Jean-Marie. M Math., M Physics, M Chemistry, Ecole Poly., Paris, 1956; CE, Ecole Ponts et Chaussees, Paris, 1959. Chief county engr. Dept. Rds. and Bridges, South Algiers, 1959-62; cons. French Ministry Fgn. Affairs, Argentina, 1962-66; sr. v.p. fin. Camea Group Pechiney Ugine Kuhlmann, Buenos Aires, 1966-70, chmn. bd., chief exec. officer, 1976-77; exec. v.p. Howmet Aluminum Corp., Greenwich, Conn., 1976-77, pres., chief operating officer, 1977-79, pres., chief exec. officer, 1980-83; corporate v.p. nuclear fuels Pechiney, Brussels, 1983-85; vice chmn., chief exec. officer Union Minière, Brussels, 1985-89; head corp. planning and devel. RTZ, London, 1989-90; pres., CEO Minorco USA, Englewood, Colo., 1990-94, also bd. dirs.; chmn. and CEO Latin Am. Gold, Inc., NYC, 1994-96, Synergex Inc., 1996—. Bd. dirs. Nevsun Resources, Inc., Meridian Gold Inc., Dynamic Materials Corp., Inc., SiVault Sys., Inc., Mag Industries; chmn., CEO, Arcadia Inc., mng. ptnr. Synergex Group LLC. Patentee low-income housing system. Served with French Air Force, 1956-57. Decorated officer Legion of Honor (France). Roman Catholic. Office: Arcadia 60 Bonner St Stamford CT 06902-6610 Office Phone: 203-316-8000.

MUNERA, PEDRO ANTONIO, child and adolescent psychiatrist; b. Granollers, Spain, May 16, 1970; s. Pedro Munera and Dolores Cordoba; m. Sherry Lynn Rowlett, Mar. 7, 2003. MD, U. Autonoma de Barcelona, Spain, 1994. Diplomate in psychiatry and in child and adolescent psychiatry Am. Bd. Psychiatry and Neurology. Child and adolescent psychiatrist Weems Cmty. Mental Health Ctr., Meridian, Miss., 2003—; clin. asst. prof. dept. psychiatry U. Miss., Jackson, 2003—. Author book reviews and case reports. Mem.: Miss. Psychiat. Assn. (assoc.; chair early career psychiatrist com., exec.coun. 2006—), Am. Acad. Child and Adolescent Psychiatry (assoc.; residents and early career psychiatrists com. 2002—03), Am. Psychiat. Assn. (assoc.). Roman Catholic. Avocations: travel, reading. Office: U Miss Med Ctr 2500 N State St Jackson MS 39216 Personal E-mail: pedromunera@comcast.net.

MUNGER, CHARLES T., diversified company executive; b. Omaha, Nebr., 1924; m. Nancy Munger; 8 children. Student, U. of Mich., 1941—42, Calif. Inst. Technol., 1943; JD, Harvard Law Sch., 1948. Joined Musick Peeler & Garrett, Los Angeles, Calif.; co-founder Munger, Tolles & Olson, 1962—, ptnr., 1962—65, Wheeler Munger & Co., LA, 1962—75; chmn., CEO, Blue Chip Stamps, 1976—; vice chmn. Berkshire Hathaway, Inc., Omaha, 1978—, also chmn., CEO Wesco Fin. subs., 1983—. Chmn. Daily Jour. Corp.; bd. dirs. Costco, 1997—. Meteorological officer USAF, World War II. Named one of Forbes' Richest Americans, 2006. Office: Berkshire Hathaway Inc 1440 Kiewit Plz Omaha NE 68131-3302 also: Munger Tolles and Olson 355 S Grand Ave Los Angeles CA 90071-1560 *

MUNGER, EDWIN STANTON, political geography educator; b. LaGrange, Ill., Nov. 19, 1921; s. Royal Freeman and Mia (Stanton) M.; m. Ann Boyer, May 2, 1970; 1 child, Elizabeth Stanton Gibson. B.Sc., U. Chgo., 1948, M.Sc., 1949, PhD, 1951. Fulbright fellow Makerere U., 1949-50; research fellow U. Chgo.; field assoc. Am. Univs. Field Staff, 1950-60; faculty Calif. Inst. Tech., Pasadena, 1961—, prof. polit. geography, 1960—. Research fellow Stellenbosch U., 1955-56; vis. prof. U. Warsaw, 1973 Author books including Afrikaner and African Nationalsim, 1968, The Afrikaners, 1979, Touched by Africa: An Autobiography, 1983, Cultures, Chess and Art: A Collector's Odyssey Across Seven Continents, Vol. 1 Sub Saharan Africa, 1996, Vol. 2, Americas, 1997, Pacific Islands and the Asian Rim, Vol. 3, 1999, 10 short stories for kids--L.A. Times on Africa, 2001-02; editor books including Munger Africana Library Notes, 1969-82; contbr. chpts. to books and numerous articles to profl. jours. Evaluator Peace Corps, Uganda, 1966, Botswana, 1967; chmn. State Dept. Evalustion Team South Africa, 1971; trustee African-Am. Inst., 1956-62; acting pres. Pasadena Playhouse, 1966; chmn. bd. trustees Crane Rogers Found., 1979-82, fellow, 1950-54; mem. exec. com. NAACP, Pasadena, 1979—, nat. del., 1984, 85; trustee Leakey Found., 1968—, pres., 1971-84; pres. Cape of Good Hope Found., 1985—; pres. Internat. Vis. Coun., L.A., 1991-93, bd. dirs., 1979-93. Recipient Alumni Citation award for pub. svc. U. Chgo., 1993, Gandhi Martin Luther King-Ikeda award Morehouse U., 2002. Fellow South African Royal Soc., Royal Soc. Arts, African Studies Assn. (founding bd. dirs. 1963-66, Martin L. King Ikeda-Mahatma Gandhi award 2002); mem. PEN USA West (v.p.), Coun. Fgn. Rels., Cosmos Club, Athenaeum Club, Twilight Club, Chess Collectors Internat. (bd. dirs. 1998—). Office: Calif Inst Tech Divsn Humanities & Social Scis 1201 E California Blvd Pasadena CA 91125-0001 E-mail: munger@hss.caltech.edu.

MUNGER, PAUL R., engineering educator; b. Hannibal, Mo., Jan. 14, 1932; s. Paul O and Anne M.; m. Frieda Anna Mette, Nov. 26, 1954; children: Amelia Ann Munger Fortmeyer, Paul David, Mark James, Martha Jane Munger Cox. BSCE, Mo. Sch. Mines and Metallurgy, 1958, MSCE, 1961; PhD in Engring. Sci., U. Ark., 1972. Registered profl. engr., Mo., Ill., Ark. Instr. civil engring Mo. Sch. Mines and Metallurgy, Rolla, 1958-61, asst. prof., 1961-65; assoc. prof. U. Mo., Rolla, 1965-73, prof., 1973-99; dir. Inst. River Studies, U. Mo., Rolla, 1976-93; exec. dir. Internat. Inst. River and Lake Systems, U. Mo., Rolla, 1984-93, interim chmn. CE dept., 1998-99, prof. emeritics of CE, 2000—. Mem. NSPE, Mo. Soc. Profl. Engr., Am. Soc. Engring. Edn., ASCE, Nat. Coun. Engring. Examiners (pres. 1983-84), Mo. Bd. Architects, Profl. Engr. and Land Surveyors (chmn. 1978-84, 95-2002).

MUNGIA, SALVADOR ALEJO, lawyer; b. Tacoma, Feb. 19, 1959; s. Salvador Alejo Sr. and Susie (Tamaki) M. BA, Pacific Luth. U., 1981; JD, Georgetown U., 1984. Bar: Wash. 1984, U.S. Dist. Ct. (we. dist.) Wash. 1985, U.S. Ct. Appeals (9th cir.) 1986, U.S. Supreme Ct. 1992. Law clk. to Justice Fred Dore Wash. State Supreme Ct., Olympia, 1984-85; law clk. to Hon. Carolyn R. Dimmick U.S. Dist. Ct. (we. dist.) Wash., Seattle, 1985-86; assoc. Gordon, Thomas, Honeywell, Malanca, Peterson & Daheim, Tacoma, 1986-91, ptnr., 1991—. Adj. prof. Pacific Luth. U., 1993-94. Vol. atty. ACLU, Tacoma, 1986—, bd. dirs., 1987-92; mem. Tacoma Human Rights Commn., 1990-96; bd. dirs. Legal Aid for Washington, 1992-96, life bd. dirs., 1997—, pres., 2002-03; dir. bd. dirs. Grand Cinema, Tacoma, 2002-04; dir. Merle Palmer Minority Scholorship Found., 2005-; trustee Lawyers Com. for Civil Rights Under the Law, 2003-04; dir. Lawyers Com. Civil Rights Under The Law, 2005-06. Recipient Am. Leadership Forum fellowship, 2001—02. Fellow: Am. Bar Found.; mem.: ABA, Pierce County Young Lawyers Assn. (trustee 1988—90), Tacoma-Pierce County Bar Assn. (pres. 1999), Fed. Bar Assn. Western Wash., Wash. State Bar Assn. (gov. 2005—), Tacoma Club, Tacoma Lawn Tennis Club. Avocations: mountain climbing, skiing, tennis, running. Office: Gordon Thomas Honeywell Malance Peterson & Daheim PO Box 1157 Tacoma WA 98401-1157 Home: 4101 N Mason Ave Tacoma WA 98407 Business E-Mail: smungia@gth-law.com.

MUNGUIA TAPIA, EMMANUEL, electrical engineer, researcher, computer scientist; b. Cd. Obregon, Sonora, Mexico, Jan. 26, 1978; s. Leonardo Munguia Xochihua and Josefina Amparo Tapia Berrelleza; m. Margarita Akiyama Gutierrez, Aug. 14, 2004. BSc, Inst. Politecnico Nac., Mex., 2000; MS, MIT, Cambridge, 2002, PhD, 2006. Rschr. Intel Rsch. Seattle, Seattle, 2004, Mitsubishi Electric Rsch. Laboratories, Cambridge, Mass., 2005, MIT, Cambridge, 2006. Dir. sensing tech. design MIT PlaceLab Living Lab., Cambridge, 2005—06; cons. in field. Recipient Presdl. award, Pres. of Mex., 2000, Best Graduating Engr. Nat. award, Nat. Assn. Schs. Engring., 2000, MIT Rsch. Assistantship award, MIT, 2002—06; fellow Telmex fellow, MIT Media Lab., 2000—06; scholar, Google, 2006. Mem.: IEEE (assoc.), Assn. for Computing Machinery (assoc.). Achievements include patents for scalable activity recognition for sensor networks; research in object-based dense sensing activity recognition. Home: 540 Memorial Dr Apt 1307 Cambridge MA 02139 Office: MIT One Cambridge Center 4F Cambridge MA 02142 Home Phone: 617-710-0300; Office Phone: 617-710-0300. Office Fax: 617-225-0027; Home Fax: 617-225-0027. Business E-Mail: emunguia@mit.edu.

MUNIR, MUHAMMAD, pain medicine physician, director; MB & Surgery, King Edwmad Med. Coll., Lahore, Pakistan, 1991—97. Diplomate Am. Bd. Anesthesiology, 2004. Fellow pain medicine Harvard Med. Sch., Brigham and Women's Hosp., Boston, 2003—04; clin. instr. Wash. U., St Louis, 2004—05; program dir. pain medicine, asst. prof. U. Cin., 2005—. Mem. exec. & edn. com. dept. anesthesiology U. Cin., 2005—06. Contbr. scientific papers. Recipient Chmns. Academic Achievement award, Dept. Anesthesiology, U. Ark. for Med. Scis., 2003; grantee Rsch. grant, Carl Koller Meml., 2002. Mem.: Am. Soc. Anesthesiology. Achievements include development of multiple new pain and anesthesia techniques. Office: Univ Cin 234 Goodman St PO Box 670764 Cincinnati OH 45267-0764

MUNISTERI, JOSEPH GEORGE, construction executive; b. Rome, Sept. 24, 1930; arrived in USA, 1934; s. Peter P. and Inez Gertrude (Ziniti) Munisteri; m. Theresa Grasso, June 7, 1952 (div. Dec. 2000); children: Joanne, Robert, Laura, Stephen, James, Richard; m. Barbra Coffman, Nov. 30, 2001. BE, Yale U., 1952. With Bechtel Corp., San Francisco, 1952-59; with The Lummus Co., NYC, London and Houston, 1959-67, gen. mgr., 1967—70; sr. v.p. sales Brown & Root, Inc., Houston, 1970—75, group v.p. power div., 1975-80, group v.p. corp. devel., 1980-81, also bd. dirs.; pres. Enserch Engrs. & Constructors, Inc., Houston, 1981-85; exec. v.p. Ford, Bacon & Davis, Inc., Dallas, 1985-87; chmn., pres., CEO Comstock Group, Inc., Danbury, Conn., 1987-88; pres. Joseph G. Munisteri Co., Houston, 1989—. Former chmn. bd. Pine-O-Pine. Former mem. Bd. dirs. Atomic Indsl. Forum; Bd. dirs. Am. Nuclear Energy Council. Mem. Atomic Indsl. Forum, Am. Inst. Chem. Engrs., Am. Nuclear Soc., Atomic Indsl. Forum, ASTM, Council Engring. Law, ASCE, Assn. Iron and Steel Engring., Assoc. Builders and Contractors (dir.), Yale Club of Houston, Yale Club of N.Y. Office: 4265 San Felipe St Ste 1100 Houston TX 77027-2998 Office Phone: 713-960-1272. Personal E-mail: jmunisteri@houston.rr.com.

MUNITZ, BARRY A., former foundation administrator; b. Bklyn., July 26, 1941; m. Anne Tomfohrde. BA, Bklyn. Coll., 1963; MA, Princeton U., 1965, PhD, 1968; cert., U. Leiden, Netherlands, 1962; doctorate (hon.), Claremont U., Calif. State Univ. Sys., Whittier Coll., U. Notre Dame. Asst. prof. lit. and drama U. Calif., Berkeley, 1966-68; staff assoc. Carnegie Commn. Higher Edn., 1968-70; acad. v.p. U. Ill. System, 1971—76; v.p., dean faculties Central Campus U. Houston, 1976-77, chancellor, 1977-82; pres., COO Federated Devel. Co., 1982-91; vice chmn. Maxxam Inc., LA, 1982-91; chancellor Calif. State U. System, Long Beach, Calif., 1991-98; prof. English lit. Calif. State U., LA, 1991—98; pres., CEO, trustee J.Paul Getty Trust, LA, 1998—2006; chmn. P-16 Edn. Council Calif. Dept. Edn., Sacramento, 2004—; trustee prof. Calif. State U., LA, 2006—. Bd. dirs. KCET-TV, SLM Holdings, KB Home; trustee Princeton U. Author: The Assessment of Institutional Leadership, also articles, monographs. Mem. art mus. vis. com. Princeton and Harvard; former chair bd. dirs. ACE; former co-chair trustees planning com. Gardner Mus.; former chair Calif. Gov. Transition Team. Recipient Disting. Alumnus award Bklyn. Coll., 1979, U. Houston Alumni Pres.'s medal, 1981; Woodrow Wilson fellow. Fellow Am. Acad. Arts and Scis.; mem. Phi Beta Kappa.

MUNIZ, FRANKIE (FRANCISCO JAMES MUNIZ IV), actor; b. Ridgewood, NJ, Dec. 5, 1985; s. Frank and Denise Muniz. Actor: (films) Lost & Found, 1999, Little Man, 1999, My Dog Skip, 2000, It Had to Be You, 2000, (voice) Dr. Dolittle 2, 2001, Big Fat Liar, 2002, Deuces Wild, 2002, Agent Cody Banks, 2003, Agent Cody Banks 2: Destination London, 2004, (voice) Racing Stripes, 2005, Stay Alive, 2006, Danny Roane: First Time Director, 2006; (TV films) To Dance with Olivia, 1997, What the Deaf Man Heard, 1997, Miracle in Lane 2, 2000; (TV series) Malcolm in the Middle, 2000— (Young Star award for Best Young Actor/Performance in a Comedy TV Series, 2000, Young Star award for Best Young Ensemble Cast - TV, 2000, Young Artist award for Best Ensemble in a Feature Film,

2001, Young Artist award for Best Performance in a TV Comedy Series - Leading Young Actor, 2002, Young Artist award for Best Ensemble in a TV Series (Comedy or Drama), 2003, Emmy nomination for Outstanding Lead Actor in a Comedy Series, 2001), (voice) The Fairly Odd Parents, 2001—03, Moville Mysteries, 2002. Office: United Talent Agy Ste 500 9560 Wilshire Blvd Beverly Hills CA 90212

MUNIZ, JORGE, composer, music educator; b. Fribourg, Switzerland, Aug. 5, 1974; s. Jose Florencio Muniz and Maria Ascension Salas; m. Jennifer Muniz, Jan. 26, 1976. MusM in Composition, Carnegie Mellon U., 2000; B in Music Composition, Royal Conservatory, Madrid, 1997; D of Musical Arts in Composition, Manhattan Sch. Music, 2004. Accompanist Conservatory of Asturias, Oviedo, Spain, 1990—95; asst. condr. Oviedo Opera Festival Chorus, Oviedo, Asturias, Spain, 1996—98; sound engr. Pitts. Digital, 1999—2000; theory faculty, coord. aural skills Manhattan Sch. Music, NYC, 2002—06; prof. music theory and composition Indiana U., South Bend, 2006—. Artistic dir., composition faculty Magistralia Summer Music Festival, Gijon, Asturias, 2005—. Composer: (opera) Germinal, (symphonic) Arche (First Grand Prize European Young Composers Competition, 1998), Piano Concerto (Second Prize Spanish Soc. of Authors Composition Competition, 1999), Areiotolmos (Joaquin Turinal Prize, 1995), In Memoriam (H.G. Archer Prize of Symphonic Composition, 2000). Named Asturian of Month, Newspaper La Nueva Espana, 2005; fellow Goodwill Amb., Rotary Internat., 2000—01, John Duffy Composers Inst., Va. Arts Festival, 2007; grantee, Atlantic Ctr. for Arts, 2003; scholar Fulbright scholar, 1998—2000. Mem.: Coll. Music Soc., Pi-Kappa-Lambda. Home: 908 Woodside St South Bend IN 46614 Office: Ernestine Raclin Sch Arts Indiana Univ 1700 Mishawaka Ave PO Box 7111 South Bend IN 46634 Business E-Mail: contact@jorgemuniz.com.

MUÑIZ, OLGA M., language educator, consultant; d. Miguel Muñiz and Inocencia González; m. Kevin E. Teegarden, Aug. 19, 1984; 1 child, Ariana R. Teegarden. MA in Spanish, Ind. U., Bloomington, 1984, MA in Italian, 1986, PhD, 1991; diploma, U. José Ortega y Gassett, Madrid, Spain, 2002, Istituto Michelangelo, Florence, Italy, 2005. Assoc. instr. Ind. U., Bloomington, 1982—91; prof. Spanish and Italian Hillsdale Coll., Mich., 1991—. Pres. GlobalReach Lang. Svcs., Hillsdale, 1995—, translator, 1995—, interpreter, 1995—. Author: La mujer en el contexto epistolar poético del Siglo de Oro Español. Scholar, Hillsdale Coll., Istituto Americano-Chicago, 1999—2006. Mem.: Am. Coun. Fgn. Lang. Tchrs. (assoc.), Am. Assn. Tchrs. Spanish and Portuguese (assoc.), Soc. Renaissance and Baroque Hispanic Poetry (assoc.). Office Phone: 617-439-1106.

MUNK, LOREN JAMES, painter, writer, critic; b. Salt Lake City, Sept. 9, 1951; s. Fredrick Harold Munk and Ida May Patrica Letz; m. Kathryn Ellen Augenblick, June 7, 1984; children: Fredrick Gilbert, Maxfield Charles. Student, Idaho State U., Pocatello, 1969—78. Art critic, art writer NYArts Mag., NYC, 1996—2001, Brooklyn Rail, NYC, 2000—. Exhibitions include Dam & Stuhltrager Gallery, Bklyn., Krief Galerie d'Art Contemporain, Paris, American Contemporary Art Gallery, Munich, Andre Zarre Gallery, NYC, Mus. Moderner Kunst, Passau, Germany, M.J. Wewerka Galerie, Berlin, Am. Contemporary Art Gallery, Munich, L'Antiquario, Sao Paulo, Brazil, Jeffrey Coploff Fine Art Ltd., NYC, Amerika-Haus, Munich, commd. mural, office Mayor of Paris. With US Army, 1972—75. Independent. Avocations: art history, bicycling. Home and Studio: 36 Tiffany Pl Brooklyn NY 11231 Home Phone: 718-858-3114; Office Phone: 718-858-3114.

MUNK, PETER, mining executive; b. Budapest, Hungary, Nov. 8, 1927; arrived in Can., 1948; s. Louis L. and Katherine (Adler) M.; m. Linda Gutterson; children: Anthony, Nina; m. Melanie Jane Bosanquet, 1973; children: Natalie, Cheyne, Marc David. BASc in Elec. Engring., U. Toronto, Ont., Can., 1953, LLD, 1995, Upsala Coll., NJ, 1991, U. Toronto, Que., Can., 1995, Bishops Coll., 1995, Concordia U., Montreal, Que., 1999. Chmn., CEO So. Pacific Hotel Corp., Sydney, Australia, 1969-81; chmn. Barrick Resources, Toronto, 1981-83, Am. Barrick Resources Corp. (now Barrick Gold Corp.), Toronto, 1983—, The Horsham Corp., Toronto, 1987-96; CEO Trizec Hahn Corp., Toronto, 1996—2000, chmn., 2001—06; chmn., pres., CEO Trizec Can. Inc., Toronto, 2002—04, chmn., CEO, 2005—06. Decorated officer Order of Can. Office: Barrick Gold Corp 161 Bay St 3700 Toronto ON Canada M5J 2S1 Business E-Mail: sfennessy@barrick.com.

MUNKVOLD, GARY P., plant pathologist, educator; BS in Forestry, U. Ill., 1986, MS in Plant Pathology, 1988; PhD in Plant Pathology, U. Calif., Davis, 1992. Grad. rsch. asst. Ill. Natural History Survey, Champaign, 1986-88; grad. rsch. asst. dept. plant pathology U. Calif., Davis, 1988-92; asst. prof., ext. plant pathologists dept. plant pathology Iowa State U., Ames, 1993-98, assoc. prof., ext. plant pathologist dept. plant pathology, 1998—. Recipient Novartis award Am. Phytopathol. Soc., 2000. Office: Iowa State U Dept Plant Pathology 317 Bessey Hall Ames IA 50010 Fax: 515-294-9420. E-mail: munkvold@iastate.edu.

MUNLEY, WILLIAM EDWARD, health services administrator; b. Scranton, Pa., Apr. 8, 1958; s. William Edward and Ann J. (McLaughlin) M.; m. Catherine Mary, Sept. 10, 1988; children: William E. III, Patrick S. BS in Gen. Sci., U. Rochester, 1981; M in Health Svcs. Adminstrn., George Washington U., 1984. cert. rehab. adminstr. Team leader-emergency Strong Meml. Hosp., Rochester, N.Y., 1979-81; adminstrv. resident Muhlenburg Med. Ctr., Bethlehem, Pa., 1983; from dir. ops. to outpatient mgr. Good Shepherd Rehab. Hosp., Allentown, Pa., 1983-86; from dir. vitality ctr. to adminstr. rehab. svcs. St. Francis Hosp., Greenville, S.C., 1988—. Home: 303 Clevington Way Simpsonville SC 29681-4641

MUNN, CECIL EDWIN, lawyer; b. Enid, Okla., Aug. 8, 1923; s. Cecil Edwin and Margaret (Kittrell) M.; m. Carolyn Taylor Culver, May 8, 1948; children: Franklin Culver, Charlotte Munn Forswall. BA, U. Okla., 1945; JD cum laude, Harvard U., 1947. Bar: Okla. 1948, Tex. 1956. Practice in, Enid, 1947-54, Ft. Worth, 1954—; partner firm Cantey & Hanger, Ft. Worth, 1960-91, of counsel, 1992—. With Champlin Petroleum Co., 1954-60, v.p., atty., 1958-60, dir., 1962-75. Fellow Am. Coll. Trial Lawyers, Am. Bar Found.; mem. ABA (chmn. natural resources law sect. 1970-71), Southwestern Legal Found. (past dir.), Tex. Bar Found., Phi Delta Theta, Phi Delta Phi. Presbyterian. Office: 2100 Burnett Plz 801 Cherry St Fort Worth TX 76102-6803 *Some things in life are better decided wrong than left undecided. It is amazing how much one can accomplish if unconcerned with who gets the credit.*

MUNN, JOHN, state agency administrator; BE, Nebr. Wesleyan U., 1970; grad., Colo. Grad. Sch. Banking, 1980. Corr. officer Nat. Bank Commerce, Lincoln, Nebr.; v.p., dir. Cattle Nat. Bank, Seward, Nebr.; sr. v.p., dir. Cornerstone Bank, N.A., York, Nebr., 1983—2001; CEO, pres., dir. First Nat. Bank & Trust, Syracuse, Nebr., 2001—05; dir. Nebr. Dept. Banking and Fin., 2005—. Bd. mem. Nebr. Ednl. Fin. Authority, Nebr. Bankers Assn., Nebr. diplomat, former chair govt. rels. com.; former instr., past pres. Schs. Banking, Inc.; founding bd. mem. Syracuse Area Econ. Devel. Corp. Office: Nebr Dept Banking & Fin PO Box 95006 Lincoln NE 68509-5006 Office Phone: 402-471-2171. Office Fax: 402-471-3062. E-mail: John.Munn@bkg.ne.gov.

MUNN, VIVIAN CAROLE, music educator, conductor; b. Bloomington, Ill., Apr. 28, 1941; d. Roger O. Johnson and Alice Marie Mehlberg; m. A. Christopher Munn, Mar. 9, 1981. Bachelor of Music Edn., Wartburg Coll., 1963; Master of Music Edn., U. Tex., El Paso, 1969; Doctor of Musical Arts, U. Okla., 1990. Dir. choirs Iowa City Schs., Burges H.S., El Paso; supr. Donne Schs., Tex.; music dir. First Luth. Ch., Edinburg, Tex., 1988—; prof. music U. Tex.-Pan Am., Edinburg, 1990—. Author: Music Reading Unlimited, 1995, 1997; editor: Songs for Sight Singing, 2002, 7 books. Recipient Outstanding Tchg. award, U. Okla., 1982, U. Tex.-Pan Am., 1999. Mem.: Phi Kappa Phi (treas.). Home: 1419 Post Oaks Rd Edinburg TX 78539 Office: Dept Music U Tex Pan Am 1201 W University Edinburg TX 78539 Office Phone: 956-381-2860. Business E-Mail: vivmunn@utpa.edu.

MUNNEKE, GARY ARTHUR, law educator, consultant; b. Cedar Rapids, Iowa, Dec. 29, 1947; s. Leslie Earl and Margaret Frances (Fortsch) M.; children: Richard Arthur, Matthew Frederick. BA in Psychology, U. Tex., 1970, JD, 1973. Bar: Tex. 1973, Pa. 1987. Asst. dean, dir. placement U. Tex., Austin, 1978-80; asst. prof., asst. dean Del. Law Sch. Widener U., Wilmington, 1980-84, assoc. prof., 1984-87; pres. Legal Info. Sys., 1987-92; prof. Sch. Law Pace U., 1988—. Contbr. articles to profl. jours. Fellow Am. Bar Found., Coll. Law Practice Mgmt.; mem. ABA (chmn. standing com. on profl. utilization and career devel. 1981-85, articles editor Legal Econs. mag. 1984-86, chmn. law practice mgmt. sect. pub. bd. 1992-95, chmn. law practice mgmt. sect. 1998-99, house dels. 2000-, bd. gov. 2006-), State Bar Tex. Office: Pace U Sch Law 78 N Broadway White Plains NY 10603-3710 Home Phone: 410-287-9084. Business E-Mail: gmunneke@law.pace.edu.

MUNOFF, GERALD J., university librarian; BA in Art and Photography, Antioch Coll., Ohio; MLS, U. Ky. Past libr. Berea Coll., Ky., U. Ky.; dir. adminstrv. svc. Ky. Dept. Libr. and Archives, dep. state libr. and dep. commr.; asst. dir. adminstrv. svc. U. Chgo. Libr., 1985—89, dept. dir., 1989—98; univ. libr. U. Calif. Irvine, 1998—. Office: U Calif Irvine 566 Main Libr PO Box 19557 Irvine CA 92623-9557 Office Phone: 949-824-5213. Office Fax: 949-824-2472. E-mail: gmunoff@uci.edu. *

MUNOZ, ANDREA LEE, human resources specialist; b. Inglewood, Calif., May 21, 1968; d. Lou and Alma Lou Munoz. BS in psychology, Lamar U., Beaumont, Tex., 1996, MS in indsl. orgnl. psychology, 2003. Store mgr. Merry-Go-Round, Beaumont, 1989—93; tech. svcs. cons. Helena Lab., Beaumont, 1993—2000; workforce devel. specialist Tex. Workforce Ctr., Port Arthur, Tex., 2000—02; spl. populations and disability coord. Lamar State Coll., Port Arthur, 2002—. Mem. bd. Workforce Devel. Ctr., Port Arthur, 2002—03; adv. bd. Lamar State Coll. Port Arthur, 2002—03. Bd. mem. S.E. Tex. Hispanic Cultural and Ednl. Ctr., Inc., 2002—, bd. dirs., 2002—04, Jefferson County Coun. on Alcohol and Drug Abuse. Grantee, Lamar U., 1987, Dr. Harry Starr Pre-Med scholarship, 1989, Maime McFadden-Ward Health Sci. scholarship, 1997. Mem.: Assn. on Higher Edn. and Disability, Disability Consortium of SE Tex., Psi Chi. Roman Catholic. Office: Lamar State Coll Port Arthur 1500 Procter St Port Arthur TX 77641 Home Phone: 409-861-2186; Office Phone: 409-984-6241.

MUÑOZ, CARLOS RAMÓN, retired bank executive; b. NYC, Dec. 8, 1935; s. Alejandro and Gladys Helena (Judah) Muñoz; m. Wilhelmina Elaine North, June 8, 1957 (div. 1993); children: Carla Christine, Kyle Alexander; m. Kassie Ohtaka, Sept. 23, 2000. BA, Columbia U., 1957, MA, 1961. Insp., ofcl. asst. Citibank N.A., NYC, 1959-64, from asst. mgr. to mgr. Dominican Republic, P.R., 1965-70, asst. v.p. NYC, 1971-72, v.p. dept. head, 1972-78; sr. v.p., regional mgr. and dir. Citicorp USA, San Francisco, 1978-81, sr. v.p. mem. credit policy com., 1982-95; exec. v.p., chief credit and risk mgmt. officer Dime Savs. Bank, NYC, 1995-2000; pres., dir. Dime Consulting Group, NYC, 1999-2000. Adv. coun. Credit Rsch. Ctr., 1994-2000. Mem. Columbia U. Senate, 2001—03; chmn. bd. dirs. Grace Ch. Cmty. Ctr., 2003—07; v.p. Episcopal Mission Soc., 1995—2000; trustee Episcopal Diocese of NY, 1994—2001, Cathedral of St. John the Divine, 1998—2004; bd. dir. Episcopal Mission Soc., NYC, 1974—2000, Inner City Scholarship Fund, 1984—95; bd. gov. Amer Contract Bridge League, 2006—, NJ/NY dist treas., 2006—. 1st lt. USAR, 1958—64. Recipient Productivity award State Senator Diane Watson, L.A., 1981, John Jay award for Disting. Profl. Achievement Columbia Coll., 2001; named Fairfield County Alumnus of Yr., 1989-90. Mem. Columbia Coll. Alumni Assn. (bd. dirs., treas. 1988-92, v.p., 1992-93, 1st v.p. 1994-96, pres. 1996-98), Columbia Club, Westchester Hills Golf Club. Republican.

MUNOZ, CELIA ALVAREZ, artist; b. El Paso, Tex., Aug. 15, 1937; d. Frank P. and Enriqueta (Limon) Alvarez; m. Andres Munoz, July 27, 1965; children: Anna Celia, Andres III. BA, U. Tex., 1964; MFA, U. North Tex., 1982. Fashion illustrator White House Dept. Store, El Paso, Tex., 1961; art instr. El Paso Pub. Schs., 1964-74, Bauder Fashion Coll., Arlington, Tex., 1984-88; lectr. U. Tex., Arlington, 1984-89. Adv. bd. Arlington Mus. Art, 1993—; design team Sky Harbor Internat. Airport, 1993, NY Percent for Art, P.S. 8, 1995—, Henry B. Gonzalez Convention Ctr. Expansion Project, 1995-98, Dallas Area Rapid Transit, 1998, Dallas Dept. Cultural Affairs Commn. Latino Cultural Ctr., 1999, Hist. Civic Ctr. River Link Project, San Antonio, 2001; lead artist Main Plz., San Antonio, 2007. Author: If Walls Could Speak, 1991, Biennial Whitney Mus. Am. Art.; one woman shows include El Paso Mus. Art, 2003; group shows include Mus. Am. History, Smithsonian Instn., 2004, Women's Mus., Dallas 2005, Sta. Mus., Houston, 2006, Mus. Contemporary Art, San Diego, 2006, Blanton Mus. Art, Austin, Tex., 2006, Art Mus. South Tex., Corpus Christi, 2007. NEA fellow, 1988, 91; recipient Outstanding Achievement in the Arts award Women's Caucus. Avocations: bicycling, walking, cinema, music, photography. Home: 5815 Arbor Valley Dr Arlington TX 76016-1522

MUNOZ, CHERYL ANN, portfolio manager; d. Roy T. and Karen Gene Willis; m. Rick Munoz, Sept. 6, 1998. MusB, Calif. State U., 1997; postgrad., Pepperdine's Graziadio Sch. Bus., 2003—06. CFA, 02; various certs. Nat. Assn. Securities Dealers. Gen. office clk. Marine & Roubidoux, Inc., Westlake Village, Calif., 1996—97, adminstrv. asst., 1998—99, portfolio adminstr., 1999—2002, portfolio mgr., strategist, 2002—05; portfolio mgr., v.p. Zephyr Investment Mgmt., Westlake Village, 2006—. Named Nat. Essay Writing Competition Winner, Big Bros./Big Sisters Orgn., 1987; Music scholar, Calif. State U. Northridge, 1991. Mem.: CFA Soc. LA, CFA Inst., Beta Gamma Sigma, Golden Key Honor Soc. Achievements include researching and creating various proprietary investment management models with the goal of reducing risk and enhancing returns. Avocations: horseback riding, skiing, clarinet, reading. Home Phone: 818-905-9883; Office Phone: 805-496-6810. Personal E-mail: chermunoz@yahoo.com.

MUÑOZ, EDUARDO RAFAEL, elementary school educator; arrived in U.S., 1961; s. Luis Alberto and Clara Luz Muñoz; m. Maria Judith Amador Muñoz, Dec. 28, 1979; children: Cristina, Rebeca. BA, U. Calif., Davis, 1974, elem. tchg. credential, secondary tchg. credential, U. Calif., Davis, 1975; MA in Edn., Santa Clara U., Calif., 1981. Elem. sch,. tchr. New Haven Unified Sch. Dist., Union City, Calif., 1975—. Sch. site coord. Decoto Elem., Union City, 1975—98, summer sch. prin., 1981, Union City, 82; PTA pres. Maloney Elem., Fremont, Calif., 1991—93. Vol. Cmty. Emergency Response Team, Fremont, Calif., 1996—. Named Outstanding Individual, Union City, 1981; recipient Gold Leaf PTA Svc. award, Fremont, 1993. Mem.: NEA, AARP, KC, Calif. Tchrs. Assn. (nominee Cesar Chavez award 2006). Democrat. Roman Catholic. Avocations: soccer, golf, baseball, hiking, audio-visual programs. Office: New Haven Unified Sch Dist 34200 Alvarado-Niles Blvd Union City CA 94587

MUÑOZ, GEORGE, investment company executive, former federal agency administrator; BBA with high honors, U. Tex., 1974; M in Pub. Policy, Harvard U., 1978, JD, 1978; LLM, DePaul U., 1984. CPA. Assoc. Gary, Thomasson, Hall & Marks, Corpus Christi, Tex., 1978-80; assoc., ptnr. Mayer, Brown & Platt, Chgo., 1980-89; mng. ptnr. GM&A Internat. Attys. & Bus. Counselors, P.C., Chgo., 1989-93; CFO, asst. sec. for mgmt. US Dept. Treasury, Washington, 1993-97; pres., CEO Overseas Pvt. Investment Corp., Washington, 1997—2001; co-founder, prin. Muñoz Group, Washington, 2001—. Mem. Coun. Fgn. Rels., 2002—. Pres. Chgo. Bd. Edn., 1984-86; trustee Chgo. Symphony Orch., Northwestern Meml. Hosp., DePaul U., Chgo. Coun. on Fgn. Rels., Ill. Internat. Port Authority, Chgo. Econ. Devel. Commn. Office: Muñoz Group 2111 Wilson Blvd Ste 850 Arlington VA 22201

MUÑOZ, HERALDO (HERALDO MUÑOZ VALENZUELA), diplomat; b. Santiago, Chile, July 22, 1948; m. Pamela Quick; 1 child. BA in Polit. sci., SUNY, Oswego; Internat. Rels. grad. with honors, Cath. U. of Chile, 1975; PhD in Internat. studies, U. of Denver, 1978; student, Harvard U.; D Honoris Causa (hon.), SUNY, 1996. Former pres. Economist Conferences, Chile, 1998—99, Latinanalyst Consultores; prof. Inst. of Internat. Studies, U. of Chile; nat. supr. People's Stores, Chile, 1973; sec. of internat. rels. Socialist Party of Chile, 1983—85; campaign chief Ricardo Lagos' senatorial race, 1989; internat. advisor of Lagos presdl. campaign and headed Internat. and Def. Commn. Chile, 1999; Chilean amb. to Brazil, 1994—98, to OAS, 1990—94; dep. fgn min. govt. of Chile, 2000—02, min. sec. gen., 2002—03; Chilean amb. and permanent rep. to UN, 2003—05. Vis. prof./lectr. several univ. and diplmatic adads. in U.S., Europe and Latin Am. Has pub. more than 20 books and dozens of essays in acad. journals. Recipient Disting. Alumnus award, Grad. Sch. of Internat. Studies, U. of Denver, 1991; fellow Resources for the Future, Ford Found., Tinker Found., Twentieth Century Fund, and MacArthur Found., PhD fellow, Brookings Inst., Washington, 1977. Achievements include founding and being dir. of fgn policy inst., Programa de Seguimiento de las Politicas Esteriores Latinoamericanas (PROSPEL), Santiago, 1983-90; co-founder of Party for Democracy. Office: Perm Mission of Chile to UN 10th Fl 305 E 47th St New York NY 10017 Business E-Mail: hmunoz@chileun.org.

MUNOZ, JOSEPH MARK, education educator, consultant; b. Zamboanga, Philippines, Apr. 19, 1966; arrived in U.S., 1999; s. Jose Edgar Cabato and Charity Judith (Schuck) Munoz; m. Melanie Salazar Bragas, Oct. 18, 1995; children: Ma.Marijka, John Paolo, Ma.Markiesha, John Marko. BS, U. Philippines, 1986; MBA, U. San Jose, Philippines, 1992, PhD in Mgmt., 1997. Retail market specialist Shell Group of Co., Manila, Philippines, 1990—92; internat. sales and mktg. dir. SGAC Retail Devel. Group, Manila, Philippines, 1992—96; country mgr. Asia Kerametal Co. Ltd., Bratislava, Slovakia, 1996—99; sr. cons. Asia Enzio Bus. Clin., Cebu, Philippines, 1997—99; acctg. dir. U.S. and Asia Ploq Rsch., NJ, 1999—2001; asst. prof. internat. bus. Millikin Univ., Decatur, Ill., 2001—; mng. dir. Munoz and Assoc. Internat., Cebu, Philippines, 2001—. Mem. of the bd. De Montaiqne Investment Banking, Sydney, 2001—, Monteland Group of Co., Cebu, Philippines, 1999—; presenter internat. bus. conferences, Hawaii, Greece, North Ireland, Malaysia, Philippines. Contbr. articles to profl. jour. Co-founder Breakfast for the World Found., Philippines, 2001. Comdr. Coast Guard, 1997—99, Philippines. Nominee Global Leader for Tomorrow, WEF; recipient Best Rsch., Enterprise Conf. Hawaii, 2003. Mem.: MBA Global Net-USA Internat. Coun. Small Bus., Internat. Exec. Svc. Corp., U.S. Assn. for Small Bus. and Entrepreurship. Roman Catholic. Achievements include research in travel executives' perceptions on the impact of globalization on contemporary business. Home: 56 Ridge Ave Decatur IL 62521 Office: Millikin Univ 1184 W Main St Decatur IL 62522 Office Phone: 217-420-6762. Business E-Mail: jmunoz@mail.millikin.edu.

MUNOZ, LAURA A., foundation administrator; d. Gilbert and Martha Munoz. BA, U. Calif., Irvine, 1996. Assoc. program dir. YMCA Orange County, Newport Beach, Calif., 1996—98, program dir., 1998—2000, sr. program dir., 2000—03, ops. dir. Tustin, 2003—06; v.p. BookEnds, West Hills, Calif., 2006—. Coach self expression and leadership Landmark Edn., LA, 2007—. Cons. Dehiwela YMCA, Dehiwela-Mount Lavinia, Sri Lanka, 2006—06. Recipient Character Counts! award, YMCA Orange County, 2000; scholar, U. Calif., 1992—93. Mem.: Assn. Fundraising Profls., Alpha Phi (scholar chair 1994—95). Avocations: travel, reading, theater.

MUNOZ, MARIO ALEJANDRO, civil engineer, retired consultant; b. Havana, Cuba, Feb. 27, 1928; arrived in US, 1961, naturalized, 1968; s. Ramón and Concepción (Bermudo) M.; m. Julia Josephine Garrofe, Jan. 17, 1970. M.Arch., U. Havana, 1954; postgrad., City Colls., Chgo., 1974, U. Wis., 1974. Owner Muñoz Bermudo-Construcciones, Havana, 1954-61; designer various cos. Chgo., 1961-65; designer Chgo. Transit Authority, Mdse. Mart, 1965-69; civil engr. Dept. Water and Sewers, City of Chgo., 1969-79; supervising engr. Dept. of Sewers, 1979-85, coordinating engr., 1985-88, asst. chief engr., 1988-93. Mem. ctrl. area subway sys. utilities com. City of Chgo., 1974-93, mem. computer graphics com., 1977-78. Mem. Am. Pub. Works Assn., Western Soc. Engrs., Chgo. Architecture Found., Theodore Thomas Soc. Chgo. Symphony, Chgo. Coun. Fgn. Rels., Soc. of the shield of Loyola, The Overture soc. of the Lyric Opera, Ground Hog Club, Execs. Club (speaker's table com.), Oak Brook Bath and Tennis Club, Barrington Polo Club. Roman Catholic.

MUNOZ, OSCAR, corporate financial executive; BS, U. So. Calif., 1982; MBA, Pepperdine U., 1986. Fin. analyst, acctg. mgr., mgr. fin. control Pepsico Inc., L.A. and Purchase, NY, 1983—86; divsn. contr., dir. fin. ops., asst. corp. contr. Coca-Cola Enterprises, L.A. and Atlanta, 1986—91, CFO, region v.p. Hollywood, Calif., 1991—96; exec. dir. Coca-Cola Co., Atlanta, 1996—97; v.p. fin., contr. USWEST Comms. Inc., Denver, 1997—99; CFO, v.p. U.S. West Retail Markets, Denver, 1999—2000; sr. v.p. fin. and adminstrn. Qwest Comms. Internat. Inc., Denver, 2000; CFO, v.p. AT&T Consumer Svcs. AT&T Corp., Basking Ridge, NJ, 2001—03; exec. v.p., CFO CSX Corp., Jacksonville, Fla., 2003—. Mem.: Fin. Execs. Inst. Office: CSX Corp 500 Water St 15th Floor Jacksonville FL 32202 *

MUÑOZ, ROMEO SOLANO, audio visual curator; b. Daraga, Philippines, July 2, 1933; s. Maximo M. and Fe (Solano) M.; m. Soledad Roselada, Jan. 2, 1964; children: Francis Vincent, Theresa Lourdes, Romualdo Romeo, Maria Cecilia, Anafe, Stephen Ignatius. BA in Psychology, Letran Coll., Manila, 1965; MS, Ea. Ill. U., 1968; MA, Gov.'s State U., 1989; EdD, No. Ill. U., 1995; postgrad., So. Ill. U. Audio visual curator Ateneo U., Quezon City, Philippines, 1962-67; audio visual dir. Olive-Harvey Coll., Chgo., 1969—. Prof. City Coll. Chgo., 1969—, prof. emeritus; cons. adminstrv. svcs., fin. City Coll. Bd. Trustees, Chgo., 1988—; v.p. Gov.'s State U., University Park, Ill. Author: Filipino Americans: From Invisibility to Empowerment, 2002. Del. AFL/CIO, Chgo., 1989, 90; deacon Archdiocese Chgo. Roman Cath. Ch., 1976—, Professed Secular Franciscan; trustee Calumet City Libr., 1993. Recipient fellowship Ea. Ill. U., Charleston, 1967-68, So. Ill. U., Carbondale, 1968-70, Gov.'s State U., Univ. Park, Ill., 1981-2000. Mem. ALA, Gov.'s State U. Alumni (bd. dirs.), Philippine Profls. Assn. (pres.), Nat. Fedn. of Filipino-Am. Orgns., Philippine Hist. Soc., Phi Delta Kappa (pres. 2000), Philippine Educators in Am. (pres.). Avocation: physical fitness. Home: 383 Hoxie Ave Calumet City IL 60409-2330 Office Phone: 708-891-3146. E-mail: rmunoz@ccc.edu, rs-munoz@yahoo.com.

MUÑOZ DONES DE CARRASCAL, ELOISA (ELOISE MUNOZ DONES), hospital administrator, pediatrician, educator; b. San Lorenzo, PR, Oct. 25, 1922; d. Pedro and Maria (Dones) Muñoz; m. José D.

Carrascal, Dec. 7, 1962; children: Lilia, Maria. BA in Edn. cum laude, BS in Chemistry cum laude, U. P.R., Rio Piedras, 1943; MD, Tulane U., 1948. Diplomate Am. Bd. Pediatrics. Intern Arecibo Charity Dist. Hosp., 1948-49; resident in pediatrics San Juan (P.R.) City Hosp., 1949-51, chief newborn svc., attending pediatrician, 1951—, dir. neonatal-perinatal medicine, 1965—, dir. fellowship tng. program, 1972—; from instr. to assoc. prof. clin. pediatrics sch. medicine U. P.R., 1951-89, prof., 1989—. Courtesy pediatrician neonatologist Tchrs. Hosp., Hato Rey, P.R., 1951-76, Ashford Presbyn. Drs. Hosp., Santurce, P.R., 1951-76, San Jorge H. H. Pavia Fernandez, Santurce, 1951-76; cons. pediatrician neonatologist Tchrs. H. Auxilio Mutuo H., Hato Rey, 1976—, Drs. H. San Jorge H. Ashford, San Juan, 1976—; mem. exec. com. San Juan City Hosp., 1976—, pres. med. faculty, 1976-77, 87-89, mem. instl. rev. bd., mem. ednl. rev. bd., mem. various coms.; lectr. in field. Contbr. articles to profl. jours. U.S. del. Care Orgn. Latin Am., 1962-63. Recipient Bronze medal Brazilian Acad. Human Scis., 1975, Hon. Cert. Internat. Yr. Women, City Mayor Lodo Carlos Romero Barceló, 1975, Hon. Cert. Disting. Svc. to Cmty., Julio Sellés Solá Elem. Sch., 1976, Pioneer Pediatrician award P.R. Pediat. Sect. Convention, 1993, Pioneer in Neonatology award P.R. Pediat. Sect. Convention, 1995, Pioneer Pediat. Critical Care award Pediat. Critical Care Assn., 1996; grantee NIH, 1962. Fellow Am. Acad. Pediatrics (neonatal perinatal sect., mem. com. fetus and newborn P.R. chpt. 1956—, sec.-treas. 1962-64, mem. com. history perinatal sect. 1992—, Plaque in Recognition Disting. Pediatrician and Tchr. 1985), Pan Am. Pediatrics; mem. Am. Med. Women Assn., P.R. Med. Assn. (pediat. sect., mem. chamber of dels. 1962-63, Bronze plaque 1967, 91, Gold Pin 1980), P.R. Med. Women Assn. (sec.-treas. 1957-60, pres. 1960-64), Pan Am. Med. Women Assn. (pres. P.R. chpt. 1960-64, P.R. del. VIII Congress Manizales Colombia 1962), Pan Am. Med. Women Alliance (vis. lectr. 1962), Tulane Med. Alumni, London Royal Soc. Health, Colegio de Químicos, Soc. Dominicana de Pediatría (hon., vis. lectr. 1971), Dominican Rep. Soc. (hon.). Avocation: poetry.

MUÑOZ FERNÁNDEZ, MICHELA, electrical engineer, researcher; arrived in US, 2000, permanent resident, 2006; d. Juan and Alicia. Diploma summa cum laude in Elec. Engring., Escuela Politécnica, U.A.H., Madrid, Spain, 1998; MS in Space Studies, Internat. Space U., Strasbourg, France, 2000; MSEE, Calif. Inst. Tech., 2001, PhD in Elec. Engring., 2005; MSEE, U. Complutense, Madrid, 2004. Registered profl. engr., Spain, 1998. Database mgmt. engr. SEMA Group Alcatel Formacion y Consultoria, Madrid, 1996; elec. engr. European Space Agy. ROSETTA mission Nat. Aerospace Inst. of Spain, Madrid, 1997—99; telecom. engr. Jet Propulsion Lab. NASA, Pasadena, Calif., 1999, rschr. Jet Propulsion Lab., 2000—06, project sys. engr. Jet Propulsion Lab., 2006—. Organizer politechnical congress Escuela Politécnica, U.A.H., Madrid, 1994—95. Contbr. articles to profl. jours. (Best paper Advanced Systems for Satellite Comm. Category award). Recipient award, Caltech/JPL, 2004; fellow, U. Politécnica, 1999, Divsn. Sci. and Engring., Calif. Inst. of Tech., 2000—01; grantee, NASA, 2002—05; scholar, European Space Agy., 1999—2000; Calvo Rodés fellowship, Nat. Aerospace Inst., 1997, Amelia Earhart fellowship, Zonta Internat. Found., 2002, 2004. Mem.: IEEE, AIAA, The Internat. Soc. Optical Engring., Athenaeum-Caltech Club. Achievements include first to new technology for high-rate coherent optical communications for deep space. Home: 158 S Madison Ave No 209 Pasadena CA 91101 Home Phone: 626-796-9731. Personal E-mail: michelamz@gmail.com. Business E-Mail: michela.munoz.fernandez@jpl.nasa.gov.

MUÑOZ-SOLÁ, HAYDEÉ SOCORRO, library administrator; b. Caguas, PR, Dec. 27, 1943; d. Gilberto Muñoz and Carmen Haydeé (Solá) de Muñoz; m. Juan M. Masini-Soler, Jan. 8, 1966 (div. 1979); children: Juan Martín Masini-Muñoz, Haydeé Milagros Masini-Muñoz. BA in Psychology, U. P.R., Río Piedras, 1965, MLS, 1970; D in Libr. Sci., Columbia U., 1985. Asst. libr. U. P.R., Río Piedras, 1964-67; dir. libr. Interam. U., Aguadilla, PR, 1974-75; head svcs. to pub. U. P.R., Aguadilla, 1975-76; cataloguer Cath. U., Ponce, PR, 1976-79, U. P.R., Río Piedras, 1982-84, head libr. and info. sci. libr., 1984-85, prof. grad. libr. sch., 1986, 99, dir. libr. sys., 1986-93, coord. external resources libr. sys., 1994-97, dir. of libr. Ponce, PR, 1997, collection devel. officer Rio Piedras, 1998, sabbatical leave, 2000-01; compiler, editor Puerto Rican Bibliography, 2001—. Dir. P.R. Newspaper Project, Río Piedras, 1986-90; mem. Adv. Com. on Pub. Librs., San Juan, 1987-93; proposal reviewer NEH, 1990—; chmn. Puerto Rican Del. to Nat. White House Conf. on Libr. and Info. Svcs., 1991. Author: La Información y la Documentación Educativa/Informe Sobre la Situación Actual en Puerto Rico, 1991, Memorias: Sequnda Pre-Conferencia de Casa Blanca Sobre Bibliotecas y Servicios de Información en Puerto Rico, 1991, Lineamientos para Colecciones Bibliograficas Nacionales, 1997, Premio por Excelencia en Investigación Aplicada y Publicación, 1997; contbr. articles to profl. jours. Mem. Ponce Sport Club, 1976—83, ARC, Ponce, 1978. Recipient plaque White House Pre-Conf. on Libr. and Info. Sci., 1990, others, Leccion Magistral Josefina del Toro Fulladosa, 2002; French Alps Study Tour scholar Assn. Caribbean Univ. Rsch. and Instl. Libr., 1989, Germany Study Tour scholar Fgn. Rels. Office, Germany, 1991, coord. So. area 1974, Lauro award 1989, Leccion Magistral Josefina del Toro Fulladosa award, 2002. Mem. ALA, Am. Mgmt. Assn., Grad. Sch. Libr. and Info. Sci. Alumni Assn. (pres. 1988-90), Seminar for Acquisitions L.Am. Libr. Materials, Iberoamerican Nat. Libr. Assn. (pres. 1992-93), Puerto Rican Libr. Soc., Assn. Caribbean U. Rsch. and Instnl. Libr. (Parchment award 1988), Asoc. para las Comunicaciones y Tecnología Educativa, Mid. States Assn. Coll. and Sch. (collaborator), Am. Women Assn., Nat. Commn. P.R. Women, Phi Delta Kappa (chair P.R. com. 1988-90, Kappan of Yr. 1990), Eta Gamma Delta. Roman Catholic. Avocations: reading, crewel work, embroidery, knitting, movies. Office: PO Box 23302 San Juan PR 00931-2302 Office Phone: 787-764-0000 2707. Business E-Mail: hmunoz@uprrp.edu.

MUNRO, BARBARA HAZARD, nursing educator, dean, researcher; b. Wakefield, RI, Nov. 28, 1938; d. Robert J. and Honore (Egan) Hazard; children: Karen Aimee, Craig Michael, Stephanie Anne. BS, MS, U. RI, Kingston; PhD, U. Conn. RN, Conn. Asst. prof. U. RI Coll. Nursing, Kingston; assoc. prof., chmn. program in nursing rsch. Yale U., New Haven; assoc. prof., asst. dir. Ctr. for Nursing Rsch. U. Pa., Phila.; dean, prof. Boston Coll. Sch. Nursing, 1991—. Presenter and workshop leader various nursing confs. and seminars in U.S. Contbr. articles and rsch. to profl. pubs. Trustee St. Elizabeth's Med. Ctr. Boston, 1994—. Recipient Nat. Rsch. Svc. award. Fellow Am. Acad. Nursing; mem. ANA, Golden Key, Sigma Theta Tau, Pi Lambda Theta, Phi Kappa Phi. Office: Boston Coll Sch Nursing Cushing Hall Chestnut Hill MA 02467-3812 Office Phone: 617-552-1710. Business E-Mail: barbara.hazard.1@bc.edu.

MUNRO, DONALD JACQUES, philosopher, educator; b. New Brunswick, NJ, Mar. 5, 1931; s. Thomas B. and Lucile (Nadler) M.; m. Ann Maples Patterson, Mar. 3, 1956; 1 child, Sarah de la Roche. AB, Harvard U., 1953; PhD (Ford Found. fellow), Columbia U., 1964. Asst. prof. philosophy U. Mich., 1964-68, assoc. prof., 1968-73, prof. philosophy, 1973—90, prof. philosophy and Asian langs., 1990-96; prof. emeritus philosophy and Chinese, 1996—; chmn. dept. Asian langs. and cultures U. Mich., 1993-95, with Ctr. Chinese Studies, 1964—; vis. rsch. philosopher Ctr. Chinese Studies U. Calif., Berkeley, 1969-70; mem. Assn. for Asian studies China and Inner Asia Coun., 1970—72; chmn. com. on studies of Chinese civilization Am. Council Learned Socs., 1979-81. Mem. Com. on Scholarly Comm. with People's Republic China, NAS, 1978-82, China Coun. of Asia Soc., 1977-80, Com. on Advanced Study in China, 1978-82; Evans-Wentz lectr. Stanford U., 1970; Fritz lectr. U. Wash., 1980; Gilbert Ryle lectr. Trent U., Ont., 1983; John Dewey lectr. U. Vt., 1989; Ch'ien Mu lectr. Chinese U. Hong Kong, 2002-03; Tang Chun I vis. prof. Chinese U. Hong Kong, 2006. Author: The Concept of Man in Early China, 1969, the Concept of Man in Contemporary China, 1977; editor: Individualism and Holism, 1985, Images of Human Nature: A Sung Portrait, 1988, The Imperial Style of Inquiry in Twentieth Century China, 1996, A Chinese Ethics for the New Century, 2005. Exec. com. Coll. Literature, Sci. and The Arts U. Mich., 1986-89. Lt. (j.g.) USNR, 1953-57. Recipient letter of commendation Chief Naval Ops.; Disting. Svc. award U. Mich., 1968, Excellence in Edn. award, 1992; Rice Humanities award, 1993-94; Nat. Humanities faculty fellow, 1971-72; John Simon Guggenheim Found. fellow, 1978-79; grantee Social Sci. Rsch. Coun., 1965-66, Am. Coun. Learned Socs., 1982-83, China com. grantee NAS, 1990; vis. rsch. scholar Chinese Acad. Social Scis. Inst. Philosophy, Beijing, 1983, dept. philosophy Beijing U., 1990. Home: 14 Ridgeway St Ann Arbor MI 48104-1739 Office: Dept Philosophy U Mich Ann Arbor MI 48104 *I believe that much knowledge is interrelated and that academic disciplinary boundaries are transitory conveniences. The human significance of any research task I undertake should be obvious to those inside and outside my professional group (a goal I seek but do not always achieve).*

MUNRO, DONALD WILLIAM, JR., non-profit organization executive; b. Phila., Dec. 27, 1937; s. Donald William and Emily McCoy (Graham) M.; m. Joyce Eleanor Thomas, Sept. 9, 1961; children: Deborah Joy, Mark William. BS, Wheaton Coll., 1959; MS, Pa. State U., 1963, PhD, 1966. Prof. biology Houghton (N.Y.) Coll., 1966-94; exec. dir. Am. Sci. Affiliation, Ipswich, Mass., 1994—2005. Adj. prof. biology Gordon Coll., Wenham, Mass., 1995-2004; chmn. biology dept. Houghton Coll., 1972-94. Capt. U.S. Army, 1960-69. Predoctoral fellow NIH, 1964-66. Mem. Am. Philatelic Soc., Houghton Stamp Club (pres. 1988-90), Elizabeth City Rotary Club. Republican. Baptist. Avocations: stamps, piano, hiking, bioethics. Personal E-mail: dandjmunro@earthlink.net.

MUNRO, JOHN HENRY ALEXANDER, economics professor, writer; b. Vancouver, BC, Can., Mar. 14, 1938; s. Hector Gordon and Blanche (Almond) M.; m. Jeanette Roberta James, May 25, 1968; children: Robert Ryder, Valerie Marlene. BA with honors, U. B.C., Vancouver, 1960; MA in History, Yale U., 1961, PhD in History, 1965. Instr. in history U. B.C., 1964-65, asst. prof. history and econs., 1965-68; assoc. prof. econs. U. Toronto, 1968-73, prof., 1973—2003, prof. emeritus, 2003—; assoc. dir. Centre for Medieval Studies, U. Toronto, 1975-78. Cons. on coinage to pub. U. Toronto Press, 1973— Author: Wool, Cloth, and Gold, 1973, Bullion Flows and Monetary Policies in England and the Low Countries, 1350-1500, 1992, Textiles, Towns and Trade: Essays in the Economic History of Late-Medieval England and the Low Countries, 1994; contbr. articles to profl. jours., essays to books; mem. editl. bd. Textile History, 1980-97, Explorations in Economic History, 1998—, Medieval Clothing and Textiles, 2005; Medieval area editor Oxford Ency. of Econ. History, 1996—2003. Can. Coun. leave fellow, Belgium, 1970-71, Social Scis. and Humanities Rsch. Coun. Can. fellow, Engl. and Holland, 1979-80, Belgium, 1986-87, Eng. and Belgium, 1992-96, 96-99, 99—, Connaught Rsch. fellow, 1993-94, 2000—01. Mem. Can. Econ. Assn., Econ. History Assn. (U.S.), Econ. History Soc. (U.K.), Medieval Acad. Am. (councillor 1990-93), Instituto Internazionale di Storia Economica (sci. com. 1999—, exec. bd. 2003—), Royal Flemish Acad. Belgium for Sci. and Arts (fgn.). Presbyterian. Home: 9 Woodmere Ct Toronto ON Canada M9A 3J1 Office: Dept Econs U Toronto 150 St George St Toronto ON Canada M5S 3G7 Office Phone: 416-978-4552. E-mail: munro5@chass.utoronto.ca, john.munro@utoronto.ca.

MUNROE, GEORGE BARBER, retired mining and manufacturing company executive; b. Joliet, Ill., Jan. 5, 1922; s. George Mueller and Ruth (Barber) Munroe; m. Elinor Bunin, May 30, 1968; children from previous marriage: George Taylor, Ralph W. Taylor. AB, Dartmouth Coll., 1943; LLB, Harvard U., 1949; BA (Rhodes scholar), Christ Church, Oxford U., Eng., 1951, MA, 1956; DHL (hon.), No. Ariz. U., 1981; LLD (hon.), Dartmouth Coll., 1993. Bar: N.Y. 1949. Assoc. Cravath, Swaine & Moore, NYC, 1949; atty. Office Gen. Counsel U.S. High Commn. Germany, Frankfurt and Bonn, 1951-53; justice U.S. Ct. Restitution Appeals Allied High Commn. Germany, Nuremberg, 1953-54; assoc. Debevoise, Plimpton & McLean, NYC, 1954-58; with Phelps Dodge Corp., 1958-87, v.p., 1962-66, pres., 1966-75, 80-82, chief exec. officer, 1969-87, chmn. bd., 1975-87, dir., 1966-94. Trustee emeritus Met. Mus. Art; chmn. emeritus bd. dirs. Acad. Polit. Sci. Served to lt. (j.g.) USNR, 1943—46. Mem. Mining and Metall. Soc. Am., Coun. Fgn. Rels., Century Assn., River Club, Univ. Club (N.Y.C.), Bridgehampton Club. Office: 444 Madison Ave Fl 19 New York NY 10022-6903 Office Phone: 212-750-4569.

MUNS, RALEIGH CLAYTON, school librarian; m. Anne Lynn Wagner, Aug. 9, 1985; 1 child, Isaac Michael Wagner-Muns; 1 child, Rachel Oriana Wagenr Muns. BA in Psychology cum laude, UCLA, 1982, MLS, 1991. Assoc. APL applications/sys. analyst Sys. Time Sharing, Inc., Woodland Hill, Calif., 1982—83; temp. assignments Digital Electronic Corp., R&B Enterprises, Bel-Air/Topa Saving and Loan, 1989; intern, Grad. Sch. Mgmt. UCLA, 1990—91, rsch. libr. desk asst., 1989—91; sole proprietor World Wide Web consulting concern, Fugax, 1995—97; reference libr., reference leadership team mem. U. Mo., St. Louis, 1991—. Spkr. in field. Contbr. articles to profl. jours. Active duty USN, 1983—87. Decorated Command Sailor of Quarter USS Rentz (FFG-46), Good Conduct medal US Navy, Sea Svc. Deployment ribbon; named an Outstanding Reference Libr., Online Computer Libr. Ctr. Inc., 1994; recipient Meritorious Svc. award, Students with disAbilities Assn., U. Mo., St. Louis, 1998, award, Nat. LATIMES.com Sportsmanship Essay Contest, 2001, URL Makers Integration award, Ovid, 2001; scholar, U. Calif. Regents, 1976—82. Office: Thomas Jefferson Libr U Mo-St Louis Saint Louis MO 63121 Office Phone: 314-516-5059. Business E-Mail: muns@umsl.edu. *

MUNSELL, DEBRA S., physician assistant, educator; b. Pt. Arthur, Tex., June 13, 1957; d. Rosemond B. and Bettie Lawrence Schoenberg; m. Lloyd Allen Foreman III, Feb. 16, 1985 (dec. Mar. 1991); m. William Peter Munsell, July 18, 1998. BS in Biology, Stephen F. Austin State U., 1979; BS in Health, U. Tex., Galveston, 1981; MPhysician Asst. Studies in Otolaryng., U. Nebr., 2000. Cert. phys. asst. Physician asst. Angleton (Tex.) Clinic, 1981-83, Tex. Dept. Corrections, Huntsville, 1983-84; physician asst. med. br. Galveston U. Tex., 1985-90, clin. instr. med. br. Galveston, 1985—2004, physician asst. M.D. Anderson Cancer Ctr. Houston, 1990—2005, dir. physician asst. student edn. program M.D. Anderson Cancer Ctr., 1996—2005; clin. assoc. prof. physician asst. edn. We. U. Health Sci., Pomona, Calif., 1999—2004; asst. prof. U. Tex. Med. Br., Sch. Allied Health Sci., Galveston, 2005—. Clin. instr. Baylor Coll. Medicine, Houston, 1999-2004. Author: (with others) Primary Care Oncology, 1999, Primary Care: A Collaborative Approach, 1999, Primary Care, A Collaborative Practice, 2d edit., 2003, The Physician Assistant Medical Handbook, 2d edit., 2004. Life mem. Brazoria County Fair Assn., Angleton, Tex., 1992—. Glaxo/Wellcome Leadership fellow Am. Acad. Physician Assts./Physician Asst. Found., 1997-98. Fellow: Assn. Physician Assts. in Oncology, Soc. Physician Assts. in Otolaryngology, Head and Neck Surgery (charter mem. 1991, bd. dirs. 1992—94, chair continuing med. edn 1994—96, pres. 1996—2000), Am. Acad. Otolaryngology, Head and Neck Surgery, Am. Acad. Physician Assts. (chair nominating com. 1998—2002, external liaison 2001—); mem.: Tex. Acad. Physician Assts., Nat. Patient Advocate Found., Houston Yacht Club. Avocations: sailing, gardening. Home: 9807 Williams Bend Ct Missouri City TX 77459-6279 Office: U Tex Med Br-Galveston SAHS 301 University Blvd Galveston TX 77553-1028 Home Phone: 281-778-7494; Office Phone: 409-772-9559. Business E-Mail: dsmunsel@utmb.edu.

MUNSELL, ELSIE LOUISE, retired lawyer; b. NYC, Feb. 15, 1939; d. Elmer Stanley and Eleanor Harriet (Dickinson) M.; m. George P. Williams, July 14, 1979. AB, Marietta Coll., 1960; JD, Marshall-Wythe Coll. William and Mary, 1972. Bar: Va. 1972, U.S. Dist. Ct. (ea. dist.) Va. 1974, U.S. Ct. Appeals (4th cir.) 1976, U.S. Supreme Ct. 1980. Tchr. Norview High Sch., Norfolk, Va., 1964-69; asst. Commonwealth atty. Commonwealth Atty.'s Office, Alexandria, Va., 1972-73; asst. U.S. atty. Alexandria, 1974-79; U.S. magistrate U.S. Dist. Ct. (ea. dist.) Va., Alexandria, 1979-81; U.S. atty. Dept. Justice, Alexandria, 1981-86; sr. trial atty. Office of Gen. Counsel, Dept. Navy, Washington, 1986-89, asst. gen. counsel installations and environ. law, 1989-91; dep. asst. environ. and safety Sec. Navy, 1991-2001, ret., 2001. Mem. USEPA Clean Air Act Adv. Com., 1997—; bd. dirs. BMT Designers & Planners. Active Va. Commn. on Status of Women, 1966-74; bd. vistors Coll. William and Mary, 1972-76; active Atty. Gen.'s Adv. Com. U.S. Attys., 1981-83; bd. dirs. Carpenter's Shelter, Inc., 1990-93; vestry St. Alban's Ch., Annandale, Va., 1996-99, 2003; fed. preservation officer Dept. Navy, 1999. Presdl. Meritorious Exec., 1999; recipient Spl. Achievement award Nat. Mil. Fish and Wildlife Assn., 2001, Disting. Civilian Svc. award, 2001. Mem. Sr. Execs. Assn., Chi Omega. Lutheran.

MUNSELL, WILLIAM A., healthcare insurance company executive; With UnitedHealth Group, Mpls., 1997—, CFO, 1997—2000, COO, 2000—03, chief adminstrv. officer, 2003—04, CEO specialized care svc., 2004—, exec. v.p., 2006—. Office: UnitedHealth Grp PO Box 1459 Minneapolis MN 55440-1459 *

MUNSEY, VIRDELL EVERARD, JR., retired utilities executive; b. Washington, Sept. 25, 1933; s. Virdell Everard and Mildred Lovenia (Wood) M.; m. Bernice Ann Wilson, Sept. 20, 1956; children: Wanda Louise, Allan Coll, Andrew Everard, Carolyn Jane. BA magna cum laude, Yale U., 1955; M.P.A., Harvard U., 1967. Reporter Washington Post, 1957-63; legis. asst. Rep. Henry S. Reuss, Washington, 1963-68; info. dir. United Democrats for Humphrey, Washington, 1968; asst. dir. public affairs Dem. Nat. Com., 1968; with Nat. Planning Assn., Washington, 1969-77, exec. v.p., 1974-76; dep. asst. sec. for public affairs Dept. Treasury, Washington, 1977-81; cons. World Bank, 1981; with Va. Electric and Power Co., 1981-86, mgr. corp. communications, 1982-83, exec. dir. pub. policy, 1983-86, v.p. pub. policy, 1986, Dominion Resources Inc., 1986-96; cons., 1996—2002. Mem. Va. Coal and Energy Commn., 1983-95. Chmn. Arlington County Dem. Party, 1967-69; mem. Arlington County Bd., 1972-75, chmn., 1973; vice chmn. No. Va. Transp. Commn., 1973, chmn., 1974; bd. dirs. Washington Met. Area Transit Authority, 1975; mem. transp. planning bd. Met. Washington Coun. Govts., 1973-75; treas. Competitive Power Policy Forum, 1990-96. Served with U.S. Army, 1955-57. Recipient Am. Political Sci. Assn. award Disting. Reporting of Public Affairs, 1962; Am. Polit. Sci Assn. Fellow, 1966—67. Mem. United Ch. Christ. Personal E-mail: everard1933@yahoo.com.

MUNSON, ALEX ROBERT, judge; b. LA, Sept. 25, 1941; s. Robert Alexander and Lillian Agnus (Hamel) M.; m. Kathleen Rae Abernathey, June 29, 1968. BA, Long Beach Coll., Calif., 1964, MA, 1965; EdD, U. So. Calif., LA, 1970; JD, Loyola U., LA, 1975. Atty. Kirtland and Packard, LA, 1978-82; chief justice High Ct. of The Trust Terr. of The Pacific Islands, Saipan, Commonwealth of the No. Mariana Islands, 1982-88; chief judge U.S. Dist. Ct. of No. Mariana Islands, Saipan, Commonwealth of the No. Mariana Islands, 1988—. Mem. ABA, Calif. Bar Assn. Republican. Home: PO Box 5356 Saipan MP 96950-5356 Office: US Dist Ct NMI PO Box 500687 Saipan MP 96950-0687

MUNSON, EDWARD HARRY, JR., medical investigator; b. Birmingham, Ala., Apr. 3, 1948; s. Edward H. Sr. and Elizabeth (W.) M.; married, Dec. 6, 1968 (div. Dec. 1985); children: Laura Davis, Kathleen DeLacy Munson, Matthew Edward; m. Patricia Beth Wool, July 29, 1989. BA in Biology, Huntingdon Coll., 1971; student, U. Mo. Law Enforcemnt Tng. Nat. cert. investigator. Investigator Montgomery (Ala.) Police Dept., 1970-81; instr. Ala. Advanced Criminal Justice Acad., 1974-80; med. investigator Ala. Bd. Med. Examiners, Montgomery, 1981—. Cons. State Bd. of Health-Controlled Substance Adv. Panel, Montgomery, 1989—, Stae Methadone Authority, Fedn. of State Med. Bds., Ft. Worth, 1990—; mem. Med. Investigator Tng. Com., chair, 1994, 97; mem. work com. prescription monitoring programs Nat. Alliance for Model State Drug Laws. Recipient Silver Star, Am. Fedn. Police, Miami, Fla., 1975, Ronald K. Williamson Meml. award Nat. Adminstrs. in Medicine, 2004; named Firearms Expert, NRA, 1978. Mem. Internat. Narcotic Officers Assn., Nat. Assn. Drug Diversion Investigators, Nat. Criminal Justice Assn., Nat. Assn. State Controlled Substance Authorities. Jewish. Avocations: travel, cooking, shooting. Office: Ala Bd Med Examiners PO Box 946 Montgomery AL 36101-0946

MUNSON, HAROLD LEWIS, education educator; b. Windham, NY, Aug. 2, 1923; s. Esmond Lewis and Gladys (Disbrow) M.; m. Evelyn Claire Moore, Sept. 8, 1946; children: Michael Lewis, Jeffrey Charles. AB, Hobart Coll., 1947; MA, SUNY, Albany, 1948; Ed.D., NYU, 1961. Tchr. social studies, counselor Cairo Ctrl. Sch., NY, 1948-50; dir. guidance Williamson Central Sch., NY, 1950-54; supr. guidance NY State Edn. Dept., Albany, 1954-59; prof. edn., chmn. Ctr. for Counseling, Family and Worklife Studies, U. Rochester, NY, 1959-85, prof. emeritus, 1985—; prof. edn. Overseas Program, Boston U., 1985-87; pres. Munson Assocs., 1988—. Vocat. cons. Social Security Adminstrn., HEW, 1962-79 Author: (with H.W. Houghton) Organizing Orientation Activities, 1956, My Educational Plans, 1959, 70, Guidance Activities for Teachers of English, Social Studies, Science, Mathematics and Foreign Languages, 1965, (with Gilbert Gockley) Career Insights and Self Awareness Games, 1973; contbg. author: Ency. of Careers, 1967, Elementary School Guidance: Concepts, Dimensions and Practice, 1970, The Foundations of Developmental Guidance, 1971, Career Education for Deaf Students: An Inservice Leader's Guide, 1975, The Land In The Sky, 2004. Served with USNR, 1944-46. Mem. Am. Counseling Assn., Nat. Career Devel. Assn., Am. Sch. Counselor Assn., Phi Delta Kappa. Home: 9 Charleston Dr Mendon NY 14506 Office Phone: 585-582-3275. *Success is whatever you want it to be. By defining it in such personal terms, everyone should be able to experience some degree of personal fulfillment through my accomplishments in helping others to define and examine their own existence.*

MUNSON, HOWARD G., federal judge; b. Claremont, NH, July 26, 1924; s. Walter N. and Helena (O'Halloran) M.; m. Ruth Jaynes, Sept. 17, 1949; children: Walter N., Richard J., Pamela A. BS in Economics, U. Pa., 1948; LL.B., Syracuse U., 1952. Bar: N.Y. With Employers' Assurance Corp., Ltd., White Plains, NY, 1949-50; mem. firm Hiscock, Lee, Rogers, Henley & Barclay, Syracuse, NY, 1952-76; judge U.S. Dist. Ct. No. Dist. N.Y., Syracuse, 1976—. Mem., pres. Syracuse Bd. Edn.; bd. dirs. Sta. WCNY-TV; chmn. ethics com. Onondaga County Legislature. Served with U.S. Army, 1943-45, ETO. Decorated Bronze Star, Purple Heart. Mem. Am. Coll. Trial Lawyers, Nat. Assn. R.R. Trial Counsel, Am. Arbitration Assn., Justinian Soc., Alpha Tau Omega, Phi Delta Phi. Office: US Dist Ct US Courthouse P O Box 7376 Syracuse NY 13261-7376 Office Phone: 315-234-8580.

MUNSON, JOHN BACKUS, computer scientist, retired data processing executive; b. Chgo., May 1, 1933; s. Mark Frame and Catherine Louise (Cherry) M.; m. Anne Lorraine Cooper, July 6, 1957; children: David B., Sharon A. BA, Knox Coll., Galesburg, Ill., 1955. With Unisys Corp., McLean, Va., 1957-93, v.p. corp. software engring., 1977-81, v.p. tech. ops., 1981-84, v.p. gen. mgr. space transp. systems, 1984-89, 89-93, v.p., gen. mgr. Space Systems divsn., 1989-94, ret., 1994. Mem. sci. adv. bd.

USAF, 1981-86, mem. USN panel on F14D issues, 1987-88. Mem. bd. advisors U. Houston, Clear Lake, 1988-93, chmn. 1990-92; bd. dirs. Bay Area YMCA, 1988-93, chmn. 1992, Clear Lake Am. Heart Assn., 1989-93; co-chmn. Bay Area United Way, 1988—, chmn., 1992; Disting. visitor IEEE Computing Soc., 1981-94. Capt. US Army, 1955-57. Recipient Exceptional Civilian Svc. award USAF, 1986, Superior Pub. Svc. award USN, 1988, cert. of appreciation NATO, 1984; named to Mgmt. Assn. Hall of Fame, 1994. Fellow IEEE (editor Trans. of Software Engring. 1982-84, bd. dirs. tech. com. software engring. 1982—); mem. AIA, Am. Astronautical Soc. (bd. dirs. S.W. sect. 1989-94), Aerospace Industries Assn. (space com. 1989-94), US Army Assn., Nat. Security Indsl. Assn., Armed Forces Comm. Electronics Assn. (pres. Houston chpt. 1987-90), S.W. Regional Coun. Corp. CEOs. Home and Office: 1018 Westcreek Ln Westlake Village CA 91362-5462 Personal E-mail: JaxG3@aol.com.

MUNSON, JOHN CHRISTIAN, acoustician; b. Clinton, Iowa, Oct. 9, 1926; s. Arthur J. and Frances (Christian) M.; m. Elaine Hendershot, Sept. 2, 1950; children: John Christian, Holly Elizabeth. BS, Iowa State Coll., 1949; MS, U. Md., 1952, PhD, 1962; Navy Dept. scholar, MIT, 1956. Electronic scientist Naval Ordnance Lab., Washington, 1949-66; tech. dir. navy portion Practice Nine, Naval Air Systems Command, 1967; supt. acoustics divsn. Naval Rsch. Lab., 1968-85; v.p. Engring. & Sci. Assocs., 1983-94; chmn. bd. dirs., 1994; ret. Asst. extension prof. elec. engring. U. Md., 1964-66; mem. Underwater Sound Adv. Group, 1969-75, U.S. Sonar Team, 1971-85, Mobile Sonar Tech. Com., 1972-85; cons., 1985-. Editor U.S. Navy Jour. Underwater Acoustics, 1983-91; patentee in field. Mem. exec. bd. DC Bapt. Conv., 1973—, chmn. fin. com., 1973, v.p., 1996-97, pres., 1997-98; trustee Midwestern Bapt. Theol. Sem., 1970-80; trustee Bapt. Sr. Adult Ministries Washington Met. Area, 1976-91, 92-04, pres., 1981-88, CEO, 1991-92; mem. Gen. Bd. Am. Bapt. Chs. USA, 1994-99; pres. Allied Silver Spring Interfaith Svcs. to Srs. Today, 1994-00, bd. dirs. 1994-03; bd. mgrs. Am. Bapt. Hist. Soc., 1996-03, sec., 1997-03; corp. mem. Am. Bapt. Homes of the West, 1999, dir., 2000-04. Fellow IEEE, Signal Processing Soc. (mem. adminstrv. com. 1974-76, chmn. underwater acoustics com. 1973-76), Acoustical Soc. Am.; mem. Sigma Xi. Home: 3118 Chartwell Crescent Ln Adamstown MD 21710-9643 E-mail: johncmunsonsr@edurostream.com. *I have a positive joy for life, and I am an incurable optimist: my basic attitude is that things will work out for the best— but only if we do our very best. Each of us has a responsibility to grow to our maximum capacity and to be of reasonable service to mankind. The proper balance among family, job, service to God, service to others, and attention to yourself is essential. Whatever you are doing, do it from the right motivation and with enthusiasm.*

MUNSON, NANCY K., lawyer; b. Huntington, NY, June 22, 1936; d. Howard H. and Edna M. (Keenan) Munson. Student, Hofstra U., 1959—62; JD, Bklyn. Law Sch., 1965. Bar: NY 1966, U.S. Dist. Ct. (ea. and so. dists.) NY 1968, U.S. Supreme Ct. 1970, U.S. Ct. Appeals (2d cir.) 1971. Law clk. to Hon. E. Merritt Weidner, Huntington, NY, 1959—66; pvt. practice, 1966. Legal adv. bd. Chgo. Title Ins. Co., Riverhead, NY, 1981—; bd. dirs., legal officer Thomas Munson Found. Trustee Huntington Fire Dept. Death Benefit Fund; pres., trustee, chmn. bd. dirs. Bklyn. Home Aged Men Found.; bd. dirs. Huntington Rural Cemetery Assn., Inc.; trustee Noyac Harbor Property Owners Assn. Mem.: DAR (trustee, treas. Ketewamoke chpt.), NRA, ABA, Federalist Soc. for Law and Pub. Policy Studies, Bklyn. Bar Assn., Suffolk County Bar Assn., N.Y. State Bar Assn., Soroptimists (past pres.). Republican. Christian Scientist. Office: 197 New York Ave Huntington NY 11743-2711 Office Phone: 631-271-8161.

MUNSON, RICHARD HOWARD, horticulturist; b. Toledo, Dec. 20, 1948; s. Stanley Warren and Margaret Rose (Winter) M. BS, Ohio State U., 1971; MS, Cornell U., 1973, PhD, 1981. Plant propagator The Holden Arboretum, Kirtland, Ohio, 1973-76; asst. prof. Agrl. Tech. Inst., Wooster, Ohio, 1976-78, Tex. Tech U., Lubbock, 1981-84; dir. botanic garden Smith Coll., Northampton, Mass., 1984-95; exec. dir. The Holden Arboretum, Kirtland, Ohio, 1995-2000; dir. botanic garden U. Mo., Columbia, Mo., 2001—04; mgr. The Conservatory, Miami U., Hamilton, Ohio, 2004—. Ret. lt. col. USAR, 1971-99. Recipient Disting. Alumnus award Ohio State U. Coll. Agr., 1998. Fellow Internat. Plant Propagator's Soc.; mem. Am. Pub. Garden Assn. (com. chmn. 1987-92, 01-03), Sigma Xi, Pi Alpha Xi, Gamma Sigma Delta. Avocations: fishing, fly-tying, golf, woodworking, gardening. Office: Miami U-Hamilton 1601 University Blvd Hamilton OH 45011 Home Phone: 513-523-5168; Office Phone: 513-785-3086. Business E-Mail: munsonrh@muohio.edu.

MUNSON, RICHARD JAY, government agency administrator; b. Hollywood, Calif., Aug. 10, 1950; s. Jay S. and Grace P. (Palmer) M.; m. Diane MacEachern; children: Daniel, Dana. BA, U. Calif., Santa Barbara, 1971; MA, U. Mich., 1973. Instr. U. Mich., Ann Arbor, 1973-75; coord. Environ. Action Found., Washington, 1975-77; exec. dir. Solar Lobby, Washington, 1977-83, N.E.-Midwest Inst., Washington, 1986—. Author: The Power Makers, 1985, Cousteau, 1988, The Cardinals of Capitol Hill, 1993, From Edison to Enron, 2005. Office: NE Midwest Inst 218 D St SE Ste A Washington DC 20003-1917 Office Phone: 202-544-5200.

MUNSON, WILLIAM LESLIE, insurance company executive; b. Chgo., Apr. 28, 1941; s. David Curtiss and Leona Ruth (Anderson) M.; m. Marian Lee Blanton, July 16, 1966; children: Katherine, Sandra, Deborah. Student, U. Md., 1959-62; BBA cum laude, Coll. of Ins., 1968. CPCU, 1967. Asst. mgr. N.Y. Fire Ins. Rating Orgn., NYC, 1959-69; br. mgr. CNA Ins. Co., NYC, 1969-75; pres., dir. Commerce & Industry Ins. Co., NYC, 1975-83; pres. Commerce & Industry of Can., 1980-83; sr. v.p., chief underwriting officer Am. Internat. Underwriters, 1983-87; exec. v.p. Home Ins. Co., 1987-93; pres., chief exec. officer Home Indemnity Ins. Co., 1987-93, also bd. dirs.; chmn. City Internat. Ins. Co. Ltd., 1991-93; pres., COO Merc. and Gen. Reins. Co. Am., 1993-97; chmn., pres., CEO Toa-Re-Ins. Co. Am. (now Toa Reins. Co. Am.), 1993—2003. Bd. dirs. USF Ins. Co., Victoria Ins. Co.; trustee Coll. of Ins., 1985—2001, Am. Inst. for Property Casualty Underwriters, 1996—2002; bd. overseers Sch. of Risk Mgmt., Ins. and Actuarial Sci. St. John's U., 2001—06; mem. bd. visitors Drew U., 2002—; mem. comml. lines. com. Ins. Svcs. Office, 1989—92. Pres. Wyckoff (NJ) Bd. Edn., 1979-82; chmn. bd. lay leaders Grace United Meth. Ch., Wyckoff, 1989-92, trustee, 1999—, pres. bd. trustees, 2005-. Past mem. Soc. CPCUs (bd. dirs. N.Y. chpt.); mem., Conf. Spl. Risk Underwriters, Reinsurance Assn. Am. (bd. dirs. 1993-2002). Clubs: John St. (N.Y.C.). Republican. Home: 762 Albemarle St Wyckoff NJ 07481-1005 Home Phone: 201-891-7834; Office Phone: 201-891-7834. Business E-Mail: wlmunson@verizon.net.

MUNT, JANET STAPLES, state senator; b. NYC, June 14, 1923; m. Plummer Coldwell Munt (dec.); 4 children. BA, Sweet Briar Coll., 1944; MS, Columbia U., 1948. Bd. cert. diplomate. Dir. maternal and child health divsn. Vis. Nurse Assn. Chittenden County, 1978—95; pvt. practice clin. social worker, 1995—. Trustee Burlington Coll., Columbia U. Sch. Social Work. Sgt. WAC, WWII. Fellow Am. Orthopsychiat. Assn., Inc.; mem. NASW, Acad. Cert. Social Workers. Democrat.

MÜNTER, LEILANI MAAJA, race car driver; b. Rochester, Minn. d. Manfred and Doris Munter. MS in Biology, U. Calif., San Diego. Lic. stock car driver Nat. Assn. Stock Car Auto Racing. Former tchg. asst. cellular biology U. Calif., San Diego; race car driver Nascar Elite divsn., 2004—; competed in ROMCO Super Late Model Series, Allison Legacy Series. Spl. corr. Nascar.com, 2004—. Photo double (for Catherine Zeta-Jones films) in Traffic and America's Sweethearts. Avocations: scuba diving, snowboarding. Office: PO Box 3335 Mooresville NC 28117 also: 5315 Highgate Dr Ste 204 Durham NC 27713 Business E-Mail: marketing@leilanimunter.com.

MUNTZ, DAVID S., information technology executive; Data sys. dir. of info. svc. Presbyn. Healthcare Sys., Dallas, v.p. info. svcs. and telecommunications, 1996; sr. v.p. info. svc. and tech. Texas Health Resources (formed in merger with Presbyn. Healthcare Sys., others), Arlington, 1997—.

MUNTZ, ERIC PHILLIP, aerospace and mechanical engineering educator, consultant; b. Hamilton, Ont., Can., May 18, 1934; came to U.S., 1961, naturalized, 1985; s. Eric Percival and Marjorie Louise (Weller) M.; m. Janice Margaret Furey, Oct. 21, 1964; children: Sabrina Weller, Eric Phillip. BASc., U. Toronto, 1956, MASc., 1957, PhD, 1961. Halfback Toronto Argonauts, 1957-60; group leader Gen. Electric, Valley Forge, Pa., 1961-69; assoc. prof. aerospace engring. and radiology U. So. Calif., Los Angeles, 1969-71, prof., 1971-87, chmn. aerospace engring., 1987-97, A.B. Freeman prof. engring., 1992—, chmn. aerospace and mech. engring., 2000—03. Cons. to aerospace and med. device cos., 1967—; mem. rev. of physics (plasma and fluids) panel NRC, Washington, 1983-85 Contbr. numerous articles in gas dynamics, micromech. sys., and med. diagnostics to profl. publs., 1961—; patentee med. imaging, isotope separation, nondestructive testing, net shape mfg., transient energy release micromachines, microscale vacuum sys., micropropulsion sys. Mem. Citizens Environ. Avc. Coun., Pasadena, Calif., 1972-76. Pilot RCAF, 1955-60. U.S. Air Force grantee, 1961-74, 82—; NSF grantee, 1970-76, 87-92; NASA grantee, 1990-94, 2001—; FDA grantee, 1980-86. Fellow AIAA (aerospace Contbn. to Soc. award 1987), Am. Phys. Soc.; mem. NAE. Episcopalian. Home: 1560 E California Blvd Pasadena CA 91106-4104 Office: U So Calif Univ Pk Los Angeles CA 90089-1191 Home Phone: 626-796-4543; Office Phone: 213-740-5366. Business E-Mail: muntz@usc.edu.

MUNYER, CHERYL, museum administrator; b. Vincennes, Ind., Apr. 27, 1970; d. Edward A. and Janet E. Munyer. BA, Ea. Ill. U., 1992, MA, 1995. Asst. curator Coles County Hist. Soc., Charleston, Ill., 1994-95, Manship Ho. Mus., Jackson, Miss., 1995-96, The Hermitage, Nashville, 1996-97; mgr. Rosalie Miss. State Soc. DAR, Natchez, 1999—2003; v.p Miss. Museums Assn., 2001—02, pres., 2002—05; dir. Hist. Jefferson Coll., Washington, Miss., 2003—. Newsletter editor Historic House Museums Affinity Group, 2000-05; bd. dirs. Natchez Hist. Soc. Editor SERA News, 1998-2002; co-founder, contbr. jour. Historia, 1992 Mem. Nat. Assn. Jr. Aux. (Natchez chpt. pres. 2005), Phi Alpha Theta, Sigma Tau Delta Democrat. Episcopalian. Avocation: visiting museums. Office: Hist Jefferson Coll PO Box 700 Washington MS 39190 E-mail: cbranyan@mdah.state.ms.us.

MUNYER, EDWARD ARNOLD, zoologist; b. Chgo., May 8, 1936; s. G. and M. Munyer; m. Marianna J. Munyer, Dec. 12, 1981; children: Robert, William, Richard, Laura, Cheryl. BS, Ill. State U., 1958, MS, 1962. Biology tchr. MDR High Sch., Minonk, Ill., 1961-63; instr. Ill. State U., Normal, 1963-64; curator zoology Ill. State Mus., Springfield, 1964-67, asst. dir., 1981-98, asst. dir. emeritus, 1998—; assoc. prof. Vincennes (Ind.) U., 1967-70; dir. Vincennes U. Mus., 1968-70; assoc. curator Fla. Mus. Natural History, Gainesville, 1970-81. Mem. Mus. Accreditation Vis. Com. Roster, 1976—. Contbr. articles to profl. jours. Mem. Am. Assn. Mus. (bd. dirs. 1990-95), Assn. Midwest Mus. (pres. 1990-92, lifetime achievement award for disting. svc. 1998), Ill. Assn. Mus. (bd. dirs. 1981-86, lifetime profl. achievement award 1998), Wilson Ornithol. Soc. (life). Office: Ill State Mus Spring & Edward Sts Springfield IL 62706-0001 Personal E-mail: eammjm@insightbb.com.

MUNZER, STEPHEN IRA, lawyer; b. NYC, Mar. 15, 1939; s. Harry and Edith (Isacowitz) M.; m. Patricia Eve Munzer, Aug. 10, 1965; children: John, Margaret. AB, Brown U., 1960; JD, Cornell U., 1963. Bar: N.Y. 1964, U.S. Supreme Ct. 1974, U.S. Dist. Ct. (so. and eas. dists.) N.Y., U.S. Ct. Appeals (3d cir.). Formerly ptnr. Pincus Munzer Bizar & D'Alessandro, 1978-83; atty., real estate investor Munzer & Saunders, LLP, 1984—. Pres. Simcor Mgmt. Corp., N.Y.C., 1984—. Lt. USNR, 1965-75. Mem. Assn. of Bar of City of N.Y., N.Y. State Bar Assn., Washington Club. Jewish. Avocations: golf, skiing. Home: 30 Lincoln Plz New York NY 10023 also: 170 Shearer Rd Washington CT 06793-1013 Office: 609 5th Ave New York NY 10017-1021 Office Phone: 212-755-0008. Business E-Mail: stephen@munzersaunders.com.

MUNZNER, ROBERT FREDERICK, biomedical engineer; s. Robert F. Munzner and Catherine E. (Appel) Gay; m. Jo Ann Goettee, Sept. 2, 1960 (div. 1980); children: Elizabeth Mae, Robert Victor, Ann Catherine; m. Karen E. Winstedt, Oct. 1, 1988. BS in Physics, Loyola Coll., Balt., 1963; PhD in Biomed. Engring., U. Va., 1976. Aerospace engr. Westinghouse Def. and Space, Balt., 1963-69; rsch. assoc. Johns Hopkins U., Balt., 1975-77; chief, neurol. devices br. U.S. FDA, Rockville, Md., 1977-97, expert sci. reviewer, 1998-99; regulatory affairs cons. Schuyler, Va., 1999—. Exec. sec. neurol. device adv. panel. U.S. FDA, Rockville, Md.; bd. standards IEEE, 1999-2001; mem. biomed. engring. adv. bd. U. N.C., Chapel Hill, 2004—. Co-author: Cerebellar Stimulation for Spasticity, 1984, The Physicians Perspective on Medical Law, 1997; contbr. articles to profl. jours. Fellow Johns Hopkins U., Balt., 1975, U. Va. fellow, Charlottesville, 1972-73, Thornton fellow, 1971. Mem. IEEE (sr., Millennium medal 2000), Biomed. Engring. Soc., Engring. in Medicine and Biology Soc. (chmn. stds. com., ad com. 1999-2005), Sigma Xi. Achievements include research in atrial mechanical stimulation producing vasomotor reflex. Home Phone: 434-263-8862; Office Phone: 434-263-8862. Business E-Mail: robert@doctordevice.com.

MUQAIBEL, ALI HUSSEIN, engineer, educator; b. Dammam, Saudi Arabia, June 8, 1974; s. Hussein Abdullah Muqaibel and Fatimah Ahmed Al-Attas. PhD, Va. Poly. Inst. and State U., Blacksburg, 2003. Lab engr. King Fahd U. Petroleum and Minerals, Dhahran, Saudi Arabia, 1996—99, lectr., 1999—2000, asst. prof., 2003—; rsch. asst. Va. Poly. Inst. and State U., 2000—01, sr. rsch. asst., 2001—03. Presenter in field. Contbr. articles to profl. publs. Recipient Best Presentor award, 2003, Short Course award, 2006. Office: King Fahd University of Petroleum and Mi Kfupm Dhahran 31261 Saudi Arabia Office Phone: +966-3-860-1595. Office Fax: +966-3-860-3535.

MURABITO, JOHN M., insurance company executive; BA in Econs., Augustana Coll., Ill., 1980; MA in Indsl. Rels., U. Iowa, 1983. With The Trane Co., Symbion, Inc.; with Frito-Lay divsn. PepsiCo; sr. v.p. human resources and corp. svcs. Monsanto; exec. v.p. human resources and svcs. CIGNA Corp., Phila., 2003—. Bd. dirs. Cornell U. Ctr. Advanced Human Resources Studies, U. SC Riegel & Emory Sch. Bus. Mem.: Human Resources Rsch. Group, Human Resources Policy Assn. Office: CIGNA Corp Two Liberty Pl 1601 Chestnut St Philadelphia PA 19192-1550 Office Phone: 215-761-1000. *

MURAD, FERID, physician; b. Whiting, Ind., Sept. 14, 1936; s. John and Josephine Murad; m. Carol Ann Leopold, June 21, 1958; children: Christine, Marianne, Carrie, Julie, Joseph. BA, DePauw U., 1958; MD, PhD, Case Western Res. U., 1965; Degree (hon.), Tirana U., 1999, Thomas Jefferson U., 2000, Case Western REs. U., 2000, State U. Ceara, 2000, Chinese U., Hong Kong, 2002, DePauw U., 2004, Charles U., 2005, Southeastern U., 2006. Diplomate Nat. Bd. Med. Examiners. Intern and resident Mass. Gen. Hosp., Boston, 1965—67; clin. assoc. NIH, Bethesda, Md., 1967—70; dir. clin. rsch. ctr. U. Va., Charlottesville, 1971—81, prof. internal medicine and pharmacology, 1975—81, Stanford U., Calif., 1981—88, acting chmn. dept. medicine, 1986—88; chief of medicine VA Med. Ctr., Palo Alto, Calif., 1981—88; v.p. pharm. divsn. Abbott Labs., 1988—92, CEO, pres. molecular geriatrics, 1993—95; prof. dept. medicine, chmn. dept. integrative biology and pharmacology U. Tex., Houston, 1997—, dir. Inst. Molecular Medicine, 1999—. Co-editor: The Pharmacological Basis of Therapeutics, 1985; contbr. articles to profl. jours. Recipient Ciba award, 1988, Albert and Mary Lasker Found. award, 1996, Nobel Prize for Medicine, 1998, others. Mem.: NAS, Inst. of Medicine, Western Assn. Physicians, Assn. Am. Physicians, Am. Soc. Clin. Investigation, Am. Soc. Physiology, Am. Soc. Biol. Chemists, Am. Soc. for Pharmacology and Exptl. Therapeutics, Am. Acad. Arts and Scis., NAS Inst. Medicine. Achievements include patents in field. Avocations: golf, carpentry. Office: U Tex Med Sch Inst Molecular Medicine 1825 Pressler Ste 530 Houston TX 77225-0708 Office Phone: 713-500-2433. Business E-Mail: ferid.murad@uth.tmc.edu.

MURADIAN, VAZGEN, composer; b. Ashtarak, Armenia, Oct. 17, 1921; arrived in U.S., 1950, naturalized, 1956; s. Grigor and Arusiak (Vardanian) Muradian; m. Arpi Kirkyasharian, Aug. 29, 1964; children: Vardges Vago, Armen Morian. Grad. professore di musica, Benedetto Marcello State Conservatory Music, Venice, Italy, 1948; studied composition with Gabriele Bianchi, studied composition with Vittoriao Giannini, studied violin with Luigi Ferro, studied viola d'amore with Renzo Sabatini. Tchr. violin, solfeggio and theory of music Collegio Armeno, Venice, Italy, 1945-50. Pvt. tchr. viola d'amore. Composer over 265 works including 69 concertos for all classical instruments and many non-traditional instruments, 57 symphonies, 12 suites for orch., 10 other works for symphonies, 4 moto perpetuos for violin or piano, 26 chamber workds for violin, viola, viola d'amore, cello or piano, 7 sonatas for solo violin, 7 sonatas for violin and piano, 2 sonatas for piano, 14 sonatas for viola d'amore, sonatas for viola d'amore, 56 songs with orch. and 8 songs for chorus and orch. in six languages on works of Shakespeare, Petrarch, Dante, Gœthe, Hugo, others; compositions performed throughout the U.S. and abroad; author articles in field; debut, N.Y. Lincoln Center, 1972; violist with various U.S. orchs. including New Orleans Symphony, Wagner Opera Co.; appeared as viola d'amore soloist, U.S. and abroad. Recipient Tekeyan prize, 1962, St. Mesrop Mashdots Medal for lifetime achievement, 1996, Saint Sahak and Saint Mesrop Medal for lifetime achievement, 2001, and numerous others. Mem.: ASCAP, Armenian Composer's Union, Viola D'amore Soc. Am. (Lifetime Achievement honor 2000, 2004). Achievements include Muradian is one of the most prolific and accomplished composers of symphonic music in history, and perhaps America's most accomplished composer in the symphonic genre; the only composer known to have written a concerto for every classical instrument as well as first ever concertos for several unusual instruments not traditionally used in classical music. Home: 269 W 72nd St Apt 11A New York NY 10023-2719

MURAI, KEVIN M., information technology executive; b. 1964; BSEE, U. Waterloo, Ontario. Former mgr. mgmt. info. svcs. Verifact, Inc., Ontario, Canada; joined Ingram Micro Inc., 1988; v.p., operations Ingram Micro Can., Canada, 1993—97, pres., 1997—2000; sr. v.p. Ingram Micro Inc., 1997—2002, exec. v.p. Santa Ana, Calif., 2000—05; pres. Ingram Micro US, 2000—01, COO, 2000—02; pres., COO Ingram Micro N. Am., 2002—05, Ingram Micro Inc., 2005—. Office: Ingram Micro Inc 1600 E St Andrew Pl Santa Ana CA 92705-4931 Office Phone: 714-566-1000. Office Fax: 714-566-7900. *

MURAI, RENE VICENTE, lawyer; b. Havana, Cuba, Mar. 11, 1945; came to the U.S., 1960; s. Andres and Silvia (Muñiz) M.; m. Luisa Botifoll, June 12, 1970; 1 child, Elisa. BA, Brown U., 1966; JD cum laude, Columbia U., 1969. Bar: Fla. 1970, N.Y. 1972, U.S. Supreme Ct. 1977. Atty. Reginald Heber Smith Fellow Legal Svcs. Greater Miami, Fla., 1969-71; assoc. Willkie, Farr & Gallagher, NYC, 1971-73; ptnr. Paul, Landy & Beiley, Miami, 1973-79; shareholder Murai, Wald, Biondo & Moreno, Miami, 1979—. Vice-chmn. Premier Am. Bank, Miami; dir. Cuban Am. Bar Assn., 1982-96, pres., 1985; vice chmn., lectr. Internat. Conf. for Lawyers of the Ams., 1982, chmn. and lectr., 1984; mem. panel grievance com. Fla. Bar, 1983-86. Mng. editor Columbia Law Rev., 1967-69. Facts About Cuban Exiles, Inc., 1982—, pres., 1989, Legal Svcs. of Greater Miami, Inc., 1980-90, pres. 1986-88, ARC, 1984-90, exec. com., 1988-90, Mercy Hosp. Found., 1985-91, Dade Cmty. Found., 1988-93, chair grants com., 1991-93, United Way, 1989-95; chmn. adminstrn. of justice com. Fla. Bar Found., 1996-98, bd. dirs., 1991-00, chmn. audit and fin. com., 1993-98, sec., 1997-98, pres. 1999-2000; mem. task force leadership Dade County Ptnrs. for Safe Neighborhoods, 1994-95, Code Enforcement Bd. City of Coral Gables, 1982-86, Bd. Adjustment, 1987-89, city mgr. selection com., 1987, charter rev. commn., 1980; trustee U. Miami, 1994-96; bd. dirs. Miami Children's Hosp., 2000—, chmn. 2004-; com. mem. Orange Bowl, 2000-, bd. dir., 2005-; bd. dir. Riviera Country Club, 2005-. Mem. Cuban-Am. Bar Assn., Dade County Bar Assn. (dir. 1987-88), Greater Miami C. of C., Miami City Club (bd. dirs. 1997—2001, pres. 2000—01). Democrat. Roman Catholic. Avocation: sports. Home: 3833 Alhambra Ct Coral Gables FL 33134-6229 Office: Murai Wald Biondo Moreno & Brochin PA 2 Alhambra Plz PH 1B Coral Gables FL 33134 Office Phone: 305-444-0101. Business E-Mail: rmurai@mwbm.com.

MURANAKA, JAMI, biology educator; m. Garett Muranaka; children: Emi, Misa. BS in Biology, UCLA; MEd, U. Hawai'i-Manoa. Cert. Nat. Bd. Profl. Tchg. Standards. Sci. tchr. Kaimuki H.S., Honolulu, 1999—. Named Honolulu Dist. Tchr. of Yr., Hawaii Tchr. of Yr., 2007. Office: Kaimuki High Sch 2705 Kaimuki Ave Honolulu HI 96816 Business E-Mail: jami_muranaka@notes.k12.hi.us. *

MURANE, WILLIAM EDWARD, lawyer; b. Denver, Mar. 4, 1933; s. Edward E. and Theodora (Wilson) M.; m. Rosemarie Palmerone, Mar. 26, 1960; children: Edward Wheelock, Peter Davenport, Alexander Phelps. AB, Dartmouth Coll., 1954; LLB, Stanford U., 1957. Bar: Wyo. 1957, Colo. 1958, D.C. 1978, U.S. Supreme Ct. 1977. Assoc. then ptnr. Holland & Hart, Denver, 1961-69; dep. gen. counsel U.S. Dept. Commerce, Washington, 1969-71; gen. counsel FDIC, Washington, 1971-72; ptnr. Holland & Hart, Denver, 1972—2000. Pub. mem. Adminstrv. Conf. of the U.S., Washington, 1978-81. Bd. dirs. Ctr. for Law and Rsch., Denver, 1973-76, Colo. Bus. Com. for Arts, 2002—; trustee Colo. Symphony Orch., 1994-2000; mem. bd. visitors Stanford U. Law Sch.; mem. vestry St. John's Cathedral, Denver, 2007-. Capt. USAF, 1958-61. Fellow Am. Coll. Trial Lawyers; mem. ABA (ho of dels. 1991-96), U. Club, Cactus Club. Republican. Avocations: fishing, classical music. Office: Holland & Hart 555 17th St Ste 2700 Denver CO 80202-3950

MURANO, ELSA A., academic and former federal agency administrator; b. Havana, Cuba; BS in Biol. Sci., Fla. Internat. U.; MS in Anaerobic Microbiology, Va. Polytechnic Inst.; PhD in Food Sci. and Tech., Va. State U. Asst. prof. Iowa State U., Ames, 1990—92, prof. in charge rsch. programs linear accelertor facility, 1992—95; various positions including dir. food safety Tex. A&M U., College Station, Tex., 1995—2001, assoc. prof. animal sci., 1995—2000, prof. dept. animal sci., 2000—01, vice chancellor, 2005—, dean agrl. & life sciences, 2005—; dir. Tex. Agrl. Experiment Station, College Station, Tex., 2005—; under sec. for food safety USDA, Washington, 2001—04. Chair food safety state initiative com. Tex. Agr. Ext. Sta., 1999—2001; nat. adv. com. meat and poultry inspection USDA, 2001; mem. Nat. Alliance for Food Safety Ops. Com., 1998—2001, chair, 2000—01; bd. dirs. Hormel Foods Corp., 2006—.

Mem.: Intenat. Assn. Food Protection, Poultry Sci. Assn., Inst. Food Technologists, Assn. Meat Sci., Am. Soc. Microbiology. Office: Tex A&M U 109 Kleberg Bldg 2042 TAMU College Station TX 77843

MURARKA, SHYAM PRASAD, science and engineering educator, administrator; b. Jaynagar, Bihar, India, Mar. 13, 1940; came to U.S., 1966; s. Bihari L. and Suti Murarka; m. Saroj Murarka, May 21, 1962; children: Sumeet, Amal. BS in Chemistry with honors, Bihar U., Muzaffarpur, 1958, MS in Chemistry, 1960; PhD in Chemistry, Agra U., India, 1970; PhD in Materials Sci. and Metals, U. Minn., 1970. Lectr., rsch. assoc. Bihar U., 1960-61; trainee Atomic Energy Est., Trombay, Maharastra, 1961-62, sci. officer, 1962-66; rsch. asst. U. Minn., Mpls., 1966-70, rsch. assoc., 1970-72; mem. tech. staff, supr. Bell Labs., Murray Hill, NJ, 1972-84; prof. Rensselaer Poly. Inst., Troy, NY, 1984—2002, dir. Ctr. for Integrated Electronics and Electronics Mfg., 1994-96, dir. Ctr. for Advanced Interconnect Sci. and Tech., 1996-2000, dir. Sematech Ctr. of Excellence, 1989-96, Elaine S. & Jack S. Parker chair engring., 1997—2002, prof. emeritus, 2002—. Cons. Bell Labs., Murray Hill, N.J., 1984-89, Applied Materials, Santa Clara, Calif., 1997-99; spkr. in field Author: Silicides for VLSI Applications, 1983, Metallization Theory and Practice for VLSI and ULSI, 1993; (with others) Electronic Materials Science and Technology, 1989, Chemical Mechanical Planarization of Microelectronic Materials, 1997, Copper Fundamental Mechanisms for Micorelectronic Applications, 2000, Interlayer Dielectrics for Semiconductor Technologies, 2003; co-editor: Advanced Metallizations in Microelectronics, 1990, Advanced Metallization and Processing for Semiconductor Devices and Circuits II, 1992, Interface Control of Electrical, Chemical, and Mechanical Properties, 1994, Advaned Metallization for Devices and Circuits, 1994, Microelectronics Technology and Process Integration, 1994, Low Dielectric Constant Materials Synthesis in Microelectronics, 1995, Interlayer Dielectrics for Semiconductor Technologies, 2003; contbr. book chpt. Transition Metal Silicides, 1983, Handbook of Semiconductor Technology, 2000, Diffusion Processes in Advanced Technological Materials, 2005; over 560 rsch. articles to profl. jours. Mem. Tri-City India Assn.'s Indian Comty. Support Group, Albany, 1996. Recipient Gold medal Bihar U., 1960; Univ. Grants Commn. scholar, 1961. Fellow IEEE, Am. Vacuum Soc., Am. Soc. Metals and Electrochem. Soc. (Thomas Callinan award 1987, Electronics Divsn. award 2001); mem. Materials Rsch Soc., Bihar U. Chem. Soc. (hon. life). Achievements include 20 patents in field.

MURASE, JIRO, lawyer; b. NYC, May 16, 1928; BBA, CCNY, 1955; JD, Georgetown U., 1958, LL.D. (hon.), 1982. Bar: D.C. 1958, N.Y. 1959. Sr. ptnr. Marks & Murase L.L.P., NYC, 1971-97, Bingham McCutchen Murase, NYC, 1997—. Legal counsel Consulate Gen. of Japan; mem. Pres.'s Adv. Com. Trade Negotiations, 1980-82; mem. Trilateral Commn., 1985—; apptd. mem. World Trade Coun., 1984-94; adv. com. internat. investment, tech. and devel. Dept. State, 1975. Editorial bd.: Law and Policy in Internat. Bus. Trustee Asia Found., 1979-83, Japanese Ednl. Inst. N.Y.; bd. dirs. Japan Soc., Japanese C. of C. in N.Y., Inc.; hon. bd. regents Georgetown U.; bd. visitors Georgetown Law Ctr.; adv. coun. Pace U., Internat. House Japan; pres. Japanese-Am. Assn. N.Y., Inc., 1996-98—, Japan Ctr. Internat. Exch., 2001—. Recipient N.Y. Gov.'s citation for contbns. to internat. trade, 1982; named to Second Order of Sacred Treasure (Japan), 1989. Mem. ABA, Assn. of Bar of City of N.Y., N.Y. State Bar Assn., N.Y. County Lawyers Assn., Maritime Law Assn., Consular Law Soc., Fed. Bar Coun., Am. Soc. Internat. Law, World Assn. Lawyers, Japanese-Am. Soc. Legal Studies, Am. Arbitration Assn., Lic. Execs. Soc., U.S. C. of C. Clubs: Nippon (dir.); Ardsley Country; N.Y. Athletic; Mid-Ocean (Bermuda). Office: Bingham McCutchen Murase 399 Park Ave New York NY 10022-4614 Office Phone: 212-705-7878. Business E-Mail: jiro.murase@bingham.com.

MURASKI, ANTHONY AUGUSTUS, lawyer; b. Cohoes, NY, July 28, 1946; s. Adam Joseph and Angeline Mary (Vozzy) M.; m. Jeanne Marie Muraski; children: Adam Peter, Emily Jo, Talia Rose, Lydia Fern, Mariah Willow, Sophia Aspen. BA, MA in Speech/Hearing, Sacramento State Coll., 1970; PhD in Audiology/ Hearing Sci., U. Mich., 1977; JD, Detroit Coll. Law, 1979. Bar: Mich. 1980, U.S. Dist. Ct. (ea. dist.) Mich. 1981, U.S. Ct. Appeals (6th cir.) 1982, U.S. Claims Ct. 1989, U.S. Supreme Ct. 1990, Pa. 1990. Asst. Kresge Hearing Research Inst. U. Mich., Ann Arbor, 1971-77; asst. prof. Wayne State U. Med. Sch., Detroit, 1979-82; assoc. Kitch, Suhrheinrich, Saurbier & Drutchas, Detroit, 1982-83; assoc. prof. Detroit Coll. Law, 1983-85; mng. ptnr. Muraski & Sikorski, Ann Arbor, 1985—. Cons. audiology Ministry of Environment, Ont., Can., 1980-81; trustee Deaf, Speech and Hearing Ctr., Detroit, 1981—; legal adv. on air WWJ Radio, Detroit, 1984—; mem. mental health adv. bd. on deafness Dept. Mental Health, 1984, vis. com. U. Mich. Sch. Edn., 1986—. Author: Legal Aspects of Audiological Practice, 1982, Hearing Conservation in Industry: Licensure, Liability and Forensics, 1985. Mem. ABA, Mich. Bar Assn., Washtenaw County Bar Assn., Am. Speech-Lang.-Hearing Assn. (sci. merit award, 1981), Ann Arbor C. of C. Avocations: photography, writing. Home: 3830 Warren Ct Ann Arbor MI 48105 Office Phone: 734-604-8765. Personal E-mail: amurphappy@cs.com.

MURAT, WILLIAM M., legislative staff member; b. Stevens Point, Wis., Dec. 4, 1957; s. James L. and Rose Murat. BS, U. Wis., Stevens Point, 1980; JD, U. Wis., Madison, 1983; MBA, Columbia U., 1992. Asst. dist. atty. to dist. atty. Portage County, Wis., 1983-88, dist. atty. Wis., 1988-91; assemblyman Wis. State Dist. 71, 1995-99; chief of staff Congressman Tammy Baldwin. Vice chmn. Portage County Dem. Com., 1976-80, chmn., 1985-86; exec. dir. Wis. Young Dems., 1978-79, pres., 1982-83; mem. exec. com. Seventh Dist. Dems., Wis., 1978-80, 82-90; adminstrv. com. Wis. Dem. Com., 1982-99; mem. Dem. Nat. Com., 1997-99; 1st vice chair Dem. Wis., 1997-99. Mem. Phi Delta Phi, Pi Kappa Delta.

MURAT, YUSEF J., plastic surgeon; b. Oaxaca, Mex., Sept. 2, 1964; arrived in U.S., 2003; s. Mateo Jiménez and Zandra Luz Murat; m. Ireri Salazar Urquiza, Nov. 29, 1997; children: Valentina, Miranda. MD, UNAM, Mexico City, 1989. Cert. plastic surgeon UNAM, 1996, Bd., 1997. Fellowship hand surgeon UNAM, Mexico City, 1997; fellowship microsurgery Hosp. Gen. Manuel Gea Gonzalez, UNAM, Mexico City, 1998, prof. plastic surgery, hand surgery, microsurgery, 1997—. Contbr. scientific papers in plastic surgery, hand surgery and microsurgery. Mem.: Assn. Dr. Ortiz-Monasterio. Avocations: tennis, golf. Office Phone: 956-544-7197. E-mail: yusmd@prodigy.net.mx.

MURATA, TADAO, engineering and computer science educator; b. Takayama, Gifu, Japan, June 26, 1938; arrived in U.S., 1962; s. Yonosuke and Ryu (Aomame) M.; m. Nellie Kit-Ha Shin, 1964; children: Patricia Emi, Theresa Terumi. BSE.E., Tokai U., 1962; MSE.E., U. Ill., 1964, PhD in Elec. Engring., 1966. Rsch. asst. U. Ill., Urbana, 1962-66; asst. prof. U. Ill. at Chgo., 1966-68, assoc. prof., 1970-76, prof., 1977—, UIC disting. prof., 2002—; assoc. prof. Tokai U., Tokyo, 1968-70. Vis. prof. U. Calif., Berkeley, 1976-77; cons. Nat. Bur. Stds., Gaithersburg, Md., 1984-85; panel mem. NAS, Washington, 1981-82, 83-85; vis. scientist Nat. Ctr. For Sci. Rsch., France, 1981; guest rschr. Gesellschaft für Mathematik und Datenverarbeitung, Germany, 1979; Hitachi-Endowed prof. Osaka (Japan) U., 1993-94. Editor IEEE Trans. on Software Engring., 1986-92; assoc. editor Jour. of Cirs., Sysems and Computers, 1990—; contbr. articles to sci. and engring. jours. Recipient C.A. Petri Disting. Tech. Achievement award Soc. Design and Process Scis., 2000; Sr. univ. scholar award U. Ill., 1990; NSF grantee, 1978—, U.S.-Spain coop. rsch. grantee, 1985-87. Fellow IEEE (life; golden core charter mem. IEEE Computer Soc., Donald G. Fink Prize award 1991), Inst. Electronics, Info. and Comm. Engrs.; mem. Assn. Computing Machinery, Info. Processing Soc. Japan, European Assn. for Theoretical Computer Sci., Upsilon Pi Epsilon. Avocations: golf, travel. Office: U Ill Dept Computer Sci m/c 152 851 S Morgan St Chicago IL 60607-7042 Personal E-mail: t.murata@ieee.org.

MURAYAMA, MAKIO, biochemist; b. San Francisco, Aug. 10, 1912; s. Hakuyo and Namiye (Miyasaka) M.; children: Gibbs Soga, Alice Myra. BA, U. Calif., Berkeley, 1938, MA, 1940; PhD (NIH fellow), U. Mich., 1953; ScD honoris causa, Open Internat. U., Sri Lanka, 1994. Rsch. biochemist Children's Hosp. Mich., Detroit, 1943, 1945—48, Bellevue Hosp., NYC, 1943—45, Harper Hosp., Detroit, 1949—54; rsch. fellow chemistry Calif. Inst. Tech., Pasadena, 1954—56; rsch. assoc. biochemistry Grad. Sch. Medicine U. Pa., Phila., 1956—58; spl. rsch. fellow Cavendish Lab. Nat. Cancer Inst., Cambridge, England, 1958; sr. rsch. biochemist NIH, Bethesda, Md., 1958—93. Author: (with Robert M. Nalbandian) Sickle Cell Hemoglobin, 1973; discovered DIPA (decompression-inducible platelet aggregation), 1975; discovered DIPA causes vascular occlusion in both acute mountain sickness and diver's syndrome, 1984. Fellow Am. Inst. Chemists; mem. AAAS, Am. Chem. Soc., Am. Soc. Biol. Chemists, Assn. Clin. Scientists, Undersea and Hyperbaric Med. Soc., Aerospace Med. Assn., Internat. Platform Assn., West African Soc. Pharmacology (hon.), N.Y. Acad. Sci., Sigma Xi. Achievements include patent for automatic amperometric titration apparatus, 1958; development of molecular mechanism of human red cell sickling and prevention of sickle cell crisis by oral prophylactic carbamide, 1972; discovery of decompression inducible platelet aggregation by means of simulation of decompression-inducible platelet aggregation of diving in frogs and mice that diver's disease and acute mountain sickness could be alleviated by piracetam and thymol, antiplatelet agents, 1986. Home: 5010 Benton Ave Bethesda MD 20814-2804 Personal E-mail: mmurayama@aol.com.

MURBURG, THELMA D., retired elementary school educator; b. Illon, NY, Jan. 24, 1924; d. Horace L. and Margaret (Kruger) White; children: Michele, Michael, John(dec.). BEd, SUNY, Oneonta, 1945; MA, William Paterson Coll., NJ, 1974, MA, 1976. Cert. tchr., adminstr. NJ. Tchr. Seaford (NY) Sch., 1945—47, Franklin Sch., Englewood, NJ, 1947—52, Bryan Sch., Cresskill, NJ, 1962, Roberge Sch., Rivervale, NJ, 1962—95, Woodside Sch., Rivervale, 1962—95; ret., 1995. Author curriculum materials in social studies and lang. arts. Negotiator Rivervale Tchrs. Union, 1990—95; vol. Hospice Pascack Valley Hospice Hosp., Emerson, 1998—, chaplain asst., 2003—06; facilitator Bereavement Groups, Hospice, Emerson, 2005—06; founder choral group, 2005; asst. pastor nursing home svcs. Named Vol. of Yr., P.U. Hospice, 2005. Avocations: music, painting, writing poetry, gardening, reading. Home (Summer): 300 Piermont Rd Norwood NJ 07648 Home (Winter): 4414 Northampton Dr New Port Richey FL 34653

MURCHISON, DAVID CLAUDIUS, lawyer; b. NYC, Aug. 19, 1923; s. Claudius Temple and Constance (Waterman) M.; m. June Margaret Guilfoyle, Dec. 19, 1946 (dec. June 2001); children: David Roderick, Brian, Courtney, Bradley, Stacy. AA, George Washington U., 1947, BA, 1949, JD with honors, 1949. Bar: DC 1949, Supreme Ct. 1955. Assoc. Dorr, Hand & Dawson, NYC, 1949-50; founding ptnr. Howrey & Simon, Washington, 1956-90, counsel, 1990—. Legal asst. under sec. army, 1949-51; counsel motor vehicle, textile, aircraft, ordinance and shipbldg. divsns. Nat. Prodn. Authority, 1951-52; assoc. gen. counsel Small Def. Plants Adminstrn., 1952-53; legal adv. and asst. to chmn. FTC, 1953-55 Chmn. So. Africa Wildlife Trust. With AUS, 1943-45, ETO. Mem. ABA (chmn. com. internat. restrictive bus. practices sect. antitrust law 1954-55, sect. adminstrv. law, sect. litigation), FBA, DC Bar Assn., NY State Bar Assn., Order of Coif, Met. Club, Chevy Chase Club, Talbot Country Club. Republican.

MURCHISON, DAVID RODERICK, lawyer; b. Washington, May 28, 1948; s. David Claudius and June Margaret (Guilfoyle) M.; m. Kathy Ann Kohn, Mar. 15, 1981; children: David Christopher, Benjamin Michael. BA cum laude, Princeton U., 1970; JD, Georgetown U., 1975. Bar: D.C. 1975, Fla. 1993. Legal asst. to vice chmn. CAB, Washington, 1975-76, enforcement atty., 1976-77; sr. atty. Air Transport Assn., Washington, 1977-80, asst. v.p., sec., 1981-85; sr. assoc. Zuckert, Scoutt and Rasenberger, Washington, 1980-81; v.p., asst. gen. counsel Piedmont Aviation, Inc., Winston-Salem, NC, 1985-88; v.p., gen. counsel, sec. Braniff, Inc., Dallas, 1988-89, chief exec. officer Orlando, 1990-94; fed. adminstrv. law judge Office of Hearings and Appeals, Charleston, W.Va., 1994-96, chief adminstrv. law judge Mobile, Ala., 1996-99, adminstrv. law judge, 1999—. Lectr. continuing legal edn. program Wake Forest U., Winston-Salem, 1988. Contbr. articles to legal jours. Lt. USNR, 1970-72. Mem. ABA, Met. Club Washington. Republican. Roman Catholic. Office: Hearings & Appeals Office 550 Government St #200 Mobile AL 36602 Office Phone: 251-441-5441.

MURDOCH, AMELIA CLARA, educational association administrator; d. Thomas Jerome and Viola Scanlan Murdoch. AB with honors, U. Pa., 1945, PhD, 1952. Instr. Juniata Coll., Huntingdon, Pa., 1950—51; linguist Nat. Security Agy., Ft. George Meade, Md., 1951—82, 1985—94; pres. and founder Nat. Mus. Lang., College Park, Md., 1998—. Mem. Tree and Landscape Bd., College Park, 1991—; chair Com. for a Better Environment, College Park, 1983—97, Vets. Meml. Improvement Com., College Park, 1991—2003. Am. Coun. Learned Socs. and Jusserand study and travel fellow, U. Pa., 1948—49. Mem.: MLA, Medieval Acad. Am., Internat. Arthurian Soc., Phi Beta Kappa (Mary Isabel Sibley fellow 1947—48). Avocations: reading, gardening. Office: Nat Museum of Language 7100 Baltimore Ave Ste 202 College Park MD 20740 Office Phone: 301-864-7071. Business E-Mail: acmurdoch@languagemuseum.org.

MURDOCH, COLIN, academic administrator; BA summa cum laude, Case Western Reserve U.; MusM, U. Ill. Faculty mem. music Lawrence U., Appleton, Wis.; dean Lawrence U. Conservatory of Music, Appleton, Wis., 1978, San Francisco Conservatory Music, Calif., 1988—92, pres. Calif., 1992—. Mem. New Orleans Symphony. Recipient Excellence Award, Pacific Musical Soc. Mem.: Nat. Assn. Schs. Music (mem. Futures Com., Commn. on Accreditation). Office: Office of the President San Francisco Conservatory of Music 50 Oak St San Francisco CA 94102-6011 Office Phone: 415-503-6230. *

MURDOCH, DAVID ARMOR, lawyer; b. Pitts., May 30, 1942; s. Armor M. and N. Edna (Jones) M.; m. Joan Wilkie, Mar. 9, 1974; children: Christina, Timothy, Deborah. AB magna cum laude, Harvard U., 1964, LLB, 1967. Bar: Pa. 1967, U.S. Dist. Ct. (we. dist.) Pa. 1967, U.S. Ct. Mil. Appeals 1968, U.S. Supreme Ct. 1990, U.S. Ct. Appeals (3d cir.) 1991. Assoc. Kirkpatrick & Lockhart Preston Gates Ellis, LLP, Pitts., 1971—78, ptnr., 1978—. Co-author: Business Workouts Manual. V.p., bd. dirs. Avonworth Sch. Dist., 1977-83; bd. dirs. Pitts. Expt., 1988-93, chmn., 1989-90; mem. Pa. Housing Fin. Agy., 1981-88, vice-chmn., 1983-87; alt. del. Rep. Nat. Conv., 1980; elder Presbyn. Ch. Sewickley, 1986-92, 2006-; past pres. Harvard Law Sch. Assn. W. Pa.; bd. adv. Geneva Coll., 1993-94, trustee, 1994-97; trustee Sewickley Pub. Libr., 1994-2002, vice-chmn., 1997-2002; trustee World Learning, Inc., 1995-04, vice chmn., 1998-2000, chmn., 2000-04, chmn. emeritus, 2004—; bd. dirs. Allegheny County Libr. Assn., 1994-96; chair Czech Working Group, Presbyn. Ch. USA, 1995-2000; bd. vis. U. Ctr. Internat. Studies, U. Pitts., 1996—; bd. advisors Ctr. for Bus., Religion, and Pub. Life, Pitts. Theol. Sem., 1997—; adv. bd. Ctr. for Internat. Legal Edn., U. Pitts. Sch. Law, 1997—; mem. Global Focus Adv. Bd., Chatham Coll., 2005—; bd. dirs., exec. com., vice-chmn. World Affairs Coun. Pitts., 1997-2007; bd. dirs. Am. Coun. Germany, 1998-2007; hon. consul Fed. Rep. Germany in Pitts., 2002—. Capt. US Army, 1968—71. Recipient Disting. Svc. award Allegheny County Libr. Assn., 2001. Fellow Am. Coll. Bankruptcy, Am. Bar Found.; mem. ABA (bus. bankruptcy com., chmn. subcom. on bankruptcy coms., trust indentures and claims trading 1991-97), Am. Law Inst. Office: Kirkpatrick & Lockhart Preston Gates Ellis LLP Henry W Oliver Bldg 535 Smithfield St Pittsburgh PA 15222-2312 Office Phone: 412-355-6472. Business E-Mail: david.murdoch@rlgates.com.

MURDOCH, ELISABETH, media company executive; b. Sydney, 1968; d. Rupert and Anna Murdoch; m. Elkin Pianim, 1993 (div.); children: Cornelia, Anna; m. Matthew Freud, 2001; 1 child, Charlotte. With News Corp.; owner, operator NBC affiliate stations, 1994—96; gen. mgr. broadcasting dept. BSkyB, 1996, dir. programming, 1996—98, mng. dir. Sky Networks, 1998—2001; founder, chmn., CEO Shine Ltd., London, 2001—. Named one of 50 Women to Watch, Wall St. Jour., 2005. Office: Shine Ltd 140 Kensington Church St London W8 4BN England

MURDOCH, JOHN, museum director; Asst. dir. collections Victoria and Albert Mus., London; dir. Gallery Courtauld, U. London, 1993—2002, Huntington Art Collections, San Marino, Calif., 2002—. Office: Huntington Art Collections 1151 Oxford Rd San Marino CA 91108

MURDOCH, LAWRENCE CORLIES, JR., retired banker, economist; b. Phila., June 3, 1926; s. Lawrence C. and Barbara (Boyd) M.; children: Lawrence C. III, Anne G.; m. 2d Eleanor M. Egan, June 16, 1970. BS Wharton Sch., U. Pa. in Econs., 1948; MBA, Wharton Sch., U. Pa., 1956. With Fed. Res. Bank Phila., 1954-92; ret., 1992. Bd. dirs. Cliveden Inc., 1981. Contbr. articles to consumer and monetary publs.; producer documentary films; spokesman (radio and TV). Lt. (j.g.) USN, 1948-54. Mem. Soc. Cin. (pres. 1990-93), Little Egg Harbor Yacht Club (Beach Haven, N.J.), Beta Gamma Sigma, Zeta Psi. Home: 115 Hilltop Rd Philadelphia PA 19118-3737

MURDOCH, ROBERT WHITTEN, lawyer; b. Pitts., Mar. 21, 1937; s. Thomas and Julia (Whitten) Murdoch; m. Eleanore L. Uram, Sept. 26, 1967; 1 child, Robert John. BA, U. Pitts., 1960; pvt. law study, 1963-67. Bar: Pa. 1967, US Dist. Ct. (we. dist.) Pa. 1968, US Ct. Appeals (3d cir.) 1978, US Supreme Ct. 1978, US Ct. Appeals (8th cir.) 1983, US Ct. Appeals (11th cir.) 1986. Ptnr. Jones, Gregg, Creehan & Gerace, Pitts., 1967-85, Grogan, Graffam, McGinley & Lucchino, P.C., Pitts., 1985-98, Zimmer Kunz P.C., 1998—2004, Rawle & Henderson LLP, 2004—. Author: Pfeifer: The Supreme Court on the Longshoremen's and Harbor Workers compensation Act and Inflation, 1983, 1984; CD, Ae Fond Kis from the Tartan Tenor. Nat. chmn. Tartan Day; bd. dirs. Scotland-Pa. Bus. Links. 2d lt. Intelligence US Army, 1960—61. Recipient Nat. Tartan Day award, 2007. Fellow: Soc. Antiquities Scotland; mem.: SAR, ABA, Am. Soc. Law and Medicine, Am. Coll. Legal Medicine, Acad. Trial Lawyers Allegheny County, Pa. Def. Inst., Def. Rsch. Inst., Maritime Law Assn. US, Allegheny County Bar Assn., Pa. Bar Assn., Pitt Varsity Letter Club, An Ceud Fear, Caledonian Found., Plymouth Herditary Soc., Continental Soc. Sons Indian Wars, Clan Donald, Nat. Soc. Sons Colonial New Eng., Descs. Colonial Clergy, Sons Union Vets. Civil War, Hon. Order Blue Goose Internat., Pitt. Golden Panthers, St. Andrews Soc. Pitts., Scottish Coalition, Phi Alpha Delta. Republican. Presbyterian. Avocations: genealogy, golf, tenor soloist. Office: Rawle & Henderson LLP Ste 1000 535 Smithfield St Pittsburgh PA 15222 Home Phone: 412-885-1703; Office Phone: 412-261-5709. Personal E-mail: tartantenor66@yahoo.com. Business E-Mail: rmurdoch@rawle.com.

MURDOCH, RUPERT (KEITH RUPERT MURDOCH), multi media company executive; b. Melbourne, Australia, Mar. 11, 1931; arrived in US, 1974, naturalized, 1985; s. Sir Keith and Dame Elisabeth Joy (Greene) M.; m. Patricia Booker, 1956 (div. 1960); 1 child: Prudence; m. Anna Maria Torv, Apr. 28, 1967 (div. June 8, 1999); children: Elisabeth, Lachlan, James; m. Wendi Deng, June 25, 1999; children: Grace Helen, Chloe. BA, BS, Oxford U.; MA, Worcester Coll., Oxford, Eng., 1953. Pub. NY Post, 1976—86, 2005; CEO News Corp., 1979—, chmn., 1991—; dir. BSkyB, 1990—, chmn., DirecTV Group, 2003—07. Owner, pub. numerous newspapers, mags. and TV ops. in U.S.A., Australia, U.K., Asia; bd. dirs. Philip Morris Cos. Inc., 1989-2002, China Netcom Group Corp. Ltd., 2001-05, chmn. STAR Group Ltd., 1993-98 Companion of the Order of Australia, 1984; Knight Order of St. Gregory the Great, 1998; named one of World's 100 Most Influential People, Time Mag. 2005, Forbes Richest Ams., 1999-, 50 Who Matter Now, CNNMoney.com Bus. 2.0, 2006, 2007, Forbes Richest People, 1999-. Avocation: sailing. Office: News Corp 8th Fl 1211 Avenue Of The Americas New York NY 10036

MURDOCH, WILLIAM WILSON, ecologist, educator; b. Glassford, Scotland, Jan. 28, 1939; came to US, 1963; m. Joan Murdoch; children: Helen, Stephen. BSc with honors in Zoology, U. Glasgow, Scotland, 1960; PhD in Population Ecology, Oxford U., Eng., 1963. Postdoctoral rschr. U. Mich., Ann Arbor, 1963—65; asst. prof. U. Calif., Santa Barbara, 1965—69, assoc. prof., 1969—74, prof. biology, 1974—, chair biol. scis. dept., 1991—95, Charles A. Storke II prof. biology, 2000—, dir. Natural Res. Sys., 2001—. Chmn. Marine Rev. Com., Santa Barbara, 1980; vis. prof. Imperial Coll., London, Adelaide U., Canberra U., Australia, U. Mich., U. Strathclyde, Glasgow, U. Calif., Berkeley, Internat. Ctr. Insect Physiology and Ecology, Nairobi, Kenya; bd. dirs. Nature Conservancy, 2000—; founding dir. Nat. Ctr. Ecol. Analysis and Synthesis, Santa Barbara. Author: Poverty of Nations, 1980; contbr. articles to sci. jours., chpts. to books; editor various sci. books; editor-in-chief Issues in Ecology, 2002-. Recipient Huffaker medal in Population Biology, U. Calif., Berkeley, Disting. Scientist award, Internat. Orgn. Biol. Control, Outstanding Svc. award, Am. Inst. Biol. Scis., 2007; grantee, NSF, 1970—; Guggenheim fellow, 1977—78. Mem. Ecol. Soc. Am. (Robert H. MacArthur award 1990-91), Brit. Ecol. Soc., Am. Soc. Naturalists (Pres.'s award 1985), Am. Acad. Arts & Scis. Office: Dept Ecology Evolution & Marine Biology U Calif Santa Barbara CA 93106-9610 Office Phone: 805-893-4887. Office Fax: 805-893-3777. E-mail: murdoch@lifesci.ucsb.edu. *

MURDOCK, CHARLES WILLIAM, lawyer, educator; b. Chgo., Feb. 10, 1935; s. Charles C. and Lucille Marie (Tracy) Murdock; m. Mary Margaret Hennessy, May 25, 1963; children: Kathleen, Michael, Kevin, Sean. BSChemE, Ill. Inst. Tech., 1956; JD cum laude, Loyola U., Chgo., 1963. Bar: Ill. 1963, Ind. 1971. Asst. prof. law DePaul U., 1968-69; assoc. prof. law U. Notre Dame, 1969-75; prof., dean Law Sch. Loyola U., Chgo., 1975-83, 86—; dep. atty. gen. State of Ill., Chgo., 1983-86; of counsel Chadwell & Kayser, Ltd., 1986-89. Vis. prof. U. Calif., 1974; cons. Pay Bd., summer 1972, SEC, summer 1973; co-founder Loyola U. Family Bus. Program; arbitrator Chgo. Bd. Options Exch., Nat. Assn. Securities Dealers, N.Y. Stock Exch., Am. Arbitration Assn.; co-founder, mem. exec. com. Loyola Family Bus. Ctr., 1990—; bd. dirs. Plymouth Tube Co., 1993—. Author: Business Organizations, 2 vols., 1996; editor: Illinois Business Corporation Act Annotated, 2 vols., 1975; tech. editor The Business Lawyer, 1989-90. Chmn. St. Joseph County (Ind.) Air Pollution Control Bd., 1971; bd. dirs. Nat. Center for Law and the Handicapped, 1973-75, Minority Venture Capital Inc., 1973-75. Capt. USMCR. Mem. ABA, Ill. Bar Assn. (cert. of award for continuing legal edn.), Chgo. Bar Assn. (cert. of award for continuing legal edn., bd. mgrs. 1976-78), Ill. Inst. Continuing Legal Edn. (adv. com.) Roman Catholic. Home: 2126 Thornwood Ave Wilmette IL 60091-1452 Office: Loyola U Sch Law 1 E Pearson St Chicago IL 60611-2055 Office Phone: 312-915-7142. Business E-Mail: cmurdoc@luc.edu.

MURDOCK, DAVID H., food products executive; b. Kansas City, Mo., Apr. 10, 1923; m. Gabriele Bryant Murdock (dec. 1985); children: Gene, David H. Jr., Justin M.; m. Tracy Vakzad. LLD (hon.), Pepperdine U., 1978; LHD (hon.), U. Nebr., 1984, Hawaii Loa Coll., 1989. Sole proprietor, chmn., CEO Murdock Holding Co. (formerly Pacific Holding Co.), LA, 1995—; chmn., CEO Dole Food Co., LA, 1985—2007, chmn., 2007—; owner, chmn. Castle & Cooke, Inc., 1985—. CEO Huntington Tile, Yankie Hill Brick, Murdock Devel. Corp., Wiscassett Mills, Flexi-Van Leasing, Goettel, Stair Co., Ventura Farms. Trustee Asia Soc., N.Y.C., L.A.; founder, bd. dirs. Found. for Advanced Brain Studies, L.A.; bd. visitors UCLA Grad. Sch. Mgmt.;bd. govs. Performing Arts Coun. of Music Ctr., L.A.; bd. govs. East-West Ctr., L.A.; patron Met. Opera, N.Y.C. With USAAC, 1943-45. Served US Army. Named one of Forbes' Richest Americans, 1999—, Forbes' Exec. Pay, 1999—, World's Richest People, Forbes mag., 2001—. Mem. Regency Club (founder, pres.) Bel-Air Bay Country Club, Sherwood Country Club (founder, pres.), Met. Club (N.Y.C.). Office: Murdock Holding Co 10900 Wilshire Blvd Ste 1600 Los Angeles CA 90024-6530 *

MURDOCK, DORIS DEAN, special education educator, program developer; b. Pacific Junction, Iowa, Feb. 7, 1913; m. Myron J. Murdock, June 28, 1933; 1 child, John Timothy. BS in Elem. Edn., So. Oreg. U., 1964; MS in Remedial Edn., U. Oreg., 1968. Primary tchr. Days Creek Elem. Sch., Oreg., 1962—66, Grants Pass Dist., 1966—67, Riddle Elem., Riddle, Oreg., 1968—71; founder, dir. Plowshare Sch., Rogue River, Oreg., 1972—78, Child Life Sanctuary, Rogue River, 1978—88; founder, dir., special education program developer Ctr. for Habilitation Living, Grants Pass, 1989—. Author: No Thank You! No Ritalin for Me Today!, 2003. Vol. Peace Corp., 1978—80. Mem.: Coun. for Exceptional Children (life). Republican. Seventh Day Adventist. Office: Ctr for Habilitative Living Inc 4493 Jerome Prairie Grants Pass OR 97527

MURDOCK, GLENN, state supreme court justice; b. Enterprise, Ala., June 25, 1956; s. Billy A. and Marita H. Murdock; m. Margaret Gilchrist; children: Emily, Bailey, John Taylor. BA summa cum laude, U. Ala., 1978; JD, U. Va. Law Sch., 1981. Law clk. United Dist. Judge (No. Ala. dist.) Clarence W. Allgood; atty. Wallace, Jordan, Ratliff & Brandt, Birmingham/Montgomery, Ala., 1992—; judge Ala. Ct. Civil Appeals, 2001—07; assoc. justice Ala. Supreme Ct., 2007—. Mem.: Ala. Bar Assn., Birmingham Bar. Assn., Birmingham Rotary Club, Phi Beta Kappa. Office: Ala Supreme Ct 300 Dexter Ave Montgomery AL 36104

MURDOCK, IAN, information technology executive; m. Debra Murdock; children: Regan, Keely, Nolan. BS in Computer Sci., Purdue Univ., 1996; attended grad. sch. in computer sci., Univ. Ariz., 1997—2000. Staff programmer Univ. Ariz., 1997—2000; co-founder, chmn., chief stategist Progeny, 2000; chief tech. officer Free Standards Group, Linux Found. (formed through merger of OSDL and the Free Standards Group); chair Linux Standard Base; chief operating platforms officer Sun Microsystems, Inc., 2007—. Founding dir. Linux Internat., 1993—95, Open Source Initiative, 1998—2001. Host (web blog) ianmurdock.com. Achievements include being founder of the Debian project in 1993. Avocations: reading, history, politics, music, gardening, investing. Office: Sun Microsystems Inc 4150 Network Circle Santa Clara CA 95054 E-mail: imurdock@imurdock.com. *

MURDOCK, PAMELA ERVILLA, travel and advertising company executive; b. LA, Dec. 3, 1940; d. John James and Chloe Conger (Keefe) M.; children: Cheryl (dec.), Kim. BA, U. Colo., 1962. Pres. Dolphin Travel, Denver, 1972-87; owner, pres. Mile Hi Tours, Denver, 1973—, MH Internat., 1987—, Mile Hi Advt. Agy., 1986—. Bd. dirs. Rocky Mountain chpt. Juvenile Diabetes Found. Internat., 1994-2000; exec. bd. Rocky Mountain Father's Day Coun., 1998, 99. Named Wholesaler of Yr., Las Vegas Conv. and Visitors Authority, 1984; recipient Leadership award Nat. Multiple Sclerosis Soc., 1996. Mem.: NAFE, Nat. Fedn. Ind. Businessmen, Am. Soc. Travel Agts. Republican. Personal E-mail: pamelaemurdock@aol.com. Business E-Mail: pamm@milehitours.com.

MURDOCK, ROBERT MEAD, curator; b. NYC, Dec. 18, 1941; s. Robert Davidson and Elizabeth Brundage (Mead) M.; m. Ellen Rebecca Olson, Apr. 22, 1967 (div.); children: Alison Mead, Anne Davidson; m. Deborah C. Ryan, Apr. 28, 1995. BA, Trinity Coll., Conn., 1963; MA, Yale U., 1965; student, Mus. Mgmt. Inst., U. Calif., Berkeley, 1980. Ford Found. intern Walker Art Center, Mpls., 1965-67; curator Albright-Knox Art Gallery, Buffalo, 1967-70; curator contemporary art Dallas Mus. Fine Arts, 1970-78; dir. Grand Rapids (Mich.) Art Mus., 1978-83; chief curator Walker Art Ctr., Mpls., 1983-85; program dir. IBM Gallery of Sci. and Art, NYC, 1985-87, 90-93; dir. exhbns. Am. Fedn. Arts, NYC, 1987-88. Panelist, cons. Nat. Endowment for Arts, 1974-90. Author: (with others) Tyler Graphics: The Extended Image, 1987, A Gallery of Modern Art, 1994, Paris Modern, The Swedish Ballet 1920-1925, 1995, Works by Leland Bell, 1950's-1991, 2001, Constellation, Pavel Zoubok Gallery, NYC, 2006; contbr. articles on David Novros, William Conlon, 1985, Bill Freeland, 1989, Nassos Daphnis, 1990, Cai Guo-Qiang, 1998, John Evans, 2004; exhbn. catalogues Early 20th Century Art from Midwestern Museums, 1981, Berlin/Hanover: The 1920's, 1977, Richard Tuttle: Books and Prints, 1996, Lesley Dill, 1998, Jim Torok, 1999, Debra Bermingham, 2002. Nat. Endowment for Arts fellow, 1973 Home and Office: 8 W 13th St 10F New York NY 10011

MURDOCK, TULLISSE ANTOINETTE (TONI MURDOCK), academic administrator; BS, MA, N. Mex. State U.; PhD, U. Ariz.; grad. HERS, Bryn Mawr Inst. Women in Higher Edn., 1988. Adminstr. Western Wyo. Coll., faculty; asst. dean coll. arts and scis. U. Ariz.; assoc. provost of programs Seattle U., 1989—97; pres. Antioch U., Seattle, 1997—. Office: Antioch U 2326 Sixth Ave Seattle WA 98121-1814

MURDOCK, WENDY JEAN, management consultant; b. Montreal, Que., Can., Aug. 28, 1952; came to U.S., 1983; d. James David and Bernice Evelyn (Dean) M. BA, McGill U., 1973; MBA, U. Western Ont., 1982. Assoc. McKinsey & Co. Inc., NYC, 1982-87, ptnr., fin. inst. practice, 1988—93; dir. strategic planning Salomon Smith Barney, NYC, 1993—98; COO, high net worth group Citicorp Asset Mgmt., NYC, 1998—2002; cons., merchant banking practice Putnam Lowell NBF, 2004—05; chief product officer MasterCard Worldwide, Purchase, NY, 2005—. Office: MasterCard Worldwide 2000 Purchase St Purchase NY 10577 *

MURDY, WAYNE WILLIAM, mining company executive, financial officer; b. LA, July 4, 1944; s. Lee Robert and Louise Marie (Kleinemas) M.; m. Diana Yvonne DeCruse, Nov. 23, 1968; children: Dawn Marie, Christopher John, Joseph William, Elizabeth Anne. AA, El Camino Coll., 1966; BS, Calif. State U., Long Beach, 1968. C.P.A., Calif. With Atlantic Richfield Co., Los Angeles, 1969-78; gen. auditor Getty Oil Co., Los Angeles, 1978-81; group v.p. Texaco Trading & Transp. Inc., Denver, 1981-87; sr. v.p., chief fin. officer Apache Corp., Denver, 1987-92, Newmont Mining Corp., Denver, 1992—99, pres., 1999—2002, CEO, 2001—07, chmn., 2002—. Mem. Am. Inst. C.P.A.s Clubs: University (Denver); Village (Cherry Hills Village, Colo.). Roman Catholic. Office: Newmont Mining Corp 1 Norwest Ctr 1700 Lincoln Ste Denver CO 80203-4500 *

MUREN, DENNIS E., special effects expert; b. Glendale, Calif., Nov. 1, 1946; s. Elmer Ernest and Charline Louise (Clayton) M.; m. Zara Pinfold, Aug. 29, 1981; children: Gregory, Gwendolen. AA, Pasadena City Coll., Calif., 1966; student, Calif. State U., LA. Freelance spl. effects expert, 1968-75; camera operator Cascade of Calif., Hollywood, 1975-76; visual effects dir. photography Indsl. Light & Magic, San Rafael, Calif., 1976-80, visual effects dir., 1980—. Guest speaker Berlin Film Festival, UCLA, Film Dept., U. Calif. Berkeley Film Series, Liverpool (Eng.) U. Film Program, Mill Valley Film Festival Program, Siggraph '86, Siggraph '87, Am. Film Inst., Portland Creative Conf. '89. Cameraman, photographer various films including Star Wars, 1977, Close Encounters of the Third Kind, 1977, Battlestar Galactica, 1978, The Empire Strikes Back, 1980 (Oscar award); visual effects supr. films include Dragonslayer, 1981 (Oscar nomination), ET: The Extraterrestrial, 1982 (Oscar award), Return of the Jedi, 1983 (Oscar award, Brit. Acad. of Film and TV award), Indiana Jones and the Temple of Doom, 1984 (Oscar award, Brit. Acad. of Film and TV award), Young Sherlock Holmes, 1985 (Oscar nomination), Captain Eo, 1986, Star Tours, 1986, Innerspace, 1987 (Oscar award), Empire of the Sun, 1987, Willow, 1988 (Oscar nomination), Ghostbusters II, 1989, The Abyss, 1989 (Oscar award), Terminator 2, 1991 (Oscar award, Brit. Film and TV award), Jurassic Park, 1993 (Oscar award, Brit. Film and TV award), Casper, 1995; visual effects supr. (TV program) Caravan of Courage (Emmy award); creative advisor Twister, 1995, Mission Impossible, 1995, Jurassic Park: The Lost World, 1997 (Academy award nomination), Star Wars: The Phantom Menace, 1999, (Acad. award nomination, Saturn award for best visual effects, Best Action Sequence award MTV), A.I., 2001 (acad. award nomination), Star Wars: The Attack of the Clones, 2002, The Hulk, 2003, The Day After Toorrow, 2004, War of the Worlds 2005 (Acad. award nomination, Hollywood Film Festival award for Best Visual Effects); prodr., dir. The Equinox, 1967. Recipient Acad. Sci./Tech. Award for the devel. of a Motion Picture Figure Mover for animation photography, 1981, Edit/VES Honors award, 2003; star on Hollywood Walk of Fame, 1999. Mem.: Visual Effects Soc. (Lifetime Achievement award 2007), Acad. Motion Picture Arts and Scis., Am. Soc. Cinematographers. Office: Indsl Light & Magic Box 29909 San Francisco CA 94129-0909

MURGATROYD, ERIC NEAL, data processing executive; b. Ware, Mass., July 30, 1950; s. Howard E. and Jean Francis M.; m. Pamela Lee Swift, Aug. 14, 1976 (div. Dec. 1992); 1 child, Lisa Nicole; m. Donna K. Goodwin, Sept. 4, 1999. Student, U. Mass, 1968—70; BSc in Computer Sci., Almeda U., 2004. Computer operator Hammond Organ Co., Chgo., 1972—73; sys. analyst Ctrl. States Health, Welfare and Pension Funds, Chgo., 1973—78; sr. analyst sys. Gould-Fluid Components Divsn., Niles, Ill., 1978—80; project leader mfg. sys. Motorola Corp., Schaumburg, Ill., 1980—85; mgr. billing sys. Cellular Billing Sys., Inc., Park Ridge, Ill., 1985—86; dir. info. sys. Leaf, Inc., Lake Forest, Ill., 1986—97; dir. applications devel. Jockey Internat., Kenosha, Wis., 1997—98; ind. IT cons. Y2K Audit, 1998—99; mgr. IT bus. processes TeleHub Network Svcs., Gurnee, Ill., 1999—2000; mgr. data warehouse Ajilon, Inc., Itasca, Ill., 2000—01; IT bus. cons. Data Warehousing, 2000—02; IT project mgr. quality mgmt., sr. EAI sys. analyst Washington Mut. Bank, FA, Vernon Hills, Ill., 2003—06; project mgr. Triple AAA Auto Club/CSAA, 2007—. Author computer programs and computer architecture. Mem. Project Mgmt. Inst., Mensa. Avocations: camping, swimming, coin collecting/numismatics, golf. Home and Office: 7147 W Desert mirage Dr Peoria AZ 85383 E-mail: emurgatroyd@yahoo.com.

MURGUIA, JANET, non-profit organization administrator; BS in Journalism, Kans. U., 1982, BA in Spanish, 1982, JD, 1985. Legis. coun. to Rep. Jim Slattery US Ho. Reps., Washington, 1987—94; various postions including dep. asst. to Pres. Clinton, dep. dir. legis. affairs, sr. liaison to Congress Washington, 1994—2000; exec. vice. chancellor univ. rels. U. Kans., 2001—04; exec. dir., COO Nat. Coun. La Raza, Washington, 2004, pres., CEO, 2005—. Bd. trustees YouthFriends. Named one of 100 Top Latinas, Hispanic mag., 100 Most Influential Hispanics, Hispanic Bus. mag., 80 Elite Hispanic Women.

MURIEL, AMADOR CRUZ, physicist; b. Marikina, Philippines, Nov. 24, 1939; came to the U.S., 1963; s. Amado and Lucena (Cruz) M.; children: Anna Christina, Rosemarie. MA, SUNY, Stony Brook, 1965, PhD, 1968. Assoc. prof. Hostos Community Coll., Bronx, N.Y., 1972-79, acting dean, 1979-80; v.p. Burlington County (N.J.) Coll., 1980-81; project mgr. Citibank, NYC, 1981-82; assoc. prof. CUNY-Baruch Coll., NYC, 1982-85; pres. Data Transport Systems, NYC, 1985—. Cons. UN, N.Y.C., Geneva, Austria, 1985—. Editor: Stellar Dynamics I, II, 1980, Stellar Evolution, 1980; contbr. articles to Phys. Rev., Physica, Physics Letters. Rockefeller Found. scholar, 1965-68, All Nations Women's Group scholar, 1957, Fulbright scholar, 1963. Mem. Am. Phys. Soc., AAAS. Achievements include discovery of occurrence of traveling depressions in density evolution of one-dimensional gravitational system; development of Prigogine results without diagrams in non-equilibrium statistical mechanics; research in molecular theory of turbulence. Home: 347 E 62nd St New York NY 10021-7755 Office: Data Transport Systems 347 E 62nd St New York NY 10021-7755 Office Phone: 347-782-1215. Personal E-mail: amador_muriel@msn.com.

MURILLO, JOSE R., JR., pharmacist; s. Jose R. and Imelda Murillo; m. Michelle U. Bui, May 21, 2005. BS, U. Tex., San Antonio, 1997; PharmD, U Tex., Austin, 2002. Pharmacy resident VA North Tex. Health Care Sys., Dallas, 2002—03; oncology pharmacy resident Audie L. Murphy Vets. Hosp., San Antonio, 2003—04; clin. pharmacist Meth. Hosp., Houston, 2004—. Mem.: Hematology Oncology Pharmacy Assn., Tex. Soc. Health-Sys. Pharmacists, Am. Soc. Health-Sys Pharmacists, Am. Coll. Clin. Pharmacy, Am. Soc. Clin. Oncology (assoc.).

MURILLO-ROHDE, ILDAURA MARIA, marriage and family therapist, consultant, educator, retired dean; b. Garachine, Panama; came to U.S., 1945; d. Amalio Murillo and Ana E. (Diaz) de Murillo; m. Erling Rohde, Sept. 19, 1959. BS, Columbia U., 1951, MA, 1953; diploma (hon.), Escuela Nat. de Enfermeria, Guatemala, 1964; MEd, Columbia U., 1969; PhD, NYU, 1971; diploma (hon.), Centro Estudios Naturista, Barcelona, Spain, 1992. RN; lic. marriage and family therapist, N.J.; cert. mental health-psychiat. nursing, ANA; lic. sex. therapist, N.J. Instr., supr. Bellevue Psychiat. Hosp., NYC, 1950-54; asst. dir., dir. psychiat. div. Wayne County Gen. Hosp., Eloise, Mich., 1954-56; chief nurse psychiat. div. Elmhurst Gen. Hosp., Queens, N.Y., 1956-58, Met. Hosp. Med. Ctr., NYC, 1961-63; psychiat. cons. to govt. of Guatemala WHO, UN, Guatemala, 1963-64; assoc. prof., chmn. psychiat. dept. N.Y. Med. Coll. Grad. Sch. Nursing, NYC, 1964-69; dir. mental health-psychiatry, asst. prof. NYU, NYC, 1970-72; assoc. prof. Hostos Coll., CUNY, NYC, 1972-76; assoc. dean. acad. affairs, prof. U. Wash., Seattle, 1976-81; prof., dean Coll. of Nursing SUNY, Downstate Med. Ctr., Bklyn., 1981-85; dean and prof. emeritus SUNY, Bklyn., 1985—. Bd. dirs. Puerto Rican Family Inst., N.Y.C., 1983—96; dir. Latin Am. Oncological Nurses Fuld Fellowships, 1989-90; psychiat. cons. Sch. Nursing, U. Antioquia, Medellin, Colombia, 1972-73, WHO; psychiat./rsch. cons. for master program Sch. Nursing, U. Panama, Project Hope, 1986; dir., leader mental-psychiat. interdisciplinary group to study the Chinese family after 30 yrs. of communism People to People Amb. Program, 1985. Editor: National Directory of Hispanic Nurses, 1981, 2d edit., 1986, 3d edit., 1994; contbr. numerous articles to profl. nat. and internat. jours., chpts. to books in field. Bd. dirs. Nat. Coalition of Hispanic Mental Health and Human Svcs. Orgns., 1974-84, chmn. bd., 1980-84; mem. Wash. State adv. com. U.S. Commn. on Civil Rights, Seattle, 1977-81; nat. adv. com. White House Conf. on Families, Washington, D.C., 1979-81; pres. King County Health Planning Coun., Seattle, 1979-81; exec. com. Puget Sound Health Systems Agy., Seattle, 1979-81; mem. bd. advisors Marquis Who's Who, 1983-91; mem. Mosby Consumer Health's Hispanic adv. bd., 1996. Univ. Honors scholar NYU, 1972; named Citizen of the Day, Radio Sta. KIXI and N.W. Airlines, Seattle, 1979, Disting. lectr. Sigma Theta Tau, 1988-89, Woman of Yr., N.Y. Gotham Club Bus. and Profl. Women, 1989; recipient 1st Nat. Intercultural Nursing award Coun. of Intercultural Nursing, ANA, New Orleans, 1984, Women's Honors in Pub. Svc. award Minority Fellowship Programs and Cabinet Human Rights, ANA, 1986, Disting. Alumna award Divsn. Nursing, NYU Alumni Assn., 1989, 1st Nat. Dr. Hildegard Peplau award for outstanding svcs. in mental health, psychiat. nursing, edn., rsch. and practice, Las Vegas conv. ANA, 1992, Practice award Tchrs. Coll., Columbia U. Nursing Edn. Alumni, 1994; designated Living Legend for leadership in practice, edn. and rsch. Am. Acad. Nursing, 1994; inducted into Nursing Hall of Fame, Columbia U., 1999; bd. advisors Marquis Who's Who, 1991-99. Fellow Am. Assn. Marriage and Family Therapy; mem. ANA (affirmative action task force 1974-84, commn. human rights, cabinet human rights, rep. ANA at ICN Cong. Tokyo 1977, spokesperson Nat. Health Ins., conceived and designed Coun. Intercultural Nursing), Am. Orthopsychiat. Assn. (bd. dirs. 1976-79, treas. 1986-89, Presdl. nominee 1980, 93), N.Y. Assn. Marriage and Family Therapy (pres. 1973-76), Nat. Assn. Hispanic Nurses (founder, 1st pres. 1976-80), Internat. Fedn. Bus. and Profl. Women (UN rep. to UNICEF London, 1987—, del. to World UN Summit for Children N.Y.C. 1990, UN N.Y. Com. for Internat. Yr. of Family 1994, Hall of Fame for Outstanding Achievements in Field of Sci., Rsch., Mental Health-Psychiatry, 4th edit., 1995), Am. Rsch. Inst. (dep. govt. 1987), NYU Club, Gotham Bus. and Profl. Women's Club. Democrat. Avocations: travel, reading, music, stamp collecting/philately, skiing. Home: 300 W 108th St Apt 12A New York NY 10025-2704 Office: SUNY Bklyn Coll Nursing Box 22 450 Clarkson Ave Brooklyn NY 11203-2056 E-mail: murillorohde@aol.com.

MURIS, TIMOTHY JOSEPH, former federal agency administrator, lawyer, educator; b. Massillon, Ohio, Nov. 18, 1949; s. George William and Louise (Hood) M.; children: Matthew Allen, Paul Austin; m. Pam Harmon, June 27, 1997. BA in economics, history, and polit. sci., San Diego State U., 1971; JD, UCLA, 1974. Bar: Calif. 1974, DC. Asst. to the dir. planning office FTC, Washington, 1974-76, dir. Bur. Consumer Protection, 1981-83, dir. Bur. Competition, 1983-85, chmn., 2001—04; exec. assoc. dir. Office Mgmt. and Budget, Washington, 1985—88, cons., 1988—89; law and economics fellow U. Chgo. Law Sch., 1979-80; asst. prof. antitrust and consumer law U. Miami Law Sch. and Law Economics Ctr., Fla., 1976-79, assoc. prof., 1979-81, prof., 1981-83; Found. prof. law George Mason U. Sch. Law, Arlington, Va., 1988—2001, 2005—, interim dean, 1996-97; of counsel Collier, Shannon, Rill & Scott, 1992—2000, Howrey, Simon, Arnold & White, 2000—01, O'Melveny & Myers LLP, Washington, 2004—, co-chair antitrust/competition practice. Dep. counsel Presdl. Task Force on Regulatory Relief, Washington, 1981; cons. Coun. on Wage and Price Stability, Washington, 1981; mem. Nat. Issues Forum, Brookings Inst., 1986-88; mem. adv. bd. Antitrust and Trade Regulation Report, 1990—; testified before numerous congressional committees on antitrust, consumer protection, and regulatory/budget issues. Assoc. editor, UCLA Law Review, 1973-74; editor: The Federal Trade Commission since 1970: Regulation and Bureaucratic Behavior, 1981; author and co-author of books, monographs and articles. Mem. Reagan-Bush transition team for FTC, Washington, 1980; sr. advisor Bush-Quayle transition team, 1988-89. Am. Bar Found. affiliated scholar, 1979 Mem. ABA (antitrust sect., 1983-, antitrust law spl. com. to study role of FTC 1988-89), Calif. Bar Assn., Order of Coif, Phi Kappa Phi, Phi Eta Sigma. Office: O'Melveny & Myers LLP 1625 Eye St NW Washington DC 20006 also: George Mason U Sch Law 3301 Fairfax Dr Arlington VA 22201 Office Phone: 202-383-5350. Office Fax: 202-383-5414. Business E-Mail: tmuris@omm.com. E-mail: tmuris@gmu.edu.

MURKETT, PHILIP TILLOTSON, human resource executive; b. Chattanooga, Apr. 3, 1931; s. Philip Tillotson and Dorothy (Ingram) M.; m. Mary Jane Brewer, Dec. 10, 1960 (dec.); children: Emmette, Mary Jane Easter, Leanne. BA, Duke U., 1954; MBA, U. Pa., 1957; postgrad., Warnboro Coll., Oxford, England, 1980. Methods engr. Westinghouse Elec. Co., Staunton, Va., 1957-60; adminstrv. mgr. Vulcan Materials Co., Birmingham, Ala., 1960-68; human resources mgr. Blount, Inc., Montgomery, Ala., 1968-74; pres. Murkett Enterprises Inc., Montgomery, 1974—. Adj. instr. Auburn U., Montgomery, Ala.; with internat. affairs Yonok Coll., Lampang, Thailand; search cons. Murkett Assocs., Montgomery, 1974—; bd. advisors Digitech Inc. Author: Use & Value of References, 1957; editor (newsletter) H.R. Quar., 1983. Pres. Montgomery Mus. Fine Art, 1982, Cmty. Concert Assn., Montgomery, 1982, Montgomery Symphony Assn., 1987; pres. Am.-Thai Edn. Devel. Found. Inc., 1991, bd. dirs. 1990; bd. dirs. Ala. World Affairs Coun., 1997; jr. warden Episcopal Ch. of Ascension, 1972. Recipient Gov.'s Arts award Ala. Arts Coun., 1983, commendation from crown princess of Thailand, 1992. Mem. Montgomery C. of C. (task chair 1983), Montgomery Country Club, Capitol City Club, Kiwanis (bd. dirs. 1972), Delta Tau Delta (chpt. v.p. 1953). Avocations: gardening, swimming, music, tennis, geneology. Office: PO Box 527 Montgomery AL 36101-0527

MURKISON, EUGENE COX, finance educator; b. Donalsonville, Ga., July 2, 1936; s. Jeff and Ollie Mae (Shores) Murkison; m. Marilyn Louise Adams, July 3, 1965; children: James, David, Jennifer. Grad., US Army JFK Spl. Warfare Sch., 1967, US Naval War Coll., 1972, US Army Command/Staff Coll., 1974; BS, U. Ga., Athens, 1959; MBA, U. Rochester, NY, 1970; PhD, U. Mo., 1986. Surveyor USDA, Donalsonville, 1956—59; commd. 2d lt. US Army, 1959, advanced through grades to lt. col., 1974, inf. bn. leader Vietnam, 1967—68; mechanized comdr. (G-3), ops. officer Brigade Exec. Officer, Korea, Europe and US, 1968—70; prof. leadership & psychology West Point, NY, 1970—73; ops. officer (J-3) Office of Chmn. Joint Chiefs of Staff, Washington, 1974—77; prof. mil. sci. and leadership Kemper Mil. Coll., 1977—81; ret. US Army, 1981; instr. U. Mo., Columbia, 1981—84; asst. prof. Ga. So. U., Stateboro, 1984—89, assoc. prof., 1989—94, prof., 1995—, chair grad. curriculum & programs task force, 1996—99. Vis. prof. mgmt. and bus. U. Tirgoviste, Romania, 1994—96, 1998—2000; vis. prof. human resource mgmt. Tech. U. Romania, Cluj-Napoca, 1998—2000; chmn. grad. programs curriculum com. GSU, 1998—2002. Author (with Gheroghe Ionescu): Human Behavior in Organizations, 2000; contbr. articles to profl. jours., chapters to books. Adminstrv. bd. Pittman Pk. Meth. Ch., Statesboro, 1986—, trustee, 1992—99, chmn., trustee, 1995—96, mem. staff parish com., 2000—04, chair memls. com., 2005—. Decorated Bronze Star with oak leaf cluster; recipient Tchg. award, U. Mo., 1983, Devel. award, Ga. So. U., 1990, Albert Burke Rsch. award, 1992, Internat. Educator of the Yr. award, Rutherford award for Excellence in Grad. Rsch. and Edn., 2006, Grad. Instrn. and Svc. award, McIntosh, 2006, others; grantee, IREX, 1994, SOROS, 1995, 1996. Mem.: VFW, Ga. Hist. Soc., Bus. History Conf., Acad. Mgmt., Internat. Acad. Bus. (program chair 1994, 1995, Best Paper award 10th Ann. Conv., McGregor Grad. Tchg. award 2006), Inst. Info. and Mgmt. Sci., So. Mgmt. Assn., Inst. Mgmt. Sci., Mil. Order World Wars, Newcomen Soc., Kiwanis Club Statesboro, Scabbard & Blade, Blue Key, Alpha Zeta, Beta Gamma Sigma. Republican. Avocations: history, hiking, boating, farming. Office: Ga So U Coll Bus Adminstrn Statesboro GA 30460-8154 Office Phone: 912-681-0318. Business E-Mail: murkison@georgiasouthern.edu.

MURKOWSKI, FRANK HUGHES, former governor, former senator; b. Seattle, Mar. 28, 1933; s. Frank Michael and Helen (Hughes) M.; m. Nancy Rena Gore, Aug. 28, 1954; children: Carol Victoria Murkowski Sturgulewski, Lisa Ann Murkowski Martell, Frank Michael, Eileen Marie Murkowski Van Wyhe, Mary Catherine Murkowski Judson, Brian Patrick. Student, Santa Clara U., Calif., 1952—53; BA in Econs., Seattle U., 1955. With Pacific Nat. Bank of Seattle, 1957-58, Nat. Bank of Alaska, Anchorage, 1959-67; asst. v.p., mgr. Nat. Bank of Alaska (Wrangell br.),

1963-66; v.p. charge bus. devel. Nat. Bank of Alaska, Anchorage, 1966-67; commr. dept. econ. devel. State of Alaska, Juneau, 1967-70; pres. Alaska Nat. Bank, Fairbanks, 1971-80; US Senator from Alaska Washington, 1981—2002; ranking mem. Com. on Energy and Natural Resources; mem. Com. on Fin., Vets Affairs Com., Indian Affairs Com., Japan-US Friendship Com.; mem. intelligence com. fgn. affairs; gov. State of Alaska, Juneau, 2002—06. Rep. nominee for U.S. Congress from Alaska, 1970; chmn. Can.-U.S. Interparliamentary Group. Former v.p. B.C. and Alaska Bd. Trade; mem. U.S. Holocaust Mus. Coun. Served with U.S. Coast Guard, 1955-57. Mem. AAA, AMVETS, NRA, Am. Legion, Ducks Unlimited, Res. Officer's Assn., Alaska World Affairs Coun., Coalition Am. Vets., Alaska Native Brotherhood, Am. Bankers Assn., Alaska Bankers Assn. (pres. 1973), Young Pres.'s Orgn., Alaska C. of C. (pres. 1977), Anchorage C. of C. (bd. dirs. 1966), Fairbanks C. of C. (bd. dirs. 1973-78), Pioneers of Alaska, Internat. Alaska Nippon Kai, Capital Hill Club, Washington Athletic Club, Elks, Lions. Republican. Catholic. Mailing: PO Box 70049 Fairbanks AK 99707 Personal E-mail: nrgdc@earthlink.net.

MURKOWSKI, LISA ANN, senator; b. Ketchikan, Alaska, May 22, 1957; d. Frank Hughes Murkowski & Nancy 9Gore); m. Verne Martell, Aug. 22, 1987; children: Nicholas, Matthew. BA in Economics, Georgetown U., 1980; JD, Willamette Coll., 1985. Dist. coun. atty., Anchorage, 1987-89; comml. atty. Hoge and Lekisch, 1989-96; pvt. law practice, 1989—96; mem. Alaska Ho. of Reps., Anchorage, 1999—2002, majority leader, 2002; U.S. Senator from Alaska, 2002—. Dir. First Bank; mem. Mayor's Task Force Homeless, 1990-91; state ctrl. com. Dist. 14 Rep. chair, 1993-98; commr. Anchorage Equal Rights Commn., 1997-2002; citizens adv. bd. Joint Com. Mil. Bases in Alaska, 1998—. Trustee Cath. Svcs.; pres. Govt. Hill Elem. PTA; dir. Alaskan Drug Free Youth; mem. YWCA, Arctic Power. Recipient Comunity Leadership award, FBI Dir., 1993, Outstanding Volunteer award, Alaska Sch. Dist., 1998, 2000, Food Safety award, Nat. Food Processors Assn., 2003. Mem. Alaska Bar Assn., Anchorage Bar Assn., Alaska Fedn. Rep. Women (bd. dirs.), Anchorage Rep. Womens Club, Midnight Sun Rep. Women. Republican. Roman Catholic. Address: 510 L St # 550 Anchorage AK 99501 Office: US Senate 709 Hart Senate Office Bldg Washington DC 20510 Office Phone: 202-224-6665. *

MURLEY, SUSAN W., lawyer; b. 1959; BA summa cum laude, Tufts Univ., 1981; JD, Univ. Va., 1986. Bar: Mass. 1986. Assoc. to ptnr., Corp. dept., mem. mgmt. com. Wilmer Cutler Pickering Hale & Dorr, Boston, 1986—. Named a Mass. Super Lawyer, Boston Mag., 2004. Mem.: Mass. Bar Assn., Boston Bar Assn., Phi Beta Kappa. Office: Wilmer Cutler Pickering Hale & Dorr 60 State St Boston MA 02109 Office Phone: 617-526-6832. Office Fax: 617-526-5000. Business E-Mail: susan.murley@wilmerhale.com.

MURNANE, MARGARET MARY, engineering and physics educator; b. Limerick, Ireland, Jan. 23, 1959; d. Matthew and Helen (Bourke) M.; m. Henry Cornelius Kapteyn, Mar. 26, 1987. MSc, U. Coll. Cork, Ireland, 1983; PhD, U. Calif., Berkeley, 1989. Postdoctoral researcher U. Calif., Berkeley, 1990; asst. prof. Wash. State U., Pullman, 1990-95; assoc. prof. U. Mich., Ann Arbor, 1996—99; prof. physics U. Colo., 1999—, fellow, Joint Inst. Lab. Astrophysics. Presdl. Young Investigator awardee NSF, 1991, Sloan Found. fellow, 1992, Presdl. faculty fellow NSF, 1993, John D. and Catherine T. MacArthur fellow, 2000. Mem. NAS, Am. Phys. Soc. (Simon Ramo award 1990, Maria Goeppert-Mayer award 1997), Optical Soc. Am., Soc. Photo-Optical Instrumentation Engrs., Assn. Women in Sci.; Fellow Am. Acad. Arts & Sciences Office: Univ Colo Joint Inst Lab Astrophysics 440 UCB Boulder CO 80309-7789

MURNION, WILLIAM EDWARD, philosopher; b. NYC, Jan. 27, 1933; s. William Edward and Frances Annie (Canavan) M.; m. Deborah Warren Cary, June 14, 1969; children: William Cary, Gregory Thomas. BA, St. Joseph's Coll., 1954; STL, Gregorian U., Rome, 1958, PhD, 1969. Ordained priest Roman Cath. Ch., 1957. Parish priest Roman Cath. Archdiocese of N.Y., 1958—68; lectr. St. John's Sem., Little Rock, 1966-67; asst. prof. Duquesne U., Pitts., 1967-68; faculty fellow Boston Coll., Chestnut Hill, Mass., 1968-69; asst. prof. Newton (Mass.) Coll., 1969-72; prof. Ramapo Coll., Mahwah, NJ, 1972-2000; writer, lectr., counselor PhilosophyWorks, Bellvale, NY, 2000—. Dir. NEH summer seminar, 1992, 95. Author: St. Thomas's Theory of Understanding, 1969; contbr. articles to profl. jours., chpts. to books. Mem. Am. Philos. Assn., Internat. Soc. Philosophy of Law and Social Philosophy, Am. Cath. Philos. Assn., Fedn. Christian Ministries. Avocations: painting, gardening, sports. Office Phone: 845-986-5406. Business E-Mail: philosophyworks@optonline.net.

MUROFF, LAWRENCE ROSS, nuclear medicine physician, educator; b. Phila., Dec. 26, 1942; s. John M. and Carolyn (Kramer) M.; m. Carol R. Savoy, July 12, 1969; children: Michael Bruce, Julie Anne. AB cum laude, Dartmouth Coll., Hanover, NH, 1964, B of Med. Sci., 1965; MD cum laude, Harvard U., Cambridge, Mass., 1967. Diplomate Am. Bd. Radiology, Am. Bd. Nuclear Medicine. Intern Boston City Hosp., Harvard, 1968; resident in radiology Columbia-Presbyn. Med. Ctr., NYC, 1970-73, chief resident, 1973; instr. dept. radiology, asst. radiologist Columbia U. Med. Ctr., NYC, 1973-74; dir. dept. nuc. medicine, computed tomography and MRI Univ. Cmty. Hosp., Tampa, Fla., 1974-94, H. Lee Moffitt Cancer Hosp., Tampa, 1994—; pres. Edn. Symposia Inc., Tampa, 1975-2001; pres., CEO Imaging Cons. Inc., Tampa, 1994—; chmn. bd. Am. Phys. Ptnrs. Inc., Dallas, 1996—98. Clin. asst. prof. radiology U. South Fla., 1974-78, clin. assoc. prof., 1978-82, clin. prof., 1982—; clin. prof. U. Fla., 1988—. Contbr. articles to profl. jours. Lt. comdr. USPHS, 1968-70. Fellow Am. Coll. Nuclear Medicine (disting. fellow., Fla. del.), Am. Coll. Nuclear Physicians (regents 1976-78, pres.-elect 1978, pres. 1979), Am. Coll. Radiology (councilor 1979-80, 91-96, 2001-06, 07, chancellor 1981-87, chmn. commn. on nuclear medicine 1981-87); mem. Am. Assn. Acad. Chief Residents Radiology (chmn. 1973), AMA, Boylston Soc., Fla. Assn. Nuclear Physician (pres. 1976), Fla. Med. Assn., Hillsborough County Med. Assn., Radiol. Soc. N.Am., Soc. Nuclear Medicine (coun. 1975-90, trustee 1980-84, 86-89, pres. Southeastern chpt. 1983, vice chmn. correlative imaging coun. 1983), Fla. Radiol. Soc. (exec. com. 1976-91, treas. 1984, sec. 1985, v.p. 1986, pres. elect 1987, pres. 1988, gold medal 1995), West Coast Radiol. Soc., Soc. Magnetic Resonance Imaging (bd. dirs. 1988-91, chmn. ednl. program 1989, chmn. membership com. 1989-93), Clin. Magnetic Resonance Soc. (pres.-elect 1995-98, pres. 1998-2000, bd. dirs. 1995—). Office: 16804 Avila Blvd Tampa FL 33613-5220 Personal E-mail: lrmuroff@hotmail.com.

MURPHEY, ARTHUR GAGE, JR., law educator; b. Macon, Miss., June 16, 1927; s. Arthur Gage and Elizabeth (Crutcher) Murphey; m. Linda Chaney, May 17, 1975; 1 stepchild, Leslie Jo Pafford;children from previous marriage: Mason Alexander, Arthur Nesbit. Student, Vanderbilt U., 1947—48; AB, U. N.C., 1951; JD, U. Miss., 1953; postgrad., London Sch. Econs., U. London, 1953—54; LLM, Yale U., 1962. Assoc. Satterfield, Ewing, Williams and Shell, Jackson, Miss., 1953; asst. prof. U. Ga., Athens, 1956-58, Emory U., Atlanta, 1958-61, U. Akron (Ohio), 1962-63, assoc. prof., 1963-67; prof. U. Ark., Little Rock, 1967-96, asst. dean Sch. Law, 1970-73, Ark. Bar Found. prof., 1996-97, Ark. Bar Found. prof. emeritus, 1997—. Vis. lectr. Case Western Res. U., Cleve., 1966; vis. prof. U. Miss., 1977. Faculty editor: Jour. Pub. Law, 1958—61; faculty advisor Ga. Bar Jour., 1958—61; contbr. articles to profl. jours. With USAAF, 1945—47. Fulbright scholar, 1953—54, Ford Found. grantee, 1964. Mem.: ABA, Phi Beta Kappa, Beta Theta Pi, Phi Delta Phi. Reformed Episcopal Ch. Home: 1918 Old Forge Dr Little Rock AR 72227-5515 Office: U Ark Sch Law 1201 McMath Ave Little Rock AR 72202-5142

MURPHEY, MURRAY GRIFFIN, history professor; b. Colorado Springs, Colo., Feb. 22, 1928; s. Bradford James and Margaret Winifred (Griffin) M.; children— Kathleen Rachel, Christopher Bradford, Jessica Lenoir. AB, Harvard U., 1949; PhD, Yale U., 1954. Asst. prof. U. Pa., Phila., 1956-61, assoc. prof., 1961-66, prof., 1966-2000, chmn. dept. Am. civilization, 1969-81, 87-94. Author: Development of Peirce's Philosophy, 1961, Our Knowledge of the Historical Past, 1973, (with E. Flower) A History of Philosophy in America, 1977, Philosophical Foundations of Historical Knowledge, 1994, C.I Lewis: The Last Great Pragmatist, 2005. Democrat. Home: 200 Rhyle Ln Bala Cynwyd PA 19004-2324

MURPHEY, ROBERT STAFFORD, pharmaceutical executive; b. Littleton, NC, Oct. 29, 1921; married; 2 children BS, U. Richmond, 1942; MS, U. Va., 1947, PhD in Organic Chemistry, 1949. Rsch. chemist in medicinal chemistry A.H. Robins & Co. Inc., Richmond, Va., 1948-53, dir. chemistry rsch., 1953-55, assoc. dir., 1955-57, dir. rsch., 1957-60, dir. internat. rsch., 1960-66, dir. sci. devel., 1966-82, asst. v.p., 1967-73, dir. sci. devel., v.p., 1973-82, v.p. sci. affairs and corp. devel., 1982-83, sr. v.p. sci. affairs and corp. devel., 1983-87, sr. v.p., dir. new bus. devel., 1983-90; sr. v.p., dir. bus. devel. E.C. Robins Internat., Inc., Glen Allen, Va., 1990—. Mem. AAAS, Am. Chem. Soc., Licensing Exec. Soc. Office: E C Robins Internat Inc 9878 Mayland Dr Richmond VA 23233

MURPHEY, SHEILA ANN, infectious diseases physician, educator, researcher; b. Phila., July 10, 1943; d. William Joseph and Sara Esther (Mallon) M. AB, Chestnut Hill Coll., 1965; MD, Women's Med. Coll. of Pa., 1969. Diplomate Am. Bd. Internal Medicine, Am. Bd. Infectious Diseases. Intern in internal medicine Mt. Sinai Hosp. of NY, 1969—70, resident in internal medicine, 1970—72, instr. internal medicine, 1971—72; fellow infectious diseases U. Pa. Sch. Medicine, Phila., 1972—74, instr. dept. medicine, 1974—75, asst. prof. dept. medicine, 1975—77; chief infectious diseases sect. Phila. Gen. Hosp., 1974—77; attending physician Hosp. U. Pa., Phila. Gen. Hosp., 1974—77; dir. divsn. infectious diseases, asst. prof. medicine Jefferson Med. Coll., Phila., 1977—80, clin. assoc. prof. medicine, 1980—2003; dir. divsn. infectious diseases Thomas Jefferson U., Phila., 1977—88; infection control officer, attending physician Thomas Jefferson U. Hosp., Phila., 1977—2003; br. chief infection control devices br., Office Device Evaluation Ctr. for Devices and Radiologic Health, FDA, Rockville, Md., 2005—. Contbr. articles to profl. jours. Fellow Coll. Physicians Phila.; mem. ACP, Am. Soc. Microbiology, Soc. Healthcare Epidemiology of Am., Infectious Diseases Soc. Am., Alpha Omega Alpha. Democrat. Roman Catholic.

MURPHREE, A. LINN, ophthalmologist; b. Houston, Miss., June 6, 1945; d. John Alan and Maxine (Linn) M. BS, U. Miss., 1967; MD, Baylor Coll., 1972. Cert. Am. Bd. Ophthalmology. Resident affiliated hosps., 1973-76, chief resident ophthalmology, 1975-76; fellow ophthalmic genetics and pediatrics The Wilmer Inst., Johns Hopkins U. Hosp., 1976-77; asst. prof. ophthalmology and pediatrics U. So. Calif., Los Angeles, 1978-83, assoc. prof., 1983—91, prof., 1991—, dir. pediatric and devel. ophthalmology Los Angeles, 1978—; head, div. ophthalmology Children's Hosp. Los Angeles, 1978—, dir. Clayton Found. Ctr. Ocular Oncology, 1978—; chief med. ops. Childrens Hosp. of Los Angeles, 1986-87. Profl. adv. com. Blind Children's Ctr., Los Angeles, 1980—; med. adv. bd. Nat. Assn. Visually Handicapped, 1980—. Contbr. numerous articles to profl. jours. Served to capt. med. corps., USAR, 1972-80. Dolly Green scholar Research to Prevent Blindness, 1984, Fulbright scholar U. Copenhagen, 1967-68; Medical Genetics fellow Baylor Coll. of Med. Affiliated Hosps., 1972-73. Mem. Calif. Assn. Ophthalmology, Calif. Med. Assn., Los Angeles County Med. Assn., Los Angeles Ophthalmol. Soc., Los Angeles Pediatric Soc., Ophthalmology Research Study Club Los Angeles, Pacific Coast Oto-Ophthalmol. Soc., Salerni Collegium, Am. Acad. Ophthalmology (honor award 1983), Am. Assn. Pediatric Ophthalmology and Strabismus, Am. Orthoptic Council, Assn. Research in Vision and Ophthalmology, Ophthalmic Genetics Study Club, Am. Bd. Ophthalmology (assoc. examiner), Internat. Soc. Genetic Eye Disease (sec. 1986—). Office: Childrens Hosp Los Angeles 4650 Sunset Blvd Mailstop 88 Los Angeles CA 90027-6016

MURPHREY, ELIZABETH HOBGOOD, history professor, librarian; b. Rocky Mount, NC, Mar. 22, 1947; d. Isaac Green and Ernestine Ragsdale (Hobgood) Murphrey. BA, U. N.C., Greensboro, 1969; MA, Duke U., 1971, PhD, 1976; postgrad., U. Fla., 1984; MLS, U. N.C., Chapel Hill, 1993. Vis. instr. history Wake Forest U., Winston-Salem, NC, 1976; asst. prof. history N.C. A&T State U., Greensboro, 1977—81; intelligence rsch. specialist U.S. Army, Fayetteville, NC, 1982—89; adj. prof. history Fayetteville State U., 1989—90; adj. instr. history Fla. Met. U. South Campus, Orlando, 2000—03, adj. history, instr. Columbia Coll. Orlando divsn., 2005, rsch. libr., 1998—. Vis. asst. prof. of history Elizabeth City State U., NC, 1993—96; adj. instr. history Colmbia Coll., 2005. Editor (guidebook): Socialist Party of America Papers, microfilm edit., 2 vols., 1973—77. Apptd. Seminole County Disiability Adv. Coun., 2005. Recipient award, NEH, 1994, 1996, 2000. Mem.: LWV (bd. dirs. Seminole County chpt. 2001—, bd. dirs. Guilford County chpt. 1978—82), ALA, Fla. Libr. Assn., Am. Hist. Assn. Home: 424 Windmeadows St Altamonte Springs FL 32701 Office: Fla Met U South Orlando Campus 9200 Southpark Center Loop Orlando FL 32819 Office Phone: 407-851-2525. Personal E-mail: emurphrey@hotmail.com.

MURPHY, ALEXIS D., auditor; b. Springfield, Ill., July 31, 1980; d. Grace A. and Raymond F. Doolin (Stepfather). BS in Acctg., U. Ill., Chgo., 2002; MS in Acctg., U. Nev., Las Vegas, 2003. CPA Ill., 2005, cert. fraud examiner, Assn. Cert. Fraud Examiners, 2006. Sr. auditor USDA Office Insp. Gen., Chgo., 2003—. Mem.: Mensa, Assn. Cert. Fraud Examiners, Alpha Phi Omega (life).

MURPHY, ANTHONY J., pharmaceutical executive; b. Cardiff, Wales; B in Psychology, Univ. Coll., Dublin, 1970; D in Psychology, U. Wales, 1975. Chartered psychologist. Lectr. indsl. rels., cons., rschr. U. Bath, England; pers. rep. Eli Lilly and Co., England, 1980—81, pers. adminstrn. mgr. Basingstoke, England, 1981—84, group mgr. adminstrn. Erl Wood England, 1984—85, adminstrn. svcs. dir. Erl Wood, 1985—86, pers. advisor Indpls., 1986—87, hosp. sales pers. mgr., 1987—88, mktg. pers. dir. Basingstoke, 1988—89, pers. dir. mfg., sales and mktg., 1989—91, pers. dir. Europe London, 1991—94, exec. dir. human resources EMA, 1994—97, exec. dir. human resources intercontinental/Japan ops., 1997—99, exec. dir. human resources European ops. and Japan, 1999—2003, exec. dir. human resources-global leadership devel. and learning, 2003—05, sr. v.p. human resources, 2005—, mem. policy and strategy com., mem. sr. mgmt. coun. Mem.: Inst. Pers. and Devel., UK. Office: Eli Lilly and Co Lilly Corp Ctr Indianapolis IN 46285 Office Phone: 317-276-2000. *

MURPHY, ARTHUR WILLIAM, lawyer, educator; b. Boston, Jan. 25, 1922; s. Arthur W. and Rose (Spillane) M.; m. Jane Marks, Dec. 21, 1948 (dec. Sept. 1951); 1 dau., Lois; m. Jean C. Marks, Sept. 30, 1954; children— Rachel, Paul. AB cum laude, Harvard, 1943; LL.B., Columbia, 1948. Bar: N.Y. State bar 1949. Asso. in law Columbia Sch. Law, NYC, 1948-49; asso. dir. Legislative Drafting Research Fund, 1956, prof. law, 1963—; trial atty. U.S. Dept. Justice, 1950-52; asso. firm Hughes, Hubbard, Blair & Reed, NYC, 1953-56, 57-58; partner firm Baer, Marks, Friedman & Berliner, NYC, 1959-63. Mem. safety and licensing panel AEC, 1962-73; mem. spl. commn. on weather modification NSF, 1964-66; mem. Presdl. Commn. on Catastrophic Nuclear Accidents, 1988-90 Author: Financial Protection against Atomic Hazards, 1957, (with others) Cases on Gratuitous Transfers, 1968, 3d edit., 1985, The Nuclear Power Controversy, 1976. Served with AUS, 1943-46. Decorated Purple Heart. Mem. ABA, Assn. of Bar of City of N.Y. (spl. com. on sci. and law) Office: Columbia Sch of Law 435 W 116th St New York NY 10027-7297

MURPHY, AUSTIN DE LA SALLE, economist, educator, banker; b. NYC, Nov. 20, 1917; s. Daniel Joseph and Marie Cornelia (Austin) M.; m. Mary Patricia Halpin, June 12, 1948 (dec. May 1974); children: Austin Joseph, Owen Gerard; m. Lee Chilton Romero, Dec. 14, 1974; stepchildren: Thomas Romero, Robert Romero (dec.). AB, St. Francis Coll., Bklyn., NY, 1938; AM (Hayden fellow 1938-40), Fordham U., 1940, PhD, 1949; PhD (hon.), Canisius Coll., 1986. Instr. econ. Fordham U., 1938-41; Instr. econ. Georgetown U., 1941-42; asst. statistician, statis. controls Bd. Econ. Warfare, 1942; sr. econ. rsch. editor NY State Dept. Labor, NY, 1947-50; lectr. econ. Fordham U. Sch. Edn., 1946-55; instr. NYU Sch. Commerce, 1949-51; dean sch. bus. adminstrn. Seton Hall U., South Orange, NJ, 1950-55; Albert O'Neill prof. Am. enterprise, dean sch. bus. adminstrn. Canisius Coll., Buffalo, 1955-62; dir. edn. dept. NAM, 1962-63; exec. v.p. Savs. Banks Assn. NY State, 1963-70; chmn., pres. River Bank Am. (formerly East River Savs. Bank), 1970-89, vice chmn., dir., 1989-96, chmn. adv. bd., 1996-98. Charter trustee Savs. Bank Rockland County, 1965-70; dir. Bank of Charleston (SC), 1989-91; chmn. bd., trustee Savs. Bank Life Ins. Fund, 1983-87; chmn. dist. I, mem. adv. coun. Conf. State Bank Supr., 1986-93; bd. dir. MSB Fund, Inc. Author (with Fleming Frasca, and Mannion): Social Studies Review Book, 1946; author: (with Bullock & Doerflinger) Leading Problems of New Jersey Manufacturing Industries, 1953; author: Reasons for Relocation, 1955, Forecast of Industrial Expansion in Buffalo and the Niagara Frontier, 1956, Metropolitan Buffalo Perspective, 1958; editor: Handbook of New York Labor Statistics, 1950. Mem. Livingston (NJ) Charter Commn., 1954—55; mem. capital expenditures com. City of Buffalo, 1957—63; trustee Fordham U., 1973—79, NY Med. Coll., 1978—81; bd. dirs. NY coun. Boy Scouts Am., 1974—, Jr. Achievement of Buffalo, 1958—63, Invest-in-Am. 1st lt. US Army, 1942—46. Named Knight of Malta, 1971. Mem. NAM (chmn. ednl. aids com. 1958-63), Am. Fin. Assn., Def. Transp. Assn. (life), Nat. Assn. Mut. Savs. Banks (bd. dir., treas. 1976-81), Friendly Sons. St. Patrick (1st v.p., 1976-77), DownTown Lower Manhattan Assn. (dir., vice chmn. 1982-93), Union League Club (pres. 1991-93), Larchmont Yacht Club, Carolina Yacht Club, KC, Alpha Kappa Psi, Pi Gamma Mu. Office: RB Asset Corp 645 5th Ave New York NY 10022-5910 *Through the various happy events and the difficult and sorrowful, loss of loved ones as well as the vagaries of business life, I have found that an ongoing prayerful relationship to God brings a certain detachment and peace that overcomes life's passing problems.*

MURPHY, BARRY AMES, lawyer; b. Summit, NJ, Mar. 3, 1938; s. Robert Joseph and Florence C. (Ames) M.; m. Leslie Lynn Smith, June 9, 1962; children— Karen Irene, Sean Patrick, Conor Brendan, Ilana Taraleigh. BA in English, Stanford U., 1960; MBA, Harvard U., 1963; JD, U. So. Calif., 1972. Bar: Calif. bar 1973, U.S. Supreme Ct 1976, U.S. Tax Ct 1976. Fin. analyst Office of Sec. Def., 1963-65; pres. Tech. Industries Inc., Los Angeles, 1966-72; invididual practice law San Mateo, Calif., 1972-74; corp. counsel Falstaff Brewing Co., San Francisco, 1974-77; sr. partner firm Levine & Murphy, San Francisco, 1978-81; v.p. Microvertics, Mountain View, Calif., 1981-86; pres. Murphy Law Corp., San Anselmo, 1987—. Mem. Am., Calif. bar assns., Calif. Trial Lawyers. Address: 28 Fern Ln San Anselmo CA 94960-1807 E-mail: barry@murphy-law.com.

MURPHY, BETTY SOUTHARD, lawyer; b. East Orange, NJ; d. Floyd Theodore and Thelma (Casto) Southard; m. Cornelius F. Murphy, May 1, 1965; children: Cornelius Francis Jr., Ann Southard Murphy; m. H. Leland Hernly, Apr. 26, 2003. AB, Ohio State U.; student, Alliance Française and U. Sorbonne, Paris; JD, Am. U. Washington Coll. Law, Washington, DC; LLD (hon.), Ea. Mich. U., Ypsilanti, 1975, Capital U., Columbus, Ohio, 1976, Seattle U., 1986; LHD (hon.), Tusculum Coll., Greenville, Tenn., 1987. Bar: D.C. Corr., free lance journalist, Europe and Asia, UPI, Washington; mem. firm McInnis, Wilson, Munson & Woods (and predecessor firm Roberts & McInnis); dep. asst. sec., adminstr. Wage and Hour Divsn. Dept. Labor, 1974-75; chmn. and mem. NLRB, 1975-79; ptnr. firm Baker & Hostetler, LLP, 1980—. Adj. prof. law Am. U., 1972-80, 99—; mem. adv. com. on rights and responsibilities of women to Sec. HHS; mem. panel conciliators Internat. Ctr. Settlement Investment Disputes, 1974-85; mem. Adminstrv. Conf. U.S., 1976-80, Pub. Svc. Adv. Bd., 1976-79; mem. human resouces com. Nat. Ctr. for Productivity and Quality of Working Life, 1976-80; mem. Presdl. Commn. on Exec. Exch., 1981-85, Ctr. for Study of the Presidency, 1998—. Trustee Mary Baldwin Coll., Staunton, Va., 1977—85, Am. U., Washington, 1980—99, George Mason U. Found., Inc., Fairfax, Va., 1993—2000, 2001—; US Constn. mem. exec com. Commn. on Bicentennial, 1985—92; chmn. internat. adv. com. Commn. on Bicentennial of US Constn., 1985—92; vice chmn. James Madison Meml. Fellowship Found., 1990—96; trustee Friends of Congl. Law Libr., 1992—, Friends of Dept. of Labor, 1984—; mediator World Intellectual Property Orgn., 1996—; nat. bd. dirs. Med. Coll. Pa., Phila., bd. corporators, 1976—85; bd. dirs. Ctr. for Women in Medicine, Phila., 1980—86, Meridian Internat. Ctr., 1992—98; bd. mem. Summer Opera Theatre, 2006—; bd. govs. St. Agnes Sch., Alexandria, Va., 1981—87. Recipient Ohio Gov.'s award, 1980, fellow award, 1981, Outstanding Pub. Service award U.S. Info. Service, 1987; named Disting. Fellow John Sherman Myers Soc., 1986, 96; fellow Nat. Acad. Human Resources, 1998. Fellow: ABA (chmn. labor law com. 1980—83, chmn. internat. and comparative law adminstrv. law sect. 1983—88, chmn. customs, tariff and trade com. 1988—90, employment law sect. 1990—2004, chmn. internat. com. dispute resolution sect. 1995—); mem.: US-Mexico Bar Assn. (US chair labor and law com. 2006—07, bd. dirs. 2007—), Am. Inns Ct. (Professionalism award 2006), Nat. Acad. Human Resources, Nat. Assn. Women Lawyers, Women's Bar Assn., Internat Bar Assn., Am. U. Alumni Assn. (Women's Leadership Award 2004), Supreme Ct. Hist. Soc., Union Internat. des Advocats (gov. bd. 1997—2000, 2003—), Rep. Nat. Lawyers Assn. (nat. v.p. 1990—95, nat. vice chmn. 1996—2000, 2001—03, co-chmn. 2003—, mem. exec. bd. 2003—, Rep. Lawyer of Yr. 2005), Am. Arbitration Assn. (bd. dirs. 1985—2000, mem. editl. bd. 1992, mem. exec. com. 1995—2000, mem. internat. arbitration com. 1997—, steering com. lawyers for Bush 2000, bd. dirs. 2001—, mem. exec. com. 2002—, bd. dirs. 2004—, trustee summer opera theater co. 2006—), Bar Assn. D.C., Inter-Am. Bar Assn. (co-chmn. labor law com. 1975—83, editor newsletter, Silver medal 1967), FBA, World Peace Through Law Ctr., Mortar Bd., Kappa Beta Pi. Republican. Office: Baker & Hostetler LLP Ste 1100 1050 Connecticut Ave NW Washington DC 20036-5304 Office Phone: 202-861-1500. Office Fax: 202-861-1783. Business E-Mail: bsmurphy@bakerlaw.com.

MURPHY, BILLY (WILLIAM H. MURPHY JR.), lawyer; b. Wilmington, Del., Apr. 22, 1943; s. William H. Murphy, Sr. BSEE, MIT, 1965; JD, U. Md., 1969. Bar: Md. 1969, US Ct. Appeals (4th cir.) 1970, US Dist. Ct. (dist. Md.). Law clk. to Judge Robert C. Murphy Ct. Spl. Appeals, Md., 1969—70; judge Cir. Ct. Balt. City, 1980—83; founder, sr. ptnr. The Murphy Firm, Balt. Recipient Charles Hamilton Houston award for Lifetime Achievement in Litig. Mem.: Md. Trial Lawyers Assn. (bd. govs.), Nat. Conf. Black Lawyers, NACDL (bd. dirs.), Md. Criminal Def. Lawyers Assn., Monumental Bar Assn., Nat. Bar Assn., ABA, Bar Assn. Balt. City. Office: The Murphy Firm 12 W Madison St Baltimore MD 21202 Office Phone: 410-735-0333. Office Fax: 410-539-6599. E-mail: billy@billymurphylaw.com. *

MURPHY, BRITTANY, actress; b. Atlanta, Nov. 10, 1977; d. Angelo Bertolotti and Sharon Murphy; m. Simon Monjack, Apr. 2007. Actor: (films) Clueless, 1995, Freeway, 1996, Drive, 1997, The Prophecy II, 1998,

Bongwater, 1998, Phoenix, 1998, Zack and Reba, 1998, Falling Sky, 1998, Drop Dead Gorgeous, 1999, Girl, Interrupted, 1999, Trixie, 2000, Angels!, 2000, Cherry Falls, 2000, The Audition, 2000, Sidewalks of NY, 2001, Summer Catch, 2001, Don't Say a Word, 2001, Riding in Cars with Boys, 2001, Spun, 2002, 8 Mile, 2002, Just Married, 2003, Uptown Girls, 2003, (voice only) Good Boy!, 2003, Little Black Book, 2004, Sin City, 2005, Neverwas, 2005, The Groomsmen, 2006, Love and Other Disasters, 2006, (voice only) Happy Feet, 2006,: (TV films) Double Jeopardy, 1996, David and Lisa, 1998, The Devil's Arithmetic, 1999, Common Ground, 2000, (TV appearances) Drexell's Class, 1991, Murphy Brown, 1991, Kids Incorporated, 1992, Parker Lewis Can't Lose, 1992, Almost Home, 1993, Blossom, 1993, Frasier, 1994, Party of Five, 1994, Sister, Sister, 1994, Boy Meets World, 1995, Murder One, 1995, The Marshal, 1995, SeaQuest DSV, 1995, Nash Bridges, 1996, Clueless, 1996, (voice only) Pepper Ann, 1997; (TV series) King of the Hill, 1997—2006. Office: Endeavor Talent Agy 9601 Wilshire Blvd Beverly Hills CA 90212 *

MURPHY, BRUCE ALLEN, government educator, law educator, writer; b. Abington, Mass., Sept. 30, 1951; m. Carol Lynn Wright, June 14, 1975; children: Emily, Geoffrey. BA, U. Mass., Amherst, 1973; PhD, U. Va., Charlottesville, 1978. Fred Morgan Kirby prof. civil rights Lafayette Coll., Easton, Pa. Author: The Brandeis/Frankfurter Connection: The Secret Political Activities of Two Supreme Court Justices, 1982, Fortas: The Rise and Ruin of a Supreme Court Justice, 1988, (with Larry Berman) Approaching Democracy, 1996, 5th edit., 2006, Wild Bill: The Legend and Life of William O. Douglas, 2003. Avocations: fishing, reading, sports. Office: Lafayette Coll Dept Govt and Law 200 Kirby Hall Civil Rights Easton PA 18042 Office Phone: 610-330-5395. Business E-Mail: murphyb@lafayette.edu.

MURPHY, CARYLE MARIE, foreign correspondent; b. Hartford, Conn., Nov. 16, 1946; d. Thomas Joseph and Muriel Kathryn (McCarthy) Murphy. BA cum laude, Trinity Coll., 1968; M in Internat. Pub. Policy, Johns Hopkins U., 1987. Tchr. English, history St. Cecilia Tchr. Tng. Coll., Nyeri, Kenya, 1968—71; reporter Brockton (Mass.) Enterprise, 1972—73; freelance corr. Washington Post, Newsweek, Sunday Times of London, et al, Luanda, Angola, 1974—76; reporter Fairfax County Washington Post, 1976—77, fgn. corr. in South Africa, 1977—82, reporter immigration issues, 1982—85, bur. chief Alexandria, Va., 1985—89, fgn. corr. Mid. East Cairo, 1989—94, religion corr. Vol. ARC, Washington, 1984, Whitman-Walker Found., Washington, 1988—89. Recipient Courage in Journalism award, Internat. Women's Media Found., 1990, George Polk award, L.I. U., 1991, Edward Weintal Journalism award, Sch. Fgn. Svc., Georgetown U., 1991, Pulitzer Prize for internat. reporting, 1991, Edward R. Murrow fellow, Coun. on Fgn. Rels., N.Y., 1994—95. Roman Catholic. Avocations: foreign languages, hiking. Office: Washington Post Fgn Desk 1150 15th St NW Washington DC 20071-0002

MURPHY, CHRISTOPHER S., congressman, former state senator; b. White Plains, NY, Aug. 3, 1973; s. Scott and Catherine Murphy. Studied at, Exeter Coll., Oxford U., 1994—95; BA with honors in Hist. & Polit. Sci., Williams Coll., 1996; JD, U. Conn., 2002. Staff mem. Conn. State Senate Majority Caucus, 1996—98; mem. Southington Planning & Zoning Commn., 1997—99, Conn. Ho. of Reps. Dist. 81, 1999—2002, mem. Environ., Judiciary & Pub. Health Com., mem. Prescription Drug Task Force; mem. Conn. State Senate Dist. 16, 2003—06, chair Pub. Health Com., 2003—; mem. US Congress from 5th Conn. dist., 2007—, mem. Fin. Svcs. and Oversight and Govt. Reform Coms. Atty. Ruben, Johnson, and Morgan, PC, Hartford, Conn. Democrat. Protestant. Office: 1 Grove St New Britain CT 06053 also: 501 Cannon House Office Bldg Washington DC 20515 Office Phone: 860-240-0567. E-mail: murphy@senatedems.ct.gov. *

MURPHY, CILLIAN, actor; b. Douglas, Ireland, May 25, 1976; m. Yvonne McGuinness, 2004. Studied Law, U. Coll. Cork. Actor: (TV miniseries) The Way We Live Now, 2001; (films) Quando, 1997, The Tale of Sweety Barrett, 1998, Eviction, 1999, At Death's Door, 1999, Sunburn, 1999, The Trench, 1999, Filleann an Feall, 2000, On the Edge, 2001, How Harry Became a Tree, 2001, Disco Pigs, 2001, 28 Days Later, 2002, Zonad, 2003, Intermission, 2003, Girl with a Pearl Earring, 2003, Cold Mountain, 2003, Batman Begins, 2005, Red Eye, 2005, Breakfast on Pluto, 2005; (plays) The Seagull, The Shape of Things, Juno and the Paycock, The Country Boy, Much Ado About Nothing, Love Song, 2006. Office: United Talent Agy 9560 Wilshire Blvd Ste 500 Beverly Hills CA 90212

MURPHY, COLEEN T., biomedical researcher, educator; BS magna cum laude in Biochemical and Biophysical Scis., U. Houston, 1992; PhD in Biochemistry, Stanford U., Calif., 1999. Postdoctoral rschr. Kenyon Lab. U. Calif., San Francisco, 2000—05; asst. prof. dept. molecular biology Princeton U. Lewis-Sigler Inst. Integrative Genomics, NJ, 2005—. Contbr. articles to profl. jours. Grantee Sloan Rsch. fellowship, 2006—; Pew Scholar in Biomedical Scis., 2006—. Office: Princeton U Lewis-Sigler Inst 148 Carl Icahn Lab Washington Rd Princeton NJ 08544-1014 Office Phone: 609-258-9396. E-mail: ctmurphy@princeton.edu. *

MURPHY, CORNELIUS B., JR., (NEIL MURPHY), academic administrator; b. July 17, 1944; m. Joanne Murphy; children: Tracy, Megan, Maureen, Michael. B in Chemistry magna cum laude, St. Michael's Coll., 1966; PhD in Chemistry, Syracuse U., 1970; DSc (hon.), Clarkson U., 1997. Joined as a lab technician O'Brien & Gere Cos., East Syracuse, NY, 1970; sr. v.p. O'Brien & Gere Engrs., Inc., East Syracuse, 1982—92, pres., 1992, chmn., chief scientist, 1998; pres. O'Brien & Gere Ltd., East Syracuse, 1996, chmn., 1999; pres. SUNY Coll. Environ. Sci. and Forestry, East Syracuse, 2000—. Mem.: AAAS, Am. Chem. Soc. Office: SUNY Coll Environ Sci and Forestry 1 Forestry Dr Syracuse NY 13210 E-mail: cbmurphy@esf.edu. *

MURPHY, DANIEL IGNATIUS, lawyer; b. Phila., Mar. 14, 1927; s. John Anthony Murphy and Irene Cooper Thorn; m. Jeanne B. Genetti, July 28, 1956 (div. Aug. 1978); children: Jewel A., Daniel I. Jr.; m. Barbara Ann Uncles, Jan. 1, 1979. BS in Econs., U. Pa., 1950; LLB, Yale U., 1953. Bar: Pa. 1954, U.S. Dist Ct. (ea. dist.) Pa. 1954, U.S. Ct. Appeals (3d cir.) 1954, U.S. Tax Ct. 1956, U.S. Supreme Ct. 1959. Assoc. Evans, Bayard & Frick, Phila., 1953-55; asst. city solicitor City of Phila., Pa., 1956-59; ptnr. Cavanaugh, Murphy & Kalodner, Phila., 1958-64, Shapiro, Stalberg, Cook, Murphy & Kalodner, Phila., 1964-66, Takiff, Bolger & Murphy, Phila., 1966-72, Waters, Gallagher, Collins & Masterson, Phila., 1972-80, Stradley, Ronon, Stevens & Young, Phila., 1980-92, ret., of counsel, 1993. Tchr. Am. Soc. CLUs, Villanova, Pa., 1956-57; mem. exec. com. Phila. Estate Planning Coun., 1958-60; lectr. Pa. Bar Inst., Harrisburg, 1974-92, Pa. Coll. Orphans Ct. Judges, Harrisburg, 1978, Pitts., 1991; apptd. spl. master for trial mgmt. of complex litigation Phila. County Ct. Common Pleas, 1994—; judge pro tem Philadelphia County Ct. Common Pleas, 2000—; arbitrator Nat. Assn. Securities Dealers, 2001-2002. Editor: Phila. Bar Assn. Mag. The Shingle, 1958-67; contbr. chpts. to manuals and articles to profl. jours. Chmn. Phila. Chpt. Am. Cancer Soc., 1956-63; mem. Com. of 70, Phila., 1968-2003, chmn., 1972-74; trustee Hahnemann U., Phila., 1983-86; bd. dirs. Covenant Ho. Pa., 2004—; trustee Easttown Libr. and Info. Ctr., Pa., 2004-2005. With USN, 1945-46. Fellow: Pa. Bar Found. (life); mem.: ABA, Colonial Soc. Pa. (bd. dirs. 2001—06), Phila. Bar Assn. (vice chmn. com. censors 1971), Pa. Bar Assn., Pa. Soc. S.R., Soc. Colonial Wars, Phila. Country Club, Union League Phila. Democrat. Roman Catholic. Avocation: U.S. Civil War history. Personal E-mail: dmurphyesq@comcast.net.

MURPHY, DANIEL J., JR., aerospace and defense manufacturing company executive, military officer; b. Newport, RI, May 30, 1948; m. Pam Murphy; children: Dan, Kate. BS, U.S. Naval Acad., 1970; M in Law and Diplomacy, Tufts U., 1981. Exec. asst. to chief of naval ops. USN; exec. asst. to Supreme Allied Comdr. Atlantic; adminstrv. aide to Sec. of Navy; plans officer Plans and Ops. Directorate; mil. analyst Bur. Intelligence and Rsch. Dept. of State; rear adm., dir. surface warfare USN, 1996-98, vice adm., comdr. Sixth Fleet, and NATO striking & support forces So. Europe, 1998—2000; group v.p., precision systems and pres. tactical systems Alliant Techsystems (ATK), Edina, Minn., 2000—03, chmn., CEO, 2003—. Comdr. Eisenhower Battle Group and Cruiser-Destroyer Group 8, comdr. Destroyer Squadron 14, commdg. officer USS Kidd, sea tours with USS Goldsborough, USS Richard L. Page, USS Edson, USN. Office: Alliant Techsystems 5050 Lincoln Dr Minneapolis MN 55436 *

MURPHY, DENNIS JOSEPH, lawyer; b. Irvington, NJ, Oct. 8, 1946; s. Joseph J. and Mary E. (Fahey) M.; m. Deborah M. Sullivan, Dec. 29, 1978. AB, Harvard U., 1968; JD, Georgetown U., 1973. Bar: N.Y. 1974, Ohio 1981, U.S. Dist. Ct. (so. dist.) N.Y. 1976. Assoc. Shearman & Sterling, NYC, 1973-81, Paris, 1977-79; ptnr. Smith & Schnacke, Cin., 1981-84, Frost & Jacobs, Cin., 1984—99; ret., 2003. Chmn. So. Ohio Dist. Export Coun., Cin., 1986-89; mem. Export Now Nat. Adv. Com., Washington, 1988-89; mem. steering com. Nat. Dist. Export Coun., Washington, 1988—. Contbr. numerous articles to profl. jours. Mem. adv. bd. Salvation Army, Cin., 1992—. Recipient E award Gov. Ohio, 1987. Mem. ABA, Internat. Bar Assn., Ohio State Bar Assn., Cin. Bar Assn., Assn. Bar of City of N.Y., No. Ky. Internat. Trade Assn. (v.p. 1992). Republican. Roman Catholic. Home: 318 Bowline Ct Fort Collins CO 80525-3116

MURPHY, DENNIS PATRICK, hotel business entrepreneur; b. Buffalo, Jan. 12, 1958; s. Dennis Charles and Dorothy E. Murphy; m. Carol Ann Klocke. B in Hospitality Mgmt., Fla. Internat. U., 1980. Cert. hotel exec. Mgr. hotel ops. Marriott Corp., Washington, 1979-80; dir. food and beverage Mariner Corp., Houston, 1980-83; corp. dir. Innco Hospitality, Wichita, Kans., 1984-86; ops. exec. Clubhouse Inns of Am., 1986-88; chmn. JLH Lodge Corp., Amherst, NY, 1988—, also bd. dirs.; founding pres. InnVest Lodging Svcs. Inc., 1990—. Bd. dirs. Hotel Baronette, Inc., Genoa Lodging, LLC, Suzuki & Son, Ltd., Penn. Investors IV, LLC; nominated Esquire mag. register, 1985; chair project devel. com. econ lodging coun. Am. Hotel/Motel Assn., 1990; dep. chair World U. Games, 1990—93; treas. World Vets. Games L/O/C, Buffalo, 1994—96, Greater Buffalo Conv. and Visitors Bur, 1992—, chmn, 1999—2001; mem. exec. com. Buffalo-Niagara Partnership, 1999—2001; trustee Gates Found., 1988—. Recipient Elsworth Statler award The Statler Found., 1978-79, Citizen of the Year award, The Buffalo News, 2002. Mem. Soc. Wine Educators (pubs. com. 1977-79), Am. Hotel and Lodging Assn., The Buffalo Club, The Buffalo Launch Club. Office: PO Box 98 Buffalo NY 14205

MURPHY, DIANA E., federal judge; b. Faribault, Minn., Jan. 4, 1934; d. Albert W. and Adleyne (Heiker) Kuske; m. Joseph Murphy, July 24, 1958; children: Michael, John E. BA magna cum laude, U. Minn., 1954, JD magna cum laude, 1974; postgrad., Johannes Gutenberg U., 1954—55, U. Minn., 1955—58; LLD, St. Johns U., 2000, U. St. Thomas, 2003. Bar: Minn. 1974, US Supreme Ct. 1980. Assoc. Lindquist & Vennum, 1974—76; mcpl. judge Hennepin County, 1976—78, Minn. State dist. judge, 1978—80; judge US Dist. Ct. for Minn., Mpls., 1980—94, chief judge, 1992—94; judge US Ct. Appeals (8th cir.), Mpls., 1994—. Chair US Sentencing Commn., 1999—2004. Bd. editors: Minn. Law Rev., Georgetown U. Jour. on Cts., Health Scis. and the Law, 1989—92. Bd. dirs. Nat. Assn. Pub. Interest Law Fellowships for Equal Justice, 1992—95, Mpls. United Way, 1985—2001, treas., 1990—94, vice-chmn., 1996—97, chmn. bd. dirs., 1997—98; bd. dirs. Bush Found., 1982—2006, chmn. bd. dirs., 1986—91; organizer, 1st chmn. adv. coun. Amicus, bd. dirs., 1976—80; chair Mpls. Charter Commn., 1973—76; bd. dirs. Ops. De Novo, 1971—76, chmn. bd. dirs., 1974—75; mem., chmn. bill of rights com. Minn. Constl. Study Commn., 1971—73; regent St. Johns U., 1978—87, 1988—98, chmn. bd., 1995—98, bd. overseers sch. theology, 1998—2001; mem. Minn. Bicentennial Commn., 1987—88; trustee Twin Cities Pub. TV, 1985—94, chmn. bd., 1990—92; trustee U. Minn. Found., 1990—, chmn. of bd., 2003—05; bd. dirs. Sci. Mus. Minn., 1988—94, vice-chmn., 1991—94; trustee U. St. Thomas, 1991—, chair exec. com., 2006—; vice chair bd. govs. U. St. Thomas Law Sch., 2001—04, chair, 2004—06; bd. dirs. Spring Hill Conf. Ctr., 1978—84; bd. govs. Hill Mus. and Manuscript Libr., 2005—; bd. dirs. Minn. Opera, 1998—2004, 2005—. Recipient Amicus Founders' award, 1980, Outstanding Achievement award, U. Minn., 1983, YWCA, 1981, Disting. Citizen award, Alpha Gamma Delta, 1985, Devitt Disting. Svc. to Justice award, 2001, Disting. Alumnus award, U. Minn. Law Sch., 2002, Woman Who Makes a Difference award, Internat. Women's Forum, 2003, Iustitia et Lex award, 2006; scholar Fulbright. Fellow: Am. Bar Found.; mem.: ABA (ethics and profl. responsibility judges adv. com. 1981—88, standing com. on jud. selection, tenure and compensation 1991—94, standing com. on fed. jud. improvements 1994—97, Appellate Judges conf. exec. com. 1996—99, chmn. ethics and profl. responsibility judges adv. com. 1997—2000), Fed. Jud. Ctr. (bd. dirs. 1990—94, 8th cir. jud. coun. 1992—94, 1992—94, convener gender fairness task force 1993, U.S. jud. conf. com. on ct. adminstrn. and case mgmt. 1994—99, chair gender fairness implementation com. 1997—98), Hist. Soc. for 8th Cir. (bd. dirs. 1988—91), Fed. Judges Assn. (bd. dirs. 1982—2003, v.p. 1984—89, pres. 1989—91), U. Minn. Alumni Assn. (bd. dirs. 1975—83, nat. pres. 1981—82), Minn. Women Lawyers (Myra Bradwell award 1996), Nat. Assn. Women Judges (Leadership Judges Jud. Adminstrn. award 1998, Honoree of Yr. 2002), Nat. Assn. Governing Bds. Univs. Colls. (dir. 1998—, vice chair 2006—), Am. Judicature Soc. (bd. dirs. 1982—93, v.p. 1985—88, treas. 1988—89, chmn. bd. 1989—91), Am. Law Inst., Hennepin County Bar Assn. (gov. coun. 1976—81), Minn. Bar Assn. (bd. govs. 1977—81), Order of Coif, Phi Beta Kappa. Office: 11 E US Courthouse 300 S 4th St Minneapolis MN 55415-1320 *

MURPHY, DONNA, actress; b. Corona, NY, Mar. 7, 1959; m. Shawn Elliott, 1990; 1 adopted child, Darmia. Student, NYU Sch. of the Arts. Actor: (Broadway plays) They're Playing Our Song, The Human Comedy, The Mystery of Edwin Drood, Passion, 1994—95 (Tony award best actress in a musical, 1994, Drama Desk award, Drama League award), 2004, The King and I, 1996 (Tony award best actress in a musical, 1996, Drama League award), Wonderful Town, 2003—04 (Tony nom. best actress in a musical, 2004, Drama Desk award best actress in a musical, 2004, Drama League award, 2004), Children & Art, 2005, LoveMusik, 2007 (Outer Critics Cir. award outstanding actress in a musical, 2007, Drama Desk award outstanding actress in a musical, 2007); (plays) Song of Singapore, Privates on Parade, Showing Off, Birds of Paradise, Little Shop of Horrors, A...My Name Is Alice, Twelve Dreams, 1995, Hello Again, 1994, Follies, 2007; (TV series) Murder One, 1995—96, Law & Order, 1993, 1997, 2000, The Practice, 1998, Ally McBeal, 1998, What About Joan, 2001, Hack, 2002—03; (TV miniseries) LIBERTY! The American Revolution, 1997; (TV films) Tales from the Hollywood Hills: A Table at Ciro's, 1987, Power, Passion and Murder, 1987, Passion, 1996, Someone Had to Be Benny, 1996 (Cable ACE award, 1996, Daytime Emmy, 1996), The Day Lincoln Was Shot, 1998, The Last Debate, 2000; (films) Jade, 1995, October 22, 1998, Star Trek: Insurrection, 1998, The Astronaut's Wife, 1999, Center Stage, 2001, The Door in the Floor, 2004, Spiderman 2, 2004, Ira and Abby, 2006, World Trade Center, 2006, The Fountain, 2006, The Nanny Diaries, 2007. Office: Innovative Artists 235 Park Ave S New York NY 10003 *

MURPHY, EDDIE, actor, comedian; b. Bklyn., Apr. 3, 1961; s. Vernon and Lillian Murphy Lynch; m. Nicole Mitchell, March 18, 1993 (div. Apr. 17, 2006); children: Bria, Myles Mitchell, Shayne Audra, Zola Ivy, Bella Zehra; 1 child with Melanie Brown, Angel Iris Student pub. schs., Bklyn. Began performing Richard M. Dixon's White House, LI, N.Y.; performed at various N.Y.C. clubs, including The Comic Strip; with Saturday Night Live, NYC, 1980-84; host 35th Ann. Emmy Awards, 1983. Actor: (films) 48 Hrs., 1982, Trading Places, 1983, Best Defense, 1984, Beverly Hills Cop, 1984, The Distinguished Gentleman, 1992, Beverly Hills Cop III, 1994, The Nutty Professor, 1996, Metro, 1997, Mulan (voice only), 1998, Dr. Dolittle, 1998, Holy Man, 1998, Bowfinger, 1999, Shrek (voice only), 2001, Dr. Dolittle 2, 2001, Showtime, 2002, The Adventures of Pluto Nash, 2002, I Spy, 2002, Daddy Day Care, 2003, The Haunted Mansion, 2003, Shrek 2 (voice only), 2004, Dreamgirls, 2006 (Best Supporting Actor, African-American Film Critics Assn., 2006, 2006 Best Supporting Actor, Critics Choice award, Broadcast Film Critics Assn., 2007, Best Performance by an Actor in a Supporting Role in a Motion Picture, Golden Globe award, Hollywood Fgn. Press Assn., 2007, Outstanding Performance by a Male Actor in a Supporting Role, SAG, 2007), Shrek the Third (voice only), 2007; actor, exec. prodr.: The Golden Child, 1986; The Nutty Professor II: The Klumps, 2000; Harlem Nights, 1989; actor(actor, prodr.): Vampire in Brooklyn, 1995; actor, prodr.: Life, 1999; actor, writer, prodr. Norbit, 2007; actor, writer Beverly Hills Cop II, 1987; Coming to America, 1988; Another 48 Hrs., 1990; actor, writer: films Boomerang, 1992; actor: (TV films) Eddie Murphy Delirious, 1983, Eddie Murphy Raw, 1987; actor (voice only), exec. prodr. (TV series) The PJ's, 1999—2001. *

MURPHY, EDWARD FRANCIS, sales executive; b. Chgo., July 30, 1947; s. Edward F. and Marjorie (Mooney) M.; m. Kay A. Worcester, Apr. 17, 1970; 1 child, Dean D. BA in Mktg., No. Ill. U., 1976. Dist. mgr. Midas Internat. Corp., Chgo., 1977-85; sales mgr. Raybestos, McHenry, Ill., 1985-89, Wagner Brakes, St. Louis, 1989-99; owner Displays of Distinction, Mesa, Ariz., 1998—. V.p. Associated Roof Structures, Mesa, 1999—. Author: Vietnam Medal of Honor Heroes, 1987, Heroes of World War II, 1990, Korea's Heroes, 1990, Dak To, 1993, Semper Fi-Vietnam, 1996, Khe Sahn-The Hill Fights, 2000; hist. cons. (book) Above and Beyond, 1985. Sgt. U.S. Army, 1965-68. Recipient Dist. Svc. award Congl. Medal of Honor Soc., 1989. Mem. Medal of Honor Hist. Soc. (founder, pres. 1975—). Republican. Avocations: writing, flying. Home: 2659 E Kael St Mesa AZ 85213-2363

MURPHY, EDWARD JOSEPH, government agency administrator; b. Washington, Aug. 17, 1948; s. Edward Conley Murphy and Pauline Anne Ehlers. BA, So. Ill. U., Carbondale, 1970; JD, Georgetown U., Washington, 1973. Bar: Washington 1973. Policy analyst US EPA, Washington, 1980—86, chief contracts policy, 1987—97, mgr. superfund contract ctr., 1997—2003, mgr. lab. analysis svc. ctr., 2003—06, dir. competitive sourcing staff, 2006—. Rep. US Civilian Agy. Acquisition Coun., Washington, 1986—92. Recipient Silver medal for Superior Svc., US EPA, 1995. Mem.: ABA (pub. contract law divsn.), Nat. Contract Mgmt. Assn., Phi Kappa Phi, Pi Sigma Alpha. Democrat. Avocations: piano, swimming, history, films, travel. Office: US EPA 1200 Penn Ave NW Washington DC 20460

MURPHY, EILEEN BRIDGET, retired mathematics and computer science professor; b. Newport, RI, Dec. 28, 1940; d. Henry Timothy and Mary Anne (Lyne) M. BA in Teaching Math., Elms Coll., 1969; MAT in Math., Purdue U., 1971; MSA in Adminstrn., U. Notre Dame, 1981; postgrad., Nova Southeastern U., 1992—96. Cert. secondary edn., math. and adminstrn. Mass. Tchr. math. Cathedral H.S., Springfield, Mass., 1961-71; tchr. Holyoke Cath. H.S., Mass., 1971-84, dept. chair, 1975-84; asst. prof., lectr. Elms Coll., Chicopee, 1984—2006, dept. chair math. scis., 1985-90, div. chair math. and sci., 1987-89; ret., 1989. Steering com. Accreditations New Eng. Assn. Secondary Schs. and Colls., Chicopee, 1991-92. Mem. Sisters of St. Joseph of Springfield, Sisters of St. Joseph Fin. Team; co-treas. Sisters of St. Joseph Festival, 1984-86; bd. dirs. Mont Marie Health Care Ctr., 1999-2005; vol. computer tchr. Hampden County Dept. Corrections; vol. tchr. math. and computer applications Elms Coll., 2006—. Recipient Econs. of Pvt. Enterprise grant Strathmore Paper Co., Springfield Coll., Mass., 1978. Mem. Assn. Computing Machinery (Western Mass. chpt. pub. rels. com. 1985-86, sec. 1986-91). Democrat. Roman Catholic. Achievements include the introduction of computers into the curriculum at Holyoke Catholic High School in 1980. Avocations: peer support for multiple sclerosis groups, knitting, puzzle solving. Home: 414 Chestnut St Apt 1204 Springfield MA 01104-3442 Home Phone: 413-737-3321. Personal E-mail: murphye@elms.edu. E-mail: murp1228@verizon.net.

MURPHY, ELAINE (FRANCES ELAINE MURPHY), musician, harpist, flutist; b. Chattanooga, July 15; MusB, Boston U., 1982; postgrad., Aspen Sch. Music, 1988; MM, Rice U., 1990; postgrad., U.S. Internat. U., 1990; DMA, U. So. Calif., 1997. Flutist Brookline (Mass.) Symphony Orch., 1982-84; piccolo player North Shore Symphony Orch., Marblehead, Mass., 1982-83, Cape Ann Symphony Orch., Gloucester, Mass., 1983-84; prin. flutist Orch. Sinfonica Del Valle, Cali, Colombia, 1984-87; flutist Pro Musica Chamber Orch., El Paso, Tex., 1987-88; prin. flutist Internat. Orchestra and Internat. Chamber Players, San Diego, 1990-91. Solo harpist Beverly Hills Hotel. Musician Scotia Festival of Music, 1988, contbr. articles to Flute Forum; participant in Festival de Hispanidad, Houston, 1990; albums Thou Shalt Play Upon the Harp, 2001. Scholar Boston U., 1978-82, Crescendo Club Boston, 1982, Aspen Music Sch., 1988, Rice U., 1988-90; recipient Shepherd Soc. Award. Mem. Nat. Flute Assn., Boston U. Alumni Assn., Mu Phi Epsilon Alumni Assn. Office: Murphy's Music PMB 449 3175 South Hoover St Los Angeles CA 90007 *

MURPHY, ELLIS, association management executive; b. Lincoln, Nebr. s. Ellis F. and Virgie (Olson) M.; m. Judy Neel, 1975; children by previous marriage: Sharon, Michael, Edward, Randall; stepchildren: Mary, Janet, Susan. BS in Agr, Purdue U., 1947; MBA, Northwestern U., 1957; postgrad., Ill. Inst. Tech., 1969-81, U. Wash., 1950-51, Mexico City Coll., 1947, U. Chgo., 1964. Assoc. editor Pacific Builder & Engr., Seattle, 1948-51; tech. editor Portland Cement Assn., 1953-55; dir. public relations Chgo. chpt. Am. Inst. Arch., 1955-56; account exec. Carrier & Jobson, Inc., Chgo., 1956-57; pres. Ellis Murphy, Inc., Chgo., 1957-73, Murphy, Tashjian & Assocs., Chgo., 1973-78; v.p. Lurie/Murphy Assocs., Inc., Chgo., 1979-83; pres. Murphy & Murphy Inc., Chgo., 1984—. Instr. mktg. Ill. Inst. Tech., Chgo., 1977-79; instr. assn. mgmt. DePaul U., Chgo., 1985—;cons. mktg. communication to various firms and trade assns., 1970—. Mem. Bd. Edn. Thornton Fractional HS Dist., Ill., 1961—67; exec. v.p. Ukrainian Am. C. of C. of Midwest, 1995—2001; trustee First Meth. Ch., Lansing, Ill., 1959—65; chmn. bd. dirs. funds com. Purdue Club, Chgo., 1990—95; docent dept. anthropology Chgo. Field Mus., 1998—2006. Maj. USMCR, 1943—46, maj. USMCR, 1950—52. Mem.: Chgo. Soc. Assn. Execs. (Disting. Svc. award 1986), Am. Soc. Assn. Execs., Am. Mktg. Assn., Public Relations Soc. Am. (citation 1963), St. Bernard Commndery (past comdr., York Rite Cross of Honor 2003), Knights Templar, Sigma Delta Chi. Avocations: gardening, canoeing. Home: 32361 Wildwood Dr Dowagiac MI 49047 Personal E-mail: ememememem@aol.com.

MURPHY, EVELYN FRANCES, economist; b. Panama Canal Zone, May 14, 1940; d. Clement Bernard and Dorothy Eloise (Jackson) M. AB, Duke U., 1961, PhD, 1965; MA, Columbia U., 1963; degree (hon.), Regis Coll., 1978, Curry Coll., Northeastern U., Simmons Coll., Wheaton Coll., Anna Maria Coll., Bridgewater State Coll., Salem State Coll., Emmanuel Coll., Suffolk U.; degree, Lasell Coll. Pres. Ancon Assocs., Boston,

1971-72; ptnr. Llewelyn-Davies, Weeks, Forrester-Walker & Bor, London, 1973-74; sec. environ. affairs Commonwealth of Mass., Boston, 1975-79, sec. econ. affairs, 1983-86, lt. gov., 1987-91; mng. dir. Brown Rudnick Freed and Gesmer, Boston, 1991-93; exec. v.p. Blue Cross/Blue Shield of Mass., Boston, 1994-98; also bd. dirs. Blue Cross Blue Shield Mass., Boston; resident scholar Brandeis U. Women's Studies Rsch. Ctr., 1999—; founder, pres. The Wage Project, Inc., 2003—. Vice-chmn., chmn. Nat. Adv. Com. on Oceans and Atmosphere, 1979-80; bd. dirs. Citizens Energy Corp., The Commonwealth Inst., Polaris Project, Nat. Ctr. on Women and Aging, chair, 1998-2002, chmn. emeritus, 2002; pres. Health Care and Policy Inst., 1997-98; resident scholar Brandeis U., 1999—; bd. trustees Regis Coll., 2003—; vice chair SBLI USA Mut. Life Ins. Author: (books) Getting Even: Why Women Don't Get Paid Like Men & What to Do About It, 2005. Recipient Dist. Svc. award New Eng. Coun., 1996, Nat. Sierra Club, 1978, Nat. Bd. Govs. Assn., 1978, Outstanding Citizen award Mass. Audobon Soc., 1978; Harvard U. fellow, 1979-80. Mem. Women Execs. in State Govt. (chair 1987), Internat. Women's Forum, 1993—. Democrat. Avocation: jogging. Personal E-mail: evmurphy1@aol.com.

MURPHY, EWELL EDWARD, JR., lawyer; b. Washington, Feb. 21, 1928; s. Ewell Edward and Lou (Phillips) M.; m. Patricia Bredell Purnell, June 26, 1954 (dec. 1964); children: Michaela, Megan Patricia, Harlan Ewell. BA, U. Tex., 1946, LLB, 1948; DPhil, Oxford U., Eng., 1951. Bar: Tex. 1948. Assoc. Baker & Botts, Houston, 1954-63, ptnr., 1964-93, head internat. dept., 1972-89. Pres. Houston World Trade Assn., 1972-74; trustee Southwestern Legal Found., 1978—2003; chmn. Houston Com. on Fgn. Rels., 1984-85, Inst. Transnat. Arbitration, 1985-89, Internat. and Comparative Law Ctr., 1986-87; mem. J. William Fulbright Fgn. Scholarship Bd., 1991-96, vice chmn., 1992-93, chmn., 1993-95; vis. prof. U. Tex. Law Sch., 1993-97; Disting. lectr., U. Houston Law Ctr., 1996—. Contbr. articles to profl. jours. Served to lt. USAF, 1952—54. Recipient Carl H. Fulda award U. Tex. Internat. Law Jour., 1980; Rhodes scholar, 1948-51 Mem.: ABA (chmn. sect. internat. law 1970—71), Internat. Law Inst. (bd. dirs. 1994—), Houston Bar Assn. (chmn. internat. law com. 1963—64, 1970—71), Coun. on Fgn. Rels., Philos. Soc. Tex., Houston C. of C. (chmn. internat. bus. com. 1964—65), Fulbright Assn. (bd. dirs. 1999—2004, v.p. 2002—04). Home and Office: 17 W Oak Dr Houston TX 77056-2117 Home Phone: 713-622-3840; Office Phone: 713-622-3840. E-mail: ewellmurphyjr@sbcglobal.net.

MURPHY, FRANCES LOUISE, II, retired newspaper publisher; b. Balt., Oct. 8, 1922; d. Carl James and L. Vashti (Turley) M.; m. James E. Wood (div.); children: Frances Murphy Wood Draper, James E. Jr., Susan Wood Barnes, David Lloyd Campbell. BA, U. Wis., 1944; BS, Coppin State Coll., Balt., 1958; MEd, Johns Hopkins U., 1963. City editor Balt. Afro-Am., 1956-57; dir. News Bur., Morgan State Coll., Balt., 1964-71; chmn. bd. dirs. Afro-Am. Newspapers, Balt., 1971-74; assoc. prof. journalism State Univ. Coll., Buffalo, 1975-85, Howard U., Washington, 1985-91; editor Washington Afro-Am., 1951-56, pub., 1987-99; editl. page editor Afro-Am. Newspapers, Balt., 1999—, columnist, 2003—. Contbr. columns in newspapers. Treas. African Am. Civil War Meml. Freedom Found.; trustee State Colls. Md., 1971-76, U. D.C., 1994-99; bd. dirs. Delta Rsch. and Ednl. Found., 1993-95; nat. bd. dirs. NACCP, 1971-76; vestry St. James' Episcopal Ch. Named one of 100 Most Influential Black Ams., Ebony mag., 1973, 74, Disting. Marylander, Gov. State of Md., 1975; recipient Ida B. Wells award Congl. Black Caucus, 1989, Public Svc. award African Methodist Episcopal Ch., 1991, Invaluable Svc. award Martin L. King Jr. Found., 1992, Black Women of Courage award Nat. Fedn. Black Women Bus. Owners, 1993, Black Awareness Ach. award Holy Redeemer Catholic Ch., 1993, Bus. of the Yr. award Bus. and Profl. Women's League, 1993, Oustanding Svc. award Capital Press Club, 1993, Black Conscious Commitment trophy Unity Nation, 1993, Dedicated Cmty. Svc. award Ward I Cmty. and DC Pub. Schs., 1994, Women of Strength award Nat. Black Media Coalition, 1994-95, Outstanding Woman of Yr. award Alpha Gamma chpt. Iota Phi Lambda, 1994, Art Carter Excellence award Capital Press Club, 1994, Excellence in Comm. award Washington Inter-Alumni Coun. United Negro Coll. Fund, 1994, 95, Disting. Cmty. Svc. award The Questers, Inc., 1995, Outstanding Journalist award Masons, 1995, Outstanding Achievement award Beta Zeta chpt. Zeta Phi Beta, 1996, award in recognition of outstanding contbns. made to youth The Soc., 1996, Disting. Black Women award BISA, 1996, Woman of 20th Century award Nat. Pol. Congress Black Women, 1999. Mem. Nat. Newspaper Pubs. Assn. (editl. com. 1987—, Merit award 1987, 89-97, First Pl. editl. writing 2003), Soc. Profl. Journalists (Disting. Svc. in local journalism award Washington chpt. 1994), Links (pres. Balt. chpt. 2004—), Capital Press Club (exec. bd. 1987-98, Outstanding Svc. award 1993, Art Carter award 1994), Delta Sigma Theta (Frances L. Murphy II Comm. award Fed. City Alumnae chpt. 1993, Fortitude Image award Prince George's County chpt. 1994, Ethel L. Payne award 1996-97), Kiwanis Club (first woman hon. 1995), Iota Phi Lambda (hon.) Democrat. Episcopalian. Avocation: bridge. Office: Baltimore 2519 N Charles St Baltimore MD 21218-4602 Address: 2406 Overland Ave Baltimore MD 21214-2440 Office Phone: 410-554-8200. Personal E-mail: frankielou@aol.com.

MURPHY, FRANCES M., federal agency administrator; MD with honors, Georgetown U., Washington, 1979; MPH, Uniformed Svcs. U. of the Health Scis., 1993. Diplomate Am. Coll. Psychiatry and Neurology. Resident in neurology Georgetown U., Washington; staff neurologist Andrews AFB, Md., 1983—87; chief cons. occupl. and environ. medicine US Dept. Veterans Affairs, Washington, dep. under-sec. for health, 1999—2002, acting under sec. for health, 2002, dep. under sec. for health policy coord., 2002—. Adj. assoc. prof. neurology Uniformed Svcs. U. of the Health Scis. Contbr. articles to profl. jours. With USAF. Office: US Dept Veterans Affairs 810 Vermont Ave NW Washington DC 20420

MURPHY, FRANCIS, language educator; b. Springfield, Mass., Mar. 13, 1932; s. Frank Edward and Sarah (O'Connor) M. BA, Am. Internat. Coll., 1953; MA, U. Conn., 1955; PhD, Harvard U., 1960; LittD (hon.), Am. Internat. Coll., 1986. Mem. faculty English lang. and lit. Smith Coll., 1959-99, assoc. prof., 1966-69, prof., 1970-99, prof. emeritus, 1999—. Vis. curator Springfield Mus. Fine Arts, 1975-76, Hudson River Mus., 1983-84. Editor: The Diary of Edward Taylor, 1964, Major Am. Poets, 1967, Form and Structure in Poetry, 1964, Edwin Arlington Robinson, 1970, Walt Whitman, 1969, The Uncollected Essays of Yvor Winters, 1973, The Complete Poems of Walt Whitman, 1975, Of Plymouth Plantation (William Bradford), 1981; author: Willard Leroy Metcalf, 1976, (with Dean Flower) A Catalogue of American Paintings, Water Colors and Drawings (to 1923) in the G.W.V. Smith Museum, 1976, The Landscape Within: J. Francis Murphy, 1982, The Book of Nature: American Painters and the Natural Sublime, 1983; co-editor: Norton Anthology of American Literature, 1979—, Mass. Rev., 1966-67.

MURPHY, FREDERICK AUGUSTUS, virologist, researcher; b. NYC, June 14, 1934; s. Frederick A. and Louise A. (Knizak) Murphy; m. Irene M. Warwas, July 2, 1960 (dec.); children: Frederick A., W. Timothy, John G., Terence D. BS in Microbiology, Cornell U., 1956, DVM, 1959; PhD in Comparative Pathology, U. Calif., Davis, 1964; MD (hon.), U. Turku, Finland, 1987; DSc (hon.), U. Guelph, Can., 2000. Chief viral pathology br. Ctrs. for Disease Control, Atlanta, 1964-78; assoc. dean Coll. Vet. Medicine Colo. State U., Ft. Collins, 1978-83; dir. divsn. viral & rickettsial diseases Ctrs. for Disease Control, Atlanta, 1983-87, dir. Nat. Ctr. for Infectious Diseases, 1987-91; dean Sch. Vet. Medicine U. Calif., Davis, 1991-96, disting. prof. Sch. Vet. Medicine, 1996—2005, disting. prof and dean emeritus, 2006—; prof. dept. pathology U. Tex. Med. Br., Galveston, 2006—. Program chair virology divsn. Internat. Union Microbiology Socs., 1978—87, chair virology divsn., 1981—84; adv. bds. Lawrence Livermore Nat. Lab., 1996—; v.p. Found. Human Rabies Edn. & Eradication, 1999—; com. mem. on Future Contributions to Public Health, Agr., Basic Rsch. Counterterrorism, Non-Proliferation Activities in Russia US Nat. Acad. Scis., 2001—03, co-chair Comm. on Occupational Health and Safety in Care of Non-Human primates, 2001—03, com. mem. on Food Safety and Nutrition, 2001—02; com. mem. on Emerging Microbial Threats to Health in 21st Century Inst. Medicine and US Nat. Acad. Scis., 2001—03, com. mem. on Transmissible Spongiform Encephalopathies, 2002—04. Editor: (book series) Advances in Virus Research, 1983—, (book) Virus Taxonomy, 1995; editor in chief: jour. Archives of Virology, 1984—2000, sr. author: book Veterinary Virology III, 1999; contbr. over 450 articles to profl. jours., reports, reviews, monographs, books, and chapters to books. Mem. Pew Trusts Nat. Vet. Edn. Program: Future Directions in Vet. Medicine, 1986—89; mem. Internat. Advisory Group Royal Vet. Coll., London, 2004—; mem. Secretary's Coun. Public Health Preparedness US Dept HHS, 2002—. Capt. US Army, 1959—62, cmdr. USPHS, 1964—68. Named elected mem., German Acad. Nat. Scis., 1985, Inst. Medicine, US Nat. Acad. Scis., 1999, Acad. Medicine Engring. Sci. Tex., 2006; recipient K.F. Meyers Gold Headed Cane, Am. Vet. Epidemiology Soc., 1986, Davis medal, U. Calif., 1998, Pres. Rank award, US Govt., 1992, Richard Moreland Taylor award, Am. Com. Arthropod-Borne Viruses, Am. Soc. Tropical Medicine & Hygeine, 2003. Fellow: Infectious Diseases Soc. Am., John Curtin Sch. Med. Rsch., Australian Nat. U. (hon.); mem.: Am. Soc. Virology (founding coun. mem.), Internat. Com. on Taxonomy of Viruses (life; pres. 1990—96), Am. Soc. Microbiology (com. public health 2006—, public and scientific affairs bd.). Democrat. Roman Catholic. Office: Univ Tex Med Br Dept Pathology 3 145 A Keiller Bldg 301 Univ Blvd Galveston TX 77555-0609 Business E-Mail: famurphy@utmb.edu.

MURPHY, GERALD, retired federal official; b. Washington, Aug. 25, 1938; s. Jeremiah T. and Jean (Curley) M.; m. Kathryn Beckman, Sept. 24, 1988; children by previous marriage: William Michael, Janet Marie, Kathleen Anne B.C.S. with honors, Benjamin Franklin U., Washington, 1960, M.C.S., 1963. C.P.A., D.C. Dep. div. dir. Dept. Treasury, Washington, 1970-71, div. dir., 1971-74, asst. commr., 1974-75, dep. commr., 1975-79, dep. fiscal asst. sec., 1979-86, fiscal asst. sec., 1986-98; sr. prin. Keane Pub. Enterprise Consulting, Washington, 1998-2000; ind. cons., 2000—. Lectr. in acctg. Southeastern U., Washington, 1965-70, Dept. Agr. Grad. Sch., Washington, 1970-76; mem. Govt. Acctg. Standards Adv. Council, 1984-89; mem. Fed. Acctg. Standards Adv. Bd., 1991-98. Served with U.S. Army, 1956 Recipient Disting. Alumni award Benjamin Franklin U., Washington, 1976. Mem. Am. Inst. C.P.A.s, Assn. Govt. Accts. (nat. pres. 1977-78, Robert W. King award 1983, Meritorious Exec. Rsch. award 1992), Sr. Execs. Assn., Fed. Exec. Inst. Alumni Assn. Roman Catholic. Personal E-mail: gmurph825@aol.com.

MURPHY, GERARD NORRIS, trade association executive; b. Washington, July 10, 1950; s. Maurice J. and Marguerite (Norris) M.; m. Jacqueline Franz, May 26, 1973; children: Anne Marie, Michael Jonathan, Kathleen Elizabeth. BA, U. Md., 1972, MA, 1975; JD, George Mason U., 1980. Mgmt. trainee Washington Area New Automobile Dealers Assn., 1972-74, asst. CEO, 1974-82, pres., CEO, 1982—; prodr. Washington Auto Show, 2003—. Bd. dirs. Met. Washington BBB, chmn., 1992—97; bd. dirs. Small Bus. Legis. Coun., 2000—; mem. exec. com. Washington Workforce Investment Coun., 2000—, vice-chmn., 2007—; chmn. Nat. Capital Area Transp. Fedn., Washington, 1990—2000. Co-founder, past chmn. Washington Regional Alcohol Program, Vienna, Va., 1983-86; trustee Nat. Automobile Dealers Assn. Sales Rep. Cert. Commn., 1995-99; sec. Boys and Girls Clubs Greater Washington, Silver Spring, 1987-02, v.p. 2002-05, bd. dirs., 2006—; trustee Greater Washington Bd. Trade PACs, Va., 2000—, Md. treas., 2003—; co-founder Montgomery Students Automotive Trades Found., Montgomery Pub. Schs., 1978, sec., 1990—. Paul Harris fellow Rotary, 1990; recipient Govs. citation Gov. William Donald Schaefer, 1990, Silver medal Boys and Girls Clubs Am., 1997; named Automotive Trade Exec. of Yr., Northwood U., 1997. Fellow Am. Soc. Assn. Execs. (cert., com. chmn. 1989-90, 96-97, 2005-06); mem. ABA, Assn. Healthcare Coalition (sec. 1995, v.p. 1996-97, pres. 1998-00), Automotive Trade Assn. Execs. (bd. dirs. 1987-88, sec., treas. 1996, v.p. 1997, pres. 1998), D.C. Bar Assn., Greater Washington Soc. Assn. Execs. (com. chmn. 1993-94, trustee Found. 1997-00, chmn. award 1994), Leadership Washington (8th class 1993-94), Rotary (sec. 1998-00, v.p. 2001-02, dist. conf. chmn. 2001, pres. 2002-03, 06, v.p. found. 2005, pres. found. 2006-07), Delta Theta Phi, Delta Tau Delta. Democrat. Roman Catholic. Office: Washington Area New Auto Dealers Assn Ste 210 5301 Wisconsin Ave NW Washington DC 20015-2015 Office Phone: 202-237-7200. Business E-Mail: gm@wanado.org.

MURPHY, GLENN T., retail executive; BA, Univ. We. Ontario. Mgmt. positions A.C. Nielsen, Loblaw Companies Ltd., Canada; pres., CEO Chapters, Canada; chmn., CEO Shoppers Drug Mart, Canada, 2001—07, The Gap Inc., San Francisco, 2007—. Office: The Gap Inc 2 Folsom St San Francisco CA 94105 *

MURPHY, GORDON JOHN, electrical engineer, educator; b. Milw., Feb. 16, 1927; s. Gordon M. and Cecelia A. (Knerr) M.; m. Dorothy F. Brautigam, June 26, 1948; children: Lynne, Craig. BS, Milw. Sch. Engring., 1949; MS, U. Wis., 1952; PhD, U. Minn., 1956. Asst. prof. elec. engring. Milw. Sch. Engring., 1949-51; systems engr. A C Spark Plug divsn. GM, 1951-52, cons., 1959-62; instr. U. Minn., 1952-56, asst. prof. elec. engring., 1956-57; assoc. prof. elec. engring. Northwestern U., Evanston, Ill., 1957-60, prof., 1960-97, head dept. elec. engring., 1960-69; pres. IPC Systems, Inc., 1975—2004; dir. Lab. for Design of Electronic Systems Northwestern U., Evanston, Ill., 1987-97, prof. emeritus, 1997—; pres. CUECOA, Inc., 2006—. Cons. numerous corps., 1959—; founder, 1st chmn. Mpls. chpt. Inst. Radio Engrs. Profl. Group on Automatic Control, 1956-57, Chgo. chpt., 1959-61; expert witness in numerous patent suits, 1997-2004. Author: Basic Automatic Control Theory, 1957, 2d edit., 1966, Control Engineering, 1959; contbr. numerous articles, papers to profl. jours.; patentee TV, electronic timers, periodontal instruments and motion control systems. Mem. indsl. adv. com. Milw. Sch. Engring., 1971-2001. Served with USN, 1945-46. Recipient ECE Centennial medal U. Wis., 1991, Outstanding Alumnus award Milw. Sch. Engring. Alumni Assn., 1974; named One of Chgo.'s Ten Outstanding Young Men Chgo. Jaycees, 1961. Fellow IEEE (for edn. and rsch. in automatic control 1967); mem. feedback control systems com. 1960-68, discrete systems com. 1962-68, adminstrv. com. profl. group on automatic control 1966-69, chmn. membership and nominating coms. 1966-67); mem. Am. Automatic Control Coun. (edn. com. 1967-69), Engr.'s Coun. for Profl. Devel. (guidance com. 1967-69), Nat. Electronic Conf. (bd. dirs. 1983-85), Am. Electronics Assn. (exec. com. M.W. coun. 1990-93), Sigma Xi, Eta Kappa Nu, Tau Beta Pi. Home: 638 Garden Ct Glenview IL 60025-4105 Office: Northwestern U Elec Engring Dept Evanston IL 60208 Office Phone: 847-491-7258.

MURPHY, GREGORY E., insurance company executive; Grad., Boston Coll.; grad. Advanced Mgmt. Program, Harvard Univ.; grad., MIT Sloan Sch. Mgmt. CPA. Joined Selective Ins. Group Inc., 1980, sr. v.p. fin., 1994—95, sr. v.p., CFO, 1995—97, COO, 1997—99, pres., 1997—, CEO, 1999—, chmn., 2000—. Bd. trustees Newton Meml. Hosp. Found. Mem.: Am. Inst. for Chartered Property Casualty Underwriters (bd. trustees), Ins. Inst. of Am. (bd. trustees). Office: Selective Ins Group 40 Wantage Ave Branchville NJ 07890 Office Phone: 973-948-3000. *

MURPHY, HAROLD LOYD, federal judge; b. Haralson County, Ga., Mar. 31, 1927; s. James Loyd and Georgia Gladys (McBrayer) M.; m. Jacqueline Marie Ferri, Dec. 20, 1958; children: Mark Harold, Paul Bailey. Student, West Ga. Coll., 1944-45, U. Miss., 1945-46; LL.B., U. Ga., 1949. Bar: Ga. 1949. Pvt. practice, Buchanan, Ga., from 1949; ptnr. Howe & Murphy, Buchanan and Tallapoosa, Ga., 1958-71; judge Superior Cts., Tallapoosa Circuit, 1971-77; U.S. dist. judge No. Dist. of Ga., Rome, 1977—. Rep. Gen. Assembly of Ga., 1951-61; asst. solicitor gen. Tallapoosa Jud. Circuit, 1956; mem. Jud. Qualifications Commn., State of Ga., 1977 With USNR, 1945-46. Fellow Am. Bar Found.; mem. ABA, Ga. Bar Assn., Dist. Judges Assn. for 11th Cir. Bar Assn., Am. Judicature Soc., Tallapoosa Cir. Bar Assn., Old War Horse Lawyers Club, Am. Inns Ct. (past pres. Joseph Henry Lumpkin sect.), Fed. Judges Assn. Methodist. Home: 321 Georgia Highway 120 Tallapoosa GA 30176-3114 Office: US Dist Ct PO Box 53 Rome GA 30162-0053

MURPHY, J. ANDREW (DREW), lawyer; b. Stanford, Calif., Jan. 21, 1961; Student, Univ. Munich, Germany; BA cum laude, Harvard Univ., 1983; JD high honors, George Washington Univ., 1987. Ptnr., head, Project Devel., Fin., Leasing Team Hunton & Williams LLP, Washington & NYC, and mem. exec. com.; exec. v.p., gen. counsel NRG Energy, Inc., Princeton, NJ, 2006—. Mem.: ABA, Am. Coll. Investment Counsel. Office: NRG Energy, Inc 211 Carnegie Ctr Princeton NJ 08540 Office Phone: 609-524-4500. *

MURPHY, JAMES EDWARD, public relations and marketing executive; Degree in Journalism, U. Ill. Sr. corp. comms. officer Owens-Corning Fiberglas, Beatrice, Merrill Lynch; exec. v.p. Burson-Marsteller, vice chmn., 1990, chmn., CEO Ams., 1991-93; chmn., CEO Murphy & Co., 1993—; chief mktg. and comm. officer Accenture (formerly known as Andersen Cons.), 1993—. Mem. bd. advisors Medill Sch. Journalism, Northwestern U.; mem. devel. bd. Coll. Comm., U. Ill.; past pres., bd. dirs. Arthur Page Soc.; chmn. PR Coalition. Mem. Inst. Pub. Rels. Rsch. (trustee), Union League Club, Belle Haven Club, Woodway Country Club, Palmetto Golf Club, Preston Mountain Club. Office: Accenture 6th Fl 1345 Avenue of the Americas New York NY 10105 E-mail: james.e.murphy@accenture.com.

MURPHY, JAMES JEFFREY, electronics executive; b. Kenosha, Wis., Nov. 4, 1954; s. Eugene C. and Thelma M. (Jensen) M.; m. Susan M. Larson, June 10, 1978. BA in Bus. Mgmt. and Labor Econs. with honors, U. Wis., 1976. Sales rep. Inland Steel, Chgo., 1976-77, product analyst, 1977; sales rep. Joerndt & Ventura, Inc., Kenosha, 1977-78; field sales rep. Applied Power Corp., New Berlin, Wis., 1978-79; Magnavox regional mgr. Philips Consumer Electronics Co., Knoxville, Tenn., 1979-87, zone mgr., 1987-89, divsn. field sales mgr., 1989-91, natl. account dir., 1991-95, v.p. merchandising, 1995—2004; mgr. VAS Portfolio, 2004—. Mem. Lincoln Continental Owners Club (treas. 1991), Vintage Radio-Phonograph Soc. Avocations: car collecting, reading, walking. Home: 2330 Stonegate Dr Cumming GA 30041-7410 Office: Philips Consumer Electronics Co 64 Perimeter Ctr E Atlanta GA 30346-2295 Office Phone: 770-821-2922. Business E-Mail: jmurphy54@bellsouth.net.

MURPHY, JAMES PAUL, lawyer; b. Jackson, Tenn., Apr. 29, 1944; s. Paul Joseph and Marjorie Mary (Smyth) Murphy; m. Marcia Mae Gaughan, Sept. 5, 1975. BA cum laude, U. Notre Dame, 1966; JD, U. Mich., 1969. Bar: Ohio 1969, D.C. 1984, Md. 1984, U.S. Dist. Ct. (no. dist.) Ohio 1970, U.S. Ct. Appeals (6th cir.) 1972, U.S. Supreme Ct. 1976, U.S. Dist. Ct. Md. 1984, U.S. Dist. Ct. D.C. 1984, U.S. Ct. Appeals (4th cir., D.C. cir.) 1984. Vol. VISTA, 1969—70; assoc. Squire, Sanders & Dempsey, LLP, Cleve., 1970—79, ptnr., 1979—. Mem.: Ohio State Bar Assn. (antitrust sect.), D.C. Bar Assn., Md. Bar Assn., Cleve. Bar Assn. (fed. ct. com.), City Club (Washington), Westwood Country Club (Rocky River, Ohio). Home: 4512 Wetherill Rd Bethesda MD 20816-1837 Home Phone: 301-229-6946; Office Phone: 202-626-6793. Business E-Mail: jmurphy@ssd.com.

MURPHY, JENNIFER H. (BUFFY MURPHY), elementary school educator; b. Columbia, SC; BA in Recreational Therapy, Clemson (SC) Univ.; MA in Edn., Univ. SC; grad. student, Coll. Charleston. Cert. Nat. Bd. Tchg. Standards, Assisting, Developing, and Evaluating Profl. Tchg. (ADEPT) evaluator. Tchr. Irmo (SC) Elem. Sch. Tchr.-in-residence and adv. bd. mem. Ctr. for Educator Recruitment, Retention and Advancement (CERRA) Inst. Higher Edn., SC; clin. adj. Univ. SC Profl. Devel. Sch. Program. Named SC Tchr. of Yr., 2007. Office: Irmo Elem Sch 7401 Gibbes St Irmo SC 29063 Business E-Mail: bmurphy@lex5.k12.sc.us. *

MURPHY, JEREMIAH T., professional sports team, construction executive; b. NYC, July 21, 1944; m. Sandra Murphy; children: Lisa, Tara, Gregory. BA, Bernard Baruch Coll. CPA Calif. Sr. ptnr. Bowman and Co., Stockton, Calif., 1971-82; CFO A.G. Spanos Companies, Stockton, Calif., 1982—; v.p. San Diego Chargers. Mem.: Calif. Soc. of CPAs, Am. Inst. of CPAs. Office: AG Spanos Companies 10100 Trinity Pky Stockton CA 95219 also: San Diego Chargers 4020 Murphy Canyon Rd San Diego CA 92123

MURPHY, JOANNE BECKER, writer; b. Detroit; d. Louis Norman and Gertrude Margaret (Kornmeier) Becker; m. Joseph A. Murphy, Jr., June 24, 1961; children: Michael Ellis, Joseph A. III. BA in Journalism, Mich. State U., 1958; MA in Humanities, Wayne State U., 1975. With pub. rels. dept. WBZ TV, Boston, 1958-60, The Jam Handy Orgn., Detroit, 1960-62, Detroit Symphony Orch., 1969-70; freelance writer, editor Detroit, 1978—90, Washington, 1990—. Contbg. writer: Affecting Change, 1986, Glass: State of the Art, 1989; editor: As Parents We Will, 1985 (1st Pl. award Pub. Svc. Nat. Found. for Alcoholism Comm.); writer, editor publs. for arts and human svcs. orgns.; contbr. articles to mags., newspapers. Program bd. Grosse Pointe (Mich.) War Meml., 1987—90; bd. dirs. Detroit Artists Market, 1982—90, Mich. Metro coun. Girl Scouts USA, 1971—78, Family Svcs. Detroit and Wayne County, 1970—76, All Hallows Guild Grounds Oversight Bd., Washington Nat. Cathedral, 1993—; bd. canvassers Grosse Pointe Sch. Sys., 1986—90; DC regional bd. Nat. Capital Area United Way, Washington, 1999—. Mem.: Washington Ind. Writers, Am. News Women's Club (bd. dirs. 1996—2001, Washington, bd. dirs. 2007—), Kappa Alpha Theta. Home and Office: 2717 O St NW Washington DC 20007-3128 Home Phone: 202-337-7856; Office Phone: 202-337-7856. E-mail: murphy.joanne@verizon.net.

MURPHY, JOHN B., portfolio manager; b. Pitts., May 30, 1947; s. John Bernard and Knolle Cordelia (Bonham) M.; m. Lauren Osa Brown, Mar. 20, 1994; children: Kira Mei Li, Anya Cai Li. BA, U. New Orleans, 1970; MBA, Columbia U., 1984. CFA 1987. Dir. La. Heritage Fair, New Orleans, 1974-75, 78-80; assoc. dir. New Orleans Jazz and Heritage Festival, 1978-80; exec. dir. New Orleans Jazz and Heritage Found. Inc., 1980; assoc. editor, analyst Value Line Pubs., NYC, 1984-86; equity analyst, v.p. Drexel, Burnham, Lambert, NYC, 1986-90; portfolio mgr., mng. dir., head convertible investments Guardian, NYC, 1990—. Mng. dir. Family Svc. Life and other Guardian subs., 1998—; mem. alumni counseling bd. Sch. Bus. Columbia U., NYC, 1986—; prodn. cons. Newport Jazz Festival, Capitol Radio Jazz Festival, Memphis Heritage Festival, 1978-80. Recipient Mayoralty Merit award City of New Orleans, 1978. Mem. Assn. Investment Mgmt. and Rsch., N.Y. Soc. Security Analysts, Beta Gamma Sigma (scholarship award 1983). Avocations: poetry, photography, golf. Home: PO Box 243 Ardsley On Hudson NY 10503-0243 Office: Guardian 7 Hanover Sq New York NY 10004-2616 Office Phone: 212-598-8104. Business E-Mail: john_murphy@glic.com.

MURPHY, JOHN CONDRON, JR., lawyer; b. Mpls., May 26, 1945; s. John Condron and Elaine Anne (Wentink) M.; m. Marie Antoinette Calcara, Aug. 17, 1968; children: Justin Peter, Jonathan Patrick. AB cum laude, Georgetown U., Washington, 1967; JD cum laude, U. Pa., 1972. Bar: Calif. 1972, D.C. 1978. Assoc. O'Melveny & Myers, LA, 1972-75; spl. counsel U.S Securities & Exch. Commn., Washington, 1975-77; assoc. Cleary Gottlieb Steen & Hamilton LLP, Washington, 1977—81, ptnr., 1982-84, 87—; gen. counsel Fed. Deposit Ins. Corp., Washington, 1984-87. Mem. bd. editors Banking Policy Report, 1988—; contbr. articles to profl. jours. Lt. (j.g.) USNR, 1968-69. Mem. ABA (subcom. chmn. banking law com., chmn. acquisitions and dispositions subcom. 1992-95), Fed. Bar Assn. (chmn. banking law com. 1992-94), Columbia Country Club (Chevy Chase, Md.). Republican. Roman Catholic. Home: 6 Newlands St Chevy Chase MD 20815-4202 Office Phone: 202-974-1580.

MURPHY, JOHN F., lawyer; b. Jersey City, May 24, 1954; s. John Francis and Helen Joan (Makowski) M.; m. Bridget Fagan, Aug. 4, 1984; children: Helen Mary, John William. BA, U. Conn., 1976; JD, Washington & Lee U., 1979. Bar: Mo. 1979, US Dist. Ct. (we. dist.) Mo. 1979, US Ct. Appeals (8th cir.) 1982, US Supreme Ct. 1991. Assoc. Shook, Hardy & Bacon LLP, Kansas City, Mo., 1979-85, ptnr., 1985—, chmn., 2003—. Bd. dirs. Lakemary Ctr. Endowment Assn., Paola, Kans., Friends of Spl. People, Starlight Theatre, Cath. Edn. Found.; pres. Waterford Homes Assn., 1994. Mem. Fedn. Defense and Corp. Counsel, Mo. Bar Assn., Kansas City Met. Bar Assn., Greater Kansas City C. of C. (bd. dirs.), Civic Coun. Greater Kans. City, Phi Beta Kappa, Phi Kappa Phi, Omicron Delta Kappa. Republican. Roman Catholic. Avocations: running, spectator sports. Office: Shook Hardy & Bacon LLP 2555 Grand Blvd Kansas City MO 64108 Office Phone: 816-474-6550. Office Fax: 816-421-5547. Business E-Mail: jmurphy@shb.com.

MURPHY, JOHN FRANCIS, law educator, consultant; b. Portchester, NY, Apr. 25, 1937; s. Francis John and Emilie (Tourtellot) M.; m. Laura S. Murphy; children: Andrew, Robert; stepchildren: Dan, Jessie, Gabriel. BA, Cornell U., 1959, LLB in Internat. Affairs, 1962. Bar: D.C. 1963, Kans. 1970, Pa. 1987. Afro-Asia Pub. Svc. fellow, India, 1962-63; assoc. Winthrop, Stimson, Putnam & Roberts, NYC, 1963-64; atty. Office Legal Adv., Dept. State, Washington, 1964-67; assoc. Kirkland, Ellis, Hodson, Chaffetz & Masters, Washington, 1967-69; assoc. prof. law U. Kans., Lawrence, 1969-72, prof. law, 1972-84, assoc. dean Sch. Law, 1975-77; vis. prof. law Villanova U., Pa., 1983-84, prof. law sch. law, 1984—. Vis. prof. law Cornell U., Ithaca, N.Y., fall 1979, Georgetown U., summer 1982, San Diego U., summer Paris, 1986, 95, Mexico City, 1988, London, 1989, La. State U. summer, Aix-en-Provence, 1990, Haifa (Israel) U., 1997; Charles H. Stockton Prof. Internat. Law, Naval War Coll., 1980-81. Author: Legal Aspects of International Terrorism: Summary Report of an International Conference, 1980, The United Nations and the Control of International Violence, 1982, Punishing International Terrorists, 1985, State Support of International Terrorism: Legal, Political and Economic Dimensions, 1989, (with Alan Swan) The Regulation of International Business and Economic Relations, 1991, Supplements, 1994, 95, 2d edit., 1999 (cert. of merit Am. Soc. Internat. Law 1992), (with James D. Dinnage) The Constitutional Law of the European Union, 1996, Supplement, 1999, The United States and The Rule of Law in International Affairs, 2004; contbr. articles, comments, book revs. to profl., popular jours.; editor (with Alona E. Evans), contbg. author: Legal Aspects of International Terrorism, 1978; bd. editors Cornell Law Quar., 1961, 62; mem. bd. editors Terrorism: An Internat. Jour., 1981-92, Terrorism and Polit. Violence, 1993-2003, The Internat. Lawyer, 1998—, Transnat. Publishers, 1999-2006; mem. editl. bd. Internat. Law Studies, Naval War Coll., 2003—. Mem.: ABA (alt. rep. to US Mission to UN 2006—07), Internat. Law Assn., Am. Soc. Internat. Law. Episcopalian. Office: Villanova U Sch Law 299 N Spring Mill Rd Villanova PA 19085 Home Phone: 610-431-1984; Office Phone: 610-519-7065. Business E-Mail: murphy@law.villanova.edu.

MURPHY, JOHN JOSEPH, manufacturing executive; b. Olean, NY, Nov. 24, 1931; s. John Joseph and Mary M.; m. Louise John; children: Kathleen A. Murphy Bell, Karen L. Murphy Rochelli, Patricia L. Murphy Smith, Michael J. AAS in Mech. Engring., Rochester Inst. Tech., 1952; MBA, So. Meth. U., 1981. Engr. Clark div. Dresser Industries, Olean, 1952-67, gen. mgr. roots blower div. Connersville, Ind., 1967-69, pres. crane, hoist and tower div. Muskegon, Mich., 1969-70, pres. machinery group Houston, 1970-75, sr. v.p. ops. Dallas, 1980, exec. v.p., 1982, pres., 1982-92, CEO, 1983—95, chmn. bd., 1983-96; mng. dir. SMG Mgmt. L.L.C., Dallas, 1997-2000. Bd. dirs. W.R. Grace & Co.; emeritus mem. Bus. Coun. With US Army, 1954—56. Office: 3838 Oak Lawn Ave Ste 224 Dallas TX 75219

MURPHY, JOHN JOSEPH, literature educator, critic, editor; b. NYC, Apr. 3, 1933; s. John and Margaret B. (Shadegg) M.; m. Sarah Marie McMahon, June 30, 1962; children: Sarah, Joseph, Willa, John, Emily. BA, St. John's U., NYC, 1956, MA, 1961. Instr. English lit. Coll. of St. Teresa, Winona, Minn., 1960-65; asst. prof. English lit. Merrimack Coll., North Andover, Mass., 1965-68, assoc. prof., 1969-84, chmn. dept. English, 1974—76, 1979—82; prof. English lit. Brigham Young U., Provo, Utah, 1984—2005, prof. emeritus, 2005—, chair Am. lit. sect. dept. English, 1986—89, assoc. dir. Ctr. for Study Christian Values in Lit., 1994—2004. Organizer and dir. Willa Cather and Nebr. 1st Internat. U. Nebr. Cather Seminar, Hastings and Red Cloud, Nebr., 1981; bd. govs. Willa Cather Meml., 1984—; mem. editl. bd. Willa Cather Scholarly Edit., U. Nebr. Press, 1986—; vis. prof. U. Leon, Spain, 2001, U. Santiago, Spain, 2003, U. Rome 3, 2005; co-dir. Willa Cather: A Writer's Worlds, 11th Internat. Cather Seminar, Paris and Provence, France, 2007; presenter in field. Author: My Antonia: The Road Home, 1989; editor: Critical Essays on Willa Cather, 1984, Willa Cather: Family, Community, History, 1990, Penguin My Antonia, 1994, Literature and Belief, 1994—2004, Death Comes for the Archbishop, 1999, Willa Cather and the Culture of Belief, 2002, Shadows on the Rock, 2005; prodr.: (TV series) KTCA TV, Great Ladies of the Am. Novel, 1963, Nathaniel Hawthorne, Am. Realist, 1964; contbr. chapters to books, articles to profl. jours. With US Army, 1958-60. Recipient R.E. Twitchell award N.Mex. Hist. Soc., 2000; NEH fellow for Coll. Tchrs, 1982. Home: 1390 Avenida Rincon # 102 Santa Fe NM 87506-6004 Office: Brigham Young U English Dept 4198 JFSB Provo UT 84602 Office Phone: 505-820-1981. Business E-Mail: john_murphy@byu.edu.

MURPHY, JOHN THOMAS, lawyer; b. Pierre, SD, July 20, 1932; s. Bernard J. and Gertrude (Loner) M.; m. Rose Marie Cogorno. LLB, U. SD, 1957. Bar: SD 1957, Calif. 1962. Pvt. practice, Stockton, Calif., 1965-75, Modesto, Calif., 1975—; atty. office gen. counsel quartermaster gen. U.S. Army, 1957-58, asst. chief counsel Sharpe Army Depot, 1958-63, gen. counsel, 1963-65; assoc. Short, Short, Scott & Murphy (and predecessor firm), 1965-68; ptnr. Hulsey, Beus, Wilson, Scott & Murphy, Stockton, 1968-70. Bd. dirs. Delta-Stockton Humane Soc., 1970-75, former dir. Tuolumne River Preservation Trust; gov. emeritus Calif. Trout Inc.; mem. Stanislaus River Task Force, Stanislaus County Water Coord. Com. Mem. State Bar Calif., ATLA, Consumer Attys. Calif., Beta Theta Pi, Phi Delta Phi, Stockton Beagler's Club (sec., dir.), Am. Kennel Club (Beagle adv. com. 1984-2004). Republican. Episcopalian. Office: 1124 11th St Modesto CA 95354-0826 Home Phone: 209-869-4464; Office Phone: 209-527-6242. Business E-Mail: bigbad@inreach.com.

MURPHY, JOHN VINCENT, investment company executive; b. Boston, July 12, 1949; s. James Gerald and Mary Lee (Dolan) Murphy; m. Kathleen Ryan, Nov. 17, 1973; children: Elizabeth Ryan, Christopher John, Carolyn Holmes. BS, Boston Coll., 1971. CPA Mass. Acct. Arthur Andersen & Co., CPAs, Boston, 1972—77; contr. Continental Investment Corp., Boston, 1977—81; v.p., contr. Torchmark Fin. Svcs. Co., Boston, 1981—85; sr. v.p. fin., CFO Liberty Fin. Svcs., Inc., Boston, 1985; exec. v.p. Mass. Mut. Life Ins. Co.; with OppenheimerFunds, Inc., 2000—, pres., 2001—07, COO, chmn., CEO, 2001—. Treas. Liberty Real Estate Corp., 1981, Torchmark Leasing Programs, Inc., Boston, 1981—85, Copley Venture Capital Inc., 1984, Liberty Asset Mgmt. Co., 1985; bd. dirs. Fiduciary Trust Co. NH, Chatham Fin. Assocs., 1983—85; bd. dirs., pres. MassMutual Instl. Funds., MML Series Funds; bd. govs. Investment Co. Inst.; del. Fin. Svcs. Roundtable; pres., bd. mem. Oppenheimer Acquisition Corp. Chmn. Alumni Capital Campaign Boston Coll. HS, 1986—87, mem. devel. adv. com. to bd. trustees; mem. Wall St. Coun. exec. com. Boston Coll.; bd. dirs. Project Rebirth, Inc., 2004—. Served in US Army, 1971—72. Named one of 30 Most Influential People in Investing, SmartMoney mag., 2001; recipient Man of Yr. award, NY Gov.'s Com. on Scholastic Achievement. Mem.: AICPA, Greater Boston C. of C. Execs. Club, Fin. Execs. Inst., Mass. Soc. CPAs, Shriver, Charitable Irish Soc., Algonquin, Blue Chips, Boston Racquet, Boston Coll Varsity (pres. 1980—82). Office: OppenheimerFunds Inc Two World Fin Ctr 225 Liberty St New York NY 10281-1008 *

MURPHY, JOSEPH ALBERT, JR., lawyer; b. Grosse Pointe, Mich., May 29, 1934; s. Joseph Albert and Isabel C. (Callahan) M.; m. Joanne Becker, June 24, 1961; children: Michael, Joseph III. BS, Georgetown U., 1956; JD, Detroit Coll. Law, Mich. State U., 1962. Bar: Mich. 1962, D.C. 1996. House counsel Blue Cross Mich., Detroit, 1964-69, gen. counsel, corp. sec., 1969-75; v.p., gen. counsel Blue Cross & Blue Shield Mich., Detroit, 1975—88; chief Washington counsel Blue Cross and Blue Shield Assn., Washington, 1989—2001; cons. eLawForum, Washington, 2002—. Chmn. Health Care Network, Southfield, Mich., 1981-85, Blue Care Inc., Southfield, 1986-88;. Editl. adv. bd. Thompson Pub., 2005—. Allocations panel United Found., Detroit, 1985-88; treas. Grosse Pointe Dem. Club, 1972-73; chmn. Health and People's Polit. Action Commn., Detroit, 1978-84; fundraiser United Way of Nat. Capital Area, 2005—. With U.S. Army, 1957-59. Mem. ABA, Mich. Bar Assn., Detroit Bar Assn., DC Bar Assn., Am. Health Lawyers Assn. (pres. 1981-82), Am. Corp. Counsel Assn., Am. Arbitrators Assn. (panel of arbitrators). Roman Catholic. Home: 2717 O St NW Washington DC 20007-3128 Personal E-mail: jamjr5@verizon.net.

MURPHY, JOSEPH EDWARD, JR., broadcast executive; b. Mpls., Mar. 13, 1930; s. Joseph Edward Murphy and Ann Hynes; m. Diana Kuske, July 24, 1958; children: Michael, John. BA, Princeton U., 1952; postgrad., U. Minn., 1956-60. Chartered fin. analyst. Dir. investment rsch. Woodward-Elwood & Co., Mpls., 1961-67; v.p. Northwestern Nat. Bank, Mpls., 1967-83; chmn. Midwest Communications, Inc., Mpls., 1990-92; ret. Dir. Midwest Comm., Inc., 1956-89, vice chmn., 1985-89. Author: Adventure Beyond the Clouds: How We Climbed China's Highest Mountain and Survived, 1986 (Friends Am. Writers award 1986), With Interest: How to Profit From Interest Rate Fluctuations, 1987, Stock Market Probability, 1988, revised edit., 1994, South to the Pole by Ski, 1990, The Random Character of Interest Rates, 1990, To the Poles by Ski and Dogsled, 1996, Bond Tables of Probable Future Yields, 1996, The Random Character of Corporate Earnings, 1997, Why the Stock Market Rises, 1998. Vice chmn. Minn. Coun. on Quality Edn., 1971-77; trustee Macalester Coll., St. Paul, 1973-87, Mpls. Soc. Fine Arts, 1977-78, Voyageur Outward Bound, 1985-92; bd. dirs. Minn. Opera Co., 1971-80, Childrens Theater Co., 1975-80, Minn. Ctr. for Book Arts, 1987-93, Greater Mpls. coun. Girl Scouts U.S.A., 1987-93, Fund for Peace, 1988-92, Minn. Nature Conservancy, 1991-96. 2d lt. U.S. Army, 1952-55. Mem. Am. Alpine Club (life, v.p. and bd. dirs. 1975-81), Himalayan Club (life), Mpls. Club. Avocations: mountain climbing, exploration. Home: 2116 W Lake Isle Minneapolis MN 55405-2425

MURPHY, JOSEPH JAMES, chiropractic physician; b. Newark, July 30, 1956; s. Joseph P. and Roberta (Nittolo) Murphy; children: Joseph Raymond, Alexandra Renee; m. Maria Elena Sileo, Feb. 17, 2002; 1 child, Sean Alfred. BA in Biology, Rider Coll., Lawrenceville, NJ, 1978; D in Chiropractic Medicine, Palmer Coll., Davenport, Iowa, 1984. Diplomate Nat. Bd. Chiropractic Examiners; cert. N.J. State Bd. Med. Examiners. Rsch. chemist Mallinkrodt, Inc., Englewood, NJ, 1979-81; staff physician Mid-Island Chiropractic, Levittown, NY, 1984; dir., chief exec. officer Suburban Chiropractic Ctr., Chatham, NJ, 1984—. Apptd. mem. N.J. Bd. Chiropractic Examiners, 2000—, sec., 2003, pres., 2006. Mem. editl. bd. Am. Chiropractor Mag., 2000—; editor-in-chief newsletter The Column. Advisor Chatham High Sch. Key Club, 1986-87; trustee Early Childhood Learning Ctr., Chatham, 1999—, sec. 2002; mem. spkrs. bur. Am. Heart Assn. D. D. Palmer scholar, 1981, 82, 83. Mem.: AAAS, APHA, Morris County Chiropractic Soc. (pres. 1987—, bd. pres. 2006), Bd. Chiropractic Examiners (apptd. mem. State of N.J.), Internat. Soc. Food Technologists, N.Y. Acad. Sci., N.J. Chiropractic Soc. (editor-in-chief Jersey Jour. 1986—, bd. dirs. 1987—, chmn. inter profl. rels. com. 1989—, 1st v.p. 1992—95, pres. 1995—, Meritorious Svc. award 1986, Disting. Svc. award 1987—97), Am. Chiropractic Assn., Am. Assn. Cereal Chemists, Chatham C. of C. (chmn. profl. rels. com. 1988—92, pres. 1989—92, Dist. Mem. Svc. award 1996), Chatham Hist. Preservation Commn. (mayor apptd. mem.), Kiwanis (bd. dirs. Chatham club 1986—89, Disting. Svc. award 1995), Tri Beta. Republican. Presbyn. Avocations: skiing, photography, model building, automobiles, bicycling. Home: 20 Squire Ct Basking Ridge NJ 07920 Office: Suburban Chiropractic Ctr 301 Main St Chatham NJ 07928-2410 Home Phone: 973-872-0175; Office Phone: 973-635-0036. Business E-Mail: drmurphy@drmurphy.com.

MURPHY, JUDITH CHISHOLM, trust company executive; b. Chippewa Falls, Wis., Jan. 26, 1942; d. John David and Bernice A. (Hartman) Chisholm. BA, Manhattanville Coll., 1964; postgrad., New Sch. for Social Research, 1965-68, Nat. Grad. Trust Sch., 1975. Asst. portfolio mgr. Chase Manhattan Bank, N.A., NYC, 1964-68; trust investment officer Marshall & Ilsley Bank, Milw., 1968-72, asst. v.p., 1972-74, v.p., 1974-75; v.p., treas. Marshall & Ilsley Invesment Mgmt. Corp., Milw., 1975-94; v.p. Marshall & Ilsley Trust Co., Phoenix, 1982—, Marshall & Ilsley Trust Co. Fla., Naples, 1985—; v.p., dir. instnl. sales Marshall & Ilsley Trust Co., Milw., 1994-97, sr. v.p., 1997-98, M&I Investment Mgmt. Corp., 1998—. Coun. mem. Am. Bankers Assn., Washington, 1984-86; govt. relations com. Wis. Bankers Assn., Madison, 1982-88. Contbr. articles to profl. jours. Chmn. Milw. City Plan Commn., 1986—97; commr. Milw. County Commn. on Handicapped, 1988—90; bd. dirs. Cardinal Stritch Coll., Milw., 1980—89, Children's Hosp. Wis., Milw., 1989—98, Milw. Ballet Co., 1996—2001, Milw. Ctr. for Independence, 1999—2004, Girl Scouts Milw. Area, 2002—06, Milw. Symphony Orch., 2002—, Alzheimers Assn., 2007—. Recipient Outstanding Achievement award YWCA Greater Milw., 1985, Sacajawea award Profl. Dimensions, Milw., 1988, Pro Urbe award Mt. Mary Coll., 1988, Vol. award Milw. Found., 1992; named Disting. Woman in Banking, Comml. West Mag., 1988. Mem. Milw. Analysts Soc. (sec. 1974-77, bd. dirs. 1977-80), Fin. Women Internat. (bd. dirs., v.p. 1976-80), Am. Inst. Banking (instr. 1975-78), TEMPO (charter), Profl. Dimensions (hon.), University Club, Woman's Club Wis., Rotary. Democrat. Roman Catholic. Home: 3622 N Lake Dr Milwaukee WI 53211-2644 Office: M&I Investment Mgmt Corp 111 E Kilbourn Ave Milwaukee WI 53202-3197 Business E-Mail: judith.murphy@micorp.com.

MURPHY, KAREN, film producer; Film prodr. Interscope Comm., LA. Prodr.: This Is Spinal Tap, 1984, True Stories, 1986, (with Nick Wechsler) Drug Store Cowboy, 1989, (with Robert W. Cort, Ted Field) The Cutting Edge, 1992, Twenty Bucks, 1993, (with Tony Allard), Waiting for Guffman, 1996, Spinal Tap: The Final Tour, 1998, Best in Show, 2000, A Mighty Wind, 2003, For Your Consideration, 2006; exec. prodr.: Magic In The Water, 1995. Office: Interscope Comm 10 Columbus Cir Ste 770B New York NY 10019-1201 Fax: 310-208-1764.

MURPHY, KAREN, sports association executive; b. 1971; With Ernst & Young, Chgo., Walt Disney Co.; contr. Chgo. Bears Football Club Inc., Lake Forest, Ill., 1999—2002, CFO & treas., 2002—. Named one of 40 Under 40, Crain's Chgo. Bus., 2006. Office: Chgo Bears Football Club Inc 1000 Football Dr Lake Forest IL 60045

MURPHY, KATHLEEN ANNE FOLEY, marketing communications executive; b. Fresh Meadows, NY, Oct. 15, 1952; d. Thomas J. and Audrey L. Finn; m. Timothy Sean Murphy, Sept. 26, 1992; 1 child, G. David. BA, Marymount Coll., 1974; postgrad., Smith Coll., 1985. V.p. acct. supr., sr. v.p. mgmt. supr., sr. v.p. group dir. Ogilvy & Mather Inc., NYC, 1974-90; sr. v.p., worldwide account dir. Young & Rubicam, San Francisco, 1990-92, sr. v.p., dir. account svcs., 1992-95, exec. v.p., dir. acct. svcs., 1995-97, exec. v.p., gen. mgr., 1997—2002, COO, 2002—03; dir. network devel. WPP, San Francisco, 2003—, dir. Western region integration, 2003—. Mem. Family Caregivers Alliance. Roman Catholic. Home: One Brookside Ave Berkeley CA 94705 Office: WPP 303 Second St S Tower 9th Fl San Francisco CA 94107

MURPHY, KATHLEEN M., lawyer; b. Evergreen Park, Ill. BA, St. Xavier Coll., 1980; MA, Loyola U., Chgo., 1982, JD, 1985. Bar: Ill. 1985, US Ct. Appeals, 7th Cir., US Ct. Appeals, Fed. Cir., US Ct. Internat. Trade, US Dist. Ct., No. Dist Ill. Ptnr., nat. chair Customs and Internat. Trade Dept. and Global Trade Adv. Group Katten Muchin Zavis Rosenman, Chgo. Mem.: ABA, Women in Internat. Trade, Midwest Importers Trade Assn., Joint Industry Group, Customs and Internat. Trade Bar Assn., Am. Assn. of Exporters and Importers.

MURPHY, KATHLEEN MARY, former law firm executive, alternative healing professional; b. Bklyn., Dec. 16, 1945; d. Raymond Joseph and Catherine Elizabeth (Kearney) Murphy. BA in Edn., Molloy Coll., Rockville Centre, NY, 1971; MS in Edn., Bklyn. Coll., 1975. Ordained minister Ch. of the Loving Servant; cert. hypnotherapist; cert. elem. sch. tchr., NY. Elem. sch. tchr. various parochial schs., LI, Bklyn., Queens, NY, 1969-80; from asst. prin. to prin. parochial sch. Queens, 1980-82; supr.-trainer Davis, Polk, Wardwell law firm, NYC, 1982-88; mgr. Schulte Roth & Zabel, NYC, 1988-95; Reiki master (alternative healing profl.), 1996—. Trainer program for new employees, 1984; speaker edn. topics, Bklyn., Queens, 1979-81. Mem.: NAFE, Reiki Alliance. Democrat. Roman Catholic. Avocations: psychic phenomenon, workings of mind, ancient histories, crossword puzzles, museums. Home: 290 14th St Brooklyn NY 11215

MURPHY, KATHRYN J., lawyer; b. Moorhead, Minn., Dec. 28, 1961; BA with honors, U. Tex., Tyler, 1986; JD, So. Meth. U., Dallas, 1989. Bar: Tex. 1989, US Dist. Ct. (no. dist. Tex.). Ptnr. Koons, Fuller, Vanden Eykel & Robertson, P.C., Plano, Tex., 1995—. Named a Tex. Super Lawyer, Tex. Monthly mag., 2003, 2004; named one of Best Lawyers in Dallas, D Mag., 2005. Fellow: Am. Acad. Matrimonial Lawyers, Collin County Bench Bar Found.; mem.: Coll. State Bar Tex., J. Reuben Clark Law Soc. (bd. dir. 1997—99), Internat. Acad. Collaborative Profl., Dallas Alliance Collaborative Law Inst. Tex., Tex. Acad. Family Law Specialists, Collin County Bar Assn., Dallas Bar Assn., ABA. Office: Koons Fuller Vanden Eykel & Robertson PC 2311 Cedar Springs Rd Ste 300 Dallas TX 75201 Office Phone: 214-871-2727. Office Fax: 214-871-0196. E-mail: Kathryn@koonsfuller.com. *

MURPHY, KENNETH F., human resources specialist; BS in Labor Rels., Cornell U., 1977. Mgr. human resources Gen. Foods Corp., 1981—85, mgr. human resources desserts divsn., 1985—94; v.p. human resources, mktg. and sales Philip Morris USA, NYC, 1996; sr. v.p. human resources and adminstrn. Altria Group, Inc., 2003—. Office: Altria Group Inc 120 Park Ave New York NY 10017-5592

MURPHY, KENYON W., lawyer; b. Rome, Ga., Nov. 28, 1956; BBA in Acctg., U. Ga., 1978; JD, Harvard U., 1981. Bar: Ga. 1981. Law clerk to Judge James C. Hill U.S. Ct. of Appeals, 11th Circuit, 1981—82; assoc. Alston & Bird, Atlanta, 1982—85; from asst. counsel to sr. v.p., gen. counsel Nat. Svc. Industries Inc., 1985—2000, sr. v.p., 2000—01, gen. coun., 2000—01; sr. v.p. Acuity Brands Inc, Atlanta, 2001—, gen. counsel, 2001—. Mem.: ABA, Am. Corp. Counsel Assn., Ga. State Bar Assn. Office: Acuity Brands Inc 1170 Peachtree St NE Atlanta GA 30309 *

MURPHY, KEVIN M., economics professor; AB, U. Calif., 1981; PhD, U. Chgo., 1986. Asst. prof. bus. economics and indsl. rels. U. Chgo., 1986—88, assoc. prof., 1988—89, prof., 1989—93, George Pratt Schultz prof., 1993—2002, George J. Stigler prof. economics, 2002—, George J. Stigler disting. svc. prof. economics, dept. economics and grad. sch. bus., 2005—. Faculty rsch. assoc. Nat. Bur. Econ. Rsch. Co-author: Social Economics: Market Behavior in a Social Environment, 2000; co-editor: Measuring the Gains from Medical Research: An Economic Approach, 2003; contbr. articles to profl. jours. Named MacArthur fellow, John D. and Catherin T. MacArthur Found., 2005; fellow, Earhart Found., 1980—81, 1983—84, Friedman Fund, 1981—83. Fellow: Econometric Soc.; mem.: Am. Acad. Arts and Scis. Office: Univ Chgo Grad Sch Bus 5807 S Woodlawn Ave Chicago IL 60637 Office Phone: 773-702-7280. Office Fax: 773-702-2699. E-mail: murphy@chicagogsb.edu.

MURPHY, KEVIN M., state agency administrator; Grad., Northeastern U., Boston, Rutgers U. Stonier Grad. Sch. Banking. Positions including bank examiner in MW and New Eng. FDIC, asst. regional dir. Mpls. regional office Washington, 1982—96; pvt. sector banking cons.; dep. commr. Minn. Dept. Commerce Fin. Svcs. Divsn., 1998—. Office: Minn Dept Commerce Fin Svcs Divsn 85 7th Place E Ste 500 Saint Paul MN 55101-2198 Office Phone: 651-296-4026. Office Fax: 651-296-8591.

MURPHY, LAWRENCE R., lawyer; b. Waterbury, Conn., Apr. 21, 1972; s. Lawrence R. and Catherine R. Murphy; m. Shannon Lee Nimmo, May 11, 1997; children: Sawyer J, Catherine Grace, Lydia Virginia. BA, St. Anselm Coll., Manchester, NH, 1994; JD, U. Tulsa, Okla., 1997. Shareholder Robinett & Murphy, Inc. P.C., Tulsa, Okla., 2004—. Republican. Roman Catholic. Office: Robinett & Murphy Inc PC 624 South Boston Ste 900 Tulsa OK 74119 Office Phone: 918-592-3699. Office Fax: 918-592-0963. Business E-Mail: lmurphy@robinettmurphy.com.

MURPHY, MARGARET A., nursing educator, adult nurse practitioner; b. NYC, Apr. 4, 1934; d. William J. and Margaret (Burchill) Allen; m. Raymond L.H. Murphy, Jr., July 12, 1958; children: Raymond L.H. III, Michael W., Ann Murphy Postell, Maureen D. Murphy Olsen, Alice M., Matthew D. BSN, St. Joseph Coll., West Hartford, Conn., 1955; MS, NYU, 1957; PhD, Boston Coll., Chestnut Hill, Mass., 1987. RN Mass., cert. adult nurse practitioner. Instr. Boston U. Sch. Nursing, 1971-72; pulmonary clin. nurse specialist Pulmonary Assocs., Boston, 1972-73; pulmonary nurse clinician Tufts U., Medford, Mass., 1973-76; from instr. prof. nursing to assoc. prof. nursing Boston Coll., 1976—2001, assoc. prof. emeritus, 2001, chmn. adult health nursing, 1988-92, dir. adult nurse practitioner program, 1987—2001, dir. Kennedy Audio Visual Resource Ctr., 1991-95, coord. MBA-MSN program, 1993-99. Rschr. in lung sound patterns in health and disease, women's attitudes toward menopause. Co-editor: Pharmacotherapeutics and Advanced Nursing Practice, 1998; co-author: (CD) Learning Lung Sounds, 2002, (CD) Learning Heart and Lung Sounds, 2005; contbr. articles to profl. jours. Fellow, USPHS, 1957—58; grantee, Uniformed Svcs. U. Health Scis., 1995—96. Fellow: Am. Coll. Nurse Practitioners; mem.: ANA, Mass. Thoracic Soc. (chmn. com. on nursing practice, counselor 1989—91), Am. Thoracic Soc., Mass. Nurses Assn. (co-chmn. cabinet on legis. 1985—88), Sigma Theta Tau (chmn. awards and scholarships com. Alpha Chi chpt. 1994—96, pres. 1996—98, newsletter editl. bd. 1998—2004, Alpha Chi chpt. Mentor award 2001). Office Phone: 617-552-4063. Business E-Mail: murphy@bc.edu.

MURPHY, MARION COLUCCI, writer, poet; b. Queens, NY, Mar. 6, 1940; s. Frank and Ida (Giotta) Colucci; children: Carrie, Maureen, Raygen, Erin. Free-lance profl. painter, N.Y., 1950's-80's; freelance costume mask designer, N.Y., 1969-78. Writer numerous poems; lyric recs. for syndicated radio shows, also, Petunia Revival, D.O.A. Dog, 1998, Fun Baby, Up Shoes, 1999; host radio poetry broadcastings Sta. WNYG-AM, 2003--. Mem.: Internat. Soc. Poets, Internat. Poetry Hall Fame. Avocations: solitude, music, innovating, walking and loving god's creations. Office Phone: 631-399-0858.

MURPHY, MARK D., lawyer, real estate developer; b. Kirksville, Mo., Sept. 12, 1961; s. Hershall and Gwendolyn J. Murphy; m. Susan L. Schelhammer, Nov. 1, 1991; children: Benjamin S., Andrew T. BS, Truman State U., Kirksville, 1983; JD with distinction, U. Mo., Kansas City, 1986. Ptnr. Mitchell, Kristl & Lieber, PC, Kansas City, 1986—95; mng. ptnr. Murphy Law Firm, PA, Overland Park, Kans., 1995—. Golf tournament com. Am. Heart Assn., Overland Park, Kans., 1995—2005. Mem.: Mo. Bar Assn., Kans. Bar Assn. Avocations: racquetball, golf. Office: Murphy Law Firm PA 6710 West 121st St Overland Park KS 66209-2002 Office Phone: 913-851-8484. Office Fax: 913-851-3737. Business E-Mail: mmurphy@mlfpa.com.

MURPHY, MARK JOSEPH, enterprise sales executive; b. Rockville Centre, NY, Aug. 5, 1960; s. John Stephen and Barbara Ann (Seeney) M.; m. Annamaria Martin, July 19, 1986; children: Dana Martine, Kelly Gabrielle. BS in Econs. and Fin., St. John's U., 1983. Sr. tech. clk. St. John's U., Jamaica, N.Y., 1979-83; sys. engr. Property and Liability Br. IBM Corp., NYC, 1983-84, sys. engr. N.Y. Ins. Br., 1984-86, mktg. rep. Manhattan Ins. Br., 1986-89, adv. mktg. staff Ea. Area, 1989, mktg. mgr. N.Y. banking, 1990-93, sys. svcs. mgr., 1993-95, mgr. client server and internet sys. mktg. N.E. area, 1995-97, client exec. fin. industry sector, 1997—2001, software sales exec., 2001—04; v.p. sales nat. accounts fin. industry sector Siemens AG, NYC, 2004—. Bd. dirs. Make-A-Wish Found., Suffolk County, N.Y., past vice-chmn., past chmn. bd. devel. com., chmn. bylaws com.; vol. Make-A-Wish Found. Mem.: Am. Mgmt. Assn. Avocations: golf, travel. Home: 134 Parkwood Rd West Islip NY 11795-3001 Office: Siemens AG 1120 Avenue of the Americas New York NY 10036 Personal E-mail: bigblue@optonline.net.

MURPHY, MARY, retired librarian; b. Hibbing, Minn., Aug. 14, 1917; d. John Philip and Ethel Robinson Murphy. BA, St. Lawrence U., Canton, NY, 1940; BSLS, U. Ill., Urbana, 1941. Map cataloger Army Map Svc. Libr., Washington, 1943—45, acquisition specialist, 1945—46, book cataloger, reviser, 1946—52, chief reference unit, asst. chief book and periodical br., 1956—65, chief document br., 1965—68; chief info. sect. Army Topographic Command, Washington, 1968—70; chief analysis br. Def. Mapping Agy. Info. Ctr., Washington, 1970—80; ret., 1980. Spkr. in field. Contbr. articles to profl. jours. Mem.: Spl. Librs. Assn. (editor Geography and Map Divsn. Bull.), Zonta Club, Phi Beta Kappa. Democrat. Episcopalian. Avocations: reading, dance, travel, photography. Home: 8102 Birnam Wood Dr Mc Lean VA 22102-2713

MURPHY, MARY, choreographer, dancer; b. Lancaster, Ohio; Grad., Ohio U. Founder & owner Champion Ballroom Acad., San Diego, 1990—; choreographer & judge So You Think You Can Dance?, 2005—. Dancer (films) Something to Talk About, 1995, Dance With Me, 1998; dance cons. (films) Marilyn Hotchkiss Ballroom Dancing & Charm School, 2005; actor: (films) Dead of Winter, 2007; judge, choreographer (TV series) So You Think You Can Dance?, 2005—. Named US Nat Prof. 9-Dance Champion, US Ballroom Dance Championships, 1996; recipient Lifetime Achievement award, Heritage Dance Classic, 2007. Office: Champion Ballroom Acad 3580 5th Ave San Diego CA 92103 *

MURPHY, MAX RAY, lawyer; b. July 18, 1934; s. Loren A. and Lois (Mink) M.; children: Michael Lee, Chad Woodrow. BA, DePauw U., 1956; JD, Yale U., 1959; postgrad., Mich. State U., 1960. Bar: Mich. 1960. Assoc. Glassen, Parr, Rhead & McLean, Lansing, Mich., 1960—67, Lokker, Boter & Dalman, Holland, Mich., 1967—69; ptnr. Dalman, Murphy, Bidol, & Bouwens, P.C., Holland, 1969—91, Cunningham Dalman, P.C., Holland, 1991—. Instr. Lansing Bus. U., 1963-67; asst. pros. atty. Ottawa County, Mich., 1967-69. Dem. candidate for Ingham County (Mich.) Pros. Atty., 1962, 1964. Mem. ABA, Ottawa County Bar Assn. (sec. 1970-71), Mich. Bar Assn. (mem. family law sect.). Home: 3169 E Crystal Waters 3 Holland MI 49424-8091 Office: 321 Settlers Rd Holland MI 49423-3778 Office Phone: 616-392-1821. Business E-Mail: mmurphy@sirus.com.

MURPHY, MEISSA BLEU, music educator, behaviorist; d. Raymond Edward and Delcia Lucille Spry; m. Hershel Ring Murphy, Sept. 22, 1990; m. Harry Angevin Rider (dec.); children: William Cary Rider, Sheri Kay Rider, B. Ann Rider, Tiffany Ann Rider. Student, Ind. Music Sch., 1954, U. of L, 1956—60, La Salle Interior Design, 1972—78; BA, Herron Art Sch., Indpls., 1987; BA in Psychology, Purdue U., 1990. Tchr. music, Indpls., pub. schs., Indpls.; behaviorist St. Vincent Hosp., New Hope-Indpls. Vocal coach, piano tchr., Indpls.; mem. faculty Am. Coll. Music, Austin, Tex.; profl. musician, guitarist and vocalist for internat. performances; chairperson Am. Coll. Musicians Nat. Auditions Piano Performance, Indpls., 2006—07. Composer: Is It Raining, 1971, Small House for Sale; composer: (music score) Christmas Mouse, 1972; composer: TV commls. Mem. Wildlife Fedn., Hist. Soc., Indpls. Zoo, Heart Drive, First Monday Symphony, Harmony Club, Symphony Womans Group. Recipient Arion award for music, 1976, Boston Mensa award, 1980, Chgo. Mensa award, 1981, Rosa Parks Tolerance award, 2002. Mem.: Indpls. Matinee Musicales, Indpls. Piano Tchrs. Assn., Musician's Union (Local 3), Am. Mensa, Indpls. Art Mus., Psi Chi (pres. 1987—89). Methodist. Avocations: flying, music, antiques, art, art history. Office: Mrs Murphys Westside Piano Studio 7988 Fishback Rd Indianapolis IN 46278 Office Phone: 317-297-1139. Personal E-mail: meissableu@aol.com.

MURPHY, MICHAEL EMMETT, retired food company executive; b. Winchester, Mass., Oct. 16, 1936; s. Michael Cornelius and Bridie (Curran) M.; m. Adele Anne Kasupski, Sept. 12, 1959; children: Leslie Maura, Glenn Stephen, Christopher McNeil. BS in Bus. Adminstrn, Boston Coll., 1958; MBA, Harvard, 1962. Financial analyst Maxwell House div. Gen. Foods Corp., White Plains, NY, 1962-64, cost mgr. San Leandro, Calif., 1964-65, controller Jacksonville, Fla., 1965-67, Hoboken, NJ, 1967-68, mgr. fin. planning and analysis, 1968-69; mgr. planning Hanes Corp., Winston-Salem, NC, 1969-70, corp. controller, 1970-72; v.p. adminstrn. Hanes Corp. (Hanes Knitwear), Winston-Salem, NC, 1972-74; v.p. fin. Ryder System Inc., Miami, Fla., 1974-75, exec. v.p., 1975-79; exec. v.p., dir. Sara Lee Corp., Chgo., 1979-93, vice chmn., 1993-97. Bd. dirs. GATX Corp., Payless Shoe Source, Inc., CNH Global N.V., Coach Inc., Bassett Furniture Industries, Inc., No. Funds. Mgmt. adviser Jr. Achievement, 1965-66; mem. exec. com. Hudson County Tax Rsch. Coun., 1967-68; trustee Boston Coll., 1980-88; chmn. Civic Fedn. Chgo., 1984-86; bd. dirs. Jobs for Youth, Chgo., 1983-86, Lyric Opera, 1986-2002; bd. dirs. Northwestern Meml. Hosp., Chgo., 1989-2000, Big Shoulders Fund, Chgo. Ctrl. Area Com., 1995—, Chgo. Cultural Ctr. Found., 1995—, Met. Pier and Exposition Authority, 2004—, Joffrey Ballet, 2006—; prin. Chgo. United, 1995-98. Mem. Nat. Assn. Mfrs. (bd. dirs. 1989-96, dir. Big Shoulders Fund 1995—), Fin. Execs. Inst., Hoboken C. of C., Winson-Salem C. of C., Miami C. of C., Internat. Platform Assn., UN Assn., Ouimet Scholar Alumni Group, Beta Gamma Sigma. Roman Catholic. Home: 1242 N Lake Shore Dr Chicago IL 60610-2361 Office: Sara Lee Corp 3 First National Plz Chicago IL 60602 Personal E-mail: mebmurphy@aol.com.

MURPHY, MICHAEL GEORGE, actor; b. Los Angeles, May 5, 1938; s. Bearl Branton and Georgia Arlyn (Money) M.; m. Wendy Crewson, 1988; children: Maggie, John (Jack) Branton. BA, U. Ariz., 1961. Former HS tchr., 1962—64. Appeared in films The Legend of Lylan Clare, 1968, The Arrangement, 1969, MASH, 1969, Brewster McCloud, 1970, McCabe & Mrs. Miller, 1971, What's Up, Doc?, 1972, Phase IV, 1973, The Autobiography of Miss Jane Pittman, 1974, Nashville, 1975, The Front, 1976, An Unmarried Woman, 1978, Manhattan, 1978, The Class of Miss MacMichael, 1978, John Cheever's O, Youth and Beauty, 1979, Strange Behavior, 1981, The Year of Living Dangerously, 1982, Cloak and Dagger, 1983, Two Marriages, 1983, Salvador, 1986, Hard Copy, 87, The Caine Mutiny Countmartial, 1987, Tanner'88, 1988, Tailspin, 1988, Shocker, 1989, Private Parts, 1997, Magnolia, 1999, Tart, 2001, Tricks, 2004, Silver City, 2004, Childstar, 2004, Heights, 2004, X-Men: The Last Stand, 2006; (TV) The Day Reagan Was Shot, 2001, Live From Baghdad, 2002, Footsteps, 2003, In The Dark, 2003, Tanner on Tanner, 2004, H2O, 2004, Hunt for Justice, 2005, Mayday, 2005, Playing House, 2006. Served with USMC, 1956-57.

MURPHY, MICHAEL JOSEPH, state official; b. Seattle, May 24, 1947; s. John Anthony and Helen Elizabeth (Domick) M.; m. Theresa Ann Smith. BA in History, Seattle U., 1969; MBA, Pacific Luth. U., 1978. Chief adjudicator vet.'s program Office of the State Treas., Olympia, Wash., 1972-75, adminstr. pub. deposit protection commn., 1975-81, internal auditor to state treas., 1981-87; treas. Thurston County, Olympia, 1987-96, State of Wash., Olympia, 1997—. Mem. adv. bd. asset/liability com. Twin County Credit Union, Olympia, 1987-96; instr. profl. orgns., govt. Treas. Thurston County Dems., 1973-77. Mem. Wash. Assn. County Treasurers (bd. dirs., officer 1987-96, legis. coord. 1989-96, Pres. award 1994), Wash. Assn. County Ofcls. (bd. dirs. 1989-90), Wash. Mcpl. Treasurers Assn. (bd. dirs. 1990—, Cert. Excellence for investment policy 1992), Wash. Fin. Officers Assn. (profl. fin. officer 1988—, bd. dirs. 1997—), Nat. Assn. State Treasurers, Olympia Yacht Club, Olympia Country and Golf Club, Valley Athletic Club. Roman Catholic. Avocations: sailing, golf, travel. Home: PO Box 1342 Olympia WA 98507-1342 Office: Legis Bldg 2d Fl Wash State Treas Olympia WA 98504-0200 *

MURPHY, MICHAEL R., federal judge; b. Denver, Aug. 1947; s. Roland and Mary Cecilia (Maloney) M.; m. Maureen Elizabeth Donnelly, Aug. 22, 1970; children: Amy Christina, Michael Donnelly. BA in History, Creighton U., 1969; JD, U. Wyo., 1972. Bar: Wyo. 1972, US Ct. Appeals (10th cir.) 1972, Utah 1973, US Dist. Ct. Utah 1974, US Dist. Ct. Wyo. 1976, US Ct. Appeals (5th cir.) 1976, US Tax Ct. 1980, US Ct. Appeals (9th cir.) 1981, US Ct. Appeals (fed. cir.) 1984. Law clk. to chief judge US Ct. Appeals (10th cir.), Salt Lake City, 1972-73; with Jones, Waldo, Holbrook & McDonough, Salt Lake City, 1973-86; judge 3d Dist. Ct., Salt Lake City, 1986-95, presiding judge, 1990-95; judge US Ct. Appeals (10th cir.), Salt Lake City, 1995—. Mem. adv. com. on rules of civil procedure Utah Supreme Ct., 1985—95, mem. bd. dist. ct. judges, 1989—90; mem. Utah State Sentencing Commn., 1993—95, Utah Adv. Com. on Child Support Guidelines, 1989—95, Utah Child Sexual Abuse Task Force, 1989—93; mem. com. on fed.-state jurisdiction Jud. Conf. of U.S., 2001—. Recipient Freedom of Info. award, Soc. Profl. Journalists, 1989, Utah Minority Bar Assn. award, 1995, Alumni Achievement citation, Creighton U., 1997; named Judge of Yr., Utah State Bar, 1992. Fellow Am. Bar Found.; mem. ABA (editl. bd. Judges' Jour. 1997-99), Utah Bar Assn. (chmn. alternative dispute resolution com. 1985-88), Sutherland Inn of Ct. II (past pres.). Office: 5438 Federal Bldg 125 S State St Salt Lake City UT 84138-1102 Office Phone: 801-524-5955. *

MURPHY, PAMELA ANN, music educator, actress, musician; b. Cooperstown, NY, June 8, 1962; d. William John and Mary Kathryn Barrett; m. Michael Francis Murphy, II, July 11, 1987; children: Michael Francis III, Sean Patrick, Timothy Andrew. MusB, SUNY, Potsdam, 1984; MS, Western Conn. State U., 1990. Permanent tchg. lic. N.Y., cert. adjudicator NYSSMA. Music tchr. Valley Ctrl. Mid. Sch., Montgomery, NY, 1984—89, Valley Ctr. Mid. Sch., Montgomery, 1999—, Valley Ctrl. H.S., Montgomery, 1991—94, Kinry Rd. Elem. Sch., Poughkeepsie, NY, 1994—97. Guest condr. for all-county chorus Dutchess County (N.Y.) Music Educators Assn., 1994; owner, music dir. Hudson Valley Conservatory Fine Arts, Walden, NY, 1995—; profl. vocalist and keyboard player for various radio commls., weddings and bands; adjudicator state and local vocal competitions. Composer: (songs) My Love, 2002; actor: New Rose Theatre, 1996—. Facilitator fundraising activities Am. Heart Assn., Otego, NY, 1995; artistic dir. Hudson Valley Parents Performing Students, Walden, 1997—; fundraiser Muscular Dystrophy Assn., Newburgh, NY, 2003. Mem.: Orange County Music Educators Assn. (guest condr. for all-county chorus 1986, 1989, 2002, govt. rels. officer), N.Y. State Sch. Assn., Music Educators Nat. Conf., Nat. Write Your Congressman. Roman Catholic. Avocations: singing, dance, acting, flute, painting. Home: 30 Browns Rd Walden NY 12586 Office: Hudson Valley Conservatory Fine Arts PO Box 704 35 E Main St Walden NY 12586 Home Phone: 845-778-0491; Office Phone: 845-778-2478. Personal E-mail: murphhvc@yahoo.com.

MURPHY, PATRICK J., congressman; b. Phila., Oct. 19, 1973; s. Jack Murphy; m. Jennifer Safford, June 17, 2006. Ed., Bucks County Cmty. coll., 1991; BS, King's Coll., Wilkes-Barre, 1996; JD, Widener U.; grad., Judge Adv. General's Sch., Charlottesville, Va., 2000. Bar: Minn. 1999, Pa. 2003, US Ct. Appeals (Armed Svc.), US Dist. Ct. (Ea. Dist. Pa.), US Supreme Ct. Intern Office of Phila. Dist. Atty.; leader Harrisburg Civil Law Clinic; legis. aide to Rep. Thomas Tangretti Pa. Ho. of Reps; assoc. Murphy & O'Connor, Phila.; judge adv. US Army Judge Adv. General's Corps; assoc. Cozen O'Connor, Pa., 2005—; mem. US Congress from 8th Pa. dist., 2007—, mem. armed svcs. com., 2007—, mem. permanent select com. on intelligence, 2007—. Asst. prof. constitutional law, values edn. officer US Mil. Acad., 2001—03; adj. prof. Am. govt. Mt. St. Mary Coll., 2000—03; lectr. US Air Force Acad., Internat. Inst. Humanitarian Rights, San Remo, Italy, Judge Adv. General's Sch.; instr. Intensive Trial Advocacy Program Widener U. Sch. Law, 2004—05. Cadet in ROTC US Army, 2nd lt. US Army, served with US Army, 2002, Bosnia, served as paratrooper 82nd Airborne Divsn. US Army, 2003—04, Baghdad, Iraq, capt. US Army, 2005—. Decorated Bronze Star; named a Rising Star, Law & Politics, 2005. Mem.: ABA, Pa. Bar Assn., Phila. Bar Assn., Bucks County Bar Assn. Democrat. Office: 414 Mill St Bristol PA 19007 Office Phone: 215-826-1963. Office Fax: 215-826-1997. *

MURPHY, PAUL REGIS, JR., business educator; b. DC, Aug. 12, 1954; m. Sheryl Anne Booher, July 4, 1995. AB, U. Notre Dame, Ind., 1972—76; MBA, U. Md., College Park, 1976—79, PhD, 1980—85. Prof. bus. logistics John Carroll U., Univ. Heights, Ohio, 1995—. Author: (textbook) Contemporary Logistics, 8th edit., 2004. Recipient Disting. Doctoral Alumnus award, Smith Sch. Bus., U. Md., 1998, Disting. Faculty award, John Carroll U., 2002. Mem.: Am. Soc. Transp. & Logistics (bd. mem. 2002—05). Office: John Carroll Univ 20700 N Park Blvd University Heights OH 44118 Business E-Mail: drmurphy@jcu.edu.

MURPHY, R. BLAIR, management consulting company executive; b. Phila., Jan. 19, 1931; s. William Beverly and Helen Marie (Brennan) M.; children: Stephen, Emily, Julia, David, Catherine. BS, Yale, 1953. Indsl. engr. DuPont Corp., Aiken, SC, 1953-55; mgr. sales can divsn. Reynolds Metals Co., Richmond, Va., 1955-69; gen. mgr. corrugated divsn. Continental Can Co., NYC, 1969-73; v.p. and gen. mgr. beverage divsn. Am. Can Co., Greenwich, Conn., 1973-75; assoc. Heidrick & Struggles, Inc., NYC, 1976-78, v.p., 1978; v.p., mng. dir. Stamford office Spencer Stuart & Assocs., 1978-84, ptnr., 1982-84; co-founder and CEO Sullivan-Murphy Assocs., 1984—. Mem. Riverside Yacht Club (Greenwich), Yale Club (N.Y.C.), Merion Cricket Club (Haverford, Pa.), Bucks Harbor Yacht Club (Brooksville, Maine). Home: 11 Indian Mill Rd Cos Cob CT 06807-1315 E-mail: rblairm69@aol.com.

MURPHY, RAMON JEREMIAH CASTROVIEJO, physician, pediatrician; b. NYC, Feb. 12, 1944; s. William J. and Angelines (Castroviejo) M.; m. Lila, Sept. 12, 1971; children: Jessica, David. BA, U. Notre Dame, 1965; MD, Northwestern U., 1969; MPH, Columbia U., 1974. Diplomate Am. Bd. Pediats. Intern in medicine Cook County Hosp., Chgo., 1969—70; resident in pediats. Children's Meml. Hosp., Chgo., 1970—71, Babies Hosp.-Columbia-Presbyn. Med. Ctr., NYC, 1971—73; resident in cmty. medicine Mt. Sinai Hosp., NYC, 1973—74, clin. asst. pediatrician, 1974—75, asst. attending pediatrician, 1975—83, assoc. attending pediatrician, 1983—, assoc. instr. cmty. medicine, 1974—75, asst. prof. clin. pediats., asst. prof. cmty. medicine, 1975—83, assoc. prof. clin. pediats., 1983—2006, clin. prof. pediat., clin. prof. preventive and cmty. medicine, 2006—; pediatrician Uptown Pediat., P.C., NYC, 1976—, pres., 1990—. Co-dir. Mt. Sinai Children's Cmty. Health, 1999—, Mt. Sinai Global Health Ctr., 2005-; dir. Mt. Sinai Off-Site Pediat. Residency Tng. Program, 1999—, Mt. Sinai Pediat. Global Health Tng. Program, 2004—; vis. clin. fellow pediat. Columbia U., Coll. Physicians and Surgeons, N.Y.C., 1971-73; pediat. cons. Oxford Health Plan, 1990-94, Children's Aid Soc., 2000—, Commonwealth Fund, 1995—. Contbr. articles to profl. jours. Co-med. dir. Benito Juarez People's Health Ctr., Chgo., 1970-71; dep. co-dir. Wagner Child Health Project, N.Y.C., 1973-75; sch. physician The Day Sch., 1984—, The Trinity Sch., 1992—, trustee, 1993-99. Fellow Am. Acad. Pediat.; mem. N.Y. Pediat. Soc. (program chmn. 1986-89, pres. 1989-90), Soc. for Adolescent Medicine, Mt. Sinai Alumni Assn. Office: 1245 Park Ave New York NY 10128-1211 Office Phone: 212-427-0540.

MURPHY, RANDALL KENT, writer, educator, consultant; b. Laramie, Wyo., Nov. 8, 1943; s. Robert Joseph and Sally (McConnell) M.; m. Cynthia Laura Hillhouse, Dec. 29, 1978; children: Caroline, Scott, Emily. Student, U. Wyo., 1961—65; MBA, So. Meth. U., 1983. Dir. mktg. Wycoa, Inc., Denver, 1967—70; dir. Comm. Resource Inst., Dallas, 1971—72; account exec. Xerox Learning Sys., Dallas, 1973—74; regional mgr. Systema Corp., Dallas, 1975; pres. Performance Assocs.; pres., dir. Acclivus Corp., Dallas, 1976—; founder, chmn. Acclivus Inst., 1982—. Author: Performance Management, Coaching and Counseling and Performance, 1980, Managing Development and Performance, 1982, Acclivus Performance Planning System, 1983, (with others) BASE For Performance, 1983, Acclivus Coaching, 1984, Acclivus Negotiation, 1985, R3 Service, 1997, BASE for Effective Presentations, 1987, BASE for Strategic Presentations, 1988, The New BASE for Excellence, 1988, Major Account Planning and Strategy, 1989, Strategic Management, 1989, Building on the BASE, 1992, Negotiation Mastery, 1995, R3 Service, 1997, Co-creating R3 Value, 2002, Getting the Meeting, 2004, R3 Interaction, 2005; co-inventor The Randy-Band multi-purpose apparel accessory, 1968. Vice chmn. bd. trustees The Winston Sch., 1994-96, chmn. bd. trustees, 1997-2000; mem. adv. bd. The Women's Ctr. of Dallas, 1995-98. With AUS, 1966. Mem. ASTD, Inst. Mgmt. Scis., Soc. Applied Learning Tech., Nat. Soc. Performance and Instrn., Assn. Mgmt. Cons., Am. Assn. Higher Edn., World Future Soc., Soc. for Intercultural Edn., Tng. and Rsch., Internat. Fedn. Tng. and Devel. Orgns., Inst. Noetic Scis., Nat. Peace Inst., Amnesty Internat., Acad. Polit. Sci., The Nature Conservancy, Theosophical Soc. Am., Children's Arts and Ideas Found., So. Meth. U. Alumni Assn., U. Wyo. Alumni Assn. Office Phone: 972-385-1277. Business E-Mail: randall.murphy@acclivus.com.

MURPHY, RICHARD A., health science association administrator; m. Elaine Murphy. AB, Coll. of the Holy Cross, Worcester, Mass.; PhD in Zoology, Rutgers U., New Brunswick, NJ. Post-doctoral studies Mass. Gen. Hosp., Boston; faculty mem., dept. cell biology and anatomy Harvard U. Med. Sch., 1976—86; chair, dept. anatomy and cell biology U. Alberta, Canada, 1986; dir. Montreal Neurological Inst., McGill U., 1992—2000, prof., neurology and neurosurgery, 1992—2000; pres., CEO Salk Inst. for Biol. Studies, La Jolla, Calif., 2000—07; interim pres. Calif. Inst. for Regenerative Medicine, San Francisco, 2007—. Bd. dr. Calif. Healthcare Inst., Inc., 2003; mem. Independent Citizen's Oversight Com. to Prop. 71, Calif. Inst. for Regenerative Medicine, 2004—07. Trustee San Diego Econ. Develop. Corp., San Diego Connect. Mem.: Dana Alliance for Brain Initiatives, Am. Soc. for Cell Biology, Soc. for Neuroscience. Office: Calif Inst for Regenerative Medicine 210 King St San Francisco CA 94107 Office Phone: 415-396-9100. Office Fax: 415-396-9141. *

MURPHY, RICHARD WILLIAM, retired diplomat; b. Boston, July 29, 1929; s. John Deneen Murphy and Jane (Diehl) Bonner; m. Anne Herrick Cook, Aug. 25, 1955; children: Katherine Anne, Elizabeth Drew, Richard McGill. Grad., Phillips Exeter Acad., 1947; AB, Harvard U., 1951, Cambridge U., Eng., 1953; postgrad. Arabic studies, U.S. Fgn. Service Inst., Beirut, 1959-60; LLD (hon.), New Eng. Coll., 1989, Balt. Hebrew U., 1992. Vice consul U.S. Consulate Gen., Salisbury, So. Rhodesia, 1955-58; consul Aleppo, Syria, 1960-63; polit. officer Am. Embassy, Jedda, Saudi Arabia, 1963-66, Amman, Jordan, 1966-68; pers. officer U.S. State Dept., Washington, 1968-69, dir. Office Arabian Peninsula Affairs, 1969-71, asst. sec. state for Near Ea. and South Asian affairs, 1983-89; U.S. amb. to Mauritania, 1971-74, to Syria, 1974-78, to the Philippines, 1978-81, to Saudi Arabia, 1981-83; sr. fellow for Middle East Coun. Fgn. Rels., NYC, 1989—2004; cons. Richard Murphy Assocs., NYC, 1993—. Chmn. Fgn. Students Svc. Coun., Washington, 1989—93, Mid. East Inst., Washington, 1993—2001, Chatham House Found., 1993—2004; mem. bd. advisors Naval War Coll., 1991—94. Trustee Am. U. of Beirut, 1995-2007; mem. vis. com. Harvard Mid. East Ctr., 1999-2002, Near East Found., 2000-2003; dir. Found. Mid. East Peace, 2000—; chmn. Friends of UN Relief and Works Agy. Assn., 2005—. Served with US Army, 1953-55. Recipient Superior Honor award, U.S. Dept. State, 1969, Pres.'s Disting. Svc. award, 1986, 88, 89. Mem. Coun. Fgn. Rels., Fgn. Svc. Assn., Century Club. Republican. Episcopalian. Avocations: tennis, scuba diving. Home: 16 Sutton Pl 9A New York NY 10022-3057 Office Phone: 212-319-6541. Home Fax: 212-421-7067. Business E-Mail: richard@rwmurphyassociates.com.

MURPHY, ROBERT, executive search consultant; b. Davenport, Iowa; s. James and Patricia M. BS, U. Ill., Chgo., 1963. Registered pharmacist, Ill. With Walgreen Co., Chgo., 1963—73; corp. mgr. Coll. Rels. & Recruiting Corp.; mgr. Human Resource Planning; corp. dir. Orgn. and Human Resource Planning & Devel.; US ptnr.-in-charge exec. search PricewaterhouseCoopers, Chgo., 1974—93; founder, chmn. Murphy Ptnrs. Internat., global exec. search firm, 1993—. Contbr. articles to profl. jours. including Wall St. Jour., Newsweek. Mem. Internat. Human Resource Assn., Soc. Human Resource Mgrs., Internat. Cons. Assn., Am. Soc. Pers. Adminstrs., Soc. Human Resource Profls., Kappa Psi. Office: 956 Shoreline Rd Barrington IL 60010-3815 Office Phone: 847-304-1599.

MURPHY, ROBERT JAMES, language educator, consultant, pianist, pipe organ performer; b. Decatur, Ind., Aug. 31, 1941; s. James William and Catherine Agnes (Schumacker) Murphy; m. Linda L. Nolan, June 28, 1975; 1 child, Christina Lyn. BS in Edn., Ball State U., Muncie, Ind., 1963, postgrad., 1972; MS in Edn., St. Francis U., Ft. Wayne, Ind., 1967; postgrad., U. Denver, 1986. Cert. English, speech, drama and journalism tchr. Ind. Speech and drama tchr. Rochester H.S., Ind., 1976—78; chair dept. English Lawrenceburg H.S., Ind., 1978—81, Holy Family H.S., Denver, 1981—86; prin. Randall-Moore Sch., Denver, 1986—87; dir. edn. Mansfield Bus. Sch., Denver, 1987—89; prin. St. John the Bapt. Cath. Sch., Ft. Wayne, Ind., 1989—94; pres., founder Murphy Ednl. Consulting, Ft. Wayne, Ind., 1995—, D/B/A Alternative Edn. Curriculum and The Learning Kaleidoscope, Pensacola, Fla., 1995—2006. Cons. Am. Printing House for Blind, Louisville, 1999—2002; cons., writer, spkr. homeschooling groups, 1995—; exec. dir., co-founder The Kaleidoscope Edn. Ctr., Ft. Wayne, Ind., 2003, co-founder, dir., 03; tchr., supr. Aurora Evening H.S., Colo., 1986—87; tchr. U. St. Francis, Ft. Wayne, 2003—; edn. coord., tchr. M.A.Y.A. Unity Ctr., Ft. Wayne, 2003; dir. edn. Phoenix Youth Ctr., 2003—06; musician Colo., Ind., Ill., 1961—. Author: All in One Big Book, 1998, The Pump Man, 1998; co-author: Teaching the Student with a Visual Impairment, 2000, author reading and writing curriculum; dir.: Firehouse Theater, 2006—. Bd. dirs. Ft. Wayne Pub. Transp. Co., 2000—, League for Blind and Disabled, Ft. Wayne, 2000—; chmn. bd. dirs. United Voice Coalition, Ft. Wayne, 2002—05; chmn. bd. dirs. State Ind. Alliance Cmty. Inclusion, 2003—05; site visitor U.S. Dept. Edn. Blue Ribbon Sch., 1991; devel. dir. Fifth Freedom Network for People with Disabilities, Ft. Wayne, 2006—07; founding bd. dirs., exec. asst. dir. Phoenix Youth Ctr.-Club Unified, Ft. Wayne, 2003—06. Named Advocate of Yr., League for the Blind and Disabled, 2002; recipient Disting. Graduate award, Decatur (Ind.) Cath. Elem. and HS, 2003. Mem.: Am. Guild Organists. Avocations: gardening, hiking, swimming, piano, organ. Home Phone: 260-493-3893; Office Phone: 260-493-3893. Personal E-mail: murphymuse@yahoo.com.

MURPHY, ROBIN ROBERSON, computer scientist, robotics engineer; b. Mobile, Ala., Aug. 25, 1957; d. Fred Blakely and Ada Lee (Wills) Roberson; m. Kevin Eddy Murphy, Aug. 27, 1982; children: Kathleen Freebern(dec.), Allan Roberson. BME, Ga. Inst. Tech., 1980, MS in Computer Sci., 1989, PhD in Computer Sci., 1992. CIMS rsch. asst. Sch. Info. and Computer Sci., Ga. Inst. Tech., Atlanta, 1987—88, grad. tchg. asst., 1989; project engr. Dow Chem. USA, Plaquemine, La., 1980-84; software project engr. Turbitrol Co., Atlanta, 1984-86; asst. prof. dept. math. and comp. sci. Colo. Sch. Mines, Golden, 1992—98, assoc. dir. Ctr. Robotics and Intelligent Systems, 1994—98; assoc. prof. Dept. Computer Sci. and Engrng. and Dept. Psychology U. South Fla., Tampa, 1998—2003, dir. Inst. Safety Security Rescue Tech. (formerly Ctr. Robot-Assisted Search and Rescue), 2002—, prof., 2003—, site dir. NSF I/UCRC Safety, Security, Rescue Rsch. Ctr., 2003—. Cons. Defense Sci. Study Group Inst. for Defense Analyses, 1998—99, cons., 2000—; ad hoc mem. USAF Sci. Adv. Bd., 2001, mem., 2001—05; mem. study on unmanned ground vehicles Nat. Rsch. Coun., 2001—02; mem. tech. adv. panel USMC Chem. Biological Incident Response Force, 2002—; mem. DARPA Info. Sci. and Tech. Study Group, 2004—07, Nat. Rsch. Coun. Study on Using Info. Tech. to Enhance Disaster Mgmt., 2005—; bd. dirs. Space Fla., 2006—; adv. bd. mem. NSF, Computer & Info. Sci. & Engring., 2006—. Author: (with others) The Handbook of Brain Theory and Neural Networks, 1995, Artificial Intelligence for Mobile Robots, 1997, AI for Mobile Robots, 1997; spl. column editor Robotics and Autonomous Systems, 1997—; contbr. articles to profl. jours. Rsch. grantee NSF, 1993—, Advanced Rsch. Projects Agy., 1994—, NASA, 1994—, Northrop Grumman, 1997—; Rockwell Internat. Doctoral fellow. Mem.: IEEE, Am. Assn. for Artificial Intelligence, Soc. Women Engrs., Soc. Photo-Optical Instrumentation Engrs., Fla. Fire Chiefs' Assn., Assn. for Unmanned Vehicle Sys. Internat., Assn. Computing Machinery. Office: Computer Sci and Engring U S Fla 4202 E Fowler Ave ENB342 Tampa FL 33620-5399 Office Phone: 813-974-3652, 813-974-5456. E-mail: murphy@cse.usf.edu. *

MURPHY, ROSEMARY, actress; b. Munich; came to U.S., 1939; d. Robert D. and Mildred (Taylor) M. Student, Paris, France and Kansas City, Mo. Broadway appearances include Look Homeward Angel, 1958, Night of the Iguana, World premier at Spoleto (Italy) Festival of Two Worlds, 1959, Period of Adjustment, 1961, King Lear, 1963, Any Wednesday, 1964-66, Delicate Balance, 1966, Weekend, 1968, Butterflies are Free, 1970, Lady Macbeth, Stratford, Conn., 1973, Ladies of the Alamo, 1977, John Gabriel Borkman, 1980, Learned Ladies, 1982, Coastal Disturbances, 1987, The Devil's Disciple, 1988, A Delicate Balance, 1996, Waiting in the Wings, 1999; motion picture appearances include To Kill a Mockingbird, 1962, Any Wednesday, 1966, Ben, 1972, Walking Tall, 1972, You'll Like My Mother, 1972, Forty Carats, 1973, Julia, 1976, September, 1987, For the Boys, 1991, And The Band Played On, 1993, The Tuskegee Airmen, 1995, Message in a Bottle, 1998, Dust, 2001, The Savages, 2006, Synecdoche New York, 2007; TV appearance Eleanor and Franklin, 1975 (Emmy award for best supporting actress 1976), George Washington, 1983 (Tony award nominations 1961, 64, 67, award Motion Picture Arts Club 1966), E-Z Streets, 1996, The Unicorn's Secret, 1998, Frasier, 1997, 99. Recipient Variety Poll award, 1961, 67. Address: 220 E 73rd St New York NY 10021-4319 Office Phone: 212-713-5294.

MURPHY, SANDRA ROBISON, lawyer; b. Detroit, July 28, 1949; m. Richard Robin. BA, Northwestern U., 1971; JD, Loyola U., Chgo., 1976. Bar: U.S. Dist. Ct. (no. dist.) Ill. 1976. Assoc. Notz, Craven, Mead, Maloney & Price, Chgo., 1976-78; ptnr. McDermott, Will & Emery, Chgo., 1978—. Mem. ABA (family law sect.), Ill. Bar Assn. (chair sect. family law coun. 1987-88), Chgo. Bar Assn. (chair matrimonial law com. 1985-86), Am. Acad. Matrimonial Lawyers (sec. 1990-91, v.p. 1991-92, pres. Ill. chpt. 1992-93, pres.-elect 1994-95, pres. 1995-96), Legal Club Chgo. Business E-Mail: smurphy@mwe.com.

MURPHY, SEAN M., lawyer; b. Ithaca, NY, Aug. 28, 1969; BA, St. Lawrence U., 1991; JD, Albany Law Sch. Union Coll., 1994. Bar: NY 1995. Ptnr. Clifford Chance LLP, NYC, 2002, Milbank, Tweed, Hadley & McCloy LLP, NYC, 2004—. Named Leading Securities Lawyer, Chambers USA, NY Super Lawyers; named one of 500 New Rising Stars, Lawdragon, Litigation's Rising Stars, The Am. Lawyer, 2007; named to Lawdragon 3000. Office: Milbank Tweed Hadley & McCloy LLP 1 Chase Manhattan Plz New York NY 10005 Office Phone: 212-530-5688. Business E-Mail: smurphy@milbank.com.

MURPHY, SHARON MARGARET, retired communications educator; b. Milw., Aug. 2, 1940; d. Adolph Leonard and Margaret Ann (Hirtz) Feyen; m. James Emmett Murphy, June 28, 1969 (dec. May 1983); children: Shannon Lynn, Erin Ann; m. Bradley B. Niemcek, Aug. 7, 1999. BA, Marquette U., 1965; MA, U. Iowa, 1970, PhD, 1973. Cert. K-14 tchr., Iowa. Tchr. elem. and secondary schs., Wis., 1959-69; dir. publs. Kirkwood C.C., Cedar Rapids, Iowa, 1969-71; instr. journalism U. Iowa, Iowa City, 1971-73; asst. prof. U. Wis., Milw., 1973-79; assoc. prof. So. Ill. U., Carbondale, 1979-84; dean, prof. Marquette U., Milw., 1984-94; prof. Bradley U., Peoria, Ill., 1994—2006, provost, v.p. acad. affairs, 1994-97, pres. Cmty. Career and Tech. Ctr., 1997-98, prof. emeritus, 2006—. Pub. rels. dir., editor Worldwide mag., Milw., 1965—68; reporter Milw. Sentinel, 1967; Fulbright sr. lectr. U. Nigeria, Nsukka, 1977—78; Fulbright sr. scholar U. Ljubljana, Slovenia, 2002. Author: Other Voices: Black, Chicano & American Indian Press, 1971; (with Wigal) Screen Experience: An Approach to Film, 1968; (with Murphy) Let My People Know: American Indian Journalism, 1981; (with Schilpp) Great Women of the Press, 1983; editor: (with others) International Perspectives on News, 1982. Mem. Peoria Riverfront Commn., 1995—2000; co-chair Peoria Race Rels. Com., 1999—2000; mem. NCA Higher Learning Commn.; bd. dirs. Dirksen Congl. Leadership Ctr., 1994—2000, Dow Jones Newspaper Fund, NYC, 1986—95, Peoria Symphony, 1996—2002. Recipient Merit medal Journalism Edn. Assn., 1976, Tchg. Excellence award Amoco, 1977, Outstanding Achievement award Greater Milw. YWCA, 1989, Paul Snider Tchg. Excellence award Bradley U., 2005; named Knight of Golden Quill, Milw. Press Club, 1977; Nat. headliner Women in Comm., Inc., 1985. Mem. Assn. Edn. in Journalism and Mass Comm. (pres. 1986-87), Soc. Profl. Journalists, Nat. Press Club, Accrediting Coun.on Edn. in Journalism and Mass Comm. (v.p. 1983-86). Democrat. Roman Catholic. Office: Bradley U Global Comm Ctr Peoria IL 61625-0001 Home: 17193 Old 61 Rd Gays Mills WI 54631 Business E-Mail: smm@bradley.edu.

MURPHY, STACIA, health service association executive; BA, Talladega Coll. With Cmty. Service Soc., N.Y. City Mission Soc., NY State Divsn. Youth, Alcoholism Coun. of N.Y.; exec. dir. NYC affiliate Nat. Coun. on Alcoholism and Drug Dependence, Inc., 1990-99, pres. NYC, 1999—2005. Office: Nat Coun Alcoholism and Drug Dependence 22 Cortlandt St Ste 801 New York NY 10007-3128 Office Phone: 212-269-7797. Business E-Mail: president@ncadd.org.

MURPHY, STEPHEN JOSEPH, III, prosecutor; b. St. Louis, Sept. 23, 1962; s. Stephen Joseph and Mary Elizabeth Murphy; m. Amy Elizabeth Uhl, June 8, 1996. BS, Marquette U., 1984; JD, St. Louis U., 1987. Bar: Mo. 1987, Mich. 1998. Trial atty. US Dept. Justice, Washington, 1987-92, asst. US atty. (ea. dist.) Mich. Detroit, 1992-2000, US atty. (ea. dist.) Mich., 2005—; asst. gen. counsel Gen. Motors Corp., Detroit, 2000—05. Adj. prof. trial practice, bus. crime U. Detroit Mercy, 1993-2000; adj. prof. evidence Ave. Maria, 2002; master of the bench Am. Inn of Ct., Detroit, 1996-99. Contbr. articles to profl. jours. Big brother Big Bros./Big Sisters of S.E. Mich., Southfield, 1993-96; co-chmn. Combined Fed. Campaign, Detroit, 1993. Recipient Commendation, Bur. ATF, 1993, Letter of Thanks from Dir. of FBI, 1996, Commendation, U.S. Secret Svc., 1998, Commendation, Detroit FBI, 1999, Commendation, Motion Picture Assn. Am., 1999. Mem. State Bar Mich. (bd. commrs. 2002-05, com. rules criminal procedure 2001-05), Fed. Bar Assn., Nat. Lawyers Assn., Pros. Attys. Assn. Mich. Roman Catholic. Office: US Attys Office 211 W Fort St #2001 Detroit MI 48226-3211 Business E-Mail: stephen.j.murphy@usdoj.gov. *

MURPHY, TERENCE MARTIN, biology professor; b. Seattle, July 1, 1942; s. Norman Walter and Dorothy Louise (Smith) M.; m Judith Baron, July 12, 1969; 1 child, Shannon Elaine Knotts. BS, Calif. Inst. Tech., 1964; PhD, U. Calif. San Diego, La Jolla, 1968. Sr. fellow dept. biochemistry U. Wash., Seattle, 1969-70; asst. prof. botany U. Calif., Davis, 1971-76, assoc. prof., 1976-82, prof. plant biology, 1982—, chmn. dept. botany, 1986-90. Author: Plant Molecular Development, 1988; co-author: Plant Biology, 1998, 2nd edit. 2006; N.Am. exec. editor, N.Am. office, Physiologia Plantarum, 1988-98; contbr. articles to profl. jours. Mem. AAAS, Am. Soc. Plant Biologists, Am. Soc. Photobiology, Scandinavian Soc. Plant Physiology. Home: 725 N Campus Way Davis CA 95616-3518 Office: U Calif Sect Plant Biology Davis CA 95616 Home Phone: 530-753-3783; Office Phone: 530-752-2413. E-mail: tmmurphy@ucdavis.edu.

MURPHY, THEODORE R., II, utilities executive; BA in Econs., Trinity Coll., 1980; MBA in Fin., Columbia U., 1986. Chartered fin. analyst. Asst. v.p., comml. loan officer Conn. Bank and Trust; dir. credit risk mgmt. Philbro Energy; v.p. power mktg. and trading AIG Trading; v.p., market risks Enron Corp., 1997—2000; sr. v.p., chief risk officer Enron Europe Ltd., 2001—02; sr. v.p. Cinergy Corp., Cin., 2002—, chief risk officer, 2002—. Mem. com. chief risk officers Cinergy Corp. Office: Cinergy Corp 139 E 4th St Cincinnati OH 45202

MURPHY, THOMAS JOHN, publishing executive; b. Lockport, NY, Mar. 29, 1931; s. Matthew J. and Mary Frances (Tracy) M.; m. Maryanne Elizabeth Stadnicki, Dec. 29, 1956; children: Kevin, Janine, Peter, Thomas. BS, SUNY-Brockport, 1952; postgrad., Boston U., 1955-57, Northwestern U., 1976. Sales rep., asst. dir. advt., mgr. sales services, dir. tng., asst. dir. mktg., dir. mktg. McGraw-Hill Co., St. Louis, NYC, 1954-73; v.p., gen. mgr. sch. dept. Holt, Rinehart & Winston pub. CBS, Inc., NYC, 1973-78; sr. v.p. CBS Sch. Pub., 1978-80, pres., 1980-82; v.p. AICPA, 1982-88; ptnr. Profl. Pub. Svcs. Co., Kensington, Conn., 1988—; pres. World Book Pubs., 1991. Contbr. articles to profl. jours. Bd. dirs. Brockport Found., 1977-83, Rec. for Blind, 1980-89, Inter-Faith Housing Assn., 1991-94; mem. social concerns com. Ch. of Assumption, Westport, 2000—05; docent New Britain Mus. Am. Art; mem. Commn. for Aging, Berlin, Conn., 2006—. Named to Heritage Hall of Fame, SUNY. Democrat. Roman Catholic. Home and Office: 145 Robindale Dr Kensington CT 06037-2053 Office Phone: 860-829-7266. Personal E-mail: pps2000@comcast.net.

MURPHY, THOMAS PATRICK, lawyer; b. Syracuse, NY, Feb. 12, 1952; s. George Edward and Sara Eileen (Murphy) M.; m. Susan Hollis Francher, Oct. 19, 1976 (div. Oct. 1992); m. Lise M. Adkins, Aug. 6, 1994; children: Casey Marie, Matthew Thomas. BS, Clarkson U., 1974; JD, Vt. Law Sch., 1978. Bar: N.Y. 1978, D.C. 1981, Md. 1988, Va. 1989. Asst. U.S. atty. U.S. Atty.'s Office, Washington, 1982—85; assoc. Highsaw & Mahoney, Washington, 1985—87, McGuire, Woods, Battle & Boothe, Washington, 1987—90; ptnr. Reed Smith Shaw & McClay, McLean, Va., 1990—99, Hunton & Williams, McLean, 1999—. Contbr. articles to profl. jours. Chmn. bd. profl. responsibility DC Ct. Appeals; mem. planning com. Va. CLE Found. With USN, 1978—82, lt. USN, 1978—81, with USNR, 1978—90. Recipient Spl. Achievement award US Dept. Justice, 1984; named one of Best Lawyers in Am. for employment law; Legal Elite Va. Bus. Mag. 2004, 05, 06, America's Leading Lawyers for Bus. Chamber's USA, Va. Super Lawyers. Mem. ABA, Fed. Bar Assn., NY State Bar Assn., DC Bar Assn. (chmn. pro se litigants com.), Md. Bar Assn., Va. Bar Assn., Fairfax County Bar Assn., Asst. US Attys., Bd. Profl. Responsibility DC Ct. Appeals (hearing com.). Office: Hunton & Williams 1751 Pinnacle Dr Ste 1700 Mc Lean VA 22102-3836 Home Phone: 202-333-9745; Office Phone: 703-714-7533. Business E-Mail: tpmurphy@hunton.com.

MURPHY, TIMOTHY F., congressman; b. Cleve., Sept. 11, 1952; s. John and Florence Murphy; m. Nanette Missign, Aug. 23, 1975; 1 child, Bevin. BS, Wheeling Jesuit U., 1974; MA, Cleve. State U., 1976; PhD in Psych., U. Pitts., 1979. Mem. Pa. State Senate from Dist. 37, Harrisburg, 1997—2002, US Congress from 18th Pa. dist., 2003—, mem. energy and commerce com., co-chair Congl. Mental Health Caucus, mem. 21st Century Healthcare Caucus. Chmn. aging and youth com. Pa. State Senate, chmn. pub. health and welfare com., comm. and high tech. com., cmty. and econ. devel. com., edn. com., health care task force; asst. prof. U. Pitts. Sch. Medicine. Author: The Angry Child, Overcoming Passive-Aggression. Bd. dirs. Head Start, Alliance for Infants, Parents Helping Parents, Korean War Vets. Western Pa. Meml. Fund; founding dir. Sr. Aides Employment Svc.; mem. St. Thomas More Ch., Bethel Park, Pa.; mem. adv. bd. Allegheny Co. Ct. of Common Pleas Family Ct. Divsn., steering com. on children's issues roundtable; mem. US Mil. Acad. Rev. Bd. Mem. Pa. Perinatal Assn. (bd. dirs.), Bethel Park C. of C., South Park C. of C., Brentwood-Baldwin-Whitehall C. of C., Greater Bridgeville C. of C., Sons of Am. Legion Republican. Roman Catholic. Office: US House Reps 322 Cannon House Office Bldg Washington DC 20515 Office Phone: 202-225-2301. Office Fax: 202-225-1844. *

MURPHY, TIMOTHY JAMES, lawyer; b. Topeka, Sept. 30, 1946; s. Miles J. and Norine D. Murphy; m. Patricia MacKinnon, Apr. 7, 1990. BA, U. Ga., 1968; JD with honors, Washington & Lee U., 1970; LLM, Harvard U., 1976. Bar: Va. 1970, Fla. 1972. Atty. Anderson, Mori & Rabinowitz, Tokyo, 1970—71, Shutts & Bowen, Miami, Fla., 1976—. Contbr. articles to profl. jours. Mem. Fla. Ho. of Reps., 1982-84; bd. dirs. Cath. Charities, Inc., 1982-97, Cath. Charities Legal Svcs., Inc., Miami, 2000—, The Barnacle soc., 1991-2002, pres. 2000-02; mem. adv. bd. Miami-Dade County Pub. Libr., 1988-2002. Col. JAG Corps USAFR, 1971-95. Mem.: Biscayne Bay Yacht Club, Army and Navy Club (Washington). Democrat. Roman Catholic. Avocation: sailing. Office: Shutts & Bowen 201 S Biscayne Blvd Ste 1500 Miami FL 33131-4308 Office Phone: 305-379-9137.

MURPHY, TIMOTHY W., music educator; b. Takoma Park, Md., Oct. 2, 1969; s. Warren and Caroline Murphy. MusB, Stetson U., 1991; MusM, La. State U., 1993. Piano tchr. Stetson U., Cmty. Sch. of Arts, DeLand, Fla., 1994—. Accompanist Datyona Beach Choral Soc., Fla., 2001—. Mem.: Nat. Guild of Piano Tchrs., Fla. Fedn. of Music Clubs, Volusia County Music Tchrs. Assn. Republican. Asembly Of God. Avocations: travel, music.

MURPHY, WILLIAM ALEXANDER, JR., diagnostic radiologist, educator; b. Pitts., Apr. 26, 1945; s. William Alexander and LaRue (Eshbaugh); m. Judy Marie Lang, June 18, 1977; children: Abigail Norris, William Lawrence, Joseph Ryan. BS, U. Pitts., 1967; MD, Pa. State U., 1971. Diplomate Am. Bd. Radiology. Intern Barnes Hosp., St. Louis, 1971-72, staff radiologist, 1975-93; radiology resident Washington U., St. Louis, 1972-75, prof. radiology, 1983-93; sec. chief Mallinckrodt Inst. Radiology, St. Louis, 1975-93; cons. Office Med. Examiner City and County St. Louis, 1993—. Radiologist, prof. radiology, John S. Dunn Sr. prof., disting. chair MD Anderson Cancer Ctr. U. Tex., 1993—, v.p. hosp. and clinics, 1996-97, COO, 1997; chmn. bd. dirs. MD Anderson Physicians Network Corp., 2001—. Fellow Am. Acad. Forensic Scis., Am. Coll. Radiology; mem. Radiol. Soc. N.Am. (1st. v.p. 1997-98), Am. Roentgen Ray Soc., Am. Soc. Bone and Mineral Rsch., Internat. Skeletal Soc., Assn. Univ. Radiologists. Methodist. Home: 4808 Bellview St Bellaire TX 77401-5306 Office: U Texas Anderson Cancer Ctr Div Dx Imaging 057 1515 Holcombe Blvd Houston TX 77030-4009 Office Phone: 713-792-4916. Business E-Mail: wmurphy@di.mdacc.tmc.edu.

MURR, JAMES COLEMAN, retired federal agency administrator; b. Lake Charles, La., Oct. 29, 1944; m. Connie Paige Chadwell, Sept. 21, 1968; children: Christopher David, Richard Reno. BA, Tex. Tech U., 1966; MPA, Am. U., 1974. With Sears, Roebuck & Co., Tex., 1971-72, Dept. Labor, Washington, 1972-74, U.S. Customs Svc., Treasury, Washington, 1975-76; legis. analyst Office Mgmt. and Budget, Washington, 1977-81, br. chief, 1982-89, assoc. dir. administrn., 1990-93, asst. dir. legis. reference, 1994-98. Capt. USAF, 1967-70. Roman Catholic. E-mail: jcmurr@cebridge.net.

MURRAH, ANN RALLS FREEMAN, historical association executive; b. Gadsden, Ala., June 23, 1932; d. Oscar William Freeman, Sr. and Annie Collier (Ralls) Freeman; m. Robert Leland Murrah, Aug. 9, 1952; children: Frances Ralls Murrah Lovett, Robert Leland Murrah Jr. Grad., Brenau U., 1954. Pres. Gen. Descendants of the Signers of the Constn., Orlando, Fla., 1991—. Rep. Fla. 8th congl. dist. Congl. Sr. Intern Program, Wash., 1998; keynote spkr. Feminist Summit for Global Peace, Taipei, Taiwan, 1995; mem. protocol & hospitality coms. for equestrian events 1996 Olympics; mem. Am. com. Ball des Rosenkavaliers, Vienna, 1989—90; bd. dir. Arnold Palmer Hosp. Bd., Orlando, Fla.; founder Nat. Constn. Ctr., Phila., 2003—; spkr. in field. Mem. women's com. N.Y. U. Downtown Hosp., 1996—99; gala chmn. Winter Pk. Health Found., Winter Pk., Fla., 1996; ball chmn. Arnold Palmer Hosp. for Women & Children, Orlando, Fla., 1997—99, 2001; mem. Orlando Regional Healthcare Found., Orlando; active Coun. of 101-Orlando Mus. Art; v. chmn. dinner com. fundraiser March of Dimes, 1998. Named First Woman Knighted in her own right, Order of St. John of Jerusalem, 1992; named to Brenau U. Alumni Hall of Fame, 2001; recipient Meritorious Svc. award, Sons of the Am. Revolution, 1986, Martha Washington medal, 1988, The Rallye Saintogeais Hunt award, Foret De La Coubre, France, 1988. Mem.: DAR (first vice-regent), Nat. Soc. So. Dames Am., Met. Opera Guild, Plantagenet Soc., Washington Soc., Gavel Soc., Fla. Opera Guild, Nat. Steeplechase Assn., Shakerag Hunt Club (awarded colors), Nat. Soc. of Colonial Dames, Daus. of the Cin., Sovereign Colonial Soc. Am. of Royal Descent, Sonsand Daus. of the Pilgrims (gov. in Ga. 1992—94, historian gen. of the U.S. 1994—97, first vice-gov.), Descs. of Knights of the Garter, Colonial Dames of Am., Colonial Order of the Crown, Magna Charta Dames (herald and courier), Alpha Delta Pi (province pres., dir. ritual and paraphernalia). Home and Office: Soc of Descendants of Signers of Constituion 903 Sussex Close Orlando FL 32804

MURRAY, ALAN ROBERT, sound editor; Sound effects editor (films) American Hot Wax, 1978, The Warriors, 1979, Escape from Alcatraz, 1979, North Dallas Forty, 1979, Bronco Billy, 1980, Any Which Way You Can, 1980, Honkytonk Man, 1982, Sudden Impact, 1983, Tightrope, 1984, Windy City, 1984, City Heat, 1984, Ratboy, 1986, South of Heaven, West of Hell, 2000, The Shrink Is In, 2001, supervising sound editor (films) Star Trek: The Motion Picture, 1979, The Postman Always Rings Twice, 1981, Zorro, the Gay Blade, 1981, Firefox, 1982, Ladyhawke, 1985, Pale Rider, 1985, Desert Bloom, 1986, Fire with Fire, 1986, Heartbreak Ridge, 1986, Lethal Weapon, 1987, Who's That Girl?, 1987, Lionheart, 1987, Fatal Attraction, 1987, Like Father Like Son, 1987, Above the Law, 1988, Bird, 1988, The Dead Pool, 1988, Scrooged, 1988, Pink Cadillac, 1989, Lethal Weapon 2, 1989, Hard to Kill, 1990, White Hunter Black Heart, 1990, Die Hard 2, 1990, The Rookie, 1990, New Jack City, 1991, Frankie and Johnny, 1991, Fried Green Tomatoes, 1991, Unforgiven, 1992, Indecent Proposal, 1993, The Thing Called Love, 1993, A Perfect World, 1993, Milk Money, 1994, Exit to Eden, 1994, The Road to Wellville, 1994, The Bridges of Madison County, 1995, Under Siege 2: Dark Territory, 1995, The Stars Fell on Henrietta, 1995, Up Close & Personal, 1996, Eraser, 1996, Absolute Power, 1997, Speed 2: Cruise Control, 1997, Midnight in the Garden of Good and Evil, 1997, Quest for Camelot, 1998, True Crime, 1999, The 13th Warrior, 1999, Dudley Do-Right, 1999, The Replacements, 2000, Heartbreakers, 2001, co-supervising sound editor (films) Lara Croft: Tomb Raider, 2001, Blood Work, 2002, Star Trek: Nemesis, 2002, Million Dollar Baby, 2004, The Legend of Zorro, 2005, Flags of Our Fathers, 2006, Letters from Iwo Jima, 2006 (Acad. award for achievement in sound editing, 2007). *

MURRAY, ALICE PEARL, data processing company executive; b. Clearfield, Pa., Aug. 4, 1932; d. James Clifford and Leah Mae (Williams) Murray. BS, Pa. State U., Univ. Park, 1954. With IBM, 1954—, sys. svc. rep. Pitts., 1954—56, computer test ctr. rep. Endicott, NY, 1956—58, edn. devel. coord., 1958—59, adv. instr. LA, 1959—63, staff instr., 1963—68, exec. edn. coord., 1968—74; sr. instr. Info. Sys. Mgmt. Inst. IBM, 1974—84; sr. edn. rep. IBM Ams. Far East Corp., 1984—87; sr. staff mem. customer exec. edn. IBM, 1989, ind. cons., 1995—. Exhibit coord. Calif. State Mus. Sci. and Industry; guest spkr. civic and profl. groups; guest instr. univs. and colls.; profl. lectr. Named hon. citizen, Tex., Alaska; recipient Distinguished Educator award, IBM, 1974, Outstanding Professionalism award, 1975. Mem.: L.A. Libr. Found., L.A. County Art Mus., Assistance League So. Calif., Wilshire Country Club, Pa. State Alumni Assn., Delta Delta Delta. Republican. Home and Office: 514 S Gramercy Pl Apt 16 Los Angeles CA 90020-4969 Office Phone: 213-384-2316.

MURRAY, ALISON ELIZABETH, microbiologist, educator, researcher; d. Richard George Murray and Gail Lair Gonzales. BS in Biochemistry, Calif. Poly. State U., San Luis Obispo, 1989; MS in Cell and Molecular Biology, San Francisco State U., 1994; PhD in Ecology, Evolution and Marine Biology, U. Calif., Santa Barbara, 1998. Postdoctoral rschr. Mich. State U., East Lansing, 1999—2001; asst. rsch. prof. Desert Rsch. Inst., Reno, 2001—06, assoc. rsch. prof., 2006—. US rep. Sci. Com. on Antarctic Rsch., 2004—. Contbr. articles to profl. jours. Recipient Peter B. Wagner medal of excellence, Desert Rsch. Inst., 2006. Mem.: Am. Soc. Limnology and Oceanography, Am. Soc. Microbiology. Avocations: skiing, hiking, ultimate Frisbee, photography, music. Office: Desert Rsch Inst 2215 Raggio Pky Reno NV 89512

MURRAY, ANDREW W., biology professor, researcher; PhD, Harvard U., 1984. Postdoctoral rschr. Harvard Med. Sch.; part-time lectr. Yale U., 1985—86; postdoctoral rschr. U. Calif., San Francisco, asst. prof. dept. physiology, 1989—94, assoc. prof., 1994—2000; prof. molecular and cell biology, dir. Bauer Ctr. Genomics Rsch. Harvard U., Cambridge, Mass., 2000—. Spkr. in field. Contbr. articles to profl. jours. Fellow, David and Lucile Packard Found., 1991. Mem.: Am. Soc. Cell Biology. Achievements include research in the function and evolution of cells; chromosome behavior during meiosis and mitosis. Office: Harvard Univ Dept Molecular and Cell Biology 16 Divinity Ave Rm 3000 Cambridge MA 02138 Office Phone: 617-496-1350. E-mail: amurray@mcb.harvard.edu.

MURRAY, ANDY, professional hockey coach; b. Gladstone, MB, Can., 1951; m. Ruth Murray; children: Braden, Jordan, Sarah. BA in Polit. Sci./Sociology, Brandon U., 1972, BA in Edn., 1974; MS in Sports Mgmt., St. Thomas U., 1986. Asst. coach Brandon U., 1974—76, head coach, 1978—81; asst. coach Hershey Bears, 1987—88; head coach Brandon Travelers, Manitoba Jr. A Hockey League, 1976—78; asst. coach Phila. Flyers, 1988-90, Minn. North Stars, 1990-92, Winnipeg Jets, 1993-95; head coach Can. Nat. Team, 1996-98, LA Kings, 1999—2006, St. Louis Blues, 2006—. Office: St Louis Blues Hockey Club Savvis Ctr 1401 Clark Ave Saint Louis MO 63103 *

MURRAY, ANNE, singer; b. Springhill, NS, Can., June 20, 1945; d. Carson and Marion (Burke) M.; m. William M. Langstroth, June 20, 1975; children: William Stewart, Dawn Joanne. B.Phys. Edn., U. N.B., 1966, D.Litt. (hon.), 1978, St. Mary's U., 1982. Rec. artist for Arc Records, Canada, 1968, Capital/EMI Records, 1969—. Appeared on series of TV spls. CBC, 1970—81, 1988—93; star CBS spls., 1981—85; toured N. Am., Japan, Englan, Germany, Holland, Ireland, Sweden, Australia and New Zealand, 1977—82. Singer: (31 albums including) A Little Good News, 1984, (albums) As I Am, 1988, Greatest Hits, vol. I, 1981, vol. II, 1989, Harmony, 1987, You Will, 1990, Yes I Do, 1991, Croonin', 1993, The Best So Far, 1994, Now and Forever, Anne Murray, 1996, An Intimate Evening with Anne Murray-Live, 1997, What A Wonderful World, 1999, What A Wonderful Christmas, 2001, Country Croonin', 2002. Hon. chmn. Can. Save the Children Fund, 1978-80. Recipient Juno awards as Can.'s top female vocalist, 1970-81; Can.'s Top Country Female Vocalist, 1970-86; Grammy award as top female vocalist-country, 1974; Grammy award as top female vocalist-pop, 1978; Grammy award as top female vocalist-country, 1980, 83; Country Music Assn. awards, 1983-84; named Female Rec. Artist of Decade, Can. Rec. Industry Assn., 1980, Top Female Vocalist 1970-86; star inserted in Hollywood Walkway of Stars, 1980; Country Music Hall of Fame Nashville; decorated companion Order of Can.; inducted Juno Hall of Fame, 1993. Mem. AFTRA, Assn. Canadian TV and Radio Artists, Am. Fedn. Musicians. Office: Bruce Allen Talent No 500 425 Carrall St Vancouver BC Canada V6B6E3 also: Emi Music 1750 Vine St Los Angeles CA 90028-5209

MURRAY, ANTHONY, lawyer; b. LA, Apr. 25, 1937; s. Bernard Anthony and Frances Louise (Simpson) M.; children— Matthew Anthony, Thomas Andrew. JD, Loyola U., LA, 1964. Bar: Calif. 1965. Ptnr. Loeb & Loeb LLP, LA, 1995—. Fellow Am. Coll. Trial Lawyers (bd. regents 1995-99, mem. ABA, Chancery Club, LA County Bar Assn., Long Beach Bar Assn., State Bar Calif. (bd. govs. 1980-83, pres. 1982-83, numerous other positions). Democrat. Office: Loeb & Loeb LLP 10100 Santa Monica Blvd Ste 2200 Los Angeles CA 90067-4120 Office Phone: 310-282-2000.

MURRAY, BILL, actor, writer; b. Wilmette, Ill., Sept. 21, 1950; s. Edward and Lucille Murray; m. Margaret Kelly, 1980 (div. 1994); children: Homer, Luke; m. Jennifer Butler, July 4, 1997; children: Jackson, Cal, Cooper, Lincoln. Student, Regis Coll., Denver, Second City Workshop, Chgo. Owner minor league baseball team the Riverdogs, Charleston, SC; co-owner Caddyshack Restaurant, Jacksonville, Fla. Performer, Second City Comedy Troupe, 1973-75; voice, Nat. Lampoon Radio Hour, 1975; actor, writer, Saturday Night Live, 1977-80; Film appearances include Next Stop, Greenwich Village, 1976, Meatballs, 1979, Mr. Mike's Mondo Video, 1979, Where the Buffalo Roam, 1980, Caddyshack, 1980, Loose Shoes, 1980, Stripes, 1981, Tootsie, 1982, Ghostbusters, 1984, The Razor's Edge, 1984, Nothing Lasts Forever, 1984, Little Shop of Horrors, 1986, Scrooged, 1988, Ghostbusters II, 1989, What About Bob?, 1991, Groundhog Day, 1993, Mad Dog and Glory, 1993, Ed Wood, 1994, Kingpin, 1996, Larger Than Life, 1996, Space Jam, 1996, The Man Who Knew Too Little, 1997, With Friends Like These, 1998, Veeck As In Wreck, 1998, Rushmore, 1998, Wild Things, 1998, The Cradle Will Rock, 1999, Scout's Honor, 1999, Hamlet, 1999, Company Man, 1999, Charlie's Angels, 2000, Speaking of Sex, 2001, The Royal Tenenbaums, 2001, Osmosis Jones, 2001, Coffee and Cigarettes, 2003, Lost in Translation, 2003 (Golden Globe for best actor in a musical or comedy, 2004, Acad. Award nomination for best actor, 2004, Screen Actors Guild Award nomination for best actor, 2004), Garfield: The Movie (voice), 2004, The Life Aquatic with Steve Zissou, 2004, Broken Flowers, 2005, The Lost City, 2005, Garfield: A Tail of Two Kitties (voice), 2006; actor, dir., prodr. Quick Change, 1990; (TV movies) The Rutles: All you Need Is Cash, 1978; (TV series) Stories from My Childhood (voice only), 1998, The Sweet Spot, 2002 Recipient Emmy award for best writing for comedy series, 1977, Sons of the Desert Comedy Performer award, 1997. Office: Creative Artists Agy care Jessica Tuchinsky 9830 Wilshire Blvd Beverly Hills CA 90212-1825

MURRAY, BRYAN CLARENCE, professional sports team executive, former professional hockey coach; b. Shawville, Que., Can., Dec. 5, 1942; s. Clarence Herbert and Rhoda (Schwartz) Murray; m. Geraldine Frances Sutton, July 8, 1967; children: Heide Alicia, Brittany. Grad., McGill U., 1964. Former athletic dir., hockey coach McGill U.; athletic dir. MacDonald Coll., Ste. Anne de Bellevue, Que., 1968-72; coach, tchr. Rockland Nat.-Pontiac HS, Rockland, Ont., 1974-76; coach Pembroke-Kings, Pembroke, Ont., 1976-79, Regina Pats, Sask., 1979-80, Hershey Bears, Pa., 1980-81; former coach Washington Capitals, Landover, Md., 1981; coach, gen. mgr. Detroit Red Wings, 1990-94; gen. manager Florida Panthers, 1994—2001; head coach Mighty Ducks Anaheim, 2001—02, sr. v.p., gen. mgr., 2002—04; head coach Ottawa Senators, 2004—07, gen. mgr., 2007—. Recipient Jack Adams award, 1984. Office: Ottawa Senators Scotiabank Place 1000 Palladium Dr Kanata ON K2V 1A5 Canada

MURRAY, CARLA MARY, sound effects artist, artist; b. North Bay, Ont., Can., Apr. 3, 1957; d. Thomas Joseph and Laura Catherine Murray; life ptnr. Paula Kathleen Fairfield. BFA, N.S. Coll. Art and Design, Halifax, Can., 1982; MFA, York U., Toronto, Ont., 1996. Cofounder, adminstrv. dir. Women's Art Resource Ctr., Toronto, 1984—91; contract art adminstr., writer, rschr. various clients Toronto, 1992—94; sound designer, sound effects editor MHz Sound Design Inc., LA, 1997—. Ways and means com., adminstr. Trinity Sq. Video, Toronto, 1987; author, exhbn. co-coord. Graphic Feminism: Graphic Art of the Ont. Women's Movement 1970-1986, (catalogue) Women's Movement Archives, Toronto, 1986; founding mem. Power Up, LA, 2000, vol. sound designer, sound effects editor, 2001—03. One-woman shows include Gallery 940, Toronto, Stride Gallery, Calgary, IDA Gallery, Toronto, exhibitions include Out of the Frame, Advocate Gallery, LA; sound designer, sound effects editor (films) A Rumour of Angels; sound designer, sound effects editor: (films) Spy Kids 3D: Game Over; Terminator 3: Rise of the Machines; The Adventures of Shark Boy and Lava Girl in 3D; Assault on Precinct 13; Sin City; Lucky Number Slevin; The Black Dahlia; sound designer: films The Reaping, 2006; sound designer, sound effects editor: (TV series) Lost, 2006—07; founding mem. editl. bd.: Matriart: A Can. Feminist Art Jour., 1990—91. Bd. dirs. A Space Gallery, Toronto, 1984; jury mem. Ont. Arts Coun., Toronto, 1994. Recipient Golden Reel award, Motion Picture Sound Editors USA, 2007; grantee, Ont. Arts Coun., 1984—91; Explorations grant, Can. Coun., 1984, Photography grant, 1992. Mem.: Motion Picture Sound Editors USA (Golden Reel award 2007), Am. Film Inst., Nat. Mus. Women in Arts, Internat. Alliance Theatrical Stage Employees, Moving Picture Technicians, Artists and Allied Crafts of the US, Its Territories and Can., Motion Picture Editor's Guild.

MURRAY, CHRISTOPHER CHARLES, III, architect; b. Bklyn., July 6, 1950; s. Christopher Charles and Gertrude Rose (Marr) M.; m. Ann Herring, Nov. 16, 1974. BArch, U. Notre Dame, 1973; MSc in Real Estate, Johns Hopkins U., 2005. Registered arch., N.Y., Md., D.C., Va., Ga., Fla., W.V., Pa., Ky. Project arch. Hibner Archs., Garden City, NY, 1973-76; project mgr. BBM Archs., NYC, 1976-79; project dir. Gensler & Assocs., NYC, 1979-84; office dir., v.p., mem. nat. mgmt. com. Gensler, Washington, 1984-96, internat. practice leader profl. svc. firms, 1996—. Prin. works include interior design Sidley & Austin Worldwide, McDermott, Will & Emery, Latham & Watkins, Baker McKenzie, Covington & Burling. Asst. v.p., bd. dirs. Nat. Capital Area Coun.; active Greater Washington Bd. Trade, 1986; bd. dirs. Archdiocese Washington. Mem. AIA, Md. Soc. Archs., Notre Dame Club, Club at Franklin Sq. Roman Catholic. Home: 12517 Knightsbridge Ct Rockville MD 20850-3732 Office: Gensler 2020 K St NW Washington DC 20006-1806 Office Phone: 202-721-5300. Business E-Mail: christopher_murray@gensler.com.

MURRAY, DANIEL CHARLES, trial lawyer; s. John Joseph and Marjorie Ellen M.; m. Martha Jane; children: Michaela, Tyler, Brian. BA in Econs., Marquette U.; JD, Loyola U., Chgo., 1976. Bar: Ill. 1976, U.S. Ct. Appeals (7th cir.) 1979, U.S. Dist. Ct. (no. dist.) Ill. 1980, U.S. Dist. Ct. (ea. dist.) Mich. 1992, U.S. Dist. Ct. (ea. dist.) Wis. 1994, U.S. Dist. Ct. (so. dist.) Ill. 2003, U.S. Dist. Ct. (ctrl. dist.) Ill. 2003. Jud. law clk. US Ct. Appeals (7th cir.) Ill., Chgo., 1976—78; asst. US atty. Office US Atty. US Dept. Justice (no. dist.) Ill., Chgo., 1978—91; shareholder, chmn. fin. crime group, chmn. pro bono program Johnson & Bell, Ltd., Chgo., 1991—. Trial instr. U.S. Atty. Gen.'s Advocacy Inst., Wash., 1989; mem. Environ. Crimes Task Force, 1991. Active Chgo. Vol. Legal Svcs. Found., 1977—, Chgo. Legal Advocacy for Incarcerated Mothers, 1995—; participant Chgo. North-of-Howard Task Force. Recipient Disting. Svc. award Chgo. Vol. Legal Svcs. Found., 1983, 87, award for significant contbns. in drug law enforcement U.S. Drug Enforcement Adminstrn., 1988, Insp. Gen.'s nat. award GSA, 1989, Spl. Achievement award U.S. Dept. Justice, 1990. Mem. Fed. Bar Assn. (bd. dirs. Chgo. chpt.), 7th Fed. Cir. Bar Assn. Office: Johnson & Bell Ltd Ste 2700 33 W Monroe St Chicago IL 60603-5404 Office Phone: 312-984-0226. Business E-Mail: murrayd@jbltd.com.

MURRAY, DANIEL RICHARD, lawyer; b. Mar. 23, 1946; s. Alfred W. and Gloria D. Murray. AB, U. Notre Dame, 1967; JD, Harvard U., 1970. Bar: Ill. 1970, U.S. Dist. Ct. (no. dist.) Ill. 1970, U.S. Ct. Appeals (7th cir.) 1971, U.S. Supreme Ct. 1974. Ptnr. Jenner & Block, Chgo., 1970—. Trustee Chgo. Mo. and Western Rlwy. Co., 1988-97; adj. prof. U. Notre Dame, 1997—. Co-author: Secured Transactions, 1978, Uniform Laws Annotated—Uniform Commercial Code Forms, 2007, Illinois Practice: Uniform Commercial Code Forms, 2007, Illinois Practice: Uniform Commercial Code with Illinois Code Comments, 2007. Bd. regents Big Shoulders Fund, Archdiocese of Chgo., Bernardin Ctr., Cath. Theol. Union. Mem.: Assn. Transp. Practitioners, Transp. Lawyers Assn., Am. Coll. Comml. Fin. Lawyers, Am. Bankruptcy Coll., Am. Law Inst., Am. Bankruptcy Inst., Cath. Lawyers Guild (bd. dirs.), Lawyers' Club Chgo. Roman Catholic. Home: 1307 N Sutton Pl Chicago IL 60610-2007 Office: Jenner & Block LLP 330 N Wabash Ave Ste 3800 Chicago IL 60611-3605 Office Phone: 312-923-2953. Business E-Mail: dmurray@jenner.com.

MURRAY, DAVID GEORGE, architect; b. Tulsa, Nov. 9, 1919; s. Lee Cloyd and Marion (Bennett) M.; m. Margaret Elizabeth Oldham, Sept. 23, 1944; children: Michael Allen, Lucy Margaret (Mrs. Norman Scheer), Patrick David. BArch, Okla. State U., Stillwater, 1942. Registered architect, Okla. Ptnr. Atkinson & Murray, Tulsa, 1949-52; prin. David G. Murray & Assocs., Tulsa, 1952-56; pres. Murray, Jones, Murray, Inc., Tulsa, 1957-85, chmn., 1986-89. Chmn., bd. govs. Licensed Architects Oklahoma City, 1964-74. Prin. works include Cities Service Technology Ctr., Broken Arrow, Okla., Terminal Bldg. Tulsa Internat. Airport, St. Patrick's Ch., Oklahoma City, Coll. of Osteopathic Medicine and Surgery, Tulsa, First Nat. Tower, Tulsa, Hillcrest Med. Ctr., Tulsa, Thomas Gilcrease Mus., Tulsa, Tulsa Civic Ctr. Bldgs. Chmn., dir. Goodwill Industries of Tulsa, 1966-87; chmn., exec. com. Downtown Tulsa Unltd., 1975-87; v.p., exec. com., dir. Met. Tulsa C. of C., 1979-85. Served to 1st lt. USAF, 1942-45. Named to Hall of Fame Coll. Engring. Okla. State U., 1969. Fellow AIA (pres. Tulsa chpt. 1964, mem. com. office practice 1983-87). Republican. Methodist. Avocations: travel, golf.

MURRAY, DIANE ELIZABETH, librarian; b. Detroit, Oct. 15, 1942; d. Gordon Lisle and Dorothy Anne (Steketee) LaBoueff; m. Donald Edgar Murray, Apr. 22, 1968. AB, Hope Coll., 1964; postgrad., Mich. State U., East Lansing, 1964-66; MLS, Western Mich. U., 1968; MM, Aquinas Coll., 1982. Catalog libr., asst. head acquisitions sect. Mich. State U. Librs., East Lansing, 1968-77; libr. tech. and automated svcs. Hope Coll., Holland, Mich., 1977-88; dir. librs. DePauw U., Greencastle, Ind., 1988-91; acquisitions libr. Grand Valley State U., Allendale, Mich., 1991—. Sec., vice chair, chairperson bd. trustees Mich. Libr. Consortium, Lansing, 1981—85. V.p. Humane Soc. Putnam County, Greencastle, 1990—91; bd. dirs. Loutit Dist. Libr., 1999—. Mem.: ALA. Methodist. Avocations: dog breeding and showing, handbell ringing. Office: Grand Valley State U Zumberge Libr Allendale MI 49401 Business E-Mail: murrayd@gvsu.edu.

MURRAY, EDWARD ROCK, insurance broker; b. Bklyn., Jan. 31, 1947; s. Garrett Francis and Anne M. (Rock) M.; m. Barbara Marie Robotti; children: Pamela Jean, Stephanie Elise. BA in Bus. Adminstrn., St. Bonaventure U., NYC, 1968. Claims examiner N.Y.C., 1970-72; agt. and mgr. John Hancock Life Ins., Albany, N.Y., 1972-76; regional dir. Colonial Life Insur, Albany, 1976-80; ptnr. Murray & Zuckerman, Inc., Schenectady, N.Y., 1980—. Bd. dirs. Northeast Mgmt. Forum, 1990—; bd. dirs., treas. The Mktg. Alliance. 1st lt. U.S. Army, 1968-70, Vietnam. Mem. Mohawk Club (past chmn.), Edison Club. Roman Catholic. Avocation: golf. Office: Murray & Zuckerman Inc 128 Erie Blvd Ste 2 Schenectady NY 12305-2283 Office Phone: 518-382-5483. Business E-Mail: emurray@mandzinc.com.

MURRAY, EILEEN K., investment company executive; BSc in acctg., Manhattan Coll., 1980. Formerly with Peat Marwick; with Morgan Stanley, 1984—2002; v.p. Morgan Stanley Group Inc., 1988—91, prin., 1991—94, mng. dir., 1994, controller and treas.; chief adminstrv. officer, instl. securities group Morgan Stanley Dean Witter & Co., 1999—2002; head of global tech, ops. & product control Credit Suisse First Boston, NYC, 2002—05; head global ops. & tech., mem. mgmt. com. Morgan Stanley, NYC, 2005—. Bd. dirs. Omgeo LLC, 2001—. Office: Morgan Stanley 1585 Broadway New York NY 10036 *

MURRAY, ELIZABETH DAVIS REID, writer, researcher; b. Wadesboro, NC, June 10, 1925; d. James Matheson and Mary Kennedy (Little) Davis; m. James William Reid, Feb. 7, 1948 (dec. June 1972); children: Michael Ernest, Nancy Kennedy Reid Baker, James William; m. Raymond L. Murray, May 12, 1979; stepchildren: Stephen, Ilah Murray Garton, Marshall. AB cum laude, Meredith Coll., 1946; postgrad., N.C. State U., 1967—68, postgrad., 1974—75. Continuity writer Sta. WPTF, Raleigh, 1946—47; program mgr., women's commentator Sta. WADE, Wadesboro, 1947—48; dir. news bur. Meredith Coll., 1948—51; state woman's news editor, columnist Raleigh News and Observer, 1951—52; exec. sec. Gov.'s Coord. Com. on Aging, 1959—61; rsch. asst. Dr. Clarence Poe, Raleigh, 1963—64; contbg. editor Raleigh Mag., 1969—72; local history corr. Raleigh Times, News and Observer, Spectator of Raleigh. Tchr. Wake history Wake Tech. Coll., Wake pub. schs. and librs.; rsch. cons. Wake County Pub. Librs., Mordecai Historic Park, State Visitor Ctr., Exec. Mansion; resource person Wake pub. schs.; dir. Capital County Pub. Co.; lectr. in field. Author: From Raleigh's Past (Cert. of Commendation Am. Assn. State and Local History), 1965, Wake: Capital County of North Carolina, vol. 1, 1983 (W.P. Peace award for best book on N.C. history 1983); editor, compilor: North Carolina's Older Population: Opportunities and Challenges, 1960; editor, contbr. Wake County Hist. Soc. newsletter, 1965-69, History of Raleigh Fire Dept., 1970; guest editor: Raleigh Mag. Wake County Bicentennial Issues, 1971; author, photographer filmstrip for Wake Pub. Schs., 1971; author sect. Windows of the Way, 1964; author instrn. materials State Exec. Mansion and Mordecai Hist. Park docents; contbr. articles to local newspaper and mags.; chpts. to books. Active Tryon Palace Commn., 1967-78, Raleigh Hist. Sites Commn., 1969-73, Raleigh City Coun., 1973, Meredith Bd. Assocs., 1976-79, Meredith Heritage Soc.; history and archives adv. com. Meredith Coll., 1995; pres. Jr. Woman's Club, 1956-56; organizing pres. Arts Coun. Raleigh; exec. com. NC Humanities Found., 1974-76; dir., officer North Carolinians for Better Libraries, 1965-69; trustee Pub. Librs., 1956-67, Meredith Coll., 1966-69; pres. Wake Meml. Hosp. Aux., 1962-63; trustee Pullen Meml. Bapt. Ch., 1975-78, chmn., 1977-78, deacon; chmn. Mayor's Com. to Preserve Hist. Objects, 1965-80; adv. coun. WUNC-FM, 1976-80, NC Art Soc.; vis. lectr. NC Mus. History Assocs., 1980; docent, lectr. NC Exec. Mansion, Mordecai Hist. Park, NC Mus. Art, 1957-1989, docent emeritus, 1989—; bd. dirs. Raleigh-Wake County Symphony Orch. Devel. Assn., 1979-83, Estey Hall Found., 1980-89, Friends of Meredith Libr., 1980-83; adv. bd. Raleigh City Mus., task force on local history, 1984-2006; bldg. adv. com. local history Wake County Pub. Libr.; com. 100 to establish Children's Mus. About World (now Exploris Mus). Recipient Outstanding Cmty. Svc. award, 1952, best all-around Jr. Woman's Club mem., 1955, Disting. Alumna award Meredith Coll., 1970, recognition for svc. award Raleigh Hist. Sites Commn., 1973, Cmty. Svc. award Raleigh Bd. Realtors, 1983, Phi Beta Kappa award Wake County, 1985, Silver Bowl award N.C. Mus. Art, 1987, Anthemion award Capital Area Preservation Inc., 1994. Mem. N. Caroliniana Soc., N.C. Soc. County and Local Historians (life), N.C. Lit. and Hist. Assn., Apex Hist. Soc. (charter), Yates Mill. Assocs., Inc. (charter), N.C. Art Soc. (Disting. Svc. citation 1979), Friends N.C. State U. Libr., Friends of Carlyle Campbell Libr. (charter, life), Wake County Geneal. Soc., N.C. African-Am. Geneal. and Hist. Soc., Friends of N.C. Archives (life), Kappa Nu Sigma. Democrat.

MURRAY, GEORGE E., lawyer; b. Mo., 1954; BA magna cum laude, Dartmouth Coll., 1976; JD cum laude, U. Mo., 1979. Bar: Mo. 1979. Ptnr. Bryan Cave LLP, St. Louis, group co-leader Real Estate Devel. Construction and Project Fin. Note and comment editor: Mo. Law Rev., 1978-79. Mem. ABA, Order of Barristers, Order of Coif. Office: Bryan Cave LLP One Metropolitan Square 211 N Broadway, Ste 3600 Saint Louis MO 63102 Office Phone: 314-259-2344. E-mail: gemurray@bryancave.com.

MURRAY, GLENN EDWARD, lawyer; b. Niskayuna, NY, Dec. 11, 1955; BA cum laude, Siena Coll., 1977; JD, Union U., Albany, NY, 1980. Bar: N.Y. 1981, U.S. Dist. Ct. (no. dist.) N.Y. 1981, U.S. Ct. Mil. Appeals 1981, U.S. Dist. Ct. (we. dist.) N.Y. 1985, U.S. Supreme Ct. 1987, U.S. Bankruptcy Ct. 1989, U.S. Ct. Appeals (2d cir.) 1992. Pvt. practice, Buffalo, 1990—; prosecutor Village of Williamsville, 1992—2002. Adj. prof. Am. constl. law Canisius Coll., 1993-94. Author: Collateral Consequences of Criminal Conduct, 1989, Civil Consequences of Criminal Conduct, 51 Am. Jr. Trials 337, 1994; contbr. articles to profl. jours. Mem. social action com. Temple Beth Am, Amherst, N.Y., 1987—; instr. Jewish Community Ctr. Greater Buffalo, 1988—; instr. police legal survival Operation Tri-Star (SWAT team conf.), Ft. Drum, N.Y., 1989-91. Capt. U.s. Army, 1981-84, mem. N.Y. Army N.G. ret. Decorated Bronze Star. Mem. ABA, N.Y. State Bar Assn. (chmn. spl. com. on mil. and vet. affairs 1991-94), Erie County Bar Assn. (instr., panelist), N.Y. Defenders Assn., N.Y. State Assn. Criminal Def. Lawyers, N.Y. Civil Liberties Union. Home: 84 Highland Dr Buffalo NY 14221-6802 Office: The Cornell Mansion 484 Delaware Ave Buffalo NY 14202-1304

MURRAY, JAMES DOYLE, accountant, educator; b. Rochester, NY, July 24, 1938; s. William Herbert and Mildred Frances (Becker) M.; m. Mary Louise Goodyear, June 22, 1962; children: William Doyle, Robert Goodyear. BS, U. Rochester, 1961. CPA, N.Y. With Ernst & Whinney, Rochester, N.Y., 1963—, ptnr., 1977-86; pvt. practice Rochester, 1986—; former mem. faculty NYSCPA. Contbr. articles to profl. jours. Treas. William Warfield Scholarship Fund, Inc.; bd. dirs. March of Dimes, Rochester chpt.; trustee B. Thomas Golisano Found.; active fund raising Boy Scouts Am., Rochester Philharm., Rochester Mus. and Sci. Ctr., U. Rochester; former bd. dirs., treas. Downstairs Cabaret; mem. Eagle bd. of rev. Boy Scouts Am.; elder Presbyn. Ch.; past pres. Egypt Vol. Fire Dept. Lt. (j.g.) USN, 1961-63. Named Acct. Adv. of Yr. for region II, SBA, 1996. Mem. N.Y. State Soc. CPAs (pres. Rochester chpt. 1982-83), Inst. Mgmt. Accts. (bd. dirs. 1978-80). Republican. Office: 349 W Commercial St East Rochester NY 14445-2407

MURRAY, JAMES JOSEPH, III, association executive; b. Boston, Dec. 31, 1933; s. James Joseph Jr. and Anne Louise (Gurvin) M.; children: James Arthur, Paul, Douglas Joseph, Laura Anne. AB, Harvard U., 1955. Regional editor Prentice Hall, Inc., 1957-60, editor, 1960-64, v.p., exec. editor, 1964-69; pres. Winthrop Pubs., Inc. subs. Prentice Hall, Cambridge, Mass., 1969-82, also bd. dirs.; spl. mng. cons. Am. Coun. Edn., Washington, 1983-84, dir. external affairs, 1984—, v.p., 1997—. Chmn. N.J. Heart Fund; spl. cons. NEH, 1975—. Mem. editorial bd. Capitol Pub., 1992—; author, editor: American Colleges and Universities, 2000. Mem. Dem. Nat. Com. from N.J., 1968; del. Dem. Nat. Conv., 1968; mem. gov. bd. Marine Mil. Acad., 1995—. 1st lt. USMCR, 1955-57. Mem. Am. Polit. Sci. Assn., Assn. Physical Plant Adminstrs. (bd. dirs.), Am. Assn. of Higher Edn., Harvard Club, Harvard Varsity Club, Pi Eta. Office: One DuPont Circle Ste 800 Washington DC 20036

MURRAY, JAMES MICHAEL, librarian, lawyer; b. Seattle, Nov. 8, 1944; s. Clarence Nicholas and Della May (Snyder) M.; m. Linda Monthy Murray. MLaw Librarianship, U. Wash., 1978; JD, Gonzaga U., 1971. Bar: Wash. 1974, U.S. Dist. Ct. (we. dist.) Wash. 1975, U.S. Dist. Ct. (ea. dist.) Wash. 1985. Reference/res. libr. U. Tex. Law Libr., Austin, 1978-81; assoc. law libr. Washington U. Law Libr., St. Louis, 1981-84; law libr., asst. prof. Gonzaga U. Sch. Law, Spokane, 1984-91; libr. East Bonner County Libr., 1991-97, U.S. Cts. Libr., Spokane, 1997—. Mem. state adv. bd. Nat. Reporter on Legal Ethics and Profl. Responsibility, 1982-91; cons. in field. Author: (with Reams and McDermott) American Legal Literature: Bibliography of Selected Legal Resources, 1985, (with Gasaway and Johnson) Law Library Administration During Fiscal Austerity, 1992; editor Tex. Bar Jour. (Books Appraisals Column), 1979-82; contbr. numerous articles and revs. to profl. jours., acknowledgements and bibliographies in field. Bd. dirs. ACLU, Spokane chpt., 1987-91, Wash. Vol. Lawyers for the Arts,

1976-78. Mem. ABA, Idaho Libr. Assn., Wash. State Bar Assn. (law sch. liaison com. 1986-88). Home: 921 W 29th Ave Spokane WA 99203-1318 Office Phone: 509-353-3293. Business E-Mail: James_Murray@lb9.uscourts.gov.

MURRAY, JEANNE See STAPLETON, JEAN

MURRAY, JEFFREY C., medical educator, pediatrician; BS, MIT, 1972; MD, Tufts Med. Sch., 1978. Pediat. resident Boston Floating Hosp.; genetics fellow U. Washington; mem. faculty U. Iowa, 1984—, prof. pediatrics, pediat. dentistry, biological sciences, epidemiology, co-chair genetics doctoral program; former dir. Cooperative Human Linkage Ctr.; dir. Comprehensive Oral Health Rsch. Ctr. of Discovery. Contbr. scientific papers, chapters to books. Recipient E. Mead Johnson award, Am. Pediat. Soc., 1997, William Geis award, Internat. Assn. Dental Rsch., 1997. Mem.: Inst. Medicine. Office: University of Iowa Iowa City IA 52241 Office Phone: 319-335-6897. E-mail: jeff-murray@uiowa.edu.

MURRAY, JOHN PATRICK, psychologist, educator, researcher; b. Cleve., Sept. 14, 1943; s. John Augustine and Helen Marie (Lynch) M.; m. Ann Coke Dennison, Apr. 17, 1971; children: Jonathan Coke, Ian Patrick. PhD, Cath. U. Am., 1970. Rsch. dir. Office U.S. Surgeon Gen. NIMH, Bethesda, Md., 1969-72; asst. to assoc. prof. psychology Macquarie U., Sydney, Australia, 1973-79; vis. assoc. prof. U. Mich., Ann Arbor, 1979-80; dir. youth and family policy Boys Town Ctr., Boys Town, Nebr., 1980-85; prof., dir. Sch. Family Studies and Human Svcs. Kans. State U., Manhattan, 1985-98, interim assoc. vice provost rsch., 1998—2000; vis. scholar Ctr. on Media and Child Health Harvard U. Med. Sch., 2004—. Scholar-in-residence Mind Sci. Found., San Antonio, 1996-97; mem. children's TV com. CBS, 1996-99. Author: Television and Youth: 25 Years of Research and Controversy, 1980, The Future of Children's TV, 1984, (with H.T. Rubin) Status Offenders: A Sourcebook, 1983, (with E.A. Rubenstein, G.A. Comstock) Television and Social Behavior, 3 vols., 1972, (with A. Huston and others) Big World, Small Screen: The Role of Television in American Society, 1992, (with C. Fisher and others) Applied Developmental Science, 1996, Children and Television: 50 Years of Research (with N. Pecora and E. Wartella), 2006; contbr. numerous articles to profl. jours. Mem. Nebr. Foster Care Rev. Bd., 1982-84; mem. Advocacy Office for Children and Youth, 1980-85; mem. Nat. Coun. Children and TV, 1982-87; trustee The Villages Children's Homes, 1986—, Menninger Found., 1996—; mem. children's TV adv. bd. CBS-TV, 1996-99. Fellow Am. Psychol. Assn. (pres. div. child youth and family svcs. 1990); mem. Internat. Comm. Assn., Soc. Rsch. in Child Devel., Royal Commonwealth Soc. (London), Manhattan Country Club. Home: 1731 Humboldt St Manhattan KS 66502-4140 Office: Kans State U 303 Justin Hall Manhattan KS 66506-1304 Office Phone: 785-532-1456. E-mail: jpm@ksu.edu.

MURRAY, JOSEPH EDWARD, retired plastic surgeon; b. Milford, Mass., Apr. 1, 1919; s. William Andrew and Mary (DePasquale) Murray; m. Virginia Link, June 2, 1945; children: Virginia, Margaret, Joseph Link, Katharine, Thomas, Richard. AB, Holy Cross Coll., 1940, DSc, 1965; MD, Harvard, 1943; DSc, Rockford Coll., Ill., 1966, Roger Williams Coll., 1986; PhD (hon.), Anna Marie Coll., 1993, SUNY, Albany, 1993, U. Suffolk, 1993, Magill U., Montreal, 1996. Diplomate Am. Bd. Surgery, Am. Bd. Plastic Surgery. Chief plastic surgeon Peter Bent Brigham Hosp., Boston, 1951—86; chief plastic surgeon Children's Hosp. Med. Center, Boston, 1972—85; prof. surgery Harvard Med. Sch., 1970—86; ret., 1986. Chmn. Am. Bd. Plastic Surgery, 1969. Maj. M.C. US Army, 1944—47. Recipient Gold medal, Internat. Soc. Surgeons, 1963, Nobel prize for medicine or physiology, 1990, Sabin award, 1994, Lifetime Achievement award, Mass. Med. Soc., 1988. Fellow: AMA, AAAS (hon.), Royal Coll. Surgeons Edinburgh, Royal Coll. Surgeons Ireland, Royal Coll. Surgeons of Eng., Royal Australasian Coll. Surgeons; mem.: NAS, ACS (regent 1970—79, v.p. 1983), Am. Acad. Arts and Scis. (Hon. award 1962), Am. Assn. Plastic Surgeons (pres. 1964—65, Hon. award 1969), Soc. U. Surgeons, Boston Surg. Soc. (pres. 1975), New Eng. Surg. Assn. (pres. 1986—87), Am. Surg. Assn. (v.p. 1979), Harvard Med. Sch. Alumni Coun. (pres. 1984), Tavern Club, Badminton and Tennis Club, Wellesley Country Club, Alpha Omega Alpha. Home: 108 Abbott Rd Wellesley MA 02481-6104

MURRAY, JULIA KAORU (MRS. JOSEPH E. MURRAY), occupational therapist; b. Wahiawa, Oahu, Hawaii, 1934; d. Gijun and Edna Tsuruko (Taba) Funakoshi; m. Joseph Edward Murray, 1961; children: Michael, Susan, Leslie. BA, U. Hawaii, 1956; cert. occupl. therapy, U. Puget Sound, 1958. Therapist Inst. Logopedics, Wichita, Kans., 1958; sr. therapist Hawaii State Hosp., Kaneohe, 1959; part-time therapist Centre County Ctr. for Crippled Children and Adults, State College, Pa., 1963; vice chmn. adv. bd. Hosp. Improvement Program East Oreg. State Hosp., Pendleton, 1974; v.p. Ind. Living, Inc., 1976—79; instr. job search; mem. adv. com. Oreg. Ednl. Coordinating Commn., 1979—82; mem. Oreg. Bd. Engring. Examiners, 1979—87; supr., occupl. therapist Fairview Tng. Ctr., Salem, Oreg., 1984—94; occupl. therapist U.S. Naval Hosp., Okinawa, Japan, 1994—99, Yokosuka, Japan, 1999—2005, occupl. therapist Misawa AB divsn., 2005—. Rep. from Umatilla County Commrs. to Blue Mountain Econ. Devel. Council, 1976-78; mem. Ashland Park and Recreation Bd., 1972-73; vice chmn. adv. bd. LINC, 1978; mem. exec. bd. Liberty-Boone Neighborhood Assn., 1979-83. Decorated Meritorious Civilian Svc. medal USN. Mem. Am. Occupational Therapy Assn., Oreg. Occupational Therapy Assn., Hawaii Occupational Therapy Assn. (sec. 1960, LWV (bd. dirs. Pendleton 1974, 77-78, pres. 1975-77; bd. dirs. Oreg. 1979-81, Ashland, Wis., 1967-71, Wis. v.p. 1970). Personal E-mail: jkfmurray@hotmail.com.

MURRAY, KATHLEEN ANNE, lawyer; b. LA, Feb. 14, 1946; d. Francis Albert and Dorothy (Thompson) M.; 1 child, Anne Murray Ladd; m. Arthur T. Perkins Jr., June 29, 1991. BA, U. Mich., 1967; JD, Hastings Coll. Law, 1973. Bar: Calif. 1973, U.S. Dist. Ct. (no. dist.) Calif. 1973, U.S. Ct. Appeals (9th cir.) 1973. Sr. staff atty Child Care Law Ctr., San Francisco, 1979—84, cons. child day care law and regulation, 1984—86; atty Epstein & Harris, San Francisco, 1985—86; gen. counsel Fisher Friedman Assocs., San Francisco, 1986—89; assoc. gen. counsel Calif. State Automobile Assn., San Francisco, 1989—98; sr. counsel Firemen's Fund Ins. Co., San Francisco, 1998—2002; prin. Mercer Health & Benefits, LLC, San Francisco, 2003—. Exec. dir., editl. adv. bd. Parenting Mag., 1985-87; chair Labor and Employment Law Com. Assn. Corp. Coun. Am., 2001-03 Editor: Child Care Center Legal Handbook; Tax Guide for California Child Care Providers; contbr. articles to profl. jours. Mem. adv. coun. Humanities West, Inc., 1986-96; vestry Episcopal Ch. of St. Mary the Virgin, 1990-92; pres. Parents' Assn., Lick-Wilmerding H.S., 1993-94; Pers. Practices Com. Episcopal Diocese of Calif., 1998-2003. Mem.: Assn. Corp. Counsel (chair labor and employment law com. 2001—03). Democrat. Episcopalian. Office: Mercer HR Cons Three Embarcadero Ctr Ste 1500 San Francisco CA 94111-4015 Business E-Mail: kathleen.murray@mercer.com.

MURRAY, KATHLEEN SARAH-JANE, literature and language professor; BA, Auburn U., Ala., 1996; diploma, Ecole Normale Superieure-lsh, 2001; PhD, Princeton U., NJ, 2003. Asst. prof. medieval lit. and french Honors Coll. Baylor U., Waco, Tex., 2003—. Co-dir. The Charrette Project Princeton (N.J.) U. and Baylor U., 1998—2003; lectr. in field. Co-author: Cultural History of Reading, 2005, Literature and Literary Studies on Their Way Towards the Digital Media—Where Are We?, 2005, Encyclopedia of Sex, Love and Culture in the Medieval World, 2006, Encyclopedia of World History, 2006; mem. editl. bd. Baylor Jour. Theatre and Performance, 2003—, Academic Exchange Quar., 2005—; contbr. articles to profl. jours. Named Outstanding Faculty Mem., Baylor U., 2006; recipient Lauréate du Concours Général des Lycées de France, French Ministry Edn., 1992, John Edward Wiatt prize, Auburn (Ala.) U., 1997, Armstrong prize, Dept. Romance Langs. and Lit. Princeton (N.J.) U., 1998, 1999, 2000, 2001, 2002, 2003; grantee, Baylor U., 2003—04, 2005—06; Alfred Foulet fellowship, Princeton (N.J.) U., 2001, Porter Ogden Jacobus fellowship, 2002—03, Donald and Mary Hyde fellowship, 2002. Mem.: MLA, Medieval Acad. Am., Princeton (N.J.) Alumni Schs. Com., Princeton (N.J.) Club, Princeton (N.J.) Assn. Grad. Alumni, Phi Mu (spirit chmn., asst. treas., panhellenic rep.). Office: Baylor University One Bear Place 97144 Waco TX 76798 Home Phone: 254-848-9585; Office Phone: 254-710-7854. Business E-Mail: sj_murray@baylor.edu.

MURRAY, LAWRENCE, management consultant; b. NYC, May 10, 1939; s. Gilbert and Edna (Blatt) M.; children: Robert, Stacy, David, Daniel, Abigail. BA, Cornell U., 1961; MBA, U. Okla., 1966; PhD, Pacific Western U., 1993. Cert. Pa. Food Mgmt. Account exec. Merrill Lynch, Paramus, NJ, 1965-69; chmn., pres. Murray, Lind & Co., Inc., Jersey City, 1969-72; dir. investor rels. IU Internat. Corp., Phila., 1972-73, dir. spl. projects, 1974-75; dir. fin. comm., mem. exec. staff of chmn. bd. ARA Svcs., Inc., Phila., 1975—78; chmn., chief exec. officer Century Mgmt. and affiliated cos., West Chester, Pa., 1976-82; chmn. bd., CEO Creative Mgmt. Corp., Bala Cynwyd and West Chester, Pa., 1982-87, Fin. Mgmt. Profl. Corp., West Chester, 1983-89; chmn. bd. dirs. Venture Frontiers Co., Denver, 1984-89; chmn. bd., CEO Fin. Intelligence Corp., West Chester, 1989-95; CEO, chmn. bd. dirs. Healthy Living Ctrs., West Chester, 1993—. Lectr. bus. orgn. and mgmt. Bergen C.C., 1971-72; chmn. bd. dirs. Med. Intelligence Corp., West Chester, 1993-95; CEO, chmn. bd. dirs. Miramax Corp.; chmn. bd. dirs., CEO, Tax Doctor Corp., West Chester, 2002-. Author: The Organized Stockbroker, 1970; A New Era in Mergers and Acquisitions, 1974; Communications: Management's Newest Marketing Skill, 1976, Powerful Tax-Saving Strategies for Honest People, 1992, Teach Your Children How to Eat Properly and Add 20 Years to Their Lives, 1999; contbr. articles to profl. jours. Pres., Congregation Beth Israel, Media, Pa., 1977-78, Parents Without Ptnrs., Valley Forge, Pa., 1982-83, PTO West Chester East HS, Pa., 2007-; v.p. Cornell U. Class of 1961, 1981-86; mem. White House Conf. on Bus. Ethics in Am., 1986; active Beth Chaim Reform Synagogue. Served to 1st lt. arty./intelligence US Army, 1963—64. Decorated U.S. Army Commendation medal. Mem. Nat. Investor Rels. Inst. (pres. Phila. chpt. 1976-78), Internat. Coun. Shopping Ctrs., Am. Health Info. Mgmt. Assn., C. of C. Greater West Chester. Home: 625 Beaumony Cir West Chester PA 19380 Personal E-mail: lmurray761@aol.com.

MURRAY, LOWELL, Canadian senator; b. New Waterford, NS, Can., Sept. 26, 1936; s. Daniel and Evelyn (Young) M.; m. Colleen Elaine MacDonald; children: William, Colin. BA, St. Francis Xavier U., Antigonish, NS, Can.; MA in Pub. Adminstrn., Queen's U., Kingston, Ont., Can.; LLD (hon.), St. Francis Xavier U., 2005. Chief of staff Minister of Justice and Minister of Pub. Works Can., Ottawa, Ont., Senator M. Wallace McCutcheon, Ottawa, Ont.; leader of opposition Can., Ottawa, Ont.; dep. minister Premier N.B. (Can.); mem. Senate of Can., Ottawa, Ont., 1979—, co-chmn. joint Senate-House of Commons com. ofcl. langs., 1980-84, chmn. standing Senate com. on banking, trade and commerce, 1984-86, chmn. standing senate com. on nat. fin., 1995—96, 1999—2004, chmn. standing senate com. on social affairs, sci. and tech., 1997-99. Bd. dirs. SONY Can. Inc.; trustee Inst. Rsch. Pub. Policy, 1984-86, mem. Trilateral Commn., 1985-86; mem. coun. Fedn. Adv. Panel Fiscal Imbalance, 2005-06. Sworn of the privy coun., appointed leader of Govt. in the Senate, 1986—93; Min. of State Fed.-Provincial Rels., 1986—91; min. responsible for Atlantic Can. Opportunities Agy., 1987—88, acting min. comms., 1988—89; nat. campaign chmn. gen. election Progressive Conservative Party Can., 1977—79, 1981—83. Progressive Conservative. Roman Catholic. Office: The Senate Ottawa ON Canada K1A 0A4

MURRAY, MARK ANDREW, food products executive, former academic administrator, economist; b. Lansing, Mich., July 5, 1954; s. John and Francoise G. (Martin) M.; m. Elizabeth J. Chapman, July 15, 1978; children: Hannah B., Laura E., Ellen T. BA, Mich. State U., 1976, M in Labor and Industrial Rels., 1979; D in Pub. Svc. (hon.), Ea. Mich. U., 2000. Economist Mich. Dept. Social Svcs., Lansing, 1978-85, Mich. Dept. Commerce, Lansing, 1985-90, dir. bus. rsch. office, 1987-90; exec. dir. Mich. Health Planning Coun., 1990-91; dep. dir. Mich. Dept. Mgmt. and Budget, 1991—94, state budget dir., 1994—98, state treas., policy advisor, 1999—2001; pres. Meijer, Inc., Grand Rapids, Mich., 2006—. Guest lectr. U. Okla. Contbr. articles to profl. jours. Named Mich. Pub. Servant of Yr., 1992; recipient Donald L. Scantlebury Award for Leadership in State Govt. Fin., 1998. Mem. Nat. Assn. Welfare Rsch. and Statistics (bd. dirs. 1984-85), Nat. Assn. State Devel. Agys. (rsch. div., bd. dirs. 1986-90), Mich. Hist. Soc., Mensa, Internat. Platform Assn., Omicron Delta Upsilon. Roman Catholic. Avocations: athletics, photography. Office: Meijer, Inc 1920 44th St SE Grand Rapids MI 49508

MURRAY, MICHAEL DENNIS, pharmacist; b. Blairsville, Pa., Apr. 13, 1952; s. Howard Jacob and Elizabeth Murray; m. Jennifer Jayne Chumbler, Aug. 4, 1979; children: Ryan Michael, Kristin Elizabeth. BSc in Pharmacy, Duquesne U., 1975, D of Pharmacy, 1977; M of Pub. Health, Ind. U., 1992. Registered pharmacist, Ind., Pa. Asst. prof. Purdue U. Sch. of Pharmacy, West Lafayette, Ind., 1982-88, assoc. prof., 1988-99, prof., 1999—2001, Bucke prof. pharmacy, 2002—. Adj. asst. prof. Purdue U. Sch. of Pharmacy, West Lafayette, 1977—82; adj. assoc. prof. Ind. U. Sch. Medicine, 1992—2001, adj. prof., 2001—; dir. rsch. Ind. Drug Evaluation and Analysis Ctr., Indpls., 1995—98; faculty Health Svcs. R&D, Indpls., 1995—98; dir. healthcare data and epidemiology Regenstrief Inst., Indpls., 1996—2004; faculty scholar Purdue U., 1999; Mescal S. Ferguson disting. prof. U. NC at Chapel Hill; dir. U. NC at Chapel Hill, Ctr. Study Pharm. Outcomes, Sch. Pharm., Chapel Hill, NC. Commr. Saints Football Club, Lawrence, Ind., 1996-97; v.p. Ind. Soccer League, Carmel, Ind., 1996-97. Fellow: Internat. Soc. Pharmacoepiemiology (sci. programs 1989—2004, membership chair 1990—93, bd. dirs. 1991—94); mem.: U.S. Pharmacopia (safe medicine use and therapeutic decision expert panels 2000—05, exec. com. coun. of experts 2005—, chair safe medication use com.), Am. Soc. Clin. Pharmacology and therapeutics (pharmacoepidemiology chair 1998—2001, chair com. on coordination of sci. sects. 2001—04, bd. dirs.). Democrat. Roman Catholic. Avocations: stained glass crafts, arts, hiking, bicycling. Office: U NC Campus Box 7360 2212 Kerr Hall Chapel Hill NC 27599-7360 Business E-Mail: mick@unc.edu.

MURRAY, MICHAEL KENT, lawyer; b. Missoula, Mont., Feb. 14, 1948; s. Paul R. and Virginia F. Murray; children: Britton M., Spencer J. BA, U. Calif., Santa Barbara, 1970; JD, U. Santa Clara, 1974. Bar: Wash. 1974, U.S. Ct. Claims 1975, U.S. Tax Ct. 1976, U.S. Dist. Ct. Wash. 1977, U.S. Ct. Appeals (fed. cir.) 1982. Trial atty. honor law grad. program U.S. Dept. Justice, Washington, 1974-76; atty. Foster Pepper & Riviera, Seattle, 1976-79, ptnr. Seattle and Bellevue, 1980-86, ptnr.-in-charge Bellevue, 1983-86; atty., pres. Michael K. Murray, P.S., Seattle, 1986—; pres. Murray & Assocs., PLLC, Eastsound, Wash., 2004—. Pres. N.W. Properties Devel. Corp., Seattle, 1986-92; of counsel Lasher Holzapfel Sperry & Ebberson, Seattle, 1992-2001; v.p. and gen. mgr. constrn. defect repair div., BELFOR USA Group, Inc., Seattle, 2001-04. Articles editor Santa Clara Lawyer, U. Santa Clara Sch. Law, 1973-74. Trustee Pacific Northwest Ballet, Seattle, 1979-81; dir. Bellevue Downtown Assn., 1984-87. Mem. Wash. State Bar Assn., King County Bar Assn. Avocations: sailing, fly fishing, bicycling, boating. Office: PO Box 10 296 Main St Ste 200 Eastsound WA 98245 Office Phone: 360-376-0306. Business E-Mail: murraylaw@orcasonline.com.

MURRAY, MICHAEL PATRICK, lawyer; b. Milw., Jan. 31, 1930; s. Michael James and Florence Mary M.; m. Allene Vereen, May 8, 1976; children: Bryan Patrick, Laura Renee. BA, Milton Coll., Wis., 1953; JD, Marquette U., 1958; LLM, John Marshall Law Sch., 1960; D of Juridicial Sci., George Washington U., DC, 1973; M of Liberal Arts, Johns Hopkins U., 1996. Bar: Wis. 1958, Calif. 1966, U.S. Supreme Ct. 1967, U.S. Ct. Appeals (9th cir.) 1982, D.C. 1989, Va. 1989, U.S. Ct. Appeals (D.C. cir.) 1989, U.S. Ct. Appeals (4th cir.) 1990. Commd. 2d lt. USMC, 1953, advanced through grades to col., 1975, prosecutor and def. counsel, 1960—66, trial judge and SJA, 1966—69, dir. policy and research Washington, 1969—72, dir. Law Ctr. Iwakuni, Japan, 1973—74; dep. legal advisor, chmn. Joint Chiefs of Staff, Washington, 1974—75; ret. USMC, 1978; trial atty. Anderson & Murphy, Milw., 1958—60; apellate judge USN Ct. of Rev., Washington, 1975—78; pvt. practice, San Diego, 1982—89; atty., counsel Clary, Lawrence, Lickstein & Moore, Falls Church, Va., 1989—91; ptnr. Michael Patrick Murray & Assocs., South Riding, Va., 1991—; asst. gen. counsel NRA, Washington, 1992—95. Assoc. prof. law Pepperdine U., Malibu, Calif., 1978-80, Marquette U., Milw., 1980-81; adj. prof. law Western State U., San Diego, 1983-88, Nat. U. Coll. Law, 1988-89; pro bono vol. atty. for indigents, San Diego, 1982-89. Author: Quarter: the Warrior's Dilemma, 1967, (law study) Eichman and Major German War Criminal Trials, 1973, O'Ryans Law, 1992, Murder By Class, 1997, Law Is a Jealous Mistress, 1999, People Needing People, 2000, Love's Mirror, 2003, Judgment in NAM, 2005, Passion, Prose and Poetry, 2005. Mem. Calif. Bar Assn., Wis. Bar Assn., D.C. Bar Assn., Va. Bar Assn., Am. Legion, First and Third Marine Div. Assn., Marine Corps Assn., Marine Mustang Assn., Phi Delta Phi. Roman Catholic. Avocations: poetry, creative writing. Office: Michael Patrick Murray & Assocs 26083 Glasgow Dr South Riding VA 20152 Office Phone: 703-327-1350. E-mail: michael.p.murray@att.net.

MURRAY, PATRICIA, electronics company executive; b. Detroit; BA, Michigan St. U.; BS, St. Louis U.; JD, U. Mich., 1986. Nurse, intensive care unit, nursing adminstr. U. Mich. Hospitals; employment litigator Morrison & Foerster, Palo Alto, Calif., until 1990; atty. human resources legal staff Intel Corp., 1990—91, mgr. human resoures legal staff, 1992—95, dir., v.p. human resources Santa Clara, 1996—97, sr. v.p., 1997—. Chmn. Intel Found. Office: Intel Corp PO Box 58119 2200 Mission College Blvd Santa Clara CA 95052-8119 E-mail: patricia.murray@intel.com.

MURRAY, PATTY (PATRICIA J. MURRAY), senator; b. Bothell, Wash., Oct. 10, 1950; d. David L. and Beverly A. (McLaughlin) Johns; m. Robert R. Murray, June 2, 1972; children: Randy P., Sara A. BA, Wash. State U., 1972. Sec. various cos., Seattle, 1972-76; citizen lobbyist various ednl. groups, Seattle, 1983-88; legis. lobbyist Orgn. for Parent Edn., Seattle, 1977-84; instr. Shoreline Community Coll., Seattle, 1984-88; mem. Wash. State Senate, Seattle, 1989-92; US Senator from Wash., 1993—. Mem. com. appropriations US Senate, com. budget, com. health, edn., labor and pensions, com. veterans affairs. Author (with Catherine Whitney): Nine and Counting: The Women of the Senate, 2000. Mem. bd. Shoreline Sch., Seattle, 1985-89; mem. steering com. Demonstration for Edn., Seattle, 1987; founder, chmn. Orgn. for Parent Edn., Wash., 1981-85; lst Congl. rep. Wash. Women United, 1983-85. Recipient Outstanding award Washing. Women United, 1986, Recognition of Svc. to Children award Shoreline PTA Coun., 1986, Golden Acorn Svc. award, 1989; Outstanding Svc. award Wash. Women United, 1986, Outstanding Svc. to Pub. Edn. award Citizens Ednl. Ctr. NW, Seattle, 1987, Wash. State Legis. of Yr., 1990, George Falcon Spike award Nat. Assn. Railroad Passengers, 2003, Person of Yr. award Wash. State VFW, 2004. Democrat. Roman Catholic. Office: US Senate 173 Russell Senate Office Bldg Washington DC 20510-0001 also: Henry M Jackson Federal Bldg Ste 2988 915 Second Ave Seattle WA 98174-4067 Office Phone: 202-224-2621, 206-553-5545. Office Fax: 202-224-0238, 206-553-0891. *

MURRAY, PETER, retired metallurgist, manufacturing executive; b. Rotherham, Yorkshire, Eng., Mar. 13, 1920; came to U.S., 1967, naturalized, 1974; s. Michael and Ann (Hamstead) M.; m. Frances Josephine Glaisher, Sept. 8, 1947; children: Jane, Paul, Alexander. BSc in Chemistry with honors, Sheffield U., Eng., 1941, postgrad., 1946-49; PhD in Metallurgy, Brit. Iron and Steel Research Bursar, Sheffield, 1948. Research chemist Steetley Co., Ltd., Worksop, Notts, Eng., 1941-45; with Atomic Energy Research Establishment, Harwell, Eng., 1949-67, head div. metallurgy, 1960-64, asst. dir., 1964-67; tech. dir., mgr. fuels and materials, advanced reactors div. Westinghouse Electric Corp., Madison, Pa., 1967-74; dir. research Westinghouse Electric Europe (S.A.), Brussels, 1974-75; chief scientist advanced power systems divs. Westinghouse Electric Corp., Madison, Pa., 1975-81, dir. nuclear programs Washington, 1981-92; sr. cons. Nuc. Programs, 1992—2001. Mem. divisional rev. coms. Argonne Nat. Lab., 1968-73; Mellor Meml. lectr. Inst. Ceramics, 1963 Contbr. numerous articles to profl. jours.; editorial adv. bd.: Jour. Less Common Metals, 1968—. Recipient Holland Meml. Research prize, Sheffield U., 1949. Fellow Royal Inst. Chemistry (Newton Chambers Research prize 1954), Inst. Ceramics, Am. Nuclear Soc.; mem. Brit. Ceramics Soc. (pres. 1965), Am. Ceramic Soc., Nat. Acad. Engring. Roman Catholic. Home: 20308 Canby Ct Montgomery Village MD 20886-4014

MURRAY, PETER See HAUTMAN, PETE

MURRAY, R. SCOTT, computer software company executive; Grad., U. We. Ont. Chartered acct. Arthur Andersen, Canada; exec. v.p., CFO The Learning Co., 1994—99; pres., COO Stream Internat., 2000—01; CEO Modus Media Internat., 2002—05; pres., CEO 3Com Corp., Marlborough, Mass., 2006—. Office: 3Com Corp 350 Campus Dr Marlborough MA 01752-3064

MURRAY, RAYMOND LE ROY, nuclear engineering educator; b. Lincoln, Nebr., Feb. 14, 1920; s. Ray Annis and Bertha (Mann) M.; m. Ilah Mae Rengler, June 16, 1941; children: Stephen, Maureen, Marshall; m. Quin Meyer, June 3, 1967; 1 stepdau., Tucker; m. Elizabeth Reid, May 12, 1979; stepchildren: Michael, Nancy, James. BS, U. Nebr., 1940, MS, 1941; PhD, U. Tenn., 1950; postgrad., U. Calif., Berkeley, 1941-43. Physicist U. Calif. Radiation Lab., Berkeley, 1942-43; asst. dept. supt. Tenn. Eastman Corp., Oak Ridge, 1943-47; research physicist Carbide & Carbon Chem. Co., Oak Ridge, 1947-50; prof. physics N.C. State U., 1950-57, Burlington prof. physics, 1957-80, prof. emeritus, 1980—, head dept. physics, 1960-63, head dept. nuclear engring., 1963-74. Acting dir. Nuclear Reactor Project, 1956-57; cons. Oak Ridge Nat. Lab., 1950-68, Los Alamos Nat. Lab., 1988-92, also to industry and govt. Author: Introduction to Nuclear Engineering, 1954, 2d edit., 1961, Nuclear Reactor Physics, 1957, Physics: Concepts and Consequences, 1970, Nuclear Energy, 1975, 5th edit., 2000, Understanding Radioactive Waste, 1982, 5th edit., 2003; mem. edit. adv. bd., U.S. exec. editor Jour. Nuclear Energy, 1963-73; adv. editor Annals Nuclear Energy, 1973—; contbr. numerous articles to profl. jours. and encys. Mem. adv. com. on radiation N.C. Bd. Health, 1958-59; mem. Gov.'s Tech. Adv. Com. on Low Level Radioactive Waste, 1980-87; mem. N.C. Radiation Protection Commn., 1979-87, chmn., 1980-82; mem., vice chmn., chmn. N.C. Low Level Radioactive Waste Mgm. Authority, 1987-93. Recipient O. Max Gardner award U. N.C., 1965; Arthur H. Compton award, 1970, Donald G. Fink award IEEE, 1988, Eugene P. Wigner Reactor Physicist award, 1994. Fellow Am. Phys. Soc., Am. Nuclear Soc. (chmn. edn. div. 1966-67, chmn. Eastern Carolinas sect. 1976-77, mem. nominating com. 1989); mem. Am. Soc. Engring. Edn. (chmn. com. on relationships with AEC 1967-68, chmn. nuclear engring. div. 1970-71, Glenn Murphy award 1976), N.C. Soc. Engrs. (Outstanding Engring. Achievement award 1975), Atomic Indsl. Forum (edn. coun.

1970-73), Inst. Nuclear Power Ops. (adv. coun. 1985-87, 89-94), Phi Beta Kappa, Sigma Xi, Pi Mu Epsilon, Phi Kappa Phi. Home: 235 Springmoor Dr Raleigh NC 27615 Home Phone: 919-848-7235. Business E-Mail: murray@eos.ncsu.edu.

MURRAY, RICHARD BENNETT, retired physics professor; b. Marietta, Ga., Dec. 5, 1928; s. William Moore and Ruth (Mozley) M.; m. Clella Bay, Apr. 1, 1956; children: Ada, Annette. BA, Emory U., 1947; MS, Ohio State U., 1950; PhD, U. Tenn., 1955. Rsch. asst. Gaseous Diffusion Plant, Oak Ridge, Tenn., 1947-48; rsch. physicist Oak Ridge Nat. Lab., 1955-66; vis. assoc. prof. physics U. Del, Newark, 1962-63, assoc. prof., 1966-69, prof., 1969-98, prof. emeritus, 1999—, acting chmn. dept. physics, 1975-76, univ. coord. for grad. studies, 1979-85, assoc. provost grad. studies, 1986-88, acting provost, v.p. acad. affairs, 1988-91, provost, 1993-94, ret., 1998. Lectr. physics U. Tenn., Knoxville, 1963-66; vis. rsch. physicist U.S. Naval Rsch. Lab., 1991-92; vis. scientist Clarendon Lab., Oxford U., 1992; cons. to industry, 1957-93; councillor Oak Ridge Associated Univs., 1979-88, bd. dirs., 1983-94, vice chmn. coun., 1983-85, chmn. coun., 1985-88; sec.-treas. NE Assn. Grad. Schs., 1982-84; dir. U. Del. Press, 1979-82. Contbr. numerous articles on exptl. nuclear and solid state physics to profl. publs., 1948-85. Trustee Sanford Sch., Hockessin, Del., 1981-85; chmn. bd. dirs. Oak Ridge Associated Univs. Found., 1989-94; bd. dirs. Del. Inst. for Med. Edn. and Rsch., 1989-91. Predoctoral fellow Oak Ridge Inst. Nuclear Studies, 1953-55; grantee AEC, NSF, Dept. Energy, 1967-84. Fellow AAAS, Am. Phys. Soc.; mem. Southeastern Univs. Rsch. Assn. (bd. dirs. 1989-97), Phi Beta Kappa, Sigma Xi, Sigma Pi Sigma, Phi Kappa Phi, Cosmos Club. Home: 4 Bridlebrook Ln Newark DE 19711-2058 Office: U Del Dept Physics & Astronomy Newark DE 19716 Business E-Mail: rmurray@udel.edu.

MURRAY, RICHARD M., engineering educator; BS with honors in elec. engring., Calif. Inst. Tech., 1985; MS in elec. engring. and computer sciences, U. Calif., Berkeley, 1989, PhD, 1991. Asst. prof. mech. engring. Calif. Inst. Tech., 1991—97, assoc. prof. mech. engring., 1997—2000, prof. mech. engring., 2000—05, chair Divsn. Engring. and Applied Sci., 2000—, prof. Control and Dynamical Sys., 2005—; dir. mechatronic systems United Technologies Rsch. Ctr., 1998—2000. Mem. info. sci. and tech. study group Def. Advanced Rsch. Projects Agy., Dept. Def., 2000—; mem. R&D strategy adv. com. Rockwell Sci. Co., 2001—; mem. Jet Propulsion Lab. adv. coun. NASA, 2001—; mem. vis. com. Dept. Mech. Engring., MIT, 2001—; chair exec. bd. Collaborative Ctr. on Control Sci., 2002—; mem. sci. adv. bd. USAF, 2002—; cons. Alphatech, Raytheon, United Technologies Rsch. Ctr., Northrop Corp. Recipient Eliahu Jury Award, U. Calif. Berkeley, 1991, Early Faculty Career Devel. Award, NSF, 1995, Young Investigator Award, Office Naval Rsch., 1995, Donald P. Eckman Award, Am. Automatic Control Coun., 1997; Richard P. Feynman-Hughes Faculty Fellowship, Calif. Inst. Tech., 1993. Achievements include patents for Actuator Bandwidth and Rate Limit Reduction for Control of Compressor Rotating Stall (with Simon Yeung), US Patent 5,984,625, Nov. 1999. Office: Control and Dynamical Systems 107-81 Calif Inst Tech MC 107-81 Pasadena CA 91125

MURRAY, RICHARD MAXIMILIAN, insurance company executive; b. Vienna, Nov. 21, 1922; came to U.S., 1955, naturalized, 1961; s. and Elizabeth Helen Peiker. Grad. in world commerce studies, U. Vienna; postgrad., Columbia U. Asst. sec. Sterling Offices Ltd. (reins. intermediaries), London, Toronto, NYC, 1951—59; v.p. Guy Carpenter, Inc. (reins. intermediaries), NYC, 1959—68, Travelers Ins. Cos., 1968—87, ret., 1987. Mng. dir. La Metropole Ins. Co., Brussels, ret., 1987; chmn. bd. Nippon Mgmt. Corp., N.Y.C., ret., 1991; chmn. bd. Travelers Marine Corp., ret., 1987; pres. Travelers Reins Co. Bermuda Ltd., ret., 1987; pres. Travelers of Asia Ltd., Hong Kong, ret., 1987; vice-chmn. bd. La Prov Corp., N.Y.C.; bd. electors Ins. Hall of Fame; bd. dirs. United Am. Inst. Co., United Am. Holdings Co., Inc.; mem. adv. bd. Firemark Global Ins. Fund, L.P.; dir. emeritus Davis Internat. Total Return Fund.; guest prof. Donau U., Krems, Austria. Contbr. articles to profl. publs. Decorated for promotion of pvt. ins. (Peru); Knight Order of St. John, Knights of Malta (ambassador at large). Mem. Internat. Ins. Coun. (chmn. 1979-81, award 1990). Home: 60 Remsen St Apt 10C Brooklyn NY 11201-3453 Office: 1 Penn Plz Ste 3600 New York NY 10119-2108 Personal E-mail: richardmurray@usa.net. Business E-Mail: nyork@gnp.com.mx.

MURRAY, ROBERT FOX, lawyer; b. Burlington, Vt., Feb. 28, 1952; s. Robert and Mary (Fox) Murray; m. Ann Marie Bevilacqua, Aug. 20, 1988. BA, Colgate U., 1974; JD, Boston U., 1978. Bar: Mass. 1978, U.S. Dist. Ct. Mass. 1979. Assoc. Law Offices of George Howard, Dedham, Mass., 1978—80; from assoc. to ptnr. Fairbanks & Silvia Koczera, Fountain, Murray, New Bedford, Mass., 1980—84; pvt. practice New Bedford, 1984—. Bd. dirs., clk. New Bedford, Inc. Mem.: Bristol County Bar Assn., New Bedford Bar Assn., Mass. Bar Assn. Democrat. Office: One Johnny Cake Hill New Bedford MA 02740 Home Phone: 508-674-5422; Office Phone: 508-993-1701. Business E-Mail: lawofficemurray@aol.com.

MURRAY, ROBERT FULTON, JR., physician; b. Newburgh, NY, Oct. 19, 1931; s. Robert Fulton and Henrietta Frances (Judd) Murray; m. Isobel Ann Parks, Aug. 26, 1956; children: Conin Charles(dec.), Robert Fulton III, Suzanne Frances, Dianne Akwe. BS, Union Coll., Schenectady, 1953; MD, U. Rochester, NYC, 1958; MS, U. Wash., Seattle, 1968. Diplomate Am. Bd. Internal Medicine, Am. Bd. Med. Genetics. Intern Denver Gen. Hosp., 1958—59; resident in internal medicine U. Colo. Med. Ctr., 1959—62; staff investigator (service with USPHS) Nat. Inst. Arthritis and Metabolic Diseases, NIH, Bethesda, Md., 1962—65; NIH spl. fellow med. genetics U. Wash., 1965—67; faculty Howard U. Coll. Medicine, Washington, 1967—74, prof. pediatrics and medicine, 1974—, grad. prof., 1976, prof. oncology, 1976, chief divsn. med. genetics, 1968—; chmn. dept. genetics and human genetics Howard U. Coll. Medicine Grad. Sch., 1976—. Nat. adv. gen. med. scis. coun. NIH, 1971—75, recombinant DNA adv. com., 1988—92; ethics adv. bd. to sec. HEW, 1978—80; chmn. Washington Mayor's Adv. Com. on Metabolic Disorders, 1980—89; mem. Med. Com. Human Rights. Co-author: Genetic Variation and Disorders in Peoples of African Origin, 1990; co-editor: Genetic, Metabolic and Developmental Aspects of Mental Retardation, 1972, Genetic Counseling: Facts, Values and Norms, 1979, The Human Genome Project and the Future of Health Care, 1996; mem. editl. bd.: Am. Jour. Clin. Genetics, 1977—93, Ency. Bioethics, 1975—77, 1993—95, Jour. Clin. Ethics, 1990. Sci. adv. bd. Nat. Sickle Cell Anemia Found.; trustee Union Coll., 1972—80. Fellow Rotary Found. fellow, 1955—56; grantee Rsch. grantee, NIH, 1969—75. Fellow: AAAS, ACP, Am. Coll. Med. Genetics, Inst. Soc., Ethics and Life Scis., Inst. Medicine; mem.: Acad. Medicine Washington, Genetics Soc. Am., Am. Soc. Human Genetics, Assn. Acad. Minority Physicians, AAUP, Neighbors Inc. D.C., Alpha Omega Alpha, Sigma Xi. Unitarian Universalist. Home: 510 Aspen St NW Washington DC 20012-2740 Office: Howard U Coll Medicine PO Box 75 Washington DC 20059-0001

MURRAY, ROBERT GRAY, sculptor; b. Vancouver, BC, Can., Mar. 2, 1936; U.S. citizen; s. John Gray and Vera (Meakin) M.; m. Cintra Wetherill Lofting, Jan. 23, 1971; children: Rebecca and Megan (twins), Claire, Hillary. Student, U. Sask., Can., 1956-58. One man shows Betty Parsons Gallery, N.Y.C., 1965, 66, 68, David Mirvish Gallery, Toronto, 1967, 68, 72, 73, 74, 75, Jewish Mus., N.Y.C., 1967, Hammarskjold Plaza, N.Y.C., 1971, Paula Cooper Gallery, N.Y.C., 1974, Janie Lee Gallery, Houston, 1977, Hamilton Gallery, N.Y.C., 1977, 79, 80, Klonaridis Inc., Toronto, 1979, 81, 82, Rice U., 1978, Dayton Mus., 1979, Columbus Mus., 1979, Lamont Gallery, Phillips Acad., Exeter, N.H., 1983, Art Gallery Greater Victoria, 1983, Gallery One, Toronto, 1985, Culturale Canadese Roma, 1985, Gallery 291, Atlanta, 1986, Richard Greene Gallery, N.Y.C.,1986, L.A., 1987, Del. Art Mus., Wilmington, 1990, Muhlenberg Coll., Allentown, Pa., 1992, Mira Godard Gallery, Toronto, Reading (Pa.) Pub. Mus., 1994, 96, Andre Zarre Gallery, N.Y.C., 1994, 04, 05, spl. showing Hillary Ground for Sculpture, Trenton N.J., 1997, retrospective, 1997, Moore Gallery, Toronto, 1999, 2001, 03, Ericson Gallery, Phila., 1999, McLaren Gallery, Barrie, 2001, Nat. Gallery of Can., Ottawa, 1999, Winchester Galleries, Victoria, 2004, Freedman Gallery, Reading, 2004; exhibited in group shows at Whitney Mus. 1996— Am., Art, N.Y.C., 1964-66, Tibor de Nagy Gallery, N.Y.C., 1965, Musée cantonal des Beaux Arts, Lausanne, Switzerland, 1966, World House Gallery, N.Y.C., 1966, Betty Parsons Gallery, 1966, Sch. Visual Arts, N.Y.C., 1967, Los Angeles County Mus., 1967, Nat. Gallery Can., Toronto, 1967, Inst. Contemporary Art, Boston, 1967, U. Toronto, 1967, Guggenheim Mus., N.Y.C., 1967, Inst. Torcuato Di Tella, Buenos Aires, 1967, Musée d'Art Moderne, Paris, 1968, Whitney Mus., 1967, Walker Art Gallery, 1969, X Sao Paulo Biennial, Brazil, 1969, Boston City Hall, 1971, Artist and Fabricator, Amherst, Mass., 1975, Met. Mus., N.Y.C., 1983, Del. Art Mus., 1990, GrandRapids (Mich.) Mus., 1994; represented in permanent collections, Montreal Mus. Fine Arts, Nat. Gallery Can., Joseph Hirshhorn Collection, Art Gallery Ont., Larry Aldrich Mus., Ridgefield, Conn., New Brunswick Mus., Whitney Mus. Am. Art, Met. Mus., N.Y.C., Columbus Mus., Dayton Art Inst., Storm King Art Centre, Del. Art. Mus., Wilmington, Muhlenberg Coll., Allentown, Pa., others; major commns. include, Everson Mus., Syracuse, N.Y., Fredonia (N.Y.) State Coll., Canadian Dept. External Affairs, Ottawa, Ont., U. Mass., U. Toronto, Ont., State Mus., Juneau, Alaska, Honeywell Corp., Mpls., CNIB, One King West, Toronto, also others. Decorated Order of Can. Home Phone: 610-869-8696; Office Phone: 610-869-4636. Fax: 610-869-4403. E-mail: rmurray601@earthlink.net.

MURRAY, ROBERT PATRICK, music educator, musician; b. Emporia, Kans., Dec. 26, 1958; s. Robert Patrick and Gloria Jacqueline Murray; m. Lauren Baker Murray, June 26, 2001. MusB, Portland State U., 1994, MusM, 1996; Mus D, U. North Tex., 2002. Asst. dir. bands U. Wash., Seattle, 1983—87; regional tng. dir. Kay-Bee Toys, Portland, Oreg., 1988—93; prof. trumpet Murray State U., Ky., 1999—2003, U. North Colo., Greeley, Colo., 2003—. Prin. trumpet Portland Musical Theater Co., Portland, Oreg., 1990—98; trumpet Dallas Brass, Dallas, 1997—2000; prin. trumpet Portland Opera, Portland, Oreg., 1998—99, Owensboro Symphony Orch., Owensboro, Ky., 1999—2003, Orquesta Sinfonica de Mineria, Mexico City, 2000—03; trumpet Harmonie del Sur, Evans, Colo., 1999—; first trumpet Rocky Mountain Brass Quintet, Greeley, Colo., 2003—. Musician: (trumpet soloist and clinician) World Association of Symphonic Bands and Ensembles, British Association of Symphonic Bands and Ensembles, (trumpet soloist and performer) International Trumpet Guild, (trumpet soloist) Owensboro Symphony Orchestra; author (lecture recital): (college music society) Synthesis and Integration: World and Electro-Acoustic Music in the Applied Studio, (nat. symposium on music instruction tech) A Global View: Applying World and Electro-Acoustic Music to the Intrumental Studio; author: (dissertation) A Performance Guide to Tomas Svoboda's Duo Concerto for Trumpet and Organ. V.p. prodn. programming Murray Civic Music Assn., Murray, Ky., 1999—2003. Recipient Spl. Commendation, Colo. House of Reps. Mem.: Hist. Brass Soc., Coll. Music Soc., Music Educators Nat. Conf., Internat. Trumpet Guild. Achievements include research in The introduction of world music and electro-acoustic music into the Applied Music Studio. Office: U Northern Colorado School Music Campus Box 28 Greeley CO 80639 Home Phone: 970-330-0317; Office Phone: 970-351-2285. Business E-Mail: robert.murray@unco.edu.

MURRAY, ROBERT WALLACE, chemistry professor; b. Brockton, Mass., June 20, 1928; s. Wallace James and Rose Elizabeth (Harper) M.; m. Claire K. Murphy, June 10, 1951; children: Kathleen A., Lynn E., Robert Wallace, Elizabeth A., Daniel J., William M., Padraic O'D. AB, Brown U., 1951; MA, Wesleyan U., Middletown, Conn., 1956; PhD, Yale U., 1960. Mem. tech. staff Bell Labs., Murray Hill, NJ, 1959-68; prof. chemistry U. Mo., St. Louis, 1968-81, chmn. dept., 1975-80, Curators' prof., 1981-2000, Curators' prof. emeritus, 2001—. Vis. prof. Engler-Bunte Inst. U. Karlsruhe, Fed. Republic Germany, 1982, dept. chemistry Univ. Coll., Cork, Ireland, 1989; cons. to govt. and industry. Co-editor: Singlet Oxygen, 1979; contbr. articles to profl. jours. Mem. Warren (N.J.) Twp. Com., 1962-63, mayor, 1963; mem. Planning Com. and Bd. Health, 1962-64, Bd. Edn., 1966-68. Served with USN, 1951-54; Lt. comdr. USNR. Grantee EPA, NSF, NIH, Office of Naval Research. Fellow AAAS, Am. Inst. Chemists, N.Y. Acad. Scis.; mem. Am. Soc. Photobiology, Am. Chem. Soc., The Oxygen Soc., Sigma Xi. Home: 1810 Walnutway Dr Saint Louis MO 63146-3659 Office: Univ Mo Dept Chemistry Saint Louis MO 63121 Personal E-mail: kinsale63@aol.com.

MURRAY, ROBIN MACGREGOR, psychiatrist, educator, consultant; b. Glasgow, Scotland, Jan. 31, 1944; s. James Alistair and Helen MacGregor Murray; m. Shelagh Harris Murray, Jan. 17, 1970; children: Graham Keith, Clare Alison. MB BChir, U. Glasgow, 1968, MD, 1974; MPhil, U. London, 1976, DSc, 1988. Sr. house officer, registrar U. Glasgow, 1969—72, Maudsley, Inst. Psychiatry, London, 1972—75; traveling fellow NIMH, Bethesda, Md., 1976—77; sr. lectr. Bethlehem, Inst. Psychiatry, London, 1978—82; dean Inst. Psychiatry, London, 1982—89, prof., head psychol. medicine, 1989—99; chair divsn. psychol. medicine GKT Sch. Medicine, London, 1998—; prof. psychiatry Inst. Psychiatry, Kings Coll., London, 1999—. Pres. European Assn. of Psychiatrists, 1995—96; cons. psychiatrist Maudsley Hosp., London. Editor: (book) Essentials of Postgraduate Psychiatry, 3d edit., 1997, The New Genetics of Mental Illness, 1991, Epidemiology of Schizophrenia, 2002. Recipient Adolf Meyer award, Am. Psychiat. Assn., 1997, Paul Hoch award, Am. Psychopathol. Assn., 1998, Dean award, Am. Coll. Psychiatrists, 1999, Robert Sommer award, 2000, Fifth Castilla del Pino award for achievement in psychiatry, 2002, Lieber prize for Schizophrenia Rsch., Nat. Alliance for Rsch. on Schizophrenia and Depression, 2003. Fellow: Royal Coll. Physicians Glasgow, Royal Coll. Physicians U.K.; mem.: (fgn.) U.S. Inst. of Med. (elected 2003), Royal Coll. Psychiatrists. Office: Inst Psychiatry Kings Coll De Crespigny Park Box 63 London SE5 8AF England Office Phone: 44 207 848 0100. Fax: 44 0 20 7701 9044. E-mail: robin.murray@iop.kcl.ac.uk.

MURRAY, RODERICK CHARLES, manufacturing executive; b. Johannesburg, S. Africa, Jan. 29, 1945; came to U.S., 1987; s. Charles Victor Murray and Yvonne Margaret Sherriffs; m. Yvonne Edna Bennett, Feb. 26, 1966; children: Sandra Leigh, Stuart Charles. BS, Witwatersrand U., 1967; MBA, Calif. Coast U., 1990. Quality assurance S. African Breweries, Johannesburg, 1971-75; tech. mgr. Hens Paper, Eerbeek, Holland, 1975-80; dir. mktg. and sales Metal Box, Barlow Rand, Johannesburg, 1980-87; v.p. mktg. ARPAC L.P., Chgo., 1987-89; pres. BMI Machinery, Milw., 1990-96; v.p. Klockner Packaging, 1990—96; CEO, pres. PPi Techs., Sarasota, Fla., 1996—. Author: Label Paper Technology, 1976, Brand Introductions, 1989; contbr. articles to profl. jours. Fellow British Bottlers; mem. Inst. Packaging Profls. (chmn. 1976), Internat. Beverage Tech. (vice chmn. 1978). Republican. Anglican. Avocations: golf, tennis, boating, travel. E-mail: rcmpp@aol.com.

MURRAY, RUSSELL, II, aeronautical engineer, security consultant; b. Woodmere, NY, Dec. 5, 1925; s. Herman Stump and Susanne Elizabeth (Warren) M.; m. Sally Tingue Gardiner, May 22, 1954; children: Ann Tingue, Prudence Warren, Alexandria Gardiner. BS in Aero. Engring, MIT, 1949, MS, 1950. Guided missile flight test engr. Grumman Aircraft Engring. Corp., Bethpage, NY, 1950-53, asst. chief operations analysis, 1953-62; prin. dep. asst. sec. of def. for systems analysis The Pentagon, Washington, 1962-69; dir. long range planning Pfizer Internat., NYC, 1969-73; dir. review Center for Naval Analyses, Arlington, Va., 1973-77; asst. sec. of def. for program analysis and evaluation Dept. of Def., The Pentagon, Washington, 1977-81; prin. Systems Research & Applications Corp., Arlington, Va., 1981-85; spl. counsellor Com. on Armed Services U.S. Ho. of Reps., 1985-89, nat. security cons., 1989—. Served with USAAF, 1944-45. Recipient Sec. of Def. Medal for meritorious civilian service, 1968; Disting. Public Service medal Dept. Def., 1981 Home: 210 Wilkes St Alexandria VA 22314-3839

MURRAY, SABINA, writer; BA, Mt. Holyoke Coll., Mass.; MA, U. of Tex. Writer-in-residence Phillips Acad., Andover, Mass., 2000—. Tchr. creative fiction and poetry. Author: (novels) Slow Burn, 1990, The Caprices, 2002 (PEN/Faulkner award for fiction, 2003), A Carnivore's Inquiry, 2004, (screenplays) The Beautiful Country, 2004. Michener Fellow, U. Texas, Bunting Fellow, Radcliffe Inst., Harvard U.

MURRAY, SHAUN MICHAEL, lobbyist, consultant; b. Gaylord, Mich., Mar. 6, 1982; s. Walter Jerome Murray, Jr. and Reinette Lucy Murray. BA in Pub. Policy, Mich. State U., East Lansing, 2004, BA in Pub. Adminstrn., 2004; MPA, Ea. Mich. U., Ypsilanti, 2007. Cert. pub. policy Inst. Pub. Policy and Social Rsch., Mich., 2004. Govtl. affairs intern Murray, Scheer & Montgomery, Washington, 1998—99; asst. legislative liaison Mich. Atty. Gen., Lansing, 2003—04; dir. govtl. affairs Allen County Govt., Ft. Wayne, 2005—06; dir. pub. andgovtl. affairs Mich. Home Builders Assn., Ann Arbor, 2006—. Campaign cons. Tom Daschle for Senate, Sioux Falls, SD, 2004. Active Mackinac Assocs., Mackinac Island, Mich., 2004—06. Mem.: Am. Assn. Polit. Consultants (assoc.), Am. League Lobbyists (assoc.), Detroit Athletic Club (assoc.), Wawashkamo Golf Club (assoc.), Mackinac Island Yacht Club (assoc.), Phi Delta Theta (life; social chmn. 2000—03). Conservative. Roman Catholic. Avocations: sailing, skiing, golf. Home: 710 W Oakdale Dr Fort Wayne IN 46807 Home Phone: 248-504-8670. Personal E-mail: murray06@hotmail.com.

MURRAY, STEPHEN JAMES, lawyer; b. Phila., Jan. 27, 1943; s. Paul Martin and Hannah (Smith) M.; m. Linda Sanders, June 20, 1970; children: Gordon Joshua, Cara Sanders. AB cum laude, Brown U., 1963; JD, Harvard U., 1966; LLM, George Washington U., 1967. Bar: N.Y. 1968, U.S. Ct. Appeals (2nd cir.) 1971, U.S. Ct. Appeals (fed. cir.) 1998, U.S. Dist. Ct. (so. and ea. dists.) N.Y. 1972, U.S. Ct. Claims 1974, U.S. Supreme Ct. 1975, Conn. 1988, U.S. Dist. Ct. Conn. 1988, U.S. Ct. Internat. Trade 1998. Spl. asst. SEC, Washington, 1966-67, Maritime Adminstrn., Washington, 1967-68; assoc. Hill, Betts & Nash, NYC, 1970-76; transp. atty. Union Carbide Corp., NYC, 1976-78, sr. transp. atty., 1978-85, chief transp. counsel Danbury, Conn., 1985—2001, group counsel, 1986—2001, chief real estate counsel, 1992—2001, comml. counsel, 1993—2001, customs and internat. trade counsel, 1997—2001; of counsel Mahoney & Keane, New York City, 2001—. Spkr. in field. Contbr. articles to profl. jours. Lt. JAGC, USN, 1968-70. Mem. ABA, Conn. State Bar Assn., U.S. Naval Inst., Navy League of U.S., Maritime Law Assn., U.S. Transp. Lawyers Assn., N.Y. State Bar Assn., Am. Corp. Counsel Assn. (co-chair real estate com. Westchester-So. Conn. chpt.), Conn. Maritime Assn., Harvard Club, Brown Club (co-pres.), Brown Faculty Club, Brown Alumni Schs. Commn. (chmn. Fairfield County), Brown Alumni Assn. (bd. govs.). Office: Mahoney & Keane 14 Pilgrim Ln Weston CT 06883 Office Phone: 203-222-1019. Personal E-mail: murraysj@optonline.net.

MURRAY, STEPHEN SANFORD, composer, lyricist, playwright; b. Putnam, Conn., Mar. 13, 1963; s. Charles Sanford and Donna Saegaert Murray; m. Ruth Werner Kaplan, Aug. 15, 1992; m. Dianne Tower, June 1982 (div. Oct. 1990); children: Daniel McCord, Benjamin Charles, Natasha Elizabeth, Jennifer Ruth. BA, Westfield State Coll., Mass., 1985; MEd, Fitchburg State Coll., Mass., 2003. Lic. tchr. Mass., 1985. Composer, lyricist, playwright: musical plays Musical! The Bard is Back! (Jackie White Meml. Nat. Children's Playwrighting award, 2000), Tortoise Vs. Hare (Anna Zornio Children's Playwriting award, 1993), Pom-Pom Zombies, Katastrophe Kate, Mother Goose, Inc. (3rd Pl. Jackie White Play Competition, 1995), The Magic Snowman. Mem.: Music Educators Nat. Conf. Personal E-mail: stevesanmu@msn.com. E-mail: stephen_murray@wayland.k12.ma.us.

MURRAY, THOMAS HENRY, bioethics educator, writer; b. Phila., July 30, 1946; s. Thomas Henry and Colombia Rita (Lucci) M.; m. Sharon Marie Engelkraut, Jan. 1968 (div. Sept. 1975); children: Kathleen Elizabeth, Dominique Maria, Peter Albert; m. Cynthia Sarah Aberle, Apr. 1, 1978; 1 child, Emily Sarah Aberle. BA in Psychology, Temple U., 1968; PhD in Social Psychology, Princeton U., 1976; MD (hon.), Uppsala U., 2003. Instr. New Coll., Sarasota, Fla., 1971-75; asst. prof. Interdisciplinary Studies Miami U., Oxford, Ohio, 1975-80, assoc. prof., 1980; assoc. social behavioral studies The Hastings Ctr., Hastings-on Hudson, NY, 1980-84; assoc. prof. Inst. Med. Humanities U. Tex. Med. Br., Galveston, 1984-86, prof., 1986-87; prof., dir. Ctr. Biomed. Ethics Case We. Res. U., Cleve., 1987-99, Susan E. Watson prof. bioethics, 1998—99; pres. The Hastings Ctr., Garrison, NY, 1999—. Mem. Nat. Bioethics Adv. Commn., 1996-2001; mem. ethical, legal and social issues working group Human Genome Project NIH/Dept. Energy, 1989-95. Author: The Worth of a Child, 1996; founder, editor Med. Humanities Rev.; mem. editl. bd. Human Gene Therapy, Cloning, Politics and the Life Scis., Hastings Cetr. Report, Jour. of Law, Medicine and Ethics; editor: Encyclopedia of Ethical, Legal, and Policy Issues in Biotechnology, (with K.W.M. Fulford and D.L. Dickenson) Healthcare Ethics and Human Values: An Introductory Text with Readings and Case Studies, 2002, (with Carol Levine) The Cultures of Caregiving: Conflict and Common Ground Among Families, Health Professionals and Policy Makers, 2004, (with M. Rothstein, G.E Kaebkick and M.A. Majunder) Genetic Ties and the Family: The Impact of Paternity Testing on Parents and Children, 2005. Fellow NEH, 1977-78, 1979-80, Aspen Inst., 1989. Fellow Hastings Ctr.; mem. APHA, Assn. Practical and Profl. Ethics, Am. Soc. Law Medicine and Ethics (bd. dirs. 1993-97), Assn. Integrative Studies (bd. dirs. 1980-87, pres. 1983), Soc. Health and Human Values (chair program dirs. sect. 1989-90, faculty assn. 1989-90, SHHV program com. 1990, pres.-elect 1992-93, pres. 1993-94), Am. Soc. Human Genetics (chair social issues com. 1998-99), Am. Coll. Ob-Gyn. (com. on ethics 1996-2001), Am. Soc. Bioethics and Humanities (pres.-elect 1998-99, pres. 1999-2000), Human Genome Orgn. (ethics com.), World Anti-Doping Agy. (chair ethical issues rev. panel 2004—). Office: The Hastings Ctr 21 Malcolm Gordon Rd Garrison NY 10524-5555 Office Phone: 845-424-4040.

MURRAY, THOMAS J., advertising executive; b. Bridgeport, Conn., Mar. 12, 1924; s. Thomas and Mary (Diskin) M.; m. Mary Elizabeth Cull, Feb. 22, 1945; children: Joshua Francis, Mary Elizabeth, Katherine Diskin. AB, Dartmouth Coll., 1947. Instr., Dartmouth Coll., 1947-48; with Warwick & Legler, NYC, 1948-68, sr. v.p., mgmt. account supr., 1964-68; sr. v.p. group supr. Gaynor & Ducas, Inc., 1968-74, exec. v.p., 1974—, chief fin. officer and gen. mgr., 1978-87; pres. TJM & Assn., 1987—. Pres., trustee Hillcrest Gen. Hosp., N.Y.C.; Westchester Inst. for tng. in Psychoanalysis and Psychotheraphy, Mt. Kisco, N.Y. Served as 1st lt. USAAF, 1942-45. Decorated D.F.C., Air medal with 4 oak leaf clusters. Mem. Nat. Wholesale Druggists Assn., Propriety Assn., Nat. Assn. Chain Drug Stores, Am. Mktg. Assn. Home and Office: 65 Norfield Rd Weston CT 06883-2213 Office Phone: 800-749-4254. E-mail: tjma@optonline.net.

MURRAY, THOMAS JAMES, financial planner, publisher; b. Jamestown, RI, Mar. 26, 1924; s. Daniel Peter and Margaret (McPartland) Murray; m. Jean Shaw, July 2, 1948 (dec. June 1985); children: Thomas, Carolyn, Elizabeth, John, Peter; m. Evelyn Ayers, Apr. 19, 1986. Student, Brown U., 1942—44; BA in Social Sci., George Washington U., 1964.

Commd. ensign USN, 1944, advanced through ranks to lt. comdr., 1964, ret., 1964; sales rep. J.D. Marsh & Assoc., Washington, 1964—78; pres. TJM Securities Inc., Chevy Chase, Md., 1985—2002, Thomas Murray Assocs. Inc., Chevy Chase, 1985—, TMA Ins., Chevy Chase, 1978—; pub. Social List Washington Inc., Kensington, 1985—; prin. Washington Securities Corp., Chevy Chase, 2002—04. Mem.: Eisenhower Found. (treas. 2003—), St. Andrew's Soc. Washington (pres. 1997—99), Knights of Malta, Am. Legion (comdr. Thad Dulin post 1975—76). Roman Catholic. Home: 10500 Rockville Pike Apt 1702 North Bethesda MD 20852-3356 Office: Social List Washington 9620 E Bexhill Dr Kensington MD 20895-3103 also: Thomas Murray Assocs 6935 Wisconsin Ave Chevy Chase MD 20815-6113 Home Phone: 301-530-0787; Office Phone: 301-657-4142. E-mail: tjm@webfirst.com.

MURRAY, THOMAS JOHN (JOCK MURRAY), physician, neurologist, educator; b. Halifax, NS, Can., May 30, 1938; m. Janet Kathleen Pottie; children: Shannon, Bruce, Suellen, Brian. Grad. pre-med, St. Francis Xavier U., 1958, LLD (hon.), 1989; MD, Dalhousie U., 1963; DSc (hon.), Acadia U., 1991; DLitt (hon.), St. Thomas U., 2004. Family physician, Nashwaaksis, N.S., 1963-65; chief medicine Camp Hill Hosp., Halifax, N.S., 1974-79; chief neurology Dalhousie U., Halifax, 1979-85, dir. multiple sclerosis rsch. unit, 1980—2003, dean medicine, 1985-92, prof. med. humanities, 1992—2003, prof. emeritus, 2003—. Mem. working group on Diability in U.S. Pres., 1994—96. Co-author: (textbook) Essential Neurology, Quotable Osler, Medicine in Quotations, Treatment and Management of MS, History of MS; author over 200 pub. works, including 7 books and contbns. to 34 textbooks. Bd. dirs. St. Francis Xavier U., Pictou Acad. Found., Robert Pope Found., Nat. Coun. on Bioethics and Health Rsch., Mus. Healthcare. Decorated officer Order Can.; recipient Neilson award Hannah Inst. for Med. History, Disting. Profl. award Discovery Ctr., 2005; named Dalhousie Alumnus of Yr., Dalhousie U., 2003; grantee 91 rsch. grants. Fellow Royal Coll. Physicians (Can. and London, Mentor of Yr. award 2002), ACP (master; gov. 1985-90, chmn. bd. govs. 1990-91, chair bd. regents 1995-97, emeritus chair, Dr. Nicholas Davies award, Laureate award, Stengel award); mem. Can. Neurol. Soc. (pres. 1982-84), Am. Acad. Neurology (v.p. 1981-83, Dr. A.B. Baker award), Can. Med. Assn., N.S. Med. Soc., Assn. Can. Med. Colls. (pres. 1991-92), Can. Med. Forum (chmn. 1992-95), Multiple Sclerosis Soc. Can. (chmn. med. adv. bd., Perkins award), Consortium of Multiple Sclerosis Ctrs. (pres. 1997-99), Can. Soc. for History of Medicine (pres. 1997-99), Canadian Acad Hlth. Scis. (fellow), FRCP (London), Rotary Internat. (Paul Harris fellow). Avocations: medical history, piano, windsurfing. Home: 16 Bobolink St Halifax NS Canada B3M 1W3 Office: Dalhousie Med Sch Clin Rsch Ctr Halifax NS Canada B3H 4H7 Home Phone: 902-443-1074; Office Phone: 902-494-1533. Business E-Mail: jock.murray@dal.ca.

MURRAY, THOMAS VEATCH, lawyer; b. Phoenix, July 17, 1947; s. Robert Morrison Jr. and Jane Veatch (Murray) Barber and Richard A. Barber; m. Cynthia Ann Burnett, June 2, 1971; children: Anne Caroline, Thomas Veatch Jr. BA, U. Kans., 1969; JD, U. Mich., 1972. Bar: Kans. 1972, U.S. Dist. Ct. Kans. 1972, U.S. Ct. Appeals (10th cir.) 1983, U.S. Supreme Ct. 1976. Assoc. Barber, Emerson, Six, Springer & Zinn, Lawrence, Kans., 1972-76; mem. Barber, Emerson, Springer, Zinn & Murray, L.C., Lawrence, Kans., 1976—2003; of counsel Lathrop & Gage L.C., Overland Park, Kans., 2004—. Adj. prof. western civilization U. Kans., 1975-77, Sch. Law., 1990-91, instr. bar rev. course, 1975-82; dir. The First Nat. Bank of Lawrence, Kans., 1980-91, The Reuter Organ Co., 1991-, Hall Ctr. for the Humanities, Lawrence, Kans., 1988-. Contbr. articles to profl. jours. Mem. adv. bd. Lawrence Consumer Affairs Assn., 1974—77, Sta. KANU, Lawrence, 1975—80; mem. Bd. Edn. Unified Sch. Dist. 497, Lawrence, 1991—95; mem. Kans. Bd. Law Examiners, 1995—, chmn., 2006—; mem. Lawrence Emergency Svcs. Coun., 1998—2002; dir. Lawrence C. of C., 1993—95; treas. Louie Holcom Baseball Assn., 1972—73; trustee First Presbyn. Ch., 1975—76. Fellow Am. Bar Found.; mem. ABA, Fedn. Def. and Corp. Counsel (regional v.p. 1994-97, dir. 1997-99), Kans. Assn. Def. Counsel (dir. 1993-97), Def. Rsch. Inst., Kans. Bar Assn. (pres. corporation, banking and bus. law sect. 1983), Kans. Bar Found. (trustee 1999-2005), Johnson County Bar Assn., Judge Hugh Means Inn of Ct., Douglas County Bar Assn., Coaches' Corner (Lawrence), Lawrence Lions Alumni Assn., The Supreme Ct. Hist. Soc., Kansas City Club, The River Club, Lawrence Country Club, The Fortnightly Club (Lawrence). Republican. Presbyterian. Avocation: classical and operatic music. Office: Lathrop & Gage LC 10851 Mastin Blvd Bldg 82 Ste 1000 Overland Park KS 66210-1669 Home Phone: 785-843-2629; Office Phone: 913-451-5100. Business E-Mail: tmurray@lathropgage.com.

MURRAY, TIMOTHY PATRICK, lieutenant governor, former mayor; b. Worcester, Mass., June 7, 1968; m. Tammy L. Sullivan; children: Helen, Katerine. BA in Am. Studies, Fordham U., 1990; JD, We. New England Sch. Law, 1994. Ptnr. Tattan, Leonard and Murray, Worcester, Mass.; councillor-at-large City of Worcester, mayor, 2002—06; lt. gov. State of Mass., Boston, 2007—. Democrat. Roman Catholic. Office Phone: 617-725-4000. Business E-Mail: ltgovoffice@state.ma.us.

MURRAY, WILLIAM BRUCE, opera singer; b. Schenectady, NY, Mar. 13, 1935; s. John Allison and Jessie Chrystal (Gray) M.; m. Nancy Lee Adams, Mar. 1, 1958; children: John Horton, Christopher Andrew, Judith Leora. BA in Music Edn., Adelphi U., 1956; Cert. di Studio, U. Perugia, Italy, 1957; grad., Goethe Inst., 1960. Opera singer Landestheater Detmold, Germany, 1960-61, Staatstheater Braunschweig, Germany, 1961-64, Nat. Theater Mannheim, Germany, 1964-66, Staatsoper München, Germany, 1966-78, Deutsche Opera Berlin, Germany, 1969—, Houston Grand Opera, 1994—. Opera singer numerous other theaters including N.Y. State Opera, Catania, Italy, Marseille, France, L.A. Opera, Teatro Reggio Torino (Italia), 1992; prof. voice Shepherd Sch. Music Rice U., Houston. Recordings include Salome, Die Bassariden, Hochzeit des Camacho, Schöne Müllerin, Die Totestadt. With U.S. Army, 1958-60. Named Kammersänger Senate Berlin Germany, 1980; Fulbright fellow, 1956. Mem. Lions Club. Avocations: hiking, cooking, swimming. Home: 113 Homeyer Rd Sparrow Bush NY 12780-8302 Office Phone: 845-665-9629. Personal E-mail: wbmurray313@hotmail.com. Business E-Mail: wbmurray@rice.edu.

MURRAY, WILLIAM MICHAEL, lawyer; b. Buffalo, Dec. 21, 1953; s. William Joseph and Mary Ann (Lichtenthal) M.; m. Suzanne M. Raynor; children: Colleen Elizabeth, William Michael Jr., Caitlin Anne, Matthew Francis Johnson. BA, U. Notre Dame, 1975; JD, U. Detroit, 1978. Bar: N.Y. 1978, U.S. Dist. Ct. (we. dist.) N.Y. 1980. Asst. county atty. Erie County, Buffalo, 1978-79; ptnr. Stamm & Murray, Williamsville, 1979-96, Renaldo Myers & Palumbo, Williamsville, 1996-98; dep. atty. Town of Amherst, 1993-96; gen. counsel Town of Amherst Indsl. Devel. Agy., 1996—2006; dep. commr. dept. environment and planning Erie County, 2006—. Adj. asst. prof. SUNY, Buffalo, 2003—; sr. counsel Hodgson Russ, LLP, 2004—06. Mem. Amherst Rep. Com., NY, 1980-2004; chmn. Amherst Zoning Bd. Appeals, 1986-93. Mem. N.Y. State Bar Assn., Erie County Bar Assn., Williamsville Bus. Assn. (bd. dirs., v.p. 1985-96), Rotary (pres. Williamsville 1989). Roman Catholic. Business E-Mail: murrayw@erie.gov.

MURRAY SHAW, JULEEN, actress; d. Marianne Polly Eileen Arnold; m. Mathew Scott Shaw, May 8, 1988; 1 child, Sophie Fay Jiaoxin Shaw. BA, Moorhead State U., Minn., 1979. Co-founder Nursery Tap, LLC, Gig Harbor, Wash., 2004—. Prodr., dir., actor, writer (performing arts dvd's for children) Nursery Tap Hip to Toe, Vol. I (George Foster Peabody award, 2005, Parents Choice Recommended award, 2005, iParenting Media award, 2005, KIDS FIRST! Endorsement, 2005, Dr. Toy's Best Products award, 2005, Creative Child Mag. Preferred award, 2005, Dove Found. Seal of Approval Highest Rating, 2004), Vol. II (Parents Choice Silver Honor award, 2006, Creative Child Mag. DVD of Yr. award, 2006, Dove Found. Seal of Approval Highest Rating, 2006). Recipient Award of Excellence, reviewcorner.com, 2005. Mem.: Screen Actor's Guild. D-Liberal. Home Phone: 253-858-8891; Office Phone: 888-855-0545. Personal E-mail: info@nurserytap.com.

MURRELL, JILL PONGRACZ, music educator, director; b. Lorain, Ohio, Mar. 10, 1956; d. Julius Albert and Donna Jean Pongracz; m. Richard Albert Murrell, Aug. 12, 1978 (div. Oct. 31, 1989); children: Rebekka Anne, Zachary Albert. MusB, Miami U., Oxford, Ohio, 1977; M in the Art of Tchg., Marygrove Coll., Mich., 1998. Choir dir. Lorain (Ohio) Hungarian Ref. Ch., 1978—; music tchr. Keystone Local Schs., LaGrange, Ohio, 1979—89; vocal music tchr., vocal music coord. Lorain City Schs., 1989—2001; choral dir. Southview HS, Lorain, 2002—; artistic musical dir. Ashland (Ohio) Symphonic Youth Chorus, 2004—. Music mentor Cleve. Opera on Tour. Musician (flutist): Patriots Symphonic Band. Com. chair Boy Scouts of Am., Sheffield Lake, Ohio, 1999—2003; trustee Lorain Internat. Assn., 1998—2006; officer Sheffield-Sheffield Lake (Ohio) Band Boosters, 1994—2003; music com. chair Lorain Hungarian Ref. Ch., 1978—2006. Mem.: Lorain Edn. Assn. (bldg. rep. 2001—06), Ohio Choral Dirs. Assn., Ohio Music Edn. Assn. (state curriculum com. 2004—06, gen. music rep. 2002—). Democrat. United Church Of Christ. Home: 219 Gayle Dr Sheffield Lake OH 44054 Office: Southview High Sch 2270 E 42nd St Lorain OH Home Phone: 440-949-6723; Office Phone: 440-277-7271 ext 114. Personal E-mail: jponmurr@hotmail.com. Business E-Mail: jmurre@lorainschools.org.

MURRELL, ROBERT GEORGE, lawyer; b. Jan. 27, 1932; s. Samuel Edwin and Myrtle Josephine (Hailey) M.; m. Bonnie Bird Robinson, Nov. 11, 1961; children: Robert George, Michele Grace, Bonnie Melissa. BA, U. Fla., 1951, JD, 1953. Bar: Fla. 1953, NY 1981, U.S. Dist. Ct. (so. dist.) Fla. 1953, U.S. Dist. Ct. (mid. dist.) Fla. 1980, U.S. Ct. Appeals (5th cir.) 1953, U.S. Ct. Appeals (11th cir.) 1981, U.S. Ct. Mil. Appeals 1958, U.S. Supreme Ct. 1958, U.S. Ct. Claims 1975, U.S. Tax Ct. 1975, U.S. Ct. Customs and Patent Appeals 1975, U.S. Ct. Appeals (DC cir.) 1989, U.S. Ct. Appeals (3rd, 4th, 6th, 7th, 8th, 9th, 10th cirs.) 1989, U.S. Ct. Appeals (2nd cir.) 1990, U.S. Ct. Vet. Appeals 1992; arbitrator Am. Arbitration Assn. Atty. Sam E. Murrell & Sons., Orlando, Fla., 1953—. Mem. Ctirus Assocs. of N.Y. Stock Exch.; pres. Colonial Mortgage Co. Fla., Inc.; dir. Weiss Realty Corp., Lake Margaret Co. With US Army, 1953—55. Mem.: ATLA, ABA, Acad. Fla. Trial Lawyers, Orange County Bar Assn., Univ. Winter Park, Elks (Orlando), Shriners, Masons. Republican. Baptist. Office: Sam E Murrell & Sons 1 N Rosalind Ave Orlando FL 32801-1682 Home: 1212 Ayrshire St Orlando FL 32803 Office Phone: 407-843-8500.

MURREN, JAMES JOSEPH, hotel executive; m. Heather Murren. BA, Trinity Coll. Chartered Fin. Analyst. Various positions Deutsche Morgan Grenfell, 1984—94; mng. dir., dir. rsch. Deutsche Bank, 1994—98; exec. v.p. MGM Mirage, Las Vegas, 1998—, CFO, 1998—, pres., 1999—, treas., 2001—. Past mem. bd. fellows Trinity Coll.; co-founder, bd. dir. Nevada Cancer Inst.; trustee Univ. Nevada Las Vegas Found., Univ. Nevada Reno Found. Office: MGM Mirage 3600 Las Vegas Blvd South Las Vegas NV 89109 *

MURRETT, ROBERT B., federal agency administrator, career military officer; b. Oct. 8, 1952; BA, U. Buffalo; M in Govt. and Strategic Intelligence, Georgetown U.; M, Def. Intelligence Coll. Advanced through ranks to vice admiral USN, 2006, watch stander and briefing officer, chief naval ops. intelligence plot, 1980—83, asst. intelligence officer, 1983—85; asst. naval attache U.S. Embassy, Oslo, 1986—89; ops. intelligence officer U.S. Pacific Fleet USN, 1989—92, asst. chief of staff intelligence for comdr, carrier group eight, 1992—95, asst. chief of staff intelligence for comdr, second fleet, 1995—97, exec. asst. to dir. naval intelligence, 1997—98, dir., intelligence directorate Office of Naval Intelligence Washington, 1998; comdr. Atlantic Intelligence Command, 1999; dir. intelligence U.S. Joint Forces Command, 2000—02; vice dir. intelligence Joint Staff USN, 2002—05, dir. naval intelligence Washington, 2005—06; dir. Nat. Geospatial-Intelligence Agy. US Dept. Def., Bethesda, Md., 2006—. Office: Nat Geospatial-Intelligence Agy 4600 Sangamore Rd Bethesda MD 20816

MURRIAN, ROBERT PHILLIP, retired federal judge, educator; b. Knoxville, Tenn., Apr. 1, 1945; s. Albert Kinzel and Mary Gilbert (Eppes) M.; m. Jerrilyn Sue Boone, Oct. 29, 1983; children: Kimberley Ann, Jennifer Rebecca, Albert Boone, Samuel Robert. BS, U.S. Naval Acad., 1967; JD, U. Tenn., 1974. Bar: Tenn. 1974, U.S. Dist. Ct. (ea. dist.) Tenn. 1975, U.S. Dist. Ct. (mid. dist.) Tenn. 2005, U.S. Ct. Appeals (6th cir.) 1982. Law clk. to judge US Dist. Ct. (ea. dist.) Tenn., Knoxville, 1974-76, magistrate judge, 1978—2002; assoc. Butler, Vines, Babb & Threadgill, Knoxville, 1976-78; ptnr. Kramer Rayson LLP, Knoxville, 2002—. Adj. prof. U. Tenn. Coll. Law, 1990-93, 95-96, 2002; trial lawyer, arbitrator, mediator, spl. master litigation. Lt. USN, 1967-71. Green scholar, 1973-74, Nat. Moot Ct. scholar, 1974; named one of Best Lawyers in Am., 2005-07. Fellow Tenn. Bar Found.; mem. ABA, Tenn. Bar Assn., Knoxville Bar Assn. (bd. govs. 1994, 2002—), Sixth Cir. Jud. Conf. (life), Order of Coif, Am. Inn of Ct. (master of the bench, pres. 1997-98), Phi Kappa Phi. Presbyterian (Elder). Office: Kramer Rayson LLP PO Box 629 Knoxville TN 37901-0629 Address: First Tennessee Plz 800 S Gay St Ste 2500 Knoxville TN 37929 Office Phone: 865-525-5134. Business E-Mail: rpmurrian@kramer-rayson.com.

MURRIN, MICHAEL J., literature educator, writer; MA, PhD, Yale U. David B. and Clara E. Stern prof. humanities U. Chgo., prof. religion and literature, Divinity Sch., prof. comparative literature and English language and literature. Author: The Veil of Allegory, 1969, The Allegorical Epic, 1980, History and Warfare in Renaissance Epic, 1994. Fellow: Am. Acad. Arts and Sciences. Office: Univ Chicago Gates-Blake Halls 315 5845 S Ellis Ave Chicago IL 60637 Office Phone: 773-702-7985. Office Fax: 773-702-8223. E-mail: m-murrin@uchicago.edu.

MURRIN, REGIS DOUBET, retired lawyer; b. Erie, Pa., July 2, 1930; s. John III and Gabrielle (Doubet) M.; m. Evelyn L. Alessio, Aug. 22, 1959; children: Catherine Shaw Murrin Hargenrader, Mary Murrin, Elizabeth Murrin Talotta, Rebecca Fielding Lamanna. BA, U. Notre Dame, 1952; JD, Harvard U., 1959; LLM, Temple U., 1968. Bar: Pa. 1959, U.S. Supreme Ct. 1971. Assoc. Murrin & Murrin, Butler, Pa., 1959-62; atty. Housing & Home Fin. Agy., Phila., 1962-64; ptnr. Baskin & Sears, Pitts., 1964-84, Reed Smith Shaw & McClay, Pitts., 1985-95, of counsel, 1995-99, counsel, 1999—2006. Trustee Pitts. Oratory, 1976—97; chmn. Zoning Bd. Adjustment, City of Pitts., 1994—2006; bd. dirs. Ellis Sch., 1991—99. Lt. USNR, 1952—55, Korea, Vietnam. Mem. Allegheny County Bar Assn., Edwin Sorin Soc. Democrat. Roman Catholic. Office: Reed Smith Shaw & McClay 435 6th Ave Ste 2 Pittsburgh PA 15219-1886 Office Phone: 412-288-3352.

MURRY, CHARLES EMERSON, lawyer, federal official; b. Hope, ND, June 23, 1924; s. Raymond Henry and Estelle Margarete (Skeim) M.; m. Donna Deane Kleve, June 20, 1948; children: Barbara, Karla, Susan, Bruce, Charles. BS, U. ND, Grand Forks, 1948, JD, 1950. Bar: ND 1950. Mem. firm Nelson and Heringer, Rugby, ND, 1950-51; dir. ND Legis. Council, 1951-75; adj. gen. with rank of maj. gen. State of ND, Bismarck, 1975-84; mgr. Garrison Diversion Conservancy Dist., 1985-93. Cons. Council State Govts.; mem. res. forces policy bd. Sec. of Def. Vice-pres. Mo. Slope Luth. Home of Bismarck, 1965-66. Served with AUS, 1942-45. Decorated D.S.M., Legion of Merit, Meritorious Service medal, Bronze Star, Army Commendation medal; Fourragere Belgium; Orange Lanyard Netherlands; recipient Sioux award U. ND, 1970; Gov.'s award of excellence, 1971; Nat. Leadership award Bismarck C. of C., 1971 Mem. Adjs. Gen. Assn. (exec. com., sec. 1983-84), Nat. Legis. Conf. (past chmn.), N.G. Assn., Am. Bar Assn., ND Bar Assn., Commrs. Uniform State Laws. Lodges: Elks, Masons. Lutheran. Office: 5505 Ponderosa Ave Bismarck ND 58503-9159

MURRY, HAROLD DAVID, JR., lawyer; b. Holdenville, Okla., June 30, 1943; s. Harold David Sr. and Willie Elizabeth (Dees) M.; m. Ann Moore Earnhardt, Nov. 1, 1975; children: Elizabeth Ann, Sarah Bryant. BA, Okla. U., 1965, JD, 1968. Bar: Okla. 1968, D.C. 1974. Asst. to v.p. U. Okla., Norman, 1968-71, legal counsel Research Inst., 1969-71; atty. U.S. Dept. Justice, Washington, 1971-74; spl. asst. U.S. Atty., Washington, 1972; assoc. Clifford & Warnke, Washington, 1974-78, ptnr., 1978-91, Howrey & Simon, Washington, 1991-98, Baker Botts LLP, Washington, 1998—. Mem. ABA, Okla. Bar Assn., D.C. Bar Assn., Fed. Bar Assn., Met. Club (Washington), Chevy Chase Club (Md.), Phi Alpha Delta. Democrat. Office: Baker Botts LLP Ste 1300 1299 Pennsylvania Ave NW Washington DC 20004-2408 Home: 3711 Village Park Dr Chevy Chase MD 20815-5745

MURTAUGH, CHRISTOPHER DAVID, lawyer; b. Darby, Pa., Oct. 25, 1945; s. John Michael and Rita (Sullivan) M.; m. Nancy R. Hanauer, Nov. 30, 1968; children: Jason C., Colin M., Alison M. AB, U. Ill., 1967, JD, 1970. Bar: Ill. 1970, Fla. 1973, U.S. Dist. Ct. (no. dist.) Ill. 1975. Assoc. to ptnr. Winston & Strawn LLP, Chgo., 1974—, capital ptnr., 1987—, real estate dept. chmn., 1994—2005. Mem. Glen Ellyn (Ill.) Capital Improvements Com., 1985-89, Glen Ellyn Plan Com., 1989-96, Met. Planning Coun., 1995—; bd. visitors U. Ill. Coll. of Law, 1998-2001. bd. dirs. LifeSource Blood Svcs., 2005—; Lt. USNR, 1971-74. Mem. ABA, Am. Coll. Real Estate Lawyers, Fla. Bar Assn., Ill. State Bar Assn., Chgo. Bar Assn., Order of Coif. Office: Winston & Strawn LLP 35 W Wacker Dr Ste 4200 Chicago IL 60601-1695 Office Phone: 312-558-5600. E-mail: cmurtaugh@winston.com.

MURTHA, JOHN PATRICK, JR., congressman; b. New Martinsville, W.Va., June 17, 1932; s. John Patrick and Mary Edna (Ray) Murtha; m. Joyce Bell, June 10, 1955; children: Donna Sue, John, Patrick. BA in Econs., U. Pitts., 1961; postgraduate student, Ind. U. Pa., 1962-65; HHD (hon.), Mt. Aloysius Jr. Coll. Mem. Pa. State Ho. Reps., 1969-73, US Congress from 12th Pa. dist., 1974—, mem. appropriations com., chmn. def. appropriations subcommittee. Author (with John Plashall): From Vietnam to 9/11: On the Front Lines of National Security, 2003. Served in USMC, as lt. 1952-55, as maj. 1966-67, USMC Res., 1955-66, 1967-90 Decorated Bronze Star, 2 Purple Hearts, Cross of Gallantry Vietnam; Recipient Pa. Disting. Svc. medal, 1978, Pa. Meritorious Svc. medal, numerous service awards for work during Johnstown flood, 1977, Iron Mike award Marine Corps League, 1988, Disting. Am. award (Nation's Capital chpt.) Air Force Assn., 1989, Outstanding Vet. award Vets. Caucus of Am. Acad. Physician Assts., 1989, Man of Steel award Cold Finished Steel Bar Inst., 1989, Pa. Disting. Svc. medal & Pa. Meritorius Svc. medal, 2000, Spirit of Hope award United Svc. Orgns., Inc., 2000, Funding Hero award Breast Cancer Rsch. Found., 2002, Profile in Courage award John F. Kennedy Libr. Found., 2006; named Man of Yr. Johnstown Jaycees, 1978 Mem.: VFW, Salvation Army, Am. Legion. Democrat. Roman Catholic. Office: US House Reps 2423 Rayburn House Office Bldg Washington DC 20515-0001 also: 647 Main St Ste 401 Johnstown PA 15901 Office Phone: 202-225-2065, 814-535-2642. Office Fax: 814-539-6229. *

MURUGAN, THIRUMAGAL ANANDHI, medical researcher; d. Murugan Sudalaiyandi; m. Vijay Ganesh Divakaran, Jan. 16, 2005; 1 child, Nitya Vijay Ganesh. MBBS, Madras Med. Coll., Chennai, India, 2000; baccalaureate in medicine and surgery, Madras MGR Med. Coll., India, 2001; MPH, U. Tex., Houston, 2003; MD, SUNY, Bklyn., 2006. Diplomate Am. Bd. Internal Medicine, 2006. Intern Madras Med. Coll., Chennai, India, 2000—01; grad. rsch. asst. U. Tex. Sch. Pub. Health, Houston, 2002; rsch. assoc. Baylor Coll. Medicine, Houston, 2002—03; grad. rsch. asst. U. Tex. MD Anderson Cancer Ctr., Houston, 2002—03; resident SUNY Downstate Med. Ctr., Bklyn., 2003—06; clin. fellow U. Tex. Med. Br., Galveston, 2006—. Contbr. articles to profl. jours. Del. Com. Interns and Residents, NYC, 2003—05. Recipient Academic Achievement Fellowship award, U. Tex. Med. Br., Galveston, 2007. Mem.: ACP, Am. Coll. Chest Physicians. Home Phone: 281-412-2795; Office Phone: 409-772-2618.

MUSA, JOHN DAVIS, information technology executive, writer; b. Amityville, NY, June 11, 1933; s. Khan Hussein and Ione Geraldine (Ryan) M.; m. Marilyn Laurene Allred, June 24, 1959. BA, Dartmouth Coll., 1954, MSEE, 1955. With AT&T Bell Labs., Murray Hill, NJ, 1958-96, mem. tech. staff, 1958-63, supr. guidance program devel., 1963-68, supr. command and control program devel., 1968-69, supr. mgmt. control and new software tech., 1969-72, supr. human factors test, 1972-74, supr. computer graphics, 1974-80, supr. computer measurements, 1980-85, supr. software quality, 1985-90, tech. mgr. software reliability engring., 1991-96. Mem. N.J. Coun. R&D; lectr., spkr. in field. Author: Software Reliability: Measurement, Prediction, Application, 1987, Software Reliability Engineering: More Reliable Software, Faster Development and Testing, 1998, Software Reliability Engineering: More Reliable Software Faster and Cheaper, 2004; editor: (book series) Software Quality Institute; contbr. over 100 articles to prof. jours. and books. Lt. USN, 1955-58. Fellow IEEE (Third Millenium medal for outstanding achievements and contbns.); mem. IEEE Computer Soc. (2d v.p. 1986, v.p. publs. 1984-85, v.p. tech. activities 1986, chair tech com. software engring. 1982-84, founding mem. editl. bd. IEEE Software Mag., Disting. lectr. 1980-83, Meritorious Svc. award 1984, 85, 87, Golden Core award, founding officer com. on software reliability engring., mem. editl. bds. Spectrum mag., 1984-86, Proc. of the IEEE 1983-90, Technique et Science Informatiques jour., sr. editor Software Engring. Inst. book series, sr. founding editor Software Quality Inst. book series, chair steering com. Internat. Conf. on Software Engring.), IEEE Reliability Soc. (Engr. of Yr. 2004), Assn. for Computing Machinery. Achievements include internat. leader in software engring. and in creation new tech. software reliability engring.; created two software reliability models; developed concepts and practice of operational profile, software-reliability engineered testing, concept of execution time; reduced operation software (ROS), and operational development; created concept of fault exposure ratio; developed approach for choosing software development strategies to meet different reliability objectives; international leader in reducing software reliability engineering to practice; organized panel and coordinated joint paper on teaching software reliability engineering. Office: 39 Hamilton Rd Morristown NJ 07960-5341 Home Phone: 973-267-2175. Personal E-mail: j.musa@ieee.org.

MUSA, SAMUEL ALBERT, university executive; m. Judith Friedman; children: Gregory, Jeffrey. BA, BSEE, Rutgers U., 1961; MS in Applied Physics, Harvard U., 1962, PhD in Applied Physics, 1965. Rsch. scientist Gen. Precision Inc., Little Falls, NJ, 1965-66; asst. prof. elec. engring. U. Pa., Phila., 1966-71; project leader Inst. for Def. Analyses, Arlington, Va., 1971-78; dep. dir. Office of Under Sec. Def., Washington, 1978-83; dir. rsch. and advanced tech. E-Systems, Inc., Dallas, 1983-86, v.p. rsch. and advanced tech., 1986-95; exec. dir. Ctr. Display Tech. and Mfg. U. Mich., 1995-99; assoc. v.p. for strategic initiative, prof. elec. and computer engring. Northwestern U., Evanston, Ill., 1999—; sr. rsch. fellow ctr. tech. and nat. security Nat. Def. U., 2005—. Mem. sci. adv. bd. USAF; mem. sci. bd. Def. Intelligence Agy., Army Sci. Bd. Contbr. articles to profl. jours.

Recipient Exceptional Civilian Svc. award, Sec. of Air Force, cert. of appreciation, Sec. Def. Fellow IEEE; mem. AIA (tech. and ops. coun. 1986-95, vice chmn. 1993, chmn. 1994), Sigma Xi, Tau Beta Pi, Pi Mu Epsilon.

MUSACCHIA, X(AVIER) J(OSEPH), physiology and biophysics educator; b. Bklyn., Feb. 11, 1923; s. Castrense and Orsolina (Mazzola) M.; m. Betty Cook, Nov. 23, 1950; children: Joseph, Mary, Thomas, Laura Ann. BS, St. Francis Coll., Bklyn., 1944; MS, Fordham U., 1947, PhD, 1949. Instr. biology Marymount (N.Y.) Coll., 1948-49; from instr. to prof. biology St. Louis U., 1949-65; prof. physiology U. Mo., Columbia, 1965-78; prof. physiology and biophysics U. Louisville, 1978-91, prof. emeritus, 1991—, dean Grad. Sch., 1978-89, assoc. provost for rsch., 1985-89. Bd. dirs. Coun. Grad. Schs., 1986-89. Author: Depressed Metabolism, 1969, Regulation of Depressed Metabolism and Thermogenesis, 1976, Survival in Cold, 1981; also articles. Bd. govs. J. Graham Brown Cancer Ctr., Louisville, 1978-83; bd. dirs. Oak Ridge Associated Univs. Served with AUS, 1943-45. Research grantee NIH; Research grantee NASA. Fellow AAAS; mem. Am. Physiol. Soc., Am. Soc. Zoologists, Am. Soc. for Space and Gravitational Biology (v.p. 1988-89, pres. 1989-90), Soc. Exptl. Biology and Medicine, Corp. Marine Biol. Lab., Sigma Xi. (past chpt. pres.) Home: 1770 East Overland Dr Fayetteville AR 72703-5202

MUSALLAM, SAMER MAKRAM, lawyer; b. Beirut, Apr. 27, 1977; arrived in US, 2000; s. Makram Fouad and Nelly Musallam; m. Eliza Jawoo Park, Nov. 5, 2005; 1 child, Carmen. BA, U. Toronto, Ont., 2000; MBA, Weatherhead Sch. Mgmt., Cleve., 2004; JD, Case Western Res. U., Cleve., 2004. Assoc. Thompson Hine LLP, Clevel, 2004—. Mem.: ABA, Cleve. Bar Assn. (mem. trial counsel 2005—, mem. ethics com. and grievances 2005—). Office: Thompson Hine LLP 3900 Key Ctr 127 Pub Sq Cleveland OH 44114

MUSANTE, TONY (ANTHONY PETER MUSANTE JR.), actor; b. Bridgeport, Conn. s. Anthony Peter and Natalie Anne (Salerno) M.; m. Jane Ashley Sparkes, June 2, 1962. BA (Baker scholar), Oberlin Coll., 1958; postgrad., Northwestern U., 1957; student, HB Studios, NYC, 1961-65. Appearances include: (off Broadway prodns.) Borak, 1960, Zoo Story, Night of the Dunce, The Collection, Match-Play, Kiss Mama, L'Histoire du Soldat, A Gun Play, Falling Man, Cassatt, Grand Magic, The Big Knife, The Taming of the Shrew, Two Brothers, The Archbishop's Ceiling, Souvenir, A Streetcar Named Desire, Double Play, Dancing in the End Zone, Snow Orchid, Wait until Dark, Widows, Anthony Rose, Mount Allegro, Frankie and Johnny in the Clair de Lune, Breaking Legs, The Flip Side, Love Letters, The Sisters, Italian Funerals and Other Festive Occasions (Broadway prodns.) PS Your Cat is Dead, 1975 (N.Y. Drama Desk nomination), Memory of Two Mondays, 27 Wagons Full of Cotton, The Lady from Dubuque; films: Once a Thief, 1964, The Incident (Best Actor award Mar del Plata Internat. Film Festival), 1967, The Detective, The Mercenary, One Night at Dinner, Bird with the Crystal Plumage, Grissom Gang, Anonymous Venetian, The Last Run, Pisciotta Case, Goodbye and Amen, Break-Up, Collector's Item, The Repenter, Devil's Hill, Appointment in Trieste, Nocturne, The Pope of Greenwich Village, The Deep End of the Ocean, The Yards, Life As It Comes, Love's Promise, We Own The Night; TV appearances include Ride with Terror, 1963, star series Toma, 1973-74 (Photoplay Gold medal award 1974), scriptwriter several episodes; star HBO series Oz, A&E series 100 Centre Street; also starred in TV miniseries and movies: Pompeii, Traffic, Exiled, The Seventh Scroll, Deep Family Secrets, A Kiss In the Dark, High Ice, Breaking Up is Hard to Do, The Baron, Legend of the Black Hand, The Story of Esther, My Husband is Missing, Nowhere to Hide, The Quality of Mercy (Emmy nominee 1975), Court Martial of Lt. William Calley, Night Heat, Rearview Mirror, Nutcracker: Money, Madness and Murder, Acapulco HEAT, Nothing Sacred, American Playhouse: Weekend, Last Waltz on a Tightrope; daytime TV (guest star): Loving, ABC, 1993, As The World Turns, CBS, 2000. Mem. SAG, AFTRA, ATAS, Actors Equity Assn., Writers Guild Am. West, Acad. Motion Picture Arts and Scis.

MUSAT, KATHERINE GADUS, retired music educator; b. Cleve., Feb. 6, 1944; d. William Martin Gadus and Catherine Ruth Salmon; m. John George Musat, July 5, 1969; children: John William, Mary Katherine Smith, Danielle Eleanor. MusB in Edn., Baldwin-Wallace Coll., Berea, Ohio, 1966; MSc in Edn., Coll. Mt. St. Joseph, Cin., Ohio, 1988. Cert. tchr. Ohio, 1996. Dir. instrumental music Parma (Ohio) City Schs., 1967—2004; ret., 2004. Studio brass tchr. Baldwin-Wallace Coll., 1985—; prin. trumpet Parma Symphony Orch., 1967—, Hermit Club Orch., 1985—. Vol. church musician various chs., 1964—. Home: 2141 Jacqueline Dr Parma OH 44134-6858 Personal E-mail: kagy@cox.net.

MUSCARI, JOSEPH CHARLES, manufacturing executive; b. Jersey City, Sept. 14, 1946; s. Joseph Vincent and Anneliese (Baumberger) M.; m. Donna Marie Veneziale, Apr. 17, 1971; children: Joseph, John, Marisa. BS in Indsl. Engring., NJ Inst. Tech., 1968; MBA, U. Pitts., 1969; LLD (hon.), Salem-Teikyo U., 1994. Indsl. engr. Alcoa, New Kensington, Pa., 1969, sr. indsl. engr. Massena, NY, 1969, chief indsl. engr., supr. Cleve., 1969, controller forging divsn., 1979, group controller Engring. Product Group, 1979, gen. mgr. powder and pigments divsn. Pitts., 1979, dir. Alcoa Mgmt. Info. Svcs., quality dir. Fin. Group, 1986, group v.p. The Stolle Corp. Ohio, 1989, pres. Alcoa Asia Japan, 1992, v.p. audit Pitts., 1997, v.p. Environ., Health and Safety, Audit and Compliance, 1997, group pres. Asia and Latin Am., 2001, exec. v.p., 2002—, head Rigid Packaging, Foil and Asia Group, 2004, CFO, 2006—, mem. exec. coun. Dir. Minerals Techs., Inc.; mem. bd. overseers NJ Inst. Tech. Recipient Spkrs. award Data Processing Mgmt. Assn. and Am. Prodn. and Inventory Control Soc., 1987. Mem. Alpha Pi Mu, Tau Beta Pi, Duquesne Club. Roman Catholic. Achievements include established Alcoa's first major operation in China and developed the company's long-term strategy there. Avocations: golf, winemaking, sports. Office: Alcoa 390 Park Ave New York NY 10022-4608 *

MUSCATINE, CHARLES, language educator, writer; b. Bklyn., Nov. 28, 1920; m. Doris Corn, July 21, 1945; children: Jeffrey, Alison. BA, Yale U., 1941, MA, 1942, PhD, 1948; L.H.D. (hon.), New Sch. for Social Research, 1982; Litt.D., SUNY, 1989, Rosary Coll., 1991. Mem. faculty dept. English U. Calif., Berkeley, 1948—, prof., 1960-91, prof. emeritus, 1991—, dir. Collegiate Seminar Program, 1974-80. Vis. prof. Wesleyan U., 1951-53; Ward Phillips lectr. U. Notre Dame, 1969; mem. com. of selection J.S. Guggenheim Found., 1969-89, chmn. 1985-89. Author: Chaucer and the French Tradition, 1957, The Book of Geoffrey Chaucer, 1963, Poetry and Crisis in the Age of Chaucer, 1972, The Old French Fabliaux, 1986, Medieval Literature, Style, and Culture, 1999; co-author, editor: Education at Berkeley, 1966, (with M. Griffith) The Borzoi College Reader, 1966, 7th edit., 1992, First Person Singular, 1973; co-editor Integrity in the Coll. Curriculum, 1985. Bd. dirs. No. Calif. chpt. ACLU, 1959-62, 63-66, Assn. Am. Colls., 1979-82, Ctr. for the Common Good, 1994-99; bd. dirs. Fedn. State Humanities Couns., 1989-94, chair, 1991-93; mem. Commn. on Humanities, Rockefeller Found., 1978-79, Calif. Coun. Humanities, 1986-94. With USNR, 1942-45. Recipient Navy Commendation ribbon, 1945, Berkeley citation, 1991; Fulbright fellow, 1958, 62, ACLS Rsch. fellow, 1958, Guggenheim fellow, 1962, NEH Sr. fellow, 1968. Fellow Am. Acad. Arts and Scis., Medieval Acad. of Am.; mem. MLA, New Chaucer Soc. (pres. 1980-81), Aircraft Owners and Pilots Assn., Phi Beta Kappa. Home: 2812 Buena Vista Way Berkeley CA 94708-2016 Personal E-mail: chasm@berkeley.edu.

MUSCATO, ANDREW, lawyer; b. Newark, Aug. 28, 1953; s. Salvatore and Bertha (Kubilus) M.; m. Ann Marie Hughes, Aug. 19, 1978; children: Amy, Andrew Joseph, Amanda. AB magna cum laude, Brown U., 1975; JD, Seton Hall U., 1978. Bar: NJ 1978, NY 1984, U.S. Dist. Ct. NJ 1978, U.S. Dist. Ct. (so. and ea. dists.) NY 1984, U.S. Dist. Ct. (no. dist.) NY 1998, U.S. Ct. Appeals (3d cir.) 1981, U.S. Ct. Appeals (2d cir.) 2005. Law clk. to presiding judge, appellate div. N.J. Superior Ct., Somerville, 1978-79; staff atty. Adminstrv. Office of Cts., Trenton, NJ, 1979-80; assoc. Simon & Allen, Newark, 1980-86; ptnr. Kirsten & Simon, Newark, 1987-89, Whitman & Ransom, Newark, 1989-93, Whitman Breed Abbott & Morgan, LLP, Newark, 1993-99; counsel Skadden, Arps, Slate, Meagher & Flom LLP, Newark, 1999—2004, NYC, 2004—; commr. N.J. Pub. Employee Rels. Commn., 1999—2002; mem. N.J. Banking Adv. Bd., 2002—. Atty. Irvington (N.J.) Rent Leveling Bd., 1980—. Author: Executing on a Debtor's Interest in a Tenancy by the Entirety, 1986. Mem. ABA, Essex County Bar Assn., Trial Attys. N.J., N.J. Inst. Mcpl. Attys., Def. Rsch. Inst. Republican. Roman Catholic. Home: 66 Addison Dr Basking Ridge NJ 07920-2202 Office: Skadden Arps Slate Meagher & Flom LLP 4 Times Sq New York NY 10036 Office Phone: 212-735-2217. Business E-Mail: amuscato@skadden.com.

MUSCHENHEIM, FREDERICK, retired pathologist; b. NYC, July 9, 1932; s. Carl and Haroldine (Humphreys) M.; m. Linda Alexander, Mar. 29, 1958; children: Alexandra Lydia, Carl William, David Henry. AB, Harvard U., 1953; MDCM, McGill U., Montreal, Can., 1963. Intern Santa Clara County Hosp., San Jose, Calif., 1963—64; resident pathology U. Colo. Med. Ctr., Denver, 1964—68, chief resident clin. pathology, 1968—69; pathologist Freeman, Hanske, Munkittrick & Foley PA, Mpls., 1969—77; clin. pathologist Union-Truesdale Hosp., Fall River, Mass., 1977—78; chief pathologist St. Clare's Hosp., Denville, NJ, 1978—83, Oneida Healthcare Ctr., 1984—99, ret., 1999; cons. pathologist St. Jude Hosp., Vieux Fort, St. Lucia, West Indies, 1999—2002. Clin. asst. prof. SUNY Health Sci. Ctr., Syracuse, 1984-90, clin. assoc. prof., 1990-97, clin. prof., 1998-99, clin. prof. emeritus, 1999-2001; chief med. staff Oneida City Hosps., 1991; pres. Sunderman Fund, Bermuda Biol. Sta. for Rsch., v.p. Madison County (NY) bd. health, 1995-96, pres., 1997-2000. Choir 1st Presbyn. Ch. of Cazenovia, NY, 1984-2000, trustee, 1985-89; choir Wayzata (Minn.) Cmty. Ch., 2001—. Mem.: Syracuse ARC Blood Svcs. (chmn. med. adv. coun. 1995—99), Minn. Soc. Pathologists (sec. 2002—05), N.Y. State Soc. Pathologists (councilor 2d dist. 1991—2000, chmn. legis. com. 1991—2000, del. to MSSNY 1998—99), N.Y. State Assn. Pub. Health Labs. (v.p. 1992—93, pres. 1993—94, edn. chmn. 1994—95), Med. Soc. Madison County (v.p. 1990—91, pres. 1991—93), Med. Soc. State N.Y. (legis. com. 1991—2000), Coll. Am. Pathologists (govt. affairs com. 1994—97, nominating com. 1995, steering com. ho. dels. 1999—2002), Assn. Clin. Scientists (v.p. 1989, pres. 1990, rec. sec. 1995—, del. Intersoc. Pathology Coun. 2004—05, Diploma of Honor 1991). Home: 1159 Hollybrook Dr Wayzata MN 55391-1364

MUSCO, LYNN ANN, music educator; b. Reedsburg, Wis., Aug. 6, 1959; d. Lewis Alan and Geraldine Ann Schmidt; m. Enrico Musco III, Dec. 31, 1999; m. Bruce John Cholka, Sept. 16, 1981 (div. Nov. 1997); 1 child, Alexander Blaine Cholka. BF A, U Wis., 1984; MusM, N.Mex State U, 1986; Mus D Fla. State U, 1994. Freelance music, Fla., 1981—, Wis., 1981—; grad. asst. tchr. N.Mex State U, Las Cruces, N.Mex., 1983—86, Fla. State U, Tallahassee, 1986—88; prof. music Stetson U Sch. of Music, Deland, Fla., 1988—. Prin. clarinet Bach Festival Orch., Winter Park, Fla., 1996—. Contbr. Tres Vientos - Music of Am. Composers. Mem.: Am. Federation of Musicians, Fla. Bandmasters Assoc. (assoc.). Democrat. Meth. Avocations: reading, remodeling old homes, sewing, gardening. Office: Stetson Univeristy School of Music 421 North Woodland Blvd Deland FL 32720 Office Phone: 386-822-8953. E-mail: lmusco59@cfl.rr.com.

MUSE, JOHN R., investment company executive; b. Ft. Worth, Feb. 24, 1951; s. Arthur C. and Betty L. (Smith) M.; m. Lyn A. Reynolds, Aug. 10, 1975; children: Michael J., J. Tyler, Whitney J. BS, USAF Acad., 1973; MBA, UCLA, 1974. Commd. 2d lt. USAF, 1973, advanced through grades to capt., resigned, 1978; sr. v.p., corp. fin. dir. Schneider, Bernet & Hickman, Dallas, 1980-84; mng. dir. Prudential Bache Capital Funding, Dallas, 1984—89; co-founder, ptnr., mem. mgmt. com. HM Capital Partners (formerly Hicks, Muse, Tate & Furst Inc.), Dallas, 1989—, chmn., 2005—. Bd. dirs. Dean Foods Co., 1997—, Swift & Co., 2002—. Bd. visitors UCLA Anderson Sch. Mgmt. Presbyterian. Office: HM Captial Ste 1600 200 Crescent Ct Dallas TX 75201 Office Phone: 214-740-7300. Office Fax: 214-720-7888. E-mail: jmuse@hmcapital.com. *

MUSFELT, DUANE CLARK, lawyer; b. Stockton, Calif., Sept. 14, 1951; s. Robert H. and Doris E. (Roth) M.; m. Linh T. To, Sept. 6, 1980. Student, U. Calif., Davis, 1969-71; BA in Econs., U. Calif., Berkeley, 1973; JD, UCLA, 1976. Bar: Calif. 1976, U.S. Dist. Ct. (cen. dist.) Calif. 1977, U.S. Ct. Appeals (9th cir.) 1980, U.S. Dist. Ct. (no. dist.) Calif. 1982, U.S. Dist. Ct. (ea. and so. dists.) Calif. 1983, U.S. Supreme Ct. 1987. Assoc. Haight, Dickson, Brown & Bonesteel, LA, 1976-77, Mori & Ota, LA, 1977-79, Lewis, D'Amato, Brisbois & Bisgaard, LA, 1979-82; ptnr. Lewis, Brisbois, Bisgaard & Smith, San Francisco, 1982—. Mem. State Bar Calif., Bar Assn. San Francisco. Democrat. Presbyterian. Avocations: tennis, skiing, bridge. Office: Lewis Brisbois Bisgaard & Smith One Sansome St Ste 1400 San Francisco CA 94104-4431 Office Phone: 415-362-2580. Business E-Mail: musfelt@lbbslaw.com.

MUSGRAVE, MARILYN N., congresswoman; b. Greeley, Colo., Jan. 27, 1949; m. Steven Musgrave, 4 children. BA, Colo. State U., 1972. Co-owner Musgrave Bale Stacking; mem. Colo. Ho. Reps., 1995—99, Colo. Senate, Dist. 1, Denver, 1998—2003; chmn. transp. com.; mem. health, environment, welfare and instns. com.; mem. state, vets. and mil. affairs com.; mem. US Congress from 4th Colo. dist., 2003—; mem. Agriculture com., Edn. & Workforce com., Resources com. & Small Bus. com. Past pres. Morgan County Rep. Women; former bd. mem. RE-3 Sch. Dist. Republican. Office: US Ho Reps 1507 Longworth Ho Office Bldg Washington DC 20515-0604 *

MUSGRAVE, R. KENTON, federal judge; b. Clearwater, Fla., Sept. 7, 1927; Student, Ga. Inst. Tech., 1945-46, U. Fla., 1946-47; BA, U. Wash., 1948; JD with distinction, Emory U., 1953. Asst. gen. counsel Lockheed Internat., 1953-62; v.p., gen. counsel Mattel, Inc., 1963-71; mem. firm Musgrave, Welbourn and Fertman, 1972-75; asst. gen. counsel Pacific Enterprises, 1975-81; v.p., gen. counsel Vivitar Corp, 1981-85; v.p., dir. Santa Barbara Applied Rsch., 1982-87; judge U.S. Ct. Internat. Trade, NYC, 1987—97, sr. judge, 1997—. Trustee The Dian Fossey Gorilla Fund, Dolphins of Sharks Bay (Australia); hon. trustee Pet Protection Soc.; mem. United Way, Save the Redwoods League; active Palos Verdes Community Assn. Mem. Internat. Bar Assn., Pan Am. Bar Assn., State Bar Calif. (chmn. corp. law sect. 1965-66, del. 1966-67), L.A. County Bar Assn., Fng. Trade Assn. So. Calif. (bd. dirs.). Office: US Ct Internat Trade 1 Federal Plz New York NY 10278-0001

MUSGRAVE, STORY, design educator, astronaut, physiologist, surgeon; b. Boston, Aug. 19, 1935; children: Lorelei Lisa, Bradley Scott, Holly Kay, Christopher Todd, Jeffrey Paul, Lane Linwood. BS in Math. and Stats., Syracuse U., 1958; MBA, UCLA, 1959; BA in Chemistry, Marietta Coll., 1960; MD, Columbia U., 1964; MS in Biophysics, U. Ky., 1966; MA in Lit., U. Houston, 1987, MA in Humanities, 1989. Surg. intern U. Ky. Med. Ctr., Lexington, 1964-65; scientist-astronaut NASA, Houston, 1967-97, backup sci.-pilot 1st Skylab mission, 1973, flew on first Challenger flight, STS-6, 1983, flew on Spacelab 2, 1985, flew on space shuttle mission STS-33, 1989, flew on STS-44, 1991, flew as payload comdr. STS61 Hubble Telescope Repair Mission, 1993, flew on STS-80 last flight, 1996; concept artist Walt Disney Imagineering, 1997—; performing artist, 1997—; designer Tupperware, Inc., 2003; prodr., dir. Lannistoria, Sydney, 2002—; innovator Applied Minds, Inc., Glendale, Calif., 2002—; landscape architect Kissimmee, Fla., 1997—. Author: numerous poems; contbr. articles to profl. jours. With USMC, 1953-56. Recipient Reese AFB Comdr.'s trophy, 1969, NASA exceptional svc. medal, 1974, 83, 90, NASA disting. svc. medal, 1992, 94, 97, NASA spaceflight medal, 1983, 85, 89, 91, 93, 96, Space award Aviation Week and Space Tech., 1997; USAF postdoctoral fellow, 1965-66, Nat. Heart Inst. postdoctoral fellow, 1966-67. Mem. AAAS, AAS, AIAA, Flying Physicians Assn. (Airman of Yr. award 1974, 83), Civil Aviation Med. Assn., N.Y. Acad. Sci., Nat. Geog. Soc., Soaring Soc. Am., U.S. Parachute Assn., Marine Corps Assn., Alpha Kappa Psi, Phi Delta Theta, Omicron Delta Kappa, Beta Gamma Sigma. Office Phone: 407-390-0221. Personal E-mail: storymusgrave@hotmail.com. *From subatomic particles, to the stardust from which I was created, from the forming galaxies, to the universes beyond our own, I live to participate physically and spiritually in every aspect of this cosmic creation and evolution.*

MUSGRAVE, THEA, composer, conductor; b. Edinburgh, May 27, 1928; m. Peter Mark, 1971. Student MusBac, Edinburgh U.; student, Paris Conservatory. Composer: (opera) The Abbot of Drimock, 1955, The Decision, 1964-65, The Voice of Ariadne, 1972-73, Mary, Queen of Scots, 1975-77, (first performed Scottish Opera) A Christmas Carol, 1978-79 (first performed Va. Opera Assn., 1979), An Occurrence at Owl Creek Bridge, 1981, Harriet, The Woman Called Moses, 1981-84 (first performed Va. Opera 1985), Simon Bolivar, Pontalba, New Orleans Opera, 2001-03, (ballet) Beauty and the Beast, 1969, (symphony and orchestral music) Obliques, 1958, Nocturnes and Arias, 1966, Concerto for Orch., 1967, Clarinet Concerto, 1968, Night Music, 1969, Scottish Dance Suite, 1969, Memento Vitae, 1969-70, Orfeo II, 1975, Soliloquy II and III, 1980, From One to Another, 1980, Peripeteia, 1981, The Seasons, 1988, (marimba concerto) Journey through a Japanese Landscape, (bass-clarinet concerto) Autumn Sonata, (oboe concerto) Helios, Phoenix Rising, 1997, (chamber and instrumental music) String Quartet, 1958, Trio for flute, oboe and piano, 1960, Monologue, 1960, Serenade, 1961, Chamber concerto No. 1, 1962, Chamber Concerto No. 2, 1966, Chamber Concerto No. 3, 1966, Music for horn and piano, 1967, Impromptu No. 1, 1967, Soliloquy I, 1969, Elegy, 1970, Impromptu No. 2, 1970, Space Play, 1974, Orfeo I, 1975, Fanfare, 1982, Pierrot, 1985, Narcissus, 1987, Niobe, 1987, (vocal and choral music) Two Songs, 1951, Four Madrigals, 1953, Six Songs: Two Early English Poems, 1953, A Suite O'Bairnsangs, 1953, Cantata for a Summer's Day, 1954, Song of the Burn, 1954, Five Love Songs, 1955, Four Portraits, 1956, A Song for Christmas, 1958, Triptych, 1959, Sir Patrick Spens, 1961, Make Ye Merry for Him That Is to Come, 1962, Two Christmas Carols in Traditional Style, 1963, John Cook, 1963, Five Ages of Man, 1963-64, Memento Creatoris, 1967, Primavera, 1971, Rorate Coeli, 1973, Monologues of Mary, Queen of Scots, 1977-86, O Caro M'e Il Sonno, 1978, The Last Twilight, 1980, Black Tambourine, 1985, For the Time Being, 1986, Echoes Through Time, 1988, Wild Winter for Viols & Voices, 1993, On the Underground Sets 1, 2 & 3, 1994, 95, (Robert Burns' poems for soprano & orch.) Songs for a Winter's Evening, 1995, (for orch.) Phoenix Rising, 1996-97, (for 3 flutes and percussion) Voices from the Ancient World, 1998, (for chorus and orch.) Celebration Day, 1998-99, (for 8 instruments) Lamenting With Ariadne, 1999, (orchestral work) Turbulent Landscapes, Boston Symphony, 2004, Journey into Light (soprano and orch.), 2004-05, Going North (childrens chorus and 2 clarinets), 2004. Office: Va Opera Assn PO Box 2580 Norfolk VA 23501-2580

MUSHAK, PAUL, toxicologist, consultant; b. Dunmore, Pa., Dec. 9, 1935; s. Steven and Mary Mushak; m. Elizabeth Orr Walker, June 30, 1973. BS in Chemistry, U. Scranton, 1961; PhD, U. Fla., 1969; postgrad., Yale U., 1969-71. Diplomate Am. Bd. Forensic Medicine, Am. Coll. Forensic Examiners, 1996. Asst. prof. U. N.C. Sch. Medicine, Chapel Hill, 1971-77, assoc. prof., 1977-85; prin. PB Assocs., Durham, NC, 1992—. Adj. prof. U. N.C. Sch. medicine, 1986-93; vis. prof. Albert Einstein Coll. of Medicine, Bronx, N.Y., 1995—; mem. com., cons. EPA Sci. Adv. Bd., Washington, 1989-97, 2000-03, 05—; mem. com. Nat. Acad. of Sci., Washington, 1989-93, 85-87, 73-75. Author and co-author chpts. to books and 175 sci. publs. in field. Mem. Environ. Affairs Bd., Durham, NC, 1990—92, Durham Housing Appeals Bd., NC, 1990—93. Recipient Pre-doctoral fellowship, NIH, 1961-67, Post-doctoral fellowship, Yale U., 1969-71; recipient Meritorious Svc. award U.S. EPA, Cin., 1981; grantee NIH, 1971-85; Hon. Mention in Colloid Chemistry Rsch., U. of S.C., 1961 Fellow Am. Coll. Forensic Examiners; mem. Soc. for Risk Analysis, Soc. of Toxicology. Achievements include Lab. methods for testing constituents of antique textiles; research in major studies on lead poisoning in children: lead vs. IQ, lead levels in remote peoples, physical chemical and biochemical determinants of metal toxicity, paths of exposure. Office: PB Assocs 714 9th St Ste 204 Durham NC 27705-4849 Office Phone: 919-286-7193. Personal E-mail: pandbmushak@cs.com.

MUSHINSKY, MARY M., state legislator; b. New Haven; m. Martin J. Waters; children: Martin Waters, Edward Waters. BA, So. Conn. State U., 1973; postgrad., Fla. Atlantic U.; MA, Wesleyan U., Middletown, Conn., 1993. Mem. Conn. Ho. of Reps., Hartford, Conn., 1981—, mem. environ., fin. revenue and bonding com., mem. select com. on children, asst. majority leader. Democrat. Home: 188 S Cherry St Wallingford CT 06492-4016 Office: Conn House of Reps Capitol Ave Hartford CT 06106 Office Phone: 860-240-8585.

MUSHLIN, ALVIN I., medical educator, researcher; b. NYC, Oct. 28, 1941; s. Max M.; m. Linda M.; children: Amy, Katey. BA, Vanderbilt U., Nashville, 1963, MD, 1966; ScM, Johns Hopkins U Sch. Hygiene, Baltimore, 1973. Diplomate Am. Bd. Internal Medicine. Instr. Johns Hopkins U., Balt., 1972-76, asst. prof., 1972-76; assoc. prof. medicine U. Rochester (N.Y.) Sch. Medicine, 1976-93; assoc. prof. U. Rochester Sch. Medicine, Rochester, NY, 1976-90, prof., 1993-99; Nanette Laitman disting. prof., chmn. dept. pub. health Cornell U. Weill Med. Coll., NYC, 1999—. With USN, 1968-70. Fax: 212-746-8544. E-mail: aim2001@mail.med.cornell.edu.

MUSICH, ROBERT LORIN, motivational speaker; b. Glendale, Calif., Feb. 15, 1969; s. Richard and Zola (Nickel) M. MBA, M, La Salle U. Sr. asst. mgr. Am. Gen. Fin., Upland, Calif., 1988-89; mgmt./corp. trainer Mortgage Link, Pasadena, 1989-94; mgr. AT&T, LA, 1994-96; owner Musich & Assocs., West Covina, Calif., 1989—. Singer (tenor) So. Calif. Mormon Choir, 1994—; cand. Calif. State Assembly, 59th Dist., 1995; vol. Am. Cancer Soc., 1994-96; coach Youth League Football, 1987-92; elder's quorum pres. LDS Ch., sec., 1992-93, 2d and 1st counselor, 1995-96, mem. stake single adult com., 1993-95, mem. regional single adult com. bi-regional chmn., 1993-95. Republican. Avocations: singing, dance, theater, volleyball, football. Office: Musich and Associates 3447 E Hillhaven Dr West Covina CA 91791-1718

MUSICK, GERALD JOE, retired entomology educator; b. Ponca City, Okla., May 24, 1940; s. Arlie A. and Leona (Beier) M.; m. Florene Ione Thompson, May 11, 1962; children: Linda Kaye, Mary Louise. BS, Okla. State U., 1962; MS, Iowa State U., 1964; PhD, U. Mo., 1969. Grad. asst. Iowa State U., 1962-64; instr. U. Mo., 1964-69; asst. prof. Ohio State U., Wooster, 1969-71, assoc. prof., 1971-76; dept. head U. Ga., Tifton, 1976-79; prof., dept. head U. Ark., Fayetteville, 1979-86, interium dir. agrl. exptl. sta., 1986-87, dean, assoc. v.p. agrl. rsch., 1987-93, univ. prof. entomology, 1993—2002, chmn.-elect faculty coun. Dale Bumpers Coll. Agrl., Food and Life Scis., 1997, chmn., 1998, prof. emeritus, 2002—, ret., 2002—; chmn. faculty coun. Dale Bumpers Coll. of Agrl. Food and Life Scis., 1998; gen. mgr. Razerback Pk. Golf Course, Fayetteville, Ark.,

2003—. Author and co-author numerous publs. Vice-chairperson com. Coop. States Rsch. Svc., 1993, So. Expt. Sta.; chairperson steering com. Midwest Food Safety Consortium, 1991-93; mem. U. Ark. Faculty Senate, 1994—, chair campus faculty, 1998-99, chair faculty senate 1999-2000, faculty exec. com., 1999—; coord. Pest Mgmt. Programs, 1998—. Mem. Entomol. Soc. Am. (pres. S.E. br. 1983-84), Ark. Acad. Sci., Ctrl. States Entomol. Soc. (v.p. 1995-96, pres. 1996-97), Sigma Xi, Gamma Sigma Delta. Lutheran. Avocation: golf. Office: Razorback Park Golf Course Fayetteville AR 72704 Personal E-mail: gjmfim@cox.net.

MUSICK, ROBERT LAWRENCE, JR., lawyer; b. Richlands, Va., Oct. 3, 1947; s. Robert Lawrence and Virginia (Brooks) M.; m. Beth Pambianchi, 1996; children: Elizabeth, Robert. BA in History with honors, U. Richmond, 1969; JD, U. Va., 1972, MA in Legal History, 1972; LLM, Coll. William and Mary, 1986. Bar: Va. 1972, U.S. Ct. Appeals (4th cir.) 1974. Law clk. Supreme Ct. Va., Richmond, 1972-73; assoc. Williams, Mullen & Christian, Richmond, 1973-78; ptnr. Williams, Mullen, Christian & Dobbins, Richmond, 1978-99, Williams Mullen, Richmond, 1999—2003, Palmer & Cay, Richmond, 2003—05; prin. Captrust Exec. Benefits Group, Richmond, 2006—. Bd. govs. estates and property sect. Va. State Bar, 1977-80, chmn., 1980. Author: RIA Non Qualified Deferred Compensation, 1997, (with others) CCH Federal Tax Service, 1989; contbr. articles to profl. jours. Trustee U. Richmond, 1991-94, Va. Intermont Coll., 2002-05; mem. Estate Planning Coun. Richmond, 1981—; bd. dirs. Va. Bapt. Homes, Inc., 1994—. Lt. col. USAR. Fellow Am. Coll. Employment Benefit Counsel, Va. Assn. Professions (pres. 1980-81), Commonwealth Club, Willow Oaks Country Club (dir. 1999-05, pres. 2002). Baptist. Avocations: tennis, skiing, golf, scuba. Office Phone: 804-672-4503. Business E-Mail: bob.musick@captrustadvisors.com.

MUSIL, ROBERT KIRKLAND, global environmental politics professor; b. NYC, Oct. 27, 1943; s. Ralph A. and Margaret Hooker (Kirkland) M.; m. Caryn Lynne McTighe, June 15, 1968; children: Rebecca M. Unruh, Emily Kirkland. BA, Yale U., 1964; MA, Northwestern U., 1966, PhD, 1970; MPH, Johns Hopkins U., 2001. Instr. Def. Info. Sch., Ft. Benjamin Harrison, Ind., 1969-71; co-dir. CCCO/An Agy. for Mil. and Draft Counseling, Phila., 1971-74; dir. mil. affairs project Ctr. for Nat. Security Studies, Washington, 1974-75; asst. prof. English and Am. studies Temple U., Phila., 1976-78; prodr., host Consider the Alternatives Radio, Phila., 1978-92; exec. dir. SANE Edn. Fund, Phila. and Washington, 1984-88, Profls. Coalition for Nuclear Arms Control, Washington, 1988-92; dir. policy and programs Physicians for Social Responsibility, Washington, 1992-95, exec. dir., CEO, 1995—2006; scholar-in-residence Am. U., 2006—. Adj. prof. Sch. Internat. Svc., Am. U., 1997—. Prodr.: (documentary series) Shadows of the Nuclear Age: American Culture and the Bomb, 1980 (NEH grantee). Bd. dirs. SANE, 1978-84, Scoville Fellowships, Washington, 1989-92, 95—, pres., 2007—; bd. dirs. Environ. Alliance, 2006—, chmn., 2007—; bd. dirs. 20/20 Vision, 2006—, Coun. for a Livable World, 2006—, Population Connection, 2006—. Capt. U.S. Army, 1969-71. Recipient Maj. Armstrong award for radio Armstrong Found., Columbia U., N.Y.C., 1988, 89. Mem. United Ch. of Christ. Home and Office: 8600 Irvington Ave Bethesda MD 20817-3604 Office Phone: 301-493-4571. Personal E-mail: bmusil1@yahoo.com.

MUSK, ELON, aerospace transportation executive; b. South Africa, June 28, 1971; m. Justine Musk; 5 children. Student, Queen's U., Kingston, Ont.; BS in Economics, U. Pa. Wharton Sch. Bus.; BS in Physics, U. Pa. With Pinnacle Rsch.; software devel. Rocket Sci., Microsoft; co-founder, chmn., CEO, chief tech. officer Zip2 Corp. (acquired by Compaq), 1995—99; co-founder, chmn., CEO X.com (changed legal name to PayPal in 2001, acquired by eBay in 2002), 1999—2002; founder, CEO, chief tech. officer Space Exploration Tech. Corp. (SpaceX), 2002—. Prin. owner, chmn. bd. Tesla Motors; primary investor, chmn. bd. Solar City; bd. dirs. The Planetary Society, 2003—. Chmn. Musk Found.; bd. trustee X-Prize Found. Named one of 50 Who Matter Now, Business 2.0, 2007. Mem.: US NAS (bd. dir, Aeronautics and Space Engring.). Office: Space Exploration Tech Corp 1310 E Grand Ave El Segundo CA 90245 *

MUSKIN, VICTOR PHILIP, lawyer; b. NYC, Mar. 1, 1942; s. Jacob Cecil and Fanya (Solomonoff) M.; m. Odette Cheryl Spreier, June 10, 1979; children: Adam James, Liana Jeanne. BA, Oberlin Coll., 1963; JD, NYU, 1966. Bar: N.Y. 1969, U.S. Dist. Ct. (so. and ea. dists.) N.Y. 1972, U.S. Ct. Appeals (2d cir.) 1974, U.S. Supreme Ct. 1974, U.S. Ct. Appeals (9th and 10th cirs.) 1978, U.S. Ct. Appeals (3d cir.) 1987. Asst. corp. counsel divsn. gen. litigation City of N.Y., 1969-73; assoc. Wolf, Popper, Ross, Wolf & Jones, NYC, 1973-74, Reavis and McGrath, NYC, 1974-78; pvt. practice NYC, 1979, 1992—2003; ptnr. Gruen & Muskin, NYC, 1980-81, Gruen, Muskin & Thau, NYC, 1981-89, Munves, Tanenhaus & Storch, NYC, 1989-90, Solin & Breimdel, NYC, 1991-92; of counsel Scheichet & Davis, P.C., 2003—. Served with Peace Corps, 1966—68; pres. Brotherhood, Ctrl. Synagogue, NYC, 1998—2002. Mem. N.Y.C. Bar Assn. (com. computer law 1982-84, com. internat. law 1996-99). Home: 529 E 84th St New York NY 10028-7330 Office: 767 Third Ave New York NY 10017 Office Phone: 212-688-3200. Business E-Mail: victor@scheichetdavis.com.

MUSMANN, KLAUS, librarian; b. Magdeburg, Germany, June 27, 1935; came to U.S., 1957; s. Ernst Hans and Eva (Grunow) M.; m. Gladys H. Arakawa, June 15, 1963 (div. 1973); children: Carlton, Michelle; m. Lois Geneva Steele, Dec. 27, 1986. BA, Wayne State U., 1962; MALS, U. Mich., 1963; MA, Mich. State U., 1967; PhD, U. So. Calif., 1981. Libr. Detroit Pub. Libr., 1962-65; asst. serials libr. Mich. State U., East Lansing, 1965-67; head of acquisitions Los Angeles County Law Libr., LA, 1968-84; coll. devel. libr. U. Redlands, Calif., 1984—2001, acting dir. Calif., 1994-96, dir. Calif., 1996—2001; dir. libr. svcs. Notre Dame de Namur U., Belmont, Calif., 2001—. Author: Helen and Vernon Farquhar Collection: A Bibliography, 1987, Diffusion of Innovations, 1989, Technological Innovations in Libraries, 1850-1950, 1993; contbr. articles to profl. jours. Grantee Coun. on Libr. Resources, 1990. Mem. ALA, Assn. Coll. and Rsch. Librs., Soc. for History of Tech. Avocations: photography, travel. Home: 975 Pizzaro Ln Foster City CA 94404 Office: Notre Dame de Namur U 1500 Ralston Ave Belmont CA 94002 Office Phone: 650-508-3745. Business E-Mail: kmusmann@ndnu.edu.

MUSMANN, LOIS S., conductor, music educator; d. Myron Roger and Lois MacNary Steele; m. Ronald Clapp, Sept. 6, 1959 (div. 1983); children: Mark Douglass Steele, Debra Clapp Walter, Holly Clapp Rogers; m. Klaus Musmann, Dec. 27, 1986. MusB, New Eng. Conservatory Music, 1984; MusM, U. Redlands, 1986; D in Musical Arts, U. So. Calif., 1989. Condr., founder Musica Viva, Redlands and Riverside, Calif., 1990—95; condr., artistic dir. Euterpe Opera Theatre, LA, 1993—; condr., founder Pacifica Chamber Orch., Redlands and Palm Springs, Calif., 1995—2001; condr. U. Calif. Choral Soc., Riverside, 1997—2000; prof. Notre Dame de Namur U., Belmont, Calif., 2001—; vis. scholar U. Calif. Beatrice Bain Rsch. Group, Berkeley, 2002—; prof. San Francisco Conservatory Music, 2003—. Lectr., founder lectr. series Redlands Symphony Orch., 1991—92, 1997—2001; chair Internat. Conf. Coll. Music Soc., Vienna, 1997; chair edn. com. San Diego Chamber Orch., La Jolla, Calif., 1997—99; mem. adv. bd. Inland Empire Chamber Music, San Bernardino, 1998—2001; mem. faculty San Francisco Conservatory Music. Contbr. articles to profl. jours.; composer: Closing Prayer, 1987; condr.: world premier opera Serafina y Arcangela. Exec. advisor Am. Coun. N.Am. Indians, Haywood, Calif., 2001—02. Recipient Fulbright Scholar, Sr. Specialist in Music, 2004, Baroque Concerto Competition Winner, New Eng. Conservatory Music, 1984; grantee, Riverside Arts Found., 1991, 1992; Postdoctoral Fellow, U. So. Calif., 1996—2001, Disting. Accomplishments award, Goodwill Industries, 1994. Mem.: Nat. League Am. Pen Women, Assn. Calif. Symphony Orchs., Pi Kappa Lambda. Avocations: travel, reading, gardening. Home: 975 Pizarro Ln Foster City CA 94404 Office: Notre Dame de Namur Univ 1500 Ralston Ave Belmont CA 94002

MUSOLF, LLOYD DARYL, political science professor, educational association administrator; b. Yale, SD, Oct. 14, 1919; s. William Ferdinand and Emma Marie (Pautz) M.; m. Berdyne Peet, June 30, 1944; children: Stephanie, Michael, Laura. BA, Huron Coll., 1941; MA, U. SD, 1946; PhD, Johns Hopkins U., 1950. Mem. faculty Vassar Coll., Poughkeepsie, NY, 1949-59, assoc. prof. polit. sci., 1955-59; chief of party adv. group Mich. State U., East Lansing, 1959-61; prof. polit. sci., 1961-63, U. Calif.-Davis, 1963-87, prof. emeritus, 1988—, dir. Inst. Govtl. Affairs, 1963-84. Vis. prof. Johns Hopkins U., Balt., 1953, U. Del., 1954, U. Mich., 1955-56; US Nat. rapporteur for Internat. Congress Adminstrv. Scis., Berlin, 1983; cons., lectr. in field. Author: Federal Examiners and the Conflict of Law and Administration, 1953, Public Ownership and Accountability: The Canadian Experience, 1959, Promoting the General Welfare, Government and the Economy, 1965, (with others) American National Government-Policies and Politics, 1971, Mixed Enterprise-A Developmental Perspective, 1972, (with Springer) Malaysia's Parliamentary System-Representative Politics and Policymaking in a Divided Society, 1979, Uncle Sam's Private Profitseeking Corporations-Comsat, Fannie Mae, Amtrak and Conrail, 1983; editor: (with Krislov) The Politics of Regulation, 1964, Communications Satellites in Political Orbit, 1968, (with Kornberg) Legislatures in Developmental Perspective, 1970, (with Joel Smith) Legislatures in Development-Dynamics of Change in New and Old States, 1979; contbr. monographs, chpts. to books, articles to profl. jours. Served to lt. USNR, 1942-45. Johnston scholar Johns Hopkins U., 1946-48; Faculty fellow Vassar Coll., 1954-55; sr. assoc. East-West Ctr., Honolulu, 1968-69; vis. scholar Brookings Instn., Washington, 1980. Mem. ASPA (exec. coun. 1967-70), Nat. Assn. Schs. Pub. Affairs and Adminstrn. (exec. coun. 1972-75), Western Govtl. Rsch. Assn. (exec. bd. 1966-68), Am. Polit. Sci. Assn., Nat. Assn. State Univs. and Land Grant Colls. (rsch. com. divsn. urban affairs 1980-81). Home: 844 Lake Blvd Davis CA 95616-2611 Office: U Calif Dept Polit Sci Davis CA 95616

MUSON, HOWARD HENRY, writer, consultant; b. Mt. Vernon, NY, Mar. 19, 1935; s. Joseph Ernest and Beatrice (Hakmaier) Muson; m. Dorothy Regina Tyor, May 21, 1967; children: Eve, Stephanie, Nickolas, Alice. AB magna cum laude, Harvard U., Cambridge, Mass., 1956; cert., Johns Hopkins Sch. Advanced Internat. Studies, Bologna, Italy, 1956-57; postgrad., U. Calif., Berkeley, 1957-58. Dir. program research CARE Inc., NYC, 1960-62; bur. chief Hartford Courant, Conn., 1962; newsman, columnist AP, Boston, 1963-66; contbg. editor Time mag., NYC, 1966-70; articles editor N.Y. Times mag., NYC, 1970-77; exec. editor Psychology Today mag., NYC, 1977-82; editor Across The Board, NYC, 1983-89; editor, pub. Family Bus. mag., Phila., 1992-2000; rsch. assoc. Lansberg Gersick & Assocs., New Haven, 1998—. Vis. lectr. in residential colls. Yale U., New Haven, 1982-83; instr. in sci. and environ. reporting program NYU, 1992; sr. writer, exec. action reports, Mid-Market Series, The Conf. Bd., 2002-. Author: Triumph of the American Spirit: Johnstown, Pennsylvania, 1989, Managing Growth: Smart Strategies for Smaller and Midsize Companies, 2000, Valuing Experience: How to Motivate and Retain Mature Workers, 2002, The Family Business Growth Handbook, 2002; co-author: Generations of Giving: Leadership and Continuity in Family Foundations, 2004; contbr. articles to profl. jours., popular mags. Dir. Project Concern/No. Westchester Walk for Mankind, Mt. Kisco, NY, 1986-90; media rels. Westchester Walk for Diabetes, 2002-03. Mem. Nat. Assn. Sci. Writers Home Phone: 914-941-1616; Office Phone: 914-941-1881. Personal E-mail: h_muson@yahoo.com.

MUSONERA, ETIENNE, finance educator, consultant; b. Nyanza, Rwanda, Sept. 25, 1961; s. Amiel Munyangeyo and Marita Nyirabakiga; m. Agnes Mukabera Musonera, Sept. 25, 1992; children: Grace, Blyss, Bercy-Dylan. BBA, Davenport U., Kalamazoo, 1990; MSc in Engring. Mgmt., We. Mich. U., Kalamazoo, 1995; PhD in Indsl. Engring. and Internat. Mktg., Wayne State U., Detroit, 2005, MSc in Indsl. Engring., 2005. Rsch. asst. Wayne State U., 1998—2005; asst. prof. mktg. Ea. N.Mex U., Portales, N.Mex., 2006—. Mfg. quality sys. engr. Gen. Motors Co., Warren, Mich., 1999—2002, HRU, Inc., Warren, 1999—2002. Author: (book) A Theoretical Model To Optimize Fdi Inflows: Wcm Best Practices And Spillovers Effect In Value Added Activities; contbr. scientific papers to profl. jours. Mem.: Phi Beta Delta (hon.). Home: 1800 N Ave O Portales NM 88130 Office: Eastern New Mexico Univ 1500 S Ave K Portales NM 88130 Home Phone: 505-356-9102; Office Phone: 505-562-2772. Personal E-mail: musonera@yahoo.com. Business E-Mail: etienne.musonera@enmu.edu.

MUSSA, MICHAEL L., economist, educator; b. LA, Apr. 15, 1944; AB, UCLA, 1966; MA, U. Chgo., 1970, PhD, 1974. Asst. prof. econs. U. Rochester, 1971—75, assoc. prof., 1975—76; assoc. prof. econs. U. Chgo., 1976—80, prof. internat. bus., 1980—91; mem. US Coun. of Econ. Advisers, 1986—88; econ. counselor, dir. Dept. Rsch. IMF, 1991—2001; sr. fellow Inst. Internat. Econs., Washington, 2001—. Rsch. fellow London Sch. Econs., 1975—76, Grad. Sch. Internat. Studies, Geneva, 1976—81; vis. prof. Asian Dept. IMF, 1980; vis. faculty mem. CUNY Grad. Ctr. Author: Argentina and the Fund: From Triumph to Tragedy, 2002; contbr. articles to profl. jours. Office: Inst Internat Econs 1750 Massachusetts Ave, NW Washington DC 20036-1903 Office Phone: 202-328-9000. Office Fax: 202-659-3225. E-mail: mmussa@iie.com.

MUSSANO, THEODORE ANTHONY, retired court services supervisor; b. Paterson, NJ, Dec. 15, 1943; s. Theodore Anthony, Sr. and Theresa Marie Mussano; m. Susan Fay Janusewski, May 24, 1980; 1 child, Theodore Edward. BA cum laude, Seton Hall U., 1965; MA, St. John's U., 1967. Probation officer Passaic County Probation Dept., Paterson, NJ, 1971-77, sr. probation officer, 1977-83; ct. svcs. supr. Superior Ct. NJ, Paterson, 1973—2005. Tchg. fellow, 1965—67, 1967—68, Weaver fellow, 1967. Mem.: Fraternal Order of Police, Probation Assn. NJ (pres. 1977), Soc. Ancient Numismatists, Am. Numis. Assn., Ancient Coin Collectors Guild, KC. Roman Catholic. Avocations: ancient and medieval studies, reading, coin collecting/numismatics, genealogy. Home: 17 Fenner Pl Wayne NJ 07470-2809 Office: Passaic County Probation Divsn 63-65 Hamilton St Paterson NJ 07505 E-mail: tmwardo@optonline.net.

MUSSEHL, ROBERT CLARENCE, lawyer; b. Washington, May 1, 1936; s. Chester Carl and Clara Cecelia (Greenwalt) Mussehl; m. Misook Chung, Mar. 22, 1987; 1 child, Omar;children from previous marriage: Debra Lee(dec.), David Lee. BA, Am. U., 1964, JD, 1966. Bar: Wash. 1967, U.S. Dist. Ct. (we. dist.) Wash. 1967, U.S. Ct. Appeals (9th cir.) 1968, U.S. Supreme Ct. 1971. Sr. ptnr. Thom, Mussehl, Navoni, Hoff, Pierson & Ryder, Seattle, 1967-78, Neubauer & Mussehl, Seattle, 1978-80, Mussehl & Rosenberg, Seattle, 1980—2001, Mussehl & Khan, 2004—06. Spkr. law convs. and other profl. orgns.; chmn. bd. dirs., CEO Seattle Smashers, 1976—80; moot ct. judge Nat. Appellate Adv. Competition, San Francisco, 1987; panel mem. ABA Symposium Compulsory Jurisdiction World Ct., San Francisco, 1987. Contbr. articles to profl. jours. Mem. Wash. Vol. Lawyers Arts, 1976—80; bd. dirs. Wash. State Pub. Interest Law Ctr., 1976—81; founder, past chair Lawyers Helping Hungry Children, bd. dirs., 1991—2007; founder, past chair Wash. State Lawyers Campaign Hunger Relief, 1991—; statewide chair Lawyers for Duming for Gov., 1976; mem. task force single adult and ch. Ch. Coun. Greater Seattle, 1976—78. Recipient Jefferson award for Cmty. and Pub. Svc., State of Wash., Am. Inst. Pub. Svc., 1997. Fellow: Am. Acad. Matrimonial Lawyers, Am. Bar Found. (life); mem.: ABA (ho. dels. 1979—91, mem. assembly resolutions com. 1979—91, chair marriage and family counseling and concilliation com. 1981—83, mem. world order under law standing com. 1983—89, chair 1986—89, chair ad hoc com. assembly 1986—89, mem. blue ribbon com. world ct. 1987—88, mem. spl. adv. com. internat. activities 1989—91, mem. standing com. dispute resolution 1992—93, mem. exec. coun. sect. dispute resolution 1993—95, asst. budget officer 1995—97, budget officer 1997—99, chair 2001—02, sect. liaison commn. racial and ethnic diversity 2002—04, ho. dels. 2003—, commn. racial and ethnic diversity 2004—06, editor Goal IX newsletter 2004—), World Assn. Lawyers World Peace through Law Ctr. (founding mem.), Am. Arbitration Assn. (panel arbitrators), Seattle-King County Bar Assn. (mem. other coms. 1970—, chmn. young lawyers sect. 1971—72, mem. family law sect. 1971—90, sec. 1972—73, trustee), Wash. State Trial Lawyers Assn., Wash. State Bar Assn. (mem. exec. com. family law sect. 1973—75, chmn. internat. law com. 1974—76, sec.-treas., mem. exec. com. world peace through law sect. 1980—, chair 1981—82, mem. editl. bd. Family Law Deskbook 1987—89), UN Assn. USA (bd. dirs. Seattle chpt. 1989—91), Heritage Club YMCA Greater Seattle (charter 1977—). Avocations: squash, bicycling, tennis, weightlifting, painting, religious studies. Office: 520 Pike St Ste 2210 Seattle WA 98101 Home: 2415 34th Ave W Seattle WA 98199 Office Phone: 206-386-7200. Personal E-mail: bobmussehl@earthlink.net.

MUSSELMAN, ERIC, former professional basketball coach; b. Ashland, Ohio, Nov. 19, 1964; s. Bill Musselman; m. Wendy Musselman; children: Michael, Matthew. BS, U. San Diego, 1987. Draft pick Continental Basketball Assn. Albany Patroons, 1987; asst. dir. scouting LA Clippers, 1987—90; asst. coach Minn. Timberwolves, 1990—91, Orlando Magic, 1998—2000, Atlanta Hawks, 2000—02, Memphis Grizzlies, 2004—06; gen. mgr. Continental Basketball Assn. Fla. Beach Dogs, 1990—98, head coach, 1991—98, US Basketball League Fla. Sharks, 1995—96, Golden State Warriors, Oakland, Calif., 2002—04, Sacramento Kings, 2006—07. Head coach Continental Basketball Assn. All-Star Game, 1990, 92, 93, 94, 97. *

MUSSELMAN, LARRY L., chemical engineer; b. Erie, Pa., Aug. 16, 1947; s. Lloyd H. and Lyda Musselman; m. Susan E., Nov. 25, 1966; children: Cheri A., Jason L., Lucy A., Gavin A., Lauren A. BSChemE magna cum laude, Akron U., 1971, MS in Engring., 1972. Rsch. engr. Timken Co., 1971-77; sr. rsch. engr. Alcoa Co., Alcoa Center, Pa., 1977-79, sr. scientist, 1979-81, staff engr., 1981-83, tech. svc. mgr., 1983-86, tech. mgr., 1986-89; dir. tech. and ops. Polymer Additives Group, Apollo, Pa., 1989-93, v.p. tech. and ops. polymer additives group, 1993—. Mem. tech. adv. com. Ohio Legislature. Author: Handbooks of Science and Technology of Alumna Chemicals, Plastics Additives; contbr. over 50 articles on polymers and fire retardants to profl. jours.; numerous patents in field. Akron U. scholar. Mem. ASME (sect. dir.), ASTM (fire testing coms.), Am. Soc. Lubrication Engrs., Soc. Plastics Engrs., Fire Retardant Chems. Assn., Soc. Plastics Industry Coms., Sigma Xi, Sigma Tau, Alpha Chi Sigma. Office: Polymer Additives Group 321 Markle Rd Apollo PA 15613-8703 Office Phone: 724-335-1120.

MUSSELMAN, P. WESTON, lawyer; BS in Mech. Engring. with high distinction, U. Va., 1981, JD, 1987. Bar: Tex. 1987, NC 1991, US Ct. Appeals (5th and fed. cirs.), US Dist. Ct. (no. dist. Tex.), US Patent and Trademark Office. Prin. Fish & Richardson, P.C., Dallas. Named a Tex. Super Lawyer, Tex. Monthly Mag., 2003—06; named one of Best Lawyers in Dallas, D Mag., 2005. Mem.: Am. Intellectual Property Law Assn., Dallas Bar Assn., Tex. Bar Assn., ABA. Office: Fish & Richardson PC 5000 Bank One Ctr 1717 Main St Dallas TX 75201 Office Phone: 214-292-4030. Office Fax: 214-747-2091. E-mail: musselman@fr.com. *

MUSSELMAN, RANDALL L., electrical engineer, educator; b. Peoria, Ill., July 27, 1958; s. Dale and Nancy Musselman; m. Kimberly Musselman; children: Alexandra, Amber. BSEE, So. Ill. U., Carbondale, 1983; MSEE, U. Colo., Colorado Springs, 1990, PhD in Elec. Engring., 1997. Cert. profl. engr., Colo., 1987; EMT Colo., 2000. Design engr. Tex. Instruments, Colorado Springs, 1983—84, 1987—90, Honeywell, 1984—87; pres. Outland Comm., 1990—92; instr. Ill. Ctrl. Coll., East Peoria, 1992—94; graduate asst. U. Colo., 1994—97; prof. elec. engring. USAF Acad., Colorado Springs, 1997—, rsch. dir. elec. engring., 1997—. Adj. faculty U. Colo., Colorado Springs; cons. RF Antenna Comm.; com. mem. Nat. Sci. Found. Contbr. 35 articles to profl. jours.; presenter to profl. socs. Vol. EMT El Paso County Search and Rescue, Colorado Springs, 1997—2006; vol. wildland firefighter El Paso County Sheriff Wildland Fire Crew. Graduate fellowship, U. Colo., 1997. Mem.: IEEE (sr.), Men's Christian Fellowship (leader), Eta Kappa Nu, Tau Beta Pi. Achievements include recognized for accomplishments in field of electro-magnetics research. Avocations: mountain climbing, rock climbing, hunting, drums. Home: 581 Tamarron Dr Colorado Springs CO 80919 Office: USAF Acad 2354 Fairchild Dr U S A F Academy CO 80840 Home Phone: 719-264-7804; Office Phone: 719-333-4211. Personal E-mail: randy@ieee.org. Business E-Mail: randall.musselman@usafa.af.mil.

MUSSENDEN, GEORG ANTONIO, electronics engineer; b. San Juan, Aug. 25, 1959; s. Gustavo Adolfo and Christa-Maria (Gotsch) M. Student, U. P.R.-Rio Piedras, 1977-79; BS in E.E. with honors, U. Fla., Gainesville, 1982; postgrad. in elec. engring., U. Fla. Electronics technician Radiotelephone Communicators of P.R. (Motorola), 1976; computer sys. programmer and operator U. P.R., Rio Piedras, 1978-79, rsch. asst. dept. physics, 1978-79; computer programmer Regional Electrocardiogram Analysis Ctr. J. Hillis Miller Health Ctr., U. Fla., Gainesville, 1981; pre-profl. engr. IBM Corp. Devel. Lab., Endicott, N.Y., 1981; sr. assoc. engr./scientist entry sys. tech. SPD, CPD and ESD design and devel. labs., Boca Raton, Fla., 1982-93; elec. hardware devel. engr. sci. Core Internat. Rsch. and Devel. Corp., Boca Raton, 1993—. Contbr. articles to profl. jours. Scholar San Jose Alumni, 1973-77, Fonalledas Found., 1977-79, Procter and Gamble, 1980; U.F. Sr. Honors scholar, 1980; scholar Nat. Fund Minority Engring., 1980, Du Pont, 1981; Nat. Consortium for Grad. Degrees for Minorities in Engring. fellow, 1981. Mem. IEEE, SMPTE, AES, N.Y. Acad. Scis., Audio-Visual Club, Amateur Radio Club, Golden Key, Eta Kappa Nu, Tau Beta Pi, Phi Kappa Phi. Roman Catholic. Achievements include 12 technological invention disclosures. Home: 3815 NW 4th Ave Boca Raton FL 33431 Office Phone: 954-723-3461. E-mail: gmussen@bellsouth.net.

MUSSINA, MICHAEL COLE, professional baseball player; b. Williamsport, Pa., Dec. 8, 1968; BA Econs., Stanford U., 1990. Pitcher Balt. Orioles, 1990-2000, N.Y. Yankees, 2001—. Player Am. League All-Star Team, 1992-94. Named Internat. League Most Valuable Pitcher, 1991, recipient 5 Am. League Gold Gloves, 5-time Am. League All-Star. Office: The New York Yankees Yankee Stadium 161st Street and River Avenue Bronx NY 10451 E-mail: csmd12000@aol.com.

MUSSMAN, WILLIAM EDWARD, III, lawyer; b. San Francisco, Jan. 31, 1951; s. William Edward and Janet Jonn (Skittone) M.; m. Carol Lynne Johnson, Jan. 9, 1988; children: Katherine Ann, Laura Lynne, Elizabeth Ashley. BS cum laude, Stanford U., 1973; JD, U. Calif.-San Francisco, 1976. Bar: Calif. 1976, US Dist. Ct. (cen. dist.) Calif. 1982, US Dist. Ct. (ea. dist.) Calif. 1998, US Dist. Ct. (no. dist.) Calif. 1976, US Ct. Appeals (9th cir.) 1987, US Supreme Ct. 1985. Assoc. Lasky, Haas, Cohler & Munter, San Francisco, 1980-82, Pillsbury, Madison & Sutro, San Francisco, 1982-84, Carr & Mussman, San Francisco, 1984-91, ptnr., 1991-95, Carr, Mussman & Harvey, LLP, San Francisco, 1996-99, Mussman & Mussman, LLP, Modesto, Calif., 2000—. Contbr. articles to profl. jours. Vol., rep., Ch. Jesus Christ Latter Day Sts., Tokyo, 1977-78. Mem.: Stanislaus County Bar Assn. (alternative dispute resolution com. Stanislaus

County Superior Ct. 2005—), Calif. State Bar Assn. (litig. sect., bus. law sect.), Stanford Alumni Assn. (life), Tau Beta Phi. Office: Mussman & Mussman LLP 1101 Sylvan Ave Ste B-4 Modesto CA 95350-1687 Office Phone: 209-577-8890. Business E-Mail: wmussman3@mussmanlaw.com.

MUSTACCHI, PIERO, preventive medicine physician, educator; b. Cairo, May 29, 1920; came to U.S., 1947; naturalized, 1962; s. Gino and Gilda (Rieti) M.; m. Dora Lisa Ancona, Sept. 26, 1948; children: Roberto, Michael. BS in Humanities, U. Florence, Italy, 1938; postgrad. in anatomy, U. Lausanne, Switzerland, 1938-39; MB, ChB, Fouad I U., Cairo, Egypt, 1944, grad. in Arabic lang. and lit., 1946; D Medicine and Surgery, U. Pisa, 1986; Degree (hon.), U. Aix-Marseille, France, 1988, U. Alexandria, Egypt, 1985. Qualified med. examiner, Calif. Indsl. Accident Commn., 1994. House officer English Hosp., Ch. Missionary Soc., Cairo, 1945-47; clin. affiliate U. Calif., San Francisco, 1947-48; intern Franklin Hosp., San Francisco, 1948-49; resident in pathology U. Calif., San Francisco, 1949-51; resident in medicine Meml. Ctr. Cancer and Allied Diseases, NYC, 1951-53; rsch. epidemiologist Dept. HEW, Nat. Cancer Inst., Bethesda, Md., 1955-57; cons. allergy clinic U. Calif., San Francisco, 1957-70, clin. prof. medicine and preventive medicine, 1970-90, clin. prof. medicine and epidemiology, 1990-96, head occupl. epidemiology, 1975-90, head divsn. internat. health edn. dept. epidemiology and internat. health, 1985-90; médecin agréé, official physician Consulate Gen. of France, San Fransisco, 1995—; sr. cons. internat. health care U. Calif., San Francisco. Med. cons., vis. prof. numerous ednl. & profl. instns., U. Marseilles, 1981—82, U. Pisa, Italy, 1983, U. Gabon, 1984, U. Siena, Italy, 1985; cons U. Calif., 1975—, sr. cons. internat. med. care, 2000—. Contbr. chpts. to books, articles to profl. jours. Editorial bd. Medecine d'Afrique Noire, Ospedali d'Italia. With USPHS USN, 1955—57. Decorated comdr. Order of Merit (Italy), officer Ordre de la Legion d'Honneur (France), Medal of St. John of Jerusalem, Sovereign Order of Malta, Order of the Republic (Egypt); Scroll, Leonardo da Vinci Soc., San Francisco, 1965; award Internat. Inst. Oakland, 1964; Hon. Vice Consul. Italy, 1971-90. Fellow ACP, Am. Soc. Environ. and Occupational Health; mem. AAAS, Am. Assn. Cancer Rsch., Calif. Soc. Allergy and Immunology, Calif. Med. Assn., San Francisco Med. Soc., West Coast Allergy Soc. (founding), Mex. Congress on Hypertension (corr.), Internat. Assn. Med. Rsch. and Continuing Edn. (U.S. rep.), Acad. Italiana della Cucina. Democrat. Avocations: music, math, languages. also: 3838 California St San Francisco CA 94118-1522 Office Phone: 415-668-2626.

MUSTAIN, DOUGLAS DEE, lawyer; b. Shreveport, La., Nov. 2, 1945; s. Reginald K. and Dorothy J. (Green) M.; m. Sharon L. Tegarden, Aug. 19, 1967; children: Kristi Kaye, Kari Dee, Kenton Douglas, Kyle Robert, Kirk Stephen, Kali Elizabeth. Student Knox Coll., 1963-64, Murray State U., 1964-66; BS, U. Ill., 1971; JD, U. Iowa, 1974. Bar: Iowa 1974, Ill. 1974; U.S. Dist. Ct. (cen. dist.) Ill. 1974, U.S. Ct. Appeals (7th cir.) 1980, U.S. Supreme Ct. 1986. Law clk. Shulman, Phelan, Tucker, Boyle & Mullin, Iowa City, 1972-74; assoc. Stuart, Neagle & West, Galesburg, Ill., 1974-76; ptnr. West, Neagle & Williamson, Galesburg, 1977-89, Mustain & Lindstrom, Galesburg, 1989—; instr. real estate law Carl Sandburg Coll., Galesburg, 1977-81. Chmn. Citizens Referendum Com., Galesburg, 1983, 1987-88; bd. dirs. YMCA, Galesburg, 1983-88, Cottage Hosp. Care Corp., Galesburg, 1984-90; trustee 1st Presbyn. Ch., Galesburg, 1984; commr. Galesburg Pub. Transp. Commn., 1985—; pres., founder Galesburg Pub. Sch. Found., 1987—. Served to SP5 U.S. Army, 1966-69, Vietnam. Decorated Army Commendation with oak leaf cluster. Mem. Knox County Bar Assn. (pres. 1980-82), ABA (comml. litigation com. 1981—), Assn. Trial Lawyers Am., Ill. Trial Lawyers Assn. Republican. Home: 1234 N Prairie St Galesburg IL 61401-1852 Office: Mustain Lindstrom & Henson 1865 N Henderson St Ste 11B Galesburg IL 61401-1377

MUSTAPHA, AZLIN, food scientist, educator; b. Johor Baru, Malaysia; PhD, U. Nebr., Lincoln, 1993. Rschr. U. Minn., St. Paul, 1994—96; asst. prof. U. Mo., Columbia, 1996—2003, assoc. prof., 2003—. Mem.: Internat. Assn. Food Protection, Am. Soc. Microbiology, Inst. Food Technologists. Office: U Mo Food Sci Program 256 WCS Wing Eckles Hall Columbia MO 65211 Office Phone: 573-882-2649.

MUSTARD, LEWIS WILLIAMS, management consultant, educator; b. Durham, NC, Sept. 4, 1942; s. Harry S. and Elizabeth (Williams) M.; divorced; children: Juliana Janice, Lewis Williams Jr. AB in English, U. NC, Chapel Hill, 1966; cert. in hosp. adminstrn., Duke U., 1970; LLB, La Salle U., Chgo., 1974; D Bus. Adminstrn., Western Coll. U., 1976; PhD in Health Adminstrn., Union Grad. Sch., Cin., 1992; MA in Humanities, Calif. State U., Dominguez Hills, 1995. Hosp. adminstr. Woodruff (S.C.) Hosp., 1968-70; exec. dir. AID, Inc., Bryn Mawr, Pa., 1970-73; sr. hosp. cons. Summerour & Assocs., Atlanta, 1975-76; regional v.p. Qualicare, Inc., New Orleans, 1976-78; regional adminstr., v.p. Triage Corp., Clearwater, Fla., 1978-80; pres. Healthcare Mgmt. Cons., Atlanta, 1980-88; CEO Healthcare Negligence Control, Inc., Chapel Hill, NC, 1993—. Legal cons., sole practitioner, 1992-; adj. prof. Ctrl. Mich. U., Mt. Pleasant, 1993-, So. Ill. U., Carbondale, 1993-, Webster U., St. Louis, 1994-, MBA program, NY Inst. Tech., 2004-, Bellevue U., Nebr., 2005-, Strayer U., 2005-, MPH program, A.T. Still U.; assoc. prof. North Ctrl. U., Prescott, Ariz., 2004-; adj. charter Oak State Coll., 2002-, New Britain, Conn., 2003-. Served with USNR Res., 1959-68. Episcopalian. Office Phone: 919-302-8865.

MUSTARD, MARY CAROLYN, financial executive; b. North Bend, Nebr., Sept. 21, 1948; d. Joseph Louis and Rosalie Margaret (Emanuel) Smaus; m. Ronald L. Mustard, Apr. 19, 1969 (div. 1988); children: Joel Jonathan, Dana Marie. Student, Creighton U., 1966—67, C.E. Sch. Commerce, 1967—68, Coll. of St. Mary, 1983—84, Met. C.C., Omaha, 1988—90, Bellevue U., 1991—92. With Platte County Dept. Pub. Welfare, Columbus, Nebr., 1968-69; sec. to plant mgr. B.L. Montague Steel Co., Sumter, SC, 1969-70; property disposal technician Property Disposal Office, Shaw AFB, SC, 1970-71; libr. technician Hdqs. Strategic Air Command Libr., Offutt AFB, Nebr., 1971-76; sec.-steno Hdqs. Strategic Air Command Comm./Frequency Mgmt., Offutt AFB, 1976-79; security specialist/program analyst Hdqs. Strategic Air Command Security Police, Offutt AFB, 1979-88; budget analyst Hdqs. Strategic Air Command Fin. Mgmt., Offutt AFB, 1988-92; funds control analyst Hdqs. Air Mobility Command, Scott AFB, Ill., 1992-93, chief hdqs. and comm. account, 1993-94, chief hdqs. relocation, transition assistance/comm. programs, 1994-95; chief base realignment and closure program Air Mobility Command, Scott AFB, 1995-96; sys. adminstr. Def. Fin. and Acctg. Svc., Kansas City, Mo., 1996-2000, fin. sys. mgmt., 2000—02, fin. ops. analyst, bus. mgmt. office, 2002—. Mem. Am. Soc. Mil. Comptrs. (SAC Budget Analyst of Yr. 1990). Democrat. Roman Catholic. Avocations: walking, reading, biking. Home: 7137 Aminda Dr Shawnee KS 66227-2117 Office: DFAS KC JBB 1500 E Bannister Rd Kansas City MO 64197-0001

MUSTION, ALAN LEE, pharmacist; b. Oklahoma City, Feb. 6, 1947; s. Granville E. and Iris E. (Graham) Mustion; m. Mary Jane Bozek, Dec. 4, 1982; children from previous marriage: Jeffrey Alan, Jennifer Chere. BS in Pharmacy, Southwestern Okla. State U., 1970. Staff pharmacist VA Med. Ctr., Oklahoma City, 1970—74, dir. pharmacy Richmond, Va., 1976—77, Iowa City, 1977—90; dir. pharmacy svcs. VA Hosp., Houston, 1990—2002; pharmacy mgr. Integris Bapt. Med. Ctr., Oklahoma City, 2002—. Clin. instr. clin./hosp. divsn. U. Iowa, 1977—90; adj. asst. prof. pharmacy practice U. Houston, 1990—2002. Contbr. articles to profl. jours. Served to lt. col. USAR. Grantee Rsch., Travenol Labs., 1980—87, VA HSR&D, 1984, 1988. Mem.: Okla. Soc. Health Sys. Pharmacists, Am. Soc. Health Sys. Pharmacists, Kappa Psi. Methodist. Office: 3300 NW Expressway Oklahoma City OK 73112 Home: 513 Winding Creek Rd Yukon OK 73099-4471 E-mail: alan.mustion@integris-health.com.

MUSTO, DAVID FRANKLIN, medical researcher, educator, historian, consultant; b. Tacoma, Jan. 8, 1936; s. Charles Hiram and Hilda Marie (Hanson) Mustoe; m. Emma Jean Baudendistel, June 2, 1961; children: Jeanne Marie, David Kyle, John Baird, Christopher Edward. BA, U. Wash., 1956, MD, 1963; MA, Yale U., 1961. Lic. physician, Conn., Pa. Clerk Nat. Hosp. for Nervous Disease, London, 1961; intern Pa. Hosp., Phila., 1963-64; resident Yale U. Med. Ctr., New Haven, 1964-67; spl. asst. to dir. NIMH, Bethesda, Md., 1967-69; vis. asst. prof. Johns Hopkins U., 1968-69; asst. prof. Yale U., 1969-73, assoc. prof., 1973-78, sr. rsch. scientist, 1978-81, prof., 1981—, exec. fellow Davenport Coll., 1983-88; mem. adv. editorial com. Yale Edits. Private Papers James Boswell, 1975—; cons. Exec. Office of Pres., 1973-75; mem. White House Strategy Coun., 1978-81; mem. panel on alcohol policy NAS, Washington, 1978-82; cons. White House Conf. on Families, 1979-80. Vis. fellow Clare Coll., Cambridge U., 1994; mem. alcohol adv. com. Nat. Assn. Broadcasters, 1994—; DuMez lectr. U. Md.; Walter Reed meml. lectr. Richmond Acad. Medicine; Galdston lectr. N.Y. Acad. Medicine; Sirridge lectr. U. Mo. Med. Sch.; Clendening lectr. U. Kans. Med. Sch. Author: The American Disease: Origins of Narcotic Control, 1973, expanded edit., 1987, 3rd edit., 1999; co-author: (with P. Korsmeyer) The Quest for Drug Control: Politics and Federal Policy in a Period of Increasing Drug Use, 1963-1981, 2002; editor: One Hundred Years of Heroin, 2002, Drugs in America: A Documentary History, 2002. Historian Pres.'s Commn. on Mental Health, 1977-78; adv. U.S. Del. to UN Commn. Narcotic Drugs, Geneva, 1978-79; mem. nat. coun. Smithsonian Instn., Washington, 1981-90, hon. mem., 1991—; hist. cons. Presdl. Commn. Human Immuno-deficiency Virus Epidemic, 1988; mem. nat. adv. com. on anti-drug program Robert Wood Johnson Found., 1989-2002; mem. nat. adv. com. on internat. narcotic policy UN Assn. of U.S.A., 1991; mem. adv. com. causes drug abuse Office Tech. Assessment, Congress U.S., 1992-94; commr. Conn. Alcohol and Drug Abuse Commn., 1992-93; bd. dirs. Coll. on Problems of Drug Dependence, 1990-94; trustee Assocs. of Cushing-Whitney Med. Libr., 1994—. With USPHS, 1967-69. Fellow: Coll. Problems of Drug Dependence, Am. Psychiat. Assn. (disting.); mem.: Soc. of Cin. in the State of Conn. (pres. 1998—2001), English-Speaking Union (pres. New Haven br. 1995—98), Am. Assn. History of Medicine (William Osler medal 1961), Am. Hist. Assn., Am. Inst. History of Pharmacy (Kraemers award 1974), New Haven County Med. Assn. (chmn. bicentennial com. 1983), Century Assn., Athenaeum Club (London), Cosmos Club. Office: Yale U PO Box 207900 New Haven CT 06520-7900 Office Phone: 203-785-4258. E-mail: david.musto@yale.edu.

MUSTO, JOSEPH JOHN, lawyer; b. Pittston, Pa., Nov. 22, 1943; s. James and Rose Musto; m. Fortunata Guidice, July 5, 1969; children: Laura, Joseph Robert. BA, King's Coll., Wilkes-Barre, Pa., 1965; JD, Dickinson Sch. Law, 1968. Bar: Pa. 1968, U.S. Ct. Appeals (3d cir.) 1968, U.S. Dist. Ct. (mid. dist.) Pa. 1971. Asst. dist. atty. City of Phila., 1968-69; assoc. Bedford, Waller, Griffith, Darling & Mitchell, Wilkes-Barre, 1969-73; ptnr. Griffith, Darling, Mitchell, Aponick & Musto, Wilkes-Barre, 1973-75; prin. Griffith, Aponick & Musto, Wilkes-Barre, 1975-90; ptnr. Rosenn, Jenkins & Greenwald, Wilkes-Barre, 1990-93; judge Ct. Common Pleas Luzerne County, 1993—94; mem. Hourigan, Kluger, Spohrer & Quinn, Wilkes-Barre, 1994—97; prin. Musto & Saunders, PC, Plymouth, Pa., 1997—. Solicitor Yatesville (Pa.) Borough, 1973—80, Pittston Area Sch. Dist., 1973—93, Duryea (Pa.) Borough, 1975—80. Mem. Luzerne County Gov. Study Com., Wilkes-Barre, 1973—74; mem., chmn. No. Luzerne Health Adv. Coun., Wilkes-Barre, 1976—80; pres., mem. Health Sys. Agy. N.E. Pa., Avoca, 1980—86; mem. civil justice reform act adv. com. Fed. Dist. Ct. Pa., 1991—95. Mem.: Wilkes-Barre Law and Libr. Assn., Pa. Bar Assn., Fed. Bar Assn. (past pres. Ctrl. Pa. chpt.). Democrat. Roman Catholic. Office: 117 W Main St Plymouth PA 18651-2926 Office Phone: 570-719-0884. Personal E-mail: jmusto@fhas.com.

MUSTOE, THOMAS ANTHONY, physician, plastic surgeon; b. Columbia, Mo., June 29, 1951; s. Robert Moore and Carolyn (Swett) M.; m. Kathryn Claire Stallcup, Aug. 13, 1977; children: Anthony, Lisa. BA cum laude in biology, Harvard Coll., 1973, MD cum laude, 1978. Diplomate Am. Bd. Otolaryngology, Am. Bd. Plastic Surgery; licensed Miss. 1985, Ill. 1991. Rsch. assoc. dept. microbiology Harvard Med. Sch., Cambridge, Mass., 1976-77; intern in medicine Mass. Gen. Hosp., Boston, 1978-79; resident in surgery Peter Bent Brigham Hosp., Boston, 1979-80; resident in otolaryngology Mass. Eye and Ear Infirmary, Boston, 1980-82, chief resident, 1982-83; resident in plastic surgery Brigham and Women;s Hosp., Children's Hosp., Boston, 1983-84, chief resident, 1984-85; asst. prof. in surgery Wash. U. Sch. Medicine, St. Louis, 1985-89, assoc. prof., 1989-91; prof., chief divsn. plastic surgery Northwestern U. Med. Sch., Chgo., 1991—; plastic surgeon Northwestern Meml. Hosp., 1991—, Evanston Hosp., 1991—, Children's Meml. Hosp., 1992—, Shriner's Hosp. Chgo., 1994—. Co-chmn. Gorden Rsch. Conf., 1995; spl. cons. FDA, 1994—98; mem. sci. adv. panel Biologies, 1997, NCI, 1998; lectr. seminars, 2001. Editl. bd. Archives of Surgery, 1992-2004, Plastic and Reconstructive Surgery, 1993-2001, Wound Repair and Regeneration, 1992—, Jour. Surg. Rsch., 1997-2006; contbr. articles to profl. jours., more than 200 publs., book chpts.; book reviewer. Harvard Nat. scholar, 1969-73; Rhodes scholar candidate, Harvard Coll., 1973. Fellow: ACS (adv. coun. plastic surgery 1999—2002, surg. forum com. 1999—2002, editl. bd. jour. 2003—, surg. biology club III); mem.: AMA, Am. Soc. Plastic Surgery (sci. program chair 2005—), Am. Bd. Plastic Surgery, Coun. Plastic Surger Org., Double Boarded Soc. (pres. 1995—98), Chgo. Surg. Soc., Chgo. Plastic Surg. Soc. (sec. 1996—97), Wound Healing Soc. (program com. 1990, audit com. 1992, program com. 1992, bd. dir. 1993—96, program com. 1994, fin. com. 1994—96, program com. 1997, pres. 1997—99), Assn. Acad. Chmn. Plastic Surgery (matching program and ctrl. application svc. com. 1994), Soc. U. Surgeons, Soc. Head and Neck Surgeons (membership com. 1993—95), Plastic Surgery Rsch. Coun. (rep. coun. acad. surgeons 1991—94, com. indsl. rels. 1992, program com. 1992—94, 1995, Judge Snyder & Crikelair awards 1991), Midwest Assn. Plastic Surgeons, Lipoplasty Soc. N.Am. (lipoplasty ednl. rsch. found. 1998—2000), Am. Assn. Plastic Surgery (rsch. and edn. com. 1994—96, chmn. 1996, mem. com. 1998—, co-chmn.ASPRS-ASAPS task force on emerging trends 1999—2000, chmn. instl. coun. com. 1999—), Am. Soc. Plastic and Reconstructive Surgery (rsch. fund proposal com. 1987—92, plastic surgery device com. 1989—93, resource book for plastic surgery residents com. 1991—93, socioecon. 1992—94, sci. program com. 1993—95, chmn. device and tecyhnique assessment com. 1994—96, co-chmn. gen. reconstruction subcom. 1995, ultrasonic lipectomy task force 1995—96, task force for outcomes and guidelines 1995—98, devices and tech. com. 1995—98, chmn. instrnl. com. 1999—2002, chmn. edn. com. 1999—, chmn. resource book com.), Aesculapian Club, Sigma Xi. Avocations: reading, golf, gardening, sports. Home: 144 Greenwood St Evanston IL 60201-4712

MUTALE, CHRISTIAN THALES, research scientist; s. Seraphin Mutale; m. Denise Chargois; 1 child, Christian Thales Jr. MSc in Engring., U. Lubumbashi, D.R. Congo, 1992; PhD, Tech. U. Clausthal, Germany, 2000. Doctor of Engineering, Tech. U. Clausthal, 2000. Jr. lectr. Universite de Lubumbashi, D.R. Congo, 1993—94; rsch. engr. Gecamines, Likasi, D.R. Congo, 1994—95; rsch. scientist Tech. U. Clausthal, Calusthal-Zellerfeld, Niedersachsen, Germany, 1996—2001; post doctoral fellow U. Pretoria, Pretoria, Gauteng, South Africa, 2001—03; rsch. assoc. CISR - MSE - Carnegie Mellon, Pitts., 2003—05; sr. scientist Alcoa Tech., Alcoa Tech. Ctr., Pa., 2005—. Mem.: Assn. Iron and Steel Tech., Electrochem. Soc., German Soc. Mining, Metallurgy, Resource and Environ. Tech., South African Inst. Mining and Metallurgy, Assn. Iron and Steel Tech., Sigma Xi. Achievements include research in research and publications in extractive ferrous & non-ferrous metallurgy, materials science and recycling of metals and alloys. Home: 40 Colony Sq Apt E Pittsburgh PA 15239-2759

MUTALIPASSI, LOUIS RICHARD, psychologist, educator; b. Kansas City, Kans., Jan. 23, 1937; s. Louie R. Mutalipassi and Cleda E. (Miller) Wolverton; m. Edalee Kenworthy, July 14, 1962 (div. 1970); 1 child, Annemarie; m. Laura Ruth Posner, July 17, 1976; 2 children: Michael and Anthony. BA in Psychology, U. Calif., Santa Barbara, 1962; MA in Psychology, UCLA, 1965, PhD in Psychology, 1969. Lic. psychologist, Calif. Staff psychologist VA Med. Ctr., LA, 1969—76, chief psychology svc. Albany, NY, 1976—80; clin. assoc. prof. psychology UCLA and U. So. Calif., LA, 1980—; chief psychology svc. VA Med. Ctr., Long Beach, 1980—97; ret., 1997; clin. psychologist in pvt. practice Cypress, Calif., 1982—. Oral commr. State Bd. Med. Examiners, Calif., 1996—. Contbr. articles to profl. jour.; presenter in field. With USAF, 1954-58. With USAF, 1954—58. Mem.: APA. Avocations: golf, photography. Office Phone: 714-507-8099. Personal E-mail: loum@roadrunner.com.

MUTH, ERIC PETER, optician, consultant; b. Munich, July 25, 1940; came to US, 1948, naturalized 1955; s. Erich Walter and Anna Lisa (Pentenrieder) M.; m. Rachel Hubbard, Apr. 4, 1971; children: Karl George, Ellen Anna. BS, Charter Oak Coll., 1978; degree (hon.), Anoka-Hennipen Tech. Coll., 1995. Sr. rsch. fellow Internat. Soc. for Philosophical Inquiry, 1991—96, pers. cons., 1996; cons. Nat. Acad. Opthamology Found. Mus., San Francisco, 1982—88, Nat. Mus. Hist. Smithsonian Inst., 1983—94, Gesell Inst. Human Devel., 1984—89; mem. adv. com. South. Cen. Cmty. Coll., Seattle, 1984—89; mem. adv. bd. internat. Scientific Inst., PR, 1989; adv. bd. Middlesex C.C. (vice chmn.)., 1989; vol. VA, West Haven, Conn., 2001—. Mem. editl. bd. Dispensing Opticians, Butterworths Heinmann, 1998, co-author 2nd edit., 1998; contbr. the Social History of Eyeglasses in Japan, 1991, die Brille, Leipzig, 1989, Thinking on the Edge Agamennon, 1993; contbr. over 250 articles to profl. jours.; contbg. editor Optical Mgmt., 1979-80, OpticScan Canada, 1981-82, Indian Optician, 1982, Prism Mag., Can., 1988, 92; tech. editor Optical Index, 1980-82; book reviewer in field. Presdl. appointment US Selective Svc. Sys., 1991-92; scoutmaster Boy Scouts Am., 1960-62; bd. dirs. ARC Conn. chpt., 1988; advisor Tri Hi-Y YMCA, 1964; founder, chmn. Korea-Vietnam Meml. com., Milford, 1985-86; organizer WWII Monument Com. 1991; trustee Conn. Visual Health Ctr., 1982-84; commr. Nat. Commn. on Opticianry Edn., 1989-93; life mem. Soc. 3d. US Inf. Div., 1987; hon. Capt. 25th Bn. Royal Fusiliers, 1999; trooper Ct. State Militia, 2d co. gov.'s horse guard, 2002-04. Served with US Army, 1957-59, Selected Reserves, 1965-69; Conn. Army N.G., 1960-64. Decorated Roman Cath. Knight Malta, Equestrian Knight of The Order of the Holy Sepulchre, Knight Comdr., Army Commendation medal; recipient Eng. Nelson/Wingate prize, 1983, Service Above Self award, Rotary, 1986, Optician of the Yr., Guild of Prescription Opticians Am., 1993, Senate Citation, State of Conn., 1993, German-Am. Friendship award, Germany, 1995, State of Conn. Justice of the Peace, 1995, cert. of appreciation, Nat. Libr. Medicine, Bethesda, Md., 1995, Med. Scis. Divsn. Nat. Mus. History, 1995, Mayoral Proclamation, Milford, Conn., 1998, Bronze medal of merit, Austrian Albert Schweitzer Soc., 1998, Chemical Corps Regimental Assn. Order of the Dragon, 1999, Oeuvre Humanitaire Croix d'Honneur, 1999, medal of merit, El Salvador Red Cross, 1999, Award of Merit, Army and Navy Union of USA, 2000, Vol. award, VA, 2003. Fellow: Conn. Opticians Assn. (pres. 1974, amb., chmn. membership and ethics coms., Optician of Yr. 1975), Opticians Assn. Am. (historian citation 1993, advancing opticianry award 1994, diploma in refractometry 1995, disting. svc. award 2000, honored fellow), Nat. Acad. Opticianry (regional membership chmn., faculty speakers bur., citation 1988), Internat. Acad. Opticianry; mem.: Nat. Contact Lens Examiners (cert.), Guild Prescription Opticians Am. (councilor 2001—02), Royal Lifesaving Soc. Can. (hon. assoc. 1998), Soc. Am. Mil. Engrs., Calif. Soc. Dispensing Opticians (hon.), Ari. Soc. Dispensing Opticians (hon.), Am. Bd. of Opticianry (master of ophthalmic optics 1972), Internat. Platform Assn., Contact Lens Soc. Am., Contact Lens Soc. Conn., Internat. Found. in Ophthalmics Optics, Conn. Guild Dispensing Opticians (pres. 1980, Optician of Yr. 1981), Charter Oak Coll. Alumni Assn. (bd. dirs. 1987, alumni citation 1995), Milford C. of C. (chmn. law and safety com. 1975, Cmty. Svc. award 1986), Disabled Am. Vets. (life; chpt. svc. officer, judge advocate, DAV-NSF commendation 2004), Am. Legion Post 196 (life; parade marshal 1998, citation 1986). Avocations: skydiving, parasailing, ballooning, motorcycling, Tae Kwon Do. Home: 25 Parkland Pl Milford CT 06460-7723 Personal E-mail: eepmuth@nyc.com.

MUTH, RICHARD FERRIS, economics professor; b. Chgo., May 14, 1927; s. Merlin Arthur and Margaret Ferris Muth; m. Helene Louise Martin, Dec. 23, 1955; children: Lisa Helene, Laurianne Martin Love. Student, USCG Acad., 1945-47; AB, Washington U., St. Louis, 1949, MA, 1950; PhD, U. Chgo., 1958; M of Theol. Studies, Emory U., 1995. Lectr. polit. economy Johns Hopkins U., Balt., 1955-56; economist Resources for Future, Washington, 1956-58; assoc. prof. urban econs. U. Chgo., 1959-64; economist Inst. Def. Analyses, Arlington, Va., 1964-66, cons., 1966-69; prof. econs. Washington U., St. Louis, 1966-70, Stanford U., Calif., 1970-83; Callaway prof. econs. Emory U., Atlanta, 1983—2001, chmn. dept., 1983-90, prof. emeritus, 2001—. Vis. assoc. prof. econs. Vanderbilt U., 1958—59; vis. sr. fellow Urban Inst., Washington, 1976—77; vis. prof. Sch. Bus. U. Calif., Berkeley, 1991. Author (with others): Regions, Resources and Economic Growth, 1960, Cities and Housing, 1969, Public Housing, 1974, Urban Economic Problems, 1975; co-author (with Allen C. Goodman): The Economics of Housing Markets, 1989. Mem. Presdl. Task Force on Urban Renewal, 1969, Presdl. Task Forces on Urban Affairs and Housing, 1980—81, Presdl. Commn. on Housing, 1981—82. With USCG, 1951—52. Libertarian. Methodist. Office: Emory U Dept Econs Atlanta GA 30322-2240 Business E-Mail: rmuth@emory.edu.

MUTHYALA, RAMAIAH, chemistry professor, researcher; b. Khammam, Andhra Pradesh, India, Feb. 10, 1946; BSc, Osmania U., Hyderabad, India, 1962; PhD, Sagar U., India, 1969, U. E. Anglia, Norwich, Eng., 1974; MBA, St. Thomas U., St. Paul, 1999. Sr. chemist Indian Drugs & Pharmaceuticals Ltd., Hyderabad, 1969—71; rsch. assoc. Schering Plough, Bloomfield, NJ, 1976—79; project leader Dow Chem. Co., Midland, Mich., 1979—89; sr. rsch. specialist 3M/imation Corp., St. Paul, 1989—99; rsch. assoc. Alzheimer's Rsch. Ctr. Regions Hosp., St. Paul, 1999—2000; assoc. prof. dept. medicinal chemistry U. Minn., Mpls., 2000—, assoc. prof. dept. exptl. clin. pharmacology, 2006—, sr. assoc. dir. Ctr. Drug Design, 2000—05, assoc. dir. Ctr. Orphan Drug Rsch., 2005—. Adj. prof. Eastern Mich. U., Ypsilanti, 1984—89; vis. prof. U. Delhi, New Delhi, 2003. Achievements include design of therapeutics related to Viral and infectiuos desease, nurological diseases such as Alzhiemers, Huntington's diseases; research in cancers and rare or neglcted and orphan diseases. Home: 699 Apache Ln Saint Paul MN 55120 Office: U Minn 2001 6th St SE MTRF Rm 4-210 Minneapolis MN 55455 Home Phone: 651-688-7382; Office Phone: 612-624-7120. Personal E-mail: ramaiah@comcast.net. Business E-Mail: muthy003@umn.edu.

MUTOMBO, DIKEMBE (DIKEMBE MUTOMBO MPOLONDO MUKAMBA JEAN JACQUE WAMUTOMBO), professional basketball player; b. Kinshasa, Zaire, June 25, 1966; m. Rose Mutombo; children: Carrie Biamba Wamutumbo, Jean Jacques Dikembe Mutombo Mplombo Jr. BA in Linguistics and Diplomacy, Georgetown U., 1991. Ctr. Denver Nuggets, 1991—96, Atlanta Hawks, 1996—2001, Phila. 76ers, 2001—02, NJ Nets, 2002—03, NY Knicks, 2003—04, Chgo. Bulls, 2004, Houston Rockets, 2004—. Founder Dikembe Mutombo Found. Named NBA

Defensive Player of Yr., 1995, 1997, 1998, 2001; named to 8 NBA All-star teams, NBA All-Rookie team, 1992; recipient President's Svc. award, Points of Light Found., 1999, Henry P. Iba Citizen Athlete award, 1999. Achievements include ranking second all-time in NBA career blocks; fluent in English, French, Spanish, Portuguese, and five African dialects. Office: c/o Houston Rockets 1510 Polk St Houston TX 77002 *

MUTTER, JOHN J., JR., writer, researcher; s. John J. Mutter, Sr. and Burnette V. Mutter; m. Karen L. Boerst, Aug. 21, 1982. Grad., Shawano Sr. H.S., Wis., 1961. Power plant operator State of Wis., Madison, Winnebago, Green Bay, Wis., 1982—2001, ret., 2001. Author: To Slay a Giant, 2000, Out in the Country, 2005; ghostwriter: I Will Sing My Songs Again, the biography of Ronnie Fuller, 2004; co-editor Shawano County Sesquicentennial 1853-2003. With USN, 1961—64, with U.S. Mcht. Marine, 1969—70, with U.S. Mcht. Marine, 1973—77, West Coast. Decorated The Vietnam Svc. Bar; recipient Outdoor Writing award, Coun. for Wis. Writers, 1990, Buzzard Buster award, Wolf Watershed Ednl. Project, 2000, 50th Bo Carter Meml. award, Waukesha Writers Group, 2002, 2d Pl. award, Al P. Nelson Feature Writing Contest, 2004. Mem.: Coun. for Wis. Writers, Wis. Regional Writers Assoc., Shawno County Hist. Soc. (life), Shawano Area Writers (pres. 2002). Avocations: writing, fishing, hunting, reading, managing woods for nature. Office: Burstone LLC N2787 McDonald Rd Shawano WI 54166-6956 Office Phone: 715-526-9277.

MUTTERPERL, WILLIAM CHARLES, lawyer, corporate financial executive; b. NYC, July 15, 1946; s. Martin and Muriel (Wurtzel) M.; m. Nancy Fay Borson, July 2, 1968; children: Matthew, Adam. BA, Dartmouth Coll., 1968; JD, Columbia U., NYC, 1971. Bar: N.Y. 1972, R.I. 1978, U.S. Dist. Ct. (so. and ea. dists.) N.Y. 1973, U.S. Dist. Ct. R.I. 1979. Assoc. atty. Cleary, Gottleib, Steen and Hamilton, NYC, 1971-77; asst. gen. counsel Fleet Nat. Bank, Providence, 1977-79, gen. counsel, 1979-85; v.p., gen. counsel, sec. Fleet Fin. Group, Inc. (now Fleet Boston Fin Inc.), Providence, 1985-89, sr. v.p., gen. counsel, sec., 1989—2001; exec. dir. ind. oversight bd. Arthur Andersen LLP, 2002; ptnr. bus. law divsn. Brown, Rudnick, Berlack, Israels, LLP, 2002; vice chmn. PNC Fin. Svcs. Group, Pitts., 2002—. Bd. mem. Black Rock, Inc., NY, Beth Israel Deaconess Hosp., Boston; former pres. Boston Bar Found. Mem. Phi Beta Kappa. Democrat. Jewish. Office: PNC Fin Svcs Group One PNC Plaza 249 Fifth Ave Pittsburgh PA 15222-2707 *

MUTTON, HOLLY BETH, psychiatrist; b. Kenmore, NY, Jan. 6, 1966; d. David Kenneth and Susan Kathleen Mutton; life ptnr. Gregory F. Smith. BFA in Applied Media Arts, Edinboro U., Pa., 1988; postgrad., Canisius Coll., 1996; DO, NY Coll. Osteo. Medicine, 2002. Freelance graphic artist HB Graphics, East Amherst, NY, 1982—; resident asst. Edinboro U., 1984—88; salesperson The Ltd. Stores, Inc., Buffalo, 1988—91; art dir., account exec. RQC Ltd., Williamsville, NY, 1990—92; sales rep. Azerty Inc., Orchard Park, NY, 1992—97; nat. account mgr. McGregor Supplies Divsn., Elma, NY, 1997—98; resident pediats. U. Buffalo Med. Sch. Hosp. Consortiums, 2002—03, resident psychiatry, 2003—05, fellow child psychiatry, 2005—. Anatomy and embryology artist, tchg. asst., student amb. N.Y. Coll. Osteo. Medicine, Old Westbury, 1999—2000; vol. Sisters Hosp. Emergency Rm., Buffalo, 1993—95. Named Hon. Letter Carrier/cert. of appreciation, U.S. Postal Svc., 1990, winner Marilyn Monroe Lookalike Contest, Bon Ton Dept. Store and Warners, 1997; recipient Humanism and Excellence in Tchg. award, Arnold P. Gold Found., 2004. Mem.: Am. Acad. Pediat. (life), Western N.Y. Osteo. Med. Soc. (life), Am. Psychiatry Assn. (life), Am. Acad. Child and Adolescent Psychiatry (life). Office: Univ at Buffalo Med Sch Hosps Buffalo NY Home Phone: 716-689-4573; Office Phone: 716-887-5800.

MUTZ, JOHN MASSIE, foundation administrator, former state official, former energy executive; b. Indpls., Nov. 5, 1935; s. John Loughery and Mary Helen (Massie) M.; m. Carolyn Hawthorne, June 21, 1958; children: Mark, Diana. BS in Advt. and Bus. Mgmt, Northwestern U., 1957, MS, 1958. Copy editor Indpls. News, summer 1953, 54; dir. public relations for residential bldg. products Aluminum Co. Am., Pitts., 1958-60; dir. advt. and public relations, sec., asst. to pres. Perine Devel. Corp., Indpls., 1960-61; instr. dept. public and environ. affairs Ind. U., Indpls., 1976-79; v.p. Circle Fin. Corp., Indpls., 1962-79, Circle Leasing Corp., Indpls., 1962-79, Fast Food Mgmt. Corp., 1978-79; mem. Ind. Ho. of Reps., 1967—70, chmn. interim sch. fin. com., 1962-69, chmn. taxation subcom. of ways and means com., 1969-70; Republican candidate state treas. Ind., 1970; mem. Ind. State Senate, 1971—80, chmn. state budget com., 1977—78; lt. gov. State of Ind., 1981-89; pres. Lilly Endowment, Inc., 1989—93, PSI Energy, 1993—99; chmn. dept. of waterworks City of Indianapolis, 2002; bd. chmn. Lumina Found., 2002—. Spkr. in field. Columnist: Indpls. Bus. Jour.; author: Fundraising for Dummies. Mem. Sch. Property Tax Control Bd. Indpls., 1975-76; bd. govs. United Way Indpls., 1978-79; mem. bd. missions United Meth. Ch., Indpls., 1976-78; bd. dirs. Suemma Coleman Agy., 1975-79, Community Services Council Indpls., 1976-77; trustee Christian Theol. Sem., 1976-79. Mem. Nat. Restaurant Assn. (dir. 1978-79), Ind. Restaurant Assn. (dir. 1977-79), Marion County Mental Health Assn., Northwestern U. Alumni Assn., Pi Alpha Mu, Deru (pres. 1956-57), Beta Theta Pi (v.p. 1956-57) Office: Lumina Found PO Box 1806 Indianapolis IN 46206-1806 Home Phone: 317-849-2677; Office Phone: 317-841-7920. Personal E-mail: j8128m@aol.com.

MUTZ, OSCAR ULYSSES, manufacturing and distribution executive; b. Edinburg, Ind., Feb. 12, 1928; s. Harold Winterberg and Laura Belle (Sawin) M.; m. Jean Greiling, Aug. 22, 1948; children: Marcia, H. William. BS, Ind. U., 1949. Vice pres. Peerless Corp., Indpls., 1954-63; v.p., gen. mgr. Space Conditioning, Inc., Harrisonburg, Va., 1964-66; v.p., treas. Cosco, Inc., Columbus, Ind., 1966-67; exec. v.p., 1967-69; pres., 1969-71; chmn. bd. Court Manor Corp., Columbus, 1971-73; pres. Jenn Air Corp., Indpls., 1973-75; pres., CEO Mutz Corp., 1975-81; pres., dir. Haag Drug Co., 1977-78; pres. Forum Group, Inc. (merger Mutz Corp. and Excepticon, Inc.), Indpls., 1981-91; chmn., CEO, bd. dirs. Capital Industries, Inc., Indpls., 1991-96; chmn. Lakeland Auto Mall, 1996—. Pres. Ct. Manor Corp., co-chmn. bd. dirs. Sargent & Greenleaf, Safemasters; pres. Security Group, Inc., 1991-2004, also bd. dirs. Nat. trustee Fellowship Christian Athletes, 1985-91, chmn. nat. conf. ctr., 1994-96; mem. pres. coun. and dean's adv. coun. Ind. U. Mem. Ind. Mfrs. Assn. (chmn. 1980), Acad. Alumnae Fellows Ind. U. Sch. Bus., Lakeland Yacht Club, Grasslands Country Club, Lone Palm Country Club. Republican. Presbyterian. Office: Mutz Corporation 5119 Lake in the Woods Blvd Lakeland FL 33813-2942

MUUSS, ROLF EDUARD, retired psychologist, author; b. Tating, Germany, Sept. 26, 1924; came to U.S., 1953, naturalized, 1992. s. Rudolf A. and Else M.; m. Gertrude Louise Kremser, Dec. 22, 1953 (dec. April 1999); children: Michael John (dec.), Gretchen Elise. Diploma, Tchr. Coll., Flensburg, Germany, 1951; student, U. Hamburg, Germany, 1951, Ctrl. Mo. State Coll., 1951—52, Columbia Tchrs. Coll., 1952; MEd, Western Md. Coll., 1954; PhD, U. Ill., 1957; Masters Degree (hon.), U. Ambrosiana, Milan, 2004. Tchr. pub. sch., Germany, 1945-46, 51, 52-53; substitute prin., 1952-53; tchr. trainee U.S. Office Edn., 1951-52; houseparent Child Study Ctr., Balt., 1953; grad. asst. U. Ill., 1954-57; rsch. assoc. prof. Iowa Child Welfare Rsch. Sta., State U. Iowa, 1957-59; rsch. cons., 1960, 61; mem. faculty Goucher Coll., 1959-95, prof. edn., 1964-95, chmn. dept., 1972-75, dir. spl. edn., 1977-92, Elizabeth C. Todd disting. prof., 1980-85, chmn. dept. sociology and anthropology, 1983-85, prof. emeritus, 1995—. Rsch. assoc. edn. Johns Hopkins, 1962-63; tchr. U.B.C., 1962, Johns Hopkins U., 1962, 65, U. Del., 1965, Towson U., 1967, U. Ill., 1967; tchg. assoc. Sheppard and Enoch Pratt Hosp., 1969-80; guest lectr. Tchrs. Coll., Kiel, Fed. Republic Germany, 1977-78; hearing officer spl. edn. cases State of Md., 1980-96. Author: First-Aid for Classroom Discipline Problems, 1962, Theories of Adolescence, 1962, 6th edit., 1996, Grundlagen der Jugendpsychologie, 1982; editor: Adolescent Behavior and Society: A Book of Readings, 1971, 5th edit., 1998; contbr. articles to profl. jours. Served with German Air Force, 1942-45. Recipient award for disting. scholarship Goucher Coll., 1979; grantee Andrew W. Mellon Found., 1976-77. Fellow Am. Psychol. Soc., Am. Psychol. Assn., Md. Psychol. Assn. (treas. 1971-73); mem. Balt. Psychol. Assn. (chmn. membership com. 1966, v.p. 1970-71), Soc. Rsch. Child Devel., Soc. Rsch. on Adolescence, Kappa Delta Pi (v.p. Alpha chpt. 1956-57), Phi Delta Kappa. Home: 1540 Pickett Rd Lutherville Timonium MD 21093-5822 Personal E-mail: rolfmuuss@yahoo.com.

MUZYKA-MCGUIRE, AMY, marketing professional, nutritionist, consultant; b. Chgo., Sept. 24, 1953; d. Basil Bohdan and Amelia (Rand) Muzyka; m. Patrick J. McGuire, June 3, 1977; children: Jonathan, Elizabeth. BS, Iowa State U., 1975, postgrad., 1978—; registered dietitian, St. Louis U., 1980. Cert. dietitian. Home economist Nat. Livestock and Meat Bd., Chgo., 1975-77; dietary cons. various hosps. and nursing homes, Iowa, 1978-79; supr. foodsvc. Am. Egg Bd., Park Ridge, Ill., 1980-83; assoc. dir., mgr. foodsvc. Cole & Weber Advt., Seattle, 1984-85; prin., owner Food and Nutrition Comms., Federal Way, Wash., 1986—. Coauthor: Turkey Foodservice Manual, 1987; editor: (newsletter) Home Economists in Business, 1975-77, Dietitians in Business and Industry, 1982-85; Food Net on Internet, 1995, Food and Culinary Profls. Newsletter, 1999-2001; contbr. articles to profl. jours. Named Outstanding Dietitian of Yr. North Suburban Dietetic Assn., 1983, Tastemaker of the Month, 2001, 02, 03. Mem. Am. Dietetic Assn., Internat. Foodsvc. Editl. Coun., Cons. Nutritionists, Internat. Assn. Culinary Profls. (CCP; chair nutritional food scis. group 2003-05). Avocations: gardening, travel, music, food and beverage tastings. Home: 5340 SW 315th St Federal Way WA 98023-2034

MWENDA, KENNETH KAOMA, legal association administrator, consultant; LLB, U. Zambia, 1990; Gr.Dip, LCCI, UK, 1991; DMS, IoC, UK, 1992; BCL, U. Oxford, UK, 1994; MBA, U. Hull, Eng., 1995; DBA, Pacific Western U., LA, 1996, PhD in Publs., 1999; PhD, U. Warwick, UK, 2000. Cert. Bar, Zambia, 1991; cert. cumpolsory edn., devels. in comml. securities, intellectual property law. With trust funds and co-financing dept. Vice-Presidency of World Bank, Washington, 1998—99, with poverty reduction, mgmt. and pub. sector reform unit, 1999; counsel legal dept. World Bank, Washington, 1999—2000, projects officer, 2000—03, sr. projects officer, 2003—04, sr. counsel, 2004—. Vis. prof. U. Miskolc Sch. Law, Hungary, 1996; lectr. U. Zambia Law Sch., 1991—95, vis. prof., 2001; lectr. Warwick U. Law Sch., 1995—98; spkr. and presenter in field. Author: Legal Aspects of Corporate Capital and Finance, 1999, Contemporary Issues In Corporate Finance and Investment Law, 2000, Banking Supervision and Systemic Bank Restructuring, 2000, Zambia's Stock Exchange and Privatization Programme, 2001, The Dynamics of Market Integration: African Stock Exchange's in the New Millennium, 2000, Banking Supervision and Microfinance Regulation: Lessons from Zambia, 2002, Principles of Arbitration Law, 2003, Frontiers of Legal Knowledge: Business and Economic Law in Context, 2003, Anti-Money Laundering Law and Practice, 2005, Legal Aspects of Financial Services Regulation and the Concept of a Unified Regulator, 2006, The Legal Administration of Financial Services in Common Law Jurisdictions: with special attention to the dual regulation system in Zambia, 2006, Combating Financial Crime: Legal, Regulatory and Institutional Frameworks, 2006, Contemporary Issues in International Economic Law, 2006, Economic Integration and Development in Africa, 2006, Comparing American and British Legal Education Systems, 2007, Made in Australia, 2007, Legal Aspects of Combating Corruption: The Case of Zambia, 2007. Tutor U. Zambia Law Sch., 1991—95. Staff Devel. fellow in law U. Zambia, 1991, U. Yale Law Faculty fellow, 1998; Rhodes scholar U. Zambia, 1992, U. Oxford, 1992-94, U. Hull, 1994-95. Fellow Royal Soc. Arts. of England, Inst. Commerce of England; mem. Internat. Bar Assn., Law Assn. of Zambia, Brit. Assn. Lawyers for Def. of Unborn. Office: The World Bank 1818 H St NW Washington DC 20433-0001 Personal E-mail: kmwenda@yahoo.com.

MYATT, WILLIAM HOWARD, theater educator, director, actor; b. Maquoketa, Iowa, Mar. 1, 1961; s. Robert Bruce and Adabelle Marie Myatt; m. Christina Marie Schnock, Aug. 10, 2002; children: Anna Marie, Alexander Ashton, Zachary Leonard. BA, U. No. Iowa, Cedar Falls, 1979—84, MA, 1985—90. Cert. 7 - 12 Libr./Media Specialist Dept. of Edn., Iowa, 2001, k - 12 Talented and Gifted Educator Dept. of Edn., Iowa, 1995. Dir., actor Meml. Union Summer Resident Theatre, Ames, Iowa, 1982—83; drama dir., tchr. Burlington HS, Wis., 1984—85, No. U. HS, Cedar Falls, Iowa, 1985—87, Clinton HS, Iowa, 1987—90, Pleasant Valley Cmty. HS, Pleasant Valley, Iowa, 1990—. Workshop presenter Tenn. Thespian Conf., Nashville, 1991, Va. Thespian Conf., 1991—94, Ednl. Theatre Assn., Regional Conf., Minneapolis, Minn., 1991, Kans. Thespian Conf., 1992; workshop presenter, adjudicator Fla. Thespian Conf., Tampa Bay, 1992; workshop presenter Iowa HS Speech Assn., Des Moines, 1997—; mainstage adjudicator Ednl. Theatre Assn., Cincinnati, Ohio, 1994—, trustee, 1996—99. Contbr. articles. Aids quilt display com. Scholar Hazel B. Strayer award, U. No. Iowa Theatre Dept., 1982. Mem.: Iowa Ednl. Theatre Assn. (Hall of Fame 2005), Ednl. Theatre Assn. (pres., v.p. 2001—05, bd. dirs. local chpt. 2005, Hall of Fame 2005). Avocations: theater, reading, science fiction. Office: Pleasant Valley Comm HS 604 Belmont Rd Bettendorf IA 52722 Office Phone: 563-332-5151. Business E-Mail: myattw@pleasval.k12.ia.us.

MYCIELSKI, JAN, retired mathematics professor; b. Wisniowa, Poland, Feb. 7, 1932; s. Jan and Helena (Bal) M.; m. Emilia Przezdziecka, Apr. 25, 1959. MS, U. Wroclaw, Poland, 1955, PhD, 1957. With Inst. Math., Polish Acad. Scis., Wroclaw, 1956-68; prof. math. U. Colo., Boulder, 1969—2002, prof. emeritus, 2002—. Vis. prof. Case Western Res. U., Cleve., 1967, U. Colo., 1967, Inst. des Hautes Etudes Scientifiques, Bures-sur-Yvette, 1978-79, dept. math. U. Hawaii, 1987; attache de recherche Centre National de la Recherche Scientifique, Paris, 1957-58; asst. prof. U. Calif., Berkeley, 1961-62, 70; long-term vis. staff mem. Los Alamos Nat. Lab., 1989-90. Author over 150 rsch. papers. Recipient Stefan Banach prize, 1965, Alfred Jurzykowski award, 1977, Waclaw Sierpinski medal, 1990. Mem. Am. Math. Soc., Math. Assn. Am., Polish Math. Soc., Assn. for Symbolic Logic. Office: U Colo Dept Math Boulder CO 80309-0395 Business E-Mail: jmyciel@euclid.colorado.edu, jan.mycielski@colorado.edu.

MYCOCK, FREDERICK CHARLES, lawyer; b. Columbus, Ga., Oct. 3, 1943; s. Edwin S. and Elaine M.M. BSBA, Boston U., 1965, LLB, 1968. Bar: Mass. 1968, U.S. Dist. Ct. Mass. 1974, U.S. Supreme Ct. 1980. Assoc. Roderick E. Smith, Hyannis, Mass., 1968-71; asst. atty. gen. State of Mass., 1972-73; ptnr. Mycock, Kilroy, Green & Mycock, Hyannis, 1972-77, Mycock, Nwewll & Morse, Barnstable, Mass., 1977-86; atty. pvt. practice, Barnstable, Mass., 1987—. Mem. ABA, Mass. Trial Lawyers Assn., Nat. Assn. Criminal Defense Lawyers, Mass. Bar Assn., Mass. Acad. Trial Lawyers, Barnstable County Bar Assn. Republican. Methodist. Home: Santuit Rd Cotuit MA 02635 Office: 3291 Main St Barnstable MA 02630-1105

MYER, DONALD BEEKMAN, architect; b. Cleve., Aug. 25, 1937; s. Beekman Walter and Jennie Helen (Gimpel) M.; m. Ellen Jane Schwartz, June 10, 1970; 1 child, Jamie Beekman. BArch, U. Ill., 1961, MArch, 1962. Registered architect Va., D.C. Supervisory architect Nat. Park Svc., Phila., Washington, Cape, Mass., 1962-65; asst. sec. Commn. Fine Arts, Washington, 1965-97; adminstrn., budget and grants cons. Keyes, Lethbridge & Condon, Architects, Washington, 1968-70; clk. of works Washington Nat. Cathedral, 1998-2001; curator bldg. and grounds Tudor Place, Georgetown, 2001—02; strategic counsel cons., 2002—. Cons. Preservation Galveston (Tex.) History Found., 1968-69, Joint Com. on Landmarks, Washington, 1969; faculty cons. Sch. of Architecture, Cath. U. Am., 1990—2005; mem. bldgs. and grounds com. Protestant Episcopal Cathedral, 2003—; mem. U.S. Capital Vis. Ctr. Arts Panel, 2004-05; bd., dirs., chair design adv. com. Adams Meml. Found., 2006—. Author: Bridges and the City of Washington, 1974, Building Potomac Aqueduct, 1975; editor: Centennial History of Washington AIA, 1987; artist: Lewis & Clark Show, Corcoran Gallery, 2006. Mem. faculty Smithsonian Resident Assocs., Washington, 1973-81; pres. Washington Archtl. Found., 1998-2000; trustee Com. of 100 on the Fed. City, 1997-2000; mem. bldgs. and grounds com., Protestant Episc. Cathedral, 2003—. Named Arch. of Yr., DC Coun. Engrng. and Archtl. Socs., 2005; named one of 77 People to Watch award, Washingtonian Mag., 1987; grantee Europa-Nostra Seminar Smithsonian Fgn. Currency Program, Poland, 1974. Fellow AIA (chair hist. resources 1976, v.p. found. 1980, chpt. pres. 1987, fellows selection jury 1998-2000, awarded Centennial Medal, Washington chpt. 2004); mem. Woodley Park Men's Club (pres. 1979-82), Lambda Alpha (hon.). Republican. Avocations: history, travel, photography, painting. Personal E-mail: aspire2@earthlink.net.

MYERBERG, MARCIA, investment banker; b. Boston, Mar. 25, 1945; d. George and Evelyn (Lewis) Katz; m. Jonathan Gene Myerberg, June 4, 1967 (div. Mar. 1994); 1 child, Gillian Michelle. BS, U. Wis., 1966. Corp. trust adminstr. Chase Manhattan Bank, NYC, 1966-67; asst. cashier Glore Forgan, Wm. R. Staats, Phoenix, 1967-68; bond portfolio analyst Trust Co. of Ga., Atlanta, 1969-72; asst. v.p. 1st Union Nat. Bank, Charlotte, NC, 1973-78; dir. cash mgmt. Carolina Power & Light Co., Raleigh, NC, 1978-79; sr. v.p., treas. Fed Home Loan Mortgage Corp., Washington, 1979-85; dir. Salomon Bros. Inc., NYC, 1985-89; sr. mng. dir. Bear, Stearns & Co. Inc., NYC, 1989-93; mng. dir. Bear, Stearns Home Loans, London, 1989-93; chief exec. Myerberg & Co., L.P., NYC, 1994—, Root Markets Inc., NYC. Home: 37 W 12th St Apt 6K New York NY 10011-3205 Office: 780 3rd Ave New York NY 10017-2024

MYEROWITZ, P(AUL) DAVID, cardiac surgeon, educator, writer; b. Balt., Jan. 18, 1947; s. Joseph Robert and Merry (Brown) M.; m. Susan Karen Macks, June 28, 1967 (div.); children: Morris Brown, Elissa Suzanne, Ian Matthew; m. Kathleen Mary Murphy, Aug. 10, 2001. BS, U. Md., 1966; MD, 1970; MS, U. Minn., 1977. Intern in surgery U. Minn., Mpls., 1970-71, resident in surgery, 1971-72, 74-77; resident in cardiothoracic surgery U. Chgo., 1977-79; practice medicine specializing in cardiovascular surgery Madison, Wis., 1979—; asst. prof. thoracic and cardiovascular surgery U. Wis., Madison, 1979-85; assoc. prof., 1985; chief sect. cardiac transplantation, 1984-85; Karl P. Klassen prof., 1985-97; chief thoracic and cardiovascular surgery Ohio State U. and Hosps., Columbus, 1985-97. Author: (book) Heart Transplantation, 1987, Heartland for Profit, 2004; contbr. articles to profl. jours. Served with USPHS, 1972-74. Mem.: ACS, Am. Assn. Thoracic Surgeons, Am. Coll. Cardiology. Jewish. Business E-Mail: hrttx1@aol.com.

MYERS, ALBERT F., aerospace executive; b. New Orleans, Jan. 11, 1946; BS in Mech. Engring., U. Idaho, 1969, MS in Mech. Engring., 1971; MS in Indl. Mgmt., MIT, 1992. Active duty U.S. Army, 1972-75; various positions Dryden Flight Rsch. Ctr., 1975-81; mgr. flight controls engring. Northrop Grumman, 1981, corp. v.p., Bus. Stategy, 1992-94, corp. v.p., treas., 1994—2003, corp. v.p., Strategy and Technology, 2003—. Mem.: NAE. Office: Northrop Grumman Corp 1840 Century Park E Los Angeles CA 90067-2101

MYERS, ALISON KAY, assistant principal; b. Tampa, Fla., Mar. 14, 1982; d. Steven Lloyd and Kay Baker Myers. BS in Elem. Edn., U. Tampa, 2003; MS in Ednl. Leadership, Nova Southeastern U., Ft. Lauderdale, Fla., 2004, EdD in Orgnl. Leadership, 2007. 4th grade tchr. Hillsborough County Schs., Tampa, 2003—04, 2nd grade tchr., 2004—06, adminstrv. resource tchr., 2006, asst. prin. elem. instrn., 2006—. Mem.: Hillsborough Assn. Sch. Adminstrs., Pi Delta Kappa.

MYERS, ALLEN RICHARD, rheumatologist; b. Balt., Jan. 14, 1935; s. Ellis Benjamin and Rosina (Blumberg) M.; m. Ellen Patz, Nov. 26, 1960; children: David Joseph, Robert Todd, Scott Patz. BA, U. Pa., Phila., 1956; MD, U. Md., 1960. Diplomate Am. Bd. Internal Medicine, Am. Bd. Rheumatology. Intern Univ. Hosp., Balt., 1960-61, resident in medicine Ann Arbor, Mich., 1961-64; fellow in rheumatology Mass. Gen. Hosp. and Harvard Med. Sch., Boston, 1966-69; dir. clin. tng. rheumatology U. Pa. Sch. Medicine, Phila., 1969-72, chief rheumatology sect., 1972-78; dep. chair medicine Temple U. Sch. Medicine, Phila., 1978-84, acting chmn. medicine, 1984-86, dean, 1991-95, prof. medicine, 1978—, assoc. v.p. Health Scis. Ctr., 1988-95. Vis. prof. Cardiothoracic Inst., U. London, 1988; mem. med. adv. bd. Scleroderma Rsch. Found., Santa Barbara, Calif., 1986. Mem. editl. bd. Arthritis & Rheumatism, 1985—90, Brit. Jour. Rheumatology, 1989—94; editor: Systemic Sclerosis, 1985, Medicine, 1986, 1993, 1996, 2000, 2004. Pres. Phila. Health Care Congress, 1994—; adv. com. Pa. Lupus Found., 1976—; bd. dirs. Phila. Conv. and Visitors Bur., 1994—. With USPHS, 1964-66. Recipient Margaret Whitaker prize U. Md. Sch. Medicine, 1960, Lindback Found. award Temple, 1981; named Physician of Yr. Temple U. Hosp., 1986. Master: Am. Coll. Rheumatology; fellow: ACP, Phila. Coll. Physicians (pres. 2000); mem.: Am. Fedn. Clin. Rsch. Avocations: walking, classical music, reading. Office Phone: 215-707-5127.

MYERS, ANGELA MICHELLE, music educator, department chairman; b. Kokomo, Ind., Nov. 29, 1978; d. Ronald Wayne Myers and Sandra Jane Myers Gaiser. BS in Instrumental Music Edn., Ball State U., Muncie, Ind., 2001. Band dir. Prince William County Sch., Stonewall Jackson HS, Manassas, Va., 2002; band dir., dept. chair Prince William County Sch., Bull Run Mid. Sch., Gainesville, Va., 2002—, presenter, 2004—, mem. music literacy com., 2006—, mem. music syllabus com., 2006—. Fine arts rep. Bull Run Mid. Sch. Adv. Council, Gainesville, Va., 2004—; curriculum cons. Prince William County Sch., Manassas, Va., 2004—, camp dir., instr., 2004—; presenter in field. Band pres. Ball State U., Sch. of Music, Muncie, Ind., 2000—01; presenter Prince William County Schs., 2004—, music literacy com. mem., 2006—, music syllabus com. mem., 2006—. Recipient Richard L. Dunham Band award, Ball State U. Marching Band, 2000, John R. Emens Leadership award, Ball State U. Sch. Music. Mem.: Sigma Alpha Iota, Va. Music Educators Assn., Music Educators Nat. Conf. Achievements include founding staff mem. Bull Run Mid. Sch., 2002.

MYERS, BETTY J., retired music specialist; b. Kansas City, Mo., Feb. 24, 1935; d. Marion O. and Jennie Lillian (Dickinson) Williams; m. Alfred M. Myers, June 6, 1958; children: Sherylyn, Douglas, Carol. BS in Edn., Cen. Mo. State U., 1956; MS in Edn. Adminstrn., CMSU, 1976. Elem. tchr. Kansas City Pub. Schs., 1956—58, elem. classrm. tchr., 1962—80, elem. music tchr., 1980—94; elem. tchr. R5 Schs., Parkville, Mo., 1958—60. Leader adult Sunday sch., 1972—. Mem. Am. Bus. Women's Assn., 1972-2000 (v.p., sec., treas., chair com. 1980-2000, pres. 1984-85, Woman of Yr. 1985), Internat. Order of The King's, Daus. and Sons (pres. Perry Crosby Cir. 1976-80 Kans. City union 1983-85, v.p. Mo. br. 1987-90, pres. 1998-2002, Mo. br. bd. dirs., 1996-2000, 2002-06, Mo. br. treas. 2004—, Delta Kappa Gamma (pres. Alpha chpt. 1984-86, pres. Kansas City area coun. 1985-87, pres. chpt. 2002-04). Baptist. Avocation: church pianist. Home: 13407 E 51st St Kansas City MO 64133-2631

MYERS, C. DAVID, manufacturing executive; BS, Pa. State U. CPA. Sr. mgr. KPMG L.L.P.; dir. fin. Airside Products Group, 1994-95; corp. contr. York (Pa.) Internat. Corp., 1995-98, v.p., fin. engineered systems group, 1998-2000, v.p., CFO, 2000—03, pres., 2003—05, CEO, 2004—05, also bd. dirs.; v.p., corp. officer, pres., bldg. efficiency bus. Johnson Controls Inc., Milw., 2005—. Office: Johnson Controls 5757 N Green Bay Ave Milwaukee WI 53209

MYERS, CHARLES EDWIN, child therapist, educator; b. Cooperstown, NY, July 8, 1966; s. Alan Wayne and Susan Foster Myers. BA in Music Edn., Marietta Coll., Ohio, 1984—88; MA in Counselor Edn., U. S.Fla., Tampa, 1999—2001. Cert. play therapy U. S.Fla., 2003; music tchr. K-6 Dept. Def. Dependents Schs., Ohio, 1988, music tchr. K-12 Fla., 1997, sch. counselor pre-K-12 Fla., 2001, counselor Nat. Bd. Cert. Counselors, 2004, disaster mental health vol. ARC, 2005, lic. profl. counselor Tex., 2005, mental health counselor Fla., 2005. Music tchr. Dept. Def. Dependents Schs., Torrejon, Spain, 1988—89; dist. exec. Boy Scouts Am., Warren, Pa., 1989—93, sr. dist. exec. Denville, NJ, 1993—95, Costa Mesa, Calif., 1995—95; security supervisor Guardsmark, San Diego, 1996—97; music tchr. Hillsborough County Sch. Dist., Tampa, Fla., 1997—2000; sch. counselor Polk County Sch. Bd., Lakeland, Fla., 2000—01, Hillsborough County Sch. Dist., Tampa, 2001—05; pvt. practice Sharp Focus Ctrs., Denton, Tex., 2005—; coord. tng. & devel. Ctr. Play Therapy, Denton, Tex., 2005—; clin. therapist mental health clinics U. N.Tex., Denton, 2005—, tchg. asst., 2006—. Contbr. chapters to books. Vol. Hurricane Katrina crisis counselor ARC, Dallas, 2005; various vol. positions Boy Scouts Am., 1984—99; water safety dir., instr. ARC, Torrejon, Spain, 1988—89, instr. Warren, Pa., 1989—93; vol. play therapist Denton Ind. Sch. Dist., 2005—; vol. Met. Ministiries, Tampa, Fla., 2002—03; vol. intercity sch. career counselor Hillsborough County Sch. Dist., Tampa, 2000; bd. dirs., instr. ARC, Marietta, Ohio, 1987—88; bd. dirs. Kiwinas Internat., Warren, Pa., 2000—03, Chatam, NJ, 2003—05. Recipient Eagle Scout award, Boy Scouts Am., 1983. Mem.: Hillsborough Counseling Assn. (mem.-at-large 2004—05), Fla. Counseling Assn. (region rep. 2000—03, leadership devel. conf. leader 2001—04), Fla. Sch. Counselor Assn. (elem. v.p. 2003—05), Fla. Assn. Play Therapy (pub. rels. chmn., Tampa Bay Chpt. 2003—04, pres. 2004—05), N.Ctrl. Tex. Counseling Assn., Tex. Assn. Play Therapy, Tex. Assn. Counselors & Supervisors, Tex. Sch. Counselor Assn., Tex. Counsleing Assn., Assn. Play Therapy (mem. clinl. comm. com. 2007—, ethics & practice com. mem. 2005—07), Am. Sch. Counselor Assn., Assn. Counseling Educators & Supervisors, Am. Counselors Assn. (assoc.), Chi Sigma Iota, Kappa Delta Pi, Phi Kappa Phi, Mensa. R-Consevative. Mem. Disciples Of Christ. Achievements include research in effectiveness of filial therapy when mothers are homeless. Avocations: sailing, photography, scuba diving, music. Office Phone: 940-381-5010. Business E-Mail: charles@sharpfocuscenters.com.

MYERS, CHRISTOPHER D., bank executive; b. Calif. BA, Harvard U.; MBA, U. Calif. Various positions including v.p., mgr. First Interstate Bank; comml. bank ctr. mgr. Bank of the West (Sanwa Bank of Calif.); chmn., CEO Mellon First Bus. Bank, LA, 1996—2006; pres., CEO, chmn. CVB Fin. Corp., Citizens Bus. Bank, 2006—. Office: CVB Fin Corp 701 North Haven Ave Ste 350 Ontario CA 91764 Office Phone: 909-980-4030. Office Fax: 909-481-2130. *

MYERS, DANE JACOB, lawyer, podiatrist; b. Murray, Utah, June 20, 1948; s. Lorin LaVar Myers and Irma Lee (Bell) Willette; m. Mary Jo Jackson, June 22, 1970; children: Troy, Chad, Melissa, Apryll, Tristan, Remington. DPM, Pa. Coll. Podiatric Medicine, 1977; BA, U. Utah, 1983; JD, U. Ark., 1986. Bar: Ark 1986. Pres. Tooele (Utah) Foot Clinic, 1977-83; owner N.W. Ark. Foot Clinic, Rogers, Ark., 1983—; pvt. practice law Fayetteville, 1986-97. Served to maj med serv corps USAR, 1977—94. Mem.: APHA, ABA, Ark. Podiatric Medicine Assn., Am. Podiatric Medicine Assn., Am. Soc. Law and Medicine, Ark. Bar Assn., Am. Diabetes Assn., Am. Coll. Foot and Ankle Surgeons (assoc.), Delta Theta Phi. Republican. Mem. Lds Ch. Avocations: golf, computers, history. Home: 2005 Oakhill Dr Springdale AR 72762 Office: NW Ark Foot Clinic 700 N 13th St Rogers AR 72756-3436 Office Phone: 479-636-1411. Personal E-mail: danejmyers@hotmail.com.

MYERS, DANIEL WILLIAM, II, lawyer; b. Camden, NJ, Mar. 21, 1931; s. Charles Rudolph II and Myrtle Henrietta (Kress) M.; m. Eileen Ethel Kohn, Nov. 22, 1959 (dec.); children: Susan Leigh, Meredith Ann Myers Winner, Kathryn Kress. BS in Commerce, U. Va., 1952, LLB, 1957. Bar: Va. 1957, N.J. 1958, U.S. Dist. Ct. N.J. 1958, U.S. Supreme Ct. 1980. Assoc. Lewis & Hutchinson, Camden, 1958-60; ptnr. Myers, Matteo, Rabii, Norcross & Landgraf and predecessors, Camden, Cherry Hill, NJ, 1960-89, Montgomery, McCracken, Walker & Rhoads, 1989-94, of counsel, 1994-98, Steven J. Jozwiak, Cherry Hill, NJ, 1998—. 1st lt. U.S. Army, 1952-54. Mem. N.J. Bar Assn., Va. Bar Assn., Camden County Bar Assn., Am. Arbitration Assn., Exch. Club (pres. Cherry Hill chpt. 1969). Republican. Lutheran. Home: 1 E Atlantic Ave Harvey Cedars NJ 08008 Office: 532 Hollywood Ave at Rte 38 Cherry Hill NJ 08002 Office Phone: 856-661-1822.

MYERS, DARLENE MARIE, dance studio owner, choreographer; b. Schenectady, NY, July 25, 1950; d. Raymond Charles and Marie (Walsh) M. Grad. high sch., Schenectady, NY. Dancer Pa. Ballet Co., Phila., 1968-70; tchr., choreographer Schenectady Civic Ballet, 1970-76, Electronic Body Arts, Albany, NY, 1978-79; dir. dance Schenectady Arts Council, 1978-79; ballet mistress, choreographer Saratoga Ballet Co., Saratoga Springs, NY, 1980-81; artistic dir. Guilderland (N.Y.) Ballet Workshop, 1980-84; head dance program SUNY, Albany, 1981-85; founder, dir. Myers Studio and Art Gallery, Schenectady, 1985—. Adj. prof. arts Union Coll., Schenectady, 1980-84, adj. prof. dance; cons. Proctors Theater, Schenectady, 1985—; dir. Myers Dance Co., Schenectady, 1985—, annual summer dance camp hiring guest tchrs. from. N.Y.C. Ballet; artistic dir. N.E. Ballet Co.; choreographer, producer annual full-length Nutcracker, Schenectady. Contbr. (jour. collection) Ariadne's Thread, 1982; choreographer ann. full-length Nutcrackers and a spring concert of new repetoire. Grantee CETA, 1978, 80, Adirondack Jr. Ballet, 1982, 83. Mem. Albany League of Arts. Avocations: hiking, walking, herbal gardening. Office: PO Box 828 Schenectady NY 12305-1102 Home Phone: 518-421-0248; Office Phone: 518-374-0376. E-mail: myersdance@aol.com.

MYERS, DOROTHY ROATZ, artist; b. Detroit, Mar. 24, 1921; d. Harry Agustus and Lola May (Kelly) Roats; children: Bruce, Leslie Ann, Douglas. Student, Antioch Coll., 1941, Corcoran Gallery Art Sch., 1943, Art Students League, 1965—. Asst. to design dir. Harper & Row Pub., NYC, 1981-87. Lectr. and writer on art-related affairs. Contbr. revs. to profl. publs.; exhibited in numerous shows including N.Y. ArtExpo, 1992, Art Miami, 1992, Cornell Med. Libr. Ann., 1992, Hellenic Art Inst. Exhbn., 1991, Vt. Inst. Natural Sci., 1983, Montserrat Gallery Internat. Exhbn. (hon. mention 1993); represented in permanent collection Ward-Nasse Gallery, N.Y.C. Recipient 1st place award for drawing Brookdale Coll., 1994, 2d place award for sculpture, 1993, Bronze medal for animal art, 1986, 20th Century award for Achievement Internat. Biog. Ctr.; apptd. Acad. Ofcl. Knight Acad. Internazionale Dept. Arts, Italy. Mem.: Academia del Verbano, Italy, N.Y. Artists Equity, Garrison Art Ctr., Hellenic Art Inst., League Sci. et Edn. Sociale, Arts, Scis., Lettres: Soc. Academique de Edn. et Encouragement, Art Students League (life), Acad. Am. Poets.

MYERS, DOUGLAS GEORGE, zoological society administrator; b. LA, Aug. 30, 1949; s. George Walter and Daydeen (Schroeder) Myers; m. Barbara Firestone Myers, Nov. 30, 1980; children: Amy, Andrew. BA, Christopher Newport Coll., 1981. Tour and show supr. Annheuser-Busch (Bird Sanctuary), Van Nuys, Calif., 1970-74, mgr. zool. ops., 1974-75, asst. mgr. ops., 1975-77, mgr. ops., 1977-78; gen. services mgr. Annheuser-Busch (Old Country), Williamsburg, Va., 1978-80, park ops. dir., 1980-81; gen. mgr. San Diego Wild Animal Park, 1981-83, dep. dir. ops., 1983-85; CEO, Zool. Soc. San Diego, 1985—. Mem. Balboa Park Cultural Partnership; mem. steering com. conservation breeding specialists group Ctrl. Balboa Park Assn.; cons. in field. Mem. pres. adv. com. Am. Mgmt. Assn.; bd. dirs. Nat. Mus. Libr. Svcs., 2007—. Mem.: Calif. Assn. Zoos and Aquariums, World Assn. Zoos and Aquariums, Am. Zoo and Aquarium Assn., Am. Assn. Museums, Rotary Club San Diego. Office: Zool Soc San Diego PO Box 120551 San Diego CA 92112-0551

MYERS, EDDIE EARL, psychologist; b. Ardmore, Okla., Nov. 24, 1937; s. Finis Weldon and Fern Durrell (Johnson) M.; m. Ineta June Moore, July 2, 1955 (div. Mar. 1988); children: Richard Weldon, Ronald Leland, Marilyn June, Rebecca Jean; m. Ann Clymer Taylor, July 15, 1988 (div. May 1996); Clark Clymer Taylor, Katy Ann Taylor; m. Katherine Call Emch, Dec. 28, 1996. BSEd, Tex. Christian U., 1958; MEd, U. N. Tex., 1967, EdD, 1969. Lic. psychologist Ohio, Nat. Drug Edn. Leadership Tng. Adelphi U., 1970. Machinist Chance Vaught Aircraft, Grand Prairie, Tex., 1957-58; 5th grade tchr., jr. high coach Ft. Worth Christian Schs., 1958-59; 6th grade tchr., jr. high coach Corpus Christi (Tex.) Ind. Sch. Dist., 1959-60; youth, music, ednl. min. Norton St. Ch. Christ, Corpus Christi, 1960-61, Procter St. Ch. Christ, Port Arthur, Tex., 1963-65; min. Cameron (Tex.) Ch. Christ, 1961-63; high sch. English tchr. Christian Schs., Inc., Dallas, 1965-66; psychology instr. Tex. Women's U., Denton, 1968-69; sr. rsch. assoc., dir. psychology dept. Ednl. Rsch. Coun. Am., Cleve., 1969-78; clin. psychologist pvt. practice Cleve., 1978—. Faculty dept. guidance anc counseling U. Oreg. Workshop, Frankfurt, German, 1972; Ea. U.S. drug abuse task force Am. Soc. Health Assn., N.Y.C., 1971-73; chmn. drug abuse and alcoholism task force Fedn. Cmty. Planning, Cleve., 1970-71; adv. bd. Freedom House Rehab. Ctr., Cleve., 1993—; adj. assoc. prof. ednl. specialists Cleve. State U., 1970-74; mem. med. staff St. John Westshore Hosp., West Lake, Ohio, Fairview Hosp., Cleve. Author: Social Isolation and Personality, 1973, Handy Asks the Psychologist, 1974, (tchr. manual) Human Persons and Use of Psychoactive Agents, 1974; co-author: (tchr. manual) New Model Me: Operator's Guide to Coping with Aggression, 1974; contbr. articles to profl. jours. R & D grantee NIMH, Washington, 1974-78, Nat. Def. Edn. Rsch. Tng. grantee U.S. Dept. Edn., Washington, 1965-69. Mem. APA, Cleve. Psychol. Assn. (bd. trustees 1981-85), Cleve. Acad. Consulting Psychologists (pres. 1984-86), Ohio Psychol. Assn. (bd. trustees 1978—), Phi Delta Kappa. Avocations: computers, golf, jet boating. Office: 3865 Rocky River Dr Ste 2 Cleveland OH 44111-4114 Office Phone: 216-251-5161. Personal E-mail: emyersbvoh@aol.com.

MYERS, ELISSA MATULIS, publishing executive, professional society administrator; b. Munich, Aug. 4, 1950; (parents Am. citizens); d. Raymond George and Anne Constance (Moley) Matulis; m. John Wake Myers, Sept. 13, 1967 (div. 1972); 1 child, Jennifer Anne Myers Bick. BA in English Lit., George Mason U., 1972, MA in English Lit., 1982. Dir. rsch. and info. Am. Soc. Assn. Execs., Washington, 1972-80, dir. mem. svcs., 1980-88, v.p., pub. Assn. Mgmt. mag., 1988-97; pres., CEO Nat. Informercial Mktg. Assn., Washington, 1997—2004, Electronic Retailing Assn., Washington, 1998—2003; chmn. Assn. Internet Radio Network. Chmn. Assn. Internet Radio Network, 2004; host weekly radio show Assn. Nation, Assn. Power and Politics. Pub. Principles of Association Management, 1976, 3d edit., 1996; columnist Footnotes, 1988-97. Bd. dirs. Ethics Resource Ctr., Washington, 1982-86; mem. Universal Postal Union Adv. Group 2000-; mem. Fed. Adv. Commn. on e-commerce; appointee DofC 1fac-4 Ecommerce, 2001-. Mem. Am. Soc. Assn. Execs. (cert.), Assn. Conv. Mktg. Execs., Greater Washington Soc. Assn. Execs. (bd. dirs. 2000—), Nat. Assn. Hispanic Mktg. Profls. (adv. bd.), Soc. Nat. Assn. Publs., Com. of 100 U.S. C. of C., Soc. Scholarly Pubs. Roman Catholic. Avocations: running, scuba diving. Home: 5315 Moultrie Rd Springfield VA 22151-1915 Office: AIR 5673 Ravnel Ln Springfield VA 22151 Home Phone: 703-321-7590; Office Phone: 703-626-9087. E-mail: elissa@elissamyers.com.

MYERS, ELLEN HOWELL, historian, educator; b. Bryan, Tex., Feb. 16, 1941; d. Douglas Wister and Ann Olive (Emory) Howell; m. William Allen Myers, Dec. 23, 1967; 1 child, William Webb. Student, Mt. Vernon Jr. Coll., 1959—61, U. Madrid, 1961—62; BA, Sophie Newcomb Coll. of Tulane U., 1963; MA, U. Va., 1965, PhD, 1970. Lectr. U. Houston, 1966—67; instr. Okla. State U., Stillwater, 1967—70; asst. prof. San Antonio Coll., 1970—73, assoc. prof., 1973—77, prof. history, 1977—. Author: (student's rev. manuals, instrs. manuals) The American Nation, 1975, 1977, 1979, 1983, 1987, Test Bank for the West Transformed, 2000; contbr. articles to profl. jours. Mem. S.W. Conf. Commn. on Higher Edn. and Campus Ministry Meth. Ch., 1978—81; bd. dirs. Family Svc. Assn., 1978—85, pres., 1983—84; bd. dirs. San Antonio Area Red Cross, 1979—85, Laurel Heights Weekday Sch., 1980—83, chmn., 1982—83. Mem.: AAUP (exec. com. San Antonio Coll. 1973—74), Conf. on L.Am. History, S.W. Conf. on L.Am. Studies (exec. com. 1974—75), Tex. C.C. Tchrs. Assn., Tues. Musical Club, Jr. League of San Antonio (bd. dirs. 1977—79), Kappa Alpha Theta, Phi Alpha Theta. Democrat. Methodist. Home: 307 Arcadia Pl San Antonio TX 78209-5950 Office: 1300 San Pedro Ave San Antonio TX 78212-4201

MYERS, ELMER, psychiatric social worker; b. Blackwell, Ark., Nov. 12, 1926; s. Chester Elmer Myers and Irene Lewis; widowed; children: Elmer Jr., Keith, Kevin. BA, U. Kans., 1951, MA, 1962; student, U. Calif., Santa Barbara, 1977-78. Lic. clin. social worker; C.C. counselor credentials. Psychiat. social worker Hastings (Nebr.) State Hosp., 1960-62, State of Calif. Bur. Social Tng. Com., Sacramento, 1962-75; supr. psychiat. social worker State of Calif., Sacramento, 1975-80, Alta Calif. Regional Ctr., Sacramento, 1980-85. Exec. dir. Tri-County Family Svcs., Yuba City, Calif., 1966-69; cons. to four convalescent Hosps., Marysville and Willows, Calif., 1969-71; lectr. Yuba Coll., Marysville, 1971-76; assoc. prof. Calif. State U., Chico, 1972-73; cons. in field, Marysville, 1985—; group and individual therapist Depot Homeless Shelter, 1996—, facilitator HIV support group, 1993-2002, counselor, 1995—; cons., therapist New Millennium Group Home, 2000. Bd. dirs. Habitat for Humanity, 1993; juror Yuba County Grand Jury, Marysville, 1965, 1987—88; sec. Y's Men's Club, Yuba City, 1964—65; chmn. Tri-County Home Health Agy., Yuba City, 1974—76; vice-chmn. Gateway Projects, Inc., Yuba City, 1974—75; bd. dirs. Yuba County Truancy Bd., Marysville, 1964—67; asst. dir. Marysville Adult Activity Ctr., 1990—; active Yuba-Sutter United Way, 1971—73, 1991—92; active, sec. Tri-County Ethnic Forum, 1991—93; steering com. Yuba County Sr. Ctr. Assn., 1992, 1995—; chmn. Yuba County Cmty. Svcs. Commn., 1997—99; bd. dirs. Yuba-Sutter Gleaners, 1997—2004, 2006—, fin. sec., 2006; chmn. Yuba-Sutter Commn. on Aging, 1996, bd. dirs., 1998, 2001; chmn. H.E.L.P. Working Group, HIV Prevention, 2000; bd. dirs. Christian Assistance Network, 1993, Golden Empire Health Sys. Agy., Sacramento, 1972—76, Youth Svcs. Bur., Yuba City, 1967, Bi-County Mental Retardation Planning Bd., Yuba City, 1972, Yuba County Juvenile Justice Commn., Marysville, 1982—90, Am. Cancer Soc., Marysville, 1985—92, Yuba County Rep. Ctrl. Com., 1983—90, Salvation Army, 1990—96, facilitator care proj., 1992—2002. Recipient Cert. Spl. Recognition, Calif. Rehab. Planning Project, 1969, Cert. Spl. Recognition, State of Calif., 1967, Cert. Spl. Recognition, Alta Calif. Regional Ctrs., 1985; named Vol. of Week, Appeal Dem. newspaper, 1999. Mem. Nat. Assn. Social Workers (cert.), Kern County Mental Health Assn. (chmn. 1978-79). Lodges: Rotary (bd. dirs. Marysville club 1975-76). Avocations: gardening, reading, computers. Home and Office: 3920 State Hwy 20 Marysville CA 95901-9003 E-mail: elm@syix.com.

MYERS, ERIC B., lawyer; BA, U. NC, Chapel Hill, 1994; JD, U. Pitts., 1997. Bar: Md., D.C., U.S. Dist. Ct. Md., U.S. Dist Ct. D.C. Law clk. Ct. Spl. Appeals, Md.; assoc. Funk & Bolton, Balt., Brown & Sheehan, Rosenberg, Martin, Funk & Greenberg, LLP; pvt. practice atty. Named one of The Top Lawyers: The Next Generation, Baltimore Mag., 2003. Mem.: ABA, Md. Bar Assn., Balt. City Bar Assn., Def. Rsch. Inst. Office: 25 S Charles St Ste 2115 Baltimore MD 21201-3305 Office Phone: 410-727-6600. *

MYERS, ERNEST M., otolaryngologist, head and neck surgeon; b. Pitts., July 9, 1945; s. Ernest H. and Ruth M. (Johnson) M.; children: Erica, Stacey, Candice, Mia; m. Patricia L. Randolph. BA, U. Pitts., 1966, MD, 1970. Diplomate Am. Bd. Otolaryngology, Head and Neck Surgery (guest examiner 1992-93). Prof. surgery Howard U. Sch. Medicine, Washington, 1979-99. Editor: (textbook) Head and Neck Oncology: Diagnosis, Treatment and Rehabilitation, 1991. Mentor, Mentors of D.C., 1989; pres. bd. dirs. Riverdance, Reston, Va., 1994. Capt. U.S. Army, 1970-74. Named one of Outstanding Otolaryngologists in The Washingtonian Mag., 1993, 95, 88. Fellow ACS; mem. Washington Acad. Surgeons, Nat. Med. Assn. (past sec. and past pres. otolaryngology sect.). Avocations: weight training, sailing, cross country skiing. Office: Howard U Hosp 2041 Georgia Ave NW Washington DC 20060-0001 Office Phone: 202-865-1431.

MYERS, EUGENE NICHOLAS, otolaryngologist, educator; b. Phila., Nov. 27, 1933; s. David and Rosalind (Nicholas) Myers; m. Barbara Labov, June 10, 1956; children: Marjorie Rose Fulbright, Jeffrey N. BS in Econs., U. Pa., 1954; MD, Temple U., 1960. Diplomate Am. Bd. Otolaryngology. Intern Mt. Sinai Hosp., NYC, 1960—61; resident Mass. Eye and Ear Infirmary, Boston, 1963—65; asst. prof. clin. otolaryngology U. Pa., 1968—72; prof. clin. oncology dept. oral pathology U. Pitts. Sch. Dental Medicine, 1975—82, prof. dept. diagnostic svcs., 1982—2000, prof. dept. oral and maxillofacial surgery, 2000—; prof., chmn., chief dept. otolaryngology U. Pitts. Med. Ctr., 1972—2005, emeritus chmn., 2005—, disting. prof. otolaryngology, 2006—. Cons. VA Med. Ctr., Pitts., 1972—, Children's Hosp., Pitts., 1972—. Editor: Cancer of the Head and Neck, 1981, 4th edit., 2003, Tracheotomy, 1985, 2d edit., 1998, Operation Otolaryngology: Head and Neck Surgery, 1997; mem. editl. bd. Laryngoscope, 1973—95, exec. editl. bd., 1995—2004, mem. editl. bd. Head and Neck Surgery, 1978—92, 1998—, AMA Archives of Otolaryngology, 1981—, Annals of Otology Rhinology and Laryngology, 1984—2005, Oncology, 1986—, European Archives of Oto-Rhino-Laryngology, 1990—97, Auris Nasus Larynx, 1996—, editor-in-chief (book) Advances in Orolaryngology, 1985—2001; co-editor: Butterworth's Intern Med. Revs., 1981—82; internat. editor Otolaryngology-Head and Neck Surgery, 1996—2005. Mem. adv. bd. Pa. Lion Hearing Rsch. Found., Pitts., 1983—99. Capt. M.C. US Army, 1965—67. Recipient Cert. of Merit Com. Rsch., Am. Acad. Otolaryngology-Salicylate Otoxicity, 1965, Award of Merit, Am. Acad. Otolaryngology-Head and Neck Surgery Inc., 1978, Robert E. Shoemaker Rsch. award, Pa. Acad. Ophthalmology and Otolaryngology, 1979, Disting. Svc. award, Am. Acad. Oto-HNS, 2001. Fellow: Am. Acad. Otolaryngology (chmn. com. on head and neck surgery 1981—83, bd. dirs. 1985—88, 1990—2003, pres. 1994—95, internat. coord. 1996—2003), Am. Laryngol. Assn. (sec. 1982—88, pres. 1989—90, mem. coun. 1990—93, James Newcomb award 1993, DeRoaldes award 2001, ALA award 2001), ACS (bd. govs. 1981—87, mem. adv. coun. 1985—87); mem.: Triological Soc. (mem. coun. 1989—92, v.p. Ea. sect. 1994—95), Am. Soc. Head and Neck Surgery (mem. coun. 1977—93, pres. 1988—90), Nat. Cancer Inst. (chmn. upper aerodigestive tract working group 1986—89), Assn. Acad. Depts. Otolaryngology (mem. coun. 1978—80), Am. Bd. Otolaryngology (bd. dirs. 1981—99, pres.-elect 1994—96, pres. 1996—98), Pitts. Athletic Assn. Republican. Jewish. Office: U Pitts Sch Med Eye and Ear Inst Ste 519 200 Lothrop St Pittsburgh PA 15213-2546 Office Phone: 412-647-2111. Business E-Mail: myersen@upmc.edu.

MYERS, FRANKLIN, oil industry executive; b. Pensacola, Fla., Nov. 2, 1952; m. Elizabeth A. Berner; children: Amanda C., Adam F., Anne Marie M., Mary Lauren Miller, Zachary J., Thomas J. BS, Miss. State U., 1974; JD, U. Miss., 1977. Bar: Miss. 1977, Tex. 1978. Ptnr. Fulbright and Jaworski, Houston, 1978-88; sr. v.p., gen. counsel Baker Hughes Inc., Houston, 1988-95; sr. v.p. Cooper Cameron Corp., Houston, 1995—, CFO, 2002—. Adj. prof. U. Tex. Sch. Law, 1990—2003; bd. dirs. InPut Output Inc., Comfort Sys., Inc. Fellow: Houston Bar Assn., Miss. Bar Assn., Tex. Bar Assn., Houston Bar Found.; mem.: Tex. Bar Found.

MYERS, GERALD EUGENE, humanities educator; b. Central City, Nebr., June 19, 1923; s. Harold W. and Mary (Ferguson) M.; m. Martha Coleman, Aug. 7, 1948; 1 son, Curt. BA, Haverford Coll., 1947; MA, Brown U., 1949, PhD, 1954. Instr. Smith Coll., 1950-52; asst. prof. Williams Coll., 1952-61; assoc. prof. Kenyon Coll., 1961-65; prof. C.W. Post Coll., L.I. U., 1965-67, Queens Coll. and Grad. Center, City U. N.Y., 1967—; also dep. exec. officer Ph.D. program Queens Coll. and Grad. Center, City U. N.Y. (Grad. Center); dir. intro. philosophy into N.Y.C. High Schs. project.; emeritus CUNY. Dir. humanities-and-dance projects, philosopher-in-residence Am. Dance Festival, Durham, N.C., 1979; project dir. African-Am. Perspectives in Am. Modern Dance, Am. Dance Festival/NEH. Author: Self, Religion and Metaphysics, 1961, Self: An Introduction to Philosophical Psychology, 1969, The Spirit of American Philosophy, 1970, William James: His Life and Thought, 1986; editor: The Black Tradition in American Modern Dance, 1988, African American Genius in Modern Dance, 1992; co-editor: Emotion Philos. Studies, 1983, Echoes from the Holocaust, 1988; cons. Free to Dancd PBS documentary, 2001; contbr. articles to profl. jours. NEH fellow, 1981-82. Mem. Am. Philos. Assn. (past sec.-treas. Western div.), Metaphys. Soc. Am., Soc. Phenomenology and Existential Philosophy, Phi Beta Kappa. Home: 36 Gardner Ave New London CT 06320-4313 Office: 33 W 42nd St New York NY 10036-8003

MYERS, HARDY, state attorney general; b. Electric Mills, Miss., Oct. 25, 1939; m. Mary Ann Thalhofer, 1962; children: Hardy III, Christopher, Jonathan. AB with distinction, U. Miss., 1961; LLB, U. Oreg., 1964. Bar: Oreg., U.S. Ct. of Appeals (9th cir.), U.S. Dist. Ct. (Dist. of Oreg.). Law clk. US Dist. Judge William G. East, 1964—65; pvt. practice Stoel Rives LLP and predecessor firms, 1965—96; atty. gen. State of Oreg., 1997—. Mem. Oreg Ho. Reps., 1975—85, spkr. of the ho., 1979—83; chair Com. on Judiciary, 1977—78, 1983—84; councilor Met. Svc. Dist. (now Metro), 1985—86. Bd. editors Oregon Law Rev. Pres. Portland City Planning Commn., 1973—74; chair Oreg. Jail Project, 1984—86, Citizens' Task Force on Mass Transit Policy, 1985—86, Oreg. Criminal Justice Coun., 1987—91, Portland Future Focus, 1990—91, Metro Charter com., 1991—92, task force on state employee benefits, 1994; co-chair gov. task force on state employee compensation, 1995; mem. Commn. on Jud. Br., 1983—85. Mem.: Multnomah County Bar Assn., Oreg. State Bar, Omicron Delta Kappa, Phi Kappa Phi, Phi Eta Sigma. Democrat. Office: Office of Atty Gen Justice Dept 1162 Court St NE Salem OR 97301-1320 Office Phone: 503-378-4732. *

MYERS, HARRY J., JR., retired publisher; b. Denver, Aug. 7, 1931; s. Harry J. and Edith M. (Reed) M.; m. Mary Kay Racine, June 21, 1958; children: Harry J., Hans R. (dec.), Peter C. BA, Colo. U., 1957; postgrad., U. Mo., 1959-60. Pub., or pub. dir. Meredith Corp., 1962-82, Geo, Archtl. Digest, Bon Appetit, Home, Sci. Am., Cowles Mag, 1982-95. Served with USMC, 1953-56. Mem. Kappa Tau Alpha, Phi Gamma Delta. Home: 46 W Ranch Trl Morrison CO 80465-9504

MYERS, IRA LEE, physician; b. Monrovia, Ala., Feb. 9, 1924; s. Ira W. and Azelea Juanita (Cobbs) Myers; m. Dorothy Will Foust, Sept. 4, 1943 (dec. June 6, 2003); children: Martha Crystal(dec.), Ira Grady, Stephen Allen, Joanna Lynn; m. Woodard H. Luker, Dec. 7, 2003. BS, Howard Coll., Birmingham, Ala., 1945; MD, U. Ala., Birmingham, 1949; postgrad., Harvard U. Sch. Public Health, Cambridge, Mass., 1953. Diplomate: Am. Bd. Preventive Medicine. Commd. officer USPHS, 1949-55; intern USPHS Marine Hosp., Seattle, 1949-50; epidemic intelligence officer Charleston, W.Va., 1950-52, Erie County Health Dept., Buffalo, 1952, Center Communicable Disease, Atlanta, 1952-55; resigned, 1955; adminstrv. health officer Ala. Dept. Health, Montgomery, 1955-63, state health officer, 1963-86. Sec. Ala. Bd. Med. Examiners, 1962-73; chmn. Ala. Bd. Registration Sanitarians, 1964-81, Ala. Air Pollution Control Commn., 1969-82; v.p. Ala. Pollution Control Fin. Authority, 1971-81; assoc. clin. prof. preventive medicine and pub. health U. Ala. Med. Sch.; mem. Ala. vol. med. adv. com. SSS, 1968-86; chmn. Ala. Health Care Hall of Fame, 1998—. Pres. Ala. div. Am. Cancer Soc., 1991-93; chmn. bd. dirs. Dalraida Health Ctr., 1992-98; chmn. Ala. Sr. Citizens Hall of Fame, 1997—. Recipient Ala. Sr. Citizens Hall of Fame Golden Eagle award, 1986, St. George medal Nat. Divisional award Am. Cancer Soc., 1989, 1st Ann. Vol. award Montgomery Bapt. Assn., 1993. Mem. AMA, Med. Assn. Ala. (William Henry Saunders award 1968, 1st annual Ira L. Myers Service award, 1986), Montgomery County Med. Soc., Ala. Pub. Health Assn. (D.G. Gill award 1967, established Ira L. Myers Scholarship Endowment), Am. Assn. Pub. Health Physicians, Assn. State and Territorial Health Officers (Arthur N. McCormick award 1976), Ala. Hosp. Assn. (hon.), State. Ala. Acad. Honor, Tuberculosis Assn. (Heacock Gold medal 1986), Montgomery Coun. of Aging (Srs. of Achievement award 1998, Gov.'s Lifetime Achievement award 1998). Lodges: Montgomery Kiwanis. Republican. Baptist. Achievements include initiating state narcotic control program, 1967, state hosp. service for indigent, 1958. Home and Office: 925 Green Forest Dr Montgomery AL 36109-1515

MYERS, JACK FREDRICK, artist, educator, writer; b. Lima, Ohio, Feb. 17, 1927; s. Harold Frank and Lesta Arvilla (Ross) M.; m. Frances Dydek, Apr. 30, 1949; children: Steven Ross, David Gene, Kevin Douglas. Student, Cleve. Inst. Art, 1947-49; MFA, Kent State U., 1980. Staff artist Bill Ripley & Assocs., Cleve., 1951-57; art dir. Premier Indsl. Corp., Cleve., 1957-70; instr. Cooper Sch. Art, Cleve., 1970-80; assoc. prof. art U. Dayton, Ohio, 1982-87; ret., 1992. Author: The Language of Visual Art, 1989, Windy Side of Care, 2002, The Greatest Gift, 2002. With USNR, 1945-46, PTO. Recipient First prize in art Newsweek/Paillard S.A., 1969. Home and Office: 22269 Country Meadows Ln Strongsville OH 44149-2000 Personal E-mail: jackms@wowway.com.

MYERS, JAMES CLARK, advertising and public relations executive; b. Chgo., Aug. 26, 1941; s. Herbert George Myers and Lenore (Goldberg) Levi; m. Judy Anne Schnitzer, Feb. 9, 1964; children: Jeffrey Stephan, Jeremy H. BA, Washington U., St. Louis, 1964. Acct. exec. Nahas, Blumberg, Zelikow, Houston, 1967-69; mgr. spl. events Houston Post, 1969-73; pres., creative dir. Motivators, Inc., Houston, 1973—2006. Vice-chmn. Internat. Sci. and Engring. Fair Coun., Washington, 1972-73; bd. dirs. Sci. Engring. Fair of Houston, 1969-73; spl. corrs. Navy Times Newspaper; pres. S.W. Houston 2000, Inc., 1999-06. Contbr. articles to newspapers. Chmn. Houston chpt. Boy Scouts Am.; mem. City of Houston Bldgs. and Stds. Commn., 2004-; dir. cmty. svcs. Brays Oaks Mgmt. Dist., Houston. Served to capt. USNR, 1964-96. Recipient Wood Badge award, Boy Scouts Am., 1979, Shofar award, 1981; named Fondren SW Citizen of Yr., 2002. Mem. Pub. Relations Soc. Am. (accredited, Silver Anvil award 1983, 87, Excalibur 2001), Bus. Adv. Fedn. (cert.) Jewish. Avocations: model railroading, square dancing, photography. Home: 8006 Duffield Ln Houston TX 77071-2017 Home Phone: 713-995-9116; Office Phone: 713-784-5560, 713-541-0447. Personal E-mail: motivators.inc@juno.com, braysoaksmd@hhcllp.com.

MYERS, JAMES M., pet products executive; BS in Acctg., John Carroll Univ. CPA. Various positions to sr. audit mgr. KPMG LLP, 1980—90; v.p., fin. to v.p., controller PETCO, San Diego, 1990—96, sr. v.p., fin., 1996—98, exec. v.p., CFO, 1998—2004, CEO, 2004—. Office: PETCO 9125 Rehco Rd San Diego CA 92121 Office Phone: 858-453-7845.

MYERS, JAMES R., lawyer; b. Valdosta, Ga., Aug. 29, 1952; s. J. Walter Jr. and Mary M.; m. Monica Faeth Myers, Sept. 19, 1992. BA cum laude, Harvard U., 1972, JD, 1975. Bar: Mass. 1975, US Dist. Ct. (DC dist.) 1976, DC 1977, US Ct. Appeals (DC cir.) 1977, US Supreme Ct. 1983, US Ct. Appeals (fed. cir.) 1991, Va. 1992, US Ct. Appeals (4th cir.) 1992. Assoc. Wald, Harkrader & Ross, Wash., 1976-77; assoc. solicitor US Dept. Energy, Wash., 1977-79; assoc. Andrews & Kurth, Wash., 1980-85; ptnr. Steele, Simmons & Fornaciari, Wash., 1985-86, Robbins & Laramie, Wash., 1986-89, Venable, Baetjer, Howard & Civiletti, Wash., 1990-97, Kilpatrick Stockton LLP, 1997—2004, Ropes & Gray LLP, 2004—. Master Giles S. Rich Am. Inn Court for intellectual property litigators; mem. editl. bd. Practical Lawyer; spkr. in field. Contbr. articles to jour. Mem.: ABA (mem. ALI-ABA bd. dirs.). Office: Ropes & Gray LLP 700 12th St NW Ste 900 Washington DC 20005 Home Phone: 301-897-9672; Office Phone: 202-508-4647. Personal E-mail: jmyers@ropesgray.com.

MYERS, JEFF L., surgeon; b. Lawton, Okla., Nov. 11, 1964; s. Lawrence Joseph and Rita Joyce Myers; m. Dahri Anna Zenker, Sept. 30, 1989; children: Connor Joseph, Cameron Marie, Tyler Gustave. MD with distinction, U. Okla., Okla. City, 2001; PhD, Georgetown U., DC, 2006. Diplomate Am. Bd. Surgery, 2002, Am. Bd. Thoracic Surgery, 2003. Chief pediatric cardiac surgery Tulane U., New Orleans, 2003—05, Lebonheur Children's Med. Ctr., Memphis, 2005—07, Mass. Gen. Hosp., 2007—; assoc. prof. surgery Harvard Med. Sch., 2007—. Dir. cardiac surg. rsch. Tulane U., 2003—05; vis. prof. surgery UCLA, 2006. Editor: (web-based textbook) E-medicine, Textbook of Pediatrics, 2005; author: articles, book chpts. Bd. govs. Operation Mend-a-Heart, New Orleans, 2004—05; mem. Children's Heartlink, Rochester, Minn., 2005. Recipient Pfizer Prize, Wash. Soc. History of Medicine, 1999. Fellow: ACS (Zehner Travelling fellowship 1999); mem.: Am. Physiol. Soc., Am. Coll. Cardiology, Internat. Soc. for Heart and Lung Transplantation, Soc. Thoracic Surgeons, Kappa Sigma (chpt. pres. 1986). Office: Mass Gen Hosp 55 Fruit St Cox 662 Boston MA 02114 Office Phone: 617-643-0172. Personal E-mail: myersjeff@yahoo.com.

MYERS, JEFFREY DANIEL, concert pianist, music educator; b. Erie, Pa., June 7, 1970; s. Neal Anthony and Beryl Diane Myers; m. Molly R. Knapp, July 3, 2004. MusB, Mercyhurst Coll., Erie, Pa., 1993; MusM, Manhattan Sch. Music, NYC, 1999; student, Chautauqua Sch. Performing Arts. Dir. Erie Piano Acad., Pa., 1999—2006; chmn. Neal A. Myers Found. Music Edn., 2004; mem. faculty Montessori Regional Charter Sch., Erie, 2006, Veritas Prep. Acad., Phoenix, 2006—; mem. faculty, chair dept. piano Ariz. Sch. for the Arts, Phoenix, 2007—. Soloist: piano recital Hubbard Hall, 1999, Cancer Benefit St. Andrews Roman Cath. Ch., 2006, performer: chamber music recital Lincoln Heights Christian Ch., 2007, piano soloist: Erie Chamber Orch., 2000, debut piano and violin concert: Classical Concert Series, Kent State U., 2002; Classical Concert Series, Kent State U., Ashtabula, Ohio, 2003. Avocations: painting, art history, travel, world history. Business E-Mail: jeff@myers-usa.com.

MYERS, JESSE JEROME, lawyer; b. Anthony, Kans., Sept. 30, 1940; s. Claud Lewis and Lucille S. (Robertson) M.; m. Claire H. Conni, Nov., 1966; children: Timothy Todd, Jessica Joy. BS, McPherson Coll., Kans., 1963; JD, Washburn U., Kans., 1970. Bar: Kans. 1970, Mo.1996, US Dist. Ct. Kans. 1970. Law clk. U.S. Dist. Ct. Judge Frank Theis, Wichita, Kans., 1970—72; individual practice law Wichita, Kans., 1972—74, 1995—; lawyer Cessna Aircraft Co., Wichita, Kans., 1974—75; v.p., dir., gen. counsel Martin K. Eby Constrn. Co., Wichita, Kans., 1975—95. Served with USN, 1963-67.

MYERS, JOHN JOSEPH, archbishop; b. Ottawa, Ill., July 26, 1941; s. M.W. and Margaret Louise (Donahue) M. BA maxima cum laude, Loras Coll., 1963; Licentiate in Sacred Theology, Gregorian U., Rome, 1967; Doctor of Canon Law, Cath. U. Am., 1977; DD (hon.), Apostolic See, Vatican City, 1987. Ordained priest Roman Cath. Ch., 1966, bishop, 1987. Asst. pastor Holy Family Parish, Peoria, Ill., 1967-70; asst. dept. internat. affairs US Cath. Conf., Washington, 1970-71; assoc. pastor St. Matthew Parish, Champaign, Ill., 1971-74; adminstr. St. Mary's Cathedral, Diocese Peoria, 1977—78, 1984; vice chancellor Cath. Diocese Peoria, 1977-78, vocation dir., 1977-87, chancellor, 1978-87, vicar gen., 1982-90, mem. Prebyteral Coun., 1968—70, 1984—90, bd. Consultors, 1978—90, coadjutor bishop, 1987-90; bishop of Peoria, Ill., 1990—2001; appointed Superior of Turks and Caicos Antilles, 2001; Archbishop of Newark, NJ, 2001—. Bd. govs. Canon Law Soc. Am., Washington, 1985-87; bd. dirs. Nat. Cath. Bio Ethics Ctr., Boston, 1999—, bd. gov.; mem. sem. com. Mt. St. Mary's Sem., Md., 1989-94; bd. trustees Cath. U. Am., Washington, 1999-, Papal Found.; seminary com., fin. com., Ad Hoc Com. for By-Laws., Cat. U. Am., Washington; seminary bd. Kenrick-Glennon of the Archdiocese of St. Louis. Author: (commentary) Book V of the Code of Canon Law, 1983; contbr. numerous articles to religious publs. Mem. Canon Law Soc. Am., Nat. Conf. Cath. Bishops. (Canonical Affairs Com., 1988-2002, Com. on Shrines and Pilgrimages, 1990-, Com. on Vocations, 1995-1998, Ad Hoc Com. on Sexual Abuse, 2002, Com. on Hispanic Affairs, 2002-, and Com. on Aid to Eastern Europe, 1999-) Roman Catholic. Office: Archdiocese of Newark 171 Clifton Ave Newark NJ 07104-0500

MYERS, JOHN T., physical therapist, educator; s. Robert and Helen Myers. BS in Gen. Sci. summa cum laude, Cleve. State U., Ohio, 1984; MBA, Heriot-Watt U., Edinburgh, Scotland, 1998. Lic. phys. therapist Ohio OTPTAT Bd., 1984. From staff phys. therapist to sr. phys. therapist, supr. phys. therapy Cleve. Clinic Found., 1984—97; program dir., assoc. prof. Lorain County C.C., Elyria, Ohio, 1997—. Team leader. on-site reviewer for phys. therapist asst. programs Commn. on Accreditation in Phys. Therapy Edn., Dept. of Accreditation, Am. Phys. Therapy Assn., Alexandria, Va., 2005—; spkr. continuing med. edn., Cleve., 1984—; cons. to musicians and orchestras regarding injury prevention and treatment, Cleve., 1988—. Author: (chpt.) Treatment Approaches in the Performer with Cervico-brachial Pain, 1992; co-reviewer (textbook) Measurement of Joint Motion: A Guide to Goniometry; contbr. articles to profl. jours. Mem. Lorain County Tech. Prep. Consortium, Ohio, 1999—2003; chair Loraine County C.C. PTA Program Cmty. Adv. Cmty., Elyria, Ohio, 1997—2006; mem. Coll. Found. Adv. Bd., Lorain, Ohio, 2000—03. Recipient Outstanding Faculty award, Lorain County C.C., 1998-1999, Faculty Excellence award, Lorain County C.C. Found., 2001; Gait and Motion Analysis Sys. for Tchg. grant, 2001. Mem.: Ohio Phys. Therapy Assn. (faculty liaison com.), Am. Phys. Therapy Assn. Achievements include design and development of structure and curriculum for the Physical Therapist Assistant Program at Lorain County Community College. Office: Lorain County CC 1005 Abbe Rd N HS 223 Elyria OH 44035 Office Phone: 440-366-7881.

MYERS, JOHN WESCOTT, air transportation executive; b. LA, June 13, 1911; s. Louis Wescott and Blanche (Brown) M.; m. Lucia Raymond, Mar. 21, 1941 (dec. Mar. 1999); children: Louis W. (dec.), Lucia R. AB, Stanford U., 1933; JD, Harvard U., 1936. Bar: Calif. 1936. Ptnr. law firm O'Melveny & Myers, LA, 1936-42; from test pilot to sr. v.p., dir. Northrop Corp., 1942-54, 1954-79; chmn. bd. Pacific Airmotive Corp., 1954-79, Airflite, Long Beach, Calif., 1970-89, Flying M Assocs., Long Beach, 1989—. Owner Flying M Ranches, Merced, Calif., 1959—. Dir. Smithsonian Nat. Air and Space Dulles Ctr. Project. Fellow Soc. Exptl. Test Pilots; mem. Calif. Bar Assn., Los Angeles Bar Assn., Inst. Aerospace Scis., Order of Daedalians (hon.). Clubs: Bohemian, California, Los Angeles Country, Los Angeles Yacht, Sunset, Aviation Country, Conquistadores del Cielo. Republican. Home: 718 N Rodeo Dr Beverly Hills CA 90210-3210 Office: 3200 Airflite Way Long Beach CA 90807-5312

MYERS, JOHN WILLIAM, lawyer; b. Aug. 8, 1941; s. Fred L. and Dossie (Huddleston) Myers; m. Jane Sutton, July 29, 1995; children: John William II, James Bryan. BS, U. Tenn., 1963, JD, 1965. Bar: Tenn. 1965. Ptnr. Myers & Bell, Attys., Newport, Tenn., 1966—. Dir. Newport Fed. Bank, 1975—, chmn., 1981—. Mem.: Tenn. Bar Assn. Republican. Episcopalian. Home: 404 6th St Newport TN 37821-3712 Office: Myers & Bell Attys PO Box 160 Newport TN 37822-0160 Office Phone: 423-623-3091. Business E-Mail: billmyers@myersbell.com.

MYERS, JULIE L., federal agency administrator; b. Shawnee, KS, 1969; m. John F. Wood, 2005. BA, Baylor U.; JD, Cornell U., 1994. Law clk. to Hon. C. Arlen Beam US Ct. Appeals (8th cir.); assoc. Mayer, Brown & Platt, Chgo., 1993—97; assoc. ind. counsel Office of Ind. Counsel Kenneth Starr, Washington, 1998—99; asst. U.S. atty. (ea. dist.) N.Y. US Dept. Justice, Bklyn., 1999—2001, chief of staff to asst. atty. gen. criminal divsn. Washington, 2003; dept. asst. sec. for money laundering and fin. crimes US Dept. Treasury, Washington, 2001—03; asst. sec. for export enforcement, Bur. Industry & Security US Dept. Commerce, Washington, 2003—05; spl. asst. to the Pres. for presdl. personnel The White House, Washington, 2005—06; asst. sec. US Immigration & Customs Enforcement US Dept. Homeland Security, Washington, 2006—.

MYERS, KENNETH RAYMOND, lawyer; b. NYC, Apr. 14, 1939; s. Cyril Burleigh and Dorothy (Podolyn) M.; m. Susan Kay Plotnick, Sept. 9, 1962; children: Lisa R., Jonathan S., Andrew C. SB, MIT, 1960; JD, Harvard U., 1963. Bar: Ill. 1963, Pa. 1968. Assoc. Ross, Hardies & O'Keefe, Chgo., 1963-68, Morgan, Lewis & Bockius, Phila., 1968-71, ptnr., 1972-2000; of counsel High, Swartz, Roberts & Seidel LLP, Norristown, Pa., 2000—. Mem. rules com. Environ. Hearing Bd., Harrisburg, Pa., 1984-89. Editor: Environmental Spill Reporting Handbook, 1992-2004; contbg. author: Environmental Law Practice Guide, 1992-2000; contbr. articles to profl. jours. Dir., past chair Water Resources Assn. Del. River Basin, Valley Forge, Pa.; dir. Albert Einstein Healthcare Network, 1997-2002, Germantown Hosp., 1998-99, Belmont Hosp., 1999-2001; pres. Am. Jewish Congress, Phila., 1996-99, mem. nat. commn., N.Y.C., 1984-99; treas. Jewish Social Policy Action Network, 2004—. Mem. ABA (rep. to U.S. Office Personnel Mgmt. 1975—), Pa. Bar Assn., Montgomery Bar Assn., Eta Kappa Nu. Home: 355 River Birch Cir Elkins Park PA 19027-1338 Home Phone: 215-635-2664; Office Phone: 610-275-0700. Personal E-mail: kmyers@highswartz.com, krmyers@alum.mit.edu.

MYERS, LISA M., broadcast journalist; b. Joplin, Mo. BA in Journalism, U. Mo., 1973. Washington, DC corr. The Chicago Sun-Times, 1977-79; White House corr. The Washington Star, Washington, 1980-81; with NBC News, 1981—, named Diplomatic Corr., 1988, Chief Congl. Corr., 1992, sr. investigative corr. NBC Investigative Unit, 2002—. Recipient Humanitas award, 1985, two time honoree, Am. Women in Radio and TV, Headliner award, 1990, Clarion award, Women in Communications, 1998, 2004, Edward R. Murrow award, 2000, Joan Barone award for exceptional reporting on the Enron scandal, 2003, Emmy award for Business and Financial Reporting, 2004, Gracie Allen Individual Achievement award, 2005, Mo. Honor Medal for Distinguished Service in Journalism, U. Mo., 2005, George Polk award for Network Television Reporting, 2006. Office: NBC News Washington Bur 4001 Nebraska Ave NW Washington DC 20016-2733 *

MYERS, LONN WILLIAM, lawyer; b. Rockford, Ill., Nov. 14, 1946; s. William H. and Leona V. (Janvrin) M.; m. Janet L. Forbes, May 14, 1968; children: Andrew, Hillary, Corwin. BA, Mich. State U., 1968; MBA, Ind. U., 1973; JD, Harvard U., 1976. Bar: Ill. 1976, U.S. Ct. of Fed. Claims 1977, U.S. Tax Ct. 1977, U.S. Ct. Appeals (7th cir.) 1977. Ptnr. McDermott Will & Emery LLP, Chgo., 1976—2005, counsel, 2006—. Served to maj. USAR, 1968—80. Mem. ABA (capital recovery and leasing com. tax sect., tax exempt fin. com. tax sect.). Episcopalian. Office: McDermott Will & Emery LLP 227 W Monroe St Chicago IL 60606-5096 Home: 1623 Glenview Rd Unit 316 Glenview IL 60025-2982 Office Phone: 312-984-7537. Business E-Mail: lmyers@mwe.com.

MYERS, MARILYN GLADYS, pediatric hematologist, oncologist; b. Lyons, Nebr., July 17, 1930; d. Leonard Clarence and Marian N. (Manning) M.; m. Paul Frederick Motzkus, July 24, 1957 (dec. Aug. 1982). BA cum laude, U. Omaha, 1954; MD, U. Nebr., 1959. Diplomate Am. Bd. Pediat. Intern Orange County Gen. Hosp., Orange, Calif., 1959-60, resident, 1960-62; fellow in hematology/oncology Orange County Gen. Hosp./Children's Hosp. L.A., 1962-64; assoc. in rsch., chief dept. hematology/oncology Children's Hosp., Orange, 1964-80, dir. outpatient dept., 1964-73, assoc. dir. leukapheresis unit, 1971-80; clin. practice hematology, oncology, rheumatology Orange, 1964-80; instr. Coll. Medicine U. Calif., Irvine, 1968-71, asst. clin. prof. pediatrics, 1971—; pvt. practice hematology, oncology, rheumatology Santa Ana, Calif., 1980—. Clin. rschr. exptl. drugs. Contbr. articles to med. jours. Med. adv. com. Orange County Blood Bank Hemophiliac Found. Grantee Am. Leukemia Soc., 1963, Am. Heart Assn., 1964. Fellow Am. Acad. Pediat.; mem. AMA, Calif. Med. Assn., LA County Med. Assn., Orange County Med. Assn., Orange County Pediat. Soc., Southwestern Pediat. Soc., LA Pediat. Soc., Internat. Coll. Pediat., Orange County Oncologic Soc., Am. Heart Assn. (Cardiopulmonary Coun.). Republican. Methodist. Avocation: reading. Office: 2220 E Fruit St Ste 217 Santa Ana CA 92701-4459 Office Phone: 714-541-3393.

MYERS, MARK D., federal official, geologist; b. Monroe, Wis., Apr. 24, 1955; s. Rhea Bowman and Ardelle Ione (Van Matre) M.; m. Alice Reding Myers, April 30, 1983; children: Justine Alice, Nathan Mark. BS in Geology and Geophysics with honors, U. Wis., 1977, MS in Geology, 1981; PhD in Geology, U. Alaska, 1994. Petroleum geologist ARCO Oil & Gas, Lafayette, La., 1981-83, ARCO Alaska, Inc., Anchorage, 1983-87; geologist, dir. Divsn. Oil & Gas, State of Alaska, Anchorage, 1988—2005; dir. US Geological Survey, US Dept. Interior, Reston, Va., 2006—. Contbr. articles to scientific jours. Lt. USAF Reserve, 1977-2003 Mem. Am. Assn. Petroleum Geologists (del. 1992—), Alaska Geological Soc. (v.p. 1993, mem. bd. dirs. 1993-95), Soc. Sedimentary Geology, Eagle River Presbyn. Ch. (pres. bd. trustees 1993—). Avocations: commercial multiengine instrument pilot ratings, skiing, fishing, sailing. Office: US Geological Survey 12201 Sunrise Valley Dr Mail Stop 100 Reston VA 20192 *

MYERS, MARY KATHLEEN, publishing executive; b. Cedar Rapids, Iowa, Aug. 19, 1945; d. Joseph Bernard and Marjorie Helen (Huntsman) Weaver; m. David F. Myers, Dec. 30, 1967; children: Mindy, James. BA in English and Psychology, U. Iowa, 1967. Tchr. Lincoln HS, Des Moines, 1967-80; editor Perfection Learning Corp., Des Moines, 1980-87, v.p., editor-in-chief, 1987-93; pres., founding ptnr. orgn. to promote Edward de Bono Advanced Practical Thinking Tng., Des Moines, 1992—; founder Myers House LLC, 2002. Pres. Innova Tng. & Cons., Inc., 2000-05. Editor: Six Thinking Hats, 1991, Lateral Thinking, 1993, Direct Attention Thinking Tools, 1997, Total Creativity, 1997 Focus on Facilitation, 2004, Simplicity, 2005; pub. A Disgrace to the Profession, 2002. Adv. bd. Sch. Bus., Econs. and Acctg., Simpson Coll., 1998—. Mem. ASTD, Am. Creativity Assn. (bd. dirs. 1997-2000, pres. 1999), Instrnl. Systems Assn. (mem. bd. dirs. 2002-04). Home: 813 56th St West Des Moines IA 50266-6314 Office: de Bono Thinking Systems 2570 106th St # A Des Moines IA 50322-3771 Home Phone: 515-225-7866; Office Phone: 515-334-2687. Business E-Mail: kmyers@debonosystems.com.

MYERS, MICHAEL TODD, accountant, telecommunications industry executive, director; s. Kelly Joe Myers and JoAnn Campbell McManus, Michael McManus (Stepfather) and René Myers (Stepmother). BBA, We. Mich. U., Kalamazoo, 1992; MBA, Ga. State U., Atlanta, 2000. CPA Ga. State Bd. Accountancy, 1998. Sr. analyst fin. Contel Cellular/GTE Mobilnet, Atlanta, 1993—96; mgr. budgets GTE Wireless, Alpharetta, Ga., 1996—2000; assoc. dir. partnership acctg. Verizon Wireless, Alpharetta, 2000—. Mem. choir St. John Neumann Adult Choir, Lilburn, Ga., 2000—07. Mem.: Mensa, Western Mich. U. Alumni Assn. (life). Democrat. Roman Catholic. Office: Verizon Wireless One Verizon Pl Alpharetta GA 30004 Home Phone: 770-931-8232; Office Phone: 678-339-5325. Personal E-mail: todd@durfee.net.

MYERS, MICHELE TOLELA, former academic administrator; b. Rabat, Morocco, Sept. 25, 1941; arrived in U.S., 1964; d. Albert and Lillie (Abecassis) Tolela; m. Pierre Vajda, Sept. 12, 1962 (div. Jan. 1965); m. Gail E. Myers, Dec. 20, 1968 (div. Oct. 2003); children: Erika, David. Diploma, Inst. Polit. Studies, U. Paris, 1962; MA, U. Denver, 1966, PhD, 1967; MA, Trinity U., 1977; LHD, Wittenberg U., 1994, Denison U., 1998, U. Denver, 1999. Asst. prof. speech Manchester Coll., North Manchester, Ind., 1967—68; asst. prof. speech and sociology Monticello Coll., Godfrey, Ill., 1968—71; asst. prof. communication Trinity U., San Antonio, 1975—80, assoc. prof., 1980—86, asst. v.p. for acad. affairs, 1982—85, assoc. v.p., 1985—86; assoc. prof. sociology, dean Undergrad. Coll. Bryn Mawr Coll., Pa., 1986—89; pres. Denison U., Granville, Ohio, 1989—98, Sarah Lawrence Coll., Bronxville, NY, 1998—2007, pres. emerita, 2007—. Comm. analyst Psychology and Commn., San Antonio, 1974—83; bd. dirs. Sherman Fairchild Found., 1992—; mem. Fed. Res. Bank Cleve., 1995—98; pres.'s commn. Nat. Collegiate Athletic Assn., 1993—97, JSTOR, 1999—, ARTSTOR, 2003—. Co-author (with Gail Myers): The Dynamics of Human Communication, 1973, The Dynamics of Human Communication, 6th and internat. edits., 1992, The Dynamics of Human Communication, French transl., 1984, Communicating When We Speak, 1975, Communicating When We Speak, 2d edit., 1978, Communication for the Urban Professional, 1977, Managing by Communicaton: An Organizational Approach, 1982, Managing by Communicaton: An Organizational Approach, Spanish transl., 1983, Managing by Communicaton: An Organizational Approach, internat. edit., 1982. Trustee Phila. Child Guidance Clinic, 1988—89; trustee assoc. The Bryn Mawr Sch., Balt., 1987—89; v.p., bd. dirs. San Antonio Cmty. Guidance Ctr., 1979—83, Bank One, Columbus, 1990—94. Recipient Chevalier de la Legion d'Honneur, 2007; fellow in acad. adminstrn., Am. Coun. Edn., 1981—82. Mem.: Am. Coun. Edn. (commn. on women in higher edn. 1990—92, bd. dirs. 1993—99, chmn. 1997—98).

MYERS, MIKE, actor, scriptwriter, film producer; b. Toronto, Ont., Can., May 25, 1963; s. Eric and Bunny (Hind) M.; m. Robin Ruzan, 1993 (separated). Stage appearences: The Second City, Toronto, 1986-88, Chgo., 1988-89; actor, writer: Mullarkey & Myers, Can., 1984-86, (TV show) Saturday Night Live, 1989-94 (Emmy award for outstanding writing in a comedy or variety series 1989), (film) Wayne's World, 1992, So I Married an Axe Murderer, 1993, Wayne's World II (also screenwriter, prodr.), 1993, Austin Powers: International Man Of Mystery (also screenwriter, prodr.), 1997, Pete's Meteor, 1998, It's a Dog's Life, 1998, 54, 1998, Austin Powers: The Spy Who Shagged Me (also screenwriter, prodr.), 1999, Austin Powers: The Animated Series, 1999, Shrek (voice), 2001, Austin Powers Goldmember (also writer, prodr.), 2002, View from the Top, 2003, Shrek 4-D (voice), 2003, The Cat in the Hat, 2003, Shrek 2 (voice), 2004, Shrek the Third (voice), 2007; actor: (TV movie) John and Yoko, 1985,

Elvis Stories, 1989, Saturday Night Live: The Best of Phil Hartman, 1998, Saturday Night Live: the Best of Mike Myers, 1998, Saturday Night Live: 25th Anniversary, 1999, Madonna: The Video Collection 93.99, 1999; screenwriter: (tv movie) Murderers Among Us: The Simon Wiesenthal Story, 1989, Saturday Night Live: The Best of Mike Myers, 1998; (video) Far Far Away Idol (voice), 2004; (video game voice) Shrek: Smash n' Crash Racing, 2006; TV appearances The Littlest Hobo, 1979, Russell Gilbert Show, 1998, Night of Too Many Stars: An Overbooked Event for Autism Edn., 2006; dir. (film) The Bacchae, 1999. Recipient Can. comedy award, 2000, MTV Generation award, 2007. *

MYERS, MILES ALVIN, educational association administrator, researcher; b. Newton, Kans., Feb. 4, 1931; s. Alvin F. and Katheryn P. (Miles) M.; m. Celeste Myers; children: Royce, Brant, Roslyn. BA in Rhetoric, U. Calif., Berkeley, 1953, MAT in English, 1979, MA in English, 1982, PhD in Lang. and Literacy, 1982. Cert. secondary tchr. English. Tchr. English Washington Union High Sch., Fremont, Calif., 1957-59, Oakland (Calif.) High Sch., 1959-67, 69-74, Concord High Sch., Mt. Diablo, Calif., 1967-69; chmn. bd. dirs. Alpha Plus Corp. Preschs., Piedmont, Calif., 1968—2002; dir. All City High, 1973-74; tchr. English Castlemont High Sch., Oakland, 1974-75; mem. faculty U. Calif., Berkeley, 1975-85, adminstrv. dir. Bay Area writing project Sch. Edn., 1976-85, adminstrv. dir. nat. writing project Sch. Edn., 1979-85; pres., CEO Calif. Fedn. Tchrs., 1985-90; exec. dir. Edschool.com of Edvantage/Riverdeep, 1999—2001; dir. Inst. Rsch. on Learning and Tchg., Berkeley, Calif., 1998—; sr. rschr. Inst. for Stds. Curricula and Assessment, United Tchrs. LA, 2000—. Co-dir. Nat. Standards Project for English Language Arts, 1992-96; adj. prof. English U. Ill., Champaign-Urbana, 1991-94; vis. lectr. at numerous colleges and Univs.; rschr. in field. Author: The Meaning of Literature, 1973; co-author: Writing: Unit Lessons in Composition, Book III, 1965, The English Book-Composition Skills, 1980; author: A Procedure for Holistic Scoring, 1980, Changing our Minds, 1996; co-author: Exemplars of Standards for English Language Arts, 3 vols., 1997, Asilomar Testing Report, 2001, CSC Professional Code for English/ELA Teachers, 2005; editor Calif. Tchr., 1966-81; contbr. articles to profl. jours. Sgt. US Army, 1953—55. Recipient cert. of Merit, Ctrl. Calif. Coun. Tchrs. of English, 1969, Commendation award Oakland Fedn. Tchrs., 1970, First Place award Internat. Labor Assn., 1971, Disting. Svc. award Calif. Coun. Classified Employees, 1991, Svc. award Nat. Writing Project, 1996. Fellow Nat. Conf. Rsch. in English; mem. Nat. Coun. Tchrs. English (exec. dir. 1990-97), Nat. Conf. on Rsch. in English, Am. Fedn. Tchrs. (legis. dir. Calif. Fedn. Tchrs. 1971-72, Union Tchr. Press awards 1969-75, 86-89, 91, Ben Rust award Calif. Fedn. Tchrs. 1994), Am. Edn. Rsch. Assn., Calif. Assn. Tchrs. English (Disting. Svc. award 86), U. Calif. Berkeley Alumni Assn. Home: 5823 Scarborough Dr Oakland CA 94611-2721 Office: Dir Inst Rsch on Learning & Tchg Berkeley CA 94704 Home Phone: 510-531-0409. Home Fax: 510-531-0409. Personal E-mail: milesmye@pacbell.net.

MYERS, PAUL WALTER, military officer, researcher, retired neurosurgeon; b. Schenectady, NY, Jan. 15, 1923; s. Roy Ferris Myers and Ruth Dorothy Mott; m. Virginia Eleanor Carman, June 17, 1944; children: Peter, Paul, Joan, Debra, Michelle. MD, Albany Med. Coll., NY, 1946, DSc (hon.), 1985; BS, Union Coll., Schenectady, NY, 1990. Bd. cert. Am. Bd. Neurol. Surgery. Intern Ellis Hosp., Schenectady, 1946—47; pvt. practice rural physician Duanesburg, NY, 1947—48; pvt. practice suburban physician Schenectady, 1948—49; commd. 1st lt. US Army, 1949; advanced through grades to lt. gen. USAF, 1978; chief profl. svcs. Ea. Air Def. Force, Stewart Field, NY, 1951—52; resident neurosurgery Albany Med. Ctr., 1952—56; chief neurosurgery USAF Hosp. Parks AFB, Livermore, Calif., 1956—58, USAF Hosp., Lackland AFB, Tex., 1958—71; comdr. Wilford Hall Med. Ctr., Lackland AFB, 1971—78; surgeon gen. USAF, Washington, 1978—82; ret., 1982. Pres. Assn. Mil. Surgeons, Washington, 1980—81, Soc. Clin. Surgery, San Antonio. Contbr. articles to profl. jours. Pvt. US Army, 1943—45, lt. gen. USAF, 1978—82. Decorated Legion of Merit USAF, Commendation medal, DSM, DSM with cluster-first oak leaf, Flight Surgeon's badge Republic of Korea, Order Nat. Security Merit Gugseon medal. Fellow: ACS; mem.: Alpha Omega Alpha. Episcopalian. Avocations: model railroading, golf, sailing, boating. Home: 5100 John D Ryan Blvd San Antonio TX 78245-3502

MYERS, PETER SCOTT, lawyer; 2 children. BA in Lit., Am. U., Washington, DC, 1981; JD, U. Calif., San Francisco, 1984. Bar: Calif. 1984, US Dist. Ct. (no. dist. Calif.) 1984, US Dist. Ct. (so. dist. Calif.) 1986, US Ct. Appeals (9th cir.) 1986, US Dist. Ct. (ea. dist. Calif.) 1987, US Dist. Ct. (ctrl. dist. Calif.) 1988, US Tax Ct. 1997. Assoc. Bartko, Tarrant & Miller, San Francisco, 1985-87, Pillsbury, Madison & Sutro, San Francisco, 1987-92; prin. Fritz & Myers, San Francisco, 1992; ptnr. Myers Law Firm, San Francisco, 1992—. Adj. prof. Hastings Coll. Law, 1988-90; del. State Bar Conf. Dels., 1992-95. Dir. Barristers' Club, San Francisco, 1993-94, Holy Family Day Home, San Francisco, 1993-94; dir., pres. Redwood Heights Improvement Assn., Oakland, Calif., 1992-94. Named a Super Lawyer, No. Calif. Super Lawyers, 2004, 05, 06; Named one of Top 100 Attys., Worth mag., 2005-06; recipient Wiley Manuel Pro Bono award State Bar Calif., 1991-92, 92-93, Outstanding Pro-Bono Atty. award BASF, 1991. Mem.: Bar Assn. San Francisco. Office: Myers Law Firm PC 100 Spear St Ste 1430 San Francisco CA 94105 Office Phone: 415-896-1500. Office Fax: 415-896-5068.

MYERS, PHILLIP FENTON, corporate financial, information technology executive; b. Cleve., June 24, 1935; s. Max I. and Rebecca (Rosenblum) M.; m. Hope Gail Strum, Aug. 13, 1961 B in Indsl. Engring., Ohio State U., 1958, MBA, 1960; D in Bus. Adminstrn., Harvard U., 1966. Staff indsl. engr. Procter & Gamble Co., Cin., 1958; sr. cons. Cresap, McCormack & Paget, NYC, 1960—61; staff assoc. Mitre Corp., Bedford, Mass., 1961; cons. Sys. Devel. Corp., Santa Monica, Calif., 1963—64; dir. long range planning Electronic Splty. Co., LA, 1966—68; chmn. Atek Industries, 1968—72; pres. Myers Fin. Corp., 1973—82; chmn. Amvid Comm. Svcs., Inc., 1975—79, Omni Resources Devel. Corp., 1979—83; chmn., pres. Am. Internat. Mining Co., Inc., 1979—83; pres. Advent Internat. Mgmt. Co., Inc., 1982—; chmn. Global Bond Mktg. Svcs., Inc., 1987—90; pres., CEO Whitehall Container Mfg. Corp., 1988—91; pres. Whitehall Motors Co., 1989—97, Allied Metamatter Tech. Corp., 1994—96; chmn. U.S. Water Resources, Inc., 1994—96; pres. Am. Tech. Venture Fund Mgmt., Inc., Advent Internat. Realty Corp., 1996—98, First Internat. Capital Corp., 1996—2000. Pres. Turbogen, Inc., 1995-98, Blue Star Material Techs. Inc., 1997-2000, founding dir. Warner Ctr. Bank, 1980-83; bd. dirs., pres. Cyber Security Systems, Inc., 2000—; lectr. bus. adminstrn. U. So. Calif., L.A., 1967-74; prof. Grad. Sch. Bus. Adminstrn. Pepperdine U., 1974-81. Trustee, treas. Chamber Symphony Soc. Calif., 1971-78; mem. campaign issues com. Reagan for Pres., 1976, 80; pub. safety commr. City of Hidden Hills, Calif., 1976-83, chmn., 1982-83; co-chmn. budget adv. com. Las Virgenes Sch. Dist., 1983-86; mem. Mayor's Blue Ribbon Fin. Com., 1981-82; mem. dean's select adv. com. Coll. Engring., Ohio State U., 1984-94; mem. state exec. com. Calif. Libertarian Party, chmn. region 61, 1989-90, chmn. strategic planning com.; dep. chmn. Los Angeles County Libertarian Party, 1991-92; chairperson campaign issues com. Marrou for Pres., 1991-92; chmn. bd. trustees WWII Hist. Soc., 1992—; first v.p. Armed Forces Cmty. Rels. Coun. Ctrl. Ohio, 2001-04. Capt. USAF, 1958-60. Ford Found. fellow, 1961-64 Mem. Soc. Automotive Engrs., Harvard Bus. Sch. Assn., Ohio State Alumni Assn., Harvard Bus. Club Columbus (bd. dirs. 1998—, pres. 1996-98), Ohio State Alumni Club (pres. 1998-99), Harvard Club Ctrl. Ohio (bd. dirs.). Personal E-mail: philmyers@wowway.com. *Personal philosophy: All out all the time. I stand for the creation of a new system of global governance which stresses individual liberty, freedom and responsibility, and which leads to a world that works for everyone with no one left out. In business, I stand for exceptional vision, creativity, innovation, and contribution.*

MYERS, PHILLIP WARD, otolaryngologist; b. Evanston, Ill., Nov. 11, 1939; s. R. Maurice and Vivian (Ward) M.; m. Lynetta Sargent, Dec. 22, 1963; children: Andrea, Ward, Alycia, Amanda, Andrew. BS, Western Ill. U., 1961; MD, U. Ill., 1965. Diplomate: Am. Bd. Otolaryngology. Intern St. Paul-Ramsey Hosp., 1965-66; resident in otolaryngology U. Louisville, 1966-68; resident Northwestern U., 1968-70, fellow, 1970-71; practice medicine specializing in otolaryngology Springfield, Ill., 1973—; clin. prof. otolaryngology So. Ill. U., Springfield, 1973—. Served to maj. M.C. AUS, 1971-73. Fellow Am. Soc. for Head and Neck Surgery, Am. Acad. Facial Plastic and Reconstructive Surgery; ACS, Am. Acad. Otolaryngology-Head and Neck Surgery. Achievements include research in perilymphatic fistulas. Home: 3423 N Oak Hill Rd Rochester IL 62563-9273 Office: So Ill Sch Medicine PO Box 19662 Springfield IL 62794-9662

MYERS, PRISCILLA A., insurance company executive; BS in Polit. Sci. and Econs., U. Mass., 1973; MBA, Suffolk U., 1978. Staff auditor The Prudential Ins. Co. Am., Boston, 1976-95, sr. v.p. and auditor, 1995-98, sr. v.p. demutualization, 1998—2002; sr. v.p., chief mktg. officer Prudential Fin., Inc., Newark, 2002—. Mem. Auditing Com. Mcpl. Excess Liability Joint Ins. Fund; trustee Inst. Internal Auditors Profl. Rsch. Found. Trustee St. Peter's Coll. Office: Prudential Fin Inc Chief Mktg Officer 213 Washington St 18th Fl Newark NJ 07102-2992

MYERS, R(ALPH) CHANDLER, lawyer; b. LA, Jan. 9, 1933; s. Ralph Cather and Winifred (Chandler) M.; m. Rebecca Blythe Borkgren, Jan. 11, 1963. BA, Stanford U., 1954, JD, 1958; LLD (hon.), Whittier Coll., 1988. Bar: Calif. 1959, U.S. Dist. Ct. (ctrl. dist.) Calif. 1959, U.S. Supreme Ct. 1971. Law clk., then assoc. Parker, Stanbury, Reese & McGee, LA, 1958-63; assoc. Nicholas, Kolliner & Van Tassel, LA, 1963-65; ptnr. Myers & D'Angelo and predecessors, L.A. and Pasadena, Calif., 1965—. Nat. panelist Am. Arbitration Assn., LA, 1964-2000; bd. visitors Stanford U. Law Sch., Calif., 1970-73; judge pro tem panel LA Mcpl. Ct., 1971-81; mem. LA County Dist. Atty.'s Adv. Coun., 1976-83. Nat. vice chmn. Keystone Gifts, Stanford Centennial Campaign, 1987—92; trustee Whittier Coll., Calif., 1973—2001, chmn. bd. trustees Calif., 1981—87, trustee emeritus Calif., 2001—; trustee Flintridge Prep. Sch., LaCanada-Flintridge, Calif., 1981—88, chmn. bd. trustees, 1985—88; co-founder Whittier Law Sch., 1975, trustee, 1975—2001, chmn. bd. trustees, 1981—87, trustee emeritus, 2001—; bd. dirs. Opera Guild So. Calif., LA, 1971—83, pres., 1980—82; bd. dirs. Guild Opera Co. L.A., 1974—83, pres., 1975—77; bd. dirs. Western Justice Ctr. Found., 1993—, pres., 2003—05; bd. dirs. L.A. Child Guidance Clinic, 1972—83, pres., 1977—79; bd. dirs. Opera Assocs. of the Music Ctr., LA, 1976—78. Recipient Stanford Assocs. award, 1984, Centennial Medallion award, 1991, Gold Spike award Stanford U., 1989, Disting. Svc. award Whittier Law Sch., 1993, Outstanding Achievement award Stanford Assocs., 1998; named R. Chandler Myers Dean's Suite in his honor Whittier Law Sch., 1997; Master's Cir. honoree Flintridge Prep. Sch., 1989. Mem. Wilshire Bar Assn. (bd. govs. 1972-81, pres. 1979-80), LA County Bar Assn. (trustee 1979-81), Stanford Law Soc. So. Calif. (bd. dirs. 1967-72, pres. 1970-71), Stanford Assocs. (bd. govs. 1992-97, treas. 1995-97), Jonathan Club, Univ. Club (Pasadena), Stanford Club LA (bd. dirs. 1963-70, pres. 1968-69). Home: La Canada 5623 Burning Tree Dr La Canada Flintridge CA 91011-2861 Office: Myers & D'Angelo 301 N Lake Ave Ste 800 Pasadena CA 91101-4108 Home Phone: 818-790-0888; Office Phone: 626-792-0007.

MYERS, REX CHARLES, historian, educator, retired dean; b. Cleve., July 1, 1945; s. Charles F. and Merial W. (Jones) M.; m. Susan L. Richards, Jan. 10, 1987; children: Gary W., Laura M. BA, Western State Coll., 1967; MA, U. Mont., 1970, PhD, 1972; postgrad., U. Wash., 1983, Harvard U., 1990. Instr. Palo Verde Coll., Blythe, Calif., 1972-75; reference librarian Mont. Hist. Soc., Helena, 1975-78; prof., divsn. chmn., dean Western Mont. Coll., Dillon, 1979-86; dean S.D. State U., Brookings, 1986-91; acad. dean Lyndon State Coll., Lyndonville, Vt., 1991-95; lectr. Western State Coll., Gunnison, Colo., 1995-98, Mesa State Coll., 1998-99, Lawrence U., 1999—2005, Northwest Coll., Powell, Wyo., 2005—. Author: Montana Symbols, 1976, Montana Trolleys, 1970, Lizzie, 1989; co-author: Marble Colorado, 1970, Montana: Our Land and People, 1978, Montana and the West, 1984; contbr. articles to profl. jours. Bd. dirs. Ctr. for Western Studies, Sioux Falls, SD, 1990—, Gunnison Arts Ctr., Gunnison County Libr., Fox Valley Arts Alliance, Meml. Park Arboretum and Gardens. Summer stipend NEH, 1973; fellow James J. Hill Library, 1985. Mem.: AAUW, Mont. Oral History Assn. (chmn. 1980—83), Am. Conf. Acad. Deans, Western History Assn. (chmn. membership com. 1980—83), N.E. Kingdom C. of C. (bd. dirs.), Masons (master 1984), Kiwanis (pres. Dillon 1983, lt. gov. 1984, 1997, 2003, pres. Gunnison 1997), Phi Alpha Theta, Phi Kappa Phi. Unitarian Universalist. Office: Nortwest Coll 231 W Sixth St Powell WY 82435 Home: PO Box 503 Powell WY 82435 Office Phone: 307-754-6172.

MYERS, RICHARD BOWMAN, former joint chiefs of staff chairman, educator; b. Kansas City, Mo., Mar. 1, 1942; m. Mary Jo Rupp; 3 children. BSME, Kans. State U., 1965; MBA, Auburn U., 1977; Diploma, Air Command/Staff Coll., Maxwell AFB, Ala., 1977, U.S. Army War Coll., 1981; postgrad., Harvard U., 1991. Commd. 2d lt. USAF, 1965, advanced through ranks to gen., 1997, ret., 2005, dir. tactical weapons & command & control acquisition programs, 1991—93, comdr. U.S. Forces Japan & 5th Air Force Yokota AFB, Japan, 1993-96; asst. to the chmn. of the Joint Chiefs of Staff US Dept. Def., Washington, 1996-97; comdr. Pacific Air Forces, Hickam AFB, Hawaii, 1997-98; comdr.-in-chief N.Am. Aerospace Def. Comm./U.S. Space Command, Peterson AFB, Colo., 1998—2000; vice chmn. Joint Chiefs of Staff, US Dept. Def., Washington, 2000—01, chmn., 2001—05; prof. mil. history & leadership Kans. State. U., Manhattan, Kans., 2006—. Bd. dirs. Northrop Grumman Corp., 2006—, Deere & Co., 2006—, United Technologies Corp., 2006—. Decorated Def. Disting. Svc. medal with three bronze oak leaf cluster, Disting. Svc. medal, Legion of Merit, Disting. Flying Cross with oak leaf cluster Air Force, Army, Navy, Coast Guard, Meritorious Svc. medal with three oak leaf clusters, Air medal with 18 oak leaf clusters, Air Force Commendation medal, others; recipient Presdl. Medal of Freedom, The White House, 2005. Office: Kans State U Dept History 208 Eisenhower Hall Manhattan KS 66506

MYERS, RICHARD BRAD, pharmacist, director; b. Ahoskie, NC, July 5, 1976; s. Richard Dale and Debra Cherry Myers; m. Sharon Renee Dean, June 25, 2002; children: Kelsea Brynn, Rhys Elliott. PharmD, U. NC, Chapel Hill, 2000. BCPS Am. Coll. Clin. Pharmacy, 2005. Pharmacy practice residency Columbus Regional Healthcare, Ga., 2000—01; critical care clin. pharmacist Columbus Regional Med. Ctr., Ga., 2001—03; pharmacy clin. coord. Sentara Healthcare Sys., Norfolk, Va., 2003—. Pharmacy residency dir. Sentara Healthcare, 2005—. Mem.: Am. Soc. Health-System Pharmacists (life), Am. Coll. Clin. Pharmacy (life). Home: 102 Windsor Ct Suffolk VA 23434 Office: Sentara Healthcare 830 Kempsville Rd Norfolk VA 23502 Home Phone: 757-934-0888; Office Phone: 757-466-3831. Home Fax: 757-466-6635. Personal E-mail: richardbradmyers@hotmail.com.

MYERS, RICHARD HEPWORTH, medical geneticist, educator; b. Austin, Nov. 1, 1947; s. Clark E. and Cora Henley (Hepworth) M.; m. Carol Anne Smith, Sept. 3, 1978; children: Margaret Anne, Madelyn Claire. BA, U. Kans., 1969; MEd, Ga. State U., 1973, MA, 1976, PhD, 1979. Diplomate Am. Bd. Med. Genetics; lic. psychologist. Asst. prof. in psychiatry Emory U., Atlanta, 1979-80; asst. prof. neurology Boston U. Sch. Medicine, 1980-87, assoc. prof. neurology, 1987—94, prof. neurology, 1994—; lectr. in neurology Harvard U. Med. Sch., Boston, 1980—; assoc. in neurology Mass. Gen. Hosp., Boston, 1980—; psychologist Univ. Hosp., Boston, 1980—. Vis. prof. MIT, Cambridge, Mass., 1993—. Contbr. articles to profl. jours. Fellow Am. Coll. Med. Genetics (founding); mem. APA, AAAS, Am. Soc. Human Genetics (mem. com. ethics of genome project 1992-94), Internat. Genetic Epidemiology Soc. Avocations: blues guitar, skiing. Office: Boston U Med Sch Dept Neurology 715 Albany St Boston MA 02118-2526

MYERS, ROBERT DAVID, judge; b. Springfield, Mass., Nov. 20, 1937; s. William and Pearl (Weiss) M.; m. Judith G. Dickenman, July 1, 1962; children— Mandy Susan, Jay Brandt, Seth William. AB, U. Mass., 1959; JD, Boston U., 1962. Bar: Ariz. 1963. Pvt. practice, Phoenix, 1963—89; judge Ariz. Superior Ct., 1989—2002; presiding judge civil dept. Superior Ct. Ariz. Maricopa County, Phoenix, 1991—92, presiding judge probate and mental health dept., 1992—95, presiding judge, 1995—2000; pro tem judge Ariz. Ct. Appeals, Phoenix; chief dep. Ariz. Atty. Gen., 2003—04; gen. counsel Ariz. Dept. Corrections, Phoenix, 2004—06. Adj. prof. Ariz. State U. Sch. Law, 1997—, Phoenix Sch. Law, 2007—; chmn. com. on exams and admissions Ariz. Supreme Ct., 1974-75, chmn. com. on character and fitness, 1975-76, mem. multi-state bar exam. com., 1976-85; bd. dirs. Nat. Conf. Met. Judges, 1997—, pres., 1998-99. Pres. Valley of Sun chpt. City of Hope, 1965-66, Cmty. Orgn. for Drug Abuse Control, 1972-73, Valley Big Bros., 1975; chmn. Mayors Ad Hoc Com. on Drug Abuse, 1974-75; bd. dirs. Maricopa County Legal Aid Soc., 1978. Recipient award for outstanding svc. and dedication to improving the legal profession and professionalism of the bar and bench Maricopa County Bar Assn., 1999, Superior Svc. award Ariz. chpt. ASPA, 2000, Justice Tom C. Clark award Nat. Conf. Metro. Cts., 2000. Mem. ATLA (nat. chmn. gov.), Ariz. Bar Assn. (gov., com. chmn., sect. pres.), Maricopa County Bar Assn. (dir., pres. 1979-80,Judge of yr., 1999, Henry S. Steven award 2000), Ariz. Trial Lawyers Assn. (pres., dir., co-editor newsletter), Phoenix Trial Lawyers Assn. (pres., dir.), Western Trial Lawyers Assn. (pres. 1977), Am. Judicature Soc. (spl. merit citation outstanding svc. improvement of adminstrn. justice 1986), Am. Bd. Trial Advocates (Phoenix chpt. Judicial Officer of Yr. award 2001), Sandra Day O'Connor Inn of Ct. (pres. 1991-92). Office Phone: 602-980-0848. Personal E-mail: bobjudge62@cox.net.

MYERS, ROBERT EUGENE, writer, educator; b. LA, Jan. 15, 1924; s. Harold Eugene and Margaret (Anawalt) M.; m. Joyce E. Daily, 1946 (div. 1949); 1 child, Kathleen; m. Patricia A. Tazer, Aug. 17, 1956; children: Edward E., Margaret A., Hal R., Karen I. AB, U. Calif., Berkeley, 1955; MA (Crown-Zellerbach fellow), Reed Coll., 1960; EdD, U. Ga., 1968. Employed in phonograph record bus., 1946-54; tchr. elem. sch. Calif., Oreg., Minn., 1954-61; rsch. asst. U. Minn., 1961-62; asst. prof. Augsburg Coll., 1962-63, U. Oreg., 1963-66; elem. tchr. Eugene, Oreg., 1966-67; assoc. prof. U. Victoria, 1968-70; assoc. rsch. prof. Oreg. System of Higher Edn., 1970-73; film maker, producer ednl. filmstrips, books, recs., 1973-77; learning resources specialist Oreg. Dept. Edn., Salem, 1977-81; with Linn-Benton Edn. Svc. Dist., Albany, Oreg., 1982-87; ret., 1987. Author: (with E. Paul Torrance) Creative Learning and Teaching (Pi Lambda Theta award 1971), 1970, La Ensenanza Creativa, 1970, Can You Imagine?, 1965, Invitations to Thinking and Doing, 1964, Invitations to Speaking and Writing Creatively, 1965, Plots, Puzzles, and Ploys, 1966, For Those Who Wonder, 1966, Stretch, 1968, Timberwood Tales, Vol. II, 1977, Stretch, 1978, Wondering, 1984, Imagining, 1985, What Next?, 1994, Facing the Issues, 1995, Cognitive Connections, 1996, Mind Sparklers, 1997, Multiple Ways of Thinking with Social Studies, 1997, Character Matters, 1999, It's Your Attitude That Counts, 2000, Mind Stretchers, 2001, Stories That Build Character, 2001, Think and Write, 2002, Now What, 2002, Spurs to Creative Thinking, 2002, Word Play, 2002, Developing Creative Thinking Skills, 2003, Learning from Nature, 2005, Exploring Character, 2005, Respect Matters, 2005 (Tchr's. Choice award 2006), Language FUNdamentals Books 1 and 2, 2005, Lively Language 1 and 2, 2005, Motivational Writing Lessons, 2005, Lessons in Writing, 2006, Writing a Persuasive Essay, 2006, Time to Write, 2006; films: Feather (CINE Golden Eagle award), 1972, The Magic Net, 1972, Elephants, 1973 Exec. bd. Nat. Assn. Gifted Children, 1974-77. With U.S. Mcht. Marine, 1944-45. Recipient CINE Golden Eagle award Coun. Internat. Non-theatrical Events, 1973. Democrat. Home: 1357 Meadow Ct Healdsburg CA 95448-3347

MYERS, ROBERT J., retail executive; Sr. v.p. Casey's General Stores, Ankeny, Iowa, 1998—2002, pres., COO, 2002—06, pres., CEO, 2006—. Office: Casey's General Stores 1 Convenience Blvd Ankeny IA 50021 *

MYERS, ROBERT JAY, retired aerospace transportation executive; b. Bklyn., Oct. 15, 1934; s. John J. and Clara S. (Martinsen) M.; m. Carolyn Erland, Aug. 10, 1963; children: Susan, Kenneth. BCE, NYU, 1955, postgrad., 1957-65; P.MD, Harvard U., 1972. With Grumman Corp., Bethpage, NY, 1964-94, v.p. resources, 1980-83, sr. v.p. bus. and resource mgmt., 1983-85, sr. v.p. corp. svcs., 1985-86; pres. Grumman Data Systems Corp., Bethpage, 1986-90; pres., chief operating officer, bd. dirs. Grumman Corp., 1991-94, ret., 1994. Sci. adv. coun. Ala. Space and Rocket Ctr., 1986-91. Adv. panel on econ. devel. N.Y. State Project 2000, 1985-86; mem. L.I. Project 2000; adv. bd. L.I. Youth Guidance, 1986-91; bd. dirs. Poly. U., 1991-98, North Shore Health System, 1994—, L.I. Mus. of Sci. and Tech., 1994-96; chmn. Huntington Hosp., 1996—2000. 1st lt. U.S. Army, 1955-57. Fellow Poly. U., 1987, Disting. Alumni award, 1989. Mem. Am. Def. Preparedness Assn. (dir. 1992-94), Navy League, Industry Exec. Bd., Nat. Space Club (bd. govs. 1986-89), Huntington Country Club (N.Y.), Audubon Country Club (Naples, Fla.). Presbyterian. Home: 200 Cheshire Way Naples FL 34110 Personal E-mail: rjm34@aol.com.

MYERS, ROBERT MANSON, language educator, writer; b. Charlottesville, Va., May 29, 1921; s. Horwood Prettyman and Matilda Manson (Wynn) M. BA summa cum laude, Vanderbilt U., 1941; MA, Columbia, 1942, Harvard, 1943; PhD, Columbia, 1948. Instr. English Yale, 1945-47; asst. prof. Coll. William and Mary, 1947-48, Tulane U., 1948-54; tchr. English Brearley Sch., NYC, 1954-56; chmn. dept. English Osbourn High Sch., Manassas, Va., 1956-59; mem. faculty U. Md., College Park, 1959—, prof. English, 1968-86, prof. emeritus, 1986—. Author: Handel's Messiah, 1948, From Beowulf to Virginia Woolf, 1952, rev., 1984, Handel, Dryden, and Milton, 1956, Restoration Comedy, 1961, The Children of Pride, 1972, abridged edit., 1984 (Carey-Thomas award 1972, Nat. Book award 1973), A Georgian at Princeton, 1976, Quintet: Five Plays, 1991, Sixes and Sevens: Three Plays, 2004, The Bostonians: A Play, 2005, Poynton Park: A Play, 2005. Mem. bd. visitors Winthrop U. Fulbright Postdoctoral Research fellow U. London, 1953-54; Fulbright lectr. Rotterdam, Netherlands, 1958-59; recipient Medal of Honor in Arts Winthrop U., 2003. Mem. Modern Lang. Assn. Am., Am. Soc. 18th Century Studies, Jane Austen Soc. N.Am., Phi Beta Kappa. Home: 3804 Deckford Pl Charlotte NC 28211-3408

MYERS, ROBERTA, editor-in-chief; b. 1960; 1 child. B, Colo. State Univ., 1982. Editl. asst. Rolling Stone Mag., 1982; mng. editor Seventeen; sr. editor In Style; editor-in-chief Tell, 1993—95; sr. articles editor Elle mag. Hachette Filipacchi Mags., 1995—97, editor-in-chief Mirabella mag. NYC, 1997—2000, editor-in-chief Elle mag., 2000—. Mem.: Am. Soc. Mag. Editors (v.p. 2007—). Office: Hachette-Filipacchi Mags Inc Elle Mag 1633 Broadway 44th Fl New York NY 10019 *

MYERS, RODMAN NATHANIEL, lawyer; b. Detroit, Oct. 27, 1920; s. Isaac Rodman and Fredericka (Hirschman) Myers; m. Jeanette Polisei, Mar. 19, 1957 (dec. 1996); children: Jennifer Myers Grabenstein, Rodman Jay. BA, Wayne State U., 1941; LLB, U. Mich., 1943. Bar: Mich. 1943, U.S. Supreme Ct. 1962. Agt. IRS, Detroit, 1943; from assoc. to ptnr. Butzel, Keidan, Simon, Myers & Graham, Detroit, 1943-90; of counsel Honigman Miller Schwartz and Cohn, LLP, Detroit, 1991—. Mem. blue ribbon task force Mich. Dept. Edn., 1988—90; founding mem., trustee Mich. chpt. Leukemia and Lymphoma Soc., founding pres., 1984—86, nat. trustee, 1984—; founding mem., trustee Detroit Sci. Ctr.; commr. Detroit Mcpl. Parking Authority, 1963—71; pres., trustee Bloomfield Twp. Pub. Libr.; trustee Temple Beth El, Bloomfield Hills, Mich.; bd. dirs. United Cmty. Svcs. of Met. Detroit, 1978—85, v.p., 1981—85, chmn. social svcs. divsn., 1982—85; bd. dirs. Children's Ctr. of Wayne County, Mich., 1963—88, pres., 1969—72. Mem. ABA, State Bar Mich. (chmn. atty. discipline panel, past vice chmn. unauthorized practice of law com., past mem. character and fitness com.). Home: 3833 Lakeland Ln Bloomfield Hills MI 48302-1328 Office: 2290 1st National Bldg Detroit MI 48226 Office Phone: 313-465-7490.

MYERS, ROLLAND GRAHAM, investment counselor; Diploma, St. Louis Country Day Sch., 1963; AB cum laude in History and Lit., Harvard U., 1966; postgrad. Faculties of Social Scis. and Law, U. Edinburgh, Scotland, 1966-67; postgrad. Fondation Nationale des Sciences Politiques and Faculte de Lettres et des Sciences Humaines, U. Paris, 1967-68. Trainee global credit dept. The Chase Manhattan Bank, N.A., NYC, 1968-69, mem. 32nd spl. devel. program, 1969, strategic planner internat. dept., 1969-70, securities analyst, mktg. rep., fiduciary investment dept., 1970; assoc. Smith, Barney & Co., Inc., NYC, 1971, account exec. N.Y. sales dept., 1971-72, instl. account exec. N.Y. internat. sales dept., 1972-74, 2nd v.p., stockholder, 1975-76; v.p., stockholder Smith Barney, Harris Upham & Co., Inc. (subs. SBHU Holdings, Inc.), NYC, 1976-78; prin. W.H. Graham & Sons, family investment office, 1977-82, investment counsel, 1982—. Ltd. ptnr. Croke Patterson Campbell, Ltd., Denver, 1975—; joint founder, gen. ptnr. Mansion Disbursements, Denver, 1979—; pres., chmn. exec. com., bd. dirs. Fifty-Five Residents Corp., N.Y.C., 1980-84; bd. dirs. Fifty-Six Danbury Rd. Assn., Inc., New Milford, Conn. Trustee, mem. corp. Bishop Rhinelander Found. (Episcopal Chaplaincy at Harvard and Radcliffe Colls.), Cambridge, 1973-75; v.p., treas., bd. dirs. The Whitehill Graham Found., St. Louis, 1976—; bd. dirs., fin. com., bylaws com., mem. corp. Eliot Pratt Edn. Ctr., Inc. (The Pratt Ctr.: Your Connection with the Natural World), New Milford, 1987-94; mem. corp. Kent (Conn.) Land Trust, Inc., 1989—, treas., 1989-93, bd. dirs., 1989-2003, adv. bd., 2003-; project financier Restoration of 1851 Samuel Curtiss Hosford House, Nat. Register Historic Dist., Falls Village, Conn., 1984-86; commr. Housatonic River Commn., Warren, Conn., 1985-93, vice chmn., 1986-87, chmn., 1988-92; commr. Conservation, Inland Wetlands and Watercourses Commn., Kent, 1988-93, vice chmn., 1988-92; mem. schs. and scholarships com., Office of Admissions and Fin. Aid, Harvard and Radcliffe Colls., 1991—. Mem. Cum Laude Soc., Mary Inst. and St. Louis Country Day Sch. Alumni Assn., Harvard Alumni Assn., Capitol Hill Club (Washington), Harvard Club (N.Y.C.), Hasty Pudding-Inst. of 1770 (Cambridge), Wyo. Bus. Alliance, Wyo. Heritage Found., St. Andrew's Soc., New Eng. Soc. in City N.Y., St. George's Soc. N.Y. Republican. Episcopalian. Office: W H Graham & Sons Investment Counsel 1818 Evans Ave Ste 207 Cheyenne WY 82001-4664

MYERS, SHARON DIANE, auditor; b. Lawrence, Kans., Sept. 18, 1955; d. Richard Paul and Helen Carol (Overbey) M. AA, Mt. San Antonio Coll., Walnut, Calif., 1981; BSBA, Calif. State U., Pomona, 1983, MBA, 1986. Cert. fraud examiner; cert. govt. fin. mgr. Revenue agt. IRS, Glendale, Calif., 1984-85; auditor Def. Contract Audit Agy., LA, 1985-92; auditor Office Inspector Gen. FDIC, Newport Beach, 1992—2002; auditor officer Inspector Gen., USPS, Portland, Oreg., 2002—. Instr. Azusa (Calif.) Pacific U., 1987, 88, West Coast U., San Diego, 1992. Musician, Sunday sch. supt. Covina (Calif.) Bapt. Temple, 1975-95, Liberty Bapt. Ch., Irvine, Calif., 1995-2002, Landmark Bapt. Ch., Olympia, Wash., 2002—. Mem. Assn. Govt. Accts. Republican. Avocations: piano, travel. Home: 2702 44th Ave NW Olympia WA 98502-3692

MYERS, SOPHIA M., writer, researcher, artist, cartographer, translator; b. Coffeyville, Kans., Oct. 25, 1928; d. Anastasios M. and Georgia A. Mardikes; m. Ralph E. Myers, Dec. 24, 1980 (dec. Oct. 5, 2006); children: George A. Vedros, Nicholas M. Vedros. Degree, Mt. St. Scholastica, 1948. Cert. tchg. Avila Coll., 1949. Tchr. elem art several Grade Schs., 1949—54; advt. mgr., artist, writer Cavanaugh Cattle Co., 1955—59, Weldwheels, 1960—64; advt. mgr. Oppenheimer Industries, 1965—71; advt. mgr., ops. mgr. The Nat. Secs. Assn., Internat., Kansas City, Mo., 1972—80; pvt. practice, 1980—. Red Herring, Potpourri; poems featured Sunday Kansas City Star; contbr. poetry, short stories, essays and articles publ. in numerous mags., anthologies and newspapers. Named to Women's Found. Greater Kansas City, 2005; recipient 1st Pl. free verse award, Springfield Writers Guild, 2002, The Vicki Millikin Bright award best poem, 2003, 2004, Winner two nat. contests. Mem.: Ptnrs. in Crime, Sisters in Crime, Okla. Writers' Fedn., Inc., The Writers' Cir., Warrensburg Writers Cir., Kans. City Press Club, Soc. Profl. Journalists, Kans. City Writers' Group, Okla. Writer's Federation, Inc., Mo. Poetry Soc., Mo. Writers Guild (1st Pl. free verse, 1st Pl. Best Lit. Poem award), Nat. League Am. Pen Women: Arts and Letters (pres. Kansas City br., 1st Pl. best poem Best Free Verse award). Avocations: painting, sculpting. Personal E-mail: smyers@kc.rr.com.

MYERS, STEPHEN HAWLEY, lawyer; b. Washington, Mar. 28, 1953; s. Robert Holt and Antoinette (Hawley) M.; children: Stephen, Hampton, Brielle; m. Laura Lee Fuller, Dec. 1, 1989. BA in Polit. Sci. with honors, Union Coll., 1976; JD, Loyola U., 1979. Bar: D.C. 1979, La. 1979, U.S. Dist. Ct. D.C. 1980, U.S. Tax Ct. 1980, U.S. Ct. Claims 1980, U.S. Ct. Appeals (fed. and D.C. cirs.) 1980, U.S. Ct. Appeals (5th cir.) 1985, U.S. Dist. Ct. (we., mid. and ea. dists.) La. 1985, U.S. Supreme Ct. 1989. Atty. advisor to hon. judge Edward S. Smith U.S. Ct. Appeals (Fed. cir.), Washington, 1979-80; assoc. Duncan Allen & Mitchell, Washington, 1980-82; atty. advisor to Judge Jules G. Körner U.S. Tax Ct., Washington, 1982-84; assoc. Davidson Meaux Sonnier & McElligott, Lafayette, La., 1984-85; ptnr. Roy Forrest, Lopresto, DeCourt & Myers and predecessor firms, Lafayette, 1985-97; pvt. practice Stephen Hawley Myers, LLC, Lafayette, La., 1997—. Lectr. for continuing legal edn. seminars on corp., bus. and sales tax litigation; chmn. Nat. Bus. Adv. Coun., Washington, 2002—; mem. La. State Police Commn., 2002—. Vice-chmn., bd. dirs. La. Coun. for Fiscal Reform, New Orleans, 1986-96; bd. dirs., treas. Acadiana Youth, Inc., Lafayette, 1986-94 Mem. ABA, Am. Platform Assn., Lafayette Bar Assn., La. Trial Lawyer's Assn., Phi Delta Phi Avocations: writing, photography, skeet shooting, sports clay shooting, hunting. Office: 600 Jefferson St Ste 401 Lafayette LA 70501-8919 Home: 105 Mill Valley Run Lafayette LA 70508-7027 Office Phone: 337-266-2225. Business E-Mail: shmyers@worldnet.att.net.

MYERS, VIRGINIA ANNE, art educator; b. Greencastle, Ind., May 8, 1927; d. Everett Clark Myers and Hurst (McKann) Bessie. BA in Fine Arts, George Washington U., Corcoran Sch. Art, 1949; MFA in Drawing and Painting, Calif. Coll. of Arts & Crafts, Oakland, 1951; postgrad. in print making, U. Ill., 1953—55, U. Iowa, Iowa City, 1955—61; studied with Stanley William Hayter, Paris, 1961—62. Rsch. asst. Sch. Art and Art History U. Iowa, Iowa City, 1958-61; instr. arts and crafts, phys. edn. Tucson Indian Tng. Sch., 1949-50; teaching asst. dept. art and architecture U. Ill., Champaign-Urbana, 1954-55; instr. printmaking U. Iowa, Iowa City, 1962-69, asst. prof. printmaking, 1969-74, assoc. prof., 1974-82, prof., 1982—. Bd. dirs. Elizabeth Found. for Arts, NY, 1994-2007, treas. 1994-2005; pres. Iowa Foil Printer Corp. Author: (manual) Creating Original Prints with Hot-Stamped foil, 1993, (hardbound) Foil Imaging...A New Art Form, 2001, Foil Imaging: The Original Editioned Prints, 2006, (limited edit.), 2006; A Time of Malfeasance (21 engravings and dry-points), 1976, The Views from Tenacre: The Seasons (66 paintings and drawings), 1979, Landscape in Iowa (36 paintings, prints and drawings), 1986, The Ghost Elm and Other Views from Tenacre, 2006; contbr. 57 paintings, drawings, prints, articles to profl. jours. Fulbright fellow, Paris, 1961-62; grantee U. Iowa, 1973, 78, 84, 89, 93, 98-99, Iowa Arts Coun., 1974-77, 80, 85, Stanley Found., 1984-88, Thorson Found., 1984, 86, Arts and Humanities Initiative, 2005, 06; elected to Iowa Women's Major Grant Archives, U. Iowa, 1999; The Virginia A. Myers Print Study Room at U. Iowa Mus. Art named in her honor, 2006. Mem. Foil Stamping and Embossing Assn. (charter), Nat. Mus. of Women in Arts (charter). Achievements include patents for Iowa Foil Printer, 1992; Underwriters Laboratories, 1997. Avocations: gardening, reading, swimming. Home: Tenacre Print 4244 210th St NE Solon IA 52333-9657 Office: Univ Iowa Sch Arts & Art History Iowa City IA 52242 Business E-Mail: virginia-myers@uiowa.edu.

MYERS, WARREN POWERS LAIRD, internist, educator; b. Phila., May 2, 1921; s. John Dashiell and Mary Hall (Laird) M.; m. Katharine Van Vechten, July 1, 1944; children: Warren Powers Laird, Jr., Anne Van Vechten Myers Evans, Duncan McNeir, Sara Myers Gormley. Grad., Episcopal Acad., 1939; BS, Yale U., 1943; MD, Columbia U., 1945; MS in Medicine, U. Minn., 1952; postgrad. (Eleanor Roosevelt Found. fellow), U. Cambridge, Eng., 1962-63. Diplomate: Am. Bd. Internal Medicine. Rotating intern Phila. Gen. Hosp., 1945-46; intern medicine Maimonides Hosp., NYC, 1948-49; resident fellow in medicine Mayo Clinic, Rochester, Minn., 1949-52; clin. asst. Meml. Hosp., NYC, 1952-54, asst. attending physician, 1954-58, assoc. attending physician, 1959, attending physician, 1959-90; instr. Cornell U. Med. Coll., 1955-56, asst. prof., 1956-59, asso. prof., 1959-68, prof. medicine, 1968-86, prof. emeritus, 1986—, assoc. dean, 1977-86; chmn. dept. medicine Meml. Sloan-Kettering Cancer Ctr., NYC, 1967-77; v.p. for ednl. affairs Meml. Hosp., 1977-81, Eugene W. Kettering prof., 1979-86; attending physician N.Y. Hosp., NYC, 1968-86; mem. Sloan-Kettering Inst. Cancer Rsch., NYC, 1969-90; mem. emeritus Meml. Sloan-Kettering Cancer Ctr., NYC, 1990—; cons. Rockefeller U. Hosp., NYC, 1977-86. Mem. clin. cancer tng. com. Nat. Cancer Inst., 1970-73, chmn., 1971-73, chmn. clin. cancer edn. com., 1975-78; adj. prof. medicine Dartmouth Med. Sch., 1987-96, prof. medicine emeritus, 1996—; cons. staff Mary Hitchcock Meml. Hosp., Hanover, N.H., 1987-96. Contbr. articles on cancer, bone metabolism, internal medicine, and med. edn. to med. jours. Bd. dirs. Rye (N.Y.) United Fund, 1969-72, chmn. budget com., 1968-69; bd. dirs. Damon Runyon-Walter Winchell Cancer Fund, 1976-86, pres., 1985-86; trustee Hitchcock Clinic, Lebanon, N.H., 1983-96, Dartmouth-Hitchcock Med. Ctr., Lebanon, 1983-95, chmn. exec. com., 1992-95, tchr.'s coll. Columbia U., 1980-86; trustee Friends of Norris Cotton Cancer Ctr., Dartmouth-Hitchcock Med. Ctr., Lebanon, 1997-2000, v.p., 1999-2000—; elder 5th Ave. Presbyn. Ch., 1969-86, Norwich Congregational Ch., deacon, 1998-2002. With M.C., USNR, 1946-47. Recipient Alumni award for research Mayo Clinic, 1952, Margaret Hay Edwards Achievement medal Am. Assn. Cancer Edn., 1993. Fellow ACP, N.Y. Acad. Medicine (v.p. 1983-85); mem. Am. Clin. and Climatological Assn., Am. Assn. Cancer Research, Endocrine Soc., Harvey Soc., Am. Fedn. Clin. Research, Practioners' Soc. of N.Y., AMA, Am. Assn. Cancer Edn. (pres. 1984-85), Am. Soc. Clin. Oncology, Founders and Patriots Pa., Yale Club, Charaka Club, Century Assn. (N.Y.C.), Alpha Omega Alpha. Presbyterian (elder 1969-86). Clubs: Yale, Charaka, Century Assn. (N.Y.C.). Address: 436 Joshua Rd White River Junction VT 05001-9028

MYERS, WILLIAM GERRY, III, lawyer; b. Roanoke, Va., July 13, 1955; AB, Coll. of William and Mary, 1977; JD, U. Denver, 1981. Bar: Colo. 1981, Wyo. 1982, DC 1987, US Supreme Ct. 1990, Idaho 1997. Assoc. Davis & Cannon, Sheridan, Wyo., 1981-85; legis. counsel US Sen. Alan K. Simpson, Wyo., 1985-89; asst. to atty. gen. US Dept. Justice, Washington, 1989-92; dep. gen. counsel for progs. US Dept. Energy, Washington, 1992-93; dir. fed. lands Nat. Cattlemen's Assn., 1993-97; exec. dir. Pub. Lands Coun., Washington, 1993-97; atty. Holland and Hart, Boise, Idaho, 1997—2001, of counsel, 2003—; solicitor US Dept. of Interior, 2001—03. Office: Holland and Hart US Bank Plz 101 S Capitol Blvd Ste 1400 Boise ID 83702-7714 Office Phone: 208-342-5000. E-mail: wmyers@hollandhart.com.

MYERS BROWN, JOAN, performing company executive; b. Phila., Dec. 25, 1931; d. Julius Thomas Myers and Nellie (Woods) Lewis Myers; m. Frederick Johnson, 1951 (div.); m. Max Brown, Nov. 18, 1967 (div.); children: Dannielle C. Brown, Marlisa J. Brown-Saint. D (hon.), U. Arts, 1994; LHD (hon.), Ursinus Coll., 2007. Dancer various prodns. U.S, Can., Caribbean, 1950—61, Pearl Bailey Prodns., nat. tour, 1961—66; choreographer Harlem Prodns., Atlantic City, 1958—67; dir., choreographer, tchr. Phila. Sch. of Dance Arts, 1960—; founder, exec. dir. Phila. Dance Co., 1970—. Bd. dirs. Univ. City Coun., 2000—, Arts and Bus. Coun., 1999—; hon. chair, founder Internat. Assn. Blacks in Dance; cons. Nat. Endowment for Arts, 1970—84, panelist, 1970—82, Ohio State Arts Coun, 1981—84, Mich. State Arts Coun., 1981—84; dance panel Pa. State Arts Coun., 1987, Md. State Arts Coun., 1990, Arts Presenters, 1995, NJ/Del. State Coun. on The Arts, 1994, The Kennedy Ctr. AAEP, 1996; advisor Nat. Dance Project, 1999—2004; dir. Wade Comm., 1983—. Mem. Mayor's Cultural Adv. Coun., 1984—; bd. dirs. Greater Phila. Cultural Alliance, Dance/USA, Citizens for Arts in Pa., Coalition of African-Am. Culture Inst., Spruce Family Planning Clinic. Named one of 50 Most Influential Women award, 1995; recipient award, Nat. Council Negro Women, 1983, Award of Merit, West Phila. C. of C., 1983, Arts and Humanities Cultural award, Phila. chpt. Continentals Socs., 1979, Philadelphians for Pub. Awareness award, 1984, Womens Way award, 1986, Theodore L. Hazlett Meml. award for excellence in the arts in Pa., 1986, Kool Achiever award, 1989, Black United Fund Arts award, 1989, Phila. Arts and Cultural award, 1989, Stella Moore Dance award, 1990, Black Unite Fund award, 1990, UNCF award, 1990, YWCA-Pioneer award, 1990, Excellence in Arts award, 1995, Arts and Business Coun. award, 1996, Chisolm award NPCBW, 1996, Keeper of the Flame award, 2003, mayoral award, Alpha Kappa Alpha, 2004, Phila. Black Profls., 2004, Theater Co. Interact, 2004, Frontiers Internat., 2004, Dance Mag. award, 2006; Nat. Endowment Arts Choreographic fellow, 1979. Democrat. Office: Phila Dance Co 9 N Preston St Philadelphia PA 19104-2299 Home Phone: 215-662-0488; Office Phone: 215-387-8200. Business E-Mail: jmb@philadanco.org. *

MYERSON, ALAN, television director, film director; b. Cleve., Aug. 8, 1936; s. Seymour A. and Vivien I. (Caplin) M.; m. Irene Ryan, June 2, 1962; 1 son, Lincoln; m. Leigh French, May 15, 1977; children: Sierra French-Myerson, Darcy French-Myerson. Student, Pepperdine Coll., 1956-57, UCLA, 1957. Mem. theater/cinema faculty U. Calif., Berkeley, 1966, San Francisco State U., 1967, Internat. Film and TV Workshops, 2002, U. So. Calif, 2005—. Dir. (Broadway, Off Broadway) including This Music Crept By Me Upon the Waters, The Committee; dir.: Second City, N.Y.C. and Chgo., 1961, 62; founder, prodr., dir. The Committee, San Francisco, L.A. and N.Y., 1963-74; dir.: (films) Steelyard Blues, 1972, Private Lessons, 1981, Police Academy 5, 1988, It's Showtime, 1976; numerous TV shows, 1975—, including Ally McBeal, Judging Amy, Joan of Arcadia, Larry Sanders Show, Friends, Frazier, Picket Fences, Miami Vice, Dynasty, Laverne and Shirley, Ed, Boston Public, Gilmore Girls, Lizzie McGuire; TV films The Love Boat, 1976, Hi, Honey, I'm Dead, 1991, Bad Attitudes, 1991, Holiday Affair, 1996. Active in civil rights, peace, anti-nuclear movements, 1957-. Recipient Emmy nomination 1997, Cable ACE award nominations, 1995, 96, 97, TV Comedy award nomination Dirs. Guild, 1997. Mem. ASCAP, Acad. Motion Picture Arts and Scis., Acad. TV Arts and Scis., Dirs. Guild Am. Home Phone: 310-463-2805; Office Phone: 310-559-7756.

MYERSON, JACOB MYER, retired diplomat; b. Rock Hill, SC, June 11, 1926; s. Solomon and Lena (Clein) Myerson; m. Nicole Neuray, June 10, 1965 (dec. Oct. 1968); 1 child, Sylvie Anne; m. Helen Hayashi, Mar. 9, 1974 (dec. Jan. 1995). Student, Pa. State Coll., 1944; BA with distinction, George Washington U., 1949, MA, 1950; grad., Fgn. Service Inst., 1953. Joined U.S. Fgn. Svc., 1950; 3d sec. Office U.S. High Commr. Germany, Berlin, 1950-52; 2d sec. U.S. Mission to NATO and European Regional Orgn., Paris, 1953-55; also mem. U.S. permanent del. to coordinating com. InterGovtl. Consultative Group on EastWest Trade; internat. economist, internat. rels. officer State Dept., 1956-60, spl. asst. to under sec. state, 1965-66; adviser U.S. del. GATT session, Geneva, 1958; ministerial session OEEC, Paris, 1958; 1st sec., chief polit. sect. U.S. Mission to European Communities, Brussels, 1960-65; officer-in-charge NATO Polit. Affairs, Dept. State, 1966-68; adviser U.S. delegation ministerial sessions North Atlantic Council, 1966-67; dep. polit. adviser, counselor U.S. Mission to NATO, Brussels, 1968-70; counselor econ. affairs U.S. Mission to European Communities, Brussels, 1970-74, minister counselor, from 1974; U.S. rep. to UN Econ. and Social Council with rank of ambassador, 1975-77; alt. U.S. del. UN Gen. Assembly, 1975—76; alt. U.S. rep. UN Conf. on Trade and Devel., 1976; minister-counselor econ. and comml. affairs Am. Embassy, Paris, 1977-80; ret., 1980; dep. sec. gen. OECD, Paris, 1980-88. With US Army, 1944—46, ETO. Decorated Bronze Star, Order of the Sacred treasure Gold and Silver medal Japan; recipient Meritorious Svc. award, State Dept., 1960. Mem.: Am. Fgn. Svc. Assn. (Rivkin award 1969), Artus, Phi Beta Kappa, Phi Eta Sigma, Pi Gamma Mu. Address: 2 rue Lucien Gaulard 75018 Paris France

MYERSON, JAY BARRY, lawyer; b. NYC; s. Martin and Sylvia Waldner Myerson; m. Barbara J.E. Myerson, June 17, 1973; children: Joshua, Jennifer M.R. Hurwitz, Matthew. BA cum laude, Georgetown U., Washington, 1973, JD, 1976. Bar: US Ct. Appeals (DC cir.) 1977, US Dist. Ct. DC 1977, DC 1977, US Ct. Appeals (fed. cir.) 1983, US Supreme Ct. 1985, Va. 1986, US Dist. Ct. Va. (ea. dist.) 1986, US Ct. Appeals (4th cir.) 1987, US Ct. Appeals (1st cir.) 1990. Assoc. Gerald M. Feder Law Offices, Washington, 1976—78; litigation, enforcement atty. Fed. Election Commn., Washington, 1978—80; assoc. Israel and Raley, Chartered, Washington, 1980—86; pvt. practice Reston, Va., 1986—. Treas. Com. for Progressive Congress, 1994—; mem. Fairfax County Environ. Quality Adv. Coun., Va., 1987—92, vice chmn. Va., 1988—89, chmn. Va., 1989—91; coach, mgr. youth baseball, 1987—96; alumni interviewer alumni admissions program Georgetown U., 1989—2004; counsel to treas. Dem. Nat. Com., 1982—86, asst. gen. counsel, 1985—86, mem. nat. lawyers coun., 1998—; gen. counsel Dem. Party Va., 1997—99, 2004—; mem. youth orgn. adult bd. B'nai B'rith, 1992—2002, chmn. No. Va. coun. adult bd., 1999—2002; bd. dirs. Congregation Beth Emeth, 1985—94, v.p., 1986—88, pres., 1988—90, trustee, 1998—2000. Master: George Mason Inn of Ct. (treas. 2002—06, pres.-elect 2006—); mem.: ABA (vice chmn. com. on election law sect. adminstrv. law and regulatory pr 1994—95, liaison standing com. on election law 1997—2000, co-chmn. com. on election law 1997—2000), Nat. Lawyers Assn., Va. Assn. Dem. Campaign Counsel, Va. Trial Lawyers Assn., Va. Bar Assn., Fairfax Bar Assn. (bd. dirs. 2004—, co-chmn. conciliation program Fairfax County Cts. 2001—02, chmn. conciliation task force Fairfax County Cts. 2002—, mem. gen. dist. ct. com. 1990—97, mem. lawyer referral svc. com. 1993—97, Pres.' award 2005). Jewish. Avocations: baseball, politics, community service, gardening. Office: 11860 Sunrise Valley Dr Reston VA 20191

MYERSON, ROBERT J., radiologist, educator; b. Boston, May 12, 1947; s. Richard Louis and Rosemarie M.; m. Carla Wheatley, Aug. 8, 1970; 1 child, Jacob Wheatley. BA, Princeton U., 1969; PhD, U. Calif., Berkeley, 1974; MD, U. Miami, 1980. Diplomate Am. Bd. Radiology. Asst. prof. dept. physics Pa. State U., State Coll., 1974-76; fellow Inst. Advanced Studies, Princeton, NJ, 1976-78; resident U. Pa. Hosp., Phila., 1981-84; assoc. prof. radiology Washington U. Sch. Medicine, St. Louis, 1984-97; prof. radiation oncology Wash. U. Sch. Medicine, St. Louis, 1997—. Contbr. articles to profl. jours. Recipient Career Devel. award Am. Cancer Soc., 1985. Fellow Am. Coll. Radiology; mem. Am. Coll. Radiation, Am. Soc. Therapeutic Radiologists, Am. Phys. Soc. Democrat. Jewish. Avocation: bicycling. Office: Washington U Radiation Oncology Ctr Box 8224 4921 Parkview Pl Saint Louis MO 63110-1001

MYERSON, ROGER BRUCE, economist, educator; b. Boston, Mar. 29, 1951; s. Richard L. and Rosemarie (Farkas) M.; m. Regina M. Weber, Aug. 29, 1982; children: Daniel, Rebecca. AB summa cum laude, Harvard U., 1973, SM, 1973, PhD, 1976. Asst. prof. decision scis. Northwestern U., Evanston, Ill., 1976-78, assoc. prof., 1979-82, prof., 1982-2001, Harold Stuart prof. decision scis., 1986-2001, prof. econs., 1987-2001; W.C. Norby prof. econs. U. Chgo., 2001—. Guest researcher U. Bielefeld, Federal Republic of Germany, 1978-79; vis. prof. econs. U. Chgo., 1985-86, 2000-01. Author: Game Theory: Analysis of Conflict, 1991, Probability Models for Economic Decisions, 2005; mem. editorial bd. Internat. Jour. Game Theory, 1982-92, Games and Econ. Behavior, 1988-97; assoc. editor Jour. Econ. Theory, 1983-93; also articles. Guggenheim fellow, 1983-84; Sloan rsch. fellow, 1984-86. Fellow Econometric Soc., Am. Acad. Arts and Scis. (Midwest v.p. 1999-2002). Office: U Chgo Dept Econs 1126 E 59th St Chicago IL 60637 Business E-Mail: myerson@uchicago.edu.

MYERSON, TOBY SALTER, lawyer; b. Chgo., July 20, 1949; s. Raymond King and Natalie Anita (Salter) M. BA, Yale U., 1971; JD, Harvard U., 1975. Bar: N.Y. 1977, Calif. 1977. Assoc. Coudert Bros., NYC, 1975-77, 81, San Francisco, 1977-81, Paul, Weiss, Rifkind, Wharton & Garrison, NYC, 1981-83, ptnr., 1983-89; mng. dir. Wasserstein Perella & Co., Inc., NYC, 1989-90; ptnr. Paul, Weiss, Rifkind, Wharton & Garrison, NYC, 1990—, co-chair, Corp. Dept. Lectr. U. Calif. Berkeley, 1979-81, Harvard U., Cambridge, Mass., 1982-83; visiting lectr. Yale U., New Haven, 1983-84; bd. dirs. Myerson, Van Den Berg & Co., Santa Barbara, Calif. Contbg. editor: Doing Business in Japan, 1983, Council on Foreign Rels., 1993—, Foreign Policy Assn., 1995—. Sec. Japan Soc., Inc., N.Y.C., 1985-89; bd. dirs. 1056 Fifth Ave. Corp., N.Y.C., 1985-88; mem. univ. resources com. Harvard U., 1997—. Mem. ABA (subcom. internat. banking, corp. and bus. law sect.), Internat. Bar Assn., N.Y. State Bar Assn., Assn. Bar City N.Y. (com. on fgn. and comparative law, chmn. 1988-89), Calif. Bar Assn. Avocations: art, music, literature, tennis, golf. Home: 1056 5th Ave New York NY 10028-0112 Office: Paul Weiss Rifkind Wharton & Garrison 1285 Ave of the Americas New York NY 10019-6065 Fax: 212-373-2753. E-mail: tmyerson@paulweiss.com.

MYHRE, BYRON ARNOLD, pathologist, educator; b. Fargo, ND, Oct. 22, 1928; s. Ben Arnold and Amy Lillian (Gilbertson) M.; m. Eileen Marguerite Scherling, June 16, 1953; children: Patricia Ann, Bruce Allen. BS, U. Ill., Champaign/Urbana, 1950; MS, Northwestern U., Evanston, Ill., 1952, MD, 1953; PhD, U. Wis., Madison, 1962. Intern Evanston Hosp., Ill., 1953-54; resident Children's Meml. Hosp., Chgo., 1956-57, U. Wis. Hosp., Madison, 1957-60; assoc. med. dir. Milw. Blood Ctr., 1962-66; sci. dir. L.A. Red Cross Blood Ctr., 1966-72; dir. Blood Bank Harbor-UCLA Med. Ctr., Torrance, Calif., 1972-85, chief clin. pathology, 1985-2000; prof. pathology UCLA, 1972-2000, prof. emeritus, 2000—. Author: Quality Control on Blood Banking, 1974; (with others) Textbook of Clinical Pathology, 1972, Paternity Testing, 1975; editor seminar procs.; contbr. articles to profl. jours., chpts. to books. With USAF, 1954—56. Mem.:

AMA, Harbor-UCLA Faculty Soc. (past pres.), Wis. Blood Bank Assn. (past pres.), LA Acad. Medicine (past pres.), Calif. Blood Bank Sys. (past pres.), Calif. Med. Assn., Assn. Clin. Scientists (past pres.), Coll. Am. Pathologists (chmn. blood bank survey com.), Am. Assn. Blood Banks (pres. 1978—79), Am. Soc. Clin. Pathology (dep. commr. commn. on continuing edn.), Palos Verdes Breakfast Club (past pres.). Home: 4004 Via Larga Vista Palos Verdes Estates CA 90274-1122 Personal E-mail: bamyhre@cox.net.

MYHRE, JANET, mathematician, educator; b. Tacoma, Wash., Sept. 24, 1932; d. Leif Christian Klippen, Thelma Gladys Klippen; m. Philip Cushman Myhre, June 12, 1954 (div. Dec. 1984); 1 child, Karin Elizabeth; m. Leon Hollerman, May 29, 1988; 1 child, Jeremy Hollerman. BA summa cum laude, Pacific Luth. U., 1954; MA, U. Wash., 1956; PhD in Math. Stats, U. Stockholm, 1968. Prof. math. Claremont McKenna Coll., Claremont, Calif., 1962—. Vis. prof. U. Stockholm, 1971—72, Swiss Fed. Inst. Tech., Zurich, 1971—72, Wash. State U., Pullman, 1978; prof. math. Claremont Grad. U., 1968—; founder, pres. Math. Analysis Rsch. Corp., Claremont, 1973—; dir. Reed Inst. for Decision Sci. Claremont McKenna Coll., Claremont, 1975—; cons. Strategic Sys. Programs USN, Washington, 1968—; cons. EPA, Washington, 1976—77. Contbr. chpts. in books, articles to profl. jours. Bd. trustees mem. The Webb Schs., Claremont, 1984—88; officer Padua Hills Homeowners Assn., Claremont, 1988—94; mem. numerous blue ribbon com. USN involving reliability, nuclear safety and risk assessment, 1972—. Recipient Austin Bonis award, Am. Soc. Quality Control, 1984; Rsch. grant, Office Naval Rsch., 1973—83. Fellow: Am. Statis. Assn. (assoc. editor Technometrics 1969—75, coun. rep. 2001—03, pres. So. Calif. chpt. 2003—05); mem.: Padua Hills Mus. Com., Phi Beta Kappa (pres. CMC chpt. 2004—). Achievements include development of models/statistical theory used since 1972 by USN Ballistic Missile Program for reliability assessments; software/theory used by Fleet Ballistic Missile Program since 1990 for safety and risk assessment. Avocations: gardening, cooking, hiking, weaving. Office: Claremont McKenna Coll Bauer Hall 9th St Claremont CA 91711 also: Math Analysis Rsch Corp 4239 Via Padova Claremont CA 91711 Office Phone: 909-621-8876, 909-624-5298.

MYHREN, TRYGVE EDWARD, communications company executive; b. Palmerton, Pa., Jan. 3, 1937; s. Arne Johannes and Anita (Blatz) M.; m. Carol Jane Enman, Aug. 8, 1964; children: Erik, Kirsten, Tor; m. 2d Victoria Hamilton, Nov. 14, 1981; 1 stepchild, Paige. BA in Philosophy and Polit. Sci., Dartmouth Coll., 1958, MBA, 1959. Sales mgr., unit mgr. Procter and Gamble, Cin., 1963-65; sr. cons. Glendinning Cos., Westport, Conn., 1965-69; pres. Auberge Vintners, 1970-73; exec. v.p. Mktg. Continental, Westport, 1969-73; v.p., gen. mgr. CRM, Inc., Del Mar, Calif., 1973-75; from v.p. mktg. to pres. Am. TV and Comm. Corp., Englewood, Colo., 1975-80, chmn. bd., CEO, 1981-88; pres. Myhren Media Inc., Denver, 1989—. V.p., then exec. v.p. Time Inc., N.Y.C., 1981-88; mem. exec. com., treas., vice chmn., then chmn. bd. dirs. Nat. Cable TV Assn., Washington, 1982-91; mem. adv. com. on HDTV, FCC, 1987-89, pres. Providence Jour. Co.; bd. dirs. Advanced Mktg. Svcs., Inc., La Jolla, Calif.; Dreyfus Founders Funds, Inc., J. D. Edwards, Inc., Verio, Inc., Nat. Cable TV Ctr., Denver, Cable Labs, Inc., Boulder, Colo., Peapod, Inc., Skokie, Ill.; pres. Myhren Media, 1989—; pres., CEO King Broadcast Co., 1991-96. Mem. Colo. Forum, 1984—, chmn. higher edn. com., 1986; bd. dirs., co-founder Colo. Bus. Com. for the Arts, 1985-91; mem. exec. coun. Found. for Commemoration U.S. Constn., 1987-90; mem. Nat. GED Task Force, 1987-90, Colo. Baseball Commn., 1989-91, Colo. Film Commn., 1989-91; trustee Nat. Jewish Hosp., 1989— (Humanitarian award 1996), R.I. Hosp., 1991-95, Lifespan Health Sys., 1994-97, U.S. Ski and Snowboard Team Found., 1998—; chmn. Local Organizing Commn. 1995 NCAA Hockey Championship; trustee, exec. com., chmn. fin. com. U. Denver, 1997—. Lt. (j.g.) USNR, 1959-63. Recipient Disting. Leader award Nat. Cable TV Assn., 1988. Mem. Cable TV Adminstrn. and Mktg. Soc. (pres. 1978-79, Grand Tam award 1985, One of A Kind award 1994), Cable Adv. Bur. (co-founder 1978), Cable TV Pioneers. Episcopalian. Address: Myhren Media Inc 280 Detroit St # 200 Denver CO 80206-4807 E-mail: trygm@earthlink.net.

MYHRVOLD, NATHAN P., technology executive; b. Seattle, Aug. 3, 1959; BS in Math., UCLA, 1979, MS in Geophysics and Space Physics, 1979; M in Math. Econs., Princeton U., 1981; D in Theoretical and Math. Physics, 1983. Fellow dept. applied math. and theoretical physics Cambridge U., 1981-83; founder, pres., CEO Dynamical Sys., 1984-86; dir. spl. projects Microsoft Corp., Redmond, Wash., 1986, v.p. applications and content; chief tech. officer Advanced Tech. and Rsch., Redmond, Wash., Microsoft Corp., Redmond, Wash., 1996—99; founder, mgr. Microsoft Rsch.; CEO Intellectual Ventures, Bellevue, Wash., 2000—. Bd. trustees Inst. Advanced Study, Princeton, N.J.; mem. Nat. Info. Infrastructure Adv. Coun.; adv. bd. Princeton U. dept. physics. Photographer America 24/7, Washington 24/7; contbr. scientific papers articles to Science, Nature, Paleobiology, Physical Review, Fortune, Time, National Geographic Traveler and online mag. Slate; provided forward Juice: The Creative Fuel that Drives World Class Inventors. Mem. United Way Million Dollar Roundtable; co-contbr. with Paul Allen SETI Found. for Allen Telescope Array, 2000. Recipient 1st and 2nd Place title, World Championship of Barbecue, Memphis, James Madison medal, Princeton U., 2005. Achievements include patents in field; patents pending in field. Avocations: mountain climbing, photography, French Cooking, Formula Car Racing. Office: Intellectual Ventures 1756 114th Ave SE Ste 110 Bellevue WA 98004

MYINT, SOE WIN, geographer, educator; s. Pe Than Tun and Khin Nu Nu; m. Susie Tin Maung Aye, Dec. 26, 1987; 1 child, Su Thinzar. BS in Forestry, Rangoon U., 1983; postgrad., Internat. Inst.Aerospace Survey and Earth Sciences, 1988—89; MS in Natural Resources, Asian Inst. Tech., 1994; PhD in Geography, La. State U., 2001. Asst. plantation officer Forest Dept., Rangoon, Rangoon Division, Burma, 1983—85; dep. mgr. Timber Corp., 1985—92; rsch. assoc. UNEP/Environment Assessment Program for Asia and the Pacific, Bangkok, 1994—96, rsch. specialist, 1996—98; asst. prof. dept. geography U. Okla., Norman, 2001—05, Ariz. State U., Tempe, 2005—. Geog. info. sci. cons. WHO, Geneva, 1999. Recipient Best Poster Presentation award, 18th Asian Conf. on Remote Sensing, 1998, Robert C. West Field Rsch. award, La. State U. Dept. Geography and Anthropology, 2000, US Geog. Sci. Scholar award, First Internat. Conf. GIScience, 2000, Best Student Paper award, Am. Soc. for Photogrammetry and Remote Sensing-Mid-South Region Meeting, 2000, William G. Haag award, La. State U., 2001, Best Student Paper award, U. Consortium Geog. Info. Scis. Assembly, 2000, Remote Sensing Speciality Group, Assn. Am. Geographers, 2001, Otis Paul Starkey award, Assn. Am. Geographers, 2001, Intergraph Young Scholar award, U. Consortium Geog. Info. Sci., 2002, Runner-up Early Career award, Remote Sensing Specialty Group, Assn. Am. Geographers, 2004; fellow, Netherlands Govt., 1988—89; grantee, NASA EPSCoR, 2001, 2002, U. Okla., 2002, Inst. Advanced Edn. Geospatial Scis., NASA, 2003—04, U. Calif., Santa Barbara, 2003, NSF, 2004—; scholar, French Govt., 1993—94, La. State U., 1999—2001; CPGIS scholar, 2005, CSISS scholar, 2003. Office: Ariz State U Dept Geography PO Box 870104 Tempe AZ 85287-0104 Home: 4175 W Shannon St Chandler AZ 85226 Home Phone: 480-459-5145; Office Phone: 480-965-6514. Office Fax: 405-325-6090, 480-965-8313. Business E-Mail: soe.myint@asu.edu.

MYLES, KEVIN MICHAEL, metallurgical engineer; b. Chgo., July 18, 1934; s. Michael J. and Ursula (May) M.; m. Joan Christine Ganczewski, Dec. 16, 1967; children: Kathleen, Gary, Jennifer. BS in Metallurgical Engring., U. Ill., 1956, PhD in Phys. Metall. Engring., 1963. Asst. mgr. nuc. fuel repossing program Argonne Nat. Lab., Ill., 1977-79, dep. dir. fossil energy program Ill., 1982-87, dir. fuel cell program Ill., 1987-88, dir. electrochem. tech. program Ill., 1988—99, assoc. dir. chem. tech. divsn. Ill., 1992—99, sr. tech. advisor Ill., 1999—. Adj. prof. materials sci. U. Ill., Chgo., 1967-69; prof. materials sci. Midwest Coll. Engring., Lombard, Ill., 1969-81; pres. Myles Engring. Consultants, Downers Grove, Ill., 1967-. Contbr. articles to Jour. Phys. Chemistry, Chem. Engring. Sci., Jour. Electrochem. Soc., Jour. Fusion Energy, Jour. Power Sources. Mem. Sch. Bd. Dist. #58, Downers Grove, Ill., 1964-70. Maj. USAR, 1956—68. Mem. Am. Soc. for Metals, AIME, Sigma Xi, Alpha Sigma Mu. Achievements include 20 patents in field. Office: Argonne Nat Lab 9700 Cass Ave Argonne IL 60439-4837 Personal E-mail: kmmyles@yahoo.com. Business E-Mail: myles@cmt.anl.gov.

MYLES, LATOYA, research scientist; b. Kosciusko, Miss. d. Steve and Lucy Luse; m. Gerald D. Myles. BS in Chemistry, Alcorn State U., Miss., 1999, BS in Biology, 1999; PhD in Environ. Sci., Fla. A&M U., Tallahassee, 2004. With student chemistry coop. edn. Grand Gulf, Port Gibson, Miss., 1997—98; phys. scientist atmospheric turbulence and diffusion divsn. NOAA, Oak Ridge, Tenn., 2004—. Mem. adv. bd. mem. Sci., Engring., & Math. Link, Inc., Atlanta, 2005. Named Outstanding Graduating Sr. Chemistry, Alcorn State U. Dept Chemistry, 1999; fellow, ednl. partnership program US Dept. Commerce NOAA, 2001—05, US EPA, 1999—2001; scholar, Nat. Merit Found.; Fortenberry Meml. scholar, Alcorn State U., 1998. Mem.: Nat. Orgn. Black Chemists Chem. Engrs., Am. Geophys. Union, Am. Meteorol. Soc., Knoxville Ebony Network (mem. exec. bd. 2005), Blacks in Govt., Beta Kappa Chi, Alpha Kappa Mu, Sigma Xi. Avocations: reading, travel.

MYLNECHUK, LARRY HERBERT, financial executive; b. Littlefork, Minn., Mar. 9, 1948; s. William and Marjorie (Raco) M.; m. Sandy L. Henderson, Mar. 14, 1970; children: Kendra Elizabeth, Scott William. BA, Lewis & Clark Coll., Portland, 1970; JD, Lewis & Clark Coll., 1974. Legal specialist Oreg. Dept. Edn., Salem, 1976-82; sr. v.p., dir. Morley Capital Mgmt. Inc., Portland, 1982-89; founder, pres. Integra Assocs., Inc., Lake Oswego, Oreg., 1989—; exec. dir. The Stable Value Assn., Inc., Lake Oswego, 1990-96; co-founder, prin. Residential Capital Mgmt., LLC, 2000; prin. Novellus Capital Mgmt., 2007—. Cons. Hueler Analytics, Inc., Mpls., 1989—, Bus. Transition LLC, 2006; conf. chmn. GIC Nat. Forum Conf., Washington, 1993-95; arbitrator NASD, NY Stock Exch.; guest lectr. Portland State U., 1978, U. Oreg., 1980; bd. dirs. SAR Found. Contbr. articles to profl. jours. Founder Woodstock Neighborhood Assn., 1975; mem. Multnomah County (Oreg.) Charter Rev. Commn., 1978, Tualatin (Oreg.) City Coun., 1980—84, Portland Com. on Fgn. Rels., 1976—98, bd. dirs., 1993—96; mem. Gov.'s Commn. on Adminstrv. Hearings, State of Oreg., 1988—89, Tchrs. Standards and Practices Commn., State of Oreg., 2000—02; mem. vestry, lay eucharistic min., del. State Episcopal Conv., 1996; mem. Diocesan Coun., 1996—98; mem. vestry Christ Ch. Parish, 1995—2000, Christ Episcopal Ch., 1998—2000; founding mem. St. Margaret's Ch., 2000—03; trustee St. Francis of Assisi Endowment Fund, 1993; bd. dirs. Patriot Found., 2002—. Fellow NEH, 1979, ednl. policy fellow George Washington U., 1980. Mem. SAR (pres. Lewis and Clark chpt.,pres. Oreg. State Soc. 1997, nat. trustee, 1997-98, v.p. Gen.-Pacific dist. 1999-2001), Western Pension Conf., Assn. Soc. Execs., World Affairs Coun. Oreg., Citizen Amb. Program to Western Europe, Gen. Soc. The War of 1812, Soc. Colonial Wars, Sons and Daus. of Pilgrims, Oregon Soc. Sons of the Revolution (co-founder, treas. 1996), Internat. Bus. Forum (mem. adv. bd. 1996), Sons of the Bench and Bar (charter), N. Am. Soc. Securities Adminstrs. (profl. stds. com. 1998), Oreg. Assn. Adminstrv. Law Judges, Soc. Magna Charta Barons, Crown of Charlegmagne Soc., Soc. Charlemagne's Descendants, Col. George Middleton Hist. Soc. (bd. dirs.) Democrat. Episcopalian. Avocations: hiking, diving. Office: Novellus Capital Mgmt LLC 601 108th Ave NE Ste 1900 Bellevue WA 98004 Office Phone: 425-467-2900.

MYLONAKIS, STAMATIOS GREGORY, research scientist, lawyer; b. Athens, Aug. 18, 1937; s. Gregory S. and Vassiliki (Charalambopoulos) Mylonakis; m. Pamela H. Morton, May 5, 1965 (dec. Mar. 1978); 1 child, Gregory (dec.). BS, Nat. U. of Athens, 1961; MS, Ill. Inst. of Tech., 1964; PhD, Mich. State U., 1970. Rsch. assoc. Ill. Inst. of Tech., Chgo., 1964—65; rsch. scientist Brookhaven Nat. Lab., Upton, NY, 1965—68; instr. U. Calif., Berkeley, 1971—73; group leader Rohm and Haas Co., Springhouse, Pa., 1973—76; supr. DeSoto, Inc., Des Plaines, Ill., 1976—79; staff scientist Borg-Warner Corp., Des Plaines, 1979—82, mgr., 1982—87; dept. head Enichem Am., Monmouth Junction, NJ, 1988—94; tech. advisor, registered patent agt. law firm Oblon, Spivak, Arlington, Va., 1994—2000; cons., patent law practitioner, 2000—; sci. fellow Nuc. Rsch. Ctr. Democritos, Athens, 1960—62. Tech. adv. bd. Ctr. Applied Polymer Rsch. Case Western Res. U., Cleve.; adv. bd. NSF Ctr. Polymer Interfaces Lehigh U. Assoc. editor: Jour. Applied Polymer Sci.; contbr. articles to profl. jours. Lt. Greek Army. Fellow Sci., Nuc. Rsch. Ctr. Democritos, Athens, Greece, 1960—62, NSF, Mich. State U., 1968—70, U. Calif., 1971—73. Mem.: AAAS, Am. Chem. Soc., N.Y. Acad. Scis., Sigma Xi. Greek Orthodox. Achievements include patents in polymer science technology. Avocations: photography, painting, travel. Home and Office: 7009 Cashell Manor Ct Derwood MD 20855-1201 Personal E-mail: mylonakis@msn.com, sgmylonakis@aol.com, sgmylonakis@yahoo.com.

MYLOTTE, JOHN ARNOLD, writer, educator; b. Phila., Pa., Aug. 26, 1942; s. Thomas Joseph and Pauline Ellen (Arnold) Mylotte; m. Eva Benda, Sept. 20, 1997; 1 stepchild, Ilya; m. Florence Ellen Noonan, Aug. 14, 1977 (div. Nov. 1992). BA in english, Villanova U., 1964; MA in english, Lehigh U., 1967; JD, Suffolk U. Law Sch., 1980; post grad, MIT, 1981. Bar: Mass. 1981. Tech. editor Naval Air Engring. Ctr., Phila., 1967—68; sr. tech. editor Navy Clothing & Textile Rsch. Lab., 1968—72, dir. tech. publ., 1973—91, dir. pub. rels., 1974—91; pres. TechWrite Assoc., 1987—. Adj. prof.,sr. lectr. Northeastern U., Boston, 1981—. Author: (book) Guide to Writing the Formal Technical Report, 1985, The Art of Technical Writing, 1987; contbr. articles to jours.; numerous appearances on TV, 2006—07. Elected mem. Framingham Town Mtg., 1975—78; Relay for Life Vol. Am. Cancer Society, 1995—; bd. mem. Big Brother-Big Sister Assn., Framingham, Mass., 1975—78, bd. pres., 1977—78. Recipient Command Hist. award, U.S. Navy Hist., 1981, Outstanding Performance award, U.S. Navy Dept., 1980—85. Mem.: Worcester County Poetry Soc., Longfellow Soc. (treas. 2005—), Soc. for Tech. Commn. (5 competitive tech. writing awards 1984—86). Independent. Unitarian Universalist. Avocation: writing. Office: TechWrite Assoc 11 Clemmons St Southborough MA 01772

MYREN, RICHARD ALBERT, criminologist, consultant; b. Madison, Wis., Aug. 9, 1924; s. Andrew Olaus and Olyanna (Olson) M.; m. Patricia Ross Hubin, June 12, 1948; children: Nina Ross Schroepfer, Tania Ellis Myren Zobel, Kristina Albee Myren Sheldon, Andrew James. BS, U. Wis., 1948; LLB, Harvard U., 1952; LLD (hon.), U. New Haven, 1976. Bar: N.C. 1954. Rsch. chemist U.S. Dept. Agr., No. Regional Rsch. Lab., Peoria, Ill., 1948-49; asst. to assoc. rsch. prof. pub. law and govt. Inst. Govt., Chapel Hill, NC, 1952-56; asst. to assoc. prof. Ind. U., 1956-66; dean, prof. Sch. Criminal Justice, State U. N.Y., Albany, 1966-76, Sch. Justice, Am. U., Washington, 1976-86, prof. emeritus, 1986—; cons. Washington, 1987—. Vis. prof. Inst. Criminology, Cambridge (Eng.) U., 1973-74, East China Inst. for Politics and Law, Shanghai, People's Republic of China, 1988; cons. law enforcement programs for children and youth Children's Bur., HEW, Washington, 1960-62; cons. Pres.'s Com. on Juvenile Delinquency and Youth Crime, 1962-64, Pres.'s Commn. on Law Enforcement and Adminstrn. Criminal Justice, 1966, U.S. Law Enforcement Assistance Adminstrn., 1968-82, N.Y. State Temp. Commn. on Constl. Conv., 1967, N.Y. State Dept. Edn., 1967, 69, Calif. Coordinating Coun. for Higher Edn., 1969-70, Nat. Adv. Commn. on Criminal Justice Standards and Goals, 1971-72, Tenn. Higher Edn. Commn., 1976, Ky. Dept. Justice, 1977-78, NSF, 1978—, U.S. Civil Rights Commn., 1978, others. Author: Coroners in North Carolina: A Discussion of Their Problems, 1953, Indiana Sheriffs' Manual of Law and Practice, rev. edit, 1959, Indiana Conservation Officers' Manual of Law and Practice, 1961; (with Lynn D. Swanson) Police Work With Children, 1962; (with Carroll L. Christenson) The Walsh-Healey Public Contracts Act: A Critical Review of Prevailing Minimum Wage Determinations, 1966, Education in Criminal Justice, 1970, Law and Justice: An Introduction, 1988, Investigation for Determination of Fact: A Primer on Proof, 1989; contbr. to: Bases for Justice Systems: Law and the Social Sciences (Gordon E. Misner), 1980, Five Year Outlook: Problems, Opportunities and Constraints in Science and Technology, 1980; assoc. editor: Jour. Criminal Justice; contbr. articles to profl. jours. Bd. dirs. Sex Info. and Edn. Coun. U.S., 1972-75. Served with inf. AUS, 1943-46, ETO; with USNR, 1954-68. Fulbright rsch. scholar to Argentina Cordoba, 1964-65 Mem. N.C. Bar Assn., Sociedad Argentina de Sociología Personal E-mail: rpmyren@peoplepc.com.

MYRICK, ALISSA B., parasitologist, science educator; b. Paris, May 3, 1976; BA, U. Calif., Berkeley, 1996; PhD, Harvard U., Boston, 2003. Program coord. Biology Scholars Program, Berkeley, Calif., 2006—. Bd. mem. minority biomedical scientists Harvard U., Boston, 1998—2001, mem. provost's interfaculty working group on diversity in the scis., 2001. Contbr. sci. edn. anthology, articles to profl. jours. Student coord. Multicultural AIDS Peer Edn. Program, Berkeley, Calif., 1994—96; elected rep. Harvard Grad. Coun., Boston, 1997—99; co-coord. Stomp Out Malaria, Boston, 2000; treas. Bldg. Diversity in the Scis., San Francisco, 2003. Recipient Grad. Opportunity prize, Harvard U., 1997—2003; Predoctoral fellow, Ford Found., 1997—2000, Gates Millenium scholar, Bill and Melinda Gates Found., 2001—03, vis. postdoctoral scholar, U. Calif., San Francisco, 2003—06, Minority Supplemental grantee, NIH, 2003—06. Mem.: AAAS, Am. Soc. Tropical Medicine and Hygiene, CAL Alumni Assn. (life). Achievements include research in validation of microsatellite markers for use in genotyping polyclonal Plasmodium falciparum infections; genomic heterogeneity in the density of noncoding single-nucleotide and microsatellite polymorphisms in Plasmodium falciparum; dynamics of Plasmodium falciparum infection after therapy; in vivo and in vitro analysis of chloroquine resistance in Plasmodium falciparum isolates from Senegal. Office: Biology Scholars Program 2075 VLSB Berkeley CA 94720-3140 Home Phone: 415-255-1060; Office Phone: 510-643-1334. Office Fax: 510-643-9961. Personal E-mail: myricka@earthlink.net. Business E-Mail: amyrick@berkeley.edu.

MYRICK, BISMARCK, diplomat, history professor; b. Portsmouth, Va., Dec. 23, 1940; m. Marie Pierre Mbaye; children: Bismarck Jr., Wesley Todd, Allison Elizabeth. BA, U. Tampa, 1972; MA, Syracuse U., 1973, postgrad., 1979-80; LHD (hon.), Spelman Coll., 2002. Enlisted U.S. Army, 1959; desk officer for Somalia, U.S. Dept. State, Washington, 1980-82; advanced through grades to maj., 1975; ret., 1979; polit. officer Am. Embassy, Monrovia, Liberia, 1982-84; action officer office strategic nuclear policy bur. politico-milit. affairs U.S. Dept. State, 1985-87, dep. dir. policy plans and coordination bur. inter-Am. affairs, 1987-89, Una Chapman Cox fellow US-African Policy, 1988-90; consul gen. Am. Consulate Gen., Durban, South Africa, 1990-93, Capetown, South Africa, 1993-95; amb. to Lesotho, Am. Embassy, Maseru, 1995-98; diplomat-in-residence Atlanta U. Ctr. at Spelman Coll., 1998-99; U.S. amb. to Liberia Dept. of State, Monrovia, Liberia, 1999—2002; univ. lectr. internat. affairs Old Dominion U., 2002—; sr. fellow Joint Forces Staff Coll., Norfolk, Va., 2002—. Adj. prof. history and polit. sci. Old Dominion U., 2002—03. Author: Three Aspects of Crisis in Colonial Kenya, 1975; contbr. chpt. to book. Decorated Silver Star, Purple Heart, 4 Bronze Stars; named to U.S. Army Hall of Fame, 1996; named Ambassador Bismarck Myrick Days, City of Portsmouth, Va., 2000; named one of Portsmouth Notable, 2006; Bismarck Myrick St. and Bismarck Myrick Crescent St. named in his honor, 2002. Mem.: World Affairs Coun. Hampton Rds. (bd. dirs. 2004—). Address: 1200 Mill Run Chesapeake VA 23322

MYRICK, SUE WILKINS, congresswoman, former mayor; b. Tiffin, Ohio, Aug. 1, 1941; d. William Henry and Margaret Ellen (Roby) Wilkins; m. Jim Forest (div.); children: Greg, Dan; m. Wilbur Edward Myrick Jr., Sept. 11, 1977. Student, Heidelberg Coll., 1959-60, LLD (hon.), 1995. Exec. sec. to mayor and city mgr., Alliance, Ohio, 1962-63; dir. br. office Stark County Ct. of Juvenile and Domestic Rels., Alliance, Ohio, 1963-65; pres. Myrick Advt. and Pub. Rels., Charlotte, NC, 1971-95; at-large mem. City Coun., Charlotte, NC, 1983—85; mayor Charlotte, NC, 1987-91; pres. Myrick Enterprises, 1992—94; mem. US Congress from 9th NC dist., 1995—. Candidate for US Senate, NC, 1992; mem. energy and commerce com. US Congress, dep. whip, 2003—, co-chair cancer caucus. Active Heart Fund, Multiple Sclerosis, March of Dimes, Arts and Scis. Fund Dr.; bd. dirs. NC Inst. Politics; v.p. Sister Cities Internat.; mem. Pres. Bush's Affordable Housing Commn.; founder, coord. Charlotte vol. tornado relief effort; lay leader, Sunday sch. tchr. 1st United Meth. Ch.; treas. Mecklenburg Ministries. Recipient Woman of Yr. award Harrisonburg, Va., 1968; named one of Outstanding Young Women of Am., 1968, Senator George L. Murphy award, 1998, Yr. of the Sr. award, 2000, Sr. Legis. Achievement award, 2000, Small Grain Leadership award, 2000, Pub. Leadership in Tech. award, 2002, Pub. Svc. Leadership award, 2002, Small Bus. Survival Com. award, 2004, Oncology Medal of Honor award, 2005. Mem. Women's Polit. Caucus, Beta Sigma Phi. Republican. Methodist. also: US House Reps 230 Cannon House Office Bldg Washington DC 20515-0001 Home and Office: 8437 Olde Troon Dr Charlotte NC 28277 Office Phone: 202-225-1976. Office Fax: 202-225-3389. E-mail: myrick@mail.house.gov.

MYRIE, LESLIE ROLCE, JR., marketing executive; s. Leslie Rolce, Sr. and Gladys Lillard Myrie. BS, Duke U., Durham, NC, 2001; MBA, U. NC, Chapel Hill, 2007. Health economist Rsch. Triangle Inst., NC, 2001—03, project mgr., 2003—05; asst. product mgr. intern Pfizer Consumer Healthcare, Morris Plains, NJ, 2006; assoc. brand mgr. Kraft Foods, East Hanover, NJ, 2007—. Fellow, Consortium For Grad. Study in Mgmt., 2005-2007. Office Phone: 973-385-2000. Business E-Mail: leslie.myrie@alumni.duke.edu.

MYRTH, JUDY G., editor; d. James Douglas and Ruth Evelyn Sheeran; children: Susanne, Evelyn. BA, SUNY Albany and U. Würzburg, Germany, 1968; MA, SUNY, Albany, 1969; postgrad., Ind. U., Bloomington, 1969—70, Free U., Berlin, 1970—71; MLS, SUNY, Albany, 1988. Cert. pub. libr. N.Y., permanent tchg. cert. in German N.Y. Tchr. English Gymnasium Landau a.d. Isar, Germany, 1971—73, Realschule Niedervie-hbach, 1973—76; editor Bibliography of the History of Art J. Paul Getty Trust, Williamstown, Mass., 1989—2000, LA, 2001—. Mem.: Coll. Art Assn. Avocations: travel, reading. Office: J Paul Getty Trust 1200 Getty Center Dr Los Angeles CA 90049 Office Phone: 310-440-6362.

MYSAK, LAWRENCE ALEXANDER, oceanographer, climatologist and mathematics educator; b. Saskatoon, Sask., Can., Jan. 1940; s. Stephen and Nettie Mysak; m. Diane Mary Eeles, Aug. 15, 1974; children: Paul Alexander, Claire Anastasia. BSc, U. Alta., Can., 1961; MSc, U. Adelaide, Australia, 1963; AM, Harvard U., 1964, PhD, 1967. Rsch. fellow Harvard U., 1966-67; mem. faculty U. B.C., Vancouver, 1967-86, prof. math. and oceanography, 1976-86; Atmospheric Environ. Svc./Natural Scis. Engring. Rsch. Coun.; sr. indsl. rsch. prof. climatology McGill U., Montreal, Que., Canada, 1986-96, dir. Climate Rsch Group, 1986-90, Can. Steamship Lines prof. meteorology, 1989—, founding dir. Ctr. for Climate and Global Change Rsch., 1990-96. Vis. rsch. assoc. Oreg. State U., summer 1968; sr.

visitor Cambridge (Eng.) U., 1971-72; vis. scientist Inst. Ocean Sci., Sidney, B.C., fall 1976, Nat. Ctr. Atmospheric Rsch., Boulder, Colo., 1977; vis. prof. U.S. Naval Postgrad. Sch., Monterey, Calif., summer 1981, Swiss Fed. Inst., Tech., Zurich, 1982-83, 2000-2001; George's Lemaître vis. prof. Cath. U. Louvain, Belgium, 1995; invitation fellowship for rsch. in Japan, Japan Soc. for Promotion of Scis., 1997; supr. 70 grad. and postdoctoral students, 1967—; vis. prof. Italian Nat. Inst. Geophysics and Volcanology, Bologna, 2001; exch. lectr. Royal Soc. Can. Nat. Acad. Scis. of Ukraine, 2002. Co-author: Waves in the Ocean, 1978; also articles in profl. jours.; assoc. editor Jour. Phys. Oceanography, 1977-92, Atmospheric-Ocean, 1988-91, Climatol. Bull., 1992-93; contbg. editor Am. Geophys. Union books on coastal and esturaine studies, 1987-2000; mem. editl. bd. Geophys. and Astrophys. Fluid Dynamics, 1983-96; series editor: Springer Atmospheric and Oceanographic Scis. Libr., 2001-. Decorated Order of Can.; recipient Patterson Disting. Svc. medal Environ. Can. Atmospheric Environment Svc., 1997, prix Michel-Jurdant, ACFAS, 2005, Marie-Victorin, prize, Que., 2006. Fellow Acad. of Sci. of Royal Soc. Can. (v.p. Acad. of Sci. 1991-93, pres. 1993-96), Am. Meteorol. Soc., Am. Geophys. Union; mem. Can. Meteorol. and Oceanog. Soc. (co-recipient Pres.'s prize 1980, J.P. Tully medal Oceanography 1997, inaugural fellow 1999), Royal Soc. Can. (life), European Geosciences Union (hon.; Alfred Wegener medal 2006), Academia Europaea (fgn.), Internat. Assn. for Phys. Scis. of Ocean (v.p. 2003-07). Office: McGill U 805 Sherbrooke St W Montreal PQ Canada H3A 2K6 Office Phone: 514-398-3768. Business E-Mail: lawrence.mysak@mcgill.ca.

MYSEN, BJORN OLAV, scientist; b. Oslo, Dec. 20, 1947; came to U.S., 1971; s. Martin T. and Randi M. (Fosser) M.; m. Susana Laya, Feb. 22, 1975; children: Joanna, Christopher. BS, U. Oslo, 1969, MA, 1971; PhD, Pa. State U., 1974. Fellow Carnegie Instn., Washington, 1974-77, sr. scientist, 1977—; lectr. Johns Hopkins U., Balt., 1975-76. Author: Structure and Properties of Silicate Melts; editor: Physico Chemical Principles of Rock-Forming Materials, 1986, Phase Diagrams for Ceramists, 1990; contbr. over 180 articles to profl. jours. Recipient Reusch medal Geol. Soc. Norway, 1979. Fellow Mineral. Soc. Am.; mem. Am. Geophys. Union, Geochem. Soc. (F.W. Clarke medal 1977), Royal Norwegian Acad. Arts and Letters. Office: Geophys Lab 5251 Broad Branch Rd NW Washington DC 20015-1305

MYSKINA, ANASTASIA, professional tennis player; b. Moscow, July 8, 1981; d. Andrey and Galina Myskina. Profl. tennis player WTA Tour, 1998—. Recipient Commitment to Cmty Award, Fla. Times-Union, 2005. Achievements include Winner 10 WTA Tour singles titles; Winner 5 WTA Tour doubles title; Winner 3 ITF Women's Circuit singles titles; Winner 3 ITF Women's Circuit doubles titles; Member Russian Olympic Team 2000, 2004. Office: c/o WTA Tour Corp Hdqs One Progress Plz Ste 1500 Saint Petersburg FL 33701 *

MYSLINSKI, NORBERT RAYMOND, medical educator; b. Buffalo, Apr. 14, 1947; s. Bernard and Amelia Joan (Lesniak) M.; m. Patricia Ann Byrne, June 19, 1970 (dec. 1980); m. René Carter, Nov. 21, 1993; children: Matthew Ryan, Kelly Lynn. BS in Biology, Canisius Coll., Buffalo, NY, 1969; PhD in Pharmacology, U. Ill., Chgo., 1973. Rsch. assoc. Tufts U., Boston, 1973—75; asst. prof. U. Md., Balt., 1975—80, assoc. prof. physiology, 1980—, co-dir. Facial Pain Clinic, 1980—84, instr. nursing, 1982—84; rsch. fellow U. Bristol, England, 1984—85; adj. assoc. prof. U. Md. Sch. Nursing, 1997—. Instr. C.C. Balt., 1980—82; dir. grad. program dept. physiology U. Md., 1981—97, mem. faculty Marine-Estuarine Environ. Scis. grad. program, 1988—97, dir. HS biomedical rsch. program, 2000—; founder, dir. Patricia Byrne Nursing Scholarship Fund Trocaire Coll., Buffalo, 1985; dir. NIH Minority Rsch. Apprentice Program Balt. Coll. Dental Surgery, 1988—; mem. grant rev. com. Nat. Inst. Nursing Rsch., 1993—94; grant reviewer Dept. Health and Human Svcs., 1993—94; cons. in field; appeared on more than 20 live TV and radio programs; founder, dir. Internat. Brain Bee, 1999—; chmn. Neuroscience Edn. Workshop, Prague, Czech Republic, 2003; mem. com. Md. Higher Edn. Commn., 2003—. Editor newsletters Med. Soc. Md. Rsch., 1977-82, Brain Storm, 1999-2005; mem. editl. bd. Jour. Environ. Neurosci. and Biomedicine; author book chpts., revs. and numerous abstracts on pharmacology and neurosci.; inventor in field; reviewer 7 jours. Rep. task force on aging U. Md., 1979—84; instr. Am. Heart Assn., Balt., 1978, ARC, Balt., 1977—83; Internat. Co. Md. chpt. ARC, 2003—; com. mem. Md. Higher Edn. Edn. Commn., 2003—; mem. Pres. Bush's Sec. of Edn. Summit on Sci., Washington, 2004; eucharistic min., pastoral visitor Cath. Ch., 1983—93; bd. dirs. Md. Brain Awareness Week, Md., 1996—, Balt. Brains Rule!, 2002—04, Md. Brain Lit. Competition, 2000—, Md. Brain Art Competition, 2000—. Capt. US Army, 1969—77. Grantee NIH, various drug cos. and founds.; USPHS fellow, 1969-73; recipient Alumni of Yr. award St. Mary's HS, Lancaster, NY, 1996, Disting. Alumni award outstanding career Canisius Coll., Buffalo, 1997, Time to Care Cmty. Svc. award U. Md., 1998, Founders Day Pub. Svc. award U. Md., 2000. Mem.: HS Neuroscience (founder 2003), Am. Soc. Pharmacology Exptl. Therapeutics, Soc. Neuroscience (pres. Balt. chpt. 1990—92, editor newsletter 1990—97, neuroscience literacy com. 1997—2001), Am. Physiol. Soc., Internat. Assn. Dental Rsch. (adv. 1980—81), Md. Soc. Med. Rsch. (exec. com. 1978—86, bd. dir. 1978—86), Internat. Brain Rsch. Orgn. (mem. sch. bd. 2007—), European Brain Behavior Soc. (hon.). Republican. Home: 9395 Carrie Way Ellicott City MD 21042-1701 Office: U Md Sch Dentistry Dept Biomed Scis 650 W Baltimore St Baltimore MD 21201-1510 Office Phone: 410-706-7258. Office Fax: 410-706-0193. Business E-Mail: nrm001@dental.umaryland.edu.

MYSTER, RANDALL WALTON, education educator, researcher; b. Rochester, Minn., Jan. 20, 1955; s. Cletis Eugene and Dorothy Walton Myster; m. Olga Vladimirovna Mironova, Feb. 21, 2003. BS, U. Minn., 1977; MS, Purdue U., 1980, Rutgers U., 1987, PhD, 1990. Rsch. scientist U. PR, San Juan, 1990—95, asst. prof., 1995—2001, U. Ctrl. Okla., 2001—. Contbr. articles to profl. jours.; author (book): Post-Agricultural Succession in the Neotropics, 2007. Recipient fellowship, Fulbright Found., 2004, Scholar of Yr., Am. Assn. U. Profls., 2005; fellowship, Nat. Sci. Found., 1987. Mem.: Ecol. Assn. Am., Assn. for Tropical Biology. Democrat. Episcopalian. Avocations: jazz, saxophone, diving, cross country skiing, backpacking. Office: U Ctrl Okla 100 N University Edmond OK 73034 Office Phone: 405-974-5909.

MYTELKA, ARNOLD KRIEGER, lawyer; b. Jersey City, July 24, 1937; s. Herman Donald and Jeannette (Krieger) M.; m. Rosalind Marcia Kaplan, Dec. 17, 1961; children: Andrew Charles, Daniel Sommer. AB, Princeton U., 1958; LLB cum laude, Harvard U., 1961; postgrad., London Sch. Econs., 1961—62. Bar: N.J. 1961, U.S. Dist. Ct. N.J. 1963, U.S. Supreme Ct. 1970, U.S. Ct. Appeals (3d cir.) 1978, U.S. Dist. Ct. (so. and ea. dist.) N.Y. 1983. Law sec. Chief Justice N.J. Supreme Ct., Newark, 1962-63; assoc. Clapp & Eisenberg, Newark, 1963-68, ptnr., 1968-94; prin. Kraemer, Burns, Mytelka, Lovell & Kulka, Springfield, N.J., 1994—. Lectr. Rutgers Law Sch., Newark, 1973; mem. Am. Law Inst., Phila., 1989—; mem. cons. group The Law Governing Lawyers, 1990-99, Restatement of Restitution and Unjust Enrichments; founding trustee Newark Legal Svcs. Project, 1965-68; trustee Edn. Law Ctr., 1974-75; chmn. dist. V ethics com. Supreme Ct. N.J., 1983-84, mem. 1981-84; trustee Legal Svcs. Found. Essex County, 1982—, pres., 1990-92; lectr. in land use law. Mem. editorial bd. N.J. Law Jour., 1991—; contbr. legal articles to profl. jours. Chmn. bd. trustees Ramapo Coll. NJ, 1979-80; mediator chancery divsn. NJ Superior Ct., 1990—, trustee, 1998-2000, 03-06, spl. fiscal agt., 1997, 2003, 2005, spl. master, 1999-00. Frank Knox Meml. fellow Harvard U., London Sch. Econs. and Polit. Sci., 1961-62. Mem.: ABA (mem. litigation sect.), N.J. State Bar Assn. (chmn. appellate practices study com. 1977—79, chmn. land use law sect. 1984—85). Home: 56 Hall Rd Chatham NJ 07928-1723 Office: Kraemer Burns Mytelka Lovell & Kulka 675 Morris Ave Springfield NJ 07081-1523 E-mail: amytelka@kraemerburns.com.

NA, TSUNG SHUN (TERRY NA), Chinese studies educator, writer; b. Beijing, Nov. 3, 1932; came to U.S., 1964; s. Chi-L and Hui (Hu) N.; m. Yen Yen Chao, 1964. BA, Taiwan Normal U., 1956; MA, U. B.C., 1970; PhD, U. Minn., 1978. Assoc. prof. Taipei Normal Coll., Taiwan, Republic of China, 1956-64; vis. lectr. Ind. U., Bloomington, 1964-66; asst. prof. U. Minn., Mpls., 1970-80; vis. prof. Sun Yat-sen U., Taiwan, 1981-84; prof., dir. Am. Inst. Chinese Studies, Charles Town, W.Va., 1985—. Author: (English books) A Linguistic Study of P'i-pa Chi, 1969, Studies on Dream of the Red Chamber: A Selected and Classified Bibliography, 1979, Supplement, 1981, Taiwan Studies on Dream of the Red Chamber: A Selected and Classified Bibliography, 1983, Chinese Studies in English: A Selected Bibliography, 1991, (Chinese) Mandarin Pronunciation, 1966, Teaching Chinese in the U.S.A., 1983, Studies on Chinese Classical Novels, 1985, A Collection of Short Stories, 1987; contbr. numerous articles, short stories, and research essays to jours. and newspapers in U.S., Taiwan, ROC, and China. Mem. MLA, Assn. Asian Studies. Office: Am Inst Chinese Studies PO Box 453 Charles Town WV 25414-0453

NAAKE, JOAN MURRAY, English professor; m. Larry E. Naake; 2 children. B in English, Emmanuel Coll., Boston; M in English Lit., Boston Coll.; grad. student in English Lit., U. Oxford, Eng. Tchr. Prince George's CC, No. Va. CC, Marymount U.; prof. English Cosumnes River Coll., Sacramento; faculty mem. to prof., chair English dept. Montgomery Coll., Germantown, Md., 1992. Recipient Nat. Inst. Staff and Orgn. Devel. award, Faculty Outstanding Svc. award, Montgomery Coll., 2002, US Prof. of Yr. award, Carnegie Found. for Advancement of Tchg. and Coun. for Advancement and Support of Edn., 2006. Office: Humanities Social Scis and Edn Montgomery Coll 20200 Observation Dr Germantown MD 20876 Office Phone: 301-353-1951. Office Fax: 301-353-7752. E-mail: joan.naake@montgomerycollege.edu. *

NABEL, ELIZABETH GUENTHNER, cardiologist, researcher; BA summa cum laude, St. Olaf Coll., Northfield, Minn., 1974; postgrad., Union Theol. Sem., 1974—75, Columbia U., NYC, 1975—77; MD, Cornell U., Ithaca, NY, 1981; DHC (hon.), Katholik U. Leuven, Belgium, 2001. Diplomate Am. Bd. Internal Medicine and cardiovascular diseases. Intern & resident in internal medicine Brigham and Women's Hosp.-Harvard Med. Sch., Boston, 1981—84, clin. and rsch. fellow cardiovasc. divsn., 1984-87; asst. prof. internal medicine U. Mich., Ann Arbor, 1987-91, assoc. prof. internal medicine, 1991-94, dir. Cardiovasc. Rsch. Ctr., 1992—99, prof. internal medicine and physiology, 1994—99, dir. divsn. cardiology, 1997-99; sci. dir. clin. rsch. Nat. Heart, Lung, and Blood Inst. NIH, Bethesda, Md., 1999—2005, dir. Nat. Heart, Lung, and Blood Inst., 2005—. Mem. sci. adv. bd. Vical Inc., San Diego, 1992-96; mem. arteriosclerosis, hypertension, and lipid metabolism adv. com. NHLBI, NIH, 1991-93, parent program project grant rev. com., 1995—, mem. task force on human gene therapy, 1992, mem. cardiology adv. com., 1993-94, mem. spl. emphasis panel arterial thrombosis, 1996; chair sci. pub. com. Am. Heart Assn., 1996-98, bd. of dir, 1996-98; chair Atherosclerosis Thrombosis and Vascular Biology Coun., 2002—, Gordon Conf. on Vascular Cell Biology, 1996; pres. N.Am. Vascular Biology Orgn., 1996-97; sci. adv.bd. Keystone Symposia, 1999—, bd. of dir. 2001—; mem. com. on space medicine Inst. of Medicine, 1991-2001; councilor and sec.-treas. Am. Soc. of Clin. Investigation, 2001—; lectr. Mayo Clinic, 1996, Yale Univ., 1997, Univ. of Texas, 1997, Womens Hosp., 1997, 2001, Univ. of Hawaii, 1980, Temple Univ., 1999, John Hopkins, 1999, 2000, 2002, Am. Heart Assn., 1999, Univ. of Mich., 2001, Vanderbilt Univ., 2001, Univ, of Va., 2002, among many others. Assoc. editor Jour. of Clin. Investigation, 1997—2002, mem. editl. bd., 2002—05, mem. bd. reviewing editors Science, 1998—2005, mem. editl. bd. New Eng. Jour. Medicine, 2001—; editor: Trends in Cardiovascular Medicine, 2001; cons. editor Circulation, Circulation Rsch., Atherial Thrombosis and Vascular Biology, 2000—05. Recipient Disting. Achievement award, Basic Cardiovascular Sciences Coun., Am. Heart Assn., Amgen-Scientific Achievement award, Am. Soc. Biochemistry and Molecular Biology. Fellow Am. Coll. Cardiology, Am. Heart Assn. (basic sci. coun., clin. cardiology coun., circulation coun., atherosclerosis coun., bd. dirs. 1996-97, sci. adv. and coord. com. 1996-97, chair sci. pub. com. 1996-97, sci. pub. com. 1994-96, sci. sessions program com. 1994-95; rsch. fellowship com. Mich. chpt. 1993-95, rsch. grant-in-aid com. 1994-96, vice chair rsch. grant-in-aid com. 1995-96, rsch. exec. com. 1995-96, rsch. com. 1995-96, chair peer rev. rsch. com. 1996-97); mem. AAAS, ACP, Am. Soc. for Biochemistry and Molecular Biology (Amgen Sci. award 1996), Am. Fedn. Clin. Rsch., Am. Soc. Investigative Pathology, Am. Soc. Clin. Investigation, N.Y. Acad. Scis., Am. Soc. Gene Therapy (bd. dirs. 1996), Assn. Am. Physicians, N.Am. Vascular Biology Orgn. (councillor 1994-95, sec., treas. 1994-95, pres. 1996-97), Inst. of Medicine, Ctrl. Soc. Clin. Rsch., Phi Beta Kappa, Alpha Omega Alpha. Office: NIH/NHLBI 31 Center Dr Bldg 31 Rm 5A52 Bethesda MD 20892 Address: NIH/NHLBI Bldg 50 Rm 4525 50 South Dr MSC 8016 Bethesda MD 20892-8016 Office Phone: 301-435-1877. Office Fax: 301-435-5295. Business E-Mail: nabel-lab@nhibi.nih.gov.

NABERS, CLAUDE LOWREY, retired periodontist, writer; b. Vernon, Tex., Mar. 29, 1924; s. John Bradford and Mae (Moore) N.; m. Blanche Lillian Eaton, Sept. 28, 1951; children: Marquis Eaton, Bradford Claude. DDS, U. Tex., 1946; MS in Dentistry, Northwestern U., 1949. Diplomate Am. Bd. Periodontology (bd. dirs. 1965-71, chmn. 1971). Civilian cons. Brook Army Hosp., 1958—84, Lackland Air Force Hosp., 1958—75, Sch. Aerospace Medicine, 1975—80; gen. mgr. Nabers Eaton Properties, San Antonio, 1983—. Nat. cons. Surgeon Gen. USAF, 1969-71; mem. ADA Coun. on Dental Rsch., Chgo., 1983-87; lectr. in field worldwide. Author: (in Japanese) Periodontal Therapy, 1980; co-author: Periodontal Therapy, 1990; originator procedures in field. Mem. devel. bd. U. Tex. Health Sci. Ctr., San Antonio, 1989-94, pres. coun., 1994—, co-chmn., 1996, U. Tex. Austin chancellor's coun. Littlefield Soc., Hermes Soc.; bd. trustees Cancer Therapy and Rsch. Ctr. Found. Bd., San Antonio, 1998-2002, bd. govs. 1999-2003; elder 1st Presbyn. Ch., San Antonio, 1960; v.p. Alamo Kiwanis, San Antonio, 1990-91; bd. dirs. The 100 Club, San Antonio, 1993-96, McFarland Tennis Found., San Antonio, 1994-97, San Antonio Salvation Army, 1998—2004. Capt. U.S. Army, 1946-48. Recipient 1st Holler's Disting. Lecturship award, San Antonio, 1984, 1st Meml. Jack Lyon Lectureship, U. Pa., 1984; recipient Outstanding Civilian Svc. medal Dept. Army, 1978, 1st Meml. G.R. Lundquist Lectureship Northwestern U., 1979, Outstanding Alumnus award U. Tex. Dental Br., Houston, 1980 Fellow Am. Coll. Dentists, Am. Acad. Periodontology (pres. 1972-73, exec. coun. 1962-74, Gold medal 1978, Master Clinician award 1990), Acad. Internat. Dentistry; mem. S.W. Soc. Periodontists (pres. 1961), San Antonio Country Club, Town Club, Conopus Club, Argyle, European Acad. Dentistry (hon.), South African Soc. Periodontology (hon.), Omicron Kappa Upsilon (hon.), Xi Psi Phi (life) Republican. Avocations: tennis, golf, hunting, bridge, travel.

NABERS, DRAYTON, JR., retired state supreme court chief justice, insurance company executive; b. Birmingham, Ala., Dec. 2, 1940; s. Drayton Sr. and Jane (Porter) N.; m. Fairfax Smathers, Dec. 31, 1965; children: Drayton III, Mary James, Fairfax Virginia. BA, Princeton U., 1962; LLB, Yale U., 1965. Law clk. to justice Hugo Black U.S. Supreme Ct., Washington, 1965-66; assoc. Cabaniss, Johnston, Gardner, Dumas & O'Neal, 1967-71, ptnr., 1971-79; sr. v.p. ops., gen. counsel Protective Life Ins. Co., 1979; pres. Empire Gen. Life Ins. Co., 1980-82; pres., COO Protective Life Corp./Protective Life Ins. Co., 1982-92; pres., CEO Protective Life Ins. Co, Birmingham, Ala., 1992-94, chmn., pres., CEO, 1994—2002; fin. dir. State of Alabama, 2002—04; chief justice Alabama Supreme Ct., 2004—06. Bd. dirs. Protective Life Corp., Protective Life Ins. Co., Am. Found. Life Ins. Co., Energen, Inc., Nat. Bank of Commerce. Chmn. Leadership Birmingham, United Way Ctrl. Ala., Am. Council Life Insurers, Cornerstone Schools of Ala. Mem. Ala. Acad. Honor, Birmingham Bar Assn., Ala. Bar Assn.

NABHOLZ, JOSEPH VINCENT, biologist, ecologist; b. Memphis, Nov. 3, 1945; s. Martin Peter and Helen Kathleen (Garbacz) N.; m. Sue Ann Winterburn, Aug. 12, 1972; children: Karen Stacey, Pamela Michelle. BS, Christian Bros. U., Memphis, 1968; MS, U. Ga., Athens, 1973, PhD, 1978. Sr. biologist EPA, Washington, 1979—. Reviewer NSF and profl. jours., 1973—, Standards Methods Com., Am. Water Works Assn., Denver 18th through 21st edits.; evaluator Office Exptl. Learning U. Md., College Park, Md., 1984-86. Author: Estimating Toxicity of Industrial Chemicals to Aquatic Organisms Using Structure Activity Relationships, 1988, 94; co-author: Methods of Ecological Toxicology, 1981, Testing for Effects of Chemicals on Ecosystems, 1981; contbr. articles to profl. jours. Bd. dirs. Comty. Assn. Rollingwood Village (4th sect.), Woodbridge, Va., 1981-90, v.p. 1981-82, pres. 1983-90, maintainence chmn. 1990—. Decorated Army Commendation medal with oak leaf cluster, US Army, Vietnam, 1969, '70. Mem. AAAS, Am. Inst. Biol. Scis. (life), Assn. Southeastern Biologists (life), Internat. Assn. Ecology, Ecol. Soc. Am. (life), Soc. Environ. Toxicology and Chemistry, Phi Kappa Phi (life). Roman Catholic. Achievements include pragmatic application of theory of chemical structure activity relationships for routine risk assessment of industrial chemicals for environmental toxicity. Home: 13627 Bentley Cir Woodbridge VA 22192-4340 Office: EPA 7403 1200 Pennsylvania Ave NW Washington DC 20460-0001 Home Phone: 703-680-4710; Office Phone: 202-564-8909. Office Fax: 202-564-9063. Business E-Mail: nabholz.joe@epa.gov.

NABI, ROBIN, communications educator; d. Saleh and Rhona Nabi. PhD, U. Pa., Phila., 1998. Asst. prof. U. Ariz., Tucson, 1998—2004, U. Calif., Santa Barbara, 2004—05, assoc. prof., 2005—. Contbr. articles to profl. jours. Mem.: Internat. Comm. Assn. (vice-chair mass comm. divsn.). Office: Univ Calif Santa Barbara 5838 Ellison Hall Santa Barbara CA 93106 Office Phone: 805-893-4531.

NABI, STANLEY ANDREW, brokerage house executive; b. Baghdad, Iraq, Sept. 17, 1930; arrived in U.S., 1947; s. Moshi S. and Victoria T. (Mukamal) N.; m. Bette E. Miller, Mar. 31, 1968; children: Deborah Susan, Lisa Meryl. BA, Columbia U., 1952; postgrad., NYU, 1954—58. Gen. ptnr. Schweickart & Co., NYC, 1954-72; gen. ptnr., chief investment officer Lazard Freres & Co., NYC, 1973-84; exec. v.p. Bessemer Trust Co., N.A., 1985-95; pres., CEO Bessemer Investors Svcs., 1985-95; vice chmn., chmn. investment policy com. Wood, Struthers & Winthrop, NYC, 1995-2000; chief investment officer DLJ Asset Mgmt. Corp., NYC, 1996-2000; mng. dir., sr. advisor Credit Suisse Asset Mgmt., 2000—03; vice chmn. Silvercrest Asset Mgmt. Group, 2004—. Lectr. New Sch. Social Rsch., N.Y.C., 1963-68; investment cons. U.S. Steel and Carnegie Pension Fund, N.Y.C., 1979—; dir. Bargain Town U.S.A., N.Y.C., 1962-69; mem. pres.'s coun. New Sch. U., N.Y.C., 1989—; adj. prof. fin. Grad. Sch. Bus., Fordham U., N.Y.C., 1992-97. Editor: weekly jour. The Analyst, 1957-72; assoc. editor: jour. The Fin. Analysts Jour., 1971-83. Trustee NABI Found., 1964—. Served with U.S. Army, 1952-54. Mem. N.Y. Soc. Security Analysts (pres. 1971-72), Inst. Chartered Fin. Analysts, Assn. for Investment Mgmt. and Rsch. Office: 1330 Ave of the Americas New York NY 10019 Home: 1 Kensington Gate (PH-1) Great Neck NY 11021-1202 Business E-Mail: snabi@silvercrestgroup.com.

NABOKOV, EVGENI, professional hockey player; b. Ust-Kamenogorsk, Kazakhstan, July 25, 1975; m. Tabitha Nabokov; 1 child, Emily. Goalie San Jose Sharks, 2000—. Player NHL All-Star Game, 2001; mem. Team Russia, Olympic Games, Torino, Italy, 2006. Named to All-Rookie Team, NHL, 2001; recipient Calder Meml. Trophy, 2001. Avocations: golf, tennis. Office: San Jose Sharks 525 W Santa Clara St San Jose CA 95113

NABORS, MARION CARROLL, retired English educator; b. Marshall, Tex., Mar. 12, 1948; d. Aldon Edgar and Iola Hall; 1 child, Inetha Iola Sheffield. MS, U. Dallas, Irving, Tex., 1993; PhD, U. North Tex., Denton, 2006. Cert. supt. Tex. Edn. Agy., 2001, prin.-EC-12 Tex. Edn. Agy., 2000, tchr. English, French Tex. Edn. Agy., 1976. English tchr. Lincoln Humanities and Comm. Magnet, Dallas, 1983—98; adminstr. Yvonne Ewell Townview Ctr., Dallas, 1998—2005; adj. prof. ElCentro CC, Dallas, 1993—98, Cedar Valley C.C., Lancaster, Tex., 2002—04; coll. prof. adj. Eastfield Coll., Mesquite, Tex., 2005—; adj. prof. Paul Quinn Coll., Dallas, 2006—; co-owner Izanhour and Nabors Tutoring Co., Dallas, 2006—. Cons. Paul Quinn Coll., Dallas, 2006—. Tutor Dallas Ind. Sch. Dist., 1986—2004. Named Tchr. of the Yr., Lincoln H.S. and Acad. Evening Sch., 1987, 1988, 1990, 1995, 1996. Mem.: Nat. Alliance of Black Sch. Educators (life). Independent. Roman Catholic. Avocations: reading, baking, cooking, chess. Home and Office: Izanhova and Nabors Tutoring Co 1438 Mirage Canyon Dr Dallas TX 75232 Home Phone: 972-228-6770; Office Phone: 972-228-6770.

NABORS, ROBERT L., military officer; b. Boston; married; children: Robert, Richard, Jonathan. BS in Systems Engring., U. Ariz.; MS in Systems Mgmt., U. So. Calif.; grad. Sr. Officials in Nat. Security, Harvard U.; grad., Armed Forces Staff Coll. Commd. 2d lt. U.S. Army, advanced through grades to maj. gen., with 67th Signal Battalion Ft. Riley, Kans., overseas tours in Vietnam and Worms, Germany, also active duty tours Ft. Dix, NJ, Aberdeen Proving Grounds, Md., aide-de-Camp for Comdg. Gen., VII Corps, 1979-81; with Office of Dir. of Plans, Programs and Policy U.S. Army Readiness Command, 1983; then comdr. 509th signal Battalion U.S. Army, Italy; spl. asst. to U.S. Army's Dir. of Info. Sys. for Command Control. Comm. and Computers; chief Integration div. Architecture Directorate U.S. Army, dep. comdr. White House Comm. Agy., comdr. 2d Signal Brigade, 1990, comdr. 5th Signal Command, 1995-98, comdr. Comm.-Electronics Command and comdr. Ft. Monmouth NJ, 1998-2001. Decorated DSM, Def. Superior Svc. medal, Legion of Merit with 4 oak leaf clusters, Bronze Star, Meritorious Svc. medal with 4 oak leaf clusters, others; recipient Roy Wilkins award of Reknown, NAACP, 2000, Fed. Asian-Pacific Am. Coun. award, 2000, others. Mem. Mensa.

NABOZNY, HEATHER, professional sports team groundskeeper; b. Milford, Mich., 1970; Grad. Turf Mgmt. Prog., Mich. State U., 1993. Groundskeeper Toronto Blue Jays spring tng. camp, Dunedin, Fla.; head groundskeeper Class A West Mich. Whitecaps, 1994, Detroit Tigers, 1999—. Named one of 40 Under 40, Crain's Detroit Bus., 2006. Achievements include becoming first female goundskeeper in Major League Baseball and World Series game. Office: c/o Detroit Tigers Comerica Park 2100 Woodward Ave Detroit MI 48201

NACE, BARRY JOHN, lawyer; b. York, Pa., Nov. 28, 1944; s. John Harrison and Mildred Louise (Orwig) Nace; m. Andrea Marcia Giardini, Apr. 28, 1973; children: Christopher Thomas, Jonathan Barry, Matthew Andrew. BS, Dickinson Coll., 1965, JD, 1969, LLD (hon.), 1994. Bar: Md. 1970, DC 1971, Pa. 1972, W.Va. 1997, U.S. Ct. Appeals (3d, 4th and DC cirs.), U.S. Supreme Ct. Ptnr. Davis & Nace, Washington, 1972-78, Paulson & Nace, Bethesda, Md., 1978—85, 1998—; sr. ptnr. Paulson, Nace & Norwind, Washington, 1986-97. Fellow: Roscoe Pound Found. (trustee); mem.: ATLA (gov. 1976—87, pres. 1993—94), Am. Bd. Profl. Liability Attys., Am. Law Inst., Internat. Acad. Trial Lawyers (bd. govs. 2003—), Trial Lawyers Pub. Justice (found. bd. govs. 2003—), Met. DC Trial Attys.

(pres. 1977—78, 1987—88, Atty. of the Yr. 1976), Montgomery County Bar Assn., DC Bar Assn., Nat. Bd. Trial Advocacy Civil Litig. (bd. govs. 2001—, pres. 2007—), Am. Inns of Ct., Lambert Soc. Avocations: golf, tennis, reading, racquetball. Home: 6208 Garnett Dr Chevy Chase MD 20815-6618 Office: Paulson & Nace 1615 New Hampshire Ave NW Washington DC 20009-2520 Home Phone: 301-657-9393; Office Phone: 202-463-1999. Business E-Mail: bjn@lawtort.com.

NACE, MORTON OLIVER, JR., human services manager; b. Tampa, Fla., June 30, 1937; s. Morton Oliver and Penelope Adele (Holland) N.; m. Eleanor Hart Moslow, June 27, 1964; children: Morton Oliver III, Jennifer Ann. BS, Boston U., 1964; MS, Syracuse U., 1974. Cert. literacy tutor Laubach Literacy Internat., Syracuse, NY. Exec. dir. Episcopal Diocese Chgo., 1964-70; dir. comm. Laubach Literacy Internat., Syracuse, N.Y., 1970-80; tng. and devel. specialist Rochester (N.Y.) Inst. Tech., 1980-96; adminstrv. asst., cons. City of Rochester, 1997—. Cons. tng. and orgn. devel., Rochester, 1982-98; facilitator retreats/tng. for new parish model The Apostle, 1990—; designer/presenter formats on discernment and daily ministry, 2000; asst. prof. Rochester Inst. Tech., Henrietta, N.Y., 1994; sales and consulting staff Human Resource Svcs., Rochester, 1995-97. Facilitator planning retreat City Coun. of Rochester, 1993; regional planning cons. Mayor-elect City Coun., Rochester, 1997, performance cons. and trainer, 1998—. With USAF, 1957-61. Mem. ASTD (Genesee Valley chpt., conf. presenter 1981-96), Profl. and Orgn. Devel. in Higher Edn. (nat. presenter on faculty/staff devel. 1993-96). Episcopalian. Avocations: photography, piano, physical exercise, history, travel. Home and Office: 2271 Westfall Rd Rochester NY 14618-3126 E-mail: mnance@frontiernet.net.

NACHMAN, GERALD WEIL, columnist, critic, writer; b. Oakland, Calif., Jan. 13, 1938; s. Leonard Calvert and Isabel (Weil) N.; m. Mary Campbell McGeachy, Sept. 3, 1966 (div. 1979). Student, Merritt Coll., 1955-57; BA in Journalism, San Jose State U., 1960. TV and humor columnist San Jose (Calif.) Mercury, 1960-63; feature writer N.Y. Post, NYC, 1963-66; drama critic Oakland (Calif.) Tribune, 1966-71; syndicated humor columnist N.Y. Daily News, 1973-79; critic and columnist San Francisco Chronicle, 1979-93. Juror Pulitzer Prize Com. to choose best play, 1991. Author: The Portable Nachman, 1960, Playing House, 1978, Out on a Whim, 1983, The Fragile Bachelor, 1989; contbr. to (book) Snooze, 1986, Raised on Radio, 1998, Seriously Funny: The Rebel Comedians of the 1950's and 1960's, 2003; contbr. articles to newspapers, mag.; author, co-lyricist (revues) Quirks, 1979, Aftershocks, 1992, New Wrinkles, 1999, 2005. Recipient Page One award N.Y. Newspaper Guild, 1965, Deems Taylor award ASCAP, 1989. E-mail: nachnach@comcast.net.

NACHMAN, RONALD JAMES, chemist, researcher; b. Takoma Park, Md., Feb. 1, 1954; s. Joseph Frank and Rosemary (Anderson) N.; m. Lita Rose Wilson, Dec. 18, 1976 (div. 1987); m. Isidora Austria Panis, May 6, 1989. BS in Chemistry, U. Calif., San Diego, 1976; PhD in Organic Chemistry, Stanford U., 1981. Rsch. asst. Scripps Inst. Oceanography, La Jolla, Calif., 1974-76; chemist Western Regional Rsch. Ctr., USDA, Berkeley, Calif., 1981-89, Vet. Toxicology and Entomology Rsch. Lab., College Station, Tex., 1989—. Vis. scientist dept. molecular biology Salk Inst., La Jolla, 1985, Scripps Rsch. Inst., La Jolla, 1988-89. Mem. editl. adv. bd. The Jour. Peptides, guest editor, 2001, 02, 03, 04; mem. organizing com. Ann. Invertebrate Neuropeptide Conf.; contbr. sci. articles to profl. jours. Recipient USDA Cert. of Merit, 1988, 1991, 1994—2001, Arthur S. Flemming award for sci. achievement, 1994. Fellow Internat. Neoropeptide Soc. (bd. dirs. 2000—); mem. AAAS, Internat. Neuropeptide Soc., Am. Chem. Soc., N.Y. Acad. Scis., Sigma Xi. Avocations: travel, photography, jogging, racquetball. Home: 14891 Pollux Dr Willis TX 77318-5079 Office: USDA Southern Plains Agrl Rsch Ctr 2881 F And B Rd College Station TX 77845-4988

NACHSHIN, ROBERT JAY, lawyer; b. NYC, June 3, 1950; s. Edward and Eleanor (Ciporin) N.; m. Monica Jane Lipkin, May 22, 1976. BA cum laude, Bucknell U., 1972; M in Internat. Affairs, JD, Columbia U., 1976. Bar: Calif. 1977, U.S. Dist. Ct. (cen. dist.) Calif. 1977. Assoc. Loeb & Loeb, LA, 1976-80, Greenberg & Gluster, LA, 1980-82, ptnr., 1982-87; ptnr., head family law dept. Jeffer, Mangels, Butler & Marmaro, LA, 1987—89; founding ptnr. Nachshin & Weston, LLP, LA, 1989—. Mediator family law L.A. Superior Ct., 1982—. Co-author (with Scott N. Weston): Do, You Do... But Sign Here: A Quick and Easy Guide to Cohabitation, Prenuptial and Postnuptial Agreements, 2004. Bd. dirs. Juvenile Diabetes Found., 1983-87. Named one of So. Calif. Super Lawyers, L.A. Magazine, 2005. Mem. ABA, L.A. County Bar Assn. (exec. com. family law sect., 1983-89), Beverly Hills Bar Assn., Calif. Bd. Legal Specialization (cert. specialist 1982—), Columbia U. Alumni Assn. (v.p. 1981—), Pi Sigma Alpha, Omicron Delta Kappa. Democrat. Avocations: hiking, running, scuba diving, skiing, travel. Office: Nachshin & Weston LLP 11601 Wilshire Blvd Ste 1500 Los Angeles CA 90025 *

NACHT, SERGIO, biochemist; came to U.S., 1965; s. Oscar and Carmen (Scheiner) N.; m. Beatriz Kahan, Dec. 21, 1958; children: Marcelo H., Gabriel A., Mariana S., Sandra M. BA in Chemistry, U. Buenos Aires, 1958, MS in Biochemistry, 1960, PhD in Biochemistry, 1964. Asst. prof. biochemistry U. Buenos Aires, 1960-64; asst. prof. medicine U. Utah, Salt Lake City, 1965-70; rsch. scientist Alza Corp., Palo Alto, Calif., 1970-73; sr. investigator Richardson-Vicks Inc., Mt. Vernon, NY, 1973-76, asst. dir. rsch., 1976-83; dir. biomed. rsch. P&G, Shelton, Conn., 1983-87; sr. v.p. rsch. and devel. Advanced Polymer Sys., Redwood City, Calif., 1987-93, sr. v.p. sci. and tech., 1993-98, sr. v.p. dermatology and skin care, 1998-2000, Cardinal Health, Redwood City, 2000—02; sr. v.p., chief sci. officer Riley-Nacht, LLC, Las Vegas, 2002—. Lectr. dermatology dept. SUNY Downstate Med. Ctr., Blkyn., 1977-87. Contbr. articles to profl. jours.; patentee in field. Mem. Soc. Cosmetic Chemists (award 1981), Dermatology Found., Am. Acad. Dermatology. Democrat. Jewish. Office Phone: 702-547-1611. Personal E-mail: sergnacht@aol.com.

NACHTIGAL, PATRICIA, lawyer; b. 1946; BA, Montclair State U.; JD, Rutgers U.; LLM, NYU. Corporate atty. Ingersoll-Rand Co., Ltd., Hamilton, Bermuda, 1979—83, dir. taxes and legal, 1983—88, sec., mng. atty., 1988—91, v.p., gen. counsel, 1991—2000, sr. v.p., gen. counsel, 2000—, bd. dirs., 2002—. Gov., trustee Rutgers, State U. N.J., 1996—, chair, 2003—04. Office: Ingersoll-Rand Co Ltd 155 Chestnut Ridge Rd Montvale NJ 07645 Office Phone: 201-573-0123.

NACKEL, JOHN GEORGE, health facility administrator; b. Medford, Mass., Nov. 4, 1951; s. Michael and Josephine (Maria) N.; m. Gail Helen Becker, Oct. 30, 1976; children: Melissa Anne, Allison Elizabeth. BS, Tufts U., 1973; MS in Pub. Health and Indsl. Engring., U. Mo., 1975, PhD, 1977. Sr. mgr. Ernst & Young, Chgo., 1977—83; nat. dir. health care cons. Cleve., 1983—87; regional dir. health industry svcs., 1987—91; mng. dir. health care Ernst & Young, Cleve., 1991—93; mng. dir. Health Consulting, LA, 1993—99, New Ventures, 1999—2000; CEO, Sogeti USA, LLC, 2000—01; chmn., CEO, Sértan Corp., Santa Fe Springs, Calif., 2002—03; exec. v.p. US Tech., Beverly Hills, Calif., 2003—05; pres., COO Salick Cardiovascular Ctrs., 2006—07; CEO Three Sixty Group, 2007—. Author: Cost Management for Hospitals, 1987 (Am. Hosp. Assn. book award 1988); mem. editl bd. Jour. Med. Systems, 1983-; contbr. articles to profl. jours Grantee Dept. Health Edn. Welfare, Washington, 1973-76. Fellow Am. Coll. Healthcare Execs., Healthcare Info. and Mgmt. Systems Soc. (articles award); mem. Inst. Indsl. Engrs. (sr.), U. Mo. Health Svcs. Mgmt. Alumni Assn. (pres.), L.A. Country Club, Annandale Golf Club. Republican. Avocations: golf, tennis, squash, paddle, photography. Home: 666 Linda Vista Ave Pasadena CA 91105-1145 Office Phone: 213-716-7771.

NACKHLA, G. HABIB, retired physician; b. Elmenia, Egypt, June 3, 1933; arrived in US, 1959; s. Habib Micheal Nackhla and Fahima Abdallah Masoud; m. Vera Louse Rodeffer, June 10, 1962; children: Jhon H., Lisa J. MB, BChir, El Abbsia Coll. Medicine, Cairo, 1957. Intern Eldemerdash U. Hosp., Cairo, 1958—59, Mercy Hosp., Hamilton, Ohio, 1959—60, resident ob-gyn., 1960—62, Good Samaritan Hosp., Cin., 1962—64; pvt. practice Hamilton Fairfield, Ohio, 1964—2000; ret., 2000. Mem.: AMA, Hamilton/Fairfield Acad. Medicine, Butler County Med. Soc.

NACLERIO, ROBERT MICHAEL, otolaryngologist, educator; b. NYC, Mar. 30, 1950; s. Albert Paul and Lee Ann (Rabinowitz) N.; m. Sharon Ann Silhan, Mar. 30, 1983; children: Jessica, Daniel. BA, Cornell U., 1972; MD with honors, Baylor U., 1976. Diplomate Am. Bd. Otolaryngology. Intern in surgery Johns Hopkins Hosp., Balt., 1976-77, resident in surgery, 1977-78; resident in otolaryngology Baylor Coll. Medicine, Houston, 1978-80, chief resident in otolaryngology, 1982-83; fellow in clin. immunology divsn. Johns Hopkins U. Sch. Medicine, Balt., 1980-82, asst. prof. medicine and otolaryngology, 1983-87, asst. prof. pediat., 1986-87, dir. divsn. pediat. otolaryngology, 1986-94, assoc. prof. otolargyngology, medicine and pediat., 1987-92, prof. otolaryngology, medicine and pediat., 1992-94; chief of otolaryngology, head and neck surgery U. Chgo., Chgo., 1994—. Cons. Richardson-Vicks Inc., 1986-89, 90, NIH, 1987, Proctor & Gamble, 1987, 94, Sandoz Rsch. Inst., 1988, Schering Rsch., 1988, Wallace Labs., 1989, Joint Rhinologic Conf., 1989, Internat. Congress Rhinology, 1991, Norwich-Eaton Pharm. Inc., 1991-92, Ciba-Geigy Corp., 1991-92, Mktg. Corp. Am., 1993—, Astra, others; mem. med. bd. Children's Ctr., 1991-94, other local comms.; reviewer Am. Jour. Rhinology, others; lectr. in field. Editor: Rhinoconjunctivitis: New Perspectives in Topical Treatment, 1988; asst. editor: Am. Jour. Rhinology, 1986—, Rhinology, 1988—; mem. editl. bd. Otolaryngology-Head and Neck Surgery, 1990-97, Laryngoscope, 1990—, Jour. Allergy and Clin. Immunology, 1992-97; contbr. numerous chpts. to books, papers and abstracts to profl. jours. and procs. Fellow ACS, Am. Acad. Otolaryngology-Head and Neck Surgery (mem. com. 1985-90, 90-92, subcom. 1987-92), Am. Laryngol., Rhinol. and Otol. Soc., Inc.; mem. Am. Acad. Allergy and Immunology (mem. com. 1983-88, 88-89, 88-95, chmn. com. 1990-91, 91—, Jerome Glazer Meml. lectureship), Am. Fedn. Clin. Rsch., Am. Soc. Pediat. Otolaryngology (mem. rsch. com. 1990-94, chmn. subcom. 1990), Soc. Univ. Otolaryngologists-Head and Neck Surgeons, Pan-Am. Assn. Otorhinolaryngology, Internat. Symposium on Infection and Allergy of the Nose (v.p.). Office: U Chgo Sect O-HNS 5841 S Maryland Ave # 1035 Chicago IL 60637-1463 E-mail: rnacleri@surgery.bsd.uchicago.edu.

NACOL, MAE, lawyer; b. Beaumont, Tex., June 15, 1944; d. William Samuel and Ethel (Bowman) N.; children: Shawn Alexander Nacol, Catherine Regina Nacol. BA, Rice U., Houston, 1965; postgrad., South Tex. Coll. Law, 1966. Bar: Tex. 1969, U.S. Dist. Ct. (so. dist.) Tex. 1969, U.S. Supreme Ct., U.S. Dist. Ct. (we. dist.), U.S. Ct. Appeals (5th cir.). Pvt. practice law, Houston, 1969—; escrow officer Land Am./Commonwealth Land Title Co., Houston; mem. bd. devel. Prosperity Bank, Houston. Author, editor ednl. materials on multiple sclerosis, 1981-85. Nat. dir. A.R.M.S. of Am. Ltd., Houston, 1984-85. Recipient Mayor's Recognition award City of Houston, 1972. Mem. Fed. Bar Assn., Houston Bar Assn. (chmn. candidate com. 1970, membership com. 1971, chmn. lawyers referral com. 1972), Assn. Trial Lawyers Am., Tex. Trial Lawyers Assn., Am. Judicature Soc. (sustaining), Houston Fin. Coun. Women, Houston Trial Lawyers Assn. Presbyterian. Office: 600 Jefferson St Ste 750 Houston TX 77002 also: 2600 S Gessner Ste 120 Houston TX 77063 Office Phone: 713-655-7055. Business E-Mail: wmnacol@sbcglobal.net.

NADAL, RAFAEL (RAFAEL NADAL PARERA), professional tennis player; b. Manacor, Mallorca, Spain, June 3, 1983; Prof. Tennis player ATP Tour, 2001—. Recipient Newcomer of the Yr., Laureus World Sports Awards, 2006. Achievements include winner, 18 career singles titles, 3 career doubles titles; winner: French Open, 2005-07, Dubai Tennis Championships, 2006, Masters Series Monte-Carlo, 2006, 2007, Open SEAT, 2006-07 Italian Open, 2006, Pacific Life Open, 2007, Mercedes Cup, 2007; winner, Davis Cup as mem. Spanish Tennis Team, 2004; record holder for consecutive men's wins on clay court; becoming the second man since 1914 to win three consecutive French Open titles. Office: c/o Carlos Costa IMG Tennis Augusta 200 4 planta 08021 Barcelona Spain

NADAS, JOHN ADALBERT, psychiatrist, educator; b. Innsbruck, Austria, Mar. 14, 1949; arrived in U.S., 1950; s. Julius Zoltan and Ibolya Erzsebet (Szöllösy) Nadas; m. Gabriella Ilona Ormay, Apr. 11, 1981; children: János, Miklós, István. BA, Case We. Res. U., 1970; MD, Duke U., 1974. Resident in psychiatry U. Chgo., 1974—77; pvt. practice Munster, Ind., 1977—84, Canton, Ohio, 1984—; instr. psychiatry Northeastern Ohio U. Coll. Medicine, Rootstown, 1985—86, asst. prof., 1986; coord. psychiat. edn. Mercy Med. Ctr., Canton, 1985—87, clin. dir. psychiat. svcs., 1990-91. Cons. Crisis Ctr., Canton, 1985—92. Author: Philosophical Basis of Depth Psychotherapy, 1983, Journey Toward Energy, 1995, Transformation, 1999. Trustee Sisters of Charity Found., Canton, 1996—2003. Named NCAA nat. collegiate epee champion, 1970; named to All-Am. Fencing Team, 1969, 1970. Mem.: AMA, Am. Psychiat. Assn., Hungarian Assn. (pres. 2000—03). Roman Catholic. Avocations: basketball, computer programming. Office: 1330 Mercy Dr NW Ste 320 Canton OH 44708-2624 Office Phone: 330-489-1495.

NADASKAY, RAYMOND, architect; b. Newark, Aug. 26, 1938; s. Charles and Marie (Roncskevitz) Nadaskay; m. Nancy Searle, 1962; 1 child, Cathy. BArch, Washington U., St. Louis, 1962. Registered architect, NJ, NY, Conn., Vt., Mass., Ill., Ohio, SC, Vt., Del.; registered planner; cert. NCARB. Designer Rotwein and Blake, Architects, Union, N.J., 1962-63, I.M. Pei, NYC, 1963-64; designer, assoc. McDowell Goldstein, Morristown, N.J., 1964-72; pres. Nadaskay Kopelson Architects, P.A., Morristown, 1972—2006. Chair Mendham Twp. Hist. Preservation Commn., NJ; mem. Mendham Twp. Roadscape Commn., Mendham Twp. Facilities Com., Mendham Twp. Open Space Com., Morristown Streetscape Com.; Blue Ribbon adv. com. Morris County Hist. Preservation Trust Fund; pres., trustee Ralston Cider Mill. Mem.: NJ Soc. Archs. (conv. chmn. 1985—86, past pres. Newark Suburban chpt. 1984, Herman Litwak award AIA Newark Suburban chpt. 2001), Porsche Club (No. NJ). Avocations: woodworking, sailing, swimming. Office: Nadaskay Kopelson Architects 95 Washington St Morristown NJ 07960-6816 E-mail: nadaskayr@nkarchitects.com.

NADEAU, JOSEPH EUGENE, health care management, information systems consultant; s. Edwin Tustin and Beatrice Margaret (Spiller) N.; m. Mary Lou Prendible, Dec. 2, 1961; children: Laura, Keith, Michael. BS in Math., Boston Coll., 1960. Cert. computer profl. Dir. sys. devel. Mass. Hosp. Assn., Burlington, 1967-72; S.E. regional mgr. Automatic Data Processing, Miami, Fla., 1972-73; S.E. regional mktg. mgr. Space Age Computer Sys., Louisville, 1973-74; prin. COMPUTERx Cons., Miami, 1974—. Asst. scoutmaster South Fla. coun. Boy Scouts Am., 1972-81. 1st lt. U.S. Army, 1960-64, Germany. Mem. Am. Hosp. Assn., Soc. Computer Medicine, Data Processing Mgmt. Assn., Hosp. Mgmt. Sys. Soc., Assn. Sys. Mgmt. (pres. 1971-72), Hosp. Fin. Mgmt. Assn. (chmn. data processing com. 1967-84), Am. Arbitration Assn. (arbitrator 1980—). Home: 10260 SW 144th St Miami FL 33176-7034 Office: COMPUTERx Consulting 9719 S Dixie Hwy Ste 1 Miami FL 33156-2834 Business E-Mail: jnadeau@computerx-consulting.com.

NADEAU, JOSEPH P., retired state supreme court justice; b. NH; AB, Dartmouth Coll.; LLB, Boston U., 1962. Pvt. practice trial atty., 1962—81; justice Durham Dist. Ct., 1968-81; judge NH Superior Ct., 1981-92, chief justice, 1992; assoc. justice NH Supreme Ct., 2000—06. Mem. Jud. Br. Adminstrv. Coun., Supreme Ct. Jud. Ednl. Svcs. Com., Supreme Ct. Accreditation Commn.; pres. Am. Acad. Jud. Edn., 1990-92; participant ct. study program former Soviet Union, facutly jud. edn. program, Latvia, study programs in Russia, Georgia, Armenia; involved in jud. edn. seminars and legis. activities in Albania, Bulgaria, Kazakhstan, Poland; former vice-chair Nat. Conference of State Trial Judges. Mem. Gov.'s Commn. on Domestic Violence. Mem.: ABA (former chair CEELI Com.), N.H. Bar Assn.

NADEAU, ROBERT BERTRAND, JR., lawyer; b. Miami Beach, Fla., July 15, 1950; s. Robert B. and Ernestine Inez (Nicholson) N. BBA magna cum laude, U. Notre Dame, 1972; JD with honors, U. Fla., 1975. Bar: Fla. 1975, U.S. Dist. Ct. (mid. dist.) Fla. 1976, U.S. Dist. Ct. (so. dist.) Fla. 1982, U.S. Ct. Appeals (11th cir.) 1982. Asst. to pres. The Fla. Bar, Tampa, 1975-76; ptnr. Akerman, Senterfitt & Eidson, P.A., Orlando, Fla., 1976—. Arbitrator Am. Arbitration Assn., Orlando, 1987—. Mem. ABA, The Fla. Bar (chmn. student edn. and admission to bar com., vice chmn. 9th cir. grievance com.), Notre Dame Club Greater Orlando (pres. 1979-80). Avocations: golf, running. Office: Akerman Senterfitt PO Box 231 Orlando FL 32802 Home Phone: 407-834-5059; Office Phone: 407-423-4000. Business E-Mail: robert.nadeau@akerman.com.

NADEL, ELLIOTT, investment company executive; b. NYC, Nov. 23, 1945; s. Archie and Faye (Braverman) N.; children: Lindsey, Amanda. BBA, Baruch Coll., 1969, MBA, 1971. Portfolio mgr. SwissRe Advisors, NYC, 1973-74; v.p., stockbroker E. F. Hutton, NYC, 1975-84, Shearson Lehman Bros., NYC, 1984-85, Oppenheimer & Co., NYC, 1985, Rooney Pace Inc., NYC, 1986-87, Philips Appel & Walden, NYC, 1987-88; sr. v.p. investments Moore, Schley & Cameron, NYC, 1988-90, Prudential-Securities, NYC, 1990-94; sr. v.p. Gilford Securities, NYC, 1994—96, SFY Investments, 1996—97, Westrock Advisor, 1997—99, Tarpon Scurry Investments, 1999—2000, Chgo. Investments Group, 2001, EN Investments, 2001—; prin. Hedge Fund. With US Army, 1969-74. Jewish. Avocations: jogging, reading, cars, golf, travel. Home Phone: 917-301-7600. E-mail: mrch1123@aol.com.

NADEL, NORMAN ALLEN, civil engineer; b. NYC, Apr. 10, 1927; s. Louis and Bertha (Julius) N.; m. Cynthia Esther Jereski, July 6, 1952; children: Nancy Sarah Frank, Lawrence Bruce. B.C.E., CCNY, 1949; postgrad., Columbia U., 1949-50. Registered profl. engr., N.Y., Conn. Engr. Arthur A. Johnson Corp., NYC, 1950-53; engr. Slattery Contracting Corp., NYC, 1953-56; mgr., estimator Hartsdale Constrn. Corp., Hartsdale, NY, 1956-59; engr. MacLean Grove & Co., Inc., Greenwich, Conn., 1959-63, project mgr., 1963-66, v.p., 1966-70, pres., 1970-94; chmn. Nadel Assocs., Inc., Brewster, NY, 1988—. Cons. tunnel and underground constrn.; mem. com. on tunneling Transp. Rsch. Bd., Washington, 1974-75; mem. U.S. Nat. Com. on Tunneling Tech., Washington, 1976-82, chmn., 1980-81; chmn. adv. com. Superconducting Super Collider Underground Tech., 1992-94. Trustee Tunnel Workers Welfare Fund, N.Y.C., 1976-88; mem. adv bd. CCNY Engring. Sch., 1992—. With USNR, 1945-46 Named Heavy Constrn. Man of Yr., United Jewish Appeal, 1984; Benjamin Wright award Conn. Soc. Civil Engrs., 1984, Townsend Harris medal City Coll. of N.Y. Alumni Assn., 1987. Fellow ASCE (Constrn. Mgmt. award 1986); mem. NAE, Conn. Acad. Sci. and Engring., The Moles (pres. 1982-83, Outstanding Achievement in Constrn. award 1985), Am. Arbitration Assn., Tau Beta Pi, Chi Epsilon. Office: Nadel Assocs Inc 420 Clock Tower Commons Brewster NY 10509-4060 Office Phone: 845-279-5516.

NADELLA, SATYA, information technology executive; b. 1967; MS in Computer Sci., U. Wis.; MBA, U. Chgo. Software devel. engr. Sun Microsystems Inc.; from group product mgr. to leader bCentral mktg. & bus. devel. Microsoft, Redmond, Wash., leader bCentral mktg. & bus. devel., 1999—2002, corp. v.p. Microsoft Bus. Solutions, 2002—. Office: One Microsoft Way Redmond WA 98052-6399

NADELMAN, MARTIN HERSHEL, college president; s. Edward and Frances Nadelman; m. Susan Lynn Cook, June 19, 1971. BS, Rensselaer Poly. Inst., 1971; MEd, U. Vt., 1972; EdD, U. Md., 1987. Dean of men Atlantic Christian Coll., Wilson, NC, 1972—76; dean of students Wor-Wic Tech CC, Salisbury, Md., 1976—91, acting pres., 1986—87; pres. Martin CC, Williamston, NC, 1991—99, Alamance CC, Graham, NC, 1999—. Mem. Cmty. Coun., Burlington, NC; pres. Martin County United Way, Williamston, 1996—98; mem. State Employees' Credit Union, Burlington, 2005—06, Women's Resource Ctr., Burlington, 2001—04; bd. dirs. United Way of Alamance County, Burlington, 2000—02, Alamance Partnership for Children, Burlington, 1999—. Named Nat. Adminstr. of the Yr., Nat. Assn. Devel. Educators, 2005. Mem.: NC Assn. Devel. Educators (exec. com. 2002—, State Adminstr. of Yr. 2004), NC Assn. C.C. Presidents (assoc.; exec com. 1998—99). Home Phone: 336-586-0528.

NADELSON, CAROL COOPERMAN, psychiatrist, educator; b. Bklyn., Oct. 13, 1936; m. Theodore Nadelson, July 16, 1965; children: Robert, Jennifer. BA magna cum laude, Bklyn. Coll., 1957; MD with honors, U. Rochester, NYC, 1961. Dir. med. student edn. Beth Israel Hosp., Boston, 1974-79, psychiatrist, 1977; assoc. prof. psychiatry Harvard U. Med. Sch., Boston, 1976-79; rsch. scholar Radcliffe Coll., Cambridge, Mass., 1979-80; prof. psychiatry Tufts Med. Sch., Boston, 1979-95; vice-chmn., dir. tng. and edn. dept. psychiatry Tufts-New Eng. Med. Ctr., Boston, 1979-93; clin. prof. psychiatry Harvard Med. Sch., Boston, 1995—; psychiatrist dept. medicine, divsn. psychiatry Brigham and Women's Hosp., Boston, 1998, dir., ptnr. office for women's careers, 1998. Cons. Peace Corps, 2000. Editor: The Woman Patient, Vols. 1, 2 and 3, 1978, 82; Treatment Interventions in Human Sexuality, 1983; Marriage and Divorce: A Contemporary Perspective, 1984, Women Physicians in Leadership Roles, 1986, Training Psychiatrists for the '90s, 1987, Treating Chronically Mentally Ill Women, 1988, Family Violence, 1988, Women and Men: New Perspectives on Gender Differences, 1990, International Review of Psychiatry Vols. 1 & 2, 1993, 96, Major Psychiatric Disorders, 1982, The Challenge of Change: Perspectives on Family, Work and Education, 1983; editor-in-chief Am. Psychiatric Press, Inc., 1986—, pres., CEO, 1995—; contbr. over 217 articles to profl. jours. Trustee Menninger Found., 1988—. Recipient Gold Medal award Mt. Airy Psychiat. Ctr., 1981, award Case Western Res. U., 1983, Elizabeth Blackwell award Am. Med. Women's Assn., 1985, Women in Medicine Leadership Devel. award Am. Assn. Med. Colls., 1999, Alexandra Symonds award 2002; Picker Found. grant, 1982-83. Fellow: Am. Psychiat. Assn. (pres. 1985—86, Seymour D. Vestermark award 1992, Disting. Svc. award 1995), Ctr. Advanced Study Behavioral Scos.; mem.: AMA (impaired physicians com. 1984, Sidney Cohen award 1988), Group for Advancement of Psychiatry (bd. dirs. 1984), Am. Coll. Psychiatrists (bd. regents 1991—94, Disting. Svc. award 1989), Phi Beta Kappa, Alpha Omega Alpha. Avocation: travel. Office: Brigham and Women's Hosp 75 Francis St PB502 Boston MA 02119 Home: 50 Longwood Ave 1114 Brookline MA 02446 Business E-Mail: carol_nadelson@hms.harvard.edu.

NADELSON, SANDRA G., nursing educator; m. Louis Nadelson. MSN, MEd, Calif. State U., LA, 1990; student, U. Nev. Las Vegas. RN Calif., 1984. Faculty mem. CC of S. Nev., Las Vegas, 2002—04, U. Nev. Las Vegas, 2005—. Mem.: MENSA, Sigma Theta Tau (assoc.; sec. 2005—06). Office Phone: 702-895-4696. Personal E-mail: sandranadelson@netscape.com.

NADER, LAURA, anthropologist, educator; b. Winsted, Conn., Sept. 30, 1930; m. Norman Milleron, Sept. 1, 1962; 3 children BA, Wells Coll., Aurora, NY, 1952; PhD, Radcliffe Coll., Cambridge, Mass., 1961. Faculty mem. U. Calif., Berkeley, 1960—, prof. anthropology; vis. prof. Yale Law Sch., New Haven, fall 1971; Henry R. Luce prof. Sch. Law Harvard Wellesley Coll., Mass., 1983-84; Henry R. Luce prof. Sch. Law Stanford U. Law Sch., 1987-89. Field work in Mex., Lebanon, Morocco and US; mem. adv. com. NSF, 1971-75; mem. cultural anthropology com. NIMH, 1968—, chmn. to 1971, chmn. social scis. rsch. tng. rev. com., 1976-78; mem. NAS-NRC assembly behavioral and social scis., 1969-71, 73-75, 75—; mem. com. Nuclear and Alternative Energy Forms, NAS, 1976-80. Editor: Law in Culture and Society, 1969, The Disputing Process, 1978, No Access to Law-Alternatives to the American Judicial System, 1980, Harmony Ideology, 1990, Naked Science, 1996, The Life of the Law, 2000; contbr. articles to profl. jours.; author edn1. films, mem. editl. com. Law and Soc. Rev., 1967—. Mem. Calif. Coun. for the Humanities, 1975—79, Carnegie Coun. on Children, 1972—77; active Coun. Librs. at Libr. of Congress, Washington, 1988—. Radcliffe Coll. grantee, 1954-59; Thaw fellow Harvard U., 1955-56, 58-59; Peabody Mus. grantee, 1954-59; Am. Philos. Assn. grantee, 1955; Mexican Govt. grantee, 1957-58; Milton Fund grantee, 1959-60, Wellness Found. grantee, 1993-96; fellow Ctr. Advanced Study in Behavioral Scis., Stanford, Calif., 1963-64; NSF grantee, 1966-68; Wenner Gren Found. grantee, 1964, 66, 73; Carnegie Corp. grantee, 1975; Woodrow Wilson fellow, 1979-80; Wells Coll. Alumnae award, 1980; Radcliffe Coll. Alumnae award, 1984. Mem.: AAAS, Soc. Women Geographers (Outstanding Achievement award 1990), Am. Acad. Arts and Scis., Ctr. for Study of Responsive Law (trustee 1968—), Law and Soc. Assn. (trustee 1967—72, Harry Kalven prize 1995), Social Sci. Rsch. Coun., Am. Anthrop. Assn. (planning and devel. com. 1968—71, 1975—76), Am. Acad. Arts and Scis. Office: U Calif Dept Anthropology 313 Kroeber Hl Berkeley CA 94720-0001 Home Phone: 510-526-3843; Office Phone: 510-642-1218. Office Fax: 510-643-8557.

NADER, NADINE ANN, social studies educator; b. Monroe, Mich., July 8, 1944; d. John Michael Nader and Marie Celeste Perrini-Nader; m. Frank Nicholas Koob, July 7, 1973; children: Paul Stephen, Peter James. BA in Social Studies and Theology, St. Mary's Coll., Notre Dame, 1966. Cert.: Roosevelt U., Chgo. (paralegal) 1983; tchr. Ill. 6th, 7th and 8th grade tchr. Our Lady Perpetual Help, Oakland, NJ, 1967—68; speech tchr. St. Thomas HS, Ann Arbor, 1968—69; tchr. Archdiocese Chgo., 1969—98; Acad. Comm. and Tech. charter tchr. Chgo. Pub. Schs., 1998—2000; sub. St. Joseph HS, Westchester, Ill., 2006—. Tutor, Chgo., 1969—88. Mem.: So. Poverty Law Ctr. (Wall of Tolerance honoree Leadership Coun. 1996—2007), Women's History Mus. (charter mem. 2003—), Smithsonian Inst. (contbg. mem. 2002—). Democrat. Roman Catholic. Avocations: theater, travel. Home: 3916 Vanburen St Bellwood IL 60104

NADER, RALPH, advocate, lawyer, writer; b. Winsted, Conn., Feb. 27, 1934; s. Nadra and Rose (Bouziane) N. AB magna cum laude, Princeton U., 1955; LLB with distinction, Harvard U., 1958. Bar: Conn. 1958, Mass. 1959, U.S. Supreme Ct. 1959. Practiced law in, Hartford, Conn., 1959—; lectr. history & govt. U. Hartford, 1961-63; founder Essential Info., 1982. Founder, Ctr. for Responsive Law, Essential Info., The Multinational Monitor Mag., Pub. Interest Research Group, Ctr. for Auto Safety, Pub. Citizen, Clean Water Action Project, Disability Rights Ctr., Pension Rights Ctr., Project for Corporate Responsibility; co-founder Princeton Project 55, 1989; lectr. to colls. and univs.; lectr. Princeton U., 1967-68 Author: Unsafe at Any Speed, 1965, Working on the System: A Manual for Citizen's Access to Federal Agencies, 1972, Action for a Change, 1972, You and Your Pension, 1973, Taming the Giant Corporation, 1976, The Lemon Book, 1980, The Big Boys, 1986, Winning The Insurance Game, 1990, No Contest: Corporate Lawyers and the Perversion of Justice in America, 1996, The Ralph Nader Reader, 2000, Crashing the Party: Taking on the Corporate Government in an Age of Surrender, 2002, In Pursuit of Justice: Collected Writing, 2000-2003, 2004, The Good Fight: Declare Your Independence and Close the Democracy Gap, 2004, Civic Arousal, 2004, The Seventeen Traditions, 2007; co-author:(with John Abbots) Menace of Atomic Energy, 1979, (with Wesley J. Smith) Collision Course:The Truth About Airline Safety, 1993; editor: Whistle Blowing: The Report on the Conference on Professional Responsibility, 1972, The Consumer and Corporate Accountability, 1973; co-editor: Corporate Power in America, 1973, Verdicts on Lawyers, 1976, Who's Poisoning America, 1981; contbg. editor: Ladies Home Jour., 1973—. Presdl. candidate, 1996, 2000, 2004; With U.S. Army, 1959. Recipient Nieman Fellows award, 1965-66; named One of 10 Outstanding Young Men of Year U.S. Jr. C. of C., 1967 Mem. ABA, AAAS, Phi Beta Kappa. Green Party. Address: Ctr for Study of Responsive Law PO Box 19367 Washington DC 20036-9367

NADER, ROBERT ALEXANDER, judge, lawyer; b. Warren, Ohio, Mar. 31, 1928; s. Nassef J. and Emily (Nader) N.; m. Nancy M. Veauthier. BA, Western Res. U., 1950, LL.B., 1953. Bar: Ohio 1953. Ptnr. Paul G. Nader, Warren, 1953-83. Pres. Warren City Police and Fire Pension Bds., 1960-66; trustee Office Econ. Opportunity, 1970-72; mem. Warren City Coun., 1960-66, pres. pro tem, 1964-66; mem. Ohio Ho. of Reps., 1971-83, chmn. reference com., 1977-81, chmn. judiciary com., 1981-83; presiding judge Trumbull County Ct. Common Pleas, 1983-91; judge Ohio 11th Dist. Ct. of Appeals, 1991-03; trustee Family Svc. Assn., 1959-65. With AUS, 1946-48. Recipient Outstanding Young Man of Yr. award, 1964, award Am. Arbitration Assn., 1965, Community Action award Warren Area Bd. Realtors, 1967, Outstanding Svc. award Kent State U., Trumbull campus, 1978, Outstanding Svc. award Children's Rehab. Ctr., 1980; named to Warren H.S. Disting. Alumni Hall of Fame, 1993, Sports Hall of Fame, 2003. Mem. Ohio State Bar Assn., Trumbull County Bar Assn. (past pres., Pres.'s award for disting. svc. 2003), Ct. Appeals Judges Assn. (chmn. legis. com. 1995-98), Trumbull County Law Libr. Assn. (trustee 1958-72), Trumbull New Theatre (past pres.), KC, Elks, Lambda Chi Alpha. Roman Catholic. Home: 798 Wildwood Dr NE Warren OH 44483-4458 Office: 11th Dist Ct of Appeals 111 High St NE Warren OH 44481 *My parents provided me with a strong moral background and the inspiration to improve. I will never feel that I have achieved success and thus may continue to improve.*

NADIG, GERALD GEORGE, retired manufacturing executive; b. Astoria, NY, May 9, 1945; s. Charles Edwin and Louise (Hahn) N.; m. Nancy Hanford Stewart, June 20, 1970; children: Sara Hanford, Jennifer Stewart. AB cum laude, Harvard Coll., 1967, MBA, 1974. Various manfacturing positions, 1974—85; dir. mfg. Toyoda Machinery USA, Arlington Heights, Ill., 1985-87, v.p., gen. mgr., 1987-88; v.p., gen. mgr. Littell div. Allied Products Corp., Chgo., 1988-89; exec. v.p. pre finish metals Material Scis. Corp., 1989-90; pres. Pre Finish Metals Materials Scis. Corp., 1990-91; pres., chief oper. officer Material Scis. Corp., Chgo., 1991-96, pres., CEO, 1997—2003, chmn. bd. dirs., 1998—2003; bd. dirs. Tokheim Corp., 2000—03; ret. Mem. adv. bd. Masters in Mgmt. Program Northwestern U. Trustee Village of Lake Barrington, 1989-91. With U.S. Army, 1966-70. Mem. Soc. Mfg. Engrs. (sr.), Nat. Assn. Corp. Dirs. (bd. dirs. Chgo. chpt. 2002—), Barrington Area Cmty. Found. (bd. dirs.) Avocations: golf, tennis, game theory. Home: 24354 N Grandview Dr Barrington IL 60010-6218 Office Phone: 847-381-3464. Personal E-mail: gerrynadig@aol.com.

NADKARNI, NALINI MORESHWAR, biology professor, researcher; b. Md., Oct. 13, 1954; d. Moreshwar Vital and Goldie Hema Nadkarni; m. John Thomas Longino, June 25, 1983; children: August Andrew Longino, Erika Jane Longino. BA, Brown U., Providence, 1972—76; PhD, U. Wash., Seattle, 1979—83. Asst. prof. U. Calif., Santa Barbara, 1983—89; dir. rsch. Marie Selby Bot. Gardens, Sarasota, Fla., 1989—92; faculty mem. Evergreen State Coll., Olympia, Wash., 1992—. Pres. Internat. Canopy Network, Olympia, Wash., 1994—2006; bd. trustees Nature Conservancy Wash., Seattle, 1999—2006. Recipient J. Stirling Morgan award, Nat. Arbor Day Found., 1997, Pres. award, Assn. Tropical Biology & Conservation, 2001—02, Disting. Vis. Prof. award, U. Miami, 2003—04; grantee Guggenheim fellowship, John Simon Guggenheim Found., 2001, fellowship, Aldo Leopold Leadership Program, 2004. Mem.: Ecol. Soc. Am. (assoc.). Home: 5031 78th Ave NW Olympia WA 98502 Office: Evergreen State Coll 2700 Evergreen Pky Lab II Olympia WA 98505 Home Phone: 360-866-9574. Business E-Mail: nadkarnn@evergreen.edu.

NADLER, DAVID A., insurance company executive; Founder, chmn., CEO Delta Consulting Group, Inc., 1980—2000; chmn., CEO Mercer Delta Consulting (following acquisition by Marsh & McLennan Cos.), 2000—05; vice chmn., mem. internat. adv. bd. Marsh & McLennan Cos.; sr. ptrn. Delta orgn. and Leadership unit Oliver Wyman (merger of Mercer Delta Consulting, Mercer Oliver Wyman and Mercer Mgmt. Consulting), 2007—. Office: Marsh & McLennan Cos 1166 Avenue of the Americas New York NY 10036 Office Phone: 212-345-5000. *

NADLER, ELLEN R., lawyer; b. Bklyn., Mar. 13, 1946; AB summa cum laude, Radcliffe Coll., 1968; JD, Yale U., 1971. Bar: NY 1972, US Ct. of Appeals (2nd, 3rd, 6th, & DC cirs.), US Dist. Ct. (so., no. & ea.,) NY, US Dist. Ct. (ea.dist.) Mich., US Supreme Ct. Lead def. counsel Saxon Securities Litig., 1982—85; mem. Kramer, Levin, Naftalis, Nessen, Kamin & Frankel, NYC; councel Kramer, Levin, Naftalis, & Frankel. Lectr. N.Y. Law Jour. Annual Civil Litigation Practice Seminar, 1983-90, co-chair, 1991-92. Recipient Gerda Richards Crosby prize Harvard U., 1967. Mem. Fed. Bar Coun. (asst. treas. 1984-85, v.p. 1987-88), NY Women's Bar Assn. (bd. dirs. 1986-87), Assn. Bar NYC (sec. state legis. com. 1973-76, com. fed. cts. 1980-83, com. on judiciary 1992—), Phi Beta Kappa, dir NY Lawyers Pub. Interest 1992-1999. Office: Kramer Levin Naftalis & Frankel 1177 Ave of Americas New York NY 10036 Office Phone: 212-715-9232. Office Fax: 212-715-9238. Business E-Mail: enadler@kramerlevin.com.

NADLER, GERALD, management consultant, educator; b. Cin., Mar. 12, 1924; s. Samuel and Minnie (Krumbein) N.; m. Elaine Muriel Dubin, June 22, 1947; children: Burton Alan, Janice Susan, Robert Daniel. Student, U. Cin., 1942-43; BSME, Purdue U., 1945, MS in Indsl. Engring, 1946, PhD, 1949. Instr. Purdue U., 1948-49; asst. prof. indsl. engring. Washington U., St. Louis, 1949-52, assoc. prof., 1952-55, prof., head dept. indsl. engring., 1955-64; prof. U. Wis., Madison, 1964-83, chmn. dept. indsl. engring., 1964-67, 71-75; prof., chmn. dept. indsl. and sys. engring. U. So. Calif., LA, 1983-93, IBM chair engring. mgmt., 1986-93, IBM chair emeritus, prof. emeritus, 1993—; v.p. Artcraft Mfg. Co., St. Louis, 1956-57; dir. Intertherm Inc., St. Louis, 1969-85. Pres. Ctr. for Breakthrough Thinking Inc., L.A., 1989—; vis. prof. U. Birmingham, Eng., 1959, Waseda U., Tokyo, 1963-64, Ind. U., 1964, U. Louvain, Belgium, 1975, Technion-Israel Inst. Tech., Haifa, 1975-76; spkr. in field. Author: The Planning and Design Approach, 1981; (with S. Hibino) Breakthrough Thinking, 1990, 2d edit., 1994, Creative Solution Finding, 1995; (with G. Hoffherr, J. Moran) Breakthrough Thinking in Total Quality Management, 1994, (with W. Chandon) Ask the Right Questions, 2003, Smart Questions, 2004; contbr. articles to profl. jours.; reviewer books, papers, proposals. Mem. Ladue Bd. Edn., St. Louis County, 1960-63, L.A. County Quality and Productivity Commn., 1997—; chmn. planning com. Wis. Regional Med. Program, 1966-69; bd. dirs. USC Credit Union, 1994—. Served with USN, 1943-45. Gilbreth medal Soc. Advancement Mgmt., 1961, Editl. award Hosp. Mgmt. Mag., 1966, Disting. Engring. Alumnus award Purdue U., 1975, Outstanding Indsl. Engr. award, 1997; Book of Yr. award Inst. Indsl. Engrs., 1983, Frank and Lillian Gilbreth award, 1992; Phi Kappa Phi Faculty Recognition award U. So. Calif., 1990, Engring. Disting. Svc. award U. Wis. Madison, 2000. Fellow AAAS, Inst. Indsl. Engrs. (pres. 1989-90), Inst. Operations Rsch. and Mgmt. Scis., Inst. for Advancement Engrs., Am. Soc. Engring. Edn.; mem. NAE, Japan Work Design Soc. (hon. adv. 1968—), World Future Soc., Acad. Mgmt., Engring. Mgmt. Soc., Sigma Xi, Alpha Pi Mu (nat. officer), Pi Tau Sigma, Omega Rho, Tau Beta Pi. Office: Univ Park GER 240 Dept Of I&se Los Angeles CA 90089-0193 Office Phone: 213-740-6415. Personal E-mail: gnadler@breakthroughthinking.com. Business E-Mail: nadler@usc.edu.

NADLER, HENRY LOUIS, pediatrician, educator, geneticist; b. NYC, Apr. 15, 1936; s. Herbert and Mary (Kartiganer) N.; m. Benita Weinhard, June 16, 1957; children: Karen, Gary, Debra, Amy. AB, Colgate U., 1957; MD, Northwestern U., 1961; MS, U. Wis., 1965. Diplomate Am. Bd. Pediatrics, Am. Bd. Med. Genetics. Intern NYU Med. Ctr., 1961-62, sr. resident pediatrics, 1962-63, chief resident, 1963-64; teaching asst. NYU Sch. Medicine, 1962-63, clin. instr., 1963-64, U. Wis. Sch. Medicine, 1964-65; practice medicine specializing in pediatrics Chgo., 1965—; fellow Children's Meml. Hosp. dept. pediatrics Northwestern U., 1964-65; assoc. in pediatrics Northwestern U. Med. Sch., 1965-66, asst. prof., 1967-68, assoc. prof., 1968-70, prof., 1970-81, chmn. dept. pediatrics, 1970-81; prof. Northwestern U. Med. Sch. (Grad. Sch.), 1971-80; mem. staff Children's Meml. Hosp., 1965-81, head div. genetics, 1969-81, chief of staff, 1970-81; dean, prof. pediatrics, ob-gyn Wayne State U. Med. Sch., Detroit, 1981-88; prof. U. Chgo., 1988-89, U. Ill., 1989—; pres. Michael Reese Hosp. and Med. Ctr., Chgo., 1988-91; market med. dir. Aetna Health Plans, Phoenix, 1993-94, mktg. v.p., CEO, 1994-95; v.p. managed care/physician integration, med. dir. Am. Healthcare Sys., San Diego, 1995. Mem. vis. staff, div. medicine Northwestern Meml. Hosp., 1972-81; staff Children's Hosp. of Mich., 1981-88. Mem. editl. bd. Comprehensive Therapy, 1973-84, Am. Jour. Human Genetics, 1979-83, Pediatrics in Rev., 1980-83, Am. Jour. Diseases of Children, 1983-91; contbr. articles to profl. jours. Recipient E. Mead Johnson award for pediatric rsch., 1973, Meyer O. Cantor award for Disting. Svc. Internat. Coll. Surgeons, 1987; Irene Heinz Given and John La Porte Given rsch. prof. pediatrics, 1970-81. Fellow Am. Acad. Pediatrics; mem. Am. Soc. for Clin. Investigation, Am. Soc. Human Genetics, Am. Pediatric Soc., Soc. for Pediatric Rsch., Midwest Soc. for Pediatric Rsch., Pan Am. Med. Assn., Alpha Omega Alpha. Home and Office: 17720 Camino de La Mitra PO Box 3665 Rancho Santa Fe CA 92067-3665 Personal E-mail: hlnadler@aol.com.

NADLER, JERROLD LEWIS, congressman, lawyer; b. Bklyn., June 13, 1947; m. Joyce L. Miller, 1976; 1 child, Michael. AB in Govt., Columbia U., 1969; JD, Fordham U. Sch. Law, 1978. Mem. Cmty. Planning Bd. Number 7, Manhattan, 1967-71; dem. leader 67th Assembly Dist. Part C, 1969-71; exec. dir. Cmty. Free Dem., 1972; dem. dist. leader 69th Assembly Dist. Part A, 1973-77; law clk. Morgan, Finnegan, Pine, Foley and Lee, 1976; mem. NY State Assembly from 69th dist., 1977-82, NY State Assembly from 67th dist., 1983-92, US Congress from NY dist., 1992, US Congress from 8th NY Dist., 1993—, mem. subcommittees on surface transp., water resources, environment, 1993—94, ranking minority mem. subcommittee on comml./adminstrv. law, 1997—2000, mem. subcommittee on constrn., 1997—2006, mem. judiciary com., chmn. constn., civil rights and civil liberties subcommittee, mem. transp. and infrastructure com., asst. whip, 2003—. Chmn. Assembly Com. on Corps, Authorities and Commn., 1991-92, Assembly Consumer Affairs and Protection Com., 1987-90, Assembly Com. on Ethics and Guidance, 1985-86, Assembly Subcom. on Mass Transit and Rail Freight, 1979-86, mem. Assembly Com. on Judiciary, Gov. Ops., Legis. Tax Study Commn.; mem. Assembly Com. Ways and Means, Housing, Real Property Tax, Health, Election Law, Ins. Founder, chmn. West Side Peace Com., 1969-71; pres. Zionist Orgn. Am. dist. 7A; active Common Cause, Met. Coun. on Housing, West Side Tenants Union; mem. nat. governing coun. Am. Jewish Congress. Recipient hon. recognition award NY State Nurses Assn., 1982, Disting. Svc. award Coalition on Domestic Violence, 1989, Legislator of Yr. award Internat. Assn. Firefighters, 2003; Pulitzer scholar Columbia U. Mem. NOW (Assembly Mem. of Yr. from NY chpt, 1980), NAACP, NY Bar Assn., NY Civil Liberties Union (honor roll), Citizens Union, League Conservation Voters, New Dem. Coalition, Ams. for Dem. Action (bd. dirs., nat. v.p.). Democrat. Office: US House Reps 2334 Rayburn House Office Bldgb Washington DC 20515-3208 Office Phone: 202-225-5635. E-mail: jerrold.nadler@mail.house.gov. *

NADLER, JUDITH, library director; b. Romania; BA in English and Romance Studies, U. Jerusalem; MLS, Israel Grad. Sch. With U. Chgo. Libr., 1966—, cataloger fgn. language materials, dir., 2004—. Office: Joseph Regenstein Libr U Chgo 1100 E 57 St 180 Chicago IL 60637 Office Phone: 773-702-8743. Office Fax: 773-702-6623. E-mail: judi@uchicago.edu. *

NADLER-HURVICH, HEDDA CAROL, public relations executive; b. Bronx, NY, June 15, 1944; d. Julius Louis and Julia Cohen; m. David George Nadler, Oct. 3, 1965 (div. 1979); 1 child, Laura Lee Nadler; m. Burton Earl Hurvich, Dec. 8, 1984. BBA, Baruch Coll., 1965. V.p., sec. Irving L. Straus Assocs., Inc., NYC, 1965-80; pres. Mount & Nadler Inc., NYC, 1999—. Avocations: aerobics, yoga. Office: Mount & Nadler 425 Madison Ave New York NY 10017-1110 Home Phone: 914-631-8834; Office Phone: 212-759-4440. E-mail: Hedda615@aol.com.

NADOLSKI, DORA J., social sciences educator, researcher; d. Harold V. and Dora H. Glidewell; m. Thomas P. Nadolski (div.); 1 child, Christopher A. MA in Social Sci., Antioch U., Yellow Springs, OH, 1965; PhD in polit. social sci., U. Mo., Kansas City, 2000. Assoc. prof. polit. sci. Northwest Nazarene Coll., Nampa, Idaho, 1966—68; lectr. Rockhurst U., Kansas City, 1995—97; prof., lectr. Park U., Kansas City, 1997—. Instr. Bedai U., Kanazawa, Japan, Kanazawa U., Peace Corps, Turkey. Co-author: Survey of U.S. Econometric Modeling Organizations; author: Special Curriculum Methods for Teaching Foreign Students; editor: Social Science Consortium Newsletter; author: The Etatist Turkish Republic and Its Political and SocioEconomic Performance from 1980-1999: A Developing State Impacted by International Organizations and Interdependence, Ottoman and Secular Civil Law International Journal of Middle East Studies, 1977. Chair Cub Scouts Am., Reston, Va., 1982—88; donor, supporter Disabled Am. Vets., Washington, 1995—. Fellow, NDEA, Soc. Sci. Rsch. Coun., U.Erfurt; grantee, NEH; scholar Fulbright, Sophia U.; Chancellor's Interdisciplinary Fellowship, U. Mo. Mem.: Am. Polit. Sci. Assn., Soc. Advancement Socio-Economics, Pi Sigma Alpha. Catholic. Avocations: cross country skiing, swimming, church choir. Personal E-mail: dora.nadolski@sbcglobal.net.

NAEGELE, PHILIPP OTTO, musician, educator; b. Stuttgart, Germany, Jan. 22, 1928; came to US, 1940; s. Reinhold and Alice (Nordlinger) N.; m. Susanne Russin (div. 1980); 1 child, Matthias Dominic; m. Barbara Wright, Mar. 1992; 1 adopted child, Olivia Kaihua. BA, Queens Coll., Flushing, NY, 1949; MFA, Princeton U., NJ, 1950, PhD, 1955. Violinist, violist Marlboro (Vt.) Music Festival, 1950—; violinist Cleve. Orch., 1956-64; from asst. prof. to William R. Kenan Jr. prof. Dept. Music Smith Coll., Northampton, Mass., 1964—2000, William R. Kenan Jr. prof. music emeritus Dept. Music, 2000—; violist Cantilena Piano Quartet, 1980-96; mem. Boccherini Ensemble, 1980-84; adj. prof. violin Amherst Coll., 2000—. Resident string quartet Kent (Ohio) State U., 1960-64; violin faculty Cleve. Inst. Music, 1961-64, Vegh String Quartet, 1977-79; rec. artist Columbia, Mus. Heritage Soc., Pro Arte, Nonesuch Records, Bis Records, Marlboro Rec. Soc., Arabesque Records, Da Camera, Spectrum Records, Bayer Records, Sony Classical, Philomusica, Qualitone Records. Author: Gustav Mahler and Johann Sebastian Bach, 1983, Marlboro Music/German Vocal Texts in Translation, An Anthology, 2006; contbr: articles to profl. jours. With US Army, 1955-56. Fellow Am. Council Learned Socs., 1949-50, Proctor fellow, 1952-53, Fulbright fellow, 1953-54. Mem. Phi Beta Kappa. Home: 57 Prospect St Northampton MA 01060-2130 Business E-Mail: pnaegele@smith.edu.

NAEGELE, TIMOTHY DUNCAN, lawyer; b. Santa Monica, Calif., Feb. 5, 1941; s. Kenneth Conrad and Lillian Alice (Duncan) N.; m. Sydene Ann Wallace, Dec. 18, 1964 (div. 1977); children: Kurt Duncan, Kirsten Ann. AB, UCLA, 1963; LLB, U. Calif., Berkeley, 1966; LLM, Georgetown U., 1969. Bar: Calif. 1966, U.S. Ct. Appeals (9th cir.) 1967, U.S. Dist. Ct. (no. dist.) Calif. 1967, U.S. Supreme Ct. 1970, D.C. 1973, U.S. Dist. Ct. D.C. 1973, U.S. Ct. Appeals (D.C. cir.) 1980, U.S. Dist. Ct. (ctrl. dist.) Calif. 1980, U.S. Ct. Appeals (10th cir.) 1987, U.S. Ct. Appeals (11th cir.) 1992, U.S. Ct. Claims 1996, U.S. Dist. Ct. Nebr. 1992. Asst. counsel U.S. Senate Banking Com., Washington, 1969-71; adminstrv. asst. Sen. Edward W. Brooke, Washington, 1971-73; ptnr. Brownstein, Zeidman & Schomer, Washington, 1973-77; mng. ptnr. Timothy D. Naegele & Assocs., Washington, 1977—. Author: A Journey Home: A Legacy of Love, 1985; contbr. articles to profl. jours. Capt. U.S. Army, 1967-69. Recipient Joint Svc. Commendation medal Def. Intelligence Agy., 1969. Mem. Fed. Bar Assn. (chmn. banking law com. 1971-74, exec. coun 1975—, vice chmn. coun. on financing 1974-75, chmn. coun. on fin. institutions and economy 1975-76), D.C. Bar Assn., Calif. Bar Assn., Ocean Reef Club (Key Largo, Fla.), Phi Delta Phi. Independent. Christian. Avocations: fishing, golf, tennis, hiking, photography. Address: PO Box 6408 Malibu CA 90264-6408 Office Phone: 805-488-6020. Personal E-mail: tdnaegele.associates@gmail.com.

NAESER, NANCY DEARIEN, geologist, researcher; b. Morgantown, W.Va., Apr. 15, 1944; d. William Harold and Katherine Elizabeth (Dearien) Cozad; m. Charles Wilbur Naeser, Feb. 6, 1982. BS, U. Ariz., 1966; PhD, Victoria U., Wellington, New Zealand, 1973. Geol. field asst. U.S. Geol. Survey, Flagstaff, Ariz., 1966; sci. editor New Zealand Jour. Geology and Geophysics, New Zealand Dept. Sci. and Indsl. Rsch., Wellington, 1974-76; postdoctoral rsch. assoc. U. Toronto, 1976-79, U.S. Geol. Survey, Denver, 1979-81, geologist, 1981—2006, scientist emeritus, 2006—. Adj. prof. Dartmouth Coll., Hanover, NH, 1985—97, U. Wyo., Laramie, 1984—91. Editor: Thermal History of Sedimentary Basins--Methods and Case Histories, 1989, Debris-Flow Hazards - Mechanics, Prediction and Assessment, 2000; contbr. articles on fission-track analysis to profl. jours. Docent, Denver Zoo, 1991-99. Fulbright fellow, New Zealand, 1967-68. Fellow Geol. Soc. Am.; mem. Geol. Soc. New Zealand, Mortar Board, Phi Kappa Phi. Methodist. Office: US Geol Survey Mail Stop 926 A 12201 Sunrise Valley Dr Reston VA 20192-0002 Office Phone: 703-648-5328. Business E-Mail: nnaeser@usgs.gov.

NAEVE, CLIFFORD MIKE, lawyer; b. Rapid City, SD, May 25, 1947; BSME, U. Tex., 1970; MPA, U. Tex., Austin, Tex., 1972; JD, George Washington, 1984. Bar: US Ct. Appeals (6th, 8th, 10th and DC cirs.) 1986. With profl. staff Senate Com. on Environment/Pub. Works, Washington, 1977-78; legis. dir. Office of Senator Lloyd Bentsen, Washington, 1978-80; mgr. fed. pub. affairs Aminoil USA, Inc., Washington, 1980-82; v.p. Mid-Continent Oil & Gas Assn., Washington, 1982-84; commr. Fed. Energy Regulatory Commn., Washington, 1985-88; ptnr., energy group Skadden, Arps, Slate, Meagher & Flom, Washington, 1988—. Mem. electricity adv. bd. to the Sec. Energy, 2002—. Contbg. author natural resources jour. The Future of the Natural Gas Market: Regulation and Prices, 1987; contr. to publications. Mem. ABA (sect. on natual resources law, sect. on pub. utility law), Fed. energy Bar Assn., Order of Coif, Tau Beta Pi, Pi Tau Sigma. Office: Skadden Arps Slate Meagher & Flom 1440 New York Ave NW Ste 600 Washington DC 20005 Office Phone: 202-371-7070. Office Fax: 202-661-8229. Business E-Mail: mnaeve@skadden.com.

NAEVE, MILO MERLE, retired curator, director; b. nr. Arnold, Kans., Oct. 9, 1931; s. Bernhardt and Fern (Yasmer) N.; m. Nancy Jammer, July 18, 1954. BFA, U. Colo., 1953; MA, U. Del., 1955. Curatorial asst. Henry Francis duPont Winterthur Mus., 1957, asst. curator, 1958, sec. of mus., 1959-63, registrar, 1963-65; editor Winterthur Portfolio, 1965-66; asst. dir. dept. collections Colonial Williamsburg, Va., 1967-69, curator, dir. dept. collections Va., 1970; dir. Colorado Springs (Colo.) Fine Arts Ctr., 1971-74; curator Am. arts Art Inst. Chgo., 1975-91; ret. Am. Arts, Art Inst. Chgo., 1991. Curator emeritus Field McCormick. Author: The Classical Presence in American Art, 1978, Identifying American Furniture: A Pictorial Guide to Styles and Terms, Colonial to Contemporary, 1981, 3rd edit., 1998, John Lewis Krimmel: An Artist in Federal America, 1987, 150 Years of Philadelphia Painters and Painting: Selections from the Sewell C. Biggs Museum of American Art, 1999; mem. editl. bd. Am. Art Jour.; contbr. articles to profl. jours. Trustee Skowhegan Sch. Painting and Sculpture, 1991-2005, Libr. Co. Phila., Nat. Coun. the Fine Arts Mus. San Francisco, 1991-2005 Recipient Robert C. Smith award for most disting. article pub. in field in U.S., Decorative Arts Soc., 1996, Chmn. Smith award, 2003. Fellow Royal Soc. Arts; mem. Coll. Art Assn. Am., Nat. Trust Hist. Preservation, Am. Assn. Museums, Museums Assn. (Eng.), Ill. Acad. Fine Arts (Lifetime Achievement award 1991), Century Assn., Grolier Club.

NAEYE, RICHARD L., pathologist, educator; b. Rochester, NY, Nov. 27, 1929; s. Peter John and Gertrude Ellen (Lookup) N.; m. Patricia Ann Dahl, June 4, 1955; children: Nancy Ellen, Susan Amy, Robert Peter. AB, Colgate U., 1951; MD, Columbia U., 1955. Diplomate: Am. Bd. Pathology. Intern N.Y. Hosp., NYC, 1955-56; resident Columbia-Presbyn. Med. Ctr., 1956-58, Mary Fletcher Hosp., Burlington, Vt., 1958-60; practice medicine, specializing in pathology Burlington, 1960-67, Hershey, Pa., 1967—; asst. attending pathologist Mary Fletcher Hosp., 1960-63; assoc. prof. U. Vt., 1963-67, prof. pathology, 1967; prof. dept. pathology M.S. Hershey Med. Ctr., Pa. State U. Coll. Medicine, 1967—, chmn. dept. pathology, 1967-97. Mem. NIH study sect. USPHS, 1968-72. Mem. editl. bd. Human Pathology, 1982-96, Pediatric Pathology, 1983-96, Pediatric and Perinatal Epidemiology, 1987-94, Modern Pathology, 1993-96, Fetal and Pediatric Pathology, 2004-; contbr. articles to med. jours. Markle scholar in acad. medicine, 1960-65. Mem. Am. Soc. Exptl. Pathology, U.S. Can. Acad. Pathology, Am. Soc. Pathologists, Am. Soc. Clin. Pathologists, Coll. Am. Pathologists, Pediatric Pathology Soc., Pa. Soc. Clin. Pathologists, Investigative Pathology. Home: 50 Laurel Ridge Rd Hershey PA 17033-2513 Office: Pa State U Coll Medicine Dept Pathology 500 University Dr Hershey PA 17033 Home Phone: 717-533-3014; Office Phone: 717-531-8352. Personal E-mail: richardnaeye@aol.com.

NAFTALI, TIMOTHY J., library director, historian, educator, writer; BA magna cum laude, Yale U., 1983; MA, Johns Hopkins U., 1987, Harvard U., 1993, PhD in History, 1993. Asst. prof. dept. history U. Hawaii, 1993—97; assoc. prof. U. Va., 1998—2006, dir. Presdl. recordings program, Kremlin decision-making project, 1999—2006; dir. Richard Nixon Presdl. Libr., Yorba Linda, Calif., 2006—. Vis. prof. Dept. History Yale U., 1996—98; hist. cons. Nazi War Crimes and Imperial Japanese Govt. Records Interagency Working Group, Nat. Archives, US Dept. Justice, 1999—, Nat. Commn. Terrorist Attacks upon US (9/11 Commn.), 2003—04; instr. Centre Counterintelligence and Security Studies, 2003—. Co-author: US-Canadian Softwood Lumber: Trade Dispute Negotiations, 1987, One Hell of a Gamble: Khrushchev, Castro and Kennedy, 1958-1964, 1997, The Presidential Recordings: John F. Kennedy, 2001, US Intelligence and the Nazis, 2004, 2005, Blindspot: The Secret History of American Counterterrorism, 2005; gen. editor Presdl. Recordings Series, 2003—; contbr. articles to profl. jours. Co-recipient Akira Iriye Prize for Internat. Hist., 1997—98; named prin. investigator, Nat. Hist. Publs. and Records Commn., 2002—; grantee MacArthur Fellowship in Internat. Security, 1990—91, Rsch. Fellowship, Kennan Inst. for Advance Russian Studies, Woodrow Wilson Internat. Ctr. for Scholars, 1996, Olin Fellowship in Nat. Security, 1996—98. Office: Richard Nixon Presdl Libr 18001 Yorba Linda Blvd Yorba Linda CA 92886 *

NAFTALIS, GARY PHILIP, lawyer, educator; b. Newark, Nov. 23, 1941; s. Gilbert and Bertha Beatrice Naftalis; m. Donna Arditi, June 30, 1974; children: Benjamin, Joshua, Daniel, Sarah. AB, Rutgers U., 1963; AM, Brown U., 1965; LLB, Columbia U., 1967. Bar: N.Y. 1967, U.S. Dist. Ct. (so. dist.) N.Y. 1969, U.S. Ct. Appeals (2d cir.) 1968, U.S. Ct. Appeals (3d cir.) 1973, U.S. Ct. Appeals (D.C. cir.) 1993, U.S. Supreme Ct. 1974. Law clk. to judge U.S. Dist. Ct. So. Dist. N.Y., 1967—68; asst. U.S. atty. So. Dist. N.Y., 1968—74, asst. chief criminal divsn., 1972—74; spl. asst. U.S. atty. for V.I., 1972—73; spl. counsel U.S. Senate Subcom. on Long Term Care, 1975, N.Y. State Temp. Commn. on Living Costs and Economy, 1975; ptnr. Orans, Elsen, Polstein & Naftalis, NYC, 1974—81, Kramer, Levin, Naftalis & Frankel, NYC, 1981—. Lectr. Law Sch. Columbia U., 1976-88; vis. lectr. Law Sch. Harvard U., 1979; mem. deptl. disciplinary com. Appellate div. 1st Dept., 1980-86. Author: (with Marvin E. Frankel) The Grand Jury: An Institution on Trial, 1977, Considerations in Representing Attorneys in Civil and Criminal Enforcement Proceedings, 1981, Sentencing: Helping Judges Do Their Jobs, 1986, SEC Actions Seeking to Bar Securities Professionals, 1995, SEC Cease and Desist Powers Limited, 1997, The Foreign Corrupt Practices Act, 1997, Prosecuting Lawyers Who Defend Clients in SEC Actions, 1998, Obtaining Reports from a Credit Bureau for Litigation May be a Crime, 1999, Encouraging Cooperation by Individual Respondents in SEC Enforcement Investigations, 2002, Navigating the Foreign Corrupt Practices Act, 2002, Fugitive Disentitlement in Civil Forfeiture Proceedings, 2002; editor: White Collar Crimes, 1980. Trustee Boys Brotherhood Rep., 1978—, Blueberry Treatment Ctr., 1981-91, Joseph Haggerty Children's Fund, 1991—; bd. dirs. The Legal Aid Soc., 2000—. Named one of 100 Most Influential Lawyers, Nat. Law Jour., 2006. Fellow: Am. Coll. Trial Lawyers; mem.: ABA (white collar crime com. criminal justice sect. 1985—, coun. criminal justice sect. 2002—05), N.Y. Coun. Def. Lawyers (bd. dirs. 2000—01), Internat. Bar Assn. (bus. crimes com. 1988—), N.Y. Bar Assn. (com. state legis. 1974—76, exec. com. comml. and fed. litigation sect.), Fed. Bar. Coun. (com. cts. 2d cir. 1974—77), Assn. of Bar of City of N.Y. (com. criminal cts. 1980—83, com. judiciary 1984—87, coun. criminal justice 1985—88, com. on criminal law 1987—90, 1997—2001), Phi Beta Kappa. Home: 1125 Park Ave Apt 7B New York NY 10128-1243 Office: Kramer Levin Naftalis & Frankel 1177 Ave of The Americas New York NY 10036 Office Phone: 212-715-9253. E-mail: gnaftalis@kramerlevin.com. *

NAFTOLIN, FREDERICK, gynecologist, educator; b. Bronx, NY, Apr. 7, 1936; s. Nathan and Jean (Pesacov) N.; children: Michael Eugene, Joshua Joseph; m. Marcie Myerson, Nov. 1, 1987. AA, UCLA, 1957; BA with honors, U. Calif., Berkeley, 1958; MD with honors, U. Calif., San Francisco, 1961; DPhil, U. Oxford, 1970. Intern King County Hosp., Seattle, 1961-62; resident in ob-gyn UCLA, 1962-66; asst. chief gynecology, reproductive endocrine fellow USPHS, Seattle, 1966-68; NIH fellow Oxford U., England, 1968-70; asst. prof. ob-gyn U. Calif., San Diego Sch. Medicine, 1970-73; assoc. prof. ob-gyn Harvard Med. Sch., 1973-75; prof., chmn. dept. ob-gyn McGill Faculty Medicine, Montreal, 1975-78, Yale Med. Sch., New Haven, 1978-2000, prof. debt. ob-gyn., 1978—2005, prof. dept. biology, 1983—2005; dir. Yale U. Ctr. for Rsch. in Reproductive Biology, 1986—2005, head reproductive neurosci. unit, 2000—03; prof. dept. ob-gyn. NYU, 2006—, dir. rsch. in reproductive biology, 2006—. Vis. prof. U. Geneva, 1982-83, Weizmann Inst., 1991-92; vis. prof. Complutense U., Spain, 1999, prof extraordinaire, 1999. Author: 15 books including: Subcellular Mechanisms in Reproductive Neuroendocrinology, 1976, Abnormal Fetal Growth, 1978, Clinical Neuroendocrinology, 1979, Dilation of the Uterine Cervix, 1980, 2-vol. series Basic Reproductive Medicine, Vol. I, Basis of Normal Reproduction, Vol. II, 1981, Male Reproduction, Vol. III, Metabolism of Steroids by Neuroendocrine Tissues, Follicle Stimulation and Ovulation Induction, 1986; mem. editl. bd.: Jour. Soc. Gynecologic Investigation, Menopause, Gynecol. Endocrinology, African Jour. Reproductive Medicine, sect. editor: Reproductive Biology, jour. Exptl. Zoology, 2002—; editor: Reproductive Divsn. Am. Jour. Zoology; contbr. more than 600 articles to med. jours. Named Fogarty Internat. fellow, 1982, John Simon Guggenheim fellow, 1983, Berlex Internat. scholar, 1991; recipient Arnaldo Bruno prize, Acad. Di Lincei, Italy, 2002; fellow ad enundem, Royal Coll. Ob-Gyn. Mem. Am. Gynecol. and Obstet. Soc., Soc. Gynecol. Investigation (pres. 1991-92, Disting. Scientist award 2003), Endocrine Soc., Internat. Soc. Neuroendocrinology, New Haven Ob-Gyn. Soc., Can. Fertility Soc., Soc. for Neurosci., N.Am. Menopause Soc. (pres. 1998-99), Internat. Menopause Soc. (exec. com. 2000—), Soc. Exptl. Biology and Medicine (coun. 2000—), Pan Am. Health and Edn. Found. (bd. trustees 2005-). Office: NYU Dept Ob-Gyn 550 1st Ave Tish 528 New York NY 10016 Business E-Mail: frederick.naptolin@med.nyu.edu.

NAFZIGER, JAMES ALBERT RICHMOND, law educator; b. Mpls., Sept. 24, 1940; s. Ralph Otto and Charlotte Monona (Hamilton) N. BA, U. Wis., 1962, MA, 1969; JD, Harvard U., Cambridge, Mass., 1967. Bar: Wis. 1967. Law clk. to chief judge U.S. Dist. Ct. (ea. dist.) Wis., 1967-69; fellow Am. Soc. Internat. Law, Washington, 1969-70, adminstrv. dir., 1970-74; exec. sec. Assn. Student Internat. Law Socs., 1969-70; lectr. Sch. Law Cath. U. Am., Washington, 1970-74; assoc. prof. law Coll. Law Willamette U., Salem, Oreg., 1977-80, prof., 1980-95, Thomas B. Stoel prof., 1995—, assoc. dean, 1985-86, dir. internat. programs, 1984—. Vis. assoc. prof. Sch. Law, U. Oreg. 1974-77; vis. prof. Nat. Autonomous U. Mex., 1978; lectr. tutor Inst. Pub. Internat. Law and Internat. Rels., Thessaloniki, Greece, 1982; scholar-in-residence Rockefeller Found. Ctr., Bellagio, Italy, 1985; cons. Adminstrv. Conf. US, 1988-90, Internat. Com. Migration, 1997—; hon. prof. East China U. of Politics and Law, 1999—; dir. rsch. ctr., Hague Acad. Internat. Law, 2005. Author: Conflict of Laws: A Northwest Perspective, 1985, Internat. Sports Law, 1988, 2d edit., 2004; editor: Procs. of Am. Soc. Internat. Law, 1977; co-editor: Law and Justice in a Multistate World, 2002; bd. dirs.: Am. Jour. Comparative Law, 1985—, mem. bd. advisors: Denver Jour. Internat. Law and Policy; contbr. articles to profl. jours. Dir. Rsch. Ctr., Hague Acad. Internat. Law, 2005; adv. com. on internat. law U.S. Dept. of State, 2001—; bd. dirs. N.W. Regional China Coun., 1987—89. 1st lt. US Army, 1962—64. Recipient Burlington No. Faculty Achievement award, 1988, Willamette U. Pres.'s award for excellence in scholarship, 2000. Mem.: UNA-USA (pres., Oreg. divsn. 1987—90, v.p. 1990—94, bd. dirs. 1990—2004, nat. coun. 2004—, chpt., divsn. pres.'s exec. com.), ACLU (pres. chpt. 1980—81, mem. state bd. 1982—88, sec. 1983—87), ABA (legal spl. ctrl. and east European law initiative 1992—), Am. Br. (human rights com. chmn. 1983—88, co dir. studies 1991—95, v.p. 1994—2000, pres. 2000—04, chmn. exec. com. 2004—), Internat. Law Assn. (rapporteur 1990—2001, mem. exec. coun. 2000—, chmn. cultural heritage law com. 2001—), Nat. Sports Law Inst. (bd. advisors 2002—), Internat. Sports Law Assn. (v.p. 1992, pres. 2004—), Oreg. Internat. Coun. (pres. 1990—92), Am. Law Inst., Assn. Am. Law Schs. (chmn. law and arts sect. 1981—83, chmn. internat. law sect. 1984—85, chmn. law and arts sect. 1989—91, chmn. immigration law sect. 1990—91, chmn. internat. law workshop 1995, com. on sects. and ann. meeting 1995—98, chmn. internat. exchs. sect. 1999—2000, chmn. conflict of laws sect. 2003—04, US Dept. of State adv. com.), Am. Coun. Learned Socs. (exec. com. 2002—, conf. adminstrv. officers), Internat. Studies Assn. (exec. bd. 1974—77, exec. coun. 2000—, internat. law sect.), Washington Fgn. Law Soc. (v.p. 1973—74), Internat. Acad. Comparative Law, Am. Soc. Comparative Law (bd. dirs. 1985—, treas. 1997—2005, chief adminstrv. officer 2005—), Am. Soc. Internat. Law (exec. coun. 1983—86, chmn. ann. meeting 1988, chmn. nominating com. 1989, exec. coun. 1992—95, exec. com. 1994—95), Phi Kappa Phi, Phi Beta Kappa. Home: 3775 Saxon Dr S Salem OR 97302-6041 Office: Willamette U Coll Law Salem OR 97301

NAGANO, KENT GEORGE, conductor, music director; b. Morro Bay, Calif., Nov. 22, 1951; BA in Sociology & Music (high honors), U of Calif., Santa Cruz, 1970—74; MA in Composition, San Francisco State U., 1974—76; studied with, Laszlo Varga. Former asst. Opera Co. Boston; former prin. guest condr. Ensemble InterContemporain & the Dutch Radio Orch.; mus. dir. & condr. Berkeley Symphony, 1978—; mus. dir. Opéra de Lyon, 1989—98; assoc. prin. & guest condr. LSO, London, 1990; mus. dir., prin. condr. designate Hallé Orch., England, 1991-94, mus. dir., prin. condr., 1994-2000, Deutsche Symphonie, Berlin, 2000—, LA Opera; mus. dir. Bavarian State Opera, Munich, 2006—, Montreal Symphony Orch., 2006—. Has performed with numerous orchestras around the world; recordings include: Songs of the Auvergne, Peter and the Wolf, Turandot and Arlecchino (Grammy nom.), La Boheme, Dialogues of the Carelites, The Death of Klinghoffer (Grammy nom.), Love for Three Oranges (Grammy nom.), Susannah (Grammy award), La damnation de Faust, The Rite of Spring, Rodrgue et chimene. Recipient Seaver/NEA Conducting award, 1985; Record of Yr. award Gramophone; named "officer" of France's Order of Arts and Letters, 1993. Office: Van Walsum Management Ltd 4 Addison Bridge Place London W14 8XP England *

NAGARAJ, DEVARAYSAMUDRAM R., engineer, researcher; Rsch. fellow Cytec Industries Inc., Stamford, Conn. Mem.: NAE. Office: Cytec Industries Inc 1937 W Main St Stamford CT 06904 Office Phone: 203-321-2200. Office Fax: 203-321-2298.

NAGARKATTI, JAI PRAKASH, chemical company executive; b. Hyderabad, India, Feb. 18, 1947; came to U.S., 1970; s. Surendranath and Shakuntala (Bai) N.; m. Linda Susan Slaughter, Mar. 14, 1975; 1 child, Shanti. BS, Osmania U., 1966, MS, 1968, Texas A&M Univ., 1973, PhD, 1976. Group leader Aldrich Chem. Co. Inc., Milw., 1977-78, supr. prodn., 1978-79, mgr. prodn., 1979-84, dir. prodn., 1985, v.p., 1985-87, pres., 1987—99; pres. fine chemicals Sigma Aldrich Corp., St. Louis, 1999—2002, pres. sci. rsch., 2002—04, pres., COO, 2004—05, pres., CEO, 2005—, bd. dir., 2005—. Lectr. chemistry V.V. Coll., Hyderabad, 1969-70. Contbr. articles to profl. jours. Robert A. Welch fellow East Tex. State U., Commerce, 1974-76. Fellow Indian Chem. Soc.; mem. Am. Chem. Soc. (chmn. membership Milw. chpt. 1981). Avocations: stamp collecting/philately, tennis. Office: Sigma Aldrich Corp 3050 Spruce St Saint Louis MO 63103 *

NAGEL, MIRIAM CARLSON, freelance/self-employed writer; d. Harold and Miriam Moll Carlson; m. James Carleton Nagel, Sept. 21, 1946; children: M. Susan, James Stevan, Janet Nagel Haley. BS, Boston U., 1962; MS, Simmons Coll., Boston, 1967. Cert. tchr. Mass., 1962, Conn., 1972. Chemistry tchr. Avon Pub. Schs., Avon, Conn., 1972—87; adj. faculty U. Hartford, 1982—89. Tech. analyst Tech. Insights Frost and Sullivan, 1998—. Contbr. articles to profl. jours. Recipient Nat. award, Chem. Mfgs. Assn., 1982. Mem.: Am. Chem. Soc., Nat. Assn. Sci. Writers. Home and Office: 152 Juniper Dr Avon CT 06001

NAGEL, SIDNEY ROBERT, physics professor; s. Ernest and Edith (Haggstrom) Nagel. BA, Columbia U., 1969; MA, Princeton U., 1972, PhD, 1974. Rsch. assoc. Brown U., Providence, 1974-76; asst. prof. physics U. Chgo., 1976-81, assoc. prof., 1981-84, prof., 1984—, assoc. dean divsn. phy. scis., 1997-2000, Louis Block prof., 1998-2000, assoc. dean divsn. phy. scis., 1997-2000, Stein-Freiler disting. svc. prof., 2001—. Contbr. articles to profl. jours. Recipient Quantrell award for Excellence in Undergrad. Tchg., U. Chgo., 1996; Klopsteg Meml. Lecture award Am. Assn. Physics Tchrs., 1998, Oliver E. Buckley prize Am. Phys. Soc., 1999; Alfred Sloan Found. fellow, 1978-82. Fellow AAAS, Am. Acad. Arts and Scis.; mem. NAS.

NAGEL, THOMAS, philosopher, lawyer, educator; b. Belgrade, Yugoslavia, July 4, 1937; came to U.S., 1939, naturalized, 1944; s. Walter and Carolyn (Baer) N.; m. Doris Blum, June 18, 1958 (div. 1973); m. Anne Hollander, June 26, 1979. BA, Cornell U., 1958; B.Phil., Oxford U., Eng., 1960; PhD, Harvard, 1963. Asst. prof. philosophy U. Calif., Berkeley, 1963-66; asst. prof. Princeton U., 1966-69, assoc., 1969-72, prof., 1972-80, NYU, 1980—, prof. philosophy and law, 1986—, Fiorello LaGuardia prof. law, 2001—03, Univ. prof., 2002—. Vis. prof. Rockefeller U., 1973, U. Mex., 1977, U. Witwatersrand, 1982, UCLA, 1986, U. Calif., Berkeley, 2004. Author: The Possibility of Altruism, 1970, Mortal Questions, 1979, The View from Nowhere, 1986, What Does It All Mean?, 1987, Equality and Partiality, 1991, Other Minds, 1995, The Last Word, 1997; author: (with Liam Murphy) The Myth of Ownership, 2002; author: Concealment and Exposure, 2002; assoc. editor: Philosophy and Public Affairs, 1970—82. Guggenheim fellow, 1966, NSF fellow, 1967-69, NEH fellow, 1978, 84-85, vis. fellow All Souls Coll., Oxford, Eng., 1990. Mem.: Am. Philos. Soc., Brit. Acad., Am. Acad. Arts and Scis., Am. Philos. Assn.

NAGEL, TREVOR W., lawyer; b. Adelaide, Australia, 1951; BA, U. Adelaide, 1973, Dip. Ed., 1974, LLB with honors, 1980; LLM, U. Chgo., 1981; SJD, Harvard U., 1984. Barrister, New South Wales, Australia 1985, Barrister, High Court of Australia 1985, bar: Mass. 1986, DC 1996. Ptnr. Shaw Pittman LLP, Washington, 1993—2006, Alston & Bird LLP, Washington, 2006—. Prof. U. Sydney Law Sch., Elton Mayo Sch. Mgmt., U. South Australia. Contbr. articles to profl. jours. Mem.: ABA, Internat. Bar Assn. Office: Alston & Bird LLP The Atlantic Bldg 950 F St NW Washington DC 20004 Office Phone: 202-756-3563. Business E-Mail: trevor.nagel@alston.com.

NAGEL, VERNON J., chemicals and eletronics executive; BBA, U. Mich. V.p. fin., CFO, treas., sec. Stericycle Inc.; exec. v.p., CFO, treas. Kuhlman Corp., 1993—99; prin. Jepson Assocs., Inc., 1999—2001; CFO Acuity Brands, Inc., Atlanta, 2001—04, vice chmn., 2004, chmn., pres., CEO, 2004—. Office: Acuity Brands Inc 1170 Peachtree St NE Atlanta GA 30309 *

NAGI, LILLIAN S., biology professor; d. Mostafa H. Nagi and Wiam Youssif. MS in Biol. Scis., Bowling Green State U., Ohio, 2002. Instr. and rsch. asst. Bowling Green State U., Ohio, 1999—2002; rsch. technician Med. Coll. Ohio, Toledo, 2002—03; prof. Owens CC, Toledo, 2002—. Guest lectr. Academic Investment in Math and Sci., Bowling Green, 2002; adj. prof. Lourdes Coll., Sylvania, 2006—. Mem.: NOW. Avocations: travel, sports, running, bicycling. Home: PO Box 464 Bowling Green OH 43402 Personal E-mail: lilliannagi@gmail.com.

NAGI, SAMUEL NJUGUNA, psychotherapist, director; b. Nairobi, Kenya, July 15, 1954; s. Jacob Nagi Njuguna and Miriam Njeri Nagi; m. Peninah Nduta Gatura, Oct. 12, 1985; children: Zawadi Njeri Njuguna, Samuel Nagi Njuguna, Baraka Kamau Njuguna. Diploma in Bible, Word Life Bible Inst., NY, 1977; BA in Bible, Moffat Bible Coll., Kijabe, Kenya, 1981; BA in Religious Edn., Citadel Coll., Ark., 1987; MA in Intercultural Studies, Columbia Bibl. Sem., SC, 1988, MDiv, 1989; D in Ministry, Columbia Internat. U., SC, 1991; degree in Edn., Converse Coll., Spartanburg, SC, 1998; PhD (hon.), Ithanga U., Kenya, 1999. Lic. profl. counselor SC Bd. Profl. Counselors, 1996, profl. counselor supr. SC Bd. Profl. Counselors, 1997, addictions counselor Nat. Bd. Addiction Examiners, 1996. Sr. pastor Africa Inland Ch., Nirobi, Kenya, 1981—85; min. edn. and counseling Bethlehem Bapt. Ch., Columbia, 1987—89; dir., min. youth and counseling NE United Meth. Ch., Columbia, 1989—91; chaplain, counselor Bapt. Med. Ctr., Columbia, 1991—93; supr. family preservation Pee Dee Mental Health Ctr., Florence, SC, 1993; dir. family svcs and cons. SC Human Svc. Assocs., Cayce, SC, 1993—99; dir. chaplaincy svcs. dept mental health G Werber Bryan Psychiat. Hosp., Columbia, 1999—; dir. clin. counseling Reach Family Counseling Svcs., PC, Columbia, 2001—. Trainer, spkr. Reach Family Counseling Svcs., 2001—; chmn. bd. dirs. Hands of Hope, Irmo, SC, 2005—. Author: Effective Parenting: A Step-by-Step Guide to Biblical Parenting, A Step-by-Step Guide to Successful Marriage: An Educational Guide for Couples and Families; contbr. scientific papers and articles to profl. jours. Named Employee of Yr., SC Human Svcs. Assn., 1998, SC Dept. Mental Health, 2002. Fellow: Am. Assn. Marriage and Family Therapists, Am. Assn. Pastoral Counselors (pastoral counselor); mem.: Kenya Christian Fellowship in Am. (editor mag. 1995—2002, dir. men's ministries 2002—04, Disting. Svc. award 2006, 2005). Avocations: boxing, soccer, basketball. Home: 131 Lordship Ln Irmo SC 29063 Office: Reach Family Counseling Svcs PC 7420 North Main St Columbia SC 29203 Home Phone: 803-238-0248. Office Fax: 803-333-9926; Home Fax: 803-333-9926. Personal E-mail: reachfamily@bellsouth.net.

NAGIN, LAWRENCE M., lawyer; b. 1941; married. BA, U. So. Calif., 1962; JD, U. Calif., Hastings, 1965. Dep. pub. defender Pub. Defender's Office, 1966-68; pvt. practice law Beverly Hills, Calif., 1968-74; spl. counsel aviation matters City Atty's. Officer, LA, 1974-76; sr. asst. city atty. L.A. Dept. of Airports, 1976; formerly v.p. Flying Tiger Line, Inc., LA, sr. v.p., gen. counsel adminstrn., from 1984; exec. v.p. corp. affairs, gen. counsel United Airlines, Inc. (UAL Corp.), Elk Grove Village, Ill., 1990-96, U.S. Airways Inc., Arlington, Va., 1996—. Office: US Airways Inc 2345 Crystal Dr Arlington VA 22227-0001

NAGIN, RAY (CLARENCE RAY NAGIN JR.), mayor; b. New Orleans, June 11, 1956; m. Seletha Smith, 1982; children: Jeremy, Jarin, Tianna. BSc in Acctg., Tuskegee U., 1978; MBA, Tulane U., 1994. With GM, 1978—81, Associates Corp., Dallas, 1981—85; contr. Cox Comm. S.E. La. cable sys., 1985—89, v.p., gen. mgr., 1989—2002; mayor City of New Orleans, 2002—. Mem. bd. dirs. United Way, Convenant Ho.; chmn. United Negro Coll. Fund Walkathon fundraising campaign; pres. 100 Black Men Metro New Orleans. Recipient Excellent Customer Svc. award, Better Bus. Bur., 1993, Disting. Bus. Ptnr. award, La. State Bd. Edn., 1994, Diversity and Role Model award, Young Leadership Coun., 1995, New Orleanian of Yr. award, Gambit weekly, 1998, Nat. Telly award, 2001, Most Influential Black Americans, Ebony mag., 2006. Office: Office of the Mayor New Orleans City Hall 1300 Perdido St Rm 2E04 New Orleans LA 70112 Office Phone: 504-565-7793. Office Fax: 504-565-6423. *

NAGLE, JAMES W., lawyer; BA magna cum laude, Georgetown Univ., 1974, JD magna cum laude, 1980; MPA, Am. Univ., 1976. Bar: Mass. 1980. Ptnr., chair, labor, employment practices group Goodwin Procter LLP, Boston. Editor: Georgetown Law Jour.; contributing editor Covenants Not to Compete: A State-by-State Survey, ABA. Mem.: ABA (individual rights, responsibilities com.), Boston Bar Assn. (chair, labor, employment law sect. 1992—94). Office: Goodwin Procter LLP Exchange Pl 53 State St Boston MA 02109 Office Phone: 617-570-1233. Office Fax: 617-523-1231. Business E-Mail: jnagle@goodwinprocter.com.

NAGLE, JEAN SUSAN KARABACZ, retired sociologist, psychologist; b. Detroit, 1936; d. Peter and Hedy (Grusczynski) Karabacz; m. Robert D. Nagle, Nov. 20, 1956; children: Carl A., Sonya L., Paula E. BS in Sociology, Wayne State U., 1956; postgrad., U. Chgo., 1953-55; MA, N.Mex. Highlands U., 1960; PhD, Union Grad. Sch., 1977; postgrad., Bryn Mawr. Inst., 1981. Diagnostic technician Vocat. Counseling Inst., Detroit,

1952; rsch. technician United Auto Workers-CIO, Detroit, 1958; clin. psychology intern N.Mex. State Hosp., Las Vegas, 1962-63; clin. psychology trainee VA Hosp., Omah and Lincoln, Nebr., 1963-64; instr. sociology N.W. Mo. State U., Maryville, 1965-70, prof. sociology and psychology, 1971-92, ret., 1992. Bd. dirs. Inst. Discourse. Grantee N.W. Mo. State U., 1981, 82. Mem. APA, Am. Sociol. Assn., Am. Psychol. Soc., Midwest Sociol. Soc., Psychology/Sociology Club, Mo. Psychol. Assn., World Federalists, Psi Chi, Pi Gamma Mu. also: 3106 E 80th St Kansas City MO 64132-3638

NAGLE, JOHN FREDERICK, physicist; b. Easton, Pa., Sept. 29, 1939; s. Edgar Eugene and Julia Elizabeth N.; m. Stephanie Tristram-Nagle; children: Julia and Lara. BA, Yale U., 1960, MS, 1962, PhD, 1965. Asst. prof. physics Carnegie-Mellon U., 1967—72, assoc. prof. physics, 1972—78, prof. physics, biol. scis., 1978—. NATO Fellow, 1965—66, Alfred P. Sloan fellow, 1969—71, Guggenheim fellow, 1979—80. Fellow Am. Phys. Soc. (chair divsn. biol. physics 1992-93); mem. AAUP, Biophys. Soc. (Avanti award 2003), Phi Beta Kappa, Sigma Xi. Office: Physics Dept Carnegie-Mellon U Pittsburgh PA 15213 Office Phone: 412-268-2764. Business E-Mail: nagle@cmu.edu.

NAGLER, BARRY, lawyer; b. NYC, Feb. 21, 1957; s. Charles and Toby (Freyman) N.; m. Laurie Beth Carter, Aug. 23, 1981; children: Daniel, Alyssa. BA magna cum laude, Franklin & Marshall Coll., 1978; JD cum laude, Harvard U., 1981. Bar: Mass. 1981. Assoc. Foley, Hoag & Eliot, Boston, 1981-87; v.p., asst. gen. coun. Reebok Internat., Stoughton, Mass., 1987-95, v.p., gen. counsel, 1995-98, sr. v.p., gen. counsel, 1998-99, Hasbro Inc., Pawtucket, RI, 2000—. Treas., mem. nat. bd. dirs. Assn. Corporate Counsel, dir. N.E. chpt., 1993—. Author: Reebok Rules for Litigation Management, 1997; contbr. articles to profl. jours. Office: Hasbro Inc 1011 Newport Ave Pawtucket RI 02862 *

NAGLER, LEON GREGORY, retired management consultant; b. Buenos Aires, Jan. 29, 1932; (parents Am. Citizens); s. Morris and Jennie (Golden) N.; m. F. Elise Charness, Dec. 20, 1953; children: Jeri Lynn, Sandra Michelle. BS cum laude, Boston U., 1953, MBA, 1954; JD, Cleve. State U., 1961. Bar: Ohio 1961. Tchr. psychology Cameron State Agrl. Jr. Coll., Lawton, Okla., 1956-57; supr. employment and tng. Jones & Laughlin Steel Corp., Cleve., 1957-65; exec. dir. indsl. rels. Charles Corp., Cleve., 1965-67; dir. personnel ITT Svc. Industries Corp., Cleve., 1967-72; v.p. personnel Builder Svcs. Corp., Clearwater, Fla., 1972-73; v.p. adminstrn. Damon Corp., Needham Heights, Mass., 1973-77; pres. Nagler & Co., Inc., Wellesley Hills, Mass., 1977-95, Nagler, Robins & Poe, Inc., 1995—2005; ret. Mem. Mayfield Heights Planning and Zoning Commn., Ohio 1965-67; sec. Mayfield Heights Zoning Bd. Appeals, 1963-65; chmn. Combined Health Fund, Mayfield Heights, 1963; pres. N.E. Ohio region, mem. nat. gov. coun. Am. Jewish Congress, 1972-73; bd. dirs. New Eng. region Anti-Defamation League, 1977-80; trustee Jewish Cmty. Ctrs. Greater Boston, 1990—; bd. dirs. Jewish Vocat. Svc., Boston, 1977—, sec., 1980-83, v.p., 1983-88; bd. dirs. Am. Friends Wingate Inst., 1987-2004, v.p. fin., 1987-2004; trustee Temple Beth Avodah, Newton, 1978-2004, v.p., 1979-83, pres., 1983-85; trustee Combined Jewish Philanthropies, Boston, 1985-1992; bd. overseers Combined Jewish Philanthropies, 1992-2004. Served with AUS, 1955-57. Mem. Boston U. Alumni Assn. (pres. N.E. Ohio 1969-73, nat. coun. 1973—), Masons, Wycliffe Golf and Country Club (bd. govs. 1999-2005, v.p. 2001-02, pres. 2003-05). Democrat.

NAGLER, STEWART GORDON, retired insurance company executive; b. Bklyn., Jan. 30, 1943; s. Henry and Mary Nagler; m. Bonnie Lawrence, Aug. 9, 1964 (dec.); children: David, Ellen; m. Ronnie Hendler, Jan. 9, 2000. BS summa cum laude, Poly. U., 1963. With Met. Life Ins. Co., NYC, 1963—2004, exec. v.p., 1983-85, sr. exec. v.p., 1985-93, sr. exec. v.p., CFO, 1993-98, vice chmn. bd., 1998—2004, CFO, 1998—2004. Fellow Soc. Actuaries, Acad. Actuaries. E-mail: stunagler@optonline.net.

NAGORSKE, LYNN A., bank executive; b. Minn., 1956; B in Acctg., Minn. State U. CPA. Sr. mgr. Audit Dept. KPMG Peat Marwick; sr. v.p. and controller TCF Bank, 1985, treas., CFO, 1986, exec. v.p., 1988, pres., 1993, pres., COO, CEO, 2006—; pres., CFO TFC Bank Minn., 1997—98. Bd. dirs. TCF Bank, 1995—. Office: TCF Financial Corp 200 Lake St E Wayzata MN 55391 *

NAGORSKI, ZYGMUNT, political scientist, writer; b. Warsaw, Sept. 27, 1912; came to U.S., 1948, naturalized, 1953; s. Zygmunt Julian and Maria Nagorski; m. Marie Bogdaszewski, Nov. 22, 1938; children: Maria, Andrew, Teresa. MA, U. Cracow, 1935; postgrad., U. Geneva, 1937-38, Internat. Inst. Trade and, Berne, Switzerland, 1937-38. Reporter Chattanooga Times, 1948; editor-in-chief Fgn. News Svc., Inc., NYC, 1949-56; chief Internat. Br. Office Rsch. USIA, Washington, 1956-59; fgn. svc. officer Cairo, 1959-61, Seoul, 1961-64, Paris, 1964-66; spl. asst. to pres. Fgn. Policy Assn., Inc., NYC, 1966-68; mem. profl. staff Hudson Inst., Inc., 1968-69; dir. members meetings program Coun. Fgn. Rels., NYC, 1969-78; v.p. Lehrman Inst., 1978-80; spl. advisor Aspen Inst. Adj. asst. prof. polit. sci. dept. Queens Coll., 1974-75; v.p. Human Resource Svcs., Inc., 1980-81; guest lectr. Wilton Park, Sussex, Eng., Fgn. Svc. Inst., Ctr. Study Human Values, Tanglewood, N.C., Experiment in Internat. Living (Vt.), also nummerous univs.; v.p., dir. exec. seminars programs Aspen Inst. Humanistic Studies, 1981-85; pres. Ctr. Internat. Leadership, N.Y.C., 1986—. Author: Armed Unemployment, 1945, The Psychology of East-West Trade, 1975, From Warsaw to Whereever, 2007; co-author U.S.-Japan Economic Relations, 1979; contbr. articles to newspapers and mags. Pres. Am. Friends Wilton Park, 1967-70, 94-96, Mid-Atlantic Club N.Y., 1972-90; bd. dirs. Scarsdale Adult Sch., 1968-72, Internat. U. Found. Served with Polish Army, 1939-45, under French and Brit. command. Decorated Brit. War medal, officer's cross Order of Merit (W. Germany); comdr. Order of Leopold II (Belgium); recipient Meritorious Svc. award USIA, 1965, Outstanding Fgn. Born Am. award Internat. Ctr. N.Y., 1988. Mem. Coun. Fgn. Rels., Am. Polit. Sci. Assn., Internat. Studies Assn., Polish Inst. Arts and Scis., Am. Fgn. Svc. Assn., Fgn. Svc. club, Nat. Press Club (Washington). Democrat. Roman Catholic. Home: Ctr for Internat Leadership Inc 3050 Military Rd NW 624 Washington DC 20015 Office Phone: 202-686-3767. Fax: 202-686-3769. E-mail: znagorski@aol.com.

NAGOURNEY, HERBERT, publishing company executive; b. NYC, Jan. 30, 1926; s. Isidor and Tillie (Burstein) N.; children: Adam, Beth, Eric, Sam. BS, Columbia U., 1946, MS, 1947. Pres. Profl. and Tech. Programs, NYC, 1951-65; v.p. Macmillan Co., NYC, 1965-69; pres. Quadrangle/New York Times Book Co., NYC, 1969-76, New York Times Book Co., NYC, 1971-76, Quartet Books, Inc., NYC and London, 1976-81, Knowledge Tree Group Inc., 1979-89; v.p., dir. Sci. DataLink, 1981-88; pres. Sci. Datalink, 1990—2000; v.p., dir. Comtex Sci., 1981-90; pres. Profl. and Tech. Pub. Inc., 1989—. Served with AUS, 1944. Home: 320 Joshuatown Rd Lyme CT 06371-3000 Office: 45 Christopher St New York NY 10014-3533 Office Phone: 212-206-9501. Personal E-mail: hnagourney@rcn.com.

NAGRA, PARMINDER, actress; b. Leicester, England, Oct. 5, 1975; Actor: (films) Bend It Like Beckham, 2002, Ella Enchanted, 2004; (TV series) Turning World, 1996, Always and Everyone, 1999, ER, 2003—; (TV films) King Girl, 1996, Donovan Quick, 1999, Twelfth Night, 2003, Second Generation, 2003.

NAGRIN, DANIEL, dancer, educator, choreographer, writer; b. NYC, May 22, 1917; s. Harry Samuel and Clara (Wexler) N.; m. Helen Tamiris, 1946 (dec. 1966); m. Phyllis A. Steele, Jan. 24, 1992. BS in Edn., CCNY, 1940; DFA, SUNY, Brockport, 1991; DHL, Ariz. State U., 1992; studied dance with Ray Moses, Martha Graham, Anna Sokolow, Helen Tamiris, Mme. Anderson-Ivantzova, Nenette Charisse and Edward Caton, 1936-56, studied acting with Miriam Goldina, Sanford Meisner and Stella Adler, 1936-56. Tchr. Silvermine Guild Art, New Canaan, Conn., 1957-66, SUNY, Brockport, 1967-71, U. Md., College Park, 1970, Davis Ctr. Performing Arts, CCNY, 1973-75, Nat. Theatre Inst., Eugene O'Neill Found., Waterford, Conn., 1974, Hartmann Theatre Conservatory, Stamford, Conn., 1975-77; long-term resident tchr., Nat. Endowment for Arts sponsorship U. Hawaii, 1978-80, tchr., 1981, Bill Evans Dance Workshop, Seattle, 1981; prof. dance dept. Ariz. State U., Tempe, 1982-92; tchr. grad. liberal studies program Wesleyan U., Middletown, Conn., 1984, Dance Workshop for Movement Rsch., NYC, 1984, Improvisation Workshop, Seattle, 1985, Improvisation, Choreography and Acting Technique for Dancers, Seattle, 1985, Dance Workshop, Glenwood Springs, Colo., 1990; prof. emeritus dance Ariz. State U., 1992. Tchr. summer sessions Conn. Coll., New London, 1959, 74; Am. Dance Festival at Conn. Coll., 1960, 77, Duke U., Durham, NC, 1978, 80, 82, 87-88, 92, Balasaraswati/Joy Ann Dewey Beinecke Chair Dising. Tchg., 1992; summer dance program Conn. Coll., 1979, E. La Tour Dance Workshop, Sedgewick, 1982, 83; dance workshop U. Minn. at Mpls., 1984, Stanford U., 1990; co-dir. Tamiris-Nagrin Summer Dance Workshop, Sedgewick, 1960-61, (with Tamiris) summer dance session C. W. Post Coll., Greenville, NY, 1962-63; dir. summer dance workshop Johnson (Vt.) State Coll., 1972-73, 75-76; lectr in field. Dancer (featured dance soloist on Broadway) Annie Get Your Gun, Lend an Ear, Touch and Go, Plain and Fancy (Billboard Donaldson award, 1954), (appearance in film) Just for You, (adapted and performed one-man theater piece) The Fall, from novel by Albert Camus, 1977—79, choreographer (solo works) Spanish Dance, 1948, Man of Action, 1948, Strange Hero, 1948, Indeterminate Figure, 1957, With My Eye and With My Hand, 1968, Jazz: Three Ways, 1958, 1966, Path-Silence, 1965, Not Me, But Him, 1965, The Peloponesian War, 1967—68, Untitled, 1974, Ruminations, 1976, Getting Well, 1978, Poems Off the Wall, 1981, Apartment 18C, 1993, Crosscurrents, 1997, Lost and Never Found, 1998, Someone for Theater X, Tokyo, Japan, What Did You Say?, 2001, others, (for groups) Faces from Walt Whitman, 1950, An American Journey, 1962, asst. choreographer (original Broadway prodns.) Up in Central Park, Stovepipe Hat, Show Boat, Annie Get Your Gun, By the Beautiful Sea, others; dir.: (off-Broadway) Volpone, 1957, The Firebugs, 1960, The Umbrella, 1961, Emperor Jones (Boston, 1963, others; (film choreography) His Majesty O'Keefe; actor: (video) The Art of Memory, 1985; (plays) Three Stories High, others; extensive touring U.S., Europe, The Pacific and Japan, 1957—84, conceived and directed (videos) Steps, 1972, The Edge is Also a Circle, 1973, Nagrin Videotape Library of Dances, 1985; author: How to Dance Forever: Surviving Against the Odds, 1988, Dance and the Specific Image: Improvisation, 1993, The Six Questions: Acting Technique for Dance Performance, 1997, Choreography and the Specific Image: Nineteen Essays and a Workbook, 2001. With spl. svcs. Army Airforce, 1942-43. Grantee Rebekah Harkness Found., 1962, Logan Found., 1965, NY State Coun. on Arts and Nat. Found. for Arts and Humanities, 1967-68, NY State Coun. on Arts, 1971-81, Anne S. Richardson Fund, 1971, 73-76, 78, Nat. Endowment for Arts, 1975, 79, 81, 83, Ariz. State U., 1983-86, 88; CAPS fellow NY State Coun. on Arts, 1977-78; fellow NEA, 1977-78, 80, 82-83, 90-91, Minn. McKnight Nat. fellow, 1996-97; commd. ballet Rebekah Harkness Ballet Found., 1986. Mem. Actors' Equity, Phi Kappa Phi (hon.). Avocation: reading. Home and Office: 208 E 14th St Tempe AZ 85281-6707 E-mail: nagrin@imap2.asu.edu.

NAGY, DONNA M., dean, law educator; BA, Vassar Coll., 1986; JD cum laude, NYU Sch. Law, 1989. Assoc. Debevoise & Plimpton, Washington, DC, 1989—94; asst. prof. U. Cin. Sch. Law, 1994—98, assoc. prof., 1998—99, prof., 1999—2001, Charles Hartsock Prof. Law, 2001—, assoc. dean faculty devel., 2002—04, interim dean, 2004—. Vis. prof. law U. Ill. Coll. Law, Urbana-Champaign, 2001; vis. scholar U. Canterbury Sch. Law, New Zealand, 2002. Co-author: Ferrara on Insider Trading and the Wall, 1995, 2002, Securities Litigation and Enforcement: Cases and Materials, 2003; contbr. articles to law jours. Recipient Howard C. Schott Publ. Prize, 2002, 2003; Order of Coif. Mem.: ABA (mem. sec. Bus. Law), Am. Assn. Law Schs. (sec. Bus. Assns., Securities Regulation, and Women in Legal Edn.), Soc. Am. Law Tchrs., ACLU, Vassar Club of Cin. (Alumni Appointments Chair 1995—99).

NAGY, ELIZABETH GARVER, artist; b. Martinsville, Ill., Jan. 14, 1928; d. Ralph Tibbs and Evelyn Fasig Garver; m. William Roger Achleman (dec.); children: Shelly Marth, Todd Jeffrey; m. Stephen Michael Nagy (dec.); children: Stephanie Nagy-Agren, Patricia Nagy Adelman. Degree in art, Studio Sch. Advt. Art, Cin., 1948. Illustrator Wolf & Dessauer, Ft. Wayne, Ind., 1949—51; freelance illustrator Ft. Wayne, 1951—; art instr. Springfield (Ohio) Art Ctr., 1968—77, Fine Line Creative Arts Ctr., St. Charles, Ill., 1986—92. Presenter in field. One-woman shows include Mountainlair Gallery, W.Va. U., Morgantown, W.Va., 1974, Clay N Caboodle Cadence, Geneva, Ill., 1993, Transylvania County Arts Ctr., Brevard, N.C., 1999, many others, exhibited in group shows at Schumacher Gallery, Columbus, Ohio, 1975, Old State Capitol Galleries, Baton Rouge, La., 1976, 1978, 1979, Greenhill, Woodmere Gallery, 1976—90, Phila. Civic Ctr., 1976—90, Port History Mus., Phila., 1976—90, Tweed Mus., Duluth, Minn., 1978, Rahr-West Mus., Manitowoc, Wis., 1979, Springfield Art Assn., Ill., 1981, 1991, 1992, Davenport Art Mus., Iowa, 1983, LA Artcore Gallery, 1988, Maurice Spertus Mus., Chgo., 1990, The Fine Line Creative Arts Ctr., St. Charles, 1993, Transylvania County Arts Coun. Gallery 7, Brevard, 1996, 1997, Transylvania County Arts Ctr., Brevard, 1999—2005, many others, Represented in permanent collections Time Temporary, Ft. Wayne, Kane County Jud. Ctr., Geneva, Bankers Club Worldwide Ho., Taipei, Taiwan, Springfield (Ohio) Art Mus., many others. Sec., bd. dirs. Springfield Art Ctr., 1969—76; mem. visual arts com. Dellora A. Norris Cultural Arts Ctr., St. Charles, 1980—88. Recipient award of excellence, Midwest Watercolor Soc., 1983, 3d award, 41st Ann. Artists Guild of Chgo., 1983, award of merit, The Anderson (Ind.) Fine Arts Ctr., 1988. Mem.: Phila. Water Color Soc. (hon. life), Transparent Watercolor Soc. Am. (signature), Watercolor West (signature), Western Ohio Watercolor Soc. (founder, 1st pres.). Avocations: creating wearable art, knitting, weaving, sewing, embroidery.

NAGY, LOUIS LEONARD, engineering executive, researcher; b. Detroit, Jan. 15, 1942; s. Alex and Helen Nagy; m. Dianna M. Skarjune, Aug. 5, 1961; children: Tammy, Kimberly, Kristine, Amanda. BSEE, U. Mich., Dearborn, 1965; MSEE, U. Mich., Ann Arbor, 1969, PhDEE, 1974. Registered profl. engr. Rsch. engr. U. Mich., Ann Arbor, 1962-69; staff rsch. engr. GM R & D Ctr., Warren, Mich., 1969-98; sr. staff rsch. engr. Delphi Rsch. Labs., Warren, 1999—. Contbr. articles to profl. jours.; patentee in field. Bd. dirs. Convergence Ednl. Found., Birmingham, Mich., 1990-97, Convergence Transp. Electronics Assn., Birmingham, 1990-97. Recipient R&D 100 award R&D Mag., 1998. Fellow IEEE; mem. Convergence Fellowship (bd. dirs. 1988-96), Vehicular Tech. Soc. (Spl. Recognition award 1979, Avant Garde award 1986, Paper of Yr. 1975), Soc. Automotive Engrs., Tau Beta Pi, Eta Kappa Nu. Avocations: electronics, antennas, radar, automotive radar, microwaves. Office: Delphi Rsch Labs MC 483-478-105 51786 Shelby Pkwy Shelby Township MI 48315 Business E-Mail: Louis.L.Nagy@delphi.com.

NAGY, STEPHEN MEARS, JR., physician, allergist; b. Yonkers, NY, Apr. 1, 1939; s. Stephen Mears and Olga (Zahoruiko) N.; m. Brenda Yu Nagy, 1966; children: Catherine, Stephen III. BA, Princeton U., 1960; MD, Tufts U., 1964. Diplomate Am. Bd. Internal Medicine, Am. Bd. Allergy and Immunology. Pvt. practice, Sacramento, Calif., 1971-2000; prof. Sch. Medicine U. Calif., Davis, 1974—. Author, editor Evaluation & Management of Allergic and Asthmatic Diseases, 1981; mem. editl. bd. Clinical Reviews in Allergy; creator Famous Teachings in Modern Medicine-Allergy Series slide collection. Capt. U.S. Army, 1966-68, Vietnam. Fellow Am. Acad. Allergy, Am. Coll. Allergy; mem. CMA, Sacramento-El Dorado Med. Soc. (bd. dirs. 1971-95, 1989-95). Avocations: bicycling, book collecting, opera, fencing. Office: 4801 J St Ste A Sacramento CA 95819-3746 Office Phone: 916-456-4782.

NAHAI, FOAD, plastic surgeon, educator; b. Teheran, Iran, Sept. 23, 1943; came to U.S., 1970; m. Shahnaz Mossanen, Aug. 4, 1969; children: Farzad R., Fariba R. BSc with honors, U. Bristol, Eng., 1966, MB ChB, 1969. Diplomate Am. Bd. Surgery, Am. Bd. Plastic Surgery. Med. and surg. intern United Bristol Hosps., 1969-70; intern in surgery Balt. City Hosps., 1970-71; resident in surgery Johns Hopkins Hosp., Balt., 1971-72; resident in gen. surgery Emory U. Affiliated Hosps., Atlanta, 1972-74, chief resident, 1974-75, fellow in hand surgery and microsurgery, 1975-76, resident in plastic surgery, 1976-77; instr. in surgery Emory U., Atlanta, 1975-76, 78, from asst. to assoc. prof., 1978-91, prof., 1991-98; pvt. practice Paces Plastic Surgery, Atlanta, 1998—. Author: (with S.J. Mathes) Clinical Atlas of Muscle and Musculocutaneous Flaps, 1979, Clinical Applications for Muscle and Musculocutaneous Flaps, 1982, (with others) Microvascular Surgery in Reconstruction of the Head and Neck, 1989, Plastic and Reconstructive Breast Surgery, 1990, Grabb's Encyclopedia of Flaps, 1990, (with Bostwick Eaves) Endoscopic Plastic Surgery, 1994, (with S.J. Mathes) Reconstructive Surgery, 1996, others; mem. editl. bd. Annals Plastic Surgery, 1984, Outlook Plastic Surgery, 1988, The Art of Esthetic Surgery, 2005; contbr. articles to profl. jours.; co-prodr. (movies) Breast Reconstruction After a Radical Mastectomy with Latissimus Dorsi Musculocutaneous Flap, 1978, The Tensor Fascia Lata Free Flap, 1979; prodr. (videotapes) TFL Neurosensory Flap for Coverage of Greater Trochanteric and Ischium, Rectus Abdominis Flap for Sternal Coverage, Gastrocnemius Muscle Flap for Coverage of Tibia, others. Recipient Gold Medal Paper Presentation Southeastern Surg. Conf., 1976, Best Paper award Atlanta Clin. Soc., 1980, award Am. Med. Writers Assn., 1983. Fellow ACS (3d Ann. Residents Competition award Ga. chpt. 1977); mem. Am. Assn. Plastic Surgeons (James Barrett Brown award 1982), Am. Soc. Aesthetic Plastic Surgery, Am. Soc. Plastic and Reconstructive Surgeons (rsch. grantee ednl. found.), Ga. Soc. Plastic Surgeons, Med. Assn. Ga., Ga. Surg. Soc., Med. Assn. Atlanta, Southeastern Soc. Plastic and Reconstructive Surgeons (Outstanding Resident award 1977), Internat. Assn. Univ. Plastic Surgeons, Plastic Surgery Rsch. Coun. (program chmn. 1988, chmn. 1989), Brazilian Coll. Surgeons (corr.), Brazilian Soc. Plastic Surgeons, Italian Soc. Plastic, Reconstructive and Aesthetic Surgery, Soc. Residents and Ex Residents of Inst. Reconstructive Surgery (hon.), Sociedad Jaime Planas de Cirurgia Plastica, Internat. Soc. Aesthetic Plastic Surgery (sec. gen. 2000-2004, 2d v.p. 2004—), Am. Soc. Aestetic Plastic Surgery (sec. 2003—). Office: Paces Plastic Surgery 3200 Downwood Cir NW Ste 640 Atlanta GA 30327-1624 Office Phone: 404-351-0051. Business E-Mail: linda@pacesplasticsurgery.com. E-mail: pacesplasticsurgery@aol.com.

NAHAT, DENNIS F., performing company executive, choreographer; b. Detroit, Feb. 20, 1946; s. Fred H. and Linda M. (Haddad) N. Hon. degree, Juilliard Sch. Music, 1965. Prin. dancer Joffrey Ballet, NYC, 1965-66; prin. dancer Am. Ballet Theatre, NYC, 1968-79; co-founder Cleve. Ballet, 1976, Sch. of Cleve. Ballet, 1972; founder, artistic dir. Sch. Cleve. San Jose Ballet, 1996; founder New Sch. of Cleve. San Jose Ballet, 1996—; founder, artistic dir. San Jose Cleve. Ballet (now Ballet San Jose), San Jose, 1985—. Co-chair Artists Round Table Dance USA, 1991; trustee Cecchetti Coun. Am., 1991; mem. adv. bd. Ohio Dance Regional Dance Am.; dir. dance USDAN Ctr. for the Creative Performing Arts, NY, 1999—. Prin. performer Broadway show Sweet Charity, 1966-67; choreographer Two Gentlemen of Verona (Tony award 1972), 1969-70; (ballet) Celebrations and Ode (resolution award 1985), 1985, Green Table, Three Virgins and a Devil (Isadora Duncan award 1985); conceived, directed, choreographed Blue Suede Shoes, PBS, 1997-98. Grantee Nat. Endowment Arts, 1978, Andrew Mellow Found., 1985; recipient Outstanding Achievement award Am. Dance Guild, 1995, 96, 2000—. Avocation: cooking. also: Ballet San Jose PO Box 1666 40 N 1st St San Jose CA 95109-1666 Office Phone: 408-288-2820 Ext.225. Business E-Mail: dnahat@balletsanjose.org. *

NAHATA, BABU L., economics professor, researcher; b. Sardarshahr, Rajasthan, India, June 2, 1944; s. Bhikam Chand and Manohari Nahata; m. Kusum Lodha, Aug. 8, 1949; children: Ritu Nahata Rowland, Rohit. BS, Birla Inst. Tech., Ranchi, India, 1967; MS, Ill. Inst. Tech., Chgo., 1970, Poly. U., Bklyn., 1974; PHD, No. Ill. U., Dekalb, 1977. Prof., co-dir., ctr. emerging market economies U. Louisville, 1978—. Vis. exch. prof. Hiroshima Shudo U., Japan, 1986—87. Fellow, Fukuoka U., Japan, 1992, Japan Soc. Promotion Sci., Tokyo, 1996—97; scholar, Indian Inst. Mgmt., Calcutta, 1989, Fukuoka U., 2000. Mem.: Am. Econ. Assn., Sigma Xi. Office: U Louisville Dept Econs COB Louisville KY 40292 Office Phone: 502-852-4864. Office Fax: 502-852-7672. Business E-Mail: nahata@louisville.edu.

NAHAVANDI, AMIR NEZAMEDDIN, retired engineering firm executive; b. Tehran, Iran, Apr. 6, 1924; arrived in U.S., 1956, naturalized, 1970; s. Ahmad and Fatima Razaghi Nahavandi. Electromech. Engring. degree, Tehran U., 1947; MS in Mech. Engring, Carnegie Inst. Tech., 1957, PhD, 1960. Registered profl. engr., Pa. Engr. Tehran U., 1948-50; head design group Nat. Iranian Oil Co., Tehran, 1950-56; adv. engr. Westinghouse Electric Corp., Pitts., 1957-66; prof., chmn. dept. mech. engring. U. Vt., 1967-68; rsch. prof. N.J. Inst. Tech., 1969-77; prof. engring. and applied Sci. Columbia U., NYC, 1977-81; chief scientist Electronic Assocs., Inc., West Long Branch, NJ, 1981-82; pres. Mazen, Inc., Long Branch, NJ, 1982-92. Decorated Sci. medal Govt. Iran. Fellow ASME; mem. N.Y. Acad. Scis., Phi Kappa Phi, Sigma Xi, Tau Beta Pi. Achievements include development of analytical models for stock market forecasting; research and development in dynamics of steam generators and boiling systems; research in thermal pollution of lakes and rivers; vibration of reactor structures; dynamic and accident analysis of conventional and nuclear power plants; solid-fluid interaction. Home: 7635 Eads Ave Unit 202 La Jolla CA 92037-4832 Personal E-mail: anahav@aol.com.

NAHIGIAN, ROBERT JOHN, real estate company executive, consultant; b. Boston, Feb. 24, 1956; s. John Moses and Theresa (Zeytoundjian) N.; m. Donna P. Dewar, Oct. 23, 1993; children: Jessica Lee, Kimberly Patricia. BA cum laude, Lehigh U., 1978; MS in Urban Planning, Columbia U., 1980. Cert. real estate mediator Mass., FRICS Royal Inst. Chartered Surveyors, 2005. Property mgr. Auburndale (Mass.) Realty Co., 1972-77; jr. planner Bethlehem (Pa.) Redevel. Authority, 1978; planner, tech. analyst Perkins & Will Archtl. Firm, NYC, 1978-80; city planner, econ. developer City of Bowie, Md., 1980-81; v.p. The Norwood Group, Inc., Burlington, Mass., 1981-88; v.p., dir. The Robbins Group, Cambridge, Mass., 1988-89; pres. Auburndale Realty Co., Newton, Mass., 1989—. Dir., lectr. real estate studies Northeastern U., Boston, 1982—93; instr. real estate Boston U., 1994—; lectr., spkr. at convs. in field; Boston U. lectr. U. of Hong Kong Polytech.; 1st SIOR spkr. at Latin America's First Real Estate Conf., Bogota, Colombia, 1998; invited lectr. Czech Republic, Poland; mem. Greater Boston Real Estate Bd. Comml. Broker Assn., Govt. and Agy. Law Task Force Affairs rep., 2002—06; mem. Comml. Overlay State Task Force; apptd. by Gov. Romney Mass. Hwy. Real Estate Rev. Bd., 2004; apptd. chmn. Mass. Realtors Comml. Investment Coun., 2005—06; arbitrator Greater Boston Real Estate Bd. Co-author: Master Office Leasing, 1993, rev. edit., 2000; contbr. articles to profl. jours., Mass. real estate sales exam book. Mem. Wang Ctr. for the Performing Arts, Boston, 1985; mem. presdl. adv. com. on Housing in Mass. Mass. Assn. of Realtors. Recipient Cert. of Appreciation, Exch. Club, 1991, Alumni award Lehigh U., 1993, N.E. Constrn. Show, So. Calif. Constrn. Show, Mex. Nat. Bd. Realtors, 1997, Disting. Achievement in cml. leasing Greater Boston Real Estate Bd., 1999; First Mass. Comml. Broker as Cert. Instr., Banker and Tradesman Top 125 Bus. Leaders in Mass. for 1999, 1st Comml Broker as Cert. Mass. Real Estate Mediator, 2001., Appreciation gift, Corenet Harvard Univ., 2005. Fellow: Royal Inst. Chartered Surveyors; mem.: Greater Boston Assn. Realtors (edn. task force, apptd. govt. affairs com.), Worcester Regional Assn. Realtors (edn. task force), Comml. Brokers Assn. (govt. affairs rep., agy. law task force to Mass. Assn. Realtors 2002—03, bd. dirs. 2002—, 2004—05, coml. overlay state task force study, Broker Achievement Bronze award 2000, Broker Achievement Gold award 2001, Indsl. Deal of Yr. award 2001, Comml. Leasing Achievement Gold award 2001, Adv. Assignment of Yr. 2003, 2004, Appreciation Gift 2005, Adv. Assignment of Yr. 2005), Nat. Assn. Indsl. and Office Parks (New Eng. chpt. membership com. 1993—96, membership com. chmn. 1996, exec. com. 1996, cert. appreciation Mass. chpt.), Am. Soc. Real Estate (counselors of real estate 1996, nat. conv. spkr. 1997, com. mem. nat. edn. com., nat. presdl. task force 1998—2000, vice chmn. pub. rels. com. 1998—2000, nat. spl. task force 2001, nat. chmn. pub. rels. and comm. 2001—02, nat. bd. dirs. 2001—04, CRE sec. New Eng./N.Y. chpt. 2005—07), Soc. Indsl. and Office Realtors (nat. vice chmn. office courses 1993—94, edn. exec. com. 1993—94, nat. regional v.p. 1994—96, nat. exec. com. 1994—96, nat. bd. dir. 1994—96, nat. chmn. instrs. com. 1994—97, nat. chmn. edn. com. 1994—98, ex officio edn. fund 1995—97, nat. chmn. edn. exec. com. 1995—97, nat. nominating com. 1995—98, Presdl. edn. task force 1995—99, bd. dir. New Eng. chpt. 1995—, pres. New Eng. chpt. 1998—99, spl. adv. and immediate past pres. 2000—01, nat. budget and fin. com. 2000—02, v.p. nat. com. programs, nat. convention co-chmn., nat. bd. dirs. 2001, nat. vice chmn. designation courses edn. com., nat. nominating com. 2002, nat. vice chmn faculty com. 2003—04, nat. vice chmn. faculty com. 2006—, site selection and facilty convention planning com. 2006—07, presdl. task force on edn. 2007, sr. instr., instrs. com. and office mktg. forum, task force indsl. office leasing handbook, property evaluation forum, expert roundtable com., Nat. Real Estate Instr. of Yr. 1994, medal of appreciation New Eng. chpt. 1998—99, Appreciation medal New Eng. chpt. 1998—99, Nat. Real Estate Instr. of Yr. 2002, 2003, 2004, cert. appreciation, cert. profl. edn. com., cert. appreciation as outgoing nat. ednl. chair), Mass. Assn. Realtors (com. mem. 2001—, agy. law task force 2003—04, comml. bd. overlay task force 2004, bd. dirs. comml. investment coun. 2005—, govt. affairs com. for CBA), Nat. Assn. Realtors (cert. of appreciation 1992, Mass. mediation officer award 2001), Algonquin Club, Lehigh Club (class '78 pres. 1993—98), Lambda Alpha (bd. dirs. Boston chpt.). Republican. Mem. Armenian Apostolic Ch. Home: 365 Highland St Weston MA 02493-2624 Office: Auburndale Realty Co PO Box 66125 335 Auburn St Newton MA 02466-1902 Home Phone: 781-894-5299; Office Phone: 617-332-6900. Business E-Mail: rob@siorcre.com.

NAHM, WALTER K., dermatologist, researcher; s. James J. and Hyun S. Nahm; m. Lauren S. Sym; 1 child, William J. BA, U. Tex., Austin, 1993; PhD, Baylor Coll., 1996, MD, 1998. Diplomate Am. Bd. Dermatology. Intern Christus St. Joseph Hosp., Houston, 1999; chief resident Boston U. Sch. Medicine, Roger Williams Med. Ctr., 2002; Mohs Micrographic Surgery fellow U. Calif., LA Sch. Medicine, 2003, cosmetic surgery fellow, 2003; staff physician Scripps Mercy Hosp., San Diego, 2003—, VA San Diego Healtcare Sys., 2003—, West LA VA Med. Ctr., 2003—04, Kindred Hosp., San Diego, 2004—05; dir. Mohs Micrographic Surgery U. Calif., San Diego, 2005—. Asst. clin. prof. U. Calif., San Diego Sch. Medicine, 2002—. Editor: PCI Jour. Named Young Investigator of Yr., Tex. Neurol. Soc. Tex. Med., 1997; recipient Excellence in Scholarly Activities award, Boston U. Sch. Medicine, 2002, Citizen's award, 2002; fellow Albert M. Kligman fellow, Soc. for Investigative Dermatology, 2002; grantee, Soc. Investigative Dermatology, 2002. Fellow: AMA (Physician's Recognition award 2005), Am. Soc. for Dermatologic Surgery (Young Investigator's Writing Competition award 2003), Am. Acad. Cosmetic Surgery (membership com. 2005—, Excellence award 2005), Am. Acad. Dermatology (Continuing Med. Edn. award 2005), Am. Coll. Mohs Micrographic Surgery and Cutaneous Oncology, Am. Soc. for Laser Medicine and Surgery; mem.: San Diego Dermatology Soc. (sec.-treas. 2007), Internat. Hyperhidrosis Soc., San Diego County Med. Soc., Calif. Med. Assn., Am. Soc. for Lipo-Sucton Surgery, San Diego Soc. for Dermatologic Surgery (pres. 2006), Soc. for Investigative Dermatology, Am. Soc. Cosmetic Dermatology and Aesthetic Surgery, Phi Beta Kappa. Office: 4060 Fourth Ave Ste 650 San Diego CA 92103 Office Phone: 619-297-1810. Office Fax: 619-297-1881. Personal E-mail: tire99@yahoo.com.

NAHMAD, ALBERT H., manufacturing executive; b. Oct. 15, 1940; m. Jane Davis; 2 children. BS in Mech. Engring., U. N. Mex., 1962; MS in Indsl. Adminstrn., Purdue U., 1963. Mgmt. cons. Arthur Young, NYC; group v.p. W.R. Grace & Co.; chmn. pres., CEO Watsco, Inc., Coconut Grove, Fla., 1973—. Bd. dirs. Am. Bankers Ins. Group, Mayor's Jewelers. Mem. Fla. Coun. 100; chmn. bd. of trustees Miami Children's Hosp.; past chmn. Fla. chpt Young Presidents' Org.; bd. dir. Cmty. Partnership for the Homeless Inc. Mem. Chief Executives Org., World Presidents' Org. Office: Watsco Inc 2665 S Bayshore Dr Ste 901 Miami FL 33133 *

NAHMAN, NORRIS STANLEY, electrical engineer; b. San Francisco, Nov. 9, 1925; s. Hyman Cohen and Rae (Levin) Nahman; m. Shirley D. Maxwell, July 20, 1968; children: Norris Stanley, Vicki L., Vance W., Scott T. BS in Electronics Engring, Calif. Poly. State U., 1951; MSE.E., Stanford U., 1952; PhD in Elec. Engring, U. Kans., 1961. Registered profl. engr., Colo. Electronic scientist Nat. Security Agy., Washington, 1952-55; prof. elec. engring., dir. electronics rsch. lab. U. Kans., Lawrence, 1955-66; sci. cons., chief pulse and time domain sect. Nat. Bur. Stds., Boulder, Colo., 1966-73, chief time domain metrology, sr. scientist, 1975-83, group leader field characterization group, 1984-85; v.p. Picosecond Pulse Labs, Inc., Boulder, 1986-90, scientific advisor, co-chair tech. adv. bd., 1990—; cons. elec. engr., 1990—; prof., chmn. dept. elec. engring. U. Toledo, 1973—75; prof. elec. engring. U. Colo., Boulder, 1966—; affiliate staff Los Alamos Nat. Lab., N.Mex., 1990—2006. Disting. lectr., prin. prof. Ctr. Nat. d'Etudes des Telcom. Summer Sch., Lanion, France, 1978; disting. lectr. Harbin Inst. Tech., China, 1982; mem. faculty NATO Advanced Study Inst., Castelvecchio, Italy, 1983, Internat. Radio Sci. Union/NRC; chmn. Internat. Intercomm. Group Waveform Measurements, 1981—90, Commn. A, 1985—86. Contbr. articles to profl. jours. Asst. scoutmaster Longs Peak coun. Boy Scouts Am., 1970—73, 1975—89. With US Mcht. Marine, 1943—46, with US Army, 1952—55. Recipient Disting. Alumnus award, Calif. Poly. State U., 1972, Order of Arrow, Boy Scouts Am., 1976; Ford Found. Faculty fellow, MIT, 1962, Nat. Bur. Stds. Sr. Staff fellow, 1978—79. Fellow: IEEE (life), Internat. Sci. Radio Union; mem.: Electromagnetic Acad., Am. Assn. Engring. Edn. (life), Instrumentation and Measurement Soc. of IEEE (mem. admnstrv. com. 1982—84, editl. bd. Trans. 1982—86, Andrew H. Chi Best Tech. Paper award 1984, Tech. Leadership and Achievement award 1987), Am. Mcht. Marine Vets., Stanford U. (life), U. Kans. (life), Calif. Poly. State U. Alumni Assn. (life), US Mcht. Marine Vets. World War II (life), Am. Radio Relay League Club (life), Am. Legion, Sigma Xi, Sigma Tau, Eta Kappa Nu, Tau Beta Pi, Sigma Pi Sigma. Achievements include patents in field. Personal E-mail: nsnahman@ieee.org.

NAHMIAS, DAVID E., prosecutor; b. Atlanta, 1964; BA summa cum laude, Duke Univ.; JD magna cum laude, Harvard Univ. Bar: Ga. 1991. Law clerk to Hon. Laurence H. Silberman US Ct. Appeals (DC cir.), 1991—92; law clerk to Justice Antonin Scalia US Supreme Ct., 1992—93; assoc. Hogan & Hartson L.L.P., Washington, 1993—95; asst. US atty. (No. dist.) Ga. US Dept. Justice, Atlanta, 1995—2001, counsel for the asst. atty. gen. criminal divsn. Washington, 2001—03, dep. asst. atty. gen. criminal divsn., 2003—04, US atty. (no. dist.) Ga., 2004—. Editor: Harvard Law Review. Office: US Attys Office 600 US Courthouse 75 Spring St SW Atlanta GA 30303-3309 *

NAHMIAS, MARIA LYNN, education educator; d. Theodore and Alexandra B. Vasiliw; life ptnr. Walter E. Rogers; children: Alysa Jeane, Jeffry Todd. PhD, Northwestern U., Evanston, Ill., 1981. Instr. U. Vt., Burlington, 1975—78; field faculty supr. Goddard Coll., Plainfield, Vt., 1977—78; adj. assoc. prof. U. Ariz., Tucson, 1981—. Cons. Pima CC, Tucson, 2006—07. US Dept. Edn. fellowship, Northwestern U., 1973—75, Project ADEPT grantee, US Dept. Edn., 1992—95, Interstellar Project grantee, 1996—2002, 2002—06. Mem.: Coun. Exceptional Children (pres. so. Ariz. chpt. 1996—97, Cert. Appreciation 2004, 2005), Pi Beta Phi. Home Phone: 520-621-0935; Office Phone: 520-621-7822.

NAHRA, KHALIL SALIM, colon and rectal surgeon; arrived in US, 1965; s. Salim Khalil Nahra and Salwa Tanios Hayek; m. Antoinette Hagop Babayan, Nov. 20, 1965 (dec.); children: Randa, Bertha. BS, Am. U., Beirut, 1957, MD, 1961. Diplomate Am. Bd. Surgery, Am. Bd. Colon and Rectal Surgery, lic. Lebanon. Intern Am. U. Hosp., Beirut, 1960—61, resident in surgery, 1961—65, NYU Med. Centre, Bellview Hosp., 1965—66; resident in cancer surgery Meml. Hosp. Cancer & Allied Disease, NYC, 1966—67; rsch. fellow in colon & rectal surgery Lahey Clinic Found., Boston, 1967—68; fellow in colon & rectal surgery St. Marks Hosp., London, 1968—69; clin. instr. Am. U., Beirut, 1969—75; attending staff divsn. colon & rectal surgery Lahey Clinic, Boston, 1975—77; asst. clin. prof. Am. U. Med. Ctr., Beirut, 1977—84; attending staff St. Mary Hosp. Livonia, Mich., 1984—, Sinai Hosp. Detroit, 1985—97, U. Mich., 1997—. Contbr. articles to profl. jours. Fellow: ACS, Am. Soc. Colon and Rectal Surgery; mem.: Crohn's and Colitis Found. Am., Detroit Surg. Assn., Oakland County Med. Soc., Mich. State Med. Soc., Internat. Acad. Proctology, Mich. Soc. Colon and Rectal Surgeons, Lebanese Surg. Soc., Lebonese Med. Soc., Am. U. Beirut Alumni Surg. Soc. N.Am. Office: 19335 Merriman Rd Livonia MI 48152

NAHRA, LYNDA J., bank executive; b. 1951; Gard., Calf. Western U., Pacific Coast Banking School. Various positions Bank of America; management Community West Bancshares, Goleta, Calif., 1997—, pres., CEO, 2000—. Dir. Women's Economic Ventures; mem., Loan Com. Community West Bancshares, mem., Asset/Liability Com., mem., Compliance Com., mem., Mgmt. Succession Com. Mem. United Way, Santa Barbara; mem., Fin. Com. Goleta Montessori Ctr. Sch. Named one of 25 Women to Watch, US Banker, 2006. Mem.: Montecito Rotary Club. Office: c/o Community West Bank 5827 Hollister Avenue Goleta CA 93117 *

NAHRSTADT, BRADLEY CHARLES, lawyer; b. Elmhurst, Ill., Oct. 21, 1967; s. William Charles and Agnes (Girvan) Nahrstadt; m. Debra Lee Snyderman, Aug. 16, 1992. BA, Monmouth Coll., 1989; JD, U. Ill., Champaign. Bar: Ill. 1992. Assoc. Williams Montgomery & John Ltd., Chgo., 1992—2001, ptnr., 2001—. Co-author: Advanced Civil Discovery for the Litigation Paralegal in Illinois, 2002, Litigation Case Management for the Illinois Paralegal, 2002, Litigation Management Techniques for the Litigation Paralegal in Illinois, 2002, Challenges in Illinois Insurance Coverage Litigation, 2004; editor: Illinois Product Liability Practice, 2005; contbr. chapters to books, articles to profl. jours. Mem. bd. trustees Monmouth Coll., 2002—. Named Outstanding Alumni, Monmouth Coll., 2000, One of 40 Ill. Attys. under 40 to Watch, Chgo. Daily Bulletin, 2006. Master: Chgo.-Lincoln Inn Ct.; mem.: Ill. Assn. Def. Trial Counsel (comml. litig. com.), Ill. State Bar Assn., Def. Rsch. Inst. (comml. litig., trial tactics and electronic discovery com.), Am. Judicature Soc. Office: Williams Montgomery John Ltd 20 N Wacker Dr Ste 2100 Chicago IL 60606

NAHRWOLD, DAVID LANGE, surgeon, educator; b. St. Louis, Dec. 21, 1935; s. Elmer William and Magdalen Louise (Lange) Nahrwold; m. Carolyn Louise Hoffman, June 14, 1958; children: Stephen Michael, Susan Alane, Thomas James, Anne Elizabeth. AB, Ind. U., Bloomington, 1957; MD, Ind. U., Indpls., 1960. Diplomate Am. Bd. Surgery, Am. Bd. Thoracic Surgery. Intern, then resident in surgery Ind. U. Med. Ctr., Indpls., 1960-65; postdoctoral scholar in gastrointestinal physiology VA Ctr., UCLA, 1965; asst. prof. surgery Ind. U. Med. Sch., 1968-70; assoc. prof. Coll. Medicine Pa. State U., 1970-73; vice-chmn. dept. surgery Pa. State U., 1971-82, assoc. provost, dean health affairs, 1981-82, prof., chief divsn. gen. surgery, 1974-82; Loyal and Edith Davis prof., chmn. dept. surgery Northwestern U. Med. Sch., Chgo., 1982-97; surgeon-in-chief Northwestern Meml. Hosp., Chgo., 1982-97; pres., CEO Northwestern Med. Faculty Found., Inc., 1996-99; prof. surgery, exec. assoc. dean clin. affairs Northwestern U. Med. Sch., 1997-99, prof. emeritus, 1999—. Mem. Nat. Digestive Disease Adv. Bd., 1985—89; bd. dirs. Am. Bd. Surgery, vice chmn., 1994—95, chmn., 1995—96; bd. dirs. Northwestern Healthcare Network, Am. Bd. Med. Specialties, 1997—2005, pres., 2002—04; mem. exec. com. Accreditation Coun. for Grad. Med. Edn., 1999—2000; bd. commrs. Joint Commn. Accreditation Healthcare Orgns., 2002—, vice chmn. bd. commrs., 2005—06, chmn. bd. commrs., 2007—; bd. dirs. Joint Commn. Resources, 2004—, vice chmn. bd. dirs., 2005—06. Editor emeritus Jour. Laparoendoscopic Surgery, 1997-2004; mem. editl. bd. Surgery, 1981-94, Archives of Surgery, 1983-93, Digestive Surgery, 1986-99, Am. Jour. Surgery, 1994-2000, Jour. Gastrointestinal Surgery, 1996-2000, Current Opinion in Gen. Surgery, Jour. Lithotripsy and Stone Disease, 1988-92; contbr. articles to profl. jours. With MC US Army, 1966—68. Recipient John P. Hubbard award, Nat. Bd. Med. Examiners, 2003. Fellow: ACS (bd. govs. 1992—98, vice chmn. 1994—96, chmn. bd. govs. exec. com. 1996—98, interim dir. 1999—2000, 1st v.p. elect 2005—06, 1st v.p. 2007—, bd. regents, Disting. Svc. award 2001), Philippine Coll. Surgeons (hon.); mem.: AMA, Chgo. Surg. Soc. (pres. 1993—94), Chgo. Med. Soc., We. Surg. Assn., Soc. Univ. Surgeons, Soc. Surgery Alimentary Tract (pres. 1989—90, trustee), Soc. Clin. Surgery (sec. 1984—88), Internat. Biliary Assn., Ill. Surg. Soc., Ill. State Med. Soc., Internat. Fedn. Surg. Colls. (hon.; treas. 1999—2002), Gastroenterology Rsch. Group, Collegium Internat. Chirurgiae Digestive (pres. U.S. chpt. 1988—90), Ctrl. Surg. Assn. (sec. 1994—97, pres.-elect 1997—98, pres. 1998—99, pres. Found. 2002—03), Assn. Surg. Edn., Assn. Acad. Surgery, Am. Surg. Assn. (2d v.p. 1993—94), Am. Phys. Soc., Alpha Omega Alpha, Sigma Xi. Office: Dept Surgery Galter 10-105 251 E Huron St Chicago IL 60611-2908 Home Phone: 847-714-1143; Office Phone: 312-695-4908. Business E-Mail: dnahrwol@nmh.org.

NAIDICH, THOMAS PAUL, neuroradiologist, educator; b. Bklyn., Apr. 8, 1944; s. James and Rose (Bitko) N.; m. Rochele Miriam Pudlowksi, Feb. 2, 1975 (div. Nov. 1981); children: 1 child, Sandra Rebecca; m. Michele W. Levin, Dec. 29, 1990. BA, Cornell U., 1965; MD, NYU, NY, 1969. Diplomate in radiology and in neuroradiology Am. Bd. Radiology. Intern Bronx Mcpl. Hosp. Ctr., NY, 1969-70; resident in radiology Montefiore Hosp., Bronx, NY, 1970-73; fellow in neuroradiology NYU Sch. Medicine, NY, 1973-75; prof. radiology and neurosurgery Mt. Sinai Med. Ctr. NYU, NY, 1998—, dir. neuroradiology NY, 1998—, vice chmn. radiology for acad. affairs, 2001—, Irving and Dorothy Regenstreif Rsch. prof. of neurosci., 2002—; asst. prof. Albert Einstein Coll. Medicine, Bronx, NY, 1975-77; from asst. prof. to assoc. prof. Mallinckrodt Inst. Radiology, St. Louis, 1978-80; from assoc. prof. to prof. Northwestern U. Sch. Medicine, Chgo., 1980-88; clin. prof. neuroradiology U. Miami Sch. Med., Fla., 1988-98; dir. neuroradiology Bapt. Hosp. Miami, Fla., 1988-98; dir Clin. Imaging Rsch. Core, Mt. Sinai Med. Ctr., Mt. Sinai, NY, 2001—05. Author: (with R. M. Quencer) Clinical Neurosonography, 1987; (with Valavanis, Schubiger) Clinical Imaging of the Cerebello-Pontine Angle, 1987; (with Daniels, Haughton) Cranial and Spinal Magnetic Ressonance Imaging, 1987, (with Duvernoy, Cattin, Fatterpeker, Raybaud, Risold, Salvolini, Scarabino) The Human Hippocampus, Anatomy, Vascularization and Serial Sections with MRAI, 3d edit., 2005; editor-in-chief Neuroradiology, 1980-91, chmn. editl. bd., 1991-93; assoc. editor Surg. and Radiol. Anatomy, 1991-97; founding editor Internat. Jour. Neuroradiology, 1994-00; contbr. articles to profl. jours. Recipient John Caffey award Soc. Pediatric Radiology, 1983. Mem. Am. Soc. Neuroradiology (treas. 1991-93, Cornelius Dyke award 1975), Am. Soc. Pediatric Neuroradiology (pres. 1994-95, Gold medal), Sociedad Ibero-latino Americana de Neurorradiologia (SILAN, Gold medal), European Soc. Neuroradiology (hon.), Brit. Soc. Neuroradiologists (hon.), Swiss Soc. Neuroradiology (hon.). Avocation: antique furniture. Office: Mt Sinai Med Ctr Dept Radiology Box 1234 1 Gustave Levy Pl New York NY 10029 Business E-Mail: thomas.naidich@mountsinai.org.

NAIDORF, LOUIS MURRAY, architect; b. LA, Aug. 15, 1928; s. Jack and Meriam (Abbott) N.; m. Dorise D. Roberts, June 1948 (div.); children: Victoria Beth Naidorf; m. Patricia Ann Shea, June 1, 1968 (div.); m. Patricia Ruth Allen, Dec. 6, 1992 (dec.); m. Sandra Chronis, Apr. 20, 2004. BA, U. Calif., Berkeley, 1949, MA, 1950; Doctorate (hon.), Woodbury U., 2000. Registered architect, Calif. Designer Welton Becket Assocs., LA, 1950-51, Pereira and Luckman, LA, 1951-52; project designer Welton Becket Assocs., LA, 1952-55, sr. project designer, 1955-59, v.p. asst., dir. design, 1959-70, sr. v.p., dir. rsch., 1970-73; sr. v.p., design prin. Ellerbe Becket Assocs., LA, 1973-95; dean Sch. Architecture and Design Woodbury U., LA, 1990-2000; prin. Allen/Naidorf Design Cons., 1995—. Mem. peer rev. panel Nat. Endowment Arts, 1995—; vis. lectr. Calif. Poly. Sch. Architecture, San Luis Obispo, 1975-82; instr. UCLA Sch. Architecture, 1985, UCLA Landscape Archtl. Program, 1980-85, Otis-Parsons, L.A., 1986-92. Prin. works include Capitol Records Bldg., Century City, Los Angeles, Hyatt Regency, Dallas, Restoration Calif. State Capitol Bldg. Bd. dir. Inst. for Garden Studies, L.A., 1986—, ARC, 2000; trustee Woodbury U., 2000. Recipient Honor award Nat. Trust for Hist. Preservation, 1985. Fellow AIA (bd. dir. L.A. chpt. 1977-79, Silver Medal 1950, Nat. Honor award 1985, Educator of Yr. 1997, Legacy award, 2005). Personal E-mail: naidorf@msn.com. *Leadership often requires decisions based on limited information. Course corrections can be made but only after action is taken because you can't steer a car that isn't moving.*

NAIFEH, STEVEN WOODWARD, writer; b. Tehran, Iran, June 19, 1952; s. George Amel and Marion (Lamphear) N. AB, Princeton U., 1974; JD, Harvard U., 1977, MA, 1978. Staff lectr. Nat. Gallery Art, Washington, 1976; assoc. Milbank, Tweed, Hadley & McCloy, NYC, 1976; v.p. Sabbagh, Naifeh and Assocs., Washington, 1980; co-founder & editor Woodward/White, Inc. (publishers of Best Lawyers in Am., Best Doctors in Am., Best Dentists in Am.), Aiken, SC, 1981. Author: Culture Making: Money, Success and the New York Art World, 1976; (with Gregory White Smith) Moving Up in Style, 1980, Gene Davis, 1981, How to Make Love to a Woman, 1982, What Every Client Needs to Know About Using a Lawyer, 1982, The Bargain Hunter's Guide to Art Collecting, 1982, Why Can't Men Open Up?: Overcoming Men's Fear of Intimacy, 1984, The Mormon Murders: A True Story of Greed, Forgery, Deceit, and Death, 1988, Jackson Pollack: An American Saga, 1989 (Nat. Book award nomination for nonfiction 1990, Pulitzer Prize for biography 1991), Final Justice: The True Story of the Richest Man Ever Tried for Murder, 1993, A Stranger in the Family: A True Story of Murder, Madness, and Unconditional Love, 1995, On a Street Called Easy, In a Cottage Called Joye, 1996, Making Miracles Happen, 1997; editor: (with Smith) The Best Lawyers in America series, The Best Doctors in America series, The Best Dentists in America series. Office: Woodward White Inc 129 First Ave SW Aiken SC 29801

NAIK, SAJO P., physicist, researcher; b. Goa, India, May 1, 1970; s. Pandharinath and Sarita Naik; m. Vinita Naik, Dec. 21, 2003; 1 child, Yasheta. BS, Goa U., 1991, MS, 1993, PhD, 1998. Lectr. St. Xaviers Coll., Mapusa, India, 1993—2001; rsch. scientist Nat. Ctrl. U., Chung-Li, Taiwan, 2001—03, U. Tokyo, 2003—05; rsch. assoc. Clarkson U., Potsdam, NY, 2005—. Patentee in field. Fellow, Univ. Grants Comn. India, 1996. Mem.: Materials Rsch. Soc. Singapore (assoc.). Office: Clarkson U Dept Physics 8 Clarkson Ave Potsdam NY 13699

NAIK, SAMEER VIJAYKUMAR, mechanical engineer, educator; arrived in U.S., 1998; s. Vijaykumar and Vijaya Naik. BSME, U. Bombay, India, 1997; MSME, Purdue U., West Lafayette, Ind., 2000; PhD, Purdue U., 2004. Grad. rsch. asst. Purdue U., West Lafayette, Ind., 1998—2004, vis. asst. prof., 2004—, sr. rsch. assoc., 2007. Finalist Chorafas award, Dmitris A. Chorafas Found., 2004; recipient Top Grad. Gold medal, U. Bombay, 1997. Mem.: AIAA, ASME, Am. Phys. Soc., Am. Soc. Engring. Edn., Am. Chem. Soc., The Combustion Inst., Optical Soc. Am. Office: Purdue Univ Mech Engring 585 Purdue Mall West Lafayette IN 47907-2088 Office Phone: 765-494-6552. Business E-Mail: naiks@ecn.purdue.edu.

NAIL, KATHY SUE See CAPSHAW, KATE

NAIL, PHIL, information technology executive; m. Sherry Nail. Co-founder, chief tech. officer, eco-green tech. internet provider Affordable Internet Svcs. Online, Inc. (AISO), Romoland, Calif. Named one of Top 25 Chief Tech. Officers, InfoWorld mag., 2007. Achievements include founding a 100% completely solar powered hosting company that does not use energy credits, and its solar panels not only power its offices but the data center and servers (since 2001). Office: AISO 25655 Louisa Ln Romoland CA 92585

NAÍM, MOISES, editor; MS, PhD, Mass. Inst. Tech. Formerly prof., dean Instituto de Estudios Superiores de Administración; exec. dir. World Bank; chmn., Latin Am. Carnegie Endowment for Internat. Peace; min. industry and trade Venezuela; now publ., editor Foreign Policy Mag. Mem. internat. bd. econ. Time Mag.; writer Fin. Times; chmn. Group of 50. Contbr. articles to numerous profl. pubs.; author: The Lost Continent, Illicit. Recipient Editorial award 100,000-250,000 circulation, Nat. Mag. awards, Am. Soc. Mag. Editors, 2007. Office: Foreign Policy Mag 1779 Massachusetts Avenue NW Washington DC 20036 *

NAIMARK, GEORGE MODELL, marketing and management consultant; b. NYC, Feb. 5, 1925; s. Myron S. and Mary (Modell) N.; m. Helen Anne Wythes, June 24, 1946; children: Ann, Richard, Jane. BS, Bucknell U., 1947, MS, 1948; PhD, U. Del., 1951. Rsch. biochemist Brush Devel. Co., Cleve., 1951; dir. quality control Strong, Cobb & Co., Inc., Cleve., 1951-54; dir. sci. svcs. White Labs., Inc., Kenilworth, NJ, 1954-60; v.p. Burdick Assocs., Inc., NYC, 1960-66; pres. Rajah Press, Summit, NJ, 1963—, Naimark and Barba, Inc., Florham Park, NJ, 1966—, Naimark & Assocs., Inc., Florham Park, NJ, 1994—; dir. Alteon, Inc., 2000—06. Author: A Patent Manual for Scientists and Engineers, 1961, Communications on Communication, 1971, 3d edit., 1987, A Man Called Skeeter, 1996, How To Be a Truly Rotten Boss, 2006, Cleaning Out My Attic, 2006, Adamant Eve Alias Myrtle Reed, 2006, How to be a Truly Rotten Driver, 2007; patentee in field; contbr. articles in profl. jours. With USNR, 1944-46. Fellow AAAS, Am. Inst. Chemists; mem. Am. Chem. Soc., N.Y. Acad. Scis., Am. Mktg. Assn. Home: 87 Canoe Brook Pky Summit NJ 07901-1404 Office: Naimark & Barba Inc 248 Columbia Tpke Ste 1 Florham Park NJ 07932-1210 Home Phone: 908-273-8725.

NAIMI, SHAPUR, cardiologist, educator; b. Tehran, Iran, Mar. 28, 1928; came to U.S., 1959; s. Mohsen and Mahbuba (Naim) n.; m. Amy Cabot Simonds, May 11, 1963; children: Timothy Simonds, Susan Lyman, Cameron Lowell. MB, ChB, Birmingham U., Eng., 1953. Diplomate Royal Coll. Physicians (London), Royal Coll. Physicians (Edinburgh), Am. Bd. Internal Medicine (subsplty. bd.cardiovascular disease). House physician Royal Postgrad. Med. Sch. London, 1955; sr. house officer Inst. Diseases of the Chest, London, 1956; fellow in grad. tng. New Eng. Med. Ctr. and MIT, 1961-64; cardiologist Tufts New Eng. Med. Ctr., Boston, 1966—, dir. intensive CCU, 1973—2001, assoc. prof., 1970-93, prof., 1993—. Contbr. articles to profl. jours. Fellow royal Coll. Physicians (Edinburgh), ACP, Am. Coll. Cardiology; mem. Am. Soc. Exptl. Biology and Medicine, AHA, Mass. Med. Soc., Country Brookline, Cohaset Yacht. Home: 265 Woodland Rd Chestnut Hill MA 02467-2204 also: 55 Lothrop Ln Cohasset MA 02025-1425 Office: 750 Washington St Boston MA 02111-1526

NAIMOLI, VINCENT JOSEPH, diversified financial services company executive; b. Paterson, NJ, Sept. 16, 1937; s. Ralph A. and Margaret R. (Calabrese) N.; children— Christine, Tory Ann, Alyson, Lindsey. BSM.E., U. Notre Dame, 1959; MSM.E., N.J. Inst. Tech., 1962; MBA, Fairleigh Dickinson U., 1964; grad. Advanced Mgmt. Program, Harvard Bus. Sch., 1974. With Continental Group, 1965-77, v.p., gen. mgr. ops., 1975-77; pres., chief oper. officer Allegheny Beverage Corp., Balt., 1977-78; sr. v.p., group exec. Jim Walter Corp., Tampa, Fla., 1978-81; group v.p. packaging Anchor Hocking Corp., Lancaster, Ohio, 1981-83; chmn. bd., pres., chief exec. officer Anchor Glass Container Corp., Lancaster, 1983-89; chmn., pres., CEO Anchor Industries Internat., Tampa, Fla., 1990—; chmn., chief exec. officer Electrolux Corp., Atlanta, 1990-91; chmn., CEO Doehler Jarvis Corp., Toledo, 1991-95; CEO Ladish, Inc., Milw., 1992-95; chmn., pres., CEO Harvard Industries, 1993-97; mng. gen. ptnr., CEO Tampa Bay Devil Rays, 1992—2005, chmn., 2006—. Bd. dirs. Strategic Materials, Inc. Roman Catholic. Office: Anchor Industries Internat 1 Tropicana Dr Saint Petersburg FL 33705-1703

NAIR, KRISHNAKUMAR R., application developer, researcher; b. Trivandrum, Kerala, India; arrived in U.S., 1990; s. Raghavan N.S. and Vijayamma R. Nair; m. Shyama R. Nair; 1 child, Srijith K. BS, U. Kerala, 1980; M of Tech., Cochin U. Sci & Tech., 1988; MS, U. Ill., Chgo., 1994. Mem. rsch. and devel. group Ctrl. Electrochem. Rsch. Inst., Karaikudi, India, 1983-90; computer cons. U. Ill., Chgo., 1990-95; from engring. intern to sr. engring. program mgr. Motorola, Inc., Boynton Beach, Fla., 1995—2005, sr. engring. program mgr., 2005—; mem. tech. staff Lucent Techs., Naperville, Ill., 1996. Referee, reviewer tech. articles Motorola, Jours., Confs. Contbr. more than 30 articles to profl. jours. Fellow: Inst. Engrs. India; mem.: AAAS, IEEE (sr.), Assn. Computing Machinery. Avocations: reading, sports, coin collecting/numismatics. Home: 4327 Juniper Ter Boynton Beach FL 33436-3024 Office: Motorola 8000 W Sunrise Blvd Plantation FL 33322-4104 Personal E-mail: kknair@hotmail.com.

NAIR, LAURA, retired music educator; d. John Henry and Elizabeth Richards Nair. MusB, Ohio Wesleyan U., Delaware, 1973. Music tchr. Saratoga Springs City Schs., NY, 1973—2007; coord. music ministries Shenendehowa United Meth. Ch., Clifton Park, NY, 1979—. Music camp dir. Skye Farm Camps, Warrensburg, NY, 1976—2006. Nominating com. mem. Troy Ann. Conf., United Meth. Ch., Saratoga Springs. Mem.: NY State United Tchrs., Choristers' Guild, Fellowship of United Methodists in Music and Worship Arts, Am. Choral Dirs.' Assn., Music Educators' Nat. Conf., Chi Omega (rush chairperson 1972—73). Methodist. Avocations: travel, golf, swimming. Home: 42 Chatsworth Way Clifton Park NY 12065 Office: Shenendehowa United Meth Ch 971 Rte 146 Clifton Park NY 12065 Home Phone: 518-788-0059; Office Phone: 518-371-7964. Office Fax: 518-373-9601. Business E-Mail: lauri@shenmeth.org.

NAIR, MIRA, film director, film producer; b. Bhubaneshwar, Orissa, India, Oct. 15, 1957; m. Mahmood Mamdani; 1 child, Zohran. Student, U. New Delhi, Harvard U. Dir., prodr. (films) Salaam Bombay, 1988 (Camera d'Or and Prix du Publique, Cannes Film Festival, Acad. Award nominee for Best Fgn. Lang. Film), Mississippi Masala, 1991 (three awards at Venice Film Festival), Kama Sutra: A Tale of Love, 1996, Monsoon Wedding, 2001 (Golden Lion Award, Venice Film Festival); dir. only (films) Jama Masjid Street Journal, 1979, So Far From India, 1982, The Perez Family, 1995, September 11, 2002, Vanity Fair, 2004; prodr. only (films) Still, the Children Are Here, 2004; dir. (TV movies) India Cabaret, 1985 (American Film Festival Award for Best Documentary of 1985), Children of a Desired Sex, 1987, My Own Country, 1998, The Laughing Club of India, 1999, Hysterical Blindness, 2002. Office: Mirabi Films Inc 5 E 16th St 12th Fl New York NY 10003

NAIR, R. SHANKAR, structural engineer; PhD in Civil Engring., U. Ill., Urbana-Champaign. Prin. Alfred Benesch & Co., Chgo., KKBNA Inc., RTKL Associates Inc., Balt.; prin., sr. v.p. Teng & Associates, Inc. Past chmn. Coun. on Tall Buildings, Urban Habitat. Contbr. articles to profl. jours. Mem.: NAE. Office: Teng & Assocs Ste 3600 205 N Michigan Ave Chicago IL 60601

NAIR, RAMACHANDRAN P.K., agroforestry educator, researcher; b. Trivandrum, Kerala, India, Mar. 12, 1942; came to U.S., 1987. s. Krishna Kittu Pillai and Parukutty Amma; m. Vimala Devi Pillai, Aug. 29, 1973; children: Bindu, Deepa, Rekha. BS in Agr., Kerala Agrl. U., 1961, MS in Agr., 1968; PhD, Pantnagar U., India, 1971; DSc in Agr., U. Goettingen, W. Germany, 1978; DSc (hon.), Kyoto U., 2002, U. Sci. and Tech., Kumasi, Ghana, 2005, U. Guelph, Ont., Can., 2006. Research asst. Kerala Agrl. U., 1961-66, lectr. in agronomy, 1966; post-doctoral fellow Rothamsted Experimental Sta., Harpenden, Eng., 1971-72; agronomist ICAR (CPCRI), Kasaragod, Kerala, 1972-76; Humboldt fellow U. Goettingen, 1976-78; prin. sci. Internat. Centre for Rsch. in Agroforestry, Nairobi, Kenya, 1978-87; prof. agroforestry U. Fla., Gainesville, 1987-2001, Disting. prof., 2001—. Cons., rschr. numerous orgns. Author: Intensive Multiple Cropping with Coconuts in India, 1979, Agroforestry Species: A Crop Sheets Manual, 1980, Soil Productivity Aspects of Agroforestry, 1984, An Introduction to Agroforestry, 1993; co-editor: Agroforestry: A Decade of Developments, 1987, Directions in Tropical Agroforestry Research, 1998, New Vistas in Agroforestry, 2004, Tropical Homegardens, 2006; editor: Agroforestry Systems in the Tropics, 1989, Agroforestry Systems, 1982—, chief editor, 1994. Recipient Internat. Soil Sci. award, 2001, Internat. Agronomy award, 2000, Internat. Crop Sci. award, 2004, Disting. Internat. Educator, U. Fla., 2004, Sci. Achievement award, Internat. Union of Forest Rsch. Orgns., 2005, Advisor/Mentoring award, U. Fla., 2006, Humboldt prize, Germany, 2006. Fellow AAAS, Am. Soc. Agronomy (chair divsn. A-6 internat. agronomy 1995-96), Nat. Acad. Agrl. Scis. India, Soil Sci. Soc. Am.; mem. Internat. Soil Sci. Soc., Internat. Soc. Tropical Foresters, Soc. Am. Foresters (Barington-Moore award, 2004). Office: U Fla 118 Newins Ziegler Hall Gainesville FL 32611-0410 E-mail: pknair@ufl.edu.

NAIR, VELAYUDHAN, pharmacologist, educator, academic administrator; arrived in U.S., 1956, naturalized, 1963; m. Jo Ann Burke, Nov. 30, 1957; children: David, Larry, Sharon. PhD in Medicine, U. London, 1956, DSc, 1976, LHD (hon.) h.c., 2003. Rsch. assoc. U. Ill. Coll. Medicine, 1956-58; asst. prof. U. Chgo. Sch. Medicine, 1958-63; dir. lab. neuropharmacology and biochemistry Michael Reese Hosp. and Med. Ctr., Chgo., 1963-68, dir. therapeutic rsch., 1968-71; prof. pharmacology FUHS/Chgo. Med. Sch., 1971—, disting. prof., 2001, vice chmn. dept. pharmacology and therapeutics, 1971—76, dean Sch. Grad. and Postdoctoral Studies, 1976—2003, v.p. rsch., 1999—2003, v.p., dean emeritus, 2003—, disting. prof., 2001. Vis. assoc. prof. pharmacology FUHS/Chgo. Med. Sch., 1963—68, vis. prof., 1968—71, Harvard U., 1994, Johns Hopkins Sch. Medicine, 1995. Contbr. articles to profl. jours. Recipient Morris Parker award, U. Health Scis./Chgo. Med. Sch., 1972. Fellow: AAAS, Am. Coll. Clin. Pharmacology, NY Acad. Scis.; mem.: AAUP, Internat. Soc. Devel. Neurosci., Am. Coll. Toxicology, Internat. Soc. Chronobiology, Soc. Neurosci., Soc. Exptl. Biology & Medicine, Pan Am. Med. Assn. (coun. on toxicology), Royal Inst. Chemistry (London), Brit. Chem. Soc., Am. Chem. Soc., Soc. Toxicology, Radiation Rsch. Soc., Am. Soc. Clin. Pharmacology & Therapeutics, Am. Soc. Pharmacology & Exptl. Therapeutics, Internat. Soc. Biochem. Pharmacology, Internat. Brain Rsch. Orgn., Cosmos Club (Washington), Alpha Omega Alpha, Sigma Xi. Office: Rosalind Franklin Univ Medicine and Sci 3333 Green Bay Rd North Chicago IL 60064-3037 Personal E-mail: velnair@comcast.net. *Success like happiness is relative and can only be gauged by one's own standards and ideals. There is probably no universal formula for either of them, but I have been guided by the following tenets: Dedication and committment to one's responsibilities and in the conduct of everyday life, honesty and sincerity in personal relations. One must have tolerance for those in less fortunate situations. As one grows older, one recognizes that no one makes it alone. As for me, I have received help from many; some of whom I can never repay except by passing on the gift which I was privileged to share. Above all, a faith that looks beyond the immediate helps to bear the inevitable ups and downs in life.*

NAIR, VELUPILLAI KRISHNAN, cardiologist; b. Kerala, India, Dec. 30, 1941; came to U.S., 1973; s. Veupillai and Bharathy Nair; m. Sathy C. Nair, Apr. 22, 1971; children: Parvathy, Pradeep. BSc, Kerala U., Trivandum, India, 1961, MB BS, 1965, MD, 1971. Diplomate Am. Bd. Internal Medicine, Am. Bd. Cardiology. Intern, resident, fellow in cardiology Bergen Pines County Hosp., Paramus, NJ; asst. prof. N.Y. Med. Coll. Lincoln Hosp., Bronx, 1979-80; cardiologist, dir. cardiology svc. Somerset (Pa.) Hosp., 1980—, chief of med. dental staff, 1990-93. V.p. bd. dirs. Somerset Hosp., 1997, Somerset Health Svcs., 2000—; clin. asst. prof. Drexel U. Coll. Medicine, 1996—; bd. dirs. Somerset Hosp., 1993—99, 2000—. Former pres. Somerset County divsn. Am. Heart Assn.; bd. dirs. Somerset Hosp. Fellow ACP, Am. Coll. Cardiology; mem. AMA, Pa. Med. Soc., Somerset County Med. Soc. (former pres.), Soc. Hypertension, Soc. Echocardiography, Cardiac Club (advisor). Avocations: reading, tennis, travel. Office: 223 S Pleasant Ave Somerset PA 15501-2188 Office Phone: 814-445-7101. E-mail: vknair@pol.net.

NAJARIAN, JOHN SARKIS, surgeon, educator; b. Oakland, Calif., Dec. 22, 1927; s. Garabed L. and Siranoush T. (Demirjian) N.; m. Arlys Viola Mignette Anderson, Apr. 27, 1952; children: Jon, David, Paul, Peter. AB with honors, U. Calif., Berkeley, 1948; MD, U. Calif., San Francisco, 1952; LHD (hon.), U. Athens, 1980; DSc (hon.), Gustavus Adolphus Coll., 1981; LHD (hon.), Calif. Luth. Coll., 1983. Diplomate Am. Bd. Surgery. Surg. intern U. Calif., San Francisco, 1952-53, surg. resident, 1955-60, asst. prof. surgery, dir. surg. research labs., chief transplant service dept. surgery, 1963-66, prof., vice chmn., 1966-67; spl. research fellow in immunopathology U. Pitts. Med. Sch., 1960-61; NIH sr. fellow and assoc. in tissue transplantation immunology Scripps Clinic and Research Found., La Jolla, Calif., 1961-63; Markle scholar Acad. Medicine, 1964-69; prof., chmn. dept. surgery U. Minn. Hosp., Mpls., 1967-93; med. dir. Transplant Ctr., clin. chief surgery Univ. Hosp., 1967-94; chief hosp. staff U. Minn. Hosp., Mpls., 1970-71, Regents' prof., 1985-95, Jay Phillips Disting. Chair in Surgery, 1986-95, prof. emeritus, prof. surgery, 1995—. Spl. cons. USPHS, NIH Clin. Rsch. Tng. Com., Inst. Gen. Med. Scis., 1965-69; cons. U.S. Bur. Budget, 1966-68; mem. sci. adv. bd. Nat. Kidney Found., 1968; mem. surg. study sect. A div. rsch. grants NIH, 1970; chmn. renal transplant adv. group VA Hosps., 1971; mem. bd. sci. cons. Sloan-Kettering Inst. Cancer Rsch., 1971-78; mem. screening com. Dernham Postdoctoral Fellowships in Oncology, Calif. div. Am. Cancer Soc. Editor: (with Richard L. Simmons) Transplantation, 1972; co-editor: Manual of Vascular Access, Organ Donation, and Transplantation, 1984; mem. editorial bd. Jour. Surg. Rsch., 1968—, Minn. Medicine, 1968—, Jour. Surg. Oncology, 1968—, Am. Jour. Surgery, 1967—, assoc. editor, 1982—; mem. editorial bd. Year Book of Surgery, 1970-85, Transplantation, 1970—, Transplantation Procs, 1970—, Bd. Clin. Editors, 1981-84, Annals of Surgery, 1972—, World Jour. Surgery, 1976—, Hippocrates, 1986—, Jour. Transplant Coordination, 1990—; assoc. editor: Surgery, 1971; editor-in-chief: Clin. Transplantation, 1986—. Bd. dirs., v.p. Variety Club Heart Hosp., U. Minn.; trustee, v.p. Minn. Med. Found. Served with USAF, 1953-55. Hon. fellow Royal Coll. Surgeons of Eng., 1987; hon. prof. U. Madrid, 1990; named Alumnus of Yr., U. Calif. Med. Sch., San Francisco, 1977; recipient award Calif. Trudeau Soc., 1962, Ann. Brotherhood award NCCJ, 1978, Disting. Achievement award Modern Medicine, 1978, Internat. Gt. Am. award B'nai B'rith Found., 1982, Uncommon Citizen award, 1985, Sir James Carreras award Variety Clubs Internat., 1987, Silver medal IXth Centenary, U. Bologna, 1988, Humanitarian of Yr. award, U. Minn., 1992, Najarian Festschrift award Am. Jour. Surgery, 1993, Jubilee medal Swedish Soc. Medicine, 1994. Fellow ACS; mem. AAAS, AMA, Internat. Pediat. Transplantation Assn. (pres. 1998-2000), Soc. Univ. Surgeons, Soc. Exptl. Biology and Medicine, Am. Soc. Exptl. Pathology, Am. Surg. Assn. (pres. 1988-89), Am. Assn. Immunologists, Transplantation Soc. (v.p. western hemisphere 1984-86, pres. 1994-96, Medawar prize 2004, Ellis Island medal of Hon, 2005), Am. Soc. Nephrology, Internat. Soc. Nephrology, Am. Assn. Lab. Animal Sci., Assn. Acad. Surgery (pres. 1969), Internat Soc. Surgery, Soc. Surg. Chairmen, Soc. Clin. Surgery, Ctrl. Surg. Assn., Minn. Med. Soc., Hennepin County Med. Socs., Minn. Surg. Soc., Mpls. Surg Soc, St. Paul Surg. Soc. Howard C. Nafziger Surg. Soc., Portland Surg Soc., Halsted Surg. Soc., Am. Heart Assn., Am. Soc. Transplant Surgeons (pres. 1977-78), Coun on Kidney in Cardiovasc. Disease, Hagfish Soc., Italian Rsch. Soc., Minn. Acad. Medicine, Minn. Med. Assn., Minn. Med. Found., Surg. Biology Club, Sigma Xi, Alpha Omega Alpha, others. Office: U Minn Surgery Dept Mayo Mail Code 195 420 Delaware St SE Minneapolis MN 55455-0374 Home Phone: 612-823-0051; Office Phone: 612-625-8444. Business E-Mail: najar001@umn.edu.

NAJEE, (JEROME NAJEE RASHEED), musician; b. NYC, Nov. 4, 1957; m. Regina Jackson, May 27, 1989; 2 children. Musician: (albums) Najee's Theme, 1986 (Soul Train Music award for Best Jazz Album, 1988), Day by Day, 1988, Tokyo Blue, 1990 (Soul Train Music award for Best Jazz Album, 1990), Just an Illusion, 1992, Share My World, 1994, Songs from the Key of Life, 1995, Morning Tenderness, 1998, Embrace, 2003, My Point of View, 2005, Rising Sun, 2007, performs with various artists including Freddie Jackson, Will Downing, Jeffrey Osborne, Marcus Miller, Paul Jackson Jr., George Duke, Prince, and others. Recipient Image award for Outstanding Jazz Artist, NAACP, 2006. Office: FAN Entertainment Group Ste 689 3940 Laurel Canyon Blvd Studio City CA 91604 also: Heads Up Internat 23309 Commerce Park Rd Cleveland OH 44122 E-mail: najee@najeeonline.com. *

NAJIB, JADWIGA S., pharmacist, educator; m. Jamal Najib; children: Daniel, Nicole. BS in Pharmacy, St. John's U., NY; PharmD, U. Minn. Lic. pharmacist State Edn. Dept., NY, 1989. Asst. prof. pharmacy practice LI U., Arnold & Marie Schwartz Coll. of Pharmacy, Bklyn., 1989—98; assoc. prof. pharmacy practice LI U. Coll. Pharmacy, Bklyn., 1998—. Clin. pharmacist St. Luke's Roosevelt Hosp. Ctr., NCY, 1989—. Contbr. articles to profl. jours. Mem. leadership coun. in local schs., NY, 2004—06. Recipient David Newton Excellence Tchg. award, LI U., 1993. Mem.: PSSNY, NYSCHP, AACP, ASHP. Achievements include research in pscyhopharmacotherapeutics. Office: Arnold & Marie Schwartz Coll Pharmacy 75 DeKalb Ave Brooklyn NY 11201 Home Phone: 212-523-8226; Office Phone: 212-523-8226. Business E-Mail: jadwiga.najib@liu.edu.

NAJIMY, KATHY, actress; Actress theater The Kathy and Mo Show, 1985-89 (also writer)(Obie award, 1989), Afterbirth: Kathy and Mo's Greatest Hits, 2004; Broadway shows Dirty Blonde, 2001; films Topsy and Bunker, Other People's Money, 1991, The Hard Way, 1991, The Fisher King, 1991, Soapdish, 1991, This Is My Life, 1992, Sister Act, 1992, Hocus Pocus, 1993, Sister Act 2: Back in the Habit, 1993, It's Pat, 1994, Jeffrey, 1995, Cats Dont' Dance, 1997, Nevada, 1997, Woman Without Implants, 1997, Hope Floats, 1998, Zack and Reba, 1998, Bride of Chucky, 1998, Attention Shoppers, 2000, Leaving Peoria, 2000, The Wedding Planner, 2001, Rat Race, 2001; TV: King of the Hill (voice), 1997-, Veronica's Closet, 1997-2001; TV movies: If These Walls Could Talk II, 2000, The Scream Team, 2002. Office: Creative Arts Agy 9830 Wilshire Blvd Beverly Hills CA 90212-1804

NAJITA, TETSUO, history professor; b. Honokaa, Hawaii, Mar. 30, 1936; s. Niichi and Kikuno (Manpuku) N.; m. Elinor Moon, Aug. 2, 1958; children: Mie Kim, Kiyoshi Young. BA, Grinnell Coll., 1958; MA, Harvard U., 1960, PhD, 1965; LLD, Grinnell Coll., 1989. Asst. prof. Carleton Coll., Northfield, Minn., 1964-66, Washington U., St. Louis, 1966-68; assoc. prof. U. Wis., Madison, 1968-69; Robert S. Ingersoll disting. prof. history/Japanese studies U. Chgo., 1969—2002, prof. emeritus, 2002—, dir. Ctr. for East Asian Studies, 1974-80, assoc. dean, 1983-87, master collegiate div. social scis., 1983-87. John A. Burns disting. visiting chair U. Hawaii, Manoa, 1994; chair dept. history U. Chgo., 1994-97; Ena H. Thompson lectr. Pomona Coll., 1996; Catherine Gould Chism vis. prof. U. Puget Sound, Tacoma; Maruyame Masao lectr. U. Calif., Berkeley, 2000; bd. dirs. Pacific Basin Inst., 2004. Author: Hara Kei in the Politics of Compromise, 1969 (J.K. Fairbank prize Am. Hist. Assn.), Intellectual Foundations of Modern Japanese Politics, 1974, Visions of Virtue in Tokugawa Japan, 1987, Tokugawa Political Writings, 1998. Grantee NEH 1973-74, 1980-81; Fulbright fellow 1961-63, 68, Guggenheim fellow 1980-81, Mellon Emeritus fellow, 2004-; recipient Yamagata Banto prize Prefecture of Osaka, 1989 Fellow Am. Acad. Arts and Scis.; mem. Am. Hist. Assn., Assn. for Asian Studies (v.p., pres. 1991-93), Phi Beta Kappa. Office: U Chgo Dept History 1126 E 59th St Chicago IL 60637-1580

NAJJAR, DIANA, elementary school educator; d. Carl and Mary Snider; children: David, Mark. BS in Elem. Edn., Ball State U., 1970; MS in Edn. with concentration in Spl. Edn., Ind. U.-Purdue U., Indpls., 1977; postgrad. in gifted edn., Purdue U., 1981—83. Cert. elem. edn. tchr. Ind. Dept. Edn. Tchr. Indpls. Pub. Schs., 1970—72, The Orchard Sch., Indpls., 1984—. Gov.'s sch. task group State Dept. of Ind., 1984—86; creator dance curriculum; dance instr., choreographer sch. musicals, plays, operettas; screenwriter math. video, 1999. Author: (book and math. kit) Namagram, 1997, (video) Factor Blocks, 1999. Catechism coach St. George Ch., Indpls., 1989—95, 2005—06. Mem.: Ind. Assn. for the Gifted (legis. team 2005—05, legis. chmn. 1979—88, Svc. award 1985). Achievements include discovery of 4 set Venn diagram; created test to measure conceptual understanding of mathematical concepts through constructions; copywright Namagram book and design. Office: The Orchard Sch 615 W 64th St Indianapolis IN 46260

NAKA, YOSHIFUMI, surgeon, researcher; b. Aug. 9, 1959; arrived in U.S., 1993; s. Yasushi and Eiko Naka; m. Kayoko Tomoda Naka, Dec. 24, 1988; 1 child, Ryoko. Completion of premed. course, Osaka U., Japan, 1980; MD, Osaka U., 1984, PhD, 1988. Cert. Japanese Bd. Surgery, lic. physician N.Y., Japan. Resident Osaka U. Hosp., 1984—86; rsch. and clin. fellow Osaka U. Med. Sch., 1986—89; resident Osaka Police Hosp., 1989—93; postdoctoral rsch. fellow dept. physiology Columbia U., NYC, 1993—96, instr. clin. dept. surgery, 1996—99, asst. prof. surgery, 1999—. Dir. cardiac transplantation and mech. circulatory support program N.Y.-Presbyn. Hosp., NYC, 2003—. Guest editor: Annals of Thoracic Surgery, 2001; author: Atherosclerosis and Coronary/Artery Disease, 1996; contbr. to profl. jours. including Jour. of Clin. Investment, Nat. Sci., Proc. Nat. Acad. Sci., 2003; author: Cardiac Surgery in the Adult, 2003. Named Herbert Irving asst. prof. surg. treatment of atrial fibrillation, Columbia U. Physicians and Surgeons, 2001—; recipient grant, Found. for Advanced of Cardiac Therapies, 2002—; grantee KO-8 grant, Vein Graft Preservation Thrombosis, and Neointimal Disease/NIH, 2001—05. Mem.: ASAIO, Soc. Univ. Surgeons, Internat. Soc. for Heart and Lung Transplantation, N.Y. Soc. Thoracic Surgeons, Am. Heart Assn. Avocations: tennis, downhill skiing, reading, cooking. Office: Milstein Hosp Bldg 7-435 177 Ft Washington Ave New York NY 10032

NAKAGAWA, KOJI, retired endocrinologist, educator; b. Sapporo, Hokkaido, Japan, June 5, 1932; s. Satosu and Michi (Yokoyama) N.; m. Keiko Hirato, Oct. 20, 1962; children: Shin, Tamao Yamaguchi. MD, Hokkaido U., 1957, PhD, 1962. Lic. endocrinologist, Japan. Staff scientist Worcester Found. for Exptl. Biology, Shrewsbury, Mass., 1964-65; rsch. staff Syntex Rsch. Ctr., Palo Alto, Calif., 1965; rsch. fellow U. Utah Med. Ctr., Salt Lake City, 1965-66; rsch. assoc. 2d dept. medicine Hokkaido U. Sch. Medicine, Sapporo, 1967-83, asst. prof., 1983-89; prof. Health Adminstrn. Ctr., Hokkaido U. Edn., Sapporo, 1989-96, dir. Health Adminstrn. Ctr., 1990-96; prof. dept. nutrition, faculty of nursing and nutrition Tenshi Coll., Sapporo, 2000—04; ret., 2004. Contbr. articles to profl. jours. Fellow Japan Endocrine Soc.; mem. Endocrine Soc., Japanese Soc. Internal Medicine, Japan Diabetes Soc. Home: 2-8 4-chome Yamanote 1-jo Nishi-ku Sapporo 063-0001 Japan

NAKAGAWARA, VAN B., optometrist, researcher; b. Honolulu, Hawaii, Mar. 8, 1947; s. Barney Hiromi and Sue Miyako Nakagawara; m. Janice Elizabeth Varner, July 29, 1979; children: Anna Elizabeth Miyako, Esther Malia Hiromi. BS in Biology, Gonzaga U., 1969; OD in Optometry, Pacific U., 1973. Lic. Bd. Examiners in Optometry, Hawaii and S.C. Optometry officer U.S. Army, Columbia, SC, 1973—76; clin. optometrist USAF, Honolulu, 1976—81; indsl. optometrist USN, Honolulu, 1981—86; rsch. optometrist FAA/Civil Aerospace Med. Inst., Oklahoma City, 1986—. Nat. adv. bd. Nat. Eye Rsch. Found., Chgo., 1992—94; mem. study group Internat. Civil Aviation Orgn., Montreal, Canada, 1999—; med. ops. cons. NASA, Houston, 1998—99. Contbr. scientific papers to profl. jours. Capt. US Army, 1972—76. Named Boss of Yr., Am. Bus. Women of Hawaii, 1982. Fellow: Am. Acad. Optometry; mem.: Armed Forces Optometric Soc., Aerospace Med. Assn., Am. Optometric Assn. (mem. aviation com. 1999—), Mike Monroney Aero. Ctr. (Asian Pacific Am. com. 1996—99), Okla. Optometric Assn. (interprofl. rels. com. 1990—95), Am. Nat. Stds. Inst. Avocations: running, stamp collecting/philately, coin collecting/numismatics, golf. Office: FAA/Civil Aerospace Med Inst PO Box 25082 Oklahoma City OK 73125 Home: 2741 SW 116th Pl Oklahoma City OK 73170-2646 Home Phone: 405-692-0489; Office Phone: 405-954-6235. E-mail: van.nakagawara@faa.gov.

NAKAJIMA, HIROSHI, education educator; b. Hiroshima, Japan, June 12, 1923; s. Iwao and Tamae (Takenaka) N.; m. Sei Sakao, May 2, 1966; children: Akihiko, Takehiko. Student, Nishogakusha Coll., 1942-44; BA, Waseda U., 1950; MA, 1954, EdD (hon.), 1989. Asst. prof. Japan women's Coll. Econs., 1954-59; lectr. Waseda U., 1954-63; asst. prof., 1963-68; prof. comparative and internat. edn., 1968-94; prof. emeritus, 1994—. Vis. prof. U. Helsinki, 1962-63; advisor Japanese Inst. Social Studies on Sweden, 1989—; vice-chmn. youth com. Higashikurumeshi, 1978-83; mem. bd. edn. Higashikurumeshi, 1983-91. Served with Japanese Army, 1943-46. Recipient Acad. Hon. Medal U. Helsinki, 1963; decorated Nat. 3rd Order, 2000. Mem.: Comparative and Internat. Edn. Soc. (mem. 1963), Finnish Acad. Sci. and Letters (fgn. 1984). Home: 1-4-37 Minamisawa Higashikurume-shi Tokyo 203-0023 Japan Office Phone: 81-3-5606-4311. Business E-Mail: nakajima@textbook-rc.or.jp.

NAKAMURA, HIROSHI, urology educator; b. Tokyo, Mar. 22, 1933; s. Yataroh and Hideko (Tanaka) N.; m. Miyoko Kodachi, Aug. 13, 1966. MD, Keio U., Tokyo, 1960, PhD, 1966. Med. diplomate. Asst. resident Mt. Sinai Hosp., NYC, 1962—63; rsch. fellow Cornell U. Med. Coll., NYC, 1966—68; asst. Sch. Medicine Keio U., Tokyo, 1968—70; chmn. urology dept. Tokyo Elec. Power Hosp., Tokyo, 1970—73; vis. asst. prof. surgery Cornell U. Med. Coll., NYC, 1973; chmn. urology Kitasato Inst. Hosp., Tokyo, 1973—77; chmn. dept., prof. urology Nat. Def. Med. Coll., Tokorozawa, Saitama, Japan, 1977—98, dir. dept. acad. affairs, 1994—96, prof. emeritus, 1999—; emeritus dir. Tokorozawa Ishikawa Clinic, 1998—. Author: Bedside Urology, 1983, Modern Clinical Point-Urology, 1993; editor: Up-to-Date Urology, 1983, Caveats & Pitfalls in Clinical Urology, 1999, Medical Ethics Q&A, 2002. Recipient Tamura award, Keio U. Sch. Medicine, 1967, All-around Med. award, Igaku-Shoin, Ltd., Tokyo, 1967, The Order of the Sacred Treasure, Emperor of Japan, 2003. Buddhist. Avocations: jazz, audiophile, travel, fishing, baseball. Home: 11-1-1204 Higashicho Tokorozawa Saitama 359-1116 Japan Office: Tokorozawa Ishikawa Clin Iseki Bldg 4F 9-22 Hiyoshicho Tokorozawa 359-1123 Japan Office Phone: 81-4-2925-7355. Business E-Mail: hiroshin@xd5.so-net.ne.jp.

NAKAMURA, ROBERT MOTOHARU, pathologist; b. Montebello, Calif., June 10, 1927; s. Mosaburo and Haru (Suematsu) N.; m. Shigeyo Jane Hayashi, July 29, 1957; children: Mary, Nancy. AB, Whittier Coll., 1949; MD, Temple U., 1954. Cert. of spl. qualification in pathologic anatomy, clin pathology, immunopathology, Am. Bd. Pathology. Prof. pathology U. Calif., Irvine, 1971-74, adj. prof. pathology, 1974-75; chmn. dept. pathology Scripps Clinic and Rsch. Found., La Jolla, Calif., 1974-92; sr. cons., 1992—; pres. Scripps Clinic Med. Group, La Jolla, 1981-91; prof. dept. immunology and exptl. and molecular medicine Scripps Rsch. Inst., 1997—; chmn. pathology Scripps Clinic, 1998-99, chmn. emeritus pathology, 1999—. Adj. prof. pathology U. Calif., San Diego, 1975-93. Co-editor: Jr. Clin. Lab. Analysis, 1989—; contbr. articles to profl. jours. Fellow: Coll. Am. Pathologists, Am. Soc. Clin. Pathologists, Assn. Clin. Scientists, Am. Coll. Nutrition; mem. Internat. Acad. Pathology. Avocation: reading. Home: 8841 Nottingham Pl La Jolla CA 92037-2131 Office Phone: 858-554-8166. Personal E-mail: rnakamura@pol.net.

NAKAMURA, SHUJI, engineering educator; b. Seto, Japan, May 22, 1954; BEE, U. Tokushima, Japan, 1977; MEE, U. Tokushima, 1979, DEng, 1994. R&D staff Nichia Chem. Industry, Ltd., 1979—84, group head R&D 1st sect., 1985—88, group head R&D 2nd sect., 1989—93, sr. rschr. dept. R&D, 1993—99; prof. materials dept. U. Calif., Santa Barbara, 1999—, dir., Solid State Lighting & Display Ctr. Vis. rsch. assoc. electronic engring. U. Fla., 1988—89. Mem. editl. bd.: Applied Physics Soc., 1998—2000; published several papers. Named Cree Prof. in Solid State Light and Display Endowed chair, 2001; recipient Nikkei Bus. Publications Engring. award, 1994, 1996, Best Paper award, Japanese Applied Physics Soc., 1994, 1997, Sakurai award, 1995, Nishina Meml. award, 1996, IEEE Lasers and Electro-Optics Soc. Engring. Achievement award, 1996, Spl. Recognition award, Soc. for Info. Display, 1996, Okochi Meml. award, 1997, medal award, Materials Rsch. Soc., 1997, Innovation in Real Materials award, 1998, C&C award, Jack A. Morton award, IEEE, 1998, Brit. Rank prize, 1998, Julius-Springer prize for applied physics, 1999, Takayanagi award, 2000, Carl Zeiss Rsch. award, 2000, Honda award, 2000, Crystal Growth and Crystal Tech. award, 2000, Asahi award, 2001, OSA Nick Holonyak award, 2001, LEOS Disting. Lectr. award, 2001, Benjamin Franklin medal in engring., Franklin Inst., 2002, Millennium Tech. prize for his inventions in light and laser tech., Millennium Prize Found., 2006. Mem.: NAE. Achievements include development of first group-III nitride-based blue/green LEDs; design of first group-III nitride-based violet laser diodes; patents in field. Office: Materials Dept Univ Calif Santa Barbara CA 93106-5050 Office Phone: 805-893-5552. E-mail: shuji@engineering.ucsb.edu. *

NAKANISHI, ALAN, ophthalmologist, state representative; b. Sacramento, Mar. 21, 1940; BA in Chem., Pacific Union Coll., 1962; MD, Loma Linda U.; MS in Health Adminstrn., Va. Commonwealth U., 1991. Intern, L.A. Coutny Med. Ctr. L.A. County Med. Ctr. U. So. Calif., 1965-66; resident, L.A. County Med. Ctr. Delta Eye Med. Group, 1966-69, ophthalmologist Stockton, Calif., 1969—; mem. Lodi City Council, 1998—2001; mayor Lodi, Calif., 2001; mem. Calif. Ho. of Reps., 2002—. Mem. com. on aging and long-term care, com. on health, com. on higher edu. & com. on public employees, retirement and social security Calif. Ho. of Reps. Maj. M.C., U.S. Army, 1969-71. Office: Delta Eye Med Group 1617 Saint Marks Plz Stockton CA 95207-6423 also: State Capital PO Box 942849 Sacramento CA 94249

NAKANISHI, DON TOSHIAKI, Asian American studies educator, writer; b. LA, Aug. 14, 1949; m. Marsha Hirano; 1 child, Thomas. BA in Polit Sci. cum laude, Yale U., 1971; PhD in Polit. Sci., Harvard U., 1978. Instr. dept. urban studies Yale U., 1971; lectr. Coun. on Ednl. Devel. UCLA, 1973, instr. Asian Am. Studies Ctr., 1974, acting asst. prof. dept. polit. sci., 1975-78; vis. scholar Sophia U., Inst. Internat. Relations, Tokyo, 1978-89; adj. asst. prof. dept. polit. sci. UCLA, 1979-82, asst. rschr. Asian Am. Studies Ctr., 1979-82, from asst. prof. to full prof. Grad. Sch. Edn., 1982—, assoc. dir. Asian Am. Studies Ctr., 1985-87, chair interdepartmental program Asian Am. studies, 1989—90, dir. Asian Am. Studies Ctr., 1990—. Co-founder and publr. Amerasia Jour., 1970-75, edtl. bd., 1975—; researcher Social Sci. Rsch. Coun. of N.Y. and the Japan Soc. for the Promotion of Sci. of Tokyo Joint-Project on Am.-Japanese Mut. Images, 1971-73; mem. Asian Am. task force for social studies guideline evaluation, Calif. State Dept. Edn., 1973; guest spkr. Ctr. for the Study of Edn. Policy, Grad. Sch. Edn., Harvard U., 1974, Metropathways, Ethni-City Sch. Desegregation Program, Boston, 1974; researcher, co-project chair Hispanic Urban Ctr., Project Sch. Desegregation, L.A., 1974; numerous coms. UCLA; numerous conf. chmns.; cons., rschr., speaker, presenter in field. Co-editor: (with Marsha J. Hirano-Nakanishi) The Education of Asian and Pacific Americans: Historical Perspectives and Prescriptions for the Future, 1983, (with Halford H. Fairchild, Luis Ortiz-Franco, Lenore A. Stiffarm) Discrimination and Prejudice: An Annotated Bibliography, 1991, (with Tina Yamano Nishida) The Asian Pacific American Educational Experience: A Sourcebook for Teachers and Students, 1995, (with James Lai) National Asian Pacific American Political Almanac, 1996, 98, 2000; contbr. numerous articles to profl. jours., monographs, book reviews and reports. Chair Yale U. Alumni Schs. Com. of So. Calif., 1978—; bd. dirs. Altamed and La Clinica Familiar Del Barrio of East L.A., 1982—; commr. Bd. Transp. Commrs., City of L.A., 1984-90; v.p. Friends of the Little Tokyo Pub. Libr., 1986-88; co-chair nat. scholars adv. com. Japanese Am. Nat. Mus., 1987—; mem., bd. govs. Assn. of Yale Alumni, 1988-91; mem. exec. coun. Mayor's LA's Best Aftersch. Program, City of Los Angeles, 1988-90. Rsch. fellow Japan Soc. for the Promotion of Sci., 1978; recipient Nat. Scholars awrd for Outstanding Rsch. Article on Asian Pacific Am. Edn., Nat. Assn. for Asian and Pacific Am. Edn., 1985, Civil Rights Impace award Asian Am. Legal Ctr. of So. Calif., 1989; grantee Chancellors' Challenge in the Arts and Humanities, 1991, Calif. Policy Seminar, 1992, U. Calif. Pacific Rim Studies, 1992; recepient numerous other research and conference grants. Mem. Nat. Assn. for Interdisciplinary Ethnic Studies (bd. dirs. 1976-79), Assn. Asian Am. Studies (nat. pres. 1983-85), Nat. Assn. for Asian and Pacific Am. Edn. (exec. bd. dirs., v.p. 1983—). Home: 4501 N Berkshire Ave Los Angeles CA 90032 Office: UCLA Asian Am Studies Ctr 3230 Campbell Ave Los Angeles CA 90024-1546 E-mail: dtn@ucla.edu.

NAKANISHI, YUKO JULIE, engineering educator, consultant; b. Westland, Mich. d. Ukyo Stanley and Tatsuko Ann Nakanishi. BA in English Lit., Harvard U., 1987; MBA, Columbia U., 1993; MSCE, CCNY, 1997; PhD in Civil Engring., Polytech U., 2004. Chair NY Area Data Coun., NYC, 1997-99; sr. tchg. assoc., cons. Rensselaer Poly. Inst., Troy, NY, 1999-2000; mgr. program Urban ITS Ctr. Poly. U., Bklyn., 2000—05; chair subcom. on tng., edn., and tech. transfer, 2003—05; prin., owner Nakanishi Rsch. and Cons., Rego Pk., NY, 2005—. Chair Freight and Intermodal Transp. Data Com., NY, 1997-2000; asst. dir. Univ. Transp. Rsch. Ctr., NYC, 1996-99; info. svc. com. Transp. Rsch. Bd., 1998—, critical transp. infrastructure protection com., chair edn., tng. and tech. transfer subcom. Contbr. articles to profl. jours. Fellow Eisenhower fellow, 1997—2000, Eno fellow, 2001. Mem. IEEE, ASCE, Inst. Transp. Engr., Intelligent Transp. Soc. N.Y. (treas., sec., bd. dirs.), N.Y. Data Coun. (bd. dirs.). Home and Office: Nakanishi Rsch and Consulting 93-40 Queens Blvd 6A Rego Park NY 11374 Office Phone: 347-512-1959. Office Fax: 347-512-1959. Personal E-mail: ynakan@aol.com. Business E-Mail: nakanishi@nrcresearch.com.

NAKARAI, CHARLES FREDERICK TOYOZO, music educator; b. Indpls., Apr. 25, 1936; s. Toyozo Wada and Frances Aileen N. BA cum laude, Butler U., 1958, Mus.M., 1967; postgrad., U. N.C., 1967-70. Organist, dir. choirs Northwood Christian Ch., Indpls., 1954-57; min. music Broad Ripple Christian Ch., Indpls., 1957-58; asst. prof. music Milligan Coll., Tenn., 1970-72; pvt. instr. organ, piano Durham, NC, 1972—. Mem. faculty piano camp U. N.C.-Greensboro, 1996, 97, 2000, 01; adjudicator N.C. Music Tchrs. Assn., N.C. Fedn. Music Clubs, Raleigh Music Tchrs. Assn., Charlotte Piano Tchrs. Forum, Chapel Hill Music Tchrs. Assn. Composer: Three Movements for Chorus, 1971, Bluesy, 1979. With USAF, 1958—64. Mem. Am. Musicol. Soc., Coll. Music Soc., Am. Guild Organists, Music Tchrs. Nat. Assn., Music Libr. Assn., N.C. Music Tchrs. Assn., Organ Hist. Soc., Durham Music Tchrs. Assn., Triangle Guitar Soc. Address: 2312 Anthony Drive Durham NC 27705

NAKASHIMA, TADAYOSHI, retired biochemist, researcher; b. Yokkaichi, Mie-ken, Japan, Dec. 1, 1922; s. Chunosuke and Hina Nakashima; m. Fukuko Kondo, Nov. 15, 1947; 1 child, Rieko. BP, Nagoya Pharm. Coll., Aichi-ken, 1941—43; BS, Taihoku Imperial U., Taihoku, 1943—46; PhD, Kyushu U., Fukuoka, 1960—61. Rsch. Scientist U. of Miami, 1964. Acting chief, rsch. lab. Sanyo Penicillin Co., Nagoya, 1946—50; assoc. prof. Kwassui Coll., Nagasaki, 1951—62; post doctoral U. of Hawaii, 1962—64; vis. rsch. scientist U. of Bonn, Germany, 1966—69; rsch. prof. Inst. for Molecular and Cellular Evolution, U. of Miami, 1964—89. Author: (molecular evolution) Journals, (protoribosomes) In Molecular Evolution and Protobiology, 1984, (genetic code) Proc. Nat. Acad. Sci., 1972, (amino acid sequence) J. Biol. Chem.1966. Mem.: Am. Chem. Soc. Home: 7400 SW 159th Ter Palmetto Bay FL 33157-2452

NAKATA, AKINORI, epidemiologist, psychologist, researcher; b. Kawasaki, Kanagawa, Japan, Feb. 23, 1967; s. Kenzo and Yoshiko Nakata; m. Sonoko Shiibashi, May 26, 2004. PhD, U. Tokyo, 1997. Domestic rsch. fellow Japan Soc. for Promotion of Sci., Kawaguchi, 1997—2000; rsch. fellow Nat. Inst. Indsl. Health, Kawasaki, 2000—, Nat. Inst. Occup. Safety Health, Cin, 2004—. Guest editor Nat. Inst. Indsl. Health, Kawasaki, 2005—; vis. rschr. U. Tokyo, 1997—2005. Contbr. articles to med. jours. Avocations: tennis, fishing, baseball. Office: Nat Inst Occup Safety Health CDC 4676 Columbia Pky Cincinnati OH 45226 Home Phone: 513-675-3088. Office Fax: 513-533-8596. Personal E-mail: nakataa-tky@umin.ac.jp.

NAKATA, GARY KENJI, lawyer; b. Okinawa, Japan, Nov. 13, 1964; arrived in U.S., 1971; s. Hiroshi Nakata and Miwako Kin; m. Jo Ann Akiko Tengan, Aug. 22, 1998. BBA in Fin., U. Hawaii, 1988; JD with distinction, U. of the Pacific, 1995. Bar: Hawaii 1996, Calif. 1996, US Dist. Ct. Hawaii, 1996; cert. mgmt. acct.; cert. fin. mgr.; cert. grad. Am. Banker's Assn. Nat. Sch. Regulatory Compliance. Credit analyst Bank of Hawaii, Honolulu, 1988-90, sr. credit analyst, 1990-92; law clk. Hawaii Atty. Gen. Tax Divsn., Honolulu, 1994; sr. assoc. Kobayashi, Sugita & Goda, Honolulu, 1995—2003; dep. corp. counsel City and County of Honolulu, 2003—04; CFO Honolulu City & County Employees Fed. Credit Union, 2004—. Mem. new product devel. adv. bd. Warren Gorham & Lamont, NYC, 1997-98. Editor-in-chief: The Transnational Lawyer, 1994, 95. Pres., enlisted adv. coun. Hawaii Air Nat. Guard, Honolulu, 1986-92; mem. ex officio alumni coun., mem. membership com., mem. membership benefits subcom. U. Hawaii Alumni Assn., Honolulu, 1990-91; mem. fin. com. and bylaws subcom. Soc. Coll. Bus. Alumni and Friends, U. Hawaii Coll. Bus. Adminstrn. Alumni Affairs, Honolulu, 1990-91, founding mem., treas., 1990-91, mem. steering com. to form alumni orgn., 1997-98, pres., 1998-2000; at-large rep., treas., legis. liaison Neighborhood Bd., Kaneohe, Hawaii, 1991-92. Mem.: ABA (bus. law sect., comml. fin. svcs. com., consumer fin. svcs. com.), Hawaii Fin. Regulatory Compliance Assn. (bd. dirs. 1997—2003, chairperson fair credit reporting act regulatory update com. 1998—2003), Inst. Cert. Mgmt. Accts. (bd. dirs. 1998—2000, dir. mem. acquisition 1998—2000), Calif. State Bar Assn., Hawaii State Bar Assn. (mem. real property and fin. svcs. sect. 1997—), Hawaii Jaycees (legal counsel 2000—01, exec. v.p. 2002, pres. 2003), Hawaii Bus. Jaycees (charter pres. 1991—92, chmn. bd. 1992—93, charter mem.). Office: Honolulu City & County Employees Fed Credit Union 2200 Kamehameha Hwy Ste 208 Honolulu HI 96819-2356 E-mail: gary@kalanet.com.

NAKAYAMA, GRANTA Y., federal agency administrator, lawyer; SB, SM, MIT, 1981; JD, George Mason U., 1994. Bar: Va. 1994, DC 1995, US Ct. Appeals (4th cir.). Chief engr. Nuclear Core Mfg., Naval Nuclear Propulsion Program, US Navy, chief quality control Welding and Nondestructive Testing Branch; ptnr. Environ. Law and Product Safety Kirkland & Ellis LLP, Washington, 1994—2005; asst. adminstr. for enforcement & compliance assurance EPA, Washington, 2005—. Writing instr. George Mason U. Sch. Law, 1993—94, adj. prof., 1998—. Contbr. articles to profl. jours. Lt. USN, 1981—86. Mem.: Soc. Automotive Engrs., Am. Welding Soc. Office: EPA 1200 Pennsylvania Ave NW Rm 3204 Washington DC 20046

NAKAYAMA, PAULA AIKO, state supreme court justice; b. Honolulu, Oct. 19, 1953; m. Charles W. Totto; children: Elizabeth Murakami, Alexander Totto. BS, U. Calif., Davis, 1975; JD, U. Calif., 1979. Bar: Hawaii 1979. Dep. pros. atty. City and County of Honolulu, 1979-82; ptnr. Shim, Tam & Kirimitsu, Honolulu, 1982-92; judge 1st Cir. Ct. State of Hawaii, Oahu, 1992-93; assoc. justice Hawaii Supreme Ct., Honolulu, 1993—. Mem. Am. Judicature Soc., Hawaii Bar Assn., Sons and Daughters of 442. Office: Hawaii Supreme Ct Ali'iolani Hale 417 S King St Honolulu HI 96813-2902 *

NAKAYAMA, WATARU, engineering educator, consultant; b. Kamakura, Kanagawa, Japan, Jan. 7, 1936; s. Shiroh and Haru N.; m. Michiko Aoyagi, Jan. 8, 1967. BS, Defense Acad., Yokosuka, Japan, 1958; MS, Tokyo Inst. Tech., 1963, DEng, 1966. Lectr. U. Sherbrooke, Que., 1969-70; rschr. Hitachi, Ltd., Tokyo, 1970-71, chief rschr. Tsuchiura, Japan, 1971-78, sr. rschr., 1978-88, sr. chief rschr., 1988-91, hon. engr., 1991-92; Hitachi chair prof. Tokyo Inst. Tech., 1989-92, prof., 1992-96; vis. prof. U. Md., 1996-98; pres. ThermTech Internat., 1998—. Lectr. in field. Author: (with others) Heat Transfer in Electronic and Microelectronic Equipment, 1990, High Performance Computing in Japan, 1992, Computers and Computing in Heat Transfer Science and Engineering, 1993; contbr. articles to profl. jours. Recipient New Tech. Innovation award Ichimura Found., 1978, best paper award Gas Turbine Soc. of Japan, 1984. Fellow IEEE (Itherm Achievement award 2000, Thermi award 2006), ASME (K-16 com. 1981—, chmn. Japanese chpt. 1990-92, Best Paper award 1981, Heat Transfer Meml. award 1992, Electronic Packaging award 1996, Achievement award 2001), InterPack (Achievement award 2001); mem. Japanese Soc. Mech. Engrs. (vice chmn. thermal engring. divsn. 1989-90, chmn. 1990-91, Best Paper award 1965, 80, Tech. award 1978, Funai Spl. award 2007), Heat Transfer Soc. Japan (pres. 1994). Achievements include patents for industrial application of heat transfer enhancement techniques to heat exchangers, rotating machinery, cooling systems of computers. E-mail: watnakayama@aol.com.

NAKAZATO, TAKUYA, ecological geneticist; b. Yokohama, Kanagawa, Japan, Sept. 9, 1972; s. Shinsuke and Mika Nakazato. PhD, Ind. U., S.Bend, 1998—2005. Postdoctoral assoc. Ind. U., 2005—. Home Phone: 812-333-3130.

NAKONECZNY, MICHAEL MARTIN, artist; b. Detroit, Oct. 30, 1952; s. Michael and Edithe (Pheil) N.; 1 child, Alysha. Student, Kent State U., 1972-74; BA, Cleve. State U., 1979; MFA, Univ. Cin., 1981. Artist in residence Pub. Sch. 1, Long Island City, NY, 1986; instr. Cuyahoga C.C., Cleve., 1987, Cleve. Inst. of Art, 1988; vis. artist Herron Sch. of Art Ind. U., Indpls., 1990, Kansas City (Mo.) Art Inst., 1991; artist in residence Bemis Found., Omaha, 1992; vis. artist Tamarind Inst., Albuquerque, 1995, Ill. State U., 1997; assoc. prof. U. Alaska, Fairbanks, 2000—. Vis. artist Mont. State U., 1998. One-man shows include Grover Thurston Gallery, Seattle, Graham Modern Gallery, NYC, 1988, Cleve. Ctr. Contemporary Art, 1993, Zolla Liberman Gallery, Chgo., 1991—93, 1996—2003, Horwitch LewAllen Gallery, Santa Fe, 1995, Purdue U., West Lafayette, Ind., 1995, Clark Gallery, Boston, 1999, Anchorage Mus. History and Art, South Bend Regional Mus. Art, 2003, Kat Kho Kong Gallery, Cambodia, 2006, U. Alaska, Fairbanks, 2007, exhibited in group shows at Corcoran Gallery Art, Washington, 1985, Alternative Mus., NY, 1986, LA County Mus. Art, 1987, Graham Modern Gallery, NYC, 1989, Machida City Mus. Graphic Arts, Tokyo, 1993, Galleria Art, Sao Paulo, Brazil, 1994, Weatherspoon Art Gallery, U. NC, 1995, Chgo. Ctr. Book & Paper Arts, Columbia Coll., 1996, Banco Ctrl., Cuenca, Ecuador, 1996, Calif. Mus. Art, Santa Rosa, 1997, U. Alaska Mus., Fairbanks. Fellow, U. Cin., 1979—81, Ohio Arts Coun., 1990, Arts Midwest NEA Regional fellow, 1994—95, Ill. Arts Coun., 1995, Visual Arts 7, 1987; Individual Artist grantee, Rasmuson Found. Address: 660 Rebecca St Apt 16 Fairbanks AK 99709-3563 Office Phone: 907-474-6545. Business E-Mail: ffmmn@uaf.edu.

NAKRA, TANUJ, plastic surgeon; b. London, Mar. 11, 1975; MD, Rush Med. Coll., Chgo., 2001. Ophthalmologist UCLA, Los Angeles, Calif., 2002—, resident in ophthal., 2005, fellow in ophthalmic and facial plastic surgery, 2007, fellow in cosmetic and reconstructive surgery, 2007. Recipient Bausch & Lomb Surgery award, UCLA, Jules Stein Eye Inst., 2005; Nat. Merit Scholar, Nat. Merit Scholar, 1993—97. Mem.: Am. Acad. Ophthalmology (assoc.), Alpha Omega Alpha, Kappa Sigma (life). Achievements include research in surgical advances in the treatment of eyelid, orbit, and facial diseases. Office: UCLA 100 Stein Plaza UCLA Los Angeles CA 90095 Office Phone: 310-825-5000. Business E-Mail: tnakra@gmail.com.

NAKU, ROLF D., gas industry executive; BS, NYU, 1973; MBA, Rensselaer Poly., 1974. With human resources and telecom. AMF, Inc.; joined Ultramar, 1983; v.p. human resources Ultramar Corp.; dir. compensation, benefits and human resources sys. Sunoco, Inc., 1998—2000, v.p. uman resources and pub. affairs, 2000—03, sr. v.p. human resources and pub. affairs Phila., 2003—. Office: Sunoco Inc Ten Penn Ctr 1801 Market St Philadelphia PA 19103-1699

NALBANDIAN, DAVID, professional tennis player; b. Cordoba, Argentina, Jan. 1, 1982; s. Norbeto and Alda. Jr. champion Jrs.-US Open, 1998; finalist Wimbledon, 2002; semi-finalist US Open, 2003, French Open, 2004; mem. Argentina Davis Cup team, 2002—04; winner Estoril Open, 2006. Nominee, Laureus World Sports Awards, 2003; named World Newcomer Yr. Achievements include highest world ranking #4, 2004. Avocations: fishing, soccer. Office: c/o Assn Tennis Profl 201 ATP Blvd Ponte Vedra Beach FL 32082

NALBANDIAN, JOHN B., lawyer; b. Fort Ord, Calif., Feb. 15, 1969; BS in Econ., U. Pa., 1991; JD, U. Va., 1994. Bar: DC 1997, Ohio 2001. Clerk Hon. Jerry E. Smith. US Ct. of Appeals Fifth Cir.; worked in Issues and Appeals Sect., Litig. Grp. Jones, Day, Reavis & Pogue, Washington; ptnr. Taft, Stettinius & Hollister LLP, Cin. Named one of Ohio's Rising Stars, Super Lawyers, 2005, 2006. Mem.: Leadership Northern Ky. (Class of 2002), Telecom. Bd. Northern Ky., Cin. Bar Assn., DC Bar Assn., Va. Bar Assn., Order of Coif. Office: Taft Stettinius & Hollister LLP 425 Walnut St Ste 1800 Cincinnati OH 45202-3957 Office Phone: 513-381-2838. Office Fax: 513-381-0205.

NALCIOGLU, ORHAN, radiologist, educator; b. Istanbul, Turkey, Feb. 2, 1944; came to U.S., 1966, naturalized, 1974; s. Mustafa and Meliha Nalcioglu. BS, Robert Coll., Istanbul, 1966; MS, Case Western Res. U., 1968; PhD, U. Oreg., 1970. Postdoctoral fellow dept. physics U. Calif., Davis, 1970-71; rsch. assoc. dept. physics U. Rochester, NY, 1971-74, U. Wis., Madison, 1974-76; sr. physicist EMI Med. Inc., Northbrook, Ill., 1976-77; prof. depts. radiol. scis., elec. engring., medicine and physics U. Calif., Irvine, 1977—, head divsn. physics and engring., 1985—, dir. biomed. magnetic resonance rsch., 1987—2002, dir. Rsch. Imaging Ctr., 1992—, vice chair dept. radiology, 2000—. Cons. UN, 1980-86; gen. chmn. IEEE Nuc. Sci. Symposium and Med. Imaging Conf., 1996, 99. Editor several books; guest editor IEEE Nuclear Sci. Symposium and Med. Imaging Conf., 1997; contbr. articles to profl. jours. Mobil scholar, 1961-66; recipient Athalie Clarke award for rsch. excellence, 2001, Outstanding Achievement in the Arts and Scis. award ATAA, 2002, Outstanding Scientist award Assembly of Turkish-Am. Assns., Washington, 2002. Fellow IEEE (pres. Nuclear and Plasma Scis. Soc. 1993-94, Millennium medal 2000, NPSS Richard Shea award 2000), Am. Assn. Physicists in Medicine, Internat. Soc. Magnetic Resonance in Medicine; mem. Nuclear and Plasma Scis. Soc., Internat. Soc. Magnetic Resonance in Medicine, Am. Assn. for Cancer Rsch., Soc. Nuc. Medicine. Office: Univ Calif Rsch Imaging Ctr Irvine CA 92697-5020 Business E-Mail: nalci@uci.edu.

NALEN, CRAIG ANTHONY, federal agency administrator; b. Montclair, NJ, Apr. 17, 1930; s. Paul Anthony and Mildred A. (Tucker) N.; m. Katherine Andrews, Dec. 30, 1953; children: Katherine M., David A., Peter H. BA, Princeton U., 1952; MBA, Stanford U., 1957. Mktg. exec. Procter & Gamble, Cin., 1957-62, Foremost-McKesson, San Francisco, 1962-64; divisional gen. mgr., corp. v.p. Gen. Mills Inc., Mpls., 1964-72; pres., also bd. dirs. Am. Photograph Corp., Great Neck, NY, 1972-75; pres., chmn. bd. dirs. STP Corp., Ft. Lauderdale, Fla., 1975-80; pres., chief exec. officer Overseas Pvt. Investment Corp. (govt. agy.), Washington, 1981-89, also bd. dirs.; chmn. AES Transpower, Washington, 1989-92. Bd. dirs. Glendale Internat. Corp., Ont., Canada, Sonex Corp. Bd. dirs., founder Children's World, Denver. Lt. USNR, 1952-55. Mem. Chevy Chase (Md.) Club, Gulf Stream Golf Club (Fla.), Gulf Stream Bath & Tennis Club (Delray Beach, Fla.), Valley Golf Club (Sun Valley, Idaho). Republican. Home: 532 Banyan Rd Gulf Stream FL 33483-7404 also: 3101 New Mexico Ave NW Apt 844 Washington DC 20016-5917 also: PO Box 2439 Ketchum ID 83340-2439

NALLI, SANDRO, research scientist, consultant; s. Rocco Nalli and Nalina Pietrandrea; m. Andrea Jane Radai, Sept. 24, 2005. B in Chem. Engring., McGill U., Montreal, 1999, M in Chem. Engring., 2001, PhD in Chem. Engring., 2005. Cert. Can. Order Engrs, 1996. Rsch. asst. McGill U., Montreal, 1999—2004; devel. engr. Cansolv Techs. Inc, Montreal, 2005; rsch. assoc. Structural Genomics Consortium, Toronto, 2005—06; devel. scientist Sanofi Pasteur, Swiftwater, Pa., 2006—. Achievements include research in advances in biotechnology and biochemical engineering; environmental impact of plastic additives; development of carbon dioxide sequestration using biocatalysts; development and scale-up of photobioreactors. Office: Sanofi Pasteur 1 Discovery Dr Swiftwater PA 18370 Home Phone: 610-438-2018. Personal E-mail: sandro.nalli@gmail.com. Business E-Mail: sandro.nalli@sanofipasteur.com.

NALLY, DENNIS MATHEW, finance company executive; b. Washington, Oct. 11, 1952; s. Thomas J. and Margaret (Allen) N.; m. Karen L. Kidder, June 18, 1977; children: Brian, Lindsay, Kathryn, Lauren. BBA, Western Mich. U., 1974; completed, Columbia U. Exec. Program, Penn State U. Exec. Program. CPA, Mich., Ohio. Staff acct. Price Waterhouse, Detroit, 1974-77, audit sr., 1977-78, audit mgr., 1978-85, audit ptnr., 1985, NYC, 1985-88, ptnr.-in-charge Dayton, Ohio, 1988—92, nat. dir. strategic planning, 1992—95, vice chmn fin. and key client svc. support, 1995—97, also mem. US firm policy com., US mgmt. com., and gen. coun. worldwide orgn., 1995—97; (Price Waterhouse merged with Coopers Lybrand in 1998); assurance and bus. adv. services leader for Americas theatre PricewaterhouseCoopers, 1996—2000, mng. ptnr. US Firm, 2000—01, chmn., sr. ptnr., 2002—, also mem. US bd. partners and principals, mem. US mgmt. com. Bd. dirs. US C. of C., US-Japan Bus. Coun.; bd. trustees St. Michael's Coll., Colchester, VT, NY POPs; mem. fin. com. Diocese of Bridgeport, Conn. Mem. AICPA, NY State Soc. CPAs. Avocations: golf, sailing, jogging, computers. Office: PricewaterhouseCoopers 300 Madison Ave New York NY 10017-6204 Office Phone: 646-471-4000. *

NAM, CHARLES BENJAMIN, demographer, sociologist, educator, writer; b. Lynbrook, NY, Mar. 25, 1926; s. Samuel and Yetta (Huff) N.; m. Marjorie Lee Tallant, Jan. 1, 1956; children: David Wallace, Rebecca Jane. BA, NYU, 1950; MA, U. N.C., 1957, PhD, 1959. Statistician U.S. Bur. Census, Washington, 1950-53, chief edn. and social stratification br., 1957-64; statistician USAF, Montgomery, Ala., 1953-54; rsch. asst. U. N.C., Chapel Hill, 1954-57; prof. sociology Fla. State U., Tallahassee, 1964—96, chmn. dept. sociology, 1968—71, disting. rsch. prof., 1994—96, disting. rsch. prof. emeritus, 1996—; rsch. assoc. Ctr. for Demography and Population Health, 1967—, dir., 1967—82; mem. population adv. com. U.S. Bur. Census, 1978-81. Cons. population divsn. Orgn. for Econ. Coop. and Devel., 1968-70, UNESCO, 1978-83, Indonesian Ministry of Population and Environment, Jakarta, 1988-90; Social Sci. Rsch. Coun., 1981-88. Author: (with John K. Folger) Education of the American Population, 1967, Population and Society, 1968, (with Susan Gustavus) Population: The Dynamics of Demographic Change, 1976, Nationality Groups and Social Stratification, 1981; (with Susan Philliber) Population: A Basic Orientation, 1983; (with Mary Powers) The Socioeconomic Approach to Status Measurement, 1983, Our Population: The Face of America, 1988, Understanding Population Change, 1994; (with Richard Rogers and Robert Hummer) Living and Dying in the USA, 2000; (with Janusz Balicki and Ewa Fratczak) Mechanisms of Population Changes and Population Policy (in Polish), 2003, The Golden Door, 2006; editor: Demography, 1972-75; co-editor: (with David Sly, William Serow) International Handbook of Internal Migration, 1990, Handbook of International Migration, 1990; mem. editl. bd. Population Research and Policy Review, 1993-94. Fellow AAAS (rep. sect. K 1999-2004); mem. Am. Sociol. Assn. (chmn. sect. on population 1976-78), Population Assn. Am. (pres. 1979), Internat. Union for Sci. Study Population, Am. Statis. Assn. (chmn. social statistics sect. 1974), So. Sociol. Soc. (pres. 1981-82), So. Demographic Assn. (vice chmn. 1974-75; fellow 2001), Soc. Study Social Biology (bd. dirs. 1996-2006, exec. com. 1998-99). Home: 820 Live Oak Plantation Rd Tallahassee FL 32312-2413 Personal E-mail: cnam@fsu.edu.

NAM, KI-BONG, mathematics professor; b. Masan, Korea, 1955; arrived in US, 1983; s. Moon-Woo and Eul-Yeon (Koo) Nam; m. Young Hee Esther Joo, May 9, 1982; children: Grace Hye-Eun, Tae-Young. BS Math., Hanyang U., Seoul, 1981; MA Math., Hanyang U., 1983; MS Math., U. Wis., Madison, 1996; PhD, U. Wis., 1998. Tchg. asst. Hanyang U., Seoul, 1981—83, Iowa State U., Ames, 1983—84; lectr. U. Wis., Whitewater, 1999—2002, asst. prof., 2003—06, assoc. prof., 2006—. Organizer Internat. Math. Conf., Jeonju City, Republic of Korea, 2004, 06; presenter Internat. Congress Math., Madrid, 2006, Beijing, 07; lectr. in field. Editor: Jour. Computational Math. and Optimization, 2005—, Jour. Applied Algebra and Discrete Structures, 2005—; assoc. editor: Internat. Jour. Applied Math. and Stats., 2005—; contbr. articles to profl. jours. Recipient Rsch. award, Coll. Letters and Scis., U. Wis., Whitewater, 2006, U. Wis., Whitewater, 2007. Mem.: Korean-Am. U. Prof. Assn., Am. Math. Soc. (reviewer). Avocations: Go, chess. Home: 468 Presidential Ln Madison WI 53711 Office: Univ Wis Dept Math 800 W Main St Whitewater WI 53190 Office Phone: 262-472-5164. Business E-Mail: namk@uww.edu.

NAM, SAE WOO, physicist; Grad. in Physics and Elec. Engring., MIT, Cambridge, 1991; MS in Physics, PhD in Physics, Stanford U., Calif., 1998. NRC postdoctoral fellowship Nat. Inst. Standards and Technology, staff scientist electronics and elec. engring. Boulder, Colo., 2001—. Contbr. articles to sci. jours. Named one of Brilliant 10, Popular Sci. mag., 2003; recipient Presdl. Early Career award for Scientists and Engrs., 2002. Office: Electronics and Elec Engring Nat Inst Standards and Tech 325 Broadway MC 815 04 Boulder CO 80305-3328 Office Phone: 303-497-3148. E-mail: saewoo.nam@nist.gov. *

NAM, SEUNG YEOB, network technician, researcher; b. Deagu, Republic of Korea, Aug. 21, 1975; s. Sang Jik Nam and Ok-Nam Hwang. BSEE, Korea Advanced Inst. Sci. and Tech., 1997, MSEE, 1999; PhD, Korea Advanced Inst.Sci. and Tech., 2004. Postdoctoral Carnegie Mellon U., Pitts., 2004—. Author: articles and conf. papers. Recipient 4th prize, Korea Math. Competition for Undergrads., 1995, Best Paper award, Asia-Pacific Conf. on Comm., 2000, Bronze Prize, Samsung Humantech Paper Contest, 2004. Mem.: ACM, IEEE. Achievements include patents for a fast convolution approximation scheme for estimating end-to-end delay performance; partitioned crossbar switch with multiple input/output buffers; patents pending for quasi-shaped output buffer type switching apparatus; method and apparatus for two-dimensional-scalable crossbar matrix switch. Avocation: skiing. Home Phone: 412-215-8089. Office Fax: 412-268-7675. Personal E-mail: nsyeob@gmail.com. Business E-Mail: synam@andrew.cmu.edu.

NAMA, GEORGE, artist; b. Pitts., 1939; BFA, MFA, Carnegie Mellon Univ. Adj. prof. Pratt Inst. Exhibitions include Atelier 17, Paris, Phila. Mus., Tibor de Nagy Gallery, NYC, Biblioteque Nationale, Paris, Jack Rutberg Gallery, L.A., Shepherd & Derom Galleries, NYC. Mem.: NAD (academician). Office: Pratt Institute 144 W 14th St New York NY 10011

NAMBU, YOICHIRO, physics professor; b. Toyko, Jan. 18, 1921; arrived in U.S., 1952; m. Chieko Hida Nambu, Nov. 3, 1945; 1 child, Jun-ichi. BS, U. Tokyo, 1942, DSc, 1952; DSc (hon.), Northwestern U., Evanston, Ill., 1987; degree (hon.), Osaka U., 1996. Research asst. U. Tokyo, 1945—49; prof. physics Osaka City U., Japan, 1950—56; mem. Inst. Advanced Study, Princeton, 1952—54; research assoc. U. Chgo., 1954—56, mem. faculty, 1956—, prof. physics, 1958, Henry Pratt Judson disting. svc. prof., 1978—91; Henry Pratt Judson Disting. Svc. prof. emeritus, dept. physics U. Chgo., Enrico Fermi Inst., 1991—. Contbr. articles to profl. jours. Recipient J. Robert Oppenheimer prize, 1976, Order of Culture, Japan Govt., 1978, US Nat. Medal Sci., 1982, Max Planck medal, German Physical Soc., 1985, Dirac medal, Internat. Centre for Theoretical Physics, 1986, Wolf prize in physics, Wolf Found., Israel, 1994, Gian Carlo Wick Commemorative medal, World Fedn. Scientists, 1995, Bogoliubov prize, Joint Inst. for Nuclear Rsch., 2003, Benjamin Franklin medal in Physics, Franklin Inst., 2005. Mem.: NAS, Georgian Acad. Sciences (fgn. fellow 1996), Am. Phys. Soc. (Sakurai prize 1994, Dannie Heineman prize for Math. Physics 1970), Am. Acad. Arts and Scis., Japan Acad. (hon.). Office: Univ of Chicago Enrico Fermi Inst 5640 S Ellis Ave EFI Box 29 RI 267 Chicago IL 60637 Office Phone: 773-702-7286. Business E-Mail: nambu@theory.uchicago.edu.

NAMDARI, BAHRAM, surgeon; b. Oct. 26, 1939; s. Rostam and Sarvar Namdari; m. Kathleen Wilmore, Jan. 5, 1976; children: Mondona, Mietra, Ariana. MD, 1966. Diplomate Am. Bd. Surgery. Resident in gen. surgery St. John's Mercy Med. Ctr., St. Louis, 1969-73; practice medicine specializing in gen. and vascular surgery Milw., 1976—. Mem. staff St. Mary's Hosp., Milw., St. Luke's Hosp., Milw.; founder, pres. Famous Mealwaukee Foods Enterprises. Contbr. articles to med. jours.; patentee med. instruments and other devices. Cardiovascular Surgery fellow with Michael DeBakey, Baylor Coll. Medicine, Houston, 1974-75. Fellow ACS, Internat. Surgeons; mem. AMA, Med. Soc. Milwaukee County, Milw. Acad. Surgery, Wis. Med. Soc., Wis. Surg. Soc., Royal Soc. Medicine Eng. (affiliate), Am. Soc. Bariatric Surgery, World Med. Assn., Internat. Acad. Bariatric Medicine (founding mem.), Am. Acad. Cosmetic Surgery, Michael DeBakey Internat. Cardiovascular Soc. Office: Great Lakes Med and Surg Ctr 6000 S 27th St Milwaukee WI 53221-4805

NAMEROW, DAVID MARK, pediatrician; b. NYC, Dec. 12, 1947; s. Nathan and Claire (Goodstein) N.; m. Pearila Brickner, June 14, 1981; children: Jordan Ilana, Evan Gabrielle, Zoe Alexandra. BS, CCNY, 1968; MD, U. Louisville, 1972. Pediatric intern Children's Hosp. Med. Ctr., Cin., 1972-73, resident in pediatrics, 1973-75; fellow in adolescent medicine U. Md. Hosps., Balt., 1975-77; pediatrician Plaza Med. Assocs., Flanders, NJ, 1977-79; dir. adolescent medicine St. Joseph's Hosp. Med. Ctr., Paterson, NJ, 1977-81; founder, pediatrician PediatriCare Assocs., Fair Lawn, NJ, 1979—. Attending pediatrician, assoc. dir. dept. pediatrics Valley Hosp., Ridgewood, N.J., 1979—; adj. asst. clin. prof. pediatrics N.Y. Hosp.-Cornell Med. Ctr., N.Y.C., 1979—; dir. dept. pediatrics Valley Hosp., 2001-05. Fellow Am. Acad. Pediatrics; mem. Soc. for Adolescent Medicine, Ambulatory Pediatric Assn. Office: PediatriCare Assocs 20-20 Fair Lawn Ave Fair Lawn NJ 07410-2319 also: 400 Franklin Tpke Mahwah NJ 07430-3516 also: 901 Rte 23 S Pompton Plains NJ 07444 Office Phone: 201-791-4545. Personal E-mail: dnamerow@optonline.net.

NAMKUNG, YOUNG, educator, researcher; b. Seoul, Republic of Korea, Sept. 7, 1979; d. Pyong Namkung and Kyungsook Baik. BS summa cum laude (hon.), Yonsei U., Seoul, 2002, MS (hon.) summa cum laude, 2004; PhD, Purdue U., West Lafayette, Ind., 2007. Exec. rschr. Rsch. Internat. Korea, Seoul, 2004; tchg. asst. Purdue U., 2005—. Rsch. asst. Purdue U., 2004—. Contbr. articles to profl. jours. Fellow Grad. Study Fellowship, Yonsei U., 2002-2004, 1998—2002. Office: Purdue U 700 W State St Stone Hall West Lafayette IN 47907 Office Phone: 765-426-7445.

NAMROW, ERIC S., lawyer; b. Washington, Aug. 16, 1967; BA cum laude, Bucknell Univ., 1989; MPhil, Oxford Univ., England, 1993; JD, Univ. Md., 1996. Bar: Md. 1996, DC 2000. Law clerk, Hon. Lawrence F. Rodowsky Ct. of Appeals, Md., 1996—97; ptnr., intellectual property litig. Venable LLP, Washington. Assoc. editor Univ. Md.The Bus. Lawyer. Mem.: ABA, Bar Assn. of DC, Md. Bar Assn., Am. Intellectual Property Law Assn. Office: Venable LLP 575 Seventh St NW Washington DC 20004 Office Phone: 202-344-4621. Office Fax: 202-344-8300. Business E-Mail: esnamrow@venable.com.

NANAGAS, MARIA TERESITA CRUZ, pediatrician, educator; b. Manila, Jan. 21, 1946; arrived in U.S., 1970; d. Ambrosio and Maria (Pasamonte) Cruz; m. Victor N. Nanagas, Jr.; children: Victor III, Valerie, Vivian. BS, U. of the Philippines, 1965, MD, 1970. Diplomate Am. Bd. Pediat. Intern, resident St. Elizabeth's Hosp., Boston, 1971-74; fellow in ambulatory pediat. North Shore Children's Hosp., Salem, Mass., 1974-75; active staff medicine Children's Med. Ctr., Dayton, Ohio, 1976—, head divsn. gen. pediat., 1988-90, 95-97, co-interim head ambulatory pediat., 1989-90, med. dir. ambulatory pediat., 1990—. Clin. asst. prof. pediat. Wright State U., Dayton, 1977-83, clin. assoc. prof. pediat., 1983—, selective dir., 1989—, assoc. prof. pediat., 2000—; clin. asst. prof. family practice Wright State U., Dayton, 1999—; dir., preceptor Wright State U. residents continuing clinic Children's Med. Ctr., 1989—, attending physician family practice programs, 1978—. Active Miami Valley Lead Poisoning Prevention Coalition, 19926. Fellow Am. Acad. Pediat.; mem. Western Ohio Pediat. Soc., Ambulatory Pediat. Assn. Office: Children's Med Ctr Health Clinic 1 Childrens Plz Dayton OH 45404-1898 Office Phone: 937-641-3500.

NANCE, ALLAN TAYLOR, retired lawyer; b. Dallas, Jan. 31, 1933; s. A.Q. and Lois Rebecca (Taylor) N. BA, So. Meth. U., 1954, LLB, 1957; LLM, NYU, 1978. Bar: Tex. 1957, N.Y. 1961. With Simpson Thacher & Bartlett, NYC, 1960-65; asst. counsel J.P. Stevens & Co., Inc., NYC, 1965-70, sec., 1970-78, asst. gen. counsel, 1970-89; counsel J.P. Stevens & Co. Inc. and WestPoint-Pepperell Inc., 1989-93; asst. gen. counsel West-Point Stevens Inc., NYC, 1993-98, ret., 1998. With USNR, 1957-59. Woodrow Wilson fellow Columbia U., 1959-60. Mem. Phi Beta Kappa. Home: 201 E 66th St New York NY 10021-6451

NANCE, FREDERICK, lawyer; b. Cleve., Oh., 1953; BA, Harvard U., 1975; JD, U. Mich., 1978. Bar: Ohio 1978, Fla. 1987, US Dist Ct., No. Dist Ohio, US Ct. Appeals Sixth Circuit. Mng. ptnr. Squire, Sanders & Dempsey, LLP, Cleve., 2002—. Mem. exec. com. Bus. Roundtable Cleve. Chmn. Cleveland Defense Indus. Alliance, 2004—05. Named one of Am. Best Corp. Lawyers, Corp. Board Mem. Mag., 2004, Best Lawyers in Am., Inside Bus. Mag, 2001—07. Mem.: ABA, US Ct Appeals Sixth Circuit Judicial Conf., Norman Minor Bar Assn., Ohio State Bar Assn. Office: Squire Sanders & Dempsey LLP 4900 Key Tower 127 Public Sq Cleveland OH 44114-1304

NANCE, JOHN JOSEPH, lawyer, writer, air traffic controller, announcer, consultant; b. Dallas, July 5, 1946; s. Joseph Turner and Margrette (Grubbs) N.; m. Benita Ann Priest, July 26, 1968; children: Dawn Michelle, Bridgitte Cathleen, Christopher Sean. BA, So. Meth. U., 1968, JD, 1969; grad., USAF Undergrad. Pilot Tng., Williams AFB, Ariz., 1971. Bar: Tex. 1970, U.S. Ct. Appeals (fed. cir.) 1994. News reporter, broadcaster, newsman various papers and stas, Honolulu and Dallas, 1957-66; news anchorman Sta. WFAA-AM, Dallas, 1966-70; newsman including on camera Sta. WFAA-TV, Dallas; pvt. practice Dallas, 1970—; news dir. Newscom Network, Dallas, 1970; airline pilot Braniff Internat. Airways, Dallas, 1975-82, Alaska Airlines, Inc., Seattle, 1985—; chmn., pres. Exec. Transport, Inc., Tacoma, 1979-85; chmn., CEO EMEX Corp., Kent, Wash., 1987—; mng. ptnr. Phoenix Ptnrs., Ltd., Tacoma, Wash., 1995—; project devel. assoc. Columbia Tristar TV, 1997—; with Nance & Carmichael, PLLC, Austin, Tex., 1997—. Spkr. Human Mgmt., 1984—, Teamwork and Comms. in the Med. Profession; airline safety, advocate Ind. Cons., earthquake preparedness spokesman Ind. Cons.; dir. steering com. Found. for Issues Resolution in Sci. Tech., Seattle, 1987-89; speaker Northwestern Transp. Ctr. Deregulation and Safety Conf., 1987; cons. NOVA Why Planes Crash, PBS, 1987, ABC World News Tonight Crash of US AIR 427, 1994; aviation analyst ABC-TV and radio, 1995—; aviation editor: ABC Good Morning Am., 1995—; broadcast analyst, 1986—; spkr. in field. Author: Scorpion Strike, 1982, Splash of Colors, 1984, Blind Trust, 1986, On Shaky Ground, 1988, Final Approach, 1990, What Goes Up, 1991, Operating Handbook USAF Air Carrier Safety and Inspection, 1991, Phoenix Rising, 1994, Medusa's Child, 1997, The Last Hostage, 1998, Blackout, 2000, Headwind, 2001, Turbulence, 2002, Skyhook, 2003, Fireflight, 2003; contbr. Transportation Deregulatio in the U.S., 1988; actor: appeared in Sheep on the Runway, 1975; (TV series) Pandora's Clock, 1996; tech. advisor (TV series) Pandora's Clock, 1996; actor: (TV series) Medusa's Child, 1997; prodr.: USAF SOC CRM Program, 1992; author: USAF SOC CRM Program, 1992, USF Video Prodns.: ANG Introduction to CRM, 1992, The Teamwork Connection, 1996; dir.: The Teamwork Connection, 1996. Pres. Fox Glen Homeowners Assn., Tacoma, 1974-77; cons. Congl. Office Tech. Assessment, Tacoma, 1987; witness air safety hearings U.S. Congress, Washington, 1986-88; bd. dirs. St. Charles Borromeo Sch., Tacoma, 1975-78, Nat. Patient Safety Found. of AMA, 1997—; mem. Mayor's Vets. Task Force, Tacoma, 1991; bd. advisors Jour. Air Law and Commerce So. Meth. Sch. Law, 1995—, exec. bd. Sch. of Law, 1998—; bd. advisors Pacific Northwest Writer's Conf., 1994—; adv. bd. supply and logistics mgmt. program Portland State U., 1997-98. Capt. USAFR, 1975-94; lt. col. Persian Gulf. Decorated Merit Svc. medal; named Airline Safety Man of Year Wash. State Div. of Aeronautics, 1987; recipient Disting. Alumni award So. Meth. U., 2002. Fellow Chartered Inst. Transport (Canberra, Australia); mem. ABA, SAG, Tex. Bar Assn., Author's Guild Am., Res. Officers Assn. (life), Aircraft Owners' and Pilots' Assn., Phi Alpha Delta, Delta Chi. Home and Office: John Nance Prodns 4512 87th Ave W Tacoma WA 98466-1920 Office: Phoenix Ptnrs Ltd PO Box 24465 Federal Way WA 98093-1465

NANCE, LIBBA L., elementary school educator; m. Dwain Nance; children: Angie N. Cannell, Bryan S., Justin M. BS in Edn., U. of Memphis, 1971. Lic. elem. edn. tchr. Tenn., 1971. Tchr. St. Louis Sch., Memphis, 1971—73, Our Lady of Sorrows Sch., Memphis, 1992—94, St. Dominic Sch., Memphis, 1994—. Sch. coord. St. Dominic Sch. Nat. Geography Bee, City Spelling Bee, Reader's Digest Word Challenge; sch. coord. St. Agnes Acad.-St. Dominic Sch. Accelerated Reader, Family Math and Sci. Night. Mem. Dominican Assoc., Memphis; Make-A-Wish chmn. SAA-SDS Sch., Memphis. Recipient Albertus Magnus Tchg. award, 2007. Mem.: Internat. Reading Assn., NCTM. Office: St Dominic School 30 Avon Rd Memphis TN 38117 Home Phone: 901-685-7564. E-mail: lnance@saa-sds.org.

NANCE, MARIONE E., biology educator; b. Tuscaloosa, Ala., May 27, 1951; d. Francis Elmond and Ella Lucinda (Dunning) Evans; m. Thomas Stanley Nance; children: Gwen Lucinda, Frances Marione. M in Biology, Samford U., Homewood, Ala., 1977. Instr. biology dept. Samford U., 1973—. Senate chmn., faculty pres., com. mem. numerous univ., coll. and departmental coms. Samford U. Vol. spokesman, asst. to veterinarian Birmingham (Ala.) Zoo, 1980—82; vol. tchr. microbiology and dissection local elem. and high schs., Homewood, Mountain Brook, and Bessemer, Ala., 1991—95; club pres., dist. sgt.-at-arms Toastmaster's Internat., Birmingham, 1981—82. Mem.: DNA Methylation Soc., Ala. Acad. Sci., Am. Bryological and Lichenological Soc., Am. Soc. Microbiology, Beta Beta Beta. Achievements include first bio-disaster drill resulting in written protocols for first responders. Avocations: reading, travel, singing, speaking. Office: Samford U Biology Dept 800 Lakeshore Dr Homewood AL 35209-2234 Home Phone: 205-942-1508; Office Phone: 205-726-2303. E-mail: menance@samford.edu.

NANCE, MARY JOE, retired secondary school educator; b. Carthage, Tex., Aug. 7, 1921; d. F.F. and Mary Elizabeth (Knight) Born; m. Earl C. Nance, July 12, 1946; 1 child, David Earl. BBA, U. North Tex., Denton, 1953; postgrad., Northwestern State U. La., Shreveport, 1974; ME, Antioch U., Seattle, 1978. Cert. bus. educator. Tchr. Port Isabel (Tex.) Ind. Sch. Dist., 1953-79; tchr. English Tex., 1965, Splendora (Tex.) H.S., 1979-80, McLeod, Tex., 1980-81, Bremond, Tex., 1981-84; ret., 1985. Vol. tchr. for Indian students, 1964—65; vol. tutor, tchr. ESL; active WAAC, 1942—43, WAC, 1945. Recipient Image Maker award Carthage C. of C., 1984; named on Meml. for Women, Washington. Mem. NEA, Tex. Tchrs. Assn., Tex. Bus. Tchrs. Assn. (Cert. of Appreciation 1978), Nat. Women's Army Corps Vets. Assn., Air Force Assn. (life), Gwinnett Hist. Soc., Hist. Soc. Panola County, Panola County Hist. & Geneal. Assn., Nat. Hist. Soc. Baptist.

NANCE, RICHARD DAMIAN, geologist, consultant; b. St. Ives, UK, Oct. 25, 1951; s. Richard William Morton and Edith Eleanor (Leach) N.; m. Rita Felice Carpenter, Aug. 28, 1982; children: André Bernard Carpenter, Sarah Marie Eleanor, Christopher Louis Morton. BS in Geology with honors, Leicester U., Eng., 1972; PhD in Geology, Cambridge U., Eng., 1978. Asst. prof. St. Francis Xavier U., Antigonish, Nova Scotia, 1976-80, Ohio U., Athens, 1980-82; sr. rsch. geologist Exxon Prodn. Rsch. Co., Houston, 1982-83; assoc. prof. Ohio U., Athens, 1983-90, dept. chmn., 1995—2000, prof., 1991—. Rsch. cons. Inst. for Environ. Studies, La. State U., Baton Rouge, 1977-81, Cominco Am. Inc., Spokane, Wash., 1984-85, Argonne Nat. Labs., Chgo., 1984-88. Author/editor 30 chpts. in books; contbr. over 100 articles to profl. jours. Grantee Geol. Survey Can., 1987-88, NSF, 90-94, 2003-06, Earthwatch, 1991-94, Nat. Geographic, 1993-95, Ohio U., 1981-92, 2001-07, US Dept. Edn., 1996-2000, Unesco, 2004—. Fellow Geol. Assn. Can.; mem. Geol. Soc. Am., Am. Geophys. Union, Am. Assn. Petroleum Geologists, Royal Geol. Soc. Cornwall, Ussher Soc., Trevithick Soc., Soc. for Indsl. Archeology, Sigma Xi. Avocations: cornish mining history, stationary steam engines, jogging. Office: Ohio U Dept Geol Scis 316 Clippinger Labs Athens OH 45701 Office Phone: 740-593-1107. Business E-Mail: nance@ohio.edu.

NANCE, ROBERT LEWIS, oil industry executive; b. Dallas, July 10, 1936; s. Melvin Renfro Nance and Ruth Natlie (Seibert) Nowlin; m. Penni Jane Warfel; children: Robert Scott, Amy Louise, Catherine Leslie. BS, So. Meth. U., 1959; LLD (hon.), Rocky Mountain Coll., 1989. V.p. geology Oliver & West Cons., Dallas, 1960-66; ptnr. Nance & Larue Cons., Dallas, 1966-69; pres., CEO Nance Petroleum Corp., Billings, Mont., 1969—. Bd. dirs. First Interstate Bank, Mont., Rocky Mountain Coll., Billings, chmn., 1986—91; mem. Nat. Petroleum Coun., 1992—94; chmn. Petroleum Tech. Transfer Coun., 1996—99. Coun. pres. Am. Luth. Ch., Billings, 1980; trustee, chmn. Deaconess Med. Ctr., Billings; chmn. Deaconess Billings Clinic Healty Sys. Recipient Hall of Fame award Rocky Mountain Coll. Alumni, 1987, Disting. Svc. Trusteeship, Assn. Governing Bds. Univs. Colls., 1988. Mem. Am. Assn. Petroleum Geologists, Ind. Petroleum Assn. Am. (exec. com., nat. bd. govs., Roughneck of Yr. 2002), Ind. Petroleum Assn. Mountain States (v.p. Mont. 1977-79, Wildcatter of Yr. 1999), Mont. Petroleum Assn., Hilands Golf Club, Billings Petroleum Club. Avocations: fly fishing, scuba diving, skiing. Office: Nance Petroleum Corp PO Box 7168 550 N 31st St Billings MT 59103 Office Phone: 406-245-6248. Business E-Mail: bnance@nancepetro.com.

NAND, SUCHA, medical educator; b. Thiriewal, Punjab, India, Feb. 3, 1948; d. Narsingh Dass and Swaran Devi; m. Surinder S. Nand, June 15, 1973; children: Ranveer, Rahul. Pre-med. student, Dayanand Ayur Vedic Coll., Amritsar, India, 1966; MB, BS, Med. Coll., Amritsar, India, 1971. Diplomate Am. Bd. Internal Medicine, Am. Bd. Hemotology, Am. Bd. Med. Oncology. Asst. prof. Stritch Sch. Medicine Loyola U., Maywood, Ill., 1981-88, assoc. prof. Stritch Sch. Medicine, 1989-95; prof. medicine, 1996—. Editor Jour. of Med. Coll., 1969-71; contbr. articles to profl. jours. Clin. fellow Am. Cancer Soc., 1981; Brilliant Student scholarships, 1962-71. Mem. Am. Soc. Hematology, Am. Soc. Clin. Oncology, S.W.

Oncology Group (mem. leukemia com. 1988—). Avocations: chess, reading, running. Office: Loyola Univ Med Ctr 2160 S 1st Ave Maywood IL 60153-3304 Office Phone: 708-327-3182.

NANDA, NAVREET K., research scientist; d. Pritpal Singh Nanda and Hardev Kaur. PhD, All India Inst. Med. Scis., New Delhi, 1985. Post-doctoral fellow U. Calif., LA, 1987—96; asst. prof. U. Ill., Chgo., 1996—2000; guest scientist NIH, Bethesda, Md., 2005—. Grantee, NSF, 1998—2000. Mem.: Am. Assn. Immunologists. Achievements include research in phenomenon of immunodominance was known for decades, its molecular basis remained unknow. Demonstrated that DM, a non-classical major histocompatibility molecule, was the underlying factor. Home Phone: 202-944-2738; Office Phone: 301-496-3842.

NANDA, VED PRAKASH, law educator, director, academic administrator; b. Gujranwala, India, Nov. 20, 1934; arrived in U.S., 1960; s. Jagan Nath and Attar (Kaur) N.; m. Katharine Kunz, Dec. 19, 1982; 1 child, Anjali Devi. MA, Punjab U., 1952; LLB, U. Delhi, 1955, LLM, 1958, Northwestern U., 1962; postgrad., Yale U., 1962-65; LLD, Soka U., Tokyo, 1997, Bundelkhand U., Jhansi, India, 2000, doctorate (hon.), 2000, Soka U., Tokyo, 1997. Asst. prof. law U. Denver, 1965—68, assoc. prof. law, 1968—70, prof. law, dir. Internat. Legal Studies Program, 1970—, Thompson G. Marsh prof. law, 1987—, Evans U. prof., 1992—, asst. provost, 1993—94, vice provost, 1994—. Vis. prof. Coll. Law U. Iowa, Iowa City, 1974—75; vis. prof. Fla. State U., 1973, U. San Diego, 1979, U. Colo., 1992; disting. vis. prof. internat. law Kent Coll. Law, 1981, Calif. We. Sch. Law, San Diego, 1983—84; disting. vis. scholar Sch. Law U. Hawaii, Honolulu, 1986—87; cons. Solar Energy Rsch. Inst., 1978—81, Dept. Energy, 1980—81; vis. prof. numerous summer programs. Co-author (with David Pansius): Litigation of International Disputes in U.S. Courts, 1987; editor: Law in the War Against International Terrorism, 2005; co-editor (with M. Cherif Bassiouni): A Treatise on International Criminal Law, 1973, Water Needs for the Future, 1977; co-editor: (with George Shepherd) Human Rights and Third World Development, 1985; co-editor: (with others) Global Human Rights, 1981, The Law of Transnational Business Transactions, 1981, World Climate Change, 1983, Breach and Adaption of International Contracts, 1992, World Debt and Human Conditions, 1993, Europe Community Law After 1992, 1993, International Environmental Law and Policy, 1995, European Union Law After Maastricht, 1996; co-editor: (with William M. Evan) Nuclear Proliferation and the Legality of Nuclear Weapons, 1995; co-editor: (with S.P. Sinha) Hindu Law and Legal Theory, 1996; co-editor: (with D. Krieger) Nuclear Weapons and the World Court, 1998; co-editor: (with George Pring) International Environmental Law and Policy for the 21st Century, 2003; co-editor: Law in the War Against International Terrorism, 2004; editor, contbr. Refugee Law and Policy, 1989, mem. editl. bd. Jour. Am. Comparative Law, Indian Jour. Internat. Law, Transnational Pubs.; columnist: Denver Post. O-chmn. Colo. Pub. Broadcasting Fedn., 1977—78; mem. Gov.'s Commn. on Pub. Telecomm., 1980—82; UN day chair State of Colo., 2000—; vice chair exec. coun. World Fedn. UN Assn., Geneva; bd. dir. various nat. and state civic orgns. Co-recipient Hyde Prize in Internat. Law, Northwestern U. Law Sch.; named Thompson G. Marsh Prof. of Law, 1987—, John Evans U. Prof., 1994—, Amb. for Peace, Interreligious and Internat. Fedn. for World Peace, 2001; recipient Univ. Gold Medal, Delhi U. Faculty of Law, Internat. Excellence award, Colo. Coun. Internat. Orgns., 1985, Burlington Northern Found. Scholar award, U. Denver, 1990, World Legal Scholar award, World Peace Through Law Ctr., Beijing, 1990, Highest honor award, Soka U., Tokyo, 1994, Alumni Faculty award, U. Denver Coll. Law, 1994, India Devel. Assn. award, 1996, Civil Right's award, Anti-Defamation League, 1996, Pioneer award, U. Denver, 1997, Medal of Honor, World Congress of Ukranian Lawyers, 1999, Rotary fellowship established in his honor, Denver Rotary, 2000, Gold Medal established in his honor, Bundelkhand U., 2000, Spl. Achievement award, Indo-Am. Assn., 2002, Cmty. Peace Bldg. award, Gandhi King Ikeda, 2004, Highest Order of Justice award, World Jurist Assn., 2005, Human Rights award, India-Can. Assn., 2006; graduate fellow, U. Delhi Faculty of Law, Yale Law Sch., Northwestern U. Law Sch. Mem. World Jurist Assn. (v.p. 1991—, pres. 1998-2000, hon. pres. 2000—), World Assn. Law Profs. (pres. 1987-93), UN Assn. (v.p. Colo. divsn. 1973-76, pres. 1986-88, 93-96, nat. coun. UNA-USA 1990—, mem. governing bd. UNA-USA 1995-2005, Arthur Goodman Leadership award 1995, Human Rights award 1997), World Fedn. UN Assns. (vice-chmn. 1995-2001), Am. Assn. Comparative Study Law (bd. dirs.), Am. Soc. Internat. Law (v.p. 1987-88, exec. coun. 1969-72, 81-84, bd. rev. and devel. 1988-91, hon. v.p. 1995-96, counselor 2000—), Assn. Am. Law Schs., U.S. Inst. Human Rights, Internat. Law Assn. (exec. com. 1986—, hon. pres. 2001—), Colo. Coun. Internat. Orgns. (pres. 1988-90), Assn. U.S. Mems. Internat. Inst. Space Law (bd. dirs., exec. com. 1980-88), Internat. Acad. Comparative Law (assoc.), Acad. Internat. Commercial and Consumer Law, Order St. Ives (pres.), Rotary, Cactus Club, Univ. Club, Colo. Athletic Club. Office Phone: 303-871-6276. Business E-Mail: vnanda@law.du.edu.

NANDEDKAR, SANJEEV DATTATRAYA, medical researcher, educator; b. Pune, India, Dec. 28, 1955; s. Dattatraya Yadav and Madhumalti Dattatraya Nandedkar; m. Anjali Sanjeev Dadhe, Dec. 27, 1978; children: Desh Sanjeev, Vishesh Sanjeev. PhD, U. of Va., 1977—83. Med. rsch. asst. prof. Duke U. Med. Ctr., 1986—90; clin. applications mgr. Oxford Instruments Med. Systems, Hawthorne, NY, 1990—. Editor: emg on cd CASA Engring., Hopewell Junction, NY, 1997—. Author, editor: multimedia text books EMG on CD: Volumes I - III, author, rschr.: articles for profl. jours., section editor: rev. chapters Textbooks on Clin. Neurophysiology. Recipient Disting. Svc., Am. Assn. of Electrodiagnostic Medicine, 2002, Excellence in Rsch. Writing, Assn. of Academic Physiatrists, 1997. Achievements include development of The Synergy Electromyograph; Multi Motor unit analysis and Median averaging; research in Computer simulations in Electromyography. Office: Oxford Instruments 12 Skyline Dr Hawthorne NY 10532 Personal E-mail: sanjeev@nandedkar.com.

NANGLE, JOHN FRANCIS, federal judge; b. St. Louis, June 8, 1922; s. Sylvester Austin and Thelma (Bank) N.; m. Jane Adams, June 7, 1986; 1 child, John Francis Jr. AA, Harris Tchrs. Coll., 1941; BS, U. Mo., 1943; JD, Washington U., St. Louis, 1948. Bar: Mo. 1948. Pvt. practice law, Clayton, 1948-73; judge US Dist. Ct. (ea. dist.) Mo., St. Louis, 1973—, chief judge, 1983-90; sr. judge US Dist. Ct. (so. dist.) Ga., 1990—. Mem. 8th Cir. Jud. Coun.; mem. exec. com. Jud. Conf. U.S.; chmn. Jud. Panel on Multidist. Litig., mem. working group on mass torts, mem. jud. resources working group; mem. ad hoc com. on asbestos. Mem. Mo. Rep. Com., 1958-73; mem. St. Louis County Rep. Cen. Com., 1958-73, chmn., 1960-61; pres. Mo. Assn. Reps., 1961, Reps. Vets. League, 1960; mem. Rep. Nat. Com., 1972-73; Grand Orator and bd. dirs. Masonic Home Mo. First Sgt. USAR, with AUS, 1943—46. Named Mo. Republican of Year John Marshall Club, 1970, Mo. Republican of Year Mo. Assn. Reps., 1971; recipient Most Disting. Alumnus award Harris-Stowe Coll., Most Disting. Alumnus award Washington U. Sch. Law, 1986. Mem. ABA, Legion of Honor DeMolay, Mo. Bar Assn., St. Louis Bar Assn., St. Louis County Bar Assn. (mem. com.). Business E-Mail: brenda_king@gas.uscourts.gov.

NANKO, RAYMOND S., physician; b. Inglewood, Calif., Feb. 13, 1962; s. John and Veronica Marie (Thunder) N. DC, Cleve. Chiropractic Coll., 1985; MD, Ross U., 1994. Diplomate Am. Bd. Disability Analysts, Am. Bd. Family Practice, Am. Bd. Chiropractic Orthopedics, Am. Bd. Pain Mgmt. With ActiveCare Med. Spine & Pain Ctr., Muncie, Ind. Fellow Am. Back Soc.; mem. AMA, Ind. State Med. Assn., Ind. State Chiropractic Assn., Am. Chiropractic Assn., Am. Acad. Orthop. Medicine, Nat. Headache Found., Ind. State Med. Assn., Ind. State Chiropractic Assn., Coun. Orthop., Acad. Chiropractic Orthopedics, Arthritis Found., Internat. Spinal Injection Soc., Am. Assn. Orthopedic Medicine. Office: Active Care Med Spine & Pain Ctr 919 W Jackson St Muncie IN 47305-1554

NANNA, MICHAEL EDWARD, chemist, researcher; b. Santa Cruz, Calif., Oct. 2, 1956; s. Herman Nanna and Patricia Strong; m. Tania N. Niedzwiecki, May 13, 1989. BS in Indsl. Tech., Calif. Poly. State U., 1988, MS in Chemistry, 1993; PhD in Polymer Sci., ND State U., 2004. R&D chemist Behr Process Corp., Santa Ana, Calif., Morton Electronics Materials, Tustin, Calif., ETI, Fields Landing, Calif., Willamette Valley Co., Pineville, La. Mem.: Fedn. Socs. for Coatings Tech. (Leo Roon award 2003). Avocations: bicycling, jogging, fishing. Office: Willamette Valley Co 100 Dixie Mae Dr Pineville LA 71361

NANNE, LOUIS VINCENT, professional hockey team executive; b. Sault Ste. Marie, Ont., Can., June 2, 1941; s. Michael and Evelyn N.; m. Francine Yvette Potvin, Aug. 27, 1962; children: Michelle, Michael, Marc, Marty. BS in Mktg., U. Minn., 1963. Mem. Minn. North Stars hockey club, 1967-78, v.p., gen. mgr., 1978-88, pres., 1988-91; sr. v.p. Piper Capital Mgmt., Mpls., 1991-95; exec. v.p. Voyageur Asset Mgmt., Mpls., 1995—. Bd. govs. Nat. Hockey League, 1981-91; mem. internat. com. USA Hockey. Bd. dirs. Mpls. C.C. Found., 1986-90, Children's Home Soc., 1998—. Recipient Lester Patrick award NHL, 1989; named among Top 50 Coll. Players in 50 Yrs.; inducted into U. Minn. Hall of Fame, U.S. Hockey Heritage Hall of Fame award, Sault St. Marie Hall of Fame, U.S. Hockey Hall of Fame, Internat. Ice Hockey Hall of Fame. Mem. Interlachen Country Club (bd. dirs. 1992-95), Spring Hill Golf Club (bd. dirs. 1996-2004). Roman Catholic. Office: Voyageur Asset Management 100 S 5th St Ste 2300 Minneapolis MN 55402-1230

NANNES, MICHAEL EDWARD, lawyer; b. Detroit, Mar. 21, 1953; s. Charles and Maxine Nannes; m. Nancy E. Everett, Apr. 7, 1979; children: Caleb, Marshall, Helena. BBA with high distinction, U. Mich., 1974; JD, Georgetown U., 1977. Bar: DC 1977, Fla. 1978, registered: US Dist. Ct. Md. 1987, US Ct. Appeals (4th cir.) 1981, US Supreme Ct. 1982. Law clk. to Hon. John H. Pratt US Dist. Ct. DC, Washington, 1977-78; ptnr. Dickstein Shapiro & Morin LLP, Washington, 1978—94, firmwide dep. mng. ptnr., 1994—2004, firmwide mng. ptnr., 2004—06; chmn. Dickstein Shapiro LLP (formerly Dickstein Shapiro & Morin LLP), Washington, 2006—. Topics editor The Georgetown Law Jour., 1976—77; co-author (with Richard J. Leveridge): Using Smart Contracting to Assure Efficiency in Resolving Complex Construction Cases, 1993; author: First of Its Kind Wastewater Privatization - A Lesson in Teamwork., 1997, Dickstein's Quest for Family Values, 1999, Leaving No One Behind, 2002. Office: Dickstein Shapiro LLP 1825 Eye St NW Washington DC 20006 E-mail: nannesm@dicksteinshapiro.com.

NANNEY, DAVID LEDBETTER, geneticist, educator; b. Abingdon, Va., Oct. 10, 1925; s. Thomas Grady and Pearl (Ledbetter) Nanney; m. Jean Kelley, June 15, 1951; children: Douglas Paul, Ruth Elizabeth Beshears. AB, Okla. Bapt. U., 1946; PhD, Ind. U., 1951; Laurea honoris causa, U. Pisa, Italy, 1994. Asst. prof. zoology U. Mich., Ann Arbor, 1951-56, assoc. prof., 1956-58; prof. U. Ill., Urbana-Champaign, 1959-76, prof. genetics and devel., 1976-86, prof. ecology, ethology and evolution, 1987-91, prof. emeritus, 1991—. NIH sr. postdoctoral fellow Ind. U., 1949—51. Author (with Herbert Stern): The Biology of Cells, 1965, Experimental Ciliatology, 1980. Named Disting. Lectr., Sch. Life Scis., U. Ill., 1981; recipient Disting. Alumnus award, Okla. Bapt. U., 1972, Preisträger, Alexander von Humboldt Stiftung, Germany, 1984. Fellow: AAAS, Am. Acad. Arts and Scis.; mem.: Soc. Protozoologists, Am. Genetic Assn. (pres. 1982), Genetics Soc. Am. Home: 703 W Indiana Ave Urbana IL 61801-4835 Office: U Ill Dept Animal Biology 505 S Gregory St Urbana IL 61801 Business E-Mail: d-nanney@life.uiuc.edu.

NANOS, GEORGE PETER, JR., science administrator, military officer, physicist; b. Torrington, Conn., Apr. 11, 1945; s. George N.; m. Joanne Louise Knowles, July 5, 1969; 1 child, George. Grad., U.S. Naval Acad., 1967; PhD in Physics, Princeton U., 1974; attended, U.S. Naval Destroyer Sch., Newport, RI, 1974, Def. Sys. Mgmt. Coll., Ft. Belvoir, Va., 1991. Joined U.S. Navy, 1967; commd. ensign USN; advanced through grades to vice admiral; antisub warfare gunnery officer USS Glennon (DD-840), 1967-69; engr. officer USS Forrest Sherman (DD-931), 1974-76; material officer mem. staff destroyer squadron 10, 1976-78; mgr. tech. devel. high energy laser program offie (NAVSEA PMS-405), 1978-82; engring. duty officer, 1980; combat sys. officer Norfolk Naval Shipyard, 1982-84; engr. officer USS America (CV-66); dep. dir. warfare sys. engring. space and naval warfare sys. cmd., 1984-86; head navigation br., 1988-90; head missile br. devel., prodn., operational support missile subsys., 1990-92; dir. tech. divsn. strategic sys. program, 1992-94; dir. strategic sys. program, 1994-98; commr. naval sea sys. command, 1998—2002, retired, 2002; prin. dep. assoc. dir. Threat Reduction Directorate Los Alamos Nat. Lab., N.Mex., 2002—03, interim dir. N.Mex., 2003, dir. N.Mex., 2003—05. Decorated Legion of Merit, Disting. Svc. medal, Meritorious Svc. medal, Navy Achievement medal.

NANTS, BRUCE ARLINGTON, lawyer; b. Orlando, Fla., Oct. 26, 1953; s. Jack Arlington and Louise (Hulme) N. BA, U. Fla., 1974, JD, 1977. Bar: Fla. 1977. Asst. state's atty. State Atty.'s Office, Orlando, 1977-78; pvt. practice, Orlando, 1979—. Columnist The Law and You, 1979—80. Auctioneer pub. TV sta., 1979; campaign coord. cen. Fla. steering com. Bob Dole for Pres., 1988; bd. dirs. Cystic Fibrosis Found. Mem. Acad. Fla. Trial Lawyers, Am. Arbitration Assn., Fellowship Christian Athletes (past bd. dirs. Cen. Fla.), Tiger Bay Club Cen. Fla., Orlando Touchdown Club, Fla. Blue Key, Omicron Delta Kappa, Phi Beta Kappa, Phi Delta Theta. Democrat. Baptist. Avocations: tennis, golf, swimming, scuba diving. Home: 1112 Country Ln Orlando FL 32804-6934 Office: PO Box 547871 Orlando FL 32854-7871 Home Phone: 407-247-4009; Office Phone: 407-246-7041. E-mail: bacfnants@earthlink.net.

NANTZ, JAMES WILLIAM (JIM NANTZ), sportscaster; b. Charlotte, NC, May 17, 1959; s. James William Jr. and Doris (Trull) N.; m. Ann-Lorraine Carlsen, Apr. 16, 1983; 1 child, Caroline Mackenzie. BA in Radio and TV, U. Houston, 1981. Radio announcer Sta. KTRH, Houston; sports announcer Sta. KHOU-TV, Houston; sports announcer, anchor Sta. KSL-TV, Salt Lake City; announcer CBS Sports, NYC, 1985—. Actor: (film) Tin Cup, 1996. Achievements include being the CBS announcer for major Sporting events including NCAA Men's Basketball Final Four, PGA Master's Tournament. Office: CBS Sports 51 W 52nd St New York NY 10019-6119 *

NANULA, RICHARD D., former heath products company executive; b. Los Angeles, 1960; married; 3 children. BA in economics, U. Calif., Santa Barbara; MBA, Harvard Bus. Sch. Joined Walt Disney Co., 1986, exec. v.p., CFO, 1991—94, pres. Disney Stores, 1994—96, CFO, 1996—98; pres., CEO Starwood Hotels and Resorts, NYC, 1998—99; chmn., CEO Broadband Sports, 1999—2001; exec. v.p., CFO Amgen Inc., 2001—07. Bd. dirs. The Boeing Co., 2005—; bd. trustees Healthcare Leadership Coun. Avocations: basketball, tennis.

NAOR, DANIEL, food products executive; b. Paris, July 1, 1960; s. Shlomo and Sarah (Puderbeutel) N.; 1 child, Nathalie. BS in Elec. Engring., MIT, 1981, MS in Elec. Engring. and Computer Sci., 1981; MBA, INSEAD, 1990. Cert. engr. Project mgr. ELOP, Rehovot, Israel, 1985-87, mktg. mgr., 1988—89; assoc. McKinsey & Co., Paris, 1990—95, prin., 1995—98, Dallas, 1998—2002; v.p. strategy, planning and bus. devel. Frito Lay N.Am., Plano, 2002—05, group v.p. bus. integration, chief strategist, 2005—, sr. v.p. transformation and strategy. Contbr. articles to profl. jours. Mem. bd. dirs. Dallas Theater Ctr. Bd., 1999-2002, Variety, 1997—. Capt. Israeli Air Force, 1981-85. Mem. IEEE, Tau Beta Pi, Sigma Xi (assoc.). Jewish. Avocations: films, theater, ballroom and Latin dancing. Office: Frito Lay N Am 7701 Legacy Dr 3A-254 Plano TX 75024 Business E-Mail: Daniel.Naor@FritoLay.com.

NAOUMOV, VIATCHESLAV I., mechanical engineer, educator; b. Kazon, Russia, Mar. 2, 1953; s. Igor P. Naoumov and Ludmila I. Naoumova; m. Irina Y. Guskova; 1 child, Anton V. Grad., Kazan Aviation Inst., Russia, 1976, PhD in AE Engring., 1981, DSWc in AE and ME Engring., 1994. Asst. prof. Kazan Aviation Inst., Russia, 1982—89, assoc. prof., 1993—96; dean coll. Kazan State Tech. U., Russia, 1995—99, prof., dept. head, 1996—2004. Vis. prof. U. Tenn., Knoxville, 2001—. Named Soros Assoc. Prof., 1995, Disting. Scientist, Russia, 1999; recipient Outstanding Rsch. award, USSR, 1998. Office: University of Tennessee 214 Perkins Hall 1506 Middle Dr Knoxville TN 37996 Home Phone: 865-946-8769; Office Phone: 865-974-7675. Business E-Mail: vnaoumov@utk.edu.

NAOUMOVA, IRINA YEVGENIEVNA, business educator, consultant; b. Omsk, Russia, Aug. 5, 1960; d. Yevgeny A. Guskov and Lydia N. Guskova; m. Viatcheslav I. Naoumov, Dec. 3, 1983; 1 child, Anton V. Naoumov. Grad., Kazan State U., Russia, 1982, PhD in Econs. and Mgmt., 1989. Asst. prof. Kazan State Tech. U., 1982—93, assoc. prof., 1993—95; assoc. prof., head Kazan State U., 1995—2002; vis. prof. U. Tenn., Knoxville, 2001—. Cons. Tatarstan C. of C., Kazan, 2000—05. Mem. Alliance of Universities for the Democracy, 2000. Grantee, Jr. Fellowship Devel. Program, 1996—97, Fulbright Assn., 2000—07. Mem.: Am. Acad. Mgmt., Internat. Acad. Edn. (corr.). Office: Univ Tenn Knoxville TN 37996 Office Phone: 865-974-1740.

NAPACK, BRIAN, publishing executive; b. 1962; Grad., Middlebury Coll.; MBA, Columbia U. Mgmt. cons. A.T. Kearney, Inc.; v.p. Paramount/Simon & Schuster; co-founder Disney Interactive Walt Disney Co., v.p., founder Disney Ednl. Publishing; CEO, founder ThinkBox; ptnr. LEK Consulting; pres. Holtzbrinck Publishers, 2006—. Office: Holtzbrinck Publishers LLC 175 5th Ave New York NY 10010-7703 Office Phone: 212-674-5151. Office Fax: 212-420-9314.

NAPIER, CAMERON MAYSON FREEMAN, historic preservationist; b. Shanghai, Dec. 5, 1931; d. Hamner Garland and Cameron Middleton (Brame) Freeman; m. John Hawkins Napier III, Sept. 11, 1964. Student, L'Ecole des Artes Municipale, Paris, 1950-51, Westhampton Coll./U. Richmond, 1951—53; BA, U. Ala., 1955. Photographer's asst. Scott, Demott & Perry, Montgomery, Ala., 1951; art dir. WCOV-TV, Montgomery, 1955; self-employed graphic designer Dallas, 1956-64; self-employed designer Alexandria, Va., 1965-71; restoration chmn. White House Assn. Ala., Montgomery, 1973-76, 1st vice regent, 1976-80, regent, 1980—. Co-founder Friends of Stratford Hall for No. Va., Alexandria, late 1960s; docent chmn. Lee's Boyhood Home, late 1960s; bd. dirs. Landmarks Found., Montgomery, 1971-75; advisor Conde Charlotte House, Mobile, Ala., 1994-95. Author, designer booklet: The First White House of the Confederacy, 1978 (nat. printers award 1979), The Struggle to Preserve the First White House of the Confederacy, 1982; contbr. to Ency. of So. Culture, 1989, Ency. of Ala.-online, 2006. Bd. dirs. English Speaking Union, Montgomery, 1980-83. Named Hon. First Lady, by the Gov.'s wife, Montgomery, Ala., 1985; recipient Award of Excellence, Advt. Artists Assn., Dallas, 1960—62, disting. svc. award, Ala. Hist. Commn., Montgomery, 1977, Cert. of Commendation, Gov. Ala., 1986, So. Patriot award, 1997, Lifetime Achievement award, Ala. Preservation Alliance, 2001, Jefferson Davis award, 1984, Winnie Davis award, United Daus. of Confederacy, 1985. Mem.: Antiquarian Soc. (pres. 1981—82), Sojourners Lit. Club (pres.), Order of Merovingian Dynasty, Militi Templi Scotia, Daus. of Barons Runnymede, Nat. Soc. Colonial Dames in Am. (hist. properties com. 1994—95, state bd. mgrs. 1998—2000, ctr. vice chmn. 1998—2000), Am. Soc. Most Venerable Order of the Hosp. St. John of Jerusalem (assoc. officer sister 1995, named Comdr. Sister 2002), Soc. Descs. of Colonial Clergy, Order of the Crown in Am., Kappa Delta. Episcopalian. Avocations: jumbles, cryptoquotes, crossword puzzles, afternoon tea. Office: First White House Confed 644 Washington St Montgomery AL 36130-3057 Office Phone: 334-242-1861.

NAPIER, JOHN HAWKINS, III, historian; b. Berkeley, Calif., Feb. 6, 1925; s. John Hawkins and Lena Mae (Tate) Napier; m. Harriet Elizabeth McGehee, Aug. 30, 1950 (dec.); m. Cameron Mayson Freeman, Sept. 11, 1964. BA, U. Miss., 1949; MA, Auburn U., 1967; postgrad., Georgetown U., 1971; D (hon.), Napier U., Edinburgh, 2000. Journalist, tchr. Picayune (Miss.) H.S., 1946; commd. 2d lt. U.S. Air Force, 1949, advanced through grades to lt. col., 1966; ret., 1977. Staff dir. Congressional Com. on S.E. Asia, 1970; faculty Air War Coll., 1971-74; Air U. Command historian, 1974-77; asst. to exec. dir. Ala. Commn. on Higher Edn., Montgomery, 1977-78; adj. history faculty Auburn U., Montgomery, 1980-85; columnist Montgomery Advertiser, 1980-87; lectr. in field. Author: Lower Pearl River's Piney Woods: Its Land and People, 1985; The Air Force Officers Guide, 30th edit., 1995, Dr. Patrick Napier: His Ancestors and Some Descendants, 1991; contbr. articles to profl. jours. With USMC, 1943-46, col. Ala. State Defense Force, 1991-97, brig. gen., dep. comdr., 1997-99. Decorated Legion of Merit; Order of St. John of Jerusalem, Milit. and Hospitaller Order of St. Lazarus of Jerusalem, Sovereign Mil. Order of Temple of Jerusalem; recipient award of merit Ala. Hist. Commn., 1976, Ala. Disting. Svc. medal, 1999, merit award English-Speaking Union U.S., 1983; Taylor medal and grad. fellow U. Miss., 1949; Storrs scholar Pomona Coll., 1942-43. Fellow: Soc. Antiquaries Scotland; mem.: S.R. SAR (pres. 1974—75), SCV (vice comdr. Ala. 1979—80), Ala. Hist. Assn. (pres. 1979—80), Royal Order Scotland, English-Speaking Union (pres. 1978—87, nat. dir. 1980—86, 1987—90, 1991—94), Scabbard and Blade, Royal Scots (Edinburgh), Mil. Order Carabao, Soc. Colonial Wars, Soc. War of 1812 (pres. Ala. 1980—82), St. Andrews Soc., Clan Napier in N.Am. (lt. to chief 1985—), Order 1st Families Va., Jamestowne Soc., Soc. Cincinnati, Ala. Assn. (pres. 1998—2001), Aztec 1847, Soc. Pioneers Montgomery (pres. 1979—80), Montgomery Country Club, Masons (32d degree), Pi Sigma Alpha, Phi Alpha Theta, Omicron Delta Kappa, Phi Kappa Phi, Sigma Chi. Democrat. Episcopalian. Home: Kilmahew 158 Mt Zion Rd Ramer AL 36069-6505

NAPLES, CAESAR JOSEPH, lawyer, educator; b. Buffalo, Sept. 4, 1938; s. Caesar M. and Fannie A. (Occhipinti) N.; children: Jennifer, Caesar; m. Sandra L. Harrison, July 16, 1983. AB, Yale U., 1960; JD, SUNY, 1963. Bar: N.Y. 1963, Fla. 1977, Calif. 1988, U.S. Supreme Ct. 1965. With Moot & Sprague, Buffalo, 1965-69; asst. dir., employee rels. N.Y. Gov. Office, Albany, 1969-71; asst. v. chancellor SUNY, Albany, 1971-75; vice chancellor and gen. counsel Fla. State U. System, 1975-82; vice chancellor Calif. State U. System, 1983-92, vice chancellor emeritus, 1992—, prof. law and fin. emeritus Long Beach, 1983—; bd. dirs., gen. counsel, corp. sec. Open U., Denver and Wilmington, Del., 1999—2003; gen. counsel Walden U., 1989—2003. Cons. Govt. of Australia, U. Nev. Sys., Assn. Can. Colls. and Univs., Que., also other univs. and colls. Contbr. articles to profl. jours.; co-author: Romanov Succession, 1989 with J. Victor Baldridge. Mem. Metlife Resources Adv. Bd., 1986-2002, chmn., 1992-2002; mem. Meml. Heart Inst. Long Beach Meml. Hosp., 1993—, bd. dirs., chmn. 1998—, found. bd., 1996—; bd. dirs. Calif. Acad. Math. and Scis., 1995—; mem. adv. bd. Incline Village Cmty. Hosp., 2004—.

Capt. U.S. Army, 1963-65. Mem. Acad Pers. Adminstrn. (founder), Nat. Ctr. for Study Collective Bargaining Higher Edn. (bd. dirs.). Avocations: opera, tennis. Fax: 310-798-0065. Business E-Mail: cjnaples@csulb.edu.

NAPLES, RONALD JAMES, manufacturing executive; b. Passaic, NJ, Sept. 10, 1945; s. James V. and Lee A. Naples; m. Suzanne Lorraine Shoudy, June 17, 1967; children: Regen Jeffrey, Marcus Jamison, Tiffany Marie. BS, U.S. Mil. Acad., 1967; MA, Fletcher Sch. Law, 1972; MBA with distinction, Harvard U., 1974. Assoc. in corp. fin. Loeb Rhoades Co., 1973; fellow, spl. asst. to counselor to Pres. The White House, 1974; spl. asst. to adminstr. Fed. Energy Adminstrn., 1975; exec. dir. Presdl. Task Force on Energy, Washington, 1975-76; v.p. internat. Hunt Mfg. Co., Phila., 1976, exec. v.p., 1980-81, vice chmn., pres., CEO, 1981-86, chmn., CEO, 1987-95; also dir.; pres. Hunt Internat. Co., 1977-82; pres., CEO Quaker Chem. Corp., 1995-97, chmn., pres., CEO, 1997—. Bd. dirs. Glatfelter Paper Co.; chmn. Fed. Res. Bank, Phila., U. of Arts. Bd. dirs. Rock Sch. Pa. Ballet, ARC, Fgn. Policy Rsch. Inst., Phila., Phila. Mus. Art, Franklin Inst. With US Army, 1967—71. Decorated Bronze star with oak leaf cluster, Army Commindation medal with oak leaf cluster, Air medal, Cross of Gallantry Vietnam; named Outstanding Young Man Am., U.S. Jaycees, 1977, CEO of Decade Bus. Equipment, Fin. World Mag., 1989; recipient Mil. Order Wars medal, U.S. Mil. Acad., 1967, Phila. Inc. Cmty. Leadership award, 1990, Human Rels. Civic Achievement award, Am. Jewish Coun., 1989, Semper Fidelis award, Marine Corps Scholarship Fedn., 1991, Stephen Girard award, Phila. Fin. Assn., 1992, Touching a Life award, Boys and Girls Club Am., 1994, Torch of Liberty award, Anti-Defamation League, 2002; Walter Heller fellow, Harvard U., 1974, White Ho. fellow, 1974—75. Mem.: Assn. Grad. U.S. Mil. Acad., Chief Execs. Orgn., World Pres.' Orgn., White Ho. Fellows Assn., Harvard Bus. Sch. Alumni Assn., Phila. Country Club, Harvard Bus. Sch. Club Phila., Pyramid Club, Racquet Club. Office: Quaker Chem Corp One Quaker Park 901 Hector St Conshohocken PA 19428

NAPLETON, ROBERT JOSEPH, lawyer; b. Evergreen Park, Ill., Jan. 13, 1963; s. Francis Edward and Elizabeth (Raynor) N.; m. Clare Therese McEnery, June 6, 1992; children: Martin Joseph, Nora Elizabeth, Patricia Clare, Francis James, Luke John. BBA, Loyola U., Chgo., 1985, JD, 1988. Bar: Ill. 1988, US Dist. Ct. (no. dist.) Ill. 1988, US Dist. Ct. (ctrl. dist.) Ill. 1995, US Dist. Ct. (we. dist.) Wis. 1998, US Dist. Ct. Colo. 2000, US Federal Ct. Claims, 2004, US Supreme Ct. 1999. Law clk. to Chief Judge James E. Murphy Circuit Ct. of Cook County, Chgo., 1985—88; mem. staff State's Atty. Office of Cook County, Markham, Ill., 1987-88; assoc. Motherway & Glenn, Chgo., 1988-98; ptnr. Motherway, Glenn & Napleton, Chgo., 1999—2002, Motherway & Napleton, Chgo., 2003—. Spkr., presenter in field. Treas. campaign Citizens to Elect James Brosnahan State Rep. for 36th Dist., Ill., 1996—; mem. Ill. Supreme Ct. Com. on Profl. Responsibility 2003, 2004, Ill. Supreme Ct. Com. on Jury Instructions in Civil Cases 2005-. Fellow Roscoe Pound Found.; mem. ATLA (aviation law com.), Am. Coll. Trial Lawyers, Ill. Trial Lawyers Assn. (bd. advocates 1993-97, bd. mgrs. 1997—, med. negligence and product liability coms. 1994—, civil practice com. 1995—), Ill. State Bar Assn. (bd. govs. 1994-2000, tort law sect. coun. 1992-95), Southwest Bar Assn., Will County Bar Assn., Chgo. Bar Assn. (trial techniques com. 1991-92), Leading Ill. Lawyer Network, Leading Am. Atty., Catholic Lawyers Guild, Brother Rice H.S. St. Thomas More Soc., Am. Bd. Trial Advocates, Soc. of Trial Lawyers. Democrat. Roman Catholic. Avocations: golf, skiing, ice hockey, reading. Home: 400 Sunset Ave La Grange IL 60525-6115 Office: Motherway & Napleton 100 W Monroe St Ste 200 Chicago IL 60603-1923 Home Phone: 708-579-1193; Office Phone: 312-726-2699. Business E-Mail: bnapleton@mnlawoffice.com.

NAPOLI, JOSEPH STEPHEN, horticulturist, conductor; b. Kansas City, Mo., Jan. 28, 1944; s. Christopher and Mary Conte Napoli; m. Margaret Jean Wright, Aug. 28, 1980. BMEd, Fla. State U., 1966; MusM in Choral Conducting, U. South Fla., 1972. Singer Metro. Opera Nat. Co., NYC, 1965—66; tchr. Adams Jr. HS, Tampa, 1967—80; nurseryman Napoli's Nursery, 1980—84, Athens Wholesale Nursery, Ga., 1984—; condr. Athens Master Chorale, 1989—. Chmn. Ga. Green Ind. Assn., 2004. Bd. Classic Ctr. Auth., Athens, 2004—. Recipient Disting. Prof. Yr., Ga. Green Ind. Assn., 2004. Mem.: So. Nursery Assn. Republican. Episcopalian.

NAPOLITANO, ANDREW P., lawyer, judge, analyst; b. Newark, June 6, 1950; s. Andrew A. and Rita (Caruso) N. AB, Princeton U., 1972; JD, U. Notre Dame, 1975. Bar: NJ 1975, U.S. Supreme Ct. 1985, U.S. Ct. Appeals (3rd cir.) 1997, U.S. Dist. Ct. NY (So. Dist.) 2000, U.S. Dist. Ct. NY (Ea. Dist.) 2001, U.S. Ct. Appeals (2nd Cir.) 2001. Atty. Riker, Danzig, Scherer & Debevoise, Newark, Winne, Banta & Rizzi, Hackensack, NJ, 1975—87; judge Superior Ct. NJ, 1987-95; news analyst Fox News Channel, NYC, 1998-2000, judge, Power of Atty., 2000—01, sr. jud. analyst, 2001—. V.p., gen. counsel Hackensack U. Med. Ctr., 1986-1987; asst. prof. law, constl. law, criminal law and procedure, and profl. ethics, Del. Law Sch. of Widener U., Wilmington, Del., 1980-81; adj. prof. law, basic and advanced constl. law, Seton Hall U., Newark, 1989-2001; faculty mem., NJ Civil Practice and Procedure, NJ Jud. Coll., Teaneck, NJ, 1989-97; lectr., NJ Civil Practice and Procedure, Constl. Law, Profl. Responsibility, Inst. for Continuing Legal Edn., New Brunswick, NJ, 1996, NJ Law Jour. Lecture Series, Newark, NJ, 1995-; legal/polit. commentator, Courtroom TV Network, NYC, 1996-97, MSNBC, Secaucus, NJ, 1997-98, Fox News Channel, NYC, 1998-2000; at-large trustee Am. Inns of Ct. Fedn.; founding pres., master, Justice Morris Pashman Am. Inn Ct., Hackensack, NJ, 1989-98; mem. NJ Supreme Ct. Com. on Civil Practice, 1982-85, 1989-94, 1996-98. Author: Constitutional Chaos: What Happens When the Government Breaks Its Own Laws, 2004; contbr. articles to profl. jours. Bd. governor Hackensack U. Med. Ctr., 1994—2002. With USAR, 1971—72. Fellow: Am. Bar Found.; mem.: Assn. Criminal Defense Lawyers NJ, Trial Attys. NJ, Assn. Trial Lawyers Am., NJ State Bar Assn., Essex County Bar Assn., Bergen County Bar Assn. Office: Fischbein Badillo Wagner Harding 909 Third Ave New York NY 10022 Address: Fox News Network LLC 1211 Avenue of the Americas New York NY 10036 Business E-Mail: anapolitano@fbwhlaw.com. *

NAPOLITANO, GRACE F., congresswoman; b. Brownsville, Tex., Dec. 4, 1936; d. Miguel and Maria Alicia Ledezma Flores; m. Frank Napolitano, 1982; 1 child, Yolando M., Fred Musquiz Jr., Edward M., Michael M., Cynthia M. Student, Cerritos Coll., LA Trade Tech, Tec Southwest Coll. Mem. Calif. Assembly, 1993-98, US Congress from 38th Calif. dist., Washington, 1999—; mem. resources com., chair water and power subcom. US Ho. Reps. Councilwoman City of Norwalk, Calif., 1986-92, mayor, 1989-90; active Cmty. Family Guidance. Mem. Cerritos Coll. Found., Lions Club. Democrat. Roman Catholic. Office: US Ho Reps 1610 Longworth Ho Office Bldg Washington DC 20515-0538

NAPOLITANO, JANET ANN, governor; b. NYC, Nov. 29, 1957; d. Leonard Michael and Jane Marie (Winer) Napolitano. BS summa cum laude, U. Santa Clara, Calif., 1979; JD, U. Va., 1983. Bar: Ariz. 1984, U.S. Dist. Ct. Ariz. 1984, U.S. Ct. Appeals (9th cir.) 1984, U.S. Ct. Appeals (10th cir.) 1988, U.S. Ct. Appeals (5th cir.), U.S. Ct. Appeals, U.S. Ct. Appeals (7th cir.), U.S. Ct. Appeals (8th cir.). Law clk. to Hon. Mary Schroeder U.S Ct. Appeals 9th Cir., 1983—84; assoc. Lewis & Roca, Phoenix, 1984—89, ptnr., 1989—93; U.S. atty. Dist. Ariz., Phoenix, 1993—97; atty. Lewis and Roca, Phoenix, 1997—98; atty. gen. State of Ariz., Phoenix, 1999—2002, gov., 2003—. Mem. Atty. Gen.'s Adv. Com., 1983—, chair, 1995—96; chair victims rights subcom. Ariz. Criminal Justice Commn.; chair Ariz. High Intensity Drug Traficking Area; mem. Ariz. Peace Officer Stds. and Tng. Bd., Ariz. Pros. Attys.' Adv. Coun.; past com. to study civil litigation abuse, cost and delay Ariz. Supreme Ct.; past pres. Ariz. Cmty. Legal Svcs. Corp.; past judge pro tem Ariz. Ct. Appeals. Contbr. articles to profl. jours. Chmn. Nucleus, 1989—91; active Phoenix Design Stds. Rev. Com., 1989—91, Ariz. Women's Forum, Charter 100; hon. chmn. Camp Fire Boys and Girls, 1999; 1st vice-chmn. Ariz. Dem. Com., 1990—92; active Dem. Nat. Com., 1990—92; chmn. Ariz. del. Dem. Nat. Conv., 1992, chmn., 2000; active Ariz. Bd. Tech. Registration, 1989—92; bd. dirs. Ariz. Fire Fighters and Emergency Paramedics Meml., Phoenix Children's Hosp., Actors' Lab Ariz., Inc., Ariz. Peace Officers Meml.; bd. regents Santa Clara U., 1992—. Named Ariz. Dem. of Yr., 1989; recipient Leader of Distinction award, Anti-Defamation League, Human Betterment award, Roots and Wings, Golden Apple award, West Valley NOW, Nat. Network To End Domestic Violence award, Woman of Distinction award, Crohns and Colitis Disease Found., Women Making History award, Nat. Mus. Women's History, Tribute to Women award, YWCA; fellow Dillard fellow; scholar, Truman Scholarship Found, 1977. Fellow: Ariz. Bar Found.; mem.: ABA, Raven Soc., Sandra Day O'Connor Inn of Ct. (barrister), Ariz. Women Lawyers Assn., Ariz. State Bar (chmn. civil practice and procedure com. 1991—92), Am. Judicature Soc., Maricopa County Bar Assn. (past long range planning com.), Ariz. Bar Assn. (past com. on minorities in law, past chmn. civil practice and procedure com.), Nat. Assn. Attys. Gen. (exec. com., tobacco bankruptcy working group, health care fraud group, co-chmn. civil rights com., stop underage smoking com., exec. working group on prosecutorial rels.), Am. Law Inst., Alpha Sigma Nu, Phi Beta Kappa. Democrat. Avocations: hiking, walking, travel, reading, films. Office: Office of Gov 1700 W Washington Phoenix AZ 85007 Office Phone: 602-542-4331. Office Fax: 602-542-7601. *

NAPOLITANO, STEVEN V., lawyer; b. NYC, June 30, 1959; BA, U. Notre Dame; attended, London Sch. Econs.; JD, Boston U., 1985. Bar: Ill. 1985. Ptnr., co-chair Private Equity practice group, mem. bd. dirs. Katten Muchin Zavis Rosenman, Chgo., NYC. Mem.: ABA, Ill. State Bar Assn., Assn. for Corp. Growth. Office: 575 Madison Ave New York NY 10022 Office Phone: 312-902-5615. Office Fax: 312-577-8749. E-mail: steven.napolitano@kmzr.com.

NAPP, GUDRUN F., artist; b. Kiel, Germany, Aug. 14, 1929; arrived in U.S., 1986; d. Walter Alexander and Erika Elisabeth (Burchard) Rode; m. Edmund Carl Napp, Dec. 29, 1951 (dec. Dec. 2001); children: Helenita F., Johann Christian, Anneke J., Florian D. Student, Art Sch., Kiel, 1949, Escuela Artes Plastias, Caracas, Venezuela, 1950, Toronto Coll. Art, Can., 1950—51. Assoc. dir. One Ear Soc., 1999—2001. Exhibited in group shows at Miami Beach Conv. Ctr., 1997, Art Expo LA, 1997, 98, Art Expo NY, 1998, Art Expo Fla., 2000, FIA Caracas Internat. Art Fair, 2003, NY Art Expo, 2006, 2007, Neocon Multimedia Show, Chgo., 2007; one-woman shows include Art Am., 1997. Recipient cert. of excellence Art Horizon, NYC, 1988, hon. mention Royal Poinciana Fiesta, Miami, 1993, The Fla. Mus. of Hispanic and L.Am. Art, Miami, 1994, Miami Watercolor Soc. exhibit, 1999, One Ear Soc. exhibit. Mem. Am. Soc. Interior Design (industry ptnr. 2005), Nat. Collage Soc., Internat. Soc. Exptl. Artists (signature mem.), Miami Watercolor Soc. (signature mem., pres. 1995-96, trustee 1997, publicity chair 1998-99, 3rd place 1990), Art Expo Fla. Lutheran. Avocation: painting. Home and Studio: Studio Gallery Napp Inc An ASID Industry Ptnr 1034 Waterside Cir Weston FL 33327-2022 Office Phone: 954-217-1722. Personal E-mail: art1100@aol.com.

NAPPIER, DENISE L., state official; BA, Va. State U., 1973; MA in Cmty. Planning, U. Cin., 1975. Analyst Office Hartford (Conn.) City Mgr.; cons. Conn. Office of Policy and Mgmt.; dir. instnl. rels. U. Conn. Health Ctr.; city treas. City of Hartford, 1989—98; treas. State of Conn., Hartford, 1999—. Exec. dir. Riverfront Recapture, Inc. Office: Office of State Treas 55 Elm St Hartford CT 06106-1746 Business E-Mail: state.treasurer@po.state.ct.us. *

NAQVI, TASNEEM ZEHRA, cardiologist, researcher, consultant; b. Karachi, Sind, Pakistan, Jan. 19, 1960; came to U.S., 1991; d. Shaiq Hussain and Laila (Rajabali) Zaidi; m. Syed Shujat A. Naqvi, June 30, 1985; children: Ali A., Kazim A. BS, St. Joseph's Coll., Karachi, 1976; MBBS, Dow Med. Coll., Karachi, 1984. Diplomate in internal medicine and cardiovasc. disease Am. Bd. Internal Medicine, Nat. Bd. Echocardiography, Am. Bd. Vascular Tech. House officer internal medicine & gen. surgery Civil Hosp., Karachi, 1984—85; resident med. officer internal medicine Aga Khan U. Hosp., Karachi, 1985—86; registrar, instr. Civil Hosp., Karachi, 1986—87; sr. house officer Lister Hosp., Stevenage, England, 1988—89; registrar Queen Elizabeth U. Hosp., Birmingham, England, 1989—91; asst. clin. instr. in medicine Stony Brook U. Hosp., NY, 1991—93; fellow in clin. cardiology Cedars Sinai Med. Ctr., LA, 1993—96, staff cardiologist, 1996—, assoc. dir. cardiac non-invasive lab, 1996—, dir. interventional echocardiography, 2003, assoc. prof. medicine and cardiology, 2004—07; prof. medicine U. Calif. Sch. Medicine, San Diego, 2007—; dir. echocardiography U. Calif., 2007—. Asst. prof. medicine UCLA Sch. Medicine, 1997-2004; mem. instl. review bd. Cedars-Sinai Med. Ctr.; spkr. in field. Reviewer Jour. Am. Coll. Cardiology, Am. Jour. Cardiology, Jour. Am. Soc. Echocardiography, Am. Jour. Med. Scis., Archives of Gen. Psychiatry, Echocardiography, Psychosomatic Medicine, Am. Heart jour., Heart (BMS), others. Co-recipient Young Investigator award Am. Heart Assn., 1995; recipient Laverna Titus Young Investigators award Am. Heart Assn., 1995, Edwards E3 award, 2005; Merck fellow, 1996-97. Fellow Am. Coll. Cardiology (cardiovasc. imaging com. 2003—, edn. com. 2003—), Am. Soc. Echocardiography (vascular task force, women's health adv. group 2003—), L.A. Soc. Echocardiography (bd. dirs. 1997—, mem. adv. bd.), Royal Coll. Physicians U.K.; mem. Pakistan Med. and Dental Coun. Office Phone: 323-442-6130. Business E-Mail: naqvi@usc.edu.

NARAEV, BORIS G., physician; b. ORenburg, Russia, Apr. 10, 1969; arrived in US, 2002; s. Genrich D. Naraev and Alexandra P. Naraeva. MD, Orenburg State Med. Acad., Russia, 1994; PhD, ORenburg State Med. Acad., Russia, 2001. Asst. prof. State Med. Acad., Orenburg, 1996—97; physician pvt. practice, Orenburg, 1997—99; med. cons. Ctr. Youth, Orenburg, 1999—2002; assoc. prof. State Inst. Arts, Orenburg, 1998—2002; attending physician State Regional Hosp., Orenburg, 2001—07; resident St. Lukes Hosp., Chesterfield, Mo., 2006—. Vis. rschr. Ho. Ear Inst., LA, 2003—05. With Russian Mil., 1987—89. Grantee, Am. Austrian Found., 2000. Mem.: Am. Coll. Physicians, Am. Acad. Otolaryngology.

NARAHASHI, TOSHIO, pharmacology educator; b. Fukuoka, Japan, Jan. 30, 1927; arrived in U.S., 1961; s. Asahachi and Itoko (Yamasaki) Ishii; m. Kyoko Narahashi, Apr. 21, 1956; children: Keiko, Taro. BS, U. Tokyo, 1948, PhD, 1960. Instr. U. Tokyo, 1951-65; research assoc. U. Chgo., 1961, asst. prof., 1962, Duke U., Durham, NC, 1962-63, 65-67, assoc. prof., 1967-69, prof., 1969-77, head pharmacology div., 1970-73, vice chmn. dept. physiology and pharmacology, 1973-75; prof., chmn. dept. pharmacology Northwestern U. Med. Sch., Chgo., 1977-94, Alfred Newton Richards prof., 1982—2005; John Evans prof. Northwestern U., Evanston, Ill., 1986—. Mem. pharmacology study sect. NIH, 1976-80; rsch. rev. com. Chgo. Heart Assn., 1977-82, vice chmn. rsch. coun., 1986-87, chmn., 1988-90; mem. Nat. Environ. Health Scis. Coun., 1982-86; rev. com. Nat. Inst. Environ. Health Scis., 1991-95. Editor: Cellular Pharmacology of Insecticides and Pheromones, 1979, Cellular and Molecular Neurotoxicology, 1984, Insecticide Action: From Molecule to Organism, 1989, Ion Channels, 1988—; specific field editor Jour. Pharmacology and Exptl. Therapeutics, 1972-97; assoc. editor Neurotoxicology, 1994—; contbr. articles to profl. jours. Recipient Javits Neurosci. Investigator award, NIH, 1986. Fellow AAAS, Acad. Toxicol. Scis.; mem. Am. Soc. for Pharmacology and Exptl. Therapeutics (Otto Krayer award 2000), Am. Physiol. Soc., Soc. for Neurosci., Biophys. Soc. (Cole award 1981), Soc. Toxicology (DuBois award 1988, Merit award 1991, Disting. Investigator Lifetime Achievement award 2001), Agrochem. Divsn. Am. Chem. Soc. (Burdick L. Jackson Internat. award 1989). Home: 175 E Delaware Pl Apt 7911 Chicago IL 60611-7745 Office: Northwestern U Med Sch Dept Mol Pharmaco Biol Chem 303 E Chicago Ave Chicago IL 60611-3008 Home Phone: 312-337-0987; Office Phone: 312-503-8284. Business E-Mail: narahashi@northwestern.edu.

NARAIN, AMITABH, aerospace and mechanical engineering educator; b. India, July 30, 1955; arrived in US, 1978, naturalized, 1984; s. Surendra and Suniti (Dayal) N.; m. Rooma Narain, July 12, 1985; children: Hursh, Jaya. BTech in Aerospace Engring., Indian Inst. Tech., Kharagpur, 1978; MS in Mechanics, U. Minn., 1980, PhD in Mechanics, 1983. Asst. prof. Mich. Technol. U., Houghton, 1983-89, assoc. prof., 1990—2006, prof., 2006—. Contbr. articles to profl. jours. Grantee, GM, 1997—2000, NSF, 2000—03, NASA, 2003—. Fellow ASME (chmn. applied mechanics divsn. com. on fluid mechanics 2000-2003, fluids engring. divsn. com. on multi-phase flows, heat transfer divsn. k-8 com.); mem. Am. Phys. Soc. Avocations: swimming, chess. Home: 1520 Brookside Dr Houghton MI 49931-2713 Office: Mich Technol U ME-EM 1400 Townsend Dr Houghton MI 49931-1200 Home Phone: 906-482-2441; Office Phone: 906-487-2555. Business E-Mail: narain@mtu.edu.

NARAIN, RALPH B., biologist; b. Wakenaam, Guyana, Feb. 22, 1968; s. Aaron and Rosie Narain. AS, Suffolk County CC, Riverhead, NY, 2001; BS, SUNY, Oneonta, 2003; postgrad. in entomology, U. Nebr., Lincoln, 2006—. Lab. tech. Aroaima Mining Co., Berbice, Guyana, 1992—96; machine operator NY Twist Drills, Bohemia, NY, 1997—2000; biologist Suffolk County Dept. Health Services, Arthropod-Borne Diseases Lab., Yaphank, 2003—. Vol. Shiv Uma Ganesh Temple, Central Islip, NY, 2000—06. Scholar, Proctor & Gamble, 2002—03; John J. New scholar, SUNY Coll., Oneonta, 2002—03. Mem.: Phi Theta Kappa. Avocation: coin collecting/numismatics. Home: 111 Lincoln Ave Holbrook NY 11741 Office: SCDHS Arthropod-Borne Disease Laboratory 335 Yaphank Ave Yaphank NY 11980 Home Phone: 631-567-2394; Office Phone: 631-852-5271. Personal E-mail: usralphn@aol.com. Business E-Mail: RNarain@suffolkcountyny.gov.

NARAINE, CHAMELI, bank executive; B in Econs., Wilfred Laurier U., Waterloo, Ont.; B in Ops. Mgmt., Conestoga Coll., Kitchener, Ont. Various sr. mgmt. positions including gen. mgr. outsourcing bus., dir. bus. devel. Asia and dir. mfg. ops. Supply Chain and Indsl. Engring. NCR Corp.; sr. v.p. acquisition and strategic sourcing Nat. City Corp., Cleve., 2002—03, dir. corp. ops. and strategic outsourcing, 2003—, sr. v.p., 2004—. Office: Nat City Corp Nat City Ctr 1900 E Ninth St Cleveland OH 44114-3484 Office Phone: 216-222-2000. *

NARASAKI, KAREN KEIKO, advocate, lawyer; b. Seattle, Apr. 4, 1958; d. Richard and Dorothy Narasaki. BA magna cum laude, Yale U., 1980; JD, UCLA, 1985. Bar: Calif. 1985, Wash. 1986, admitted to practice: US Supreme Ct., US Ct. Appeals (9th Cir.). Law clk. to Judge Harry Pregerson US Ct. Appeals (9th Cir.), LA, 1985-86; sr. assoc. Perkins Coie, Seattle, 1986-92; Washington Rep. Japanese Am. Citizens League, 1992-94; pres. and exec. dir. Nat. Asian Pacific Am. Legal Consortium, Washington. Chairperson Nat. Council of Asian Pacific Americans, Asian Pacific Am. Media Coalition, Nat. Network Against Anti-Asian Violence, Washington, 1993—; chairperson, compliance/enforcement com. Leadership Conf. on Civil Rights, Washington, 1995—. Named one of 100 Most Powerful Women, Washingtonian Mag., 2001; recipient Community Award, Asian Pacific Am. Labor Alliance, 1999, Citizen Vol. Svc. Award, US Dept. Justice, 2000, Ruth Standish Baldwin Award, Greater Sacramento Urban League, 2004, We the People Award, Internat. Channel, 2004, Spirit of Excellence Award, ABA, 2005. Mem.: Nat. Assn. Pacific Am. Women's Forum, Nat. Asian Pacific Am. Bar Assn. (founding mem., bd. dir., Trailblazers Award 1994). Office: Nat Asian Pacific Am Legal Consortium 1140 Connecticut Ave NW Washington DC 20036-4001

NARASIMHAN, PADMA MANDYAM, physician; b. Bangalore, India; came to U.S., 1976; d. Alasingracher Mandyam and Alamela Mandyam Narasimhan; 1 child, Ravi. MD, Maulana Azad Med. Coll., New Delhi, 1970. Diplomate Am. Bd. Internal Medicine. Intern in internal medicine Flushing Hosp., NYC, 1976-77; resident in internal medicine Luth. Med. Ctr., NYC, 1977-79; fellow hematology, oncology Beth-Israel Med. Ctr., NYC, 1979-81; asst. prof. King Drew Med. Ctr., LA, 1983-87, Harbor UCLA, Torrance, 1987—2000, USC, 2003—. Mem. editorial bd. Jour. Internal Medicine, 1986—. Mem. ACP, AAPI, Am. Soc. Clin. Oncology, So. Calif. Acad. Clin. Oncology. Hindu. Avocations: travel, reading, meeting people, music, walking. Home: 6604 Madeline Cove Dr Palos Verdes Peninsula CA 90275-4608 Office Phone: 310-377-9555. Personal E-mail: padmanarasim@yahoo.com.

NARAYAN, BEVERLY ELAINE, lawyer; b. Berkeley, Calif., June 19, 1961; d. Jagjiwan and Alexandra Mataras Narayan; m. James Dean Schmidt, Jan. 7, 1989 (div. May 2002); children: Sasha Karan Narayan-Schmidt, Kaiya Maria Narayan-Schmidt; m. Corey Kryst Boe, Dec. 28, 2002. Student, San Francisco State U., 1979—80; BA, U. Calif., Berkeley, 1983; JD, U. Calif., San Francisco, 1987. Bar: Calif. 1987, U.S. Dist. Ct. (no. dist.) Calif. 1987, U.S. Dist. Ct. (ctrl. dist.) Calif. 1988. Atty. Daniels Barratta & Fine, LA, 1988-89, Kornblum Ferry & Frye, LA, 1990-91, Clapp Moroney Bellagamba Davis & Vucinich, Menlo Park, Calif., 1991-93; pvt. practice Burlingame, Calif., 1993—2002; mng. dir. KarmaTek, Burlingame, 1999—2000; sr. trial atty. Allstate Ins. Co., San Jose, 2002—03, lead counsel; staff counsel Encompass and Allstate Ins. Cos., San Jose, 2003—. Arbitrator Nat. Assn. Securities Dealers, San Francisco, 1987-2003, Pacific Exch., San Francisco, 1994—; mediator Peninsula Conflict Resolution Ctr., San Mateo, Calif., 1995—; appellate mediator First Dist. Ct. Appeals, 2000—; neutral San Mateo County Multi-Option ADR Project; judge pro tem San Mateo County Superior Ct. Candidate Sch. Bd. San Mateo (Calif.) Unified Sch. Dist., 1993; mem. San Mateo County Task Force Violence Against Women. Recipient U. Calif. Hastings Coll. Law Achievement award, 1986; named Barrister of Yr., San Mateo County, 1996. Mem. ABA, San Mateo County Bar Assn. (co-chair women lawyers 1995, bd. dirs. 1994-96), South Asian Bar Assn., Nat. Women's Polit. Caucus (bd. dirs., diversity chair 1993-96), San Mateo County Barristers Club (bd. dirs. 1993-99, child watch chair 1995-99). Avocations: baking, cooking, reading, travel, motorcycles. Office: 1740 Technology Dr Ste 250 San Jose CA 95110 Office Phone: 408-392-6962. E-mail: bnara@allstate.com.

NARAYAN, RAMESH, astronomy educator; b. Bombay, Sept. 25, 1950; came to U.S., 1983; s. G.N. and Rajalakshmi (Sankaran) Ramachandran; m. G.V. Vani, June 6, 1977. BS in Physics, Madras U., 1971; MS in Physics, Bangalore U., 1973, PhD in Physics, 1979. Rsch. scientist Raman Rsch. Inst., Bangalore, India, 1978-83; postdoctoral fellow Calif. Inst. Tech., 1983-84, sr. rsch. fellow, 1984-85; assoc. prof. astronomy U. Ariz., Tucson, 1985-90, prof., 1990-91; prof. astronomy Harvard U., Cambridge, Mass., 1991—2003, chmn. dept., 1997-2001, Thomas Dudley Cabot prof. natural scis., 2003—. Sr. astronomer Harvard-Smithsonian Ctr. for Astrophysics, 1991—, assoc. dir., 1996-97; adv. bd. Inst. Theoretical Physics U. Calif., Santa Barbara, 1994-98, chmn., 1996-97; com. gravitational physics NRC, 1997-99; chmn. adv. bd. Ctr. for Gravitational Wave Physics, Pa. State U., 2001—; mem. adv. bd. Max Planck Inst. for Astrophysics, 2002-05, chmn., 2003-05. Contbr. articles to profl. jours. Named NSF Presdl. Young Investigator, 1989, George Darwin lectr. Royal Astron. Soc.,

2002. Fellow: Royal Soc. London; mem.: AAAS, Internat. Astron. Union (mem. U.S. nat. com. 2000—03), Am. Astron. Soc. (mem. exec. com. High Energy Astrophys. Divsn. 2002—04). Achievements include research in the general area of theoretical astrophysics, specializing in accretion disks, black holes, gravitational lenses, gamma-ray bursts, radio pulsars, image processing and scintillation. Office: Harvard-Smithsonian Ctr Astrophysics 60 Garden St # 51 Cambridge MA 02138-1516

NARAYANAMURTI, VENKATESH, health science association administrator; b. Bangalore, Karnataka, India, Sept. 9, 1939; came to U.S., 1961; s. Duraiswami and Janaki (Subramaniam) N.; m. Jayalakshmi Krishnayya, Aug. 23, 1961; children: Arjun, Ranjini, Krishna. BSc, MSc, St. Stephen's Coll., Delhi, India, 1958; PhD, Cornell U., 1965. Instr., rsch. assoc. Cornell U., Ithaca, NY, 1965-68; mem. tech. staff AT&T Bell Labs., Murray Hill, NJ, 1968-76, dept.head, 1976-81, dir., 1981-87; v.p. rsch. Sandia Nat. Labs., Albuquerque, 1987-92; dean engring. U. Calif., Santa Barbara, 1992-98; dean engring. and applied scis. Harvard U., Cambridge, Mass., 1998—. Chmn. condensed matter and materials phys. panel NRC, 1996-99; mem. U. Calif. Pres.' Coun. for Nat. Labs., 1995-98; mem. NAE Pub. Info. Adv. Bd., 1993-94, NSF Dir.'s Strategic Planning Bd., 1994-98; mem. adv. bd. Miller Inst. for Basic Sci., U. Calif. Berkeley, 1999-2006. Author more than 190 publs.; patentee in field. Fellow IEEE, AAAS, Am. Phys. Soc., Indian Acad. Scis.; mem. NAE, Royal Swedish Acad. Engring. Scis. (fgn.). Avocations: long distance running, squash. Office: Harvard Univ SEAS Pierce Hall 217 29 Oxford St Cambridge MA 02138-2901 Office Phone: 617-495-5829. Business E-Mail: venky@harvard.edu.

NARAYANAMURTI, VENKATESH, engineering educator, physics professor; BSc, Univ. Delhi, 1958, MSc in Physics, 1960; PhD in Physics, Cornell Univ., 1960. With AT&T Bell Labs., 1968, dir., Solid State Electronics Rsch. Lab., 1981—87; v.p. rsch., exploratory tech. Sandia Nat. Lab., 1987—92; dean, coll. engring. Univ. Calif., Santa Barbara, 1992—98; dean, engring., applied sci. Harvard Univ., 1998—2006, dean, phys. sci., 2003—06, John A. and Elizabeth S. Armstrong prof., engring., applied sci., 2006—. Fellow: AAAS, Royal Swedish Acad. Engring Sci., IEEE, Am. Physical Soc., Am. Acad. Arts & Scis.; mem.: NAE. Office: Engring & Applied Sci Harvard -Pierce 217A 29 Oxford St Cambridge MA 02138 Office Phone: 617-495-5829. Business E-Mail: venky@deas.harvard.edu.

NARAYEN, SHANTANU, computer software company executive; BS in Elec. Engring., Osmania Univ., India; MS in Computer Sci., Bowling Green Univ.; MBA, Haas Sch. Bus. Sr. mgr. Apple Computer, Inc.; dir. desktop and collaboration products Silicon Graphics, Inc.; co-founder Pictra, Inc.; with Adobe Sys., Inc., San Jose, Calif., 1998—2001, v.p., gen. mgr. engring. group, 2001—05, pres., COO, 2005—. Office: Adobe Sys Inc 345 Park Ave San Jose CA 95110-2704 Office Phone: 408-536-6000.

NARDELL, EDWARD ANTHONY, pulmonologist, researcher; s. Carl Edward and Frances Elizabeth Nardell; m. Madeline Sylvia Crivello, Sept. 23, 1978; children: Maria Francesca, Anthony Joseph. MD, Hahnemann U., Phila., 1975. Chief pulmonary medicine Cambridge Hosp., Mass., 1981—2005; pulmonologist, rschr. Brigham & Women's Hosp., Boston, 2005—. Recipient Chadwick medal, Mass. Thoracic Soc., 2006. Fellow: Am. Coll. Chest Physicians. Office Phone: 617-432-6937. Business E-Mail: enardell@pih.org.

NARDELLI, ROBERT LOUIS, automotive executive, former consumer home products company executive; b. Old Forge, Pa., May 17, 1948; m. Sue Nardelli, 1971; 4 children. BS in Bus., Western Ill. U., 1971; MBA, U. Louisville, 1975; D in Bus. Adminstrn. (hon.), U. Louisville, 2001; LLD (hon.), Siena Coll., 2001; LHD (hon.), Western Ill. U., 2002. With GE, 1971-88; exec. v.p., gen. mgr. worldwide parts and components Case Corp., Racine, Wis., 1988-91; pres., CEO Can. Appliance Mfg. Co. subs. GE, Toronto, Ont., Canada, 1991-92, GE Transp. Sys., Erie, Pa., 1992-95, GE Power Sys., 1995-2000, The Home Depot, Atlanta, 2000—07, chmn., 2002—07; chmn., CEO Chrysler LLC, Auburn Hills, Mich., 2007—. Bd. dirs. The Home Depot, 2000—07, The Coca-Cola Co, 2002—05. Named Exec. of Yr., Schenectady County C of C, 2000, Alumnus of Yr., U. Louisville, 2001; recipient Disting. Pennsylvanian Award, Gannon U., 1995, Disting. Alumni Award, Western Ill. U. Coll. Bus. & Tech., 1998. Mem.: President's Coun. on Service and Civic Participation, 2003. Office: Chrysler LLC 1000 Chrysler Dr Auburn Hills MI 48326 *

NARDI RIDDLE, CLARINE, lawyer, federal official; b. Clinton, Ind., Apr. 23, 1949; d. Frank Jr. and Alice (Mattioda) Nardi; children: Carl Nardi, Julia Nardi. AB in Math with honors, Ind. U., 1971, JD, 1974; LHD (hon.), St. Joseph Coll., 1991. Bar: Ind. 1974, U.S. Dist. Ct. (so. dist.) Ind. 1974, Conn. 1979, Fed. Dist. Ct. Conn. 1980, U.S. Supreme Ct. 1980, U.S. Ct. Appeals (2d cir.) 1986, U.S. Ct. Appeals (D.C. cir.) 1994. Staff atty. Ind. Legis. Svc. Agy., Indpls., 1974-78, legal counsel, 1978-79; dep. corp. counsel City of New Haven, 1980-83; counsel to atty. gen. State of Conn., Hartford, 1983-86, dep. atty. gen., 1986-89, acting atty. gen., 1989, atty. gen., 1989-91, judge Superior Ct., 1991-93; assn. exec., sr. v.p., gen. counsel Nat. Multi-Housing Coun., Nat. Apartment Assn., 1995—2003; chief of staff Senator Joseph I. Lieberman, Washington, 2003—. Asst. counsel state majority Conn. Gen. Assembly, Hartford, 1979, legal rsch. asst. to prof. Yale U., New Haven, 1979; legal counsel com. on law revision Indpls. State Bar Assn., 1979; mem. Chief Justice's Task Force on Gender Bias, Hartford, 1988-90; mem. ethics and values com. Ind. Sector, Washington, 1988-90; co-organizer Ind. Continuing Legal Edn. Forum Inst. Legal Drafting Legislature and Pvt. Practice; Internat. Women's Yr. panelist Credit Laws and Their Enforcement; mem. Atty. Gen.'s Blue Ribbon Commn., Chief Justice's Com. Study Publs. Policy Conn. Law. Jour., Law Revision Commn. Adminstrv. Law Study, Chief Justice's Task Force Gender, Justice and Cts., Gov.'s Task Force Fed. Revenue Enhancements; mem. exec. com. Jud. Dept.; mem. panel arbitrators Am. Arbitration Assn., 1994; gen. counsel Nat. Multi Housing Coun.; lectr. in field. Author: (with F.R. Rembusch) Drafting Manual for the Indiana General Assembly, 1976; sr. editor Ind. U. Law Sch. Interdisciplinary Law Jour.; contbr. articles to profl. jours. Bd. visitors Ind. U., Bloomington, 1974-92; mem. Gov.'s Missing Children Com., Hartford, Conn. Child Support Guidelines Com., Gov.'s Task Force on Justice for Abused Children, Hartford, 1988-90; mem. Mayor's City of New Haven Task Force Reorganization Corp. Counsel's Office, Gov.'s Child Support Commn., Mayor of New Haven's Blue Ribbon Commn.; former bd. dirs. New Haven Neighborhood Music Sch.; bd. dirs., mem. youth adv. com. Gov.'s Partnership Prevent Substance Abuse Workforce-Drugs Don't Work; mem. Blue Ribbon Com. Army War Coll., 2006. Recipient Women in Leadership Recognition award Hartford Region YWCA, 1986, Award of Merit, Women & Law Sect. Conn. Bar Assn., 1989, Fellowship award South End Ladies Dem. Club, 1989, Woman of Yr. award Greater Hartford Fedn. of Bus. & Profl. Women's Clubs, 1990, Conn. Original award Somers-Mabelle B. Avery Sch., 1990, Cert. of Recognition, Consortium Law-Related Edn., 1990, Citizen award Conn. Task Force Children's Constl. Rights, 1991, Ann. award Hartford Assn. Women Attys., 1993; named Conn. History Maker, U.S. Dept. Labor, Women's Bur. & Permanent Commn. Status Women, 1989, Impact Player, The Conn. Law Tribune, 1992; inductee Ind. U. Sch. Law Alumni Acad. Fellow, 1999. Mem. ABA, Conn. Bar Assn. (chair com. on gender bias, Citation of Merit women and law sect. 1989), Nat. Assn. Attys. Gen. (chair charitable trusts and solicitation 1988-90), New Haven Neighborhood Music Sch. (bd. dirs.), Am. Arbitration Assn. (arbitration panel 1994), Ind. Bar Assn., Conn. Bar Assn. (chair com. gender bias legal profession), Indpls. Bar Assn., Ind. Civil Liberties Union (bd. dirs., mem. exec. com., chair long range planning com., mem. women's rights project, membership v.p., Disting. Svc. award), Conn. Consortium Law and Citizenship Edn., Inc. (bd. dirs.), Conn. Judges Assn. (mem. legislation com.), Ind. U. Law Sch. Alumni Assn. (bd. dirs.), Enomene Hon. Soc., Pleiades Hon. Soc., Mortar Bd. (nat. fellow), Alpha Lambda Delta. Democrat. Presbyterian. Office: 706 Hart Senate Office Bldg Washington DC 20510 Office Phone: 202-224-4041. Business E-Mail: clarine_nardi_riddle@lieberman.senate.gov.

NARDOZZI, PETER MICHAEL, pharmacist, clinical educator, lecturer, entrepreneur; b. Brockton, Mass., Nov. 6, 1937; s. Michael John Nardozzi and Doris M. (MacLea) Worthington; m. Sandra Scott Boyatsis (div. 1975); 1 child, Mark; m. Sandra Scafani, Dec. 31, 1984; 1 child, Cody Abernathy. BS in Pharmacy, Northeastern U., 1960; MS in Nutrition, Hawaii Inst. for Health, Diet and Nutrition, 1982; PharmD, Southeastern Coll. Pharm. Scis., Miami, Fla., 1992. Registered pharmacist, Fla., Maine, Mass.; lic. cons. pharmacist, Fla. Exec. v.p. Nardozzi Rexall Drug and other firms, Fla., 1960-77, Mass., 1960—77; propr. Bonnie & Clyde's Tavern, Brockton, Mass., 1974—76; treas. Columbian Enterprises Importing/Emeralds, Caribbean Salvage Diving Co., Boston, 1975-77; ptnr., v.p., pharmacist Oceanside Drug, Pompano Beach, Fla., 1965-87; pharmacist mgr. Grand Union Pharmacy Dept., Hialeah, Fla., 1977-78; chief pharmacist Shoppers Drug Mart, Ft. Lauderdale, Fla., 1978-80; pres. Carribean Salvage, Inc., Pompano Beach; dir. pharm. services Bodee Med. Facilities, Pompano Beach, 1981; founder, exec. v.p. Hawaii Diet Plan, Honolulu, 1982-84; founder, pres. Innovative Bus. Devel. Group, Albuquerque, 1984-85; pharmacist, mgr. Cunningham Drug, Singer Island, Fla., 1986-87, Popular Pharmacy, Miami, 1987—89, Pharmor Drug, Miami, 1989—93; pharmacist, clin. educator Rite Aid Corp., Bath, Maine, 1994—. Mem. Rite Aid Adv. Coun. Region 66, 2004; assoc. Achievement Rsch. & Verification Systems, Albuquerque, 1984-85; bd. dirs. Alliance Enterprises, Albuquerque, Zyne Design, Taos, N.Mex.; founder, pres. ITOCAM-Alternative Medicine Cons. Co.; mem. Pharmacy in the Amazon Rainforest, Pharmacy on the Belize Reef, Internat. Expdns., Nat. Pharmacist Response Team divsn. FEMA, 2004-05; comty. medicine advocate for Maine Medicare Edn. Partnership, 2005-06; lectr. and trainer Rite Aid Medicare Part D Outreach, 2005; steering com. Franklin County Health Acess Rx Consortium, 2006-07; part-time traveling pharmacist and cons.; founder Alternative Pharm. Care; promoter Internat. Sports Road Trips, 2007; lectr. in field Author weight loss booklet, 1985; editor Nat. Nutrition Newsletter, 1982-84; health columnist; co-patentee nutritional diet supplement. Youth counselor Hawaii Supreme Ct., Honolulu, 1982; lectr. drug abuse Nat. Assn. Retail Druggists. Fellow Am. Soc. Cons. Pharmacists; mem. Am. Pharm. Assn., Am. Mktg. Assn., Nat. Small Bus. Assoc., Maine Pharmacy Assn., Fla. Pharm. Assn., Hawaii Soc. Corp. Planners, Ctr. for Entrpreneurial Mgmt., Soc. Integrative Medicine, Soc. Natural Pharmacy, Venture Founders, Mortar and Pestle Soc. E-mail: docn@gwi.net.

NARENDRA, KUMPATI SUBRAHMANYA, electrical engineer, educator; b. Madras, India, Apr. 14, 1933; came to U.S., 1954, naturalized, 1974; s. Subrahmanya and Sarada (Alladi) Kumpati; m. Barbara Lamb, Nov. 3, 1961. BEE with honors, U. Madras, India, 1954; MS, Harvard U., Cambridge, Mass., 1955, PhD, 1959; MA (hon.), Yale U., New Haven, 1968; DSc (hon.), Anna U., Madras, 1995, Nat. U. Ireland, Dublin, 2007. Lectr., postdoctoral asst. Harvard U., Cambridge, Mass., 1959-61, asst. prof., 1961-65; assoc. prof. Yale U., New Haven, 1965-68, prof. elec. engring., 1968—, Harold W. Cheel prof. elec. engring., 2003—, chmn. dept. elec. engring., 1984-87, dir. Neuroengring. and Neurosci. Ctr., 1995-96. Cons. to comml. firms, 1961—; dir. Ctr. for Systems Sci., 1981—; disting. lectr. Tex. A&M Coll., 1997; disting. vis. scientist Jet Propulsion Lab., 1994—95; hon. vis. prof. Anna U., Madras, India, 1993—; mem. adv. bd. Inst. Advanced Engring., Republic of Korea; disting. lectr. U. N.Mex., 1999, U. Va., 2001; plenary spkr. Am. Control Conf., 2000; keynote spkr. Conf. on Intelligent Control, U. Va., 2001, Internat. Conf. of Soc. of Indsl. and Control Engring., Osaka, Japan, 2002; Hamilton lectr. Hamilton Inst., Ireland, 2003. Author: Frequency Domain Criteria for Absolute Stability, 1973, Stable Adaptive Systems, 1989, Learning Automata-An Introduction, 1989; editor: Applications of Adaptive Control, 1980, Adaptive and Learning Systems: Theory and Applications, 1987, Advances in Adaptive Control, 1991; editor issue on learning automata Jour. Cybernetics and Info. Sci., vol. I, 1977. Recipient John R. Ragazzini Edn. award Am. Automatic Control Coun., 1990, Leadership award Neural Network Soc., 1994, Hendrik W. Bode prize/Lectr. award Control Sys. Soc., 1995, Richard E. Bellman Control Heritage award 2003, Walton Visitor award Sci. Found. Ireland, 2007. Fellow AAAS, IEEE (life, Franklin V. Taylor award 1973, George S. Axelby award 1988, Outstanding Paper of neural network coun. 1991), Inst. Elec. Engrs. (U.K.); mem. Conn. Acad. Sci. and Engring., Sigma Xi. Home: 35 Old Mill Rd Woodbridge CT 06525-1523 Office: Yale U Ctr Systems Sci PO Box 2157 New Haven CT 06520-2157 Business E-Mail: kumpati.narendra@yale.edu.

NARENDRANATH, NEELAKANTAM V., microbiologist, researcher; b. Chennai, TamilNadu, India, Aug. 28, 1971; s. Neelakantam V. Varadarajulu and NagamaDevi Cherukuri; m. Srividya Adusumilli, Mar. 1, 2002; 1 child, Vishnu. BS in Agr., Tamil Nadu Agrl. U., Coimbatore, India, 1992, MS in Agrl. Microbiology, 1995; PhD, U. Sask., Saskatoon, Can., 2000. Postdoctoral rschr. Alltech, Inc., Nicholasville, Ky., 2001—02, coord. alcohol rsch., 2002—04, coord. alcohol rsch., grad. student affairs, 2003—04, coord. yeast physiology rsch., grad. student affairs, 2004—05; fermentation rsch. dir. POET Rsch., Inc., Sioux Falls, SD, 2005—. Author: Bacterial Contamination and Control in Ethanol Production; contbr. articles to profl. jours. Scholar, U. Sask., 1995—99; Merit scholar, Tamil Nadu Agrl. U., 1988—92, Jr. Rsch. fellow, 1993—95. Mem.: Soc. Indsl. Microbiology, Am. Soc. Microbiology. Home: 3909 W 84th St Sioux Falls SD 57108 Home Phone: 605-271-0248.

NARIN, STEPHEN B., lawyer; b. Phila., Nov. 23, 1929; s. Bernard E. and Anne (Lipsius) N.; m. Sandra C. Goldberg, Sept. 29, 1963; children: Howard Glen, Brenda Teri. BS, Temple U., 1951, LL.B., 1953; LL.M. in Taxation, NYU, 1960. Bar: Pa. 1954, U.S. Supreme Ct. 1958; CPA, Pa. Dep. atty. gen. Commonwealth of Pa., Harrisburg, 1955-57; instr. acctg. Temple U., Phila., 1954-55; lectr. in law grad. legal studies div. Temple U. Sch. Law, Phila., 1976-85; lectr. Practicing Law Inst., 1967-69; ptnr. Narin & Chait, Phila., 1970-89, Predecessor Ptnrships., Phila., 1955-70; v.p., gen. counsel Travelco Assocs., Phila., 1989-90; of counsel Krekstein, Wolfson & Krekstein, Phila., 1989-92; v.p., gen. counsel Eagle Nat. Bank, 1990-91; counsel Schachtel, Gerstley, Levine & Koplin, Phila., 1993-98; pvt. practice Rosemont, Pa., 1998—. Mem. Phila. County Bd. Law Examiners, 1961-65. Nat. governing coun. Am. Jewish Congress, 1963-84, nat. exec. com., 1978-84, pres. Greater Phila. council, 1965-67; active Nat. Commn. on Law and Social Action, 1964-84. Mem. Phila. Bar Assn., Phi Alpha Delta. Home and Office: 1459 County Line Rd Bryn Mawr PA 19010-1604 Home Phone: 610-527-0665. Personal E-mail: cahduh@aol.com.

NARITA, HIRO, cinematographer; b. Seoul, Republic of Korea, June 26, 1941; arrived in Japan, 1945, arrived in U.S., 1957; s. Masao and Masako (Kojima) Morikawa; m. Barbara Parker, Sept. 8, 1971. BFA in Design, San Francisco Art Inst., 1964. Lectr. Mill Valley Film Festival, 1984, Hawaii Internat. Film Festival, 1984, San Jose State U., 2006. Dir. photography: (films) Farewell to Manzanar, 1976 (Emmy nomination, 1976); Never Cry Wolf, 1983 (Best Cinematography award Nat. Soc. Film Critics, 1983); Solomon Northrup's Odyssey, 1984; Go Tell It on the Mountain, 1985; Amerika, 1987; Honey, I Shrunk the Kids, 1989; The Rocketeer, 1991; Star Trek VI, 1992; Hocus Pocus, 1993; White Fang II, 1994; James & The Giant Peach, 1995; The Arrival, 1995; Stones & Paper, 1997; Conceiving Ada, 1998; Shadrach, 1998; I'll Be Home for Christmas, 1998; Dirty Pictures, 1999 (Emmy nomination, 2000); Half Past Autumn, 2001 (Emmy nomination, 2001); Technolust, 2002; The Darwin Awards, 2005; The Valley of the Heats' Delight, 2006; Strange Culture, 2007. With US Army, 1964—66. Mem.: Acad. Motion Picture Arts and Scis., Am. Soc. Cinematographers, Internat. Photographers Guild. Office Phone: 707-763-5358. Personal E-mail: phnarita@comcast.net.

NARRON, JERRY AUSTIN, former professional baseball manager; b. Goldboro, NC, Jan. 15, 1956; 1 child, Connor. Catcher NY Yankees, 1979, Seattle Mariners, 1980—81, 1987, Calif. Angels, 1983—86; mgr. Orioles' sys., 1989—92; mgr. minor league Double-A Hagerstown, 1990—91; mgr. minor league Triple-A Rochester, 1992; 3nd base coach Tex. Rangers, 1994, interim mgr., 2001, mgr., 2001—02, Cin. Reds, 2005—07. *

NASCA, THOMAS JOSEPH, dean; b. Bklyn., June 1, 1949; m. Jean S. Styslinger; children: Patrick T., Brian J. children: Thomas J, Andrew J. BS, U. of Notre Dame, Ind., 1971; MD, Jefferson Med. Coll., Phila., 1975. Diplomate Am. Bd. Internal Medicine 1978, Am. Bd. Nephrology 1982. Intern Mercy Hosp. of Pitts., 1975—76, resident in internal medicine, 1976—79; fellow in nephrology RI Hosp.-Brown U., Providence, 1979—81; coord. of clin. services, dept. of medicine Mercy Hosp. of Pitts., 1981—85, chmn. and residency program dir., dept. of medicine, 1985—92; vice chmn., dept. of medicine Jefferson Med. Coll., Phila., 1992—97, assoc. dean for edn. and rsch., 1997—2000, acting dean, 2000—01, dean, 2001—; sr. v.p. Thomas Jefferson U., Phila., 2001—; pres. Jefferson U. Physicians, Phila., 2001—. Chmn. Residency Rev. Com. for Internal Medicine, Chgo., 2001—. Contbr. over 40 articles to profl. jours. Named White Plains H.S. Citizen of the Yr., Nat. Exch. Club, 1967; recipient Caduceus Award for Exemplary Leadership, Mercy Hosp. of Pitts., 1986, W.W.G. Mclauchlan Award for Exemplary Contbns. in Edn., 1993, The Christian R. and Mary F. Lindback Award for Disting. Tchg., Jefferson Med. Coll., 1994, Presentation of Portrait to Thomas Jefferson U., Class of 2000, Jefferson Med. Coll., 2000, Sister M. Ferdinand Clark Outstanding Alumnus Achievement Award, Mercy Hosp. of Pitts., 2001. Fellow: ACP, Coll. of Physicians of Phila.; mem.: Myasthena Gravis Assn. Western Pa. (bd. dirs. 1990—92), Assn. of Program Dirs. in Internal Medicine (mem. coun. 1990—2001, sec.-treas. 1995—99, pres. 2000—01), Chester Valley Golf Club, Pyramid Club, Alpha Omega Alpha. Avocations: golf, photography, basketball, marine aquarist, rugby. Office: Jefferson Med Coll 1025 Walnut St Philadelphia PA 19107 E-mail: thomas.nasca@jefferson.edu.

NASER, SALEH A., medical researcher, educator; PhD, N.Mex State U., 1993. Prof. U. Ctrl. Fla., Orlando, 1995—. Achievements include research in Crohn's disease etiology. Office: U Ctrl Fla 4000 Central Florida Blvd Orlando FL 32816 Home Phone: 407-823-0955.

NASGAARD, ROALD, museum curator; b. Denmark, Oct. 14, 1941; s. Jens Larsen and Petra (Guldbaek) N.; m. Lori J. Walters. BA, U. B.C., 1965, MA, 1967; PhD, Inst. Fine Arts, N.Y. U., 1973. Lectr., asst. prof. U. Guelph, 1971-75; curator contemporary art Art Gallery of Ont., Toronto, 1975-78, chief curator, 1978-89, deputy dir., chief curator, 1989-93, sr. curator rsch., 1993; chair dept. art Fla. State U., Tallahassee, 1995—2006, prof. art history, 2006—; co-dir. programming Inst. of Modern and Contemporary Art, Calgary, Alta., Canada. Vis. lectr. U. Guelph, York U.; vis. lectr., adj. prof. U. Toronto; rsch. fellow Nat. Gallery Phila. Libr. and Archives (summer), 2002. Author, curator: Ron Martin: World Paintings, 1976, Structures for Behavior, 1977, Garry Neill Kennedy: Recent Work, 1978, Ten Canadian Artists in the 1970's, 1980, Yves Gaucher: A Fifteen Year Perspective, 1978, The Mystic North: Symbolist Landscape Painting in Northern Europe and North America, 1890-1940, 1984, Gerhard Richter: Paintings, 1988, Individualites: 14 Contemporary Artists from France, 1991, Free Worlds: Metaphors and Realities in Contemporary Hungarian Art, 1991, Concealing/Revealing: Voices from the Canadian Foothills, 1997, Pleasures of Sight and States of Being: Radical Abstract Painting, 2001, Abstract Painting in Canada, 2007, co-organizer: The European Iceberg: Creativity in Germany and Italy Today, 1985. Mem. Toronto Pub. Art Commn., Gershon Iskowitz Found. Can. Council fellow, 1967-68, 70-71 Mem. Coll. Art Assn., Univ. Art Assn. Can., Assn. Can. Studies in U.S Office Phone: 850-383-1110. Business E-Mail: rnasgaar@mailer.fsu.edu.

NASH, ALICIA LARDÉ, application developer, physicist; b. San Salvador, Jan. 1, 1933; came to U.S., 1944; d. Carlos Roberto and Alicia (Lopez-Harrison) Larde; m. John Forbes Nash, Jr., Feb. 16, 1957; children: John Charles Martin Nash. BS in Physics, MIT, 1955, postgrad., 1959. Physicist Nuclear Devel. Corp. of Am., White Plains, NY, 1956-57, Tech. Ops., Burlington, Mass., 1957-58; rsch. assoc. MIT Computation Ctr., Cambridge, Mass., 1958-59; physicist, aerospace engr. R.C.A. Astro Divsn., Hightstown, NJ, 1960-66; programmer, analyst Mgmt. Data Processing, NYC, 1972-74, Con Edison, NYC, 1974-80, Blue Cross Blue Shield of N.Y., NYC, 1980-82; systems/analyst programmer specialist N.J. Transit, Newark, 1983—. Mem. AAUW, MIT Club of Princeton (past pres., bd. dirs.), Soc. of Women Engring. Achievements include being the subject for the role of Alicia Nash in the movie "A Beautiful Mind". Home: 932 Alexander Rd Princeton Junction NJ 08550-1002 Office: NJ Transit One Penn Plaza East Newark NJ 07105 E-mail: alroad932@hotmail.com.

NASH, ANTHONY J., military analyst; b. Edina, Minn., Apr. 9, 1974; s. James Allen Nash and Maureen G. Mendelsohn; m. Bethany Lynn Clough, Aug. 1, 1998. BS in Liberal Studies cum laude, Excelsior Coll., Albany, NY, 2002; AAS in Comm. Applications Tech., CC of Air Force, Denver, 2006. Prodn. mgr. Northstar Home Improvement, St. Louis Park, Minn., 1995—96; lead intelligence and ops. support Logos Techs., Arlington, Va., 2006—. Varsity football coach Meade HS, Ft. Meade, Md., 2005—07. Sgt. USAF, 1997—2006. Decorated Air Force Good Conduct medal USAF, Air Force Achievement medal, Armed Forces Expeditionary medal, Air Force Expeditionary medal, Global War on Terrorism Svc. medal, Global War on Terrorism Expeditionary medal, Air and Space Campaign medal, Combat Readiness medal, Air Force Commendation medal, Joint Svc. Achievement medal; recipient John Levitow award, 2000. Office: Logos Techs 3811 N Fairfax Dr Ste 100 Arlington VA 22203 Home Phone: 410-305-0785; Office Phone: 301-404-4885.

NASH, BOB J., political organization worker; b. Texarkana, Ark., 1947; m. Janis F. Kearney, 1994; 2 children. ABA Sociology, U. Ark., 1969; MA Urban Studies, Howard U., 1972. Asst. to dep. mayor, Washington, 1970-71; asst. to city mgr. Fairfax, Va., 1971-72; adminstrv. officer Nat. Tng. and Devel. Svc., Washington, 1972-74; dir. cmty. and regional affairs Ark. Dept. Planning, 1974-75; v.p. Winthrop Rockefeller Found., Little Rock, 1975-83; sr. exec. asst. econ. devel. Office Ark. gov., 1983-89; pres. Ark. Devel. Fin. Authority, Little Rock, 1989-92; under sec. agr. for small cmty. and rural devel. USDA, Washington, 1993-1995; asst. to Pres., dir. presdl. pers. White House, Washington, 1995—2001; vice chmn. Shore-Bank Corp., Chgo., 2001—07; deputy campaign mgr. for 2008 presidential race Hillary Clinton, 2007—. Office: Hillary Clinton for President 4420 N Fairfax Dr Arlington VA 22203 *

NASH, CYNTHIA JEANNE, journalist; b. Detroit, Dec. 24, 1947; d. Frederick Copp and Carolyn (Coffin) N.; 1 child, Lydia Anne Maza; m. Richard Zahler, July 22, 1994. BA, U. Mich., 1969. Reporter Detroit News, 1970-75, sports columnist, 1975-77, Life Style columnist 1977-79, Life Style editor, 1979-82; news features editor Seattle Times, 1983; asst. mng. editor Sunday Seattle Times, 1983-86, assoc. mng. editor, 1986-97, dir. content devel., 1986-2000, dir., brand and content devel., 2000—. Mem. Harbor Sq. Club. Office: Seattle Times PO Box 70 Fairview Ave N & John St Seattle WA 98111-0070 E-mail: cnash@seattletimes.com.

NASH, DAVID BRET, physician; b. NYC, Nov. 15, 1955; s. Albert J. and Charlotte Nash; m. Esther Jean Nash; children: Rachel and Leah (twins), Jacob. BA, Vassar Coll., 1977; MD, U. Rochester, 1981; MBA, U. Pa., 1986. Internship The Graduate Hosp., U. Pa., 1981-82, residency, 1982-84; med. dir. Health Evaluation Ctr., Hosp. U. Pa., Phila., 1988-90; chair, dept. health policy Jefferson Med. Coll., Phila., 1990—. Editor: Future Practice Alternatives, 1987, Providing Quality Care, 1989. Fellow ACP; mem. Phi Beta Kappa. Office: Thomas Jefferson U 115 Curtis Bldg 1015 Walnut St Philadelphia PA 19107-5005 Office Phone: 215-955-6969.

NASH, DAVID J., engineering and construction company executive, retired military officer; BSEE, Ind. Inst. Tech., Ft. Wayne, 1965; MS in Fin. Mgmt., Naval Postgraduate Sch., Monterey, Calif., 1977; student in Exec. Prog., Carnegie Mellon U., Pitts. Advanced through ranks to rear adm. USN, comdr. Naval Constrn. Bn. Ctr. Port Hueneme, Calif., comdr. Pacific Divsn. Naval Facilities Command, comdr. naval facilities engring., chief civil engrs.; with Parsons Brinkerhoff Constrn. Svcs., dir. automotive/indsl. divsn.; prog. dir. tech. ctr. campus GM, Warren, Mich.; pres. PB Bldgs., 2002; v.p. govt. ops. BE&K, 2003—04, pres. govt. grp. Birmingham, Ala., 2004—; dir. Iraq Prog. Mgmt. Office, 2003—04, Iraq Reconstruction Mgmt. Office, 2004, Project and Contracting Office, 2004. Named one of Top 25 Newsmakers, Engring. News-Record, 2004; recipient Henry L. Michel award for Industry Advancement of Rsch., 2001, John I. Parcel-Leif J. Sverdrup award for Civil Engring. Mgmt., ASCE, 2004, Golden Eagle award, Soc. Am. Mil. Engrs., 2005, Golden Beaver award, 2005. Mem.: Nat. Acad. Constrn., NAE. Office: BE&K Govt Grp 2000 International Park Dr Birmingham AL 35243

NASH, DONALD GENE, federal investigator, economist; b. Paris, Ill., July 20, 1945; s. Lelan and Mildred (Washburn) N.; m. Jo Ann Bellew, Aug. 29, 1964; children: Stacey Alan, Ryan Christopher, Shaun Christian BS, So. Ill. U., 1967, MS, 1969; postgrad., DePaul U., Chgo., 1970-71. Farm mgr., test farms So. Ill. U., Carbondale, 1968-69; economist Commodity Futures Trading Commn., Chgo., 1969-77; v.p.-ops. Mid. Am. Commodity Exch., Chgo., 1977-86; sr. futures trading investigator Commodity Futures Trading Commn., Chgo., 1986—. Bd. trustees Friends of Danada, Wheaton, Ill., 2001—, pres., 2007. With N.G. US Army, 1968—74. Recipient Outstanding Mktg. award Wall St. Jour., 1966, award of merit Am. Farm Econ. Assn., 1967, cert. of merit Commodity Exch. Authority, merit award Naperville Art League, 1994, Honorable Mention award Danada Nature Show, 1995, 2002. Methodist. Avocations: photography, woodworking, sketching. Home: 923 Bainbridge Dr Naperville IL 60563-2002 Office: Commodity Futures Trading Commn 525 W Monroe St Ste 1100 Chicago IL 60661 Business E-Mail: dnash@cftc.gov.

NASH, EDWARD L., advertising executive; b. NYC, Nov. 8, 1936; s. Irving and Mina (Koppel) N.; m. Diana R. Kithcart, June 2, 1968; 1 child, Amelia. BA, CCNY, 1953. Dir. advt. Crowell, Collier, Macmillan, Inc., NYC, 1961-62; v.p. mktg. LaSalle Extension U., Chgo., 1962-64; pres. Capitol Record Club, Inc., Los Angeles, 1964-69; founder, pres. Nash Pub., Los Angeles, 1969-74; exec. v.p. Rapp & Collins, NYC, 1975-82; pres., chief exec. officer BBDO Direct, NYC, 1982-86; owner, pres. Nash Direct Inc., NYC, 1986-91; chmn. Nash, Wakeman & de Forrest, Inc., 1991-92; exec. v.p. Bozell, Jacobs, Kenyon & Eckhardt, NYC, 1992-95; CEO, mng. ptnr. Team Nash, Inc., NYC, 1996—. Lectr. in field; chmn. Direct Mktg. Day, N.Y.C., 1985, Internat. Direct Mktg. Conf., 1996; instr. NYU, 1998—, Va. Commonwealth U., 1998—. Author: Direct Marketing: Strategy/Planning/Execution, 1982, 2d edit., 1986, 3d edit., 1995, 4th edit., 2000; editor: The Direct Marketing Handbook, 1984, 2d edit., 1991, Database Marketing, 1993. Mem. Direct Mktg. Assn. (chmn. mktg. coun. 1980-82), NY Direct Mktg. Club (Silver Apple award 1999). Office: Team Nash Inc 245 E 58th St #21E New York NY 10022-1356 Office Phone: 646-497-0297. Business E-Mail: ednash@teamnash.com.

NASH, HENRY WARREN, marketing educator; b. Tampa, Fla., Sept. 19, 1927; s. Leslie Dikeman and Mildred (Johnson) N.; m. Frances Lora Venters, Aug. 20, 1950; children: Warren Leslie, Richard Dale. BS in Bus. Adminstrn, U. Fla., 1950, MBA, 1951; postgrad., Ind. U., 1951-53; PhD, U. Ala., 1965. Student asst. U. Fla., 1948-50, grad. asst., 1950-51, Ind. U., 1951-53; salesman Field Enterprises, Inc., Chgo., 1953; assoc. prof. bus. and econs. Miss. Coll., 1953-57; assoc. prof. marketing Miss. State U., 1957-66, prof., head dept., 1966-96; emeritus prof. mktg.; emeritus head dept. mktg., quantitative analysis, bus. law; dir. Coll. Bus. and Industry Acad. Advising Ctr., 1995-2000; ptnr. Southland Cons. Assos., 1968-84; bd. dirs. Govt. Employees Credit Union, 1969-92, v.p., 1969-73, pres., 1973-78; ret., 2000. Author: (with others) Principles of Marketing, 1961 Served with USNR, 1945-46. Loveman's Merchandising fellow U. Ala., 1961-62 Mem. Am. Mktg. Assn., Am. Acad. Advt., Acad. Internat. Bus., So. Econ. Assn., So. Mktg. Assn. (sec. 1974-75, pres. 1976-77), Sales and Mktg. Execs. (internat. chmn. educators com. 1967-70), Miss. Retail Mchts. Assn. (bd. dirs.), Pi Sigma Epsilon (nat. educator, v.p. 1967-69, nat. pres. 1969-71), Kiwanis (treas. Starkville club 1969-70, v.p. 1973-74, pres. 1974-75, lt. gov. 1977-78, gov. 1982-83), Blue Key, Beta Gamma Sigma, Omicron Delta Kappa, Mu Kappa Tau (nat. v.p. 1977-79, 86-88, pres. 1979-81, 88-90), Alpha Kappa Psi, Phi Kappa Phi (v.p. Miss. State U. 1990-91, pres. 1991-92). Baptist (tchr., deacon). Home: 2800 W Main St Cottage 302B Tupelo MS 38801-3027

NASH, HORACE LYONS, lawyer; b. San Jose, Calif., Dec. 19, 1955; BA with honors, U. Chgo., 1975; PhD, Stanford U., 1982; JD cum laude, Harvard U., 1985. Bar: Calif. 1985. Ptnr. Fenwick & West LLP, Mountain View, Calif., chair securities group. Named a Dealmaker of the Yr., Am. Lawyer mag., 2006. Mem.: State Bar Calif. Office: Fenwick & West LLP Silcon Valley Ctr 801 California St Mountain View CA 94041 Office Phone: 650-988-8500, 650-335-7934. Office Fax: 650-938-5200. E-mail: hnash@fenwick.com.

NASH, JAMES LEE, poet, security official; b. Lynchburg, Va., Oct. 1, 1957; s. James Belvy and Marjorie Lea Glden (Campbell) N. Grad., Brookville H.S., Lynchburg, 1977. VIP info. aide de camp Greater Ft. Lauderdale Broward County Conv. Ctr. Author: (poetry) Casus Belli, 1993, Enduring Significance, 1996; contbg. author: T.P.O.A., 1994, Treasure the Moment, 1996, A Shadow in the Light, 1999, Love and Other Observations, 1999, Melodies and Madness, 1999, Explanations, 2000, Other Planets are Places Too, 2000, The Erotic Adventures of a White Trash Southern Boy, 2002, Faces and Places on Capitol Hill, 2004, I Try Not to Cuss, 2006. Mem. at large Dem. Exec. Com., Broward County, Fla., 1997-2000; mem. Croissant Park Civic Assn., Ft. Lauderdale, Fla., 1997-2000. Mem. Titanic Hist. Soc., Soc. Am. Magicians. Home: 1114 F St NE #402 Washington DC 20002 Office: Taverna: The Greek Islands 305 Pennsylvania Ave SE Washington DC 20003 E-mail: chg4600@aol.com.

NASH, JESSIE MADELEINE, journalist, science writer; b. Elizabeth City, NC, Sept. 11, 1943; d. John V. and Jessie B.; m. E. Thomas Nash, June 9, 1970. AB in History magna cum laude, Bryn Mawr Coll., 1965. Clip girl to sec. Time Mag., NYC, 1965-66, reporter rschr., 1966-70, stringer Bonn, Germany and Chgo., 1970-74, staff corr. Chgo., 1974-87, sr. sci. corr., 1987—. Mem. adv. com. on pub. infor. Am. Inst. of Physics, 1993-95. Contbr. articles to mags. Recipient Page One award Newspaper Guild of N.Y., 1981, award Leukemia Soc. Am., 1994, Popular Sci. Writing award, Am. Astronomical Soc., 1997. Mem. AAAS (Westinghouse award 1987, 90, Sci. Journalism award 1987, 91, 96,), Nat. Assn. Sci. Writers, Author's Guild, Sigma Xi (hon. mem). Avocation: travel. Office: Time Mag 303 E Ohio St Chicago IL 60611-3373

NASH, JILL, communications executive; BA, San Diego State U. Head corp. comm. Transamerica Life Companies; with KPMG; v.p. corp. comm. Charles Schwab Corp.; v.p. global comm. Gap Inc.; sr. v.p., chief comm. officer Yahoo! Inc., 2007—. Past pres. Orgn. of Women Executives. Recipient multiple Gold Quill awards. Office: Yahoo Inc 701 1st Ave Sunnyvale CA 94089 *

NASH, JOHN DAVIDSON, JR., economist; b. Houston, Apr. 12, 1953; s. John Davidson and Virginia (Bryant) Nash; m. Sarah Hendrickson, June 26, 1962; children: Scott, Rachel. BS, Tex. A&M U., College Station, 1975; MA, U. Chgo., 1978, PhD, 1982. Asst. prof. econ. Tex. A&M U., College Station, 1980—83; economist Bur. Econ. FTC, Washington, 1982—83; dep. asst. dir. consumer protection FTC, 1983—84, asst. dir. trade regulation rules, 1984—86, advisor to chmn., 1986; from agrl. sector economist agrl. products divsn. to lead economist L.Am. and Caribbean The World Bank, 1986—2007, lead economist sustainable devel. dept. L.Am. and Caribbean, 2007—. Author (with others): Strategic Minerals for Defense Needs, 1979, Colombia: External Sector and Agriculture Policies for Adjustment and Growth, 1985, Best Practices in Trade Policy Reform, 1991, Trade Policy and Exchange Rate Reform in Sub-Saharan Africa, 1997, Trade Policy Reform: Lessons and Implications, 1998, Food and Agricultural Policy in Russia: Progress to Date and The Road Forward, 2002, Agriculture and the WTO: Creating a Trading System for Development, Liberalizing Agricultural Trade: Issues and Options for Sub-Saharan Africa in the WTO, 2003, Agricutura, Comercio y Desarcello: Multilateralism vs Proteccionism, 2005; author: Reforming Agricultural Trade for Developing Countries, 2 vols.; contbr. articles to profl. jours. Mem.: So. Econ. Assn., We. Econ. Assn., Am. Econ. Assn., Omicron Delta Epsilon, Phi Kappa Phi, Phi Eta Sigma. Libertarian. Avocations: scuba diving, tennis, running. Home: 3307 Brandy Ct Falls Church VA 22042-3705 Office: The World Bank 18th And H Sts NW Washington DC 20433-0001 E-mail: jnash1@worldbank.org.

NASH, JOHN FORBES, JR., mathematician, researcher; b. Bluefield, W.Va., 1928; BS in Math., MS in Math., Carnegie-Mellon U., Pitts., 1948, ScD (hon.), 1999; PhD, Princeton U., New Brunswick, NJ, 1950; PhD (hon.), U. Athens, Greece, 2000, U. Naples, Italy, 2003, U. Charleston, W.Va., 2003; DSc (hon.), W.Va. U., Morgantown, 2006; PhD in Applied Econ. (hon.), U. Antwerp, Belgium, 2007. Rsch. asst., instr. Princeton (N.J.) U., 1950—51; Moore instr. MIT, 1951—53, asst. prof., 1953—57, assoc. prof., 1957—59; sr. rsch. mathematician Princeton U. Cons. RAND Corp., 1950, 52, 54; vis. mem. Inst. Advanced Study Princeton U., 1956—57, 1961—62, 1963—64; rsch. assoc. math. MIT, 1966—67. Co-recipient Nobel Prize in Econ. Scis., 1994, Bus. Week award, Erasmus U., Rotterdam, 1998, Leroy P. Steele prize in math., 1999; recipient von Neumann Theory prize, Ops. Rsch. Soc. Am., Pres.'s award, Nat. Alliance for the Mentally Ill, 1999, Herbert Simon award, New Eng. Complex Sys. Inst., 2006; Sloan fellow, NSF fellow, Westinghouse scholar. Fellow: Am. Acad. Arts and Scis., Econometric Soc.; mem.: NAS. Office: Princeton U Fine Hall Math Dept Princeton NJ 08544-0001

NASH, KATIE C., archivist; b. Honolulu, Nov. 13, 1979; d. Malcolm P. and Patricia G. Nash; m. Anders B. Selhorst, May 21, 2005. BS in Anthropology, Appalachian State U., Boone, NC, 2002; MLS, U. NC, Greensboro, 2004. Libr. tech. asst. U. NC, Greensboro, 2004—05; archives asst. Greensboro Hist. Mus., 2004—05; archivist Belk Libr. Elon U., NC, 2005—, libr. spl. collections Belk Libr., 2005—. Contbr. book revs. to profl. jours. Mem.: ALA (assoc.), Soc. Am. Archivists (assoc.), Libr. and Info. Sci. Alumni Assn. U. NC Greensboro (assoc.; sec. 2005), NC Preservation Consortium (assoc.; mem. instl. membership com. 2005, contact com. 2005), Soc. NC Archivists (assoc.), NC Libr. Assn. Roundtable Spl. Collections (assoc.; sec. 2005, treas. 2005), Pi Gamma Mu (life). Avocations: exercise, reading, gardening, travel, baking. Office: Elon Univ Belk Libr PO Box 187 Elon NC 27244 Office Phone: 336-278-6681. Office Fax: 336-278-6638. Business E-Mail: knash@elon.edu.

NASH, LEONARD KOLLENDER, retired chemistry professor; b. NYC, Oct. 27, 1918; s. Adolph and Carol (Kollender) N.; m. Ava Byer, Mar. 3, 1945; children: Vivian C., David B. BS, Harvard, 1939, MA, 1941, PhD, 1944. Rsch. asst. Harvard U., Cambridge, Mass., 1943-44, instr., 1946-48, asst. prof., 1948-53, assoc. prof., 1953-59, prof. chemistry, 1959-86, chmn. dept., 1971-74; rsch. assoc. Columbia, 1944-45; instr. U. Ill., 1945-46; ret. Staff Manhattan Project, 1944-45 Author: Elements of Chemical Thermodynamics, 1962, The Nature of the Natural Sciences, 1963, Stoichiometry, 1966, Elements of Statistical Thermodynamics, 1968, ChemThermo, 1972. Recipient Mfg. Chemists' award, 1966; James Flack Norris award, 1975 Home: 1443 Beacon St Apt 614 Brookline MA 02446-4712

NASH, MELVIN SAMUEL, lawyer; b. Atlanta, Aug. 26, 1949; s. Ralph Samuel and Mary Pauline (Quarles) N.; m. Cynthia Joanna Hamrick, Aug. 21, 1980 (dec.); m. Kristine Marie Clark, Nov. 22, 1997. A.B., Ga. State U., 1974; J.D., U. Fla., 1976. Bar: Ga. 1977, U.S. Ct. Claims 1983, U.S. Ct. Internat. Trade 1983, U.S. Tax Ct. 1982, U.S. Ct. Appeals (5th cir.) 1978, U.S. Ct. Appeals (11th cir.) 1981, U.S. Supreme Ct. 1985. Asst. solicitor State Ct., Cobb County, Marietta, Ga., 1977-78; assoc. Milam & Smith, Austell, Ga., 1978; ptnr. Milam, Smith & Nash, Austell, 1978-79; sole practice, Marietta, 1979—; spl. master Cobb Superior Ct., 1982—; dir. Nash Trucking Co., Inc., Marietta, Security Fiedelity Mortgage, Marietta, Nash Properties, Marietta. Magistrate Prohac Vice State Ct. Cobb County, Marietta, 1980-82; candidate state rep. State of Ga. Dist. 21, Marietta, 1982. Served with USAF, 1967-71. Mem. ABA, Acad. Fla. Trial Lawyers, Assn. Trial Lawyers Am., Nat. Assn. Criminal Def. Lawyers, Ga. Assn. Criminal Def. Lawyers, Cobb County Bar Assn. (com. 1983-84), Cobb Criminal Def. Bar Assn. (sec., Seminar award 1984), State Bar Ga. (fee arbitrator 1982—), Atlanta Ski Club, Atlanta Track (Marathon finisher), Atlanta Lawyers Club. Democrat. Presbyterian. Office Phone: 770-422-0878. E-mail: melvinsnash@msn.com.

NASH, NICHOLAS DAVID, retail executive; b. Mpls., June 11, 1939; s. Edgar Vanderhoef and Nancy (Van Slyke) N. AB, Harvard U., 1962; MEd, Bowling Green State U., 1970; PhD, U. Minn., 1975. Head lower sch. Maumee Valley (Ohio) Country Day Sch., 1965-71; assoc. dir. Univ. Council for Ednl. Adminstrn.; adj. asst. prof. Ohio State U., 1975-78; v.p. programming Minn. Public Radio, St. Paul, 1978-82, Am. Pub. Radio, St. Paul, 1982-85; pres. The Nash Co., 1985—. Bd. dirs. Artspace Projects, Inc. Contbr. articles to profl. jours. Bd. dirs. Nash Found., 1975-04, Humane Soc. Companion Animals, 2002—06. Mem. Univ. Club St. Paul. Episcopalian. Home: 1340 N Birch Lake Blvd Saint Paul MN 55110-6716 Office: 2179 4th St Ste 2H Saint Paul MN 55110-3041 Business E-Mail: nicholasnash@post.harvard.edu.

NASH, PAUL LENOIR, lawyer; b. Poughkeepsie, NY, Jan. 29, 1931; s. George Matthew and Winifred (LeNoir) Nash; m. Nancy Allyn Thouron, Dec. 30, 1961; children: Andrew Gray, Laurie LeNoir, Daphne Thouron. BA, Yale U., 1953; LLB, Harvard U., 1958. Bar: N.Y. 1959. Assoc. Dewey Ballantine, NYC, 1958-66, ptnr., 1966—. Pres. bd. trustees Peck Sch., Morristown, N.J., 1978-82. Served to capt. USMC, 1953-55; Japan. Mem. Assn. of Bar of City of N.Y. Republican. Home: 4 Westminster Pl Morristown NJ 07960-5810 Office: Dewey Ballantine LLP 1301 Avenue Of The Americas New York NY 10019-6022 Office Phone: 212-259-7100. Business E-Mail: pnash@deweyballantine.com. E-mail: pnash65131@aol.com.

NASH, RICHARD EDIN, publishing executive; b. Limerick, Republic of Ireland, June 30, 1970; came to U.S., 1988; s. Richard Oliver and Katherine Victoria (Sheehan) N. BA, Harvard U., 1992. Adv. Soft Skull Press, Manhattan, 1999—2001, pub. Bklyn, 2001—. Asst. dir. Yeats Drama Found., Dublin, Atlanta, 1991. Author, director, actor plays: Hair of the Dogma, 1990, The Frenzy of Sweeney, 1991, The Visit of the Old Lady, 1992. Recipient Gold medal for letter writing UNESCO, 1986, Young Writers award Dublin Sunday Tribune, 1991; Miriam Bass award for Creativity in Independent Pub. Assn. Am. Pub., 2006 Avocations: rugby, skiing.

NASH, STEVE, professional basketball player; b. Feb. 7, 1974; Degree, Santa Clara Coll., 1996. Player Phoenix Suns, 1996, Dallas Mavericks, 1998—2004, Phoenix Suns, 2004—. Named a Man of Yr., GQ mag., 2005; named MVP, NBA, 2005—06; named one of 100 Most Influential People, Time Mag., 2006; named to Western Conf. All-Star Team, NBA, 2002, 2003, 2005, 2007, All-NBA Third Team, 2003, 2002, All-NBA First Team, 2005, 2006, 2007; recipient Best NBA Player, ESPY awards, 2005. Achievements include leading NBA in assists and assists per game (884, 11.6), 2007. Office: c/o Phoenix Suns 201 E Jefferson St Phoenix AZ 85004 *

NASH, THOMAS, physician; b. NYC, Apr. 11, 1953; s. Eric Quinn and Lilliane Nash; m. Elizbeth Nash, July 11, 1981; 1 child, Katherine. BA in Biology, Swarthmore Coll., Pa., 1974; MD, NY U., NYC, 1978. Intern NY Hosp., Cornell Reed Ctr., NYC, 1978—81, fellow in infectious diseases, 1981—83, chief resident, 1984—85, asst. attending physician, 1985—; fellow in pulmory medicine Meml. Sloan Kellering, 1983—89. Asst. prof. clin. medicine NY Hosp., Cornell Reed Ctr., 1985—. Fellow: ACP, Am. Coll. Chest Physicians. Office: 72nd Street Medicine Assoc 310 E 72nd St New York NY 10021

NASH, WILLIAM ARTHUR, civil engineer, educator; b. Chgo., Sept. 15, 1922; s. William A. and Rose (Keck) N.; m. Verna Lucile Baer, Aug. 8, 1953; children: Rebecca Ann, Phillip Arthur. BSCE, Ill. Inst. Tech., Chgo., 1944, MS, 1946; PhD, U. Mich., 1949. Rsch. engr. David W. Taylor Model Basin, Navy Dept., Washington, 1949-54; mem. faculty U. Fla., Gainesville, 1954-67, head dept. engring. mechanics, 1964-67; prof. civil engring. U. Mass., Amherst, 1967—. Hon. prof. Shanghai Inst. Tech., 1985; pres. Cons. Engring., Amherst, 1992—; cons. in field. Author: Theory and Outline of Strength of Materials, 4th edit., 1998 (translated into 10 langs.), Statics and Mechanics of Materials, 1991, Hydrostatically Loaded Structures, 1995; contbr. over 100 articles to profl. jours.; editor Internat. Jour. Nonlinear Mechanics. Recipient Humboldt US Sr. Scientist award, Fed. Republic Germany, 1986. Fellow ASME; mem. Internat. Assn. Shell and Spatial Structures, Am. Soc. Engring. Edn. (Curtis W. McGraw Rsch. award 1961), AIAA, Earthquake Engring. Rsch. Inst. Congregationalist. Office: 235 Marston Hall U Mass Amherst MA 01003 Office Phone: 413-534-4510.

NASH, WILLIAM LEWIS, III, retired music educator; b. Kingston, Pa., July 5, 1946; s. Ray S. and Margaret (Zimmerman) N.; m. Janet Nossal, Dec. 29, 1979; children: Adrienne, William James. B of Music Edn., Westminster Choir Coll., 1968; MA in Music Performance, Trenton State Coll., 1970; PhD, Columbia State U., 1997. Cert. elementary and secondary edn. educator. Music tchr. Milford Mid. Sch. Quakertown (Pa.) Cmty. Sch. Dist., 1968-98, coord. of music, 1974-98. Organist, choirmaster St. John's Luth. Ch., Boyertown, Pa., 1968-87; organist, music dir., dir. concert series Emmanuel Luth. Ch., Pottstown, Pa., 1987—; organist Am. Legion Baseball World Series, Boyertown, Pa., 1990—; organist St. David's Soc., 1998—, v.p., 2000, pres., 2001. Mem. Bucks County Music Educators Assn. (pres. 1978-80), Antique Classic Boat Soc. (N.E. chpt. founder, bd. dirs., pres. 1991-94, pres. 2002), Pa. Music Educators Assn. (Citation of Excellence, 1997, bd dirs. 1992-2004) Republican. Avocations: restoration of antique cars, boats, antique furniture, painting, fishing gardening, cooking, composing music. Home: 285 E Moyer Rd Pottstown PA 19464-1534 Office: Emmanuel Lutheran Ch Hanover and Walnut Sts Pottstown PA 19464 Personal E-mail: nashr455@aol.com.

NASHAT, GUITY, historian, education educator, researcher; b. Bagdad, Iraq, July 28, 1937; arrived in U.S., 1956; d. Muhammad Sadegh Nashat-Mirdamad and Qamar Afshar; m. Gary S. Becker, Oct. 31, 1979; children: Michael, Cryus Claffey stepchildren: Judy, Catherine. BA, Barnard Coll., NYC, 1958; MS journalism, Columbia Univ., NYC, 1959; PhD hist., Univ. Chgo., Chgo., 1974. Vis. asst. prof. Loyola Univ., Chgo., 1974—75; asst. prof. Univ. Ill., Chgo., 1975—83, assoc. prof., 1983—2006. Rsch. fellow Hoover Inst., Stanford Univ., 1995—. Author: The Origins of Modern Reform in Iran 1870-1880, 1982, Middle Eastern History Selected Reading Lists and Course Outlines from American Colleges and Universities, 1988; editor: Women and Revolution in Iran, 1984; co-author: Women in the Middle East and North Africa, 1999; co-editor: The Economics of Life, 1996, Women in Iran From the Rise of Islam to 1800, 2003, Women in Iran from 1800 to the Islamic Republic, 2003. Grantee Ford Found. Grant, Univ. Chgo., 1968—69, Soc. Sci. Rsch. Coun. summer grant, 1978, Soc. Sci. Rsch. Coun. grant, 1976—77; Ford Found. fellowship, Columbia Sch. of Journalism, 1958—59. Mem.: Mont Pelerin Soc., Qajar Studies Assn., Iranian Studies (exec. bd. mem. 1986—89), Middle Eastern Studies Assn. Office: Univ Ill at Chgo 601 S Morgan St Chicago IL 60607-7109 Office Phone: 312-996-3144. E-mail: gnashat@uic.edu.

NASHED, M. ZUHAIR, mathematics professor, editor; b. Aleppo, Syria, May 14, 1936; s. Zaki Nashed and Nabiha Mosalati; m. Ragda Yagan, Dec. 23, 1959; children: Ziad, Zaki, Zane, Nadia. SB in Elec. Engring., MIT, 1957, SM in Elec. Engring., 1958; MS in Math., PhD in Math., U. Mich., 1963. Asst. prof. Ga. Inst. Tech., Atlanta, 1963—65, assoc. prof., 1965—69, prof., 1969—76; prof. math. and elec. engring. U. Del.; prof., chair U. Ctrl. Fla., Orlando, 2002—. Assoc. prof. Am. U. Beirut, Lebanon, 1967—69; vis. prof. U. Mich., U. Wis., European and Middle Eastern univs. Editor: Jour. Numerical Functional Analysis & Optimization, 1979—, Jour. Integral Equations, 1987—; mem. editl. bd.: 15 jours., exec. editor: 2 book series; author: over 120 papers in math. and engring. jours.; editor: 7 books; contbr.: numerous books. Recipient Sigma Xi Rsch. award, Ga. Tech., 1966, 1974, Lester Ford award, Math. Assn. Am., 1969; grantee rsch. and conf. grants, U.S. Army Rsch. Office and USAF Rsch. Mem.: Am. Math. Soc. (chair, VLP program 2000—), Soc. Indsl. & Applied Math. (education com. 2000—). Office: Univ Central Florida 209 MAP Bldg Orlando FL 32816 Business E-Mail: znashed@mail.ucf.edu.

NASKY, H(AROLD) GREGORY (HAROLD GREGORY NASKY), lawyer; b. Titusville, Pa., June 9, 1942; s. Harold G. and Majella Marie (Beck) N.; m. Rosanne Guson, July 22, 1967. AB, St. Bonaventure U., 1964; JD, U. Notre Dame, 1967. Bar: Pa. 1967, Nev. 1972, Hawaii, 2003. Assoc. Eaton & Hill, Warren, Pa., 1967-68, Vargas, Bartlett & Dixon, Reno, 1972-73; ptnr. Vargas & Bartlett, Las Vegas, Nev., 1974-94, mng. ptnr., 1981-91; of counsel Kummer, Kaempfer, Bonner & Renshaw, 1994—2006; prin. Resort Devel. Cons., 1998—; ptnr. Goodsill Anderson Quinn & Stifel, Honolulu, 2006—. Corp. sec. Showboat, Inc. (NYSE-SBO), Las Vegas, 1978-98, bd. dirs., 1983-98, exec. v.p., 1995-98; bd. dirs. U. Notre Dame Law Assn., 1990-2000; mem. adv. bd. U. Nev. Sch. Medicine.; chmn. 1993, bd. dirs. Author: Inter Alia Jour. of State Bar of Nevada, A Glimpse of China, 1986; Nev. contbg. author: Real Property, Probate & Trust Law Jour., Disposition of Rents, 1981. Legal advisor Nev. Dance Theatre, Las Vegas, 1977-94, bd. dirs. 1988-2000; legal com. Nev. Resort Assn., Las Vegas, gaming regulations com. 1990-93; bd. dirs. Boulder Dam coun. Boy Scouts Am., Las Vegas, 1986-93; del. People to

People Citizen Ambassador Program, People's Republic China, 1985, New Zealand/Australia, 1987, Hungary, Czechoslovakia and Poland, 1990, Russia and Estonia, 1992. Served to capt. JAGC, U.S. Army, 1968-72, Vietnam. Decorated Bronze Star, 1970. Mem. ABA (bus. sect. task force conflicts interest com. 1993-95), State Bar Nev. (chmn. fee dispute com. 1983-89, exec. com. mem. Gaming Law Sect. 1985-93), Am. Soc. Corp. Secs., Internat. Assn. Gaming Attys., Notre Dame Club Las Vegas (past pres. 1978-79), U. Nev. Las Vegas Found. (president's assocs. 1993, chmn.). also: Resort Devel Cons PMB A14 Ste 105 9101 W Sahara Ave Las Vegas NV 89117 Office: Goodsill Anderson Quinn and Stifel 1099 Alakea St Ste 1800 Honolulu HI 96813 Home: 4340 Pahoa Ave 8A Honolulu HI 96816 Home Phone: 702-496-5583; Office Phone: 808-547-5600. Business E-Mail: gnasky@goodsill.com.

NASLUND, HOWARD RICHARD, geological science educator; b. Green Hills, Ohio, Nov. 25, 1950; married, 1979; 5 children. BS, U. Ill., 1972; MS, U. Oreg., 1977, PhD, 1980. Leader East Greenland Expeditions, 1985, 1986, 1988, 1989; igneous petrologist Ocean Drilling Program, 1991, 97; asst. prof. Dartmouth Coll., 1979-87; assoc. prof. dept. geol. scis. and environ. studies SUNY, Binghamton, 1987-95, assoc. chmn. geol. scis. and environ. studies, 1987-88, dir. grad. studies geol. scis., 1988-92, prof. dept. geol. scis. and environ. studies, 1995—, chmn. geol. scis. and environ. studies, 1992-95,97-2000. Vis. prof. Departamento de Geologia, U. Chile, 1995-96, vis. prof. Departamento de Ingenieriá en Minas, U. de Santiago, Chile, 2001-02; outside rev. com. dept. geology SUNY, New Paltz, 1995, sponsored programs adv. coun., 1994-97, grad. coun., 1994-97, chair adv. com. on scholarship and rsch., 1994-97, material rsch. inst., 1991—, faculty senate, 1988-90, 96-98, 2005—; trustee Glenn G. Bartle Meml. Fund, 1988-90, 96-98, 2004-06; exec. com. of faculty Dartmouth Coll., 1982-85, com. on stds., 1981-86. Contbr. articles to profl. jours. J. William Fulbright scholar, 1995-96; rsch. grant USSAC, 1991, 92, 97, 98, 2005, NSF, 1982, 88, 90, 99, 2004, equipment grant NSF, 1990, 91. Mem. Geol. Soc. of Am. (Penrose Rsch. award 1974, 76), Mineralogical Soc. Am., Am. Geophys. Union, Sociedad Geologica de Chile, NY State Geol. Assn. (pres. 1997-98), Internat. Assn. Volcanology Chemistry Earth Interior. Office: Geol Scis SUNY Binghamton NY 13902-6000 Home Phone: 607-786-0430; Office Phone: 607-777-4313. Business E-Mail: Naslund@Binghamton.edu.

NASON, CHARLES TUCKEY, retired diversified financial services company executive; b. Apr. 22, 1946; s. Raymond W. and Helen (Tuckey) Nason; m. Elizabeth Lucille Rabun, May 1, 1999; children: Rebecca Ann, Jill Nicole. BA, Washington and Jefferson Coll., 1968; MBA, U. Pitts., 1969. Cert. fin. planner, chartered fin. cons. Dist. sales mgr. Met. Life Ins. Co., Pitts., 1971-77; mng. dir. Acacia Grp. Cos., Pitts., 1977-88; founder, pres. Coordinated Capital Ltd., Pitts., 1982-85; pres., CEO Acacia Life Ins. Co., Washington, 1988—2003, chmn., 1988—2005, Acacia Fed. Savings Bank, Calvert Grp., Ltd. Chmn. devel. coun. exec. com. Washington and Jefferson Coll., 1982—85, trustee, 1988—, chmn. Nat. Ann. Giving Fund, 1992—96; trustee Washington Fed. City Coun., 1988—; bd. dirs. Greater Washington Bd. Trade, chmn.-elect, 1993, chmn., 1994; bd. dirs. Washington Real Estate Investment Trust, Medstar Inc., Blue Cross Blue Shield Washington, 1991—93, Greater Washington Boys and Girls clubs, Am. Coun. Life Ins., 1993—2000, Medlantic Healthcare Group, 1997—98. Lt. USAF, 1970—71. Mem.: Ins. Marketplace Stds. Assn. (bd. dirs. 1999—, chmn.-elect 2001, chmn. 2002), Inst. Cert. Fin. Planners (bd. dirs.), Nat. Assn. Securities Dealers, Estate Planning Coun. (bd. dirs.), Am. Soc. CLUS (pres. 1981—82), Gen. Agts. and Mgrs. Assn. (pres. 1984—85), Fiddlesticks Golf and Country Club, Talbout Country Club, Congl. Country Club, Burning Tree Club. Republican. Roman Catholic. Mailing: c/o Acacia Fed Savings Bank PO Box 6430 Falls Church VA 22040-9825

NASON, DAVID GEORGE, federal agency administrator; b. 1970; m. Nicole R. Nason; children: Alexandra, Abigail. BS in Fin., Am. U., 1992; JD, Washington Coll. Law, 1995. Law clk. to Hon. Marvin J. Garbis US Dist. Ct. Md.; atty. Covington & Burling LLP; counsel SEC; dep. asst. sec. for fin. institutions policy US Dept. Treasury, under sec. for domestic fin., 2005—07; asst. sec. for fin. institutions US Dept Treasury, 2007—. Bd. dirs. Nat. Consumer Cooperative Bank, 2007—. Office: US Dept Treasury 1500 Pennsylvania Ave NW Rm 2326 Washington DC 20220 Office Phone: 202-622-2610. Office Fax: 202-622-2027. E-mail: david.nason@do.treas.gov. *

NASON, DOLORES IRENE, computer company executive, social welfare administrator, minister; b. Seattle; d. William Joseph and Ruby Irene Lockinger; m. George Malcolm Nason, Jr.; children: George Malcolm III, Scott James, Lance William, Natalie Joan. Student, Long Beach City Coll., Calif.; cert. in Religious Edn. for elem tchrs., Immaculate Heart Coll., cert. teaching, cert. secondary teaching; attended, Salesian Sem. Buyer J. C. Penney Co., Barstow, Calif.; prin. St. Cyprian Confraternity of Christian Doctrine Elem. Sch., Long Beach; prin. summer sch. St. Cyprian Confraternity of Christian Doctrine Elem. Sch., Long Beach; pres. St. Cyprian Confraternity Orgn., Long Beach; dist. co-chmn. L.A. Diocese; v.p. Nason & Assocs., Inc., Long Beach, 1978—; pres. L.A. County Commn. on Obscenity & Pornography, 1984—; eucharistic minister St. Cyprian Ch., Long Beach, 1985—; bd. dirs. L.A. County Children's Svcs., 1988—; assoc. dir. social svcs. Disabled Resources Ctr., Inc, Long Beach, 1992—. Scholarship com. Long Beach City Coll., 1984—90, Calif. State U., Long Beach, 1984—90; chmn. bd. dirs. LA County Access Svcs. Inc., 2004—. Active Long Beach Civic Light Opera, 1973—96, Assitance League Long Beach, 1976—; vol. Meml. Children's Hosp., Long Beach, 1977—; pres. St. Cyprian's Parish Coun., 1962—. Mem.: KC (Family of Month award 1988), U. Pacific Club. Roman Catholic. Avocations: physical fitness, theater, choir, travel.

NASON, LEONARD YOSHIMOTO, lawyer, writer; b. NYC, Feb. 17, 1954; s. Leonard Hastings and Mary Yukiko (Yoshimoto) N.; m. Linda Thayer, Sept. 26, 1981; children: Victoria, Kelsey, Jennifer. BA, Tufts U., 1975; JD, Northeastern U., Boston, 1979. Bar: Mass. 1979, U.S. Dist. Ct. 1979, U.S. Ct. Appeals (1st cir.) 1985. Assoc. Ricklefs & Uehlein, Natick, Mass., 1979-84; ptnr. Uehlein, Nason & Wall, Natick, 1985-95, Nason, Wall & Wall, P.C., Lexington, Mass., 1995—2005; of counsel Curtin, Murphy & O'Reilly, PC, Boston, 2005—; pvt. practice Bedford, Mass., 2005—. Pres. Legal Info. Svcs., Inc., Lexington, 1986—; interviewer admissions Tuft U.; mem. SBANE HR com. Author: (handbook) Mass. Workers' Compensation, 1986, (statute book) Mass. Workers' Compensation, 1987; co-author: Massachusetts Practice Series, Vol. 29, 1989, 95, 2002, 04, lead author, Vol. 29, 3rd edit.; contbg. author: A Judicial Guide to Labor and Employment Law, 1990, SBANE HR Guide for 2002. Coach soccer, basketball and softball, Little League. Mem. ABA (vice-chair and webmaster tort and ins. practice sect., workers' compensation and employee liability law com. 2004), Mass. Bar Assn., Boston Bar Assn., Assn. Trial Lawyers Am. Avocations: tennis, sailing, softball, music. Office: Curtin Murphy & O'Reilly PC Ste 320 31 Saint James Ave Boston MA 02116-4185 Home Phone: 781-861-7112; Office Phone: 781-271-9296. E-mail: lnason@nasonlaw.com, LNASON1750@aol.com.

NASON, NICOLE R., federal agency administrator; b. LI, NY, Aug. 12, 1970; m. David G. Nason; children: Alexandra, Abigail. Grad., Am. U., Washington, 1992; JD, Case Western Res. U., Cleve., 1995. Counsel to Rep. Henry Hyde House Judiciary Subcom. on Crime, Washington, 1995—99; govt. affairs counsel Met. Life Ins. Co., 1999—2000; comm. dir., counsel to US Rep. Porter J. Goss House Intelligence Com., 2000—02; asst. commr. Office of Congl. Affairs, U.S. Customs Svc., Washington, 2002—03; asst. sec. for govtl. affairs US Dept. Transp., Washington, 2003—06, adminstr., Nat. Hwy. Traffic Safety Adminstrn., 2006—. Office: Nat Hwy Traffic Safety Adminstrn US Dept Transp 400 7th St Washington DC 20590 *

NASON, ROCHELLE, conservation organization administrator; b. Oakland, Calif., May 21, 1959; d. Milton and Ann Frances (Reed) Nason. BA, U. Calif., Berkeley, 1984; JD, U. Calif., San Francisco, 1987. Bar: Calif. 1987. Law clk. to Chief Justice Malcolm Lucas Supreme Ct. of Calif., San Francisco, 1987-88; litigation assoc. Morrison & Foerster, San Francisco, 1988-92; staff lawyer League to Save Lake Tahoe, South Lake Tahoe, Calif., 1992-93, exec. dir., 1993—. Adj. instr. Sierra Nev. Coll., Incline Village, 1992—94, Lake Tahoe C.C., 1992—96. Editor: The Traynor Reader, 1987; sr. rev. editor: Hastings Law Jour., 1986—87; editor: (jour.) Keep Tahoe Blue, 1992—; columnist: newspaper Tahoe Daily Tribune; contbr. articles to profl. jours. Mem. leadership coun. Tahoe-Truckee Regional Econ. Coalition, Stateline, Nev., 1992—94; v.p., bd. dirs. Jewish Cmty. South Lake Tahoe/Temple Bat Yam, 1992—99; bd. dirs. Tahoe Ctr. Sustainable Future, Glenbrook, Nev., 1995—98, Earthshare Calif., 2002—. Mem.: Thurston Soc., Order of Coif. Jewish. Avocations: backpacking, skiing. Office: League to Save Lake Tahoe 955 Emerald Bay Rd South Lake Tahoe CA 96150-6410

NASR, NADIA, library and information scientist; b. Houston, Apr. 2, 1977; d. Ghazi Said Nasr and Patricia Maureen Moye. BA in French, Miss. Coll.; MS in Info. Sci., U. So. Miss., 2005. Cert. publ. libr. Md. Digitization specialist McCain Libr. and Archives, Hattiesburg, Miss., 2002—05; libr., digitization supr. Enoch Pratt Free Libr., Balt., 2005—, coord. Md. Digital Cultural Heritage Project. Named one of the Movers & Shakers, Libr. Jour., 2007. Mem.: ALA, Miss. Libr. Assn., Md. Libr. Assn., Soc. Am. Archivists, Spl. Librs. Assn. Office: Enoch Pratt Free Libr 400 Cathedral St Baltimore MD 21201 Home Phone: 443-846-1996; Office Phone: 410-545-6342. Business E-Mail: nnasr@epfl.net.

NASRAOUI, OLFA, computer scientist, educator, electrical engineer; b. Tunis, Tunisia, July 6, 1968; d. Ezzeddine Zidane Nasraoui and Fatma Braiek; m. Hichem Frigui, Apr. 3, 1993; children: Yasmine Frigui, Sara Frigui. BS in Computer Engring. with honors, U. Mo., Columbia, 1990, BSEE with honors, 1990, MSEE, 1992, PhD in Computer Engring. and Computer Sci., 1999. Asst. prof. dept. elec. and computer engring. U. Memphis, 2000—04; endowed chmn. e-commerce dept. computer sci. and computer engring. U. Louisville, 2004—, founder, dir. Knowledge Discovery and Web Mining Rsch. Lab., 2004—. Panel organizer internat. confs., outreach/sci. fair activities; reviewer rsch. proposals NASA; mem. program com., organizing com. various internat. confs.; reviewer internat. jours. in field. Editor conf. procs. Faculty advisor local chpt. Soc. Women Engrs., Memphis, 2000—04. Recipient Best Paper award for Theoretical Developments in Computational Intelligence, Procs. Artificial Neural Networks in Engring., 2001, Career award, NSF, 2002; grantee, 2002—, So. Consortium for Elec. Engring. Edn., 2002—03, NASA, 2004—, Innovative Productivity Inc., 2006. Mem.: IEEE, IEEE Women in Engring., Internal Adv. Bd. Logistics and Distbn. Inst., MentorNet, Assn. Computing Machinery. Office: U Louisville Sch Engring CECS Dept Speed Louisville KY 40292 Home Phone: 901-491-3851; Office Phone: 502-852-0191.

NASRULLAH, MOHAMMED JALEEL, research scientist; s. Abdul Subhan Jaleel and Puthli Begum; m. Rabiya Shabnam, May 14, 2006. PhD, Indian Inst. Tech., Madras, 2001. Polymer engr. Neopad Tech. Corp, Sunnyvale, Calif., 2004—05; rsch. assoc. ND State U., Fargo, 2005—. Mem.: Am. Chem. Soc. Home: 208 University Village Fargo ND 58102 Personal E-mail: jaleelmn@yahoo.com.

NASS, HERBERT EVAN, lawyer; b. NYC, May 31, 1959; s. Samuel and Edna (Kadin) N. BA, Swarthmore Coll., 1981; JD, NYU, 1984. Bar: NY 1985. Assoc. Paul, Weiss, Rifkind, Wharton & Garrison, NYC, 1984-87, Tenzer, Greenblatt, Fallon & Kaplan, NYC, 1987-89; pvt. practice law NYC, 1989—. Mem. Vol. Lawyers for Arts, NYC, 1987—. Editor-in-chief NYU Jour. Internat. Law and Politics, 1983-84; author: Wills of Rich & Famous, 2000; contbr. articles to profl. jours. Named one of Top 100 Attys., Worth mag., 2005—06. Mem. ABA, Assn. of Bar of City of NY, Horace Mann Alumni Coun. Democrat. Jewish. Avocations: visiting museums and art galleries, running, tennis, travel. Home: 16 Justin Rd Harrison NY 10528-1210 Office: 230 Park Ave Ste 2525 New York NY 10169-0005 Home Phone: 914-967-5267; Office Phone: 212-370-0777. Personal E-mail: herbnass@nasslaw.net.

NASS, MERYL J., physician, writer, research scientist; b. Rockville Ctr., NY, Apr. 6, 1951; d. Leonard Ira and Irene Shirley Nass; m. John Duncan Abernethy, Aug. 13, 1977 (div. 1987); children: Abraham David Abernethy, Jacob Duncan Abernethy. BS in Biology, MIT, 1974; MD, Univ. Miss., 1980. Diplomate Am. Bd. of Internal Medicine, 1986. Physician hosp. and health care ctrs., 1985—98; self-employed, 1999—. Mem. adv. bd. Alliance for Human Rsch. Protection, NYC, 2001—, Nat. Vaccine Info. Ctr., Vienna, 2000—, Inst. for Molecular Medicine, Huntington Beach, Calif., 2000—; cons. Interamerican Devel. Bank, Washington, 2001—; presenter testimony on anthrax vaccine reaction NAS Inst. Medicine, U.S. Congress, major mass media, 1998—. Contbr. scientific papers to profl. jour., articles over 30 to profl. jour. Achievements include development of assessment and treatment strategies for fibromyalgia, Gulf War syndrome, chronic fatigue sydrome; discovery of first use of biological weapons in modern times; high rate of severe reactions to anthrax vaccine; research in establishing long-term safety and efficacy for vaccines and drugs before licensure and widespread use; improving criteria to distinguish between naturally occurring and deliberate outbreaks of disease; development of comprehensive epidemiologic surveillance to identify questionable disease outbreaks; research in mitigation of bioterrorism events. Office: Mount Desert Island Hosp 10 Wayman Lane Bar Harbor ME 04609 Office Phone: 207-288-5082 x220. Personal E-mail: mnass@gwi.net. Business E-Mail: mnass@anthraxvaccine.org.

NASS, RUTH, pediatric neurologist; b. NYC, Apr. 14, 1947; d. Samuel and Edna (Kadin) N.; m. Theodore Gross, Aug. 28, 1977; 1 child, Nora Gross. BA, Brandeis U., 1969; postgrad., MIT, 1969-70, Brandeis U., 1970-72; MD, Einstein Coll. Medicine, 1975. Diplomate Nat. Bd. Med. Examiners, Am. Bd. Pediatrics, Am. Bd. Psychiatry and Neurology with spl. competence in child neurology; lic. physician, N.Y. Resident pediatrics N.Y. Hosp., NYC, 1975-77; resident neurology Columbia Presbyn. Hosp., NYC, 1977-80; clin. rsch. fellow in neurology/neuropsychology Cornell U. Med. Coll., NYC, 1980-82, instr. pediatrics, 1981-82, asst. prof., 1982-88, asst. prof. neurology, 1982-89; asst. attending pediatrics and neurology N.Y. Hosp., NYC, 1982-89; divsn. chief pediatric neurology N.Y. Hosp.-Cornell Med. Ctr., NYC, 1986-89, assoc. attending pediatrician, 1988-91; assoc. prof. clin. pediatrics Cornell Med. Coll., NYC, 1988-89, assoc. prof. neurology and pediatrics, 1989-91; assoc. attending neurologist N.Y. Hosp., NYC, 1989-91; assoc. prof. neurology and pediatrics NYU Med. Ctr., NYC, 1991—; assoc. attending pediatrician, neurologist Tisch Hosp., Bellevue Hosp., N.Y. U. Med. Ctr., 1991—; dir. learning diagnostics program NYU Med. Ctr., 1991—. Neurologic cons. N.Y. Foundling Hosp., N.Y.C., 1980-83; dir. Learning Disability Ctr. N.Y. Hosp.-Cornell Med. Ctr., 1983-91; neurologic cons. St. Mary's Hosp., Bklyn., 1984-86, Englewood (N.J.) Hosp., 1986, Hosp. for Spl. Surgery, N.Y.C., 1987-91; acting chief divsn. pediatric neurology N.Y. Hosp.-Cornell Med. Ctr., 1985-86; chief neurology Blythedale Children's Hosp., 1989-91; adj. assoc. prof. pediatrics N.Y. Hosp.-Cornell U. Med. Ctr., 1991—; NIH ad hoc site com. Nosology of Learning Disabilities, Washington, Isabelle Rapin, P.I., 1987, N.Y.C., 1988; external rev. panel Child Neurology Soc. Nosology Project in Presch. Child, 1989; ad hoc NIH site com. at Boston Children's Hosp. Program Project on Learning in At Risk Groups, 1990, ad hoc NIH site com. for Ctr. and Program Project on Neurobiology of Dyslexia, 1992; mem. written bds. com. Am. Acad. Psychiatry and Neurology, 1992-93; mem. NIH Consensus Com. on Early Identificaiton of Hearing Impairment, 1993; lectr. univs., hosps, orgns., workshops and symposiums. Ad hoc reviewer Neurology, Annals of Neurology, Cognitive Neurosci., Psychol. Bull., Pediatrics, Psychoneuroendocrinology, Jour. Neuro-oncology, Epilepsia; contbr. articles to profl. jours., chpts. to books. Mary Putnam Jacobie fellow, 1981; grantee NIH Nat. Rsch. Svc., 1980-83, NIH Biomed. Rsch., Cornell U. Med. Coll., 1983-84, March of Dimes, 1984-95, United Cerebral Palsy, 1984-87, Rita G. Rudel Found., 1986-88, NIH Ctr., 1991—; recipient Rockefeller Bros. Clin. Scholarship N.Y. Hosp.-Cornell Med. Coll., 1983-84. Mem. Am. Neurol. Assn., Am. Acad. Neurology, Am. Acad. Pediatrics (develop. disabilities com. 1992-93), Assn. for Rsch. in Nervous and Mental Diseases, Child Neurology Soc. (sci. selection com. 1988-89, 91-93, clin. practice com. 1991-93, award com. 1990-92), Internat. Child Neurology Soc., Am. Epilepsy Soc., Am. Acad. Cerebral Palsy, N.Y. Acad. Sci., Orton Dyslexia Soc., Soc. for Children with Attention Deficit Disorder. Office: NYU Med Ctr Rusk Rsch 212 550 1st Ave New York NY 10016-6402

NASSAR, RAJA, statistics educator, researcher, consultant; b. Lebanon, 1936; came to U.S., 1958; naturalized, 1971; m. Ita G. Schaeffer, 1965; 1 child, Mark BS, Am. U., Beirut, Lebanon, 1958; MS, U. Idaho, 1960; PhD, U. Calif., Davis, 1963. Rsch. fellow U. Idaho, Moscow, 1958—60; rsch. asst. U. Calif., Davis, 1960—63, rsch. assoc., 1963—64; mem. vis. faculty U. Minn., St. Paul, 1964—66; asst. prof. Kans. State U., Manhattan, 1966—68, assoc. prof., 1968—74, prof. stats., 1974—; prof. emeritus La. State U., 2007—. Maxfield prof. math. and stats. Kans. State U., 1995-2007; vis. prof. Govt. Research Inst., Hamburg, Germany, 1969-70, Nat. Research Inst., Toulouse, France, 1974-75, U. Kiel, Germany, 1982-83, U. Giessen, Germany, 1992-93 Contbr. numerous articles to sci. jours.; editor sci. jours. Alexander von Humboldt fellow, 1969, 82, French Govt. fellow, 1974; rsch. grantee Greek Orthodox. Avocations: tennis, travel, piano, reading. Office: La Tech U Math and Stats 305 Wisteria St Ruston LA 71270-4235 Business E-Mail: nassar@coes.latech.edu.

NASSAR, SUSAN D., lawyer; d. Reda E. Fidurski. AS, Johnson & Wales Coll. Culinary Arts, Providence, RI, 1983; BS (hon.), U. Houston, TX, 1995—97; JD, U. Houston Law Ctr., TX, 1997—2000. Lic.: Tex. State Bar 2001. Exec. pastry chef Four Seasons Hotel, Austin, Tex., 1986—93; briefing atty. Justice Sarah B. Duncan, Tex. Fourth Ct. of Appeals, San Antonio, 2000—02; law clk. Unitied States Dist. Ct. Judge Sam A. Lindsay, Dallas, 2002—03; assoc. atty. Godwin Pappas, Dallas, 2003—05, Elrod PLLC, Dallas, 2005—07. Co-chair Ask-A-Lawyer Com., Dallas Assn. Young Lawyers, Dallas, 2005—06; contbr. Publ. Com. Dallas Bar Assn., Dallas, 2006—07. Mem.: Tex. Bar, Dallas Bar Assn., Phi Kappa Phi. Independent. Christian. Avocations: embroidery, cooking. Office: Elrod PLLC 500 N Akard Ste 3000 Dallas TX 75201 Home Phone: 214-855-5188; Office Phone: 214-855-5188.

NASSAR, WILLIAM MICHAEL, lawyer; b. Methuen, Mass., June 5, 1958; s. William M. and Catherine M. Nassar; m. Ermelinda Amezcua, June 26, 1982; children: Brandon Michael, Elyse Renae. AAS, R.I. C.C., 1978; BSBA, U. Redlands, 1980; JD, Western State Coll. of Law, 1986. Legal adminstr. Bourns Inc., Riverside, Calif., 1988-90, dir. worldwide contracts adminstr., 1990-94, dir. worldwide contracts/legal counsel, 1994-97, sr. legal counsel, 1997-2000; v.p., gen. counsel Standard MEMS, Inc., Burlington, Mass., 1999—2002; ptnr. Law Offices William M Nassar & Assoc., Redlands, Calif., 2005—. Bd. dirs. Advanced Med. Inc., Riverside, Calif., Global Pathways Inc., Riverside; v.p. Bourns Employees Fed. Credit Union, bd. dirs. Adv. bd. Ronald McDonald House, Loma Linda, Calif., 1994-98. Roman Catholic. Avocations: sailing, boating, skiing, reading. Home: 13015 Burns Ln Redlands CA 92373-7415 Office: 300 E State St Ste 200 Redlands CA 92373 Office Phone: 909-798-6179. E-mail: william.nassar@verizon.net.

NASSAU, DAVID L., engineer; b. Chgo., Feb. 20, 1918; s. Julius and Anna Nassau; m. Enid Carol Nassau, Jan. 7; children: Lawrence D., Bruce A., Anne L. BSME, Purdue U., West Lafayette, Ind., 1940. Named East Chgo. Hall Fame, 2003. Mem.: East Chgo. Male Chorus (pres. 1974), Ind. Hist. Soc., East Chgo. C. of C., Kiwanis (pres. 1990—96), Harbor Lodge Masonic Lodge, East Chgo. Elks. Avocations: ping pong/table tennis, golf, bridge.

NASSAU, MICHAEL JAY, lawyer; b. NYC, June 3, 1935; s. Benjamin and Belle (Nassau) N.; m. Roberta Bluma Herzlich, June 26, 1971; children: Stephanie Ellen, William Michael. BA summa cum laude, Yale U., 1956, LLB cum laude, 1960. Bar: NY 1960, US Ct. Appeals (2d cir.) 1963, US Tax Ct. 1963, US Supreme Ct. 1965, US Dist. Ct. (so. dist.) NY 1978. Asst. instr. in constl. law Yale U., 1959-60; law clk. judge US Ct. Appeals 2d Cir., 1960-61; assoc. tax dept. Paul, Weiss, Rifkind, Wharton & Garrison, NYC, 1961-73; ptnr. Kramer Levin Naftails & Frankel LLP, and predecessor, NYC, 1974—. Mem. adv. bd. Matthew Bender Fed. Pension Law Service, 1975-76; mem. adv. com. NYU Ann. Inst. Employee Plans Exec. Compensation, 1976-79; mem. steering com. Am. Pension Conf., 1981-83; lectr. field; chair PLI Seminars, Deferred Compensation after Treasury Guidance, 2005, 2007; panelist various seminars employee benefits; mem. N.E. region pension liaison group IRS. Mem. editl. bd. Bank Corp. Governance Law Reporter, 1989—; contbr. chpts. to books and articles to profl. jours. Recipient Excellence in Benefits award lifetime achievement benefits svc., Worldwide Employee Benefits Network, 2003. Charter fellow Am. Coll. Employee Benefits Counsel; mem. ABA (sect. taxation, employee benefits com. 1993—), NY State Bar Assn. (co-chmn. employee benefits sect. taxation 1976-78, mem. exec. com. sect. taxation 1976-79), Assn. Bar City NY (chmn. subcom. pension legis. of com. taxation 1975-76, employee benefits com. 1987-92), WEB (NY chpt. bd. dirs. 1990—, pres. 1993-94), Phi Beta Kappa. Office: Kramer Levin Naftalis & Frankel LLP 1177 Ave of the Americas New York NY 10036 Office Phone: 212-715-9416. Business E-Mail: mnassau@kramerlevin.com.

NASSER, JACQUES, banker, former automotive company executive; b. Beirut, Dec. 12, 1947; Degree in Bus. studies, Royal Melbourne Inst. Tech. With Ford of Australia, 1968-73; mem. fin. staff N. Am. truck ops. Ford Motor Co., 1973, mgr. profit analysis, product programming, 1973-75, with Asia-Pacific and Latin-Am. ops., 1970—80, dir., v.p. fin. and adminstrn., Autolatina joint venture, 1987-90, chmn. Ford Europe, 1993—99, pres. Ford automotive ops., exec. v.p., 1996—99, v.p., 1993-96, pres., CEO Dearborn, Mich., 1999—2001, Ford of Australia, 1990-93; sr. ptnr. One Equity Partners LLC, NYC, 2002—; non-exec. chmn. Polaroid Corp., Waltham, Mass., 2002—. Office: One Equity Partners LLC 320 Park Ave 18th Fl New York NY 10022

NASSER, JENNIFER ANN, nutritionist, researcher, healthcare educator; d. Joseph J. Nasser and Eleanor M. Gilmartin. BA, Elmira Coll., NYC, 1974; MS, Lehigh U., Bethlehem, Pa., 1978; PhD, Rutgers U., New Brunswick, NJ, 1998. Registered dietitian Commn. Dietetics Registration, 2004, clin. chemistry techonologist Nat. Registry Clin. Chemists, 1981, cert. dietitian-nutritionist N.Y. State Dept Edn., 2003. Rsch. scientist, Bridgewater, NJ, 1979—91; rsch. assoc. N.Y. Obesity Rsch. Ctr., NYC, 1998—. Reviewer Appetite, Obesity Rsch. Jour. Am. Dietetic Assn., 2000—; adj. asst. prof. nutrition Hunter Coll., NYC, 2002—; cons. CURA Hospitality, Allentown, Pa., 2004—. Contbr. articles to profl. jours. Bd. mem. Am. Singers Opera Project, NYC, 1998—2000. Fellow, NIH,

1999—2002; grantee, Van Slyke Rsch. Soc., 1991, NIH, 2000—, Internat. Life Scis. Inst., 2004—. Mem.: NAASO, The Obesity Soc., Am. Soc. Clin. Nutrition, Am. Dietetics Assn. Achievements include patents for immunopharmaceuticals. Avocation: professional musician. Office: St Lukes Roosevelt Hosp Ctr WH1020 NY Obesity Rsch Ctr 1111 Amsterdam Ave New York NY 10025 Office Phone: 212-523-3357. Office Fax: 212-523-4830. E-mail: jnasser@chpnet.org; jnasser@att.net.

NASSER, JOSEPH YOUSEF, public safety administrator, consultant; b. Welch, W.Va., Mar. 19, 1943; s. Joseph H. and Betty Anne (Caldwell) N.; m: Janis Halligan Nasser; children: Robert, Eric, Melanie, Matthew, Michelle. BS, Pacific Western U., 1989, PhD, 1991. Patrolman, firefighter, emergency med. technician Mich. Dept. Pub. Safety, Oak Park, 1962-75; patrolman Daytona Beach (Fla.) Police Dept., 1975-76; lt., capt., dir. Volusia County (Fla.) Sheriff's Dept., 1976-90; pres., founder, owner Ctr. for Pub. Safety Studies, Ormond Beach, Fla., 1990—97; sr. v.p. RCC Cons., Inc, 1997—. Pres. Associated Pub. Safety Comm. Officer, Inc., 1987-88, Land Mobile Comm. Coun., Washington, 1988-89; chmn. Nat. Pub. Safety Planning Com./F.C.C., 1987-88; life mem. APCO, Inc. Past chmn. Fla. State Standards and Telecommunicator Cert. Com., Fla. State Emergency Mgmt. 9-1-1 Com.; past mem. exec. coun. Volusia County Emergency Med. Found.; past chmn. Volusia County Emergency Med. Svcs. Trust Fund Adv. Bd. Recipient Dayton Beach Cooper-Taylor Pub. Safety Achievement award, 1985, Nat. Achievement award Pub. Safety Comm. Coun., 1987, FCC Recognition award, 1987, APCO Life Mem. award, 1988, Emergency Mgmt. Recognition award State of Fla., 1989, Appreciation award Emergency Med. Found., 1990, Disting. Svc. award Volusia County Sheriff's Dept., 1990. Fellow Radio Club of Am.; mem. Associated Pub. Safety Comms. Ofcls. Internat. (life, Outstanding Achievement in Pub. Safety, 2001), Internat. Mcpl. Signal Assn. (sustaining, Journalistic Excellence award 1991). Republican. Methodist. Avocations: fishing, bowling, jogging, horseback riding. Home: 4507 Rangewood Dr Tallahassee FL 32309-8965 Office Phone: 850-224-4451. Personal E-mail: jynasser@comcast.net.

NASSERIPOUR, MOHAMMAD MICHEL, artist, architect; b. Teheran, Iran, Sept. 9, 1942; arrived in U.S., 1982; s. Moussa and Zari Nasseripour; m. Nooshazar Mary Sanei, Nov. 7, 1974; children: Melanie, Pearl. M in Art and Arch., Teheran U., 1971. Exhibitions include France, Paris, 1981, Art Gallery, NYC, 1988, Am. U., Washington, 1988, George Washington U., 1988, Beaux Art Mus., Teheran, 1996, Silk Road Festival, Smithsonian Instn., 2002, Opening Minds, Washington, 2003, NY Art Expo, 2006; author: The Life and Work of Behzad, 1999; co-author: Splendors of Iran: Lacquer Work Section, 2002, Guide to Iran: Persian Miniatures and Artists, 2003. Recipient Agha Khan award, Agha Khan Found., 2001, Silk Road Festival award, Smithsonian Inst., 2002, Opening Mind award, Iranian Am. Tech. Coun., 2003. Mem.: Internat. Coun. Mus., Am. Inst. for Conservation. Office Phone: 202-489-4050.

NASSETTA, CHRISTOPHER J., hotel facility executive; Various positions Oliver Carr Co., 1984-91, chief devel. officer; pres. Bailey Realty Corp., 1991-95; exec. v.p. Host Hotels and Resorts Inc., 1995—97, COO, 1997—2000, pres., CEO Bethesda, Md., 2000—. Dir. CoStar Group Inc.; trustee Prime Group Realty Trust. Adv. bd. McIntire Sch. Commerce, U. Va. Office: Host Hotels & Resorts Inc Ste 1500 6903 Rockledge Dr Bethesda MD 20817-1118

NASSIF, PAUL S., facial plastic and reconstructive surgeon; b. LA, Calif., June 6, 1962; m. Adrienne Nassif; 1 child, Galvin Paul. BS in Bus., U. So. Calif., LA, 1984; attended, U. Health Sciences Chgo. Med. Sch., 1988—89; MD, U. So. Calif. Sch. Medicine, 1992. Diplomate Am. Bd. Otolaryngology-Head and Neck Surgery, 1998, Am. Bd. Facial Plastic and Reconstructive Surgery, 2000, lic. Calif., Nevada. Intern, general surgery U. N.Mex. Health Sciences Ctr., 1992—93, resident, otolaryngology-head and neck surgery, 1993—96, chief resident, otolaryngology-head and neck surgery, 1996—97; fellowship, facial plastic and reconstructive surgery Am. Acad. Facial & Plastic & Reconstructive Surgery, J. Regan Thomas, MD, Preceptor St. Louis U. Sch. Medicine, Dept. Otolaryngology-Head and Neck Surgery, Mo., 1997—98; instructor,, Dept. Otolaryngology-Head and Neck Surgery St. Louis U. Sch. Medicine, 1997; attending, Divsn. Facial Plastic & Reconstructive Surgery, Dept. Otolaryngology-Head and Neck Surgery VA Med. Ctr., West LA, Calif., 1998; clin. asst. prof., Divsn. Facial Plastic & Reconstructive Surgery, Dept. Otolaryngology-Head and Neck Surgery U. So. Calif. Sch. Medicine, LA, 1998, UCLA Sch. Medicine, 1998; rhinoplasty specialist, co-owner Spaulding Drive Cosmetic Surgery & Dermatology, Beverly Hills, Calif., 1999—. Presenter in field; hospital affiliations include Cedars-Sinai Med. Ctr., LA County, U. So. Calif. Med. Ctr., West LA VA, UCLA Med. Ctr. Contbr. articles to peer-reviewed jours.; featured on Dr. 90210, mem. editl. adv. bd. Plastic Surgery Products Mag., 2002—05, guest appearances NBC Nightly News, Inside Edition, CBS Healthbeat, Entertainment Tonight, EXTRA, Good Morning America, Tom Brokaw, Peter Jennings and other members of the media, interviewed by People Mag., USA Today, LA Times, Wall Street Journal and AP, Anti-Gravity Facelift featured on Good Morning America and Entertainment Tonight. Participates Face to Face, Lymphoma Rsch. Found. Am., Race to Erase MS, Coach for Kids, Arthritis Found., Portraits of Hope; mem., Salerni Collegium U. So. Calif. Sch. Medicine. Fellow: ACS, Am. Acad. Facial Plastic & Reconstructive Surgery (mem. Face-to-Face (anti-domestic violence) com. 2000—, mem. new technologies and devices com., chmn. young physicians com. 2002—05, mem. strategic develop. com., mem. ethics com.), Am. Acad. Otolaryngology-Head and Neck Surgery; mem.: Calif. Soc. Facial Plastic Surgery (membership chmn. 1999—2004), LA Soc. Otolaryngologists, AMA, Calif. Soc. Facial Plastic Surgery, Alpha Omega Alpha (sec. 1991—92). Achievements include development of the Anti-Gravity Facelift, leaves no visible scars and achieves natural-looking results with a short recovery time. Avocations: golf, tennis, water-skiing, boating, snow skiing, scuba diving, fishing. Office: Spalding Drive Cosmetic Surgery & Dermatology 120 S Spalding Dr Ste 315 Beverly Hills CA 90212 Office Phone: 310-275-2467. Office Fax: 310-275-6651. *

NASSTROM, ROY RICHARD, educational consultant; b. Oakland, Calif., Oct. 28, 1930; s. Roy Richard and Edith Dolores (Spilman) N.; m. Sally Louise Shaw, Aug. 29, 1964; children: Karen, Eric. AA, U. Calif., Berkeley, 1955, BA, 1956, MA, 1964, PhD, 1971. Asst. to supt. Ravenswood Sch. Dist., East Palo Alto, Calif., 1964-65; acting instr. edn. U. Calif., Berkeley, 1965-68; asst. prof. ednl. adminstrn. U. Ky., Lexington, 1969-70; asst. prof. edn. Purdue U., West Lafayette, Ind., 1971-76; mediator, fact finder Ind. Edn. Employment Rels. Bd., 1974-76; asst. grad. dean Winona (Minn.) State U., 1976-77, chmn. ednl. adminstrn. dept., 1976-88, prof., 1976-01, prof. emeritus, 2001—, chmn. ednl. leadership dept., 1998-01; ednl. polit. cons. R. Nasstrom, 2002—. Cons., spkr. various orgns. and schs., 1969—; mem. bd. abstractors Ednl. Adminstrn. Abstracts, 1976-83; dir. post-masters studies, Winona State U., 1992-99. Editor Ravenswood Report, 1964-65, U. Calif.-Berkeley Sch. Edn. Newsletter, 1965-68; bd of editors AASA Prof., 1979-82; manuscript reviewer various jours. and pubs, 1983-87; contbr. articles and revs. to profl. jours., chpts. to books. List mgr. Winona On-line Democracy, 2005—, mem. steering com., 2003—. With US Army, 1952—54. Recipient numerous grants, 1969-98. Mem.Am. Ednl. Rsch. Assn. (paper reviewer 1983-2000), Calif. Alumni Assn., Am. Assn. Colls. for Tchr. Edn. (instnl. rep., paper reviewer), Nat. Assn. Scholars, Learning Club, Pi Sigma Alpha Avocation: photography. Home: 1702 Edgewood Rd Winona MN 55987-2149 Personal E-mail: nasstrom@cal.berkeley.edu. Business E-Mail: rnasstro@hbci.com.

NAST, DIANNE MARTHA, lawyer; b. Mount Holly, NJ, Jan. 30, 1948; d. Henry Daniel and Anastasia (Lovenduski) N.; m. Joseph Francis Roda, Aug. 23, 1980; children: Michael, Daniel, Joseph, Joshua, Anastasia. BA, Pa. State U.; JD, Rutgers U., 1976. Bar: Pa. 1976, U.S. Dist. Ct. Pa. 1976, N.J. 1976, U.S. Dist. Ct. N.J. 1976, U.S. Ct. Appeals (3d, 5th, 6th, 7th, 8th and 11th cirs.) 1976, U.S. Supreme Ct. 1982, U.S. Dist. Ct. Ariz. 1985. Dir., v.p. Kohn, Nast & Graf, P.C., Phila., 1976-95, Roda & Nast, P.C., Lancaster, Pa., 1995—. Mem. lawyers adv. com. U.S. Ct. Appeals (3d cir.), 1982-84, chmn., 1983-84, mem. com. on revision jud. conf. conduct rules, 1982-84; mem. Third Cir. Task Force on Selection of Class Clunsel, 2001-02mem. U.S. Ct. Appeals for the 3d Cir. Jud. Conf. Permanent Planning Com., 1983-90; bd. dirs. 3d Cir. Hist. Soc., Phila. Pub. Def., 1980-89, Fed. Jud. Ctr. Found., 1992-2002, chmn. 1997-2002; chmn. lawyers adv. com. U.S. Dist. Ct. (ea. dist.) Pa., 1982-90. Pres. Hist. Soc., 1988-91. Fellow ABA (coun. litigation sect. 1986-89, co-chmn. anti-trust com. litigation sect. 1984-86, div. dir. 1990-91, practical litigation editl. bd. 1989—, ho. of dels. 1992-94, mem. task force state justice initiatives, mem. task force state of justice system, 1993, mem. task force long range planning com. 1994), Am. Law Inst. (chair internat. professionalism com. 1991-94, civil justice task force 1993-95), Am. Arbitration Assn. (bd. dirs., mem. alt. dispute resolution and mass torts task force), Am. Judicature Soc., Pa. Bar Assn. (bd. of dels. 1983-95), N.J. Bar Assn., Pa. Trial Lawyers Assn., Phila. Bar Assn. (bd. govs. 1985-87, chmn., bicentennial com. 1986-87, chmn. bench bar conf. 1988-89), Lancaster Bar Assn. (co-chair civil litigation and rules com. trial law sect.), Rutgers Law Sch. Alumni Assn. Home: 1059 Sylvan Rd Lancaster PA 17601-1923 Office: Roda & Nast PC 801 Estelle Dr Lancaster PA 17601-2130 Home Phone: 717-397-3059; Office Phone: 717-892-3000. Business E-Mail: dnast@rodanast.com.

NAST, EDWARD PAUL, cardiothoracic surgeon, vascular surgeon; b. Balt., Dec. 13, 1958; s. Richard Cecil and Lenora (Heilig) N.; m. Lauren Jean Nast; children: Bennett Ross, Jaclyn Rose, Jacob Martin. BS, Emory U., 1979; MD, U. Md., 1984. Diplomate Am. Bd. Thoracic Surgery, Am. Bd. Surgery. Intern Georgetown U. Med. Ctr., Washington, 1984-85, resident in gen. surgery, 1985-86, 88-91; fellow in cardiac surgery NIH, Bethesda, Md., 1986-88; resident in thoracic and cardiovascular surgery U. Md. Med. Sys., Balt., 1991-93; attending cardiothoracic surgeon St. Joseph's Hosp. Health Ctr., Syracuse, NY, 1993—2002; cardiothoracic surgeon Arnot Ogden Med. Ctr., Elmira, NY, 2001—, chief, med. dir. cardiothoracic and vascular surgery, 2006—. Asst. attending cardiothoracic surgeon NY Presbyn. Hosp., Columbia U. Med. Ctr., NYC, 2002—; asst. clin. prof. cardiothoracic surgery Columbia U., NYC, 2002—. Contbr. articles to profl. jours. Named one of Outstanding Young Men of Am., 1996, 98. Fellow ACS, Am. Coll. Cardiology, Am. Coll. Chest Physicians; mem. Soc. Thoracic Surgeons, Phi Beta Kappa. Office: 600 Ivy St Ste 201 Elmira NY 14905 Home: 14 Prospect Ridge Horseheads NY 14845 Office Phone: 607-737-7780. Personal E-mail: enast@stny.rr.com. Business E-Mail: enast@aomc.org.

NASTA, DEEP, real estate agent and broker; b. Austin, Tex. Lic. Tex. Mortgage Broker. Realtor, Austin, Tex., 1994—; founder Deep in the Heart of Texas Realty & Mortgage, Inc., Austin. Active in Young Men's Bus. League, Austin, Ballet Austin Barre, Austin Symphony BATS, Leadership Austin. Recipient Austin Under 40 award for Real Estate, 2006. Office: Deep in the Heart of Texas Inc Ste G100 3420 Executive Ctr Austin TX 78731 Office Phone: 512-345-7653.

NASTASI, ALDO A., judge; b. NYC, Sept. 18, 1932; s. Anthony and Santina N.; m. Marie A. Nastasi, Dec. 26, 1954; children: Aldo, Robert, Marc, Anthony, David. B in Social Sci., Fordham U., 1954, LLD, 1959. Bar: N.Y. 1960, U.S. Supreme Ct. 1974. City ct. judge, Yonkers, N.Y., 1975-79; judge Westchester County Ct., N.Y., 1980-83, N.Y. State Supreme Ct., 1984-97, 98—. Councilman City of Yonkers, 1972-75, selected coun. majority leader. 1st lt. USMC, 1954-56. Mem. N.Y. State Lawyers Trial Assn., Westchester County Bar Assn., Columbia Lawyers Assn. (bd. dirs. 1992-98), Forham Law Alumni Assn. (Gov. Malcolm Wilson Disting. Alumnu award 2004) Republican. Roman Catholic. Avocations: golf, reading. Office: 9th Jud Dist Ct NY Westchester County Ct House 111 MLK Jr Blvd White Plains NY 10601 Office Phone: 914-824-5427.

NATALE, BARBARA GUSTAFSON, retired librarian; b. Hartford, Conn., Jan. 12, 1938; d. Carl William and Gertrude Fallon Gustafson; m. John Charles Natale, Sept. 12, 1959; children: Linda Skehan, John A., Mary Ellen. BA, U. Conn., 1959; MLS, So. Conn. State U., 1977. Libr. media specialist Windsor (Conn.) Pub. Schs., 1976—82; pub. svcs. libr. Manchester (Conn.) C.C., 1982—90, dir. libr. svcs., 1990—98, ret., 1998. Vice chmn. campus master planning com. Manchester (Conn.) C.C., 1992—98; mem. coun. librs. Conn. C.C.s, Hartford, Conn., 1992—98, chmn. coun. librs., 1993—95; evaluator New Eng. Assn. Schs. and Colls., Bedford, Mass., 1994—95; bd. dirs. Sea Call Supporters, Inc., sec., 2003—. Vol. Snow Libr., Orleans, Mass., 2003—05; sec. Friends of N.W. Park, 1981—87, vice chair, 1988—89; Windsor mayor's rep. Riverfront Recapture, Hartford, 1992—96; dist. capt., campaign coord. Windsor (Conn.) Dem. Com., 1978—92. Recipient Ednl. Excellence and Disting. Svc. award, Conn. C.C., 1994, Leadership Women award, Women's Caucus, Manchester (Conn.) C.C., 1994. Fellow: LWV, Wellfleet Garden Club; mem.: Conn. Libr. Assn. (bd. coll. and univ. sect. 1984—86, mem. ref. and adult svcs. com. 1986—90, chmn. 1989—90). Democrat. Avocations: travel, reading, gardening, bicycling, photography. Home: PO Box 1467 11 Pleasant View Dr East Orleans MA 02643

NATALE, PATRICK J, professional society administrator; m. Sheila Natale; 2 children. BS in Civil Engring., Newark Coll.of Engring.; MS in Engring. Mgmt., NJ Inst. of Tech.; grad., exec. mgmt. program, Yale U. Lic. profl. engr., NJ; cert. Assn. Exec. (CAE). Various mgmt. positions PSE&G, NJ; v.p., northeast region Nat. Soc. Profl. Engr., exec. dir., 1999—2002; exec. dir., chief staff officer, sec. Am. Soc. Civil Engr., 2003—. Pres. Am. Soc. Civil Engr. Found., 2003—. Chmn. Reston, Va., 2002—. Pres. Am. Soc. Civil Engr. Found., 2003—. Chmn. Goodwill Ind. of NJ; bd. dir. C. of C., Am. Red Cross; asst. dist. commr. Boy Scouts of Am. Office: Exec Dir Am Soc Civil Engr 1801 Alexander Bell Dr Reston VA 20191-4400

NATALE, RONALD BRUNO, oncologist; b. Detroit, Mich., Nov. 18, 1948; MD, Wayne State U. Sch. Medicine, Detroit, 1974. Cert. Internal Medicine, Med. Oncology. Intern, medicine Wayne State U. Affiliate Hosp., 1974—75, resident, hematologic oncology, 1975—77; fellow, med. oncology Meml. Sloan-Kettering, NYC, 1977—80; rsch. fellowship Nat. Cancer Inst.-Navy Med. Oncology Branch, Bethesda, Md.; attending physician Cedars-Sinai Med. Ctr., LA, 1997—, dir., Nat. Lung Cancer Rsch. Program, sr. rsch. advisor, Solid Tumor Program for Aptium Oncology. Various faculty positions Keck Sch. Medicine, U. So. Calif., U. Mich. Contbr. articles to profl. jours. Named one of Best Cancer Doctors, LA Mag., Top Cancer for Women, Good Housekeeping, Top Lung Cancer Specialists, America's Top Doctors for Cancer. Office: Cedars-Sinai Comp Cancer Ctr 8700 Beverly Blvd Los Angeles CA 90048 *

NATALICIO, DIANA SIEDHOFF, academic administrator; b. St. Louis, Aug. 25, 1939; d. William and Eleanor J. (Biermann) Siedhoff. BS in Spanish summa cum laude, St. Louis U., 1961; MA in Portuguese lang., U. Tex., 1964, PhD in Linguistics, 1969. Chmn. dept. modern langs. U. Tex., El Paso, 1973-77, assoc. dean liberal arts, 1977-79, acting dean liberal arts, 1979-80, dean Coll. Liberal Arts, 1980-84, v.p. acad. affairs, 1984-88, pres., 1988—. Bd. dirs. El Paso br. Fed. Res. Bd. Dallas, chmn., 1989; mem. Presdl. Adv. Commn. on Ednl. Excellence for Hispanic Ams., 1991; bd. dirs. Sandia Corp., Trinity Industries; bd. dirs. Nat. Action Coun. for Minorities in Engring., 1993—; mem. Nat. Sci. Bd. 1994-2000; mem. NASA Adv. Coun., 1994-96; bd. mem. Fund for Improvement of Post-Secondary Edn., 1993-97; bd. dirs. Fogarty Internat. Ctr. of NIH, 1993-96; bd. chair Am. Assn. Higher Edn., 1995-96; bd. dirs. U.S.-Mexico Commn. for Ednl. and Cultural Exch., 1994—. Co-author: Sounds of Children, 1977; contbr. articles to profl. jours. Bd. dirs. United Way El Paso, 1990-93, chmn. needs survey com., 1990-91, chmn. edn. divsn., 1989; chmn. Quality Edn. for Minorities Network in Math. Sci. and Engring., 1991-92; chairperson Leadership El Paso, Class 12, 1989-90, mem. adv. coun., 1987-90, participant, 1980-81; mem. Historically Black Colls. and Univs./Minority Instns. Consortium on Environ. Tech. chairperson, 1991-93; trustee Rockefeller Found. Recipient Harold W. McGraw. Jr. prize in edn., 1997, Torch of Liberty award Anti-Defamation League B'nai B'rith, 1991, Conquistador award City of El Paso, 1990, Humanitarian award El Paso chpt. NCCJ, 1990; named to El Paso Women's Hall of Fame, 1990, Tex. Women's Hall of Fame, 1998. Mem. Philos. Soc. Tex. Avocations: hiking, bicycling, skiing, skating. Office: U Tex at El Paso Office of the Pres 500 W University Ave El Paso TX 79968-0001

NATARAJAN, ARUNA, physician, educator, researcher; b. Madras, Tamilnadu, India, Nov. 5, 1960; came to U.S., 1994; d. R. and Bama N.; m. Rajiv N. Sheth, July 12, 1998. BS, MB, Armed Forces Med. Coll., Poona, Maharashtra, India, 1984. Diplomate Am. Bd. Pediatrics Critical Care. Chief resident, instr. Dartmouth Med. Sch., Hanover, NH, 1995-96; fellow pediat. intensive care U. Tex. Southwestern Med. Ctr., Dallas, 1996-99; asst. prof. pediat. Georgetown U. Med. Ctr., Washington, 1999—. Co-author: Clinics in Primary Care, 1995, Journal of Molecular & Cellular Cardiology, 2001, Portman's Text Book Pediatric Hypertension, 2004, Pediatric Research, 2004; contbr. articles to prof. jours. Mem. Soc. Critical Care Medicine. Avocations: reading, writing, listening to indian classical music. Office: Georgetown U Med Ctr CCC Bldg Rm 5414 3800 Reservoir Rd Washington DC 20007 Home Phone: 202-444-2757. Business E-Mail: an5@gunet.georgetown.edu.

NATARAJAN, GITHA, elementary school educator; b. Toronto; m. Arun Natarajan. Tchr. Prince George's County, 1998—99, John Eaton Elem. Sch., Washington, 1999—. Named DC Tchr. of Yr., 2007. Office: John Eaton Elem Sch 3301 Lowell St NW Washington DC 20008 E-mail: githadn@aol.com. *

NATARUS, BURTON F., land use consultant, lawyer; b. Wausau, Wis., Nov. 7, 1933; BS in Polit. Sci., U. Wis., 1956, JD, 1960; postgrad., John F. Kennedy Sch. Govt., 1993. Chair qualified arbitrator: Cir. Ct. Cook County, Ill. Pvt. practice law, Chgo.; alderman 42d Ward, Chgo., 1971—2007, elected democratic committeeman, 2004; chmn. Chgo. City Coun. Com. Traffic Control and Safety, 1997—2007; mem. Chgo. Plan Com. State St. Com., 1997—. Mem. Mayor's Zoning Reform Commn.; mem. Ctrl. Area Planning Task Force, Ill. Regional Transp. Task Force, State Street Coun. Mem. Chgo. Trade Del. to China. Capt. USAR, ret. Fellow Acad. Polit. Sci.; mem. Internat. Soc. Poets, City Club, Greater North Michigan Ave. Assn., Streeterville C. of C., River North Assn., North Dearborn Assn., Gold Coast Neighbors Dr. Assn., Streeterville Orgn. Active Residents. Address: 30 N La Salle St Ste 2900 Chicago IL 60602-2584

NATCHER, STEPHEN DARLINGTON, retired lawyer, electronics executive; b. San Francisco, Nov. 19, 1940; m. Carolyn Anne Bowman, Aug. 23, 1969; children: Tanya Michelle, Stephanie Elizabeth. AB in Polit. Sci., Stanford U., 1962; JD, U. Calif., San Francisco, 1965. Bar: Calif. 1966. Assoc. firm Pillsbury, Madison & Sutro, San Francisco, 1966-68; counsel Douglas Aircraft div. McDonnell Douglas Corp., Long Beach, Calif., 1968-70; v.p., sec. Security Pacific Nat. Bank, 1971-79; asst. gen. counsel Security Pacific Corp., 1979-80; v.p., sec., gen. counsel Lear Siegler, Inc., Santa Monica, Calif., 1980-87; v.p., gen. counsel Computer Sci. Corp., El Segundo, Calif., 1987-88; exec. v.p., gen. counsel, sec. CalFed Inc., 1989-90; sr. v.p. adminstrn., gen. counsel, sec. Wyle Electronics, Irvine, Calif., 1991-98; gen. counsel VEBA Electronics LLC, Santa Clara, Calif., 1998—2002, ret., 2002. With USCG, 1965-71. Mem.: St. Francis Yacht Club (San Francisco). Republican. E-mail: snatcher@starstream.net.

NATH, JOGINDER, genetics and biology educator, researcher; b. Joginder Nagar, Panjab, India, May 12, 1932; arrived in U.S., 1957; s. Moti Ram and Vira Wali (Khorana) N.; m. Charlotte Lynn Reese, Apr. 5, 1969; children— Pravene, Brian BS with honors, Panjab U, Amritsar, India, 1953, MS with honors, 1955; PhD, U. Wis., 1960. Research assoc. Am. Inst. Biol. Research, Madison, Wis., 1960-63; asst. prof. So. Ill. U., Carbondale, Ill., 1964-66; from asst. to assoc. prof. W.Va. U., Morgantown, 1966-72, prof., chmn. dept. genetics and devel. biology, 1972—. Contbr. articles on cytogenetics, mutagenesis, biochem genetics and cryobiology to profl. jours. Chmn. bd. Morgantown Day Sch., 1977—79. Recipient Alexander Hollaender award, Environ. Mutagen Soc., 1997, Edn. and Student Mems. Com. award, 2000, Mehra Meml. award, Panjab U., 2000; grantee, NSF, 1967—68, DOE, 1992—95, Nat. Inst. Occupl. Safety and Health, 1985—95, NIH, 2002—. Mem. Soc. Cryobiology, Environ. Mutagen Soc., Sigma Xi. Office: WVa U Coll Agr Dept Genetics & Devel Biology Morgantown WV 26506 Office Phone: 304-293-6256.

NATHAN, ANDREW JAMES, political science educator; b. NYC, Apr. 3, 1943; s. Paul S. and Dorothy (Goldeen) N.; children: Chloe Armann Nathan, Oliver Paul Bauer-Nathan, Isabel Rae Bauer-Nathan; 1 stepchild Alexandra Witke. BA summa cum laude, Harvard U., 1963, MA in East Asian Regional Studies, 1965, PhD in Polit. Sci., 1971. Lectr. U. Mich., Ann Arbor, 1971; research assoc. Ctr. for Chinese Studies, 1970; asst. prof. polit. sci. Columbia U., NYC, 1971-75, assoc. prof., 1975-82, prof., 1982—2001; dir. East Asian Inst. Columbia U., NYC, 1991-95, prof. political sci., 2001—; prof. polit. sci. Class of 1919, 2001—. Mem. steering com. China Internat. Bus. Project, 1978—; mem. nat. com. on U.S.-China rels., 1987—; chair adv. com. Human Rights Watch/Asia, 1995-2000; cons. Ambrica Prodns., Nat. Endowment for Democracy, others; lectr. in field. Author: A History of the China International Famine Relief Commission, 1965, Modern China, 1840-1972, An Introduction to Sources and Research Aids, 1973, Peking Politics, 1918-1923: Factionalism and the Failure of Constitutionalism, 1976, Chinese Democracy, 1985 (Levenson prize 1987), (with others) Human Rights in Contemporary China, 1986, China's Crisis, 1990; co-editor Popular Culture in Late Imperial China (with Robert S. Ross), 1985, The Great Wall & the Empty Fortress: China's Search for Security, 1997, China's Transition, 1997; co-editor: The Tiananmen Papers, 2001; contbr. book revs. to publs.; manuscript reviewer U. Calif. Press., Columbia U. Press, Harvard U. Press, others; coord. The Tienanment Papers, 2001; contbr. numerous articles to profl. jours. and current popular publs. Guggenheim fellow, 1973-74; fellow Am. Coun. Learned Soc.-Social Sci. Rsch. Coun., 1977-78, NEH fellow 1986-87, 1992-93; grantee Luce Found., 1979-82, 91-93, 92-95, Chiang Ching-Kuo Found., 1992, 1995-96, 1995-97, NSF, 1993-96 and others. Mem. Am. Polit. Sci. Assn., Assn. for Asian Studies, Coun. Fgn. Rels. Office: Polic Sci Dept Columbia U 420 W 118th St New York NY 10027-7213 E-mail: ajn1@columbia.edu.

NATHAN, ARTHUR M., lawyer; b. Houston, July 20, 1951; s. Herman Nathan and Doris (Samuelson) Abramson; m. Arlene Kissner, May 29, 1988; children: Robert Michael Kissner, Jeffrey David Kissner, M. Douglas Kissner. BA magna cum laude, U. Tex., 1972, JD cum laude, 1975. Bar: Tex. 1975, admitted to practice: US Tax Ct. 1976, US Claims Ct. 1976, US Dist. Ct. (So. Dist.) Tex. 1976, US Ct. Appeals (5th Cir.). Assoc. Foreman, Dyess, Prewett, Rosenberg & Henderson, Houston, 1975-80; ptnr. Foreman & Dyess, Houston, 1980-81, Porter & Clements, Houston, 1981-90; ptnr., bus. and tax planning, mergers and acquisitions Haynes and Boone, LLP,

Houston, 1990—, bd. dir. Author (seminar books): Advanced Tax Law Course, 1991, Building Blocks of A Business Law Practice, 1992; co-author (seminar book): Corporate, Partnership and Business Law, 1994, 95. Mem. Tax Law Exam Commn., 1999—2005. Fellow: Tex. Bar Found. (bd. dir.); mem.: ABA (corp. taxation com., taxation sect. 1987—, negotiated acquisitions com., bus. law sect. 1995—), State Bar Tex. (chmn. corp. tax problems com., tax sect. 1981—83, chmn. bus. tax. com. 1983—85, mem. coun. tax sect. 1985—87, venture capital com., bus. law sect. 1991—), Phi Eta Sigma, Phi Kappa Phi, Phi Beta Kappa, Order of Coif. Jewish. Office: Haynes and Boone LLP 1 Houston Ctr 1221 Mc Kinney Ste 2100 Houston TX 77010 Office Phone: 713-547-2009. Office Fax: 713-236-5551. Business E-Mail: arthur.nathan@haynesboone.com.

NATHAN, CHERIE-ANN OLYMPIA, surgeon, educator; b. Bombay, India, Dec. 17, 1963; d. Jeffrey Victor and Gema Maria Menezes; m. Raghu Parthasarathy Nathan, Dec. 29, 1991; children: Sean, Neil. MD, Bombay U., 1986. Diplomate Am. Bd. Otolaryngologist; lic. La. State Bd. Med. Examiners; bd. cert. otolaryngology/head and neck surgery. Intern U. Bombay, 1986—87, resident in otolaryngology, 1987—88; postdoctoral rsch. fellow Johns Hopkins U., 1988—89; intern in gen. surgery Butterworth Hosp. Mich. State U., 1989—90; resident in otolaryngology U. Calif., San Diego, 1990—94, clin. instr. head and neck fellow, 1994—95; chief of ENT VA Med. Ctr. La. State U. Health Sci. Ctr., Shreveport, 1995—97, asst. prof., dir. head and neck cancer surgery, 1997—99, assoc. prof. otolaryngology, dir. head and neck oncologic surgery, 1999—2003; prof., vice chmn. La. State U. Health Sci. Ctr., Dept. Otolar. Head and Neck Surgery, Shreveport, 2004—; dir. head and neck surgery Feist-Weller Cancer Ctr. Contbr. chpts. to books, numerous articles to profl. jours. Bd. dirs. Sci. Port Discovery Ctr., 2006—08, South highland Found.; chmn. media com. Shreveport Med. Soc. Recipient Travel awards, 1991, 93; NIH grantee, 1999, NIH R01 award, 2005-. Fellow Am. Coll. Surgeons; mem. AMA, AAAS, ACS, Am. Rhinol. Soc., Am. Assn. Cancer Rsch., Soc. U. Otolaryngologists Head and Neck Surgeons, S.W. Oncology Group, So. Med. Soc., Am. Acad. Otolaryngology Head and Neck Surgery, North Am. Skull Base Soc.(bd. dirs.), Shreveport Med. Soc. Roman Catholic. Avocations: piano, dance, hiking, ping pong/table tennis. Office: La State U Health Sci Ctr Dept Otolaryngol Head Neck 1501 Kings Hwy Shreveport LA 71103-4228 Home Phone: 318-861-1758; Office Phone: 318-675-6262. Personal E-mail: aray@lsuhsc.edu. Business E-Mail: cnatha@lsuhsc.edu.

NATHAN, DAVID GORDON, pediatrician, educator; b. Boston, May 25, 1929; s. E. Geoffrey and Ruth (Gordon) Nathan; m. Jean Louise Friedman, Sept. 1, 1951; children: Deborah, Linda, Geoffrey. BA, Harvard U., 1951; MD, Harvard Med. Sch., 1955. Diplomate Am. Bd. Internal Medicine, Am. Bd. Pediat. Intern dept. medicine Peter Bent Brigham Hosp., Boston, 1955—56, sr. resident, 1958—59; jr. assoc. in medicine Brigham and Women's Hosp., Boston, 1961—67, sr. assoc. in medicine, 1967—; assoc. in medicine, hematology Childrens Hosp., Boston, 1963—68, chief, divsn. hematology, 1968—73, chief divsn. hematology and oncology, 1974—84; pediatrician-in-chief Dana Farber Cancer Inst., Boston, 1974—85; Robert A. Stranahan prof. pediat. Harvard Med. Sch., Boston, 1977—95; physician-in-chief Childrens Hosp., Boston, 1985—95; pres. Dana-Farber Cancer Inst., Boston, 1995—2000; Richard and Susan Smith prof. medicine Harvard Med. Sch., Boston, 1996—2000, prof. pediat., 1996—2000, Robert A. Stranahan Disting. prof. pediat., 2001—. Chair NIH Panel on Clin. Rsch., 1995—98; pres. emeritus Dana Farber Cancer Inst., 2001—. Author: Genes, Blood and Courage, 1994; editor: Hematology in Infancy and Childhood, 1993, 1997. With USMC, 1948—49. Recipient Nat. medal Sci., NSF, 1990. Fellow: AAAS; mem.: Am. Philos. Soc., Am. Soc. Hematology (pres. 1986), Am. Soc. Clin. Investigators, Assn. Am. Physicians, Soc. Pediatric Rsch., Am. Pediatric Soc., Am. Acad. Arts and Scis., Inst. Medicine NAS, Phi Beta Kappa (hon.). Avocations: tennis, hiking, sailing. Office: Dana-Farber Cancer Inst 44 Binney St Boston MA 02115-6084 E-mail: david_nathan@dfci.harvard.edu.

NATHAN, FREDERIC SOLIS, lawyer; b. NYC, June 24, 1922; s. Edgar Joshua and Mabel (Unterberg) N.; m. Frances E., Oct. 28, 1956; children: Jean E., Frederic S. Jr., William E. BA, Williams Coll., Williamstown, Mass., 1943; LLD, Yale U., 1948. Bar: N.Y. 1948, U.S. Dist. Ct. (so. and ea. dists) N.Y. 1948, U.S. Ct. Appeals (2d cir.) 1953, U.S. Supreme Ct. 1968. Instr. Williams Coll., Williamstown, 1948; assoc. Rathbone Perry Kelley & Drye, NYC, 1948-53; asst. U.S. atty. U.S. Attys.' Office (so. dist.) N.Y., NYC, 1953-56; assoc. Greenbaum, Wolff & Ernst, NYC, 1956-58, ptnr., 1959-65, 70-82; 1st asst. corp. counsel N.Y.C. Law Dept., NYC, 1966-69; ptnr. Kelley, Drye & Warren, NYC, 1982—. Mem. N.Y. Rep. County Com., N.Y.C., 1948-65; trustee Mt. Sinai Hosp., N.Y.C., 1970—; chmn. bd. FOJP Svc. Corp., N.Y.C., 1977-85, bd. dirs., 1979—; bd. dirs., v.p. Am. Jewish Soc. for Svc., N.Y.C., 1950—; bd. dirs. Everybody Wins Found., Inc., 1992—. With U.S. Army, 1943-45, ETO. Fellow Am. Coll. Trial Lawyers; mem. ABA, Assn. of Bar of City of N.Y. (exec. com. 1979-81), Fed. Bar Council (pres. 1975-76), Clubs: Century Assn., Yale of N.Y.C.; Sunningdale Country. Republican. Jewish. Home: 180 East End Ave New York NY 10128-7763 Office: Kelley Drye & Warren 101 Park Ave New York NY 10178-0062 Office Phone: 212-808-7840. Business E-Mail: fnathan@kelleydrye.com.

NATHAN, GERALD DALE, retired psychologist, researcher, writer; b. Norfolk, Nebr., Oct. 1, 1938; s. Raymond John and Esther Marie (Neuwerk) N.; m. Jo Anne Williams, Aug. 19, 1993; 1 child, Jerald John; stepchildren: Rodney Wade, Erica Wren. Student, Wayne State Coll., Nebr., 1956—57, Yale U., 1959—60; BA, U. Nebr., 1966, MA, 1968, PhD (NDEA fellow), 1970. Diplomate Am. Bd. Sexology; lic. marriage counselor, Calif., lic. marital therapist, Oreg.; cert. sex educator, sex therapist; lic. psychologist, Oreg. Cons. psychologist Calavaras County Edn. Dept., San Andreas, Calif., 1970—72; pvt. practice sex and marital therapy, lifestyle stress mgmt. Salem, Oreg., 1972—2000; ret., 2000. Cons. psychologist Cmty. Counseling Center, Salem, 1972-73, William Temple House, Portland, Oreg., 1974-77; sex educator Oreg. Dept. Continuing Edn., Salem, 1972-74; vis. prof. Willamette U., Salem, 1981; bd. dirs. Morrison Charter H.S., Dallas, Oreg.; adj. instr. Chemeketa C.C., Salem, 2001-04 Active Salem Cmty. Chorus, 1978-84, pres., 1980-81; active Festival Chorale Oreg., 1986, 96, 2001-05; adv. bd. Friends Oreg. Area, 1997-98. With USAF, 1959-63 Fellow Am. Bd. Sexology; mem. APA, Am. Assn. Marriage and Family Therapy, Am. Assn. Sex Educators, Counselors and Therapists, Oreg. Assn. Marriage and Family Therapists (dir. 1976-77), Soc. Sci. Study Sex, Salem Psychol. Soc. (co-chmn. 1981-82), Nature Conservancy, Union Concerned Scientists, Am. Farmland Trust, Am. Minor Breeds Conservancy, World Wildlife Fund Office: 18075 Oakdale Rd Dallas OR 97338-9108 Personal E-mail: j_nathan1977@hotmail.com.

NATHAN, JERRY E., lawyer; b. Bluefield, W.Va., Aug. 15, 1948; BS summa cum laude, Ohio State U., 1970; JD, Yale U., 1973. Bar: Ohio 1973. Asst. sec. Rickenbacker Port Authority, 1980—90; ptnr. Bricker & Eckler, Columbus, Ohio, 1973—. Adj. asst. prof. Ohio State U. Coll. Edn., 1999. Recipient Hon. Nat. Merit Scholar, 1970, State Farm Found. Scholar, 1973. Mem. ABA, Ohio State Bar Assn., Ohio Coun. Sch. Bd. Attys. (exec. com. 1986—, chmn. 1992), Columbus Bar Assn., Beta Gamma Sigma, Phi Eta Sigma, Pacesetters honoraries, Nat. Sch. Bds. Assn. Coun. Sch. Attys., Sphinx hon. (treas.). Address: Bricker & Eckler 100 S 3rd St Columbus OH 43215-4236 Office Phone: 614-227-2358. Office Fax: 614-227-2390. Business E-Mail: jnathan@bricker.com.

NATHAN, PAUL S., retired editor, writer; b. Oakland, Calif., Apr. 2, 1913; s. Alfred Jacobs and Frances (Strause) N.; m. Dorothy Goldeen, July 14, 1935 (dec. Dec. 1966); children: Andrew J., Carl F., Janet D. Souza; m. Ruth Wilk Notkins, May 26, 1972 (dec. 2005). BA, U. Calif., Berkeley, 1934. Reporter Oakland Post-Enquirer, 1929-36; asst. play editor Paramount Pictures, NYC, 1937-48; Hosp. pub. rels. Will, Folsom & Smith, NYC, 1948-61; sci. editor Nat. Cystic Fibrosis Rsch. Found., NYC and Atlanta, 1963—73; columnist Rights and Permissions (subsequently Rights) Pubs. Weekly, NYC, 1946-98. US liaison Jerusalem Internat. Book Fair, 1976-77 Author: (play) Ricochet, 1980 (Edgar Allan Poe award of Mystery Writers Am. for best play of 1980), Texas Collects: Fine Arts, Furniture, Windmills & Whimseys, 1988; co-editor: (anthology) View: Parade of the Avant-Garde, 1991; author: (novels) Protocol for Murder, 1994, No Good Deed, 1995, Count Your Enemies, 1997; columnist Pub. News, London, 1998-2003; contbr. fiction and articles to Story, NY Times mag., Saturday Evening Post, Saturday Rev., others. Mem.: PEN, Mystery Writers Am., Authors League, Authors Guild, Dramatists Guild, Phi Beta Kappa. Home and Office: 141 E 33rd St New York NY 10016-4606 Personal E-mail: paulnathanny@aol.com.

NATHAN, PETER E., psychologist, educator; b. St. Louis, Apr. 18, 1935; s. Emil and Kathryn (Kline) N.; m. Florence I. Baker, Nov. 26, 1959; children: David Edward, Anne Miller, Laura Carol, Mark Andrew. AB, Harvard U., 1957; PhD, Washington U., 1962. Research fellow psychology Harvard U., 1962-64, research asso., 1964-68, asst. prof. psychology, 1968-69; research psychologist Boston City Hosp., 1964-68, dir. alcohol study unit, 1967-70; prof. Rutgers U., New Brunswick, NJ, 1969-89, dir. clin. psychology tng., 1969-87, dir. Alcohol Behavior Research Lab., 1970-87, chmn. dept. clin. psychology, 1976-87, dir. Ctr. Alcohol Studies, 1983-89, Henry and Anna Starr prof. psychology, 1983-89; sr. program officer, health program MacArthur Found., 1987-89; v.p. acad. affairs, found. disting. prof. psychology U. Iowa, 1990—, dean faculties, 1990-93, provost, 1993-95, acting pres., 1995. Mem. advisory council VA, 1972-76; chmn. alcoholism com. Nat. Inst. on Alcohol Abuse and Alcoholism, 1973-76, co-chmn. spl. rev. com., 1985, mem. nat. adv. coun., 1990-94; mem. psychol. scis. fellowship rev. com. NIMH, 1977-79; chmn. N.J. State Community Mental Health Bd., 1981-84; mem. working group substance use disorders, DSM-IV. Author: Cues, Decisions, and Diagnoses, 1967, Psychopathology and Society, 1975, 2d edit., 1980, Experimental and Behavioral Approaches to Alcoholism, 1978, Alcoholism: New Directions in Behavioral Treatment and Research, 1978, Clinical Case Studies in the Behavioral Treatment of Alcoholism, 1982, Professionals in Distress, 1987, Neuropsychological Deficits in Alcoholism, 1987, Introduction to Psychology, 1987, 2d edit., 1990, Abnormal Psychology, 1992, 2d edit., 1996, A Guide to Treatments that Work, 1998, 2d edit., 2002; exec. editor: Jour. Studies Alcohol, 1983—90; assoc. editor Am. Psychologist, 1977—85, Contemporary Psychology, 1991—97, Prevention and Treatment, 1998—2001, Psychol. Bull., 2002—, mem. editl. bd. Jour. Clin. Psychology, 1969—95, Jour. Cons. Clin. Psychology, 1973—95, Profl. Psychology, 1976—89. Fellow Am. Psychol. Assn. (chmn. sect. 3 div. 12 1976-77, rep. to council 1976-79, 82-85, pres. div. 12 1984-85; Disting. Contbns. to Knowledge award 1999). Democrat. Jewish. Home: 248 Black Springs Cir Iowa City IA 52246-3800 Office: Univ Iowa E119 Seashore Hall Iowa City IA 52242-1316 Business E-Mail: peter-nathan@uiowa.edu.

NATHAN, RICHARD P(ERLE), political science professor; b. Schenectady, NY, Nov. 24, 1935; s. Sidney Robert and Betty (Green) N.; m. Mary McNamara, June 5, 1957; children: Robert Joseph, Carol Hewitt. AB, Brown U., 1957; M in Pub. Adminstrn., Harvard U., 1959, PhD, 1966. Legis. asst. U.S. Senator Kenneth B. Keating, Washington, 1959-62; dir. domestic policy rsch. Nelson A. Rockefeller, 1963-64; rsch. assoc. The Brookings Instn., Washington, 1966-69, sr. fellow, project dir. monitoring studies gen. revenue sharing, community devel. block grant and pub. svc. employment programs, 1972-79; associated staff The Brookings Inst., Washington, 1980-85; asst. dir. U.S. Office of Mgmt. and Budget, Washington, 1969-71; dep. undersec. U.S Dept. Health, Edn. and Welfare, Washington, 1971-72; prof. pub. and internat. affairs Woodrow Wilson Sch. Pub. and Internat. Affairs Princeton (N.J.) U., 1979-89, also dir. Princeton Urban and Regional Rsch. Ctr., 1979-89; Disting. prof. polit. sci. and pub. policy SUNY, Albany, 1989-97; provost Rockefeller Coll. Pub. Affairs and Policy, Albany, 1989-98. Dir. Rockefeller Inst., 1989-2004, co-dir., 2005—; assoc. dir. Nat. Adv. Commn. on Civil Disorders, 1967-68; vis. prof. govt. and fgn. affairs U. Va., 1972-77; chmn. Nixon Adminstrn. Transition Task Forces on Poverty and Intergovtl. Fiscal Rels., 1968, Domestic Coun. Com. on Welfare Reform Planning, 1969-70; mem. Commn. on Orgn. Govt. of D.C., 1970-72; bd. overseers New Sch. for Social Rsch., 1982-88; mem. working seminar on family and welfare Marquette U., 1986-87; selection com. Rockefeller Pub. Svc. Awards Program, 1976-78; income maintenance task force Nat. Urban Coalition, 1975-78; treas. Manpower Demonstration Rsch. Corp., 1974-81, chmn., 1981-98; mem. coun. scholars U.S. Libr. of Congress, 1989—; mem. N.Y. State Temp. Commn. Constl. Revision, 1993-94; mem. U.S. Adv. Commn. on Intergovtl. Rels., 1995-96; vis. fellow GAO, 1998-2000; cons. U.S. Gen. Acctg. Office, 1994-96. Author: Jobs and Civil Rights, The Role of the Federal Government in Promoting Equal Opportunity in Employment and Training, 1969, The Plot That Failed: Nixon and the Administrative Presidency, 1975, Monitoring Revenue Sharing, 1975, Revenue Sharing, The Second Round., 1977, Monitoring the Public Service Employment Program, 1978, America's Government: A Fact Book of Census Data on the Organization, Finances, and Employment of Federal, State, and Local Governments, 1979, Public Service Employment: A Field Evaluation, 1981, The Administrative Presidency, 1983, Reagan and the States, 1987, Social Science in Government Uses and Abuses, 1988, A New Agenda for Cities, 1992, Turning Promises into Performance: The Management Challenge of Implementing Workfare, 1993; co-author: (with Thomas L. Gais) Implementing the Personal Responsibility Act: A First Look, 1999, Social Science in Government, 2000; (with Gerald Benjamin) Regionalism and Realism, A Study of Governments in the New York Metropolitan Area, 2001; contbr. chpts. to books; editor: (with Harvey S. Perloff) Revenue Sharing and the City, 1968; (with John D. DiJulio, Jr.) The View From the States, Making Health Reform Work, Brookings Instn., 1994; mem. editl. bd. Urban Affairs Quar., 1978-85. Eisenhower fellow European Econ. Commn., 1977. Mem. ASPA (Intergovtl. Mgmt. award 1985), Nat. Acad. Social Inst., Nat. Acad. Pub. Adminstrn. (James E. Webb award 1986), Am. Pub. Human Svcs. Assn. (bd. dirs. 2000-02), Am. Polit. Sci. Assn. (Charles E. Merriam award 1987), Assn. for Pub. Policy Analysis and Mgmt.(pres.-elect 2000— pres. 2003-04), Ft. Orange Club, Phi Beta Kappa, Theta Delta Chi. Republican. Jewish. Avocations: reading, travel, movies. Office: SUNY Rockefeller Inst Office of Co-Dir 411 State St Albany NY 12203-1003 Office Phone: 518-443-5831. Business E-Mail: nathanr@rockinst.org.

NATHAN, STEVEN D., pulmonologist; s. Arthur H. and Carmen K. Nathan; m. Romy K. Gunter, Nov. 11, 1965; children: Jack, Max. MBBcH, U. Witwatersrand, Johannesburg, South Africa, 1981. Med. dir. lung transplant and advanced lung disease program Inova Fairfax Hosp., Falls Church, Va., 1996—. Mem. Wash. Regional Transplant Consortium, Washington. Recipient 75th Jubilee medal award Disting. Achievements, U. Witwatersrand, 1997. Fellow: Am. Coll. Chest Physicians (network interstitial lung disease 2003—07). Office: Inova Fairfax Hosp 3300 Gallows Rd Falls Church VA 22042 Home Phone: 703-776-3610; Office Phone: 703-776-3610. Personal E-mail: steven.nathan@inova.vom. E-mail: steven.nathan@inova.org.

NATHANSON, DAVID, communications executive; b. 1977; Grad., U. Pa. Corp. analyst Comcast Cable Comm.; mgr., Strategic Planning Cablevision Systems Corp.; dir., Mktg. News Corp.; dir., Broadband Strategy Fox Cable Networks Grp., 2000, v.p., Broadband Strategy and Channel Devel., 2001; gen. mgr. Fox Sports Digital Nets, 2001; sr. v.p., gen. mgr. TVG Network, 2005—. Mem. Cable & Telecom. Assn for Mktg. Cable Network ITV Coun.; chmn. CablePositive, LA. Named one of 100 Most Influential Executives in Cable TV, Cable Fax Mag., 2000—01, 40 Executives Under 40, Multichannel News, 2006. Office: TVG Network 19545 NW Von Neumann Dr Ste 210 Beaverton OR 97006

NATHANSON, HARVEY CHARLES, electrical engineer; b. Pitts., Oct. 22, 1936; s. David Benjamin and Ella (Sachs) N.; m. Esther Janet Mishelevich, Oct. 13, 1963; children: Marc Elliot, Elinor Sharon. BSEE, Carnegie Inst. Tech., 1958, MSEE, 1959, PhD, 1962. Sr. engr. Junction Device Physics, Westinghouse, Research/Devel. Center, Pitts., 1962-67, fellow engr., 1968-72, mgr. silicon junction physics, 1972-77, mgr. microelectronics dept., 1978-90, chief scientist electronic div., 1990-95; chief scientist Northrop Grumman Sci. Tech. Ctr., 1996—2001; cons. Northrop Grumman, 2002—. Instr. Carnegie Inst. Tech., Pitts., 1959-60; chmn. Westinghouse Sat. Sci. Honors Inst. for High Sch. Students, 1970-76; mem. adv. group on electron devices U.S. Dept. Def., 1976-86; adviser to Nat. Materials Bd., 1986-87. Contbr. articles to profl. jours.; mem. editorial bd. Solid State Electronics, 1985—; patentee in field. Bd. dirs. Temple Sinai, 1981-83, 95-97; pres. Brotherhood, 1993-95. Recipient IR100 award, 1965, hon. mention Outstanding Young Engr. award Eta Kappa Nu, 1967, Best Display Paper award Soc. Info. Display, 1972, Carnegie-Mellon Alumni award, 1982, Westinghouse Top Corp. Patent award, 1990; named to Westinghouse Order of Merit, Westinghouse Electric Corp., 1987, named Pitts. Inventor Yr., 2002. Fellow IEEE (editl. bd. Spectrum mag. 1989-91, 3e Millennium medal 2000); mem. IEEE Electron Device Soc. (pres. 1978-80), Fedn. Materials Socs. (bd. dirs. 1987-90), Sigma Xi, Eta Kappa Nu. Democrat. Jewish. Home: 5635 Marlborough Rd Pittsburgh PA 15217-1404 Office: Northrop Grumman Sci-Tech Ctr Advanced Tech Lab PO Box 1521-MS 3B10 Baltimore MD 21203 Business E-Mail: harvey.c.nathanson@ngc.com.

NATHANSON, LARRY, medical educator; b. Boston, Dec. 23, 1928; s. Robert Bernard and Leah (Rabin) N.; m. Anna Bloch, May 27, 1962; children: Andrew, Aran, Nicholas. AB, Harvard Coll., 1950; MD, U. Chgo., 1955. Diplomate Am. Bd. Internal Medicine, Am. Bd. Med. Oncology. Instr. medicine Harvard Med. Sch., Boston, 1966-68; from asst. to prof. Tufts U. Sch. Medicine, Boston, 1968-79; prof. medicine SUNY Stony Brook Sch. of Medicine, 1980-96, prof. emeritus, 1996—. Pres., CEO Oncology Cons., Cambridge, Mass., 1996—; cons. John Wayne Cancer Inst., Santa Monica, Calif., 1996—; councilor Cambridge Hist. Soc.; bd. dirs. Mass. Soc. for Med. Rsch. Editl. bd. Cancer, 1977—, Jour. Clin. Oncology, 1995-98, Seminars in Oncology, 1979-83, Med. & Pediat. Oncology, 1977-96, Jour. Cancer Edn., 1986-92; editor 6 books; contbr. 283 articles to profl. jours. Trustee Cold Spring Harbor Lab., 1990-94, Soc. Preservation L.I. Antiquities, Setauket, N.Y., 1982-92, Cambridge Sch. of Weston, 1997—, Mass. Soc. Med. Rsch., 2002—; active Herreshoff Marine Mus., Bristol, R.I., 2000—, Reliance Soc. Capt. U.S. Army Med. Corps., 1956-58. Recipient Disting Svc. award Cancer Rsch., Vet. Affairs Rev. Bd., 1974—78, Disting Svc. award, Winthrop U. Hosp., 1993, Disting Alumni award, Cambridge Sch. Weston, 2006; grantee, Nat. Cancer Inst., 1964—80. Fellow ACP; mem. Mass. Soc. Med. Rsch. (trustee 2002—), Harvard Club (Boston, N.Y.), Seawanhaka Corinthian Yacht Club (race com. 1990-96), Harvard Faculty Club, Sigma Xi. Avocations: sailing, squash, tennis, history. Office: Oncology Cons 3 Gray Gdns E Cambridge MA 02138-1401 Office Fax: 617-441-0043. Personal E-mail: larrymd1@comcast.net.

NATHANSON, LINDA SUE, publishing executive, writer; b. Washington, Aug. 11, 1946; d. Nat and Edith (Weinstein) N.; m. James F. Barrett. BS, U. Md., 1969; MA, UCLA, 1970, PhD, 1975. Tng. dir. Rockland Rsch. Inst., Orangeburg, NY, 1975—77; asst. prof. psychology SUNY, 1978—79; pres. Cabri Prodns., Inc., Ft. Lee, NJ, 1979—81; rsch. supr. Darcy, McManus & Masius, St. Louis, 1981—83; mgr. software tng., documentation On-Line Software Internat., Ft. Lee, 1983—85; pvt. practice Ft. Lee, 1985—87; founder, exec. dir. Edin. Group, Inc., Gillette, NJ, 1987—98; founder, pres. Edin Books, Inc., Gillette, 1994—. Sr. tech. trainer Schering-Plough, 2002—. Author: (with others) Psychological Testing: An Introduction to Tests and Measurements, 1988; (with S.J. Thayer) Interview with an Angel, 1997, The Heart of Interview with an Angel, 1998; publ. A Funny Thing Happened at the Interview (G.F. Farrell), 1996, Angel Talk (R. Crystal), 1996; (audiobook with W. Barnes) I Built the Titanic: Past-Life Memories of a Master Shipbuilder, 1999, Thomas Andrews, Voyage into History, 2000; (audio book on CD with W. Barnes and F. Baranowski) My Life and Death: A Past-Life Interview with Titanic's Designer, 2005. Recipient Rsch. Svc. award 1978; Rsch. fellow Albert Einstein Coll. Medicine, 1978-79. Jewish. Home and Office: 102 Sunrise Dr Gillette NJ 07933-1944 Home Phone: 908-647-3346. Business E-Mail: edinbooks@patmedia.net.

NATHANSON, MELVYN BERNARD, academic administrator, mathematician, educator; b. Phila., Oct. 10, 1944; s. Israel and Sophia (Manstein) N.; m. Marjorie Jane Frankel, Jan. 29, 1978; children: Alexander Philip, Rebecca Anne. BA, U. Pa., 1965; postgrad., Harvard U., 1965-66; MA, U. Rochester, 1968, PhD, 1972. Prof. So. Ill. U., Carbondale, 1971-81; dean Rutgers U., Newark, 1981-86; provost, v.p. acad. affairs Lehman Coll. CUNY, Bronx, 1986-91, prof. math. Grad. Sch., 1986—; pres. Short Hills Math. Vis. prof. Moscow State U., USSR, 1972-73, Inst. for Advanced Study, Princeton U., N.J., 1974-75, 76, 90-91, 99-2000, Harvard U., Cambridge, Mass., 1977-78, Rockefeller U., 1982-85, Rutgers U., 1991-93, Tel Aviv U., 2001. Author, editor fifteen books; contbr. articles to profl. jours. Fellow N.Y. Acad. Sci.; mem. AAAS, Am. Math. Soc., Math. Assn. Am., Assn. Mems. Inst. for Advanced Study (pres.). Office: CUNY Lehman Coll Dept Math Bronx NY 10468 Office Phone: 973-921-9615. Personal E-mail: melnathanson@hotmail.com. Business E-Mail: melvyn.nathanson@lehman.cuny.edu.

NATHANSON, NEAL, virologist, epidemiologist, educator; b. Boston, Sept. 1, 1927; s. Robert B. and Leah (Rabinowitch) N.; m. Constance Allen, June 8, 1954; children: Katherine L., John A., Daniel R.; m. Phoebe Starfield, Oct. 7, 1984. BA, Harvard U., 1949, MD, 1953. Chief polio surveillance unit USPHS, 1955-57; rsch. assoc., asst. prof. anatomy Johns Hopkins U., Balt., 1957-63, assoc. prof. epidemiology, 1963-68, prof., 1968-79; chmn. dept. microbiology U. Pa., Phila., 1979-93, vice dean rsch., 1993-95, dir. Office of AIDS Rsch., 1998-2000, vice provost rsch., 2000—03; assoc. dean Global Health Programs, 2003—. Editor-in-chief: Am. Jour. Epidemiology, 1964-79, Microbial Pathogenesis, 1985-88. Achievements include research in pathogenesis, immunology, and epidemiology of viral infections. Home: 1600 Hagys Ford Rd Apt 9W Narberth PA 19072-1049 Office Phone: 215-898-0848. E-mail: nathanson@mail.med.upenn.edu.

NATHANSON, PAUL S., lawyer, educator; b. 1943; BA, Tulane U., 1964; JD, Duke U., 1967; MCL, U. Chgo., 1969. Bar: Calif., N. Mex. Assoc. O'Melveny & Myers, LA; founding dir. Nat. Sr. Citizens Law Ctr., LA, 1972—80; rsch. prof. U. N.Mex Sch. Law, 1980—2005, rsch. prof. emeritus, 2005—, dir. Inst. Public Law, 1983—2005; assoc. provost academic affairs U. N.Mex. Mem. bd. dir. Nat. Sr. Citizens Law Ctr., Internat. Ctr. for Not-For-Profit Law, Nat. Com. Preserve Social Security & Medicare, 1998—, vice chmn., 2001—03, chmn., 2003—; chmn. bd. KNME PBS TV, N.Mex.; mem. bd. dir. N.Mex Legal Aid Found. Mem.: ABA (founding mem., Commn. on Elderly), Am. Soc. Aging (past pres.), Gray Panthers (past nat. sec.). Office: UNM School of Law MSC11 6070 1 University of New Mexico Albuquerque NM 87131-0001 Office Phone: 505-277-1046. Business E-Mail: nathanson@law.unm.edu. *

NATHANSON, SAUL DAVID, oncologist, surgeon, educator; b. Johannesburg, Dec. 12, 1943; came to U.S., 1975; s. Hymie Barnett and Freda Charlotte (Weinberg) N.; m. Maxine Elaine Zacks, Nov. 29, 1966 (div. Sept. 1978); children: Laurence Cecil, Joshua Russel; m. Jerrilyn Marie Burke, Feb. 18, 1979; children: Abigail Mary, Alison Megan. MD, U. Witwatersrand, Johannesburg, 1966. Diplomate Am. Bd. Surgery. Resident in surgery U. Witwatersrand, 1967-74; fellow in immunology UCLA, 1975-77, fellow in surg. oncology, 1977-80; chief resident in surgery U. Calif.-Davis, Sacramento, 1980-82; surg. oncologist Henry Ford Health Sys., Detroit, 1982—, dir. breast cancer ctr., 1995—; prof. surgery Case Western Res. U., Cleve., 1993—2005. Assoc. clin. prof. surgery U. Mich., Ann Arbor, 1985—2000; adj. assoc. prof. med. physics Oakland U., Rochester, Mich., 1993—; cancer liaison physician, Commn. on Cancer; prin. investigator for HFHS, ACS Oncology Group; endowed chair Breast Cancer Rsch., 2001. Author: Ordinary Miracles, 2006; contbr. over 200 articles and abstracts to sci. jours., chpts. to books. Recipient Outstanding Tchr. awards U. Mich., 1982-2000, Humanitarian Cancer award, 2006; named Resident Tchr. of Yr., Henry Ford Health Sys. Dept. Surgery, 2006; NIH grantee Nat. Cancer Inst., 1989. Fellow ACS, Soc. Surg. Oncology, Royal Coll. Surgeons; mem. Am. Soc. Clin. Oncology, Western Surg. Assn., Am. Assn. Cancer Rsch., Wayne County Med. Soc. (alt. del. 1994—96). Office: Henry Ford Health Sys 2799 W Grand Blvd Detroit MI 48202-2608 Home Phone: 248-594-0045; Office Phone: 313-916-2917. Business E-Mail: dnathan1@hfhs.org.

NATION, DAVID ARTHUR, retired computer scientist, sculptor; s. Harold Stanley and Martha Elizabeth (Loonan) N.; m. Jean Lea Bielefeldt, Aug. 9, 1969 (div. May 1979); 1 child, Justin David; m. Rebecca L. Johnson, Oct. 27, 1979. BS in Computer Sci., Iowa State U., 1970; MS, Johns Hopkins U., 1979. Computer scientist U.S. Govt., Washington, 1975—2001; ret., 2001. Author mapping software, pattern classification software, Web software, information visualization software; sculptor;solo shows: Dave Nation's Art Gallery, 1995—; Bay Country Art Guild Member Show, 2000, Treas., Emmanuel United Meth. Ch., Dorsey, md., 1987-2006. Sgt. USAF, 1970—73. Mem. SAG, Assn. for Computing Machinery. Democrat. Unitarian Universalist. Achievements include 4 patents in field. Avocations: sculpting, birdwatching, genealogy, photography, community theater. Personal E-mail: dave@davenation.com.

NATION, EARL F., retired urologist, educator; b. Zephyr, Tex., Jan. 16, 1910; s. Joseph Madison and Alma Emily (Johnson) N.; m. Evelyn Stapp Poynter, Aug. 11, 1936; children: William Earl, Robert Joseph. BA, San Diego State U., 1931; MD, Western Res. U., 1935. Lic. urologist, Calif.; diplomate Am. Bd. Urology. Internship, resident in urology Los Angeles County Gen. Hosp., 1935-39; pvt. practice Pasadena, Calif., 1941-90; ret., 1990. Instr., assoc. prof. urology U. So. Calif., L.A., 1941-55; sr. attending staff Huntington Meml. Hosp., Pasadena, 1941—, St. Luke Hosp., Pasadena, 1941—, also past pres.; pres. Pasadena Dispensary, 1946; lectr. Coll. Med. Evangelists (now Loma Linda U.), 1941-48. Mem. editorial bd. Jour. of Urology, 1958-66, Calif. Medicine, 1965-69, Forum on Medicine; contbr. articles to profl. jours., contbg. author to numerous books. Sec.-treas. Pasadena Breakfast Forum, 1970-73, pres. 1974-75. Crile rsch. scholar Western Res. U., 1931; recipient Monty award San Diego (Calif.) State U., 2005, Zeilstra award Huntington Hosp., 2005; honoree Am. Osler Soc. Mem. ACS, AMA, Am. Urol. Assn. (past pres., Ramon Guiteras award 2002), Am. Osler Soc. (past pres.), L.A. County Med. Assn., Calif. Med. Assn., Pasadena Hist. Soc., So. Calif. Hist. Soc., Am. Soc. Clin. Urologists, Pasadena U. Club, Zamorano Club (v.p. L.A. chpt. 1991), Twilight Club, Alpha Omega Alpha. Republican. Avocations: book collecting, reading, writing, gardening, fishing. Home: # E 311 E Sierra Madre Blvd Apt E Sierra Madre CA 91024-2669 Personal E-mail: enoitan@gte.net.

NATIONS, HOWARD LYNN, lawyer; b. Dalton, Ga., Jan. 9, 1938; s. Howard Lynn and Eva Earline (Armstrong) Lamb; m. Ella Lois Johnson, June 4, 1960 (div. Nov. 1976); children: Cynthia Lynn Nations Garcia, Angela Jean Gordon Hernandez. BA, Fla. State U., 1963, JD, 1966. Bar: Tex. 1966; cert. trial atty. Tex. Bd. Legal Specialization. Assoc. Butler, Rice Cook & Knapp, Houston, 1966-71; pres. Nations & Cross, Houston, 1971—; v.p., dir., co-founder Ins. Corp. Am., Houston, 1972—; pres. Caplinger & Nations Galleries, Houston, 1973—, Nations Investment Corp., Houston, 1975—, NCM Trade Corp., Houston, 1975; v.p. Delher Am. Inc., Houston, 1975—; pres. Howard L. Nations, PC, Houston, 1971—, Trial Focus, Inc., 1995—. Founder Nations Found.; adj. prof. So. Tex. Coll. Law, Houston, 1967—; speaker in field. Author: Structuring Settlements, 1987; co-author: Texas Workers' Compensation, 1988, (with others) The Anatomy of a Personal Injury Lawsuit, 3rd rev. edit. 1991; editor: Maximizing Damages in Wrongful Death and Personal Injury Litigation, 1985; contbr. articles to profl. jours. Chmn., trustee Nat. Coll. Advocacy, Washington, 1985-92. With M.I. Corps, U.S. Army, 1957-60. Recipient Gene Cavin Excellence award State Bar Tex., 2000. Fellow Tex. Bar Found., Houston Bar Found. (life); mem. ATLA (exec. com. 1991-95), Nat. Bd. Trial Advocacy (diplomate civil trial advocacy), So. Trial Lawyers Assn. (pres. 1994-95), Tex. Trial Lawyers Assn. (pres. 1992-93). Office: The Sterling Mansion 4515 Yoakum Blvd Houston TX 77006-5821 Office Phone: 713-807-8400.

NATIVIDAD, IRENE, women's rights advocate; b. Manila, Philippines, Sept. 14, 1948; m. Andrea Cortese; 1 child, Carlo Natividad Cortese. BA, LI Univ., 1971; MA, Columbus U., 1973, MPhil, 1978; LHD (hon.), LI Univ., 1989, Marymount Coll., 1994. Pres. Globe Women, Inc., Washington, Nat. Women's Political Caucus, 1985—89; chmn. Nat. Commn. on Working Women, 1989—98. Dep. vice chair Dem. Party Asian Caucus, 1982—84; pres. Global Summit of Women; co-chair Corp. Women Dir. Internat.; exec. dir. Philippine Am. Found.; bd. dir. Nat. Mus. Women in Arts, Nat. Assn. Corp. Dir., Sallie Mae; adv. bd. Cigna, Wyndham Internat. Exec. editor Asian American Almanac, 1995, frequent commentator, panelist on TV news shows; contbr. columns in newspapers. Named one of 100 Most Power Women in Am., Ladies Home Jour., 1988, 74 Women Changing Am. Politics, Campaigns & Elections Mag., 1993, 25 Most Influential Working Mothers, Working Mother Mag., 1997, 21 Leaders for the 21st Century, Women's eNews, 2004, Top 25 Influental Asian Americans, A. Mag.; recipient Women Making History award, Women's Congl. Caucus, 1985, Magnificent 7 award, Bus. & Profl. Women/USA, 1995, Women of Genius award, Trinity Coll., Washington, DC, 2001. Office: Natividad Assn 504 1211 Connecticut Ave NW Washington DC 20036 Business E-Mail: president@globewomen.com.

NATIVI NICOLAU, JUAN JOSE, industrial engineer; b. Panama City, Panama, Aug. 13, 1981; s. Jose Napoleon Nativi Peart and Ruth Elvira Nicolau Perez. BS in Indsl. Engring., U. Cath. Santa Maria Antigua, Panama City, 2004; MS in Indsl. and Sys. Engring., Tex. A&M U., Coll. Sta., 2007. With Citibank, N. Am. Panama Br., Panama City, Panama, 2002—03, mgmt. info. sys., 2003—05; tech. planning engr. Ga. Tech. Authority, Atlanta, 2006. Contbr. articles to profl. jours. Vol. Simon Bolivar Elder Ho., Panama City, Panama, 2004, Ctr. for Spl. Children, Panama City, Panama, 2000. Fulbright Grant, 2005. Mem.: Soc. Engring. and Mgmt. Sys., Soc. Indsl. and Applied Math., Inst. Indsl. Engrs., Inst. Ops. Rsch. and Mgmt. Sci. Avocations: sports, travel, reading.

NATOLI, JOSEPH, language educator; b. Bklyn., Aug. 24, 1943; m. Elaine Tuminelli, June 6, 1970; children: Amelia, Brenda. BA, Bklyn. Coll., 1965, MA, 1968; PhD, SUNY, Albany, 1973. Asst. prof. English New Eng. Coll., Henniker, NH, 1971-73, 1973-75; acting dir. libr., adj. lectr. English Bluefield State Coll., W.Va., 1975-77; head reference and bibliography libr. Wake Forest U., Winston Salem, NC, 1977-81; bibliographer, adj. lectr. humanities U. Calif., Irvine, 1981-83, Mich. State U., East Lansing, 1983—, dir. study abroad program Europe, 1996—. Series editor SUNY Press Postmodern Culture, Albany, 1990—. Author: Mots D'Ordre, 1992, Hauntings, 1994, Primer to Postmodernity, 1997, Speeding to the Millenium, 1998, Postmodern Journeys, 2000, Memory's Orbit, 2003, This is a Picture and Not the World, 2007; editor: Twentieth Century Blake Criticism, 1982, Psychological Perspectives on Literature, 1984, Psychocriticism, 1984, Tracing Literary Theory, 1987, Literary Theory's Future(s), 1989, A Postmodern Reader, 1993, Postmodernism: The Key Figures, 2002. Office: Mich State Univ Writing Rhetoric Am Culture Dept 241 Bessey Hall East Lansing MI 48824 Business E-Mail: natoli@msu.edu.

NATOLI, JOSEPH T., financial administrator, former publishing executive; b. NYC; m. Jennifer Natoli; children: Danielle, Joey. Grad., U. South Fla.; MBA, Nova U. Joined Knight Ridder as staff acct., 1976; v.p. ops. Miami Herald Pub. Co., gen. mgr., 1993—94, pres., 1994—2001; pres., pub. San Jose Mercury News, 2001—03; pub., chmn. Phila. Inquirer, 2004—06, Phila. Daily News, 2004—06; CFO, sr. v.p. bus. & fin. U. Miami, 2006—. Bd. mem. CEO Coun. for Growth. Bd. mem. Franklin Inst., Greater Phila. C. of C., United Way of Southeastern Pa., campaign chair, 2005; mem. cmty. adv. bd. Knight Found. Office: U Miami Miami FL 33124

NATORI, JOSIE CRUZ (JOSEFINA ALMEDA CRUZ NATORI), apparel executive; b. Manila, Philippines, May 9, 1947; arrived in US, 1964; d. Felipe F. and Angelita A. (Almeda) Cruz; m. Kenneth R. Natori, May 20, 1972; 1 child, Kenneth E.F. BA in Econs., Manhattanville Coll., 1968; Degree (hon.), Acad. Art Coll., San Francisco, 2003. With Bache Securities, NYC; joined Merrill-Lynch Co. as an investment banker, 1971; v.p., 1976—77; owner, CEO The Natori Co., NYC, 1977—. Bd. dirs. The Alltel Corp., 1995—. Bd. dirs. Philippine Am. Found., Jr. Achievement, Inc., 1992, Ednl. Found. for Fashion Industries; trustee Manhattanville Coll., Asian Cultural Coun.; commr. White House Conf. on Small Bus., 1993. Recipient Human Relations award Am. Jewish Com., NYC., 1986, Harriet Alger award Working Woman, NY, 1987, Castle award Manhattanville Coll., Purchase, 1988, Galleon award Pres. Philippines, 1988, NYC Asian-Am. award, Friendship award Philippine-Am. Found., Hall of Fame award Mega Mags., Salute to Am. Fashion Designers award Dept. of Commerce, Ellis Island medal of Honor, 1994, Presdl. Awards for Filipino Individuals and Orgns. Overseas, Pamana ng Pilipino award Philippine Consulate Gen., 2002; named Bus. Woman of Yr. NYC Partnership and C. of C., 1998. Mem. CFDA, Young Pres.'s Orgn., Fashion Group, Com. of 200. Avocations: pianist, tennis player. Home: 45 E 62nd St New York NY 10021-8025 Office: The Natori Company 180 Madison Ave # 19 New York NY 10016-5267

NATSIOS, ANDREW STEPHEN, diplomat, former federal agency administrator; b. Phila., Pa., Sept. 22, 1949; s. Basil Andrew and Eta (Lappas) Natsios; m. Elizabeth E. Macdonald; children: Emily, Alexander, Phillip. BA, Georgetown U., 1971; MPA, Harvard U., 1979. Treas. Holliston Indsl. Devel. Commn., 1973—75; chmn. Holliston Rep. Town Com., 1974—75; mem. Mass. Ho. Reps. from Dist. 8, 1975—87; exec. dir. Northeast Pub. Power Assn., Milford, Mass., 1987—89; dir. Office of Fgn. Disaster Assistance US Agy. Internat. Devel., 1989—91, asst. adminstr. Bur. Food and Humanitarian Assistance, 1991—93, adminstr. Washington, 2001—05; v.p. World Vision US, 1993—98; sec. adminstrn. & fin. Commonwealth Mass., 1999—2000; chmn. Mass. Turnpike Authority, 2000—01; Disting. Prof in the Practice of Diplomacy and Advisor on Internat. Devel., Edmund A. Walsh Sch. Fgn. Svc. Georgetown U., 2006—. Spl. coord. for Internat. Disaster Assistance & Spl. Humanitarian Coord. for Sudan The White House, 2004; spl. envoy to pursue ending the violence in the Darfur region of Sudan US Dept. State, 2006—. Author: U.S. Foreign Policy and the Four Horsemen of the Apocalypse, 1997, The Great North Korean Famine, 2001. Served in USAR, 1972—95. Named Legis. of Yr., Mass. Mcpl. Assn., 1978, Mass. Assn. Sch. Committees, 1986, Citizens for Limited Taxation, 1986; fellow Jennings Randolph Fellowship, US Inst. Peace, 1998—99. Office: Edmund A Walsh Sch Fgn Svc 301 Intercultural Ctr 37th & O St NW Washington DC 20057 E-mail: asn8@georgetown.edu. *

NATTEL, STANLEY, cardiologist, research scientist; b. Haifa, Israel, Jan. 28, 1951; arrived in Can., 1952; s. William and Julie (Zwirek) N.; m. Celia Anne Reich, Sept. 25, 1973; children: Jonathan, Ilana, Daniel, Sarah. BSc magna cum laude, McGill U., 1972, MD, 1974. Diplomate Am. Bd. Internal Medicine, Am. Bd. Cardiology. Intern in medicine Royal Victoria Hosp., 1974-75, resident in internal medicine, 1975-76; resident in clin. pharmacology Montreal Gen. Hosp., Que., Canada, 1976-78, cardiologist, clin. pharmacologist, 1981-87, dir. coronary care unit, 1983-87; fellow in cardiology Ind. U., 1978-80; fellow in physiology U. Pa., 1980-81; asst. prof. pharmacology, medicine McGill U., Montreal, 1981-87, assoc. prof., 1987—; cardiologist Montreal Heart Inst., 1987—, dir. rsch. ctr., 1990—2004; prof. dept. medicine U. Montreal, 1995—, Paul-David chair in cardiovasc. electrophysiology, 2003—. External reviewer Med. Rsch. Coun., 1981—, Ont. Health Ministry, 1983-84, NSF, 1992, others; chmn. libr. com. dept. pharmacology McGill U., 1982-86, mem. grad. com., 1984-89, chmn. grad. tng. com., 1986-89, departmental rep. grad. faculty coun., 1989-91, coord. grad. tchg. pharmacology, 1989-91; mem. oper. grants com. Can. Heart Found., 1983-86; chmn. clin. trials com. Montreal Gen. Hosp., 1983-87, chmn. pharmacy and therapeutics com., 1984-87, sec. clin. chemistry rev. com., 1984, course dir. drug therapy, 1984-87, acting dir. divsn. clin. pharmacology, 1984-85, mem. various coms., 1985-87; mem. fellowship awards com. FRSQ, 1988-90, mem. ctr. grants pharmacology/pharmacy com., 1989-90; chmn. pharmacology com. Montreal Heart Inst., 1988-90, mem. search com. pharmacist-in-chief, 1989-90, mem. ethics com., 1991-2004, chmn. internal rsch. com., 1991-2004, mem. consultative com. exec. dir., 1991-2004, chmn. consultative com. rsch. ctr., 1991-2004; cons. coun. pharmacology Province of Quebec, 1989-90; mem. safety monitoring com. CAMIAT Study, 1990-95; assoc. prof. medicine U. Montreal, 1991-95, prof. 1995—, chmn. search com. dir. rsch. Sacré-Coeur Hosp., 1991, mem. rsch. com. Cormes faculty medicine, 1991—2002, mem. rsch. com. dept. medicine, 1991-2004; chmn. search com., dir. rsch. Maisonneuve Rosemont Hosp., 1996; mem. site visit team program project grant NIH, 1991, cons. program project grant, 1993, spl. reviewer cardiovascular study sect., 1993, 95, 97, 98; mem. oper. grants com. Med. Rsch. Coun. Can., 1988-93, chmn., 2002-05; mem. sr. pers. awards com. Can. Heart Found., 1994-96; lectr. in field. Assoc. editor Can. Jour. Physiology and Pharmacology, 1990-95, Br. Jour. Pharmacology, 2000-2005; mem. editl. bd. Jour. Cardiovasc. Electrophysiology, 1991—, Drugs, 1993—, Cardiovasc. Drugs and Therapy, 1993-2001, Circulation Rsch., 1995—, JACC, 1995-2000, Cardiovascular Rsch., 1999-2002, others; manuscript reviewer Am. Jour. Cardiology, Nature, Nature Medicine, Nature Genetics, New Eng. Jour. Medicine, PNAS, Science, others; contbr. chpts. to books and articles to profl. jours. Chmn. edn. com. Hebrew Acad. Sch., Montreal, 1991-92. Grantee Que. Heart Found., 1981—, Nordic Pharms., 1985-87, Knoll Pharms., 1991-93, others; fellow Med. Rsch. Coun. Can., 1979-81; McGill U. scholar, 1967-74, Sir Edward Beatty scholar McGill U., 1967-70, Rsch. scholar Med. Rsch. Coun., 1982-87, Sr. Rsch. scholar Fonds de la Recherche en Santé du Quebec, 1990-93; recipient Career Rsch. Achievement award Can. Cardiovasc. Soc., 2001. Fellow Am. Coll. Cardiology, Royal Coll. Physicians Can. (cert. medicine, cardiology), Acad. Scis. Royal Soc. Can.; mem. Am. Heart Assn. (coun. basic sci., leadership com. 2003-05), Royal Soc. Can., Heart Rhythm Soc., Am. Soc. Pharmacology and Exptl. Therapeutics, Can. Cardiovasc. Soc. (councilor 1992-95), Can. Soc. Clin. Pharmacology (Kenneth M. Piafsky Young Investigator award 1985), Pharm. Soc. Can. Biophys. Soc., Am. Heart Assn. (leadership com.). Avocations: studying jewish religious works, sports. Home: 5609 Alpine Ave Côte Saint Luc PQ Canada H4V 2X6 Office: Montreal Heart Inst 5000 Belanger St E Montreal PQ Canada H1T 1C8 Home Phone: 514-482-0715; Office Phone: 514-376-3330. Personal E-mail: stanleynattel@aol.com. Business E-Mail: stanley.nattel@icm-mhi.org.

NAU, DAVID PAUL, pharmacist, educator; b. Toledo, Ohio, Mar. 17, 1966; s. Paul and Mary Lou Nau; m. Martha Evans, June 7, 1997; children: Jena Mason, Paige Mason, Madison. BS in Pharmacy, Ohio No. U., Ada, 1989; MS in Pharm. Scis., U. Toledo, 1991; PhD in Pharmacy Health Car Adminstrn., U. Fla., Gainesville, 1997. Cert. Healthcare Quality Certification Bd. Asst. prof. U. W.Va., Morgantown, 1997—2001; assoc. prof. U. Mich., Ann Arbor, 2001—06, U. Ky., Lexington, 2006—. Cons. Pharmacy Quality Alliance, Washington. Chmn. Mich. Medication Safety Coalition, Lansing, 2005. Recipient Excellence in Rsch. award, Blue Cross Blue Shield Mich. Found., 2006. Mem.: AcademyHealth, Internat. Soc. Pharmacoeconomics and Outcomes Rsch., Acad. Managed Care Pharmacy, Ky. Pharmacists Assn., Am. Pharmacists Assn. Achievements include development of quality measures for pharmacy services. Office: U Ky 725 Rose St Lexington KY 40536-0082 Office Phone: 859-257-4523. Business E-Mail: dnau2@email.uky.edu.

NAUGHTON, EILEEN T., Internet company executive; b. White Plains, NY, Dec. 21, 1957; d. Patrick J. Naughton; m. Craig Allen Chesley, Aug. 29, 1987; 3 children. BA in Internat. Rels., Univ. Pa., 1979, MBA, 1987; MA, Lauder Inst. Internat. Studies, 1987. Joined Time Inc., 1989, gen. mgr., Fortune mag. NYC, 1993—97, v.p., dir. fin., 1997—99; pres. Time Inc. Interactive, 1999—2000; v.p. investor rels. AOL Time Warner, 2000—02; pres., Time mag. Time Inc., 2002—05; head, advt. sales Google Inc., NYC, 2006—. Bd. dirs. The Knot, Inc., 2006—. Bd. dir. Volunteers of Am. of NY, Fragile X Rsch. Found. (FRAXA). Named a Woman to Watch, Advt. Age, 2007. Office Phone: 212-624-9600. *

NAUGHTON, JAMES, actor; b. Middletown, Conn., Dec. 6, 1945; s. James Joseph and Rosemary (Walsh) N.; m. Pamela Parsons, Oct. 1968; children: Gregory J., Keira P. BA, Brown U., 1967; MFA, Yale U., 1970. Broadway appearances include Edmund in Long Day's Journey Into Night, 1971 (Theatre World award, N.Y. Drama Critics award, Vernon Rice award 1971), Stone in City of Angels (Tony award 1990, Drama Desk award), I Love My Wife, 1977, Whose Life Is It Anyway, 1980, Chicago, 1996 (Tony award, 1997); films include Paper Chase, 1972, Second Wind, 1975, A Stranger is Watching, 1981, Cat's Eye, 1982, The Glass Menagerie, 1987, The Good Mother, 1988, First Kid, 1996, The First Wives Club, 1996, The Proprietor, 1996, Oxygen, 1999, Labor Pains, 2000, Fascination, 2004, The Devil Wears Prada, 2006; TV appearances include: (series) Faraday and Company, 1973-74, Planet of the Apes, 1974, Making the Grade, 1982, Trauma Center, 1983, The Cosby Mysteries, 1994; (movies) F. Scott Fitzgerald and "The Last of the Belles", 1974, The Last 36 Hours of Dr. Durant, 1975, The Bunker, 1981, My Body, My Child, 1982, Parole, 1982, The Last of the Great Survivors, 1984, Between Darkness and the Dawn, 1985, Sin of Innocence, 1986, Necessity, 1988, Blown Away, 1990, The Birds II: Land's End, 1994, Couples, 1994, Cagney & Lacey: The Return, 1994, Cagney & Lacey: Together Again, 1995, Mixed Blessings, 1995, The Truth About Jane, 2000; dir. (plays) Surface to Air, 2007. Recipient Tony award Leading Actor in a Musical, 1997. *

NAUGHTON, JAMES LEE, internist; b. 1946; AB, Dartmouth Coll., 1968; MD, Harvard U., 1972. Intern U. Calif. Moffitt Hosp., San Francisco, 1972-73; resident in medicine U. Calif. Affiliated Hosps., San Francisco, 1973-75, San Francisco Gen. Hosp., 1975-76; fellow in nephrology U. Calif., San Francisco, 1976-77, assoc. clin. prof. medicine, 1982—; pvt. practice internal medicine, ptnr. Alliance Med. Group, Pinole, Calif., 1982—. Mem. Am. Bd. Internal Medicine (bd. dirs. 1995-2002, exec. com. 1997-2002, trustee found. 2000—). Office: Alliance Med Group 2160 Appian Way Ste 200 Pinole CA 94564-2524

NAUGHTON, JAMES MARTIN, journalist; b. Pitts., Aug. 13, 1938; s. Francis Patrick and Martha Ann (Clear) N.; m. Diana Marie Thomas, Sept. 5, 1964; children: Jenifer Mary Naughton Genovesi, Lara Marie, Michael Thomas, Kerry Marie. BA cum laude, U. Notre Dame, 1960. Reporter, photographer Painesville (Ohio) Telegraph, summer, 1955-60; reporter Cleve. Plain Dealer, 1962-69; Washington corr. N.Y. Times, 1969-77; nat. editor Phila. Inquirer, 1977-79, met. editor, 1979-83, assoc. mng. editor, 1980-86, dep. mng. editor, 1986-90, mng. editor, 1990-91, exec. editor, 1991-96; pres. The Poynter Inst. for Media Studies, St. Petersburg, Fla., 1996—2003, pres. emeritus, 2003—. Marsh prof. U. Mich., Ann Arbor, 1977; Pulitzer prize juror, 1998—99; Heinz award juror, 2005—07. With USMC, 1960—62. Recipient Disting. Svc. award Sigma Delta Chi, 1973. Roman Catholic. Home: 2500 Coffee Pot Blvd NE Saint Petersburg FL 33704-3466 E-mail: swamijim@mac.com.

NAUGHTON, JOHN PATRICK, cardiologist, educator; b. West Nanticoke, Pa., May 20, 1933; s. John Patrick and Anne Frances (McCormick) N.; children: Bruce, Marcia, Lisa, George, Michael, Thomas. AA, Cameron State U., Lawton, Okla., 1952; BS, St. Louis U., 1954; MD, Okla. U., 1958; MD (hon.), Kosin U., 1995. Intern George Washington U. Hosp., Washington, 1958-59; resident U. Okla. Med. Center, 1959-64; asst. prof. medicine U. Okla., 1966-68; assoc. prof. medicine U. Ill., 1968-70; prof. medicine George Washington U., 1970-75, dean acad. affairs, 1973-75, dir. div. rehab. medicine and Regional Rehab. Research and Tng. Center, 1970-75; dean Sch. Medicine SUNY, Buffalo, 1975-96, prof. medicine, physiology, social, preventive and rehab. medicine Sch. Medicine, 1975—, acting v.p. for health scis., 1983-84, v.p. clin. affairs, 1984-96, interim chmn. rehab. medicine, 2003—. Dir. Nat. Exercise and Heart Disease Project, 1972-83; chmn. policy adv. bd. Beta-blocker Heart Attack Trial Nat. Heart, Lung and Blood Inst., 1977-82; pres. Western N.Y. chpt. Am. Heart Assn., 1983-85, v.p. N.Y. State affiliate, 1985, pres. N.Y. State affiliate, 1988-90; chmn. clin. applications and preventions adv. com. Nat. Heart, Lung and Blood Inst., 1984; mem. Fed. COGME working group on consortia, 1996-97, N.Y. Gov.'s Commn. on Grad. Med. Edn., 1985, N.Y. State Coun. on Grad. Med. Edn., 1988-90, chmn. 1996—; pres. Assoc. Med. Schs. N.Y., 1982-84, mem. adminstrv. com. Coun. of Deans, 1983-89; mem. N.Y. State Dept. of Health Adv. Com. on Physician Recredentialing; mem. exec. coun. Nat. Inst. on Disability and Rehab. Rsch. 1991-92; v.p. James H. Cummings Found. Author: Exercise Testing and Exercise Training in Coronary Heart Disease, 1973, Exercise Testing: Physiological, Biomechanical, and Clinical Principles, 1988 Career devel. awardee Nat. Heart Inst., 1966-71; recipient Brotherhood-Sisterhood award in medicine NCCJ, N.E. Minority Educators award, 1990, Acad. Alumnus of Yr. award Okla. U., 1990, award for svc. to minorities in med. edn., 1991, Frank Sindelar award N.Y. State Am. Heart Assn., 1995, James Platt White Soc. award, 1995, Outstanding Contbns. in the field of Health Care award Sheehan Meml. Hosp., 1995, Chancellor Charles P. Norton medal, SUNY, Buffalo, 1997, AMS Disting. Svc. award, 2001. Fellow ACP, Am. Coll. Cardiology, Am. Coll. Sports Medicine (pres. 1970-71, Citation award 2000), Am. Coll. Chest Physicians; Am. Coll. Preventive Medicine, Am. Heart Assn. (epidemiology coun. 2000—, coun. on nutrition, phys. activity and metabolism), Acad. Health Profls. Ins. Assn. (hon.). Office: SUNY Buffalo 128 Farber Hall 3435 Main St Buffalo NY 14214-3099 Home Phone: 716-668-3753. Business E-Mail: jpn@buffalo.edu.

NAUGLE, LOUIS A., lawyer; b. Plainfield, NJ, Aug. 6, 1950; BA in polit. sci./history, Williams Coll., 1972; JD, Georgetown U., 1975. Bar: Pa. 1975, NY 1985, US Ct. Appeals 3rd Cir., US Supreme Ct., US Dist. Ct. We. Dist. Pa., US Dist. Ct. Mid. Dist. Pa., US Dist. Ct. Ea. Dist. Pa., US Dist. Ct. We. Dist. NY. Asst. atty. gen./asst. counsel Bur. Litig. Pa. Dept. Environ.

Resources, 1975—84; asst. atty. gen. Environ. Protection Bur. NY Dept. Law, 1984—86; ptnr. Hodgson, Russ, Andrews, Woods & Goodyear, 1986—88; joined Reed Smith LLP, Pitts., 1988, ptnr., 1990—, also practice group leader environ. group. Vice chair Allegheny County Air Pollution Adv. Com.; adv. com. mem. Cert. Program in Environ. Law, Sci. & Policy U. Pitts. Law Sch. Mem.: ABA, Allegheny County Bar Assn., Pa. Bar Assn. Office: Reed Smith LLP 435 Sixth Ave Pittsburgh PA 15219 Office Phone: 412-288-8586. Office Fax: 412-288-3063. Business E-Mail: lnaugle@reedsmith.com.

NAUHEIM, STEPHEN ALAN, lawyer; b. Washington, Nov. 17, 1942; s. Ferdinand Alan and Beatrice Lillian (Strasburger) N.; children: Terry Beth, David Alan. BS in Acctg., U. N.C., 1964; JD, Georgetown U., 1967; LLM, George Washington U., 1970. Bar: D.C. 1968, U.S. Ct. Claims 1968, U.S. Tax Ct. 1971. Atty. adviser office chief counsel IRS, Washington, 1967-71, asst. br. chief, 1970-71; assoc. Surrey & Morse, Washington, 1971-75, ptnr., 1975-81; prin. Anderson, Hibey, Nauheim & Blair, Washington, 1981-91, Schall, Boudreau & Gore, Washington, 1991-93; pres., gen. counsel CMW Group, Ltd., Washington, 1994-96; mng. dir. Pricewaterhouse Coopers LLP, 1996—. Mem. adv. bd. World Trade Inst., N.Y.C., 1978—, Tax Mgmt. Adv. Bd., Washington, 1980—. Mem. editl. bd. Internat. Tax Jour., N.Y.C., 1982—; contbr. to profl. publs. Mem. ABA (former com. chmn. taxation sect.), Internat. Fiscal Assn., D.C. Bar Assn. (mem. steering com. tax sect. 1987-92, chmn. tax sect. 1990-92), Am. Coll. of Tax Counsel. Avocations: travel, sailing. Office: PricewaterhouseCoopers 1301 K St NW Ste 800W Washington DC 20005-3333 Home Phone: 202-466-2151; Office Phone: 202-414-1524. Business E-Mail: stephen.a.nauheim@us.pwc.com.

NAULT, WILLIAM HENRY, publishing executive; b. Ishpeming, Mich., June 9, 1926; s. Henry J. and Eva (Perrault) N.; m. Helen E. Matthews, Nov. 28, 1946; children: William Henry, Rebecca Nault Marks, Ronald, George, Peter, Julia Nault Doyle, Robert, David. AB, No. Mich. U., 1948, LittD (hon.), 1988; MA, U. Mich., 1949; EdD, Columbia U., 1953, LHD (hon.), 1980, LLD (hon.), 1986, LittD (hon.), 1988. Dir. adult edn., Battle Creek, Mich., 1948—49; guidance counselor, 1949-50; prin. W.K. Kellogg High Sch., Battle Creek, 1950-53; research assoc. Columbia U., 1953-54; asst. supt. Ridgewood, NJ, 1954-55; adj. prof. William Patterson U. N.J., 1954—55; dir. research World Book, Inc. (formerly Field Enterprises Edn. Corp.), Chgo., 1955-63, v.p., 1963-66, sr. v.p., editorial dir., 1966-68, exec. v.p. and editorial dir., 1968-83; pres., pub., chief operating officer World Book, Inc., 1983-84, gen. chmn. editorial adv. bds., 1968-99, pub., 1983-95, pub. emeritus, 1995—. Past vice chmn. Govt. Adv. Com. on Internat. Library and Book Programs, U.S. Dept. State; past mem. nat. adv. bd. Ctr. on Ednl. Media and Materials for Handicapped; past mem. exec. bd. Comm. Instns. Higher Edn., North Central Assn. Colls. and Secondary Schs.; mem. dean's adv. council Coll. Bus. and Pub. Adminstrn., U. Mo., Columbia; mem. nat. council Inst. Internat. Edn. Author material on courses of study. Mem. alumni com. Columbia Tchrs. Coll. Capital Campaign; mem. White House Conf. on Youth, White House Conf. on Librs., White House Conf. on Edn.; pres. Oak Park (Ill.) Bd. Edn., 1960-63; v.p. LaGrange (Ill.) Libr. Bd.; bd. regents Lincoln Acad., Ill.; past trustee Adler Planetarium, De Paul U., Chgo. Geol. Soc.; bd. dirs. H.V. Phalin Found. Grad. Study, World Book, Inc., A.J. Nystrom Co., Field Edn. Co., Libr. Movens, Inc.; mem. adv. bd. Rosary Coll.; mem. liberal arts and scis. adv. council De Paul U. Served with F.A., AUS, 1944-45. Recipient Columbia U. Tchrs. Coll. medal for disting. svc. in edn.; named Disting. Alumnus No. Mich. U., U. Mich., Columbia U. Fellow AAAS; mem. ALA, Chgo. Planetarium Soc. (trustee), Chgo. Geog. Soc. (dir.), Am. Acad. Polit. and Social Sci., Am. Edn. Rsch. Assn., Am. Assn. Sch. Adminstrs., ASCD, Chgo. Pubs. Assn. (past pres.), Ill. Assn. Sch. Adminstrs., Ill. Acad. Sci., NSTA, Nat. Council Tchrs. English, Assn. Am. Geographers, Assn. Childhood Edn. Internat., NAESP, Nat. Assn. Secondary Sch. Prins., Council for Advancement Sci. Writing, Internat. Platform Assn., Nat. Council Social Studies, Nat. Soc. Study Edn. Clubs: Mid-Am, Mchts. and Mfrs. Roman Catholic. Office: World Book Inc 525 W Monroe St Chicago IL 60661-3629 Personal E-mail: naultwh@aol.com, naultwh@comcast.net.

NAULTY, SUSAN LOUISE, archivist; b. Abington, Pa., May 28, 1944; d. Charles J. and Ruth E. (Schick) N. BA, Whittier Coll., 1967; MA, Loyola U., LA, 1972. Tchr. history and English, Whittier (Calif.) H.S., 1968-70; from libr. asst. to asst. curator Huntington Libr., San Marino, Calif., 1972-91; archivist Richard Nixon Libr. and Birthplace, Yorba Linda, Calif., 1991—.

NAUMAN, BRUCE, artist; b. Ft. Wayne, Ind., Dec. 6, 1941; m. Judy Nauman, 1964 (div.); 2 children; m. Susan Rothenberg, 1989. BFA, U. Wis.-Madison, 1964; MFA, U. Calif., Davis, 1966; studied with, Italo Scango, William Wiley, Robert Arneson, Frank Owen, Stephen Kaltenbach.; DFA (hon.), San Francisco Art Inst., 1989; ArtsD (hon.), Calif. Inst. Arts, 2000. Tchr. asst. to Wayne Thiebaud, 1964; instr. San Francisco Art Inst., 1966-68; instr. sculpture U. Calif., Irvine, 1970 Author: Pictures of Sculptures in a Room, 1966, Clear Sky, 1968, Burning Small Fires, 1968; one man shows include Nicholas Wilder Gallery, L.A., Sacramento State Coll., 1968, Galerie Konrad Fischer Dusseldorff, 1968, Los Angeles County Mus. Art (retrospective), 1972, U. Calif., Irvine, 1973, Stadtische Kunsthalle (retrospective), Dusseldorf, W. Ger., Art/Voir, Centre Beaubourg, Paris, 1974, Sculpture Am. Directions 1945-1975, Nat. Collection of Fine Arts, Smithsonian Inst., 1975, Body Works, Mus. Contemporary Art, Chgo., 1975, Drawing Now, Mus. Modern Art, N.Y.C., 1975, 200 Years Am. Sculpture, Whitney Mus., N.Y.C., 1976, The Artist and the Photograph, Israel Mus., 1976, Sculpture, Munster, W. Ger., 1977, A View of a Decade, Mus. Contemporary Art, Chgo., 1977, Made by Sculptors, Stedelijk Mus., Amsterdam, 1978, Words Words, Mus. Bochum, W. Ger., 1979, The Broadening of the Concept of Reality in the Art of the 60s and 70s, Mus. Haus Lange Krefeld, W. Ger., 1979, Albright-Knox Art Gallery, Buffalo, 1975, U. Nev., 1976, Mpls. Inst. Arts, 1978, Portland Center for Visual Arts, 1979, Leo Castelli Gallery, N.Y.C., 1982, Sperone Westwater Fischer, N.Y.C., 1982, Sperone Westwater, N.Y.C., 1990, 96, 2001, 02, Dia Ctr. for Arts, N.Y.C., 2002, DIA Ctr. Arts, N.Y.C., 2002, Corcoran Gallery Art, Washington, 2002-03, Ludwig Mus. Cologne, Germany, 2003, Deutsche Guggenheim, Berlin, 2003-04, Tate Modern, London, 2004-05, others; group exhbns. include Fischbach Gallery, William Geis, Bruce Nauman, San Francisco Art Inst., 1966, Am. Sculpture of the Sixties, Los Angeles County Mus. Art, 1967, Documenta IV, Kassel, W. Ger., 1968, When Attitudes Become Form, Kunsthalle, Berne, Switzerland, toured, Europe, 1969, Kompass IV, Van Abbermuseum, Eindohoven, Netherlands, 1969, Corcoran Gallery Art, Washington, 1969, Anti-Illusion: Procedures-Materials, Whitney Mus. Art, N.Y.C., 1969, Soloman R. Guggenheim Mus., N.Y.C., 1969, Holograms and Lasers, Mus. Contemporary Art, Chgo., 1970, Conceptual Art and Conceptual Aspects, N.Y. Cultural Center, 1970, Am. Art Since 1960, Princeton U., 1970, Info, Mus. Modern Art, N.Y.C., 1971, Diagrams and Drawing, Rijksmuseum Kroller-Mueller, 1972, USA West Coast, Kunstverein, Hamburg, W. Ger., 1972, Documenta V, Kassel, W. Ger., 1972, Gilder, Objedte, Filme, Konzepte, Stadische Galerie, Munich, 1973, Art and Image in Recent Art, Art Inst., Chgo., 1974, Carol Taylor Art, Dallas, 1983, Kunsthalle, Basel, Switzerland, 1986, Carnegie Mus. Art, 1991-92, La. Mus. Art, 1997-98, Henry Art Gallery, Seattle, 2000, Art Gallery NSW, 2001, Donald Young Gallery, Chgo., 2002, Austin Mus. Art, Austin, Tex., 2003, others; group show 64th Whitney Biennial, 1987; represented in permanent collections: Whitney Mus. Am. Art, Los Angeles County Mus. Art; prodr. numerous video works. Nat. Endowment Arts grantee, 1968; Aspen Inst. Humanistic Studies, grantee, 1970; recipient Wolf Prize in arts (xculpture) Wolf Found., Israel, 1993, Praemium Imperiale award, Japan, 2004; named Best Internat. Artist, Beaux-Arts Mag., Paris, 2004. Fellow: Am. Acad. Arts and Scis.; mem.: Am. Acad. Arts and Letters. Avocation: horseback riding. Office: Sperone Westwater 415 W 13 St New York NY 10014

NAUMANN, JOSEPH F., archbishop; b. St. Louis, June 4, 1949; BA, Cardinal Glennon Coll., St. Louis, 1971; degree in theology, Kenrick Sem., St. Louis, 1975. Ordained priest, St. Louis, 1975; transitional deacon St. Christopher's Parish, Florissant, Mo., 1974-75; assoc. pastor St. Dominic Savio Parish, Affton, Mo., 1975-79, Our Lady of Sorrows Parish, St. Louis, 1979-84; part-time assoc. pastor Most Blessed Sacrament Parish, St. Louis, 1984-89; pastor Ascension Parish, Normandy, Mo., 1989-94; vicar gen., 1994—97; auxiliary bishop, 1997—2004; titular bishop Caput Cilla, 1997—; coadjutor archbishop Archdiocese of Kansas City, Kans., 2004, archbishop Kans., 2005—. Office: Archdiocese of Kansas City 12615 Parallel Pkwy Kansas City KS 66109

NAUMER, CAROLA, art historian, educator; d. Helmuth and Tomee Naumer. BA, San Francisco State U., 1983, MA, 1987; PhD, Fla. State U., 1998. Instr. Fla. A&M U., Tallahassee, 1989—95, Bainbridge Coll., Ga., 1995—96, Tallahssee C.C., 1995—98; grad. tchg. asst. Fla. State U., Tallahassee, 1998—98; prof. Truckee Meadows C.C., Reno, 1999—. Participant NEH Summer Seminar, Naples, Italy, 2000. Contbr. articles to profl. jours. Mem.: Coll. Art Assn., Archaeol. Inst. Am. Home Phone: 775-322-4229; Office Phone: 775-673-8269. Office Fax: 775-674-4853. Business E-Mail: cnaumer@tmcc.edu.

NAURATH, DAVID ALLISON, engineering psychologist, researcher; b. Houston, Mar. 11, 1927; s. Walter Arthur and Joy Frances (Bradbury) N.; m. Barbara Ellen Coverdell; children: Kathleen Ann, David Allen, Cynthia Ellyn, Randall Austin. BA, Simpson Coll., Indianola, Iowa, 1948; MA, Southern Meth. U., 1949; postgrad., U. Denver, 1955-57. Job analyst U.S. Air Force, San Antonio and Denver, 1951-55, rsch. psychologist Lowry AFB, Colo., 1955-60, Navy, Life Scis. & Systems div., Point Mugu, Calif., 1960-76; engrng. psychologist Navy Systems Engrng., Point Mugu, 1976-83; ret. Presenter at profl. socs. and orgns. in field. Contbr. articles to Jour. Engrng. Psychology, jour. Soc. for Info. Display, jour. Soc. Photo-optical Instrument Engrs. With USAAF, 1944-46. Mem. AAAS (life), IEEE (sr.), Am. Psychol. Assn., N.Y. Acad. Sci. (emeritus), Human Factors Soc. (panel mem. Certification of Human Factors Engrs. 1976), Soc. Engrng. Psychologists, Soc. for Info. Display (life). Methodist. Home: 5633 Pembroke St Ventura CA 93003-2200

NAVAB, APHRODITE DESIREE, artist, educator, writer; b. Esfahan, Iran, Oct. 31, 1971; arrived in U.S., 1980; d. Ali and Katina Navab; m. Richard C. Foltz, Aug. 21, 1994; children: Shahrzad Foltz-Navab, Bijan Foltz-Navab. BA magna cum laude, Harvard U., 1993; MA, EdM, Columbia U., 2000, EdD, 2004. Asst. prof. U. Fla., Gainesville, 2004—. Adj. asst. prof. U. Fla., 2000—02, grad. faculty supr., 2000—, faculty minority mentor, 2001—02, vis. asst. prof., 2002—04, faculty advisor undergrad. photography, 2002—, chair photography Sch. Arts & Art History, 2003—04. Contbr. articles to profl. jours.; one-woman shows include Bernice Steinbaum Gallery, Miami, Brown Gallery, Duke U., Durham, N.C., Charles Culpeper Photography Gallery, NYC. Recipient David McCord prize Outstanding Visual Artist, Harvard U., Cambridge, Mass., 1993. Mem.: Soc. Internat. Studies, Nat. Art Edn. Assn., Coll. Art Assn. Avocations: travel, languages, literature. E-mail: dnavab@ufl.edu.

NAVAR, LUIS GABRIEL, physiology educator, director, researcher; b. El Paso, Tex., Mar. 24, 1941; s. Luis and Concepcion (Najera) N.; m. Randa Ann Bumgarner, Oct. 15, 1965; children: Tonia, Tess, Gabriel, Daniel. BS, Tex. A&M U., 1962; PhD, U. Miss., 1966, postdoctoral study, 1966-69. Instr. dept. physiology/biophysics U. Miss., Jackson, 1966-67, asst. prof., 1967-71, assoc. prof., 1971-74, U. Ala., Birmingham, 1974-76, prof., 1976-88, assoc. prof. Nephrology Rsch. and Tng. Ctr., 1979-83, prof., 1983-88; prof., chmn. dept. physiology Tulane U. Med. Sch., New Orleans, 1988—, co-dir. Hypertension and Renal Ctr. of Excellence, 2001—. Vis. scientist Duke U. Med. Ctr., Durham, N.C., 1972-73; adv. bd. NIH Ctr. Sci. Rev., 1998-99; bd. dirs. Fedn. Am. Socs. Exptl. Biology, 1997-01. Assoc. editor News in Physiol. Scis., 1994-2000, Am. Jour. Physiology, 1983-89, mem. editl. bd., 1982-83, 97—; mem. editl. bd. Kidney Internat., 1976-87, Kidney, 1992—, Clin. Sci., 1994-99, Jour. Am. Soc. Nephrology, 1996-2001, Jour. Am. Soc. Nephrology, 1996-2001, Am. Jour. Kidney Disease, 1997-2001, Am. Jour. Hypertension, 1999—, Hypertension, 1980-83, 2002-04, assoc. editor, 1993-2000, cons. editor, 2006—; contbr. chpts. to books, articles to profl. jours. Cardiovascular and renal study sects. NIH, 1998—2000, chmn., 2000—02; bd. dirs. Consortium for Southeastern Hypertension Control, 1998—2000. Recipient Rsch. Career Devel. award, Nat. Heart, Lung and Blood Inst., 1974—79, Merit award, 1988—97, Bodil M. Schmidt Nielson Disting. Mentor and Scientist award, 2006, Lifetime Achievement award, COSEHC, 2006, Robert W. Berliner award for excellence in renal physiology, 2007; vis. scholar Pfizer/ACCF, 2002. Fellow: AAAS; mem.: High Blood Pressure Rsch. Am. Heart Assn., Assn. of Am. Med. Coll. (administrv. bd. of coun. of academic soc. 2004—), Assn. Chmn. Depts. Physiology (councillor 1993—95, pres.-elect 1995—96, pres. 1996—97, Disting. Svc. award 2003), Interam. Soc. Hypertension (chair awards com. 2003—), Am. Soc. Hypertension (coun. 1992—94, chmn. basic. sci. com. 1997, treas. 1997—2001, Richard Bright award 2001), Internat. Soc. Nephrology, Am. Soc. Nephrology, Am. Heart Assn. (chmn. cardiorenal rsch. study com. 1994—95, nat. rsch. com. 1994—99, Lewis K. Dahl Lectr. 1997, profl. and pub. edn. com. 1999—, chmn. coun. high blood pressure rsch. 2006—, kidney, high blood pressure couns., vice chmn. leadership com. coun. high blood pressure rsch., Sci. Coun. Disting. Achievement award 1999, Corcoran Lectr. award 2001), Am. Physiol. Soc. (coun. 1991—94, Gottschalk Disting. Lectr. Renal Physiology 1997, pres.-elect 1997—98, pres. 1998—99, Bodil M. Schmidt-Nielson Disting. Mentor and Sci. award 2006, Robert W. Berliner award 2007). Democrat. Roman Catholic. Home: 10020 Hyde Pl New Orleans LA 70123-1522 Office: Tulane U Med Sch Dept Physiology 1430 Tulane Ave New Orleans LA 70112-2699 Home Phone: 504-738-5547; Office Phone: 504-988-5251. Business E-Mail: navar@tulane.edu.

NAVARRA, TOVA, writer, artist; b. Newark, July 10, 1948; d. Joe and Rose Leslie Treihart; m. John G. Navarra Jr., Aug. 26, 1967 (div. 1998); children: Yolanda, John G. III; m. Robert B. Kern, July 10, 2004. BA magna cum laude, Seton Hall Univ., 1974; AAS, Brookdale C.C., Lincroft, NJ, 1984; postgrad., Fairleigh Dickinson U. Elem. sch. tchr., Jersey City, 1967-69; corr. Village Times, Long Island, NY, 1974-75; tchr. music, humanities, German, art, art history Seton Hall Prep. Sch., South Orange, NJ, 1975-78; entertainment, feature writer, press corr. Asbury Park Press, Neptune, NJ, 1978-85, feature writer, art critic, family writer, 1985-92; feature writer, art columnist Two River Times, Red Bank, NJ, 1993-94. Psychiatric charge nurse, 1985; supr. grant rsch. Vis. Nurse Assn. Ctrl. Jersey, Red Bank, NJ, 1993-94; art coord. Monmouth Players, Navesink, NJ; lectr. at writing confs; instr. Bayshore fitness and Wellness Ctr., Hazlet, NJ, 2005. Author: The New Jersey Shore: A Vanishing Splendor, 1985, Jim Gary: His Life and Art, 1987, Your Body: Highlights of Human Anatomy, 1990, Playing It Smart: What to Do When You're on Your Own, 1989, also, pub. On My Own: Helping Kids Help Themselves, (translated into Italian, Portuguese and Hebrew) 1994, 2d edit., 2003, An Insider's Guide to Home Health Care: An Interdisciplinary Approach (with Margaret Lundrigan), 1995, Wisdom for Caregivers, 1995; (staged readings) Through the Kunai Grass with Dad, 1988, Don't Cry, Pandora, 1989; (with Myron A. Lipkowitz and John G. Navarra) Therapeutic Communication: A Guide to Effective Interpersonal Skills for Health Care Professionals, 1990, Encyclopedia of Vitamins, Minerals, and Supplements, 1995, 2d edit., 2004; (with Lipkowitz), Allergies A-Z, 1994; Images of America: Howell and Farmingdale 1996; (with Lundrigan) Image of America: Levittown: The First Fifty Years, 1997, Staten Island, 1997, Staten Island II, 1998, Levittown II, 1998; Toward Painless Writing, 1998; The American Century: Staten Island (with Lundrigan), 1999; Seton Hall University: A Photographic History, 1999, Monmouth University, 2001, A Kids Guidebook: Great Advice to Help Kids Cope, 2002, Encyclopedia of Asthma and Respiratory Disorders, 2003, Young People/Tough Problems, 2003, Encyclopedia of Allergies 2d edit., 2004, Encyclopedia of Complementary and Alternative Medicine, 2004; illustrator Drugs and Man, 1973; editor in chief Shore Affinity, 1979-81; contbg. editor Am. Jour. Nursing, 1990-94, "d." Mag., Red Bank, NJ, 2007; staff writer, illustrator, photographer NJ Music and Arts, 1978-81; editor Associated Univ. Presses, 1981-82; copywriter, photographer Jersey Shore Med. Ctr., 1985; feature writer, columnist Copley News Svc., 1988-93; health trend columnist Personal Fitness, 1989-90; assoc. editor The Courier, Middletown, NJ, May-Dec. 1998; assoc. contbg. editor M.A.R. Mag., Red Bank, 2005; lifestyle editor The Two River Times, Red Bank, May 1999-2000; contr. to Nursing Spectrum Mag.; photography exhbns. in NY, NJ, Pa. Mid-Atlantic Riviera Magazine, 2005; guest various radio and TV programs; contbr. photographs to books, articles and photogs. to mags., newspapers; solo exhibits include Atlantic City Art Ctr., 1982, O.K. Harris Works of Art, NYC, 1990, Gallery Axiom, Phila., 1991, Monmouth U., 1991, M. Thomson Kravetz Gallery, Bay Head, NJ, Oceanic Pub. Libr., 2000, Navesink Libr. Theater, 2004, 05; two-person exhbn. Tova Navarra and Santo Pezzutti: Two Visions at 800 Gallery, Monmouth U., 2007, AAA World's Photo Contest award, 2006; group shows at Art Forms, Red Bank, 1991, Moravian Coll., Bethlehem, Pa., 1992. Mem. Gov.'s Coun. on Alcoholism and Drug Abuse Prevention, co-chair Later Childhood subcom., 1992 Mem. NJ Playwrights Workshop (charter), NJ State Nurses Assn. Avocations: singing, guitar, piano, dance, crafts. Office: Sanford J Greenburger Assocs care Faith H Hamlin 55 5th Ave New York NY 10003-4301

NAVARRETE, JORGE EDUARDO, ambassador; b. Mexico City, Apr. 29, 1940; s. Gabriel and Lucrecia (Lopez) N.; m. Marie Bolaños, 1965 (dec. Sept. 1985); 1 child, Federico Navarrete Linares; m. Angeles Salceda, July 31, 1986. BA in Econs., U. Mexico, 1970. Head econ. studies Nat. Fgn. Trade Bank, Mexico City, 1967-72; Mexican ambassador to Venezuela, 1972-75, Austria, 1976, Yugoslavia, 1977-78, UN, 1979; undersec. econ. affairs Ministry Fgn. Affairs, Mexico City, 1979-85; ambassador to Eng. London, 1986—. Author: Latin American External Debt, 1987. Avocation: chess.

NAVARRO, BRUCE CHARLES, lawyer; b. West Lafayette, Ind., Oct. 30, 1954; s. Joseph Anthony and Dorothy Gloria (Gnazzo) N.; children: Philip Joseph, Joanna Christina; m. Andrea Fox; children: Christi Renee, Karina Michelle. BA, Duke U., 1976; JD, Ind. U., 1980. Bar: D.C. 1980. Asst. counsel U.S. Senate Labor Subcom., Washington, 1981; acting dep. undersec. for legis. affairs Dept. Labor, Washington, 1984—85; atty. advisor EEOC, Washington, 1985—86; dir. Office of Congl. Rels. Office of Pers. Mgmt., Washington, 1986—89; prin. dep. asst. atty. gen. for legis. U.S. Dept. of Justice, Washington, 1989—91; spl. asst. to gen. counsel U.S. Dept. HHS, Washington, 1991; expert cons. U.S. Dept. Def., Washington, 1992; counsel to the vice chmn. U.S. Consumer Product Safety Commn., Bethesda, Md., 1992—95; prin. Navarro Regulatory and Legis. Affairs, Washington, 1995—, Fabiani & Co., Washington, 2005—. Mem. Arlington County (Va.) Rep. Com., 1983; bd. dirs. Prince William Cmty. Safe Kids Coalition, 1997-99, 2005—. Mem. D.C. Bar Assn. Roman Catholic. Avocations: music, golf. Home: 12631 Magic Springs Way Bristow VA 20136 Office: Fabiani and Co 1101 Pennsylvania Ave NW Ste 700 Washington DC 20004 also: 1250 Connecticut Ave Ste 200 Washington DC 20036 Office Phone: 202-955-6006, 202-756-4583. Personal E-mail: nlra@verizon.net. Business E-Mail: bnavarro@fabiani-co.com.

NAVARRO, DAVE (DAVID MICHAEL NAVARRO), musician, recording artist; b. Santa Monica, Calif., June 7, 1967; s. James Raul 'Mike' and Constance Colleen (Hopkins) Navarro; m. Carmen Electra, Nov. 22, 2003 (div. Feb. 20, 2007). Mem. band Jane's Addiction, 1986-91, 1997, Red Hot Chili Peppers, 1993—97, Spread; working with the band The Panic Channel. Recordings include (with Jane's Addiction) Jane's Addiction, 1987, Nothing's Shocking, 1988, Ritual de lo Habitual, 1990, (with Red Hot Chili Peppers) One Hot Minute, 1995, (solo album) Trust No One. 2001; composer (Films) Ugly Meets the People, 1995, Twister, 1996, Private Parts, 1997, Bringing Out the Dead, 1999, Ordinary Decent Criminal, 2000, Anger Management, 2003, S.W.A.T., 2003, Torque, 2004, (video) Soul Kiss, 1989 (also actor), Gift, 1993 (also actor), (video game) Grand Theft Auto: San Andreas, 2004; prodr., exec. prodr. Three Days, 1999; actor (TV mini series) House of Style, 1996-, I Love the 80s Strikes Back, 2003, Til' Death Do Us Part: Carmen & Dave, 2004, I Love the 90s, 2004, I Love the 90s Part Deux, 2005, (TV) Set in Skin, 2002, Carmen & Dave: An MTV Love Story, 2002, The Osbourne Family Christmas Special, 2003, (film) Sexual Intent, 1994, Floundering, 1994, Uptown Girls, 2003; co-host, Rock Stars 2005-; performer Camp Freddy, Lollapalooza, 2003-04; appeared in music video for Moby, "We Are All Made of Stars"; guest appearances include: Martial Law, 1999, Charmed, 2001, Punk'd, 2004, Celebrity Poker Showdown, 2004,Celebrity Blackjack, 2004 and MADtv, 2004 and several others; author Dont' Try This At Home, 2004. Office: care Warner Bros Records 3300 Warner Blvd Burbank CA 91505-4632

NAVARRO, GUILLERMO, cinematographer; b. Mexico City, Mex., 1955; Cinematographer: (films) El Salvador: Another Vietnam, 1981, Una Moneda en el Aire, 1990, Bathroom Intimacy, 1990, Dollar Mambo, 1993, Blade II, 2002; photographer (films) Amor a la Vuelta de la Esquina, 1986, dir. photography Morir en el Golfo, 1989, Cabeza de Vaca, 1992, Vinaya, 1993, Cronos, 1994, Four Rooms, 1995, Desperado, 1995, The Long Kiss Goodnight, 1996, Spawn, 1997, Jackie Brown, 1997, Dream For An Insomniac, 1998, Stuart Little, 1999, The Devil's Backbone, 2001, Broken Silence, 2001, Imagining Argentina, 2004, Hellboy, 2004, Zathura: A Space Adventure, 2005, Pan's Labyrinth, 2006 (Best Cinematographer, NY Film Critics Circle award, 2006, Best Cinematography, Acad. award, 2007), Night At the Museum, 2006, camera operator, dir. photography From Dusk Till Dawn, 1996, actor, dir. photography Spy Kids, 2001. *

NAVARRO, JOSEPH ANTHONY, retired statistician, consultant; b. New Britain, Conn., July 6, 1927; s. Charles C. and Josephine V. (Bianco) N.; m. Dorothy G. Gnazzo; children: Kenneth M., Bruce C., Joseph S. BS, Cen. Conn. State U., 1950; MS, Purdue U., 1952, PhD, 1955. Rsch. staff, cons. GE, 1955-59; rsch. staff, mgmt. IBM, 1962-64; sr. staff mem., asst. dir. Inst. Def. Analyses, Alexandria, Va., 1964-72; pres., chief oper. officer System Planning Corp., Arlington, Va., 1972-86; dep. undersec. test and evaluation Dept. Defense, Washington, 1986-87; now pvt. practice cons., 1987—2005; pres. Wackenhut Applied Technologies Ctr., Fairfax, Va., 1989-90; ret., 2005. Contbr. articles to profl. jours. Mem. Bd. Trade, Washington, 1983-85. Mem. Internat. Test and Evaluation Assn. Clubs: COSMOS (Washington). Republican. Roman Catholic. Home: 8010 Grand Teton Dr Potomac MD 20854-4074 Personal E-mail: jadgnav@comcast.net.

NAVARRO, MONICA, lawyer; b. 1967; arrived in US, 1984; m. Mark Crane. BA in Polit. Sci. and Internat. Rels., Fla. Internat. U., 1990; JD, U. Mich. Law Sch., 1993. Bar: Ill., Mich., US Supreme Ct., US Ct. of Appeals Sixth Cir., US Dist. Ct. Eastern Dist. Mich., US Dist. Ct. Western Dist. Mich. Judicial clerk Hon. Julian Abele Cook, Jr., US Dist. Ct., Eastern Dist. Mich.; atty. Frank, Haron; prin. mem., ptnr. Frank, Haron, Weiner and Navarro, 2004—. Mem., HIPAA Compliance Com. Troy Chamber of Commerce; trustee Mich. Psychoanalytic Found. Guest Hospitals and

Physicians: Friends and Foes, Bloomfield Cmty. TV, 2006. Named one of Top 10 Qui Tam Lawyers in Country, Corp. Crime Reporter, 40 Under 40, Crain's Detroit Bus., 2006; recipient Am. Jurisprudence award in Adminstrv. Law, Best Oralist award. Fellow: Oakland County Bar Found.; mem.: State of Mich. Bd. Psych., Mich. Trial Lawyers Assn., Assn. Trial Lawyers Am., Oakland County Women's Bar Assn. (Work Life balance award 2006), Oakland County Bar Assn. (Med./Legal Com.), Mich. Assn. Health Lawyers (mem. Tech. Subcommittee), Hispanic Bar Assn. Mich., Am. Health Lawyers Assn. Office: Frank, Haron, Weiner and Navarro 5435 Corporate Dr Ste 225 Troy MI 48098 Office Phone: 248-952-0400. Office Fax: 248-952-0890. Business E-Mail: mnavarro@fhwnlaw.com.

NAVARRO, RICHARD, banker; BA in Econs.; MSc in Fin., Fla. Internat. U., 1996. Chartered fin. analyst. Investment ops. analyst Loan Am. Fin. Corp., Miami Lakes, Fla., 1992-93, trader, 1993-95; credit analyst Eurobank, Coral Gables, Fla., 1995-97; sr. credit analyst Banco Santander Internat., Miami, Fla., 1997-98, pvt. banking officer, 1998—. Address: 18342 SW 33rd St Miramar FL 33029-1625

NAVAS, WILLIAM ANTONIO, JR., civilian military employee and retired officer; b. Mayaguez, PR, Dec. 15, 1942; s. William Antonio Sr. and Ethel Ines (Marin) N.; m. Wilda Margarita Cordova Navas, Aug. 7, 1965; children: William Antonio III, Gretchen Maria. BSCE, U. P.R., 1965; MS in Engring. Mgmt., U. Bridgeport, 1979. Registered profl. engr., P.R. Commd. 2d. lt. U.S. Army, 1966, advanced through grades to maj. gen., 1990, ret., 1998; served in U.S. Army Corps of Engrs., 1966-70; project engr. Empresas Navas, Inc., Mayaguez, P.R., 1970-72; ptnr., prin. W.A. Navas Jr. & Assocs., Mayaguez, 1972-80; dir. Navas & Moreda, Inc., Mayaguez, 1973-81; with Interamerican Def. Coll., Washington, 1981-82; dir. ops. P.R. Army Nat. Guard, San Juan, 1982-84, 84-87; comdr. Engr. Task Force, Panama, 1984; dep. dir. Army Nat. Guard, Washington, 1987-97; vice chief Nat. Guard Bur., 1990; mil. exec. reserve. forces policy bd. US Dept. Def., 1992-94, dep. asst. sec., 1994-95; dir. Army Nat. Guard, 1995—98; asst. sec. for manpower & reserve affairs, Dept. Navy US Dept. Def., Washington, 2001—. Chmn. Dept. of Army Hispanic Employment Commn., Washington, 1988. Decorated Knight Eq. Order of Holy Sepulchre. Mem. Nat. Guard Assn. of the U.S. (del. 1980-86), Nat. Guard Assn. of P.R., Soc. of Am. Mil. Engrs. Roman Catholic. Avocations: militaria collection, reading, running, travel, tennis. Office: US Dept Defense Manpower Reserve Affairs 1000 Navy Pentagon Washington DC 20350-1000 E-mail: bnavas@aol.com.

NAVASKY, VICTOR SAUL, publisher; b. NYC, July 5, 1932; s. Macy and Esther Blanche (Goldberg) N.; m. Anne Landey Strongin, Mar. 27, 1966; children: Bruno, Miri, Jenny. AB, Swarthmore Coll., 1954; LL.B., Yale U., 1959. Spl. asst. to Gov. G. Mennen Williams, Mich., 1959-60; editor, pub. Monocle Mag., 1961-65; editor NY Times mag., 1970-72, The Nation mag., NYC, 1978-94, pub., gen. ptnr., 1995—2005, pub. emeritus, 2005—; Delacorte prof. of mag. journalism Columbia U., NYC, 1999—; and chmn. Columbia Journalism Rev. Vis. scholarRussell Sage Found., 1975—76; Ferris prof. journalism Princeton U., 1976—77. Author: Kennedy Justice, 1971 (Nat. Book Award nominee), Naming Names, 1980 (Nat. Book award 1981), rev. edit., 1991, 2003, A Matter of Opinion, 2005 (recipient George S. Polk book award, 2006); editor: (with C. Cerf) The Experts Speak, 1984; playwright: (with Richard R. Lingeman) Starr's Last Tape, 1999. Mem. bd. mgrs. Swarthmore Coll., 1991-94; bd. trustees The New Sch. Served with U.S. Army, 1954-56. Guggenheim fellow, 1974-75; fellow Inst. of Politics, Harvard U., 1994; Sr. fellow Freedom Forum, 1994. Mem. Author's Guild (coun.), Com. To Protect Journalists (exec. com.), Phi Beta Kappa; fellow Am. Acad. Arts & Sciences Democrat. Jewish. Office Phone: 212-209-5411. Business E-Mail: vic@thenation.com.

NAVATTA, ANNA PAULA, lawyer; b. Hackensack, NJ, Jan. 7, 1956; d. Jack Anthony and Natalie (Pretto) N. BA, Rutgers U., 1978, MA, 1979; JD, Seton Hall U., 1982. Bar: N.J. 1983, U.S. Dist. Ct. N.J. 1983, U.S. Ct. Appeals (3d cir.) 1986. Law clk. to presiding justice Superior Ct. N.J., Hackensack, 1982-83; staff atty. Bergen County Legal Svcs., Hackensack, 1983—. Instr. Am. Inst. Paralegal Studies, Mahwah, N.J., 1986-95; atty. Lyndhurst (N.J.) Planning Bd., 1987-89. Mem. ABA, Fed. Bar Assn., N.J. State Bar Assn., Bergen County Bar Assn., Emblem Club. Democrat. Roman Catholic. Office: Northeast NJ Legal Svcs 61 Kansas St Hackensack NJ 07601-5351 Office Phone: 201-487-2166.

NAVE, J. L., performing company executive; b. Nashville, May 4, 1972; BA Conducting, Belmont U., 1994; MA Arts Adminstrn., U. Cin., 1997, MBA, 1997. Orch. mgr. Northeastern Pa. Philharm.; orch. mgmt. fellow Am. Symphony Orch. League; pres., CEO Baton Rouge Symphony Orch., 2000—. Ops. chair First Night Scranton; grant rev. panelist Pa. Coun. on Arts. Office: Baton Rouge Symphony Orch PO Box 14209 Baton Rouge LA 70898 Office Phone: 225-383-0500. E-mail: jlnave@brso.org.

NAVETTA, CHRISTOPHER J., metal products executive; BBA, Mich. State U., East Lansing, 1969. Cert. mgmt. acct. Acctg. trainee Gary Works US Steel, Ind., 1969—72, various fin. positions Chems. Divsn. Pitts., 1972—75, mgr. acctg. Molded Plastic Products Ind., 1975—76, mgr. acctg. West Coast Products Divsn. Alameda, Calif., 1976—79, staff asst. Ctrl. Steel Divsn. Chgo., 1979—81, staff supr. comml. analysis Pitts., 1981, various managerial acctg. positions, 1981—85, mgr. acctg. Fairless Works Pa., 1985—87, dir. analysis and gen. acctg. Pitts., 1987—89, gen. mgr. adminstrn., group comptr. Diversified Group, 1989—92, comptr. raw materials Diversified Bus. and Joint Ventures, 1992—94, gen. mgr. plate products Gary Works, 1994—2001, exec. v.p. US Steel Kosice, 2002—03, pres. US Steel Kosice, 2003—05, sr. v.p. procurement, logistics & diversified businesses, 2005—; pres. USX Engrs. and Consultants, Inc., 2001—02. Mem.: Inst. Mgmt. Accts. Office: US Steel 600 Grant St Pittsburgh PA 15219-2800 Office Phone: 412-433-1121. *

NAVIS, TIMOTHY JAMES, music minister; b. Sheboygan, Wis., Nov. 18, 1982; s. John Allen and Marge Mary Navis; m. Leslie Lou Dekker, Aug. 20, 2005; 1 child, Evan Cole. Grad., Oostburg HS, Wis., 2001. Asst. organist Oostburg Reformed Ch., 1999—, Hingham Reformed Ch., Wis., 1999—, 1st Reformed Ch., Oostburg, 1999—; landscaper McKay Nursery, Oostburg, 1999—; dir. music ministries Hope Reformed Ch., Sheboygan, 2001—; piano tchr. Sheboygan, 2001—; organist, bell dir. St. Luke's Meth. Ch., Sheboygan, 2005—. Organist McDowell Club of Milw., 2004. Mentor Luth. Social Svcs., Mantiwoc, Wis., 2004. Music scholar, Silver Lake Coll., Manitowoc, 2004—, music performance scholar, 2004—. Mem.: Am. Guild Organists, Music Educators Nat. Conf. (sec. 2004—). Home: 2405A Cleveland Ave Sheboygan WI 53081

NAVLAKHA, JAINENDRA, computer scientist, educator, dean; arrived in US, 1974; m. Surekha Jain, Sept. 14, 1980; children: Saral, Saket. B in Engring. with honors, Birla Inst. Tech. and Sci., Pilani, India, 1972; M in Tech., Indian Inst. Tech., Kanpur, India, 1974; PhD, Case Western Res. U., Cleve., 1977. Prof. computer sci. Sch. Computing and Info. Scis. Fla. Internat. U., Miami, 1987—, dir. Sch. Computer Sci., 1999—2002, assoc. dean grad. studies Coll. Engring. and Computing, 2006—. Mem. del. computer software specialists and engrs. People to People, China, 1983. Contbr. articles to profl. jours. Named Commr., Fla. Hurricane Loss Projection Methodology, CEO, State Fla., 2005—; Fulbright Sr. Scholar Specialist, Fulbright, 2004—. Mem.: IEEE Computer Soc. (Disting. Visitor 1984), Assn. Computing Machinery. Office: Florida International University College of Engineering and Computing Miami FL 33199 Home Phone: 305-271-6235; Office Phone: 305-348-2026. Office Fax: 305-348-6142. Business E-Mail: navlakha@fiu.edu.

NAVON, IONEL MICHAEL, mathematics professor; b. Bucharest, Romania, Apr. 28, 1940; s. David and Sarah (Schwartzman) N.; m. Lily Marcu, May 11, 1967; children: Daria, Livia. BSc in Math., Hebrew U. Jerusalem, 1967, MSc in Atmospheric Scis., 1971; PhD in Applied Math., U. Witwatersrand, Johannesburg, South Africa, 1979. Sr. rsch. meteorologist Israel Meteorol. Office, Tel Aviv, 1973-74; head applied math. sect. Tamam/Israel Aircraft Industry, Tel Aviv, 1974-76; sr. rsch. officer Counc. Sci. and Indsl. Rsch., Pretoria, South Africa, 1976-78, chief rsch. officer, 1979-80, sr. chief rsch. officer, 1981-83; sr. vis. scientist NASA/Goddard Space Flight Ctr., Greenbelt, Md., 1983-84; cons. NASA/Goddarad Space Flight Ctr., Greenbelt, Md., 1984-85; sr. specialist researcher Coun. Sci. and Indsl. Rsch., Pretoria, 1984-85; assoc. rsch. scientist Supercomputer Rsch. Inst., Tallahassee, Fla., 1985-87; assoc. prof. math. Fla. State U., Tallahassee, 1987-1990, prof., 1991—, program dir. optimization and optimal control, 1993—, hon. prof. dept. meteorology Supercomputer Rsch. Inst., 1987—, faculty assoc. Supercomputer Computation Rsch. Inst., 1988—, faculty assoc. Geophys. Fluid Dynamics Inst., 1989—, dir. applied math dept. math, 1998—. Dir. applied math. Fla. State U., 1998—; cons. Ctr. Analysis Prediction of Storms, Norman, Okla., 1989, French Navy, 1995; leader Argonne Nat. Lab.; co-organizer Internat. Conf. Element Methods in Geophysics, Tallahassee, 1991; summer lecture series scientist NASA, 1991—; mem. panel nat. experts to rev. and conduct site visiting Okla. Sci. and Tech. Ctr.; keynote spkr. Internat. Conf. on Finite Element Methods, South Africa, 1992, Internat. Conf. on Optimization Techniques and Applications, Singapore, 1992, Assimilation of Meteorological and Oceanographic Observations, France, 1993. Editor spl. issues Computer and Math. with Applications; editor Monthly Weather Rev., 1991-94; assoc. editor Monthly Weather Rev., 2001, Jour. for Numerical Linear Algebra with Applications, 1991, Computational Fluid Dynamics Jour., 1992; chief editor spl. issue Dynamics of Atmospheres and Oceans, 1998; spl. editor Internat. Jour. on Computational Fluid Dynamics, 2003; contbr. over 95 refereed articles to sci. jours. Lt. Israel Civil Def., 1960-63. Grantee NSF, 1988, 91, 94—, 98-2001, 2002, 2003-06, NASA, 1991, 94, 97-99, 2006-; rsch. grantee Air Force Office Sci., 1989, 91, 94. Fellow Am. Meteorol. Soc.; Nat. Rsch. Coun. NASA/GSFC Delta Assimilation Office, 2000 (sr.); mem. Am. Math. Soc., Am. Geophys. Union, Soc. Indsl. and Applied Math. (organizer symposiums 2004-05), Israel Assn. Profl. Engrs., Am. Computing Machinery Assn. Avocations: ping-pong, photography, books. Home: 3138 Ferns Glen Dr Tallahassee FL 32309-2304 Office: Fla State U Ditac Sci Library Bldg Rm 483 Tallahassee FL 32306 Office Phone: 850-644-6560. Business E-Mail: navon@ses.fsu.edu.

NAVRATILOVA, MARTINA, professional tennis player; b. Prague, Czech Republic, Oct. 18, 1956; came to US, 1975, naturalized, 1981; d. Miroslav Navratil and Jana Navratilova. Student, schs. in Czechoslovakia; Hon. doctorate, George Washington U., 1996. Tennis commentator/broadcaster HBO Sports, 1995-99; Profl. tennis player, 1973-94, 2003—06. Player Czech Fed. Cup Team, 1975, U.S. Fed Cup Team, 1982, 86, 89, 95, 2003; mem. World Team Tennis, 1990—. Author: (with George Vecsey) Martina, 1985; (with Liz Nickles) The Total Zone, 1995, Breaking Point, 1996, Killer Instinct, 1997, Shape Your Self: My 6-Step Diet and Fitness Plan to Achieve the Best Shape of Your Life, 2006; columnist. Co-founder Rainbow Card. Winner Czechoslovak Nat. singles, 1972-74, U.S. Open singles, 1983, 84, 86, 87, U.S. Open doubles, 1977, 78, 80, 83, 84, 87, 90, U.S. Open mixed doubles, 1987, 2006, Va. Slims Championsips, 1978, 83, 84, 85, 86, Va. Slims Championships, 1991, Wimbledon singles, 1978, 79, 82, 83, 84, 85, 86, 87, 90, Wimbledon women's doubles, 1976, 79, 81, 82, 83, 84, 86, Wimbledon mixed doubles, 1985, 93, 95, 2003, French Open singles, 1982, 84, Australian Open singles, 1981, 83, 85, Australian Doubles (with Betsy Nagelsen) 1980, (with Pam Shriver), 1982, 84, 85, 87, 88, 89, Australian Mixed Doubles, 2003, Roland Garros (with Pam Shriver), 1985, 87, 89, Italian Open doubles (with Gabriela Sabatini), 1987, (with Pam Shriver) COREL WTA Tour doubles team of yr., 1981-89, triple Crown at U.S. Open, 1987; recipient Women's Sports Found. Flo Hyman award, 1987, BBC Lifetime Achievement Award, 2003; named Female Athlete of the Decade (1980s) The Nat. Sports Review, UPI, and AP, WTA Player of Yr., 1978-79, 82-86, Women's Sports Found. Sportswoman of Yr., 1982-84, Hon. Citizen of Dallas, AP Female Athlete of Yr., 1983; named to Internat. Tennis Hall of Fame, 2000; Martina Navratilova Day proclaimed in Chgo., 1992 Mem. Women's Tennis Assn. (dir., exec. com., pres.), Women's Tennis Assn. Tour Player's Assn. (pres. 1979-80, 83-84, 94-95). Achievements include being the holder of 167 singles titles and 173 doubles titles; holder of record of singles-match wins (1,309), 1991; holds record for 109 consecutive doubles matches won (with Pam Shriver).

NAWAB, AKHTAR, chef; Attended, Calif. Culinary Acad. Chef Gramercy Tavern, NYC; sous chef Craft, NYC, 2001; exec. chef Craftbar, EU, NYC. Named one of NYC's Rising Stars, StarChefs.com, 2007. Office: EU 235 E 4th St New York NY 10009 Office Phone: 212-254-2900. *

NAWROCKI, DAVID NORMAN, finance educator; b. East Chicago, Ind., Jan. 9, 1950; s. Arnold Norman and Jean (Kettring) N.; m. D. Christine Thomas, June 7, 1975; children: Jodi Lynmarie, Bryan Christopher. BS in Fin., Pa. State U., 1970, MBA, 1972, PhD, 1976. Econ. analyst Girard Bank, Phila., 1972-73; cons. Morgan Guaranty Trust, NYC, 1974-75; instr. Pa. State U., University Park, 1971-75; asst. prof. fin. Drexel U., Phila., 1975-81; prof. fin. Villanova U., Pa., 1981—; Katherine M. and Richard J. Salisbury Jr. prof. fin. Villanova U., Pa., 2004—. Dir. Inst. for Rsch. in Advanced Fin. Tech., 2004—; pres. Computer Handholders, Arcola, Pa., 1982—, The Q Insight Group, San Diego, 1994—; vis. prof. San Diego State U., 1991-92. Contbr. articles to fin. jours., 1973—; author (software) Portfolio Mgmt., 1983, CAPBUD, 1985; assoc. editor Fin. Rev., 1992-98, Internat Rev. of Fin. Analysis, 1992—; mem editl. adv. bd. Jour. of Fin. Planning, 1997—. Den leader Cub Scout Pack 119, Evansburg, Pa., 1990-95; adult leader Boy Scout Troop, 119, Evansburg, 1995-97, assoc. leader Explorer Post 119, 1997-99. Recipient Order of the Four Chaplains, Chapel of the Four Chaplains, Phila., 1981; Ben Franklin grantee State of Pa., Harrisburg, 1991. Mem. Am. Econ. Assn., Am. Fin. Assn., Ea. Fin. Assn., Beta Gamma Sigma, Phi Kappa Phi. Avocations: piano, flying, computers, travel. Office: Villanova U Fin Dept 800 Lancaster Ave Villanova PA 19085-1603 Mailing: Computer Handholder %D Nawrocki 96 Fenwick Cir Collegeville PA 19426-3414 E-mail: David.Nawrocki@villanova.edu.

NAYAK, LAXMEESH MIKE, plastic surgeon; b. Effingham, Ill. BS in Molecular Biophysics and Biochemistry summa cum laude, Yale U., New Haven, 1994; MD, Washington U. Sch. Medicine, St. Louis, 1998. Cert. Am. Bd. Facial Plastic and Reconstructive Surgery, Am. Bd. Otolaryngology/Head and Neck Surgery, Nat. Bd. Med. Examiners, lic. NJ, NY, Ill., Mo. Intern gen. surgery Harvard Med. Sch., Mass. Gen. Hosp., Boston, 1998—99; resident otolaryngology/head and neck surgery Harvard Med. Sch., Mass. Eye and Ear Infirmary, Boston, 1999—2003; fellowship Am. Acad. Facial Plastic and Reconstructive Surgery, Glasgold Group, Highland Pk., NJ, 2003—04; dir. divsn. facial plastic and reconstructive surgery, asst. prof. otolaryngology/head and neck surgery St. Louis U. Sch. Medicine, 2004—06, clin. asst. prof. divsn. facial plastic and reconstructive surgery, 2006—. Clin. instr. otology and laryngology Harvard Med. Sch., 1998—2003; vol. clin. instr. surgery U. Medicine and Dentistry NJ U. Hosp., Newark, 2003—04, attending in surgery otolaryngology/head and neck surgery, 2003—04, Robert Wood Johnson U. Hosp., 2003—04; attending otolaryngology/head and neck surgery St. John's Hosp., 2004—, St. Louis U. Hosp., 2004—06, Cardinal Glennon Children's Hosp., St. Louis, 2004—06; dir. facial and cosmetic surgery Nayak Plastic Surgery; presenter in field. Contbr. articles to profl. jours. Named Clin. Prof. of Yr., St. Louis U. Sch. Medicine, 2006; recipient Resident Rsch. award, Triological Soc., 2002, Jack Anderson prize for Scholastic Excellence, 1st Runner Up, Am. Bd. Facial Plastic Surgery, 2004. Mem.: AMA, Am. Acad. Aesthetic Lipodissolve, Am. Acad. Otolaryngology/Head and Neck Surgery, Am. Acad. Facial Plastic and Reconstructive Surgery, Alpha Omega Alpha, Phi Beta Kappa (Alpha of Conn.). Avocations: music, scuba diving, digital media, fitness, wind instruments, singing. Office: 763 S New Ballas Rd Ste 204 Saint Louis MO 63141 Office Phone: 314-991-5438. Office Fax: 314-991-2914. *

NAYAR, BALDEV RAJ, political science professor; b. Gujrat Dist., India, Oct. 26, 1931; arrived in Canada, 1964; s. Jamna Das and Durga Devi (Marwah) N.; m. Nancy Ann Skinner, Aug. 27, 1961; children— Sheila Jane, Kamala Elizabeth, Sunita Maria. BA, Punjab U., 1953; MA, 1956, U. Chgo., 1959, PhD, 1963. Asst. prof. Calif. State Coll., Hayward, 1963-64; mem. faculty dept. polit. sci. McGill U., 1964-94, assoc. prof., 1966-71, prof., 1971-94, prof. emeritus, 1996—, assoc. chmn., 1990-93. Rsch. assoc. Internat. Devel. Rsch. Centre, 1978 Author: Minority Politics in the Punjab, 1966, National Communication and Language Policy, 1969, The Modernization Imperative and Indian Planning, 1972, American Geopolitics and India, 1976, India's Quest for Technological Independence, 1983, India's Mixed Economy, 1989, The Political Economy of India's Public Sector, 1990, Superpower Dominance and Military Aid, 1991, The State and International Aviation in India, 1994, The State and Market in India's Shipping, 1996, Globalization and Nationalism, 2001, India and the Major Powers After Pokhran II, 2001; co-author: India in the World Order, 2003, The Geopolitics of Globalization, 2005, India's Globalization, 2006. Bd. dirs. Shastri Indo-Canadian Inst., 1970-72, sr. fellow, 1978, 86. Recipient Watumull prize Am. Hist. Assn., 1966; Charles E. Merriam fellow, 1957; Carnegie Study New Nations fellow, 1962; Can. Council sr. fellow, 1967, 74; SSHRC leave fellow, 1982 Mem. Can. Asian Studies Assn. Office: McGill Univ Dept Polit Sci Montreal PQ Canada H3A 2T7 Home Phone: 514-932-3373. E-mail: baldev.nayar@mcgill.ca.

NAYDAN, MICHAEL M., foreign language educator; b. Trenton, NJ, Oct. 20, 1952; s. William and Anna (Yaremko) N.; m. Roxanne Robak; 1 child Liliana Marika. BA magna cum laude, The American U., Washington, 1973, MA, 1975; MPh, Columbia U., NYC, 1980, PhD, 1984. Asst. prof. Yale U., New Haven, 1982-86; vis. asst. prof. Rutgers U., New Brunswick, NJ, 1986-88; asst. prof. Pa. State U., Univ. Park, 1988-90, assoc. prof., 1990—96, prof., 1996—. Gen. asst. Columbia U. Bakhmeteff Archive of Russian and East European History and Culture, 1979-81; adj. instr. Russian Rutgers U., Newark, 1982; preceptor and instr. Russian, Columbia Univ., 1980-82; acting instr. Russian Yale U., 1982-84; head of instruction Yale Russian and Slavic Summer Lang. Inst., 1984-86; panelist, lectr. on Russian and Slavic poets at convs. and meetings of nat. and internat. orgns. Translator: (books) The Poetry of Lina Kostenko: Wanderings of the Heart, 1990, Marina Tsvetaeva's After Russia, 1992, From Three Worlds: New Writing from Ukraine, 1996, Yuri Vynnchuk's The Windows of Time Frozen and other Stories, 2000, Pavlo Tychyna's The Complete Early Poetry Collections of Pavlo Tychyna, 2000, A Hundred Years of Youth: A Bilingual Anthology of Ukrainian Poetry, 2000, Landscapes of Memory: Selected Later Poetry of Lina Kostenko, 2002, Olga Sedakova's Poems and Elegies, 2003, Igor Klekh's A Country the Size of Binoculars, 2004, Yuri Andrukhovych's Perverzion, 2005, Viktor Neborak's The Flying Head and Other Poems, 2006, The Grand Harmony, 2007; contbr. articles and reviews to profl. jours. and encyclopedias, translations in book chpts., journals and periodicals; contbr. poetry to Monmouth Review, 1975, Poet Lore, 1977, Bitterroot, 1979; editor-in-chief Slavic and East European Jour., 1993-98; assoc. editor Comparative Literature Studies, 1990—; assoc. editor and co-founder Ulbandus Review: A Jour. of Slavic Langs. and Lits., 1977-84. Recipient Pushkin prize, 1975, 76, 81, Columbia U., Eugene Kayden Meritorious Achievement award in translation, U. Colo., 1993, Mihaly-Mogilat fellowship, Columbia U., 1979; grantee Schevchenko Scholarly Soc., 1980, Moore Fund, 1983-84, NJ Dept Higher Edn., 1987-88 (2), Woskob Fellow in Humanities, Nat. Endowment for the Humanities, 1991-92, 95. Mem. Am. Assn. for Advancement of Slavic Studies, Am. Assn. Tchrs. of Slavic and East European Langs., Am. Assn. Ukrainian Studies (v.p.), Phi Kappa Phi. Avocations: tennis, squash. Office: Pa State Univ Germanic andSlavic Studies Dept 311 Burrowes Bldg University Park PA 16802-5201

NAYERI, ALI, physicist, educator; Rsch. scientist MIT, Cambridge, 1999—2002; rsch. assoc., lectr. Harvard U., Cambridge, 2004—. Mem. Iranian Studies Grp. MIT, 2002. Mem.: Am. Phys. Soc. Achievements include research in string cosmology, gravity in higher dimensions. Office: Harvard Univ 17 Oxfordt St Cambridge MA 02138

NAYLON, MICHAEL EDWARD, retired army officer; b. Rochester, NY, Jan. 15, 1943; s. Edward M. and Patricia (Brennan) N.; m. Beverly Marzano, Mar. 27, 1965; children: Michelle A. Faber, Colleen M. Burgos. BA, John Carroll U., 1965; MBA, Marymount U., 1986; grad., U.S. Army War Coll., 1989. Indsl. rels. specialist Gen. Ry. Signal Co., Rochester, Farrell Co., Rochester; manpower adminstr. City of Rochester; employment mgr. U. Rochester; pers. dir. Interstate Brands Corp., Rochester; office mgr., dir. adminstrn., regional tng. coord. Nat. Machine Tool Builders Assn., McLean, Va.; chief U.S Army Res. Hdqs. Dept. of Army, Washington; staff officer Joint Chiefs of Staff, col., sr. res. advisor Dept. Def., Washington; with U.S. So. Command, Panama City, Panama; col. U.S. Army, ret. Dir. ops. Nat. Assn. Ret. Fed. Employees; nat. exec. dir. AMVETS; exec. dir. Presdl. Spl. Oversight Bd., Dept. Def. investigations of Gulf War chem. and biol. incidents; chief of staff Nat. Com. Employer Support of Guard and Res., Arlington, Va.; dep. dir. Office of Asst. Sec. of Def. for Res. Affairs, Pentagon, Washington. Mem. VFW, AMVETS, U.S. Army War Coll. Alumni Assn., John Carroll U. Alumni Assn., Res. Officers Assn. USA, Ret. Officers Assn., Am. Legion, Vietnam Vets. Home: 1434 Aldenham Ln Reston VA 20190-3901 E-mail: naylonmike@juno.com.

NAYLOR, C. DAVID, academic administrator; b. Woodstock, Ont., Canada, 1954; s. Thomas and Edna Anne (Aziz) Naylor; m. Ilse Treurnicht; children: Karli, Melinda, Sam, Max. MD (hon.), U. Toronto, 1978; Rhodes Scholar, Oxford U., 1979; DPhil, 1983. Fellow Royal Coll. Physicians & Surgeons, 1986; trainee in gen. internal medicine U. Western Ontario, 1983—86; fellow in clin. epidemiology Med. Rsch. Coun. Can., Toronto, 1986—87; asst. prof. dept. medicine U. Toronto, 1988—92, assoc. prof., 1992—96, prof., 1996—, dean of medicine, 1999—2005, vice provost, Relations with Health Care Institutions, 1999—2005, pres., 2005—. Head rsch. program Sunnybrook Health Sci. Ctr., Toronto, 1990—96; CEO Inst. Clin. Evaluative Sciences, 1991—98; sr. scientist Med. Rsch. Coun. Can., 1999; editorial bd. Jour. Am. Med. Assn., Brit. Med. Jour., 1996—98, Can. Med. Assn. Jour., 1996—2000. Co-author approximately 300 scholarly publications. Chair Nat. Adv. Com. on SARS & Pub. Health, Canada, 2003. Decorated officer Order of Can.; recipient John Dinham Cottrell medal, Royal Australasian Coll. Physicians, 1996, Malcolm Brown award, Royal Coll. Physicians & Surgeons, 1996, Michael Smith award, Med. Rsch. Coun., 1999, Rsch. Achievement award, Can. Cardiovascular Soc., 2002, Defries award, Can. Pub. Health Assn., 2005. Fellow: Royal Soc. Can.; mem.: Inst. Medicine (fgn. assoc.). Office: UToronto Office of the President 27 King's College Circle Toronto ON Canada M5S 1A1 Home Phone: 416-929-3800; Office Phone: 416-978-2121. E-mail: president@utoronto.ca.

NAYLOR, JAMES CHARLES, psychologist, educator; b. Chgo., Feb. 8, 1932; s. Joseph Sewell and Berniece (Berg) N.; m. Georgia Lou Mason, Feb. 14, 1953; children— Mary Denise, Diana Darice, Shari Dalice. BS, Purdue U., 1957, MS, 1958, PhD, 1960. Asst. prof. Ohio State U., 1960-63, asso. prof., 1963-67, prof. vice chmn. dept. psychology, 1967-68; prof.

Purdue U., Lafayette, Ind., 1968-86, head dept. psychol. scis., 1968-79; prof., chmn. dept. psychology Ohio State U., Columbus, 1986-98, prof. emeritus, 1999—. Fulbright rsch. scholar, Umea, Sweden, 1976; Disting. scholar, vis. scientist Flinders U., South Australia, 1982-83, UNESCO ednl. cons. to Hangzhou U., Peoples Republic of China, 1984; chmn. Coun. Grad. Depts. Psychology, 1993-94; lead reviewer Psychology Program Rev., State U. Sys. Fla., 1996. Author: Industrial Psychology, 1968, A Theory of Behavior in Organizations, 1980; founder, editor: Organizational Behavior and Human Decision Processes; mem. editorial bd.: Prof. Psychology; Contbr. articles to profl. jours. Served with USN, 1950-54. Fellow AAAS, Am. Psychol. Soc., Am. Psychol. Assn.; mem. Psychonomic Soc., Psychmetric Soc., Internat. Assn. Applied Psychology, Soc. Organizational Behavior (founder), Midwestern Psychol. Assn. (coun. 1994-97), Phi Beta Kappa, Sigma Xi. Home: 176 Tucker Dr Columbus OH 43085-3064 Office: Ohio State U Dept Psychology Columbus OH 43210 E-mail: naylor.2@osu.edu.

NAYLOR, JEFFREY GORDON, retail executive; b. Montreal, Que., Can., Nov. 15, 1958; s. Gordon Charles and Patricia Grace (Pryde) N.; m. Shawn Elizabeth Baker, Oct. 6, 1984; 1 child, Madeleine Baker Naylor. BA in Econs., Northwestern U., 1980, MBA, 1982. CPA, Ill. Pub. acct. Deloitte, Haskins & Sells, Chgo., 1982-86; assoc. N.Am. Venture Capital, Chgo., 1986-88; mgr. mergers and acquisitions A.C. Nielsen, Northbrook, Ill., 1988-90, dir. fin. analysis, 1990-91; dir. fin. Kraft Foods Sales, Northfield, Ill., 1991-93, Kraft Foods Corp., Northfield, 1993-95; v.p. credit divsn. Sears Roebuck & Co., Hoffman Estates, Ill., 1995; v.p., contr The LimitedInc; CFO, sr. v.p. fin. Dade Behring, Dearfield, Ill., 2000—01; sr. v.p., CFO Big Lots Inc., 2001—04; sr. exec. v.p. TJX Companies Inc., Framingham, Mass., 2004—, CFO, 2004—07, chief adminstrv. officer, bus. develop. officer, 2007—. Prof. acctg. Keller Grad. Sch. Mgmt., Chgo., 1987-91. Treas. Episcopal Ch. of Northwestern U., Evanston, 1996; mem. Brookfield Zoo, 1995, Northwestern U. "N" Club, 1980. Mem. AICPA, Ill. CPA Soc. Episcopalian. Avocations: swimming, gourmet cooking, reading, ice skating. Office: TJX Cos 770 Cochituate Rd Framingham MA 01701 *

NAYLOR, MAGDALENA RACZKOWSKA, psychiatrist, educator; b. Warsaw, Aug. 4, 1950; arrived in U.S., 1981; d. Wlodzimierz Raczkowski and Urszula Raczkowska-Cieslik; m. Thomas Herbert Naylor, Dec. 14, 1985; 1 child, Alexander Watkins. MD, Warsaw Med. U., Poland, 1976, PhD, 1987. Diplomate psychiatry and neurology Nat. Bd. Certification in Psychiatry and Neurology, 1994. Asst. prof. Warsaw Med. U., 1977—83; rsch. assoc. Med. Coll. Va., Richmond, 1981—82; resident psychiatry Duke U., Durham, NC, 1984—88; pvt. practice psychiatry Richmond, Va., 1988—93; attending physician psychiatry Fletcher Allen Health Care, Burlington, Vt., 1993—; asst. prof. U. Vt., Burlington, 1993—99, assoc. prof., 1999—. Rsch. assoc. Med. Coll. Va., Richmond, Va., 1981—82; med. dir. women's program Psychiat. Inst. Richmond, Va., 1991—92; med. dir. partial hospitalization program Charter Westbrook Hosp., 1992—93; med. dir. psychiat. unit Flecher Allen Health Care, Burlington, Vt., 1994—97; dir. mindbody medicine clinic U. Vt. Med./Flecher Allen Health Care, 1998—; assoc. dir. clin. neuroscience rsch. unit U. Vt. Med.; spkr. on search for meaning and integration of mind, body and spirit into med. practice. Author (with Thomas Naylor and William Willimon): The Search for Meaning, 1994, The Search for Meaning Workbook, 1994; contbr. articles to profl. jours. Com. mem. Vt. Pain & Symptom Mgmt. Com.; mem. Gailer Sch., Shelburn, Vt., 2001—03. Recipient Best Tchr. of Yr. Dept. of Psychiatry, U. Vt. Med. Sch., 1996, 1998; grantee, NIH, 2002, 2004, 2005, U. Vt. Med. Sch., 2004. Mem.: Am. Pain Soc., Vt. Med. Assn. Achievements include research in coping skills training for patients in chronic pain, obesity and chemical dependence. Home: 202 Stockbridge Rd Charlotte VT 05445 Office: U Vt UHC 1 S Prospect St Burlington VT 05401 Home Phone: 802-425-4133; Office Phone: 802-847-2673. Business E-Mail: magdalena.naylor@vtmednet.org.

NAYLOR, MARY D., medical professor, director; BSN, Villanova U.; PhD, MSN, U. Penn. Assoc. dean, dir. undergrad. studies U. Penn. Sch. Nursing, Philadelphia, 1986—98, founder, dir. Living Independently for Elders (LIFE) program, 1998—, Marian S. Ware prof. gerontology; dir. RAND/Hartford Ctr. Inderdisciplinary Geriatric Health Care Rsch. U. Penn., Philadelphia. Named to Nat. Honor Soc. Nursing; recipient Lenore Williams award, U. Penn., Outstanding Alumni award, U. Penn. Sch. Nursing., Claire Fagin Disting. Rsch. award, U. Penn. Sch. Nursing, 2003, Disting. Lectr. award, Sigma Theta Tau, Pa. Nurses Assn. Nursing Rsch. award, Nightingale Award of Pa., McCann Scholar award, Joy McCann Found., 2004; Nat. Leadership Fellowship, W.K. Kellogg Found. Fellow: Leonard Davis Inst. Health Economics, Am. Heart Assn.; mem.: Inst. Medicine. Office: UPenn Sch Nursing Rm 364 NEB 420 Guardian Dr Philadelphia PA 19104-6069 Office Phone: 215-898-6088. E-mail: naylor@nursing.upenn.edu.

NAYLOR, PAUL DONALD, retired lawyer; b. St. Bernard, Ohio, May 28, 1925; s. David Frederick and Erna Helen (Miller) N.; m. Geraldine L. Lacy, Jan. 20, 1945; children: Linda S., Paul Scott, Todd L. JD, U. Cin., 1948. Bar: Ohio 1948. Ptnr. Pulse & Naylor, Cin., 1949-65; pvt. practice Cin., 1965—2003; ret., 2003. Mem. Nat. Rep. Com. Lt. (j.g.) USN, 1943-46. Recipient Svc. to Mankind award Sertoma Internat. Mem. Cin. Bar Assn. (real property com. 1966-86), Ohio Bar Assn., Cin. Lawyers Club (pres. 1955), Order of the Coif. Home: 304 Amherst Ave Terrace Park OH 45174-1104

NAYLOR, PHYLLIS REYNOLDS, writer; b. Anderson, Ind., Jan. 4, 1933; d. Eugene Spencer and Lura Mae (Schield) Reynolds; m. Thomas A. Tedesco, Jr., Sept. 9, 1951 (div. 1960); m. Rex V. Naylor, May 26, 1960; children: Jeffrey, Michael. Diploma, Joliet Jr. Coll., 1953; BA, Am. U., 1963. Author: Crazy Love: An Autobiographical Account of Marriage and Madness, 1977, Revelations, 1979, A String of Chances, 1982 (ALA notable book), The Agony of Alice, 1985 (ALA notable book), The Keeper, 1986 (ALA notable book), Unexpected Pleasures, 1986, Send No Blessings, 1990 (YASD best book for young adults), Shiloh, 1991 (ALA notable book, John Newbery medal, 1992), The Fear of Place, 1994, Sang Spell, 1998, Walker's Crossing, 1999, Blizzard's Wake, 2002, After, 2003, others. Recipient Golden Kite award, Soc. Children's Book Writers Am., 1985, Child Study award, Bank St. Coll., 1983, Edgar Allan Poe award, Mystery Writers Am., 1985, 2004, Internat. Book award, Soc. Sch. Librs., 1988, Christopher award, 1989; Nat. Endowments Arts Creative Writing fellow, 1987. Mem.: PEN, Authors Guild, Soc. Children's Book Writers, Children's Book Guild Washington (pres. 1974—75, 1983—84), Amnesty Internat., Physicians for Social Responsibility, Coun. for a Livable World. Unitarian Universalist. Avocations: theater, swimming. Home and Office: 401 Russell Ave Apt 713 Gaithersburg MD 20877

NAYLOR, THOMAS HERBERT, economist, educator, consultant; b. Jackson, Miss., May 30, 1936; s. Thomas Hector and Martha (Watkins) N.; m. Magdalena Raczkowska, Dec. 14, 1985; children: Susanne, Alexander. BS in Math., Millsaps Coll., 1958; BS in Indsl. Engring., Columbia U., 1959; MBA in Quantitative Bus. Analysis, Ind. U., 1961; PhD in Econs., Tulane U., 1964. Instr. Sch. Bus. Adminstrn. Tulane U., 1961-63; asst. prof. econs. Duke U., 1964-66, assoc. prof. econs., 1966-68, prof. econs., 1968-93, prof. emeritus econs., 1994—. Vis. prof. U. Wis., 1969-70, Middlebury Coll., 1993-94, U. Vt., 1994-96; pres. Social Systems, Inc., 1971-80; mng. dir. Naylor Group, 1980; cons., lectr. in over 30 countries. Co-author: (with Eugene Byrne) Linear Programming, 1963, (with Joseph L. Balintfy, Donald S. Burdick and Kong Chu) Computer Simulation Techniques, 1966, translated into Japanese, Portuguese and Spanish, (with John Vernon) Microeconomics and Decision Models of the Firm, 1969, translated into Spanish, (with James Clotfelter) Strategies for Change in the South, 1975, (with John M. Vernon and Kenneth Wertz) Managerial Economics: Corporate Economics and Strategy, 1983, (with William H. Willimon) The Abandoned Generation: Rethinking Higher Education, 1995, Downsizing the U.S.A., 1997, (with Rolf Österberg and William H. Willimon) The Search for Meaning in the Workplace, 1996, others; author or co-author of 30 books including: Computer Simulation Experiments with Models of Economic Systems, 1971, translated into Spanish, Polish, and Russian, Corporate Planning Models, 1979, Strategic Planning Management, 1980, The Corporate Strategy Matrix, 1986, translated into Hungarian, The Gorbachev Strategy, 1988, The Cold War Legacy, 1991, (with William H. Willimon and Magdalena R. Naylor), The Search for Meaning, 1994; editor: The Impact of the Computer on Society, 1967, The Design of Computer Simulation Experiments, 1969, The Politics of Corporate Planning and Modeling, 1978, Simulation Models in Corporate Planning, 1979, Simulation in Business Planning and Decision Making, 1981, others; co-editor: (with H. Brandt Ayers) You Can't Eat Magnolias, 1972, (with Michele H. Mann) Portfolio Planning and Corporate Strategy, 1983, (with Celia Thomas) Optimization Models for Strategic Planning, 1984, (with John DeGraff and David Wann), Affluenza, 2001, translated into French, German, Japanese and other langs., The Vermont Manifesto, 2003, others; contbr. numerous articles to profl. publs.; mem. editl. bd. jours. Exec. dir., founder. L.Q.C. Lamar Soc., Washington, 1969-73; founder Second Vt. Republic, 2003. Named to Lambda Chi Alpha Alumni Hall of Fame, 1996. Mem.: Beta Gamma Sigma, Omicron Delta Kappa. Home: 202 Stockbridge Rd Charlotte VT 05445-9358 Office Phone: 802-425-4133.

NAZAIRE, MICHEL HARRY, physician; b. Jérémie, Haiti, Sept. 29, 1939; s. Joseph and Hermance Nazaire; m. Nicole Lamarque, Dec. 28, 1968 (div.); children: Hannick, Carline. BS, DOE, Port-Au-Prince, Haiti, 1959; MD Faculty of Medicine and Pharmacology, State U. Haiti, 1966. Intern State U. Hosp., Port-Au-Prince, Haiti, 1965-66; resident physician Sanitarium, Port-Au-Prince, Haiti, 1966-68; physician pneumology, 1966-68; physician pneumo-phtisiology Port-Au-Prince, 1966—; fellow Klinik Havelhohe and Heckeshorn, Berlin, 1969-70, 89-91; attending physician Sanitarium, Port-Au-Prince, 1976-91. Dep. mem. Internat. Parliament for Safety and Peace, envoy-at-large Internat. State Parliament, mem. global environ. technol. network WHO. Contbr. articles to profl. jours. Recipient Physician's Recognition award, Am. Med. Assn., 2002, AMA, 2002, 2005. Fellow Internat. Soc. for Respiratory Protection, Am. Coll. Chest Physicians (recognition award, 2006); mem. AMA (Physician's Recognition award 2002, 2005), APHA, Am. Conf. Govtl. Indsl. Hygienists, Internat. Union Against Tb, Internat. Platform Assn., Physicians for Social Responsibility, European Respiratory Soc. Home: 12 B St NE Apt 103 Auburn WA 98002 Home Fax: 253-333-6520. Personal E-mail: michharnazamed@msn.com.

NAZARETH, ANNETTE LAPORTE, commissioner, lawyer; b. Providence, Jan. 27, 1956; d. George Robert and Dolores (LaPorte) Nazareth; m. Roger Walton Fergunson, May 3, 1986; 2 children. AB magna cum laude, Brown U., 1978; JD, Columbia U., 1981. Assoc. Davis Polk & Wardwell, NYC, 1981-86; gen. ptnr., gen. counsel Mabon, Nugent & Co., NYC, 1986-91; mng. dir., gen. counsel Mabon Securities Corp., NYC, 1991—94; sr. v.p. Lehman Brothers, Inc., NYC, 1994—97; mng. dir., dep. head Salomon Smith Barney, NYC, 1997—98; sr. counsel to chmn. SEC, Washington, 1998—99, acting dir., Divsn. Investment Mgmt., dir., Divsn. Mkt. Regulation, 1999—2005, commr., 2005—. Mem.: Securities Industry Assn., Phi Beta Kappa. Office: SEC 100 F St NE Washington DC 20549 Office Phone: 202-551-6551.

NAZARI, KOUROSH, ophthalmologist; s. Abbas and Shoukat Nazari. MD, Med. Coll. Ga., August, 1998. Physician Fla. Eye and Surg. Ctr., Orlando, 2002—. Author: (motivational book) Lessons from East and West. Congl. reelection com. Rep. Party, Washington, 2003—04. Fellow: Am. Acad. Ophthalmology (assoc.). Conservative. Office: Florida Eye and Ambulatory Surgical Cent 160 Boston Ave Altamonte Springs FL 32701 Home Phone: 321-271-6220; Office Phone: 407-834-7776.

NAZARIAN, LAWRENCE FRED, pediatrician; b. NYC, May 17, 1940; s. Samuel George and Winifred Lucia (Zotian) N.; m. Sharon Louise Carlson, June 22, 1963; children: Douglas, Stephen, Sarah. BA, Yale U., 1960; MD, U. Rochester, 1964. Cert. Am. Bd. Pediatrics 1970. Pediatrician Panorama Pediatric Group, Rochester, NY, 1969—2004; clin. prof. pediatrics U. Rochester Sch. Medicine and Dentistry, 1969—. Bd. dirs. James P. Wilmot Found., Rochester. Assoc. editor Pediatrics in Rev. Jour., 1990-2004, editor-in-chief, 2005-; contbr. articles to profl. jours. Mem. troop com. Boy Scouts Am., Penfield, N.Y., 1978-88; mem. coun. com. Luth. Ch. of Reformation, Rochester, 1969—. Maj. USAR, 1967-69. Recipient Nat. Pediatric Tchg. award, Ambulatory Pediatric Assn., 2002. Fellow Am. Acad. Pediatrics; mem. Med. Soc. State of N.Y., Ctrl. N.Y. Pediatric Club, Monroe County Med. Soc., Rochester Acad. Medicine, Rochester Pediatric Soc. Avocations: hiking, camping, canoeing, gardening, cross country skiing. Office: U Rochester Med Ctr 601 Elmwood Ave Box 777 Rochester NY 14642 Office Phone: 585-275-0225.

NAZARIAN, MANUCHER, surgeon; arrived in US, 1962; s. Eliahoo and Seemeen Nazarian; m. Sara Lili Nazarian, Dec. 27, 1978; children: Michel, Rachel, Rebekah. BS, Hadaff Sch., Tehran, Iran, 1956; MD, U. Tehran, 1962. Gen. surgery Harvard Med. Sch.-Beth Israel Hosp., Boston, 1968; cardiothoracic surgery SW Med. Sch., Dallas, 1970; surgeon Harris Meth., Ft. Worth, 1971—, Baylor Med. Ctr.-All Saint, 1973—, Plaza Med. Ctr., Ft. Worth, 1975. Contbr. articles to profl. jours. Recipient Terrell award, All Saint Health Found., 2002, Med. Hero award, Ft. Worth Press, 2033. Mem.: Ft. Worth Surg. Soc., Tex. Med. Assn. Avocations: stamp collecting/philately, music. Office: 757 8th Ave Fort Worth TX 76104-2522

NAZARIAN, SAM, film producer; b. Tehran, Iran, 1975; CEO, chmn. SBE Entertainment Group, 2003—. Owner Area, Hyde and Privilige. Exec. prodr.: (films) Home of Phobia, 2004, The Beautiful Country, 2004, Trespassing, 2004, Waiting..., 2005, Down in the Valley, 2005, Five Fingers, 2006, The Last Time, 2006, Pride, 2007. Office: SBE Entertainment Group 8000 Beverly Blvd Los Angeles CA 90048 *

NAZARYAN, HOVAKIM, mathematician, researcher, atmospheric scientist; b. Yerevan, Armenia, Apr. 20, 1974; arrived in U.S., 2000; s. Roland and Eli Nazaryan. MS in Math., Yerevan State U., 1994; PhD in Math., Byurakan Astrophysical Observatory, Yerevan State U., 1998. Rsch. assoc. Byurakan Astrophysical Observatory, Armenia, 1998—99; postdoctoral position U. Padua, Italy, 1999—2001; postdoctoral rsch. fellow Hampton U., 2003—. Contbr. articles to profl. jours. Mem.: Am. Geophys. Union. Avocation: painting. Office: Hampton U Ctr Atmospheric Scis 23 Tyler St Hampton VA 23668 Office Phone: 757-728-6368. Business E-Mail: hovakim.nazaryan@hamptonu.edu.

NAZARYAN, VAHAGN, physics researcher, consultant; s. Roland and Eli Nazaryan. MS, Yerevan State U., 1999; PhD, Coll. William and Mary, Williamsburg, Va., 2004. Postdoctoral rsch. assoc. Coll. William and Mary, Williamsburg, 2004—05, Hampton U., Va., 2005—07, supr. Med. Physics Rsch., 2007—. Contbr. articles to profl. jours. Recipient Rolf G. Winter award for Excellence in Tchg., Coll. William and Mary, Va., 2003; grantee Biologically Optimized Treatment Planning for Hadron Radiotherapy, Varian Med. Systems, Inc., 2007—; Alikhanov — Alikhanian Bros. fellow for Academic Excellence, Yerevan Physics Inst., Armenia, 1997—99. Mem.: Am. Assn. for Cancer Rsch., Am. Assn. Physicists in Medicine (assoc.), Nat. Soc. Collegiate Scholars (life). Achievements include patents for proton beam treatment planning with adequate biological weighting; accelerated partial breast irradiation with shielded MammoSite applicator and method of use. Avocations: travel, tennis, music. Office: Hampton University Physics Department OLIN 102 Hampton VA 23668 Office Phone: 757-727-5893. Business E-Mail: vahagn.nazaryan@hamptonu.edu.

NAZEM, FEREYDOUN F., venture capitalist, entrepreneur; b. Tehran, Iran, Dec. 29, 1940; came to US, 1960; naturalized, 1976; s. Hassan and Afsar N.; m. Susie Gharib, Jan. 20, 1973; children: Alexander, Taraneh. BS, Ohio State U., 1964; MSc, U. Cin., 1967; MBA, Columbia U., 1971. Sr. rsch. chemist Matheson Coleman & Bell, Norwood, Ohio, 1967-68; asst. v.p., investment analyst Irving Trust Co., NYC, 1969-74; v.p., venture capital officer Charter NY, NYC, 1974-75; mng. dir. Collier Enterprises, NYC, 1976-81; mng. ptnr. Nazem & Co. I, II, III and IV, NYC, 1981—, Explorer Fund, NYC, 1997—, Transatlantic Venture Fund, 1998—, Hedgeworth, L.L.C., NYC, 2003—; founder, chmn., CEO Flagship Global Health, NYC, 2004—. Bd. dirs. ETRIALS, Carey, NC. Author: The Chemical Industry and Energy Shortage, Hedgeworth Market Letter. Recipient Ellis Island Medal of Honor, 2007. Avocations: fine arts, sports, music, building trend-setting technology companies. Office: 220 W 42nd St New York NY 10036 Home Phone: 212-570-6757; Office Phone: 212-340-9110. Business E-Mail: ffn@naezm.com. E-mail: fnazem@flagshipglobalhealth.com. *You can have success and serenity at the same time. Become a possibilitarian- spend time solving problems, not worrying about them.*

NAZEMETZ, PATRICIA, human resources specialist; BA, MA, Fordham U. Benefits analyst W.R. Grace and Co.; various positions in human resources including benefits ops. mgr. Xerox Corp., Stamford, Conn., 1979—99, v.p. human resources, 1999—. Bd. dirs., chair human resources com. Nat. Bus. Group Health and Human Svcs., Long Island; trustee, vice-chmn. bd. Fordham U. Office: Xerox Corp 800 Long Ridge Rd Stamford CT 06904 Office Phone: 203-968-3000. Office Fax: 203-968-3218.

NAZETTE, RICHARD FOLLETT, lawyer; b. Eldora, Iowa, July 27, 1919; s. Hilmer H. and Genevieve A. (Follett) N.; m. Joan Chehak, June 20, 1942; children— Ronald D., Randall A. BA, U. Iowa, 1942, JD with distinction, 1946. Bar: Iowa bar 1946. Practiced in, Cedar Rapids, 1946—; partner firm Nazette, Marner, Wendt, Knoll & Usher, 1968—; asst. atty. Linn County, Iowa, 1951-56; county atty., 1957-63. Dir. United States Bank, Cedar Rapids, 1968-91, State Surety Co., Des Moines, 1966-78 Bd. dirs. Linn County Health Center, 1968-73, chmn., 1968-69; mem. Iowa Bd. Parole, 1981-84. Served with AUS, 1942-44. Fellow Am. Bar Found., Iowa Bar Assn. (bd. govs. 1972-76), Iowa State Bar Found.; mem. Linn County Bar Assn. (pres. 1963), Iowa County Attys. Assn. (pres. 1959), Iowa Acad. Trial Lawyers (pres. 1964), Masons (33rd degree Scottish Rite), Shriners, Jesters, Elks, Optimists (internat. v.p. 1955), Sigma Phi Epsilon. Republican. Presbyterian. Office: 100 1st St SW Cedar Rapids IA 52404-5701 Home Phone: 319-363-0640; Office Phone: 319-364-0124. Business E-Mail: rfnazette@nazmar.com.

NCHEKWUBE, EMEKA J., neurologist, surgeon; b. Lagos, Nigeria, Mar. 27, 1946; s. Matthias and Georgina A. Nchekwube; m. Donna Nissley, Oct. 23, 1973; children: Uche S., Chukwuemeka Jr., Obi D. MD, Wayne State U., Detroit, 1974. Diplomate Am. Bd. Neurol. Surgery, 1984. Intern Ind. U., 1975; resident in neurosurgery Wayne State U., 1979; neurosurgeon E&D Nchekwube, MD, Inc., San Jose, Calif., 1979—; med. dir. Immune Modulation, Inc., Bloomington, 1997—. Mem. staff Good Samaritan Hosp., San Jose Regional Hosp., Calif., Valley Med. Ctr., Los Gatos Cmty. Hosp., St. Louise Regional Hosp. Author: True Wealth; contbr. articles to profl. pubs. Named Top Doc, Guide to America's Top Doctors, 1998—2002, Top Physician, Guide to America's Top Pysicians, 2003—06. Mem.: AMA, Congress Neurol. Surgeons, Calif. Assn. Neurol. Surgeons, Am. Assn. Neurol. Surgeons, Santa Clara County Med. Soc., Calif. Med. Assn. Achievements include patents for hypoestoxides, derivitives, and agonists thereof for use as antiparasitic agents; patents pending for hypoestoxides: multiple other use. Office: E&D Nchekwube MD Inc 18550 DePaul Dr #203 Morgan Hill CA 95037 Office Phone: 408-782-6575. Office Fax: 408-782-6590.

NDURA, ELAVIE, literature and language educator; d. Melchior Ndura and Angela Mudende; children: Star Shahuri, Queen Shahuri. EdD, No. Ariz. U., Flagstaff, 1994. Tchr. secondary sch. English Ministry Edn., Bujumbura, Burundi, 1983—88; instr. English Am. Cultural Ctr., Bujumbura, 1987—89; asst. prof. U. Burundi, Bujumbura, 1988—89; tchr. French Phoenix Country Day Sch., Paradise Valley, Ariz., 1994—95; tchr. English, French Mesa Pub. Schs., Ariz., 1995—2001; asst. prof. multicultural edn. U. Nev., Reno, 2001—05; assoc. prof. edn. George Mason U., Fairfax, Va., 2005—. Adj. faculty No. Ariz. U., Phoenix, 1990—2001. Contbr. articles to profl. jours. Founder, coord. Reach Out Burundi Schools Project, 2006; pres., founder no. Nev. chpt. Nat. Assn. Multicultural Edn., Reno, 2001—05; mem. at large Peace Spl. Interest Group, Am. Ednl. Rsch. Assn., 2006. Recipient Programming award, NAU Office Residence Life, 1991, 1993, Cmty. Devel. award, 1993, Brown v. Bd. Edn. 50th Anniversary award, Reno-Sparks NAACP, 2004; scholar, US Info. Svc., Fulbright Commn., 1988, 1989—94; Abba Schwartz Rsch. fellow, John F. Kennedy Libr., 2005, Brit. Coun. scholar, England, 1986—87. Mem.: TESOL, Nat. Assn. Black Sch. Educators, Internat. Peace Rsch. Assn., Comparative and Internat. Edn. Soc., Am. Ednl. Rsch. Assn. (mem. at large 2006), Peace and Justice Studies Assn. (bd. mem. 2005), Nat. Assn. Multicultural Edn. (founder, chpt. pres. 2001—05). Home Phone: 703-590-3524; Office Phone: 703-993-9424. E-mail: endura@gmu.edu.

NEAL, A. MICHAEL, utilities executive; BS, Ga. Inst. Tech., 1975. V.p., gen. mgr., Vendor Fin. Svcs, G.E. Capital, 1987—90, gen. mgr., Comml. Equip. Financing, 1990—94; sr. v.p. G.E. Co., 1993—; exec. v.p. G.E. Captial, 1994—2000; pres., COO G.E. Capital, 2000—02; pres., CEO G.E. Comml. Fin., 2002—. Mem. adv. bd. European Inst. Bus. Adminstrn. Bd. trustees Fairfiled U.; trustee Ga. Tech. Found.; chmn. GE Captial United Way campaign. Office: GE Commercial Fin 260 Long Ridge Rd Stamford CT 06927

NEAL, ALAINE (DIANN NEAL), nursing administrator; b. Seaside, Oreg., Jan. 25, 1942; d. Alan Welch Jr. and Beatrice June (Wisdom) Smith; m. Kelly Sayre Neal Jr., July 31, 1965; children: Kelly III, Karter B. BS, U. Portland, 1964; MS, U. Ariz., 1970. RNC in in-patient obstetrics, nursing adminstrn. advanced. Head nurse Family Childbirth Ctr. St. Joseph's Hosp. and Med. Ctr., Phoenix, 1982-87, nurse mgr. maternal-newborn svcs., 1987-90, dir. nursing women's and children's svcs., 1990-95; dir. pediatrics and nursery, pediatric intensive care Desert Samaritan Med. Ctr., Mesa, Ariz., 1995-2000; dir. women and infants svcs. St. Joseph's Hosp., Carondelet Health Network, Tucson, 2000—. Author: (with others) High-Risk Intrapartum Nursing, 1992. Capt. Nurse Corps, U.S. Army, 1964-67. Mem. Sigma Theta Tau. Episcopalian. Avocations: equestrian, genealogy, cooking. Office: 350 N Wilmart Rd Tucson AZ 85711 E-mail: dneal@carondelet.org.

NEAL, CAROLYN V., librarian; b. Jan. 19, 1964; MLS, Clark Atlanta U., 1999. US Customs Svc. Inspector; libr. Cleve. Pub. Libr., project coord. North Coast SeniorsConnect. Named one of the Movers & Shakers, Libr. Jour., 2007; recipient Diversity Fair Best of Show award, ALA, 2004. Office: Cleveland Public Library 325 Superior Ave NE Cleveland OH 44114 Office Phone: 216-623-2800, 216-623-2902. Office Fax: 216-623-7015. E-mail: cneal@cpl.org.

NEAL, DARWINA LEE, federal agency administrator; b. Mansfield, Pa., Mar. 31, 1942; d. Darwin Leonard and Ina Belle (Cooke) N. BS, Pa. State U., 1965; postgrad., Cath. U, 1968-70. Registered landscape architect. Landscape architect nat. capital region Nat. Pk. Svc., 1965-69, office of White House liaison, 1969-71, office of profl. services, 1971-74, div. design svcs., 1974-89, chief design svcs., 1989-95, chief landscape arch. office of stewardship and partnership Washington, 1996-98, chief cultural resource preservation svcs. nat. capital reg., 1998—. Judge numerous award juries. Contbr. articles to profl. jours.; co-author sects. of profl. bull., mag.; author introduction to book Women, Design and the Cambridge School; columnist: Land monthly, 1975-79. Recipient Merit award Landscape Contractors Met. Washington; recipient hon. mention Les Floralies Internat. Montreal, 1980 Alumni Achievement award Pa. State U. Arts and Architecture Alumni Soc., 1981 Fellow Am. Soc. Landscape Architects (v.p. 1979-81, pres. elect 1982-83, pres. 1983-84, trustee 1976-77, nat. treas. 1977-79, legis. coord. 1975-79, sec. Coun. Fellows 1988-90, del. to Internat. Fedn. Landscape Architects 1989-92, 00-03, ex-officio rep. to U.S./internat. coun. on monuments and sites 1985-98, liaison to historically black coll. and univ. program Dept. Interior, chair internat. task force 1999-2000, Pres.' medal 1987), U.S. Internat. Coun. on Monuments and Sites (treas. 1998-2004, trustee 2004-07), Internat. Fed. Landscape Architects (sec. West Region, 2003-06, v.p. Am.'s Region 2006—); mem. Landscape Archtl. Accreditation Bd. (roster vis. evaluators), Nat. Recreation and Parks Assn., Nat. Soc. Park Resources (bd. dirs. 1978-80), Nat. Trust Hist. Preservation, Pa. State U. Alumni Assn. (Washington met. chpt. trustee 1972-74), Am. Arbitration Assn. (nat. panel arbitrators), Com. 100 for the Fed. City, Preservation Action, Nat. Assn. Olmsted Parks, Beekman Pl. Condominium Assn. (bd. dirs. 1985-91, archtl. control com. 1977-00, landscape com. 2000-02), Alliance for Historic Preservation, Garden Conservancy, Scenic Am., Preservation Action, Preservation Roundtable, Hist. Soc. Washington Office: Nat Park Svc/Nat Capital Region Off Lands Resources & Plan 1100 Ohio Dr SW Washington DC 20242-0001

NEAL, DENNIS MELTON, elementary school educator; b. Lakeland, Fla., Feb. 7, 1966; s. M. H. and Alice Marie (Twiddy) N.; m. Christine Anne Rufo, Oct. 21, 1989; children: Lauren Elizabeth, Waverly Rose, Emma Katherine. AA, Polk C.C., Winter Haven, Fla., 1987; BS, Fla. So. Coll., 1991; MEd, Stetson U., 1995. Cert. elem. tchr., ednl. leader, prin., Fla. Guest svcs. Cypress gardens, Winter Haven, 1985-86; entertainer Boardwalk and Baseball, Baseball City, Fla., 1986-88; guest svcs. Hilton Walt Disney World, Orlando, Fla., 1988-91; tchr. Deltona (Fla.) Middle Sch., 1991-95, asst. prin., 1995-99, Heritage Middle Sch., Deltona, Fla., 1999-2000; prin. intern Pine Ridge H.S., 2000—. Chair correlate com., team leader Deltona Middle Sch., sch. adv. coun. Tchr. Lith. Ch. of Providence, Orange City, Fla., 1992-93; active Parent, Tchr., Student Assn. Named One of Top 100 Beginning Tchrs. in Nation, Sallie Mae Student Loan Assn., 1992. Avocations: soccer, racquetball, drawing, painting.

NEAL, DIANE L., retail executive; BS in Retailing, Mich. State U., 1979. Various positions to pres. of Target subs. Mervyn's Target Corp., 1985—2001, pres. Mervyn's, 2001—04; sr. v.p. merchandising Gap Inc., 2004—05, pres. Gap Inc. Outlet, 2005—06; pres., COO Bath and Body Works Limited Brands Inc., 2006—. Bd. dirs. Nautilus Inc., 2004—. Mem. corp. fundraising com. San Francisco Museum Modern Art. Office: Bath and Body Works Inc Seven Limited Pkwy Reynoldsburg OH 43068 *

NEAL, DIANNE M., consumer products company executive; B in acctg., Univ. NC, Greensboro, 1981, MBA, 1988. CPA NC. Acctg. positions Forsyth Mem. Hosp., Winston Salem, NC; fin. mgmt. positions R.J. Reynolds Tobacco, Winston Salem, NC, 1988—94, dir. fin. planning & acctg., 1994—97, v.p., controller, 1997—99, v.p. investor rels., 1999—2003; exec. v.p., CFO R.J. Reynolds Tobacco Holdings & R.J. Reynolds Tobacco, Winston Salem, NC, 2003—04, Reynolds American Inc., Winston Salem, NC, 2004—. Mailing: Reynolds American Inc PO Box 2990 Winston Salem NC 27102-2990 *

NEAL, EDWARD GARRISON, lawyer; b. Abingdon, Va., Mar. 20, 1940; s. James Wiley Neal and Edna Mae (Felty) Millsap; m. Diane T. Neal, Feb. 16, 2002; children: Jay Garrison, Heather Leigh. BA, Fla. State U., Tallahassee, 1962; JD, U. Balt., 1966; LLM, George Washington U., Washington, 1969. Bar: Md. 1966, US Dist. Ct. Md. 1968, US Supreme Ct. 1972. Asst. trust officer Md. Nat. Bank, Balt., 1964-66; gen. counsel Hatch Act Study Commn., Washington, 1967; exec. asst. U.S. Sen. Daniel Brewster, Washington, 1966-68; asst. states atty. Office of States Atty., Balt., 1968-71; chief criminal div. States Atty. Prince George's County, Upper Marlboro, Md., 1971-76; assoc. county atty. Prince George's County Office of Law, Upper Marlboro, 1976-79; pvt. practice College Park, Md., 1979—. Law lectr. Prince Georges County and Md. State Police Acads., 1971—76; law lectr. U.S. Secret Svc. Fed. Law Enforcement Tng. Ctr., 2000—; legal advisor Office Tech. Assistance US Treasury Dept., Moldova, 1999; spl. reporter Md. criminal rules com. Prince Georges County and Md. State Police Acads. Vice chmn. Women's Sexual Assault Commn., Upper Marlboro, Md., 1974—75; pres. PTA Concordia Luth. Sch., Hyattsville, Md., 1976—77; Dem. precinct chmn. University Park, Md., 1972—80; pres. bd. trustees Rossborough Festival, Kapell Internat. Piano Competition, College Park, 1986—89, 1989—. Recipient cert. of Appreciation, Prince George's County Coun., Upper Marlboro, Md., 1975. Mem.: Daniel O'Connell Law Soc., Marlborough Inn of Ct., Daniel O'Coanell Law Soc., Marlborough nn of Ct., Nat. Dist. Attys. Assn. (scholarship award 1968, 1970, 1975, 1976), Md. State's Attys. Assn. (legislative liaison Md. Gen. Assembly 1972—76), Md. State Bar Assn. (various coms.), George Washington U. Alumni Assn. (bd. dirs. 1980—), Fla. State U. Varsity Club, Kiwanis, Phi Alpha Delta (dist. v.p. 1962—, pres. 1963). Episcopalian. Avocations: music, reading, tennis, basketball, bridge. Office: 7309 Baltimore Ave Ste 117 College Park MD 20740-3200 Home: 849 Singing Hills Ct Annapolis MD 21401-7337 Personal E-mail: gnealesq@aol.com.

NEAL, GAIL FALLON, physical therapist, educator; b. New Haven, May 6, 1938; d. Edward Francis and Ruth Alexina (Hutchinson) Fallon; m. Marcus Pinson Neal Jr.; children: Sandra Neal Dawson, Marcus Pinson III, Ruth-Catherine Neal Perkins. Student, Mary Washington Coll., 1955-57; BS in Phys. Therapy, Med. Coll. Va., 1959. Lic. phys. therapist. Staff phys. therpist Univ. Hosps., U. Wis., Madison, 1959-61; chief phys. therapy Stoughton (Wis.) Cmty. Hosp., 1961-63; vol. phys. therapy Cerebral Palsy Ctr., Richmond, Va., 1963-64; pvt. practice Richmond, 1965—68; interim dir. Stuart Cir. Hosp., Richmond, 1968-69; phys. therpist on call St. Mary's Hosp., Richmond, 1968-74; pres., owner Capital Phys. Therapy Assocs., Richmond, 1989—. Phys. therapist St. Mary's Hosp., Richmond, 1975-88; lectr. Med. Coll. Va., Richmond, 1992-93, John Tyler C.C., Richmond, 1992-94; adv. bd. phys. therapy Va. State Bd. Medicine, 1990-96, vice chmn., 1992-93, chmn. 1995-96. Adv. bd. Va. Opera, 1979—; bd. visitors Mary Washington Coll., Fredericksburg, Va., 1980-82, rector bd. visitors, 1982-84; pres. Richmond Symphony Orch. League, 1986-88. Named Clubwoman of Yr., Richmond Newsleader, 1972. Mem. Am. Phys. Therapy Assn., Richmond Acad. Medicine Aux. (pres. 1967-68), Med. Soc. Va. Alliance (pres. 1980-81), Med. Coll. Va. Hosps. Aux. (pres. 1973-75), Va. Cultural Laureate Soc. Avocations: reading, music, skiing, indian folklore. Home: Pony Bluffs 7301 Riverside Dr Richmond VA 23225-1066 Office: Capital Phys Therapy Assocs Pony Bluffs Richmond VA 23225 Office Phone: 804-330-2440. Personal E-mail: gfncpta@hotmail.com.

NEAL, HOMER ALFRED, physics professor, researcher, academic administrator; b. Franklin, Ky., June 13, 1942; s. Homer and Margaret Elizabeth (Holland) Neal; m. Donna Jean Daniels, June 16, 1962; children: Sharon Denise, Homer Alfred Jr. BS in Physics with honors, Ind. U., 1961; MS in Physics (John Hay Whitney fellow), U. Mich., 1963, PhD in Physics, 1966. Asst. prof. physics Ind. U., 1967—70, assoc. prof., 1970—72, prof., 1972—81, dean research and grad. devel., 1976—81; prof. physics SUNY, Stony Brook, 1981—87, provost, 1981—86; prof. physics, chmn. U. Mich., Ann Arbor, 1987—93, v.p. rsch., 1993—97, interim pres., 1996—97, prof. of physics, 1987—2000, Samuel A. Goudsmit disting. prof. physics, 2000—, dir. of atlas project, 1997—. Bd. dirs. Ford Motor Co.; mem. Nat. Sci. Bd., 1980—86; mem. adv. coun. Oak Ridge Nat. Lab., 1993—99; mem. external adv. coun. Nat. Computational Sci. Alliance, 1997—; mem. applications strategy coun. Univ. Corp. for Advanced Internet Devel., 2000—; chmn. Argonne Zero Gradient Synchrotron Users Group, 1970—72; trustee Argonne Univs. Assn., 1971—74, 1977—80; physics adv. panel NSF, 1976—79, chmn. physics adv. panel, 1987—89; high energy physics adv. panel U.S. Dept. Energy, 1977—81. Contbr. articles to profl. jours. Mem. bd. regents Smithsonian Instn., 1989—2001; trustee Ctr. for Strategic and Internat. Studies, 1990—2000, Oak Ridge Nat. Lab., Tenn., 1993—99; mem. Smithsonian Coun. on the Nat. Mus. African Am. History and Culture, 2004—; mem. bd. overseers Superconducting Super Collider, 1989—93; trustee Environ. Rsch. Inst. of Mich., 1994—96, Lounsbery Found., 2005—. NY Sea Grant Inst., 1982—86. Recipient Stony Brook medal, 1986, Ind. U. Disting. Alumni award, 1994; fellow NSF, 1966—67, Sloan, 1968, Guggenheim, 1980—81. Fellow: AAAS, Am. Acad. Arts and Scis., Am. Phys. Soc.; mem.: Univs. Rsch. Assn. (trustee), Sigma Xi. Office: Dept Physics Rm 2477 Randall Lab 450 Church St Ann Arbor MI 48109-1040

NEAL, IRENE COLLINS, artist, educator; b. Greensburg, Pa., May 14, 1936; d. Oliver Shupe and Betsey Cowap (Mann) Collins; m. Paul Whitaker Neal, Nov. 24, 1960; children: Paul Collins Gordon, Betsey Whitaker. BA, Wilson Coll., Chambersburg, Pa., 1958; student, Sch. Visual Arts, Rio de Janeiro, 1976-77, Memphis Sate U., Tenn., 1979-80, U. Bridgeport, Conn., 1982-83; participant, Triangle Art Workshop, Pine Plains, NY, 1985. Guest spkr. Coll. Santa Fe, Albuquerque, 1994. One-woman shows include Allied Chem. Corp., Morristown, NJ, 1975, Planetarium Rio de Janeiro, 1977, Pat Ackerman Gallery, Memphis, 1980, Westmoreland Mus. Art, Greensburg, 1986, Wilson Coll., 1993, Cooper Classics Collections, NYC, 2001—02, Trans-Lux Cocteau Corp., Santa Fe, 2003, Acton Pub. Libr., Conn., 1007, St. Ann's Episcopal Ch., 2007, exhibited in group shows at Jersey City Mus., 1975, NJ State Mus., 1975, Somerset Tri-State Mus., NJ, 1975, Nat. Arts Club, NYC, 1975, Garden State Watercolor Soc., 1975, Salao de Marinhas, Rio de Janeiro, 1977, Stamford Mus., 1984—85, 1989, Branchville Soho Gallery, Ridgefield, Conn., 1984, Silvermine Guild, New Canaan, Conn., 1984, Stamford Libr., 1985, Shippee Gallery, NYC, 1986, 110 Greene St., 1986, Wilton Libr., Conn., 1986, Aldrich Mus. Contemporary Art, Ridgefield, 1987, Visual Arts Festival, Edmonton, Atla., Can., 1989, Mus. Art, Ft. Lauderdale, Fla., 1991—92, Salander-O'Reilly Galleries, Inc., NY, 1994, Vanderleele Gallery, Edmonton, 1996, Galerie Piltzer, Paris, 1996, Fine Art 2000 Gallery, Stamford, 1996—97, York Coll., Queens, NY, 1997, Ctr. Performing Arts, Stamford, 1997, Mus. Contemporary Art, Palm Beach, Fla., 1997, Griffis Art Ctr., New London, 1997, Vero Beach Mus., Fla., 1998, Flint Inst. Art, Mich., 1999, Mus. Contemporary Art, Denver, 1999, Gelabert Studios Gallery, NYC, 2000, Hotel de Ville, Brussels, 2000, 69th Regiment Armory, NYC, New New Painters, Real Avant Garde, 2000, Nat. Gallery, Prague, Czech Republic, 2001—02, Galerie Anne-Lettrie, Paris, 2001, Durst Orgn., NYC, 2002—03, Musee du Bas-Saint Laurent Riviere de Lupe, Que., Can., 2002—03, Scope NY Stevenson Fine Art, Dylan Hotel, NYC, 2003, Mus. au Bus, St. Laurant, Que., 2003, Elfsar Collection, Ltd., Vancouver, BC, 2003, Juten Gallery, Toronto, 2003, Anew Found., Ft. Lauderdale, Fla., 2004, Westport Arts Ctr., Conn., 2004, Realtra, Cork, Ireland, 2005, Lurie Gallery, Miami, 2005, Pthalo Gallery, 2005, Diane Birdsall Gallery, Old Lyme Conn., 2005, Troy Gallery, Stamfod, 2005—06, A.N.E.W. Found., Ft. Lauderdale, Lurie Gallery, Miami, Diane Birdsall Gallery, Lyme, A New Found. Arts, 2006, Seth Jason Beitler Gallery, 2007, U. Alta., Can., 2007, New Day Contemporary Mus., Beijing, 2007, Represented in permanent collections Planetarium, Rio de Janeiro, Internat. Paper, NYC, Westmoreland Mus. Art, Greensburg, Pa., Pepperdine U., Malibu, Calif., Newport Harbor Art Mus., Newport Beach, Calif., Hoover Instn. Stanford U., St. Matthew's Episcopal Ch., Wilton, Columbia U., Ctr. Arts, Vero Beach, Fla., Mus. Art, Ft. Lauderdale, Alamo Rent A Car, Denver Ctr. Performing Arts, Flint Inst. Art, Mich., Nat. Gallery, Prague, Wilson Coll., Chambersburg, Pa., Appleton Mus. Art, Ocala, Fla., Nat. Mus. Women Arts; pub., contr.: New New Painting, 1996, catalog, 2000, Cooper Classics Collection, 2001—02. Recipient Tift award, Wilson Coll., Chambersburg, Pa., 2003. Republican. Episcopalian. Avocations: ocean diving, tennis, golf, gardening. Home and Office: 98 Maple Ave Old Saybrook CT 06475 Office Phone: 860-388-9291. Personal E-mail: icneal@aol.com.

NEAL, JAMES G., university librarian; BA in Russian Studies, Rutgers U., 1965—69; MA in History, Columbia U., 1969—71, MS in Libr. Sci., 1972—73. Cert. in advanced Librarianship Columbia U., 1978. Social sciences libr. Queensborough Cmty. Coll., CUNY, 1973—76; head collection develop. dept. U. Notre Dame, 1977—79, head collection mgmt. dept., 1979—82, asst. dir. pub. services, 1982—83; asst dean & head reference Pa. State U. Libraries, 1983—89; dean univ. libraries Ind. U., 1989—95; Sheridan Dir. Milton S. Eisenhower Libr. Johns Hopkins U., 1995—2001, dean libraries, 1998—2001; v.p. info. services & univ. libr. Columbia U., NYC, 2001—. Bd. dirs. Nat. Info. Standards Orgn.; chair bd. dirs. Rsch. Libraries Group; chair steering com. Scholarly Pub. and Academic Resources Coalition; editl. bd. Coll. and Rsch. Libraries, 1990—96, Jour. Libr. Adminstrn., 1995—2003, portal: Libraries and the Academy, 2000—; editl. adv. bd. The Bottom Line: Mng. Libr. Finances, 1993—98. Bd. trustees Freedom to Read Found., 2007—. Named Outstanding Librarian of Yr., Indiana Libr. Fedn., 1993, Academic/Rsch. Libr. of Year, Assn. Coll. and Rsch. Libraries, ALA, 1997; recipient Hugh C. Atkinson Meml. award, ALA, 2007. Mem.: Baltimore Bibliophiles, Grolier Club. Office: Columbia U 517 Butler Libr 535 W 114th St New York NY 10027 Office Phone: 212-854-2247. Office Fax: 212-854-4972. Business E-Mail: jneal@columbia.edu. *

NEAL, JAMES PRESTON, state senator, project engineer; b. Cin., July 1, 1935; s. James Preston and Desha Frank (Thompson) N.; m. Nancy Joan Tyner, June 11, 1961; children: Leslie Neal Driscoll, Karen Desha, James P. BSME, U. Ill., 1960. Registered profl. engr., Del. Project engr. DuPont Co., 1960-92; dir. Tetra Tech Inc., Christiana, Del., 1992-95; pres. Tech. Mgmt., 1994—2001. Mem. Del. Ho. of Reps., 1978-80; mem. Del. Senate, 1980-94; trustee U. Del., 2002—. Patentee in field. Councilman City of Newark, 1973-78; elder Presbyn. Ch.; bd. dirs. Christina Conservancy, 2004—; mem. Gov.'s Task Force on Sch. Librs., 2003—. With U.S. Army, 1954-56. Recipient Disting. Svc. award Forum to Advance Minorities in Engring., 1989, Disting. Svc. citation Del. Libr. Assn., 1994, Appreciation award Del. Autistic Program, 1999. Mem. Am. Legis. Exch. Coun. (sr. fellow, nat. officer 1991-94, Outstanding Leader 1989, Outstanding Legis. mem. 1994), Del. Engring. Soc. (Engr. of Yr. 1989), Del. Acad. Scis. (bd. dirs. 1996—), Torch Club of Del., Lincoln Club (bd. dirs. 2006—). Republican. Presbyterian. Avocations: photography, reading. Home and Office: 50 Bridlebrook Ln Newark DE 19711-2061

NEAL, JOAN BURKES, librarian; b. Phenix City, Ala., Feb. 27, 1928; d. George Ashby and Maybelle Ethel (Barnes) Burkes; m. Charles A. Land, May 25, 1944 (dec. Sept. 1947); 1 child, Jo Sandra Land; m. Ray Verlin Neal, Dec. 25, 1952 (dec. May 8, 1996); children: Jo Griffeth, J. Kim, Roger Verlin, Kathy Brown. BS in Edn., U. Ga., Athens, 1951, postgrad., 1966. Dir. kindergarten Fayetteville First Bapt. Ch., Ga., 1958-63; tchr. 3d grade Fayetteville Elem. Sch., 1964-67, libr., 1967—91. Bd. dirs. Ga. PTA, 1977-80; spkr. Silver Haired Legis. Mem. Ga. State Dem. Party, Atlanta, 1977—; sec. ARC, Fayetteville, 1979-83; pres. Band and Athletic Boosters, Fayetteville, 1968-70. Mem. Fayette County Assn. Educators (pres., v.p., sec. 1963—), Ga. Assn. Educators (governing bd. Ga. chpt. 1976-79, legis. chair 1981, 83), Fayette County Bus. and Profl. Women (pres. 1976-78, treas., sec.), Kappa Kappa Iota (pres. Fayetteville chpt. 1970-72). Avocations: reading, golf, politics, walking. Home: 432 Forrest Ave Fayetteville GA 30214-1327 Personal E-mail: joann2271@bellsouth.net.

NEAL, JOSEPH LEE, vocational school educator; b. Memphis, Feb. 17, 1948; s. James Henry and Minnie Rue (Waldrop) N.; children: Janice Celeste Neal, Mary Joanne; m. Lou Alice Smith, Apr. 10, 1999. AAS, N.W. C.C., Senatobia, Miss., 1979, AS in Bus., 1980; BS, U. S. Miss., 1984, MS, 1986. Cert. tchr. Miss. Police officer City of W. Memphis, Ark., 1970-72; customer svc. rep. Biomed. Labs., Little Rock, Ark., 1972-75; sales, svc. rep Moore Ford Co., N. Little Rock, 1975-77; electronics technician N.W. Miss. C.C., Senatobia, 1979-82, electronics inst., 1982-83; electronics engr. U. So. Miss., Hattiesburg, 1983-85; electronics instr. Tex. State Tech. Inst., Sweetwater, 1985-87, De Soto County Vo-Tech. Ctr., Southaven, Miss., 1988-97, South Panola H.S., Batesville, Miss., 1997—. Cons. engr. various radio ops., Hattiesburg, 1982-85; mem. curriculum com. De Soto County Schs., 1990-95; steering com. N.W. Miss. Tech. Prep., Senatobia, 1992-95, participant in Learn to Work Workshop Miss. St. U. and Pealey Electronics, 1997, tchr. trainer for Tech. Discovery, 1998, 99. Bd. dirs. Optimist Club, Sweetwater, Tex., 1987. Named Outstanding Tchr., Horn Lake So. C. of C., 1992. Mem. Am. Vocat. Assn., Miss. Trade and Tech. Assn. (v.p. 1994-95, pres. 1995-96), Miss. Assn. Vocat. Educators (pres. dist. 1 1991-92, 95-96, bd. dirs. 1991-92, 95-96, sec. dist. 1 1993-94, v.p. 1994-95), Vocat.-Indsl. Clubs of Am. (100% Advisor 1990, 91, 92, VICA state advisor of yr. 1993), N.Am. Hunting Club (life). Baptist. Avocations: hunting, fishing, public speaking. Office: South Panola HS Batesville MS 38606 Home: 1578 Freeman Rd Como MS 38619-2852

NEAL, LARRY DWIGHT, retired economic historian, educator; b. Twin Falls, Idaho, May 11, 1941; s. Fred Roy and Fay Margaret (Stacy) N.; m. Margaret Anne Doherty, June 14, 1963; children: Kathryn, Elizabeth, Christopher. BA, Stanford U., 1962; PhD, U. Calif., Berkeley, 1968. Asst. prof. U. Ill., Urbana, 1967-73, assoc. prof., 1973-78, prof., 1978—2005, prof. emeritus, 2005—. Economist Orgn. for Econ. Cooperation and Devel., Paris, 1970—72. Author: Rise of Financial Capitalism, 1990, Economics of Europe, 2007; editor Explorations in Econ. History, 1982-98. Pres. Bus. History Conf., 2001. Fellowship Alexander von Humboldt Found., 1982, Fulbright Rsch., 1996-97, Guggenheim, 1996-97. Mem. Cliometrics Soc. (trustee, Clio award), Econ. History Assn. (v.p. 1991-92, pres. 2001). Roman Catholic. Avocation: sailing. Office: U Ill 1407 W Gregory Dr Urbana IL 61801-3606 Business E-Mail: lneal@uiuc.edu.

NEAL, LARRY P., library director; MBA, Oakland Univ., 1991; MS, Univ. Mich., 2001. Asst. dir. Clinton-Macomb Pub. Libr., Clinton Twp., Mich., interim dir., 2005—06, dir., 2006—. Named one of the Movers & Shakers, Libr. Jour., 2007. Mem.: ALA (mem. recruitment assembly), Pub. Libr. Assn. (chmn. recruitment of pub. libr. com. 2003—05), Mich. Libr. Assn. (past chmn. libr. tech. div.), Macomb County C. of C. Office: Clinton-Macomb Pub Libr 40900 Romeo Plank Rd Clinton Township MI 48038 Office Phone: 586-226-5011. Business E-Mail: larry@cmpl.org.

NEAL, LEORA LOUISE HASKETT, social services administrator; b. NYC, Feb. 23, 1943; d. Melvin Elias and Miriam Emily (Johnson) Haskett; m. Robert A. Neal, Apr. 23, 1966; children: Marla Patrice, Johnathan Robert. BA in Psychology and Sociology, City Coll. N.Y., 1965; MS in Social Work, Columbia U., 1970, cert. adoption specialist, 1977; IBM cert. community exec. tng. program, NYC, 1982. Cert. social worker NY, 1970; lic. master social worker, NY, 2004, clin. social worker, NY, 2005. Caseworker N.Y.C. Dept. Social Service, 1965-67, Windham Child Care, NYC, 1967-73; exec. dir., founder Assn. Black Social Workers Child Adoption Counseling and Referral Service, NYC, 1975-96; adoption tng. specialist Ctr. for Devel. Human Svcs., SUNY-N.Y. State Office Children and Family Svcs., Yonkers, 1996—. Cons. in field; founder Haskett-Neal Publs., Bronx, N.Y., 1993. Co-author: Transracial Adoptive Parenting: A Black/White Community Issue, 1993; contbr. articles to profl. jours. Pres. bd. dirs., founder Fountain Ave. Cmty. Devel. Corp.; bd. dirs. Grandparents Advocacy Project, 2000—. Child Welfare League Am. fellow, 1976; recipient No Time to Lose cert. NY State Dept. Social Svcs., 1989, Pyramid award NY Assn Black Social Workers, 2005. Mem. NAFE, Nat. Assn. Black Social Workers (co-chair task force on foster care and adoption 1994—, Outstanding Cmty. Svc. award 1994), Columbia U. Alumni Assn., CCNY Alumni Assn., Missionary Com. Revival Team (outreach chair 1982-88). Democrat. Avocations: writing, religious studies, travel, cultural activities, history. Office: NY State Office of Children and Family Svcs SUNY 525 Nepperhan Ave Yonkers NY 10703-2857 Office Phone: 914-377-2079.

NEAL, MARCUS PINSON, JR., radiologist, educator; b. Columbia, Mo., Apr. 22, 1927; s. M. Pinson and Mathilda (Evers) N.; m. Gail S. Fallon, May 27, 1961; children: Sandra G. Neal Dawson, M. Pinson III, Ruth-Catherine Neal Perkins. AB, U. Mo., 1949, BS, 1951; MD, U. Tenn., 1953. Intern Med. Coll. Va., Richmond, 1953—54; resident U. Wis. Hosp., Madison, 1954—57; instr. dept. radiology Sch. Medicine U. Wis., Madison, 1957—59; mem. staff U. Wis. Hosps., Madison, 1957—63; asst. prof. radiology, dir. dept. radiology Ctrl. Wis. Colony, Madison, 1959—63; radiologist Wis. Diagnostic Ctr., Madison, 1962—63; mem. staff Med. Coll. Va. Hosps., Va. Commonwealth U., 1963—99; assoc. prof. radiology Med. Coll. Va., Va. Commonwealth U., 1963—66, prof. radiology, 1966—97, prof. emeritus, 1997—, dir. postgrad. edn. dept. radiology, 1964—73, chmn. divsn. diagnostic radiology, 1965—68, asst. dean Sch. Medicine, dir. grad. med. edn., dir. regional med. program, 1968—71, dir. continuing edn. Sch. Medicine, 1969—72, interim dean Sch. Medicine, 1971, asst. v.p. health scis., 1971—73, provost Health Scis. campus, 1973—78, assoc. dean for continuing med. edn. and quality assurance Sch. Medicine, 1978—79, dir. housestaff edn., dept. radiology, 1979—93, dir. section genitourinary radiology, dept. radiology, 1981—92; prof. emeritus Va. Commonwealth U., 1993—. Cons., radiologist Va. Hosp., Madison, 1962-63, USAF Hosp., Truax Field, Madison, 1962-63, McGuire VA Hosp., Richmond, 1963-99; bd. forestry Commonwealth Va., 1990-94, chmn. bd. forestry, 1993-94. Editor: Emergency Interventional Radiology: Practical Aspects, 1988; contbr. articles to profl. jours. Pres. Oxford Civic Assn., Richmond, 1965-67, Three Ridges Condominium Assn., Wintergreen, Va., 1979-84. Served as pharmacist mate USNR, 1945-47. Fellow Oak Ridge Inst. Nuc. Studies, Am. Coll. Radiology (fellow emeritus, councilor Va. chpt. 1977-83, 85-91, 93-97); mem. AMA, Radiol. Soc. N.Am., Am. Roentgen Ray Soc., Med. Soc. Va., So. Med. Assn. (pres. 1982-83, Disting. Svc. award 1994), Richmond Acad. Medicine, Commonwealth Club, Bull and Bear Club, Willow Oaks Country Club, Sigma Xi. Avocations: hunting, fishing, gardening. Home: 7301 Riverside Dr Richmond VA 23225-1242 Personal E-mail: dr.neal@comcast.net.

NEAL, MICHAEL A., corporate financial executive; BS, Ga. Inst. Tech., 1975. With General Electric Co., 1979—; v.p. & gen. mgr., vendor fin. svcs. GE Capital, 1987—90, gen. mgr., comml. equip. financing, 1990—94, exec. v.p., 1994—99, pres., COO, 2000—02; pres. & CEO GE Comml. Fin., 2002—; vice chmn. General Electric Co., 2005—. Trustee Fairfield Univ., Ga. Tech. Found.; bd. mem. Soundwaters, Stamford, Conn.; mem. U.S. adv. bd. European Inst. Bus. Adminstrn. Mailing: General Electric Co 3135 Easton Tpke Fairfield CT 06828 *

NEAL, PHIL HUDSON, JR., retired manufacturing executive; b. Birmingham, Ala., Nov. 17, 1926; s. Phil Hudson and Amy (Gross) N.; m. Sarah Swift Britton, Sept. 19, 1959; children: Amy Neal Ager, Phil Hudson, III, Samuel Abney Britton. AB, Duke U., 1950; MBA, Harvard U., 1952. Investment analyst First Nat. Bank, Birmingham, 1952-55; procedures analyst Gen. Electric Co., Hendersonville, NC, 1955-58; with Ala. By-Products Corp., Birmingham, 1958-79, asst. treas., 1964-68, treas., 1968-79; dir., v.p. Utility Tool Co., Birmingham, 1979-86; dir., pres. Nutec Metal Finishing Inc., Birmingham, 1986-92, chmn., 1992—2005; ret., 2005. Trustee Advent Episcopal Sch., 1967—, pres., 1968-89, trustee charitable endowment trust, 1981—; treas. Cathedral Ch. of Advent, 1981-82, mem. chpt., 1983-85, 86-89; bd. dirs. Greater Birmingham Ministries, 1975-77, Advent Episcopal Assn. for Edn., 1968-89, Jefferson County chpt. Ala. Soc. Crippled Children and Adults, Inc., 1977-79; trustee Ala. Found. for Hearing and Speech, 1967-74, v.p., 1968-69, pres., 1969-71. Served with USNR, 1945-46. Mem. Newcomen Soc. N.Am., Birmingham Country Club, The Club, The Summit Club, Phi Beta Kappa, Sigma Nu, Phi Eta Sigma. Episcopalian (vestryman, sr. warden). Home: 3336 Hermitage Rd Birmingham AL 35223-2004 also: 81 Old Duck Hole Rd East Orleans MA 02643

NEAL, RICHARD EDMUND, congressman, former mayor; b. Worcester, Mass., Feb. 14, 1949; s. Edmund J. and Mary H. (Garvey) N.; m. Maureen Conway, Dec. 20, 1975; children: Rory, Brendan, Maura, Sean BS, Am. Internat. Coll., Springfield, Mass., 1972; M.P.A., U. Hartford, Conn., 1976; postgrad., U. Mass., Amherst, 1982. Adminstrv. aide to Mayor City of Springfield, Mass., 1973-78, mem. city council Mass., 1978-83, mayor Mass., 1984-88; mem. U.S. Congress from 2nd. Mass. dist., 1989—, mem. ways & means com., budget com., social security subcommittee. Lectr. history and politics Springfield Tech. Community Coll., Mass., 1973-83; lectr. bus. and govt. Western New Eng. Coll., Springfield, 1979-82; project dir. Springfield Tech. Community Coll., 1979-82 Trustee ARC, YMCA, Springfield Named to Outstanding Young Men in Am., U.S. Jr. C. of C., Springfield; recipient John F. Kennedy award & Amb.'s award, Holyoke, Mass. St. Patrick's Day Com., Internat. Leadership award, Am. Ireland Fund, 2002. Mem. Am. Internat. Coll. Alumni Assn. (pres. 1980, Alumni Achievement award 1985). Springfield Library and Mus. Assn. (trustee) Clubs: Valley Press. John Boyle O'Reilly (Springfield). Democrat. Roman Catholic. Office: US Ho Reps 2266 Rayburn Ho Office Bldg Washington DC 20515-2102 *

NEAL, STEPHEN CASSIDY, lawyer; b. San Francisco, Mar. 26, 1949; AB, Harvard U., 1970; JD, Stanford U., 1973. Bar: Ill 1973, Calif. 1993. Ptnr. Kirkland & Ellis, Chgo.; ptnr., bus. litigation Cooley Godward Kronish LLP (formerly Cooley Godward LLP), Palo Alto, Calif., 1995—, chmn., CEO, 2001—. Named one of 100 Most Influential Lawyers, Nat. Law Jour., 2006. Fellow: Am. Coll. Trial Lawyers. Office: Cooley Godward Kronish LLP 5 Palo Alto Square #400 3000 El Camino Real Palo Alto CA 94306-2155 Office Phone: 650-843-5182. Office Fax: 650-857-0663. Business E-Mail: nealsc@cooley.com. *

NEALE, ERNEST RICHARD WARD, retired university official, consultant; b. Montreal, Que., Can., July 3, 1923; s. Ernest John and Mabel Elizabeth (McNamee) N.; m. Roxie Eveline Anderson, June 3, 1950; children: Richard Ward, Owen Curtis. B.Sc., McGill U., Montreal, 1949; MS, Yale U., 1950, PhD, 1952; LL.D. (hon.), Calgary U., Alta., Can., 1977; DSc (hon.), Meml. U., Nfld., Can., 1989. Asst. prof. geology U. Rochester, N.Y., 1952-54; sect. chief Geol. Survey Can., Ottawa, Ont., 1954-63, div. chief, 1965-68, Calgary, 1976-81; commonwealth geol. liaison officer London, 1963-65; prof., head geology Meml. U., St. John's, Nfld., Can., 1968-76, v.p. acad., 1982-87; cons., Calgary, Alta., Can., 1987—. Chmn. nat. adv. bd. on sci. publs. NRC-Natural Scis. and Engring. Rsch. Coun., Ottawa, 1982-88. Author: Geology and Geophysics in Canadian Universities, 1980. Editor: Some Guides to Mineral Exploration, 1967, Geology of the Atlantic Region, 1968, The Geosciences in Canada, 1980; editor: Can. Jour. Earth Sci., 1974-79. Bd. dirs. Unitarian Ch. Calgary, 1993—, pres., 1995-96. Petty officer Royal Can. Navy, 1943-45. Decorated officer Order of Can.; recipient Queen's Jubilee medal, Govt. Can., 1977, 125 medal Can., 1992, Golden Jubilee medal Can., 2002, Integrity award, Calgary Rotary, 2003, William Irvine award, Unitarian Ch. Calgary, 2004, Alta. Centennial medal, 2005. Fellow Royal Soc. Can. (coun. 1972-75, chmn. com. pub. awareness of sci. 1987-91, Bancroft medal 1975), Geol. Assn. Can. (pres. 1973-74, Ambrose medal 1986, 1st E.R. Ward Neale medal 1995), Can. Geosci. Coun. (pres. 1975-76, R.T. Bell medal Can. Mining Jour. 1977), Geol. Soc. Am.; mem. Assn. Earth Sci. Editors, Nat. Def. (chmn. biol. and chem. def. rev. com. 1990-93), Univ. Club Calgary, Chancellor's Club, Crows Nest Club, Calgary Sci. Network (pres. 1989), Sigma Xi (nat. lectr. New Haven 1976, chmn. Avalon chpt. 1986). Avocations: golf, cross country skiing, hiking, canoeing. Home and Office: 5108 Carney Rd NW Calgary AB Canada T2L 1G2

NEALE-MAY, DONOVAN, marketing executive; Degree in journalism, Rhodes U., South Africa. Leader pub. rels. ops. Ogilvy & Mather, Calif.; founder, mng. ptnr. GlobalFluency, Inc.; founder, exec. dir. Chief Mktg. Officer (CMO) Coun. Mem. adv. bd. pub. rels. degree program San Jose State U., Calif.; cons. with various clients; several acct. mgmt., sr. exec. positions comm. agys., England. Mem. bd. Travelzoo.com; mem. bd. Rhodes U. Charitable Trust. Scholar Cape Times. Office: GlobalFluency 4151 Middlefield Rd Palo Alto CA 94303 Office Phone: 650-433-4200. Office Fax: 650-328-5016. E-mail: donovan@globalfluency.com, donovan@cmocouncil.org. *

NEALON, WILLIAM JOSEPH, federal judge; b. Scranton, Pa., July 31, 1923; s. William Joseph and Ann Cannon (McNally) N.; m. Jean Sullivan, Nov. 15, 1947; children: Ann, Robert, William, John, Jean, Patricia, Kathleen, Terrence, Thomas, Timothy. Student, U. Miami, Fla., 1942-43; BS in Econs, Villanova U., 1947; LL.B., Cath. U. Am., 1950; LL.D. (hon.), U. Scranton, 1975. Bar: Pa. 1951. With firm Kennedy, O'Brien & O'Brien (and predecessor), Scranton, 1951-60; mem. Lackawanna County Ct. Common Pleas, 1960-62; U.S. dist. judge Middle Dist. Pa., 1962—, chief judge, 1976-88, sr. judge, 1989—. Mem. com. on adminstrn. of criminal law Jud. Conf. U.S., 1979—; lectr. bus. law and labor law U. Scranton, 1951-59; mem. jud. council 3d Cir. Ct. Appeals, 1984—; dist. judge rep. from 3d Cir. Jud. Conf. of U.S., 1987—. Mem. Scranton Registration Commn., 1953-55; hearing examiner Pa. Liquor Control Bd., 1955-59; campaign dir. Lackawanna County chpt. Nat. Found., 1961-63; mem. Scranton-Lackawanna Health and Welfare Authority, 1963—; assoc. bd. Marywood Coll., Scranton; pres. bd. dirs. Cath. Youth Center; pres. Father's Club Scranton Prep. Sch., 1966; chmn. bd. dirs. Mercy Hosp., 1991-95; chmn. bd. trustees U. Scranton; vice chmn. bd. trustees Lackawanna Jr. Coll., Scranton; bd. dirs. St. Joseph's Children's and Maternity Hosp., 1963-66, Lackawanna County unit Am. Cancer Soc., Lackawanna County Heart Assn., Lackawanna County chpt. Pa. Assn. Retarded Children, Scranton chpt. ARC, Lackawanna United Fund, Mercy Hosp., Scranton, 1975—; trustee St. Michael's Sch. Boys, Hoban Heights; adv. com. Hosp. Service Assn. Northeastern Pa. Served to 1st lt. USMCR, 1942-45. Recipient Americanism award Amos Lodge B'nai B'rith, 1975; Cyrano award U. Scranton Grad. Sch., 1977; Disting. Service award Pa. Trial Lawyers Assn., 1979; named one of 50 Disting. Pennsylvanians Greater Phila. C. of C., 1980, Outstanding Fed. Trial Judge Assn. Trial Lawyers Am., 1983 Mem. Pa. Bar Assn., Lackawanna County Bar Assn. (Chief Justice Michael J. Eagen award 1987), Friendly Sons St. Patrick (pres. Lackawanna County 1963-64), Pi Sigma Alpha. Clubs: Scranton Country (Clarks Summit, Pa.) (bd. dirs.). Lodges: K.C. Office: US Courthouse PO Box 1146 Scranton PA 18501-1146

NEAMAN, MARK ROBERT, hospital administrator; b. Buffalo, Oct. 22, 1950; married. B, Ohio State U., 1972, MHA, 1974. Adminstrv. asst. Evanston (Ill.) Hosp., 1974-76, asst. to v.p., 1976-78, asst. v.p., 1978-80, v.p., 1980-84, sr. v.p., 1984-85, pres., exec. v.p., 1985-90, pres., 1990-92, pres., CEO, 1992—. Chmn. Am. College of Healthcare Execs., 2002—; bd. trustees Healthcare Leadership Coun. Fellow Am. Coll. Healthcare Execs. (chmn., RS Hudgens award 1988). Office: Evanston Northwestern Healthcare 1301 Central St Evanston IL 60201-1781

NEAR, TIMOTHY, theater director; Grad., San Francisco State U., Acad. Music and Dramatic Art, London. Artistic dir. San Jose Repertory Theatre, 1987—. Past actress, dir. with numerous prestigious theaters including The Guthrie Theatre, Berkeley (Calif.) Repertory Theater, La Jolla (Calif.) Playhouse, The Alliance Theatre, Atlanta, The Mark Taper Forum, L.A., Ford's Theatre, Washington, Repertory Theatre of St. Louis, N.Y. Shakespeare Festival, Stage West, Mass., A.C.T., Seattle. Dir. Ghosts on Fire, La Jolla Playhouse (Drama League award), Singer in the Storm, Mark Taper Forum (Drama League award), Thunder Knocking on the Door (Drama League award). Recipient 1997 Woman of Achievement in the Arts, San Jose Mercury News and The Woman's Fund. Office: San Jose Repertory Theatre 101 Paseo De San Antonio San Jose CA 95113-2603

NEARINE, ROBERT JAMES, educational psychologist; b. Fitchburg, Mass., May 15, 1930; s. Raymond Johns and Beatrice Aileen (Strickland) N.; children: Luke, Martha, Amy. BS, Fitchburg State Coll., 1951; EdM, Tufts Coll., 1952; MA, U. Conn., 1965, profl. diploma, 1996; EdD, Boston U., 1973. Cert. advanced grad. specialization Boston U. Tchr. pub. schs., Holbrook, Mass., 1952-54, Groton, Mass., 1954-55, Winchester, Mass., 1955-59, supr. Inverness, Mont., 1959-60, guidance counselor Manchester, Conn., 1961-66, supr. of evaluation, 1966-73, adminstr. for funding and evaluation, 1973-76, spl. asst. for funding Hartford, Conn., 1976-78; spl. asst. for evaluation rsch. and testing Bd. Edn., Hartford, 1978-93; ednl. cons. Glastonbury, Conn., 1993—. Mem. requirements adv. com., 1991-92. Contbr. articles to profl. jours. Col. ret. US Army. NDEA fellow Boston U., 1960-61, GE fellow Syracuse U., 1971, Ednl. Policy Inst. fellow George Washington U., 1979-80. Mem. APA, Am. Ednl. Rsch. Assn., Nat. Coun. on Measurement in Edn., Res. Officers Assn. (nat. councilman 1994—), Amvets, Civitan (pres. 1998-99), Conn. state com. employee support of Guard and Res.), Am. Legion (post comdr. 2006—), Victory Svcs. Club U.K., Assn. of U.S. Army, NG Assn. U.S., Gov.'s Foot Guard, Freemasons, Scottish Rite, York Rite, Shriners, Jesters, Phi Delta Kappa. Avocations: military history, travel. E-mail: rjnear@sbcglobal.net.

NEARY, DANIEL P., insurance company executive; b. Carroll, Iowa, 1952; m. Shirley Neary; 4 children. Degree, U. Iowa, 1974. With Mut. of Omaha, 1975—, exec. v.p. group benefit svcs., 1999—2003; pres., bd. dirs. Mut. of Omaha and United of Omaha, 2003—05, CEO, chmn., 2005—. Bd. dir. Comml. Fed. Bank, Comml. Fed. Corp., America's Health Ins. Plans, Creighton U. Bd. dirs. United Way, Midlands and Am. Red Cross; mem. Boy Scouts Am. Mid-Am. Coun.; chmn. Walk to Cure Diabetes Juvenile Diabetes Rsch. Found., 2004; bd. trustees Strategic Air & Space Mus. Mem.: Soc. Actuaries. Office: Mut of Omaha Mutual of Omaha Plz Omaha NE 68175 *

NEARY, PATRICIA ELINOR, ballet director; b. Miami, Fla. d. James Elliott and Elinor (Mitsitz) N. Corps de ballet Nat. Ballet of Can., Toronto, Ont., 1957-60; prin. dancer N.Y.C. Ballet, 1960-68; ballerina Geneva Ballet, Switzerland, 1968-70, ballet dir., 1973-78; guest artist Stuttgart Ballet, Germany, 1968-70; asst. ballet dir., ballerina West Berlin Ballet, 1970-73; ballet dir. Zurich Ballet, Switzerland, 1978-86, La Scala di Milano ballet co., Italy, 1986-88; tchr. Balanchine ballets, Balanchine Trust, 1987—.

NEAS, JOHN THEODORE, investment company executive; b. Tulsa, May 1, 1940; s. George and Lillian J. (Kaspar) N.; m. Sally Jane McPherson, June 10, 1966; children: Stephen, Gregory, Matthew. BS, Okla. State U., 1967, MS, 1968. With acctg. dept. Rockwell Internat., 1965; with contr.'s dept. Amoco Prodn. Co., 1966—67; audit and tax staff Deloitte, Haskins & Sells, 1968—75; pres. Nat. Petroleum Sales, Inc., Tulsa, 1975—; prin. Neas Investments Ltd. Partnership, 1997—, Sebring Investments Ltd. Partnership, 1997—, Stockholder N-H Dealership Investments, Inc., 1996—; mem. Coun. Oak Bldg. Mgmt., LLC, 1997—; mem. Brad Noe Autoplex, LLC, 1997—, Vet. Properties, LLC, 1994—, Honda Automobiles, Bartlesville, 2006—; asst. instr. U. Tulsa, 1974; bd. dirs. Summit Bank. Mem. AICPA, Inst. Mgmt. Accts., Okla. Soc. CPAs, McClellan-Kerr Arkansas River Nav. Sys. Hist. Soc., Okla. Heritage Assn., Okla. State U. Pres.'s Club, Okla. State U. Coll. Bus. Adminstrn. Assocs. (v.p. memberships 1989-91, Hall of Fame 1991, Acctg. Dept. Hall of Fame 1993), Southern Hills Country Club, Gol Club Okla. Republican. Lutheran. Office: Nat Petroleum Sales Inc 5401 S Harvard Ave Ste 200 Tulsa OK 74135-3861

NEASMAN, ANNIE RUTH, health facility administrator; b. Moore Haven, Fla., Oct. 24, 1947; d. Nathan and Daisy Mae Miles; children: Beatrice Daizine, Barry Anthony. BSN, Fla. A&M U., 1969; MS, Fla. Internat. U., 1976. Registered Nurse, Fla. Dept. Health, Bd. Nursing. Staff nurse Jackson Meml. Hosp., Miami, 1969—71, adminstr., nursing R&D, 1976—84; adminstr. Jackson Meml. Health Sys., North Dade Health Ctr., Miami, 1984—90; adminstr., dept. health Fla. Dept. Health, Rehabilitative Svcs., Miami, 1990—92, dep. dist. adminstr., 1992—96; adminstr. Fla. Dept. Health, Miami, 1996—99, divsn. dir., family health svc. Tallahassee, 1999—2001, dep. sec., state nursing dir., 2001—04; pres., CEO Econ. Opportunity Health Ctr., Miami, 2004—. Bd. mem. Fla. Am. Lung Assn., Jacksonville, 2004—06; mem. Mt. Hermon AME Ch., Miami Gardens, Fla., 2004—06; bd. mem. Fla. Ctr. for Nursing, Orlando, 2002—04; mem. Fla. Nurses Assn., Orlando, 1976—2006, Black Nurses Assn., Miami, 2004—06. Named to Nursing Hall of Fame, Fla. A&M, 1996; recipient Woman of Yr., Pub. Health, 1994, Sr. Mgmt. Svc. award, Health and Rehab. Svcs., 1996. Mem.: Black Nurses Assn., Fla. Nurses Assn., Chi Eta Phi Nursing Sorority (Humanitarian award 1994), Delta Sigma Theta Sorority. Democrat-Npl. Ame. Avocations: travel, walking, reading. Home: 6799 Brookline Dr Miami FL 33015 Office: Econ Opportortunity Family Health Ctr Inc 700 S Royal Poinciana Blvd Ste 300 Miami Springs FL 33166 Home Phone: 305-816-0154; Office Phone: 305-805-1710. Office Fax: 305-805-1715. Personal E-mail: aruthmg47@aol.com. Business E-Mail: aneasman@hcnetwork.org.

NEAVEL, CELIA BETH, medical association administrator; b. Blommington, Ind., Aug. 30, 1959; d. Richard Charles and Nancy Trager Neavel; m. Jose Carlos Cortez; children: Elizabeth, Elena, Geordi. BA with honors in liberal arts, U. Tex., 1981; MD, Baylor Coll. of Medicine, 1985. Diplomate Am. Bd. of Family Medicine, cert. Added Qualification, Adolescent Medicine. Asst. prof. Dept. of Family Medicine, Cin., 1989—91; contract physician Austin Regional Clin., Austin, Tex., 1991—92; clin. asst., prof. of Pediat. Scott and White, Temple, Tex., 1991—95; physician adv. Easter Seals Ctrl. Tex., Austin, Tex., 1995—; faculty Austin Med. Edn. Program, Austin, Tex., 1995—2006; dir., adolescent medicine Ctr. for Adolescent Health at People's Cmty Clin., Austin, Tex., 1994—. Med. dir. Lifeworks St. Outreach Clin., Austin, Tex., 1996—, RGK Downtown Ctr. for Health Clin., Austin, Tex., 1996—, Phoenix Acad. Off-Site Clin., Austin, Tex., 2003—; dir. Devel. Behavioral Primary Care Program, People's Cmty. Clin., Austin, Tex., 2004—; clin. asst. prof. pediat. UTMB, Austin, 2006—. Co-author: (monograph) Integrating Child and Adolescent Mental Health Into Primary Care, 2002. Vol. lectr. Camp Disabled Children, Center Point, Tex., 1990—2005, physician, 1990—2005. Named Tex. Super Doctor, Tex. Monthly Mag., 2004; grant, Healthy Tomorrows from HRSA, 2005. Mem.: AMA, Physicians for Social Responsibility, Soc. of Adolescent Medicine, Tex. Med. Assn., Travis County Managed Care Regional Adv. Com. Office: Ctr for Adolescent Health People's Cmty Clin 2909 NIH 35 Austin TX 78722 Office Phone: 512-478-4939. Office Fax: 512-320-0702. E-mail: ibappmd@aol.com.

NEAVES, WILLIAM BARLOW, cell biologist, educator; b. Spur, Tex., Dec. 25, 1943; s. William Fred and Revvie Lee (Hefner) N.; m. Priscilla Wood, Jan. 28, 1965; children: William Barlow, Clarissa D'laine. AB magna cum laude, Harvard U., 1966; postgrad., Med. Sch., 1966-67, PhD, 1969. Lectr. vet. anatomy U. Nairobi, 1970-71, vis. prof., 1978; lectr. anatomy Harvard U., 1972; asst. prof. cell biology U. Tex. Health Sci. Ctr., Dallas, 1972-74, assoc. prof., 1974-77, prof., 1977—, Doris and Brian Wildenthal Prof. of Biomed. Sci., 1993—, dean Grad. Sch. Biomed. Scis., 1980-88, interim dean Southwestern Med. Sch., 1986-88, dean Southwestern Med. Sch., 1989-98, exec. v.p. acad. affairs, 1998—2000; prof. medicine U. Mo., Kans. City, 1998—2000; pres., CEO, bd. dirs. Stowers Inst. Med. Rsch., Kans. City, 2000—. Dir. Cerner Corp., Midwest Rsch. Inst., Kans. City Area Life Scis. Inst.; trustee Wash. U.; mem. nat. coun. Wash. U. Sch. Medicine; rsch. assoc. herpetology Los Angeles County Mus., 1970-73; vis. lectr. U. Chgo., 1976-77. Assoc. editor Anat. Record, 1975-87; mem. editl. bd. Biology of Reprodn., 1983-86, Jour. Andrology, 1987-89; contbr. chpts. to books, articles to profl. jours. Bd. dirs. Dallas Zool. Soc., 1989-94, Dallas Mus. Natural History, 1993-95, Damon Runyan-Walter Winchell Cancer Fund, 1986-92, v.p., 1990-92, Sarnoff Endowment, 1998—. Rockefeller Found. fellow, 1970-71; Milton Fund grantee, 1970-71; Population Council grantee, 1973-75; NIH grantee, 1973-89; Ford. Found. grantee, 1976-78. Fellow AAAS; mem. Am. Assn. Anatomists, Am. Soc. Andrology (Young Andrologist award 1983), Dallas Assembly, N.Y. Acad. Scis., Soc. Study of Reprodn., Liaison Com. on Med. Edn. (joint com. of AMA and Assn. Am. Med. Colls.), Sigma Xi, Alpha Omega Alpha. Methodist. Office: Stowers Inst Med Rsch 1000 East 50th St Kansas City MO 64110 Office Phone: 816-926-4040. Business E-Mail: wbn@stowers-institute.org.

NEAVOLL, GEORGE FRANKLIN, writer; b. Lebanon, Oreg., Aug. 20, 1938; s. Jesse Hunter and Mazie Maude (Meyer) N.; m. Laney Lila Hunter Hough, June 21, 1969 (dec. Nov. 2000); m. Joanne Darlen MacRoberts, May 4, 2002. BS, U. Oreg., 1965. Reporter, photographer Lebanon (Oreg.) Express, 1969-70; state editor Idaho State Jour., Pocatello, 1970-72; editorial writer The Jour.-Gazette, Ft. Wayne, Ind., 1972-75, Detroit Free Press, 1975-78; editorial page editor The Wichita (Kans.) Eagle, 1978-91, Portland (Maine) Press Herald, Maine Sunday Telegram, 1991-99. Vol. Peace Corps, India, 1967-69; bd. councilors Save-the-Redwoods League, 1980—; bd. dirs. Population Inst., 2002—. Recipient Edward J. Meeman award Scripps-Howard Found., 1973, Honor Roll award Izaak Walton League Am., 1974, Jamaica Daily Gleaner award Inter Am. Press Assn., 1985, Disting. Citizen award Bethany Coll., 1985, Servant Leadership award Southwestern Coll., 1987, Global Media award Population Inst., 1996, Henri A. Benoit award Greater Portland (Maine) C. of C., 1999, Restoration Leadership award Restore the North Woods, 2005; named Hon. Park Ranger, Nat. Park Svc., 1988 Mem.: Nat. Press Club. Home: 1000 SW Vista Ave No 801 Portland OR 97205-1163 Personal E-mail: gneavoll@comcast.net.

NEBEKER, FRANK QUILL, judge; b. Salt Lake City, Apr. 23, 1930; s. J. Quill and Minnie (Holmgren) N.; m. Louana M. Visintainer, July 11, 1953; children: Caramaria, Melia, William Mark. Student, Weber Coll., 1948-50; BS in Polit. Sci, U. Utah, 1953; JD, Am. U., 1955. Bar: D.C. 1956. Corr. sec. The White House, 1953-56; trial atty. Internal Security div. Justice Dept., Washington, 1956-58; asst. U.S. atty. US Dept. Justice, 1958-69; judge DC Ct. Appeals, Washington, 1969-87, sr. judge, 2000—; dir. Office Govt. Ethics, Washington, 1987-89; chief judge US Ct. Appeals Vets. Claims, Washington, 1989-2000. Cons. Nat. Commn. on Reform of Fed. Criminal Laws, 1967-68; adj. prof. Am. U. Washington Coll. Law, 1967-85. Mem. Am., D.C. Bar Assn., Am. Law Inst. Office: DC Ct Appeals 500 Indiana Ave NW Washington DC 20001-2131

NEBENZAHL, KENNETH, rare book and map dealer, author; b. Far Rockaway, NY, Sept. 16, 1927; s. Meyer and Ethel (Levin) N.; m. Jocelyn Hart Spitz, Feb. 7, 1953; children: Kenneth (dec.), Patricia Suzanne Nebenzahl, Margaret Spitz Nebenzahl Quintong, Suzanne Spitz Nebenzahl Nichol. Student, Columbia U., 1947-48; L.H.D. (hon.), Coll. William and Mary, 1983. Solicitor new bus. United Factors Corp., NYC, 1947-50; sales rep. Fromm & Sichel, Inc., NYC, 1950-52; v.p. Cricketeer, Inc., Chgo., 1953-58; pres. Kenneth Nebenzahl, Inc., Chgo., 1957—. Bd. dirs. Imago Mundi, Ltd., London; cons. Rand McNally and Co., 1966-97. Author: Atlas of the American Revolution, 1974, Bibliography of Printed Battle Plans of the American Revolution, 1975, Maps of the Holy Land, 1986 (German edit. 1995), Atlas of Columbus and the Great Discoveries, 1990, also edits. in Spanish, German, Italian, Portugese and French langs., Mapping Asia: The Silk Road and Beyond, 2,000 Years of Exploring the East, 2004, also edits. in French and Japanese langs.; contbr. articles to profl. jours. Trustee Glencoe Pub. Libr., 1963-69, pres., 1966-69; bd. dirs. North Suburban Libr. System, 1966-69, Beverly Farm Found., Godfrey, Ill., 1961-67, Nature Conservancy of Ill., 1980-88; trustee Adler Planetarium, 1969—, chmn., 1977-81; mem. exec. com. Northwestern U. Libr. Coun., 1973-75; sponsor Kenneth Nebenzahl Jr. lectures history cartography Newberry Libr., Chgo., 1965—; trustee John Crear Libr., Chgo., 1976-84; trustee U. Chgo., 1982—, mem. vis. com. to libr., 1978-96, chmn., 1987-95; co-chair Phillips Soc.-Libr. of Congress, Washington, 1995-98; bd. dirs. Evanston Hosp. Corp., 1978-85, Am. Himalayan Found., 1994—; mem. U.S. nat. adv. coun. World Wildlife Fund, 1993-2006; founding pres. Ill. Ctr. for Book, 1986-88. With USMCR, 1945-46. Recipient IMCoS-Tooley award (London), 1984. Fellow Royal Geog. Soc., Royal Soc. for Asian Affairs; mem. Manuscript Soc. (dir. 1965-71), Am. Library Trustees Assn. (nat. chmn. com. intellectual freedom 1967-68), Bibliog. Soc. Am., Newberry Library Assocs. (bd. govs. 1965-78, chmn. 1976-78), Newberry Library (trustee 1978-2003, vice chmn. 1994-2003, life trustee 2003—), Antiquarian Booksellers Assn. Am. (bd. govs. 1965-67, v.p. 1975-77), Am. Antiquarian Soc. (gov. 1981-85), Soc. History Discoveries (dir. 1974-76), Chgo. Map Soc. (dir. 1976-86), Caxton Club (Chgo.) (bd. govs. 1961-68, 74-80, pres. 1964-66), Wayfarers Club (Chgo.) (pres. 1979-80), Lake Shore Country Club, Century Assn. (NYC), Grolier Club (NYC) (bd. govs. 1998-99). Office: PO Box 370 Glencoe IL 60022-0370

NEBERT, DANIEL WALTER, molecular geneticist, research administrator; b. Portland, Oreg., Sept. 26, 1938; s. Walter Francis Nebert and Marie Sophie (Schick) Kirk; m. Myrna Sisk, Mar. 12, 1960 (div. 1975); children: Douglas Daniel, Dietrich Andrew; m. Kathleen Dixon, Aug. 15, 1981 (div. 1997); children: Rosemarie Dixon, Rebecca Frances, David Porter, Lucas Daniel; m. Lucia Jorge Fung, Mar. 6, 2000. BA, Wesleyan U., 1959; BS and MS in Biochemistry, U. Oreg., 1964, MD, 1964. Lic. physician, Ohio; bd. qualified in pediats. and human genetics; Am. Bd. Pediat. and Human Genetics. Pediat. intern UCLA Hosps., 1964—65, resident pediat., 1965—66; postdoctoral fellow Nat. Cancer Inst., NIH, Bethesda, Md., 1966—68; sr. investigator Nat. Inst. Child Health and Human Devel., Bethesda, 1968—71, sect. head, 1971—74, lab. chief, 1974—89; prof. dept. environ. health U. Cin. Med. Ctr., 1989—, prof. dept. pediat. and molecular devel. biology, 1991—. Faculty bd. cert. in human genetics NIH, 1981-89; coord. med. genetics program US-China Coop. Med. Health Protocol, 1982-89; Pfizer lectr. U. Vt., Burlington, 1978, Stanford U., 1979; Wellcome vis. prof. biochemistry and molecular biology U. SD, Vermillion, 1991; assoc. dir. physician scientist tng. program MD/PhD, U. Cin. Med. Ctr., 1994-98; nat. adv. Environ. Health Scis. Coun., 2000-04; external adv. bd. Howard U. Cancer Ctr., Wash., 1998-, U.

Lisbon, 1998-, Inst. DNA and Human Genomics U. Panama, 1999-2004; dir. Ctr. Environ. Genetics, 1992-97 Mem. editl. bd. Molecular Pharmacology, 1972-1984, Biochem. Pharmacology, 1972-, Archives of Biochemistry and Biophysics, 1973-76, Archieves Internationales de Pharmacodynamie et de Therapie, 1975-81, Jour. Environ. Scis. and Health, 1976-81, Chemico-Biol. Interactions, 1977-83, Teratogenesis, Carcinogenesis and Mutagenesis, Devel. Pharmacology and Therapeutics, 1980-86, Anticancer Rsch., 1981-83, DNA and Cell Biology, 1986—2003, Jour. Exptl. Pathology, 1986-1994, Molecular Endocrinology, 1988-1992, Endocrinology, 1989-2002, Molecular Toxicology, 1990-92, Pharmacogenetics Genomics, 1991—, Mutation Rsch., 1996-2001, Environ. Health Prospectives, 1997-, European Jour. Pharmacology, 2002-, Human Genomics, 2003—; assoc. editor DNA and Cell Biology, 1987-2003, Biochem. Pharmacology (N.Am.), 1994-2001, Environ. Health Perspectives, 1997—; commn. edit. Human Mutation, 2005-; contbr. more than 560 articles to profl. jours. Capt. USPHS, 1966-89 Recipient Meritorious Svc. medal USPHS, 1978, Frank Ayrey fellow award in clin. pharmacology, U.K., 1984, Bernard B. Brodie award, 1986, Ernst A. Sommer Meml. award, 1988; GM scholar, 1956-59, Lawrence Selling scholar, 1961, 63, Disting. Rsch. Professorship award, U. Cin., 1998, George Rieveschl Jr. award for disting. sci. rsch., U. Cin., 1999 Fellow AAAS; mem. Am. Soc. Human Genetics, Am. Soc. Pharmacology and Exptl. Therapeutics, Am. Soc. Biochemistry and Molecular Biology, Am. Soc. Clin. Investigation (emeritus 1984-), Soc. Toxicology (Disting. Lifetime Toxicology Scholar award, 2005), Human Genome Variation Soc. (founder), Sigma Xi Republican. Episcopalian. Avocations: gardening, golf, piano, art. Home: 20 Oliver Rd Cincinnati OH 45215-2631 Office: Univ Cin Med Ctr Dept Environ Health PO Box 670056 Cincinnati OH 45267-0056 Office Phone: 513-821-4664.

NEBLETT, CAROL, soprano; b. Modesto, Calif., Feb. 1, 1946; m. Philip R. Akre; 3 children. Studies with, William Vennard, Roger Wagner, Esther Andreas, Ernest St. John Metz, Lotte Lehmann, Pierre Bernac, Rosa Ponselle, George London, Jascha Heifetz, Norman Treigle, Sol Hurak, Dorothy Kirsten, Maestros Julius Rudel, Claudio Abbado, Daniel Barenboin, Erich Leinsdorf, James Levine, others. Soloist with Roger Wagner Chorale; performed in U.S. and abroad with various symphonies; debut with Carnegie Hall, 1966, N.Y.C. Opera, 1969, Met. Opera, 1979; sung with maj. opera cos. including Met. Opera, N.Y.C., Lyric Opera Chgo., Balt. Opera, Pitts. Opera, Houston Grand Opera, San Francisco Opera, Boston Opera Co., Milw. Florentine Opera, Washington Opera Soc., Covent Garden, Cologne Opera, Vienna (Austria) Staatsoper, Paris Opera, Teatro Regio, Turin, Italy, Teatro San Carlo, Naples, Italy, Teatro Massimo, Palermo, Italy, Gran Teatro del Liceo, Barcelona, Spain, Kirov Opera Theatre, Leningrad, USSR, Dubrovnik (Yugoslavia) Summer Festival, Salzberg Festival, others; rec. artist RCA, DGG, EMI; appearances with symphony orchs., also solo recitals, (film) La Clemenza di Tito; filmed and recorded live performance with Placido Domingo, La Fancuilla del West; numerous TV appearances.

NECCO, ALEXANDER DAVID, lawyer, educator; b. Gary, Ind., Jan. 31, 1936; s. Alesandro Necco and Mary Millonovich; m. Caroline Chappel, Apr. 20, 1958 (dec. Mar. 1978); 1 child, Laurie Ann Necco Stansbury; m. Edna Joanne Painter, July 1, 1989. BA in Philosophy, U. Nev., 1958; JD, Oklahoma City U., 1965. Bar: Okla. 1965, U.S. Dist. Ct. (we. dist.) Okla. 1965, U.S. Ct. Appeals (10th cir.) 1987), U.S. Ct. Claims 1989, U.S. Ct. Vets. Appeals 1994. Assoc. Robert Jordan, Oklahoma City, 1965-66, Stuckey & Witcher, Oklahoma City, 1968-69; atty. Okla. Hwy. Dept., Oklahoma City, 1966, Oklahoma City Urban Renewal, 1966-67; ptnr. Stuckey & Necco, Oklahoma City, 1969-71, Necco & Dyer, Oklahoma City, 1978-82, Dyer, Necco & Byrd, Oklahoma City, 1982-88; pvt. practice Oklahoma City, 1965—; ptnr. Necco & Byrd, Oklahoma City, 1988—. Adj. prof. Oklahoma City U. Sch. Bus., 1965—, Webster U., 1995—. Cubmaster Boy Scouts Am., Oklahoma City. With USMC, 1953-82, lt. col. Res. ret. Named Pro-bono Atty. of Month Okla. County. Mem.: ABA, Okla. Trial Lawyers Assn., Marine Corps Res. Officers Assn. (pres. Oklahoma City chpt. 1984—85), Sigma Nu, Phi Delta Phi. Republican. Roman Catholic. Avocations: golf, swimming, tennis. Office: Necco & Byrd PC Landmark Towers W 3555 NW 58th St Ste 130 Oklahoma City OK 73112-1662 Office Phone: 405-948-8140. Personal E-mail: dnecco@cox.net. Business E-Mail: dnecco@neccoandbyrd.com.

NECHEMIAS, STEPHEN MURRAY, lawyer; b. St. Louis, July 27, 1944; s. Herbert Bernard and Toby Helen (Wax) N.; m. Marcia Rosenstein, June 19, 1966 (div. Dec. 1981); children: Daniel Jay, Scott Michael; m. Linda Adams, Aug. 20, 1983. BS, Ohio State U., 1966; JD, U. Cin., 1969. Bar: Ohio 1969. Ptnr. Taft, Stettinius & Hollister, Cin., 1969—. Adj. prof. law No. Ky. U., Chase Coll. Law. Tax comment author: Couse's Ohio Form Book, 6th edit., 1984. Mem. Ohio State Bar Assn. (former chmn. taxation com.), Cin. Bar Assn. (former chmn. taxation sect. 1985), Legal Aid Soc. Cin. (former pres., trustee), Am. Bar Assn. (taxation sect.) Democrat. Jewish. Home: 2490 Royalview Ct Cincinnati OH 45244 Office: 1800 US Bank Tower 425 Walnut St Cincinnati OH 45202-3923 Office Phone: 513-357-9392.

NECHIN, HERBERT BENJAMIN, lawyer; b. Chgo., Oct. 25, 1935; s. Abraham and Zelda (Benjamin) Nechin; m. Susan Zimmerman (div.); 1 child, Jill Rebecca; m. Roberta Fishman, Oct. 24, 1976; 1 child, Stefan. BA with distinction and with honors in History, Northwestern U., Evanston, Ill., 1956; JD, Harvard U. Law Sch., Cambridge, Mass., 1959. Bar: Ill. 1960. From assoc. to ptnr. Brown Fox & Blumberg, Chgo., 1960-75; ptnr. Taussig Wexler & Shaw, Chgo., 1975-79, Fink Coff Stern, Chgo., 1979-81, Holleb & Coff, Chgo., 1981-2000; of counsel Levin & Schreder, Ltd., Chgo., 2000—04; assoc. dir. gift planning Northwestern U., Evanston, Ill., 2004—. Contbr. articles to profl. jours. Pres. Emanuel Congregation, Chgo., 1994—97. Staff sgt. USAR, 1960—66. Mem.: ABA, Am. Coll. Trust and Estate Counsel, Chgo. Bar Assn. (chmn. trust law com. 1990—91), Ill. Bar Assn., Cliff Dwellers Club, Phi Beta Kappa. Office: Northwestern U Office Alumini Rels and Devel 2020 Ridge Ave 3rd Fl Evanston IL 60208-4307 Home Phone: 773-929-5889; Office Phone: 847-491-7394. Business E-Mail: h-nechin@northwestern.edu.

NEDERLANDER, JAMES LAURENCE, theater producer; b. Detroit, Jan. 23, 1960; s. James Morton and Barbara (Smith) N. Student, Cranbrook Prep, Boston U. Asst. mgr. Pineknob, Clarkston, Mich., producer NYC; v.p. Nederlander, NYC, now pres. Trustee Comprehensive Cancer Ctr. Wake Forest U.; bd. dirs. Comprehensive Cancer Ctr. Wake Forest U. Bapt. Med. Ctr. Assoc. prodr.: (plays) The Tragedy of Carmen, 1984 (Tony award, 1984); Starlight Express, 1989; Cafe Crown, 1989; A Mid Summer Night's Dream, 1996; The Capeman, 1997, Private Lives, 2002 (Tony award); (with Kathleen Turner) Who's Afraid of Virginia Woolf?, 2005; prodr.: (shows) Mort Sahl, 1988, (musicals) On Your Toes, 1987, Billy Joel and Twyla Tharp's Movin Out, 2002 (Touring Broadway award, Best New Musical, Leaugue Am. Theaters & Prodn., 2005), Thoroughly Modern Millie, 2002 (Tony award), (with Fred Molina) Fiddler on the Roof, 2004, La Cage Aux Folles, 2004, Twyla Tharp and Bob Dylan's The Times They Are A-Changin', 2006, Legally Blonde, 2007, A Moon for the Misbegotten, 2007; co-prodr.: (concerts) Kenny Loggins, 1988, Barry Manilow, 1989, Billy Joel, Yankee Stadium, 1990, Harry Connick Jr., 1990, Yanni, 1993, Pink Floyd, Yankee Stadium, 1994, U2, Yankee Stadium, 1994, Basia, 1994, Shari Lewis and Lambchop, 1994, Laurie Anderson, 1995, Ray Davies-20th Century Man, 1996, 42. Mem. Com. Am. Candlelite Vigil, 1990; bd. trustees Intrepid Museum, 1990, Fizher Ctr. for Alzheimer's Rsch. Found.; bd. dirs. Midtown Mgmt. Group, 1996; exec. com. N.Y.C. Vis. Bur.; bd. dirs. ASPCA. Mem. Exec. League N.Y. Theatres.

NEDERLANDER, JAMES MORTON, theater executive; b. Detroit, Mar. 31, 1922; s. David T. and Sarah L. (Applebaum) N.; m. Charlene Saunders, Feb. 12, 1969; children: James Laurence, Sharon, Kristina. Student, Detroit Inst. Tech. Chmn. Nederlander Orgn., Inc. (formerly Nederlander Producing Co. Am., Inc., NYC, 1966—. Owner and operator of numerous theaters including Palace Theatre, Lunt-Fontanne Theatre, Nederlander Theatre, Brooks Atkinson Theatre, Gershwin Theatre, Neil Simon Theatre, Marquis Theatre, Minskoff Theatre, Richard Rodgers Theatre, N.Y.C., Greek Theatre, Pantages Theatre, Henry Fonda Theatre, L.A., Shubert Theatre, Chgo., Fisher Theatre, Masonic Temple, Detroit, Aldwych Theatre, Adelphi Theatre, Dominion Theatre, London; producer numerous shows for Broadway including She Loves Me, Will Rogers Follies, Me and My Girl, Orpheus Descending, Les Liaisons Dangereuses, Nicholas Nickleby, Annie, La Cage aux Folles, Nine, Applause, Not Now Darling, See Saw, Oliver, Abelard and Heloise, Sherlock Holmes, Treemonisha, Habeus Corpus, Otherwise Engaged, Whose Life is it Anyway?, Betrayal, Woman of the Year, Lena Horne: The Lady and Her Music, The Dresser, Noises Off, Merlin, Night and Day, My Fat Friend, Shirley MacLaine on Broadway, Sweet Charity, Benefactors, Breaking the Code; numerous road show prodns.; revivals: Peter Pan, She Loves Me, Hello Dolly, Porgy and Bess, The Music Man, I Do! I Do!, Oklahoma, On a Clear Day You Can See Forever, Fiddler on the Roof. Office: Nederlander Orgn Inc 1450 Broadway Fl 6 New York NY 10018-2201

NEDERLANDER, ROBERT E., entertainment and television executive, lawyer; b. Detroit, Apr. 10, 1933; s. David T. and Sarah (Applebaum) N.; m. Caren Berman (div.); children: Robert E. Jr., Eric; Gladys Rackmil, Jan. 1, 1988. BA in Econs., U. Mich., 1955, JD, 1958, LLD (hon.), 1990. Ptnr. Nederlander, Dodge & Rollins, Detroit, 1960-90; pres. Nederlander Co. LLC (formerly Nederlander Orgn. Inc.), NYC, 1981—, Nederlander TV & Film Prodns., NYC, 1985—. Mng. gen. ptnr. N.Y. Yankees, 1990-91. Regent U. Mich., Ann Arbor, 1969-84; trustee Am. Health Found., 1989—; chmn. Gateway Am., 1991—. Recipient Disting. Alumni Svc. award U. Mich., 1985; named Man of Yr. by Gov.'s Com. on Scholastic Achievement, N.Y.C., 1991. Fellow ABA, Mich. Bar Assn. Avocations: tennis, baseball. Office: Nederlander Co LLC 1450 Broadway Ste 2000 New York NY 10018

NEDOM, H. ARTHUR, petroleum consultant; b. Lincoln, Nebr., Aug. 19, 1925; s. Henry Arthur and Pearle Bertrick (Swan) N.; m. Patricia Margaret Rankin, July 4, 1974; children: Richard A., Robert L., Nicole C. BS, U. Tulsa, 1949, MS, 1950; postgrad. in bus. adminstrn., Northwestern U., Evanston, Ill., 1968. Chief engr. Amerada Petroleum Corp., Tulsa, 1961-65, v.p., 1965-70, Natomas Co., San Francisco, 1971-74; also dir.; pres. Norwegian Oil Co., Houston, 1974-75; pres., mng. dir. Weeks Petroleum Ltd., Westport, Conn., 1975-82; cons., 1982—; chmn. bd. arbitration Prudhoe Bay Unit, 1983-85. Chmn. Offshore Tech. Conf., 1971; bd. dirs. Engrs. Joint Council, 1978 Contbr. articles to profl. jours. Served with inf. U.S. Army, 1943-45, ETO. Decorated Bronze Star; named Disting. Alumnus U. Tulsa, 1972 Mem. Soc. Petroleum Engrs. (dir. 1965-68, pres. 1967, Disting. Lectr. 1973, Disting Svc. award 1978, DeGolyer Disting. Svc. medal 1981, Disting. mem. 1983, Disting. lectr. emeritus 1989, Legion of Honor 1998, v.p. SPE Found. 1988-89), AIME (dir. 1966-69, 76-79, pres. 1977, hon. mem. 1982, Disting. Svc. award 1993), Am. Assn. Engring. Soc. (dir. 1980-82, chmn. 1981, Spl. award 1979, Engring. Svc. award 1980). Home: 9924 S Sandusky Ave Tulsa OK 74137-5311 Personal E-mail: artnedom@aol.com.

NEDZBALA, MICHAEL, lawyer; b. Washington, Feb. 2, 1962; BA in Econ., Govt., Univ. Va., 1984; JD, UNC, 1987. Ptnr. Hunton & Williams LLP, Charlotte, NC, 1995—, co-head, asset securitization group, mem. global capital mkts. team. Mem.: Va. State Bar Assn., NC State Bar Assn., Mecklenburg Co. Bar Assn., UNC Banking Inst. (bd. adv.). Office: Hunton & Williams LLP Bank of Am Plz Ste 3500 101 S Tryon St Charlotte NC 28280 Office Phone: 704-378-4703. Office Fax: 704-378-4890. Business E-Mail: mnedzbala@hunton.com.

NEECE, OLIVIA HELENE ERNST, investment company executive, consultant; b. LA, Jan. 3, 1948; d. Robert and Beatrice Pearl Ernst; m. Huntley Lee Bluestein, 1967 (div. 1974); children: Melissa Dawn, Brendon Wade; m. Anthony Ray Neece, Mar. 20, 1976. BSBA, U. So. Calif., 1990; MBA, UCLA, 1993; postgrad., Claremont U., 1998—2004. Cert. interior designer Calif. Coun. for Interior Design, UCLA, 1975; lic. gen. contractor, real estate broker, Calif. Staff designer Frances Lux Designs, LA, 1974; project designer Yates Silverman Inc., LA, 1974-77; owner Olivia Neece Planning & Design, Tarzana, Calif., 1977-86; v.p. project devel. Design Svc. /Aircoa, Englewood, Colo., 1986-87; v.p. project adminstrn. Hirsch-Bedner Assoc., Santa Monica, Calif., 1987—; treas.-sec. EON Corp., LA, 1980—87; owner Olivia Neece Planning & Design, Tarzana, 1980—88; dir. ops. The Ernst Group, LA, 1988—2005; pres. Neece Assocs., 2003—. Instr. ext. program UCLA, 1981—83; part-time prof. Calif. State U., Northridge, 1994—99; acad. rschr. Jet Propulsion Lab., 2000—02; spkr. in field. Co-author: A Step by Step Approach to Hotel Devel., 1988; contbr. chapters to books, articles to profl. jours. Co-chair LA Master Chorale Gala; mem. Hollywood Bowl Soc.; vol. restoration of San Diego R.R. Mus., 1985—92; patron LA Philharm., LA Opera Soc.; Found. of Music Ctr. of Los Angels; fellow circle Ctr. Theatre Group; donor, patron Costume Coun. LA County Mus. Art; deacon First Presbyn. Ch., Encino, Calif.; bd. dir., historian Master Choral Assoc., 1995—2005; bd. mem. Music Ctr. Club 100. Recipient Holiday Inn Devel. award, Foster City, Calif., 1986, Warwick, R.I., 1988, 1st and 2d pl. awards, Lodging Hospitality Designers Ctr., 1987, Gold Key award, Russell St. Inn, 1986, Best Paper award, Am. Conf. on Info. Systems, 2002. Mem. Am. Soc. Interior Designers (1st pl. portfolio competition 1974), Acad. of Mgmt. (Best Paper award 2002), Fin. Mgmt. Assn., Internat. Inst. Designers & Arch. (profl., v.p., bd. dir.), We. Acad. Mgmt., Assn. Info. Sys., Inst. Ops. Rsch. and Mgmt. Sci, Beta Gamma Sigma. Office: Neece Assoc 18200 Rosita St Tarzana CA 91356-4622 Personal E-mail: oneece@yahoo.com.

NEEDELL, BENJAMIN F., lawyer; b. Rahway, NJ, 1941; BA, Rutgers U., 1963; LLB, St. John's U., 1966. Bar: NY 1967. Ptnr. real estate Skadden, Arps, Slate, Meagher & Flom LLP, NYC. Bd. dir. Rock and Roll Hall of Fame, 1986—, mem., 1990—, Wenner Media, inc., 1978—. Mem. St. John's Law Rev. Chmn. Stratton Mountain Sch., 1988—93, mem., 1980—; mem., chmn. NY Restoration Project, 2002—; mem. Westchester Land Trust, 2001—. Office: Skadden Arps Slate Meagher & Flom LLP 4 Times Sq New York NY 10036

NEEDHAM, GEORGE AUSTIN, investment banker; b. Beverly, Mass., Jan. 27, 1943; s. Everett Austin and Edith Strode (Walton) N.; m. Ellen Ann Levin, July 9, 1978; children: Michael Austin, Sarah Elisabeth, Paul Everett. BS in Bus. Adminstrn., Bucknell U., 1965; MBA, Stanford U., 1971. Portfolio mgr. Bankers Trust Co., NYC, 1967-69; mng. dir. First Boston Corp., NYC, 1971-84; chmn., CEO Needham & Co. Inc., NYC, 1985—. Trustee Stanford Bus. Sch. Trust, Palo Alto, Calif., 1983-89. Served to 1st lt. U.S. Army, 1965-67. Mem. Fin. Analysts Fedn., Bond Club N.Y., The Links, Univ. Club, Sleepy Hollow Country Club, Coral Beach Club. Republican. Home: 79 E 79th St New York NY 10021-0202 Office: Needham & Co Inc 445 Park Ave New York NY 10022-2606 Office Phone: 212-705-0307. Business E-Mail: gneedham@needhamco.com.

NEEDHAM, GEORGE MICHAEL, association executive; b. Buffalo, July 3, 1955; s. Paul James and Dolores Ann (Duffy) N.; m. Joyce Elaine Leahy, Nov. 28, 1992; 1 stepchild, Katherine Cillian. BA in English, SUNY, Buffalo, 1976, MLS, 1977. Various profl. positions Charleston (S.C.) County Libr., 1977-84; dir. Fairfield County Dist. Libr., Lancaster, Ohio, 1984-89; mem. svcs. dir. Ohio Libr. Assn., Columbus, 1990-92; exec. dir. Pub. Libr. Assn., Chgo., 1993-96; state librarian State of Mich., Lansing, 1996-99; v.p. mem. svcs. OCLC Online Computer libr. Ctr., Dublin, Ohio, 1999—. Trustee Learning Point Assocs, 2004-. Co-author: A Director's Checklist for Connecting Public Libraries to the Internet, 1995; author (book revs.) Booklist, 1994-2002 (video revs.), Libr. Jours., 1979-94. Bd. dirs. Fairfield County chpt. ARC, Lancaster, 1984-88, Mt. Prospect Theatre Soc., Mt. Prospect, Ill., 1993-96, Lib. Media Project, 1997-2007. Mem. ALA, Pub. Libr. Assn., Ohio Libr. Assn. Achievements include 2 time Jeopardy champion. Avocations: acting, traditional folk music, writing. Office: OCLC Online Computer Libr Ctr 6565 Kilgour Pl Dublin OH 43017-3395 Home Phone: 614-761-0372; Office Phone: 614-761-5173. E-mail: needhamg@oclc.org.

NEEDHAM, GLEN RAY, entomology and acarology educator, researcher; b. Lamar, Colo., Dec. 25, 1951; s. Robert Lee and Evor Elaine (Kern) N.; m. Karla Marie Lohr, May 28, 1983; children: Kathleen Marie, John Harrison, Elizabeth Anne. BS, S.W. Okla. State U., 1973; MS, Okla. State U., 1975, PhD, 1978. Grad. rsch. asst. Okla. State U., Stillwater, 1974-78; asst. prof. Ohio State U., Columbus, 1978-84, assoc. prof., 1984—, co-organizer and coord. acarology summer program. Co-editor: Africanized Honey Bees and Bee Mites, 1988, Acarology IX: Proceedings and Symposia. Donor ARC, Columbus. Recipient Dist. Alumnus award Okla. State U., 1992; Christian fellow Ohio State U. Mem. Acarology Soc. Am. (pres. 1994), Ohio Acad. Sci., Ohio Asthma Coalition, Ctrl. Ohio Asthma Coalition, Lions Club, Gamma Sigma Delta. Methodist. Achievements include research in tick and dust mite biology and control. Office: Ohio State U 318 W 12th Ave Columbus OH 43210 Office Phone: 614-688-3026. Business E-Mail: needham.1@osu.edu.

NEEDHAM, KEITH ALAN, language educator; b. Bay City, Tex., Jan. 5, 1967; s. Douglas Earl and Melba Louise Needham. BA, Tex. State U., 1991, MA, 1993. Cert. secondary English Tex. State U., 1991. Tchg. asst. Tex. State U., San Marcos, 1991—93; tchr. Austin Ind. Sch. Dist., Tex., 1993—94; instr. English Lamar U., Beaumont, Tex., 1994—. Dir. TAL-Hent On Wheels, Beaumont, Tex., 2001—04, Adopt-A-Grandchild, Beaumont, 2004—, P.A.L.S. Unite!, Beaumont, 2006—. Recipient Julie and Ben Rogers Outstanding Cmty. Svc. award, 2004. Office: Lamar Univ PO Box 10023 Beaumont TX 77710 Office Phone: 409-880-8579. E-mail: KNForest34@aol.com.

NEEDHAM, RICHARD LEE, magazine editor; b. Cleve., Jan. 16, 1939; s. Lester Hayes and Helen (Bender) N.; m. Irene Juechter, Aug. 7, 1965; children: Margaret, Richard, Trevor. BA, Denison U., 1961; MA, U. Mo., 1967. Copy editor Sat. Rev., NYC, 1967-68; editor-in-chief Preview Internat., NYC, 1968-69; financial and N.Y. editor Instns. mag.; also editor Service World Internat., NYC, 1969-70; copy dir. American Home mag., NYC, 1970-71; exec. editor Ski Mag., NYC, 1971-74, editor, 1974-92, editor-in-chief, 1992-94, sr. contbg. editor, 1994—; contbg. editor Yachting Mag., NYC, 1996; editor Ency. of Skiing, 1978, Ski Fever, 1995; editl. dir. Times Mirror Mags. Conservation Coun., 1994-96; editor-in-chief Inside Tracks, 1996—2002; automotive writer Gannett Suburban Newspapers, 1995—; editor Arthritis Advisor, 2002—, Skiing Heritage, 2002—. Broadcaster: Ski Spot, CBS Radio, N.Y.C., 1978-83, On the Slopes, Audio Features Syndicate, 1984-87; author: Ski--50 Years in North America, 1992, Ski Fever!, 1995. Served to lt. USNR, 1961-65. Recipient Lowell Thomas award, 1985 Mem. N.Am. Ski Journalists Assn., Ea. Ski Writers Assn., Internat. Assn. Ski Journalists, Internat. Skiing History Assn. (Lifetime Achievement award). Home and Office: 481 Sandy Point Ave Portsmouth RI 02871-3515 E-mail: richardneedham@cox.net.

NEEDLEMAN, ALAN, mechanical engineering educator; b. Phila., Sept. 2, 1944; s. Herman and Hannah (Goodman) N.; m. Wanda Sapolsky, Apr. 12, 1970; children: Deborah, Daniel BS, U. Pa., 1966; MS, Harvard U., 1967, PhD, 1970. Instr. applied math. MIT, Cambridge, 1970-72, asst. prof., 1972-75; asst. prof. engring. Brown U., Providence, 1975-78, assoc. prof., 1978-81, prof., 1981—, dean engring., 1988-91, Florence Pirce Grant Univ. prof. Vis. asst. prof. Tech. U. Denmark, Lyngby, 1973; vis. fellow Clare Hall, U. Cambridge, Eng., 1978; vis. prof. MIT, Cambridge, 1991. Contbr. articles to profl. jours. Guggenheim fellow, 1977. Fellow ASME, Am. Acad. Mechanics, Danish Ctr. for Applied Math. and Mechanics (fgn.), Groupe Francais de Macanique des Materiaux (hon.), Am. Acad. Arts & Scis.; mem. NAE. Home: 24 Elton St Providence RI 02906-4106 Office: Brown U Div Engring Providence RI 02912-0001 E-mail: Alan_Needleman@brown.edu.

NEEDLEMAN, HERBERT LEROY, psychiatrist, pediatrician; b. Phila., Dec. 13, 1927; s. J. Joseph and Sonia Rita (Shupak) Needleman; m. Shirley Weinstein, Sept. 12, 1948 (div. 1957); 1 child, Samuel; m. Roberta Pizor, June 2, 1963; children: Joshua, Sara. BS, Muhlenberg Coll., Allentown, Pa., 1948; MD, U. Pa., 1952. Intern Phila. Gen. Hosp., 1952—54; resident in pediat. Children's Hosp. of Phila., 1957—58, chief resident in pediat., 1958—59; resident in psychiatry Temple U. Med. Ctr., Phila., 1962—65, asst. prof. psychiatry, 1967—71; spl. fellow in psychiatry NIMH, Bethesda, Md., 1965—67; assoc. prof. psychiatry Harvard Med. Sch., Boston, 1971—81; prof. psychiatry and pediat. U. Pitts. Sch. Medicine, 1981—. Cons. air lead criteria document EPA, Washington, 1977; editor Ctrs. for Disease Control, Atlanta, 1978; mem. adv. com. on childhood lead poisoning prevention, 90; chmn. devel. toxicology subpanel NAS, 1986. Editor: Low Level Lead Exposure: The Clinical Implications of Current Research, 1980; contbr. articles to profl. jours. Chmn. Alliance to End Childhood Lead Poisoning, Washington, 1991—92, Com. of Responsibility, Boston, 1966—75; bd. dirs. Mass. Advocacy Ctr., Boston, 1972—80. Capt. US Army, 1955—57. Recipient Sarah L. Poiley Meml. award, N.Y. Acad. Scis., 1985, The Charles A. Dana award, 1989, NAS IOM, 1990, H. John Heinz award, 1995, Edward Barsky award, Physicians' Forum, 1997, Disting. Grad. award, U. Pa. Sch. Medicine, 1999, Prince Mahidol award in pub. health, Bangkok, 2003, Vernon Houk award, Soc. Occupl. Environ. Health. Fellow: Am. Acad. Pediat.; mem.: Am. Acad. Pediat. Com. on Environ. Hazards, Am. Acad. Child and Adolescent Psychiatry, Am. Pediat. Soc., Soc. of Toxicology, Sigma Xi, Phi Beta Kappa. Democrat. Jewish. Avocations: trout fishing, carpentry. Office: Univ Pitts Sch Medicine 3520 5th Ave Pittsburgh PA 15213-3320 Office Phone: 412-383-3128. Business E-Mail: hlnlead@pitt.edu.

NEEDLEMAN, JACK, education educator, researcher; b. NYC, May 12, 1948; s. Charles and Bella Needleman; m. Barbara Berney, May 30, 1981; children: Rachel Berney Needleman, David Berney Needleman. BS, CCNY, 1969; MA, Syracuse U., NY, 1973; PhD, Harvard U., Cambridge, Mass., 1995. V.p. Lewin/ICF, Washington, 1973—90; asst. prof. Harvard U. Sch. Pub. Health, Boston, 1995—2003; assoc. prof. UCLA Sch. Pub. Health, 2003—. Mem. nursing adv. coun. Joint Commn. Accreditation Healthcare Orgns., Oakbrook Terrace, Ill., 2003—. Recipient Health Svcs. Rsch. Impact award, Acad. Health, 2006; numerous grants, NIH, US Agy. Healthcare Rsch. and Quality and Robert Wood Johnson Found. Mem.: Phi Beta Kappa. Jewish. Achievements include conducted widely-cited landmark studies on the association of hospital nurse staffing and quality of care. Office: UCLA Sch Pub Health PO Box 951772 Los Angeles CA 90095-1772 Home Phone: 310-820-8698; Office Phone: 310-267-2706. Business E-Mail: needlema@ucla.edu.

NEEDLEMAN, JACOB, philosophy educator, writer; b. Phila., Oct. 6, 1934; s. Benjamin and Ida (Seltzer) Needleman; m. Carla Satzman, Aug. 30, 1959 (div. 1989); children: Raphael, Eve; m. Gail Anderson, Dec. 1989. BA, Harvard U., 1956; grad., U. Freiburg, 1957-58; PhD, Yale U., 1961. Clin. psychology trainee West Haven (Conn.) Veterans Hosp. Adminstrn.,

1960-61; rsch. assoc. Rockefeller Inst., NY, 1961-62; from asst. prof. to assoc. prof. philosophy San Francisco State U., 1962-66, prof philosophy, 1967—, chair dept. philosophy, 1968-69. Vis. scholar Union Theol. Seminary, 1967-68; dir. Ctr. Study New Religions, 1977-83; lectr. psychiatry, cons. med. ethics U. Calif., 1981-84. Author: Being-in-the-World, 1963, The New Religions, 1970, Religion for a New Generation, 1973, A Sense of the Cosmos, 1975, On the Way to Self-Knowledge: Sacred Tradition and Psychotherapy, 1976, Lost Christianity, 1980, Consciousness and Tradition, 1982, The Heart of Philosophy, 1982, Sorcerers, 1986, Sin and Scientism, 1986, Lost Christianity: A Journey of Rediscovery to the Centre of Christian Experience, 1990, Money and the Meaning of Life, 1991, Modern Esoteric Spirituality, 1992, The Way of the Physician, 1993, The Indestructible Question, 1994, A Little Book on Love, 1996, Time and the Soul, 1998; The American Soul, 2002, The Wisdom of Love, 2005, Why Can't We Be Good?, 2007; (trans.) The Primary World of Senses, 1963, Essays on Ego Psychology, 1964; editor Care of Patients with Fatal Illness, 1969, The Sword of Gnosis, 1973, Sacred Tradition and Present Need, 1974, Understanding the New Religions, 1978, Speaking of My Life: The Art of Living in the Cultural Revolution, 1979, Real Philosophy: An Anthology of the Universal Search for Meaning, 1991, The American Soul, 2002; contbr. Death and Bereavement, 1969, To Live Within, 1971, My Life with a Brahmin Family, 1972, The New Man, 1972, The Universal Meaning of the Kabbalah, 1973, The Phenomenon of Death. Grantee Religion in Higher Edn., Marsden Found., 1967—68, Ella Lymna Cabot Trust, 1969, Far West Inst., 1975. Office: San Francisco State U Dept Philosophy 1600 Holloway Ave San Francisco CA 94132-1722 Office Phone: 415-338-2216. Business E-Mail: jneedle@sfsu.edu.

NEEDLEMAN, PHILIP, cardiologist, pharmacologist; b. Bklyn., Feb. 10, 1939; m. Sima Needleman. BS in Pharmacology, Phila. Coll. Pharm. & Sci., 1960, MS in Pharmacology, 1962; PhD in Pharmacology, U. Md. Med. Sch., 1964. Fellow Sch. Medicine Washington U., St. Louis, 1965—67, from asst. prof. to prof. Sch. Medicine, 1967—75, prof. Sch. Medicine, 1975—89, adj. prof., 1976—89, chmn., dept. pharmacology, 1989, chief scientist, 1991, assoc. dean, spl. projects, 2004; sr. v.p., chief scientist Monsanto, 1989—93; pres. Searle Pharma. Co., 1993—2000; sr. exec. v.p., chief scientist, chmn. R&D Pharmacia (fomerly Monsanto/Searle), 2000—03; ptnr. Prospect Ventures Ptnrs., 2003—. Served on com. NIH study sects.; adv. com. FDA, NIH, Nat. Coun. Washington Univ. Med. Sch. Contbr. numerous articles to profl. jours. Bd. trustee Washington U.; bd. dir. Barnes-Jewish Hosp., St. Louis Plant and Biotechnology consortium, St. Louis Sci. Ctr.; sci. advisor to pres. for R&D Ben Gurion U., 2002—, bd. trustee; mem. adv. com. for the creation of Nat. Inst. for Biotechnology in the Negev; bd. trustee Donald Danforth Plant Sci. Ctr. Recipient John Jacob Abel award, Am. Pharmacology Soc., 1974, Rsch. Career Devel. award, NIH, 1974, 1976, Wellcome Creesy award in clin. pharmacology, 1977, 1978, 1980, 1987, Cochems Thrombosis Rsch. prize, 1980, Rsch. Achievement award, Am. Heart Assn., 1988, Second Century award, 1994, C. Chester Stock award Lectureship, Meml. Sloan Kettering Cancer Ctr., 2001, Indsl. Rsch. Inst. medal, 2001, Am. Soc. Exptl. Therapeutics award, Dart/NYU Biotechnology Achievement awards, Biotechnology Study Ctr. NYU Sch. Medicine, 2005. Mem.: IOM, NAS (chair phamacology-physiology sect. 2001—04, bd. trustee NAS Coun. 2004, award for Indsl. Application of Sci. 2005). Achievements include pioneering studies on the role of Cox 1 and Cox 2 enzymes in inflammation, cardiovascular and renal disease, and in tumor progression; developing the first angiotensin receptor antagonist, the first thromboxane synthetase inhibitor; discovering atriopeptin, the atrial natriuretic factor, a novel endocrine peptide that allows the heart to communicate with the kidneys and blood vessels. Office: Prospect Venture Ptnrs 435 Tasso St Ste 200 Palo Alto CA 94301 Office Phone: 650-327-8800. Office Fax: 650-324-8838.

NEEL, HARRY BRYAN, III, surgeon, scientist, educator; b. Rochester, Minn., Oct. 28, 1939; s. Harry Bryan and May Birgitta (Bjornsson) N.; m. Ingrid Helene Vaga, Aug. 29, 1964; children: Carlton Bryan, Harry Bryan IV, Roger Clifton. BS, Cornell U., 1962; MD, SUNY-Bklyn., 1966; PhD, U. Minn., 1976. Diplomate Am. Bd. Otolaryngology. Intern Kings County Hosp., Bklyn., 1966-67; resident in gen. surgery U. Minn. Hosps., Mpls., 1967-68; clin. assoc. NCI/NIH, 1968—70; resident in otolaryngology Mayo Grad. Sch. Medicine Mayo Clinic, Rochester, Minn., 1970-74, cons. in otorhinolaryngology, 1974—2005, cons. in cell biology, 1981—2005, assoc. prof. otolaryngology and microbiology Med. Sch., 1979-84, prof., 1984—, also chmn. dept. otolaryngology. Mem. sci. adv. com. Pitts. Eye and Ear Found.; lifetime vis. prof. Hunan U., China, 2003—. Author: Cryosurgery for Cancer, 1976; contbr. chpts. to books, articles to profl. jours. V.p. bd. dirs. Minn. Orch. in Rochester, Inc., 1982, pres., chmn., 1983—84; mem. devel. com. Minn. Orchestral Assn., 1983, Mayo Found., 1983—86; bd. dirs. Mayo Health Plan, 1986—92, chmn., 1990—92; mem. bd. Mayo Mgmt. Svcs., Inc., 1992—94; mem. bd. regents U. Minn., 1991—2003, chair faculty staff, student affairs com., 1993—95, 1999, vice chmn. bd., 1995—97, chmn. fin. and ops. com., 1999, mem. audit com., 1995—2000, chair litigation review com., 2001—03, chair facilities com., 2001—03; bd. dirs. Greater Rochester Area Univ. Ctr., 1993—2003; trustee U. Minn. Found., 1996—2005, mem. fin. com., 1999—2005; chmn. U. Minn. Investment Adv. Com., 1999—2003; mem. State Commn. on U. Minn. Excellence, 2002; founder U. Minn.-Rochester Neel Scholarship Endowment Fund Health Scis., 2003. With USPHS, 1968—70. Recipient travel award Soc. Acad. Chmn. Otolaryngology, 1974, Ira J. Tresley rsch. award Am. Acad. Facial and Reconstructive Surgery, 1982, Master Tchr. award in surgery Alumni Assn. Coll. Medicine, SUNY, Health Sci. Ctr., Bklyn., 1991, Notable award Nat. Assn. Collegiate Women Athletic Adminstrs., 1992; name one of Best Drs. in Am., Good Housekeeping, 1991, Best Drs. in Am., Woodward/White, 1992—, Best Drs. in Minn., Minn. Monthly, 2003, Cmty. Leaders of World, Am.'s Top Physicians, Consumers' Rsch. Coun. Mem. AMA, ACS (bd. govs. 1985-90, devel. bd. 1988—, treas. 1990-98, sec.-treas. Minn. chpt. 1983-85, pres. 1988-89), Am. Acad. Otolaryngology-Head and Neck Surgery (prize for basic rsch. in otolaryngology 1972, bd. dirs. 1988-91, established Neel Disting. Rsch. Lectureship Endowment Fund 1994, audit com. 1998-2000, chair investment adv. com. 1995—, chmn. audit com. 1999-2000), Minn. Med. Assn. (com. on adminstrn. and fin. 2003—05, Cmty. Svc. award for outstanding cmty. svc. 2003, Pub. Svc. Achievement award 2003), Zumbro Valley Med. Soc., Am. Broncho-Esophagological Assn. (pres. 1989-90), Am. Laryngological, Rhinological and Oto. Sco. (Mosher award 1980, pres.-elect 1995-96, centennial pres. 1996-97, investment com. 1994—, historian, 2001—), Am. Laryngological Assn. (Casselberry award 1985, sec. 1988-93, v.p. 1994, pres. 1994—, Newcomb award 1996, Baker lectr. 1998), Assn. for Rsch. in Otolaryngology, Assn. Acad. Depts. in Otolaryngology (sec.-treas. 1984-86, pres.-elect 1986, pres. 1988-9), Alumni Assn. Cornell U. (Outstanding Alumni award 1985), Collegium ORL Amicitiae Sacrum (bd. dirs., 2d sec. 2000—), Am. Bd. Otolaryngology (bd. dirs. 1986-2005, treas. 1998-2004), Am Laryngol. Voice Rsch. and Edn. Found. (charter bd. dirs. 1996-2003), Rochester Golf and Country Club. Republican. Presbyterian. Home: 828 8th St SW Rochester MN 55902-6310 Office: Mayo Clinic 200 1st St SW Rochester MN 55905-0002 Home Phone: 507-282-0035.

NEEL, JOHN DODD, cemetery executive; b. McKeesport, Pa., Aug. 7, 1923; s. Harry Campbell and Anna (Dodd) N.; m. Daisy Jean Wyatt, Feb. 11, 1948; children: Harry C., John Dodd II, W. Wyatt (dec.), Jeffrey J BA, Pa. State U., 1946. From salesman to pres. Jefferson Meml. Park, Pitts., 1946-88, chmn. bd. dirs., 1988—; chmn. Jefferson Meml. Funeral Home. Former mem., and chmn now alt. Zoning Hearing Bd., Pleasant Hills, Pa., 1970—. Mem. adv. bd. Pa. State U., Greater Allegheny; former mem. Pa. State Real Estate Commn. 1st lt. USAAF, 1943-45 Decorated Air medal with 4 clusters, D.F.C.; recipient George Washington cert. Freedom Found., 1974 Mem. Pa. Cemetery Fun. Assn. (pres. 1963-65), Internat. Cemetery and Funeral Assn. (pres. 1973-74), West Jefferson Hills C. of C. (pres. 1984), VFW, Am. Legion 57th Bomb Wing Assn., South Hills Country Club, Indian Lake Golf Club, Aero Club, OX-5CLUB, Kiwanis (pres. 1959), Masons, Shriner, Tau Kappa Epsilon, Delta Sigma Pi Presbyterian. Office: 401 Curry Hollow Rd Pittsburgh PA 15236-4636 Office Phone: 412-655-4500.

NEEL, JUDY MURPHY, management consultant; b. Rhome, Tex. d. James W. and Linna B. (Vess) Neel; m. Ellis F. Murphy, Jr., Dec. 30, 1975; children from previous marriage: Mary B. Schmidt, Janet E. Hollingsworth, Susan E. Salinas. BS, Northwestern U., 1977; MBA, Roosevelt U., 1983. V.p. Murphy, Tashjian & Assocs., Chgo., 1960-73; exec. dir. Automotive Affiliated Rep. Assn., Chgo., 1973-78; mgr. Automotive Svc. Ind. Assn., Chgo., 1978-80; exec. dir. Am. Soc. Safety Engrs., Des Plaines, Ill., 1980-98, Am. Assn. Diabetes Educators, 1999—2003; mgmt. cons., 2003—. Recipient Assn. Leadership Award Bus. Women's Network/Assn. Trends Mag., 1998. Mem. Chgo. Soc. Assn. Execs. (bd. dirs. 1979—, pres. 1985—, Shapiro award 1991), Am. Soc. Assn. Execs. (sec.-treas. 1994, found. dir. 1986-90, bd. dirs. 1990-95, Key award 1986). Republican. Personal E-mail: jneelcae@aol.com.

NEEL, RICHARD EUGENE, economist, educator; b. Bluefield, Va., Jan. 7, 1932; s. Charles Richard and Zell LaVerne (Bowling) Neel; m. Binnie Jo LeFever, June 10, 1961; children: Jeffrey Richard, Cynthia Jo. BS, U. Tenn., 1954, MS, 1955; PhD, Ohio State U., 1960. Instr. econs. Ohio State U., 1958-60; asst. prof. econs. Coll. William and Mary, 1960-61; asst. prof. U. South Fla., 1961-63, assoc. prof., 1963-66, chmn. econs. and fin. programs, 1964-66, acting chmn. grad. program Coll. Bus Adminstrn., 1965-66; dir. instl. planning Fla. Tech. U., 1966-68, chmn. dept. econs., prof. econs., 1968-69; assoc. dean Sch. Bus. Adminstrn. Ga. State U., 1969-77, dean grad. studies Sch. Bus. Adminstrn., 1973-77, prof. econs. Sch. Bus. Adminstrn., 1969-78; dean Coll. Bus. Adminstrn. U. NC, Charlotte, 1978-93, prof. econs., 1978-97, dean emeritus Belk Coll. Bus. Adminstrn., 1997—, prof. econs. emeritus, 1997—. Author (contbg auth): (book) The Case Study of Off-Campus Postsecondary Education on Military Bases, 1980; contbr. articles, monographs to profl publs; editor: (book) Readings in Price Theory, 1973. Mem.: Beta Gamma Sigma, Phi Kappa Phi. Presbyterian. Office: U NC at Charlotte Dept Economics Charlotte NC 28223 Office Phone: 704-687-4122. Business E-Mail: reneel@uncc.edu.

NEELEMAN, DAVID G., air transportation executive; b. Sao Paulo, Brazil, Oct. 16, 1959; s. Gary and Rose Neeleman; m. Vicki Vranes, 1981; 9 children. Student, U. Utah, 1977—80. Co-founder, exec. v.p. Morris Air Corp., 1984—88, pres., 1988—94; mem. exec. planning com. Southwest Airlines, 1994; CEO Open Skies, 1995—98; co-founder WestJet, 1996—99; founder JetBlue Airways Corp., Forest Hills, NY, 1998—, CEO, 1998—2007, chmn., 2002—. Bd. dirs. WestJet, 1996—99. Named Travel Industry Innovator, Time mag., 2000; named one of Top Ten Entrepreneurs of 2000, Bus. Week Mag., Most Influential Bus. Travel Execs., Bus. Travel News, 2000; recipient NY Ten awards, Exec. Coun., 2004. Office: JetBlue Airways Corp 118-29 Queens Blvd Forest Hills NY 11415 *

NEELEY, BEVERLY EVON, sociologist, consultant; b. Oakland, Calif., June 14, 1947; d. Chester Arthur Neeley Jr. and Thalia Evon Neeley-Littlefield; m. Niles Bruce, Sept. 13, 1970 (div. Aug. 1977); 1 child, Autumn Yvonne Curd BA, U. Calif., Berkeley, 1970, MPH, 1972; PhD, U. Calif., San Diego, 1983. Eligibility supr. W. Oakland Health Ctr., 1970-72; health edn. supr. San Diego County Drug Edn., 1972-74; proposal writer, cons. Cmty. Crisis Ctr., San Diego, 1974-77; sociologist, dir., sec., treas. Image Mind, Inc., Oakland, 1993—. Instr. Calif. State U., San Diego, 1976; health planner Health Sys. Agy., San Diego, 1978; mem. adv. bd. Help Other People Evole Inst., Oakland, 2000—; sr. acad. cons. Hercules NAACP Saturday Sch., 2002; tchrs., rschr. Oakland Pub. Schs., 1983—. Author: The Ethiopian Grail: On the Origin of Cultural Excellence, 1994, Ancient Ethiopian Egyptian Cultural Excellence, 2003. Founder S.E. Drug Coalition, San Diego, 1974, Nu-Way Youth Svc. Ctr., San Diego, 1976. Mem. NAACP, Sojourner Truth Tenants Assn., Nat. Assn. Negro Bus. and Profl. Women's Clubs Inc. Avocations: reading, walking, cooking. Home and Office: 5915 Martin Luther King Jr Way B10 Oakland CA 94609 Office Phone: 510-653-7561. E-mail: drbneeley3@hotmail.com.

NEELEY, SHIRLEY J., school system administrator; 1 child, Brandy. BA, U. Houston, EdD in Curriculum and Instrn.; MA, Prarie View A&M U. Supt. Galena Park Independent Sch. Dist., Tex., 1995—2004; commr. Tex. Edn. Agency, 2004—. Former pres. Tex. Assn. of Suburban and Mid-Urban Schs.; mem. So. Regional Edn. Bd., 2003; supt. Tex. Assn. of Sch. Bd.'s, 2003. Bd. mem. Harris County Youth Program, Tex. Academic Decathlon; bd. dirs. North Channel Area C. of C. Mem.: Houston Livestock Show (life; com. mem.), Rotary Club. Avocations: motorcycling, cross stitch, cattle-ranching. Office: Tex Edn Agency 1701 N Congress Ave Austin TX 78701-1494 Office Phone: 512-463-8985. E-mail: commissioner@tea.state.tx.us.

NEELIN, J. DAVID, meteorologist, educator; arrived in U.S., 1983; BS with honors, U. Toronto, 1981, MS, 1983; PhD, Princeton U., NJ, 1987. Postdoctoral assoc. dept. Earth, atmospheric and planetary scis. MIT, Cambridge, Mass., 1987—88, vis. assoc. prof., 1994—95; asst. prof. dept. atmospheric scis. UCLA, 1988—92, assoc. prof., 1992—95, prof., 1995—. Mem. Inst. Geophysics and Planetary Physics, LA, 1995—; vice chair dept. atmospheric and oceanic scis. UCLA, 2004—. Contbr. articles to profl. jours.; assoc. editor: Jour. Climate, 1996—. Recipient Presdl. Young Investigator award, 1991—96, Spl. Creativity award, NSF, 1999—2000; grantee Guggenheim fellowship, 2007. Fellow: Am. Meteorol. Soc. (C. L. Meisinger award 1996), Royal Meteorol. Soc.; mem.: AAAS, Can. Meteorol. and Oceanog. Soc., Am. Geophys. Union. Office: Dept Atmospheric and Oceanic Scis UCLA 405 Hilgard Ave Los Angeles CA 90095-1565 Office Phone: 310-206-3734. E-mail: neelin@atmos.ucla.edu. *

NEELY, ALEXIS, lawyer; 2 children. Grad., Georgetown U. Law Ctr. Founding ptnr. Martin Neely & Assocs., Redondo Beach, Calif., 2003—. Founder Family Wealth Planning Inst. Named a Rising Star, LA Mag.; named one of Top 100 Attys., Worth mag., 2005—06. Office: Martin Neely & Assocs 417 Beryl St Redondo Beach CA 90277 Office Phone: 310-697-0411. Office Fax: 310-531-7395. E-mail: alexis@martinneely.com. *

NEELY, CHARLES B., JR., lawyer; b. Raleigh, NC, Dec. 11, 1943; AB with honors, U. N.C., 1965; JD, Duke U., 1970. Bar: N.C. 1970. Lawyer Maupin Taylor P.A., Raleigh. Mem. 4th Cir. Jud. Conf. Mem. N.C. Ho. of Reps., 1995-99. Capt. USNR, JAGC, 1965-89. Fellow Am. Bar Found.; mem. ABA (taxation sect.), N.C. Bar Assn. (chmn. law office mgmt. sect. 1986-88, bd. govs. 1995-98), Inst. for Profls. in Taxation. Address: Maupin Taylor PA PO Drawer 19764 Ste 500 3200 Beechleaf Ct Raleigh NC 27619 E-mail: cneely@maupintaylor.com.

NEELY, JOHN GAIL, otolaryngologist; b. Oklahoma City, Dec. 10, 1939; MD, U. Okla., 1965. Intern U. Oreg. Med. Ctr., Portland, 1965-66; resident in surgery Baylor Hosp., Houston, 1968-69, resident in otolaryngology, 1969-72; fellow Otologic Med. Group, LA, 1972-73; staff Barnes Hosp., St. Louis, 1992—, Jewish Hosp., St. Louis, 1992—; prof., dir. rsch. Washington U., St. Louis, 1992—. Mem. ACS, Am. Neurotology Soc., Am. Otol. Soc., Am. Acad. Otolaryngology, Head and Neck Surgery, Soc. Univ. Otolaryngologists, Triologic Soc. Office: Washington U Sch Medicine Dept Oto Head-Neck Surgery 660 S Euclid Ave Box 8115 Saint Louis MO 63110-1010 Office Phone: 314-362-7344. Business E-Mail: neelyg@ent.wustl.edu.

NEELY, MARK EDWARD, JR., writer; b. Amarillo, Tex., Nov. 10, 1944; s. Mark Edward and Lottie (Wright) N.; m. Sylvia Eakes, June 15, 1966. BA, Yale U., 1966, PhD, 1973; LHD (hon.), Lincoln Coll., 1981. Visiting instr. Iowa State U., 1971—72; dir. Louis A. Warren Lincoln Library and Museum, Ft. Wayne, Ind., 1972—92; John Francis Bannon Prof. History and Am. Studies Saint Louis U., 1992—98; McCabe-Greer Prof. Civil War History Pa. State U., University Park, 1998—. Vis. instr. Iowa State U., Ames, 1971-72; editor Lincoln Lore, 1973—; mem. adv. bd. Ind. Historical Bureau, 1980—; mem. editorial adv. com. Ind. Mag. of History, 1981—; mem. editorial bd. Ulysses S. Grant Assn., 1981—. Author: The Abraham Lincoln Encyclopedia, 1981, The Lincoln Family Album: Photographs From The Personal Collection of a Historic American Family, 1990, The Fate of Liberty: Abraham Lincoln and Civil Liberties, 1991 (Pulitzer Prize for history 1992), The Last Best Hope on Earth: Abraham Lincoln and the Promise of America, 1993, Southern Rights: Political Prisoners and the Myth of Confederate Constitutionalism, 1999, The Union Divided: Party Conflict in the Civil War North, 2002, The Boundaries of American Political Culture in the Civil War Era, 2005; (with Harold Holzer and Gabor S. Boritt) The Lincoln Image: Abraham Lincoln and the Popular Print, 1984, The Confederate Image: Prints of the Last Cause, 1987; (with R. Gerald McMurty) The Insanity File: The Case of Mary Todd Lincoln, 1986; (with Holzer) Mine Eyes Have Seen the Glory: The Civil War in American Art, 1993. Mem. Abraham Lincoln Assn., Soc. Ind. Archivists (pres. 1980-81), Ind. Assn. of Historians (pres. 1987-88).

NEELY, RICHARD, lawyer; b. Aug. 2, 1941; s. John Champ and Elinore (Forlani) N.; m. Carolyn Elaine Elmore, 1979; children: John Champ, Charles Whittaker. AB, Dartmouth Coll., 1964; LLB, Yale U., 1967. Bar: W.Va. 1967. Practiced in, Fairmont, W.Va., 1969-73; chmn. Marion County Bd. Pub. Health, 1971-72; mem. W.Va. Ho. of Dels., 1971-73; justice, chief justice W.Va. Supreme Ct. of Appeals, Charleston, 1973-95; ptnr. Neely & Hunter, Charleston, 1995—2007, Neely & Callaghan, Charleston, 2007—. Chmn. bd. Kane & Keyser Co., Belington, W.Va., 1970-88. Author: How Courts Govern America, 1980, Why Courts Don't Work, 1983, The Divorce Decision, 1984, Judicial Jeopardy: When Business Collides with the Courts, 1986, The Product Liability Mess: How Business Can Be Rescued from State Court Politics, 1988, Take Back Your Neighborhood: A Case for Modern-Day Vigilantism, 1990, Tragedies of our Own Making: How Private Choices have Created Public Bankruptcy, 1994; contbr. articles to nat. mags. Mem. bd. advisors BNA Class Action Litigation Report. Capt. US Army, 1967-69. Decorated Bronze Star, Vietnam Honor medal 1st Class. Mem.: Am. Legion, VFW, Internat. Brotherhood Elec. Workers, W.Va. Bar Assn., Fourth Cir. Jud. Conf. (life), Moose, Phi Sigma Kappa, Phi Delta Phi. Episcopalian. Office: Neely & Callaghan 159 Summers St Charleston WV 25301-2134 Office Phone: 304-343-6500. Business E-Mail: rneely@neelycallaghan.com.

NEELY, SALLY SCHULTZ, lawyer; b. LA, Mar. 2, 1948; BA, Stanford U., 1970, JD, 1971. Bar: Ariz. 1972, Calif. 1977. Law clk. to judge U.S. Ct. Appeals (9th cir.), Phoenix, 1971-72; assoc. Lewis and Roca, Phoenix, 1972-75; asst. prof. Law Sch. Harvard U., Cambridge, Mass., 1975-77; assoc. Shutan & Trost, P.C., LA, 1977-79; ptnr., sr. counsel Sidley Austin LLP (and predecessor firms), LA, 1980—. Co-chair Am. Law Inst.-ABA Chpt. 11 Bus. Reorgns., 1989-95, 97—, Banking and Comml. Lending Law, 1997-99, Nat. Conf. Bankruptcy Judges, 1988, 90, 95, 96, 97, 99, 02, 06 Fed. Jud. Ctr., 1989, 90, 94-95, Southeast Bankruptcy Law Inst., 2002, 2006 Workshop Bankruptcy and Bus. Reorgn. NYU, 1992—; rep. 9th cir. jud. conf., 1989-91; mem. Nat. Bankruptcy Conf., 1993—, co-chair com. on legis., 2001—, mem. exec. com. Chair Stanford U. Law Sch. Reunion Giving, 1996; bd. vis. Stanford U. Law Sch., 1990-92; mem. bd. dir. LA Children's Chorus, 2006-. Mem.: ABA, Calif. Bar Assn., Am. Coll. Bankruptcy (mem. bd. regents 1998—2003, bd. dirs. 2003—05, co-chair ednl. programs com. 2003—, v.p. 2005—). Office: Sidley Austin LLP 555 W 5th St Ste 4000 Los Angeles CA 90013-3000 Office Phone: 213-896-6024. Business E-Mail: sneely@sidley.com.

NEELY, STEPHANIE, librarian; 4 children. M in Libr. and Info. Sci., U. Tex., Austin, 1989. Tel. reference rschr. Austin Pub. Libr., Tex., 1985, mng. dir. Little Walnut Creek br., 1997, mng. libr. Daniel E. Ruiz br. Recipient NY Times Libr. award, 2006. Mem.: Tex. Libr. Assn. Office: Daniel E Ruiz Br Austin Pub Libr 1600 Grove Blvd Austin TX 78741 Office Phone: 512-836-8975. E-mail: Stephanie.Neely@ci.austin.tx.us.

NEELY, WILLIAM CHARLES, chemistry professor, consultant, research scientist; b. Cave City, Ark., Nov. 22, 1931; s. Kenneth Andrew and Sara Virginia Neely; m. Betty Jean Tibi, Dec. 7, 1956; children: Virginia Stringfellow, William(dec.). PhD, La. State U., 1962. Rsch. chemist Chemstrand Rsch. Ctr. Inc., Research Triangle Park, NC, 1962—66; prof. Auburn (Ala.) U., 1962—. Cons. Auburn Chem. Co. Inc., 1986—, Sci. Applications Internat., San Diego, 1995—. Contbr. articles to profl. jours.; inventor in field. Chmn. Bd. Zoning Adjustment, Auburn, 1986—96. With US Army, 1954—56, Germany. Mem.: Sigma Xi (life). Home: 415 Hare Ave Auburn AL 36830 Office: Auburn U Dept Chemistry 257 Chemistry Bldg Auburn AL 36849 Office Phone: 334-844-4043. Business E-Mail: neelywc@auburn.edu.

NEER, CHARLES SUMNER, II, orthopedic surgeon, educator; b. Vinita, Okla., Nov. 10, 1917; s. Charles Sumner and Pearl Victoria (Brooke) N.; m. Eileen Meyer, June 12, 1990; children: Charlotte Marguerite, Sydney Victoria, Charles Henry. BA, Dartmouth Coll., 1939; MD, U. Pa., 1942. Diplomate Am. Bd. Orthopaedic Surgery (bd. dirs. 1970-75). Intern U. Pa. Hosp., Phila., 1942-43; asso. in surgery N.Y. Orthopedic-Columbia-Presbyn. Med. Center, NYC, 1943-44; instr. in surgery Coll. Physicians and Surgeons, Columbia U., NYC, 1946-47, instr. orthopaedic surgery, 1947-57, asst. prof. clin. orthopaedic surgery, 1957-64, asso. prof., 1964-68, prof. clin. orthopaedic surgery, 1968-90, prof. clin. orthopaedic surgery emeritus, spl. lectr. orthopaedic surgery, 1990—. Attending orthopaedic surgeon Columbia-Presbyn. Med. Ctr., N.Y.C.; chief adult reconstructive svc. N.Y. Orthopaedic Hosp.; chief shoulder and elbow clinic Presbyn. Hosp.; cons. orthopaedic surgeon emeritus N.Y. Orthopaedic-Columbia-Presbyn. Med. Ctr., 1991—; chmn. 4th Internat. Congress Shoulder Surgeons; chmn. Internat. Bd. Shoulder Surgery, 1992—. Founder, chmn. bd. trustees Jour. Shoulder and Elbow Surgery, 1990—; contbr. articles to books, tech. films, sound slides. Served with U.S. Army, 1944-46. Recipient Disting. Svc. award Am. Bd. Orthopaedic Surgeons 1975. Fellow ACS (sr. mem. nat. com. on trauma), Am. Acad. Orthop. Surgeons (com. on upper extremity, shoulder com.); mem. AMA, ACS (mem. com. trauma), Am. Bd. Orthop. Surgeons (bd. dirs. 1970-75, Disting. Svc. award 1975), Am. Shoulder and Elbow Surgeons (inaugural pres.), Am. Assn. Surgery Trauma, Am. Orthop. Assn., Mid-Am. Orthop. Assn. (hon.), N.Y. Acad. Medicine, Allen O. Whipple Surg. Soc., N.Y. State Med. Soc., N.Y. County Med. Soc., Pan Am. Med. Assn., Am. Trauma Soc., Soc. Latino Am. Orthop. y Traumatology, Internat. Soc. Orthop. Surgery and Traumatology, Va. Orthop. Soc. (hon.), Carolina Orthop. Alumni Assn. (hon.), Conn. Orthop. Club (hon.), Houston Orthop. Assn. (hon.), Soc. Française de Chirurgie Orthop. et Traumatology (hon.), Soc. Italiana Orthop. Etravmatologia e Traumatologia; patron, Shoulder and Elbow Soc. Australia, South African Shoulder Soc., Giraffe Club, Internat. Bd. Shoulder Surgery (chmn. 1992—), Alpha Omega Alpha, Phi Chi.

Home and Office: 231 S Miller St Vinita OK 74301-3625 Office Phone: 918-256-6673. E-mail: elmcreekacres@junct.com. *Forever grateful I could be a doctor and especially to work in the exciting area of shoulder surgery.*

NEERMAN, SANDRA M., library director; BA in Religion and Philosophy, St. Andrews Coll., Laurinburg, NC; MLS, George Peabody Coll., Nashville. Br. mgr. Greensboro Pub. Libr., NC, 1976, asst. dir. mktg. and ext., 1986, interim dir., 1996, dir., 1996—. Dir. NC Libr. Assn., 1993—95. Mem. adv. com. YWCA; bd. mem. Family Life Coun., 2003—05. Mem.: ALA (mem. literacy com. 2000, 2003), Pub. Libr. Assn. (Charlie Robinson award 2006), Rotary Club Greensboro. Office: Greensboro Pub Libr 219 N Church St Greensboro NC 27402-3178 Office Phone: 336-373-2699. Office Fax: 336-333-6781. E-mail: sandy.neerman@greensboro-nc.gov.

NEFF, AMY HANCOCK, elementary school educator; b. Phila., Dec. 1, 1961; d. Vance and Doris (Kroesser) Hancock; m. Ernest William Neff, July 18, 1987; 1 child, Kaylee. BS in Edn., Bloomsburg U., 1983; MEd, Beaver Coll., 1990. Elem. tchr. Archdiocese of Phila., 1983-85; contract specialist GSA, 1985-86; elem. tchr. Neshaminy Sch. Dist., Langhorne, Pa., 1987—. Bldg. sci. rep. K-12 Sci. Adv. Com., Langhorne, 1987-99, 2001-2002; mem. Sci. Textbook Selection Com., Langhorne, 1991; sch. sci. fair coord., 1992-94; participant NASA Ednl. Workshop for Elem. Sch. Tchrs., Kennedy Space Ctr., Fla., 1990, Johnson Space Ctr., Houston, 1991; Project LABS participant Rohm and Haas Corp., summer, 1994, presenter Delaware Valley Sci. Week; presenter dist.-wide space and physics workshops, 1990-94; participant Sci. Lesson Study, 2004-2005; mem. Grade 4 Curriculum Devel. Com. for Social Studies, sci. program pilot tchr., 2006-. Rider Am. Cancer Soc., Bike-a-Thons, 1989-92, MS 150 Bike Tour, 1992; vol. Action Team, Langhorne, 1991. Mem. Am. Fedn. Tchrs., Nat. Sci. Tchrs. Assn. (dist. rep. nat. conv. 1991-93), Bucks County Sci. Tchrs. Assn., Phila. Area Elem. Sci. Tchrs. Assn., Kappa Delta Pi (v.p. 1981-82). Avocations: guitar, bicycling, singing, aerobics, yoga. Home: 12 Amaryllis Ln Newtown PA 18940-1246 Office: Oliver Heckman Elem Sch Cherry St Langhorne PA 19047

NEFF, BONITA DOSTAL, communication development facilitator; b. Grinnell, Iowa, Aug. 16, 1942; d. Lester Ernest and Mary Margaret (Hudnut) Dostal; m. Gregory Pall Neff, Apr. 27, 1974; 1 child, Kristiana. BA, U. N. Iowa, 1964, MA, 1966; PhD, U. Mich., 1973; AA cum laude, Lansing C.C., Mich., 1980. Cert. cycling instr. Edn. leadership fellow George Washington U., Washington, 1976-77; specialist Mich. State U., East Lansing, 1977-80, co-investigator family and child inst. energy rsch. team, 1980-82; asst. prof. comm. Purdue U., Hammond, Ind., 1982-87; pres. Pub. Comm. Assocs., Munster, Ind., 1986—; assoc. prof. comm. Valparaiso (Ind.) U., 1991—; tchr., scholar Nat. Comm. Assn., Inst. for Faculty Devel., 2006. Co-organizer European Comm. Conf., Dubrovnik, Croatia, 2002—; vis. prof. grad. comm. program U. Kadar, Croatia, 2003, Sogang U., Seoul, Republic of Korea, 2005; co-founding mem. Internat. Interdisciplinary and Intercultural Annual Conf. in Pub. Rels., Sogang; adv. bd. Australian Ctr. Pub. Comm.; presenter, cons. in field. Co-author: Public Relations: From Theory to Practice; mem. adv. bd., reviewer Jour. Applied Comm. Rsch.; mem. editl. bd. Jour. Promotional Mgmt., Jour. Pub. Rels. Rsch., Pub. Rels. Rev., on-line jour. multicultural comm. from Cyprus; reviewer Mgmt. Comm. Quar.: An Internat. Jour.; editor procs. on accreditation for nat. conf.; contbr. chpts. in books, profl. articles and poetry to jours. Mem. Nat. Steering Commn. for Revision of Pub. Rels. Curriculum, 1996—; chair nat. benchmark study on pub. rels. edn.; mem. Nat. Task Force Pub. Rels. Conf. 1998; mem. Lake County (Ind.) Cmty. Devel. Bd., 1984—; bd. dirs. Big Bros. and Big Sisters N.W. Ind., 1984, 87; pres., chmn. bd. dirs. N.W. Ind. Youth Chorus, 1985—; bd. dirs., mktg. com. N.W. Ind. Symphony, bd. dirs. Lakeshore Pub. TV(PBS56-Ind.), sec. exec. com., 2000—, chair cmty. adv. bd. 2007; pub. rep. Nat. PBS Adv. Bd. Faculty Rsch. grant U. Mich., 1971, Consumer Product Safety Coun. grant, 1976-77, Ind. Arts Commn./Nat. Endowment for Arts grant, 1990-92, Valparaiso U. Diversity grant, 1996 Mem.: Nat. Commn. on Undergrad. and Grad. Pub. Rels. Curriculum (nat. task force for conf. 1998), Pub. Rels. Soc. Am. (advisor 2001—, sec. internat. divsn. 2005—, established student chpt.), Internat. Acad. Bus. Disciplines (co-chair pub. rels. divsn.), World Comm. Assn., Assn. Educators in Journalism Mass Comm. (chair internat. com. 1994—96, scholarly liaison com. 1995—, chair pub. rels. divsn. 2007), Ctrl. States Comm. Assn. (founder and chmn. 1988—89, pub. rels. officer 1989—92), Nat. Comm. Assn. (founder and twice chair of pub. rels. divsn. 1988, chmn. nat. Pub. Rels. Rsch. awards com. PRIDE 1988, nat. legis. coun. rep. 1993—96, seminar leader 2006, nat. com. on convs. allied orgns., task force on nat. policy), Internat. Pub. Rels. Assn., Internat. Comm. Assn. (chmn. task force on accreditation 1988, newsletter editor 1997, chair planning pub. rels. divsn. internat. conf. South Korea, chair dissertation thesis award com. pub. rels. divsn., founding mem., chair), Assn. Women in Comm. (assoc.; pres. Calumet chpt. 1985—90, advisor Valparaiso Student AWC, Inc. 1994—, advisor PRSSA student chpt. and PR agy., Outstanding Communicator 1990, Nat. Outstanding chpt. advisor 1999). Democrat. Roman Catholic. Avocations: ballet, tap, piano, reading, professional clown. Home: 8320 Greenwood Ave Munster IN 46321-1813 Office: Pub Comm Assocs 8320 Greenwood Ave Munster IN 46321-1813 Office Phone: 219-464-6827. Business E-Mail: bonita.neff@valpo.edu.

NEFF, DANIEL A., lawyer; b. Phila., Jan. 7, 1953; AB magna cum laude, Brown U., 1974; JD, Columbia U., 1977. Bar: N.Y. 1978, D.C. 1980. Ptnr., corp. dept. Wachtell, Lipton, Rosen & Katz, NYC, mng. ptnr. of firm. Notes and comments editor: Columbia Law Rev., 1976-77. Named in Dealmaker of the Year article, Am. Lawyer mag., 2001. Mem. ABA, Phi Beta Kappa. Office: Wachtell Lipton Rosen & Katz c/o Gail Edelman 51 W 52nd St Fl 29 New York NY 10019-6150 Office Phone: 212-403-1218. Office Fax: 212-403-2218. Business E-Mail: daneff@wlrk.com.

NEFF, DAVID M., lawyer; b. Allentown, Pa., Nov. 18, 1960; BSJ, Northwestern Univ., 1982; JD, DePaul Univ., 1985. Bar: Ill. 1985, US Dist. Ct. (no. Ill., ea. & we. Wis., we. Mich. dist.). Law clk. Judge Robert E. Ginsberg, US Bankruptcy Ct., no. dist. Ill., 1985—86; ptnr., co-chmn. Lodging & Timeshare practice group DLA Piper US LLP, Chgo. Contbr. articles to profl. jours. Mem.: Internat. Soc. Hospitality Consultants (chmn.), ABA (co-chmn. publications, Bankruptcy & Insolvency subcommittee.), Am. Bankruptcy Inst., 7th Cir. Bar Assn. (Ill. bankruptcy liason), Chgo. Bar Assn. (chmn. bankruptcy & reorganization com. 1998—99). Office: DLA Piper US LLP Suite 1900 203 N LaSalle St Chicago IL 60601-1293 Office Phone: 312-368-4042. Office Fax: 312-630-2758. Business E-Mail: david.neff@dlapiper.com.

NEFF, DONALD LLOYD, news correspondent, writer; b. York, Pa., Oct. 15, 1930; s. Harry William and Gertrude Marie N.; m. Abigail Trafford; 1 son, Gregory Harry. Student, Trinity Coll., San Antonio, 1949, York Coll., 1950-52, N.Y. U., 1953. Reporter York Dispatch, 1954-56, L.A. Mirror-News, 1956-57, UPI, LA, 1957-61; with L.A. Times, 1961-64, bur. chief Tokyo, 1964; with Time mag., 1965-81, corr. Vietnam, 1965-66, writer NYC, 1966-68, bur. chief Houston, 1968-70, LA, 1970-73, Jerusalem, 1975-78, NYC, 1978-79, sr. editor, 1973-75; news svcs. editor Washington Star, 1979-80; Wash. correspondant Mid. East Internat., London, 1991—2001. Author: Warriors at Suez: Eisenhower Takes America into the Middle East, 1981, Warriors for Jerusalem, The Six Days That Changed the Middle East, 1984; Warriors Against Israel, 1988, Fallen Pillars; U.S. Policy Toward Palestine and Israel since 1945, 1995, 2d edit., 2002, Fifty Years of Israel, 1998. Served with AUS, 1948-50. Recipient Theta Sigma Phi Matrix award, 1962, Calif.-Nev. AP Writing Contest best met. spot news story award, 1962, Overseas Press Club award for best fgn. article in a mag., 1979; finalist Am. Book Award History category, 1982. Mem. Fgn. Press Assn. (Israel pres. 1977, v.p. 1978)

NEFF, FRED LEONARD, lawyer; b. St. Paul, Nov. 1, 1948; s. Elliott Ira and Mollie (Poboisk) N.; m. Christa Ruth Powell, Sept. 10, 1989; 1 child, Lena. BS with high distinction, U. Minn., 1970; JD, William Mitchell Coll. Law, 1976. Bar: Minn. 1976, ND 1994, US Dist. Ct. Minn. 1977, US Ct. Appeals (8th cir.) 1985, US Supreme Ct. 1985, Wis. 1986, US Dist. Ct. (ea. and we. dists.) Wis. 1992. Tchr. Hopkins Pub. Schs., Minn., 1970-72; instr. U. Minn., Mpls., 1974-76; pvt. practice Mpls., 1976-79; asst. county atty. Sibley County, Gaylord, Minn., 1979-80; mng. atty. Hyatt Legal Svcs., St. Paul, 1981-83, regional ptnr., 1983-85, profl. devel. ptnr., 1985-86; pres. Neff Law Firm, PA, Mpls., 1986—; CEO Profl. Devel. Inst. Inc., Edina, Minn., 1994—, also bd. dirs. Instr. Inver Hills Coll., 1973-77; counsel Am. Tool Supply Co., St. Paul, 1976-78; cons. Nat. Detective Agy., Inc., St. Paul, 1980-83; CEO A Basic Legal Svc., Bloomington, 1990—; CEO, bd. dirs. Profl. Devel. Inst., Inc., Edina, Minn., 1994—; lectr., guest instr. U. Wis., River Falls, 1976-77; spl. instr. Hamline U., St. Paul, 1977; vis. lectr. Coll. St. Scholastica, Duluth, Minn., 1977; program. faculty, cons. Employment Law Seminar for Colo., Fla., La., Oreg., Employment and Labor Law Seminar for Ala., Alaska, Calif., Conn., Ind., NC, Ohio, Va., NC Safety and Health at the Workplace, SC Labor Law, Ohio Safety at the Workplace; bd. dirs. Acceptance Ins. Holdings, Inc., Omaha; active Internat. Confederation Jurists, 1993; mem. faculty sem. Ariz. Safety at Workplace, Hawaii Employment & Labor, Miss. Employment & Labor Law, Del. Employment & Labor, Alaska Employment and Labor Law, Ga. Employment & Labor Law, NJ Employment & Labor, Wash. Employment Law, Mass. Employment & Labor Law, 1995—, Ark. Employment and Labor Law, Mo. Employment and Labor Law, Iowa Employment and Labor Law, Utah Employment and Labor Law; pres. Martial Arts Bookstore Internat., Inc., 1998; pres. Endless Fist Soc., Inc., 1998. Author: Fred Neff's Self-Defense Library, 1976, Everybody's Self-Defense Book, 1978, Karate Is for Me, 1980, Running Is for Me, 1980, Lessons from the Samurai, 1986, Lessons from the Art of Kempo, 1986, Lessons from the Western Warriors, 1986, Lessons from the Fighting Commandos, 1990, Lessons from the Ancient Japanese Masters of Self-Defense, 1990, Lessons from the Eastern Warriors, 1990, Mysterious Persons of the Past, 1991, Great Mysteries of Crime, 1991; host TV series Great Puzzles In History; co-host TV series Great Unsolved Crimes, Minn.; asst. editor: Hennepin County Lawyer, 1992—. Advisor to bd. Sibley County Commrs., 1979-80; speaker civic groups, 1976-82; mem. Hennepin County Juvenile Justice Panel, 1980-82, Hennepin County (Minn.) Pub. Def. Conflict Panel, 1980-82, 86—, Hennepin County Bar Assn. Advice Panel Law Day, 1987, mem. dist. ethics com., 1990-2004; mem. Panel Union Privilege Legal Svcs. div. AFL-CIO, 1986—, Signature Legal Svcs., 2003—, Montgomery Wards Legal Svcs. Panel, 1986—, Edina Hist. Soc., Decathlon Athletic Club; charter mem. Commn. for the Battle of Normandy Mus.; founding sponsor Civil Justice Found., 1986—; mem. com. for publ. Hennepin County Lawyer, 1992; pres. Endless Fist Soc., Inc., 1998—, martial arts website, 2007. Recipient Outstanding Tchr. award Inver Hills Coll. Student Body, 1973, St. Paul Citizen of Month award Citizens Group, 1975, Kempo Club award U. Minn., 1975, U. Minn. Student Appreciation award Kempo Club, 1978, Sibley County Atty. Commendation award, 1980, Good Neighbor award WCCO Radio, 1985, Lamp of Knowledge award Twin Cities Lawyers Guild, 1986, NW Cmty. TV Commendation award, 1989-91, Presdl. Merit medal Pres. George Bush, 1990, NW Cmty. TV award, 1991, HLS Leadership award, 1984, Mng. Attys. Guidance award, 1985, Creative Thinker award Regional Staff, 1986, HLS Justice award, 1986, Honors cert. for Authors, Childrens Reading Round Table of Chgo., 1988, Wisdom Soc. Wisdom award, 1998; numerous martial arts awards. Fellow Roscoe Pound Found., Nat. Dist. Attys. Assn.; mem. ABA, ATLA, Minn. Bar Assn. (com. on ethics 1994-2004, com. on alternative dispute resolution 1994—), Minn. Trial Lawyers Assn., Hennepin County Bar Assn. (dist. ethics com. 1990—2004, Wis. Bar Assn., Ramsey County Bar Assn., Am. Judicature Soc., Internat. Platform Assn., Am. Arbitration Assn. (panel of arbitrators 1992), Minn. Martial Arts Assn. (pres. 1974-78, Outstanding Instr. award 1973), Nippon Kobudo Rengokai (bd. dirs. North Ctrl. States 1972-76, regional dir. 1972-76), Endless Fist Soc. (pres. 1998), Internat. Confedn. Jurists, Edina C. of C., Southview Country Club, Masons, Kiwanis, Scottish Rite, Sigma Alpha Mu. Avocations: reading, far eastern and oriental studies, civic activities, physical conditioning. also: 1711 County Road B W Ste 340N Roseville MN 55113-4077 Office: 7400 Metro Blvd Ste 390 Edina MN 55439 Home: 4908 Poppy Ln Minneapolis MN 55435-4013 Office Phone: 952-831-6555. Business E-Mail: nefflawfirm@yahoo.com.

NEFF, JOHN BROWN, financial portfolio manager; b. Wauseon, Ohio, Sept. 19, 1931; s. John Franklin Neff and Barbara (Brown) Hutton; m. Lillian Elizabeth Tulak, Oct. 4, 1935; children: Lisa, Stephen. BBA summa cum laude, U. Toledo, 1955; MBA, Case Western Reserve U., 1958; MA (hon.), U. Pa., 1984. Chartered fin. analyst. Asst. v.p. security analysis Nat. City Bank of Cleve., 1955-63; mng. ptnr., sr. v.p., portfolio mgr. Wellington Mgmt. Co., Valley Forge, Pa., 1963—95. Bd. dirs. Gen. Accident Ins., Crown Holdings, Inc., Amkor Tech., Inc., Chrysler Corp., Assn. Investment Mgmt. and Rsch. Author (with S.L. Mintz): John Neff on Investing. Charter trustee U. Pa., Phila.; trustee Case Western U. Served with USN, 1951-53. Recipient Giving Forward award, Phil. Edn. Fund, 1995. Mem. Chartered Fin. Analysts Fedn., Fin. Analysts of Phila. Avocations: tennis, golf, travel, history.

NEFF, MARIE TAYLOR, museum director, artist; d. James Arthur Taylor and Pearl Jackson; m. Edward Lewis Neff, June 24, 1946 (dec. July 1, 1994); children: James Edward, Charles Lewis(dec.). Degree in art and photography, Western Tex. Coll., 1985. Studio artist, Post, 1943—; art instr. Neff Art Sch., Post, 1963—78; co-owner retail bus. Post, 1963—88; art instr. Post Art Guild, Kids n Art, Post, 1975—85; dir. OS Ranch Found. Mus., Post, 1991—. Represented in permanent collections, pvt. collections. Pres., bd. dirs. Post Commerce and Tourism Bur., 1994—2002; dir., coord. Tex. Plains Trail Region, 2002—04, treas., 2004—. Named Queen Panhandle South Plains, Mrs. Tex. Sr. Pageant, 1999. Mem.: North Tex. Mus. Assn. (pres. 2001—04), Tex. Assn. Mus. (planning bd. state conv. 1997—2001, trustee-sec. 2000—05), Post C. of C. (designer commemorative coin 1976, Woman of Yr. 1972), Post Art Guild (pres., founding mem. 1974—2003), Rotary. Avocations: archaeology, photography, reading, travel. Office: OS Ranch Found Mus Ste 3 201 E Main St Post TX 79356 E-mail: mtneff@caprock-spur.com.

NEFF, MARY ELLEN ANDRE, retired elementary school educator; b. Indiana, Pa., July 6, 1943; d. Frank Vincent and Marie Isabel (Elrick) Andre; children: Gary V. Jr., Traci Dawn. BS, Indiana U. Pa., 1965, MEd, 1971. Elem. sch. tchr. Blairsville (Pa.)-Saltsburg Sch. Dist., Derry (Pa.) Area Sch. Dist.; ret., 2002. Zone chmn. Lions Dist. 14E; bd. mem. Ind. County Tourist Bur. Mem.: PTA, NEA, Pa. State Edn. Assn., Derry Area Hist. Soc. (bd. dirs.), Saltsburg Hist. Soc. (pres.), Nat. Soc. DAR (vice regent), Westmoreland County Hist. Soc. (bd. dirs., sec.), Latrobe Lions Club (pres., dist. zone chmn.), Delta Kappa Gamma (pres. 1986—90, treas. 1992—2000). Home: 17 Carriage Rd Greensburg PA 15601-9014 Personal E-mail: meneff@infionline.net.

NEFF, MICHAEL ALAN, lawyer; b. Springfield, Ill., Sept. 4, 1940; s. Benjamin Ezra and Ann (Alpert) N.; m. Lin Laghi, Mar. 26, 1977; 1 son, Aaron Benjamin. Student, U. Ill., 1958-61; BA, U. Calif., Berkeley, 1963, postgrad., 1963-64; JD, Columbia U., 1967. Bar: NY 1967, US Dist. Ct. (so. and ea. dists.) NY 1969, US Ct. Appeals (2d cir.) 1988, US Supreme Ct. 1988. Congl. intern US Ho. of Reps., 1965; assoc. Spear, Gray, Todd & Sims, NYC, 1967-74, Fellner & Rovins, NYC, 1974-75; ptnr. Poier, Tulin, Clark & Neff, NYC, 1976-77; pvt. practice NYC, 1977-83; pres. private practice, 1983—. Counsel St. Dominic's Home, 1971-74, Louise Wise Svcs., 1976-77, Edwin Gould Svc. for Children, 1969-79, 76—, Family Svc.of Westchester, Inc., 1977-87, The Children's Village, 1977-84, Brookwood Child Care, 1980—, Forestdale, 1988—, Fam. Support Sys. Unlimited, 1990—, Ednl. Assistance Corp., 1990-95, Coalition for Hispanic Family Svcs., 1992-93, Soc. Children and Families, 1996—, Pius XII Youth and Family Svcs., 2000—, Child Devel. Support Corp, 2001—, Hale House Ctr., Inc., 2001—; tchg. asst. U. Calif., 1963-64; instr. Social Welfare Policy and Law, Marymount Manhattan Coll., 1973; mem. Indigent Defendant's Legal Panel, Appellate Div., First Dept., 1974-84; participant NY State Conf. on Children's Rights, 1974; asst. sec. Edwin Gould Svcs. for Children, 1977—; cons. NY Task Force on Permanency Planning For Children in Foster Care, 1985-90, NY State Foster and Adoptive Parent Assn., Inc., 1988—, NY Spaulding for Children, 1988-90, Ct. Appointed Spl. Advs., 1988-91; instr. adoption law in NY, City Bar Ctr. for CLE, 2001—; mem. Adoption Adv. Com. NY State Dept. Social Svcs., 1997-98; advisor Nat. Resource Ctr. for Foster Care and Permanency Planning, 2000—; trainer Inst. for Families and Children, 1992-95, NYC Adminstrn. for Children's Svcs., 1996-97; facilitator Parenting Journey, 2000—; group leader Model Approach to Partnerships in Parenting, 2001—. Author: Freeing Foster Children for Adoption, A Child's Right to a Plan of Permanency, 1972, Permanent Neglect Proceedings, 1980, Adoption Proceedings, Basic Matrimonial Practice in New York, 1980, Foster Parenting Handbook, 1997 Adopting Foster Children: A Handbook for Foster Parents, 1999, Permanency Planning ASFA, Best Practices: A Handbook for Caseworkers, 2000; Contbr. articles to profl. jours. Mem. Protestant Bd. of Guardians, 2001—. Mem. ABA, Am. Acad. Adoption Attys., Assn. Bar City of NY (mem. com. on children and law, family law sect.). Home: 5 W 86th St Apt 6B New York NY 10024-3664 E-mail: manpc@aol.com.

NEFF, P(AUL) SHERRILL, venture capitalist; b. Balt., Dec. 18, 1951; s. Paul Heston and Mary (Poulnot) N.; m. Sarah B. Barrett, June 20, 1976 (div. 1985); 1 child, Jacob Colin; m. Alicia Phyll Felton, May 26, 1988; children: Michael Felton, Jonathan Felton. BA, Wesleyan U., 1974; JD magna cum laude, U. Mich., 1980. Bar: Pa. 1980. Atty. Morgan Lewis & Bockius, Phila., 1980—84; investment banker Alex Brown & Sons, Inc., Balt., 1984—93, mng. dir., 1992—93; sr. v.p. corp. devel. U.S. Healthcare, Blue Bell, Pa., 1993—94; pres., CFO Neose Techs., Inc., Horsham, 1994—2000, pres., COO, 2000—02; mng. ptnr. Quaker Bio Ventures, Phila., 2002—. Bd. dirs. Amicus Therapeutics, Biolex, Inc., Resource Capital Corp., Regado Bioscis., Inc., WXPN-FM, Biotech. Inst., Neuronetics, Inc., Optherion, Inc., University City Sci. Ctr.; bd. dirs., past chmn. Greater Phila. Venture Group. Mem. Pa. Biotech. Assn. (bd. dirs. 1996-2002, pres. 1998-99). Democrat. Jewish. Home: 619 Revere Rd Merion Station PA 19066-1007 Office: Quaker Bio Ventures 1811 Chestnut St Philadelphia PA 19103

NEFF, ROBERT MATTHEW, lawyer, finance company executive; b. Huntington, Ind., Mar. 26, 1955; s. Robert Eugene and Ann (Bash) N.; m. Lee Ann Loving, Aug. 23, 1980; children: Alexandra, Graydon, Philip. BA in English, DePauw U., 1977; JD, Ind. U., Indpls., 1980. Bar: Ind. 1980, U.S. Dist. Ct. (so. dist.) Ind. 1980, U.S. Supreme Ct., 1993. Assoc. Krieg, DeVault, Alexander & Capehart, Indpls., 1980-85, ptnr., 1986-88, Baker & Daniels, Indpls., 1988-92; of counsel, 1993-96; dept. to chmn. Fed. Housing Fin. Bd., Washington, 1992-93; pres., CEO Circle Investors, Inc., Indpls., 1993-97, also bd. dirs.; chmn., CEO Senex Fin. Corp., Indpls., 1998—2007; pres., CEO Clarian Health Ventures, Inc., Indpls., 2007—. Mem. faculty Grad. Sch. of Banking of South, 1988—1990; chmn. Liberty Bankers Life Ins. Co., 1995—1998, Am. Founders Life Ins. Co., Laurel Life Ins. Co., Aztek Life Assurance Co., 1996—1997; bd. dirs. Quanta Specialty Lines Ins. Co., CH Assurance Ltd., Clarian Health RRG, Unified Fin. Svcs., Inc., Conseco Strategic Income Fund. Exec. editor Ind. Law Rev., 1979-80. Participant Lacy Exec. Leadership Conf., Indpls., 1985-86; trustee DePauw U., 1977-80; bd. govs. Riley Children's Found., 1999-; del. White House Conf. on Aging, 2005. Mem. ABA (chmn. bus. law com. young lawyers divsn. 1988-90, banking law com. 1990-92), Ind. Bar Assn. (chmn. corps. banking and bus. law sect. 1987-88), DePauw Alumni Assn. (bd. dirs. 1982-88), Phi Kappa Psi, Phi Beta Kappa. Avocations: golf, fishing. Home: 7202 Merriam Rd Indianapolis IN 46240 Office: Clarian Health Ventures 10 W Market St No 400 Indianapolis IN 46204 Office Phone: 317-656-8511. Business E-Mail: rmneff@clarian.org.

NEFF, ROBERT WILBUR, academic administrator, educator, minister; b. Lancaster, Pa., June 16, 1936; s. Wilbur Hildebr and Hazel Margaret (Martin) N.; m. Dorothy Rosewarne, Aug. 16, 1959; children: Charles Scott, Heather Lynn. BS, Pa. State U., 1958; BD, Yale Div. Sch., 1961, MA, 1963, PhD, 1969; DD, Juniata Coll., 1978, Manchester Coll., 1979; DHL, Bridgewater Coll., 1979. Asst. prof. Bridgewater Coll., 1964-65; mem. faculty dept. Bibl. studies Bethany Theol. Sem., 1965-77, prof., 1973-77; gen. sec. Ch. of the Brethren, Elgin, Ill., 1978-86; pres. Juniata Coll., 1986-98, pres. emeritus, 1998—. Vis. prof. Pa. State U., 1998-2003; assoc. for resource devel. The Village at Morrison's Cove, 1999-, coord. chaplaincy svc., 2006-; mem. faculty North Park Sem., No. Bapt. Sem., Theol. Coll. No. Nigeria; bd. dirs. Mellon Bank (Ctrl.) Nat. Assn., exec. com., 1989, chair exec. com., 1993, chair CRA com., 1994-2001; mem. pres.'s com. NCAA, 1996-99; bd. dirs. Susquehanna Valley Ministry Ctr., 2002-, chair, 2004-; adj. faculty Bethany Theol. Sem., 1999—; cons. Archdiocese (Altoona/Johnstown), 2003—; lectr. Young Ctr. at Elizabethtown Coll., 2002; mem. USDA Del. to Baltic States, 2000. Mem. governing bd. Nat. Coun. Chs. of Christ, 1976-86, mem. exec. com., 1979-86; mem. Mid-East panel, 1980, 2d v.p., 1985-86; mem. ctrl. com. World Coun. Chs., 1983-92; rep. Assembly of World Coun. Chs., 1983, mem. exec. com. on interch. rels., 1980-84, mem. del. to China, 1981, chmn. presdl. panel, 1982-84; bd. dirs. Bethany Theol. Sem., 1978-86, So. Alleghenies chpt. ARC, 2004—; campaign chmn. United Way, Huntington County, 1989; chair higher edn. com. Ch. of Brethren, 1993-98. Danforth fellow, 1958-69. Mem. Soc. Bibl. Lit., Soc. Old Testament Study, Chgo. Soc. Bibl. Rsch., Soc. Values in Higher Edn., Coun. Ind. Colls. (nat. bd. dirs. 1991-94, treas. 1995-98), Pa. Coun. Ind. Colls. and Univs. (exec. com. 1988-90, 92-96, chair ann. conf. nominating com. 1993-94), Mid Atlantic Athletic Conf. (sec., mem. exec. com. 1994-97). Democrat. Office: Village at Morrisons Cove 429 Market St Martinsburg PA 16662 Home: 3221 Shellers Bend Rd Unit 827 State College PA 16801 Home Phone: 814-235-1656; Office Phone: 814-793-5207.

NEFF, SEVERINE, music educator; b. Waterbury, Conn., Dec. 17, 1949; d. Victor and Evangeline Josephine Neff; m. Joel Stanley Feigin, June 7, 1986. AB, Barnard Coll., 1971; MA, Yale U., 1972; MFA, Princeton U., NJ, PhD, 1979. Asst. prof. Bates Coll., Lewiston, Maine, 1979—80, U. Hawaii, Honolulu, 1980—81, Barnard Coll., NYC, 1983—91; fellow Cornell U., Ithaca, NY, 1981—83; assoc. prof. Cin. Coll.-Conservatory, 1991—92, prof., 1993—95; prof. music U. NC, Chapel Hill, 1995—2003, Eugene Falk disting. prof., 2004—. Author: Coherence, Counterpoint, Instrumentation, Instruction in Form, 1994, The Musical Idea, 1995, 2nd edit., 2006, Norton Critical Score, Second String Quartet, Op. 10 by Arnold Schoenberg, 2006; editor: Theory and Practice, 1991—93, Music Theory Spectrum, 1999—2002. Fellow, Mellon Found., 1981; grantee, NEH, 1993, Arnold Schoenberg Ctr., 2004, Korea Found., 2005; scholar, Fulbright Found., 1998—99; Tchg. fellow, Mannes Inst., 2005—07. Mem.: Soc. Music Theory (sec. 1991—94, revs. editor 2000—02, bd. dirs.), Coll. Music Soc. (theory rep. 2001—04, bd. dirs.). Achievements include discovery of two unknown works of Arnold Schoenberg. Avocation: antiques. Office: U NC CB 3320 Chapel Hill NC 27599

NEFF, TERRY ANN R., art director, consultant; b. Chgo., Apr. 24, 1944; d. Henry H. and Elaine T. Rothschild; m. John H. Neff, Dec. 27, 1967 (div. Apr. 20, 1984); children: John H. Neff, Jr., Henry H., Victoria H.; m.

Sheldon Gerald Zimmerman, July 29, 1994; children: Jodii Zimmerman, Anita Zimmerman. BA, Wellesley Coll., Mass., 1965; MA, Harvard U., Cambridge, Mass., 1967. Editor Detroit Inst. Arts, 1974—78; freelance editor Art Inst, Chgo., 1978—83, Mus. Contemporay Art, Chgo., 1978—83; publs. coord. Mus. Contemporary Art, 1983—86; pres. T. A. Neff Assocs., Inc., Tucson, 1986—. Consulting vol. Sch. Art, U. Ariz., Tucson, 1995—. Editor: (exhibition catalogue) Biedermeier: The Invention of Simplicity (Most Beautiful Book award, Vienna Art Week, 2007), Leonardo da Vinci and The Splendor of Poland: A History of Collecting and Patronage. Art bd. mem. Sch. Art, U. Ariz., 1995—2007, art. bd. pres., 1999—2002. Recipient Spirit of Philanthropy award, Am. Fundraising Profls., 2001. Office: T A Neff Assocs Inc 5970 E Terra Grande Tucson AZ 85750-10

NEFF, THOMAS JOSEPH, search firm executive; b. Easton, Pa., Oct. 2, 1937; s. John Wallace and Elizabeth Ann (Dougherty) N.; m. Susan Culver Paull, Nov. 26, 1971 (dec.); children: David Andrew, Mark Gregory, Scott Dougherty; m. Sarah Brown Hallingby, Jan. 20, 1989; stepchildren: Brooke, Bailey BS in Indsl. Engring., Lafayette Coll., 1959; MBA, Lehigh U., 1961. Assoc. McKinsey & Co., Inc., NYC and Australia, 1963-66; dir. mktg. planning Trans-World Airlines, NYC, 1966-69; pres. Hosp. Data Scis., Inc., NYC, 1969-74; prin. Booz, Allen & Hamilton, Inc., NYC, 1974-76; regional ptnr. Spencer Stuart, Inc., NYC, 1976-79; bd. dirs. Spencer Stuart & Assocs., NYC, 1976-79, pres., 1979-96, also bd. dirs., chmn. U.S., 1996—. Bd. dirs. Lord Abbett Mut. Funds, Ace Ltd., Hewitt Assocs., Inc.; chmn. Brunswick Sch., 1991-95. Co-author: Lessons From the Top, 1999, You're in Charge--Now What: The 8-Point Plan, 2005. Trustee, emeritus Lafayette Coll., 2004—. 1st lt. US Army, 1961-63. Mem. Links Club, Blind Brook Club, Quogue (NY) Beach Club, Quogue Field Club, Round Hill Club, Coral Beach Club, Quantuck Beach Club, Nat. Golf Links, Lost Tree Club, McArthur Golf Club. Republican. Roman Catholic. Office: Spencer Stuart & Assocs 277 Park Ave 29th Fl New York NY 10172-2998 Business E-Mail: tneff@spencerstuart.com.

NEFSKE, DONALD JOSEPH, engineer; b. Detroit, Dec. 18, 1938; s. Frank J. and Esther M. N.; m. Susan Sung, Dec. 10, 1983. BS magna cum laude, U. Detroit, 1962; MS, U. Mich., 1964, PhD, 1969. Engr. Ford Motor Co., Dearborn, Mich., 1960—61; rsch. engr. GM, Warren, Mich., 1969—70, sr. rsch. engr., 1970—85, sr. staff engr., 1985—93, prin. engr., 1993—2003, tech. fellow, 2003—05; dir. Engring. Mechanics Group, Troy, Mich., 2005—. Contbr. articles profl. jour., chapters to books. Fellow ASME; mem. AIAA, Acoustical Soc. Am., Soc. Automotive Engr., Sigma Xi. Roman Catholic. Achievements include research in CAE methods for automotive vehicle noise and vibration, airbag safety systems. Office: Engring Mechanics Group 4178 Drexel Dr Troy MI 48098

NEGELE, JOHN WILLIAM, physics professor, consultant; b. Cleve., Apr. 18, 1944; s. Charles Frederick and Virgil Lea (Wettich) N.; m. Rose Anne Meeks, June 18, 1967; Janette Andrea, Julia Elizabeth. BS, Purdue U., 1965; PhD, Cornell U., 1969. Research fellow Niels Bohr Inst., Copenhagen, 1969-70; vis. asst. prof. MIT, Cambridge, 1970-71, faculty mem., 1971—, prof. physics, 1979—, William A. Coolidge prof., 1991—, head nuclear and particle theory divsn., 1988-89, dir. Ctr. for Theoretical Physics, 1989-98. Cons. Los Alamos Sci. Lab., Brookhaven Nat. Lab., Lawrence Livermore Nat. Lab., Oak Ridge Nat. Lab.; mem. physics div. rev. com. Argonne Nat. Lab., (Ill.), 1977-83; mem. nuclear sci. div. rev. com. Lawrence Berkeley Lab., (Calif.), 1982—; mem. adv. bd., steering com. Inst. for Theoretical Physics, U. Calif.-Santa Barbara, 1982-86; mem. adv. bd. inst. for Nuclear Theory U. Washington, 1990—, chair 1992-94; program adv. com. Tandem Van de Graaff Accelerator, Brookhaven Nat. Lab., 1977-78, Bates Linear Accelerator, 1977-80, Los Alamos Meson Prodn. Facility, 1986-89, Brookhaven Alternating Gradient Synchraton, 1987-90, mem. exec. com. on computational resources lattice QCD, Dept. Energy, 1999—. Author: Quantum Many Particle Systems, 1987; contbr. articles to profl. jours.; editor: Advances in Nuclear Physics, 1977—. Grantee NSF, 1965-69; grantee Danforth Found., 1965-69, Woodrow Wilson Found., 1965, Alfred P. Sloan Found., 1979, Japan Soc. for Promotion Sci., 1981, John Simon Guggenheim Found., 1982; Alexander von Humboldt Found. fellow, 1998. Fellow Am. Phys. Soc. (program com. 1980-82, editorial bd. Phys. Rev. 1980-82, exec. com. 1982-84, Bonner prize com. 1984-85, exec. com. topical group on computational physics 1992-93, chair divsn. of computational physics 1992-93, exec. com. 1992-94, fellowship com. 2007—, Bethe prize com., 2007—), AAAS (nominating com. 1987-91, mem. physics sect. com. 1991—), Fedn. Am. Scientists. Home: 70 Buckman Dr Lexington MA 02421-6000 Office: MIT Dept Physics 6-315 77 Massachusetts Ave Dept 6-308 Cambridge MA 02139-4307

NEGER, PETER C., lawyer; b. NYC, Dec. 23, 1955; s. Edward B. Neger and Cherie M. (Oltarsh) Stahl; m. Melinda Beck, Sept. 12, 1982; children: Emily, Hillary. BA, Yale U., 1977; JD, Fordham U., 1981. Bar: N.Y. 1982, U.S. Dist. Ct. (so. and ea. dists.) N.Y. 1982, U.S. Ct. Appeals (2d cir.) 1982, U.S. Supreme Ct. 1986, U.S. Ct. Appeals (7th cir.) 1996. Assoc. Shea & Gould, NYC, 1981-89, ptnr., 1990-94, Richards & O'Neil, LLP, NYC, 1994—, Bingham McCutchen LLP, NYC, co-chmn. product liability practice group. Mem.: Fed. Bar Coun., N.Y. State Bar Assn., Assn. Bar City N.Y., ABA (product liability com.), Food & Drug Law Inst., Defense Research Inst. (product liability com., drug & med. devices com.). Office: Bingham McCutchen LLP 399 Park Avenue New York NY 10022-4689 Office Phone: 212-705-7226. Office Fax: 212-752-5378. Business E-Mail: peter.neger@bingham.com.

NEGI, DEVENDRA S., communications services company administrator; b. Varanasi, Uttar Pradesh, India, Aug. 8, 1953; s. Vidya Wati and (Deceased) Balwant S Negi. B of Mech. Engring., Indian Inst. Tech., 1974; MS in Indsl. Engring, Kans. State U., 1981, PhD in Indsl. Engring, 1989. Engr. trainee Bharat Heavy Electricals Ltd., Hardwar, Uttar Pradesh, India, 1975—76, engr., 1976—79; grad. rsch. asst. Kans. State U., Manhattan, 1980, 1986—89; systems analyst Patso Co., Inc, Houston, 1981—82; indsl. engr. Millar Instruments, Inc., 1882—1984; ops. rsch. analyst Phillips Petroleum Co., Bartlesville, Okla., 1990—97; sr. tech. staff mem. AT&T, Florham Park and Murray Hill, NJ, 1997—2001, dist. mgr. Florham Park, 2001—04, group mgr. Middletown and Florham Park, 2004—07, assoc. dir. Middletown, NJ, 2007—. Vis. asst. prof. Ohio U., Athens, 1989—90. Mem.: Inst. Ops. Rsch. and Mgmt. Scis., Inst. Indsl. Engrs. Avocations: travel, movies, tennis. Home: 1428-1432 South Ave Apt 1-H Plainfield NJ 07062 Office: AT&T 180 Park Ave Florham Park NJ 07932 Office Phone: 732-420-0370. Personal E-mail: dsnegi@att.net, negids@gmail.com. Business E-Mail: dsnegi@homer.att.com.

NEGINSKY, ROSINA, literature educator, writer, poet; BA in Lit., U. Paris III, 1984, MA in Lit., 1986; PhD, U. Ill., Urbana-Champaign, 1991. Assoc. prof. U. Ill., Springfield, 2000—. Curator Pregel: A Search for Self Exhibit. Author: Zinaida Vengerova: in Search of Beauty. A Literary Ambassador between East and West, 2d edit., (poetry) Under the Light of the Moon, Dancing Over the Precipice; contbr. articles to profl. jours. Grantee, NEH, 1994, 2003. Mem.: Soc. Midland Authors (life). Office: Univ Ill One University Plz Springfield IL 62703 Home Phone: 217-414-8224; Office Phone: 217-206-6962.

NEGISHI, EI-ICHI, chemistry professor; arrived in U.S., 1960; BS in Organic Chemistry, U. Tokyo, 1958; PhD in Organic Chemistry, U. Pa., 1963. Rsch. chemist Teijin Ltd., 1958-65; postdoctoral assoc. Purdue U., 1966-68, asst. to H.C. Brown, 1968-72; asst. prof. Syracuse (N.Y.) U., 1972-76, assoc. prof., 1976-79; prof. Purdue U., West Lafayette, Ind., 1979-99, Herbert C. Brown disting. prof., 1999—. Lectr. in field. Recipient A. von Humboldt Rschr. award 1998—; Fulbright scholar, 1960-63. Mem.: Royal Soc. Chemistry (Sir E. Frankland Prize lectureship 2000), Japan Chem. Soc. (award 1997), Am. Chem. Soc. (Organometallic Chemistry award 1998), Sigma Xi, Phi Lambda Epsilon. Office: Purdue U Chem Dept 560 Oval Dr West Lafayette IN 47907-2084 Home Phone: 765-463-4439; Office Phone: 765-494-5301. Business E-Mail: negishi@purdue.edu.

NEGRON-GARCIA, ANTONIO S., law educator, former territory supreme court justice; b. Rio Piedras, P.R., Dec. 31, 1940; s. Luis Negron-Fernandez and Rosa M. Garcia-Saldana; m. Gloria Villardefrancos-Vergara, May 26, 1962; 1 son, Antonio Rogelio. BA, U. P.R., 1962, LL.B., 1964. Bar: P.R. bar 1964. Law aide and lawyer legal div. Water Resources Authority, 1962-64; judge Dist. Ct., 1964-69, Superior Ct., 1969-74; justice P.R. Supreme Ct., San Juan, 1974—2001; administrating judge, 1969-71; exec. officer Constl. Bd. for Revision Senatorial and Rep. Dists., 1971-72; mem. Jud. Conf., 1974—2000; first exec. sec. Council for Reform of System of Justice in P.R., 1973-74; prof. InterAmerican U. Puerto Rico, 2001—. Chmn. Gov.'s Advisory Com. for Jud. Appointments, 1973-74; lectr. U. P.R. Law Sch., 1973-74; columnist El Nuevo Dia newspaper, 2000. Mem. P.R. Bar Assn., Am. Judicature Soc. Roman Catholic. Office: Univ InterAmericana de Puerto Rico Apartado 70351 San Juan PR 00936-8351

NEGROPONTE, JOHN DIMITRI, federal agency administrator, former national intelligence director, ambassador; b. London, July 21, 1939; s. Dimitri John and Catherine (Coumantaros) Negroponte; m. Diana Mary Villiers, Dec. 14, 1976; children: Marina, Alexandra, John, George, Sophia. BA, Yale U., 1960. Commd. fgn. svc. officer U.S. Dept. State, 1960; vice consul Hong Kong, 1961—63; 2nd sec. Saigon, 1964—68; mem. U.S. Del. to Paris Peace Talks on Vietnam, 1968—69; mem. staff NSC, 1970—73; polit. counselor Am. Embassy, Quito, Ecuador, 1973—75, consul gen. Thessaloniki, Greece, 1975—77; dep. asst. sec. for oceans & fisheries affairs US Dept. State, Washington, 1977—79, dep. asst. sec. for East Asian and Pacific affairs, 1980—81, U.S. amb. to Honduras Tegucigalpa, 1981—85, asst. sec. for oceans and internat. environ. and sci. affairs Washington, 1985—87; dep. asst. to Pres. for nat. security affairs NSC, Washington, 1987—89; US amb. to Mexico US Dept. State, Mexico City, 1989—93, US amb. to The Philippines Manilla, 1993—96, spl. coord. for post-1999 U.S. presence in Panama, 1996—97; exec. v.p. global markets McGraw-Hill Cos., NYC, 1997—2001; permanent U.S. rep. to UN US Dept. State, NYC, 2001—04, US amb. to Iraq Baghdad, 2004—05; dir. Office Nat. Intelligence, Washington, 2005—07; dep. sec. US Dept. State, Washington, 2007—. Co-pres. U.S./Mex. Commn. for Ednl. and Cultural Exch., 1997—2001; chmn. The French-Am. Found., 1998—2001; mem. exec. com. U.S. Coun. for Internat. Bus., 1998—2001. Recipient Golden Plate award, Acad. Achievement, 2006. Mem.: Fgn. Policy Assn., Am. Acad. Diplomacy, Coun. on Fgn. Rels., Am. Fgn. Svc. Assn. Greek Orthodox. Office: US Dept State 2201 C St NW Rm 7220 Washington DC 20520 *

NEGROPONTE, NICHOLAS, media specialist, educator; m. Elaine Negroponte. Founding chairman, dir. MIT Media Lab., Cambridge, Mass., 1986—; faculty MIT, Cambridge, Mass., 1966-86, Wiesner prof., media tech. Founder, Architecture Machine Group, MIT; bd. dirs. Motorola; spl. gen. ptnr. in a venture capital firm; founder, sr. columnist WiReD mag.; angel investor for over 40 start-ups, including three in China. Author: Being Digital, 1995 (NY Times Bestseller, translated into over 40 languages) Helped establish, chmn. 2BI Found., 1996-; chmn., One Laptop per Child (OLPC), 2005-. Named one of 50 Who Matter Now, Business 2.0, 2007. First to announce at the World Economic Forum at Davos, Switzerland in January 2005, the MIT Media Lab's research initiative to develop the world's first working $100 laptop for a non-profit program, One Laptop Per Child (OLPC). The computer allows hundreds of millions of underprivileged students worldwide to gain access to knowledge and modern forms of education. Office: MIT Media Lab Bldg E15 77 Massachusetts Ave Cambridge MA 02139-4307 also: MIT Media Lab Wiesner Building, E15 20 Ames St Cambridge MA 02139-4307 Office Phone: 617-253-5960. Office Fax: 617-258-6264. Business E-Mail: nicholas@media.mit.edu. *

NEHAMAS, ALEXANDER, philosophy educator; b. Athens, Greece, Mar. 22, 1946; came to U.S., 1964; s. Albert and Christine (Yannuli) N.; m. Susan Glimcher, June 22, 1983; 1 child, Nicholas Albert Glimcher. BA, Swarthmore Coll., 1967; PhD, Princeton U., 1971; D in Philosophy (hon.), Athens, 1993. Asst. then assoc. prof. philosophy U. Pitts., 1971-81, prof., 1981-86; prof. philosophy U. Pa., 1986-90; vis. prof. Princeton (N.J.) U., 1978-79, 89, Edmund Carpenter prof. humanities, 1990—, prof. philosophy and comparative lit., 1990—, chair humanities coun., 1994—2002, chmn. program in Hellenic studies, 1994—2002. Dir. Princeton Soc. Fellow in Liberal Arts, 1999-2002; Mills vis. prof. U. Calif., Berkeley, 1983; Sather vis. prof., 1993; vis. prof. U. Calif., Santa Cruz, 1988; bd. dirs. Princeton U. Press; trustee Nat. Humanities Ctr., 1996-99, Athens Coll., 1996—; Tanner lectr., 2001. Author: Nietzche: Life as Literature, 1985, The Art of Living: Socratic Reflectionsfrom Plato to Foucault, 1998, Virtues of Authenticity: Essays on Plato and Socrates, 1999, Only a Promise of Happiness, 2007; translator Plato's Symposium, 1989, Plato's Phaedrus, 1995; co-editor: Aristotle's Rhetoric: Philosophical Essays, 1994; contbr. articles to profl. jours.; mem. editl. bd. Am. Philos. Quar., 1981-86, History of Philosophy Quar., 1983-88, Ancient Philosophy, 1984—, Jour. Modern Greek Studies, 1986—, Arion, 1989—, Philosophy and Lit., 1989—, Philosophy and Phenomenological Rsch., 1990—. Recipient Lindback Found. Tchg. award, U. Pa., 1989, Behrman award in humanities, Princeton U., 1999, Ann. prize in Hellenic Studies Acad., Athens, 2000, Internat. Nietsche prize, 2001, Mellon Disting. Achievement award, 2001; grantee Guggenheim fellow, 1983, NEH, 1978. Mem.: MLA, N.Am. Nietzsche Soc. (exec. com. 1988—91), Am. Soc. Aesthetics, Modern Greek Studies Assn. (exec. com. 1983—89), Am. Philos. Assn. (chmn. program 1982—83, exec. com. 1990—92, v.p. 2002, pres. 2003), Phi Beta Kappa (vis. prof. 1989, vis. scholar 1995). Office: Princeton U Dept Philosophy Princeton NJ 08544-0001

NEHLS, RICHARD CHARLES, lawyer; b. Detroit, Oct. 26, 1951; s. Edward J. and Helen (Hecker) N.; m. Sharon Kay Scudder, Mar. 29, 1975; children: Christopher, Jeffrey. BA, Miami U., Oxford, Ohio, 1973; JD, U. Chgo., 1976. Bar: Colo. 1976. Ptnr. Lirtzman & Nehls, Boulder, Colo., 1976—2006, Packard Dierking, LLC, Boulder, Colo., 2006—. Trustee Legal Aid Found., 1995-2003. Mem. Colo. Bar Assn. (trustee 1996-2002), Boulder County Bar Assn. (trustee 1990-95, pres. 1994-95). Democrat. Avocations: skiing, bicycling. Home: 385 Overlook Dr Boulder CO 80305-5258 Office: Packard Dierking 2595 Canyon Blvd Ste 200 Boulder CO 80302 Office Phone: 303-447-0450. Business E-Mail: rich@packarddierking.com.

NEHRA, GERALD PETER, lawyer; b. Detroit, Mar. 25, 1940; s. Joseph P. and Jeanette M. (Bauer) N.; m. children: Teresa, Patricia; m. Peggy Jensen, Sept. 12, 1987. BIE, Gen. Motors Inst., Flint, Mich., 1962; JD, Detroit Coll. Law, 1970. Bar: Mich. 1970, N.Y. 1972, Colo. 1992, U.S. Dist. Ct. (ea. dist.) Mich. 1970, U.S. Dist. Ct. (so. dist.) N.Y. 1972, U.S. Dist. Ct. (no. dist.) N.Y. 1976, U.S. Ct. Appeals (6th cir.) 1978. Successively engr., supr., gen. supr. Gen. Motors Corp., 1958-67; mktg. rep. to regional counsel IBM Corp., 1967-79; v.p. gen. counsel Church & Dwight Co., Inc., 1979-82; dep. chief atty. Amway Corp., 1982-83; dep. gen. counsel, 1983-92; dir. legal div., 1989-91; sec., dir. corp. law, 1991-92; v.p. gen. counsel Fuller Brush, Boulder, Colo., 1991-92; pvt. practice, 1992—. Adj. instr. Dale Carnegie Courses, 1983-91. Recipient Outstanding Contbn. award Am. Cancer Soc., 1976. Mem. ABA, Mich. Bar Assn., Colo. Bar Assn., N.Y. State Bar Assn. Home and Office: 1710 Beach St Muskegon MI 49441-1008 Home Phone: 231-755-3800; Office Phone: 231-755-3800. Business E-Mail: gnehra@mlmatty.com.

NEHRBASS, SETH MARTIN, lawyer; b. Lafayette, La., Nov. 10, 1960; s. Neil Martin and Janet (Himbert) N.; m. Mary Elizabeth Dennis, Aug. 12, 2000; children: Gabriel, Fabian. Student, U. Catholique de l'Ouest, Angers, France, 1980, U. Paul Valéry, Montpellier, France, 1981; BS in Physics summa cum laude, U. Southwestern La., 1982; JD cum laude, Loyola U., 1990. Bar: U.S. Patent & Trademark Office 1984, La. 1990, U.S. Dist. Ct. (ea., mid., and we. dists.) La. 1990, U.S. Ct. Appeals (5th and fed. cirs.) 1990, U.S. Supreme Ct. 2006; cert. notary public, La. Patent examiner U.S. Patent & Trademark Office, 1982-84; patent agt. with law firm New Orleans, 1986-87; assoc. Pravel, Hewitt, Kimball & Krieger, New Orleans, 1987-97, shareholder, 1997-98, Garvey, Smith, Nehrbass & North, L.L.C., Metairie, La., 1998—. Adj. law faculty Tulane Law Sch., 1997—; judge practice round moot ct. teams Loyola Law Sch., 1992—; preparer questions patent bar exam PTO Q & A Bd., 1992-93; presenter in field. Contbr. articles to profl. jours. Den leader 2d grade Cub Scouts, Boy Scouts Am., Lusher Sch., Audubon Dist., 1991-92, 3d grade, 1994-95, asst. den leader 3d grade, 1992-93, 4th grade, 1993-94; soccer coach Carrollton Booster Club, New Orleans, 1993-95, Lakeview Soccer Club, New Orleans, 1995-96; adv. mem. La. Ctr. for Law and Civic Edn., 1996-98; mem. New Orleans Citizen Diplomacy Coun., 2000—. Recipient Hornbook award West Pub. Co., 1986-87, 87-88, Corpus Juris Secundum award, 1986-87, Am. Jurisprudence awards (2), 1986; scholar La. State U. Alumni Fedn., 1978, Coun. Devel. French La./French Govt., 1980-81, Loyola Law Sch., 1986. Mem. ABA (sect. law, sci., tech. 1988-91, law student divsn. liaison patent trademark and copyright law 1988-90, intellectual property law sect. 1988—, chmn. law student com. 1996-98, chmn. spl. com. drug crisis 1990-93, co-chmn. ann. meeting arrangements com. 1993-94, internat. treaties and laws com. 1994—, co-chmn. young lawyers com. 1998-99), Am. Intellectual Property Law Assn. (ADR com., internat. and fgn. law com., patent law com. 1994-2000), La. Bar Assn. (internat. law sect. 1992—, intellectual property law sect. 1996—, vice chmn. 1997-98, chair-elect 1998-99, chair 1999-2000), New Orleans Bar Assn. (interim chmn. ad hoc com. drug crisis 1991-92, chmn. intellectual property law com. 1991-95, chmn. law related edn. com. 1995-97), Round Table Club, Plimsoll Club, Loyola Law Sch. Moot Ct. Alumni Assn., Sigma Pi Sigma, Pi Delta Phi, Alpha Sigma Nu. Democrat. Roman Catholic. Avocations: gardening, photography, travel, hunting, fishing. Home: 453 Audubon Blvd New Orleans LA 70125-3503 Office: 3838 N Causeway Blvd Ste 3290 Metairie LA 70002 Office Phone: 504-835-2000. Business E-Mail: nehrbass@gsnn.us. E-mail: Nehrbass@aol.com.

NEHRING, RONALD E., state supreme court justice; b. Wis., 1947; BA in History, Cornell U., 1976; JD, U. Utah, 1978. Bar: Utah 1978. Atty. Utah Legal Svcs.; shareholder Prince, Yeates and Geldzahler, Salt Lake City, 1982—94; judge U.S. Dist. Ct. (3d dist.) Utah, 1995—2003, Utah Supreme Ct., Salt Lake City, 2003—. Chmn. Bd. Dist. Ct. Judges; mem. adv. com. rules profl. conduct Utah Supreme Ct. Fellow: ABA. Office: Utah Supreme Ct PO Box 140210 Salt Lake City UT 84114-0210 *

NEHRIR, M. HASHEM, electrical engineer, educator; b. Shiraz, Fars, Iran, Aug. 16, 1946; s. Mohammad Hossein Nehrir; m. Maryam Nehrir, Oct. 15, 1970; children: Ali Reza, Sara, Amin Reza. BSEE, Oreg. State U., 1969, MSEE, 1971, PhD, 1978. Instr. Shiraz U., 1971—75, asst./assoc. prof., 1978—86; vis. scholar Univ. Idaho, 1986—87; asst./assoc. prof. Mont. State U., Bozeman, 1987—96, prof., 1996—. Invited lectr. Selisian U. Tech., Gliwice, Poland, 1995, Dresden U., Germany, 1997, Kumamoto U., 1998, vis. rsch. fellow, 98, Curtin U. Tech., Australia, 2001, 04, invited lectr., 01, 04, Chongquing U., China, 2007. Author: Basic Electric Circuits, 1981, Hybrid Simulation of Engineering Systems, 1986 (Mont. State U. Alumini Assn. and Bozeman Area C. of C. award of excellence, 2001); contbr. numerous articles to profl. jours. Rsch. grantee, NSF, 1992—95, 1997—2006, US Dept. Energy, 1994—2000, 2002—, Mont. State U., 1997, 2000. Mem.: IEEE (sr.), Am. Soc. Engring. Edn. Avocations: travel, hiking. Office: Mont State U Elec and Computer Engring Dept Bozeman MT 59717 Business E-Mail: hnehrir@ece.montana.edu.

NEHS, (WILLIAM) SCOTT, lawyer; b. Janesville, Wis., Mar. 7, 1966; m. Jacqueline Nehs. BA, Northwestern U., 1988; JD, U. Wis., Madison, 1991. Bar: Ill. 1991, Wis. 1991, US Dist. Ct. No. Dist. Ill. 1991, US Dist. Ct. We. Dist. Wis. 1991, US Dist. Ct. Ea. Dist. Wis. 1993. Assoc. Wildman, Harrold, Allen & Dixon, Chgo., 1991—99; dep. gen. counsel Pepsi-Cola Gen. Bottlers Inc., Rolling Meadows, Ill., 2000—01; asst. gen. counsel PepsiAmericas Inc. (formerly Whitman Corp.), Rolling Meadows, Ill., 2000—01, v.p. legal, 2001—, chief compliance officer. Pro bono work Legal Clinic for the Disabled, 1992—, Les Turner ALS Found., 1995—. Named one of The Top 40 Lawyers Under 40 in Ill., Chgo. Daily Law Bulletin, 2004. Mem.: Assn. of Corp. Counsel, Wis. State Bar, Chgo. Bar Assn. Office: Pepsiamericas Caribbean Inc 1475 E Woodfield Rd Ste 1300 Schaumburg IL 60173-5482 *

NEIBERGER, RICHARD EUGENE, pediatrician, nephrologist, educator; b. Onaga, Kans., Nov. 16, 1947; s. Earl Edward and Margaret Bell (Grim) N.; m. Mary June Chamberlin, Oct. 31, 1971; children: Ami, Eric, Chris, Robert. BS in Physics, U. Ctrl. Fla., 1971; PhD, U. Louisville, 1979, MD, 1982. Diplomate Am. Bd. Pediat., Nat. Bd. Med. Examiners. Intern, then resident in pediat. Albert Einstein Coll. Med., Bronx, N.Y., 1982-85, fellow in pediat. nephrology, 1985-88; asst. prof. U. Fla. Coll. Med., Gainesville, 1988-93, assoc. prof., 1993—; med. dir. pediatrics Renal Stone Disease Clinic, 1996—. Assoc. med. dir. Children's Kidney Ctr., Gainesville, 1989—; co-investigator on 6 rsch. studies, dir. Pediatric Rsch. Stone Disease Clin. U. Fla., rsch. peer rev. com. Am. Heart Assn., 1997-99; physician advisor Fla. Med. Quality Assurance, Tampa, 1994-2002. Contbr. articles to profl. jours. Active Children's Home Soc., Gainesville, 1994—2002, Ronald McDonald House, 1996—. Named one of Best Drs. in Am., Best Drs. in Fla., Best Pediatricians in Am.; grantee, CoInvest, Bethesda, Md., 1995—. Mem. AMA, Fla. Med. Assn., So. Med. Assn., Am. Soc. Nephrology, Internat. Pediat. Nephrology Assn., Am. Soc. Pediat. Nephrology, Fla. Soc. Pediat. Nephrology (pres. 1998). Republican. Methodist. Avocations: camping, skiing, travel. Office: HD 216 Univ Fla Coll Med Pediats 1300 Archer Rd Gainesville FL 32610-0296 Office Phone: 352-392-4434. Business E-Mail: neibere@peds.ufl.edu.

NEIDELL, MARTIN H., lawyer; b. Bklyn., Apr. 5, 1946; s. Sidney B. and Sophie (Goldstein) N.; m. Suzan C. Rucker, June 23, 1968; children: Michael, Sari. BA magna cum laude, Lehigh U., 1968; JD cum laude, NYU, 1971. Bar: N.Y. 1972, U.S. Dist. Ct. (ea. and so. dists.) N.Y. 1973, U.S. Ct. Appeals (2d cir.) 1973. Law clk. to presiding justice U.S. Dist. Ct. (ea. dist.) N.Y., Bklyn., 1971-73; assoc. Stroock & Stroock & Lavan LLP, NYC, 1973-79, ptnr., corp., securities law, 1980—, mem., operating exec. com. Editor NYU Law Rev., 1971. Trustee North Shore Synagogue, Syosset, N.Y., 1984-90. Office: Stroock & Stroock & Lavan LLP 180 Maiden Ln New York NY 10038-4925 Home Phone: 516-624-8006; Office Phone: 212-806-5836. Office Fax: 212-806-7836. Business E-Mail: mneidell@stroock.com.

NEIDHARDT, FREDERICK CARL, microbiologist, educator; b. Phila., May 12, 1931; s. Adam Fred and Carrie (Fry) N.; m. Elizabeth Robinson, June 9, 1956 (div. Sept. 1977); children: Richard Frederick, Jane Elizabeth; m. Germaine Chipault, Dec. 3, 1977; 1 son, Marc Frederick. BA, Kenyon Coll., 1952, DSc (hon.), 1976; PhD, Harvard U., 1956; DSc (hon.), Purdue U., 1988, Umea U., 1994. Research fellow Pasteur Inst., Paris, 1956-57; H.C. Ernst research fellow Harvard Med. Sch., 1957-58, instr., then assoc.,

1958-61; mem. faculty Purdue U., 1961-70, assoc. prof, then prof., assoc. head dept. biol. scis., 1965-70; mem. faculty U. Mich., Ann Arbor, 1970—, chmn. dept. microbiology and immunology, 1970-82, F.G. Novy disting. univ. prof., 1989-99, F.G. Novy disting. univ. prof. emeritus, 2000—, assoc. dean faculty affairs, 1990-93, assoc. v.p. for rsch., 1993-96, acting v.p. for rsch., 1996-97, interim v.p. for rsch., 1997, v.p. for rsch., 1998. Cons. Dept. Agr., 1964-65; mem. grant study panel NIH, 1965-69, 88-92; mem. commn. scholars Ill. Bd. Higher Edn., 1973-79; mem. test com. for microbiology Nat. Bd. Med. Examiners, 1975-79, chmn., 1979-83; mem. sci. adv. com. Neogen Corp., 1982-92; mem. basic energy scis. adv. com. U.S. Dept. Energy, 1994-98; Wellcome vis. prof. in microbiology U. Ky., 1986. Author books and papers in field; mem. editorial bd. profl. jours. Recipient award bacteriology and immunology Eli Lilly and Co., 1966; Alexander von Humboldt Found. award for U.S. sr. scientist, 1979; NSF sr. fellow U. Copenhagen, 1968-69 Mem. Am. Soc. Microbiology (pres. 1981-82), Am. Acad. Arts and Scis., Am. Soc. Biochemistry and Molecular Biology, Am. Inst. Biol. Scis., Genetics Soc. Am., Bavarian Acad. Sci., Soc. Gen. Physiology, Waksman Found. for Microbiology (bd. dirs. 1996—, pres. 2001—), Phi Beta Kappa, Sigma Xi. Office: U Mich Med Sch Dept Microbiology and Immunology Ann Arbor MI 48109-0620 Home Phone: 734-995-2951; Office Phone: 734-763-1209. E-mail: fcneid@umich.edu.

NEIDHART, JAMES ALLEN, oncologist, educator; b. Steubenville, Ohio, Aug. 30, 1940; s. James Leonard and Mary Jane (Daniels) N.; m. Patricia Irene Harpkamp, Aug. 16, 1966 (div. Apr. 1985); children—James, Jeffrey, Jennifer; m. Mary Gagen, Feb. 1986; children: Andrew, Rae Ann. BS, Union Coll., Alliance, Ohio, 1962; MD, Ohio State U., 1966. Diplomate Am. Bd. Internal Medicine, Am. Bd. Hematology and Oncology. Intern Bronson Hosp., Kalamazoo, Mich., 1966-67; resident Ohio State U., Columbus, Ohio, 1969-71; postdoctoral fellow Coll. Medicine, Ohio State U., Columbus, 1972-74, asst. prof. medicine, 1974-78, assoc. prof., 1978-84, dir. interdisciplinary oncology unit Comprehensive Cancer Ctr., 1975-80, dep. dir. Comprehensive Cancer Ctr., 1980-84; prof. medicine U. Tex.-Houston-M.D. Anderson Hosp. and Tumor Inst., 1984-86, Hubert L. and Olive Stringer prof. oncology, 1984-86, dep. head div. medicine, 1984-86, chmn. dept. med. oncology, 1984-86; dir. Cancer Rsch. and Treatment Ctr., U. N.Mex., Albuquerque, 1986-96, chief hematology and oncology, 1986-91; dir. Cancer Rsch. and Treatment Ctr. San Juan Regional Cancer Ctr., 1996—. Contbr. chpts. to Recent Advances in Clinical Therapeutics, Clinical Immunotherapy Former mem. bd. dirs. Am. Cancer Soc., Columbus; former v.p. Ohio Cancer Research Assocs. Served to lt. USN, 1967-69, Vietnam Mem. Am. Soc. Hematology, Am. Soc. Clin. Oncology, Am. Assn. Cancer Research, ACP, S.W. Oncology Group, Wilderness Soc., Sierra Club Home: 66 Road 2577 Aztec NM 87410-1020 Office: San Juan Regional Cancer Ctr Farmington NM 87401

NEIDICH, BROOKE GARBER, foundation administrator, art patron; m. Daniel Neidich. BA, NYU. Founder, chmn. NYU Child Study Ctr. Trustee Chapin Sch., Mt. Sinai - NYU Health Care Sys., NYU Med. Sch. Found.; bd. dir. Lincoln Ctr. Theater, Lubovitch Dance Co.; adv. coun. Children's Defense Fund - NY; vice chmn. Whitney Mus. Am. Art. Recipient Health Care Leadership Award distinguished cmty. svc., United Hosp. Fund., 1999. Mailing: c/o Whitney Mus Am Art 945 Madison Ave New York NY 10021

NEIDICH, GEORGE ARTHUR, lawyer; b. NYC, Feb. 22, 1950; s. Hyman and Rosalyn N.; m. Alene Wendrow, Jan. 10, 1982; 1 child, Hannah Lauren. BA, SUNY, Binghamton, 1971; JD magna cum laude, SUNY, Buffalo, 1974; MLT, Georgetown U., 1981. Bar: N.Y. 1975, D.C. 1979, Va. 1996, Conn. 1990. Assoc. Runfola & Birzon, Buffalo, 1973-75, Duke, Holzman, Yaeger & Radlin, Buffalo, 1975-77; gen. counsel subcom. on capital, investments and bus. opportunity, com. on small bus. U.S. Ho. of Reps., Washington, 1977-79, subcom. on gen. oversight, 1979-80; sr. legal advisor Task Force Product Liability and Accident Compensation Office of Gen. Counsel, Dept. Commerce, Washington, 1980-81; assoc. Steptoe & Johnson, Washington, 1981-86, of counsel, 1986-89; gen. counsel, sr. v.p. Preferred Health Care, Ltd., Wilton, Conn., 1989-93; COO Value Behavioral Health, Inc., Falls Church, Va., 1993-95; counsellor at law, 1995—; gen. counsel CareAdvantage, Inc., Iselin, NJ, 1999—. Adj. prof. Georgetown U. Law Ctr., 1985—87. Office: 9301 Morison Ln Great Falls VA 22066-4153 Office Phone: 703-757-2820. Personal E-mail: gneidich@aol.com.

NEIDICH-RYDER, CAROLE LOUISE, curator, educator; b. Bronx, Dec. 17, 1950; m. Richard D. Ryder. BS in Biology, Molloy Coll., Rockville Centre, NY, 1972; MS in Biology, Adelphi U., Garden City, NY, 1974. Mus. curator Nassau County Dept. Pks., Recreation and Mus., Seaford, NY, 1972—; adj. asst. prof. Nassau CC, Garden City, 2000—. Pres. WindRyder Resources, Ltd., Hicksville, NY, 2005—. Col. NY Guard, 1986—2006. Decorated Conspicuous Svc. medal NY State, Divsn. Mil. and Naval Affairs; named Woman Yr., LWV Nassau County, 1996; recipient Leadership award, NY State Outdoor Edn. Assn., 1988, Pathfinder award for excellence in govt., Town Hempstead, NY, 2000, Women Distinctionaward, Town Oyster Bay, NY, 2001, Lifetime Achievement award, Nassau County Exec., NY, 2001, Govs. award for excellence, NY Divsn. for Women, Nassau County Adv. Coun., 2002, Def. Liberty medal, NY State, Divsn. Mil. and Naval Affairs, 2002. Mem.: Sigma Chi Sci. Roman Catholic. Avocations: nature, geocaching, hiking. Home Phone: 516-938-5675; Office Phone: 516-938-5675.

NEIDORFF, MICHAEL F., health care executive; b. Phila., Nov. 19, 1942; s. A. Harvey and Shirley R. (Rubin) N.; m. Noemi Karpati. BS, Trinity U., 1965; MA, St. Francis Coll., 1966. Mgr. Miles Labs., Ltd., 1969-75, dir., 1967-85; pres., CEO Physician Health Plan, 1985-95, Group Health Plan, Inc., St. Louis, 1995—96; treas. Centene Corp., St. Louis, 1996—2001, pres., CEO, 1996—2004, chmn., pres., CEO, 2004—. Bd. dirs. Mark Twain Bank, St. Louis. Bd. trustees St. Louis Symphony Orch., St. Louis; bd. dirs. St. Louis Area coun. Boy Scouts Am., Grand Ctr., St. Louis. Mem. Mo. Managed Healthcare Assn. Office: Centene Corp 7711 Carondelet Ave Saint Louis MO 63105 *

NEIER, ARYEH, author, human rights organization administrator; b. Berlin, Apr. 22, 1937; came to U.S., 1947, naturalized, 1955; s. Wolf and Gitla (Bendzinska) N.; m. Yvette Celton, June 22, 1958; 1 son, David. BS, Cornell U., 1958; LL.D. (hon.), Hofstra U., 1975, Hamilton Coll., 1979, SUNY, Binghamton, 1988. Exec. dir. League Indsl. Democracy, NYC, 1958-60; assoc. editor Current mag., NYC, 1960-63; exec. dir. N.Y. Civil Liberties Union, NYC, 1965-70; field devel. officer ACLU, NYC, 1963-64, exec. dir., 1970-78; adj. prof. law NYU, NYC, 1978—; dir. 20th Century Fund Project on Litigation and Social Policy, 1978-81; exec. dir. Human Rights Watch, NYC, 1981-93; pres. Open Soc. Fund and Inst., NYC, 1993—. Lectr. Police Acad., NY, 1969-70. Author: Dossier, 1975, Crime and Punishment: A Radical Solution, 1976, Defending My Enemy, 1979, Only Judgment, 1982; co-editor series of handbooks on rights of Americans, 1972-78; mem. editorial bd. The Nation, 1978-86, columnist, 1990—. Commr. juvenile justice standards project Am. Bar Assn.— Inst. for Judicial Adminstrn. Recipient Gavel award Am. Bar Assn., 1974 Fellow Am. Acad. Arts & Scis. Address: Open Society Institute 400 W 59th St Fl 4 New York NY 10019-1105 *

NEIKIRK, WILLIAM ROBERT, journalist; b. Irvine, Ky., Jan. 6, 1938; s. Lewis Byron and Nancy Elizabeth (Green) N.; m. Ruth Ann Clary, Sept. 10, 1960; children: Paul Gregory, John Stuart, Christa Lynn. BA in Journalism, U. Ky., 1960. Reporter Lexington (Ky.) Herald, 1959-60; state capital corr. AP, Frankfort, Ky., 1961-66, Baton Rouge, 1966-69; econ. corr. AP (Washington Bur.), 1970-74; nat. econ. writer Chgo. Tribune, Washington, 1974-83, White House corr., 1977, 94-98—, econ. columnist, 1980—, news editor Washington bur., 1983, fin. editor, 1988-91, sr. writer, 1991—, chief Washington corr., 1998—. Author: The Work Revolution, 1983, Volcker: The Money Man, 1987. Recipient Beck award Chgo. Tribune, 1975, Bus. Writing award U. Mo., 1978, 80, Bus. Writing award Amos Tuck Grad. Sch. Bus., Dartmouth Coll., 1980, John Hancock Bus. Writing award Wharton Sch. Fin., U. Pa., 1979, finalist, 1990, 91, John Hancock Bus. Writing award U. Houston, 1980, Loeb Bus. Writing award UCLA Grad. Sch. Mgmt., 1979, Chgo. Headliner Club award, 1979, 84, Raymond Clapper Meml. award, 1981, Barnet Nover award, 1994, Merriman Smith award, 1995, White House Correspondents Assn.; named to Ky. Journalism Hall of Fame, 1998, One of Top 100 Bus. News Luminaries of the Century, TJFR mag., 2000; co-recipient Pulitzer Prize, 2001. Mem.: Gridiron Club (pres. 2007). Mem. Christian Ch. (Disciples Of Christ). Home: 5121 38th St N Arlington VA 22207-1827 Office Phone: 202-824-8214. Business E-Mail: wneikirk@tribune.com.

NEIL, ROBERT F., broadcast executive; Program dir. WYYY-FM, WSYR-AM, 1983, ops. mgr., 1983—84, WYAY-FM, Gainesville, Ga., 1984—86; station mgr. WSB-AM/FM, 1986—88, v.p. & gen. mgr., 1989—92; joined Cox Broadcasting, 1986, v.p. east, 1989—92, exec. v.p. radio, 1992—96; pres. CEO Cox Radio, 1996—. Named Radio Exec. of Yr., Radio Ink, 2003. Office: Cox Radio Inc 6205 Peachtree Dunwoody Rd Atlanta GA 30328

NEIL, SANDRA EILLEEN SILVERBERG, psychologist; b. NYC, Sept. 30, 1945; d. Marcus and Pearl (Bloom) Glickfeld; m. Robert Silverberg; children: Gerard David, Simonne Elizabeth, Julien Richard, Shari Beth Silverberg. BA, LaTrobe U., Melbourne, Australia, 1974, BEd in Counseling, 1976; MA in Clin. Psychology, U. Melbourne, 1986, PhD in Medicine, 1993. Registered clin. and forensic psychologist 1979, cert. family therapist Avanta Virginia Satir Network, 1987. Rsch. asst. dept. ednl. psychology U. Melbourne, 1965—68; clin. psychologist Janefield Hosp., Melbourne, 1975—77, Prince Henry Hosp., Melbourne, 1977—79, Cairnmillar Inst., Melbourne, 1979—83; pvt. practice Melbourne, 1983—; clin. psychologist St. Vincent's Hosp., Melbourne, 1986—93; clin. psychologist and family therapist, founding dir. Satir Centre Australia, Armadale, Victoria, Australia, 1993—. Forensic psychologist Supreme Ct., Melbourne, 1976—87; media psychologist, 1977—; sworn marriage counsellor Atty. Gen.'s Dept., Melbourne, 1978—. Author: The Persistence of Obesity, 1986, The Psychodynamics of Obesity, 1993, The Family Chessboard, 1995; editor: A Matter Of Life: Psychological Theory, Research And Practice, 1999; author: A Journey Through Three Continents And Four Generations: A Family Reconstruction, 2001. Active Opera Australia. Fellow: Australian Psychol. Soc. (chmn. pub. and media rels. Victorian br. 1983—2004); mem.: APA, Internat. Coun. Psychologists (pres. 1997—2000, chair internat. rels. and human rights interest group 1990—, named World Area Chair 2000—), Internat. Acad. Family Psychology (Australian nat. rep. 1997—), Patron Opera Australia, Avanta, The Virginia Satir Internat. Network. Office: Satir Centre of Australia Suite 2 1051-A/B High St Armadale VIC 3143 Australia Office Phone: 61-3-9824-7755. Office Fax: 61-3-9824-7865. Personal E-mail: icp@netspace.net.au, drneil@satiraustralia.com.

NEIL, STUART, management consultant, real estate broker; s. Judith Gottlieb; m. Christine Anne Kessler; children: Jaime Cameran, Glenn Skyler. BA, Marist Coll., Poughkeepsie, NY, 1971—73; MA, Fairfield U., Conn., 1974—76. Cert. Secondary English Tchr. N.Y. Bd. Edn., 1975, Bus. Edn. The U. of State of N.Y., 1975, School Counselor The U. of State of N.Y., 1982, Human Resource Profl. Soc. Human Resource Mgmt., 1993. Sr. ptnr. Interact Human Resources, Fort Collins, Colo., 1989—; broker/owner Stuart Neil Ltd., Fort Collins, 1993. Safety cons. SunBlest Mgmt., Fort Lupton, 2001—; safety & human resource cons. Colorstar Growers of Colo., Fort Lupton; safety & human resource mgmt. cons. SunValley Farms, Loveland, 2004—. With US Army, 1963—66. Decorated Parachutist badge US Army, Purple Heart, Combat Infantrymans badge. Mem.: Soc. Human Resource Mgmt., Colo. Assn. Realtors, Disabled Vets., Mil. Order of Purple Heart, Am. Legion. Office: Interact Human Resources PO Box 270226 Fort Collins CO 80527 Home Phone: 970-980-3983; Office Phone: 303-753-5855. Personal E-mail: iamus@juno.com. Business E-mail: interact@consultant.com.

NEILAN, AIDAN JOSEPH, radiologist; b. Galway, Ireland, Sept. 30, 1923; arrived in U.S., 1950; s. John and Honoria Killeen Neilan; m. Nuala Mary McCarthy, June 1, 1959; children: Katherine Rosemary, Rosemary Collette, David Aidan. MD, Nat. U. Ireland, 1948. Diplomate Am. Bd. Radiology. Intern New Rochelle Gen. Hosp., 1950—51; resident Wadsworth VA Hosp., 1970—74; chief orthop. radiology Wadsworth Hosp., LA; prof. radiology UCLA, LA, 1979, prof. emeritus. Pres., CEO AJNCO, Inc., LA, 1958. Capt. US Army, 1953—55, France. Mem.: AMA, Irish Med. Assn., Brit. Med. Assn. Republican. Roman Cath. Avocations: piano, swimming, reading. Home: 30639 Rue Langlois Rancho Palos Verdes CA 90275 Personal E-mail: neilan@cox.net.

NEILL, DENIS MICHAEL, management consultant; b. Grand Rapids, Mich., Apr. 27, 1943; s. Thomas Patrick and Agnes Josephine (Weber) N.; m. Mary Kathleen Golden, June 11, 1966; children: Mark, Erin. AB cum laude, St. Louis U., 1964, JD cum laude, 1967. Bar: Mo. 1967, D.C. 1969. Gen. atty. Office of Asst. Regional Counsel IRS, Newark, 1967-68; assoc. Arent, Fox, Kintner, Plotkin & Kahn, Washington, 1969-71, Morgan, Lewis & Bockius, Washington, 1971-72; atty. advisor office gen. counsel AID, Washington, 1972-73, asst. gen. counsel legis. and policy coordination, 1973-75, asst. adminstr. legis. affairs, 1975-77; sr. v.p., gen. counsel Aeromaritime Internat. Corp., Washington, 1977-80; counsel Surrey & Morse, Washington, 1980-81; sr. ptnr. Neill & Shaw, Washington, 1981-92; sr. law ptnr. Dalley, Neill, Assevero, Carroll & Nealer, Washington, 1992-93; pres. Neill & Co., Inc., Washington, 1981—; counsel Fin. Markets Internat., Inc., 1998—. Bd. dirs. Barker Found., 1981-86, Fed. City Nat. Bank, Washington, 1987. Lt. USCG, 1968-71. Recipient Superior Unit Citation AID, 1976, Disting. Honor award, 1977. Mem. ABA, FBA, D.C. Bar Assn., Mo. Bar Assn., Nat. Security Indsl. Assn. (bd. dirs. 1982-90), Capitol Hill Club, Columbia Country Club (Chevy Chase, Md.), Jefferson Islands Club. Democrat. Home: 5945 Searl Ter Bethesda MD 20816-2022 Office: Neill & Co 5945 Searl Ter Bethesda MD 20816-2022 E-mail: denisneill@aol.com.

NEILL, MONTY, educational association administrator; PhD, Harvard U. Dir. Nat. Ctr. Fair & Open Testing, Cambridge, Mass., 1987—; leader Nat. Forum on Assessment in developing Principles and Indicators for Student Assessment Systems; chair Forum Ednl. Accountability. Author: Failing Our Children, Implementing Performance Assessments: A Guide to Classroom School and System Reform, Testing Our Children: A Report Card on State Assessment Systems. Office: FairTest 342 Broadway Cambridge MA 02139 Office Phone: 617-864-4810. Office Fax: 617-497-2224. *

NEILL, RICHARD ROBERT, retired publishing executive; b. NYC, June 20, 1925; s. Robert Irving and Mildred Mary (Hall) N.; m. Patricia Mae Robinson, Dec. 27, 1952; 1 son, Robert Kenneth. AB summa cum laude, Princeton U., 1948; MA, N.Y. U., 1953. With Prentice-Hall, Inc., NYC and Englewood Cliffs, NJ, 1948-85, advt. mgr., 1953-58, v.p. advt., 1958-62; pres. Executive Reports Corporation, 1962-85, ret., 1985. Regional chmn. Princeton Alumni Giving, Yonkers, N.Y., 1960-63, Tarrytown-Irvington, N.Y., 1977-80 Pres. Tarrytown (N.Y.) Jr. High Sch. PTA, 1971-72; bd. dirs. Martling Owners, Tarrytown, 1980-84, 89-93. Lt. (j.g.) USNR, 1943-46, PTO. Mem. USN Meml. Found., Princeton Terrace Club (bd. govs. 1986-92), Phi Beta Kappa. Republican. Mem. Reform Ch. Home: 3306 Kendal Way Sleepy Hollow NY 10591-1066 *A thought acquired from one of my first bosses: "Everything happens for the best - or can be made to do so." This has been a lifelong help.*

NEILL, WILLIAM HAROLD, JR., science educator, researcher; b. Wynne, Ark., Oct. 21, 1943; s. William H., Sr. and Shirley A. (Ellis) N.; m. Charlotte A. Jackson, 1964; 1 child, Amanda K. BS in Zoology, U. Ark., 1965, MS in Zoology, 1967; PhD in Zoology/Statis., U. Wis., 1971. Rsch. fishery biologist Southwest Fisheries Ctr. Nat. Marine Fisheries Svc., Honolulu, 1971—74; prin. investigator Tex. Agrl. Expt. Sta., 1975—; assoc. prof. Tex. A&M U., College Station, Tex., 1975—83, prof., 1983—, interim head, dept. Wildlife and Fisheries Sci., 1992—93, interim assoc. head grad. programs and rsch., dept. Wildlife and Fisheries Sci., 2006—07. Organizing com. Advanced Rsch. Inst. on Mechanisms Fish Migration, NATO, 1980-82; tech. com. So. Regional Aquaculture Ctr., USDA, 1987-89; sci.-tech. adv. com. Corpus Christi Bay Nat. Estuary Program, 1994-97; mem. Tex. Sea Grant adv. bd., 1998-2005; faculty Sloan, 2005—. Editor Tex. Jour. Sci., 1983-85; mem. editl. adv. bd. Critical Revs. in Aquatic Sci., 1986-90; assoc. editor Transactions of the Am. Fisheries Soc., 1995-97; contbr. numerous articles to sci. jours. and books. Grantee numerous orgns., 1975—. Fellow Tex. Acad. Sci.; mem. Am. Fisheries Soc. (life, Award of Excellence com. 1987, 89, chair Publ. Awards com. 1993, editl. bd. 1995), Am. Inst. Fishery Rsch. Biologists, Phi Beta Kappa, Sigma Xi, Phi Sigma, Gamma Sigma Delta. Office: Texas A&M U Dept Wildlife & Fisheries Sci 2258 TAMUS College Station TX 77843-2258 Office Phone: 979-845-5759. Business E-Mail: w-neill@tamu.edu.

NEILSEN, CRAIG H., hotel executive; b. 1942; MBA, JD, U. Utah. Pres. Cactus Pete, Inc., Jackpot, Nev., 1984—, Ameristar Casino Vicksburg, Miss., 1993—. Pres. & chmn. bd. dir. Cactus Pete's Inc. Named best performing CEO, Am. Gaming Assn., 2002. Office: Ameristar Casinos Inc 3773 Howard Hughes Pkwy Las Vegas NV 89109

NEILSON, ERIC GRANT, physician, educator, health facility administrator; b. Bklyn., Sept. 14, 1949; s. Jack Drew and Lynette Elsie (Lundquist) N.; m. Linda Rae Apolzon, May 27, 1972; children: Tinsley, Sigrid. BS magna cum laude, Denison U., 1971; MD magna cum laude, U. Ala., 1975; MA (hon.), U. Pa., 1987. Asst. prof. U. Pa., Phila., 1980-87, assoc. prof., 1987-91, prof., 1991-98, C. Mahlon Kline prof., 1993-98, chief renal-electrolyte & hypertension divsn. dept. medicine, 1988-98; Hugh Jackson Morgan prof., chmn. dept. medicine Vanderbilt U. Med. Ctr., Nashville, 1998—. Attending physician Hosp. of U. Pa., 1980-98; physician-in-chief Vanderbilt U. Hosp., 1998—; cons. in field. Med. editl. bds. on sci. jours.; assoc. editor Kidney Internat., 1997-2006; editor-in-chief Jour. Am. Soc. Nephrology, 2007-; contbr. numerous articles to profl. jours. Chmn. med. adv. bd. Lupus Found. of Phila., 1985-95; chmn. pathology A study sect. NIH, Bethesda, Md., 1990-92; chmn. grant rev. com. Nat. Kidney Found. of Delaware Valley; mem. adv. coun. NIDDK, NIH; mem. bd. sci. advisors Polycystic Kidney Found., 1997-2000; mem. postdoctoral fellowship com. Howard Hughes Med. Inst., 1997-2000. Recipient Clin. Scientist award Am. Heart Assn., 1980, Young Investigator award Am. Soc. Nephrology/Am. Heart Assn., 1985, Established Investigator award Am. Heart Assn., 1985-90, President's medal Am. Soc. Nephrology, 1994, AN Richard Disting. Achievement award U. Pa., 1998, John P. Peters award, Am. Soc. Nephrology, 2005; named Disting. Alumnus, U. Ala., Birmingham, 2006. Fellow: ACP; mem.: Internat. Soc. Nephrology (treas. 2003—), Assn. Prof. Medicine (chmn. rsch. com. 2000—), Assn. Subsplty. Profs. (pres. 1994—96, Disting. Prof. award 2003), Am. Assn. Immunologists, Am. Clin. Climatol. Assn., Am. Soc. Nephrology (John P. Peters award 2005), Assn. Am. Physicians, Am. Soc. Clin. investigation. Mem. Soc. Of Friends. Office: Vanderbilt U Med Ctr Dept Medicine D3100 Med Ctr N Nashville TN 37232-0001 Office Phone: 615-322-3146. Business E-Mail: eric.neilson@vanderbilt.edu.

NEILSON, WINTHROP CUNNINGHAM, III, retired communications executive, financial consultant, photographer; b. NYC, Jan. 7, 1934; s. Winthrop Cunningham, Jr. and Frances Fullerton (Jones) N.; m. Ilse Rossenbeck, Jan. 4, 1957; children: Luise R., Victoria F.; m. Demaris King Hetrick, July 5, 1985; 1 child, Whitney C. C.; stepchildren: Norman P. Hetrick Jr., D. Page Hetrick. BA, Harvard U., 1956; grad. in security analysis, N.Y. Inst. Finance, 1963. Asst. prodr., asst. dir. Rangley Lakes Theater, 1955; gen. assignment reporter Albany (N.Y.) Times-Union, 1959—60; pub. info. writer, spkr. Consol. Edison, 1960—61; asst. dir. pub. rels. Union Svc. Corp., 1962; with Georgeson & Co., NYC, 1962—81, prin., 1969—81; sr. v.p. D.F. King & Co. Inc., NYC, 1982—86; founder, mng. dir. Krone Comm., Harrisburg, Pa., 1986—87; pres. Krone Group Inc., Harrisburg, 1987—89; mng. dir. Neilson/Hetrick Group, Montclair, NJ, 1990—93, Harrisburg, Pa., 1993—97, chmn. Chambersburg, Pa., 1987—2006; guest lectr. NYU, 1991; profl. nature photographer, 2001—. Author: series Aunt Jane, 1971, 73, The Reluctant Marriage, 1978, Investorism, 1981, Annual Reports, The Agony and the Ecstasy, 1985, Individual Investors, a Counterbalance to Institutional Investors, 1986; writer, assoc. editor: Trends, 1965-81; contbr. articles to profl. jours. Mem. Mountain Lakes (N.J.) Econ. Devel. Council, 1974-79, chmn., 1977-79; pres. Robert A. Taft Republican Club, Queens, N.Y., 1964-65, chmn., 1966-67; treas. 23d Assembly Dist. Rep. Party, 1966-67; county committeeman, 1964-67; del. N.Y. State Nominating Conv., 1966; campaign mgr. for 2 assemblymen and state senator; mem. exec. com. Chambersburg Cmty. Theater, Inc., 2002-03. Served with AUS, 1956-59. Recipient Investor Edn. Disting. Service award Nat. Assn. Investors Clubs, 1986. Mem. Nat. Investor Rels. Inst. (dir. 1980-84, v.p. manpower 1980-81, v.p. long-range planning 1981-84), Pub. Rels. Soc. Am. (charter, exec. com. investor rels. 1982-90, chmn. 1987, Pres. award 1987, charter inductee into Hall of Fame for Investor Rels.), Corp. Rels. Soc. Ctrl. Pa. (v.p. 1986-89, pres. 1994-95), Ctrl. Pa. Entrepreneurial Assn. (bd. dirs. 1988-89, adv. bd. tech. coun. Ctrl. Pa. 1994-96), DU Club, Hershey Mills Golf Club, Hasty Pudding Club, Ausable Club. Lutheran. Home (Summer): Ausable Club 14 Neilson Way Saint Huberts NY 12943

NEIMAN, JOSEPH BRUCE, dermatologist; b. NYC, July 28, 1947; s. Nathan and Sarah N.; BA, NYU, 1968; MD, U. Tenn., 1972; m. Karen Marcia Simon, Aug. 31, 1975. Intern, Brown U., Providence, 1973-74; resident SUNY, Buffalo, 1974-75, 76-78, chief resident, 1977; dir. adult health services, head cmty. health screening Erie County Health Dept., Buffalo, NY, 1975-76; practice medicine specializing in dermatology and dermatologic surgery Boston, 1978-79, Williamsville, NY, 1980—; mem. staffs Buffalo Gen. Hosp., Millard Fillmore Hosp., Buffalo, Sisters of Charity Hosp., Buffalo; clin. asst. prof. dept. dermatology SUNY, Buffalo, 1980—; cons. USPHS, Buffalo, 1979-81. Fellow Am. Acad. Dermatology; mem. AMA, Internat. Soc. Dermatologic Surgery, Internat. Soc. Hair Restoration Surgery, Am. Soc. Dermatologic Surgery, N.AM. Soc. Phlebology, NY State Soc. Dermatology, Buffalo-Rochester Dermatol. Soc., Erie County Med. Soc., NY State Med. Soc. Home: 48 Brandywine Dr Buffalo NY 14221-1804 Office: Neiman Ctr for Dermatology & Hair Restoration 1140 Youngs Rd Williamsville NY 14221-3625 Personal E-mail: jneimanmd@aol.com.

NEIMAN, KENNETH PAUL, judge; b. NYC, July 4, 1945; s. Julius and Gertrude (Fox) N.; m. Jan Dumond, May 24, 1987; children: Jennifer Gottlieb, Anna L. Neiman, J. Matthew Gowdy, Kerri Escudero. BA, Tufts U., 1967; JD, Harvard Law Sch., 1971. Bar: N.Y. 1972, Mass. 1974, U.S. Dist. Ct. Mass. 1974, U.S. Ct. Appeals (1st cir.) 1981, U.S. Supreme Ct. 1978. Staff atty. Mental Health Info. Svcs., NYC, 1971, Ctr. Social Welfare, Policy & Law, NYC, 1971-73; rsch. fellow Legal Svcs. Corp. Rsch. Inst., Washington, 1978; mng. atty. Western Mass. Legal Svcs., Holyoke,

1973-81; ptnr. Fierst & Neiman, Northampton, Mass., 1981-94; U.S. magistrate judge Dist. Mass., Springfield, 1995—. Mem. ABA, Mass. Bar Assn., Mass. Bar Found., Hampshire County Bar Assn. Office: US Dist Ct 1550 Main St Springfield MA 01103-1422

NEIMAN, LEROY, artist; b. St. Paul, June 8, 1921; s. Charles and Lydia (Serline) Runquist; m. Janet Byrne, June 22, 1957. Student, Sch. Art Inst., Chgo., 1946-50, U. Ill., 1951, DePaul U., 1951; LittD (hon.), Franklin Pierce Coll., 1976; D (hon.), St. John's U., 1980, Iona Coll., 1985, Hofstra U., 1997, St. Francis Coll., 1998, St. Bonaventure U., 1999, Sch. Art Inst., Chgo., 2006. Instr. Sch. Art Inst. Chgo., 1950-60, LeRoy Neiman master classes, 2006—07; instr. Saugatuck Summer Sch. Painting, Mich., 1957-58, 63, Sch. Arts and Crafts, Winston-Salem, NC, 1963; instr. painting Atlanta Youth Coun., 1968-69; printmaker-graphics, 1971—; artist Olympics, ABC-TV, Munich, 1972, ofcl. artist Montreal, 1976, US Olympics, 1980, 84; computer artist CBS-TV (Superbowl), New Orleans, 1978; ofcl. artist Goodwill Games CNN-TV, Moscow, 1986; 1st ofcl. artist Ky. Derby, Louisville, 1997; ofcl. artist Mardi Gras, New Orleans, 2002. Mem. adv. com. LeRoy Neiman Ctr. Print Studies Sch. of the Arts Columbia U., 1995; mem. adv. com. for NYC Commn. Cultural Affairs, 1995, UCLA LeRoy Neiman Ctr. Study of Am. Soc. and Culture, 1998; established LeRoy Neiman Art Ctr. for Youth, San Francisco, 2000, 05, Watsonville, Calif., 2002. One-man shows include Oehlschlaeger Gallery, Chgo., 1959, 61, O'Hana Gallery, London, Gallerie O. Bosc, Paris, 1962, Hammer Gallery, NYC, 1963, 65, 67, 70, 72, 76, 78-79, 81-83, 85-87, 89, 92, 94, 97, 2000, 03, Huntington-Hartford Gallery Modern Art, NYC, 1967, Heath Gallery, Atlanta, 1969, Abbey Theatre, Dublin, Ireland, 1970, Museo de Bellas Artes, Caracas, Indpls. Inst. Arts, 1972, Hermitage Mus., Leningrad, Tobu Gallery, Tokyo, 1974, Springfield Mus. Fine Arts, Mass., 1974, 84, Knoedler Gallery, London, 1976, Casa gratica, Helsinki, 1977, Renée Victor, Stockholm, 1977, Okla. Art Ctr., Oklahoma City, 1981, Harrod's, London, 1982; retrospective show, Minn. Mus. Art, St. Paul, 1975, Meredith Long Galleries, Houston, 1978, Hanae Mori Gallery, Tokyo, 1988, New State Tretyakov Mus., Moscow, 1988, Butler Inst., Youngstown, Ohio, 1990, Galerie Marcel Bernheim, Paris, 1993, Ky. Derby Mus., Louisville, 1995, 1997, Marlborough Gallery, NYC, 2000, The Fairfield, Sturgeon Bay, Wis., 2001, Nat. Art Mus. Sport, Ind. U.-Purdue U., 2001, Wildlife Experience, Parker, Colo., 2003; two-man show, Neiman-Warhol, LA Inst. Contemporary Art, 1981; exhibited in group shows at Art Inst. Chgo., 1954-60, Carnegie Internat., 1956, Corcoran Gallery Am., Washington, Walker Art Center, Mpls., 1957, Ringling Mus., Sarasota, Fla., 1959, Salon d'Art Mus., Paris, 1961, Nat. Gallery Portraiture, Smithsonian Instn., Washington, Minn. Mus. Art, 1969, Rotunda Della Basana, Milan, Italy, 1971, Royal Coll. Art, London, 1971, Minn. Mus. Art Nat. Tour, 1976-77, Whitney Mus., 1985; Master Prints of 19th and 20th Centuries, Hammer Gallery, NY, 1987, Salon d'Automne, Paris, 1992-93, Newport Art Mus., 2004; represented in permanent collections Mpls. Inst. Arts, Ill. State Mus., Springfield, Joslyn Mus., Omaha, Wodham Coll., Oxford, Eng., Nat. Art Mus. Sport, NYC, Museo De Ballas Artes Caracas, Hermitage Mus., Indpls. Inst. Arts, U. Ill., Balt. Mus. Fine Art, The Armand Hammer Collection, LA, Edwin & Ruth Kennedy Mus. Am. Art at Ohio U., Midwest Mus. Am. Art, Elkhart, Ind., Nat. Art Mus. Sport, Indpls.; executed murals at Merc. Nat. Bank, Hammond, Ind., Continental Hotel, Chgo., Swedish Lloyd Ship S.S. Patricia, Stockholm, ceramic tile mural, Sportsmans Park, Chgo., The Muhammad Ali Ctr., Louisville, 2005, Polo Mural, Southampton, NY, 2005; author: LeRoy Neiman—Art and Life Style, 1974, Horses, 1979, LeRoy Neiman. Posters, 1980, LeRoy Neiman. Catalogue Raisonné, 1980, Carnaval, 1981, LeRoy Neiman: Winners, 1983, Japanese translation, 1985, LeRoy Neiman, Monte Carlo Chase, 1988, The Prints of LeRoy Neiman, 1980-90, Big Time Golf, 1992, LeRoy Neiman, An Am. in Paris, 1994, LeRoy Neiman on Safari, 1997, The Prints of LeRoy Neiman 1991-2000, LeRoy Neiman, Five Decades, 2003, deluxe ltd. edit. The LeRoy Neiman Sketchbook, 2004, Playboy Femlin, LeRoyn Neiman, 2007; illustrator: 12 paintings deluxe edit. Moby Dick, 1975, 35 charcoal drawings deluxe edit. Casey at the Bat, 2000, trade edit., 2002. Served with AUS, 1942-46. Recipient 1st prize Twin City Show, 1953, 2nd prize Minn. State Show, 1954, Clark Meml. prize Chgo. Show, 1957, Hamilton-Graham prize Ball State Coll., 1958, Mcpl. prize Chgo. Show, 1958, Purchase prize Miss. Valley Show, 1959, Gold medal Salon d'Art Modern Paris, 1961; award of merit as nation's outstanding sports artist AAU, 1976; Olympic Artist of Century award, 1979, Gold Medal award St. John's U., 1985; named to Internat. Boxing Hall of Fame, 2007. Address: 1 W 67th St New York NY 10023-6200

NEIMAN, RICHARD H., state agency administrator; BA, Am. U., Washington; JD, Emory U. Spl. asst. to chief counsel Comptr. Currency; v.p., counsel including gen. counsel global equities group Citicorp, 1979—89; dir. regulatory adv. svcs. Price Waterhouse, LLP, 1990—94; exec. v.p., gen. counsel TD Waterhouse Group, 1994—2006; chmn., pres., CEO TD Bank USA, N.A., 2006—07; supt. banks NY State Banking Dept., 2007—. Office: Supt Banks NY State Banking Dept One State St New York NY 10004-1417 Office Phone: 212-709-3501. Office Fax: 212-709-3520. E-mail: richard.neiman@banking.state.ny.us.

NEIMAN, SHIRAH, prosecutor; b. 1943; BA cum laude, Barnard Coll., 1965; JD magna cum laude, Columbia Univ., NYC, 1968. Bar: NY 1968. Law clk. to Hon. William B. Herlands US Dist. Ct. (So. dist.) NY, law clk. to Milton Pollack; asst. US atty. (So. dist.) NY US Dept Justice, 1970—, dep. chief criminal divsn., chief major crimes unit, dep. US atty., 1993—2002, chief counsel, 2002. Asst. spl. prosecutor Watergate Spl. Prosecution Force; mem. Atty Gen. Advisors Com., 1996—97; guest faculty mem. Harvard Law Sch., NYU, Fordham Law, Cardozo Univ. Mem.: ABA, PLI, NIT, Fed. Bar Coun., NYC Bar Assn. Office: US Attys Office SDNY Rm 834 One St Andrews Plz New York NY 10007

NEIMS, ALLEN HOWARD, pediatrician, educator, dean, researcher; b. Chgo., Oct. 24, 1938; s. Irving Morris and Ruth (Geller) N.; m. Myrna Gay Robins, June 18, 1961; children: Daniel Mark, Susan Roberta, Nancy Elizabeth. BA, BS, U. Chgo., 1957; MD, Johns Hopkins U., 1961, PhD, 1966. Intern, resident in pediatrics Johns Hopkins Hosp., 1961-62, 66-68; research asso. Lab. Neurochemistry, NIH, 1968-70; asst. prof. physiol. chemistry and pediatrics Johns Hopkins Med. Sch., 70-72; assoc. prof. McGill U., 1972-77, prof. pharmacology and pediatrics, 1977-78; dir. Roche developmental pharmacology unit, 1972-78; prof., chmn. dept. pharmacology and therapeutics, prof. pediatrics U. Fla., Gainesville, 1978-89, dean Coll. Medicine, 1989-96, prof. pharmcology, pediat., 1996—; dir. Ctr. for Spirituality and Health, 2002—. Dir. Ctr. Spirituality and Health; Fulton Bequest prof. U. Melbourne, Australia, 1974; mem. human embryology and devel. study sect. NIH, 1979-83; sci. cons. Can. Found. for Study of Sudden Infant Death, 1974-77, Nat. Soft Drink Assn., 1976-78, Internat. Life Scis. Inst., 1978-89; bd. sci. counsellors Nat. Inst. Child Health and Human Devel., 1984-89. Contbr. chpts. to books, articles to med. jours. Served to comdr. USPHS, 1968-70. NIH, Can. Med. Research Council grantee. Mem. Can. Assn. Research in Toxicology (pres. 1976-78), Am. Soc. Pharmacology and Exptl. Therapeutics (past mem. exec. coms. clin. pharmacology and drug metabolism), Am. Pediatric Soc., Am. Acad. Pediatrs. Democrat. Jewish. Office: U Fla Coll Medicine PO Box 100267 Gainesville FL 32610-0267 Office Phone: 352-392-0687. Business E-Mail: ahneims@ufl.edu.

NEINAS, CHARLES MERRILL, sports association executive, consultant; b. Marshfield, Wis., Jan. 18, 1932; s. Arthur Oscar and Blanche Amelia (Reeder) N.; children: Andrew, Toby. BS, U. Wis., 1957. Asst. exec. dir. Nat. Collegiate Athletic Assn., Kansas City, Mo., 1961-71; commr. Big Eight Conf., Kansas City, 1971-81; exec. dir. Coll. Football Assn., 1981—97; Dr. Patricia L. Pacey prof. econs. U. Colo., Boulder, 1981—85; with Pacey Ecometrics Group, Inc., 1985—. Adviser Am. Football Coaches Assn., 1997—; cons. NCAA Football, 1997—. Served with USNR, 1952-54. Office: Neinas Sports Svcs 6630 Gunpark Dr Boulder CO 80301-3372 Home: 5344 Westridge DR Boulder CO 80301-6501

NEIS, ARNOLD HAYWARD, pharmaceutical company executive; b. NYC, Feb. 13, 1940; s. Harry H. and Mary Ruth (Bishop) N.; children: Nancy R., Robert C. BS cum laude, Columbia U., 1960; MBA, NYU, 1967. With Scott Chem. Co., 1960—64; v.p. Odell, Inc., NYC, 1964—71, pres. Thayer Knomark divsn., 1969—71; pres., chief exec. officer E.T. Browne Drug Co., Inc., Englewood Cliffs, NJ, 1971—, chmn., 2000—. Dir. Esquire A.B. Stockholm, Knomark Can. Ltd., E.T. Browne Internat. Fellow Royal Soc. Chemists, Royal Geog. Soc., Am. Inst. Chemists, NY Acad. Scis.; mem. AAAS, Am. Chem. Soc., Am. Pharm. Assn., New Eng. Soc. (pres., bd. dirs.), Explorers Club (v.p., bd. dirs., Sweeney medal 1997), Chemists Club, Lotos Club, Soldiers, Sailors and Airmans Club (bd. dirs.), St. Georges Soc. (bd. dirs.), Ch. Club (bd. dirs.), Pilgrims of the US, Order St. John. Episcopalian. Home: 898 Park Ave New York NY 10021-0234 Office: PO Box 1613 440 Sylvan Ave Englewood Cliffs NJ 07632-2700

NEIS, ARTHUR VERAL, healthcare and development company executive; b. Lawrence, Kans., May 30, 1940; s. Veral Herbert and Louise (Schlegel) N.; m. Fleeta Weigel, Apr. 12, 1969 (dec. 1999); children: Frederich Arthur, Benjamin Jason, Sarah Louise. BS in Bus., U. Kans., 1962, MS in Acctg., 1963. CPA, Kans., Iowa. Mgmt. cons. Arthur Andersen & Co., Kansas City, Mo. and Mpls., 1963-74; chief corp. acctg. Carlson Co., Mpls., 1974-76; contr. The Fullerton Cos., Mpls., 1976-78; asst. treas. Fru-Con Corp., St. Louis, 1978-80, asst. contr., 1981, contr., 1982-86; corp. contr. LCS Holdings, Inc. (Weitz Corp. and Subs.), Des Moines, 1986-87, v.p., treas., CFO, 1987—2007, v.p., treas., CFO, mem. exec. com., 1995—2007, also bd. dirs., trustee retirement plan; treas., CFO Weitz Co., Des Moines, 1987-93, Life Care Svcs. LLC, Des Moines, 1987—2007; pres. Alliance Minerals N.Am., LLC, 2007—. Adv. group Nat. Assn. Ins. Com., 1990—93; treas., exec. com. bd. Villa de Maria Montessori Sch., St. Louis, 1984—86; trustee Fin. Execs. Rsch. Found., 1994—2000, chair audit com., 1997—98, vice chair rsch., 1998—2000, chmn., 2000—01; mem. Internat. Acctg. Standards Bd.; trustee Plymouth Congl. Ch., 1997—97, found. trustee, 1998—2001, chair, 2000—01; active Des Moines Poetry Festival, 2000—04, treas. bd. dirs., 2003—04; bd. dirs. Inst. Humane Studies, George Mason U., Fairfax, Va., 1971—2006, exec. com., 1975—83, chmn., 1978—83; bd. dirs. Lake Country Sch., Mpls., 1973—78, Alliance for Arts and Understanding, co-chair, 1993—96, bd. trustees, 1993—2002, chair, 1996—2002. Named to Bus. and Industry Hall Fame, AICPA, 2007; recipient Amb. award, Iowa Asian Alliance, 2004. Mem. AICPA (pvt. co. fin. pvt. task force 2004, mem. task force pvt. co. reporting generally accepted acctg. practices 2004, mem. nominating com. 2006—07), Kans. Soc. CPAs, Iowa Soc. CPAs, Fin. Execs. Inst. (bd. dirs. Iowa chpt. 1986, 88-94, sec. 1988-90, v.p. 1990-91, pres. 1991-92, com. on pvt. cos. stds. subcom. 2005—). Avocations: history, Asian art. Office: 1575 NW 106th St Clive IA 50325 E-mail: veral01@att.net.

NEIS, JAMES MICHAEL, lawyer; b. Chgo., Mar. 3, 1946; BA, DePaul U., 1969, JD, 1973. Bar: Ill. 1973, U.S. Tax Ct. 1974. Ptnr. Winston & Strawn LLP, Chgo., 1977-93, 2006—, mng. ptnr., 1993—2006. Adj. prof. law DePaul U., 1979-86; dir. Attys.' Liability Assurance Soc. Ltd., Bermuda, 2001-. Mem. ABA, Ill. State Bar Assn., Chgo. Bar Assn. Office: Winston & Strawn LLP 35 W Wacker Dr Ste 4200 Chicago IL 60601-1695 Office Phone: 312-558-5636. Business E-Mail: jneis@winston.com.

NEISER, BRENT ALLEN, foundation executive, public affairs and personal finance speaker, consultant; b. Cin., 1954; s. Rodger and Hazel Neiser; m. Marion, Apr. 1, 1978; children: Christy Jean, Steven José, April Reneé. BA in Pub. Affairs, George Washington U., 1976; MA in Urban Studies, Occidental Coll., 1978; MBA, U. Louisville, 1979; M in Global Studies Internat. Security, U. Denver, 2005. Cert. fin. planner, 1985; cert. assn. exec., 1994; cert. in Homeland Security U. Denver, 2005; cert. in exec. edn. performance measurement Harvard Bus. Sch., 2006; chartered mut. fund counselor, 1996; accredited asset mgmt. specialist, 1998. Project mgr., analyst Legis. Research Com., Frankfort, Ky., 1978-84; pres. Moneyminder, Denver and Frankfort, 1983-91; dir. edn., govt. affairs Inst. Cert. Fin. Planners, Denver, 1985-91, exec. dir., 1991-94; pub. affairs, govt. rels. bus. strategies cons. The Brent Neiser Co., Englewood, Colo., 1994—; dir. collaborative programs Nat. Endowment for Fin. Edn., 1995—. Mng. dir. Fin. Products Stds. Bd., Denver, 1985-91; co-creator Personal Econ. Summit '93, Washington; spkr. in field. Author: EPCOT/World Showcase External Directions, Walt Disney Imagineering, 1977, Personal Management, 1996, 2000, 03, Ignoring the Obvious: Public Diplomacy U.S. Foreign and Defense Policy, 2005; mem. editl. adv. bd. Jour. Fin. Planning, 2007. Vol., v.p. Big Bros./Big Sisters, Frankfort, 1982; del. Colo. Model Constn. Conv., 1987; mem. citizens budget rev. com. Greenwood Village; mem. long range planning com. Adoption Exch., Denver, 1992-93, bd. dirs., 1993-99; polit. action dir. Frankfort NAACP, 1983, legis. chmn. state conf., 1984; troop com. mem., asst. scoutmaster Boy Scouts Am., Englewood, 1993-99; bd. dirs. Young Ams. Bank Edn. Found., 1993-99, chair edn. coun.; mem. Leadership Denver, 1994; vol. host com. Denver Summit of the Eight, 1997; nat. spokesperson Protect our Children Campaign, 1996; active Annie E. Casey Found.: Nat. Foster Care Awareness Project, 1999-02; citizen's panelist News Hour with Jim Lehrer (PBS), 1998—; founding ptnr. Social Venture Ptnrs., Denver, 2000-04, Colo. Coun. of Advisors on Consumer Credit, 2000—, chmn., 2005-; mem. CFP bd. Consumer Adv. Coun. on Fin. Planning, 2001-03, 05-; bd. advisors Coll. Visual and Performing Arts, Winthrop U., 2002-05; mem. cmty. rels. bd. Daniels Coll. Bus., 2006-, U. Denver; mem. Leadership Program of Rockies, 2007. Lt. (j.g.) USNR, 1985-92. Recipient award of Excellence, Assn. Advance Am., 1996, 98, Summit award, Am. Soc. Assn. Exec., 2004; Pub. Affairs fellow Coro Found., 1976-77; fellow Ctr. for Social Innovation Stanford U., 2003, exec. seminar Aspen Inst., 2006. Mem. Denver World Affairs Coun., Denver Coun. on Fgn. Rels., Investors Edn. Assn. Colo. (bd. dirs. 1995-01), Nat. Assns. in Colo., Denver C. of C. (pub. affairs coun.), N.Am. Securities Adminstrs. Assn. (investment adviser and fin. planner adv. com.), Nat. Soc. Compliance Profls. (bd. dirs. 1987-89), Am. Film Inst. (writers workshop), Am. Polit. Items Collectors, Fin. Planning Assn. (Foresight Group, chair awards task force, judge Fin. Frontier Awards), Alliance for Investor Edn., Nat. Eagle Scout Assn., Snowboard Outreach Soc. Achievements include co-inventor Trivia Express Game, Denver, 1986; developer over 100 projects for disaster victims, low income families and children. Avocations: snowboarding, drums (jazz) and latin percussion music, golf, swimming, modern design. Office: 5860 Big Canyon Dr Englewood CO 80111-3516 Office Phone: 303-224-3501. E-mail: ban@nefe.org.

NEISSER, HORST, library director, writer; b. Nuernberg, Germany, July 30, 1943; s. Heinrich and Eleonore (Mergner) Neisser. Student, U. Frankfurt, Germany, 1965-68; DPhil, U. Tuebingen, Germany, 1973. Subject specialist EKZ, Reutlingen, Germany, 1973-76; dir. City Libr. Saarbrücken, Germany, 1976-86, City Libr. Cologne, Germany, 1986—. Lectr Fochhochschule für Sozialwesen, Esslingen, Germany, 1973—76, Fachhochschule für Bibliotheken, Cologne, Germany, 1987—; adv. in field. Author: (book) Die Jugendzeitschrift, 1975, Diskotheken in Deutschland, 1979, Traumzeiten, 1984, Der Gott der Ameise, 1993, Centratur, 1996, Centratur II, 1997. Mem.: Verband Deutscher Schriftsteller. Avocations: painting, music. Office: City Libr Cologne Josef-Haubrich-Hof 1 50676 Cologne Germany Business E-Mail: neisser@centratur.de.

NEITER, GERALD IRVING, lawyer; b. LA, Nov. 11, 1933; s. Harry and Ida Florence (Alperin) N.; m. Margaret P. Rowe, Mar. 5, 1961; children: David, Karen, Michael. BSL, JD, U. So. Calif., 1957. Bar: Calif. 1958. Judge pro tem Mcpl. Cts., L.A. and Beverly Hills, 1970-94, Calif. Superior Ct., L.A. County, 1974-94, family law mediator, 1976—; prin. Gerald I. Neiter, P.C., LA, 1981—. Lectr. State Bar of Calif., 1968, 76, 79, 81; former referee State Bar Ct.; arbitrator Am. Arbitration Assn.; mediator L.A. Superior Ct. Mem. ABA, Los Angeles County Bar Assn. (arbitrator), Beverly Hills Bar Assn., State Bar Calif. Office: 1925 Century Park E Ste 2000 Los Angeles CA 90067-2701 Office Phone: 310-277-2236. E-mail: Neitlaw@aol.com.

NEITHERCUT, DAVID J., real estate company officer; BA, St. Lawrence U.; MBA, Columbia U. With real estate dept. Continental Bank; with comml. mortgage banking div. Draper & Kramer, Inc.; sr. v.p. fin. Equity Group Investments; joined Equity Residential, 1993, CFO, 1995—2004, exec. v.p. corp. strategy, 2004—05, pres., 2005—, CEO, 2006—. Office: Equity Residential Properties Trust 2 N Riverside Plz Ste 450 Chicago IL 60606-2600 *

NEITHERCUT, MARK EDWARD, foundation consultant; b. Flint, Mich., June 26, 1951; s. Edward John and Elizabeth Koegel Neithercut; m. Helen Patrick Lownie, Oct. 6, 1990. BA with high honors in history, U. Mich., 1974; MA, Mich. State U., East Lansing, 1977; PhD, U. BC, Vancouver, Can., 1984. From instr. to asst. prof. U. Ala., Tuscaloosa, 1982-85; dir. Mich. Met. Info. Ctr. Wayne State U., Detroit, 1985-93, assoc. prof. rsch., 1993; program officer Kresge Found., Troy, Mich., 1993-95; v.p. program Cmty. Found. for Southeastern Mich., Detroit, 1995—2005; prin. Neithercut Advs. LLC, Detroit, 2005—. Adj. prof. urban planning Wayne State U., Detroit, 1990—95; chmn. Mich. Nonprofit Rsch. Program, Aspen Inst., Washington, 2003—06; membership com. Coun. on Founds., Washington, 1999—; bd. dirs. Anna Paulina Found., 2005—. Chmn. Detroit Area Grantmakers, 2001-2003; mem. cmty. found. leadership team Coun. of Found., 2001-2004; mem. adv. com. John S. and James L. Knight Found., Detroit, 2002-06; mem. bd. govs. Cranbrook Schs., 2003—; bd. dirs. Detroit Inst. Arts, 2005—. Named NSFRE Vol. of Yr., Detroit Inst. Arts, 1994; grantee Kresge Found., 1998—2004; James B. Angell scholar, U. Mich., 1974, Internat. Schoolboy fellow, English Spkg. Union, 1969—70, doctoral fellow, U. B.C., 1978—80. Mem. Grosse Pointe Club, Flint Rainbow Club, Detroit Athletic Club, Phi Beta Kappa. Avocations: steelhead fly fishing, tennis. Office: 300 River Pl Ste 5000 Detroit MI 48207 Office Phone: 313-568-9000. Business E-Mail: mark@neithercutadvisors.com.

NEITZKE, ERIC KARL, lawyer; b. Mobile, Ala., Dec. 10, 1955; s. Howard and Otti S. Neitzke; m. Kathryn Sloan; children: Kyle, Blake, Blaire. BA, U. Fla., 1979, JD, 1982. Bar: Fla. 1982, U.S. Dist. Ct. (mid. dist.) Fla. 1987. Asst. state atty. 7th Jud. Cir., State Atty., Daytona Beach, Fla., 1982; assoc. Dunn, Smith & Withers, Daytona Beach, 1982—88, Monaco, Smith, Hood and Perkins, Daytona Beach, 1988—2003; sole practice Daytona Beach, 2003—. Adj. faculty family law and criminal law Daytona C.C.; chmn. adv. com. Juvenile Detention Ctr. Contbr. articles to profl. jours. Mem. ATLA, Fla. Acad. Trial Lawyers, Volusia Bar Assn., Fla. Assn. Criminal Def. Lawyers, Phi Beta Kappa. Avocations: water sports, shooting, travel. Home: 19 Lost Creek Ln Ormond Beach FL 32174-4840 Office: Eric K Neitzke Pa 412 N Wild Olive Ave Daytona Beach FL 32118 Home Phone: 386-323-1900; Office Phone: 386-672-9283. Personal E-mail: knightmas@aol.com.

NEJELSKI, PAUL ARTHUR, retired judge, freelance writer; b. Chgo., Feb. 24, 1938; s. Leo Lawrence and Rena Grace (Martin) N.; m. Marilyn Ray Mills, Oct. 2, 1965; children: Nicole Rena, Stephen Downing. BA magna cum laude, Yale U., 1959, LLB, 1962; MPA, Am. U., 1969; cert. of theol. studies, Georgetown U., 1989. Bar: N.J. 1963. Law clk. appellate div. N.J. Superior Ct., 1962-63; asst. U.S. atty. U.S. Dist. Ct. N.J., 1964-65; atty., later chief immigration unit Dept. Justice, Washington, 1965-69; chief cts. desk Nat. Inst. Justice, Washington, 1969-70; asst. dir. Criminal Justice Ctr., Harvard U., 1970-71; dir. planning phase Inst. Jud. Adminstrn.-ABA Juvenile Justice Standards Project, NYC, 1971-73; dir. Inst. Jud. Adminstrn., NYU, 1973-76; dep. ct. adminstrn. Conn. Jud. Dept., Hartford, 1976-77; dep. asst. atty. gen. Office for Improvements in Adminstrn. Justice, Dept. Justice, Washington, 1977-79; dir. Action Commn. to Reduce Ct. Costs and Delay, ABA, Washington, 1979-81; cir. exec. 3rd Cir., Phila., 1981-84; ct. adminstr. U.S. Tax Ct., 1984-89; immigration judge Dept. Justice, Arlington, Va., 1989-98. Mem. faculty law NYU, 1972-74, U. Conn., 1976-77, U. Md., 1981-82; cons. Author: (with C.O. Philip) Where Do Judges Come From?, 1976; editor: Social Research in Conflict With Law and Ethics, 1976; contbr. articles to profl. and popular jours. With US Army, 1963—65, with USN, 1965—68. Home: 4628 Western Ave Bethesda MD 20816-2749

NEKRITZ, EDWARD STEVEN, lawyer; b. Chgo., Nov. 11, 1965; s. Barry Benjamin and Susan Ellen (Moss) N.; m. Wendy Nekritz, children: Jessica, Matthew AB, Harvard U., 1987; JD, U. Chgo. Law Sch., 1990. Bar: Ill. 1990. Assoc. Mayer, Brown & Platt (formerly Mayer, Brown, Rowe & Maw), Chgo., 1990-95; v.p. asset mgmt. Security Capital Indsl. Trust, Aurora, Colo., 1995-98; sr. v.p., gen. counsel, sec. ProLogis, Aurora, Colo., 1998—. Mem. Harvard Club of Chgo. (dir. 1989—). Office: ProLogis 14100 E 35th Place Aurora CO 80011

NELDNER, SUMMER D., athletic trainer; d. Robert Neldner and Ruby Dye. AA in Sports Medicine, Jones Co. Jr. Coll., Ellisville, Miss., 2000; BS cum laude in Phys. Edn., U. Ala., Birmingham, 2002; MSc in Health and Human Performance, U. Tenn., Chattanooga, 2005. Cert. Atc NATA Bd. Cert., 2004. Grad. asst. athletic trainer U. Tenn., 2003—05; athletic trainer, sports medicine dept. Trinity Med. Ctr., Birmingham, Ala., 2005—. Mem.: Southeastern Athletic Trainers' Assn., Ala. Athletic Trainers' Assn., Nat. Athletic Trainers' Assn., U. Ala. Alumni Soc. (assoc.), U. Ala. Student Athletic Trainers Club (sec. 2001—02), Phi Kappa Phi, Golden Key. Avocations: softball, bowling, exercise, swimming.

NELIPOVICH, SANDRA GRASSI, artist; b. Oak Park, Ill., Nov. 22, 1939; d. Alessandro and Lena Mary (Ascareggi) Grassi; m. John Nelipovich Jr., Aug. 19, 1973. BFA in Art Edn., U. Ill., Champaign/Urbana, 1961; postgrad., Northwestern U., Evanston, Ill., 1963, Gonzaga U., Florence, Italy, 1966, Art Inst. Chgo., 1968; diploma (hon.), Accademia Universale Alessandro Magno, Prato, Italy, 1983. Tchr. art Edgewood Jr. High Sch., Highland Park, Ill., 1961-62, Emerson Sch. Jr. High Sch., Oak Park, 1962-77; batik artist Calif., 1977—; illustrator Jolly Robin Publ. Co., Anaheim, Calif., 1988—2001, Assistance League of Anaheim, Calif., 2000—. Supr. student tchrs., Oak Park, 1970-75; adult edn. tchr. ESL, ceramics, Medinah, Ill., 1974; mem. curriculum action group on human dignity, EEO workshop demonstration, Oak Park, 1975-76; guest lectr. Muckenthaler Ctr., Fullerton, Calif., 1980, 92, Niguel Art Group, Dana Point, Calif., 1989, Carlsbad A.A., 1990, Art League, Oceanside Art Group, 1992; 2d v.p. Anaheim Hills Women's Club, 1990-91, rec. sec. 1991-92; fabric designer for fashion designer Barbara Jax, 1987; illustrator Assistance League Anaheim (Calif.), 2000—, muralist Lincoln Sch. Ill., 2002-2003. One-Woman shows include Lawry's Calif. Ctr., L.A., 1981-83, Whittier (Calif.) Mus., 1985-86, Anaheim Cultural Ctr., 1986-88, Ill. Inst. Tech., Chgo., 1989, Muckenthaler Cultural Ctr., Fullerton, 1990; also gallery exhibits in Oak Brook, 1982, La Habra, Calif., 1983, Millard Sheets Gallery, Pomona, Calif., 1996; represented in permanent collections McDonald's Corp., Oak Brook, Glenkirk Sch., Deerfield, Ill., Emerson Sch., Oak Park, Calif., Ogden Ave. Sch., LaGrange, Ill.; poster designer Saratoga Fine Arts. Active Assistance League, Anaheim, Calif., 1992—, 2d v.p. ways and means com., 1995—96, 1997—98, 2d v.p. ways and means, 2004—05, 2005—06, historian, 2002—03, Anaheim Arts Coun., 2002—, 2004—; chairwoman Arturo Toscanini Guild Orange County Performing Arts Ctr., 2006—. Recipient numerous awards, purchase prizes, 1979—; featured in Calif. Art Rev., Artists of So. Calif., Vol. II, Nat. Artists' Network, 1992, Batik for Artists and Quilters, 2001. Mem. AAUW (hospitality chmn. 1984-85), Soc. Children's Book Writers and Illustrators, Assistance League Anaheim, Orange Art Assn. (jury chmn. 1980). Roman Catholic. Avocations: cooking, gardening, travel. Home and Office: 5922 E Calle Cedro Anaheim CA 92807-3207 Personal E-mail: sgneli@roadrunner.com.

NELKIN, BARRY DAVID, oncology researcher and educator; b. New Orleans, Dec. 12, 1951; s. Joseph William and Bertha (Washastrom) N.; m. Deborah Ann Medetsky, June 4, 1975; children: Moshe, Aryeh, Yehuda, Esther, Yisroel, Rivka, Bina, Yaakov, Miriam, Shira. BS, Johns Hopkins U., 1972; PhD, George Washington U., 1979. Postdoctoral fellow Johns Hopkins U. Sch. Medicine, Balt., 1979—82, instr. oncology, 1982—84, asst. prof., 1984—90, assoc. prof., 1990—2004, prof., 2004—. Mem. ad hoc study sect. U.S. Nat. Cancer Inst., Bethesda, 1989-; grant reviewer Dutch Cancer Soc., 1990, VA, 1990. Author: (with others) Tumor Cell Heterogeneity, vol. 4, 1982, Progress in Nonhistone Protein Research, 1985; editor: Genetic Mechanisms in Multiple Endocrine Neoplasia Type 2, 1996; mem. editl. bd. oncology rep., 1997-98; contbr. articles to profl. jours. Nat. Cancer Inst. grantee, 1988-. Mem. Am. Assn. Cancer Rsch., Am. Soc. Microbiology. Achievements include the cloning of human calcitonin gene; demonstration of oncogene mediated differentiation of medullary thyroid carcinoma cells; isolation of ras oncogene responsive transcriptional element in human calcitonin gene; cloning of human BARX2 and RREB transcription factor genes. Home: 3831 Labyrinth Rd Baltimore MD 21215-1505 Office: Johns Hopkins Sch Medicine 1650 Orleans St Baltimore MD 21231 Home Phone: 410-358-4975; Office Phone: 410-955-8506. Business E-Mail: bnelkin@jhmi.edu.

NELLEMANN, LYNNE O'SHEA, management consultant; b. Chgo., Oct. 18, 1955; d. Edward Fisk and Mildred Lessner O'Shea. BA, BJ in Polit. Sci. and Journalism, U. Mo., MA in Info. Theory, 1971; PhD in Consumer Cultures, Northwestern U., 1978; postgrad., Sch. Mgmt. and Strategic Studies, U. Calif., 1988. Congl. asst., Washington, 1968—70; brand mgr. Procter & Gamble Co., Cin., 1971-73; v.p. Foote, Cone & Belding, Inc., Chgo., 1973-79; v.p. corp. comms. Internat. Harvester Co., Chgo., 1979-82; dir. mktg. and comms. Arthur Andersen & Co., Chgo., 1983-86; v.p. bus. devel. Gannett Co., Inc., Chgo., 1987-94; pres., chief oper. officer Shalit Place L.L.C., 1995—98; exec. v.p. Mus. Broadcast Comm., Chgo., 1996-97; dir. A.T. Kearney, Chgo., 1998—2005; pres. Ill. Women's Forum, 2005—; head Women's Leadership Initiative, Dominican U., 2007—. Prof. mktg. U. Chgo. Grad. Sch. Bus., 1979—80, Kellogg Grad. Sch. Mgmt., 1983—84, 1994—95; co-chair Fed. Glass Ceiling Commn., 1991—95; exec.-in-residence, prof. Kellstadt Grad. Sch. Bus., DePaul U., 2000—03; founder Women's Leadership Inst. Dominican U., 2006—; bd. dirs. AskRex.com, Clark/Bardes Inc., Motown Snacks, Robison Securities/Fleet Bank, Internat. Leadership Found. Co-chair Fed. Glass Ceiling Commn., 1991—95, Com. 21st Century, 1992—; bd. dirs. Internat. Forum Found., Off-the-St. Club, Chgo., 1977—86; adv. bd. U. Ill. Coll. Commerce, 1980—2000, Chgo. Crime Commn., 1987—90, DePaul U., 1989—95, Roosevelt U., 1994—2000, St. Mary's U., 1995—98. Named Advt. Women of the Yr., Chgo. Advt. Club, 1989; named one of Top 100 in Tech., 2003; recipient numerous Eagle Fin. Advt. awards, Silver medal, Am. Advt. Fedn., 1989; fellow, Internat. Leadership Forum, 2005—. Mem.: Chgo. Network, Social Venture Network, Women's Forum Chgo., Internat. Women's Forum (v.p. devel., v.p. comm., mem. exec. com., bd. dirs.), Women's Athletic Club Chgo., Mid-Am. Club (bd. govs. 1990—92). Office: 1703 Shoreline Dr Saint Charles IL 60174-5562 Home Phone: 630-587-6180; Office Phone: 847-778-8411. Personal E-mail: lynneoshea@juno.com.

NELLES, SHARON, lawyer; b. 1965; AB, Mount Holyoke Coll., 1987; MA, NYU, 1990; JD, Boston Coll. Law Sch., 1993. Bar: Mass., NY. Clerk US Dist. Ct., NH, 1993—95; faculty Franklin Pierce Law Ctr., 1995—96; ptnr. Sullivan & Cromwell LLP, NYC. Dir. The Acting Co. Named one of Litigation's Rising Stars, The Am. Lawyer, 2007. Mem.: Assn. of Bar of City of NY. Office: Sullivan & Cromwell LLP 125 Broad St New York NY 10004-2498 Office Phone: 212-558-4000. Office Fax: 212-558-3588.

NELLESSEN, JAMES EDWARD, environmental scientist, consultant; b. Nov. 21, 1956; BS in Biology, U. Minn., St. Paul, 1979; MS in Plant Pathology, Va. Tech., Blacksburg, 1982; PhD in Botany, Ohio U., Athens, 1989. With Environ. Rsch. and Tech. and NUS Corp., 1977, U. Minn. Herbarium, 1978—79; rsch. asst. Va. Poly. Inst. and State U., 1980—83; tchg. assoc. Ohio U., 1984—89; postdoctoral rsch. asst. U. Okla., 1989—93, asst. prof., 1994; environ. specialist Air Quality Bur. N.Mex. Environ. Dept., 1994—99; hwy. environmentalist environ. sect. Preliminary Design Bur. N.Mex. State Hwy. and Transp. Dept., 1999—2000; biologist, environ. scientist Taschek Environ. Cons., 2000—. Adj. faculty Rose State Coll., Okla., 1993; part-time faculty Santa Fe C.C., 1996—97; mem. N.Mex. Rare Plant Tech. Coun.; conservation chair Native Plant Soc. N.Mex.; presenter in field. Contbr. articles to profl. jours. Grantee, Nat. Fish and Wildlife Found., 2006. Mem.: Southwestern Assn. Naturalists, Am. Soc. Mining and Reclamation, Soc. for Ecol. Restoration, Am. Inst. Biol. Scis. Home: 7553 Ottawa Dr NE Rio Rancho NM 87144-8430

NELLETT, GAILE H., adult education educator; b. Ottawa, Ill., Nov. 5, 1941; d. Edwin Edward and Mabel Delia (Higgins) Hausman; m. Henry H. Nellett. BSN, Governors State U., University Park, Ill., 1993; MS in Nursing Adminstrn., Loyola U., Chgo., 1995, PhD, 1998. RN, Ill. ELNEC (End of Life Nursing Edn. Consortium) certified, 2001. Staff nurse med.-surg. and psychiat. units Cmty. Hosp. Ottawa, 1974-75, asst. head nurse, 1975-77, head nurse psychiat. unit, 1977-79, head nurse psychiat. and chem. dependency units, 1979-84, nursing mgr. psychiat. and chem. dependency units, 1984-92, program mgr. psychiat. and chem. dependency units, 1987-92, part-time home health nurse, 1992-94; rsch. asst. Loyola U., 1993-96; asst. prof. U. St. Francis, 1997—2005, sr. chmn. Conah, 2000—04, assoc. prof., 2005—, co-project dir. RRF grant, 2003—. Bd. dirs. Ottawa area United Way, 1976-92, v.p., 1985, sec., 1984, 86. Nursing Adminstrn. fellow Edward Hines Jr. VA, Hines, Ill., 1994, tuition fellow Loyola U., 1993-96. Mem. ANA, Ill. Nurses Assn. (bd. dirs. dist. 4 1974-80), Nat. Gerontologic Nurses Assn., Peer Assistance Network for Nurses (regional support person dist. 2 1988-), Midwest Nursing Rsch. Soc., Sigma Theta Tau. Soc., Rogerian Scholars Roman Catholic. Avocations: archery, hunting, handcrafts, reading. Home: 2768 E 2551st Rd Marseilles IL 61341 Office Phone: 815-740-3668. E-mail: gnellett@stfrancis.edu.

NELLIGAN, WILLIAM DAVID, III, professional association executive; b. Halstead, Kans., Aug. 10, 1926; s. William D. and Katherine (Roberts) N.; m. Dorothy Meyer, Aug. 17, 1952; children: Richard, Arthur, Mark. Student, U. Wichita, 1944-46; BS, U. Kans., 1949. Display advt. salesman Kansas City Star and Times, Mo., 1949-51; mgr. SW Kans. Extension Ctr. U. Kans., Garden City, 1951-55, exec. dir. dept. postgrad. med. edn. Sch. Medicine Kansas City, Kans., 1955-64; asst. to pres. Med. Coll. Ga., Augusta, 1964-65; exec. v.p. Am. Coll. Cardiology, Bethesda, Md., 1965-92; v.p. Marion Merrell DOW, Inc., Kansas City, Mo., 1992-94; exec. dir. Am. Soc. Nuc. Cardiology, Bethesda, 1994-2001, Cert. Bd. Nuclear Cardiology, Damascus, Md., 1996—2004, Soc. Cardiovasc. CT, Damascus, Md., 2005—06, Soc. Atherosclerosis Imaging and Prevention, Damascus, Md., 2005—. Mem. Nat. Commn. Diabetes, 1975-76, adv. coun. Nat. Diabetes and Digestive and Kidney Diseases, 1987-88; bd. dirs. Arthur E. Hertzler Research Found., Halstead, Kans., 1961—. Recipient Man with a Heart award NY Cardiol. Soc., 1970, Presdl. citation Am. Coll. Cardiology, 1975, Disting. Svc. award Am. Coll. Cardiology, 1986, CLC Hall of Leaders award, 1986. Fellow Am. Coll. Cardiology; mem. AMA (citation of layman for disting. svc. 1993), Profl. Conv. Mgmt. Assn. (pres. 1974-75, Disting. Svc. award 1990), Am. Med. Writers Assn. (dir., exec. com., treas. 1970-78, Harold Swanberg Disting. Svc. award), Am. Soc. Assn. Execs. (cert., dir. 1975-78, sec.-treas. 1987-88, Key award 1984), Am. Assn. Med. Soc. Execs. (pres. 1986-87), Brit. Cardiac Soc. (hon.), Alliance for Continuing Med. Edn. (Pres.'s award 1994), Masons.

NELLY, (CORNELL HAYNES JR.), rap artist; b. Austin, Tex., Nov. 2, 1974; s. Cornell Haynes and Rhonda Mack; children: Chanel, Cornell III. Formed St. Lunatics, 1993; co-owner, co-founder, spokesperson Vokal Clothing Co., St. Louis, 1997—; co-owner, founder Apple Bottoms, 2003—; co-owner Billy Ballew Motersports, NASCAR racing team, 2003—; CEO Derrty Entertainment, 2003—; co-owner Charlotte Bobcats, 2004—. Performer: (albums) Country Grammar, 2000 (Album of Yr., Source Hip-Hop Music awards, 2001), (with St. Lunatics) Free City, 2001, Nellyville, 2002 (Grammy award for best make rap solo performance, 2002, Grammy award best rap/sung collaboration for "Dilemma," featuring Kelly Rowland, 2002), Da Derrty Versions: The Reinvention, 2003, Iz U, 2004, Sweat, 2004, Suit, 2004, (singles) E.I., 2001, Ride With Me, 2001, (songs) Shake Ya Tailfeather (with P. Diddy and Murphy Lee), Bad Boys II soundtrack, 2003 (Grammy award best rap performance by a duo or group, 2003); actor: (films) Snipes, 2001, The Longest Yard, 2005. Founder 4sho4kids. Recipient New Artist of Yr., Source Hip-Hop Music Awards, 2001, Best New Artist, BET awards, 2001, Best R&B/Soul or Rap New Artist, Soul Train Music Awards, 2001, Favorite Artist-Rap/Hip-Hop, Am. Music Awards, 2002, Source Found. Image Award, Source Hip-Hop Music Awards, 2003, Artist of Yr., 2003, Sammy Davis Jr. Entertainer of Yr., Soul Train Music Awards. Office: Uptown/Universal Records 1755 Broadway New York NY 10019 also: The 4Sho4Kids Found Inc 9648 Olive Blvd Ste 230 Saint Louis MO 63132 also: Vokal Clothing 1835 Belt Way Dr Saint Louis MO 63114-5815 Office Phone: 314-531-3346.

NELMS, DAVID W., finance company executive; BS, Univ. Fla.; MBA, Harvard Univ., 1987. Mgmt. positions through exec. v.p. & vice-chmn. MBNA Am. Bank, 1991—98; pres., COO Discover Fin. Services div., Morgan Stanley, Riverwoods, Ill., 1998—2004, chmn., CEO, 2004—, Discover Bank. Mem. Chgo. Bd. Juvenile Diabetes Rsch. Found. Office: Discover Fin Services 2500 Lake Cook Rd Riverwoods IL 60015 *

NELON, ROBERT DALE, lawyer; b. Shawnee, Okla., Aug. 8, 1946; s. Cecil Eugene and Neata Madelyn (Fox) N.; m. Freddie Anne Tipton, Aug. 2, 1975; children: Lindsay Anne, Gregory Tipton. BA, Northwestern U., 1968; JD, U. Okla., 1971. Bar: Okla. 1971, U.S. Dist. Ct. (we., no. and ea. dists) Okla. 1971, U.S. Ct. Appeals (10th cir.) 1971, (8th cir.) 1992, (2d cir.) 1993, U.S. Ct. Appeals for the Armed Forces 1972, U.S. Supreme Ct. 1989. Law clk. Okla. Atty. Gen., Oklahoma City, 1966-70; mem. Andrews, Davis, Legg, Bixler, Milsten & Price, Oklahoma City, 1971-95, Hall Estill Hardwick Gable Golden & Nelson, Oklahoma City, 1995—. Served to capt. USMCR, 1972-74. Mem. ABA, Okla. Bar Assn., Am. Judicature Soc. Democrat. Methodist. Office: Hall Estill Hardwick Gable Golden & Nelson Chase Tower Suite 2900 100 N Broadway Ave Oklahoma City OK 73102-8865 Home Phone: 405-721-8501; Office Phone: 405-553-2828. Business E-Mail: bnelon@hallestill.com.

NELP, WIL B., physician, medical educator; s. Wil B. and Olive E. (Edwards) Nelp; m. Barbara M. Monroe; children: Todd, Nancy, Paige, Blaine. BA cum laude, Franklin Coll.of Ind., 1951; MD, Johns Hopkins U., 1955; DSc (hon.), Franklin Coll., Ind., 1967. Lic. Md., 1955, Wash., 1962, cert. Am. Bd. Nuc. Medicine, 1972, Am. Bd. Internal Medicine. Intern asst. resident Johns Hopkins Hosp., Osler Med. Svc., Md., 1955—60; rsch. fellow Johns Hopkins Hosp., Dept. Medicine and Radiology, Divsn. Nuc. Med., Md., 1960—62; instr. Johns Hopkins U., Medicine and Radiology Dept., Md., 1961—62; asst. prof., assoc. prof., and prof. U. Wash., Dept. Medicine and Radiology, 1962—95; head dept. U. Wash., Nuc. Medicine, 1962—95; co-dir. U. Hosp., Thyroid Clin., Wash., 1978—83; attending physician Endocrine Thyroid Clin., Wash., 1983—; prof. emeritus U. Wash., Dept. Medicine and Radiology, 1996; assoc. staff Veterans Adminstrn. Hosp., Wash., Harborview Med., Seattle; cons. in nuc. medicine Group Health Coop. of Puget Sound, Providence Hosp., Northwest Hosp., Children's Orthopedic Hosp., Seattle, Madigan Army Hosp., Tacoma. Cons. Nat. Heart and Lung Inst., 1968—74; cons. to commr. FDA Radiopharmaceuticals, 1970—74, usp adv. panel, 1970—80; adv. to Romanian govt. UN Nuc. Medicine, IAEA, 1971—72; diagnostic rsch. adv. group Nat. Cancer Inst., 1977—81; usp adv. panel Radiopharmaceuticals, 1982—86; sec. coun. for nuc. medicine AMA, 1982—88; mem. adv. com. Electro-magnetic Isotope Enrichment Facility, Oak Ridge Nat. Lab., Oak Ridge, 1986, Nuc. Regulatory Commn., Med. Uses of Isotopes, 1993—99. Dir. U. Wash. residency Nuc. Medicine Tng. Program, 1964—96; chmn., organizer U. Wash. Med. Ethics, Human Use, Review Sys. in Exptl. Rsch., 1967—71; mem. Med. Staff Exec. Com., 1973—80; com. mem. Los Alamos Sci. Lab., N.Mex., 1976—80; coun. mem. AMA, Nuc. Med. Sect., 1976—79; affiliate mem. Assn. of Governing Bd. of U. and Coll., 1996—. Capt., acting chief med. svc. Offult AFB USAF, 1957—59, Nebr. Named Outstanding Young Man of Am. Award, 1964; recipient NIH rsch. fellow, 1960—62, Disting. Scientist Award, Soc. of Nuc. Medicine, Western Region, 1980, Creative Devel. Award, NASA, 1980, Korean Soc. of Nuc. Medicine Honoree, 1990. Fellow: ACP, Am. Coll. Nuc. Physicians; mem.: Seattle Acad. Internal Med., Soc. Nuc. Med. (v.p. 1970—71, nat. pres. 1973—74), Am. Bd. of Nuc. Medicine (life; dir. 1984, treas. 1986, vice chmn. 1987), Johns Hopkins Med. Surg. Assn.

NELSEN, HART MICHAEL, sociologist, educator; b. Pipestone, Minn., 1938; s. Noah I. and Nova Nelsen; m. Anne Kusener, June 13, 1964; 1 dau., Jennifer. BA, U. No. Iowa, 1959, MA, 1963; M.Div., Princeton Theol. Sem., 1963; PhD (NSF faculty fellow), Vanderbilt U., 1972. Asst. prof. sociology Western Ky. U., Bowling Green, 1965-70, assoc. prof., 1970-73, Catholic U. Am., 1973-74, prof., 1974-81, chmn. dept. sociology, 1974-77, mem. Boys Town Ctr. for Study Youth Devel., 1974-81; prof. sociology La. State U., Baton Rouge, 1981-84, chmn. dept. sociology, head dept. rural sociology, 1981-84, coordinator rural sociology research, 1981-84; dean Coll. Liberal Arts Pa. State U., 1984-90, prof. sociology, 1984—2004, prof. emeritus, 2004—. Author: (with Anne K. Nelsen) Black Church in the Sixties, 1975; co-author: The Religion of Children, 1977, Religion and American Youth, 1976; editor: (with others) The Black Church in America, 1971; adv. editor: Sociol. Quar, 1976-82; assoc. editor: Sociol. Analysis, 1977-80, Rev. Religious Research, 1977-80, 84—, editor, 1980-84; mem. editorial bd.: Social Forces, 1983-86. Co-rec. sec. Capitol Hill Restoration Soc., 1979-80, v.p., 1980-81; mem. exec. bd. Lafitte Hills Assn., 1983-84; pres. Midtown Sq. Condo. Assn., 1996-99, treas., 1999-2001; v.p. Market Sq. West Condominium Assn., 2006-. Presbyterian Chs. grantee, 1966-69; NIMH co-grantee, 1969-72; Russell Sage Found. co-grantee, 1972-73; La. Gov.'s Commn. on Alcoholism and Drug Abuse grantee, 1982 Mem. Assn. Sociology Religion (exec. coun. 1974-76, 78-82, v.p. 1978-79, pres. 1980-81), Religious Rsch. Assn. (dir. 1977-80, pres.-elect 1985-86, pres. 1987-88), Soc. Sci. Study Religion (coun. 1981-83, exec. sec. 1984-87), Am. Sociol. Assn., So. Sociol. Soc. (chmn. membership com. 1983-85), AAAS (rep. 1984-2000). Mem. United Ch. Of Christ. Home: Residence 1121 Market Sq Residences 801 Pennsylvania Ave NW Washington DC 20004-2615 E-mail: hmnelsen@mindspring.com.

NELSEN, WILLIAM CAMERON, educational consultant; b. Omaha, Oct. 18, 1941; s. William Peter and Ellen Lucella (Cameron) N.; m. Margaret Leone Rossow, May 30, 1981; children by previous marriage: William Norris, Shawna Lynn; 1 adopted dau., Sarah Ruth. BA, Midland Luth. Coll., Fremont, Nebr., 1963; MA, Columbia U., 1966; PhD, U. Pa., 1971; Fulbright scholar, U. Erlangen, W. Ger., 1964; D (hon.), Midland Luth. Coll., 1995. Program exec. Danforth Found., St. Louis, 1970-73; asst. dean, then v.p., dean coll. St. Olaf Coll., Northfield, Minn., 1973-80; dir. Project on Faculty Devel. Assn. of Am. Colls., 1979; pres. Augustana Coll., Sioux Falls, SD, 1980-86, Scholarship Am., St. Peter, Minn., 1986—2004; v.p. develop. NC Wesleyan Coll., Rocky Mount, NC, 2004—. Bd. dirs. 1st Nat. Bank and Bancommunity Svc. Corp., St. Peter, Minn., Learning Cmtys. Coalition, USA Funds. Author: Effective Approaches to Faculty Development, 1980, Renewal of the Teacher Scholar, 1981, also articles. Bd. dirs. S.D. Symphony, 1980-85, Sioux Falls YMCA, 1980-86, Luth. Ednl. Conf. N.Am., 1982-86, Sioux Falls United Way, 1983-86; nat. bd. advisors Coun. Aid to Edn.; mem. nat. coun. Connect Am., Points of Light Found., 1998-2003; chmn. bd. U.S. Dream Acad., 1999-2004; mem. exec. bd. Nat. Assembly, 2001-2004; bd. dirs. Nat. Scholarship Providers Assn., 1999-2004, chmn. bd., 2003-04; dir. Learning Cmtys. Coalition; mem. Registry of Coll. and Univ. Pres.; interim v.p. devel. N.C. Wesleyan Coll.; bd trustees Midland Luth. Coll. Recipient McKee award Nat. Assn. Ptnrs. in Edn., 1999, award Freedoms Found., 2003; Danforth Grad. fellow, 1963, Woodrow Wilson fellow, 1963. Mem. Assn. Am. Colls. (bd. dirs. 1984-86), Shoreland Country Club (pres. 1996-99), Consortium for Advancement of Pvt. Higher Edn., Coun. of Ind. Colls., Nat. Dollars for Scholars, Rotary Club. Republican. Lutheran.

NELSON, ALICE CARLSTEDT, retired nursing educator; b. Strandquist, Minn., May 25, 1921; d. Peter Gustaf and Florence Olivia (Berg) Carlstedt; m. Armour Halstead Nelson June 5, 1954 (dec. Dec. 1993). RN, Bethesda Hosp., St. Paul, Minn., 1944; BS, Augustana Coll., Rock Island, Ill., 1948; MA, U. Chgo., 1954. RN, Minn., Ill., N.D., Iowa, Calif.; cert. lactation educator, cert. lifetime cmty. coll. tchr. Ob nurse Moline Luth. Hosp., Ill., 1943—44; asst. night supr. Bethesda Hosp., St. Paul, 1944—45; with Army Nurse Corps, 1945—46; ob nurse Miller Hosp., St. Paul, 1947; nurse intermediate grade Wadsworth VA Hosp., LA, 1947—48; head nurse Crippled Children's Sch., Jamestown, ND, 1948—50; head nurse Sch. Handicapped Children U. Iowa, Iowa City, 1950—51; clin. instr. Chgo. Lying-In Hosp., 1951—54, St. Luke's Hosp., Fargo, ND, 1954—60; tchr., supr. lab. pre-sch. N.D. State U., Fargo, 1962—64; coll. health svc. Calif. Luth. U., Thousand Oaks, 1968—74, faculty dept. nursing, 1982—85; pvt. duty nurse Thousand Oaks, 1976—81; ret., 1990. State sec. League for Nursing, N.D., 1956-64; team mem. preparation Nat. Achievement Test in Nursing of Children, NY, 1959 Author: Post-War Europe Through The Eyes of Youth, 2002; editor: The Conquest of Chicago, 2004; contbr. articles to profl. jours. Various offices including Ch. Coun. Holy Trinity Luth. Ch., Thousand Oaks, Calif., 1964-90; founding bd. dirs. Honey Tree Pre-Sch., Thousand Oaks, Calif., 1972; mem. task force on aging S.W. Pacific Luth. Synod Office, LA, 1979; parent-aide, hotline, etc. Child Abuse & Neglect, Ventura County, Calif., 1979-82; bd. dirs. La Serena Retirement Ctr., Thousand Oaks, Calif., 1985-88; mem. ch. choir Salemsborg Luth. Ch., Smolan, Kans., 1990-2000, mem. ch. coun., 1996-2000, tchr. adult classes, 1996-99 Recipient award writing contests Am. Jour. Nursing, 1969, Calif. Nurse, 1987, Outstanding Vol. award Ventura County Child Abuse & Neglect, 1982. Mem. Bethany Bibliophiles Book Club, Writer's Cramp Group Democrat. Avocations: travel, reading, writing.

NELSON, ALISON R., lawyer; BS in Criminal Justice, Mich. State U., 1987, JD, 1990. Atty., environ. Ford Motor Co., Dearborn, Mich., mng. counsel, consumer litig., 1994—. Former asst. gen. counsel Mich. State Coun. NAACP. Mem.: State Bar Mich., Nat. Bar Inst. (bd. dir., Presdl. award), Wolverine Bar Assn. (pres. 2000—01, Trailblazer award), ABA (bd. govs. 2005—, Gavel Awards Com.), Legal Aid and Defenders Assn. Mich. Office: Consumer Litig Ford Motor Co American Rd Dearborn MI 48121-1899 Office Phone: 313-322-3000.

NELSON, ALLEN F., proxy solicitation company executive; b. Portland, Oreg., Oct. 17, 1943; s. Roy August and Mildred Mary (Jensen) N.; m. Johanna Molenaar, Dec. 8, 1973. BS, U. Iowa, 1965, MA, 1968. V.p. Shareholder Comm. Corp., NYC, 1970-72; v.p. Trafalgar Capital Corp., NYC, 1973; pres. Nelson, Lasky & Co., Inc., NYC, 1974-76; account exec. Corp. Comm., Inc., Seattle, 1976-77; pres. Allen Nelson & Co., Inc., Seattle, 1977—. Mem. Fin. Analysts Fedn., Nat. Investor Rels. Inst., Nat. Security Traders Assn., Practicing Law Inst. (U.S. Presdl. rank rev. bd.), Pub. Rels. Soc. Am., Am. Soc. Corp. Secs., Can. Corp. Secs., Rainier Club, Montana Club, Vancouver Club. Home: 4400 Beach Dr SW Seattle WA 98116-3937 Office: Allen Nelson & Co Inc PO Box 16157 Seattle WA 98116-0157 Office Phone: 206-938-5783.

NELSON, ALLEN W., lawyer, insurance claims management company executive; b. 1964; m. Amy Nelson; children: Katie, Teddy. BA with honors, Duke U., Durham, NC, 1986, JD, 1989. Assoc. Troutman, Sanders, Lockerman & Ashmore, Atlanta, 1989—91; atty. Hawkins & Parnell, Atlanta, 1991—97; chief compliance counsel BellSouth Corp., 1997—2005; exec. v.p., gen. counsel, corp. sec. Crawford & Co., Atlanta, 2005—. Bd. mem. Ga. Trust for Hist. Preservation, Atlanta Ballet. Office: Crawford & Co PO Box 5047 Atlanta GA 30302-5047 Office Phone: 800-241-2541.

NELSON, ALLYSON LYN, lawyer; b. Honolulu, June 16, 1976; d. Craig E. and Pamela K. Nelson. BA in Polit. Sci. and Russian, U. Ala., 1998; JD, U. Miss. Sch. Law, 2002. Bar: U.S. Ct. Appeals (5th cir.) 2002, U.S. Dist. Ct. (no. and so. dists.) Miss. 2002, Miss. Supreme Ct. 2002. Legislative intern U.S. Senator Richard Shelby, Washington, 1996—96; law clk. U.S. Dept. of Justice, Hon. Charles E. Pazar, Memphis, 2001—01; atty. and com. counsel Miss. Ho. of Representatives, Jackson, Miss., 2002—03; assoc. atty. Rushing & Guice, PLLC, Biloxi, Miss., 2003—04; asst. dist. atty. Office of the Hinds County Dist. Atty., Jackson, 2004—. Mem. Sexual Assault Response Team, Jackson, Miss., 2004—, Hinds County Multi-Disciplinary Child Abuse Rev. Team, Jackson, Miss., 2004—. Recipient Outstanding Student award, Oil and Gas Law, 2001, Energy Law, 2001; scholar Heidelberg & Woodliff Excellence award, 2001, Study in Prague, Czech Republic scholar, The Fund for Am. Studies, 1997, Scholarship for study in Russia, U.S. Dept. of State, 1999, Jeffery P. Reynolds, P.A. Environ. Law scholar, 2001, IOLTA scholar, Miss. Bar Found., 2000; Strong scholarship for Outstanding Freshman in Russian, 1995. Mem.: ABA, Jour. of Nat. Security Law, Miss. Bar Assn., Hinds County Bar Assn., Miss. Prosecutors Assn., Nat. Dist. Attorneys Assn., Dobro Slovo, Phi Delta Phi, Gamma Beta Phi. Avocation: travel, politics, history, government, foreign languages. Home Phone: 601-352-1079; Office Phone: 601-968-6568. Personal E-mail: allyson_76@hotmail.com. E-mail: allysonnelson@co.hinds.ms.us.

NELSON, ANNE, media consultant, educator, writer; b. Fort Sill, Okla., Nov. 26, 1954; married; 2 children. BA, Yale U. Reporter Central Am., 1980—83; dir. Com. to Protect Journalists, 1988—92; dir. Internat. Programs, Graduate Sch. Journalism Columbia U., 1995—2003; adj. assoc. prof., Internat. Media Sch. Internat. and Public Affairs, 2005—. Editor (and co-author): Twenty Years and Forty Days, 1985; author: (book) Murder Under Two Flags, 1989, (screenplays) The Guys, 2002, (plays), 2001, Paprika, 2005, Dependence Day, 2006, Savages, 2006, Petra, 2007, numerous essays, articles, and reports. Mem. editl. bd. Episcopal New Yorker, 2004—; bd. dir. Bridging the Gap Arab-American Dialogue, 2006, New Harmony Project, Salzburg Sem., 2007. Recipient Audie award for

Best Recorded Play, 2003, Livingston award for Internat. Reporting, 1989, Thomas More Storke award, 1989; Guggenheim fellow, 2005—06, New Harmony Dramatists fellow, 2004, 2005. Independent. Protestant. Mailing: 202 Riverside Dr New York NY 10025 Home Phone: 212-666-9909. Business E-Mail: an115@columbia.edu.

NELSON, ARTHUR HUNT, real estate company executive; b. Kansas City, Mo., May 21, 1923; s. Carl Ferdinand and Hearty (Brown) N.; m. Eleanor Thomas, Dec. 27, 1954; children: Carl F., Frances, Pamela. AB, U. Kans., 1943; JD, Harvard U., 1949. Bar: Mass. 1949. Staff radiation lab. MIT, 1943-44; sr. engr., cons. Raytheon Mfg. Co., Boston, 1948-52; pvt. practice Boston, 1949; v.p., treas., dir. Gen. Electronic Labs., Inc., Cambridge, Mass., 1951-64, chmn. bd., 1959-63; treas., dir. Sci. Electronics, Inc., Cambridge, 1955-64, Assocs. for Internat. Rsch., Inc., Cambridge, 1954—, pres., 1968—; treas., dir. Victor Realty Devel., Inc., Cambridge, 1959-76, pres., 1972-76, gen. ptnr., 1976—, Prospect Hill Exec. Office Park, Waltham, Mass., 1977—; chmn. Nelson Cos., 1990—, Cambridge Devel. Lab., Cambridge, 1994—2001. Bd. dirs. Internat. Data Group, Inc., Sterling Bank. Pres., trustee Tech. Edn. Rsch. Ctrs., Inc., 1965—; trustee Winsor Sch., Boston, 1978-88, treas., 1978-82; bd. dirs. Charles River Mus. Industry, Waltham, 1986—, pres. 1994—, pres., dir. 128 Bus. Coun. Inc., 1987—, Hist. Waltham Inc., 1996—, Am. Computer Fedn. Inc., 1996—, Charles River Pub. Internet Ctr. Inc., 1996—. Ensign USNR, 1944-46. Recipient Ernst & Young New Eng. Master Entrepreneur of Yr. award, 1999. Mem. ABA, Mass. Bar Assn., Boston Bar Assn., Boston Computer Soc. (bd. dirs. 1985-97, chmn. 1994-97), Greater Boston C. of C., Harvard Club Boston, Beta Theta Pi, Phi Beta Kappa, Sigma Xi. Home: 75 Robin Rd Weston MA 02493-2436 Office: 75 3rd Ave Waltham MA 02451-7528

NELSON, AUDREY MAY, physician; b. Austin, Minn., Apr. 1, 1940; d. Glen Stanley and Clara May (Torgerson) N. BA, U. Minn., Mpls., 1962, BS, 1963, MD, 1965. Diplomate in internal medicine and rheumatology Am. Bd. Internal Medicine. Assoc. cons. Mayo Clinic, Rochester, Minn., 1972, cons. in internal medicine and rheumatology, 1972—2002; instr. medicine Mayo Med. Sch., Rochester, 1973—76, from asst. prof. to assoc. prof. medicine, 1976—2000, prof., 2000—02, prof. emeritus, 2002—, chair pediat. rheumatology, 1993—2001; cons. staff Shriners Hosp. for Children, Mpls., 1985—2006. Bd. govs. Mayo Clinic, 1982-89; trustee Mayo Found., 1982-93, v.p., 1989-92. Trustee Christ United Meth. Ch., Rochester, 1995—2002, vice chair, 1999—2001, chair, 2001—02. Recipient Woman of Achievement award YWCA, Alumni Recognition award U. Minn. Alumni Med. Soc., 2002; named Woman Physician of Yr., Alpha Epsilon Iota. Master: Am. Coll. Rheumatology; fellow: ACP, Am. Coll. Pediat., Am. Coll. Rheumatology (bd. dirs. 1995—99, master 2006, Disting. Svc. award 2002); mem.: AMA (del. 1984—2002), Am. Group Practice Assn. (trustee 1991—96, v.p. 1995, pres.-elect 1996), Am. Med. Group Assn. (chair elect 1996—97, bd. dirs. 1996—99, chair bd. dirs. 1997—98), Minn. Med. Assn. (trustee 1985—2002, Disting. Svc. award 1999), Phi Beta Kappa, Alpha Omega Alpha. Avocation: sailing. Home (Summer): 2105 Valkyrie Dr NW Rochester MN 55901-8117 Office: Mayo Clinic 200 1st St SW Rochester MN 55905-0002

NELSON, BARBARA KASZTAN, marketing professional; d. Eugeniusz and Danuta Kasztan; m. Kelley Nelson, June 26, 2004. B in Mktg., Seton Hall U., 1998, MBA magna cum laude, 2004. Mktg. rsch. assoc. Schering Plough Pharms., Kenilworth, NJ, 1997—99, analyst, mktg. rsch., 1999—2001; sr. analyst, mktg. rsch. Novartis Pharms., East Hanover, NJ, 2001—03, mgr., mktg. rsch., 2003—05, assoc. dir. mktg. rsch., 2005—. Participant Habitat For Humanity, NJ, 2003—05. Mem.: Healthcare Businesswomens Assn., Am. Mktg. Assn., Beta Gamma Sigma, Panhellenic Coun. (pres. 1996—97), Alpha Sigma Tau. Office: Novartis Pharms One Health Pl East Hanover NJ 07936 Home Phone: 732-423-7243. E-mail: barbara.nelson@novartis.com.

NELSON, (EARL) BEN(JAMIN), senator, former governor, lawyer; b. McCook, Nebr., May 17, 1941; s. Benjamin Earl and Birdella Ruby (Henderson) N.; m. Diane C. Gleason, Feb. 22, 1980; children from a previous marriage: Sarah Jane, Patrick James; stepchildren: Kevin Michael Gleason, Christine Marie Gleason. BA in Philosophy, U. Nebr., 1963, MA in Philosophy, 1966, JD, 1970; LLD (hon.), Creighton U., 1992, Peru State Coll., 1993. Bar: Nebr. 1970. Instr. dept. philosophy U. Nebr., Lincoln, 1963-65; supr. Dept. Ins. State of Nebr., Lincoln, 1965-72; dir. ins., 1975-76; asst. gen. counsel, gen. counsel, sec., v.p. The Ctrl. Nat. Ins. Group Omaha, 1972-75, exec. v.p., 1976-77, pres., 1978-81, CEO, 1980-81; of counsel Kennedy, Holland, DeLacy & Svoboda, Omaha, 1985-90, Lumson, Dugan and Murray, Omaha, 1999—2001; gov. State of Nebr., Lincoln, 1991—99; US Senator from Nebr., 2000—. Com. rules and adminstrn. US Senate, com. commerce, sci. and transp., com. armed services, com. agr., nutrition and forestry. Co-chmn. Carter/Mondale re-election campaign, Nebr., 1980; chair Nat. Edn. Goals Panel, 1992-94; co-founder Gov.'s Ethanol Coalition, chair, 1991, 94; pres. Coun. of State Govs., 1994; bd. trustee Wesley House Found., Omaha, 1970-76. Recipient Friends of Nebr. Broadcasters award Nebr. Broadcasters Assn., 1993, Disting. Eagle award Nat. Eagle Scout Assn., 1994; named Amb. Plenipotentiary, 1993. Mem. ABA, Nat. Assn. Independent Insurers, Nat. Assn. Ins. Commrs. (exec. v.p. 1982-85), Nebr. Bar Assn., Consumer Credit Ins. Assn., Midwestern Govs. Assn. (chair 1994), Western Govs. Assn. (vice chair 1994, chair 1995), Happy Hollow Club, Omaha Club, Hillcrest Country Club. Democrat. Methodist. Avocations: reading, hunting, fishing. Office: US Senate 720 Hart Office Bldg Washington DC 20510 also: District Office Ste 205 7602n Pacific St Omaha NE 68114 Office Phone: 202-224-6551, 402-391-3411. Office Fax: 202-224-0012, 402-391-4725. *

NELSON, BILL (CLARENCE WILLIAM NELSON), senator, former state treasurer; b. Miami, Fla., Sept. 29, 1942; s. C.W. and Nannie (Merle) N.; m. Grace H. Cavert, Feb. 19, 1972; children: C. William, Nan Ellen. BA, Yale U., 1965; JD, U. Va., 1968. Bar: Fla. 1968. Atty. Nelson, Normile and Dettmer, Melbourne, Fla., 1970-79, Maguire, Vorrhis and Wells, Pa., 1991—94; mem. Fla. Ho. of Reps., 1972-78, US Congress, 1979-91; payload specialist 1 Space Shuttle Columbia seventh orbital mission, 1986; treas. State of Fla., Tallahassee, 1995—2000; US Senator from Fla., 2001—; vice chmn. Dem. Senatorial Campaign com., 2000—. Mem. com. armed services US Senate, com. budget, com. commerce, sci., transp., com. fgn. relations, spl. com. aging. Author: Mission: An American Congressman's Voyage to Space, 1988. Bd. dirs. Am. Astronautical Soc.; mem. Fla. Space Bus. Roundtable. Served to capt. USAR, 1965—75, served with US Army, 1968—70. Recipient Public Svc. award, Nat. Crystallography Assn., 1988, Debus award, Nat. Space Club, Fla. Com., 1993, President's award, Fla. State Conf. NAACP, 2001. Mem.: Fla. Bar Assn., Brevard County Bar Assn., Assn. Space Explorers. Democrat. Episcopalian. Office: US Senate 716 Hart Sen Office Bldg Rm 716 Washington DC 20510 Address: Landmark Ctr Two Ste 610 N Robinson St Orlando FL 32801 Office Phone: 202-224-5274, 407-872-7161. Office Fax: 202-228-2183, 407-872-7165. *

NELSON, BILL, broadcast executive; b. 1949; CPA. Audit supr. Ernst & Young, NYC, 1975—79; dir. external reporting & risk mgmt. Time Inc., 1979—84; v.p. & asst. controller HBO, 1984—85, v.p. & controller, 1985—91, sr. v.p. & CFO, 1991—94, exec. v.p. fin., info., ops. tech. & bus. affairs, 1994—2002, COO, 2002—07, chmn. & CEO, 2007—. Office: HBO 1 Time Warner Ctr New York NY 10019-8016 Office Phone: 212-484-8000. *

NELSON, BRUCE (MURRAY BRUCE NELSON), former consumer products company executive; m. LaVaun Nelson; children: Suzanne, Connor. Grad., ID State U., 1968. Sr. mgmt. positions Boise Cascade, 1968-90; pres., CEO BT Office Products USA, 1991-94, Viking, 1995—98; pres. Office Depot Inc., Delray Beach, Fla., 1998—2000, CEO, 2000—04, chmn., 2001—04.

NELSON, CALEB EDWARD, law educator; b. Cleve., Sept. 20, 1966; s. David Aldrich and Mary Dickson Nelson; m. Elizabeth Kristol, Aug. 11, 1991; children: Maxwell David, Katherine Ellen. AB, Harvard U., 1988; JD, Yale U., 1993. Bar: Ohio 1993. Mng. editor and other editl. positions The Pub. Interest, Washington, 1988—90; law clk. to judge Stephen F. Williams U.S. Ct. of Appeals for the D.C. Circuit, Washington, 1993—94; law clk. to justice Clarence Thomas U.S. Supreme Ct., Washington, 1994—95; assoc. litig. dept. Taft, Stettinius & Hollister, Cin., 1995—98; prof. U. Va. Sch. Law, Charlottesville, 1998—. Vis. prof. Harvard Law Sch., 2006. Contbr. articles to profl. jours. Named Winner Scholarly Papers Competition, Assn. Am. Law Schs., 2000; recipient Paul M. Bator award, Federalist Soc., 2006. Mem.: Phi Beta Kappa. Republican. Office: Univ Virginia School Law 580 Massie Rd Charlottesville VA 22903-1789 Office Phone: 434-924-7372.

NELSON, CAREY BOONE, sculptor; b. Lexington, Mo. d. William M. and Carey (Butler) Boone; m. Kenneth Warwick Nelson; children: Caren, Kenneth Warwick II, Kimberley, Keith, Kyle, Craig. Student, U. Mo.; BA, Wellesley Coll.; MS in Edn., Wagner Coll. Cert. tchr., NYC, NY State. Tchr. NYC Pub. Schs.; instr. sculpture Snug Harbor Cultural Ctr., NYC, 1982—84. Per diem col., artist USAF, 1974—; artist USCG, 1974—. One-woman shows include Pietrantonio Galleries, NYC, St. Bartholomew's, Salmagundi Club, Poly. Prep. Country Day Sch., Bklyn., Snug Harbor Cultural Ctr., NYC, Epiphany Libr., Nat. Arts Club, exhibited in group shows at Internat. Art Exch., Monte Carlo, Paris, Cannes, Athens, Victoria Mus. Libr., Melbourne, Australia, Represented in permanent collections Victoria Libr. Mus., Australia, Esperanza, Antarctica, Durban Mus., South Africa, John Noble Maritime Mus., SI, NY, Vanderbilt Collection, NY, Wright-Patterson A.F. Mus., Dayton, Ohio, Sheldon Swope Mus., Terre Haute, Ind., Internat. Mus. Cartoon Art, Boca Raton, Fla., numerous others, commd., Am.-Israel Friendship House, NYC, Mildred McAffee Horton, Wellesley Coll., Everett Barnes, Colgate U., Chuck Yeager for USAF, Daniel Boone for Rotunda of Mo. State Capitol, Jimmie Doolittle for USAF, Franklin Mineral Mus., NJ, 1989, Munro Monument USCG, 1989, George Vaughn Coll. Aeronautics, LaGuardia Airport, NYC, 1991, James Madison Monument, Montpellier, Va., 1992, Subway Riders, Internat. Mus. Cartoon Art, 1996, Sentinel of the Sea, Noble Collection Snug Harbor, SI, Reading is Fundamental Inc., Washington, Dr. William M. Boone Monument, Highland, Kans., 2001, SI U. Hosp., 2001, Cesar Chavez Monument, Chavez Found./Detroit, 2004. Bd. dirs. Cerebral Palsy Assn., S.I., NY, Vis. Nurse Assn., S.I. Named Woman of Achievement, Wagner Coll., 1978, Hon. Life Artist, Catharine Lorillard Wolfe Art Club, 1990; recipient awards, Salmagundi, 1995, 1996, 1997, 1998, 1999, 2000, award, 2003, awards, 2004, Anna Hyatt Huntington award, Catharine Lorillard Wolfe Art Club, Horsehead Trophy, 1980, Coun. of Am. Artists award, Hudson Valley, 1996, Medal of Achievement, USCG, 1991, Nat. Arts Club award, 1998, Salmagundi Peter Helch award, 1998, 1st Pl. Sculpture award, 1999, M. Soroka Meml. award, 1999, Cert. of Appreciation, USCG, 1999, Achievement award, 1999, George Gray award, 1999, Louis A. Magnini award, 2003, Eliot Liskin award, 2003, Lila Sawyer award, 2005. Fellow Am. Artists Profl. League (cert. of appreciation 1999, awards 2003, 05, When We Were Very Young award 2005); mem. Nat. Arts Club (life, award 1998), Royal Soc. Arts (London, life), Composers, Authors and Artists Am. (nat. bd. dirs. 1981-90, 1st pl. award 1982, 84, 86), Soc. Illustrators, Burr Artists (bd. dirs.), Catharine Lorillard Wolfe Art Club (pres. 1978-81, bd. dirs., sculpture chmn., Creative Hands award 1987, Artist of Yr. 1985, tour US Mus., Colls., 1996—), Nat. League Am. PEN Women (pres. NYC br. 1981-84, Manhattan-NYC br. 1990-94, 96-98, Woman of Achievement award 1988), Wellesley Coll. Club (pres. SI), Salmagundi Club (Meml. award 2006), Kappa Kappa Gamma (Woman of Achievement award 1978). Episcopalian. Avocations: jewelry design, snorkeling, travel. Home: 282 Douglas Rd Staten Island NY 10304-1526

NELSON, CARL, journalist; Assoc. sports editor The New York Times. Mem.: Assoc. Press Sports Editors (ASPE) (assoc.). Office: NY Times Sports Desk 229 W 43rd St New York NY 10036 Office Phone: 212-556-7371.

NELSON, CARL ALFRED, writer, international business educator; b. Pitts., Oct. 11, 1930; s. Alfred Helge Nelson and Isabel Alice (Younger) Newbauer; m. Barbara Long, June 2, 1956 (dec.); children: Jennifer, Allison, Monica; m. Dolores Hansen, Apr. 8, 2006. BS, U.S. Naval Acad., 1956; MS, U.S. Naval Post Grad., 1967; student, US Naval War Coll., 1970; D of Bus. Adminstrn., U.S. Internat. U., 1984. Enlisted USN, 1949, advanced through grades to capt., 1956-82; comdg. officer USS Worden CG-18, 4 others; v.p., dir. AMMEX Cons., Chula Vista, Calif., 1985-86; pres. Global Bus. & Trade, San Diego, 1982—. Prof. Calif. Sch. Internat. Mgmt.; lectr. in field. Author: Your Own Import-Export Business: Winning the Trade Game, 1988, Global Success, 1990, Managing Globally; A Complete Guide to Competing Worldwide, 1993, Protocol for Profit, 1998, International Business, 1998, Exporting, 1999, The Advisor, 1999, Secret Players, 2003, Import-Export: How to Get Started in International Trade, 4th edit., 2007; contbr. articles to profl. jours.; contbr. short stories to popular mags. Pres. Chula Vista Boys Club, 1988; exec. bd. dirs. Calif. Dem. Party, 1992-97, pres. S.D. Writers/Editors Guild, 1998—; dir. Vietnam Vets.; active Econ. Devel. Commr., Chula Vista, 2000-06. Decorated Legion of Merit, Bronze Star, Air medals, combat commendations; named Outstanding Alumni of Yr., U.S. Internat. U., 1989, Disting. Grad. Carrick HS, Pltts., 2006; recipient Disting. Global Educator award Calif. Sch. Internat. Mgmt., 2003. Mem. Assn. Global Bus., Acad. Internat. Bus., Authors's Guild of Am., Chula Vista C. of C. (dir. 1984-90, Internat. Focus award 1988), Optimist Club, 50 Yr. Mason (32 deg.). Home: 1385 Don Carlos Ct Chula Vista CA 91910-7130 Office Phone: 619-421-9094. E-mail: canelson56@cox.net.

NELSON, CARL ROGER, retired lawyer; b. Gowrie, Iowa, Dec. 26, 1915; s. Carl Helge and Inez Olivia (West) N.; m. Elizabeth Boswell Campbell, Apr. 27, 1946; children: Thomas C., Nancy L. AB, Grinnell Coll., 1937; MA, Columbia, 1938, LLB, 1941. Bar: N.Y. 1941, D.C. 1947, U.S. Supreme Ct. 1947. Law clk. to Chief Justice Stone, 1941-42; Washington assoc. firm Root, Ballantine, Harlan, Bushby & Palmer, 1946-51; mem. firm Purcell & Nelson, Washington, 1951-80, Reavis & McGrath, 1980-83, Nelson Thurston Jones & Blouch, 1984-86. Mem. Adminstrv. Conf. U.S., 1967—73. Served to capt. AUS, 1942-46. Fellow Am. Bar Found.; mem. ABA (mem. ho. dels. 1964-66, mem. coun. 1960-66, chmn. sect. adminstrv. law 1963-64), Chevy Chase (Md.) Club, Lawyers Club (Washington), Met. Club (Washington), Phi Beta Kappa. Mem. United Ch. of Christ. Personal E-mail: nelsoncrn@comcast.net.

NELSON, CAROL EVELYN, retired pre-school educator; b. Grand Meadow, Minn., May 25, 1939; d. Charles Henry and Evelyn Hazel Lockwood; m. Loren Dean Nelson, Feb. 6, 1960; children: Sonia Jayne, Barrett Christopher, Bryce Phillip. BS, U. Minn., 1962. Cert. tchr., Minn. Substitute tchr. mil. schs. Camp Darby, Livorno, Italy, 1960—61; tchr. St. Paul Pub. Schs., 1962-63, Caledonia (Minn.) Pub. Schs., 1963-64, Rochester (Minn.) Pub. Schs., 1964-67, 83-87; early childhood educator Kids' Tree House, Rochester, 1987—2004; owner, mgr. CEN, Inc., Kids' Tree House, Rochester, 1988—99; ret., 2004. Mentor entrepreneurial tng. pilot program Minn. Women's Network, 1990-99. Canvasser, Rochester United Way, 1978-84; mem. climate control com., Elton Hills PTA, Rochester, 1983-85; leader Northwest Notables 4-H Club, Rochester, 1977-86. Mem. AAUW (Rochester, Minn. br. pres. 2002-04, chair Upper Midwest Regional Conf. Biannual Conf. 2004), Women Ind. Bus. Owners, Rochester Edn. Assn., S.E. Minn. Assn. for Edn. of Young Children, Rochester Civic Music Guild, Stock Club. Republican. Lutheran. Avocations: singing, reading. Personal E-mail: cenelson60@msn.com.

NELSON, CAROL KOBUKE, bank executive; m. Ken Nelson; 2 children. BA in fin. magna cum laude, Seattle U., Wash., 1978, MBA, 1984; attended grad. sch. Credit & Fin. Mgmt., Santa Clara U., Calif. With SeaFirst Bank (now Bank of Am.); sr. v.p., No. regional consumer exec. Bank of Am.; pres., COO Cascade Fin. Corp., Everett, Wash., 2001—02, pres., CEO, 2002—, Cascade Bank, Everett, Wash., 2001—. Exec. adv. bd. Albers Sch. Bus. and Economics Seattle U. Chair bd. dirs. United Way, Snohomish County; bd. dirs. Boys and Girls Club, Snohomish County, Econ. Devel. Coun., Snohomish County; adv. bd. Leadership Snohomish County; bd. pub. facilities dist. Washington States Baseball Stadium. Named One of 25 Women to Watch, U.S. Banker Mag., 2003; named one of The 25 Most Powerful Women in Banking, 2004, 2005. Mem.: Wash. Bankers Assn. (bd. dirs.), Wash. Fin. League (bd. dirs.). Office: Cascade Financial Corp 2828 Colby Ave Everett WA 98201

NELSON, CAROLYN, state legislator; b. Madison, Wis., Oct. 8, 1937; m. Gilbert W. Nelson; children: Paul, John, Karla. BS, N.D. State U., 1959, MS, 1960. Sr. lectr. emeritus N.D. State U., 1968—; mem. N.D. Ho. of Reps., 1986-88, 92-94, N.D. Senate from 21st dist., 1994—; mem. judiciary com., vet. affairs com. N.D. Senate, minority caucus leader, 2000—. Mem. N.D. State Investment Bd., 1989-92. Mem. Bd. Edn., Fargo, N.D., 1985-91, pres., 1989-90; trustee N.D. Tchrs. Fund for Retirement, 1985-92, pres., 1990-92; mem. N.D. PTA, pres., 1978-81, N.D. Women's and Children's Caucus. Recipient Merit Svc. award Gamma Phi Beta, 1978, 90, Legis. Voices award Children's Caucus, 1995; named Legislator of Yr., N.D. Bar Assn., 2000, N.D. Student Assn., 2001. Mem. LWV, Am. Guild English Handbell Ringers (area chmn. 1982-84, nat. bd. dirs. 1982-90), Nat. Fedn. Music Clubs (bd. dirs. 2003—, legis. chair 2003-07, regional v.p. 2005—07, 1st v.p. 2007-), N.D. Fedn. Music Clubs (life, pres. 1997-2001, nat. bd. mem. 2005—, legis. chair, Rose Fay Thomas fellow 2001), Gamma Phi Beta, Phi Kappa Phi, Sigma Alpha Iota. Office: ND Senate State Capitol Bismarck ND 58505 Address: One 2d St S 5 402 Fargo ND 58103-1959 Business E-Mail: cnelson@nd.gov.

NELSON, CARY ROBERT, language educator; b. Phila., May 15, 1946; s. Aaron and Sophie (Cohen) N. BA, Antioch Coll., 1967; PhD in English, U. Rochester, 1970. Asst. prof. English U. Ill., 1970-75, assoc. prof. English, 1975-82, prof. English and Criticism and Interpretive Theory, 1982—, prof. Ctr. for Writing, 1991—, Jubilee prof. liberal arts and scis., 1991—. Project dir. Nat. Endowment for the Humanities grants U. Ill., 1983-85, founding dir. unit for criticism and interpretive theory, 1981-85, 96, coord. faculty criticism seminar 1977-82, 96; governing bd., exec. com. Abraham Lincoln Brigade Archives, 1994—, vice chair 1995—; cons. in field. Author: The Incarnate Word: Literature as Verbal Space, 1973, Our Last First Poets: Vision and History in Contemporary American Poetry, 1981, Repression and Recovery: Modern American Poetry and THe Politics of Cultural Memory 1910-1945, 1989, Shouts from the Wall: Posters and Photographs Brought Back from the Spanish Civil War by American Volunteers, 1996, Manifesto of a Tenured Radical, 1997, Academic Keywords: A Devil's Dictionary for Higher Education, 1999; editor: Theory in the Classroom, 1986, W.S. Merwin: Essays on the Poetry, 1987, Regions of Memory: Uncollected Prose, 1949-82, 1987, Marxism and the Interpretation of Culture, 1988, Edwin Rolfe: A Biographical Essay and Guide to the Rolfe Archive at the University of Illinois at Urbana-Champaign, 1990, Cutural Studies, 1992, The Collected Poems of Edwin Rolfe, 1993, Higher Educaton Under Fire: Politics, Economics, and the Crisis of the Humanities, 1994, Trees Became Torches: Selected Poems of Edwin Rolfe, 1995, Trees Became Torches: Selected Poems of Edwin Rolfe, 1995, Madrid 1937: Letters of the Abraham Lincoln Brigade from the Spanish Civil War, 1996, Disciplinarity and Dissent in Cultural Studies, 1996, Will Teach for Food: Academic Labor in Crisis, 1997, The Aura of the Cause: A Photo Album for North American Volunteers in the Spanish Civil War, 1997, An Anthology of Modern American Poetry, 1999; editl. adv. bd. Literature and Psychology, 1985—, Academe: Bull. of the AAUP, 1996—, Jour. of Midwest MLA, 1996—; editl. bd. Coll. Lit., 1990—, Works and Days, 1995—; contbr. numerous articles to profl. jours. Fellowships U. of Ill. Ctr. for Advanced Study, 1978, 85-86, U. Ill. coll. of Liberal Arts and Scis. Faculty Study in a Second Discipline, 1987-88, Program for the Study of Cultural Values and Ethics, 1993-94, Program for Rsch. in Humanities, 1999—; grantee NSF, 1996. Mem. MLA (exec. coun. 1999—, 2d v.p. 1996-97, pres. 1996-97), Midwest MLA (pres. 1998), AAUP (nat. coun. 1995—, 2nd v.p. 2005-06, pres. 2006-), Tchrs. for a Dem. Culture, Kenneth Burke Soc., Ernest Hemingway Soc., Nat. Coun. of Tchrs. of English. Home: 808 S Lynn St Champaign IL 61820-6313 Office: English Dept U of Ill 608 S Wright St Urbana IL 61801-3668 E-mail: crnelson@uiuc.edu.

NELSON, CHARLOTTE BOWERS, public administrator; b. Bristol, Va., June 28, 1931; d. Thaddeus Ray and Ruth Nelson (Moore) Bowers; m. Gustav Carl Nelson, June 1, 1957; children: Ruth Elizabeth, David Carl, Thomas Gustav. BA summa cum laude, Duke U., 1954; MA, Columbia U., 1961; MPA, Drake U., 1983. Instr. Beaver Coll., 1957-58, Drake U., Des Moines, 1975-82; office mgr. LWV of Iowa, Des Moines, 1975-82; exec. asst. Iowa Dept. Human Svcs., Des Moines, 1983-85; exec. dir. Iowa Commn. on Status of Women Dept. Human Rights, Des Moines, 1985; pub. adminstr. State of Iowa, 1983—. Bd. dirs., pres. LWV, Beloit, Wis., 1960-74; bd. dirs. LWV, Des Moines, 1974-82, Westminster House, Des Moines, 1988-97, pres. 1996-97. Recipient Gov.'s Golden Dome award as Leader of the Yr., 2002; named Visionary Woman, Young Women's Resource Ctr., 1994. Mem. Am. Soc. Pub. Adminstrn. (mem. exec. coun. 1984-92, 98-99, past pres., Mem. of Yr. 1993), Phi Beta Kappa, Pi Alpha Alpha. Home: 1141 Cummins Cir Des Moines IA 50311-2113 Office: Human Rights Dept Lucas State Office Bldg Des Moines IA 50319-0001 Office Phone: 515-281-4467. E-mail: charlotte.nelson@iowa.gov, nelson514@aol.com.

NELSON, CHRIS A., state official; b. Mitchell, SD, Aug. 18, 1964; m. Penny Pfeifle; 1 child, Rebekah; 1 stepchild. BS in Animal Sci., SD State U., 1987. Self-employed farmer/rancher, 1981—; UCC supr. State of SD, Pierre, 1987—89, state election supr., 1989—2002, asst. sec. state, 2002—03, sec. state, 2003—. Nat. Govs. Assn. rep. US Election Assistance Commn. Bd. Advs., 2005. Recipient Excellence in SD Mcpl. Govt. award, SD Mcpl. League, 2003, Hazeltine/Taylor award, SD Kids Voting, 2004. Republican. Office: Office Sec State 500 E Capitol Ave Ste 204 Pierre SD 57501 Office Phone: 605-773-3537. Fax: 605-773-6580. *

NELSON, CHRISTINA GERRISH, lawyer; b. Kalispell, Montana, June 5, 1975; BA in English Lit., Pepperdine Univ., Malibu, Calif., 1994; JD, Gonzaga Univ., 1999. Bar: Wash. 1999. Former fed. pub. defender Spokane; assoc. atty., construction, real estate litig. Short Cressman & Burgess PLLC, Seattle. Contbr. articles to numerous profl. jours. Named Wash. Rising Star, SuperLawyer Mag., 2006. Mem.: ABA, Spokane Co. Bar Assn., King Co. Bar Assn., Wash. State Bar Assn. Office: Short Cressman & Burgess PLLC Ste 3000 Wells Fargo Ctr 999 Third Ave Seattle WA 98104-4088

NELSON, CHRISTOPHER GRANT, dermatologist; b. Peoria, Ill., Feb. 11, 1946; s. Grant Leonard and Shirlee Ann (Brunnenmeyer) N.; m. Mary Jo Donnelly, June 30, 1972; children: Christopher Jr., Andrew Anthony. BS, U. Iowa, 1968, MD, 1971. Diplomate Am. Bd. Dermatology; cert. clin.

trial investigator. Intern Ball Meml. Hosp., Muncie, Ind., 1971-72; resident in dermatology U. Tex. Med. Br., Galveston, 1974-77; staff Bayfront Med. Ctr., St. Petersburg, 1977—, St. Anthony's Hosp., St. Petersburg, 1977—; tchr. Bayfront Med. Ctr., 1977—; affiliate assoc. prof. U. South Fla. Coll. Medicine, 1977—; staff Tampa Gen. Hosp., 2001—. Contbr. articles to profl. jours. Vol. Am. Cancer Soc. Mem. ACP, So. Med. Assn., Fla. Med. Assn., Am. Acad. Dermatology (fellow), Am. Soc. Dermatologic Surgery, Soc. Investigative Dermatology, Pinellas County Med. Soc., Fla. West Coast Soc. Dermatology (sec.-treas. 1982-84, pres. 1984-87), Fla. Soc. Dermatologic Surgery, St. Petersburg Yacht Club (bd. dirs. 1989-95, entertainment chmn. 1989-92, house and grounds com. 1987-95), Dragon Club, Masons, Royal Order of Jesters. Presbyterian. Avocations: sailing, scuba diving, photography, amateur ham radio. Office Phone: 727-895-8131.

NELSON, CRAIG ALAN, management consultant; b. San Rafael, Calif., July 11, 1961; s. Kenneth Alfred and Anne Catherine (Laurie) N. BS in Fin., San Diego State U., 1984. Loan assoc. Union Bank, San Diego, 1984-85, comml. loan officer, 1985-86, corp. banking officer, 1986-87, asst. v.p., 1987-89, v.p. corp. banking, 1989-93; v.p. Alexander & Alexander, San Diego, 1993-95; sr. assoc. Goreham-Moore & Assocs., San Diego, 1995-98; v.p. Sedgwick Tech. Group Sedgwick of Calif., Inc., San Diego, 1998; v.p., dir. tech. Marsh Inc., La Jolla, Calif., 1998—; regional v.p. Comerica Tech. Banking Group, San Diego; regional v.p., sr. mgr. Bank of the West, San Diego, 2002—05; exec. v.p. First Nat. Bank. V.p. Sedgwick Tech. Group, 1997; pres. MIT Enterprise Forum, San Diego. Community group chair San Diego chpt. Am. Cancer Soc., 1989; mem. com. Juvenile Diabetes Assn.; bd. dirs. San Diego State Found., 1989—; pres. Am. Lung Assn., San Diego and Imperial counties, San Diego State U. Athletic Found., 2004-. Mem. San Diego State U. Young Alumni Assn. (pres. 1988-89, bd. dirs. emeritus 1989). Home: 429 Santa Dominga Solana Beach CA 92075 Office: First Nat Bank 401 W A St Ste 200 San Diego CA 92101 Office Phone: 619-235-1205. Personal E-mail: cnelson_madison@hotmail.com. Business E-Mail: cnelson@banksandiego.com.

NELSON, CRAIG T., actor; b. Spokane, Wash., Apr. 4, 1944; m. Robin Nelson (div. 1978); m. Doria Cook-Nelson, 1987. Attended, U. Ariz., Ctrl. Washington U. Appeared in (feature films) And Justice for All, 1979, The Formula, 1980, Where the Buffalo Roam, 1980, Private Benjamin, 1980, Stir Crazy, 1981, Poltergeist, 1982, Man, Woman, and Child, 1983, The Osterman Weekend, 1983, All the Right Moves, 1983, The Killing Fields, 1984, Silkwood, 1984, Poltergeist II: The Other Side, 1986, Red Riding Hood, 1987, Action Jackson, 1988, Me and Him, 1988, Troup Beverly Hills, 1989, Rachel River, 1989, Turner & Hooch, 1989, I'm Not Rappaport, 1996, Ghosts of Mississippi, 1996, Devil's Advocate, 1997, Wag the Dog, 1997, The Skulls, 2000, All Over Again, 2001, The Incredibles (voice), 2004, The Family Stone, 2005, Blades of Glory, 2007; (stage prodns.) Friends, 1983-84, Ah, Wilderness!, 1998, (TV films) How the West Was Won, 1978, Diary of a Teenage Hitchiker, 1979, Rage, 1980, Inmates: A Love Story, 1981, Murder in Texas, 1981, Paper Dolls, 1983, Alex: The Life of a Child, 1986, The Ted Kennedy, Jr. Story, 1986, Murderers Among Us: The Simon Wiesenthal Story, 1989, Extreme Close-Up, 1990, Drug Wars: The Camarena Story, 1990, The Josephine Baker Story, 1991, The Fire Next Time, 1993, Probable Cause, 1994, Top of the World, 1997, The Fifty, 1998, Creature, 1998, To Serve and Protect, 1999, Family Shield, 1999, Dirty Pictures, 2000; (TV series) Heroes: Made in the U.S.A. (host), 1986, Coach, 1989-97 (Emmy award, Leading actor in a comedy series, 1992), The District, 2000—04; producer (film documentaries) American Still; screenwriter (TV shows) The Lohman and Barkley Show, The Tim Conway Show, The Alan King Special, (miniseries) Creature, 1998, To Serve and Protect, 1999; prodr., writer (TV) Ride With the Wind, 1994; TV appearances include WKRP in Cincinnati, 1978, The Mary Tyler Moore Show, 1970, The White Shadow, 1978. *

NELSON, DARRELL WAYNE, retired academic administrator, research scientist; b. Aledo, Ill., Nov. 28, 1939; s. Wayne Edward and Olive Elvina (Peterson) N.; m. Nancyann Hyer, Aug. 27, 1961; children: Christina Lynne, Craig Douglas. BS in Agriculture, U. Ill., 1961, MS in Agronomy, 1963; PhD in Agronomy, Iowa State U., 1967. Cert. profl. soil scientist. Div. chief U.S. Army Chem. Corps., Denver, 1967-68; asst. prof. Purdue U., West Lafayette, Ind., 1968-73, assoc. prof., 1973-77, prof. agronomy, 1977-84; dept. head U. Nebr., Lincoln, 1984-88, dean for agr. rsch. and dir. Nebr. Agrl. Experiment Sta., 1988—2005; ret., 2005. Cons. U.S. EPA, Washington, 1977-79, Ind. Bd. of Health, Indpls., 1977-83, Eli Lilly Co., Indpls., 1976. Editor: Chemical Mobility and Reactivity in Soils, 1983. Served to capt. U.S. Army, 1967-68. Fellow AAAS, Am. Soc. Agronomy (bd. dirs., pres.-elect, pres. 2001, past pres. 2002, CIBA-Geigy award 1975, Agronomic Achievement award 1983, Environ. Quality Rsch. award 1985), Soil Sci. Soc. Am. (bd. dirs., pres. elect 1992, pres. 1993, past. pres. 1994); mem. Internat. Soil Sci. Soc., Lions Lodge (treas. 1980-83, Lafayette, Ind. chpt.). Presbyterian. Avocations: fishing, skiing, jogging. Office: Univ of Nebr Agrl Rsch Divsn Lincoln NE 68583-0704 Business E-Mail: dnelson1@unl.edu.

NELSON, DAVID ALDRICH, former federal judge; b. Watertown, NY, 1932; s. Carlton Low and Irene Demetria (Aldrich) Nelson; m. Mary Dickson, 1956; 3 children. AB, Hamilton Coll., 1954; postgrad., Cambridge U., Eng., 1954—55; LLB, Harvard U., 1958. Bar: Ohio 1958, NY 1982. Atty.-advisor Office of the Gen. Counsel, Dept. of the Air Force, 1959—62; assoc. Squire, Sanders & Dempsey, Cleve., 1958—67, ptnr., 1967—69, 1972—85; judge US Ct. Appeals (6th cir.), Cin., 1985—99, sr. judge, 1999—2006. Gen. counsel US Post Office Dept., Washington, 1969—71; sr. asst. postmaster gen., gen. counsel US Postal Svc., Washington, 1971; nat. coun. Ohio State U. Coll. Law, 1988—98. Trustee Hamilton Coll., 1984—88. Served to maj. USAFR, 1959—73. Recipient Benjamin Franklin award, US Post Office Dept., 1969; Fulbright scholar, 1954—55. Fellow: Am. Coll. Trial Lawyers; mem.: Ohio Bar Assn., Fed. Bar Assn., Emerson Lit. Soc., Ct. of Nisi Prius (sgt. emeritus), Phi Beta Kappa. *

NELSON, DAVID LEONARD, data processing executive; b. Omaha, May 8, 1930; s. Leonard A. and Cecelia (Steinert) N.; m. Jacqueline J. Zerbe, Dec. 26, 1952; 1 child, Nancy Jo. BS, Iowa State U., 1952. Mktg. adminstr. Ingersoll Rand, Chgo., 1954-56; with Accuray Corp., Columbus, Ohio, 1956-87, exec. v.p., gen. mgr., 1967, pres., 1967-87, chief exec. officer, 1970-87; pres. process automation bus. unit Combustion Engring., Inc., Columbus, 1987-90; pres. bus. area process automation Asea Brown Boveri, Stamford, Conn., 1990-91, v.p. customer satisfaction Ams. region, 1991-93, v.p. customer support Ams. region, 1994-95; chmn. bd. dirs. Herman Miller Inc., Zeeland, Mich., 1995-2000, counsel, 2000—04. Served to capt. USMCR, 1952-54. Mem. IEEE, Instrument Soc. Am., Newcomen Soc. N.Am., Tau Beta Pi, Phi Kappa Phi, Phi Eta Sigma, Delta Upsilon. Achievements include patents in field. Home: 1113 Roundhouse Ln Alexandria VA 22314-5935 Office Phone: 703-299-4588. Business E-Mail: david-nelson@hermanmiller.com.

NELSON, DAVID LOREN, geneticist, educator; b. Washington, June 25, 1956; s. Erling Walter and Marlys Joan (Jorgenson) N.; m. Claudia Jane Hackbarth, July 31, 1982; children: Jorgen William, Erik Alexander. BA, U. Va., 1978; PhD, MIT, 1984. Staff fellow NIH, Bethesda, Md., 1985-86; sr. assoc. Baylor Coll. Medicine, Houston, 1986-89, instr., 1989-90, asst. prof., 1990-94, assoc. prof., 1994-99, prof., 1999—. Dir. Human Genome Ctr., 1995-96. Editor: Genome Data Base, 1992-2000; assoc. editor Genomics, 1994-2002. Achievements include development of Alu PCR; discovery of fragile X syndrome gene (FMR-1), new form of genetic mutation (simple repeat expansion); identification of gene defects in Lowe Syndrome and Incontinentia Pigmenti. Office: Baylor Coll Dept Medicine Molecular & Human Genetics 1 Baylor Plz Houston TX 77030-3411 Personal E-mail: nelson@bcm.edu.

NELSON, DEAN B., media company executive; Process ctrl. engr. Shell Oil Co., 1981—83; with Boston Consulting Group, 1985—98, sr. v.p., 1998—2000; founder Capstone Consulting LLC, 2000, CEO, 2000—; chmn. PRIMEDIA Inc., NYC, 2003—, pres., CEO, 2005—. Bd. dirs. PRIMEDIA Inc., 2003—. Office: PRIMEDIA Inc 745 Fifth Ave New York NY 10151 Office Phone: 212-745-0100. Office Fax: 212-745-0121.

NELSON, DEBORAH JANE, family and consumer science educator; d. Roy Irvin and Jane Maurine Nelson. BS in Vocat. Home Economics Edn., Colo. State U., Fort Collins, 1983; MA in Ednl. Psychology, U. Colo. at Denver, 1991. CFCS Am. Assn. of Family & Consumer Sciences, 1986. Tchr. home econ. Cripple Creek-Victor Sch., Colo., 1983—84; tchr. family and consumer scis. Jefferson H.S., Edgewater, 1984—2000, Alameda H.S., Lakewood, 2000—. Mem. career devel. focus team Jefferson County Pub. Schs., Golden, Colo., 2004—; mem. state stds. rev. team family and consumer scis. Colo. Cmty. Colleges Sys., Denver, 2002—04; state star event chair and evaluator Family, Career & Cmty. Leaders Am., 1983—. Contbr. articles to profl. jours. Walkamerica vol. Mar. of Dimes, Denver, 1974—; clarinetist Denver Concert Band, 1986—; supporter 4-H Clubs, El Paso County, 1991—; judge Job's Daughters, Denver, 1995. Named Colo. FACS Profl. of Yr., Colo. Assn. Family and Consumer Scis., 1995; named an Outstanding Tchr., Colo. Tchr. Awards, 1996. Mem.: NEA, Internat. Fedn. Home Econ., Assn. Career and Tech. Edn. (sec. Colo. divsn. 1999—2001, CATFACS Outstanding Tchr. 2003), Am. Assn. Family and Consumer Scis. (v.p. svcs. 2003—05). Avocations: swimming, scrapbooks, travel, clarinet, piano. Office: Alameda HS 1255 S Wadsworth Blvd Lakewood CO 80232-5406 Home Phone: 303-969-9473.

NELSON, DIANE W., broadcast executive; BS in Comm., Syracuse U. Dir. nat. promotions Walt Disney Records; dir. worldwide corp. promotions Warner Brothers Pictures, 1996—98, v.p. worldwide corp. promotions, 1998—2001, sr. v.p. family entertainment, 2001—02, exec. v.p. domestic mktg., 2002—04, exec. v.p. global brand mgmt., 2004—. Named one of 100 Most Powerful Women in Entertainment, Hollywood Reporter, 2006. Mailing: Warner Bros Pictures 4000 Warner Blvd Burbank CA 91522 Office Phone: 818-954-6000. *

NELSON, DONALD ARVID (NELLIE NELSON), professional basketball coach; b. Muskegon, Mich., May 15, 1940; m. Joy Wolfgram, June 19, 1991; children: Julie, Donn, Christie, Katie, Lee. Student, U. Iowa. Player Chgo. Zephyrs, 1962-63, LA Lakers, 1963-65, Boston Celtics, 1965-76; asst. to head coach Milw. Bucks, 1976-87, dir. player pers.; exec. v.p., part owner, gen. mgr. Golden State Warriors, Oakland, Calif., 1987-95, head coach, 1988-95, 2006—, NY Knicks, 1995-96; head coach, gen. mgr. Dallas Mavericks, 1997—2005. Head coach NBA Western Conf. All-Star Team, 1992; head coach US Nat. Team World Championships (gold medal), Toronto, 1994. Named NBA Coach of Yr. 1983, 85, 92; named one of Top 10 Coaches in NBA Hist., 1997. Achievements include winning NBA Championships as a member of the Boston Celtics, 1966, 68, 69, 74, 76. Mailing: Golden State Warriors 1011 Broadway Oakland CA 94607 *

NELSON, DONALD FREDERICK, retired physics educator, researcher; b. East Grand Rapids, Mich., July 4, 1930; s. Paul Vine and Florence Dorothea (Atchison) N.; m. Margaret Ellen Fuerstenau, Dec. 18, 1954; children: Elizabeth Ellen, Julia Karen Nelson-Gal. BS, U. Mich., 1952, MS, 1953, PhD, 1958. Postdoctoral fellow U. Mich., Ann Arbor, 1958-59; mem. tech. staff Bell Telephone Labs., Murray Hill, N.J., 1959-67; prof. U. So. Calif., LA, 1967-68; mem. tech. staff AT&T Bell Labs., Murray Hill, 1968-87; prof. Worcester Poly. Inst., Mass., 1997—2000, prof. emeritus, 2000—. Vis. lectr. Princeton (N.J.) U., 1976. Author: Electric, Optic, and Acoustic Interactions in Dielectrics, 1979; contbr. articles to profl. jours. Mem. Gov.'s Sci. Adv. Com., Trenton, N.J., 1982-87, N.J. Noise Control Coun., Trenton, 1983-87; councilman Common Coun., Summit, N.J., 1981-84. Fellow Am. Phys. Soc.; mem. Optical Soc. Am., Acoustical Soc. Am. Achievements include patents in end pumped optical maser; development of first continuously operating ruby laser, first optical modulator in optical waveguide; prediction and measurement of lower symmetry of elasto-optic tensor; prediction of lower symmetry of stiffness tensor. Home: RR 1 Box 475P Edgartown MA 02539-9733 Office: Worcester Poly Inst 100 Institute Rd Worcester MA 01609-2280 Personal E-mail: dnelson@wpi.edu.

NELSON, DONNA GAYLE, state representative; b. Paducah, Tex., June 13, 1943; d. Jack Harold Williams and Hazel Louise (Cooper Moss) Stephens; m. Douglas Caldwell Nelson, June 24, 1966 (div. 1976); children: Kellye Lou Fetters, Robert Kreg Nelson, J. Graigory. AB, South Plains Coll., Levelland, Tex., 1963; BBA, West Tex. A&M U., Canyon, 1965, MBA, 1967. Founder Evergreen Mut., McMinnville, Oreg., 1975; co-founder Evergreen Life Line, McMinnville, 1978—; founder, corp. dir. AAA Profl. Promotions, McMinnville, 1977—; pres. Evergreen Bus. Mgmt. Co., McMinnville, 1978—; sr. v.p. Evergreen Helicopters, Inc., McMinnville, 1978—, Evergreen Internat. Aviation, Inc., McMinnville, 1978—; mem. Oreg. State Ho. of Reps., 2000—, chair veterans commn., vice chair edn. bus. com., vice chair govt. com., vice chair agr. com. Bd. dirs. Evergreen Air Ctr., Inc., Marana, Ariz., Evergreen Aircraft Sales & Leasing Co., Evergreen Aviation Ground Logistics Enterprises, Inc.; sr. v.p., bd. dirs. Evergreen Internat. Aviation, Inc., McMinnville; speaker Nat. Speakers' Assn., Phoenix, 1986—; mem. adv. bd. Chemeketa Community Coll., McMinnville, 1984-85; owner 3N & Assocs. Inc., Donna G. Nelson Auctions, LLC; founder Yamhill Co. Market; teacher Tex., Calif., and Oregon; author, journalist. Poet World's Most Beloved Poetry, 1985 (Silver poet); writer Aviation/Space Writers' Assn., 1989-90; columnist It Takes Grit. Mem. Team 100 Rep. party, Washington, 1989; co-founder Poyama Land Treatment Ctr., Independence, Oreg., 1973; den mother, sustained membership chmn. Boy Scouts Am., McMinnville, 1977-79; dr. mem. March of Dimes, Heart Fund, McMinnville, 1973-75; sr. mem. transportation, budget and parks com., Yamhill Co. Budget Parks, Elks Lions, Red Cross, NRA, N7IB Farm Bur.; founder Newcomers Club, Fund for Hope, Free Enterprise Fund for Kids; bd. dirs. Humane Soc., Linfield Chamber Orch., WOU Found., Salvation Army. Named Woman of Excellence, Portland, Oreg., 1985. Mem. DAR, C. of C., McMinnville Duplicate Bridge Assn. (founder), Soroptimists Club, Elks, Lions, Beta Sigma Phi (pres. 1974-75, Woman of Yr. 1990). Republican. Baptist. Avocations: music, sports, bridge, writing, fishing, speaking, travel, fishing, charity auctioneer. Home and Office: 2150 St Andrews Dr Mcminnville OR 97128-2436 Home Phone: 503-472-7446; Office Phone: 503-472-8015. Business E-Mail: donnanelson@state.or.us.

NELSON, DONNIE, professional sports team executive; b. Sept. 10, 1962; s. Don Nelson; m. Lotta Nelson; children: Christie, D.J. Grad., Wheaton Coll., Ill., 1986. Regional scout Milw. Bucks, 1984—86; asst. coach Golden State Warriors, 1986—94, Phoenix Suns, 1994—97; asst. coach, dir. player pers. Dallas Mavericks, 1998—2002, acting head coach, 2001, 2002, pres. basketball ops., 2002—, gen. mgr., 2005—. Asst. coach Lithuanian Nat. Team, 1990—; scout at World Championships USA Basketball, Toronto, Canada, 1994; founder Global Games, Dallas; hon. amb. League of Industries; chief adv. Chinese Nat. Basketball Team. Founder Assist Youth Found. (now combined with Heroes), 2002. Named to Wheaton Coll. Hall of Honor, 1997; recipient Grand Cross of the Comdr., Pres. of Lithuania, 2004. Office: Dallas Mavericks The Pavilion 2909 Taylor St Dallas TX 75226 E-mail: dcn@dallasmavs.com. *

NELSON, DOROTHY WRIGHT, federal judge; b. San Pedro, Calif., Sept. 30, 1928; d. Harry Earl and Lorna Amy Wright; m. James Frank Nelson, Dec. 27, 1950; children: Franklin Wright, Lorna Jean. BA, UCLA, 1950, JD, 1953; LLM, U. So. Calif., 1956; LLD (hon.), Western State U. Coll. Law, 1980, U. So. Calif., 1983, Georgetown U., 1988, Whittier U., 1989, U. Santa Clara, 1990, U. San Diego, 1997, Pepperdine U. Sch. of Law, 2003. Bar: Calif. 1954. Rsch. assoc. fellow U. So. Calif., 1953—56, instr., 1957, asst. prof., 1958—61, assoc. prof., 1961—67, prof., 1967—, assoc. dean., 1965—67, dean., 1967—80; judge US Ct. Appeals (9th cir.), 1979—95, sr. judge, 1995—. Com. to consider stds. for admission to practice in fed. cts. Jud. Conf. US, 1976—79; cons. project STAR Law Enforcement Assistance Adminstrn.; select com. on internal procedures Calif. Supreme Ct., 1987—; co-chair Sino-Am. Seminar on Mediation and Arbitration, Beijing, 1992. Contbr. articles to profl. jours.; author: Judicial Adminstration and The Administration of Justice, 1973; author: (with Christopher Goelz and Meredith Watts) Federal Ninth Circuit Civil Appellate Practice, 1995. Co-chair Confronting Myths in Edn. for Pres. Nixon's White House Conf. on Children, Pres. Carter's Commn. for Pension Policy, 1974—80; pres. Reagon's Madison Trust; mem. Nat. Spiritual Assembly of Bahais of US, 1967—; bd. dirs. Dialogue on Transition to a Global Soc., Weinacht, Switzerland, 1992; bd. vis. US Air Force Acad., 1978; bd. dirs. Coun. on Legal Edn. for Profl. Responsibility, 1971—80, Constl. Right Found., Am. Nat. Inst. for Social Advancement; adv. bd. Nat. Ctr. for State Cts., 1971—76; adv. com. to promote equality for woman and men in cts. Nat. Jud. Edn. Program; bd. dirs. Pacific Oaks Coll., Childrens Sch. & Rsch. Ctr., 1996—98; adv. bd. World Law Inst., 1997—, Tahirih Justice Inst., Washington, 1998—; chmn. bd. Western Justice Ctr., 1986—; chair 9th Cir. Standing Com. on Alternative Dispute Resolution, 1998—. Named Law Alumnus of Yr., UCLA, 1967, Woman of Yr., Times, 1968, Disting. Jurist, Ind. U. Law, 1994; recipient Profl. Achievement award, 1969, AWARE Internat. award, 1970, Ernestine Stalhut Outstanding Woman Lawyer award, 1972, Humanitarian award, U. Judaism, 1973, Pax Orbis ex Jure medal, World Peace thru Law Ctr., 1975, Pub. Svc. award, Coro Found., 1978, Hollzer Human Rights award, Jewish Fedn. Coun., 1988, Medal of Honor, UCLA, 1993, Emil Gumpert Jud. ADR Recognition award, LA County Bar Assn., 1996, Julia Morgan award, YWCA, 1997, Samuel E. Gates Litigation award, Am. Coll. Trial Lawyers, 1999, Bernard E. Witkin award, State Bar Assn. Calif., 2000, Judge of Yr. award, Pasadena Bar Assn., 2002, Thurgood Marshall Career Achievement award, 2005, Harry Sheldon award, Pasadena Human Relations Comm., 2006; fellow, Davenport Coll.; Lustman fellow, Yale U., 1977. Fellow: Davenport Coll., Am. Bar Found.; mem.: ABA (sect. on jud. adminstrn., chmn. com. on edn. in jud. adminstrn. 1973—89, D'Alemberte/Raven award 2000), Assn. Am. Law Schs. (chmn. com. edn. in jud. adminstrn.), Am. Judicature Soc. (bd. dirs., Justice award 1985), Bar Calif. (bd. dirs. continuing edn. bar commn. 1967—74), Order of Coif (nat. v.p. 1974—76), Phi Beta Kappa. Office: US Ct Appeals Cir 125 S Grand Ave Ste 303 Pasadena CA 91105-1621 Office Phone: 626-229-7400. Business E-Mail: dorothy-nelson@ca9.uscourt.gov. *

NELSON, DOUGLAS W., foundation administrator; b. 1946; BA, U. Ill., 1968; MA in History, U. Wyoming. Asst. secy. health and social svcs. State of Wis., Madison, 1967-85; dep. dir. Ctr. for Study Policy, Washington, 1985-90; with The Annie E. Casey Found., Greenwith, Conn., 1990—97, now exec. dir., pres., 1997—. Vice chair, bd. of trustees Foundation Ctr., NYC; co-chair, bd. of trustees Jim Casey Youth Opportunities Initiative; trustee Balt. Campaign for Children and Youth, Balt. Community Found., Wis. Child Abuse and Neglect Trust Fund; bd. mem. E. Balt. Develop., Inc., Nat. Acad. on Aging; bd. mem., former chair Living Cities; chair NYC Special Adv. Panel on Child Welfare; prog. adv. Edna McConnell Clark Found. Recipient Jane Addams Disting. Leadership award. Office: The Annie E Casey Found 701 Saint Paul St Baltimore MD 21202-2311

NELSON, EDITH ELLEN, dietician; b. Vicksburg, Mich., Sept. 26, 1940; d. Edward Kenneth and Anna (McManus) Rolffs; m. Douglas Keith Nelson; children: Daniel Lee, Jennifer Lynn. BS, Mich. State U., 1962; MEd in Applied Nutrition, U. Cin., 1979. Lic. dietitian, Fla. Clin. dietitian Macon (Ga.) Gen. Hosp., Blodgett Meml. Hosp., Grand Rapids, Mich.; grad. teaching asst. U. Cin., 1978-79; dir. nutrition svcs. Dialysis Clinic, Inc., Cin., 1979-88; cons. dietitian Panama City Devel. Ctr., Ft. Walton Beach Devel. Ctr., Fla., 1988-94; renal dietitian Dialysis Svcs. Fla., Ft. Walton Beach, 1989-92; cons. dietitian N.W. Fla. Community Hosp., Chipley, Fla., 1993-94, Beverly Enterprises, Panama City Beach, 1994-96, pvt. practice, Panama City, Fla., 1996—. Mich. Edn. Assn. scholar, 1958; Nat. Kidney Found. grantee, 1986. Mem. Am. Dietetic Assn., Fla. Dietetic Assn., Panhandle Dist. Dietetic Assn., Nat. Kidney Found. (coun. on renal nutrition, Fla. coun. on renal nutrition), Omicron Nu. Home and Office: 3522 Fox Run Blvd Panama City Beach FL 32408-7151 Personal E-mail: ediepcb@aol.com.

NELSON, EDWARD GAGE, brokerage house and bank executive, consultant; b. Nashville, May 17, 1931; s. Charles and Polly (Prentiss) N.; m. Carole Olivia Frances Minton, Sept. 17, 1960; children: Carole Gervais, Emily Minton, Ellen Prentiss BA in Polit. Sci., U. of South, Sewanee, Tenn., 1952. Exec. v.p. Clark, Landstreet & Kirkpatrick, Inc., Nashville, 1955-64, Commerce Union Bank, Nashville, 1968-72, pres., 1972-82, cons., 1985—, chmn., CEO, 1982-84; chmn., pres. Nelson Capital Corp., Nashville, 1985—. Hon. consul gen. Japan; bd. dirs. Werthan Packaging, Consumers Ins., Franklin Industries, Trans Arabian Investment Bank, Ctrl. Parking Sys., Ohio Star Forge, Bucyrus Internat., Inc.; mem. 1st adv. coun. Japan/Tenn. Soc. Trustee Vanderbilt U., Nashville, 1979—, chmn. med. ctr. bd., 1984-2003. Spl. agt. U.S. Army, 1955, Japan. Mem. Belle Meade Country Club, River Club (N.Y.C.). Republican. Episcopalian. Home: 1305 Chickering Rd Nashville TN 37215-4521 Office: Nelson Capital Corp 3401 W End Ave Ste 300 Nashville TN 37203-1085

NELSON, EDWARD HUMPHREY, architect; b. Winchester, Mass., Sept. 2, 1918; s. Richard MacDonald and Evelyn Miller (Humphrey) N.; m. Lois Whitaker Renouf, Sept. 24, 1948 (dec.); children: Susan, David, Sarah; m. Miriam P. Ketcham, Jan. 2, 1988. Grad., Lenox Sch., 1936; B.Arch., Yale, 1950. Pvt. archtl. practice, Tucson, 1953-61; sr. v.p. CNWC Architects, Tucson, 1961-88, pres., 1989-94; ret., 1994. Mem. adv. com. U. Ariz. Coll. Architecture, 1984-93. Works include: design for Tucson Community Ctr. Pres. Tucson Cmty. Coun., 1969-71, Tucson Art Ctr., 1960; bd. dirs. Tucson Housing Found., 1969-06, Estes Gardens Low Rent Sr. Housing, 2004-05, Tucson Symphony, 1977-84, Tucson United Way, 1980, NBA Tucson Housing, 2002-05, Tucson Art Mus., 1960-74, Tucson Trade Bur., 1976-91, pres., 1984; trustee Green Fields Sch., 1960-74; vestry St. Philips Episc. Ch., 1967-69, sr. warden, 1987-90, parish warden, 1993-94; convenor Episcopal Interparish Coun., 1990-92; mem. Episcopal Diocese of Ariz., S.W. Regional Parish; 1st Phila. City Troop, 1940—, horse cavalry, 1940-42. Served to capt. AUS, 1940-41, WWII, ETO. Decorated Bronze Star with oak leaf cluster, Purple Heart; recipient Disting. Citizen award U. Ariz., 1981, St. Philips medal St. Philips Episc. Ch., 2000. Fellow: AIA (pres. So. Ariz. chpt. 1962, emeritus 1994, chmn. Ariz. Fellows 1986—94); mem.: Ariz. Soc. Archs. (pres. 1963), U. Ariz. Pres.'s Club, Yale Club (pres. Tucson chpt. 1962, 1983, dir. 1979—). Home: 7500 N Calle Sin Envidia # 7101 Tucson AZ 85718-7359 E-mail: miriamned@msn.com.

NELSON, EDWARD SHEFFIELD, lawyer, retired utilities executive; b. Keevil, Ark., Feb. 23, 1941; s. Robert Ford and Thelma Jo (Mayberry) N.; m. Mary Lynn McCastlain, Oct. 12, 1962; children: Cynthia, Lynn (dec.), Laura. BS, U. Cen. Ark., 1963; LLB, Ark. Law Sch., 1968; JD, U. Ark., 1969. Mgmt. trainee Ark. La. Gas Co., Little Rock, 1963-64, sales engr., 1964-67, sales coordinator, 1967-69, gen. sales mgr., 1969-71, v.p., gen.

sales mgr., 1971-73, pres., dir., 1973-79, pres., chmn., chief exec. officer, 1979-85; ptnr., chmn. bd., chief exec. officer House, Wallace, Nelson & Jewel, Little Rock, 1985-86; pvt. practice law Little Rock, 1986—; of counsel Jack, Lyon & Jones, P.A., 1991—. Bd. dirs. Fed. Res. Mem. N.G., 1957-63, Fellowship Bible Ch.; bd. dirs. U. Ark., Little Rock, vice chmn. bd. visitors, 1981; bd. dirs. Philander Smith Coll., 1981; chmn. Ark. Indsl. Devel. Commn., 1987, 88; past chmn. Little Rock br. Fed. Res. Bd. St. Louis; chmn. Econ. Expansion Study Commn., 1987—; bd. dirs. Ark. Ednl. TV Found., Ark. Game and Fish Commn. Found.; founder, 1st pres. Jr. Achievement Ark., 1987-88; Rep. nominee for Gov. of Ark., 1990, 94; co-state chmn. Ark. Reps., 1991-92, nat. committeeman Ark. GOP, 1993-2000; mem. Ark. Higher Edn. Coord. Bd., 1997-99; apptd. commr. Ark. Game and Fish Commn., 2000-07, chmn., 2007-. Named Ark.'s Outstanding Young Man Ark. J. C. of C., 1973; One of Am.'s Ten Outstanding Young Men U.S. Jr. C. of C., 1974; Citizen of Yr. Ark. chpt. March of Dimes, 1983; Humanitarian of Yr. NCCJ, 1983; Best Chief Exec. Officer in Natural Gas Industry Wall Street Transcript, 1983; recipient 1st Disting. Alumnus award U. Cen. Ark., 1987. Mem. Am., Ark., Pulaski County Bar Assns., Ark. C. of C. (dir.), Little Rock C. of C. (dir., pres. 1981), Sales and Mktg. Execs. Assn. (pres. 1975, Top Mgmt. award 1977), U. Ark. Law Sch. Alumni Assn. (pres. 1980), Sigma Tau Gamma (Ben T. Laney Leadership award for leadership and achievement 2000), Ark. Wildlife Fedn. (Conservationist of Yr. 2002), Am. Lung Assn. (Philanthropist of Yr. 2003). Fellowship Bible Ch. Office: 6th and Broadway 3400 TCBY Bldg Little Rock AR 72201 Office Phone: 501-375-1122. Personal E-mail: esn@jlj.com.

NELSON, ELAINE EDWARDS, lawyer; b. Waco, Tex., Sept. 16, 1947; d. Bedford Duncan and Joyce (Harlan) Edwards; m. David A. Nelson, Apr. 12, 1969; children: Carol Christine, Harlan Claire. BA, Baylor U., 1969, JD, 1978. Bar: Tex. 1978. Gen. counsel Austin Industries, Inc., Dallas, 1978—. Office: Austin Industries Inc 3535 Travis St Ste 300 Dallas TX 75204-1466 also: PO Box 2879 Dallas TX 75221-2879

NELSON, ELIZABETH HAWKINS, not-for-profit association administrator; b. Rockville Centre, NY, Jan. 27, 1931; arrived in Eng., 1951; d. Harry Dadmun and Gretchen (Hawkins) N.; m. Ivan Piercy, Dec. 7, 1960 (div. 1972); children: Catherine, Christopher, Nicholas; m. Claude Jacob Esterson, July 26, 1975 (div. 1998). BA, Middlebury Coll., 1951; PhD, U. London, 1953; DSc (hon.), City London U., 1993; PhD (hon.), Open U., 2003. Rsch. psychologist Mars Ltd., London, 1954-55; dir., mng. dir. rsch. unit Benton & Bowles, London, 1955-64; dir. Mass Observation Ltd., London, 1964-65; founder dir., chmn. Taylor Nelson/Sofres plc, London, 1965-92; chief exec. The Princess Royal Trust for Carers, London, 1992-95; chair coun. U. Roehampton, 1995—2001; chmn. South West London Cmty. NHS Trust, 1997—2002. Non-exec. dir. Royal Bank Scotland, Edinburgh, 1988—97; chmn. bd. UK Ecolabelling, 1992—98; pres. World Assn. Pub. Opinion Rsch., 1990—92; coun. mem. City & Guilds, 1998—; mem. adv. com. on degree awarding powers Quality Assurance Agy., 1998—; chmn. Stargate Capital Investment Group Ltd., 2004—; CEO, Chronic Granulomatous Disorder Rsch. Trust, 2004—; dir. Bright Talk Ltd., 2004—. Vice chair coun. Open U., Milton Keynes, England, 1991—2001; dir. U.S. Open U., 1998—2001; non exec. dir. Bright Talk Ltd.; trustee Jeans for Genes, 2006, Immigration Adv. Svcs., 2005; mem. Doctors and Dentists Pay Rev. Bd., London, 1992—97. Decorated Order Brit. Empire; hon. fellow City & Guilds, 1994, U. Surrey, Roehampton, 2003. Fellow: Royal Soc. Arts, Market Rsch. Soc. (hon.); mem.: Freedom City of London, Internat. Women's Forum (bd. mem. 2001—05), First Forum U.K. Avocations: choral singing, opera, bridge. Home: 57 Home Park Rd London SW19 7HS England Office: 62 Trafalgar Sw London WC2N 5DY England Office Phone: 44 0 208 946 2317. Personal E-mail: liznlson53@aol.com.

NELSON, ELMER KINGSHOLM, JR., (KIM NELSON), political scientist, educator, writer, mediator, consultant; b. Laramie, Wyo., Sept. 14, 1922; s. Elmer Kingsholm and Alice (Downey) N.; m. Jane Beckwith Oliver, Aug. 4, 1945; 1 son, Elmer Kingsholm III (Kirk). BA, U. Wyo., 1943, JD, 1948, MA, 1949; Dr. Pub. Adminstrn., U. So. Calif., 1959. Instr. psychology U. Wyo., 1947-49; psychologist, staff psychologist dept. probation Contra Costa County, Calif., 1949-51; sr. psychologist Cal. State Dept. Corrections, San Quentin and Chino Prisons, 1951-52; asst. prof. criminology U. B.C., Can., 1952-54, assoc. prof., 1954-56, head criminology div., 1953-56; warden Haney Correctional Instn., B.C., 1956-58; assoc. dir. Youth Studies Ctr. U. So. Calif., 1958-59, dir. Youth Studies Ctr., 1959-64, assoc. prof. pub. adminstrn., 1958-61, prof., 1961—, dean Sch. Pub. Adminstrn., 1971-76, prof., co-dir. Sacramento Pub. Affairs Ctr.; head Bay Area Research Center, Berkeley, 1979—; prof. emeritus U. So. Calif. Dep. adminstr. Youth and Adult Corrections Agy., State of Calif., Sacramento, 1964-65; interim exec. dir. Office Criminal Justice Planning, spring 1975; dir. Nat. Study Probation and Parole, 1976-77; chmn. task force on corrections, asso. dir. Pres.'s Commn. on Law Enforcement and Adminstrn. of Justice, Washington, 1966-67; dir. nat. study of correctional adminstrn. U. So. Calif. for Joint Commn. on Correctional Manpower and Tng., 1967-69 Co-author: Corrections in America, 1975; contbr. articles, monographs, research reports to profl. jours. Advisor on mgmt. Boys Republic, Chino, Calif., 1967—; bd. dirs., v.p. Am. Justice Inst., Sacramento; bd. dirs. Human Interaction Rsch. Inst., L.A. Recipient Disting. Alumnus award U. Wyo., 1975, Exemplary Alumni award U. Wyo. Coll. Arts and Scis., 1994; Ford Found. Travel Study grantee, 1970-71; E. Kim Nelson endowed doctoral fellowship established at U. So. Calif., 1987. Sr. fellow Nat. Acad. Pub. Adminstrn.; mem. Wyo. Bar Assn., Alpha Tau Omega, Phi Beta Kappa, Phi Kappa Phi, Psi Chi. Home: 355 St Augustine Ct Benicia CA 94510-2866 Personal E-mail: eknscarq@aol.com.

NELSON, ERIC JOHN, lawyer; BA, Eastern U., St. Davids, Pa., 1996; JD, Hamline U. Sch. Law, 2001. Bar: Minn. 2001. Jud. law clk. First Jud. Dist.; founding ptnr. Halberg Criminal Def., Bloomington, Minn. Contbg. author: DWI Desk Book. Named a Rising Star, Minn. Super Lawyers mag., 2006. Mem.: Hennepin County Bar Assn., Minn. Bar Assn., Nat. Assn. Criminal Def. Lawyers. Office: Halberg Criminal Def Northland Plz Ste 1590 3800 American Blvd W Bloomington MN 55431 Office Phone: 952-224-4848. E-mail: enelson@halbergdefense.com. *

NELSON, ETHELYN BARNETT, civic worker; b. Bessemer, Ala., Jan. 16, 1925; d. Laurence McBride and Ethel Victoria Fortesque (King) Barnett; m. Stuart David Nelson, May 6, 1949; children: Terryl Lynn, Cynthia Dianne, Jacqueline Margo. Student, Huntingdon Coll., 1943, U. Ala., 1948, George Washington U., 1948—49, student, 1974. Sec. U.S. Air Force, Montgomery, Ala. and Panama Canal Zone, 1944—49; sec. to dep. undersec. U.S. Dept. State, Washington, 1951—53, U.S. Ho. of Reps. and U.S. Senate, 1959—60; adminstrv. asst. editl. divsn. Nat. Geog. Soc., Washington, 1962—65; rec. sec. Dist. IV Nat. Capital Area Fedn. Garden Clubs, Inc., Washington, 1981—83. Mem. Women's Com. Nat. Symphony Orch. Mem.: Nat. Trust for Historic Preservation, Salvation Army Aux., Am. Scandinavian Assn., Landon Woods Garden Club (pres. 1978—80), Congl. Country Club. Republican. Methodist. Achievements include patentee. Home: 6410 Maiden Ln Bethesda MD 20817-5612

NELSON, FREDA NELL HEIN, librarian; b. Trenton, Mo., Dec. 16, 1929; d. Fred Albert and Mable Carman (Doan) Hein; m. Robert John Nelson, Nov. 1, 1957 (div. Apr. 1984); children: Thor, Hope. Nursing diploma, Trinity Luth. Hosp., Kansas City, Mo., 1950; B. Philosophy, Northwestern U., 1961; MS in Info. and Libr. Sci., U. Ill., 1986. RN. Operating rm. nurse Trinity Luth. Hosp., Kansas City, Mo., 1950-52, Johns Hopkins Hosp., Balt., 1952, Wesley Meml. Hosp., Chgo., 1952-58, Tacoma Gen. Hosp., 1958-59, Chgo. Wesley Hosp., 1959-61; libr. asst. Maple Woods Campus Met. Community Colls., Kansas City, 1987-89, libr., libr. mgr. Blue Springs Campus, 1989-96; ret., 1996. Co-founder Coll. for Kids, Knox Coll., Galesburg, Ill., 1982. Nurses scholar Edgar Bergen Found., 1947; recipient Award of Merit, Chgo. Bd. Health, 1952. Avocations: swimming, walking, cross-word puzzles. Home: 5708 N Polk Dr Kansas City MO 64151

NELSON, FREDERICK DICKSON, judge; b. Cleve., Oct. 19, 1958; s. David Aldrich and Mary Ellen (Dickson) N. AB, Hamilton Coll., 1980; JD, Harvard U., 1983. Bar: Ohio 1984. Majority counsel subcom. on criminal law U.S. Senate Judiciary Com., Washington, 1983-85; spl. asst. to asst. atty. gen., Office of Legal Policy U.S. Dept. Justice, Washington, 1985-86, dep. asst. atty. gen., Office of Legal Policy, 1986-87; assoc. Taft, Stettinius & Hollister, Cin., 1988-89, of counsel, 1991-93; assoc. counsel to Pres. of U.S. The White House, Washington, 1989-90. Advisor to govts. of Ukraine and Russia, ABA Ctrl. and East European Law Initiative, 1992-93; adj. prof. constl. law Salmon P. Chase Coll. Law, U. No. Ky., 1994; chief of staff, legal coun. U.S. Rep. Steve Chabot, 1995-97; cons. Constnl. Commn. Albania, per Internat. Rep. Inst., 1998; pres. Civic Solutions, LLC, Cin., 1998-2002; co-creator, panelist Hotseat, Sta. WCPO-TV, (Cin. Channel 9), 2000-02; judge Hamilton County Ct. of Common Pleas, 2003—. Exec. editor Harvard Jour. of Law and Pub. Policy, 1982-83. Mem. Hamilton County Rep. Policy and Appts. Coms., 1999-2002; cons. Chabot for Congress Campaign, Cin., 1994, 98; mem. Ohio Bd. Uniform State Laws, Nat. Conf. Commrs. on Unifort State Laws, 2001—. Harry S. Truman Found. scholar, 1978-81. Mem. NATAS (Ohio Valley chpt.), Federalist Soc., Harvard Club. of Cin. (bd. dirs. 1989, 2001-2005), Phi Beta Kappa. Republican. Office Phone: 513-946-5840. E-mail: fnelson1@cinci.rr.com.

NELSON, GEORGE DRIVER, astronomer, educator, former astronaut; b. Charles City, Iowa, July 13, 1950; s. George Vernon and Evelyn Elenor (Driver) N.; m. Susan Lynn Howard, June 19, 1971; children: Aimee Tess, Marti Ann. BS, Harvey Mudd Coll., 1972; MS, U. Wash., 1974, PhD, 1978; DSc (hon.), U. Colo., 2000; LHD (hon.), Towson U., 2001. Astronaut NASA, Houston, 1978-89; mission specialist Space Shuttle flight, 1984, 86, 88; assoc. vice provost for rsch., assoc. prof. astronomy U. Wash., Seattle, 1989-96; dir. project 2061 AAAS, Washington, 1996—2000; dir. sci., math., and tech. edn. Western Wash. U., Bellingham, 2002—. Adj. assoc. prof. edn. U. Wash., 1989-96. Recipient Haley Space Flight award AIAA, 1989. Unitarian Universalist. Avocations: reading, athletics, guitar. Office: SMATE Western Wash Univ 516 High St Bellingham WA 98225-9155 Office Phone: 360-650-3637. Business E-Mail: george.nelson@wwu.edu.

NELSON, GERALDA, language educator; b. Jan. 4, 1960; MEd, Ga. Southwestern, Americus, 2003; DEd, Ga. Southern, Statesboro, 2007. Tchr. Sumter County Sch., Americus, Ga., Marion County Sch., Buena Vista, Ga., ESL coord.; project coord. Habitat for Humanity, Brazil, Nicaragua, Philippines. Bd. mem. Ct. Appointed Spl. Advocate. Mem.: Profl. Assn. Ga. Educators.

NELSON, GLEN DAVID, health products executive, physician; b. Mpls., Mar. 28, 1937; s. Ralph and Edna S. Nelson; m. Marilyn Carlson, June 30, 1961; children: Diana, Curtis, Wendy. BA, Harvard U., Cambridge, Mass., 1959; MD, U. Minn., 1963. Diplomate Am. Bd. Surgery, also sub-bd. bariatric and peripheral vascular surgery; cert. Am. Bd. Surgery, 1970. Intern Hennepin County Gen. Hosp., Mpls., 1963—64, resident in gen. surgery, 1964—69; staff surgeon Park Nicollet Med. Ctr. (formerly St. Louis Park Med. Ctr.), Mpls.; practiced surgery, 1969—86; chmn., pres. and CEO Park Nicollet Med. Ctr., 1975—86; chmn. and CEO Am. MedCenters, Inc., 1984—86; dir. Medtronic, Inc., 1980—2002, exec. v.p., 1986—88, vice chmn., 1988—2002; chmn., prin. owner GDN Holdings, LLC, Minnetonka, Minn., 2002—. Bd. dirs. Am.Carlson Cos., Inc., Advanced BioSurfaces, Inc., Cardiovascular Systems, Inc., Carlson Holdings, Inc., DexCom, Inc., Evera Med., Inc., Guided Delivery Sys., Inc., Harvard U. Com. on Sci.-Allston, Johns Hopkins Medicine Bd. of Advisors, Inspire Med. Sys., LLC, MinuteClinic, Inc. (wholly owned subs. CVS Pharmacy), chmn.; bd. dirs., trustee and chmn. Am. Pub. Media/Minn. Pub. Radio; sr. advisor CVS Pharmacy, Perth Corp., Red-Brick Health, Regent Aviation, chmn., Reliant Technologies, Inc., Stemedica Cell Technologies, Inc., Travelers Cos., Inc.; emeritus clin. prof. surgery, U. Minn. Trustee Am. Pub. Media/Minn. Pub. Radio, chmn.

NELSON, GORDON LEIGH, chemist, educator; b. Palo Alto, Calif., May 27, 1943; s. Nels Folke and Alice Virginia (Fredrickson) N. BS in Chemistry, U. Nev., 1965; MS, Yale U., 1967, PhD, 1970; DSc (hon.), William Carey Coll., 1988. Staff research chemist corp. research and devel. Gen. Electric Co., Schenectady, NY, 1970-74, mgr. combustibility tech. plastics div. Pittsfield, Mass., 1974-79, mgr. environ. protection plastics div., 1979-82; v.p. materials sci. and tech. Springborn Labs. Inc., Enfield, Conn., 1982-83; prof., chmn. dept. polymer sci. U. So. Miss., Hattiesburg, 1983-89; dean Coll. Sci. and Liberal Arts, prof. chemistry Fla. Inst. Tech., Melbourne, 1989—, mem. coun. sci., soc. pres., sec., 1989-90, chair-elect, 1991, chair, 1992. Cons. in field. Author: Carbon-13 Nuclear Magnetic Resonance for Organic Chemists, 1972, Carbon-13 Nuclear Magnetic Resonance for Organic Chemists, 2d edit., 1980; co-author: Polymeric Materials-Chemistry for the Future, 1989, Carbon Monoxide and Human Lethality, 1993; editor: Fire and Polymers-Materials and Tests for Hazard Prevention, 1990, 1995; co-editor: Fire and Polymers-Materials and Solutions for Hazard Prevention, 2001, Fire and Polymer IVs-Materials and Solutions for Hazard Prevention, 2005, editor books on coating sci. tech.; contbr. articles to profl. jours. Mem.: ASTM (E5 cert. of appreciation 1985, D1 1997), Soc. Advancement of Scandinavian Study, Coun. Colls Arts and Scis., Soc. Plastics Industry (structural plastics divsn., Man of Yr. 1979), Internat. Electrotech. Commn. (U.S. tech. adv. group on info. processing equipment), So. Soc. for Coatings Tech., Ctr. Sci. Tech. and the Media (bd. dir. 1991—94), Info. Tech. Industry Coun. (chmn. plastics task group), Am. Chem. Soc. (bd. dirs. 1977—85, 1987—89, pres. 1988, bd. dirs. 1992—94, 1st Nelson award Orlando sect. 1996, Charles Holmes Herty medal Ga. sect. 1998), Am. Inst. Chemists, Nev. Hist. Soc., Yale Chemists Assn. (pres. 1981—), Sigma Xi. Republican. Presbyterian. Avocations: travel, western U.S. history. Office: Fla Inst Tech Coll Sci & Liberal Arts 150 W University Blvd Melbourne FL 32901-6975 Office Phone: 321-674-7260.

NELSON, GRANT STEEL, law educator; b. Mitchell, SD, Apr. 18, 1939; s. Howard Steel and Clara Marie (Winandy) N.; m. Judith Ann Haugen, Sept. 22, 1962; children: Mary Elizabeth, Rebekah Anne, John Adam. BA magna cum laude, U. Minn., 1960; JD cum laude, 1963. Bar: Minn. 1963, Mo. 1971. Assoc. Faegre & Benson, Mpls., 1963-67; mem. law faculty U. Mo., Columbia, 1967-91, assoc. prof., 1970-72, prof., 1972-91, Enoch H. Crowder prof. law, 1974-91; prof. UCLA, 1991—2007; William H. Rehnquist prof. law Pepperdine U., Malibu, Calif., 2007—. Bd. legal advisors Gt. Plains Legal Found., 1978-85; vis. asst. prof. U. Mich., Ann Arbor, 1969-70, Brigham Young U., Provo, Utah, 1976; vis. prof. U. Minn., Mpls., 1981-82, UCLA, 1989-90; disting. vis. prof. Pepperdine U., 1987-88, 2006; vis. endowed Campbell prof. U. Mo., Columbia, 1996-98; commr. Nat. Conf. Commrs. Uniform State Laws, 1983-91; adv. bd. West Pub. Law Sch Author: (with Van Hecke and Leavell) Cases and Materials on Equitable Remedies and Restitution, 1973; (with Whitman) Cases and Materials on Real Estate Finance and Development, 1976, Cases and Materials on Real Estate Transfer, Finance and Development, 1981, (with Osborne and Whitman) Real Estate Finance Law, 1979, (with Leavell and Love) Cases and Materials on Equitable Remedies and Restitution, 1980; (with Whitman) Land Transactions and Finance, 1983, 4th edit., 2004, Real Estate Finance Law, 1985, 4th edit., 2001, Cases and Materials on Real Estate Transfer, Finance and Development, 1987, 7th edit., 2006; (with Leavell, Love and Kovacic-Fleischer) Cases and Materials on Equitable Remedies, Restitution and Damages, 1986, 7th edit., 2005; (with Browder, Cunningham, Stoebuck and Whitman) Basic Property Law, 1989; (with Stoebuck and Whitman) Contemporary Property, 1996, rev. edit., 2002; co-reporter ALI Restatement of Property-Mortgages; contbr. articles to profl. jours. 1st lt. AUS, 1964-65. Recipient award for meritorious service and achievement U. Mo. Law Sch. Found., 1974, Disting. Faculty Svc. award U. Mo.-Columbia Alumni Assn., 1978, Disting. Faculty award, 1986, Disting. Non-Alumnus award, 1991, Rutter award UCLA Law Sch., 2000, Disting. Tchg. award UCLA Alumni Assn., 2002. Mem. Am. Law Inst., Assn. Am. Law Schs. (sect. chmn. 1976-77), Am. Coll. Real Estate Lawyers, Am. Coll. Mortgage Attys., Mo. Bar Assn. (vice chmn. property law com. 1974-75, chmn. 1975-77), Order of Coif, Phi Beta Kappa, Phi Delta Phi. Office: Pepperdine Sch Law 24255 Pacific Coast Hwy Malibu CA 90263 Office Phone: 310-506-4676. Business E-Mail: grant.nelson@pepperdine.edu.

NELSON, H. WAYNE, gerontologist, advocate; s. Hubert Wayne Nelson and Sandra Lynn Scott; m. Ela A. Alivio, Aug. 8, 2005; children: Cameron W., Sarah E. MA in History, Portland State U., 1980; MA in Humanities, Calif. State U., Dominguez Hills, 1982; MBA, City Coll., Bellevue, Wash., 1984; PhD, Oreg. State U., 1993. Asst. to Gov. Victor Atiyeh Gov.'s Office, Salem, Oreg., 1983—85; dep. state long-term care ombudsman Oreg. Office Long-Term Care Ombudsman, Salem, 1985—87, acting state ombudsman, 1987—89, dep. dir., 1987—98; assoc. prof. dept. health sci. Towson (Md.) U., 1998—. Cons. Nat. Citizen's Coalition Nursing Home Reform, Nat. Long-Term Care Ombudsman Resource Ctr., Washington, 1998—; cons, commd. report author Natonal Assn. State Ombudsman Programs, Washington, 2002—; cons., trainer numerous state aging programs; spkr. in field. Author: (book) Elder Advocacy: Essential Practice and Skills Across Settings, 2007; contbr. entries to encys., articles to profl. jours. Dep. comdr. 10th med. regiment Mil. Dept. Md., Pikesville Military Reservation, 2001—06; founder Balt. County Med. Emergency Volunteers, 2003—06. Decorated Oreg. N.G. Commendation medal Gov., Oreg. N.G. Meritorious Svc. medal, Oreg. N.G. Exceptional Svc. medal, Wash. Army N.G. Commendation medal Mil. Dept. Wash., Md. State Active Duty medal Mil. Dept. Md., Md. N.G. Meritorioius Svc. medal with Oak Leaf Cluster Gov.; recipient Iris award, Ky. Cabinet Human Resources; fellow, Nat. Inst. Aging, 1996. Fellow: Gerontol. Soc. Am. (life; chair elect fellowship com., social rsch. and pub. policy sect. 2002—06). Avocation: emergency public health service. Office: Towson U 8000 York Rd Towson MD 21252 Home Phone: 410-821-7843; Office Phone: 410-704-4845. Personal E-mail: wnelson@towson.edu.

NELSON, HAROLD E. (BUD NELSON), fire protection engineer; Grad., Ill. Inst. Tech. Registered profl. engr. Dir. accident and fire prevention divsn. GSA, 1958—75; sr. rsch. engr., group mgr. Nat. Inst. Stds. and Tech., 1975—92; with Hughes Assocs., Inc., 1992—2002. Contbr. articles to profl. publs. Recipient Gold Medal award, Commerce Dept., GSA, Stds. medal, Nat. Fire Protection Assn., 2005 Nat. Engring. award, Am. Assn. Engring. Socs., 2006. Fellow: Soc. Fire Protection Engrs. (former pres., Harold E. Nelson award 1987); mem.: Internat. Assn. Fire Safety Sci. (founding mem., Kawagoe Gold medal 1999). Home: 4217 Kings Mill Ln Annandale VA 22003-2033 *

NELSON, HERBERT LEROY, psychiatrist; b. Eddyville, Iowa, June 15, 1922; s. Albert and Bessie Mae (Durham) Nelson; m. Carol Lorayne Hofert, Dec. 23, 1943; children: Richard Kent, Vicki Lurae, Thadeus Leroy, Cylda Vermae. BA, U. Iowa, 1943, MD, 1946. Diplomate Am Bd Psychiatry and Neurology. Intern Univ Hosps. of U. Iowa, Iowa City, 1946-47; resident Brooke Army Med. Ctr, Fort Sam Houston, Tex., 1947-49, U.S. VA Hosp., Knoxville, Iowa, 1949-51, Oreg. State Hosp., Salem, 1951-52, clin. dir., 1952-63; asst. prof. psychiatry U. Iowa, Iowa City, 1963-66, assoc. prof., 1966-73, prof., 1973-84, prof. emeritus, 1984—; dir. Iowa Mental Health Authority, Iowa City, 1968-82; med. dir. Mideast Iowa Community Mental Health Ctr., Iowa City, 1969-84. Adj prof Tulane Univ, New Orleans, 1974—77. Co-author: 4 monographs; contbr. articles to profl jours. Served as capt MC US Army, 1947—49. Fellow: Am Psychiat Asn; mem.: AMA, Am Col Mental Health Adminrs, Am Asn Psychiat Adminrs, Johnson County Med Soc, Iowa Psychiat Soc (pres 1970—71, chmn subcom psychiat care 1973—77). Republican. Methodist. Avocations: gardening, fishing, woodworking, painting, travel. Home and Office: Melrose Meadows #1009 350 Dublin Dr Iowa City IA 52246 E-mail: hlnelson@mchsi.com.

NELSON, HOWARD JOSEPH, geographer, educator; b. Gowrie, Iowa, Jan. 12, 1919; s. Joseph A. and Hannah (Swanson) N.; m. Betty Marie Garlick, June 18, 1944; children: Linda Ann, James Allan. BA with high honors, Iowa State Tchrs. Coll., 1942; MA, U. Chgo., 1947, PhD, 1949. Mem. faculty UCLA, 1949—, prof. geography, 1963-86, prof. emeritus, 1986—, chmn. dept., 1966-71. Author: (with W.A.V. Clark) Los Angeles, The Metropolitan Experience, 1976, The Los Angeles Metropolis, 1983. Served with AUS, 1943-46. Mem. Assn. Am. Geographers (regional councillor 1968-71), Sigma Xi. Home: 3939 Walnut Ave #162 Carmichael CA 95608 Office: Univ Calif Dept Geography Los Angeles CA 90024

NELSON, IVORY VANCE, academic administrator; b. Curtis, La., June 11, 1934; s. Elijah H. and Mattie (White) N.; m. Patricia Robbins, Dec. 27, 1985; children: Cherlyn, Karyn, Eric Beatty, Kim Beatty. BS with distinction, Grambling U., La., 1959; PhD with distinction, U. Kans., Lawrence, 1963. Assoc. prof. chemistry So. U., Baton Rouge, 1963-67, head div. sci., 1966-68; prof. chemistry Prairie View A&M U., Tex., 1968-83, asst. acad. dean Tex., 1968-72, v.p. rsch. Tex., 1972-82, acting pres. Tex., 1982-83; exec. asst. Tex. A&M U. System, College Station, 1983-86; chancellor Alamo C.C. Dist., San Antonio, 1986-92; pres. Ctrl. Wash. U., Ellensburg, 1992-99, Lincoln U., Pa., 1999—. DuPont teaching fellow U. Kans., 1959; rsch. chemist Am. Oil Co., 1962; sr. rsch. chemist Union Carbide Co., 1969; vis. prof. U. Autonomous Guadalajara, Mex., 1966, Loyola U., 1967; Fulbright lectr., 1966; cons. evaluation coms. Oak Ridge Assoc. Univs., Tenn., NSF, Nat. Coun. for Accreditation Tchr. Edn., So. Assn. Colls. and Schs.; mem. regional policy coms. on minorities Western Interstate Com. on Higher Edn., 1986-88; mem. exec. com. Nat. Assn. State Univs. and Land Grant Colls., 1980-82. Contbr. articles to profl. jours. Bd. dirs. Target 90, Goals San Antonio, 1987-89, coun. of pres.NAIDA,(1993-96) Commn. on Student Learning, Wash., 1992—, United Way San Antonio, 1987-89, Alamo Area coun. Boy Scouts Am., 1987-89, San Antonio Symphony Soc., 1987-91, Key Bank of Wash.; mem. bd. dirs. assn. Western U., (1995—) mem. com. for jud. reform State of Tex., 1991; mem. edn. adv. bd. Tex. Rsch. Park, 1987-89; bd. givs. Am. Inst. for character Edn., Inc., 1988-91; mem. pres.'s bd. advisors on HBCUs, 2006-; mem. adv. com. Tex. Ho. of Reps., 1978; chmn. United Way Campaign Tex. A&M U. System, 1984, others. Staff sgt. USAF, 1951-55, Korea. T.H. Harris scholar Grambling State U., 1959; fellow Nat. Urban League, 1969; finalist Pulitzer for general non-fiction, 1992. Mem. AAAS, Am. Chem. Soc., Tex. Acad. Sci., NAACP, Phi Beta Kappa, Sigma Xi, Phi Lambda Upsilon, Beta Kappa Chi, Alpha Mu Gamma, Kappa Delta Pi, Sigma Pi Sigma, Omega Psi Phi, Sigma Pi Phi, Phi Kappa Phi. Avocations: fishing, photography, sports. Office: Lincoln U Office of Pres PO Box 179 Lincoln University PA 19352-0999 Office Phone: 484-365-8000. Business E-Mail: inelson@lincoln.edu.

NELSON, JACK LEE, education educator; b. Cheyenne, Wyo., Nov. 2, 1932; s. Myron Alfred and Mary Elizabeth (Baker) N.; m. Gwen Margret Names, Mar. 13, 1953; children: Barbara Louise Nelson Vollmer, Steven Lee. BA, U. Denver, 1954; MA, Calif. State U.-Los Angeles, 1958; Ed.D.,

U. So. Calif., 1961. Tchr. pub. schs., Riverside, Calif., 1956-58; instr. Calif. State U., Los Angeles, 1958-59, asst. prof., 1959-63; instr. Citrus Community Coll., Glendora, Calif., 1959-63; assoc. prof. SUNY, Buffalo, 1963-68, chmn. dept., 1966-68; prof. edn. Rutgers U., New Brunswick, NJ, 1968—, Disting. prof., 1975; dean, prof. Sch. Edn. San Jose (Calif.) State U., 1986-87. Chmn. dept. sci. and humanities edn. Rutgers U., 1972-75; vis. prof. Cambridge U., Eng., 1974, 75, 79, 80, 83, 84, 85; vis. scholar U. Calif., Berkeley, 1975-76, Stanford U., 1982-83, Western Australia Inst. Tech., 1985, U. Colo., 1989, U. Wash., 1993, U. Sydney, Australia, 1994-95, 2003, Edith Cowan U., Australia, 1997; cons. editor Random House Inc., McGraw-Hill Inc., Primis Pubs.; cons. author Scott, Foresman Publs.; mem. adv. coun. New World Dictionary; mem. San Diego County Supt. Com. on Tchr. Quality, 2000—. Author: (with J. Michaelis) Secondary Social Studies, 1980, (with V. Green) International Human Rights, 1980, (with Frank Besag) Foundations of Education, 1984, (with S. Palonsky and M. McCarthy) Critical Issues in Education, 1990, 6th edit., 2007; contbr. numerous articles to profl. jours.; editor: Social Sci. Rsch., 1964-68, Theory and Rsch. in Social Edn., 1982-85. Mem. exec. bd. ACLU, Middlesex County, NJ, 1968-83; mem. Erie County Dem. Com., 1967-68, NJ Gov.'s Task Force on Rehab. Edn. for Prisoners, 1970-74, Highland Park Bd. Edn., NJ, 1972-75, pres., 1974-75; mem. Highland Park Hist. Commn., 1980-86, NJ Rural Adv. Commn., 1992—, Carlsbad Sister Cities Commn., 2002-05, Carlsbad Sr. Citizen Commn., 2005—, vice chair 2006-07, chair, 2007-; mem. nat. panel Project Censored, 1976—. Commissioned 2d lt. US Army, 1954—55, Ft. Lee, Va., commissioned 2d lt. US Army, 1955—56, Ft. Hood, Tex., 1st lt. US Army, 1956, with Civil Affairs USAR, 1956—63, capt. USAR, 1959. Robert Taft Found. grantee Inst. in Govt., 1970, 86; Inst. for World Order grantee Rutgers U., 1973; Rutgers U. grantee; SUNY-Buffalo grantee, 1967-68; ACLU of N.J. grantee, 1972-73; U.S. Office Edn. grantee, 1967-68; N.J. Dept. Higher Edn. grantee, 1985-86 Mem. Am. Acad. Polit. and Social Sci., AAUP (editorial bd. 1977-80, rep. nat. council 1982-85, com. on acad. freedom and tenure 1983-86, com. on legis. affairs 1992-95, 96-99, exec. bd., state confs. 1996-98), Am. Ednl. Research Assn., Internat. Studies Assn., Nat. Council for Social Studies, Social Sci. Edn. Consortium (bd. dirs. 1983-85), Phi Delta Kappa Democrat. Home: 1360 Las Flores Dr Carlsbad CA 92008-1031 Office: Rutgers U Grad Sch Edn Rutgers U Grad Sch Edn New Brunswick NJ 08903 Business E-Mail: junelson@rci.rutgers.edu.

NELSON, JAMES ALONZO, radiologist, educator; b. Cherokee, Iowa, Oct. 20, 1938; s. Joe George and Ruth Geraldine (Jones) N.; m. Katherine Metcalf, July 16, 1966; children: John Metcalf, Julie Heaps. AB, Harvard U., 1961, MD, 1965. Asst. prof. radiology U. Calif., San Francisco, 1972-74; assoc. prof. U. Utah, Salt Lake City, 1974-79, prof., 1979-86, U. Wash., Seattle, 1986-2000, prof. emeritus, 2000—04; ptnr. Integra Ventures, Seattle, 2004. Dir. radiol. rsch. U. Calif./Ft. Miley VA Hosp., 1973—74, U. Utah, 1974—85, U. Wash., 1986—98; mem. bd. sci. advisors NeoVision, 1995—96, Oreg. Life Scis., 1995—; co-founder Circulation, Inc., 1996; mem. adv. panel on non-radioactive diagnostic agts. USP, 1984—96; mem. NIH RSN study sect., 1998—; RSN study sect., 1998—2004. Contbr. chpts. to books, articles to Am. Jour. Roentgenology, Radiology, Investigative Radiology, others. Capt. USAF, 1967-69. John Harvard scholar, 1957-61, James Picker Found. scholar, 1973-77; recipient Mallinckrodt prize Soc. Body Computerized Tomography, 1990, Roscoe Miller award Soc. Gastrointestinal Radiology, 1991. Fellow Am. Coll. Radiology (diplomate); mem. Radiol. Soc. N.Am., Assn. Univ. Radiology. Achievements include patents (with others) for Non-Surgical Peritoneal Lavage, Recursive Band-Pass Filter for Digital Angiography, for Unsharp Masking for Chest Films, Oral Hepatobiliary MRI Contrast Agent, non-surgical myocardial revascularization, magnetic gut motility monitor, k-edge brachy therapy enhancement, self-debriding catheter. Office: Integra Ventures 300 E Pine Seattle WA 98122 Home Phone: 206-523-4546; Office Phone: 206-832-1995. Business E-Mail: jalonzonel@comcast.net, nelson@integraventures.net.

NELSON, JAMES AUGUSTUS, II, real estate company executive, architect; b. Damrascotta, Maine, July 26, 1947; s. Robert Maynard and Margret Rebbeca (Harmision) Nelson; 1 child, Jennifer Alexandria. BArch, Columbia U., 1973, MBA, 1974. Resident v.p. Citibank, NYC, 1974-77; group v.p. Bank of Am., San Francisco, 1977-82; assoc. John Portman and Assocs., Atlanta, 1983-85; pres. J.A. Nelson and Assocs., LA, 1986-88; dir. real estate planning and devel. Universal Studios, LA, 1988-94; founder Mother Co., Hollywood, Calif., 1995. Master planner, Internat. Gateway of the Ams., San Yisedro, Calif. Author: Banker's Guide to Construction, 1978, Doing Business in Saudi Arabia, 1979. Chmn. Eco. Dev. Com., L.A. Conservancy-Broadway Iniative, Laurel Canyon Coalition, L.A.; bd. dirs. Laurel Canyon Assn., Hollywood Heritage, Hillside Fedn., L.A., Lookout Mountain Assocs., L.A.; developer Universal CityWalk Project. Recipient Innovative Design award for Universal CityWalk, Internat. Coun. Shopping Ctrs., 1994, best new home of yr. award Metro. Home, 1989, commendation and pres.'s award Hillside Fedn., 1989, 1992. Avocations: gardening, architecture. Office: Mother Co 8306 Grand View Dr Los Angeles CA 90046-1918 E-mail: motherco@aol.com.

NELSON, JAMES C, state supreme court justice; b. Moscow, Idaho, Feb. 20, 1944; m. Chari Werner; 2 children. BS, U. Idaho, 1966; JD cum laude, George Washington U., 1974. Fin. analyst SEC, Washington, 1970—73; pvt. practice Werner, Nelson and Epstein, Cut Bank, Mont., 1974—93; county atty. Glacier County, 1980—93; assoc. justice Mont. Supreme Ct., 1993—. Former mem. State Bd. Oil and Gas Conservation, also chmn.; former mem. State Gaming Adv. Counsel, Gov. Adv. Coun. on Corrections and Criminal Justice Policy; liaison to Commn. of Cts. of Ltd. Jurisdiction, mem. adv. com. Ct. Assessment Program. Former pres. Cut Bank Chamber of Commerce. First lieutenant US Army, 1966—69. Office: Supreme Ct PO Box 203004 Helena MT 59620 *

NELSON, JAMES CARMER, JR., writer, editor, advertising executive; b. Denver, Nov. 10, 1921; s. James Carmer and Helen (McClelland) N.; m. Mary-Armour Ransom, Sept. 9, 1950; children: James Carmer III, Marie-Louise Nelson Graves, Jeffrey Armour, Sophia McClelland (dec.), Rebecca McClelland Nelson Sylla. AB, Yale, 1943. Mktg. editor Bus. Week mag., NYC, 1946-48, illustration editor, 1948-52; freelance author Sonoma, Calif., 1952-57; copy chief Hoefer, Dieterich & Brown, Inc., San Francisco, 1957-59, v.p., creative dir., 1959-66, exec. v.p., 1966-76, pres., 1976-79, vice chmn., 1979-80; ptnr. John H. Hoefer & Assocs., 1972—82; vice chmn. Chiat/Day/Hoefer, 1980; pvt. advt. cons., 1980—87. Bd. dir. McKinney, Inc., Phila.; instr. Golden Gate Coll., San Francisco, 1958-59, Nat. Advt. Rev. Bd., 1971-75. Author: The Trouble With Gumballs, 1957, Great Cheap Wines: A Poorperson's Guide, 1977, Great Wines Under $5, 1983, Killing Dave Henderson, etc., 2007; contbr. articles and fiction to popular mags. Mem. Harold Brunn Soc. Med. Rsch., Mt. Zion Hosp., San Francisco; bd. assocs. Linus Pauling Inst. Sci. and Medicine, Palo Alto, Calif.; mem. Colony Found., New Haven; trustee Coro Found., 1965-75, Marin Art Complex; bd. mgrs. Marin County YMCA. Served with USNR, 1942-46. Mem. ASCAP. Clubs: Villa Taverna (San Francisco). Home: 649 Idylberry Rd San Rafael CA 94903-1231

NELSON, JIM, editor; b. Greenbelt, Md., Mar. 8, 1963; BA in American Studies, U. Notre Dame. Editor Harper's Mag., 1994—97; sr. editor GQ Mag., 1997—2002, co-exec. editor, 2002—03, editor-in-chief, 2003—. Former writer, producer CNN. Contbr. Nominee Am. Soc. Mag. Editors, 2003; recipient Feature Writing award, Nat. Mag. awards, Am. Soc. Mag. Editors, 2007. Office: GQ Mag 17th Fl 4 Times Square New York NY 10036 Office Phone: 212-286-5960. *

NELSON, JOELLE GRACE KENNEY, lawyer; b. Augusta, Maine, Dec. 4, 1973; d. Meylon Grant and Lois Marie Kenney; m. Christopher Caldwell Nelson, May 6, 2006; 1 child, Jocelyn Grace. BS, U. So. Maine, Portland, 1996; JD, South Tex. Coll. Law, Houston, 2000. Bar: Tex. 2001. Law clk. Justice Eric Andell First Dist. Ct. Appeals, State of Tex., Houston, 1999—2000; briefing atty. for Justice John S. Anderson 14th Dist. Ct. Appeals, State of Tex., Houston, 2000—01; med. malpractice assoc. McGehee & Pianelli, LLP, Houston, 2001—03; comml. litig. assoc. Johnson DeLuca Kennedy & Kurisky, P.C., Houston, 2003—. Author law seminar South Tex. Coll. Law, 2003, U. Houston Law Ctr., 2003; spkr. in field. Vol. Spl. Olympics, Houston, 1999—2006; participant bike tour Nat. Multiple Sclerosis Soc., Houston, 2005—06. Student advocacy scholar, South Tex. Coll. Law, 1998—2000. Mem.: Houston Young Lawyers Assn., Houston Bar Assn., Tex. Trial Lawyers Assn. (adv. 2001—06). Democrat. Rman Catholic. Avocations: marathon running, cycling, camping, travel. Office: Johnson DeLuca Kennedy & Kurisky PC 1221 Lamar St Ste 1000 Houston TX 77010 Home Phone: 832-265-6888; Office Phone: 713-652-2525. Office Fax: 713-652-5130. Business E-Mail: jnelson@jdkklaw.com.

NELSON, JOHN C., obstetrician, gynecologist; b. 1944; m. Linda Nelson; 8 children. MPH, U. Utah, 1993, MD. Diplomate Am. Bd. Ob-Gyn. Intern Providence Hosp., Portland, Oreg.; resident U. Utah Sch. of Medicine. Charter mem. Prospective Payment Assessment Commn.; dep. dir. Utah's Dept. of Health; leader govs. task force on child abuse and neglect, teenage pregnancy prevention. Com. mem. Utah Domestic Violence adv. com.; former bd. mem. Salt Lake City Boys and Girls Club. Served in US Army. Recipient Light of Learning award Utah State Office of Edn. Fellow Am. Coll. of Ob-Gyn.; mem. AMA (bd. trustees 1994-, sec-treas. 2002-04, pres-elect 2004, pres. 2004-05, immediate past pres. 2005-), Utah Med. Assn. (former pres.), Salt Lake County Med. Soc. (past pres.), Motion Picture Assn. Am. TV Parental Guidelines Monitoring Bd. Office: 370 9th Ave Ste 101 Salt Lake City UT 84103-3186 also: AMA 515 N State St Chicago IL 60610-4325

NELSON, JOHN HARRISON, mathematics educator; b. Lubbock, Tex., Apr. 3, 1954; s. Orval Earl and Nancy Ann Nelson. BS, U. Montevallo, Ala., 1983—85. Cert. tchr. Tex. State Bd., 1999. Chemistry tchr. Russellville HS, Ala., 1985—86; sci. tchr. Brandon Hall Sch., Atlanta, 1987—93; math./sci. tchr. Iola HS, Tex., 1994—. Sgt. US Army, 1972—75, Neu-Ulm, Germany. Recipient Sr. Elite, U. Montevallo, 1985. Avocations: tennis, coin collecting/numismatics, puzzles. Home: 502 Southwest Pky #902 College Station TX 77840 Office: Iola HS 7237 Fort Worth St Iola TX 77861 Home Phone: 832-878-7282. Personal E-mail: jnelson3454@hotmail.com. Business E-Mail: jnelson@iolaisd.net.

NELSON, JOHN HOWARD (JACK HOWARD NELSON), journalist; b. Talladega, Ala., Oct. 11, 1929; s. Howard Alonzo and Barbara Lena (O'Donnell) N.; m. Virginia Dare Dickinson, Aug. 4, 1951 (div. Nov. 1974); children: Karen Dare, John Michael, Steven Howard; m. Barbara Joan Matusow, Dec. 7, 1974. Student, Ga. State Coll., 1953—57. Reporter Biloxi (Miss.) Daily Herald, 1947-51, Atlanta Constitution, 1952-65; so. bur. chief L.A. Times, Atlanta, 1965-70, with Washington bur., 1970—, Washington bur. chief, 1975-96, chief Washington corr., 1996—2002. Author: (with Gene Roberts, Jr.) The Censors and the Schools, 1963, (with Jack Bass) The Orangeburg Massacre, 1970, (with R.J. Ostrow) The FBI and the Berrigans, 1972, Captive Voices, Shocken Books, 1974, Terror in the Night, 1993. With AUS, 1951-52. Recipient Pulitzer prize for local reporting under deadline pressure, 1960; Drew Pearson award for gen. excellence in investigative reporting, 1974; Nieman fellow Harvard U., 1961-62, Shorenstein fellow Harvard U., 2002. Mem. The Gridiron Club. Home: 4 Wynkoop Ct Bethesda MD 20817-5936

NELSON, JOHN WOOLARD, neurology educator, physician; b. Hagerstown, Ind., Mar. 9, 1928; s. John Hans and Marvel May (Woolard) N.; m. Nancy Louise Elam, July 21, 1966; 1 son, John Hancock. AB, Earlham Coll., 1950; MD, Ind. U., 1953. Diplomate Am. Bd. Psychiatry and Neurology. Instr. neurology U. Tenn. Coll. Medicine, 1959-61; asst. prof. neurology W. Va. U. Sch. Medicine, 1961-63; assoc. prof. neurology U. Tenn., 1963-66; assoc. prof. to prof. Med. Coll. Wis., Milw., 1966-72; clin. prof. neurology U. Minn., Duluth, 1972-73; prof., head dept. neurology U. Okla. Coll. of Medicine, Oklahoma City, 1973-88, prof. emeritus neurology, 1989—. Served with M.C. U.S. Army, 1955-56. Mem. Okla. County Med. Soc., Okla. Med. Soc., AMA, Am. Acad. Neurology, Am. Electroencephalographic Soc., Am. Med. Electroencephalographic Soc.

NELSON, JONATHAN M., finance capital executive; b. Providence, May 18, 1956; s. Eugene M. and Jane S. N.; m. Britt Anette Ansnars; m. Alexandra, Rebecca, Katja. AB, Brown U., 1977; MBA, Harvard U., 1983. Export mgr. Wellman, Inc., Boston, 1977-79, also bd. dirs.; pres. Longlife Co., Stockholm, 1979-83; v.p. NCC, Providence, 1983-88; co-chmn. Narragansett Capital, Inc., Providence, 1988; CEO Providence Equity Partners. Co-chmn., pres. Narragansett TV, Inc., Providence; co-chmn. bd. dirs. Born In Pub., Inc., Numerous Companion; mem. bd. dirs. Metro-Goldwyn-Mayer Inc., Warner Music Group, Yankees Entertainment and Sports Network, LLC; dir. Trinity Repertory Co. Bd. govs. Gordon Sch., East Providence, R.I., 1984; bd. trustees Brown U. Avocation: skiing. Office: Providence Equity Partners Inc 18th Floor 50 Kennedy Plaza Providence RI 02903 *

NELSON, JULIE LOFTUS, lawyer; b. Milw., Jan. 14, 1967; BA, U. Wis., Madison, 1996; JD cum laude, Hamline U., 2002. Bar: Minn. 2002, US Ct. Appeals (8th cir.) 2004, US Dist. Ct. (dist. Minn.) 2005. Jud. clk. to Judge R.A. Randall Minn. Ct. Appeals; jud. clk. to Judge P. Hunter Anderson Dist. Ct.; assoc. Frederic Bruno & Assocs., Mpls. Named a Rising Star, Minn. Super Lawyers mag., 2006. Mem.: Minn. Assn. Criminal Def. Attys., Minn. State Bar Assn. (sec. criminal law sect.). Office: Frederic Bruno & Assocs 5500 Wayzata Blvd Ste 1450 Minneapolis MN 55416 Office Phone: 763-545-7900. E-mail: julie@brunolaw.com. *

NELSON, K. BONITA, literary agent; b. Austin, Minn., July 5, 1945; d. Wallace Arthur and Opal Rebecca (Lastine) N. BA, Hunter Coll., 1969; B in laws, LaSalle U., 1982. Lit. agt. Am. Play Co., Inc., NYC, 1970-75; legal sec., reviewer Eastman & DaSilva, Esqs., NYC, 1975-79; founder, pres. BK Nelson Literary Agy., NYC, 1983—, BK Nelson Lect. Bureau, NYC, 1994—; pres., publ. Internat. Media Comm., Inc., 1998. Bd. dirs. Dynaray, N.Y.; founder BK Nelson, Inc., 1995; founder Literacy Inst. for Edn. (Life) Inc., 1996. Collaborator: Looking for Canterbury, 1994; author: My Literary Agent, 1998; co-prodr. (movies) Dancing Dan's Christmas, 2006, (musical) Packed Full of Miracles, 2006, Mem. Authors Guild (assoc.), NAFE (assoc.), Nat. Assn. Campus Activities (assoc.), AAUW, (assoc.), Dramatists Guild (assoc.), Minority and Woman Owned Businesses. Avocations: yoga, stamp collecting/philately, automobiles. Office: Bk Nelson Lecture Bureau 1565 Paseo Vida Palm Springs CA 92264-9508 Office Phone: 760-778-8800. E-mail: bknelson4@cs.com.

NELSON, KATHY, broadcast executive; Sr. v.p., gen. mgr. MCA Records Inc.; pres. film music The Walt Disney Motion Picture Group, 1996—2001, Universal Music Group & Universal Pictures, 2001—. Bd. dir. Women in Film. Named one of 100 Most Powerful Women in Entertainment, Hollywood Reporter, 2006. Office: Universal Music Group 1755 Broadway New York NY 10019 *

NELSON, KEITH A., federal agency administrator; BA, U. Tex.; MA, U. Calif. Berkeley; MBA, U. Calif. LA. Sports journalist Dallas Morning News, Tyler Morning Telegraph; sr. mgr. bus. devel. Dow Jones & Co.; with US Dept. Labor, Washington, 2000—05, acting dep. chief info. officer, 2003—04, assoc. dep. sec. mgmt., 2004—05; asst. sec. adminstrn. US Dept. Housing & Urban Devel., 2005—. Office: HUD 451 7th St SW Washington DC 20410 Office Phone: 202-710-1112.

NELSON, KEVIN, statistician; b. NYC, Dec. 29, 1964; s. Phillip Jacob and Lucie Anne Nelson. BA, U. Chgo., 1987; MA, Wesleyan U., Middletown, Conn., 1991; MPH, U. Ala., Birmingham, 1993; PhD, Med. U. SC., Charleston, 1998. Maternal and child health epidemio Mich. Dept. Pub. Health, Lansing, 2005—06; pub. health analyst US Health Resources and Svcs. Adminstrn., Rockville, Md., 2006—. Functional analyst Lockhead-Martin, Alexandria, Va., 2003. Fellow, Nat. Heart, Lung, and Blood Inst., 1998—2000, Nat. Cancer Inst., 2000—01. Mem.: Am. Statis. Assn. (assoc.), Mu Sigma Rho (assoc.). Home: 3205 Weeping Willow Ct Apt 43 Silver Spring MD 20900 Office: Health Resources and Services Administra 5600 Fishers Ln Rockville MD Home Phone: 301-460-4837. Personal E-mail: knelson@hrsa.gov.

NELSON, KIMBERLY TERESE, computer software company executive, former federal agency administrator; b. Phila., 1956; B, Shippensburg U.; M, U. Pa. Spl. asst. to sec., spl. asst. to deputy sec. adminstrn., spl. asst. deputy sec. field ops. Pa. Dept. Environ. Resources, 1987—95; dir. program integration and effectiveness then chief info. officer Pa. Dept. Environ. Protection, 1999—2001; asst. adminstr. for environ. info. EPA, Washington, 2001—05; exec. dir. e-govt. Microsoft Corp., Redmond, Wash., 2006—. Office: Microsoft Corp 1 Microsoft Way Redmond WA 98052

NELSON, KRISTIN SCHAD, cosmetic surgeon; b. Ashland, Wis., Jan. 3, 1968; d. John Edward Schad and Lynda Jean Zeise; m. Brent David Nelson, June 23, 2002; 1 child, Lake Mattias. BS in Engring. Mechanics, U. Wis., 1990; MS in Engring., U. Ala., 1992; DO, Kirksville Coll. Osteo. Medicine, 1999. Diplomate Kirksville Coll. Osteo. Medicine, 1999. Resident Northeast Regional Med. Ctr., Kirksville, Mo., 1999—2004; cosmetic surgeon Scottsdale, Ariz., 2005—06; cosmetic surgeon, pres. Zen Surgical Aesthetics, Boise, 2006—. Supv. physician free health clinic Golden Gate Cmty. Ctr., Phoenix, 2004—05; vol. physician Kirksville Coll. Osteo. Medicine, Belize, 2000—03. Fellow, The Body Sculpting Ctr., Scottsdale, 2004—05. Mem.: AMA, Am. Osteo. Assn., Am. Acad. Otolaryngology, Am. Osteo. Coll. Ophthalmology and Otolaryngology, Am. Acad. Cosmetic Surgery. Avocations: travel, yoga, hiking, bicycling, running. Office: Zen Surg Aesthetics 6077 N Eagle Rd Boise ID 83713 Office Phone: 208-939-2949.

NELSON, LARRY A., statistics educator, consultant; b. Omaha, Oct. 28, 1932; s. Rudolph Lawrence and Elizabeth Coleman (Lewis) N. BS in Agronomy, Iowa State U., 1954; MS in Soil Sci., Tex. A&M U., 1958; PhD in Soil Sci.-Stats., N.C. State U., 1961. Soil scientist Iowa Agrl. Exptl. Sta., Ames, 1954-55; soils instr. Tex. A&I Coll., Kingsville, 1955; rsch. soil scientist Tex. A&M Rsch. Found., College Station, 1956; soils lab. instr. Tex. A&M U., College Station, 1956-58; rsch. asst. N.C. State U., Raleigh, 1959-61; asst. specialist in land classification Land Study Bur., U. Hawaii, Honolulu, 1961-64; asst. prof. exptl. stats. N.C. State U., Raleigh, 1964-66, assoc. prof. exptl. stats., 1966-71, prof. stats., 1971-89, prof. emeritus stats., 1989—, coord. Concade Project (Bolivia), 1999—2003, interim coord. internat. programs Coll. Agr. and Life Scis., 2002—03, asst. dean for internat. programs Coll. Agr. and Life Scis., 2003—07. Spl. advisor head dep. stats. Kasetsart U., Bangkok, Thailand, 1973; evaluator quantitative skills IADS, Bangladesh, 1984; mem. rev. team Ctr. for Agrl. Econs. and Ctr. for Data Processing, Winrock Internat., Indonesia, 1985; statis. cons. PROCAFE, El Salvador, 1993-96, ICRAF, Nairobi, Kenya, 1991-95; cons. Potash and Phosphate Inst. Can., China and India, 1990, 94, 96; ptnr. Statis. Rsch. Assocs., Honolulu, 1962-63; bd. dirs. Meadowlands Environ. Rsch. Inst., NJ, 2005-; lectr., tchr., cons. in field Assoc. editor Geoderma, 1976-84, Agronomy Jour., 1981-87; contbr. numerous articles to profl. publs. Mem. bd. NC-Bolivia Ptnrs. of Ams., 2007—. NATO fellow Data Analysis Lab., Lyngby, Denmark, 1978. Fellow AAAS, Am. Statis. Assn. (mem. biometrics sect. com. 1989-90, mem. com. on internat. rels. in stats. 1996-98), Am. Soc. Agronomy, Soil Sci. Soc. Am.; mem. Statis. Assn. Thailand (life), Internat. Biometric Soc. (bus. mgr. and treas. 1969-79, awards com. 1987-94, chmn. 1990-93, com. on edn. 1997-99), Internat. Statis. Inst., Sigma Xi, Gamma Sigma Delta (internat. pres. 1984-86, award of merit 1973-74, rep. to AAAS 1978-86), Phi Kappa Phi, Sigma Iota Rho. Baptist. Avocations: music, genealogy, diving, bicycling, travel. Home: 2816 Wycliff Rd Raleigh NC 27607-3035 Office: NC State U Coll of Agrl and Life Sci Office Internat Programs PO Box 7608 Raleigh NC 27695-7608 Office Phone: 919-515-2665. Personal E-mail: lnelson460@worldnet.att.net. Business E-Mail: larry_nelson@ncsu.edu.

NELSON, LARRY DEAN, telecommunications and computer systems company executive, consultant; b. Newton, Kans., Aug. 5, 1937; s. Carl Aaron and Leta V. (Van Eaton) N.; m. Linda Hawkins, June 2, 1972. BA, Phillips U., 1959; MS, Kans. State U., 1962; PhD, Ohio State U., 1965. From rsch. asst. to rsch. assoc. Rsch. Found., Ohio State U., Columbus, 1962—65; mathematician II Batelle Meml. Inst., Columbus, 1962—65; from mem. tech. staff to supr. math. dept., data sys. devel. Bellcomm, Inc., Washington, 1965—72; supr. mgmt. info. sys. dept. Bell Telephone Labs., Murray Hill, NJ, 1972—77; supr. rate and tariff planning divsn. AT&T, NYC, 1977—79; dep. adminstr. rsch. and spl. programs adminstrn. U.S. Dept. Transp., Washington, 1979—81; pres. MCS, Inc., Washington, 1981—; supr. govt. comm. ctr. AT&T Bell Labs., 1985—89; mgr. govt. mktg. AT&T Network Sys., 1989—90, supr. secure info. sys. engring., 1990—94, disting. mem. tech. staff, secure sys. engring., 1995—96; tech. cons. AT&T Labs, Info. Security Ctr., AT&T, 1996—98; prin. network security engr., cons. mem. tech. staff Lucent Tech. Integrated Solutions Inc., 2003—, v.p. sys. engring. and integration, 2004—. Cons. Contel Info. Sys., Denver, 1982-85, Martin Marietta Corp., Denver, 1982-85; mem. info. assurance task force, info infrastructure group, intrusion detection task force, cybercrime subgroup Nat. Security Telecomms. Adv. Com. Contbr. articles to profl. jours. Organizer, sponsor Odd Jobs Club, Washington, 1967-72; pres. Mountain County Condominiums Assn., Dillon, Colo., 1975-83, 85—; treas. Chris' Landing Condominium Assn., 1986-90; del. or rep. to numerous confs. Mem. ABA (assoc., info. security com. 1991-99), Am. Nat. Stds. Inst. (info. tech. security tech. stds. com. 1997-2001, internat. rep. tech. com. on info. tech. security mgmt.), IEEE (sec. D.C. sect. 1982, cert. appreciation 1968), Sys., Man and Cybernetics Soc. (sec. 1981, v.p. 1982-83), Math. Programming Soc, Am. Math Soc., N.Y. Acad. Scis., Assn. Computing Machinery, Sigma Xi, Phi Kappa Phi, Pi Mu Epsilon Democrat. Mem. Disciples of Christ. Current work: information assurance, networks and network management, digital signature, public key infrastructure, and electronic commerce technology. Subspecialties: secure information technology systems and networks; systems engineering. Office: 5220 Pacific Concourse Dr Ste 200 Los Angeles CA 90045 Home Phone: 310-373-3176; Office Phone: 310-297-5436. Business E-Mail: ldnelson1@cox.net.

NELSON, LARRY GENE, professional golfer; b. Ft. Payne, Ala., Sept. 10, 1947; m. Gayle; 2 sons. Student, Kennesaw Jr. Coll. Profl. golfer, 1971—. Named to World Golf Hall of Fame, PGA Tour, 2006. Winter Jackie Gleason-Inverrary Classic, 1979, Western Open, 1979, Ryder Cup, 1979, 81, Atlanta Classic, 1980, U.S. PGA Championship, 1981, 87, Greensboro Open, 1981, U.S. Open, 1983; Sr. Tour wins include Fleet-Boston Classic, 2000, 2001, Foremost Insurance Championship, 2000, Bank One Sr. Championship, Vantage Championship, MasterCard Championship, 2001, Royal Caribbean Championship, Farmers Charity Classic,

SBC Championship, Constellation Energy Classic, 2003, Greater Hickory Classic, FedEx Kinko's Classic, 2004, Administaff Small Bus. Classic. Office: care PGA 100 Avenue Of Champions Palm Beach Gardens FL 33418-3653

NELSON, LAWRENCE EVAN, manufacturing executive, consultant; b. Chgo., Dec. 3, 1932; s. Evan Thomas and Elizabeth Marie (Stettka) N.; m. Jean H. Clayton, July 11, 1953; children: Lori Jean, Lawrence Evan. BS with honors, So. Ill. U., 1959; MBA, U. Chgo., 1969. CPA, Ill. Sr. acct. Price Waterhouse & Co., CPA's, Chgo., 1959-65; sec.-treas. Bradner Cen. Co., Chgo., 1965-73; pres. Protectoseal Co., Bensenville, Ill., 1973-84, Plan Ahead Inc., Palos Park, Ill., 1984—. Author: (book) Personal Financial Planning, 1985. Treas. City of Palos Heights, Ill., 1964-68, alderman, 1970-71; trustee Palos Heights FPD, 1977-1995. Served with USNR, 1952-56. Mem. Am. Inst. CPA's, Ill. Soc. CPA's. Office: Plan Ahead Inc PO Box 164 Palos Park IL 60464-0164 Office Phone: 708-448-8569.

NELSON, LEON, retired data processing professional; b. Arkadelphia, Ark., Aug. 17, 1947; s. Freeman and Jewellene Nelson. BA in Fine Arts, Henderson State U., Arkadelphia, 1969; BFA in Fine Art and Design, Sch. of the Art Inst., Chgo., 1994. Adminstrv. asst. to dir. rsch. Ency. Britannica, 1972—73; CRT operator, svc. order processor Ill. Bell Tel., 1973—77; data entry specialist Stivers Temporary Pers., 1979—80; supr. computerized TWX and data processsing rm. Katz Comm., 1980—83; data entry specialist Norrel Employment, 1983—86, Chgo. Housing Authority, 1987—96. Bd. dirs. Alumni Assn. of Sch. of Art Inst., 1994—98. Served with US Army, 1967. Mem.: ACLU. Baptist. Avocations: music, painting, drawing, desktop publishing, computer animation. Home: 354 Jones St Arkadelphia AR 71923 Personal E-mail: leonnelson@peoplepc.com.

NELSON, LINDA J., state legislator; b. Plentywood, Mont., June 12, 1942; m. Roger Nelson. Grad., Medicine Lake H.S. Farmer, rancher; mem. Mont. Ho. of Reps., 1989-94, Mont. Senate, Dist. 49, Helena, 1994—2004; mem. ethics com., mem. rules com., mem. fin. and claims com.; mem. agr., livestock and irrigation com.; mem. jt. appropriations subcom. natural resources/commerce; minority whip Mont. Senate, 1999—2002, dean of senate, 2003—04. Mem. Medicine Lake (Mont.) Sch. Bd., 1981-88, chair, 1984-88; active Mont. Dem. Party; dir. Nemont Tel. Coop.; bd. mem., chair Mont. Oil and Gas Conservation; mem. Mont. ELCA Synod Coun. Mem. N.E. Mont. Land and Mineral Owners Assn., Sheridan County Dem. Women. Democrat. Lutheran. Home: 469 Griffin Medicine Lake MT 59247-9708

NELSON, LIONEL M., otolaryngologist; BA Physics, CUNY Queens, 1965; MD, Yale U., 1969. Diplomate Am. Bd. Otolaryngology, 1974. Pvt. practice, otolaryngology-head and neck surgery Lionel M. Nelson, MD, San Jose, Calif., 1974—; clin. faculty Stanford U. Sch. Medicine, Calif., 1986—2004; co-founder and med. dir. Apneon, Inc., Cupertino, Calif., 2003—; med. advisor Gyrus ENT, Bartlett, Tenn., 2001—05; med. dir. Somnus Med. Technologies, Inc, Sunnyvale, Calif., 1998—2001. Guest lectr. Sleep apnea treatments. Contbr. articles to profl. jours. Col. USAR, 1984—2001. Recipient Outstanding Tchr. Recognition Award, Am. Acad. Family Practice, 1987—91; Jonas Salk Med. Rsch. Scholar, City of NY, 1965. Fellow: ACS, Am. Acad. Otolaryngology-Head and Neck Surgery; mem.: Soc. U.S. Flight Surgeons, Am. Acad. Sleep Medicine, Alpha Omega Alpha, Phi Beta Kappa. Achievements include patents for Airway Implants for Sleep Apnea Treatment; Radiofrequency surgical instrumentation; invention of Airway implants for sleep apnea; development of Surgical and radiofrequency devices. Office: 2505 Samaritan Dr Ste 510 San Jose CA 95124 Home Phone: 408-488-5217; Office Phone: 408-358-6163. Business E-Mail: lnelson580@aol.com.

NELSON, MARILYN CARLSON, hotel executive, travel company executive; b. Mpls. m. Glen Nelson; children: Diana, Curtis C., Wendy. Student, U. Sorbonne, Paris, Inst. Hautes Etudes Econ., Geneva; degree in internat. econs. with honors, Smith Coll., 1961; DBA (hon.), Johnson & Wales U.; DHL (hon.), Coll. St. Catherine, Gustavus Adolphus Coll. Securities analyst Paine Webber, Mpls.; pres., COO Carlson Cos., Inc., Mpls., 1998—2003, CEO, chmn., 1998—, also bd. dirs. Co-chair Carlson Holdings, Inc., 2000—; co-chair Carlson Wagonlit Travel, 1994-2003; disting. vis. prof. Johnson & Wales U.; bd. dirs. Exxonmobil Corp., Mayo Clinic Found., Com. to Encourage Corp. Philanthropy; chmn. Nat. Women's Bus. Coun., 2002-05; vice chair U.S. Travel and Tourism Adv. Bd.; bd. mem. Singapore Tourism Bur. Pres. United Way Mpls., campaign chair, 1984; bd. dirs. United Way Am., 1984-90, U.S. Nat. Tourism Orgn., 1996-98, Ctr. for Internat. Leadership, 1989-2003; mem. disting. adv. coun. Coll. of St. Catherine, 1991-94; hon. bd. dirs. Svenska Inst., Stockholm, 1993—; mem. adv. bd. Hubert H. Humphrey Inst. Pub. Affairs, 1992-96; co-founder Minn. Women's Econ. Roundtable, 1974—; chair Minn. Super Bowl Task Force, 1984-92; chair, founder Midsummer Internat. Festival of Music, 1992; co-chair New Sweden '88; past bd. dirs. Guthrie Theatre, Greater Mpls. Girl Scout Coun., Jr. Achievement, Jr. League Mpls., KTCA Pub. TV, Minn. Econ. Assn., Minn. Congl. Award, Minn. Opera Co., Women's' Assn. Minn. Symphony Orch.; trustee Smith Coll., Northampton, Mass., 1980-85, Macalester Coll., St. Paul, 1974-80; mem. adv. bd. Minn. Women's Yearbook; trustee Curtis L. Carlson Family Found. Named Sales Exec. of Yr., Sales and Mktg. Exec. Mpls., Woman of Yr., Minn. Exec. Women in Tourism, 1991—92, Outstanding Individual in Tourism, Minn. Office Tourism, 1992, Woman of Yr., Roundtable Women in Food Svc., 1995, #1 Most Powerful Women in Travel, Travel Agent Mag., 1997—2003, Businesswoman of World, Bus. Women's Network, 2001, Swedish Am. of Yr., King and Queen of Sweden, 2003, Minnesotan of Yr., Minn. Monthly mag., 2003, Businesswoman of Yr., US Commerce Dept. Small Bus. Adminstrn., 2005, Life Dir., Minn. Orchestra, 2006; named one of Exec. Yr. Corp. Report Minn., 1999, Forbes Richest Americans, 2006, Am.'s Best Leaders, US News and World Report, 2006; named to Hall of Fame, Sales and Mktg. Execs. Mpls., 2003; recipient Minn. Congl. award for initiative and svc. to cmty., Commendation cert., State of Minn., Cmty. Svc. award, YWCA, Independence award, Vinland Nat. Ctr., Cmty. Svc. award, Park-Nicollet Med. Ctr., Outstanding Mktg. Exec. of Yr. award, Minn. Distributive Edn. Club Am., Career Achievement award, Sales and Mktg. Execs. Mpls., Outstanding Achievement award, United Way Mpls., Extraordinary Leadership award, Greater Mpls. C. of C., Disting. Svc. award, United Way of Am., 1984—90, Nat. Caring award, Caring Inst., 1995, Outstanding Bus. Leader award, Northwood U., 1995, Disting. Svc. award (highest vol. honor), United Way Minn., 1998, Good Neighbor award, WCCO Radio, 1999, Caring Heart award, Larry King Cardiac Found., 1999, Svc. Above Self award, Rotary Club Downtown, Minn., 1999, Northwest Airlines Disting. World Traveler award, Hospitality Sales and Mktg. Assn. Internat., 2000, Responsible Capitalism award, FIRST mag., 2001, Glass Ceiling award, Minn. Women's Consortium, 2001, Great Swedish Heritage award, Swedish Coun. Am., 2002, Lifetime Achievement award, Internat. Investment Forum, 2002, Athena award, Athena Found., 2004, Lifetime Achievement award, Hospitality Sales and Mktg. Assn. Internat., 2004, 18th Ann. Lucia Travel award, 2005, Chevalier knight, French Legion Honor, 2006, Icon award, Nat. Bus. Travel Assn., 2006, Leadership award, Multicultural Devel. Ctr., 2006. Mem. World Econ. Forum, World Travel and Tourism Coun., Travel Industry Assn. Am. (bd. dirs.), Hennepin County Med. Soc. Aux., Bus. Roundtable, Smith Coll. Alumni Assn., Smith Club Mpls., Woodhill Country Club, Mpls. Club, N.W. Tennis Club, Nat. Ctr. Social Entrepreneurs, Com. of 200, Hospitality Sales and Mktg. Assn. Internat. (Lifetime Achievement award 2004), Minn. Orchestral Assn., Orphei Dranger, Alpha Kappa Psi. Office: Carlson Cos Inc 701 Carlson Pkwy Minnetonka MN 55305 Office Phone: 763-212-5000. *

NELSON, MARIO, physiatrist; b. Port-Au-Prince, Haiti, Mar. 4, 1954; arrived in US, 1981; s. Edner Nelson and Adeline Saint-Louis; m. Hildegarde Ledan, May 28, 1983; 1 child, Mario Emmanuel. MD, U. Haiti, 1978. Resident in surgery U. Haiti, 1981—85; resident in phys. rehab. NY Med. Coll., Valhalla, 1985, instr., 1986—87, asst. prof., 1987—95, assoc. prof., 1995—, assoc. dir. rehab. medicine dept., 1992—96. Contbr. articles to profl. jours., chpt. to book. Named Best Dr. in NY, NY Mag., 2006, Top Dr. in Westchester, Westchester Mag., 2005—06. Mem.: Am. Acad. Phys. Medicine and Rehab. (mem. health policy and legalizaiton com.). Home: 59 Westchester View Ln White Plains NY 10607

NELSON, MARK D., music educator, arts education administrator; b. NYC, June 4, 1954; s. Harry D. and Sylvia Allen Nelson. BA, Yale U., 1976; MusM, U. Ill., 1980; PhD, Princeton U., 1995. Asst. prof. music Lake Forest (Ill.) Coll., 1986—93; asst. prof., chmn. music dept. Wabash Coll., Crawfordsville, Ind., 1993—95; performing arts chmn., tchr. music, cultural history Hawken Upper Sch., Gates Mills, Ohio, 1998—2001, Ross Sch., East Hampton, NY, 2004—06, Webb Sch., Claremont, Calif., 2006—. Composer: Arboreal, 1985 (NJ Arts Coun. grant, 1985), Song Lines, 1998, 2d edit., 2006. Recipient William L. Dunn award for Outstanding Tchg. and Scholarly Promise., Lake Forest Coll., 1990. Mem.: Phi Kappa Phi, Soc. for Ethnomusicology, Coll. Music Soc., Phi Beta Kappa. Independent. Avocations: backpacking, photography, music of India and Java. Home and Office: Webb Schs 1175 W Baseline Rd Claremont CA 91711 Personal E-mail: mdnelson@wesleyan.edu.

NELSON, MARTHA JANE, editor; b. Pierre, SD, Aug. 13, 1952; d. Bernard Anton and Pauline Isabel (Noren) Nelson. BA, Barnard Coll., NYC, 1976. Mng. editor Signs: Jour. of Women in Culture, NYC, 1976—80; staff editor Ms. Mag., NYC, 1980—85; editor-in-chief Women's Sports and Fitness Mag., San Francisco, 1985—87; exec. editor Savvy, NYC, 1988—89, editor-in-chief, 1989—91; asst. mng. editor People, 1993; founding editor In Style Mag., NYC, 1993—2002, exec. prodr. TV program Celebrity Weddings, 1997—2002, exec. prodr. TV programs Celebrity Moms, Celebrity Homes, 2001; mng. editor People Mag., NYC, 2002—06; editor People Group Time Inc., NYC, 2006—. Editor: Women in the American City, 1980; editor: (cons. editor) Who Weekly, 1992; contbr. articles to profl. jours. Bd. dirs. Painting Space 122, NYC, 1982—85, 1995—96, Urban Athletic Assn., 1986, ACRIA, AIDS Comm. Rsch. Inst. Am., Am. Soc. Mag Editors, Accessories Coun., 1999—2001, Athletic and Swim Club, 2000—07, Actor's Fund, 2006—, Drama Dept., NYC Theatre Co.; adv. bd. NYU Grad. Sch., 2000—07. Named One of the Top 25 Most Influential People in Media, Brill's Content, 1999; named one of 100 Most Powerful Women, Forbes Mag., 2004—06; recipient Child Victimization in the News award, Nat. Ctr. for Missing and Exploited Children, 2003, Achiever award, Cosmetic Exec. Women, 2000, Inspiration award, Women's Step Up Network, 2004, Matrix award, NY Women in Comm., Inc., 2004. Mem.: NY Women in Comm., Women in Film, Am. Soc. Mag. Editors. Office: People Group Rockefeller Ctr 1271 Ave of the Americas New York NY 10020 *

NELSON, MARVIN DALE, JR., radiologist, educator; b. Hastings, Nebr., June 16, 1954; s. Marvin Dale Sr. and Patricia J. (Pingenot) N.; m. Mary C. Baron, Sep. 30, 1990; children: Kevin James, Andrew John. BS, MD, Loma Linda U., 1978; MBA, U. So. Calif., 1999. Diplomate Am. Bd. Radiology, Am. Bd. Daignostic Radiology, Am. Bd. Pediat. Radiology, Am. Bd. Neuroradiology. Intern, resident in radiology Loma Linda U. Med. Ctr., 1978-82; fellow in neuroradiology Nat. Hosp. for Nervous Disease, London, 1985-86, Rothschild Founds., Paris, 1986; fellow in pediat. neuroradiology Children's Mem. Hosp., Chgo., 1986-87; asst. prof. radiology Children's Hosp.-USC Sch. Med., 1987-93, assoc. prof., 1993-2001; chmn. dept. radiology Children' Hosp., LA, 1998—, prof., 2001—, John L. Gwinn prof. pediat. radiology, 2002—. Maj. USAF, 1982-85 Recipient Cornelius Dyke award for original rsch. Am. Soc. Radiology, 1990, Gabriel Wilson award for best paper Western Neuroradiol. Soc., 1997 Fellow Am. Coll. Radiology; mem. Am. Soc. Neurol. Radiology, Am. Soc. Pediat. Neuroradiology (pres. 2004-05), Western Neuroradiog. Soc. (pres. 2001). Office: Children's Hosp 4650 W Sunset Blvd Los Angeles CA 90027-6062 Office Phone: 323-361-4572. E-mail: mdnelson@chla.usc.edu.

NELSON, MARVIN RAY, retired life insurance company executive; b. Thornton, Iowa, Aug. 29, 1926; s. Clarence Anton and Rose Bessie (Nicolet) N.; m. Juanita Mae Brown, May 26, 1951; children: Nancy, Kenneth. BS, Drake U, 1951. Actuary Security Mut. Life Ins. Co., Lincoln, Nebr., 1951-58; assoc. actuary Life Ins. Co. N.Am., Phila., 1958-59; group actuary Bankers Life of Nebr., Lincoln, 1959-66; actuary Mut. Service Life Ins. Co., St. Paul, 1966-68; sr. v.p. Horace Mann Educators Corp., Springfield, Ill., 1968-77, Security Life of Denver, 1977-83, exec. v.p., 1988-91; pres., chief oper. officer, dir., mem. investment com. Midwestern United Life Ins. Co., Ft. Wayne, Ind., 1983-89; ret., 1991. Bd. dirs., treas. Ft. Wayne Urban League, 1983-87; bd. dirs. Taxpayers Research Assn., Ft. Wayne, 1984-88; pres. Shalom Pk. Men's Group, 2006-. With US Army, 1946—47. Fellow Soc. Actuaries; mem. Am. Acad. Actuaries, Pi Kappa Phi. Home: 5224 S Shalom Pk Cir Aurora CO 80015-2263

NELSON, MARY CARROLL, artist, writer; b. Bryan, Tex., Apr. 24, 1929; d. James Vincent and Mary Elizabeth (Langton) Carroll; m. Edwin Blakeley Nelson, June 27, 1950; children: Patricia Ann, Edwin Blakely. BA in Fine Arts, Barnard Coll., NYA, 1950; MA, U. N.Mex., Albuquerque, 1963. Juror Am. Artist Golden Anniversary Competition, 1987. Guest instr. continuing edn. U. N.Mex., 1991; conf. co-organizer Affirming Wholeness, The Art and Healing Experience, San Antonio, 1992, Artists of the Spirit Symposium, 1994. Exhibited in group shows at N.Mex. Mus., 1987, Art is for Healing, The Universal Link, San Antonio, 1992, Fuller Lodge Art Ctr. Los Alamos, N.Mex., 1993, Layering, Albuquerque, 1993, Crossings, Bradford, Mass., 1994, The Layered Perspective, Fayetteville, Ark., 1994, Tree of Life, San Miguel de Allende, Mex., 1996, (honoree Magnifico, Albuquerque, 1997, Bravos award Excellence in Arts 2004, Achievement award Masterworks, 2005), Guardian Spirits, Marlborough, Eng., 1997, Memories in Multi-Media, Columbus, Ohio, 1998, Agora Gallery, NYC, 1998, Celtic Connections, Mass., 1998, Bridging Time and Space, Calif., 1999, Musings on the Millennium, Ohio, 2000, Layerists in Multi-Media/Affirming Wholeness, Albuquerque, 2000, The Birth of Wisdom, N.M.and Gordes, France, 2000, Tides of Change, Tex., 2001, EarthSpirit, Ohio, 2001, Shadow & Light, Albuquerque, 2001, Landscape and Memory, Sedona, Ariz., 2002, dsg Gallery, Albuquerque, 2002, Albuquerque Mus., 2003, 07, Fire in the Heart, Ashland, Oreg., 2003, Layered Images, Albuquerque, 2003, Masterworks Miniatures, Albuquerque, 2004 (1st award Mixed Media, Juror Masterworks award 2005), 2006-07, Get the Lead Out, Los Alamos U., 2005, Weynich Gallery, Alburquerque, 2006, N.Mex. State U., Las Cruces, 2006, Soul Shrines, Las Cruces, 2006, Mus. Fine Arts, Las Cruces, 2006, Rock, Paper, Scissors, Los Alamos, N.Mex., 2006, Connections: We Are All One, Lexington, Ky., 2006, Art of Space, Las Cruces, 2006, Exploring Multiple Dimensions, Albuquerque, 2007; represented in pvt. collections; author: American Indian Biography Series, 1971-76, (with Robert E. Wood) Watercolor Workshop, 1974; (with Ramon Kelley) Ramon Kelley Paints Portraits and Figures, 1977, The Legendary Artists of Taos, 1980, (catalog) American Art in Peking, 1981, Masters of Western Art, 1982, Connecting, The Art of Beth Ames Swartz, 1984, Artists of the Spirit, 1994, Doris Steider, A Vision of Silence, 1997, Beyond Fear, A Toltec's Guide to Freedom and Joy, 1997, Layering, An Art of Time and Space, 1985, (catalog) Layering/Connecting, 1987; contbg. editor Am. Artist, 1976-91, Southwest Art, 1987-91; editor (video) Layering, 1990; arts corr. Albuquerque Jour., 1991-93; contbr. One Source Sacred Journeys, 1997, Lightstream, 2003; co-author: Bridging Time and Space, Essays on Layered Art, 1998, Toltec Prophecies of Don Miguel Ruiz, 2003; co-editor The Art of Layering: Making Connections, 2004, Crop Circles, An Art of Our Time, 2007. Mem. Albuquerque Arts Bd., 1984—88. Mem. Soc. Layerists in Multi-Media (founder 1982, coord. symposium 2007). Home: 1408 Georgia St NE Albuquerque NM 87110-6861 Personal E-mail: mcn50@comcast.net.

NELSON, MARY KATHRYN, bilingual counselor, small business owner, real estate agent, artist, insurance agent; b. Chgo., May 28, 1954; d. James C. Nelson and Leila R. Cooke. BS in Social Work, So. Ill. U., 1978; MS in Rehab. Counseling, U. Ariz., 1982. Cert. rehab. counselor, Ariz.; nat. cert. counselor; lic. real estate agt., Ariz., lic. ins. agent Allstate, Ariz., 2006. Bilingual counselor Ill. Migrant Council, 1975-76; social worker Child Protective Svcs., 1980-85; bilingual clinician pvt. nonprofit agys., 1985-96; bilingual counselor contractor, counselor Suprme Ct. Ariz., Phoenix, 1995—; owner, mgr. Bilingual Svcs., LLC, Phoenix, 1985—, owner Peoria, Ariz., 1994—; real estate agt. Liberty Properties, Inc., Ariz., 2003—05, Ken Meade Realty, Sun City, Ariz., 2005—06; bilingual agent Am. Farmer's Ins., Peoria, Ariz., 2006—, Weinstein-Fehris Realty, Scottsdale, Ariz., 2006—; agt. Assurant Ins. Co., 2006—; ins. agt. Mutual of Omaha, Ariz., 2007—; realtor Liberty Properties, Inc., 2007—. Exhibited in group shows at Franciscan Renewal Ctr., Scottsdale, 2001, exhibitions include Artareas.com, 2001—, Fountain Hills Ariz. Art Exhibit, 1995, Channel 22 Phoenix Cable Amateur Hr., Spanish Songs, 1996, Iberoamericana Internat. Art Exhibit, Miami, Fla., 1997, Phoenix K Lite Radio TV Commn., 1997, Peoria Sportscomplex Art Fair, Ariz., 1998, Franciscan Renewal Ctr. Art Fair, Scottsdale, Ariz., 1999, 2001, ArtAreas.com, portrait artist, Send. Kyle Ariz., 2007, Sen. McCain Ariz., 2007, Sen. Collins Ariz., 2007; performer: Talent Show at Crossroads, 1999—2001; singer: Franciscan Renewal Ctr., 2000—01. Vol. Big Bros.-Big Sisters, Tucson, 1999; family advocate Cesar Chavez Farmworkers Union Labor Movement; art donor Ariz. Foster Care Assn., Paradise Valley, Ariz., 2001, donor original oil painting with World Trade Ctr. motif, 2001; founder Morris Dee's Ctr. for Justice/Civil Rights Mtml. Ctr.; mem. So. Poverty Law Ctr.; vol. campaign worker Jon Kyle for Senator, Phoenix, 1996—2007; fundraiser John Shadeg for Congressman, Ariz., 2002, Women Reps. for Kyl, 1996—2006; choir mem. Franciscan Renewal Ctr., Paradise Valley, Ariz., 1999—2002. Recipient humanitarian award Inst. Arts Plastiques, 1997; named to Martin Luther King Meml. Wall of Tolerance, 2003. Mem. Drama Beat Acting Club. Republican. Avocations: singing, comedy, acting. Home: 12667 W Maya Way Peoria AZ 85383-2829 Home Phone: 623-478-9149. E-mail: marynelsonsc@aol.com.

NELSON, MATTHEW, graphics designer; b. 1979; BA Graphic Design, Keene State Coll., 2001; MBA Direct Mktg., Mercy Coll., 2005—. Graphic designer Staff Devel. for Educators, 2001—05, graphic & multimedia sr. designer, 2005—06, creative supervisor, 2006; graphics & website mgr. Mt. Sunapee Resorts, 2006—; designer & mktg. cons. Nelson Design Studios, 2003—. Named one of 40 Under 40, Advt. Age, 2007. Office: Nelson Design Studios 54 Sawmill Rd Hillsboro NH 03244 Office Phone: 603-325-2429. E-mail: mnelson@nelsondesignstudios.com. *

NELSON, MAURICE SANDY, JR., metal products company executive; BS in Indsl. Engring., Ga. Inst. Tech.; MS in Indsl. Engring., U. Tenn.; D (hon.), Marycrest Coll. Pres. aerospace and comml. div. Aluminum Co. of Am., 1987—92; pres., CEO, COO Inland Steel Co., 1992—96, Earle M. Jorgensen Co., Brea, Calif., 1997—. Chmn. adv. bd. Ga. Tech.; chmn. The Steel Svc. Ctr. Inst. Named Exec. of Yr., Metals Svc. Ctr. mag., 2001. Office: Earle M Jorgensen Co 10650 Alameda St Lynwood CA 90262-1754

NELSON, MERLIN EDWARD, retired management consultant, lawyer; b. Fargo, ND, Jan. 30, 1922; s. Theodore G. and Eva C. (Hultgren) Nelson; m. Nancy Ellen Craig, 1952 (div. June 1962); children: Craig Edward, Brian Anthony; m. Janet April Pope, Aug. 30, 1963; children: Claudia Jane, Rolf Merlin. BS in Polit. Sci., U. Oreg., 1943; postgrad., Fordham U., 1943-44; JD, Yale U., 1948. Bar: Oreg. 1948, N.Y. 1954, U.S. Dist. Ct. DC 1954. Atty. Office Gen. Counsel, ECA, Washington, Paris, 1949-52; assoc. Davis, Polk, Wardwell, Sunderland & Kiendl, 1952-59; exec. asst. to v.p. AMF, Inc., NYC, 1960-62; chmn., mng. dir. AMF Internat., Ltd., London, 1962-63; v.p., group exec. AMF, Inc., 1963-70, exec. v.p., vice chmn., dir., 1970-84; ret., 1984. Mem., chmn. Coun. Fgn. Rels.; nat. leadership coun. Trust for Pub. Land; bd. dirs. Mitsui Found., Mizuho Found., chmn. Decorated Purple Heart. Mem.: Phi Beta Kappa. Home and Office: 16 W 77th St Apt 12E New York NY 10024-5126 Office Phone: 212-579-0064. Personal E-mail: nelsonmj@earthlink.net.

NELSON, MICHAEL UNDERHILL, educational association administrator; b. Balt., May 5, 1932; s. Cyril Arthur and Elise (Macy) N.; m. Barbara Gail Hutchins, June 25, 1960; children: Kevin Underhill, Bronwyn Hastings, Gayle Hutchins, Corey Williams. AB, Rutgers U., 1957, EdM, 1968. Salesman J & N Distbg. Co., New Brunswick, NJ, 1957-59; extension assoc. Univ. Coll., Rutgers U., New Brunswick, 1959-61; asst. dir. summer session Rutgers U., 1961-68; asst. dean sch. continuing edn., dir. summer sch. Washington U., St. Louis, 1969-81, dir. div. of profl. and community programs sch. continuing edn., 1975-78; exec. sec. N.Am. Assn. Summer Sessions, 1979—; account exec. Trio Printing Co., 1982-84; sr. procedures analyst McDonnell Douglas Corp, St. Louis, 1984-96. Bd. dirs. Adult Edn. Council of Greater St. Louis, 1975-78. Served with USMC, 1951-54. Mem. North Ctrl. Conf. Summer Schs. (pres. 1974-75), Am. Assn. Univ. Adminstrs., Assn. Univ. Summer Sessions, Am. Summer Sessions Senate, N.Am. Assm. Summer Sessions (pres. 1978), Alpha Sigma Lambda, Phi Delta Kappa. Episcopalian. Home and Office: 43 Belanger Dr Dover NH 03820-4602 Home Phone: 603-740-9880; Office Phone: 603-740-9880. Personal E-mail: NAASS@aol.com.

NELSON, NORMAN DANIEL, government official; married; 2 children. BSBA, U. Fla., 1991; MBA, U. Miami, 1997; MA, Georgetown U., 2000. Intern corp. fin. divsn. mergers and acquisitions Commerzbank AG, Frankfurt, 1992; intern corp. fin. divsn. internat. leasing and new stock issues Deutsche Bank AG, Frankfurt, 1992; commd. 2d lt. disting. mil. grad. USAR, 1991, advanced through grades to maj., C.E. and Civil Affairs, 2007; econ. plans and program officer US Dept. State, 1997—2001, fgn. svc. officer, 2001; pres., CEO Nelson Systems Internat. Corp., 1998—2000. Decorated Army Commendation medal (3); recipient Meritorious Honor award U.S. Dept. State, 2003; Fed. Chancellor scholar Alexander-von-Humboldt Found., 1991-92. Mem. Sigma Chi. Personal E-mail: texas_florida@hotmail.com.

NELSON, PATRICIA L., lawyer; d. Charles Patrick McGerald and Inez Gallagher; m. Bruce Neil Nelson, May 29, 1980; 1 child, Adam. BA in Political Sci., U. Vt., 1980; JD magna cum laude, Suffolk U., 1999, cert. of distinction in intellectual property law. Bar: Mass. 1999. Rights mgr. Addison-Wesley Pub. Co., Reading, Mass., 1990—99; atty. Palmer & Dodge LLP, Boston, 1999—2001, Hill & Barlow, Boston, 2001—03, Fish & Richardson PC, Boston, 2003—. Trustee Arts/Boston, 2003—; vol. Lawyers for the Arts, Boston, 2002—. Named Super Lawyer Rising Star, Law & Politics/Boston Mag., 2005, 2006. Mem.: Licensing Execs. Soc., Copyright Soc. USA. Avocations: skiing, horseback riding. Office: Fish & Richardson PC 225 Franklin St Boston MA 02210-2809

NELSON, PAUL D., retired religious organization administrator; m. Elaine Nelson. Grad., Adelphi Coll. Joined Focus on the Family, 1985, exec. v.p., COO; pres. Evang. Coun. for Fin. Accountability, 1994—2006.

Mem. Nat. Panel on Nonprofit Sector, 2004. Named Exec. of Year, NonProfit Times, 1996. Office: Evang Coun for Fin Accountability Ste 130 440 W Jubal Early Dr Winchester VA 22601

NELSON, PHILIP EDWIN, food scientist, educator; b. Shelbyville, Ind., Nov. 12, 1934; s. Brainard R. and Alta E. (Pitts) N.; m. Sue Bayless, Dec. 27, 1955; children: Jennifer, Andrew, Bradley. BS, Purdue U., 1956, PhD, 1976. Plant mgr. Blue River Packing Co., Morristown, Ind., 1956-60; instr. Purdue U., West Lafayette, Ind., 1961-76, head dept. food sci., 1983—2003, Scholle chair prof., 2004—. Cons. PEN Cons., West Lafayette, 1974; chair Food Processors Inst., Washington, 1990-93; mem. adv. bd. USDA, 2002-06. Editor: Fruit Vegetable Juice Technology, 1980, Principles of Aseptic Processing and Packaging, 1992. Recipient Pers. Achievement award USDA, 1997, World Food Prize Laureate, 2007. Fellow Inst. Food Techs. (pres. 2001-02, Indsl. Achievement award 1976, Nicholas Appert award 1995, 49'er Svc. award 1995, Tanner lectr. 1999), Internat. Acad. Food Sci. and Tech. (USDA specialty crops com. 2005-07); mem. AAAS, Sigma Xi, Phi Tau Sigma (pres. 1976-77). Achievements include 11 U.S. and foreign patents. Office: Purdue U Dept Food Sci 745 Ag Mall Drive West Lafayette IN 47907-2009 E-mail: pen@purdue.edu.

NELSON, PHILIP FRANCIS, musicologist, consultant, conductor; b. Waseca, Minn., Feb. 17, 1928; s. Elmer Philip and Frances (Bretzke) Nelson; m. Georgia Ann Yelland, June 5, 1950; children: Curtis Ann, Philip Francis Jr. AB, Grinnell Coll., 1950; AM, U. N.C., 1956, PhD, 1958; Diplome (Fulbright scholar), U. Paris, 1957; student, Conservatoire Nat. de Paris, 1956-57; MA (hon.), Yale U., 1971; LHD (hon.), Grinnell Coll., 1981. Asst. prof. Ariz. State U., 1958-62, assoc. prof., 1962-63; prof., chmn. dept. music SUNY, Binghamton, 1963-70; prof., dean Sch. Music, Yale U., 1970-81; prof., provost, dean U. Calif., Santa Cruz, 1981-83; chmn. trustee com. Curtis Inst., 1982-83; sr. v.p. AED, NYC, 1984-87; v.p. Aspen Inst. Humanistic Studies, 1987-89; interim chancellor Sch. Arts U. N.C., 1989-90, interim vice chancellor Chapel Hill, 1991, chmn. grad. sch. adv. coun., 1993-96, cons. arts and humanities, 1996—; assoc. fellow Nat. Humanities Ctr., 1990-91; cons. edn., arts, 1992-93; interim dir. N.C. Sch. Sci. and Math., 1999-2000; sr. cons. U. N.C. and Nat. Humanities Ctr., 2000—; cons. Park Found., 2003—; trustee N.C. Sch. Arts, 2005—. Music critic Phoenix Gazette, 1959—62; music cons. Tallesin West, 1959—63; chmn. Nat. Screening Com. Fulbright Awards in Musicology, 1965—68; cons. Nat. Endowment Arts, 1984—90; vis. lectr. Duke U., 1992—. Contbg. editor: College and Adult Reading List, 1962, Nicolas Bernier, Principles of Composition, 1964, Recherches sur la musique Française classique, 1979, 1980; co-author: Groves Dictionary of Music, 6th edit.; editor: Aspen Inst. Humanities, 1987—89. Bd. dirs. various symphonies, chamber music socs., arts groups; trustee Curtis Inst. Music, Phila., 1980—83; bd. dirs. Conn. Hospice, 1983—87, Nat. Soc. Prevent Blindness, 1987—93, bd. dirs., v.p., 1987—93; mem. Chapel Hill Arts Ctr., 1992—, Triangle J. Coun. Govt., 1992—95; trustee N.C. Sch. Arts, 2005; mem. exec. com. Conn. State Golf Assn., 1975—81; founder Seven Springs Soc., 1975. Lt. comdr. USCGR, 1952—72. Found. grantee. Mem.: Soc. Ethnomusicology, Société Française de Musicologie, Coll. Music Soc. (nat. coun., editor jour. 1966—69), Internat. Musicol. Soc., Am. Musicol. Soc., U.S. Srs. Golf Assn., Chapel Hill Country Club, Finley Golf Club, Yale Golf Club, Carolina Club, Elizabethan Grads. Club, Yale Club (N.Y.C.), Mory's Club (New Haven). Home: 621 Greenwood Rd Chapel Hill NC 27514-5921 Office Phone: 919-968-6486. *Keep casting bread on the waters-it may come back as French toast.*

NELSON, PRINCE ROGERS **See PRINCE**

NELSON, RALPH ALFRED, physician; b. Mpls., June 19, 1927; s. Alfred W. and Lydia (Johnson) N.; m. Rosemary Pokela, Aug. 7, 1954; children: Edward Ancher, Audrey Anne, Elizabeth Marie, Andrew William, Evan Robert. BA, U. Minn., 1949, MD, 1953, PhD, 1961. Diplomate Am. Bd. Internal Medicine. Intern Cook County (Ill.) Hosp., 1953-54; resident U. Minn. Hosps., Mpls., 1954-55, U. Minn., Mpls., 1955-56; fellow in physiology Mayo Grad. Sch., Rochester, Minn., 1957-60, resident in internal medicine, 1976-78; practice medicine specializing in internal medicine and clin. nutrition Sioux Falls, SD, 1978-79, Urbana, Ill., 1979—. Bd. dirs. Scott Research Lab., Fairview Park Hosp., Cleve., 1962-67; assoc. in physiology Western Res. U., Cleve., 1962-67; asst. prof. physiology Mayo Grad. Sch., 1967-73, Mayo Med. Sch., 1973, assoc. prof. nutrition, 1974; cons. in nutrition Mayo Clinic, 1967-76; assoc. prof. medicine U. S.D. Sch. Medicine, Sioux Falls, 1978-79; prof. nutrition U. Ill. Coll. Medicine, Urbana-Champaign, 1986—2002, chmn. dept. medicine prof. nutritional sci., physiology, biophysics dept. food sci. Sch. Agr., 1979-2002, also prof. medicine, exec. head dept. internal medicine, 1989-2002, exec. head four sites of Coll. Medicine, 2002, emeritus prof. internal medicine, emeritus prof. nutritional scis.; dir. med.research Carle Found. Hosp., Urbana, 1979—; cons. nutritional support service Danville (Ill.) VA Hosp., 1980—. Co-author: The Mayo Clinic Renal Diet Cookbook, 1974; contbr. articles on nutrition, physiology, and hibernation to sci. jours.; editor: Geriatrics, 1980—2002, The Physician and Sportsmedicine, 1980-88, Am. Jour. Clin. Nutrition, 1980-83. Cons. in nutrition Nat. Cancer Inst., 1976; cons. in nutrition HEW, 1976, 79, 89, Nat. Heart and Lung Inst., 1976. Served with USAF, 1945-47. Fulbright scholar, Morocco, 1988. Fellow ACP; mem. Am. Physiol. Soc., Am. Inst. Nutrition, Am. Soc. Clin. Nutrition, Central Soc. Clin. Research, Am. Gastroent. Assn. Lutheran. Home: 2 Illini Cir Urbana IL 61801-5813 Office: Carle Found Hosp Dir Med Rsch 611 W Park St Urbana IL 61801-2529 Office Phone: 217-344-4676. Personal E-mail: ralph.nelson@carle.com.

NELSON, RALPH STANLEY, lawyer; b. Mpls., Mar. 15, 1943; s. Stanley L. and Louise M. Nelson; m. Judy E. Nelson, July 8, 1867; children: Sara C., Amy E., David A. BS in Bus. Adminstrn., U. Minn., 1966; JD with honors, Drake U., 1972. Bar: Minn. 1973, Wash. 1982, Tex. 1985, Ga. 2003. Assoc. Wiese and Cox, Ltd., Mpls., 1973-76; atty. Burlington No. R.R., St. Paul, 1976-81; sr. corp. counsel Burlington No. Inc., Seattle, 1981-85; v.p. law and adminstrn. Burlington Motor Carriers Inc., Ft. Worth, 1985-88, exec. v.p. and gen. counsel, 1988-93, sr. v.p., gen. counsel Daleville (Indpls.), Ind., 1993-96, Trism Inc., Kennesaw, Ga., 1996-2001, exec. v.p., gen. counsel, 2001—03; sr. v.p., gen. counsel Tango Transport Inc., Shreveport, La., 2003—. Mem. law rev. Drake U. Mem. Order of the Coif. Office: 6009 Financial Plz Shreveport LA 71129-2615 Office Phone: 318-683-6605. Personal E-mail: ralphnelso@yahoo.com.

NELSON, RAYMOND JOHN, language educator, dean; b. Waterbury, Conn., Sept. 5, 1938; s. Raymond John and Eileen (McGrath) N.; m. Claudine Eva Ligot, Aug. 20, 1972; children: Sylvie, Christopher. BA, U. Conn., 1965; MA, Stanford U., 1967, PhD, 1969. Prof. English U. Va., Charlottesville, 1969—, dean faculty arts and scis., 1989-97. Author: Van Wyck Brooks: A Writer's Life, 1981, Kenneth Patchen and American Mysticism, 1984 (Melville Cane award Poetry Soc. Am. 1984); also articles. With USCG, 1958-62. Woodrow Wilson fellow, 1965-66, fellow NEH, 1971-72. Mem. Colonnade Club (U. Va.), Phi Beta Kappa. Avocation: photography. Office: U Va Dept English 219 Bryan Hall Charlottesville VA 22903

NELSON, REGINALD (BOB) WENON, JR., minister; b. Troy, NC, Nov. 20, 1944; s. Reginald Wenon and Helen Lucile Nelson; m. Marie Staley Nelson, Mar. 20, 2005; m. Dianne Garner Nelson (dec.); children: Reginald Wenon III, Robert Monte. A in Applied Sci., Montgomery Tech. Inst., Troy; BS, United Wesleyan Coll., Allentown, Pa.; PhD, Am. Coll. Metaphys. Theology, Mpls. Cert. criminal justice officer NC, 1974, Eagle Springs, 1984. Min. Wesleyan Ch., Kearnersville, NC, 1963—68; police officer, sgt. Mt. Gilead, Troy Star, NC, 1970—80; behavior specialist criminal justice, Eagle Springs, NC, 1980—2002; sr. min. New Life Ministry, Inc., Troy, 1995—. Fireman Troy Fire Dept., 1970—91; behavior specialist criminal justice, Eagle Springs, NC, 1984—2002; cons. New Life Ministry, Inc., Troy, 1995—. Sp4 US Army, 1968—69, Vietnam. Decorated Bronze Star medal US Army, Vietnam, Combat Inf. badge, Air medal with 3 bronze stars. Mem.: Am. Coll. Metaphysical Theology. Independent. Avocations: target shooting, camping, travel.

NELSON, RICHARD ARTHUR, lawyer; b. Fosston, Minn., Apr. 8, 1947; BS in Math., with distinction, U. Minn., 1969, JD magna cum laude, 1974. Bar: Minn. 1974, U.S. Ct. Appeals (D.C. cir.) 1975, U.S. Dist. Ct. Minn. 1975. Law clk. U.S. Ct. Appeals (D.C. cir.), Washington, 1974-75; ptnr. Faegre and Benson, Mpls., 1975—, group head employee benefits group, 2002—. Seminar lectr. in employee benefits and labor laws, 1983—. Note and articles editor Minn. Law Rev., 1973-74. Active Dem.-Farmer-Labor Party State Cen. Com., Minn., 1976—, del. dist. and local coms. and convs., 1970—, state exec. com., 1990—; student rep. bd. regents U. Minn., Mpls., 1973-74; mem. IRS employee plans adv. couns., Mid-States Key Dist., 1996-2000, Ctrl. Mountains Region TE/GE, 2001-05, IRS Great Lakes Region TE/GE, 2006-; chair Mpls. Pension Coun., 1999-00; Minn. State Bd. Continuing Legal Edn., 2000-06, chair, 2005-06. With US Army, 1970—72. Mem. ABA, Minn. Bar Assn. (chair employee benefits sect. 1997-98), Order of Coif, Tau Beta Pi. Lutheran. Office: Faegre and Benson 90 S 7th St Ste 2200 Minneapolis MN 55402-3901 Office Phone: 612-766-7321. Business E-Mail: rnelson@faegre.com.

NELSON, RICHARD DAVID, lawyer; b. Chgo., Jan. 29, 1940; s. Irving E. and Dorothy (Apolsky) N.; m. Davida Distenfield, Dec. 17, 1960; children: Cheryl, Laurel. BS in Acctg., U. Ill., 1961, LLB, 1964. Bar: Ill. 1964. Ptnr. Defrees & Fiske Law Offices, Chgo., 1964-81; ptnr., counsel Heidrick & Struggles, Inc., Chgo., 1981—2001, chief fin. officer, 1981—97, chief adminstrv. officer, 1981—2001; pres. Galrk Sheridan, Inc., Highland Park, Ill., 2001—. Bd. dirs., exec. com. Heidrick & Struggles, Inc., Chgo., 1981-99. Pres. Jewish Cmty. Ctrs. of Chgo., 1987-89; chmn. Sign Graphics Task Force, Highland Park, Ill., 1986-88; mem. bus. and econ. devel. commn., Highland Park, 1993-96, 2000-, chmn. 2004-06, Ft. Sheridan Joint Plan Commn., 1997-2000. Mem. Ill. State Bar Assn., Chgo. Bar Assn., Standard Club, Northmoor Country Club. Office: Galrk Sheridan Inc 1896 Sheridan Rd Ste 200 Highland Park IL 60035-4635

NELSON, ROBERT EDDINGER, retired management consultant; b. Mentone, Ind., Mar. 2, 1928; s. Arthur Irven and Tural Cecile (Eddinger) N.; m. Carol J., Nov. 24, 1951; children: Janet K., Eric P. BA, Northwestern U., 1949; LHD, Iowa Wesleyan Coll., 1969, North Ctrl. Coll., 1987. Asst. dir. alumni rels. Northwestern U., Evanston, Ill., 1950-51; v.p., dir. pub. rels. Iowa Wesleyan Coll., Mt. Pleasant, 1955-58; vice chancellor for devel. U. Kansas City, 1959—61; v.p. instl. devel. Ill. Inst. Tech., Chgo., 1961-68; pres. Robert Johnston Corp., Oak Brook, Ill., 1968-69, Robert E. Nelson Assocs., Inc., Oak Brook, 1969—2004; ret., 2004. Bd. dirs. Chautauqua Workshop in Fund Raising and Instl. Relations, Continental Bank Oak Brook Terr., Sun Cos.; nat. conf. chmn. and program dir. Am. Coll. Pub. Relations Assn., 1961; trustee Iowa Wesleyan Coll., 1962-68, Have a Heart Found.; faculty mem. Ind. U. Workshops on Coll. and Univ. Devel., 1963-65, Lorretto Heights Summer Inst. for Fund Raising and Pub. Rels., 1964-68; pub. rev. panel for grants programs Lilly Endowment, Inc., 1975. Contbr. chpt. to Handbook of College and University Administration, 1970. With U.S. Army, 1951-54. Mem.: Chgo. Soc. Fundraising Execs., Nat. Small Bus. Assn., Nat. Soc. Fundraisers, Pub. Rels. Soc. Am., Coun. Fin. Aid to Edn. (bd. dirs. 1957—63), Union League, Internat. Club (Chgo.), Blue Key, Execs. Club, Club Internat., DuPage Club, Econ. Club, Masons, Delta Tau Delta. Methodist. Home: 5 Oakbrook Club Dr N101 Oak Brook IL 60523-1348

NELSON, ROBERT LOUIS, lawyer; b. Dover, NH, Aug. 10, 1931; s. Albert Louis and Alice (Rogers) N.; m. Rita Jean Hutchins, June 11, 1955; children: Karen, Robin Andrea. BA, Bates Coll., Lewiston, Maine, 1956; LLB, Georgetown U., 1959. Bar: D.C. 1960. With U.S. Commn. Civil Rights, 1958-63, AID, 1963-66; program sec. U.S. Mission to Brazil, 1965-66; exec. dir. Lawyers Com. Civil Rights Under Law, 1966-70; dep. campaign mgr. Muskie for Pres., 1970-72; v.p. Perpetual Corp., Houston, 1972-74; sr. v.p., gen. counsel Washington Star, 1974-76; pres. broadcast div. Washington Star Communications, Inc., 1976-77; asst. sec. of army U.S. Dept. Def., 1977-79; spl. advisor to chief N.G. Bur., Dept. Def., 1980-85; pres., dir. Mid-Md. Communications Corp., 1981-85; ptnr. Verner, Liipfert, Bernhard, McPherson and Hand, 1979-87; gen. counsel Paralyzed Vets. Am., 1988-99, sr. counsel, 2000—04; prin. Non-Profit Advisors, 2005—. Vice chmn. D.C. Redevel. Land Agy., 1976-77; bd. dirs. Friends of Nat. Zoo, 1975—89, pres., 1982-84; bd. dirs. Downtown Progress, 1976-77, Fed. City Coun., 1976-77, 83-87, Pennsylvania Ave. Devel. Corp., 1976-77, Cmty. Found. Greater Washington, 1977-78, Pep Direct, 2003-04, Friends of Perry's Eagle Island; trustee Wolfe's Neck Farm Found., 2001—. Served with AUS, 1953-54. Mem. Army Navy Club, Washington. Democrat. Episcopalian. Home (Summer): Robins Nest Orrs Island ME 04066 Home (Winter): 11 Zeitler Farm Rd Brunswick ME 04011 Office Fax: 207-725-8482. E-mail: nonprofitadvisors@msn.com.

NELSON, ROBERT LOUIS, education educator, consultant; b. Manitowoc, Wis., Sept. 14, 1927; s. Louis Robert and Germaine Emily (Moser) N.; m. Catherine Mary Wojtanowska, Oct. 2, 1948; children: Karen Marie, Christine Mary, Robert Stephen. B of Edn., U. Wis., Whitewater, 1959; MS, U. Wis., Madison, 1968; MA, Ohio State U., 1969; PhD, Mich. State U., 1974. Tchr., prin., adminstr. Bark River Elem. Sch., Nashotah, Wis., 1952-68; tchr. Ctrl. High Sch., West Allis, Wis., 1969-71, Hale High Sch., West Allis, Wis., 1972-77; lectr. Cardinal Stritch Coll., Milw., 1975-77, Milw. Area Tech. Coll., 1972-74; lectr., counselor U. Wis., LaCrosse, 1977-89; freelance speaker, cons. Manitowoc, Wis., 1990—. Cons., lectr. Luth. Hosp., LaCrosse, 1987-89. Author: Downhill to Uphill, 1980, Teaching Vocabulary in Sensible Ways, 1984; contbr. articles to profl. jours. Vol. guide Pinecrest Hist. Village, Manitowoc, 1990—; libr. asst. Manitowoc Pub. Libr., 1990—. With U.S. Army, 1945-46. Mich. State U. scholar, 1966, Calif. State U. scholar, 1967; Ohio State U. fellow, 1968-69. Mem. Internat. Reading Assn., Nat. Coun. Tchrs. English, Wis. Hist. Soc., Manitowoc County Hist. Soc., Retired Tchrs. Assn., Phi Delta Kappa. Avocations: travel, photography, model trains, walking, biking. Home: 1129 S 12th St Manitowoc WI 54220-5221

NELSON, ROGER HUGH, corporate financial executive, educator, consultant; b. Spring City, Utah, Mar. 7, 1931; s. Hugh Devere and Maudella Sarah (Larsen) N.; m. DeEtte Munk, Aug. 26, 1955 (dec. Sept. 1998); children: Steven R., Deanne, Mark L. BS, MS, U. Utah, 1953; Ed.D., Columbia U., 1958. Mem. faculty U. Utah Coll. Bus., 1953-97; mem. faculty Utah Mgmt. Inst., 1968-75; asst. dean U. Utah Coll. Bus., 1969-74, prof. mgmt., 1970-97, chmn. mgmt. dept., 1976-82, dir. programs in emerging bus., 1989-97, dir. MBA integrative field studies, 1993-96, prof. emeritus, 1997—; v.p. Computer Logic Corp., 1970-73; pres. Oil Resources, Inc., 1980-88, Puma Energy Corp., 1981-88, The Ultimate Choice Catalog Co., 1986—, David Eccles Sch. of Bus. Faculty, 1995-96; chmn. bd. Am. Recreation & Sports, 1996—. Fin. and mgmt. cons., 1965—; founder Utah Small Bus. Devel. Ctr., U. Utah, 1979; trustee Utah Tech. Fin. Corp., 1998-2003. Author: Personal Money Management, 1973, The Utah Entrepreneur's Guide, 1995, also articles, reports, manuals. Active local Am. Heart Assn., Am. Cancer Soc. campaigns; mem. exec. bd. Utah Opera Co., 1981-85, gen. bd., 1985-89. Danforth Teaching fellow, 1957 Mem. Acad. Mgmt., Adminstrv. Mgmt. Soc., NEA, AAUP, Phi Kappa Phi, Beta Gamma Sigma, Phi Delta Kappa, Delta Phi Epsilon. Inventor comml. color separation camera and related dye-transfer processes. Home: 2662 Skyline Dr Salt Lake City UT 84108-2855

NELSON, RON, composer, educator, conductor; b. Joliet, Ill., Dec. 14, 1929; s. Walter E. and Lois (Fulton) N.; m. Helen Mitchell, 1954 (dec. 1967); children: Marc W., Kristen R.; m. Michele Miller, 2004. Mus.B., Eastman Sch. Music, 1952, MusM, 1953, MusD, 1956; postgrad., L'École Normale, Normale, Paris, 1954-55; MA, Brown U., 1959; MusD (hon.), Oklahoma City U., 2006. Prof. Brown U., Providence, chmn. dept. music, 1963-73, Acuff chair of excellence in creative arts, 1991, prof. emeritus, 1993—. Film composer: HEW, Eastman Kodak, ARC, Columbia Pictures, commns. from, Cin. Symphony, Lima Symphony, Rochester Philharm., R.I. Philharm., Am. Bapt. Soc., U. Minn., Dartmouth Coll., Brown U., New Music Ensemble, LaSalle Coll., Western Mich. U., Classic Chorale, U.S. Air Force Band, Nat. Symphony Orch.; composer (for orch.) Savannah River Holiday, 1954, Sarabande: For Katherine in April, 1954, (opera) The Birthday of the Infanta, 1956; (cantata) The Christmas Story, 1958: (for orch.) Tocatta for Orchestra, 1963; (oratorio) What is Man?, 1964; (orch./wind ensemble) Rocky Point Holiday, 1968-69; This is the Orchestra; (orch. and tape trilogy) Trilogy: JFK-MLK-RFK, 1969; (choral) Prayer of Emperor of China, 1973; (choral) Thy Truth is Great, 1973; (choral) Psalm 95, 1974; (orch.) Five Pieces for Orchestra after Paintings by Andrew Wyeth, 1975; (choral) Prayer of St. Francis of Assisi, 1976; (orch.) Meditation and Dance for Orch., 1976; (choral) Six Pieces for Chamber Ensemble, 1977, Four Choral Pieces After the Seasons, 1978, Three Autumnal Sketches, 1979, Here We Come As in The Beginning, 1979, Mass in Honor of St. LaSalle, 1981, Three Nocturnal Pieces, 1982, Three Seasonal Reflections, 1982; composer: Fanfare for a Celebration, 1982; (choral) On Christmas Night, 1982; Medieval Suite, 1983; (choral) Dreams, 1982; (band) Fanfare for a Celebration, 1983; (cello-piano) And the Moon Rose Golden, 1983; (band) Medieval Suite, 1983; composer: Aspen Jubilee, 1984; (organ-brass) Pebble Beach Sojourn, 1984; (chorus-band) Te Deum Laudamus, 1985; (choral) Lost and Found, 1985, Light Years, 1985, Three Settings of the Moon, 1985, (strings-trumpet) Elegy, 1986, (brass) Brevard Fanfare, 1986, (chorus/band) Prime: The Hour of Sunrise, 1987, (choral) White, 1987, (choral) Another Spring, 1987, (choral) Miniatures from a Bestiary Parts I and II, 1988, (saxophone-band) Danza Capriccio, 1988, (choral) Three Pieces after Tennyson (1988), (choral) Three Mountain Ballads, 1989, (brass-winds-percussion) Fanfare for the Hour of Sunrise, 1989, (band) Morning Alleluias for the Winter Solstice, 1989, (band) Resonances, 1990; (chorus) And This Shall Be for Music, 1990, Invoking the Powers, 1991, Songs of Praise and Reconciliation, 1991, (band) Lauds: Praise High Day, 1992, To the Airborne, 1991, Passacaglia (Homage on B-A-C-H), 1992, Chaconne (In Memoriam), 1994, Sonoran Desert Holiday, 1994, (band), Epiphanies (Fanfares and Chorales bands), 1995, Courtly Airs and Dances, 1995, (orch.) Resonances II, 1996, (orch., band) Resonances III, 1996,(orch.) Panels (Epiphanies II), 1996, The Music of Ron Nelson, 1996, (euphonium and winds) Night Song, 1998, (band) Fanfare for the New Millennium, 1999, Proclaim This Day for Music, 2002, (choral) Let Us Find a Meadow, 2006, (band) Pastorale: Autumn Rune, 2006. Recipient ASCAP awards, 1962-20047, Found. award for World tour, 1965-66, Nat. Band Assn. award, 1992, John Philip Sousa medal of merit, 1994; Fulbright fellow, 1954; Ford Found. commn., 1962, NEA grantee, 1973, 76, 79; awarded Acuff Chair of Excellence on the Creative Arts, 1991; winner Am. Bandmasters Assn. Ostwald Contest, 1993, Am. Band Assn. contest, 1992, Sudler Internat. Wind Band Competition, 1993.

NELSON, RONALD L., travel services company executive, former film company executive; MBA, UCLA; B, U. Calif., Berkeley. Exec. v.p., CFO Paramount Comm. Inc. (formerly Gulf & Western Inc), 1987-94, bd. dirs., 1992; CFO, founding mem. DreamWorks SKG, Univeral City, Calif., 1994—2003; sr. exec. v.p. fin. Cendant Corp., NYC, 2003, CFO, 2003—06, pres., 2004—06; chmn., CEO Avis Budget Group, Parsippany, NJ, 2006—. Bd. dir. Advanced Tissue Scis., Inc., 1997, PHH Corp. Office: Avis Budget Group 6 Sylvan Way Parsippany NJ 07054 *

NELSON, ROY HUGH, JR., mediator, arbitrator, lawyer; b. St. Paul, May 13, 1955; s. Roy H. and Helen S. Nelson; m. MaryJean G. Froehlich, Aug. 13, 1994; children: Benjamin, Calla. BS, U. Wis., Milw., 1979, MS, 1985; JD, U. Wis., 1988. Bar: Wis. 1988, U.S. Dist. Ct. (ea. and we. dists.) Wis. 1988, U.S. Dist. Ct. (ea. dist.) Mich. 1991, U.S. Ct. Appeals (7th cir.) 1988, U.S. Ct. Appeals (fed. cir.) 1996, U.S. Supreme Ct. 1999. Police officer City of Brookfield, Wis., 1978-88; assoc. Borgelt, Powell, Peterson & Frauen, Milw., 1988-92; shareholder, dir. Petrie & Stocking SC, Milw., 1992—2003; pvt. practice, 2003—. Mem. Wis. Bar Assn., Wis. Assn. Mediators. Lutheran. Office Phone: 414-333-0364.

NELSON, ROY JAY, retired French educator; b. Pitts., July 27, 1929; s. Roy J. and Ruth Brown (Bainbridge) N.; m. Anita Lee Chandler, Aug. 16, 1954; children: Wendy Nelson Wilson, Barbara Nelson Videira. BA, U. Pitts., 1951; MA, Middlebury Coll., 1952; PhD, U. Ill., 1958. Instr. French, U. Mich., Ann Arbor, 1957-60, asst. prof., 1960-65, assoc. prof., 1965-72, prof., 1972-94, prof. emeritus, 1994—. Author: Péguy poète du sacré, 1960, Causality and Narrative in French Fiction from Zola to Robbe-Grillet, 1989; editor: 20e siècle: La Problématique du discours, 1986; contbr. articles to French Rev. Recipient Ruth Sinclair counseling award U. Mich., 1982, cert. for outstanding tchg., 1986; faculty tchg. award Amoco Found., 1992. Mem. MLA, Am. Assn. Tchrs. French Avocation: writing fiction. Office: U Mich Dept Romance Langs and Lits Ann Arbor MI 48109-1275 Personal E-mail: rnelson01@comcast.net.

NELSON, RUSSELL MARION, surgeon, educator; b. Salt Lake City, Sept. 9, 1924; s. Marion C. and Edna (Anderson) N.; m. Dantzel White, Aug. 31, 1945 (dec.); children: Marsha Nelson McKellar, Wendy Nelson Maxfield, Gloria Nelson Irion, Brenda Nelson Miles, Sylvia Nelson Webster, Emily Nelson Wittwer (dec.), Laurie Nelson Marsh, Rosalie Nelson Ringwood, Marjorie Nelson Helsten, Russell Marion Jr.; m. Wendy Lee Watson, April 6, 2006. BA, U. Utah, 1945, MD, 1947; PhD in Surgery, U. Minn., 1954; ScD (hon.), Brigham Young U., 1970; DMS (hon.), Utah State U., 1989; LHD (hon.), Snow Coll., 1994. Diplomate: Am. Bd. Surgery, Am. Bd. Thoracic Surgery (dir. 1972-78). Intern U. Minn. Hosps., Mpls., 1947, asst. resident surgery, 1948-51; first asst. resident surgery Mass. Gen. Hosp., Boston, 1953-54; sr. resident surgery U. Minn. Hosps., Mpls., 1954-55; practice medicine (specializing in cardiovascular and thoracic surgery), Salt Lake City, 1959-84; staff surgeon LDS Hosp., Salt Lake City, 1959-84, dir. surg. research lab., 1959-72, chief cardiovascular-thoracic surg. div., 1967-72, also bd. govs., 1970-90, vice chmn., 1979-89; staff surgeon Primary Children's Hosp., Salt Lake City, 1960; attending in surgery VA Hosp., Salt Lake City, 1955-84, Univ. Hosp., Salt Lake City, 1955-84; asst. prof. surgery Med. Sch. U. Utah, Salt Lake City, 1955-59, asst. clin. prof. surgery, 1959-66, asso. clin. prof. surgery, clin. prof., 1966-69, research prof. surgery, 1970-84, clin. prof. emeritus, 1984—; staff services Utah Biomed. Test Lab., 1970-84. Dir. tng. program cardiovascular and thoracic surgery at Univ. Utah affiliated hosps., 1967-84; mem. policyholders adv. com. New Eng. Mut. Life Ins. Co., Boston, 1976-80 Contbr. articles to profl. jours. Mem. White House Conf. on Youth and Children, 1960; bd. dirs. Internat. Cardiol. Found.; bd. govs. LDS Hosp., 1970-90, Deseret Gymnasium, 1971-75, Promised Valley Playhouse, 1970-79; mem. adv. com. U.S. Sec. of State on Religious Freedom Abroad, 1996-99. lst lt. to capt. M.C., AUS, 1951-53. Markle scholar in med. scis., 1957-59; Fellowship of Medici Publici U. Utah Coll., 1967; Gold Medal of Merit, Argentina, 1974; named Hon. Prof. Shandong Med. U., Jinan, People's Republic of China, 1985; Old People's U., Jinan, 1986; Xi-an (People's Republic of China) Med. Coll., 1986, Legacy of Life award,

1993. Fellow A.C.S. (chmn. adv. council on thoracic surgery 1973-75), Am. Coll. Cardiology, Am. Coll. Chest Physicians; mem. Am. Assn. Thoracic Surgery, Am. Soc. Artificial Internal Organs, AMA, Dirs. Thoracic Residencies (pres. 1971-72), Utah Med. Assn. (pres. 1970-71), Salt Lake County Med. Soc., Am. Heart Assn. (exec. com. cardiovascular surgery 1972, dir. 1976-78, chmn. council cardiovascular surgery 1976-78), Utah Heart Assn. (pres. 1964-65), Soc. Thoracic Surgeons, Soc. Vascular Surgery (sec. 1968-72, pres. 1974), Utah Thoracic Soc., Salt Lake Surg. Soc., Samson Thoracic Surg. Soc., Western Soc. for Clin. Research, Soc. U. Surgeons, Am., Western, Pan-Pacific surg. assns., Inter. Am. Soc. Cardiology (bd. mgrs.), Phi Beta Kappa, Sigma Xi, Alpha Omega Alpha, Phi Kappa Phi, Sigma Chi. Mem. Ch. of Jesus Christ of Latter-day Saints (pres. Bonneville Stake 1964-71, gen. pres. Sunday sch. 1971-79, regional rep. 1979-84, Quorum of the Twelve Apostles 1984—). Office: 47 E South Temple Salt Lake City UT 84150-1200

NELSON, SANDRA E., information technology executive; d. Samual Aaron and Nelia Mary Aronson; children: Ryan Dagen, Kyle Degn. Mgmt. of Tech., Kennedy Western U., Thousand Oaks, CA, 2000—02. Career & Tech. Edn. Wash., 2005. Curriculum devel. asst. SW Regional Sch. Dist., Dillingham, Alaska, 1985—89; media specialist Sumner Sch. Dist., Wash., 1989—95; dir. of its Fed. Way Pub. Schs., Federal Way, Wash., 1995—. Cons. in field, 1999—2005; prin., cons. Leadership upward, Tacoma, 1999—2005; trainer Aha Process, Baytown, Tex., 2000—05. Master: Assn. Computer Profls. in Edn. (pres. 2002—03); fellow: Wash. Assn. Sch. Administrs. (presenter 2002—05); mem.: Advancing Leadership (presenter 2003—05), Fed. Way C of C. Home Phone: 253-945-2110; Office Phone: 253-945-2111. E-mail: snelson@fwps.org.

NELSON, SARAH MILLEDGE, archaeology educator; b. Miami, Fla., Nov. 29, 1931; d. Stanley and Sarah Woodman (Franklin) M.; m. Harold Stanley Nelson, July 25, 1953; children: Erik Harold, Mark Milledge, Stanley Franklin. BA, Wellesley Coll., 1953; MA, U. Mich., 1969, PhD, 1973. Instr. archaeology U. Md. extension, Seoul, Republic Korea, 1970-71; asst. prof. U. Denver, 1974-79, assoc. prof., 1979-85, prof. archaeology, 1985—2004, rsch. prof., 2004—, chair dept. anthropology, 1985-95, dir. women's studies program, 1985-87, John Evans prof., dir. Asian studies, 1996, vice provost for rsch., 1998—2002, interim vice provost grad. studies and rsch., 2001—02. Vis. asst. prof. U. Colo., Boulder, 1974; resident Rockefeller Ctr. in Bellagio, Italy, 1996. Author: Archaeology of Korea, 1993, Gender in Archaeology: Analyzing Power and Prestige, 1997, 2d rev. edit., 2004, Shamanism in East Asian Archaeology, 2007; (novel) Spirit Bird Journey, 1999, Ancient Queens: Archaeological Perspectives, 2003, Jade Dragon, 2004, Shaman Queen, 2007; co-author: Denver: An Archaeological History, 2001; editor: The Archaeology of Northeast China, 1995, Ancestors for the Pigs: Pigs in Prehistory, 1998, Handbook of Gender in Archeology, 2006, Women in Antiquity: Theoretical Approaches to Gender and Archaeology, 2007, Worlds of Gender, The Archaeology of Women's Lives Around the Globe, 2007; co-editor: Powers of Observation, 1990, Equity Issues for Women in Archaeology, 1994, Archaeology of the Russian Far East, 2005, In Pursuit of Gender: Worldwide Archaeological Perspectives, 2001, Korean Social Archaeology, 2005, Archeology of the Russian Far East, 2006, Integrating the Diversity of the 21st Century Anthropology, 2006. Active Earthwatch, 1989. Recipient Outstanding Scholar award U. Denver, 1989; grantee S.W. Inst. Rsch. on Women, 1981, Acad. Korean Studies, Seoul, 1983, Internat. Cultural Soc. Korea, 1986, Colo. Hist. Fund, 1995-97, Rockefeller Found. Residency, Bellagio, Italy, Wenner-Gren Found., 2000-02, Nat. Geographic Soc., 2000—. Fellow Am. Anthrop. Assn.; mem. Soc. Am. Archaeology, Assn. Asian Studies, Royal Asiatic Soc., Sigma Xi (sec.-treas. 1978-79), Phi Beta Kappa. Democrat. Avocations: travel, gardening. Home: 5878 S Dry Creek Ct Littleton CO 80121-1709 Office: U Denver Dept Anthropology Denver CO 80208-0001 Office Phone: 303-871-2682. Business E-Mail: snelson@du.edu.

NELSON, STEPHEN D., music educator; b. Clearwater, Fla., Apr. 5, 1957; adopted s. Brasher Parker and Catherine Land (Kit) Nelson. BA, U. Cen. Fla., 1982. Dir. music 1st Presbyn. Ch. Apopka; performer, co-founder Ars Antiqua - an Early Music Ensemble, Orlando, 1986—; dir. music 1st Presbyn. Ch. Apopka, 1983—; creative music cons. Nelson Music Svcs., Apopka, 1976—. Musician orch. arrangement of ednl. mus. materials, composer 2 For The Road; contbr. Arrangements for Harcourt Texts, 1995; musician: (ednl. video) Ars Antiqua - Music from a Distant Tyme, 1996. Mem.: Bears of Cen. Fla. (pres. 2001—02). Office: Park Maitland Sch 1450 S Orlando Ave Maitland FL 32751 Personal E-mail: nelsonmusic@cfl.rr.com.

NELSON, STEVEN CRAIG, lawyer; b. Oakland, Calif., May 11, 1944; s. Eskil Manfred and Florence Lucille (Boatman) N.; m. Kathryn Cassel Stoltz, Nov. 30, 1974 (div. Apr. 1997); children: Carleton Philip, Whitney Cassel. BA in Econs. with exceptional distinction, Yale U., 1966, LLB, 1969. Bar: DC 1969, Minn. Supreme Ct. 1975, U.S. Supreme Ct. 1973, Hong Kong 2000. From atty. adviser to asst. legal adviser U.S. Dept. State, Washington, 1969-74; from assoc. to ptnr. Oppenheimer, Wolff, Foster, Shepard & Donnelly, St. Paul and Mpls., 1975-85; ptnr., internat. practice group Dorsey & Whitney LLP, Mpls., 1985—, co-chmn., Asia practice Hong Kong & Mpls. Mem. bd. appeals NATO, Brussels. 1977-2003; adj. prof. law U. Minn, 1980-86; spkr. in field. Contbr. articles to profl. jours. Mem. ABA (chmn. internat. law and practice 1988-89), Minn. Bar Assn., Internat. Bar Assn. (mem. coun. 1996-2000, mem. WTO Working Group, 2000-present), Inter-Pacific Bar Assn., Minikahda Club. Avocations: golf, tennis, skiing, sailing. Office: Dorsey & Whitney 3008 One Pacific Pl 88 Queensway Hong Kong SAR China Office Phone: 852 2105 0211. Business E-Mail: nelson.steve@dorsey.com.

NELSON, STEVEN DWAYNE, lawyer; b. Austin, Minn. m. Vicky L. Staab, July 6, 1990. BA in English, SUNY, Buffalo, 1972; JD, U. Mont., 1978. Bar: Mont. 1978, U.S. Dist. Ct. Mont. 1978. Atty., Bozeman, Mont., 1978—90; city prosecutor City of Bozeman, 1979-82; city atty. City of Ennis, Mont., 1980-82; prof. U. Great Falls, Mont., 1990—, mediator Mont., 1998—. Mem. Mont. State Bar Assn., Phi Delta Phi. Avocations: fishing, skiing, hiking. Home and Office: 4590 Maiden Rock Rd Bozeman MT 59715-7769 Business E-Mail: snelson@ugf.edu.

NELSON, STUART OWEN, agricultural engineer, researcher, educator; b. Pilger, Nebr., Jan. 23, 1927; s. Irvin Andrew and Agnes Emilie (Nissen) N.; m. Carolyn Joye Fricke, Dec. 27, 1953 (dec. Nov. 1975); children: Richard Lynn, Jana Sue; m. Martha Ellen White Fuller, Apr. 8, 1979. BS in Agrl. Engring., U. Nebr., 1950; MS in Agrl. Engring., 1952; MA in Physics, U. Nebr., 1954; PhD in Engring., Iowa State U., 1972; DSc (hon.), U. Nebr., 1989. Grad. asst. U. Nebr., Lincoln, 1952-54, rsch. assoc., 1954-60, assoc. prof., 1960-72, prof., 1972-76. Project leader Farm Electrification Rsch., Agrl. Rsch. Svc., USDA, Lincoln, 1954-59, rsch. investigations leader, 1959-72, rsch. leader 1972-76, rsch. agrl. engr. Russell Rsch. Ctr., Athens, Ga., 1976—; adj. prof. U. Ga., 1976—; sci. adv. coun. Am. Seed Rsch. Found.; mem. CAST Task Force on Irradiation for Food Preservation and Pest Control; adv. com. grain moisture measurement Nat. Coun. Weights and Measures; mem. sci. bd. 4th Internat. Conf. on Phys. Properties Agrl. Materials, Prague, 1985. Assoc. editor Jour. Microwave Power 1975-76, 95-2000; contbr. more than 600 articles to sci. and tech. jours. With USN, 1946-48. Recipient HM Crops and Soils award Am. Soc. Agronomy, 1966, Founders Gold medal Fed. Engr. of Yr. NSPE, 1985, Superior Svc. award USDA, 1986, Profl. Achievement Citation Engring. award Iowa State U., 1987, Ga. Engring. Found. medal of honor, 1999; named to U. Nebr. Biol. Systems Engring. Hall of Fame, 1999, USDA-ARS Sci. Hall of Fame, 2002. Fellow IEEE, Am. Soc. Agrl. Engrs. (Tech. Paper award 1965, 94, 2005, 07, Engr. of Yr. award Ga. sect. 1988, chmn. Ga. sect. 1988-89, Cyrus Hall McCormick-Jerome Increase Case Gold Medal award 2000), Internat. Microwave Power Inst. (Decade award 1981), AAAS; mem. The Electromagnetics Acad., Internat. Soc. Agromaterials Sci. and Engring., Internat. Dielectric Soc., Ga. Soc. Profl. Engrs. (Engr. of Yr. in Govt. award 1991, Engr. of Yr. 1998), Nat. Acad. Engring., Nat. Soc. Profl. Engrs., Orgn. Profl. Employees of Dept. of Agrl. (pres. Athens area chpt. 1984-86, nat. coun. rep. 1988-95, Profl. of Yr. award 1987), Athens Optimist (pres. 1980-81, 2000-2001, lt. gov. Ga. dist. 1983-84, Optimist of Yr. award 1982, disting. and outstanding lt. gov. Ga. dist. 1985), Assn. for Microwave Power in Europe for Rsch. and Edn., Sigma Xi, Sigma Tau, Gamma Sigma Delta, Tau Beta Pi. Methodist. Home: 270 Idylwood Dr Athens GA 30605-4635 Office: USDA Agrl Rsch Svc Russell Rsch Ctr PO Box 5677 Athens GA 30604-5677

NELSON, SUE GRODSKY, humanities educator, consultant; b. Bklyn., Apr. 1, 1943; d. Juliette Dorfman and Louis Grodsky; m. Michael R. Nelson, Nov. 23, 1968; children: Andrew Robert, John Samuel. BA, Allegheny Coll., Meadville, Pa., 1964; EdM, John Carroll U., University Heights, Ohio, 1995. Cert. tchr. Ohio, 1988. Asst. prodn. mgr. CBS, NYC, 1964—65; tchr./dept. chair of English, honors English, reading, journalism, French Cleve. Bd. of Edn., 1965—71; group home foster parent Jewish Children's Bur., Shaker Heights, Ohio, 1971—75; tchr. of English, inclusion English/learning cmty., career edn., journalism East Cleve. Bd. of Edn., 1972—98; adj. instr., reading cons. Cuyahoga CC, Cleve. Mem. tchr. rev. panel McDougal, Littell & Co., Evanston, Ill., 1990—92; presenter Cons. - Multiple Intelligences Workshops, Ohio, 1994—99; mem. adv. com. John Carroll U., University Heights, Ohio, 1995—97; mem. Newbury Bd. of Edn., Ohio, 2000—04, past pres. Author: (instruction manual) Getting Elected to Public Office; contbr. anthology Humanities Programs Today; co-author/editor (instruction manual) Multiple Intelligences at Work!; editor: (inspirational lessons) Zen Shin Talks. Chairperson Social Action Coun., 2005—, People for Polensek, Cleve., 1977—90; vice chairperson and sec. Cuyahoga County Dem. Party, Cuyahoga County, Ohio, 1982—89; vol. coord. Boyle for Senate, Cleveland, Ohio, 1997—98; trustee Suburban Temple-Kol Ami, 2005—. Recipient Ashland Achievement award, Ashland Oil, Inc., 1992; Coach of State Champion - Oratorical Interpretation, Ohio H.S. Speech League, 1986. Mem.: NEA (life), East Cleve. Edn. Assn. (pres. 1982—83), Ohio Sch. Bd. Assn., Ohio Edn. Assn. (life; chairperson svc. coun. 1980—81). Democrat. Jewish. Avocations: reading, exercising, interior decorating, political activism, travel. Home: 10450 Bell St Newbury OH 44065 Office: Cuyahoga CC 2900 Community College Avenue Cleveland OH 44114 E-mail: m.s.nelson@juno.com.

NELSON, SUSAN RHODES, media specialist, educator; b. Birmingham, Ala., June 27, 1948; d. Horace and Evelyn Vines Rhodes; m. Roger Hudson Nelson, Dec. 19, 1970; children: Jay Matthew, Jon Bradley. BS, Auburn U., 1970; MA, U. Ala., Birmingham, 1973, EdS, 1985; MLIS, U. Ala., Tuscaloosa, 1997, EdD, 2001. Cert. tchr. Ala. Tchr. Jefferson County Bd. of Edn., Birmingham, 1970—94, media specialist, 1994—; adj. prof. U. Ala., Tuscaloosa, 2001—. Adv. bd. Jefferson County Librarians, Birmingham, 2001—; chmn. Jefferson County Elem. Librarians, Birmingham, 2003—; mem. bldg. leadership team Hueytown (Ala.) Elem. Sch., 1994—, tech. coord., 1994—; cons., rschr. Learning Through Sports, Birmingham, 2003—; leader People to People Ambassador Program, Birmingham, 2004—; online facilitator Ala. State Dept. Edn. Bd. dirs. Daycare, Bessemer, Ala., 2000—05. Named Leader of the Yr., Jefferson County 4-H, 1975, Tchr. of Yr., Hueytown Elem. Sch., 2003; recipient Exemplary Libr. Program award, Libr. and Media Professionals, 1999, 2003, Most Exemplary Elem. Libr. award, Jefferson County Libr. Links for Success, 2004. Mem.: ALA (assoc.), NEA (assoc.), Ala. Libr. Assn. (assoc.), Alpha Delta Kappa (treas. 2002—), Kappa Delta Pi (assoc.), Kappa Delta Epsilon (assoc.). Republican. Avocations: travel, music, reading, sports. Home: 11227 Apple Valley Rd Mc Calla AL 35111-2448 Office: Hueytown Elem Sch 112 Forest Rd Hueytown AL 35023 Home Phone: 205-938-9485; Office Phone: 205-379-4123. Personal E-mail: nelsonsr2@bellsouth.net. Business E-Mail: snelson@jefcoed.com.

NELSON, THOMAS ADAMS, electrical engineer, consultant; b. Berkeley, Calif., Aug. 26, 1921; s. Thomas Fleming and Mabel Margaretta (Adams) N.; m. Mary Anne Mares, July 12, 1958. AA, LA City Coll., 1942; BS, U. So. Calif., 1949, MS, 1953; postgrad. cert. bus. mgmt., UCLA, 1970. Registered profl. elec. and quality engr., Calif. Design engr. LA Dept. Water and Power, 1950—53, quality assurance engr., resident engr. factories in U.S., Europe and Japan, 1953—65, asst. chief quality assurance engr., 1965—68, chief quality assurance engr., 1968—72, sr. engr. in charge oper. engring., 1972—77, prin. engr., mgr. comm., transmission lines, sta. maintenance and distbn. trouble, 1977—80, rail transp. cons. on coal delivery to elec. generating stas. Ariz. and Nev., 1973-79, rep. to Calif. Power Pool, 1975-77; cons. engr., transp. cons. LA, 1980—. Reviewer rail transit plans So. Calif. Rapid Transit Dist., LA County Transp. Commn., LA County Met. Transp. Authority, Orange County Transit Dist., Caltrans, San Diego Met. Transit Devel. Bd., 1978—. Editor, maj. author Railroad Chronology Compendium, 1976, 50 Years of Railroading in Southern California, 2001; editor Jour. Pacific R.R. Soc., 1980-84, 87-94, cons. editor, 1994-2005; contbr. articles to profl. jours., academic publs. and newspapers, 1970—. Mem. Citizens Adv. Commn. for Met. Rail, Hollywood, Calif., 1982-84, Met. Rail CORE Forum, 1987; advisor Beijing ofcl. regarding rail transit, 2002, Spokane Transit Authority, 2003, 2006. Served to capt. USAAF, 1942-45, ETO. Mem. IEEE (sr.), Vehicular Tech. Soc., Pacific R.R. Soc. (bd. dirs. 1977-80, 82-85, v.p. 1986, pres. 1987-89, publs. mgr. 1981-94), Eta Kappa Nu, Tau Beta Pi, Phi Kappa Phi.

NELSON, THOMAS C., manufacturing executive; BS in Indsl. Engring., Stanford U.; MBA, Harvard U. Investment banker Morgan Stanley & Co.; spl. asst. to Sec. of Def. Richard B. Cheney U.S. Dept. Defense, Washington, 1992; gen. ptnr. Wakefield Group, 1988; CEO, pres. Nat. Gypsum, Charlotte, 1999—, chmn, 2005—. Vice-chmn, policy advisory bd. Harvard U. Joint Ctr. for Housing Studies, 2003—. Office: Nat Gypsum Co 2001 Rexford Rd Charlotte NC 28211

NELSON, THOMAS G., federal judge; b. Idaho Falls, Idaho, 1936; Student, U. Idaho, 1955—59, LLB, 1962. Ptnr. Parry, Robertson, and Daly, Twin Falls, Idaho, 1965—79, Nelson, Rosholt, Robertson, Tolman and Tucker, Twin Falls, 1979; judge US Ct. Appeals (9th cir.), Boise, Idaho, 1990—2003, sr. judge, 2003—. With Idaho Air N.G., 1962—65, with USAR, 1965—68. Mem.: ABA, Idaho Law Found., Am. Bd. Trial Advocates (pres. Idaho chpt.), Idaho Assn. Def. Counsel, Idaho State Bar (pres., bd. commrs.), Am. Coll. Trial Lawyers, Am. Bar Found., Phi Alpha Delta. Office: US Ct Appeals 9th Circuit 304 N Eighth St Boise ID 83702 *

NELSON, THOMAS JOHN, music educator, musician; b. Ft. Monmouth, NJ, Mar. 17, 1970; s. John David and Barbara Stephanie Nelson; m. Lori Ann Roupp, June 18, 1994; children: Jonathan Michael, Taylor Foster, Jaclyn Claire. BS in Music Edn., West Chester U., 1992; MusM, Mansfield U., 1998. Gen. music tchr. St. Joe's Cath. Sch., North Plainfield, NJ, 1992—93; asst. band dir. Allentown HS, NJ, 1992—93; 4-12 band dir. Williamson HS, Tioga, Pa., 1993—2000, Liberty Schs., Pa., 2000—. Pvt. percussion tchr. Robert M. Sides Music Ctr., Williamsport, Pa., 1993—2000, Liberty, 2000—; co-owner TC Prodns. Rec., Liberty, 1996—; tchr. Vic Firth Corp., Boston, 2003—. Author: (website) tomnelsondrums.com, 2003—; nat. rec. artist tomnelsondrums.com; composer: tomnelsondrums.com. Nominee Disney Hands Tchr. of Yr., 2004; Tchr. of Yr., So. Tioga Sch. Dist., 2004. Mem.: Music Educators Nat. Conf., Nat. Educators Assn., Arnot Sportsmen Club. Republican. Roman Catholic. Avocations: hunting, fishing, skiing, composing, reading. Home: 896 Decoursey Rd Liberty PA 16930 Office: Liberty HS PO Box 135 Liberty PA 16930

NELSON, TROY ALAN, music educator, church musician; b. Iowa City, Apr. 9, 1969; s. Verne Franklyn and Johanna Pearl Nelson; m. Kari Marie Urevig, Feb. 18, 1971; children: Haley Marie, Hannah Elizabeth, Ryan Laurence. BA, Luther Coll., 1991; MEd, Oakland U., 1998. Music educator grades 6-12 Eagle Grove Schs., Eagle Grove, Iowa, 1991—93, Clarenceville Schs., Livonia, Mich., 1993—; dir. music and worship St. John Luth. Ch., Farmington, 1993—. Scheduling chair Clarenceville H.S. Block Scheduling Com., Livonia, Mich., 2000—02; participant Oakland Leadership Acad. Aspiring Principals, Waterford, 2001—01; adj. faculty Marygrove Coll., Detroit, 2001—. Dir.: (musicals) Oliver, L'il Abner, All-American, Oklahoma, The Music Man, Pirates of Penzance, Guys and Dolls, Anything Goes, Once Upon A Mattress, Meet Me in St. Louis, Annie Get Your Gun, My Fair Lady, Damn Yankees; actor: (video) NCA Transitions Informational Video; choral director (song) (Overall Mixed Choir Trophy, St. Louis Festivals of Music, 1992), 1 high sch. choral dir. (songs) (Overall Divsn. One Rating, 2001, 2005, 2006, 2007). Recipient cert. appreciation, Clarenceville Schools Bd. Edn., 1999, 2002. Mem.: NEA, ASCD, Mich. Elem. Mid. Sch. Prin. Assn., Assn. Luth. Ch. Musicians, Mich. Sch. Vocal Music Assn., Am. Choral Dirs. Assn. Lutheran. Avocations: running, reading, skiing, home improvement. Home: 36694 Saxony Rd Farmington MI 48335 Office: Clarenceville Schs 20155 Middlebelt Rd Livonia MI 48152 Home Phone: 248-476-7498; Office Phone: 248-919-0408 x 223. Personal E-mail: luthergrads@aol.com. E-mail: tnelson@clarenceville.k12.mi.us.

NELSON, VITA JOY, editor, publisher; b. NYC, Dec. 9, 1937; d. Leon Abraham and Bertha (Sher) Reiner; m. Lester Nelson, Aug. 27, 1961; children: Lee Reiner, Clifford Samuel, Cara Ritchie. BA, Boston U., 1959. Promotion copywriter Street & Smith, NYC, 1958-59; asst. to mng. editor Mademoiselle Mag., NYC, 1959-60; mcpl. bond trader Granger & Co., NYC, 1960-63; founder, editor, pub. Westchester Mag., Mamaroneck, NY, 1968-80, L.I. Mag., 1973-78; founder, editor, pub., pres. Moneypaper, 1981—. Pub. The Guide to Dividend Reinvestment Plans, Direct Investing; founder MP63 Fund; pres. Moneypaper Advisor Inc., 1999—. Author: (with Donald Korn) Create and Manage Your Own Mutual Fund, 1994. Bd. dirs. United Way of Westchester/Putnam County, 1998—2002; bd. govs., v.p. Am. Jewish Com., Westchester, 1979—89. Recipient citation Coun. Arts, 1972, Media award Pub. Rels. Soc. Am., 1974. Mem. Women in Comms. (Outstanding Communicator award 1983). Democrat. Home: Pleasant Ridge Rd Harrison NY 10528-1004 Office: The Moneypaper Inc 555 Theodore Frend Ave Rye NY 10580 Office Phone: 914-925-0022. E-mail: vitajoy@aol.com.

NELSON, WALTER GERALD, retired insurance company executive; b. Peoria, Ill., Jan. 2, 1930; s. Walter Dennis and Hazel Marie (Tucker) Nelson; m. Mary Ann Olberding, Jan. 28, 1952 (dec. Nov. 1989); children: Ann Larkin, Michael, Susan Boor, Patrick, Thomas, Timothy, Molly Edwards; m. Mary Jo Sunderland, Apr. 6, 1991. Student, St. Benedict's Coll., Atchison, Kans., 1947-49, Bradley U., Peoria, Ill., 1949; JD, Creighton U., Omaha, 1952. Bar: Nebr 1952, Ill 1955. Practice in, Peoria, 1955-56; with State Farm Life Ins. Co., Bloomington, Ill., 1956—, counsel, 1968—, v.p., 1970-96. Past dir Ill Life Ins Coun; past chmn legal sect Am Coun Life Ins; spkr in field. Contbr. articles to profl jours. Mem.: ABA, Nat. Orgn. Life and Health Ins. Guaranty Assn. (past pres.), Assn. Life Ins. Counsel (past pres.), Nebr. Bar Assn., Ill. Bar Assn., Bloomington Country Club, KofC. Republican. Roman Catholic. Personal E-mail: WGN1930@aol.com.

NELSON, WILLIAM EUGENE, lawyer; b. Roland, Iowa, Sept. 23, 1927; s. Sam J. and Katherine A. (Coffey) N.; m. Sherlee M. Stanford, July 11, 1959; children: Anne, Kristin, William. BA, U. Iowa, 1950; JD, Drake U., 1957. Bar: Iowa 1957, D.C. 1965, Md. 1976, W.Va. 2004. Trial atty. civil divsn. U.S. Dept. Justice, 1957—65, asst. chief tort sect., 1966—70, chief r.r. reorgn. unit, 1970—71; gen. counsel Cost of Living Coun. Phase I, 1971, chief econ. stblzn. sect., 1971—74; ptnr. Nelson and Nelson, LLP, Washington, Bethesda, Md., 1975—. Gen. counsel the Communicators, Inc., Myersville, Md. Assoc. editor Drake Law Rev., 1955-57. With USN, 1945—46. Recipient Atty. Gen.'s Disting. Svc. award, 1972. Mem.: Omicron Delta Kappa, Order of Coif. Home: 511 Colston Dr Falling Waters WV 25419 Office: Nelson & Nelson LLP 3 Bethesda Metro Ctr Ste 700 Bethesda MD 20814-6300 Office Phone: 301-961-1958. Personal E-mail: reg1927@aol.com.

NELSON, WILLIE HUGH, musician, lyricist; b. Abbott, Tex., Apr. 30, 1933; children: Jacob, Lukas, Paula Carlene, Amy, Lana, Susie, Billy. Student, Baylor U. Salesman; announcer, host country music shows local Tex. stas.; bass player Ray Price's band; formed own band; personal appearances at Grand Ole Opry, Nashville, throughout U.S., 1964—; rec. artist Atlantic, Columbia and RCA records; founder Pedernales Studios, Spicewood, Tex., Pedernales Records, Austin, Tex., 2007; owner Pedernales Golf Club/Willie Nelson's Cut-N-Putt. Co-founder Willie Nelson's Biodiesel. Musician: (albums) Love & Pain, 1961, And Then I Wrote, 1962, Here's Willie Nelson, 1963, Country Willie: His Own Songs, 1965, Country Favorites: Willie Nelson Style, 1966, Live Country Music Concert, 1966, Make Way for Willie Nelson, 1967, Texas in My Soul, 1968, Good Times, 1968, My Own Peculiar Way, 1969, Both Sides Now, 1970, Laying My Burdens Down, Yesterday's Wine, 1971, Willie Nelson & Family, 1971, The Willie Way, 1972, The Words Don't Fit the Picture, 1972, Shotgun Willie, 1973, Phases and Stages, 1974, Red Headed Stranger, 1975 (Grammy award Best Country Vocal Performance for song "Blue Eyes Crying In The Rain", 1975), Willie Nelson Live, 1976, The Sound in Your Mind, 1976, The Troublemaker, 1976, To Lefty from Willie, 1977, Stardust, 1978 (Grammy award Best Country Vocal Performance for song "Georgia on My Mind", 1978), Waylon & Willie, 1978 (Grammy award Best Country Vocal Performance By A Duo Or Group for song "Mammas Don't Let Your Babies Grow Up to Be Cowboys", 1978), Willie and Family Live, 1978, The Electric Horseman, 1979, Sings Kris Kristofferson, 1979, One for the Road, 1979, Pretty Paper, 1979, San Antonio Rose, 1980, Honeysuckle Rose, 1980 (Grammy award Best Country Song for "On The Road Again", 1980), Blue Skies, 1981, Somewhere over the Rainbow, 1981, Pancho & Lefty, 1983 (Vocal Duo Yr. (with Merle Haggard) Country Music Assn. Awards, 1983), Old Friends, 1982, Always on My Mind, 1982 (Grammy award Best Country Vocal Performance for song "Always On My Mind", 1982, Country Music Assn. awards: Album Yr., 1982, Single Yr. for "Always On My Mind", 1982), Tougher Than Leather, 1983, Without a Song, 1983, Take It to the Limit, 1983, Music from Songwriter, 1984, Portrait in Music, 1984, Angel Eyes, 1984, City of New Orleans, 1984, Me and Paul, 1985, Half Nelson, 1985 (Vocal Duo Yr. (with Julio Iglesias) Country Music Assn. Awards, 1984), Brand on My Heart, 1985, Funny How Time Slips Away, 1985, Partners, 1986, The Promiseland, 1986, Island in the Sea, 1987, Seashores of Old Mexico, 1987, What a Wonderful World, 1988, Horse Called Music, 1989, Born for Trouble, 1990, The IRS Tapes: Who'll Buy My Memories?, Willie Nelson, 1993, Across the Borderline, 1993, Moonlight Becomes You, 1994, Healing Hands of Time, 1994, Pancho, Lefty and Rudolph, 1995, Six Hours at Pedernales, 1995, Just One Love, 1996, Spirit, 1996, How Great Thou Art, 1996, Christmas with Willie Nelson, 1997, Hill Country Christmas, 1997, Teatro, 1998, Life's Railway to Heaven, 1998, Back to Back: Willie Nelson and Patsy Cline, 1998, Night and Day, 1999, Clean Shirt, 2000, Outlaws, 2000, Memories of Hank Williams, Sr., 2000, Me and the Drummer, 2000, Milk Cow Blues, 2000, Good Ol' Country Singin', 2000, Rainbow Connection, 2001, Tales Out of Luck, 2001, The Great

Divide, 2002, Home is Where You're Happy, 2002, All of Me Live...in Concert, 2002, Stars & Guitars, 2002 (Grammy award (with Lee Ann Womack) Best Country Collaboration With Vocals for song "Mendocino County Line", 2002), Night Life, 2002, Country Willie, 2002, Is There Something on Your Mind, 2002, On the Road Again, 2002, Honky Tonk Heroes, 2003, Broken Promises, 2003, Reunion - Can't Get the Hell Out of Texas, 2003, Willie Nelson and Friends: Live and Kickin', 2003, Standard Time, 2003, Keepsake, 2003, Run That By Me One More Time, 2003, I Just Don't Understand, 2003, Live in Amsterdam, 2004, Music Legends: The Best of Willie Live, 2004, Live at Billy Bob's Texas, 2004, It Always Will Be, 2004, Songs for Tsunami Relief, 2005, Countryman, 2005, You Don't Know Me, 2006, Just a Couple of Outlaws, 2006, All American Country, 2006, Last of the Breed, 2007; appeared on (album by Waylon Jennings) Good Hearted Woman, 1972 (Single Yr. (with Waylon Jennings) Country Music Assn. Awards, 1976), appeared with various artists (albums) Wanted: The Outlaws, 1976 (Vocal Duo Yr. (with Waylon Jennings) Country Music Assn. (CMA) Awards, 1976, Album Yr. (with Waylon Jennings, Tompall Glaser, Jessi Colter) Country Music Assn. Awards, 1976); actor: (films) The Electric Horseman, 1979, Honeysuckle Rose, 1980, Thief, 1981, Barbarosa, 1982, Songwriter, 1984, Red-Headed Stranger, 1986, Starlight, 1996, Gone Fishin', 1997, Wag the Dog, 1997, Stardust, 2000, The Journeyman, 2001, The Big Bounce, 2004, The Dukes of Hazzard, 2005; (film appearances include) Anthem, 1997, Dill Scallion, 1999, Austin Powers: The Spy Who Shagged Me, 1999; actor, co-writer musical score: (TV films) Stagecoach, 1986; performer: (theme song for film) Welcome Home, 1989, (songs) Cowboys Are Frequently, Secretly (Fond of Each Other), 2006, (movie soundtrack, Brokeback Mountain) He Was a Friend of Mine, 2005; (TV films appearances include) Where the Hell's That Gold, 1988, Once Upon a Texas Train, 1989, A Pair of Aces, 1990, Born for Trouble, 1990, Another Pair of Aces: Three of a Kind, 1991, Big Country, 1994, Big Dreams and Broken Hearts: The Dottie West Story, 1995, The Beach Boys: Nashville Sounds, 1996, Starlight, 1996, Farm Aid '96, 1996, Outlaw Justice, 1998; author: (autobiography) I Didn't Come Here (and I Ain't Leavin'), 1988; co-author (with Turk Pipkin): (memoir) The Tao of Willie, 2006. Served in USAF. Named Entertainer Yr., Country Music Assn. (CMA), 1979; named to, Nashville Songwriters Assn. Hall Fame, 1973, Country Music Hall Fame, 1993; recipient citation for Top Album Artist, Billboard mag., 1976, Special Humanitarian award, Nat. Farmers Orgn., 1986, Grammy Lifetime Achievement award, 1989. Achievements include performing Cowboys Are Frequently, Secretly (Fond of Each Other), which may be the first gay cowboy song by a major recording artist. Office: care Mark Rothbaum & Assocs Inc PO Box 2689 Danbury CT 06813-2689 Address: William Morris Agency 150 El Camino Beverly Hills CA 90212 Home: Austin TX

NELSON-KAUFFMAN, WENDY, history educator; b. Evanston, Ill., Mar. 7, 1961; d. Wayne Keith Nelson and Jane Van Dellen; m. Matthew William Kauffman, Oct. 5, 1961; children: David Alexander Nelson Kauffman, Sam VanDellen Nelson Kauffman. BS, Dartmouth Coll., Hanover, NH, 1983; MS, Northwestern U., Evanston, IL, 1984; MS in History, So. Conn. State U., New Haven, 1990. Cert. tchr. Conn., 1990. Tv news anchor, reporter WAOW-TV, Wausau, Wis., 1984—86; tv reporter WTNH-TV, New Haven, 1986—88; adult educator New Haven and Hartford Adult Edn., 1990—96; tchr., chair dept. Bloomfield H.S., 1996—2004; history educator Met. Learning Ctr., 2004—. Mem. closing achievement gap task force Conn. Dept. Edn., Hartford, 2003—04; advisor Student Abolitionists Stopping Slavery, Bloomfield, 2004—06; mem. conn. task force revise state social studies stds. Conn. Dept. Edn., 2005—06; tchr. adv. bd. Unitarian Universalist Ch., West Hartford, 2005—06. Recipient Conn. Tchr. of Yr. award, 2003, All-Star Tchg. Team awaqrd, USA Today, 2004, Kidger award for outstanding history tchr. in New Eng., 2004, Conn. History Tchr. of Yr., 2005. Mem.: Nat. Coun. History Edn., Nat. Coun. Social Studies, Conn. Coun. Social Studies (assoc.; bd. mem. 2004—06). Unitarian Universalist. Avocations: travel, reading, gardening, physical fitness. Home: 101 Four Mile Rd West Hartford CT 06107 Office: Metropolitan Learning Center 1551 Blue Hills Ave Bloomfield CT 06002 Home Phone: 860-561-8854; Office Phone: 860-242-7834. Personal E-mail: wnkauffman@yahoo.com. E-mail: wnelson-kauffman@crec.org.

NELSON-WALKER, ROBERTA, management software company executive; b. NYC, Sept. 1, 1936; d. Richard E. and Esther (McBride) Martin; m. Robert L. Nelson, July 20, 1957 (div.); children: Carol, Craig, Robert H.; m. Dan Walker, Nov. 1978 (div.). BA, DePaul U., 1976, MS in Mgmt. with distinction, 1977. Dir. devel. Ray Graham Assocs., Elmhurst, Ill., 1970-76; dir. human resources Nat. Easter Seal Soc., Chgo., 1979-81; v.p. Butler Walker Inc., Oak Brook, Ill., 1981-85; pres. CNR, Inc., Oak Brook, Ill., 1985-91; spl. agt. Prudential Ins., Oak Brook, Ill., 1991-95; mng. dir. Visimark L.L.C., Oak Brook, Ill., 1995—. Author: Creating Acceptance for Handicapped People, 1975, Creating, Planning, and Financial Housing for Handicapped People, 1979. Founder, organizer Found. for Handicapped, 1970-76,; pres. DuPage County Pub. Health Coun., 1974; bd. dirs. DuPage County Mental Health Assocs., 1970, Forest Found. DuPage County, 1976-86, Shakespeare Globe, London and Chgo., 1982—; mem. DuPage County Bd. Health, 1975, Ill. Gov.'s Com. for Handicapped, 1976, women's coun. Chgo. Heart Assn., 1979—. Recipient Meritorious Svc. award, Chgo. Heart Assn., 1968, 70, Fond du Coer award AHA, 1968, Cursade of Mercy Achievement awards, 1974-76, State of Ill. procalmation by Gov. James Thompson, Ill. Epilepsy Assn., 1978. Home: 71293 Country Club Dr Rancho Mirage CA 92270-3536

NELSONWILLIAMS, CECELIA ELAINE, dietician, nutritionist; d. Henry Austin Williams and Geraldine Jackson; m. Reverend John Alexander Nelson, Aug. 26, 1995. MS, CUNY, 1982. Registered dietitian-nutritionist SUNY Edn. Dept., 1996. Food svc. dir., clin. nutritionist Sheepshead Nursing Home, Bklyn., 1987—93; nutrition cons. Met. Jewish Hospice Greater NY, 1994—; correctional health care nutritionist, 2002—. Adj. lectr. NYU Sch. Contunining Edn., NYC, 1992—96. Trustee N.Y. ann. conf. United Meth. Ch., White Plains, 1999—. Recipient Devoted and Loyal Svc. award, John Wesley United Meth. Ch., 1994, Vol. Am. Heart Assn. Recognition award, 1997. Mem.: Am. Dietetic Assn. (assoc.). Democrat. Methodist. Avocations: swimming, tennis, antique buyer, reading, travel. Home: PO Box 415 Mount Vernon NY 10552 Office: Health Edn Inst 100 Stevens Ave Mount Vernon NY 10550 Home Phone: 914-699-7308. Office Fax: 914-664-4797. Personal E-mail: ceceliard@aol.com.

NELTNER, MICHAEL MARTIN, lawyer; b. Cin., July 31, 1959; s. Harold John and Joyce Ann Neltner; m. Barbara Ann Phair, July 9, 1988; children: Brandon August, Alexandra Nicole. BA, Mercy Coll., 1981; MA, Athenaeum of Ohio, 1987; JD, U. Cin., 1994. Bar: Ohio 1994, U.S. Dist. Ct. (so. dist.) Ohio 1995. Tchr. Elder H.S., Cin., 1985-91; ins. agt. Ky. Ctrl., Cin., 1987-91; mediator City of Cin., 1992-94; tchg. asst. Ohio Gov.'s Inst., Cin., 1992; legal extern to Chief Justice Thomas Moyer Ohio Supreme Ct., 1993; assoc. Eagen, Wykoff & Healy, LPA, Cin., 1994-99, Thompson Hine & Flory, Cin., 1999-2000, Freund, Freeze & Arnold, Cin., 2000—03, Green & Green, Dayton, Ohio, 2003—. Editor-in-chief Mercy Coll. Lit. Mag., 1980-81, U. Cin. Law Rev., 1993-94. Campaign coord. Rep. Orgn. Detroit, 1980. Recipient Merit scholarship Cin. Enquirer, 1977-81, Sage scholarship Mercy Coll., 1980, Am. Jurisprudence award Lawyers Coop. Publishing, 1994. Mem ABA, Ohio Bar Assn., Cin. Bar Assn. (mem. acad. medicine com. 1995—, chair Ct. Appeals com. 1998-2000), Downtown Bar Assn. (chair appellate practice com. 2004-06). Home: 3344 Milverton Ct Cincinnati OH 45248-2865 Office: Green & Green 109 N Main St Dayton OH 45402 Office Phone: 937-224-3333. Business E-Mail: mmneltner@green-law.com.

NEMAT-NASSER, SIA, engineering educator, researcher; b. Tehran, Apr. 14, 1936; married. BS, Calif. State U., Sacramento, 1960; MSCE, U. Calif., Berkeley, 1961, PhD in Structural Mechanics, 1964. Asst. prof. civil engring. Calif. State U., Sacramento, 1961—62; postdoctoral fellow Northwestern U., Evanston, Ill., 1964—65, prof. civil engring. and applied math., 1970—85; tchg. fellow U. Calif., Berkeley, 1963—64, asst. prof. applied mechanics San Diego, 1966—69, assoc. prof. applied mechanics, 1969—70, prof. applied mechanics and engring. scis., 1985—99, prof. mech. and aerospace engring. dept., 1999—, disting. prof. mechanics and materials, 2004—. Dir. U. Calif. Ctr. Excellence Advanced Materials, San Diego, 1986—; founding dir. materials sci. and engring. grad. program U. Calif., San Diego, 1989—94, dir. Inst. Mechanics and Materials, 1998—2000; cons. Jet Propulsion Lab., Pasadena, Calif., 1967—67, Systems Exploration, San Diego, 1967—67, Gulf-General Atomic, San Diego, 1969—69, BDM Corp., McLean, Va., 1983—83, S-Cubed, La Jolla, Calif., 1985—89, Anatech Rsch. Corp, La Jolla, Calif., 1989—95, TRW, Redondo Beach, Calif., 1990—91, Engring. Sci. Software Inc, Smithfield, RI, 1992—92, Trans-Science Corp., La Jolla, Calif., 1987—98, Sandia Nat. Laboratories, Albuquerque, 1993—98, Alpha Star Corp., West Los Angeles, Calif., 1995—97, Gen. Atomics, San Diego, 1995—97, BP Exploration, Houston, 1998—99, Logicon, Albuquerque, 1998—2000; vis. prof. Tech. U. Denmark, Lyngby, 1972—73. Author: (book) On Elastic Stability Under Nonconservative Loads, 1972; editor: Mechanics Today, Vol. 1, 1974, Mechanics Today, Vol. 2, 1975, Mechanics Today, Vol. 3, 1976, Mechanics Today, Vol. 4, 1978, Mechanics Today, Vol. 5, 1980, Mechanics Today, Vol. 6, 1981, (seven book series) Mechanics of Elastic and Inelastic Solids, 1980, (book) Three Dimensional Constitutive Relations and Ductile Fracture, 1981, Hydraulic Fracturing and Geothermal Energy, 1983, Theoretical Foundation for Large-Scale Computations of Nonlinear Material BehaviorDordrecht, 1984, Large Deformations of Solids: Physical Basis and Mathematical Modeling, 1986; author: Micromechanics: Overall Properties of Heterogeneous Materials, 1993, Micromechanics: Overall Properties of Heterogeneous Materials, 2d edit., 1999, Plasticity: A Treatise on Finite Deformation of Heterogeneous In Elastic Materials, 2004. Named John Dove Isaacs Chair in Natural Philosophy, U. of Calif. San Diego, 1995—2000; recipient Alburz Ednl. Found. prize, Iran, 1975, Gold medal, Tech. U. of Crete, Greece, 1997, Willard F. Rockwell medal, Internat. Tech. Inst., 2003, Faculty Rsch. Lectr. award, U. Calif., San Diego, 2005; fellow Arthur Gould Tasheira fellow, 1962—63, Forth Found., 1963—64, Tech. U. of Denmark, 1972—73, Danish Ctr. for Applied Math. and Mechanics, 1987. Fellow: ASME (chair-materials divsn. 1997—98, Lifetime Membership Certification and Life Fellow Designation 2001, Nadai medal 2002, Adaptive Structures and Materials Sys. Best Paper award 2003, Hon. mem. award 2005, Robert Henry Thurston Lecture award 2006), Soc. Engring. Sci. (dir. 1976—82, v.p. 1978—79, pres. 1979—80, William Prager medal in Solid Mechanics 2002), Am. Acad. Mechanics (sec. 1988—94, pres. 1996—97); mem.: ASM, ASCE, NAE, Soc. for Exptl. Mechanics (B.J. Lazan award 2007), Internat. Soc. for Optical Engring., Minerals, Metals and Materials Soc., World Innovation Found. Office: U Calif San Diego 9500 Gilman Dr La Jolla CA 92093-0416 Business E-Mail: sia@ucsd.edu.

NEMAZEE, HASSAN, investment banker; b. Washington, Jan. 27, 1950; AB, Harvard U., 1972. Chmn., CEO Nemazee Holdings, 1972—79, HN Properties, 1979—87, Nemazee Capital Corp., Washington, 1987—. Chmn. Iran Found., Shiraz Waterworks; mem., vis. com. U. Resources Harvard U., 1986—2002, mem., Mid. East Ctr. Adv. Coun., 1990—94, mem., Internat. Affairs Planning Com., 1990—95, mem., vis. com. Ctr. Internat. Affairs, 1998—2005; vice chmn. Encyclopedia Iranica, Columbia U., 1990—98; mem. Am. Iranian Coun., 2001; mem., policy adv. bd. Asia Soc., mem., bd. trustees, 2003; mem. Coun. Fgn. Rels., 2004; mem., adv. bd. Fgn. Policy Leadership Coun., 2004, RAND Ctr. Mid. East Pub. Policy, 2006; co-chair Carret Asset Mgmt. Grp. LLC, Brean Murray Carret & Co.; mem., bd. dirs. Iranian Am. Polit. Action Com., NYC. Chmn. Nemazee Hosp., Nemazee Sch. Nursing; bd. trustee Shiraz U., Spence Sch., 1993—97, Brain Trauma Found., 1996—. Office: 770 Park Ave New York NY 10021 *

NEMAZIE, SIAMACK, nephrologist, consultant; s. Farrokh and Fazileh Nemazie; m. Ammu Joyce James Gopalan, Nov. 3, 2000. MBBS, Kasturba Med. Coll., Manipal, India, 1998. Diplomate Am. Bd. Internal Medicine, 2004. House officer Rainy Hosp., Madras, 1998—99; resident house officer Apollo Specialty Hosp., Madras, 1999—2000, Harvey Heart Hosp., Madras, 2000—01, 2000—01; resident Brookdale Hosp. and Med. Ctr., Bklyn., 2001—04, chief resident internal medicine, 2003—04, nephrology fellow, 2004—. Hosp. del. Com. Interns and Residents, Bklyn., 2004—05. Named Best First Yr. Resident, Alumni Assn., 2002. Mem.: AMA, ACP, Am. Soc. Hypertension (cert. specialist in clin. hypertension 2005), Am. Soc. Nephrology (assoc.). Achievements include research in platelet dysfunction in hemodialysis patients. Avocation: travel. Office: Brookdale Hosp and Med Ctr Divsn Nephrology 1 Brookdale Plz Brooklyn NY 11236 Home Phone: 718-485-0097; Office Phone: 718-240-5615. E-mail: snemazie@hotmail.com.

NEMEC, CHRISTOPHER E., music educator; b. Park Ridge, Ill., July 31, 1962; s. Emil F. Nemec and Barbara A. Hamilton. MusB in Edn., U. Memphis, 1985, postgrad., 1998. Children's choir leadership cert. progra, Choristers Guild. Organist-music adminstr., dir. children's and youth music Lindenwood Christian Ch., Memphis, 1983—. With Lindenwood Concerts, Memphis, 1982—; accompanist, assoc. condr. Gary Beard Chorale, Memphis, 1987—; intern Am. Boychoir, Princeton, NJ, 1996; singer Carnegie Hall, NYC, 1997—2004; music dir. Gold Strike Casino, Tunica, Miss., 2003—04. Composer: (choral-orchetsral composition) Be Strong; prodr.: (musical productions) Producer of Lindenwood Concerts; performer: (CDs) Do You Remember? The Piano Stylings of Chris Nemex, Simply Delicious, The Very Best Time of Year. Meal deliverer Memphis Interfaith Assn., Memphis, 2003—05; tutor Hollywood Elem. Sch., Memphis, 2003—04; vol. St. Jude's Children's Rsch. Hosp., 2007. Mem.: Chorus USA, Am. Choral Dirs. Assn., Choristers Guild (Five Exceptional Children's Choir Leaders 2007), Am. Guild Organists. Democrat. Mem. Christian Ch. (Disciples Of Christ). Avocations: travel, yoga. Office: Lindenwood Christian Ch 2400 Union Ave Memphis TN 38112 Home: 2263 Tunis Cove Memphis TN 38104 Home Phone: 901-725-7409; Office Phone: 901-458-1652. Office Fax: 901-458-0145; Home Fax: 901-458-0145. Personal E-mail: chrisnemec@bellsouth.net. Business E-Mail: chris.nemec@lroom.org.

NEMEC, JOSEF, retired organic chemist, researcher; b. Ostresany, Czechoslovakia, Sept. 7, 1929; came to U.S., 1969; s. Josef Nemec and Marie (Joskova) Nemcova; m. Anna Pastush, Aug. 29, 1975; 1 child, Marketa. MS, Inst. Chem. Tech., Prague, Czechoslovakia, 1954; PhD, Czechoslovak Acad. Scis., Prague, 1958. Organic chemist Inst. Chem. Tech., Prague, 1954-61; sr. rsch. chemist Czechoslovak Acad. Scis., Prague, 1961-69; rsch. fellow in organic chemistry Wayne State U., Detroit, 1969-70; sr. rsch. scientist Squibb Inst. Med. Rsch., New Brunswick, NJ, 1970-75; staff mem. St. Jude Children's Rsch. Hosp., Memphis, 1975-84; sr. scientist Nat. Cancer Inst.-Program Resources, Inc. Cancer R&D Ctr., Frederick, Md., 1984-95; ret., 1995. Adj. prof. med. chemistry U. Tenn., Memphis, 1979-91; external examiner U. Zimbabwe, Harare, 1994—; cons. in field. Contbr. articles to scholarly and profl. jours. Grantee Nat. Cancer Inst., 1975-85. Mem. AAAS, Am. Chem. Soc., Royal Soc. Chemistry, Czechoslovak Soc. Arts and Scis. Achievements include patents in fields of anticancer agents, organic chemicals, semimicroequipment in organic chemistry; research in natural products, synthetic anticancer agents, monosaccharides, experimental semimicrotechniques in organic chemistry.

NEMECEK, ALBERT DUNCAN, JR., retail executive, investment banker, management consultant; b. Helena, Mont., Mar. 10, 1936; s. Albert Duncan and Geneva (Reindle) N.; m. Marilyn Ann Shaughnessy, Sept. 7, 1963 (div.); children: Maureen Ann, Steven Mathew; m. Judith Eileen Swift, Sept. 18, 1981 (div.); 1 child, Jennifer Eileen. BS, U. Md., 1960, postgrad. in econs., 1961. Agt. IRS, Washington, 1961-65; tax dir. Macke Co., Washington, 1965-69; tax dir., then sec. Garfinckle, Brooks Bros., Miller & Rhoads, Inc., Washington, 1969-76, treas., 1976—, v.p., 1979—; mng. ptnr. Nemecek & Falleroni, 1987, Nemecek & Jacknis, investment bankers, mgmt. cons., Falls Church, Va., 1989; founder Nemecek & Co., Inc., Falls Church, 1990. Founder Entreprenurial Growth Fund, Falls Church, 1990. Founder The Leadership Group, 1996. Home: PO Box 21 Occoquan VA 22125-0021 Personal E-mail: fixit00001@aol.com. *A man's success is measured by the respect he has gained from his peers, his understanding and compassion, respect for the feelings of others, appreciation of the world's beauty, and his attempts to leave the world better than he found it.*

NEMECEK, GEORGINA MARIE, molecular pharmacologist; b. Mineola, NY, Aug. 27, 1946; d. George and Frances Valerie (Masaryk) N. AB, Mt. Holyoke Coll., 1968; PhD, U. Pa., 1972; Master's cert. in Project Mgmt., George Washington U., 2000. Cert. project mgmt. profl. Project Mgmt. Inst., 2005. Rsch. assoc. dept. biochemistry U. Mass. Med. Sch., Worcester, 1972-73, postdoctoral fellow of Am. Heart Assn., dept. biochemistry, 1974, asst. prof., 1974-80, assoc. prof., 1981-83; sr. scientist platelet dept. Sandoz Pharm. Corp., East Hanover, NJ, 1983-85, mem. sr. sci. staff, platelet dept., 1986, fellow, sect. head molecular biology, 1987-91, fellow diabetes, 1991-93, study dir. regulatory toxicology, 1993-96; team rep. internat. project preclin. safety Novartis Pharm. Corp., East Hanover, 1997, assoc. dir. project mgmt., 1997-2000, dir. project mgmt., 2000—02, dir. integrative compound and product profiling, 2002—03, dir. project review, biomarker devel., 2003—04, dir. neurosci. project mgmt., biomarker devel., 2004—. Vis. scientist dept. molecular biology, Princeton (N.J.) U., 1987, Sea Pharm. Inc., 1985, NATO, U. Libre, Brussels, 1979, biotechnology dept. Sandoz AG, Basel, Switzerland, 1988. Contbr. articles to profl. jours. Named Nat. Heart, Lung, and Blood Inst. Young Investigator, NIH, 1977-81. Mem. Am. Soc. Pharmacol. Exptl. Therapeutics, N.Y. Acad. Scis. (chmn. biochem. sect. 1992-94), Project Mgmt. Inst., Sigma Xi. Avocations: boating, gardening, riding, needlecrafts. Office: Novartis Pharm Corp 1 Health Plz East Hanover NJ 07936-1005 Home Phone: 973-598-1231; Office Phone: 862-778-2342. Business E-Mail: georgina.nemecek@novatis.com.

NEMEROFF, CHARLES BARNET, neurobiology and psychiatry educator; b. Bronx, NY, Sept. 7, 1949; s. Philip Peace and Sarah (Greenberg) N.; m. Melissa Ann Pilkington, May 24, 1980 (div.); children: Matthew P. (dec. 1997), Amanda P., Sarah-Frances P.; m. Gayle Applegate, June 11, 2001. BS, CCNY, 1970; MS, Northeastern U., 1973; PhD, U. N.C., 1976, MD, 1981. Diplomate Am. Bd. Psychiatry and Neurology; lic. physician, N.C., Ga. Rsch. asst. ichthyology Am. Mus. Natural History, NYC, 1968-71; neurochemistry lab. McLean Hosp., Belmont, Mass., 1971-72; rsch. assoc. surgery Beth Israel Hosp., Boston, 1972-73; tchg. asst. biology Northeastern U., 1972-73; postdoctoral fellow Biol. Scis. Rsch. Ctr., U. N.C., Chapell Hill, 1976-77, rsch. fellow, 1977-83, clin. instr. psychiatry, 1983; resident psychiatry N.C. Meml. Hosp., Chapel Hill, 1981-83; asst. prof. dept. psychiatry and pharmacology Duke U., Durham, NC, 1983-85, assoc. prof. psychiatry, 1985-89, assoc. prof. pharmacology, 1986-89, prof. depts. psychiatry and pharmacology, 1989-91, chief divsn. biol. psychiatry, 1988-91; prof., chmn. dept. psychiatry and behavioral scis. Emory U. Sch. Medicine, Atlanta, 1991—, Reunette W. Harris prof. psychiatry and behavioral scis., 1994—. Vis. prof. physiology Cath. U., Santiago, Chile, 1978; sci. coun. Nat. Alliance for Rsch. Schizophrenia and Depression, 1997—; mem. coun. NIMH, 1999-2002; mem. biomed. rsch. coun. NASA, 2000-03; bd. dirs. George West Mental Health Found., 1999—, Cypress Bioscis. Inc., 2001—05, NovaDel Pharma, 2005—. Editor: (with A.J. Prange Jr.) Neurotensin, a Brain and Gastrointestinal Peptide, 1982, (with A.J. Dunn) Peptides, Hormones and Behavior, 1984, (with P.T. Loosen) Handbook of Clinical Psychoneuroendocrinology, Neuropeptides in Psychiatric and Neurological Disorders, 1987, Neuropeptides in Psychiatric Disorders, 1991, Neuroendocrinology, 1992, (with P. Kitabgi) The Neurobiology of Neurotensin, 1992, (with A.F. Schatzberg) Textbook of Psychopharmacology, 1995, 3d edit., 2004, (with A. F. Schatzberg) Recognition and Treatment of Psychiatric Disorders, 1999, The Corsini Encyclopedia of Psychology and Behavioral Science, 3d edit., vols. 1-4, 2001, (with W.E. Craighead) concise edit. 2004, (with Dennis S. Charney) The Peace of Mind Prescription, 2004 (Ken award Nat. Alliance of The Mentally Ill), (with David Purselle and Arthur Jongsmia) The Psychopharmacology Treatment Planner, 2003, (with Jeffrey Kelsey and D. Jeffrey Newport) Principles of Psychopharmacology for Mental Health Professionals 2006; editor-in-chief: Depression, 1993-00, Psychopharmacology Bull., 2001-02, Neuropsychopharmacology, 2001-06; co-editor-in-chief: Critical Revs. in Neurobiology, 1992-01; contbr. chpts. to books and articles and abstracts to profl. jours. Recipient Michiko Kuno award U. N.C., 1978, 79, Merck award for acad. excellence, 1981, Merck award for young investigators Am. Geriatrics Soc., 1985, 2nd prize Anna Monica Found. for Rsch. in Endogenous Depression, 1987, Merit award NIMH, 1987, rsch. prize World Fedn. Socs. Biol. Psychiatry, 1991, Edward J. Sachar award Columbia U., 1993, Edward A. Strecker prize Instnl. Pa. Hosp., 1993, Outstanding Alumni award in health scis. Northeastern U., 1995, Disting. Alumni award U. NC Sch. Medicine, 1999, George Ham Alumni award dept. psychiatry U. NC, 2000, Charles Burlingame prize Inst. Living, 2002, Alumni award U. NC, 2006; grantee Nat. Inst. Aging, 1982-83, NIMH, 1983—, NIDA, 1996-98; predoctoral fellow Schizophrenia Rsch. Found., Soc. Scottish Rite, Lexington, Mass., 1975-76, postdoctoral fellow Nat. Inst. Neurol., Communicative Disorders and Stroke, 1977, Nanaline Duke fellow Duke U. Med. Ctr., 1985-87. Fellow Am. Coll. Neuropsychopharmacology (Mead Johnson Travel award 1982, Efron award 1987, coun. 1993—99, pres. 1997), Am. Coll. Psychiatrists (chmn. contbns. com. 1991-93, 95—, edn. com. 1993-96, 96—, bd. regents 1994-97, 1st v.p. 1999, pres.-elect 2000, pres. 2001, chair sci. program com. 2005-07, Mood Disorders Rsch. award 1998, Bowis award 1999, Dean award 2004); mem. AAAS, AMA, Soc. Neurosci. (program com. 1993-95), Internat. Soc. Psychoneuroendocrinology (pres. 1993-96, Curt P. Richter award 1985), Internat. Soc. Neuroendocrinology, Internat. Soc. Neurochemistry, Am. Soc. Neurochemistry (Jordi-Folch-Pi award 1987), Endocrine Soc., Soc. Neuroendocrinology, Soc. Biol. Psychiatry (A.E. Bennett award 1979, Gold medal award 1996), Am. Fedn. Clin. Rsch., Am. Pain Soc., Am. Psychiat. Assn. (coun. rsch. 1993-98, 02-04, chmn. 1994-95, bd. dirs. rsch. inst. 1999—2007, chair coun. rsch. subcom. on psychiat. treatments 1999-2003, Kempf award 1989, Samuel Hibbs award 1991, Rsch. prize 1996, Rsch. Mentoring award 2006, Vestermark award 2006, Disting. Psychiatrist lectr. Ann. Meeting 1999, 2003), Am. Coll. Physicians (William C. Menninger award 2000), Argentine Assn. Psychoneuroendocrinology (sci. coun.), Nat. Depressive and Manic Depressive Disorders Assn. (vice chair 1996-98, bd. dirs. 1999—2002, chair 1999-2000, Gerald L. Klerman Lifetime Achievement award 1997), Anxiety Disorder Assn. Am. (chmn. sci. adv. bd. 2001-2003), NY Acad. Scis., Am. Found. for Suicide Prevention (sci. adv. bd. 1997—, bd. dirs. 1998—, v.p. 2006, pres. Sci. Coun. 2007—, Rsch. prize 2001), Inst. Medicine, Sigma Xi, Alpha Omega Alpha. Democrat. Jewish. Office: Emory U Sch Medicine Dept Psychiatry 101 Woodruff Cir Atlanta GA 30322-0001 Home Phone: 404-236-0372; Office Phone: 404-727-8382. Business E-Mail: cnemero@emory.edu.

NEMEROFF, MICHAEL ALAN, lawyer; b. Feb. 16, 1946; s. Bernard Gregor and Frances (Gotleib) N.; m. Sharon Lynn Leininger, Sept. 22, 1974; children: Theodore, Patrick, James. BA, U. Chgo., 1968; JD, Columbia U., 1971. Asst. counsel Subcom. on Juvenile Delinquency of Senate Jud. Com., Washington, 1971-73; assoc. Sidley Austin LLP, Washington, 1973-78, ptnr., 1978—. Treas. Friends of Jim Sasser, 1978-96, Andy Ireland Campaign Com., 1984-92. Office: Sidley Austin LLP 1501 K St NW Washington DC 20005 Office Phone: 202-736-8000.

NEMEROWICZ, GLORIA, academic administrator; 2 children. BA, MA, Rutgers U., PhD in Sociology. Assoc. prof. sociology Monmouth Coll., NJ, provost NJ; exec. dir. Women's Leadership Inst. Wells Coll., Aurora, NY, 1993—96; pres. Pine Manor Coll., Chestnut Hill, Mass., 1996—. Author: (books) Children's Perceptions of Gender and Work Roles; co-author (with Eugene Rosi): Professionalism in Unpaid Work; contbr. op-ed pieces to newspapers. Office: Pine Manor Coll 400 Health St Chestnut Hill MA 02467

NEMES, ATTILA, soil scientist, researcher; b. Miskolc, Hungary, Nov. 14, 1970; s. Zoltán Nemes and Hedvig Sárossy; m. Anikó Ildikó Kádár, Aug. 31, 2002. MSc, Agrl. U. Gödöllö, Hungary, 1994; PhD, Wageningen U. and Rsch. Ctr., Netherlands, 2003. Rsch. assoc. Rsch. Inst. for Soil Sci. and Agrl. Chemistry of the Hungarian Acad. Scis., Budapest, 1994—97; vis. scientist Purdue U., West Lafayette, Ind., 1996; rsch. assoc. The Winand Staring Ctr., Wageningen, 1997—98; vis. scientist U. Calif., Riverside, 1999, postdoctoral scientist, 2005—; rsch. assoc. ALTERRA Green World Rsch. Inst., Wageningen, 1999—2003; vis. scientist Hydrology and Remote Sensing Lab., US Dept. Agr., Beltsville, Md., 2003—. Contbr. articles to profl. jours., chapters to books. Mem., regional co-chair, nat. bd. mem. Assn. Student Housing Orgn., Budapest, 1991—93; mem., regional chair Assn. Agrl. and Rural Youth and 4H Clubs, Budapest, 1991—94. TEMPUS European Union fellow, European Union, 1993, 1996, Eötvös fellow, Hungarian Nat. Fellowship Bd., 1997, Internat. Agrl. Ctr. fellow, Ministry of Agr. Nature Mgmt. and Fisheries, The Netherlands, 1998, 2000, 2001, Huygens fellow, Netherlands Orgn. for Internat. Cooperation in Higher Edn., 1999. Mem.: Am. Geophys. Union, Soil Sci. Soc. Am. (assoc. editor, mem. editl. bd. jour., Editor's citation 2004), Crop Sci. Soc. Am., Agronomy Soc. Am., Toastmasters Internat. Avocations: travel, hiking, swimming, basketball, curling. Office: Crop Sys and Global Change Lab 10300 Baltimore Ave Bldg 001 Beltsville MD 20705 Home Phone: 301-725-9737; Office Phone: 301-504-5177. Business E-Mail: attila.nemes@ars.usda.gov.

NEMETH, PATRICIA MARIE, lawyer; b. Flint, Mich., Sept. 18, 1959; d. Gyula Nemeth and Marie (Glaska) Adkins. BA, U. Mich., 1981; JD, Wayne State U., 1984, LLM, 1990. Bar: Ill. 1987, Mich. 1984, U.S. Ct. Appeals (6th cir.), U.S. Dist. Ct. (ea. dist.) Mich., U.S. Dist. Ct. (we. dist.) Mich. Teaching asst. Wayne State U., Detroit, 1982; intern. U.S. Dist. Ct. (ea. dist.) Mich., Detroit, 1983; assoc. Bloom & Bloom, Birmingham, Mich., 1984-85, Stringari, Fritz, Kreger, Ahearn, Bennett & Hunsinger, Detroit, 1985-92; prin. Law Offices of Patricia Nemeth, P.C., Detroit, 1992-97, Nemeth Burwell PC, Detroit, 1992—. Lectr. in field; adj. prof. Walsh Coll., 1992—94. Guest appearance (TV) Straight Talk, 1994, 95, 2002, You and the Law, 2005, Detroit Newsmakers, 2005; contbr. articles to profl. jours. Mem. adv. bd. Vista Maria, 2001-02, bd. dirs., 2002—, vice chair exec. bd., 2003—; mem. pers. com. Met. Detroit coun. Girl Scout Am., 2002—. Named Winner Orgnl. Performance Category, Crain's/IRI, 2003; named one of Top10 Best Places to Work in Southeastern Mich., 2001, 2003, Best and Brightest Cos. to Work For, 2001—06, Top 50 Women Super Lawyers Mich., 2006—07; recipient Dist. Vol. for Vista Maria, Assn. Fundraising Profls., 2005. Mem. ABA (labor sect.), Mich. Bar Assn. (labor sect.), Ill. Bar Assn., Nat. Order Barristers, Nat. Assn. Women Bus. Owners (internat. com. sec., exec. bd., bd. dirs., named One of Top Ten Women Bus. Owners of Distinction 2002), Women's Econ. Club (strategic com. 2002-03), Lawyers Assn. Mich., Detroit Bar Assn., Health Care Assn. of Mich. Roman Catholic. Avocations: sailing, rollerblade. Office: 200 Talon Centre Detroit MI 48207- Office Phone: 313-567-5921. Business E-Mail: pnemeth@nemethburwell.com.

NEMETZ, PETER NEWMAN, economist, researcher, policy analysis educator; b. Vancouver, BC, Can., Feb. 19, 1944; s. Nathan Theodore and Bel Nemetz; m. Roma E.S. Kellock, July 16, 1994; 1 stepchild, Fiona Susan. BA in Econs. and Polit. Sci., U. BC, Can., 1966; AM in Econs., Harvard U., Cambridge, Mass., 1969, PhD in Econs., 1973. Tchg. fellow, tutor Harvard U., Cambridge, Mass., 1971-73; lectr. Sch. Planning U. BC, Vancouver, 1973-75, asst. prof. to assoc. prof. policy analysis, 1975-96, prof., 1996—, chmn., 1984-90. Non-resident faculty Green Coll., 1993-94, 95-97, St. John's Coll., 1997-2002; vis. scientist, rschr., collaborator Dept. Health Scis. Rsch. Mayo Clinic, 1986—; cons. consumer and corp. affairs, Can., 1977-80, BC Hydro, 2000-02; program chmn. The Vancouver Inst., 1987—; mem. bd. advisors evidence-based practice ctr. rsch. project U. Calif., San Francisco, 2000-01; mem. sr. faculty Ctr. Health Svcs. and Policy Rsch., U. BC, 1990-, dept. resource mgmt. and environ. studies, 1979—, Ctr. Japanese Studies, 1992—; mem. Inst. for Resources and Environment, U. BC, 1997—, selection com. Rhodes Scholarship, 1991-99, mem. senate, 1998-2002, mgmt. com. Ctr. Southeast Asia Rsch., 1992-99, assoc. mem. Faculty Medicine dept. health care and epidemiology faculty medicine, 1995—; bd. dirs. U. BC Press, 1993-2002; assoc. Ctr. Pacific Basin Monetary and Econ. Studies, Econ. Rsch. Dept., Fed. Reserve Bank of San Francisco, 1991—. Editor Jour. Bus. Adminstrn., 1978-04, Sustainable Resource Management: Reality or Illusion?, 2007; mem. editl. bd. Jour. Internat. Bus. Edn., 2001—; contbr. articles to sci. jours. Life mem. BC-Yukon divsn. Can Nat. Inst. for Blind. Recipient Tchg. Excellence award Commerce Undergrad. Soc., 2006-07; grantee Natural Scis. and Engring. Rsch. Coun. Can., 1976-92, Consumer and Corp. Affairs Can., 1978-80, Econ. Coun. Can., 1979-80, Max Bell Found., 1982-84; postdoctoral fellow Westwater Rsch. Ctr., Vancouver, 1973-75. Mem. Am. Econ. Assn., Internat. Epidemiol. Assn., Harvard Club of BC (pres. 1986-94), Vancouver Club. Jewish. Avocations: swimming, photography. Office: Univ BC Sauder Sch Bus Vancouver BC Canada V6T 1Z2 Home Phone: 604-224-5383; Office Phone: 604-822-8443. Business E-Mail: peter.nemetz@sauder.ubc.ca.

NEMFAKOS, CHARLES PANAGIOTIS, defense industry executive, strategic consultant; b. Athens, Greece, Oct. 21, 1942; s. Panagiotis Soterios and Mirka (Kyriakakis) N.; children: Mirka Leigh, Charles Jr.; m. Pamela Durrant; 1 child, Alexandra. BA, Pan Am. U., 1964; MA, Georgetown U., 1982. Cert. in nat. security. Health advisor USPHS, Washington, 1965-66; fed. mgmt. intern Dept. Navy, Washington, 1966-67; budget analyst Naval Ordnance Systems Command, Washington, 1967-71; supervisory budget analyst Naval Ship Systems Command, Washington, 1971-73; sr. budget analyst Office of Sec. of Def., Washington, 1973-75; divsn. dir. Office Budget and Reports Dept. Navy, Washington, 1975-76, assoc. dir., 1976-93, dep. asst. sec., 1994-95, dep. undersec., 1995—2001, sr. civilian ofcl. for fin. mgmt., comptr., 1998—2001; dir. internal programs devel. Lockheed Martin Corp., Manassas, Va., 2001—03; organizing mem. Nemfakos Ptnrs., LLC, Arlington, Va., 2003—07; sr. fellow Rand Corp., 2007—. Bd. dirs. First Command Ednl. Found., Am. Automar and Atlantic Marine; mem. adv. bd. Advanced Tech. Inst., Global Maritek; adj. Rand Corp., Logistics Mgmt. Inst.; lectr. Naval Postgrad. Sch., Monterey, Calif., 1984—, Georgetown U., Washington, 1987—, Ind. U. Grad. Sch., 1996—, Def. Acquisition U., 2001—; mem. base structure com. Dept. Navy, Washington, 1990-91, mem. sr. advisors group, 1991-92, vice-chmn. base structure com., 1992-95; gen. adminstrn. bd. USDA Grad. Sch., 2000—; bd. advisors, chmn. disaster relief and humanitarian assistance com. SOLE Internat. Contbr. articles to profl. jours. Coach McLean (Va.) Youth Soccer, 1978-93, chmn., 1982-85; bd. dirs. McLean Youth, Inc., 1980-84; registrar Va. Youth Soccer Assn., 1984-86. Recipient Dept. Navy Superior Civilian Svc. award Asst. Sec. of Navy, 1980, Dept. Navy Disting. Civilian Svc. award Sec. of Navy, 1985, 87, 93, 2000, 01, Dept. Def. Disting. Civilian Svc. award Sec. of Def., 1990, 2000, 01, Dept. Navy Disting. Pub. Svc. award Sec. of Navy, 1995, Roger W. Jones award exec. leadership Am. U., 2000; named to Rank of Disting. Exec. Pres. of U.S., 1986, 95, to Rank of Meritorious Exec., Pres. of U.S., 1981, 91; named Career Civilian Exemplar Sec. of Def., 2004. Mem. Am. Assn. Budget and Program Analysis (dir.-at-large 1980-83), Am. Soc. Mil. Comptrs. (v.p. 1988-90), Fed. Execs. Inst. Alumni Assn., Tau Kappa Epsilon (chpt. pres. 1964-65). Greek Orthodox. Avocations: golf, tennis, soccer. Home Phone: 703-362-6391; Office Phone: 703-413-1100 x5660. Business E-Mail: charles_nemfakos@rand.org.

NEMIR, DONALD PHILIP, lawyer; b. Oakland, Calif., Oct. 31, 1931; s. Philip F. and Mary (Shavor) N. AB, U. Calif., Berkeley, 1957, JD, 1960. Bar: Calif. 1961, U.S. Dist. Ct. (no. dist.) Calif. 1961, U.S. Ct. Appeals (9th cir.) 1961, U.S. Dist. Ct. (ctrl. dist.) Calif. 1975, U.S. Supreme Ct. 1980. Pvt. practice, San Francisco, 1961—. Home: PO Box 1089 Mill Valley CA 94942-1089 Home Phone: 415-381-8469; Office Phone: 415-421-0400. Personal E-mail: dnemir@earthlink.net.

NEMIRO, BEVERLY MIRIUM ANDERSON, author, educator; b. St. Paul, May 29, 1925; d. Martin and Anna Mae Anderson; m. Jerome Morton Nemiro, Feb. 10, 1951-75; children: Guy Samuel, Lee Anna, Dee Martin. Student, Reed Coll., 1943-44; BA, U. Colo., 1947; postgrad., U. Denver. Tchr. Seattle Pub. Sch., 1945-46; fashion coord., dir. Denver Dry Goods Co., 1948-51; fashion dir. Denver Market Week Assn., 1952-53; free-lance writer Denver, 1958—. Moderator TV program Your Presch. Child, Denver, 1955-56; instr. writing and comm. U. Colo. Denver Ctr., 1970—, U. Calif., San Diego, 1976-78, Met. State Coll., 1985; dir. pub. rels. Fairmont Hotel, Denver, 1979-80; freelance fashion and TV model. Author, co-author: The Complete Book of High Altitude Baking, 1961, Colorado a la Carte, 1963, Colorado a la Carte, Series II, 1966, (with Donna Hamilton) The High Altitude Cookbook, 1969, The Busy People's Cookbook, 1971 (Better Homes and Gardens Book Club selection 1971), Where to Eat in Colorado, 1967, Lunch Box Cookbook, 1965, Complete Book of High Altitude Baking, 1961, (under name Beverly Anderson) Single After 50, 1978, The New High Altitude Cookbook, 1980. Co-founder, pres. Jr. Symphony Guild, Denver, 1959-60; active Friends of Denver Libr., Opera Colo.; mem. Friends of Painting and Sculpture, Denver Art Mus. Recipient Top Hand award Colo. Authors' League, 1969, 72, 79-82, 100 Best Books of Yr. award NY Times, 1969, 71; named one of Colo. Women of Yr., Denver Post, 1964. Mem. Am. Soc. Journalists and Authors, Colo. Authors League (dir. 1969-79), Authors Guild, Friends Denver Libr., Denver Women's Press Club, Kappa Alpha Theta. Address: Park Towers 1299 Gilpin St Apt 15W Denver CO 80218-2556

NEMIROFF, MAXINE CELIA, small business owner, art historian; b. Chgo., Feb. 11, 1935; d. Oscar Bernard and Martha (Mann) Kessler; m. Paul Rubenstein, June 26, 1955 (div. 1974); children: Daniel, Peter, Anthony; m. Allan Nemiroff, Dec. 24, 1979. BA, U. So. Calif., 1955; MA, UCLA, 1974. Sr. instr. UCLA, 1974-92; dir., curator art gallery Doolittle Theater, Los Angeles, 1985-86; owner Nemiroff Deutsch Fine Art, Santa Monica, Calif. Leader of worldwide art tours; cons. L'Ermitage Hotel Group, Beverly Hills, Calif., 1982—, Broadway Dept. Stores, So. Calif., 1979—, Security Pacific Bank, Calif., 1978—, Am. Airlines, Calif. Pizza Kitchen Restaurants; art chmn. UCLA Thieves Market, Century City, 1960—, L.A. Music Ctr. Mercado, 1982—; lectr. in field. Apptd. bd. dirs. Dublin (Calif.) Fine Arts Found., 1989; mem. Calif. Govs. Adv. Coun. for Women, 1992; mem. art selection com. Calif. State Office Bldgs., 1997—. Named Woman of Yr. UCLA Panhellenic Council, 1982, Instr. of Yr. UCLA Dept. Arts, 1984; recipient Woman of Achievement award Friends of Sheba Med. Ctr., 2003; elected to Fashion Circle of the Costume Coun., L.A. County Mus. Art, 1997—; honoree L.A. Art Core 15th Ann. Awards Benefit, 2003. Mem. L.A. County Mus. Art Coun., UCLA Art Coun., UCLA Art Coun. Docents, Alpha Epsilon Phi (alumnus of yr. 1983). Avocations: tennis, horseback riding, skiing, piano and guitar. Personal E-mail: mumseyart@aol.com.

NEMMERS, JOSEPH M., JR., pharmaceutical executive; b. Dec. 22, 1954; B in History, Ariz. State U. Numerous positions in comml. ops., mfg. and materials mgmt. Abbott Labs., Abbott Park, Ill., 1980—99, v.p., exec. dir. Clara Abbott Found., 1999—2000, divisional v.p. Acquisition Integration Mgmt., 2001—02, corp. v.p., 2001—02, v.p. hosp. products bus. sector, 2002, v.p. global comml. ops., 2002—03, sr. v.p. diagnostic ops., 2003—06, exec. v.p. diagnostics & animal health, 2006—. Mem. supervisory bd. Abbott Mgmt. GmbH and Abbott Holding GmbH. Chmn. bd. dirs. United Way Lake County, Carmel H.S.; bd. dirs. Ct. Appointed Spl. Advs., Boys and Girls Club Waukegan. With USAR. Office: Abbott Labs 100 Abbott Park Rd Abbott Park IL 60064-6400 *

NEMO, ANTHONY JAMES, lawyer; b. St. Paul, May 18, 1963; s. Joseph Marino Jr. and Dianne Marie (Wegner) N.; m. Mary Rose Mazzitello, July 17, 1987; children: Anne Marie, Katherine Mary, Anthony James Jr. BA in English Lit., U. St. Thomas, 1986; JD, William Mitchell Coll. Law, 1991. Bar: Minn. 1991, U.S. Dist. Ct. Minn., U.S. Dist. Ct. Ariz., U.S. Dist. Ct. (ea. dist.) Wis., U.S. Ct. Appeals (4th cir.), U.S. Supreme Ct. Account exec. div. info. svcs. TRW, Mpls., 1986-90; ptnr. Meshbesher & Spence, Ltd., St. Paul, 1990—. Assoc. editor William Mitchell Law Rev., 1988-90; author law rev. note. Recipient R. Ross Quaintance award, Douglas K. Amdahl-Mary O'Malley Lyons Trial Advocacy award. Mem. ABA, Minn. Trial Lawyers Assn., Assn. Trial Lawyers Am., Minn. State Bar Assn., Hennepin County Bar Assn., John P. Sheehy Legal History Soc. Roman Catholic. Home: 2125 Heath Ave N Oakdale MN 55128-5207 Office: Meshbesher & Spence Ltd 1616 Park Ave Minneapolis MN 55404

NEMSER, EARL HAROLD, lawyer; b. NYC, Jan. 17, 1947; s. Harold Summers and Eleanor Patricia (Beckerman) N.; m. Randy Lynn Lehrer, June 17, 1974 (div.); children: Eliza Sarah, Maggie Lehrer. BA, NYU, 1967; JD magna cum laude, Boston U., 1970. Bar: N.Y. 1970, U.S. Supreme Ct. 1975, U.S. Claims Ct. 1979, U.S. Tax Ct. 1985. Law clk. Hon. Collins J. Seitz chief judge U.S. Ct. Appeals 3rd Cir., 1970-71; ptnr. Cadwalader, Wickersham & Taft, NYC, 1971-95, Swidler Berlin Shereff Friedman, LLP, NYC, 1996—2001, sr. of counsel, 2002—04; pres. Park and 76th Street Co., Inc., NYC, 1998—2007; spl. counsel Dechert LLC, NYC, 2005—. Vice chmn. Interactive Brokers Group, Inc., Greenwich, Conn., 1995—; dir. Timber Hill, LLC, Greenwich, Caribbean Cellular Telephone Ltd., Tortola, BVI, 1997-02; solicitor gen. H.C., Guana Island, BVI. Spl. town atty. Town of Southampton, NY, 2002—; mem. bd. advisors Lenox Hill Hosp., Greenwich Land Trust. Mem. Assn. Bar City NY; dir. The Quiogue Assn., Greenwich Riding Trails Assn. (dir. 2005-). Office: Interactive Brokers Group Inc One Pickwick Plz Greenwich CT 06830

NEMUNAITIS, JOHN J., oncologist, medical association administrator; BA, Case Western Res. U., Cleve., 1978, MD, 1982. Bd. cert. internal medicine 1987. Asst. prof. medicine U. Wash., Seattle, 1991—92; dir. hematopoiesis program Western Pa. Hosp., Pitts., 1992—93; dir. clin. rsch. Tex. Oncology, P.A., Dallas, 1993—2004; exec. med. dir. Mary Crowley Med. Rsch. Ctr., Dallas, 1995—. Bd. mem. instl. biosafety com. WIRB, 2001—. Contbr. articles to profl. jours. Mem.: Internat. Soc. for Cell and Gene Therapy (mem. cancer coun. 2005—). Office: Mary Crowley Medical Research Center Ste 6000 1717 Main St Dallas TX 75201 Office Phone: 214-658-1964.

NENNEMAN, RICHARD ARTHUR, retired publishing executive; b. Chgo., Oct. 13, 1929; s. William T. and Fannie (Peterson) N.; m. Katherine Ann LaBrunerie, June 29, 1954; children: Ann Walker, Mary Lisa, Katherine Conley. AB magna cum laude, Harvard U., 1951, MA in Internat. Affairs, 1953. With No. Trust Co., Chgo., 1957-58; v.p., treas., dir. First Fed. Savs. & Loan Assn., St. Joseph, Mo., 1958-60; with Valley Nat. Bank, Phoenix, 1960-65; asst. v.p., 1963-65; bus. and fin. editor Christian Sci. Monitor, Boston, 1965-74; v.p., dir. investment rsch. Girard Bank, Phila., 1974-77, sr. v.p., chmn. trust investment policy com., 1977-82; mng. editor Christian Sci. Monitor, Boston, 1983-86; editor, exec. prodr., TV broadcasting Christian Sci. Pub. Soc., Boston, 1987; editor-in-chief Christian Sci. Monitor, 1988-93; ret., 1993. Mem. investment com. Gen. Accident Ins. Group., until 1982; dir. DLB Fund Group, 1994—. Contbr. to Understanding Our Century, 1984; editor: (with Earl Foell) How Peace Came to the World, 1986, The New Birth of Christianity, 1992, Persistent Pilgrim: The Life of Mary Baker Eddy, 1997. Trustee Barnes Found., until 1982; selectman Town of Weston, Mass., 1973-74. Served with AUS, 1954-57. Mem.: Coun. on Fgn. Rels. Home: PO Box 641 Lincoln MA 01773

NENOV, IVO P., mathematical and software researcher; b. Nikolaevo, Bulgaria, May 5, 1964; arrived in U.S., 1995; s. Panayot Nenov Ivanov and Maria Todorova Ivanova; m. Albena Dragomirova Stoilova-Nenova, Aug. 16, 1987 (div. Apr. 7, 1994); 1 child, Lubomir Ivov. MS, Tech. U. Sofia, Bulgaria, 1990, PhD (hon.), 2003; cert. in internat. bus. mgmt., U. Del., 1992. Rschr. Microprocessor Control Lab., Sofia, Bulgaria, 1986—86; rschr., developer CAD R&D Ctr. Ltd., Sofia, 1990—92; developer, technologist DataMap- Europe Ltd., Sofia, 1993—94; self-employed rschr., developer, cons. Calif., 1995—. Participated, set up European br. Frontline Sys., Inc., Incline Village, Nev., 2003; presenter in field. Contbr. articles to profl. jours. Capt. arty. Bulgarian armed forces, 1982—84. Recipient prize, Nat. Olympiad of Math., 1985, prize for tech., Nat. Competition for Tech., Sofia, 1989, award for extraordinary ability in sci., INS, 2000. Mem.: Am. Owners and Pilots Assn., Soc. Indsl. and Applied Math. Bulgarian Orthodox. Avocation: flying. Home and Office: 3337 Saxonville Way Antelope CA 95843 Office Phone: 916-334-3465. Personal E-mail: inenov@sbcglobal.net.

NENSTIEL, SUSAN KISTHART, fundraising professional; b. Hazleton, Pa., Aug. 21, 1951; d. Frank W. and Mary A. (Price) Kisthart. BS, Pa. State U., 1973; MBA, Wilkes Coll., Pa., 1982. Cert. fund raising exec. Control mgr. Barrett, Haentjens & Co., Hazleton, 1973-79, export mgr., 1979-86; exec. dir. Leadership Hazleton, 1986-87; devel. officer Planned Parenthood of NE Pa., Wilkes-Barre, 1986-87; ins. broker, office mgr. Nenstiel & Nenstiel, West Hazleton, Pa., 1988-96; assoc. dir. devel. Hospice St. John, 1996-97; devel. assoc. Luth. Svcs. N.E., 1997-98, reg. dir. devel., 1998-2000; exec. dir. LWV of Pa., 2000—01; sr. v.p. devel. Easter Seals Ea. Pa., 2001—03; dir. major gifts Albright Coll., 2003—05; devel. dir. Kutztown U., 2005—. Pres. YWCA, Hazleton, 1983-85, Women's Coalition of Greater Hazleton, 1987-91; sec. Govt. Study Commn., Hazleton, 1986; trustee Hazleton Area Pub. Libr., sec., 1987-89, v.p., 1990-91, pres., 1991-93; chmn. Luzerne County Commn. for Women, 1988-91; mem., chmn. Hazleton City Zoning Bd., 1988-92; treas. Pa. Women's Campaign Fund, 1987-91, pres., 1991-92; mem. Leadership Hazleton Adv. Coun., 1988-92; mem. Pa. Pub. Libr. Project, 1992-94; bd. dirs. Hazleton Health Care Found., 1992-2000, chairperson, 1994-99, Cmty. Banks, Inc., 1996-2001; mem. Greater Hazleton Health Alliance Bd., 1995-2000, sec., 2000; mem. Luzerne County Regional Bd. Cmty. Banks, N.A., 1993-2000, YWCA adv. coun., 1998-2000. Named one of Outstanding Women Penns Woods Coun. Girl Scouts USA, 1977, Outstanding Young Women in Am., 1985, Woman of Yr. Soroptimist Internat., 1984, Greater Hazleton Jaycee Disting. Svc. award, 1990; recipient Luzerne County Pathfinder's award, 1990, Hon. P.E.A.R.L. award YWCA, 1996; named to Pa. Honor Roll of Women, 1996. Mem. AAUW (br. pres. 1977-79, 97-2000, state sec. 1981-83, state treas. 1983-85, state pres. 1992-96, state bd. dirs. 2005, Br. Outstanding Woman of Yr. 1980, assn. program com. 1995-97, ednl. found. bd. dirs. 1999—2003, ednl. found. devel. v.p. 2001-03, mem. state bd., 2005—), Assn. Fund Raising Profls. (chpt. v.p. 2003-05, pres.-elect 2006—), Greater Hazleton C. of C. (bd. dirs. 1995-2000, treas. 1998-2000).

NEPALES, RUBEN VIADO, journalist; b. Calasiao, Pangasinan, Philippines, June 6, 1957; s. Pedro Parajas and Socorro Viado Nepales; m. Janet Susan Rodriguez Nepales, Aug. 2, 1985; children: Bianca Nicole Rodriguez, Rafaella Angelica Rodriguez. BA in Comm. Arts, U. Santo Tomas, Manila, Philippines, 1977. Contbg. writer Manila Bull., Philippine Daily Express and Times Jour., 1977—85; exec. editor Manila Extra Mag., LA, 1996—97; L.A. corr., columnist Philippine Daily Inquirer, Makati, 1997—. Contbr. essays and articles to publs. Named Outstanding Pangasinan Artist, Provincial Govt. of Pangasinan, 1984, Outstanding Profl. in the field of journalism, Celebrity Chronicle mag., 2004. Mem.: Hollywood Fgn. Press Assn. Roman Catholic. Avocation: travel. Home and Office: 11011 Whitegate Ave Sunland CA 91040 Home Phone: 818-352-6608; Office Phone: 818-352-6608. Personal E-mail: rvnepales@yahoo.com. Business E-Mail: rnepales@hfpa.org.

NEPHEW, EDMUND A., physicist, retired mayor; b. Kinsman, Ohio, Apr. 26, 1928; s. Seward Ralph Nephew and Carrie Alice Bascom; m. Maria Theresia Goebhardt, Sept. 1, 1956; children: Thomas, Robert. BS, Youngstown State U., Ohio; MS, Ohio State U.; grad. studies, U. Gottingen, Germany, U. Tenn. With Oak Ridge (Tenn.) Nat. Lab., 1959—89, City of Oak Ridge (Tenn.), 1984—89. Physicist Oak Ridge (Tenn.) Nat. Lab., 1959—89; councilman Oak Ridge (Tenn.) City Council, 1989—97, mayor, 1991—95. Mem., officer Sister Cities Orgn., Oak Ridge, Tenn., 1990—; chmn. ACLU (local chpt.), Oak Ridge, Tenn., 1998; commr. Oak Ridge (Tenn.) Regional Planning Assn., Oak Ridge, Tenn., 1984—88. Pvt. US Army, 1950—52. Democrat. Unitarian Universalist. Avocations: gardening, travel, reading, languages. Home: 119 Netherlands Rd Oak Ridge TN 37830

NEPHEW, JULIA ANNE, language educator; d. Albert Henry and Elizabeth Anne Nephew; m. Eric W. Bergman; 1 stepchild, Emily. BA in French, Gustavus Adolphus Coll., St. Peter, Minn., 1988; MA in French, U. Mich., Ann Arbor, 1990; PhD in French Lit., U. Wis., Madison, 1998. Instr. French Gustavus Adolphus Coll., 1994—96; prof. French Rockford Coll., 1998—2003; adj. prof. French Dominican U., 2003—. Adj. prof. Benedictine U., Lisle, Ill., 2007—. Co-founder and dir. Jane Addams Tenant Resource Ctr., Rockford, Ill., 2001—03. Grantee Summer Travel, Rockford Coll., 1999, Summer Rsch., 2001, Cmty. Engagement, Ill. Campus Compact, 2001—02, Partners in Action, 2002—03; scholar, Whiteside Scholarship Fund, 1984—88. Mem.: Betsy-Tacy Soc. (hon. bd. mem.), Medieval Assn. of Midwest, Sixteenth Century Studies, Christine de Pizan Soc. (treas. 2003—), Pi Delta Phi, Phi Sigma Iota. Avocations: travel, cross country skiing, reading, bicycling. Personal E-mail: nephewja@yahoo.com.

NEPPL, WALTER JOSEPH, retired retail executive; b. Halbur, Iowa, June 15, 1922; s. Frank and Anna (Halbur) N.; m. Marian Maher, Oct. 15, 1945; children: Eugenie Neppl Kauffman, Marilee Neppl Cumming, Deborah Neppl Johnson, John, Thomas (dec.), Christina Neppl Totino, Nancy Neppl Tripucka. With J.C. Penney Co., Inc., 1940—, mgr. store Albuquerque, 1954-55, dist. mgr. Pitts., 1955-61, store coordination mgr. NYC, 1961-64, asst. to dir. dist. mgmt. dept., 1964-65, gen. mdse. mgr. hard lines, 1965-67, v.p., 1967-68, gen. sales and mdse. mgr., 1968-71, dir. merchandising, 1971-72, exec. v.p., 1972-76, pres., chief operating officer, 1976-81, vice-chmn. bd., 1981-82, ret., 1982, dir., 1968-85. Bd. dirs.

emeritus J.C. Penney Co. Inc. Trustee emeirtus Geraldine R. Dodge Found. Served to capt. USAAF, 1943-45. Decorated D.F.C. Roman Catholic. Home: The Enclave 5345 Annabel Ln Plano TX 75093-3428

NEPPLE, JAMES ANTHONY, lawyer; b. Carroll, Iowa, Jan. 5, 1945; s. Herbert J. and Cecilia T. (Irlmeier) N.; m. Jeannine Ann Jennings, Sept. 9, 1967; children: Jeffrey B., Scott G., Carin J., Andrew J. BA, Creighton U., 1967; JD, U. Iowa, 1970; postgrad. in bus., Tex. Christian U., 1971; LLM in Taxation, NYU, 1982. Bar: Iowa 1970, Ill. 1973, U.S. Dist. Ct. (so. dist.) Iowa 1972, U.S. Dist. Ct. (cen. dist.) Ill. 1972, U.S. Dist. Ct.(no. dist.) Iowa 1975, U.S. Ct. Appeals (7th and 8th cirs.) 1975, U.S. Supreme Ct. 1975, U.S. Ct. Claims 1976, U.S. Tax Ct. 1976. Tax acct. Arthur Young & Co., Chgo., 1970; v.p., treas., bd. dirs. Stanley, Rehling, Lande & VanDerKamp, Muscatine, Iowa, 1972-92; pres. Nepple, VanDerKamp & Flynn, P.C., Rock Island, Ill., 1992-98, Nepple Law P.L.C., 1999—. Scoutmaster Boy Scouts Am., Muscatine, 1982—85, dist. chmn., 2005—; trustee State His. Soc. Iowa, 1986—92, vice-chmn., 1991—92; bd. dirs. Iowa Hist. Found., 1988—95, pres., 1991—93; trustee Musser Pub. Libr., 2000—04; pres. Muscatine Hist. Preservation Commn., 2001—, chmn., 2001—04. Recipient Gov.'s Vol. award State of Iowa, 1988, 90, Jr. Achievement of the Quad Cities Bronze award, 1996, Silver award, 2000. Fellow: Ill. Bar Found., Iowa Bar Found., Am. Bar Found., Am. Coll. Trust and Estate Counsel; mem.: ABA (tax sect. 1972—, chair bus. coop. & agrl. tax com. 2001—03), Iowa Bar Assn. (mem. tax sect. 1978—91, chmn. tax sect. 1988—91), Quad City Estate Planning Coun. (pres. 1987), Iowa Assn. Bus. and Industry (tax com. 1978—, chmn. 1986—88), Rock Island County Bar Assn., Scott County Bar Assn., Muscatine Bar Assn. (pres. 1982—83), Ill. Bar Assn. (fed. tax. sect. coun. 1993—99, chair 1997—98, bus. advice and fin. planning sect. coun. 2000—, vice chair 2006), Fed Bar Assn., Muscatine C. of C. (pres. 1985), Geneva Golf and Country Club (pres. 1990—91), Elks, Kiwanis (pres. Muscatine chpt. 1978). Republican. Roman Catholic. Home: 2704 Mulberry Ave Muscatine IA 52761-2746 Home Phone: 563-264-3887; Office Phone: 563-264-6840. Office Fax: 563-264-6844. Personal E-mail: nepple@machlink.com. Business E-Mail: jim@nepplelaw.com.

NEREM, ROBERT MICHAEL, engineering educator, consultant; b. Chgo., July 20, 1937; s. Robert and Borghild Guneva (Bakken) Nerem; m. Jill Ann Thomson, Dec. 21, 1958 (div. 1977); children: Robert Steven, Nancy Ann Nerem Chambers; m. Marilyn Reed, Oct. 7, 1978; stepchildren: Christina Lynn Maser, Carol Marie Maser. BS, U. Okla., 1959; MS, Ohio State U., 1961, PhD, 1964; D (hon.), U. Paris, 1990. Asst. prof. Ohio State U., Columbus, 1964-68, assoc. prof., 1968-72, prof., 1972-79, assoc. dean Grad. Sch., 1975-79; prof. mech. engring., chmn. dept. U. Houston, 1979-86; Parker H. Petit prof. Ga. Inst. Tech., Atlanta, 1987—, Inst. prof., 1991—, dir. Inst. for Bioengring. and Biosci., 1995—; dir. Ga. Tech/Emory Ctr. for the Engring. of Living Tissues NSF Engring. Rsch. Ctr., Atlanta, 1998—. Mem. Ga. Gov.'s Adv. Coun. on Sci. and Tech. Devel., Atlanta, 1992—95; Alza disting. lectr. Biomed. Engring. Soc., 1991; ASME Thurston lectr., 94; mem. sci. bd. FDA, 2000—03; sr. adv. for bioengring. Nat. Inst. Biomed. Imaging and Bioengring., 2003—06. Contbr. articles to profl. jours. Fellow: AAAS, ASME, Instn. Mech. Engrs., U.K. (hon.), Am. Inst. Med. and Biol. Engring. (founding pres. 1992—94); mem.: NAE, Royal Swedish Acad. Engring. Scis., Polish Acad. Scis., U.S. Nat. Com. on Biomechanics (chmn. 1988—91), Japanese Soc. for Med. & Biol. Engring. (hon.), Internat. Fedn. for Med. and Biol. Engring. (pres. 1988—91), Internat. Union for Phys. and Engring. Scis. in Medicine (pres. 1991—94), Inst. Medicine, Biomed. Engring. Soc., Am. Acad. Arts and Scis. Home: 2950 Waverly Ct SE Atlanta GA 30339-4200 Home Phone: 770-434-8985; Office Phone: 404-894-2768. Business E-Mail: robert.nerem@ibb.gatech.edu.

NERI, MANUEL, sculptor, educator; b. Sanger, Calif., Apr. 12, 1930; s. Manuel and Guadalupe (Penilla) N.; children: Raoul Garth, LaTicia Elizabeth, Noel Elmer, Maximilian Anthony, Ruby Rose Victoria, Julia Marjorie, Gustavo Manuel Student, San Francisco City Coll., 1949-50, U. Calif., Berkeley, 1951-52, Calif. Sch. Arts and Crafts, 1952-57, Calif. Sch. Fine Arts, 1957-59; D (hon.), San Francisco Art Inst., 1990, Calif. Coll. Arts and Crafts, 1992, Corcoran Sch. Art., Washinton, 1995. Mem. faculty art Calif. Sch. Fine Arts, San Francisco, 1959—65; prof. art U. Calif., Berkeley, 1963—64, Davis, 1965—90. One-man shows of sculpture, from 1957, recent exhbns. include, Oakland Mus. Art, Oakland, Calif., 1976, Western Assn. Art Mus. Travelling Exhbn., 1980-83, Seattle Art Mus., 1981, Charles Cowles Gallery, N.Y.C., 1981, 82, 86, 89, 93, 95, 97, 2002, 2003, Middendorf Gallery, Washington, 1983, 84, Gimpel-Hanover & Andre Emmerich Galerien, Zurich, Switzerland, 1984, San Francisco Mus. Modern Art, 1989, Dia Ctr. for the Arts, Bridgehampton, N.Y., 1993, 1997, Corcoran Gallery Art, Washington, D.C., 1997, Palm Springs (Calif.) Desert Mus., 1998, Riva Yares Gallery, Scottsdale, Ariz., 2002, 05, Hackett Freedman Gallery, San Francisco, 2001, 2003, 05, Fresno (Calif.) Art Mus., 2005; numerous group shows, from 1955, including San Francisco Mus. Modern Art, 1980, 83, 84, 85, 86, Am. Acad. Arts and Letters, N.Y.C., 1981, 82, 84, Oakland Mus. (Calif.), 1982, 84, 85, Seattle Art Mus., 1983, 84, Inst. Contemporary Art, Richmond, Va., 1983, Hirshhorn Mus., 1984, Contemporary Arts Ctr., Cin., 1985, Mus. Fine Arts, Houston, 1987, Bronx Mus. Arts, 1988, Whitney Mus., N.Y., 1992, 95, The White Ho., Washington, D.C., 1994, 99, Mus. Moderner Kunst, Vienna, 1997, Isetan Mus., Japan, 1999; represented in permanent collections: Oakland Mus., Seattle Art Mus., San Francisco Mus. Modern Art, Honolulu Acad. Arts, Des Moines Arts Ctr., also numerous pvt. collections including Verlaine Found., New Orleans, Bank Am. Corp., San Francisco, Lannan Found., L.A., Portland (Oreg.) Art Mus., Fine Arts Mus. San Francisco, Calif., San Jose (Calif.) Mus. Art, others Recipient 1st Award in Sculpture Oakland Art Mus., 1953, Nat. Art Found. award, 1965, award San Francisco Art Inst., 1963, award in art Am. Acad. and Inst. Arts and Letters, 1982, award of merit in sculpture San Francisco Arts Commn., 1985; Guggenheim fellow, 1979; Nat. Endowment for the Arts grantee, 1980 Roman Catholic.

NERLOVE, MARC LEON, economics professor; b. Chgo., Oct. 12, 1933; s. Samuel Henry and Evelyn (Andelman) N.; children: Susan, Miriam. BA, U. Chgo., 1952; MA, Johns Hopkins U., 1955, PhD, 1956. Analytical statistician USDA, Washington, 1956-57; assoc. prof. U. Minn., Mpls., 1959-60; prof. Stanford (Calif.) U., 1960-65, Yale U., 1965-69; prof. econs. U. Chgo., 1969-74; F.W. Taussig rsch. prof. Harvard Coll., Cambridge, Mass., 1967-68; vis. Cook prof. Northwestern U., Evanston, Ill., 1973-74, Cook prof., 1974-82; prof. econs. U. Pa., Phila., 1982-86, Univ. prof., 1986-93; prof. agr. and resource econs. U. Md., College Park, 1993—. Author: Dynamics of Supply, 1958, Distributed Lags and Demand Analysis, 1958, Estimation and Identification of Cobb-Douglas Production Functions, 1965, Analysis of Economic Time Series: A Synthesis, 1979, Household and Economy: Welfare Economics of Endogenous Fertility, 1987, Essays on Panel Data Econometrics, 2002; contbr. numerous articles to profl. jours. 1st lt. AUS, 1957-59. Recipient award Am. Farm Econ. Assn., 1956, 58, 61, 79, P.S. Mahalanobis medal Indian Econ. Soc., 1975. Fellow Am. Statis. Assn., Econometric Soc. (v.p. 1980, pres. 1981), Am. Acad. Arts and Scis., Am. Agrl. Econ. Assn.; mem. NAS, Am. Econ. Assn. (mem. exec. com. 1977-79, John Bates Clark medal 1969), Royal Econ. Soc., Phi Beta Kappa, others. Achievements include research on economics of agriculture with particular reference to developing countries, population and economic growth; analysis of categorical data, particularly business and household surveys. Office: U Md Dept Agr and Resource Econs College Park MD 20742-0001 E-mail: mnerlove@arec.umd.edu.

NERN, CHRISTOPHER CARL, lawyer; b. NYC, Sept. 30, 1944; s. William Francis and Jule Anne (Allison) N.; m. Kathleen Jean Brogan, Aug. 24, 1974 (div. Nov. 1985). BA, Mich. State U., 1967; JD, Wayne State U., 1972. Bar: Mich. 1973, U.S. Dist. Ct. (ea. and we. dists.) Mich. 1973, U.S. Ct. Appeals (6th cir.) 1974, U.S. Supreme Ct. 1979. Asst. atty. gen. State of Mich., Lansing, 1972-73; staff atty. corp. affairs div. Detroit Edison Co., 1973-74, sr.atty. rates and regulatory div., 1975-78, gen. atty. regulatory affairs div., 1978-82, assoc. gen. counsel, mgr., 1982-89, asst. v.p., asst. gen. counsel, 1989-93, v.p., gen. counsel, 1993-2000, DTE Energy, 1993-2000; adj. prof. St. Mary's Coll., 2002—. Adj. prof. Lawrence Tech. U., 2002—. Mem. allocation com. United Found., Detroit, 1983, 86-87; bd. dirs. Oakland Parks Found., Oakland County, Mich., 1985, Mich. Opera Theatre, 1996—; trustee Music Hall Ctr. for the Performing Arts, 1987-93. Served with USAF, 1967-69. Mem. ABA (bd. trustees), Detroit Met. Bar Assn. (trustee found.), Am. Corp. Counsel Assn. (pres. Mich chpt. 1986-88), Econs. Club (Detroit), Detroit Golf Club, Detroit Athletic Club. Roman Catholic. Home: 1052 Stratford Ln Bloomfield Hills MI 48304-2930 E-mail: nernchris@aol.com.

NERO, SHONDEL J., language educator; arrived in US, 1984; d. Edward P. and Stells V. Nero; m. Louis J. Parascandola, July 1, 2000. BA in French and Spanish, Concordia U., Montreal, 1984; MA in TESOL, Columbia U., NYC, 1990, MEd in Applied Linguistics, 1994, EdD in Applied Linguistics, 1997. Cert. ESL NY. Reservation agt. Air Can. Airlines, NYC, 1985—90; ESL and French tchr. Manhattan Ctr. for Sci. and Math., 1990—91; instr. LI U, Bklyn., 1991—95, asst. prof., 1995—98, St. John's U., Queens, 1998—2001, assoc. prof., 2001—. Asst. dir. ctr. Literacy Vol. NYC, 1990—92; cons. NYC Dept. Edn., 2001—. Author: (book) Englishes in Contact: Anglophone Cubban Students in an Urban College, 2001; editor: Dialects, Englishes, Creoles and Educators, 2006. Mem.: TESOL (chain caucus leadership coun. 2001—, chair black caucus 2003—05), Nat. Conf. Tchrs. English. Avocations: travel, languages, pottery. Home: 69-09 108th St #510 Forest Hills NY 11375

NERODE, ANIL, mathematician, educator; b. LA, June 4, 1932; s. Nirad Ranjan and Agnes (Spencer) N.; m. Sondra Raines, Feb. 12, 1955 (div. 1968); children: Christopher Curtis, Gregory Daniel; m. Sally Riedel Sievers, May 16, 1970; 1 child, Nathanael Caldwell. BA, U. Chgo., 1949, BS, 1952, MS, 1953, PhD, 1956. Group leader automata and weapons systems Lab. Applied Sci., U. Chgo., 1954-57; mem. Inst. for Advanced Study, Princeton, 1957-58, 62-63; vis. asst. prof. math. U. Calif. at Berkeley, 1958-59; mem. faculty Cornell U., 1959—, prof. math., 1965—, Goldwin Smith prof. math., 1990—, chmn. dept. math., 1982-87, dir. Math. Sci. Inst., 1986-97; acting dir. Center for Applied Math., 1965-66; vis. prof. Monash U., Melbourne, Australia, 1970, 74, 78, 79, U. Chgo., 1976, M.I.T., 1980, U. Calif., San Diego, 1981; disting. vis. scientist EPA, 1985-87; dir. Ctr. for Found. of Intelligent Sys. Cornell U., 1997—2001. Prin. investigator numerous grants; mem. sci. adv. bd. EPA, 1988-93, chair tech. adv. panel Global Change, 1990-92; mem. sci. adv. bd. Ctr. for Intelligent Control, Harvard-MIT-Brown U., 1988-94; cons. to govt. and industry; co-founder Clearsight Corp., 1995. Author: (with John Crossley) Combinatorial Functors, 1974, (with Richard Shore) Logic for Applications, 2d edit., 1996, (with G.A. Metakides) Principles of Logic and Logic Programming, 1996, (with B. Khoussainov) Automata Theory and its Applications, 2001; editor Advances in Mathematics, 1967-70, Jour. Symbolic Logic, 1967-82, Annals of Pure and Applied Logic, 1983-96, Future Generation Computing Systems, 1983-97, Jour. Pure & Applied Algebra, 1988-2005, Annals of Math. and Artificial Intelligence, 1989—, Logical Methods in Computer Sci., 1991-94, Computer Modelling and Simulation, 1991—, Constraints, 1995-2001, Grammers, 1997-2001, (with J. Remmel, S. Goncharov, Y. Ershov) Handbook of Recursive Algebra, 1998. Mem. AIII, IEEE, Assn. Computing Machinery, Am. Math. Soc. (assoc. editor procs. 1962-65, v.p. 1991-94), Soc. Indsl. and Applied Math., Math. Assn. Am., Assn. Symbolic Logic, European Assn. for Theoretical Computer Sci. Home: 406 Cayuga Heights Rd Ithaca NY 14850-1402 Office: Cornell U 545 Mallott Hall Dept Math Ithaca NY 14853-4201 E-mail: anil@cornell.edu.

NÉRON, MARTIN, musician; s. Raymond Néron and Louise Chiricota. B Music, U. Montreal, 1990; MusM, Westminster Choir Coll., Princeton, NJ, 1996; D in Musical Arts, Manhattan Sch. Music, NYC, 2001. Collaborative pianist Westminster Choir Coll., Princeton, 1997—. Musician (pianist): (compact disk) Greek Songs for Romantics and Realists, L'Heure Exquise. Recipient 1st prize, Can. Music Competition, 1989; grantee, Fonds les Amis de l'Arts Awards, 1990—92, Canadian-Italian Profl. and Businessmen Assn., 1991—93, Conseil des Arts du Québec, 1992, 1994, 1996; scholar, Manhattan Sch. Music, 1996—98. Mem.: Nat. Assn. Tchrs. Singing. Home Phone: 609-452-0272. Personal E-mail: mneron@msn.com.

NESBIT, SANDI MICHELLE, corporate financial executive; b. Marietta, Ga., Aug. 30, 1963; d. Walter DeForest (Stepfather) and Linda S. Van Fleet, William E. Ray; m. Eric James E Nesbit, Oct. 11, 1998; 1 child, Cora Helene. Title Insurance Agent Tenn., 2002; Notary Public at Large Tenn., 2000. Ceo/founder NNBS, Inc., Anytime Services.com, Rockford, Tenn., 1999—; mgr. Nationwide Homes, Alcoa, Tenn., 1998—2000. Author: (educational workbook) The Title Searchers Handbook. Hon. chmn. Nat. Rep. Congl. Com., 2003. Pentacostal. Avocations: travel, reading, music, animals. Office: NNBS Inc 3532 Calvert St Rockford TN 37853-3926 Office Phone: 865-977-8808.

NESBIT, WILLIAM TERRY, small business owner, consultant; b. Pitts., Jan. 30, 1945; s. William Frank and Glenna (Cleeton) N.; 2 children. Owner, CEO Narrow Gauge Car Shop, Evergreen Outdoor Ctr., Shiremanstown, Pa., 1972—; mem. faculty Millersville (Pa.) U., 1976-81, Temple U., Phila., 1979, Nat. Aquatic and Small Craft Sch., Bemis Point, NY, 1980, Harrisburg (Pa.) Area C. C., 1981-82, 91, Dickinson Coll., Carlisle, Pa., 1982-83. Judge 32d Capital Area Sci., Engring. Fair, Dickinson Coll., Carlisle, Pa., 1989; mem. tech. briefs reader adv. panel NASA, 2000—. Co-developer ARC basic and whitewater canoeing programs for instrn., 1977-79; inventor, developer The Z Drag for Boat Rescues, 1980; developer, mfr. first HOn3 ready-to-run plastic rolling stock having NMRA warrant; contbg. author: The Brown Book, 2d edit., 1982. Vol. ARC, 1961—; contbr. A.C. Kalmbach Meml. Libr., Chattanooga; benefactor Carlyton Sch. Dist. Libr., Carnegie, Pa. Recipient award for Humanity ARC, 1967, award for 30 Yrs. Vol. Svc., 1991; named Class I Radiol. Protection Officer, U.S. Dept. Def. and NRC, 1993. Mem. Math. Assn. Am., Nat. Assn. Canoe Liveries and Outfitters (founding), Nat. Model Railroad Assn. (life, mid-eastern region bd. dirs. 1997-2001, supt. Susquehanna divsn. 1996-2000, edn. chair 2002-), Nat. Railroad Assn., Conewago Canoe Club (canoe tng. officer 1999—), Canoe Club of Greater Harrisburg (founding mem.). Episcopalian. Avocation: ferroequinology. Office: Evergreen Outdoor Ctr PO Box 3081 Shiremanstown PA 17011-3081 Business E-Mail: william.nesbit@dla.mil.

NESBITT, CHARLES RUDOLPH, lawyer, energy executive, consultant; b. Miami, Okla., Aug. 30, 1921; s. Charles Rudolph and Irma Louise (Wilhelmi) N.; m. Margot Dorothy Lord, June 6, 1948; children: Nancy Margot Nesbitt Nagle, Douglas Charles, Carolyn Jane Nesbitt Gresham-Fiegel. BA, U. Okla., 1942; JD, Yale U., 1947. Bar: Okla. 1947, U.S. Supreme Ct. 1957. Pvt. practice, Oklahoma City, 1948-62, 67-69, 75-91, 95—; atty. gen. Okla., 1963-67; mem. Okla. Corp. Commn., 1968-75, chmn., 1969-75; sec. of energy State of Okla., 1991-95; pvt. practice Oklahoma City, 1995—. Okla. rep., v.p. Interstate Oil and Gas Compact. Trustee endowment fund St. Gregory's Coll.; pres. Hist. Preservation, Inc.; pres. bd. trustees Okla. Mus. Art; v.p., bd. dirs. Western History Collections Assocs., U. Okla. Librs.; mem. panel arbitrators Am. Arbitration Assn., NASD, NYSE. With AUS, 1942-46. Mem. ABA, Okla. Bar Assn., Oklahoma City C. of C., Phi Beta Kappa, Phi Delta Phi. Episcopalian.

NESBITT, DEETTE DUPREE, small business owner, investor; b. Houston, May 5, 1941; d. Raymond Benjamin DuPree and Alice Lula (Cade) Foster; children: Alice L., Charles S. Massey Nesbitt; m. Ernest V. Nesbitt, Aug. 20, 1971 (dec.). Student, Sam Houston State U., 1960-61, U. Houston, 1961-62, 81-83. Contbr. articles to various publs. Former trustee Pace Soc. Am., Inc., 1992-95, Inc.; bd. dirs. Evergreen Friends, Inc., 1991-92; dir., sec. competitive swim team Dad's Club YMCA, Houston, 1981-83; vol. adminstrv. asst. numerous orgns., Houston; patron Houston Jr. League. Recipient Varina Howell Davis medal Mil. Order Stars and Bars, 1992, Silver Good Citizenship medal SAR, 1992, Honor award Tex. SCV, 1992; featured on Eyes of Texas, NBC, 1992, Nat. Honor award Hereditary Soc. Cmty., 2003; Ky. Col. Mem.: Hereditary Soc. (cmty. cons. 2006—), Nat. Soc. Colonial Dames Am. in Commonwealth of Va., Nat. Soc. Sons and Daus. Antebellum Planters 1607-1861, Harris County Hist. Commn., Freedoms Found. Valley Forge (George Washington Honor medal 1994), United Daus. Confederacy (Confederate Ball com. 1985—95, co-chmn. ball 1988, adv. to chmn. 1989, 1990, hon. chmn. Houston's confederate ball 1995, So. Heritage Ball com. 2005—, Charleston chpt. #4, Jefferson Davis Hist. award, Winnie Davis medal, Spl. Recognition award), Daus. Rep. Tex. (Appreciation award 1996), Nat. Gavel Soc., Nat. Jamestown Soc. (mem. coun. 1993—95, auditor gen. 1995—97, lt. gov. gen. 1997—98, gov. gen. 1998—2000, Resolution of Appreciation, Outstanding Leadership 2000), Soc. First Families of S.C. 1670-1700 (life; sec. 2003—05, 3rd v.p. 2005—07, pres. gen. 2007—), Order of First Families of Va. 1607-1624 (life; mem. coun. 2001—, rec. sec. 2005—), Order of First Families of Miss. 1699-1817 (life), Nat. Soc. DAR, Huguenot Soc. Am., S.C. Soc. Descs. of Colonial Clergy, Nat. Soc. Magna Charta Dames (Houston colony historian 1992—95), Plantagenet Soc., Am. Royal Descent, First Tex. Co. Jamestowne Soc. (lt. gov., gov. 1985—93, hon. gov. emerita), Dames of Colonial Cavaliers 1640-1660 (organizing dep. gov. gen. 2001—03, gov. gen. 2003—05, life hon. gov. gen. emerita), Colonial Dames Am. (pres. chpt. VIII 1995—97), Sons and Daus. of Pilgrims (nat. com. 1993—97), Galveston Yacht Club, Petroleum Club Houston, Order Descendants Colonial Cavaliers (organizing gov. gen. 2007—). Republican. Episcopalian. Home: 15411 Old Stone Trail Houston TX 77079-4206

NESBITT, JOHN ARTHUR, recreational therapist, writer, educator, researcher; b. Detroit, Mar. 29, 1933; s. John Jackson and Anna Maye (Hartley) N.; children: John Arthur, and Victoria Bowen. Attended, Howe Mil. Sch., 1945-51, Olivet Coll., 1952-53; BA, Mich. State U., 1955; MA, Columbia Univ., 1961, EdD, 1968. Registered hosp. recreation dir.; cert. therapeutic recreation splty. Program dir. Jaycees Internat., Miami, Fla., 1957-60; therapeutic recreation specialist Rusk Inst. Rehab. Medicine, N.Y.U., Bellevue Med. Ctr., 1960-61; dir. World Commn. on Vocat. Rehab., Rehab. Internat., NYC, 1963—65; dep. dir. gen. World Leisure and Recreation Assn., NYC, 1964—66; asst. sec. gen. Rehab. Internat., NYC, 1966-68; assoc. prof., coord. rehab. svc., leisure studies San Jose State U., Calif., 1968—72; prof., chmn. recreation edn. program U. Iowa, Iowa City, 1972-76, prof. therapeutic recreation, 1977—91, prof. emeritus, 1991—. Pres., CEO Spl. Recreation disABLED Internat., Inc., 1978—; dir., vice chair People to People Com. Disability, 1964-2000; chmn. sub com. recreation and leisure U.S. President's Com. on Employment of Handicapped, 1972-81; dir. Internat. Ctr. on Spl. Recreation, 1978—; webmaster Global Vision of Rehab. and Recreation for People with Disabilities in the 21st Century. Author, editor books in field; editor Alert Mag., 1956; Jaycees Internat. World, 1957-60; Internat. Rehab. of Disabled Rev., 1965-68; Therapeutic Recreation Jour., 1968-70; Jour. Iowa Parks and Recreation, 1974-76; Play, Recreation, and Leisure for People Who Are Disabled, 1977; Fed. Funding for Spl. Recreation, 1978; New Concepts and New Processes in Spl. Recreation, 1978; New Horizons in Profl. Tng. in Recreation Svc. for Handicapped Children and Youth, 1983; Nisbet, Nesbitt Family Surname Assn. Newsletter, 1983-86; Spl. Recreation for DisABLED Digest, 1983-89; U.S.A. Ban Fireworks and Fireworks Safety Campaign Bul., 1988—; UNAGRAM, 1997-99; sr. editor Recreation and Leisure Svc. for Disadvantaged, 1969 (Nat. Recreation Lit. award); editor, compiler Spl. Recreation Compendium of 1,500 Resources for Disabled People, 3d edit., 1989; Special Recreation for Disabled Press, Iowa, 1989; webmaster Global Vision Rehab. and Recreation for People with Disabilities Stop Fireworks Victimization Campaign. Bd. dirs. United Cerebral Palsy Assn., San Mateo and Santa Clara County, 1970-72; bd. dirs. Harold Russell Found., 1971-73; Goodwill Industries Santa Clara County, 1969-72; rehab. counselor, master therapeutic recreation specialist; bd. dir. Hawkeye Area Poverty Cmty. Action Program, Iowa; Iowa Pk. and Recreation Assn., Am. Leisure and Recreation Assn., Washington, others; bd. dirs., state v.p. Iowa Aging Coalition, Iowa; bd. dirs., founding pres. Santa Clara County Assn. on Recreation Handicapped, Iowa; bd. dirs., tech. adv. Disability Internat. Found., 1997—. Served in USAFR, 1955-57; maj. Ret. Recreation Svc. Ill. and Handicapped fellow; recipient numerous awards and citations for work with handicapped, including Torch of Gold Award, Nat. Boy Scouts Am.; Appreciation Award Philippines Found. Mem. Nat. Therapeutic Recreation Soc. (pres. 1970-71, Disting. Svc. Award), Nat. Rehab. Assn.; Am. Assn. Leisure and Recreation (bd. dir. 1977-80, Tommy Wilson svc. Handicapped Youth award); Nat. Consortium on Phys. Edn. and Recreation for Handicapped (pres. 1976-77, Nat. Scholarship award); Nat. Forum Comml. Recreation and Handicapped (chmn. 1979); Iowa Parks and Recreation Assn. (bd.dir. 1973-75, 89-90); Nat. Rehab. Counseling Assn.; Council Exceptional Children; Pi Sigma Epsilon. Presbyterian. Avocations: art, travel, genealogy, cmty. svc. Office Phone: 319-466-3192.

NESBITT, MITZI EVALEE, voice educator, director; d. Sylvan Julian and Mildred Evelyn (Moe) Nylander; divorced; 1 child, Travis Orlo. AA in Music, N.W. Coll., Kirkland, Wash., 1970; BA in Music, Calif State U., Hayward, 1975; MA in Music, Dance, Drama, Calif State U., Fullerton, 1994. Cert. tchr. Calif. Music tchr. Christian Ctr. Sch., Dublin, Calif., 1972—76; vocal music tchr. Phoenix Elem. Schs., 1976—79, Placentia (Calif.) Unified Sch. Dist., 1979—85, Corona/Norco (Calif.) Unified Sch. Dist., 1988—92, 1997—, 4th grade tchr., 1992—97. Pvt. practice, Norco, Calif., 1985—; adv. bd. Nat. Orff Schulwerk, Redlands, Calif., 1994. Author, composer: Oh California, 1994, Lion, Witch, and the Wardrobe, 1994. Music dir. Children's Theatre Experience, Chatsworth, Calif., 1996—; pianist Calvary Christian Ctr., Corona, 1987—97. Named Tchr. of Yr., Stallings Elem. Sch., 2004, Bravo award finalist, 1995; recipient Mentor Tchr. award, Corona Norco Unified Sch. Dist., 1994—96. Mem.: Am. Orff Schulwerk (sec. 1993—2006). Avocations: jogging, photography, sewing, yoga, tennis.

NESBITT, PAUL EDWARD, historian, author, educator; b. Balt., Dec. 25, 1943; s. William Ervin and Margaret Caroline (Shaw) N.; m. Donna Jean Coppock, Aug. 15 1966 (dec. 1972); children: Erik-Paul A., Janelle M.; m. Pamela Jean Lichty, May 25, 1974 (div. 1983); m. Anita Louise Wood, Dec. 8, 1984 (div. 1989); m. Paula Jane Sawyer, May 7, 1994. AB, U. Wash., 1965; MA, Wash. State U., 1968, PhD (hon.), 1970; PhD, U. Calgary, Alta., Can., 1972. Reader anthropology U. Wash., 1965; grad. rschr.-tchr. Wash. State U., 1966-68; instr. Tacoma C.C., Wash., 1968-69; grad. rschr.-tchr. U. Calgary, 1969-71; exec. Hudson's Bay Co., Calgery, 1971; prof. Western Oreg. U., Monmouth, 1971-74; state historian State of Calif., Sacramento, 1974-97; ret., 1997. Dir. Am. Sch. of Interior Design, San Francisco, 1974, HBC Bow Fort Rsch., Morley, Atla., 1970-71; instr. Am. River Coll., Sacramento, 1980-86. Contbr. articles to profl. jours. Exec. mgr. Calif. State Govt. United Way Campaign, 1986, 87, also bd. dirs., mem. fiscal and comm. coms., El Dorado County and Sacramento chpts., 1988—; designer, cultural rsch. cons. pvt. contracts western states, 1960—; exec. dir. Heritage Areas Assn., 1993—, pres. bd. dirs., 1994—. Fellow Am. Anthropol. Assn.; mem. Calif. Hist. Soc., Am. Inst. Interior

Designers (profl. 1974-77, bd. dirs. energy planning and devel. cos. 1986-88), AIA (Ctrl. Valley chpt. 1975-77), Rotary. Home: 3177 Clark St Placerville CA 95667-6405 Office Phone: 530-626-8697. Personal E-mail: pnesbitt@sbcglobal.net. E-mail: heritage@innercite.com.

NESBITT, RICHARD, stock exchange executive; b. Oct. 7, 1955; BA in bus. adminstrn., Univ. Western Ontario, Can.; MBA, Univ. Toronto, 1985; MSc in acctg. and fin., London Sch. Economics. Position at Mobil Oil Can. Ltd., CIBC Wood Gundy; pres. and CEO HSBC Securities Can.; pres. and COO BayStreetDirect Inc.; gov. Toronto Stock Exch., 1996—99, pres. TSX Markets, 2001—04, CEO TSX Group Inc., 2004—. Former lectr. Univ. Western Ontario Sch. Bus.; bd. dirs. World Fedn. of Exchanges, Market Regulation Services, CanDeal, Frontier Coll., Prostate Cancer Rsch. Found. of Canada. Office: TSX Group Inc PO Box 450 130 King St W 3rd Fl Toronto ON Canada Office Phone: 416-947-4670. Office Fax: 416-947-4662.

NESCI, VINCENT PETER, lawyer; b. New Rochelle, NY, Feb. 27, 1947; s. Vincent S. and Carmela (DeMasi) N.; m. Donna M. Dahlgren, July 21, 1968; children: Vincent P. Jr., Joseph E., Patricia A. BA, Sacred Heart U., 1969; JD, St. John's U., 1971. Bar: N.Y. 1972, U.S. Dist. Ct. (ea. dist.) N.Y. 1973, U.S. Dist. Ct. (so. dist.) N.Y. 1978), U.S. Supreme Ct. 1976. Assoc. Campbell, Hyman & Lang, New Rochelle, 1972-76; ptnr. Lang & Nesci, P.C., New Rochelle, 1976-79; pvt. practice Yonkers, N.Y., 1980-93. Gen. counsel Liberty Lines, Yonkers, 1979-93; CEO Specialized Risk Mgmt., White Plains, N.Y., 1993—; mgr. ptnr. Nesci Keane Piekarski Keogh & Corrigan, White Plains, 1993—; cons. Summit Investment, Queensland, Australia, 1992—. Avocation: auto racing. Home: RR 2 Bedford NY 10506-9802 Office: 245 Main St Ste 600 White Plains NY 10601 Home Phone: 914-234-9415; Office Phone: 914-993-6200. Business E-Mail: vnesci@nesci-keane.com.

NESHAT, SHIRIN, artist; b. Qazvin, Iran, 1957; MFA, U. Calif. Berkeley, 1979—82. Hon. prof. Berlin Inst. Arts, 2004. One-woman shows include Woman of Allah, 1993—97, Tate Gallery, London, 1998, Whitney Mus. Am. Art, Phillip Morris Branch, NY, 1998, Maison Europeene de las Photographie, Paris, 1998, Tensta Konsthall, Spanga, Sweden, 1999, Henie Onstad Artsentre, Oslo, Norway, 1999, Galerie Jerome de Noirmont, Paris, 1999, D'Amelio Terras, NY, 1999, Patrick Painter Gallery, LA, 1999, Art Inst. Chgo., 1999, Wexner Ctr., Columbus, Ohio, 2000, Matrix, Berkeley Art Mus., Calif., 2000, Dallas Mus. Art, 2000, Lia Rumma, Milan, 2000, Kunsthalle Wien, Vienna, 2000, Pitti Discovery, Florence, 2000, Serpentine Gallery, London, 2000, Barbara Gladstone Gallery, NY, 2001, Kanazawa Contemporary Art Mus., Kanazawa, Japan, 2001, Patrick Painter, Santa Monica, 2001, Irish Mus. Modern Art, Dublin, 2001, Musee d'Art Contemporain de Montreal, Passage, Regina Gouger Miller Gallery, Carnegie Mellon U., 2002, Banco di Brasil, Rio de Janeiro, 2002, Castello di rivoli, Turin, 2002, Walker Art Ctr., Mpls., 2002, Contemporary Arts Mus., Houston, 2003, Museo de Arte Moderno, Mexico City, 2003, Lumen Travo Gallery, Amsterdam, 2003, Galeria Filomena Soares, Lisbon, 2003, Miami Art Mus., 2003, Tooba, Asia Soc. Mus., NY, 2003, Auckland Art Gallery, New Zealand, 2004, Hiroshima City Mus. Contemporary Art, 2005, Museo de Arte Contemporaneo, Leon, Spain, 2005, Hamburger Bahnhof, Mus. Fur Gengewart, Berlin, 2005, exhibited in group shows at Documenta XI, Venice Biennale, 1999 (Golden Lion award), Whitney Biennale, 2000; prodr.: (films) Turbulent, 1998, Rapture, 1999, Fervor, 2000, Zarin, 2005. Recipient Infinity award, Internat. Ctr. Photography, 2002, Hiroshima Freedom prize, 2005, Dorothy and Lillian Gish prize, 2006. Office: Storefront for Art and Architecture 97 Kenmara St New York NY 10012 Office Phone: 212-431-5795. Office Fax: 212-431-5755. *

NESHEIM, ROBERT OLAF, retired food products executive; b. Monroe Center, Ill., Sept. 13, 1921; s. Olaf M. and Sena M. (Willms) Nesheim; m. Emogene P. Sullivan, July 13, 1946 (div.); children: Barbara Mowry, Susan Yost(dec.), Sandra Rankin; m. Doris Howes Calloway, July 4, 1981 (dec.). BS, U. Ill., 1943, MS, 1950, PhD, 1951; postgrad., Harvard U., 1971. Farm mgr. Halderman Farm Mgmt. Svc., Wabash, Ind., 1946-48; instr. U. Ill., 1951; mgr. feed rsch. The Quaker Oats Co., Barrington, Ill., 1952-64; prof., head of dept. animal sci. U. Ill., 1964-67; dir. nutrition rsch. The Quaker Oats Co., Barrington, Ill., 1967-69, v.p. R & D, 1969-78, v.p. sci. & tech. Chgo., 1978-83; sr. v.p. sci. & tech. Avadyne, Inc., Monterey, Calif., 1983-85; pres. Advanced Healthcare, Monterey, 1985-91; ret., 1991. Food and nutrition bd. NAS, 1972—78, chmn. com. in mil. nutrition rsch. FNB, 1982—97; chmn. Bioscis. Info. Svcs., 1982—84. Capt. U.S. Army, 1943-46, South Pacific. Fellow Am. Inst. Nutrition (treas. 1983-86), AAAS; mem. Inst. Food Technologists, Fed. Socs. Exptl. Biologists (treas. 1973-79), APHA, Corral de Tierra Club (Salinas, Calif.). Avocations: gardening, golf. Home: Apt 407 200 Glenwood Cir Monterey CA 93940

NESIN, JEFFREY DAVID, academic administrator; b. NYC; m. Diane Garvey, 1968; children: Kate Dillon, Sarah Grace. BA in Eng. Lit., Hobart Coll., 1966; MA in Eng. Lit, SUNY, Buffalo, 1971, MA in Am. Studies, 1973. Faculty dept. humanities & scis. Sch. Visual Arts, NYC, 1974-91; pres. Memphis Coll. Art, 1991—. Asst. to pres. Sch. Visual Arts, 1982-91; cons. Smithsonian Instn., IBM, 1st Tenn. Bank; panelist, speaker in field. Contbg. editor: High Fidelity, Creem; contbr. reviews, interviews, essays to mags.; adv. editor Jour. Popular Music and Society. Recipient Thomas W. Briggs Found. Cmty. Svc. award, 1998. Mem. Am. Studies Assn., Met. Am. Studies Assn. (past pres.), Assn. Ind. Colls. Art & Design (bd. dirs. 1991—), Nat. Assn. Schs. Art & Design (chair commn. on accreditation, exec. com. and bd. 1999—), Ctr. for So. Folklore (bd. and exec. com. 2000—), Memphis Rotary. Avocations: mystery novels, baseball, music. Office: Memphis Coll Art Office of President 1930 Poplar Ave Memphis TN 38104-2756 Office Phone: 901-272-5101. E-mail: jnesin@mca.edu. *

NESLAGE, JOHN E., lawyer; b. Pampa, Tex., Aug. 13, 1946; AA cum laude, N.Mex. Milit. Inst., 1966; BBA magna cum laude, Tex. Tech. U., 1969; JD cum laude, U. Houston, 1972. Bar: Tex. 1972. Mem. Baker Botts L.L.P., Houston. Mem. ABA, State Bar Tex., Houston Bar Assn., Phi Kappa Phi, Phi Alpha Delta, Order of the Barons. Office: Baker Botts LLP One Shell Plz 910 Louisiana Houston TX 77002-4995 Office Phone: 713-229-1342.

NESMITH, RICHARD A., education educator, consultant; b. Lakeland, Fla., Jan. 13, 1959; s. Wendell B. and Patricia A. NeSmith; m. Melissa M. NeSmith; children: Ricky A., Wendell C. BS, Hyles-Anderson Coll., 1983, MRE, 1984; D in Ministry, Bethany Theol. Sem., 1986; BS, USC, 1991, MEd, 1993; specialists in edn., Augusta State U., 1997; PhD, Curtin U. Tech., 2003. Tchg. cert. biology SC. State Dept. Edn., 1991, educator cert. biology, edn. leadership, mid. grade Ga. State Dept. Edn., 1995, curriculum validator Western Australia Curriculum Coun., 2000, cert. prin., supt. Ill. Dept. Edn., 1981. Secondary sci. tchr. SC. Dept. Edn., Lexingington, 1992—93; sch. prin. Winfield Heights Christian Sch., Williston, SC, 1994—95; secondary sci. tchr. Ga. Pub. Schs., Ga., 1995—98; head sci. and math dept. Maranatha Christian Coll., Perth, Australia, 1999—2001; asst. prof. edn. Ea. Ill. U., Charleston, 2003—06; asst. prof. of edn. Lake Erie Coll., Painesville, Ohio, 2002—03; dean edn. North Greenville U., Tigerville, SC, 2006—. Bd. examiners Ohio State Dept. Edn., Columbus, 2002—03; textbook reviewer Alyn-Bacon Pub. Sci. author, cons.: BioSci. Edn., 1996—, mid-level editor: Ill. Sci. Tchrs. Assn. Jour. (Spectrum), Mem.: Assn. Childhood Edn. Internat. (assoc.; v.p. Ill. chpt.), Am. Rsch. Ednl. Assn. (assoc.), NSTA (assoc.; reviewer), Nat. Mid. Sch. Assn. (assoc.), Phi Delta Kappa (assoc.). Baptist. Achievements include research in middle school students perception of effective teaching and learning; various approaches to improving the curriculum and teaching of science in secondary schools; professional development using multimedia DVD technology. Avocations: hiking, travel, computers, writing. Office: North Greenville U 7801 N Tigerville SC 29688

NESPOLI, PAOLO ANGELO, astronaut; b. Milan, Apr. 6, 1957; s. Luigi and Maria Nespoli. BS in Aerospace Engring., Poly. U. N.Y., 1988, MS in Aeronautics and Astronautics, 1989; laurea in ingegneria meccanica, U. degli Studi di Firenze, Italy, 1990. Registered profl. engr.; lic. pvt. pilot, advanced scuba diver, NitrOx diver, master parachutist, cert. parachutist instr., jump master, demolition expert. Non-commd. officer, parachute instr. Scuola Militare de Paracudutismo, Pisa, Italy, 1977—80; spl. forces operator 9° Btg d'Assalto "Col Moschin", Livorno, Italy; mem. multinat. peacekeeping force Italian Army, Beirut, 1982—84, ret., 1987; design engr. Proel Tecnologie, Florence, Italy, 1989—91; mem. astronaut tng. divsn., European Astronaut Ctr. European Space Agy., Cologne, Germany, 1991—98; mem. EUROMIR project European Space Tech. Ctr., Noordwijk, Netherlands, 1995—96; mem. spaceflight tng. divsn. NASA, Johnson Space Ctr., Houston, 1996—98; astronaut Italian Space Agy., 1998; joined European Space Agy. European astronaut corps European Astronaut Ctr., Colonge, Germany, 1998; astronaut, mission specialist candidate NASA, Johnson Space Ctr., Houston, 1998—. Temporary assignment Gagarin Cosmonaut Tng. Ctr., Star City, Russia, 2004; mission specialist STS-120 to Internat. Space Station, 2006. Avocations: scuba diving, aircraft piloting, assembling computer hardware and electronic equipment, computer software. Office: Astronaut Office NASA Johnson Space Ctr Houston TX 77058 Address: European Space Agy 8-10 rue Mario Nikis 75738 Paris France

NESS, ANDREW DAVID, lawyer; b. San Francisco, Oct. 29, 1952; s. Orville Arne and Muriel Ruth (Trendt) N.; m. Rita M. Kobylenski, May 25, 1980; children: Katherine, Austin, Emily. BS, Stanford U., 1974; JD, Harvard U., 1977. Bar: Calif. 1977, D.C. 1979, Va. 1986, U.S. Dist. Ct. (No. Dist.) Calif. 1977, U.S. Dist. Ct. D.C. 1983, U.S. Dist. Ct. (Ea. Dist.) Va. 1988, U.S. Ct. Appeals (4th Cir.) 1989. Law clk. U.S. Dist. Ct., San Francisco, 1977-78; assoc. Lewis, Mitchell & Moore, Vienna, Va., 1979-82, ptnr., 1982-87, Morgan, Lewis & Bockius LLP, Washington, 1987-2000, Thelen Reid Brown Raysman & Striver LLP, Washington, 2000—; mng. ptnr. D.C. office Thelen Reid & Priest LLP, Washington, 2001—, mem. partnership coun. and exec. com., 2003—. Instr. U. Md., College Park, 1987-90; mem. faculty constrn. exec. program Stanford (Calif.) U., 1984-87. Co-editor Fed. Govt. Construction Contracts, 2003; contbr. chpts. to books, articles to profl. jours. Mem. ABA (forum on constrn. industry, pub. contract law sect.). Avocations: hiking, bicycling. Office: Thelen Reid Brown Raysman & Steiner LLP 701 Eighth St NW Washington DC 20001 Office Phone: 202-508-4368. Business E-Mail: adness@thelen.com.

NESS, BERNICE HAGIE, retired music educator; b. Mpls., Sept. 4, 1926; d. John Leonard and Mathilda Caroline Hagie; m. Elmo Vernon Ness, Aug. 3, 1974. BS, U. Minn., Mpls., 1948, MEd, 1950. Elem. music supr. Lake Co. Schs., Two Harbors, Minn., 1950—51, Mounds View Dist. #621, New Brighton, Minn., 1951—54; tchr., choral music & music theory Mounds View H.S., New Brighton, Minn., 1954—81, tchr., choral music & French, 1981—83; ret., 1983. Mem. adv. bd. U. Minn. Alumni Band, Mpls., 1949—51, coun. mem., 1996—98; dir., arranger Mounds View Alumni Choir, New Brighton, Minn., 1996—2006. Singer: Mounds View Alumni Choir, 1996—, (TV series) KARE 11 TV, 2007—. Chair, music com. Abiding Savior Ch., Mounds View, Minn., 1985—94; mem., music com. Christ the King Ch., New Brighton, Minn., 1995—97. Recipient Pillar award, Mounds View H.S., 2005. Personal E-mail: enbns@msn.com.

NESS, DAVID MICHAEL, lawyer; b. Mpls., July 9, 1969; BA, Gustavus Adolphus Coll., 1991; JD with distinction, Thomas M. Cooley Law Sch., 1998. Bar: Minn. 1998. Assoc. Bernick & Lifson, P.A., Mpls., 2001—. Assoc. editor: Thomas M. Cooley Jour. of Practical and Clin. Law. Named a Rising Star, Minn. Super Lawyers mag., 2006; recipient Am. Jurisprudence awards, Gaming Law, Computer Assisted Legal Rsch. and Estate Planning. Mem.: ABA, Minn. State Bar Assn., Hennepin County Bar Assn. Office: Bernick & Lifson PA Colonnade Ste 1200 5500 Wayzata Blvd Minneapolis MN 55416 Office Phone: 763-546-1200. E-mail: dness@bernick-lifson.com. *

NESS, NORMAN FREDERICK, retired astrophysicist, educator, administrator; b. Springfield, Mass., Apr. 15, 1933; s. Herman and Eva N.; children: Elizabeth Ann, Stephen Andrew. BS, Mass. Inst. Tech., 1955, PhD, 1959. Space physicist, asst. prof. geophysics UCLA, 1959-61; NAS-NRC postdoctoral rsch. assoc. NASA, 1960-61; rsch. physicist in space scis. Goddard Space Flight Center, Greenbelt, Md., 1961-86, head extraterrestrial physics br., 1968-69, chief Lab. for Extraterrestrial Physics, 1969-86; pres. Bartol Rsch. Inst. U. Del., Newark, 1987—2000, prof. Bartol Rsch. Inst., 1987—2005, prof. emeritus, 2005—; dir. NASA Space Grant Coll. Consortium, Del., 1991—2005. Lectr. math. U. Md., 1962-64, assoc. rsch. prof., 1965-67; vis. prof. U. Rome, 1968-69; liasion scientist US Office Naval Rsch., London, 1984-85. Contbr. articles profl. jours. Recipient Exceptional Sci. Achievement award NASA, 1966, 81, 86, Arthur S. Flemming award, 1968, Space Sci. award AIAA, 1971, Disting. Svc. medal NASA, 1986, Nat. Space Club Sci. award, 1993, Emil Wiechert medal German Geophys. Soc., 1993, Space Sci. award COSPAR, 1996. Fellow Am. Geophys. Union (John Adam Fleming award 1965); mem. US-NAS, Acad. Nat. dei Lincei. Achievements include research in publications reporting on experimental studies of interplanetary and planetary magnetic fields by satellites and space probes. Personal E-mail: nfnudel@yahoo.com.

NESSEL, EDWARD HARRY, swimming coach; b. Roselle, NJ, 1945; s. Irving Meyer Nessel and Ruth Elliott; m. Eileen Robin Berstein, 1973; children: Lee Allyson, Jason Eric(dec.), Matthew Scott(dec.). BS in Chemistry, Rutgers U., 1967, degree in Pharmacy Chemistry, 1968; post grad., Jersey City State, 1970, Rutgers U., 1971; MS in Bacteriology, Wagner Coll., 1978, MPH, 1978. Registered pharmacist Calif., NJ, Fla.; cert. US swimming coach. Rschr., product developer Mennen Co., Morris Plains, NJ, 1967; pharmacist supr. Pathmark Pharmacies, NJ, 1968—79; pharmacist, mgr. Roxy Drug Co., Inc., Irvington, NJ, 1979—90. Diet and nutrition cons. Fanwood Scotch Plaines YMCA, 1985—91, masters swim coach, 1984—91, swimming and racing cons., head age group coach, asst. sr. coach, 1989—91; head swim coach Jewish Cmty. Ctr. Metrowest, West Orange, 1991—2001; head masters swim coach Rutgers U., New Brunswick, 2000—04; head swim coach Maccabi, 1990—91, 1992, 93, 94; head coach swimming USA Nat. Team World Maccabi Games, Israel, 1997; coach NJ Masters Swimming, 1981—2004; physiology and sports medicine cons. Nat. Health and Fitness; health and fitness chmn. NJ Masters Swimming; nat. masters swimming coaches com. Nat. Com. Sports Medicine; nat. libr. US Masters Swimming; chair NJ Masters Swimming Com.; pres. Jersey Masters Swimming Inc.; sports chair age group and masters swimming Garden State Games; summer coord. long-course 50 meter swim season Rayway YMCA, 1987—2004. Contbr. articles to profl. jours.; patents adjustable hand-swim paddle. Athletic and swimming cons. NJ Spl. Olympics, 1986; cons. Essex County Narcotic Strike Force; ofcl. Garden State Games, chair gov. coun. phys. fitness swimming events, 1989—96. Named winner, NJ State Pentathlon champion Masters Swimming, 1986—87, YMCA Masters Nat. Swim champion, 1988, 1991, 1995, 1998, 2000—04, Masters All Am. Relay, 1998—99, 2002—03, head swim coach, US Jr. Nat. Swim Team, 1997, Coach of the Yr., US Masters Swimming, Inc., 1998, mentor coach, 2000, 2003, USMS Nat. champion 100 meter breast stroke, 2003; recipient Presdl. Series award, 1986, Nat. Svc. award, US Masters Swimming, 1999. Mem.: NRA (disting. expert rating pistol shotting), NJ Masters Swimming Inc. (chmn. 1999—2003), Masters Aquatic Coaches Assn. Am. (pres.), Master Swim Coaches Assn. Am., US Swimming Coaches Assn. (masters swimming coaches and sports medicine coms., cert. level five), Am. Masters Aquatic Coaches Assn. (pres. 1999—2003), Internat. Practical Shooters Confedn. (NJ State champion 1982, 1983), NJ Guild Pharmacists, NJ Pharm. Assn., Am. Assn. Microbiologists, Am. Med. Athletic Assn. (life; clin. cons., contbg. editor quar. 1993—, clin. advisor 1996—2006), Am. Swimming Coaches Assn. (life master level cert. level five coach, cert. level four YMCA), Rutgers Coll. Pharmacy Alumni Assn., South River Pistol Club, Willow Grove Swim Club (bd. dirs. 1986—90). Avocations: clarinet, saxophone, flute, mus. quality ship builder. Home: 1950 Crane Creek Blvd Viera FL 32940-6831 Personal E-mail: Ednessel@aol.com.

NESSMITH, H(ERBERT) ALVA, dentist; b. Miami, Fla., Nov. 27, 1935; s. William Boyd and Florence Editha (Lowe) N.; m. Paula Ann Fox, Oct. 1, 1960 (div. 1984); children: Amy Susan, Lynn Margaret, Mark Alva. Student, U. Miami, Fla., 1953-56; DDS, Northwestern U., 1960. Gen. practice dentistry, Tequesta, Fla., 1963—; dental cons. Palm Beach-Martin County Med. Ctr., Jupiter, Fla., 1970—; rsch. assoc. Colgate Palmolive Co., 1997—. Calibrated caries examiner, cons. Colgate Dental Rsch., 1997—. Mem. advminstrv. bd. United Meth. Ch. Tequesta, Jupiter, 1970—, chmn., 1988-90; pres. Meth. Men, 1982; chmn. Coun. on Ministries, 1992-94, mem. staff parish rels. com. 1999—; pres. Jupiter Elem. PTO, 1972; clarinetist Symphonic Band of Palm Beaches, Fla. Concert Band; pianist and clarinetist United Meth. Ch.; active Village of Tequesta Hist. Commn., 1992-96, Jupiter (Fla.) Cmty. Resource Ctr., 1994—; mem. adminstrv. bd., v.p. Christian Dental Soc., 1994—, v.p., 1995—, Andean Rural Health Care, 1999—. Mem. ADA, North Palm Beach County Dental Soc., Fla. Dental Assn., Jupiter-Tequesta-Juno Beach C. of C. Lodges: Kiwanis (pres. Jupiter/Tequesta chpt. 1980-81). Democrat. Avocations: mission dentistry, latin american studies, gardening, music, travel. Home: 196 River Dr Tequesta FL 33469-1934 Office: Inlet Profl Bldg 175 Tequesta Dr Jupiter FL 33469-2733

NESTELL, GALINA PETROVNA, paleontologist, researcher; d. Petr Prokhorovich Tsibin and Lidiya Alekseevna Tsibina; m. Valeriy Yanovich Vuks, July 6, 1979 (div. Aug. 18, 1987); 1 child, Yan Valerievich Vuks; m. Victor Ivanovich Pronin, Sept. 26, 1987 (div. Nov. 5, 1996); m. Merlynd Keith Nestell, Feb. 28, 1997. BS, Leningrad Mining Inst., Leningrad, 1979; PhD, All Russia Geol. Rsch. Inst., St. Petersburg, Russia, 1990. Sr. scientist All Russia Geol. Rsch. Inst., St. Petersburg, 1976—2001, Earth Crust Inst., St. Petersburg State U., 2001—; adj. prof. U. Tex., Arlington, 1997—. Contbr. numerous articles to profl. jours., abstracts in field. Recipient diploma, Soros Found., 1993. Mem.: Grzybowski Found. (corr.), Paleontol. Soc. Russia (corr.). Office Phone: 817-272-2983. Office Fax: 817-272-2628. Business E-Mail: gnestell@uta.edu.

NESTER, WILLIAM RAYMOND, JR., retired academic administrator; b. Cin., Feb. 19, 1928; s. William Raymond and Evelyn (Blettner) N.; m. Mary Jane (dec.); children: William Raymond, Mark Patrick, Brian Philip, Stephen Christopher. BS, U. Cin., 1950, EdM, 1953, PhD, 1965, DHL (hon.), 2005, No. Ky. U., 2001, U. Nebr., 2002, U. Cin., 2005. Dir. student union U. Cin., 1952-53, asst. dean of men, 1953-60, dean of men, 1960-67, assoc. prof. edn., 1965-70, dean of students, 1967-69, vice provost student and univ. affairs, 1969-76, prof. edn., 1970-78, assoc. sr. v.p., assoc. provost, 1976-78; v.p. student svcs. Ohio State U., Columbus, 1978-83, prof. edn., 1978-83; pres. Kearney State Coll., Nebr., 1983-91, prof. edn. Nebr., 1983-93; chancellor U. Nebr., Kearney, 1991-93, prof. emeritus, chancellor emeritus, 1993—; v.p. univ. rels. devel. No. Ky. U., 1996-99. Pres. emeritus Mus. Nebr. Art, 1991—; cons. on higher edn., 1993—. Pres. Metro-Six Athletic Conf., 1975-76. Mem. Am. Assn. State Colls. and Univs. (bd. dirs.), Ctrl. States Intercollegiate Conf. (pres. 1986-89), Nat. Assn. Student Pers. Adminstrs. (past regional v.p., mem. exec. com.), Am. Assn. Higher Edn., Ohio Assn. Student Pers. Adminstrs. (past pres.), Nat. Intrafrat. Conf. (pres. 1991-92), Frat. Scholarship Officers Assn. (past pres.), Mortar Bd., Pi Kappa Alpha (nat. pres. 1978-80, pres. nat. interfrat. conf. 1988-89, past pres. Pi Kappa Alpha Ednl. Found.), Omicron Delta Kappa, Phi Delta Kappa, Phi Alpha Theta, Phi Eta Sigma, Sigma Sigma. Episcopalian. Home: 7674 Coldstream Dr Cincinnati OH 45255-3932 E-mail: wrnchanem@cs.com.

NESTLER, JOHN EDWIN, endocrinology educator; b. Passaic, NJ, Sept. 24, 1952; m. Michelle Dumont, Dec. 29, 1990. BA in Chemistry (with honors) and German, Haverford Coll., Pa., 1975; MD, U. Pa., Phila., 1979. Diplomate Am. Bd. Internal Medicine, Am. Bd. Endocrinology and Metabolism; cert. Nat. Bd. Med. Examiners. Intern Med. Coll. Va., Richmond, 1979-80, resident, 1980-82, chief med. resident, instr. in medicine, 1982-83, fellow in endocrinology, 1985-86, asst. prof. medicine, 1986-91, assoc. prof. medicine, 1991—, dir. med. affairs, BioClin, 1991-95, prof. medicine, 1995—, chmn. divsn. endocrinology and metabolism, 1997—, vice chmn. dept. internal medicine, 2003—; fellow in endocrinology U. Pa., Phila., 1983-85. Reviewer various profl. jours.; vis. prof. Dalhousie U., Halifax, N.S., 1991; invited speaker several major confs. including NIH/NICHD Conf. on Polycystic Ovary Syndrome, Bethesda, Md., 1990. Author numerous original publs., book chpts., abstracts. Recipient Sandra Tate Russell Meml. Rsch. award Am. Diabetes Assn. Va. affiliate, 1986, Clin. Assoc. Physician award NIH, 1985-87, rsch. trainee awards Phila. Endocrine Soc., 1984, 85. Fellow Am. Coll. Physicians; mem. AAAS, Internat. Diabetes Found., European Assn. for Study of Diabetes, Cen Va. Assn. Diabetes Educators, Am. Assn. Diabetes Educators, Am. Diabetes Assn. (pres. 1990—), Am. Fedn. Clin. Rsch., Internat. Soc. for Androgenic Disorders, The Endocrine Soc., So. Soc. for Clin. Investigation. Achievements include research on diabetes, polycystic ovary syndrome, steroids, and insulin. Home: 5800 Three Chopt Rd Richmond VA 23226-2337 Office: Med Coll Va Div Endocrinology PO Box 980111 Richmond VA 23298-0111 Office Phone: 804-828-9696.

NESTLER, PATRICIA C., English professor; BA, Gettysburg Coll., 1972; MA, U. NC, Chapel Hill, 1973. Faculty mem. to assoc. prof. English Montgomery County CC, Pa., 1977—. Recipient US Prof. of Yr. award, Carnegie Found. for Advancement of Tchg. and Coun. for Advancement and Support of Edn., 2006. Office: English Dept Montgomery County CC 101 College Dr Pottstown PA 19464 Office Phone: 215-641-6369. E-mail: pnestler@mc3.edu. *

NESTOR CASTELLANO, BRENDA DIANA, real estate company executive; b. Palm Beach, Fla., Nov. 10, 1948; d. John Joseph and Marion O'Connor Nestor; m. Robert Castellano. Student, U. Miami, Fla., 1978. Lic. real estate broker, Fla. Salesman Oscar E Dooley, Inc., Miami, Fla., 1978-80; prin. Brenda Nestor Assocs, Inc., Miami Beach, Fla., 1980—. Exec. v.p., bd. dirs. D.W.G. Corp., 1988-94, N.V.F. Corp., Salem Corp., 1988-97, Southeastern Pub. Svc., Graniteville Corp., 1988-94, Essex Ins., Chesapeake Ins.; exec. v.p., dir. Security Mgmt. Bd. dirs. Vizcayan Mus.; dir. Miami's Jackson Meml. Found. Named Ms. Charity, City of Miami, 1985, Lady Comdr., State of Fla. Mem. Miami Beach Bd. Realtors (bd. dirs. 1984—), Real Estate Securities and Exch. Com., Knights of Malta, Doubles Club (N.Y.C.), La Gorce Country Club, Fisher Island Club, Surf Club, Ocean Reef Club, Carnegie Abbey (R.I.) Espicopalian. Avocations: golf, tennis, boating. Home and Office: 39 Palm Ave Miami FL 33139-3263 E-mail: ladybnestor@aol.com.

NETA, BENY, mathematics educator, researcher; b. Tripoli, Libya, Nov. 2, 1945; arrived in USA, 1975, naturalized, 1984; s. Shalom and Ahuva (Vittori) N.; m. Tamar Cerklevitz, Aug. 15, 1971; children: Itay, Leeor, Maital. BSc, Tel Aviv U., 1967, MSc, 1971, PhD, Carnegie-Mellon U., 1977. Asst. prof. math. No. Ill. U., De Kalb, 1977-80; asst. prof. numerical analysis Tex. Tech U., Lubbock, 1980-84; assoc. prof. Naval Postgrad.

Sch., Monterey, Calif., 1985-92, prof., 1992—. Rsch. adv. Nat. Rsch. Coun. Nat. Academics. Guest editor Geophys. and Astrophys. Fluid Dynamics, Computers and Math. with Applications, Mathematical and Computer Modelling; editl. bd. Electronic Jours. of Theoretical Physics, Advanced Studies in Theoretical Physics; contbr. articles to profl. jours. Pres. Lubbock chpt. PTA, 1983-84. Grantee Nat. Acad. Scis., 1984-85. Mem. AIAA, Internat. Assn. for Math. and Computers in Simulation, N.Y. Acad. Scis.; fellow Am. Inst. Aeronautics and Astronautics (assoc.). Home: 1410 Augusta Pl Monterey CA 93940-6403 Office: Naval Postgrad Sch Dept Appl Math Code MA/Nd Monterey CA 93943 Office Phone: 831-656-2235. Business E-Mail: bneta@nps.edu.

NETHERCOTT, MARK A., physics educator; Secondary tchg. cert. Named Wy. Tchr. of Yr., 2007. Mem.: Am. Assn. Physics Tchrs., Geology Soc. Am., Nat. Sci. Tchr.'s Assn. Office: Star Valley High Sch 455 West Swift Creek Ln PO Box 8000 Afton WY 83110 Business E-Mail: mnethercott@lcsd2.org. *

NETHERCUTT, GEORGE RECTOR, JR., lawyer, consultant, former congressman; b. Spokane, Wash., Oct. 7, 1944; s. George Rector and Nancy N.; m. Mary Beth Socha Nethercutt, Apr. 2., 1977; children: Meredith, Elliott. BA in English, Wash. State U., 1967; JD, Gonzaga U., 1971. Bar: D.C. 1972. Law clk. to Hon. Raymond Plummer U.S. Dist. Ct. Alaska, Anchorage, 1971; staff counsel to U.S. Senator Ted Stevens Washington, 1972; chief of staff to U.S. Senator Ted Stevens, 1972-76; pvt. practice Spokane, Wash., 1977-94; mem. 104th-108th Congresses from 5th Wash. dist., Washington, 1995—2005; ptnr. Lundquist, Nethercutt & Griles, LLC, Washington, 2005—. Mem. house appropriations and sci. coms.; mem. bd. Heola Mining Co., ISR Arcadis Co., Washington Policy Ctr., Juvenile Diabetes Rsch. Found. Internat., 2005—; chmn. U.S. sect. Permanent Joint Bd. Def., U.S., Can., 2005— Chmn. Spokane County Rep. Party, 1990-94, co-founder Vanessa Behan Crisis Nursery, pres. Spokane Juvenile Diabetes Found., 1993-94. Mem. Masons (lodge #34), Lions Club (Spokane Ctrl.), Sigma Nu. Republican. Presbyterian. Avocations: running, handball, squash. Office: Lundquist Nethercutt & Griles LLC 400 N Capital St Ste 475 Washington DC 20001 Home Phone: 703-827-2203; Office Phone: 202-589-0015. Business E-Mail: gnethercutt@lngassociates.com.

NETHERLAND, JOSEPH H., manufacturing executive; BS in Indsl. Engring., Ga. Inst. Tech.; MBA, U. Pa. Bus. planner machinery group FMC Technologies, 1973-78, ops. mgr. ordnance divsn., 1978-83, mgr. fluid control divsn., 1983-84, mgr. wellhead divsn., 1984-85, gen mgr. wellhead divsn., 1985-89, gen. mgr. specialized machinery group, 1989-99, pres., 1999—2006, chmn., CEO, 2001—06, chmn., 2006—. Bd. dirs. Am. Petroleum Inst. Mem. adv. bd. Dept. Engring. Tex. A&M Univ.; mem. Pres. Council Ga. Inst. Tech. Recipient Don E. Waggener Butch Griffin award, Spindletop Internat., 2002. Office: FMC Technologies 1803 Gears Rd Houston TX 77067 *

NETHERY, JOHN JAY, government official, military officer; b. Mpls., June 4, 1941; s. Ronald Jay and Mary Vesta (McVeety) N.; m. Sonya Elisabeth Magin, July 27, 1968; children: William Jay, Mary Elisabeth (dec.), Sarah Ann. BA, U. Denver, 1963, MPA, 1968. Mgmt. intern USAF Logistics Command, San Antonio, 1969-71, budget analyst Dayton, Ohio, 1971-72; chief, fiscal analysis USAF Hdqrs., Washington, 1973-80, chief, investment div., 1980-81, chief budget mgmt., 1981-85; dep. asst. sec. programs and budget Dept. of USAF, Washington, 1986-88, asst. to undersecretary, 1988-89, dep. asst. sec. fin. ops., 1989—. Mem. Air Force bd. for the correction of mil. records, Washington, 1980—. Recipient Gov.'s Scholastic award Gov. of Colo., 1968, Presdl. Rank award, 1988. Mem. Sr. Execs. Assn., Air Force Assn. Presbyterian. Avocations: history, military miniatures. Office: Dept USAF SAF/FM The Pentagon Washington DC 20330-1130 E-mail: Jnethery@aol.com.

NETRAVALI, ARUN N., communications executive; b. Bombay, May 26, 1946; m. Chitra Netravali; 2 children. BS in Tech. with honors, Indian Inst. Tech., Bombay, 1967; MS, Rice U., 1969, PhD, 1970; PhD (hon.), Ecole Polytechnique Federale, Lausanne, Switzerland, 1994. With NASA, Orlando, Fla., 1970-72; mem. tech. staff AT&T Bell Labs., Holmdel, NJ, 1972-78, head visual comm. rsch. dept. Murray Hill, NJ, 1978-83, dir. computing systems rsch., 1983-92, exec. dir. rsch., comm. scis. divsn., 1992-94; pres. Bell Labs., Murray Hill, NJ, 1999—2001; chief scientist Lucent Tech. (formerly Bell Labs.), Murray Hill, NJ, 2001—04; mng. ptnr. Omni Capital, LLC, NJ, 2004—. Former adj. prof. media lab. MIT, Cambridge, Mass; lectr. City Coll. N.Y., Columbia U., MIT, Rutgers U.; advisor Ctr. for Telecomm. Rsch. of Columbia U., 1987—, EPFL Swiss Fed. Inst. Tech., Lausanne, 1986—, Beckman Inst. of U. Ill. Co-author: Digital Pictures: Representation and Compression, 1987, Visual Communication Systems, 1989, Digital Video: An Introduction to MPEG-2, 1996; contbr. 100 tech. papers to sci. jours. Mem. N.J. Govs. Com. on Schs. Program. Recipient Journal award Soc. of Motion Pictures and TV Engrs., 1982, Ann. Asian Am. Corp. Employees award Orgn. Chinese Ams., 1991, Engr. of Yr. award Assn. Engrs. of India, 1992, Nat. Medal of Tech. Laureate, 2001, Padma Bhushan award Govt. of India, 2001. Fellow IEEE (editor Communications 1984—, mem. editorial bd. Proceedsings of IEEE 1980-84, Fink prize 1980, L.G. Abraham prize 1985, 91, Alexander Graham Bell medal 1991, mem. digitals TV com.), AAAS; mem. NAE, Tau Beta Pi, Sigma Xi. Achievements include patents in field. Avocation: tennis. Office Phone: 908-304-4083. Business E-Mail: arunnetravali@omnivc.com.

NETSIRI, CHAIYAPOJ, research scientist; b. Bangkok, May 29, 1964; arrived in US, 2001, permanent resident, 2005; s. Chote and Patcharin Netsiri. BSEE, King Mongkut's Inst. Tech., Bangkok, Thailand, 1986; MS in Computer Sci., Chiba U., Japan, 1996; PhD in Elec. Engring., U. Tokyo, 1999. Prodn. engr. Kang Yang Electric MFG Co., Ltd., Samutprakarn, Thailand, 1987—89; elec. engr. Tom Tech Co., Ltd., Bangkok, 1990—92; R&D engr. Yamada Kikai Kogyo Co., Ltd., Chiba, Japan, 1992—94; rsch. assoc. U. Cambridge, England, 1999—2001, Albert Einstein Coll. Medicine, Bronx, NY, 2001—03; sr. staff assoc. Columbia U., NYC, 2003—04; rsch. scientist Rice U., Houston, 2004—05; sr. applications engr. MicroMRI, Inc., Phila., 2005—06; rsch. scientist NexTech Solutions Inc., Austin, Tex., 2006—07, Bend Tree Group LLC, Georgetown, Tex., 2007—. Fellow, U. Cambridge, 1999—2001; grantee, Royal Soc., 2000—01; scholar, Nagai Found., 1994—95, Japanese Govt., 1995—99. Mem.: Soc. Neurosci. (assoc.), IEEE (assoc.). Buddhist. Avocation: tennis. Office: Bench Tree Group LLC PO Box 1878 Georgetown TX 78627-1878 Personal E-mail: netsiri_c@hotmail.com.

NETTELBECK, FRED ARTHUR, poet; b. Chgo., Nov. 9, 1950; s. Manfred Emil Nettelbeck and Thelma Anderson; m. Billy Joe Nettelbeck, July 17, 1999; children: James, Danny, Amandla. Student, El Camino Coll., 1969—71. Author: The Quick and The Dead, 1970, Spectator, 1977, Large Talk, 1983, Americruiser, 1983, The Kiss Off, 1984, Hands on a Mirror, 1987, Albert Ayler Disappeared, 1989, Ecosystems Collapsing, 1992, Hurting Music, 1998, All Fell Down, 2003, Everything Written Exists, 2004, (with John M. Bennett) Lap Gun Cut, 2006, others; editor: This is Important mag., 1980—. Democrat. Avocations: fishing, entheogenic plants. Home and Office: PO Box 69 Beatty OR 97621 Office Phone: 541-533-2486. Personal E-mail: fanettelbeck@fanettelbeck.com.

NETTELHORST, ROBIN PAUL, academic administrator, writer; b. Ohio, Mar. 14, 1957; s. Paul Merrit and Naomi Jean (Saylor) N.; m. Ruth Williamson, June 25, 1983; children: Vanessa Rachel, Nichole Antoinette, Sarah Brittany. BA, L.A. Bapt. Coll., 1979; MA, UCLA, 1983. Lectr. Christian Heritage Coll., El Cagon, Calif., 1984; lectr. Old Testament and bibl. langs. LA Bapt. Coll., 1984—87; novelist, 1987—; v.p. Quartz Hill Sch. Theology, Calif., 1992—. Webmaster Quartz Hill Sch. Theology, 1996—. Editor Quartz Hill Jour. Theology, 1994—; author short stories; contbr. articles to mags.; host (internet and FM Radio broadcast) Beyond the Box, 1999-2004; writer weekly column Ridge Rider News; author: What Dreamers Be These Rocks: Tableland, Book I, 2000, Dreams of Nothingness: Tableland, Book II, 2000, Awakens the Dreamer: Tableland, Book III, 2000, The Wrong Side of Morning, 2000, With a Rod of Iron, 2000, Antediluvian, 2000, Somewhere Obscurely, 2000, The Complaint of Jacob, 2005, Does God Have a Long Nose? 2006, Somewhen Obscurely, 2006, Inheritance, 2006, The Bible's Most Fascinating People: An Illustrated Collection: Stories from the Old and New Testaments, 2007. Ordained deacon Quartz Hill Cmty. Ch., 1989—. Mem. Am. Acad. Religion, Soc. Bibl. Lit. Baptist. Avocations: camping, reading, stamp collecting/philately, coin collecting/numismatics. Office: Quartz Hill Sch Theology 43543 51st St W Quartz Hill CA 93536-5608 Office Phone: 661-722-0891. Business E-Mail: robin@theology.edu. *To hold the hand of God, to listen to his heart, to feel his pain, to taste his joys, to long for his happiness—that is to love God.*

NETTELS, ELSA, English language educator; b. Madison, Wis., May 25, 1931; d. Curtis Putnam and Elsie (Patterson) Nettels. BA, Cornell U., 1953; MA, U. Wis., 1955, PhD, 1960. From instr. to asst. prof. English Mt. Holyoke Coll., South Hadley, Mass., 1959—67; from asst. prof. to prof. English Coll. William and Mary, Williamsburg, Va., 1967—97, prof. emeritus, 1997—. Author: James and Conrad, 1977 (South Atlantic MLA award, 1975), Language, Race and Social Class in Howells' America, 1988, Language and Gender in American Fiction: Howells, James, Wharton, and Cather, 1997; contbr. articles to profl. jours. Fellow, NEH, 1984—85. Mem.: MLA, South Atlantic MLA (mem. editl. bdl. 1977—83), Henry James Soc. (mem. editl. bd. 1983—). Office: Coll William and Mary Dept English Williamsburg VA 23187 Office Phone: 757-221-3905. Business E-Mail: exnett@wm.edu.

NETTELS, GEORGE EDWARD, JR., retired mining executive; b. Pittsburg, Kans., Oct. 20, 1927; s. George Edward and Mathilde A. (Wulke) N.; m. Mary Joanne Myers, July 19, 1952; children: Christopher Bryan, Margaret Anne, Katherine Anne, Rebecca Jane. BSCE, U. Kans., Lawrence, 1950. With Black & Veatch Engrs., Kansas City, Mo., 1950-51, Spencer Chem. Co., Kansas City, Mo., 1951-55, Freeto Constrn. Co., Pittsburg, 1955-57; pres. Midwest Minerals, Inc., Pittsburg, 1957—; chmn. bd. McNally Pittsburg Mfg. Corp., 1970-76, pres., CEO, 1976-87, ret., 1987. Past chmn. bd. Nat. Limestone Inst.; bd. dirs. Pitts. Indsl. Devel. Com. Mem. bd. advisors U. Kans. Endowment Assn.; mem. Kans. U. Chancellor's Club, Kans., Inc.; past pres. Bd. Edn. 250, Pittsburg; past chmn. bd. trustees Mt. Carmel Hosp.; past mem. Kans. Commn. Civil Rights; chmn. Kans. Republican Com., 1966-68; Kans. del. Rep. Nat. Conv., 1968, Kans. Bus. and Industry Com. for Re-election of Pres., 1972. With AUS, 1946-47. Recipient Disting. Svc. citation U. Kans., 1980, Disting. Engring. citation U. Kans., 1985; named Kansan of Yr. Natives Sons and Daus. Kans., 1986. Mem. ASCE, NAM (past. dir.), Kans. C. of C. and Industry (dir., chmn. 1983-84), Kans. Right to Work (dir.), Pittsburg C. of C. (past dir.), Kans. U. Alumni Assn. (pres. 1977), Kans. Leadership Com., Crestwood Country Club, Wolf Creek Golf Club (Olathe), Tau Beta Pi, Omicron Delta Kappa, Beta Theta Pi. Office: Midwest Minerals Inc 509 W Quincy St Pittsburg KS 66762-5689 Business E-Mail: george@midwestminerals.com.

NETTERFIELD, KYLE, lawyer; b. Surrey, BC, Sept. 4, 1970; BA, Moody Bible Inst., 1992; JD magna cum laude, Seattle Univ. Sch. Law, 1997. Bar: Wash. 1997, U.S. Supreme Ct., U.S. Dist. Ct., Western Dist. Wash., Northern Dist. Ill. 1997. Assoc. atty., comml. litig., constrn. law Ellis, Li & McKinstry, Seattle. Contbr. articles to numerous profl. jours. Mem.: ABA, Wash. State Bar Assn. Office: Ellis Li and Mckinstry Ste 4900 Two Union Sq 601 Union St Seattle WA 98101-3906

NETTL, BRUNO, anthropologist, musicologist, educator; b. Prague, Czechoslovakia, Mar. 14, 1930; s. Paul and Gertrud (Hutter) N.; m. Wanda Maria White, Sept. 15, 1952; children: Rebecca Nettl-Fiol, Gloria Roubal. AB, Ind. U., 1950, PhD, 1953; MA in L.S, U. Mich., 1960; LHD (hon.), U. Chgo., 1993; LHD (hon.), U. Ill., 1996, Carleton Coll., 2000, Kenyon Coll., 2002. Mem. faculty Wayne State U., Detroit, 1953-64, asst. prof., 1954-64, music librarian, 1958-64; mem. faculty U. Ill., Urbana, 1964—, prof. music and anthropology, 1967—, chmn. div. musicology, 1967-72, 75-77, 82-85. Vis. lectr., Fulbright grantee U. Kiel, Fed. Republic of Germany, 1956-58; cons. Ency. Brit., 1969—; cons. on ethnomusicology to various univs.; vis. prof. Williams Coll., 1971, Washington U., 1978, U. Louisville, 1983, U. Wash., 1985, 88, 89, 93, 95, 98, 2000, Fla. State U., 1988, Harvard U., 1989, U. Alta., 1991, Colo. Coll., 1992, Northwestern U., 1993, U. Minn., 1994, U. Chgo., 1996, 2006, Carleton Coll., 1996, U. So. Calif., 2002, U. Denver, 2005. Author: Theory and Method in Ethnomusicology, 1964, Music in Primitive Culture, 1956, Folk and Traditional Music of the Western Continents, 1965, 2nd edit., 1973, Eight Urban Musical Cultures, 1978, The Study of Ethnomusicology, 1983, new edit., 2005, The Western Impact on World Music, 1985, The Radif of Persian Music, 1987, rev. edit., 1992, Blackfoot Musical Thought, 1989, Comparative Musicology and Anthropology of Music, 1991, Heartland Excursions, 1995, In the course of Performance, 1998, Encounters in Ethnomusicology, a Memoir, 2002; co-author Excursions in World Music, 1992, 3rd edit., 2000, 5th edit., 2007; editor Ethnomusicology, 1961-65, 98-2002, Yearbook of the International Folk Music Council, 1975-77; sr. adv. editor Garland Ency. of World Music; contbr. articles to profl. jours. Recipient Koizumi prize in ethnomusicology, Tokyo, 1994; named hon. prof. Ctrl. Conservatory Music, Beijing, 2007. Fellow Am. Acad. of Arts and Scis.; mem. Soc. Ethnomusicology (pres. 1969-71), Am., Internat. musicol. socs., Internat. Coun. for Traditional Music, Coll. Music Soc, Am. Musicological Soc. (hon.), Soc. for Ethnomusicology (hon.) Home: 1423 Cambridge Dr Champaign IL 61821-4958 Office: U Ill Sch Music Urbana IL 61801 Office Phone: 217-333-9613. Business E-Mail: b-nettl@uiuc.edu.

NETTLES, BERT SHEFFIELD, lawyer; b. Monroeville, Ala., May 6, 1936; s. George Lee and Blanche (Sheffield) N.; m. Elizabeth Duquet, Sept. 16, 1967; children: Jane, Mary Katherine, Susan, Anne. BS, U. Ala., Tuscaloosa, 1958, JD, 1960. Bar: Ala. 1960. Asst. atty. gen. State of Ala., Montgomery, 1961-62; ptnr. Johnston, Johnston & Nettles, Mobile, Ala., 1962-69, Nettles & Cox, Mobile, 1969-81, Nettles, Barker, Janecky & Copeland, Mobile, 1981-89, Spain, Gillon, Grooms, Blan & Nettles, Birmingham, Ala., 1989-94, London & Yancey, Birmingham, 1995—2003, Haskell Slaughter Young @ Rediker, LLC, Birmingham, 2003—. Counsel Ala. Ins. Underwriting Assn., 1986—. Contbr. articles to profl. jours. Mem. Ala. Ho. of Reps., 1969-74; bd. dirs. U. South Ala. Med. Sci. Found., Mobile, 1982-89, U. So. Ala. Health Svcs. Found., 1985-89; chancellor Episcopal Diocese of Cen. Gulf Coast, Mobile, 1983-88; asst. chancellor Episcopal Diocese of Ala., 2000-03. 2d lt. inf. U.S. Army, 1960-61, capt., inf. Res., 1960-67. Recipient Exceptional Performance citation Def. Rsch. Inst. and ATLA, 1987; named to Best Lawyers in Am. for Ins. Mem. ABA (chmn. standing com. on legis. 1978), Ala. Bar Assn. (chmn. young lawyers divsn. 1966-67, chair task force on appellate restructuring 1988-91), Am. Right of Way Assn. (sr.), Ala. Def. Lawyers Assn. (pres. 1986-87), Ala. Supreme Ct. (com. on pattern jury instructions/civil, 1990—, standing com. rules of appellate procedure 2001—, appellate practice sect. 2004—). Republican. Avocation: reading. Home: 1416 Windsor Cir Birmingham AL 35213-3434 Office: Haskell Slaughter Young & Rediker LLC 2001 Park Pl N Ste 1400 Birmingham AL 35203 Office Phone: 205-251-1000. Business E-Mail: bsn@hsy.com.

NETTLES, JENNIFER, singer; b. Atlanta, Ga., Sept. 12, 1974; BA, Agnes Scott Coll., Decatur, Ga. Lead singer Soul Miner's Daughter, 1996, Jennifer Nettles band, Sugarland, 2002—. Signed to Mercury Records. Singer: (albums) (solo albums) Story of Your Bones, 2000, (with Sugarland) Twice the Speed of Life, 2004, Enjoy the Ride, 2006, (songs) Want To, 2006 (Duo Video of Yr., Country Music TV, 2007), (with Bon Jovi) Who Says You Can't Go Home, 2005 (Collaborative Video of Yr., Country Music TV, 2006, Grammy award, Best Country Collaboration with Vocals, 2007). Recipient Ind. Musician of Yr. award, 2001, New Duo/Group award, Acad. Country Music, 2006. Office: Gail Gellman Mgmt 23852 PCH 920 Malibu CA 90265 Office Phone: 310-456-2620. Office Fax: 310-456-1415. E-mail: gellmanmgmt@aol.com, sugarlandmail@aol.com. *

NETTLES, JOHN BARNWELL, obstetrics and gynecology educator; b. Dover, NC, May 19, 1922; s. Stephen A. and Estelle (Hendrix) N.; m. Eunice Anita Saugstad, Apr. 28, 1956; children: Eric, Robert, John Barnwell; m. 2d, Sandra Williams, Sept. 14, 1991; stepchildren: Steven Williams, Clayton Williams. BS, U. S.C., 1941; MD, Med. Coll. S.C., 1944. Diplomate: Am. Bd. Obstetrics and Gynecology. Intern Garfield Meml. Hosp., Washington, 1944-45; research fellow in pathology Med. Coll. Ga., Augusta, 1946-47; resident in ob-gyn. U. Ill. Rsch. and Ednl. Hosps., Chgo., 1947-51; instr. to asst. prof. ob-gyn. U. Ill. Coll. Medicine, Chgo., 1951-57; asst. prof., assoc. prof., prof. ob-gyn. U. Ark. Med. Ctr., Little Rock, 1957-69; dir. grad. edn. Hillcrest Med. Ctr., Tulsa, 1969-73; prof. ob-gyn Coll. Medicine, U. Okla., Oklahoma City, 1969-78; chmn. dept. ob-gyn. U. Okla.-Tulsa Med. Coll., 1975-80, prof., 1980—, mem. coun. on residency edn. in ob-gyn., 1974-79. Dir. Tulsa Obstet. and Gynecol. Edn. Found., 1969-80; Coordinator med. edn. Nat. Def., Ark., 1961-69; mem. S.W. regional med. adv. com. Planned Parenthood Fedn. Am., 1974-78; mem. adv. com. Health Policy Agenda Am. People, 1982-85, rev. com. Accrediation Coun. for Continuing Med. Edn., 1987-92. Contbr. articles on uterine malignancy, kidney biopsy in pregnancy, perinatal morbidity and mortality, human sexuality sch. age pregnancy to profl. jours. Served as lt. (j.g.) M.C. USNR, 1945-46; as lt. 1953-54. Recipient Nat. Faculty award. Fellow Am. Coll. Ob-Gyn. (dist. sec.-treas. 1964-70, dist. chmn. exec. bd. 1970-73, v.p. 1977-78, Disting. Svc. award 1998, Dist. VII Outstanding Clin. Prof. award 1989, Nat. Tchr. award 1992), ACS (bd. govs. 1969-71, program com. 1970-71, Surg. forum 1977-84, adv. com. gyn/ob 1985-92), Royal Soc. Health, Royal Soc. Medicine; mem. Ark. Obstet. and Gynecol. Soc. (exec. sec. 1959-69), Ctrl. Assn. Obstetrics and Gynecology (exec. com. 1966-69, pres. 1978-79), Internat. Soc. Advancement Humanistic Studies in Gynecology, Assn. Mil. Surgeons U.S., AMA (sect. coun. on obstetrics and gynecology 1975-96, chmn. 1982-96, del. from Am. Coll. Obstetricians and Gynecologists 1987-96, governing coun. sr. physicians group 2003—, Young at Heart award Young Physicians sect. 1994), Nurses Assn. So. Med. Assn. (chmn. obstetrics 1973-74), Okla. Med. Soc. (Ed L. Calhoun Leadership in Organized Medicine award, 2004), Tulsa County Med. Soc., Chgo. Med. Soc., Am. Assn. for Maternal and Infant Health, Assn. Am. Med. Colls., APHA, Am. Assn. Sex Edn. Counselors and Therapists (S.W. regional bd. 1976-79), Soc. for Gynecol. Investigation, AAAS, Am. Soc. for Study Fertility and Sterility, Internat. Soc. Gen. Semantics, So. Gynecol. and Obstet. Soc. (pres. 1981-82), Am. Cancer Soc. (pres. Okla. div. 1979-83, St. George's medal 1991), Com. on In-Tng. Exam. in Ob-Gyn, Am. Coll. Nurse Midwives (governing bd. examiners 1979-83), Sigma Xi (pres. Tulsa chpt. 1992-93), Phi Rho Sigma. Lutheran. Office: U Okla Health Sci Ctr 1145 S Utica Ave Ste 600 Tulsa OK 74104-4070 Office Phone: 918-582-0955. Business E-Mail: John-Nettles@ouhsc.edu. *To live life fully, with faith and trust in God and his people, working with others to make our world a little better, and willing to fill the gaps wherever they are.*

NETTLES, SAUNDRA R. MURRAY, psychologist, writer, educator; b. Atlanta, Ga., Jan. 6, 1947; d. Edna Lewis and George Halbert Rice; m. Donald Gaines Murray, Mar. 14, 1972 (div.); m. Reginald Nettles (div.); children: Alana Denise Murray, Kali Nicole Murray. BA, Howard U., 1963—67; MS, U. of Ill. Grad. Sch. of Libr. and Info. Sci., 1967—68, Howard U., 1972—74, PhD, 1972—76. Prof. and dept. chair Coll. of Edn., Ga. So. U., 2004—; assoc. prof. of human devel. U. of Md., 1994—2003; prin. rsch. scientist Johns Hopkins U. Ctr. for Social Orgn. of Schools, Balt., 1988—99; dir., office of field services United Planning Orgn., Washington, 1983—87; sr. rsch. scientist Am. Inst. for Rsch., Washington, 1978—82. Contbr. articles to profl. jours. Mem. Jack and Jill of Am., Columbia, Md., 1989—92; rsch. scholars panel Pathways to Coll. Network, Boston, 2001—04. Mem.: APA, APA Sect. on the Psychology of Black Women (pres. 1986—87), Environ. Design Rsch. Assn., Am. Ednl. Rsch. Assn. Office: Georgia Southern Univ Po B 8144 Statesboro GA 30460-8144 Office Phone: 912-681-0672. Office Fax: 912-681-5091. E-mail: snettles@georgiasouthern.edu.

NETTO, AMBA CECILE, military officer; b. Lafayette, La., Aug. 3, 1980; d. Michael R. Netto and DeciAmba C. Morgan; m. Terry J. Meadows, June 25, 2003 (div.); children: Kailly M. Paulson, Kayne M. Paulson. Commd. lt. USAF, 1999, advanced through grades to staff sgt., 2003, security forces Albuquerque, 1999—2004, info. mgr. Columbus, Miss., 2004—06. Tng. assessor police reform directorate USAF, Kabul, Afghanistan, 2005—. Named Non-Commisioned Officer of Qua., 14th Comm. Squadron Comdr., USAF, 2005. Home Phone: 662-241-9573; Office Phone: 662-434-7096.

NETTO, PAUL V., critical care nurse; b. Santa Cruz, Calif., Oct. 1, 1951; s. Joseph and Mary C. Netto; m. Patricia L. Jaynes-Netto (dec.); children: Paul V. Jr., Joseph P., Matthew R.; m. Cathy J. Montgomery-Netto, Aug. 12, 1984. ASN, Sierra Coll., Rocklin, Calif., 1985, AA in Art, 1993; BA in Studio Art cum laude, Calif. State U., 2000. RN Calif., critical care RN. RN supr. Carmichael (Calif.) Convalescent, 1986—87; supr., dir. Mt. Olivette Care Ctr., Carmichael, 1988—89; RN, clin. mgr. Roseville (Calif.) Cmty. Hosp., 1989—95; asst. dir. Hilltop Manor, Auburn, Calif., 1993—95; RNII CICU/MSICU Sutter Roseville Med. Ctr., 1995—. Nurse rep. Calif. Nurses Assn., Sacramento, 1998—. Author: Brothers and Friends, 2001; author: (illustrator) The Birds In The Hand, 2005; composer, performer (audio album) Pearls and Swine, 1991. Mem.: NRA (life), Jews for Preservation of Firearms Ownership, Golden Key Nat. Honor Soc. Libertarian. Avocations: travel, scuba diving, fishing, target shooting, writing. Home: PO Box 756 Meadow Vista CA 95722 Office: Sutter Roseville Med Ctr 1 Medical Ctr Plz Roseville CA 95561 Office Phone: 916-781-1522.

NETZEL, PAUL ARTHUR, fundraising management executive, consultant; b. Tacoma, Sept. 11, 1941; s. Marden Arthur and Audrey Rose (Jones) Netzel; m. Diane Viscount, Mar. 21, 1963; children: Paul M., Shari Ann. BS in Group Work Edn., George Williams Coll., 1963. Program dir. S. Pasadena-San Marino YMCA, 1963—66; exec. dir. camp and youth programs Wenatchee YMCA, 1966—67; exec. dir. Culver-Palms Family YMCA, Culver City, Calif., 1967—73; v.p. met. fin. devel. YMCA Met. LA, 1978—78, exec. v.p. devel., 1979—85; pres. bd. dirs. YMCA Employees Credit Union, 1977—80; founding chmn. N. Am. Fellowship of YMCA Devel. Orricers, 1980—83; chmn., CEO Netzel Assocs., Inc., 1985—; pvt. practice cons., fund raiser. Adj. faculty U. So. Calif. Coll. Continuing Edn., 1983—86, Loyola Marymount U., 1986—90, Calif. State U., 1991—92, UCLA Extension, 1991—2002. Bd. mgrs. Culver-Palms YMCA, Culver City, 1985—2002, chmn., 1989—91, 1991—93; mem.

Culver City Bd. Edn., 1975—79, pres., 1977—78; mem. Culver City Edn. Found., 1982—91, Culver City Redevel. Agy., 1980—88, chmn., 1983—84, 1987—88, vice chmn., 1985—86; chmn. bd. dirs. Calif. Youth Model Legislature, 1987—92; mem. World Affairs Coun., 1989—92; mem. adv. bd. Automobile Club So. Calif., 1996—2002; mem. Culver City City Coun., 1980—88, vice mayor, 1980—82, 1984—85, mayor, 1983—84, 1986—87; bd. dirs. L.A. Psychiat. Svc., 1971—74, Goodwill Industries of So. Calif., 1993—97, L.A. County Sanitation Dists., 1982—83, 1985—87, Western Region United Way, 1986—93, vice chmn., 1991—92. Recipient Man of Yr. award, Culver City C. of C., 1972. Mem.: Assn. Fundraising Profls. (v.p. bd. dirs. Greater L.A. chpt. 1986—88, pres. bd. dirs. 1989—90, nat. bd. dirs. 1989—91, vice chmn. 1994, Profl. of Yr. 1983), Mountain Gate Country Club, Rotary Internat. (L.A. # 5 pres. 1992—93, treas. L.A. found. 1995—96, gov. dist. 5280 1997—98, worldwide bd. dirs. 2007—, chmn. L.A. conv., founding chmn. internat. convention 2008 host orgn. com., named to Dist. 5280 Hall Fame 2005), Calif. Club. Office: Netzel Assocs Inc 9696 Culver Blvd Ste 105 Culver City CA 90232-2753 Home: 12336 Ridge Cir Los Angeles CA 90049-1151

NETZER, DICK, economics professor; b. NYC, May 14, 1928; s. Solomon and Sue (Dick) Netzer; m. Carol Risika, Dec. 30, 1945; children: Jenny, Katherine. BA, U. Wis., 1946; MA, MPA, Harvard U., 1948, PhD, 1952. Successively economist, sr. economist, asst. v.p. Fed. Res. Bank Chgo., 1948-60; econ. cons. Regional Plan Assn., NYC, 1960-80; assoc. prof. N.Y. U., 1961-64, prof. econs., 1964—, dean Grad. Sch. Pub. Adminstrn., 1969-82, dir. Urban Research Center, 1981-86. Cons. in field, 1960—. Author: Economics of the Property Tax, 1966, The Economics of Public Finance, 1974, The Subsidized Muse, 1978, Urban Politics New York Style, 1990; editor: N.Y. Affairs, 1973—88. Mem. Mayor N.Y.C. Fiscal Adv. Com., 1969—73; treas. Colony-South Bklyn. Houses, 1968—73; mem. Mcpl. Securities Rulemaking Bd., 1978—81, vice chmn., 1980—81; bd. dirs. Mcpl. Assistance Corp., NYC, 1975—97, Citizens Union Found.; bd. dirs., treas. Adolph and Esther Gottlieb Found., 1975—, v.p., 1979—88, pres., 1989—. Fellow: Am. Inst. Cert. Planners; mem.: Nat. Tax Assn., Regional Sci. Assn., Am. Econs. Assn., Assn. Cultural Econs. Internat. (pres. 1993—94). Home: 41 Huckleberry Ln East Hampton NY 11937-2830 Office: 295 Lafayette St New York NY 10012 Office Phone: 212-998-8750. Business E-Mail: dick.netzer@nyu.edu.

NETZER, NANCY, museum director, art historian, educator; b. Pitts., July 25, 1951; m. Robert A.S. Silberman, Nov. 10, 1974. MA, Harvard U., 1978, PhD, 1986; LittD (hon.), U. Ulster, No. Ireland, 2000. Asst. curator Mus. Fine Arts, Boston, 1982-90; prof. art history Boston Coll., 1990—; dir. McMullen Mus. Art, 1990—. Bd. advs. Internat. Ctr. Medieval Art., N.Y.C., 1990-94; dir. Internat. Ctr. Medieval Art, 1995-2000 Author: Medieval Objects in the Museum of Fine Arts, 1986, vol. II, 1991, Cultural Interplay in the Eighth Century, 1994, Memory and the Middle Ages, 1995, Fragmented Devotion, 2000, Secular Sacred, 2006. Bd. advisors Woodrow Wilson Nat. Fellowship Found.; gov. appointee bd. dirs. Mass. Found. Humanities; bd. dirs. ICMA, 1995. Fellow: Soc. Antiquaries. Office: McMullen Mus Devlin Hall #423 140 Commonwealth Ave Chestnut Hill MA 02467-3800 Business E-Mail: netzer@bc.edu.

NEU, CHARLES ERIC, historian, educator; b. Carroll, Iowa, Apr. 10, 1936; s. Arthur Nicholas and Martha Margaret (Frandsen) N.; m. Deborah Dunning, Sept. 2, 1961 (div. 1978); children: Hilary Adams, Douglas Bancroft.; m. Sabina deWerth Tuck, Mar. 27, 1999. BA, Northwestern U., 1958; PhD, Harvard U., 1964. Instr. history Rice U., 1963-64, asst. prof., 1964-67, asso. prof., 1968-70; asso. prof. history Brown U., Providence, 1970-76, prof., 1976—2003, prof. emeritus, 2003—, chmn. dept. history, 1995—98, 1999—2002. Dir. summer seminar NEH, 1979, 1986—87, 1989, 92, 2005; adj. prof. history U. Miami, 2004—. Author: An Uncertain Friendship: Theodore Roosevelt and Japan, 1906-1909, 1967, The Troubled Encounter: The United States and Japan, 1975, America's Lost War: Vietnam, 1945-1975, 2005; co-editor: The Wilson Era: Essays in Honor of Arthur S. Link, 1991, Artists of Power: Theodore Roosevelt, Woodrow Wilson, and Their Enduring Impact on U.S. Foreign Policy, 2006; editor: After Vietnam: Legacies of a Lost War, 2000. Adv. coun. Vietnam Ctr. Tex. Tech. U. Recipient, Woodrow Wilson Found. fellowship, 1958—59, Am. Coun. Learned Socs. fellowship, 1975—76, Charles Warren Ctr. fellowship, 1971—72, Howard Found. fellowship, 1976—77, Guggenheim fellowship, 1981—82, Barrett Hazeltine citation for disting. undergrad. tchg., 1998; fellow, NEH, 1968—69, Woodrow Wilson Ctr., 2007; guest scholar, 1988. Mem. Am. Hist. Assn., Orgn. Am. Historians, Soc. Historians of Am. Fgn. Policy, Phi Beta Kappa. Democrat. Home: 4929 SW 71st Place Miami FL 33155 Home Phone: 305-668-7978. Personal E-mail: cneu@bellsouth.net.

NEU, DAVID C., lawyer; b. May 30, 1971; BA in Bio., Tulane Univ., New Orleans, La., 1992; MS in Fisheries Bio., Auburn Univ., 1995; JD summa cum laude, Seattle Univ. Sch. Law, 2002. Bar: Wash. 2002. Former investment wholesaler SAFECO; assoc. atty., bankruptcy and real estate Preston Gates & Ellis LLP, Seattle. Contbr. articles to numerous profl. jours. Named Wash. Rising Star, SuperLawyer Mag., 2006. Mem.: King Co. Bar Assn., Wash. State Bar Assn. Office: Preston Gates and Ellis LLP Ste 2900 925 Fourth Ave Seattle WA 98104-1158

NEUBAUER, JOSEPH, food services company executive; b. Oct. 19, 1941; s. Max and Herta (Kahn) Neubauer; children: Lawrence, Melissa. BS in Chem. Engring, Tufts U., 1963; MBA in Fin, U. Chgo., 1965. Asst. treas. Chase Manhattan Bank, 1965—68, asst. v.p., 1968—70, v.p., 1970—71; asst. treas. Pepsico Inc., Purchase, NY, 1971—72, treas., 1972—73, v.p., 1973—76; v.p. fin. and control Wilson Sporting Goods Co., River Grove, Ill., 1976—77, sr. v.p., gen. mgr. team sports divsn., 1977—79; exec. v.p. fin. and devel., CFO, dir. ARA Svcs., Inc., Phila., 1979—81; pres., COO, dir. ARA Services, Inc., Phila., 1981—83, pres., CEO, 1983—84; chmn., CEO ARA Svcs., Inc. (in 1994, name changed to ARAMARK Corp.), Phila., 1984—. Bd. dirs. Wachovia Corp., Verizon Corp., Federated Dept. Stores; trustee Penn Mut. Life Ins. Co. Chmn., CEO Phila. Orch. Assn., Mann Music Ctr., Inroads/Phila., Inc.; trustee Hahnemann U., Tufts U., Mus. Am. Jewish History, Greater Phila. First Corp., Com. Econ. Devel., U. Chgo.; bd. govs. Joseph H. Lauder Inst. Mgmt. and Internat. Studies, U. Pa.; dir. The Barnes Found. Mem.: Bus. Roundtable, Bus. Coun., Phila. C. of C., Locust Club, Union League Club. Office: ARAMARK Corp 1101 Market St Philadelphia PA 19107 *

NEUBAUER, PETER BELA, psychoanalyst; b. Krems, Austria, July 5, 1913; came to US, 1941, naturalized, 1946; s. Samuel and Rose (Blau) N.; m. Susan Rachlin, Nov. 25, 1953 (dec.); children: Joshua Rachlin, Alexander Lewis. MD, U. Berne, 1938. Intern Lawrence Meml. Hosp., New London, Conn., 1941, Beth-El Hosp., Bklyn., 1942; resident in psychiatry Bellevue Hosp., NYC, 1943-45; dir. Child Devel. Ctr., Jewish Bd. Family Children's Svcs., NYC, 1951-83; clin. prof. psychiatry Psychoanalytic Inst., NYU, 1979—. Lectr. child psychoanalysis Psychoanalytic Inst. Tng. Research Columbia U., 1973 Author: Children in Collectives: Child Rearing Aims and Practices in Kibbutzim, 1965, Early Child Day Car, 1974, Process of Child Development, 1976, (with Alexander Neubauer) Nature's Thumbprint, 1990; contbg. author: Fathers and Their Families, 1989; mem. editorial bd. Psychoanalytic Study of the Child, 1978. Recipient Hulse award NY Council Child Psychiatry, 1975, Heinz Hartmann award NY Psychoanalytic Soc., 1981, Mary S. Sigourney award, 1994. Mem. Am. Psychoanalytic Assn., Am. Acad. Child Psychiatry, Assn. Child Psychoanalysis, Internat. Assn. Child and Adolescent Psychiatry, Assn. Child Psychoanalysis (pres. 1974-76). Office: 33 E 70th St New York NY 10021-4941 Office Phone: 212-288-2348.

NEUBAUER, RICHARD A., library science educator, consultant; b. Meadville, Pa., Oct. 9, 1933; s. Carl Gustave and Velma Winston (Watson) N.; m. Janice Ernest; children: David, Lynda, Karl, Jennifer; m. Carol Barton. BS, Clarion U., Pa., 1955; MLS, SUNY, Geneseo, 1966; attended, Kent State U., Ohio, 1966-68, Simmons Coll., Boston, 1970-72. Cert. profl. libr., sch. libr., tchr. Tchr. geography Franklin Sch. Dept., Pa., 1957-58, N. Bedford County Schs., Woodbury, Mass., 1958-60; tchr. history Hornell Jr. H.S., NY, 1960-62, sch. libr. NY, 1962-65; prof. libr. sci. Edinboro U., Pa., 1965-68, assoc. libr. Hamilton Libr. Pa., 1965-68; dir. sch. librs. Duxbury Sch. Dept., Mass., 1968-69; dir., cons. Pub. Libr., Lincoln, Mass., 1969-70; prof. libr. sci. Bridgewater State Coll., Mass., 1969-78, chair dept. libr. sci. Mass., 1978-80, prof. libr. sci. Mass., 1980-91, coord. libr. media program Mass., 1991-95; prof. emeritus libr. sci., 1996—. Adj. prof. libr. sci. U. R.I., Kingston, 1975-88; cons. Tabor Acad., Marion, Mass., 1970-71, Abington (Mass.) Pub. Libr. Trustees, 1973-76, Duxbury Free Libr., 1968-72. Author: Planning the Elementary School Library, 1968; author, editor Exploring the U.S.-Northeast, 1994. Chmn. Mass. Dept. Edn. Cert., Quincy, 1989-90; resource cons. Project Contemporary Competitiveness, Bridgewater, Mass., 1973-83. 1st lt. USMC, 1955-57. Inst. grantee HEA of 1965 Edinboro U., 1968. Mem. NEA, Am. Libr. Assn., Intellectual Freedom Found., Mass. Assn. of Edn. Media, Mass. Sch. Libr. Media Assn., Mass. Tchrs. Assn. Democrat. Avocations: gardening, woodworking, reading. Home: 22 Pleasant St Carver MA 02330-1013

NEUBERG, HANS W., internist, educator; b. Hannover, Germany, Mar. 26, 1921; came to U.S., 1937, naturalized, 1943. s. Georg and Gertrud (Dux) N.; m. Birgit Aron, Apr. 8, 1949; children: Peter G., Gerald W. BS, Wagner Coll., 1941; MD, Columbia U., 1950. Diplomate Am. Bd. Internal Medicine. Intern Presbyn. Hosp., NYC, 1950-53, asst. resident, NRC fellow in medicine, 1953-54, asst. attending physician, 1966-80, assoc. attending physician, 1980-91, attending physician, 1992—; pvt. practice, 1954-83. Instr. medicine Columbia U. Coll. Phys. and Surg., N.Y.C., 1954-63, assoc. in medicine, 1963-67, asst. prof. clin. medicine, 1967-80, assoc. clin. prof. medicine, 1980-91, clin. prof. medicine, 1992—, mem. Instnl. Rev. Bd. With AUS, 1943-46. Fellow ACP; mem. Alpha Omega Alpha. Mem. Am. Diabetes Assn. Home: 3213 Kendal Way Sleepy Hollow NY 10591 Office: 620 W 168th St New York NY 10032-3702 Personal E-mail: Neubergh@aol.com.

NEUBERGER, JOHN WILLIAM, mathematics professor; b. Ventura, Iowa, Aug. 14, 1934; s. John Mitchell and Pearl (Ax) N.; m. Barbara Ann Osher, July 7, 1959; children: John Michael, Sandra Ann. BA, U. Tex., 1954, PhD, 1957. Spl. instr. U. Tex., Austin, 1956-57; instr. Ill. Inst. Tech., Chgo., 1957-59; asst. prof. U. Tenn., Knoxville, 1959-63; assoc. prof. Emory U., Atlanta, 1963-67, prof., 1967-77, U. North Tex., Denton, 1977-87, regents prof. math., 1987—2005, modified svc., 2005—. Cons. Inst. for Def. Analyses/Ctr. Comms. Rsch., 1973—; cons. Inst. for Def. Analyses/Sci. Tech. Divsn., Alexandria, Va., 1986—, Oak Ridge (Tenn.) Nat. Lab., 1978-89, Nat. Security Agy, 1995-, Los Alamos Nat. Lab., 1999-, others. Editor Houston Jour. of Math., 1975-90, Internat. Jour. of Math., 1977-92; mem. editl. bd. Electronic Jour. Differential Equations, 1993—, Comms. on Applied Non-linear Analysis, Jour. Abstract and Applied Analysis; contbr. articles to profl. publs. Sr. cons. Ednl. Advancement Found. Alfred P. Sloan Found. rsch. fellow, 1967-69. Mem. Am. Math. Soc., Math. Soc. Am., London Math. Soc., Soc. Indsl. and Applied Math., Phi Beta Kappa. E-mail: jwn@unt.edu.

NEUBORNE, BURT, law educator; b. 1941; AB, Cornell U., 1961; LLB, Harvard U., 1964. Bar: NY 1965. Assoc. Casey, Lane & Mittendorf, NYC, 1964-67; staff counsel NY Civil Liberties Union, NYC, 1967-72; asst. legal dir. ACLU, NYC, 1972-74, legal dir., 1983—86; assoc. prof. NYU Sch. Law, 1974-76, prof., 1976—, John Norton Pomeroy prof. of law, 1994—2005, Inez Milholland professor of civil liberties, 2005, dir. Brennan Ctr. for Justice, 1994—. Spl. counsel NOW Legal Def. and Edn. Fund, 1991-; commr. NYC Commn. Human Rights, 1988-93. Co-author: Political and Civil Rights in the United States, Vol. I, 1976, Vol. II, 1979. Named one of 100 Most Influential Lawyers, Nat. Law Jour., 2006. Master: Am. Acad. Arts & Sciences. Office: NYU Sch Law Vanderbilt Hall Rm 307 40 Washington Sq S New York NY 10012-1099 Office Phone: 212-998-6172. E-mail: burt.neuborne@nyu.edu. *

NEUENSCHWANDER, PIERRE FERNAND, medical educator; BS in Chemistry, 1985; PhD in Biochemistry & Molecular Biology, SUNY, Stony Brook, 1990. Lab. tchg. asst. SUNY, Stony Brook, 1985-86, lecture tchg. asst. in biochemistry, 1986, 87; assoc. rsch. scientist Cardiovascular Biology Rsch. Program Okla. Med. Rsch. Found., Oklahoma City, 1990-93, sr. rsch. scientist, 1993-94, found. rsch. scientist, 1994-95, asst. mem., 1995-2001; assoc. prof. biochemistry U. Tex. Health Ctr., Tyler, 2001—. Co-editor Trigger newsletter; rev. Jour. Biol. Chemistry; contbr. articles to profl. jours. Recipient Am. Heart Assn. Travel stipend, 1994, Internat. Soc. Haematology Travel award, 1992, Am. Soc. Hematology Travel award, 1989, 90. Mem. Am. Heart Assn. (coun. on thrombosis), Am. Chem Soc. (divsn. biol. chemistry), Internat. Soc. Thrombosis and Haemostasis, Sigma Xi, Alpha Chi Sigma. Office: Univ Tex Health Ctr Biomed Rsch Lab C8 11937 US Hwy 271 Tyler TX 75708 Office Phone: 903-877-7678. E-mail: Pierre.Neuenschwander@uthct.edu.

NEUER, PHILIP DAVID, lawyer, real estate consultant; b. Bklyn., May 31, 1946; s. Murray and Adele (Jacobs) Neuer; m. Rena Donna Levine, July 30, 1972 (div. 1987); children: Jeremy Evan, Linzy Michelle, Sari Faith. BBA, CCNY, 1968; postgrad., Boston U., 1968-69; JD, Seton Hall U., 1976. Bar: N.J. 1976, U.S. Dist. Ct. N.J. 1977, U.S. Supreme Ct. 1980. Asst. town atty. Town of West Orange, NJ, 1976-77; assoc. Margolis and Bergstein, Verona, 1979-80; ptnr. Slavitt and Slavitt, West Orange, 1980-81; assoc. Mandelbaum and Targan, West Orange, 1981-83; ptnr. Margolis Neuer, Verona, 1984-91; of counsel Slavitt Simon & Neuer, Parsippany, 1991-2000; exec. v.p., gen. counsel Safer Textiles Group, Safer Devel. and Mgmt. Co., Newark, 1993—; of counsel Lum, Danzis, Drasco, Positan & Kleinberg, LLC, Roseland, 2000—02. Faculty mem. NYU Grad. Sch. Real Estate, NYC, 2004—; mem. Zoning Bd. Adjustment, West Orange, 2006—. Mem. editl. bd. Internat. Jour. Corp. Real Estate, 1998—2004. With USN, 1969—73. Named to, Inst. Corp. Real Estate Hall of Fame, 2002. Mem.: ABA, Urban Land Inst., Inst. Corp. Real Estate (bd. dirs., pres. 1998—2002), Internat. Assn. Corp. Real Estate Execs. (pres., bd. dirs., gen. counsel NJ chpt., internat. bd. dirs. 1993—2002, Assoc. Mem. of Yr. 1993, N.J. Corp. Real Exec. of the Yr. 1993), Essex County Bar Assn., N.J. State Bar Assn., Mensa. Office: 1875 McCarter Hwy Newark NJ 07104-4211 Home Phone: 973-669-0666; Office Phone: 973-482-0840. E-mail: pdn@neuerlaw.com, pdneuer@aol.com.

NEUFELD, ELIZABETH FONDAL, biochemist, educator; b. Paris, Sept. 27, 1928; married, 1951. PhD, U. Calif., Berkeley, 1956; DHc (hon.), U. Rene Descartes, Paris, 1978; DSc (hon.), Russell Sage Coll., Troy, NY, 1981; DSc (hon.), Hahnemann U. Sch. Medicine, 1984; DSc (hon.), Queens Coll., 1996. Asst. rsch. biochemist U. Calif., Berkeley, 1957—63; with Nat. Inst. Arthritis, Metabolism and Digestive Diseases, Bethesda, Md., 1963—84, research biochemist, 1963—73, chief sect. human biochem. genetics, 1973—79, chief genetics and biochem. br., 1979—84; prof. Dept. Biol. Chemistry Sch. Medicine U. Calif., 1984—, chmn. Dept. Biol. Chemistry Sch. Medicine, 1984—2004. Named Passano Found. sr. laureate, 1982, Calif. Scientist of Yr., 1990; recipient Dickson prize, U. Pitts., 1974, Hillenbrand award, 1975, Gairdner Found. award, 1981, Albert Lasker Clin. Med. Rsch. award, 1982, William Allan award, 1982, Elliott Cresson medal, 1984, Wolf Found. prize, 1988, Christopher Columbus Discovery award for biomed. rsch., 1992, Nat. Medal of Sci., 1994. Fellow: Fellow AAAS; mem.: NAS, Am. Soc. Gene Therapy, Am. Soc. Clin. Investigation, Am. Soc. Cell Biology, Am. Soc. Biochemistry and Molecular Biology (pres. 1992—93), Am. Chem. Soc., Am. Soc. Human Genetics, Am. Philos. Soc., Am. Acad. Arts and Scis, Inst. Medicine of NAS. Office: UCLA David Geffen Sch Medicine Dept Biol Chemistry 33-257 CHS 33-355 CH Box 951737 Los Angeles CA 90095-1737 Business E-Mail: eneufeld@mednet.ucla.edu.

NEUFELD, MICHAEL JOHN, curator, historian; b. Edmonton, Alta., Can., July 7, 1951; s. Henry John and Isabel Grace (Mitchell) N.; m. Sheila Faith Weiss, May 29, 1983 (div. Dec. 1992); m. Karen Lee Levenback, June 14, 1994. BA with 1st class honors, U. Calgary, Alta., 1974; MA, U. B.C., Vancouver, Can., 1976, Johns Hopkins U., 1980, PhD in History, 1984. Hist. rschr. Dept. Supply and Svcs., Ottawa, Ont., Canada, summer 1973, 74; teaching asst. Johns Hopkins U., Balt., 1979-80; instr. Clarkson U., Potsdam, NY, 1983-84, from part-time instr. to part-time asst. prof., 1983-85; vis. asst. prof. SUNY, Oswego, 1985-86, Colgate U., Hamilton, NY, 1986-88; Verville fellow Nat. Air and Space Mus., Washington, 1988-89, Smithsonian postdoctoral fellow, 1989-90, curator aeronautics, 1990-99, curator space history, 1999—, chair space history divsn., 2007—. Curator Air Power in WWII series, 1991-94; sr. lectr. Johns Hopkins U., 2001. Author: The Skilled Metalworkers of Nuremberg, 1989, The Rocket and the Reich, 1995, Von Braun, 2007; editor: Planet Dora, 1997; co-editor: The Bombing of Auschwitz, 2000; contbr. articles and book revs. to profl. jours. Recipient History Manuscript award AIAA, 1995, Dexter Prize SHOT, 1997, NSF Scholar's award History of Sci. and Tech. Program, 1989-90. Mem. German Studies Assn., Soc. Mil. History, Soc. for History Tech., History of Sci. Soc., Amnesty Internat. Avocation: amateur astronomy. Office: Nat Air & Space Mus Divsn Space History MRC 311 Smithsonian Instn PO Box 37012 Washington DC 20013-7012 Office Phone: 202-633-2434. E-mail: neufeldm@si.edu.

NEUFELD, PETER, lawyer; b. Bklyn. BA, U. Wis.; degree (hon.), Northeastern U. Sch. Law; LLD (hon.), Gonzaga U. Ptnr. Cochran, Neufeld & Scheck LLP, NYC. Co-founder, dir. The Innocence Project, Benjamin Cardoza Sch. Law, Yeshiva U., NYC, 1992—; mem. N.Y. State's Commn. Forensic Sci. Co-author (with Barry Scheck and Jim Dwyer): Actual Innocence: Five Days to Execution and Other Dispatches from the Wrongly Convicted, 2000. Named one of the Top 100 Influential Lawyers in Am., Nat. Law Jour., 2000. Office: Cochran Neufeld & Scheck LLP 99 Hudson St 8th fl New York NY 10013 Address: Benjamin N Cardozo Sch Law Yeshiva Univ Brookdale Ctr 55 Fifth Ave (at 12th St) New York NY 10003

NEUFELD, RONALD DAVID, environmental engineer, educator; b. NYC, Feb. 10, 1947; s. Milton and Norma Neufeld; m. Toby Heringer, Aug. 31, 1968; children: Steven, Todd, Jennifer. B Engring. in Chem. Engring., Copper Union, 1967; MS in Chem. Engring., Northwestern U., 1969, PhD in Civil & Environ. Health Engring., 1973. Registered profl. engr., Pa.; diplomate Am. Acad. Environ. Engrs. Asst. prof. U. Pitts., 1973-77, assoc. prof., 1977-82, prof. civil engring., 1982—. Chmn. environ. sci. com. Fulbright Coun. Internat. Exch. Scholars; mem. Effluent Guidelines Task Force EPA, 1992—; mem. indsl. waste com. WEF, 1992—, program com.; mem. edn. com. Am. Acad. Environ. Engring, 1992; program evaluator ABET Environ.; apptd. Pa. Cleanup Sci. Adv. Bd., 1995—; former dir. Green Constrn. and Sustainable Devel. Program; expert witness in field; cons. in field. Contbr. articles to profl. jours. Fulbright sr. scholar, 1983-84. Mem. ASCE (bd. dirs. Pits. sect. 1984-87, chmn. energy divsn., chmn. energy divsn. specialty conf. 1991, mem. nat. energy policy com. 1995—), Am. Inst. Chem. Engrs., Internat. Assn. Water Pollution Rsch., Assn. Environ. Engring. Profs., Assn. Engring. Educators, Water Environ. Fedn., Sigma Xi (pres. Pitts. chpt. 1997-99), Chi Epsilon. Achievements include research in biotechnology for remediation of liquid and solid wastes and soils containing fuel hydrocarbons, electrochemical sludge dewatering, heavy metals, and PCBs; environmental process engineering, environmental engineering for energy development, environmental implication of high fly ash content cellular concrete; stabilization of hazardous wastes with high lime content fly ash, ceramic membrane microfiltration for combined sewer overflows; aluminum containing acid rock discharge, high rate oxidation of acid mine drainage. Home: 6558 Bartlett St Pittsburgh PA 15217-1834 Office Phone: 412-624-9874. Business E-Mail: neufeld@engr.pitt.edu.

NEUGEBAUER, CYNTHIA A., lawyer; b. Queens, NY, Apr. 26, 1964; BA, SUNY, Buffalo, 1986; MA, SUNY, Stony Brook, 1987; JD, Touro Coll., 1994. Bar: NJ 1995, NY 1996, US Dist. Ct. Ea. Dist. NY, US Dist. Ct. No. Dist. NY, US Dist. Ct. So. Dist. NY. Ptnr. Wilson, Elser, Moskowitz, Edelman & Dicker LLP, NYC. Mem. appellate courts com. State of NY. Mem.: ABA. Office: Wilson Elser Moskowitz Edelman & Dicker LLP 23rd Fl 150 E 42nd St New York NY 10017-5639 Office Phone: 212-490-3000 ext. 2496. Office Fax: 212-490-3038. Business E-Mail: neugebauerc@wemed.com.

NEUGEBAUER, MARCIA, physicist, researcher; b. NYC, Sept. 27, 1932; d. Howard Graeme MacDonald and Frances (Townsend) Marshall; m. Gerry Neugebauer, Aug. 25, 1956; children: Carol, Lee. BS, Cornell U., 1954; MS, U. Ill., 1956; D of Physics (hon.), U. New Hampshire, 1998. Grad. asst. U. Ill., Urbana, 1954-56; vis. fellow Clare Hall Coll., Cambridge, Eng., 1975; sr. research scientist Jet Propulsion Lab. Calif. Inst. Tech., Pasadena, 1956-96, disting. vis. scientist, 1996—2003; vis. prof. planetary sci. Calif. Inst. Tech., Pasadena, 1986-87. Mem. com. NASA, Washington, 1960-96, NAS, Washington, 1981-94; Regents lectr. UCLA, 1990-91; adj. sr. rsch. sci. Lunar & Planetary Lab., U. Ariz., 2002-; bd. dirs. Acad. Svcs. Corp., Ariz. Sr. Acad., pres., 2004—. Contbr. numerous articles on physics to profl. jours. Named Calif. Woman Scientist of Yr. Calif., Mus. Sci. and Industry, 1967, to Women in Tech. Internat. Hall of Fame, 1997; recipient Exceptional Sci. Achievement medal NASA, 1970, Outstanding Leadership medal NASA, 1993, Disting. Svc. medal NASA, 1997, COSPAR award for space sci., 1998. Fellow Am. Geophys. Union (sec., pres. solar planetary relationships sect. 1979-84, editor-in-chief Rev. Geophysics 1988-92, pres.-elect 1992-94, pres. 1994-96) mem. governing bd. Amer. Inst. Physics, 1995-97. Democrat. Home: 7519 S Eliot Ln Tucson AZ 85747-9627 Office: U Ariz Lunar & Planetary Lab 1629 E Univ Blvd Tucson AZ 85721 Business E-Mail: nmeugeb@lpl.Arizona.edu.

NEUGEBAUER, RANDY (ROBERT R. NEUGEBAUER), congressman; b. St. Louis, Dec. 24, 1949; m. Dana Collins; 2 children. BBA in Acctg., Tex. Tech U., Lubbock, 1972. Mgr. Sentry Property Mgmt., Lubbock, Tex., 1972—75; instr. South Plains Coll., Lubbock, 1975—78; v.p. First Nat. Bank, Lubbock, 1975—82; pres. Prestige Homes, Lubbock, 1983—87; pres., CEO Lubbock Land Co., 1987—2003; mem. US Congress from 19th Tex. dist., 2003—, mem. agr. com., 2006—, mem. fin. svcs. com. Chair Ports-to-Plains Trade Coalition, 1996—2003. Mem. City Coun., 1992—98; mayor pro tempore, 1994—96. Mem.: West Tex. Home Builders Assn. (pres. 1990). Republican. Baptist. Office: US Ho Reps 429 Cannon Ho Office Bldg Washington DC 20515 Office Phone: 202-225-4005. *

NEUHAUS, JOSEPH EMANUEL, lawyer; b. Glen Ridge, NJ, Aug. 17, 1957; s. Gottfried and Helen (Bull) N.; m. Cynthia Ann Loomis. BA, Dartmouth Coll., 1979; JD, Columbia U., 1982. Bar: NY 1986, DC 1986, US Dist. Ct. (so. and ea. dists.) NY 1987, US Ct. Appeals (2d cir.) 1995, US Ct. Appeals (fed. cir.) 1995, US Ct. Appeals (10th cir.) 1996, US Supreme Ct. 1998. Law clk. to sr. judge U.S. Ct. Appeals, Washington, 1982-83; law clk. to Hon. Lewis F. Powell, Jr. U.S. Supreme Ct., Washington, 1983-84; legal asst. Iran-U.S. Claims Tribunal, The Hague, Netherlands, 1984-85; assoc. Covington & Burling, Washington, 1986-87,

Sullivan & Cromwell, NYC, 1987-91, ptnr., 1992—. Co-author: Guide to the UNCITRAL Model Law on International Commercial Arbitration, 1989. Mem. Assn. Bar City N.Y. (com. sec. 1989-92), NY State Bar Assn. (com. chair 2005—). Office Phone: 212-558-4240. E-mail: neuhausj@sullcrom.com.

NEUHAUS, PHILIP ROSS, investment banker; b. Houston, Dec. 25, 1919; s. Hugo Victor and Kate Padgitt (Rice) N.; m. Elizabeth Lacey Thompson, Oct. 31, 1942 (div. 1967); children: Philip Ross (dec.), Lacey Neuhaus Dorn, Elizabeth Neuhaus Armstrong, Joan Neuhaus Schaan; m. Barbara R. Haden, Aug. 14, 1968; 5 stepchildren. Grad., St. Mark's Sch., Southborough, Mass., 1938; BA, Yale, 1942. With Nat. City Bank of Cleve., 1946-47, McDonald & Co., Cleve., 1947; with Neuhaus & Co., 1947; chmn. Underwood, Neuhaus & Co., Inc., Houston, 1948-89; hon. chmn. Lovett Underwood Neuhaus & Webb, Houston, 1989-92; sr. v.p. Kemper Securities Inc., Houston, 1992-95, Everen Securities, Inc., Houston, 1995-99, Wachovia Securities Inc. (formerly First Union Securities, Inc.), Houston, 1999—. Chmn. bd. Voss-Woodway, Inc., 1994-2007. Mem. adv. bd. Tex. Children's Hosp., 1973-; assoc. Rice U.; advisory bd. Salvation Army, Houston, 1969-91. Served to capt., cav. AUS, 1942-45. Mem. Securities Industry Assn. Am. (bd. govs., chmn. Tex. dist. 1973, exec. com. 1975), Houston Soc. Financial Analysts (pres. 1959), Stock and Bond Club Houston (past pres.), Nat. Fedn. Financial Analysts (v.p. 1963, dir.) Clubs: Bayou, Houston Country, Houston, Eagle Lake Rod and Gun. Home: 407 Thamer Ln Houston TX 77024-6939 Office: Wachovia Securities Inc Ste 1100 909 Fannin Houston TX 77010-1001 Office Phone: 713-853-2221.

NEUHAUS, RICHARD JOHN, priest, research institute president; b. Pembroke, Ont., Can., May 14, 1936; Came to U.S., 1950; s. Clemens Henry and Ella Carolina (Prange) N. M Div., Concordia Sem., 1960; DD (hon.), Benedictine Coll., 1985, Gonzaga U., 1985, Valparaiso U., 1986, Nichols Coll., 1986, Boston U., 1988. Ordained to ministry Luth. Ch., 1960; ordained priest Roman Cath. Ch., 1991. Pastor St. John The Evangelist, Bklyn., 1961-78; sr. editor Worldview Mag., NYC, 1972-82; dir. Rockford Inst. Ctr. on Religion and Soc., NYC, 1984-89, Inst. on Religion and Pub. Life, NYC, 1989—. Author: Freedom for Ministry, 1979, The Naked Public Square, 1984, The Catholic Moment, 1987, America Against Itself, 1992, Doing Well & Doing Good, 1992, Evangelicals and Catholics Together, 1995, The End of Democracy?, 1997, Appointment in Rome, 1998; The Eternal Pity, 2000, Death on a Friday Afternoon: Meditations on the Last Words of Jesus, 2000; As I Lay Dying: Meditations Upon Returning, 2002; Catholic Matters: Confusion, Controversy, And the Splendor of Truth, 2006; editor-in-chief First Things Mag., N.Y.C., 1990—. Bd. dirs. U.S. Inst. Peace, 1986-91, Inst. on Religion and Democracy, 1981—, Ethics and Pub. Policy Ctr., 1982—. Named one of The 25 Most Influential Evangelists in Am., Time mag., 2005, New York's Influentials, New York Mag., 2006. Mem.: Becket Fund Adv. Bd. Office: Inst Religion & Pub Life 156 5th Ave New York NY 10010 Office Phone: 212-627-2288. *

NEUHAUSER, DUNCAN VONBRIESEN, medical educator; b. Phila., June 20, 1939; s. Edward Blaine Duncan and Gernda (vonBriesen) Neuhauser; m. Elinor Toaz, Mar. 6, 1965; children: Steven, Ann. BA, Harvard U., 1961; MHA, U. Mich., 1963; MBA, U. Chgo., 1966, PhD, 1971. Rsch. assoc. U. Chgo., 1965—70; asst. prof. Sch. Pub. Health, Harvard U., Boston, 1970—74, assoc. prof., 1974—79; cons. in medicine Mass. Gen. Hosp., Boston, 1975—80; assoc. dir. Health Systems Mgmt. Ctr. Case Western Res. U., Cleve., 1979—85, prof. epidemiology, biostats., orgnl. behavior, 1979—, prof. medicine, 1981—, prof. family medicine, 1990—, Charles Elton Blanchard prof. health mgmt., 1995—, co-dir. Health Systems Mgmt. Ctr., 1985—. Mem. biomed. staff Metrohealth Med. Ctr., 1981—; adj. mem. med. staff Cleve. Clinic Found., 1984—99; vis. prof. Vanderbilt U. Sch. Nursing, 1998—, Karolinska Med. Sch., Stockholm, 2002—. Author: numerous books, sci. papers; editor (jours.): Health Matrix, 1982—90, Med. Care, 1983—97. Vice chmn. bd. dirs. Vis. Nurse Assn. Greater Cleve., 1983—84, chmn., 1984—85; bd. dirs. New Eng. Grenfell Assn., Boston, 1972—, Braintree Hosp., Mass., 1975—86; trustee Internat. Grenfell Assn., St. Anthony, Nfld., Canada, 1975—83, Blue Hill Hosp., Maine, 1983—94, Hough Norwood Health Ctr., 1983—94, chmn., 1993—94; mem. vis. com. Columbia U. Sch. Nursing, 2000—; founding bd. dirs. Acad. for Healthcare Improvement, 2004—. Recipient E.F. Meyers Trustee award, Cleve. Hosp. Assn., 1987, Hope award, Nat. Multiple Sclerosis Soc., 1992, Neuhauser lectr., Soc. Pediatric Radiology, 1982, Freedlander lectr., Ohio Permanente Med. Group, 1986, Univ. medal, Tohoku Med. U., Sendi, Japan, 2001, Arthur Shapiro Best Book of Yr. Hypnosis award, 2003, McAuley lectr., Georgetown U., 2007; scholar Keck Found., 1982—; Kellogg fellow, U. Chgo., 1963—65, Duncan Neuhauser Endowed chair in cmty. health improvement at Case Western Res. U. and MetroHealth Med. Ctr., 2003. Mem.: Soc. for Clin. Decision Making, Inst. Medicine NAS, Cleve. Skating Club, Kollegewidgwok Yacht Club (Blue Hill) (commodore 1991—93), St. Botolph Club (Boston), Beta Gamma Sigma. Home (Summer): PO Box 932 Blue Hill ME 04614-0932 Office: Case Western Reserve U Med Sch 10900 Euclid Ave Cleveland OH 44106-4945 Home: 2641 Idlewood Rd 1st Fl Cleveland OH 44118-4249 Home Phone: 216-321-1327; Office Phone: 216-368-3726. Office Fax: 216-368-3970. Business E-Mail: dvn@cwru.edu.

NEUHOFER, MARY DOROTHY, archivist, librarian; d. Joseph Peter and Helen Frances Neuhofer. BS, Barry Coll., Miami, 1964; MALS, Rosary Coll., River Forest, Ill., 1965; MChA in Canon Law, Cath. U. Am., Washington, DC, 1977; PhD in Libr. Studies, Fla. State U., Tallahassee, 1998. Elem. sch. tchr. Fla. Cath. Sch., Sarasota, 1950—64; elem. sch. prin. Epiphany Cath. Sch., Venice, Fla., 1959—63; ref. libr. St. Leo U., St. Leo, 1965—75, 1990—98, dir. libr. svc., 1975—88, 1999—2006, archivist, 1990—, archivist, spl. collections libr., 2007—; prioress Holy Name Monastery, St. Leo, 1972—75. Author: (book) In the Benedictine Tradition, 1999. Mem. Order St. Benedict. Fellow: Am. Benedictine Acad. (exec. bd. 1972—86, pres. 1982—84, awards com. 2006—); mem.: Tampa Bay Libr. Consortium (pres. 1987—88, mem. exec. bd. 1980—89, sec. 1980—81), Pasco County Hist. Preservation Com., Canon Law Soc. Am., Soc. Am. Archivists, Cath. Libr. Assn. (exec. bd. 1999—2007, pres. 2003—05, mem. strategic planning com. 2007—, mem. constitution and bylaws com. 2007—), Assn. Coll. and Rsch. Libr., Am. Libr. Assn. Avocation: gardening. Home: Holy Name Monastery 33201 State Rd 52 Saint Leo FL 33574 Office: St Leo U 33701 State Rd 52 Saint Leo FL 33574

NEUKOM, WILLIAM H., lawyer; b. Chgo., Nov. 7, 1941; s. John Goudey and Ruth (Horlick) N.; m. Diane McMakin, Dec. 28, 1963 (div. Jun. 1977); children: Josselyn, Samantha, Gillian, John. BA, Dartmouth Coll., 1964; LLB, Stanford U., 1967. Bar: Calif., Wash., U.S. Dist. Ct. (we. dist.) Wash., U.S. Dist. Ct. (no. dist.) Calif., U.S. Ct. Appeals (9th cir.) 1968, U.S. Supreme Court 1974. Atty. MacDonald, Hoague & Bayless, Seattle, 1968—77; ptnr. Preston, Gates & Lucas (formerly Shidler, McBroom, Gates & Lucas), Seattle, 1978—85; v.p., law, corp. affairs Microsoft Corp., Redmond, Wash., 1985—93, exec. v.p. law & corp. affairs, sec., 1994—2002; ptnr. Bus. Practice Group Preston Gates & Ellis LLP, Seattle, 2002—, mem. exec. com.; chair Preston Gates & Ellis LLP (now Kilpatrick & Lockhart Preston Gates Ellis), Seattle, 2004—. Wash. State Delegate House of Delegates, 1999—2005; chair Decennial Governance Commn. Trustee Seattle Art Mus., 1993-99; mem. Assn. Gen. Counsel, 1994—; bd. dirs. Greater Seattle C. of C., 1987—, exec. com. 1988—, YMCA Greater Seattle, 1988—, Corporate Coun. Arts, 1988—, exec. com. 1993—, Nature Conservance (Wash. chpt.), 1991-99, Oreg. Shakespeare Festival, 1993-99. Fellow: ABA (chmn. young lawyers divsn. 1977—78, ho. of dels. 1978—80, sec. 1983—87, ho. of dels. 1983—98, pres.-elect 2006—); mem.: Wash. State Trial Lawyers Assn., Wash. State Bar Assn., Seattle-King County Bar Assn. (chmn. young lawyers divsn. 1972—73). Avocations: fly fishing, skiing, running, golf, jazz. Office: Kilpatrick & Lochart Preston Gates & Ellis LLP 925 Fourth Ave Seattle WA 98104 Office Phone: 206-370-8120. Office Fax: 206-370-6165. E-mail: bill.neukom@klgates.com. *

NEUMAIER, GERHARD JOHN, environmental services administrator, consultant; b. Covington, Ky., July 27, 1937; s. John Edward and Elli Anna (Raudies) N.; m. Ellen Elaine Klepper, Oct. 24, 1959; children: Kevin Scott, Kirsten Lynn. BME, Gen. Motors Inst., 1960; MA in Biophysics, U. Buffalo, 1963. Research ecologist, project mgr. Cornell Aero. Lab., Buffalo, 1963-70; pres., chief exec., chmn. bd. Ecology and Environment Inc., Buffalo, 1970—. Recipient Theodore Roosevelt Citizen of Yr. award City of Buffalo, 1990, Paul McClennan Environ. Citizen of Yr. award Erie County, 2000. Mem. APHA, Air Pollution Control Assn., Internat. Assn. Gt. Lakes Research, Inst. Environ. Scis., Ecol. Soc. Am., Am. Inst. Biol. Scis., Urban Land Inst., Arctic Inst. N.Am., Nat. Parks and Conservation Assn., Defenders of Wildlife, Nat. Wildlife Fedn., Wilderness Soc., Am. Hort. Soc., Smithsonian Assocs., Nat. Audubon Soc. Home: 284 Mill Rd East Aurora NY 14052-2805 Office: Ecology & Environment Inc 368 Pleasant View Dr Lancaster NY 14086-1316 Office Phone: 716-684-8060.

NEUMAN, CHARLES P., electrical and computer engineering educator; b. Pitts., July 26, 1940; s. Daniel and Frances G. Neuman; m. Susan G. Neuman, Sept. 4, 1967 BSEE honors, Carnegie Inst. Tech., 1962; SM, Harvard U., 1963, PhD in Applied Math., 1968. Tchg. fellow Harvard U., Cambridge, Mass., 1962—64, rsch. asst., 1964—67; mem. tech. staff Bell Tel. Labs., Whippany, NJ, 1967—69; asst. prof. elec. engring. Carnegie-Mellon U., Pitts., 1969—71, assoc. prof., 1971—78, prof. elec. engring., 1978—83, prof. elec. and computer engring., 1983—, undergrad. advisor, 1994—. Mem. editl. bd. Internat. Jour. Modelling and Simulation, Control and Computers; contbr. numerous articles to profl. jours Mem. IEEE (sr., assoc. editor Trans. on Systems, Man and Cybernetics), AAAS, Inst. Mgmt. Scis., Instrument Soc. Am. (sr.), Soc. Harvard Engrs. and Scientists, Soc. Indsl. and Applied Math., Sigma Xi, Phi Kappa Phi, Tau Beta Pi, Eta Kappa Nu Office: Carnegie-Mellon U Dept Elec & Computer Engring Pittsburgh PA 15213 Office Phone: 412-268-2460. Business E-Mail: cpn@ece.cmu.edu.

NEUMAN, CLIFFORD, computer scientist, educator; s. Peter H-X. Neuman and Barbara Diane (Allen) Gordon; m. Grace Ruth (Kwok) Neuman. BS Computer Sci. and Engring., MIT, 1985; MS Computer Sci., U. Wash., 1988, PhD Computer Sci., 1992. With MIT Project Athena, Cambridge, 1985—86; sr. rsch. scientist U. So. Calif., Info. Scis. Inst., Marina del Rey, 1991—; rsch. assoc. prof. U. So. Calif., Dept. Computer Sci., LA, 1992—; chief scientist CyberSafe Corp., Issaquah, 1992—2001; dir. U. So. Calif., Ctr. Computer Sys. Security, Marina del Rey, 2002—. Participant Internet Rsch. Task Force, 1991—, Internet Engring. Task Force, 1991— Co-designer Kerberos computer security sys., designer Prospero distributed computer sys., NetCheque elec. payment sys.; contbr. articles to profl. jours Mem. King County (Wash.) Search and Rescue, 1987-91; bd. dirs. Beth Shir Sholom, 2006—, Ladera Heights Civic Assn., 2006—. Named Top Ten Tech. Innovators, InfoWorld Mag., 2002. Mem.: IEEE, Usenix Assn., Internet Soc., Assn. Computer Machinery. Achievements include development of Kerberos authentication sys; NetCheque electronic payment sys; Prospero Directory Svc. Avocations: flying, hiking, skiing, photography, cooking, amateur radio. Office: U So Calif Information Scis Inst 4676 Admiralty Way Marina Del Rey CA 90292 Office Phone: 310-822-1511. E-mail: ww07@clifford.neuman.name.

NEUMAN, EDWARD GEORGE, mathematician, educator; b. Rydultowy, Katowice, Poland, Sept. 19, 1943; arrived in U.S., 1984; s. Emanuel and Matylda Neuman; children: Emanuel Karol, Magdalena Natalia. Diploma, U. Wroclaw, Poland, 1967, PhD in Math., 1972. Asst. prof. U. Wroclaw, 1976—84; assoc. prof. So. Ill. U., Carbondale, 1986—89, prof. math., 1989—. Chmn. numerical analysis dept. U. Wroclaw, 1981—84. Mem. editl. bd.: Australian Jour. Mathematical Analysis and Applications, 2005—, Internat. Jour. Applied Math. and Statis., 2005—; mem. editl. bd. Jour. Math. Inequalities, 2007—; contbr. articles to profl. jours. Fellow Summer Undergrad. Tchg. fellow, So. Ill. U., Carbondale, 1999; grantee, Polish Acad. Scis., 1974—84. Mem.: Polish Math. Soc. (assoc.), Rsch. Group in Math. Inequalities and Applications (assoc.), Soc. for Indsl. and Applied Math. (assoc.). Achievements include research in spline theory, special functions and mathematical inequalities. Office: So Ill Univ Carbondale Dept Math Neckers 385 Carbondale IL 62901-4408 Office Phone: 618-453-6592. Business E-Mail: edneuman@math.siu.edu.

NEUMAN, ISABEL, mathematics educator; b. NYC, Dec. 3, 1939; d. J. Morton and Irene Finke; m. David Wagner Neuman, June 18, 1960; children: Randi Levin, Leslie Spillman, Andrea Malkin. BS, Syracuse U., 1960; MA, Ariz. State U., 1978. Cert. Edn. Specialist Ariz. State U., 1980, in Elem. Edn. Ariz. Dept. Edn. Tchr. Westwood Sch., Park Forest, Ill., 1960—62, Little Friends, NYC, 1968—70, Holiday Park, Phoenix, 1976—2002, math coach, tchr., 2002—. Pres. Hadassah, Phoenix, 1980—82. Named Tchr. of Yr., Walmart, Tempe, Ariz., 2002; recipient Vol. award, 4-H, 2003, Urban Forest award, Phoeniz Pk. and Recreation, 2003; grantee, Wells Fargo, 1999, 2001. Mem.: Nat. Coun. Tchrs. Math. Avocations: reading, music box collecting, travel, music. Home: 15806 W Acapulco Ln Surprise AZ 85379

NEUMAN, LINDA KINNEY, retired state supreme court justice, lawyer; b. Chgo., June 18, 1948; d. Harold and Mary E. Kinney; m. Henry G. Neuman; children: Emily, Lindsey. BA, U. Colo., 1970, JD, 1973; LLM, U. Va., 1998. Ptnr. Betty, Neuman, McMahon, Hellstrom & Bittner, 1973-79; v.p., trust officer Bettendorf Bank & Trust Co., 1979-80; dist. ct. judge, 1982-86; supreme ct. justice State of Iowa, 1986—2003; ptnr. Betty Neuman & McMahon. L.L.P., Davenport, Iowa, 2003—05. Mem. adj. faculty U. Iowa Law Sch., 2003-; part-time jud. magistrate Scott County, 1980-82; mem. Supreme Ct. continuing legal edn. commn.; chair Iowa Supreme Ct. commn. planning 21st Century; mem. bd. counselors Drake Law Sch., time on appeal adv. com. Nat. Ctr. State Cts.; mem. Uniform State Laws Commn., 2004. Trustee St. Ambrose U.; commnr. Nat. Conf. Commr. on Uniform State Laws, 2004-. Recipient Regents scholarship, U. Colo. award for disting. svc. Fellow ABA (life; chair appellate judges conf. 1995); mem. Am. Judicature Soc., Iowa Bar Assn., Scott County Bar Assn., Dillon Am. Inn of Ct. (pres. 2003-04), Am. Acad. ADR Attys (pres. 2006-07). Office Phone: 563-289-3255. Office Fax: 563-289-3255. Business E-Mail: lkn@neumanadr.com.

NEUMAN, MAXINE DARCY, cellist, educator; b. Phila., July 1, 1948; d. Marvin Memorial and Helga (Henningson) Neuman; m. Reinhard Humburg, Oct. 16, 1987; children: Julia Vera, Mark Daniel Humburg. MusB, Manhattan Sch. Music, NY, 1968, MusM, 1969. Cellist N.J. Symphony Orch., Newark, 1969-71; cellist with variety of groups including Mozart Festival, Am. Ballet Theatre, "Y" Chamber Symphony, Bklyn. Philharm., Am. Composers Orch., NYC, 1971—80; cellist Walden Trio (Vanguard Records), Leonia, NJ, 1972—, Contemporary Trio, Crest Records, NYC, 1975—80; cellist, U.S., European and Mexico tours Crescent Quartet (Leonarda Records) U.S., European and Mexico tours, NYC, 1979—; cellist St. Luke's Chamber Ensemble, NYC, 1981—; prof. music Bennington Coll., Bennington, 1981-95, chmn. dept. music, 1985—86, 1990—91; prof. music Williams Coll., Mass., 1994-95, 98—; mem. faculty Sch. for Strings, NYC, 1996—, Hoff-Barthelson Sch., NYC, 2003—; cellist Claremont Duo (Artek Records), Germany, 1998—, Belmont Trio (Thorofon Records), Germany, 2003—, Por el Tango, 2005—, Cutting Edge Ensemble, 2006, Trio Maximo, 2007, Westchester Philharm., NY, 2007—. Touring solo cellist Europe, Mex., S.Am., Japan, 1980—, Montreux Jazz Festival, 1993, 94, NY Film Festival, 1995, Manchester Music Festival, 2007—; mem. faculty Chamber Music Conf. N.E., Bennington, 1982—, bd. dirs.; founder Bennington Cello Quartet; panelist Chamber Mus. Am. nat. conv., 2000, Jazz at Lincoln Ctr., 2001, Leipzig Media Awards, 2005. Rec. artist: Swiss, French, Australian, German, Italian, Ecuadorian, Colombian radio and TV, 1980—, Columbia, Orion, CRI, Opus One, Albany Records. Sony/Virgin, Koch Internat., CBS World, Nonesuch, AMC, Biddulph Records, B.E. Records, Angel, Mus. Heritage, CBS Records, Deutsche Grammophon, PBS Gt. Performers, 1995—2005; rec. artist Gt. Performances, 2006, Trio Maximo, 2007; performer: Sat. Night Live, 1998, Live from Lincoln Ctr., 2000, 2002, Elgar Concerto, 2005, Dvorak Concerto, 2005, Ecce cor Meum, Sir Paul McCartney, 2006. Bd. dirs. Bronx (N.Y.) Opera Co., 1972—85. Recipient Double award of Merit, Nat. Fedn. Music Clubs, 1976, award, Internat. Congress Women in Music, UN, 1990, prize, Am. Soc. Jewish Music, 1998, Grammy award, 1988, 1991, 2003, award, St. Luke's, 2005, Carnegie Mellon Found. award, 2005, 2007; Ford Found. grantee, 1971—72. Mem.: BMI, Rec. Musicians Am., Am. Fedn. Musicians, Kulturforum (artistic advisor), Bohemians, Chamber Music Conf. of East (bd. dirs.). Avocations: photography, travel, cooking, hiking. Home: 200 Claremont Ave Apt 52 New York NY 10027-4070 also: 799 Park St North Bennington VT 05257 Office Phone: 212-222-7896. Personal E-mail: cellomax@aol.com.

NEUMAN, NANCY ADAMS MOSSHAMMER, civic leader; b. Greenwich, Conn., July 24, 1936; d. Alden Smith and Margaret (Mevis) Mosshammer; m. Mark Donald Neuman, Dec. 23, 1958; children: Deborah Adams, Jennifer Fuller, Jeffrey Abbott. BA, Pomona Coll., 1957; LLD, 1983; MA, U. Calif., Berkeley, 1961; LHD, Westminster Coll., 1987. Disting. lectr. Am. govt. Pomona Coll., 1990; disting. vis. prof. Washington and Jefferson Coll., 1991, 94, Bucknell U., 1992. Editor: A Voice of Our Own: Leading American Women Celebrate the Right to Vote, 1996, True to Ourselves: A Celebration of Women Making a Difference, 1998. Pres. Lewisburg (Pa.) LWV, 1967-70; bd. dirs. LWV Pa., 1970-77, pres., 1975-77; bd. dirs. LWV U.S., 1977-90, 2nd v.p., 1978-80, 1st v.p., 1982-84, pres., 1986-90; mem. Pa. Gov.'s Commn. on Mortgage and Interest Rates, 1973, Pa. Commonwealth Child Devel. com., 1974-75, Nat. Commn. on Pub. Svc., 1987-90; bd. dirs. Housing Assistance Coun., Inc., Washington, 1974—2003, pres., 1978-80; bd. dirs. Nat. Coun. Agrl. Life and Labor, 1974-79, Nat. Rural Housing Coalition, 1975-95, Pa. Housing Fin. Agy., 1975-80, Jud. Inquiry and Rev. Bd. Pa., 1989-93; disciplinary bd. Supreme Ct. Pa., 1980-85; mem. Pa. Gov.'s Task Force on Voter Registration, 1975-76, Nat. Task Force for Implementation Equal Rights Amendment, 1975-77; mem. adv. com. Pa. Gov.'s Interdepartmental Coun. on Seasonal Farmworkers, 1975-77; mem. Appellate Ct. Nominating Commn. Pa., 1976-79; mem. Fed. Jud. Nominating Commn. Pa., 1977-85, chmn., 1978-81, 82-83; mem. Pa. Gov.'s Study Commn. on Pub. Employee rels., 1976-78; del. Internat. Women's Yr. Conf., 1977; bd. dirs. ER-America, Inc., 1st v.p., 1977-79, Nat. Low Income Housing Coalition, 1979-82; Rural Am., 1979-81, Fed. Home Loan Bank Pitts., 1979-82; mem. Nat. adv. Com. Women, 1978-79; mem. nat. adv. com. Pa. Neighborhood Preservation Support Sys., 1976-77; bd. dirs. Pa. Women's Campaign fund, 1984-86, 92-2002, pres., 1992-96, 2001-02, Rural coalition, Washington, 1984-90, Com. on the Constitutional Sys., 1988-90, Am. Judicature Soc., 1989-93; exec. com. Leadership Conf. Civil Rights, 1986-90; bd. dirs. Pennsylvanians for Modern Cts., 1986—; trustee Citizen's Rsch. Found., 1989-99; mem. mid. dist. Pa. adv. com. judicial and U.S. atty. nominations, 1993-94; bd. dirs. Pathmakers, 1993-97, pres. 1993-95; bd. dirs. Capital Concerts, 1997—. Virginia Travis lectureship Bucknell U., 1982; Woodrow Wilson vis. fellow, 1993-2000; recipient Disting. Alumna Award MacDuffle Sch. Girls, 1979, Liberty Bell award Pa. Bar Assn., 1983, Barrows Alumni Award Pomona Coll., 1987, Disting. Daus. of Pa. award, 1987, Thomas P. O'Neill Jr. award for Exemplary Pub. Svc., 1989. Mem. ABA (com. election law and voter participation 1986-90, accreditation com. 1990-96, coun. sect. legal edn. 1997-03), Disting. Daughters Pa. (pres. 2005—), Cosmos Club. Home: 190 Verna Rd Lewisburg PA 17837-8747 Business E-Mail: neuman@bucknell.edu.

NEUMAN, ROBERT STERLING, art educator, artist; b. Kellogg, Idaho, Sept. 9, 1926; s. Oscar C. and Katherine (Samuelson) N.; m. Helen Patricia Feddersen, Apr. 6, 1947 (div. 1971); children— Ingrid Alexandra, Elizabeth Catherine; m. Sunne Savage, June 3, 1979; 1 dau., Christina Mary. Student, U. Idaho, 1944-46; BAA., M.F.A., Calif. Coll. Arts and Crafts, 1947-51; student, San Francisco Sch. Fine Arts, 1950-51, Mills Coll., 1951. Assoc. prof. art Brown U., 1962-63; lectr. drawing Carpenter Center for Visual Arts, Harvard, 1963-72; prof. art, chmn. dept. Keene (N.H.) State Coll., 1972-90. Exhbns. include, Mus. Modern Art, Whitney Mus. Am. Art, Carnegie Internat., Fogg Mus. Art, Harvard U., San Francisco Mus. Art, Boston Mus. Fine Arts, Worcester (Mass.) Art Mus., Fogg Mus./Harvard U., Sunne Savage Gallery, Allan Stone Gallery, NYC, 1956—, also Japan and Europe. Served with AUS and USAAF, 1945-46. Recipient Howard Found. award for painting, 1967; Fulbright grantee, 1953-54; Guggenheim fellow, 1956-57; Bender grantee San Francisco Art Assn., 1952. Home: 135 Cambridge St Winchester MA 01890-2411

NEUMAN, SHLOMO P., hydrologist, educator; b. Zilina, Czechoslovakia, Oct. 26, 1938; came to U.S., 1963, naturalized, 1970; s. Alexander Neumann and Klara (Pikler) Lesny; m. Yael B. Neuman, Jan. 30, 1965; children: Gil, Michal, Ariel. BSc in Geology, Hebrew U., Jerusalem, 1963; MS in Engring. Sci., U. Calif., Berkeley, 1966, PhD in Engring. Sci., 1968. Cert. profl. hydrogeologist. Acting asst. prof., asst. rsch. engr. dept. civil engring. U. Calif., Berkeley, 1968-70, vis. assoc. prof. dept. civil engring., 1974-75; sr. scientist, assoc. rsch. prof. Inst. Soil and Water Agrl. Rsch. Orgn., Bet-Dagan, Israel, 1970-74; prof. hydrology dept. hydrology and water resources U. Ariz., Tucson, 1975-88, Regents' prof. dept. hydrology and water resources, 1988—. Cons. to U.S., Can. and Swedish govts. on hydrologic issues concerning nuc. waste disposal; vis. scientist dept. isotope Weizmann Inst. Sci., Rehovot, Israel, 1976; maitre de rsch. Ctr. d'Informatique Geologique, Ecole Mines Paris, Fountainebleau, France, 1978, dir. rsch., 1981; vis. prof. dept. fluid mechanics and heat transfer Tel-Aviv U., 1981; hon. appointment concurrent prof. Nanjing U., China; disting. lectr. in field; hon. prof. Nanjing Hydraulic Rsch. Inst., China, 1998—. Mem. editl. bd. Jour. Hydrology, 1977—84, Water Sci. and Tech. Libr. (The Netherlands), 1983—86, Stochastic Environmental Research and Risk Assessment, 1992—, Water Resources Rsch. Jour., 2006—, Hydrogeology Jour., 1999—2004, guest editor spl. issue in memory of Eugene S. Simpson, 1997—98; contbr. more than 300 profl. publs. including papers, books and reports. Hebrew U. scholar, 1962-63, Edwin Letts Oliver scholar, 1965-66; Jane Lewis fellow, 1966-68; recipient Cert. of Appreciation award USDA, 1975, C.V. Theis award Am. Inst. Hydrology, 1990. Fellow Geol. Soc. Am. (O.E. Meinzer award 1976, Birdsal Disting. Lectr. 1987), Am. Geophys. Union (4th Walter B. Langbein lectr. hydrology 1996, Robert E. Horton award 1969, Robert E. Horton medal, 2003), mem. ISI highly cited rschrs. database, Soc. Petroleum Engrs. of AIME, NAE, Assn. Groundwater Scientists and Engrs. of Nat. Well Water Assn. (Sci. award 1989), Ariz. Hydrol. Soc., Internat. Assn. Hydrogeologists. Jewish. Office: U Ariz Dept Hydrology & Water Resou Tucson AZ 85721-0001 Business E-Mail: neuman@hwr.arizona.edu.

NEUMANN, DONALD A., physical therapist, educator; BS in Phys. Therapy, U. Fla.; MS in Sci. Edn., U. Iowa, 1986, PhD in Exercise Sci. and Phys. Edn., 1986. Phys. therapist Woodrow Wilson Rehab. Ctr., Fishersville, Va., 1976, coord. clin. edn. Phys. Therapy Dept.; faculty mem. to prof. phys. therapy dept. Marquette U., Milw., 1986—. Tchr. kinesiology

Kaunas Med. Sch., Lithuania, 2002; tchr. kinesiology Phys. Therapy Prog. Semmelweis U., Budapest, Hungary, 2005. Contbr. articles to profl. jours.; assoc. editor: Jour. Orthop. & Sports Phys. Therapy; author: Kinesiology of the Musculoskeletal System: Foundations for Physical Rehabilitation, 2002. Recipient Steven J. Rose Endowment award for Excellence in Orthop. Phys. Therapy Rsch., Am. Phys. Therapy Assn., Eugene Michels New Investigator award for Outstanding Rsch. by a Young Investigator, Dorothy J. Baethke - Eleanor J. Carlin award for Excellence in Acad. Tchg., Jack Walker award for Best Article on Clin. Rsch. Published in Phys. Therapy, 1999, Fulbright Sr. Specialist award, 2005, US Prof. of Yr. award, Carnegie Found. for Advancement of Tchg. and Coun. for Advancement and Support of Edn., 2006; grantee Fulbright scholarship, 2002. Office: Coll Health Scis Marquette U PO Box 1881 Milwaukee WI 53201-1881 Office Phone: 414-288-3319. E-mail: donald.neumann@marquette.edu. *

NEUMANN, EDWARD SCHREIBER, transportation engineering educator; b. Harvey, Ill., Mar. 6, 1942; s. Arthur Edward Schreiber and Adeline Ruth (Spenks) N.; m. Carole Ann Dunkelberger, Apr. 19, 1969; children: Edward Schreiber, Jonathan David. BSCE, Mich. Technol. U., 1964; MS, Northwestern U., 1967, PhD, 1969, Cert. in Prosthetics, 2000. Registered profl. engr., W.Va., Nev.; cert. prosthetist Am. Bd. Certification. Mem. faculty W.Va. U., Morgantown, 1970-90, prof. transp. engring., 1980-90, interim dir. Harley O. Staggers Nat. Transp. Ctr., 1982-95, dir., 1985-90; prof. U. Nev., Las Vegas, 1991—, chmn. dept., 1991-99, dir. Transp. Rsch. Ctr., 1991-98, dir. Ctr. Disability and Applied Biomechanics, 2003—. Founder Human Kinetics Engring., LLC; chair rsch. edn. com. Am. Acad. Orthotists and Prosthetists. Editor numerous conf. procs.; contbr. articles and rsch. reports to profl. lit. Bd. dirs. Mason Dixon Hist. Park Assn., 1978-90; chmn. new transp. systems and tech. com. transp. rsch. bd. mem, 1998-2004, emeritus, 2004. Capt., C.E., AUS, 1969-70. Resources for Future fellow, 1969. Fellow Inst. Transp. Engrs.; mem. ASCE (chmn. com. on automated people movers, chmn. exec. com. urban planning and devel. divsn., chmn. exec. com. urban transp. divsn., James Laurie prize 1996), Nat. Soc. Profl. Engrs., Am. Soc. Engring. Edn., OITAF-NACS, Advanced Transit Assn. (bd. dirs., pres. 1988-90), Sigma Xi, Tau Beta Pi, Phi Kappa Phi, Phi Eta Sigma, Chi Epsilon. Presbyterian. Home: 935 E Eldorado Ln Las Vegas NV 89123-0515 Office: UNLV Dept Civil Environ Engring Las Vegas NV 89154-4015 Office Phone: 702-895-1072. Business E-Mail: neumann@ce.unlv.edu.

NEUMANN, FORREST KARL, retired health facility administrator; b. St. Louis, Oct. 7, 1930; s. Metz Earl and Ruth (McGhee) N.; m. Erika Stefanie Turkl, Feb. 11, 1955; children: Tracey Neumann Liberson, Karen Neumann Kruger, Scott, Lisa. BS, Roosevelt U., 1953; MS in Hosp. Adminstrn., Northwestern U., 1955. Adminstrv. resident Louis A. Weiss Hosp., Chgo., 1954-55; mem. staff Sparrow Hosp., Lansing, Mich., 1958-90; CEO, pres., dir. Edward W. Sparrow Hosp., Lansing, 1962-90; pres., chief exec. officer, dir. Mason Gen. Hosp., Mich., 1973-85; chmn. bd. Caymich Ins. Co. Ltd., Cayman Islands, 1979-91, emeritus dir. Cayman Islands, 1991—; chmn. bd. Caymich Ins. Co. (Barbados) Ltd., 1986-91; pres., CEO, Mich. Hosp. Assn. Ins. Co., 1990-96; dir. Mich. Hosp. Assocs. Ins. Co., 1976-98; pres., CEO, Sparrow, Inc., 1984-90. Chmn. bd. Mich. Hosp. Assn. Ins. Co., 1979-90; dir. First of Am. Bank Corp., 1980-95, Auto Owners Ins. Co., 1980-90. Chmn. hosp. div. United Community Chest, 1965-68, chmn. budget steering com., 1970-71, bd. dirs., mem. exec. com., 1969-75; mem. adv. com. Capitol Area Comprehensive Health Planning Assn., 1969, bd. dirs., 1971-75, treas., 1974-75; mem., vice chmn. Mich. Arbitration Adv. Com., 1975-80; bd. dirs. Grad. Med. Edn., Inc., 1971-80, pres., 1972-73, treas. 1973. 1st lt. Med. Svcs. Corps USAF, 1955—58. Fellow Am. Coll. Hosp. Adminstrs. (life); mem. Southwestern Mich. Hosp. Council (trustee 1968-73, pres. 1970-71), Am. Hosp. Assn. (del. 1979-87), Mich. Hosp. Assn. (1st v.p. 1972-73, bd. dirs., exec. com., treas. 1974-75, chmn. 1976-77, Meritorious Key award 1979), Rotary.

NEUMANN, HENRY W., JR., energy executive; B in Acctg. and Bus. Adminstrn., Ill. State U., Normal. With Kinder Morgan, Houston, 1976—, various positions in acctg. and info. tech., v.p. sys. devel., v.p., chief info. officer. Office: Kinder Morgan 500 Dallas St Ste 1000 Houston TX 77002 Office Phone: 713-369-9000. *

NEUMANN, HERSCHEL, retired physics professor; b. San Bernardino, Calif., Feb. 3, 1930; s. Arthur and Dorothy (Greenhood) N.; m. Julia Black, June 15, 1951; 1 child, Keith. BA, U. Calif., Berkeley, 1951; MS, U. Oreg., 1959; PhD, U. Nebr., 1965. Theoretical physicist GE, Richland, Wash., 1951—57; instr. physics U. Nebr., Lincoln, 1964—65; asst. prof. physics U. Denver, 1965—71, assoc. prof. physics, 1971—85, prof. physics, 1985—2006; ret., 2006; chmn. physics and astronomy U. Denver, 1985—97, assoc. chmn. physics and astronomy, 2001—04, interim chmn. physics and astronomy, 2004—06, chmn. physics and astronomy, 2006. Contbr. over 20 articles to profl. jours. Dir. numerous pub. outreach programs in physics. Mem. Am. Assn. Physics Tchrs. Home: 964 Salem Aurora CO 80011-6344 Office: U Denver Dept Physics Astronomy Denver CO 80208-2238 Home Phone: 303-366-0315. Business E-Mail: hneumann@du.edu.

NEUMANN, JEFFREY JAY, photographer, minister; b. Cleve., Aug. 6, 1948; s. Fred and LaVerne (Vavra) N.; m. Charlene Rose Sparrow, Apr. 21, 1968 (dec.); children: Stephan, Corene, Lara; m. Carolyn Hannah, Nov. 4, 1972; 1 son, Jeffrey. Ordained to ministry, 1962. Lithographer, camera operator Advertype, Inc., Cleve., 1972; lab. technician Vista Color Lab., Cleve., 1972-73; prodn. mgr. Mort Tucker Photography, Cleve., 1973-78; owner, photographer Photography by Jeffrey Neumann, Wadsworth, OH, 1978—. Lectr. in field. Author: Thirty Years as Jehovah's Slave, 1999, Forty Years as Jehovah's Willing Slave, 2002, 120 Years Preaching the Good News of the Kingdom, 2002, To Have and Remember the Perfect Wedding, 2003, Unlocking the Secrets to Mankind's Mysterious Past, 2007. Mem. Sm. Bus. Mgmt. Adv. Com., 1980-83. Mem. Internat. Platform Assn., Profl. Photographers Am. (awards), Wedding and Portrait Photographers Internat. (awards), Profl. Photographers Ohio (awards). Jehovahs Witness. Home and Office: 9960 Mount Eaton Rd Wadsworth OH 44281-9028 E-mail: jneumann@neo.rr.com.

NEUMANN, LINDA KAY, marketing professional; b. Wyandotte, Mich., Feb. 5, 1959; d. Michael and Raelene Fern (Bongart) Goldman; m. David Dewain Neumann, Mar. 31, 1980; children: Rachel Anne, Kyle Wayne. Student, Mesa CC, San Diego, 1976—86; grad. with honors, Bank Mktg. Sch., 1991. Mail clk., securities clk. Hawaiian Trust Co. Ltd., Honolulu, 1977-78, supr., 1979-81; securities vault clk., bank card clk. Union Bank Calif., San Diego, 1981-82, sales adminstrv. asst., 1983-86, mktg. adminstrv. asst., mktg. officer, 1986-88, from mktg. asst. v.p. to mktg. v.p., 1992-94, mktg. v.p., mgr., 1994-96, bus. and sales planning mgr., v.p., 1996—2002; pres. Brilliant Mktg. Ideas, Inc., San Diego, 2002—. Chmn. San Diego Ednl. Coun., Am. Banking Assn., Am. Inst. Banking, 1996—97; chmn. adv. coun. for mktg. program Alliant Internat. U., 2007—. Pres. Rolling Hills Elem. PTA, 1995—96; parliamentarian Deer Canyon Elem. PTA; nat. del. San Diego Imperial Coun. Girl Scouts, 2002—05; mem. NC C. of C.; chmn. bd. dirs. San Diego Safety Coun., Pacific Safety Coun., 2000—05; bd. dir., pres. Westview Found., 2001—06; bd. dirs., sec. Difference Makers Internat., 2004. Mem.: Calif. Activity Dirs. Assn., San Diego Employers Assn., Nat. Soc. Fundraising Execs., Advt. Splty. Inst. Promotional Products Assns., Bank Mktg. Assn., San Diego Direct Mktg. Assn., Advt. Club San Diego, Direct Mktg. Assn., Am. Soc. Autism. Office: Brilliant Mktg Ideas inc PO Box 721419 San Diego CA 92172-1419 Personal E-mail: ideas@adexec.com. Business E-Mail: linda@brilliantmarketingideas.com.

NEUMANN, MARK W., former congressman, real estate developer; b. Waukesha, Wis., Feb. 27, 1954; m. Sue; 3 children. BS, U. Wis., Whtiewater, 1975; MS, U. Wis., River Falls, 1977. Real estate developer Neumann Devels. (now Neumann Corp.), 1980—; mem. 104th and 105th Congresses from 1st Wis. dist., 1994-97; candidate Wis. State Senate, 2004. Mem. appropriations, nat. security, vets. affairs, HUD and ind. agys., budget coms. Address: W330 N6233 Hasslinger Dr Nashotah WI 53058-9432

NEUMANN, NANCY RUTH, film studio educator; b. LA, Feb. 1, 1948; d. Robert Thomas and Frances Andersen; m. Bernd Fritz Dietmar Neumann, June 26, 1971; children: Peter, Christina, Linda, Christoph, Karin. BA, U. Calif., Riverside, 1969; MA, Sorbonne U., Paris, 1971; credentials, Calif. State U., San Bernardino, 1985. Cert. community coll. tchr., various subjects, Calif., studio tchr., Calif. Missionary, reading instr., Maroua, Cameroon, South Africa, 1971-73; instr. Pasadena City Coll., Calif., 1974-75, Riverside CC, 1988; secondary tchr. Riverside Christian Sch., Calif., 1985-86; studio tchr. Vista Films, Culver City, 1986, A&M Recs., 1987, Hollywood Studios, Calif., 1986-88, Paramount Studios, Hollywood, Calif., 1986—2006, MGM - Lorimar Prodns., Culver City, Calif., 1986-91, MCA/Universal Studios, Universal City, Calif., 1986—99, R.J. Louis Prodns., Burbank, Calif., 1987, Michael Landon Prodns., Culver City, 1987-88, Carsey-Werner Prodns., LA, 1988, Bob Booker Prodns., Hollywood, 1988-90, ABC, 1990—95, NBC Prodns., Burbank, 1990—2003, Fox TV, 1990—2006, New Line Cinema, 1991—2006, 20th Century Fox, 1993—2004, Warner Bros., 1991—2005, RCA, 1997—98, CBS, 1991—2006, Sony Pictures, 1999—2004, Walt Disney Prodns., Burbank, 2000—06, Christian Film Group, 2005; exec. prodr. Am. Pictures, Riverside, 1989—. Pvt. tutor, Riverside, L.A., 1987—; drama coach Grace Ch., Riverside, 1981-82, Magnolia Ave. Bapt. Ch. Riverside, 1986-89. Author: several plays, 1981-89; writer 80 songs, 1968—2004; pub. access TV prodr. Nancy Norway Presents: Windmills, L.A. and Riverside, 1994-2004; TV prodr., 1994-2006. Coach mock trial Riverside Christian HS, 1994-06, TV prodr., 1994-07; choir dir. Riverside Christian Sch., 1985-86; Sunday Sch. tchr. Grace Bapt. Ch., Harvest Christian Fellowship, Riverside, Magnolia Ave. Bapt. Ch., 1968-92, Wheat, Oil and Wine Christian Fellowship, Riverside, Sunday sch. supt., 1992-93; children's choir dir. Grace Bapt. Ch., 1981-82; Christian edn. coord., Sunday sch. tchr., and vacation Bible sch. dir. First United Meth. Ch., Riverside, 2002-03. Recipient Golden Star Halo award, Star Sapphire Halo award, Jeanie Golden Halo award for acting and teaching So. Calif. Motion Picture Coun., 1994. Mem. Nat. Assn. Christian Educators, Internat. Alliance of Theatre and Stage Employees, Internat. Platform Assn., Greater L.A. World Trade Ctr. Assn., Sons of Norway (study scholar 1967), Delta Phi Alpha. Democrat. Avocations: photography, music, travel, production of films and videos. Home: 1244 SE Seaport Cir Corvallis OR 97333-3110 Home Phone: 541-753-1075; Office Phone: 818-618-2948. Personal E-mail: nrneumann@yahoo.com.

NEUMANN, PETER GABRIEL, computer scientist; b. NYC, Sept. 21, 1932; s. J.B. and Elsa (Schmid) N.; m. Elizabeth Susan Neumann; 1 child, Helen K. AB, Harvard U., 1954, SM, 1955; Dr rerum naturarum, Technische Hochschule, Darmstadt, Fed. Republic Germany, 1960; PhD, Harvard U., 1961. Mem. tech. staff Bell Labs, Murray Hill, NJ, 1960-70; Mackay lectr. Stanford U., 1964, U. Calif., Berkeley, 1970-71; prin. scientist SRI Internat., Menlo Park, Calif., 1971—. Adj. prof. U. Md., 1999. Author: Computer-Related Risks, 1995. Recipient Nat. Computer Sys. Security award, 2002; Fulbright grantee, 1958—60. Fellow AAAS, IEEE, Assn. for Computing Machinery (editor jour. 1976-93, chmn. com. on computers and pub. policy 1985—). Avocations: music, tai chi. Office: SRI Internat EL-243 333 Ravenswood Ave Menlo Park CA 94025-3493 Business E-Mail: pneumann@acm.org.

NEUMANN, RITA NUNEZ, lawyer; b. New Brunswick, NJ, Apr. 23, 1944; d. Arno Otto and Florence (Alligier) N. BA in Math., Trenton State Coll., 1965; MS in Math., Stevens Inst. Tech., 1970; JD, Seton Hall U., 1976; LLM in Tax Law, U. San Diego, 1983. Bar: D.C. 1984, U.S. Tax Ct. 1984, N.Y. 1985, N.J. 1986, U.S. Supreme Ct. 1989, Mont. 1990, U.S. Ct. Appeals (9th cir.) 1991. Instr. math. Middlesex County Coll., Edison, N.J., 1971-74; tax cons. Evan Morris Esq. Offices, Woodland Hills, Calif., 1975-85; asst. to editor Jour. Taxation, NYC, 1985-86; pvt. practice law New Brunswick, 1986-94, Las Cruces, N.Mex., 1994—; mcpl. prosecutor Manville, N.J., 1987. Adj. instr. bus. law and fin. L.A. C.C. Dist., 1976-82; adj. instr. law and bus. calculus Ventura (Calif.) C.C. Dist., 1977-82; adj. prof. bus. calculus Calif. State U., Northridge, 1981-83; adj. instr. internat. law Laverne U. and San Fernando Valley Coll. Law, 1983-85; disting. lectr. in law and mgmt. Troy State U., Holloman AFB/White Sands Missile Range.; atty. Ability Ctr. of Las Cruces; candidate Ct. of Appeals of N.Mex., 2000; candidate Dist. Ct. Judge, 2004. Author: Doing Business in North America, 1994, various edits., 95—, Legal Aspects of Doing Business in North America, 1995, 11th edit., 2005; contbr. articles to profl. publs. Vol. to farm workers ctr., Moorpark, Calif., 1979; instr. community extension ctr. for women, Calif., 1980; vol. atty. for N.J. Vietnam Vets., 1986; organizer 10-kilometer run to benefit ill children, Manville, N.J., 1986; guest lectr. taxes Second Ann. Bus. Seminar for Vets. and Non-Vet. Am. Indians of N.W. U.S., Billings, Mont., 1988; candidate for freeholder, Middlesex County, 1988; active with numerous Am. Indian tribes thoughout the U.S. in bus. devel. and Indian rights. Recipient Outstanding Contbn. for Individuals with Disabilities award, N.Mex. Bar Assn., 2004; fellow, NSF, 1968—71. Mem. Kappa Delta Phi. Avocation: running. Office: 1850 N Solano Dr Las Cruces NM 88001-1851 Office Phone: 505-647-3778. E-mail: justy.neumann@lycos.com.

NEUMANN, RONALD DANIEL, nuclear medicine physician, educator; b. Watertown, Wis., Oct. 10, 1947; BS summa cum laude, Carroll Coll., 1970; MD with highest honors, Yale U., 1974. Diplomate Nat. Bd. Med. Examiners, Am. Bd. Nuclear Medicine; lic. physician, Md. Resident in pathology Yale-New Haven Hosp., 1974-77, resident in nuc. medicine, 1977-79, chief resident in nuc. medicine, 1978-79, attending physician, 1979-85; asst. prof. diagnostic radiology Sch. Medicine Yale U., 1979-83, assoc. prof. diagnostic radiology and pathology, 1983-86; dep. chief dept. nuc. medicine NIH, Bethesda, Md., 1985-88, chief. dept. nuc. medicine, 1988—, dir. nuclear medicine residency tng. program, 1986-92; clin. prof. diagnostic radiology and nuc. medicine Sch. Medicine George Washington U., Washington, 1986—92. Chmn. med. isotopes and radiation safety com. West Haven VA Med. Ctr., 1979-85; mem. clin. rsch. panel Nat. Inst. Diabetes and Digestive and Kidney Diseases, 1987-88; mem. radiation safety com. NIH and Nat. Ctr. for Health Stats., 1987-89. Patentee Antigen-specific composition and in-vivo methods for detecting and localizing an antigenic site and for radiotherapy; contbr. over 200 articles and abstracts to med. and sci. jours., 30 chpts. to books and conf. proceedings. Nat. Merit scholar; NASA summer fellow. Fellow Am. Coll. Chest Physicians; mem. AAAS, Am. Soc. for Investigative Pathology, Soc. Nuclear Medicine (co-chmn. C.M.E. program 1995-96, pres.-elect 1997, pres. Mid.-Atlantic chpt. 1998), Internat. Acad. Pathology (U.S. and Can. divsns.), European Assn. Nuclear Medicine, Sigma Xi., Delta Sigma Nu. Office: NIH CC Dept Nuclear Medicine Bethesda MD 20892-1180 Office Phone: 301-496-6455.

NEUMANN, ROY COVERT, architect; b. Columbus, Nebr., Mar. 1, 1921; s. LeRoy Franklin and Clara Louise (Covert) N.; children: Tali, Scott; m. Donna Corwin, Oct. 11, 2003. Student, Midland Coll., 1939-40, U. Calif.-Berkeley Armed Forces Inst., overseas, 1942-43; AB, U. Nebr., 1948, BArch, 1949; MA, Harvard U., 1952; postgrad., U. Wis., Iowa State U. Registered profl. architect, Iowa, Nebr., Kans., Minn., S.D., N.Y., Mass., Ohio, Pa., Tenn., Ky., Va., W.Va., Ga., Mich., Mo., Ill., Wis., Tex., Colo. Ptnr., architect R. Neumann Assocs., Lincoln, Nebr., 1952-55; officer mgr. Sargent, Webster, Crenshaw & Folley, Schenectady, NY, 1955-59; dir. architecture, ptnr. A.M. Kinney Assocs., Cin., 1959-65; officer mgr. Hunter, Campbell & Rea, Johnstown, Pa., 1965-66; dir. architecture, ptnr. Stanley Cons., Muscatine, Iowa, 1966-76; pres., chmn. bd. Neumann Monson P.C., Iowa City, 1976—. Ptnr. Clinton St. Ptnrs., Iowa City, 1983—, Iris City Devel. Co. Mt. Pleasant, Iowa, 1986, Linn Mar Elem./Mid. Sch., Marion, Iowa. Prin. works include Harbour Facilities, Antigua, W.I., S.C. Johnson Office Bldg., Racine, Wis., Iowa City Transit Facility Bldg., addition to Davenport Ctrl. High Sch., V.A. Adminstrv. Office Bldg., Iowa City, Johnson County Office Bldg., Iowa City Mercer Park Aquatic Ctr., Iowa City, Coll. Bus. U. Iowa, Iowa City, renovation Lawrence County Courthouse, Deadwood, S.D., H.S. and Elem. Schs., Mt. Pleasant, Iowa, Riverview Ctr., Muscatine, Iowa, Muscatine County Adminstv. Bldg., Iowa. Mem. bd. edn. Muscatine Community Sch. Dist., 1974-76. Served with USN, 1942-46, PTO. Recipient Honor award Portland Cement Assn., 1949, Lorraine D. Wright award for outstanding constrn. Camanche (Iowa) H.S., 1998-99. Mem. AIA (Honor award 1975), Constrn. Specifications Inst. (pres. 1974-76, Honor award 1983, 84, 85, 86), Soc. Archtl. Historians, Archtl. Assn. London, U. Nebr. Alumni Assn., Harvard U. Alumni Assn., Iowa City C. of C., Phi Kappa Psi, Univ. Athletic Club (Iowa City), Masons, Ea. Star, Elks Republican. Presbyterian. Avocations: golf, fishing, medieval history, big band music. Home: 312 Locust St Muscatine IA 52761-3510 Office: Neumann Monson Architects 111 E College St Iowa City IA 52240-4012 Office Phone: 319-338-7878. E-mail: roy@neumannmonson.com.

NEUMANN, SERINA ANN LOUISE, psychologist, researcher; b. Fitchburg, Mass., Dec. 29, 1970; d. James Martin Neumann and Annette Marie Rooney; m. Mark Cardiff, Feb. 19, 1973. BS in Psychology and Bus. cum laude, U. Pitts., 1992; MA in Clin. Psychology and Behavioral Medicine, U. Md., Balt., 1999, PhD in Clin. Psychology and Behavioral Medicine, 2001. Lic. psychologist Bur. Profl. Occupl. Affairs, Pa., 2003, Va., 2006. Postdoctoral scholar, cardiovasc. behavioral medicine rsch. tng. program U. Pitts., 2001—04, rsch. asst. prof., 2004—05; ast. prof. psychiatry and behavioral scis. Eastern Va. Med. Sch., 2006—. Author articles and papers in field. Fellow Ruth L. Kirschstein Nat. Rsch. Svc. award, NIH, Nat. Heart, Lung, and Blood Inst., 2001-2004; Loan Repayment Program grant, NIH, 2002—, Grant (NIMH) Kiosk award, 2005—. Mem.: APA (mem. Health Psychology Divsn. 38), Internat. Soc. Behavioral Medicine, Soc. Behavioral Medicine, Am. Psychosomatic Soc. (program com. student mem. 2000—01, Citation award 2005), Phi Kappa Phi. Achievements include discovery of preliminary evidence of an association between genetic variation in the choline transporter gene and parasympathetic-cardiac function, depressive symptomatology; corticolimbic reactivity and subclinical measures of atherosclerosis. Office: Eastern Va Med Sch Dept Psychiatry 825 Fairfax Ave Norfolk VA 23501 Home Phone: 724-861-5023; Office Phone: 757-446-5888. Business E-Mail: neumansa@evms.edu.

NEUMANN, THOMAS WILLIAM, archaeologist; b. Cin., Aug. 30, 1951; s. William Henry and Virginia Marie Neumann; m. Mary Louise Spink, Sept. 3, 1988. BA in Anthropology, U. Ky., 1973; PhD in Anthropology, U. Minn., 1979. Instr. U. Minn., Mpls., 1977-79; asst. prof. Syracuse U., 1979-86, dir. archaeology field program, 1979-86; sr. ptnr. Neumann & Sanford Cultural Resource Assessments, Syracuse, 1985-87; sr. scientist R. Christopher Goodwin & Assocs., Inc., Frederick, Md., 1987-92. Rsch. assoc. Terrestrial Environ. Specialists, Phoenix, N.Y., 1980-83, SUNY Rsch. Found., Potsdam, 1985-87; external reviewer NSF, Washington, 1982-85; dir. Ctr. for Archaeol. Rsch. and Edn., Houston, Minn., 1982-84; vis. assoc. prof. Emory U., 1991-93, 96-2000, 2002-06, U. Ga., 1997; ind. cons., 1991—; mgr. Diachronics divsn. Pocket Park-Wentworth Analytical Facility, 1993—. Author, co-author more than 80 monographs including 2 winners of the Anne Arundell County Hist. Preservation award; asst. editor Amanuensis, 1972-73; contbr. more than 40 articles to profl. jours. Nat. Trust Historic Preservation honor award. Recipient Oswald award U. Ky., 1973; co-recipient Vt. Gov.'s medal for Stonewalls and Cellarholes; grantee Am. Philos. Soc., 1981, Appleby-Mosher Found., 1983, Landmarks Assn. Ctrl. N.Y., 1984. Mem. AAAS, N.Y. Acad. Sci., Soc. for Am. Archaeology, Ea. States Archaeol. Fedn., Mid. Atlantic Archaeol. Conf., Ga. Coun. Profl. Archaeologists, Register of Profl. Archaeologists, Phi Beta Kappa. Roman Catholic. Achievements include development of use of vegetation successional stages for cultural resource assessments; identification of cause of passenger pigeon extinctions, microlithic compound tool industry in the eastern prehistoric U.S., contingency planning budget system for Archdiocese of Atlanta. Home and Office: Ind Archeol Cons 3859 Wentworth Ln SW Lilburn GA 30047-2260

NEUMANN, WILLIAM ALLEN, retired state supreme court justice; b. Minot, ND, Feb. 11, 1944; s. Albert W. and Opal Olive (Whitlock) N.; m. Jaqueline Denise Buechler, Aug. 9, 1980; children: Andrew, Emily. BSBA, U. N.D., 1965; JD, Stanford U., 1968. Bar: N.D. 1969, U.S. Dist. Ct. N.D. 1969. Pvt. practice law, Williston, ND, 1969-70, Bottineau, ND, 1970-79; judge N.D. Judicial Dist. Ct., N.E. Judicial Dist., Rugby and Bottineau, 1979-92; justice N.D. Supreme Ct., Bismarck, 1993—2005; exec. dir. State Bar Assn., ND, 2005—. Chmn. elect N.D. Jud. Conf., 1985-87, chmn. 1987-89. Mem. ABA, State Bar Assn. N.D., Am. Judicature Soc. (bd. dirs. 1998-2004). Lutheran. Office: ND State Bar Assn 504 N Washington St Bismarck ND 58501 Office Phone: 701-255-1404.

NEUMEIER, JOHN, choreographer, ballet company director; b. Milw., Feb. 24, 1942; s. Albert and Lucille N. BA, Marquette U., 1961, DFA (hon.), 1987; student, Stone-Camryn Ballet Sch., Chgo., 1957-62, Royal Ballet Sch., London, 1962-63; student of Vera Volkova, Copenhagen, 1962-63. Dancer Sybil Shearer Co., Chgo., 1960-62, Stuttgart (Fed. Republic Germany) Ballet, 1963-69; artistic dir. Frankfurt (Fed. Republic Germany) Opera Ballet, 1969-73, Hamburg (Fed. Republic Germany) State Opera Ballet, 1973—; prof. City of Hamburg, 1987; dir. Hamburg Ballet, 1996, ballettintendant, 1997—. Found. ballet sch. Hamburg State Opera, 1978; found. ballet ctr. John Neumeier, ballet sch., Hamburg State Opera co. tng. under one roof., 1989. Guest choreographer for various cos. including Am. Ballet Theatre, Royal Ballet London, Royal Danish Ballet, Nat. Ballet Can., Royal Winnipeg Ballet, Stuttgart Ballet, Munich Opera, Vienna Opera, Ballet du XX siecle, Brussels, Opera de Paris, Opera of Stockholm, Mariinsky Theatre, St. Petersburg; guest opera dir. Otello, Munich Opera, Hamburg State Opera; ballet dir. (films) Rondo, 1971 (Prix Italia 1972), Third Symphony of Gustav Mahler (Golden Camera award 1978), Legend of Joseph, Wendungen (String Quintet in C major by Schubert), 1979, Scenes of Childhood, The Lady of the Camellias, 1986, Othello, 1987, Illusions - Like Swan Lake, 2002, Death in Venice, 2004, St. Matthew Passion and Sylvia, 2005; choreographer Romeo and Juliet, The Nutcracker, 1971, Daphnis and Chloé, 1972, Third Symphony of Gustav Mahler, 1975, Illusions-Like Swan Lake, 1976, A Midsummer Night's Dream, 1977, Sleeping Beauty, The Lady of the Camelias, 1978, Matthaeus-Passion, 1981, Giselle, 1983, Sixth Symphony of G. Mahler, 1984, Peer Gynt, 1989, Fifth Symphony of G. Mahler, 1989, Requiem, 1991, A Cinderella Story, 1992, Odyssee, 1995, Vivaldi Or What You Will, 1996, Sylvia, 1997, Images from Bartók, 1998, Messias, 1999 (Danza Danza award 2001), Nijinsky, 2000, Giselle, 2000, Sounds of Empty Pages, Winterreiwse, 2001, The Seagull, 2002, Death in Venice, 2003, Preludes CV, 2003, The Little Mermaid, a homage to Hans Christian Andersen for his 200th birthday celebrations, 2005, Songs of the Night, 2005. Decorated knight's cross Danebrog Order (Denmark); recipient Dance mag. award, 1983, Fed. German Cross of Merit, 1987, German Dance prize, 1988; title of Prof. conferred by City of Hamburg, 1987, Deutscher Tanzpreis, Fed. Republic of Germany, 1988; recipient Prix

Diaghilev award, France, 1988, Order Des Arts et des Lettres award French Minister Culture, 1991, Carina Ari award, Stockholm, 1994, Nijinsky medal Polish Minister Culture, 1996, Danebrog Order in Gold, Denmark, 2000, Bayerischer Theaterpreis, 2001, First prize for best contemporary choreography, Vasva 2002, Wilhelm Hansen prize, 2002, Medal for Art and Science, 2003; named Hon. Mem. Semper Opera, 2002, Knight of the Region of Knox French President Jacques Chirac, 2003, Porselli prize, Italy, 2004, Hans Christian Andersen Embassador, 2004, 05; Saeculum prize for his lifework, Dresden, 2005, Steffen Kempe prize, 2005; Hamburg John Neumeier Found. named in his honor, 2006, Nijinsky award for lifetime achievement, 2006, Citizen of Yr. Hamburg, 2006, Honorary Citizen of Hamburg, 2007. Mem. Acad. der Kuenste Hamburg, Acad. der Kuenste Berlin, Golden Mask, 2002 (Medal for Sci, 2003). Roman Catholic. Office: Ballettzentrum Hamburg Caspar-Voght-Strasse 54 D-20535 Hamburg Germany E-mail: intendanz@hamburgballett.de, presse@hamburgballett.de.

NEUMEIER, MATTHEW MICHAEL, lawyer, educator; b. Racine, Wis., Sept. 13, 1954; s. Frank Edward and Ruth Irene (Effenberger) N.; m. Annmarie Prine, Jan. 31, 1987; children: Ruthann Marie, Emilie Irene, Matthew Charles. B in Gen. Studies with distinction, U. Mich., 1981; JD magna cum laude, Harvard U., 1984. Bar: NY 1987, Mich. 1988, Ill. 1991, US Dist. Ct. (ea. dist.) Mich. 1988, US Dist. Ct. (ea., no. dists. and trial bar) Ill. 1991, US Ct. Appeals (7th cir.) 1992, US Ct. Appeals (fed. cir.) 1998, US Supreme Ct. 1991. Sec.-treas. Ind. Roofing & Siding Co., Escanaba, Mich., 1973-78; mng. ptnr. Ind. Roofing Co., Menominee, Mich., 1977-78; law clk. to presiding justice US Ct. Appeals (9th cir.), San Diego, 1984-85; law clk. to chief justice Warren E. Burger US Supreme Ct., Washington, 1985-86; spl. asst. to chmn. US Constn. Bicentennial Commn., Washington, 1986; assoc. Cravath, Swaine & Moore, NYC, 1986-88; spl. counsel Burnham & Ritchie, Ann Arbor, Mich., 1988; assoc. Schlussel, Lifton, Simon, Rands, Galvin & Jackier, P.C., Ann Arbor, Mich., 1988-90, Skadden, Arps, Slate, Meagher & Flom, Chgo., 1990-96; ptnr. Jenner & Block, Chgo., 1996—2007, Howrey LLP, Chgo., 2007—. Adj. prof. computer law and high tech. litig. John Marshall Law Sch., Chgo., 1999—. Editor: Harvard Law Rev., 1982—84. Pres., bd. dirs. Univ. Cellar Inc., Ann Arbor, 1979-81; bd. dirs. Econ. Devel. Corp., Menominee, 1978-79, Midwestern divsn. Am. Suicide Found., sec., 1992-97, Commonwealth Plaza Condominium Assn., dir., 1999—, pres., 2000—; dir. Harvard Law Soc. Ill., 2003-, sec., 2005-07, treas., 2007—; mem. vestry Ch. Our Savior, 1997-2000; bd. dirs. Chgo. Children's Mus., 1999-, sec., 2003-; chmn. Harvard Law Sch. 15 Yr. Reunion Gift Fund, 1999; vice chair Harvard Law Sch. 20 Yr. Reunion Gift Fund, 2003-04. Mem. ABA, State Bar Mich., Assn. of Bar of City of NY, Chgo. Bar Assn., Ill. State Bar Assn., Def. Rsch. Inst., The 410 Club, Econ. Club Chgo., City Club of Chgo. Republican. Avocations: classic automobiles, piano, choir. Office: Howrey LLP 321 N Clark St Chicago IL 60610 Office Phone: 312-846-5640. E-mail: neumeierm@howrey.com.

NEUMEYER, JOHN LEOPOLD, chemistry professor; b. Munich, July 19, 1930; came to U.S., 1945, naturalized, 1950; s. Albert and Martha (Stern) N.; m. Evelyn Friedman, June 24, 1956; children: Ann Martha, David Alexander, Elizabeth Jean. BS, Columbia U., 1952; PhD, U. Wis., 1961. Rsch. chemist Ethicon Inc., New Brunswick, NJ, 1952-57, FMC Corp., Princeton, NJ, 1961-63; sr. staff chemist Arthur D. Little, Inc., Cambridge, Mass., 1963-69; prof. medicinal chemistry, chemistry Northeastern U., Boston, 1969-91, dir. grad. sch., 1978-85, univ. disting. prof., 1982—92, univ. disting. prof. emeritus, 1992—; chmn. bd., chief sci. officer, co-founder Rsch. Biochem. Internat., Natick, 1981-97; pres., co-founder Brain Rsch. Labs., Inc., 1999—2002. Mem. com. of revision U.S. Pharmacopeia, 1970-85; lectr. in psychiatry dept. psychiatry Harvard Med. Sch., 1996—; Boudewijn Tieboel vis. prof., Groningen-Utrecht Inst. for Drug Exploration, Holland, 1997, dir. medicinal chemistry program Alcohol and Drug Abuse Rsch. Ctr. McLean Hosp., Belmont, Mass., 1996—; vis. prof. chemistry U. Konstanz, Germany, 1975-77cons. in field. Contbr. articles to profl. jours., chapters to books; patentee in field. Mem. Bd. Health, Wayland, Mass., 1968-75, Pesticide Bd., Mass., 1972-75; mem. panel to sec. HEW Commn. on Pesticides and their Relationship to Environ. Health, 1969; mem. Mass. Tech. Collaborative, 1996-2002. Served to cpl. U.S. Army, 1953-55. Recipient Lunsford Richardson award, 1961, Marie Curie award in Nuclear Medicine, 1992; sr. Hayes Fulbright fellow, 1975-76, Henry A. Hill award for Outstanding Contbns. to the Northeastern Sect., Am. Chem. Soc., 1998. Fellow: AAAS (mem. at large 1983—87, chmn. pharm. sci. sec. 1992—93), Am. Assn. Pharm. Scis. (Rsch. Achievement award in medicinal chemistry 1982); mem.: Am. Chem. Soc. (bd. editors Jour. Medicinal Chemistry 1974—88, chmn. divsn. med. chem. 1982, councilor 1985—, trustee 1989—93, N.E. sect. chmn.-elect 2002, chmn. 2003), Am. Soc. Exptl. Pharm. and Exptl. Therapeutics, Am. Soc. Neurosci., Acad. Pharm. Scis. Office: Harvard Med Sch/McLean Hosp ADARC 115 Mill St Belmont MA 02478-1041 E-mail: jneumeyer@mclean.harvard.edu.

NEUNER, FRANK X., JR., lawyer; b. Baton Rouge, May 23, 1951; s. Frank X. and Mary Frances (Ellis) N.; m. Tracy Owens, May 27, 1972; children: Gretchen, Hearin, Trip, Mary Frances. BS in Mgmt., La. State U., 1972, JD, 1976. Bar: La. 1976, Tex. 1993; U.S. Dist. Ct. (Ea. Dist. La.) U.S. Dist. Ct. (We. Dist. La.), U.S. Ct. Appeals (5th cir.). Assoc. Franklin, Moore & Walsh, Baton Rouge, 1976-77; ptnr. Onebane, Donohoe, et al, Lafayette, La., 1977-87, Laborde & Neuner, Lafayette, 1987—. Pres. United Way Acadiana, campaign chmn.; chmn. bd. dirs. Our Lady of Lourdes Regional Med. Ctr., Lafayette; Lafayette adv. bd. Iberia Bank Corp.; founding mem. bd. dirs. Cmty. Found. Acadiana; co-chmn. Lafayette Outreach for Civil Justice. Bd. dirs. United Way, Lafayette, chmn. leadership campaign, 1992; pres. Cathedral Carmel Found., Lafayette, 1987-91; bd. dirs. Nike La. Open, Lafayette, 1992-93. Mem. ABA (mem. House of Delegates), Lafayette Parish Bar Assn. (pres. 1988), La. State Bar Assn. (mem. House of Delegates 1980-96, past chmn. professionalism and quality of life com., bd. gov. 1997-99, treas. 2002-04, pres. 2005-06; David A. Hamilton Lifetime Achievement award 2004, Professionalism award 2006, Pres. award 2006), Lafayette Parish Bar Assn. (past pres.), Maritime Law Assn., Def. Rsch. Inst., La. Assn. Def. Counsel, Internat. Assn. Def. Counsel, Southeastern Admiralty Law Inst., Fedn. Def. and Corp. Counsel, Acadiana Inns of Ct. (past pres., team leader). Republican. Roman Catholic. Office: Laborde & Neuner Ste 200 1001 W Pinhook Rd Lafayette LA 70505-2828 Office Phone: 337-237-7000. Office Fax: 337-233-9450. Business E-Mail: fxnjr@ln-law.com. *

NEUNER, LYNN K., lawyer; b. Providence, July 15, 1967; BA summa cum laude, Williams Coll., 1989; JD, Yale U., 1992. CLU U.S. Supreme Ct., 2001; bar: Conn. 1992, N.Y. 1994, U.S. Dist. Ct. (so. dist.) NY 1996, U.S. Dist. Ct. Conn. 2001, US Dist. Ct. (ea. dist.), NY 2001, U.S. Ct. Appeals (2nd cir.) 2004. Law clk. Hon. H. Lee Sarokin, U.S. Dist. Ct., Dist. N.J., 1992—93, Hon. John M. Walker Jr., U.S. Ct. Appeals, second cir., 1993—94; ptnr. Simpson Thacher & Bartlett LLP, NYC, 1994—, co-chmn. recruiting com., litig. training com. & diversity com. Mem. bd. editors, co-author Ins. Coverage News Bull. Named one of Litigation's Rising Stars, The Am. Lawyer, 2007. Mem.: Yale Law Sch. Alumni Fund (mem. bd. dirs.), Conn. Bar Assn., ABA (co-chmn. property ins. sub-com.), N.Y. State Bar Assn., Assn. Bar City N.Y. (fed. ct. com. 2003—). Office: Simpson Thacher & Bartlett LLP 425 Lexington Ave New York NY 10017-3954 Office Phone: 212-455-2696. Office Fax: 212-455-2502. Business E-Mail: lneuner@stblaw.com. *

NEUNZIG, CAROLYN MILLER, elementary, middle and high school educator; b. LI, May 5, 1930; kd. Stanley and Grace (Walsh) Miller; m. Herbert Neunzig, May 28, 1955; children: Kurt Miller, Keith Weidler. BA, Beaver Coll., Glen Side, Pa., 1953; MSSc, Syracuse U., 1989; postgrad., Adelphi U.; Cert., N.C. State U., Raleigh. Cert. in elem. edn., reading, history and English, N.C., permanent cert. in secondary English, N.Y., leader, Great Books Found. Reading tchr. grades K-6 St. Timothy's Sch., Raleigh, N.C., 1971-83, 5th grade tchr., 1983-88, 5th grade lead tchr., 1986-88; tchr. English and geography 7th grade St. Timothy's Mid. Sch., Raleigh, 1991—; tchr Am. govt. 12th grade St. Timothy's Mid. Sch./Hale H.S., Raleigh, 1991-93. Instr. continuing edn. program history Meredith Coll., Raleigh, 1990-91, spl. high sch. registration commr., 1991-93, instr. presdl. classroom, 1998-2007; mem. Ctr. Study of Presidency, 1998-2005. Asst. election ofcl. Wake County, N.C., 200, 04. Mem. AAUW, Acad. Polit. Sci.

NEURAUTER, ELIZABETH STRAIN, secondary school educator; b. Indpls., Mar. 7, 1959; d. Edward Richard Strain and Elizabeth Meyer (Strain) Gunn; m. Ronald Otto Neurauter, July 7, 1984; children: Stacy Marie, Ronald Paul, Beatrice Grace, Clara Helen. BA, Elmhurst Coll., Ill., 1981; EdM, Nat. Louis U., Wheeling, Ill., 2004; cert. advanced studies ednl. leadership, Nat. Louis U., 2005. Cert. tchr. English, ESL and psychology Ill. Staff asst. for vol. affairs ESL/ABE dept. Coll. DuPage, Glen Ellyn, Ill., 1991—94, ESL tchr. H.S. summer credit program, 2002—06; tutor English lang. learner, asst. dir. student activities Glenbard South H.S., Glen Ellyn, 1994—. Presenter in field; adj. faculty adult and family svcs. Joliet Jr. Coll., Ill., 2006—. Legis. apptd. mem. Ill. Literacy Coun., 1998. Nominee Golden Apple award, 2000; named Person of Character, Glen Ellyn Character Counts Coalition, 2004. Mem.: AAUW, NEA, ASCD, Ill. Edn. Assn., Nat. Coun. Tchrs. English, Archaeol. Conservancy. Republican. Avocations: archaeology, real estate. Home: 22W521 Burr Oak Dr Glen Ellyn IL 60137 Office: Glenbard South HS 23W200 Butterfield Rd Glen Ellyn IL 60137 Office Phone: 630-469-6500.

NEUREITER, NORMAN P., science association director; b. Jan. 24, 1932; m. Georgine Reid; 4 children. BS in Chemistry, U. Rochester, 1952; PhD in Organic Chemistry, Northwestern U., 1957. With Humble Oil & Refining Co., 1957—63, NSF Internat. Affairs Office, 1963—65; dep. sci. attache U.S. Dept. State, Bonn, 1965—67, sci. attache Warsaw, 1967—69; with White House Office Sci. and Tech. Policy, 1969—73, Tex. Instruments, 1973—96, v.p. corp. staff, 1980—89, dir. Japan, v.p. Asia, 1989—96; sci. and tech. adv. to U.S. Sec. of State, 2000—03; dir. ctr. sci., tech., and security policy AAAS, 2004—. Disting. presdl. fellow NAS Internat. Affairs, 2003—; space studies bd. NAS/Nat. Rsch. Coun., 2004—. Fellow: Am. Acad. Arts & Scis. Office: AAAS 1200 New York Ave NW Washington DC 20005 Home Phone: 703-535-9655; Office Phone: 202-326-6493. Business E-Mail: neureit@aas.org. *

NEUROHR, SHIRLEY ANN, retired special education educator; b. Chgo., Nov. 18, 1936; d. Anton and Anna (Ludvik) Sedlak; m. Joseph Henry Neurohr, Apr. 7, 1956 (dec. 1995); children: Debora Neurohr-Wearne, Kathleen Neurohr Rodenhauser, Jacqueline Neurohr Rueden; m. James Brennan, 2001. AA in Edn., Morton Coll., 1955; BA Psychology/Sociology summa cum laude, Mundelein Coll., 1977; MS in Edn. Adminstrn. with dept. honors, Winona State U., 1983. Cert. elem. edn tchr., learning disabilities edn., behavioral disorders edn., elem. adminstrn. Elem. tchr. St. Mary's Cath. Sch., Tomah, Wis., 1978-80, elem. prin., 1980-85; secondary tchr. behaviorally disordered Sparta (Wis.) Sr. H.S., 1985-86, 86—; elem. tchr. behaviorally disordered Tomah Area Sch. Dist., 1986-87, secondary tchr. behaviorally disordered, 1987-90, secondary tchr. learning disabled, 1990—2001; ret., 2001. Mem. Edn. for Employment Coun., Tomah, 1990-95, Spl. Edn. Transition Task Force, Tomah, 1988-93, Sch. to Work Task Force, Tomah, 1990-95. Troop leader, program cons., v.p. coun. Girl Scouts DuPage County Coun., DuPage, Ill., 1963-77; lay min. Diocese of LaCrosse, Wis., 1985; mem. St. Mary's Coun. Cath. Women, 1977—. Recipient Thanks Badge, DuPage County coun. Girl Scouts U.S., 1976; named Woman of Yr., St. Joseph's Coun. of Cath. Women, 1977. Mem. AAUW (Tomah br. 1977-95, v.p., past sec.-treas.), ASCD, Nat. Coun. Tchrs. English, Midwest Reading Coun., Tomah Edn. Assn. (bldg. rep. 1986, asst. v.p., pres. 2000), Sierra Club Nat. Wildlife Found., Crane Found., Monroe County Ret. Tchrs. Assn (pres. 2007), Master Gardeners Assn., Delta Kappa Gamma (past sec. Alpha Upsilon chpt., past pres.). Democrat. Roman Catholic. Avocations: travel, gardening, birding. Home: 23584 Emblem Ave Tomah WI 54660-9731 Personal E-mail: shirlgym@charter.net.

NEUTRA, DION, architect; b. LA, Oct. 8, 1926; s. Richard Joseph and Dione (Niedermann) N.; m. Lynn Smart; children: Gregory, Wendy, Haig, Nicholas. Student, Swiss Inst. Tech., 1947-48; B.Arch. cum laude, U. So. Calif., 1950. With Richard J. Neutra (architect), Los Angeles, 1942-55; assoc. Neutra & Alexander, Los Angeles, 1955-60; assoc. Robert E. Alexander, Los Angeles, 1960-62; prin. Richard & Dion Neutra, Architects and Assos., Los Angeles, 1962—; pres. Richard J. Neutra, Inc., 1970—. Exec. cons. Neutra Inst. for Survival Through Design, LA; lectr. Calif. State U., LA, Sacramento City Coll., Mira Costa State U., Cabrillo State U., Soka U., Tokyo, San Diego City Coll., Germany, Switzerland, England, Austria, SFA, Paris, 2006; vis. prof. Calif. State U., Pomona, 1970, 1985—86, Va. Commonwealth U., 1998; vis. lectr. U. Minn., 2000, Fullerton U., 2001, Nat. Bldg. Mus., 2002, SHPO, Puerto Rico, 2003, U. So. Calif. Prin. works include various residential, ednl., religious and instnl. facilities including Am. Embassy Karachi, Pakistan, Gettysburg Cyclorama Ctr., Simpson Coll. Libr., Adelphi Univ. Libr., Libr. and Resource Ctr. for City of Huntington Beach, Calif., Treetops Townhouses, 1980; exhbns. View from Inside, 1984, 86, 92, 98, 99, travelling show, 2000, Visions & Evies, Vienna, 1995, Am. Century Art and Culture, Whitney Mus., NYC, 1999. Mem. Silver Lake-Echo Park Dist. Plan Adv. Com., Master Plan City of LA, 1970-71; mem. Citizens to Save Silver Lake, 1973-76; dir. Child Care and Devel. Services, 1970-71, Preservation and Maintenance of Existing Neutra Projects. Served with USNR, 1944-46. Street named Neutra Place in firm's honor, Silverlake, 1992; Neutra Centennial, 1992, Firm's 80th Anniversary Celebration, 2006; fellow Neutra Inst. for Survival Through Design, 2004. Mem. AIA, Nat. Council Archtl. Registration Bds., Alpha Rho Chi. Studio: Richard & Dion Neutra 2440 Neutra Pl Los Angeles CA 90039-4400 Office Phone: 323-666-1806. E-mail: dion@neutra.org.

NEUWIRTH, ALAN JAMES, lawyer; b. NYC, July 4, 1943; s. Bernard and Audrey (Hattenbach) N.; m. Patricia E. Neuwirth, Sept. 4, 1966; children: John A., Daniel P. BA, Lehigh U., 1965; JD, NYU, 1969. Bar: N.Y. 1970, U.S. Dist. Ct. (so. and ea. dists.) N.Y. 1972, U.S. Ct. Appeals (2d cir.) 1972, U.S. Ct. Internat. Trade 1983, U.S. Ct. Appeals (Fed. cir.) 1984, U.S. Supreme Ct. 1988. Assoc. Miller & Summit, NYC, 1970-72, Ratheim, Hoffman, Kassel & Silverman, NYC, 1973-75; ptnr. Kassel, Neuwirth & Geiger, NYC, 1976-86, Webster & Sheffield, NYC, 1987-90; mng. ptnr. Tokyo Office Morgan, Lewis & Bockius LLP, sr. ptnr., bus. & fin. practice group, 1990—. With U.S. Army, 1969-74, USAR. Mem. ABA, Assn. of Bar of City of N.Y., Internat. Trade Commn., Trial Lawyers Assn. Office: Morgan Lewis & Bockius LLP 101 Park Ave New York NY 10178-0060 Office Fax: 212-309-6001. Business E-Mail: aneuwirth@morganlewis.com.

NEUWIRTH, BEBE (BEATRICE NEUWIRTH), dancer, actress; b. Newark, Dec. 31, 1958; d. Lee Paul and Sydney Anne Neuwirth; m. Paul Dorman, 1984 (div.); m. Michael Danek. Student, Juilliard Sch., 1976-77. Appeared: (on Broadway) A Chorus Line (as Sheila), 1975-90, Dancin', 1978-82, Little Me, 1982, Sweet Charity, 1986-87 (Tony award for best featured actress in a musical, 1986), Damn Yankees, 1994-95, Chicago, 1996 (Tony award for best actress in a musical, 1997, Outer Critics Circle award for best actress in a musical, 1997, Drama League Award for disting. performance, 1997, Drama Desk Award for outstanding actress in a musical, 1997, Astaire Award for best female dancer, 1997), Fosse, 1999-2001, Funny Girl, 2002, Here Lies Jenny, 2004, Chicago, 2007; (off Broadway) include West Side Story, 1981, Upstairs at O'Neal's, 1982-83, The Road to Hollywood, 1984, Just So, 1985, Waiting in the Wings: The Night the Understudies Take the Stage, 1986, Showing Off, 1989, Kiss of the Spider Woman (London), 1993, Pal Joey, 1995, Here Lies Jenny, 2004. Prin. dancer on Broadway Dancin', 1982; leading dance role Kicks, 1984. Actor: (TV series) The Edge of Night, 1981, Cheers, 1986-93 (Emmy award for Best Supporting Actress in a Comedy Series 1990, 91), (voice) Aladdin, 1993, (voice) All Dogs Go to Heaven: The Series, 1996, Deadline, 2000-01; (TV series guest appearances) Frasier, 1994-2003; (TV miniseries) Wild Palms, 1993; (TV films) Without Her Consent, 1990, Unspeakable Acts, 1990, Dash and Lilly, 1999, Cupid & Cate, 2000, Sounds From a Town I Love, 2001; (films) Say Anything, 1989, Green Card, 1990, Bugsy, 1991, The Paint Job, 1992, Malice, 1993, Jumanji, 1995, (voice) All Dogs Go to Heaven 2, 1996, The Adventures of Pinocchio, 1996, The Associate, 1996, Dear Diary, 1996, Celebrity, 1998, The Faculty, 1998, (voice) An All Dogs Christmas Carol, 1998, Summer of Sam, 1999, Liberty Heights, 1999, Getting to Know You, 1999, Tadpole, 2002, How to Lose a Guy in 10 Days, 2003, Le Divorce, 2003, The Big Bounce, 2004. Vol. performances for March of Dimes Telethon, 1986, Cystic Fibrosis Benefit Children's Ball, 1986, Ensemble Studio Theater Benefit, 1986, Circle Repertory Co. Benefit, 1986, all in N.Y.C. Democrat.

NEUWIRTH, MICHAEL G., orthopedist, surgeon, educator; b. NYC, Oct. 9, 1948; BA with distinction, Cornell U.; MD cum laude, SUNY Downstate Med. Sch., 1974. Cert. Am. Bd. Orthopaedic Surgery, 1980, lic. NY. Intern, dept. surgery Kings County Hosp., Bklyn., 1973—74; resident orthopaedics Hosp. For Joint Diseases Orthopaedic Inst., NYC, 1974—78, attending, orthopaedics, 1979, chief scoliosis svc., 1988, chief spine svc., 1991; fellow spinal surgery rsch. Rush-Presbyn.-St. Luke's Med. Ctr., Chgo., 1978—79; spinal cons. City Hosp. Ctr. at Elmhurst, NY, 1979—83; attending, orthopaedics Beth Israel Med. Ctr., NY, 1979; assoc. attending NYU/Tisch, NYC, 1995; dir. Spine Inst. of NY, Beth Israel Med. Ctr., NYC, 1996—. Asst. clin. prof. orthopaedics Mount Sinai Sch. Medicine, 1979; assoc. clin. prof. orthopaedics NYU Sch. Medicine, 1995—. Author: The Scoliosis Sourcebook; contbr. articles to med. jours. Fellow: ACS, Am. Acad. Orthop. Surgeons, Scoliosis Rsch. Soc. (bd. mem. 1996, chmn., instrumentation com. 1990, sect. leader, core curriculum 1999); mem.: Scoliosis Assn., NY State Soc. Orthop. Surgeons, NY State Med. Soc., NY County Med. Soc., NY Acad. Medicine, Alpha Omega Alpha. Office: Spine Inst of NY Beth Israel Med Ctr 10 Union Square E Ste 5P New York NY 10003 Office Phone: 212-844-8680. Office Fax: 212-844-8681. *

NEUWIRTH, ROBERT SAMUEL, obstetrician, gynecologist, educator; b. NYC, July 11, 1933; s. Abraham Alexander and Phyllis Neuwirth; children from previous marriage: Susan, Jessica, Laura, Michael, Alexander. BS, Yale U., 1955, MD, 1958. Intern Presbyn. Hosp., NYC, 1958-59, resident, 1959-64; asst. prof. ob-gyn. Columbia U., NYC, 1964-68, assoc. prof., 1968-71, prof., 1972-2001, Babcock prof., 1977-2001, Babcock prof. emeritus, 2001—. Dir. ob-gyn. Bronx Lebanon Hosp., NYC, 1967-72, Woman's Hosp., NYC, St. Luke's Hosp. Ctr., 1974—, St. Luke's Roosevelt Hosp., 1981-91; prof. Albert Einstein Coll. Medicine, 1971-72; cons. WHO, NIH, AID, FDA; interim dir. St. Luke's Roosevelt Hosp., 1998-2000. Author: Hysteroscopy, 1975; contbr. articles to profl. jours. Mem.: ACOG, Assn. Vol. Sterilization (chmn. biomed. com. 1971—), Am. Assn. Profs. Ob-Gyn., NY Obstet. Soc., Soc. Gynecol. Investigation, Am. Gynecol. and Obstet. Soc. Office: St Lukes Roosevelt Hosp 1000 10th Ave Dept Ob New York NY 10019-1147 Office Phone: 212-523-8368.

NEVAI, LUCIA, writer; b. Des Moines, Sept. 11, 1945; d. Darwin Thomas and Ruth Marcella (Courson) Lynner; m. Andrew Nevai, July 6, 1968 (div. Sept. 1984); children: Nandor, Matthew. BA, New Sch. Social Rsch., 1967. Author: (novels) Seriously, (short stories) Normal, Star Game (Winner of The Iowa Short Fiction Award 1987), (anthologies) New Stories from The South 2002, The Year's Best, Francis Ford Coppola's Zoetrope: All Story, Fault Lines: Stories of Divorce, The Algonkian, The Way We Write Now: Short Stories from the AIDS Crisis, Closing: An Anthology of American Short Fiction on The Art of Selling, American Fiction Award Anthology No. 4, The Iowa Award: The Best Stories from Twenty Years, Best of the South, 2005, Best of Tin House, 2006, (short stories) Glimmer Train, 2006, My Father Married Your Mother: Writers Talk About Stepparents, Stepchildren, and Everyone in Between, 2006; contbr. articles in numerous profl. jours. Recipient Iowa Award For Lit., Iowa Review, 2001, Winner PEN Syndicated Fiction Award, Chgo. Tribune Mag., Am. Fiction Award, American Fiction No. 4, Best Fiction, Newsday Mag., State Mag.

NEVANS, ROY NORMAN, food products executive, producer; b. NYC, July 1, 1931; s. Al Nevans and Lillian (Schiff) Margolis; m. Virginia Place, Dec. 31, 1961; children: Lisa Ann, Laurel Sue, Judith Lynn. BS, U. Pa., 1953; MBA, Columbia U., 1957. Mgmt. trainee Henningsen Foods, Inc., NYC, 1958-60, mgr. export sales div., 1960-65, mgr. nat. sales div., 1965-70, v.p. mktg. White Plains, NY, 1970-90; mng. dir. Henningsen Van Den Burg, Waalyk, Holland, 1979-90, Henningsen Nederland B.V., Waalyk, 1984-90, Henningsen Foods, Ltd., London, 1977-90; pres. Royco Internat. Inc., Stamford, Conn., 1991—. Pres Royal Productions, Ltd, New York, NY, 1966, New York, 73, Int TV Productions, Ltd, London, 1978—; exec producer NCM Entertainment, Inc, New York, NY, 1982—; bd dirs Global Educ Mgt, Wall St Inst, World Trade Club. Prodr.: (Broadway plays) Gandhi, 1969, Solitaire Double Solitaire, 1972; (TV series) Juke Box, 1978—79; exec. prodr.: (TV miniseries) Roots of Rock and Roll, 1981. Lt comdr USN, 1953—56. Mem.: NATAS, US Naval Order, US Naval War Col, Univ Pa Club, Jaguar Touring Club, River Club. Avocations: classic cars collector, boating, theater. also: 1945 Gulf of Mexico Dr #108 Longboat Key FL 34228 also: 302 W 12th St New York NY 10014 Office: Royco Internat Inc 1177 High Ridge Rd Stamford CT 06905-1203 E-mail: roycointl@att.net.

NEVELLE, PHYN, actress, judge; d. Gerhard and Brigitte Susanne Lohmeier. Grad., Gymnasium Tettnang, Germany, 1991; state exam., U. Konstanz, Germany, 1996; judge, Justizministerium Baden-Wuerttemberg, Germany, 1998. State exam.: Baden-Wuerttemberg, Germany 1998. Legal rschr. County Ct., Waldshut-Tiengen, 1996—97, Local Civil Ct., Waldshut-Tiengen, 1996; lawyer, rschr. Victor Grazelli, Ravensburg, Baden-Wuerttemberg, 1997, Kues & Ptnr., Konstanz, Baden-Wuerttemberg, 1997—98; lawyer Landratsamt Waldshut-Tiengen, Baden-Wuerttemberg, 1997; state atty. rep. in ct. State Attorney's Office, Waldshut-Tiengen, 1997; lawyer, rschr. Ferdie & Gouz, Miami, 1998. Voice-over prodr., 2000—; conf. chair Animation Conf. 2002, London, 2002; alternate dir. bd. dirs. Network Rail CP Finance plc, SFM Dirs. Ltd., SFM Dirs. (No. 2) Ltd., SFM Corp. Svcs. Ltd., SFM Nominees Ltd. Actor: (films) Rope Art; (plays) Woman in the Moon, The Yiddish Queen Lear. Sponsor BornFree Found., London, 2004; youth group leader Gemeinde Meckenbeuren, Baden-Wuerttemberg, 1986—88; sponsor Philipinien Hilfe, Tettnang, Baden-Wuerttemberg, Germany, 1994—2002; dog walker Tierheim, Konstanz, Baden-Wuerttemberg, 1991—97. Mem.: Brit. Actors Equity. Avocations: scuba diving, martial arts, nature and philosophy studies, skydiving, ballroom dancing. Personal E-mail: phynnevelle@hotmail.com.

NEVELOFF, JAY A., lawyer; b. Bklyn., Oct. 11, 1950; m. Arlene Sillman, Aug. 26, 1972; children: David, Kevin. BA, Bklyn. Coll., 1971; JD, NYU, 1974. Bar: N.Y. 1975, D.C. 1992, U.S. Dist. Ct. (so. and ea. dists.) N.Y. 1975, U.S. Ct. Appeals (2d cir.) 1975, U.S. Supreme Ct. 1982. Assoc. Marshall, Bratter, Greene, Allison & Tucker, NYC, 1974-82,

Rosenman, Colin, Freund, Lewis & Cohen, NYC, 1982-83, ptnr., 1983-88, Kramer, Levin, Naftalis, Nessen, Kamin & Frankel, NYC, 1988—. Editor N.Y. Real Property Service. Mem. planning bd. Briarcliff Manor, 1995—. Mem. ABA (vice chmn. com. partnerships, joint ventures and other investment vehicles 1988-95), Am. Law Inst., Am. Coll. Real Estate Attys., Am. Coll. Mortgage Attys., NY State Bar Assn. (financing com.), Endeavor Global Adv. Bd., Practising Law Inst. (lectr. 1988—, mem. adv. bd. 1991—), Assn. Bar City NY (real property law com., lectr. 1984-88), Law Jours. Seminars (lectr. 1987—), Strategic Resources Inst. (lectr. 1994-98), Internat. Health Network Soc. (vice chmn. 1995-2000), Inst. Internat. Rsch. (lectr. 1994—), Info. Mgmt. Network (lectr. 2004-), Am. Conf. Inst. (lectr. 2006-). Home: 134 Alder Dr Briarcliff Manor NY 10510-2218 Office: Kramer Levin Naftalis & Frankel LLP 1177 Ave of the Americas New York NY 10036 Office Phone: 212-715-9290. Business E-Mail: jneveloff@kramerlevin.com.

NEVES, DAVID, musician, educator; b. Central Falls, RI, Aug. 7, 1955; s. Joaquim Almeida and Maria Rosa N.; m. Janice Poulin, Aug. 6, 1977; children: Kristin Marie, Jennifer Anne, Amanda Michaela. B in Music Edn., Berklee Coll. Music, 1976; MAT in Saxophone, R.I. Coll., 1981. Cert. music tchr., music supr., RI. Choral dir. Scituate (R.I.) High Sch., 1976-79, band dir., supr. music, 1979—. Prin. saxophone Am. Band, 1978—. Mem. Gov.'s Arts Task Force State of RI., 1999-00. Recipient Milken Edn. award Milken Family Found., 1991; named RI Tchr. of Yr., 2002. Mem. Nat. Band Assn., Nat. Edn. Assn., RI. Music Educators Assn. (mem. band, pres. 1985-87, treas. 1996-98, editor 1989-91, Meritorious Svc. award 1994, guest condr. concert band 1994, guest condr. jazz 1997). Avocation: computers. Home: 260 Phenix Ave Cranston RI 02920-4018 Office: Scituate High Sch 94 Trimtown Rd Scituate RI 02857-1947 *

NEVES, KERRY LANE, lawyer; b. San Angelo, Tex., Dec. 19, 1950; s. Herman Walter and Geraldine (Ball) N.; m. Sharon Lynn Briggs, July 28, 1973; 1 child, Erin Lesli. BBA, U. Tex., 1975, JD, 1978. Bar: Tex. 1978, U.S. Dist. Ct. (so. and ea. dists.) Tex. 1979, U.S. Ct. Appeals (5th cir.) 1979, U.S. Dist. Ct. (we. dist.) 1980; cert. personal injury trial law, Tex. Bd. Legal Specialization, 1994. Ptnr. Mills, Shirley, Eckel & Bassett, Galveston, Tex., 1978—93, Neves & Crowther, Galveston, Tex., 1993—2002; pvt. practice Law Offices of Kerry L. Neves, Galveston, 2002—06, Dickinson, Tex., 2007—. Vice-chmn. Bldg. Stds. Commn., Dickinson, Tex., 1991—98; mem. City Coun., Dickinson, 1998—; chmn. Galveston County Rep. Party, 2007—; bd. dirs. Houston-Galveston Area Coun., 2002—. Sgt. USMC, 1969—72. Fellow Tex. Bar Found. (life); mem. ABA, State Bar Tex. (grievance com. 1989-92, disciplinary rules profl. conduct com. 1990-92, dir. dist. 5 1997-2000), Galveston County Bar Assn. (pres. 1989-90), U. Tex. Law Alumni Assn. (pres. 1991-92). Avocations: gardening, wine, reading. Home: RR 2 Box 95 Dickinson TX 77539-9204 Home Phone: 281-337-4006; Office Phone: 281-337-5414. Personal E-mail: bkwds@aol.com.

NEVIASER, ROBERT JON, orthopaedic surgeon, educator; b. Washington, Nov. 21, 1936; s. Julius Salem and Jane Frances (Gibbons) N.; m. Anne Maclean Shedden, Dec. 3, 1966; children: Jeanne Nicole, Robert Jon Jr., Ian Maclean, Andrew Shedden. Grad., Phillips Acad., Andover, Mass., 1954; AB, Princeton U., 1958; MD, Jefferson Med. Coll., 1962. Diplomate Am. Bd. Orthop. Surgery with cert. of added qualification in surgery of hand. Intern NY Hosp., Cornell Med. Ctr., NYC, 1962-63, asst. resident, 1963-64; asst. resident in orthopaedic surgery NY Orthop. Hosp., Columbia-Presbyn. Med. Ctr., NYC, 1964-66, jr. Annie C. Kane fellow, resident, 1966-67; fellow in surgery of the hand Orthop. Hosp., LA, 1969-70; asst. prof. divsn. orthop. and hand surgery, chmn. dept. U. Conn., Hartford, 1970-71; assoc. prof. orthop. surgery George Washington U., Washington, 1971-76, prof., 1976—, dir. orthop. edn., assoc. chmn. dept. orthop. surgery, 1984-87, chmn. dept. orthop. surgery, 1987—; chmn. governing bd. Med. Faculty Assocs. George Washington U. Med. Ctr., 1995-98, trustee, 2000—03, 2005—. Editor-in-chief Jour. of Shoulder and Elbow Surgery, 1997—; contbr. articles in field to profl. jours. Lt. comdr. USNR, 1967-69. Fellow Am. Soc. Surgery of the Hand, Am. Acad. Orthop. Surgeons, Ea. Orthop. Assn., Am. Shoulder and Elbow Surgeons, Am. Orthop. Assn., Princeton Club (NY), Manor Country Club, Cosmos Club, Club at Four Streams, Alpha Omega Alpha. Republican. Office: 2150 Pennsylvania Ave NW Washington DC 20037-3201 Home Phone: 301-869-1919; Office Phone: 202-741-3301. Business E-Mail: rneviaser@mfa.gwu.edu.

NEVILL, WILLIAM ALBERT, chemistry professor; b. Indpls., Jan. 1, 1929; s. Irwin Lowell and Mary Marie (Barker) N.; m. Nancy Neiman (Roll), May 19, 1979; children: Paul David, John Michael, Steven Joseph, Anne Marie, Deborah Ruth. BS, Butler U., 1951; PhD, Calif. Inst. of Tech., 1954. Rsch. chemist Procter and Gamble, Cin., 1954; chemistry prof., chmn. dept. Grinnell Coll., 1956-67; prof. chemistry Ind. U., Purdue, Indpls., 1967-83, chmn. dept., 1967-72, dean sch. sci., 1972-79, dir. grad. studies, 1979-83; pres. B and N Cons. Co., 1972-93; vice chancellor acad. affairs La. State U., Shreveport, La., 1983-85, prof., 1983-94; pres. Catoctin Assoc., 1993—. Arbitrator, mediator, Ind. Employment Rels. Bd., 1975-83. Author: Gen. Chemistry, 1967, Expt. in Gen. Chemistry, 1968. Bd. dir. Indpls. Sci. and Engring. Found., 1972-75, 79-82, Westminster Found., Lafayette, Ind., 1972-74, Am. Chem. Soc., 1986-92. With U.S. Army, 1954-56; col., USAR, 1956-84. Grantee NSF, 1959-74; Grantee NIH, 1963-70; Grantee Office Naval Rsch., 1953 Mem. Ind. Acad. Sci., Am. Chem. Soc., chmn. sect. 1972, counselor 1973-92. Presbyterian.

NEVILLE, AARON, musician; b. New Orleans, La., Jan. 24, 1941; m. Joel; 1 d., Ernestine; 3 s., Aaron, Jr., Ivan, Jason. Singer (singles): Over You, 1959, Tell It Like It Is, 1966, 91; (albums): Greatest Hits, 1967, Orchid in the Storm, 1990, The Classic: My Greatest Gift, 1990, Tell It Like It Is, 1991, Warm Your Heart, 1991, The Grand Tour, 1993, Aaron Neville's Soulful Christmas, 1993, The Tatooed Heart, 1995, Can't Stop my Heart, 1995, Doing It Their Own Way, 1996, To Make Me Who I Am, 1997, Uptown Rulin'-Best of Neville, 1999, Valence Street, 1999, Very Best of Aaron Neville, 2000, Devotion, 2000, Aaron Neville: Ultimate Collection, 2001, Aaron Neville: The Best of, the Millenium Collection, 2002, Gospel Roots, 2003, Love Songs, 2003, Believe, 2003, Nature Boy, 2003, Aaron Neville Christmas Prayer, 2005; singles (with Linda Ronstadt) Don't Know Much, 1990 (Grammy award, Best Pop Duo with Linda Ronstadt, 1989), All My Life, 1990(Grammy award, Best Pop Duo with Linda Ronstadt, 1990), featured on Midnight at St. Jude's; albums (with Neville Brothers) Wild Tchoupatoulas, 1976, The Neville Brothers, 1977, Fiyo On the Bayou, 1981, Nevillization, 1984, Treacherous: A History of the Neville Brothers (vol. 1), 1986, Uptown, 1987, Yellow Moon, 1989, Brother's Keeper, 1990, Treacherous vol. 2, 1992, Family Groove, 1992, Live on Planet Earth, 1994, Mitakuye Oyasin, 1996, The Very Best of the Neville Brothers, 1997, Valance Street, 1999, Uptown Rulin, 1999, Walkin' In the Shadow of Life, 2004; guest appearances Superbowl XXIV, New Orleans, 1990, Superbowl XL, New Orleans, 2006. Recipient Grammy award with Neville Brothers, Best Pop Instrumental Performance for Healing Chant, 1989, Down Beat Blues, Soul, R&B Group award, 1990, Grammy award, Best Country Collaboration with vocals with Trisha Yearwood for I Fall to Pieces, 1994; co-recipient with Neville Brother, Chairman's award, NAACP Image awards, 2006; named Best Male Singer, Rolling Stones critics poll (2 years in row) Address: c/o William Morris Agy 151 El Camino Drive Beverly Hills CA 90212

NEVILLE, BRUCE DAVID, librarian; b. Painesville, Ohio, June 14, 1955; s. Wayne Foster and Barbara Lee (Naughton) N. BS, U. Miami, 1977; MLS, Fla. State U., 1992. Biologist Gen. Devel. Corp., Miami, 1977-83; assoc. scientist Environ. Sci. & Engring., Miami, 1983-86; environ. scientist Kimley-Horn & Assocs., West Palm Beach, Fla., 1986-87, Gaby & Gaby, Inc., South Miami, Fla., 1987-90; libr. Terra Inc., Tallahassee, Fla., 1990-92, U. Tex., El Paso, 1992-96, U. N.Mex., Albuquerque, 1996—. Co-author: The Wentletrap Book, 1999, New Mexico Bird Finding Guide, 3d edit., 2002, Science and Technology Research Writing Strategies for Students, 2002; contbr. articles to profl. jours. Elected bd. dirs. Tropical Audubon Soc., Miami, 1982-89. Mem. N.Mex. Ornithological Soc. (bd. dirs. 1998-2006), Fla. Ornithological Soc. (sec. 1985-93), Am. Soc. for Engring. Edn., Conchologists of Am., High Desert Shell Club (founder 1998—), Beta Phi Mu. Avocation: avid birder and conchologist. Office: Centennial Libr MSC05-3020 U Nmex Albuquerque NM 87131-0001 Office Phone: 505-277-4760. Business E-Mail: bneville@unm.edu.

NEVILLE, DAVID, apparel designer; b. Eng. m. Gucci Westman. Grad., Wellington Coll., Eng. With US equity markets divsn. ING, NYC; co-founder, head designer Rag & Bone, NYC, 2001—. Recipient Ecco Domani Fashion Found. award, 2006, Swarovski award for Emerging Talent Menswear, Coun. Fashion Designers Am., 2007. Office: Rag & Bone LLC 80 W 40th St New York NY 10018 Office Phone: 212-278-8214. Office Fax: 212-287-8242. *

NEVILLE, ELIZABETH EGAN, artist, educator; b. Albany, NY, May 16, 1937; d. Philip Sidney and Harriet Rust Egan; m. Robert Cummings Neville, June 8, 1963; children: Naomi Louise, Leonora Alice. BA, Smith Coll., 1959; MA in Tchg., Harvard U., 1961. Dir. Neville Art Enterprises, Milton, Mass., 1969—. Art instr. Town of Huntington, NY, 1982—88, Adelphi U., Garden City, NY, 1983—85; dir. Milton Art Mus., 1993—97, art instr., 1998—2006; lectr. in field. Art critic: Art N.Eng., 1998—2006; Represented in permanent collections Heckscher Mus., Huntington, L.I., Fine Arts Mus. L.I., Hempstead, N.Y., Maritime Mus., State U. N.Y., Throgs Neck, Katonah Gallery, N.Y., Hudson-Athens Lighthouse Preservation Soc., Symbols of Jesus, 2001, Boston Confucianism, 2000, The God Who Beckons, 1999, The Cosmology of Freedom, 1995, Creativity and God, 1995, God the Creator, 1992, Eternity and Times Flow, 1993, A Theology Primer, 1991, Behind the Masks of God, 1991, Recovery of the Measure, 1989, The Butterfly as Companion, 1989, The Puritan Smile, 1987, solo exhbns., Neville Gallery, 2004, Boston U. Sch. Theology, 1998, Claremont Sch. Theology, Calif., 1997, 1995, 1991, Sturdy Meml. Hosp. Gallery, Attleboro, Mass., 1997, Weston Theol. Inst., Mass., 1995, U. Mass. Med. Ctr. Gallery, Worcester, 1994, Kaaterskill Gallery, Columbia-Greene C.C., Hudson, N.Y., 1992, Milton Art Mus, Mass., 1990, NoHo Gallery, NYC, 1981, 1983. Mem. Newport Art Mus., RI, 2002—, Capt. Robert Forbes Mus., Milton, 1989—2007; pres. bd. trustees Milton Art Mus., 2001—06, 2003. Grantee, Henry Luce Found., 1990, Milton Cultural Arts Coun., 1995, 1996, 1997, 2006. Mem.: Nat. Mus. Women in Art (charter mem.), Women's Caucus for Art, Harvard Club Boston (adv. bd. fine arts com. 1998—2007), Smith Coll. Club Boston, Milton Garden Club (chair Smithsonian garden history 2001—07), Alpha Kappa XI. Democrat. Avocations: landscape architecture, photography, history, citrus horticulture.

NEVILLE, HELEN J., psychology professor, neuroscientist; BA in Psychology, Univ. BC; MA, Simon Fraser Univ.; PhD in Neuropsychology, Cornell Univ. Dir., brain devel. lab. Univ. Oreg., 1995—, prof., psychology, neuroscience, 1995—, assoc. dir., Inst. Neuroscience, 1998—2005, dir., Ctr. Cognitive Neuroscience, 1998—. Recipient Justine and Yves Sergent award, Montreal, 2000, Claude Pepper award, 1993—97. Fellow: Am. Psychological Soc., Am. Acad. Arts & Scis.; mem.: Soc. Exptl. Psychologists. Office: Brain Devel Lab 1227 Univ Oregon Eugene OR 97403-1227 Office Phone: 541-346-4248. Business E-Mail: neville@uoregon.edu. *

NEVILLE, JACK L. (DREW), JR., lawyer; b. Okla. City, Okla., July 29, 1947; BA, Univ. Okla., 1969, JD, 1972. Bar: Okla. 1972, Okla. Supreme Ct., US Dist. Ct. (we., no., ea. dist. Okla., so. dist. NY, so. dist. Fla., Colo., no., ea. dist. Tex.), US Ct. Appeals (5th, 7th, 10th, 11th cir.). Legis. asst. U.S. Senate, 1974—75; asst. U.S. atty. we. dist. Okla., 1975—76; atty, pvt. practice, 1976—2000; ptnr., litigation practice Hartzog Conger Cason & Neville, Okla. City, Okla., 2000—. Mem. adv. com. US Ct. Appeals (10th cir.). Master: Luther Bohanon Am. Inn of Ct.; fellow: Am. Coll. Trial Lawyers; mem.: ABA, Fed. Bar Assn. (past pres. Okla. City chpt.), Okla. Bar Assn., Okla. County Bar Assn. (dir.). Office: Hartzog Conger Cason & Neville Ste 1600 201 Robert S Kerr Ave Oklahoma City OK 73102 Office Phone: 405-235-7000. Office Fax: 405-996-3403. Business E-Mail: dneville@hartzoglaw.com.

NEVILLE, JAMES MORTON, retired lawyer, consumer products company executive; b. Mpls., May 28, 1939; s. Philip and Maurene (Morton) N.; m. Judie Martha Proctor, Sept. 9, 1961; children: Stephen Warren, Martha Maurene Hereford. BA, U. Minn., JD magna cum laude, 1964. Bar: Minn. 1964, Mo. 1984. Assoc. Neville, Johnson & Thompson, Mpls., 1964-69, ptnr., 1969-70; assoc. counsel Gen. Mills, Inc., Mpls., 1970-77, sr. assoc. counsel, 1977-83, corp. sec., 1976-83; v.p., sec., asst. gen. counsel Ralston Purina Co., St. Louis, 1983-84, v.p., gen. counsel, sec., 1984-96, v.p., gen. counsel, 1996-2000, v.p., sr. counsel, 2000-01; ret., 2001. Lectr. bus. law. U. Minn., 1967-71; chmn. The Thompson Ctr., 2002. Bd. mem. Haven of Grace, 1997—2000. Named Man of Yr., Edina Jaycees, 1967. Mem. ABA, Mo. Bar Assn., U.S. Supreme Ct. Bar Assn., St. Louis Bar Assn., U. Minn. Law Sch. Alumni Assn., Old Warson Country Club, Ladue Racquet Club, Order of Coif, Phi Delta Phi, Psi Upsilon. Episcopalian. Avocation: bridge. Home: 9810 Log Cabin Ct Saint Louis MO 63124-1133 Home Phone: 314-993-6607. Personal E-mail: jnev57@aol.com.

NEVILLE, PHOEBE, choreographer, dancer, educator; b. Swarthmore, Pa., Sept. 28, 1941; d. Kennith R. and Marion (Eberbach) Balsley; m. Philip E. Hipwell, June 21, 1969 (dissolved Sept. 1978); m. Philip Corner, Nov. 3, 1996. Student, Wilson Coll., 1959-61. Cert. practitioner body mind centering, registered somatic movement therapist. Instr. Bennington (Vt.) Coll., 1981-84, 87-88; vis. lectr. UCLA, 1984-86. Dancer, choreographer Judson Meml. Ch., N.Y.C., 1966—70, Dance Uptown Series, 1969, Cubiculo Theatre, 1972—75, Delacorte Dance Festival, 1976, Dance Umbrella Series, 1977, Riverside Dance Festival, 1976, 1978, N.Y. Seasons, 1979—, dancer, artistic dir. Phoebe Neville Dance Co., N.Y.C., 1975—, Jacob's Pillow Splash! Festival, 1988—, Dance Theater Workshop Winter Events, 1988—, Mersdith Wonk Benefit, 1994, performances with Philip Corner: Venice, Genoa, San Michele al' Adige, 1996—, BBB Festival, Thailand, Genoa, Salso Maggiore, Terme, 1997—, Seoul NY Max Festival, N.Y.C., 1998, Malpartida de Caseras, Spain, Caserano, Italy, 1998, Besancon, France, 1998, Paris, Lyon, 1999, Saluggia, Italy, 1999, Performance Festival, Odense, Denmark, 1999, 2001, Bassano del Grappa, Genoa, Italy, 2000, 2001, 2002, Novarra, Italy, 2002—; performances with, Ghent, Belgium, 2002—; performances with: Castelvetro di Modena, 2003; Argos Festival, 2003. Recipient Creative Artist Public Svc. award, 1975; Nat. Endowment for Arts fellow, 1975, 79, 80, 85-87, 92-94, Choreographic fellow N.Y. Found. for Arts, 1988. Mem.: Internat. Assn. Healthcare Practitioners, Internat. Somatic Movement Edn. and Therapy Assn. (registered), Body-Mind Centering Assn. (cert. practitioner and tchr.). Buddhist.

NEVILLE, ROY GERALD, research scientist, chemical executive, consultant; b. Bournemouth, Dorsetshire, Eng., Oct. 15, 1926; came to U.S., 1951, naturalized, 1957; s. Percy Herbert and Georgina Lallie (Jenkins) N.; m. Jeanne Frances Russ, July 26, 1952; children: Laura Jean, Janet Marilyn. BSc with honors, U. London, 1951; MSc, U. Oreg., 1952, PhD, 1954; FRIC, Royal Inst. Chemistry, London, 1963, DSc (hon.), 1973. Research chemist Monsanto Chem. co., Seattle, 1955-57; sr. chem. engr. Boeing Co., Seattle, 1957-58; sr. research scientist Lockheed Missiles & Space Co., Palo Alto, Calif., 1958-61; sr. staff scientist Aerospace Corp., El Segundo, Calif., 1961-63; prin. scientist Rockwell Internat. Corp., Los Angeles, 1963-67; head dept. materials Scis. Lab., Boeing Sci. Research Labs. Boeing Co., Seattle, 1967-69; sr. environ. engring. specialist Bechtel Corp., San Francisco, 1969-73; pres. Engring. & Tech. Cons., Inc., Redwood City, Calif., 1973—. Contbr. numerous sci. articles on inorganic and organic synthesis, thermally stable polymers, pollution control processes to profl. jours. and books; many U.S. and fgn. patents in field; associateship Southampton U., England, 1951. Founder, dir. R.G. Neville Hist. Chem. Libr. The Chem. Heritage Found., Phila.; dir. Sequoia Hosp. Found., Redwood City, Calif. Fulbright scholar to U.S., 1951; USPHS fellowship, 1951-52, Research Corp. fellow, 1952-54; chartered chemist, London. Fellow AAAS, Royal Soc. Chemistry (London), Am. Inst. Chemists; mem. AIChE, Am. Chem. Soc., History Sci. Soc., Soc. Study Early Chemistry, Royal Instn. Great Britain, Rsch. Soc. Am., Soc. Mining Engrs. of AIME, Calif. Mining Assn., Sigma Xi. Office: ETC Inc 1552 Viscaino Rd Pebble Beach CA 93953-3303

NEVILLE, THOMAS LEE, food service company executive; b. Columbus, Ind., Jan. 1, 1947; s. Frank Thomas and Esquline Coons (Davis) N.; m. Shavona Rose Lagneau, Aug. 10, 1966; children: Timothy David, Sherry Lynn. AAS, Austin Peay State U., Clarksville, Tenn., 1994. Cert. exec. chef; cert. food exec. Enlisted U.S. Army, 1966, apptd. WO1, 1976, commd. CW3, 1986; food advisor Army Food Rsch., Devel. and Engring. Ctr., Natick, Mass.; ret. U.S. Army, 1990; gen. mgr. KCA Corp., Hopkinsville, Ky., 1990—. Mem. Warrant Officers Assn., 1976-90. Mem. Ret. Officers Assn., Am. Soc. Quality Control, Am. Culinary Fedn., Am. Mgmt. Assn., Internat. Food Svc. Execs. Assn., Masons. Home: 1728 Clara Ct Clarksville TN 37040-7823 Office: KCA Corp PO Box 641 Hopkinsville KY 42241-0641 Office Phone: 270-886-5551. Business E-Mail: tneville@kcacorp.com.

NEVIN, CROCKER, investment banker; b. Tulsa, Mar. 14, 1923; s. Ethelbert Paul and Jennie Crocker (Fassett) N.; m. Mary Elizabeth Sherwin, Apr. 24, 1952 (div. 1984); children: Anne, Paul, Elizabeth, Crocker; m. Marilyn Elizabeth English, Nov. 3, 1984; 1 child, Jennie Fassett. Grad. with high honors, St. Paul's Sch., 1942; AB with high honors, Princeton U., 1946. With Vick Chem. Co., 1949-50, John Roberts Powers Cosmetic Co., 1950-52; with Marine Midland Grace Trust Co. of N.Y., 1952—, exec. v.p., 1964-66, pres., 1966-70, chmn. bd., chief exec. officer, 1968-73; also dir.; vice chmn. bd. Evans Products Co., NYC, 1974-76, Drexel Burnam Lambert Co., investment bankers, NYC, 1976-88; chmn. bd., chief exec. officer CF & I Steel Corp., Pueblo, Colo., 1985-93. Dir. Magnatck, Inc. Chmn. exec. com. ACCION Internat. Lt. (j.g.) AC USN, 1942-46. Mem. Riverside Yacht Club, N.Y. Yacht Club (N.Y.C.), Blind Brook Club. Home: 20 Hope Farm Rd Greenwich CT 06830

NEVIN, JOHN ROBERT, business educator, consultant; b. Joliet, Ill., Jan. 27, 1943; s. Robert Charles and Rita Alice (Roder) N.; m. Jeanne M. Conroy, June 10, 1967; children: Erin, Michael. BS, So. Ill. U., 1965; MS, U. Ill., 1968, PhD, 1972. Asst. prof. bus. U. Wis., Madison, 1970—77, assoc. prof. bus., 1977—83, prof. bus., 1983—, Grainger Wis. disting. prof. bus., 1989—, exec. dir. Grainger Ctr. for Supply Chain Mgmt., 1992—, assoc. dean masters program, 1999—2002, exec. dir. Ctr. Brand and Product Mgmt., 2003—07. Mem. investment adv. com. Venture Investors of Wis., Inc., Madison, 1986-99. Author: International Marketing: An Annotated Bibliography, 1983; mem. editl. bd. Jour. of Mtg. Channels, The Haworth Press, Inc., 1991—; contbr. articles to profl. jours. Bd. dirs. Madison Civic Ctr., 1983—99. Mem. Am. Mktg. Assn. (bd. dirs. PhD consortium 1979, editorial bd. Jour. of Mktg. Chgo. chpt. 1983-97), Assn. for Consumer Rsch. Avocations: golf, skiing, running. Home: 7514 Red Fox Trl Madison WI 53717-1860 Office: U Wis Grainger Ctr Supply Chain Mgmt 975 University Ave Madison WI 53706-1324 Office Phone: 608-262-8912. E-mail: jnevin@bus.wisc.edu.

NEVIN, PHILLIP, professional baseball player; b. Fullerton, Calif., Jan. 19, 1971; First baseman San Diego Padres, 1999—2005, Anaheim Angles, 1998—99, Detroit Tigers, 1995—97, Houston Astros, 1995—95, Tex. Rangers, 2005—06, Chgo. Cubs, 2006, Minn. Twins, 2006—. Office: Minn Twins H Humphrey Metrodome 900 S Fifth St Minneapolis MN 55415

NEVIN, ROBERT CHARLES, information systems executive; b. Dayton, Ohio, Nov. 4, 1940; s. Robert Steely and Virginia (Boehme) N.; m. Linda Sharon Fox, Apr. 16, 1966; children: Heather, Andrew. BA, Williams Coll., 1962; MBA, U. Pa., 1970. Fin. planning mgr. Huffy Corp., Dayton, Ohio, 1971-72, asst. treas., 1972-73, treas., 1973-75, v.p. fin., 1975-79, exec. v.p., 1982-85; pres., gen. mgr. Frabill Sporting Good, Milw., 1979-82; exec. v.p. Reynolds & Reynolds, Dayton, Ohio, 1985-88, pres. bus. forms divsn., 1988-97; pres. automotive group, 1997—. Bd. dirs. Reynolds & Reynolds, Olympic Title Ins. Co. Bd. dirs., pres. Camp Fire Girls, Dayton, 1975; bd. dirs. ARC, 1977; participant, then trustee Leadership Dayton, 1986-95; vice chmn. Med. Am. Corp.; trustee, treas. Victory Theater Assn., 1985-91, Dayton Mus. Natural History, 1982-96; trustee, chmn. Alliance for Edn., Dayton Art Inst. 1st lt. USN, 1962-70. Mem. Beta Gamma Sigma, Racquet (Dayton), Dayton Country, Country Club of the North. Republican. Episcopalian.

NEVINS, ARTHUR GERARD, JR., lawyer; b. Bklyn., Dec. 23, 1948; s. Arthur Gerard Sr. and Gertrude Anna May (Schlueter) N.; m. Reine T. Hughes, June 26, 1982; m. Amanda Mitchell, May 16, 1989. BS, Cornell U., 1971; JD, Fordham U., 1974. Bar: N.Y. 1975, N.J. 1976. Assoc. Lester, Schwab, Katz & Dwer, NYC, 1975-77, Law Offices of Peter De Blasio, NYC, 1977-80, Law Offices of Robert Ginsberg, NYC, 1980-82; pvt. practice NYC, 1982—. Mem. ABA, N.Y. State Bar Assn., N.J. Bar Assn., N.Y. County Bar Assn., Hudson County Bar Assn., Phi Gamma Delta. Roman Catholic. Home: 41 Charlestown Rd Hampton NJ 08827-2781 Office: Plz 78 56 State Rt 173 W Hampton NJ 08827 also: 225 Broadway Ste 3111 New York NY 10007-3001 Home Phone: 908-730-6984; Office Phone: 212-406-2062, 908-713-6666.

NEVINS, JOHN J., bishop; b. New Rochelle, NY, Jan. 19, 1932; Student, Iona Coll., NYC, Cath. U. Washington, Tulane U. Ordained priest Roman Cath. Ch., 1959. Ordained titular bishop of Rusticana and aux. bishop Diocese of Miami, 1979—84; first bishop Diocese of Venice, Fla., 1984—. Office: PO Box 2006 1000 Pinebrook Rd Venice FL 34292

NEVINS, LYN (CAROLYN A. NEVINS), school disciplinarian; b. Chelsea, Mass., June 9, 1948; d. Samuel Joseph and Stella Theresa (Maronski) N.; m. John Edward Herbert, Jr., May 1, 1979; children: Chrissy, Johnny. BA in Sociology, Edn., U. Mass., 1970; MA in Women's Studies, George Washington U., 1975. Cert. tchr., trainer. Tchr. social studies Greenwich (Conn.) Pub. Schs., 1970-74; rschr. career/vocat. edn. Conn. State Dept. Edn., Hartford, 1975-76; rschr., career/vocat. edn. Area Coop. Edn. Svcs., Hamden, Conn., 1976-77; program mgr., trainer career edn. and gender equity Coop. Ednl. Svcs., Norwalk, Conn., 1977-83, trainer, mgr., devel., Beginning Educator Support and Tng. program Trumbull, Conn., 1987—; state coord. career edn. Conn. State Dept. Edn., Hartford, 1982-83; supr. Sacred Heart U., Fairfield, 1992—. Bias com. Conn. State Dept. Edn., Hartford, 1981—; vision com. Middlesex Mid. Sch., Darien, Conn., 1993-95; ednl. quality and diversity com. Town of Darien, 1993-95; cons., trainer career devel./pre-retirement planning Cohen and Assocs., Fairfield, 1981—, Farren Assocs., Annandale, Va.,

1992—, Tracey Robert Assocs., Fairfield, 1994—; freelance cons., trainer, Darien, 1983-87; presenter Nat. Conf. GE, 1980, Career Edn., 1983, Am. Edn. Rsch. Assn., 1991, Nat. Conf. New Tchr. Induction, 2006, 07, Nat. Cof. Beginning Tchrs., 2007; mem. statewide B.E.S.T. adv.com., 2006; lectr. in field. Tennis coach Spl. Olympics, 1993—, Darien (Conn.) Girls' Softball League, 1992-96, tennis coord. Spl. Olympics Summer Games, 1997—; tennis coach Unified Ptnr. Spl. Olympics Nat. Games, 2005-06; tennis coach, Conn. delegation Nat. Games for Spl. Olympics, 2005—06; bldg. com. Darien HS, 1999—. Mem. NOW (founder, state coord. edn. 1972-74), ASCD. Avocations: tennis, running, walking, golf, travel. Home: 4 Hollister Ln Darien CT 06820-5404 Office: Coop Ednl Svcs 40 Lindeman Drive Trumbull CT 06611-4723 Business E-Mail: nevinsl@ces.k12.ct.us.

NEVINS, PATRICK FREDRICK, librarian; b. Oak Park, Ill., Jan. 21, 1950; s. George Howard and Mary Jane Nevins; m. Barbara Ann Borowski, July 30, 1977; children: Kimberly J., Timothy P. BA, U. Ill., Chgo., 1972; MA in Libr. Sci., Rosary Coll., River Forest, Ill., 1976. Libr. student asst. U. Ill., Chgo., 1969-72, math. libr. supr., 1972-76; libr. tech. asst. Northeastern Ill. U., Chgo., 1972; head libr. Markham Pub. Libr., Ill., 1976-78, Grande Prairie Pub. Libr., Hazel Crest, Ill., 1978-79, Richton Park Pub. Libr., Ill., 1980—. Adv. com. rep. Suburban Libr. Sys., Burr Ridge, Ill., 1984, 97-99; bldg. cons. Homewood Pub. Libr., Ill., 1997; rep. Swan Coun., 2003—. Leisure svcs. com. mem. Homewood-Flossmoor Pk. Dist., Ill., 1989-92, 93-96, pk. commr., 1997—, v.p., 1999-2002, pres., 2002-06; softball and baseball coach Homewood Baseball, Ill., 1990-97; vol. Cancer Support Ctr., Homewood, 1997—, bd. mem., 2001-2003. cmty. vol., 2003—; co-chair Walk for Hope 2002-. Recipient Cmty. Svc. award Ill. Assn. Pk. Dists. and Ill. Pk. and Recreation Assn., 1993, 2004, Thomas R. Jones Humanitarian award, 2005. Mem. ALA, Ill. Libr. Assn., Ill. Assn. Pk. Dists. Avocations: reading, basketball, storytelling. Home: 1343 187th St Homewood IL 60430-3831 Office: Richton Pk Pub Libr Dist 4045 Sauk Trl Richton Park IL 60471-1239 Office Phone: 708-481-5333.

NEVINS, SHEILA, television producer; b. NYC; d. Benjamin and Stella Nevins; m. Sidney Koch, 1972; 1 child, David Andrew. BA, Barnard Coll.; MFA, Yale U. TV prodr. Great Am. Dream Machine, NET, 1971-73, The Reasoner Report, ABC, 1973, Feeling Good, Children's TV Workshop, 1975-76, Who's Who, CBS, 1977-78; dir. documentary & family programming HBO, NYC, 1978-82, v.p. documentary programming, 1986-95, sr. v.p. original programming, 1998-99, exec. v.p. original programming, 1999—2003, pres. documentary & family programming, 2004—. Bd. dirs. Film Forum, Creative Capital, Ind. Feature Project. Prodr.: Gang War: Bangin' in Little Rock, 1994, Taxicab Confessions, 1995, The Celluloid Closet, 1995, Going, Going, Almost Gone! Animals in Danger, 1995, One Survivor Remembers, 1995, 5 American Kids - 5 American Handguns, 1995, How Do You Spell God?, 1996, Without Pity: A Film About Abilities, 1996, Smoke Alarm, 1996, Paradise Lost, 1996, Kids of Survival, 1996, Heart of a Child, 1997, Wonderland, 1997, Mumia Abu-Jamal: A Case for Reasonable Doubt?, 1997, Little Dieter Needs to Fly, 1997, 4 Little Girls, 1997, Talked to Death, 1997, Thug Life in DC, 1998, Kids are Punny, 1998, Lenny Bruce: Swear to Tell the Truth, 1998, Dead Blue: Surviving Depression, 1998, King Gimp, 1999, Goodnight Moon & Other Sleepytime Tales, 1999, American Hollow, 1999, Cancer: Evolution to Revolution, 1999, Punitive Damage, 1999, Through a Blue Lens, 1999, Half Past Autumn: The Life & Works of Gordon Parks, 2000, Children in War, 2000, Paradise Lost 2, 2000, Bach in Auschwitz, 2000, Legacy, 2000, Dwarfs: Not a Fairy Tale, 2001, Living Dolls: The Making of a Child Beauty Queen, 2001, Through a Child's Eyes: September 11, 2001, Journeys with George, 2002, In Memoriam: New York City, 2002, Amandla!, 2002, Sister Helen, 2002, Secret Lives: Hidden Children & Their Rescuers During WWII, 2002, Telling Nicholas, 2002, Born Rich, 2003, Unchained Memories: Readings from the Slave Narratives, 2003, America Undercover, 2003, Death in Gaza, 2004, Last Letters Home, 2004, Happy to be Nappy & Other Stories of Me, 2004, Elaine Stritch at Liberty, 2004, I Have Tourrette's But Tourette's Doesn't Have Me, 2005, Classical Baby, 2005, Baghdad ER, 2006, All Aboard! Rosie's Family Cruise, 2006, When the Levees Broke: A Requiem in Four Acts, 2006, Friends of God, 2007. Bd. dirs. Women's Action Alliance. Named Woman of Achievement, YMCA, 1991; named one of Top 25 Women in TV, Emmy mag., 1996, Top 25 Smartest Women Am., Mirabella Mag., 1999, Top 50 Women in TV, Hollywood Reporter Mag., 2005, 100 Most Powerful Women in Entertainment, 2006; named to Broadcasting & Cable Hall of Fame, 2000; recipient Peabody award, 1986, 1992, 1995, 1996, 1997, 1999, 2000, 2003, 2004, Glaad Media award, 1989, Acad. Award for Documentary, 1993, 1996, 1998, 1999, 2000, 2001, 2003, Emmy award, 1994, 3 Emmy awards, 1995, Emmy award, 1996, 1998, 1999, 2003, 2002, 2 Emmy awards, 1997, 2000, 2004, 2005, 2006, Media award, Mental Health Assn. NYC, 1996, Personal Peabody award, 1999, NATAS Silver Cir., 2000, Wellness Cmty. award, 2001, Humanitarian award, Nat. Bd. Rev., 2002, Lucy award, Women in Film, 2003, Three Arts award, Lifetime Achievement award, News & Documentary Emmy Awards, 2005, Alfred I. DuPont-Columbia U. award, 2007. Mem.: Internt. Documentary Assn. (Vision award 1998), NY Women in Film (Muse award 1998), Writers Guild Am. *

NEVINS, WILLIAM J., oil and gas brokerage executive, consultant; b. Yonkers, NY, Sept. 16, 1952; s. Francis Robert and Alice Frances (Stager) N.; m. Joan Evelyn Leach, June 8, 1975 (div. June, 1980). BA in English Lit. and Fin., U. Miami, Coral Gables, Fla., 1974; postgrad. studies in Law, Western State U., Fullerton, Calif., 1974-75. CEO Nevins Enterprises Ltd., various cities, U.S., 1976—; CEO, pres. Century 21, Heritage Realty, Inc., North Miami, Fla., 1985-87, N&Z, Heritage Realty, Inc., Miami, 1987-96; sr. assoc., registered rep. Texakoma Fin. Oil and Gas, 1996-98; oil and gas broker Western Am. Securities, Reef Exploration, Inc., 1998—2001, v.p., 1998-2001, sr. v.p., 2001—, Geo Cos. of N.A. Inc., 2002—; oil and gas broker, sr. v.p. GeoSecurities Inc., 2002—, Geo Natural Resources, Inc., 2002—; sr. v.p. Geo Cos. of N.Am., Inc., 2002—03, Prolific Energy, LLC, 2003; exec. dir. Am. Landmark Securities, Inc./ Prodigy Oil & Gas, LLC, 2004—. V.p., bd. dirs. Pyramid Fin. Svcs., Inc., North Miami Beach, Fla., 1982; cons. Park West Overtown Devel. Com., Miami, 1984—85, Miami Beach Developers and Investors Conf., 1985—90; exec. dir. Plummer Securities, Inc., 2006—, Chestnut Energy Ptnrs., Inc., 2006—, Petroleum, Inc., 2006—, Chestnut and Chestnut Energy Ptnrs., Inc., 2006—. Author: Oil Patch and Oilmen, 2004. Vol. asst. mgr. John V. Lindsay Miami Dem. Primary Campaign. 1972; founder Universal Children's Found. Inc., 1995. Mem. Nat. Assn. Security Dealers (registered rep.), Security Investment Protection Corp. Orgn., Nu Beta Epsilon. Roman Catholic. Avocations: game fishing, antique autos, coin collecting/numismatics, travel, yachting. Office: Nevins Enterprises Ltd 13237 Montfort Dr Ste 438 Dallas TX 75240-1117 Office Phone: 305-453-9260. Personal E-mail: wjnevins@yahoo.com.

NEVLING, HARRY REED, human resources consultant; b. Rochester, Minn., Sept. 15, 1946; s. Edwin Reid and Ruth Margaret (Mulvihill) N.; m. Joanne Carol Meyer, Nov. 26, 1976; 1 son, Terry John. AA, Rochester C.C., 1973; BA cum laude, U. Winona, 1974; MBA, U. Colo., 1990. Pers. rep. Rochester Meth. Hosp., 1974-75; dist. mgr. Internat. Dairy Queen Corp., 1975-76; with David Realty Corp., Littleton, Colo., 1976-83, v.p., 1979-83, gen. mgr., 1981-83, Longmont United Hosp., Colo., 1977-99, pers. dir. Colo., 1977-87, dir. human resources Colo., 1988-95, v.p. human resources Colo., 1995-99; prin. HR Cons., Rochester, Minn., 1999—. Cons. Front Range C.C. Denver, 1983-85; prin. Harry R. Nevling-Broker, 1983-85, 95-97; v.p. Realty Mart Internat., Inc., 1985-93, Dist. chmn. Am. party, 1973-74, St. Vrain Valley Sch. Dist., Health Occupations Adv. Com. 1977-99, chmn. 1979-85, Vocat. Edn. Adv. Coun. 1986-91, pres. 1986-91; with Citizen Amb. People to People Program, Hungary, Czech Republic, Germany, 1991; exec. com. Nat. Health Care Skills Stds. Project, 1993-95; spkr., presenter in field. Co-author: Healthcare Reform: The Human Resources Cornerstone to Successful Reform, 1992. Adv. bd. Olmsted County Cmty. Social Svcs., 2007—. Capt. US Army, 1965-72; Vietnam. Decorated D.F.C., Bronze Star with oakleaf cluster, Air medal (22, valor device); recipient Rescue citation for lifesaving Boeing Co., 1969, Helping Hand award United Way, 1974, Outstanding Svc. award, 1979, cert. of appreciation, 1982, Disting. Young Alumni award Winona State U., 1989. Mem. VFW (past post comdr.), Longmont Area Human Resources Assn., 1980-89, Boulder Area Human Resource Assn., 1978-00, Mountain States VHA (pers. com. 1989-96, chmn. 1989-93), Colo. Healthcare Assn. Human Resources Mgmt. (hon. life, sec. 1980, pres. elect 1981, pres. 1981-82, exec. com. 1986-00), Am. Soc. for Healthcare Human Resources Adminstrn. (hon. life, ann. meeting chmn. 1985-86, regional dir. 1986-90, legis. and labor liaison 1988-90, chpt. rels. com. 1990-91, pres. elect 1991-92, exec. com. 1991-95, pres. 1992-93, bylaws com. 1992-93, 96-99, chmn. nominating com. 1994-95, chmn. conflict of interest com., 1994-95, immediate past pres. 1994-95, nat. nominating com. 1996, Disting. Svc. award 1996), Soc. Human Resource Mgmt., Human Resource Cert. Inst. (life, sr. profl. in human resources), Vietnam Helicopter Pilots Assn., Bus. Dependent Care Assn. (pres. 1996, chmn. 1997-98), Region 10 Stakeholders (VOICE rev. quality assurance team mem. 2003—, mentor 2004—, leader brain injury com. 2003—, Rochester area brain injury cmty. com. 2002—, co-chair 2005-06, chair, 2006—), Region 10 Quality Assurance Commn.(treas. 2006—, chair pers. com. 2006—, abilities unltd. program com. 2003—, adv. coun. 2004—), Olmstead County Cmty. Social Svcs. Adv. Bd. Home and Office: 1916 Century Hills Dr NE Rochester MN 55906-7623

NEW, MARIA IANDOLO, pediatrician, educator; b. NYC; d. Loris J. and Esther B. (Giglio) Iandolo; m. Bertrand L. New, 1949 (dec. 1990); children: Erica, Daniel, Antonia. BA, Cornell U., 1950; MD, U. Pa., 1954; degree in medicine (hon.), U. degli Studi di Roma, Rome, 1999, U. di Parma, Italy, 2000. Diplomate Am. Bd. Pediat. Med. intern Bellevue Hosp., NYC, 1954-55; resident in pediat. N.Y. Hosp., 1955-57; fellow NIH, 1957-58, 61-64; practice medicine specializing in pediat. NYC, 1955—; mem. staff N.Y. Hosp., dir. Pediatric Endocrine and Metabolism Clinic, 1964—2004, attending pediatrician, 1971-80; pediatrician-in-chief N.Y.-Presbyn. Hosp., 1980—2002, dir. pediatric endocrinology, 1998—2002; prof. pediat. Mt. Sinai Sch. Medicine, NYC. Asst. prof. dept. pediat. Joan and Sanford Weill Med. Coll. of Cornell U., N.Y.C., 1963-68, assoc. prof., 1968-71, prof., 1971-2004, Harold and Percy Uris prof. pediatric endocrinology, 1978-2004, prof., 1980-2004, chmn. dept. pediat., 1980-2002; program dir. Childrens Clin. Rsch. Ctr., 1996-2002; assoc. dir. Pediatric Clin. Rsch. Ctr., 1980-88; adj. faculty prof. Rockefeller U., 1981—; career scientist N.Y.C. Health Rsch. Coun., 1966-75; adj. attending pedatrician dept. pediat. Meml. Sloan-Kettering Cancer Ctr., 1979-93; cons. United Hosp., Port Chester, N.Y., 1977—, North Shore Univ. Hosp., 1982-97, dept. pediat. Cath. Med. Ctr. Bklyn. and Queens, N.Y., 1987—; vis. physician Rockefeller U. Hosp., N.Y.C., 1973-87; mem. endocrine study sect. NIH, 1977-80, Gen. Clin. Rsch. Ctrs. Adv. Com.; chmn. Divsn. Rsch. Resources Gen. Clin. Rsch. Ctrs. Com. NIH, 1987-88; bd. dirs. Robert Wood Johnson Clin. Scholars Program; mem. N.Y. State Gov.'s Task Force on Life and Law, 1985—; mem. NIH Reviewers Res.; mem. FDA endocrinology and metabolism drug adv. com., 1994—; panelist ACGME bd. appeals, 1994—; cons. Meml. Sloan-Kettering Cancer Ctr., 1993—, Meml. Hosp. for the Cancer and Allied Diseases, 1993—; hon. mem. pediat. dept. Blythedale Children's Hosp., Valhalla, N.Y., 1992—; mem. rsch. adv. com. Population Coun. Ctr. for Biomed. Rsch., 1991-97. Editor-in-chief Jour. Clin. Endocrinology and Metabolism, 1994-99; mem. editl. adv. coun. Jour. Endocrinological Investigation, 1995—; mem. editl. bd. Jour. Women's Health, 1993, Endotext; corr. editor Jour. Steroid Biochemistry, 1985; mem. adv. bd. pediatric anns., assoc. editor Metabolism. Trustee Irma T. Hirschl Trust. Recipient Mary Jane Kugel award Juvenile Diabetes Found., 1977, Katharine D. McCormick Disting. Lectureship, 1981, Robert H. Williams Disting. Leadership award, 1988, Albion O. Bernstein award Med. Soc. State N.Y., 1988, medal N.Y. Acad. Medicine, 1991, Disting. Grad. award U. Pa. Sch. Medicine, 1991, Optimate Recognition award Assn. Student-Profl. Italian-Ams., 1991, Outstanding Woman Scientist award N.Y. chpt. Am. Women in Sci., 1986, Maurice R. Greenberg Disting. Svc. award, 1994, Humanitarian award Juvenile Diabetes Found., 1994, Rhône Poulenc Rorer Clin. Investigator Lecture award, 1994, Dale medal Brit. Endocrine Soc., 1996, MERIT award USPHS, NIHCHD, 1998, 11th Ann. award for excellence in clin. rsch. USPHS, NIH, 1998; grantee; named to Hall of Honor, NICHD, 2003. Fellow AAAS, Italian Soc. Endocrinology (hon.); mem. NAS (sr. mem. Inst. Medicine), AAAS, APHA, Am. Soc. Human Genetics, Am. Acad. Pediat., Soc. for Pediatric Rsch., Harvey Soc., Endocrine Soc. (mem. coun. 1981-84, pres. 1991-92, Fred Conrad Koch award 2003), Lawson Wilkins Pediatric Endocrine Soc. (pres. 1985-86), Am. Soc. Nephrology, Am. Soc. Pediatric Nephrology, Am. Pediatric Soc., Am. Fedn. Clin. Rsch., Am. Diabetes Assn., European Soc. Pediatric Endocrinology, Soc. for the Advancement of Women's Health Rsch. (basic sci. award 1996), Am. Coll. Clin. Pharmacology, Am. Clin. and Climatol. Assn., N.Y. Acad. Scis., Pan Am. Med. Assn., Assn. Am. Physicians, Am. Fertility Soc., U.S. Pharmacopeial Conv. (elected), Am. Acad. of Arts and Scis. (elected 1992), Alpha Omega Alpha. Office: Mt Sinai Sch Medicine Box 1198 1 Gustav L Levy Pl New York NY 10029 Office Phone: 212-241-7847. E-mail: maria.new@mssm.edu.

NEW, ROSETTA HOLBROCK, retired secondary school educator, retired department chairman, retired nutrition consultant; b. Aug. 26, 1921; d. Edward F. and Mabel (Kohler) Holbrock; m. John Lorton New, Sept. 3, 1943; 1 child, John Lorton Jr. BS, Miami U., Oxford, Ohio, 1943; MA, U. No. Colo., 1971; PhD, Ohio State U., 1974; student, Kantcentrum, Brugge, Belgium, 1992, Lesage Sch. Embroidery, Paris, 1995, Kent State U., 1998. Cert. tchr. Colo. Tchr. English and sci. Monahans (Tex.) H.S., 1943—44; emergency war food asst. USDA, College Station, Tex., 1945—46; dept. chmn. home econs., adult edn. Hamilton (Ohio) Pub. Schs., 1946—47; tchr., dept. chmn. home econs. East H.S., Denver, 1948—59, Thomas Jefferson H.S., Denver, 1959—83; ret., 1983. Exec. bd. Denver Pub. Schs.; lectr. in field; exec. dir. Ctr. Nutrition Info. U.S. Office Edn. Grantee, Ohio State U., 1971—73. Mem.: Internat. Platform Assn., Fairfield (Ohio) Hist. Soc., Ohio State Home Econs. Alumni Assn., Ohio State U. Assn., Hamilton Hist. Soc., Am. Vocat. Assn., Am. Home Econs. Assn., Nat. Trust for Hist. Preservation, Cin. Art Mus., Internat. Old Lacers, Embroiders Guild Am., Rep. Club Denver, Order White Shrine of Jerusalem, Daus. of the Nile, Masons, Order of Ea. Star, Phi Upsilon Omicron. Presbyterian.

NEWBAUER, JOHN ARTHUR, JR., editor; b. Newport, RI, Apr. 24, 1928; s. John Arthur and Theo Caroline (Trewhella) N.; m. Marilyn Mahler, Oct. 14, 1956; children: April, Dana, Miranda. BA, U. Calif., Berkeley, 1951. Sr. editor and writer sci. and engring., rocket devel. dept. U.S. Naval Ordnance Test Sta., China Lake, Calif., 1951-56; editor in chief Astronautics and Aeronautics jour., NYC, 1963-83; adminstr. sci. publs. AIAA, 1983-91, cons. editor, 1991—; editor in chief Aerospace Am., 1983-87, aquisitions editor, 1987-89. Fellow AIAA (assoc.), Brit. Interplanetary Soc. Office Phone: 718-768-7697.

NEWBERG, ESTHER, literary agent; d. Marion Newberg. MA, Wheaton Coll., Norton, Mass., 1963, degree, 2003. Worked with Robert F. Kennedy, Bella Abzug, Morris Udall Presdl. Campaign, 1976; joined Internat. Creative Mgmt., NYC, 1976, v.p., co-dir. lit. dept., 1988, sr. v.p., co-dir. lit. dept. Named one of 100 Most Powerful Women in Entertainment, Hollywood Reporter, 2006; recipient Matrix Award, N.Y. Women in Comm., 1997. Office: Internat Creative Mgmt 40 W 57th St New York NY 10019 E-mail: enewberg@icmtalent.com.

NEWBERG, JOSEPH H., lawyer; b. Middletown, Conn., May 20, 1947; s. Mendel and Annette (Gold) N.; m. Alice V. Melnikoff, Sept. 23, 1973; children: Mark, Emily. BA, U. Mich., 1969; JD, Harvard U., 1972; LLM in Taxation, Boston U., 1976. Bar: Mass. 1972, US Tax Ct. 1975. Assoc. Sullivan & Worcester, Boston, 1972-80, ptnr., 1980; stockholder Hutchins, Wheeler & Dittmar, Boston; ptnr. Gotshal & Manges, Boston, 2002—. Lectr. grad. tax prog. Boston U, 1982-84, adj. asst. prof. Bentley Grad. Tax Prog., Waltham, Mass., 1985-86, spkr. in field. Contbr. articles to profl. jour. Chmn. Planning Bd. of Town of Belmont. Mem. ABA, Boston Bar Assn. (co-chmn. internat. tax com.). Office: Gotshal & Manges 100 Federal St Fl 34 Boston MA 02110 Office Phone: 617-772-8350, 617-772-8333. Business E-Mail: joseph.newberg@weil.com.

NEWBERN, WILLIAM DAVID, retired state supreme court justice; b. Oklahoma City, May 28, 1937; s. Charles Banks and Mary Frances (Harding) N.; m. Barbara Lee Rigsby, Aug. 19, 1961 (div. 1968); 1 child, Laura Harding; m. Carolyn Lewis, July 30, 1970; 1 child, Alistair Elizabeth. BA, U. Ark., 1959, JD, 1961; LL.M., George Washington U., 1963; MA, Tufts U., 1967. Bar: Ark. 1961, U.S. Dist. Ct. (we. dist.) Ark. 1961, U.S. Supreme Ct. 1968, U.S. Ct. Appeals (8th cir.) 1983. Commd. 1st lt. advanced to maj. U.S. Army JAGC, 1961-70; Prof. law U. Ark., Fayetteville, 1970-84; adminstr. Ozark Folk Ctr., Mountain View, Ark., 1973; judge Ark. Ct. Appeals, Little Rock, 1979-80; assoc. justice Ark. Supreme Ct., Little Rock, 1985-99. Mem. faculty sr. appellate judges seminar NYU, 1987-91; panel chmn. com. on profl. conduct Ark. Supreme Ct., 2001—05. Editor Ark. Law Rev., 1961; author: Arkansas Civil Practice and Procedure, 1985, (with John J. Watkins) 4th edit., 2006. Mem. Fayetteville Bd. Adjustment, 1972-79; bd. dirs. Decision Point, Inc., Springdale, Ark., 1980-85, Hot Springs Music Festival, 2000—03, Little Rock Wind Symphony, 1993-2001, pres. 1993-95. Named a Disting. Alumnus, Fulbright Coll. Arts and Scis., U. Ark., 2004. Fellow Ark. Bar Found.; mem. Ark. Bar Assn., Am. Judicature Soc. (bd. dirs. 1985-89), Inst. Jud. Adminstrn., Ark. IOLTA Found. (bd. dirs. 1985-87). Democrat. Avocations: string band-guitar, mandolin, banjo and brass quintet-tuba. Personal E-mail: dnewbern@aristotle.net.

NEWBERRY, CONRAD FLOYDE, aerospace engineering educator; b. Neodesha, Kans., Nov. 10, 1931; s. Ragan McGregor and Audra Anitia (Newmaster) N.; m. Sarah Louise Thonn, Jan. 26, 1958; children: Conrad Floyde Jr., Thomas Edwin, Susan Louise. AA, Independence Jr. Coll., Kans., 1951; BEME with aero. sequence, U. So. Calif., LA, 1957; MSME, Calif. State U., LA, 1971, MA in Edn., 1974; D.Environ. Sci. and Engring., UCLA, 1985. Registered profl. engr., Calif., Kans., NC, Tex.; chartered engr., UK. Mathematician LA divsn. N.Am. Aviation Inc., 1951-53, jr. engr., 1953-54, engr., 1954-57, sr. engr., 1957-64; asst. prof. aerospace engring. Calif. State Poly. U., Pomona, 1964-70, assoc. prof. aerospace engring., 1970-75, prof. aerospace engring., 1975-90, prof. emeritus, 1990—; staff engr. EPA, 1980-82; engring. specialist space transp. sys. divsn. Rockwell Internat. Corp., 1984-90; prof. aeronautics and astronautics Naval Postgrad. Sch., Monterey, Calif., 1990—2002, prof. emeritus, 2002—, acad. assoc. space sys. engring., 1992-94. Recipient John Leland Atwood award as outstanding aerospace engring. educator AIAA/Am. Soc. Engring. Edn., 1986, Fred Merryfield Design award ASEE, 1997. Fellow: AIAA (dep. dir. edn. region VI 1976—79, dep. dir. career enhancement 1982—91, chmn. L.A. sect. 1989—90, chmn. Point Lobos sect. 1990—91, chmn. acad. affairs com. 1990—93, dir. tech. aircraft sys. 1990—93, chmn. Point Lobos sect. 1999—2001, Disting. Svc. award 2006); mem.: IEEE, ASME, NSPE, Am. Soc. Naval Engrs., Calif. Water Pollution Control Assn., Assn. Unmanned Vehicle Sys. Internat., Soc. Allied Weight Engrs., Soc. Automotive Engr., Water Environ. Fedn., Exptl. Aircraft Assn., Inst. Environ. Scis., Air and Waste Mgmt. Assn., Soc. Naval Architects and Marine Engrs., Am. Helicopter Soc., US Naval Inst., Am. Meteorol. Soc., Am. Soc. Engring. Edn. (trustee 1999—2002, cert. air pollution control engr., aerospace divsn. exec. com. 1976—80, chmn. aerospace divsn. 1979—80, exec. com. ocean, marine engring. divsn. 1982—85, exec. com. 1989—95, program chmn. 1991—93, chmn. 1993—95, chmn. Profl Interest Coun. 1995—97, bd. dirs. 1995—97), Am. Acad. Environ. Engrs., Calif. Soc. Profl. Engrs., Royal Aero. Soc., Inst. Advancement Engring., Brit. Interplanetary Soc., Planetary Soc., Kappa Delta Pi, Sigma Gamma Tau, Tau Beta Pi. Democrat. Achievements include research on aircraft, spacecraft, missiles, and engine design, waveriders, aircrew centered system design and related impacts on exergy, quality, concurrent engineering, cost and environmental controls. Home: 9463 Willow Oak Rd Salinas CA 93907-1037 Personal E-mail: cfnacmdesign@msn.com.

NEWBERRY, EDWARD J., lawyer; b. Schenectady, NY, Sept. 25, 1962; BA, BS, George Mason Univ., 1984; JD, Georgetown Univ., 1989. Former staff mem. U.S. Rep. Frank Wolf, Washington, U.S. Ho. Rep. Appropriations Com., Washington, 1984—91; ptnr., Public Policy, Mcpl. Representation, dep. mng. ptnr., mem. exec. and mgmt. com. Patton Boggs LLP, Washington, 1991—. Office: Patton Boggs LLP 2550 M St NW Washington DC 20037-1350 Office Phone: 202-457-5285. Office Fax: 202-457-6315. Business E-Mail: enewberry@pattonboggs.com.

NEWBERRY, STEPHEN G., semiconductor equipment company executive; BS, USNA, Annapolis, 1975; MBA, Harvard Univ. Mgmt. positions through group v.p. global ops. & planning Applied Materials Inc., 1980—97; exec. v.p., COO Lam Rsch. Corp., Fremont, Calif., 1997—98, pres., COO, 1998—2005, pres., CEO, 2005—. Bd. dir. Nextest Systems Corp., Semiconductor Equip. & Materials Internat. Office: Lam Rsch Corp 4650 Cushing Pkwy Fremont CA 94538 *

NEWBOLD, JOHN LOWE, retired banker, financial consultant; b. Washington, Dec. 26, 1935; s. John Lowe and Katharine Emily (Wilkins) N.; m. Judith Allen Bourne, June 20, 1959; children: Jennifer Hathaway, Timothy Bourne, Michael Fleming. BS, Yale U., 1957; MBA, NYU, 1963; sr. execs. program cert., MIT, 1970. Asst. v.p., credit instr. Citibank, N.A., NYC, 1968-69, v.p. retail trade unit, 1969-70, v.p. info. svcs. dept., 1970-72, v.p., corp. bank head Tokyo, 1972-73, v.p., country head Singapore, 1974-76, sr. v.p., shipping dept. head NYC, 1976-85, divsn. exec., Global Shipping Divsn., 1985—97, divsn. exec., Global Transp. Divsn., 1989—93; ret., 1997; chmn., dir. Mchts. Fund, Inc., Bethesda, Md., 1981—2003. Bd. dirs. Castalia Ptnrs. Ltd. Trustee Reeves Reed Arboretum, Summit, NJ, 1999-2002, Summit Area Cmty. Coun., 1983-86, United Way, Summit, 1984-92; pres. PTA Presidents' Coun., Summit, 1981-83; pres. Abel's Hill Assn., 2006; pres., dir. One Fifth Ave. Apt. Corp., 2001-06, Friends of Chilmark Libr., Mass., 2006—, vice-chmn., 2003-06; mem. vestry, treas., Grace Ch., NYC, 2006—. Lt. (j.g.) USNR, 1957-63. Mem. Yale Club of Ctrl. N.J. (trustee 1980-85). Home: 1 Fifth Ave 11J New York NY 10003 Home Phone: 212-529-9220; Office Phone: 212-674-5881. Personal E-mail: jocknewb@aol.com.

NEWBOLD-COCO, RAIN L., social services administrator; d. Clyde and June M. Newbold; m. Christopher D. Coco, Aug. 20, 2005. Diploma with disting. grad. honors, Webster U., 2002; PhD, Capella U., Mpls., 2006. Cert. bd. cert. behavior analyst. Performance improvement dir., cons., regional team lead STAR Cons., Inc., Altamonte Springs, Fla., 2000—06; founder, prin. Lighthouse Mentoring Group, Satellite Beach, Fla., 2006—; Brevard supr. KidsPeace, Cocoa, Fla., 2006—. Adj. prof. Argosy U. Author: Lighting the Way for Success: Mentoring Black Professional Women; contbr. articles to profl. jours. Named Overlay Employee of Quarter, Human Services Associates, Inc., 2001; grantee, Bonner Elem.

Sch., 2002, Frangus Elem. Sch., 2002. Mem.: Nat. Career Devel. Assn. (assoc.), Fla. Assn. Behavior Analysis (assoc.), Soc. Consulting Psychology (assoc.), Soc. Indsl. and Orgnl. Psychology, Inc. (assoc.). Office: Lighthouse Mentoring Group PO Box 372866 Satellite Beach FL 32937 Home Phone: 321-773-6202; Office Phone: 321-947-1939. Personal E-mail: newboldcoco@aol.com. Business E-Mail: lightmentorgroup@aol.com.

NEWBORG, GERALD GORDON, state archives administrator; b. Ada, Minn., Dec. 13, 1942; s. George Harold and Olea (Halstad) N.; m. Jean Annette Gruhl, Aug. 14, 1964; children: Erica, Annette. BA, Concordia Coll., Moorhead, Minn., 1964; MA, U. N.D., 1969; MBA, Ohio State U., 1978. Cert. archivist. Tutor, preceptor Parsons Coll., Fairfield, Iowa, 1964-67; state archivist Ohio Hist. Soc., Columbus, 1968-76; v.p. Archival Systems Inc., Columbus, 1978-81; state archivist State Hist. Soc. of N.D., Bismarck, 1981—. Instr. Franklin U., Columbus, 1974; adj. prof. Bismarck State Coll., 1985-86. Co-author: North Dakota: A Pictorial History, 1988. Recipient Resolution of Commendation Ohio Ho. of Reps., Columbus, 1976. Mem. Soc. Am. Archivists, Nat. Assn. Govt. Archives & Records Adminstrs. (bd. dirs. 1984-86, sec. 1994-99), Midwest Archives Conf., N.D. Libr. Assn. (exec. bd. 1985-86). Home: 1327 N 18th St Bismarck ND 58501-2827 Office: State Hist Soc 612 E Boulevard Ave Bismarck ND 58505-0660

NEWBORN, ANDREA R., publishing executive, lawyer; b. NYC, Jan. 14, 1963; BA magna cum laude, Brown U., 1984; JD, Columbia U., 1987. Bar: NY 1988. Assoc. Fried, Frank, Harris, Shriver & Jacobson LLP, 1987—89, Herzog, Calamari & Gleason, NYC, 1989—91; sr. atty. The Reader's Digest Assn., Inc., Pleasantville, NY, 1991—98, asst. gen. counsel, 1998—2000, v.p., assoc. gen. counsel, 2000—07, v.p., gen. counsel, 2007—. Mem. Columbia Law Rev., 1986—87, notes & comments editor, 1986—87. Scholar Harlan Fiske Stone, 1984—86, James Kent, 1986—87. Office: Reader's Digest Assn Inc Reader's Digest Rd Pleasantville NY 10570 Office Phone: 914-238-1000. Office Fax: 914-241-5644. *

NEWBORN, JUD, anthropologist, writer, curator, educator, historian; b. NYC, Nov. 8, 1952; s. Solomon and Rita Newborn. BA magna cum laude in Anthropology and English, NYU, 1974; postgrad., Clare Hall, Cambridge U., 1974-75; MA in Anthropology, U. Chgo., 1977, PhD with distinction, 1994. Free-lance writer, NYC, Munich, Chgo., 1974—; publicist Oxford U. Press, NYC, 1975-76; founding historian, co-creator Mus. Jewish Heritage (N.Y. Holocaust Meml. Commn.), NYC, 1986-92, 96-00. Spl. cons. Cinema Arts Ctr., 1986—2005; cons., spkr., lectr. in field; cons. Holocaust Resource Ctr. CUNY, Queensborough; dir. devel., spl. projects curator Cinema Arts Centre, LI, 2005—. Author: Shattering the German Night: The Story of the White Rose Anti-Nazi Resistance, 1986, Herder Verlag, 2002, Sophie Scholl and the White Rose, 2006; contbg. editor Diplomatic World Obs., UN, 1999-00; freelance writer, lyricist. Fulbright fellow, 1980-82; Newcombe fellow, 1984-85. Mem. ASCAP, Am. Anthrop. Assn., Am. Hist. Assn., Authors Guild, Assn. Holocaust Orgns., N.Y. Old Growth Forest Assn. (bd. mem.), Nat. Arts Club (hon. mem.), Phi Beta Kappa.

NEWBRANDER, WILLIAM CARL, health economist, management consultant; b. Irumagawa, Japan, Sept. 14, 1951; parents Am. citizens; s. Virgil Ray and Ella Jeannette (Rae) N.; m. Nancy Sharon Wilson, June 15, 1974; children: Sharon, Billy, Andrew, Jonathan, Daniel. BA, Wheaton Coll., 1973, M of Hosp. Adminstrn., 1975; M of Applied Econs., U. Mich., 1981, PhD, 1983. Tchg./rsch. asst. U. Mich., Ann Arbor, 1979—83; mgmt. specialist VA-HSR&D, Ann Arbor, 1980—83; hosp. adminstr. Whittaker Corp., Tabuk, Saudi Arabia, 1983—85; health economist WHO, Geneva, 1985—92; dir. health financing program Mgmt. Scis. for Health, Cambridge, Mass., 1992—2001; adv. to minister of health Afghanistan Health Program, Cambridge, 2002—. Author: Health Policy and Planning, 1988, 5th edit., 1994, Health Planning and Mgmt., 1988, 5th edit., 2007, Decentralization in a Developing Country, 1991, Hospital Economics and Financing in Developing Countries, 1992, World Health Forum, 1994, Modelling in Health Care Finance: A Compendium of Quantitative Techniques for Health Care Financing, 1999, Private Health Sector Growth in Asia: Issues and Implications, 1997, Extending Access to Health Care Through Public-Private Partnerships: The PROSALUD Experience, 2000, Ensuring Equal Access to Health Services: User Fee Systems and the Poor, 2001. Eagle Scout advisor, troop com. chmn. Boy Scouts Am., Geneva and Hopkinton, Mass., 1990-2004; mgr. Little League baseball team, Geneva and Hopkinton, 1990-2000; elder First Congl. Ch., Hopkinton, 1995-99; chmn. bd. dirs. Pioneers, U.S., Orlando, Fla., 1997-2000. Capt. U.S. Army, 1975-79. VA Rsch. fellow, 1981-83. Fellow Am. Coll. Healthcare Execs. Home: 33 Valleywood Rd Hopkinton MA 01748-1634 Office Phone: 617-250-9500. Personal E-mail: wnewbrander@yahoo.com.

NEWBRUN, ERNEST, oral biology and periodontology educator; b. Vienna, Dec. 1, 1932; came to U.S., 1955; s. Victor and Elizabeth (Reichl) N; m. Eva Miriam, June 17, 1956; children: Deborah Ann, Daniel Eric, Karen Ruth. BDS, Sydney U., Australia, 1954; MS, U. Rochester, 1957; DMD, U. Ala., 1959; PhD, U. Calif., San Francisco, 1965; Odont. Dr. (hon.), U. Lund, Sweden, 1988; DDSc (hon.), U. Sydney, 1997. Cert. periodontology, 1983. Rsch. assoc. Eastman Dental Ctr., Rochester, NY, 1955-57, U. Ala. Med. Ctr., Birmingham, 1957-59; rsch. fellow Inst. Dental Rsch., Sydney, Australia, 1960-61; rsch. tchr. trainee U. Calif., San Francisco, 1961-63, postdoctoral fellow, 1963-65, assoc. prof., 1965-70, prof. oral biology, 1970-83, prof. oral biology and periodontology, 1983-94, prof. emeritus, 1994—. Cons. FDA, 1983—. Author: Cariology, 1989, Pharmacology and Therapeutics for Dentistry, 2004, (with others) Pediatrics, 1991; editor: Fluorides and Dental Caries, 1986; mem. editl. bd. Jour. Periodontal Rsch., 1985-90, Jour. Periodontology, 1990-2005. Bd. dirs. Raoul Wallenberg Dem. Club, San Francisco, 1987-92. Fellow AAAS (chmn. dental section, 1988-89), Internat. Assn. Dental Rsch. (pres. 1989-90) Jewish. Avocations: gardening, hiking, skiing, opera, theater. Office Phone: 415-476-1004. Business E-Mail: ernest.newbrun@ucsf.edu.

NEWBURGER, BETH WEINSTEIN, communications executive; b. Schenectady, July 8, 1937; d. H. Edward and Shirley (Diamond) Weinstein; m. Alan C. Newburger, Jan. 23, 1963 (dec. Oct. 1980); children: Mark, Lori, Eric, Jill; m. Richard Schwartz, May 26, 1989. BA, Cornell U., 1959. Dir. advt. New Republic, Washington, 1974-77; mktg. mgr. Washington Post, 1977-84; pres. Owlcat/Digital Rsch., Inc., Monterey, Calif., 1984-86; pres., CEO Corabi Internat. Telemetrics, Inc., Alexandria, Va., 1986-95; assoc. adminstr. Gen. Svcs. Adminstrn., Washington, 1996—2001; dir. comm. Nat. Trust for Hist. Preservation, 2001—04; pres., CEO Epoch Comm. LLC, 2004—. Chmn. bd. Health Street, Inc., Bethesda, Md., 1985—95; mem. NASA adv. coun. Tech. Commercialization Adv. Com., 1995—98; co-chmn. President's Comm. on Celebration of Women in Am. History, 1998—2000; commr., exec. dir. Women's Progress Commemorative Commn., 2000—01; bd. dirs. Nat. Women's History Project, 2000—02; adv. bd. Eleanor Roosevelt Papers, 2000—; bd. dirs. Nat. Women's Hall of Fame, 2001—04; trustee Jewish Women's Archives, 2002—. Chmn. bd. Capital Children's Mus., Washington, 1994—98, trustee, 1984—2005; trustee, exec. com. Nat. Childrens Mus., 2005—; bd. dirs. Arena Stage, Washington, 1993—, BOAT/U.S., 1990—. Named Woman of Yr., Svc. Guild, Washington, 1972, 73. Mem. Women in Advt. and Mktg. (bd. dirs. 1986-89). Home: 1401 N Oak St Arlington VA 22209-3648 Business E-Mail: beth@epoch1.net.

NEWBURGER, HOWARD MARTIN, psychoanalyst; b. NYC, May 16, 1924; s. Bernhard and Bertha (Travers) N.; m. Doris Schekter, July 3, 1949; children: Amy, Barry, Cary. BA, NYU, 1948, MA, 1950, PhD, 1952; tng. in Jungian, Neo-Freudian and Horneyian psychoanalysis. Cert. in group psychotherapy and psychodrama. Rotating intern N.J. Dept. Instns. and Agys., 1948-49; chief psychologist N.J. State Instn., Annandale, 1949-52; dir. psychoanalysis Div. Social Def. UN, 1952; pvt. practice in psychoanalysis and group psychotherapy, 1952—; dir. rsch. HEW, 1958; rsch. assoc. Beth Israel Hosp., 1958-69. Staff mem. St. Agnes Hosp., White Plains, 1991-93; lectr., adj. assoc. prof. NYU, 1951-60, chmn. dept. exceptional child and youth, 1954-62; chmn. faculty and supr. treatment Inst. Applied Human Dynamics, 1960-99; prelect prof. psychology John Jay Coll. Criminal Justice, 1969-72; chmn. bd. dirs. Inst. Applied Human Dynamics, N.Y.C. and Westchester, N.Y., 1960-81, exec. v.p., 1983-85; dean faculty IAHD, 1999-2002; forensic examiner N.Y.S. Supreme Ct., 2005-06; lectr., cons. in field. Co-author: Winners and Losers. Assoc. editor: Excerpta Medica, 1951-62. Contbr. articles and papers to tech. jours. Trustee Acad. Jewish Religion, 1991-96. Served with AUS, World War II, ETO; with AUS, MTO. Recipient Outstanding Service to Humanity award Inst. Applied Human Dynamics for Handicapped, 1970 Mem. Am. Psychol. Assn., Am. Soc. Group Psychotherapy and Psychodrama (sec.-treas. 1954-55). Office: 4 Timber Trl Rye NY 10580-1935 Office Phone: 914-967-4011. *Our country affords tremendous opportunity. Through the development of our inner resources, and their assertion, we can all have happy and effective lives.*

NEWBY, EARL FERNANDO, education educator; b. Louisville, Apr. 14, 1948; BS, Tenn. State U., 1970; MA, U. Louisville, 1972; EdD, Spalding U., 1998; MA, Vanderbilt U., 2002. Cons., tchr. edn. Ky. Dept. Edn., Frankfort, 1970; tchr., prin. Jefferson County Schs., Louisville, 1971-75, Greater Clark County Schs., Jeffersonville, Ind., 1975-98; cons., computer tech. Newby & Assocs., Louisville, 1996—; asst. prof. Morehead (Ky.) State U., 1998—. Adj. prof. Western Ky. U., Bowling Green, 1998; prof. Eastern Ky. U., 1999-2004; assoc. prof. Austin Peay State U., Clarksville, Tenn., 2004-2006; apptd. to serve on many scholastic audit sch. rev. teams, 2002—; presenter So. Regional Coun. Ednl. Adminstrs., 2004, Nat. Coun. Profs. of Ednl. Adminstrs., 2004, Internat. Conf. Profs. of Black Sch. Educators, 2004, Am. Assn. Sch. Adminstrs. Nat. Conf. (presentation and session convener), 2005. Author: Leadership Perspectives, 2004; contbr. articles to profl. publs. Named to Order Ky. Cols. Mem. Am. Assn. Sch. Adminstrs. (presenter confs.), NAESP (presenter ann. internat. conf. San Diego, Calif. 2001), So. Regional Coun. Ednl. Adminstrs., Nat. Coun. Profs. Ednl. Adminstrn. (presenter nat. conf. Houston 2001, Sedona, Ariz. 2003), Nat. Assn. Black Sch. Educators, Ky. Assn. Sch. Adminstrs., Ky. Assn. Black Sch. Educators, Lexington Assn. Black Sch. Educators, Kappa Alpha Psi, Phi Delta Kappa, Pi Lambda Theta (presenter profl. assn. in edn. ann. conf. Mpls. 2001), Sigma Rho Sigma. Democrat. Methodist. Avocations: tennis, basketball, reading, bowling, golf. Home: PO Box 211 Harrods Creek KY 40027-0211 Office: Austin Peay State U Educational Leadership Studies Coll Profl Programs and Social Scis Clarksville TN 37044 also: Va State Univ Coll Liberal Arts and Edn Petersburg VA Fax: 859-622-1126.

NEWBY, JOHN ROBERT, metallurgical engineer; b. Kansas City, Mo., Nov. 17, 1923; s. Merritt Owen and Gladys Mary (McCleery) N.; m. Audry Marie Loniker, Sept. 21, 1963 (div. 1980); children: Deborah A., Walter J., William F., Matthew O., Robert J. BA, U. Mo., Kansas City, 1947; BS in Metall. Engring., Colo. Sch. Mines, 1949; MS, U. Cin., 1963. Cert. profl. engr. Chemist Bar Rusto Plating Corp., Kansas City, 1949; supr. United Chromium, Ferndale, Mich., 1949-52; prin. rsch. metallurgist Armco Inc., Middletown, Ohio, 1952-85; prin. John Newby Cons., Middletown, 1985—; mem. The Edison Materials Tech. Ctr., Dayton, Ohio, 2001—. Cons. Phoenix Cons., Inc., Cin., 1988—. Author, editor: Formability 2000, 1982, Metallic Materials, 1978, Sheet Metal Forming, 1976; editor: Mechanical Testing, Vol. 8, 9th edit., 1985. Scoutmaster Boy Scouts Am., Middletown, 1952-86, now asst. dist. commr.; chmn. Safety Coun., Middletown, 1978-80. Staff sgt. USAF, 1943-46, PTO. Fellow ASTM (chmn. 1963—, chmn. E-28 com. on mech. testing 1998-2002, Award of Merit 1984), ASM (sustaining mem., chpt. chmn. 1970, Award of Merit 1980); mem. SAE (sect. chmn. 1984). Democrat. Achievements include patent for high strength formable steel sheet; development of interstitial free steel, strain analysis process for metallic sheet formability. Home and Office: 100 Marymont Ct Middletown OH 45042-3735

NEWBY, PAUL MARTIN, state supreme court justice; b. Asheboro, NC, May 5, 1955; s. Samuel O. and Ruth (Parks) N.; m. Macon Tucker, Apr. 16, 1983. BA in Public Policy studies magna cum laude, Duke U., 1977; JD, U. NC, 1980. Bar: NC 1980, US Dist. Ct. (we. dist.) NC 1981, US. Dist. Ct. (mid. dist.) NC 1983, US Dist. Ct. (ea. dist.) NC. 1985, US Ct. Appeals (4th cir.) 1986. Research & teacher asst. U. N.C. Sch. of Law, 1979—80; assoc. Van Winkle, Buck, Wall, Starnes & Davis, Asheville, NC, 1980-84; v.p., gen. counsel Cannon Mills Realty & Devel. Corp., Kannapolis, NC, 1984-85; asst. atty. (ea. dist.) N.C. US Dept. Justice, Raleigh, 1985—2004, chief fin. litigation (ea. dist.) N.C., 1994—99; assoc. justice NC Supreme Ct., 2004—. Chmn. bd. dirs. Pregnancy Life Care Ctr., Raleigh, 1986. Mem. NC Bar Assn., Christian Legal Soc. Avocation: tennis. Office: NC Supreme Ct PO Box 1841 Raleigh NC 27602

NEWBY-ALEXANDER, CASSANDRA LYNN, history professor; d. James Edward Newby Jr. and Claytea Baker Newby; m. William Henry Alexander, Dec. 28, 1996. BA in Am. Govt. and African Am. Studies, U. Va., 1980; tchg. cert., Norfolk State U., 1982; MA, Old Dominion U., 1984; PhD, Coll. William and Mary, Williamsburg, Va., 1992. Tchr. Norfolk Pub. Schs., Norfolk, Va., 1988—92; assoc. prof. Norfolk State U., Norfolk, Va., 1992—. Grad. tchg. and rsch. asst. Coll. William and Mary, Williamsburg, 1984—88. Author: (book) Black America Series: Portsmouth, 2003. Bd. mem. Norfolk Sister City Assn., Norfolk, Va., 2006, Supreme Ct. Va. Hist. Commn., Richmond, 2006. Mem.: S.E. Va. Arts Assn. (Pioneer award 2006). Office: Norfolk State Univ 700 Park Ave Norfolk VA 23504 Business E-Mail: clnewby-alexander@nsu.edu.

NEWCOM, JENNINGS JAY, lawyer, director; b. St. Joseph, Mo., Oct. 18, 1941; s. Arden Henderson and Loyal Beatrice (Winans) N.; m. Cherry Ann Phelps, Apr. 4, 1964; children: Shandra Karine, J. Derek Arden. BA, Graceland U., Lamoni, Iowa, 1964; JD, Harvard U., 1968; LLD (hon.), Graceland U., 1999. Bar: Ill. 1968, Calif. 1973, Mo. 1979, Kans. 1981, Colo. 1999. Atty. McDermott, Will & Emery, Chgo., 1968-73; ptnr. Rifkind, Sterling & Lockwood, Beverly Hills, Calif., 1973-79, Shook, Hardy & Bacon L.L.P., Kansas City, Mo., 1979-99, Davis, Graham & Stubbs, LLP, Denver, 1999—; gen. counsel Lovell Minnick Ptnrs. LLC, LA, 1999—; dir. Skillpath Seminars, Overland Park, Kans.; bd. dirs. Duff & Phelps Acquisitions LLC, N.Y.C., Atlantic Asset Mgmt. LLC, Stamford, Conn., Berkeley Capital Mgmt., LLC, San Francisco, ClariVest Asset Mgmt. LLC. Trustee Hubbard Found., Linde Found. Mem. Denver Bar Assn., State Bar Assn. Calif. Office: Davis Graham & Stubbs LLP 1550 17th St Ste 500 Denver CO 80202-1500 Office Phone: 303-892-7318. Business E-Mail: j.newcom@dgslaw.com.

NEWCOMB, ELDON HENRY, retired botany educator; b. Columbia, Mo., Jan. 19, 1919; s. Ernest Henry and Ruby Josephine (Anderson) N.; m. Joyce Bright Rieling, June 21, 1949; children: Norman Robert, Barbara Pauline, Cynthia Irma. Student, U. Kansas City, 1936-38; AB, U. Mo., 1940, A.M., 1942; PhD, U. Wis., 1949; DS honoris causa, U. Mo., Columbia, 1993. Asst. prof. botany U. Wis.-Madison, 1949-54, assoc. prof., 1954-58, prof., 1958-90, prof. emeritus, 1990—; dir. Inst. Plant Devel., 1979-88; chmn. dept. botany U. Wis.-Madison, 1982-88, Folke Skoog prof. botany, 1987—90; ret., 1990. Cons. Shell Devel. Co., 1954-59; mem. expdn. to Great Barrier Reef, 1973. Sr. author: Plants in Perspective, 1963; mng. editor Protoplasma, 1969-73; mem. editorial bd. Ann. Rev. Plant Physiology, 1965-69, Protoplasma, 1973-99, Planta, 1981-90; contbr. articles to profl. jours. Served with AUS, 1942-45. NRC predoctoral fellow U. Wis., 1946-49; Guggenheim Found. fellow U. Calif. at Berkeley, 1951-52; Sci. Faculty fellow Harvard, 1963-64; Fulbright Sr. Research scholar Australian Nat. U., Canberra, 1976 Mem. NAS, Am. Soc. Cell Biologists, Am. Acad. Arts and Scis., Bot. Soc. Am., Am. Soc. Plant Physiologists, Soc. Devel. Biology, Phi Beta Kappa (pres. Wis. Alpha chpt. 1978-79), Sigma Xi. Home: 52 Oak Creek Trl Madison WI 53717-1510 Personal E-mail: enewcomb@wisc.edu.

NEWCOMB, MARTIN EUGENE, JR., chemistry professor; b. Mishauaha, Ind., Nov. 17, 1946; s. Martin Eugene and Yolanda Frances (Saliani) N.; 1 child, Jennifer Ruth. BA, Wabash Coll., 1969; PhD in Chemistry, U. Ill., 1973. Asst. prof. Tex. A&M U., College Station, 1973-81, assoc. prof., 1981-85, prof. chemistry, 1985-91, Wayne State U., Detroit, 1991-2001; prof. U. Ill., Chgo., 2001—. Contbr. articles to Accounts of Chem. Rsch., 1988, Jour. Am. Chem. Soc. 1989— Named Dreyfus Tchr.-Scholar, Camille and Henry Dreyfus Found., 1980-85. Mem. AAAS, Am. Chem. Soc.(Arthur C. Cope Scholar award, 1994, James Flack Norris award in Physical Organic Chemistry, 2000). Office: U Ill Chgo Dept Chemistry Chicago IL 60607

NEWCOMB, ROBERT WAYNE, electrical engineer educator; b. Glendale, Calif., June 27, 1933; s. Robert Dobson and Dorothy Opal (Bissinger) Newcomb; m. Sarah Eleanor Fritz, May 22, 1954; children: Gail E., Robert W. BSEE, Purdue U., 1955; MS, Stanford U., 1957; PhD, U. Calif., Berkeley, 1960. Registered profl. engr., Calif. Rsch. intern Stanford Rsch. Inst., Menlo Park, Calif., 1957-60; tchg. assoc. U. Calif., Berkeley, 1957-60; asst. and tenured assoc. prof. Stanford U., 1960—70; prof. elec. engring. U. Md., College Park, 1970—. Bd. dirs. PARCOR Rsch. program, Universidad Politecnica de Madrid, Spain. Author: Linear Multisport Synthesis, 1966, Active Integrated Circuit Synthesis, 1968, Concepts of Linear Systems and Control, 1968, Network Theory, 1967; editor: Neurocomputing Letters, 2002—06. Recipient IEEE CAS Edn. award, 2001; Fulbright fellow, 1963; Fulbright-Hays fellow, 1976; Robert Wayne Newcomb Lab. opened at U. Politecnica Madrid, 1995. Fellow IEEE (life, golden jubilee medal 1999), Am. Inst. Med. and Biol. Engrs.; mem. Soc. Indsl. and Applied Math., Math. Assn. Am., Acad. Am. Poets. Avocations: films, literature, poetry, guitar. Home: 13120 Two Farm Dr Silver Spring MD 20904-3418 Office: U Md Microsystems Lab Elec/Computer Engring College Park MD 20742-0001 Office Phone: 301-405-3662. Business E-Mail: newcomb@eng.umd.edu.

NEWCOMBE, NORA, psychology professor; BA in Psychology, Antioch Coll., Ohio, 1972; PhD in Psychology and Social Relations, Harvard U., 1976. Asst. prof. Dept. Psychology Pa. State U., 1976—81; assoc. prof. Dept. Psychology Temple U., 1981—87, prof., 1987—, dir. undergrad. studies, 1981—86, assoc. chair Dept. Psychology, 1986—89, dir. Cognitive Divsn., 1995—99, James H. Glackin Disting. faculty fellow, 2003—. Vis. scholar U. Pa., 1986—87, 1993—94, Princeton U., 1999—2000; vis. scholar Spatial Cognition Group Wissenschaftskolleg, Berlin, 2003—04; editor Jour. Exptl. Psychology: Gen., 1996—2001; guest editor spl. issues on early memory Jour. Exptl. Child Psychology, 1993—94; assoc. editor Psychological Bull., 1990—94; cons. editor Child Develop., 1982—96, Developmental Psychology, 1981—87, Jour. Cognition and Develop., 2002—, Psychological Sci., 2004—; reviewer Behavioral and Brain Sciences, Jour. Exptl. Psychology: Learning, Memory, and Cognition, Psychological Rev., Psychonomic Bull. and Rev., Science. Co-editor (with L.S. Liben and A.H. Patterson): (book) Spatial representation and behavior across the life span, 1981; author: Child development: Change over time, 1996; co-author (with J. Huttenlocher): Making space: The development of spatial representation and reasoning, 2000; contbr. articles to profl. journals, chapters to books. Adv. bd. Cornell Inst. Rsch. on Children, 2003—. Recipient Paul W. Eberman Faculty Rsch. award, Temple U., 2004; fellow James McKeen Cattell, 1999—2000. Fellow: Am. Psychological Soc., APA (chair early career award com. 1995, publications and comm. bd. 1998—2000, chair coun. elders 1999—2000, exec. com. divsn. 1 1999—2000, pres. divsn. 7 2001—02, com. scientific awards 2004—06, George A. Miller award 2004), AAAS (sec. sect. psychology 2002—06), Am. Acad. Arts and Sciences; mem.: Soc. Rsch. Child Develop. (program com. 1993—99, co-chair program com. 1995—97), Sigma Xi, Psychonomic Soc. (governing bd. 2002—06), Jean Piaget Soc., Internat. Soc. Study of Behavioral Develop., Internat. Soc. Infant Studies, Cognitive Neuroscience Soc., Cognitive Develop. Soc. (bd. dirs. 2003—). Office: Dept Psychology Temple Univ 1701 N 13th St Rm 565 Philadelphia PA 19122-6085 Office Phone: 215-204-6944. Office Fax: 215-204-8100. E-mail: newcombe@temple.edu.

NEWELL, BARBARA ANN, coatings company executive; b. Portland, Oreg., Mar. 20, 1945; d. John Wesley and Marion Josephine (Hill) Clausen; children: Shamaz, Hukam (dec.), Mardana. BA, Lindenwood Coll. for Women, 1968; MA, Portland State U., 1972; PhD, Summit U., 2000. Owner Shamaz Trading Co., Ukiah, Calif., 1974-77; mgr. small bus. dept. Ernst & Ernst, Portland, 1977-78; CFO All Heart Lumber Co., Ukiah, 1978-83; CFO, CEO Performance Coatings Inc., Ukiah, 1983—, chmn. bd. dirs., 1992—. Chmn. bd. dirs. Rural Visions Found.; treas. chmn. fin. com. Mendocino County Health Clinic, chmn. bd. dirs., 2001-03; CEO, chmn. bd. dirs. Dusky Rose & Assoc., Botanics of Calif.; founder Potter Valley Cafe, 2000; owner Hukam Maj Arabian Horse Ranch, 1998—. Founder, chair Penofin Jazz Festival; chmn. bd. dirs. Mendocino Ballet Co.; bd. dirs. Potter Valley Youth and Cmty. Ctr. Mem. Nat. Paint and Coatings Assn., Golden State Paint and Coatings Assn., Ukiah C. of C. (mem. econ. devel. com. 1993-94), Women in Coatings (Leadership award 1994), Leadership Mendocino. Avocations: showing Arabian horses, reading, children, organic gardening, dance. Office: Penofin-Performance Coatings Inc PO Box 1569 Ukiah CA 95482-1569 Home Phone: 707-489-0241; Office Phone: 707-462-3023. Business E-Mail: ceo@penofin.com.

NEWELL, BRUCE, library director; BS, Sch. Cmty. Services and Pub. Affairs, U. Oreg., 1975; MLS, U. Washington, 1979. Haines branch libr., Baker County, Oreg., 1979; temp. county libr., 1980; online searching libr., libr. develop. & reference libr. (title varied) Mont. State Libr., 1980—84, dir., Mont. Libr. Network, 1999—; info. sys. planner, info. services divsn., dept. adminstrn. State Mont., 1984—86; pub. & network services libr. Lewis & Clark Libr., 1986—99. Bd. dir. Natural Resource Info. Systems Adv. Com., 1996—99, Alternative Energy Resources Orgn., 1984—87, chair bd. dirs., 1986; bd. trustee Online Computer Libr. Ctr., Inc., Dublin, 2007—. Contbr. articles to profl. jours. Mem.: Mont. Libr. Assn. (pres. 1999, western dir.-at-large 1996). Office: Mont Libr Network Mont State Libr 1515 E Sixth Ave PO Box 201800 Helena MT 59620-1800 Address: Online Computer Libr Ctr Inc 6565 Kilgour Pl Dublin OH 43017-3395 Office Phone: 406-444-9816. Office Fax: 406-444-5612. Business E-Mail: bnewell@state.mt.us. *

NEWELL, CHARLDEAN, public administration educator; b. Ft. Worth, Oct. 14, 1939; d. Charles Thurlow and Mildred Dean (Looney) Newell. BA, U. North Tex., Denton, 1960, MA, 1962; PhD, U. Tex., 1968; cert., Harvard U., Cambridge, Mass., 1988. Instr. U. North Tex., Denton, 1965-68, asst. prof., 1968-72; assoc. prof., dir. Fedn. North Tex. Area Univs., Denton, Dallas, 1972-74; assoc. prof., assoc. v.p. acad. affairs U. North Tex., Denton, 1974-76, assoc. prof., chair dept. polit. sci., 1976-80, prof. polit. sci., 1980-92, assoc. v.p., spl. asst. to chancellor, 1982-92, regents prof. pub. adminstrn., 1992—2002, prof. emerita, 2002—. Cons. Miss. Bd. Trustees State Instns. Higher Learning, Jackson, 1983—84, Ednl. Testing Svc., Princeton, NJ, 1980, Princeton, 82, Princeton, 85, Spear

Down & Judin, Dallas, 1994—95, North Tex. Inst. Edn. Visual Arts, Denton, 1993—94; bd. regents Internat. City/County Mgmt. Assn., Washington, 1994—98, vol. credentialing adv. bd., 2002—; trainer Emergency Leaders Program, 2005—. Author (with others): City Executives: Leadership Roles, Work Characteristics and Time Management, 1989, The Effective Local Government Manager, 2004, Texas Politics, 2005; author: Essentials of Texas Politics, 2007; contbr. articles to profl. jours. Chmn. Denton Charter Rev. Com., 1978—79; mem. Denton CSC, 1989—97, chmn., 1992—97; active Denton Blue Ribbon Capital Improvements Com., 1995—96; mem. Denton Devel. Plan Com., 1996—97, Denton Pub. Utilities Bd., 1997—, chmn., 2002—; v.p. Denton Christian Pre-Sch. Bd., 2001—02, pres., 2002—05, mem., 2005—07, City Coun. Ethics Com., 2004; v.p. Our Daily Bread, 2005—, vice-chair, 2005—06; mem. exec. coun. Episcopal Diocese Dallas, 1985—88. Recipient Elmer Staats Career Pub. Svc. award, Nat. Assn. Sch. Pub. Affairs Adminstrn., 1993. Fellow: Nat. Acad. Pub. Adminstrn.; mem.: Am. Soc. for Pub. Adminstrn. (sect. chmn. 1982—83, mem. editl. bd. 1985—88, Donald C. Stone award 2004), Internat. City/County Mgmt. Assn. (hon.), Pi Alpha Alpha (exec. coun. 1995—99), Pi Sigma Alpha (exec. coun. 1988—92). Democrat. Avocations: spectator sports, reading. Home: 2008 Tremont Cir Denton TX 76205-7408 Business E-Mail: newellc@verizon.net.

NEWELL, DAVID L., curator; s. James W. and Lola M. Newell. BA, U. N.Tex., Denton, 1975—80; MFA, So. Meth. U., Dallas, 1980—83; MA, Tex. Tech U., Lubbock, 1988—91. Collections mgr. Tex. Fashion Collection, Denton, 1992—95; curator collections & exhibitions Dallas Hist. Soc., 1995—97; asst. curator decorative & fine arts Colo. Hist. Soc., Denver, 1998—99, dir. design & prodn., 1999—2005; curator exhibitions Gilcrease Mus., Tulsa, 2005—. Designer/curator (exhibitions) The Many Faces of Edward Sherriff Curtis, designer John James Audubon: American Artists and Naturalist, Lines of Discovery: 225 of American Drawing, designer/coordinator American Art in Miniature, 2006, Rendezvous, 2006. Mem.: Costume Soc. Am. (nat. bd. dirs. 2000—03, chair 2001, editor csa series 2004—, southwestern regional pres. 2005—, regional pres. 2005—06, bd. mem. 2000—03, Richard Martin award 2001). D-Liberal. Office: Thomas Gilcrease Mus Assn 1400 N Gilcrease Museum Rd Tulsa OK 74127-2100 Home Phone: 918-592-4222. Business E-Mail: dnewell@gilcrease.org.

NEWELL, ELIZABETH CAROLYN, retired secondary school educator; b. Georgetown, Ky., Mar. 26, 1940; d. George M. Newell, Sr. and Pearl Carlton Newell. BA in Speech and Drama, Georgetown Coll., 1961; student in Speech, Hist. and Theater, U. Ky., 1963—64; MA magna cum laude in Secondary Guidance and Counseling, Georgetown Coll., 1971. Tchr. Jefferson County Pub. Sch. Sys., 1961—97, ret., 1997, substitute tchr., 1997—; mutuel clk. Keeneland Downs, 2005—; clk. Churchill Downs, 2005—. Coach championship debate club Butler HS, dir. championship drama club, coach championship future problem-solving club. Editor: History of Butler Traditional High School: 50 Years of Excellence, 2004. Co-coord. crisis team JCTA, 1976. Named Tchr. of Yr., Ky. H.S. Speech League, 1965, Elizabeth C. Newell Day, JC Judge Exec. David Armstrong, 1997; recipient Tchr. Recognition award, Butler H.S., 1968; grantee, Capitol Holding, WAVE TV, 1992. Mem.: Svc. Employees Internat. Union, Jefferson County Tchrs. Assn. Retired, Ky. Edn. Assn. Avocations: horses, cats, U.K. ballgames, travel, genealogy. Home: 12001 Running Creek Rd Louisville KY 40243-1932

NEWELL, ERIC JAMES, financial planner, retired insurance company executive; b. Toronto, Ont., Can., Sept. 24, 1930; came to U.S., 1959, naturalized, 1970; s. James and Anne (Brown) N.; m. Essie Miskelly, Sept. 30, 1950; 1 son, Eric Wayne. Student, U. Toronto, 1951-53. Pub. acct. W.J. Wilcox & Co., Toronto, 1949-53; chief acct. Toronto Mut. Life Ins. Co., 1953-57; asst. sec. Holland Life Ins. Co., Toronto, 1957-59; with Penn Mut. Life Ins. Co., Phila., 1959-86, assoc. controller, 1965-70, 2d v.p., controller, 1970-84, v.p., controller, 1984-86, ret., 1986; fin., tax cons., 1986—; dir. Hotel Brunswick, Lancaster, Pa., 1982-85. Mem. Traffic and Transp. Bd., Cherry Hill, N.J., 1971-73, Zoning Bd., 1975-78; vice chmn. Cherry Hill Econ. Devel. Bd., 1973-75; pres. Greater Kingston Civic Assn., Cherry Hill, 1970-76; Democratic committeeman, Camden County, 1976-79; vice chmn. Dem. Party, Cherry Hill, 1976. Fellow Life Mgmt. Inst., Royal Commonwealth Soc.; mem. Fin. Execs. Inst., Am. Inst. Corp. Contrs., N.Y. Ins. Accts. Club (chmn. 1984), Nat. Soc. Tax Profls., Royal Black Knights of Ireland, Loyal Orange Assn. (past master), Scotch-Irish Soc. of U.S. (mem. coun., pres. 1999), Am. Legion, Masons. Presbyterian (deacon 1969-72). Home and Office: 20 Wordsworth Street Galloway NJ 08205

NEWELL, LIONEL L., III, treasurer; Grad., Ohio State U. CPA. Fin. exec. Pizza Hut; dir. internal audit Pillsbury Co., v.p. food and internat. retailing audit, v.p., controller; CFO Pillsbury N.Am., 1991—98; sr. v.p. strategy and bus. devel. RJR Nabisco, Inc., 1998—99; sr. v.p., controller PepsiCo Inc., Purchase, NY, 1999, sr. v.p., CFO, sr. v.p., treas., 1999—. Bd. dirs. Am. Electric Power Co., 2004—, Church & Dwight. Mem. dean's adv. bd. Fisher Coll. Bus., Ohio State U. Mem.: AICPA, Ohio Society of CPAs, Fin. Exec. Inst., Exec. Leadership Coun. Office: PepsiCo. Inc 700 Anderson Hill Rd Purchase NY 10577 *

NEWELL, MARK E., lawyer; m. Jo Ann Newell; 2 children. BA summa cum laude, Albion Coll., 1977; MPP, Kennedy Sch. of Govt., 1981; JD magna cum laude, Harvard Univ., 1981. Bar: DC 1983. Law clk. Judge Malcolm R. Wilkey, US Ct. of Appeals, DC Cir., 1981—82, Justice Lewis F Powell Jr., US Supreme Ct., 1982—83; joined Latham & Watkins, 1983—, mng. ptnr. Washington, 1993—2000, chief operating ptnr., 2000—. Editor and treas. Harvard Law Rev., 1981. Mem.: ABA, DC Bar, Phi Beta Kappa. Office: Latham & Watkins Ste 1000 555 Eleventh St NW Washington DC 20004-1304

NEWELL, MARTIN EDWARD, computer scientist; b. Eng. m. Sandra Newell. PhD, U. Utah, 1975. Mem. computer sci. faculty U. Utah, 1977—79; with Xerox Palo Alto Rsch. Ctr., Calif.; founder Ashlar, Inc., 1988; Adobe fellow Adobe Systems Inc., San Jose, Calif. Contbr. articles to sci. jours. Mem.: NAE. Achievements include creating the Utah Teapot, a 3D model that has become a standard reference object in the computer graphics community; patents in field. Office: Adobe Systems Inc 345 Park Ave San Jose CA 95110-2704 *

NEWELL, MIKE, film director; b. St. Albans, England, Mar. 28, 1942; m. Bernice Stegers; 3 children. Attended, Cambridge U. Films include: The Awakening, 1980, Bad Blood, 1983, Dance With a Stranger, 1985, The Good Father, 1986, Amazing Grace and Chuck, 1987, Soursweet, 1988, Enchanted April, 1991, Into the West, 1992, Four Weddings and a Funeral, 1994, An Awfully Big Adventure, 1995, Donnie Brasco, 1997, Pushing Tin, 1999, Mona Lisa Smile, 2003, Harry Potter and the Goblet of Fire, 2005; exec. prodr. (films) Photographing Fairies, 1997, 200 Cigarettes, 1999, Best Laid Plans, 1999, High Fidelity, 2000, Traffic, 2000; TV films include: Big Soft Nellie, Mrs. Mouse, Baa Baa Blacksheep, The Melancholy Hussar, Ready When You Are Mr. McGill, Destiny, The Man in the Iron Mask, 1977, The Gift of Friendship, Blood Feud, 1983, Common Ground, 1990; exec. prodr., dir. (TV series) The Branch, 2003, dir. (TV movie) Jo, 2002. Office: Dogstar UK 5 Sherwood St London W1V 7RA England Address: ICM Ste 219 8942 Wilshire Blvd Beverly Hills CA 90211

NEWELL, PAUL HAYNES, JR., engineering educator; b. Nashville, July 1, 1933; s. Paul Haynes Newell; m. Martha A. Newell; children: Paul Haynes III, Mike, Nan. B.M.E., U. Tenn., 1958, M.M.E., 1961; Mech.E., Mass. Inst. Tech., 1964, PhD, 1966. Registered profl. engr., Ala., Tenn., Tex., N.J. Student asst. mech. engrng. U. Tenn., 1957, instr. mech. engrng., 1958-62; NSF sci. faculty fellow MIT, 1962-65; asso. prof. U. Ala. Coll. Engrng., 1966-69; prof. mech. Tex. A&M U., 1969-72, asso. dean engrng., 1972, prof., head indsl. engrng. dept., 1972-74, prof., head combined programs of behavioral engrng., bioengrng., cybernetic engrng., hygiene and safety engrng., indsl. engrng., 1972-74; prof. biomed. engrng., dept. phys. medicine Baylor Coll. Medicine, 1969-74, prof. biomed. engrng., dept. physiology, 1970-74, prof. biomed. engrng., dept. community medicine, 1972-74, prof. biomed. engrng., dept. rehab., 1972—, mem. grad. faculty, 1970-74, prof. Houston, from 1971; pres., prof. Newark Coll. Engrng., NJ Inst. Tech., 1974-78; prof. Adminstrn. Prosthetics Ctr., NY, 1973-75, VA Hosp., Houston, 1972-75; pres. Newell Engrng., Greenbrier, Tenn., 1979—. Bd. dirs. NJ Bell Tel. Co., Mid Atlantic Nat. Bank, Thomas-Betts Corp. Contbr. articles to profl. jours., chapters to books. Mem. liaison com. NSF, Newark Transp. Coun., N.J. Safety Coun.; sec. exec. com. coun. Boy Scouts Am., Birmingham, Ala., 1966—68; bd. dirs. N.J. State Opera, United Hosps. Newark. With USMCR, Korea. NSF Sci. Faculty fellow. Mem.: NSPE, ASME, AAAS, N.J. Soc. Engrs., Am. Fluid Power Soc., Pres.'s Assn., Soc. Engrng. Sci., Soc. Advanced Med. Sys., Internat. Soc. Prosthetics and Orthotics, Inst. Engrng. Deans, Biomedical Engrng. Soc., Am. Soc. Engrng. Edn., Am. Soc. Artificial Internal Organs, Am. Inst. Indsl. Engrs., Am. Heart Assn., Am. Congress Rehab. Medicine, Ala. Acad. Scis., N.Y. Acad. Scis., Am. Soc. Tool and Mfg. Engrs., Rotary, Sigma Xi, Pi Tau Sigma, Phi Kappa Phi, Tau Beta Pi. Home and Office: Newell Engrng 1855 Lake Rd Greenbrier TN 37073-4619

NEWELL, STEVEN WAYNE, secondary school educator, consultant; m. Sandra Kay Johnson, Feb. 7, 1976 (div. Jan. 12, 1977); m. Sara Josephine Rawland-Staurland, Jan. 18, 1983 (div. Oct. 17, 1988). BA in Biology, Drake U., Des Moines, 1982, MA in Tchg., 1984. Registered EMT Mo. Divsn. Health, 1978; cert. pub. sch. tchr., grades 7-12 Iowa Bd. of Ednl. Examiners, 1984, pub. sch. tchr., grades 6-12 Ill. Bd. Edn., 2000, pub. sch. tchr. in biology grades 7-12 Mont. Bd. Edn., 1990, NY Bd. Edn., 1998. Sr. clk. adminstrn. Goldman, Sachs & Co., 1986—87; per diem substitute tchr. Kansas City, Mo., 1988—89; bus. cons. Iowa City and Des Moines, 1990—93, Chgo., 1995; substitute tchr. West Des Moines, 1994, Iowa City, 1996—97; per diem biology tchr. Bklyn., 1998—99; bus./tech. cons. NYC, 1999—2000; substitute tchr. Grant Wood Area, Iowa City, 2000—07; asst. mgr. and treas. Images of Iowa, Inc., 2002—03; bus. cons. and IT and treas. PA TV Channel 18, Iowa City, 2004—06; ins. agt. HBW Life Ins., Iowa City, 2005—06; per diem substitute tchr. sci. Cedar Rapids, 2006—07; rep. ins. and fin. svcs. Life Investors-Aegon Ins., Strellner Agy., Cedar Rapids, 2007—. Dir.(writer): (TV series) The Professor Noodle Show on Science and Human Values (Excellence award, 2006); author: Dreams of Allon, 1987, Shadow of My Dream: The Allon National, 2000. Com. mem. Johnson County Dem. Party, Iowa City, 2006—07; treas. bd. dir. Pub. Access TV Channel 18, Iowa City, 2003—07. Sgt. USAR, 1982—99, Des Moines. Democrat. Avocations: tai chi, meditation, reading. Office: S Newell Inst 308 E Burlington St 257 Iowa City IA 52240 Office Phone: 319-393-6526. Business E-Mail: snewellinstitute@aol.com.

NEWEY, WHITNEY K., economist, educator; b. July 17, 1954; married; 5 children. BA in Econs., Brigham Young Univ., 1978; PhD, MIT, 1983. Asst. prof., econs. Princeton Univ., 1983—88, assoc. prof., 1988—90; tech. staff Bell Comm. Rsch., 1988—90; prof., econs. MIT, 1990—2004, Jane Berkowitz Carlton and Dennis William Carlton prof., 2004—; internat. fellow Univ. Coll. London, 2004—. Grantee Alfred P. Sloan Rsch. Fellowship, 1987—91. Fellow: Am. Acad. Arts & Scis. Office: MIT Dept Economics E52-262D 50 Memorial Dr Cambridge MA 02142-1347 Office Phone: 617-253-6420. Business E-Mail: wnewey@mit.edu. *

NEWHALL, DAVID, III, retired federal official; b. Phila., Dec. 6, 1937; s. David, Jr. and Jane Martyn (Dunn) Newhall. AB in Politics, Princeton U., 1961. Mgr. Bell Tel. Co. of Pa., Norristown, 1961-63; adminstrv. asst. U.S. Rep. R.S. Schweiker, Washington, 1963-69; chief of staff U.S. Senator R.S. Schweiker, Washington, 1969-81, HHS, Washington, 1981-83; pres. Marmion Plantation Co., King George, Va., 1983—85; prin. dep. asst. sec. def.(health affairs) U.S. Dept. Def., Washington, 1985-90, acting asst. sec. def. (health affairs), 1989-90; gen. ptnr. Marmion Partnership Restorations, 1990—. Bd. dirs. Western Healthcare Alliance, Phoenix, 1995—97; chmn. compliance com., lead dir. TrailBlazer Health Enterprises, LLC, Dallas, 1997—2007; outside dir. First Coast Svc. Options, Inc., Jacksonville, 2007—. Mem.: Princeton Tower Club. Republican. Episcopalian. Home and Office: 7382M Marmion Ln King George VA 22485-7300

NEWHALL, JANE WARD, psychologist; b. South Orange, NJ, Feb. 16, 1940; d. Norman S. Ward and Dorothy Ward (Williams) Gordon; m. John Harrison Newhall, July 15, 1961; children: Carol, Thomas, Daniel. BA, Bryn Mawr Coll., 1962, MA in Edn. and Child Devel., 1984, PhD in Human Devel., 1987; respecialization in clin. psychology, Pacific Grad. Sch. Psychology, 1989. Cert. sch. psychologist; lic. psychologist. Staff psychologist Bryn Mawr (Pa.) Child Study Inst., 1986-87; psychologist Agoraphobia & Anxiety Treatment Ctr., Bala Cynwyd, Pa., 1990-91; staff psychologist Phila. Child Guidance Ctr., 1991-93, inpatient unit mgr., 1993—96, chief psychologist inpatient svcs, 1995—96; pvt. practice specializing in therapy, psychol. testing and consulting, 1991—96; assoc. faculty dept. psychiatry U. Pa. Sch. Medicine, Phila., 1993—96; psychologist Bryn Mawr Coll., 1996—, dir. psychotherapy svcs., 2002—. Lectr. grad. dept. psychology Bryn Mawr Coll., 2002—. Bd. dirs. The Crossroads Sch., Paoli, Pa., 2004—. Mem. APA, Pa. Psychol. Assn., Orton Dyslexia Soc., Gulph Mills Golf Club, Merion Cricket Club. Avocations: tennis, swimming, golf. Home: 414 Righters Mill Rd Penn Valley PA 19072-1423 Office: Bryn Mawr Coll Child Study Inst 101 N Merion Ave Bryn Mawr PA 19010-4322 Office Phone: 610-527-5090. Personal E-mail: jnewhall@verizon.net.

NEWHALL, JOHN HARRISON, retired business executive, management consultant; b. Phila., Sept. 29, 1933; s. Blackwell and Mary Large (Harrison) N.; m. Jane Carol Ward, July 15, 1961; children: Carol Newhall Neilson, Thomas Blackwell, Daniel Ward. BA, Williams Coll., 1955; MBA, Harvard U., 1960. Product mktg. mgr. Campbell Soup Co., Camden, NJ, 1960—67; product group mgr. Gen. Foods Corp. (now Kraft Corp.), White Plains, NY, 1967—70; dir. corp. planning, gen. mgr. Europe H.J. Heinz Co., Pitts., 1970—77; v.p. mktg. Sunoco Corp., Phila., 1977—81; chmn., CEO Aitkin-Kynett Co. (subs. Foote Cone & Belding), Phila., 1981—84; mng. dir., exec. v.p. Campbell-Ewald Co., NYC, 1984—86; prin. mgmt. cons. SRI Internat., Menlo Park, Calif., 1987—90; mng. dir. Strategic Directions, Narberth, Pa., 1990—99; pres. Advanced Promotion Techs., Deerfield Beach, Fla., 1992—93; CEO The Newcomen Soc. of the U.S., Exton, Pa., 1999—2003; ret., 2003. Mem. devel. coun. Williams Coll., Williamstown, Mass., 1977-87, regional vice chmn. capital campaign, 1991-93; mem. Com. of 70, Phila., 1981-84; bd. dirs. Bryn Mawr (Pa.) Hosp., 1982-88, The Haverford (Pa.) Sch., 1980-86, mem. headmaster selection com., 1992, mem. strategic planning com., 1994; bd. dirs. World Affairs Coun., Phila., 1982-86, Found. for Vascular Hypertension Rsch., Phila., 1982-2001, chmn., 1987; bd. dirs. Jr. Achievement, Phila., 1977-81, vice chmn., 1981; bd. dirs. SE chpt. ARC, Phila., 1981-84; bd. dirs. Pa. Economy League, 1981-84; vestryman, lay reader Episcopal Ch., 1964-70, chmn. ann. campaign, 1992, vice chmn. capital campaign, 1994; mem. bd. overseers Hospitality Hall of Honor, 2000-2003; bd. dirs. M.D.I. Drug and Alcohol Abuse Found., 2005—. Lt. USN, 1955—58. Recipient Cert. of Merit Chapel of Four Chaplains, 1983, 85, Alumni Svc. award Haverford Sch., 2006. Mem. Assn. Nat. Advertisers (exec. com. 1977-81), Harvard Bus. Sch. Club Phila. (pres. 1994-96, chmn. 1996-98), Merion Cricket Club (Haverford), Gulph Mills (Pa.) Golf Club, Harbor Club (Seal Harbor, Maine), Union League Club Phila. Republican. Episcopalian. Avocations: skiing, gardening, sailing, swimming. Home: 414 Righters Mill Rd Narberth PA 19072-1423 Personal E-mail: jnewhall@verizon.net.

NEWHART, BOB (GEORGE ROBERT NEWHART), entertainer; b. Oak Park, Ill., Sept. 5, 1929; m. Virginia Quinn, Jan. 12, 1963; 4 children. BS, Loyola U., Chgo., 1952. Acct. U.S. Gypsum Co.; copywriter Fred Niles Film Co.; star TV variety show Bob Newhart Show, 1961; star TV series The Bob Newhart Show, 1972—78, Newhart, 1982-90, Bob, 1992, George & Leo, 1997. Rec. artist (album) The Button Down Mind of Bob Newhart, 1960, The Button Down Mind Strikes Back, 1961, Behind the Button Down Mind, 1961, The Button Down Mind on TV, 1962, Bob Newhart Faces Bob Newhart, 1964, Windmille Are Weakening, 1965, This Is it, 1967, The Best of Bob Newhart, 1971, Very Funny Bob Newhart, 1973; royal command performance, London, 1964; appeared in films Hell is for Heroes, 1962, Hot Millions, 1968, Catch 22, 1970, On a Clear Day You Can See Forever, 1970, Cold Turkey, 1971, First Family, 1980, Little Miss Marker, 1980, In and Out, 1997, Rudolph the Red-Nosed Reindeer: The Movie (voice), 1998, Legally Blonde 2: Red, White & Blonde, 2003, Elf, 2003; TV films include Thursday's Game, 1974, Marathon, 1980, The Librarian: Quest for the Spear, 2004; TV appearances (1960-) include The Ed Sullivan Show (a.k.a. Toast of the Town, (8 Times), Jack Parr Show, 1960, The Andy Williams Show, 1962, 1964, & 1966, The Dean Martin Show (24 Times), Rowan & Martin's Laugh-In, 1968 & 1969, The Tonight Show Starring Johnny Carson (also guest host), It's Garry Shandling's Show, 1990, Late Night with David Letterman, 1993, Murphy Brown, 1994, The Simpsons (voice), 1996, Mad TV, 2001, ER, 2003, Saturday Night Live (host 1980, 1995), Desperate Housewives, 2005, (PBS) Bob Newhart: Unbuttoned (Honored Am. Master 2005), 2005, and numerous others. Grand marshall Tournament Roses Parade, 1991. With U.S. Army, 1952-54. Recipient Emmy award, 1961, Peabody award, 1961, Sword of Loyola award, 1976, Legend to Legend award, 1993, three Grammy awards 1960, Kennedy Ctr. Mark Twain award, 2002, Icon award, TVLand, 2005; named to TV Acad. of Arts & Sci. Hall of Fame, 1993; honored as an American Master (Bob Newhart: Unbuttoned), PBS, 2005. Best Known Trademarks: Stammering delivery while talking; Telephone monologues as part of act; One-sided conversations. Office: c/o Capell Rudolph 11601 Wilshire Blvd Ste 1840 Los Angeles CA 90025-1759

NEWHOUSE, ALAN RUSSELL, retired federal official; b. NYC, Feb. 27, 1938; s. Russell Conwell and Clara Lucille (Scovell) N.; m. Margo Stiles Hicks, Feb. 3, 1960; children: Daryl, Jeffrey, William. BEE, Cornell U., 1960. Engr. Bur. of Ships, Washington, 1964-66; nuc. power engr., chief West Milton field office AEC, Schenectady, NY, 1966-69; sr. exec. AEC, ERDA, U.S. Dept. Energy, Washington, 1969-92; dep. asst. sec. Space and Def. Power Systems Office Nuc. Energy, Washington, 1992-93; dir. Office Space and Def. Power Systems, 1993-95; dir. Project Prometheus Office of Exploration, NASA, 2003—04; ind. cons., 1995—. Composer numerous musical works. Mem. Cmty. Orchestra So. Md. in Concert. Lt. USN, 1960-64. Mem.: AIAA, IEEE, Am. Nuc. Soc. Unitarian Universalist. Home and Office: 24670 Greenview Dr Hollywood MD 20636-4823 E-mail: consultant@arnewhouse.com.

NEWHOUSE, BENJAMIN REED, composer, educator; b. Stroudsburg, Pa., July 19, 1976; s. Dean Gregory and Norma Jean Newhouse. MusB, Eastman Sch. Music, Rochester, NY, 1998; MBA, U. So. Calif., LA, 2006. Composer Alan Ett Music Group, LA, 1999—2002; prof. Burklee Coll. Music, Boston, 2002—04. Author: Producing Music with Digital Performer, 2004; editor: Royalty Week, 2007. Recipient Howard Hanson award, Eastman Sch. music, 1998; Pete Carpenter fellow, BMI, 1999. Mem.: Mensa.

NEWHOUSE, DONALD E., newspaper publishing executive; b. 1930; s. Samuel Irving Newhouse Sr. and Mitzi Epstein; married; 3 children. Student, Syracuse U. With Advance Publs. Inc., Staten Island, NY, 1951—, pres., 1979—; chmn. The Associated Press, NYC, 1997—2002. Treas. Herald Am., Syracuse, 1960—, The Post Standard, Syracuse, 1960—, The Syracuse Herald Jour., 1960—, The Herald Co. Inc., 1960—; co-founder Metro-Suburbia, Inc., NYC, 1963; prin. The Trenton (N.J.) Times, Times of Trenton Pub. Corp.; pres. The Star Ledger, Newark. Named one of Forbes Richest Americans, 1999—, World's Richest People, Forbes Mag., 1999—. Office: Advance Publications Inc 950 Fingerboard Rd Staten Island NY 10305-1453 *

NEWHOUSE, JEFFREY H., radiologist, educator; b. NY, Dec. 10, 1942; s. Edward and Dorothy DeLay Newhouse; m. Nancy Hargadon, June 4, 1983; children: Amy Lee, Edward Walter. AB, Princeton U., NJ, 1963; MD, Harvard U., Boston, 1967. Diplomate Am. Bd. Radiology, 1972. Intern gen. surgery Roosevelt Hosp., NYC, 1967—68; resident diagnostic radiology Mass. Gen. Hosp., Boston, 1968—72; instr. radiology Med. Sch. Harvard U., Boston, 1974—78, asst. prof. radiology Med. Sch., 1978—83; assoc. prof. radiology Columbia-Presbyn. Med. Ctr. Columbia Coll. Physicians and Surgeons, NYC, 1983—88, chief divsn. abdominal radiology, 1983—; prof. radiology and urology Columbia Coll. Physicians and Surgeons/NY Presbyn. Hosp., 1988—; vice chmn. dept. radiology N.Y. Presbyn. Hosp., 1998—. Disting. scientist Armed Forces Inst. Pathology, Washington, 1996. Co-author: Understanding MRI, Essentials of Uroradiology, Textbook of Uroradiology; editor: Urologic Radiology and General Abdomen, MRI of the Urinary Tract, Clinical MRI, Gamuts in Radiology; contbr. 172 scientific papers. Maj. med. corps. US Army, 1972—74. Recipient Best Sci. Paper award, Soc. Uroradiology, 1981, online jour., 2002, Tchr. of Yr. award, Dept. Urology, Columbia U. Med. Ctr., 2000, Dept. Radiology, Columbia U. Med. Ctr., 2004; scholar, Gen. Motors, 1959—63, James Picker Found., 1969—72. Fellow: Am. Coll. Radiology (chmn. com. appropriateness criteria 2002—05); mem.: Bronxville Field Club, Union Boat Club. Avocations: skiing, tennis, sailing, sculling. Home: 10 Hilltop Road Bronxville NY 10708 Office: Columbia University Medical Center 177 Fort Washington Avenue New York NY 10032 Office Phone: 212-305-7898. Business E-Mail: jhn2@columbia.edu.

NEWHOUSE, JOSEPH PAUL, economist, educator; b. Waterloo, Iowa, Feb. 24, 1942; s. Joseph Alexander and Ruth Linnea (Johnson) Newhouse; m. Margaret Louise Locke, June 22, 1968; children: Eric Joseph, David Locke. BA, Harvard U., 1963, PhD, 1969; postgrad (Fulbright scholar), Goethe U., Frankfurt, Germany, 1963—64. Staff economist Rand Corp., Santa Monica, Calif., 1968—72, dep. program mgr., health and biosci. rsch., 1971—88, sr. staff economist, 1972—81, head econs. dept., 1981—85, sr. corp. fellow, 1985—2001; John D. MacArthur prof. health policy and mgmt., dir. div. Health Policy Rsch. and Edn., Harvard U., 1988—. Lectr. UCLA, 1970—83, adj. prof., 1983—88; mem. faculty Rand Grad. Sch., 1972—88; dir. Rand-UCLA Ctr. for Study Health Care Fin. Policy, 1984—88, co-dir., 1988—92; prin. investigator health ins. study grant HHS, 1971—86; chmn. health svcs. rsch. study sect. HHS-Agy. for Health Care Policy and Rsch., 1989—93; mem. Nat. Commn. Cost Med. Care, 1976—77; mem. health svcs. devel. grants study sect. HEW, 1978—82, Inst. Medicine of NAS, 1978—, mem. coun., 1991—97; mem. Physician Payment Rev. Commn., 1993—96; chmn. Prospective Payment Assessment Com., 1996—97; vice chair Medicare Payment Assessment Commn., 1997—2001, mem., 2001—; bd. regents Nat. Libr. Medicine, 1999—; bd. dirs. Aetna, ABT Assocs., Nat. Com. Quality Assurance. Author: The Economics of Medical Care, 1978, The Cost of Poor Health Habits, 1991, A Measure of Malpractice, 1993, Free for All?, 1993, Pricing the Priceless, 2002; editor: Jour. Health Econs., 1981—; assoc. editor: Jour. Econ. Perspectives, 1992—98, mem. editl. bd.: New Eng. Jour. Medicine, 2003—; contbr. articles to profl. jours. Recipient David Kershaw award and prize, Assn. Pub. Policy and Mgmt., 1983, Baxter Am. Found. prize, 1988, Adminstr.'s citation, Health Care Fin. Adminstrn., 1988, Hans Sigrist Found. prize, 1995, Elizur Wright award, 1995, Zvi Griliches award, 2000, Kenneth Arrow award, 2001, Paul A. Samuelson Excellence cert., TIAA CREF, 2003. Fellow: AAAS, Am. Acad. Arts and Scis.; mem.: Am. Soc. Health Economists (pres. 2005—), Internat. Health Econs. Assn. (pres. 1996—98, bd. dirs. 1996—2002), Econometric Soc., Royal Econ. Soc., Am. Econ. Assn., Assn. for Health Svcs. Rsch. (bd. dirs. 1991—, pres. 1993—94, Article of Yr. award 1989). Office: Harvard U Health Policy Rsch and Edn 180 Longwood Ave Boston MA 02115-5821

NEWHOUSE, MARK WILLIAM, publishing executive; b. NYC, Oct. 14, 1948; s. Norman Nathan and Alice (Gross) Newhouse; m. Lorry A. Whitehead, June 1, 1974; children: Jesse Louis, Charlotte Ann. BA, Yale U., 1969. V.p., gen. mgr. The Star-Ledger, Newark, 1980—. Bd. dirs. Newspaper Assn. Am., 2005—. Bd. dirs. N.Y.C. Opera, 1992—, pres., 1993—; bd. dirs. Audit Bur. Circulations, 1995—2004, Glimmerglass Opera, 1997—, N.Y.C. Outward Bound Ctr., 2004—. Office: Newark Morning Star Ledger Co One Star Ledger Plz Newark NJ 07102-1200

NEWHOUSE, SAMUEL IRVING, JR., (SI NEWHOUSE JR.), publishing executive; b. Nov. 8, 1927; s. Samuel Irving Newhouse Sr. and Mitzi Epstein; m. Jane Franke (div.); 3 children; m. Victoria Carrington Benedict de Ramel. Pub. Vogue mag., 1964; chmn. Condé Nast Publs. Inc., NYC, 1975—; also chmn. bd. dirs., CEO Advance Publs. Inc., SI, NY, 1979—. Named one of Top 200 Collectors, ARTnews Mag., 2004, 2006, Forbes Richest Americans, 1999—, World's Richest People, Forbes Mag., 1999—; recipient Henry J. Fisher award, Mag. Pubs. Assn., 1985. Avocation: Collector of Modern and contemporary art. Address: Advance Pubs Inc 950 Fingerboard Rd Staten Island NY 10305-1453 *

NEWICK, CRAIG DAVID, architect; b. Orange, NJ, Feb. 14, 1960; s. Russel Forester and Helen (Welch) N.; m. Linda Hammer Lindroth, June 6, 1987; 1 child, Zachary Eran. BA in Architecture, Lehigh U., 1982; MArch, Yale U., 1987. Registered architect, Conn. Designer, draftsman The Archtl. Studio, Easton, Pa., 1983-84; job capt., project designer Svigals & Assocs., New Haven, 1985; designer, draftsman Centerbrook (Conn.) Architects, 1986; job capt., project designer Allan Dehar Assocs., Architects & Planners, New Haven, 1988-90; ptnr. Lindroth & Newick, New Haven, 1991—; designer Cesar Pelli & Assocs., Inc., New Haven, 1992; project arch. Tai Soo Kim Ptnrs., Hartford, Conn., 1995—2001; prin. Newick Archs., New Haven, 2001—. Vis. faculty Vis. Critics Studio, Lehigh U., 1993; vis. critic Wesleyan U., 1990-2005, R.I. Sch. Design, 1988, Yale U., 2000-05; faculty Creative Arts Workshop, New Haven, 1991, 92; co-dir. Eyebeam Competition, N.Y.C. Exhibitions include Out Of Bounds; author: Simultaneous Space (first prize artists books, 1994). Recipient 1st place award Am. Visionary Set Design Competition, 1989, 3d place award Astronauts Meml. Design Competition, 1988, ID Mag. Ann. Design Rev. award, 1990, 2d prize African Burial Ground Competition Mcpl. Arts Soc. N.Y., 1994, 1st place drawing award Conn. Soc. Architects, 1997, AIA Conn. honor award, 2000. AIA Conn. Design award, 2005, Nat. AIA Design citation, 2006; grantee New Eng. Found. for Arts, 1992, NEA Interarts grantee Rockefeller Found., 1989-90, Found. for Contemporary Performance Art, 1989, 90, Humanities Coun. of Fairfield U., 1995, AIA Conn. Designer award, 2006; New Eng. Found. for Arts Regional fellow, 1993, Conn. Commn. on the Arts fellow, 1998, others. Mem. Architecture League N.Y. (young architects forum 1991, emerging voices, 1996). Office: Newick Archs 85 Willow St New Haven CT 06511

NEWILL, JAMES WAGNER, accounting executive; b. Greensburg, Pa., Dec. 22, 1934; s. James Meyers and Ruth Elizabeth (Wagner) N.; m. Helene Margaret Dolibois, Feb. 18, 1957; 1 child, J. Eric. BBA, St. Vincent Coll., Latrobe, Pa., 1962. CPA, Pa., Ohio, Fla. Staff acct. George Conti & Co., CPA, Greensburg, 1962-65; internal auditor Duquesne Light Co., Pitts., 1965-67; supr. accounts payable and gen. ledger Kennametal, Inc., Latrobe, 1967-71; asst. controller Glosser Stores, Inc., Johnstown, Pa., 1971-73; controller, asst. treas. Meridian Plastics, Inc., Byesville, Ohio, 1973-76; regional controller Friendly Ice Cream Corp., Wilbraham, Mass., 1976-79; pres. J.W. Newill Co., Troy, Ohio, 1979-92; pvt. practice Fla., 1993—. Bd. dirs. 1st Commonwealth Fin. Corp., Indiana, Pa., 1999—. Elected town commr. Highland Beach, 2005—; v.p. bd. dirs. Troy-Hayner Cultural Ctr., Troy, Ohio, 1982—85, fin. adv. bd. Highland Beach, Fla., 2003—05. To staff sgt. USAF, 1954—58. Mem. AICPA, Pa. Inst. CPAs, Ohio Soc. CPAs, Fla. Inst. CPAs, Nat. Assn. Accts., Sea Ranch Club Boca (bd. dirs. 1999-2001), Masons, Shriners, Scottish Rite, Rotary (chmn. com., Paul Harris fellow), Elks. Republican. Presbyterian. Avocations: travel, tennis, theater. Office Phone: 561-395-0987.

NEWITT, JOHN GARWOOD, JR., lawyer; b. Charlotte, NC, Apr. 9, 1941; s. John Garwood and Sarah Elizabeth (Stratford) N.; m. Catherine Elizabeth Hubbard, Aug. 28, 1965; children: Catherine Stratford, Elizabeth Blake BA, Wake Forest U., 1963, JD, 1965; postgrad., U. Va., 1966—68; CBA Bus. Mgmt., Ctrl. Piedmont C.C., 2001. Bar: NC 1965, US Ct. Mil. Appeals 1965, US Dist. Ct. (we. dist.) NC 1968, US Ct. Claims 1968, US Tax. Ct. 1968, US Ct. Appeals (4th cir.) 1984. Ptnr. Newitt & Newitt, Charlotte, 1968—73; sr. ptnr. Newitt & Bruny, Charlotte, 1973—. Lectr. The Judge Advocate Gen.'s Sch., 1965-68, United Way Vol. Leadership Devel. Program, 1986-93. Contbr. articles to profl. jours Chmn. Bd. Zoning Adjustment, 1971-77; bd. dirs. Carolina Group Homes, 1992-95. Recipient awards ASCAP Mem. NC Bar Assn., Mecklenburg County Bar Assn., NC Coll. Advocacy (cert. competency), Charlotte Bus. Roundtable, Myers Park Country Club (past pres., bd. dirs.), Selwyn Men's Fellowship (past pres.), Good Fellows, Phi Delta Phi (past sec.) Republican. Presbyterian. Avocations: jogging, golf. Home: 3216 Ferncliff Rd Charlotte NC 28211-3259 Office: Newitt & Bruny 417 East Blvd Ste 104 Charlotte NC 28203-5163 Office Phone: 704-372-6181. Personal E-mail: johnnewitt@cs.com. Business E-Mail: newittbru@cs.com.

NEWKIRK, INGRID, animal rights activist; b. Surrey, Eng., July 11, 1949; m. Steve Newkirk, 1967 (div. 1980). Former animal protection officer and dep. sheriff, Md.; poundmaster Washington, 1978; former chief of animal disease control Commn. on Public Health, Washington; dir. cruelty investigations Washington Humane Soc., Washington, 1978-80; pres., co-founder (with Alex Pacheco) People for the Ethical Treatment of Animals (PETA), Washington, 1980—. Author: Save the Animals! 101 Easy Things You Can Do, 1990, Kids Can Save the Animals! 101 Easy Things You Can Do, The Compassionate Cook, 250 Things You Can Do to Make Your Cat Adore You, You Can Save the Animals: 251 Simple Ways to Stop Thoughtless Cruelty, Making Kind Choices; TV appearances include The Today Show, The Oprah Winfrey Show, Nightline, 20/20. Office: PETA 501 Front St Norfolk VA 23510

NEWKIRK, JOHN BURT, retired metallurgical research administrator; b. Mpls., Mar. 24, 1920; s. Burt Leroy and Mary Louise (Leavenworth) N.; m. Carolyn Mae Jordan, Aug. 4, 1951; children: Jeffrey Burt (dec.), John Jordan, Victoria Louise Lierheimer, Christina Newkirk Seldomridge. B in Metall. Engring., Rensselaer Poly. Inst., 1941; MS, Carnegie Inst. Tech., 1947, ScD, 1950. Metall. investigator Bethlehem Steel Co., Pa., 1941-42; Fulbright postdoctoral fellow Cambridge (Eng.) U., 1950-51; research metallurgist research lab. Gen. Electric Co., Schenectady, 1951-59; prof. Cornell U., 1959-65; Phillipson prof. U. Denver, 1965-74, prof. phys. chemistry, 1975-84, Phillipson prof. emeritus, 1984—; pres. Denver Biomaterials, Inc., 1969-86, Colo. Biomed., Inc., 1987-2000; ret., 2000. Editor Rews. on High Temperature Materials, 1973-78; co-editor: 16 ann. volumes Advances in X-Ray Analysis; contbr. articles profl. jours. Lt. USNR, 1942-46. Fellow Am. Soc. Metals (life); mem. Kiwanis, Sigma Xi, Tau Beta Pi, Phi Kappa Phi, Alpha Sigma Mu (internat. pres. 1950), Alpha Tau Omega. Republican. Baptist. Personal E-mail: jack@snowvalley.org.

NEWKIRK, THOMAS CHARLES, lawyer; b. NYC, June 6, 1942; s. Rudolph H. and Ruth H. (Wilson) N.; m. Nancy W., Dec. 23, 1965; children: Jennifer L., Christopher T. BA, Cornell U., 1964, LLB with distinction, 1966. Bar: N.Y. 1966, D.C. 1976, U.S. Ct. Appeals (2d cir.) 1968, U.S. Ct. Appeals (D.C. cir.) 1974. Assoc. Donovan Leisure Newton & Irvine, NY, 1966-72; asst. chief counsel Securities Industry Study, U.S. Senate, Washington, 1972; assoc. Donovan Leisure Newton & Irvine, Washington, 1973-75; sr. atty. Office of Legal Counsel, Dept. Justice, Washington, 1975-78; asst. gen. counsel US Dept. Energy, Washington, 1978-79, dep. gen. counsel, 1979-85, chief counsel for jud. litigation, 1985; chief litig. counsel SEC, Washington, 1986-93, assoc. dir. div. of enforcement, 1993—2004; ptnr. Jenner & Block LLP, Washington, 2004—. Lectr. in field. Contbr. articles to profl. jours. Recipient Presdl. Meritorious Exec. award Pres. of U.S., 1980, 92, Exceptional Svc. award Sec. of Energy, 1985, Outstanding Svc. medal Sec. of Energy, 1981. Mem. ABA, Assn. Bar City of N.Y. Avocations: skiing, sailing, tennis, opera. Office: Jenner & Block LLP 601 13th St NW Ste 1200 S Washington DC 20005 Home Phone: 301-320-5007; Office Phone: 202-639-6099. Business E-Mail: tnewkirk@jenner.com.

NEWLAND, CHESTER ALBERT, public administration educator; b. Kansas City, Kans., June 18, 1930; s. Guy Wesley and Mary Virginia (Yoakum) N. BA, U. N. Tex., Denton, 1954; MA, U. Kans., 1955, PhD, 1958. Social Sci. Rsch. Coun. fellow U. Wis. and U.S. Supreme Ct., 1958-59; instr. polit. sci. Idaho State U., Pocatello, 1959-60; mem. faculty U. North Tex., Denton, 1960-66, prof. govt., 1963-66, dir. dept. govt., 1963-66; prof. polit. sci. U. Houston, 1967-68; dir. Lyndon Baines Johnson Libr., Austin, Tex., 1968-70; prof. pub. adminstrn. U. So. Calif., 1966-67, 68-71, 76-82, 84-92, Duggan disting. prof. pub. adminstrn., 1992—; prof. George Mason U., Fairfax, Va., 1982-84. Faculty Fed. Exec. Inst., 1971-76, dir. 1973-76, 80-81; mgr. task force on fed. labor-mgmt. rels. US Pers. Mgmt. Project, Pres.'s Reorgn., Washington, 1977-78. Editor in chief Pub. Adminstrn. Rev., 1984-90; contbr. articles to profl. jours. Chmn. Mcpl. Rsch. Coun., Denton, 1963-64; city councilman, Denton, 1964-66; mem. Pub. Sector Commn. on Productivity and Work Quality, 1974-78; trustee Sacramento (Calif.) Mus. History, Sci. and Tech., 1993-95; mem. UN Devel. Program Kazakhstan, 1997-2000, strategy review program, 2002, Moldova, 1994, Kuwait, 1991, 95-96; cons. Poland, 1990-91, Hungary, 1991, Czech and Slovak Republics, 1992, Bank of Greece, 1999-2002, 04, Taiwan, 2001. Fellow Nat. Acad. Pub. Adminstrn., (trustee 1979-82, nominating com. 2006—); mem. Southwestern Social Sci. Assn. (chmn. govt. sect. 1964-65), Am. Soc. Pub. Adminstrn. (pres. Dallas-Ft. Worth chpt. 1964-65, nat. coun. 1976, 78-81, editl. bd. jour. 1972-76, chmn. publ. com. 1975-79, program chmn. 1977, nat. pres. 1981-82, Dimock award 1984, Van Riper award 2002, Waldo Lifetime Scholarly Pubs. award 2007), Am. Polit. Sci. Assn., Internat. Pers. Mgmt. Assn. (program chmn. 1978, Stockberger award 1979), Am. Acad. Polit. and Social Sci., Internat. City Mgmt. Assn. (hon., Calif. bd. 2003—, credentialing adv. bd. 2006—), Nat. Assn. Schs Pub. Affairs and Adminstrn. (Staats Pub. Svc. award 1989). Office: Univ Southern California 1800 I St Sacramento CA 95811-3004

NEWLAND, RUTH LAURA, small business owner; b. Ellensburg, Wash., June 4, 1949; d. George J. and Ruth Marjorie (Porter) N. BA, Cen. Wash. State Coll., 1970, MEd, 1972; EdS, Vanderbilt U., 1973; PhD, Columbia Pacific U., 1981. Tchr. Union Gap (Wash.) Sch., 1970-71; owner Newland Ranch Gravel Co., Yakima, Wash., 1998; ptnr. Arnold Artificial Limb, Yakima, 1981-86, owner, pres. Yakima and Richland, Wash., 1986—. Owner Newland Ranch, Yakima, 1969—. Contbg. mem. Nat. Dem. Com., Irish Nat. Caucus Found.; mem. Pub. Citizen, We The People, Nat. Humane Edn. Soc.; charter mem. Nat. Mus. Am. Indian. George Washington scholar Masons, Yakima, 1967. Mem. NAFE, NOW, Am. Orthotic and Prosthetic Assn., Internat. Platform Assn., Nat. Antivisection Soc. (life), Vanderbilt U. Alumni Assn., Peabody Coll. Alumni Assn., Columbia Pacific U. Alumni Assn., World Wildlife Fund, Nat. Audubon Soc., Greenpeace, Mus. Fine Arts, Humane Soc. U.S., Wilderness Soc., Nature Conservancy, People for Ethical Treatment of Animals, Amnesty Internat., The Windstar Found., Rodale Inst., Sierra Club (life), Emily's List. Democrat. Avocations: reading, gardening, sewing, handcrafts. Home: 2004 Riverside Rd Yakima WA 98901-8540 Office: Arnold Artificial Limb 9 S 12th Ave Yakima WA 98902-3106 *Personal philosophy: God first. Then be politically and socially conservative but liberal in your concern for others.*

NEWLIN, CHARLES FREMONT, lawyer; b. Palestine, Ill., Nov. 18, 1953; s. Charles Norris and Regina Helen (Correll) N.; m. Jean Bolt, Jan. 6, 1975; children: Christian N., Charles W., Ethan A. BA in Polit. Sci. summa cum laude, Ill. Wesleyan U., 1975; JD cum laude, Harvard U., 1978. Bar: Ill. 1978, US Dist. Ct. (no. dist.) Ill. 1978, US Tax Ct. 1980. Law clk. Sugarman, Rogers, Barshak & Cohen, Boston, 1976-78; assoc. Mayer, Brown & Platt, Chgo., 1978-84, ptnr., 1985-94, Sonnenschein, Nath & Rosenthal, 1994—2002, McGuire Woods LLP, 2002—03, Harrison & Held LLP, Chgo. Research asst., Harvard Law Sch., Mass., 1976, adj. prof. law DePaul U., Chgo., 1986-90, adminstr. Wealth Mgmt.(trusts, estates and found. practice area), 1989-1994. Contbg. author: Am. Law of Property, 1975, Trust Adminstrn. Ill., 1983, 87, 92, 99, Bogert on Trusts, 1986-91, The Lawyer's Guide to Retirement, 1991, 94; contbr. articles to profl. jours. Scouting coord. DuPage area coun. Boy Scouts Am., Woodridge, Ill., 1984-86; bishop's counselor Mormon Ch., Woodridge, 1984-86; mem. planned giving com. Ill. divsn. Am. Cancer Soc., 1988—, chair, 1997—; active Boys and Girls Clubs of Chgo., 1993—; mem. bd. dirs. Suburban Chgo. Planned Giving Coun., 1997, Ill. Inst. for Continuing Legal Edn., 1999—, vol. legal cons. The Tower Chorale, Westner Springs, Ill., 1989-91. Listed in Who's Who in Am., Who's Who in Am. Law, Who's Who of Emerging Leaders in Am., Who's Who in Practicing Atty., Internat. Who's Who Profl., named Leading Ill. Atty., Am. Research Corp., 1997. Fellow Am. Coll. Trust and Estate Counsel; mem. Chgo. Bar Assn., 1982-, Chgo. Estate Planning Coun., Tech. Practice Com., 1991-2000, Elder Law Com., 1995-, Probate Practice Com., U Club Chgo., 1986-1992, Met. Club Chgo., 1994-2000. Democrat. Mem. Lds Ch. Office: Harrison & Held LLP 333 W Wacker Dr Ste 950 Chicago IL 60606 Office Phone: 312-322-3940. Office Fax: 866-406-9515. Business E-Mail: mnewlin@harrisonheld.com.

NEWLIN, STEPHEN DORE, chemicals executive; b. Pierre, SD, Feb. 8, 1953; s. Douglas M. and Mary Newlin; m. Terry Ochsner, Aug. 17, 1975; children: Grant, Scott. BSCE, S.D. Sch. Mines & Tech., 1975; Advanced Mgmt. Program, Harvard U., 1990. Dist. rep. Nalco Chem. Co., Naperville, Ill., 1976-80, sales rep., 1980-82, dist. mgr. Watergy group, 1982-84, sales mgr. Watergy group, 1984-87, gen. mgr. Watergy group, 1987-90, gen. mgr. Unisolv group, 1990-92, gen. mgr. pulp & paper group, 1992-93, v.p.-pres. Nalco Pacific, 1993-94, pres. Nalco Europe, 1994, pres. specialty divsn., 1996, pres., 1998, COO, vice chmn., 2000; chmn. Nalco Exxon Energy Chemicals, 2000—01; private investor and bus. advisor, 2001—03; pres. indsl. ctr. Ecolab Inc., 2003—06; chmn., pres., CEO PolyOne Corp., Avon Lake, Ohio, 2006—. Bd. dirs. Black Hills Corp., 2004—. With USPHS. Mem. Paper Industry Mgrs., Triangle Alumni Assn. Avocation: sports. Office: PolyOne Corp 33587 Walker Rd Avon Lake OH 44012 *

NEWLIN, WILLIAM RANKIN, lawyer; b. Pitts., Dec. 1, 1940; s. Theodore F. Newlin and Elizabeth Crooks; m. Ann Kleinschmidt, Aug. 25, 1962; children: Steffler Ann, Shelley Kay, William Rankin II. AB, Princeton U., 1962; JD, U. Pitts., 1965; DBA (hon.), Robert Morris Coll., 1997. Bar: Pa. 1965. Assoc. Buchanan Ingersoll, Pitts., 1965-71, ptnr., 1971—2003, mng. dir., 1980—2003; mng. gen. ptnr. CEO Venture Fund, Pitts., 1985—2000; chmn. bd. Kennametal Inc., Latrobe, Pa., 1996—2002, exec. v.p., 2003—, chief adminstrv. officer, 2003—. Bd. dirs. bd. Nat. City Bank Pa., Pitts., Pitts. Regional Alliance, Colson Corban, (hon.) British Consul, Pitts. Editor in chief U. Pitts. Law Rev., 1963; contbr. articles to profl. jours. Chmn., Gov. Thornburgh's Corp. Adv. Com., 1980-82; bd. dirs. Mfr. Studies Bd. nat. Rsch. Coun., Washington, 1988-89, Pitts. High Tech. Coun., 1982—, Pa. Tech. Coun. Recipient Entrepreneur of Yr. award Ernst & Young, Inc. Mag./ Merrill Lynch, 1991. Fellow Am. Bar Found., Pa. Bar Found.; mem. ABA (corp. banking, bus. law sect.), Pa. Bar Assn. (mem. coun. corp. banking and bus. law sect. 1973-82, chmn. sect. 1979-81, Spl. Achievement award 1982), Allegheny County Bar Assn., Assn. of Bar of City of N.Y., Am. Law Inst., Pa. S.W. Assn. (trustee), Greater Pitts. C. of C. (bd. dirs.), Duquesne Club (dir. 1982-85), Laurel Valley Golf Club (bd. dirs. 2003—), Allegheny Country Club (bd. dirs. 1988-2002). Office: Dicks Sporting Goods Inc 306 Industry Dr Pittsburgh PA 15275 Business E-Mail: bill.mewlin@dscs.com.

NEWMAN, ANDREA FISCHER, air transportation executive; AB, U. Mich., Ann Arbor, 1979; JD, George Washington U., 1983. With Patton, Boggs, Washington; dept. asst. to V.P. George Bush The White House; spl. counsel to asst. sec. def. for acquisitions and logistics Dept. Def.; sr. ptnr Miller, Canfield, Paddock and Stone, Detroit; v.p. state and local affairs NW Airlines Corp., sr. v.p. govt. affairs Detroit, 2001—. Bd. regents U. Mich., Ann Arbor, 1994—; vice chmn. George W. Bush for Pres. Campaign, co-chmn. fin. com. Mich., 2000; bd. dirs. Mich. Econ. Devel. Corp. Found., Mich. Thanksgiving Day Parade Found., Isiah Thomas Found. Mem.: Detroit Econ. Club (v.p.). Office: NW Airlines Detroit Met Airport 2601 WorldGateway Pl Detroit MI 48242 Office Phone: 734-955-3428. E-mail: afnewman@umich.edu. *

NEWMAN, ANDREW EDISON, restaurant manager; b. St. Louis, Aug. 14, 1944; s. Eric Pfeiffer and Evelyn Frances (Edison) N.; m. Peggy Gregory, Feb. 14, 1984; children: Daniel Mark, Anthony Edison. BA, Harvard U., 1966, MBA, 1968. With Office of Sec. Def., Washington, 1968-70; with Edison Bros. Stores, Inc., St. Louis, 1970-95, v.p. ops. and adminstrn., 1975-80, dir., 1978-96, exec. v.p., 1980-86, chmn., 1987-95; chmn., CEO Race Rock Internat., St. Louis, 1995—. Bd. dirs. Lee Enterprises, Davenport, Iowa. Trustee Washington U. Office: 8000 Maryland Ave Saint Louis MO 63105-3752

NEWMAN, ANDY, journalist; Bklyn. Bur. reporter New York Times. Author: (articles) Serving Gays who Serve God, 2005 (Art Feature award, Association of Alternative Newsweeklies, 2003), Fire Dept. Chaplain Resigns After Remarks About 9/11, 2005. Office: The New York Times 229 W 43rd St New York NY 10036

NEWMAN, BARBARA MILLER, psychologist, educator; b. Chgo., Sept. 6, 1944; d. Irving George and Florence (Levy) Miller; m. Philip R. Newman, June 12, 1966; children: Samuel Asher, Abraham Levy, Rachel Florence. Student, Bryn Mawr Coll.; AB with honors in Psychology, U. Mich., 1966, PhD in Devel. Psychology, 1971. Undergrad. research asst. in psychology U. Mich., 1963-64, research asst. in psychology, 1964-69, teaching fellow, 1965-71, asst. project dir. Inst. for Social Research, 1971-72, univ. lectr. in psychology and research assoc., 1971-72; asst. prof. psychology Russell Sage Coll., 1972-76, assoc. prof., 1977-78; assoc. prof. and chair dept. family rels. and human devel. Ohio State U., 1978-83, prof. and chair, 1983-86, assoc. provost for faculty recruitment and devel., 1987-92, prof., 1992-2000; prof., chair dept. human devel. and family studies U. R.I., 2000—06, prof., 2006—. Author: Development Through Life, 1975, 9th edit., 2006; author: (with P. Newman) Living: The Process of Adjustment, 1981, Understanding Adulthood, 1983; author: Adolescent Development, 1986, When Kids Go to College, 1992, Childhood and Adolescence, 1997; author: (with P. Newman, L. Landry-Meyer and B. Lohman) Life Span Development: A Case Book, 2003; author: Theories of Human Development, 2007; contbr. articles to profl. jours. Vis. scholar, UCLA, 2006—07. Mem.: AAAS, APA, Soc. Rsch. in Child Devel., Am. Psychol. Soc., Nat. Coun. Family Rels., Groves Conf. on Marriage and Family, Soc. for Rsch. on Adolescence. Office: U RI Human Devel and Family Studies 112 Transition Ctr Kingston RI 02881 Home Phone: 401-783-3904; Office Phone: 401-874-7135. Business E-Mail: bnewman@uri.edu.

NEWMAN, BARRY INGALLS, retired bank executive; b. NYC, Mar. 19, 1932; s. M.A. and T.C. (Weitman) N.; m. Jean Short, Mar. 6, 1965; children: Suzanne, Cathy, David. BA, Alfred U., 1952; JD, NYU, 1955. Bar: N.Y. 1957, Ohio 1958, U.S. Supreme Ct. 1967, Calif. 1990; practice in N.Y.C., 1957. Assoc., then ptnr. firm Shapiro Persky Marken & Newman, Cleve., 1957-63; asst. v.p. Meinhard & Co. (now Meinhard Comml. Corp.), NYC, 1963-65; v.p. Amsterdam Overseas Corp., NYC, 1966-68; pres. No. Fin. Corp., LA, 1968-72; sr. v.p. Aetna Bus. Credit, Inc., Hartford, Conn., 1972-78; exec. v.p. Security Pacific Fin. Group, San Diego, 1978-81, chmn., pres., CEO, 1981-82; sr. exec. v.p. Gt. Am. Bank, 1982—88, ret., 1988. Chmn. bd. dirs. San Diego County Capital Asset Leasing Corp., 1984-2000. Chmn. San Diego County Treasury Oversight com., 1995—; bd. govs. San Diego Found.; pres. San Diego County Civil Svc. Commn.; vice chmn. planning commn. City of Escondido; judge pro tem Superior Ct., 2001—; mem. pub. utilities adv. commn. City of San Diego; dep. foreman County Grand Jury, 1999—2000; treas. The Episcopal Diocese of San Diego, 1993—2001, v.p. bd. dirs., 2006—. Recipient Disting. Svc. award Cleve. Jr. C. of C., 1961. Mem. ABA, N.Y. State Bar Assn., Calif. Bar Assn., San Diego Bar Assn., San Diego County Taxpayers Assn. (past pres.), Univ. Club of San Diego (past pres.), Masons. Republican. Home: 3308 Avenida Sierra Escondido CA 92029-7937 Home Phone: 760-743-2982; Office Phone: 760-743-5005. Personal E-mail: BNewmanlaw@aol.com.

NEWMAN, BARRY MARC, pediatric surgeon; b. NYC, Dec. 13, 1951; s. Sheldon and Miriam Newman; m. Jane Post, July 2, 1989; 1 child, Alexander Ross. BA, U. Pa., 1973; MD, SUNY, Stony Brook, 1976. Diplomate Nat. Bd. Med. Examiners, Am. Bd. Surgery, Am. Bd. Pediatric Surgery. Resident in surgery N.Y. Med. Coll., NYC, 1976-78; sr. resident in surgery SUNY, Stony Brook, 1978-81; chief resident pediatric surgery Childrens Hosp. of Buffalo, 1981-83, fellow pediatric surgery and gastroenterology, 1983-84; asst. prof. surgery U. Va., Charlottesville, 1984-88, U. Ill., Chgo., 1988-93; dir. pediatric surgery Luth. Gen. Children's Hosp., Park Ridge, Ill., 1991-96; clin. assoc. prof. surgery U. Chgo., 1993-95; dir. pediatric surg. svcs. Loyola U. Med. Ctr., Maywood, Ill., 1996—, co-dir. surg. laparoscopy lab., 1996-97, assoc. prof. surgery and pediatrics, 1996—2004, prof. surgery and pediatrics, 2004—. Instr. Adv. Trauma and Life Support, ACS, Chgo., 1984—. Contbr. articles to profl. jours., chapters to books. Grantee, NIH, 1982—83, 1987—88. Fellow ACS, Am. Coll. Chest Physicians, Am. Acad. Pediatrics; mem. Am. Gastroenterol. Assn., Am. Pediatric Surg. Assn., Am. Coll. Physician Execs. Democrat. Jewish. Avocations: wine collecting, scuba diving, underwater photography, personal computing. Office: Loyola U Med Ctr Dept Surgery 2160 S 1st Ave Dept Surgery Maywood IL 60153-3304 Home Phone: 847-835-1478; Office Phone: 708-327-2782. Business E-Mail: bnewma1@lumc.edu.

NEWMAN, BRUCE MURRAY, retired art gallery owner; b. NYC, Jan. 27, 1930; s. Meyer and Evelyn (Kantor) Newman; m. Judith S Brandus, June 26, 1965; 1 child, Emily Rachel. BA, Pratt Inst., 1953, D (hon.), 1997, BFA (hon.), 1998, degree (hon.) in fine arts, 1997. Pres. Newel Art Galleries Inc., NYC, 1975—2001. Lectr mus and univs; mem regional adv bd Chase Manhattan Bank; mem regional adv bd J P Morgan Chase Bank. Author: Fantasy Furniture, 1989, Don't Come Back Until You Find It,

2006; featured numerous TV & radio programs, mags, and other publs, guest CBS Morning Show, 1988. Assoc mem Mt Sinia Med Ctr, 1988—; bd dirs New York City Ctr, 1988—90; trustee Pratt Inst, Brooklyn, NY, 1983—. Named Man of the Yr., Pratt Inst., 1993; recipient Designer Award, Art Dirs. Club, 1984. Mem.: Victorian Soc Am, Am Soc Interior Designers (bd dirs 1989—). Avocations: golf, reading, jogging, travel.

NEWMAN, CAROL L., lawyer; b. Yonkers, NY, Aug. 7, 1949; d. Richard J. and Pauline Frances (Stoll) N. AB/MA summa cum laude, Brown U., 1971; postgrad., Harvard U. Law Sch., 1972-73; JD cum laude, George Washington U., 1977. Bar: D.C. 1977, Calif. 1979. With antitrust divsn. U.S. Dept. Justice, Washington and L.A., 1977-80; assoc. Alschuler, Grossman & Pines, LA, 1980-82, Costello & Walcher, LA, 1982-85, Rosen, Wachtell & Gilbert, LA, 1985-88, ptnr., 1988-90, Keck, Mahin & Cate, LA, 1990-94; pvt. practice LA, 1994—. Adj. prof. Sch. Bus., Golden Gate U., spring 1982. Commr. L.A. Bd. Transp. Commrs., 1993—98, v.p., 1995—96; pres. Bd. Taxicab Commrs., 1999—2001; candidate for State Atty. Gen., 1986; bd. dirs. Women's Progress Alliance, 1996—98. Mem. State Bar Calif., L.A. County Bar Assn., L.A. Lawyers for Human Rights (co. pres. 1991-92), Log Cabin (bd. dirs. 1992-97, 2003-06, pres. 1996-97), Calif. Women Lawyers (bd. govs. 1991-94), Order of Coif, Phi Beta Kappa. Office Phone: 818-225-0056. E-mail: cnewman540@aol.com.

NEWMAN, CHARLES ANDREW, lawyer; b. LA, Mar. 18, 1949; s. Arthur and Gladys Newman; m. Elizabeth F.; children: Anne R., Elyse S. BA magna cum laude, U. Calif., 1970; JD, Washington U., 1973. Bar: Mo. 1973, DC 1981, Ill. 2001, Wis. 2003, NY 2006, US Dist. Ct. (ea. dist.) Mo. 1973, US Dist. Ct. (so. dist.) Ill. 2001, US Dist. Ct. (ctrl. dist.) Ill. 1996, US Dist. Ct. (ea. dist.) Mich. 2002, US Ct. Appeals (8th cir.) 1975, US Supreme Ct. 1976, US Tax Ct. 1981, US Claims Ct. 1981, US Ct. Appeals (11th cir.) 1994, US Ct. Appeals (9th cir.) 1995, US Ct. Appeals (3d, 5th, 7th and 10th cirs.) 1996, US Ct. Appeals (6th cir.) 1997, US Dist. Ct. (so. dist.) Ill. 2001, US Dist. Ct. (ea. dist.) Wis. 2003, US Ct. Appeals (1st & 4th cirs.) 2006, US Ct. Appeals (2d cir.) 2006, US Ct. Appeals (DC cir.) 2006. From assoc. to ptnr. Thompson & Mitchell, St. Louis, 1973-96; ptnr. Thompson Coburn, St. Louis, 1996-97, Bryan Cave LLP, St. Louis, 1997—. Lectr. law Washington U., St. Louis, 1976-78. Bd. dirs. Hawthorn Found., 1997-2000; trustee Mo. Bar Found., 1990-96, mem. Mo. Bar Bd. Govs, 1980-84; bd. dirs. United Israel Appeal, N.Y.C., 1990-93, Coun. Jewish Fedns., N.Y.C., 1992-95, United Jewish Appeal Young Leadership Cabinet, N.Y.C., 1985-88, Ctr. for Study of Dispute Resolution, 1985-88, Legal Svcs. Ea. Mo., 1985-94, St. Louis Community Found., 1992-2001, vice-chmn. 1997-99, St. Louis chpt. Young Audiences 1993-95, Planned Parenthood St. Louis, 1986-89, Jewish Fedn., St. Louis, 1986-98, asst. treas., 1989-90, v.p. fin. planning, 1990-93, asst. sec., 1994-95; v.p. Repertory Theatre, St. Louis, 1986-89, sr. v.p., 1990-91; pres. St. Louis Opportunity Clearinghouse, 1974-78. Recipient Lon O. Hocker Meml. Trial award Mo. Bar Found., 1984, What's Right with the Region award, FOCUS St. Louis, 2005. Mem. Bar Assn. Met. St. Louis (Merit award 1976). Democrat. Avocations: golf, reading, music, sailing. Office: Bryan Cave LLP One Metropolitan Square Saint Louis MO 63102-2750 Home Phone: 314-725-4199; Office Phone: 314-259-2000. Business E-Mail: canewman@bryancave.com.

NEWMAN, CHARLES MICHAEL, mathematician, physicist, educator; b. Chgo., Mar. 1, 1946; s. Harry M. and Dorothy Thelma (Pollack) N.; m. Arlene Milgram, July 5, 1970; children: Jennifer, Serena. BS in Physics, BS in Math., MIT, Cambridge, Mass., 1966; MA, Princeton U., NJ, 1968, PhD in Physics, 1971. Asst. prof. NYU, NYC, 1971-73, prof., 1989—, dir. grad. studies, 1996—98, dept. chair, 1998—2001, dir. Courant Inst. Math. Scis., 2002—06; asst. prof. Ind. U., Bloomington, 1973-75, assoc. prof., 1975-79; prof. U. Ariz., Tucson, 1979-90, regents prof., 1990-91. Editor book series on probability and applications, 1988—; assoc. editor: Annals of Probability, 1985-90, Annals of Applied Probability, 2006—; author: Random Matrices and Their Applications, 1986, Topics in Disordered Systems, 1997; contbr. articles to Nature, Comm. Math. Physics, Physical Rev. Letters and others. J.S. Guggenheim fellow, 1984-85, A.P. Sloan fellow, 1978-81, NATO fellow, 1975-76; NSF grantee, 1974—, U.S.-Israel Binational grantee, 1978-81. Fellow Inst. Math. Stats., Am. Acad. Arts & Scis.; mem. NAS, Internat. Assn. Math. Physicists, Am. Math. Soc. Achievements include co-invention of cascade model of community food web structure, of model for three dimensional wetting phase transition; mathematical demonstration of consistency of neo-Darwinian evolution with fossil record patterns of punctuated equilibria; research concerning discontinuity of certain phase transitions; nature of spin glass models; full scaling limit of two-dimensional percolation. Office: Dept Math Warren Weaver Hall 1117 251 Mercer St New York NY 10012 Business E-Mail: newman@cims.nyu.edu.

NEWMAN, CONSTANCE BERRY, federal agency administrator; b. Chgo., July 8, 1935; d. Joseph Alonzo and Ernestine (Siggers) B.; m. Theodore Roosevelt Newman, July 25, 1959 (div. 1980). AB, Bates Coll., 1956; BSL, U. Minn., 1959; JD (hon.), Bates Coll., 1972, Amherst Coll., 1980; LHD (hon.), Central State U., 1991. Dir. VISTA, Washington, 1971-73; commr. Consumer Product Safety Commn., Washington, 1973-76; asst. sec. U.S. HUD, Washington, 1976-77; pres. The Newman & Hermanson Co., Washington, 1977-82; cons. Govt. of Lesotho, 1987-88; dir. nat. voter coalition Bush-Quayle '88, Washington, 1988; dir. Office Pers. Mgmt., Washington, 1989-92; under sec. Smithsonian Instn., Washington, 1992-2000; vice chair D.C. Fin. Responsiblity and Mgmt. Assistance Authority, 1994—2000; ptnr. Upstart Ptnrs., 2000—01; asst. adminr. bur. for Africa USAID, Washington, 2001—04; asst. sec. for African affairs US Dept. State, 2004—. Mem. adj. faculty John F. Kennedy Sch. Govt., Harvard U., Cambridge, Mass., 1979-82. Contbr. articles to profl. jours. Mem. Adminstrn. Conf. U.S., Washington, 1973-76, 1989—; commr. M.L. King Fed. Holiday Commn., Washington, 1989; chmn. Def. Adv. Com. on Women in the Svcs., Washington, 1985-86; trustee Community Coll. Balt., 1985-89; adv. to chmn. 1988 Rep. Nat. Conv., New Orleans, 1988; bd. overseers Morehouse Coll. Sch. Medicine, Atlanta, 1976-77; bd. dirs. Brookings Instn., Aspen Inst., Coun. for Excellence in Govt. Recipient Pub. Svc. award Ohio State U., 1991. Mem. NAACP, Exec. Women in Govt. (founding mem.), Internat. Repub. Inst., 1998-2000. Republican. Avocation: photography. E-mail: newmancb@state.gov.

NEWMAN, DANNY MERRIL, lawyer; BA, U. Ariz., 1997; JD, Capital U. Law Sch., 2002. Bar: Ohio 2002, US Dist. Ct. Southern Dist. Ohio 2002, Commonwealth Ky. 2003, US Dist. Ct. Western Dist. Ky. 2003, US Dist. Ct. Eastern Dist. Ky. 2003, US Ct. of Appeals, Sixth Cir. 2003. Jud. clerk Franklin County Probate Ct. Judge; atty. Reminger & Reminger Co., Cin. Named one of Ohio's Rising Stars, Super Lawyers, 2006. Mem.: Ohio Assn. Civil Trial Attorneys, Assn. Cert. Fraud Examiners, Ky. Bar Assn., Def. Rsch. Inst., FBA, Assn. Trial Lawyers Am., ABA, Ohio State Bar Assn., Clermont County Bar Assn., Cin. Bar Assn. Office: Reminger & Reminger Co 525 Vine St Ste 1700 Cincinnati OH 45202 Office Phone: 513-721-1311. Office Fax: 513-721-2553.

NEWMAN, DAVA JEAN, aerospace engineering educator, director; b. Helena, Mont., Aug. 11, 1964; d. Daniel L. Newman and Deanna A. (Mack) Elliott. BS in Aerospace Engring., U. Notre Dame, 1986; MS in Tech. and Policy, MIT, 1989, MS in Aeronautics and Astronautics, 1989, PhD in Aerospace Biomed. Engring., 1992. Engr. Boeing Co., Seattle, 1986; cons., lectr. Internat. Space U., Strasbourg, France, 1987—; rsch. fellow NASA Ames Rsch. Ctr., Mountain View, Calif., 1989-92; asst. prof. U. Houston, 1992-93; C.S. Draper asst. prof. aerospace engring. MIT, Cambridge, Mass., 1993-95, prof. aeronautics, astronautics and engring. sys., 1998—2004, full prof. aeronautics, astronautics and engring. sys., 2004—, dir. Tech. and Policy Program, 2003—. Bd. dirs. Aeronautics and Space Engring. Nat. Acad.; cons. NASA Hdqs., Washington, 1995-96, Trotti and Assocs., Inc., Boston, 1996—, Nascent Technologies, Inc., 1999; affiliate faculty Health, Scis. and Tech. Harvard/MIT. Author: Interactive Aerospace Engineering and Design, 2002; contbr. author: Fundamentals of Space Life Sciences, 1997; contbr. over 100 articles to profl. jours.; author, prodr. U.S./Russian Astronaut Training Video, 1996. Bd. dirs. OMNISport 2001, 1990-2004; advisor KEYS To Empowring Youth, Cambridge, 1995—. Named Prof. of Yr., U. Houston, Soc. Automotive Engrs., 1993; recipient Manned Space Flight award NASA, 1995, Nat. Aerospace Educator award Women in Aerospace, 2001; numerous rsch. grants NASA, 1993—. Fellow AIAA (assoc.); mem. Am. Soc. for Engring. Edn., Internat. Soc. Biomechanics, Union Concerned Scientists, NY Acad. Scis., Soc. Women Engrs. Democrat. Achievements include rsch. in astronaut biomechanics and energetics for space flight and on the moon and Mars; world record holder of women's human-powered hydrofoil speed record; working with team to develop better design for astronaut suit. Office: MIT Rm 33-307 77 Massachusetts Ave Cambridge MA 02139-4307 Office Phone: 617-258-8799. Office Fax: 617-253-4196. Business E-Mail: dnewman@mit.edu. *

NEWMAN, DAVID WHEELER, lawyer; b. Salt Lake City, Apr. 5, 1952; s. Donnell and Vera Mae (Siratt) N.; m. Mahnaz Navai, Mar. 14, 1981; 1 child, Anthony Dara. BA magna cum laude, Claremont Men's Coll., 1973; JD, UCLA, 1977; LLM in Taxation, NYU, 1979. Bar: Calif. 1978, US Dist. Ct. (ctrl. dist. Calif.) 1978, US Tax Ct. 1979. Tax ptnr. Mitchell, Silberberg & Knupp, LLP, LA, 1982—. Mem. exec. com. tax sect. L.A. County Bar, 1991-2000. Trustee New Visions Found., 1995—; trustee, pres. New Rds. Sch., 2000—. Named one of Top 100 Attys., Worth mag., 2005. Mem. Calif. Club, Men's Garden Club L.A. (dir. 2000—). Avocations: tennis, skiing, gardening. Office: Mitchell Silberberg & Knupp 11377 W Olympic Blvd Los Angeles CA 90064-1625 Office Phone: 310-312-3171. Office Fax: 310-231-8371. E-mail: dwn@msk.com. *

NEWMAN, DEAN GORDON, business consultant; b. North Branch, Iowa, Mar. 17, 1929; s. Floyd William and Hazel Jane (Covault) N.; m. Maggie Newman; children: Gary Dean, Craig William. BA, Simpson Coll., 1950; MBA, Stanford U., 1952. From trainee to mgr. GE, Syracuse, NY, Chgo., Milw., 1952—62, mgr. employee and cmty. rels. DeKalb, 1963—69; v.p. employee and pub. rels. United Nuclear Corp., Elmsford, NY, 1969—71; v.p. employee rels. Apache Corp., Mpls., 1971-83, v.p. human resources and comm., 1983-87; v.p. mktg. Nelson Cons. Group, Mpls., 1989-92; chmn., CFO Linear Fitness Systems, Inc., Allenspark, Colo., 1998—2004. Pres. Apache Found., 1973—87; v.p., bd. dirs. Boys Clubs, Mpls., 1978—85; chmn. Boys and Girls Club Mpls., 1985—88, exec. com., 1988—89; v.p. fin., bd. Boys and Girls Club Larimer County, 1993—96; vice chmn. Bus. Econs. Edn. Found., 1986—88, chmn. fin. com., 1988—89; com. mem., treas. Allenspark Sr. Adv. Com., 1999—2003; treas. Allenspark Fire Protection Dist., 2000—05, bd. dirs., 2000—05, Aging Svcs. Found., 2006—. With USNR, 1952—55, Korea. Nat. Meth. scholar, 1946—50, Hicks fellow, 1952. Mem.: Nat. Assn. Mfrs. (dir. 1981—87), Allenspark Area Club (bd. dirs., treas. 2000—03, Founder's award 2002, Boulder County Honoring Our Elders award 2003), Pi Gamma Mu, Sigma Tau Delta, Epsilon Sigma, Alpha Tau Omega. Republican. Methodist. Home and Office: 2930 Bryn Mawr Pl Longmont CO 80503 Personal E-mail: mdnewman85@msn.com.

NEWMAN, DIANA S., foundation administrator, consultant; b. Toledo, June 15, 1943; d. Fred Andrew and Thelma Elizabeth (Hewitt) Smith; m. Dennis Ryan Newman, Feb. 15, 1964; children: Barbara Lynn Newman LaBine, John Ryan, Elizabeth Anne. Student, Oberlin Coll., 1961-64. Asst. treas. Marble Cliff Quarries Co., 1964-68; cmty. vol., 1968-83; dir. Ohio Hist. Found., Columbus, 1983-90; v.p. advancement The Columbus (Ohio) Found., 1990-95; pres. Philanthropic Resource Group, Columbus, 1995—. Author: Opening Doors: Pathways to Diverse Donors, 2002 (AFP/Skystone Ryan prize for rsch., 2003), Nonprofit Essentials: Endowment Building, 2005. Bd. dirs. Leader Inst., Inc., 2001-04; mem. governing bd. First Cmty. Ch., 1983-88, chair, 1987-88; bd. dirs. LWV Ctrl. Ohio, 1968-72, Ohio Mus. Assn., 1985-90, Crittenton Family Svcs., Columbus, 1992-95; founder Franklin County Com. on Criminal Justice, Columbus, 1972; pres. Jr. League Columbus, 1980-81. Mem. Assn. Fundraising Profls. (bd. dirs. Ctrl. Ohio chpt. 1985-88, 2004-, nat. rsch. coun. 2003—, Outstanding Profl. Fundraiser 2004), Ctrl. Ohio Planned Giving Coun. (bd. dirs. 1990-2001, pres. 1998), Columbus Female Benevolent Soc. (bd. dirs. 1984—). Office: Philanthropic Resource Group 926 Augusta Glen Dr Columbus OH 43235-5097 Office Phone: 614-486-4787. Business E-Mail: diana@diananewman.com.

NEWMAN, DIANE, publishing executive; 3 children. Grad., NYU, 1982. Sr. level advt. mgmt. position Scholastic, Prevention, YM; assoc. pub. Redbook, Family Circle; pub. Fitness; sr. v.p., group pub. Active Lifestyle Group Am. Media Internat.; v.p., pub. Parents mag. Meredith Corp., NYC, 2007—. Office: Parents Meredith Corp 375 Lexington Ave 10th Fl New York NY 10017 Office Phone: 212-499-2000. *

NEWMAN, DONALD LYNN, psychologist, consultant; b. Jeffersonville, Ind., Jan. 5, 1951; s. Mason Lynn and Rita Scott Newman; m. Kathy Jean Hopkins, July 28, 1993; children: Higgens McPheaters, Isabella Catalina, Fannie Jean. BA in Sociology, U. Ariz., 1974; MSW, Ariz. State U., 1976; M in Sch. Psychology, No. Ariz. U., 1996. LCSW Ariz.; cert. sch. psychologist Ariz. Dept. Edn. Founder, CEO Family Preservationists: Counseling Assocs., Phoenix, 1991—94, AmeriPsych, Inc., Phoenix, 1994—2005; exec. dir. Gen. Health Corp. ResCare Inc. (formerly AmeriPsych, Inc.), Phoenix, 2005—. Author: PREP-R: Parenting and Resource Education Program-Revised. Exec. dir. Cmtys. in Need, Phoenix, 1991—2005; pres. Children with Challenges, Phoenix, 1995—2005. Grantee State of Ariz., 1995—2005. Mem.: Nat. Assn. Sch. Psychologists (life). Democrat. Buddhist. Avocations: running, travel, fly fishing, gardening, food preserving. Office: AmeriPsych Inc 3877 N 7th St Ste 220 Phoenix AZ 85014 Home Phone: 602-264-4381; Office Phone: 602-728-0630. Fax: 602-728-0632. Business E-Mail: dnewman@ameripsych.com.

NEWMAN, EDWIN HAROLD, news commentator; b. NYC, Jan. 25, 1919; s. Myron and Rose (Parker) N.; m. Rigel Grell, Aug. 14, 1944; 1 child, Nancy (Mrs. Henry Drucker). BA, U. Wis., 1940; postgrad. (fellow), La. State U., 1940. With Washington bur. Internat. News Svc., 1941, U.P., 1941-42, 45-46, N.Y. Daily PM, 1946-47; ind. Washington news bur., 1947; asst to Eric Sevareid at Washington bur. CBS, 1947-49; freelance writer, broadcaster London, 1949-52; with European Recovery Program, 1951-52, NBC, 1952—, chief news bur. London, 1956-57, Rome, 1957-58, Paris, 1958-61, news commentator NYC, 1961-83; columnist King Features Syndicate, 1984-89. Moderator 1st Ford-Carter Debate, 1976, 2d Reagan-Mondale debate, 1984; moderator ann. conf. former secs. of state, 1983—, former secs. of def., 1987—. Narrator: TV spls. including Japan: East is West, 1961, Orient Express, 1964, Who Shall Live?, 1965, Pensions-The Broken Promise, 1972, Violence in America, 1977, I Want It All Now, 1978, Spying for Uncle Sam, 1978, Oil and American Power, 1979, The Billionaire Hunts, 1981, Congress: We the People, 1983-84, On Television, 1985-86, Freud, 1987, The Borgias, 1988; host Saturday Night Live, 1984; drama critic WNB C-TV, 1965-71 (Emmy awards 1966, 68, 70, 72, 73, 74, 82, Peabody award 1966); author: Strictly Speaking: Will America Be The Death of English?, 1974, A Civil Tongue, 1976, Sunday Punch, 1979, I Must Say, 1988; contbr. articles and revs. to various periodicals, U.S., Can. and Eng.; chmn. usage panel Am. Heritage Dictionary, 1975-80. Served from ensign to lt. USNR, 1942-45. Decorated chevalier Legion of Honor France; recipient awards Overseas Press Club, 1961, awards U. Wis. Sch. Journalism, 1967, awards U. Mo. Sch. Journalism, 1975 Mem. AFTRA, Authors Guild, Screen Actors Guild.

NEWMAN, EILEEN, not-for-profit organization executive; 1 child. Exec. dir. Film/Video Arts, NYC, 1998—. Program officer New Visions for Pub. Schs. Mem.: The N.Y. Film/Video Coun. (bd. dirs.), N.Y. Women in Film and TV (bd. dirs., past v.p.), Educators for Social Responsibility (v.p.).

NEWMAN, FREDRIC SAMUEL, lawyer, communications executive; b. York, Pa., June 22, 1945; s. Nat. Howard and Josephine (Farkas) N.; m. Mary E. Kiley, May 19, 1973; children: Lydia Ann, Anne Marie, Pauline. AB cum laude, Harvard U., 1967; JD, Columbia U., 1970; cert. the exec. program, U. Va., 1984. Bar: N.Y. 1971, U.S. Dist. Ct. (so. and ea. dists.) N.Y. 1972, U.S. Ct. Appeals (2d cir.) 1974, U.S. Ct. Claims 1993. Assoc. White & Case, NYC, 1970-80; asst. gen. counsel Philip Morris Cos., NYC, 1981-87; gen. counsel, v.p., sec. Philip Morris, Inc., NYC, 1987-90; chief exec. officer TeamTennis, Inc., 1991; prin. Law Office of Fredric S. Newman, NYC, 1992-95; founding ptnr. Hoguet Newman & Regal, LLP, 1996—; pres., CEO, Pathe Comm. Corp., NYC, 1993-97. Bd. dirs. Exel Ins. Co., Bermuda. Trustee Calhoun Sch., N.Y.C., 1985-88; bd. dirs. N.Y. Fire Safety Found., N.Y.C., 1985-88; treas. Clean Water/Clean Air Bond Act Com., 1996. Fellow Am. Bar Found.; mem. Columbia Law Sch. Assn. (bd. dirs. 1999-2001). Office: 10 E 40th St New York NY 10016-0200 Office Phone: 212-689-8808.

NEWMAN, GARY, broadcast executive; BA, Yale U.; JD, U. Southern Calif. Law Ctr. Bus. affairs dept. exec. NBC; exec. v.p. Twentieth Century Fox TV, pres., 1999—2007, chmn., 2007—; co-creator Fox21, 2004. Office: Twentieth Century Fox TV Bldg 103 Rm 5286 10201 W Pico Blvd Los Angeles CA 90035 Office Phone: 310-369-1000. Office Fax: 310-369-8726. E-mail: gary.newman@fox.com. *

NEWMAN, J. BONNIE, political science professor, former federal official; b. Lawrence, Mass., June 2, 1945; d. William Michael and Louise Catherine (Casey) Newman BA, St. Joseph's Coll., Maine, 1967; MEdn, Pa. State U., 1969; LHD (hon.), Rivier Coll., Nashua, NH, 1983; LLD (hon.), Notre Dame Coll., Manchester, NH, 1984, Keene State Coll., NH, 1987; LHD (hon.), St. Joseph's Coll., Standish, Maine, 1990. Exec. dir. Forum on NH's Future, 1978-80, dir, 1980-82; asst. dean students U. NH, Durham, 1969—72, dean of students, 1972-78, interim dean Whittemore Sch. of Bus. and Econs., 1998—99, interim pres., 2006—07; chief of staff to Rep. Judd Gregg US Congress, 1981-82; assoc. dir. Office Presdl. Pers. The White House, Washington, 1982-84; asst. sec. econ. devel. US Dept. Commerce, Washington, 1984-85; asst. to the Pres. for mgmt. & adminstrn. The White House, Washington, 1989—91; exec. dean Kennedy Sch. Govt., Harvard U., 2000—05, sr. fellow. Bd. dirs. NH Charitable Found., Citizens Advisors, Lumina Found., Markem Corp.; chmn. US Navy Acad. Bd. of Visitors. Bd. dirs. Gov.'s Econ. Devel. & Land Use Com., 1979-80. Named Alumni Fellow, Pa. State U.; recipient Granite State Award, Yankee Award, Pub. Rels. Soc., Lifetime Achievement Award, Bus. and Industry Assn. of NH, New England Coun.'s Leadership Award, Abigail Adams Award, Mass. Women's Polit. Caucus, 2005. Mem.: Bus. and Industry Assn. NH (pres. 1985—88), Econ. Club of NY. Republican. Roman Catholic. Office: Kennedy Sch Govt Mailbox 67 79 JFK Street Cambridge MA 02138-5801 Office Phone: 603-964-1917. E-mail: J.BonnieNewman@comcast.net. *

NEWMAN, JAMES MICHAEL, judge, lawyer; b. Bklyn., Apr. 3, 1946; s. Sheldon and Ethel (Silverman) Newman; m. Lee Galen; children: Danielle Carl, Matthew Evan, Merrie Lee, Cindy Joy, Bradley Curtis. BA, Queens Coll., 1966; JD, NYU, 1969, LLM, 1975. Bar: NY 1970, NJ 1977, cert.: N.J. (matrimonial atty.). Assoc. Kramer, Marx, Greenlee & Backus, NYC, 1970-73, Forsyth, Decker, Murray & Broderick, NYC, 1973-74; ptnr. Tommaney & Newman, NYC, 1975-82, Goldzweig, Reilly, Grossman & Newman, Marlboro, NJ, 1978-79, Canarick & Newman, Freehold, NJ, 1979-97, Newman, Scarola & Assocs., Freehold, 1998—2001, Newman Scarola & Schneider, Freehold, 2001—05, Newman Scarola, Freehold, 2005—; pub. defender Marlboro Twp., NJ, 1984-86, judge, 1986—2006, Englishtown Borough, 1990—, Farmingdale Borough, 1991—2006, Manalapan Township, 1993—, Borough Fair Haven, 1996—2002, 2006—, Borough of Highstown, 2006—. Dep. mayor Marlboro Twp., 1975—79, dir. econ. develop., 1975—79, dir. commuter affairs, 1974; interim commr. Monmouth Utilities Authority, 1977; mem. Ctrl. N.J. Transp. Bd., 1974—76. Fellow: Am. Acad. Matrimonial Lawyers; mem.: Am. Judges Assn. (bd. govs.), Monmouth County Judges Assn. (pres. 1995), Monmouth County Bar Assn. (co-chair family law comt 1996—98, trustee 1999—2006, sec. 2006—07), N.J. Bar Assn., Masons. Jewish. Office: 64 W Main St Freehold NJ 07728-2142 Home Phone: 732-536-8822; Office Phone: 732-431-0150. Business E-Mail: jnewman@monmouthlaw.com.

NEWMAN, JOAN MESKIEL, lawyer; b. Youngstown, Ohio, Dec. 12, 1947; d. John F. and Rosemary (Scarmuzzi) Meskiel; children: Anne R., Elyse S. BA in Polit. Sci., Case-Western Reserve U., 1969; JD, Washington U., St. Louis, 1972, LLM in Taxation, 1973. Bar: Mo. 1972. Assoc. Lewis & Rice, St. Louis, 1973-80, ptnr., 1981-90, Thompson Coburn, St. Louis, 1990—2005. Adj. prof. law Washington U. Sch. Law, St. Louis, 1975-92; past pres. St. Louis chpt., mem. Midwest Pension Conf. Mem. nat. coun. Washington U., Sch. Law, 1988—91; chmn. bd. dir. Great St. Louis Coun. Girl Scouts USA, 1975—92, officer, 1978—92; mem. cmty. wide youth svcs. panel United Way Greater St. Louis, 1992—96; fin. futures task force Kiwanis Camp Wyman, 1992—93; chmn. staff blue ribbon fin. com. Sch. Dist., Clayton, 1986—87; vol. Women's Self Help Ctr.; bd. dirs. Parents as Teachers, 2001—04; bd. dir., exec. com. Girl Scouts USA, 1993—99, nat. treas., 1996—99; bd. dirs. Met. Employment and Rehab. Svcs., 1980—2001, chmn. bd. dir., 1994—96, Women of Achievement, 1993—96; bd. dirs. Jewish Ctr. Aged, 1990—92, bd. dir., 1999—2001, Jewish Fedn. St. Louis, 1991—96, City Mus., 1998—2001, United Way Greater St. Louis, 2000—, Oasis, 1999—2001; chair bd. dirs. MERS/Goodwill Industries, 2007—, chmn. bd. dirs., 2007—; bd. dirs. Walker Scottish Rite Ctr., 2002—. Named Woman of Achievement St. Louis, 1991. Mem. Mo. Bar Assn. (staff pension and benefits com. 1991—), Bar Met. St. Louis (past chmn. taxation sect.), St. Louis Forum, Order of Coif (hon.). Home Phone: 314-781-3002; Office Phone: 314-645-5001. Business E-Mail: joan@joannewmanassociates.com.

NEWMAN, JOHN M., JR., lawyer; b. Youngstown, Ohio, Aug. 15, 1944; BA, Georgetown U., 1966; JD, Harvard U., 1969. BAr: Ill. 1970, Calif. 1972, Ohio 1976. Law clerk ctrl. dist. U.S. Dist. Ct., Calif., 1969-70, asst. U.S. Atty. ctrl. dist. Calif., 1970-75; ptnr. Jones, Day, Cleve. Fellow Am. Coll. Trial Lawyers; mem. Phi Beta Kappa. Office: Jones Day North Point 901 Lakeside Ave E Cleveland OH 44114-1190 Office Phone: 216-586-7207. Business E-Mail: jmnewman@jonesday.com.

NEWMAN, JOHN NICHOLAS, naval architect educator; b. New Haven, Mar. 10, 1935; s. Richard and Daisy (Neumann) N.; m. Kathleen Smedley Kirk, June 16, 1956; children— James Bartram, Nancy Kirk, Carol Ann. BS Mass. Inst. Tech, 1956, MS, 1957, Sc.D., 1960; postgrad., Cambridge U., Eng., 1958-59; D Technicae honoris causa, U. Trondheim, Norway, 1992. Research naval architect David Taylor Model Basin, Navy Dept., Washington, 1959-67; assoc. prof. naval architecture MIT, Cambridge, 1967-70, prof., 1970—, prof. emeritus. Vis. prof. U. New South Wales, Australia, 1973, U. Adelaide, Australia, 1974, Tech. U. Norway, 1981-82; cons. Navy Dept., Dept. Justice, pvt. firms. Author: Marine Hydrodynamics, 1977; Contbr.: articles to profl. jours., including Sci. Am. Recipient prize Am. Bur. Shipping, 1956; Walter Atkinson prize Royal Instn. Naval

Architects, 1973, also Bronze medal, 1976; Guggenheim fellow, 1973-74; research grantee Office Naval Research; NSF. Mem. AAAS, NAE, Soc. Naval Architects and Marine Engrs. (Davidson medal 1988), Norwegian Acad. Sci. Home: 1 Bowditch Rd Woods Hole MA 02543-1201 Business E-Mail: jnn@mit.edu.

NEWMAN, JON O., federal judge; b. NYC, May 2, 1932; s. Harold W. Jr. and Estelle L. (Ormond) Newman; m. Martha G. Silberman, June 19, 1953 (dec. Feb. 8, 2005); children: Leigh, Scott, David; m. Ann Z. Leventhal, Jan. 1, 2007. Grad., Hotchkiss Sch., 1949; AB magna cum laude, Princeton U., 1953; LLB, Yale U., 1956; LLD (hon.), U. Hartford, 1975, U. Bridgeport, 1980, Bklyn. Law Sch., 1995, NY Law Sch., 1996. Bar: Conn. 1956, DC 1956. Law clk. to Hon. George T. Washington US Ct. Appeals, 1956—57; sr. law clk. to Hon. Earl Warren US Supreme Ct., 1957—58; ptnr. Ritter, Satter & Newman, Hartford, Conn., 1958—60; counsel to majority Conn. Gen. Assembly, 1959; spl. counsel to gov. Conn., 1959—61; asst. to sec. HEW, 1961—62; adminstrv. asst. to U.S. senator, 1963—64; U.S. atty. Dist. of Conn., 1964—69, U.S. dist. judge, 1972—79; pvt. practice, 1969—71; U.S. cir. judge US Ct. Appeals (2d cir.), 1979—93, chief judge, 1993—97, sr. judge, 1997—. Co-author: Politics: The American Way, 1964, A Genealogical Chart of Greek Mythology, 2003. With USAR, 1954—62. Recipient Learned Hand medal, Fed. Bar Coun., 1987. Fellow: Am. Bar Found.; mem.: ABA, Am. Judicature Soc., Conn. Bar Assn., Am. Law Inst. Democrat. Office: US Ct Appeals 2d Cir 450 Main St Hartford CT 06103-3022 *

NEWMAN, JOSEPH HERZL, advertising executive, consultant; b. NYC, Dec. 1, 1928; s. Max A. and Tillie C. (Weitzman) N.; m. Ruth Zita Marcus, Dec. 19, 1954 (div. Feb. 1987); children: Deborah Lynn, David Alan, Mark Jonathan; m. Nancy Rose Kramer Deutschman, Aug. 19, 1990 (dec. Feb. 2005); stepchildren: Pamela Sue Deutschman, Douglas Hayes Deutschman, Cindi Elaine Deutschman-Ruiz. AB, Bethany Coll., W.Va., 1949; MS Grad. Sch. Bus., Columbia U., NYC, 1956. With 20th Century Fox Film Corp., NYC, 1949—53; media supr. Fred Wittner Advt. Agy., NYC, 1953—56; media dir. O.S. Tyson & Co., NYC, 1956—64; v.p., media dir. Marsteller Inc., NYC, 1965—85; v.p., assoc. media dir. HBM/Creamer, NYC, 1985—87, Della Femina, McNamee, Inc., NYC, 1987—89; pres. Newman And Assocs., Cleve., 1989—. Mem. faculty Advt. Age Media Workshop, 1972; past chmn. media mgrs. adv. com. Bus. Publs. Audit of Circulation Inc., NYC; condr. profl. media planning seminars, 1989-99. Contbr. articles to profl. jours. Past chmn. bus.-to-bus. media com. Am. Assn. Advt. Agys.; vice chmn. tax incentive rev. coun. City of Mayfield Heights, Ohio, 1994-97, chmn., 1997-2005, co-vice chmn., 2005-06; mem. master plan adv. com. City of Mayfield Heights, 2003-04, mem. mayor's cmty. coun., 2006—; rep. Mayfield Heights to Euclid Creek Watershed Coun., 2003-. With US Army, 1950-52. Mem. Bus. Mktg. Assn. (past mem. media comparability coun., media data form com. and rsch. resource com., Agy. Exec. of Yr., NY chpt. 1960, 66, 71, 73, cert. bus. communicator). Home and Office: 6338 Woodhawk Dr Mayfield Heights OH 44124-4153 Office Phone: 440-449-1804. E-mail: nknewmansion@aol.com.

NEWMAN, KEITH DAVID, surgeon; b. Dallas, July 14, 1960; s. Sylvan Roy and Barbara Anne Newman; m. Katherine Elaine Newman. BS in Psychology, Tex. A&M U., College Station, 1982, BS, 1983, MD, 1987. Resident Mayo Clinic, Rochester, Minn., 1987—89; chief resident Duke U., Durham, NC, 1989—93. Fellow: Am. Coll. Surgeons; mem.: Am. Urologic Assn. Avocations: music, piano, bicycling. Office: Tex Med & Surg Assocs 8440 Walnut Hill Ln 400 Dallas TX 75231

NEWMAN, KENNETH E., lawyer; b. NYC, Sept. 28, 1946; s. Stanley and Muriel (Orenstein) N.; m. Michele M. Jette; children: Douglas C., Jason B., Gregory R. BA, Queens Coll., NYC, 1967; JD, St. John's U., NYC, 1971. Bar: N.Y. 1972, U.S. Supreme Ct. 1976, U.S. Ct. Appeals (2nd cir.) 1974, U.S. Ct. Appeals (D.C. cir.) 1974, U.S. Ct. Appeals (3d cir.) 1980, U.S. Ct. Appeals (10th cir.) 1982, (4th cir.) 1988, U.S. Dist. Ct. (so. dist.) N.Y. 1974, (ea. dist.) N.Y.) 1979. Trial atty. U.S. Dept. Justice, Washington, 1971-73, atty. gen. honors program appointee; assoc. Donovan Leisure Newton & Irvine, NYC, 1973-80, ptnr., 1980-95; sr. v.p., ea. regional counsel Walt Disney Co., NYC, 1995—. Trial faculty Practicing Law Inst., N.Y.C., 1983-94. Dir. Jr. Achievement NY. Mem. ABA, Fed. Bar Coun., Assn. Bar City of N.Y. Office: The Walt Disney Co 77 W 66th St New York NY 10023

NEWMAN, KIMBERLY EILEEN, adult education educator; d. James Benjamin and Eileen Wages Newman. BEE, Ga. Inst. Tech., Atlanta, 1992, PhD, 1999. Asst. prof. microprocessor systems, HDL, sensor networks Rochester Inst. Tech., NY, 2000—01, U. Denver, 2001—. Judge Computer Soc. Internat. Design Competition IEEE Computer Soc., Washington, 2001—06. Recipient Best Transactions Paper award, IEEE Edn. Soc., 2003. Mem.: IEEE (sr.). Achievements include patents for inspection system and method for bond detection and validation of surface mount devices. Office: University of Denver 2390 S York St Denver CO 80208 Office Phone: 303-871-3436. Office Fax: 303-871-4450. Business E-Mail: kinewman@du.edu.

NEWMAN, LAWRENCE, lawyer, educator; b. NYC, May 31, 1931; s. Herman and Sarah (Steinsaltz) N.; m. Helaine J. Glickstein, June 6, 1954; children: Debra, Daniel, Karen. AB, Dartmouth Coll., 1952; LL.B., Yale U., 1955; S.JD, N.Y. Law Sch., 1963. Bar: N.Y. 1956. Law clk. to Hon. Lawrence E. Walsh U.S. Dist. Ct., NYC, 1955-57. Adj. prof. U. Pa. Law Sch., Phila., 1969—, Yale U. Law Sch., 1983—85; Everett B. Birch adj. prof. wills and estate planning Columbia U. Law Sch., NYC, 1994—. Author: (with Albert Kalter) Postmortem Estate Planning, 1976, 2d edit., 1994. Mem. exec. com. Am. Friends of Hebrew U., chmn. bd., 1994-98. Fellow Am. Bar Found., Am. Coll. Trust and Estate Coun.; mem. ABA (chmn. sect. legal edn. 1979-80, chmn. com. estate & gift taxation 1976-78), Estate Planning Council N.Y.C. (pres. 1979-80), N.Y. State Bar Assn. Office: NYU Sch Law 435 West 116th St New York NY 10027-7297 Office Phone: 212-854-2640. E-mail: lnewman@law.columbia.edu.

NEWMAN, LAWRENCE WALKER, lawyer; b. Boston, July 1, 1935; s. Leon Bettoney and Hazel W. (Walker) N.; children: Timothy D., Isabel B., Thomas H. AB, Harvard U., 1957, LL.B., 1960. Bar: DC 1961, NY 1965. Atty. US Dept. Justice, 1960-61, Spl. Study of Securities Markets and Office Spl. Counsel on Investment Co. Act Matters, U.S. SEC, 1961-64; asst. US atty. So. Dist. NY, 1964-69; assoc. Baker & McKenzie, NYC, 1969-71, ptnr., 1971—. Mem. internat. adv. coun. World Arbitration Inst., 1984-87; adv. com. Asia Pacific Ctr. for Resolution of Internat. Trade Disputes, 1987—; adv. bd. Inst. for Transnat. Arbitration, 1988—; chmn. U.S. Iranian Claimants Com., 1982—; adv. bd. World Arbitration and Mediation Report, 1993-2002, co-chmn., 2002—; bd. adv. to Corporate Counsel's Internat. Adviser, 1995—. Co-author: The Practice of Internat. Litigation, 1992, 2d edit. 1998, Litigating Internat. Commercial Disputes, 1996; columnist NY Law Jour., 1982—; bd. advisors Corp. Counsel's Internat. Adviser; contbr. articles to profl. jours., chpts. to books; editor: Enforcement of Money Judgments, Attachment of Assets, Internat. Arbitration Checklists; chmn. editl. bd. Juris Pub., Inc.; co-editor: Revolutionary Days: The Iran Hostage Crisis and the Hague Claims Tribunal, A Look Back, 1999, Take the Witness: The Experts Speak on Cross-examination, 2006. Mem. Internat. Bar Assn. (com. dispute resolution, com. constrn. litigation), Inter-Am. Bar Assn., Fed. Bar Coun., Am. Fgn. Law Assn., Maritime Law Assn. US, Assn. Bar City NY (com. on arbitration and alternative dispute resolution 1991-94, com. internat. comml. dispute resolution, 2000—, chmn. 2003—), Am. Arbitration Assn. (corp. counsel com. 1987—, panel internat. arbitrators), US Coun. Internat. Bus., Ct. Arbitration of Polish Chamber Fgn. Trade (panel of arbitrators), Brit. Col. Internat. Comml. Arbitration Ctr., Am. Law Inst., Bar Assn. City NY (inaugural mem. com. on internat. comml. dispute resolution, chmn. 2003-07). Office: Baker & McKenzie 1114 Avenue of the Americas New York NY 10036 Office Phone: 212-891-3970. E-mail: lwn@bakernet.com.

NEWMAN, LEONARD JAY, retail jewel merchant, gemologist; b. Milw., Oct. 25, 1927; s. David and Pia Goldie (Smith) N.; m. Louise Shainberg, Jan. 14, 1951; children: Shelley, Marty, Alan, Heidi, Dee. BS, Purdue U.; postgrad., Washington U., St. Louis. Owner, mgr. Newman's Diamond Ctr., Jasper, Ind., 1951—; tchr. The Jasper Ctr., Ind., 1970-80. Bd. dirs. Sta. WFIU Pub. Radio, VUJC Found., State Bd. Health Systems Agy., sub area Health Systems Agy., Internat. Harp Competition, Bloomington United Way, Ind. U. Hillel Found.; consellor Sr. corps Re. Execs.; 1st v.p. Vincennes Univ. Found.; past pres. Jasper Community Arts Commn.; pres. Friends of Arts; commnr. Boy Scouts Am.; mem. Dubois County Mental Health Assn.; lay adv. bd. Convent Immaculate Conception Sisters of St. Benedict, Ferdinand, Ind,; adv. bd. Jasper Hist. Soc., German Club, Young Abe Lincoln Soc., WFIU pub. radio; bd. dirs. Dubois County Crippled Children's Soc., Bloomington (Ind.) Symphony, Patoka Valley Vocat. Coop., Patoka Valley Rehab., Beth Shalom, Monroe County Purdue Alumni, Camerata Orch., Ind. U. Friends of Music, Ind. Jewish Hist. Soc., Hillel Found.; pres. Jasper Edn. Fund; mem., chmn. nominee com. Raintree Coun. Girl Scouts U.S.A., bd. dirs.; Midwest bd. dirs. Anti-Defamation League. Recipient Outstanding Citizenship award Purdue U. Alumni Assn., 1980 Outstanding Alumni award Jasper High Sch., Ronald Reagan Medal, 1994, Outstanding Community Svc. award Bloomington, Ind. C. of C., 2000, 01, Gov.'s award Sagamore of the Wabash, 2001. Mem. Nat. Assn. Jewelry Appraisers (sr.), Ind. Jewelers Orgn. Am., Retail Jewelers Am., Jasper C. of C., Jaycees (Rooster, past pres., past nat. bd. dirs., Disting. Svc. award 1957), Monroe County Purdue Alumni Club (bd. dirs.), Nat. Soc. Arts and Letters (bd. mem.), Svc. Corp. Ret. Execs. (pres.), Purdue Agrl. Alumni Assn. (hon.), Skull and Crescent (hon.), Hadassah, Sigma Alpha Mu, Alpha Phi Omega, Lions, Masons, Shriners (past pres.), B'nai Brith, Temple Beth Shalom (pres.). Office: Newman's Diamond Ctr 3 D Pl Jasper IN 47546 Home: 3754 Villa Glen Ct Bloomington IN 47401 E-mail: newmangem@insightbb.com.

NEWMAN, LESLÉA, writer; m. Mary Vazquez. BS in Edn., U. Vt., 1977; cert. in poetics, Naropa Inst., Boulder, Colo., 1980. Author: A Letter to Harvey Milk, 1988, Heather Has Two Mommies, 1989, In Every Laugh a Tear, 1992, Fat Chance, 1994, Too Far Away to Touch, 1995, Remember That, 1996, Still Life with Buddy, 1997, Out of the Closet and Nothing to Wear, 1997, Matzo Ball Moon, 1998, Girls Will Be Girls, 2000, Signs of Love, 2001, Cats, Cats, Cats!, 2001, Dogs, Dogs, Dogs!, 2002, Runaway Dreidel, 2002;: She Loves Me, She Loves Me Not, 2002, Felicia's Favorite Story, 2002, Pigs, Pigs, Pigs!, 2003, Best Short Stories of Leslea Newman, 2003, The Best Cat in the World, 2004 (Muse Medallion Best Children's Book award Cat Writers Assn., awards), The Boy Who Cried Fabulous, 2004, A Fire Engine for Ruthie, 2004, Where is Bear?, 2004, Hachiko Waits, 2004 (Henry Bergh Children's Book Honor award), Jailbait, 2005, The Eight Nights of Chanukah, 2005, Skunk's Spring Surprise, 2007, Daddy's Song, 2007. Recipient fiction award Highlights for Children, 1992; fellow Mass. Artists Fellowship, 1989, NEA, 1997. Mem. Author's Guild, Poets and Writers, Soc. Children's Book Writers and Illustrators, Pub. Triangle. Jewish. Avocations: crossword puzzles, bowling, collage-making. Address: PO Box 815 Northampton MA 01061-0815

NEWMAN, LIBBY, painter, printmaker, curator; b. Rockland Del., Nov. 17, 1925; d. Hyman and Dora (Horowitz) Goldberg; children: Don, Andrea Newman Orsher. BFA U. Arts; postgrad. U. Pa., Villanova U. Mem. visual arts panel Pa. Council on Arts, 1971-76; artist-in-residence/curator exhbns. University City Sci. Ctr., Phila., 1975—; co-curator sculpture Gov.'s Mansion, Harrisburg, Pa., 1979—88; one-woman shows Phila. Art Alliance, 1971, 2003, Mangel Gallery, Phila., 1972, 75, 78, 84, 88, 92, 95, 99, 2004-05, University City Sci. Ctr. Gallery, Phila., Tianjin Fine Arts Coll., China, 1988-89, Biblioteca Alexandrina, Egypt, 2006, Paper Mus., Tokyo, 2007; group shows include Mangel Gallery, 1972-2000, Pa. Acad. Fine Arts, Phila., Peale Galleries of Pa. Acad. Fine Arts, Woodmere Art Mus., Chestnut Hill, Pa., Moore Coll. Art, Phila., Fritz Miller Gallery, NYC, William Penn State Mus., Harrisburg, Pa., Fountain Gallery, Portland, Oreg., Del. Art Mus., Wilmington, Phila. Mus. Art, Circle Gallery, NYC, Chgo., So. Alleghenies Mus. Art, Loretto, Pa., Mus. Phila. Civic Ctr., Moore Coll. Art, Phila., 1982, Sichuan Fine Arts Inst., Changging, People's Republic China, 1985, Tianjin Fine Arts Coll., People's Republic China, 1986, Art in City Hall, Phila., 1986, King St. Mus., Szekesherva, Hungary; represented in permanent collections Phila. Mus. Art, Nat. Mus. Belgrade (Yugoslavia), Mus. Modern Art, Buenos Aires, Argentina, U. Pa. Law Sch., Mus. Phila. Civic Ctr., Temple U. Law Sch., Phila., Glassboro State Coll., NJ, Free Libr. Phila., University City Sci. Ctr., Phila., St. Joseph's Coll., Phila., St. Charles Borromeo Sem., Overbrook, Pa., Temple U. Health and Sci. Ctr., Phila., Nationalities Svc. Ctr., Phila., Phila. Assn. Clin. Trials., Mus. Andropologico, Guayagui, Equador, Indus Valley Sch. Arts and Architecture, Karachi, Pakistan; Editor: R. Buckminster Fuller Sketchbook, 1981; A City Sketched: A Guide to the Art and History of Philadelphia, 1976. Mem. Mayor's Com. for Sci. and Tech., 1979-82. Recipient Fleischer Art Meml. award; Cheltenham Nat. Graphic award; Best Pictures of the Yr. award Phila. Art Alliance; Carl Zigrosser Nat. Meml. award Am. Color Print Exhbn., Disting. Daus. Pa. award, 1992; chosen for vis. artist project Brandywine Graphics, 1984; Nat. Endowment grantee, 1973; Pa. Acad. of Fine Arts fellow, Perry Owens award, Mayor's citation City of Phila., 1995. Mem. Artists Equity Assn. (pres. Phila. chpt. 1969-71), Am. Color Print Assn., Phila. Art Alliance, Phila. Watercolor Club. Home: 2401 Pennsylvania Ave Apt 7b34 Philadelphia PA 19130-3029 Office Phone: 215-765-4555. Personal E-mail: libby2401@aol.com.

NEWMAN, MALCOLM, mechanical and civil engineering consultant; b. NYC, June 29, 1931; m. Estelle Ruth Glotzer, June 11, 1955. BSCE, CCNY, 1952; MSCE, Columbia U., 1957; D in Engrng. Sci., NYU, 1962. Registered profl. engr., N.Y. Chief structural mechanics Republic-Fairchild Hiller Corp., Farmingdale, N.Y., 1962-65, staff cons., 1970-71; dir. structural mechanics Harry Belock Assocs. Inc., Great Neck, N.Y., 1965-69; dir. structural mechanics and design Analytical Mechanics Assn., Jericho, N.Y., 1969-70; prof. mech. engrng. Tel Aviv U., 1972-75; pres., tech. dir. Inter-City Testing and Cons., Mineola, NY, 1976—2004. Pres. Athletic Safety Products Inc., Mineola, 1985—; adj. prof. engrng. Cooper Union. Contbr. over 80 articles to profl. jours.; patentee in field. Bd. dirs. Cinema Arts Ctr., Huntington, N.Y., 1989—. Mem. NSPE, Am. Soc. Safety Engrs., Nat. Assn. Profl. Accident Reconstruction Specialists, Soc. Automotive Engrs., System Safety Soc. (pres. 1983-85). Office: Inter-City Testing & Cons 167 Willis Ave Ste 2 Mineola NY 11501-2680 E-mail: exptl@aol.com.

NEWMAN, MARIE STEFANINI, law librarian, educator; b. Boston, Aug. 30, 1951; d. Mario and Elizabeth (Just) S.; m. Gary Nathaniel Newman, Sept. 30, 1978; children: Alexander, Elizabeth. AB, Smith Coll., 1973; MS, Columbia U., 1974; JD, Rutgers U., 1983. Bar: N.Y. 1984. Jr. librarian Bayonne (N.J.) Pub. Library, 1974-75; editor Microfilming Corp. Am., Glen Rock, N.J., 1975-78; circulation librarian SUNY Downstate Med. Ctr, Bklyn., 1979-80; head reference svcs. N.Y. Law Sch., NYC, 1984-90, adj. assoc. prof. law, 1985-90; assoc. dir. Pub. Svcs., lectr. U. Pa. Law Sch., 1991-93; dep. libr. dir. and adj. prof. law Pace U. Sch. Law, White Plains, N.Y., 1993-99, libr. dir., assoc. prof. law, 1999—. Database mgr. Inst. Internat. Comml. Law, 1994—. Mem. Am. Assn. Law Libraries. Office: Pace Law Libr 78 N Broadway White Plains NY 10603-3710 Business E-Mail: mnewman@law.pace.edu.

NEWMAN, MARK S., electronics company executive; BA, SUNY, Binghampton; MBA, Pace Univ. CPA. Mgmt. positions through CFO DRS Technologies Inc., Parsippany, NJ, 1974—94, pres., CEO, 1994—95, chmn., pres., CEO, 1995—. Bd. dir. Congoleum Corp., Refac Optical Group, EFJ Inc., NJ Tech. Council; bd. gov. Aerospace Ind. Assn.; past chmn. Am. Electronics Assn. Mem.: Surface Navy Assn., Assn. U.S. Army, Nat. Defense Indsl. Assn., Navy League U.S., Bus. Executives for Nat. Security (bd. dir.). Office: DRS Technologies Inc Five Sylvan Way Parsippany NJ 07054 *

NEWMAN, MICHAEL RODNEY, lawyer; b. NYC, Oct. 2, 1945; s. Morris and Helen Gloria (Hendler) Newman; m. Cheryl Jeanne Anker, June 11, 1967; children: Hillary Abra, Nicole Brooke. Student NASA Inst. Space Physics, Columbia U., 1964; BA, U. Denver, 1967; JD, U. Chgo., 1970. Bar: Calif. 1971, U.S. Dist. Ct. (cen. dist.) Calif. 1972, U.S. Ct. Appeals (9th cir.) 1974, U.S. Dist. Ct. (no. dist.) Calif. 1975, U.S. Supreme Ct. 1978, U.S. Dist. Ct. (so. dist.) Calif. 1979, U.S. Tax Ct. 1979, U.S. Dist. Ct. (ea. dist.) Calif. 1983. Assoc. David Daar, 1971-76; ptnr. Daar & Newman, 1976-78, Miller & Daar, 1978-88, Miller, Daar & Newman, 1988-89, Daar & Newman, 1989—; judge pro-tem L.A. Mcpl. Ct., 1982—, L.A. Superior Ct., 1988—. Vice chmn., bd. dirs. German-Am. C. of C., 2001—02; bd. govs., fin. and phys. devel. com. U. Haifa, Israel; bd. dirs., mem. adv. bd., chmn. bus. generation com. Consulegis EEIG, 1995—; founder, facilitator 1st, 2d and 3d Ann. German-Am. Strategic Partnership Confs., 1992—2000; guest lectr. Calif. State U., Fullerton, 2006, 07; lectr. in field. Mem. L.A. Citizens Organizing Com. for Olympic Summer Games, 1984, mem. govtl. liaison adv. commn., 1984; mem. So. Calif. Com. for Olympic Summer Games, 1984; cert. ofcl. Athletics Congress of U.S., co-chmn. legal com. S.P.A.-T.A.C., chief finish judge; trustee Massada lodge B'nai Brith; bd. dirs. Ctr. for the Study of Emerging Markets, Calif. State U. Fullerton Grad. Sch. Bus. and Econs., 1997—. Recipient Maths. award, USN Sci., 1963. Mem.: TAC (bd. dirs., Disting. Svc. award 1988), ABA (multi-dist. litigation subcom., com. on class actions), German Am. Lawyers Assn. So. Calif. (mem. bd.), Lawyers Profl. Liability Bar Assn., Conf. Ins. Counsel, Los Angeles County Bar Assn. (chmn. attys. errors and omissions prevention com. 1995—2005, mem. cts. com., mem. internat. law sect., state cts. coord. com. litigation sect., exec. com.), Rotary Club (internat. com.), City Club on Bunker Hill, Breakfast Club, Porter Valley Country Club. Office: Daar & Newman 865 S Figueroa St Ste 2300 Los Angeles CA 90017-2567 Office Phone: 213-892-0999. Business E-Mail: mnewman@daarnewman.com.

NEWMAN, MURIEL KALLIS STEINBERG, art collector; b. Chgo., Feb. 25, 1914; d. Maurice and Ida (Nudelman) Kallis; m. Albert H. Newman, May 14, 1955; 1 son by previous marriage, Glenn D. Steinberg. Student, Art Inst. Chgo., 1932-36, Ill. Inst. Tech., 1947-50, U. Chgo., 1958-65. Hon. life trustee, benefactor Met. Mus. Art, N.Y.C., vis. com. dept. 20th Century Art, acquisitions com., 1981—, decorative arts com., 1989, Costume Inst. Dir., 20th Century Painting and Sculpture Com., Art Inst. Chgo., 1955-80, governing mem. inst., 1955—; pioneer collector Am. abstract expressionist art, 1949—, major show of collection, Met. Mus. Art, N.Y.C., 1981, personal collection of costumes and jewelry, 1981. Bd. govs. Landmarks Preservation Council, Chgo., 1966-78; woman's bd. U. Chgo., 1960-81, Art Inst. Chgo., 1953—, 20th century com., Asian com.; trustee Mus. Contemporary Art, 1970, benefactor, 1970; trustee Chgo. Sch. of Architecture Found., 1971, Archives Am. Art, 1976; bd. dirs. Bright New City Urban Affairs Lecture Series, 1966—; trustee Art Inst. Chgo., African and American art com. Recipient Scroll Recognition of Pub. Svc., U.S. Dept. State, 1958; named Disting. Benefactor, Art Inst. Chgo., 1998. Mem. Antiquarian Soc. of Art Inst. Chgo., Chgo. Hist. Soc. (mem. guild 1958—), Arts Club Chgo., Casino Club Chgo., Arts Club (Chgo.), Casino Club (Chgo.) *Searching for truth is a given for a life of value. For me visual art ontologically reveals the truth of the search. Striving for excellence is the spearhead with which to proceed.*

NEWMAN, MURRAY ARTHUR, aquarium administrator; b. Chgo., Mar. 6, 1924; emigrated to Can., 1953, naturalized, 1970; s. Paul Jones and Virginia (Murray) N.; m. Katherine Greene Rose, Aug. 8, 1952; 1 child, Susan. BSc, U. Chgo., 1949; postgrad., U. Hawaii, 1950; MA, U. Calif., Berkeley, 1951; PhD, U. B.C., Vancouver, Can., 1960. Curator fisheries UCLA, 1951-53; curator fisheries Ichthyology Mus. U. B.C., 1953-56; curator Vancouver Pub. Aquarium, 1956-66, dir., 1966-93; pres. Mana Aquarium Cons. Fgn. adv. Nat. Mus./Aquarium Project, Taiwan; past chmn. adv. com. Western Can. Univs. Marine Biol. Soc.; co-chmn. Enoshima (Japan) Internat. Aquarium Symposium, 1997; spl. advisor Enoshima Aquarium, 1998, Port of Nagoya Pub. Aquarium, 1999, 2000; hon. com. Fifth Internat. Congress, Monaco, 2000, Sixth Internat. Congress, Monterey, 2004, grand opening new Enoshima Aquarium, 2004. Author: Life in a Fishbowl: Confessions of an Aquarium Director, 1994, People Fish and Whales The Vancouver Aquarium Story, 2006. Served with USN, 1943-46. Decorated Order of Can., Order of British Columbia, 2006; recipient Man of Yr. award City of Vancouver, 1964; Centennial award Govt. Can., 1967, cert. of merit, 1988; Harold J. Merilees award Vancouver Visitors Bur., 1976, 75 Achievers award, 1987, Silver Bravery medal Royal Soc. Can., 1992, Can. 125 medal, 1992, Golden Jubilee medal, 2002. Mem. Am. Assn. Zool. Parks and Aquariums, Internat. Union Dirs. Zool. Gardens, Can. Assn. Zool. Parks and Aquariums (pres. 1978-79), Vancouver Club, Round Table Club. Office: Vancouver Pub Aquarium PO Box 3232 Vancouver BC Canada V6B 3X8

NEWMAN, NORMAN RICHARD, lawyer; b. Indpls., Dec. 10, 1934; s. Irving and Anne Newman; m. Pauline Nelson, Dec. 28, 1958; children: Anne Leslie Smeltzer, Mark Alan, Eric Daniel. AB, Ind. U., 1956, LLB, 1960. Bar: Ind. 1960. Ptnr. Dann, Pecar, Newman&Kleiman, P.C., Indpls., 1965—. Mem. Am. Coll. of Real Estate Lawyers, Washington, 1983—; spkr. in field; counsel to major nat. and regional real estate developers Projects Mall of Am. and Circle Ctr. Mall. Author: (legal commentary) Indiana Continuing Legal Education Forum, ALI/ABA - The Practical Lawyer. Recipient Listed in Best Lawyers in Am., 1983—, Named an Ind. Super Lawyer, 2004—. Avocation: golf. Office: Dann Pecar Newman&Kleiman PC One American Sq Ste 2300 Indianapolis IN 46282 Home Phone: 317-581-9989; Office Phone: 317-632-3232. E-mail: nnewman@dannpecar.com.

NEWMAN, PAUL, actor, food products executive, race car driver; b. Cleve., Jan. 26, 1925; s. Arthur S. and Theresa (Fetzer) N.; m. Jacqueline Witte, Dec. 1949 (div. 1958); children: Scott (dec. 1978), Susan, Stephanie; m. Joanne Woodward, Jan. 29, 1958; children: Elinor, Melissa, Clea. BA, Kenyon Coll., 1949; postgrad., Yale U. Sch. Drama, 1951; student (with Lee Strasberg), The Actor's Studio; LHD (hon.), Yale U., 1988. Founder, pres. Newman's Own Food, Inc., Westport, Conn., 1982—; co-founder Double H Ranch, 1992—; owner, ptnr. Dressing Room: A Homegrown Restaurant, Westport, Conn., 2006—. Appeared on Broadway in: Picnic, 1953-54, Desperate Hours, 1955, Sweet Bird of Youth, 1959, Baby Want a Kiss, 1964; Actor (films) The Silver Chalice, 1954, Somebody Up There Likes Me, 1956, The Rack, 1956, The Helen Morgan Story, 1957, Until They Sail, 1957, The Long Hot Summer, 1958 (Best Actor award Cannes Internat. Film Festival, 1958), The Left Handed Gun, 1958, Cat on a Hot Tin Roof, 1958, Rally 'Round the Flag Boys!, 1958, The Young Philadelphians, 1959, From the Terrace, 1960, Exodus, 1960, The Hustler, 1961 (British Film Acad. award for best foreign actor, 1961), Paris Blues, 1961, Sweet Bird of Youth, 1962, Hemingway's Adventures of a Young Man, 1962, Hud, 1963, A New Kind of Love, 1963, The Outrage, 1964, The Prize, 1964, What a Way to Go!, 1964, Lady L, 1965, Harper, 1966, Torn Curtain, 1966, Hombre, 1967, Cool Hand Luke, 1967, The Secret War of Harry Frigg, 1968, Winning, 1969, Butch Cassidy and the Sundance Kid,

1969, WUSA, 1970, Pocket Money, 1972, The Life and Times of Judge Roy Bean, 1972, The MacIntosh Man, 1973, The Sting, 1973, The Towering Inferno, 1974, The Drowning Pool, 1975, Buffalo Bill and the Indians or Sitting Bull's History Lesson, 1976, Slap Shot, 1977, Quintet, 1979, When Time Ran Out, 1980, Fort Apache, The Bronx, 1981, Absence of Malice, 1981, The Verdict, 1982, The Color of Money, 1986 (Acad. award for best actor, 1987, Nat. Bd. of Review award for best actor, 1987), Fat Man and Little Boy, 1989, Blaze, 1989, Mr. and Mrs. Bridge, 1989, The Hudsucker Proxy, 1994, Nobody's Fool, 1994 (NY Film Critics Circle award for best actor, Nat. Soc. of Film Critics award for best actor, 1994, Berlin Film Fest. Silver Bear for best actor, 1995), Super Speedway, 1997, Twilight, 1998, Message in a Bottle, 1999, Where the Money Is, 2000, Sweet Dreams, 2001, Road to Perdition, 2002, (voice only) Cars, 2006; actor, dir., writer, Harry and Son, 1984; actor, dir. Sometimes A Great Notion, 1971; actor (TV movies) Come Along With Me, 1982, Our Town, 2003; (TV series) Tales of Tomorrow, 1951, The Aldritch Family, 1952-53; (TV mini-series) Empire Falls, 2005 (Emmy award for outstanding supporting actor in a miniseries or a movie, 2005, best performance by an actor in a supporting role in a series, miniseries or motion picture made for TV, Hollywood Fgn. Press Assn. (Golden Globe award), 2006, outstanding performance by a male actor in a TV movie or miniseries, Screen Actors Guild award, 2006); dir., prodr, (films) Rachel, Rachel, 1968 (Golden Globe Award for best dir., Prodrs. Guild of Am. Award for best motion picture prodr., NY Film Critics Circle award for best dir., 1968), The Effect of Gamma Rays on Man-in-the-Moon Marigolds, 1973, The Shadow Box, 1980, Glass Menagerie, 1987 Served with AC USNR, 1943-46. Recipient Theatre World Award, 1953, Man of Yr. award Hasty Pudding Theater, Harvard U., 1968, Cecil B. DeMille award, 1984, Acad. award for lifetime achievement, 1985, SAG lifetime achievement award, 1985, D.W. Griffith Best Actor award Nat Bd. Rev. Motion Pictures, 1986, Kennedy Center Honors lifetime achievement award, 1992, Jean Hersholt Humanitarian award Acad. Motion Pictures Arts and Scis., 1993; named World Film Favorite, Hollywood Foreign Press, 1963, 65, 67. Best Motion Picture Prodr. of Yr., Prodrs. Guild of Am., 1968. Address: Newman's Own Inc 246 Post Rd E Westport CT 06880-3615

NEWMAN, PAULINE, federal judge; b. NYC, June 20, 1927; d. Maxwell Henry and Rosella Newman. BA, Vassar Coll., 1947; MA, Columbia U., 1948; PhD, Yale U., 1952; LLB, NYU, 1958. Bar: NY 1958, US Supreme Ct. 1972, US Ct. Customs and Patent Appeals 1978, Pa. 1979, US Ct. Appeals (3d cir.) 1981, US Ct. Appeals (fed. cir.) 1982. Research chemist Am. Cyanamid Co., Bound Brook, NJ, 1951—54; mem. patent staff FMC Corp., NYC, 1954—75, Phila., 1975—84, dir. dept. patent and licensing, 1969—84; judge US Ct. Appeals (fed. cir.), Washington, 1984—; Disting. prof. George Mason Law Sch., 1995—. Program specialist Dept. Natural Scis. UNESCO, Paris, 1961—62; mem. State Dept. Adv. Com. on Internat. Indsl. Property, 1974—84; lectr. in field. Contbr. articles to profl. jours. Trustee Phila. Coll. Pharmacy and Sci., 1983—84; bd. dirs. Med. Coll. Pa., 1975—84, Midgard Found., 1973—84. Mem.: ABA (coun. sect. patent trademark and copyright 1983—84), Coun. Fgn. Rels., U.S. Trademark Assn. (bd. dirs. 1975—79, v.p. 1978—79), Pacific Indsl. Property Assn. (pres. 1979—80), Am. Inst. Chemists (bd. dirs. 1960—66, 1970—76), Am. Chem. Soc. (bd. dirs. 1972—81), Am. Patent Law Assn. (bd. dirs. 1981—84), Yale Club, Vassar Club, Cosmos Club. Office: US Ct Appeals Nat Cts Bldg 717 Madison Pl Washington DC 20439-0002 *

NEWMAN, PHILIP ROBERT, psychologist; b. Dec. 17, 1942; s. Samuel M. and Sara Rose (Dumain) N.; m. Barbara Miller, June 12, 1966; children: Samuel Asher, Abraham Levy, Rachel Florence. AB with high distinction, U. Mich., 1964, PhD, 1971. Asst. prof. psychology U. Mich., Ann Arbor, 1971-72, Union Coll., Schenectady, NY, 1972-76; dir. human behavior curriculum project APA, Washington, 1977-81; pvt. practice psychology Columbus, Ohio, 1978-2000, South Kingston, RI, 2000—. Adj. prof., sr. rschr. young scholars program Ohio State U., 1990-98; adj. prof. human devel. and family studies U. R.I., 2000—; cons. Agy. Instrnl. TV, 1979; vis. scholar psychology, UCLA, 2006-. Author: (with B. Newman) Development through Life: A Psychosocial Approach, 1975, 9th edit., 2006; Infancy and Childhood Development and Its Context, 1978, An Introduction to the Psychology of Adolescence, 1979, Personality Development through the Life Span, 1980, Living: The Process of Adjustment, 1981, Understanding Adulthood, 1983, Principles of Psychology, 1983, Adolescent Development, 1986, When Kids Go to College: A Parents Guide to Changing Relationships, 1992, Childhood and Adolescence, 1997, (with B. Newman, L. Landry-Meyer, B. Lohman) Life Span Development: A Case Book, 2003, Theories of Human Development, 2007; editor: (with B. Newman) Development Through Life: A Case Study Approach, 1976. Woodrow Wilson fellow U. Mich., 1964, Univ. fellow, 1964-66, Horace H. Rackham Rsch. scholar, 1969-71. Mem. APA, APHA, Internat. Assn. Applied Psychology, Internat. Sociol. Assn., Soc. Psychol. Study Social Issues, Am. Sociol. Assn., Nat. Coun. Family Rels., Groves Conf. Marriage and Family, Ea. Psychol. Assn., N.Y. Acad. Sci., Gerontol. Soc. Am., Am. Orthopsychiat. Assn., Am. Statis. Assn., Soc. for Rsch. on Child Devel., Soc. for Rsch. on Adolescence, Soc. Study Human Devel., Phi Beta Kappa, Sigma Xi, Phi Kappa Phi. Office Phone: 401-559-1245. Personal E-mail: prn10@yahoo.com.

NEWMAN, PHYLLIS, counselor, therapist, hypnotist; b. NYC, Aug. 20, 1933; d. Max and Frieda Yetta (Pechter) Hershkowitz; BS, Mercy Coll., 1977; MS, LIU, 1979; m. Milton Newman, Dec. 28, 1952; children: Renee Holly, Eileen Sharon, Jeffrey Mark. Pvt. practice hypnosis and therapy, Peekskill, NY, 1977—89; lectr. Pepsico Fitness Ctr., Purchase, NY, 1984, Purdue U., 1986, 88, Girl Scouts' Coun., local radio; dir. counseling Hypnosis Group, 1979—89; featured local TV, 2004, 60 Minutes 2, 2004, Ivanhoe Broadcasting Co., 2005, Purdue Alumnus Mag., 2005. Mem. parents exec. bd. Purdue U., 1978-83, mem. pres.' council, 1982—89; bd. dirs. Hand to Mouth Players, Garrison, NY, Yorktown Cmty. Players, NY, 1988-89; v.p., prodr. Tempe Little Theatre, 1990-95; pres. Tempe Welcome Wagon Social Club, 1990-91; v.p. bd. dirs. Temple Emanuel Tempe, Ariz., 1996-; chair Beit Am. (Ho. of People), 2003-, healing svc. 2005-; active for Normal Pressure Hydrocephalus Support Group, Barrows Neurol. Inst., Phoenix, 2005—, Hydrocephalus Assn., San Francisco, 2005—; lectr. Ahwautukee Cancer Assn., 2002; leader meditation JCC, 1994-2001; liaison Union of Reform Judaism, SW Coun. Jewish Family Concerns, 2006—. Mem. Am. Assn. Counseling and Devel., Am. Mental Health Counselors Assn., NY Soc. Ericksonian Hypnosis, Am. Assn. Profl. Hypnotherapists. Contbr. articles to profl. jours. Address: 4333 W Walton Way Chandler AZ 85226 Personal E-mail: phylnew820@cox.net.

NEWMAN, R. DONALD, paper company executive; V.p., resident mgr. Bowater, Inc., Calhoun, Tenn., 1987; v.p. Bowater, Inc., Canadian Newsprint Oper., 1998—2001; v.p., strategic planning Bowater, Inc., 2001—02, exec. v.p., COO Greenville, SC, 2002—. Office: Bowater Inc 55 E Camperdown Way Greenville SC 29602

NEWMAN, RACHEL, editor; b. Malden, Mass., May 1, 1938; d. Maurice and Edythe Brenda (Tichell) Newman; m. Herbert Bleiweiss, Apr. 6, 1973 (div. Apr. 1989); m. Michael Lucas, Feb. 24, 2004. BA, Pa. State U., University Park, 1960; cert., NY Sch. Interior Design, NYC, 1963. Accessories editor Women's Wear Daily, NYC, 1964—65; designer, publicist Grandoe Glove Corp., NYC, 1965—67; assoc. editor McCall's Sportswear and Dress Merchandiser mag., NYC, 1967; mng. editor McCall's You-Do-It Home Decorating, 1968—70, Ladies Home Jour. Needle and Craft mag., NYC, 1970—72; editor-in-chief Am. Home Crafts mag., NYC, 1972—77; fashion dir. Good Housekeeping mag., NYC, 1977—78, home bldg. and decorating dir., 1978—82; editor-in-chief Country Living mag., NYC, 1978—98; founding editor Country Cooking mag., 1985—90, Dream Homes mag., 1989—2000, Country Kitchens mag., 1990—93, Country Living Gardener Mag., 1993—2000, Healthy Living mag., 1996—2000. Bd. dirs. Mothers and Others for a Livable Planet. Named Disting. Alumna, Pa. State U., 1988; recipient Cir. of Excellence award, Internat. Furnishings and Design Assn., 1992, YMCA Hall of Fame, 1992; Pa. State U. Alumni fellow, 1986. Mem.: Am. Soc. Mag. Editors, Am. Soc. Interior Designers, Nat. Home Fashions League, N.Y. Fashion Group. E-mail: Rachelsfree@earthlink.net.

NEWMAN, RANDY, singer, songwriter, musician; b. LA, Nov. 28, 1943; s. Irving and Adele N.; m. Gretchen Newman; children: Amos, Eric, John, Patrick, Alice. Degree, U. Calif. Arranger, singer, songwriter, musician various record firms; singer-composer: (albums) including Randy Newman, 1968, Twelve Songs, 1969, Live, 1971, Sail Away, 1972, Good Old Boys, 1974, Little Criminals, 1977, Born Again, 1979, Trouble In Paradise, 1983, Land of Dreams, 1988, Bad Love, 1999; (with others) Randy Newman's Faust, 1995; appeared in film: Ragtime, 1981; also TV and concert engagements; music composer for films: Performance, 1970, Pursuit of Happiness, 1971, Cold Turkey, 1971, Ragtime, 1981, The Natural, 1984 (Grammy award for Best Instrumental Composition, 1984), Three Amigos (also co-wrote screenplay), 1986, Parenthood, 1989, Avalon, 1990, Awakenings, 1990, Toy Story, 1995 (Annie award for Individual Achievement in Music, 1995), Michael, 1996, James and the Giant Peach, 1996, Cats Don't Dance, 1997 (Annie award for Feature Video Prodn. Music, 1997), A Bug's Life, 1998 (Grammy award for Best Instrumental Composition for Motion Picture, 2000), Pleasantville, 1998, Toy Story 2, 1999 (Grammy award for Best Song Written for Motion Picture, 2001, Annie award for Outstanding Individual Achievement for Music in an Animated Feature Prodn., 2000), Meet the Parents, 2000, Monsters, Inc., 2001 (ASCAP award for Top Box Office Film, 2001, Acad award for Best Original Song, 2002, Grammy award for Best Song Written for Motion Picture, 2003), Mike's New Car, 2002, Seabiscuit, 2003 (ASCAP award for Top Box Office Film), Mr. 3000, 2004, Meet the Fockers, 2004 (ASCAP award for Top Box Office Film, 2005), Cars, 2006 (Grammy award for Best Song Written for Motion Picture, 2007, ASCAP award, 2007); composer for TV Series: Monk, 2002 (Emmy award for Outstanding Main Title Theme Music, 2004, ASCAP award for Top TV Series, 2005); recorded 30 Years of Randy Newman (4 CD set), 1998. Named to Songwriters' Hall of Fame, 2002. Office: c/o Sacks & Co 427 W 14th St New York NY 10014 also: c/o Gorfaine/Schwartz Agy Inc Ste 509 4111 W Alameda Ave Burbank CA 91505 *

NEWMAN, RICHARD G., engineering company executive; BSCE, Bucknell U.; MSCE, Columbia U.; grad. Exec. Mgmt. Program, UCLA. Former CEO AECOM Tech. Corp., LA, 2002—, chmn. Bd. dirs. Southwest Water Co., 13 mutual funds under Capital Rsch. and Mgmt. Co., Sempra Energy, San Diego, 2002—, mem. audit and corp. governance coms. Fellow: Inst. for Advancement of Engring.; mem.: NSPE, Am. Soc. Civil Engrs., Chief Executives Orgn. Office: AECOM Tech Corp 555 S Flower St Ste 3700 Los Angeles CA 90071-2300 Office Phone: 215-593-8000. Office Fax: 213-593-8729.

NEWMAN, ROBERT GABRIEL, physician; b. The Netherlands, Oct. 26, 1937; came to U.S., 1939; s. Randolph H. and Eva E. (Feilchenfeld) N.; m. Seiko Kusuba, Oct. 26, 1968; children: Henry Seiji, Hana Marie. BA, NYU, 1958; MD with honors, U. Rochester, 1963; MPH, U. Calif.-Berkeley, 1969. Intern and resident in surgery Univ. Hosps., Cleve., 1963-65; dist. health officer N.Y.C. Health Dept., 1968; dir. Nat. Nutrition Survey of N.Y.C., 1969-70; asst. commr. N.Y.C. Health Dept., 1970-74; health cons., 1974-76; assoc. gen. dir. Beth Israel Med. Ctr., NYC, 1976-78, CEO, pres., 1978-97; prof. dept. community medicine Mt. Sinai Sch. Medicine, NYC, 1982-94; prof. depts. epidemiology and social medicine/psychiatry Albert Einstein Coll. of Medicine, 1994—; CEO, pres. Continuum Health Ptnrs. Inc. (formerly Greater Met. Health), NYC, 1997—2000, pres. emeritus; dir. Baron Edmond de Rothschild Chem. Dependency Inst., NYC, 2000—. Cons. addiction problems Govt. of Hong Kong, 1975-85 Author book in field of methadone treatment; contbr. articles to profl. jours. Trustee U. Rochester, NY, 1994—2002. With USAF, 1965—67. WHO fellow, 1972 Fellow N.Y. Acad. Medicine, Am. Coll. Preventive Medicine; mem. Public Health Assn. N.Y.C., Hosp. Assn. N.Y. State (past chmn. 1992), Greater N.Y. Hosp. Assn. (past chmn. bd.), Am. Public Health Assn. Office: Continuum Health Ptnrs Inc 555 W 57th St Fl 18 New York NY 10019-2925 E-mail: rnewman@icaat.org.

NEWMAN, RUTH GALLERT, psychologist; b. NYC, June 16, 1914; d. Ernest Ezra and Belle (Cohen) Gallert; m. James R. Newman (July 27, 1940 (dec.); children: Jeffrey Frederick, Brooke Anne. BA, Rtugers U., 1937; MA, George Washington U., 1942; PhD, U. Md., 1950. Tchr. Emerson Sch., NYC, 1938-40; remedial tutor Remedial Edn. Ctr., Washington, 1942-45; remedial tchr. Geroge Wahsington Day Sch., Washington, 1948-51; clin. tchr., supr. Children's Hosp., Washington, 1955-60; pvt. practice group therapy Washington Sch. Psychiatry, 1960—. Mem. AKPice Group Rels.; speaker in field; cons. in field. NIMH grantee. Democrat. Address: c/o Brooke Newman 273 Roaring Fork Dr Aspen CO 81611-2238 Personal E-mail: thelittletern@hotmail.com.

NEWMAN, RYAN, race car driver; b. South Bend, Ind. Degree in vehicle structure engring., Purdue U., 2001. Racecar driver Penske Racing So., 2001—. Named winner, All-Am. Midget Series, 1993, Rookie of the Yr., USAC Nat. Midget Series, 1995, USAC Silver Crown Series, 1996, Sprint Car, 1999, winner, USAC Coors Light Silver Bullet Series, 1999, Pepsi Automobile Racing Club Am. 200, 2000, Automobile Racing Club Am. Ky. Speedway, 2000, Automobile Racing Club Am. Lowe's Motor Speedway, 2000; recipient, Roger Penske 500, 2002, 2005, Sylvania 300, 2005; scholar Rich Vogler Meml. scholar, 2001.

NEWMAN, SAMUEL, retired trust company executive; b. NYC, Mar. 12, 1938; s. Aaron and Rachel (Hershkowitz) Newman; m. Carolyn Gropper, Oct. 27, 1963; children: Marci Ann, Jodi Robin, Michael David. BBA, CUNY, 1971; grad. Advanced Mgmt. Program, Harvard U., 1982. Methods analyst Bankers Trust Co., NYC, 1960-67; project leader Clark O'Neill SVC Corp., Fairview, NJ, 1967-68; sr. v.p. Irving Trust Co., NYC, 1968-85; sr. v.p., gen. mgr. trade svcs. and GEOSERVE legal and regulatory support Mfrs. Hanover Trust (merger with Chem. Bank 1992), NYC, 1985-92; sr. v.p., gen. mgr. funds transfer and trade svcs. Chem. Bank, NYC, 1992-93; sr. v.p. and bus. head payment products First Fidelity Bank NA, Newark, 1993-95; head dept. project support Fleet Pa. Svcs. Inc., Scranton, Pa., 1995-98; dir. new bus. devel., mgr. customer svc., internat. fin. instns. Fleet Bank, NYC, 1998—2001; dir. float mgmt. Fleet Nat. Bank, Melville, NY, 2001—03. Past chmn. bd. dirs. SWIFT Terminal Svcs.; past chmn. NY Clearing House funds transfer com.; speaker industry confs. Contbr. articles to profl. jours. Advisor Nat. Conf. of Commrs. on Uniform State Laws; former mem. US coun. Internat. Banking Exec. Com., US del. to Uncitral Working Group on Internat. Payments; former chief US del. to tech. com. 168 Internat. Standards Orgn. Mem. Soc. Worldwide Fin. Telecom. (bd. dirs. 1978-92, dep. chmn 1989-92), Internat. Fin. Svcs. Assn. (bd. dirs. 2001—03). Avocation: foreign currency note collection. Office: 39 Wyandanch Ave Wyandanch NY 11798 Personal E-mail: wallstrbkr@aol.com.

NEWMAN, SANDRA SCHULTZ, lawyer, former state supreme court justice; b. Nov. 4, 1938; BS, Drexel U., 1959; MA, Temple U., 1969; JD, Villanova U., 1972; D (hon.), Gannon U., 1996, Widener U., 1996, Clarion U., 2000, Drexel U., 2001. Bar: Pa., U.S. Dist. Ct. (ea. dist.) Pa., U.S. Ct. Appeals (3d cir.), U.S. Supreme Ct. Asst. dist. atty. Montgomery County, Pa., 1972—74; pvt. practice, 1974—93; judge Commonwealth Ct. of Pa., 1993—95; justice Pa. Supreme Ct., 1995—2006; ptnr., head appellate practice Cozen O'Connor, Phila., 2007—. Past chair bd. consultors Villanova U. Law Sch.; mem. jud. coun. Supreme Ct. of Pa., liaison to the 3rd cir. task force on mgmt. of death penalty litigation, liaison to Pa. lawyers fund for client security bd., liaison to domestic rels. procedural rules com.; liaison Pa. Bar Inst.; jud. work group HHS; mem. adv. com. Nat. Ctr. for State Cts., Am. Law Inst.; mem. Drexel U. Coll. Bus. and Adminstrn.; lectr. and spkr. in field. Author: Alimony, Child Support and Counsel Fees, 1988; contbr. articles to profl. jours. Named named Disting. Daughter of Pa.; recipient Phila. award for Super Achiever, Pediatric Juvenile Colitis Found. Jefferson Med. Coll. and Hosp, 1979, award for Dedicated Leadership and Outstanding Contbns. to the Cmty. and Law Employment, Drexel 100 award, Police Chiefs Assn. of Southeastern Pa., 1993, Medallion of Achievement award, Villanova U., 1993, Susan B. Anthony award, Women's Bar Assn. Western Pa., 1996, award, Justinian Soc., 1996, Tau Epsilon Law Soc., 1996, Legion of Honor Gold Medallion award, Chapel of Four Chaplain, 1997, honored by, Women of Greater Phila., 1996, Person of Yr. award, Shomrim of Phila., 1998, Women of Distinction award, Greater Phila. Council of Jewish Women Internat., 2005, Person of Yr. award, Pa. State Constables Assoc., 2005. Fellow: Pa. Bar Found., Am. Bar Found.; mem.: Montgomery Bar Assn., Nat. Assn. Women Judges, Am. Law Inst. Office: Cozen O'Connor 1900 Market St Philadelphia PA 19103 *

NEWMAN, SHERRYL HOBBS, former district secretary; BA in Chemistry, Rutgers U., 1986, BA in Economics, 1986; MBA in Management, Lubin Graduate Sch. of Bus. Pace Univ., White Plains, NY, 1992. Acting dep. dir.-Taxpayer Assistance Divsn. NYC-Dept. of Finance, 1992—93, city collector-Property Bureau, 1993—96; dir. Customer Svc. Adminstrn.-Office of Tax and Revenue, Washington, 1997—99, Citywide Customer Svc. Adminstrn.-Office of the City Adminstr., Washington, 1999, Dept. of Motor Vehicles, Washington, 1999—2003; sec. dist. DC Govt., 2003—05, dep. CFO, Office Tax & Revenue, 2005—. Democrat. Office: DC Office of Tax & Revenue 941 N Capitol St NE Ste 800 Washington DC 20002 Business E-Mail: shnewman@dc.gov.

NEWMAN, SLATER EDMUND, psychologist, educator; b. Boston, Sept. 8, 1924; s. Max and Gertrude (Raphael) N.; m. Corrine Lois Silfen, June 18, 1950 (div. 1968); children: Kurt Douglas, Jonathan Mark, Eric Bruce; m. Patricia Ellen Christopher Thomas, July 2, 1969; 1 stepchild, Arthur C. Thomas III. BS, U. Pa., 1947; MA, Boston U., 1948; PhD, Northwestern U., 1951. Research psychologist U.S. Air Force, 1951-57; mem. faculty N.C. State U., Raleigh, 1957—2003, prof. emeritus psychology, 2003—. Vis. fgn. mem. Exptl. Psychology Soc. U.K., 1973-74, 82-83, 90. Contbr. chpts. to books, articles to profl. publs. Bd. dirs. ACLU, 1992—97, mem. biennial conf. com., 1994—97, mem. task force internat. human rights, 1994—2005, mem. spl. nominating com., 1996, mem. constn. com., 1996—97, mem. youth affairs com., 1997, mem. nat. adv. coun., 1998—; organizing com. NC Civil Liberties Union, 1965, pres., 1980—82, exec. com., 1986—87, bd. dirs., 1969—73, 1976—82, 1984—90; chair Com. on Internat. Human Rights, 1988—; chair founding com. Wake County chpt. ACLU, 1969, pres., 1969—72, 1984—86, bd. dirs., 1969—73, 1976—82, 1984—90, life mem., 2002—; founding mem. North Carolinians Against the Death Penalty, 1967, bd. govs., 1967—73; mem. Mayor's Com. UN Week, Raleigh, 1986—95; active Amnesty Internat.; co-founder, coord. Com. to Reverse Arms Race, 1982—; co-founder, mem. steering com. North Carolinians Against Apartheid, 1985—87; mem. Wake County Com. Bicentennial US Constn., 1987—89; co-founder, co-chair NC Com. for Celebration of Human Rights, 1989—97; mem. Human Rights Week Com., NC State U., 1993—99, founder, 1993, chair, 1993—96; co-founder Human Rights Coalition NC, 1997—, co-chair, 1997—; co-founder North Carolinians for Ratification, Conv. on Elimination of All Forms of Discrimination Against Women, 1997; chair North Carolinians for Ratification, Com. on Elimination of All Forms of Discrimination Against Women, 1998—; mem. civil rights adv. bd. NC Mus. History, 2001—05. Served with USAF, 1943—46, 2d lt. USAF, 1952—53. USPHS spl. rsch. fellow U. Calif.-Berkeley, 1965-66; U. London hon. rsch. fellow, 1973-74, 82-83, 90; recipient W.W. Finlator award ACLU of Wake County, 1997, Norman Smith award ACLU of NC, 1998; recipient Frank Porter Graham Award, ACLU of NC, 2004, Human Rights award, Wake County and West Triangle Chpts., UN Assn., 2007; Slater Newman annual debate established by Wake County ACLU, 2006. Fellow: APA, AAAS, Assn. for Psychol. Sci.; mem.: AAUP (pres. N.C. State U. chpt. 1968—69), Carolinas Conf. for Undergrad. Rsch. in Psychology (co-founder 1976, co-advisor), Ea. Psychol. Assn., N.C. Cognition Group (founder 1972), S.E. Psychol. Assn. (exec. com. 2001—07, sec.-treas. 2004—07), S.E. Workers in Memory (founder 1969), So. Soc. Philosophy and Psychology, Psychonomic Soc., UN Assn. (bd. dirs. Wake County chpt. 1991—95), Psi Chi (v.p. southea. region 1990—94, nat. coun. 1990—94, nat. pres.-elect 1996—97, nat. coun. 1996—99, nat. pres. 1997—98, nat. past pres. 1998—99), Sigma Xi. Home: 315 Shepherd St Raleigh NC 27607-4031 Office: NC State U Dept Psychology Raleigh NC 27695-7650 Office Phone: 919-515-1728. Business E-Mail: slater_newman@ncsu.edu. E-mail: slaterpat@mindspring.com.

NEWMAN, STACEY CLARFIELD, artist, curator; b. NYC, July 21, 1956; d. Wallace J. Clarfield and Elinor (Kandel) Clarfield-Toberoff; m. Fredric Alan Newman, Nov. 27, 1983; children: Benjamin Clarfield, Marissa Paige, Alexandra Brooke Student, Franklin & Marshall, 1974—76; BS Labor Rels. and Mgmt., U. Bridgeport, 1978. Dir. ops. Nat. Rec. and Video Studios, NYC, 1978—80; cons., client rep./MTV VCA/Teletronics, NYC, 1979—84, dir. tech. ops., 1980—82, exec. prodr., 1982—85, dir. tech ops. prodr.; artist, art curator Stacey Clarfield Newman Studios, Scarsdale, NY, 1986—. Merchandise cons. Tahari Fashions, NYC, 1985—86; artist mem., jury com. You Gotta Have Art program White Plains Hosp. Ctr., NY, 1990—92; art tchr. collage Scarsdale Adult Edn. Program, 1993—95; artist in residence Scarsdale Elem. Schs., 1995—97; art cons., curator Manhattan Transfer, Inc., NYC, 1997—2000; mem. faculty Young at Art enrichment program, Scarsdale, 2002—; juror Figure and Form Edward Hopper House Mus., NYC, 2004. One-person shows include Quogue Gallery, NY, 1986, Piermont Fine Arts Gallery, NY, 1997-98, 2001, Manhattan Transfer, Inc., 1997, J&W Gallery, New Hope, Pa., 1999, Studio 4 West, 1999, 93 South Gallery, 2000, Adele Greenberg Salon, Cambridge, Mass., 2000, Amb. Galleries, Palm Beach, Fla., 2001, Viridian Gallery, NYC, 2001, 02, 05, Viridian Gallery @ Chelsea, 2002, 04, 05; exhibited in juried group shows: Piermont Fine Art Gallery, 1995, 96, 98, 99, 2000, 01, Anaya Gallery, Scarsdale, 1986, Katonah Gallery, NY, 1986, Gallery at Jamaica, Stratton Mountain, Vt., 1987, CDS Contemporary Art, Albuquerque, 1989, Mari Galleries, Mamaroneck, NY, 1992, Manhattan Transfer, Inc., 1993, 98, 93 South Gallery, Nyack, NY, 1998-99, Bibro Fine Arts Gallery, Chelsea, NY, 1998, Weber Fine Art, Scarsdale, 1998, 2000, J&W Gallery, New Hope, 1998, 99, 2001, 02, Studio 4 West, Hewlett Mus., 2000, Amb. Gallery, Palm Beach, 2000, Viridian Gallery, NYC, 2000-04, Adele Greenberg Salon, 2000, 01, A Pirate Space, Denver, 2001, Contemporary Art Oasis, Denver, 2001, Manhattanville Coll. Gallery, 2002, Nat. Assn. Women Artists, NYC, 2003, Chgo. Fine Arts Bldg. Gallery, 2003, Inklings, Viridian Artists, Chelsea, 2005, 06, News Art, Virdian Artists, 2005, John Jay Coll. Pres.'s Gallery, 2005, Fountain St. Gallery, Cape Girardeau, Mo., 2006, City Lights, Veridian Artists Inc., NYC, 2006, Viridian Artists Inc., 2007, A Reality, Viridian Artists Inc., NY, 2007; commd. Am. Soc. Plastic and Reconstructive Surgeons, LA Conv. Ctr., 1988, White Plains Hosp. Ctr., 1989, 90, Cystic Fibrosis Found., NYC, 1990, Joan Kroc Found., Calif., 1989-91. 1st v.p., bd. dirs. Internat. Coll. Surgeons Aux., Chgo., 1988—90; mem. Gala com. Juvenile Diabetes Found., 2000; Regional v.p. Am. Cancer Soc., White Plains, 1986—88; bd.

dirs. White Plains Hosp. Ctr. Aux.; fund raiser, event planner Holocaust Commn., NYC, 1998; active Scarsdale Tremont Synagogue Gala, 2001, 2002; fund-raiser Alternative Arts and Music Events, Scarsdale Teen Ctr., 2003—; liaison Scarsdale H.S. PTA, Alternative Art and Music Events, Scarsdale Teen Ctr., 2003—05; bd. dirs. com. on spl. edn. Scarsdale Sch. Dist. Mem. Internat. Platform Assn., Nat. Mus. Women in Contemporary Arts, Nat. Assn. Women Artists, Inc., Katonah Mus., Nat. Mus. Women in Arts (artist), Nat. Arts Club Avocations: piano, photography, tennis, kayaking, skiing. Personal E-mail: staceyscn21@aol.com.

NEWMAN, STEPHEN MICHAEL, lawyer; b. Buffalo, Jan. 12, 1945; s. Howard A. and Mildred (Ballow) N.; m. Gayle Mallon, May 24, 1969; children: Holly, Deborah. AB, Princeton U., 1966; JD, U. Mich., 1969. Bar: N.Y. 1969, Fla. 1976. Assoc. Hodgson, Russ, Andrews, Woods & Goodyear, Buffalo, 1969-73; ptnr. Hodgson Russ, LLP (formerly Hodgson, Russ, Andrews, Woods & Goodyear), Buffalo, 1973—2004, Nixon Peabody, LLP, Buffalo, 2005—. Lectr. in field. Bd. dirs. Leukemia Soc., United Jewish Fedn. Buffalo Inc., Jewish Ctr. Greater Buffalo Inc., Temple Beth Zion; bd. dirs., chpt. chmn., exec. com. Am. Jewish Com., Buffalo chpt.; bd. advisors Am. Lung Assn., Southeast Fla. chpt. Fellow Am. Coll. Trusts and Estates Coun.; mem. ABA (personal svc. corps. com. tax sect.), N.Y. State Bar Assn. (chair trusts and estates law sect. 2001), Princeton Club of Fla. Office: Nixon Peabody LLP 7121 Fairway Dr Ste 203 Palm Beach Gardens FL 33418 Home Phone: 716-634-0951; Office Phone: 561-626-3011. Business E-Mail: snewman@nixonpeabody.com.

NEWMAN, STEVEN DAVID, psychologist, consultant; b. Oxford, Ohio, Sept. 5, 1961; s. David William Newman and JoAnne Marie Slighting; m. Mary Christine Schaefer, May 27, 1985; children: Anna, Hayley. BA, Miami U., 1983; PsyD, Hahnemann U., Phila., 1988. Diplomate Am. Bd. Profl. Psychology, 2000. Psychologist Pauline W. Lewis Ctr., Cin., 1988—91; clinical psychologist United Samaritans Med. Ctr., Danville, Ill., 1991—2002, Mountain Regional Svcs., Cheyenne, Wyo., 2003—. Cons. psychologist pvt. practice, Crawfordsville, Ind., 2000—03. Fellow: Acad. Clinical Psychology; mem.: APA. Office: Mountain Regional Svcs 115 Evelyn Dr Cheyenne WY 82003

NEWMAN, STEVEN HARVEY, insurance company executive, director; b. Bklyn., Apr. 26, 1943; s. Charlotte Newman Bart; m. Lenore Blaustein, June 14, 1964; children: Richard, Michael, Stephanie. BS, Bklyn. Coll., 1963. Actuarial asst. Royal Globe Ins. Co., NYC, 1963-65; asst. sec. Ins. Rating Bd., NYC, 1965-69; v.p., sr. casualty actuary Am. Internat. Group, NYC, 1969-82; exec. v.p. Home Ins. Co., NYC, 1982-85, pres., 1985-86, also bd. dirs.; chmn., CEO Underwriters Reinsurance Co., Woodland Hills, Calif., 1987—2001; now chmn. Platinum Underwriters Holdings, Ltd., Bermuda, 2002—. Chmn. GCR Holdings, 1993-97, Reins. Assn. Am., 1995-96. Fellow Casualty Actuarial Soc. (pres. 1981-82); mem. Am. Acad. Actuaries, Internat. Actuarial Assn.

NEWMAN, STEVEN L., health care executive; BA, Rutgers U., NJ; MBA, Tulane U., New Orleans; MD, U. Tenn. Intern to resident to fellow Emory U. Sch. Medicine, Atlanta; assoc. prof. pediat. and medicine Wright State U. Sch. Medicine, Dayton, Ohio, 1979—90; dir. gastroenterology and nutrition support Children's Med. Ctr., Dayton, Ohio, 1979—90; sr. v.p., chief med. officer Touro Infirmary, New Orleans, 1990—97; pres., CEO Louisville Healthcare Network Columbia/HCA, 1997—98, pres. Omega Divsn., 1998—99; CEO Audubon Hosp., 1997; v.p. ops. Gulf States Region in Ala., La. and Miss. Tenet Healthcare Corp., 1999—2000, sr. v.p. ops., 2000—03, sr. v.p. Calif. ops., 2003—07, COO. Mem. exec. com. of bd. dirs. Calif. Hosp. Assn. Office: Tenet Healthcare Corp PO Box 809088 Dallas TX 75380-9088 Office Phone: 469-893-2200. Office Fax: 469-893-8600. *

NEWMAN, STUART, lawyer; b. Hackensack, NJ, June 7, 1947; s. Joseph and Rose (Wilenski) N.; m. Tina Gilson; children: Leslie, Dara, Mindy, Robert, Jessica. BA, SUNY, Cortland, 1971; JD cum laude, Albany Law Sch., 1974. Bar: N.Y. 1975, Ga. 1978. Assoc. Dewey, Ballantine LLP, NYC, 1974-76; from assoc. to ptnr. Jackson, Lewis LLP, Atlanta, 1976—. Lectr. U. Ala., Tuscaloosa, 1980-84, Auburn U., 1986—. Dir. Ruth Mitchell Dance Co. of Atlanta, 1986-88; sec., bd. trustees N.Y. Mil. Acad., 2000-. Mem. ABA, Atlanta Bar Assn., Ga. Bar Assn., Lawyers Club Atlanta, Commerce Club, Shakerag Hounds, Inc., Bear Creek Hounds, Inc. Office: Jackson Lewis LLP 1900 Marquis One Tower 245 Peachtree Center Ave NE Atlanta GA 30303-1222

NEWMAN, TERRY E., lawyer; b. Chgo., Jan. 15, 1947; BA, Loyola U., Ill., 1969; JD, DePaul U., 1977. Bar: Ill. 1977, U.S. Dist. Ct. (no. dist.) Ill. 1977, D.C. 1991. Asst. states atty. Cook County, 1977-78; ptnr. Katten Muchin Zavis Rosenman, Chgo. Sec. bd. trustees City Coll. Chgo., 1989. Mem. ABA, Ill. State Bar, D.C. Bar, Chgo. Bar Assn. (real estate tax sect.). Office: Katten Muchin Zavis Rosenman 525 W Monroe St Ste 1600 Chicago IL 60661-3649 Office Fax: 317-577-8781.

NEWMAN, THEODORE ROOSEVELT, JR., judge; b. Birmingham, Ala., July 5, 1934; s. Theodore R. and Ruth L. (Oliver) N. AB, Brown U., 1955, LL.D. (hon.), 1980; JD, Harvard U., 1958. Bar: D.C. 1958, Ala. 1959. Atty. civil rights div. Dept. Justice, Washington, 1961-62; practiced law in Washington, 1962-70; assoc. judge D.C. Superior Ct., 1970-76; judge D.C. Ct. Appeals, 1976-91, chief judge, 1976-84, sr. judge, 1991—; bd. dirs. Nat. Center for State Cts., v.p., 1980-81, pres., 1981-82. Visiting lecturer Harvard Law Sch.; adjunct prof. Howard U. Sch. of Law, Georgetown Law Ctr. Trustee Brown U. With USAF, 1958-61. Fellow Am. Bar Found.; mem. Nat. Bar Assn. (past pres. jud. coun., C. Francis Stradford award 1984, William H. Hastie award 1988). E-mail: tnewman@dcca.state.dc.us.

NEWMAN, THOMAS DANIEL, archaeologist, school system administrator, minister; b. London, May 12, 1922; s. Frederick and Margaret (O'Leary) N.; m. Louise Johannah Albertano, Apr. 1, 1963; 1 dau., Susan (Mrs. Alan J. Rennie). Student, Glasgow Sch. Accounting, 1946, Unity Sch. Christianity, 1962-66, Harvard Div. Sch., 1967—; DSc, Alma Coll., 1975. Ordained to ministry Ch. of Christ, 1966. Mng. dir. Thomas Newman (Printers) Ltd., 1945-49; mng. dir. H. & M.J. Pubs. Ltd., 1947-49, Forget-Me-Not Greeting Cards Ltd., 1949-61, Diplomat Greetings Ltd., 1957-61, Nevill's Ltd., 1955-57; pastor Christ's Ch., Springfield, Mo., 1966-67, Longwood, Brookline, Mass., 1967-99; adminstrv. dir. Am. Schs. Oriental Rsch., 1968, treas., 1970—, trustee, 1972—. Pastor Jefferson (N.H.) Cmty. Chapel, 2000—; founder Carthage Rsch. Inst., Khereddine, Tunisia, 1975, Cyprus Archaeol. Rsch. Inst., Nicosia, 1977; cons. Joint Archeol. Expdns. to, Ai, 1969-73, to; Tell-El-Hesi, 1970-73, to, Idalion, 1970-73; mem. Joint Archeol. Expdn. to, Caesarea Maritima, 1971, to; Carthage, 1975; dir. Logistics Survey Qu'Rayyah, Saudi Arabia, 1973; pub. cons. (Dead Sea Scrolls Com.), 1968-73; Trustee Allbright Inst. Archeol. Rsch., Jerusalem.; Am. Center Oriental Rsch., Amman, Jordan. Served with RAF, 1940-45. Mem. Archeol. Inst. Am., Soc. Bibl. Lit., Soc. O.T. Studies, Masons, Harvard Faculty Club, Univ. Club Boston. Home and Office: 359 Ivy Terrace Dahlonega GA 30533 Office Phone: 706-864-5853. Personal E-mail: revtomn@alltel.net.

NEWMAN, URSULA IRENE, music educator; b. Toledo, May 24, 1954; d. Lowell Cauffiel and Ursula Irene Zulka; m. Bruce Lee Newman, Nov. 15, 1986; 3 children. Attended, Mary Manse Coll., Toledo, Columbia U., NYC. Lic. realtor. Owner Ursula Cauffiel Sch of Music, Toledo, 1980—90. Adv. Ursula Cauffiel Sch. of Music, Toledo, 1990—; music dir. Temple Beth Israel, Phoenix, 1999—2001, asst. music dir. Children's Choir. Founder PracticeAthon, 2004—. Mem.: Music Tchr. Nat. Assn. (scholarship chair 2005—). Avocations: swimming, acting. Home: 10201 N 109th Pl Scottsdale AZ 85259-4809 Personal E-mail: grandpiano2002@aol.com.

NEWMAN, WILLIAM ARTHUR, lawyer; b. Dupont, Pa., Oct. 10, 1947; s. Jerome Mager and Doris Evelyn (Ross) N.; m. Pamela Jane Schneider, May 19, 1974; children: Romy S., T. R. BA, Yale U., 1969; JD, U. Mich., Ann Arbor, 1973. Bar: NY 1973, US Dist. Ct. So. Dist. NY 1973. Assoc. Debevoise & Plimpton, NYC, 1973-77, Richards, O'Neil & Allegaert, NYC, 1977-79, ptnr., 1979—90; prin. Blumenthal & Lynne PC, 1990—98; shareholder Greenberg Traurig, NYC, 1998—99; now ptnr. McGuire-Woods LLP, NYC, co-mng. ptnr. NYC office. Bd. dirs. On2.com Inc., 2000—. Office: McGuireWoods LLP 7th Fl 1345 Ave of the Americas New York NY 10105-0106 Office Phone: 212-548-2160. Office Fax: 212-548-2170. Business E-Mail: wnewman@mcguirewoods.com.

NEWMAR, JULIE CHALENE, actress, dancer, real estate businesswoman; b. Hollywood, Calif. d. Donald Charles and Helene (Jesmer) Newmeyer; m. J. Holt Smith, Aug. 5, 1977 (div. Apr. 1986); 1 child, John Jewl Smith. Student, UCLA. Actress TV series, plays, movies. Mem. Actors Studio, N.Y. and Los Angeles. Appeared on Broadway in Marriage Go Round (Tony award), Damn Yankees, Guys and Dolls, Irma La Douce, Stop the World, L'il Abner, Dames At Sea; films: Seven Brides for Seven Brothers, Marriage Go Round, Mackenna's Gold, The Maltese Bippy, Streetwalkin', 1985, Dance Academy, 1987, Ghosts Can't Do It, Oblivion I and II, To Wong Foo, Thanks for Everything, Julie Newmar; TV: Rhoda the Robot in My Living Doll, Catwoman on Batman, guest starred on Get Smart, The Monkees, Bewitched, Route 66, Hart to Hart, Love American Style, Star Trek, Twilight Zone, Beverly Hillbillies, Columbo, Fantasy Island, Melrose Place, Hope & Gloria, The Making of Seven Brides for Seven Brothers, 1997, According to Jim; prima ballerina with L.A. Opera Co.; video: Too Funky (George Michael); (model) Thierry Mugler high fashion shows, Paris; author (e-book) The Very Last How To Book (or) The Concious Catwoman Explains Life on Earth. Recipient Antoinette Perry award. Avocations: gardening, piano.

NEWMARK, CRAIG ALEXANDER, communications executive; b. Morristown, NJ, Dec. 6, 1952; s. Leon and Joyce Newmark. BS, Case Western Reserve U., 1975, MS in Computer Sci., 1977. Computer programmer IBM, NJ, 1979—93; systems security architect, gen. cons. Charles Schwab, Calif., 1993—95; ind. contractor, software sys. architect Bank of America, Calif., 1995—97, Intel, Calif., 1995—97, Sun Microsystems, Calif., 1995—97; founder, chmn., customer service rep. Craigslist, San Francisco, 1995—. Featured in AP, Wall Street Journal, NY Times, LA Times, USA Today, Business Week, Time Mag., and Esquire Mag. Adv. bd. Climate Theatre, Haight-Ashbury Food Program; supporter of local writers through Grotto Nights. Named #1 Most Efficient US Job Site, Forrester Rsch. Report, Wall St. Jour., 2000, Best Cmty. Website - People's Voice, Webby Awards, 2001, The Elite of the Online Employment Industry, WEDDLE's User's Choice Awards, 2004, 50 online destinations for the quarterlifer, Hatch Mag., 2004, 50 Coolest Websites, Time mag., 2004, Person of the Year, Webby Awards, The Internat. Acad. Digital Arts and Sciences, 2005, Webby Person of Yr., 2005; named one of World's 100 Most Influential People, Time Mag., 2005, 26 Most Fascinating Entrepreneurs, Inc.com, 2005. Achievements include millions of people use Craigslist to research subjects such as: jobs, housing, goods & services, events, friendships, and advice; first commercial transmission of a website into space by Deep Space Communications Network, March 11, 2005. Office: Craigslist 1319 9th Ave San Francisco CA 94122-2308 Office Phone: 415-566-6394. Office Fax: 415-504-6394. Business E-Mail: craig@craigslist.org. *

NEWMARK, EMANUEL, ophthalmologist; b. Newark, May 25, 1936; s. Charles Meyer and Bella (Yoskowitz) Newmark; m. Tina Steinberg, Aug. 25, 1957; children: Karen Beth, Heidi Ellen, Stuart Jeffrey. BS in Pharmacy, Rutgers U., Newark, 1959; postgrad., U. Amsterdam, The Netherlands, 1960-63, Armed Forces Inst. Pathology, Washington, 1971; MD, Duke U., Durham, NC, 1966; postgrad., Harvard U., Cambridge, Mass., 1967. Diplomate Am. Bd. Ophthalmology. Intern George Washington U. Hosp., Washington, 1966; trainee NIH rsch. U. Fla., Gainesville, 1967—70; resident ophthalmology U. Fla. Hosp., 1967—70; instr. dept. ophthalmology U. Fla., 1970; cons. ophthalmology Gainesville VA Hosp., 1970; clin. instr. ophthalmology U. Tex. Med. Sch., San Antonio, 1971—72; cons. ophthalmology Kerrville VA Hosp., Tex., 1971—72; asst. chief ophthalmology svc. Brooke Army Gen. Hosp., Fort Sam, Tex., 1971—72. Clin. asst. prof. ophthalmology Bexar County Hosp. and Clinics, San Antonio, 1971—72; tchg. faculty Joint Commn. Allied Health Pers. in Ophthalmology, commr., 2004—; sec., treas. Palm Beach Eye Assocs., Atlantis, Fla., 1973—98; pharm. adv. com. Agy. Health Care Adminstrn. Bd. Optometry, 1991—; mem. adv. bd. Fla. east coast chpt. Nat. Sjorgren's Syndrome; chief ophthalmology JFK Med. Ctr., 1984, chmn. CME and edn. com., 2004—06; staff ophthalmologist West Palm Beach VA Hosp., 2005—, Regional Eye Inst., 1998—2006. *Dr. Newmark's research has led to a treatment for mycotic kerititis. During his military service, he received the Army Commendation Medal for his excellence as a teacher, surgeon, and clinician. He is committed to the education of allied health personnel in ophthalmology and was editor of "Refinements" and is the executive editor of the fourth edition of "Ophthalmic Medical Assisting" national publication for ophthalmic technicians. He is featured in Guide to America's Top Physicians, Guide to America's Top Ophthalmologist and Castle Connolly guide to the Best Florida Doctors. He is the recipient of the Secretariat award.* Contbr. chapters to books, articles to profl. jours.; exec. editor Ophthalmic Medical Assisting: An Independent Study Course, 2006. Alumni assoc. Rutgers Coll. Pharmacy, 1990—, chmn. reunion, 1986, 2001, Duke U. Med. Alumni Assn., NC, 1967—; centurian Davison Club-Duke U. Med. Sch., NC, 1982—; campaign chmn., nat. vice chmn. Israel Bonds, Palm Beach County, Fla., 1988—90; participant charitable orgns.; v.p. Palm Beach Liturgical Culture Found., 1994—2000, pres., 2000—01. Decorated Lion of Judea State of Israel; recipient Gates of Jerusalem medal, 1991, Jerusalem medal, 1996, Recognition award, Joint Commn. Allied Health Personnel in Ophthalmology, 2001, 2006, US Army Commendation medal. Fellow: ACS, Am. Acad. Ophthalmology (del. to coun. 1996—2001, allied health edn. com. 1997—2002, editor Refinements 1998—2000, rep. to joint com. allied health pers. in ophthalmology 2004—, Fla. state chmn. cdnl. trust, Achievement award 2001, Councillors award 2001, Secretariat award 2005); mem.: AMA, Fla. Soc. Ophthalmology (ethics chmn. 1985—90, pres. 1990—91, James W. Clower Jr. Cmty. Svc. award 1995, Shalov Richardson, MD Svc. to Medicine award 2007), Palm Beach County Ophthal. Soc. (pres. 1984—85, Ophthalmologist of Yr. 2004), Palm Beach County Med. Soc. (chair ethics com. 1997—2000, vice chair ethics com. 2002, bd. dirs. 2003, bd. dirs. mem.-at-large 2003—, coun. on ethical and jud. affairs 2004—06, trustee 2005, v.p. svcs. bd.), Fla. Med. Assn. (ho. dels. 1993—95, 2001—06), Am. Orgn. for Rehab. Through Tng. Fedn. (nat. exec. com.-campaign cabinet 1987, pres. 1987—90, Palm Beach Men's Achievement award 1988, Pres. award 1989), Founder's Soc. Duke U. Jewish. Avocation: travel. Home: 180 Palm Cir Atlantis FL 33462-6627 Office: West Palm Beach Vets Med Ctr 7305 Military Trail West Palm Beach FL 33410 Home Phone: 561-969-3262; Office Phone: 561-422-8690. Personal E-mail: mannynewmark@msn.com.

NEWMARK, LEONARD DANIEL, linguistics educator; b. Attica, Ind., Apr. 8, 1929; s. Max Jacob and Sophie (Glusker) N.; m. Ruth Broessler, Sept. 16, 1951; children: Katya, Mark. AB, U. Chgo., 1947; MA, Ind. U., 1951, PhD, 1955. Instr. English U. Ill., Urbana, 1951; vis. asst. prof. linguistics U. Mich., Ann Arbor, 1961; assoc. prof. English Ohio State U., 1954-62; assoc. prof. linguistics Ind. U., Bloomington, 1962-63; prof. linguistics U. Calif., San Diego, 1963-91, prof. emeritus, 1992—, chmn. dept., 1963-71, 79-85, head program in Am. lang. and culture, 1979-84, rsch. linguist Ctr. for Rsch. in Lang., 1992—. Author: Linguistic History of English, 1963, Spoken Albanian, 1997, Standard Albanian, 1982, Albanian-English Dictionary, 1998, Albanian Handbook, 1999; founding editor UCSD Emeriti Newsletter: Chronicles, 2001-2004. Mem. Linguistics Soc. Am., Dictionary Soc. N.Am., Phi Beta Kappa. Achievements include invention of memory aid device. Business E-Mail: ldnewmark@ucsd.edu.

NEWMARK, MARILYN, sculptor; b. NYC, July 20, 1928; d. Edward Ellis and Mabel (Davies) Newmark; m. Leonard J. Meiselman, Mar. 15, 1952. Student, Adelphi Coll., 1945—47, Alfred U., NYC, 1949. Sculpture specializing in horses, equestrian figures, dogs, foxes. Exhibited in group shows Derby Mus., Fleischer Mus., Scottsdale, Leigh Yawkey Woodson Art Mus., Wis., Bennington Ctr. for Arts, Vt., NAD, NYC, Nat. Arts Club, NYC, Smithsonian Instn., Washington, Mus. of Horse, Ky., Port of History Mus., Pa., Marietta/Cobb Mus. Art, Wildlife Experience, Denver, Nat. Geog. Soc., Washington, Allegheny Colls. Galleries, Butler Inst. Am. Art; represented in permanent collections Nat. Mus. Racing, Saratoga, NY, Internat. Mus. Horse, Ky. Horse Park, Brookgreen Gardens, S.C., also pvt. collections. Recipient Anna Hyatt Huntington award, 1970-72, 75, 78, 80-83, 86, 88, 90, 97, 2002, Gold medal, 1973, award Coun. Am. Artists Socs., 1972, 73, 79, 80, Hudson Valley John Newington award, 1973, 77, Gold medal, 1979, Elliot Liskin Meml. award, 1989, 96, Academician NAD Ellin P. Speyer award, 1974, 93, 99, Artist Fund award, 1982, Michael Gressel award, 2006. Fellow Nat. Sculpture Soc. (coun. 1973-75, rec. sec. 1976, sec. 1977-79, coun. 1981-83, 92-97, 2006-, Bronze medal 1986, Mildred Victor Meml. award 1996, Leonard Meiselman Meml. award 2003), Audubon Artists (Elliott Liskin Meml. award 2000, 02), Am. Artists Profl. League (Gold medal 1974, 77, medal of hon. 1987), Allied Artists Am. (Gold medal 1981, 93, In Memorium award 1994), Pen & Brush Club (Gold medal 1977, Salmagundi Club award 1982, 83, 91, C. Dunwiddie Meml. award 1999, 2004), Soc. Animal Artists (jury of admissions 1972-75, 90—, v.p. 1998—, Legacy award 2002), Am. Acad. Equine Art (founding mem., dir. sculpture 1980—), Nassau Suffolk Horsemans Assn. (dir. 1968-82), Catherine Lorillard Wolfe Art Club, Smithtown Hunt Club, Meadowbrook Hunt Club. Address: 22 Woodhollow Rd Roslyn Heights NY 11577-2217 Office Phone: 516-621-5914.

NEWMARK, RICHARD ALAN, chemist; b. Urbana, Ill., Nov. 11, 1940; s. Nathan M. and Anne Mae (Cohen) N.; m. Joan Friedman, July 4, 1965; children: David, Merel. AB, Harvard Coll., 1961; PhD, U. Calif., Berkeley, 1964. Postgrad. fellow Mass. Inst. Tech., Cambridge, 1964-66; asst. prof. U. Colo., Boulder, 1966-69; rsch. chemist 3M, St. Paul, 1969-72, rsch. specialist, 1972-76, sr. rsch. specialist, 1976-81, staff scientist, 1981-92, corp. scientist, 1992—2001; cons., 2002—. Councilor Minn. section Am. Chem. Soc., Washington, 1992-94. Contbr. articles to profl. jours. Chair Dist. 1 Cmty. Coun., St. Paul, 1984-88; co-chair St. Paul Sch. Bd. Commn. of Gifted and Talented, 1986-88; treas. Neighborhood Energy Consortium 2004-05, treas. St. Paul Audubon Soc. 2004—. Recipient award 3M Carlton Soc., 1993, Minn. award Am. Chem. Soc., 2000. Mem.: Sigma Xi, Phi Beta Kappa. Jewish. Avocations: skiing, bicycling. Office: 3M 201-bs 05 Saint Paul MN 55144-0001 Home Phone: 651-340-3487; Office Phone: 651-270-9345. E-mail: neumarque@comcast.com.

NEWMARK, WILLIAM D., conservation biologist; b. St. Louis, Mo., Feb. 22, 1952; s. Philip and Marjorie Newmark. BA with distinction, U. of Colo., 1974, BA with distinction, 1977; MS, U. of Mich., 1980, PhD, 1986. Tech. adviser Coll. of African Wildlife Mgmt., Mweka, Tanzania, 1987—91; vis. scholar U. of Calif., San Diego, 1991—92, U. of Utah, Salt Lake City, 1993—94; rsch. curator Utah Mus. of Natural History, Salt Lake City, 1994—. Team leader Usambara Forest Fragmentation Project, Tanzania, 1987—; tech. cons. Norwegian Internat. Devel. Agy., Dar es Salaam, 1993—94; vis. sr. lectr. global environment faculty U. of Dar es Salaam, Tanzania, 1996—97; tech. cons. World Bank, African Families, Washington, 2000—; stap expert UNEP -Global Environment Facility, NYC, 2003—. Author: (book) The Conservation of Mount Kilimanjaro, 1991, Conserving Biodiversity in East African forests: A Study of the Eastern Arc Mountains, 2002. Recipient rsch. grant, NSF, MacArthur Found., Nat. Geog. Soc., Earthwatch Inst., Critical Ecosys. Partnership. Mem.: Soc. for Conservation Biology, Ecol. Soc. of Am., Am. Soc. for the Advancement of Sci. Achievements include research in Reserve And Corridor Design; Patterns Of Extinction And Movement Of Vertebrate Species; Conservation And Development. Office: Utah Mus of Natural History 1390 E Presidents Cir Salt Lake City UT 84112 Home Phone: 801-363-9749; Office Phone: 801-581-6927. E-mail: bnewmark@umnh.utah.edu.

NEWMEYER, FREDERICK JARET, linguist, educator; b. Phila., Jan. 30, 1944; s. Alvin S. and Fritzie B. (Nisenson) N.; m. Carolyn V. Platt, Apr. 28, 1968 (div. 1974); m. Marilyn M. Goebel, Dec. 25, 1993. BA, U. Rochester, 1965, MA, 1967; PhD, U. Ill., 1969. Asst. prof. linguistics U. Wash., Seattle, 1969-75, assoc. prof., 1975-81, prof., 1981—, chair, 1990-2000. Vis. prof. U. London, 1979, Cornell U., 1981, U. Md., 1982, UCLA, 1982-83, La Trobe U., Australia, 1987. Author: English Aspectual Verbs, 1975, Linguistic Theory in America, 1980, Grammatical Theory, 1983, Politics of Linguistics, 1986, Generative Linguistics, 1995, Language Form and Language Function, 1998, Possible and Probable Languages, 2005; editor: Linguistics: The Cambridge Survey, 1988, Natural Language and Linguistic Theory, 1987-2003; assoc. editor: Language, 1980-85. NEH fellow, 1973-74. Fellow AAAS; mem. Linguistic Soc. Am. (sec.-treas. 1989-94, v.p. 2001, pres. 2002). Avocation: gardening. Home: 4621 NE 107th St Seattle WA 98125-6947 Office: 1068 Seymour St Vancouver BC V6B 3M6 Canada Home: 428 Beach Crescent # 1505 Vancouver BC V6Z 3G1 Canada E-mail: fjn@u.washington.edu.

NEWPORT, ELISSA L., psychology professor; b. St. Louis, July 3, 1947; d. Eugene and Anita Evelyn (Ginsberg) N.; m. Theodore Supalla, Oct. 12, 1980; children: Susanna, Zachary. Student, Wellesley Coll., 1965-67; BA, Barnard Coll., 1969; MA, U. Pa., 1974, PhD, 1975. Asst. prof. U. Calif. San Diego, La Jolla, 1974-79; assoc. prof., prof. U. Ill., Champaign, 1979-88; prof. U. Rochester, 1988—, George Eastman prof. brain and cognitive scis. and linguistics, chair dept. brain and cognitive scis., 1998—. Mem. editorial bd. Cognitive Psychology, 1981-1996, Language Acquisition, 1989-2004. Editor: (book series) MIT Press, 1982—; contbr. articles to profl. jours. Alfred P. Sloan Found. fellow MIT, 1981, U. Pa., 1982; NIH rsch. grantee, 1980—; recipient Arnold O. Bediman Rsch. award U. Ill., 1982-83, William Bonsall Vis. Chair in Humanities Stanford U., 1984, Claude Pepper award of excellence, NIH. Fellow Am. Acad. Arts and Scis.; mem. AAAS (chair section J, 2004-2006), NAS,Cognitive Sci. Soc. Office: Univ Rochester Dept Psychology Meliora Hall 414 Rochester NY 14627-0268 Office Phone: 585-275-8689. E-mail: newport@bcs.rochester.edu.

NEWQUIST, JUDY LYNNE ROOS, elementary school educator, education educator; d. John Peter and June Janette (Johnson) Roos; m. Russell Duane Newquist, Mar. 6, 1976; children: Nichole, Matthew, Jennifer. BS, Iowa State U., Ames, 1976; BA in Edn., Buena Vista U., Storm Lake, Iowa, 1998; MA in Edn., Morningside Coll., Sioux City, Iowa, 2005. Med. social worker Ottumwa Regional Health Ctr., Iowa, 1976—2000; tchr. 7th grade social studies Ottumwa Cmty. Schs., 1998—. Mem. parent adv. com. Cardinal Cmty. Schs., Eldon, Iowa, 1996—2005. Sunday sch. tchr. Agency (Iowa) Meth. Ch., 1981—2000, mem. adminstrv. bd., 1982—83. Mem.: Alpha Delta Kappa. Avocations: reading, travel, genealogy, quilting, gardening. Office: Evans Mld Sch 812 Chester Ave Ottumwa IA 52501 Business E-Mail: newquist@aea15.k12.ia.us.

NEWSOM, CAROLYN CARDALL, management consultant; b. South Weymouth, Mass., Feb. 27, 1941; d. Alfred James and Bertha Virginia (Roy) Cardall; m. John Harlan Newsom, Feb. 4, 1967; children: John Cardall, James Harlan. AB, Brown U., Providence, RI, 1962; MBA, U. Pa., 1978, PhD, 1985. Systems engr. IBM, Seattle, 1964-70, Newsom S.E. Services, Seattle, 1970-76; instr. U. Pa. Wharton Sch., Phila., 1978-81; v.p., prin. sr. cons. PA Cons. Group, Princeton, NJ, 1981-88; pres. Newsom Assocs., Yardley, Pa., 1988; ptnr. Bus. Strategy Implementation, Princeton, NJ, 1989-90; pres. Strategy Implementation Solutions, Yardley, Pa., 1990—. Examiner N.J. Gov.'s Performance Excellence Award, 1993, sr. examiner, 1994—2002, judge, 2003—06; examiner Malcolm Baldrige Nat. Quality Award, 2003—05. Trustee St. Mary Hosp., Langhorne, Pa., 1986—94; sec. bd. dir. Gordonstown Am. Found., 1999—2005; bd. dir. Chandler Hall, 1980—87. Mem.: Quality N.J. (vice chair 1998—99), Am. Soc. for Quality, Am. Acad. Mgmt., Brown Alumni Assn. (pres.-elect 1993—95, pres. 1995—97). Office: Strategy Implementation Solutions 1588 Woodside Rd Yardley PA 19067-2611

NEWSOM, DAVID DUNLOP, ambassador, educator; b. Richmond, Calif., Jan. 6, 1918; s. Fred Stoddard and Ivy Elizabeth (Dunlop) N.; m. Jean Frances Craig, Nov. 17, 1942; children: John, Daniel, Nancy, David, Catherine. AB, U. Calif., 1938; MS, Columbia U., 1940; LLD, U. Pacific, 1979. Pulitzer traveling scholar, 1940-41; pub. Walnut Creek (Calif.) Courier-Jour., 1946-47; 3d sec., info. officer Am. embassy, Karachi, Pakistan, 1948-50; 2d sec., vice consul Oslo, 1950-51; pub. affairs officer Baghdad, Iraq, 1952-55; officer-in-charge Arabian peninsula affairs Dept. State, Washington, 1955-59; with Nat. War Coll., 1959-60; 1st sec. Am. embassy, London, 1960-62; dep. dir. Office No. African Affairs, Dept. State, Washington, 1962-63, dir., 1963-65; U.S. ambassador Libya, 1965-69; asst. sec. state for African affairs, 1969-74; U.S. ambassador Indonesia, 1974-77, Philippines, 1977-78; undersec. state of polit. affairs Washington, 1978-81; dir. Inst. Study of Diplomacy, Sch. Fgn. Svc., Georgetown U., 1981-90, Marshall Coyne rsch. prof. diplomacy, 1989-91; interim dean Sch. Fgn. Svc. Goergetown U., 1995-96; Cumming Meml. prof. internat. rels. U. Va., 1991-98; spl. adviser U.S. del. UN Gen. Assembly, 1972, 78, 79, 80. Sr. fellow The Miller Ctr., U. Va., 1999-2003; mem. com. on sci., tech. and health aspects of fgn. policy Nat. Rsch. Coun., 1999. Author: (book) Soviet Brigade in Cuba, Diplomacy and The American Democracy, The Public Dimension of Foreign Policy, The Imperial Mantle. Served to lt. USNR, 1942-46. Recipient Commendable Service award USIS, 1955; Dept. State Meritorious Service award, 1958; Nat. Civil Service League award, 1972; Rockefeller Pub. Service award, 1973; Lifetime award Am. Fgn. Svc. Assn., 2000. Mem. U.S. Fgn. Svc. Assn., Coun. Fgn. Rels., Cosmos Club. Presbyterian. Home: 500 Crestwood Dr 2504 Charlottesville VA 22903

NEWSOM, GAVIN, mayor; b. San Francisco, Oct. 10, 1967; s. William and Tessa Newsom; m. Kimberly Guilfoyle Newsom, Dec. 8, 2001. BA in Polit. Sci., Santa Clara U., 1989. Founder PlumpJack Wines Mgmt. Group, San Francisco, 1992—; pres. Pkg. and Traffic Commn., San Francisco, 1996—97; supr. Office of Bd. Suprs., San Francisco, 1997—2004; mayor City of San Francisco, 2003—. Office: City Hall Room 200 1 Dr Carlton B Goodlett Place San Francisco CA 94102 *

NEWSOM, GERALD HIGLEY, astronomy educator; b. Albuquerque, Feb. 11, 1939; s. Carroll Vincent and Frances Jeanne (Higley) N.; m. Ann Catherine Bricker, June 17, 1972; children: Christine Ann, Elizabeth Ann. BA, U. Mich., 1961; MA, Harvard U., 1963, PhD, 1968. Research asst. McMath-Hulbert Obs., Pontiac, Mich., summers 1959, 61; research asst. astronomy dept. U. Mich., Ann Arbor, 1959-61; research asst. Shock Tube Lab. Harvard U., Cambridge, Mass., 1962, 64-68; research asst. dept. physics Imperial Coll., London, 1968-69; asst. prof. astronomy Ohio State U., Columbus, 1969-73, assoc. prof., 1973-82, prof., 1982—2004, acting chmn. dept. astronomy, 1991-93, vice chmn. dept. astronomy, 1993—2004, acting asst. dean, 1985-86; sr. post-doctoral research asst. Physikalisches Institut, Bonn, Fed. Republic of Germany, 1978. Author: Astronomy, 1976, Exploring the Universe, 1979; contbr. articles to profl. jours. Fellow Woodrow Wilson Found., 1961-62, NSF, 1961-63; grantee Noble Found., 1961-64. Mem.: Am. Astron. Soc., Internat. Astron. Union. Home: 46 W Weisheimer Rd Columbus OH 43214-2545 Office: Ohio State U Dept Astronomy 140 W 18th Ave Columbus OH 43210-1173 Home Phone: 614-263-8240; Office Phone: 614-292-2632. Business E-Mail: gnewsom@astronomy.ohio-state.edu.

NEWSOM, JAMES THOMAS, lawyer; b. Carrollton, Mo., Oct. 6, 1944; s. Thomas Edward and Hazel Love (Mitchell) N.; m. Sherry Elaine Retzloff, Aug. 9, 1986; stepchildren: Benjamin A. Bawden, Holly K. Bawden. AB, U. Mo., 1966, JD, 1968. Bar: Mo. 1968, US Supreme Ct. 1971. Assoc. Shook, Hardy & Bacon, London and Kansas City, Mo., 1972, ptnr., 1976—. Mem. Mo. Law Rev., 1966-68. Lt. comdr. JAGC, USNR, 1968-72. Mem. ABA, Kansas City Met. Bar Assn., U. Mo. Law Sch. Law Soc., U. Mo. Jefferson Club, Order of Coif, Perry (Kans.) Yacht Club, Stone Horse Yacht Club (Harwich Port, Mass.). Avocations: skiing, sailing, auto racing. Office: Shook Hardy & Bacon 2555 Grand Blvd Kansas City MO 64108-2613 Home Phone: 913-381-5605; Office Phone: 816-474-6550. Business E-Mail: jnewsom@shb.com.

NEWSOM, JOHN HARLAN, physician; b. Worland, Wyo., May 6, 1940; s. John Cecil and Arlene Zelda (Finch) N.; m. Carolyn Cardall, Feb. 4, 1967; children: John Cardall, James Harlan. BS, U.S. Naval Acad., 1963; MD, U. Wash., 1971. Diplomate Am. Bd. Family Practice. Intern Doctors Hosp., Seattle, 1971-72; physician in pvt. practice, Newport, Oreg., 1972-73; physician Group Health, Seattle, 1973-74; pvt. practice Yardley, Pa., 1974—; mem. med. staff St. Mary Med. Ctr., 1974—, chmn. family practice dept., 1978-80, pres. med. staff, 1980-81, 2006—07, v.p. med. affairs, 1983—85, 1999—2004. Trustee St. Mary Hosp., Langhorne, Pa., 1981-83; bd. dirs. Pennswood Village, Newtown, Pa., 1978-81; clin. asst. prof. Temple U. Sch. Medicine, 1978-91; clin. instr. Pa. State Med. Sch., 2000-01. Contbr. articles to profl. jours. Pres. Parents at Lawrenceville, N.J., 1989-90. Lt. USN, 1963-67. Decorated Bronze Star; named a Top Doc, Phila. Mag., 2002. Fellow Am. Acad. Family Physicians; mem. U. Wash. Alumni Assn. (pres. Del. Valley chpt. 1989-90), Pa. Med. Soc. (del. 1985), Coll. Physicians Phila., Bucks County Med. Soc. (pres. 1985). Office: 1588 Woodside Rd Yardley PA 19067-2611

NEWSOM, KEVIN, federal official, lawyer; b. 1972; m. Deborah Elizabeth Wilgus Newsom; children: Marshall James, Chapman Bethea, Grad., Samford U., Harvard Law Sch., 1997. Clerk US Ct. of Appeals, US Supreme Ct., 2000; assoc. Covington & Burling, Washington; solicitor gen. State of Ala., 2003—. Named one of Litigation's Rising Stars, The Am. Lawyer, 2007; recipient Best Brief award, Nat. Assn. Attorneys, 2005, 2006. Mem.: Am. Law Inst. *

NEWSOME, FREDERICK V., medical educator; b. Charleston, W.Va., July 7, 1946; s. Moses and Ruth (Bass) N.; children: Akasemi, Imhotep, Nubia, Hatshepsut. BA in Chemistry, Harvard U., 1968; MD, W.Va. U., 1972; MSc in Tropical Medicine, London Sch. Hygiene & Tropical Medicine, 1981. Diplomate Am. Bd. Internal Medicine. Instr. in medicine Coll. of Physicians and Surgeons Columbia U., NYC, 1975-78; instr. in medicine Albert Einstein Med. Sch., Bronx, 1979-80; sr. lectr. in medicine U. Jos, Nigeria, 1981-88; clin. prof., head dept. of medicine Coll. of Health Scis. Usmanu Danfodio U., Sokoto, Nigeria, 1988-90; chief ambulatory medicine The Meth. Hosp., Bklyn., 1991-92; asst. prof. medicine Columbia U. Coll. Physicians & Surgeons, NYC, 1992—. Author: An African American Philosophy of Medicine, 2005; contbr. articles to profl. jours. Fellow ACP, West African Coll. Physicians, Royal Soc. Tropical Medicine and Hygiene; mem. Nat. Med. Assn., Assn. for Study Afro-Am. Life and History. Office: Harlem Hosp Dept Medicine Rm 14131 135th St & Malcolm X Ave New York NY 10037 Office Phone: 212-939-1411. E-mail: fvn1@columbia.edu.

NEWSOME, JAMES E., mercantile exchange executive; m. Mei Mei Newsome; children: Molly, Riley. BS in Econ., U. Fla., 1982; MS in Agr., Miss. State U., 1985, PhD in Animal sci./Agrl. Econs., 2001. Mem. U.S. Commodity Futures Trading Commn., Washington, 1998-01; chmn. Commodity Futures Trading Commn., Washington, 2001—04; pres., CEO NY Mercantile Exch., Inc., NYC, 2004—. Mem. Pres. Working Group on Fin. Markets; mem. U.S. Corp. Fraud Task Force; exec. v.p. Miss. Cattlemen's Assn. and Beef Coun., chmn. Miss. Agribus. Coun., mem. Gov's. Task Force on Future Miss. Agrl., pres. Fla. Future Farmers Am., pres. U. Fla. Agrl. Coun. Mem. Assn. Miss. Agrl. Orgns. (pres.). Office: NYMEX World Fin Ctr One N End Ave New York NY 10282-1101 *

NEWSOME, JOHN DAVID, JR., music educator; b. Fitzgerald, Ga., Apr. 6, 1969; s. John David Newsome and Linda Hair Scurlock; m. Leanne Paige McMichen, Aug. 4, 2001; children: Sandra Elizabeth, Sarah Danielle; m. Melissa Diane Presley (div.). MusB, Troy State U., 1987—91. Band dir. Clinch County H.S., Homerville, Ga., 1991—94, Tattnall County H.S., Reidsville, Ga., 1994—97, Treutlen H.S., Soperton, Ga., 1997—2004, Fitzgerald H.S., 2004—. Composer: Atlantic Coast Overture, 2002, Discata Mexicana, 2002, Le Pelea del Toro, 2004, The Fighting 50th Regiment, 2005. Recipient John Phillip Sousa award, Instrumentalist Mag., 1987. Mem.: Profl. Assn. Ga. Educators, Ga. Music Educators Assn. Avocations: golf, web site design. Office: Fitzgerald HS Marching Canes 601 W Cypress St Fitzgerald GA 31750

NEWSOME, OZZIE, professional sports team executive; b. Muscle Shoals, Ala., Mar. 16, 1956; s. Ethel Newsome and Ozzie Newsome Sr.; m. Gloria Jenkins. BS, U. Ala. Tight end Cleve. Browns, 1978-90; v.p. player pers. Balt. Ravens, 1996—99, sr. v.p. football ops., 1999—2002, exec. v.p., gen. mgr., 2002—. Active Big Bros., Athletes in Action; bd. dirs. Police Athletic League. Named Ala. Amateur Athlete of Yr., Ala. Sportswriters Assn., 1977; named to AFC Pro-Squad, 1981, Outstanding Team Player, 1981, All Pro, Pro-Football Writers Assn. and Sporting News, 1979; Cleveland Browns All-Time Leading Receiver, MVP on Offense, Cleve. TD Club (three times); ranked among NFL's top 10 in receptions; became 14th player in NFL history to make over 500 receptions; all-time leading tight end in NFL history; leading receiver in AFC, 1984; inducted into Coll. Football Hall of Fame, 1994; Inductee Pro Football Hall of Fame, 1999, Canton Ohio. Mem. Fellowship of Christian Athletes. Office: Balt Ravens Owings Mills Tng Facility 1 Winning Dr Owings Mills MD 21117 Office Phone: 410-701-4000. *

NEWSOME, RANDALL JACKSON, judge; b. Dayton, Ohio, July 13, 1950; s. Harold I. and Sultana S. (Stone) N. BA summa cum laude, Boston U., 1972; JD, U. Cin., 1975. Bar: Ohio 1975, U.S. Dist. Ct. (so. dist.) Ohio 1977, U.S. Ct. Appeals (6th cir.) 1979, U.S. Supreme Ct. 1981. Law clk. to chief judge U.S. Dist. Ct. (so. dist.) Ohio, 1975-77; assoc. Dinsmore & Shohl, Cin., 1978-82; judge U.S. Bankruptcy Ct. (so. dist.) Ohio, 1982-88, U.S. Bankruptcy Ct. (no. dist.) Calif., Oakland, 1988—2004, chief judge, 2004—. Faculty mem. Fed. Jud. Ctr., ALI-ABA, 1987—; mem. Nat. Conf. of Bankruptcy Judges, 1983—, mem. bd. govs., 1987-88, pres., 1998-99. Contbg. author: Chapter 11 Theory and Practice, 1994—, Collier on Bankruptcy, 1997—. Fellow Am. Coll. Bankruptcy; mem. Am. Law Inst., Phi Beta Kappa. Democrat. Office: US Bankruptcy Ct PO Box 2070 Oakland CA 94604-2070 Office Phone: 510-879-3530.

NEWSTEAD, JENNIFER G., lawyer; b. 1969; AB, Harvard U., 1991; JD, Yale Law Sch., 1994. Mng. editor Yale Law Jour.; editor Yale Jour. Internat. Law; law clk. to Hon. Laurence H. Silberman US Ct. Appeals (DC Cir.), 1994—95; law clk. to Justice Stephen G. Breyer US Supreme Ct., 1995—96; assoc. Davis Polk & Wardwell LLP, NYC, 1997—2001, coun., 2005—06, ptnr. Litig. Dept., 2006—; dep. asst. atty. gen., Office of Legal Policy US Dept. Justice, Washington, 2001—02, prin. dep. asst. atty. gen., Office of Legal Policy, 2002; assoc. coun. The White House, Washington, 2002—03; gen. counsel Office Mgmt. & Budget, Exec. Office the Pres., Washington, 2003—05. Adj. prof. law, national security law Georgetown U. Law Ctr., 2002; exec. branch liaison to ABA section on Adminstrv. Law & Regulatory Practice, 2004—05. Office: Davis Polk & Wardwell LLP 450 Lexington Ave New York NY 10017 Office Phone: 212-450-4999. Office Fax: 212-450-3999. Business E-Mail: jennifer.newstead@dpw.com.

NEWTON, ALEXANDER WORTHY, lawyer; b. Birmingham, Ala., June 19, 1930; s. Jeff H. and Annis Lillian (Kelly) N.; m. Sue Aldridge, Dec. 22, 1952; children: Lamar Aldridge Newton, Kelly McClure Newton Hammond, Jane Worthy Newton, Robins Jeffry Newton. BS, U. Ala., 1952, JD, 1957. Bar: Ala. 1957. Pvt. practice law, Birmingham; assoc. Hare, Wynn & Newell, Birmingham, 1957; ptnr. Hare, Wynn, Newell & Newton, Birmingham, 1961—. Del. U.S. Ct. Appeals (11th cir.) Jud. Conf., 1988, 89, 90, 91; mem. Jefferson County Jud. Nominating Com., 1983-89; mem. Birmingham Airport Authority, 1991-2006; founding dir. First Comm. Bank. Co-author: (with others) Federal Appellate Procedure, 11th Circuit, 1996. Vice chmn. Birmingham Racing Commn., 1984-87; v.p. U. Ala. Law Sch. Found., 1978-79, pres., 1980-82, exec. com., 1987—; mem. Leadership Ala. Class IV; trustee Ala. Trust Fund, 2002; bd. dirs. St. Vincent Hosp. Found.; mem. Jefferson Met. Healthcare Authority, 2005-06. Capt. inf. U.S. Army, 1952-54. Recipient Disting. Alumnus award Farrah Law Soc. U. Ala., 1984, Sam W. Pipes Disting. Alumnus award 1982 Fellow Am. Coll. Trial Lawyers (state chmn. 1983-84, regents' nominatin com. 1984-85), Internat. Soc. Barristers (bd. dirs. 1974-75, sec.-treas. 1976-77, v.p. 1977-78, pres. 1979-80), Internat. Acad. Trial Lawyers (bd. dirs. 1998—); mem. ABA, ATLA, Am. Bar Found., Ala. State Bar (chmn. practices and procedures subsect. 1965, governance com. and pres.'s task force 1984-86, pres.'s com. 1987-88), Birmingham Bar Assn. (exec. com. 1967), Ala. Trial Lawyers Assn. (sec.-treas. 1958-65), Am. Judicature Soc., 11th Cir. Hist. Soc. (trustee 1988—), Shoal Creek Club, Birmingham Country Club, Capital City Club (Atlanta), Garden of the Gods Club (Colorado Springs, Colo.), Univ. Club (N.Y.C.), Sigma Chi. Democrat. Presbyterian. Home: 2837 Canoe Brook Ln Birmingham AL 35243-5908 Office: Hare Wynn Newell & Newton 800 Massey Bldg 2025 3d Ave N Birmingham AL 35203-3330 Office Phone: 205-328-5330.

NEWTON, CINDY LYNN, elementary school educator, media specialist; b. Frankfort, Ind., Nov. 1, 1954; d. William Max and Barbara Lois Cline; m. Robert Allen Newton, Dec. 28, 1974; children: Amber Lynne Robinson, Amanda Joy Fredericks. BSc, Ind. U., 1994; M in Edn., Ind. Wesleyan U., 1999. Reading Endorsement Ind. U., 1994, Academy of Leadership for Teachers Ind., 1999. Elem. tchr. Eastview Elem., Connersville, Ind., 1994—2007; media specialist Connersville Mid. Sch., 2007—. Tech. bldg. go-to Eastview Elem., Connersville, Ind.; armstrong educator Ind. U., 2005—; supervising tchr. Ind. U. East, 1995—; state reading dist. rep. Ind. State Reading Assn., 1998—2006; staff devel. inservice provider Eastview Elem., Connersville, Ind., 1995—. State officer rep. Ind. State Read Assn., 1998—2000; tchr. yr. selection com. Fayette County Schs., Connersville, 2000—07; Sunday sch. tchr. Pk. Pl. Ch. of God, 1981—, dir. 40 Days of Purpose, 2005. Recipient Ind. U. Armstrong Tchr. Educator award, Ind. U., 2005, Citizen's Adv. Achievement award, 3Rivers SWM Dist., 2005, Outstanding Svc. award, Ind. State Reading Assn., 2003, Christel DeHann's Excellence in Edn., Project e, 2000, Outstanding Profl. award, Ind. Wesleyan U., 1999, Tchr. of Yr., Fayette County Sch. Corp., 1998, Three Rivers Solid Waste Mgmt. Environ. Citizen's award; fellow Gifted and Talented Action Rsch. grant, State of Ind., 2000. Master: Connersville Area Reading Coun. (assoc.); mem.: ASCD, Internat. Reading Assn. (assoc.), Ind. Computer Educators (assoc.), Ind. State Reading Assn. (assoc.; sec. 2001—02, Outstanding Svc. award 2003), Delta Kappa Gamma. Achievements include development of elementary computer clubs. Office: Connersville Mid Sch 1900 N Grand Ave Connersville IN 47331 Office Phone: 765-825-1139. Business E-Mail: cnewton@fayette.k12.in.us.

NEWTON, DON ALLEN, economic development consultant; b. Laurel, Miss., Oct. 19, 1934; s. Wilfred L. and Mary (McMullan) N.; m. Coleta Farrell, Oct. 11, 1958; children: Don Jr., Coleta Midge Rast. AA, Meridian CC, Miss., 1954; BA, U. Ala., 1956; postgrad. in Assn. Mgmt., U. NC; postgrad. in Econ. Devel., U. Okla. Asst. mgr. Meridian C. of C., 1956; mgr. Winston County C. of C., Louisville, Miss., 1960—61; asst. dir. Delta Coun. Indsl. and Cmty. Devel. Bd., Stoneville, Miss., 1961—62, dir., 1963—70; exec. v.p. Met. Devel. Bd., Birmingham, Ala., 1970—74; pres. Birmingham Regional C. of C., 1974—99; pub. Birmingham Mag., Birmingham Bus. Mag., 1974—99; pres. Birmingham Area C. of C. Found., Inc., 1988-99, Devel. Assocs. Econ. Devel., 1999. Contbr. articles to profl. jours., newspapers. Former appointee Ala. Export Coun.; bd. dirs. Birmingham Met. Devel. Bd., Ala. Sports Found. Lt. USNR, 1957-60. Named Ala. Mktg. Man of Yr., 1972. Mem.: Sigma Chi. Home: 4156 Glenbrook Dr Birmingham AL 35213 Office: Development Assocs PO Box 530093 Birmingham AL 35253-0093 Home Phone: 205-879-9088.

NEWTON, ESTHER MARY, anthropologist, educator; b. NYC, Nov. 28, 1940; d. Saul B. and Virginia Newton. BA, U. Mich., 1962; MA, U. Chgo., 1964, PhD, 1968. Asst. prof. CUNY, Queens, 1968-71; from asst. prof. to assoc. prof. anthropology SUNY, Purchase, 1971-92, prof. anthropology, 1992—, Kempner disting. professorship, 1999; adj. prof. Am. culture and women's studies U. Mich., Ann Arbor, 2004—. Coord. women's studies program SUNY, Purchase, 1984-86; vis. prof. Yale U., 1970, U. Amsterdam, 1993; affiliated scholar CUNY, 1992-93; scholar in residence U. Calif., Santa Cruz, 1993; curator exhbn. Gay and Lesbian Cmty. Svcs. Ctr., 1993. Author: Mother Camp: Female Impersonators in America, 1972, reprinted with new introduction, 1979, Cherry Grove, Fire Island: Sixty years in America's First Gay and Lesbian Town, 1993, Margaret Meade May Me Gay, 2000; co-author: (with Shirley Walton) Womanfriends, 1976; contbr. to anthologies including The Lesbian Issue: Essays from Signs, 1985, Hidden from History: Reclaiming the Gay and Lesbian Past, 1989, International Gay Studies: The Amsterdam Conference, 1994, History of Homosexuality in Europe and America, 1994, Writing Lesbian and Gay Culture, 1995; mem. editl. bd. The Cutting Edge: Lesbian Life and Literature Series, Between men, Between Women: Lesbian and Gay Studies Series, GLQ: Jour. of Queer Studies, Jour. of Homosexuality, Jour. Sexuality in History; contbr. to books including Amazon Expedition, 1973, Anthropology and American Life, 1974, Symbolic Anthropology: A Reader in the Study of Symbols and Meaning, 1977, Strategies des femmes, 1984, Pleasure and Danger: Exploring Female Sexuality, 1984, Homosexuality, Which Homosexuality? Vol. 2, 1987, The Lesbian and Gay Studies Reader, 1993; contbr. articles to mags. and jours. La Verne Noyes scholar U. Chgo., 1962-63; training grantee NIH, 1963-65, faculty support grantee SUNY, Purchase, 1987, 92; pre-doctoral fellow NIMH, 1965-67; recipient experienced faculty travel award SUNY, 1987, 91; Rockefeller Humanities fellow, 1999. Mem. Am. Anthrop. Assn. (cochair commn. lesbian and gay issues, 1994-96). Avocation: dog training. Office: Divsn Social Sci SUNY Purchase NY 10577

NEWTON, FLOYD CHILDS, III, lawyer; b. Griffin, Ga., Feb. 4, 1955; s. Floyd Childs Jr. and Jean (Hunt) N.; m. Katrina Dalton, Aug. 30, 1986; children: Stephanie, Amanda, Natalie. BA, Princeton U., NJ, 1977; JD, U. Ga., 1980. Bar: Ga. 1980, U.S. Dist. Ct. (no. dist.) Ga. 1980, U.S. Ct. Appeals (11th cir.) 1980. Ptnr. King & Spalding, Atlanta, 1980—. Mem. Nat. Assn. Bond Lawyers (pres. 1998-99). Office: King & Spalding 1180 Peachtree St Atlanta GA 30309 Office Phone: 404-572-4600. Business E-Mail: fnewton@kslaw.com.

NEWTON, FRANCIS CHANDLER, JR., lawyer; b. Boston, Oct. 25, 1925; s. Francis C. and Helen L. (Prentiss) N.; m. Elizabeth White, June 8, 1950; children— James W., Francis C., III. B.A., Amherst Coll., 1949; J.D., Boston U., 1952. Bar: Mass. 1952, U.S. Dist. Ct. Mass. 1953, U.S. Ct. Claims 1969, U.S. Ct. Mil. Appeals, 1959, U.S. Ct. Appeals (1st cir.) 1969, U.S. Supreme Ct. 1959. Trial counsel Powers and Hall, P.C., Boston, 1952-61, ptnr., 1962-66; individual practice, Boston, 1966-1996, Judge ODAR SSA, 1996-. Served as Col. JAGC, USAR, 1943-82. Mem. ABA, Boston Bar Assn., Assn. Trial Lawyers Am., Mass. Bar Assn., Ancient and Hon. Arty. Co. Home Phone: 978-443-6000; Office Phone: 617-523-4550 ext. 3049. Business E-Mail: francis.c.newton@ssa.gov.

NEWTON, JIM, editor; b. Palo Alto, Calif. m. Karlene Goller; 1 child, Jack. BA with high honors, Dartmouth Coll., 1985. Clk. for James Reston at NY Times, with fgn. desk; reporter Atlanta Journal-Constitution, LA Times, 1989—92, LA Police Dept. reporter, 1992—97, Calif. govt. & politics editor, 2001, city-county bur. chief, editl. page editor, 2007—. Author: Justice for All: Earl Warren & the Nation He Made, 2006. Co-recipient Pulitzer Prize, 1992, 1994; named Times Mirror Journalist of Yr., 1995; John Jacobs fellow, Inst. Govtl. Studies, 2003—04. Office: LA Times 202 W 1st St Los Angeles CA 90012 E-mail: jim.newton@latimes.com. *

NEWTON, JOHN MILTON, academic administrator, psychologist, educator; b. Schenectady, Feb. 25, 1929; s. Harry Hazleton and Bertha A. (Lehmann) N.; m. Elizabeth Ann Slattery, Sept. 11, 1954; children: Patricia, Peter, Christopher. BS, Union Coll., Schenectady, 1951; MA, Ohio State U., 1952, PhD, 1955. Lic. psychologist, Nebr. Rsch. psychologist Electric Boat divsn. Gen. Dynamics Corp., Groton, Conn., 1957-60; mem. faculty U. Nebr., Omaha, 1960—, prof. psychology, 1966-99, chmn. dept., 1967-74, acting vice chancellor acad. affairs, 1994-95, prof. emeritus, 1999—, dean Coll. Arts and Scis., 1974-94, dean emeritus, 1999—. Cons. in field, 1960-72 Author research papers in field. Served to 1st lt. Med. Service Corps, AUS, 1955-57. Mem. Am. Psychol. Assn., Psychonomic Soc., Midwestern Psychol. Assn. Home: 5611 Jones St Omaha NE 68106-1232 Office: Univ of Nebr-Omaha Dept Psychology Omaha NE 68182-0274 Business E-Mail: jnewton@mail.unomaha.edu.

NEWTON, LISA HAENLEIN, philosopher, educator; b. Orange, NJ, Sept. 17, 1939; d. Wallen Joseph and Carol Bigelow (Cypiot) Haenlein; m. Victor Joseph Newton, June 3, 1972; children: Tracey, Kit, Cynthia Perkins, Daniel Perkins, Laura Perkins. Student, Swarthmore Coll., 1957-59; BS in Philosophy with honors, Columbia U., 1962, PhD, 1967. Asst. prof. philosophy Hofstra U., Hempstead, NY, 1967-69; from asst. prof. to assoc. prof. Fairfield (Conn.) U., 1969—78, prof., 1978—, dir. program applied ethics, 1983—, dir. program environ. studies, 1986—2007; lectr. in medicine Yale U., 1984—. Lectr., cons. in field. Author: Ethics and Sustainability, 2002, Ethics in America, Study Guide, 2d edit., 2003, Ethics in America Source Reader, 2d edit., 2003, Business Ethics and the Natural Environment, 2004, Permission to Steal, 2006; co-author: Watersheds, 1994, 4th edit., 2005, Wake-Up Calls, 2d edit., 2003; co-editor: Taking Sides: Controversial Issues in Business Ethics, 2006; contbr. articles to profl. jours. Mem. exec. bd. Conn. Humanities Coun., 1979—83. Mem.: Internat. Soc. Environ. Ethics (mem. exec. bd.), Assn. Practical Prof. Ethics (exec. bd.), Soc. Bus. Ethics (past pres.), Am. Soc. Bioethics and Humanities, Soc. Ethics Across Curriculum, Am. Soc. Polit. and Legal Philosophy, Am. Philos. Assn., Am. Soc. Value Inquiry (past pres.), Phi Beta Kappa (local sec.). Home: 1870 Redding Rd Fairfield CT 06824 Office: Fairfield U Program Applied Ethics Fairfield CT 06824 Office Phone: 203-254-4128. Business E-Mail: lhnewton@mail.fairfield.edu.

NEWTON, NELL JESSUP, dean, law educator; b. St. Louis, Apr. 30, 1944; d. Robert Edward and Marcella (Boehm) Mier. BA, U. Calif., Berkeley, 1973; JD, U. Calif., Hastings, 1976. Bar: Calif., Washington, U.S. Ct. Appeals (9th crct.), U.S. Supreme Ct. Prof. Cath. U. Sch. Law, 1976-92; prof. Washington Coll. Law Am. U., Washington, 1992—98; dean U. Denver Law Sch., 1998—2000, U. Conn. Sch. Law, Hartford, 2000—06, U. Calif. Hastings Coll. Law, San Francisco, 2006—. Lectr. Internat. Law Inst., Washington, 1984-89; prof. Pre-Law Summer Inst. for Native Am. Students, U. N.Mex. Law Sch., Albuquerque, 1990, 91, 93; panelist, speaker NEH, 1981; presenter S.W. Intertribal Ct. of Appeals, 1990; panelist Orgn. Am. Historians, 1991; vis. prof. Boston Coll. Law Sch., Hastings Law Sch. Co-author: American Indian Law, 3d edit., 1991; contbr. articles to profl. jours. NEH fellow Harvard Law Sch., 1980. Life fellow Am. Bar Found., Conn. Bar Found.; mem. Soc. of Law Teachers, Law & Soc. Assn., Law Sch. Admissions Coun. Assn., Am. Law Schs. (Native Am. rights sect., mem. exec. com. 1987—, chair 1987-88, oral argument newsletter editor 1987—, mem. women in legal edn. sect. 1987—, chair profl. devel. workshop com. 1992, sec. 1993), Balt.-Washington-Va. Women Law Tchrs. Group (planning com. Symposium on Scholarship I 1985, II 1986), Thurston Soc., Order of Coif. Office: U Calif Hastings Coll Law 200 McAllister St San Francisco CA 94102 Office Phone: 415-565-4700. E-mail: newtonn@uchastings.edu. *

NEWTON, PAUL GEORGE, musician, retired librarian; b. Syracuse, NY, Dec. 1, 1930; s. Wayland LeRoy and Georgia Crumrine Newton; m. Dahlia Lorraine Brazell, Dec. 24, 1961; children: Jessica Suzanne, Roy Christopher. MusB cum laude, Syracuse U., 1952; MusM, Ind. U., 1954; PhD, U. North Tex., 1968; MLS, U. N.C., 1974. Instr. Augustana Coll., Sioux Falls, SD, 1954—56; prof. Wayland Bapt. Coll., Plainview, Tex., 1956—58, 1960—64; asst. prof. N.W. La. State Coll., Natchitoches, 1958—59, Stephen F. Austin State U., Nacogdoches, Tex., 1964—65, Ark. State U., Jonesboro, 1965—66; orch. dir. Forsyth County Schs., Winston-Salem, NC, 1968—69; music libr. Mars Hill (N.C.) Coll., 1969—83; libr. dir. Martin Meth. Coll., Pulaski, Tenn., 1983—93. Violist Asheville (N.C.) Symphony Orch., 1979—83; archivist Mars Hill Coll., 1979—83. Recipient Merit award, Kennedy-Douglass Mus., Florence, Ala., 1994. Mem.: So. Appalachian Mineral Soc., Am. Musicol. Soc., Ark. Archaeol. Soc. Avocations: travel, art, archaeology, geology, photography. Home: 114 S Sam Davis Ave Pulaski TN 38478 Office: 94 W Ridge Rd Mars Hill NC 28754 E-mail: pgnewton@energize.net.

NEWTON, RHONWEN LEONARD, writer, data processing executive, consultant; b. Lexington, NC, Nov. 13, 1940; d. Jacob Calvin and Mary Louise (Moffitt) Leonard; children: Blair Armistead Newton Jones, Allison Page, William Brockenbrough III. AB, Duke U., Durham, NC, 1962; MS in Edn., Old Dominion U., Norfolk, Va., 1968. French tchr. Hampton Pub. Schs., Va., 1962-65, Va. Beach Pub. Schs., 1965-66; instr. foreign lang. various colls. and univs., 1967-75; foreign lang. cons. Portsmouth Pub. Schs., Va., 1973-75; dir. The Computer Inst., Inc., Columbia, S.C., 1983; pres., founder The Computer Experience, Inc., Columbia, 1983-88, RN Enterprises, Columbia, 1991—. Author: WordPerfect, 1988, All About Computers, 1989, Microsoft Excel for the Mac, 1989, Introduction to the Mac, 1989, Introduction to DOS, 1989, Introduction to Lotus 1-2-3, 1989, Advanced Lotus 1-2-3, 1989, Introduction to WordPerfect, 1989, Advanced WordPerfect, 1989, Introduction to Display/Write 4, 1989, WordPerfect for the Mac, 1989, Introduction to Microsoft Works for the Mac, 1990, Accountant, Inc for the Mac, 1992, Introduction to Filemaker Pro, 1992, Quicken for the MAC, 1993, Quicken for Windows, 1993, WordPerfect for Windows, 1993, Advanced WordPerfect for Windows, 1993, Lotus 1-2-3 for Windows, 1993, Introduction to Quick Books, 1994, Quick Book for Windows, 1994, Introduction to Word for Windows, 1995, Introduction to File Maker Pro 4.0, 1998, Introduction to Microscoft Word, 1999, Introduction to Microsoft Excel, 1999, Introduction to AOL, 1999, Introduction to Excel, 1999, Using America OnLine, 1999. Mem. Columbia Planning Commn., 1980-87; bd. dirs. United Way Midlands, Columbia, 1983-86, Assn. Jr. Leagues, NYC, 1980-82, SC Wildlife Fedn., 1997-98; trustee Heathwood Hall Episcopal Sch., Columbia, 1979-85; active SC Episcopal Home Bd., 1999-2005, chmn., 2001-2003; vestry Trinity Cathedral, 1999-02; active SC Real Estate Appraisers Bd., 2000, sec., 2002—. Mem. Investment Club (pres. 1995-97, regional coun.), Nat. Assn. Investors Corp. (dir. S.C. Midlands regional coun. 1998-02). Republican. Episcopalian. Avocations: golf, walking. Home and Office: 1635 Kathwood Dr Columbia SC 29206-4509 Personal E-mail: rhonwenln@yahoo.com.

NEWTON, TERRY FERNANDO, health facility specialist, writer; b. Miami, Fla., Dec. 10, 1956; s. Julius Lee Newton and Frances Louise Cason; children: Torrence Levine, Patrick Fernando. Student, Fla. Montanari, 1976—78; BATh, 2007. Specialist child care Montanari Clin. Sch., Hialeah, Fla., 1976—79; technician mental health Miami Variety Children's Hosp., Coral Gables, Fla., 1979—80; psychiat. nurse technician Cedars of Lebanon Hosp., Miami, Fla., 1980—82; from office asst. dir. of safety to health info. specialist II Jackson Hosp., Miami, 1982—83, health info. specialist II, 1983—. Bd. dir. Body Mind & Soul Inc., Miami; 1st v.p. Lip Tongue & Ear Prodn., Miami, 1999—. Author: A Composition in Verse, 1996, A Cascade of Memories, 1998, America at the Millenium, 2000, Earthbeat, 2002, Theatre of the Mind, 2003, The Dream of Time, 2007. Active media rep. Concern & Committed Bros. Inc., Miami, 2002; bd. dir. BMS Movement, 2001—. Named African Am. Achiever, JM Family Enterprise, Inc., 1998—2003, Cmty. Achiever, Macedonia Ch., 1999; named to Internat. Poetry Hall of Fame, 1997, Miami Dade Office of Mayor, Bd. County Commrs.; recipient Accomplishment award, Gov. Lawton Chiles, 1997, Renaissance award, Macedonia Ch., 2006, Unsung Hero award, Coconut Grove Negro Women Club, 2006. Mem.: Fla. State Poetry Hosts Coalition (promotor 2003), Concern Bros. Inc. Poetry Club (dir. 2001, Mentor award 1997). Avocations: reading, performing, basketball, birdwatching. Home: 10762 SW 145th St Miami FL 33176 Office Phone: 786-222-2791. E-mail: renee@jazzandpoetry.net.

NEWTON, VIRGINIA, archivist, historian, librarian; d. John Walter and Reba Catherine Newton; m. Alvin Ellis Schmid, 2003. Student, Inst. Tecnológico y de Estudios Superiores de Monterrey, Nuevo Leon, Mex., 1957; AA in Bus. Adminstrn., Stephens Coll., 1958; BA in History, Okla. State U., 1960; M of Librarianship, U. Wash., 1963; cert. in libr. sci., U. Tex., 1968, MA in Latin Am. Studies, History, Archives and Libr. Sci., 1975, PhD in Latin Am. Studies, History, Archives and Libr. Sci., 1983. Libr. Inst. Pub. Affairs U. Tex., Austin, 1963-65, libr. Art Libr., 1965-67; coord. Sr. Cmty. Svcs. Program Econ. Opportunities Devel. Corp., San Antonio, 1968-69; archivist, spl. collections libr. Trinity U., San Antonio, 1969-73; spl. collections and reference libr. Pan Am. U., Edinburg, Tex., 1974-77; archivist records analyst Alaska State Archives and Records Svc., 1983-84, dep. state archivist, 1984-87; state archivist Alaska State Archives & Records Mgmt. Svcs., 1988-93; dir. Columbus Meml. Libr. OAS, Washington, 1993—2001. Archives cons. Ford Found. for Brazilian Archivists Assn., 1976, Soc. for Ibero-Latin Thought, 1980, Project for a Notarial Archives Computerized Guide, 1980; chair Alaska State Hist. Records Adv. Bd., 1988-93, coords. steering com., 1991-93; cons. Puerto Rican Hist. Records Adv. Bd., 1997-99. Author: An Archivists' Guide to the Catholic Church in Mexico, 1979; contbr. articles to profl. publs. Founder jail libr. Bexar County Jail, San Antonio; hon. dep. sheriff Bexar County, 1972-75; mem. Dem. party; chair Dems. Abroad in Mex., 1979-81; mem. Dems. Abroad Del. The Dem. Nat. Conv., N.Y., 1980; vice- chair Bill Egan Forum Greater Juneau Dem. Precinct, 1986-88 Recipient Commendation award Gov. of Alaska William Sheffield, 1985, Disting. Alumnae award U. Tex. Sch. Libr. and Info. Sci., 1998; Masonic Scholarship for internat. rels. George Washington U., 1960-61; univ. fellow U. Tex.-Austin, 1982-83, post masters fellow U.S. Dept. Edn.-U. Tex., Austin, 1967-68; scholar Orgn. Am. States, 1980, 81, Fulbright-Hays scholar, 1979, 80, scholar Nat. Def. Fgn. Lang.-U. Tex., Austin, 1978-79, scholar Calif. State Libr., 1962-63. Mem. AAUW (bd. dirs. 1983-86, scholar 1983), Nat. Assn. Govt. Archives and Records Adminstrs. (bd. dirs. 1989-93, chair membership com. 1989-93), Alaska Hist. Soc. (bd. treas. 1988-94), Alaska Libr. Assn., Acad. Cert. Archivists (cert. 1989), Rotary, Phi Kappa Phi. Democrat. Avocations: skiing, dance, researching, reading, hiking. Office: 206 Laurel Heights Place San Antonio TX 78212

NEWTON, WAYNE (CARSON WAYNE NEWTON), entertainer, actor, recording industry executive; b. Norfolk, Va., Apr. 3, 1942; s. Patrick and Evelyn (Smith) N.; m. Elaine Okamura, June 1, 1968 (div. 1985); 1 child, Erin; m. Kathleen McCrone, April 9, 1994; 1 child, Lauren Ashley. L.H.D. (hon.), U. Nev.-Las Vegas, 1981; Doctorate (hon.), William Woods U. Owner Tamiment Internat. Resort. Appearances include Sands, Caesar's Palace, Desert Inn, Flamingo and Frontier hotels, Las Vegas, Harrah's Club, Reno and Lake Tahoe, I Love N.Y. Concert, Americana Hotel, N.Y.C., Talk of the Town, London, London Paladium, Grand Ole Oprey House, Nashville, 4th of July, Washington, Astrodome, Houston, Hollywood (Calif.) Bowl, Melodyland, Anaheim, Calif., Circle Star, San Francisco, Sea World, Orlando, Fla., Sherman House, Chgo., Wis. State, Iowa State fairs, Valley Forge Music, Westbury Music fairs, Deauville and Eden Roc hotels, Miami Beach, Carlton Club, Bloomington, Minn., hotels Atlantic City, N.J., before U.S. troops, Vietnam, Beirut, & Persian Gulf; TV appearances include Red, White & Wow, A Christmas Card, (TV miniseries) North and South: Book II, 1986, TV spls. Opryland, 1973, Joys, 1976, Happy Birthday, Las Vegas, 1977, The Wayne Newton Special, 1982, The Real Las Vegas (TV series), 1996, Las Vegas on Ice, 1997, Feed the Children, 1997, Elvis Meets Nixon, 1997, VH1 Divas Las Vegas, 2002; film appearances in 80 Steps to Jonah, 1969 (also composer), Licence to Kill, 1989, The Adventures of Ford Fairlane, 1990, The Dark Backward, 1991, Best of the Best II, 1993, Night of the Running Man, 1994, Vegas Vacation, 1997, Ocean's Eleven, 2003, Smokin' Aces, 2006; video appearances in Who's Your Daddy?, 2003; host, prodr. The Entertainer, 2005; guest appearances include Jackie Gleason and His American Scene Magazine, 1962. 1964, The Mike Douglas Show, 1964, The Lucy Show, 1965, Bonanza, 1966, Here's Lucy, 1968, 1970, The Tonight Show Starring Johnny Carson, 1971, 1972, The Dean Martin Show, 1971, 1974, Switch, 1976, Vega$, 1979, 1981, The Highwayman, 1988, Full House, 1990, L.A. Law, 1991, Roseanne, 1991, Perfect Strangers, 1992, Renegade, 1994, 1995, Tales from the Crypt, 1994, The Fresh Prince of Bel-Air, 1995, Ellen, 1997, Ally McBeal, 1998, The Pretender, 2000, Las Vegas, 2003, 7th Heaven, 2004, The Tonight Show with Jay Leno, 2004, Larry King Live, CBS This Morning, E! Entertainment Television, Entertainment Tonight and others; albums include Danke Schoen, 1963, In Person!, 1964, Wayne Newton in Person!, 1964, Summer Wind, 1965, Red Roses for a Blue Lady, 1965, Now!, 1966, It's Only the Good Times, 1967, Old Rugged Cross, 1966, One More Time, 1968, Walking on New Grass, 1968, Can't You Hear the Song?, 1972, Change of Heart, 1978, Daddy Don't You Walk So Fast, 1972, Coming Home, 1989, God Is Alive, 1991, Showstoppers, 1992, Rock of Ages, 1992, A Merry Little Christmas, 1992, Moods & Moments, 1992, Christmas Song, 1995, Branson City Limits, 1998, Real Thing, 2004, Song of the Year: Wayne Newton Style, Tomorrow; author (with Dick Maurice): Once Before I Go, 1989; performer Dancing With the Stars, 2007. A supporter St. John's Indian Mission, Levene, Ariz.; chmn. USO Celebrity Circle. Recipient citation as distinguished recording artist and humanitarian, 1971; Freedom Lantern award Commonwealth of Mass., 1979, Entertainer of Yr. award Variety Clubs So. Nev., 1973, Gov.'s award Commonwealth of Mass., 1976, cert. of appreciation Gov. of Nev., 1978, Founders award St. Judes Childrens Hosp., Humanitarian award Am. Cancer Soc. Cancer Research Ctr., Lifetime Achievement award, First Am. in the Arts, 2000, Congl. medal, Honor Soc. Citizenship award, medal of honor, Dept. Def., US Legion of Valor's Citizen award, Jimmie E. Howard Meml. award, Medal of Honor, City Las Vegas, Ellis Island Medal of Honor, 1999, American Legend award, Washington, D.C., 1999, VFW Hall of Fame award, Am. Legion Exceptional Citizen award, star on the Hollywood Walk of Fame, award for Daddy Don't Walk So Fast ASCAP, platinum record for Danke Schoen, also gold album and gold records; named one of 10 Outstanding Young Men of Am. Nat. Jaycees, 1976; named Most Disting. Citizen of Yr. NCCJ, Outstanding Indian Entertainer of Yr. Navajo Nation, 1980, Entertainer of Yr., Nev. Mag., Casino Player Mag., 1999, Top Three Entertainers of the Century in Nev. and Around the World, Reno Gazett Jour., Amb. Goodwill, State of Nev, Veteran Fgn. Wars of US, Hon. Vietnam Veteran, Hon. Green Beret, 1999; knighted, 1998; renamed in his honor Las Vegas' McCarran Internat. Airport main thouroghfare Wayne Newton Blvd.; inducted Gaming Hall of Fame, Am. Gaming Assn. *

NEWTON, WILLIAM ALLEN, JR., pediatrician, pathologist; b. Traverse City, Mich., May 19, 1923; s. William Allen and Florence Emma (Brown) N.; m. Helen Patricia Goodrich, Apr. 21, 1945; children: Katherine Germaine, Elizabeth Gale, William Allen, Nancy Anne. BSc cum laude, Alma Coll., Mich., 1943; MD, U. Mich., 1946. Diplomate: Am. Bd. Pathology, Am. Bd. Pediatrics. Intern Wayne County Gen. Hosp., Detroit, 1947; resident in pediatric pathology/oncology/hematology Children's Hosp. Mich., Detroit, 1948-50; resident in pediat. Children's Hosp. Phila., 1950; dir. labs. Children's Hosp. Columbus, Ohio, 1952-88, rsch. pathologist Ohio, 1989—; mem. faculty Coll. Medicine, Ohio State U., 1952—, prof., 1965—, chief pediatric pathology, 1952-89, chief divsn. pediatric hematology, 1952—82, prof. emeritus, 1989—. Chmn. pathology com. Children's Cancer Study Group, 1965-91; chmn. Pathology Com. Intergroup Rhabdomyosarcoma Study Group; chmn. pathology com. Late Effects Study Group. Contbr. articles to med. jours. Trustee, exec. com. Ohio divsn. Am. Cancer Soc., 1972-86; adv. com. on childhood cancer Am. Cancer Soc.; chmn. exec. com. Consortium for Cancer Control Ohio, 1982-86; sci. adv. com. Armed Forces Inst. Pathology; pres. Internat. Consortium for Cure of Childhood Cancer in China, 2000—. Served to capt. M.C. U.S. Army, 1950-52, brig. gen. Res. ret. Mem. Ohio State Med. Assn. (com. on cancer), Midwest Soc. Pediatric Research (mem. council 1960-63, pres. 1964-65), Soc. Pediatric Research, Am. Pediatric Soc., Pediatric Pathology Club (pres. 1968-69), Am. Soc. Clin. Oncology, Internat. Soc. Pediatric Oncology, Sigma Xi, Phi Sigma Pi. Republican. Baptist. Home: 2500 Harrison Rd Johnstown OH 43031-9540 Office: PO Box 6957 Columbus OH 43205 Office Phone: 614-722-3269. Business E-Mail: wnewton@chi.osu.edu.

NEWTON-JOHN, OLIVIA, singer, actress; b. Cambridge, Eng., Sept. 26, 1948; arrived in Australia, 1954, arrived in England, 1964, arrived in Am., 1975; d. Brin and Irene (Born) Newton-John; m. Matt Lattanzi, Dec. 1984 (div. 1995); 1 child, Chloe Rose Lattanzi. Student pub. schs. Co-owner Koala Blue, 1982—. Singer, actress in Australia, Eng. and US, 1965—; actress: (films) Funny Things Happen Down Under, 1965, Tomorrow, 1970, Grease, 1978, Xanadu, 1980, Two of a Kind, 1983, It's My Party, 1996, Sordid Lives, 2000; (TV) Timeless Tales from Hallmark, 1990, A Mom for Christmas, 1990, A Christmas Romance, 1994, Snowden on Ice (voice), 1997, The Christmas Angel: A Story on Ice, 1998, The Wilde Girls, 2001; singer: (albums) If Not for You, 1971, Let me Be There, 1973, If You Love Me Let Me Know, 1974, Long Live Love, 1974, First Impressions, 1974, Have You Ever Been Mellow, 1975, Clearly Love, 1975, Come on Over, 1976, Don't Stop Believin', 1976, Making a Good Thing Better, 1977, Greatest Hits, 1977, Totally Hot, 1978, Grease, 1978, Xanadu, 1980, Physical, 1981, Greatest Hits, 1982, (with John Travolta) Two of a Kind, 1984, Soul Kiss, 1985, The Rumour, 1988, Warm And Tender, 1989, Back To Basics-The Essential Collection, 1992, Gaia, 1994, Heathcliff, 1995, Back With A Heart, 1998, The Main Event, 1998, Two, 2002, Indigo-Women of Song, 2004, Stronger Than Before, 2005; TV prodn. In Australia, 1988. Decorated as Officer, Order Brit. Empire, 1979, Order of Australia, 2006; named one of 50 Most Beautiful People in the World, People mag., 1998, one of 100 Greatest Women of Rock N Roll, VH1.; recipient Acad. Country Music, 1973, Country Music Assn. U.K., 1974-75, Country Music Assn. award, 1974, Grammy award, 1973-74, AGVA award, 1974, Billboard Mag. award, 1974-75, People's Choice award 1974, 1976, 1979, Record World award, 1974-76, 1978, Nat. Assn. Retail Merchandisers/Cashbox, 1974-75, Am. Music award 1974-76, Nat. Juke Box award, 1980, Lifetime Achievement award, Australian Record Industry Assn., 2002. Address: PO Box 2710 Malibu CA 90265-7710 Office: MCA 70 Universal City Plz North Hollywood CA 91608-1011

NEWTOWN, THANDIE, actress; b. Lusaka, Zambia, Nov. 6, 1972; m. Ol Parker, July 11, 1998; 1 child, Ripley. Actor: (films) Flirting, 1991, Pirate Prince, 1991, The Young Americans, 1993, Loaded, 1994, Interview with the Vampire: The Vampire Chronicles, 1994, Jefferson in Paris, 1995, The Journey of August King, 1995, The Leading Man, 1996, Gridlock'd, 1997, Beloved, 1998, Besieged, 1998, Mission: Impossible II, 2000, It Was an Accident, 2000, The Truth About Charlie, 2002, Shade, 2003, The Chronicles of Riddick, 2004, Crash, 2004 (recipient, Outstanding Performance by a Cast in a Motion Picture, SAG awards, 2006); (TV series) ER, 2004.

NEXSEN, JULIAN JACOBS, lawyer; b. Kingstree, SC, Apr. 14, 1924; s. William Ivey and Barbara (Jacobs) N.; m. Mary Elizabeth McIntosh, Jan. 28, 1948; children: Louise Ivey (Mrs. Heyward Harles Bouknight, Jr.), Julian Jacobs Jr. At, The Citadel, Charleston, SC, 1941—43; BS magna cum laude, U. SC, Columbia, 1948, JD magna cum laude, 1950. Bar: S.C. 1950, U.S. Supreme Ct. 1960. Ptnr. firm Nexsen Pruet, LLC, Columbia, SC. Trustee Richland County Pub. Libr., chmn., 1976-77; trustee Providence Hosp., chmn., 1984-86; trustee Providence Found., Providence Ministries, Sisters of Charity of St. Augustine Health Sys.; past bd. dirs. Columbia Music Festival Assn., ARC Richland-Lexington Counties, Ctrl. Carolina Cmty. Found.; mem. U.S.C. Law Sch. partnership bd.; elder Eastminster Presbyn. Ch., trustee Congaree Presbytery, 1967-87, Synod, S.C., 1969-74, mem. Trinity Presbytery Coun. Lt. inf. AUS, 1943-46, ETO, capt., 1950-51, Korea. Decorated Bronze Star with oak leaf cluster; recipient Compleat Lawyer award U. SC Sch. Law, Disting. Pub. Svc. award Order of Coif, 2007. Mem. ABA, SC Bar (treas., bd. govs. 1974-79, House of Dels. 1980-92), Richland County Bar Assn. (pres. 1974-75, Disting. Svc. award 1987), Am. Bar Found., SC Bar Found. (pres. 1971-72), SC Law Inst. (coun., exec. com. 1986—), Am. Law Inst., Am. Coll. Trust and Estate Counsel (regent 1973-82), Am. Judicature Soc., Forest Lake Country Club, Palmetto Club, Kiwanis (bd. dirs. 1972-74, 77-79), Phi Beta Kappa. Home: 2840 Sheffield Rd Columbia SC 29204-2332 Office: Nexsen Pruet LLC Drawer 2426 1230 Main St Columbia SC 29202-2426 Office Phone: 803-253-8247. Business E-Mail: jnexsen@nexsenpruet.com.

NEXSEN, JULIAN JACOBS, JR., lawyer; b. Columbia, SC, Sept. 22, 1954; s. Julian J. and Mary Elizabeth (McIntosh) N.; m. Christine Spigner Johnston, Feb. 25, 1984; children: Elizabeth Kincaid, Julian J. III, Sarah Ivey. BA, Washington and Lee U., 1976; JD, U. S.C., 1979. Bar: S.C. 1979, U.S. Ct. Appeals (4th cir.) 1982. Assoc. Nexsen, Pruet, Jacobs & Pollard, Columbia, S.C., 1979-84; assoc. in house counsel, asst. sec. Greenwood (S.C.) Mills, Inc., 1984-95, exec. v.p., 1999—2001; exec. v.p., COO Greenwood Devel. Corp., 1995-99, pres., CEO, 1999—. Bd. dirs. CountyBank, Greenwood Devel. Corp., Ctrl. Trust Co., Partnership for a Greater Greenwood, Greenwood Genetic Ctr.; trustee Self Family Found. Self Regional Healthcare Ctr.; trustee First Presbyn. Ch. Bd. visitors Lander Coll., 1985-87; bd. dirs. Edn. Enrichment Found., 1986-89, Greenwood United Way, 1989-92, Greenwood Community Theatre, 1989-93, Greenwood Uptown Devel. Corp., 1991-93; bd. deacons 1st Presbyn. Ch., 1990-93, session, 1993-96; trustee Self Meml. Hosp., 1992-98; bd. dirs. Greenwood County Econ. Alliance, 1999-2001. Mem. ABA, Am. Corp. Counsel Assn., S.C. Bar Assn., Greater U. S.C. Alumni Assn. (bd. govs. 2004—), Forest Lake Club, Greenwood Country Club, S.C. C. of C. (bd. dirs. 1990-93). Presbyterian. Home: 512 E Henrietta Ave Greenwood SC 29649-3142 Office: Greenwood Devel Corp PO Box 1546 Greenwood SC 29648-1546 Business E-Mail: jnexsen@greenwooddevelopment.com.

NEY, EDWARD N., ambassador, advertising and public relations executive; b. St. Paul, May 26, 1925; s. John Joseph and Marie (Noonan) N.; m. Suzanne Hayes, 1950 (div. 1974); children: Nicholas, Hilary, Michelle; m. Judith I. Lasky, May 24, 1974. BA (Lord Jeffrey Amherst scholar 1942), Amherst Coll., 1947. With Young & Rubicam, Inc., NYC, 1951-86, chmn., pres. CEO, 1970-86; chmn. Paine Webber/Young & Rubicam Ventures, NYC, 1987-89; vice-chmn. Paine Webber, Inc., NYC, 1987-89; amb. to Can., Am. Embassy, Ottawa, Ont., 1989-92; chmn. bd. advisors Burson-Marsteller, NYC, 1992-98; chmn. Marsteller Advt.; chmn. emeritus Young & Rubicam Advt., NYC, 1999—. Mem. Coun. on Fgn. Rels., 1975—; mem. adv. bd. Ctr. for Strategic and Internat. Studies (C.S.I.S.), 1986—; honorary chmn. Advt. Coun.; mem. Advt. Hall of Fame. Life Trustee Amherst Coll., 1979—; Trustee Bush Presidential Libr. Found., James A. Baker III Inst. for Public Policy, Rice U., Museum of TV/Radio (MTR), 1982—. Office: Young Rubicam Advt 285 Madison Ave New York NY 10017-6486 Business E-Mail: ed_ney@yr.com.

NEY, PETER ERNEST, mathematician, educator; b. Brno, Czech Republic, July 6, 1930; s. Paul E. and Katherine B. Ney; m. Irene Paulu Ney, July 28, 1993; children: Paul A., Christine E. BS, MIT, Cambridge, 1951; MA, Columbia U., NYC, 1952, PhD, 1961. Instr., math. Cornell U., Ithaca, NY, 1958—60, asst. prof., opers. rsch., 1960—63, assoc. prof., opers. rsch., 1963—65; vis. asst. prof., stats. Stanford U., Calif., 1963—64; assoc. prof., math. U. Wis., Madison, 1965—67, prof., math., 1967—2000, chmn., dept. math., 1974—77, emeritus prof., math., 2000—. Author: Branching Processes, 1971; editor: Advances in Probability, 1971—84, Annals of Probability, 1988—90; contbr. articles to profl. jours. Fellow, Guggenheim Found., 1971—72, Fulbright Found., 1984, Humboldt Found., 1991, 1994. Fellow: Inst. Math. Stats. (coun. mem.); mem.: Internat. Stats. Soc., Am. Math. Soc. Home: 104 Riverside Dr Unit C606 Cocoa FL 32922 Office: Dept Math Univ Wis 480 Lincoln Dr Madison WI 53706 Office Phone: 608-263-3054. Business E-Mail: ney@math.wisc.edu.

NEYER, JEROME CHARLES, consulting civil engineer; b. Cin., July 15, 1938; s. Urban Charles and Marie Helen (Hemsteger) N.; m. Judy Ann Drolet, June 17, 1961; children: Janet, Karen. BCE, U. Detroit, 1961; MCE, U. Wash., 1963. Registered profl. engr. 16 states. Facilities engr. Boeing Co., Seattle, 1961-62; found. engr. Metro Engrs., Seattle, 1962-65; project engr. Hugo N. Helpert Assocs., Detroit, 1965-70; pres. NTH Cons. Ltd., Farmington Hills, Mich., 1970—. Adj. prof. U. Detroit, 1973-79. Contbr. articles to profl. jours. Mem. mineral well adv. bd., Lansing, Mich., 1975, mem. constrn. safety stds. bd., 1982; chmn. bldg. appeals bd. City of Farmington Hills, 1983. Mem. ASTM, ASCE (br. pres. 1973-74), Engring. Soc. Dtroit, Cons. Engrs. Mich. (pres. 1981), Mich. Soc. Profl. Engrs. (bd. dirs. 1980), Assn. Engring. Firms Practicing in the Geoscis. (pres. 1991). Roman Catholic. Avocations: golf, tennis. Home: 26478 Ballantrae Ct Farmington Hills MI 48331-3528 Office: NTH Consultants Ltd 38955 Hills Tech Dr Farmington MI 48331-3434 Home Phone: 734-459-5952; Office Phone: 248-553-6300. Business E-Mail: jneyer@nthconsultants.com, jneyer007@comcast.net.

NEZU, VICTOR A., lawyer; b. NYC, Mar. 2, 1964; BA, SUNY, Stony Brook, 1987; JD, Boston U., 1994, MBA, 1995. Legal counsel Sunburst Comm., LLC, Palisades Park, NJ, 1996—99; atty. Law Offices Victor A. Nezu, P.C., NYC, 1999—. Pres. Winthrop Apartments Corp., Forest Hills,

NY, 2005—. Mem.: Phi Beta Kappa. Office: Law Offices Victor A Nezu PC 1001 Avenue of the Americas 4th Fl New York NY 10018 Home Phone: 212-790-9464; Office Phone: 212-790-9464. Office Fax: 212-790-9465; Home Fax: 212-790-9465. Business E-Mail: victor@nezulaw.com.

NG, DAVID, electrical engineer; b. Far Rockaway, NY, Feb. 3, 1963; s. Tom Yoke and Nung Chan (Choi) N.; m. Francine Mae Gruby, July 22, 1989 (div. Dec. 1993); 1 child, Elizabeth Marie. BSEE, SUNY, Buffalo, 1985. Registered profl. engr., 06. Electronics engr. 485 Engring. Installation Group/EITX, Griffiss AFB, N.Y., 1986-88, 1991-95, Naval Electronic System Sec. Ctr., Washington, 1988-91; test engr. Tellabs, Inc., Hauppauge, N.Y., 1996-98; electronics engr. Dept. Army, New Orleans, 1995-96; compliance engr. switch mode power supplies Lambda Electronics, 1999—2001; prin. engr. Hazen & Sawyer, P.C., NY, 2006—. Network security officer 485 Engring. Installation Group/EITX, Griffiss AFB, 1991-95. Mem. IEEE. Avocations: various sports, computer programming, music, movies. Home: PO Box 901507 Far Rockaway NY 11690-1507 Office: 498 7th Ave New York NY 10018 Office Phone: 212-777-8400. Personal E-mail: dave11691@yahoo.com.

NG, DOMINIC, bank executive; b. Hong Kong, Jan. 24, 1959; BBA in Acctg., U. Houston, 1980. CPA Calif., Texas. Dir. Chinese bus. svcs., sr. mgr. Deloitte & Touche, LLP, L.A., Houston, 1980—90; pres., CEO Seyin Investment, Inc., LA, 1990—92, East-West Fed. Bank f.s.b., San Marino, Calif., 1992—. Bd. dirs. Fed. Res. Bank, San Francisco, LA, Mattel Inc. Office: East West Bank 135 N Los Robles Ave 7th Fl Pasadena CA 91101 Office Phone: 626-768-6800. Business E-Mail: carmen.pan@eastwest.com.

NG, JOHN DANIEL, ophthalmologist, educator; s. Andre Jose and Theresa Ng; m. Patti Adams Ng, June 21, 1986; children: Coral Janelle, Fisher Ward. BS in Neurosci., U. Rochester, 1983; MS in Physiology, Georgetown U., 1984; MD, George Washington U., 1988. Diplomate Am. Bd. Ophthalmology. Flight surgeon U.S. Army, Ft. Sheridan, Ill., 1989—91, comprehensive ophthalmologist Ft. Gordon, Ga., 1994—95, faculty oculoplastic surgeon Ft. Sam Houston, Tex., 1997—2000; assoc. prof. Casey Eye Inst., Portland, Oreg., 2000—. Contbr. articles to profl. jours.; reviewer Ophthalmology jour., 1995—. Recipient Meritorious Svc. award, U.S, Army. Fellow: Am. Acad. Ophthalmology (Achievement award), Am. Soc. Ophthalmic Plastic Reconstructive Surgery (thesis com. 2003—); mem.: Health for Humanity, Elks. Baha'I. Avocations: bicycling, hiking, scuba diving, snow shoeing, tai chi. Office: Casey Eye Inst 3375 SW Terwilliger Blvd Portland OR 97239 Office Phone: 503-494-3010.

NG, KIM (KIMBERLY J. NG), professional sports team executive; b. Wu Peiqin, China, Nov. 17, 1968; m. Tony Markward. BA in Pub. Policy, U. Chgo., 1990. Front office arbitration intern Chgo. White Sox, 1990, spl. projects analyst, 1991, asst. dir., baseball ops., 1991—95; dir. waivers, player records MLB Am. League, 1995—97; asst. gen. mgr. NY Yankees, 1998—2001; asst. gen. mgr., v.p. baseball ops. LA Dodgers, 2001—. Office: Los Angeles Dodgers 1000 Elysian Park Ave Los Angeles CA 90012-1199

NG, LAWRENCE MING-LOY, pediatrician; b. Hong Kong, Mar. 21, 1940; arrived in U.S., 1967, naturalized, 1977; s. John Iu-cheung and Mary Wing (Wong) N.; m. Bella May Ha Kan, June 25, 1971; children: Jennifer Wing-mui, Jessica Wing-yee. MBBS in Medicine, U. Hong Kong, 1965. Diplomate Am. Bd. Pediatrics. House physician Queen Elizabeth Hosp., Hong Kong, 1965-66, med. officer, 1966-67; resident physician Children's Hosp. of Los Angeles, 1967-68, Children's Hosp. Med. Ctr., Oakland, Calif., 1968-70; fellow in pediatric cardiology, 1970-72; now mem. tchg. staff; practice medicine specializing in pediat. and pediatric cardiology, San Leandro, Calif., 1972—, Oakland, Calif., 1982—; mng. ptnr. Pediatric Med. Assocs. of East Bay, 1990—. Chief pediat. Oakland Hosp., 1974-77, Meml. Hosp., San Leandro, 1986-88; chief pediat. Vesper Meml. Hosp., 1977-79, sec. staff, 1984, v.p. staff, 1985; founder Pediatric Assocs. of East Bay, 1990. Active Republican Party. Recipient Small Bus. Leadership award, Oakland Chinatown C. of C., Comty. Svc. award, Ethnic Health Inst., Family Bridges Comty. Svc. award, Spl. Congl. Recognition cert., 2004. Fellow: Am. Acad. Pediatrics; mem.: AMA, Chancellor's Assocs. U. Calif. at Berkeley, Children's First Healthcare Network (bd. dirs. 1997—, sec. 2006—), Oakland Chinatown C. of C. (bd. dirs. 1986—91, 1986—91, adv. bd. 1992—, Cmty. Spirit award 2000), Ethnic Health Inst. (bd. dirs. 1998—, Frank Stagger Sr. Cmty. svc. award 2004), Fedn. Chinese Med. Socs. (dir. 1998—2006, sec. 2006—), Chinese-Am. Physicians Soc. (sec. 1980, pres. 1983, exec. dir. 1997—2001, bd. dirs. 2003—), Chinese-Am. POlit. Assn. (life), Orgn. Chinese Ams. (chpt. pres. 1984), Smithsonian Assocs., L.A. Pediat. Soc., Alameda County Assn. Primary Care Practitioners (membership chmn. 1993—97, sec.-treas. 1994—97), Am. Heart Assn., Calif. Med. Assn., Family Bridges Inc. (bd. dirs. 2002—, Kenneth Hoh award for cmty. svc. 2004, Outstanding Vol. award 2006), Stanford U. Alumni Assn. (life), Consumer's Union (life), Hong Kong U. Alumni Assn. (sec. No. Calif. chpt. 1992—96, pres. 1997—2000, chair 2001—), Friends of Hong Kong U. (bd. dirs. 2001—, treas. 2003—), Oakland Asian Cultural Ctr. (dir. 1996—99, treas. 1996—99), U.S. Golf Assn., San Leandro Golf Club, No. Calif. Golf Assn., Commonwealth Club, PGA Tour Ptnrs. Club (life). Republican. Buddhist. Avocations: golf, photography, web design. Office: 345 9th St Ste 204 Oakland CA 94607-4206 also: 101 Callan Ave Ste 401 San Leandro CA 94577-4523 Home Phone: 510-351-4225; Office Phone: 510-357-7077. E-mail: larryn@pedmed.com.

NG, WING CHIU, accountant, educator, application developer, lawyer, advocate; b. Hong Kong, Oct. 14, 1947; came to U.S., 1966; s. Bing Nuen and Oi Ying (Lee) Ng. BS, MS, Yale U., 1969; PhD, NYU, 1972; JD, U. Hawaii, 2000. Bar: Hawaii 2001; CPA, Hawaii. Rsch. assoc. SUNY, Stony Brook, 1972-74; asst. prof. U. Md., College Park, 1974-76; rsch. physicist U. Bonn, Fed. Republic of Germany, 1976-78; chartered acct. Richter, Usher & Vineberg, Montreal, Can., 1978-80; pvt. practice Honolulu, Hawaii, 1980—; pres. Bowen, Ng & Co., Honolulu, 1983-84, Asia-Am. Investment, Inc., Honolulu, 1983—, Mathematica Pacific, Inc., Honolulu, 1984—. Part-time prof. U. Hawaii, Honolulu, 1982—; ptnr. Advance Realty Investment, Honolulu, 1980—; dir. S & L Internat., Inc., Honolulu, 1987—. Creator: (computer software) Time Billing, 1984, Dbase General Ledger, 1987, Dbase Payroll, 1987, Dbase Accounts Receivable, 1989; co-author: Draft Constitution of the Federal Republic of China (http://frchina.blogspot.com), 1994. Dir. Orgn. of Chinese Ams., Honolulu, 1984-86, Fedn. for a Dem. China, Honolulu, 1990—, Hong Kong, 1991—; dir. Alliance Hong Kong Chinese in U.S., 1995—. Included in Prominent People of Hawaii, Delta Pub. Co., 1988. Mem. AICPA, Hong Kong Soc. Accts., Hawaiian Trail & Mountain Club (auditor 1987—). Democrat. Buddhist. Avocations: hiking, the internet. Office: 1149 Bethel St Ste 306 Honolulu HI 96813-2210

NGAAGE, DUMBOR LAATEH, cardiothoracic surgeon; b. Bori, Ogoni, Rivers State, Nigeria, Sept. 3, 1963; s. Leonard and Esther Ngaage; m. Queen Chinedum Uzodinma; children: SanyieBari, Kadilobari, Letom children: LedibaBari. MBBS, U. Benin, Nigeria, 1985. Sr. house officer U. Port Harcourt Tchg. Hosp., Rivers State, Nigeria, 1989—91, registrar, 1991—93, sr. registrar, 1993—95; registrar Caithness Gen. Infirmary, Wick, 1995—97; sr. house officer Glasgow Western Infirmary, Scotland, 1997—98; specialist registrar Leeds Gen. Infirmary, England, 1998—. Chief surg. resident U. Port Harcourt, 1993—94; co-med. dir. Queen Esther's Specialist Hosp., Port Harcourt, 1994—; chief surg. resident Caithness Gen. Hosp., Wick, 1996—97; chief cardiothoracic surg. resident Castle Hill Hosp., Hull, East Yorkshire, England, 1999—2000. Pres. Assn. Resident Drs., Port Harcourt, 1992—93; fin. sec. Nigeria Med. Assn., Port Harcourt, 1993—94. Fellow: European Bd. Thoracic and Cardiovascular Surgery, W. African Coll. Surgeons, Royal Coll. Surgeons (Edinburgh, cardiothoracic surgery); mem.: European Assn. Cardiothoracic Surgeons. Achievements include discovery of a safe technique for removing extensive renal cell tumors; invention of transmitral cardiopulmonary endoscopy; cardiopulmonary endoscopy. Avocations: travel, music, swimming, soccer, poetry. Office: Divsn Cardiovasc Surgery Mayo Clinic Rochester MN 55905 Home Phone: 44 113 2680104.

NGO, CHIU Y., electrical engineer; s. Hor and Wai-Yau Ngo; m. Christy Lao; children: Vincent, Lawrence. BSEE (hon.), U. Hong Kong, 1984; M in Engring., Philips Internat. Inst., Eindhoven, The Netherlands, 1986; MSc, U. So. Calif., LA, 1991, MSc in Applied Math., 1993, PhD in Elec. Engring., 1995; MSc in Mgmt., Poly. U., NYC, 2001. Sr. mem. rsch. staff, project leader Philips Rsch., Briarcliff Manor, NY, 1995—2002; prin. engr. Samsung Electronics, San Jose, Calif., 2002—. Mem.: IEEE, IET (chartered engr.). Achievements include patents in field. Office: Samsung Electronics 75 W Plumeria Dr San Jose CA 95134 Home Phone: 408-544-5633.

NGO, VAN TAN (TAN VAN), financial planner, poet; b. Dai Loc, Quang Nam, Vietnam, June 17, 1952; s. Hoa Ngo and Thi Ta Tran; m. Kim Phuong Thi Do-Phan, Apr. 2, 1987. Diploma in Fin. Planning, Quebec Inst. Fin. Planning, 1996. Cert. fin. planner IQPF, 1996. Translator, instr. USN, Saigon, Vietnam, 1972—75; fin. planner, fin. security advisor Sun Life Fin., Montreal, Que., Canada, 1978—; chartered adminstr. Order of Chartered Adminstrs., Que., 1994; profl. mgr. Can. Inst. Mgmt., 1995. Mem. Chamber of Fin. Sec. Que.; pres. conf. attendant representing Montreal city Clarica, 2005. Editor: Vietnam-Can. Newspaper, 1982—86, (website) Vietnamville.ca, author poems worldwide in numerous lit. mags. and websites, cited in Vietnamese and English. Campaign organizer Tsunami, 2005; organizer NGO Humanitarian & Development projects in the third-world countries, Chanchu Typhoon Relief Campaign for Vietnam, 2006, Xangsane Typhoon Relief Campaign for Vietnam, 2006; founder Quang Da Assn.; project initiator for creation of Vietnamtown in Montreal. Recipient Citation award, US Naval Support Facility Comdr., Vietnam, 1972, Achievement award, Naval Advisory Group Comdr., Saigon, 1974, Macaulay Club award, Sun Life Ins. Co. Can., 1995, Five Star Club award, 1995, Nat. Quality award, Chamber Fin. Sec. Que., 1998, Outstanding Poetry award, Internat. Soc. Poets, 2004, Award of Excellence, Clarica, 2005, Order of Merit, 2006. Mem.: PEN Canada, World Movement for Prosperity (pres., found. 1992—), Vietnam-Can. Found. (pres., found. 1982—), Montreal Fin. Security Chamber (Nat. Quality Award 1998). Achievements include development of poetry therapy, initative for creation of Duy Tan University; helped bring internat. co-operation to reogranization and consolidation of Univ. Danang, Vietnam. Office: Sun Life Fin 1001 Dorchester Sq Ste 600 Montreal PQ H3B 1N1 Canada Office Phone: 514-866-5811 Ext.202. Office Fax: 514-731-9782. Personal E-mail: ngovantan@yahoo.com. Business E-Mail: van.tan.ngo@sunlife.com.

NGUYEN, ANN CAC KHUE, pharmaceutical and medicinal chemist; b. Kieu Moc, Sontay, Vietnam, Nov. 12, 1949; d. Nguyen Van Soan and Luu Thi Hieu. BS, U. Saigon, 1973; MS, San Francisco State U., 1978; PhD, U. Calif., San Francisco, 1983. Tchg. and rsch. asst. U. Calif., San Francisco, 1978-83, postdoctoral fellow, 1983-86, rsch. scientist, 1987—. Contbr. articles to profl. jours. Recipient Nat. Rsch. Svc. award, NIH, 1981-83; Regents fellow U. Calif., San Francisco, 1978-81. Mem. AAAS, Am. Chem. Soc., N.Y. Acad. Scis., Bay Area Enzyme Mechanism Group, Am. Assn. Pharm. Scientists. Roman Catholic. Home: 1488 Portola Dr San Francisco CA 94127-1409 Office: U Calif PO Box 446 San Francisco CA 94143-0001 Personal E-mail: ann94143@yahoo.com. Business E-Mail: ann.cac.k.nguyen@ucsf.edu.

NGUYEN, CHARLES CUONG, engineering educator, researcher, dean; b. Danang, Vietnam, Jan. 1, 1956; arrived in U.S., 1978, naturalized, 1978; s. Buoi and Tinh Thi Nguyen; m. Kim-Bang Pham, Aug. 5, 1989; children: Carissa Kim Thuy Duong, Olivia Quynh Duong, Dylan Nhat Khang, Parker Duy Khang. Diploma, Konstanz U., Fed. Rep. Germany, 1978; MS with distinction, George Washington U., 1980, DSc with superiour performance, 1982. Engr. Siemens Corp., Erlangen, Germany, 1977-78; lectr. George Washington U., Washington, 1978-82; asst. prof. engring. Cath. U. Am., Washington, 1982-85, assoc. prof. elec. engring., 1985-92, prof., 1992—, chmn. dept. elec. engring. and computer sci., 1997-2001, dean Sch. Engring., 2001—. Cons. Mitre Corp., Meridian Corp., Jet Propulsion Lab., others; dir. Ctr. Artificial Intelligence and Robotics, 1985—; mem. organizing coms. various robotics confs.; sr. rsch. assoc. NAS, 1990—; program vice chair IEE-Internat. Conf. Robotics 2d Automation, 1997, Internat. Symposium and Robotic Automation, 1997; chmn. organizing com. Robotics Internat., Internat. Symposium Robotics and Mfg. Founding editor, editor-in-chief: Jour. Intelligent Automation and Soft Computing (10th Anniversary award, 2006); editor: (book) Robotics and Manufacturing, Vol. 5, 1994, Intelligent Automation and Soft Computing, Vol. 1, 1994, Intelligent Automation and Soft Computing, Vol. 2, 1994; mem. editl. bd.: Jour. Intelligent and Fuzzy Sys., Engring. Design and Automation, assoc. editor: Computers and Elec. Engring.: An Internat. Jour., 1992—, guest editor: Jour. Robotic Sys., —; contbr. scientific papers to profl. jours. Apptd. by Pres. Bus to bd. dirs. Vietnam Edn. Found., 2004—07. Recipient Rsch. Initiation award, Engring. Found., 1985, Disting. Alumni Scholar award, George Wash. U., 2002, Lifetime Achievement award, World Automation Congress, 2004, Cmty. Svc. award in Edn., Asia Entertainment Inc., 2004, Excellence in Cmty. Svc. award, Vietnamese Med. Rsch. Found., 2007; fellow, NASA-Am. Soc. Elec. Engring., 1985, 1986, NASA-Am. Soc. Elec. Engring. Summer, Goddard Space Flight Ctr., 1994. Mem.: IEEE (sr.; program v.p. Washington chpt.), Soc. Mfg. Engrs. (sr. Robotics Internat.), Internat. Soc. Mini-and Microcomputers, Tau Beta Pi (faculty advisor), Sigma Xi. Roman Catholic. Avocations: guitar, singing, tennis, skiing, ping pong/table tennis. Business E-Mail: nguyen@cua.edu.

NGUYEN, CLIFFORD HAM-THIEM, telecommunications engineer; b. Saigon, Vietnam, Nov. 7, 1962; came to U.S., 1982; s. Nghi Duc Nguyen and Lien Kim Hoang; m. Julie Thach Pham. BSEE, Poly. U., 1988, MSEE, 1989; MA in Stats., Columbia U., 1998. Electronics engr. DoD-ARDEC, Dover, N.J., 1989-91; switch engr. Bell Atlantic/NYNEX, NYC, 1991-96, sr. engr., 1996-99, sr. specialist, 1999, Lucent, 1999-2000; ops. mgr. Bell Labs, 2000—, mem. tech. staff. Achievements include research in telecommunications infrastructures; methodologies and tolls for wireline and wireless network planning, design, and deployment decisions; development of network performance analysis on data, voice, optical; planning, designing, engineering telecommunication networks with broad range of technologies and products.

NGUYEN, DONG, computer scientist, researcher, software engineer, educator; s. Dao Nguyen and Khau Thi Le; m. Dung Xuan Phi, Dec. 30, 1976; children: Henry Huy, Huy Tuan. BS in Computer Sci. and Engring., Calif. State U., Long Beach, 1985, MS in Computer Sci., 1988; PhD in Computer Engring. and Applied Math., Claremont Grad. U., 2000, exec. MBA, 2002, MS in Math., 1997. Software engr. Info. Internat., Inc., Culver City, Calif., 1984—86; sr. software engr. CALCOMP, Anaheim, Calif., 1986—90; sr. programmer analyst Sys. Divsn. Ball Aerospace, Huntington Beach, Calif., 1985—87; sr. firmware engr. Micro Tech., Inc., Anaheim, Calif., 1990—92; sr. software engr., sys. engr. Beckman Instruments, Brea, 1990—97; sr. staff engr. B/E Aerospace, Irvine, Calif., 1997—2001; sr. adv. engr., rschr. Kofax Image Products, Irvine, Calif., 2001—03; software engr. mgr. Celerity Group, Inc., Yorba Linda, 2003—. Lectr. Cal State Univ., Longweach, 1998—2000, in field. Prodr.(music concerts): Young Love, 1992—94. Achievements include research in reliability modeling and evaluation in real-time distributed multimedia systems; recovery blocks in real-time distributed systems; failure mode and effect analysis in software reliability; reliability modeling and evaluation in computer networks and distributed systems; development of rasterization algorithm which greatly improved the speed of converting the vector data to raster data in printers/plotters; dynamic camera calibration algorithm for the scanner's automatic camera calibration in real-time without manual operations from users. Personal E-mail: nguyendg@aol.com.

NGUYEN, HAN VAN, mechanical engineer; b. Danang, Vietnam, June 10, 1956; came to U.S., 1974; s. Tien Van Nguyen and Dieu Anh Khoa Nguyen; m. Thien-Tam Trang, Jan. 7, 1995; children: Brandon Huy, Bryan Minh. BSME with distinction, Iowa State U., 1979; MSME, Purdue U., 1981, PhD, 1986. Registered profl. engr., Calif., Wash. Grad. rsch. asst. Purdue U., West Lafayette, Ind., 1979—83; sr. engr. Westinghouse Electric Corp., Sunnyvale, Calif., 1983—87; assoc. tech. fellow Boeing Co., Downey and Huntington Beach, Calif., 1987—. Mem. adj. faculty Calif. State Poly. U., Pomona, 1995-97. Contbr. articles to profl. jours. (recipient Meritorious Invention awards, 1998, 2000). Bd. dir. L.A. Coun. Engrs. and Scientists, 2000-01, Asian Am. Profl. Assn., 2002-04. Recipient Cert. Appreciation, Rockwell Internat. Corp., 1989, 94, Instant Compensation award, 1992, 94, Group Achievement award NASA, 1992; Iowa State U. scholar; Purdue U. fellow. Fellow: AIAA (assoc.; conf. session chair 2002, 2003, 2005, 2006, Disting. Svc. cert. 2006), Inst. Advancement Engring.; mem.: Sigma Xi, Golden Key, Phi Eta Sigma, Pi Mu Epsilon, Eta Kappa Nu, Pi Tau Sigma, Tau Beta Pi, Phi Kappa Phi. Achievements include development of numerous thermo-fluid models to evaluate the design and predict the performance of launch vehicle propulsion systems, and publications in space propulsion. Office: The Boeing Co MC H012-B201 5301 Bolsa Ave Huntington Beach CA 92647-2048 Business E-Mail: han.v.nguyen@boeing.com.

NGUYEN, HUONG TRAN, former elementary and secondary language educator, former district office administrator; b. Haiphong, Vietnam, Nov. 16, 1953; came to the U.S., 1971; d. Joe (Quang) Trong Tran and Therese (Nguyet-Anh) (Do) Dotran; m. Tony (Phu) The Nguyen; children: Long Tran Nguyen, Ty Tran Nguyen. B in Liberal Studies, San Diego State U., 1976, tchg. credential grades K-12, 1977; M in Curriculum Devel., Point Loma Coll., 1984; lang. devel. specialist cert., Calif. Commn. Credentialing, 1991; PhD in Edn., Curriculum & Instrn., U. Calif. Riverside, 2004. ESL tchr. San Diego (Calif.) Job Corps, 1978-80; resource tchr. grades K-12 San Diego (Calif.) Unified Sch. Dist., 1980-82; resource tchr. SEAL project grades K-12 Long Beach (Calif.) Unified Sch. Dist., 1982-83, ESL specialist, 1983-85, 85-92, English lang. devel. tchr., chair, 1992-95; adminstr., 1996-98; sr. fellow officer U.S. Dept. Edn., Office Bilingual & Minority Lang. Affairs, Washington, 1995-96; from disting. tchr.-in-residence to asst. prof. Calif. State U., Long Beach, 1998—2004, asst. prof., 2003—. Instr. curriculum PhD Program Calif. State U., 2004. Named Outstanding Tchr. of 1994, Disney Co. Am. Tchr. Awards, Washington, 1994, Outstanding Tchr. in Fgn. Lang./ESL, Disney Co. Am. Tchr. Awards, Washington, 1994. Mem.: Pacific Am. Edn., Calif. Assn. Asian Pacific Bilingual Edn., Calif. Coun. Tchr. Edn., Am. Ednl. Rsch. Assn., Nat. Coun. Tchrs. English. Avocations: reading, travel, gardening, meditation, yoga. Office: Calif State U Coll Edn Dept Tchr Edn 1250 N Bellflower Blvd Long Beach CA 90840-0001 Office Phone: 562-985-4536. Business E-Mail: hnguye10@csulb.edu.

NGUYEN, KHANH GIA, medical educator; b. Hanoi, Vietnam, Dec. 17, 1940; arrived in Can., 1972; s. Lien Bich and Lan Chi Nguyen; m. Nga Thi Ho, Dec. 30, 1940; children: Van Thanh Nguyen-Ho, Phong Nguyen-Ho. Cert. of physics, chemistry and biology, Saigon U., 1961, MD, 1969. Diplomate Am. Bd. Pathology, Am. Bd. Pathology in Cytopathology, cert. pathologist Royal Coll. Physicians and Surgeons, Can. Asst. prof. pathology U. Sask., Saskatoon, Canada, 1978—82; pathologist Plains Health Ctr., Regina, Canada, 1978—80; pathologist, head provincial cytology lab. Pasqua Hosp., Regina, Canada, 1980—82; asst. prof. pathology U. Alta., Edmonton, Alberta, Canada, 1982—84, assoc. prof. pathology, 1984—92, prof. lab. medicine and pathology, 1992—2006, prof. emeritus lab. medicine and pathology, 2006—; pathologist U. Alta. Hosp., Edmonton, Alberta, Canada, 1982—2006, pathologist and head of electron microscopy, 1987—2000, pathologist and head of cytology, 1997—2004; pathologist BC Cancer Agy., Vancouver, Canada, 2006—. Cons. pathologist Can. Tumor Reference Ctr., Ottawa, Ontario, Canada, 1982—87. Author: Essentials of Aspiration Biopsy Cytology, 1991, Essentials of Exfoliative Cytology, 1992, Essentials of Cytology: An Atlas, 1993, Critical Issues in Cytopathology, 1996; mem. editl. bd.: Acta Cytologica Jour., 1985—2006, Vietnamese Med. Jour., 2001—06; contbr. articles to profl. jours. Accreditation com. for Can. sch. cytotechnology Can. Med. Assn., Ottawa, Ont., Canada, 1992—2000. Recipient Med. Excellency award, Vietnamese Am. Rsch. Found., Westminster, CA, USA, 2004. Fellow: Internat. Acad. Cytology (assoc.; membership com. 1989—92, editl. com. 1992—95, exam. bd. 1995—2002); mem.: European Acad. Scis., Royal Coll. Physicians and Surgeons of Can., Can. Soc. Cytology (hon.; chmn. 1984—85, sec.-treas. 1985—89), Papanicolaou Soc. Cytopathology (assoc.; member-at-large 1991—99). Achievements include research in cytopathology, pathology, patient care. Personal E-mail: khanhnguyen1730@hotmail.com. Business E-Mail: gknguyen@bccancer.bc.ca.

NGUYEN, KHUE VU, molecular biologist, researcher; b. Ha Noi, Vietnam, Sept. 24, 1952; arrived in France, 1974; s. Cang Van Nguyen and Dy Thi Vu; m. Martine Françoise Juilleret, Sept. 18, 1979; 3 children. BS in Biochemistry, U. Louis Pasteur, Strasbourg, France, 1979, MS in Molecular Biology, 1980, PhD in Macromolecular Phys. Chemistry, 1983, PhD (D d'Etat) in Phys. Scis., 1986. Postdoctoral rschr. Faculty Medicine, Strasbourg, 1986-87; rsch. scientist Anda Biols. Co., Strasbourg, 1987-97, Neurofit Co., Strasbourg, 1998-99, U. Calif. San Diego Sch. Medicine, 1999—2001, Vista Biols. Corp., Carlsbad, Calif., 2001—. Contbr. articles to profl. jours.; patentee in field. Mem. AAAS, Am. Soc. Microbiology, Am. Chem. Soc., NY Acad. Scis. Address: 14652 Acacia St Westminster CA 92683 Office Phone: 760-438-0230. Personal E-mail: kv52nguyen@yahoo.com.

NGUYEN, LAM HUY, electronics engineer; arrived in US, 1979; s. Quyen Huy Nguyen and Cuc Thi Pham; m. Kim Thu Phan, May 24, 2003; children: Vy Lam, Kim Linh. BSEE, Va. Poly. Inst. and State U., Blacksburg, 1984; MSEE, George Washington U., Washington, 1991; MS in Computer Sci., Johns Hopkins U., Balt., 1994. Design engr. GE, Portsmouth, Va., 1984—85; electronics engr. Harry Diamond Lab., Adelphi, Md., 1985—92; team leader signal processing, microwave br. Army Rsch. Lab., Adelphi, 1992—. Contbr. articles to profl. jours., chapters to books. Recipient R&D Achievement award, US Army, 2006, Sci. and Engring. Excellence award, Army Rsch. Lab., 2005, 2007. Mem.: IEEE, Eta Kappa Nu, Phi Kappa Phi, Tau Beta Pi. Achievements include design and development of several versions of ultra-wideband radar; development of algorithms for SAR signal and image processing. Avocations: guitar, photography. Home: 11568 Jamestown Ct Laurel MD 20723 Office: Army Rsch Lab AMSRD-ARL-SE-RU-Microwave Br 2800 Powder Mill Rd Adelphi MD 20783-1197

NGUYEN, LAN THI HOANG, physician, educator; b. Hai-Duong, Vietnam, July 18, 1950; came to U.S., 1975; d. Thua Nang and Niem Thi (Do) N.; m. Khanh Vinh Quoc, Oct. 15, 1981. MD, U. Kans., 1983. Intern St. Mary Med. Ctr./UCLA, Long Beach, Calif., 1983-84; resident City of Faith Med. Rsch. Ctr.-Oral Roberts Sch. Medicine, Tulsa, 1986-88; fellow VA Med. Ctr.-Wadsworth-UCLA, 1988-90; physician Santa Ana (Calif.) Med. Ctr., Doctors Hosp. Santa Ana, Fountain Valley (Calif.) Regional

Med. Ctr. Clin. assoc. prof. family medicine Keck Sch. Medicine U. So. Calif., LA, 2002—. Contbr. articles to profl. jours. V.p. Vietnamese Am. Med. Rsch. Found. Kans. Med. scholar, 1979-81. Fellow: ACP, Am. Coll. Endocrinology, Am. Coll. Nutrition; mem.: Am. Assn. Clin. Endocrinologists (charter). Office: 14971 Brookhurst St Westminster CA 92683-5556 Office Phone: 714-839-5898.

NGUYEN, RU, entomologist; b. Nhatrang, Khanh Hoa, Vietnam, Dec. 12, 1944; s. Tam Nguyen and Van Thi Le; m. Kim-Dung Thi Nguyen, Jan. 28, 1981; 1 child, Kim-Anh. BS, Coll. Agr., Saigon, Vietnam, 1966; PhD, U. Fla., 1975. Asst. entomologist U. Fla., Gainesville, 1976—78; rsch. fellow Alexander von Humboldt-Stiftung/U. Bonn, Germany, 1978—79; rsch. entomologist, leader USDA-APHIS-PPQ, Ft. Lauderdale, Fla., 1980—82; rsch. entomologist divsn. plant industry Fla. Dept. Agr., Gainesville, 1982—. Mem. Caribbean fruit fly tech. com. Fla. Dept. Agr., 1983—; mem. citrus leafminer task force U. Fla., Gainesville, 1994—98; mem. nat. genetic resources adv. coun. USDA, Washington, 2000—04. Contbr. articles to profl. jours.; author: (book) Catalog of Aleyrodidae on Citrus and Their Natural Enemies, 1993. Recipient Disting. Svc. to Agr. award, Gamma Sigma Delta Honor Soc. of Agr., 1995, Outstanding Achievement award in developing Fly Free Zone, Fla. Dept. Agr. and Consumer Svcs., 1984. Mem.: Fla. Entomol. Soc. (Team Rsch. award 1997, 2007, Achievement award for rsch. 2002), Internat. Orgn. for Biol. Control, Entomol. Soc. Am. Office: Fla Dept Agr Divsn Plant Industry PO Box 147100 Gainesville FL 32614 Personal E-mail: runguyen@aol.com. Business E-Mail: nguyenr@doacs.state.fl.us.

NGUYEN, SAN DUY, psychiatrist, educator; b. Langson, Vietnam, Sept. 25, 1932; arrived in Can., 1971, naturalized, 1977; s. Nguyen Duy and Tran Tuyet, Quyen (Trang) San; m. Eddie Jean Ciesielski, Aug. 24, 1971; children: Thuan Le San, Megan Thuloan San, Muriel Mylinh San, Claire Kimlan San, Robin Xuanlan San, Baodan Edward San. MD, U. Saigon, 1960; postgrad, U. Mich., 1970. Intern Cho Ray Hosp., Saigon, 1957—58; resident Univ. Hosp., Ann Arbor, Mich., 1968—70, Lafayette Clinic, Detroit, 1970—71, Clarke Inst. Psychiatry, Toronto, Ont., Canada, 1971—72; chief of psychiatry S. Vietnamese Army, 1964—68; sr. psychiatrist Queen St. Mental Health Ctr., Toronto, 1972—74; unit dir. Homewood San., Guelph, Ont., 1974—80; cons. psychiatrist Guelph Gen. Hosp., Guelph, 1974—80, St. Joseph's Hosp., Guelph; practice medicine specializing in psychiatry Guelph, 1974—80; unit dir. inpatient svc. Royal Ottawa Hosp., Ont., Canada, 1980—84, dir. psychiat. rehab. program, 1985—87; asst. prof. psychiatry U. Ottawa Med. Sch., 1980—85; assoc. prof. psychiatry, 1985—87; bd. dir. Hong Fook Mental Health Svc., Toronto, 1987—; dir. East-West Mental Health Ctr., Toronto, 1987—; chmn., bd. dir. Access Alliance Multicultural Health Ctr., Toronto, 1988—; cons. UN High Commr. for Refugees, 1987—. Author: Etude du Tetanos au Vietnam, 1960, Psycholsomatic Medicine: Theoretical, Clinical, and Transcultural Aspects, 1983, Uprooting, Loss and Adaptation, 1984—87, S.E. Asian Mental Health, 1985, Ten Years Later: Indochinese Communities in Can., 1988, Refugee Resettlement and Well-Being, 1989; co-author: The Psychology and Physiology of Stress, 1969. Served, 1953—68, Army Republic of Vietnam. Mem.: NY Acad. Sci., Internat. Soc. Hypnosis, Am. Soc. Clin. Hypnosis, Am. Psychiat. Assn., Can. Psychiat. Assn., Can. Med. Assn. Buddhist. Office: 2238 Dundas St W Ste 306 Toronto ON Canada M6R 3A9

NGUYEN, THACH NGOC, cardiologist; b. Feb. 2, 1953; s. Sau Ngoc Nguyen and Hanh Hong Tran. Diploma, Hue Med. Sch., 1978. Diplomate Am. Bd. Internal Medicine, Am. Bd. Cardiovasc. Diseases and Interventional Cardiology. Resident internal medicine Bklyn. Hosp., 1982-85, fellow cardiology, 1985-87; clin. asst. prof. medicine Ind. U. Sch. Medicine, 1992—; dir. cardiovascular rsch. St. Mary Med. Ctr., Hobart, Ind., 1997—, dir. cardiology, 2001—, pres. med. staff, 2002—04, 2006—. Editl. cons. Jour. of Interventional Cardiology, 1998, Vietnamese Med. Jour., 2001; sect. editor Mgmt. of Patients, Lesion & Complication; hon. prof. Inst. Geriatric Cardiology, Chinese PLA Ctrl. Hosp., Beijng, 2004—, Chao Yang Red Cross Hosp., 1998—, Beijing Friendship Hosp., Nanjing U. Hosp., 2006. Editor: Cardiology Today, 1995, Advances and Challenges in Today's Cardiology, 1997, Management of Complex Cardiovascular Problems: The Consultant's Approach, 2002, Spanish edit., 2002, Vietnamese edit., 2002, Practical Handbook of Advanced Interventional Cardiology, 2000;: 3d edit., 2007, Management of Complex Cardiovascular Problems: The Evidence-Based Medicine Approach, 2007; co-editor: Jour. Geriatric Cardiology, 2003. Fellow: ACP, Soc. Cardiovasc. Angiography and Intervention; mem.: Am. Coll. Cardiology (internat. membership task force 2007, internat. com. 2006—). Roman Catholic. Address: 200 E 86th Pl Merrillville IN 46410-6258 Home Phone: 219-872-7275; Office Phone: 219-756-1400. E-mail: thachnguyen2000@yahoo.com.

NGUYEN, THANH TRUC THI, computer animator, educator; d. Chi Thi Tran. MEd, U. Hawaii, 2000, BA, 1993; EdD, U. So. Calif., 2007. Instrnl. designer CRDG, U. Hawaii, Honolulu, 2003—06; asst. specialist CRDG, U.Hawaii, Honolulu, 2006—. Owner TTN Consulting, Honolulu, 1998—. Pres. Roosevelt 1992 Alumni Assn., Honolulu, 2006—07. Recipient John P. Craven Visionary award, Marine Option Program, U. Hawaii, 1996; scholar Bachman scholar, U. Hawaii, Manoa, 1992—94, Unity Ho., 1994—95. Mem.: ASCD, NEA (assoc.), Hawaii Ednl. Rsch. Assn. (pres. 2007), Assn. Ednl. Computing and Tech. (assoc.), Internat. Soc. Tech. in Edn. (assoc.). Office: CRDG Univ Hawaii 1776 University Ave WA 1-101 Honolulu HI 96822 Home Phone: 808-256-6671; Office Phone: 808-956-6507. Office Fax: 808-956-0814. Business E-Mail: nguyen@hawaii.edu.

NGUYEN, THANH-VAN, otolaryngologist; b. Apr. 28, 1966; BS, Stanford U., Calif., 1989; MD, U. Calif., San Francisco, 1993. Diplomate Am. Bd. Otolaryngology. Ear, nose and throat resident Baylor Coll. Medicine, Houston, 1994—2000; pvt. practice Fountain Valley, Calif., 2000—. Mem. editl. rev. bd.: Otolaryngology - Head and Neck Surgery Jour., 1995—99. Recipient 1st pl. residenct basic sci. award, Am. Acad. Otolaryngology, 1996; Outstanding Resident Rsch. grantee, 1995. Fellow: ACS. Office: 10760 Warner Ave Ste 201 Fountain Valley CA 92708

NGUYEN, TUAN, physics educator; BA in Philosophy, U. Detroit Mercy, 1999. Chemistry and physics educator St. Mary's Acad., New Orleans, 2004—05; physics educator MAX Sch., New Orleans, 2005—06, St. Augustine HS, New Orleans, 2006—. Mem. MAX Academic Coun. Mem.: ASCE, AIAA (assoc.; educator assoc. 2005). Business E-Mail: tnguyen@purpleknights.com.

NGUYEN, VAN THUAN, finance educator; s. Bich Van and Om Thi Nguyen. BA in Econ., Odense U., Denmark, 1995—99; MS in Econ., U. So. Denmark, Odense, 1999—2001; PhD in Fin., U. Miss., Oxford, 2001—05. Intern European Commn., European Union, Brussels, 1999—2000; rsch. & tchg. asst. U. Miss., 2001—05; asst. prof. fin. Fairleigh Dickinson U., Madison, NJ, 2005—07, Morgan State U., Balt., 2007—. Author: (book series) Advances in Quantitative Analysis of Finance and Accounting; contbr. articles to profl. jours. Rsch. grant, European Commn., 1999, Standard & Poors, 2004, Travel grant, U. Miss., 2004. Mem.: Profl. Risk Mgrs. Internat. Assn. (assoc.), Fin. Mgmt. Assn. (assoc.), Am. Fin. Assn. (assoc.), Beta Gamma Sigma.

NGUYEN-DINH, THANH, internist, geriatrician, acupuncturist; b. Saigon, Vietnam; s. Bam and Chanh (Thi Duong) Nguyen-Dinh; m. Kim-Chi Nguyen-Dinh; children: Trung, Kim-Trang, Kim-Trinh, Trong. MD, Free U. Brussels, 1974; Tropical MD, Antwerp Tropical Med. Inst., 1975. Diplomate Am. Bd. Internal Medicine, Am. Bd. Geriat. Medicine, Am. Bd. Forensic Examiners, Am. Bd. Forensic Medicine, Coll. Acupuncture and Neuromuscular Therapy, Am. Assn. Integrative Medicine. Asst. prof. medicine Howard Med. Svc., Washington, 1981—2004; physician dir. St. Elizabeth Unit, D.C. Gen. Hosp., Washington, 1983-94. Co-dir. Howard U. Md. Clinics, D.C. Gen. Hosp., 1990-96. Contbr. articles to profl. jours. Fellow ACP, Am. Assn. Integrative Medicine (diplomate). Avocations: chess, swimming. Office: 611 S Carlin Springs Rd Ste 211 Arlington VA 22204-1078 Personal E-mail: drtnd@yahoo.com.

NIBLOCK, ROBERT A., consumer home products company executive; b. Fla., 1962; m. Melanie Niblock; 2 children. BA in Acctg., U. NC. Acct. Ernst & Young, 1986—93; dir. tax Lowe's Companies Inc., Mooresville, NC, sr. dir. tax Mooreville, NC, v.p., treas., 1997—99, sr. v.p. fin. Mooresville, NC, 1999—2000, sr. v.p., CFO, 2000—01, exec. v.p., CFO, 2001—03, pres., 2003—, CEO, chmn., 2005—. Bd. dirs. Lowe's Companies Inc., 2004—. Office: Lowe's Companies Inc 1000 Lowe's Blvd Mooresville NC 28117 *

NICASTRI, ANN GILBERT, science educator; b. NYC, May 26, 1934; d. Ralph and Ruth Gilbert; m. Anthony D. Nicastri, July 2, 1960; children: RuthAnn, Christina, Catherine, Daniel. BA magna cum laude, Bklyn. Coll., 1954; MA, Columbia U., NYC, 1956. Tchg. asst. Barnard Coll., NYC, 1954—55, Columbia Coll., NYC, 1955; tchr. Midwood HS, Bklyn., 1955—60, tchr. AP biology, rsch., 1986—2004; tchr. Balt. Jr. HS, 1960—61, Balt. Jr. Coll., 1961—62, Julia Richman HS, NYC, 1962—63; adj. faculty fellows program, cons. Bklyn. Coll., 2004—. Sci. judge NYC Sci. and Engring. Fair, 2001—; rsch. coord. student projects Midwood H.S., Bklyn., 2003—04. Recipient ISEF Mentor award, USAF, 2004; fellow, NSF, 1957—58, 1959. Mem.: N.Y. Acad. Sci., Kappa Delta Pi, Phi Beta Kappa. Home: 164 Beach 143rd St Neponsit NY 11694 Personal E-mail: agnicastri@aol.com.

NICCHI, VINCENT, JR., cardiologist; b. Bklyn., Nov. 16, 1955; s. Vincent Sr. and Rosalie (Martino) N.; m. Kathleen Mary Healy, May 26, 1985; children: Kristina Rose, Lisa Marie, Michelle Kathleen, Vincent Michael. BS in Chemistry, Bklyn. Coll., 1977; MD, U. Noreste, Tampico Tamps, Mex., 1981. Diplomate Am. Bd. Internal Medicine, Am. Bd. Cardiovasc. Diseases, Am. Bd. Nuc. Cardiology. Intern Maimonides Med. Ctr., Bklyn., 1982-83, resident, 1983-85; fellow in cardiology Deborah Heart Lung Ctr., Browns Mills, NJ, 1985-87; invasive/interventional cardiologist Ariz. Heart Inst., 1987-96; founder Cardiac Care Consultants, Sun City, Ariz., 1996—; mem. staff Boswell Hosp., Sun City. Past chmn. credential com. Del Webb Hosp., Sun City West, Ariz., past mem. med. exec. com. Fellow: Am. Coll. Cardiology; mem.: AMA. Roman Catholic. Office: Cardiac Care Consultants 13188 N 103d Dr Ste 201 Sun City AZ 85351

NICCOL, BRIAN, marketing executive; b. 1974; Brand officer Proctor & Gamble, 1995—2005; v.p. strategic mktg. Pizza Hut, 2005—07; v.p. mktg., strategy and consumer insights Pizza Hut, Yum Brands, 2007—. Named one of 40 Under 40, Advt. Age, 2007. Office: Pizza Hut Inc 14841 Dallas Pkwy Dallas TX 75254 Office Phone: 972-338-7700.

NICCOLLS, WESLEY OLIVER, SR., retired electronics engineering technician; b. Star, Idaho, Jan. 17, 1918; s. Herbert Oliver Niccolls and Hazel Katherine Gillaspy; m. Doris Louise Ball, June 1, 1946; children: James Leslie, Wesley Oliver, Douglas Eldon, Jeffry Herbert, Linda Jane, Barbara Louise, John William. Student, L.A. City Coll., 1938—39, Modesto Jr. Coll., Calif., 1940—42, U.S. Navy Electronics, Treasure Island, Calif., 1943. Radio tech. U.S. Navy Reserve, PTO, 1942—45; tech. advisor electronics supply office U.S. Navy, North Chgo., Ill., 1946—51; electronics engr. tech. Diamond Ordnance Fuze Lab., Washington, 1951—70. Co-author: Natural Breakdown of Planar Jets. Achievements include design and construction of production inspection instrumentation for Smart Bomb fuze; design of electronic circuits in TOW anti-tank missile; fluidics pitch-a-yaw sensing device; patent for the latest major class of direct current motors known as brushless DC motors first used in all space vehicles and the robotics industry; patents for neon photoconductor ring oscillator circuit; photoelectric ring oscillator circuit with voltage doubler; low and high pressure steam whistle; patents pending in fields of desalinization and nuclear waste disposal. Home: 508 S 25th St Arlington VA 22202 Fax: 703-418-1829.

NICE, CARTER, conductor; b. Jacksonville, Fla., Apr. 5, 1940; s. Clarence Carter and Elizabeth Jane (Hintermister) N.; m. Jennifer Charlotte Smith, Apr. 4, 1983; children: Danielle, Christian, Olivia. MusB, Eastman Sch. Music, 1962; MusM, Manhattan Sch. Music, 1964. Asst. condr., concert master New Orleans Philharm., 1967-79; condr., music dir. Sacramento Symphony, 1979-92; music dir., condr. Bear Valley Music Fest., 1985—. Office: 579 Kevington Ct Sacramento CA 95864 Office Phone: 916-973-1138. Personal E-mail: ccniii@aol.com.

NICELY, DONNA D., library director; BA, Boston U., 1969; MA in Tchg., Emory U., 1970, M in Librarianship, 1975, diploma in Librarianship, 1987. Asst. dir. DeKalb County Pub. Libr., Decatur, Ga., 1982—91, 1991—95; dir. Nashville Pub. Libr., 1995—. Del. mems. coun. Online Computer Libr. Ctr.; chair exec. bd. Urban Librs. Coun. Contbr. articles to profl. publs. Mem. edn. com. Country Music Found., bd. dirs., Downtown Nashville Partnership, NashvilleREAD, African Am. Hist. Found. Nashville, Inc., Nashville Alliance Pub. Edn. Office: Nashville Pub Libr 615 Church St Nashville TN 37219 Office Phone: 615-862-5760. E-mail: donna.nicely@nashville.gov.

NICHOL, GENE RAY, JR., academic administrator, law educator; b. Dallas, May 11, 1951; s. Gene R. and Dolores (Dumas) N.; m. Janet Castle, Aug. 20, 1973 (div. 1978); m. Glenn George, Nov. 25, 1984. BA in Philosophy, Okla. State U., 1973; JD, U. Texas, 1976. Bar: Alaska 1978. Assoc. Ely, Guess and Rudd, Anchorage, 1976-78; asst. prof. W.Va. U., Morgantown, 1978-80, assoc. prof., 1980-82; prof. law U. Fla., Gainesville, 1983-84; Cutler prof. law, dir. Inst. of Bill of Rights Law Coll. William and Mary, Williamsburg, W.Va., 1984-88; dean U. Colo. Law Sch., 1988-95; dean, Burton Craige prof. law U. NC Sch. of Law, 1999—2005; pres. Coll. William & Mary, Williamsburg, Va., 2005—. Host Culture Wars, KBDI T.V., Denver, 1995-96. Author: (with M. Redish) Federal Courts; columnist: Rocky Mt. News, 1999-2000, Raleigh News and Observer, 2000-04; contbr. articles to profl. jours. Posten research grantee U. W.Va., 1980, 81, 82. Mem. Nat. Lawyers Guild (coms. 1978, vice chair Colo. reapportionment commn.), Am. Law Inst., ACLU (coms. 1978—), Am. Bar Found. Fellows, Order of Coif. Roman Catholic. Avocation: back packing. Office: Coll of William and Mary Office of Pres PO Box 8795 Williamsburg VA 23187-8795 E-mail: gnichol@wm.edu. *

NICHOLAS, ARTHUR SOTERIOS, manufacturing executive; b. Grand Rapids, Mich., Mar. 6, 1930; s. Samuel D. and Penelope A. (Kalapodes) N.; m. Bessie Zazanis, Aug. 25, 1957; children: Niki Stephanie, Arthur S., Thomas. BS in Chem. Engring, U. Mich., 1953; BA in Indsl. Mgmt, Wayne State U., 1957. Registered profl. engr., Mich. Project engr. B.F. Goodrich Co., 1953-54; plant mgr. Cadillac Plastics and Chem. Co., 1954-69; pres., chief exec. officer Leon Chem. and Plastics, Inc., Grand Rapids, 1960-69; with U.S. Industries, Inc., 1969-73, pres., chief operating officer, 1973; now pres. The Antech Group. Bd. dirs. ERO Industries, Inc. Patentee in field. Judge Jr. Achievement, Chgo. Served with USNR, 1948-49. Recipient Distinguished Alumni award Grand Rapids Jr. Coll., 1970 Mem. Young Pres. Orgn., Soc. Plastic Engrs., Mich. Acad. Sci., Arts and Letters, Chgo. Coun. on Fgn. Rels., Pres.' Assn. Mem. Greek Orthodox Ch. Clubs: Chgo. Athletic Assn. (Chgo.), Executives (Chgo.). Office: 2300 Barrington Rd # 411 Hoffman Estates IL 60195-2082 Home: 467 Park Barrington Barrington IL 60010 Personal E-mail: anicholas@aol.com.

NICHOLAS, BLAIR, lawyer; b. Mesa, Ariz., July 9, 1970; BA in Economics, U. Calif., Santa Barbara, 1992; JD, U. San Diego, 1995. Bar: Calif. 1995, US Dist. Ct., Southern Dist. Calif. 1996, US Dist. Ct., Northern Dist. Calif. 1996, US Dist. Ct., Ctrl. Dist. Calif. 1996, US Dist. Ct., Ariz., US Ct. of Appeals, Ninth Cir. 1996. Ptnr. Bernstein Litowitz Berger & Grossmann LLP, San Diego. Named one of Litigation's Rising Stars, The Am. Lawyer, 2007. Mem.: Consumer Attorneys of San Diego, Assn. Bus. Trial Lawyers, San Diego Fed. Bar Assn. (v.p.), San Diego County Bar Assn. Office: Bernstein Litowitz Berger & Grossmann LLP 12481 High Bluff Dr Ste 300 San Diego CA 92130 Office Phone: 858-793-0070. Office Fax: 858-793-0323. *

NICHOLAS, FREDERICK M., lawyer; b. NYC, May 30, 1920; s. Benjamin L. and Rose F. (Nechols) Nicholas; m. Eleanore Berman, Sept. 2, 1951 (div. 1963); children: Deborah, Jan, Tony; m. Joan Fields, Jan. 2, 1983. AB, U. So. Calif., 1947; postgrad., U. Chgo., 1949-50; JD, U. So. Calif., 1952. Bar: Calif. 1952, US Dist. Ct. Calif. 1952, US Ct. Appeals (9th cir.) 1952. Assoc. Loeb & Loeb, LA, 1952-56; ptnr. Swerdlow, Glikbarg & Nicholas, Beverly Hills, Calif., 1956-62; pvt. practice Beverly Hills, 1962-80; pres., atty. Hapsmith Co., Beverly Hills, 1980—. Gen. counsel Beverly Hills Realty Bd., 1971—79; founder, pres. Pub. Counsel, LA, 1970—73. Author: Setting Up a Shopping Center, 1960, Commercial Real Property Lease Practice, 1976. Chmn. Mus. Contemporary Art, LA, 1987—93, life trustee, 2002—; chmn. com. Walt Disney Concert Hall, LA, 1987—95; trustee Music Ctr. Los Angeles County, 1987—95, L.A. Philharm. Assn., 1987—95, Mus. Flying, Santa Monica, Calif., 1991—2002, Frederick R. Weisman Art Found., 2003—, Frederick R. Weisman Philanthropic Found., 2003—, Pitzer Coll., 1992—95, Art Ctr. Coll. Design, 2003—; chmn. Calif. Pub. Broadcasting Commn., Sacramento, 1972—78; pres. Maple Ctr., 1977—79; co-developer Ronald Reagan Bldg., Washington, 1998; adminstr. Estate of Sam Francis, 1996—. With US Army, 1941—46, capt. US Army, 1946. Named Citizen of the Yr., Beverly Hills Bd. Realtors, 1978, Man of the Yr., Maple Ctr., 1980, Outstanding Founder in Philanthropy, Nat. Philanthropy Day Com., 1990; recipient Pub. Svc. award, Coro Found., 1988, Medici award, LA C. of C., 1990, Founders award, Pub. Counsel, 1990, Trustees award, Calif. Inst. Arts, 1993, City of Angels award, LA Ctrl. Bus. Assn., Disting. Svc. award, U. So. Calif. Law Sch. Class of 1952, 2002, Parkison Spirit of Urbanism award, U. So. Calif. Archtl. Guild, 2004, Equal Justice Advocacy award, ACLU Found., 2005, AIA LA Cmty. Svc. award, 2006. Mem.: Beverly Hills Bar Assn. (bd. govs. 1970—76, Disting. Svc. award 1974, 1981, Exceptional Svc. award 1986, 2004), Beverly Hills C. of C. (Man of the Yr. 1983). Home: 1001 Maybrook Dr Beverly Hills CA 90210-2715 Office: Hapsmith Co 3844 Culver Center St Ste B Culver City CA 90232 Business E-Mail: fmnicholas@hapsmithco.com.

NICHOLAS, HENRY THOMPSON, III, former electronics company executive; b. 1959; BSEE, MSEE, UCLA, PhD in EE. With TRW; dir. microelectronics PairGain Techs.; co-founder, pres., CEO Broadcom Corp., Irvine, Calif., 1991—2003. Named one of Top 20 Entrepreneurs, 1997 Red Herring, 1997, World's Top Cyber Elite, 1997 Time Digital Mag., 1997; recipient Engrepreneur of the Yr. award, Ernst & Young, 1996, Forbes Richest Americans, 2006.

NICHOLAS, LAWRENCE BRUCE, company executive; b. Dallas, Nov. 9, 1945; s. J. W. and Helen Elouise (Whiteacre) N.; m. Virginia Pearl Farmer, Aug. 5, 1967; children: Helen Brooke, John Lawrence, Alexis Bradlee. BBA, So. Meth. U., 1968. Mem. sales staff Nicholas Machinery Co., Dallas, 1963-69; sales mgr. Indsl. and Comml. Rsch. Corp., Dallas, 1969-74; v.p. Precision Concepts Corp., Dallas, 1974-76, gen. mgr., 1976-78, pres. Addison, Tex., 1978-86, INCOR Inc., Addison, 1974-91, dir.; pres. The Octagon Group Corp., 2006—. Pres., dir. Multiple Axis Machine Corp., 1981-96, Investment Svcs. Corp., 1991-93; mem. adv. bd. Consultores Patrimoniales, Mex. City, 1992-2007; pres. Equity Capital Interests, Inc., San Antonio, Tex., 1993—; chmn. bd. dirs. Cross Securities Internat. Corp., San Antonio, 1993-94; pres. Worldwide Exec. Aviation, San Antonio, 1996—; bd. dirs. Sea Hawke Yachte Ltd., Can., 2003-. Served as officer Ordnance Corps, U.S. Army, 1968, N.G., 1968-74. Mem. NRA, Soc. Mfg. Engrs., Nat. Shooting Sports Found., Safari Club Internat., World Affairs Coun. San Antonio, Petroleum Club San Antonio.

NICHOLAS, LEONARD G., music educator; b. Phila., May 1, 1957; m. Jan Lee Wilson, July 20, 1985; children: Leonard Charles, Christopher Lee. MusB, B in Music Edn., U. Arts, Phila., 1980; MS in Applied Tech., Chestnut Hill Coll., Pa., 2002. Cert. K-12 music tchr. Pa., 1980, NJ, 1980. Lead tchr. instrumental music dept. Lenape HS, Medford, NJ, 1980—. Condr. (mid. sch. symphonic band) All S. Jersey Band & Orch. Dirs., Glassboro, NJ, (HS jazz band) All S. Jersey Jazz Educator Assn., Medford, NJ. Recipient Tchr. of Yr. award, Lenape Regional HS Dist., 2001—02; Pair & Share grant, NJ Dept. Edn., 2000, Tech. grant, Bell Atlantic, 1997. Mem.: Tech. Inst. Music Educators, Internat. Assn. Jazz Educators (auditions chmn. 1997—), Music Educator Nat. Conf. Office: Lenape HS 235 Hartford Rd Medford NJ 08055 Business E-Mail: lnicholas@irhsd.org.

NICHOLAS, LYNN B., medical association administrator; b. Tenn. BS in med. tech., Tenn. Wesleyan Coll.; M in mgmt., Cent. Mich. U., 1983. Bd. cert. fellow Am. Coll. Healthcare Exec. (ACHE). Med. technologist to sr. v.p. clinical and ambulatory svc. Morristown Meml. Hosp., NJ; exec. v.p., COO NJ Hosp. Assn., 1995—2000; pres., CEO La. Hosp. Assn., 2000—04; CEO Am. Diabetes Assn., Alexandria, Va., 2004—. Mem. bd. gov. Am. Coll. Healthcare Exec.; chair La. Health Works Commn.; mem. La. Health Care Commn.; rep. La. hosp. Am,. Hosp. Assn. Recipient Early Career Healthcare Exec. award (first recipient in NJ), Am. Coll. Healthcare Exec. Office: Am Diabetes Assn 1701 N Beauregard St Alexandria VA 22311 Office Phone: 703-549-1500, 800-342-2383. Office Fax: 703-739-9346.

NICHOLAS, LYNN HOLMAN, historian, researcher, writer; b. New London, Conn., Nov. 11, 1939; d. William Grizzard Holman and Carol (Ackiss) Wakelin; m. Robert Carter Nicholas III, Dec. 20, 1965; children: William C., R. Carter, Philip H. Student, Radcliffe Coll., 1957-59; diploma, U. Madrid, 1960; BA, Oxford U., Eng., 1964. Mem. adv. panel Presdl. Commn. on Holocaust Assets in the U.S., 1999. Author: The Rape of Europa: The Fate of Europe's Treasures in the Third Reich and the Second World War, 1994 (Nat. Book Critics Circle award 1995), Cruel World: The Children of Europe in the Nazi Web, 2005. Decorated chevalier Légion d'Honneur (France); named Amicus Poloniae, Govt. of Poland, 2003. Personal E-mail: lynnick105@aol.com.

NICHOLAS, NICHOLAS CONSTANTINE, retired military officer; b. Balt., Apr. 20, 1929; s. Constantine and Helene (Kalymnin) Nicholas; m. Sammie Ruth Vick (div.); children: Carolyn H., Lois E. stepchildren: Deborah L., Jana D.; m. Linda Lee Elkins, Sept. 2, 1977. BA, U. Md., 1952; MA, U. Okla., 1973; attended, USAF Sch. Aviation Medicine, 1956, USAF Sch. Aerospace Medicine, 1975. Commissioned 2d lt. USAF, Coll. Pk., Md., 1952; observor B-36 and B-52 aircraft Ramey AFB, PR; observor B-36 and B-52 Aircraft Carswell AFB, Tex., 1954; comdr. 4th Physiological Tng. Flight, Carswell AFB, Tex., 1956—63; chief physiological tng. unit Little Rock AFB, Ark., 1963—66; command coord. aerospace physiology Hdqs. Strategic Air Command, Omaha, 1966—70, Pacific Air Force and Comdr. 15th Physiological Training Unit Kadena AFB, 1970—72;

chief dept. medicine USAF Sch. of Health Care Scis. Sheppard AFB, 1972—76; chief med. sys. div. Office of Se. of Def., Washington, 1976—78; chief Health Policy and Programs Divsn., 1978—84, Biomed. Sci. Corps., 1981—84. Cons. aerospace physiology Surgeons General USAF, Wash., DC, 1977—88, cons. med. edn. and tng., 1977—88; cons. MedTech Comm. Inc., NYC. Author: Use of Modified Partial Pressure Suits to Aleviate Orthostatic Hypotension, 1962; co-author: Human Decompression Tests for B-58 Escape Capsule System, 1964, USAF/USN Physician Assistant Program: Military Medicine, 1977. Pres. Young Dem. Club, Coll. Pk, Md., 1950—52; delegate State Convention Young Dem. Club, Anapolis, Md., 1951, Nat. Convention Young Dem. Club, St. Louis, 1951; mem. Inauguaral Gala for Pres. Truman, Wash., DC, 1949. Col. USAF, 1952—84. Decorated Commendation medals (2) Air Force, Meritorious Svc. medals, Air medal, Outstanding Unit awards (4) Air Force, Outstanding Unit award, Armed Forces Expeditionary medal, Joint Svc. Commendation medal, Legion of Merit, Nat. Defense Svc. medal, Vietnam Svc. medal with 5 Clusters, Vietnam Gallantry Cross with one Bronze Star, Vietnam Campaign medal with one Silver Star; recipient Men's League award Outstanding Achievement and Svc. to U., U. Md., 1950. Mem.: Arnold Air Soc., Scabbard and Blade, Aerospace Physiologist Soc., Assn. Mil. Surgeons of US, Mil. Officers Assn. (life), Air Force Assn. (life), Aerospace Medicine Assn. (life), Phi Alpha Theta, Omicron Delta Kappa, Phi Kappa Tau. Episcopalian. Avocations: walking, reading. Home: 8724 Racquet Club Dr Fort Worth TX 76120 Personal E-mail: nicholasn101@charter.net.

NICHOLAS, PETER M., medical products executive; married; 3 children. BS, Duke U.; MS, U. Pa. Former corp. dir. mktg., gen. mgr. med. products divsn. Millipore Corp.; various sales, mktg., and gen. mgmt. positions Eli Lily and Co.; co-chmn. bd. Boston Sci., Natick, Mass., 1979—95, CEO, 1979—99, chmn. bd., 1995—. Chmn. bd. trustees, mem. bd. exec. com. Duke U.; mem. Mass. Bus. Roundtable, Mass. Bus. High Tech. Coun., CEOs for Fundamental Change in Edn., Boys and Girls Club Boston. Named one of World's Richest People, Forbes Mag., 2001—04. Fellow: Nat. Acad. Arts and Scis. (trustee); mem.: Boys and Girls Club, Boston, CEOs Fundamental Change Edn., Mass. Bus. High Tech. Coun., Mass. Bus. Roundtable. Office: Boston Sci 1 Boston Sci Pl Natick MA 01760-1537 *

NICHOLAS, RALPH WALLACE W., anthropologist, educator; b. Dallas, Nov. 28, 1934; s. Ralph Wendell and Ruth Elizabeth (Oury) N.; m. Marta Ruth Weinstock, June 13, 1963. BA, Wayne U., 1957; MA, U. Chgo., 1958, PhD, 1962. From asst. prof. to prof. Mich. State U., East Lansing, 1964-71; prof. anthropology U. Chgo., 1971—, chmn. dept., 1981-82, dep. provost, 1982-87, dean of coll., 1987-92, dir. Ctr. Internat. Studies, 1984-95, William Rainey Harper prof. anthropology and social scis., 1992-2000, William Rainey Harper prof. emeritus, 2000—; pres. Internat. House of Chgo., 1993-2000. Cons. Ford Found., Dhaka, Bangladesh, 1973 Author: (with others) Kinship Bengali Culture, 1977, The Fruits of Worship, 2003; editor: Jour. Asian Studies, 1975-78. Sec. Coun. Am. Overseas Rsch. Ctrs., 2005—; v.p. Am. Inst. Indian Studies, 1974—76, treas., 1993—2001, pres.-elect, 2001—02, pres., 2002—; trustee Bangladesh Found., 1972—2005; dir. Indo-Am. Ctr., Chgo. Ford Found. fgn. area tng. fellow, India, 1960-61; Sch. Oriental and African Studies research fellow, London, 1962-63; sr. Fulbright fellow, West Bengal, India, 1968-69 Fellow AAAS, Am. Anthrop. Assn., Royal Anthrop. Inst. (Eng.); mem. Assn. Asian Studies, India League of Am. Found. (trustee). Office: U Chgo Dept Anthropology 1126 E 59th St Chicago IL 60637-1580 also: Am Inst Indian Studies 1130 E 59th St Chicago IL 60637

NICHOLAS, ROBERT A., lawyer; BA magna cum laude, Amherst Coll., 1976; JD, Columbia U., 1980. Bar: NY 1981, Pa. 1985. Asst. dist. atty. Manhattan Dist. Atty.'s Office, 1980—85; with Reed Smith LLP, 1985—, former head Del. Valley Region litig. group, mng. ptnr. Phila. and Wilmington offices, 2000—07, mem. exec. com., mng. ptnr. NY office, 2007—. Bd. mem. World Affairs Coun. of Phila. Office: Reed Smith LLP 599 Lexington Ave 29th Fl New York NY 10022 Office Fax: 212-521-5450. *

NICHOLAS, STEPHEN J., orthopedic surgeon, sports medicine physician; BA in Biology, Harvard U., Cambridge, Mass., 1982; MD, NY Med. Coll., Valhalla, NY, 1986. Dir. Nicholas Inst. Sports Medicine and Athletic Trama, Lenox Hill Hosp., NYC, 2001—; chief, bioskills lab. Lenox Hill Hosp., NYC. Mem. adv. bd., Med. Leadership Coun. Lenox Hill Hosp.; worked extensively with profl. and collegiate athletes; orthopaedist NY Jets, NY Islanders, Hofstra U., & NJ Galdiators. Mem. NYC Sports Commn.; mem. alumni adv. bd. NY Med. Coll. Mem.: AMA, Am. Orthopaedic Assn., Quigley Orthopedic Soc., Med. Soc. State NY, Greater Met. Sports Medicine Soc., Am. Orthopedic Soc. for Sports Medicine (mem. publs. com.), Am. Acad. Orthopedic Surgeons. Office: 130 E 77th St New York NY 10021 Office Phone: 212-737-3301.

NICHOLAS, THOMAS ANDREW, artist; b. Middletown, Conn., Sept. 26, 1934; s. Michael and Lena (Sequenzia) N.; m. Gloria R. Spencer, Oct. 11, 1958; 1 child, Thomas Michael. Student of Ernst Lohrmann, 1949-53; scholarship student, Sch. Visual Arts, NYC, 1953-55. Instr. Famous Artists Schs., Inc., Westport, Conn., 1958-60; instr. painting, Rockport, Mass., 1963-66. Commd. by Franklin Mint Gallery Am. Art to produce lithographs of Am. coastline, 1977; one-man shows include Grand Cen. Galleries, NYC, 1962, 64, 66, 68, 70, 78, I.F.A. Galleries, Washington, 1964-92, A. Huney Gallery, San Diego, 1980, 82;, Carolyn Hill Gallery, Soho, NYC, 1988-89, 3 person show, 1992; represented in permanent collections Butler Inst. Am. Art, Youngstown, Ohio, Ga. Mus., Athens, New Britain Art Mus., Conn., U. Utah, Adelphi U., Greenshields Mus., Montreal, Can., Farnsworth Mus., Rockland, Maine, Springfield Art Mus., Mo., Ranger Collection at NAD, Peabody Mus., Salem, Mass., Hispanic Soc. Am., Peter A. Juley and Son Collection, Nat. Mus. Am. Art, Smithsonian Inst., Washington, NYC. Recipient Key to City, Middle-Sex County C. of C., 1989, Gold medal honor New Eng. Watercolor Soc., Boston, 1985, Acad. Artists Assn., 1985, Emile Lowe award Am. Watercolor Soc. 1961, watercolor prize 1964, Gold medal honor 1969, Clare Stout award 1971, Mary S. Litt award 1972, medal honor for watercolor Knickerbocker Artists 1962, Purchase award watercolor Butler Inst. Am. Art 1962, Henry Ward Ranger Fund purchase watercolor NAD 1962, 71, Obrig prize watercolor 1964, 66, 79, 87, Gold medal honor watercolor Allied Artists Am. 1962, Grumbacher prize 1978, Today Mag. Art medal 1970, 74, Gold medal honor watercolor Am. Artists Profl. League 1964, best landscape award 1974, Gold medal 1978, Edwin S. Webster award honor watercolor Boston Soc. Watercolor 1964, gold medal honor watercolor Hudson Valley Art Assn. 1964, 74, DuMond Meml. award 1971, Isabel Stinschneider Meml. award 1972, Herman Wick Meml. award Salmagundi Club, NYC, 1966, 2d prize 1966, June Justin J. Impasto award 1972, Arthur T. Hill prize 1973, Arthur T. Hill Meml. prize 1975, Louis Z. Seley prize 1978, Gwynne Lennon prize 1979, Gold medal honor oil Rockport Art Assn. 1966, 1969, 1976, 1985, 1996, 1997, 1999, 2002, 03, 04, 07, cash award Wichita Centennial Watercolor 1970, Providence Art Club prize 1972, Gold medal Franklin Mint Competition 1974, Gold medal Honor Acad. Assn. 1976, Grumbacher award watercolor, Acad. Artists Assn., 1990, Grumbacher Gold medal Gouache New Eng. Watercolor Soc., 1992, Gouache Transparent Watercolor, 1995, others; named Knickerbocker Honoree Artist of Yr., 1989; Elizabeth Greenshields grantee, 1961, 62. Mem. NAD (assoc. 1963-70, academician, 1970-, cert. merit watercolor 1992), Am. Watercolor Soc. (ea. v.p. 1994—, Dolphin fellow), Boston Watercolor Soc., Conn. Watercolor Socs., Allied Artists Am., Knickerbocker Artists (dir.'s prize 1971, Gold medal 1989), Boston Guild Artists (Grumbacher Gold medallion award watercolor 1988, No. Shore Arts Assn. award oil 1991), Rockport Art Assn. (George O. Davies Meml. Silver medal 1988, 94, Darrand award oil 1992, Cirino award 1st prize Gouache 1992, Clark Polupar award Gouache 1992, Cooley award graphics 1995, Clark Popular award Gouache 1995, Cirino award Gouache 1995, Davis Meml. award watercolor 1996, Mills Meml. award Gouache 1996), Hudson Valley Artists (Gold medal 1974, 85, 94, Huntington Meml. award oil 1995, Bohnert Meml. award oil 1996), Hudson Valley Art Assn. (honoree 2000). Office: Tom Nicholas Gallery 65 Main St Rockport MA 01966-1512 Office Phone: 978-546-9647. Personal E-mail: tangallery@aol.com. *I have been fortunate to have been encouraged by my family at an early age and have a number of people to thank for their support, especially my wife. I feel artists must never compromise their ideals and principles, no matter how high their standards. Originality and professional ethics with one's work make goals achieved meaningful. On the one hand, an artist should inwardly feel that there is little he can't accomplish, and yet he must learn to work within his realized limitations.*

NICHOLAS, THOMAS PETER, municipal official; b. Laramie, Wyo., Dec. 6, 1948; s. Thomas Lloyd Nicholas and Frances (Collins) Chambers; m. Tanya Michelle Villont; 1 child, Ja'el Michelle. AA in Fine Arts, Cabrillo Coll., 1970; BA in English, U. Colo., 1972; MS in Librarianship and Info. Sci., U. Denver, 1982. V.p. Nicholas Properties, Denver, 1971—77; real estate salesperson Sun Country, Lakewood, Colo., 1972—74; libr. City of Aurora, Colo., 1975—80, sys. support mgr. Colo., 1981—83, dir. libr. and TV svcs. Colo., 1984—95, dir. libr., recreation & TV svcs., 1995—2000, dir. libr., recreation and cultural svcs., 2000—. Pres. bd. Irving Libr. Network Inc., Denver, 1985; adv. CL Sys. Inc., Boston, 1985; acting pers. dir. City of Aurora. Exec. prodr. TV progs.: Election Night 85 (Franny award 1986), Miss Plumjoy's Pl., 1988 (Starwards 1988), Aurora's Can't Afford Not To, 1988 (Starwards 1988). Mem. exec. bd., chmn. Arapahoe Pub. Access to Librs., 1984-85; site coord. Am. Cancer Soc., Aurora, 1988; adv. Youth at Risk, Aurora, 1989; bd. dirs. Ctrl. Colo. Libr. Sys., Lakewood, 1985-87; mem. exec. bd. Colo. Libr. Legis. Com., Denver, 1988; pres. Greater Metro Cable Consortium, 1992; acting dep. city mgr. City of Aurora, 1993. Recipient Denver Regional Coun. Govt. award for Cmty. Svc. and Govt. Coop., 1995. Mem. ALA, Colo. Libr. Assn. (adv. 1982-83, dir. libr., recreation and TV 1995, Programming award 1982, 1st Colo. Childrens Prog. award 1983, 88), Nat. Assn. Telecom. Officers and Advs. (regional pres. 1983-84, TV Prog. award 1986), Rotary (prog. chmn. 1987-88, v.p. 1997-98), Eastgate Lions Club (pres. 1989-90), pres. elect Gatway Rotary, 1998. Democrat. Greek Orthodox. Avocations: art, poetry, auto restoration, martial arts. Office: Aurora Pub Libr 14949 E Alameda Pky Aurora CO 80012-1500 Office Phone: 303-739-6600. E-mail: library@auroragov.org.

NICHOLAS, WILLIAM RICHARD, lawyer; b. Pontiac, Mich., June 19, 1934; s. Reginald and Edna Irene (Bartlett) N.; m. Diana Lee Johnson, Aug. 20, 1960; children: Susan Lee, William Richard Jr. BS in Bus., U. Idaho, 1956; JD, U. Mich., 1962. Bar: 1963. Of counsel Latham & Watkins, Los Angeles, 1962-96. Contbr. numerous articles on taxation. Lt. (j.g.) USN, 1956-59. Mem. Calif. Bar Assn., Los Angeles County Bar Assn., Am. Coll. Tax Counsel. Home: 1808 Old Ranch Rd Los Angeles CA 90049-2207 Office: Latham & Watkins 633 W 5th St Ste 4000 Los Angeles CA 90071-2005 Office Phone: 310-485-1234.

NICHOLL, JEFFREY SCOTT, neurologist, educator; b. Stamford, Conn., Aug. 13, 1949; s. Robert George and Helen Holmes (Wilson) N.; m. Katherine Maris Mattes, Mar. 2, 1996; 1 child, Colleen Marie. BA, U. Pa., 1970; MD, Georgetown U., 1974. Diplomate in psychiatry, neurology, and clin. neurophysiology Am. Bd. Psychiatry and Neurology, Am. Bd. Emergency Medicine, Am. Bd. Clin. Neurophysiology. Intern Hosp. of the Good Samaritan, LA, 1974—75; resident in psychiatry UCLA, 1975—77, 1978—79, fellow in epilepsy, 1998—2000; fellow in consultation-liaison psychiatry U. Calif., Irvine, 1979—80; emergency physician various instns, Calif., 1979—87, Kaiser-Permanente, San Diego, 1987—95; resident in neurology Tulane U., New Orleans, 1995—98, assoc. prof. clin. neurology and psychiatry, 2000—; clin. instr. neurology UCLA, 1998—2000. Avocations: sailing, swimming. Office: Tulane U Sch Medicine TB 52 1440 Canal St New Orleans LA 70112 Office Phone: 504-988-6669. Personal E-mail: jsnichollmd@yahoo.com.

NICHOLLS, PETER J., academic administrator; BS in Math., London U., 1967; PhD in Math., Cambridge U., Eng., 1970. Prof. math. scis. No. Ill. U., 1971—91, acting dean Coll. Liberal Arts and Scis., 1988—89, assoc. dean Coll. Liberal Arts and Scis., 1987—88, 1989—91; dean Coll. Arts and Scis. Kans. State U., 1991—2002, prof. math., 1991—2002; provost, acad. v.p. Colo. State U., Ft. Collins, 2002—05; provost, exec. v.p. U. Conn., Storrs, 2005—. Office: Office of the Provost U Conn 352 Mansfield Rd Unit 2086 Storrs Mansfield CT 06269-2086 Office Phone: 860-486-4037.

NICHOLLS, RALPH WILLIAM, physicist, researcher; b. Richmond, Surrey, Eng., May 3, 1926; s. Williams James and Evelyn Mabel (Jones) Nicholls; m. Doris Margaret McEwen, June 28, 1952. BSc, Imperial Coll., U. London, 1945, PhD, 1951, DSc in Spectroscopy, 1961. Sr. demonstrator in astrophysics Imperial Coll., U. London, 1945-48; instr. physics U. Western Ont. (Can.), London, 1948-50, lectr. physics, 1950-52, asst. prof. physics, 1952-56, assoc. prof., 1956-58, prof., 1958-63, sr. prof., 1963-65; prof. York U., Toronto, 1965—, Disting. Rsch. prof. physics, 1983-96, Disting. Rsch. prof. physics emeritus, 1996—, chmn. dept. physics, 1965-69; dir. Centre for Rsch. in Earth and Space Sci., 1965-92, dir. emeritus, 1996—; dir. atmospheric physics lab. Inst. for Space and Terrestrial Sci., 1987-94. Vis scientist Nat. Bur. Stds., 1959; vis. prof. Stanford U., 1964, 68, 73, 90. Author (with B. H. Armstrong): (book) Emission, Absorption and Transfer of Radiation in Heated Atmospheres, 1972; editor: Can. Jour. Physics, 1986—92; editor: (assoc. editor) JQSRT Jour., 1960—; contbr. Decorated officer Order of Can.; Walter Gordon rsch. fellow, York U., 1982—83. Fellow: U.K. Inst. Physics, Can. Aero. and Space Inst., Am. Phys. Soc., Optical Soc. Am., Royal Soc. Can. Home: 9 Pinevale Rd Thornhill ON Canada L3T 1J5 Office: York U 4700 Keele St North York ON Canada M3J 1P3 Home Phone: 905-889-5093; Office Phone: 416-736-5247. Business E-Mail: nicholls@yorku.ca.

NICHOLLS, RICHARD AURELIUS, retired obstetrician, gynecologist; b. Norfolk, Va., Aug. 12, 1941; s. Richard Beddoe and Aurelia (Gill) Nicholls; m. Geri Bowden, Feb. 24, 1986. BS in Biology, Stetson U., Deland, Fla., 1963; MD, Med. Coll. Va., 1967. Diplomate Am. Bd. Ob-Gyn. Ret., 1998; intern Charity Hosp. Tulane divsn., New Orleans, 1967—68, resident in ob-gyn., 1968—71; asst. prof. ob-gyn. Tulane Med. Sch., New Orleans, 1973—74, clin. asst. prof., 1974—83; pvt. practice specializing in ob-gyn. Pascagoula, Miss., 1974—89, Ocean Spring, Miss., 1989—98; ret. Mem. staff Singing River Hosp., chmn. surg. and ob-gyn. depts., 1979—80, chmn. ob-gyn. dept., 1984; mem. staff Ocean Springs Hosp., laser com., pharmacy com. and therapeutics com., chmn. ob -gyn. dept., mem. exec. bd., 1990—91, sec., treas. staff, 1991—92, exec. bd., 1991—92, chief staff, 1993—94. Contbr. articles to profl. jours. Bd. dirs. Miss Racing Assn. Maj. US Army, 1971—73. Fellow: ACS, ACOG; mem.: Am. Cancer Soc. (bd. dirs. Jackson County br.), Am. Veneral Disease Soc., Conrald Collins Ob-Gyn Soc., Gulf Coast Ob-Gyn. Soc., New Orleans Ob-Gyn Soc., New Orleans Grad. Me4d. Assembly, So. Med. Soc., AMA, Am. Assn. Gynecol. Laparoscopists, Am. Fertility Soc., Singing River Med. Soc., Miss. State Med. Soc. Personal E-mail: nichollg1@bellsouth.net.

NICHOLS, ALBERT L., economic consultant; b. Poughkeepsie, NY, Feb. 13, 1951; s. Albert and Margaret (Schaefer) N.; m. Eve Kaufman, June 16, 1973; children: Matthew, Elizabeth. AB, Stanford U., 1973; M of Pub. Policy, Harvard U., 1975, PhD, 1981. Assoc. prof. Harvard U., Cambridge, Mass., 1977-83, 85-88, dir. adminstrv. planning, 1988-89; dir. econ. analysis EPA, Washington, 1983-85; v.p. Nat. Econ. Rsch. Assocs., Cambridge, 1989—2004; dir. LECG, LLC, Cambridge, 2004—. Author: Targeting Economic Incentives for Environmental Protection, 1984; contbr. numerous articles to profl. jours. Nat. Merit scholar, 1969. Mem. ABA, AAAS, Am. Econ. Assn., Phi Beta Kappa. Avocation: woodworking. Home: 14 Baskin Rd Lexington MA 02421-6929 Office Phone: 617-761-0152. E-mail: anichols@lecg.com.

NICHOLS, ALBERT MYRON, retired minister; b. Creston, Iowa, Oct. 17, 1914; s. Albert Maurice and Lou (Myers) N.; m. Phyllis Cochran, June 28, 1939; children: Byron Albert, Phillip Garrett. AB, UCLA, 1936; BS, San Francisco Theol. Sem., 1940; DD, Occidental Coll., 1952. Ordained to ministry United Presbyn. Ch. in U.S.A., 1940. Pastor chs., North Hollywood, Calif., 1940-43; assoc. pastor Pasadena (Calif.) Presbyn. Ch., 1943-57; pastor 1st Presbyn. Ch., Pendleton, Oreg., 1957-82, ret., 1982. Chmn. gen. assembly com. on responsible marriage and parenthood United Presbyn. Ch. in U.S.A., 1959-62, mem. Bd. Christian Edn., 1969-72; mem. 1st coun. Synod of Pacific; moderator Oreg. Synod, 1968, 69; stated clk. Ea. Oreg. Presbytery, 1975-99. Pres. Pasadena Child Guidance Clinic, 1955-57, Glen Eddy Residents Assn., 2004; trustee San Francisco Theol. Sem., 1963-84; life trustee Lewis and Clark Coll., Portland, Oreg.; active Pendleton City Recreation Commn., 1965-2001; founding bd. dirs. Presbyn. Intercommunity Hosp., Whittier, Calif.; mem. State of Oreg. Health Coun., 1985-88, State Trauma Adv. Bd., 1987-91; chmn. City of Pendleton Capital Improvements Commn., 1983-2001. Named 1st Citizen of Pendleton, 1984. Home: 114 Glen Eddy Dr Niskayuna NY 12309 Personal E-mail: nicholsm@gleneddy.com.

NICHOLS, C. WALTER, III, retired trust company executive; b. NYC, Aug. 25, 1937; s. Charles Walter and Marjorie (Jones) N.; m. Anne Sharp, Aug. 8, 1959 (dec. Nov. 1996); children: Blair, Sandra, Walter, Hope; m. Helga Faulenbach, Aug. 24, 2002. V.p. Citibank, NYC, 1962-78, J.P. Morgan & Co., NYC, 1979-93; 1st v.p. Republic Nat. Bank N.Y., NYC, 1994. Bd. dirs. Nichols Found., Inc., 1959—, Greenwich House, 1969-94, Westport River Watershed Alliance, 2004—; trustee Choate Rosemary Hall, 1972-77, 82-89, Westover Sch., 1979-81, ea. N.Y. chpt. Nature Conservancy, 1978-87; Caramoor Music Festival, 1980-90, John Jay Homestead, 1980-2000, Nat. Audubon Soc., 1983-87; mem. adv. bd. Wildlife Conservation Soc. (Bronx Zoo), 1987-94; trustee Guillain-Barré Syndrome Found. Internat., 2004—. Served to 1st lt. U.S. Army, 1960-62. Decorated Army Commendation medal. Mem. Naturist Soc., Nat. Assn. Railroad Passengers (bd. dirs. 1996-98), Am. Assn. for Nude Recreation, Yale (N.Y.C.) Club. Home: 1 Bent Oak Run Westport MA 02790-5179

NICHOLS, CARL WHEELER, retired advertising agency executive; b. Ottawa, Kans., Oct. 9, 1923; s. Carl Wheeler and Cora Merle (Hanks) N.; children: Christine, Carl Wheeler, Nancy, Matthew; m. Anna Norris, Apr. 18, 1992. Student, Baker U., 1940-41, U. Mo., 1941-43; BA, U. Mich., 1944. Research analyst Cunningham & Walsh, Inc. (advt. agy.), NYC, 1946-49, copywriter, 1949-58, co-creative dir., v.p., 1958-59, dir. account mgmt., 1959-61, pres., 1961-69, chmn., chief exec. officer, 1969-85, chmn. emeritus, 1986. Trustee Vero Beach Mus. Art, 1996, chmn. bd. trustees, 2002—03. Capt. USMCR, 1943-46, 50-52, Korea. Named to Advt. Hall of Fame, 1986. Mem. N.Y. Advt. Coun. (bd. dirs. 1974-85), Am. Advt. Fedn. (dir. 1972—, chmn. 1975-76), Advt. Ednl. Found. (bd. dirs., sec., treas. 1983-91), Birchwood Farms Golf Club, John's Island Club, Sigma Xi. Presbyterian (elder). Home: 241 Island Creek Dr Vero Beach FL 32963-3304

NICHOLS, CLYDE RICHARD, minister, consumer products company executive; b. NYC, Apr. 15, 1945; s. William and Novella Nichols; m. Marsha A. Wade, Oct. 11, 1986; children: Forest, Marvin, Anthony, Gerald. BS, Met. State Coll., Denver, 1985; ThD, Berean Bible Coll., Dallas, 1994. Ordained pastor and bishop Fellowship of Deliverance Chs., Inc. Correction officer City and County Denver, 1981-92; sr. pastor, founder Redeeming Love Ch., Denver; sr. dir. M&C Enterprises, Inc., Denver; exec. dir. Josie M. Bedford Found. Dir. membership Greater Metro Denver Ministers Alliance Orgn., Denver, 1997-99. Bd. dirs. Denver Opportunities for Outreach and Reflection 2000—. Recipient award for outstanding cmty. work Cheyenne br. NAACP, Wyo., 1982, award for outstanding cmty. activities 24th Syl Morgan Acad. Arts, Denver, 1992, Juanita Gray award. Avocations: travel, reading, computers. Home and Office: PO Box 31092 Aurora CO 80041-0092 Business E-Mail: mcenterpr31092@aol.com. E-mail: rev98crn@aol.com.

NICHOLS, DANA, language educator; d. Don and Jean Nichols. AA in English and Fgn. Langs., Gainesville State Coll., Ga., 1995; BA in English and Spanish, Mercer U., Macon, Ga., 1997; MA in English, Ga. State U., Atlanta, 1998, PhD in English, 2006. Instrnl. lab asst. Gainesville State Coll., Ga., 1997—2002, asst. prof. English, Spanish, 2002—. Scholar, Phi Theta Kappa, 1995—97. Mem.: Popular Culture Assn. Am., Soc. Study So. Lit. Avocations: travel, horseback riding. Office: Gainesville State Coll PO Box 1358 Gainesville GA 30503 Office Phone: 678-717-3471. Business E-Mail: dnichols@gsc.edu.

NICHOLS, DAVID GREGORY, anesthesiologist, pediatrician, educator; b. Hampton, Va., Oct. 1, 1951; MD, Mt. Sinai Sch. Medicine, 1977. Diplomate Am. Bd. Anesthesiology, Am. Bd. Pediatrics, Am. Bd. Critical Care Medicine. Intern Children's Hosp., Phila., 1977-78, resident in pediatrics, 1978-80; resident in anesthesiology U. Pa. Hosp., Phila., 1981-83; fellow in anesthesiology Critical Care Children's Hosp., Phila., 1983; assoc. prof. anesthesiology, critical care & pediatric medicine Johns Hopkins U. Sch. Medicine, Balt., 1991—98, prof. anesthesiology, critical care & pediatric medicine, 1998—, vice dean edn., 2000—. Dir. Pediat. ICU, Johns Hopkins U. Hosp., Balt., 1991-97, Pediat. Anesthesiology and Critical Care Medicine, 1997—. Mem. Am. Soc. Anesthesiology, Soc. for Pediat. Rsch., Soc. Critical Care Medicine, Am. Thoracic Soc. Office: John Hopkins Sch Medicine 733 N Broadway Ste 115 Baltimore MD 21205

NICHOLS, DENNIS WITT, rector; b. Bedford, Va., Oct. 20, 1955; s. Heenan Witt and Betty C. Nichols; m. Linda Jean Wintersteen, Aug. 8, 1958; children: Ashley Corinne, Ande Catherine. BME magna cum laude, Shenandoah U., Winchester, Va, 1978; MDiv magna cum laude, Gen. Theol. Sem., NYC, 1992. Tchr. Holy Cross Regional Sch., Lynchburg, Va., 1979—85, Bedford County Pub. Schs., Va., 1985—89; pastoral asst. Grace Episcopal Ch., Manhattan, NY, 1990—91; episcopal deacon St. Mark's Episcopal Ch., Queens, NY, 1991—92; organist asst. Gen. Theol. Sem., NYC, 1991—92; organist, choir master St. Marks Episcopal Ch., Queens, 1991—92; rector St. John Wilderness, Gibbsboro, NJ, 1992—95, St. Peter's Episcopal Ch., Clarksboro, NJ, 1995—. Dean Woodbury Episcopal Convocation, Diocese of NJ, NJ, 2001—04; mem. alumni exec. com. Gen. Theol. Sem., 2003—05. Contbr. articles to profl. jours. Del. Oxford Round Table, England, 2007. Scholar, Louise Wilkens Found., 1971—78. Liberal. Episcopalian. Avocations: golf, swimming, chess, travel. Home Phone: 609-221-5829. Personal E-mail: dn4116@comcast.net. E-mail: stpetes10@verizon.net.

NICHOLS, DONALD ARTHUR, economist, educator; b. Madison, Conn., Dec. 20, 1940; s. Edward Charles and Ruth (Nilson) Nichols; m. Linda Powley, Aug. 19, 1962 (dec. Oct. 1982); children: Charles Spencer, Elizabeth Clarke; m. Barbara Jakubowski Noel, May 22, 1983 (dec. Dec. 26, 2000); m. Jane Bartels, Sept. 26, 2001. BA, Yale U., 1962, MA, 1963,

PhD, 1968. Mem. faculty dept. econs. U. Wis., Madison, 1966—2006, prof., 1977—2006, chmn. dept. econs., 1983-86, 88-90, mem. exec. com. faculty senate, 1987-90, chmn., 1989-90, dir. Robert M. LaFollette Sch. Pub. Affairs, 2002—06, Wis. Idea fellow, 2004—06, emeritus prof., 2006—; lectr. Yale U., 1970—71; sr. economist Senate Budget Com., Washington, 1975—76; dep. asst. sec. for econ. policy and rsch. Dept. Labor, Washington, 1977-79; dir. Ctr. for Rsch. on Wis. Economy. Econ. advisor to gov. State of Wis., 1983—86; exec. sec. Gov.'s Coun. Econ. Advisors, 1983—86; mem. Gov.'s Export Strategy Commn., 1994—95, Gov.'s Econ. Growth Coun., 2003—; mem. acad. adv. coun. Fed. Res. Bank of Chgo., 2004—; bd. dirs. Thompson, Plumb Funds, 1987—, Sustainable Woods Co-operative, 2001—03; dir. Ctr. for World Affairs and Global Economy, 1995—2000; affiliate Christensen Assocs., Madison, 1999—; cons. in field. Author: (with Clark Reynolds) Principles of Economics, 1970, Dollars and Sense, 1994; contbr. articles to profl. jours. Trustee U. Wis. Bookstore, 1990-95; bd. advisors Am. Players Theatre, Spring Green, Wis., 1993-2001, Taliesin Coun., 2001-04. NSF fellow, 1963-66, 70-72; Nat. Commn. Employment Policy rsch. grantee, 1980-82; recipient William H. Kiekhofer Meml. Teaching prize U. Wis., 1973 Mem. Am. Econ. Assn., Royal Econ. Soc. Office: Univ Wis 1180 Observatory Dr Madison WI 53706

NICHOLS, DONNA MARDELL, nurse anesthetist; b. Mpls., Mar. 24, 1936; d. Donald Burma and Lucille Elvera Nichols. Diploma, Northwestern Hosp. Sch. Nursing, Mpls., 1957, Mpls. Sch. Anesthesia, 1959; BS in Nurse Anesthesia, U. Minn., 1977. RN Minn., 1957. Nurse anesthetist Hennepin County Med. Ctr., Mpls., 1959—60, Eden Twp. Hosp., Castro Valley, Calif., 1960—63, Bethesda Hosp., St. Paul, 1963—64, Meml. Bapt. Hosp., Houston, 1964—67, St. Joseph's Hosp., St. Paul, 1967—95; ret., 1995. Mem.: Minn. Assn. Nurse Anesthetists (bd. dirs. 1975—77), Am. Assn. Nurse Anesthetists (emeritus, cert. anesthetists). Avocations: golf, gardening, antiques. Home: 10427 Upton Ave S Bloomington MN 55431

NICHOLS, EDIE DIANE, real estate broker; b. Grahamstown, Eastern Cape Province, Republic of South Africa, Mar. 28, 1939; arrived in U.S., 1963; d. Cyril Doughtry and Dorothy Ethel (Nottingham) Tyson; m. John F. Nichols, Dec. 16, 1962 (div. Dec. 1978); 1 child, Ian Tyson. Adminstrv. asst. Am. Acad. Medicine, NYC, 1963-64, Jack Lenor Larsen, Inc., NYC, 1964-70; v.p. John Scott Fones, Inc., NYC, 1971-76, Howard J. Rubenstein Assocs. Inc., NYC, 1976-80; dir. comm. Carl Byoir & Assocs., NYC, 1981-83; account supr. Hill and Knowlton, NYC, 1983-85; broker Cross & Brown Co., NYC, 1986-88; v.p. Marc Nichols Assocs., Inc., NYC, 1989-95; mng. ptnr. Nichols Brown Internat., NYC, 1995—2004; real estate broker Citi-Habitats, NYC, 2005—; v.p. J.C. DeNiro & Assoc., NYC. Trustee Ctrl. Pk. Hist. Soc., N.Y.C., 1978-80. Mem. NOW, Internat. Assn. Corp. and Profl. Recruitment, N.Y. Women in Comm. (pub. rels. chair 1980-81, v.p., programs bd. dirs. 1985-87), Fin. Women's Assn. of N.Y. (bd. dirs. 1997-98), City Club of N.Y. (trustee, v.p., fin. and devel. 1987-89). Democrat. Episcopalian. Home: 16 Stuyvesant Oval Apt 10F New York NY 10009 Office: JC DeNiro & Assoc 34 8th Ave New York NY 10014 Office Phone: 212-561-0690. E-mail: ednny@aol.com.

NICHOLS, ELIZABETH GRACE, nursing educator, dean; b. Tehran, Iran, Feb. 1, 1943; d. Terence and Eleanor Denny (Payne) Quilliam; m. Gerald Ray Nichols, Nov. 20, 1965; children: Tina Lynn, Jeffrey David. BSN, San Francisco State U., 1969; MS, U. Calif., San Francisco, 1970, D of Nursing Sci., 1974; MA, Idaho State U., Pocatello, 1989. Staff nurse Peninsula Hosp., Burlingame, Calif., 1966-72; asst. prof. U. Calif.-San Francisco Sch. Nursing, 1974-82; chmn. dept. nursing Idaho State U., Pocatello, 1982-85; assoc. dean Coll. Health Scis. Sch. Nursing U. Wyo., Laramie, 1985-91, asst. to pres. for program revs., 1991-95; dean Coll. Nursing U. N.D., 1995—2004, Mont. State U., Bozeman, 2004—. Cons. U. Rochester, NY, 1979, Carroll Coll., Mont., 1980, divsn. Nursing Dept. HHS, Washington, U. Maine, Ft. Kent, 1992, Stanford Hosp. Nursing Svc., Calif., 1981—82, Ea. N.Mex. U., 1988, Met. State U., Minn., 1998, U. Nev.-Reno, 2003; cons. evaluator Higher Learning Commn., 1993—2004; site visitor CCNE, 1998—; mem. accreditation review com. The Higher Learning Commn., 2001—04, budget com. Contbr. articles to profl. jours. Mem. adv. bd. dir. U. Calif. Home Care Svc., San Francisco, 1975—82, Ombudsman Svc. of Contra Costa Calif., 1979—82, Free Clin. of Pocatello, 1984; mem. bd. of rev. coun. baccalaureate & higher degree programs, 1990—92; mem bd. dirs. United Way of Grand Forks/East Grand Forks, 2000—04. Recipient Jo Eleanor Elliott award, 1994; fellow ACE, U. Maine Sys., 1990—91. Fellow: Am. Acad. Nursing, Gerontol. Soc. Am. (chmn. clin. medicine sect. 1987, sec. 1990—93); mem.: ANA, Western Inst. Nursing (chmn. 1990—92, bd. govs., bd. dir. mid-west alliance), Idaho Nurses Assn. (dist. 51 adv. bd. dir. 1982—84), ND Nurses Assn. (pres. 2003—04), Oakland Ski Club. (1st v.p. 1981—82), Sigma Theta Tau. Democrat. Home Phone: 406-586-2298; Office Phone: 406-994-3784. Business E-Mail: egnichols@montana.edu.

NICHOLS, EUGENE DOUGLAS, mathematics professor; b. Rovno, Poland, Feb. 6, 1923; came to U.S., 1946, naturalized, 1951; s. Alex and Anna (Radchuk) Nichiporuk; m. Alice Bissell, Mar. 31, 1951. BS, U. Chgo., 1949, postgrad., 1949-51; MEd, U. Ill., 1953, MA, 1954, PhD, 1956. Instr. math. Roberts Wesleyan Coll., North Chili, N.Y., 1950-51, U. Ill., 1951-56; assoc. prof. math. edn. Fla. State U., 1956-61, prof., head dept., 1961-73; dir. Project for Mathematical Devel. of Children, 1973-77; dir. math program NSF, 1958-61; dir. Math. Inst. Elem. Tchrs., 1961-70; pres. Nichols Schwartz Pub., 1992—; prof. math. edn. Fla. State U., 1974-90. Chmn. U. Ill. Com. on Sch. Math., 1954-55; cons. editor math McGraw-Hill Book Co., 1956 Co-author: Modern Elementary Algebra, 1961, Introduction to Sets, 1962, Arithmetic of Directed Numbers, 1962, Introduction to Equations and Inequalities, 1963, Introduction to Coordinate Geometry, 1963, Introduction to Exponents, 1964, Understanding Arithmetic, 1965, Elementary Mathematics Patterns and Structure, 1966, Algebra, 1966, Modern Geometry, 1968, Modern Trigonometry, 1968, Modern Intermediate Algebra, 1969, Analytic Geometry, 1973, Holt Algebra 1, 1974, 78, 82, 86, 92, Holt Algebra 2, 1974, 78, 82, 86, 92, Holt Geometry, 1974, 78, 82, 86, Holt School Mathematics, 1974, 78, 81, Holt Pre-Algebra Mathematics, 1980, 86, Holt Mathematics, 1981, 85, Elementary School Mathematics and How to Teach It, 1982, Geometry, 1991, Holt Pre-Algebra, 1992, Mathematics Dictionary and Handbook, 1993, 95, 98, 99; author: Pre-Algebra Mathematics, 1970, Introductory Algebra for College Students, 1971, Mathematics for the Elementary School Teacher, 1971, College Mathematics, 1975, College Mathematics for General Education, rev. edit., 1975. Named Fla. State U. Disting. Prof., 1968-69; recipient Disting. Alumni award U. Ill. Coll. Edn., 1970. Mem. Am. Math. Soc., Math. Assn. Am., Sch. Sci. and Math. Assn., Nat. Coun. Tchrs. Math., Coun. Basic Edn., Text and Acad. Authors Assn., Pi Mu Epsilon, Phi Delta Kappa. Home: 3386 W Lakeshore Dr Tallahassee FL 32312-1305 Office Phone: 570-253-9362. Personal E-mail: eunichols@aol.com. *Do not look for a career--look for opportunities to do kind things for others. Be honest with yourself and with those around you.*

NICHOLS, GEORGE LEON, JR., minister; b. Phila., Mar. 7, 1938; s. George Leon Sr. and Elva Grace (Berger) N.; m. K. Diane Hunt, Sept. 21, 1963; children: Katherine J., Stephen J. BS in Bible, Phila. Coll. Bible, 1961; postgrad., Reformed Episcopal Sem., Phila., 1961-63; DD, Fla. Bible Coll, Hollywood, 1976; D of Ministry, Luther Rice Sem., Jacksonville, Fla., 1979; MA, Liberty U., 1988. Ordained to ministry Bapt. Ch., 1961; cert. Christian counselor. Pastor Nicetown Bapt. Ch., Phila., 1961-64, 1st Bapt. Ch., Elmer, N.J., 1964-67; sr. pastor Pennsville Bapt. Ch., Mt. Pleasant, Pa., 1967-87, Faith Bapt. Ch., Wilmington, Del., 1987—. Trustee Phila. Biblical U., Langhorne, Pa., 1987; trustee, v.p. Out-Island Ministries, St. Petersburg, Fla., 1973, pres.; bd. dirs. Mil. Evangelism, Aberdeen, Md., Sandy Cove Ministries, N.E. Md. Mem. Am. Assn. Christian Counselors, United Assn. Christian Counselors (bd. dirs., pres. Harrisburg, Pa.), Bibl. Archeol. Soc., Evang. Theol. Soc. Office: Faith Bapt Ch 4210 Limestone Rd Wilmington DE 19808-2099 Home: 17 Cauline Ct Newark DE 19711 *To enjoy life we must have a theology that is practical and practiced.*

NICHOLS, GUY WARREN, retired institute and utilities executive; b. Colchester, Vt., Oct. 27, 1925; s. Guy W. and Gladys (Tomlinson) N.; m. Shirley Hibbard, June 21, 1947; children: Pamela, Gail, Sally. BSCE, U. Vt., 1947; postgrad., Worcester Poly. Inst. Sch. Indsl. Mgmt., 1953-56; MS in Bus. Adminstrn., MIT, 1961. With New. Eng. Electric System, Westborough, Mass., 1947-84, exec. v.p., 1968-70, pres., 1970-84, chief exec. officer, 1972-84, chmn. bd., 1978-84. Bd. dirs. Ameresco Inc. Chmn., trustee Woods Hole Oceanographic Instn., 1985-95. Sloan fellow, MIT, 1961. Fellow Am. Acad. Arts and Scis. Office: 25 Research Dr Westborough MA 01582-0001 Personal E-mail: looncall99@comcast.net.

NICHOLS, HENRY ELIOT, lawyer, realtor, banker, columnist; b. NYC; m. Frances Griffin Morrison, Aug. 12, 1950 (dec. July 1978); children: Clyde Whitney, Diane Spencer; m. Mary ann Wall, May 31, 1987. BA, Yale U., 1946; JD, U. Va., 1948. Bar: DC 1950, US Dist. Ct. 1950, US Ct. Appeals 1952, US Supreme Ct. 1969. Assoc. Frederick W. Berens, Washington, 1950-52; sole practice Washington, 1952—. Real estate columnist Washington Star, 1966-81; pres., gen. counsel Hamilton Fed. Savs. & Loan Assn., 1971-74; vice chmn. bd. Columbia 1st Bank (formerly Columbia 1st Fed. Savs. & Loan Assn.), Washington, 1974-90, bd. dirs.; pres. Century Fin. Corp., 1971-90; regional v.p. Preview, Inc., 1972-78; bd. dirs., exec. com. Columbia Real Estate Title Ins. Co., Washington, 1968-78. Contbr. articles to profl. jours. Nat. adv. bd Harker Prep. Sch., 1975-80; exec. com. Father Walter E. Schmitz Meml. Fund, Cath. U., 1982-83; bd. dirs. Vincent T. Lombardi Cancer Rsch. Ctr., 1979-84; del. Pres. Johnson's Conf. LAw and Poverty, 1967; vice chmn. Mayor's Ad Hoc Com. Housing Code Problems, Washington, 1968-71; mem. Commn. Landlord-Tenant Affairs Washington City Coun., 1970-71; vice chmn. Washington Area Realtors Coun., 1970; exec. com., dir. Downtown Progress, 1970; bd. dirs. Washington Mental Health Assn., 1973, Washington Med. Ctr., 1975. Capt. USAAF, 1942-46. Mem. Am. Land Devel. Assn., Nat. Assn. Real Estate Editors, Washington Bd. Realtors (pres. 1970, Realtor of Yr. 1970, Martin Isen award 1981), Greater Met. Washington Bs. Trade (bd. dirs. 1974-80), US League Savs. Assns. (attys. com. 1971-80), Washington Savs. and Loan League, ABA, DC Bar Assn., Internat. Real Estate Fedn., Yale Club, Cosmos Club, Rolls Royce Club, Antique Auto Club, St. Elmo Club, Omega Tau Rho. Episcopalian. Home: Apt 905 4550 N Park Ave Chevy Chase MD 20815 Office Phone: 301-718-7888.

NICHOLS, HENRY LOUIS, lawyer; b. Collin County, Tex., Nov. 7, 1916; s. Jesse Cleveland and Leva (Stiff) N.; m. Elaine Guentherman, May 17, 1949; children: David Michael, Martha Marie. LL.B., So. Meth. U., 1940. Bar: Tex. 1939. Asst. city atty., Dallas, 1946-50; pvt. practice, 1951—. Mem. adv. bd. Ctr. for Legal Mcpl. Studies. Served to lt. col. AUS, 1941-46; col. USAR ret. Rsch. fellow Southwestern Legal Found., 1964. Fellow Am. Bar Found.; mem. ABA, Dallas Bar Assn. (pres. 1963), State Bar Tex., Tex. Bar Found. (charter), Park City Club. Home: 3131 Maple Ave Apt 13H Dallas TX 75201-1206 Office: 1800 Lincoln Plz Dallas TX 75201 Office Phone: 214-965-9900. Business E-Mail: hnichols@njdhs.com. *As a night-school graduate (Law School), I believe the opportunities in America are unlimited for anyone willing to work. Nowhere in the world are such opportunities available. We who live in the U.S.A. are blessed and the most fortunate of all people. We should strive to maintain that which our fathers preserved for us.*

NICHOLS, IRIS JEAN, retired illustrator; b. Yakima, Wash., Aug. 2, 1938; d. Charles Frederick and Velma Irene (Hacker) Beisner; (div. June 1963); children: Reid William, Amy Jo; m. David Gary Nichols, Sept. 21, 1966. BFA in Art, U. Wash., 1978. Freelance illustrator, graphic designer, Seattle, 1966—2004; med. illustrator, head dept. illustration Swedish Hosp. Med. Ctr., Seattle, 1981-86; owner, med. and sci. illustrator Art for Medicine, Seattle, 1986—2003; ret., 2003. Med. illustrator U. Wash., Seattle, 1966-67; part-time med. illustrator, graphic coord. dept. art The Mason Clinic, 1968-78; instr. advanced illustration Cornish Coll. Arts, Seattle, 1988-90; organized, coordinated and gifted the artwork of Prof. Glen E. Alps of U. Wash. after his death in 1996 Illustrator various books including Bryophytes of Pacific Northwest, 1966, Microbiology, 1973, 78, 82, 94, 98, Introduction to Human Physiology, 1980, Understanding Human Anatomy and Physiology, 1983, Human Anatomy, 1984 Regional Anesthesia, 1990, many other med. and sci. books, and children's books on various subjects; exhibited in group shows at Seattle Pacific Sci. Ctr., summer 1979, 82, Am. Coll. Surgeons (1st prize 1974), N.W. Urology Conf. (1st prize 1974, 76, 2d prize 1975); pub. illustrations Constellation Pk. and Marine Res., City Seattle Pk., 1999, Whale Tail Park, Seattle. Pres. ArtsWest (formerly West Seattle Arts Coun.), 1983; chmn. West Seattle (Wash.) H.S. Art Acquisition Com., 2003—. Named to West Seattle H.S. Alumni Hall of Fame, 1986, Matrix Table, 1986-96. Mem. Assn. Med. Illustrators (Murial McLatchie Fine Arts award 1981), Nat. Mus. Women in the Arts (Wash. state com., bd. dirs. 1987-95, pres. 1993-94), Women Painters of Wash. (pres. 1987-89), U. Wash. Alumni Assn., Lambda Rho (pres. alumni assn. 1995-98, treas. 2002-04) Avocations: artwork, printmaking, small books.

NICHOLS, J. GARY, state librarian; Libr. Maine State Libr., Augusta. Named Libr. of Yr., 2005. Mem.: ALA, Chief Officers of State Libr. Agencies (pres. 2006—08). Office: State Library of Maine 64 State House Section Augusta ME 04333 Office Phone: 207-287-5600. Office Fax: 207-287-5615. Business E-Mail: gary.nichols@maine.gov. *

NICHOLS, JAMES RICHARD, civil engineer, consultant; b. Amarillo, Tex., June 29, 1923; s. Marvin Curtis and Ethel (Nichols) N.; m. Billie Louise Smith, Dec. 24, 1944; children: Judith Ann, James Richard Jr., John M. BS in Civil Engring., Tex. A&M U., 1949, MS in Civil Engring., 1950; DHum (hon.), Tex. Wesleyan U., 1990. Registered profl. engr., Tex., Okla., N.Mex. Ptnr. Freese & Nichols, Inc., Cons. Engrs., Fort Worth, 1950-76, pres., 1977-88, chmn., 1988—. Former chmn., dir. emeritus Tex. Bd. Profl. Engrs. Former chmn. Ft. Worth Conv. and Visitors Bur.; bd. dirs. Pub. Comm. Found. North Tex., Tex. A&M Rsch. Found., Tex. Wesleyan U.; co-chmn. Metroplex Mission with Billy Graham. With US Army, 1943—46. Fellow: Am. Cons. Engrs. Coun.; mem.: NSPE, ASCE (hon.), Tex. Water Conservation Assn., Ft. Worth C. of C. (bd. dirs., adv. coun.), Rotary, Ft. Worth Club, Exch. Club. Methodist. Home: 4821 Overton Woods Dr Fort Worth TX 76109-2429 Office: Freese & Nichols Inc 4055 Internat Plz Ste 200 Fort Worth TX 76109-4895 Office Phone: 817-735-7300. Personal E-mail: jrn@freese.com.

NICHOLS, JANET HILDRETH, elementary school educator, childbirth and parenting educator; b. Glenwood Springs, Colo., July 1, 1948; d. Pershing Loveland and Myrna Jean Nichols; children: Carrie Christine Schultz, Taylor James Pruss. BA, U. NColo., 1971, MA, 1973. Lic. childbirth educator Lamaze Internat., 1982, cert. prenatal parenting instr. Prenatal Parenting, 2003. Spl. edn. tchr., kindergarten tchr. Ouray Pub. Schs., Colo., 1971—72; spl. edn. tchr. Jefferson County Schs., Lakewood, Colo., 1973—74; child find evaluator St. Vrain Pub. Schs., Longmont, Colo., 1979—80, tchr. physically handicapped, 1985—87; lead tchr. Mountain View Presch., Boulder, Colo., 1983—84; pre-acad. tchr. Boulder Valley Schs., 1987—92; kindergarten tchr. Douglass Elem. Sch., 1992—2006; tchr. Rocky Mt. Sch. for Gifted and Creative, 2006—. Childbirth & parenting instr. Boulder Cmty. Hosp., 1990—. Contbr. Head Start, Boulder, 1988—89. Grantee Math Edn. grant, Found. Boulder Valley Schs., 1995, Reading Comprehension grant, 2002, Map Making grant, 2003. Mem.: Lamaze Internat. (assoc.). Home: 1775 Holeman Dr Erie CO 80516 Home Phone: 303-926-1017. Business E-Mail: jan.nichols@bvsd.org. E-mail: jannichols548@yahoo.com.

NICHOLS, JOHN DOANE, diversified manufacturing corporation executive; b. Shanghai, 1930; m. Alexandra M. Curran, Dec. 4, 1971; children: Kendra E., John D. III. BA, Harvard U., 1953, MBA, 1955. Various operating positions Ford Motor Corp., 1958-68; dir. fin. controls ITT Corp., 1968-69; exec. v.p., COO Aerojet-Gen. Corp., 1969-79, Ill. Tool Works Inc., Chgo., 1980-81, CEO, dir., 1982-95, chmn., 1986-96; pres., CEO Marmon Group Inc., Chgo., 2002—. Bd. dirs. Household Internat., Philip Morris Cos., Inc., Rockwell Internat.; overseer Harvard U., 1994-99, vis. com. Sch. Edn., com. athletics, com. univ. resources. Trustee U. Chgo., 1987-93, Lyric Opera Chgo., Mus. Sci. and Industry, Jr. Achievement Chgo., Chgo. Commerce Club Civic Com.; life trustee Chgo. Symphony Orch.; bd. dirs. Art Inst. Chgo., past chmn.; mem. bd. govs. Argonne (Ill.) Nat. Lab., 1988-93; vice chmn. exec. com. Chgo. Cmty. Trust, 1997—. Mem. Harvard Club (NY, Chgo.), Indian Hill Club (Winnetka, Ill.), Chgo. Club, Comml. Club, Econ. Club Chgo. Office: Marmon Group Inc 225 W Washington St Chicago IL 60606

NICHOLS, KATIE, investment company executive; b. Des Moines, May 19, 1940; d. Gardner (Mike) and Lois (Thornburg) Cowles; m. Julian Strauss, June 11, 1960 (div. 1971); children: Elizabeth Lois Strauss Grossi, Gwen Beatrix STrauss Jenkins, Kate Anne Strauss Long; m. Roger Marvin Nichols, Sept. 1, 1973 (div. 1981); m. H. E. Rummel, Mar. 27, 1983 (div. 1994). Student, Cornell U., 1957—61. Ptnr., v.p. The Rummel Group, Inc., St. Petersburg, Fla., 1985—2003, chmn., 2003—, pres., 2003—, CEO, 2003—. Trustee Cowles Charitable Trust, NYC, 1985—. Vol. Hosp. Albert Schweitzer, Deschapelles, Haiti, 1961—63; vice chmn. Fla. Human Rels. Commn., Tallahassee, 1974—75, Fla. Corrections Commn., 1994—98; Dem. candidate Fla. Pub. Svc. Commn., 1976, commr., 1981—89, chmn., 1987—89; bd. dirs. Nat. Coun. Crime and Delinquency, San Francisco, 1990—, chmn., 1997—98; bd. dirs. HAS2000 Campaign Hosp. Albert Schweitzer, Haiti. Recipient Honor award, Fla. Human Rels. Commn., 1985. Mem.: NOW, League Women Voters Fla., Emily's List. Democrat. Episcopalian. Avocations: reading, needlepoint. Home: 1682 Oceanview Dr Tierra Verde FL 33715-2500 Office: The Rummel Group Inc 1641 1st Ave N Saint Petersburg FL 33713-8935

NICHOLS, MICHAEL COOPER, food products executive, lawyer; b. Birmingham, Ala., Feb. 4, 1952; s. F.W. and Jeanette (Cooper) N.; m. Marcia Couch, Sept. 23, 1976; children: Joshua, Jessica, Zachary, Anna. BA with honors, Brown U., 1974; JD, Emory U., 1977. Bar: Ga. 1977, Tex. 1981. Mem. Ga. Ho. of Reps., Atlanta, 1977-81; chief adminstrv. officer Appletree Mktg., Houston, 1988-91; gen. counsel SYSCO Corp., Houston, 1981-88, v.p., 1991—98, v.p., sec., gen. counsel, 1998—, sr. v.p., gen. counsel, corp. sec., 2006—. Pres. Houston Food Bank, Houston, 1990—92; trustee Houston Police Officer Pension Fund; chmn. Houston Civil Svc. Commn., co-chmn.; bd. dirs. Congregation Beth Israel, 1986. Home: 12155 Maple Rock Houston TX 77077 Office Phone: 281-584-1471. E-mail: nichols.mike@corp.sysco.com.

NICHOLS, MIKE, stage and film director; b. Berlin, Nov. 6, 1931; s. Nicholaievitch and Brigitte (Landauer) Peschowsky; m. Patricia Scott, 1957 (div.); m. Margot Callas, 1974 (div.); 1 child; m. Annabel Davis-Goff (div.); 2 children; m. Diane Sawyer, Apr. 29, 1988. Student, U. Chgo., 1950-53; student acting, Lee Strasberg. Ptnr. with Elaine May in comedy act; first appeared at Playwrights Theatre Club, Compass Theatre, Chgo.; N.Y. debut An Evening with Mike Nichols and Elaine May, 1960; acted in A Matter of Position, Phila., 1962; dir.: (plays) Barefoot in the Park, 1963 (Tony award best dir.), The Knack, 1964, Luv, 1964 (Tony award best dir.), The Odd Couple, 1965 (Tony award best dir.), The Apple Tree, 1966, The Little Foxes, 1967, Plaza Suite, 1968 (Tony award best dir.), The Prisoner of 2d Avenue, 1971 (Tony award best dir.), Uncle Vanya (co-adapted), 1973, Streamers, 1976, Comedians, 1976, The Gin Game, 1977, (L.A. Drama Critics award), Drink Before Dinner, 1978, Lunch Hour, 1980, Fools, 1981, The Real Thing, 1984 (Tony award 1984,), Hurlyburly, 1984, Social Security, 1984, Elliot Loves, 1990, Death and the Maiden, 1992, Monty Python's Spamalot, 2005 (Outer Critic Cir., outstanding direction of a musical, 2005, Julia Hansen award for excellence in directing, Drama League, 2005, Tony award for best direction of a musical, 2005), (Julia Hansen Award excellence in directing, The Drama League, 2005); (films) Who's Afraid of Virginia Woolf?, 1966, (Academy award nomination best director 1966), The Graduate, 1967 (Academy award best director 1967), Catch-22, 1970, Carnal Knowledge, 1971, The Day of the Dolphin, 1973, The Fortune, 1975, Heartburn, 1986, Biloxi Blues, 1987, Working Girl, 1988 (Academy award nomination best director 1988), Wolf, 1994; dir., prodr.: Silkwood, 1983 (Academy award nomination best director 1983), Postcards From the Edge, 1990, Regarding Henry, 1991, The Birdcage, 1996, Primary Colors, 1998, What Planet Are You From?, 2000, Closer, 2004; prodr. All the Pretty Horses, 2000; prodr.: (musical) Annie, 1977; (TV movie) dir., exec. prodr. Wit, 2001, (miniseries) dir. Angels in America, 2003 (Emmy award Outstanding Directing for a Miniseries, Movie or Dramatic Special, 2004); performed at N.Y. musical Pres. Johnson's Inaugural Gala, 1965.

NICHOLS, RALPH ARTHUR, lawyer; b. Clinton, NY, Jan. 27, 1919; s. Arthur Britcher and Carrie Lena (Pitcher) N.; m. Pamela Crow Bermingham, May 3, 1947 (dec. Feb. 1980); children: Jeremy Nichols Pierce, Ralph A. Jr., Melinda Nichols Mayer; m. Victoria Requa Lalli, Sept. 5, 1981. AB, Hamilton Coll., 1940; LLB, Yale U., 1947. Bar: Conn. 1949, N.Y. 1947, U.S. Dist. Ct. (so. dist.) N.Y. 1949, U.S. Dist. Ct. Conn. 1950, U.S. Supreme Ct. 1959. Assoc. Burke & Burke, NYC, 1947-49, Maguire, Walker & Middleton, Stamford, Conn., 1949-54; assoc., then ptnr. Cummings & Lockwood, Stamford, 1954—. Founder, former bd. dirs. Stamford Land Conservation Trust; former bd. dirs. Conservationists Stamford, Inc., Stamford YMCA; former bd. dirs., sec. Stamford Area Commerce and Industry; trustee Stamford YMCA. Lt. USNR, 1942-46, ETO, PTO. Fellow: Am. Coll. Trust and Estate Counsel; mem.: ABA, Yale Club (N.Y.C.), Woodway Country Club (Darien, Conn.), Phi Delta Phi. Republican. Episcopalian. Office: Cummings & Lockwood 6 Landmark Sq Stamford CT 06901 Home: 32 Bank St New Canaan CT 06840-6238 Home Phone: 203-966-6325. E-mail: rnichols@cl-law.com.

NICHOLS, ROB (ROBERT STANLEY NICHOLS), think-tank executive, former federal agency administrator; b. Seattle; m. Rebecca Nichols; 1 child Henry Alexander BS in Polit. Sci., George Washington U. Press advance rep. Office of Presdl. Advance The White House, Washington, staff asst. to Chief of Staff John Sununu; personal aide to sec. US Dept. Transport., Washington; mgr. campaign US Rep. Jennifer Dunn, 1994; polit. dir. Wash. State Rep. party, 1995; press sec. U.S. Rep. Jennifer Dunn, 1996-97; comms. dir. US Senator Slade Gordon, Electronic Industries Alliance; dep. asst. for pub. affairs US Dept. Treasury, Washington, asst. sec. for pub. affairs, 2003—05; pres., COO Fin. Services Forum, Washington, 2005—. Office: Fin Services Forum 601 Thirteenth St NW Ste 750 S Washington DC 20005 Fax: (202-224-9393.

NICHOLS, ROBERT LEIGHTON, civil engineer; b. Amarillo, Tex., June 24, 1926; s. Marvin Curtis and Ethel Nichols; m. Frances Hardison, June 8, 1948; children: Eileen, William C., Michael L. BSCE, Tex. A&M U., Coll. Station, 1947, MSCE, 1948. Grad. asst., instr. Tex. A&M U., 1947-48; assoc. Freese & Nichols (and predecessors), Ft. Worth, 1948-50, ptnr., 1950-77, v.p., 1977-88, pres., 1988-91, vice chmn., 1991-92, pres. emeritus, 1992—. Mem. Bldg. Stds. Commn., 1956—62; pres. Tri-State

Water Resource Coalition, 2003—. Chmn. Horn Frog dist. Boy Scouts Am., pres. Longhorn coun., 1990—93, Ozark Trails coun., 1998—99; mem. City Coun., Webb City, Mo., 2004—06. Mem.: NSPE (pres. 1977—78, pres. Ednl. Found.), ASCE, Environ. Task Force Jasper and Newton Counties (pres. 2003—), Tri-state Water Resource Coalition (pres. 2002—), Nat. Inst. Engring. Ethics (pres. 1995—97), Tex. Pub. Works Assn., Tex. Water Utilities Assn., Am. Pub. Works Assn., Water Environ. Assn. Tex. (pres. 1962—63), Water Environ. Fedn., Tex. Water Conservation Assn., Am. Water Works Assn., Tex. Soc. Profl. Engrs. (pres. 1965—66), C. of C. Webb City, Mo. (exec. dir. 1997—2001), Masons, Chi Epsilon, Tau Beta Pi. Methodist. Office Phone: 417-673-7151. Business E-Mail: rln@freese.com.

NICHOLS, ROBERT LYMAN, retired foreign service officer, lecturer; b. Milw. s. Malcolm Strong and Ruth Mary (Lyman) N.; m. Virginia Lee Straghan, Sept. 7, 1947 (dec. 1989); children: Robert Gibbs (dec.), Nancy Lee, Peter Lyman. Student, Swarthmore Coll., 1942-43; BA, Tufts U., 1949; MA, Fletcher Sch. Law & Diplomacy, Medford, Mass., 1950; diploma, U.S. Army War Coll., Carlisle, Pa., 1969. Fgn. svc. officer U.S. Dept. State, The Philippines, 1951-53, USIA, Italy, 1954—56, Holland, 1956—58, Taiwan, 1959—61, 1969—71, Hong Kong, 1961—65, Singapore, 1971—74; dir. Chinese divsn. Voice of America, 1966-69; dep. dir. East Asia Cultural Afairs U.S. Dept. State, Washington, 1974-76; dep. dir. East Asia USIA, Washington, 1977-79; ret., 1979; part-time faculty Cape Cod C.C., Barnstable, Mass., 1981—2004; tchr. of Chinese Light House Charter Sch., Orleans, Mass., 1997. China tour leader Chinese Ednl. Travel, Nat. Com. US-China Rels. and Smithsonian, 1980—95, 1999; tchr. Chinese Cape Cod Acad.; lectr. in field. Contbr. articles various newspapers Bd. dirs. Cape Cod Human Svcs., Hyannis, Mass., 1987-2004, chmn., 1990-91. Quartermaster 1st class, USN, 1943-46, Pacific. Episcopalian. Avocations: boating, fishing, theater acting, yoga. Home: Po Box 1180 South Yarmouth MA 02664-0180 Personal E-mail: rlnichols@comcast.net.

NICHOLS, RONALD LEE, surgeon, educator; b. Chgo., June 25, 1941; s. Peter Raymond and Jane Eleanor (Johnson) N.; m. Elsa Elaine Johnson, Dec. 4, 1964; children: Kimberly Jane, Matthew Bennett. MD, U. Ill., 1966, MS, 1970. Diplomate Am. Bd. Surgery (assoc. cert. examiner, New Orleans, 1991), Nat. Bd. Med. Examiners. Intern U. Ill. Hosp., Chgo., 1966-67, resident in surgery, 1967-72, instr. surgery, 1970-72, asst. prof. surgery, 1972-74; assoc. prof. surgery U. Health Scis. Chgo. Med. Sch., 1975-77, dir. surg. edn., 1975-77; William Henderson prof. surgery Tulane U. Sch. Medicine, New Orleans, 1977—2002, vice chmn. dept. surgery, 1982-91, staff surgeon, 1977—2002, prof. microbiology, immunology, 1979—, William Henderson prof. surgery emeritus, 2003—; sr. vis. surgeon Med. Ctr. La., New Orleans, 1988—. Cons. surgeon VA Hosp., Alexandria, La., 1978-93, Huey P. Long Hosp., Pineville, La., 1978-2002, Lallie Kemp Charity Hosp., Independence, La., 1977-85, Touro Infirmary, New Orleans, Monmouth Med. Ctr., Long Branch, NJ, 1979-88; sr. vis. surgeon Med. Ctr. La., New Orleans, 1988—; mem. VA Coop. Study Rev. Bd., 1978-81, VA Merit Rev. Bd. in Surgery, 1979-82; sci. program com. 3d Internat. Conf. Nosocomial Infections, Ctr. Disease Control, sci. program and fundraising com. 4th Internat. Conf.; bd. dirs. Nat. Found. Infectious Diseases, 1989-2003, v.p., 1994-97, pres.-elect., 1997-99, pres., 1999-2001, trustee, 2003—; hon. fellow faculty Kasr El Aini Cairo U. Sch. Medicine, 1989; adv. com. on infection control Ctrs. for Disease Control, 1991-97; disting. guest. vis. prof. Royal Coll. Surgeons Thailand, 1989, 1992; infectious diseases adv. bd. Roche Labs., 1988-95, Abbott Labs., 1990-92, Kimberly Clark Corp., 1990-99, SmithKline Beecham Labs., 1990-95, Fujisawa Pharm., chmn., 1990-99, Bayer Pharm., 1994-2001, Merck Sharpe Dohme, 1996, Depotech, 1996, Zeneca Pharm., 1997-2000, Rhone-Poulenc Rorer, 1997-99, Wyeth-Ayrest Labs., 1998-2003, Pfizer Pharm., 1999, Searle Pharm., 1999-2001, GlaxoWellcome, 1999, Aventis, 1999-2000, Cubist Pharm., 2000—05, Regent Med., 2003—06, others; study group Prophylaxis Antibiotic Project La. Health Care Rev., Inc., 1995-2000, Nat. Com. Study Blood Borne Disease Transmission make Nat. Policy, Rockefeller Brothers Fund, 2001-03; apptd. by gov. La. commn. HIV and AIDS, 1999-2007; lectr. Royal Coll. Physicians and Surgeons, Can., 1998, Internat. Infectious Disease Soc. Ob-gyn., 1998, 20th NY State Surg. Symposium, 1998, Dept. Surgery, U. Ark., 1998; nat. policy com. study innovative surgery reg. Greenwall Found., 2003—06; lectr. in field. Author: (with Gorbach, Bartlett and Nichols) Manual of Surgical Infection, 1984; author, guest editor: (with Nichols, Hyslop Jr. and Bartlett) Decision Mking in Surgical Sepsis, 1991; guest editor, author: Surgical Sepsis and Beyond, 1993; mem. editl. bd. Current Surgery, 1977—, Hosp. Physician, 1980—2006, Infection Control, 1980-86, Guidelines to Antibiotic Therapy, 1976-81, Am. Jour. Infection Control, 1981-99, Internat. Medicine, 1983—, Confronting Infection, 1983-86, Current Concepts in Clin. Surgery, 1984—, Fact Line, 1984-91, Host/Pathogen News, 1984—, Infectious Diseases in Clin. Practice, 1991—, surg. sect. editor, 1992—, Surg. Infections: Index and Revs., 1991—, So. Med. Jour., 1992-97, ANAEROBE, 1994—, Surg. Infections, 1998—, Clin. Infectious Diseases, 1999—; editl. adv. bd. MD Consult Infectious Diseases, 2002-04; mem. adv. bd. Physician News Network, 1991-95; patentee (with S.G. schoenberger and W.R. Rank) Helical-Tipped Lesion Localization Needle Device; patentee in field. Elected faculty sponsor graduating class Tulane Med. Sch., 1979-80, 83, 85, 87, 88, 91-92; apptd. La. Commn. HIV and AIDS, 1999-2007. Maj. USAR, 1972-75. Recipient House Staff tchg. award U. Ill. Coll. Medicine, 1973, rsch. award bd. trustees U. Health Scis., Chgo. Med. Ctr., 1977, Clin. Prof. of Year U. Health Sci., 1977, Tchg. award Owl Club, 1980-86, 90, Douglas Stubbs Lectr. award Nat. Med. Assn. Surg. Sect., 1987, Prix d'Elegance award Men of Fashion, New Orleans, 1993; named Prof. of Yr. U. Health Sci., Chgo. Med. Sch., 1977, Clin. Prof. of Yr. Tulane U. Sch. Medicine, 1979, Brit. Jour. Surgery Lectr., 1997, 1st Ann. Warren Cole Lectr., 2001; elected to Wall of Fame, Lakeview HS, Chgo., 2006. Fellow Infectious Disease Soc. Am. (mem. FDA subcom. to develop guidelines in surg. prophylaxis 1989-93, co-recipient Joseph Susman Meml. award 1990), Am. Acad. Microbiology, Internat. Soc. Univ. Colon and Rectal Surgeons, ACS (mem. oper. rm. environ. com. 1978-80, vice chair oper. rm. environ. com. 1980-81, chmn. oper. rm. environ. com. 1981-83, sr. mem. oper. rm. environ. com. 1983-87, mem. internat. rels. com. 1987-93, sr. mem. internat. rels. com. 1993-97); mem. AMA, Nat. Found. for Infectious Diseases (bd. dirs.), Joint Commn. on Accreditation of Health Care Orgn. (Infection Control adv. group, 1988-98, sci. program com. 3d internat. conf. nosocomial infections CDC/Nat. Found. Infectious Diseases 1990, FDA Subcom. to Develop Guidelines in Surg. Prophylaxis, 1989-93; prophylactic antibiotic study group La. Health Care Rev. Inc. 1996-2000, clin. advisor, mem., 2001—, AIDS commr. State of La. 1992-94, mem. 1999-2007), 5th Nat. Forum on AIDS (sci. program com.), US Pharmacopeial Convention Inc. (adv. panel surg. drugs and devices 1995-2000, nominating com. The Heinz Awards 1995-96), Assn. Practitioners in Infection Control (physician adv. coun. 1991-98), Internat. Soc. Anaerobic Bacteria, So. Med. Assn. (vice chmn. sect. surgery 1980-81, chmn. 1982-83), Assn. Acad. Surgery, NY Acad. Sci., Warren H. Cole Soc. (pres.-elect 1988, pres. 1989-90), Assn. VA Surgeons, Soc. Surgery Alimentary Tract, Inst. Medicine Chgo., Midwest Surg. Assn., Ctrl. Surg. Assn., Ill. Surg. Soc., European Soc. Surg. Rsch., Collegium Internationale Chirugiae Digestivae, Chgo. Surg. Soc. (hon.), New Orleans Surg. Soc. (bd. dirs. 1983-87), Soc. Univ. Surgeons, Surg. Soc. La., Southeastern Surg. Soc., Phoenix Surg. Soc. (hon.), Hellenic Surg. Soc. (hon.), Ctrl. NY Surg. Soc. (hon.), Tulane Surg. Soc., Alton Ochsner Surg. Soc., Am. Soc. Microbiology, Soc. Internat. de Chirugie, Surg. Infection Soc. (sci. study com. 1982-83, fellowship com. 1985-87, ad hoc sci. liaison com. 1986-89, program com. 1986-87, chmn. ad hoc com. rels. with industry 1990-93, mem. sci. liaison com. 1995-96), Soc. for Intestinal Microbial Ecology and Disease, Soc. Critical Care Medicine, Am. Surg. Assn., Kansas City Surg. Soc., Bay Surg. Soc. (hon.), Cuban Surg. Soc. (hon.), Panhellenic Surg. Soc. (hon.), Tacoma Surg. Club (hon.), Sigma Xi, Alpha Omega Alpha. Episcopalian. Home: 1521 7th St New Orleans LA 70115-3322 Office: 1430 Tulane Ave New Orleans LA 70112-2699 Office Phone: 504-988-5168. Personal E-mail: rlnmd@yahoo.com. Business E-Mail: ronald.nichols@tulane.edu.

NICHOLS, SHARON LOUISE, educator, researcher; b. Williamsport, Pa., June 12, 1969; d. William Nichols and Patricia Ann Thompson. BA, Bucknell U., 1991; MA, U. Ariz., 1997, PhD, 2003. Postdoctoral rsch. fellow Ariz. State U., Phoenix, 2003—04; asst. prof. ednl. psychology U. Tex., San Antonio, 2004—. Co-author (with Tom Good): America's Teenagers Myths and Realities: Media Images, Schooling, and the Social Costs of Indifference; co-author: (with David Berliner) Collateral Damage: How High Stakes Testing Corrupts America's Schools, 2007. Mem.: APA, Am. Ednl. Rsch. Assn. (chair adolescence spl. interest group 2005—). Office: U Tex at San Antonio 501 W Durango Blvd Ste DB 4342 San Antonio TX 78207 Office Phone: 210-458-2035. Business E-Mail: sharon.nichols@utsa.edu.

NICHOLS, STEPHEN GEORGE, Romance languages educator; b. Cambridge, Mass., Oct. 24, 1936; s. Stephen George and Marjorie (Whitney) N.; m. Mary Winn Jordan, June 22, 1957 (div. 1972); children: Stephen Frost (dec.), Sarah Winn; m. Edith Karetzky, 1972; stepchildren: Laura Natalie Karetzky, Sarah Karetzky Rothman. AB cum laude, Dartmouth Coll., 1958; PhD, Yale U., 1963; LittD (hon.), U. Genève, 1992. Asst. prof. French UCLA, 1963-65; assoc. prof. comparative lit. U. Wis.-Madison, 1965-68, chmn. dept., 1967-68; prof. Romance langs. and comparative lit. Dartmouth Coll., 1968-84, chmn. dept. comparative lit., 1969-72, 74, 79-82, chmn. dept. romance langs., 1974-77, Edward Tuck prof. French, 1984-85, chmn. dept. French and Italian, 1982-85, liaison officer Sch. Criticism and Theory, 1983-85; faculty Dartmouth Inst., 1980-85, faculty dir., 1984-85; prof. romance langs. U. Pa., 1985-86, Edmund J. Kahn Disting. prof. humanities, 1986-92; James M. Beall prof. French and humanities Johns Hopkins U., Balt., 1992—; grad. group chmn. French and Italian U. Pa., 1986-88, chmn. dept. romance langs., 1987-88, assoc. dean for humanities, 1988-91; acting chair French, 1993-94; dir. grad. studies dept. French The Johns Hopkins U., Balt., 1992-94; R. Champlin and Debbie Sheridan interim dir. Eisenhower Libr., Johns Hopkins U., 1994-95, chmn. dept. French, 1995—. Dir. sch. Criticism and Theory, 1995-2000; vis. prof. U. Tel Aviv, 1977, NYU, 1979-81, Exeter (Eng.) U., 1980, Ariz. State U., 1982, U. Calif., Irvine, 1985, Sch. Criticism and Theory, 1989, 95, Humanities Rsch. Inst. U. Calif., 1990, Ecole Pratique des Hautes Etudes, Paris, 1995, U. Pa., 1995, Dartmouth Coll., 1995-96, Cornell U., 1996—, Ecole Normale Superieure, Paris, 1996, 98, 2000, 02, U. Paris, 1997; rev. panelist NEH, 1979-81, 84, 91, Guggenheim fellow, 1987-88; ACLS sr. fellow, 2001-02; Phi Beta Kappa vis. scholar, 1983-84; Lauder fellow Aspen Inst. for Humanistic Study, 1988; adv. bd. Inst. d'Etudes Francaises d'Avignon, Bryn Mawr Coll., 1965—; dir. seminar NEH, 1975-79, Mellon summer seminar in humanities Johns Hopkins U., 1993, 94; exec. com. Ea. Comparative Lit. Conf.; mem. adv. coun. dept. comparative lit. Princeton U., 1982-88, chmn., 1984-88; co-dir. Ctr. Cultural Study, U. Pa., 1986-92; co-dir. Louis Marin Ctr. for French Studies, 1992—; advisor Waverly Consort, 1987-95; adv. bd. Soc. Humanities Cornell U., 1993—; reviewer Guggenheim Fellowship applications, medieval sect., 1995—, French, 1996—; chair task force on artifact in libr. collections Coun. on Libr. Info. Resources, 1999-2001. Author: Formulaic Diction and Thematic Composition in the Chanson de Roland, 1961, The Songs of Bernard de Ventadorn, 1962, 2d edit., 1968, Le Roman de la Rose, 1967, 72, Comparists at Work, 1968, The Meaning of Mannerism, 1972, Mimesis: From Mirror to Method, Augustine to Descartes, 1982, Medieval and Renaissance Theories of Representation, 1984, Romanesque Signs: Early Medieval Narrative and Iconography, 1983, 85, Images of Power: History/Text/Discourse, 1986, The Legitimacy of the Middle Ages, 1988, The New Philology, 1990, Boundaries and Transgressions, 1991, The New Medievalism, 1991, Commentary as Cultural Artifact, 1992, Medievalism and the Modernist Temper: On the Discipline of Medieval, 1996, The Whole Book: Miscellany and Order in the Medieval Manuscript, 1996, The Evidence in Hand: The Artifact in Library Collections, 2001, L'Altérité du Moyen Age, 2003; editor: (book series) Parallax: Revisions of Culture and Society, 1987—; asst. editor French Rev., 1968-88; mem. editl. bd. Olifant, 1974-94, Medievalia et Humanistica, 1974-95, Medievalia, 1975—, Comparative Lit. Studies, 1986, Publ. of the MLA, 1988-89, Recentiores, 1991—, Modern Lang. Notes, 1992; adv. bd. Colleagues Press, 1986-96, Exemplaria: A Jour. Medieval Theory, 1987—; adv. com. PMLA, 1980-84; adv. editor Romanic Rev., 1986—, Storia della Storiographia, 1992—. Rotary Found. fellow U. d'Aix Marseilles, France, 1958-59; fellow Inst. Rsch. in Humanities, 1966-67, NEH fellow, 1978-79, sr. fellow Sch. of Criticism and Theory, 1988—. Fellow Medieval Acad. Am.; mem. Acad. Lit. Studies (nominating com. 1974-78, sec.-treas. 1978-87), Dante Soc., Internat. Comparative Lit. Assn., New Eng. Medieval Assn. (adv. com. 1981-85), MLA (chmn. com. on careers 1985-86, James Russell Lowell prize com. 1986-88, com. on profl. ethics 1987-88, del. assembly 1994-97), Medieval Acad. Am., Soc. Rencesvals (sec.-treas. Am. sect. 1964-69). Home: 5 Saint Martins Rd Baltimore MD 21218-1815 Office: Johns Hopkins Univ Romance Languages and Lit 3400 N Charles St Baltimore MD 21218 Office Phone: 410-516-4736. E-mail: stephen.nichols@jhu.edu.

NICHOLS, STEVEN PARKS, mechanical engineer, educator, academic administrator, lawyer; b. Cody, Wyo., July 1, 1950; s. Rufus Parks Nichols and Gwen Sena (Frank) Keyes; m. Mary Ruth Barrow, Aug. 5, 1990; 1 child, Nicholas Barrow Nichols. PhD, U. Tex., Austin, 1975, JD, 1983. Assoc. dir. Tex. Space Grant Consortium, Austin, 1989-91, dir. Design Projects Program, 1989—2002; dep. dir. Ctr. for Energy Studies, U. Tex., Austin, 1988-91, dir. of Ctr., 1991-99, acting dir. Ctr. for Electromechanics, 1994-99, assoc. prof. mech. engring., 1996—2000, prof. mech. engring., 2004—, assoc. chair dept. mech. engring., 1999—2002, dir. Ctr. for Energy and Environ. Resources, 1998—, fellow Ctr. for Nano and Molecular Scis., 1998—, dir. Chair of Free Enterprise, 2001—, fellow, 2001—, assoc. v.p. rsch., 2002—06, ASME Internat. vision and strategy task force, 2006—, prof. IC2, 2006—. Bd. dirs. Assn. Mfg. Excellence; chmn. Nat. Coun. Space Grant Dirs., NASA, 1989-92; bd. dirs. So. Coalition for Advanced Transp., 1994-99, chair elect 1998-99, chair 1998-00; bd. dirs. Nat. Inst. for Engring. Ethics, 1996-01; chmn. mgmt. divsn. ASME Internat., 1999-01, exec. com. engring. and tech. mgmt., 1999-; rsch. integrity officer, 2004-2006. Patentee (with others) pulsed welding techniques, railgun igniter, inert burner, rail thruster, other patents pending. Recipient Olympus Innovation award, 2005. Fellow ASME (Disting. Lectr. award 2004-06), IC2 Inst. (sr.), Ctr. Nano and Biotech.; mem. NSPE, ABA, ASCE (anti-corruption task force 2006-), Am. Soc. Engring. Edn. (Fred Merryfield Design award 2001, Kauffman Outstanding Entrepreneurship award 2007), Nat. Inst. Engring. Ethics (bd. govs. 1987-93, 96-01), NY Acad. Scis. (gov.'s task force on technology communicalization, 2006—, dir. global idea product program, 2003—). Home: 1400 Lorrain St Austin TX 78703-4023 Office: U Tex Dept Mech Engring Austin TX 78712

NICHOLS, VICKI ANNE, financial consultant, librarian; b. Denver, June 10, 1949; d. Glenn Warner and Loretta Irene (Chalender) Adams; m. Robert H. Nichols, Oct. 28, 1972 (div.); children: Christopher Travis, Lindsay Meredith. BA, Colo. Coll., 1972; postgrad., U. Denver, 1976-77. Treas., controller, dir. Polaris Resources, Inc., Denver, 1972-86; controller Inter-Cap Devel. Corp., 1986-87; treas., controller, dir. Transnat. Cons., Ltd., 1986-91; web coord. Jefferson County Pub. Libr., Colo., 1986—. Dir., owner Nichols Bus. Services. Home: 4305 Brentwood St Wheat Ridge CO 80033-4412 Office: 10200 W 20th Ave Lakewood CO 80215 Business E-Mail: vnichols@jefferson.lib.co.us.

NICHOLS, WILLIAM CURTIS, psychologist, educator, marriage and family therapist, consultant; b. Fayette, Ala., Apr. 16, 1929; s. William Curtis and Eva (Hargett) N.; m. Alice Louise Mancill, May 29, 1954 (dec. 1990); children: Alice Camille, William Mancill, David Paul; m. Mary Anne Pace, Feb. 29, 1992. AB, U. Ala., 1953; EdD, Columbia U., 1960. Diplomate Am. Bd. Profl. Psychology. Asst. prof. sociology U. Ala., Birmingham, 1960-63; postdoctoral fellow Merrill-Palmer Inst., 1963-64, mem. psychotherapy faculty, 1965-69; prof. sociology Samford U., Birmingham, Ala., 1963-65; pvt. practice clin. psychology and marital and family therapy Grosse Pointe, Mich., 1969-73, 76-87; pvt. practice psychology, marital and family therapy Birmingham, Mich., 1976-87; prof. home and family life, dir. marriage and family counseling Fla. State U., 1973-76; exec. dir. Gov.'s Constituency Children, Fla., 1987-89; pvt. practice marital and family therapy S.E. Family Inst., 1989-90; pres. William Nichols Assocs., Organizational Cons., 1990-91; cons., marital and family therapist Atlanta, 1992—97; cons. in field, 1997-98; with The Nichols Group, Inc., 1998. Adj. prof. clin. psychology U. Detroit, 1976-83; adj. prof. family therapy Fla. State U., 1990-91; adj. prof., grad. faculty child and family devel. dept. U. Ga., 1992-05, founder, chair adv. com. Family Therapy Archives, 1993—, The Nichols Group, Inc., 1998-99. Author: Treating People in Families: An Integrative Framework, 1996, Marital Therapy: An Integrative Approach, 1988, Treating Adult Survivors of Childhood Sexual Abuse, 1992, The AAMFT: Fifty Years of Marital and Family Therapy, 1992, Family Therapy Around the World: A Festschrift to Florence Kaslow, 2004; co-author: Systematic Family Therapy, 1986; editor: (with others) Handbook of Family Development and Intervention, 2000; editor The Family Coord., 1970-75, Jour. Marriage and Family Counseling, 1974-76, Contemporary Family Therapy: An Internat. Jour., 1986-2006, Family Therapy News, 1986-91, The Internat. Connection, 1996-99; mem. editl. bd. Internat. Jour. Family Therapy, 1977-85, Jour. Divorce and Remarriage, 1976-83, 85—, Sage Family Studies Abstracts, 1977-99, Family Systems Medicine, 1982-96, Jour. Marital and Family Therapy, 1984—, Jour. Family Psychotherapy, 1990—, Jour. Family Psychology, 1986-90. Mem. mental health and health coms. Detroit Mayor's Commn. on Children and Youth, 1966-69; bd. dir. Family and Children's Svc., Oakland, Mich., 1977-87, chmn., 1984-86, dir. emeritus, 1987—. With C.E., U.S. Army, 1948-49. Recipient Svc. award Ala. Assn. for Mental Health, 1962, Spl. award for Outstanding Contbns. Fla. Assn. Marriage and Family Therapy, 1977, 82, 90; NSF fellow U. Colo., 1963, Disting. Svc. Families award Southeastern Coun. on Family Rels., 1996. Fellow: APA, Am. Assn. Marriage and Family Therapy (dir. 1969—72, founding editor Jour. Marital and Family Therapy 1974—76, chmn. accreditation com. 1976—77, pres.-elect 1979—80, dir. 1979—83, pres. 1981—82, Spl. awards 1976, 1978, Disting. Leadership awards 1982, 1983, Disting. Leadership award 1991, Orgnl. Contbns. award 1992), Am. Psychol. Soc.; mem.: Am. Family Therapy Acad., Internat. Family Therapy Assn. (bd. dirs. ex-officio 1996—98, editor Internat. Connections 1996—99, pres.-elect 1998—99, pres. 2000—01), Ga. Assn. for Marriage and Family Therapy (pres.-elect 1994—95, pres. 1996), Mich. Bd. Marriage Counselors (chmn. 1980—87), Nat. Coun. on Family Rels. (bd. dir., exec. com. 1969—78, pres. 1976—77), Mich. Assn. Marriage Counselors (pres. 1969—71, chmn. profl. liaison com. 1972—73), Mich. Inter-Profl. Assn. on Marriage, Divorce and Family (com. chmn. 1968—71, 1976—86, trustee 1977—80, Orgnl. Contbn. award 1992), Assn. Marital and Family therapy Regulation Bds. (MFT examination adv. bd. 1989—92), Am. Assn. Marriage and Family Therapy Edn. and Rsch. Found. (trustee 1992—94). Home: 755 W Lake Dr Athens GA 30606 Personal E-mail: nicholsw@aol.com.

NICHOLS, WILLIAM FORD, JR., foundation, health science association administrator, educator; b. Palo Alto, Calif., July 4, 1934; s. William Ford and Elizabeth (Woodyatt) N.; m. Rosemary Peterson, 1988; children: Deborah, John, Andrew. AB, Stanford U., 1956, MBA, 1958. CPA, Calif. With Price Waterhouse, San Francisco, 1958-69, Price Waterhouse & Co., Sydney, Australia, 1966; asst. contr. Saga Corp., Menlo Park, Calif., 1969-72, contr., 1972—, asst. treas., 1981-83; assoc. prof. San Jose State U., 1983-88; treas. William and Flora Hewlett Found., Menlo Park, 1985-2000. Trustee Investment Fund for Founds., 1991-2001. Bd. dirs. Lucile Packard Found. for Children's Health, Palo Alto, Calif., 1999—2006; trustee Oreg. Shakespeare Festival Endowment Fund, 2005-. Mem. AICPA, Calif. Soc. CPA's, Inst. Mgmt. Accts. (nat. v.p. 1974-75, bd. dirs.), Fin. Execs. Inst. (pres. Santa Clara Valley chpt. 1979-80), Palo Alto Club, Alpha Omega Alpha (asst. treas. 1985—). Home: 620 Sand Hill Rd Apt 220-D Palo Alto CA 94304-2098

NICHOLS, WILLIAM OWEN, conservationist; b. Appleton, Wis., Mar. 11, 1939; s. Freeman Alfred and Lila (Arvidson) N.; m. Susan Karen Babbitt, Oct. 20, 1962; children: Sarah Kay, John Freeman. BS in Biology, U. Wis., 1961. Park ranger Yellowstone Nat. Park, 1960-61, Shenandoah Nat. Park, 1964-70; supr. park ranger Mammoth Cave Nat. Park, 1970-73; chief park ranger Cumberland Gap Nat. Park, 1973-82; supt. Abraham Lincoln Birthplace, 1982-85, Vicksburg (Miss.) Nat. Mil. Park, 1985—. Pres. United Way of West Ctrl. Miss., Vicksburg, 1990-91; bd. dirs. Miss. Children's Home Soc., Jackson, 1986—; trustee Vicksburg-Warren County Libr., 1992—. Mem. Rotary (pres. Vicksburg club 1989-90). Presbyterian. Avocations: gardening, bird watching, walking, reading. Office: Vicksburg Nat Mil Park 3201 Clay St Vicksburg MS 39183-3469 Address: Nichols 1004 Windy Lake Dr Vicksburg MS 39183-8751

NICHOLSON, BERNICE LOUGHRAN, art educator; b. Newark, June 8, 1919; d. Harvey Whitfield and Carolyn (Augenstein) Bingham; m. Joseph S. Loughran, Mar. 31, 1947 (dec. 1977); children: Kevin, Mary Ann Loughran Rundell; m. Loren Lee Nicholson, Feb. 26, 1983. BS in Art Edn., Kean Coll., 1940; MA in Art, Ohio State U., 1946; EdD in Art and Edn., Stanford U., 1958. Art tchr. elem. sch., Irvington, N.J., 1940-43; instr. Johnson (Vt.) State Coll., 1943-47; tchr. elem. sch. Redwood City, Calif., 1954-56; prof. art Calif. Poly. State U., San Luis Obispo, 1958-88, prof. emerita art, 1988—. Co-dir. Integrated Arts for the Classroom Workshops, 1991—. Author: Art Experiences: An Experimental Approach, 1963, Experiences in Twentieth Century Art, 1970, revision, 1990. Mem. com. state curriculum visual and performing arts, 1980-82. Recipient Award of Excellence, Calif. State Fair "Calif. Works", 1989, Bernice Loughran Nicholson Endowment for Arts Edn. Calif. Polytechnic State U., 2005. Mem. Calif. Humanities Assn. (state pres. 1978-80), Inst. Noetic Sci. (leader local study group 1992-98). Congregationalist. Avocations: travel, dance. Home and Office: 156 Del Norte Way San Luis Obispo CA 93405-1508

NICHOLSON, BRADLEY JAMES, lawyer; b. Montebello, Calif., Sept. 22, 1958; s. Thomas Edwin and Charlotte Elizabeth (Knight) N.; m. Anne Marie Dooley, Oct. 6, 1990. BA, Reed Coll., 1983; JD, U. Pa., 1990. Bar: Oreg. 2001. Atty. Wilson, Sonsini, Goodrich & Rosati, Palo Alto, Calif., 1990-91; law clk. to Hon. Morris S. Arnold U.S. Dist. Ct., Ft. Smith, Ark., 1991-92; atty. Coudert Bros., San Jose, Calif., 1992-94; law clerk to Hon. Morris S. Arnold U.S. Cir. Ct., Little Rock, 1994-96; atty. Brown & Bain, Palo Alto, Calif., 1997-98; staff atty. ctrl. legal staff Nev. Supreme Ct., Carson City, 1998-99, prin. staff atty., ctrl. legal staff, 1999-2000; appellate staff atty. Oreg. Supreme Ct., Salem, Oreg., 2000—. Contbr. articles to profl. jours. Mem. Federalist Soc.(vice chmn. publications Litigation practice group, 1997-98, pres. Little Rock lawyers chpt. 1995-96). Avocation: classical guitar. Office: Oreg Supreme Ct 1163 State St Salem OR 97301-2563

NICHOLSON, BRUCE ALLEN, lawyer; b. Phila., Nov. 12, 1949; s. Charles Glanz and Jean (Billman) N.; m. Linda King Barton, Apr. 22, 1972; children: Jessica Ann, James Barton. BA, Cornell U., 1971; JD cum laude,

Boston Coll., 1975. Bar: Pa. 1975. Staff asst. Mass Bar Assn., Boston, 1973-75; assoc. Duffy, North, Wilson, Thomas & Nicholson, LLP, Hatboro, Pa., 1975-78; ptnr., 1978—. Solicitor Mongomery County (Pa.) Redevel. Authority, 1993—. Pres. Main St. Hatboro Revitalization Com., 1995-2000; mem. Hatboro Boro Coun., 1984-88; chmn. Hatboro Hist. Commn., 1981-83; bd. mgrs. Hatboro Area YMCA, 1984-95, bd. chmn., 1990, 91; pres., Comet Class Yacht Racing Assn., 1979-80; chmn., Washington District, Cradle of Liberty Coun., Boy Scouts of Am., 2004-. Named YMCA Vol. of Yr., 1989, 92. Mem. ABA, Pa. Bar Assn., Montgomery Bar Assn., greater Hatboro C. of C. (v.p., bd. dirs.), Rotary, Yacht Club Stone Harbor (N.J.), Riverton Yacht Club (N.J.). Office: Duffy North Wilson Thomas & Nicholson LLP 104 N York Rd Hatboro PA 19040-2699 Home: 104 N York Rd Hatboro PA 19040-2609 E-mail: banicholson@duffynorth.com.

NICHOLSON, BRUCE J., insurance company executive; BS, St. Olaf Coll., Northfield, Minn., 1968. With Ministers Life Ins. Co., Mpls., 1975-1984, Towers Perrin Co, Mpls., 1984-1990; exec. v.p., CFO Lutheran Brotherhood, Mpls., 1990—97, exec. v.p., COO, 1997—99, pres., COO, 1999—2000, pres., CEO, 2000—02, Thrivent Fin. for Lutherans, Mpls., 2002—05, chmn., pres., CEO, 2005—. Mem. bd. regents St. Olaf Coll.; bd. mem. Luther Sem., Minn. Orchestral Assn., Minn. Bus. Partnership, Fox Cities C. of C. Fellow: Soc. of Actuaries; mem.: Am. Acad. of Actuaries. Office: Thrivent Financial for Lutherans 625 4th Ave S Minneapolis MN 55415 *

NICHOLSON, COY LEE, English educator, writer; b. Hanford, Calif., Sept. 15, 1936; s. Coy Hargrove and Retha Alice Nicholson. AA, Little Rock Jr. Coll., 1955; BA, Millsaps Coll., Jackson, Miss., 1957; MA, U. Miss., 1959. General Secondary Certificate in Teaching State of Calif., 1960. Tchr. Turlock HS, 1959—64; instr. Modesto Jr. Coll., Calif., 1964—96. Author: (book) Common Ground, 2000; author: (and illustrator) Speakeasy, 2005. Mem. Democratic Nat. Com.; founder of Retha Alice Medley Nicholson prize Yellville-Summit H.S., Ark., 2001. Recipient Cert. of Recognition for Achievment in Lit. Arts, Stanislaus County Arts Coun., Calif., 2001; Wallstreet Jour. fellow, Fresno State U., 1961, scholar, Nat. Endowment for the Humanities, 1964, 1978. Mem.: Acad. Am. Poets (assoc.). Avocation: calligraphy. Home: The Stratford at Beyer Pk 3529 Forest Glenn Dr Apt 218 Modesto CA 95355

NICHOLSON, DIANE M., special education educator; BS in Psychology, Ga. Coll., 1977; MEd in Behavior Disorders, West Ga. Coll., 1989, EDs in behavior disorders, 1993. Cert. K-12 in behavior disorders, learning disabilities, mental retardation and inter-related TSS, early childhood edn. 2005. Behavior disorder/learning disability resource room instr. Whitesburg Elem. Sch., Carroll County Bd. Edn., 1980—87, 1988—91; academic therapist Burwell Psychoeducational Ctr., Carrollton, Ga., 1987—88; behavior disordered program instr. Ctrl. Mid. Sch. Carroll County Bd. Edn., 1991—92; grad. asst., tchg. asst. spl. edn. dept. West Ga. Coll., Carrollton, 1992—93, tchng. asst. for seminar for pre-tchrs., 1993, adj. instr., 1993—95, instr., 1994, adj. instr., 1995; resource tchr. for emotional and behavior disorders/learning disabled/mildly mentally handicapped Carroll County Bd. Edn., Ga., 1993—. Consultant, team mem. (book) Language Movement Strategies, 1983. Recipient Spirit award, Carroll County C. of C., 2005. Mem.: Phi Delta Kappa. Avocations: reading, computers. Home: 25 Agean Way Whitesburg GA 30185

NICHOLSON, DOUGLAS ROBERT, accountant; b. Avon, NY, Dec. 4, 1921; s. Robert William and Ruth (Neff) N.; m. Gertrude Jane Scott, Apr. 24, 1944; children— Laurie, Scott, Susan, Steven. AB, U. Rochester, 1942, MS, 1948. Baseball player St. Louis Cardinal Farm Teams, 1942, 46; staff acct. Oliver & Clapp, 1948-49; sr. acct. Charles L. Clapp & Co., 1949-51; tchr. income taxes U. Rochester, 1950-61; office mgr. Williams, Clapp & Co., 1951-53, ptnr., 1953-56; prin. Haskins & Sells, CPA's, Rochester, N.Y., 1956-59, ptnr., 1959-67, ptnr.-in-charge Rochester office, 1967-82. Author: After Reagan-Bush is it Too Late, 2002. Pres. Estate Planning Coun. Rochester; team capt. YMCA capital fund dr., 1961, Rochester Inst. Tech. new campus fund dr., 1964; chmn. spl. gifts com. U. Rochester, 1965, group leader 38 million capital fund campaign, 1966; mem. acctg. adv. bd. Syracuse U., 1968; adv. com. M.S. program Rochester Inst. Tech. Bd. Dirs.; treas. Highland Hosp., Rochester; bd. dirs. Hosp. Computer Ctr. Rochester, Rochester Regional Rsch. Libr. Coun.; mem. deferred giving adv. coun. Rochester Inst. Tech.; mem. N.Y. State Bd. Pub. Accountancy, 1977-82. Lt. USN, 1942-45, WWII. Decorated two battle stars; recipient Gannett Newspapers awards, 1956, SUNY Empire State medal for philanthropy, 1999. Mem. AICPA, N.Y. State Soc. CPAs (past pres. Rochester), Nat. Assn. Accts., Am. Acctg. Assn., Am. Mgmt. Assn., Rochester C. of C., Beta Alpha Psi. Democrat. Unitarian (trustee). Clubs: Oak Hill Country, University, Genesee Valley. Home and Office: 312 Kidd Castle Way Webster NY 14580-1966

NICHOLSON, ELLEN ELLIS, clinical social worker; b. Boston, Apr. 1, 1940; d. George Letham and Mary Stirling (Money) McIver; divorced; 1 child, Matthew Norman Ellis. Dental Hygienist, Forsyth Coll., 1959; BS, Northeastern U., 1973, MEd in Counseling, 1974; MSW, Boston U., 1984. Registered dental hygienist, Mass. Dental hygienist, 1959—66; clin. coord., pvt. dental practice Forsyth Dental Ctr., Boston, 1966—70; dir. vol. counseling Solomon Mental Health Ctr., Lowell, Mass., 1974—75; social worker East Boston Social Ctrs., Inc., 1976—77, dir. youth family counseling, 1977—79; supr. family svc. Boston Housing Authority, 1979—81; social worker Mass. Soc. Prevention Cruelty to Children, Hyannis, 1984—86, supr., 1986—93, clinic dir., 1993—95; dir. profl. svcs. Child and Family Svc. of Cape Cod, Hyannis, 1995—98, dir., 1998—2005, dir. Abuse Prevention Svcs., 1995—96, dir., 1995—2005; cons., therapist Child & Family Svcs. Cape Cod, 2005—. Psychotherapist Riverview Sch., Sandwich, Mass., 1989-93. Advisor youth group Christ Episcopal Ch., Needham, Mass., 1960-64, St. Paul's Ch., Newburyport, Mass., 1964-65; vol. counselor Solomon Mental Health Ctr., Lowell, 1972-74; chair Barnstable County Children's Task Force, 1994-96; chmn. adv. com. Barnstable County Sexual Abuse Intervention Network, 1994-96; mem. task force Barnstable County Juvenile Firesetters, 1995-96, mem. steering com., 1996—; mem. adv. bd. Cape and Islands Child Advocacy Ctr.; mem. Cape & Islands Domestic Violence Coun. Bd., 1998—. Mem. NASW, Am. Profl. Soc. on Abuse of Children, Assn. for Treatment of Sexual Abusers, Sigma Phi Alpha, Sigma Epsilon Rho, Kappa Delta Pi. Avocations: travel, ballroom dancing, skiing. Office: Child and Family Svc Cape Cod 1019 Rt 132 Hyannis MA 02601-1839

NICHOLSON, HENRY HALE, JR., retired surgeon; b. Statesville, NC, June 22, 1922; s. Henry Hale and Martha Haseltine (Miller) N.; m. Freda Hyams, Sept. 24, 1956; children: Henry Hale III, Thomas Dalton Miller, John Christie, Michael Witherspoon, Freda Amanda, W. Stuart Cooper. BA in Chemistry, Duke U., 1944, MD, 1947; grad., USAF Sch. Aviation Medicine, 1952. Diplomate Am. Bd. Gen. Surgery, Am. Bd. Colon and Rectal Surgery. Rotating intern U. Wis. Gen. Hosp., Madison, 1947-48; resident in gen. surgery Med. Coll. Va., Richmond, 1948-49, Alton Ochsner Hosp. and Clinic, New Orleans, 1949-51, 53-55, inaugeral resident in colon and rectal surgery, 1955-56; resident in gen. surgery Tulane U., La. Charity Hosp., New Orleans, 1949-51, 53-55; pvt. practice gen., colon and rectal surgery, aerospace medicine Charlotte, NC, 1956—2002; sr. surg. staff mem. Carolinas Med. Ctr. and Mercy Hosp., Charlotte; ret., 2002. Sr. active staff Presbyn. Hosp., Charlotte; sr. active teaching staff Carolinas Med. Ctr., 1956-85, cons. staff, 1985—; surg. cons. Surgeon Gen. USAF, 1971-82. Mem. Airport Authority Charlotte/Douglas Internat. Airport, 1992—; mem. Mayor's Com. of 100 to study regional transp. and make appropriate recommendations, 1993-94; sr. examiner FAA, 1952-2007; mem. athletic-med. bd. N.C. Shrine Bowl, 1980-2003. With U.S. Army, 1943-46. Maj. flight surgeon USAF, 1951-53, Korea; col. USAFR, 1961-82. Decorated Legion of Merit, Disting. Svc. medal NC; named Flight Surgeon of Yr., USAF N.G., 1981, 1st Alternate Flight Surgeon of Yr. award USAF, 1982. Fellow ACS, Am. Soc. Colon and Rectal Surgeons; mem. Mecklenberg County Med. Soc. (pres. 1972), Charlotte Surg. Soc. (pres. 1987), Shriners, Masons (32 degree), Jesters, Alton Ochsner Surg. Soc., Hazel Creek Trout Club, Robert Burns Soc., St. Andrews Soc. of Carolina, Air Force Assn., Hound Ears Club (Blowing Rock, N.C.), Charlotte Country Club, Alpha Tau Omega, Phi Chi, Omicron Delta Kappa. Methodist. Avocations: golf, skiing, fly fishing, travel, painting.

NICHOLSON, JACK, actor; b. Neptune, NJ, Apr. 22, 1937; raised by John and Ethel May N.; m. Sandra Knight, June 17, 1962 (div. Aug. 8, 1968); children: Jennifer, Lorraine Broussard. Acting debut: (Hollywood stage prodn.) Tea an Sympathy; actor: (films) Cry-Baby Killer, 1958, Studs Lonigen, 1960, Little Shop of Horrors, 1960, Ensign Pulver, 1964, The Trip, 1967, Easy Rider, 1969 (Acad. award nomination best supporting actor), Five Easy Pieces, 1970, Carnal Knowledge, 1971, A Safe Place, 1971, The Last Detail, 1974 (Cannes Film Festival prize, BAFTA award best actor), Chinatown, 1974 (BAFTA award best actor, Acad. award nomination, NY Film Critics Circle award, Golden Globe award best actor), Tommy, The Passenger, 1975, The Fortune, 1975, One Flew Over the Cuckoo's Nest, 1975 (Golden Globe award best actor, Acad. award best actor, NY Film Critics Circle award, BAFTA award best actor), The Missouri Breaks, 1976, The Last Tycoon, 1976, The Shining, 1980, The Postman Always Rings Twice, 1981, Reds, 1981 (BAFTA award best supporting actor, Acad. award nomination best supporting actor), The Border, 1982, Terms of Endearment, 1983 (Acad. award best supporting actor, Golden Globe award best actor), Prizzi's Honor, 1985, Heartburn, 1986, The Witches of Eastwick, 1987, Broadcast News, 1987, Ironweed, 1987 (Acad. award nomination best actor), Batman, 1989, Man Trouble, 1991, A Few Good Men, 1992, Hoffa, 1992, Wolf, 1994, The Crossing Guard, 1995, Mars Attacks!, 1996, The Evening Star, 1996, Blood and Wine, 1996, As Good As It Gets, 1997 (Acad. award best actor, Golden Globe award best actor, SAG award best actor), The Pledge, 2001, About Schmidt, 2002 (Acad. award nomination best actor, Golden Globe award best actor), Anger Management, 2003, Something's Gotta Give, 2003, The Departed, 2006 (MTV Movie award best villain, 2007); prodr.: Head, 1968, Ride the Whirlwind, The Shooting; dir.: Drive, He Said, 1971; dir., actor: (films) Goin' South, 1978, The Two Jakes, 1990. Co-recipient (with Bobby McFerrin) Grammy award for best recording for children, 1987; recipient Life Achievement award, Am. Film Inst., 1994, Cecil B. DeMille award, 1999. Office: Bresler Kelly & Assocs 11500 W Olympic Blvd Ste 510 Los Angeles CA 90064-1578

NICHOLSON, JAMES M., chemicals executive; b. 1967; Worked for Amerisure Cos., Aon Corp.; v.p. PVS Chemicals Inc., Detroit, 1995—; mgr. Chantland Material Handling Solutions. Named one of 40 Under 40, Crain's Detroit Bus., 2006. Mem.: Mich. Mfg. Assn. (chmn. 2005). Office: PVS Chemicals Inc 10900 Harper Ave Detroit MI 48213 Office Phone: 313-921-1200. Office Fax: 313-921-1378.

NICHOLSON, JIM (ROBERT JAMES NICHOLSON), secretary of veterans affairs, former ambassador; b. Struble, IA, Feb. 4, 1938; s. Don and Helen Nicholson; m. Suzanne Nicholson; children: Nick, Katie, R.J. BA, U.S. Mil. Acad., West Point, 1961; MA in Pub. Policy, Columbia U., 1969; JD, U. Denver, 1972; PhD in Pub. Svc. (hon.), Regis U., 2001; PhD (hon.), John Cabot U., 2002. Atty., Denver, 1973-78; founder Nicholson Enterprises, Inc., 1978, Renaissance Homes, Denver, 1987; committeeman from Colo. Rep. Nat. Com., 1986—2000, vice chmn, 1993—97, chmn., 1997—2001; US amb. to The Holy See US Dept. State, Rome, 2001—04; sec. US Dept. Veterans Affairs, Washington, 2005—. Chmn. task force presdl. primaries and caucuses Rep. Nat. Com., 1996, chmn. rules com., 1993-97, mem. budget com. Author: (non-fiction) The United States and the Holy See-The Long Road, 2002. Bd. dirs. Daniels Fund. With US Army, 1961—69, with USAR, 1969—91. Decorated Bronze Star, Combat Infantryman's Badge, Meritorious Svc. medal with oak leaf cluster, Vietnamese Cross for Gallantry, 2 Air medals, Horatio Alger award, 2000, Pres. medal, Georgetown U., 2003; inducted as a Knight in the Sovereign Mil. Order of Malta, 1999, named a Knight of the Grand Cross of the Order of Pius IX, 2003. Office: US Dept Veterans Affairs 810 Vermont Ave Washington DC 20420 *

NICHOLSON, JOSEPH BRUCE, real estate developer; b. San Jose, Calif., Jan. 21, 1940; s. Wilmot Joseph and Ruth (Russell) N.; m. Susan Knight, Nov. 1963 (div. 1972); children: Kelsey Erin, Craig Wilmot; m. Linda Mirassou, Aug. 1992. BArch, U. Oreg., 1963. Exec. v.p. Nicholson-Brown Inc., Santa Clara, Calif., 1967-80; prin. Nicholson Assocs., Aptos, Calif., 1977—; v.p., gen. mgr. Nicholson-Wilson Co., Santa Clara, 1980-83; prin. The Nicholson Co., Campbell, Calif., 1984—; v.p. Pacific Property Ventures Inc., Campbell, 1988—; pres. Nicholson Constrn. Inc., Campbell, 1989—; v.p. Nicholson Property Mgmt. Inc., Campbell, 1989—; pres. The Nicholson Family Found., 1996—. Bd. dirs. Transmetrics Inc., San Jose. Bd. dirs. Triton Mus., Santa Clara, 1979, Hope Rehab. Svc., San Jose, 1979, United Way Ctrl. Area, San Jose, 1991. Devel. Engring. Rsch. Inst., Carmel, Calif., 1999—, Tannery Art Ctr., Santa Cruz, 2003—; pres. adv. bd. de Saisset Mus., Santa Clara U., 1991; trustee Mus. of Art and History, Santa Cruz, 1993; pres. Cabrillo Festival of Contemporary Music, Santa Cruz, Calif., 2000—. Lt. USN, 1963—67. Mem. Rotary, Commonwealth Club (San Francisco), Santa Cruz Yacht Club, Tennis Club Rio Del Mar. Republican. Avocations: travel, reading, art, painting, tennis. Home: 218 Shoreview Dr Aptos CA 95003-4621 Business E-Mail: brucenicholson@thenicholsonco.com.

NICHOLSON, LELAND ROSS, retired utilities executive, energy consultant; b. Carrington, ND, Feb. 21, 1924; s. Malcom and Lena May (Kerlin) N.; m. Virginia E. Blair, Mar. 16, 1946; children: Heather Le Nicholson Studebaker, Leland B., Holly Kay. Student, Northwestern U., 1940-41; BSEE, U. N.D., 1949; postgrad. in utility mgmt., U. Minn., 1952. Planning and mktg. engr. Minkota Power Coop., Grand Forks, ND, 1949-54; dir. new bus. Kans. Power & Light Co., Topeka, 1954-64, v.p. mktg., 1964-76, sr. v.p., 1976-80, exec. v.p., 1980-83, also bd. dirs.; pres. Kans. Power & Light Gas Service, Topeka, 1985-88, ret., 1988; pres., chief operating officer The Gas Service Co., Kansas City, Mo., 1983-85. Pres. Indsl. Devel. Corp., Topeka; chmn. Kans. Coun. on Electricity and Environment; exec. com. Kansas City Labor Mgmt. Coun., 1986-89; mem. Mktg. Execs. Conf.; bd. dirs. Gas Service Energy Corp., Kansas City, Merchants Nat. Bank, Topeka. Idea innovator heat pump water heater, photo cell controlled yard light, hydrogen fuel cell, electric grill. Bd. dirs., area relations com. Kansas City Area Econ. Devel. Coun., Mo., 1983-89; bd. dirs. Kansas City Pvt. Industry Coun., 1986-89, Kansas City Downtown Coun.; trustee U. Mo., Kansas City, 1984-91; mktg. chmn. Kansas City Full Employment Council; past chmn., mem. Topeka-Shawnee County Planning Commn.; adult adv. com. Sea Scouts. Master sgt. USMC, 1942-46. Mem. Am. Gas Assn., Midwest Gas Assn. (bd. dirs. 1985-89), Mo. Valley Electric Assn. (chmn. 1979-81), Edison Electric Inst. (mktg. chmn. 1978-80), Assoc. Industries of Mo., Kans. Assn. Commerce and Industry, Greater Kansas City (Mo.) C. of C. (bd. dirs. 1979-82), US Marine Corps League (life), Shawnee Yacht Club (Topeka) (commodore 1972-74), Lake Gaston Assn. (pres. 1993-97), Kansas City Club, Rotary. Republican. Congregationalist. Avocations: sailing, canoeing, fishing, reading, electronics.

NICHOLSON, MARILYN LEE, arts administrator; b. San Jose, Calif., Feb. 7, 1949; d. John Hart Nicholson and Betty Ann (Price) Shepardson; m. Neal Luit Evenhuis. BA in English and History, U. Ariz., 1972; BFA in Studio, U. Hawaii-Manoa, Honolulu, 1977, MA in English, 1977, AS, 1984. Edn. coord., dir. Bishop Mus. Arts and Crafts Sch., Honolulu, 1977-79; owner Fiber Arts Store, Kailua, Hawaii, 1978-82; field coord. Hawaii State Found. on Culture and Arts, Honolulu, 1981-85; exec. dir. Sedona (Ariz.) Arts Ctr., 1986-92, Volcano (Hawaii) Art Ctr., 1992—. Mem. bd. artist selection com. Ariz. Indian Living Treasures, 1988-92; bd. dirs., treas. Sedona Cultural Arts Ctr., 1987-92; conf. speaker Nat. Assembly Arts Agys., 1988. Founding Chmn. Sedona Gallery Assn., 1990-92; mem. com. Sedona Acad., 1986-92; mem. steering com. community plan City of Sedona, 1989-91; commr. Arts & Cultural Ctr., Sedona, 1989-91; mem. exec. com. planning Volcano Community Assn., 1993-96. Recipient Mayor's award for Disting. Svc., Sedona City Coun., 1992. Mem. Hawaii Mus. Assn. (bd. dirs. 1995-00), Cooper Ctr. Coun. (bd. dirs. 1992—), Aloha Festivals-Hawaii Island (bd. dirs. 1992-99). Office: Volcano Art Ctr PO Box 129 Volcano HI 96785

NICHOLSON, MYREEN MOORE, artist, researcher; b. Norfolk, Va., June 2, 1940; d. William Chester and Illeen (Fox) Moore; m. Roland Quarles Nicholson Jr., Jan. 9, 1964 (dec. 1986); children: Andrea Joy, Ross (dec. 1965); m. Harold Wellington McKinney II, 1981; 1 child, Cara Isadora. AA, William and Mary Coll., 1960; BA, Old Dominion U., 1962, MA, 1997; MLS, U. N.C., Chapel Hill, 1971; postgrad., The Citadel, 1968-69, Hastie Sch. Art, 1968, Chrysler Mus. Art Sch., 1964, Contemporary Art Ctr., Va., 1972, Old Dominion U., 1997—2000. LCSW Va., 1965, S.C., 1967; cert. tchr. English, art and media Va. English tchr., Chesapeake, Va., 1962-63; dept. head Portsmouth Bus. Coll., Va., 1963-64; tech. writer City Planning/Art Commn., Norfolk, 1964-65; art tchr. Norfolk pub. schs., 1965-67; prof. lit. art Palmer Jr. Coll., Charleston, S.C., 1968; tchr. Penn Sch., John's Island, SC, 1968; libr. Charleston Schs., 1968-69; asst. to asst. dir. City Libr. Norfolk, 1970-72; art and audio-visual libr., 1972-75; rsch. libr., 1975-83; libr. dept. fiction, 1983-90; prof. Ctrl. Tex. Coll., 1998—; dir. W. Ghent Arts Alliance, Norfolk, 1978—, Gyaden SAT's, 2006—. Poet-in-schs., Virginia Beach, Va., 1987. Book reviewer Art Book Revs., Libr. Jour., 1973-76; editor, illustrator Acquisitions Bibliographies, 1970—, (play) Eldorado: The Poes in Norfolk, 1996, West Ghent newsletter, 1995-96; juried exhibits various cities including Grand Hyatt, Mayflower, Washington, by Joan Mondale, Nohra Haime, curator of Freer Gallery, by sr. curator Nat. Mus. Am. Art, curator Phillips Collection, asst. curator, White House and by dir. of Nat. Portrait Gallery; group shows include Contemporary Art Ctr., Va., Va. Beach, 1993, 98, Yorktown Small Works Show, 1996, Hampton Arts Commn. and Tidewater Artists Assn. Portfolio Show, 1996, Suffolk Artists and Writers Invitational Exhibit, 1996, Artists in Virginia, 1996, Peninsula Ann, Juried Art Exhibit, 1996, Hampton Bay Day Juried Art Exhibit, 1996, Trinity Ch. Stations of the Cross, Portsmouth Mus., 1996-97, Hermitage Mus., 1996, 98, Yorktown (Va.) On-The-Hill, 1997, 98,(First Place, IPA Printmaking), Wakefield Art Ctr., 1998, Norfolk Internat. Airport, 2002-04, 07; contbr. art and poetry to various publs. and anthologies. Mem. Charleston Artists Guild, 1968-70, Virginia Beach Arts Ctr., 1978-98, Suffolk Art League, 1990-2003; bd. dirs. W. Ghent Art/Lit. Festival, 1979; poetry reader Poetry Soc. Va., Va. Ctr. for Creative Arts, Sweetbriar, 1989, Walden Books, 1991, Christopher Newport U., 1994-95, J.M. Prince Books and Coffeehouse, 1995—, Statues St. Mark's Cath. Ch., 1991-92, Statue City of Hampton Va. Devel., 2004-05, Statue of St. Bridget, Oreg., 2005, Gaia Fest, 2006; graphics of hundreds of celebrities from life; curator Va. Winter Show Life Saving Mus., 1991-92; judge Bornstein art scholarship Chrysler Mus., 1992; mem. staff Mid-Atlantic Antiques Mag., 1993—; Nat. Endowment Arts grantwriter, 1975; bd. dirs. Tidewater Literacy Coun., 1971-72, Maine Antiques Digest, 2007; poetry reader GaiaFest, 2006-. Recipient awards various art and poetry contests; Coll. William and Mary art scholarship, 1958, Tricentenial award for Contbns. to the Arts in Va., 1993; recipient Cert. for Vol. Contbns. to Va. by Gov., 1984. Mem. ALA (poster sessions rev. com. 1985-96, pub. relations judge, subcom. com. 1988-90), Pub. Libr. Assn. (com. bylaws and orgns. 1988-90), Va. Libr. Assn. (pub. rels. com. 1984-86, grievance and pay equity com. 1986-88, co-winner Paraprofl. Logo award 1985, chair Pub. Documen ts Forum 1992-93), Southeastern Libr. Assn. (Rothrock award com. 1986-88, com. on coms. 1991-92), Poetry Soc. Va. (v.p. 1986-89, nominating com. 1989-90, editor newsletter 1990-93, dir. publicity 1993-95, 70th Anniversary plaque for Wren Bldg., commn. 75th anniversary poster), Art Librs. Soc. N.Am., Tidewater Artists Alliance (bd. dirs. 1989—, chair grantwriting com. 1990—, pres. 1991-92), Southeastern Coll. Art Assn., Irene Leache Soc., Norfolk Historical Soc., Internat. Platform Assn. (artists assn.), Old Dominion U. Alumni Assn. (artistic dir. Silver Reunion), Southeastern Soc. Archtl. Historians, Ikara (pres. 1989—), D'Art Ctr. (bd. dirs. 1991-92), Ex Libris Soc. (charter), Va. Writers Club. Home and Office: West Ghent Arts Office 1404 Gates Ave Norfolk VA 23507-1131 Office Phone: 757-282-6982. Personal E-mail: mnicholson9@cox.net.

NICHOLSON, R. STEPHEN, former cultural organization administrator; b. Radford, Va., Mar. 4, 1926; s. Roy S. and Ethel Dovie (Macy) Nicholson; m. Carol Peterson; 1 child, Suzanne Carpenter. AB, Marion Coll., 1950; MA, Syracuse U., NY, 1956; PhD, Mich. State U., East Lansing, 1971. Pres. Daley Coll., Chgo., 1969-71; prof. Lansing C.C., Lansing, Mich., 1963-66, acad. dean, 1971—76; pres. Clark County C.C. (now So. Nev. C.C.), 1971—76, Mt. Hood C.C., 1976—85; chancellor Oakland C.C., 1985-90; vice chancellor Higher Colls. of Tech., United Arab Emirates, 1990-92; CEO Internat. Christian Leadership, 1992-93, Mercy Corps Internat., 1994—95, chmn. bd. dirs., 1997—2004; corp. bd. dirs. Green Plains Renewable Energy, 2005—. Pres. Creative Futures; bd. dirs. MCI, Green Plains Renewable Energy Corp., 2004—. Sr. fellow for higher edn. M.J. Murdock Trust, 1993—95, 1996—99; chair bd. dir. N.W. Autism Found., 2000—02; bd. dir. Green Plains Reusable Energy, Inc., 2004—. Mem.: World Affairs Coun., Am. Acad. Polit. and Social Scis., Am. Sociology Assn., Am. Sch. Adminstrs. Assn., N.W. Assn. Cmty. and Jr. Coll.s (pres. 1976), Am. Assn. Cmty. and Jr. Colls. (pres. Pres.'s Acad. 1982, bd. dirs. 1985—87), Am. Futurist Soc., Japan-Am. Soc., Gresham C. of C. (dir. 1977—79), Rotary Club (pres. 1983, Paul Harris fellow 1986), Phi Delta Kappa. Home and Office: 9685 Irvine Bay Ct Las Vegas NV 89147-8365 E-mail: stephenicholson@earthlink.net.

NICHOLSON, RALPH LESTER, botanist, educator; b. Lynn, Mass., Aug. 25, 1942; s. Nathan Aaron and Muriel Spinney (Buxton) N. BA, U. Vt., 1964; MS, U. Maine, 1967; PhD, Purdue U., 1972. Prof. dept. botany and plant pathology Purdue U., West Lafayette, Ind., 1972—. Contbr. chpts. to books, more than 100 articles to profl. jours. Active Big Bros./Big Sisters, Lafayette, Ind., 1974—. Fellow Am. Phytopathol. Soc. Office: Purdue U Botany and Plant Pathology Lafayette IN 47907 E-mail: nicholson@btny.purdue.edu.

NICHOLSON, RICHARD SELINDH, educational association administrator; b. Des Moines, Apr. 5, 1938; s. George Eugene and Margaret (Selindh) N.; m. Mary Lou Weisbrod, Aug. 1, 1958 (div. 1971) 1 child, Jeffrey Richard; m. Lois Ann Karls, Aug. 15, 1976; 1 child, Gregory Michael. BS, Iowa State U., 1960; PhD, U. Wis., 1964; LHD (hon.), CUNY, 1994, CUNY-Mt. Sinai Med. Ctr., 1994. Rsch. assoc. U. Wis., Madison, 1963-64; asst. prof. Mich. State U., East Lansing, 1964-67, assoc. prof., 1967-70; program dir. NSF, Washington, 1970-77, dir. 1977-82, chief of staff, 1983-85, asst. dir., 1985-89; exec. dir. Nat. Sci. Bd. Commn., Washington, 1982-83; exec. officer, pub. Science AAAS, Washington, 1989—. Cons. on sci. affairs Pres. of U.S., Washington, 1978-79; exec. sec. Pres.' Com. on Nat. Medal Sci., Washington, 1976-84; mem. Pres.' Nat. Commn. on Superconductivity, 1989; vice chair Commn. on Phys. Scis.,

Math and Resources NRC, 1989—, Edn. Coordinating Coun., 1991—, com. on environ. rsch., 1991-92, co-chair coun. on competitiveness, 1993—; mem. statutory vis. com. Nat. Inst. of Stds. and Tech., 1990-93; vis. com. chemistry dept. Harvard U., 1989—; bd. dirs. Quality Edn. for Minorities Network, 1989—; trustee Gordon Rsch. Conf., 1989—; sci. policy adv. com. com. space, sci. and tech. U.S. Ho. Reps., 1992—; co-chair Coun. on Competitiveness, 1993—, Dept. of Energy Panel on Basic Rsch., 1995—; chmn. edn. adv. com. Genentech, 1993—. Mem. editorial bd. Analytical Chemistry, 1980-82, Chem. and Engring. News, 1985-88; contbr. articles to profl. jours. and chpts. to books. Served as seaman USN, 1956-63. Recipient Presdl. Disitng. Ranking, Pres. Reagan, 1982, Alumni Citation Merit award Iowa State U., 1983. Fellow AAAS; mem. Am. Chem. Soc. (chmn. Mich. State U. sect. 1968-70), Chem. Soc. Washington (nominations com. 1977), Cosmos Club, Nat. Press Club. Avocations: sports, tennis, reading. Office: AAAS 1200 New York Ave NW Ste 100 Washington DC 20005-3941 Home: 6009 Villa Roma Bonsall CA 92003-6220

NICHOLSON, ROBERT ARTHUR, college president; b. Pepin, Wis., Oct. 13, 1923; s. Arthur W. and Ethel (Weeden) N.; m. Dorothy Nelis, June 17, 1944; children: Paul, Gary. BS, Anderson U., Ind., 1944; MA, NYU, 1946, PhD, 1953. With Anderson U., 1945-90, successively instr., asst. prof., assoc. prof. music, chmn. dept., asst. to dean, 1945-58, dean, 1958-83, v.p., 1964-83, pres., 1983-90, pres. emeritus, 1990—. Author: Handbook to the Hymnal of the Church of God, 1953, So I Said Yes! A Personal Memoir, 2006; editor: Hymnal of the Church of God, 1953, 71. Interim CEO Ch. of God Ministries, Inc., 1998, cons., 1997-99; interim exec. pastor, Park Place Ch. of God, 1995; interim min. of music, 1999-2002; mem. pub. bd. Ch. of God, 1955-80, chmn. commn. higher edn., 1963-70, 83-86, vice chmn., 1970-83, cons., 1990-96; cons. Warner Pacific Coll., Oreg., 1990-98, N.Ind. United Meth. Found., Inc., 1992-95, Anderson Pub. Libr., 1994-95, United Faith Housing Corp., 1994, Hopewell Ctr., 1996, Alexandria Cmty. Ctr., Inc., 1997, Family Network Agy., Inc., 1997-2000, Wilson Boys and Girls Club, 1997, Cmty. Found. Grant County, 1998, United Way Anderson and Madison County, Ind., 1998, 2000, Anderson Area C. of C., 1998, 2001, Christian Ctr., 2001; bd. dirs. Anderson Symphony Orch., 1974-87, 93-94, United Way Madison County, 1985-89, 91-94, Minnetrista Cultural Found., 1988-2002; bd. dirs., v.p. Anderson Internat., 1990-93; bd. dirs. Cmty. Hosp. Madison County, 1986-95, vice chmn., 1988-94, interim pres., CEO, 1991; mem. Madison County Comty. Found., Inc., 1991-2003, pres., 1991-98. Mem. Associated Colls. of Ind., Ind. Colls. and Univs. of Ind. (chmn. 1988-89), Anderson Area C. of C. (bd. dirs. 1985-90, vice chmn. and chmn. elect 1988, chmn. 1989). Home: 2727 Crown Pointe Cir Apt 127 Anderson IN 46012-3265

NICHOLSON, WILL FAUST, JR., bank executive; b. Colorado Springs, Colo., Feb. 8, 1929; s. Will Faust and Gladys Olivia (Burns) N.; m. Shirley Ann Baker, Nov. 26, 1955; children: Ann Louise Nicholson Naughton, Will Faust III. S.B., M.I.T., 1950; MBA, U. Denver, 1956. V.p. Van Schaack & Co., Denver, 1954-66; pntr. N. G. Petry Constrn. Co., Denver, 1966-70; sr. v.p. Colo. Nat. Bankshares, Inc., Denver, 1970-75, pres., 1975-95, chmn. bd., chief exec. officer, 1985-95; chmn. Rocky Mountain Bankcard Sys., Denver, 1995—2001. Bd. dirs. Boys and Girls Clubs of Metro Denver; active Downtown Denver, Inc., Colo. Assn. of Commerce and Industry, chmn. 1990-91, Denver Urban Renewal Authority, 1958-59, Denver Bd. Water Commrs., 1959-65, pres. 1964, 65; Nat. Western Stock Show. With USAF, 1950-53. Mem. Assn. Bank Holding Cos. (bd. dirs. 1979-87, 89-91, exec. com. 1980-85, vice chmn. 1981-82, chmn. 1983-84), US C. of C. (bd. dirs. 1990-2005, chmn. 1999-2000), US Golf Assn. (exec. com. 1974-82, v.p. 1978, 79, pres. 1980, 81), Denver Country Club, Univ. Club Colo., Univ. Club NY, Castle Pines Golf Club, Royal and Ancient Golf Club (St. Andrews, Scotland), Augusta (Ga.) Nat. Golf Club. Republican. Episcopalian. Home: 37 Polo Club Cir Denver CO 80209-3307 Office: Rocky Mountain BankCard Sys Inc PO Box 5168 Denver CO 80217-5168

NICHOLSON, WILLIAM JOSEPH, energy and environmental consultant; b. Tacoma, Aug. 24, 1938; s. Ferris Frank and Athyleen Myrtle (Fesenmaier) Nicholson; m. Carland Elaine Crook, Oct. 10, 1964; children: Courtney, Brian, Kay, Benjamin. SB in ChemE, MIT, Cambridge, Mass., 1960, SM in ChemE Practice, 1961; PhD in ChemE, Cornell U., Ithaca, NY, 1965; MBA, Pacific Luth. U., Tacoma, Wash., 1969. Registered profl. chem. engr., Wash. Sr. devel. engr. Hooker Chem. Co., Tacoma, 1964—69, Battelle N.W., Richland, Wash., 1969—70; planning assoc. Potlatch Corp., San Francisco, 1970—75, mgr. corp. energy svc., 1976—94, dir. corp. energy and environ. svcs., 1994—2002, ind. energy and environ. cons., 2002—; chair energy coun. Am. Forest and Paper Assn., Washington, 1998—2002. Mem. MIT Ednl. Coun., 1971—; U.S. expert environ. labeling Internat. Stds. Orgn., 1994—2000; adv. bd. Forest Products lab. U. Calif., Richmond, 1992—2003, chmn. adv. bd., 1993—95, 2003, adv. bd. Coll. Natural Resources, 1993—95; adv. com. Fed. Biomass, 2000—05; project peer reviewer USDOE, 2004—. Mem.: AAAS, AIChE (assoc.), Am. Chem. Soc., Commonwealth Club (San Francisco), Sigma Xi. Republican. Avocations: history, genealogy. Home and Office: PO Box 1114 Ross CA 94957-1114 Office Phone: 415-457-2425. Personal E-mail: nicholsonhome@aol.com.

NICHOLSON, WILLIAM NOEL, clinical neuropsychologist; b. Detroit, Dec. 24, 1936; s. James Eardly and Hazel A. (Wagner) N.; m. Nancy Ann Marshall, June 15, 1957; children: Anne Marie, Kristin, Scott. AB, Wittenberg U., 1959; MDiv, Luth. Theol. Sem., Phila., 1962; PhD, Mich. State U., 1972. Diplomate Am. Bd. Forensic Examiners, Am. Bd. Med. Psychotherapists; lic. clin. psychologist, Mich.; ordained to ministry Luth. Ch., 1962; cert. Nat. Register Health Care Providers in Psychology, Assn. of State and Provincial Psychology Bds. Parish pastor Our Saviour Luth. Ch., Saginaw, Mich., 1962-69; intern in psychology Ingham Mental Health Bd., 1971-72; resident in psychology Bay-Arenac Mental Health Bd., 1972-74; dir., psychologist Riverside Ctr., Bay City, Mich., 1974-75; pastor, psychologist Psych Studies and Clergy Consultation of Mich., 1989—2003. Pres. Bay Psychol. Assocs., P.C., Bay City, 1975—2002; cons. Gov.'s Office of Drug Abuse, 1972-74. Author: A Guttman Facet Analysis of Attitude-Behaviors Toward Drug Users by Heroin Addicts and Mental Health Therapists, 1972, An Episcopalian Guide to the Augsburg Confession, 1997; contbr. articles to profl. jours. Mem. APA, Mich. Psychol. Assn. Office: 820 Arlington Ave Ste 2 Petoskey MI 49770 Home Phone: 231-347-0117; Office Phone: 231-347-4700. Personal E-mail: fatherbill36@hotmail.com.

NICITA, RICK, agent; m. Paula Wagner, 1984. Agent Creative Artists Agy., co-chmn. Beverly Hills, Calif., 1995—. Chmn. Am. Cinematheque; former vice-chmn. Am. Film Inst. Named one of most influential people in Hollywood, Entertainment Weekly mag., Premiere mag. Office: Creative Artists Agy 9830 Wilshire Blvd Beverly Hills CA 90212-1825

NICKEL, ALBERT GEORGE, advertising agency executive; b. Pitts., July 12, 1943; s. Frank George and Dorothy (Wiefling) N.; m. Dana Cooper; children: Mark, Grace, Olivia. AB, Washington and Jefferson Coll., 1965; MBA, Ind. U., 1967. Mktg. rsch. analyst Pfizer, Inc., NYC, 1967, prof. svc. rep., 1967-68, mktg. rsch. mgr., 1968-69, product mgr., 1969-70, USV Internat., Tuckahoe, NY, 1970-71; account supr. Sudler & Hennessey, NYC, 1973-77; sr. v.p. mgmt. group supr. Young and Rubicam, NYC, 1977-79; chmn., pres., COO Dorritie Lyons & Nickel, Inc., NYC; chmn., pres., CEO HMC Group Omnicom, Inc., 1999—; pres., chmn., CEO Lyons, Lavey, Nickel, Swift, Inc., 2000—. Trustee Wilton YMCA, Five Town Found.; bd. dirs. Cancer CARE; bd. dirs., exec. com. Wilton LaCrosse Assn.; trustee Dominican Coll., Healthcare Businesswoman's Assn., Wilton HS Long Range Planning Team, Am. Coun. on Sci. and Health, Cancer Care; co-chmn. TBWA WorldHealth. Capt. USAF, 1969. Recipient Ellis Island medal of honor and honor soc., 2002. Mem. Pharm. Rsch. and Mfrs. Assn. (bd. dirs.), Healthcare Mktg. and Comm. Coun. (bd. dirs.), Vis. Nurses Assn. (sec. found. bd.), Midwest Healthcare Mktg. Assn., Wilton Riding Club (pres.), Shore and Country Club, Silver Spring Country Club. Home: 65 Keelers Ridge Rd Wilton CT 06897-1608 E-mail: anickel@llns.com.

NICKEL, HENRY V., lawyer; b. Chgo., Aug. 8, 1943; AB, U. Va., 1965; JD, George Washington U., 1968. Bar: D.C. 1968. Mem. Hunton & Williams LLP, Washington, ptnr., resources, regulatory, environ. law, 1976, head adminstrv. law group, 1994. Rsch. editor: George Washington Law Rev., 1967-68. Mem. Order of Coif. Office: Hunton & Williams LLP 1900 K St NW Washington DC 20006-1109 Office Phone: 202-955-1561. E-mail: hnickel@hunton.com.

NICKEL, JANET MARLENE MILTON, retired geriatrics nurse; b. Manitowoc, Wis., June 9, 1940; d. Ashley and Pearl Milton; m. Curtis A. Nickel, July 29, 1961; children: Cassie, Debra, Susan. Diploma, Milw. Inst., 1961; ADN, N.D. State U., 1988. Nurse Milw. VA, Wood, Wis., 1961-62; supervising nurse Park Lawn Convalescent Hosp., Manitowoc, 1964-65; newsletter editor Fargo Model Cities Program, ND, 1970—73; supervising night nurse Rosewood on Broadway, Luth. Hosps. and Homes, Fargo, 1973-92; assoc. dir. nursing Elim Care Ctr., Fargo, 1992-94, night nurse, 1994—2005; ret., 2005. Night nurse Elim Care Ctr., 2007—. Mem. Phi Eta Sigma.

NICKELL, JAKE, internet retail executive, apparel designer, web site designer; b. Crown Point, Ind., 1980; m. Shondi Nickell, 2004. Attended, Ill. Inst. Art, 1998—2001. Co-founder & pres. SkinnyCorp, Chgo., 2000—. Co-creator (SkinnyCorp websites) Threadless, 2000, Naked & Angry, OMG Clothing, Extra Tasty, Yay Hooray!, 15 Megs of Fame. Named one of 40 Under 40, Crain's Chgo. Bus., 2006. Office: SkinnyCorp Ste 101 5225 N Ravenswood Ave Chicago IL 60640 Office Phone: 773-878-3557. Office Fax: 888-595-3258. E-mail: info@skinnycorp.com.

NICKELL, JOE, paranormal expert; b. Lexington, Ky., Dec. 1, 1944; s. James Wendell and Ella Kathleen (Turner) Nickell; m. Diana Harris, 2006; 1 child, Cherette. BA, U. Ky., 1967, MA, 1982, PhD, 1987. Profl. stage magician, Toronto, Ont., Canada, 1968-73; pvt. investigator, 1973-75; mus. exhibit designer Dawson City (Yukon) Mus., 1975-76; freelance investigative writer, 1976—; tchg. asst. U. Ky., Lexington, 1980-87, instr., 1987-95; sr. rsch. fellow Com. for Skeptical Inquiry, Amherst, NY, 1995—. Author: Inquest on the Shroud of Turin, 1983, Secrets of the Supernatural, 1988, The Magic Detectives, 1989, Pen, Ink and Evidence, 1990, Wonder Workers!, 1991, Ambrose Bierce Is Missing, 1992, Mysterious Realms, 1992, Looking for a Miracle, 1993, Camera Clues, 1994, Entities, 1995, Detecting Forgery, 1996, Real Life X-Files, 2001, The Mystery Chronicles, 2004, Unsolved History, 2005, Secrets of the Sideshows, 2005, Relics of the Christ, 2007, Adventures in Paranormal Investigation, 2007; co-author (with Robert A. Baker): Missing Pieces, 1992; co-author: (with John F. Fischer) Crime Science, 1999; co-author: (with Benjamin Radford) Lake Monster Mysteries, 2006; editor: Psychic Sleuths, 1994, The Outer Edge, 1996; co-editor: The UFO Invasion, 1997. Office: Ctr for Inquiry 3965 Rensch Rd Amherst NY 14228-2743 Office Phone: 716-636-1425 310.

NICKELL, ROBERT E., electric power industry executive; b. Reedley, Calif. s. Ernest and Selma Helen (Mullen) N.; m. Margaret Mary Harrold, July 18, 1964; children: Steven Dana, Kristen Elena. BS, U. Calif., Berkeley, 1963, MS, 1964, PhD, 1967. Mem. tech. staff Rohm & Haas Co., Huntsville, Ala., 1967-68, Bell Tel. Labs., Whippany, NJ, 1968-71, Sandia Nat. Labs., Albuquerque, 1973-77; vis. assoc. prof. Brown U., Providence, 1971-73; v.p. Pacific Tech., Del Mar, Calif., 1977-79; cons. to pres. Applied Sci. and Tech., Poway, Calif., 1978—; prog mgr. Electric Power Rsch. Inst., Palo Alto, Calif., 1980-84. Tech. dir. SGI Internat., La Jolla, Calif., 1992-95. Assoc. editor Computer Methods in Applied Mechanics and Engring; contbr. numerous articles to profl. publs. Bella Zellerbach Cross scholarship, 1962-63; recipient Structural Mechanics award ONR/AIAA, 1972; NDEA Title IX fellowship, 1964-66. Fellow ASME, AAAS; mem. ASCE, NAE, Am. Nuc. Soc., Pressure Vessel Rsch. Coun., Nat. Coal Coun., Internat. Assn. Structural Mechanics in Reactor Tech., Phi Kappa Phi, Tau Beta Pi (treas. 1962), Chi Epsilon, Sigma Xi, Upper Divsn. Honor Students Soc. Home: 2500 6th Ave Apt 204 San Diego CA 92103-6629 *

NICKELS, GREG, mayor; b. Chgo., Aug. 7, 1955; s. Bob and Kathie Nickels; m. Sharon Nickels; children: Jacob, Carey. Legis. asst. to Council member Norm Rice City of Seattle, 1979—87; mem. King County Coun., 1987—2002; mayor City of Seattle, 2002—. Chair Seattle/King County Bd. Health, 1996—2001; mem. exec. com. & bd. dirs. Dirs. of Sound Transit. Office: City Hall PO Box 94749 Seattle WA 98124-4749 E-mail: gjnickels@seattle.gov. *

NICKELS, THOM, writer, journalist; b. Darby, Pa., Oct. 12, 1947; s. Thomas Clavey Nickels and Teresa Marie Muldoon. Diploma in journalism, Charles Morris Price Sch. Advt.and Journalism, 1967; BA, Eastern Coll., Batl., 1968. Ordained priest Sts. Cyril and Methodius Ch., 2001, apptd. archpriest Orthodox Ch. Far Isles, 2002. Station editor TV Guide, 1978; editor Soc. Hill Towers Newsletter, Phila., 1981—83; gay issues columnist Welcomat, Phila., 1983—94; resume and grant writer, 1990—94; commetary columnist Phila. Inquirer, 1998—2001; newspaper columnist, feature writer Weekly/Univ. City Press, Phila., 1999—. Book reviewer Lambda Books Report, Washington, 1996—, Gay and Lesbian Rev., Boston, 1999—; commentary columnist Phila. Daily News, 1999—2001; feature writer Philly Style Mag., Phila., 2000—01; weekly issues columnist PrideVisionTV, Toronto, Que., Canada, 2001—; freelance arts and entertainment writer, reviewer TPI Metro, Phila., 2001—. Author: Manayunk, 2001, Gay and Lesbian Philadelphia, 2002, Tropic of Libra, 2002, Philadelphia Architecture History, 2005 (Phila. AIA Lewis Mumford Architecture Journalism award, 2005), (plays) Z for Shelter, 1967 (Hon. Mention Samuel French Young Playwrights Contest, 1968), (novels) The Cliffs of Aries, 1988, Two Novellas: Walking Water & After All This, 1989 (Nominated for a Hugo award and a Lambda Literary award), The Boy on the Bicycle, 1992, (anthology) The Boy on the Bicycle (reissue), 1993, Out in History, 2005; contbg. editor Weekly University City Press, 2004, critic, architect Metro, 2005, columnist Star Publications; columnist: www.LincolninLouisville.com, 2007—. Vol. Lyndon B. Johnsom Presdl. Campaign, West Chester, Pa., 1964; founder Coalition Phila. Art, 1998—2002; mem. Boston Gay Liberation Front, 1968—69. Mem.: Nat. Lesbian and Gay Journalist Assn. Home and Office: 2643 Mercer St Philadelphia PA 19125

NICKENS, HARRY CARL, medical association administrator; b. Monterey, Tenn., June 25, 1944; s. Van B. and Martha (Winningham) N.; m. Alicia Beck, Aug. 26, 1967; children: Kimberly, Cassidee, Brad. BS, Tenn. Tech. U., 1966, MS, 1968; EdD, U. Tenn., 1972. Counselor Va. Western C.C., Roanoke, 1972-76, dir. student devel., 1977-78, dean students, 1979-84, exec. dir. community devel. and tng., 1985-89; pres. Coll. Health Scis., Roanoke, 1989—2001; v.p. cmty. rels. and devel. Ephraim McDowell Health, Danville, Ky., 2002—07, v.p. cmty. rels., 2007. Chair Roanoke Valley Chamber's Sch., originator Grad, Ctr.; pres. Ephraim McDowell Health Care Found., 2003-06. Pres. Roanoke Valley Career Edn.; bd. dirs. Va. Cares, Adult Care Ctr., Am. Heart Assn., Va. Amateur Sports, Salvation Army; bd. suprs. Roanoke County; trustee St. Catherine Coll. Mem. Kiwanis (pres. Roanoke chpt. 1990, pres. Danville chpt. 2006, vice chmn. cmty. devel. coun.). Baptist. Avocation: gardening. Home: 107 Patrick Henry Ct Danville KY 40422 Office: Ephraim McDowell Health 217 South 3rd St Danville KY 40422 Office Phone: 859-239-2632. Business E-Mail: hnickens@emhealth.org.

NICKENS, JACKS CLARENCE, lawyer; b. McCamey, Tex., Feb. 7, 1949; s. Jacks C. Nickens and Elsie Louise (Jordan) Donohue; m. Linda M. Colangelo, June 13, 1970 (div.1984); 1 child, Marie Louise; m. Melinda Jo Hubbert, Oct. 13, 1990; 1 child, Charles Clay. AB magna cum laude, Harvard U., 1971, JD cum laude, 1975. Bar: Tex. 1975, US Dist. Ct. (so., ea. & no., dists.) Tex. 1975, US Ct. of Appeals (3rd, 5th, 7th, & 9th cir.), US Supreme Ct. Jud. clk.hon. Robert M. Hill US Dist. Judge (no. dist.) Tex.; assoc. Vinson & Elkins, Houston, 1975-79; ptnr. Scott Douglass & Keeton (now Miller, Bristow & Brown), Houston, 1979-90; prin. Jacks C. Nickens & Assocs., Houston, 1990-91; ptnr. Mayer, Brown & Platt, Houston, 1991-94, Clements, O'Neill, Pierce & Nickens, L.L.P., Houston, 1994—, Nickens Keeton Lawless Farell & Flack LLP. Recipient Paul Revere Frothingham Prize; grantee Henry Russell Shaw Fellowship. Mem.: Houston Bar Assn. (antitrust sect.) (vice-chair), State Bar Tex. dist. 4 Grievance Com. (chmn.), Fellow Houston and Tex. Bar Found. Office: Nickens Keeton Lawless Farell & Flack LLP 600 Travis Ste 7500 Houston TX 77002 Office Phone: 713-353-6668. Office Fax: 713-571-9652. Business E-Mail: jnickens@nickenskeeton.com.

NICKERSON, DON C., lawyer, retired prosecutor, judge; married; 3 children. JD, Drake U., 1977. Bar: Iowa 1977, admitted to practice: US Ct. Appeals (8th Cir.) 1977, US Dist. Ct. (So. Dist.) Iowa 1977. US atty. US Dist. Ct. (So. Dist.), Iowa, 1993—2001; assoc. gen. counsel Wellmark Blue Cross & Blue Shield, Iowa, 2001—03; judge Dist. Ct. (5th Dist.), Iowa, 2003—. Bd. mem. Urban Dreams, United Way of Central Iowa, Cmty. Focus, Inc., Des Moines Enterprise Cmty. Recipient Medal of Honor, Drake U., Cmty. Svc. award, Iowa State Bar Assn. Mem.: Commn. on Planning for the 21st Century, Polk County Bar Assn., Iowa Nat. Bar Assn., Iowa State Bar Assn. Office: State of Iowa Dist Ct 5C Polk County Courthouse 500 Mulberry Rm 212 Des Moines IA 50309 Office Phone: 515-245-4500, 515-286-3391. Office Fax: 515-286-3858.

NICKERSON, GARY LEE, educational consultant; b. Cleve., Nov. 7, 1942; s. Alto Lee and Louisa Evelyn (Watson) Nickerson; m. Barbara Marie Butler, Aug. 17, 1968; 1 child, L'Oreal. BS, Ohio U., Athens, 1966; MA, Atlanta U., 1971. Cert. secondary tchr. Ohio. With Cleve. Pub. Schs., 1966-98; sci. dept. chmn. John F. Kennedy High Sch., Cleve., 1985-98; youth edn. coord. Cleve. Bot. Garden, 1999—2002; sci. mgr. Cleve. Mcpl. Schs., 2002—04; ednl. cons. Ohio Dept. Edn., 2004—. Sci. instr. Std. Oil Elem. Tchg. Retraining Program, 1986, Cleve. Ednl. Found. Elem. Tchg. Retraining Program, 1990—, Baldwin Wallace U. Upward Bound Program, 1992; physics instr. Case Western Res. U., Cleve., 1988, engring. project instr. MEIOP Summer Program, 91; mem. adv. panel Ednl. Devel. Ctr., Inc., Newton, Mass., 1989—98; tchr. trainer Kent State U. Trivet Program, 1991—98; sci. tchr. Gov.'s Inst. Gifted and Talented Cleve. State U., 1992—98. Co-author: curriculum guides. Trustee N.E. Ohio Sci. and Engring. Fair, 2001—04. Recipient cert. of Excellence in Tchg., Rotary, 1990. Mem.: NAACP, Sci. Edn. Coun. Ohio, Nat. Sci. Tchrs. Assn., Cleve. Regional Coun. Sci. Tchrs. (bd. dirs. 1986—87, pres. 2002—), Metrocabse Assn., Urban League, Kappa Alpha Psi. Democrat. Baptist. Avocations: ice skating, tennis, swimming, singing, weightlifting. Home: 5871 White Pine Dr Cleveland OH 44146-3075 Personal E-mail: ganickers@aol.com.

NICKERSON, GUY ROBERT, lumber company executive; b. Salt Lake City, May 20, 1956; s. Charles Augustus and Florence May (Fogel) N.; m. Maggie Rose McDonnell, May 30, 1992; children: Melissa Marie, Rebecca Rose. B Acctg., U. Utah, 1977, M Profl. Accountancy, 1978. CPA, Utah. Sr. mgr. Deloitte Haskins & Sells, Salt Lake City and NYC, 1978-87; v.p. fin. Anderson Lumber Co., Ogden, Utah, 1987-96, v.p. ops., 1996—2001; pvt. investor Salt Lake City, 2001—.

NICKERSON, JAMES FINDLEY, retired education educator; b. Gretna, Nebr., Dec. 16, 1910; s. Elmer Samuel and Lulu Perkins (Patterson) Nickerson; m. Juanita M. Bolin, Mar. 3, 1934; children: Ann Rogers Nickerson Lueck, Maria De Miranda. BS, Nebr. Wesleyan U., 1932; MA, Columbia Tchrs. Coll., 1940; PhD, U. Minn., 1948; ScD (hon.), Yankton Coll., SD, 1971. Tchr. pub. schs., Giltner, Nebr., 1932-35; sch. music supr. Gordon, Nebr., 1936-38, Bayshore, LI, 1939-41, Grand Island, Nebr., 1941-42; instr. Coll. Edn., music supr. HS U. Minn., 1942-46, vis. prof. Coll. Edn., 1948; asst. prof. music edn. U. Kans., 1946-48, assoc. prof., 1948-53; prof. psychology, dean edn., dir. summer quar. Mont. State U., 1954—64, head dept. psychology, 1954—56; rsch. assoc. Electronics Rsch. Lab., 1958—64; v.p. acad. affairs N.D. State U., Fargo, 1964—66; pres. Minn. State U., Mankato, 1966—73, disting. svc. prof., pres. emeritus, 1973—76. Mem. vis. com. Schola Cantorum, NYC, 1938—39, Choral Arts Soc., Washington, 1969—71, Harvard Grad. Sch. Edn., 1970—76; rsch. assoc. dept. psychology U. So. Calif.; with human factors divsn. USN Electronics Lab., San Diego, 1953—54; bd. dirs. Svc. Mems. Opportunity Colls.; mem. steering com. Pacific N.W. Coun. Higher Edn., 1962; cons. pub. edn. Office Gov. Wash., 1964; exec. sec., study dir. interim com. edn. Wash. Legislature, 1959—60; chmn. regional conf. womanpower Nat. Manpower Coun. and Mont. State Coll., 1957; mem. adv. com. sci. edn. NSF, 1968—71, chmn., 1970—71. Stringbass Mont. State Coll. Symphonette, 1959—63, Mankato Symphony Orch., 1967—73, 1983—93, bd. dirs., 1987—90; author: Out of Chaos, 2006. Named Nicerkson Conf. Rm. in his honor, Student Union, Minn. State U., 2003; named to Internat. Adult and Continuing Edn. Hall of Fame, 1999; recipient Alumni award, Nebr. Wesleyan U., 1968, Sec. Def. medal for Outstanding Pub. Svc., 1981, citation, Am. Coun. Edn., 1981, James F. Nickerson medal of Merit for Outstanding Svc. to Mil. Edn., Am. Assn. Sr. Colls. and Univs., 1981; Danforth Found. Adminstrn. grantee, 1969. Mem.: Edn. Commn. States (commr. 1967—73, mem. task force coord., governance and structure postsecondary edn. 1973), Assn. Minn. Colls. (pres. 1972), Am. Assn. Higher Edn. (chmn. resolutions com. 1974), Am. Assn. Colls. Tchr. Edn. (bd. dirs. 1969—71), Am. Assn. State Colls. and State Univs. (bd. dirs. 1966—71), Nat. Assn. Student Univs. and Land Grant Colls. (senate, chmn. divsn. tchr. edn. 1962—65, sec. coun. acad. officers 1965), Sigma Xi, Phi Mu Alpha Sinfonia. Home and Office: 77 Stadium Rd Apt 23 Mankato MN 56001-1022

NICKERSON, JERRY EDGAR ALAN, business executive; b. North Sydney, NS, Can., Apr. 28, 1936; s. Jeremiah Beldon and Jean Frances (Innes) N.; m. Jean Frances Ritcey, Sept. 20, 1958; children: Mark Alan, Jerry Ross. B.Commerce, Dalhousie U., 1958. Chmn. bd. H.B. Nickerson & Son, Ltd., North Sydney. Bd. dirs. Gt. West Life & Annuity, Gt. West Life Assurance Co., Great-West Lifeco Inc., London Ins. Group, London Life Ins., Power Fin., Inc., Power Corp. Can., Can. Life Fin. Corp., Can. Life Assurance Co., Can. Life Capital Corp Mem. Chief Execs. Orgn., Zeta Psi. Office: HB Nickerson & Sons Ltd PO Box 130 North Sydney NS Canada B2A 3M2 Office Phone: 902-794-8008. Personal E-mail: jeanickerson@aol.com.

NICKERSON, JOHN MITCHELL, political science professor; b. Lewiston, Maine, July 1, 1937; s. Elmer Winfield and Marion Gertrude (Howard) N. BA, U. Maine, 1959; MA, Wash. State U., 1966; PhD, U. Idaho, 1971. Commd. 2d lt. US Army, 1959, advanced through grades to capt., resigned, 1967; rsch. assoc. Bur. Pub. Adminstrn. U. Maine, Orono, 1967—68, mem. grad. faculty, 1970—88, asst. prof., assoc. prof. polit. sci. Augusta, 1970—81, prof., 1981—, developer 10 baccalaureate degrees pub. adminstrn.; dir. New Eng. Govtl. Rsch. Inst., Inc., Waterville, Maine, 1971. Lectr. Colby Coll., Waterville, Maine, 1979, Maine State Dedimus Justice; cons. in field. Author: The Control of Civil Disturbances, 1968;

Municipal Police in Maine - A Study of Selected Personnel Practices with Emphasis on Recruit Selection and Training, 1969; (with others) A Study of Policy-Making: The Dynamics and Adaptability of the United States Federal System, 1971; editor, author foreward: Is the Municipality Liable for Insufficiently Trained Police? (James P. Murphy), 1968; contbr. articles to profl. jours. Mem. Maine State Police Planning Adv. Group, 1984-87, Maine State Bd. Assessment Rev., 1981-84, Maine Hwy. Safety Com., 1984-87; vice chmn. adv. bd. Salvation Army, Augusta, 1980-85; trustee, treas. Lithgow Library, 1980-85; incorporator Kennebec Valley Med. Ctr., Augusta, 1980-97. Dept. Justice grantee, 1967. Mem. Am. Polit. Sci. Assn., New Eng. Polit. Sci. Assn., Northeastern Polit. Sci. Assn., Acad. Polit. Sci. (life), Am. Acad. Polit. and Social Sci. (life), Am. Soc. for Pub. Adminstrn., ACLU (life), Kennebec Hist. Soc. (life), Kennebec Valley Humane Soc. (life), Maine Civil Liberties Union (life, legis. com.), Pi Sigma Alpha, Pi Alpha Alpha. Home: 190 Capitol St Apt 216 Augusta ME 04330-6237 Office: U Maine at Augusta 46 University Dr Augusta ME 04330 Office Phone: 207-621-3287. Business E-Mail: john.nickerson@maine.edu.

NICKLAUS, JACK WILLIAM, professional golfer; b. Columbus, Ohio, Jan. 21, 1940; s. Louis Charles, Jr. and Helen (Schoener) N.; m. Barbara Bash, July 23, 1960; children: Jack William II, Steven Charles, Nancy Jean, Gary Thomas, Michael Scott. Student, Ohio State U., 1957-62, D (hon.) of Athletic Arts, 1972; LLD (hon.), U. St. Andrews, 1984. Chmn., CEO Golden Bear Internat., Inc. Player U.S. Ryder Cup Team, 1969, 71, 73, 75, 77, 81, 83, 87. Author: My 55 Ways to Lower Your Golf Score, 1964, Take a Tip From Me, 1968, The Greatest Game of All, 1969, Jack Nicklaus' Lesson Tee, 1972, Golf My Way, 1974, Jack Nicklaus' Playing Lessons, 1976, On and Off the Fairway, 1978, Play Better Golf, Vols. 1-3, 1980, 81, 83, The Full Swing, 1982, My Most Memorable Shots in the Majors, 1988. Chmn. Ohio divsn. Am. Cancer Soc., 1967; chmn. sports divsn. Nat. Easter Seal Soc., 1967. Named PGA Player of Year, 1967, 72, 73, 75, 76, Dunlop Profl. Athlete of Yr., 1972, Golfer of Year Profl. Golfers Assn., 1973, Byron Nelson award, 1964, 65, 72, 73, Bob Jones award, 1975; named Sportsman of Yr., Sports Illus. mag., 1978; named to World Golf Hall of Fame; named Athlete of the Decade for 1970-79, 1979, Golfer of the '70s, 1979, Golfer of the Century, 1988; recipient Presdl. Medal of Freedom, The White House, 2005. Mem. President's Club Ohio State U., Phi Gamma Delta. Achievements include playing on over 105 golf courses on 5 continents, 12 ranked in US Top 100; hosted 185 profl. tournaments 1973—; won 73 ofcl. tournaments; maj. tournaments won include Tournament of Champions, 1963, 64, 71, 73, 77, US Amateur, 1959, 61, US Open, 1962, 67, 72, 80, US Masters, 1963, 65, 66, 72, 75, 86, Brit. Open, 1966, 70, 78, PGA Championship, 1963, 71, 73, 75, 80, Internat. Pro-Amateur, 1973, Tournament Players Championship, 1974, 76, 78, Australian Open, 1964, 68, 71, 75, 76, 78, World Series of Golf, 1962, 63, 67, 70, 76, PGA Seniors Championship, 1991, US Senior Open, 1991, 93. Office: Golden Bear Realty Inc 11684 US Hwy #1 North Palm Beach FL 33408

NICKLE, DENNIS EDWIN, electronics engineer, consultant, deacon; b. Sioux City, Iowa, Jan. 30, 1936; s. Harold Bateman and Helen Cecilia (Killackey) H. BS in Math., Fla. State U., 1961. Ordained deacon Roman Cath. Ch., 1979. Reliability mathematician Pratt & Whitney Aircraft Co., West Palm Beach, Fla., 1961-63; br. supr. Melpar Inc., Falls Church, Va., 1963-66; prin. mem. tech. staff Xerox Data Sys., Rockville, Md., 1966-70; sr. tech. officer WHO, Washington, 1970-76; software tech. mgr. Melpar divsn. E-Sys., Inc., Falls Church, 1976-95; software process improvement mgr. Bell Atlantic, Arlington, Va., 1996-97; sr. software mgr. Litton Denro, Gaithersburg, Md., 1997—2001; cons., 2001—. Lectr. in field; coord. D.C. Software Process Improvement Network, 1995—2001, chair, 1997—2002. Author: Stress in Adolescents, 1986; co-author: Handbook for Handling Non-Productive Stress in Adolescence, Standard for Software Life Cycle Processes, IMPEESA Junior Leader Training Guide, Standard for Software Quality Assurance, 1984-91, Standard for Developing Software Life Cycle Processes, Configuration Management Procedures, Software Quality Assurance Procedures, Software Development Procedures; editor: Mama's Good Italian Cookbook, 2004; contbr. to profl. jours. Chief judge for computers Fairfax County Regional Sci. Fair, 1964-88; scoutmaster, commr. Boy Scouts Am., 1957-92; youth custodian Fairfax County Juvenile Ct., 1973-87; chaplain No. Va. Regional Juvenile Detention Home, 1978-88; moderator Nocturnal Adoration Soc.; parochial St. Michael's Ch., Annandale, Va., 1979-89, Christ the Redeemer, Sterling, Va., 1990-93. With U.S. Army, 1958-60. Recipient Eagle award, Silver award, Silver Beaver award, other awards Boy Scouts Am.; Ad Altare Dei, St. George Emblem, Diocese of Richmond. Mem. Assn. Computing Machinery, Computer Soc., Am. Soc. for Quality Control, CODSIA (chmn. working groups), ORLANDO II (Govt./industry working group), Old Crows Assn., Rolm Mil-Spec Computer Users Group (internat. pres.), San Antonio I (select industry coord. group), Nat. Security Indsl. Assn. (conv. com. 1985-96, software quality assurance subcom., regional membership chmn. 1981-89, nat. exec. vice-chmn. 1989-94, chmn. 1994-96), Am. Security Coun., IEEE (sr., stds. working group in computers 1983—, Outstanding Vol. award 1993, Golden Core 1996), Def. Software Devel. Stds. Adv. Bd. (chmn. 1991-96), Soc. Software Quality, Hewlett-Packard Users Group, Smithsonian Assn., Internat. Platform Assn., NRA (endowment), Nat. Eagle Scout Assn. (life), KC (4 deg.), Alpha Phi Omega (life), Sigma Phi Epsilon. Home: 43245 Preston Ct Ashburn VA 20147-5307 Office Phone: 703-729-2653.

NICKLES, DON (DONALD LEE NICKLES), former senator; b. Ponca City, Okla., Dec. 6, 1948; s. Robert C. and Coeweene (Bryan) N.; m. Linda L. Morrison, Sept. 5, 1968; children— Donald Lee II, Jennifer Lynn, Kim Elizabeth, Robyn Leigh. BA in Bus. Adminstrn., Okla. State U., 1971. Owner, operator Don Nickles Profl. Cleaning Svc., Stillwater, Okla., 1968-71; v.p., gen. mgr. Nickles Machine Corp., Ponca City, 1972—80; mem. Okla. Senate, 1979-80, U.S. Senate from Okla., 1981—2005; founder, prin. The Nickles Group lobbying, 2005—. Asst. majority whip, 1996-2003; chmn. Senate Rep. policy com., mem. com. on energy and natural resources, com. on rules and adminstrn., com. on budget fin., budget com., mem. arms control observer group, rural health caucus, world climate conv. observer group, Rep. task force on nat. security and regulatory reform, senate budget com., 2003-05; passed legislation to provide for econ. and employment impact statement for all new laws and regulations; mem., bd. dirs. Valero Energy Corp., 2005- Chmn. platform com. Rep. Nat. Conv., 1992; bd. dirs. Ponca City United Way; bd. advisors Close Up Found.; mem. Kay Coun. for Retarded Children, Ponca City, St. Mary's Roman Cath. Parish Coun.; mem. adv. bd. Salvation Army, Ponca City. With USNG, 1970-76. Named one of Outstanding Young Men of Am., U.S. Jaycees, 1983. Mem. Fellowship Christian Athletes, Ponca City C. of C. Clubs: Rotary. Republican.

NICKLES, I. MACARTHUR, librarian; b. Pittsfield, Mass., Feb. 5, 1944; s. Irving J. and Elsie (Hutchinson) N.; m. Rosalie M. Cangialose, Jan. 14, 1978; 1 child, Vincent Charles Nickles. BA, SUNY, Albany, 1965, MA, 1968, MLS, 1971. Asst. libr. SUNY Coll. at Oneonta, 1971-77; jr. libr. Passaic (N.J.) Pub. Libr., 1978; dir. Garfield (N.J.) Pub. Libr., 1979—. Pres. Bergen County Coop. Libr. System, Hackensack, N.J., 1993. Gate attendant Tanglewood, Lenox, Mass., 1965—; mem. Garfield Sta. N.J. Transit Arts Com., 1999—; participant Oxford U. Round Table on Freedom of Speech and Press, 2005. With U.S. Army, 1969-70. Mem. ALA, N.J. Libr. Assn., Garfield Rotary (pres. 1981-82, 2001-02, Paul Harris fellow 1992), Garfield C. of C., N.J. Transit Arts Com. Garfield Sta. Avocations: reading, classical music. Office: Garfield Pub Libr 500 Midland Ave Garfield NJ 07026-1606 E-mail: mac@bccls.org.

NICKLES, SHELLEY KAPLAN, curator, educator; b. Kingston, NY, Apr. 3, 1964; d. Jerome Allen and Leah (Maskowsky) Kaplan; m. John Peter Nickles, Sept. 3, 1995; 1 child, Kealani Rose. BA in History, Cornell U., 1986; MA in Early Am. Culture, U. Del., 1990; PhD in history, U. Va., 1999. Instr. Parsons Sch. Design, NYC, Washington, 1996—2002; mus. curator Nat. Mus. Am. History Smithsonian Instn., Washington, 1999—2006. Adj. asst. prof. George Washington U., 2002—04. Editor: (exhibit rev.) Home Cultures Jour., 2003—04; contbr. articles to profl. jours. Fellow, Winterthur and Hagley Mus., Wilmington, 1993, Wolfsonian Mus., Miami Beach, 1994, Smithsonian Instn., 1995—97; Lois F. McNeil fellow, Winterthur Mus., Wilmington, 1988—90. Mem.: Am. Studies Assn., Soc. Winterthur Fellows, Orgn. Am. Historians.

NICKLIN, EMILY, lawyer; b. Cooperstown, NY, June 24, 1953; d. George Leslie Jr. and Katherine Mildred (Aronson) N.; m. Jay Schleusener, Dec. 28, 1974; children: Max, Lucas, Anna. BA, U. Chgo., 1975, JD, 1977. Bar: Ill. 1977, US Dist. Ct. (no. dist. Ill.) 1979, US Ct. Appeals (7th cir.) 1979. Law clk. to judge US Dist. Ct. (no. dist. Ill.), Chgo., 1977-79; assoc. Kirkland & Ellis, Chgo., 1979-83, ptnr., 1983—, mem. firm mgmt. com., 1995—. Tchr. Ill. Continuing Legal Edn. Bar Prog., Chgo., 1983—; fellow Salzburg Seminar, Austria, 1983; dep. corp. counsel City of Chgo., 1989-91; mem. bd. trustees, U. Chgo., lectr. law, 2001. Named one of Am. Top 50 Women Litigators, Nat. Law. Jour., 2001, 30 Tough Lawyers, Chgo. Mag. Mem. Nat. Inst. Trial Advocacy (tchr., team leader 1982—), Order of Coif, Phi Beta Kappa. Office: Kirkland & Ellis LLP 200 E Randolph Dr Fl 54 Chicago IL 60601-6636 Office Phone: 312-861-2387. Office Fax: 312-861-2200. E-mail: enicklin@kirkland.com. *

NICKLIN, GEORGE LESLIE, JR., psychoanalyst, educator, physician, writer; b. Franklin, Pa., July 25, 1925; s. George Leslie and Emma (Reed) N.; m. Katherine Mildred Aronson, Sept. 30, 1950 BA, Haverford Coll., 1949; MD, Columbia U., 1951; cert. in psychoanalysis, William A. White Inst., NYC, 1962. Diplomate Am. Bd. Psychiatry and Neurology. Resident, then chief resident Bellevue Psychiat. Hosp., NYC, 1953-56; pvt. practice specializing in psychoanalytic psychiatry, 1956—; staff Bellevue Hosp., 1956—; assoc. clin. prof. psychiatry NYU Med. Sch., 1970—; dir. LI Inst. Psychoanalysis, 1978-88, dir. emeritus, 1988—, dir. emeritus. Mem. Com. to Award Martin Luther King Peace Prize. Author: Doctors In Peril, 2000, War Stories, 2005. Mem. Corp. Haverford Coll., 1957-2003; founder, trustee Westbury Friends Sch., 1957-2006; founder Friends World Coll., 1958. With AUS, 1943-46, ETO. Decorated Purple Heart (3) with oak leaf cluster (3), Bronze Star with oak leaf cluster and three battle stars. Fellow Am. Acad. Psychoanalysis, Am. Psychiat. Assn. (disting. life fellow, 2003); mem. AAAS, NAACP, Soc. Med. Psychoanalysts (pres. 1986-87), White Psychoanalytic Soc., Assn. for World Edn. (charter trustee, treas. 1970-78), 9th Inf. Divsn. Assn., Vets. of the Bulge, Mil. Order of the Purple Heart. Clubs: Gardiner's Bay Country (Shelter Island, NY). Mem. Soc. Of Friends. Home (Summer): PO Box 88 Shelter Island NY 11964-0088 Home (Winter): The Medford L Way Medford NJ 08055 *Education is essential to the future evolution of human society. But education alone is not enough. Integrity, creative thinking and informed action open the path to the future.*

NICKOLOFF, EDWARD LEE, radiology physicist; m. Diane Zambetti; children: Andrea Lee, Edward Jr Lee. BS, Lebanon Valley Coll., Annville, Pa., 1965; MS, U. of N.H., 1968; DSc, Johns Hopkins U., 1977. Lic. nuclear medicince physics and diagnostic radiology physics Am. Bd. Radiology, cert. health physicist Am. Bd. Health Physics, lic. diagnostic imaging physics Am. Bd. Med. Physics. Asst. prof. of radiology, acting dir. of physics and engring. dept. radiology Johns Hopkins Med. Instns., Balt., 1977—81; prof. of clin. radiology, chief hosp. physicist dept. radiology Columbia U. Physicians and Surgeons, NYC, 1982—. Contbr., tchr., adviser Columbia U.; presenter in field. Contbr. articles and abstracts to profl. jours., chpts. to books. Fellow: Am. Coll. Radiologists (life), Am. Coll. Med. Physics (chmn.), Am. Assn. Physicists Medicine. Independent. Achievements include research in image quality and radiation dosimetry. Avocations: hiking, gardening, reading, theater. Office: Columbia U Physicians and Surgeons 177 Fort Washington Ave New York NY 10032-3784 Business E-Mail: eln1@columbia.edu.

NICKON, ALEX, chemist, educator; b. Poland, Oct. 6, 1927; came to U.S., 1955, naturalized, 1961; s. Steve and Maria (Nickon); m. Beulah Monica Godby, Aug. 22, 1950; children— Dale Beverly, Linda Cheryl, Leanne Marie. B.Sc., U. Alta., 1949; MA, Harvard U., 1951, PhD, 1953. Vis. lectr. Bryn Mawr Coll., 1953; postdoctoral fellow Birkbeck Coll., U. London, England, 1953-54, NRC, Ottawa, Canada, 1954-55; NSF sr. fellow; Imperial Coll., London, 1963-64; U. Munich, Germany, 1971-72; mem. faculty Johns Hopkins, 1955—, prof. chemistry, 1964-94, Vernon K. Krieble prof. chemistry, 1975-94, prof. emeritus, 1994—. Vis. assoc. Am. Chem. Soc. on Profl. Tng., 1975-95; mem. medicinal chem. panel NIH, 1966-70; postdoctoral panel NRC, 1968-69. Sr. editor Jour. Organic Chemistry, 1965-71; Am. exec. editor: Tetrahedron Reports, 1978-96. Recipient Md. Chemist award, 1990; Sloan Found. fellow, 1957-61 Fellow N.Y. Acad. Scis.; mem. Am. Chem. Soc. (nat. awards com. 1974-76), Brit. Chem. Soc. Home: 770 Knoll Rd Lewisville TX 75077 Personal E-mail: nickontx@yahoo.com.

NICOARA, ANDREEA CARINA, mathematics professor; d. Ioan Lucian Nicoara and Ana Eugenia Bursan. BS in Math. (hon.), Stanford U., Calif., 1997; MA in Math., Princeton U., NJ, 1999, PhD in Math., 2002. Benjamin Peirce asst. prof. math. Harvard U., Cambridge, Mass., 2002—. Contbr. articles to profl. jours. Recipient Boothe prize for Excellence in Writing, Stanford U., 1994, Firestone medal for Excellence in Rsch., 1997, Robert M. Golden medal for Excellence in the Humanities, 1997; Luce fellow, Princeton U., 1997—99, Postdoctoral fellow, NSF, 2003—06. Mem.: Am. Math. Soc. (Waldemar J. Trjitzinsky Meml. Fund award 1996), Kokikai Aikido (instr. 2004, black belt 2004), Phi Beta Kappa. Democrat. Roman Catholic. Avocations: art history, comparative religion, Aikido, fencing, travel. Home Phone: 617-945-9415; Office Phone: 617-495-2482.

NICOGOSSIAN, ANRAULD E.T., education educator; b. Dniepropetrovsk, Ukraine; naturalized U.S. citizen, 1972; m. Barbara Ann Gallagher; 4 children. Student, Coll. St. Louis, Teheran, Iran, 1953; B in Biology, Lycee Franco-Iranian Razi, Teheran, 1956; MD, Teheran U., 1964; MS in Aerospace Medicine, Ohio State U., 1972. Diplomate Am. Bd. Preventive Medicine. Resident in medicine Pahlavi U. Hosp., Teheran U., 1963-65; intern Sydenham City Hosp., NYC, 1965-66; resident in medicine Mt. Sinai Hosp. Svcs., Elmhurst, NY, 1966-68; chief med. resident, 1968-69, fellow pulmonary medicine, 1969-70; resident in aerospace and preventive medicine Ohio State U., Columbus, 1970-72; med. rsch. officer cardiovascular br. NASA Johnson Space Ctr., Houston, 1971-76, Apollo-Soyuz test project crew surgeon, 1974-75, chief med. ops. life scis. divsn. Washington, 1976-78, mgr. operational medicine office life scis. divsn., 1978-83, chief space medicine br. life scis. divsn., 1983—, chief med. officer office space flight, 1992—; pvt. practice Fairfax (Va.) Immediate Care Ctr., 1984-91; dir. Office Internat. Med. Policy, Disting. rsch. prof. George Mason U., Fairfax, Va., 2005—. Chmn. med. policy bd. NASA, 1979-2001, mem. rev. team for human presence in space, space sta. redesign and space sta. transition, 1992-93, mem. hdqrs. contingency action team, 1992-2001, dep. assoc. adminstr. for ops. and space flight for life and microgravity scis. and applications, 1993-2000, assoc. adminstr. for life and microgravity scis. and applications, 2000-2001, chief health and med. officer, 2001, sr. advisor for health to NASA adminstr.; staff physician Barnett Gen. Hosp., Patterson, N.J., 1967-68, LaGuardia Hosp., Queens, N.Y., 1968-70; vis. physician student health ctr. Ohio State U., Columbus, 1970-72, clin. instr. dept. internal medicine, 1971-72; assoc. clin. prof. dept. cmty. medicine Wright State U., Dayton, Ohio, 1978-84; affiliate faculty ACLS and ATLS tng. ctr. Georgetown U. Hosp., Washington, 1980-84; asst. prof. dept. preventive medicine Uniformed Svcs., U. Health Scis., Washington, 1977—; vis. faculty; lectr. in physiology and medicine Moscow State U., 1995. Co-author: Space Physiology and Medicine, 1983, 3d edit., 1994, Life Sciences Considerations for Long Duration Missions, 1994; contbr. articles to profl. jours., chpts. to books; mem. editl. bd. Aviation, Space and Environ. Medicine Jour., 1978-93, 96, ATA, 2005—. Scholar Nat. TB and Respiratory Disease Assn., 1970, Link Found., 1970-71; recipient Meritorious Svc. medallion Am. Heart Assn., 1980, 82, Jeffries Med. Rsch. award AIAA, 1982, Past Pres. award No. Va. chpt. Am. Heart Assn., 1983, Strughold award Aerospace Med. Assn., 1984, Tech. Publs. award Aerospace Med. Assn., 1985, Yuri Gagarin medal USSR Fedn. Cosmonautics, 1987, Disting. Svc. award Am. Soc. Gravitational and space biology, 1989, Allan D. Emil Meml. award Internat. Aero. Fedn., 1990, Life Scis. award internat. Acad. Astronautics, 1990, Cert. Appreciation Coun. Mins., Armenia, 1990, Commemorative award and medal Yuri Gagarin Cosmonaut Tng. Ctr., 1990, Presdl. Letter of Commendation for Cmty. Svcs., 1990, S.P. Korolev medal Russian Fedn. Cosmonautics, 1993, Internat. Cooperation award AIAA, 1993, Cert. of Appreciation Russian Space Agy., 1994, Achievement award 1995, 2 Disting. Svc. medals NASA, numerous others. Fellow ACP, Am. Coll. Preventive Medicine, Am. Astron. Soc. (chmn. awards com. 1990-93, bd. dirs. 1988—, Melbourne W. Boyton award 1984, W. Randolph Lovelace II award 1993), Aerospace Med. Assn., Am. Astronautical Soc.; mem. AAAS, Nat. Assn. Residents and Interns, Am. Thoracic Soc., Tex. Thoracic Soc., Internat. Acad. Astronautics (Tech. Publs. award 1985, chair life scis. sect. 1995), Internat. Union Physiol. Socs., Korean Aeromed. Soc. (hon.), Acad. Scis. of Armenian Republic (fgn. mem.). Office: Sch Pub Policy George Mason Univ 4400 Univ Dr Fairfax VA 22030 Office Phone: 703-728-7277. E-mail: anicogoss@gmu.edu.

NICOL, DOMINIK, writer, photographer; b. northern Oltenia, Romania, Sept. 25, 1930; arrived in US, 1969, naturalized, 1976; s. Dumitru and Valentina (Sandulescu) Nicolaescu-Stroe. Diploma in Chemistry and Tech. of Antibiotics, The Tech. Sch., Bucharest, Romania, 1954. Photo-reporter Agerpress, Bucharest, 1950-51; med. photographer Cantacuzino Hosp., Bucharest, 1955-68; ret., 1995. Author, editor: Self Encounter, 1979, Ten Oneiric Sketches, 1980, Rendes-Vous sau Intalnire cu mine insumi, 1987; (play) Vacuum (Colocviu de abis), 1979, Vacuum-Void, 1988, Pe portativul vietii, 1992. Home: 334 W 49th St Apt 4FE New York NY 10019-7308

NICOLADIS, MICHAEL F., engineering company executive; b. New Orleans, Aug. 15, 1960; s. Frank and Peggy (Yemelos) N. B in Engring. magna cum laude, Vanderbilt U., 1982; MBA, Duke U., 1984. Assoc. N-Y Assocs., Inc., Metairie, La., 1984-85, v.p., 1985-97, COO, sr. v.p., 1997—. Mem. Holy Trinity Greek Orthodox Cathedral, New Orleans. Fuqua scholar, Conoco scholar Duke U. Mem.: ASCE, Am. Pub. Works Assn., Am. Coun. Engring. Cos., Soc. Am. Mil. Engrs., Chi Epsilon, Tau Beta Pi. Avocations: tennis, reading, travel. Office: N Y Assocs Inc 2750 Lake Villa Dr Metairie LA 70002-6786 Office Phone: 504-885-0500. Business E-Mail: mnicoladis@n-yassociates.com.

NICOLAIDES, MARY, retired lawyer; b. NYC, June 7, 1927; d. George and Dorothy Nicolaides. BCE, CUNY, 1947; MBA with distinction, DePaul U., 1975, JD, 1981. Bar: Ill. 1982, U.S. Dist. Ct. (no. dist.) Ill. 1982, U.S. Patent Office 1983. Sr. design engr. cement subs. U.S. Steel Corp., NYC, then Pitts., 1948-71; sole practice Chgo., 1982—2006; ret., 2007. Republican. Greek Orthodox. Address: 233 E Erie St Apt 1804 Chicago IL 60611-2903

NICOLAOU, K. C., chemistry professor; b. Karavas, Kyrenia, Cyprus, July 5, 1946; came to U.S., 1972; s. Costa and Helen (Yettimi) N.; m. Georgette Karayianni, July 15, 1973; children: Colette, Alexis, Christopher, Paul. BSc, Bedford Coll., London, 1969; PhD, U. Coll., London, 1972; DSc, U. London, 1994; PhD (hon.), U. Athens, 1995. Rsch. assoc. Columbia U., NYC, 1972-73, Harvard U., Cambridge, Mass., 1973-76; from asst. prof. to Rhodes-Thompson prof. chemistry U. Pa., Phila., 1976-89; prof. chemistry U. Calif. at San Diego, La Jolla, 1989—; Darlene Shiley prof. chemistry, chmn. dept. The Scripps Rsch. Inst., La Jolla, Calif., 1989—; Aline W. & L.S. Skaggs prof. Skaggs Inst. for Chemical Biology, Scripps Rsch. Inst., 1996—. Vis. prof. U. Paris, 1986; mem. exec. com. Diann. Cyprus Conf. on Drug Design; mem. med. study sect. D, NIH, 1988-90; mem. internat. adv. bd. Angewandte Chemie, 1994—. Author: (with N. A. Petasis) Selenium in Natural Products Synthesis, 1984, (with E. J. Sorensen) Classics in Total Synthesis, 1996; co-editor: Synthesis, Germany, 1984-90, Chemistry and Biology, 1994; editl. bd. Prostaglandins, Leukotrienes and Medicine, 1978-88, Synthesis, 1990—, Accounts of Chem. Rsch., 1992—, Carbohydrate Letters, 1993—, Chemistry-A European Jour., 1994—, Perspectives in Drug, Discovery and Design, 1994—, Indian Jour. of Chemistry, Sect. B, 1995—; mem. bd. consulting editors Tetrahedron Publs., 1992—; mem. adv. bd. Contemporary Organic Synthesis, 1993—; mem. regional adv. bd. J. C. S. Chem. Comm., 189—, J. C. S. Perkin I, 1991—; contbr. articles to profl. jours.; patentee in field. Recipient Japan Soc. for Promotion Sci. award 1987-88, U.S. Sr. Scientist award Alexander von Humboldt Found., 1987-88, Alan R. Day award Phila. Organic Chemists Club, 1993, Pfizer Rsch. award, 1993-94, Paul Janssen Prize, 1994, Alexander the Great Award Hellenic Cultural Soc. of San Diego, 1994, Rhone-Poulenc medal Royal Soc. of Chemistry, 1995, Chem. Pioneer Am. Inst. of Chemists, 1996, Inhoffen Medal of Gesellscaft fur Biotechnologische Forschung mbH (GBF) Tech. U. of Braunschweig, 1996, Linus Pauling award, 1996, Schering prize, Aspirin prize, Max Tischler Lecture prize, Yamada prize, Nagoya medal, Centenary medal, Royal Soc., Paul Karrer medal, Esselen award, Nobel Laureate Signature award, Petrahedron prize; fellow A.P. Sloan Found., 1979-83, J. S. Guggenheim Found., 1984; Camille and Henry Dreyfus scholar, 1980-84, Arthur C. Cope scholar, 1987. Fellow N.Y. Acad. Scis., AAAS; mem. Nat. Acad. Scis., Am. Chem. Soc. (Creative Work in Synthetic Organic Chemistry award 1993, William H. Nichols medal N.Y. sect. 1996, Ernest Guenther award in chemistry of natural products 1996), Chem. Soc. London, German Chem. Soc., Japanese Chem. Soc. Office: Scripps Rsch Inst Dept Chemistry 10550 N Torrey Pines Rd La Jolla CA 92037-1000

NICOLAS, KENNETH LEE, import/export company executive; s. Norman L. and Bernice L. (Hameister) N.; m. Anne Vanderwielen, July 5, 1992 (dec.); children: Juliana M., Camille G. BA in Polit. Sci., Calif. State U., Fullerton, 1968; MA in Legis. Affairs/Econs., George Washington U., 1975. Exec. asst. Congressman Richard T. Hanna, Washington, 1970-72; sr. staff assoc. Nat. Assn. Ednl. Broadcasters, Washington, 1972-74; founder, pres. Nicolas Assocs. Internat., Inc., 1972—80; exec. dir. Am. Coll. Nuc. Physicians, Washington, 1974-77; aide to the Pres. White House, Washington, 1977-80; v.p. McSweeney & Co. Consulting, Newport Beach, Calif., 1980-83, L.E. Peterson & Co. Investment Banking, Costa Mesa, Calif., 1983-85; founder, pres. Fin. Strategies Group, Inc., Newport Beach, 1985—; CEO Tradex Internat., Inc., Newport Beach, 1988-94; founder, CEO Trade Access Group, Inc., 1994—. Adj. prof. Orange Coast Coll., Costa Mesa, 1983-97, internat. MBA program U. So. Calif., 1989-90, Thunderbird Sch. Internat. Bus., Orange County, 1990-92, U. Calif., Riverside and Irvine, 1996-98; adj. prof. internat. bus. MBA program Webster U., 1998—. Author: (article series) Business to Business Mag., 1984-87 (Excellence award 1984-87). Bd. dirs., v.p. Leukemia Soc. Am., Orange County, Calif., 1982-88; chmn. Holiday Project, 1992-94; mem. bd. mgrs., chmn. capital devel. com. Orange County YMCA, 2001—, gen. campaign chmn., fedn. chief parent/child program, 2002-; nation chief Orange Blossom Nation, Indian Princess Program; bd. gov. YMCA, 2006-; investment advisor, City of Irvine, Calif., 2006-; democratic party canidate,

Orange County, 2007-. With U.S. Army, 1968-70, Vietnam. Recipient Outstanding Svc. award Nat. Holiday Project, 1993, Nat. Svc. Appreciation award Pres. Jimmy Carter, 1980, Excellence award Leukemia Soc. Am., 1988. Mem. Japan Am. Soc. (Orange County chpt. chmn. bd. dirs. 1997-99), Japan Am. Soc. So. Calif. (exec. bd. 1996-98), Surfrider Assn. Democrat. Episcopalian. Avocations: Karate, sailing, travel, chess, swimming.

NICOLAU, SIOBHAN, cultural organization administrator; Grad., Goucher Coll., Latin Am. Inst. Former sr. program officer Ford Found.; pres., founder Hispanic Policy Develop. Project, 1981—; pres. Nat. Film Archive of Philanthropy. Trustee Ewing Marion Kauffman Found., 1993—2002, 2003—; bd. mem. Public/Private Ventures, Enterprise Found. Office: Hispanic Policy Develop Project 122 E 42nd St New York NY 10168 Office Phone: 646-723-0750. E-mail: siobhan96@aol.com.

NICOLETTI, PAUL LEE, retired veterinarian, educator; b. Goodman, Mo., Oct. 26, 1932; s. Felix and Clarice N.; m. Earlene Blackburn, June 6, 1954; children: Diana, Julie, Nancy. BS in Agr., U. Mo., 1956, DVM, 1956; MS, U. Wis., 1962. Diplomate Am. Coll. Vet. Preventive Medicine. Veterinarian USDA, Mo., Wis., NY, 1956-68, UN FAO, Tehran, Iran, 1968-72, USDA, Jackson, Miss., 1972-75, Gainesville, Fla., 1973-78; prof. vet. medicine U. Fla., Gainesville, 1978—2003, prof. emeritus, 2003—. Recipient awards from Fla. Cattleman's Assn., 1978, Dairy Farmers, Inc., 1978, Borden award, 1979, Gold Star award Fla. Veterinary Medicine Assoc., 1981, 86, U. Austral, Chile, 1981, P.R. Dairy Assn., 1978, faculty alumni award U. Mo., 1987; named Basic Scis. Tchr. of Yr. Nat. Student Am. Vet. Med. Assn., 1994, Alumnus of Yr. award, U. Mo., 2000, U. Fla. Disting. Svc. award, 2003. Mem. Am. Vet. Medicine Assn. (internat. prize 1991), Fla. Vet. Medicine Assn. (pres. 1995-96, veterinarian of yr. 1994, Disting. Svc. award 1999, Lifetime Achievement award 2004), Am. Coll. Vet. Preventive Medicine (pres. 1997-98), Phi Zeta (nat. pres. 1997-99). Home: 2552 SW 14th Dr Gainesville FL 32608-2042 Office: Univ of Fla Coll Vet Medicine PO Box 110880 Gainesville FL 32611-0880 Office Phone: 352-392-2239 ext. 5860. Business E-Mail: nicolettip@vetmed.ufl.edu.

NICOLL, EDWARD J., information technology company executive; b. Aug. 13, 1953; JD, Yale U., 1997. Co-founder, pres. Waterhouse Investor Svcs., Inc. (sold to Toronto-Dominion Bank and became TD Waterhouse), 1979—96; chmn., CEO Datek Online Holdings, Corp., Iselin, NJ, 1999—2002, Instinet, LLC, 2002—07, chmn., 2007—. Trustee New Cmty. Found. Fellow Yale U. Achievements include first to to attend Yale Law without a college degree. *

NICOLS, HOWARD J.C., lawyer; b. Woodhaven, NY, 1956; BA summa cum laude, SUNY, Albany, 1978; JD cum laude, Cornell U., 1981. Bar: Ohio 1981, NY 2000, US Ct. Appeals, 2nd, 6th, 9th, 10th Circuits 2003, US Dist. Ct. 2003, Northern Dist. Ohio 2003. Ptnr., litigation Squire, Sanders & Dempsey, LLP, Cleve., mem. mgmt. com. Master bencher Judge Anthony J. Celebrezze Am. Inn Ct.; chancellor Cornell Moot Ct. Bd.; presenter in field. Bd. editor Cornell Internat. Law Jour.; co-author: Taxes on Profits of Multinational Companies and Implications for Russia, 2004. Mem.: Cleve. Bar Assn. Office: Squire Sanders & Dempsey LLP 4900 Key Tower 122 Public Sq Cleveland OH 44114-1304 Office Phone: 216-479-8743. Office Fax: 216-479-8780. Business E-Mail: hnicols@ssd.com.

NICOLSON, DAN HENRY, retired plant taxonomist; b. Kansas City, Mo., Sept. 5, 1933; s. John Whitley and LeOna Johanna (Teget) N.; m. Alice Black Crawford, Aug. 22, 1959; children: John Crawford, Sarah Whitley, David Teget. AB, Grinnell Coll., 1955; MBA, Stanford U., 1957; MSc, Cornell U., 1959, PhD, 1964. Asst. curator Smithsonian Instn., Washington, 1964-65, assoc. curator, 1965-74, curator, 1974—2006; ret., 2006. Author: Flora of Dominica, 1991; co-author: An Interpretation Van Rheede's Hortus Malabaricus, 1988, The Forsters and the Botany of the Second Cook Expedition (1772-1775), 2004; co-editor: Flora of the Hassan District, 1976. Mem. Internat. Assn. Plant Taxonomy (v.p. 1987-93, pres. 1993-99, past pres. 1999-2005), Washington Biologists Field Club (treas. 1981-97), Washington Bot. Soc. (pres. 1989-90, treas. 1997-2006). Office: Dept Botany MRC-166 Nat Mus Natural History Smithsonian Instn Washington DC 20013-7012 Office Phone: 202-633-0910. Business E-Mail: nicolson@si.edu.

NIDECKER, ANDREAS CORNELIS, radiologist, educator; b. Tiel, The Netherlands, Oct. 1, 1947; s. Hans Jakob and Rosemarie (Huggenberg) Nidecker; children from previous marriage: Florian, Maja, Eva. MD, Med. Sch. U. Basel, Switzerland, 1973. Diplomate Am. Bd. Radiology. Internship Lawrence Gen. Hosp., Toronto, Canada, 1973—74, 1976—79; asst. prof. radiology U. Basel, 1985-99, prof., 1999—; pvt. practice Basel, 1982—. Mem. Arbeitsgruppe Knochentumoren, Deutsches Krebsforschungsfentrur; co-owner IMAMED Radiologie Nordwest, Basel. Mem. exec. com., past pres. Internat. Physicians Prevention Nuc. War, 1982—; mem. constl. coun. Basel Canton. Mem.: Swiss Soc. Radiology, Radiol. Soc. N.Am., Internat. Soc. Skeletal Radiology. Avocations: hiking, skiing, travel, music. Office: IMAMED Radiologie Nordwest Untere Rebgasse 18 4058 Basel Switzerland E-mail: anidecker@bluewin.ch, andreas.nidecker@imamed.ch.

NIDES, THOMAS RICHARD, diversified financial services company executive; s. Mr. and Mrs. Arnold R. Nides BA, U. Minn. Campaign staffer, midwest region polit. and fin. div. Mondale-Ferraro presdl. campaign, 1984; polit. action com. dir. Dem. Congressional Campaign Com., 1985—86; spl. asst. Tony Coelho, House Majority, 1986—89; exec. asst. to spkr. Ho. of Reps. Thomas Foley, 1989—93; chief of staff Michael Kantor, US Trade Rep., 1993—94; v.p. housing impact Fannie Mae, 1995—96, sr. v.p. human resources, 1997—2001; prin., head of corp. affairs Morgan Stanley, NYC, 1996—97; campaign mgr., vice-presidential campaign Joe Lieberman, 2000; global chief adminstrv. officer Credit Suisse First Boston LLC, NYC, 2001—04, mem., oper. com.; pres., CEO Burson-Marsteller, NYC, 2004—05; chief adminstrv. officer Morgan Stanley, NYC, 2005—. Office: Morgan Stanley 1585 Broadway New York NY 10036

NIDETZ, MYRON PHILIP, health care delivery systems consultant; b. Chgo., Dec. 29, 1935; s. David J. and Rose Y. (Yudell) N.; m. Linda Freeman, Dec. 18, 1960; children: Julia, Allison. BS, U. Ill., 1958; M in Bus. and Commerce, Hamilton Inst., Phila., 1972; MPA, Roosevelt U., 1981. Diplomate Am. Acad. Med. Adminstrs. Dir. Union Coop. Eye Care Ctr., Chgo., 1961-65; dir. med. admistrv. svcs. Michael Reese Hosp. and Med. Ctr., Chgo., 1965-75; assoc. dir. program to imrpove med. care and health svcs. AMA, Chgo., 1975-79; exec. dir. North Ctrl. Dialysis Ctrs., Chgo., 1979-92; pres. Myron P. Nidetz & Assocs., Inc., Chgo., 1992—. Disting. vis. lectr. health care adminstrn. Roosevelt U., Chgo., bd. govs., 1992—2005, pres. pub. adminstrn. coun., 1993—2005, mem. curriculum rev. com. pub. adminstrn., 1992—97, chair admissions com., 1992—2005, chair coun. and chpt. leadership com., 1998—; vis. lectr. Ind. U. N.W., 2003—, arts cons., 2005—; Nat. Inst. Corrections tech. cons. U.S. Dept. Justice, 1978—90; adj. prof., program chair Calumet Coll., St. Joseph U., Whiting, Ind., 1997—99. Mem. adv. bd. Inst. of Medicine, 1979—2000; active Health Planning Facilities Bd., Ill., 1979—93, Ill. Dept. Pub. Aid, 1992—99, Ill. Dept. Aging, 1992—99; mem. adv. bd. Am. Kidney Fund, chmn. Midwest core group, 1979—92; mem. adv. bd. Nat. Kidney Found., 1992—99; Met. area satellite group, state legis. com., 1992—99; cmty. coord. AARP, 1992—98; pres. bd. dirs. Suburban Area Agy. on Aging, 1997—99, sr. adv. cons., 1999—2004; mem. Munster Area Rotary Club, Humane Soc. of the Calumet Area, Friends of Theatre at the Ctr., Munster Hist. Soc., Lake County Devel. Com.; bd. dirs., mem. ethics com. Hospice of Calumet Area; counselor Svc. Core of Ret. Execs., 1992—2002; bd. dirs. Active Srs. Found., 1999—2003, chair bd. devel. com.; regional rev. panelist Ind. Arts Commn., 2002; bd. dirs. Lake County Pub. Libr. Found., Friends of Emerson Sch. for Visual and Performing Arts, 2005—; v.p. South Shore Arts Assn.; chmn. Ind. Regional Arts Coun. With US Army, 1959—60. Fellow: APHA, Am. Acad. Med. Adminstrs., Royal Soc. Health; mem.: AMA, Humane Soc. of Calumet Area, 21st Century Fund (trustee), Lake County Libr. Found. (bd. dirs.), Humane Soc. of the Calunet Area, Hospice of the Calunet Area, Ind. Pub. Health Assn., Ill. Pub. Health Assn., Am. Mgmt. Assn., Assn. U. Programs Health Adminstrn., Gerontol. Soc., Inst. Soc. Ethics and Life Scis., Am. Mgmt. Assn., Am. Hosp. Assn., Am. Geriatrics Soc., Am. Acad. Polit. and Social Sci., Nat. Renal Adminstrs. Assn. (govt. affairs com.), Am. Assn. Kidney Patients, Nat. Dialysis Assn. (sec.), Assn. Hosp. Med. Edn., Munster Hist. Soc., Friends of the Theatre, Ind. Regional Arts Commn. (commr.), Munster Rotary Club, Ind. U. Northwest Ctr. for Cultural Discovery & Learning Group, Ind. U. Northwest Theatre Patron, Ind. U. Northwest (curatorate), Books, Brushes & Bands (bd. dir.), Munster Ednl. Found. (bd. dir.), Hammond Cmty. Concerts Assn. Soc., Hammond Cmty. Concerts Assn., No. Ind. Arts Assn. (bd. dir., devel. com.), Lyric Opera Chpt., Auditorium Bldg. Soc., NW Ind. Excellence in Theatre Found. (bd. dir.), Ill. Theatre Ctr. Guild (chmn. 1990—91), Ill. Theatre Ctr., Northwest Ind. Symphony Soc. (bd. dirs.), No. Ind. Arts Assn. (bd.dir.).

NIE, GUOJUN, research scientist; b. Huangmei, Hubie, China, Apr. 12, 1963; parents Songshan Nie and Shuie Yan; m. Jinghua Feng, July 7, 1987; children: Pingting, George F., Derek H. BS, Hubei Normal U., Huangshi, China, 1984; MS, Chinese Acad. Scis., Changchun, Jilin, 1987; PhD, Utah State U., Logan, 1999. Asst. prof. Wuhan Inst. Chem. Tech., Hubei, 1987—94; rsch. scientist U. Kans. Med. Ctr., Kansas City, 1999—2001, Baxter Biosci., Columbia, Md., 2001—. Contbr. articles to profl. jours. Scholar E.L. and Inez Waldron Biotech. Endowment Fund Biotech. Ctr. Utah State U. Mem. ACS, ASME, Chinese Student and Scholar Assn. Achievements include invention of WZ-2 reducing agent for fuel oil viscosity; WZ-1 emulsifier for heavy oil. Avocations: basketball, tennis, soccer, fishing. Home: 14213 Reed Farm Way North Potomac MD 20878 Office: Baxter Biosci 1015 Old Columbia Rd Columbia MD 21046

NIEBRUEGGE, MICHAEL E., lawyer; b. Alton, Ill., Mar. 21, 1952; BA, Harvard U., 1974; JD, Cornell U., 1977. Bar: Ill. 1977, U.S. Dist. Ct. (no. dist.) Ill. 1977, Tex. 1982, U.S. Dist. Ct. (so dist.) Tex. 1988. Lectr. bus. law Northwestern Univ., Chg., Ill., 1979—80; v.p., gen. counsel Gulf Coast Royalty Co., Houston, 1981—82; atty. Mayer, Brown, Rowe & Maw LLP, Chgo., 1977—81, Houston, 1982—84, ptnr., 1984—, ptnr.-in-charge, 1995—. Lectr. Northwestern U., Chgo., 1979-80. Mem. State Bar Tex., Tex. Assn. Bank Counsel. Office: Mayer Brown Rowe & Maw LLP Ste 3600 700 Louisiana St Houston TX 77002-2730 Office Phone: 713-546-0507. Office Fax: 713-632-1800. Business E-Mail: mniebruegge@mayerbrownrowe.com.

NIEBUHR, DAVID WILLIAM, epidemiologist, educator; b. Mineola, NY, Apr. 14, 1959; s. Henry William and Nancy Elizabeth Niebuhr; m. Stacey B. Baszkowski, June 12, 1982; children: Tiffany Elaine, Nicole Elizabeth, Brieanna Lynn. BA, Johns Hopkins U., Balt., 1981, MPH, 1985; MD, George Washington U., DC, 1985; MS, U. Wash., Seattle, 1995. Cert. Am. Coll. Preventive Medicine, Am. Acad. Family Physicians. Chief dept. epidemiology Walter Reed Army Inst. Rsch., Silver Spring, Md., 2000—. Adj. asst. prof. dept. biometrics and preventive medicine Uniformed Services U. Health Scis., Bethesda, Md., 2004—; presenter in field. Author: Textbook of Military Medicine in Recruit; contbr. articles to profl. jours. Lay leader Immanuel Ch., Silver Spring, 2000—. Lt. col. US Army, 2000—07. Decorated Order of Military Med. Merit. Achievements include research in genetic and environmental associations with the development of psychotic disorders. Avocation: travel. Office: Walter Reed Army Institute of Research 503 Robert Grant Ave Silver Spring MD 20910-7500 Office Phone: 301-319-9833. Office Fax: 301-319-9104. Business E-Mail: david.niebuhr@us.army.mil.

NIEBYL, JENNIFER ROBINSON, obstetrician, gynecologist, educator; BSc, McGill U., Mont., 1963; MD, Yale U., 1967. Diplomate Am. Bd. Ob-Gyn., Am. Bd. Maternal and Fetal Medicine. Intern in Internal Medicine N.Y. Hosp.-Cornell Med. Ctr., 1967-68, resident in ob-gyn., 1968-70, Johns Hopkins Hosp., Balt., 1970-73, fellow in maternal and fetal medicine, 1976-78, mem. staff, 1973—88, U. Iowa Hosps. and Clinics, Iowa City, 1988—; prof., head ob-gyn. dept. U. Iowa Sch. Medicine, Iowa City, 1988—. Mem. ACOG, Am. Gynecol. and Obstetrical Soc., Soc. Gynecol. Investigation, Soc. Maternal Fetal Medicine, Inst. Medicine of NAS. Office: U Iowa Hosps & Clinics 200 Hawkins Dr Iowa City IA 52242 Office Phone: 319-356-1976.

NIED, THOMAS HERMAN, retired media specialist; b. Queens, NY, May 4, 1942; s. Herman Joseph and Margaret (Jos) N.; m. Carol J. Thomas, June 6, 1964; children: Stacey, Allison. BA, Rutgers U., 1964, LLB, 1967; LLM in Taxation, NYU, 1972. CPA, N.J., Ga. Tax mgr. Ernst & Young, NYC, Atlanta, Newark and Trenton, N.J., 1968-77; v.p. taxation N.Y. Times Co., NYC, 1977-97; v.p. fed. tax Universal Music Group (formerly Polygram Holding Inc.), NYC, 1997—2004, ret., 2004. Founder Media Tax Group, 1979, mem., 1979-99. Mem. ABA, AICPA, Tax Execs. Inst. (bd. dirs. 1986-2004, pres. N.Y. chpt. 1991-92, exec. com. 1992-93), Newspaper Assn. of Am. (chmn. tax com. 1995-97, chmn. ind. contractor task force 1995-97, mem. pub. policy com. 1995-97). Avocations: travel, reading, stamp collecting/philately, birding. Home: 31 Vreeland Ct Princeton NJ 08540-6760 Personal E-mail: tomnied@aol.com.

NIEDERAUER, DUNCAN L., stock exchange executive; b. Sept. 7, 1959; BA cum laude in Economics, Colgate U., 1981; MBA, Emory U., 1985. Joined Goldman Sachs, 1985, equities divsn., 1987, ran the Equities E-Commerce effort, global head of portfolio trading, and spent three years in Tokyo in Derivatives and Japanese products, mng. dir., 1997, ptnr., 2000, relocated to the headquarters of Spear, Leeds & Kellogg, 2000, co-head equities divsn. execution services franchise, 2005—07; pres., co-COO NYSE Group Inc., NYC, 2007; pres., co-COO, head US cash markets NYSE Euronext, NYC, 2007—. Bd. dirs. EzeCastle Software, 2000—. Bd. trustees Colgate U. Mem.: Omicron Delta Epsilon. Office: NYSE Euronext 11 Wall St New York NY 10005 *

NIEDERAUER, GEORGE H., bishop; b. LA, June 14, 1936; s. George and Elaine N. BA Philosophy, St. John's Seminary, Camarillo, CA, 1959; BA Sacred Theology, Catholic U., Washington, DC, 1962; MA English Lit., Loyola U., LA, 1962; PhD English Lit., USC, 1966. Ordained priest 1962, named prelate of honor (monsignor) 1984, named bishop Diocese of Salt Lake City, 1994. Asst. pastor Our Lady of the Assumption Parish, Claremont, Calif., 1962—63; priest in residence Holy Name of Jesus Parish, Los Angeles, 1963—65; instr. English Lit. St. John's Seminary Coll., Camarillo, Calif., 1965—79; instr. of English Lit. Mt. St. Mary's Coll., Los Angeles, 1967—74; English Dept. chmn. St. John's Seminary Coll., Camarillo, 1968—77, spiritual dir., 1972—79; part-time instr. of Spiritual Theology St. John's Seminary Theologate, 1976—79, full-time instr. of Spiritual Theology, 1979—87; part-time instr. of English Lit. St. John's Seminary Coll., 1979—92; rector St. John's Seminary, 1987—92, spiritual dir., 1979—95; co-dir. Cardinal Manning House of Prayer for Priests, Los Angeles, 1992—95; bishop Salt Lake City, 1995—. Mem. Nat. Fedn. of Spiritual Dirs., pres., 1975—77; mem. bd. of the Comm. of Priests' Retreat Archdiocese L.A.; mem. select comm. for revision of U.S. Cath. Conf. "Program for Priestly Formation" 3rd edit.; mem. Vatican Visitation Team for Theologates; spkr. World Vision Internat., Fuller Theol. Sem., Calif. Lutheran Coll. Mem.: Camarillo Ministerial Assn., Western Assn. of Spiritual Dirs. (pres. 1973—75), Alpha Sigma Nu (Jesuit Honor Soc. - LMU chpt.). Avocations: classical music, stamp collecting/philately, reading, film appreciation. Office: Chancery Office 27 C St Salt Lake City UT 84103-2302

NIEDERBERGER, JANE, information technology executive; m. Mark Niederberger; children: Amy, Sarah. BS in nutrition, Simmons Coll., 1982; MBA in health care adminstrn., Northeastern U. Various mgmt. positions Harvard Pilgrim Health Care, Boston, 1983—96; with IT divsn. Anthem, Inc., Indpls., 1997, acting chief info. officer, 1998—99, sr. v.p., chief info. officer, 1999—. Bd. dir. Managed Care Exec. Group. Bd. mem. Jr. Achievement, Indpls. Recipient Women and Hi Tech Leading Light award, 2002.

NIEDERHUBER, JOHN EDWARD, federal agency administrator, oncologist, surgeon, immunologist; b. Steubenville, Ohio, June 21, 1938; s. William Henry and Helen (Smittle) N.; m. Tracey J. Williamson (dec. Dec. 2001); children: Elizabeth Ann, Matthew John. BS, Bethany Coll., 1960; MD, Ohio State U., 1964. Diplomate Am. Bd. Surgery. Internship, surgery Ohio State U. Hosp., Columbus, 1964-65; from resident surgery to prof. U. Mich. Med. Ctr., Ann Arbor, 1967—80, prof. surgery, prof. microbiology and immunology, 1980-87, chief divsn. surg. oncology sect. gen. surgery, 1983—86, assoc. dean rsch., 1982—85, sr. assoc. dean med. sch., 1983—85; cons. Wayne County Gen. Hosp., Mich., 1973-84; cons. surgery Ann Arbor VA Hosp., 1973-87; prof. surgery, oncology, molecular biology and genetics The Johns Hopkins U. Sch. Med., Balt., 1987-91; Emile Holman prof. surgery, chair, dept. surgery, head sect. surgical scis. Stanford (Calif.) U. Sch. Medicine., 1991-95, prof. microbiology and immunology, 1991-97; chief of surgery Stanford (Calif.) U. Hosp., 1991-95; dir. planning Comp. Cancer Ctr. Stanford (Calif.) Med. Ctr., 1991-95; prof. surgery and oncology Sch. Medicine U. Wis., Madison, 1997—2005, asst. dean oncology, dir. Comprehensive Cancer Ctr., 1997—2002; dep. dir. for translational & clin. sciences, COO Nat. Cancer. Inst., NIH, Bethesda, Md., 2005—, acting dir., 2006—. Vis. prof. Howard Hughes Med. Inst. dept. molecular biology and genetics Howard Hughes Med. Inst., The Johns Hopkins U. Sch. Medicine, Balt., 1986-87; cons. in field. Author books on cancer and surgery; mem. editl. bd. Jour. Immunology, 1981-85, Jour. Surg. Res., 1989-95, Current Opinion in Oncology, 1989—95, Cure, 2002-04, Annals of Surgery, 1991—97, Surg. Oncology, 1991—, Jour. Clin. Oncology, 1993, Annals of Surg. Oncology, 1993—, Jour. ACS, 1994—, The Oncologist, 1995—, Surgery, 1999-2004; contbr. articles to profl. jours. Active bd. sci. councilors NCI divsn. Cancer Treatment, 1986-91, chmn., 1987-91, Gen. Motors Cancer Rsch. Found. Awards Assembly, 1988-92, 98-2003; chmn. nat. cancer adv. bd. NCI, 2002—05; mem. C-Change, 2001—, mem. planning and budget com., vice-chair cancer ctrs. constituency com., vice-chair rsch. com., 2005-, mem. CEO Roundtable, 2003—. Served to capt. U.S. Army, 1965-67 Recipient USPHS Rsch. Career Devel. award Nat. Inst. Allergy and Infectious Disease, 1974-79, Disting. Faculty Svc. award U. Mich., 1978, Alumni Achievement award Ohio State U. Coll. Medicine, 1989, Alumni Achievement award in Medicine Bethany Coll., 1995; vis. rsch. fellow divsn. immunobiology Karolinska Inst., Stockholm, 1970-71, Am. Cancer Soc. Jr. Faculty Clin. fellow, 1977-79. Fellow ACS; mem. Am. Soc. Transplant Surgeons, Transplantation Soc., Am. Surg. Assn., Am. Assn. Immunologists, Am. Assn. Cancer Insts. (v.p. 1999-2001, pres. 2001-03), Coller Surg. Soc., Soc. Univ. Surgeons, Assn. Acad. Surgeons, Soc. Surg. Oncology (v.p. 1999-2001, pres. 2001-02), Ctrl. Surg. Soc., Am. Assn. Cancer Rsch., Am. Soc. Clin. Oncology, Soc. Clin. Surgery, Biology Club II, Robert M. Zollinger-Ohio State U. Surg. Soc., Pacific Coast Surg. Assn., Soc. Surgery of the Alimentary Tract. Avocations: golf, gardening. Office: Nat Cancer Inst NIH Bldg 31 Room 11A03 31 Center Dr MSC 2590 Bethesda MD 20892-2590 Office Phone: 301-496-6511. Business E-Mail: niederhj@mail.nih.gov.

NIEDERMAN, JAMES CORSON, retired internist, educator; b. Hamilton, Ohio, Nov. 27, 1924; s. Clifford Frederick and Henrietta (Corson) N.; m. Miriam Camp, Dec. 12, 1951; children— Timothy Porter, Derrick Corson, Eliza Orton, Caroline Noble. Student, Kenyon Coll., 1942—45, DSc (hon.), 1981; MD, Johns Hopkins U., 1949. Intern Osler Svc. Johns Hopkins Hosp., Balt., 1949-50; asst. resident in medicine Yale-New Haven Med. Center, 1950-51, assoc. resident, 1953-55; med. ctr. practice specializing in internal medicine, infectious disease and clin. epidemiology New Haven, 1955-97; instr. Yale U., 1955-58, asst. prof., 1958-66, assoc. prof., 1966-76, clin. prof. medicine and epidemiology, 1976-97, emeritus clin. prof. medicine and epidemiology, 1997—, clin. prof. emeritus epidemiology and pub. health, 1998; mem. Nat. Coun. for Johns Hopkins Medicine. Trustee Kenyon Coll., 1974-97, trustee emeritus, 1997—; bd. counselors Smith Coll., 1970-77. Served to 1st lt. M.C. U.S. Army, 1951-53. Fellow Silliman Coll., Yale U. Fellow Am. Coll. Epidemiology; mem. Infectious Diseases Soc. Am., Am. Epidemiol. Soc., Johns Hopkins Med. and Surg. Assn.; mem. The Kenyon Rev. Bd. Trustees, Conn. Soc. Arts and Scis. Clubs: Yale (N.Y.C.); New Haven Lawn. Democrat. Episcopalian. Achievements include research in clin. epidemiology of Epstein Barr virus infections and demonstration of its causal relationship of infectious mononucleosis. Home: 429 Sperry Rd Bethany CT 06524-3544 Home Phone: 203-393-3538. Home Fax: 203-393-1902. E-mail: jcniederman@sbcglobal.net.

NIEDERMAN, MICHAEL STEVEN, physician, educator; b. NYC, Mar. 30, 1953; s. L. Louis and Betty Doris N.; m. Ronna Diane Kay, Aug. 15, 1976; children: Alex, Eric. AB, Boston U., 1974, MD, 1977. Intern Northwestern U. Med. Sch., Chgo., 1977-78, resident, 1978-80; pulmonary medicine fellow Yale U. Sch. Med., New Haven, 1980-83; dir. Med. ICU Winthrop U. Hosp., Mineola, N.Y., 1983-97, chief pulmonary and critical care medicine, 1997—; assoc. prof., then prof. medicine SUNY, Stony Brook, 1990—. Dir. Microbiology Assembly, Am. Thoracic Soc., N.Y.C., 1990-91. Editor: Respiratory Infections (textbook), 1994; editor-in-chief Clin. Pulmonary Medicine, 1994-2005; mem. editl. bd. Am. Jour. Respiratory and Cridical Care Medicine, 1994—, Chest, 1994—, Critical Care Medicine; contbr. numerous articles to profl. jours. Fellow ACP, Am. Coll. Chest Physicians (credentials com. 1991—), Coll. Critical Care Medicine; mem. Phi Beta Kappa, Alpha Omega Alpha. Avocations: skiing, tennis, golf, jazz music. Office: Winthrop Univ Hosp 222 Station Plz N Ste 509 Mineola NY 11501-3893 Office Phone: 516-663-2381. E-mail: mniederman@winthrop.org.

NIEDERMAYER, SCOTT, professional hockey player; b. Edmonton, Alta., Can., Aug. 31, 1973; m. Lisa Niedermayer; children: Logan, Jackson, Joshua. Defenseman NJ Devils, 1991—2005, Anaheim Ducks (formerly Mighty Ducks of Anaheim), 2005—, capt., 2005—. Mem. Team Can., Olympic Games, Nagano, Japan, 1998, Salt Lake City, 2002, Team Can., World Cup of Hockey, 1996, 2004; player NHL All-Star Game, 1998, 2001, 04. Named to All-Rookie Team, NHL, 1993, Second All-Star Team, 1998, First All-Star Team, 2004, 2006, 2007; recipient James Norris Meml. Trophy, 2004, Mark Messier Leadership Award, 2006, Conn Smythe Trophy, 2007. Achievements include being a member of Stanley Cup Champion New Jersey Devils, 1995, 2000, 2003, Anaheim Ducks, 2007; being a member of gold medal winning Canadian Hockey Team, Salt Lake City Olympic games, 2002; being a member of World Cup Champion Team Canada, 2004. Office: c/o Anaheim Ducks 5695 E Katella Ave Anaheim CA 92806 *

NIEHAUS, MARY C., lawyer; b. 1961; BA with honors, Grinnell Coll., 1985; JD cum laude, Northwestern U., 1988. Bar: Ill. 1988, U.S. Dist. Ct. (no. dist.) Ill. 1988, U.S. Tax Ct. 1989. With Sidley & Austin, Chgo.,

1988—, ptnr., 1996—. Mem. editl. staff Northwestern U. Law Rev., 1987-88. Mem. Order of Coif, Phi Beta Kappa. Office: Sidley & Austin Bank One Plz 10 S Dearborn St Chicago IL 60603 Fax: 312-83-7036. E-mail: mniehaus@sidley.com.

NIEHOFF, KARL RICHARD BESUDEN, finance company executive; b. Cin., May 11, 1943; s. Karl George and Jean (Besuden) N.; children: K. Richard B. Jr., Kelly B. BA, U. Cin., 1967. Corp. trust ops. officer 5th-3d Union Trust, Cin., 1968-74; v.p., gen. mgr. Sabina Water Co., Ohio, 1974-76; v.p., sec. Weil, Roth and Irving, Inc., 1974-76; co-mgr., mcpl. fin. dept. Thomson McKinnon Securities, Cin. and NYC, 1976—78; chmn. Cin. Stock Exch., Inc., Cin., 1975, pres., trustee, seat owner, 1976—89; exch. rep., founding mem. Consol. Quote, Consol. Tape Oper. Coms., 1979-90, alt., 1991-92; pres. Fin. Instruments Svcs. Corp., Cin., Chgo., London, 1985-90; sr. v.p. Trading, Trans. and Market Svcs. NASDAQ, Inc., 1990—92; v.p. D.E. Shaw & Co., NYC, 1992-94; pres. D.E. Shaw Securities, LLC, NYC, 1992—94; pres., mng. ptnr. Niehoff and Assocs., NYC, 1994-99; mng. dir., chief of party OTC Capital Mkt. Devel. Project, Ceto, Warsaw, 1994—96; advisor Ministry Mass Privatization, Republic of Poland, Warsaw, 1994—96; v.p., dir. Third Market Trading Corp., Chicago, 1994-98; pres., dir. SBX Inc., Cin., Princeton, NJ, 1997-2000; mng. dir. trading and tech. Unified Mgmt. Corp., Indpls., 1999—2000; pres. VSX Techs. Inc., NYC, Indpls., 1999—2000, Mark Securities, Inc., Pelham Manor, NY, 2002—; pres., CEO Webix, Inc., NYC, 2000—02; chmn. The X-Change Corp., NYC, 2002, pres., 2002; founder, chmn. US OTC Markets, Inc., NYC, 2005—; dir., pres., sec., treas. Schuyler Pk. Manor Coop., Pelham Manor, NY, 2000—. Witness U.S. Ho. Reps. Consumers Protection and Fin. Com., 1977, other gen. oversight, GAO com. panels and inquiries, 1987—94; v.p. Wit Capital Corp., NYC, 1998—99; pres., COO DSM-Wit, 1998—99; mem. Cin. Stock Exch., 1974—89, trustee, 1974—90, chmn. bd. trustees, 1975; mem. trading com. Inter-Market, 1980—90; mem. chief execs. com. Stock Exch., 1988—90; mem. task force com. GLOBEX, 1988—89; founding charter mem. Easdaq, Brussels, 1994—96; vis. lectr. U. Cin. Coll. Bus. Adminstrn., Xavier U. Bus. Adminstrn. Coll., Cin.; long-term planning com. Chgo. Bd. Options Exch., 1987—88; pres. Digital Stock Market, NYC, 1998—99; vis. com. U.S. Info. Agy., NYC, 1992—95; mng. dir. trading and tech. Unified Mgmt. Corp., Inc., Indpls and NYC, 1999—2000; pres. WEBIX, Inc., 1999—2002; bd. dirs., audit com. Equity Analysts, L.L.C., Cin.; instl. trading com. Boston Stock Exch., instl. adv. com., 2004. Trustee, sec. Contemporary Arts Ctr., Cin., 1975-83; mem. Young Mens Mercantile Libr. Assn., 1974-90, adv. com., 1974-77; devel. com. Tangeman Gallery of Art, 1981-82; pres., dir. Bermuda Condominium High Assn., Delray Beach, Fla., 1999-06. Mem.: Boston Securities Traders Assn., Securities Traders Assn. N.Y. (chmn. listed trading com. 1993, OTC Bull. Bd. 2002—04, com. chmn. STA trading subcom. 2002—04), India House, Keeneland Assn., Stone House Club, Nat. Arts Club, NYAC Yacht Club (Pelham Manor), N.Y. Athletic Club, Cin. Stock and Bond Club (trustee and 1st v.p. 1974—90), Queen City Mcpl. Bond Club (trustee 1974—80), Phi Alpha Theta.

NIEHOFF, LEONARD MARVIN, lawyer; b. St. Louis, Dec. 2, 1957; s. Leonard Marvin and May (Gordon) Niehoff; m. Lisa Rudgers. BA with high distinction, U. Mich., 1981, JD, postgrad., U. Mich., 1984. Bar: Mich. 1984, U.S. Dist. Ct. (ea. dist.) Mich., 1985, U.S. Dist. Ct. (we. dist.) Mich. 1985, U.S. Ct. Appeals (6th cir.) 1985, U.S. Supreme Ct. 1988. Research asst. U. Mich. Law Sch., Ann Arbor, 1983; shareholder Butzel Long, Detroit, 1984—. Adj. prof. law U. Detroit Law Sch., 1988—, Wayne State U. Law Sch., 1989—, U. Mich. Law Sch., 2002—. Editor U. Mich. Jour. Law Reform, 1983-84. Bd. advisors C.S. Mott Children's Hosp.; bd. dirs. Mich. Theatre Found. Named to 40 Under 40, Crain's Detroit Bus., 1996. Mem. ABA (forum com. on comms. law 1985—), Fed. Bar Assn. (exec. bd. 1995—), State Bar Mich. (chmn. constl. law com., law and media com., bar jour. adv. bd.), Detroit Bar Assn., Washtenaw Bar Assn. (chmn. trial practice sect., Patriot award 2004), U. Musical Soc. (bd. dirs.). Avocations: fishing, hunting, hiking. Office: 350 S Main St Ste 300 Ann Arbor MI 48104-2131

NIEHOFF, PHILIP JOHN, lawyer; b. Beaver Dam, Wis., Dec. 31, 1959; s. John Henry and Muriel Jean (Moore) Niehoff. BBA with distinction, U. Wis., 1982, JD cum laude, 1985; LLM in Securities Regulation, Georgetown U., 1988. Bar: Wis. 1985, U.S. Dist. Ct. (we. dist.) Wis. 1985, Ill. 1991. Atty. SEC, Washington, 1985-90; assoc. Mayer, Brown, Rowe & Maw, LLP, Chgo., 1990-95, ptnr., 1996—. Co-author: Current Law of Insider Trading, 1990, Public Offerings, securities law handbook, 1997; contbg. author: Securitization of Financial Assets, 1991. Fed. Bar Assn. scholar, 1988. Mem. ABA, State Bar Wis., State Bar Ill., Chgo. Bar Assn., Order of Coif, Golden Key Honor Soc., Beta Gamma Sigma, Phi Kappa Phi, Phi Eta Sigma. Republican. Lutheran. Avocations: fishing, computers, reading, travel. Home: 2800 N Lake Shore Dr Apt 2416 Chicago IL 60657-6248 Office: Mayer Brown Rowe & Maw LLP 71 S Wacker Dr Chicago IL 60606 Office Phone: 312-701-7843. E-mail: pniehoff@mayerbrown.com.

NIEHUSS, JOHN MARVIN, lawyer; b. Ann Arbor, Mar. 7, 1937; s. Marvin Lemmon Niehuss and Lois Celicia Markham; m. Rosemary Juliette Neaher, June 30, 1973 (div. Mar. 1991); children: Juliette, John. BA, Amherst Coll., 1958; JD, U. Mich., 1962. Assoc. atty. Sullivan & Cromwell, NYC, 1966-69; legal advisor Govt. of Zambia, Lusaka, 1969-71; loan officer, dir. World Bank, Washington, 1971-73, 90-91; dep. asst. sec. U.S. Treasury Dept., Washington, 1974-77, 89-90; v.p. Merrill Lynch, NYC, 1977-89; gen. counsel Inter-Am. Devel. Bank, Washington, 1992-99, Export-Import Bank U.S., Washington, 1999—2001; dir. Pvt. Fin. of Infrastructure Ctr., Internat. Law Inst., Washington, 2005—; adj. prof. U. Mich. Law Sch., Ann Arbor, 2007—. Mem. adv. bd. Internat. Law Inst., Washington, 1977—. Mem. Coun. Fgn. Rels., Met. Club. Avocations: golf, hiking, fly fishing. Home: 3019 45th St NW Washington DC 20016-3523 Office Phone: 202-362-1164. Personal E-mail: niehuss@gmail.com.

NIELSEN, FORREST HAROLD, research nutritionist; b. Dancy, Wis., Oct. 26, 1941; s. George Adolph and Sylvia Viola (Blood) N.; m. Emily Joanne Currie, June 13, 1964; children: Forrest Erik, Kistin Emily. BS, U. Wis., 1963, MS, 1966, PhD, 1967. NIH grad. fellow, dept. biochemistry U. Wis., Madison, 1963-67; rsch. chemist, Human Nutrition Rsch. Inst. USDA, Beltsville, Md., 1969-70, rsch. chemist Human Nutrition Rsch. Ctr. Grand Forks, ND, 1970-86, ctr. dir. and rsch. nutritionist, 1986-2001, rsch. nutritionist, 2001—. Adj. prof. dept. biochemistry and molecular biology, U. N.D., Grand Forks, 1971—, speaker in field. Assoc. editor Magnesium and Trace Elements Jour., 1990-93; mem. editl. bd. Jour. Trace Elements in Exptl. Medicine, 1988—2004, Biol. Trace Element Rsch. Jour., 1979—, Jour. Nutrition, 1984-88, Biofactors, 1997—; contbr. articles to profl. jours. Capt. U.S. Army, 1967-69. Recipient Klaus Schwarz Commemorative medal and award Internat. Assn. of Bioinorganic Scientists; named Scientist of Yr. U.S. Dept. Agrl., 1993. Mem. Internat. Soc. Trace Element Rsch. in Humans (gov. bd. 1989—, pres. 1992-95), Soc. for Exptl. Biology and Medicine, Am. Soc. Nutrition, N.D. Acad. Sci. (pres. 1988-89), Internat. Bone and Mineral Soc., Sigma Xi (pres. U. N.D. chpt. 1976-77). Lutheran. Achievements include patent for use of Boron Supplements to Increase in Vivo Production of Hydroxylated Steroids; discovery of the nutritional essentiality of the trace elements boron and nickel. Office: USDA ARS GFHNRC 2420 2 Ave N Stop 9034 Grand Forks ND 58202-9034 Home Phone: 701-775-2798; Office Phone: 701-795-8455. Business E-Mail: forrest.nielsen@ars.usda.gov.

NIELSEN, GEORGE LEE, architect; b. Ames, Iowa, Dec. 12, 1937; s. Verner Henry and Verba Lucile (Smith) N.; m. Karen Wall, Feb. 28, 1959; children: David Stuart, Kristina, Melissa. B.Arch., Iowa State U., 1961; M.Arch., M.I.T., 1962. Registered arch., Mass., Ohio, N.Y., Ill., Ind., Ky., Miss., Kans., Colo., Mich., Nat. Coun. Archtl. Registration Bds. Designer Perry, Shaw, Hepburn & Dean, Boston, 1961-64, F.A. Stahl & Assos., Cambridge, Mass., 1964-65; project architect Peirce & Pierce, Boston, 1965-70; project mgr. A.M. Kinney Assos., Cin., 1970—, partner, 1978—; sec. A.M. Kinney Assocs., Inc., Ill., 1993—, also dir. Cin.; v.p. A.M. Kinney Inc., Cin., 1992-94, pres., 1994-99, also dir.; sr. prin. A.M. Kinney Inc. Assocs., 1999—. Architect prin. works include Avco Rsch. Lab., Cin. Children's Hosp. Med. Ctr., Square D. Corp., Nalco Chem. Co., Olin Corp., Mead Johnson/Bristol Myers Squib, Cin. Gas and Elec. Co., Novartis Pharm. Corp., Hoechst Celanese, Hoechst Marion Roussel, Martek Bioscis., Witco Corp., Sotheby's, Shell Chem. Co., Bayer Corp., U. Ky. Biomed./Biol. Scis. Rsch. Bldg., U. Ky. Chandler Med. Ctr. Patient Care Facility, Wright Patterson Environ. Hazzards Bldg. and Edwards AFB Sci. Rsch. Bldg. With US Army, 1962—64. Mem.: AIA (design awards 1970—71, 1974, 1978, 1981, 1991, 1994, 1995, 2001, 2002). Episcopalian. Home: 5680 Windridge View Cincinnati OH 45243-2518 Office: A M Kinney Inc 150 E 4th St Fl 6 Cincinnati OH 45202-4131 Office Phone: 513-421-2265.

NIELSEN, GREG ROSS, lawyer; b. Provo, Utah, Sept. 24, 1947; s. Ross T. and Carma (Peterson) N.; m. Jo Rita Beer, Sept. 3, 1971; children: Jennifer, Jerilyn, Eric Michael, Brittany Anne. BA in Polit. Sci. magna cum laude, Brigham Young U., 1971; JD cum laude, Harvard U., 1975. Bar: Ariz. 1975, U.S. Dist. Ct. Ariz. 1975, U.S. Ct. Appeals (9th cir.) 1977, Utah 1990, Nev. 2003. Assoc. Snell & Wilmer, Phoenix, 1975-80, ptnr., 1981—2004, mng. ptnr. Salt Lake City, 1991—2002, adminstrv. coord. real estate practice group Phoenix, 1988-90; gen. counsel franchise fin. GE Comml. Fin., Scottsdale, Ariz., 2004—. Mem. dist. com. Theodore Roosevelt coun. Boy Scouts Am., 1988-90; trustee Utah Heritage Found., 1998-2000, Swaner Nature Preserve, 2002-04. Hinckley scholar Brigham Young U., 1970; fellow Ford Found., 1970. Mem. ABA. Republican. Mem. Lds Ch. Office: GE Comml Fin Franchise Fin 8377 E Hartford Dr Ste 200 Scottsdale AZ 85255 Home Phone: 480-290-0917; Office Phone: 480-585-2234. Business E-Mail: greg.nielsen@ge.com.

NIELSEN, HARALD CHRISTIAN, retired chemist, researcher; b. Chgo., Apr. 18, 1930; s. Svend Aage and Seena (Hansen) N.; m. Eloise Wilma Soule, Dec. 19, 1953; children: Brenda Mae, Paul Erick, Gloria Lynn, Judy Ann (dec.). BA, St. Olaf Coll., Northfield, Minn., 1952; PhD, Mich. State U., East Lansing, 1957. Cereal grain protein chemist Nat. Ctr. for Agrl. Utilization Rsch. (formerly No. Regional Rsch. Ctr.), Agrl. Rsch. Svc., USDA, Peoria, Ill., 1957—87; ret., 1987. Contbr. articles to profl. jours. Mem. Peoria Area Combined Fed. Campaign Coord. Com., 1980—87; pres. local 3247 Am. Fedn. Govt. Employees, AFL-CIO, 1977—86; active Peoria Prostrate Cancer Support Group, 1996—2005, editor newsletter, 2000—05. Mem.: Nat. Assn. Ret. Fed. Employees (officer chpt. 268 1989—92, pres. chpt. 268 1991, editor chpt. newsletter 1999—2004), Am. Assn. Cereal Chemists. Democrat. Lutheran. Home: 2318 N Gale Ave Peoria IL 61604-3229

NIELSEN, JAKOB, computer interface engineer; b. Copenhagen, Oct. 5, 1957; arrived in U.S., 1990, naturalized, 2001; s. Gerhard and Helle (Hofner); m. Hannah Kain, Feb. 18, 1984. MS in Computer Sci., Aarhus U., Denmark, 1983; PhD in Computer Sci., T.U. of Denmark, 1988. Rsch. fellow Aarhus U., 1983-84; vis. scientist IBM User Interface Inst., Yorktown Heights, NY, 1985; adj. asst. prof. T.U. Denmark, Lyngby, 1986-90; mem. rsch. staff Bell Comm. Rsch., Morristown, NJ, 1990-94; disting. engr. Sun Microsystems, Mountain View, Calif., 1994-98; principal Nielsen Norman Group, Fremont, Calif., 1998—. Author: Hypertext and Hypermedia, 1990, Usability Engineering, 1993, Multimedia and Hypertext: The Internet and Beyond, 1995, Designing Web Usability: The Practice of Simplicity, 2000, Homepage Usability: 50 Websites Deconstructed, 2001, Prioritizing Web Usability, 2006; editor: Coordinating User Interfaces for Consistency, 1989, Designing User Interfaces for International Use, 1990, Usability Inspection Methods, 1994, International User Interfaces, 1996, Eyetracking Web Usability, 2007; mem. editl. bd.: Behavior and Info. Tech., 1989—, Hypermedia Jour., 1989—95, Interacting with Computers, 1989—, Internat. Jour. Human-Computer Interaction, 1989—, Internat. Jour. Man-Machine Studies, 1991—94, ACM Networker, 1997—2000, Personal Technologies, 1997—2004; contbr. articles to profl. jours. Mem.: Assn. for Computing Machinery (papers co-chair internat. conf. 1993, editl. bd. Networker 1997—2000, spl. interest group on computer human interaction). Achievements include holder 79 patents in field; founding of discount usability engineering approach; invention (with R. Molich) of heuristic evaluation method for cost-effective improvement of user interfaces; demonstration (with T.K. Landauer) that user testing and heuristic evaluation both follow same mathematical model; definition of the parallel design method for rapidly exploring user interface alternatives; patents for.

NIELSEN, JENNIFER LEE, molecular ecologist, researcher; b. Balt., Mar. 21, 1946; d. Leo Jay and Mary Marriott (Mules) N.; divorced; children: Nadja Wilson, Allisha Ochs MFA, Ecole des Beaux Arts, Paris, 1968; BS, Evergreen State Coll., 1987; MS, U. Calif., Berkeley, 1990, PhD, 1994. Artist, Seattle, 1969-78; fish biologist Weyerhaeuser Co., Tacoma, 1978-89; resource cons. Berkeley, 1989-90; rsch. biologist USDA-Forest Svc., Albany, Calif., 1990-99; vis. scientist Stanford U., Pacific Grove, Calif., 1994-99; supr. fisheries Alaska Sci. Ctr., Anchorage, 1999—. Rsch. assoc. Calif. State U. Mosslanding Marie Sta., 1995-99; adj. prof. integrated biology U. Calif., Berkeley, 1998; adj. prof. U. Alaska, Fairbanks, 1999—, U. Alaska Anchorage, 2001-; supervisory rsch. fishery biologist U.S. Geol. Svc., Alaska Sci. Ctr., Anchorage, 1999—. Editor-in-chief: Reviews in Fish Biology and Fisheries, 1999—; editor: Evolution and the Aquatic Ecosystem, 1995, Advisory Editor Environment Biology of Fishes, 1998—; contbr. over 100 articles to profl. jours.; paintings exhibited at Metro. Mus. Modern Art, 1966; represented in numerous pvt. collections, U.S. and Europe. Mem. Am. Fisheries Soc. (pres. chpt. 1993-94, genetics sect. pres. 1999-2001, pres.-elect of society 2005, pres. 2006-), Molecular Marine Biology and Biotech. (regional editor 1995), Animal Behaviour Soc. (policy com. 1993-94). Avocations: painting, cooking, gardening, skijoring. Office: USGS Alaska Sci Ctr 1011 E Tudor Rd Anchorage AK 99503-6119 Office Phone: 907-786-3670. E-mail: jennifer_nielsen@usgs.gov.

NIELSEN, LEON, animal scientist; b. Viby, Denmark, Apr. 26, 1937; s. Melitha Marie and adopted s. Jens Peter Nielsen; m. Jill Ruth Turcott, Nov. 29, 1985; 1 child, Logan Turcott. Undergrad. in Equine Care, Colo. State U., Ft. Collins, 1973, undergrad. in Care of Captive Wild and Exotic Animals, 1973; undergrad. in Ecology, Atabasca U., Edmonton, Alta., Can., 1976. Cert.: Wis. Dept. Justice (law enforcement standards bd.) 1978. Forestry wildlife officer Alta. Dept. Lands & Forests, High Level, Canada, 1966—70; exec. dir. Calgary Humane Soc., 1970—77, Wis. Humane Soc., Milw., 1977—90; wildlife biologist Safe Capture Internat., Mt. Horeb, Wis., 1990—95; exec. dir. Peninsula Humane Soc., San Mateo, Calif., 1991; dir. St. Maarten Zool. Garden, Phillipsburg, Netherlands Antilles, 1992—93; exec. dir. Conroe Humane Soc., Tex., 1993—95; writer, 1995—. Rschr. (nonfiction) Robert E. Howard - A Collectors Bibliography, Arkham House - A Collector's Guide, Chemical Immobilization of Wild and Exotic Animals, Translocation of Wild Animals, Chemical Immobilization of North American Wildlife; contbr. papers to prof. jours. and pubs. 1st lt. spl. ops. force Danish Army, 1956—67, Denmark. Mem.: Wis. Humane Soc. (bd. dirs., sec. 1980—90). Democrat. Roman Catholic. Achievements include design of radio tracking of rhinoceros with horn implants. Avocations: writing, military history, reading, gardening. Office: Leon Nielsen PO Box 1654 Brookfield WI 53008-1654 Business E-Mail: lnielsen@wi.rr.com.

NIELSEN, LINDA MILLER, councilman; b. Cedar Falls, Iowa, Apr. 13, 1948; d. Donald Hugh and Mary I. (Hansen) Miller; m. Kenneth Andrew Nielsen, Aug. 22, 1970; children: Annette Marie, Kirsten Viola. BS in Home Econs., Iowa State U., 1970, MS in Food Sci., 1972. Rsch. asst. Iowa State U., Ames, 1970-72, rsch. assoc., 1972-74, instr., 1975-76; city councilwoman City of Charleston, W.Va., 1988—; minority leader Charleston City Coun., 2003—; dir. profl. devel. and cmty. svc. W.Va. State Cmty. and Tech. Coll., 1998—. Leader Girl Scouts U.S.A., 1978-96; chair environ. and recycling com. of Charleston, 1991-2003, realignment com. of Charleston, 1992-94, 2002, mcpl. planning com., 1988—, fin. com., 1995—, storm water com., 1997-99, 2003—, parks and recreation com., 1988-95; classroom vol. Kanawha County Schs., Charleston, 1978-90; mem., officer Forest Hills Comm. Assn., Charleston, 1983-87. Contbr. articles to profl. publs. Mem. NICS (bd. dirs. 1994—), Sigma Xi, Iota Sigma Pi, Omicron Nu. Republican. Avocations: hiking, camping, reading, sewing, cooking. Personal E-mail: nielsen413@suddenlink.net.

NIELSEN, LYNN CAROL, lawyer, educational consultant; b. Perth Amboy, NJ, Jan. 11, 1950; d. Hans and Esther (Pucker) N.; m. Russell F. Baldwin, Nov. 22, 1980; 1 child, Blake Nielsen Baldwin. BS, Millersville U., 1972; MA, NYU, 1979; JD, Rutgers U., 1984. Bar: N.J. 1984; cert. tchr. handicapped, reading specialist, learning disability tchr. cons., elem. edn. supr. Instr. Woodbridge (N.J.) Twp. Bd. Edn., 1972-83; legal intern appellate sect. divsn. criminal justice Atty. Gen. State N.J., Trenton, 1983, dep. atty. gen. divsn. civil law, 1985; assoc. Kantor & Kusic, Keyport, NJ, 1984-86, Kantor & Linderoth, Keyport, NJ, 1986-92. Officer Fords (N.J.) Sch. # 14 PTO, 1974-75; elder First Presbyn. Ch. Avenel, N.J., 1985-88, Flemington (N.J.) Presbyn. Ch., 1997-99; bd. dirs. New Beginnings Nursery Sch., Woodbridge, 1989-90, Flemington Presbyn. Nursery Sch., 1991-93; elder Flemington Presbyn. Ch., 1997-99; bd. mem. Woodside Farms Homeowners Assn., 1996-99. Mem. ABA, N.J. Bar Assn., Monmouth County Bar Assn., Hunterdon County Bar Assn. Avocations: reading, skiing, sailing. Home and Office: 3 Buchannan Way Flemington NJ 08822-3205

NIELSEN, MARK D., former state legislator; b. Hartford, Conn., Aug. 25, 1964; s. E. Kenneth and Janet (Worrad) N.; m. Jane Hamilton, 1988. AB magna cum laude, Harvard U., 1986, JD cum laude, 1989. Atty., Danbury, Conn.; mem. Conn. Ho. of Reps., 1993-94, Conn. State Senate, 1995-99; chief legal counsel State House Boston, Boston, 2002—. Mem. Danbury Rep. Town Com., 1990—. Dir. Literacy Vols. of Am., 1991—. Mem. Danbury Bar Assn., Lions Club. Office: State House Boston Rm 271 Boston MA 02133 Office Phone: 617-727-2065. Office Fax: 617-727-8290.

NIELSEN, MARY TANZY, literature and language professor, department chairman; b. Columbus, Ohio, Dec. 19, 1951; d. Conrad Eugene and Regina Roth Tanzy; m. Charles Edward Nielsen, Aug. 2, 1995; children from previous marriage: Geoffrey Crume, Maria Crume. BA, Fla. State U., Tallahassee, 1973; MEd, U. Fla., Gainesville, 1977, EdS, PhD, U. Fla., Gainesville, 1988; postgrad., Ga. State U., Millegeville, 1999. Editor U. Fla., Gainesville, 1977—88; assoc. prof. English and reading Brevard C.C., Titusville, Fla., 1988—96, E. Ga. Coll., Swainsboro, 1996—99, Dalton State Coll., Ga., 2000—07, chair divsn. humanities, 2004—. Recipient Dist. Prof. award, Ga. Bd. Regents, 1996—99. Mem.: Ga. Assn. Depts. English, Nat. Assn. Depts. English. Home: 1203 Rio Vista Dr Dalton GA 30720 Office: Dalton State Coll 650 College Drive Dalton GA 30720

NIELSEN, MORTEN ØRREGAARD, economics professor; b. Herning, Denmark, Nov. 14, 1976; arrived in U.S., 2003; s. Jens Ørregaard and Inga Irene Skytte Nielsen. BS in Econs., U. Aarhus, Denmark, 1998, MSc in Econs., 2001, PhD in Econs., 2003; MSc in Econometrics and Math. Econs., London Sch. Econs. and Polit. Sci., 1999. Postdoctoral rsch. fellow Dept. Econ. U. Aarhus, Denmark, 2003—03; asst. prof. econ. Dept. Econ. Cornell U., Ithaca, NY, 2003—. Contbr. articles to profl. jours. Mem.: Inst. Math. Stats., Am. Econ. Assn., Econometric Soc. Office Phone: 607-255-6338.

NIELSEN, NANCY H., health organization executive; m. Don Nielsen; 5 children. BA, W.Va. U., 1964; MS in Microbiology, Cath. U., 1967, PhD in Microbiology, 1969; MD, SUNY Medicine and Biomedical Scis., Buffalo, 1967. Past chief med. officer N.Y. State Dept. Health Western Region; former pres. med. staff Buffalo Gen. Hosp.; asst. dean med. edn., clin. prof. medicine U. Buffalo Sch. Medicine and Biomed. Sci., Buffalo; apptd. to serve US Dept. Health and Human Svcs. Adv. Com. on Regulatory Reform, 2002; assoc. med. dir. for quality, interim chief med. officer Independent Health Assn., NY, now chief med. officer NY; clin. prof. medicine, sr. assoc. dean med. edn. SUNY. Bd. dir. Med. Liability Mut. Ins. Co., Kaleida Health, Nat. Patient Safety Found.; former trustee SUNY; former mem. Commn. for the Prevention of Youth Violence, Task Force on Quality and Patient Safety. Bd. dirs. Nat. Patient Safety Found. Recipient Samuel P. Capen award, U. Buffalo Alumni Assn., 1996. Fellow: ACP; mem.: AMA (vice speaker Ho. of Dels. 2000—03, speaker Ho. of Dels. 2003—, pres.-elect 2007—, bd. trustee, former mem. Coun. on Sci. Affairs, del. med. sch. sect., liaison to the Coun. on Med. Edn.), Inst. Medicine (Consumer Empowerment Com. of America's Health Information Cmty., Roundtable on Evidence Based Medicine), NY State Soc. Internal Medicine (bd. dir.), Med. Soc. State of NY (spkr. ho. dels. 1995—2000), Erie County Med. Soc. (former pres.). Office: Independant Health Assn 511 Farber Lakes Dr Buffalo NY 14221 also: AMA 515 N State St Chicago IL 60610 Business E-Mail: nielse@buffalo.edu. *

NIELSEN, NIELS CHRISTIAN, JR., retired religious studies educator; b. Long Beach, Calif., June 2, 1921; s. Niels Hansen and Frances (Nofziger) N.; m. Erika Kreuth, May 10, 1958; children: Camilla Regina, Niels Albrecht. BA, George Pepperdine Coll., LA, 1942; BD, Yale U., 1946, PhD, 1951. Ordained to ministry Meth. Ch., 1946. Pastor Woodbury (Conn.) Meth. Ch., 1944-46; instr. religion Yale U., New Haven, 1948-51; faculty Rice U., Houston, 1951—, J. Newton Rayzor prof. religious studies., prof. emeritus, 1991—; Amax presdl. prof. humanities Colo. Sch. Mines, Golden, 1982-83. Author: Philosophy and Religion in Contemporary Japan, 1957, Geistige Landerkunde USA, 1960, A Layman Looks at World Religions, 1962, God in Education, 1966, Solzhenitsyn's Religion, 1975, The Religion of Jimmy Carter, 1977, The Crisis of Human Rights, 1978, Religions of the World, 1982, Revolutions in Eastern Europe: The Religious Roots, 1991, Fundamentalism, Mythos and World Religions, 1993; editor: Religion After Communism in Russia, 1994; contbr. articles to profl. jours. Mem. Am. Acad. Religion, Am. Philos. Soc., Am. Soc. Study Religion (sec. 1977-89), Soc. European Culture, Soc. for Values in Higher Edn. Democrat. Home and Office: 2424 Swift Blvd Houston TX 77030-1806 Office Phone: 713-667-0783. Personal E-mail: niels@rice.edu.

NIELSEN, PAUL DOUGLAS, engineering executive, retired military officer; s. Jack Alton and Shirley Mae (Gillette) N.; m. Dorothy Webb Spragins, May 3, 1975. BS in Physics and Math., USAF Acad., 1972; MS in Applied Sci., U. Calif., Davis, 1973, PhD in Plasma Physics, 1981; MBA, U. N.Mex., 1977; postgrad., Nat. War Coll., 1988-89. Physicist Nat. Security Agency Ft. George G. Meade, Md., 1973—75; space sys. procurement officer nuc. techs. Air Force Weapons Lab., Kirtland AFB, N.Mex., 1975—77; sys. programs mgmt. officer nuc. techs. Air Force Sys. Command, Andrews AFB, Md., 1977—78, aide to comdr., 1977—78;

space sys. procurement mgmt. officer Hdqrs. AFSC, Andrews AFB, Md., 1978; mil. rsch. assoc. Dept. Energy Lawrence Livermore Nat. Libr., 1978—81; asst. chief advanced sys., chief Satellite Attitude Control br., Satellite Engring. divsn., sec. Air Force Office Spl. Projects, L.A. Air Force Sta., Calif., 1981—84; sys. program dir. electronics sys. divsn. Command Ctr. Processing and Display Sys. Replacement Program, Hanscom AFB, Mass., 1984—85; sys. program dir. Space Def. Ops Ctr., 1985—87; chief engr. Strat. Sys. Deputate, ESD, Hanscom AFB, Mass., 1987—88; mil. asst., col. Office of Asst. Sec. Def., Washington, 1989-92; comdr. Rome Lab., Griffiss AFB, 1992-95; command dir. Cheyenne Mountain Ops. Ctr., Cheyenne Mountain Air Sta, Colo., 1995—96, chief ops., 1996-97; brig. gen., dir. plans N.Am. Aerospace Def. Command, Peterson AFB, Colo., 1997-99; vice comdr. Aero. Systems Ctr., AFMC, Wright-Patterson AFB, Ohio, 1999-2000; comdr. Air Force Rsch. Lab., Wright-Patterson AFB, 2000—04; CEO, dir. Software Engring Inst. Carnegie Mellon U., Pitts., 2004—. With USAF, 1972, ret. USAF, 2004, 2d lt., 1972, 1st lt., 1974, capt., 1976, major, 1981, lt. col., 1986, col., 1989, brigadier gen., 1997, major gen., 2001. Decorated Def. Superior Svc. medal with oak leaf cluster, Meritorious Svc. medal with two oak leaf clusters, Disting. Svc. medal, Legion of Merit, Def. Meritorious Svc. medal; fellow Hertz Found., Livermore, Calif., 1972-73, 78-81. Fellow AIAA (Hap Arnold award 2002), IEEE; mem. Armed Forces Comm. and Electronics Assn., Air Force Assn. Office: Software Eng Inst Carnegie Mellon Univ 4500 Fifth Ave Pittsburgh PA 15213-3890 Home: 30 Wedgewood Ln Pittsburgh PA 15215-1560 Office Phone: 412-268-7740. Business E-Mail: nielsen@sei.cmu.edu.

NIELSEN, PHILIP EDWARD, physicist, research manager; b. Chgo., July 18, 1944; s. John Edward and Doris Anne (Roessler) Nielsen; m. Mary Jane Hill, Aug. 21, 1971; children: Aaron P., June E., David C. BS in Physics, Ill. Inst. Tech., Chgo., 1966; MS in Physics, Case Western Res, U., Cleve., 1968, PhD, 1970. Commd. 2d lt. USAF, 1970, advanced through ranks to col., 1988; ret., 1996; chief, interaction physics group AF Weapons Lab., Kirtland AFB, N.Mex., 1970-74; assoc. prof. physics AF Inst. Tech., Wright-Patterson AFB, Ohio, 1974-79; dep. dir. Directorate of Aerospace Studies, Kirtland AFB, 1980-84; dep. chief, missile divsn. AF Studies and Analyses, Pentagon, Washington, 1984-86, chief, force analyses divsn., 1986-87; dir. tech. Fgn. Tech. Divsn., Wright-Patterson AFB, 1988-92; chief, tech. requirements HQ AF Materiel Command, Wright-Patterson AFB, 1992-96; v.p. ops. MacAulay-Brown, Inc., Dayton, Ohio, 1996—. Author: Effects of Directed Energy Weapons, 2000. Pres. Shadowbrook Homeowners Assn., Mt. Vernon, Va., 1986-87. Recipient USAF R & D award, 1975, Supr. Rsch. award Air Command and Staff Coll., Montgomery, Ala., 1980, Disting. Govt. Svc. award Albuquerque-Santa Fe Fed. Exec. Bd., 1983, Devel. Planning cert. of merit AF Systems Command, Washington, 1983. Mem. AAAS, Am. Phys. Soc., Inst. Ops. Rsch. and Mgmt. Sci., Mil. Ops. Rsch. Soc. Achievements include co-discovery (with P.L. Taylor) of an effect in the low-temperature thermoelectric power of metals and alloys now known as the "Nielsen-Taylor" or "N-T" effect; resolution of many puzzling results in the laser-induced breakdown thresholds of clean and aerosol-laden atmospheres; analysis of solid response to laser radiation which provided insights needed to extrapolate small scale experiments to large scale applications. Home: 9138 Payne Farm Ln Dayton OH 45458-9388 Office: MacAulay-Brown Inc 4021 Executive Dr Dayton OH 45430-1062

NIELSEN, SUE M., elementary school educator; b. Dec. 6, 1955; m. Jim R. Nielsen. BS, Winona State U., Minn., 1993, MEd, 1994. Tchr. grade 6 Rochester Sch. Dist., Minn., 1993—. Recipient Milken Nat. Educator award, 2001.

NIELSEN, TOD, information technology executive; BS, Cent. Wash. U. Various mgmt. positions Microsoft Corp., 1988—2000; CEO CrossGain (acquired by BEA Systems, Inc.), 2000—01; sr. v.p. developer programs BEA Systems, Inc., San Jose, Calif., 2001, exec. v.p. engring., chief mktg. officer, 2001—05; sr. v.p., global sales support Oracle Corp., Redwood Shores, Calif., 2005; pres., CEO Borland Software Corp., Cupertino, Calif., 2005—. Office: Borland Software Corp 20450 Stevens Creek Blvd Ste 800 Cupertino CA 95014 Office Phone: 800-817-4BEA, 408-570-8000, 408-863-2800. Office Fax: 408-570-8901.

NIELSEN, VANCE GIRARD, anesthesiologist, researcher; b. Mpls., Feb. 23, 1961; s. Francis Knud and Katheryn Mary Nielsen; m. Loriellen Louise Liska, Jan. 12, 1991; children: Mary Grace, Sarah Ann, Hannah Elizabeth. BS, Loyola Marymount U., LA, 1983; postgrad., St. Louis U., 1983—85; MD, U. So. Calif., LA, 1987—87. Cert. anesthesiologist Am. Bd. Anesthesiology, 1992. Asst. prof. dept. anesthesiology U. Ala., Birmingham, 1992—97, assoc. prof. dept. anesthesiology, 1997—2005, prof. dept. anesthesiology, 2005—. Grantee, Am. Heart Assn., 1998—2000. Mem.: Internat. Anesthsia Rsch. Soc. Republican. Office: Univ Ala Birmingham 619 South 19th St Birmingham AL 35249 Office Phone: 205-934-4696. Office Fax: 205-975-5033. Business E-Mail: vnielsen@uab.edu.

NIELSEN-JONES, IAN RICHARD, lottery and gaming executive, consultant; b. Winchester, Eng., Jan. 24, 1950; arrived in Can., 1950, arrived in US, 1995; s. Richard and Jean-Marie (Edwards) Nielsen-J.; m. Linda Ann George, June 10, 1972; children: Christopher James, Alison Leigh, Eric Philip. BA in Econs., Loyola Coll., 1971; MA in Econs., McMaster U., 1972. From investigator to dep. dir. investigation & rsch. Competition Bur., Ottawa, Ont., Canada, 1972-89; pres. Ont. Lottery Corp., Toronto, Sault Ste. Marie, Canada, 1989-93; mng. dir. nat. lottery Rank Orgn. Plc, London, 1993-94; pres. gaming and recreation Rank Canada Ltd., Toronto, 1994-95; pres., COO CUE Network Corp., Irvine, Calif., 1995-97; pres., CEO Online Internat. Corp., Smithtown, NY, 1997-99, Gaming Mgmt. Corp., Del., 1999-2000, Entertainment Mgmt. Group Ltd., British Virgin Islands, 2001—04; asst. deputy commr. competition Competition Bureau, Toronto, Ontario, Canada, 2006—. Bd. dirs. Lotto4U.com, Calif., Computer Radio Network, Ltd., Toronto, Granada Empresarial, S.A., Dominican Republic, LotCo Plc, London, Interprovincial Lottery Corp., 1989-93, Econ. Devel. Corp., Sault Ste. Marie, 1992-93; adv. com. Consumers Coun. Can., Toronto. Hon. bd. dirs. Bushplane Mus., Sault Ste. Marie, Ont.; bd. dirs. United Way, 1990-93, Plummer Hosp., 1991-93, Algoma U. Coll., 1991-93. Named newsmaker of yr., Gaming and Wagering Mag., 1992. Avocations: writing, music, running, coin collecting/numismatics, travel. Home: 8 Zinfandel Ct RR5 Niagara-on-the-Lake ON Canada L0S 1J0 Office Phone: 416-954-8165. Personal E-mail: iannielsenjones@sympatico.ca.

NIEMANN, CHESTER S., JR., retired band director, customer service administrator; b. Belleville, Ill., Apr. 27, 1941; s. Chester S. and Louise S. Niemann; m. Judith Ann Houton, Mar. 16, 1980; children: Laura L., Daniel E., C. Scott, Sheryl L., Austin G., Shaun P. B in Music Edn., U. Ga., 1964; M in Arts Edn., Murray State U., 1972. Cert. tchr. Fla. From lt. to capt. US Army, 1964—69; band dir. Habersham County Schs., Clarksville, Ga., 1969—71, Caldwell County Schs., Princeton, Ky., 1971—73, Morgan County Schs., Sturgis, Ky., 1974—75, Brevard County Schs., Titusville, Fla., 1975—79, St. Lucie County Schs., Ft. Pierce, Fla., 1979—86, Volusia County Schs., Deland, Fla., 1986—89; quality control mem. GIS Mktg., Deland, 1989—92; band didr. Calvary Christian Acad., Ormond Beach, Fla., 1992—96, Trinity Christian Acad., Deltona, Fla., 1996—2004. Composer: Folk Song Ste., 1990, Lord of the Dance, 1994. Organizer, founder Treasure Coast Symphony Orch., 1984. Named Tchr. of Yr., Trinity Christian Acad., 2000. Avocations: model trains, gardening. Home: 3120 Hickory Tree Ln Deland FL 32724 Personal E-mail: cniemann427@aol.com.

NIEMEIER, CHARLES D., accountant; b. 1956; BBA, Baylor U.; JD, Georgetown U. Bar: 1995. Ptnr. Williams & Connolly LLP, Washington, 1988—99; chief acct. enforcement divsn., co-chair fin. fraud task force SEC, 1999—2002; bd. dirs. Pub. Acctg. Oversight Bd., 2002—, acting chmn., 2003. Office: Pub Co Acctg Oversight Bd 1666 K St NW Washington DC 20006-2803 Office Phone: 202-207-9100. Office Fax: 202-862-8430.

NIEMETH, CHARLES FREDERICK, lawyer; b. Lorain, Ohio, Nov. 25, 1939; s. Charles Ambrose and Christine Cameron (Mollison) N.; m. Anne Marie Meckes, Oct. 12, 1968. BA, Harvard U., 1962; JD, U. Mich., 1965. Bar: Calif. 1966, N.Y. 1984. Assoc. O'Melveny & Myers, Los Angeles, 1965-72, ptnr., 1973—2005, Baker & McKenzie, NYC, 2005—. Mem. leadership com. Corp. Fund of Lincoln Ctr. Mem. nat. com. Mich. Law Sch. Fund; trustee Challengers Boys and Girls Club, 1968-83; mem. bus. adv. coun. UCLA, 1979-83; mem. exec. com. Internat. Student Ctr., 1979-83; bd. dirs. Olympic Tower Condominium, 1986-92, N.Y. Philharm.; bd. visitors Mich. Law Sch., mem. Tri-Bar Opinion Com. Mem. Riviera Tennis Club, Regency Club, N.Y. Athletic Club, Field Club (Greenwich, Conn.), Harvard Club (NYC). Democrat. Roman Catholic. Home: 70 Oneida Dr Greenwich CT 06830-7131 Office: Baker & McKenzie 1114 Avenue of the Americas New York NY 10036 Home Phone: 203-622-9312; Office Phone: 212-891-3568. E-mail: charles.f.niemeth@bakernet.com.

NIEMEYER, PAUL VICTOR, federal judge; b. Princeton, NJ, Apr. 5, 1941; s. Gerhart and Lucie (Lenzer) Niemeyer; m. Susan Kinley, Aug. 24, 1963; children: Jonathan K., Peter E., Christopher J. AB, Kenyon Coll., 1962; student, U. Munich, Federal Republic of Germany, 1962—63; JD, U. Notre Dame, 1966. Bar: Md. 1966, US Dist. Ct. Md. 1967, US Ct. Appeals (4th cir.) 1968, US Supreme Ct. 1970, US Dist. Ct. (so. dist.) Tex. 1977, US Ct. Appeals (5th cir.) 1978, US Ct. Appeals (3d cir.) 1980. Assoc. Piper & Marbury, Balt., 1966—74, ptnr., 1974—88; U.S. dist. judge US Dist. Ct. Md., Balt., 1988—90; circuit judge US Ct. Appeals (4th cir.), Balt., 1990—. Lectr. advanced bus. law Johns Hopkins U., Balt., 1971—75; lectr. Md. Jud. Conf., Md. Ct. Clks. Assn.; sr. lecturing fellow in appellate advocacy Duke U. Sch. of Law, 1994—; mem. standing com. on rules of practice and procedure cts. appeals, 1973—88; atty. grievance com.-hearing panel, 1978—81; select com.-profl. conduct, 1983—85; adv. com. on Fed. Rules of Civil Procedure, 1993—2000; chmn., 1996—2000. Author: (book) A Path Remembered, 2006; co-author: Maryland Rules Commentary, 1984, 3d. edit., 2003, Maryland Rules Commentary supplement, 1988; contbr. articles to profl. jours. Recipient Spl. Merit citation, Am. Judicature Soc., 1987. Fellow: Am. Law Inst., Md. Bar Assn. (Disting. Svc. award litigation sect. 1981), Md. Bar Found., Am. Bar Found., Am. Coll. Trial Lawyers; mem.: Lawyers' Round Table, Wednesday Law Club. Republican. Episcopalian. Office: US Cir Ct Md US Courthouse 101 W Lombard St Ste 910 Baltimore MD 21201-2611 *

NIEMEYER, PETER EDUARD, history educator; b. Balt., Apr. 4, 1972; s. Paul V. and Susan K. Niemeyer; m. Kathryn A. Foley, Oct. 18, 1997; children: Walker, Maya. AB magna cum laude, Kenyon Coll., Gambier, Ohio, 1994; MDiv, Harvard U., Cambridge, Mass., 1998. Cert. tchr. secondary sch. history and social studies Mass. Tchr. Watson Ho. Group Home, Cambridge, Mass., 1997—99, coord. edn., 1998—99; tchr. social studies Mt. Greylock Regional H.S., Williamstown, Mass., 1999—. Firefighter Williamstown Fire Dept., Mass., 2002—. Grantee, Carnegie Harvard Children's Studies, 1997. Mem.: Nat. Coun. Social Studies, Gale Hose Co. (2d asst. foreman 2002—). Office: Mount Greylock Regional High Sch 1781 Cold Spring Rd Williamstown MA 01267

NIEMI, BEATRICE NEAL, social services professional; b. Fitchburg, Mass., July 23, 1923; d. Albert G. and Florence E. (Copeland) Neal; m. Walter V. Niemi, Oct. 21, 1944 (div. 1970); children: Karen Smith-Gary, Gail Niemi Shaw. AS, Colby-Sawyer Coll., 1942; BS in Psychology, Northeastern U., 1972; MA in Counseling Psychology, Assumption Coll., 1974. Diplomate in psychotherapy Am. Psychotherapy Assn. Dir. homemaker svcs. Children's Aid and Family Svcs., Inc., Fitchburg, 1965-73; founder, exec. dir. Home Health Aide Svc. of North Cen. Mass., Inc., Fitchburg, 1973-85, Ctr. for Well Being, Inc., Fitchburg, 1985—; instr. Touch for Health Found., Pasadena, Calif., 1977—; tchr., 7th degree master The Radiance Technique Assn. Internat., St. Petersburg, Fla., 1986—; Outreach trainer The Monroe Inst., Faber, Va., 1990—. V.p. Mass. Coun. for Homemaker-Home Health Aide Svcs., Inc., 1973-81. Pres. Children's Aid and Family Svcs., Inc., Fitchburg, 1964-65; bd. dirs. United Way of Greater Fitchburg, Inc., 1964-70, Leominster (Mass.) Vis. Nursing Assn, 1972-78; chmn. adv. bd. Salvation Army, Fitchburg, 1970-72; v.p. Fitchburg Coun. of Girl Scouts. Mem. ACA, Am. Psychotherapy Assn. (diplomate), Assn. Comprehensive Energy Psychology, Am. Mental Health Counselors Assn., Am. Holistic Health Assn., Am. Holistic Med. Found., Mass. Assn. Cmty. Health Agys. (bd. dirs. 1970-83), Mass. Mental Health Counselors Assn., Assn. for Transpersonal Psychology, Nat. Guild Hypnotists, N.E. Holistic Counselors Assn., Touch For Health Kinesiology Assn., others. Avocations: yoga, meditation, travel. Office: Ctr for Well Being Inc 70 Bond St Fitchburg MA 01420-2251 Office Phone: 978-345-5964.

NIEMI, JANICE, retired lawyer, state legislator, judge; b. Flint, Mich., Sept. 18, 1928; d. Richard Jesse and Norma (Bell) Bailey; m. Preston Niemi, Feb. 4, 1953 (div. 1987); children: Ries, Patricia. BA, U. Wash., 1950, LLB, 1967; postgrad., U. Mich., 1950-52; cert., Hague Acad. Internat. Law, The Netherlands, 1954. Bar: Wash. 1968. Assoc. firm Powell, Livengood, Dunlap & Silverdale, Kirkland, Wash., 1968; staff atty. Legal Svc. Ctr., Seattle, 1968-70; judge Seattle Dist. Ct., 1971-72, King County Superior Ct., Seattle, 1973-78; acting gen. counsel, dep. gen. counsel SBA, Washington, 1979-81; mem. Wash. State Ho. of Reps., Olympia, 1983-87, chmn. com. on state govt., 1984; mem. Wash. State Senate, 1987-95; sole practice Seattle, 1981-94; superior ct. judge King County, 1995-2000; chief criminal judge, 1997-2000; ret., 2000; mem. Wash. State Gambling Commn., 2002—. Mem. White Ho. Fellows Regional Selection Panel, Seattle, 1974—77, chmn., 1976, 77; incorporator Soudn Savs. & Loan, Seattle, 1975. Bd. visitors dept. psychology U. Wash., Seattle, 1983—87, bd. visitors dept. sociology, 1988—98; mem. adv. bd. Tacoma Art Mus., 1987—; mem. Wash. State Gender and Justice Commn., 1987—89; Bd. dirs. Allied Arts, Seattle, 1971—78, Ctr. Contemporary Art, Seattle, 1981—83, Women's Network, Seattle, 1981—84, Pub. Defender Assn., Seattle, 1982—84, Artist's Trust, 2002—05. Named Woman of Yr. in Law, Past Pres.'s Assn., Seattle, 1971, Woman of Yr., Matrix Table, Seattle, 1973, Capitol Hill Bus. and Profl. Women, 1975. Mem. Wash. State Bar Assn., Wash. Women Lawyers, Am. Arbitration Assn. (panel 2003—). Democrat. Home: PO Box 20516 Seattle WA 98102-1516 Personal E-mail: janicen@aol.com.

NIEMI, RICHARD GENE, political science educator; b. Green Bay, Wis., Jan. 10, 1941; s. Eugene H. and Dorothy M. (Stevens) N.; m. Shirley A. Gill, Aug. 4, 1962; children: Nancy, Patricia, Jennifer, Julie. BA, Lawrence Coll., 1962; PhD, U. Mich., 1967. Asst. prof. polit. sci. U. Rochester, NY, 1967-71, assoc. prof. NY, 1971-75, prof., 1975—99, disting. grad. tchg. prof. NY, 1983-86, chmn. dept. polit. sci. NY, 1979-83, assoc. dean NY, 1986-89, sr. assoc. dean NY, 1989-91, Watson prof. NY, 1999—, now assoc. dept. chair and dir. undergraduate studies NY. Vis. prof. U. Lund, Sweden, 1974, 81, U. Iowa, 1985; vis. rschr. Kobe U., Japan, 1991. Co-author (with M. Kent Jennings): (poliical science book) The Political Character of Adolescence, 1974; author: Generations and Politics, 1981, How Generations Perceive Each Other, 1974; co-author (with others): Minority Representation and the Quest for Voting Equality, 1992; co-author: (with Jane Junn) (Education Book) Civic Education: What Makes Students Learn, 1998; co-author: (with others) (Political Science Book) Term Limits in the States, 1999; co-editor (with Harold Stanley): (Polit. Sci. Book) Vital Statistics on American Politics, 2003, 9th edit.; co-editor: (with Herbert Weisberg) (Politic. Sci. Book) Controversies in Voting Behavior, 2001; co-editor: (Polit. Sci. Book) Comparing Democracies, 1996, 2d edit. 2002; co-author: Trends in Public Opinion. Fellow, Guggenheim Found., 1983—84, Ctr. for Advanced Study in Behavioral Sci., 1989; grantee, NIMH, 1969—70, Ford Found., 1972—73, NSF, 1974—77, 1980—86, 1994—, Am. Ednl. Rsch. Assn., 1997—98, U.S. Dept. Edn., 1997—99, 2001—02. Fellow Am. Acad. Arts & Scis.; mem. Am. Polit. Sci. Assn., Phi Beta Kappa. Lutheran. Home: 45 Boniface Dr Rochester NY 14620-3333 Office: U Rochester Dept Polit Sci Rochester NY 14627-0146 E-mail: niemi@rochester.edu. *

NIEMI, ROBERT JAMES, adult education educator, writer; b. Fitchburg, Mass., Apr. 17, 1955; s. Anita Niemi; m. Gretchen Lynn Feeser, Dec. 23, 1993; 1 child, Elena Rose Moore-Niemi. PhD, U. Mass., Amherst, 1990. Assoc. prof. St. Michael's Coll., Colchester, Vt., 1997—. Home: 35 Breer Rd Barre VT 05641-8675 Office: St Michaels College 1 Winooski Pk Colchester VT 05439 Home Phone: 802-479-5599; Office Phone: 802-654-2569. Office Fax: 802-654-2610. Personal E-mail: rniemi@charter.net. Business E-Mail: rniemi@smcvt.edu.

NIEMIEC, DAVID WALLACE, investment company executive; b. Midland, Mich., Dec. 17, 1949; s. George G. and Eleanor (Yack) N.; m. Melanie Taveau Mason, Oct. 4, 1975; children: Elizabeth Street, Margaret Johnson AB, Harvard U., 1972, MBA, 1974. Assoc. Dillon, Read & Co., Inc., NYC, 1974-78, v.p., 1979-81, sr. v.p., chief adminstrv. officer, 1982-83, mng. dir., chief adminstrv. officer, 1984-97, vice chmn., 1991-97; mng. dir. Saratoga Ptnrs., NYC, 1998—2001, adv., 2001—. Bd. dirs. Emeritus Corp., Seattle, OSI Pharms., Melville, NY; bd. dirs., trustee Templeton Funds, Ft. Lauderdale. Trustee Nightingale-Bamford Sch., N.Y.C., 1993-2004; bd. govs. The Mannes Coll. of Music, N.Y.C., 1996—. Mem. Union Club N.Y.C. Republican. Unitarian Universalist. Office: Saratoga Ptnrs 535 Madison Ave New York NY 10022-4212 Office Phone: 212-906-7044.

NIEMIEC, EDWARD WALTER, retired professional association executive; b. Detroit, Nov. 1, 1936; s. Walter A. and Mary N.; m. Nancy M. Bennett, Aug. 25, 1962; children: Lisa, Julie, Brenda. BS, U. Detroit, 1959, MBA, 1961. With Paine Webber Jackson & Curtis, NYC, 1959-80, exec. v.p., dir. adminstrv. divsn., to 1980; v.p., bd. dirs. Moseley, Hallgarten, Estabrook, Weeden, Inc., 1980-82; also bd. dirs. Moseley, Hallgarten, Estabrook & Weeden Holding Corp.; pres., CEO, dir., mem. exec. com. Securities Settlement Corp. (subs. The Travelers 1982), NYC, 1980-87; pres., dir. Inc. Trading Co. subs. Instinet Corp., 1988-89; COO Instinet Corp. subs. Reuters Holdings Plc., 1988-89; group v.p. AICPA, NYC, 1989—2001. Served with U.S. Army. Roman Catholic.

NIENHUIS, ARTHUR WESLEY, physician, researcher; b. Hudsonville, Mich., Aug. 9, 1941; s. Willard M. and Grace (Prince) Nienhuis; children: Carol Elizabeth, Craig Wesley, Kevin Robert, Heather Grace. Student, Cornell Coll., 1959-61; MD, UCLA, 1963-68. Am. Bd. Internal Medicine, Am. Bd. Hematology. Intern Mass. Gen. Hosp., Boston, 1968-69, asst. resident, 1969-70; clin. assoc. NHLBI, NIH, Bethesda, Md., 1970-72; clin. fellow hematology Children's Hosp., Boston, 1972-73; chief. clin. svc. Molecular Hematology NIH, Bethesda, Md., 1973-77; dept. clin. dir. NHLBI, NIH, Bethesda, Md., 1976-93, chief clin. Hematology Branch, 1976-93; dir. St. Jude Children's Rsch. Hosp., Memphis, 1993—2004. Editor BLOOD-J Am. Soc. Hematology, Bethesda, Md., 1988-92; chmn. Hematology Bd. Am. Bd. Internal Med., Phila., 1988-92. Editor: Molecular Basis of Blood Diseases, 1986, 93. Mem. Am. Soc. Hematology (pres. 1994), Am. Soc. Clin. Investigation, Assn. Am. Physicians, Nat. Cancer Adv. Bd. Office: St Jude Children's Rsch Hosp 332 N Lauderdale St Memphis TN 38105-2729 E-mail: Arthur.Nienhuis@stjude.org.

NIEPORENT, DREW, restaurant group executive; Grad in Hotel Mgmt., Cornell U., 1977. Mgmt. Maxwell's Plum, NYC, Tavern On The Green, NYC, Le Périgord, NYC, La Grenouille, NYC, Le Plaza Athénée, NYC; owner Montrachet, NYC, 1985—; co-owner Tribeca Grill, NYC, 1990—; pres., owner Myriad Restaurant Group, NYC, 1993—, Nobu, NYC, Next Door Nobu, NYC, Nobu 57, NYC, Centrico, NYC, Crush Wine and Spirits, NYC, Pulse, NYC, The Coach House, NYC. Guest lectr. Cornell U., NYU, NYC, Syracuse U., New Eng. Culinary Inst., NY Restaurant Assn., New Sch., NYC; dir. American Inst. of Wine and Food. Hon. co-chairperson, master ceremonies Starfish Found., 1995; co-chair Share Our Strength's Taste Nation, NYC, 1997—99; guest honor Tourette Syndrome Assn. Dinner, 1997; culinary chair Momentum Project; hon. chair City Harvest Food Coun.; bd. dirs. Citymeals on Wheels. Named Man of the Yr., Food Beverage Assn., 1993, Humanitarian of the Yr., James Beard Found., 2000, Restaurateur of the Yr., Bon Appetit Mag., 2000; recipient Gates Jerusalem medal, Israel Bonds, 1994, Oustanding Svc. award, James Beard Awards, 1995. Mem.: Am. Inst. Wine and Food (bd. dirs.). Office: Myriad Restaurant Group 180 Franklin St New York NY 10013 Office Phone: 212-219-9500. Office Fax: 212-219-2380. *

NIERVA, MAGDELENA LAVESORES, mathematics educator; b. Merida, Leyte, Philippines; arrived in US, 2003; d. Juanito and Maria Lavesores; m. Honorio Nierva, July 28, 1985; children: Mark Lester, Agnes, Kristine, Manny, Oliver, Emmanuel, Jose, Lucky. BSEd in Math., Ateneo de Zamboanga U., Philippines, 1985, MA in Math., 1999. Cert. tchr. Philippines, tchr. math. NY. Tchr. math. Olutanga Nat. HS, Olutanga, Philippines, 1985—89, Ateneo de Zamboanga U. HS, Zamboanga City, 1989—2003, NYC Bd. Edn., 2003—. Supr. Ateneo de Zamboanga U. HS, 1994—2003; coach, trainer Cath. Edn. Assn. Philippines, Zamboanga City, 1995—2003. Named Most Outstanding Tchr., Pvt. Edn. Retirement Annuity Assn., 1999. Home: 949 Sherman Ave #3 Bronx NY 10456-6467

NIESEN, JAMES LOUIS, theater director; b. St. Louis, Feb. 15, 1946; s. James Louis and Emily Elise (Brennecke) N. BFA, Ill. Wesleyan U., 1968; MFA, Ohio U., 1974. Actor Stage South, Columbia, S.C., 1974-75, Long Wharf Theatre, New Haven, 1977-78, Geva Theater, Rochester, N.Y., 1978-79; freelance dir., 1980-83; stage mgr. Roundabout Theater, NYC, 1982-83; artistic dir. Irondale Ensemble Project, NYC, 1983—. Panelist N.Y. Found. on the Arts, N.Y., 1988-89. Author: (book) Game Guide, 1988; contbr. articles to profl. jours.; dir. (play) St. Joan of the Stockyards, 1993, Danton's Death, 1994, You Can't Win, 1994, Andrew Carnegie Presands the Jew of Malta, 1996, The Mother, 1997, Degenerate Art, 1998, The Murals of Rockefeller Center, 2002, The Pope and the Witch, 2000, Brecht on Brecht, 2000, Jungle of Cities, 2001, Peter Pan, 2001, Seuss Centennial Tour, 2004, Outside the Law, 2004. Mem. Actors Equity Assn. Avocations: folk music, country music, tennis. Home: 419 Pacific St Brooklyn NY 11217-2204 Office: Irondale Ensemble Project PO Box 150604 Brooklyn NY 11215-0604 Office Phone: 718-488-9233. E-mail: jim@irondale.org.

NIETO, JUAN MANUEL, emergency medicine physician; b. Alpine, Tex., Sept. 24, 1949; s. Edmundo Miguel and Socorro (Herrera) N.; children: Ana Raquel, Cristina Marie. BS, U. Notre Dame, 1970; MD, U. Colo., 1974. Intern LA County, U. So. Calif. Med. Ctr., 1974-75; physician Cmty. Health Found., LA, 1975-77; physician emergency dept. Physicians Med. Group, Marina Del Ray, Calif., 1977-78; resident in emergency medicine Denver Gen.-St. Anthony Hosp. Sys., 1978-80; mem. staff North Colo. Med. Ctr., Greeley, 1980-83; emergency physician, med. dir. emergency dept. Brackenridge Hosp., Austin, Tex., 1984-85; practice medicine Austin, 1983—. Emergency physician Emergency Physicians

Affiliates, 1986-89; assoc. prof. U. Tex. Health Sci. Ctr., San Antonio, 1994—; mem. planning com. Starflight Helicopter Air Transport, 1985; instr. advanced cardiac life support, 1977; bd. dirs. Nat. Chicano Health Orgn., 1971-74; advisor East Los Angeles Hypertension Screening Program, 1978; med. advisor Weld County Ambulance Service, 1980-83; med. dir. Air Life, 1980-83; med. dir. Alamo Heights Emergency Med. Svc., 1988-90, med. dir. AMR Ambulance, 1991-98; amb. Nat. Health Svc. Corps, 2003—. Del. Colo. Med. Soc., 1983. Fellow: Nat. Hispanic Med. Assn., Am. Acad. Emergency Medicine, Am. Coll. Emergency Physicians, NYU Wagner Sch. (leadership fellow 2001); mem.: APHA, Nat. Hispanic Medicine Assn., Soc. Academic Emergency Medicine, Physicians for a Nat. Healthcare Program, Nat. Hispanic Med. Assn., Travis County Med. Soc., Tex. Med. Assn., Nat. Hispanic Med. Assn. (leadership fellow, advisor, board mem. 2001—, mem. adv. bd. 2003—, Leadership award 2006), Amnesty Internat. Office Phone: 210-358-2078. Personal E-mail: jnietomd@sbcglobal.net, juan-nieto@msn.com.

NIEUWENDYK, JOE, retired professional hockey player, consultant; b. Oshawa, Ontario, Can., Sept. 10, 1966; m. Tina Nieuwendyk; children: Kaycee, Tyra, Jackson. Student, Cornell U., 1984-87. Center Calgary Flames, Calgary, 1987—95, Dallas Stars, 1995—2002, NJ Devils, 2002—03, Toronto Maple Leafs, 2003—05, Fla. Panthers, 2005—06, spl. cons. to gen. mgr., 2007—. Mem. Team Can., Olympic Games, Nagano, Japan, 1998, Salt Lake City, 2002; player NHL All-Star Game, 1988—90, 1994. Named Ivy League Rookie of Yr., 1985, NHL Rookie of Yr., Sporting News, 1988; named to East First All-American Team, NCAA, 1986, 1987, First-Team All-Conference Team, ECAC, 1986, 1987, All-Rookie Team, NHL, 1988; recipient Dodge Ram Tough Award, 1988, Calder Meml. Trophy, 1988, King Clancy Meml. Trophy, NHL, 1995, Conn Smythe Trophy, 1999. Achievements include being a member of Stanley Cup Champion Calgary Flames, 1989, Dallas Stars, 1999, NJ Devils, 2003; being a member of gold medal Canadian Hockey team, Salt Lake City Olympic Games, 2002. Office: c/o Florida Panthers 1 Panther Parkway Sunrise FL 33323 *

NIEUWSMA, MILTON JOHN, writer, journalist; b. Sept. 5, 1941; s. John and Jean (Potter); m. Marilee Gordon, Feb. 1, 1964; children: Jonathan, Gregory, Elizabeth. BA, Hope Coll., Holland, Mich., 1963; postgrad., Wayne State U., 1963—65; MA, U. Ill., 1978. Pres. Trans. Am. Syndicate, Inc., Chgo., 1988—97; vis. prof. Rutgers U., New Brunswick, NJ, 1990—95, St. Xavier U., Chgo., 1996—97. Author: Kinderlager, 1998, Surviving Auschwitz, 2005, Defying Hitler, 2006; writer, co-prodr.: Children of The Shoah, PBS, 2005 (2 Emmy awards, 2006); contbg. editor: Chgo. Tribune, L.A. Times, others. Home: 2421 Central-Idlewood Beach Holland MI 49424-2277 Personal E-mail: mmnieuwsma@hotmail.com.

NIEVAR, M. ANGELA, social sciences professor; d. William Haywood and Nadean Pittman Jones; m. Richard L. Casady (div.); children: Richard William Casady, Margaret Casady, Robert Casady; m. Billy Wayne Nievar, Dec. 27, 2002. BFA, U. Okla., Norman, 1983; MS in Family Ecology, U. Utah, Salt Lake City, 2001; PhD in Family and Child Ecology, Mich. State U., E. Lansing, 2004. Prof. U. N. Tex., Denton, 2004—. Mem. Cmty. Workgroup for Devel. Nat. Child Care Accreditation Stds., 1997—98. Contbr. chapters to books, articles to profl. jours. Adv. Utah Kids Coalition, Salt Lake City, 1998—99; coun. and dist. roundtable Boy Scouts Am., Salt Lake City, 1996—2000, unit commr. Lansing, Mich., 2001—04, Denton, Tex., 2004—07. Recipient Legis. Advocacy award, Gov. Michael Leavitt, Utah Assn. for the Edn. of Young Children and Utah Office of Child Care, 1998; fellow, Mich. State U., 2000—04. Mem.: Profl. Family Child Care Assn. (bd. dirs. 1995—99), Tex. Assn. Infant Mental Health (univ. adv. com. 2005—06), Nat. Coun. Family Rels. (cert. family life educator, Outstanding Poster 2002), Soc. Rsch. in Human Devel., Am. Ednl. Rsch. Assn., Phi Kappa Phi. Mem. Lds Ch. Office: Development and Family Studies Univ North Texas PO Box 311335 Denton TX 76203

NIEVEEN, TERESA J., elementary school educator; b. Grand Island, Nebr., Aug. 24, 1960; d. Arthur E. and Dixie L. Ostermeier; m. Jay K. Nieveen; children: Timothy J., Jerod M. EdB, U. Nebr., Lincoln, 1982, MEd in Curriculum and Instrn., 1989. Cert. tchr. Nebr., 1982. Tchr. Filley Consol. Schs., Nebr., 1983—84, Adams Pub. Schs., Nebr., 1984—98, Freeman Pub. Schs., Adams, 1998—. Lang. arts chmn. Freeman Pub. Schs., Adams, 1995—, co-chmn. steering com., 2002—. Asst. leader Nemaha Valley 4-H Club, Adams, 1996—2007; youth choir dir. Pella Ref. Ch., Adams, 1996—2007, mem. worship task force, 1998—2007. Mem.: Nat. Coun. Tchrs. English, Internat. Reading Assn., Nebr. State Reading Assn. (liason to Nebr. Dept. Edn. 2006—07), Ea. Nebr. Reading Coun. (past pres. 2006—07). Republican. Avocations: music, reading, sewing, quilting, gardening. Home: 2088 S 176 Rd Adams NE 68301 Office: Freeman Pub Schs PO Box 259 415 8th St Adams NE 68301 Home Phone: 402-988-2035; Office Phone: 402-988-2525.

NIEWIAROSKI, TRUDI OSMERS (GERTRUDE NIEWIAROSKI), social studies educator; b. Jersey City, Apr. 30, 1935; d. Albert John and Margaret (Niemeyer) Osmers; m. Donald H. Niewiaroski, June 8, 1957; children: Donald H., Donna, Margaret Anne, Nancy Noel. AB in History and German, Upsala Coll., East Orange, NJ, 1957; MEd, Montgomery County Pub. Schs., Rockville, Md., 1992. Cert. tchr. Md. Tchr. geography Colego Americano, Quito, Ecuador, 1964-66; bd. dirs. Cotopaxi Acad., Quito, 1964-65; tchr. speed reading Escuela Lincoln, Buenos Aires, Argentina, 1966-67; substitute thcr. Montgomery County Pub. Schs., Rockville, 1978-83, tchr. social studies, 1984—. Del. Eisenhower People to People Educators' Del. Vietnam, 1993; pres. Fulbright Meml. Fund Program, 1997; resident tchg. fellow Russia-Ukraine Excellence in Tchg. Program, 1997; resident scholar in Korea The Korea Soc., 1999; Ethiopia site visit Global Poverty Project, 2007. Author curricula; contbr. chpts. to books, articles to profl. jours.; lectr. at workshops. Bd. dirs. Cotopaxi Acad., Quito, 1964-65; pres. Citizens Assn., Potomac, Md., 1977-81; leader Girl Scouts U.S., 1975-76; adv. coun. Milken Found; pres. Fulbright Meml. Fund Program Japan Alumni, 1999—. Recipient Md. Tchr. of Yr. award State of Md. Edn. Dept., 1993, finalist nat. Tchr. of Yr., 1993, Disting. Alumni award Upsala Coll., 1993, Nat. Educator award Milken Found., 1994, Summer Fellowship Korean Studies Program, 1999, Joseph Malone fellowship Sultanate of Oman, 2003, Goethe Inst. fellowship, Germany, 2003; Fulbright fellow, India, 1985, China, 1990, Japan Keizai Koho Ctr. fellow, 1992, Fulbright Meml. Fund Tchr. Program fellow, Japan, 1997, Fulbright fellow, South Africa, 2001, Malone fellow, Oman, 2003, U. Tex. Mideast Inst. fellow, 2005; UMBC-U. Mex. Art and Culture scholar, 1995; mem. Cuba Study Tour, 2004, Dar Al Islam Study Tour, Iran, 2004; fellow U. Pitts. and Freeman Found., China, 2004; Fulbright fellow, China, 2004; Egypt fellow U. Tex. Middle East Inst., 2005. Mem. AAUW, ASCD, Nat. Coun. Social Studies, Md. Coun. for Social Studies, Asia Soc., Smithsonian Instn., Montgomery County Hist. Soc., Spl. Interest Groups-China, Japan and Korea, Md. Bus. Roundtable for Edn., Nat. Social Studies Suprs. Assn., Kappa Delta Pi. Avocations: cake and cookie decorating, travel. Office: R Montgomery High Sch Rockville MD 20852 Office Phone: 301-279-8442. Personal E-mail: niewiaroski.dandt@aol.com. Business E-Mail: trudi_niewiaroski@fc.mcps.k12.md.us.

NIFONG, MICHAEL BYRON, former prosecutor; b. Wilmington, NC, Sept. 14, 1950; s. Julius Lee and Shirley S. Nifong; m. Cy Gurney; children: Bryan Gabriel, Sarah Katherine. AB in Polit. Sci., U. NC, Chapel Hill, 1971; JD, U. NC, 1978. Bar: NC 1978. Math. tchr., boys phys. ed. tchr., Southport, NC, 1971—72; social worker New Hanover County Dept. Social Services, Wilmington, NC, 1972—75; atty. Durham County Dist. Atty. Office, NC, 1978—79, asst. dist. atty. NC, 1979—2005, dist. atty. NC, 2005—07. District attorney in the Duke lacrosse sexual assault case, 2006; ethics charges lead to disbarment in 2007. Democrat.

NIGAM, HEMANSHU, lawyer, Internet company executive; BA in Polit. Theory, Wesleyan U., Conn., 1987; JD, Boston U. Sch. Law, 1990. Dep. district atty. LA County Dist. Atty. Office, 1990—97; trial atty., criminal divsn. US Dept. Justice, Washington, 1997—2000; v.p., dir. worldwide internet enforcement Motion Picture Assn./Motion Picture Assn. Am., 2000—02; corp. atty., criminal compliance, security & law enforcement affairs, digital integrity group, Microsoft law and corp. affairs Microsoft Corp., Redmond, Wash., 2002—06, dir., consumer security outreach and child safe computing; chief security officer, MySpace.com News Corp., NYC, 2006—. Spkr. in field. Mem.: Washington State Bar Assn., Calif. State Bar Assn. Achievements include being a proven leader in online safety and security; served as a federal prosecutor against Internet child exploitation for the US Department of Justice; an advisor to a Congressional commission on online child safety; an advisor to the White House on cyber stalking. Office: News Corp 1211 Avenue of Americas 8th Fl New York NY 10036

NIGBOR, DONALD E., electronics executive; BS engineering, MS engineering, Rensselaer Polytechnic Institute; MBA, Amos Tuck School of Business, Dartmouth College. Manufacturing analyst Intermedics, 1980—84; gen. mgr. Benchmark Electronics Inc., 1984—90, bd. dir., 1986—, pres., 1986—2001, CEO, 2001—05, chmn., 2001—. Office: c/o Benchmark Electronics 3000 Technology Dr Angleton TX 77515

NIGHTINGALE, EDMUND JOSEPH, clinical psychologist, educator, consultant; b. St. Paul, Jan. 10, 1941; s. Edmund Anthony and Lauretta Alexandria (Horejs) N.; m. Marie Arcara, Apr. 9, 1978 (dec. April 1992); 1 child, Edmund Bernard. Student, Nazarath Hall Prep. Sem., 1959—61; AB, St. Paul Sem., 1963; AB magna cum laude, Cath. U. Louvain, Belgium, 1965, MA, 1967, STB cum laude, 1967; postgrad., U. Minn., 1971; MA, Loyola U., Chgo., 1973, PhD of Clin. Psychology, 1975. Lic. clin. psychologist, Ill., Minn., cert. Nat. Registry Health Svc. Providers in Psychology; diplomate clin. psychology Am. Bd. Profl. Psychology. With Cath. Archdiocese St. Paul and Mpls., 1967—73; intern clin. psychology Michael Reese Hosp. and Med. Ctr., Chgo., 1973—74; with West Side VA Hosp., Chgo., 1974—75; staff psychologist Student Counseling Ctr., Loyola U., Chgo., 1975; staff psychologist, clin. coord. inpatient unit Drug Dependency Treatment Ctr., 1975—80; chief psychology VA Med. Ctr., Danville, Ill., 1980—86, VA Med. Ctr. Mpls., 1986—2006; ret., 2006; cons., 2006—. Mem. pers. bd. Archdiocese St. Paul and Mpls., 1968-70; lectr. psychology, Loyola U., Chgo., 1975; asst. professorial lectr. psychology, St. Paul Xavier Coll., Chgo., 1975-78; adj. asst. prof. psychology in psychology, Abraham Lincoln Sch. Medicine, Med. Ctr. U. Ill., Chgo., 1977-82; adj. prof. psychology Purdue U., 1981-87; asst. prof. psychology Med. Sch., U. Minn., 1987—, clin. assoc. prof. psychology Coll. Liberal Arts, 1986-90; adj. asst. prof., 1990—; clin. asst. prof. U. Ill. Sch. Medicine, Urbana/Champaign, 1982-87; mem. grad. faculty counseling psychology Ind. State U., Terre Haute, 1983-86 Founding editor: Louvain Studies, 1966; editor: VA Dir. Psychology Staffing and Svcs., 1982, 83, 84, 85, 87; mem. editl. bd. Psychol. Svcs., 2006-. Bd. dirs. Inst. Postgrad. Studies, Ill. Psychol. Assn Recipient Exemplary Career award, US Dept. VA, 2006. Fellow APA (clin. psychology, psychotherapy, pub. svc., psychol. hypnosis, sec. treas. pub. svc. 1990-91, coun. reps. 1999-2004, pres. elect pub. svc. 2006, pres. pub. svc 2007, mem. com. on accreditation, 2006-07, Karl F. Heiser Presdl. award for Adv. 2002, divsn. Psychologists Pub. Svc. Disting. Contbns. award 2002); mem. AAAS, Am. Psychol. Soc., Assn. for Advancement Psychology, Ill. Psychol. Assn. (clin. psychology and acad. sects., sec. 1982-83, pres.-elect 1983-84, pres. 1984-85), Am. Group Psychotherapy Assn., Am. Soc. Clin. Hypnosis, Minn. Psychol. Assn. (pub. svc.- pres. 1997-99), Eagle Scout Assn., Assn. VA Chief Psychologists (sec., treas. 1987-90, pres.-elect 1990-91, pres. 1991-92, past pres. 1992-93, Outstanding Leadership award 1992), Minn. Soc. Clin. Hypnosis (bd. dirs. 1999-2001), Nat. MS Soc. (bd. trustees, Minn. chpt., 2005-). Home: 28 W Marie Ave West Saint Paul MN 55118 Business E-Mail: night002@umn.edu.

NIGHTINGALE, ELENA OTTOLENGHI, pediatric geneticist, academic administrator, educator; b. Livorno, Italy, Nov. 1, 1932; arrived in U.S., 1939, naturalized; d. Mario Lazzaro and Elisa Vittoria (Levi) Ottolenghi; m. Suart L. Nightingale, July 1, 1965; children: Elizabeth, Marisa. AB summa cum laude, Barnard Coll., 1954; PhD, Rockefeller U., 1961; MD, NYU, 1964. Asst. prof. Cornell U. Med. Coll., NYC, 1965—70, Johns Hopkins U., Balt., 1970—73; fellow in clin. genetics and pediat. Georgetown U. Hosp., Washington, 1973—74; sr. staff officer NAS, Washington, 1975—79, sr. program officer Inst. Medicine, 1979—82, sr. scholar-in-residence, 1982—83; spl. advisor to pres. Carnegie Corp. N.Y., NYC, 1983—94, sr. program officer, 1989—94; scholar-in-residence Inst. of Medicine, NAS, Washington, 1995—. Vis. assoc. prof. Harvard Med. Sch., Boston, 1980—84, vis. lectr., 1984—95; adj. prof. pediat. Georgetown U. Med. Ctr., 1984—, George Washington U. Med. Ctr., 1994—; mem. recombinant DNA adv. com. NIH, Bethesda, Md., 1979—83. Editor: The Breaking of Bodies and Minds: Torture, Psychiatric Abuses and the Health Professions, 1985, Prenatal Screening, Policies and Values: The Example of Neural Tube Defects, 1987, Promoting the Health of Adolescents: New Directions for the 21st Century, 1993, Adolescent Risk and Vulnerability: Concepts and Measurement, 2001; co-author: Before Birth: Prenatal Screening for Genetic Disease, 1990; contbr. numerous sci. articles to profl. publs. Bd. dirs. Amnesty Internat., U.S.A., Washington, 1989—91, Ctr. for Youth Svcs., Washington, 1980—84, Sci. Svc., Inc., Washington, 1985—96. Fellow: AAAS (chmn. com. on sci. freedom and responsibility 1985—88), N.Y. Acad. Scis.; mem.: Inst. Medicine of NAS (chmn. com. on health and human rights 1987—90), Genetics Soc. Am., Am. Soc. Human Genetics (social issues com. 1982—85), Am. Soc. Microbiology, Sigma Xi, Phi Beta Kappa. Office: NAS 500 5th St NW Washington DC 20001 Business E-Mail: enightin@nas.edu.

NIGHTINGALE, STUART LESTER, public health service officer; b. NYC, Jan. 26, 1938; s. Lester M. Nightingale and Beatrice L. N. (Liebowitz) Helpern; m. Elena Ottolenghi, July 1, 1965; children: Elizabeth S., Marisa O. BA, Yale U., 1959; MD, NYU, 1964. Diplomate Am. Bd. Internal Medicine. Intern in medicine and surgery Montefiore Hosp. and Med. Ctr., Bronx, 1964—65, resident in internal medicine, fellow in adolescent medicine, 1965—66, resident internal medicine, fellow adolescent medicine, 1967—69, asst. attending physician, 1969—70; resident in anatomical pathology NYU Sch. Medicine, 1966—67; med. dir. drug abuse adminstrn. Dept. Health and Mental Hygiene State of Md., Balt., 1971—72; chief treatment and rehab., office of programs, spl. action office for drug abuse prevention Exec. Office of Pres., Washington, 1972—74, chief office treatment and rehab., spl. action office for drug abuse prevention, 1974—75; dir. divsn. resource devel. Nat. Inst. on Drug Abuse, Rockville, Md., 1974—76; asst. to dir. Bur. Drugs, FDA, Rockville, 1976—79; dep. assoc. commr. for health affairs FDA, Rockville, 1979—82, acting assoc. commr. for health affairs, 1979—82, assoc. commr. for health affairs, 1982—2000; sr. med. adv. to dir. global health affairs and chief med. officer Office of the Asst. Sec. for Planning and Evaluation Dept. HHS, Washington, 2000—04, chief med. officer Office Pub. Health Emergency Preparedness, 2004—, dep. asst. sec. Office Pub. Health Emergency Preparedness, 2005—. Vis. physician Balt. City Hosps., 1970-72; clin. instr. dept. medicine Coll. Medicine SUNY, Bklyn., 1970; asst. physician out-patient dept., instr. dept. medicine Johns Hopkins U. Sch. Medicine, Balt., 1970-72, med. dir. drug abuse ctr., 1970-71, instr. dept. med. care and hosps. Sch. Hygiene and Pub. Health, 1971-74, rsch. program mgr. health svcs. rsch. and devel. ctr., 1970-71; chmn. rsch. involving human subjects com. FDA, 1979-84; liaison mem. Commn. on Fed. Drug Approval Process, U.S. Congress, 1980-81; mem.-at-large U.S. Pharmacopeial Conv., Inc., 1985-95; bd. trustees The Milton Helpern Libr. of Legal Medicine, N.Y.C., 1982-2000; bd. dirs. Nat. Coun. on Patient Info. and Edn., Washington; mem. forum on drug devel. and regulation Inst. Medicine, NAS, Washington, 1986-2000. Contbg. author Jour. AMA, 1985-99, Am. Family Physician, 1986-99. Capt. M.C., USAR, 1966-72; with USPHS. Recipient Disting. Svc. Spl. Action Office for Drug Abuse Prevention award Exec. Office of Pres., 1975, Pub. Health Superior Svc. award, 1983, Disting. Contbn. award Nat. Coun. Patient Info. and Edn., 1987, Achievement award Am. Assn. Physicians for Human Rights, 1990, Presdl. Meritorious Exec. Rank award, 1990, 2005, Pub. Health Svc. Spl. Recognition award, 1993, Sec.'s Recognition award Dept. HHS, 1999. Fellow ACP; mem. AMA, Sr. Execs. Assn., Cosmos Club. Office: Dept Health and Human Svcs 200 Independence Ave SW Washington DC 20201-0004 Office Phone: 202-205-2882. Business E-Mail: stuart.nightingale@hhs.gov.

NIGHTINGALE, SUZANNE M., management consultant; d. Stanley Wren and Ann Mary Nightingale; m. Kathleen P. Clementson, May 20, 2004. BA in Econ., U. San Francisco, 1985. Cert. sys. engr. Microsoft Corp., Redmond WA, 2000; spiritual healer Okla. City, Okla., 1985; lic. pvt. pilot, single engine land FAA, 1989. Project mgr. Lockheed Missiles and Space Co., Sunnyvale, Calif., 1982—89. Constrn. project mgr. Nightingale Assoc., The Sea Ranch, Calif., 1983—89, prin., Cape Coral, Calif., 1989—; data base analyst Lockheed Missiles and Space, Sunnyvale, Calif., 1987—89; corr. Door County Adv., Sturgeon Bay, Wis., 1991—94. Dir. Interfaith Events to Promote Cmty. Unity, Fort Myers, 1997—2002, Quality Life Acad., Fort Myers, 2004—05; founder Wash. Island Aviation Libr., Washington Island, Wis., 1990—94. Achievements include invention of purifier for diesel fuel using magnetic technology; design of major contribution to data base dictionary of first national security project employing artificial intelligence for intelligence analysis. Avocations: writer, artist, pilot. Home and Office: Nightingale Assocs 309 Cape Coral Pky W #206 Cape Coral FL 33914-5973 Home Phone: 239-945-2579; Office Phone: 239-945-2579.

NIGHTINGALE, WILLIAM JOSLYN, management consultant; b. Mpls., Sept. 16, 1929; s. William Isaac and Gladys (Joslyn) N.; children: Paul, Sara, William Joslyn, Jr., Margaret. BA, Bowdoin Coll., 1951; MBA, Harvard U., 1953. Mktg. mgr. Gen. Mills Inc., Mpls., 1957-66; sr. assoc. Booz, Allen & Hamilton Inc., NYC, 1966-68; v.p. fin. Hanes Corp., Winston-Salem, NC, 1969; pres. Bali Co. Inc., NYC, 1970—95; founder, pres., chmn., sr. adviser Nightingale & Assocs. LLC, Stamford, Conn., 1975—2000. Bd. dirs. Ring's End Inc.; trustee Naragansett Tax Free Bond Fund. Active numerous charitable orgns.; vestryman St. Luke's Episcopal Ch., 1975-78, sr. warden, 1989-91; mem. Darien Representative Town Meeting, 1971-74. Lt. (j.g.) USNR, 1953-57. Mem. Wee Burn Country Club, Noroton, Conn., Yacht Club, Harvard Club, NYC. Republican. Home: 195 Rowayton Ave Norwalk CT 06853-1237

NIGHY, BILL FRANCIS, actor; b. Surrey, England, Dec. 12, 1949; life ptnr. Diana Quick; 1 child, Mary. Spokesperson Nat. Soc. for Epilepsy; amb. DebRA, 2006—. Actor: (films) Death Watch, 1979, Eye of the Needle, 1981, Curse of the Pink Panther, 1983, Little Drummer Girl, 1984, The Phantom of the Opera, 1989, Being Human, 1993, True Blue, 1996, Indian Summer (Alive and Kicking), 1996, Fairy Tale: A True Story, 1997, Still Crazy, 1998 (Evening Standard Peter Sellers award, 1998), Guest House Paradiso, 1999, Blow Dry, 2001, The Lawless Heart, 2001 (Best Supporting Actor, LA Critics Cir. award, 2002), Lucky Break, 2001, AKA, 2002, I Capture the Castle, 2003 (Best Supporting Actor, LA Critics Cir. award, 2004), Love Actually, 2003 (Best Supporting Actor, Brit. Acad. Film and TV Arts, LA Critics Cir. award, London Film Critics award, 2004, Best Comdey Performance, Evening Standard Peter Sellers award, 2004), Underworld, 2003, Shaun of the Dead, 2004, Enduring Love, 2004, The Magic Roundabout, 2005, The Hitchhiker's Guide To The Galaxy, 2005, The Constant Gardener, 2005, Underworld: Evolution, 2006, Pirates Of the Caribbean - Dean Man's Chest, 2006, Stormbreaker, 2006, Flushed Away, 2006, Notes on a Scandal, 2006, Disgrace, 2006, Pirates of the Caribbean: At World's End, 2007 (Choice Movie: Villain, Teen Choice Awards, 2007); (TV films) Deasey, 1979, Fat, 1979, Little Lord Fauntleroy, 1980, Dreams of Leaving, 1980, Writing On the Wall, 1990, Antonia and Jane, 1991, The Girl In The Café, 2005, Gideon's Daughter, 2006 (Satellite award, 2006, Best Performance by an Actor in a Mini-Series or Motion Picture Made for TV, Golden Globe award, Hollywood Fgn. Press Assn., 2007); (TV series) Agony, 2d season, 1980, Making News, 1989, The Lost Prince, 2003 (Best Actor, Broadcasting Press Guild award, 2003), The Young Visitors, 2003 (Best Actor in a TV Film, Broadcasting Press Guild award, 2003); (TV miniseries) Reilly - Ace of Spies, 1983, The Last Place on Earth, 1985, The Men's Room, 1991, Eye of the Storm, 1993, God's Messengers, 1994, The Canterbury Tales, 1998, State of Play, 2003 (Best Actor, Brit. Acad. Film and TV Arts, 2004, Best Actor, Broadcasting Press Guild award, 2003), The Canterbury Tales, The Wife Of Bath, 2003, He Knew He Was Right, 2004; (Broadway plays) The Vertical Hour, 2007 (Theatre World award, 2007). Office: c/o Markham and Froggatt Ltd Personal Management 4 Windmill St London W1T 2HZ England *

NIGO, fashion designer; b. Japan; Stylist, editor Popeye Mag.; founder, owner Nowhere Ltd., Tokyo, 1993—, Bathing Ape brand, Tokyo, 1993—, BAPE CUTS hair salon, BAPE cafe and gallery, APE SOUNDS, 2000—, BAPE TV; co-owner Billionaire Boys Club clothing line. BAPE/Pepsi camouflaged can, Pepsi Co.; featured in DUB Mag. Recipient Asia's Heroes award, Time Asia. Achievements include owner of many clothing stores across Tokyo, Kyoto, Osaka, London, NYC. Avocation: art and Hollywood memorabilia collecting. Office: Bathing Ape 91 Greene St New York NY 10013

NIGRO, KENNETH MICHAEL, music educator, musician; b. Waterbury, Conn., Nov. 27, 1954; s. Ugo Mario and Antoinette Rose Nigro; m. Karen Lynn Milo, July 17, 1976; 1 child, Kyle Michael. BS in Music Edn., Ctrl. Conn. State U., 1976; MusM in Applied Music, U. Miami, 1980; degree in Adminstrn., Sacred Heart U., 2000. Cert. educator Conn., administrator Conn. Freelance musician, 1979—; lectr. Ctrl. Conn. State U., New Britain, 1982—87; lectr. saxophone, improv and combo, dir. saxophone ensemble U. Conn., Storrs, 1987—2004; tchr. music Wilby HS, Waterbury, Conn., 1997—; woodwind lectr. Naugatuck Valley CC, Waterbury, 2004—. Clinician, performer Yamaha Corp. Am., Indpls., 1998—. Author: The Complete Saxophone; musician: White Nights Jazz Festival, 1995, Fifty-third Presdl. Inaugural, 1997, (albums) New Millenium Jazz Ensemble CD, 1998; composer: (songs) Big Schleps, 2001, 84 Again, 2004, The Complete Saxophone, 2005; contbr. articles to profl. jours. Recipient Saxophone Svc. Performance award, Saxophone Jour., 1977; scholar, U. Miami, 1979—80. Mem.: Nat. Assn. Coll. Wind & Percussion Instrs, Pi Kappa Lambda, Phi Beta Mu. Avocations: bicycling, swimming, running. Home Phone: 203-753-0015. Personal E-mail: kyamasax@aol.com.

NIGRO, RUSSELL M., former state supreme court justice; b. Phila., Mar. 23, 1946; BA, Temple U.; JD, Rutgers U., 1973. Atty. priv. practice, Phila., 1974—87; judge Phila. Ct. of Common Pleas, 1987; justice Pa. Supreme Ct., Phila., 1996—2006. Former chmn. staffing com. Phila. Ct. of Common Pleas, established Arbitration Appeals Program; lecturer civil law Pa. Bar

Inst.; lecturer Temple U. James E. Beasley Sch. of Law; chair Pa. Supreme Ct. Capital Case Standards Com.; mem. Pa. Futures Commn. on Justice in 21st Century. Mem.: Pa. Bar Assn. (William J. Brennan Jr. Disting. Jurist award 2002). *

NIGUIDULA, FAUSTINO NAZARIO, surgeon, educator; b. June 27, 1926; came to U.S., 1953, naturalized, 1970; s. Aquilino Uriarte and Encarnacion (Nazario) N.; children: David, Diane, Susan, John, Stephan, Daniel, Nancy, Kathy; m. Barbara Ann Brooks, Dec. 17, 1977; children: Andrew, Nicole. Intern Arnot-Ogden Meml. Hosp., Elmira, N.Y., 1953-54; resident in surgery Strong Meml. Hosp., Rochester, N.Y., 1954-59; instr. surgery U. Rochester, 1958-59; resident in thoracic surgery Buffalo Gen. Hosp., 1959-61; fellow in pediatric cardiothoracic surgery Children's Hosp., Buffalo, 1961-62, Hosp. Sick Children, Toronto, Ont., 1963-64; clin. instr. U. Buffalo, 1965-66; asst. prof. Temple U., Phila., 1967-70, assoc. prof. surgery, pediat., 1970-75; clin. assoc. prof. Rutgers U., 1979-83; prof. surgery, prof. pediat. N.Y. Med. Coll., 1983—. Chief pediatric cardiothoracic surgery St. Christopher's Hosp. Children, Phila., 1967-75, Westchester Med. Ctr., Valhalla, N.Y., 1983—; dir. pediatric cardio-thoracic surgery Deborah Heart and Lung Ctr., Browns Mills, N.J., 1975-83. Mem. ACS, AAAS, Soc. Thoracic Surgeons, Am. Heart Assn., Assn. Thoracic and Cardiovasc. Surgeons Asia, Soc. Philippine Surgeons Am., Cardiology Soc. Poland (hon., 7th commemorative medal 1982), N.Y. State Med. Soc., N.Y. Acad. Scis., Westchester County Med. Soc., Westchester Acad. Medicine. Presbyterian. Office: Westchester Med Ctr 95 Grasslands Rd Valhalla NY 10595 Home: 48 Roma Orchard RD Peekskill NY 10566-4870

NIGUIDULA, KATHLEEN ANN, music educator, musician; b. Upper Darby, Pa., Apr. 5, 1972; d. Faustino Nazario Niguidula and Brenda Marie Maybury; m. Christopher Jordan O'Neill, Aug. 30, 2004; children: Luke O'Neill, Jacquelyn O'Neill. B in Music Edn., Eastman Sch. Music, 1994; MusM in Piano Performance, Boston Conservatory, 1998. Cert. K-12 music tchr. N.Y., Tex., Mass. Music tchr., choir dir. grades 6-8 Aldine Ind. Sch. Dist., Houston, 1994—95; music tchr., choir dir. grades 7-8 Norwood Pub. Schs., Mass., 1998—99; music tchr. K-8 Music On The Move, Chelsea, Mass., 1999—2001; piano tchr. Timeline Music, Wakefield, Mass., 1998—2001; music tchr. Wolf Sch., Providence, 2001—05; piano tchr. Music Sch. R.I. Philharm., Providence, 2001—, registrar, 2005—. Freelance accompanist, Boston, 1996—; choir dir. K-5 after-school programs Wolf Sch., Providence, 2001—05; coord. early childhood music Music Sch. R.I. Philharmonic, 2002—04. Music dir., organist Islington Cmty. Ch., Westwood, Mass., 1999—2004. Finalist piano, Florida Concerto Competition, 1989; recipient Excellence in Music award, Sarasota Visual and Performing Arts, 1990, 1st prize Composition, Women's Soc. Sarasota, 1990, 1st prize Music Performance, Shriner's Club, 1990; scholar, Eastman Sch. Music, 1990—94. Mem.: Orff-Schuwerk Assn., Music Educators Nat. Conf., Music Tchrs. Nat. Assn., New Eng. Piano Tchrs. Assn., Chopin Club. Home Phone: 401-359-0545. Personal E-mail: kathleen-o@cox.net.

NII, SHIRO, director, virologist, educator; b. Naruto, Tokushima, Japan, Jan. 12, 1932; parents Atsushi and Toyo (Toyota) N.; m. Etsuko Tada, Mar. 29, 1960; children: Satoshi, Keiko Maeda, Yoshiko Fujita. MD, Osaka U., 1956, PhD, 1961. Lic. physician. Rsch. assoc. Rsch. Inst. for Microbial Diseases Osaka U., Japan, 1961—66, assoc. prof. Rsch. Inst. for Microbial Diseases, 1966—78; prof. Okayama U. Med. Sch., Japan, 1978—97, dean, 1993—95; prof. emeritus Okayama U., 1997—; prof. Kawasaki Coll. Allied Health Professions, Kurashiki, Japan, 1997—98; pres. Niimi Coll., Japan, 1998—2002; academic adminstr. CAC Rehab. Coll., Hiroshima, 2002—03, dir., 2003—06, dir. emeritus, 2006—. Councilor Okayama U., 1990-92; hon. prof. Jiangxi Med. Coll., China, 1993; guest prof. Dalian Med. Coll., China, 1994; expert adviser Sci. and Tech. Com., 1994; pres. Univ. and Coll. Assn. Okayama Prefecture, 1995, 43d Ann. Meeting of Japanese Virologists, 1995. Co-author: (book) Virology, 1997; editor, co-author: (book) Essentials of Microbiology, 1983, 98; contbr. articles to sci. jours. Mem.: Japanese Assn. Infectious Diseases (auditor 1995—98), Japanese Soc. Virology (hon.). Avocations: reading, baseball, walking. Home: 372-1-206 Hama Okayama 703-8256 Japan Office: 372-1-206 Hama Okayama 703-8256 Japan E-mail: snii@po12.oninet.ne.jp.

NII, YUKO, artist; b. Tokyo, Toshima-ku, Japan, Oct. 22, 1942; arrived in US, 1963; d. Satoshi and Chieko Nii. BFA, Macalester Coll., St. Paul, Minn., 1965; MFA, Pratt Inst., Bklyn., 1969. Residency Yaddo, Saratoga Springs, NY, 1980, 1982; artist (painter); founder, dir. Williamsburg Art and Hist. Ctr., Bklyn., 1996—. Costume and stage set designer Chiang Ching Dance Company, NYC, 1977—78, Zignal I at La-Mama, 1978—79; contbr. N.Y. Jour., Japan, 1982—83, NY Arts Mag., 2002, 11211 mag., 2004, Friends and Mentors Art Show catalog, 2001. One-woman shows include Elaine Benson Gallery, L.I., 1977, 1986, 1994, Fairleigh Dickenson U., N.J., 1978, Berkshire Mus., Mass., 1979, Monique Lnowlton Gallery, N.Y.C., 1979, Vered Internat. Gallery, L.I., 1979, Haber Theodore Gallery, N.Y.C., 1980, Internat. Monetary Fund, Washington, 1980. Recipient Woman of Yr., Office of Bklyn Borough Pres. Howard Golden, 1998, Office of Gov. of N.Y. State George Pataki, 2001, Office of Bklyn Borough Pres. Marty Markowitz, 2003, Outstanding Citizen award, N.Y.C. Coun., 2003; fellow, Pratt Inst., Bklyn., 1966—69; scholar, Macalester Coll., St. Paul, Minn., 1963—65. Home: 385 Clinton Ave Brooklyn NY 11238 Office: Williamsburg Art & Hist Ctr 135 Broadway Brooklyn NY 11211 Home Phone: 718-486-6012; Office Phone: 718-486-7372. Home Fax: 718-486-6012. Personal E-mail: wahcenter@earthlink.net.

NIJHUIS, MICHELLE, freelance journalist; BA, Reed Coll., Portland, Oreg., 1996. Biol. tech. US Geo. Survey, 1994—97; staff reporter High Country News, 1998—99, sr. editor/assoc. editor, 1999—2001, contributing editor, 2003—; corr. Orion mag.; freelance writer, 2001—. Recipient John M. Collier award for Journalism in Forest and Conservation History, 2005, Best Profile award, American Soc. Journalists and Authors, 2006, Walter Sullivan award for Excellence in Sci. Journalism, Am. Geophys. Union, 2006, AAAS Sci. Journalism award (small newspaper), 2006. Mem.: Phi Beta Kappa.

NIJINSKY, TAMARA, actress, puppeteer, author, librarian, educator; b. Vienna; arrived in U.S., 1961; d. Waslaw and Romola (de Pulszky) Nijinsky; widowed; 1 child, Kinga Maria Szakats-Gaspers. Student, Europe; postgrad. studies in U.S. Mem., actress Nat. Theater of Budapest; owner, tchr. Tamara Nijinsky Performing Art Studio, Montreal; tchr. speech/drama, French and German, libr. Cath. H.S., Phoenix; founder, exec. dir. Waslaw and Romola Nijinsky Found., Inc., 1991—. Lectr. in field. Author: Nijinsky and Romola, 1991. Decorated chevalier de l'Ordre des Arts et des Lettres, officier de l'Ordre des Arts et des Lettres (France); recipient Nijinsky medal, Pagart, Poland, Polish Order of Arts and Letters, 1997, La Medaille Vermeil de Paris, 2000. Roman Catholic. Avocations: reading, computer, swimming. Office: Nijinsky Foundation Inc PO Box # 15981 Phoenix AZ 85060-5981 Office Phone: 602-840-9605.

NIJMAN, JAN, geographer, educator; b. Heemskerk, The Netherlands, Oct. 15, 1957; arrived in U.S., 1987; BA in Human Geography, U. Amsterdam, 1980, MA in Human Geography, 1985; PhD in Geography, U. Colo., 1990. Freelance journalist, Netherlands, 1981—87; cons., rschr. Regioplan, Amsterdam, 1985, U. Amsterdam Sch. Environ. Scis., 1986; tchg. asst. dept. geography U. Ill., Champaign-Urbana, 1987—88; instr. dept. geography U. Colo., Boulder, 1988—90; asst. prof. geography U. Miami, Fla., 1990—94, assoc. prof. geography Fla., 1994—98, prof. dept. geography and regional studies Fla., 1998—, dir. internat. studies program Coll. Arts and Scis. Fla., 1993—98. Cons. internat. dvisn. Moran, Stahl & Boyer, Boulder, 1989—90; disting. vis. rsch. prof. Amsterdam Study for the Met. Environment U. Amsterdam, 1996; mem. sr. panel geography and regional sci. program NSF, Washington, 1998—2000; mem. com. for rsch. and exploration Nat. Geog. Soc., Washington, 2001—; presenter in field. Author: The Geopolitics of Power and Conflict: Superpowers in the International System, 1993, The Global Moment in Urban Evolution, 1996; editor (with R. Grant): The Global Crisis in Foreign Aid, 1998, 2000. Grantee, U. Miami, 1990—92, 1993, 1996, 1997, 2000, 2002, 2002, Assn. Am. Geographers, 1997, Nat. Geog. Soc., 1998—2000, NSF, 1998—2001, 1999, 2002—, 2003—; Knight Jr. fellow, U. Miami, 1990—92, John Simon Guggenheim Meml. Found., 2003. Mem.: Koninklijk Nederlands Aardrijkskundig Genootschap, Internat. Studies Assn., Assn. Am. Geographers (Warren Nystrom award 1991). Office: Univ Miami Dept Geography and Regional Studies PO Box 8067 Coral Gables FL 33124-2221

NIJMAN, JENNIFER T., lawyer, department chairman; b. Aug. 27, 1962; BA, U. Ill., 1984; JD, U. Chgo., 1987. Bar: Ill. 1987, US Dist. Ct. (no. dist.) Ill. 1987. Assoc. to ptnr. Winston & Strawn LLP, Chgo., 1994—, co-chmn. environ. dept. Co-chmn. diversity com. Winston & Strawn LLP, Chgo., mem. hiring com.; bd. dirs. Pub. Interest Law Initiative, Ctr. Conflict Resolution; chair Ill. Legal Needs Study, Ill. Coalition Equal Justice. Contbr. articles to profl. jours. Mem.: ABA (mem. environ. litigation com.), Economic Club Chgo., Ill. State Bar Assn., Chgo. Bar Assn. (pres. 2002—03). Office: Winston & Strawn LLP 35 W Wacker Dr Chicago IL 60601-9703 Office Phone: 312-558-5771. Office Fax: 312-558-5700. Business E-Mail: jnijman@winston.com.

NIKAIDO, HIROSHI, microbiologist; b. Tokyo, Mar. 26, 1932; arrived in U.S., 1962; s. Tatsuya and Ryo Nikaido; m. Kishiko Jokura, Mar. 11, 1963; children: Michio, George. MD, Keio U., Tokyo, 1955, D in Med. Sci., 1961. Assoc. bacteriology Harvard Med. Sch., Boston, 1963-64, asst. prof., 1965-69; assoc. prof. U. Calif., Berkeley, 1969-71, prof., 1971—. Sci. adv. Essential Therapeutics, Mountain View, Calif., 1992—2002. Co-author: Microbial Biotechnology, 1995; contbr. articles to profl. jours. Recipient Paul Ehrlich award, Paul Ehrlich Found., 1969, Freedom to Discover Achievement award, Bristol-Myers Squibb, 2004. Fellow: Am. Acad. Microbiology; mem.: Am. Acad. Arts and Scis., Am. Soc. Biochemistry and Molecular Biology, Am. Soc. Microbiology (editor Jour. Bacteriology 1998—2002, Hoechst-Roussel award 1984).

NIKAIDOH, HISASHI, pediatric cardiac surgeon, professor; b. Tokyo, Sept. 21, 1934; s. Tatsuya and Ryo Nikaidoh; m. Lynn Ann Zuttermeister, Oct. 21, 1952; children: Kimi Lynn, Ken Paul. MD, U. Tokyo, 1959. Diplomate Am. Bd. Surgery, 1967, Am. Bd. Thoracic Surgery, 1976, lic. physician Japan, 1960, DC, 1966, Ill., 1970, Tex., 1977. Postgrad. trainee Branch Hosp., Faculty Medicine, U. Tokyo, 1960, asst., 1967—69; rotating intern USN Hosp., Yokosuka, Japan, 1959—60; asst. resident Mt. Sinai Hosp., NYC, 1960—64, sr. resident, 1964—65; rsch. fellow Children's Meml. Hosp., Chgo., 1965, resident, 1966—67; assoc. dept. surgery Northwestern U. Med. Sch., Chgo., 1969—71, asst. prof., 1971—77; sr. resident Case Western Res. U., Cleve., 1974—75; assoc. prof. dept. surgery U. Tex. Southwestern Med. Ctr., Dallas, 1978—85, clin. assoc. prof., 1985—99, clin. prof. dept. cardiothoracic surgery, 1999—2002, prof., 2002—. Attending surgeon divsn. thoracic and cardiovasc. surgery Dallas County Hosp. Dist. (Parkland Meml. Hosp.), St. Paul Univ. Hosp.; active attending surgeon divsn. thoracic surgery Children's Med. Ctr., Dallas. Recipient Robert Moore, MD Disting. Svc. award in Medicine, Children's Med. Ctr. Dallas, 2000; Fullbright Travel grante, 1960. Fellow: ACS (mem. Leadership Soc. 2005), Am. Acad. Pediatrics; mem.: AMA, Tex. Med. Assn., Dallas County Med. Soc., Ctrl. Surg. Assn., Am. Pediatric Surg. Assn., Soc. Thoracic Surgeons. Office: Univ Tex Southwestern Med Ctr Dallas Pediat Cardiothoracic Surgery 1935 Motor St Ste C-320 Dallas TX 75235 Office Phone: 214-456-5000. Office Fax: 214-456-5015. Business E-Mail: hisashi.nikaidoh@utsouthwestern.edu.

NIKAS, RICHARD JOHN, lawyer; b. Long Beach, Calif., Sept. 9, 1968; s. John Nikolas and Dorothy (Bernardo) N. BA in Internat. Rels., U. So. Calif., 1991, JD, 1995. Bar: Calif. Spl. projects coord. Vessel Assist Assn. Am., Newport Beach, Calif., 1989-94; ptnr. Herrick Nikas, LLP, Costa Mesa, Calif., 2003—. Guest lectr. maritime law U. So. Calif., L.A., 1998—; lectr. admiralty and maritime law Calif. Maritime Acad., Vallejo; chmn. USCG Working Group on Nat. Maritime Incident Reporting Sys., Washington, 1997—, designated proctor in admiralty, The Maritime Law Assn. of the U.S.A. Author: Benedict on Admiralty, 1998, Moore's Federal Practice, 1998, The Last Yankee, 1999, Recreational Boating Law, 2000, Admiralty Practice and Procedure, 2000. Head football coach Ocean View H.S., Huntington Beach, 1995; mentor Huntington Beach Unified Sch. Dist., 1997—; pitcher Greek Olympic Baseball Team, Atlantic City Surf Profl. Baseball Club; mng. gen. ptnr. Old Reliable Baseball, LLC; bd. govs. The Am. Mariner, Loyola U., 1999. Recipient Best Oralist award Spong Nat. Invitational Moot Ct., Williamsburg, Va., 1995, Meritorious Pub. Svc. medal USCG. Mem. Calif. State Bar Assn., Maritime Law Assn., Soc. Naval Architects and Marine Engrs. (chmn. panel 0-38), Assn. Profl. Ball Players Am. Avocation: baseball.

NIKIAS, CHRYSOSTOMOS L. (MAX NIKIAS), engineering educator; b. Cyprus, Greece; arrived in US, 1979; m. Niki Nikias. Diploma in elec. and mech. engring., Nat. Tech. U., Athens, Greece, 1977; MS in elec. engring., SUNY, Buffalo, 1980, PhD in elec. engring., 1982; PhD (hon.), U. Cyprus, 2000. Prof. elec. and computer engring. U. Conn., Northeastern U.; prof. elec. engring.-systems U. So. Calif., 1991—, assoc. dean engring., 1992—2001, founding dir. Integrated Media Systems Ctr., 1996—2001, dean Andrew and Erna Viterbi Sch. Engring., 2001—05, Zohrab A. Kaprielian Chair in Engring., provost, sch. engring., sr. v.p. academic affairs, 2005—. Bd. dirs. Lord Found., Calif., Alfred Mann Inst. Biomedical Engring. Bd. trustees Chadwick Sch., Palos Verde Peninsula, Calif. Recipient Outstanding Tchr. Award, Nat. Technol. U., 1993. Fellow: Calif. Coun. on Sci. and Tech., IEEE (Signal Processing Best Paper Award 1988, Fred W. Ellersick Award of Outstanding Unclassified Paper at Mil. Comm. 1992, AH Reeves Premium Award 2002); mem.: Russian Acad. Nat. Sci. (fgn. mem.), Phi Kappa Phi. Office: U So Calif Sch Engring Office of the Dean Los Angeles CA 90089-1450

NIKIRK, SUSAN SILVA (SUSAN SILVA), minister, writer, dancer, consultant; b. NYC, Mar. 13, 1947; d. Victor and Lina Silva; m. Gerald Eugene Nikirk, Jan. 29, 1988. English, City Coll. of N.Y., NYC, 1966; fashion mktg., Fashion Inst. Tech., NYC, 1967; Biblical studies, Heart to Heart Internat., Norwich, Conn., 1993. Rev. Ordination Kingsway Fellowship Internat., Iowa, 1992; championship cert. nat. adjudicator Nat. Dance Coun. Am., 2006, master cert. dance tchr. Nat. Dance Tchrs. Am., 85, Nat. Dance Tchrs. Am., 2006, championship cert. dance tchr. N. Am. Dance Tchrs. Assn., 2006, cert. examiner Arthur Murray Internat., 2007. Profl. dancer Broadway, Off Broadway Theatre & TV, NYC, 1964—72; dir. fashion merchandising sch. Barbizon Sch. of Queens, Rego Pk., Queens, NY, 1973—75; mgmt. cons. RTW Mgmt., NYC, 1975—77; Theatrical Exhbn., Am. Ballroom Dance Champion in US Competitions Fred Astaire, Arthur Murray, 1977—86; profl. ballroom dancer and tchr. Fred Astaire, Arthur Murray, various ind. dance studios, 1977—89; night club act Hamilton & Silva, 1980—85; examiner, coach Arthur Murray Internat., 2007—; profl. ballroom nat. adjudicator Nat. Dance Coun. of Am., Arthur Murray Internat., 2006—; choreographer Ind. Dance Teams, 1977—89; author & mktg. cons. Arthur Murray Internat., Coral Gables, Fla., 1985—89; cosmetic cons. Estee Lauder, Inc., Conn., 1989—91; co-founder, ordained min., v.p. bd. dirs. Nikirk Ministries, Colchester, Conn., 1992—; Theatrical Ballroom coach and choreographer, 2006—. Ordained min., nat. & internat. speaker inter Denom. chs. and confs., USA, Holland, Belgium, Switerland, Germany, Iceland, 1992—; pastor VINE Tng. and Worship Ctr., 1997—2005; dir. founder Watchmen Sch. of Prayer, Colchester, Conn., 1998—. Dancer (discotheque) Beatles Tour, 1965; author: (tchg. video, manual) Arthur Murray Bronze Theatrical Ballroom Syllabus, 1986—88, (tchg. video) Watchmen Sch. of Prayer, 2002; co-host (TV series) Voice In New Eng. T.V. Broadcast, 1996—; dance dir. Cinemystic Film; contbr. articles pub. to profl. jour. Recipient Profl. Dance Devel. award, Arthur Murray Studios, 1986. Mem.: Arthur Murray Nat. Dance Bd., Nat. Dance Coun. Am., N.Am. Dance Tchrs. Assn., Nat. Dance Tchrs. Assn., Kingsway Fellowship Internat. Messianic Jew. Avocations: gardening, dance. Office: Nikirk Ministries PO Box 211 Colchester CT 06415 Office Phone: 860-537-5881. Business E-Mail: snikirk@nikirkvoice.org.

NIKITIN, ALEXANDER YU., pathologist; b. St. Petersburg, Russia, Sept. 28, 1960; s. Yurii V. Nikitin and Valentina D. Nikitina; m. Andrea Flesken-Nikitin, Feb. 24, 1995; children: Dmitrii Yu., Maria Yu. Nikitina. MD (hon.), Acad. Pavlov First Med. Inst., St. Petersburg, Russia., 1983; PhD, Prof. Petrov Rsch. Inst. Oncology, St. Petersburg, Russia, 1988. Asst. prof. rsch. dept. molecular medicine Univ. Tex. Health Sci. Ctr., San Antonio, 1999—2000; asst. prof. pathology Cornell U., Ithaca, NY, 2000—. Contbr. articles to profl. jours. Vice chair pathology and lab. medicine standing com. Mouse Models of Human Cancers Consortium, Bethesda, Md., 1999—2004; organizer Ann. Practical Workshop on Pathology of Mouse Models for Human Disease, Bar Harbor, Maine, 2002—. Recipient Midcareer award in Mouse Pathobiology, NIH, 2002—; grantee, 2002—, Dept. of Def., 2001—04, 2000—03. Mem.: AAAS, Soc. Toxicologic Pathology, Am. Assn. Cancer Rsch. Achievements include first to develop a novel genetic model of human ovarian cancer; development of new classification of mouse proliferative pulmonary lesions; discovery of syndrome of multiple endocrine neoplasia in Rb +/- mice. Office: Cornell Univ T2014AVRT Ithaca NY 14850 Home Phone: 607-256-8697.

NIKOLAI, LOREN ALFRED, accounting educator; b. Northfield, Minn., Dec. 14, 1943; s. Roman Peter and Loyola (Gertrude) N.; m. Anita Carol Baker, Jan. 15, 1966; children: Trishia, Jay. BA, St. Cloud State U., 1966, MBA, 1967; PhD, U. Minn., 1973. CPA, Mo. Asst. prof. U. N.C., Chapel Hill, 1973-76; assoc. prof. U. Mo., Columbia, 1976-80, prof., 1980-82, Ernst & Young Disting. prof. Sch. Accountancy, 1982—, dir. masters programs, 2002—. Author: Financial Accounting: Concepts and Uses, 1988, 3d edit., 1995, Intermediate Accounting, 1980, 10th edit., 2007, Accounting Information for Business Decisions, 2000, updated 2d edit., 2007. Recipient Faculty award of merit Fedn. Schs. of Accountancy, 1989, Disting. Alumni award St. Cloud U., 1990, Coll. of Bus. Faculty Mem. of Yr. award, 1991, Mo. Outstanding Acctg. Educators award, 1993; Kemper fellow U. Mo., 1992, Alumni award MU Faculty, 1996, UM Presdl. awd. for Outstanding Teaching, 1999; Coll. of Bus. Teacher of the Yr., 1999. Mem. AICPA, Am. Acctg. Assn., Mo. Soc. CPAs, Fedn. Schs. of Acctg. (pres. 1994). Office: U Mo Sch Accountancy 303 Cornell Hall Columbia MO 65211-0001 Business E-Mail: nikolai@missouri.edu.

NIKOLOV, ZHORRO, engineering educator, director; arrived in US, 2000; s. Stefan Nikolov and Milka Poushkarova; m. Galia Nikolov; m. Snejanka Kortcheva (div.); children: Milena Perrine, Mariela Nikolova. MS in Physics, Sofia U., Bulgaria, 1976, PhD in Physics, 1982. Rsch. asst. prof. physics Sofia U., 1982—86, asst. prof. physics, 1887—1993, assoc. prof. physics, 1993—2000; hon. rsch. fellow Queen's U. of Belfast, Northern Ireland, 1991—93; jsps invited scholar chemistry Hiroshima U., Japan, 1997—98; rsch. assoc. prof. U. Utah, Salt Lake City, 2000—05; dir. materials characterization facility Coll. Engring. Drexel U., Phila., 2005—. Contbr. more than 60 articles to profl. publs. Fellow hon. rsch. fellow, Commn. European Cmty., 1993; rsch. fellow, Nat. Sci. and Engring. Rsch. Coun., UK, 1991—92, sr. scholar fellow, Japanese Soc. Promotion Sci., 1997—98, vis. prof. scholar, Venture Bus. Lab., Hiroshima U., 1998. Mem.: Am. Chem. Soc. Achievements include first to first total internal reflection Raman setup to study water structure at the liquid/solid interface; development of nonlinear optics laboratory with sum-frequency spectroscopy and second harmonic generation capabilities to study interfaces. Office: Drexel U 3141 Chestnut St Philadelphia PA 19104 Office Phone: 215-895-1293.

NIKOPOULOS, BETH, educational association administrator; BA in English, U. Tex., Arlington; MA in Human Services, Nat. U., San Diego. Dir., tutorial services Brookhaven Coll., Dallas, 1998—. Mem.: Assn. Tutoring Profession (pres. 2007—), Coll. Reading Learning Assn., Tex. Tutors' Assn. (former pres.), Nat. Tutoring Assn. (chair, constn. and by-laws 1998—2003). Office: Brookhaven College Bldg S Rm S255 3939 Calley View Ln Farmers Branch Dallas TX 75244-4997 Office Phone: 972-860-4672. *

NIKOUI, HOSSEIN REZA, quality assurance professional; came to U.S., 1977; s. Gholam Reza and Monireh (Jahanshahi) Nikoui; m. Niki Forouzi, Nov. 3, 1983; children: Neda Lili, Amir Reza. BSChemE, Arya-Mehr Univ., Tehran, 1971; MEng in Ops. Rsch., U. Toronto, 1981; cert. in quality assurance, Ryerson Univ., Toronto, 1983; cert. sys. approach/quality improvement, Madonna U., Livonia, Mich., 1996; MSBA in Quality and Ops. Mgmt., Madonna U., 1998; cert. in lean mfg., U. Mich., 2001. Registered profl. engr., 1981, cert. quality engr., Am. Soc. for Quality, 1981, quality auditor, 1990, quality mgr., 1995, quality mgmt. sys. lead auditor, Registrar Accreditation Bd., 1995, skill examiner, 2006, Six Sigma Black Belt, Ford Motor Co., 2007. Quality engr. Gen. Motors, Tehran, 1971-72, supt. supplier quality assurance, 1973-74, mgr. quality assurance, 1975-78, resident materials mgr. Oshawa, Ont., Can., 1978-79; mgr. quality control G.S. Woolley, Toronto, 1979-82, mgr. quality assurance, 1982-85; dir. corp. quality assurance The Progressive/Woolley Group, Toronto, 1985-88, Manchester Plastics, Troy, Mich., 1988-97; dir. quality assurance Collins & Aikman Plastics, Manchester, Mich., 1997-99; dir. corp. quality assurance Oakwood Group, Dearborn, Mich., 1999-2000, dir. ops., 2000-01; lean mfg. coach Ford Motor Co., 2001—02, paint area mfg. super., 2002—03, quality oper. system leader, 2003—04, lead assessor quality operating sys., 2005—06, supplier tech. assistance, 2006—. Instr. Centennial Coll., Toronto, 1984-88; cons. Can. Post Corp., Toronto, 1985-86; faculty Coll. Grad. Bus. and Mgmt. U. Phoenix Online, 2002-. Contbr. articles to profl. jours. Recipient Frank E. & Bessie Angileri Quality award, 1997. Fellow Am. Soc. for Quality; mem. Soc. Automotive Engrs., Engring. Soc. Detroit, Inst. of Quality Assurance. Avocations: travel, tennis, reading, classical music, collecting stamps and coins. Home: 5539 Pinecrest Estates Dr Ann Arbor MI 48105-9351 Personal E-mail: hrnikoui@aol.com.

NIKSIC, GWEN M., biology professor; d. Thomas and Kathleen Niksic; m. Lucian Babiarz, Aug. 28, 2006. BS in Animal Sci., U. Ill., Urbana, 1990; MS in Animal Sci., U. Nev., Reno, 1993; postgrad. in Animal Sci., U. NH, Durham, 1996; PhD, U. ND, Grand Forks, 2005—. Tutor hearing impaired program Whitney Young Magnet HS, Chgo., 1985—86; grad. asst. U. Nev., Reno, 1991—93; tchg. and rsch. asst. U. NH, Durham, 1993—96; clk. Melroe, Bismarck, ND, 1997—2001; prof. math. and sci. tutor and lab instr. U. of Mary, Bismarck, 2001—04, asst. prof., 2004—. Recipient Quality Cost/Improvement award, Melroe, 1998. Mem.: Riverside Readers, Sigma Xi. Avocation: reading. Office: U of Mary 7500 University Dr Bismarck ND 58504 Home Phone: 701-224-1155; Office Phone: 701-355-8198.

NIKU, SOHEIL DANIEL, urologist; b. Tehran, Iran, Nov. 20, 1963; s. Saleh and Sara Niku; m. Doris Aghari Niku. BS, UCLA, 1985, MD, 1989. Diplomate Am. Bd. Urology, 1997. Urologist resident U. Calif., San Diego, 1989—95. Mem.: Am. Coll. Surgeons, Am. Urol. Assn. Office: 14901

Rinaldi St #205 Mission Hills CA 91345 Office Phone: 818-365-0259. Business E-Mail: sonurology@msn.com.

NILAKANTAN, VANI, medical educator, consultant, research scientist; m. Sudip Mukerji, June 28, 1992; children: Sharad Mukerji, Shefali Mukerji. BS in Zoology, U. Delhi, India, 1986; MS in Marine Biology, Annamalai U., India, 1988; MS in Environ. Engring. Sci., U. Fla., 1991; PhD, U. Ky., Lexington, 1997. Instr. Med. Coll. Wis., Milw., 2005—06, asst. prof., 2006—. Adj. asst. prof. Marquette U., Milw., 2003—05. Grantee, Med. Coll. Wis., 2005, NIH, 2007—; Nat. Merit scholar, U. Grants Commn., India., 1987—88, Rsch. fellow, U. Ky., 1992—97. Mem.: Am. Soc. Nephrology, Soc. Free Radicals in Biology and Medicine, Am. Soc. Transplantation. Achievements include research in research and development in new clinical strategies for treatment for acute renal failure. Office Phone: 414-456-4819.

NILES, JOHN GILBERT, lawyer; b. Dallas, Oct. 5, 1943; s. Paul Dickerman and Nedra Mary (Arendts) N.; m. Marian Higginbotham, Nov. 21, 1970; children: Paul Breckenridge, Matthew Higginbotham. BA in History, Stanford U., 1965; LLB, U. Tex., 1968. Bar: Tex. 1968, Calif. 1969, U.S. Dist. Ct. (cen. dist.) Calif. 1973, U.S. Ct. Appeals (9th cir.) 1973, U.S. Dist. Ct. (so. dist.) Calif. 1977, U.S. Supreme Ct. 1979, U.S. Dist. Ct. (no. dist.) Calif. 1983. Assoc. O'Melveny & Myers, Los Angeles, 1973-77, ptnr., 1978-99; of counsel, 1999—. Judge pro tem mcpl. ct. L.A.; spkr., panel mem. Practicing Law Inst., Calif. C.E.B. Served to lt. comdr. USNR, 1968-72, Vietnam. Mem. ABA, Los Angeles County Bar Assn., Am. Judicature Soc. Clubs: Bel-Air Bay (Pacific Palisades, Calif.); Calif. (Los Angeles). Avocation: sailing. Home: 1257 Villa Woods Dr Pacific Palisades CA 90272-3953 Office: O'Melveny & Myers 400 S Hope St Los Angeles CA 90071-2899 Office Phone: 213-430-6050.

NILES, THOMAS MICHAEL TOLLIVER, former business association executive; b. Lexington, Sept. 22, 1939; s. John Jacob and Rena (Lipetz) N.; m. Carroll C. Ehringhaus, July 22, 1967; children: John Thomas, Mary Chapman. BA, Harvard U., 1960; MA, U. Ky., 1962. Commd. fgn. service officer US Dept. State, Washington, 1962, U.S. ambassador to Can., Ottawa, 1985-1989; then permanent rep. EEC, Brussels; asst. sec. Europe and Can. US Dept. State, Washington, 1991-93, amb. to Greece Athens, 1993-97; v.p. Nat. Def. U., 1997-98; pres. U.S. Coun. Internat. Bus., 1999—2005. Recipient Superior Honor award Dept. State, 1982, 85, Presdl. award, 1988, 89, 94. Mem. Phi Beta Kappa

NILLES, JOHN MATHIAS (JACK NILLES), futurist; b. Evanston, Ill., Aug. 25, 1932; s. Elmer Edward and Hazel Evelyn Nilles; m. Laila Padorr, July 8, 1957. BA magna cum laude, Lawrence Coll., 1954; MS in Engring., UCLA, Los Angeles, 1964. Sr. engr. Raytheon Mfg. Co., Santa Barbara, Calif., 1956-58; section head. Ramo-Woodridge Corp., LA, 1958-59; project engr. Space Technology Lab., LA, 1960; dir. The Aerospace Corp., LA, 1961-67; sr. systems engr. TRW Systems, LA, 1967-69; assoc. group dir. The Aerospace Corp., LA, 1969-72; dir. interdisciplinary programs U. So. Calif., LA, 1972-81, dir. info. technology program, 1981-89; pres. JALA Internat. Inc., LA, 1980—. Coord. EC Telework Forum, Madrid, 1992-00; dir. Internat. Telework Assocs., & Coun., 1991-97, pres., 1993-94; chmn. Telecommuting Rsch. Inst., Inc., L.A., 1990—. Author: The Telecommunications Transportation Tradeoff, 1976, rev. edit., 2007, Japanese edit., 1977, Exploring the World of the Personal Computer, 1982, French edit., 1985, Micros and Modems, 1983, French edit., 1986, Making Telecommuting Happen, 1994, Portuguese edit., 1997, Managing Telework, 1998, Polish edit., 2003; mem. editl. bd. Revista Portuguesa de Gestao, 2000—. Capt. USAF, 1954-56. Recipient Rod Rose award Soc. Rsch. Adminstrs., 1976, Environ. Pride award L.A. Mag., 1993, Environ. Achievement award Renew Am., 1994-96, Commendation, L.A. County Bd. Suprs., 1997; inducted into Telework Hall of Fame, 1998. Mem. IEEE, IEEE Computer Soc., AAAS, Assn. Computing Machinery, Inst. Ops. Rsch. and Mgmt. Scis., World Future Soc., Calif. Yacht Club. Avocations: sailing, photography. Office: JALA Internat Inc 971 Stonehill Ln Los Angeles CA 90049-1412 Business E-Mail: info@jala.com.

NILLES, JOHN MICHAEL, lawyer; b. Langdon, ND, Aug. 20, 1930; s. John Joseph and Isabel Mary (O'Neil) N.; m. Barbara Ann Cook, June 22, 1957; children: Terese M., Daniel J., Marcia L., Thomas M., Margaret J. BA cum laude, St. Johns U., 1955; JD cum laude with distinction, U. N.D., 1958. Bar: N.D. 1958, U.S. Dist. Ct. N.D. 1958, U.S. Ct. Appeals (8th cir.) 1958, Minn. 1991. Shareholder, dir., pres. Nilles, Hansen and Davies, Ltd., Fargo, ND, 1958-90, of counsel, 1990-95; exec. v.p., gen. counsel Met. Fin. Corp., Mpls., 1990-95, First Bank F.S.B., Mpls., 1995; ret., 1996. Pres., bd. dirs. Legal Aid Soc. N.D., Fargo, 1970-76, Red River Estate Planning Coun., 1980-87; vice-chmn. disciplinary bd. Supreme Ct. N.D., 1984-90. Bd. editors N.D. Law Rev., 1957-58. Mem. exec. bd. Red. River Valley coun. Boy Scouts Am., 1959-70; bd. regents U. Mary, Bismarck, N.D., 1967-77; pres., bd. dirs. Cath. Charities, Fargo, 1959-65, Southeast Mental Health Ctr., Fargo, 1972-80. Staff sgt. USAF, 1951-54. Fellow Am. Coll. Trust and Estate Counsel (state dir. 1979-90); mem. ABA, State Bar Assn. N.D., Minn. Bar Assn., Order of Coif. Republican. Roman Catholic. Avocations: tennis, downhill skiing, cross country skiing, hunting, gun collecting. Home: 10412 Fawns Way Eden Prairie MN 55347-5117

NILLES, LAILA PADORR, musician, music company executive; b. Chgo., July 25, 1929; d. Abraham Leonard Ginsburg and Jeanette Padorr; m. Jack Mathias Nilles, July 8, 1957. MusB, Northwestern U., 1947, B of Music Edn., 1947, MusM, 1949; postgrad., Julliard Sch. Music, 1950—51, Ecoles d'Art Am. Fontainebleau, France, 1953. Founder, dir. Padorr Trio, Chgo. and LA, 1951—55, 1956—72; dir. Concerts at the Mt., LA, 1958—60; mgr., dir. Concerts West, LA, 1965—75; freelance musician LA, 1975—77; asst. dir. Protone Records, LA, 1977—82, assoc. dir., 1992—2000; v.p. Jala Internat., Inc., LA, 1982—; freelance A&R prodr., editor LA, 2000—. Dir. design for Sharing UCLA, L.A., 1984-89, Friends of Music U. So. Calif., 1984-90, Am. Youth Symphony, 1981-88. Soloist on record: Music for Flute and Piano by Four Americans, 1976; co-prodr.: 42 records, cassettes and compact discs, 1977—2001. Recipient First prize Coleman Auditions, 1956, Young Artists League, 1956. Mem. Audio Engring. Soc., Nat. Acad. Recording Arts and Scis., Musicians Union Local 47. Clubs: Calif. Yacht (Marina Del Ray). Avocations: photography, sailing, astronomy. Home and Office: 971 Stonehill Ln Los Angeles CA 90049-1412 Personal E-mail: lnilles@jala.com.

NILSEN, ARTHUR CHRISTIAN, lawyer; b. Rockville Centre, NY, Dec. 30, 1946; s. Arthur and Lillian Alfheld (Christiansen) N.; m. Linda Marie Rom Oleschlager, July 27, 1966 (div. Jan. 1977); children: Christopher James, Karla Lynn; m. Donna Jean Holmes, Apr. 22, 1978; children: Arthur Christian, Arthur Jorgen, Johanna Blanche. BS, Cornell U., 1969; MBA in Fin., JD, Samford U., 1986. Bar: Ala., Ga. Dir. ops. M.D. Anderson Tumor Inst., Houston, 1976-78; dir. exec. svcs./ops. PFM, Inc., St. Louis, 1978-83; atty. Roe & Rowell, Birmingham, Ala., 1983-86; regional ptnr. Hyatt Legal Svcs., Atlanta, 1986-88; atty. Law Offices of Frederick Hanna, Atlanta, 1988-89; mng. atty. Siler & Jonap, Atlanta, 1989-92, Law Offices of Kenneth S. Nugent, P.C., Atlanta, 1995—96, Attys. Kaufman & Assocs., P.A., Atlanta, 2003—06, Dover Law Firm, P.C., Atlanta, 2006—; mng. ptnr. Jonap & Assocs., Atlanta, 1992-94; mng. ptnr., cons. A.C. Nilsen & Assocs., Atlanta, 1994—; CEO, CFO Thomas W. Malone, P.C., Atlanta, 2001—02. Bd. dirs. Law Offices Richardson, Phoenix, Ariz. Active nat. and local Rep. coms., 1975; mem. Roswell United Meth. Choir, 1978, Bd. Stewards. Mem. ABA, ATLA, Ga. Trial Lawyer's Assn., Masons, Men's Club. Republican. Methodist. Avocations: golf, swimming, fishing, reading, writing. Office: A C Nilsen & Assocs PO Box 243 Roswell GA 30077-0243 Home: 190 Riding Trail Ct Roswell GA 30075-1758 Office Phone: 770-518-1133. Business E-Mail: artn@doverlawfirm.com.

NILSON, GEORGE ALBERT, lawyer; b. NYC, Jan. 15, 1942; s. Howard Seth and Beatrice Ethyl (McCurdy) N.; m. Elizabeth Hughes Logan, July 18, 1942; children: Scott Logan, Douglas George. BA, Yale U., 1963, LLB, 1967, M of Urban Studies, 1967. Bar: Md. 1967, U.S. Dist. Ct. Md., U.S. Ct. Appeals (4th cir.), U.S. Supreme Ct. Assoc. Piper & Marbury, Balt., 1967-73, ptnr., 1982—2006; asst. atty. gen. Md. State Law Dept., Balt., 1973-76, dep. atty. gen., 1976-82; city atty. Legal Dept., Baltimore, Md., 2006—. Chmn. Gen. Assembly Compensation Commn., Annapolis, Md., 1984-93, Commn. to Rev. Md. Elections Laws, Annapolis, 1986-87. Pres. Guilford Assn., Balt., 1990-92. Mem. Rule Day Club, The Wranglers, Sergeants Inn. Democrat. Avocations: fishing, golf. Office: Baltimore City Dept Law City Hall Ste 101 100 N Holliday St Baltimore MD 21201

NIMBACH, LAWRENCE THOMAS, securities trader, researcher; b. Mt. Clemens, Mich., May 7, 1974; s. Marian Therese McLaughlin and Thomas Nimbach; 1 child, Laura Therese. BA in Econs., U. Mich., Ann Arbor, 1996. Gen. Securities Prin. NASD, 2005. Fixed income trader H&R Block Fin. Advisors, Detroit, 1996—. Fellow: Mensa; mem.: NRA, Detroit Bond Club (assoc.). Conservative. Avocations: travel, running, skiing, hockey. Home Phone: 586-775-5768; Office Phone: 313-628-1883.

NIMETZ, MATTHEW, lawyer, investment company executive; b. Bklyn, June 17, 1939; s. Joseph L. and Elsie (Botwinik) N.; children: Alexandra Elise, Lloyd. BA, Williams Coll., 1960, LL.D. (hon.), 1979; BA (Rhodes scholar), Balliol Coll., Oxford U., Eng., 1962, MA, 1966; LL.B., Harvard U., 1965. Bar: NY 1966, DC 1968. Law clk. to Justice John M. Harlan, US Supreme Ct., 1965-67; staff asst. to Pres. Johnson, 1967-69; assoc. firm Simpson Thacher & Bartlett, NYC, 1969-74, ptnr., 1974-77; counselor Dept. of State, Washington, 1977-80, acting coord. refugee affairs, 1979-80, under sec. of state for security assistance, sci. and tech., 1980; ptnr. firm Paul, Weiss, Rifkind, Wharton & Garrison, NYC, 1981-2000; mng. dir. Gen. Atlantic LLC, Greenwich, Conn., 2000—. Commr. Port Authority NY and NJ, 1975-77; dir. Wais Markets, Inc.; mem. NY State Adv. Coun. on State Productivity, 1990-92; presdl. envoy Greece-Macedonian Negotiations, 1994-95, spl. rep. UN Sec. Gen., 1999—. Trustee William Coll., 1981-96; chmn. UN Devel. Corp., 1986-94; bd. dir. Charles H. Revson Found., 1990-98, NY State Nature Conservancy, 1997-2005; chmn. Carnegie Forum in US, Greece and Turkey, 1996-98; chmn. Ctr. for Democracy and Reconciliation in S.E. Europe, 1998—; trustee Ctrl. European U., Budapest, Hungary, 2005—, Levin Inst., 2005—. Mem. Assn. of Bar of City of NY, Coun. on Fgn. Rels. Clubs: Harvard (NYC). Office: Gen Atlantic LLC 3 Pickwick Plz Greenwich CT 06830-5538 E-mail: mnimetz@generalatlantic.com.

NIMKARN, SAROJ, endocrinologist, researcher; MD (hon.), Mahidol U., Bangkok, 1991. Lic. Am. Bd. of Pediats. and Subboard Pediat. Endocrinology. Clin. instr. pediats. dept. pediats. Siriraj Hosp., Mahidol U., Bangkok, 2001—03, asst. prof. pediats. dept. pediats. faculty medicine, 2003—04; asst. prof. pediats. Med. Coll. of Wis., Milw., 2004—05, Mt. Sinai Sch. of Medicine of NYU, NYC, 2005—. Recipient Recognition Winning Poster award, Nat. Coop. Growth Study, 1999, Fellowship Rsch. Tng. grant, Lilly Rsch. Labs., Divsn. of Eli Lilly & Co., 1999, Endocrine Soc. Endocrinology award, Endocrine Soc. of Thailand, 2003, Investigator award, 11th Asian Congress of Pediat. and 1st Asian Congress of Pediat. Nursing, 2003, Free Paper award, 44th Siriraj Sci. Ann. Meeting, Faculty of Medicine, Siriraj Hosp., 2004, grant for rsch. devel., Faculty of Medicine, Siriraj Hosp., 2001. Mem.: Pediat. Endocrine Soc. of Thailand, Asia Pacific Pediat. Endocrine Soc., Lawson Wilkins Pediat. Endocrine Soc., Med. Coun. of Thailand, The Endocrine Soc. Office: Mt Sinai Sch Medicine Box 1198 1 Gustave LLevy Pl New York NY 10029 Office Phone: 212-241-8210. Office Fax: 212-241-5405. Business E-Mail: saroj.nimkarn@mssm.edu.

NIMNI, MARCEL EPHRAIM, biochemistry educator; b. Buenos Aires, Feb. 1, 1931; came to U.S., 1955; s. Sam and Sarah Dora (Freedman) N.; children: Elizabeth, Brian Sam; m. Fabiola Cordoba, Dec. 21, 1996. BS in Pharmacy, U. Buenos Aires, 1954, PhD, 1960; MS, U. So. Calif., 1957; MD honoris causae (hon.), Maimonides U., 2002. Cert. nutrition specialist. Rsch. fellow U. So. Calif., LA, 1960-61, asst. prof. biochemistry, 1963-66, assoc. prof., 1966-72, prof., 1972—, prof. surgery, 1990—, prof. orthop., 1980—; dir. biology Don Baxter Labs., Glendale, Calif., 1962. Cons. Hancock Labs., Glendale, Calif., 1962; cons. Hancock Labs., Anaheim, Calif., 1970-78, pathobiochemistry study sect. NIH, 1980-85, orthopaedics and biomechanics study sect., 1987-90; mem. NASA Tissue Engring. Rev. Bd., 2002—; dir. biochemistry rsch. Orthopaedic Hosp., L.A., 1980-91; cons. Tillots Pharma Labs., Basle, Switzerland, 1986-94; dir. surg. rsch. Chidlren's Hosp. of L.A., 1991-98, dir. Tissue Engring. Lab., 1998—; mem. adv. bd. Maimonides U., Buenos Aires. Editor: Collagen: Biochemistry, Biotechnology and Molecular Biology, Vols. I-V,1987-91; editor Matrix, 1980-93, Connective Tissue Rsch., 1973-91, Jour. Orthopaedic Rsch., 1989-94; patentee collagen tech., transderman drug delivery. Recipient Merit award NIH, 1987; rsch. grantee NIH Arthritis Inst., 1966-94, NIH Aging Inst., 1982-2000. Fellow AAAS, Am. Coll. Nutrition, Soc. Biomaterials (Founders award 1986); mem. Am. Inst. Nutrition, Am. Assn. Biochem. and Molecular Biology. Office: Univ So Calif EDM-191 Keck Sch Medicine Los Angeles CA 90033 Office Phone: 323-224-5067. Personal E-mail: nimni007@aol.com.

NIMOITYN, PHILIP, cardiologist; b. Phila., Pa., Mar. 6, 1951; s. Benjamin Solomon and Edith (Ornstein) N.; m. Hillary Rachel Saul, June 11, 1989. BS in Biology with distinction, Phila. Coll. Pharmacy and Sci., 1972; MD, Thomas Jefferson U., 1976. Cert. Nat. Bd. Med. Examiners, Am. Bd. Internal Medicine, Am. Bd. Cardiovascular Disease. Intern Hahnemann U. Hosp., Phila., 1976-77; resident in internal medicine Thomas Jefferson U. Hosp., Phila., 1977-79, cardiovascular disease fellow, 1979-81, instr. medicine, 1981-90, clin. asst. prof., 1990—; attending physician Pa. Hosp., Phila., 1995—; cons. physician Wills Eye Hosp., Phila., 1981—; attending physician Penn. Hosp., Phila., 1995—. Author: (with others) Artificial Cardiac Pacing, 1984, Quick Reference to Cardiovascular Disease, 1987, Cardiac Emergency Care, 1991; contbr. articles to profl. jours. Recipient Cert. of Merit for Sci. Exhibits AMA, 1974, 2d prize for sci. exhibits Ind. State Med. Assn., 1974. Fellow Am. Coll. Cardiology; mem. AMA, Pa. Med. Soc., Phila. County Med. Soc. Office: 1128 Walnut St Ste 401 Philadelphia PA 19107-5568 Home Phone: 610-525-8734; Office Phone: 215-629-1158. Business E-Mail: philip.nimoityn@mail.tju.edu.

NIMS, ARTHUR LEE, III, federal judge; b. Oklahoma City, Jan. 3, 1923; s. Arthur Lee and Edwina (Peckham) N.; m. Nancy Chloe Keyes, July 28, 1950; children: Chloe, Lucy. BA, Williams Coll., 1945; LLB, U. Ga., 1949; LLM in Taxation, NYU, 1954. Bar: Ga. 1949, NJ 1955. Practice law, Macon, Ga., 1949-51; spl. atty. Office Chief Counsel, IRS, NYC and Washington, 1951-55; assoc. McCarter & English, Newark, 1955-61, ptnr., 1961-79; judge US Tax Ct., Washington, 1979-88, chief judge, 1988-92, sr. judge, 1992—. Mem. standing com. Episcopal Diocese of Newark, 1971-75; pres. Colonial Symphony Soc., Madison, NJ, 1975-78. Served to lt. (j.g.) USNR, 1943-46. Recipient Kellogg award Williams Coll., 1990, Career Achievement award The Tax Soc. NYU, 1990. Fellow Am. Coll. Tax Counsel; mem. ABA (sec. sect. taxation 1977-79), NJ Bar Assn. (chmn. sect. taxation 1969-7l, Am. Law Inst., J. Edgar Murdock Am. Inn of Ct. (pres. 1988-92). Office: US Tax Ct 400 2nd St NW Washington DC 20217-0002 *

NING, SHOUCHENG, cancer biologist, head and neck surgeon; b. Gao-Qing, Shandong, China, Aug. 1, 1951; came to U.S., 1988; s. Yun-You and Shu-Zheng (Gao) N.; m. Ling-Yi Zhang, Sept. 10, 1979; 1 child, Kevin X.B. MD, Shanghai 2d Med. U., 1978, MS, 1982, PhD, 1986. Asst. prof. Shanghai 2d Med. U., 1978-81, attending surgeon, 1982-88, assoc. prof., vice chief surgeon, 1988—; rsch. fellow Stanford (Calif.) U. Med. Sch., 1988-93, rsch. scientist, 1993—. Author: Modern Treatment in Internal Medicine, 1987, China Yearbook of Stomatology, 1988; contbr. articles to Internat. Jour. Radiation Oncology and Biol. Physics, Jour. Cellular Physiology. Recipient award for outstanding young scientists Shanghai Assn. Sci. and Tech., 1985, nat. award in cancer rsch. China Ministry Pub. Health, 1986, nat. award for advancement of sci. and tech. China. Nat. Coun. for Edn., 1994. Mem. Am. Assn. for Cancer Rsch., N.Am. Hyperthermia Soc., Chinese Med. Assn. Office: Stanford U Med Ctr A010 300 Pasteur Dr Palo Alto CA 94304-2203

NING, TAK HUNG, physicist, microelectronic technologist; b. Canton, China, Nov. 14, 1943; came to U.S., 1964; s. Hong and Kwai-Chan (Lee) N.; m. Yin Ngao Fan; children: Adrienne, Brenda. BA in Physics, Reed Coll., 1967; MS in Physics, U. Ill., 1968, PhD in Physics, 1971. IBM Rsch. Div., Yorktown Heights, N.Y., 1973-78, mgr. bipolar devices and cirs., 1978-82, mgr. Advanced Silicon Technology Lab., 1982-83, mgr. silicon devices and technology, 1983-90, mgr. VLSI design and tech., 1990-91; IBM fellow, 1991—. Patentee in field. Fellow IEEE (assoc. editor Trans. on Electron Devices 1988-90, J.J. Ebers award 1989, Jack a. Morton award 1991), Am. Phys. Soc.; mem. NAE (Pan Wen-Yuan award 1998). Home: 3085 Weston Ln Yorktown Heights NY 10598-1962 Office: IBM T J Watson Research Ct Yorktown Heights NY 10598

NING, XUE-HAN (HSUEH-HAN NING), physiologist, researcher; b. Peng-Lai, Shandong, People's Republic of China, Apr. 15, 1936; came to U.S., 1984; s. Yi-Xing and Liu Ning; m. Jian-Xin Fan, May 28, 1967; 1 child, Di Fan. *Grandfather Xi-Quan was a doctor of traditional Chinese medicine and master of Si-Nai-Tang (the meaning is "seek truth from facts") Chinese Pharmacy. Father was the general manager of Li-Hua Textile Mill, Tsingdao, China. Wife, MD Shanghai First Medical College, 1960 an emeritus doctor and associate research professor in Shanghai Research Institute of Sports Science. She was a medical and physiological researcher in the Research and Training Group of high jumper Zhu Jian-Hua, who broke the world record 3 times.* MD, Shanghai 1st Med. Coll., People's Republic of China, 1960; post grad., Chinese Traditional Medicine Coll. for Advanced Study, 1960—61; postgrad. in Physiology, U. Mich., 1984—87. Rsch. fellow, rsch. assoc., leader cardiovasc. rsch. group Shanghai Inst. Physiology, Acad. Sinica, 1973—83, head, assoc. prof. cardiovasc. rsch. unit, 1960—87, prof. and chair hypoxia dept., 1988-90, vice chairperson academic com., 1988-90; NIH internat. rsch. fellow U. Mich., Ann Arbor, 1984-87; prof. and dir. Key Lab of Hypoxia Physiology Academia Sinica, Shanghai, 1989-90. Acting leader, High Altitude Physiology Group, Chinese mountaineering and sci. expdn. team to Mt. Everest, 1975; leader High Altitude Physiology Group, Dept. Metall. Industry of China and Ry. Engring. Corps, 1979; vis. prof. dept. physiology Mich. State U., East Lansing, U. Mich., U. Wash. Med. Sch., 1989-97; affiliate prof., U. Wash., 1997—; rsch. scientist Children's Hosp. and Regional Med. Ctr., Seattle, 1997—. Author: High Altitude Physiology and Medicine, 1981, Reports on Scientific Expedition to Mt. Qomolungma, High Altitude Physiology, 1980, Environment and Ecology of Qinghai-Xizang (Tibet) Plateau, 1982, Self-Health Care at High Altitude, 2006; mem. editl. bd. Chinese Jour. Applied Physiology, 1984-1992, Acta Physiologica, 1988-90, Chinese Jour. Physiology (Taiwan) 2004-; contbr. articles to profl. jours. Recipient Merit award Shanghai Sci. Congress, 1977, All-China Sci. Congress, Beijing, 1978, Super Class award Academia Sinica, Beijing, 1986, 1st Class award Nat. Natural Scis., Beijing, 1987, 2d Class award Acad. Sinica Sci. and Technol. Achievements, Beijing, 1992, # 1 Best Article award Tzu-Chi Med. Jour., Taiwan, 1995. Mem. Am. Physiol. Soc., Am. Heart Assn., Internat. Soc. Heart Rsch., Royal Soc. Medicine, Internat. Soc. for Mountain Medicine. Achievements include first to electrocardiography record at summit of Mt. Everest; research in predictive evaluation of mountaineering performance; characteristics for high altitude adaptation and acclimatization; effect of medicinal herbs on cardiac performance; cardiovascular adaptation and resistance to hypoxia and ischemia; injury threshold of short-cycle-intermittent hypoxia and gene expression in heat; the critical temperature 30 degrees celsius "temperature protectine threshold" for modulating myocardial energy, metabolic pathways, and gene expression to resist ischemia and hypoxia; the 28 degrees celsius "temperature injury threshold" for cardiac contractility in the beating heart in vivo; hypothermic cross adaptation protects heart from subsequent ischema and hypoxia by preserving signaling for mitochondrial biogenesis, activating stress pathways and inactivating apoptosis to maintain myocardial stability and improve functional recovery during reperfusion and reoxygenation. Home: 7033 43rd Ave NE Seattle WA 98115-6015 Office: Wash Dept Pediats CHRMC 4800 Sand Point Way NE Box G0035 Seattle WA 98105-0371 Business E-Mail: xh@u.washington.edu.

NINIVAGGI, DANIEL A., lawyer, manufacturing executive; b. NYC, June 27, 1964; m. Katie Ninivaggi; children: Caleb, Matthew, Jane, Jack. BA, Columbia U., 1986; MBA, U. Chgo., 1988; JD, Stanford U., 1991. Bar: Ill. 1991, NY 1995, Mich. 2003. Assoc. Skadden, Arps, Slate, Meagher & Flum, Winston & Strawn, LLP, NYC, 1992—98, ptnr., 1998—2003; v.p., sec., gen. counsel Lear Corp., Southfield, Mich., 2003—04, sr. v.p., sec., gen. counsel, 2004—06, exec. v.p., sec., gen. counsel, 2006—. Office: Lear Corp 21557 Telgraph Rd PO Box 5008 Southfield MI 48086-5008 Office Phone: 248-447-1500. Business E-Mail: dninivaggi@lear.com. *

NINOW, KEVIN J., chemicals executive; With Huntsman Corp., Salt Lake City, 1989—, project engr., process control group leader, mgr. tech., ops. mgr. C4's; plant mgr. C4's; plant mgr. oxides and olefins Huntsman Corp., v.p. internat. mfg., v.p. European Petrochemicals, sr. v.p. European Petrochemicals, 1999—2003, divsn. pres. base chems. and polymers, 2003—. Office: Huntsman Corp 500 Huntsman Way Salt Lake City UT 84108 Office Phone: 801-584-5700. *

NIRENBERG, DARRYL D., lawyer; b. Middletown, NY, Sept. 23, 1959; s. Alex Jack and Sandra (Levine) N. BA cum laude, Colgate U., 1981; JD, George Washington U., 1987. Legis. asst. Senator S.I. Hayakawa, Washington, 1981-82; profl. staff Agr. Com. US Senate, 1983-86, assoc. Rep. counsel Fgn. Rels. Com. US Senate, 1987-89; Rep. dep. staff dir. Fgn. Rels. Com. US Senate, 1990-91; chief of staff Senator Jesse Helms, Washington, 1991-95; ptnr., Public Policy, Def. and Nat. Security practices, and hiring ptnr. Patton Boggs LLP, Washington; vice chmn. NY State Coll. Reps., 1979-80, Fairfax County Young Rep., Va., 1982-83, campaign aide Sen. Jacob K. Javits, 1980; counsel Rep. Platform Com. 2000, Presd. Inauguration Com. 2001; mem. Nat. Moot Ct. Team George Washington U. Mem. Phi Alpha Theta. Jewish. Office: US Senate Com on Fgn Relations 452 Dirksen Bldg Washington DC 20510-0001 also: Patton Boggs LLP 2550 M St Nw Washington DC 20037-1350 Office Phone: 202-457-6022. Office Fax: 202-457-6315. Business E-Mail: dnirenberg@pattonboggs.com.

NIRENBERG, LOUIS, mathematician, educator; b. Hamilton, Ont., Can., Feb. 28, 1925; arrived in U.S., 1945, naturalized, 1954; s. Zuzie and Bina (Katz) Nirenberg; m. Susan Blank, Jan. 25, 1948; children: Marc, Lisa. BSc, McGill U., Montreal, 1945, DSc (hon.), 1986; MS, NYU, 1947, PhD, 1949; DSc (hon.), U. Pisa, Italy, 1990, U. Paris Dauphine, 1990, McMaster U., Can., 2000. Mem. faculty NYU, 1949—, prof. math., 1957—, dir. Courant Inst., 1970—72. Visitor Inst. Advanced Study, 1958; hon. prof. Nannkai U., Zhejiang U. Author rsch. articles. Recipient Crafoord prize,

Royal Swedish Acad., 1982, Nat. medal of Sci., 1995; fellow NRC, 1951—52, Sloan Found., 1958—60, Guggenheim Found., 1966—67, 1975—76, Fulbright, 1965. Mem.: NAS, Ukrainian Acad. Sci. (fgn.), Accademia de Scienze e Lettere (fgn.), Istituto Lombardo, Accademia dei Lincei (fgn.), French Acad. Scis. (fgn.), Am. Philos. Soc., Am. Math. Soc. (v.p. 1976—78, M. Bocher prize 1959, L.P. Steele prize 1994), Am. Acad. Arts and Scis., European Acad. Scis. (hon.). Home: 221 W 82nd St New York NY 10024-5406 Office: Courant Inst 251 Mercer St New York NY 10012-1185 Home Phone: 212-724-1069. Business E-Mail: nirenl@cims.nyu.edu.

NIRENBERG, MARSHALL WARREN, biochemist; b. NYC, Apr. 10, 1927; s. Harry Edward and Minerva (Bykowsky) Nirenberg; m. Perola Zaltzman, July 14, 1961. BS in Zoology, U. Fla., 1948, MS, 1952; PhD in Biochemistry, U. Mich., 1957. Postdoctoral fellow Am. Cancer Soc. at NIH, 1957—59; postdoctoral fellow USPHS at NIH, 1959—60; mem. staff NIH, 1960—; rsch. biochemist, chief lab. biochem. genetics Nat. Heart, Lung and Blood Inst., NIH, Bethesda, Md., 1962—. Co-recipient Louisa Gross Horowitz prize Columbia, 1968, Nobel prize in physiology or medicine, 1968; recipient Molecular Biology award, NAS, 1962, award in biol. scis., Washington Acad. Scis., 1962, medal, HEW, 1964, Modern Medicine award, 1963, Harrison Howe award, Am. Chem. Soc., 1964, Nat. Medal Sci., Pres. Johnson, 1965, Hildebrand award, Am. Chem. Soc., 1966, Research Corp. award, 1966, A.C.P. award, 1967, award merit, Gairdner Found., Can, 1967, Prix Charles Leopold Meyer, French Acad. Scis., 1967, Franklin medal, Franklin Inst., 1968, Albert Lasker Med. Research award, 1968, Priestly award, 1968. Fellow: AAAS, NY Acad. Scis.; mem.: NAS, Pontificial Acad. Scis., Leopoldina Deutsche Akademie der Naturforscher, Soc. Devel. Biology, Soc. for Study Devel. and Growth, Washington Acad. Scis., Harvey Soc. (hon.), Biophys. Soc., Am. Acad. Arts and Scis., Am. Chem. Soc. (Paul Lewis award enzyme chemistry 1964), Am. Soc. Biol. Chemists. Achievements include research in mechanism protein synthesis, genetic code, nucleic acids, regulatory mechanisms in synthesis macromolecules, and neurobiology.

NIRMEL, KRISHNA, neurosurgeon; b. Kenya, Sept. 5, 1950; BSc with honors, McGill U., Montreal, Que., Can., 1972, MD, 1976. Diplomate Am. Bd. Neurol. Surgery, Nat. Bd. Med. Examiners, lic. Med. Coun. Can., physician Mass., Pa. Intern in surgery Royal Victoria Hosp., McGill U., Montreal, 1976—77; resident in neurosurgery NYU/Bellevue Med. Ctr., NYC, 1977—79, Mass. Gen. Hosp., Harvard Med. Sch., Boston, 1980—82, chief resident, asst. in neurosurgery, 1983; resident in neurology Longwood Ave. VA Neurology Program, Harvard Med. Sch., Boston, 1979—80; fellow in pediat. neurosurgery Children's Hosp. of Phila., U. Pa., 1982; clin. practice neurosurgery, 1984—. Clin. fellow in neurology Harvard U., 1979—80, clin. fellow in surgery, 1980—83; clin. and rsch. fellow in neurosurgery Mass. Gen. Hosp., 1984; mem. staff dept. surgery-neurosurgery Boston U. Med. Ctr., 1984—; cons. in neurosurgery John Graham Headache Rsch. Ctr., Faulkner Hosp., Boston, 1984—90; dir. Pain Mgmt. Ctr. Metrowest, Med. Ctr., Natick, Mass., 1991—93. Contbr. articles to profl. jours. Fellow: ACS, Am. Back Soc.; mem.: AMA, New Eng. Pain Assn., New Eng. Neurosurg. Soc., Mass. Neurosurg. Soc., Joint Sect. on Neurotrauma and Critical Care, Congress Neurol. Surgeons, Am. Heart Assn., Am. Assn. for Study of Headache, Am. Assn. Neurol. Surgeons (joint sec. tumors, pediat. sect.). Office: The Nirmel Neurol Inst Inc 10 Union St Natick MA 01760 Office Phone: 508-650-1022. Office Fax: 508-653-7420. Business E-Mail: tnni@verizon.net.

NIRO, CHERYL, lawyer; b. Feb. 19, 1950; d. Samuel James and Nancy (Canezaro) Ippolito; m. William Luciano Niro, July 1, 1979; children: Christopher William, Melissa Leigh. BS with highest honors, U. Ill., 1972; JD, No. Ill. U., 1980. Bar: Ill. 1981, U.S. Dist. Ct. (no. dist.) Ill. 1981, U.S. Ct. Appeals (7th cir.) 1990, U.S. Supreme Ct. 1999, cert.: negotiator, mediator, facilitator, arbitrator. Ptnr. Quinlan & Carroll, Chgo., 1999—2005; pres. Judicial Dispute Resolution, Inc., Chgo.; exec. dir. commn. on professionalism Ill. Supreme Ct., Chgo., 2006—. Spl. counsel to Atty. Gen., 1996—99; tchg. asst. program instrn. lawyers mediation and negotiation workshops and guest lectr. Harvard Law Sch. Program of Instrn. for Lawyers Harvard U.; mem. appt. panel U.S. Ct. Appeals (7th cir.); found. dir. Nat. Ctr. for Conflict Resolution Edn.; mem. copyright arbitration royalty panel U.S. Libr. of Congress, 2000—05; mem. London Ct. of Internat. Arbitation. Named 100 Women Making A Difference, Today's Chgo. Woman Found., 2001; named one of Ten Most Influential Women Lawyers in Ill, Am Lawyer Media, 2000; named to Today's Chgo. Woman Mag. Hall of Fame, 2002. Mem.: ATLA, ABA (comm multijurisdictional practice, standing comt bar servs, dispute resolution sect coun, house delegs), Nat. Caucus State Bar Assns. (pres.-elect), Internat. Ctr. for Healing the Law (mem. bd. adv.), Internat. Bar Assn., Ill. State Bar Assn. (mem assembly 1993, bd govs 1994—97, treas 1995—96, 2d vpres 1997—98, pres 1999—2000, standing comt legal-related educ pub), Ill Trial Lawyers Asn. Home: 633 N East Ave Oak Park IL 60302-1715 Office: Prudential Plz 180 N Stetson Ave Ste 1950 Chicago IL 60601 Office Phone: 312-363-6210. Office Fax: 312-365-6218. Business E-Mail: cheryl.niro@ilsccp.org.

NIRSCHL, ROBERT PHILLIP, orthopedic surgeon; b. South Milwaukee, Wis., Aug. 28, 1933; s. Boyd A. and Helen (Wozny) N.; m. Mary Ann Oleniczak, June 21, 1958; children: Suzanne, Robert C., Julie. Student, Coll. Holy Cross, 1951-53, Marquette U., 1953-54; MD, Med. Coll. Wis./Marquette U., 1958; MS, U. Minn., 1965. Diplomate Am. Bd. Orthop. Surgery. Intern St. Mary's Hosp., Duluth, Minn., 1958-59; resident in orthop. Mayo Clinic, Rochester, Minn., 1959-63; lt. comdr. USN, Washington, 1963-65; pvt. practice Arlington, Va., 1965—. Attending orthop. surgeon Va. Hosp. Ctr., Arlington, dir. Hand Surgery Svc., 1975—85, v.p. med. staff, 1980—83, mem. hosp. med. exec. com., 2006—; chief orthop. surgery No. Va. Cmty. Hosp., 1971—82; founding dir. Nirschl Orthop. Ctr. for Sports Medicine and Joint Reconstrn., 1974—, Nirschl Orthop. Sport Med. Ctr. Orthop. Sports Medicine Fellowship Program Va. Hosp. Ctr., Arlington, 1987—; mem. clin. faculty Georgetown U. Med. Ctr., 1965—; orthop. cons. Pres.'s Coun. Phys. Fitness, Washington, 1981—87; mem. sports sci. com. USTA, NYC, 1987—94; chief orthopedic sports med. cons. Athletic Dept. Marymount U., 2006—; course dir. numerous symposia in field. Author: Arm Care, 1981, rev. edit., 1996, Isoflex Exercise System, 1983; chief med. editor Orthop. Today, 1983-93; mem. editl. bd. The Physician and Sportsmedicine, 1992-2005, The Med. Sentinel, 1996-02, Orthopedics Today, 2003-; creator 9 video programs; contbr. chpts. to books and over 125 articles to profl. publs.; patentee in field. Chmn. Jeffersonian Health Policy Found., Williamsburg, Va., 1994—97; mem. Va. Bd. Medicine, 2000—04; trustee Marymount U., Arlington, 2005—. Grantee Pfizer Inc., 1992-93, Sano Corp, 1993-94, Iomed Corp., 1999-2000. Mem.: AMA, Am. Orthop. Assn., VA Orthop. Soc. (Lifetime Career award 2005), Arlington County Med. Soc. (pres. 1977, chmn. legis. com. 1987—2004, Welburn award 1995), Med. Soc. Va. (chmn. sports medicine com. 1973—84, trustee polit. action com. 1990—2002, legis. com. 1995, liability com. 2005—, trustee polit. action com. 2006—), Va. Orthop. Soc. (pres. 1998—99, career award 2005), Washington Orthop. Soc., Ea. Orthop. Assn., Soc. Tennis Medicine and Sci. (exec. com.), Am. Orthop. Soc. Sports Medicine (ethics com. 1992—97, bd. dels. 2002—), Am. Acad. Orthop. Surgery (health fin. com. 1994—2000, comm. and state soc. coms. bd. of counselors 2000—03, bd. counselors 2000—06), Washington Golf and Country Club. Republican. Roman Catholic. Avocation: fitness activities. Office: Nirschl Orthop Ctr Sports Medicine & Joint Reconstrn 1715 N George Mason Dr Ste 504 Arlington VA 22205-3670 Home Phone: 703-237-8706; Office Phone: 703-525-2200. Personal E-mail: nirschlorthopaedics@comcast.net.

NISBET, TOMA A., nursing administrator; Diploma with honors, St. Mark's Hosp. Sch. Nursing, 1967; BSN with honors, No. Ill. U., 1969, MSN with honors, 1973. Internship Winnebago County Dept. Pub. Health-Health Adminstrn. & Family Planning; night staff nurse Sycamore Municipal Hosp., Ill., 1967-68; evening relief supr., charge nurse DeKalb County Nursing Home, Ill., 1969; pub. health nurse DeKalb County Health Dept., Ill., 1969-71; divsn. dir. nursing svcs. Winnebago County Dept. Pub. Health, Rockford, Ill., 1974-84; pub. dir. nursing svcs. divsn. of health & med. svcs. State of Wyo., Cheyenne, 1985-87, policy devel. & spl. projects state program mgr. divsn. of health & med. svcs., 1987-88, state bd. nursing exec., 1988—. Spokesperson for NLX D-A-Y Pub. Rels. for Burroughs Welcome, N.Y.C., 1987; project coord. for health svcs. No. Ill. U. Sch. Nursing, DeKalb, 1973-74, instr. 1979-84. Author of numerous articles. Awarded numerous rsch. grants. Mem. ANA, Nat. Coun. State Bds. of Nursing (del. 1988-95, AEC com. mem. 1990-94, mem. nomination com. 1991-92, ednl. program task force 1994-95, alternate examination com. 1994-95), Wyo. Commn. on Nursing & Nursing Edn., Wyo. Orgn. Nurse Execs., Wyo. State Bd. of Nursing Home Adminstrs. (sec. 1988-89, vice-chmn. 1990-95), Wyo. Advanced Practitioner of Nursing Orgn.

NISBETT, ROBERT F., music educator, consultant; b. Niles, Ohio, Aug. 12, 1937; s. Joes and Miriam Alice (Rex) Nisbett; m. Ellen Ruth Stoken, June 4, 1966; children: Heath, Tamara. BS in Piano and Music Edn., Kent State U., Ohio, 1960, MA in Piano and Music History, 1963; PhD in Music History, Ohio State U., Columbus, 1979; study in piano, Cleve. Inst. Music, 1956—57. Music tchr. Ohio Pub. Sch., Warren, 1959—60, North Canton, 1960—63; piano tchr. Kent State U., 1963—64; asst. Ohio State U., Columbus, 1964—65; instr. to asst. prof. Colo State U., Ft. Collins, 1965—82, assoc. prof., 1982—, asst. dept. chmn., 1988—89, chair dept. music, theater, and dance, 1989—94. Vis. prof. U. Wales, Swansea, 1986; spkr. in field. Contbr. articles to profl. jours., chapters to books. Recipient Am. Music Rsch. award, Sinfonia Found., 1976, Rsch. award for study in black music, NEH, 1982. Home: 6336 Little Elm St North Las Vegas NV 89031

NISENHOLTZ, MARTIN ABRAM, telecommunications executive, educator; b. Phila., Apr. 1, 1955; s. Louis William and Rhoda Greta (Koenig) N.; m. Anne Ermine Stockler, July 26, 1987; children: Johanna, Marjorie. BA, U. Pa., 1977, MA, 1979. Research scientist NYU, NYC, 1979-83; mgr. Ogilvy & Mather, NYC, 1983-84, v.p., 1984-89, sr. v.p., 1989-94; dir. content strategy Ameritech Corp., Chgo., 1994-95; pres. N.Y. Times Electronic Media Co., 1995-99; CEO N.Y. Times Digital, 1999—2005; sr. v.p. digital ops. The N.Y. Times Co., 2005—. Mem. ops. Ogilvy & Mather Direct, 1992—94; adj. assoc. prof. NYU, 1983—; bd. dirs. internet advtsg. bur. Ctr. for Comm., 1999; bd. dirs. Yellow Pages Group. Mem. Annenberg Sch. Alumni Bd., 1996—; bd. dirs. N.Y. Leukemia and Lumphoma Soc., 2005—. Recipient Merrill Panott Citizenship award, 1997, Ten award, 2003; grantee Nat. Endowment Arts, 1981. Mem.: Online Pubs. Assn. (founding chmn. 2001—04), Interactive Svcs. Assn. (dir. 1985—94, chmn. 1991, Disting. Svc. award 1994). Office: NY Times Co 820 8th Ave New York NY 10018

NISH, WAYNE PAUL, chef, restaurant owner; b. NYC, July 23, 1951; s. John and Dorothy (Bugelli) N.; children: Caitlin Nicola, Alexandra Jane. Student, Long Island U., 1969-70, Cornell U., 1972-73, CCNY, 1973-74; diploma, N.Y. Restaurant Sch., 1983. Assoc. chef The Quilted Giraffe, NYC, 1984-87; pvt. chef Anne Bass, NYC, 1987-88; exec. chef La Colombe d'Or, NYC, 1988-89; chef, co-owner March Restaurant, NYC, 1990—. Adv. bd. mem. N.Y. Restaurant Sch., 1991—. Fund raiser Women's Camapign Fund, 1992, 93, 94. Recipient Three Stars award N.Y. Times, 1988, 92, 95, Forbes Mag., 1989, Four Stars award Forbes Mag., 1993, 94; named Am.'s top Restaurant Zagat Survey, 1993, 94, 95. Mem. Am. Inst. Wine and Food, James Beard Found. Democrat. Roman Catholic. Avocations: cooking, photography, driving. Office: March Restaurant 405 E 58th St New York NY 10022-2302 Home: 405 E 58th St New York NY 10022-2302

NISHIMURA, JOSEPH YO, retired retail executive, accountant; b. Berkeley, Calif., Nov. 4, 1933; s. Masamoto and Kimiko (Ishihara) N.; m. Joyce Toshiye Mori, Sept. 1, 1956; children: Brenda Joyce, Stephen Lloyd. AB cum laude, Princeton U., 1956; MBA, Stanford U., 1961. CPA, Calif., N.Y.; cert. Employee Benefit Specialist. Audit supr. Touche Ross & Co., San Francisco, 1961-66; contr. Scott Co. of Calif., Oakland, 1966-67, Purity Stores, Inc., Burlingame, Calif., 1967-69; pres. Cubit Sys. Corp., Burlingame, 1969-72; sr. v.p. Golden West Fin. Corp., Oakland, 1972-73; exec. v.p. Victory Mkts., Inc., Norwich, NY, 1973-90; gen. ptnr. Mori Enterprises, 1994—2005. Dir. Carl's Drug Co., Rome, N.Y., 1988-90, mem. site devel. com., Wakefern Food Corp., Edison, N.J., 1996—. V.p., bd. dirs. Chenango Meml. Hosp., Norwich, 1981-87; bd. dirs. United Fund, Norwich, 1984-90, N.Y. State Food Mchts. Assn., 1988-90, Binghamton (N.Y.) Philharmonic, 1988-98, treas., 1990-93; cons. Mori Charitable Unitrust, 2005-. Served to lt. (j.g.) USN, 1956-59; Japan. Mem. AICPA, Calif. Soc. CPAs, Marbella Country Club, Princeton (N.Y.C.) Club. Democrat. Presbyterian.

NISHIMURA, PETE HIDEO, oral surgeon; b. Hilo, Hawaii, Aug. 7, 1922; s. Hideichi and Satsuki N.; m. Tomoe Nishimura, June, 1949; children— Dennis Dean, Grant Neil, Dawn Naomi. Student, U. Hawaii, 1940-44; D.D.S., U. Mo., 1947; MSD., Northwestern U., 1949. Practice dentistry specializing in oral surgery, Honolulu, 1952—; pres. Oral Surgery Group, 1978—. Mem. coun. Nat. Bd. Dental Examination; dir. Hawaii Dental Svc., 1962-85, pres., 1970-72, 76-78; pres. State Bd. Dental Examiners, Delta Sigma Delta, Fedn. Dentaire Internat. Served with U.S. Army, 1952-54. Named Disting. Alumni, U. Mo. Hawaii, 2004; recipient Citation for outstanding pub. svc. toward the devel. of state plan for emergency mgmt. resources, Dir. Emergency Planning, Exec. Office of Pres. of U.S., 1968, Lifetime Achievement award, Hawaii Dental Assn. Fellow Am. Coll. Dentists, Internat. Coll. Dentists; mem. ADA, Hawaii Dental Assn. (past pres., Lifetime Achievement award 2006), Delta Dental Plans Assn. (dir.), Honolulu County Dental Soc., Hawaii Soc. Oral Surgeons, Am. Assn. Oral and Maxillofacial Surgeons, Western Soc. Oral and Maxillofacial Surgeons, Am. Assn. Dental Examiners, Pierre Fauchard Acad. (citation for oustanding contbn. to arts and sci. of dentistry 1987). Democrat. Home: Apt 606 4389 Malia St Honolulu HI 96821 Office: 848 S Beretania St Honolulu HI 96813-2551 Personal E-mail: hilopete@aol.com.

NISHIYAMA, CHIAKI, economist, educator; b. Fukuoka-ken, Japan, Aug. 9, 1924; s. Michiki and Teruko (Tsuji) N.; m. Shigeko Okabe, June 9, 1957; children: Keita, Mikiko. BA in Econs., Rikkyo U., Tokyo, 1950; MA in Polit. Sci., U. Chgo., 1952, PhD in Social Thought, 1960, postgrad. in econs., 1959-60. Instr. U. Chgo., 1955—56, lectr. econs., 1956—57; assoc. prof. Rikkyo U., 1962-64, prof. econs., 1964-90, prof. emeritus, 1990—. Sr. rsch. fellow Hoover Instn., Stanford U., 1977—; prof. econs. Grad. Sch. Internat. Mgmt., U. Japan, 1994-97; lectr. Tng. Inst., Min. Trade and Industry, Japanese Govt., 1964-66, Gakushuin U., 1970-71, Waseda U., 1972-74; exec. dir. Assembly on US-Japan Econ. Policy, 1972-76; prime minister's spl. envoy to White House, 1971, 75; specialist counselor Japan Employers' Assn., 1975-85; fellow Woodrow Wilson Internat. Ctr. for Scholars, 1978-79; del. European Assembly, Strasbourg, France, 1982; world travel for Japanese Min. Fgn. Affairs, Japan External Trade Orgn., 1968-82; lectr. various univs., US and Europe, 1976-94; mem. Am. Citizen to Citizen Econ. and Fin. Mgmt. Del. to USSR, 1991; spl. envoy of Japan to Germany, Czechoslovakia, Hungary, Bulgaria, Ukraine, Russia, 1991. Author numerous books including: Lecture on Modern Economics, 1964, Free Economy, Its Policies and Principles, 1974, The Price for Prosperity, 1974, A Monetary History and Analysis of the Japanese Economy 1968-70, 1974, Reflection on Japanese Economy, 1976, Monetarism, 1976, The Last Chance for Creativity, Liberty and Prosperity, 1981, Human Capitalism, 1982, The Fourth Philosophy, Vol. I, 1982, Vol. II, 1983, No Limits to Growth, 1984, The Essence of Hayek, 1984, The Japanese Economy, 1987, Paradigm Shift, 1987, Japanese Economy and Life Tomorrow, 1988, A New Economics Under a New Paradigm, 1991, The End of Recession, 1994, Depression or New Prosperity, 1998, Market Economy: New Way, 1999, Chicago Boys, 2003, Japan in the New Century and Blackship, 2005, Reason and Its Limits from Asian Paradigm, 2005; editl. bd. Jour. Internat. Money and Fin., 1981—. Hon. fellow Inst. Econ. Affairs, London, 1976—; mem. adv. bd. Econ. Inst. Paris, 1984-86, Carl Menger Inst., Wien, 1984; councilor The Daiwa Securities Welfare Found., 1994—. Recipient Japan Econ. Lit. award Japan Econ. Jour., 1974; Eahart fellow, 1960-61, E.C. Nef fellow, 1958-59; grantee Relm, 1962-64, Ford, 1965-66, Lilly, 1966-67, Bank of Japan, Bankers Assn. Japan, other fin. orgns., 1978-83. Mem. Am. Enterprise Inst. (adj. scholar), Am. Econ. Assn., Econometric Soc., Japan Econs. Assn., Econ. Assn., Statis. Soc., Mont Pelerin Soc. (pres. 1980-82, sr. v.p. 1982-85, hon. v.p. 1986-88), Japan Econ. Rsch. Ctr. (spl. mem. 1964). Episcopalian. Office: Nishiyama-Kenkyushitsu 5-15-18 Kamiuma Setagaya-ku 154-0011 Tokyo Japan Personal E-mail: nichiko@classicmsn.com.

NISKANEN, WILLIAM ARTHUR, JR., economist, think-tank executive; b. Bend, Oreg., Mar. 13, 1933; s. William Arthur and Nina Elizabeth (McCord) Niskanen; m. Kathryn Washburn; children: Lia, Pamela, Jaime. BA, Harvard U., 1954; MA, U. Chgo., 1955, PhD, 1962. Staff economist RAND Corp., Santa Monica, Calif., 1957—62; staff dir. U.S. Dept. Def., Washington, 1962—64; divsn. dir. Inst. Def. Analyses, Washington, 1964—70; asst. dir. Office of Mgmt. and Budget, Washington, 1970—72; prof. U. Calif., Berkeley, 1972—75; chief economist Ford Motor Co., Dearborn, Mich., 1975—80; prof. UCLA, 1980—81; mem. Coun. Econ. Advisers, Washington, 1981—85; chmn. CATO Inst., Washington, 1985—. Author: Bureaucracy and Representative Goverment, 1971, Reaganomics, 1988, Policy Analysis and Public Choice, 1998, Going Digital, 1998, Autocratic, Democratic and Optimal Government, 2004, After Enron: Lessons for Public Policy, 2005; editor: Regulation mag., 1990—96. Founder Nat. Tax Limitation Com. Mem.: Atlantic Econ. Assn. (past pres.), Pub. Choice Soc. (past pres.), Am. Econ. Assn. Republican. Office: Cato Inst 1000 Massachusetts Ave NW Washington DC 20001-5400 Home Phone: 202-546-1097; Office Phone: 202-789-5236. Business E-Mail: wniskan@cato.org.

NISSEN, DAVID R., corporate financial executive; B, Northwestern U., 1975; MBA, U. Chgo. Staff strategic planning and bus. devel. G.E. Captial, 1981—83; mktg. G.E. Card Svcs., 1983—87, gen. mgr., 1987—90, G.E. U.S. Consumer Fin. Svcs., 1990—93; officer G.E., 1996—2001, sr. v.p., 2001—; pres., CEO G.E. Consumer Fin., 2002—. Named one of Ten Retail Banking Heros, Retail Banker Internat., 2003. Avocations: golf, jet skiing, tennis. Office: GE Global Consumer Fin 1600 Summer St Stamford CT 06927 *

NISSEN, STEVEN E., cardiologist, researcher; b. Toledo, Ohio, 1949; m. Linda Butler. BS, U. Mich., Ann Arbor; MD, U. Mich. Sch. Medicine, Ann Arbor. Intern internal medicine Univ. Calif. Davis, Sacramento, resident internal medicine; fellowship in cardiology Chandler Med. Ctr. Univ. Ky., Lexington; cardiologist Cleveland Clinic, 1992—, dir. coronary ICU, 1992—97, sect. head clinical cardiology, 1992—2002, vice chmn. dept. cardiology, 1993—2002, interim chmn., dept. cardiovascular med., 2006, chmn., dept. cardiovascular med., 2006—, dir., Joseph J. Jacobs Ctr. for Thrombosis and Vascular Biology; prof. medicine Ohio State U. Mem. and chmn. CardioRenal adv. panel US FDA; spl. govt. employee US FDA Committees; mem. med. & sci. adv. bd. Forbes Medi-Tech Inc.; vis. prof. at med. colleges and universities internationally and nationally. Contbr. articles to profl. jours., chapters to books; mem. editl. bd. Internat. Jour. Cardiac Imaging, Cardiology Today, Clinical Cardiology; editor: Current Cardiology Reports, 2006—; sr. consulting editor Journal of American College of Cardiology, 2002—. Named one of The World's Most Influential People, TIME Mag., 2007; recipient Award for Outstanding Rsch. in Cardiovascular Rsch., Gill Heart Inst., U. Ky., 2004. Mem.: Am. Coll. Cardiology (pres., chmn. bd. trustees 2006—, ednl. products com., info. tech. com.). Achievements include development of intravascular ultrasound imaging; published rsch. on cardiovascular problems caused by Cox-2 inhibitor drugs, such as Vioxx & Celebrex. Avocation: bicycling. Office: Cleveland Clinic Mailcode F 15 9500 Euclid Ave Cleveland OH 44195 Office Phone: 216-445-6852. Business E-Mail: nissens@ccf.org. *

NISSEN, VARINA, employment services executive; MBA, Melbourne Bus. Sch., Australia. Dir. corp. svcs. Sydney Airports Corp. Ltd.; CEO Australia, exec. dir. Asia Pacific Burson-Marsteller; mng. dir. Australia and New Zealand Manpower, Inc., 2003—06, sr. v.p. global mktg. and comm., 2006—. Bd. mem. Essendon, Bankstown, Hoxton Pk., Camden Airports, Australia; dir. Com. Econ. Devel., Australia. Office: Manpower Inc 5301 N Ironwood Rd Milwaukee WI 53217 Office Phone: 414-961-1000. *

NISSENBAUM, ROBERT JAY, law librarian, educator; b. NYC, July 31, 1952; s. I. Joseph and Lillian E. (Spingeld) N. BA in internat. affairs, George Washington U., 1973; MLS, Pratt Inst., 1976; JD, Western New Eng. Coll., 1980. Bar: Mass. 1980, Tex. 1982, U.S. Dist. Ct. (fed. dist.) Mass. 1981, U.S. Dist. Ct. (fed. dist.) Conn. 1981, U.S. Ct. Appeals (1st cir.) 1981, U.S. Ct. Appeals (5th cir.) 1984. Law/legis. ref. libr. Conn. State Libr., Hartford, 1980-81; law libr. ref. dept. U. Tex., Austin, 1981-82, libr. collection mgmt./reference, lectr. law, 1982-83, head reference svc., lectr. law, 1983-84; dir. law libr., assoc. prof. law Cleve. State U., 1984-88; dir. law libr., prof. law Loyola Law Sch., LA, 1988—2004; prof. law, dir. Leo T. Kissam Meml. Libr. Fordham U. Sch. Law, NYC, 2004—. Vis. prof. law U. Tex., Austin, summer 1992, U. Internat. Bus. and Econs., Beijing, 1995; chmn. govt. documents spl. interst sect. Ad Hoc Com. on Citation Reform, 1983-94. Author: (with Saltalamachia) Fundamentals of Legal Research Assignments and Instructor's Manual, 3d edit., 1985; book rev. editor Criminal Law Bull., 1995%; contbr. articles to profl. jours., chpts. to books. Matthew Bender scholar, 1984. Mem. Assn. Am. Law Schs. (law libr. jour. com. 1983-84, chmn. com. on stds. 1985-87, rep. to Am. Nat. Stds. Inst. 1986-87, mem. nat. com. law libr. resources 1985-87, chmn. spl. com. citation form 1986-87), Assn. Jesuit Colls. and Univs. (treas. conf. law librs. 1993-94, chmn.-elect conf. 1994-95), Order of Coif, Beta Phi Mu. Jewish. Avocations: theater, classical music, rare books. Office: Fordham U Sch Law 140 W 62nd St New York NY 10023 Office Phone: 212-636-7609. Office Fax: 212-930-8818. E-mail: rnissenbaum@law.fordham.edu.

NISSENSON, ALLEN RICHARD, physician, educator; b. Chgo., Dec. 10, 1946; s. Harry and Sylvia Lillian (Chapnitsky) N.; m. Charna H. Karp, May 28, 1978; 1 child, Ariel Rose. BS in Medicine, Northwestern U., 1967, MD, 1971. Diplomate Am. Bd. Internal Medicine, bd. cert. internal medicine and nephrology. Intern in medicine Michael Reese Hosp. and Med. Ctr., Chgo., 1971-72, resident in internal medicine, 1972-74; fellowship in nephrology Northwestern U., Chgo., 1974-76; assoc. medicine Northwestern U. Med. Sch., Chgo., 1976-77; asst. prof. medicine UCLA Sch. Medicine, 1977-82, assoc. prof. medicine, 1982-88, prof. medicine, 1988—; dir. dialysis program UCLA Ctr. for the Health Scis., 1977—, med. dir. renal mgmt. strategies, assoc. dean David Geffen Sch. Medicine, 2006—. Adj. attending physician Northwestern Meml. Hosp., Chgo., 1976-77; asst. attending physician UCLA Ctr. for Health Scis., 1977-82, assoc. attending physician, 1988—; attending physician nephrology Wadsworth VA Hosp., 1978—; cons. on peritoneal dialysis Baxter-Travenol Labs., 1981—; mem. nephrology adv. com. Nephrology Nursing Edn.

Grant, Calif. State U., 1983-90; vice chmn. Forum of End Stage Renal Disease Networks, 1988-91; mem. sci. adv. bd. Nat. Kidney Found., 1989-91, chmn. coun. on clin. nephrology, dialysis and transplantation, 1989-91; cons. on End Stage Renal Disease reimbursement Rand Corp., 1990—, others. Editor-in-chief Advances in Renal Replacement Therapy, 1993—, Hemodialysis Internat., 2004—, Medscape Nephrology, 2006; mem. editl. bd. Dialysis and Transplantation, 1978—, UCLA Health Insights, 1981-89, Perspectives in Peritoneal Dialysis, 1983—, Internat. Jour. Artificial Organs, 1984—, Seminars in Dialysis, 1987—, Am. Jour. Nephrology, 1989—, Am. Jour. Kidney Diseases, 1989—, Geriat. Nephrology and Urology Jour., 1989—; mem. editl. adv. bd. Contemporary Dialysis, 1983—, Nephrology Practice Today, 1989—, Hematopoietic Therapy Index and Revs., 1993—, Primary Care Reports, 1994—; editl. cons. Am. Jour. Nephrology, 1981-88; contbr. chpts. to books, abstracts and articles to profl. publs. Recipient Nat. Kidney Found. So. Calif. Cmty. Svc. award, 1981, Pres.'s award Nat. Kidney Found., 1998, Lifetime Achievement award in hemodialysis U. Mo., 2007; Robert Wood Johnson policy fellow Office of Sen. Paul Wellstone, 1994-95. Fellow ACP; mem. Am. Soc. for Artifical Internal Organs, Am. Fedn. for Clin. Rsch., Am. Soc. Nephrology, Internat. Soc. Nephrology, Internat. Soc. Artificial Organs, Western Soc. for Clin. Investigation, European Dialysis and Transplant Assn., N.Am. Soc. for Dialysis and Transplantation, Renal Physicians' Assn. (bd. dirs. 1993—, sec. bd. dirs. 1994—, pres. 1999-2001), Calif. Renal Physicians (bd. dirs. 1987—). Office: UCLA Med Ctr Dialysis Ctr Ste 565-59 200 Medical Plaza Los Angeles CA 90024-6945 E-mail: anissenson@mednet.ucla.edu.

NISSINEN, MIKKO PEKKA, dancer, performing arts company executive, artistic director; arrived in U.S., 1987; Grad., Finnish Nat. Ballet Sch., 1977; postgrad., Leningrad Acad. Ballet Sch., 1979-80. Mem. corps de ballet Finnish Nat. Ballet, Helsinki, 1977-79, soloist, 1980-82; grand sujete Dutch Nat. Ballet, Amsterdam, The Netherlands, 1982-84; soloist Basel (Switzerland) Ballet, 1984-87, San Francisco Ballet, 1987-88, prin. dancer, 1988-96; artistic dir. Marin Ballet, 1996-97, Alberta Ballet, Calgary, Canada, 1998—2002, Boston Ballet, 2001—. Guest artist La Bayadere Nat. Ballet Can., 1989; guest artist Oberlin Dance Collective, 1993; bd. dirs. Le Don Des Etoiles; guest tchr. Royal Acad. Danciang, 1993, Kennedy Ctr. Ednl. Program, 1994, Nat. Ballet Sch., Toronto, 1994; lectr. on dance history and state of dance today Stanford U., Lethbridge U., St. Mary's Coll., Christensen Soc.; artistic com. N.Y. Choreographic Inst.; juror Prix de Lausanne, Benois de la Danse, Helsinki Internat. Ballet Competition. Dancer Sleeping Beauty, San Francisco Ballet, Swan Lake, Bizet Pas de Deux, Handel-a Celebration, Haffner Symphony, Variations de Ballet, Rodin, Rodeo, Con Brio, Ballet d'Isoline, Giuliani: Variations on a Theme, Tchaikovsky Pas de Deux, Symphony in C, Theme and Variations, Ballo della Regina, The Nutcracker, Airs de Ballet, Maelstrom, Dark Elegies, Harvest Moon, Napoli, Job, The Wanderer Fantasy, In the middle, somewhat elevated, Calcium Light Night, Le Corsaire Pas de Deux, Dreams of Harmony, Pulcinella, The Dream, Don Quixote, Giselle, A Midsummer Night's Dream, Les Biches, Sleeping Beauty, Pyrrich Dances, Masse, Le Tombeau de Couperin, Symphony in C, The Four Temperaments, The Prodigal Son, Rodin, Pierrot Lunaire, La Fille mal gardée, Swan Lake, Henze, Five Tangos, In and Out, Bits and Pieces, Jeu de Cartes, Gala Des Etoiles, Can. Internat. Ballet Gala, 1989, 1990, 1991, 1992, 1993, 1994, 1995, Reykjavik Arts Festival, 1990, Internat. Ballet Gala, Kuopio, Finland, 1992, Vail, Colo., 1993, Night of Stars Ballet Gala, Helsinki, 1993; profiled in nat. and internat. radio and TV programs CNN Worldwide Report, 1992, featured on cover Dance Mag., 1992; choreographer Full Evening Nutcracker, Marin Ballet, 1996, Alta. Ballet, 2000, Nutcracker, 2003—04, Swan Lake, 2004. Recipient 1st prize Nat. Dance Competition, Kuopio, Finland, 1978; fellowship exec. program for non-profit leaders, Stanford Univ. Mem.: Artistic Com. NY Coreographic Inst. Office: Boston Ballet 19 Clarendon St Boston MA 02116-6100 *

NISSL, COLLEEN KAYE, lawyer; b. McMinnville, Oreg., June 3, 1950; d. Anton Arthur and Luella Elaine (Kerr) N.; m. Roger Philip Sugarman; children: Jordan Elizabeth, Zachary Max. BA, Ohio Wesleyan U., 1972; JD, U. Toledo, 1975. Bar: Ohio 1975, U.S. Dist. Ct. (so. dist.) Ohio 1977, U.S. Supreme Ct. 1980. Litigation sect. chief Atty. Gen. Ohio, Columbus, 1976-82; sr. counsel Battelle Meml. Inst., Columbus, 1982-84; v.p., asst. gen. counsel Borden Chemical, Inc., Columbus, 1984—. Mem. ABA, Ohio Bar Assn., Columbus Bar Assn. (chmn. alt. dispute resolution com.). Democrat. Roman Catholic. Avocations: skiing, bicycling, antiques. Office: Borden Inc 180 E Broad St 27th Fl Columbus OH 43215

NISSLY, KENNETH L., lawyer; b. Mesa, Ariz., Oct. 25, 1952; m. Marjorie J. Nissly, Aug. 17, 1974; children: Jennifer, Peter. BA, San Diego State U., 1974; JD, U. Calif., San Francisco, 1977. Bar: Calif. 1977, US Dist. Ct. (No. Dist.) Calif., US Dist. Ct. (Ea. Dist.) Calif., US Ct. Appeals (9th Cir.), US Dist. Ct. (Ea. Dist.) Tex., US Dist. Ct. (Ea. Dist.) Va., US Dist. Ct. (Dist. Del.), US Ct. Appeals (Fed. Cir.). Assoc. Thelen, Marrin, Johnson & Bridges, San Jose, Calif., 1977-85, ptnr., 1985—98; ptnr., litig. dept. Thelen Reid & Priest LLP, 1998—, mng. ptnr. Silicon Valley office. Mem.: Calif. State Bar Assn., Santa Clara County Bar Assn. (judge pro tem neighborhood small claims ct. program 1985—), ABA, Order of Coif, Phi Beta Kappa. Avocation: flying. Office: Thelen Reid & Priest LLP 225 W Santa Clara St Ste 1200 San Jose CA 95113-1723 Office Phone: 408-292-5800. Office Fax: 408-287-8040. Business E-Mail: kennissly@thelenreid.com.

NISSOV, MORTEN, telecommunications industry executive; arrived in US, 1998; s. Per Nissov and Rose Loehndorf; m. Susanne Christiansen, Nov. 18, 1995; children: Morten Christian, Sarah Christina. MEE, Tech. U. Denmark, Lyngby, 1994, PhD, 1997; student in Business, NYU, NYC, 2007—. Sr. mem. tech. staff Tyco Telecom., Eatontown, NJ, 1998—2000, dir., 2000—. Contbr. chapters to books. Mem.: IEEE. Achievements include 11 patents in field. Office: Tyco Telecomms 250 Industrial Way West Eatontown NJ 07724

NITECKI, JOSEPH ZBIGNIEW, librarian; b. Dabrowa Górnicza, Poland, Jan. 31, 1922; came to U.S., 1951, naturalized, 1956; s. Henryk W. and Antonina S. N.; m. Sophie V. Zboinski, June 17, 1945; children: Zbigniew H., Danuta A. BA in Philosophy, Wayne State U., 1955; MA, Roosevelt U., 1959; MA in L.S., U. Chgo., 1963. Various profl. and adminstrv. positions in libraries U. Chgo., 1961-63, Chgo. City Coll., 1963-66, U. Wis., Milw., 1967-70, Temple U., Phila., 1970-78; prof., exec. dir. libraries U. Wis., Oshkosh, 1978-80; dir. libraries SUNY, Albany, 1980-88, vis. prof. Sch. Info Sci. and Policy, 1988-90, prof. emeritus, 1990—. Cons. library issues. Author, editor compiler and reviewer in field; ref. and manuscript reader. Served with Polish Armed Forces under Brit. command, 1939-48. Recipient 1st. prize Polish Émigré Poetry Contest, 2001. Mem. ALA, Beta Phi Mu. Home: 430 Coburg Village Way Rexford NY 12148-1461 E-mail: jzniteckisr@aol.com.

NITHOO, ROVINDRANATH, pharmacist; b. Souillac, Mauritius, Nov. 29, 1967; came to U.S., 1988; s. Mohunlall and Taramanee (Khooblall) N.; m. Veena Ramyead, Apr. 19, 1997. BS in Pharmacy, Mass. Coll. Pharmacy, 1993. Registered pharmacist. Pharmacist cons. CVS/Revco Drug, Youngstown, Ohio, 1994—. Recipient Cert. of Accreditation of Diabetes Care, Nat. Inst. Pharmacist Care Outcomes, 1999. Mem. Am. Pharm. Assn. Home: 466 Tailor Way Lansdale PA 19446-4036

NITIKMAN, FRANKLIN W., lawyer; b. Davenport, Iowa, Oct. 26, 1940; s. David A. and Janette (Gordon) N.; m. Adrienne C. Drell, Nov. 28, 1972. BA, Northwestern U., 1963; LLB, Yale U., 1966. Bar: Ill. 1966, US Dist. Ct. (no. dist.) Ill. 1967, US Tax Ct. 1972, Fla. 1977, DC 1981. Assoc. McDermott, Will & Emery, Chgo., 1966-72, ptnr., 1973—2006, counsel, 2007—. Co-author: Drafting Wills and Trust Agreements, 1990. Bd. dirs. Owen Coon Found., Glenview, Ill., 1985—, Jewish Fedn. Met. Chgo., Jewish United Fund, 1994—2003, Spertus Inst. Jewish Studies, Chgo., 1991—, chmn. bd., 1999—2002. Fellow Am. Coll. Trust and Estate Coun., Am. Bar Found.; mem. Standard Club, Arts Club (Chgo.). Home: 365 Lakeside Pl Highland Park IL 60035-5371 Office: McDermott Will & Emery LLP 227 W Monroe St Ste 4700 Chicago IL 60606-5096 Office Phone: 312-984-7614. Business E-Mail: fnitikman@mwe.com.

NITOWSKY, HAROLD MARTIN, physician, educator; b. Bklyn., Feb. 12, 1925; s. Max and Fannie (Gershowitz) N.; m. Myra Heller, Nov. 28, 1954; children— Fran Ellen, Daniel Howard. AB, N.Y. U., 1944, MD, 1947; MS, U. Colo., 1952. Intern Mt. Sinai Hosp., NYC, 1947-48; resident pediats. U. Colo. Med. Center, 1948-50; USPHS postdoctoral fellow U. Colo., 1950-51; staff Sinai Hosp., Balt., 1953-67, dir. pediat. rsch., 1960-67; faculty Johns Hopkins Sch. Medicine, 1953-67, assoc. prof. ob-gyn., pediats., molecular genetics, 1962-67; prof. pediats. and genetics Albert Einstein Coll. Medicine, 1967—. Cons. Nat. Inst. Child Health and Human Devel., 1966—; Sr. surgeon USPHS, 1951-53 Contbr. articles on nutrition, metabolism, genetics to profl. jours. Mem. Am. Pediat. Soc., Soc. Pediat. Rsch., Am. Soc. Human Genetics. Home: 25 Devonshire Rd New Rochelle NY 10804-3925 Office: Albert Einstein Coll Med Dept Ob-Gyn Divsn Reproductive Genetics 1695 Eastchester Rd Bronx NY 10461-2374 Personal E-mail: nidoc@aol.com.

NITSCHKE-SHAW, DEBRA ANN, education educator, dean; d. Edward John and Mary Elizabeth Nitschke; m. Edward Houghton Shaw II, Aug. 9, 1975; children: Nathaniel Houghton Shaw, Lindsay Ludlow Shaw. BA, New England Coll., Henniker, NH, 1975; MEd, Keene State Coll., Keene, NH, 1977; PhD, Fielding Univ., Santa Barbara, Calif., 1997. Special edn. tchr. Dame Sch., Concord, NH, 1975—81, kindergarten tchr., 1981—98, Henniker Cmty. Sch., 1983—85; dir. tchr. edn. New Eng. Coll., 1985—. Tchr. cons. Campus Compact NH, 1996—; adv. bd. mental health Henniker Br. Concord NH; sch. bd. mem., chair Henniker Sch. Bd., 1987—93. Author: The Partnership Development Tool Kit, 1998; contbr. chapters to books. Sch. bd. mem. Henniker Sch. Dist., 1987—93, sch. bd. chair, 1991—93. Recipient Tchr. of the Yr., New Eng. Coll., 1999, Henniker Sch. Dist., 1984. Mem.: CEC, ASCD. Office: New Eng Coll Box 22 Ctr Ednl Henniker NH 03242 Business E-Mail: dnitschke@nec.edu.

NITTOLY, PAUL GERARD, lawyer; b. Bklyn., July 13, 1948; s. Edward Joseph and Philomena (Lorenzo) Nittoly; m. Maryann Racioppi, May 31, 1970; children: Melissa Beth, Matthew Edward. AB, Rutgers U., 1970; JD, NYLS, 1973. Bar: N.J., U.S. Dist. Ct. NJ 1973, U.S. Supreme Ct. 1979, U.S. Ct. Appeals (3d cir.) 1990, U.S. Dist. Ct. (so. and ea. dist.) NY 1998, cert.: NJ Supreme Ct. (trial atty. civil and criminal law). Asst. prosecutor, sr. trial atty. Essex County Prosecutor's Office, Newark, 1974-79; ptnr. Shanley & Fisher, P.C., Morristown, NJ, 1979-99, Drinker Biddle & Shanley LLP, Florham Park, NJ, 1999—2003, Drinker Biddle & Reath, LLP, Florham Park, 2003—. Moot trial ct. judge Seton Hall Law Sch., Newark, 1982—; lectr. symposium perinatal malpractice ACOG and Rutgers U. Med. Sch., Morristown, NJ, 1984; mem. practitioner's adv. group U.S. Sentencing Commn., 1992—2002. Author: Readings in White Collar Crime, 1991; mem. editl. adv. bd. Corporate Criminal Liability Reporter; contbr. chapters to books. Pres. C. Willard Heckel Am. Inn. of Ct., 1995—97, master; del. adv. Am. Bd. Trial Advs.; pres. Legal Svcs. Found. Essex County. Capt. US Army, 1972. Mem.: ABA, Assn. Fed. Bar State N.J. (trustee 2000—), Trial Attys. N.J. (pres. 2005—06), Assn. Criminal Def. Attys. N.J., Nat. Assn. Criminal Def. Lawyers, Morris County Bar Assn., Essex County Bar Assn. (pres. 1998—99, Samuel S. Saiber Profl. Achievement award 2005), N.J. Bar Assn., Park Ave. Club (Morristown), Delta Upsilon. Roman Catholic. Home: 275 Meetinghouse Ln Mountainside NJ 07092-1305 Office: Drinker Biddle & Reath LLP 500 Campus Dr Fl 4 Florham Park NJ 07932-1047 Office Phone: 973-549-7180. Business E-Mail: paul.nittoly@dbr.com.

NITZARIM, YOEL DAVID, language educator; b. Chgo., Aug. 29, 1949; s. Maurice and Elaine Pearl Smith; m. Esther Marsha Nitzarim; children: Rachel Sarah, Gavriella Leebah. BA, Northeastern Ill. U., Chgo., 1974, MEd, 1983. Cert. secondary edn. in English Ill. ESL tchr. Kibbutz Newe Eitan Regional H.S., Israel, 1976—77, Kibbutz Maoz Haim Elem. Sch., Israel, 1976—77, Morton Jr. Coll., Cicero, Ill., 1988; ESL tchr. Soviet refugees Truman Coll./ The Jewish Vocat. Svc. Temple Menorah, Chgo., 1989, 1991—92; ESL instr. Rogosin H.S., Migdal Ha'Emeq, Israel, 1978—79, ORT Israel Vocat. H.S., Osefia, Israel, 1978—79; adult English seminar tchr. Cultural Ctr. Kfar Tabor, Israel, 1978—79; prep. seminar course biology Oranim Coll., Tivon, Israel, 1979; Hebrew and Jewish social studies tchr. Jewish Reconstructionist Congregation, Evanston, Ill., 1982—83; Jewish social studies tchr. B'nai Tikvah, Deerfield, Ill., 1982—83; English tchr. Aquinas Cath. H.S., Chgo., 1980—82, St. Benedict H.S., Chgo., 1984—86, Austin Career Edn. Ctr., Chgo., 1989—92; writing tchr. Columbia Coll., Chgo., 1988; asst. prof. English East-West U., Chgo., 1999—2002; instr. English Benedictine U., Lisle, Ill., 2002—03; instr. English composition Coll. Lake County, Grayslake, Ill., 2005—07, 2007, McHenry County Coll., Crystal Lake, Ill., 2006—. Author: (essays, poetry, photography, short stories) Affair of the Mind; contbr. articles to profl. jours. Founding mem. Nat. Campaign for Tolerance, a project of the So. Poverty Law Ctr., 2005—; charter mem. US Holocaust Meml. Mus.; founding sponsor Martin Luther King, Jr. Nat. Meml., Washington. Mem.: English Teachers Assn. of Israel, US Holocaust Meml. Mus. Jewish. Avocations: reading, writing, music, travel, dogs. Office Phone: 847-543-2550. Personal E-mail: Ynitzari1@aol.com.

NITZE, WILLIAM ALBERT, government official, lawyer, not-for-profit developer, energy executive; b. NYC, Sept. 27, 1942; s. Paul Henry and Phyllis (Pratt) N.; m. Ann Kendall Richards, June 5, 1971; children: Paul Kendall, Charles Richards. BA, Harvard U., 1964, JD, 1969; BA, Oxford U., 1966. Bar: N.Y. 1970, U.S. Supreme Ct. 1987. Assoc. Sullivan and Cromwell, NYC, 1970-72; v.p. London Arts, Inc., NYC, 1972-73; counsel Mobil South, Inc., NYC, 1974-76; gen. counsel Mobil Oil Japan, Tokyo, 1976-80; asst. gen. counsel exploration and producing divsn. Mobil Oil Corp., NYC, 1980-87; dep asst. sec. for environment, health and natural resources U.S. Dept. State, Washington, 1987-90; pres. Alliance to Save Energy, Washington, 1990-94, Gemstar Group, Washington, 2001—05; asst. adminstr. for internat. activities U.S. EPA, Washington, 1994-2001; chmn. GridPoint, Inc., Washington, 2003—. Chmn. Oceana Energy Co., Washington, 2006—; mem. adv. com. Sch. Advanced Internat. Studies, Washington, 1982—95, professorial lectr., 1993—94, 2001—; vis. scholar Environ. Law Inst., Washington, 1990. Trustee Aspen Inst., Queenstown, Md., 1988—, Krasnow Inst., Fairfax, Va., 1996—2001, mem. adv. bd., 2004—; bd. dirs. Charles A. Lindbergh Fund, Mpls., 1990—94, Nat. Symphony Orch. Assn., Washington, 1990—2002, Atlantic Coun. US, Washington, 2002—, Galapagos Conservancy, Falls Church, Va., 2001—, vice chmn., 2002—03, chmn., 2003—; bd. dirs. Climate Inst., Washington, 2001—, vice chmn., 2001—02, chmn., 2002—, Alliance to Save Energy, 2001—. Mem.: Coun. on Fgn. Rels., Assn. Bar City NY, Links Club, Cosmos Club, Met. Club. Republican. Episcopalian. Avocations: running, piano, collecting art. Home: 1537 28th St NW Washington DC 20007-3059 Office: Ste 100 1785 Mass Ave NW Washington DC 20036 Office Phone: 202-331-2485. Business E-Mail: wnitze@gridpoint.com.

NITZKI-GEORGE, DIANE M., pharmacist, medical writer; d. Rosemary F. and Edward H. Nitzki, Raymond F. Nitzki (Stepfather); m. Gerald J. George, May 22, 1982; 1 child, Michael L. George. B in Chemistry, No. Ill. U., 1976; B in Pharmacy, Creighton U., 1980; MBA, Keller Grad. Sch., 1992. Registered pharmacist Nebr., 1980, Ill., 1982. Staff pharmacist Bishop Clarkson Meml. Hosp., Omaha, 1980—82, Luth. Gen. Hosp., Park Ridge, Ill., 1982—87; inpatient pharmacy mgr. U.S. Naval Hosp., Great Lakes, Ill., 1987—89; pharmacy mgr. Parkside Luth. Hosp., Park Ridge, Ill., 1989; clin. info. mgr. Baxter Healthcare Corp., Deerfield, Ill., 1990—2002; med. writer DNG Consulting, Deerfield, Ill., 2002—; clin. pharmacist Evanston Hosp. Home Infusion Svc., Evanston, Ill., 2003—. Author: Generic Alternatives to Prescription Drugs, Extended Stability for Parenteral Drugs, 3d edit. Vol. webmaster Holy Cross Sch. & Ch., Deerfield, Ill., 1999—; vol. middle sch. sci. fair judge, 1999—2003, 2005—; active Highland Park Music Club, 2003—. Recipient Achievement award, Baxter Healthcare Corp., 1991—97, Svc. award, Rho Chi Honor Soc., 1980, Pres.'s award for Sci. Achievement, Arnar-Stone Labs., 1978, others. Mem.: Am. Soc. Health-Sys. Pharmacist, Am. Med. Writers Assn. Achievements include worked closely with FDA to import an injectable multivitamin drug to the U.S. during a period of national shortage in which patients were at risk of injury (1997). Avocation: singing. Office: DNG Consulting 401 Locust Place Deerfield IL 60015 E-mail: dngconsulting@comcast.net.

NIVARTHI, RAJU NAGA, anesthesiology educator; b. Nandyal, India, June 16, 1964; came to U.S., 1993; s. Kameswara Sarma and Suseelamma Nivarthi; m. Aparna Nagaraju Nivarthi; children: Nidhi, Aditya. BSc with Chemistry, Zoology and Botany, Sri Venkateswara U., Tirupati, India, 1984; MSc in Biochemistry, Sri Kirshnadevaraya U., Anantapur, India, 1986; PhD, U. Hyderabad, 1996. Fellow Sch. Life Scis., U. Hyderabad, India, 1987-93; rsch. asst. prof. dept. anesthesiology NYU Med. Ctr., NYC, 1996, scientist, 1996-99, Wyeth-Ayerst Rsch., Pearl River, NY, 1999-2001; sr. scientist, mgr. analytical biochemistry Bristol-Myers Squibb, Syracuse, NY, 2001—05, mgr. immunology and molecular biology, biologics quality control, 2005—. Contbr. articles to profl. jours. Jr. Rsch. fellow Coun. Sci. and Indsl. Rsch., India, 1987, Sr. Rsch. fellow Coun. Sci. and Indsl. Rsch., 1990, Postdoctoral fellow NIH, 1998; recipient cert. of merit Pharmacia & Biotech Prize for Young Scientists, 1997, named 2000 Outstanding Scientist of 20th Century, 1998, Internat. Biographical Ctr. Mem. AAAS, Acad. Med. Cmty., Am. Chem. Soc., Am. Soc. Anesthesiologists, Am. Soc. Biochemistry and Molecular Biology, Internat. Anesthesia Rsch. Soc., Internat. Soc. for Study of Xenobiotics, Nat. Geographic Soc., N.Y. Acad. Scis. Office: Bristol-Myer Squibb 6000 Thompson Rd East Syracuse NY 13057-5050 Home: 161 North Way Camillus NY 13031-1253 Office Phone: 315-432-9612. Personal E-mail: rnivarthi@yahoo.com.

NIVEN, JAMES GRAHAM, auctioneer, art appreciator, philanthropist; b. London, 1945; s. David and Primula (Rollo) Niven; m. Fernanda Wetherill (div. 1995); children: Eugenie, Fernanda; m. Lee Auchincloss, Oct. 22, 2005. BA, Harvard Coll. Gen. ptnr. Pioneer Associates Co., 1982—98; chmn. bd. Global Natural Resources, 1989—94; auctioneer Sotheby's (North & South Am.) Holdings, Inc., NYC, 1997—, sr. v.p., dir. bus. devel., 1997—2000, vice chmn, 2000—. Trustee MoMA, NYC, 1988—, chmn. trustee com. on film and media; trustee Ralph Lauren Ctr. Cancer Care & Prevention, NYC; founding mem., spl. projects com. Meml. Sloan-Kettering Cancer Ctr., NYC, overseer, mgr., 1978—. Luncheon co-chmn. United Hosp. Fund Honors, 2006. Recipient Award for Excellence in Philanthropy, Soc. Meml. Sloan-Kettering Cancer Ctr., 2005. Office: Sothebys 1334 York Ave New York NY 10021 Office Phone: 212-606-7549.

NIVISON, DAVID SHEPHERD, language educator, philosopher; b. Farmingdale, Maine, Jan. 17, 1923; s. William and Ruth (Robinson) N.; m. Cornelia Green, Sept. 11, 1944; children: Louise, Helen Thom, David Gregory, James Nicholas. AB summa cum laude, Harvard U., 1946, MA, 1948, PhD, 1953. Instr. Chinese Stanford U., 1948-52, Ford Found. faculty fellow, 1952-53, instr. Chinese and philosophy, 1953-54; Fulbright research scholar Kyoto, Japan, 1954-55; lectr. philosophy Stanford U., 1955-58, asst. prof. Chinese and philosophy, 1958-59, assoc. prof., 1959-66, prof., 1966-88, Walter Y. Evans-Wentz prof. Oriental Philosophies, Religions and Ethics, 1983-88, chmn. dept. philosophy, 1969-72, 75-76, acting chmn. dept. Asian langs., 1985-86, emeritus, 1988—. Author: The Life and Thought of Chang Hsüeh-ch'eng, 1738-1801, 1966, Chinese trans., 2003, The Ways of Confucianism: Investigations in Chinese Philosophy, 1996, Chinese trans., 2006; co-author: Chinese Language, Thought and Culture: Nivison and His Critics, 1996; editor, co-compiler: Stanford Chinese Concordance Series, 1979; co-editor: Confucianism in Action, 1959, Studies on the Modern Text of the Bamboo Annals (in Chinese), 2002; contbr. articles to profl. jours. and encys. Served with AUS, 1943-46. Recipient Prix Stanislas-Julien Inst. de France, 1967; Am. Council Learned Socs. fellow, 1973; John Simon Guggenheim fellow, 1973-74 Mem. Assn. Asian Studies, Am. Philos. Assn. (v.p. Pacific div. 1978-79, pres. 1979-80), Am. Oriental Soc. (Western br. v.p. 1964-65, sec. 1965-70, pres. 1971-72), AAUP (pres. No. Calif. Conf. 1964-66), Internat. Acad. Chinese Culture (Beijing, Peoples Republic of China), Phi Beta Kappa. Home: 1169 Russell Ave Los Altos CA 94024-5066 Business E-Mail: dnivison@stanford.edu.

NIX, EDMUND ALFRED, lawyer; b. Eau Claire, Wis., May 24, 1929; s. Sebastian and Kathryn (Keirnan) N.; m. Mary Kathryn Nagle Daley, Apr. 27, 1968; children: Kim, Mary Kay, Norbert, Edmund Alfred, Michael. BS, Wis. State U., 1951; LL.B., U. Wis., 1954, postgrad. in speech, 1956-57. Bar: Wis. 1954. Practice in, Eau Claire, 1954-65; dist. atty. Eau Claire County, 1958-64; U.S. atty. Western Dist. Wis., Eau Claire, 1965-69, U.S. magistrate, 1969-70; dist. atty. La Crosse County, Wis., 1975-77; mcpl. judge City of La Crosse, 1992—. Co-chmn. United Fund, Eau Claire, 1958; Pres. Young Democrats Wis., 1951-53; mem. adminstrv. bd. Wis. Dem. party, 1953-54; chmn. 10th Congl. dist., 1965; sec. Kennedy for Pres. Club Wis., 1959-60. Served with AUS, 1954-56. Mem. Fed. Bar Assn., Wis. Bar Assn. (state chmn. crime prevention and control com.), La Crosse County Bar Assn. (pres.), Nat. Dist. Attys. Assn., KC. Roman Catholic.

NIX, J. ELMER, retired orthopedist, surgeon; b. Ellisville, Miss., Oct. 24, 1931; s. Robert Leroy and Gladys Jane (Strahan) Nix; m. Rosemary Jane Cochrane, Nov. 16, 1956; children: Georgia Miller, Susan Hill, James Elmer Jr., Robert L. II. MD, Jefferson Med. Coll., Phila., 1956. Diplomate Am. Bd. Orthop. Surgery, 1965. Intern Hermann Hosp., Houston, 1956—57, resident in internal medicine, 1959—63; orthop. surgeon Am. Acad. Orthop. Surgeons, Chgo., 1965—2007; ret., 2007. Asst. prof. orthop. surgery U. Miss. Sch. Medicine, 1963—. Pres. N.Am. Spine Soc., Chgo., 1986—87; AMA del. Miss. Spine Soc., 1987—99, N.Am. Spine Soc., 1987—99; pres. Clinical Orthop. Soc., 1995—96, Miss. State Med. Soc., Jackson, 1990—91. Capt. USAF, 1957—59. Named Intern of Yr., Hermann Hosp., Houston, 1957, Violet Keller Outstanding Resident, 1963; named one of Am. Top Surgeons, Consumer Rsch. Coun. Am., 2002; recipient Clinical Surgery award, Jefferson Med. Coll., 1956, David Selby award, N.Am. Spine Soc., 1997. Fellow: Am. Bd. Orthop. Surgery, Am. Acad. Orthop. Surgery; mem.: N.Am. Spine Soc. (founder), Walter Scott Club. Republican. Presbyterian. Avocations: golf, reading, poetry, football. Home: 420 St Andrews Dr Jackson MS 39211

NIX, JAMES RAYFORD, nuclear physicist, consultant; b. Natchitoches, La., Feb. 18, 1938; s. Joe Ebbin and Edna (Guin) N.; m. Sally Ann Wood, Aug. 19, 1961; children: Patricia Lynne, David Allen. BS in Physics, Carnegie Inst. Tech., 1960; PhD in Physics, U. Calif., Berkeley, 1964. Summer physicist Lawrence Livermore Nat. Lab., Calif., 1961; rsch. asst. Lawrence Berkeley Lab., 1961-64, postdoctoral physicist, 1966-68; NATO postdoctoral fellow Niels Bohr Inst., Copenhagen, 1964-65; mem. staff Los Alamos (N.Mex.) Nat. Lab., 1968-77, 89-94, group leader, 1977-89, fellow, 1994-98, sci. cons., 1998—. Vis. prof. Centro Brasileiro de

Pesquisas Fisicas, Rio de Janeiro, 1974; cons. Calif. Inst. Tech., Pasadena, 1976, 79; chmn. Gordon Research Conf. Nuclear Chemistry, New London, NH, 1976; chmn. physics divsn. adv. com. Oak Ridge (Tenn.) Nat. Lab., 1976, 97; chmn. nuc. sci. divsn. vis. com. Lawrence Berkeley Lab., 1979—80. Contbr. articles to numerous publs. Recipient Alexander von Humboldt Sr. U.S. Scientist award, Univ. Munich and Max-Planck Inst. for Nuc. Physics, 1980—81; fellow, Phi Kappa Phi, Berkeley, 1960—61; scholar, Alfred P. Sloan Found., Pitts., 1956—60. Fellow: Am. Phys. Soc. (exec. com. 1973—75); mem.: AAAS, Phi Kappa Phi, Sigma Xi. Democrat. Home and Office: 12 Los Pueblos Los Alamos NM 87544-2659 Personal E-mail: j_r_nix@hotmail.com.

NIX, JERRY W., automotive executive; Sr. v.p. fin., CFO Genuine Parts Co., Atlanta, 1979—2000, exec. v.p. fin., CFO, 2000—05, vice-chmn., exec. v.p. fin., CFO, 2005—. Office: Genuine Parts Co 2999 Circle 75 Pkwy SE Atlanta GA 30339-3050 *

NIX, KEMIE RICHARDS, educational association administrator, editor; b. Atlanta, Dec. 10, 1938; d. James McDowell and Evelyn Knight Richards; m. John Arthur Nix, July 22, 1961; children: Mary Evelyn Nix Hollowell, John Arthur Jr. EdB, Emory U., 1960, EdM, 1970. Tchr. Westminster Schs., Atlanta, 1961—87; founder, dir. Children's Lit. for Children, Atlanta, 1986—2002, Reader-to-Reader, Atlanta, 1986—2002; co-founder, co-dir. Reader-to-Patient, Atlanta, 1990—2000; co-founder Biblioteca Juvenil de Mayaguez, PR, 1991—2001; dir. Reader-to-Reader: Africa, 1990—. Children's book editor Atlanta Jour./Constn., 1976—91, Parents' Choice, 1978—, corr. editor Jour. African Youth and Children's Lit., 1995—. Bd. dirs. US Bd. Books Young People, Wilmington, Del., 1996—98, Children's Lit. Children, Atlanta, 1996—, Mt. Kenya Acad., Nyeri, Kenya, 2002—. Named to Coca-Cola Centennial Olympic Wall, Atlanta, 1996, Kemie Nix Libr. named in her honor, Primary Sch., Nyeri, 1992, Mt. Kenya Acad., Nyeri, 2001. Mem.: ALA (Newbery com. 1994, Notable Books com. 1998—99, Newbery com. 2002, Caldecott com. 2006), Internat. Reading Assn. Democrat. Presbyterian. Avocations: birdwatching, animals, reading. Home and Office: Reader-to-Reader: Africa 104 Madison Ave Peachtree City GA 30269

NIX, PATRICIA, artist; d. Nobe Astin Briggs and Lela Mae (Lucas) Rockstrom; m. (dec.); children: Pandora Nix Shaw, William Riley Jr., John Houston. BA, NYU, 1982. One-woman shows include Tower Gallery, Southampton, N.Y., 1978—82, 1985, NYU, 1980, Sutton Gallery, N.Y.C., 1982—83, Baumgartner Gallery, Washington, 1984, S.I. (N.Y.) Mus., 1986, Andre Zarre Gallery, N.Y.C., 1987, S.I. (N.Y.) Mus., 1988, Nerlino Gallery, N.Y.C., 1988, Andre Zarre Gallery, 1991, U. Windsor (Ont., Can.) Mus., Griffin McGear Modern Gallery, N.Y.C., 1989, San Angelo (Tex.) Mus. of Art, 1991, Hurlbutt Gallery, Greenwich, Conn., 1990, Galerie Donguy, Paris, 1994, Dillon Gallery, N.Y.C., 1994—98, numerous group shows including most recently, exhibited in group shows at Merill Chase Galleries, Chgo., 1999, Am. Embassy, Rome, Italy, 1999, Hilligoss Galleries, 2000—03, Tex. Tech. Mus., Lubbock, 2000, Dillin Gallery, NYC, 2006, Ann Norton Mus. Sculptor Garden, West Palm Beach, Fla., 2007; represented in numerous permanent collections, designer sets and costumes (ballets) Petrushka, Pulcinella, Jeu de Cartes, 2002, Totem Altar, Saint Peters Ch., N.Y.C., 2004, Gallerie Mary Claude Goinnard, Paris, France, 2005, Totem Altar, St. John the Devine Cathedral., N.Y.C., 2005, Mary Claude Goinnard, Paris, France, 2005. Office Phone: 212-686-3512.

NIXDORF, DONALD, dentist, researcher; DDS, U. Alta., Edmonton, Can., 1996. Asst. prof. U. Minn., Mpls., 2005—. Office: Univ Minn 6-320 Moos Tower 515 Delaware Str SE Minneapolis MN 55455 Office Phone: 612-626-0140.

NIXON, ARLIE JAMES, gas and oil company executive; b. Ralston, Okla., May 22, 1914; s. James Gordon and Wella May (Platt) N.; m. Wylie Elizabeth Jones, Apr. 21, 1939 (div May 1950); children: Cole Jay, Kathleen (Mrs. S. Brent Joyce); m. Lisa Marie Grant, Dec. 7, 1981 (div. June 1989). BS, Okla. State U., 1935. Airline capt. Trans World Airlines, NYC, 1939-74; pres. Crystal Gas Co., Jennings, Okla., 1960—, Blackburn Gas Co., Jennings, 1964—, Blackberry Oil Co., Jennings, 1969—. Represented U.S. in several ofcl. dels. to internat. aviation tech. meetings, also represented Internat. Fedn. Air Line Pilots Assns. at internat. confs. *His degree, at Oklahoma State (1931-35), was in Dairy Science. There he helped pioneer the homogenization of milk and the artificial insemenation of dairy cows. He has been an enlisted man and officer in both the army and navy. He was Oklahoma's first naval aviator. In 1955 he researched "flying over the pole" and was Captain on the World's very first commercial polar flight...Los Angeles to Frankfurt, Germany. In 1966 he helped design the present North Atlantic Air Traffic System. In 1997, he graduated from Central Oklahoma Votech and received an unrestricted, Class A Commercial Driver's License at age 83.* Lt. (j.g.) USNR, 1935-63. Mem. Internat. Fedn. Air Line Pilots Assn. (regional v.p. 1972), Internat. Platform Assn., Wings Club. Democrat. Office: PO Box 68 Jennings OK 74038-0068 Office Phone: 918-454-2241.

NIXON, BRENDA JOYCE, elementary school educator, small business owner; b. Hazlehurst, Miss., Feb. 6, 1949; d. Archie C. Ashley, Sr. and Joyce B. Ashley; m. W.B. (Benny) Nixon, Jr. (div.); children: Ashley Michelle Nixon Rogers, Christopher Jarrett. BA, William Carey Coll., Hattiesburg, Miss, 1971; post grad., 1987—. CPA; lic. educator Miss. Group leader Ga. Bapt. Children's Home, Palmetto, Ga.; tchr. grade 6 Union Academy, Georgetown, Miss., 1987—95, Windsor Academy, Macon, Ga., 1993—2000, Crystal Springs Mid. Sch., Crystal Springs, Miss., 2000—. Tchr. participant So. Regional Edn. Bd., lead tchr. lang. arts 6th grade; pres. club rep. Avon, 2001—. Vol. fund raiser Bethel Vol. Fire Dept., Hazlehurst, 2004; state level judge Pre Teen Am. Program, 1994—96; music dir. Bethel Bapt. Ch., Hazlehurst, 2000—, mission action dir., 2003—. Named Tchr. of Yr., Macon/Bibb County Fire Dept., 1997—98, Macon Sheriff's Dept., 1998—99, Nat. Honor Roll Outstanding Am. Tchr., 2006. Avocations: reading, painting, music. Office: Crystal Springs Mid Sch 2092 S Pat Harrison Dr Crystal Springs MS 39059-3038 Home: 8157 Hwy 472 Hazlehurst MS 39083 Office Phone: 601-892-2789. Personal E-mail: abcnixon@aol.com.

NIXON, CHARLES WILLIAM, retired acoustician; b. Wellsburg, W.Va., Aug. 15, 1929; s. William E. and Lenora S. (Treiber) Nixon; m. Barbara Irene Hunter, May 19, 1956; children: Timothy C., Tracy Scott. BS, Ohio State U., 1952, MS, 1953, PhD, 1960. Tchr. spl. edn. Ohio and W.Va. Pub. Schs., Wheeling, 1954—56; rsch. audiologist Aeromed Lab., Wright Patterson AFB, Ohio, 1956—67; supervisory rsch. audiologist Armstrong Lab., Wright Patterson AFB, 1967—96, Veridian, Dayton, 1996—2004. Chair W4 Am. Nat. Stds. Inst., NYC, 1968—96; U.S. rep. hearing protection Internat. Stds. Orgn., Geneva, 1968—96; USAF rep. NRC-NAS Hearing Com., Washington, 1976—94; chair robotics panel Joint Dirs. Labs., Washington, 1987—88. Author: reports and book chpts. Cpl. US Army, 1953—55. Recipient Meritorious Svc. medal, U.S. Dept. Def., Dayton, Ohio, 1986, Outstanding Civilian Svc. award, 1996. Fellow: Acoustical Soc. Am.; mem.: Rsch. Soc. Am. Achievements include research in noise exposure, voice communications, hearing protection, sonic boom, active noise reduction, 3-D audio displays, others. Home: 4316 Sillman Pl Dayton OH 45440-1141

NIXON, CYNTHIA, actress; b. NYC, Apr. 9, 1966; d. Walter and Anne Nixon; children: Samantha Mozes, Charles Ezekiel Mozes. BA in English, Barnard Coll., 1988. Founding member The Drama Dept., 1996. Actor: (plays) The Philadelphia Story, 1980 (Theatre World Award, 1981), The Real Thing, 1984, Hurly Burly, 1984, Indiscretions, 1996 (Tony Award nom., 1996, Tony award, best performance by leading actress in a play, 2006), Rabbit Hole, 2006, The Prime of Miss Jean Brodie, 2006; (films) Little Darlings, 1980, Prince of the City, 1981, Tattoo, 1981, I Am the Cheese, 1983, Amadeus, 1984, The Manhattan Project, 1986, O.C. and Stiggs, 1987, Let It Ride, 1989, Through an Open Window, 1992, The Pelican Brief, 1993, Addams Family Values, 1993, Baby's Day Out, 1994, The Cottonwood, 1996, 'M' Word, 1996, Marvin's Room, 1996, Advice From a Caterpillar, 1999, The Out-of-Towners, 1999, Igby Goes Down, 2002, The Paper Mache Chase, 2003; (TV series) Sex and the City, 1998—2004 (Emmy nom. for Outstanding Supporting Actress in a comedy series, 2002, Emmy award Outstanding Supporting Actress in a Comedy Series, 2004); (TV miniseries) Tanner '88, 1988; (TV films) The Seven Wishes of a Rich Kid, 1979, The Private History of a Campaign That Failed, 1981, Rascals and Robbers: The Secret Adventures of Tom Sawyer and Huck Finn, 1982, My Body, My Child, 1982, Fifth of July, 1982, The Murder of Mary Phagan, 1988, Women & Wallace, 1990, Love She Sought, The, 1990, Face of a Stranger, 1991, Love, Lies and Murder, 1991, Kiss-Kiss, Dahlings!, 1992, Sex and the Matrix, 2000, Papa's Angels, 2000, Stage on Screen: The Women, 2002, Tanner on Tanner, 2004, Warm Springs, 2005. Office: William Morris Agency One William Morris Place Beverly Hills CA 90212

NIXON, DANIEL WALKER, oncologist, researcher; b. Brunswick, Ga., Sept. 8, 1943; s. Marvin Elesberry and Mildred Anita (Whitehead) N.; m. Sandra Gayle Brakefield, July 18, 1970; children: William B., Marvin A. BS, U. Ga., 1965, MD, 1969. Diplomate Am. Bd. Internal Medicine, Am. Bd. Med. Oncology; lic. physician S.C. Asst. prof. Med. Coll. Ga., Augusta, 1973-75; from assoc. prof. to prof. Emory U., Atlanta, 1975-87; assoc. dir. divsn. cancer prevention and control, Nat. Cancer Inst. NIH, Bethesda, Md., 1987-89; v.p., prof. edn. Am. Cancer Soc., Atlanta, 1989-94; Folk prof., assoc. dir. prevention and control Hollings Cancer Ctr., Med. U. S.C., Charleston, 1994—99; pres. Inst. Cancer Prevention, NYC, 1999—2004. Mem. sci. bd. Cancer Treatment Rsch. Found., chmn. bd. sci. counselors, 1999—. Author: Cancer Recovery Eating Plan, 1994; editor: Cancer Chemoprevention, 1994; editor-in-chief Preventive Medicine, 1999—2004; contbr. more than 100 articles to med. jours. Capt. USNR. Recipient several found. awards; grantee NIH, 1975—2004. Mem. Nutrition Oncology Adjuvant Therapy Soc. (pres. 1996), Army and Navy Club, Druid Hills Country Club. Achievements include research in cancer prevention and nutrition; chemoprevention and cancer metabolism. Office: 125 Doughty St Ste 280 Charleston SC 29403 Personal E-mail: dnixonun@aol.com.

NIXON, DAVID, dancer; b. Windsor, Ont., Can. Student, The Nat. Ballet Sch. Dancer Nat. Ballet Can., 1978—82, 1st soloist, 1982—84; prin. dancer Deutsche Opera Ballet, Berlin, 1985—90, Komische OperaBallet, Berlin, 1991—93; artistic dir. Ballet met., Columbus, Ohio, 1995—2001, No. Ballet Theatre, England, 2001—. Various guest appearance including Munich Ballet, 1990-91, Staatsoper, Berlin, 1990, Birmingham Royal Ballet, 1990-93. Dancer Bayerisches Staatsoper Ballet Munich, 1990—91, Alexander Godunov and Stars, 1982, Milw. Ballet, 1984, Sydney Ballet Australia, 1984, World Ballet Festival Tokyo, 1985, 1988, Hamburg Ballet, 1988, 1989, Staatsoper Berlin, 1988—91, Bayerisches Staatsballet, 1988—90, Komische Opera Berlin, 1990—93; prodr.: David Nixon's Dance Theatre, Hebbel Theatre Berlin, 1990, 1991; choreographer Butterfly, 1983, La Follia, 1984, Dangerous Liaisons, 1990, 1996, African Fantasy, 1990, Celebrate Mozart, 1991, Sudden Impulse, 1994, A Summer's Night Reflections, 1995, Full-Length Nutcracker, 1995, Butterfly, 1996, Beauty and the Beast, 1997, Carmen, 1997, Romeo and Juliet, 1998, Swan Lake, 1998, Dracula, 1999, A Midsummer Nights Dream, 2000—03, A Celebration of Dance with Music by Gershwin, 2001, Wuthering Heights, 2002, Peter Pan, 2004, Undine, 2006. Recipient Ollivier award, 2005, Best Dir. award, 2004, 2006. Office: Northern Ballet Theatre West Park Centre Spen Ln Leeds LS16 5BE England

NIXON, EUGENE RAY, chemist, educator; b. Mt. Pleasant, Mich., Apr. 14, 1919; s. William S. and Grace (Brookens) N.; m. Phyllis R. Jones, June 10, 1945; children— Cynthia L., Emily E. Sc.B. summa cum laude, Alma Coll., 1941; PhD, Brown U., 1947. Research chemist Manhattan Project, 1942-46; instr. chemistry Brown U., 1947-49; mem. faculty U. Pa., Phila., 1949-85, prof. chemistry, 1965-85, vice dean grad. sch., 1958-62, acting chmn. dept. chemistry, 1965-66, dir. materials research lab., 1969-72, prof. emeritus, 1985—. Vis. prof. U. London, 1963-64; vis. lectr. Bryn Mawr Coll., 1957-58 Mem. Am. Chem. Soc., Am. Phys. Soc., Soc. Applied Spectroscopy (Jour. award 1965, Spectroscopist of Yr. award Del. Valley sect. 1988), Coblentz Soc. (bd. mgrs.), Sigma Xi. Research, publs. on phys. chemistry, molecular structure and molecular spectroscopy, properties of crystals, intermolecular interactions, laser spectroscopy and laser chemistry. Home: 35 Julio Dr Apt 106 Shrewsbury MA 01545-3049

NIXON, JEREMIAH W. (JAY), state attorney general; b. DeSoto, Mo., Feb. 13, 1956; s. Jeremiah and Betty (Lea) Nixon; m. Georganne Nixon; children: Jeremiah, Will. BS in Polit. Sci., U. Mo., 1978, JD, 1981. Ptnr. Nixon, Nixon, Breeze & Roberts, Jefferson County, Mo., 1981—86; mem. Mo. State Senate from Dist. 22, 1986—93; atty. gen. State of Mo., 1993—. Chmn. select com. ins. reform; creator video internat. devel. and edn. opportunity prog. Named Outstanding Young Missourian, Jaycees, 1994, Outstanding Young Lawyer, Barrister's Mag., 1993; recipient Conservation Fedn. Mo award, 1992. Mem.: Mo. Assn. Trial Attys., Midwest Assn. Attys. Gen., Nat. Assn. Attys. Gen. Democrat. Methodist. Office: Office of Atty Gen Supreme Ct Bldg 207 W High St Jefferson City MO 65101 *

NIXON, JUDITH MAY, librarian; b. Gary, Ind., June 14, 1945; d. Louis Robert Sr. and Mable Sophia (Reiner) Vician; m. Cleon Robert Nixon III, Aug. 20, 1967; 1 child, Elizabeth Marie. BS in Edn., Valparaiso U., 1967; MA in LS, U. Iowa, 1974. Tchr. U.S. Peace Corps, Tonga, 1968—69; popular books libr. Lincoln Libr., Springfield, Ill., 1971—73; ref. libr. Cedar Rapids (Iowa) Pub. Libr., 1974—76; ref.coord. U. Wis., Platteville, 1976—82; bus. libr. U. Ariz., Tucson, 1982—84; consumer and family sci. libr. Purdue U., West Lafayette, La., 1984—93, Krannert mgmt. and econs. libr., 1993—2005, humanities, social sci. and edn. head libr., 2005—. Editor: Industry and Company Information, 1991, Organization Charts, 1992, 2d edit., 1996, Hotel and Restaurant Industries, 1993; editor quar. serial Lodging and Restaurant Index, 1985-93. Leader Girl Scouts U.S., Lafayette, 1985—2005. Recipient John H. Moriarty award Purdue U. Librs., 1989. Mem. ALA (chair bus. reference and svcs. sect. 1995-96, GALE Rsch. award for excellence in bus. librarianship 1994). Home: 2375 N 23rd St Lafayette IN 47904-1242 Office: Purdue U Libraries Humanities Social Sci Edn Libr 504 W State St West Lafayette IN 47907-2058 Office Phone: 765-494-2834. Business E-Mail: jnixon@purdue.edu.

NIXON, MARNI, singer; b. Altadena, Calif., Feb. 22, 1930; d. Charles and Margaret (Wittke) McEathron; m. Ernest Gold, May 22, 1950 (div. 1969); m. Lajos Frederick Fenster, July 23, 1971 (div. July 1975); m. Albert David Block, Apr. 11, 1983. Student, L.A. City Coll., UCLA, U. So. Calif., Tanglewood, Mass. Dir. vocal faculty Calif. Inst. Arts, Valencia, 1970-72; pvt. tchr., vocal coacn, condr. master classes, 1970—; pvt. voice tchr., coach, condr. master classes, 1970—; head apprentice divsn. Santa Barbara Music Acad. of West, 1980; formerly dir. opera workshop Cornish Inst. Arts, Seattle. Tchr. in field; judge Met. Opera Internat. Am. Music Awards, Nat. Inst. Music Theatre, 1984—87; dialect dir., opera recs. Actor: (musicals) Pasadena (Calif.) Playhouse, 1940—45; (films) Sound of Music, 1964, I Think I Do, 1996; (TV series) Boomerang, 1975; (Broadway plays) My Fair Lady, 1964, 2007, Taking My Turn, 1983, Opal, 1992—94, Cabaret, 1998, Ballymore, 1999, Follies, 2000—01, James Joyce's The Dead, 1999—2001, Nine, 2003; singer (soloist): Roger Wagner chorale, 1947—53; singer: (Operas) New Eng. Opera Co., LA Opera Co., Ford Found. TV Opera, 1948—63, San Francisco Spring Opera, 1966, Seattle Opera, 1971—73, classical recitals and appearances with symphony orchs. throughout U.S., Can., Eng., Israel, Ireland; voice dub: (films) My Fair Lady; The King and I; An Affair to Remember; West Side Story; Disney's Mulan; others; singer: (albums) Columbia, Mus. Heritage Records, Capital, RCA Victor, Ednl. Records, Reference Recs., Varese-Sarabande, Nonesuch; author: I Could Have Sung All Night: My Story, 2006. Nominee Drama Desk award, 2 Grammy award, NARAS; recipient 4 Emmy awards for best actress, 2 Action for Childrens TV awards, 1977, Chgo. Film Festival award, 1977, 2 Gold Records for Songs from Mary Poppins and Mulan, VERA award, Voice Found., Phila., 2007. Mem.: Nat. Assn. Tchrs. Singing (pres. N.Y. chpt. 1994—97, panelist new music).

NIXON, PATRICIA SAUNDERS, music educator, actress; b. Norfolk, Va., Nov. 22, 1955; d. John Edward Saunders and Marie Ewing; m. Jimmie Larry Nixon, July 7, 1979; children: Jimmie Larry Jr.(dec.), Annette Marie. BS in Music Edn., Norfolk State U., 1978, MusM in Vocal Performance, 1988; postgrad. in Vocal Performance, Shenandoah U. Conservatory, 2002—. Music instr. VA Sch. for Deaf, Blind and Multi-Disabled, Hampton, Va., 1978—2000; choral dir. Norview Mid. Sch. Norfolk Pub. Schs., 2000—01; choral dir. Wilson H.S. Portsmouth (Va.) Pub. Schs., 2001—02; vocal instr. Norfolk State U., 2002—, dir. jazz vocal ensemble, 2003—. Choir dir., pianist intermediate choir Ebenezer Bapt. Ch., Portsmouth, 1991—. Photography, D-Day (pub., 2002), Whose in the Drivers Seat Now?, 2003; actor: Porgy and Bess; musician: Va. Symphony Pops, I. Sherman Green Chorale, others; singer: Let My People Go. Mem. Brighton/Prentice Pk. Civic League, Portsmouth, 1998—, Va. and Nat. Minority Caucus, 1990—2002. Recipient Apple for the Tchr. award, Alpha Chi chpt. Iota Phi Lambda Sorority, Inc., 1993, Christian Svc. award, Ebenezer Bapt. Ch. Vacational Bible Sch., 2000—01, 2001 Team Ptnr. Recognition award, U. S. Olympic Com., 2001, We Teach the Children Whole Village award, Va. Edn. Assn., 2001, Outstanding Performance in A Tribute to African Am. Sacred Music award, Parkview United Meth. Ch., 2001, Black Educators' award, Delicados, Inc. Portsmouth Chpt., 1997, A Salute to Black Achievers in the Tidewater Area award, Martin Luther King, Jr. Meml. Ch. Choir, 1996, A Tribute to Excellence award in classical voice category, Area II NAACP ACT-SO Coalition, 2005; grantee VTAG, Shenandoah U., 2002. Mem.: AAUP, NEA (del. 1999—2000), NAACP (A Tribute to Excellence award), Nat. Assn. Teachers and Singing, Am. Choral Directors Assn., Intercolligiate Music Assn., Va. Choral Dirs. Assn., Hampton Edn. Assn. (pres. 1998—2000), Va. Edn. Assn., Portsmouth Edn. Assn. (assoc.), Norfolk Edn. Assn. (assoc.; del. 2000), The Am. Choral Directors Assn. (assoc.), Nat. Assn. of Negro Musicians Tidewater Area Musicians Chpt. (assoc.), Music Educators Nat. Conf. (assoc.), VA Sch. at Hampton Edn. Assn. (assoc.; pres. 1998—2000, del. 1999—2000), Chancel Choir of Ebenezer Bapt. Ch. (assoc.), Va. Opera Guild (assoc.), Alpha Kappa Alpha (co-chmn. music 49th Mid-Atlantic Regional Conf. 2002, Leadership Excel award 2000), Gamma Delta Omega Chpt. of Alpha Kappa Alpha Sorority, Inc. (assoc.; publicity chmn. 1998—99, Cert. of Appreciation 1999). Democrat. Avocations: performing, crafts, photography, computer technology, travel. Home: 1019 Centre Ave Portsmouth VA 23704-7005 Office: Norfolk State U 700 Park Ave Norfolk VA 23504 Personal E-mail: psnixon@aol.com. Business E-Mail: psnixon@nsu.edu.

NIXON, RONDA LYNN, paralegal; b. Ashland, Ky., Jan. 9, 1971; d. Ronnie Dewey and Sadie Francis Bishop; m. Norman Brian Nixon, May 1, 2004; children: Darren Connors, Shelby Connors, Roni Nixon. AAS in Paralegal Tech., Miller Motte Bus. Coll., Clarksville, Tenn., 1995; BS in Paralegal Studies, Kaplan U., Chgo., 2007. Cert. Paralegal Nat. Assn. of Legal Asst., 2005. Paralegal Pruitt & Thorner, Catlettsburg, Ky., 2003—; legal sec. Robinson & Rice, Ashland, Ky., 2003. Advocate CASA, Ashland, Ky., 2004—06. Mem.: Nat. Assn. of Legal Assistants, Assn. of Trial Lawyers of Am. Home: 102Township Rd 286 Chesapeake OH 45619 Office: Pruitt & Thorner P O Box 352 Catlettsburg KY 41129

NIXON, SANDRA L., retired registrar; b. Kansas City, Mo., Feb. 23, 1944; d. C. Harold and Anna Pearl Scott-Mann; m. Hiram Luttmers Jr., Mar. 6, 1965 (div. Aug. 1973); children: Hiram Charles, Gerald Lee; m. Douglas L. Nixon, July 16, 1976; children: Karen, Katherine, Raymond. Student, Cen. Mo. State U., 1962-63, Nat. Coll., 1991-93. Credit clk. Harzfeld's, Kansas City, Mo., 1963-65; typist/receptionist Powers Regulator Co., Overland Park, Kans., 1965-69; ins. typist Comml. Union Ins. Co., Kansas City, Mo., 1969-73; typist Social Security Admin., Kansas City, Mo., 1973-78; dir. of Mothers Day Out Birchwood Bapt. Ch., Independence, Mo., 1978-80; accompanist K.C. Mo. Sch. Dist., Kansas City, Mo., 1979-81; registrar Northeast Mid. Sch., Kansas City, Mo., 1981-2000; ind. fashion coord. Weekenders aka Sandi's Butterfly Boutique, 2001—. Mem. ABWA (pres. 1990-91, Woman of Yr. 1992-93), VFW Aux. Post 4242 (sr. v.p. 2000-2001, pres. 2001-2004, sr. v.p. 2004-2005). Baptist. Avocations: piano, square dancing, precious moments. Office Phone: 816-260-4538. E-mail: sandy.nixon@fellowship.net.

NIXON, SCOTT SHERMAN, lawyer; b. Grosse Pointe, Mich., Feb. 7, 1959; s. Floyd Sherman and Marjorie Jane (Quermann) N.; m. Cathryn Lynn Starnes, Aug. 27, 1983; children: Jeffry Sherman, Kelsy Jane, James Robert. BABA, Mich. State U., 1981; JD, U. Denver, 1984. Bar: Colo. 1984, U.S. Dist. Ct. Colo. 1984, U.S. Ct. Appeals (10th cir.) 1984. Assoc. Pryor, Carney & Johnson, P.C., Englewood, Colo., 1984-89, shareholder, 1990-95; pres., shareholder Pryor Johnson Carney Karr Nixon, P.C., Greenwood Village, Colo., 1995—. Officer, bd. dirs. Luth. Brotherhood Br. 8856, Denver, 1993-99, Mark K. Ulmer Meml. Native Am. Scholarship Found., Denver, 1994—; officer, mem. coun. Bethan Luth Ch., Englewood, 1993-95. Mem.: ABA, Colo. Def. Lawyers Assn., Denver Bar Assn., Colo. Bar Assn. Avocation: music performance. Home: 6984 S Pontiac Ct Centennial CO 80112-1127 Office: Pryor Johnson et al Ste 1200 5619 DTC Pky Greenwood Village CO 80111 Home Phone: 303-770-2608; Office Phone: 303-773-3500. Business E-Mail: snixon@pjckn.com.

NIXON, SCOTT WEST, oceanography science educator; b. Phila., Aug. 24, 1943; s. Robert Scott West and Elizabeth (Wright) West Nixon; m. Pendleton Hall, (div.); children: Carter Hall, Elizabeth Pendleton; m. Virginia Lee. BA, U. Del., 1965; PhD, U. N.C., 1970. Prof. oceanography U. R.I., Kingston, 1970—, dir. sea grant coll. program, 1983-2000. Mem. ocean studies bd. NRC, 1999-2004. Author: (with others) A Coastal Marine Ecosystem, 1978, The New England High Salt Marshes, 1982; co-editor-in-chief Estuaries, 1988—2006; also articles. Recipient Ketchum award Woods Hole Oceanographic Inst., 1992, Achievement award New Eng. Estuarine Rsch. Soc., 2000, Achievement award Nat. Sea Grant Assn., 2001, Lifetime appointment Nat. Assn. of Nat. Academies, 2002; grantee NSF, NOAA, EPA, Office Water Resources Rsch., State of R.I. Mem. Am. Soc. Limnology and Oceanography (governing bd. 1984-87), Estuarine Rsch. Fedn. (Odum award 2003) Office: U RI Bay Campus Dept Of Oceanography Narragansett RI 02882 Office Phone: 401-874-6803. Business E-Mail: swn@gso.uri.edu.

NIXON, TIMOTHY FRANCIS, lawyer; b. Two Rivers, Wis., Mar. 15, 1958; AS in Maritime Sci. with high honors, Northwestern Mich. Coll., 1979; BS in Pub. and Environ. Adminstrn. cum laude, U. Wis., Green Bay, 1987; MA in Pub. Policy and Adminstrn.; JD with honors, U. Wis., Madison, 1990. Bar: Wis., NY, US Dist. Ct. (ea. and we. dists.) Wis., US Dist. Ct. (we. dist.) Mich., US Dist. Ct. (no. and ctrl. dists.) Ill., US Dist. Ct. (cen. dist.) Ill., US Dist. Ct. (so. and ea. dists.) NY, US Ct. Appeals (7th cir.), US Supreme Ct. Cadet sailor Cleve. Cliffs Iron Co., 1977, US Steel Corp., 1978, 1979, Am. Steamship Co., 1978, US Mcht. Marine Officer, lic.

1st class pilot and Gt. Lakes mate Buffalo, 1979—85, Bethlehem Steel Corp., Seven Hills, Ohio, 1986, 1987; law clk. Office of Adminstrv. Legal Svcs., U. Wis., Madison, 1989—90; law clk. Godfrey & Kahn, S.C. (formerly LaFollette Sinykin, LLP), Green Bay, Wis., 1990, assoc. atty., 1991—96, shareholder, ptnr., 1997—. Intern Exec. Office of Pres., Office Mgmt. and Budget, Washington, 1988; lead atty. bus. fin. and restructuring team Godfrey & Kahn, S.C., 2002—; mem. adj. faculty U. Wis., Green Bay, 2001—, instr. outreach and ext., 2002—06; instr. Criminal Justice Dept. Exec. Devel. Inst., Fox Valley Tech. Coll., 2001—04, police mgmt. assessor, criminal justice dept., 2000—05; spkr. in field. Co-author: No Small Change: The Bankruptcy Abuse Prevention and Consumer Protection Act of 2005, Inside the Minds, Bankruptcy and Financial Restructuring, Settlements and Negotiations; asst. editor Voyageur Mag., 2004—; contbr. articles to profl. jours. Pres. Village of Waunakee, Wis., 1997—2001, chair planning commn., econ. devel. com., mem. growth task force, EMS dist. bd., pres. Cmty. Devel. Authority, 1998—2001, pres. fire dist., 1999—2001, pres. Waunakee Tax Increment Dist. Nos. 2 and 3 Bd. Rev., 2000, rep. Am. Pub. Power Assn. Legis. Rally Washington, 2000—01, village trustee, 1995—97, chair pers. com., police com., indsl. devel. com., planning commn., stormwater mgmt. com., boundary agreement com., utility commn., mem. citizen adv. com., 1993—95, v.p. police commn., mem. zoning appeals bd., mem. utility commn.; bd. dirs. Green Bay Area C. of C., 2004—; mem. water commn. City of Green Bay, 2003—, v.p., 2003—04, pres., 2004—, lead negotiator suburban water sales agreements; trustee Wis. Maritime Mus., 2004—05, chair audit com., mem. collections com., co-chair dir. search com.; bd. edn. Notre Dame Acad., Green Bay, 2003—06, chair fin. com., 2004—06; mem. DOT Roadway Grant Adv. Com. League of Wis. Municipalities, 2000, mem. legis. com., 2000—01; vice chair Dane County North Mendota Pky. Planning Com., 2000—01; gov.'s appointee South Ctrl. Wis. Regional Planning Commn. Study Com., 2000—01; account exec. Dane County United Way, 1998, 2000, cabinet mem., cmtys. divn. chair, 1999; asst. den leader, merit badge coord., mem. troop com. Boy Scouts Am., 1998—2003; alt. gov.'s appointee Wis. Patients Compensation Panel, 1983—85; mem. parish coun., maintenance com., facilities com., pub. rels. com., catechist, KC, cantor St. John the Bapt. Parish, Waunakee, 1999—2001. Named a Wis. Super Lawyer, Milw. Mag., 2005—06; named one of 50 People You Should Know in Green Bay, Bay Bus. Jour., 2005; recipient George B. Rector Cmty. Svc. award, Gt. Lakes Maritime Acad. Alumni Assn., 2000. Mem.: KC, ABA, Am. Soc. Litig. Counsel (charter fellow), State Bar NY, Turnaround Mgmt. Assn., St. Thomas More Lawyers Soc. of Wis., Comml. Law League of Am., Hon. Robert J. Parins Inn of Ct., Am. Soc. Pub. Adminstrn., Am. Bankruptcy Inst., Western Dist. Wis. Bar Assn., Ea. Dist. of Wis. Bar Assn., 7th Cir. Ct. Appeals Bar Assn., Milw. County Bar Assn., Dane County Bar Assn., Brown County Bar Assn., Western Dist. Bankruptcy Bar (v.p. 1997—98, pres. 1998—99), State Bar Wis. (bd. dirs. bankruptcy, insolvency and creditors rights sect. 2004—, chair creditor edn. com.), INSOL Internat., U. Wis. Green Bay Law Alumni Assn. (founder), Order of Coif. Roman Catholic. Avocations: Great Lakes history, genealogy, travel. Office: Godfrey & Kahn SC 333 Main St Ste 600 Green Bay WI 54301 Office Phone: 920-436-7693. Fax: 920-436-7988. E-mail: tnixon@gklaw.com.

NIYEKAWA, AGNES MITSUE, foreign language professor; b. Tokyo, May 9, 1924; came to U.S., 1949, naturalized; d. Basil Zensaku and Irene (Kano) N.; m. Roy C. Calogeras (div. 1964); children: Erik, Meagan. BA in English, Tokyo Women's U., 1945; BA in Sociology, U. Hawaii, 1952; MA in Psychology, Bryn Mawr Coll., 1954; PhD in Psychology, NYU, 1960; postdoc. in Linguistics, Columbia U., MIT, U. Wash., 1963. Rsch. assoc. psychology dept. NYU, 1959-61; asst. prof. ednl. psychology U. Hawaii, Honolulu, 1964-67, from prof. human devel. to chmn. East Asian langs., 1971-81, prof. East Asian langs. and lit., 1973-91, prof. emeritus, 1992—; assoc. prof. ednl. psychology Northeastern U., Boston, 1968-69; from sr. specialist Inst. Advanced Rsch. to assoc. dir. Culture Learning Inst. East West Ctr., Honolulu, 1969-71. Vis. scholar Columbia U., N.Y.C., 1961-63, MIT, Cambridge, 1967-68, Harvard U., Cambridge, 1987, U. Tokyo, 1982, U. Vienna, Austria, 1986-87. Author: Minimum Essential Politeness, 1992, (with others) Cross-Cultural Learning, 1977, Design for Cross-Cultural Learning, 1987; contbr. numerous articles to profl. jours. USPHS fellow, 1961-63; grantee U.S. Office Edn., 1965-67, Am. Coun. Learned Socs., 1962, 67-68, Fulbright, 1981-82, Social Sci. Rsch. Coun.; recipient Order of the Sacred Treasure (Gold Rays with Rosette), Japanese govt., 1998 Mem. Chamber Music Hawaii (bd. dirs.), Austrian Assn. Hawaii (bd. dirs.). Home: 500 University Ave Apt 2003 Honolulu HI 96826-4941 Personal E-mail: agnesmn@hawaiiantel.net.

NIYOGI-SALHI, RUMA, science educator; b. Calcutta, India, Dec. 23, 1972; d. Dipak and Maya Niyogi; m. Muhannad Adnan Salhi, Dec. 16, 2004. BA, U. Calif., LA; MA, U. Chgo., PhD, 2005. Asst. prof. St. Xavier U., Chgo., 2004—. Office: Saint Xavier Univ 3700 W 103rd St Chicago IL 60655 Office Phone: 773-298-3758.

NJOKU, SCHOLASTICA IBARI, retired college librarian, writer; d. David Mgbahuruike Njoku and Elizabeth Ekeoma Ukaegbu; divorced; children: Anthony, Emelia, Martina, Iheanyi, Chinedu, Onyekachi. BA cum laude in English, Wiley Coll., 1963; MLS, U. Oreg., 1965, MS in Edn., 1967, PhD in Edn., 1969; diploma in writing for children and teenagers, Inst. Children's Lit., Conn., 1996. Ref. libr. Knapp Libr. Project, Portland, Oreg., 1965—66; asst. edn. libr. Portland State U., 1969—70; assoc. prof. edn. Miss. Valley State Coll., Itta Bena, 1970—72; ref. cons. Oreg. State Libr., Salem, 1974—81, on-line cataloger, 1981—86; ref. libr. Portland C.C., 1986—2003; ret., 2003. Multicultural mentoring com. Portland C.C., 1996—2003, edn1. adv. coun. com., 1999—2003, women history planning com., 1999—2003. Author: The Miracle of A Christmas Doll, 1986, Dog What?, 1989; contbr. poems to poetry anthologies; author (writer, recorder): (CD) Smiling Faces in My Class At School, 2006. Recipient 3d prize Poetry award, Ann. Reader's Digest, United Negro Coll. Fund, 1963. Mem.: ALA, The Willamette Writers, Pacific NW Libr. Assn., Oreg. State Poetry Assn., Am. Assn. Higher Edn., Oreg. Libr. Assn., Delta Sigma Theta (Sisterhood award 2006). Democrat. Roman Catholic. Avocations: gardening, story telling, reading, writing. Home: 307 NE Holland St Portland OR 97211

NKANSAH, FRANKLIN DANIEL, electrical engineer, educator; s. John Benjamin and Rachel Endurance Nkansah; m. Mercy Ekfui Yongkuma, Dec. 27, 1991; children: Claribel, Franklin. PhD, Lehigh U., Pa., 2000. Mem. tech. staff AT&T Bell Labs., Allentown, Pa., 1988—93; wireless device mgr. Motorola Inc, Austin, Tex., 1993—2000; engring. mgr. Advanced Micro Devices, Austin, 2000—06; pres., CEO FDN Enterprises LLC, Buda, Tex., 2002—; prof. elec. engring. Prairie View A&M U., Tex., 2002—. Tech. cons. AWET Group and Holdings, Accra, Ghana, 1999—, overseer strategic directions, 2000—. Contbr. articles to profl. jours. Active Bekom Orphan Ho., Bekom, Cameroon, 2003—07. Mem.: IEEE. Achievements include patents for integrated circuit structure and method therefore; method for forming trench isolation; method of making a semiconductor device using chemicalmechanical polishing having a combination-step process; method of integrated circuit fabrication having planarized dielectrics. Office Phone: 512-312-2429.

NKOY, FLORY LUMU, medical educator; s. Olenga Mkoy and Zizita Esale; m. Annie Dioko Nkoy, Dec. 18, 1993; children: Joshua A., Jason A. B, U. Kinshasa, Democratic Republic of the Congo, 1984, MD, 1988; MS, MPH, U. Utah, Salt Lake City, 2005. Attending physician gen. medicine Epharza Med. Ctr., Kinshasa, 1989—94; attending physician internal medicine Kimtambo Hosp., Kinshasa, 1989—94; coord. Milcreek Women's Ctr., Salt Lake City, 1996—97; rsch. assoc. Utah Valley Regional Med. Ctr., Provo, Utah, 1997—99; oncology rschr. Intermountain Health Care, Salt Lake City, 2001—06; rsch. asst. prof., rsch. dir. U. Utah, Salt Lake City, 2006—. Cons. Incodx, Phoenix, 2005. Contbr. articles to profl. jours. Fellow, Intermountain Health Care, 1999—2001; grantee, Deseret Found., Salt Lake City, 2002, 2004. Mem.: Internat. Soc. Quality Life Rsch., Am. Fedn. Med. Rsch., Am. Med. Informatics Assn. Avocations: reading, travel, exercise.

NOACK, HAROLD QUINCY, JR., lawyer; b. San Francisco, May 1, 1931; m. Ann Crosby, Nov. 1952 (div. Sept. 1974); children: Stephen Tracy, Peter Quincy, Andrew Crosby; m. Susan K. Sherwood, Dec. 1975 (div. Jan. 1983); m. Penny Jo Orth, Apr. 2, 1988 (div. May 1989); m. Linda F. Killeen, Mar. 15, 1994 (div. May 1996). BA, U. Calif., Berkeley, 1953; LLB, U. Calif., San Francisco, 1959. Bar: Calif. 1960, Idaho 1969, U.S. Dist. Ct. Idaho 1969. Assoc. Fernoff & Wolfe, Oakland, Calif., 1959-64, Cooley, Crowley, Gaither, Godward, Castro & Huddleson, San Francisco, 1964-65; pvt. practice Oakland, 1965-66; ptnr. Oliphant, Hopper, Stribling & Noack, Oakland, 1966-69; assoc. Eberle, Berlin, Kading & Turnbow, Boise, Idaho, 1969-70; pvt. practice Boise, 1970-83, 85-88; assoc. Anthony Parks, Boise, 1970-75; ptnr. Noack & Korn, Boise, 1970-75, Noack & Hawley, Boise, 1983-85, Lyons & Noack, Boise, 1988-89; pvt. practice law Boise, 1989—. Contbr. articles to profl. jours. Bd. dirs., pres. Idaho Planned Parenthood, Boise, 1970-72; bd. dirs. Idaho Heart Assn., Boise, 1975. 2d lt. U.S. Army, 1954-55. Mem. ABA, Calif. Bar Assn., Idaho Bar Assn. (fee grievance com. 1986—), Boise Bar Assn., Rotary (bd. dirs. Boise club 1980). Avocations: running, walking, fishing, cooking. Home: PO Box 875 1915 N 24th St Boise ID 83702-0204 Home Phone: 208-336-2480; Office Phone: 208-336-9292. Business E-Mail: Pete@noacklaw.com.

NOAH, CHRISTOPHER RAY, history educator; b. Campinas, Brazil, Dec. 17, 1972; s. Melvin Ray and Frances Browning Noah; m. Jennifer Nichole Pike, June 22, 2001; 1 child, Sawyer Ray. BA in Secondary Edn., Asbury Coll., Wilmore, Ky., 1996; MA in Ednl. Splty., U. Louisville, 2006, MA in Ednl. Adminstrn., 2004. Tchr. Lexington Christian Acad., Ky., 1996—98, Portland Pub. Schs., Oreg., 2001, Jefferson County Pub. Schs., Louisville, 2001—. Social studies dept. chair Iroquois Mid. Sch., Louisville, 2002—03; sch. hospitality chair Kammerer Mid. Sch., Louisville, 2003—04, mentor, 2003—, sch. budget com. chair, 2005—. Vol. Jefferson County Tchrs. Assn., Louisville, 2006—. Republican. Avocations: ancient numismatics, travel, ancient history readings, soccer. Office: Kammerer Mid Sch 7315 Wesboro Rd Louisville KY 40222

NOAH, JAMES WILLIAM, biochemist, researcher; s. James C. Palocsay and Margaret M. Noah, Theodore G Noah; m. Diana Lee North, June 13, 1992; children: Hannah Rose, Sarah Grace. BS, Ohio State U., Columbus, 1992; PhD, NC State U., Raleigh, 1999. Rsch. assoc. DNX Biotherapeutics, Princeton, NJ, 1992—94, Apex Biosciences, Inc., Durham, NC, 1994—95; rsch. prof. U. Tex., Austin, 2004—05; rsch. biochemist So. Rsch. Inst., Birmingham, Ala., 2005—; adj. prof. U. Ala., Birmingham, 2007—. 1st lt. US Army NG, 1987—95. Decorated German Efficiency Badge US Army; GAANN fellow, NC State U., 1996, NRSA fellow, NIH, 2001—04. Mem.: Soc. Antiviral Rsch. (assoc.). Independent. Achievements include research in catalytic RNA and influenza antivirals. Office: So Rsch Inst 2000 9th Ave South Birmingham AL 35205 Home Phone: 205-678-4559; Office Phone: 205-581-2804. Office Fax: 205-581-2726. Business E-Mail: j.noah@sri.org.

NOAKES, WILLIAM S., JR., lawyer; b. 1956; BA, U. Notre Dame, 1978; MA, U. Chgo., 1981, JD, 1982. Bar: Mich. 1982. Sr. assoc. independent counsel Office of Independent Counsel Donald Smaltz; ptnr. Jaffe, Raitt, Heuer & Weiss, Detroit; mem. Meijer Inc., Grand Rapids, Mich., 1999—, sr. v.p., gen. counsel, CIO, sec. Legal commentator CourtTV, WDIV Channel 4 News, Detroit. Capt. & judge advocate USAF. Mem.: Wolverine Bar Assn., State Bar Mich. Office: Meijer Inc Legal Dept 2929 Walker Ave NW Grand Rapids MI 49544-9428

NOAM, ELI MICHAEL, telecommunications industry executive, educator; b. Jerusalem, Aug. 22, 1946; came to U.S., 1963; s. Ernst and Lotte (Dahn) N.; m. Nadine Strossen, 1980. AB, Harvard U., 1970, AM, 1972, PhD in Econs., 1975, JD, 1975. Bar: N.Y. 1996, D.C. 1997. Asst. prof. Princeton (N.J.) U., 1975-76, Columbia Bus. Sch., NYC, 1981-84, prof. finance and econ., 1984—; commr. N.Y. State Pub. Svc. Commn., NYC, 1987-90. Dir. Columbia Inst. for Tele-Info., N.Y.C., 1983-87, 1990—; contbr. articles, Financial Times Online, 2003-, appointed to White House IT advisory com., 2003-. Author or editor: Telecommunications Regulation: Today and Tomorrow, 1982, Video Media Competition, 1985, Law of International Telecommunications in the United States, 1988, The Cost of Libel, 1989, Television in Europe, 1991, Telecommunications in Europe, 1991, Telecommunications in Western Asia, 1997, Telecommunications in Latin America, 1998. Telecommunications in Africa, 1998. Bd. dirs. IRS Computer Modernization, Washington, D.C., 1988-89, Fed. Telecom System FTS-2000 Selection, Washington, 1990—. With Israel Air Force, 1967, 73. Grantee NSF, 1982, 85, 86; fellow German Marshall Fund U.S., 1983-84. 1966-68, Mideast Wars; Fellow Freedom Forum Media Center, 1996. Mem. Coun. on Fgn. REls., Phi Beta Kappa. Jewish. Avocations: flying, skiing, diving. Office: Columbia U Inst Tele-Info 809 Uris Hall New York NY 10027

NOBACK, RICHARDSON KILBOURNE, medical educator; b. Richmond, Va., Nov. 7, 1923; s. Gustav Joseph and Hazel (Kilborn) N.; m. Nan Jean Gates, Apr. 5, 1947; children: Carl R., Robert K., Catherine E. MD, Cornell U., 1947; BA, Columbia U., 1993. Diplomate Am. Bd. Internal Medicine. Intern N.Y. Hosp., 1947-48; asst. resident Cornell Med. div. Bellevue Hosp., NYC, 1958-50, chief resident, 1950-52; instr. medicine Cornell U., NYC, 1950-53; asst. prof. medicine SUNY Upstate Med. Ctr., Syracuse, 1955-56; assoc. prof. medicine U. Ky. Med. Ctr., Lexington, 1956-64; exec. dir. Kansas City (Mo.) Gen. Hosp. and Med. Ctr., 1964-69; assoc. dean, prof. medicine U. Mo. Sch. Medicine, Columbia, 1964-69, founding dean Kansas City, 1969-78, prof. medicine, 1969-90, prof. and dean emeritus, 1990—. Cons. U. Tenn., U. Mich., U. Del., Northeastern Ohio Group, U. Mo., Eastern Va. Med. Sch., Tex. Tech. U. Author Realism, Standards, and Performances: Three Essentials in Assessment, Planning, and Action, 2005; contbr. numerous articles to profl. jours. Bd. dirs. Kansas City Gen. Hosp., Truman Med. Ctr., Wayne Miner Health Ctr., Jackson County Med. Soc., The Shepherd's Ctr., Am. Fedn. Aging Rsch., Mo. Gerontol. Inst., The Shepherd's Ctrs. of Am.; dir. Mo. Geriatric Edn. Ctr., 1985-88. With US Army, 1943—46, with USAF, 1953—55. Recipient medal of honor Avila Coll., Kansas City, 1968, merit award Met. Med. Soc., 1991, recognition award Mo. Soc. Internal Medicine, 1993. Mem. AMA, Mo. Med. Assn. (former mem. ho. of dels., v.p. 1992), Am. Geriatric Soc., Alpha Omega Alpha, Phi Kappa Phi. Avocations: photography, writing, travel. Home: 2912 Abercorn Dr Las Vegas NV 89134-7440 Personal E-mail: nanori@earthlink.net.

NOBE, KEN, chemical engineering professor; b. Berkeley, Calif., Aug. 26, 1925; s. Sidney and Kiyo (Uyeyama) N.; m. Mary Tagami, Aug. 31, 1957; children: Steven Andrew, Keven Gibbs, Brian Kelvin. BS, U. Calif., Berkeley, 1951; PhD, UCLA, 1956. Jr. chem. engr. Air Reduction Co., Murray Hill, NJ, 1951-52; instr. engring. UCLA, 1955—57, asst. prof. chem. engring., 1957-62, assoc. prof., 1962-68, prof., 1968—, chmn. dept. chem., nuclear and thermal engring., 1978-83, founding chmn. chem. engring., 1983-84. Mem. tech. staff Ramo-Wooldridge Corp., El Segundo, Calif., 1958-59 Div. editor: Jour. Electrochem. Soc. 1967-91, Electrochimica Acta, 1977-85 With US Army, 1944—46. Recipient Disting. Tchg. award, UCLA, 1962. Mem. Electrochem. Soc. (Henry B. Linford award 1992), Am. Chem. Soc., Internat. Soc. Electrochemistry, Am. Electroplaters Surfacing Fin. Soc. (Abner Brenner Gold medal 2000), Sigma Xi. Office: UCLA Dept Chemical Engring Los Angeles CA 90095-1592 Business E-Mail: nobe@seas.ucla.edu.

NOBEL, JOEL J., biomedical researcher; b. Phila., Dec. 8, 1934; s. Bernard D. and Golda R. (Nobel) Judovich; m. Bonnie Sue Goldberg, June 19, 1960 (div.); children: Erika, Joshua; m. Loretta Schwartz, Oct. 28, 1979 (div.); 1 child, Adam. AB, Haverford Coll., 1956; MA, U. Pa., 1958; MD, Thomas Jefferson Med. Coll., Phila., 1963. Intern Presbyn. Hosp., Phila., 1963-64; resident in surgery Pa. Hosp., Phila., 1964-65; resident in neurosurgery U. Pa. Hosp., 1965-66; practice medicine specializing in biomed. engring. rsch. and healthcare tech. assessment, hosp. planning and mgmt., Phila., 1968—; dir. research Emergency Care Research Inst., Plymouth Meeting, Pa., 1968-71, dir., pres., 1971—2001; pres. Plymouth Inst., 1979—2002; founder and pres. emeritus ECRI, 2001—; founder, pres. ECRI Bhd, Malaysia, 2001—; CEO The Nobel Group, 2002—, chmn. Arab Health award, 2004—05. Chmn. tech. policy com., exec. bd., chmn. strategic planning com. Consumers Union; cons. in field. Publisher Health Devices, 1971-2001, Health Devices Alerts, 1977-2001; contbr. articles to profl. jours. With USNR, 1966—68. Smith, Kline & French fgn. fellow, 1962; grantee HEW, 1968-72; grantee Am. Heart Assn., 1965-66 Mem. AMA, APHA, Assn. Advancement Med. Instrumentation, Critical Care Med. Soc., Pa. Med. Assn., Navy League, US Naval Inst., Brit. Officers Club Phila. Office: ECRI 5200 Butler Pike Plymouth Meeting PA 19462-1298 Home: 361 Righters Mill Rd Gladwyne PA 19035 Business E-Mail: jjnobel@ecri.org.

NOBER, ROGER, rail transportation executive; married; 3 children. BA, Haverford Coll., Pa., 1986; JD, Harvard Law Sch., 1989. With Skadden, Arps, Slate, Meagher & Flom, NYC; various positions Com. on Transp. and Infrastructure US House Reps., 1993—97, chief counsel Com. on Transp. and Infrastructure, 1997—2001; counselor to dep. sec. Michael Jackson US Dept. Transp.; chmn. Surface Transp. Bd., 2002—06; ptnr. Steptoe & Johnson, LLP, Washington, 2006; exec. v.p. law, sec. Burlington No. Santa Fe Corp., 2007—. Chmn. Surface Transp. Bd., 2002—06. Republican. Office: Burlington No Santa Fe Corp PO Box 961056 Fort Worth TX 76161-0056 Office Phone: 817-867-6100. *

NOBIL, JAMES HOWARD, JR., real estate investor, developer, broker, consultant; b. Columbus, Ohio, Mar. 21, 1955; s. James Howard Nobil and Carol Mae (Wiesenberger) Greenbaum; m. Elizabeth Ann Corro, Apr. 16, 1983 (div. 1998); children: Jonathan James Michael, Jennifer Carrie Lee. BA in Polit. Sci., Tufts U., Medford, Mass., 1975; postgrad., George Washington U., Washington, DC, 1978—80. Lic. real estate broker Md., Va., D.C., Fla.; cert. leasing specialist ICSC. Account exec. Riviere Securities Corp., Washington, 1977-78; v.p. ops. Fed. Realty Investment Trust, Bethesda, Md., 1978-83; mng. gen. ptnr. NRW Devel. Co., Vienna, Va., 1983-84; v.p. acquisitions Oxford Nat. Properties Corp., Bethesda, 1984-85; 1st v.p. Washington Real Estate Investment Trust, Bethesda, 1985-86; pres. Washington Comml. Properties, Inc., McLean, Va., 1986—, Rent Verification Svcs. (subs. of Washington Comml. Properties, Inc.), McLean, 1986—. Mem. Internat. Coun. Shopping Ctrs., Nat. Assn. Realtors, DC Area Comml. Brokers Coun. Avocations: running, boating, skiing, tennis. Office: Washington Comml Properties Inc 1420 Beverly Rd Mc Lean VA 22101

NOBLE, ALICE L., writer, researcher; b. Rome, Ga., Apr. 20, 1934; d. Bruce Gary Landers and Lucille Mae Pyle-Landers; m. Donald Eugene Noble, May 28, 1998. Student, Anthony's Real Estate Sch., Fresno, Calif., 1967—69, Calif. Chrsitian Coll., 1970—73, Internat. Assn. Assessing Officers, Chgo., 1980—81, Writers Digest Sch., LA, 1999—2001. Real estate agt., Fresno, Calif., 1965—73; owner White Fang Pub., Delta Junction, Ark., 2003—. Author: (novels) Elusive Autumn, 2003, On the Kenai, 2003. Mem.: Creative Writers Anchorage. Republican. Presbyterian. Avocations: hiking, stamp and coin collecting, writing. Mailing: PO Box 1307 Pahrump NV 89041 Office Phone: 775-727-9359. Business E-Mail: alice.noble@sbcglobal.net.

NOBLE, DOUGLAS, architecture educator; BS in Architecture, Calif. State Poly. U., 1981, BArch, 1982; MArch, U. Calif., Berkeley, 1983, PhD in Architecture, 1991. Registered Calif., 1985. With Cashion-Horie-Cocke-Gonzalez Architects, 1978—84; tchg. asst. U. Calif., Berkeley, 1983—88, lectr., 1988—91, rsch. asst., 1988—89; prof. U. So. Calif., 1991—; with Kenneth S. Wing and Assocs., 1985—86. Co-editor: Software for Architects; A Guide to Software for the Architectural Profession, (conf. procs.) Mission, Method, Madness; Computer Supported Design in Architecture, 1992. Fellow: AIA; mem.: Assn. for Computer Aided Design in Architecture (pres. 1998), Phi Kappa Phi. Office: 204 Watt Hall U So Calif Sch Architecture Los Angeles CA 90089-0291 Business E-Mail: dnoble@usc.edu.

NOBLE, ERNEST PASCAL, pharmacologist, biochemist, educator, psychiatrist; b. Baghdad, Iraq, Apr. 2, 1929; came to U.S., 1946; s. Noble Babik and Barkev Grace (Kasparian) Babikian; m. Inga Birgitta Kilstromer, May 19, 1956; children: Lorna, Katharine, Erik BS in Chemistry, U. Calif.-Berkeley, 1951; PhD in Biochemistry, Oreg. State U., 1955; MD, Case Western Res. U., 1962. Diplomate Nat. Bd. Med. Examiners. Sr. instr. biochemistry Western Res. U., Cleve., 1957-62; intern Stanford Med. Ctr., Calif., 1962-63, resident in psychiatry Calif., 1963-66, research assoc., asst. prof. Calif., 1965-69; assoc. prof. psychiatry, psychobiology and pharmacology U. Calif.-Irvine, 1969-71, prof., chief neurochemistry, 1971-76, 79-81; dir. Nat. Inst. Alcohol Abuse and Alcoholism HEW, 1976-78, assoc. adminstr. sci., alcohol, drug abuse and mental health, 1978-79; Pike prof. alcohol studies, dir. Alcohol Research Ctr. UCLA Sch. of Medicine, 1981—. Mem. various med./sci. jour. editorial bds.; contbr. numerous articles to profl. jours., chpts. to books V.p. Nat. Coun. on Alcoholism 1981-84; pres. Internat. Commn. for the Prevention of Alcoholism and Drug Dependency, 1988. Fulbright scholar, 1955-56; Guggenheim fellow, 1974-75; Sr. Fulbright scholar, 1984-85; recipient Career Devel. award NIMH, HEW, 1966-69 Fellow Am. Coll. Neuropsychopharmacology; mem. Internat. Soc. Neurochemistry, Am. Soc. Pharmacology and Exptl. Therapeutics, Research Soc. on Alcoholism. Office: UCLA 760 Westwood Plz Los Angeles CA 90095-8353 Business E-Mail: epnoble@ucla.edu.

NOBLE, JAMES WILKES, actor; b. Dallas, Mar. 5, 1922; s. Ralph Byrne and Lois Frances (Wilkes) N.; m. Carolyn Owen Coates, May 19, 1956; 1 child: Jessica Katherine. Student, North Tex. Coll., Arlington, 1939-41, So. Methodist U., Dallas, 1941-43, 1946-47. Lectr. acting and mime Am. Acad. Dramatic Art, 1956-59. Mem. Lydia Tarnower Modern Dance Co., 1937-39; title role in 1st TV drama, The Egoist on Dumont TV, 1943; 1st NY Stage appearance Helena's Room, 1947; 1st Broadway appearance: The Big Knife, 1949; others include: The Velvet Glove, 1949; Medea, 1951; Come of Age, 1952; A Far Country, 1961; Strange Interlude, 1963; 1776, 1971; The Runner Stumbles, 1976; mem. Am. Mime Theatre, 1952-59; appeared in TV dramas and soap operas; appeared in more than 200 plays in theatres throughout the world including Stratford Characters in Stratford-Upon-Avon, England, T.S. Eliot in The Poet's Theatre, Cambridge, Mass., 1996, Out of Order, Calgary, Alta., Can., 1997, Moon Over Buffalo, Edmonton, Alta., 1998, Intelejunt Dezyne, 2007; (TV) role of Governor on Benson, 1979-86, series First Impressions, 1987, series Archies, 1990, Law and Order, 1991; (films) Dragonfly, 1965; The Sporting Club, 1967, 1776, 1972; Promises in the Dark, 1978; Ten, 1979; Being There, 1979; Airplane II, 1983; You Talkin' To Me?, 1986; Tiger's Tale, 1987, Chances Are, 1988, Absent Minded Professor, 1989, Law and Order, 1991, All My Children, 1992, others; prodr. Glacier Bay, 2006.

Active Lee Strasberg Theater, Theatre Artists Workshop. Served as lt. USNR, 1943-46, P.T.O. Named Hon. Gov., N.J., N.Y., 1982; appreciation award Am. Heart Assn., 1983. Mem. Actors Studio (life), Actors Equity, SAG, AFTRA. Democrat. Roman Catholic. Avocation: photography. Office: Paradigm Agy 10100 Santa Monica Blvd Los Angeles CA 90067-4003

NOBLE, JOSEPH VEACH, retired museum director; b. Phila., Apr. 3, 1920; s. Joseph Haderman and Helen Elizabeth (Veach) N.; m. Olive Ashley Mooney, June 21, 1941 (dec. Sept. 1978); children: Josette, Ashley, Laurence; m. Lois Cook Cartwright, Oct. 27, 1979. Student, U. Pa., 1942. Cameraman, dir. DeFrenes and Co. Studios, Phila., 1939-41; studio mgr. WPTZ, Philco TV Sta., Phila., 1941-42, DeFrenes and Co. Studios, 1946-49; gen. mgr. Murphy-Lillis Prodns., NYC, 1949-50; exec. v.p. Film Counselors, Inc., NYC, 1950-56, dir., 1950-82; operating adminstr. Met. Mus. Art, 1956-67, vice dir. adminstrn., 1967-70; dir. Mus. City NY, 1970-85, dir. emeritus; exec. dir. Soc. Medalists, 1985-95. Photog. salon exhibitor, from 1936; lectr. CCNY, 1949-51 Author: The Techniques of Painted Attic Pottery, 1965, The Historical Murals of Maplewood, 1961, Forgery of the Etruscan Terracotta Warriors, 1961; Contbr.: Ency. Brit, 1970. Trustee Corning Mus. of Glass, 1970—; mem. Morrow Meth. Ch., pres. trustees, 1972-77; chmn. NY State Bd. Hist. Preservation 1972-76; co-chmn. Save Venice, Inc., 1972; trustee Brookgreen Gardens, 1971—, pres., 1976-90, chmn., 1990-95, chmn. emeritus, 1995—. With AUS, 1942-46. Recipient Venice Film Festival medal for photography in sci., 1948, Sigma Xi award 1963, Maple Leaf award Maplewood, NJ, 1966, 87, Gold medal for The Big Apple NY Film Festival, 1979, Disting. Svc. award Maplewood C. of C., 1987. Fellow Soc. Antiquaries London, Am. Numismatic Soc.; mem. NY State Assn. Museums (pres. 1970-72), NAD (medal 1976), Nat. Sculpture Soc. (medal 1978, 91), Artists' Fellowship (medal 1978), Archeol. Inst. Am. (treas. 1963-70), Museums Coun. NYC (chmn. 1965-67), Am. Assn. Museums (pres. 1975-78, Disting. Svc. Awd., 1991, named to Centennial Honor Roll, 2006), Cultural Instns. Group NYC (chmn. 1984-85), Soc. Promotion Hellenic Studies; Am. Watercolor Soc. (medal 1982). Clubs: Maplewood Country; Explorers (NUC), Century Assn. (NYC). Office: Brookgreen Gardens PO Box 3368 Pawleys Island SC 29585-3368 Home: 7226 Williams Dr S Saint Petersburg FL 33705-6158 *As a classical archaeologist I always have been guided by the ancient saying, "Let the light of the past illumine a pathway to the future.".* *

NOBLE, LAWRENCE ALAN, artist; b. Tampa, Fla., Nov. 11, 1948; s. Clymer Marlay and Mary Alice (Cortes) N.; m. Elizabeth Wearden, May 22, 1982; children: Casey Josephine, John Marlay. Student, Tex. Acad. Art, 1969, Houston Mus. Fine Art Sch., 1974-75. Illustrator U.S. Army, Ft. Sheridan, Ill., 1970, San Francisco, 1971; staff artist, promotion dept. The Houston Chronicle, Houston, 1972; art dir., designer, illustrator Middaugh Assocs., Houston, 1973; freelance illustrator Noble Studio, Houston, 1973-88, designer, sculptor Crestline, Calif., 1988—. Sculptor, com. mem. San Bernardino County Peace Officers Meml. Com., San Bernardino, 1995—, designer sculptor Victor Salmones galleries, 1995—, sculptor, com. mem. Jack Benny Meml. Com., 1992-93, Ft. Sheridan Centennial Com., 1989-90. Sculptor, designer various art galleries. Hon. firefighter City of Redlands Fire Dept., 1997; marshall 4th July Parade Crestline Resorts C. of C., 1996, vol. McGovern for Pres., Dem. party, 1972. With U.S. Army, 1969-71. Recipient 4th U.S. Army Leadership and Integrity medal, 1986. Mem. Nat. Sculptors Soc., Internat. Sculpture Ctr., Calif. Profl. Firefighters, Star Wars Fan Club, Star Trek Fan Club. Republican. Roman Catholic. Avocations: surfing, reading, history. Office: Noble Studio PO Box 2229 Crestline CA 92325-2229

NOBLE, MARY C., state supreme court justice; b. Jackson, Ky., 1949; m. Larry Noble. B., Austin Peay State U., Clarksville, Tenn., 1971, M., 1975; JD, U. Ky. Coll. Law, 1981. Pvt. practice, 1981—91; domestic rels. commr., 1989—91; cir. judge for Fayette County Fayette Cir. Ct., 1991—2006, chief regional cir. judge, 1998—2002; assoc. justice for 5th Supreme Ct. Dist. Supreme Ct. Ky., 2007—; co-founder Ky. Drug Courts, Drug Ct. judge, 1996—2006. Mem.: Nat. Assn. Drug Ct. Professionals (mem. & former pres. congress state drug cts., bd. dirs.). Office: Supreme Ct Ky 155 E Main St Ste 200 Lexington KY 40507 Office Phone: 859-246-2220. *

NOBLE, RALPH C., animal scientist, department chairman; s. Willie G. Noble; m. Debra Tazewell; 1 child, Rachel C. BS, Tuskegee U., Ala., 1973, MS, 1975; PhD, U. Ill., Champaign-Urbana, 1981. Cert. artificial insemination technician Ala., forage mgmt. Coop. Ext., Ala., beef quality assurance Coop. Ext., Ala. Instr. Tuskegee U., 1975—77, from asst. to assoc. prof., 1982—2005, acting coord. George Washington Carver agrl. expt. sta., 1985—86, coord. of CSREES animal sci. rsch. program, 1986—97, coord. animal, poultry and vet. scis. program, 2002—05; rsch./tchg. asst. U. Ill., Champaign-Urbana, 1978—81; chmn. dept. animal scis. NC A&T State U., Greensboro, 2005—. Cons. Heifer Internat., Gainsville, Fla., 1990—2005; dir. strategic alliance for the Ala. goat industry Tuskegee U., 2001—05; advisor Ala. Farmers Fedn. Meat Goat and Sheep subcom., Montgomery, 2002—05; bd. dirs. NRCS-AL Grassland Res. com., Auburn, Ala., 2003—05; mem. adv. com. U.S. Poultry & Egg Assn., Atlanta, 2002—03; advisor Nat. Pre-Vet. Medicine Assn., Stillwater, Okla., 2002—04; chair livestock com. Macon County Farmers Orgn., Inc., Tuskegee, 1988—2005; mem. planning com. farmers conf. Tuskegee U. Coop. Ext. Program, 1982—2005; contbg. editor Am. Assn. Animal Sci., Urbana, 1985—86. Vol. eyeglass collection Lions Club, Tuskegee, 1986—90; sec. Sigma Xi, Tuskegee; pres., sec. Gamma Sigma Delta, Tuskegee; mem. Humane Soc. of the Piedmont, Greensboro, 2006—; mem. adv. com. to the bishop ELCA SE Luth. Ch., Atlanta, 1986—88; bd. dirs. St. Luke Luth. Ch., Tuskegee, 1988—98. Recipient Outstanding Faculty Performance award for tchg., Tuskegee U., 1987, 1997, Outstanding Faculty Performance award for svc., 2002, Outstanding Recognition award for tech. assistance to small farmers in the Southea. US, Heifer Project Internat., 2002, Alumni Merit Honor, Tuskegee U. Vet. Alumni Assn., 2005. Mem.: Phi Kappa Phi (licentiate). Office: NC A&T State U Webb Hall Ste 101 1601 E Market St Greensboro NC 27411 Home Phone: 336-337-7549; Office Phone: 336-334-7547. Office Fax: 336-334-7288. E-mail: rcnoble@ncat.edu.

NOBLE, RONALD KENNETH, secretary general of Interpol; b. Ft. Dix, NJ, Sept. 24, 1956; BA cum laude, U. NH, 1979; JD, Stanford U., 1982. Bar: Pa. 1983, NJ, 1983. Sr. law clk. to Hon. A. Leon Higginbotham Jr. US Ct. Appeals 3rd Cir., Phila., 1982-84; asst. US atty. ea. dist. Pa. Office Atty. Gen., Phila., 1984-88; spl. counsel & chief of staff criminal divsn. US Dept. Justice, Washington, 1988-89, dep. asst. atty. gen., 1989; asst. prof. law NYU Sch. Law, 1990—92, assoc. prof., 1992—99, prof., 1999—; asst. sec. for enforcement US Dept. Treasury, Washington, 1993-94, under sec. for enforcement, 1994-96; sec. gen INTERPOL, Lyon, France, 2000—. Pres. Fin. Action Task Force, 1994—; mem. exec. com. INTERPOL, 1994—; mem. Root-Tilden Scholar Selection Bd., 1990—; chmn. Customs Ops. Adv. Com., 1993—; chmn. Bank Secrecy Act Adv. Com., 1993—. Articles editor Stanford Law Rev., 1981-82. Mem. Am. Law Inst. Office: NYU Sch of Law Vanderbilt Hall 40 Washington Sq S Rm 420 New York NY 10012-1099 also: INTERPOL Gen Secretariat 200 quai Charles de Gaulle 69006 Lyons France

NOBLES, LAURENCE HEWIT, retired geology educator; b. Spokane, Wash., Sept. 28, 1927; s. Harry and Florence (Giffin) N.; m. Barbara Joanne Smith, Aug. 28, 1948; children: Heather C., Laurence F. BS, MS, Calif. Inst. Tech., 1949; PhD, Harvard, 1952. Instr. geology Northwestern U., 1952-55, asst. prof., 1955-61, assoc. prof., 1961-67, prof., 1967-90, prof. emeritus, 1990—, also asst. dean Coll. Arts and Scis., 1966-67, asso. dean, 1968-70; acting dean Northwestern U. (Coll. Arts and Scis.), 1970-72, dean adminstrn., 1972-81, v.p. adminstrn. and fin. planning, 1981-86. Trustee Adler Planetarium, 1980-86, Chgo. Acad. Scis., 1967-87, pres., 1973-78, hon. trustee, 1987—; faculty rep. Big Ten Conf., 1976-81; active Port Ludlow Village Coun., 2005—, pres., 2007—. Mem. Am. Geophys. Union, Geol. Soc. Am. Personal E-mail: lnobles@cablespeed.com.

NOBLITT, HARDING COOLIDGE, political scientist, educator; b. Marion, NC, Oct. 31, 1920; s. Walter Tate and Nellie Mae (Horton) N.; m. Louise Hope Lester, July 3, 1943; 1 son, Walter Thomas. BA, Berea Coll., 1942; MA, U. Chgo., 1947, PhD, 1955. Mem. faculty Concordia Coll., Moorhead, Minn., 1950-90, prof. polit. sci., 1956-90, Wije Disting. prof., 1979-82, chmn. dept., 1964-72, prof. emeritus, 1990. Mem. editorial bd.: Discourse: A Review of the Liberal Arts, 1957-67, acting editor, 1959-60. Democratic candidate Congress, 1962; del. Dem. Nat. Conv., 1964; chmn. Profs. for Johnson-Humphrey, Minn., 1964; chmn. platform com. Dem. State Conv., 1968; mem. Gov.'s Citizens Council on Aging, 1963-68; mem. City Charter Commn., Moorhead, 1985—; mem. Minn. Higher Edn. Coordinating Bd., 1971-81, sec., 1974-75, pres., 1979-80. Served with AUS, 1943-46, ETO. Recipient 1st ann. Great Tchr. award Concordia Coll., 1960; recipient Flaat Disting. Service award Concordia Coll., 1982 Mem. Am. Polit. Sci. Assn., Am. Legion, Phi Kappa Phi, Pi Gamma Mu, Tau Kappa Alpha, Pi Kappa Delta Presbyterian (elder). Home: 2014 4th St S Moorhead MN 56560-4131 Office: Concordia Coll Dept Polit Sci Moorhead MN 56560

NOBLITT, NANCY ANNE, aerospace engineer; b. Roanoke, Va., Aug. 14, 1959; d. Jerry Spencer and Mary Louise (Jerrell) N. BA, Mills Coll., Oakland, Calif., 1982; MS in Indsl. Engring., Northeastern U., 1990; JD, Coll. William and Mary, 2003. Cert. quality auditor, ASQ, 2006. Data red specialist Universal Energy Sys., Beaver Creek, Ohio, 1981; aerospace engr. turbine engine divsn. components br. turbine group aero-propulsion lab. Wright-Patterson AFB, Ohio, 1982-84, engine assessment br. spl. engines group, 1984-87; lead analyst cycle methods computer aided engr. GE, Lynn, Mass., 1987-90, Lynn PACES project coord., 1990-91; software sys. analyst Sci. Applications Internat. Corp., with artificial intelligence McLean, Va., 1991-92, software engring. mgr., intelligence applications integration Hampton, Va., 1992-93, mgr. test engring. and sys. support, 1993-94, mgr. configuration mgmt., 1994, mgmt. asst. to TBMCS program mgr., 1994-95; sr. simulation engr. Chem Demil, 1995-98; supervisory engr. Analytical Mechanics Assocs., Hampton, 1998-99; sr. project engr. Newport News (Va.) Shipbuilding Inc., 1999-00; quality assurance mgr. Sci. Applications Internat. Corp., 2005—. Tutor math. and sci. Centerville Sch. Bd., Ohio, 1982-86; tutor math. and physics Marblehead Sch. Bd., Mass., 1988-90; tutor math., chemistry and physics Poquoson Sch. Bd., Va., 1994—; rep. alumnae admissions Boston area Mills Coll., 1987-91, trustee, bd. govs., 1995-98; mem. Citizens for Hilton Area Revitalization, 1994—. Math. and sci. tutor Centerville Sch. Bd., Ohio, 1982-86, math. and physics tutor Marblehead (Mass.) Sch. Bd., 1988-90; tutor math., chemistry and physics Poquoson Sch. Bd., Va., 1994—; rep. alumnae admissions Mills Coll., Boston area, 1987-91, trustee/bd. govs., 1995-98; mem. Citizens for Hilton Area Revitalization, 1994—. Recipient Notable Achievement award USAF, 1984, Spl. award Fed. Lab. Consortium, 1987. Mem. Soc. Mfg. Engrs., Sports and Entertainment Law Soc., Phi Alpha Delta. Avocation: book collecting. Home: 58 Hopkins St Newport News VA 23601-4034 Office: SAIC Suffolk VA 23535 Office Phone: 757-686-9815.

NOBUMOTO, KAREN S., prosecutor; BA, U. Hartford, 1973; JD Southwestern U., 1989. Dep. dist. atty. County of L.A. Named Unsung Hero, KFWB Radio, 1997, Prosecutor of Yr., Century City Bar Assn., 1998, Person of Yr., Met. News-Enterprise, 2001, Lawyer of Yr., Calif. Lawyer Mag., 2003, Alumna of Yr., Southwestern U., 2003, Super Lawyer, L.A. mag., 2004. Mem.: L.A. County Bar Assn., Calif. Assn. Black Lawyers, Assn. Dep. Dist. Attys., Black Women Lawyers L.A., Women Lawyers Assn. L.A., John M. Langston Bar Assn. (pres. 1997), State Bar Calif. (pres. 2001—02), Coalition 100 Black Women, Breakfast Club, Chancery Club. Office: LA Dist Attys Office 210 W Temple St Ste 18000 Los Angeles CA 90012-3210 Home Phone: 323-440-2385; Office Phone: 310-288-1246. E-mail: karennobu@aol.com.

NOCE, DAVID D., judge; b. 1944; AB, St. Louis U., 1966; JD, U. Mo., Columbia, 1969. Bar: Mo. Law clk. to Hon. H. Kenneth Wangelin US Dist. Ct. (ea. and we. dists.) Mo., 1972-73; law clk. to Hon. John F. Nangle US Dist. Ct. (ea. dist.) Mo., 1973-75; asst. US atty. (ea. dist.) Mo US Dept. Justice, St. Louis, 1975-76; magistrate judge US Dist. Ct. (ea. dist.) Mo., St. Louis, 1976—. Adj. prof. law St. Louis U. Sch. Law, Washington U. Sch. Law, St. Louis. Author: Jury Instructions Drafting Workbook West, 1999. Served with U.S. Army, 1970-72. Mem. ABA, Mo. Bar, Bar Assn. Met. St. Louis, Fed. Magistrate Judges Assn. Office: US Courthouse 17th Flr N 111 S 10th St Saint Louis MO 63102 Office Phone: 314-244-7630.

NOCE, DONNA, retail executive; With Petrie Stores, Lerner NY; merchandising v.p. separates, dresses and suits Ann Taylor Stores, 1996—2000; v.p. merchandising and planning AnnTaylor.com, 2000—02; v.p. Ann Taylor Factory Stores, 2002, sr. v.p.; exec. v.p. merchandising and design Ann Taylor LOFT, 2006—. Office: Ann Taylor Stores Corp 7 Times Square 15th Fl New York NY 10036

NOCE, WALTER WILLIAM, JR., hospital administrator; b. Neptune, NJ, Sept. 27, 1945; s. Walter William and Louise Marie (Jenkins) N.; m. Susan Harris, Nov. 6, 2005; children: Krista Suzanne, David Michael. BA, LaSalle Coll., Phila., 1967; M.P.H., UCLA, 1969. Regional coordinator USPHS, Rockville, Md., 1969-71; v.p. Hollywood Presbyn. Hosp., LA, 1971-75; sr. v.p. Hollywood Presbyn. Med. ctr., 1975-77; v.p. adminstrn. Huntington Meml. Hosp, Pasadena, Calif., 1977-83; pres., CEO St. Joseph Hosp., Orange, Calif., 1983-90, Children's Hosp., LA, 1995—2006, vice chmn., 2006—; pres. so. Calif. region St. Joseph Health Sys., 1987-90, exec. v.p., 1990-94. Preceptor UCLA Health Svcs. Mgmt. Program, 1977—; chmn. bd. Health Plan of Am., 1985-91; chmn. Hosp. Coun. So. Calif., 1989. Exec. v.p. Mental Health Assn. in LA County, 1979-82; regional v.p. Calif. Mental Health Assn., 1982-83; vice chmn., bd. trustees Children's Hosp. LA, 2006-. W. Glenn Ebersole finalist Assn. Western Hosp., 1969; recipient USPHS letter commendation, 1971, leadership in health affairs award Healthcare Assn. So. Calif., 1997. Mem. Am. Coll. Hosp. Adminstrs., Am. Hosp. Assn. (ho. of dels. 1994—), Nat. Assn. Children's Hosps. (bd. dirs. 1995—), Calif. Assn. Cath. Hosps. (chmn. 1990-91), Calif. Assn. Hosps. and Health Sys. (chmn. 1992), UCLA Hosp. Adminstrn. Alumni Assn. (pres. 1979-80), Pasadena C. of C. (v.p. 1980-82). Home: 1012 Glen Oaks Blvd Pasadena CA 91105-1108 Office: Childrens Hosp LA 4650 Sunset Blvd Los Angeles CA 90027 Home Phone: 626-796-3809; Office Phone: 323-671-1779. Business E-Mail: wnoce@chla.usc.edu. *Ambition is necessary for success, but success achieved at the expense of others is failure.*

NOCEK, JANET, library director; Dir. Portland Pub. Libr., Conn. Recipient Outstanding Librarian award, Ct. Libr. Assn., 2006, ProQuest-SIRS State and Regional Achievement award, ALA Intellectual Freedom Round Table, 2007, Paul Howard award for Courage, ALA, 2007. Achievements include challenging the constitutionality of FBI National Security Letters and gag orders imposed under the USA PATRIOT Act, as one of four Connecticut "John Does". Office: Portland Library 20 Freestone Ave Portland CT 06480 Office Fax: 860-342-6778.

NOCERA, JOSEPH, editor, writer; b. May 1952; married; 3 children. BS in Journalism, Boston U. Contbg. editor Newsweek; exec. editor New England Monthly, Fortune Mag.; editorial dir.; editor Wash. Monthly; columnist The Profit Motive column, GQ, Esquire, 1988—90; sr. editor Tex. Monthly Mag.; editor-at-large Fortune Mag.; columnist Money Mag., 1998; fin. columnist NY Times, 2005—. Anchor PBS Frontline Documentary, Betting on the Market, 1997; master's project adv., grad. sch. journalism Columbia Univ. Contbr. articles to Wall Street Journal, Newsweek, Wash. Monthly; author: Bidness: The Booms and Busts of the Texas Economy, 1986, A Piece of the Action: How the Middle Class Joined the Money Class, 1994 (NY Pub.Libr.Helen Bernstein award for best nonfiction book of yr., 1995). Named one of 100 Business News Luminaries of the Century, The Journalist and Financial Reporting, 2000; recipient John Hancock award, 1983, 1984, 1991, Gerald Loeb award, 1993, 1996. Office: Columnist NY Times 229 W 43rd St New York NY 10036

NOCHIMSON, DAVID, lawyer; b. Paterson, NJ, June 19, 1943; s. Samuel S. and Mildred (Singer) N.; m. Roberta Maizel, June 5, 1966 (div. 1972); m. Gail Burgess, May 26, 1978. BA, Yale U., 1965; LLB, Columbia U., 1968; LLM, Australian Nat. U., Canberra, 1969. Bar: N.Y. 1970, Calif. 1977. Assoc. Paul, Weiss, Rifkind, Wharton and Garrison, NYC, 1970-72; sr. v.p. Comprop Equities Corp., NYC, 1972-76; assoc. Mitchell, Silberberg and Knupp, LA, 1977-80, ptnr., 1980-83, Ziffren, Brittenham, Branca, Fischer, Gilbert-Lurie & Stiffelman, LA, 1983—. Adv. com. UCLA Entertainment Symposium, 1979-99, co-chmn., 1981-82. Contbr. articles to Encyclopedia of Investments, 1982, profl. jours. Pres. Friends of the L.A. Free Clinic, 1994-96; trustee Santa Monica (Calif.) Mus. of Art, 1995—. Fulbright scholar, Australia, 1968-69. Mem. ABA (forum com. on entertainment and sports industries 1982—, editor The Entertainment and Sports Lawyer 1982-89, chmn. 1989-92), Internat. Bar Assn. (Vice chmn. entertainment com. 1986-90), Am. Bar Found., Beverly Hills Bar Assn. Democrat. Jewish. Avocations: tennis, racquetball, yoga, playing piano, hiking. Office: Ziffren Brittenham Branca Fischer Gilbert-Lurie and Stiffelman 1801 Century Park W Los Angeles CA 90067-6406 Office Phone: 310-552-3388.

NOCHMAN, LOIS WOOD KIVI (MRS. MARVIN NOCHMAN), retired literature educator; b. Detroit, Nov. 5, 1924; d. Peter K. and Annetta Lois (Wood) Kivi; m. Harold I. Pitchford, Sept. 6, 1944 (div. May 1949); children: Jean Wood Pitchford Scott, Joyce Lynn Pitchford Undiano; m. Marvin A. Nochman, Aug. 15, 1953; 1 child, Joseph Asa. AB, U. Mich., 1946, AM, 1949. Tchr. adult edn., Honolulu, 1947, Ypsilanti (Mich.) H.S., 1951—52; spl. instr. English Wayne State U., Detroit, 1953—54; tchr. Highland Park (Mich.) Coll., 1950—51, instr. English, 1954—83; ret., 1983. Mem. exec. bd. Highland Park Fedn. Tchrs., 1963—66, 1973, del. to nat. conv., 64, 1971—74; rep. higher edn. Mich. Fedn. Tchrs. Exec. Com., 1972—76; mem. faculty adv. com. Gov's Commn. Higher Edn., 1973—. Contbr. articles to profl. jours. Tchr. Baha'i Schs., Davison, Mich., 1954—55, 1958—59, 1963—66, Beaulac, Que., Canada, 1960, Greenacre, Maine, 1965; sec. local spiritual assembly Baha'is, Ann Arbor, Mich., 1953, sec. Detroit, 1954, chmn., 1955; mem. nat. com. Baha'is U.S., 1955—58; sec. com. and coun. Baha'i Schs., Davison, Mich., 1956, 1958, 1963—68; Baha'i lectr. subject of local TV show Senior Focus, 1992. Recipient Women's Movement plaque, Women Lawyers Assn. Mich., 1975. Mem.: MLA, NOW, Nat. Soc. Lit. and Arts, Am. Fedn. Tchrs., Mich. Coll. English Assn., Nat. Coun. Tchrs. English, Women's Equity and Action League (sec. Mich. chpt. 1975—79), Alpha Gamma Delta, Alpha Lambda Delta. Avocation: U.S. Swimming Master Champion.

NODDINGS, NEL, education educator, writer; b. Irvington, NJ, Jan. 19, 1929; d. Edward A. Rieth and Nellie A. (Connors) Walter; m. James A. Noddings, Aug. 20, 1949; children: Chris, Howard, Laurie, James, Nancy, William, Sharon, Edward, Vicky, Timothy. BA in Math., Montclair State Coll., 1949; MA in Math., Rutgers U., 1964; PhD in Edn., Stanford U., 1973; PhD (hon.), Columbia Coll., SC, 1995; LLD (hon.), Queen's U., Can., 2006; LHD (hon.), Montclair State U., 2006; PhD (hon.), Lewis & Clark Coll., Portland, Oreg., 2007. Cert. tchr. Calif., NJ. Tchr. Woodbury (N.J.) Pub. Schs., 1949-52; tchr. math. dept. Matawan (N.J.) High Sch., 1958-62, chair, asst. prin., 1964-69; curriculum supr. Montgomery Twp. Pub. Schs., Skillman, NJ, 1970-72; dir. precollegiate edn. U. Chgo., 1975-76; asst. prof. Pa. State U., State College, 1973; from asst. prof. to assoc. prof. Stanford (Calif.) U., 1977-86, prof., 1986—, assoc. dean, 1990-92, acting dean, 1992-94, Lee L. Jacks prof. child edn., 1992-98, prof. emeritus, 1998—; prof. philosophy and edn. Columbia U., NYC, 1998—. Bd. dirs. Ctr. for Human Caring Sch. Nursing, Denver, 1986-92; cons. NIE, NSF and various other sch. dists. Author: Caring: A Feminine Approach to Ethics and Moral Education, 1984, Women and Evil, 1989; author: (with W. Paul Shore) Awakening the Inner Eye: Intuition in Education, 1984; author: (with Carol Witherell) Stories Lives Tell, 1991; author: The Challenge to Care in Schools, 1992, Educating for Intelligent Belief or Unbelief, 1993, Philosophy of Education, 1995, Starting at Home: Caring and Social Policy, 2002, Educating Moral People, 2002, Happiness and Education, 2003; editor (with Suzanne Gordon and Patricia Benner): Caregiving, 1996; editor: (with Michael Katz and Kenneth Strike) Justice and Caring, 1999; editor: Educating Citizens for Global Awareness, 2005, Critical Lessons: What Our Schools Should Teach, 2006, When School Reform Goes Wrong, 2007. Mem. disting. women's adv. bd. Coll. St. Catherine. Recipient Anne Roe award for Contbns. to Profl. Devel. of Women, Harvard Grad. Sch. Edn., 1993, medal for disting. svc. Tchrs. Coll. Columbia, 1994, Willystine Goodsell award, 1997, Laureate chpt. Kappa Delta Pi, Pi Lambda Theta award, 1999, award for disting. leadership in edn. Rutgers U., 2004; Spencer Mentor grantee, Spencer Found., 1995-97. Fellow Philosophy of Edn. Soc. (pres. 1991-92); mem. Am. Ednl. Rsch. Assn. (Div B, 2000, Lifetime achievment award), Am. Philos. Assn., Nat. Acad. Edn. (pres. 2001—), John Dewey Soc. (pres. 1994-96), Phi Beta Kappa (vis. scholar). Avocation: gardening. Home Phone: 732-988-9695; Office Phone: 732-988-9695. Business E-Mail: noddings@stanford.edu.

NODDINGS, SARAH ELLEN, lawyer; b. Matawan, NJ; d. William Clayton and Sarah Stephenson (Cox) Noddings; children: Christopher, Aaron. BA in Math., Rutgers U., New Brunswick, NJ, 1965, MSW, 1968; JD cum laude, Seton Hall U., Newark, NJ, 1975; postgrad., UCLA, 1979. Bar: Calif. 1976, Nev. 1976, NJ 1975, US Dist. Ct. (ctrl. dist.) Calif. 1976, US Dist. Ct. NJ 1975. Social worker Carteret (N.J.) Bd. Edn., 1970-75; law clk. Hon. Howard W. Babcock, 8th Jud. Dist. Ct., Las Vegas, Nev., 1975-76; assoc. O'Melveny & Myers, LA, 1976-78; atty. Internat. Creative Mgmt., Beverly Hills, Calif., 1978-81, Russell & Glickman, Century City, Calif., 1981-83; from atty to v.p. Lorimar Prodns., Culver City and Burbank, Calif., 1983—93; atty., v.p. Warner Bros. TV, Burbank, Calif., 1993—2001, sr. atty., 1999-2001; pvt. practice, 2001—. Dir. county youth program, rsch. analyst Sonoma County People Econ. Opportunity, Santa Rosa, Calif., 1968-69; VISTA vol. Kings County Cmty. Action Orgn., Hanford, Calif., 1965-66; officer, PTA bd. West H.S., Casimir Mid. Sch. and Arlington Elem. Sch. Mem.: Media Dist. Intellectual Property Bar Assn. (bd. dir. 1999—2001), LA County Bar Assn. (intellectual property sect.), Friends of Madrona Marsh (bd. dirs. 2007—), Women in Film, Acad. TV Arts and Scis. (nat. awards com. 1994—96), LA Copyright Soc. (trustee 1990—91), Women Entertainment Lawyers, US Tennis Assn. (capt. 2006—07), South Bay Marine League (B-2 rep.). Avocations: travel, tennis, bicycling, swimming, bridge.

NODDLE, JEFFREY, retail and food distribution executive; BA, U. Iowa. Various positions, including pres. 2 food divsns. Supervalu Inc., Eden Prairie, Minn., 1976-92, exec. v.p., 1992-95, exec. v.p. mktg.; pres., COO wholesale food cos., 1995-99, pres., COO, 2000-01, pres., CEO, 2001—04, chmn., CEO, 2004—. Bd. mem. Ind. Grocers Alliance

Inc., Food Industry Ctr., U. Minn., Acad. Food Mktg., St. Joseph's U., Pa.; corp. bd. Donaldson Co. Inc.; chmn. bd. Food Mktg. Inst. Bd. dir. Greater Twin Cities United Way; bd. overseers U. Minn. Carlson Sch. Mgmt.; exec. com. Minn. Bus. Partnership. Office: Supervalu Inc 11840 Valley View Rd Eden Prairie MN 55344-3691 *

NODEEN, JANEY PRICE, information technology executive; b. Scotland Neck, NC, Nov. 7, 1959; d. Wade Hampton and Joyce Ann (Councill) P.; m. Thomas Nodeen. BS in Info. Sci., Christopher Newport Coll., 1987; grad., Def. Sys. Mgmt. Coll., 1994; grad. advanced mgmt. program, Nat. Def. U., 1995; grad. owner president's program, Harvard Bus. Sch., 2003. Engring. analyst Newport News Shipbldg., Va., 1978-86; mgr. submarine info. resources and computer ops. Dept. of the Navy, Washington, 1986-93, mem. exec. devel. program, 1993-96, sr. staff Navy Acquisition Reform Exec., 1995, dep. program exec. officer Submarines for Acquisition, 1996-97; prin. Burke Consortium, Inc., Springfield, Va., 1997—. Mil. legis. fellow for Congressman Sam Gejdenson, 1994; sr. exec. fellow John F. Kennedy Sch. Govt. Harvard U., class officer, 1994. Office: Burke Consortium Inc Ste 510 5500 Cherokee Ave Alexandria VA 22312

NODIFF, JACK, artist, retired pharmacist; s. Isadore Abraham and Sarah Nodiff; m. Ruth Abrin Nodiff, July 12, 1954; children: Debra, Eric, David. BA in Sci., NYU, 1945; BS in Pharmacy, LI U., 1951. Pharmacist, NY, 1948—51. Exhibitions include Welles Gallery, Lenox, Mass., 1991, E. Rockaway Libr., 1978, Village Gallery, Hewlett, NY, 1980, Malverne Gallery, NY, 1982, E. Rockaway Libr., 1989, NY, Berkshires, grp. exhibitions, Abraham & Straus, Hempstead, NY, 1981, Towns Music & Art Found., Woodmere, NY, 1981—84, Long Beach Mus. Art, NY, 1983 (1st prize, 1983), Internat. Arts Festival, E.Rockaway, 1983, Salmagundi Club, NY, 1983, Chung-Cheng Art Gallery, Queens, NY, 1984, Shelter Rock Libr., Albertson, NY, 1985, Long Beach Mus. Art, NY, 1986, Nassau County. Mus. Fine Arts, Roslyn, NY, 1986, Garden City Pub. Libr., NY, 1986, Freeport Meml. Libr., 1986—87 (Grumbacher Silver award, 1987), Salmagundi Club, 1987, Syosset Pub. Libr., 1987, Chelsea Art Ctr., Muttontown, NY, 1992, Sheffield Art League, Mass., 1992—94 (1st prize, 1992), Nassau County. Mus. Fine Arts, 1994. Mem. NY Dept. Cultural Affairs, NY, 1987, E.Rockaway Cultural Arts Coun., NY. Mem.: Tri-county Artists, Housatonic Valley Art League. Jewish. Avocations: chess, music, golf. Home: 6 Emmet Ave East Rockaway NY 11518 Personal E-mail: jnodiff@verizon.net.

NODLER, CHARLES EDWARD, JR., archivist, history professor; b. Urbana, Ill., Jan. 13, 1949; s. Charles Edward Nodler, Sr. and Beatrice June Nodler. AA, Crowder Coll., 1973; BA in History, Mo. So. State Coll., Joplin, 1975; MA in History, U. Tex., Arlington, 1978; MA in Libr. Sci., U. Mo., Columbia, 1995. Cert. archival Adminstrn. U. Tex., Arlington, 1979, archivist Acad. Cert. Archivists, 2002. Archivist Mo. So. State U., Joplin, 1978—. Project archivist George Washington Carver Nat. Monument, Diamond, Mo., 1981—82; history prof. SW Bapt. U., Kelley U. Coll., Joplin, 1989—90; adj. history prof. Mo. So. State U., Joplin, 2005—06; exec. bd. Gene Taylor Libr. and Mus., Sarcoxie, Mo., 1990—; v.p. George Wash. Carver Birthplace Dist. Assn., Diamond, 1994—; archival cons. Newton County, Mo., Neosho, 2006. Author: Bracing the Cornerpost, 1992, Field of Teams; Baseball in Neosho, 2006; contbr. Committeeman Rep. Party, Neosho, 2002—06; lay leader United Meth. Ch., Neosho, 2000—06. With US Army, 1969—71. Named Outstanding Alumnus, Crowder Coll., 2007; grantee Digitization Grant Riches from the Earth: Geol. and Indsl. History of Jasper County, Libr. Svcs. and Tech. Grant Act, Digital Imaging Grant Program, 2006; Digitization Grant Mining the History SW Mo., Environ. Task Force Jasper and Newton County, 2005—06. Mem.: Pub. History Alliance Mo., Acad. Cert. Archivists, Soc. SW Archivists, Midwest Archives Conf., Soc. Am. Archivists, Newtonia Battlefields Protection Assn. (life), Phi Alpha Theta. Conservative. Methodist. Avocations: collect old sports cards (baseball and football), weight training, running. Home: 1215 Northwest Blvd Neosho MO 64850 Office: Missouri Southern State University 3950 E Newman Rd Joplin MO 64801 Office Phone: 417-625-9552. Office Fax: 417-625-9734. Business E-Mail: nodler-c@mssu.edu.

NOE, ELIZABETH HARDY, lawyer; b. Albertville, Ala., Sept. 24, 1964; d. John William and Nancy Jo (Luther) Hardy; m. George McRae Noe, Nov. 6, 1993. BA, Agnes Scott Coll., 1986; JD, U. Va., 1989. Bar: La. 1989, Ga. 1996. Assoc. Jones, Walker, Waechter, Poitevent, Carrere & Denegre, New Orleans, 1989-94; atty. Paul, Hastings, Janofsky & Walker, Atlanta, 1995—, co-chmn. atty. devel., ptnr., 2001—. Mem. ABA, La. Bar Assn., Ga. Bar Assn. Office: Paul Hastings Janofsky & Walker 600 Peachtree St NE Ste 2400 Atlanta GA 30308-2265 Office Phone: 404-815-2287. Business E-Mail: elizabethnoe@paulhastings.com.

NOE, ELNORA (ELLIE NOE), retired chemicals executive; b. Evansville, Ind., Aug. 23, 1928; d. Thomas Noe and Evelyn (West) Dieter. Student, Ind. U.-Purdue U., Indpls. Sec. Pitman Moore Co., Indpls., 1946—60; with Dow Chem. Co., Indpls., 1960-90, pub. rels. asst. then mgr. employee comm., 1970-87, mgr. cmty. rels., 1987-90, DowBrands, Inc., Indpls., 1986-90, vice chmn. Indpls. C. of C. corp. affairs discussion group, 1988—89, chmn., 1989-90; mem. steering com. Learn About Bus. Recipient 2d pl. award as Businesswoman of Yr., Indpls. Bus. and Profl. Women's Assn., 1980, Indpls. Profl. Woman of Yr. award Zonta, Altrusa, Soroptomist & Pilot Svc. Clubs, 1985, DowBrands Great Things Cmty. Svc. award, 1991. Mem. Am. Bus. Women Assn. (Woman of Yr. award 1965, past pres.), Ind. Assn. Bus. Communicators (hon., Communicator of Yr. 1977), Assn. Women in Comm. (Louise Eleanor Kleinhenz award 1984), Zonta (dist. pub. rels. chmn. 1978-80, area dir. 1980-82, pres. Indpls. club 1977-79, bd. dirs. 1993-95, 2000-02, 04-06, v.p. 2006—), Dow Indpls. Retiree Group (pres. 1995—). Personal E-mail: elenoe@aol.com.

NOE, GUY, retired social services administrator; b. Brussels, Jan. 28, 1934; came to U.S., 1955, naturalized, 1961; s. Marinus Cornelis and Johanna Dorothea (Beijne) N.; 1 child, Jeanette Sue. BS, Regional Agrl. Sch., Loiret, France, 1954. Social worker State of Wyo., Casper, 1962-66; dir. Natrona County (Wyo.) Dept. Public Assistance, Casper, 1966-79, Wyo. Div. Mental Health, Cheyenne, 1979-82, asst. adminstr. Divsn. of Youth Svcs., 1992-95; former mgr. Platte County Office Pub. Assistance and Social Svcs., Wheatland, Wyo., dir. low income energy assistance programs, 1994-95. Lectr. in field. V.p. Wyo. chpt. Big Bros., 1976-77; chmn. adv. coun. social svcs. State of Wyo., 1969-79; bd. dirs. Casper United Way, 1970—, Casper Salvation Army, 1970—, Casper chpt. ARC, 1977—; mem. Gov.'s Drug Abuse Adv. Bd., 1992—; pres. State Employees Assn. Named Outstanding Adminstr. State of Wyo., 1976; recipient Youth Svcs. award Wyo. Human Resources Confedn., 1988; named to Wyo. Dept. Family Svcs. Hall of Fame, 2005. Mem. ASPA, Am. Public Welfare Assn. (Wyo. membership chmn.), Wyo. State Employees Assn. (pres. 1996-97), Toastmasters. Democrat. Home: 2731 Deming Blvd Cheyenne WY 82001-5709

NOE, JAMES ALVA, retired judge; b. Billings, Mont., May 25, 1932; s. James Alva Sr. and Laura Madlen (Parmenter) N.; m. Patricia Arlene Caudill, Aug. 4, 1956; children: Kendra Sue, Jeffrey James, Bradley John, Kirkwood Merle. BA in Polit. Sci., U. Wash., 1954, LLB, 1957; LittD hon., Christian Theol. Sem., 1986. Bar: Wash. 1958, U.S. Dist. Ct. (we. dist.) Wash. 1958, U.S. Ct. Appeals (9th cir.) 1959. Dep. prosecuting atty. King County, Seattle, 1958-61; trial lawyer Williams, Kastner & Gibbs, Seattle, 1961-67; judge Seattle Mcpl. Ct., 1967-71, King County Superior Ct., 1971-96; ret., 1996. Moderator Christian Ch. (Disciples of Christ) in the U.S. and Can., 1977-79. Fellow: Am. Bar Found. (life); mem.: ABA (ho. of dels. 1976—78, chmn. nat. conf. state trial judges 1981—82, ho. of dels. 1982—87, chmn. jud. divsn. 1988—89, bd. govs. 1991—94, ho. of dels. 1991—96, sr. lawyers divsn. coun. 2001—, ho. of dels. 2003—, chmn. elect 2007—), Nat. Jud. Coll. (trustee 1988—91, 1995—2001, chair 1999—2001), Wash. State Superior Ct. Judges Assn. (pres. 1984—85, Wash. State Jurist of Yr. award 1991). Home: 8250 SE 61st St Mercer Island WA 98040-4902

NOE, JOHN, validation engineer; BS in Biomedical & Elec. Engring., U. So. Calif., LA, 1999—2002. Validation engr. Mission Pharmacal Co., San Antonio, 2002—. Mem.: Am. Mensa, Lambda Chi Alpha. Personal E-mail: john_noe@alumni.usc.edu.

NOECKERT, ROBERT J., ophthalmologist, educator; b. Nyack, NY, June 30, 1964; s. Robert and Carolyn Noecker; m. Georgette Pascale, Oct. 29, 2004; 1 child, Bianca Noecker. BS in Biology, MIT, Cambridge, Mass., BS in Materials Sci. and Engring., BS in Humanities and Engring.; MD, U. NC, Chapel Hill; MBA, U. Ariz., Tucson. Lic. physician and surgeon Pa., 2003, Mass., 1993, Ariz., 1992. Vice chmn. eye ctr. dept. ophthalmology sch. medicine U. Pitts., dir. glaucoma svc. eye ctr. dept. ophthalmology sch. medicine, assoc. prof. ophthalmology sch. medicine; staff physician VA Med. Ctr., Tucson, staff physician dept. ophthalmology Boston; staff physician Kino Cmty. Hosp., Tucson; ophthalmologist U. Med. Ctr., Tucson; staff physician St. Elizabeth's Med. Ctr., Boston, dir. New Eng. Eye Ctr.; ophthalmologist New Eng. Eye Ctr. New Eng. Med. Ctr., Boston; asst. prof. ophthalmology sch. medicine Tufts U., Boston; dir. clin. studies unit dept. ophthalmology U. Ariz., dir. glaucoma svc. dept. ophthalmology, assoc. clin. prof. ophthalmology sch. medicine, asst. prof. ophthalmology sch. medicine. Residency dir. sch. medicine U. Ariz., assoc. chmn. clin. activities, mem. faculty biomed. engring. interdisciplinary program sch. medicine, assoc. residency dir. sch. medicine. Office: UPMC Eye Ctr 203 Lothrop St Ste 820 Pittsburgh PA 15213 Office Phone: 412-647-2152. Office Fax: 412-647-5119. Business E-Mail: noeckerrj@upmc.edu.

NOEL, ALFRED, mathematics professor; Grad., Collège Roger Anglade, Port-au-Prince, Haiti, 1976; BEE, Centre Pilote de Formation Technique, Port-au-Prince, Haiti, 1980; math. teaching cert., Institut Pédagogique National, Port-au-Prince, Haiti, 1982; MSc in Applied Math, Northeastern Univ., Boston, 1986, PhD, 1997. High sch. math. tchr., Port-au-Prince, 1979—82; software engr. Computervision, Bedford, Mass., 1987—94; adj. lectr., statistics Roxbury Comty. Coll., Boston, 1986—87; lectr., math, computer sci. Northeastern Univ., Boston, 1984—98, supr. coop. learning in math., 1993—96; sr. engr. Peritus Software Svcs., Billerica, Mass., 1997—98; asst. prof. math. Univ. Mass., Boston, 1998—2005, assoc. prof. math., 2005—. Vis. scholar Harvard Univ., 2006, MIT, 2006; vis. prof. Université de Poitiers, France, 2006. Mem.: Haitian Sci. Soc. (founding mem.), Nat. Assn. Mathematicians, Am. Math. Soc. Achievements include being one of 18 top mathematicians and computer scientists (Atlas of Lie Groups Project) from the US to successfully map E8, one of the largest and most complicated structures in mathematics. Office: Sci Bldg Fl 03 Rm 00175 Univ Mass Boston 100 Morrissey Blvd Boston MA 02125-3393 Office Phone: 617-287-6458. Office Fax: 617-287-6433. Business E-Mail: anoel@cs.umb.edu. *

NOEL, BARBARA HUGHES MCMURTRY, retired music educator; b. Mt. Vernon, Wash., Feb. 27, 1929; d. Lowell Robinson and Mary Evelyn (Hayton) Hughes; children: Sarah Kathleen, Martha Elizabeth. BM, U. Ky., 1951, MM, 1952; PhD, U. Ill., 1972; student, Oberlin Conservatory, 1947-49. Instr. music Union Coll., Barbourville, Ky., 1952-54; instr. music and fine arts Annie Wright Sem., Tacoma, 1957-63; organist, choirmaster Episc. churches, Calif., Wash., 1954-66; chmn. music dept. U. Richmond (Va.), 1971-76, Mankato (Minn.) State U., 1976-78; dean coll. humanities and fine arts Tex. Woman's U., Denton, 1978-81; dean coll. visual and performing arts U. Mass. Dartmouth, North Dartmouth, 1981-89; prof. music U. Mass., Dartmouth, 1990—96, ret., 1996. Cons. for various music orgns. and univs., 1976—, textbook pubs., 1980—; reviewer Nat. Endowment for the Humanities. Book reviewer Providence Sunday Jour., 1984—; contbr. articles to music jours.; contbr. New Grove Dictionary of Music, 1974. Bd. dirs. Community Symphony Orchs., Mankato, 1976-78, New Bedford, Mass., 1981-87. Grad. fellow Danforth Found., U. Ill., 1966-71. Mem. Coll. Music Soc. (treas. 1983-87, v.p. 1979-83, coun. mem.), Nat. Assn. Schs. Music (undergrad. commr. 1978-81). Episcopalian. Avocations: reading, travel, hiking. Home: 301 Linden Ponds Way BC 521 Hingham MA 02043

NOEL, CAROL ADELE, music educator, opera singer; d. Albert Edgar and Adelaide L. Noel. MusB, Boston Conservation of Music, 1962; MusM, Northwestern U., Ill., 1970. Cert. K-12 tchr. Ill., Tex., music and elem. edn. K-9th grade. Opera singer State Opera House of Rendsburg & Hagen Germany, 1965—67; music tchr. Chgo. Pub. Schs., 1971—; wind ensemble Chgo. Wind Ensemble, 1977; soloist Southwest Allied Arts Assn., Chgo., 1982; opera singer Lyric Opera of Chgo., 1963. Choir dir. Posen Sch. Choir, Ill., 1982; music dir. Grant Cmty. Acad., Chgo., 1995—98; chorus dir. Thorp Elem. Sch., Chgo., 2005—. Recipient Alderman Pacini award, First Pl. in vocal; grantee Voice Scholarship, Rosary Coll. Mem.: AARP, Chgo. Tchrs. Union, Music Educators Nat. Conf., German Theatre Union, Actors Equity Assn., Am. Guild of Musical Artists. Avocations: travel, theater, dance, concerts, museums. Home: 6629 S Whipple St Chicago IL 60629-2915 Personal E-mail: cancatlady11@aol.com.

NOEL, DON OBERT, JR., retired editor, columnist; b. Elizabeth, NJ, Nov. 27, 1931; s. Don O. and Catherine (Pyle) N.; m. Elizabeth Bradford Foulds, Aug. 29, 1953; 1 child, Emily Rebecca. BA in Am. Studies, Cornell U., 1954. Reporter Hartford (Conn.) Times, 1958-68, asst. mng. editor, 1968-69, editorial page editor, 1969-74, editor in chief, 1974-75; sr. corr. WFSB-TV, host Face the State Post-Newsweek Stas., 1975-84; polit. columnist op-ed page Hartford Courant, 1984-97, ret., 1997. Author: Jamaica memoir, Near a Far Sea, 2006. Bd. sec. Blue Hills Civic Assn., Hartford, 1988-05; bd. dirs. ACLU of Conn., 1998-, chair, 2005-. Served alt. mil. duty Am. Friends Svc. Com., Tokyo, 1954-56. Recipient Sevellon Brown Meml. award New England AP, 1964, Nat. Journalism award AMA, 1972, Nat. Journalism award Am. Soc. Planning Officials, 1972, 74; fellow Alicia Patterson Found., 1966-67; finalist Pulitzer Prize for non-deadline reporting, 1964. Mem. Soc. Of Friends. Avocations: gardening, birdwatching, language study. Home: 141 Ridgefield St Hartford CT 06112-1837 Office Phone: 860-247-2080. Personal E-mail: dononoel@yahoo.com.

NOEL, EDWIN LAWRENCE, lawyer; b. St. Louis, July 11, 1946; s. Thomas Currie and Christine (Jones) N.; m. Nancy Carter Simpson, Feb. 7, 1970; children: Caroline, Edwin C. BA, Brown U., 1968; JD cum laude, St. Louis U., 1974. Bar: Mo. 1974, U.S. Dist. Ct. (ea. dist.) Mo. 1974, U.S. Ct. Appeals (8th cir.) 1974, U.S. Ct. Appeals (6th cir.) 1978, U.S. Ct. Appeals (7th cir.) 1994, U.S. Supreme Ct. 1986. Ptnr. Armstrong, Teasdale, LLP, St. Louis, 1974—, mng. ptnr., 1993-97. Bd. dirs. Corley Printing Co., St. Louis, Home Fed. Savs. Bank of Mo., 1988—93. Bd. dirs. Edgewood Children's Ctr., St. Louis, 1982-92, St. Louis Assn. for Retarded Citizens, 1984-87, Churchill Sch., 1988-94, Whitfield Sch., 1991-95; chmn. Mo. Clean Water Com., Jefferson City, 1982-88. Mem. Mo. Bar Assn., Bar Assn. Met. St. Louis, Attys. Liability Assurance Soc. (bd. dirs. 1995—, chmn. 2006—). Republican. Episcopalian. Home: 301 S Mcknight Rd Saint Louis MO 63124-1884 Office: Armstrong Teasdale LLP 1 Metropolitan Sq Ste 2600 Saint Louis MO 63102-2740 Office Phone: 314-621-5070. Business E-Mail: enoel@armstrongteasdale.com.

NOEL, FRANKLIN LINWOOD, judge; b. NYC, Dec. 7, 1951; s. Charles Alexander and Mayme (Loth) N.; m. Ellen Barbara Perl, Sept. 15, 1979; children: Kate Alexandra, Charles David. BA, SUNY, Binghamton, 1974; JD, Georgetown U., 1977. Bar: D.C. 1977, U. S. Dist. Ct. D.C. 1978, U.S. Ct. Appeals (D.C. cir.) 1978, Pa. 1979, Minn. 1983, U.S. Ct. Appeals (8th cir.) 1983, U.S. Dist. Ct. Minn. 1984. Assoc. Arnold & Porter, Washington, 1977-79; asst. dist. atty. Phila. Dist. Attys. Office, 1979-83; asst. U.S. atty. U.S. Attys. Office, Mpls., 1983-89; U.S. magistrate judge U.S. Dist. Ct., Mpls., 1989—. Legal writing instr. U. Minn., Mpls., 1989-92, adj. prof. Law Sch., 1996—. Mem. League Am. Bicyclists, Phi Beta Kappa. Episcopalian. Avocation: bicycling. Office: US Dist Ct 300 S 4th St Minneapolis MN 55415-1320

NOEL, MARY MARGARET, nutritionist, educator; b. Tacoma, July 13, 1948; d. Webster Young and Mary Leize Barth; m. George W. Noel, June 30, 1973; children: Katherine Mary, Joseph William. BS in Dietetics, Mich. State U., 1969; MPH, U. Mich., 1973; PhD in Family Ecology, Mich. Sate U., 1988. Registered dietitian. Intern in dietetics Barnes Med. Ctr., St. Louis, 1970; nutrition cons. Vis. Nurse Assn., St. Louis, 1970-72; clin. nutritionist U. Mich., Ann Arbor, 1973-76; instr. dietetics Mich. State U., East Lansing, 1975-76; cons. in nutrition East Lansing, 1976-86; exec. dir. Dairy Coun. of Mich., Okemos, 1986-88; asst. prof. dept. family practice, Coll. Human Medicine Mich. State U., East Lansing, 1988-93, assoc. prof., 1993—2000, prof., 2000—, assoc. chair dept., 1997—. Vol. Neighborhood Assn., East Lansing, 1983-97; bd. dirs., treas. Downtown Devel. Authority, East Lansing, 1986-96; vol. East Lansing Pub. Schs., 1982-98. Grantee, NIH, 1997—2001. Mem. Am. Dietetic Assn. (sect. sec. 1970—), Mich. Dietetic Assn. (parliamentarian 1972—, nominating com., Recognized Young Dietitian 1977), Soc. for Tchrs. of Family Medicine, Vis. Nurses of Lansing (vice chair, then chair 1987-91) Office: Mich State U Dept Family Practice Coll Human Medicin B101 Clin Ctr East Lansing MI 48824 Business E-Mail: noel@msu.edu.

NOEL, NICHOLAS, III, legal company executive, lawyer; b. Pottstown, Pa., June 5, 1952; s. Nicholas Jr. and Elaine (Buckwalter) Noel; m. Karen Bean Schomp, Oct. 28, 1978; children: Carol Elaine, Nicholas IV. BA magna cum laude, Lehigh U., 1974; JD, U. Detroit, 1977. Bar: Pa. 1977, U.S. Dist. Ct. (ea. dist.) Pa. 1979, U.S. Ct. Appeals (3d cir.) 1980, U.S. Supreme Ct. 1986, U.S. Dist. Ct. (mid. dist.) Pa. 1989, cert.: Am. Arbitration Assn. (comml. arbitrator). Assoc. Hahalis Law Office, Bethlehem, Pa., 1977-84; assoc. Teel, Stettz, Shimer & DiGiacomo, Easton, Pa., 1984-87; ptnr. Teel, Stettz, P.C., Easton, 1987-2000, sr. litig. ptnr., 1989-2000, v.p., 1998-2000, pres., 2000, Noel & Kovacs, P.C., Easton, 2000—04, Noel, Kovacs & McGuire, P.C., Easton, 2004—. Solicitor Chiefs Police Assn. Mid. Ea. Pa., 1977—2005, Palmer Twp. Zoning Hearing Bd., Easton, 1989—, Housing Authority Easton, Pa., 2005; spl. counsel City of Reading Police Diversity Bd., Pa., 2005—; adj. prof. Northampton County CC, Bethlehem, 1990, Bethlehem, 97, Bethlehem, 2000; lectr. Pa. Bar Inst., 2001; presenter Conf. of Invited Attys., Toronto, Canada, 2004, Savannah, Ga., 06. Contbr. to several books. Mem. Palmer Moravian Day Sch. Bd., 1991—94, 1999—2000, Pa. Ho. Dels., 1998—; trustee Palmer Twp. Moravian Ch., 1985—97, 1999—2004, 2006—, pres., 1986—92, sec. bldg. expansion com., 1998—2001; mem. Moravian Ch. No. Province Ch. and Soc. Com., 1990—. Named Outstanding Young Man Am., 1974. Fellow: Pa. Bar Found.; mem.: ABA, Northampton County Bar Assn. (mem. legal ethics and responsibility com. 1987—94, bd. govs. 1991—99, treas. 1995, v.p. 1996, pres.-elect 1997, pres. 1998, past pres. 1999), Pa. Bar Assn. (profl. stds. com. 1983, civil rights chair 1989—92, vice-chmn. legal edn. com. 1992, ho. dels. 1998—), Lehigh U. Alumni Assn. (Class of 1974 treas.). Avocations: sports, swimming, hiking. Home: 2840 Green Pond Rd Easton PA 18045-2504 Office: Noel Kovacs & McGuire PC 2505 Newburg Rd Easton PA 18045-1963 Home Phone: 610-258-0134; Office Phone: 610-258-0866. Business E-Mail: nnoel@noelandkovacs.com. E-mail: nn6552@yahoo.com.

NOEL, RANDALL DEANE, lawyer; b. Memphis, Oct. 19, 1953; s. D.A. and Patricia G. Noel; m. Lissa Johns, May 28, 1977; children: Lauren Elizabeth, Randall Walker. BBA with honors, U. Miss., 1975, JD, 1978. Bar: Miss. 1978, U.S. Dist. Ct. (no. and so. dists.) Miss. 1978, Tenn. 1979, U.S. Dist. Ct. (we., mid. and ea. dists.) Tenn. 1979, U.S. Ct. Appeals (5th and 6th cirs.) 1984, U.S. Supreme Ct. 1986. Assoc. Armstrong/Allen, PLLC, Memphis, 1978-85, ptnr., 1985—, mgr. litig. practice group, 1990-94; mgmt. com. Armstrong, Allen, Prewitt, Gentry, Johnston & Holmes, Memphis, 1994—97; chief mem. Armstrong/Allen, PLLC, Memphis, 2002—04; ptnr. Butler, Snow, O'Mara, Stevens & Cannada, 2004—, litig. dept. chair, 2007—. Fin. com. Memphis in May Internat. Festival, 1980-81; pres. Carnival Memphis, 1996; bd. dirs. Christ United Meth. Ch., Memphis, 1984-87, 89-91, chmn. bd. trustees, 1995; mem. Leadership Memphis, 1994-95. Fellow Am. Bar Found., Tenn. Bar Found., Memphis Bar Found.; mem. ABA (young lawyers divsn., fellow dir. 1988-90, editor The Affiliate newsletter 1987-88, dir. Affiliate Outreach project 1988—, vice-chmn. Award of Achievement com. 1986, ALI-ABA bd. 1992-97, div. dir. litig. sect., 2002, coun. litig. sect., mem. House of Dels., standing com. fed. judiciary), Am. Counsel Assn. (pres. 1997), Tenn. Bar Assn. (pres. young lawyers divsn. 1990, pres. litig. sect. 1988, bd. govs. 1989—, pres. 1999, Pres.'s Disting. Svc. award 1988-89), So. Conf. Bar Pres. (pres. 2000), Memphis and Shelby Bar Assn. (mem. jud, recommendations, law week nominations and membership coms.), Miss. Bar Assn., Def. Rsch. Inst., Tenn. Def. Lawyers Assn., Am. Judicature Soc. (bd. dirs. 1992-96), Tenn. Legal Cmty. Found. (pres. 1999-2001), Tenn. Supreme Ct. Hist. Soc. (bd. dirs. 2005). Home: 2938 Tishomingo Ln Memphis TN 38111-2627 Office: Butler Snow O'Mara Stevens & Cannada PLLC Ste 500 Crescent Ctr 6075 Poplar Ave Memphis TN 38119 Business E-Mail: randy.noel@butlersnow.com.

NOËLDECHEN, JOAN MARGUERITE, writer; b. West Islip, NY, May 20, 1963; d. Warren G. Noëldechen and Joan M. Walter. BA in Drama and English, Flagler Coll., St. Augustine, Fla., 1985. Author: (books) Bedside Prayers, 1997, Bless the Day, 1998, House Blessings, 2004, Beyond Katrina, 2005, Pocket Prayers, 2005, Everyday Blessings, 2006, Forever in Love, 2006, Miracles of Motherhood, 2007, To Have and To Hold: Blessings for Newlyweds, 2007, Takoma Poems, 2007, (novel) Dreamers Out of Step, 2000, (poetry) Ashes & Embers: Complete Poems, 2000, (novella) Eve's Song, 2000, (screenplays) Takoma Blue, 2003, Borrowed Starling, 2004; co-author: (screenplays) (with Silvi M. Richardson) And the Angels Sing, 1995, Shadowdance, 1996, Pasaquan Daze, 1996, (play) And the Angels Sing, 1996; apprentice: Flat Rock Playhouse, NC, 1985. Sponsor Old Vic Theatre. Recipient Thespian award, Internat. Thespian Soc., 1980, 1981. Episcopalian. Avocations: reading, cooking, gardening, hiking, photography. Office Phone: 518-653-6063. Business E-Mail: jnoeldechen@flagler.edu.

NOFFSINGER, NANCY LEIGH, retired special education educator; b. Princeton, Ky., Oct. 20, 1948; d. Charlie H. and Margaree (Oates) N. BS, Murray State U., Ky., 1980, masters equivalent, 1982, postgrad., 1987. LPN, 1974. Sch. nurse, then spl. edn. tchr. Dawson Springs Bd. Edn., Ky., 1980-83; spl. edn. substitute tchr. various counties, Ky., 1983-85; spl. edn. tchr. Critten County Bd. Edn., Marion, Ky., 1985—98, Christian County Bd. Edn., Hopkinsville, Ky., 1998—2003; ret., 2003; sub. tchr., 2004—. Mem. NEA, ACLU, Ky. Edn. Assn. Ret. (1st dist. pres. 1996-97, human and civil rights state com. 1994—, chair 1997-98), Second Dist. Edn. Assn. Ret., Crittenden County Edn. Assn. (pres. 1992-95, 97-98, chair KePAC legis. chair 1995-97), Christian County Edn. Assn. (bldg. rep. 1998-2003), Nature Conservancy, World Wildlife Fund, Sierra Club, Nat. Wildlife Fedn. Democrat. Home: 200 N Franklin St Apt 303 Princeton KY 42445-1684 Office Phone: 270-365-6504. Personal E-mail: nancy@noffsinger.net.

NOGALES, LUIS GUERRERO, investment company executive; b. Madera, Calif., Oct. 17, 1943; s. Alejandro Cano and Florence (Guerrero) N.; children: Alicia Fipp, Maria Cristina. BA in Polit. Sci., San Diego State U., 1966; JD, Stanford U., 1969. Asst. to pres. Stanford U., Calif., 1969-72; White House fellow, asst. to sec. U.S. Dept. Interior, Washington, 1972-73; exec. v.p., dir. Golden West Broadcasters, LA, 1973-80; pres. Nogales, Bermudex, Chase and Tamayo, LA, 1981-82; chmn., chief exec. officer UPI, Washington, 1983-86; pres. ECO Internat. News Svc., 1987, Univision, 1987-88; gen. ptnr. Nogales Castro Ptnrs., 1989-90; mng. ptnr. Nogales Investors Mgmt. LLC, LA, 1990—. Bd. mem. Edison Internat., KB Home, Arbitron Inc. Bd. dirs. State of Calif. Bd. Higher Edn., Sacramento, 1973-79, LA Redevelopment Agy., 1973-76, United Way Am., Alexandria, Va., 1984-88; trustee Claremont U. Ctr. and Grad. Sch., 1987; chmn. MALDEF, 1980-82; bd. trustees J. Paul Getty Trust, LA, 2000-, Mayo Clinic, Rochester, Minn., 2003-. Office: Nogales Investors Mgmt LLC Ste 900 9229 W Sunset Blvd Los Angeles CA 90069 Office Phone: 310-276-7439. Office Fax: 310-276-7405.

NOGAY, ARLIE R., lawyer; m. Mary J. Hackett; children: Walter, Robert. AB in anthropology, Brown U., 1981; JD magna cum laude, U. Pitts., 1987. Bar: Pa. 1987. Assoc. Reed Smith LLP, Pitts., 1987—96, ptnr., 1996—, practice group leader corp. & securities group, 2002—. Mem.: Allegheny County Bar Assn., Pa. Bar Assn., ABA. Office: Reed Smith LLP 435 Sixth Ave Pittsburgh PA 15219 Office Phone: 412-288-4594. Office Fax: 412-288-3063. Business E-Mail: anogay@reedsmith.com.

NOGEE, JEFFREY LAURENCE, lawyer; b. Schenectady, NY, Oct. 31, 1952; s. Rodney and Shirley Ruth (Mannes) N.; m. Freda Carolyn Wartel, Aug. 31, 1980; children: Rori Caitlen, Amara Sonia, Jaden Gwynn. BA cum laude, Bucknell U., 1974; JD, Boston U., 1977. Bar: NY 1978, US Dist. Ct. (so. and ea. dists.) NY 1978. Assoc. Hale Russell & Gray, NYC, 1977—83; sr. atty. Ebasco Svcs. Inc., NYC, 1984—88, dir. Countertrade unit, 1985—88; sr. ptnr. Fogh & Nogee Assocs., 1988; ptnr. Brauner, Baron, Rosenzweig, Bauman & Klein, NYC, 1988—90; sr. ptnr. Nogee & Wartel, Garden City, NY, 1990—; sr. counsel Citigroup, Inc., 2006—. Pvt. counsellor for internat. bus. firms, 1987—; cert. mediator comml. divsn. NY State Supreme Ct., Nassau County, 2002—. Prin. bassoonist, bd. dirs. The Band of LI, 1997—, sec., 1997-99, pres., 1999—; prin. bassoonist Rockway-Five Towns Symphony Orch., 1998-99, Lawrence Philharm., 2000—, South Shore Wind and Percussion Ensemble, 2002—, St. Martin of Tours Orch., 2005—; assoc. bassoonist South Shore Symphony, 2002—; pvt. bassoon instr., 2000—. Trustee Temple Emanu-el of East Meadow, 1995-99, v.p., 1996-97; bd. dirs. Glory House Recovery Inc., 2005—, LI Arts Coun., Freeport, 2007-. Mem. ABA, Am. Arbitration Assn., Assn. of Bar of City of NY, Nassau County Bar Assn., Internat. Platform Assn., NY New Media Assn., Phi Beta Kappa, Pi Sigma Alpha. Avocations: fencing, bassoon, racquet sports, hiking, astronomy. Office: Ste 705 585 Stewart Ave Garden City NY 11530 Office Phone: 516-222-6575. Business E-Mail: jnogee@nogeelaw.com.

NOGHAIDELI, ZURAB, Prime Minister of Georgia; b. Kobuleti, Georgia, Oct. 22, 1964; m. Nino Tsintsabadze; 1 child. Grad., Moscow Lomonosov State U. Mem. parliament Govt. Georgia, chair Environment Protection and Natural Resources Com., 1992, chair Tax and Income Com., 1999, min. fin., 2000—02, 2004—05, prime min., 2005—. Mem. supr. com. People's Bank, 2002—03. Office: Office of Govt Ingorovka 7 380018 Tbilisi Georgia *

NOGINOV, MIKHAIL A., physicist, researcher, educator; b. Dolgoprudnyi, Russia, May 28, 1962; arrived in U.S., 1991; s. Anatolii M. and Lidia V. (Platonova) N.; m. Natalia Noginova (Chernova), July 3, 1982; children: Maxim M., Julia M. MSEE, Moscow Inst. Physics and Tech., 1985; PhD in Physics and Math., USSR Acad. Scis., Moscow, 1990. Engr., from jr. staff rschr. to staff rschr. Gen. Physics Inst. of USSR Acad. Scis., 1985—91; rsch. assoc. MIT, Cambridge, 1991-93; from asst. to assoc. rsch. prof. dept. physics Ala. Agrl. Mech. U., Huntsville, 1993-97; assoc. rsch. prof. Ctr. for Materials Rsch., Norfolk (Va.) State U., 1997—99, from asst. to assoc. prof. dept. physics, 1999—2000. Grant proposal reviewer NSF, CRDF; panel reviewer NSF; jour reviewer sci. jours. including Optical Soc. Am., Am. Phys. Soc., others; mem., chmn. various conf. coms. Author: Solid-State Randm Lasers, 2005; contbr. over 90 articles to profl. jours., chapters to books. Mem.: SPIE (chair and tech. program com. mem. conf.), IEEE, Am. Phys. Soc., Optical Soc. Am. (faculty adv. student chpt. Norfolk State U. 2003—, chair and tech. program com. mem. conf.), Sigma Xi. Achievements include research in spectroscopic characterization and study of energy transfer processes in laser and nonlinear optical materials; energy transfer upconversion in laser materials, optimization of solid-state laser materials, nonlinear optics, holographic recording; photorefraction mechanisms and holographic currents in dielectric and semiconductor crystals; intrinsic optical bistability in broad variety of materials with different mechanisms and nonlinearity; stimulated emission in ensembles of micro-size, nano-size particles with optical gain, potential miniature light sources for integrated optics; optoelectronics and nanoscale devices (random lasers). Avocations: travel, windsurfing. Office: Norfolk State U Ctr for Materials Rsch 700 Park Ave Norfolk VA 23504-3993 Personal E-mail: mnoginov@hotmail.com. Business E-Mail: mnoginov@nsu.edu.

NOGLOWS, WILLIAM P., electronics executive; BS in Chem. Engring., Ga. Inst. Tech. From various mgmt. positions to exec. v.p. Cabot Corp., Aurora, Ill., 1984—98, exec. v.p., 1998—2003; chmn. Cabot Microelectronics Corp., Aurora, 2003—, pres., 2003—, CEO, 2003—. Office: Cabot Microelectronics Corp 870 N Commons Dr Aurora IL 60504

NOGUCHI, HIDEO, insurance company executive; b. Kyoto, Jan. 17, 1945; s. Tasao and Ishiko (Tsujii) Noguchi; m. Eleanor Kazuko Horii, May 7, 1970; children: Mark H.Y., Mitchell H.Y. BBA, U. Hawaii, 1969. Buyer RCA Purchasing Co., Tokyo, 1969—73; ins. specialist Continental Ins. Agy., Honolulu, 1973—82; CEO Noguchi & Assocs., Inc., Honolulu, 1983—. Cons. in field. Named to Coll. Bus. Adminstrn. Alumni Hall of Honor, U. Hawaii, 2004; recipient Nat. New Agt. Leadership award, CNA Corp., 1974, Key Club award, CNA Co., 1975, 1979—81, Nat. New Agt. Leader II, Continental Assurance Co., Can Co., 1975, Aloha Club award, 1983, VIP Club award, Pacific Guardian Life, 1984—86, Persistency Leader of Region award, 1984. Mem.: Hawaii Ind. Ins. Agents Assn., Urasenke Hawaii Assn. Profl. Ins. Agents, Rotary (bd. dirs. 1980). Office: 1314 S King St Ste 560 Honolulu HI 96814-1978 Office Phone: 808-596-2700.

NOGUCHI, SOICHI, astronaut; b. Yokohama, Japan, Apr. 15, 1965; married; 3 children. Bachelor in Aero. Engring., U. Tokyo, 1989, M in Aero. Engring., 1991. Flight instructor cert. as CFII and MEI. Mem. mfg. dept. Ishikawajima-Harima Heavy Industries Co., Ltd., Japan, 1991—96; astronaut Nat. Space Devel. Agy. Japan (merged with Inst. of Space & Astronautic Sci. and Nat. Aerospace Lab. of Japan and renamed Japan Aerospace Exploration Agy. in 2003), 1996—; tech. specialist Astronaut Office Space Sta. Br. Johnson Space Ctr., Houston, 1996, qualified mission specialist, 1998—; participated in the basic tng. course for Russian manned space systems Gagarin Cosmonaut Tng. Ctr., 1998; assigned tech. duties to support Japanese Experiment Module (Kibo) develop. tests Johnson Space Ctr., Houston, mission specialist, STS-114/ULF-1(Utilization and Logistics Flight), 2001—. Mem.: Japan Soc. Aero. and Space Scis. Will serve as MS-1 (mission specialist) and EV-1 on the Return To Flight Mission of STS-114 (Discovery), during which the crew will test and evaluate new procedures for flight safety and shuttle inspection and repair techniques in July, 2005; second Japanese astronaut ever to walk the void of three spacewalks. Office: NASA Johnson Space Ctr Astronaut Office/CB Houston TX 77058

NOGUCHI, THOMAS TSUNETOMI, writer, pathologist; b. Fukuoka, Japan, Jan. 4, 1927; arrived in U.S., 1952; s. Wataru and Tomika Narahashi Noguchi. Doctorate of Medicine, Nippon Med. Sch., Tokyo, 1951; DSc (hon.), Worcester State Coll., 1985. Dep. med. examiner LA County Dept. Chief Med. Examiner, 1961-67, coroner, 1967-82; prof. forensic pathology U. So. Calif. Med. Sch., LA, 1982-99; prof. emeritus forensic pathology, 1999—. Author: Coroner, 1983 (N.Y. Times Bestseller, 1984), Coroner at Large, 1985, Unnatural Causes, 1988, Physical Evidence, 1990. Recipient Imperial medal Order Sacred Treasure, His Majesty the Emperor of Japan, 1999, Helpern Laureate medal, Nat. Assn. Med. Examiners, 2006. Fellow: Am. Acad. Forensic Sci. (chmn. sect. 1966, Disting. Fellow award 2007); mem.: AMA, AAAS, World Assn. Med. Law (treas.), Calif. Assn. Criminalists, Calif. State Coroners Assn. (pres. 1974—75), Nat. Assn. Med. Examiners (pres. 1983), Internat. Acad. Legal and Social Medicine, Am. Soc. Law, Medicine and Ethics, Am. Coll. Legal Medicine. Republican. Avocations: fine arts, gourmet oriental cooking, painting stills and abstracts. Office: U So Calif Med Ctr 1200 N State St Rm 2520 Los Angeles CA 90033-1029 Business E-Mail: noguchi@hse.usc.edu.

NOGUERAS, JUAN JOSE, surgeon; b. Rio Piedras, PR, Apr. 23, 1956; s. Juan Jose and Agustina (Soroeta) N.; m. Michele LeMoal, Sept. 22, 1984; children: Nicole, John, Robert. AB in Biochemistry, Princeton U., 1978; MD, Jefferson Med. Coll., 1982. Diplomate Am. Bd. Surgery, Am. Bd. Colon and Rectal Surgery, Nat. Bd. Med. Examiners. Instr. surgery Wilford Hall Air Foce Med. Ctr., San Antonio, 1987-90; staff dept. colorectal surgery Cleveland Clin. Fla., Weston, 1991—, chmn. divsn. surgery, 2000—. Presenter in field. Contbg. author: Current Controversies in Breast Cancer, 1984, Pre-test Self Assessment and Review, 1987, Textbook and Atlas of Laparaoscopic Colorectal Surgery, Intestinal Stomas, 1993; reviewer: Surgical Endoscopy, 1993—, So. Med. Jour., 1993—; contbr. articles to profl. jours. Maj. M.C., U.S. Army, 1987-90. Recipient A.W. Martin Marino Sr. M.D. award N.Y. Soc. Colon and Rectal Surgeons, 1991; Fellow U. Minn., 1990-91. Fellow ACS, Am. Soc. Colon and Rectal Surgeons, Soc. Am. Gastrointestinal Endoscopic Surgeons, Crohn's and Colitis Found. Am. (chmn. med. adv. com. 1992-96), Dominican Coll. Surgeons (hon.), Midwest Soc. Colon and Rectal Surgeons (pres. 1993-94). Home: 2505 Poinciana Dr Weston FL 33327-1415 Business E-Mail: noguerj@ccf.org.

NOGUERE, SUZANNE, trade association executive, poet; b. Bklyn., Dec. 1, 1947; d. Eugene R. and Virginia Helene (Braun) N.; m. Henry Grinberg, June 5, 1983. BA in Philosophy magna cum laude with honors, Columbia U., NYC, 1969. Classified ad mgr. Printing News, Melville, NY, 1973—2006, sr. acct. exec., 1999—2006; sr. dir. mem. svcs. Nat. Assn. for Printing Leadership, Paramus, NJ, 2006—. Author: (children's books) Little Koala, 1979, Little Raccoon, 1981, (poetry collection) Whirling Round the Sun, 1996; poet (with artist Miriam Adams): (exhibitions) Leaf Lines, 1998, poet (with artist Lesley Nishigawara): (exhibitions) Left Out, 2003; co-author (with James V. Hatch): The Stone House, A Blues Legend, 2000; co-author: (plays) Klub Ka, The Blues Legend, U. Iowa, 2002, La MaMa E.T.C., 2004, U. Md., 2006. Recipient Discovery award The 92nd St. Y Unterberg Poetry Ctr. and The Nation mag., 1996. Mem. Acad. Am. Poets, Poetry Soc. Am. (Gertrude B. Claytor Meml. award 1989), Poets House, Dramatists Guild Am., Authors Guild. Home: 27 W 96th St Apt 12B New York NY 10025-6614 Office: Nat Assn for Printing Leadership 75 W Century Rd Paramus NJ 07652 Office Phone: 800-642-6275 ext. 6304. Personal E-mail: snoguere@napl.org.

NOH, JUN-YONG, computer scientist, researcher; b. Seoul, Republic of Korea, Feb. 14, 1971; s. Hae-Kyu Noh and Yoo-im Bang. Bachelor magna cum laude, U. So. Calif., 1994, Master, 1996, PhD, 2002. Rschr. on brain-like computer Info. Scis. Inst., Marina del Rey, Calif., 1997; rschr. facial animation U. So. Calif., LA, 1998—. CEO Digital Clone Lab., LA, 2002—. Pvt., 1999, Seoul. Achievements include patent for expression cloning. Avocations: scuba diving, travel.

NOHR, MATTHEW RYAN, information technology analyst; b. Green Bay, Wis., Nov. 2, 1978; s. Ronald M. and Jean M. Nohr; m. Katie J. Trunnell, Aug. 20, 2005. BA in Computer Sci., U. Wis., Eau Claire, 2001; MS in Software Engring., U. St. Thomas, St. Paul, Minn., 2005. Java Cert. Programmer Sun Microsys., Calif., 2005. IT analyst 3M, St. Paul, 2001—. Mem.: Assn. Computing Machinists, Mensa.

NOHR, MONICA CAROL, art educator, sculptor; b. Waupaca, Wis., Sept. 16, 1976; d. Carol Joy and Raymond Earl Nohr. BFA in 3-D Studio Art, Cardinal Stritch U., Milw., 2001, BA in Art Edn. pre-K to grade 12, 2001; MFA in Visual Arts/Clay, Marywood U., Scranton, Pa., 2006. Studio asst. for profl. artist Ellie Burke Original Glasswork, Milw., 1997—2001; youth art program art instr. continuing edn. dept. Cardinal Stritch U., Milw., 1999—2000; art educator grades 7-12 Suring Pub. Schs., Wis., 2001—03; visual arts instr. grades K-12 French Woods Festival the Performing Arts, Hancock, NY, 2004—; art educator grades 7-12 Pioneer Westfield HS and Mid. Sch., Wis., 2006—07; art instr. grades K-3 21st Century Clubhouse After Sch. Program, Westfield Elem. Sch., 2006—07. Guest tchr. Little Wolf H.S. Talented and Gifted Art Program, Manawa, Wis., 2001—02; traveling artist asst. for glass artist Ellie Burke Wash. Craft Show, 2003—05, Phila. Mus. Art Craft Show, 2005. Exhibitions include No. Nat. Juried Art Competition, WEA Trust Art Educators Showcase Juried Exhbn., Madison, SHELTERED Regional Juried Art Exhibition, Easton, Pa., MFA Graduate Exhbn., Scranton, Pa. Mem.: Coll. Arts Assn., Alpha Epsilon Lambda, Delta Epsilon Sigma, Kappa Gamma Pi, Kappa Delta Pi Internat. Edn. Honor Soc. Avocations: travel, hiking, photography, linguistics, films. Home Phone: 920-373-1976. Personal E-mail: monica.c.nohre@gmail.com.

NOHRNBERG, JAMES CARSON, language educator; b. Berkeley, Calif., Mar. 19, 1941; s. Carson and Geneva Gertrude (Gibbs) N.; m. Stephanie Payson Lamport, June 14, 1964; children: Gabrielle L., Peter Carson L. Student, Kenyon Coll., 1958-60; BA, Harvard Coll., 1962, postgrad., 1965-68; PhD, U. Toronto, 1970. Tchg. fellow dept. English U. Coll., U. Toronto, 1963-64; jr. fellow Soc. of Fellows Harvard U., 1965-68; acting instr. dept. English Yale U., New Haven, 1968-69, lectr., 1969-70, asst. prof., 1970-75, assoc. prof., 1975; prof. English U. Va., Charlottesville, 1975—. Adj. instr. English Harvard U., Cambridge, 1967; Gauss Seminars in Criticism lectr. Princeton U., 1987; lectr. various univs., 1974—. Author: The Analogy of The Faerie Queene, 1976, 80, Like Unto Moses: The Constituting of an Interruption, 1995; mem. editl. bd. Spenser Ency., 1977-90, Spenser Studies, 1977—, Manchester Spenser, 2007—; contbr. articles to profl. jours. and poems to mags.; editor vols. on allegory, Bible, Homer, Dante, Boiardo, Spenser, Shakespeare, Milton, Thomas Pynchon, Northrop Frye, among others. Recipient Am. Acad. Poets prize Harvard U., 1962; Woodrow Wilson fellow, 1962, jr. fellow Harvard U., 1965-68, Morse fellow Yale U., 1974-75, U. Va. Ctr. for Advanced Studies fellow, 1975-78, Guggenheim fellow, 1981-82, Ind. U. Inst. for Advanced Studies fellow, 1991, U. Va. Sesquicentennial fellow, 2003-2004. Mem.: MLA, Am. Comparative Lit. Assn., Milton Soc., Spenser Soc., Phi Beta Kappa. Presbyterian. Avocations: poetry, collecting books and records. Home: 1874 Wayside Pl Charlottesville VA 22903-1631 Office: U Va Dept English Bryan Hall Charlottesville VA 22903 Office Phone: 434-924-6629. Business E-Mail: jcn@virginia.edu.

NOJI, ERIC K., epidemiologist; MD, U. Rochester; MPH, Johns Hopkins Bloomberg Sch. Pub. Health, 1987. Prof. Johns Hopkins U. Sch. Med., Baltimore, Md.; attending emergency physician Johns Hopkins Hosp., Baltimore, Md.; with CDC, Atlanta, 1989—, asst. branch chief emergency response, 1989, chief disaster assessment & epidemiology, 1990—95, assoc. dir. bioterrorism preparedness & response, 2001—; chief of Emergency Health Intelligence Unit, WHO Health Information Network for Advanced Planning (HINAP), Geneva, 1996—2000; med. expert White House Office of Homeland Security, Washington, 2001—; dep. chief Med. & Pub. Health Unit, US Humanitarian Assistance Mission for Operation Iraqi Freedom, Washington, 2003—; prof. internat. health Tulane U. Sch. Pub. Health & Tropical Medicine. Sr. fellow Homeland Security Policy Inst., George Washington U.; sr. policy advisor CDC, Washington, Dept. Homeland Security (FEMA), Washington, Pentagon's Chemical & Biological Def. Program, Washington. Author: over 200 scientific articles & publications, The Public Health Consequences of Disasters, 1997. Pres. Soc. Alumni Johns Hopkins Bloomberg Sch. Pub. Health. Recipient Woodrow Wilson award for Disting. Govt. Svc., 2005. Mem.: Inst. Medicine.

NOKES, JEFFERY D., history professor; b. Murray, Utah, Sept. 2, 1966; s. Vernon Doyle and Tava Lee Nokes; m. Gina Park, Dec. 21, 1990; children: Carly J., Mandy T., Kelsey G., Caleb Jeffery, Joseph Jeffery, Isaac Thomas. BA, Brigham Young U., Provo, Utah, 1991; MEd, Utah State U., Logan, 1996; PhD, U. Utah, Salt Lake City, 2005. Cert. Tchr. Utah State Office Edn., 1991. History tchr. Bingham HS, South Jordan, Utah, 2001—05; instr. Brigham Young U., 2005—. Adult hs tchr. Southpointe HS, Sandy, Utah, 1997—. Missionary LDS Ch., Stockholm, 1985—87, various leadership roles in local congregations Riverton, Utah, 1990—2006. Named HS History Tchr. of Yr., Utah Coun. for the Social Studies, 2005. Mem.: NEA. R-Liberal. Mem. Lds Ch. Achievements include research in effective methods of teaching. Avocations: camping, fishing, reading. Office: Brigham Young Univ 201 MCKB Provo UT 84062 Home Phone: 801-254-1594.

NOLAN, ALAN TUCKER, lawyer, writer, arbitrator; b. Evansville, Ind., Jan. 19, 1923; s. Val and Jeannette (Covert) N.; m. Elizabeth Clare Titsworth, Aug. 26, 1947 (dec. Nov. 1967); children: Patrick A., Thomas C., Mary F., Elizabeth T., John V.; m. Jane Ransel DeVoe, Feb. 7, 1970; adopted children: John C. DeVoe, Ellen R. DeVoe, Thomas R. DeVoe. AB in Govt. with honors, Ind. U., Bloomington, 1944, LHD, 1993; LLB, Harvard U., Cambridge, Mass., 1947. Bar: Ind. 1947. Law clk. U.S. Ct. Appeals (7th Cir.), Chgo., 1947-48; assoc. Ice, Miller, Donadio & Ryan, Indpls., 1948-58, ptnr., 1958-93, ret., 1993—. Chmn. Disciplinary Commn. Supreme Ct. Ind., Indpls., 1966-73. Author: The Iron Brigade, 1961, As Sounding Brass, 1964, Lee Considered, 1991; editor (with S. Vipond) Giants in Tall Black Hats, 1998, (with Gary Gallagher) The Myth of the Lost Cause and Civil War History, 2000, Rally Once Again, 2000; contbg. editor The Civil War, 1985-89; contbr. numerous articles to profl. jours. Life mem. NAACP Indpls., v.p., 1950-54; bd. dirs., founder Ind. Civil Liberties Union, Indpls., 1953-60; bd. dirs. Indpls. Art League, 1981-87; chmn., bd. trustees Ind. Hist. Soc., Indpls., 1986-98; trustee Eiteljorg Mus., Indpls., 1987-93. Fellow Co. Mil. Historians, Am. Bar Found., State Hist. Soc. Wis.; mem. ABA, ACLU, Ind. Bar Assn., Indpls. Bar Assn. (bd. mgrs. 1958-60, chmn. Grievance Com. 1960-64), Indpls. Civil War Round Table, Ensemble Music Soc. (bd. dirs. 1999—), Phi Beta Kappa. Democrat. Roman Catholic. Avocations: travel, gardening, reading. Home and Office: 3307 Bay Road North Drive Indianapolis IN 46240 Office Phone: 317-585-1988. Personal E-mail: indynolan@sbcglobal.net.

NOLAN, DEANNA NICOLE, professional basketball player; b. Flint, Mich., Aug. 25, 1979; d. Virginia Nolan and Phillip Murphy. Grad. in Child and Family Devel., U. Ga., Athens, 2001. Guard-forward Detroit Shock, 2001—; player (off-season) Zaragoza, Spain, 2003—04, Ramat Hasharon, Israel, 2005—06. Mem. USA Women's Sr. Nat. Team. Named to All-WNBA Second Team, 2003, Ea. Conf. All-Star Team, WNBA, 2003, 2005—07, All-WNBA First Team, 2005, WNBA All-Defensive Second Team, 2005, WNBA All-Defensive First Team, 2007. Achievements include won WNBA Championships as a member of the Shock, 2003, 06. Mailing: Detroit Shock Palace Sports & Entertainment 5 Championship Dr Auburn Hills MI 48326 *

NOLAN, J. MICHAEL, JR., retired lawyer; b. Newark, June 19, 1949; BA with honors, St. Vincent Coll., 1971; JD, Villanova U., 1975. Bar: N.J. 1975. Law clk. Hon. Samuel Allcorn, Jr. appellate divsn. Superior Ct. N.J., 1975-76; asst. prosecutor Essex County, N.J., 1976-77; spl. coun. N.J. Supreme Ct., 1984-85; ptnr. Pitney, Hardin, Kipp & Szuch, Morristown, NJ, 1977—. Fellow Am. Bar Found.; mem. N.J. State Bar Assn. (chmn. casino law sect. 1987-88). Office: Pitney Hardin Kipp & Szuch PO Box 1945 Park Ave at Morris County Morristown NJ 07962-1945

NOLAN, JAMES PAUL, internist, educator, researcher; b. Buffalo, June 21, 1929; s. James Paul and Isabel (Curry) N.; m. Christa Paul, July 23, 1956; children— Lisa, James, Christopher, Thomas. BA, Yale U., 1951, MD cum laude, 1955. Diplomate Am. Bd. Internal Medicine. Instr. in medicine Yale U., New Haven, 1961-63; intern Grace-New Haven Hosp., 1955-56, resident, 1958-60, chief med. resident, 1961-62, asso. physician, 1962-63; asst. prof. medicine SUNY, Buffalo, 1963-67, asso. prof., 1967-69, prof., 1969—, vice-chmn. dept. medicine, 1973-77, acting chmn. dept., 1978-79, chmn. dept., 1979-95, disting. svc. prof., 1996—; chief of medicine Buffalo Gen. Hosp., 1969-80, attending, 1969—; asso. attending Edward J. Meyer Meml. Hosp., Buffalo, 1963-68, attending, 1968-71, cons., 1971—; cons. physician Millard Fillmore Hosp., 1981—, Deaconess Hosp., 1973—. Attending Buffalo VA Hosp., Children's Hosp. Buffalo; cons. Roswell Park Meml. Inst., 1970—; acting dir. dept. medicine Erie County Med. Center, 1978-80, dir. dept., 1980—; trustee Buffalo Gen. Hosp., 1974—; bd. dirs. Kaleid Health, ACP Found. Editl. adv. bd. Jour. Medicine Exptl. and Clin, 1971—; reviewer: Gastroenterology, 1973—; contbr. numerous articles to med. and sci. jours. Served to lt. comdr., M.C. USN, 1956-58. NIH grantee, 1979-86; Hartford Found. grantee, 1981 Mem. ACP (master, chair bd. regents 1994-95), Am. Fedn. Clin. Rsch., AAAS, Am. Gastroent. Assn. (procedures com.), Am. Assn. Study of Liver Disease, Reticuloendothelial Soc., N.Y. Acad. Sci., Am. Clin. and Climatol. Assn., Interurban Club, Ctrl. Soc. Clin. Rsch., Internat. Assn. Study of Liver, Assn. Am. Physicians, Assn. Profs. Medicine (pres. 1993-94), Phi Beta Kappa, Alpha Omega Alpha. Office: 462 Grider St Buffalo NY 14215-3021 Address: 213 Burbank Dr Snyder NY 14226-3938 E-mail: jpnolanmd@yahoo.com.

NOLAN, JAMES W., food products executive; BS, Ithaca Coll., NY. With Procter & Gamble; various positions including chief customer officer PepsiCola N.Am. and sr. v.p. sales and market devel. PepsiCola N.Am. PepsiCo; with PepsiAmericas, 2001—05, exec. v.p. US ops.; CEO Foodservice, exec. v.p. Sara Lee Corp., 2005—. Office: Sara Lee Corp 3500 Lacey Rd Downers Grove IL 60515 Office Phone: 630-598-6000. *

NOLAN, JANIECE SIMMONS, health facility administrator; b. Ft. Worth; d. James Coleman and Berenice Johnson Simmons; m. Robert L. Nolan; children: Douglas, Patricia, Nancy, Margaret, Sheffield, Gemini Janiece. BA, U. Tex., 1961, MA, 1963; PhD, Tulane U., 1968; MPH, U. Calif., Berkeley, 1975. Diplomate Am. Coll. Healthcare Execs. Rsch. scientist Tex. Nuc. (Nuc. Chgo.), Austin, 1963-65; head cell biology Gulf South Rsch. Inst., New Orleans, 1968-70; postdoctoral fellow dept. physiology/anatomy U. Calif., Berkeley, 1970-72; rsch. physiologist, acting assoc. chief of staff for rsch. VA Hosp., Martinez, Calif., 1970-75; COO, v.p. adminstrn. John Muir Med. Ctr., Walnut Creek, Calif., 1977-97;

pres., CEO John Muir Physician Network, Walnut Creek, 1997—. Commr. State Commn. Emergency Svcs., Sacramento, 1997; mem. corp. adv. bd. for grad. program in health mgmt. rsch. U. Calif., Berkeley, 2003; mem. industry adv. bd. Ctr. for Health Mgmt. Rsch., 2004—. Capt. USNR, (ret.). Woodrow Wilson fellow, 1960; named Woman of Yr., Women Health Care Execs., San Francisco, 1989; recipient Navy Commendation medals (3), Humanitarian Svc. medal, 2 Armed Forces Res. medals (2). Mem.: Ind. Physician Assn., Med. Group Mgmt. Assn., Am. Mil. Surgeons of the U.S., Assn. Integrated Health Delivery Systems, Rotary (Paul Harris fellow), Phi Beta Kappa (No. Calif. Assn. bd. dirs. 2005—). Avocations: international travel, genealogy. Office: John Muir Physician Network 1340 Treat Blvd Ste 450 Walnut Creek CA 94597 Office Phone: 925-952-2880. Business E-Mail: Janiece.Nolan@johnmuirhealth.com.

NOLAN, JEANADA H., retired state agency administrator, social worker, educator; b. Fresno, Calif., Aug. 6, 1915; d. John Andrew and Lucille Wallace Hamilton; children: Jay Hamilton, Thomas Joseph. BA, Fresno State Coll., Calif., 1938; MA, Sacramento State Coll., Calif., 1953; PhD, Union Grad. Sch., Cin., 1977. Social worker Fresno County Welfare Dept., Calif., 1935—42; social welfare agt. State Dept. Social Welfare, Sacramento, 1942—45; coord. parent and preschool edn. Sacramento City Unified Sch. Dist., 1951—66, coord. Project Head Start, 1965; chief bur. preschool edn. programs Calif. State Dept. Edn., 1966—72, asst. to assoc. supt. early childhood edn., 1972—74; ret., 1974. Mem. Gov.'s Adv. Commn. Children and Youth, Sacramento, 1959—65; exec. sec. Gov.'s Adv. Com. Child Devel. Programs, 1966—72; parent involvement specialist Nat. Head Start, 1966—69; adv. bd. Parent Participation Preschools Internat., 1966—70; co-chmn., leader child devel. com. Wilson Riles Early Childhood Edn. Program, 1972; vis. lectr. in orgn., mgmt. and adminstrn. preschool and child care programs U. Calif. Ext., 1974—79; prodr. radio series Families are Our Bus., 1954; mem. State Bd. Mgrs. Calif. Congress Parents and Tchr. Contbr. articles to profl. jours. Mem.: Sacramento Mental Health Assn. (charter mem.), Calif. Assn. Edn. Young Children, Nat. Assn. Young Children, UN-USA, Ret. Tchrs. Assn., Soroptimist Internat.

NOLAN, JOHN BLANCHARD, lawyer; b. Providence, Aug. 30, 1943; s. John O'Leary and Elizabeth Rita (Blanchard) Nolan; m. Marguerite Ruth Hartley, Mar. 1, 1969 (dec. Aug. 1988); children: Suzanne, Caroline, Danielle; m. Lillian B. Prestley, 1989. AB, Brown U., 1965; JD, Georgetown U., 1968. Bar: Conn. 1968, NY 1974, US Dist. Ct. Conn. 1969, US Dist. Ct. (so. dist.) NY 1973, US Dist. Ct. Ariz. 1994, US Ct. Appeals (2d cir.) 1969, US Ct. Appeals (1st cir.) 1991, US Supreme Ct. 1995. Assoc. Day, Berry & Howard, Hartford, Conn., 1969-76, ptnr., 1976—2006, Day Pitney, LLP, Hartford, Conn., 2007—. Bd. dirs. Spiritus Wines, Inc.; chmn. local rules practice adv. com. U.S. Bankruptcy Ct., 1981—. Corporator St. Francis Hosp. Med. Ctr., Hartford, 1982—; bd. dirs. Greater Hartford Arts Coun., Inc., 1993—, v.p., mem. exec. com.; mem. parish coun. Ch. St. Timothy; trustee St. Mary Home Found., 1983—, U. Hartford Art Sch., 1988—94. Fellow: Conn. Bar Found.; mem.: ABA, Insolvency Internat., Hartford County Bar Assn., Conn. Bar Assn., Am. Bankruptcy Inst., Loomis Chaffee Sch. Alumni Assn., Hartford Golf Club (bd. dirs. 2000—03, v.p. 2004—06, pres. 2007—). Democrat. Roman Catholic. Avocations: golf, opera, travel, wines. Home: 34 Northmoor Rd West Hartford CT 06117-1709 Office: Day Pitney LLP 185 City Place Hartford CT 06103-3499 Office Phone: 860-275-0100. Business E-Mail: jbnolan@daypitney.com.

NOLAN, JOHN EDWARD, lawyer; b. Mpls., July 11, 1927; s. John E. and Teresa (Franey) Nolan; m. Joan Dobbins, June 3, 1950; children: Carol N. Klatt, John Edward III(dec.), Kelly N. Spencer, Richard Clark, Patricia N. McNeill. BS, U.S. Naval Acad., 1950; JD, Georgetown U., 1955. Bar: DC 1955, US Supreme Ct. 1959, Md. 1961. Law clk. to Justice Clark U.S. Supreme Ct., 1955-56; adminstrv. asst. to Atty. Gen. Robert F. Kennedy, 1963-64; assoc. Steptoe & Johnson, Washington, 1956-62, ptnr., 1962—63, 1965—. Assoc. counsel Cuban families com. Cuban Prisoners Exch., Havana, 1962—63; spl. counsel refugee subcom. Senate Jud. Com., Vietnam, 1967—68; mem. CPR Panel Disting. neutrals, Washington; mediator U.S. Ct. Appeals DC cir.; mem. exec. com. Lawyers Com. Civil Rights Under Law; vis. fellow Wolfson Coll., Cambridge (Eng.) U., 1987, 92; bd. dirs. Iomega, Inc. Trustee Robert F. Kennedy Meml., 1969—; moderator Aspen Inst., 1980—; gen. counsel, bd. dirs. U.S. Naval Acad. Found., 1997—; bd. dirs. Fund Dem. Majority. Served from 2d lt. to capt. USMC, 1950—54, Korea. Decorated Silver Star, Bronze Star with combat V, Purple Heart. Mem.: ABA, Am. Law Inst., DC Bar Assn., U.S. Naval Acad. Alumni Assn. (bd. counsel, trustee 1997—), Univ. Club (N.Y.C.), Congl. Club, Met. Club (Washington). Democrat. Roman Catholic. Office: 1330 Connecticut Ave NW Washington DC 20036-1704 Personal E-mail: jnolan@steptoe.com.

NOLAN, JOHN MICHAEL, lawyer; b. Conway, Ark., June 21, 1948; s. Paul Thomas and Peggy (Hime) N. BA, U. Tex., 1970, JD, 1973; LLM in Taxation, George Washington U., Washington, DC, 1976. Bar: Tex. 1973, DC 1975, US Ct. Mil. Appeals 1973, US Ct. Appeals (DC cir.) 1975, US Tax Ct. 1975, US Supreme Ct. 1975. Chief counsel to chief judge US Ct. Mil. Appeals, Washington, 1976-77; assoc. Winstead, McGuire, Sechrest & Minick PC, Dallas, 1977-81; shareholder Winstead Sechrest & Minick PC, Dallas, 1981—2006, Winstead, Dallas, 2007—. Editor in chief The Advocate, 1973-76. Capt. JAGC, US Army, 1973-76. Named one of Outstanding Young Men in Am. US Jaycees, 1976; Keeton fellow Chancellor Coun.; named among Best Lawyers in Am. Tex. Super Lawyer. Fellow Dallas Bar Found. (life), Tex. Bar Found. (life); mem. ABA (real property, probate and trust sect., real property com., partnerships, joint ventures, and other investment vehicles), Tex. Bar Assn. (real property, probate and trust sect.), DC Bar Assn., Dallas Bar Assn. (real estate group), Tex. Coll. Real Estate Lawyers, Am. Coll. Real Estate Lawyers, Coll. State Bar Tex., Real Estate Coun. (bd. dirs.), Salesmanship Club Dallas, Royal Oaks Country Club. Presbyterian. Home: 6681 Crest Way Ct Dallas TX 75230-2868 Office: Winstead 5400 Renaissance Tower 1201 Elm St Ste 5400 Dallas TX 75270-2199 Office Phone: 214-745-5251. Business E-Mail: jnolan@winstead.com.

NOLAN, JOSEPH THOMAS, journalism educator, communications consultant; b. Waterbury, Conn., Apr. 11, 1920; s. Thomas Francis and Mary Margaret (Gaffney) N.; m. Virginia Theodate Tappin, May 6, 1943; children— Carol Nolan Rigolot, David J. AB, Holy Cross Coll., 1942; MA in English Lit., Boston U., 1945; PhD in Econs, NYU, 1973. Washington corr. UPI, 1943-49; writer, copy editor N.Y. Times, NYC, 1949-55; mgr. editorial and press services RCA Corp., NYC, 1955-62; sr. v.p. corporate communications Chase Manhattan Bank, NYC, 1962-74; prof. journalism and pub. affairs U. S.C., Columbia, 1974-76; v.p. pub. affairs Monsanto Co., St. Louis, 1976-85; Gannett vis. prof. communications U. Fla., 1985-86; prof. communications U. North Fla., Jacksonville, 1986-92; adj. prof. bus. and comm. Flagler Coll., St. Augustine, Fla., 1985—95. Contbr. articles to various mags. Fellow Pub. Rels. Soc. Am. Roman Catholic. Home: 30 Park Terrace Dr Saint Augustine FL 32080-5334

NOLAN, LESLIE MARIAN, artist; b. Portland, Mar. 11, 1948; d. John Edward Nolan and Marion May Lindseth; m. K. Steven Halter, May 30, 1979; children: Ryan, Edward, Douglas. BA in French, Portland State U., 1970; MS in spl. studies, George Washington U., DC, 1975; MS in nat. security, Nat. Def. U., DC, 1997. Chief fgn. activities U.S. Info. Agy., Washington, 1979—82, dep. chief physical security, 1982—87, chief overseas support, 1987—93, chief security svc., 1993—96, resource analyst, 1997—99; chief attestation officer of U.S. U.S. Dept. of State, Washington, 1999—2004; artist self-employed, Herndon, Va., 2004—. V.p. programs Fairfax Art League, Va., 2000—04; co-chair hanging Art League, Alexandria, Va., 2005—06. Logo, Fairfax Art League, 2003. Mem.: League of Reston Artists, Potomac Valley Watercolorists, So. Watercolor Soc., League of Women Voters. Avocations: reading, travel, hiking. Home: 11660 Gilman Ln Herndon VA 20170

NOLAN, MIKE, professional football coach; b. Balt., Md., Mar. 7, 1959; s. Dick Nolan; m. Kathy Nolan; children: Michael, Christopher, Laura, Jennifer. Attended, U. Oreg. Asst. coach U. Oreg., 1981—82, Stanford U., 1982—83, Rice U., 1984—85; head coach LSU, 1986; linebackers coach, spl. teams asst. Denver Broncos, 1987—92; def. coord. NY Giants, 1993—96, Wash. Redskins, 1997—99, NY Jets, 2000; wide receivers coach Balt. Ravens, 2001, def. coord., 2002—04; head coach San Francisco 49ers, 2005—. Office: San Francisco 49ers Marie P DeBartolo Sports Ctr 4949 Cetennial Blvd Santa Clara CA 95054 *

NOLAN, OWEN, professional hockey player; b. Belfast, Northern Ireland, Feb. 12, 1972; m. Diana Nolan; 1 child, Jordan. Right wing Cornwall Royals, 1988—90, Halifax Citadels, 1990—91, Que. Nordiques, 1990—95, Colo. Avalanche, 1995, San Jose Sharks, 1995—2003, Toronto Maple Leafs, 2003—04, Phoenix Coyotes, 2006—. Player NHL All-Star Game, 1992, 96, 97, 2000, 02; mem. Team Can., Olympic Games, Salt Lake City, 2002. Recipient Emms Family Award, OHL, 1989, Jim Mahon Meml. Trophy, 1990. Achievements include being the first overall draft pick in NHL entry draft, 1990; being a member of gold medal Canadian Hockey team, Salt Lake City Olympic Games, 2002. Office: Phoenix Coyotes Hockey Club 5800 W Glenn Dr, Ste 350 Glendale AZ 85301

NOLAN, PETER JOHN, physics professor; b. NYC, Mar. 25, 1934; s. Peter John and Nora (Gleeson) Nolan; m. Barbara Nolan, 2000; children from previous marriage: Thomas, James, John, Kevin. BS in Physics, Manhattan Coll., 1956; cert. in Meteorology, UCLA, 1958; MS in Physics, Adelphi U., 1966, PhD in Physics, 1974. Engr. various corps., NJ, NY, 1956-63; systems analysis engr. on lunar module Gruman Aircraft Engring. Corp., Bethpage, NY, 1963-66; asst. prof. physics SUNY, Farmingdale, 1966-68, assoc. prof. physics, 1968-71, prof. physics, 1971—. Chmn. physics dept. SUNY, Farmingdale, 1970—77. Author: Experiments in Physics, 1982, 2d edit., 1995, Electromagnetic Theory for Electrical Technology Students, 1995, Fundamentals of College Physics, 1993, Italian Version, Fundementi Di Fisica, 1996. Mem.: Am. Assn. Physics Tchrs. Home: 59 Parnell Dr Smithtown NY 11787-2428 Office: SUNY Dept Physics Farmingdale NY 11735 Office Phone: 631-420-2271. Personal E-mail: pjnolan@optonline.net. Business E-Mail: nolanpj@farmingdale.edu.

NOLAN, RICHARD THOMAS, clergyman, educator; b. Waltham, Mass., May 30, 1937; s. Thomas Michael and Elizabeth Louise (Leishman) N.; life ptnr. Robert C. Pingpank, Sept. 14, 1955. BA, Trinity Coll., 1960; Diploma in Theol. Studies, Berkeley Div. Sch., 1960; MDiv. in Theol. Studies, Hartford Sem. Found., 1963; postgrad. in Religious Edn., Union Theol. Sem., 1963; MA in Religion, Yale U., 1967; PhD in Philosophy of Religion, NYU, 1973; postgrad. in Career Assessment, Ctr. Career Devel. and Ministry, 1987; postgrad. in Biomed. Ethics, Harvard U., 1991. Ordained deacon Episcopal Ch., 1963, priest, 1965; cert. in clinical pastoral edn. Conn. Valley Hosp., 1962, in death, dying and bereavement Waterbury Hosp. Health Ctr., Conn., 1977. Instr. Latin and English Watkinson Sch., Conn., 1961-62; instr. math. Choir Sch. of Cathedral of St. John the Divine, NYC, 1962-64; instr. math. and religion, assoc. chaplain Cheshire Acad., Conn., 1965-67; instr. Hartford Sem. Found., Conn., 1967-68, asst. acad. dean, lectr. philosophy and edn., 1968-70; instr. Mattatuck C.C., Waterbury, Conn., 1969-70, asst. prof. philosophy and history, 1970-74, assoc. prof., 1974-78, prof. philosophy and social sci., 1978-92, prof. emeritus, 1992—; vicar St. Paul's Parish, Bantam, Conn., 1974-88, pastor emeritus, 1988—; pres. Litchfield Inst., Conn. and Fla., 1984-96; adj. lectr. in philosophy Palm Beach C. C., Fla., 2000—02. Ethics com. Waterbury Hosp. Health Ctr., 1984—88; vis. and adj. prof. philosophy, theology and religious studies Trinity Coll., Conn., L.I. U., U. Miami, St. Joseph Coll., Conn., Pace U., Teikyo Post U., U. Conn., Hartford Grad. Ctr., Ctrl. Conn. State U., 1964—95, Broward C.C., Fla.; lectr. philosophy and theology Barry U., Fla., 1973, 1989—92, 1997—98; adj. assoc. in continuing edn. Berkeley Div. Sch. Yale U., 1987—89; Rabbi Harry Halpern Meml. lectr., Southbury, Conn., 1987; adj. prof. philosophy Fla. Atlantic U., 1998—99; adj. prof. The Union Inst., Fla., 1999; faculty of cons. examiners Charter Oak State Coll., Conn., 1990—93; assoc. for edn. Christ Ch. Cathedral, Hartford, Conn., 1988—94, hon. canon, 1991—; cons. Dept. Def. Activity Non-Traditional Ednl. Support, Ednl. Testing Svc., Princeton, NJ, 1990; vis. scholar Coll. Preachers, Washington Nat. Cathedral, 1994; supply priest Episcopal Diocese of S.E. Fla., 1994—2002; ret. priest-in-residence St. Andrew's Ch., Lake Worth, Fla., 2002—; soc. regents Cathedral Ch. St. John the Divine, 2002—. Author (with H. Titus and M. Smith): Living Issues in Philosophy, 7th edit., 1979, Indonesian edit., 1984, 8th edit., 1986, 9th edit., 1995; author: (with F. Kirkpatrick) Living Issues in Ethics, 1982, 2d edit., 2000, Chinese edit., 1988 (Honored Author for Books Exceeding 100,000 Copies award Wadsworth Pub. Co., 1986); editor, contbr. Diaconate Now, 1968, host Conversations With..., 1987—89; author (with Robert C. Pingpank): Soul Mates: More Than Partners (online), 2004. Notary pub., Fla. Recipient Founder's Day award, NYU, 1973; Rsch. fellow Med. Ethics, Yale, 1978, Bus. Ethics, 1987. Mem. Am. Acad. Religion, Am. Philos. Assn., Authors Guild, Hemlock Soc. Fla. (adv. bd. 1998—), Interfaith Alliance, Integrity, Boston Latin Sch. Alumni Assn., Tabor Acad. Alumni Assn., McCook Fellows Soc. Trinity Coll., Cavalier King Charles Spaniel Club, Yale Legacy Partners, Harwood Soc. Cheshire Acad., Society of The Torch of NYU, Founders Soc. of the Wash. Nat. Cathedral, Lambda Legal, Compass Lake Worth Fla., Phi Delta Kappa. Independent. Episcopalian. Home: 2527 Egret Lake Dr West Palm Beach FL 33413-2161 Personal E-mail: canon@rtnolan.com. *Who am I? By baptism I am a resurrected child of God born to love and be loved; my pilgrimage among others is lived within this baptismal identity, more enduring than any achievement.*

NOLAN, SHARON THERESA, nurse, educator; b. Hackensack, NJ; d. Louis and Doris Marzitelli; m. Kevin Nolan, Sr., Sept. 4, 1982; 1 child, Kevin Jr. AA in Edn., Bergen CC, Paramus, NJ, 1972; RN, Felician Coll., Lodi, NJ, 1976; BS in Health Edn., Fairleigh Dickinson U., Rutherford, NJ, 1980. RN NJ, 1977, NY, 1982. Staff nurse Hackensack U. Med. Ctr., 1975—79, children's diabetic health educator, 1979—81; staff nurse Tri Cities Nursing, Albany, NY, 1982—84; sch. nurse, tchr. Clifton Pub. Schs., NJ, 1981—96, Middlesex Pub. Schs., NJ, 1998—2001; tchr. health occupations Old Bridge HS, Matawan, NJ, 2004—. Recipient Hon. Commn., Congl. Youth Leadership Coun., DC, 2006. Mem.: Middlesex County Edn. Assn., N.J. Edn. Assn. Catholic. Office: Old Bridge HS 4207 Rt 516 Matawan NJ 07747

NOLAN, STANTON PEELLE, surgeon, educator; b. Washington, May 29, 1933; s. James Parker and Ellen Dubose (Peelle) N.; m. Marion Faro, June 16, 1955; children: Stanton Peelle Jr., Tiphanie Ravenel Clarke. BA, Princeton U., NJ, 1955; MD, U. Va., Charlottesville, 1959, MS, 1962. Diplomate Am. Bd. Surgery, Am. Bd. Thoracic Surgery. Intern U. Va. Med. Ctr., Charlottesville, 1959-60, asst. resident gen. surgery, 1960-61, research fellow surgery, 1961-62, sr. asst. resident gen. surgery, 1962-64, chief resident gen surgery, 1964-65, chief resident thoracic cardiovascular surgery, 1965-66; sr. rsch. assoc. Clinic of Surgery Nat. Heart Inst., NIH, Bethesda, Md., 1966-68; asst. prof. surgery U. Va. Med. Ctr., Charlottesville, 1968-70, assoc. prof. surgery, 1970-74, surgeon in charge div. thoracic cardiovascular surgery, 1970-93, prof. surgery, 1974-81, Claude A. Jessup prof. surgery, 1981-98, clin. prof. surgery, 1998—2004, prof. surgery, 2004—06, med. dir. Thoracic Cardiovascular post-operative unit, 1989-93, prof. emeritus of surgery, 2006—. Established Investigator Am. Heart Assn., 1969-74; mem. surgery A study sect. NIH, Washington, 1972-76, surgery and bioengring. study sect. 1984-87, chmn. 1985-87; cons. thoracic cardiovascular surgery VA Hosp., Salem, Va., 1968-98, Am. Bd. Surgery cons. to qualifying examination com., 1988-91; surg. cons. Bur. Crippled Children, Charlottesville, 1968-93; vis. cons. cardiothoracic surgery Aga Khan U., Karachi, Pakistan, 1995, vis cons. Vol. Health Svcs., Madras, India, 1997, cons. So. Petrochem. Industries Corp. SPIC, Chennai, India 2000; vis. prof. U. Hanover, Germany, 1990; vis. prof. Cardiac Surgerey, U. Wis. 1992; visiting/invited lectr. and keynote spkr., 1999-2002. Mem. editl. bd. Jour. Surg. Rsch., 1973-79, Annals of Thoracic Surgery, 1979-88; mem. sci. adv. bd. Jour. for Heart Valve Disease, 1993—2006; mem. editl. adv. bd. ECRI Operating Rm. Risk Mgmt., 1992-2006; co-editor: Comprehensive Thoracic Surgery Curriculum, TSDA, 1995; contbr. articles to profl. jours., chpts. to books. Bd. mgrs. Ctrl. Va. Health Network, 2000—05; active Westminster Canterbury Blue Ridge, chmn. Residents' Assn., 2004—06; bd. dirs. Piedmont Liability Trust, 1989—2005, chmn. claims com., 1989—2006, chmn. bd., 1991—2004. Recipient John Horsley Meml. prize U. Va. Med. Sch., 1962, Merit award Rsch. Forum of Am. Coll. Chest Physicians, 1968, Clyde Watson Disting. Svc. award Pastoral Care and Edn., 2006, Stanton P. Nolan Professorship Thoracic and Cardiovascular Surgery, U. Va. Bd. Visitors, 2006; Rsch. fellow Va. Heart Assn., 1961-62, Am. Cancer Soc., 1963-64; grantee NIH, 1968-84, Am. Heart Assn., 1970-73, Medtronic Corp., 1975-81. Fellow ACS (com. allied health pers. 1996—2004, exec. com. 1997-2000, vice chair), Am. Coll. Cardiology, Am. Surg. Assn.; mem. Am. Assn. Thoracic Surgery, Am. Heart Assn. (coun. on cardiovasc. surgery 1969-99, anesthesiology, radiology and surgery study com. 1991-94), Andrew G. Morrow Soc., Assn. Acad. Surgery, Assn. Advancement of Med. Instrumentation (chair 1998-2000, co-chmn. cardiac valve prostheses stds. com. 1974-2005, mem. internat. stds. strategy com. 1989—2005, bd. dirs. 1990-2000, stds. bd. 1991—2005, edn. com. 1992-93, nominating com. 1996-2000, chair 1998-2000, exec. com. 1996-2000, govt. rels. com. 1996-2000), Internat. Stds. Orgn. (chmn. subcom. on cardiovascular surg. implants 1982-2004), Assn. Clin. Cardiac Surgeons, Halsted Soc. (exec. com. 1985-89), Coord. Com. on Perfusion Affairs (chmn. 1990-2000), Internat. Assn. Cardiac Biol. Implants (sci. com. 1994), Am. Assn. for Vascular Surgery, Muller Surg. Soc. (pres. 1979), Soc. Internat. de Cirurgie, Soc. Vascular Surgery, Soc. Thoracic Surgeons (ad hoc com. on industry rels. 1992-97, stds. and ethics com. 1993-95, 98-2001, edn. and resources com. 1996-97), Soc. Univ. Surgeons, Southeastern Surg. Congress, So. Surg. Assn. (2d v.p. 1982), Thoracic Surgery Found. Rsch. and Edn. (chair New Century Soc. com. 1997-2000), Va. Surg. Soc. (v.p. 1980-83, pres. 1984), Va. Vascular Soc. (exec. coun. 1985-86), Soc. Critical Care Medicine, Raven Soc., Assn. Am. Med. Colls. (rep. coun. acad. socs. 1992-01), Chevy Chase Club, Alpha Omega Alpha, Omicron Delta Kappa. Home: #5204 250 Pantops Mountain Rd Charlottesville VA 22911-8702 Office: U Va TCV Surgery PO Box 800679 Charlottesville VA 22908-0679 Business E-Mail: snolan@virginia.edu.

NOLAN, TED (THEODORE JOHN NOLAN), professional hockey coach; b. Sault Ste. Marie, Ont., Can., Apr. 7, 1958; m. Sandra Nolan; children: Brandon, Jordan. LLD (hon.), Laurentian U., 2002. Player Detroit Red Wings, 1981—84, Pitts. Penguins, 1985—86; head coach Sault Ste. Marie Greyhounds, 1988—94; asst. coach Hartford Whalers, 1994-95; head coach Buffalo Sabres, 1995—97; head coach, dir. hockey ops. Moncton Wildcats, 2005—06; head coach NY Islanders, 2006—. Pres., CEO Ted Nolan Found. Named Sault Ste. Marie Citizen of Yr., 1990—91; recipient Order of Ontario, 1993, National Aboriginal Achievement Award, 1994, Jack Adams Award, NHL, 1997. Office: NY Islanders Nassau Veterans Meml Coliseum 1255 Hempstead Turnpike Uniondale NY 11553

NOLAN, THERESA A., retired judge, mediator, arbitrator; b. Washington, Dec. 10, 1930; d. Peter James Sr. and Mary Dorothea (Gerhardt) Hagan; m. Bernard A. Nolan, Jr. (dec.); children: Patrick, Theresa Davis, Mary Ellen Purcell, Joanne Kowalczyk, Frances McKeever, Bernard, Christine, Thomas, Barbara Kristek, William, Kathleen, Joseph; m. Walter G. Planet (dec.). BA, U. Balt., 1973; LLB, U. Balt. Sch. Law, 1975. Bar: Md. 1976. Legal sec. Law & Sinclair, Upper Marlboro, Md., 1961—68, McGrane, Casey, Miller, Lanham, 1968—72; legis. asst. Prince George's County Office Law, Upper Marlboro, 1972—76; ptnr. Sherry, Boyer & Nolan, Bowie, 1977—79; sole practitioner, 1979—80; master domestic rels. causes 7th Jud. Cir. Ct. Md., Upper Marlboro, 1981—85; judge 4th Dist. Ct. Md., 1985—97, civil coordinating judge, 1991—2000; judge 7th Jud. Cir. Ct. Md., 1997—2000; mediator Md. Ct. Sys., 2000—. Instr. paralegal program Prince George's Cmty. Coll., 1980—88, USDA, 1980—88, U. Md. U. Coll., 1985—2000; family law sect. coun. Md. State Bar Assn., 1982—85; mem. Gov.'s Coun. Child Support Enforcement, 1983—86; mem. adv. bd. Dist. Pub. Defender, Upper Marlboro, 1984—; bd. govs. Md. State Bar Assn., 1985—87, 1989—91, local bar liaison, 1986—88; com. on criminal law procedure Md. Jud. Conf., 1987—88, dist. ct. edn. com., 1988—89, exec. com., 1990—91, chair dist. ct. edn. com., 1990—91, faculty, 1990—2000, vice chair, 1991—92, chair, 1992—93, civil law and procedures com., 1992—94, adminstrv. judges com., 1995—96, pub. rels. com., 1996—2000; pres. Prince George's County Women Lawyers Caucus, 1979—80, treas., 1981—82, exec. com., 1989—91; mem. Commn. Future of Md. Cts., 1995—96, chair criminal, juvenile and family matters sub-com. Charter mem. Law Found. Prince George's County; chmn. Prince George's County Cable Television Commn., 1978; mem. sodality Sacred Heart Parish; bd. dir. Prince George's Hosp., Cheverly, Md., 2000—03, Md. Vol. Lawyers Svcs., Inc., 1986—93; adv. bd. Family Crisis Ctr., Prince George's County Hotline and Suicide Prevention Ctr. Named a Woman of History, 1990, Woman of Achievement, Prince George's County, 1994; named one of Md. Top 100 Women, 1998; named to Women's Hall of Fame, Prince George's County, 1993; recipient Fabulous Forties award, Prince George's Cmty. Coll., 1998, Disting. Svc. award, Prince George's County, 2000, Salute to Women award, Gtr. Bowie C. of C., 2000. Mem.: Am. Judges Assn., Inns of Ct., Md. Cir. Judges Assn., Women's Bar Assn. Md. (pres.-elect 1994—95, treas. 1981—82, bd. dir. 1982—94, nominating com. 1985—87, chmn. elections 1986, exec. com. 1989—90, chmn. awards com. 1989—93, Rita Davidson award 1993), Nat. Assn. Women Judges (sec. 4th dist. 1991—92, treas. 1993—94, pres. 1995—97, chair women in prison com. 2000, women in prison com. 2000—, ret. mem.), Prince George's County Bar Assn. (criminal liaison com. 1978, bd. dir. 1978—90, domestic rels. com. 1980—90, treas. 1981—82, sec. 1982—83, pres.-elect 1983—84, pres. 1984—85, budget com. 1984—86, chair social com. 1985—98, chmn. ABA-MSBA liaison com. 1986, nominating com. 1989—90). Democrat. Roman Catholic. Avocations: dance, golf, theater, book club, travel. Home: 2802 Berth Ter Annapolis MD 21401-7103

NOLAN, VAL, JR., retired biologist, lawyer; b. Evansville, Ind., Apr. 28, 1920; s. Val and Jeannette (Covert) N.; m. Susanne Howe, Dec. 23, 1946 (div. Aug. 29, 1980); children: Val, Ann Clare, William Alan; m. Ellen D. Ketterson, Oct. 17, 1980. AB, Ind. U., 1941, JD, 1949. Bar: Ind. 1949. Dep. U.S. marshal, 1941; agt. White House Detail, U.S. Secret Service, 1942; asst. prof. law Ind. U., 1949-52, assoc. prof., 1952-56, prof., 1956-85, prof. emeritus, 1985—, research scholar in zoology, 1957-68, prof. zoology, 1968-77, prof. biology, 1977-85; prof. emeritus, 1985—; acting dean Sch. Law, 1976, 80. Author: (with F.E. Horack, Jr.) Land Use Controls, 1955, Ecology and Behavior of the Prairie Warbler, 1978; editor Ind. Law Jour., 1945-46, Jour. Avian Biology, 1998—2005, Current Ornithology, 1994-2004. Served with USNR, 1942-46. Guggenheim fellow, 1957; recipient Ind. U. Disting. Alumni Svc. award, 1987; named to Acad. Law Alumni Fellows, Ind. U., 1988. Fellow AAAS, Am. Ornithologists Union (v.p. 1989-90, Brewster Meml. award 1986), Animal Behavior Soc.; mem. Brit.

Ornithologists Union, Cooper Ornithol. Soc., Wilson Ornithol. Soc. (co-recipient (with Ellen D. Ketterson) Margaret M. Nice award 1998), Assn. Field Ornithologists, Ecol. Soc. Am., Am. Soc. Naturalists, Deutsche Ornithologen-Gesellschaft, Nederlandse Ornithologische Unie, Soc. Study of Reprodn., Phi Beta Kappa, Sigma Xi. Democrat. Home: 4675 E Heritage Woods Rd Bloomington IN 47401-9312 E-mail: vnolan@indiana.edu.

NOLAN, VICTORIA, theater director; b. Portland, Maine, June 15, 1952; d. Herbert Wallace and Diane Katharine (Kremm) N.; m. Clarkson Newell Crolius, Aug. 30, 1980; children: Covey Emmeline, Wilhelmina Adams. BA magna cum laude, U. Maine, 1976. Publicity asst. Loeb Drama Ctr. Harvard U., Cambridge, Mass., 1975; pub. rels. asst. to dir. Sch. Arts Boston U., 1975-76; mgmt. asst. TAG Found., NYC, 1976-77; mng. dir. Ram Island Dance Co., Portland, 1977-78; dir. devel. Ctr. Stage, Balt., 1979-81, assoc. mng. dir., 1981-87; mng. dir. Ind. Repertory Theatre, Indpls., 1988-93; dep. dean, mng. dir. and prof. Yale Sch. Drama Yale Repertory Theatre, New Haven, 1993—. Program evaluator Nat. Endowment Arts, Washington, 1988—, panelist, 1991—; mem. Indpls. Cultural Consortium, v.p., 1991-93; bd. dir. Greater Indpls. Progress Com., Indpls. Urban League, Arts Coun. Indpls.; mem. nat. bd. Theatre Comm. Group, N.Y.C., treas., 1995-99; bd. dir. New Haven Arts Industry Coalition, co-chair, 1997-99, treas., 1999-2002. Mem. exec. com. League Resident Profl. Theatres, 2000-04. Nat. Performing Arts Mgmt. fellow Exxon, Doner Fedn. and NEA, 1978; Elizabeth L. Mahaffey arts adminstrn. fellow Conn. Commn. on the Arts, 2000; recipient SetonElm Ivy award Yale U. and City of New Haven, 2005. Home: 120 Rimmon Rd Woodbridge CT 06525-1915 Office: Yale Repertory Theater PO Box 208244 Yale Station 222 York St New Haven CT 06520-8244

NOLAN, WILLIAM C., JR., oil industry executive; b. 1939; BA, Yale U., New Haven, 1961, JD, 1964. Mem. law dept. Murphy Oil Corp., El Dorado, Ark., 1964—69, chmn. bd. dirs., 2002—; founding ptnr. Nolan and Alderson, Attys., El Dorado, 1969—; pres. Noalmark Broadcasting. Office: Murphy Oil Corp PO Box 7000 El Dorado AR 71731-7000 also: Nolan and Alderson Attys 202 W 19th St El Dorado AR 71730 *

NOLAN, WILLIAM JOSEPH, III, banker; b. NYC, Apr. 6, 1947; s. William J. Jr. and Alice Nettleton (Edwards) N.; m. Wendy Collison French, Mar. 21, 1981; children: William J. IV, Anina Chrysler. Student, Hackley Sch., Tarrytown, NY, 1958-65; E.S.U. scholar, Eastbourne Coll., UK, 1966; BA, Colgate U., 1970; MBA, Stanford U., 1973. V.p. Bankers Trust Co., NYC, 1973-83; mng. dir. Becker-Paribas, NYC, 1983-84; exec. v.p., treas. PaineWebber, NYC, 1984-2001. Bd. trustees Adirondack Mus. (Blue Mountain), 1996—, (treas. 2000—). Mem. Pub. Securities Assn. (money market exec. com. 1985-89, chmn. 1987, bd. dirs. 1988-91, treas. 1990), Adirondack League, Piping Rock Club, Union Club of N.Y.C. Home: 1088 Park Ave New York NY 10128-1132

NOLAND, CHRISTINE A., judge; b. 1945; BA, JD, La. State Univ. Law clk. to Hon. John V. Parker U.S. Dist. Ct. (La. mid. dist.), 5th circuit, magistrate judge Baton Rouge, 1987—. Mem. ABA, La. State Bar, La. trial Lawyers Assn., Baton Rouge Bar Assn., Dean Henry George McMahon Inn of Ct. (counselor 1995-97). Office: Russell B Long Fed Bldg & Courthouse 777 Florida St Rm 278 Baton Rouge LA 70801-1717 Office Phone: 225-389-3592.

NOLAND, KENNETH CLIFTON, artist; b. Asheville, NC, Apr. 10, 1924; s. Harry C. and Bessie (Elkins) N.; m. Cornelia Langer (div.); children: Cady, William L., Lyndon; m. Stephanie Gordon, 1967 (div.); m. Peggy Schiffer; children: Samuel Jesse (div.); m. Paige Rense, 1994. Student, Ozzip Zadkine, Paris, 1948-49; studied, Black Mountain Coll., NC, summers, 1950, 51. Tchr. Inst. Contemporary Arts, 1950-52, Cath. U., 1951-60. One man shows include Galerie Creuze, Paris, 1949, Tibor de Nagy Gallery, N.Y.C., 1957, 58, Jefferson Pl. Gallery, 1958, French & Co., N.Y.C., 1959, Bennington Coll., 1961, Andre Emmerich Gallery, N.Y.C., 15 shows from 1960-83, Andre Emmerich Gallery, Zurich, Switzerland, 1973, 76, 79, 82, David Mirvish Gallery, Toronto, Can., 1965, 67, 74, 76, Jewish Mus., 1965, Salander O'Reilly Galleries, N.Y.C., 1989, Leo Castelli Gallery, N.Y., 1995, Gana Art Gallery, Seoul, 1995-96, also other galleries in Milan, Italy, Paris, Zurich, Dusseldorf, Hamburg and Cologne, Fed. Republic Germany, London, Montreal and Toronto, Can.; retrospective show Guggenheim Mus., N.Y.C., 1977; group shows include Kootz Gallery, N.Y.C., 1954, Norman Mackenzie Art Gallery, Regina, Sask., Can., 1963, Corcoran Gallery, Washington, 1956, 59, 63, 64, 67, 70, 75, Corcoran Gallery Biennial in Italy, 1964, Fogg Art Mus., Cambridge, Mass., 1965, 72, Mus. Modern Art, N.Y.C., 1965, 68, Nat. Gallery, Washington, 1968, U.S. Pavilion Expo 67, Montreal, Art Inst. Chgo., 1962, 70, 72, 76, Balt. Mus., 1957, 70, 77, Jewish Mus., 1963, Tate Gallery, London, 1964, 74, Guggenheim Mus., 1961, 66, 70, 73-74, 76-77, L.A. County Mus., 1964, Inst. Contemporary Art, Boston, 1964, 65, 67, Whitney Mus., N.Y.C., 1961-67, 69-73, 76, Met. Mus. N.Y.C., 1968, 70, Mus. Fine Arts, Boston, 1972, Albright-Knox Gallery, Buffalo, 1978, 80, Ameringer Howard Fine Art, NY, 99; Meredith Long Gall., Houston,Tex., 99; Andre Emmerich, CLosing Exhibition of Gall., NY, 99; CHAC-Mool Gall., CA, 99, Ameringer/Howard Gall., N.Y.C, 1999-2001, Farnsworth Mus. Art, Maine, 2002, Naples (Fla.) Mus., 2002; represented in permanent collections Salander O'Reily Galleries, N.Y.C., Mus. of Fine Arts, Houston, 1994, Ft. Lauderdale, 1994; Arte Metro Roma, Rome Colosseum Ctrl. Subway Mosaic Installed, 1995. Trustee Bennington (Vt.) Coll. Recipient 1st prize Premio Nacional Internat., Inst. Torcuato de Tella, Buenos Aires, 1964, Creative Arts award Brandeis U., 1965, 4th prize Corcoran Biennale, 1967; recipient The N.C. Award/medal of arts, 1995. Office Phone: 207-372-9684. Personal E-mail: kcnbridge@aol.com.

NOLAND, KEVIN M., school system administrator; BA, Univ. Ky., 1974, JD, 1978. Gen. coun. Ky. Dept. Edn., 1991—, dep. commr. edn., 1991—, interim commr. edn., 2006—07. Mem.: Nat. Coun. State Edn. Attorneys (former chmn.), Ky. Bar Assn. (former chairperson educ. law sect.). Office: 500 Mero St 1st Fl CPT Frankfort KY 40601-1957 *

NOLAND, MARIAM CHARL, foundation executive; b. Parkersburg, W.Va., Mar. 29, 1947; d. Lloyd Henry and Ethel May (Beare) Noland; m. James Arthur Kelly, June 13, 1981. BS, Case Western Res. U., 1969; M in Edn., Harvard U., 1975. Asst. dir admissions, fin. aid Baldwin-Wallace Coll., Berea, Ohio, 1969-72; asst. dir. admissions Davidson (N.C.) Coll., 1972-74; case writer Inst. Edn. Mgmt., Cambridge, Mass., 1975; sec., treas., program officer The Cleve. Found., 1975-81; v.p. The St. Paul Found., 1981-85; pres. Community Found. for S.E. Mich., 1985—. Trustee Coun. Mich. Founds., 1988-98, Coun. on Founds., 1994-99, Henry Ford Health System, 1994-2002, 2004— Alma Coll., 1994-2004, John S. and James L. Knight Found., 2002—, Detroit Riverfront Conservancy, 2003—; commr. Detroit 300, 2000-01. Office: Community Found SE Mich 333 W Fort St Ste 2010 Detroit MI 48226-3134 Office Phone: 313-961-6675. Business E-Mail: mnoland@cfsem.org.

NOLAND, MARY RICHERSON, retired management consultant; b. Lebanon, Ky., Aug. 6, 1925; d. Thomas Wesley and Mary Suda Richerson; m. James Russell Noland, Jr., Dec. 22, 1945; children: James Russell III, Ellen Gay, Mary Elise. BA in Sociology and Psychology, U. Louisville, Ky.; student in Sociology and Psychology, New Haven State U., Conn., 1946—47; student, U. Houston, 1969—70. Exec. dir. vol. svcs. Meml. City Hosp., Houston, 1971—73; exec. cons. Mgmt. Techs., Inc., Houston, 1975—78, CEO, chmn., 1978—98; chmn. Personalysis Corp. (formerly Mgmt. Techs., Inc.), Houston, 1998—. Editor: Real Estate Focused Newsletter, 1973—75. Organizer, dir. Heart of Houston, 1965—66. Methodist. Avocations: reading, history, politics, music, piano. Home: 13303 Havershire Houston TX 77079 Office: Personalysis Corp 5847 San Felipe 650 Houston TX 77079

NOLAND, THOMAS TURLEY, JR., managed healthcare company executive; b. Norwalk, Conn., July 16, 1953; s. Thomas Turley and Judy (Kwis) N.; m. Vivian Ruth Sawyer, July 17, 1982; children: Andrew Montgomery, Sidney Victoria. Student, Duke U., 1971-73; BA magna cum laude, Yale U., 1975. Staff writer Anniston Star newspaper, Anniston, Ala., 1976-79; spl. correspondent Atlanta Constitution newspaper, Paris, 1979-84; instr. English and journalism Am. Coll. in Paris, 1979-81; inst. English Centre de Perfectionnement Linguistique, Paris, 1981-84, co-dir. Am. dept., 1982-84; mgr. pub. affairs Humana Inc., Louisville, 1984-85, sr. mgr. pub. affairs, 1985-87, dir. communications, 1987-91, v.p. communications, 1991-93; pub. Health Care Industry Group, The Cobb Group, Louisville, 1993-95; pub. Vertical Mkts. Group The Cobb Group, Louisville, 1995-97; v.p. corp. comms. Humana Inc., Louisville, 1997-99, sr. v.p. corp. comms., 1999—. Author: The Permissive Will of God, 1979, The Celestine Travesty, 1996; co-author (play) Columbia Preserved, 1983, (play) The Neglected Few, 2000; editor (book) September 11 2001: Stories from 55 Broad Street, 2002; co-editor Remembering Wendell Cherry, 2003, The Dacian Chronicles, 2006. Chmn. bd. Ky. chpt. Nat. Multiple Sclerosis Soc., Louisville, 1987-88, bd. dirs., 1985-90; bd. dirs. Ky. Shakespeare Festival, 1986-91, U.S.A. Harvest, Louisville, 1989-94; bd. dirs., Filson Club Hist. Soc., Louisville, 1991—, treas., 1994-96. v.p., 1997, pres., 1998-03; bd. dirs., Cabbage Patch Settlement House, Louisville, 1994-97, Ky. Ctr. African-Am. Heritage, 1999-, Yale in Ky., 2000-, Ky. Opera, 2002-05; mem. Leadership Louisville Class, 1989-90, Leadership Louisville Found., Inc., 1989-90; vestry Calvary Episc. Ch., 1990-92, jr. warden, 1995, sr. warden, 1996-97, vestry St. Francis in Fields Episc. Ch., 2004—. Recipient 1st place feature writing Ala. AP Assn., 1978, Silver Anvil awrd Pub. Rels. Soc. Am., 1985. Mem. Health Ins. Assn. Am. (pub. rels. policy com. 1989-93), Am. Assn. Health Plans (strategic Commns. com. 1997-). Republican. Episcopalian. Avocations: history, travel, French language and literature, running, racquetball. Office: Humana Inc 500 W Main St Louisville KY 40202-4268 Home Phone: 502-895-9635; Office Phone: 502-580-3674. Business E-Mail: tnoland@humana.com.

NOLD, AURORA RAMIREZ, finance company executive; b. Honolulu, Apr. 21, 1958; m. Allan Jeffrey Nold, Aug. 1, 1995. BSBA cum laude, St. Louis U., 1969, MS in Bus. Adminstrn. magna cum laude, 1975, PhD summa cum laude, 1986. Exch. prof., dept. chairperson mgmt. St. Louis U., Baguio City, Philippines, 1980-86, dean Coll. Bus., 1980—86; rsch. asst. East/West Ctr. for Am. Studies, Honolulu, 1986-87; dir. Am. studies USIS, Washington, 1987-89; fin. cons. Shadow Hill Samaritan, Long Beach, Calif., 1989-93; dir. A&A Edu Care Consultancy Programs, Inc., Las Vegas, Nev., 1993—; prin., owner Felocor Diversified Funding, Las Vegas, Nev., 2005—. Bd. advisors Am. Biog. Inst., Raleigh, N.C., 1995—, Internat. Biog. Ctr., Cambridge, Eng., 1995—; rschr. S.H.S. Inc., Las Vegas, 1995—; prof. econs., bus and mgmt. C.C. So. Nev.; prof. stats. U. Nev., Las Vegas; tutor C.C. So. Nev.; pres., founder Felocor Diversified Funding Co Author: Business Education in the Philippines, 1986; contbr. articles to profl. jours. Pres. Rep. Presdl. Task Force, Las Vegas, 1995—. Cultural Exch. grant Fulbright Am. Studies, 1987, scholarship grant St. Louis U., 1979-86; recipient Appreciation award Nat. Humane Edn. Soc., 1996, Nat. Park Trust, 1996, Nat. Law Enforcement Officers Meml. Fund, 1997, Oustanding Cmty. and Profl. Achievement Commemorative medal Am. Biog. Inst., 1997, internat. cultural diploma of honor, 2000. Mem. AAUW, NAFE, Asian Am. Studies Assn., U.S. Profl. Bookkeepers Assn., Am. Cash Flow Assn., Las Vegas C. of C., Nev. Faculty Alliance Republican. Mem. Lds Ch. Avocations: collecting rare coins, writing, reading, music and coin collecting. Office Phone: 702-242-6020. Personal E-mail: auroranold@aol.com.

NOLD, CARL RICHARD, museum administrator; b. Mineola, NY, Nov. 26, 1955; s. Carl Frederick and Joan Catherine (Heine) N.; m. Mary Beth Krivoruchka (div.). BA in History magna cum laude, St. John's U., Jamaica, NY, 1977; MA in History Mus. Studies, SUNY, Oneonta, 1982. Pres. Gregory Mus., Hicksville, N.Y., 1977; registrar N.Y. State Hist. Assn., Cooperstown, 1978-80; dir., curator Gadsby's Tavern Mus., Alexandria, Va., 1980-84; dir. State Mus. Pa., Harrisburg, 1984-91; exec. dir. Mackinac State Hist. Parks, Lansing, Mackinac Island, Mich., 1992—2003; pres., CEO Historic New Eng. (Soc. Preservation New England Antiquities), Boston, 2003—. Grant reviewer Inst. Mus. Svcs., Washington, 1982-90, 95—, mus. assessment prog. reviewer, 1985—, panelist, 1992-94; panelist mus. grant program Nat. Endowment for Humanities, 1990-93, panelist challenge grant program, 1997. Co-author: Gadsby's Tavern Mus. Interpretive Master Plan, 1984; contbr. articles to profl. jours. Mem. adv. bd. for Grad. History George Mason U., Fairfax, Va., 1982-84, Ctr. for Great Lakes Culture, Mich. State U., 2000-2002; adv. com. Susquehanna Mus. Art, Harrisburg, 1989-91; bd. dirs. Harrisburg-Hershey-Carlisle Tourism and Visitor Bur., 1987-91, bd. sec., 1990-91; mem. mayor's adv. bd. city of Mackinac Island, 1993-2003; mem. task force Mich. Cultural Tourism, 1998—; mem. Essex Nat. Heritage Comm., 2003-06. Mem. Assn. of Midwest Mus. (treas. 1998-2000, pres. 2000-2002, Mich. Mus. Assn. (bd. dirs. 1995-98, bd. sec. 1999-2001, Dist. Svc. award, 2002, 06), Am. Assn. Mus. (vis. com. mus. accreditation 1989—, chmn. coun. of regions 2000-01, MAP adv. com. 2002-, bd. dirs. 2003—, chair fin. com.), Am. Assn. for State and Local History (elections chmn. 1990, mem. performance measurement program task force 2002-03), Cooperstown Grad. Assn. (bd. dirs. 1985-87), St. Botolph Club(Boston). Home: 21 Grove St Winchester MA 01890-3837 Office: Hist New Eng 141 Cambridge St Boston MA 02114-2702

NOLEN, ROY LEMUEL, retired lawyer; b. Montgomery, Ala., Nov. 29, 1937; s. Roy Lemuel Jr. and Elizabeth (Larkin) N.; m. Evelyn McNeill Thomas, Aug. 28, 1965; 1 child, Rives Rutledge. BArch, Rice U., 1961; LLB, Harvard U., 1967. Bar: Tex. 1968, U.S. Ct. Appeals (5th cir.) 1969. Law clk. to sr. judge U.S. Ct. Appeals (5th cir.), 1967-68; assoc. Baker Botts LLP, Houston, 1968-75, ptnr., 1976-2000; co-head Corp. Dept., 1985-90; mem. exec. com., 1988-91; adminstrv. ptnr., 1997-2000; ret., 2001. Cmty. rep. instnl. animal care and use com. M.D. Anderson Cancer Ctr., 2001—06. Bd. dirs. Houston Ballet Found., 1980-92, Rice Design Alliance, 1995-96; exec. com. Contemporary Arts Mus., 1990-96, 97-2002; exec. com. Houston Symphony Soc., 1994-99, gen. counsel, 1994-98; trustee Menil Found. (Menil Collection), 1999—, sr. warden Christ Ch. Cathedral, 1991-92, chancellor, 2003—; chmn. Houston area devel. initiative Episcopal Diocese of Tex., 1997. 1st lt. USMC, 1961-64. Mem.: State Bar Tex., Briar Club, Paul Jones Dancing Club, Allegro, Coronado Club. Episcopalian. Office: Baker Botts LLP One Shell Plz 910 Louisiana St Houston TX 77002-4995 Office Phone: 713-229-1216. Personal E-mail: roynolen@aol.com.

NOLEN, SAMUEL AUGUSTUS, lawyer; b. Circleville, Ohio, Nov. 18, 1954; s. Jake Thomas and Amelia Aerl (Maverick) N.; m. Gail Anne McCurdy, May 17, 1980; children: S. Maverick, Maury McCurdy. Student, U. Regensburg, 1974-75; BA cum laude, Vanderbilt U., 1976; JD, Washington and Lee U., 1979. Bar: Del. 1979, US Dist. Ct. Del. 1980, US Ct. Appeals (3d cir.) 1985, US Supreme Ct. 2004. Law clk. Del. Ct. Chancery, Wilmington, 1979-80; assoc. Richards, Layton & Finger, Wilmington, 1980-86, mem., 1986—. Bd. dirs. Lex Mundi Pro Bono Found., 2006—. Mem. ABA, Internat. Bar Assn. (sect. bus. law), Del. Bar Assn. (sect. corp. law), Coun. Sect. Corp. Law, World Affairs Coun. Wilmington, Inc. (bd. dirs.), Lex Mundi Ltd. (bd. dirs. 2002—, exec. com. 2003—), Greenville Country Club. Republican. Episcopalian. Office: Richards Layton & Finger 1 Rodney Sq Wilmington DE 19801-3305 Office Phone: 302-651-7752.

NOLEN, WILLIAM GILES, lawyer, accountant; b. Fayetteville, Ark., Aug. 4, 1931; s. William Jefferson and Marie (Giles) N.; m. Carole Turner, Aug. 25, 1957; children: Kathy, Thomas (dec.). BSBA, U. Ark., Fayetteville, 1960; JD, U. Houston, 1980. Bar: Tex. 1980; CPA, Tex. Auditor Arthur Anderson & Co., Houston, 1960-66; sec., treas. Brown & Root (U.K.) Ltd., London, 1966-69; v.p. Highlands Ins. Co., Houston, 1969-73, sr. v.p., 1973-80, dir., 1973-88; v.p. Halliburton Co., Dallas, 1980-82; sr. v.p. Brown & Root, Inc., Houston, 1982-86; exec. v.p. Highlands Ins. Co., Houston, 1986-88; of counsel Whitmore, Sheppard & Pollicoff, Houston, 1988-92, Policoff, Smith & Myres LLP, Houston, 1992-95, Policoff, Smith, Myres & Remels LLP, Houston, 1995-2000, Pollicoff, Smith & Remels, Houston, 2000—02. Maj. USAF, 1951-56. Mem. Am. Assn. Atty. CPAs (past pres., bd. dirs.), Tex. Soc. CPAs (Tex. CPA of Yr. 1961), Mensa. Presbyterian.

NOLET, GUUST, geophysicist; MSc cum laude in Geophysics, Utrecht U., Netherlands, 1972, PhD cum laude, 1976. Tchg. asst. dept. med. physics Utrecht U., Netherlands, 1967—68, tchg. asst. depts. physics and geophysics, 1969—72, mem. faculty earth sci. dept., 1976—85, prof., 1985—91; prof. dept. geosciences Princeton U., NJ, 1991—97, George J. Magee prof. geophysics and geol. engring., 1997—; rsch. assoc. Netherlands Orgn. for Advancement of Pure Rsch., 1972—75. Head dept. geophysics Utrecht U., 1985—87, assoc. dean faculty of earth scis., 1987—88; dir. Internat. Sch. Applied Geophysics, Erice, Italy, 1986—87; vis. prof. Inst. Geophysics and Planetary Physics U. Calif., San Diego, 1988—89; v.p. European Seismol. Commn., 1990—92; vis. prof. U. Nice, France, 1997—98, 2005; mem. com. seismology NRC, 2000—04; assoc. chair dept. geosciences Princeton U., 2001—; vis. prof. LGIT U. Joseph Fourier, Grenoble, France, 2004; mem. EarthScope Sci. and Edn. Com., 2005. Contbr. articles to profl. jours.; editor: Geophys. Jour. Royal Astron. Soc., 1982—86, Modern Approaches to Geophysics, 1988—2002, Jour. Seismology, 1998—2001; assoc. editor: Jour. Geophys. Rsch., 1993—95. Recipient Lagrange prize, Royal Acad. Scis., Humanities and Fine Arts Belgium, 1980, Vening Meinesz prijs, Netherlands Orgn. for Advancement of Pure Rsch., 1983, Beno Gutenberg medal, European Geophys. Soc., 2006, Bownocker medal, Ohio State U., 2006; grantee Cecil H. and Idan Green fellowship, 1988. Fellow: Am. Geophys. Union (pres. seismology sect. 1998—2000), Am. Acad. Arts & Scis.; mem.: Academia Europaea, Royal Netherlands Acad. Scis. (corr.; earth sci. coun. 1990—91). Office: Dept Geosciences Princeton U 320 Guyot Hall Princeton NJ 08544 E-mail: nolet@princeton.edu.

NOLF, DAVID M., financial consultant; b. Hartford, Conn., Nov. 25, 1942; s. Richard A. and Erreld I. (Manstan) N.; m. Linda J. Anderson, June 20, 1964; 1 child, Cristina E. BSChemE, Lafayette Coll., 1964; MBA, U. Conn., 1968. Prodn. engr. Am. Cyanamid, Wallingford, Conn., 1664-66; adminstrn. supr. Electric Boat Div. Gen. Dynamics, Groton, Conn., 1966-71; chief fin. and adminstrv. officer, corp. sec. Analysis and Tech. Inc., North Stonington, Conn., 1971—99; cons., 2001—. Bd. dirs. Reflexite Corp. Chmn. Ch. Fin. Com., Westerly, R.I., 2002—; trustee Westerly Hosp., 1993—, chmn. 2003—; bd. dirs. The Day Newspaper, 1997—. Mem.: Beta Gamma Sigma, Tau Beta Pi. Avocations: fishing, golf. Home: 347 Lantern Hill Rd Mystic CT 06355-3623

NOLFI, EDWARD ANTHONY, lawyer; b. Warren, Ohio, Sept. 30, 1958; s. Eugene Vincent Sr. and Margaret Joyce (Futey) N.; m. Sheri Ann Loue, June 5, 1982. AB, Brown U., 1980; JD, U. Akron, 1983. Bar: Ohio 1983, N.Y. 1986, U.S. Dist. Ct. (no. dist.) Ohio 1987, U.S. Tax Ct. 1987, U.S. Ct. Appeals (6th cir. 1989), U.S. Supreme Ct. 1989. Instr. Sch. One, Providence, 1980; tech. writer Drs.' Hosp., Massillon, Ohio, 1982; pvt. practice Warren, 1983—84, Akron, Ohio, 1987—2003, Portage County, Ohio, 2003—; assoc. editor Lawyers Coop. Pub. Co., Rochester, NY, 1985—87. Prof. Acad. Ct. Reporting, Akron, 1988-91; prof. Kent State U., 1993, Mt. Aloysius Coll., Cresson, Pa., 1996; product developer and lead case law editor LexisNexis, Miamisburg, Ohio, 1999-06; prof. Remington Coll., Cleve., 2006-. Author: The Master Juggler, 1980, Basic Legal Research, 1993, Basic Wills, Trusts, and Estates, 1995; articles editor Am. Law Reports, Fed., 1986-87. Roman Catholic. Avocation: juggling. Home and Office: 4965 State Rte 14 Ravenna OH 44266-9622 Business E-Mail: enolfi@neo.rr.com.

NOLKER, DAVID BRETT, music educator; s. James Leroy and Glenda Jeanne Nolker; m. Jill Brewer Puyear, July 13, 1985; children: Daniel Aaron, Allison Jeanne. B Music Edn., Ctrl. Meth. Coll., 1985; M Music Edn., Wichita State U., 1989; PhD, U. Mo., Columbia, 2001. Dir. music Bent County Schools, Las Animas, Colo., 1985—87, Westminster Coll., Fulton, Mo., 1994—96; dir. vocal music Gasconade County Schools, Hermann, Mo., 1988—93; dir. music edn. Augustana Coll., Rock Island, Ill., 1996—2002; asst. prof. music edn. U. NC, Greensboro, 2002—. Rschr. Music Rsch. Inst., Greensboro, 2004—; dir. music Hermann United Meth. Ch., 1989—93, Trinity Episcopal Cathedral, Davenport, Iowa, 1999—2001. Contbr. articles to profl. publs. Named Hon. U. Marshal, U. NC, Greensboro, 2004; New Faculty Rsch. grantee, 2003. Mem.: NC Music Educators Assn. (chmn. tchr. edn. 2003—06), Nat. Assn. Music Edn. (chmn. spl. rsch. interest group social scis. 2002—04), Kappa Delta Pi, Omicron Delta Kappa, Pi Kappa Lambda, Phi Mu Alpha Sinfonia (province gov. 1999—2001), Sigma Alpha Iota (hon.). Avocation: equestrian trail riding. Home Phone: 336-342-3503; Office Phone: 336-334-3642.

NOLL, AMY, secondary educator; b. Madison, Wis., Sept. 12, 1956; d. David John and Eva Joyce (Tappen) N. BA, Milton Coll., Wis., 1978; MA, L.I. U., 1990. Tchr. orch. Sun Prairie (Wis.) Pub. Schs., 1979-85; freelance violinist NYC, 1985—; tchr. orch. Hicksville (N.Y.) Pub. Schs., 1987—. Violinist Akron (Ohio) Symphony Orch., 1979-80, Canton (Ohio) Symphony Orch., 1979-80, Madison (Wis.) Symphony Orch., 1980-85; conducting debut Lincoln Ctr., 1999; violinist Nepethe Ensemble, 1994—. Recipient Tchr. Excellence award, Hicksville Pub. Schs, 1989, PTSA Founders Day award, 1994—95, Paul Vetrano Tchr. of the Yr. award, 2000. Mem. Nat. Sch. Orch. Assn., Am. String Tchrs. Assn., Music Educators Nat. Conf., Nassau Music Educators Assn. Avocations: travel, reading, theater, opera. Office: Hicksville Pub Schs Division Ave Hicksville NY 11801 Home: 5 Dorchester St Huntington Station NY 11746-8407

NOLL, JEANNE C., retired music educator; b. Reading, Pa., Aug. 12, 1935; d. Carl Foreman and Barbara Rebecca (Mengel) Winter; m. Clair W. Noll; children: Eric W., Douglas C. BS Music Edn., Lebanon Valley Coll., Annville, Pa., 1957; music student, West Chester U., Milligan U., Lehigh U., MIT. Cert. tchr. Pa., 1961. Tchr. elem. music North Coventry Elem. Sch., Chester County, Pa., Yokohama Army Sch., Japan, 1957—58; tchr. vocal jr. H.S. Reading Sch. Dist., Pa., 1959—61; organist, choir dir. St. Paul's United Ch. of Christ, Fleetwood, Pa., 1967—2001, organist/choir dir. emerita, 2002—; tchr. vocal music elem., jr. and sr. H.S. Kutztown Area Sch. Dist., Pa., 1981—94. Dir. show choir Kutztown Area Sch. Dist., 1981—94; accompanist Kutztown Cmty. Choir, 1999—2001, organist, mem., 2001—. Del. 17th congl. dist. Rep. Nat. Conv., NY, 2004, del. 6th congl. dist. Phila., 2000; com. mem. Berks County Rep. Com., Fleetwood, 1982—, vice chmn.; committeewoman Pa. Rep. state com., Harrisburg, 1998—; active Berks Area Muhlenberg Coun. Rep. Women, 1996, 2d v.p., 2005; vice chair Berk County Rep. Com., 2005—, vice chair, acting chair, 2007—. Mem.: East Penn Valley Kiwanis Club (Dir., Key Club Advisor

1994—, Kiwanian of the Year 2000). Mem. United Ch. Of Christ. Avocations: travel, music, reading, politics.

NOLL, MARK A., history professor; BA in English, Wheaton Coll.; MA, Trinity Evangelical Div. Sch., Ill.; PhD in History of Christianity, Vanderbilt Univ., 1975. Faculty Wheaton Coll., Ill., 1979—, McManis prof. Christian Thought Dept. History, 2006, co-founder and dir. Inst. Study Am. Evangs., 2006; Francis A. McAnaney prof. history U. Notre Dame, 2006—. Vis. lectr. Harvard Div. Sch., Chgo. Div. Sch., Westminster Theol. Sem., Regent Coll., Vancouver, BC. Contbr. articles to religious journals. Recipient Nat. Humanities Medal, NEH, 2006. Fellow: Am. Acad. Arts & Sci. Office: Dept History U Notre Dame 219 OShaughnessy Hall Notre Dame IN 46556 Office Phone: 574-631-7574. E-mail: Mark.Noll.8@nd.edu. *

NOLL, RICHARD A., apparel executive; BBA, Pa. State Univ.; MBA with distinction, Carnegie Mellon Univ. CEO U.S. sock bus. Sara Lee Corp., Chgo., 1992—2002, COO bakery group, 2002—03, CEO bakery group, 2003—05, sr. v.p., pres. & COO branded apparel, 2005—06, CEO branded apparel, 2006; CEO Hanesbrands Inc., Winston Salem, NC, 2006—. Office: Hanesbrands Inc 1000 E Hanes Mill Rd Winston Salem NC 27105

NOLL, RICHARD DEAN, JR., psychologist, educator, historian; b. Detroit, Oct. 27, 1959; s. Richard Dean and Betty Ann (Adamczak) Noll. BA, U. Ariz., 1979; MA, New Sch. for Social Rsch., 1982; PhD, New Sch. for Rsch., 1992. Lic. clin. psychologist, Pa. Staff clin. psychologist Ancora Psychiat. Hosp., Hammonton, NJ, 1985-88; clin. psychologist in pvt. practice Phila., 1988-92; instr. dept. psychology West Chester U., Pa., 1992-94; postdoctoral fellow Harvard U., Cambridge, Mass., 1994-96, Lectr. in History of Sci., 1997-98; resident fellow Dibner Inst. History of Sci. and Tech. MIT, 1995-96; assoc. prof. psychology De Sales U., 2000—. Lectr. in field. Author: The Encyclopedia of Schizophrenia and the Psychotic Disorders, 1992, 3d rev. edit., 2006, Vampires, Werewolves and Demons: Twentieth Century Case Reports in the Psychiatric Literature, 1992, The Jung Cult, 1994 (Best Book in Psychology Assn. Am. Publishers 1994), The Aryan Christ, 1997; contbr. articles to profl. jours. Rsch. grant Wenner-Gren Found. for Anthropol. Rsch., 1993, vis. scholar MIT, 1995-96. Office Phone: 610-282-1100 ext. 1268. Business E-Mail: richard.noll@desales.edu.

NOLL, ROGER GORDON, economist, educator; b. Monterey Park, Calif., Mar. 13, 1940; s. Cecil Ray and Hjordis Alberta (Westover) Noll; m. Robyn Schreiber, Aug. 25, 1962 (dec. Jan. 2000); 1 child, Kimberlee Elizabeth; m. Ann Seminara, Dec. 2, 2001. BS, Calif. Inst. Tech., 1962; AM, Harvard U., 1965, PhD in Econs, 1967. Mem. social sci. faculty Calif. Inst. Tech., 1965-84, prof., 1973-82, inst. prof., 1982-84, chmn. div. humanities and social scis., 1978-82; prof. econs. Stanford U., 1984—2006, Morris M. Doyle centennial prof. of pub. policy, 1990—2002, dir. pub. policy program, 1986—2002, dir. Am. Studies Program, 2001—02, dir. Ctr. for Internat. Devel., 2002—06, prof. emeritus, 2006—; Jean Monnet prof. European U. Inst., 1991; vis. fellow Brookings Instn., 1995-96, non-resident sr. fellow, 1996—2000, vis. scholar, 2003. Sr. staff economist Coun. Econ. Advisors, Washington, 1967—69; sr. fellow Brookings Instn., Washington, 1970—73; mem. tech. adv. bd. Com. Econ. Devel., 1978—82; mem. adv. coun. NSF, 1978—89, NASA, 1978—81, SERI, 1982—90; mem. Pres.'s Commn. Nat. Agenda for Eighties, 1980; chmn. L.A. Sch. Monitoring Com., 1978—79; mem. Commn. Behavioral Social Scis. and Edn. NAS, 1984—90, mem. bd. sci., tech. and econ. policy, 2000—06; mem. energy rsch. adv. bd. Dept. Energy, 1986—89; mem. Sec. Energy Adv. Bd., 1990—94, Calif. Coun. Sci. and Tech., 1995—2000; mem. bd. on sci., tech. and econ. policy NRC, 2001—. Author: (book) Reforming Regulation, 1971, The Economics and Politics of Deregulation, 1991, The Economics and Politics of the Slowdown in Regulatory Reform, 1999; co-author: Economic Aspects of Television Regulation, 1973, The Political Economy of Deregulation, 1983, The Technology Pork Barrel, 1991; editor: Government and the Sports Business, 1974, Regulatory Policy and the Social Sciences, 1985, Challenges to Research Universities, 1998; co-editor: Constitutional Reform in California, 1995, Sports, Jobs and Taxes, 1997, A Communications Cornucopia, 1998; supervisory editor: Info. Econs. and Policy Jour., 1984—92. Recipient 1st ann. book award, Nat. Assn. Ednl. Broadcasters, 1974; fellow Guggenheim, 1983—84; grantee NSF, 1973—82. Mem.: Am. Econ. Assn. Democrat. Home: 4153 Hubbartt Dr Palo Alto CA 94306-3834 Office: Stanford U Dept Econs Stanford CA 94305 Office Phone: 650-723-2297. Business E-Mail: rnoll@stanford.edu.

NOLLEN, MEG (MARGARET ROACH NOLLEN), food products executive; b. St. Louis, May 3, 1963; d. Jerry Burns and Mary Judith (Moreau) Roach; m. Frederick Walter Nollen II, Jan. 16, 1988; children: Jacob Burns, Patrick James. BBA in Fin., U. Tex., 1984; MBA, S.W. Tex. State U., 1990. Mktg. officer First City-Clear Lake, Houston, 1984-85; corp. svcs. officer, mgr. point of sales svcs. First City-Austin, Austin, Tex., 1985-87; investment officer NCNB Tex. Nat. Bank, Austin, Tex., 1987-89; fin. analyst U. Tex. System, Austin, Tex., 1989-91; dir. adminstrn. for external affairs Rice U., Houston, 1991-92; sr. fin. analyst for corp. fin., risk mgmt. and pensions Transco Energy Co., Houston, 1992-95; dir. fin. and adminstrn. Houston Symphony Soc., Houston, 1995-96; dir. investor rels. Enron Corp., Houston, 1996-98; sr. v.p. investor rels. Dynegy Inc., Houston, 1998—2002; v.p. investor rels. Georgia-Pacific Corp., Atlanta, 2003—05, CapitalSource Fin. LLC, Chevy Chase, Md., 2006—07, H. J. Heinz Co., Pitts., 2007—. Patentee in field of comml. monetary payment. Mem. NAFE, U. Tex. Exes, S.W. Tex. State U. Alumni Assn. Office: H J Heinz Co 600 Grant St Pittsburgh PA 15219

NOLLY, ROBERT J., pharmacist, educator, health facility administrator; married; 3 children. BS in Pharmacy, Albany Coll. Pharmacy, NY, 1970; MS in Hosp. Pharmacy, Ohio State U., Columbus, 1979. Pharmacist Park Row Drugs, Canajoharie, NY, 1970—71, asst. mgr., 1971—72; staff pharmacist Mary Imogene Bassett Hosp., Cooperstown, NY, 1972—74, 1975—77; med. svc. rep. Dista Products Co., Eli Lilly and Co., Indpls., 1974-75; resident hosp. pharmacy Grant Hosp., Columbus, Ohio, 1977-79; asst. dir. pharmacy svcs. City of Memphis Hosp., 1979-81, U. Tenn. Bowld Hosp., Memphis, 1982, dir. pharmacy svcs. and materials mgmt., 1982-85, asst. adminstr. pharmacy svcs. and materials mgmt., 1985—90, adminstr., 1991—92, adminstr. ops., 1992—98, exec. dir., 1999—2002. Asst. prof. Coll. Pharmacy U. Tenn., Memphis, 1979-92, assoc. prof. 1992-2005; prof. 2005; bd. dir. Tenn. Hosp. Assn. Solution Group, 1997-2000; trustee, Diversified Svcs., Inc., Tenn. Hosp. Assn., 1990-94, mem. pharmacy adv. com., 1990; bd. dirs. Ava Marie Nursing Home, chmn. nom. com., 1988, 89, mem. long-range planning com., 1989, 90, mem. constn. and by-laws com., 1990, mem. govtl. rels. com., 1991-93; presenter in field. Editor U. Tenn. Bowld Hosp. Pharmacy Newsletter, 1987-91; mem. editl. bd. Drug and Therapeutics Newsletter, U. Tenn. Coll. Pharmacy, 1989, 90. Mem. adv. bd. Trinity Home Care and Hospice, Memphis Managed Care Formulary, Memphis and Shelby County Pub. Libr.; mem. cmty. adv. bd. Hope Health Care. Recipient Med. Staff Disting. Svc. award, U. Tenn. Bolwd Hosp. Mem. Parenteral Drug Assn., Am. Assn. Pharmaceutical Scientists, Tenn. Soc. Health Sys. Pharmacists (mem. com. 1980, constn. and by-laws com. 1985, 88, 89, 90, chmn. nominating com. 1989, orgn. and goals com. 1991, strategic planning com. 1992, 98, 2005, pharmacy tech. task force 1988, 89, 90, chmn. tech. curriculum com. 1991, tech. edn. accreditation com. 1994, 95, Technician Edn. Com. 1991, 92, 93), Memphis Area Soc. Hosp. Pharmacists (pres.-elect 1984, pres. 1985, past pres. 1986, chmn. nominating com. 1991), Memphis Area Pharmacists Society, Tenn. Hosp. Assn. (liaison Tenn. Med. Assn. com. 1993), Kappa Psi, Rho Chi. Office Phone: 901-448-1144. Business E-Mail: rnolly@utmem.edu.

NOLT, STEVEN M., historian; b. Pa., 1968; m. Rachel S. Miller, 1992; children: Lydia, Esther. BA, Goshen Coll., Ind., 1990; MA in Theol. Studies, Associated Mennonite Bibl. Sem., Elkhart, Ind., 1994; MA, U. Notre Dame, Ind., 1996, PhD, 1998. Asst. prof. history Goshen Coll., 1999—2003, assoc. prof. history, 2003—07, prof. history, 2007—. Vis. asst. prof. history U. Notre Dame, 1998—99. Author: (book) Foreigners in Their Own Land: Pennsylvania Germans in the Early Republic, 2002, A History of the Amish, rev. edit., 2003; co-author: Through Fire and Water: An Overview of Mennonite History, 1996, Amish Enterprise: From Plows to Profits, 2d edit., 2004 (Choice Outstanding Academic Title (for first edit.), 1995), An Amish Patchwork: Indiana's Old Orders in the Modern World, 2005, Plain Diversity: Amish Cultures and Identities, 2007, Mennonites, Amish and the American Civil War, 2007, Amish Grace: How Forgiveness Transcended Tragedy, 2007. Office: Goshen Coll 1700 S Main St Goshen IN 46526 Home Phone: 574-534-6438; Office Phone: 574-535-7460.

NOLTE, NICK, actor; b. Omaha, Feb. 8, 1941; m. Sheila Page, 1966 (div. 1971), m. Sharon Haddad, May 10, 1978 (div. 1983); m. Rebecca Linger, Feb. 19, 1984 (div. 1995); 1 child, Brawley King. Student, Ariz. St. Univ., Eastern Ariz. Coll., Pasadena City Coll., Phoenix City Coll.; studies with, John Paul, Allen Dutton. Actor: (play) The Last Pad, 1973, (TV movies) Winter Kill, 1974, The California Kid, 1974, Death Sentence, 1974, (TV series) Adams of Eagle Lake, 1975, (TV movies) The Treasure Chest Murder, 1975, The Runaway Barge, 1975, (mini-series) Rich Man, Poor Man, 1976; (films) Return to Macon County, 1975, The Deep, 1977, Who'll Stop the Rain, 1978, North Dallas Forty, 1979, Heart Beat, 1980, Cannery Row, 1982, 48 Hours, 1982, Under Fire, 1983, The Ultimate Solution of Grace Quigley, 1984, Teachers, 1984, Down and Out in Beverly Hills, 1986, Weeds, 1987, Extreme Prejudice, 1987, Farewell to the King, 1988, Three Fugitives, 1988, New York Stories, 1989, Everybody Wins, 1989, Q & A, 1990, Another 48 Hours, 1990, Prince of Tides, 1991, Cape Fear, 1991, Lorenzo's Oil, 1992, The Player, 1992, Blue Chips, 1994, I'll Do Anything, 1994, I Love Trouble, 1994, Jefferson in Paris, 1995, Mulholland Falls, 1996, Mother Night, 1996, Nightwatch, 1997, Afterglow, 1997, U-Turn, 1997, Affliction (also exec. prod), 1998, Thin Red Line, 1998, The Best of Enemies, 1999, Simpatico, 1999, Breakfast of Champions, 1999, The Golden Bowl, 2000, Trixie, 2000, Investigating Sex (also prod.), 2001, The Good Thief, 2002, Northfork, 2003, The Hulk, 2003, (voice) Over the Hedge, 2006, Peaceful Warrior, 2006.

NONIS, DAVID, professional sports team executive; b. Burnaby, BC, Can., May 25, 1966; m. Susan Nonis; 1 child, Nicholas. BA, U. Maine, 1988, MBA, 1990. Asst. corp. contracts, computer scouting and team svcs. Vancouver Canucks, 1990—94, sr. v.p., dir. hockey ops., 1998—2004, gen. mgr., 2004—; mgr. hockey ops. NHL, 1994—98. Office: Vancouver Canucks 800 Griffiths Way Vancouver BC Canada V6B 6G1

NONNA, JOHN MICHAEL, lawyer; b. NYC, July 8, 1948; s. Angelo and Josephine (Visconti) N.; m. Jean Wanda (Cleary), June 9, 1973; children: Elizabeth, Caroline, Marianne, Timothy. BA, Princeton U., 1970; JD, NYU, 1975. Bar: NY 1976, US Dist. Ct. (so. dist.) NY, 1978, US Ct. Appeals (2d cir.) 1978, US Ct. Appeals (9th cir.) 1980, US Ct. Appeals (5th cir.) 1997, US Dist. Ct. Conn. 1988, US Supreme Ct. 1998. Law asst. to Hon. D.L. Gabrielli N.Y. Ct. Appeals, Albany, 1975-77; assoc. Reid and Priest, NYC, 1977-84; ptnr. Werner and Kennedy, NYC, 1984-99, LeBoeuf, Lamb, Greene, and MacRae, NYC, 1999—. Contbr. articles to profl. jours. Dep. mayor, trustee Pleasantville, NY, 1990-95; mayor, 1995-2003; acting justice, 1983-89; bd. trustees Lawyers Com. for Civil Rights Under the Law. With USNR, 1970-75. Mem. U.S. Olympic Team, 1972, 1980; Paul Harris fellow Rotary Internat. Fellow Am. Bar Found. (life), Am. Coll. Trial Lawyers; mem. ABA (torts and ins. practice sect. com. chair 1986-87, 92-93), NY State Bar Assn. (chair comml. and fed. litig. sect. 1998-99, co-editor in chief 2000, NY ins. law practice), Assn. Bar City NY, NY Fencers Club (pres. 1990-93). Avocations: fencing, running, piano. Office: LeBoeuf Lamb Greene & MacRae 125 W 55th St New York NY 10019-5369 Home Phone: 914-769-8961; Office Phone: 212-424-8311. Business E-Mail: jnonna@llgm.com.

NONOGAKI, HIROFUMI, research scientist; b. Nagoya, Aichi, Japan, July 22, 1976; s. Masao and Miyako Nonogaki; m. Reiko Kubo; 1 child, Yuna Natalie. BS in Marine Biology, Zoology (hon.), U. Wales Bangor, Gwynedd, UK, 2000; MS in Fish Physiology, Towson U., Md., 2003. Lab. asst., Ctr. Marine Biotechnology U. Md. Biotechnology Inst., Balt., 2004, rsch. asst., Ctr. Marine Biotechnology, 2004—. Asst. aquarist Balt. Aquarium, 2004—. Contbr. articles to profl. jours. Achievements include development of fish meal and fish oil free diets for carnivorous fish species; research in toxin extraction and purification from harmful marine algae; comparison analysis on fatty acid profiles between wild and farm raised organisms for production quality and enhancement; dietary history analysis in fish by use of stable isotopes in otoliths. Office: U Md 701 East Pratt St Ste 236 Baltimore MD 21202 Home Phone: 410-296-9636; Office Phone: 410-234-8830. Office Fax: 410-234-8896. Business E-Mail: nonogaki@umbi.umd.edu.

NOONAN, DANIEL W., archivist; b. West Allis, Wis., Jan. 1, 1962; s. James Patrick and Mary Margaret Noonan; m. Carolee Watkins, June 29, 1996; children: Benedict, Cordelia. BS in Constrn. Adminstrn., U. Wis., Madison, 1985; MLS, Rutgers U., New Brunswick, NJ, 2001. Appraiser Am. Appraisal Assocs., Milw., 1985—90, engagement mgr. Princeton, NJ, 1990—93; sr. tech. cons. Valuation Resource Mgmt., Ft. Washington, Pa., 1993—98; digital documents libr. NJ Inst. Tech., Newark, 2001; supr. electronic records mgmt. State NJ, Trenton, 2001—06; electronic records mgr., archivist Ohio State U., Columbus, 2006—. Mem. adv. and steering coms. NJ Digital Hwy., Trenton, 2002—06. Preservation com. Trenton Hist. Soc., 2001—03; pres. Glen Afron Cmty. Assocs., Trenton, 2003—06; ticket mgr. Trenton Film Festival, 2004—06. Recipient Eagle Scout, Boy Scouts Am., 1979; Leadership Trenton fellow, Thomas Edison State Coll., 2003. Mem.: Beta Phi Mu (pres. Omicron chpt. 2006). Avocations: reading, bicycling, stained glass, needlecrafts, model building. E-mail: dw.noonan@yahoo.com.

NOONAN, JACK, analytics software and solutions company executive; With field engring. and sys. devel. IBM Corp., 1967—77; from with software devel., mktg., customer svc. to v.p. product support Amdahl Corp., Santa Clara, Calif., 1977—85; v.p. Product Group Candle Corp., 1985—90; pres., CEO Microrim Corp., 1990—91; pres. SPSS Inc., Chgo., 1992—, CEO, 1992—, bd. dir. Bd. dir. Morningstar, Inc., Repository Technologies, Inc., Fortel Inc.; adv. com. Geneva Tech. Ptnrs., Inc. Office: SPSS Inc 233 S Wacker Dr 11th Fl Chicago IL 60606 *

NOONAN, JACQUELINE ANNE, pediatrician, educator; b. Burlington, Vt., Oct. 28, 1928; BA, Albertus Magnus Coll., New Haven, Conn., 1950; MD, U. Vt., Burlington, 1954, DSc (hon.), 1980. Diplomate Am. Bd. Pediatrics, Am. Bd. Pediatric Cardiology. Intern N.C. Meml. Hosp., Chapel Hill, 1954-55; resident in pediatrics Children's Hosp., Cin., 1955-57; rsch. fellow Children's Med. Ctr., Boston, 1957-59; asst. prof. pediatrics State U. Iowa Sch. Medicine, 1959-61; asst. prof. pediatrics cardiology U. Ky. Coll. Medicine, Lexington, 1961-64, assoc. prof., 1964-69, prof., 1969-99, chmn. dept. pediatrics, 1974-92, emeritus prof., 1999—. Mem. embryology and human devel. study sect. NIH, 1973-78; mem. US-USSR Symposium on Congenital Heart Disease, 1975; mem. sub. bd. pediatric cardiology Am. Bd. Pediatrics, 1977-82; examiner, mem. test. com. Nat. Bd. Med. Examiners, 1984-90, exec. com., 1991-95; participant various confs. in field; vis. prof. Vanderbilt U., Nashville, 1987; spkr. in field. Contbr. articles, revs. to med. publs.; mem. editl. bd. Am. Jour. Diseases Children, 1970-80, Am. Jour. Med. Edn., 1975-78, Pediatric Cardiology, 1978-90, Am. Heart Jour., 1994-96, Clin. Pediatrics, 1990-99. Fellow: Royal Coll. Irish Physicians (hon.); mem.: AMA, So. Soc. Pediat. Rsch. (pres. 1972), Soc. Pediat. Rsch., NIH Alumni Assn., Ky. State Med. Assn., Irish-Am. Pediat. Soc. (pres. 1999—2001), Fayette County Pediat. Soc., Am. Pediat. Soc., Assn. Med. Sch. Pediatrics (dept. chmn. exec. com. 1978—81), Am. Coll. Cardiology (gov. Ky. chpt. 1989—92), Am. Acad. Pediatrics (chmn. cardiol. sect. 1972—74). Business E-Mail: jnoonan@uky.edu.

NOONAN, JAMES C., lawyer, mediator, arbitrator; b. Chgo., July 16, 1928; s. T. Clifford and Ethel (Jennett) N.; m. Carol Colbert, Nov. 24, 1954 (div. June 1975); children: James, Christopher, Mary, Anne, Catherine; m. Ardis Niemann, May 24, 1986. AB, U. Notre Dame, 1953, MA in Criminology, 1954; JD, William Mitchell Coll. Law, St. Paul, 1962. Bar: Minn. 1962, U.S. Dist. Ct. Minn. 1963, U.S. Ct. Appeals (8th cir.) 1971, U.S. Supreme Ct. 1969. Probation officer Ramsey County Juvenile Ct., St. Paul, 1954-57; supt. Woodview Detention Home, St. Paul, 1957-63; assoc. Firestone, Fink, Krawetz, Miley, O'Neill, St. Paul, 1963-67; ptnr. Firestone Fink, Krawetz, Miley, Maas and Noonan, St. Paul, 1967-70, Magistad & Noonan, St. Paul, 1971-75; owner James C. Noonan and Assocs., St. Paul, 1975—. Mem. adv. bd. Home of Good Shepherd, St. Paul, 1958-74; mem. citizen adv. bd. Detention and Corrections Authority, St. Paul, 1966-80. Mem. ABA, Minn. State Bar Assn., Ramsey County Bar Assn., St. Paul Amateur Radio Club, Am. Radio Relay League. Roman Catholic. Avocation: amateur radio (w9osn). Home (Winter): 2015 E Edison St Tucson AZ 85719-3801 Home Phone: 651-222-3310, 520-318-6222. Personal E-mail: w9osn@arrl.net.

NOONAN, JOHN DANIEL, plastic surgeon; b. Bklyn., Aug. 2, 1947; s. William Jerome and Eleanor F. (Kells) N.; m. Barbara Shea, June 11, 1972; children— Kristen, John, Brendan, William, Kathleen. BA., Marist Coll., 1969; M.D., SUNY-Bklyn., 1973. Cert. Am. Bd. Plastic Surgery, Am. Soc. Aesthetic Plastic Surgeons, Nat. Bd. Med. Examiners. Diplomate Am. Bd. Surgery, Am. Bd. Plastic Surgery. Resident Albany Med. Ctr. (NY), 1973-77, Ea. Va. Med. Ctr., Norfolk, 1977-80; practice medicine specializing in plastic surgery, Albany, 1981—; co-dir. Albany Med. Burn Unit, 1980-81; cons. Albany VA Hosp., Sunnyview Rehab. Ctr., Schenectady, Regional Emergency Med. Orgn., Albany; assoc. prof. clin. surgery Albany Med. Coll., 1984—, dir., Cranio-Facial Ctr., St. Peter's Hosp. Contbr. articles to med. jours. Fellow ACS; mem. Albany County Med. Soc., Am. Soc. Plastic Surgeons, Soc. Plastic Surgeons Upstate NY, Med. Soc. State of NY, Operation Smile. Club: Rotary. Office: Plastic Surgery Group Ste 200 1365 Washington Ave Albany NY 12206-1098 Office Phone: 518-438-0505. *

NOONAN, JOHN T., JR., federal judge, educator; b. Boston, Oct. 24, 1926; s. John T. and Marie (Shea) Noonan; m. Mary Lee Bennett, Dec. 27, 1967; children: John Kenneth, Rebecca Lee, Susanna Bain. BA, Harvard U., 1946, LLB, 1954; student, Cambridge U., 1946—47; MA, Cath. U. Am., 1949, PhD, 1951, LHD, 1980, Holy Cross Coll., 1980, Loyola U., Chgo., 1999; LLD, U. Santa Clara, 1974, U. Notre Dame, 1976, Loyola U. South, 1978, St. Louis U., 1981, Duquesne U., 1995, Valparaiso U., 1996, U. San Diego, 1999, Gonzaga U., 1986, U. San Francisco, 1986. Bar: Mass. 1954, US Supreme Ct. 1971. Mem. spl. staff Nat. Security Council, 1954-55; pvt. practice Herrick & Smith, Boston, 1955-60; prof. law U. Notre Dame, 1961-66, U. Calif., Berkeley, 1967-86, chmn. religious studies, 1970-73, chmn. medieval studies, 1978-79; judge US Ct. Appeals (9th cir.), San Francisco, 1985-96, sr. judge, 1996—. Oliver Wendell Holmes, Jr. lectr. Harvard U. Law Sch., 1972; Pope John XXIII lectr. Cath. U. Law Sch., 1973; Cardinal Bellarmine lectr. St. Louis U. Div. Sch., 1973; Ernest Messenger lectr. Cornell U., 1982; John Dewey Meml. lectr. U. Minn., 1986; Baum lectr. U. Ill., 1988; Strassberger lectr. U. Tex., 1989; chmn. bd. Games Rsch., Inc., 1961—76; overseer Harvard U., 1991—97; Maguire chair in ethics Libr. of Congress, 2002; vis. prof. U. Catania, Sicily, Italy, 2002; vis. Disting. prof. kaw Emory U., 2000; Erasmus lectr. U. Notre Dame, 2003. Author: The Scholastic Analysis of Usury, 1957, Contraception: A History of Its Treatment by the Catholic Theologians and Canonists, 1965, Power to Dissolve, 1972, Persons and Masks of the Law, 1976, The Antelope, 1977, A Private Choice, 1979, Bribes, 1984, The Responsible Judge, 1993, Professional and Personal Responsibilities of the Lawyer, 1997, Canons and Canonists in Context, 1997, The Lustre of Our Country, 1998, Narrowing the Nation's Power, 2002, A Church That Can and Cannot Change, 2005; editor: Natural Law Forum, 1961—70, Am. Jour. Jurisprudence, 1970, The Morality of Abortion, 1970. Chmn. Brookline Redevel. Authority, Mass., 1958—62; cons. Papal Commn. on Family, 1965—66, Ford Found., Indonesian Legal Program, 1968, NIH, 1973, 1974; expert Presdl. Commn. on Population and Am. Future, 1971; pres. Thomas More-Jacques Maritain Inst., 1977—; trustee Population Coun., 1969—76, Phi Kappa Found., 1970—76, U. San Francisco, 1971—75; mem. com. theol. edn. Yale U., 1972—77; cons. U.S. Cath. Conf., 1979—86; sec., treas. Inst. for Rsch. in Medieval Canon Law, 1970—88; trustee Grad. Theol. Union, 1970—73; exec. com. Cath. Commn. Intellectual and Cultural Affairs, 1972—75; bd. dirs. Ctr. for Human Values in the Health Scis., 1969—71, S.W. Intergroup Rels. Coun., 1970—72, Inst. for Study Ethical Issues, 1971—73. Recipient St. Thomas More award, U. San Francisco, 1974, Christian Culture medal, 1975, Laetare medal, U. Notre Dame, 1984, Campion medal, Cath. Book Club, 1987, Alemany medal, Western Dominican Province, 1988; fellow Guggenheim fellow, 1965—66, 1979—80, Ctr. for Advanced Studies in Behavioral Scis. fellow, 1973—74, Wilson Ctr. fellow, 1979—80, Kluge chair in Am. law and govt., Libr. Congress Ctr. for Scholars, 2002. Fellow: Am. Acad. Arts and Scis., Am. Soc. Legal Historians (hon.); mem.: Am. Law Inst., Canon Law Soc. Am. (gov. 1970—72), Am. Soc. Polit. and Legal Philosophy (v.p. 1964), Phi Beta Kappa (senator United chpts. 1970—72, pres. Alpha of Calif. chpt. 1972—73). Office: US Ct Appeals 9th Cir 95 7th St San Francisco CA 94103-1526 *

NOONAN, JOSETTE MARIE, music educator; b. Melrose Park, Ill., Mar. 6, 1955; d. Frank Eugene and Barbara Ann Noonan. ADN, Waubonsee Coll., Ill., 1984; MusB, DePaul U., 1990. Registered Profl. Nurse, Ill., 1984; cert. musikgarten educator 1999, dir. music ministries 2005. Music dir. St. Mary's Ch., West Chgo., Ill.; RN surg. resource team Children's Meml. Med. Ctr., Chgo., 1985—90; singer Grant Pk. Symphony Chorus, 1985—90; artist in residence Coll. of DuPage, Glen Ellyn, Ill., 1987—88; asst. dir. Light Opera Works, Evanston, Ill., 1990—91; RN rehab. Oak Pk. Hosp., Ill., 1992—97; soprano soloist and sect. leader First United Meth. Ch. at Chgo. Temple, Chgo., 1993—2004, children's choir dir., 1999—2003; voice tchr. No. Ill. U. Cmty. Sch. of Music, DeKalb, Ill., 1999—2002; music and movement tchr. No. Ill. U. Suzuki Sch., DeKalb, 1999—2002; tchr. voice and strings Countryside Music Sch., Elburn, Ill., 1999—; music tchr. Creative Beginning Presch., 2005—06. Violist Celebration String Quartet, Arlington Heights, Ill., 2000—04; dir. Countryside Players, Elburn, Ill., 2002—, Kindechor and Angeli Musicali Children's Choirs St. Mary's, West Chgo., Ill., 2005—06; founder and adminstr. Patrick Edgar Triplett Meml. Scholarship Program; rehabilitative music specialist Healing Harps, DeKalb, Ill., 2000—03; guest artist German Song Text Workshop, Vienna, 2004—, Assisi Music Festival, Italy, 2005—06, Mladi Fest, Medjugorje, Bosnia-Herzegovina, 2005, Accademia Voci d'Estate, Verona, Italy, 2006, Art Song Festival, 2006. Composer: (songs) Songs for Children's Worship; arranger (musical) From Mozart to Moulin

Rouge; singer: (improvisatory music for dance troupe) The Death of the King, author of poems. Past pres. Ill. Collegiate Music Educators, Mokena, Ill., 2000—01; canvas voters to encourage passage of referendum for schs. Save our Schs., West Chgo., Ill., 1970; fed and clothed homeless people First United Meth. Ch. at Chgo., Chgo., 2000—02; care and concern ministry First United Meth. Ch. at Chgo. Temple, Chgo., 2002—04; mem. Pax Christi, 2005—06, Christian Peacemaker Team, 2005—06, Kairos Retreat Leadership Team, 2006. Recipient Invitation to sing for Martin Katz, DePaul U., 1987, Invited to sing for John Wustman, 1988, Invitation to sing Honors Recitals, 1985—88, Invited to sing and speak at a meml. concert honoring composer, Moses Hogan, Abyssinian Bapt. Ch. NY, 2002, First prize, Italian Cultural Soc. Voice Competition, 1988. Mem.: Nat. Assn. Pastoral Musicians, Nat. Guild Hypnotists (assoc.), Am. Choral Dirs. Assn. (assoc.; treas. local chpt. 1999—2001), Music Educator's Nat. Conf. (assoc.; pres. of ill. collegiate assn. 2000—01), Healing Harps (assoc.). Independent. Achievements include Specialist in German Lied interpretation; development of music program for autistic children at Northern Illinois University; Set up music and movement program for local preschool; Planned, executed and evaluated a weekend workshop for music education students in the state of Illinois entitled, What I didn't learn in music school. Avocations: backpacking, german language and culture, scuba diving, fiddling, hypnosis. Home: 324 Church St West Chicago IL 60185 Office: St Mary's Church 140 North Oakwood Avenue West Chicago IL 60185 Home Phone: 630-231-3075; Office Phone: 630-231-0013. Office Fax: 630-293-2671. E-mail: scotchdiva@aol.com.

NOONAN, PATRICK FRANCIS, conservation executive; b. St. Petersburg, Fla., Dec. 2, 1942; s. Francis Patrick and Henrietta (Donovan) Noonan; m. Nancy Elizabeth Peck, Aug. 15, 1964; children: Karen Elizabeth(dec.), Dawn Wiley. BA, Gettysburg Coll., 1965; M in City and Regional Planning, Catholic U. Am., 1967; MBA, Am. U., 1971. V.p., pres. The Nature Conservancy, 1968—80; founder, dir., chmn. Am. Farmland Trust, 1980—97; chmn., pres. The Conservation Fund, 1985—2003, chmn. emeritus, 2003—. Trustee Nat. Geog. Soc., 1990—; vice chmn. Nat. Geog. Edn. Found., 1995—; trustee Gettysburg Coll., 1978—91, Duke U. Sch. Environment, 1979—, Ind. Sector, 1984—91, Am. Conservation Assn., 1986—, Natural Resources Coun. Am., 1996—2002; dir. Ashland, 1991—2006, Internat. Paper, 1993—2004, Saul Ctrs., 1993—; mem. Pres.' Commn. on Am. Outdoors, 1985—87, Pres.' Commn. on Environ. Quality, 1991—93, Pres.' Commn. on White House Fellows, 2001—. MacArthur Found. fellow, 1985—90. Home: 3553 Hamlet Pl Chevy Chase MD 20815

NOONAN, PATRICK SUTTON, management educator; b. Springfield, Ill., July 11, 1955; s. Patrick Arthur and Julia Ann (Sutton) N.; m. M. Jo Howarth, Apr. 27, 1985; children: Paul Howarth, William Prindiville. BS in Engring. Sci., Yale U., 1977, MBA, 1984; MS in Engring. Sci., Harvard U., 1989, PhD in Decision Scis., 1992. Dir. and gen. mgr. East River Consort, Boston, 1977—80; pres. Greenpeace New Eng., Boston, 1980-82; assoc. McKinsey & Co., Inc., NYC, 1984-88; prin. Planning Techs. Group, Inc., Lexington, Mass., 1990—98; assoc. prof. Emory U., 1993—; Fulbright sr. specialist, 2005. Prodr. record albums, including Laurasia, 1978, Undiscovered Country, 1988, Beat Noir, 1996, Scott's Red Star, 2000; prodr. film Journey to Georges Bank, 1982. Office Phone: 404-727-0549.

NOONAN, PEGGY, writer; b. Bklyn., Sept. 7, 1950; d. Jim and Mary Jane (Byrne) N.; m. Richard Kahn, Nov. 27, 1985 (div. 1990); 1 child, Will. BA in English Literature & Journalism, Fairleigh Dickinson U., Rutherford, NJ, 1974, PhD in Humane Letters (hon.), 1990. Premium adjuster Aetna Ins. Co., Newark, 1968-70; student Antiwar Protester of Vietnam; temp. agency sec. NYC, 1974; news staffer WEEI Radio (CBS station), Boston, 1974, editl. dir., 1975-77; writer, editor CBS News, NYC, 1977-80, commentary for Walter Cronkite and Dan Rather, 1980-81, full time commentary writer for Dan Rather, 1981-84; White House speech writing tech. Ronald Reagan, Washington, 1984-86; White House speech writer George Bush, Washington, 1988-89; contbg. editor The Wall St. Jour., Time, Good Housekeeping. Bd. dir. The Manhattan Inst. Author: What I Saw at the Revolution: A Political Life in the Reagan Era, 1990, Life, Liberty, & the Pursuit of Happiness, 1995, Simply Speaking: How to Communicate Your Ideas With Style, Substance, and Clarity, 1998, The Case Against Hillary Clinton, 2000, When Character was King: A Story of Ronald Reagan, 2001, A Heart, a Cross and a Flag, 2003, John Paul the Great: Remembering a Spiritual Father, 2005; contbr. articles to Forbes, Mirabella, Newsweek, N.Y. Times, O Mag., Time, Wash. Post. Coll. Guest Editor Mademoiselle, 1990; Mother of Yr. award, 1990; Nat. Mother's Day Com., 1990. Mem. Judson Welliver Soc. Republican. Roman Catholic. Office: ICM 40 W 57th St Fl 16 New York NY 10019-4001

NOONAN, ROBERT HARRY, art and music educator; b. Mpls., Sept. 18, 1924; s. William Earl and Nellie Morene Noonan. BS in Chemistry, Northwestern State Coll., 1948; MusB in Music Edn., Centenary Coll., 1963. Cert. tchr. music, chemistry, sci., math., visually talented and musically talented La. Sr. chemist Ark. Fuel Oil Co., Shreveport, La., 1948-53; grad. asst. U. Wyo., Laramie, 1953-54; asst. chief chemist Atlas Processing Co., Shreveport, 1955-58; Frenh horn player Shreveport Symphony Orch., 1948-72; sch. sys. employee East Baton Rouge Sch. Sys., Baton Rouge, 1972-81; pub. sch. tchr. Ascension Parish Schs., Donaldsonville, La., 1981-95; tchr. visually and musically talented St. James Parish Schs., Lutcher, La., 1997—2001. Composer, arranger: music One Step from the Edge, 1999—2000, I Am Your Child, 2000—01, Finding My Way, 2001—02; composer: symphony for Yalley Youth Orch., 2002, three string quartets, a piano trio, a sonata for clarinet and piano, music for voices and strings, theater, 2003; one-man shows include Jones Creek Libr., Baton Rouge, 1993, Donaldsonville HS, La., 1994, Galvez Libr., La., 1994, Westbank Libr., Harvey, La., 1995, Bruno Gallery, New Orleans, 1997, exhibited in group shows, Baton Rouge, Jackson, Plaquemine, Morgan City, numerous others, Represented in permanent collections, La., Tex., Miss., Ala., Okla., others. Chmn. La. Sch. Employees Coun.l, 1977—81; art gallery mgr. Blue Sage Ctr. for Arts, Paonia, Colo. With Air Corps US Army, 1943—46. Grantee Goals 2000, State of La., 1995—96, Spl. Arts, 1997—99. Mem.: Jefferson Art Guild, St. Bernard Art Guild (pres. 1999—2001), New Orleans Art Assn. (v.p. 1998—2000, art gallery mgr. Blue Sage Ctr. for the Arts), Am. Chem. Soc. (sr. grade chemist 1948—58), La. Partnership for the Arts. Avocations: outdoor painting, writing article for newspapers. Home and Office: 433 Delta Ave Paonia CO 81428-8413 Personal E-mail: robmusart@paonia.com.

NOONAN, TIMOTHY PAUL, musicologist, educator; b. Milw., Apr. 30, 1960; s. James J. and Betty J. Noonan; m. Jill A. Ehn; children: Christopher, Paul. BA, U. Wis., Milw., 1982, MusM, 1984; PhD, U. Wis., Madison, 1996. Lectr. music U. Wis., Milw., 1996—. Spkr. at confs. in field. Mem.: Haydn Soc. N.Am, Am. Beethoven Soc., Soc. Eighteenth-Century Music, Mozart Soc. Am., Am. Musicological Soc. Democrat. Roman Catholic. Office: U Wis Milw Music Dept 2600 E Kenwood Blvd Milwaukee WI 53212

NOONAN, WILLIAM DONALD, lawyer, physician; b. Kansas City, Mo., Oct. 18, 1955; s. Robert Owen and Patricia Ruth Noonan. AB, Princeton U., NJ, 1977; JD, U. Mo., Kansas City, 1980; postgrad., Tulane U., 1981-83; MD magna cum laude, Oreg. Health Scis. U., 1991. Bar: Mo. 1980, U.S. Ct. Appeals (5th cir.) 1982, U.S. Patent & Trademark Office 1982, U.S. Ct. Appeals (D.C. cir.) 1984, Oreg. 1985, U.S. Ct. Appeals (9th Cir.) 1985. Assoc. Shurgue, Mion, Zinn, Washington, 1983-84, Keaty & Keaty, New Orleans, 1984-85; ptnr. Klarquist, Sparkman LLP, Portland, Oreg., 1985—; intern in internal medicine Portland Providence Med. Ctr., 1993-94; resident in ophthalmology Casey Eye Inst., Portland, 1994-95. Adj. prof. patent law Tulane U., New Orleans, 1984-85, U. Oreg., 1992-93. Casenotes editor U. Mo. Law Rev., 1979. Nat. Merit scholar. Mem. ABA, AMA (Leadership award 1994), Alpha Omega Alpha (pres. Oreg. chpt. 1990-91). Independent. Avocations: raising horses, running, travel, genealogy. Office: 1600 World Trade Ctr 121 SW Salmon St Portland OR 97204-2901 Office Phone: 503-226-7391.

NOONE, LAURA PALMER, academic administrator, lawyer; BBA, U. Dubuque; MBA, JD, U. Iowa; PhD in higher edn. adminstrn., Union Inst. Atty gen. civil practice, Iowa, Ariz.; judge City of Chandler, Ariz.; faculty mem. U. Phoenix, 1987—91, dir. acad affairs, 1991—94, provost, sr. v.p. acad. affairs, 1994—2000, pres., 2002—06, pres. emerita, 2006—. Adj. faculty Grand Canyon Univ., Chandler-Gilbert Cmty. Coll.; mem. Ariz. State Bd. for pvt. postsecondary edn.; trustee Phoenix Internat. Sch. Law. Mem.: ABA, Ariz. State Bar Assn., Maricopa County Bar Assn. Office: University of Phoenix 4615 E Elwood St Phoenix AZ 85040 *

NOONE, R. BARRETT, plastic surgeon; b. Scranton, Pa., Oct. 30, 1939; s. Robert Patrick and Margaret Ann (Barrett) N.; m. Barbara Ellen Atkins, May 29, 1965; children: Robert B. Jr., Megan J., Genevieve C., Rebecca B., Theresa Ann. BS, U. Scranton, 1961; MD, U. Pa., 1965. Diplomate Am. Bd. Surgery, Am. Bd. Plastic Surgery. Rotating intern Hosp. of U. Pa., Phila., 1965-66, resident in surgery, 1966-71, resident in plastic surgery, 1971-73; asst. prof. surgery Sch. Medicine, U. Pa., Phila., 1974-83, clin. assoc. prof. surgery, 1983-89, clin. prof. surgery, 1989—; head sect. on plastic surgery Pa. Hosp., Phila., 1974-80; chief svc. plastic surgery Bryn Mawr (Pa.) Hosp., 1977—2005, chmn. dept. surgery, 1991—2001; chief svc. plastic surgery Lankenau Hosp., Phila., 1980-91; exec. dir. Am. Bd. Plastic Surgery, 1997—. Bd. dirs. Am. Bd. Plastic Surgery, Phila., 1987-94, vice chmn. 1993-94; bd. dirs. Plastic Surgery Ednl. Found., Chgo., 1981-91, pres. 1989-90. Contbr. articles to profl. jours. Bd. dirs., trustee Rosemont Sch. of the Holy Child, Pa., 1983-87, U. Scranton, 1998—2004. Capt. USAF, 1967-69. Recipient Frank J. O'Hara Disting. Alumnus award U. Scranton, 1986, Magee-Woodruff award Bryn Mawr Hosp. Fellow ACS (bd. govs. 1994-98); mem. AMA (del. plastic surgery 1986-88), Am. Soc. Plastic and Reconstructive Surgery (bd. dirs. 1989-90, 92-95, chmn. bd. trustees 1994-95), Am. Assn. Plastic Surgeons (sec. 1995-98, v.p. 1998-99, pres.-elect 1999-2000, pres. 2000-01, disting. fellow 2006), Northeastern Soc. Plastic Surgeons (pres. 1985-86), Robert H. Ivy Soc. (pres. 1982-83), Merion Cricket Club, Phila. Country Club, Eagles Mere Country Club. Republican. Roman Catholic. Avocations: golf, tennis, photography, swimming, travel, reading. Home: 234 Cheswold Hill Rd Haverford PA 19041-1814 Office: Plastic & Reconstructive Surg Assocs 888 Glenbrook Ave Bryn Mawr PA 19010-2506 Office Phone: 610-527-4833. E-mail: RBNoone@aol.com.

NOONKESTER, JAMES RALPH, retired college president; b. Flatridge, Va., June 10, 1924; s. Reggie L. and Arcie (Parks) N.; m. Naomi Hopkins, June 10, 1947; children: Myron Craig, Lila. BA, U. Richmond, 1944, LLD, 1968; ThM, So. Bapt. Theol. Sem., 1947, PhD, 1949; LHD (hon.), Blue Mountain Coll., 1982; postgrad., Harvard U., 1980. Minister edn. 1st Bapt. Ch., Charlottesville, Va., 1950-52; prof., head div. religion and philosophy William Carey Coll., Hattiesburg, Miss., 1952-53, acad. dean, 1953-56, pres., 1956-89, pres. emeritus, 1989—. Pres. Miss. Found. Ind. Colls.; mem. Edn. commn. So. Bapt. Conv., chmn., 1983; bd. dirs. Miss. Sch. Bds. Assn. Workers Compensation Trust, 1993-95, chmn., 1994. Chmn. bd. dirs. Am. Cancer Soc., Miss. divsn., 1966; campaign chmn. United Givers Fund, 1975-76, pres. 1976-77; coun. chmn. Boy Scouts Am., dir. Planned Giving Pine Burr area Boy Scouts Am., 1990-93; trustee Hattiesburg Pub. Schs., 1990-95, pres. bd. trustees, 1992-95 Named Outstanding Grad. English U. Richmond, 1944, Hattiesburg's Outstanding Young Man of 1956, Sales and Mktg. Execs. Man of Yr., 1983; recipient Silver Beaver award Boy Scouts Am., 1981, HUB award, 1983 Mem. NEA, Miss. Edn. Assn., Hattiesburg Concert Assn. (bd. dir.), So. Assn. Bapt. Colls. and Schs. (pres.), Miss. Assn. Colls. (pres.), Hattiesburg C. of C. (pres. 1966), Kiwanis, Phi Beta Kappa, Phi Delta Kappa, Chi Beta Phi, Omicron Delta Kappa. Home: 100 Lesley Ln Hattiesburg MS 39402-2922

NOOR, RONNY, language educator, writer; MA, Tech. U., Berlin, 1986, Okla. State U., 1989, PhD, 1994. Lectr. Salisbury State U., Md., 1995—96; sr. lectr. U. Tex., Brownsville, 1996—98, asst. prof., 1999—2004, assoc. prof., 2004—. Contbr. essays, short stories, articles to profl. jours. Recipient Exceptional Merit award, 2001, Wall of Tolerance honoree, Civil Rights Meml. Ctr., Montgomery, Ala., 2005, Faculty Appreciation award, Student Support Svcs. Program/A Support Program in Reaching Excellence, 2005, 2006. Mem.: Nat. Writers Assn., South Ctrl. MLA, Popular Culture Assn. Achievements include research in literature and linguistics. Avocations: piano, tennis. Office Phone: 956-882-8239. Personal E-mail: noorronny@yahoo.com.

NOORDERGRAAF, ABRAHAM, biophysics educator; b. Utrecht, Netherlands, Aug. 7, 1929; s. Leendert and Johanna (Kool) N.; m. Geertruida Alida Van Nee, Sept. 6, 1956 (div. Jan. 2001); children: Annemiek (Mrs. James A. Young), Gerrit Jan, Jeske Inette, Alexander Abraham. B.Sc., U. Utrecht, 1953, MS, 1955, PhD, 1956; MA (hon.), U. Pa., 1971. Teaching asst. U. Utrecht, 1949-50, asst. dept. physics, 1951-53, research asst. dept. med. physics, 1953-55, research fellow dept. med. physics, 1956-58, sr. research fellow dept. med. physics, 1959-65; tchr. math. and physics Vereniging Nijverheidsonderwijs, Utrecht, 1951; research asst. U. Amsterdam, Netherlands, 1952; vis. fellow dept. therapeutic research U. Pa., Phila., 1957-58; assoc. prof. biomed. engring. Moore Sch. Elec. Engring., U. Pa., 1964-70, acting head electromed. div., 1968-69, prof. biomed. engring., 1970-97, assoc. dir. biomed. engring. tng. program, 1971-76, asso. dir. sch., 1972-74, chmn. grad. group in biomed. electronic engring., 1973-75, chmn. dept. bioengring., 1973-76, chmn. grad. group bioengring., 1975-76, dir. systems and integrative biology tng. program, 1979-84; prof. physiology Sch. Vet. Medicine U. Pa., 1976-97, prof. Dutch culture Sch. Arts and Scis., 1983-97, prof. anesthesia Med. Sch., 1990-97, prof. emeritus, 1997—. Vis. prof. biomed. engring. U. Miami, 1970-79, Erasmus U. Med. Sch., Rotterdam, The Netherlands, 1970-71, Tech. U., Delft, 1970-71, Polish Acad. Scis., Warsaw, 1975; hon. vis. prof. physiology U. Ljubljana, 1994—; mem. cardiovasc. study sect. NIH, 1985-89, temp. mem., 1998—; cons. sci. affairs divsn. NATO, 1973—; participant numerous internat. confs. in field. Author: (with I. Starr) Ballistocardiography in Cardiovascular Research, 1967, Circulatory System Dynamics, 1978; contbg. author: Biological Engineering, 1969; Editor: (with G.N. Jager and N. Westerhof) Circulatory Analog Computers, 1963, (with G.H. Pollack) Ballistocardiography and Cardiac Performance, 1967, (with E. Kresch) The Venous System: Characteristics and Function, 1969, (with J. Baan and J. Raines) Cardiovascular System Dynamics, 1978, (with Reichenbach-Consten) Two Hundred Years of Netherlands-American Interaction; sci. editor Biophysics and Bioengring. Series, 1976-94; contbr. numerous articles to profl. jours.; Referee: Biophys. Jour., 1968—, Physics in Medicine and Biology, 1969—, Bull. Math. Biophysics, 1972-84, Circulation Research, 1973—; mem. editorial adv. bd.: Jour. Biomechanics, 1969-84; assoc. editor: Bull. Math. Biology, 1973-84. V.p. Haverford Friends Sch. PTA, 1968—70. Recipient S. Reid Warren Jr. award U. Pa. Sch. Engring. and Applied Sci., 1986, Christian and Mary Lindback award U. Pa., 1988, Lifetime Achievement award, 2001, Internat. Order of Merit, 2003, Arthur C. Guyton award, 2003. Fellow IEEE (life, mem. adminstrv. com. engring. in medicine and biology group 1967-70, mem. edn. com. group biomed. engring. 1968-70, sec. Phila. chpt. 1974-75, mem. regional coun. profl. group engring. in medicine and biology 1974-77), AAAS, N.Y. Acad. Scis., Explorers Club, Coll. Physicians Phila., Am. Coll. Cardiology, Royal Soc. Medicine London; mem. Nederlandse Natuurkundige Vereniging, Ballistocardiograph Research Soc. U.S.A. (sec.-treas. 1965-67, pres. 1968-70), Biophys. Soc. (charter), European Soc. for Noninvasive Cardiovascular Research (co-founder 1960, sec.-treas. 1960-61, mem. com. on nomenclature 1960-61, officer 1961-62, Herman C. Burger award 1978, Disting. Rsch. Award, 1993), Cardiovascular System Dynamics Soc. (co-founder 1976, pres. 1976-80, hon. life 1986), Franklin Inst., John Morgan Soc., Biomed. Engring. Soc. (founding mem., chmn. membership com. 1978-79, dir. 1972-75), Am. Heart Assn., Instrument Soc. Am. (sr. mem.), Soc. Math. Biology (charter mem.), Am. Physiol. Soc., Microcirculatory Soc., Am. Assn. Med. Systems and Informatics, Pa. Acad. Sci., Sigma Xi, Phi Zeta. Presbyterian. Achievements include discovery (with Maximilian Moser) of impedance-defined flow, generalizing William Harvey's 1628 theory of blood circulation; research in properties of impedance-defined flow, especially with respect to venous return and cardiopulmonary resuscitation. Home: 620 Haydock Ln Haverford PA 19041-1208 Office: U Pa 101 Hayden Hall Philadelphia PA 19104-6392 Office Phone: 215-898-5881. Business E-Mail: anoor@seas.upenn.edu.

NOOYI, INDRA KRISHNAMURTHY, food products executive; b. Madras, India, Oct. 28, 1955; m. Raj K. Nooyi; 2 children. BS, Madras Christian Coll., India, 1976; MBA, Indian Inst. Mgmt., Calcutta, 1978; M Pub. and Pvt. Mgmt., Yale U., 1980. Product mgr. Johnson & Johnson, India, Mettur Beardsell, Ltd., India; dir. internat. corp. strategy projects Boston Cons. Group, 1980—86; bus. devel. exec. Motorola, Inc., v.p., dir. corp. strategy and planning, 1986—90; sr. v.p. strategy, planning and strategic mktg. Asea Brown Boveri, 1990—94; sr. v.p. strategic planning PepsiCo, Inc., Purchase, NY, 1994-2000, sr. v.p., CFO, 2000-01, pres., CFO, 2001—06, pres., CEO, 2006—07, chairwoman, pres., CEO, 2007—. Bd. dir. Phoenix Home Life Mut. Ins. Co. Bd. dir. PepsiCo Found.; trustee Convent of Sacred Heart Sch., Greenwich, Conn. Named an Outstanding American of Choice, US Dept. State, 2007; named one of 50 Women to Watch, Wall St. Jour., 2005, 2006, 100 Most Powerful Women, Forbes mag., 2005, Forbes Mag., 2006, 50 Most Powerful Women in Bus., Fortune mag., 2006, The World's Most Influential People, TIME mag., 2007, 50 Who Matter Now, Business 2.0, 2007. Achievements include being the first woman CEO for PepsiCo, Inc. Office: PepsiCo Inc 700 Anderson Hill Rd Purchase NY 10577-1444 *

NOPAR, ALAN SCOTT, lawyer; s. Myron E. and Evelyn M. Nopar; m. Angela P. Yancey, Aug. 26, 2000. BS, U. Ill., 1976; JD, Stanford U., Calif., 1979. Bar; Ariz. 1979, US Dist. Ct. Ariz. 1980, US Ct. Appeals (9th cir.) 1980, US Supreme Ct. 1982, Calif. 1989; CPA, Ill. Assoc. O'Connor, Cavanagh, Anderson, Westover, Killingsworth & Beshears P.A., Phoenix, 1979-85, ptnr., 1985-87; of counsel Tower, Byrne & Beaugureau, Phoenix, 1987-88; ptnr. Minutillo & Gorman, San Jose, Calif., 1989-91, Bosco, Blau, Ward & Nopar, San Jose, 1991-96; exec. v.p., gen. counsel, dir. AmeriNet Fin. Systems, Inc., Ontario, Calif., 1996-97; sole practice law Palo Alto, Calif., 1998-99; ptnr. Bosco, Ward & Nopar, Palo Alto, 2000—04, Bosco & Nopar, Palo Alto, 2004—07, Nopar & Assocs., Palo Alto, 2007—. Mem. Ariz. Rep. Caucus, Phoenix, 1984-88. Mem. AICPA, ABA (bus. law and law practice mgmt. sects., mem. forum com. on franchising), Ariz. Bar Assn. (bus. law sect.), Calif. State Bar Assn. (bus. law sect.). Avocations: golf, skiing, tennis, bicycling. Office: 425 Sherman Ave Ste 100 Palo Alto CA 94306-1849

NORA, AUDREY HART, physician; b. Picayune, Miss., Dec. 5, 1936; d. Allen Joshua and Vera Lee (Ballard) H.; m. James Jackson Nora, Apr. 9, 1966; children: James Jackson Jr., Elizabeth Hart. BS, U. Miss., 1958, MD, 1961; MPH, U. Calif., 1978. Diplomate Am. Bd. Pediat., Am. Bd. Hematology and Oncology. Resident in pediat. U. Wis. Hosp., Madison, 1961-64; fellow in hematology/oncology Baylor U., Tex. Childrens Hosp., Houston, 1964-66, asst. prof. pediat., 1966-70; assoc. clin. prof. pediat. U. Colo. Sch. Medicine, Denver, 1970—; dir. genetics Denver Childrens Hosp., 1970-78; commd. med. officer USPHS, 1978, advanced through grades to asst. surgeon gen., 1983, cons. maternal and child health Denver, 1978-83, asst. surgeon gen. regional health adminstr., 1983-92, dir. maternal & child health bur., health resources and svc. adminstrn., 1992-99. Mem. adv. com. NIH, Bethesda, 1975-77; mem. adv. bd. Metronet Health, Inc., Denver, 1986-92; mem. adv. bd. Colo. Assn. Commerce and Industry, Denver, 1985-92, WIC program USDA, 1989-99; mem. adv. coun. NICHD, 1992-99; bd. mem. RMC for Health Promotion and Edn., pres., 2004-05. Author: (with J.J. Nora) Genetics and Counseling in Cardiovascular Diseases, 1978, (with others) Blakiston's Medical Dictionary, 1980, Birth Defects Encyclopedia, 1990, (with J.J. Nora and K. Berg) Cardiovascular Diseases: Genetics, Epidemiology and Prevention, 1991; contbr. articles to profl. jours. Recipient Virginia Apgar award Nat. Found., 1976. Fellow Am. Acad. Pediat.; mem. Am. Pub. Health Assn. (governing coun. 1990-92, coun. mem. maternal and child health 1990—), Commd. Officers Assn., Am. Soc. Human Genetics, Teratology Soc., Western Soc. Pediatric Rsch. Presbyterian. Avocations: cooking, hiking, quilting. Office: 1973 S Kenton Ct Aurora CO 80014-4709

NORA, JAMES JACKSON, physician, writer, educator; b. Chgo., June 26, 1928; s. Joseph James and Mae Henrietta (Jackson) N.; m. Barbara June Fluhrer, Sept. 7, 1949 (div. 1963); children: Wendy Alison, Penelope Welbon, Marianne Leslie; m. Audrey Faye Hart, Apr. 9, 1966; children: James Jackson Jr., Elizabeth Hart Nora. AB, Harvard U., 1950; MD, Yale U., 1954; MPH, U. Calif., Berkeley, 1978. Diplomate Am. Bd. Pediat., Am. Bd. Cardiology, Am. Bd. Med. Genetics. Intern Detroit Receiving Hosp., 1954-55; resident in pediat. U. Wis. Hosps., Madison, 1959-61, fellow in cardiology, 1962-64; fellow in genetics McGill U. Children's Hosp., Montreal, Canada, 1964-65; assoc. prof. pediat. Baylor Coll. Medicine, Houston, 1965-71; prof. genetics, preventive medicine and pediat. U. Colo. Med. Sch., Denver, 1971—, prof. emeritus, 1986. Dir. genetics Rose Med. Ctr., Denver, 1980—; dir. pediatric cardiology and cardiovasc. tng. U. Colo. Sch. Medicine, 1971-78; mem. task force Nat. Heart and Lung Program, Bethesda, Md., 1973; cons. WHO, Geneva, 1983—; mem. U.S.-U.S.S.R. Exch. Program on Heart Disease, Moscow and Leningrad, 1975. Author: The Whole Heart Book, 1980, 2d rev. edit., 1989; author: (with F.C. Fraser) Medical Genetics, 4th Rev. edit., 1994; author: Genetics of Man, 2d rev. edit., 1986, Cardiovascular Diseases: Genetics, Epidemiology and Prevention, 1991, The Upstart Spring, 1989, The Psi Delegation, 1989, The Hemingway Sabbatical, 1996, Songs from a Brazen Bull, 2001, Panacea, 2002, What Every Senior Needs to Know About Health Care, 2004, Half-Open Windows, 2005, Progress Notes, 2005, The 9/11 Dialogues, 2006. 2nd lt. USAAC, 1945—47. Grantee Nat. Heart, Lung and Blood Inst., Nat. Inst. Child Health and Human Devel., Am. Heart Assn., NIH; recipient Virginia Apgar Meml. award. Fellow: Am. Coll. Med. Genetics, Am. Coll. Cardiology; mem.: Poets and Writers, Acad. Am. Poets, Mystery Writers Am., Authors League Am., Authors Guild. Democrat. Presbyterian. Avocations: writing fiction, poetry.

NORA, LOIS MARGARET, neurologist, educator, academic administrator, dean; BS in Biology with honors, U. Ill., 1976; MD, Rush Med. Coll., Chgo., 1979; JD, U. Chgo., 1987; MBA, U. Ky., 2002. Fellow Am. Bd. Neurology, Am. Bd. Electrodiagnostic Medicine; bar: Ill. 1988, D.C. 1988. Intern in family medicine Cmty. Meml. Gen. Hosp., LaGrange, Ill., 1980; resident in neurology Rush-Presbyn.-St. Luke's Med. Ctr., Chgo., 1981-84, chief resident in neurology, 1983-84, fellow electromyography and neuromuscular disease, 1984-85; asst. prof. dept. neurology, asst. dean clin. curriculum Rush Med. Coll., Chgo., 1987-94, assoc. prof. dept. neurology, 1994-95; fellow Ctr. for Clin. Med. Ethics U. Chgo., 1993-95; assoc. dean acad. affairs, assoc. prof. dept. neurology U. Ky. Coll. Medicine, 1995—2002; prof. neurology U. Ky. Coll. Law, 1996—2002; pres. Northeastern Ohio Univ. Coll. of Med., 2002—, dean, 2002—. Spkr. in field. Contbr. articles to profl. jours., chpts. to books. Vice chair Epilepsy Found. of Greater Chgo., 1988-90, chair, 1991, chair strategic planning com. 1990-91, bd. dirs., 1987-94; bd. dirs. Epilepsy Found. of Am.,

1992-95, co-chair quality standards com. 1992-94; mem. needs assessment com. United Way of Chgo., 1989-90; camp physician children's summer camp program Muscular Dystrophy Assn., 1984-86; vol. tchr. Christ the King Elem. Sch., 1996—2002. Mem. AMA (mem. dean's com. on family violence curriculum 1993, mem. report and resolutions subcom. for reference com. C 1997), Am. Acad. Neurology (mem. ethics com. 1997—2002), Am. Assn. Electrodiagnostic Medicine (chair profl. practice com. 1991—97, sec., treas., 1999-2002, pres.-elect, 2002-03, pres. 2003-04), Soc. Clin. Neurologists. Office: Northeastern Ohio U Coll Med PO Box 95 4209 St Rt 44 Rootstown OH 44272

NORAH, PATRICIA ANN, retired music educator; b. Columbus, Ga., Sept. 1, 1946; d. Tommy T. and Mary Farley Norah; 1 child, Terrence D. Murphy. Student, Spelman Coll., 1964—65, U. Fla., 1972; B Music Edn., Columbus State U., 1971, MEd, 1978. Cert. tchr. Ga. Gen. music tchr. South Columbus Elem. Sch., 1971—78, Matthew Elem. Sch./Ft. Benning Pub. Schs., Columbus, 1986—87; choral dir. Ft. Mid. Sch., Columbus, 1978—84, Baker HS, Columbus, 1987—91, Carver HS, Columbus, 1991—2006; ret., 2006. Vocal coach, Columbus, 1995—; asst. min. music St. Benedict Cath. Ch., Columbus, 1999—; workshop dir. Franchise Ch., Phenix City, Ala., 2004. Performer Columbus Consol. Gov. One Columbus, 2003; active Keep Columbus Beautiful. Named to Most Outstanding Women Am., 1974; recipient Outstanding Ga. Citizen award, Sec. of State Cathy Cox, 2000, Outstanding African-Am. award, Carver HS, Music Tchr. Excellence award, Nat. League Am. Pen Women (Columbus chpt.), 2006. Mem.: NEA, Nat. Music Educators Assn., Ga. Assn. Educators, Ga. Music Educators Assn. (mem.-at-large elem. coun. 1974). Avocations: reading, travel, music. Office: Carver HS 3100 8th St Columbus GA 31906 Home: 3633 St Mary's Rd Columbus GA 31906 Personal E-mail: pnorah@bellsouth.net.

NORBACK, CRAIG THOMAS, writer; b. Pitts., Nov. 14, 1943; s. Howard George and Maybelle Veronica Montaigne (Cosse) Norback; m. Judith Carol Shaul, Oct. 12, 1976. BS, Washington U., St. Louis, 1967; postgrad., Drew U., 1986—. Author, co-author, compiler, producer over 150 books, including: The Misspeller's Dictionary, 1972, Everything You Can Get from the Government for Free or Almost for Free, 1975, The Dream Machine: The Golden Age of American Automobiles 1946-65, 1976, Great Songs of Madison Avenue, 1976, Great North American Indians, 1977, The Health Care Directory, 1977, The Older American's Handbook, 1977, The Educational Marketplace, 1978, Famous American Admirals, 1978, Newsweek Travel Guide to the U.S., 1978, The Dow Jones-Irwin Guide to Franchising, 1979, The Horseman's Catalog, 1979, The Must Words, 1979, The Practical Inventor's Handbook, 1979, ABC Complete Book of Sports Facts, 1980, ABC Monday Night Football, 1980-81, 1982, The Bible Almanac, 1980, Check Yourself Out, 1980, The Signet Book of World Winners, 1980, The TV Guide Almanac, 1980, The World's Great News Photos (1840-1980), 1980, The Allergy Encyclopedia, 1981, American Expressions, 1981, The Computer Invasion, 1981, The Consumer's Energy Handbook, 1981, 500 Questions New Parents Ask, 1982, Business Week Almanac, 1982, The International Yellow Pages, 1982, The Puzzle King's Bafflers, 1982, The Associated Press Sunday Crossword Puzzle Book, 1983, Chilton's Job Textbook Series: Advertising Management, 1983, Office Management, 1983, It's a Fact, 1983, National Education Association Parent and Child Success Library: Helping Your Child Read, 1983, How Letters Make Words, 1983, How to Prepare Your Child for School, 1983, Learning the Alphabet, 1983, Learning to Add, 1983, The Ultimate Toy Catalog, 1983, U.S. Publicity Directory, various years, Advertising and Promotion Management, 1983, America Wants to Know, 1983, Certified Professional Secretary modules I through VI, 1984, East Coast Publicity Directory, 1984, Human Resources Yearbook, 1987, 88, 89, 90, Princeton Area Job Finder, 1986-87, Career Encyclopedia, 1987, Travel Publicity Directory, 1987, 88, 89, 90, Arthur Young Guide to Venture Capital, 1987, Hazardous Chemicals on File, 1988, Joint Ventures, 1992. Home: 3112 Kaitlyn Ct Princeton Junction NJ 08550-5349

NORBECK, GEORGE, psychiatrist, consultant; b. Vermillion, SD, Jan. 15, 1937; s. Kermit George and Winfree Virginia Norbeck; m. Joyce Erickson (div.); children: John, Kari, Kirsten, Tyra; m. Mary Jeanette Moore, June 5, 1977. BA, St. Olaf Coll., Northfield, Minn., 1959; BS, MD, U. Minn., Mpls., 1964; M Social Psychiatry, UCLA, 1971. Diplomate Am. Bd. Psychiatry and Neurology, 1976. Flight surgeon USAF, Beale AFB, Calif., 1965—67; resident psychiatry UCLA, 1970; staff psychiatrist St. John's Hosp., Santa Monica, Calif., 1970—71, Ulleraker Psychiat. Rsch. Hosp., Uppsala, Sweden, 1971—72, Karolinska Psychiat. Outpatient Clinic, Stockholm, 1972—73; chief inpatient psychiat. dept., outpatient psychiat. dept. Palo Alto VA Med. Ctr., Calif., 1973—95; med. cons. Social Security Disability, Oakland, Calif., 2000—. Treas. Santa Clara County Psychiat. Soc., 1976—78, pres., 1978; state air surgeon Calif. Air N.G., 1985—93; mem. San Mateo County Mounted Patrol Search and Rescue, 1980—. Col. USAF, 1975—93. Fellow: Am. Psychiat. Assn. (disting.); mem.: No. Calif. Psychiat. Soc. Avocations: horseback riding, singing, Broadway shows, trombone.

NORBECK, JACK CARL, library exhibitor; b. Greensburg, Pa., Dec. 8, 1940; Cert., Opticians Inst., 1971; Cert. U. Conn., Ratcliffe Hicks Sch. Agr., 1964. Founder, pres. Norbeck Rsch., Coplay, Pa., 1978—. Designer 71 mag. covers. Author: The Encyclopedia of American Steam Traction Engines; contbr. articles to profl. jours.; more than 240 photo exhibits in 42 countries. Mem. YMCA. Named Internat. Man of the Yr., 2000—01; recipient 20th Century award, Am. Medal of Honor, 2001, Noble prize, 2001, Internat. Ambs. medal and Gold Record of Achievement, 2001. Mem.: USA Gymnastics, Am. Legion, Union Hist. Fire Soc., The Authors Guild, Am. Soc. Agrl. Engrs., Hist. Steam Assns. Lutheran. Achievements include design using his photos on 74 magazine covers. Home: 117 N Ruch St 8 Coplay PA 18037-1712

NORBECK, JANE S., retired nursing educator; b. Redfield, SD, Feb. 20, 1942; d. Sterling M. and Helen L. (Williamson) N.; m. Paul J. Gorman, June 28, 1970. BA in Psychology, U. Minn., 1965, BSN, 1965; MS, U. Calif., San Francisco, 1971, DSN, 1975. Psychiat. nurse Colo. Psychiat. Hosp., Denver, 1965-66, Langley Porter Hosp., San Francisco, 1966-67; pub. health nurse San Francisco Health Dept., 1968-69; prof. U. Calif. Sch. of Nursing, San Francisco, 1975—2003, dean, 1989-99, dept. chair, 1984-89, prof. and dean emeritus, 2003. Chair study sect. Nat. Inst. of Nursing Rsch., 1990-93, mem. editl. bd. Archives of Psychiat. Nursing, 1985-95, Rsch. in Nursing and Health, 1987-2003. Co-editor: Annual Review of Nursing Research, 1996-97; contbr. articles to profl. jours. Mem. ANA, Am. Acad. Nursing, Inst. of Medicine, Sigma Theta Tau.

NORBECK, TIMOTHY BURNS, medical association executive; b. Buffalo, June 29, 1938; s. Carl Francis N. and Helene Smith (Comstock) Browne; children: Carl, Kim, Karin; m. Michèle R. Mathieu, Mar. 24, 1990. BA, Hamilton Coll., 1960. Sales rep. Nat. Steel Corp., Detroit, Milw., Chgo., 1960-67; regional dir. AMA, Chgo., St. Louis, Chgo., 1967-73; exec. dir. RI Med. Soc., Providence, 1973-77, Conn. State Med. Soc., New Haven, 1977—. Bd. dirs., treas. Conn. Med. Mgmt., Inc., Wallingford, 1984-; asst. treas. Conn. Med. Ins. Co., Wallingford, 1984-; cons. Vt. State Med. Soc., Montpelier, 1987; cons. RI Med. Soc., Providence, 1986; bd. dirs. MD Advantage. Contbr. articles profl. jours. Chmn. bd. dirs. Am. Cancer Soc. Conn. Div., Wallingford, 1985-87, mem. nat. com. on field svcs., 1989—, bd. dirs. Conn. div.; bd. dirs. St. Louis County Narcotics Commn., 1967-70; bd. dirs. New Haven Regional Mental Health Assn., 1980-83; pres. Conn. Physicians Guild; exec. com. Gaylord Hosp., Wallingford, Conn., 1998-. Recipient Nat. Bronze medal Am. Cancer Soc., 1987, hon. MD, Conn. State Med. Soc., Med. Exec. Achievement award, AMA, 2005 Mem. Am. Soc. Assn. Execs., Am. Assn. Med. Soc. Execs. (bd. dirs., pres.), Rotary. Democrat. Presbyterian. Avocations: public speaking, reading, writing speeches and articles, tennis. Office: Conn State Med Soc 160 Saint Ronan St New Haven CT 06511-2312 E-mail: tnorbeck@csms.org. *

NORBERG, ARTHUR LAWRENCE, JR., historian, physicist, educator; b. Providence, Apr. 13, 1938; s. Arthur Lawrence Sr. and Margaret Helen (Riley) N.; children: Catherine E. Norberg Morin, Patricia A. Norberg Fetta, Timothy E., Gregory T. BS in Physics, Providence Coll., 1959; MS in Physics, U. Vt., 1962; PhD in History of Sci., U. Wis., 1974. Asst. prof. physics St. Michael's Coll., Winooski, Vt., 1961-63, 64-68; assoc. scientist Westinghouse Electric Co., Pitts., 1963-64; instr. in physics U. Wis., Whitewater, 1968-71; rsch. historian U. Calif., Berkeley, 1973-79; program mgr. NSF, Washington, 1979-81; dir. Charles Babbage Inst. for History of Info. Processing U. Minn., Mpls., 1981—93, 1999—2006, prof. history of sci. and tech., 1995—2005, assoc. prof. computer sci., 1981-95, prof. computer sci., 1995—2005, prof. emeritus, 2005—, consulting historian, 2006—. Del. Am. Coun. Learned Socs., N.Y.C., 1981-87; mem. adv. coun. NASA, Washington, 1988-93; endowed ERA Land Grant chair U. Minn., 1989-93, 99—2006. Editor: Annals of the History of Computing, 1982-93; adv. editor Tech. and Culture, 1985-92, (books) Transforming Computer Technology: Information Processing for the Pentagon, 1996, Computers and Commerce, 2005; contbr. articles to profl. jours Founding pres. City Works-A Tech. Ctr., Mpls., 1987-90; exec. dir. Charles Babbage Found., 1984-94; trustee Charles Babbage Found., 1993-96. Fellow AAAS; mem. History of Sci. Soc. (treas. 1975-80), Brit. Soc. for History of Sci., Soc. for History of Tech., Sigma Xi. E-mail: norberg@cs.umn.edu.

NORBERG, RICHARD EDWIN, physicist, researcher; b. Newark, Dec. 28, 1922; s. Arthur Edwin and Melita (Roefer) N.; m. Patricia Ann Leach, Dec. 27, 1947 (dec. July 1977); children: Karen Elizabeth, Craig Alan, Peter Douglas; m. Jeanne C. O'Brien, Apr. 1, 1978. BA, DePauw U., 1943; MA, U. Ill., 1947, PhD, 1951. Research assoc., control sytems lab. U. Ill., 1951-53, asst. prof., 1953; vis. lectr. physics Washington U., St. Louis, 1954—, mem. faculty, 1955—, prof. physics, 1958—, chmn. dept., 1962-91. Mem. editl. bd. Magnetic Rsch. Rev. Served with USAAF, 1942-46. Co-recipient ISMAR prize, 2004. Fellow Am. Phys. Soc., Internat. Soc. Magnetic Research. Home: 7134 Princeton Ave Saint Louis MO 63130-2308 Office: Washington U Dept Physics PO Box 1105 Saint Louis MO 63188-1105 Business E-Mail: ren@wuphys.wustl.edu.

NORCEL, JACQUELINE JOYCE CASALE, educational association administrator; b. Nov. 19, 1940; d. Frederick and Josephine Jeanette (Bestafka) Casale; m. Edward John Norcel, Feb. 24, 1962. BS, Fordham U., 1961; MS, Bklyn. Coll., 1966; 6th yr. cert., So. Conn. State U., 1980; postgrad., Bridgeport U. Elem. tchr. NYC Pub. Schs., 1961-80; prin. Coventry (Conn.) Schs., 1980-84, Trumbull (Conn.) Schs., 1984—2003, Frenchtown Elem. Sch., 2003—. Guest lectr. So. Conn. State U., 1980; cons. Monson (Mass.) Schs., 1984; mem. Conn. State Prin. Acad. Adv. Bd., 1986-88; mem. adj. faculty Sacred Heart U., Fairfield, Conn., 1985—, So. Conn. State U., summer 1991; fed. rels. coord. Nat. Assn. Elem. Sch. Prins., Conn., 1999-2002. Editor: Best of the Decade, 1980; mem. editl. adv. bd. Principal Matters; contbr. articles to profl. jours. Chmn. bldg. com. Trumbull Bd. Edn., 1978-80; chmn. Sch. Benefit Com., Trumbull, 1985-86; catechist Bridgeport Diocese, Roman Cath. Ch., Conn., 1975-85, youth min., 1979-84, coord., evaluator leadership tng. workshops for teens and adults, 1979-84; mem. St. Stephen's Parish Coun., 1993-97, trustee, 1997—, Eucharist min., 1999—, lector, 1990-; com. mem. New Sch. Bldg. Town of Trumbull, 2001-05. Recipient Town of Trumbull Svc. award, 1982, Nat. Disting. Prin. award, 1988, Joseph Formica Disting. Svc. award EMSPAC, 1994. Mem.: ASCD, Assoc. Tchrs. Math. in Conn., New Eng. Coalition Ednl. Leaders, Ea. Conn. Coun. Internat. Reading Assn., Conn. Assn. Elem. Sch. Prins., Trumbull Adminstrs. Assn. (pres.-elect 1989—91, pres. 1991—93, 2002—), Conn. Assn. Supervision and Curriculum Devel., Nat. Assn. Elem. Sch. Prins. (del. to gen. assemblies 1984—90, zone I dir. 1987—90, del. to gen. assemblies 1999—), Hartford Area Prins. and Suprs. Assn. (local pres. 1981—82), Conn. Assn. Schs. (bd. mem. 2000—05), Adminstrn. and Supervision Assn. (sec. 1980—81, pres. 1981—82, exec. bd. 1982—93), Elem. Mid. Sch. Prins. Assn. (pres. 1985—86, state elected rep. 1989—90, fed. rels. coord. 1990—94, dists. 1, 2 and 3 dir. 1995—98, commr. 1997—2000, fed. rels. coord. 1999—2002, Citizen of Yr. award 1991, Pres.'s award 1981—85), N.E. Regional Elem. Prins. Assn. (rep. 1984—86, sec. 1986—87), Delta Kappa Gamma (v.p. 1996—2000), Pi Lambda Theta, Phi Delta Kappa (v.p. rsch. and projects 1993—95, Disting. Fellow award 1992). Home: 5240 Madison Ave Trumbull CT 06611-1016 Office: Frenchtown Elem Sch 30 Frenchtown Rd Trumbull CT 06611 Office Phone: 203-452-4227. Personal E-mail: norcelJ98@yahoo.com.

NORCIA, STEPHEN WILLIAM, advertising executive; b. NYC, Jan. 21, 1941; s. William Matthew and Amelia (Marrone) N.; m. Martha Elizabeth Whelan, Apr. 22, 1978; children: Matthew F., Daniel P., Anne E. BA, U. Conn., 1962. Media planner and buyer SSC&B, NYC, 1965-66; account exec. McCann-Erickson Co., Chgo., 1966-68, v.p., dep. mgr. Milw., 1971-72, v.p., mgmt. supr. NYC, 1972-74, sr. v.p., gen. mgr. Atlanta, 1974-78, exec. v.p., gen. mgr. NYC, 1978-81; exec. v.p., mem. exec. policy com., mem. mgmt. com. Lintas, NYC, 1981-94, exec. v.p., 1989-95, world wide client dir., dir. bus. devel., 1991-94, also bd. dirs.; mng. ptnr. Earle Palmer Brown, NYC, 1994-96; dir. global account DDB, NYC, 1996-99, mng. dir., 1998-2000; v.p. bus. devel. Agency.com, 2000—; owner cons. co. Norcia Group, 2002—; founder, prin. Topsail Group, 2003. Account exec. Needham, Harper & Steers, Chgo., 1968-70; dir. mktg. product devel. workshop Interpub., N.Y.C., 1970-71; bd. dirs. Communication Counselors Network; adj. prof. Fordham U., Iona Coll. Bd. dirs. U. Ga. Master of Br. Mgmt. Program, 1985, 86, 87, Advt. Edn. Found., 1999-2007; bd. dirs. Spirial Frog, 2006—. 1st lt. U.S. Army, 1962-65. Recipient Robert E. Healy award Interpub. Group Cos., 1975, Effie award Am. Mktg. Assn., 1985, Grand Effie award Am. Mktg. Assn., 1984. Mem. Am. Assn. Advt. Agys., Advt. Club N.Y., Am. Yacht Club, Essex Yacht Club, Old Lyme Country Club. Republican. Roman Catholic. Avocations: tennis, boating, skiing, bicycling. Home: 53 Otter Cove Dr Old Saybrook CT 06475 Office: Topsail Group PO Box 488 Old Saybrook CT 06475 Office Phone: 914-921-3351.

NORCOTT, FLEMMING L., JR., state supreme court justice; b. New Haven, Oct. 11, 1943; BA, Columbia U., 1965, JD, 1968; LLD (hon.), U. New Haven, 1993, Albertus Magnus Coll., 2004. Bar: Conn. 1968. Peace corps vol. U. East Africa, Nairobi, Kenya; legal staff Bedford-Stuyvestant Restoration Corp.; asst. atty. gen. Office Atty. Gen., V.I.; judge Superior Ct., 1979-87, Appellate Ct., 1987-92; assoc. justice Conn. Supreme Ct., Hartford, 1992—. Hearing examiner Conn. Commn. Human Rights and Opportunities; co-founder, exec. dir. Ctr. Advocacy, Rsch. and Planning, Ind., New Haven; lectr. Yale U. Bd. govs. U. New Haven; bd. dirs. Dixwell Community House, Ea. Collegiate Football Officials. Assn., New Haven Football Officials Assn., Long Wharf Theatre; assoc. fellow Calhoun Coll., Yale U.; bd. trustees Yale-New Haven Hosp. Mem. Omega Psi Phi Office: Conn Supreme Ct 231 Capital Ave Hartford CT 06106 *

NORCROSS, MARVIN AUGUSTUS, veterinarian, researcher, retired federal official; b. Tansboro, NJ, Feb. 8, 1931; s. Marvin A. and Katherine V. (McGuigan) N.; m. Diane L. Tuttle, Nov. 22, 1956 (div. 1991); children: James, Janet. Student, Rutgers U., 1954-55; VMD, U. Pa., 1959, PhD, 1966. Pathologist Merck Sharp & Dohme Rsch. Labs., Rahway, NJ, 1966-69, dir. clin. research, 1969-72, sr. dir. domestic vet. research, 1972-75; dir. div. vet. med. rsch. Ctr. Vet. Medicine, FDA, Rockville, Md., 1975-78, assoc. dir. for rsch., 1978-82, assoc. dir. for human food safety, 1982-84, assoc. dir. for new animal drug evaluation, 1984-87; asst. dep. adminstr., then dep. adminstr. Sci. and Tech., Food Safety and Inspection Svc. USDA, Washington, 1987-93, exec. asst. to the adminstr., 1993-94; U.S. coord. for Codex Alimentarius USDA, Washington, 1994-96, sr. sci. advisor to adminstr., 1996; cons. vet. medicine and food safety, 1996—. Adj. prof. Va.-Md. Regional Coll. Vet. Medicine, Blacksburg, 1980-85 Contbr. articles to profl. jours. Trustee Scotch Plains (NJ) Cmty. Fund, 1969-72. Lt. AUS, 1952-54; col. Res., 1954-83 (ret.) Recipient FDA Merit award, 1978, Meritorious Presdl. Rank award, 1989; named to Artillery OCS Hall of Fame, 2000. Mem. AAAS, Am. Vet. Med. Assn., Assn. Mil. Surgeons US, Civil Affairs Assn., Nat. Assn. Fed. Veterinarians, NJ Acad. Sci., NY Acad. Scis., Res. Officers Assn., Soc. Toxicologic Pathology, Sigma Xi. Home and Office: 14304 Brickhowe Ct Germantown MD 20874-3431 Office Phone: 877-899-9426. Personal E-mail: mjnorcross@bww.com.

NORD, HENRY J., transportation executive; b. Berlin, May 1, 1917; came to U.S., 1937, naturalized, 1943; s. Walter and Herta (Riess) N.; children: Stephen, Philip. Student, U. Oxford, Eng., 1934, Northwestern U., 1938-40, Ill. Inst. Tech., 1942; JD, De Paul U., 1949. CPA, Ill. Apprentice in export, Hamburg, Germany, 1935- 37; with GATX Corp., Chgo., 1938-85, comptroller, 1961-67, v.p., 1967-71, exec. v.p., 1971-78, sr. v.p., 1978-80, v.p., 1980-82, cons., 1982-84, fin. cons., 1982—, dir., 1964-78. Dir. Planned Lighting, Inc. to 1988. Trustee DePaul U. Served to 1st lt. AUS, 1943—46. Mem. Internat. Law Assn. Clubs: Tavern (Chgo.). Home: 1000 N Lake Shore Pl Chicago IL 60611-1308 Office: 111 N Wabash Ave Chicago IL 60602-1936

NORD, MYRTLE SELMA, writer, researcher; b. Lane, SD, Mar. 13, 1918; d. Carl Frederick Schaefer and Minna Anna (Meyer) Scandrett; m. Warren E. Nord, Aug. 10, 1938. BA, Fort Lewis Coll., 1972. Sec. Anaconda Mining, Robeau, SD, 1935; waitress Rapid City, SD, 1935-38; office mgr. Farmers Ins. Group, Durango, Colo., 1947-62, ret., 1962. Author: Tell Me a Story, 1956, Inspiring Stories, 1975, Prospectives on Mass Communications, 1982, Main Currents in Communications, 1986, Leadville's Chicken Bill, 1977, The Searcher, 1993-94, Hot Flashes From Writing, 2005, Sestina and Haiku, 2005, The Searcher, 2006, Observations, 2006, To Kill A Bird, 2006, Murder 101, 2006, View Points, 2007, Kip, Boy Pioneer of Am. West, 2007; (plays) Five Under Cover 6, 1983, Celebrations 6, 1986, Virtue of Necessity, 1982, (stage plays) Tomorrow = X2,19, 1968, Sound Another Trumpet, 1976, (serials) Children's Friend, Missing Red Envelope, 1950-51, The Blue Triangle, 1952-53, (musicals) Getting It 2-Gether, 1982, No Patsy Like a Dame, 1985, High Blonde Pressure, 1986, Katie's Capers in the Mining Camp, 1989, (poetry) Hold Dear a Long Time Love, 1998, Story, Out-Guessing Ourselves, 1999 (Palomar Showcase); contbr. articles to popular mags.; chpts. to books. Mem. Nat. League of Am. Pen Women (state pres. 1966-68), Mystery Writers of Am. Avocations: herbs, music, outdoors. Home: Apt 213 11 E Orange Grove Rd Tucson AZ 85704-5555 Personal E-mail: myrtle.nord747@comcast.net.

NORD, PAUL ELLIOTT, lawyer, accountant; b. Mar. 22, 1936; s. Abe and Rose (Guss) N.; m. Marcia B. Gross, June 13, 1965; children: Howard, Aimee, Samuel. Student, U. Utah, 1952-56; JD, John F. Kennedy U., 2000. CPA, Calif.; bar: Calif., 2000, U.S. Tax Ct., U.S. Ct. Appeals (9th cir.). Staff acct. Robinson, Nowell & Co. (merged with Muncy McPherson & Co.), 1966-73, ptnr., 1973-81, mng. ptnr., 1981-87; ptnr. BDO Seidman, 1988-95, sr. ptnr., 1995—2000; pvt. practice Walnut Creek, Calif., 2000—. Bd. dirs. Congregation Beth Sholom, San Francisco, 1969-87, pres. 1979-81; mem. budget and allocations com. Jewish Fedn., East Bay, 1981-84. With U.S. Army, 1957-58, 61-62. Ford Found. scholar. Mem. Am. Inst. CPAs (acctg. standards exec. com. 1979-81), Calif. Soc. CPAs (chmn. sub-com. acctg. principles 1981-83), Club Sport. Jewish. Home: 931 Walnut Ave Walnut Creek CA 94598-3738 Office: 3075 Citrus Cir Ste 155 Walnut Creek CA 94598 Office Phone: 925-906-9300. Business E-Mail: paulnordlaw@gmail.com.

NORD, ROBERT EAMOR, lawyer; b. Ogden, Utah, Apr. 11, 1945; s. Eamor Carroll and Ella Carol (Winkler) N.; m. Sherryl Ann Smith, May 15, 1969; children: Kimberly, P. Ryan, Debra, Heather, Andrew, Elizabeth. BS, Brigham Young U., 1969; JD, U. Chgo., 1972. Bar: Ill. 1972, U.S. Dist. Ct. (no. dist.) Ill. 1972, U.S. Ct. Appeals (D.C. cir.) 1974, U.S. Dist. Ct. (mid. dist.) Fla. 1976, U.S. Ct. Appeals (7th cir.) 1977, U.S. Dist. Ct. (no. dist.) Ind. 1978, U.S. Dist. Ct. (no. dist.) Fla. 1979, U.S. Supreme Ct. 1981, U.S. Dist. Ct. (ea. dist.) Mich. 1984, U.S. Ct. Appeals (11th cir.) 1985, U.S. Ct. Appeals (3d cir.) 1996, U.S. Ct. Appeals (2d cir.) 2002. Assoc. Chadwell & Kayser, Chgo., 1972-75; from assoc. to ptnr. Hinshaw & Culbertson, Chgo., 1975—2002, of counsel, 2003—. Assoc. internat. legal counsel, Area Presidency LDS Ch., Moscow, 2005, Frankfurt, Germany, 2006. Republican. Home: 481 Woodlawn Ave Glencoe IL 60022-2175 Office: Hinshaw & Culbertson 222 N La Salle St Ste 300 Chicago IL 60601-1081 Office Phone: 312-704-3120. Personal E-mail: robertnord@gmail.com.

NORD, WALTER ROBERT, business administration educator, researcher, consultant; b. Mt. Kisco, NY, July 2, 1939; s. Arthur William and Elizabeth (Reimstedt) N.; m. Ann Feagan, June 10, 1967. BA in Econs., Williams Coll., 1961; MS in Organizational Behavior, Cornell U., 1963; PhD in Social Psychology, Washington U., St. Louis, 1967. Asst. prof. organizational psychology Washington U., 1967-70, assoc. prof., 1970-73, prof., 1973-89; prof. mgmt. U. South Fla., 1989—, Disting. Univ. prof., 2001; vis. prof. faculty commerce Northwestern U., 1981, U. B.C. (Can.), Vancouver, 1975-76. Author: (with S. Tucker) Implementing Routine and Radical Innovations, 1987; editor: Concepts and Controversy in Organizational Behavior, 1972, rev. edit, 1976; (with P. Frost and V. Mitchell) Organizational Reality, 1978, rev. edit., 1982, 86, 92; (with H. Meltzer) Making Organizations Humane and Productive, 1982; (with P. Frost and V. Mitchell) Managerial Reality, 1989, HRM Reality, 1992; (with A. Brief) Meanings of Occupational Work, 1990, (with S. Clegg and C. Hardy) Handbook of Organization Studies, 1996 (George Terry Book award 1997), 2d edit., 2006, (with P. Frost and L. Krefting) Managerial and Organization Reality, Stories of Life and Work, 2004, (with S. Clegg, C. Hardy and T. Lawrence) Sage Handbook of Organization Studies, 2006. Fellow APA; mem. Acad. Mgmt. (named Disting. Educator 2002). Home: 6004 Pratt St Tampa FL 33647-1043 Office: U South Fla Sch Bus Tampa FL 33620-5500 Business E-Mail: wnord@coba.usf.edu.

NORDBY, EUGENE JORGEN, orthopedic surgeon; b. Abbotsford, Wis., Apr. 30, 1918; s. Herman Preus and Lucille Violet (Korsrud) N.; m. Olive Marie Jensen, June 21, 1941; 1 child, Jon Jorgen BA, Luther Coll., Decorah, Iowa, 1939; MD, U. Wis., 1943. Diplomate Am. Bd. Orthopaedic Surgery. Intern Madison Gen. Hosp., Wis., 1943-44, asst. in orthopedic surgery Wis., 1944-48; practice medicine specializing in orthopedic surgery Madison, Wis., 1948—. Pres. Bone and Joint Surgery Assocs., S.C., 1969—91; chief staff Madison Gen. Hosp., 1957—63; assoc. clin. prof. U. Wis. Med. Sch., 1961—; bd. dirs. Wis. Physicians Svcs., Norwegian Am. Geneal. Ctr., Naeseth Libr.; chmn. Wis. Physicians Svcs., 1979—; dir. Wis. Regional Med. Program, Chgo. Madison and No. R.R.; bd. govs. Wis. Health Care Liability Ins. Plan; chmn. trustees S.M.S. Realty Corp.; mem. bd. attys. Profl. Responsibility of Wis. Supreme Ct., 1992—. Mem. editl. bd. Clin. Orthopaedics and Related Research, 1964—, Spine, 1994-2000. Pres. Vesterheim Norwegian Am. Mus., Decorah, Iowa, 1968-97, pres. emeritus, 1997—. Served to capt. M.C., AUS, 1944-46 Decorated Knight 1st class Royal Norwegian Order St. Olav; named Notable Norwegian Dane County Norwegian-Am. Fest, 1995; recipient Disting. Svc. award Internat. Rotary,1 987, Den Hoyeste Aere award Vesterheim, 1993, Lyman

Smith, M.D. and Eugene J. Nordby, M.D. award for minimally invasive spine surgery established N.Am. Spine Soc., 1998, The Nordby Bldg. designated Wis. Phys. Svc. Health Ins. Co., 1998, Internat. Therapy Soc. Lifetime Achievement award, 2006. Fellow Wisdom Hall of Fame; mem. Acad. Orthop. Surgeons (bd. dirs. 1972-73, 1st chmn. bd. councilors 1972), Clin. Orthop. Soc., Assn. Bone and Joint Surgeons (pres. 1973), Internat. Soc. Study Lumbar Spine, State Med. Soc. Wis. (chmn. 1968-76, treas. 1976-97, Coun. award 1976), Am. Orthop. Assn., N.Am. Spine Soc., Internat. Intradiscal Therapy Soc. (sec. 1987-99, exec. dir. 1996-2006, exec. dir. emeritus 2006—, Eugene J. Nordby Rsch. award established in his honor 1993, Lifetime Achievement award 2006), Wis. Orthop. Soc., Dane County Med. Soc. (pres. 1957), Nat. Exch. Club, Madison Torske Klubben (founder, pres. 1978-98, pres. emeritus 1998—), Norwegian-Am. Orthop. Soc., Am. Acad. Orthop. Surgeons, Am. Orthop. Assn., Norwegian Am. Found. (mem. geneal. ctr. bd. 2006), Norwegian-Am. Geneal. Ctr. (bd. mem. 2006), Phi Chi. Lutheran. Home: 7824 Courtyard Dr Madison WI 53719 Office: 304 S Whitney Way Madison WI 53705 Home Phone: 608-831-2356; Office Phone: 608-831-2356. Personal E-mail: ejnor@charter.net. *We must remember no matter how dedicated we are to the accumulation of knowledge, it isn't always what you know that matters but what you can think of in time.*

NORDEEN, JON K., retail executive; With Dayton Hudson Corp.; chief info. officer Spiegel Inc., Downers Grove, Ill., 1996—2001, sr. v.p., 2000—01; with Kohl's Corp., Menomonee Falls, Wis., 2001—, sr. v.p., chief info. officer, exec. v.p. planning and allocation, 2004—. Office: Kohls Corp N56 W17000 Ridgewood Dr Menomonee Falls WI 53051-5660 Office Phone: 262-703-7000. *

NORDELL, HANS RODERICK, journalist, retired editor; b. Alexandria, Minn., June 26, 1925; s. Wilbur Eric and Amelia (Jasperson) N.; m. Joan Projansky, Apr. 30, 1955; children: Eric Peter, John Roderick, Elizabeth Sabin. AB magna cum laude, Harvard U., 1948; B Litt, U. Dublin, 1951. Exec. editor World Monitor: The Christian Science Monitor Monthly; with Christian Sci. Monitor, Boston, 1948-93, arts editor, 1968-73, asst. chief editorial writer, 1973-83, home forum editor, 1983-85, feature editor, 1985-87; exec. editor World Monitor: The Christian Science Monitor Monthly, Boston, 1988-93. Bd. dirs. Cmty. Music Ctr., Boston, 1970-94, corp. chair, 1994—; bd. dirs. Young Audiences, 1970-88; mem. Com. for Harvard Theatre Collection, 1977-91; trustee Berklee Coll. Music, 1970-97, trustee emeritus, 1997—. With USMCR, 1943-46. Fellowship Rotary Found., 1950-51. Mem.: Harvard Musical Assn., St. Botolph Club, Phi Beta Kappa. Christian Scientist. Home: 25 Meadow Way Cambridge MA 02138-4635

NORDENBERG, MARK ALAN, academic administrator, law educator; b. Duluth, Minn., July 12, 1948; s. John Clemens and Shirley Mae (Tappen) N.; m. Nikki Patricia Pirillo, Dec. 26, 1970; children: Erin, Carl, Michael. BA, Thiel Coll., 1970; JD, U. Wis., 1973. Bar: Wis. 1973, Minn. 1974, U.S. Supreme Ct. 1976, Pa. 1985. Atty. Gray, Plant, Mooty & Anderson, Mpls., 1973—75; prof. law Capital U. Law Ctr., Columbus, Ohio, 1975—77, U. Pitts., 1977—, acting dean Sch. Law, 1985—87, dean Sch. Law, 1987—93, interim sr. vice chancellor & provost, 1993—94, Disting. Svc. prof., 1994—, interim chancellor, 1995—96, chancellor, 1996—. Mem. U.S. Supreme Ct. Adv. Com. on Civil Rules, Washington, 1988-93, Pa. Supreme Ct. Civil Procedure Rules Com., Phila., 1986-92; reporter civil justice adv. group U.S. Dist. Ct., Pitts., 1991-96; bd. dirs. Bank of NY Mellon Corp. Author: Modern Pennsylvania Civil Practice, 1985, 2d edit., 1995. Bd. dirs. Allegheny Conf. on Cmty. Devel., Pitts., Pitts. Coun. on Higher Edn., Pa. Assn. Colls. and Univs., Assn. Am. Univs.; trustee Thiel Coll., Greenville, Pa., 1987—97; bd. dirs. Pitts. Life Scis. Greenhouse, The Tech. Collaborative. Named Vectors Pitts. Person of Yr. in Edn., 1996, Person of Yr., 1997, Pitts. Mag. Person of Yr., 2001, Hon. Consul for Great Britain. Fellow Am. Bar Found.; mem. ABA, Pa. Bar Assn., Allegheny County Bar Assn., Pitts. Athletic Assn., Duquesne Club. Office: U Pitts Cathedral of Learning Pittsburgh PA 15260 Office Phone: 412-624-4200. Business E-Mail: norden@pitt.edu.

NORDGREN, RONALD PAUL, retired engineering educator, researcher; b. Munising, Mich., Apr. 3, 1936; s. Paul A. and Martha M. N.; m. Joan E. McAfee, Sept 12, 1959; children: Sonia, Paul. BS in Engring., U. Mich., 1957, MS in Engring., 1958; PhD, U. Calif., Berkeley, 1962. Rsch. asst. U. Calif., Berkeley, 1959-62; mathematician Shell Devel. Co., Houston, 1963-68, staff rsch. engr., 1968-74, sr. staff rsch. engr., 1974-80, rsch. assoc., 1980-90; Brown prof. civil and mech. engring. Rice U., Houston, 1989-2000, prof. emeritus, 2001—. U.S. nat. com. on theoretical and applied mechanics NRC, 1984-86, U.S. nat. com. for rock mechanics, 1991-95. Contbr. articles to profl. jours.; assoc. editor Jour. Applied Mechanics, 1972-76, 81-85; patentee in field. Fellow: ASME; mem.: NAE, Sigma Xi. Home: 492 Utica Ave Boulder CO 80304-0754 Home Phone: 303-440-1047. Business E-Mail: nordgren@rice.edu.

NORDHAUS, ROBERT RIGGS, lawyer; b. Albuquerque, Mar. 27, 1937; s. Robert J. and Virginia (Riggs) N.; m. Jean Friedberg, June 27, 1964; children: Ronald E., Hannah E. BA, Stanford U., 1960; LLB, Yale U., 1963. Bar: N.Mex. 1963, D.C. 1981, U.S. Supreme Ct. 1982. Asst. counsel U.S. House Reps., Washington, 1963-74, counsel interstate and fgn. commerce com., 1975-76; asst. adminstr. FEA, Washington, 1977; gen. counsel Fed. Energy Regulatory Commn., Washington, 1977-80; ptnr. Van Ness, Feldman & Curtis, Washington, 1981-93; gen. counsel Dept. of Energy, Washington, 1993-97; ptnr. Van Ness Feldman, Washington, 1997—. Professorial lectr. George Washington Law Sch., Washington, 2001—. 2d. lt. U.S. Army, 1960. Mem. Fed. Energy Bar Assn. (bd. dirs. 1989-92). Office: Van Ness Feldman Ste 700 1050 Thomas Jefferson St NW Washington DC 20007-3877 Office Phone: 202-298-1800.

NORDLAND, GERALD, museum administrator, historian, consultant; b. LA; AB, JD, U. So. Calif. Dean of faculty Chouinard Art Sch., LA, 1960-64; dir. Washington Gallery of Modern Art, 1964-66, San Francisco Mus. Art, 1966-72, Frederick S. Wight Art Galleries, UCLA, 1973-77, Milw. Art Mus., 1977-85; ind. curator, author, editor Chgo., 1985—. Author: Paul Jenkins, 1972, Gaston Lachaise/The Man and His Work, 1974, Richard Diebenkorn, 1987, rev. edit., 2001, Frank Lloyd Wright: In the Realm of Ideas, 1988, Zhou Brothers, 1994, Ynez Johnston, 1996, Lev Syrkin, 1998, Twentieth Century American Drawings, 1998, Jon Schueler: To The North, 2002, In the Spirit of the Times, 2003, Emerson Woelffer: A Solo Flight, 2003, Richard Drebenkorn in New Mexico, 2007, Breaking the Mold, 2007. Gaston Lachaise Found. grantee, 1973-74; John Simon Guggenheim Found. fellow, 1985-86. Home and Office: 645 W Sheridan Rd Chicago IL 60613-3316 Office Phone: 773-348-5133. Personal E-mail: geraldnordland@sbcglobal.net.

NORDLEY, GERALD DAVID, investor, writer; b. Mpls., May 22, 1947; s. V. Gerald and Evelyn May (Whitesel) N.; (div. 1973); 1 child, Sharon; m. Gayle Ann Wiesner, May 9, 1976; children: Jeffrey Goldberg, Andrew Nordley. BA in Physics, Macalester Coll., 1969; MS in System Mgmt., U. So. Calif., LA, 1980. Enlisted USAF, 1969, commd. 2nd lt., 1970, advanced through grades to maj., 1982; inter-range ops. officer Network Ops. Div., Sunnyvale AFB, Calif., 1973-76; chief orbital ops. br. Def. Satellite Communications Directorate, L.A. AFB, 1976-81; chief spacecraft engr. br. DSCS III Program Office, L.A. AFB, 1981-82; battle dir. Mangilsan Liason Annex, Mang Il San, South Korea, 1983; chief advanced propulsion br. A.F. Rocket Propulsion Lab., Edwards AFB, Calif., 1984-86; rsch. staff mgr. ARIES office Astronautics Lab., Edwards AFB, 1986-89; ret. USAF, 1989; writer, pvt. investor Sunnyvale, 1990—. Mem. dir. Macalester Coll. Rep. Club, St. Paul, 1967-68; pres. Park Knowles Estates Property Owners Assn., Boron, Calif., 1988; co-chair Silicon Valley Writers Workshop, Cupertino, Calif., 1992, 93; treas. CONTACT: Cultures of the Imagination, 1997—. Decorated Air Force Commendation medal with 4 oak leaf clusters, Meritorious Svc. medal with 1 oak leaf cluster; recipient Anlab award Analog Mag., 1992, 93, 2000. Fellow Brit. Interplanetary Soc.; mem. AIAA (sr.; elec. propulsion com. 1984-86), Air Force Assn., Sci. Fiction Writers Am., Whensday People Writers Group, Space Access Soc., Am. Legion. Unitarian Universalist. Avocation: amateur astronomy. E-mail: gdnordley@aol.com.

NORDLIE, ROBERT CONRAD, biochemistry educator; b. Willmar, Minn., June 11, 1930; s. Peder Conrad and Myrtle (Spindler) N.; m. Sally Ann Christianson, Aug. 23, 1959; children: Margaret, Melissa, John. BS St. Cloud State Coll., Minn., 1952; MS, U. N.D., 1957, PhD, 1960. Tchg., rsch. asst. biochemistry U. N.D. Med. Sch., Grand Forks, 1955-60, James J. Hill rsch. prof. biochemistry, 1962-74, Chester Fritz disting. prof. biochemistry, 1974—, Cornatzer prof., chmn. dept. biochemistry and molecular biology, 1983-2000, Chester Fritz disting. emeritus prof., 2000—. Hon. prof. San Marcos U., Lima, Peru, 1981, 82—; emeritus prof., 2000-; NIH fellow Inst. Enzyme Rsch., U. Wis., 1960-61; mem. biochemistry study sect. NIH; merit rev. com. VA, 1994—; cons. enzymology Oak Ridge, 1961—; vis. prof. Tokyo Biomed. Inst., 1984; mem. predoctoral fellowship rev. group Howard Hughes Inst., 1990-93. Mem. editorial bd.: Jour. Biol. Chemistry, Biochimca et Biophysica Acta. Research publs. on enzymology relating to metabolism of various carbohydrates in mammalian livers, regulation blood sugar levels. Served with AUS, 1953-55. Recipient Disting. Alumnus award St. Cloud State U., 1983; recipient Sigma Xi Rsch. award, 1969, Golden Apple award U. N.D., 1968, Edgar Dale award U. N.D., 1983, Burlington No. Faculty Scholar award, 1987, Thomas J. Clifford Faculty Achievement award for excellence in rsch. U. N.D. Found., 1993, Hippocratic Dignity award, 2005. Mem. AAAS, Am. Soc. Biol. Chemistry and Molecular Biology, Am. Chem. Soc., Internat. Union Biochemists, Soc. Exptl. Biology and Medicine, Am. Inst. Nutrition, Sigma Xi, Alpha Omega Alpha. Home: 162 Columbia Ct Grand Forks ND 58203-2947 Office Phone: 701-777-2751. Business E-Mail: rnordlie@medicine.nodak.edu.

NORDLINGER, GERSON, investor; b. Washington, Feb. 2, 1916; s. Gerson and Camille (Bensinger) N. BA, George Washington U., 1935; BCS, Benjamin Franklin U., 1939. Head Navy Dept. Bur. Aeros. Budget, 1946-50; trustee Washington Real Estate Investment Trust, 1961-98; pres. Nordlinger Investment Corp., Washington, 1955—. Chmn. D.C. Arts Commn., 1965-67; v.p. Nat. Symphony Assn., 1953—, Nat. Ballet, 1966-70, Alliance Francaise, 1980—; pres. Prevention of Blindness Soc., 1960-67; treas. Friendship House, 1951-69; vice chmn. D.C. Recreation Bd., 1960-67; trustee Washington Performing Arts Soc., Mt. Vernon Coll., Washington Opera, Cathedral Choral Soc., Phillips Collection; life trustee Nat. Symphony Orch., 1952—; state com. Republican Party, 1952-64. Lt. comdr. Supply Corps, USNR, 1941-46, PTO. Recipient Angel of Arts award, 2001. Mem. D.C. Inst. CPAs, Cosmos Club, Met. Club. Home: 2700 Calvert St NW # 515 Washington DC 20008-2621 also: 3900 Galt Ocean Dr Fort Lauderdale FL 33308-6631 Personal E-mail: gersonn@aol.com.

NORDLOH, DAVID JOSEPH, literature and language professor, dean; b. Cin., May 3, 1942; s. Joseph Westerman and Josephine (Fusz) N.; m. Barbara Jane Beddow, June 29, 1968; children: Geoffrey David, Jennifer Ellen Blum. AB in English, Coll. of Holy Cross, 1964; PhD in English, Ind. U., 1969. From asst. prof. to prof. emeritus English Ind. U., Bloomington, 1969—2007, prof. emeritus English, 2007—, assoc. dean faculties, 2003—06. Vis. assoc. prof. U. Va., Charlottesville, 1978; dir. Am. Studies Program, Ind. U., 1987-94. Gen. editor: A Selected Edition of W.D. Howells, 1974—; editor: Twayne's United States Author's Series, 1978-90; co-editor: American Literary Scholarship, 1986—; mem. editl. bd. Walter Scott Edition, 1984—; adv. bd. The Writings of James Fenimore Cooper, 1995—. Pres. Bloomington Symphony Orch., 1986-88, 93-94. Fulbright scholar, 1982-83. Mem. Am. Lit. Assn. Home: 1600 Morganton Rd L-3 Pinehurst NC 28374 Personal E-mail: nordloh@indiana.edu.

NORDLUND, DONALD CRAIG, lawyer, electronics executive; b. Chgo., May 23, 1949; s. Donald E. and Jane (Houston) N.; m. Sally Baum, Sept. 7, 1975; children: Courtney Elizabeth, Michael Andrew, Laurie Katherine. AB in Polit. Sci. and Journalism, Stanford U., 1971; JD, Vanderbilt U., 1974. Assoc. Ware & Freidenrich, Palo Alto, Calif., 1974-77; atty. Hewlett-Packard Co., Palo Alto, 1977-87, assoc. gen. counsel, sec., dir., 1987-99; sr. v.p., gen. counsel, sec. Agilent Technologies, Inc., 1999—. Panelist inn. disclosure doc. seminar Practicing Law Inst., 1982—2005, co-chmn., 2002—04; bd. dirs. Addison Ave. Fed. Credit Union, 1985—; sec., dir. Agilent Tech. Found. and various Agilent Tech. subsidiaries, 1999—; mem. corp. law com. ABA, 2005—. Chmn. bd. dirs. Santa Clara County chpt. Jr. Achievement, 1995-97. Mem.: Assn. Gen. Counsel (pres. 2006—07), Assn. Corp. Counsel (bd. dirs. San Francisco chpt. 1984—2000, pres. 1989—90, nat. bd. dirs. 1995—2001, Founding dir. Bay Area Chapter), Soc. Corp. Sec. and Governance Profl. (pres. San Francisco region 1986—88, bd. dirs. 1987—90, mem. exec. com. 1988—89, chmn. securities law com. 1995—98, nat. chmn. 1999—2000). Avocations: tennis, skiing, sailing, golf. Office: Agilent Technologies Inc 5301 Stevens Creek Blvd Santa Clara CA 95051

NORDMAN, CHRISTER ERIC, chemistry professor; b. Helsinki, Finland, Jan. 23, 1925; came to U.S., 1948, naturalized, 1960; s. Eric Johan and Gertrud (Nordgren) N.; m. Barbara Lorraine Neal, Nov. 28, 1952 (div. 1993); children: Christina, Aleta, Eric, Carl; m. Outi Marttila, Dec. 28, 1994. Dipl. Ing., Finnish Inst. Tech., Helsinki, 1949; PhD, U. Minn., 1953. Research asso. Inst. Cancer Research, Phila., 1953-55; mem. faculty U. Mich., Ann Arbor, 1955—, prof. chemistry, 1964-95; prof. emeritus, 1995—. Mem. U.S. Nat. Com. Crystallography, 1970-72. Served with Finnish Army, 1943-44. NIH spl. fellow, 1971-72; recipient A.L. Patterson award, 1997. Fellow AAAS; mem. Am. Chem. Soc., Am. Phys. Soc., Am. Crystallographic Assn., Finnish Soc. Scis. and Letters. Home: 27 Haverhill Ct Ann Arbor MI 48105-1406 Office: Univ Mich Dept Chemistry Ann Arbor MI 48109 Business E-Mail: cnordman@umich.edu.

NORDSIECK, KAREN ANN, custom apparel company executive; b. Ft. Campbell, Ky., Nov. 2, 1955; d. Reuben James and Shirley Jean (Walters) Simpson; m. Kenneth M. Farber, Mar. 5, 1977 (div. July 1982); children: Carissa Ann, Laurie Jean; m. Derrell E. Hiett, May 10, 1985 (div. May 1989); m. Michael Louis Nordsieck, June 2, 1989. Student, El Paso C.C., 1976, student, 1984. Sales clk. Busy B Gift Shop, El Paso, Tex., 1973; svc. rep. Bell Sys., El Paso and Seattle, 1974-85; substitute tchr. Cleburne County Elem. Sch., Heflin, Ala., 1986; credit clk. Wakefields, Anniston, Ala., 1986-87; svc. rep. Ala. Power, Anniston, 1986-88; beauty cons. May Kay Cosmetics, El Paso and Heflin, 1983-88; mgr. Rock's T-Shirts & Screen Printing, El Paso, 1988-92; owner Custom Designs and Promotions, Richmond, Mo., 1992-96; svc. rep. New AT&T, Kansas City, Mo., 1993—; owner Kreations by Karen, Independence, 1996—. Past matron Eastgate #367 Order of Ea. Star, 2003; liaison for ptnrs. in edn. El Paso Ind. Sch. Dist., Rock's T-Shirts and Screen Print, El Paso, 1990-1992; co-chairperson quality of work life com. Southwestern Bell, El Paso, 1984; union steward Communication Workers Am., El Paso, 1974-75. Troop leader Brownies, Girl Scouts U.S.A., troop # 126, Heflin, 1985-88, mag. chair, 1986; v.p. Clendenin Elem. PTA, El Paso, 1989-90, pres., 1990-92; family support leader Ft. Bliss Family Support, El Paso, 1990-91; strategic planning com. El Paso Ind. Sch. Dist., 1990-91; campus improvement com. Clendenin Elem., 1991-92, vol. pub. schs., 1989-92; parent adv. com. ctrl. area El Paso Ind. Sch. Dist., 1989-92; mem. Richmond PTA, 1992-1998, Battlefield Piece Makers Quilt Guild, 1995—; com. mem. Richmond A-Plus Sch. Planning, 1994-95; co-chair Jr. Class Parents After Prom/Project Graduation, 1995-96; chmn., editor CWA Local 6327 newsletter, The Localizer, 1997-98, union steward, 1996-98; mem. Southwestern Bell/CWA United Way com., 1997-98; chair office improvement com. Southwestern Bell Kansas City Soc., 1997-98. Recipient Outstanding Troop Leader award Girl Scouts U.S.A., Anniston, 1987, cert. outstanding svc. Clendenin PTA, El Paso, 1990-92; cert. of honor Clendenin Elem. Sch., 1990-92, Cert. of Appreciation, 1991-92; Cert. of Appreciation, Ft. Bliss Army Family Support, 1991, plaque Vols. in Pub. Sch., El Paso, 1991-92, Ptnrs. in Edn., El Paso Ind. Sch. Dist., 1991-92, Desert Storm vol. pin Ptnrs. in Edn., 1991, Pres. Appreciation award S.W. Bell, 1997 Mem.: Battlefield Piecemakers Quilt Guild (sec. 2000—01, chair newsletter 2000—01), Tel. Pioneers, Order Ea. Star (Worthy Matron 2004, grand chpt. com. 2005). Mem. Assembly Of God Ch. Avocations: sewing, painting, reading, sailing, quilting. Office: Kreations by Karen 15601 E 3rd Street Ct S Independence MO 64050-1970 Business E-Mail: mknordsk@swbell.net.

NORDSTRAND, NATHALIE ELIZABETH JOHNSON, artist; b. Woburn, Mass., Nov. 6, 1932; d. Edward N. and Ruth Peterson Johnson; m. Robert I. Nordstrand, Jan. 12, 1962. AA, Bradford Jr. Coll., 1952; BA, Columbia U., 1954, Barnard Coll., 1954; studied with with Jay Connaway, Don Stone, Roger Curtis, Paul Strisik. Rsch. assoc. Gerontology Age Ctr. of New Eng., Boston, 1955-64; clk. corp. dir. Johnson Bros. Greenhouses, Inc., Woburn, 1958-84; owner Nordstrand Gallery, Rockport, Mass., 1970-99. Exhibited at Nat. Acad. Galleries, NYC, Springfield Mus. Fine Arts, Hammond Mus., North Salem, NYC, Bhulabha Meml. Inst., Bombay, India, Copley Soc. at Boston Symphony Hall, Hermann Fine Arts Ctr., Marietta, Ohio, Am. C. of C., Hong Kong, 1975-76, Silvermine Guild, Conn., 1976, Wall of Fame, Balt. Watercolor Soc., 1976, Ann. Copley Masters Exhbn. Boston, others; one woman shows include Rockport (Mass.) Art Assn., 1969, Laura Knotts Art Gallery, Bradford Coll., 1982, Reading Pub. Libr. Found., 1997; several invited exhibitions; paintings in Nat. Mus. Am. Art, Smithsonian Inst., 1994, Best of Watercolors, 1995, Best of Oil Painting, 1996, Landscape Inspirations, 1997, Gallery of Marine Art, 1998. Planning bd. North Suburban Art Festival, 1963—68; chair. planned giving Barnard Coll., NYC, 2003—04. Named Citizen of Yr., Reading chpt. Am. Cancer Soc., 1983; recipient Louis E. Seley award, Salmagundi Art Club, 1974, Excellence in Watercolor award, Rockport Art Assn., 1997, Philip Isenberg Meml. award, Salmagundi Club, 1997, more than 180 awards in nat. and regional competition, 1960—. Fellow Am. Artist Profl. League (Gold medal 1971, 75, award 1978-79); mem. Acad. Artists Assn. (Watercolor awards 1973-74, 76-77, New Eng. Heritage award 1993), Copley Soc. Boston (master artist), Hudson Valley, North Shore (bd. dirs. 1964-67, 86-95), Rockport Art Assn. (Lifetime Dedication to Promotion of Art award 1999, Joseph Santoro Meml. award 2005, Robert Dunnelly Meml. award 2007), Affiliated Art Assn. Mass. (v.p. 1980), Reading Art Assn. (charter, program chmn. 1960-86, Pres.'s awards 1973-80), Am. Watercolor Soc. (juror internat. exhbn. 1992), Allied Artists Am. (Watercolor Gold medals 1973-74), New Eng. Watercolor Soc. (2d v.p. 1984-90), Boston Watercolor Soc. (award 1975), Guild Boston Artists (bd. dirs. 1986-99, A. Lassall Ripley award 1993), Reading Assn. Fine and Performing Arts (charter, bd. dirs. 1993), Nat. Mus. Women in Arts (charter mem.), Salmagundi Art Club (40 awards including MacGowin Tuttle Meml. award 1976, 78-79, Elliot Liskin Meml. award 1988, Steven Blackman award 1988, Joseph Hartley award 1989, 2001, 2002, Mortimer Freehof Meml. award 1991, Bruce Crane award 1994, Rita Duis Meml. award 2001, Margery Saroka Meml. award 2003, Thomas Moran award 2004, Ogden Pleissner Meml. award 2006). Methodist. Address: 384 Franklin St Reading MA 01867-1036 Office Phone: 751-944-4252. Personal E-mail: nordstrands@aol.com.

NORDSTROM, BLAKE W., retail executive; b. 1960; With Nordstrom, Inc., Seattle, 1974—, v.p. & gen. mgr. Wash./Alaska region, 1991—95, co-pres. Seattle, 1995—2000, pres., 2000—, bd. dir., 2005—. Office: Nordstrom Inc 1617 Sixth Ave Seattle WA 98101-1742 *

NORDYKE, ELEANOR COLE, demographer, researcher, public health nurse; b. LA, June 15, 1927; d. Ralph G. and Louise Noble (Carter) Cole; m. Robert Allan Nordyke, June 18, 1950 (dec. 1997); children: Mary Ellen Nordyke-Grace, Carolyn Nordyke Cozzette, Thomas J., Susan Nordyke Bell., Gretchen Nordyke Worthington. BS, Stanford U., 1950; P.H.N. accreditation, U. Calif.-Berkeley, 1952; MPH, U. Hawaii, 1969. RN. Pub. health nurse San Francisco Dept. Health, 1950-52; nurse-tchr. Punahou Sch., Honolulu, 1966-67; clinic coordinator East-West Population Inst., East-West Ctr., Honolulu, 1969-75, population rschr., 1975-82, rsch. fellow, 1982-92. Cons. Hawaii Commn. on Population, Honolulu, 1970-83; mem. Hawaii Policy Action Group for Family Planning, Honolulu, 1971-89, chmn., 1976-77; nurse-cons. vol. Straub Clinic and Hosp., 2001--. Author: The Peopling of Hawaii, 1977, 2d rev. edit., 1989, A Profile of Hawaii's Elderly Population, 1984; author: (with Robert Gardner) The Demographic Situation in Hawaii, 1974; author: Pacific Images-Views from Captain Cook's Third Voyage, 1999; editor: I'm Third-An American Boy of Depression Years - Memoirs of Robert A. Nordyke, MD, 2003; mem. editl. bd. Hawaiian Jour. History, 1980—; contbr. articles to profl. jours. Bd. dirs. YMCA, Honolulu, 1970-85, YMCA Camp Erdman Br., 1985—, vice-chmn. 1978-79, chmn. YMCA Camp Erdman, 1989-92; bd. dirs. Hawaii Planned Parenthood, 1974-78, Friends of Libr. of Hawaii, 1985-87, 2002-2005; trustee Hawaiian Hist. Soc., 1978-82, Arcadia Retirement Residence, Honolulu, 1978-87; mem. liberal arts coun. Hawaii Pacific U., 1988—. Mem. Population Reference Bur., Hawaii Econ. Assn., Hawaiian Hist. Soc., Friends of East-West Ctr., Friends of Univ. Hawaii Sch. Medicine, Stanford Nurses Alumni Assn., Stanford Alumni Assn. (bd. dirs. Hawaii chpt.), U. Hawaii Sch. Pub. Health Alumni Assn. (life), Gen. Fed. Women's History Club, Adventure Club of Honolulu, Book Reading Clubs, Captain-Cook Soc., Outrigger Canoe Club, Morning Music Club, Caledonian Soc., Phi Beta Kappa. Democrat. Congregationalist. Avocations: music, art, swimming, Hawaiian books, travel. Home: 2013 Kakela Dr Honolulu HI 96822-2158 Personal E-mail: rnordyke@aol.com.

NORELL, MARK ALLEN, paleontologist, curator; b. St. Paul, July 26, 1957; s. Albert Donald Norell and Helen Louise Soltau; m. Vivian Pan, Nov. 1, 1991; 1 child, Inga Pan. BS, Long Beach State U., 1980; MS, San Diego State U., 1983; PhD, Yale U., 1988. Assoc. curator Am. Mus., NYC, 1989—99, chmn. dept., 1996—99, divsn. chmn., curator, 1999—2005. Adj. assoc. prof. dept. biology Yale U., New Haven, 1991-99; adj. prof. Columbia U., 1995—; lectr. in the field. Author: All You Need to Know About Dinosaurs, 1991, Discovering Dinosaurs, 1995, 2d edit., 2000 (recipient Young Readers Book of Yr. award, Scientific American), Searching for Velociraptor, 1996, A Dinosaur and Its Nest, 1999, Unearthing the Dragon, 2005, and several others; contbr. articles to profl. jours. Named Disting. Alumnus, Long Beach State U., 2000, NYC Leader of Yr., NY Times. Fellow: Explorer's Club, Willi Hennig Soc.; mem.: Soc. Vertebrate Paleontology (Romer prize 1987). Achievements include contributing to the investigation of unearthing the remains of a perfectly preserved 130 million-year-old new species of dinosaur in China, which provides a look at how prehistoric creatures slept. Office: Am Museum of Natural History 79th at Central Park W New York NY 10024-5192 Home Phone: 917-710-6399; Office Phone: 212-769-5804. Business E-Mail: norell@amnh.org.

NORELLI, TERIE THOMPSON, state legislator; b. Orange, NJ, July 7, 1952; d. George Russell and Iverna C. (Weber) Thompson; m. Allen M. Norelli, Dec. 31, 1973; children: Gina Marie, Daniel Thompson. BS in Math. summa cum laude, U. NH, 1985. Tchr. math. Winnacunnet H.S., Hampton, NH, 1985—95; mem. NH Ho. of Reps., Concord, 1996—, sci., tech. and energy com., 1996—2003, telecomm. oversight com., 1997—2003, ho. Dem. leadership, 1998—, asst. Dem. whip, 2002—04, asst. Dem. leader, 2005—, chair clean air subcom., 1998—2003, electric utility restructuring oversight com., 1998—2003, pub. works and hwys. com., 2003—05, rules com., 2003—05, co-chair reproductive rights caucus, 1996—, mem. legis. caucus for children, 1997—2002, mem. fin. com., 2005—. Participant in devel. series geometry insvc. workshops U. NH, 1986-89. Area team Nat. Abortion Rights Action League of NH, Portsmouth, 1990-94, bd. dirs., Concord, 1996-2000; chair Naral-Prochoice NH Pac, 2001-; bd. dirs. Sexual Assault Support Svcs., Portsmouth, 1992-96, pres. bd., 1993-95; del. to Joint US-China Conf. on Women's Issues, Beijing, 1995; organizing com. Bringing Back Beijing '95, Statewide Women's Conf., Concord, 1996, Beijing +5 Tri-State Preperation Conf., 1999; adv. bd. Feminist Health Ctr. Ports, Portsmouth, 1996-97; mem. Leadership Seacoast, 1995. Recipient NH Women's Lobby Meritorious Svc. award, 2002, Naral Pro-Choice N.H. Champion for Choice award, 2003, NASW-NH Legislator of Yr. award, 2004. Mem. Phi Beta Kappa, Phi Kappa Phi, Pi Mu Epsilon. Avocations: travel, arts and culture, running. Office: Rm 210 LOB State St Concord NH 03301 Office Phone: 603-271-2136.

NOREM, RICHARD FREDERICK, SR., musician, educator; b. Joliet, Ill., June 28, 1931; s. Oscar Lewis and Mabel Vera (Meyer) N.; m. Sally Lou Jarvis, July 24, 1954; 1 son, Richard Frederick II. Mus.B., U. Rochester, 1953, Mus.M., 1958; postgrad., Guildhall Sch., London, 1974. Instr. Joliet Musical Coll., Ill., 1951-53; tchr. Rochester Pub. Schs., NY, 1956-57; mem. faculty La. State U., Baton Rouge, 1957-95, prof., asst. dean music, 1969-84, prof. emeritus Baton Rouge, 1995. Dir., sec.-treas. Bank Commerce, 1983-97; bd. dirs., sec.-treas. NBC Fin. Corp., 1988-97; adv. bd. First Am. Tenn. Bank., 1997-99, AmSouth Bank, 1999-2003; ptnr. Am. Train Yard. Musician: Jackson Symphony, 1960—65, Lake Charles Symphony, 1966—69. Mem. Baton Rouge Symphony Orch., 1957—, Timm Woodwind Quintet, 1957-95; founder La. State U. Faculty Brass Quintet (now named Norem Brass Quintet of La. State U.), 1999. With USMC Band, 1953-56. Mem. Am. Legion (past post comdr.), Rolls-Royce Owners Club (sec.-treas. So. Delta region 1982-98, regional chmn. 1997-99), Norwegian Club Baton Rouge, La. State U. Faculty Club, Baton Rouge Model R.R. Club, Rotary (Paul Harris fellow). Republican. Episcopalian. Home: 4821 Sweetbriar St Baton Rouge LA 70808-8660 Office: La State U Sch Music Baton Rouge LA 70803-0001 Business E-Mail: richard@clamp.net. *I have been blessed by the divine creator with an artistic talent in music to which I have dedicated my life. Early during my performing career I knew I must share with others the knowledge I had obtained in music; consequently my goals have been to train and educate the hundreds of music students I have taught during my teaching career. I have also continued to bring beauty to our world in my own way as an active performing musician in the Baton Rouge Symphony Orchestra.*

NOREN, MARC B., lawyer; b. Balt., 1955; married; 2 children. BA, U. Balt., 1990, JD, 1994. Bar: Md. 1995. Dept. head clk.'s office Cir. Ct. Balt. City, dir. case mgmt., 1994—96; with Adelberg, Rudow, Dorf & Hendler, Balt., 1996—, assoc., mem., 2002—. Cons., lectr. in field. Co-author: Civil Practice Manual: Circuit Court for Baltimore City. Named one of Top Lawyers of the Next Generation, Balt. Mag., 2003. Mem.: ABA, Balt. County Bar Assn. (mem. family law com.), Bar Assn. Balt. City (past co-chair family law sect., jud. adminstrn. com.), Md. State Bar Assn. Office: Adelberg Rudow Dorf & Hendler 7 St Paul St Ste 600 Baltimore MD 21202 Office Phone: 410-539-5195. E-mail: MNoren@AdelbergRudow.com. *

NORFLEET, LEONTINE SANDRA, retired biologist; d. James Edward and Dorothy Calloway Norfleet. BS, CUNY, NYC, 1957; MA in Biol. and Physiol. Scis., Hunter Coll., NYC, 1964; MBA in Human Resources Mgmt., Adelphi U., Garden City, NY, 1994. Clin. microbiologist Bklyn. Jewish Hosp., 1957—63; asst. bacteriologist Byrd S. Coler Hosp., Roosevelt Island, NY, 1963—64; med. rschr. LI Jewish Hosp., Ney Hyde Pk., NY, 1964—67; biochemistry assoc. Endo Labs./Dupont-Merck/Bristol Meyers Squibb, Garden City, 1967—2004, quality assurance specialist, scientist, auditor, quality engr. Vol. NYC Ballet, 2004—. Mem.: Met. Opera Guild, Am. Ballet Theater Guild, NYC Ballet Guild. Democrat. Roman Catholic. Avocations: exercise, ballet, reading, movies. Home: 111-39 201 St Saint Albans NY 11412

NORGAARD, RICHARD BRUCE, economist, educator, consultant; b. Washington, Aug. 18, 1943; s. John Trout and Marva Dawn (Andersen) N.; m. Marida Jane Fowle, June 19, 1965 (div.); children: Kari Marie, Marc Anders; m. Nancy A. Rader, June 5, 1993; children: Addie Nelle, Mathiesen Rader. BA in Econs., U. Calif., Berkeley, 1965; MS in Agrl. Econs., Oreg. State U., 1967; PhD in Econs., U. Chgo., 1971. Instr. Oreg. Coll. Edn., 1967-68; asst. prof. agrl. and resource econs. U. Calif., Berkeley, 1970-76, assoc. prof., 1976-77, 80-87, assoc. prof. energy and resources, 1987-92, prof. energy and resources, 1992—. Project specialist Ford Found., Brazil, 1978-79; environ. cons. to internat. devel. agencies; sci. com. on problems of the environment U.S. Nat. Rsch. Coun.; founding chmn. bd. Redefining Progress, 1993-97; sci. adv. bd. US EPA, 2000-04; mem. ind. sci. bd. Calif. Bay-Delta Authority. Author: Development Betrayed: The End of Progress and a Coevolutionary Revisioning of the Future, 1994; chpt. rev. editor Millenium Ecosys. Assessment, 2004-05; mem. editl. bd. numerous academic jours.; contbr. articles to profl. jours. Active civil rights, environ., and peace orgns. Mem. AAAS, Am. Econs. Assn., Internat. Soc. Ecol. Econs. (pres. 1998-2001, past pres. 2002-2003), Fedn. Am. Scientists, Assn. Environ. and Resource Econs., Am. Inst. Biol. Scis. (bd. dirs. 2000-, treas. 2004—). Home: 1198 Keith Ave Berkeley CA 94708-1607 Office: U Calif Energy & Resources Program 310 Barrows Hall Berkeley CA 94720-3050 Business E-Mail: norgaard@berkeley.edu.

NORGARD, KAREN-SAM, art educator; b. Plainfield, NJ, June 6, 1952; d. Arthur Denver and Geneva Rae (Lasares) Norgard; m. David Lee Golden, May 2, 1987; children: William Golden, Max Golden. BFA, U. NC, Greensboro, 1974; MFA, U. Cin., 1976. Asst. prof. Chestnut Hill Coll., Pa., 1983—87; lectr. Cazenovia Coll., 1993—94; prof. Savannah Coll. Art & Design, Ga.; assoc. prof. U. Wis., Whitewater, 2003—. One-woman shows include J.R. Kortman Design Ctr., 2004, West Bend Art Mus., 2006, New Vision Gallery, 2007, over 70 exhbns. Mem.: The Guild, Founds. Art Theory and Edn., Soc. N.Am. Goldsmiths. Office: U Wis Dept Art 800 W Main St Whitewater WI 53190 Personal E-mail: karensamnorgard@mac.com.

NORGLE, CHARLES RONALD, SR., federal judge; b. Mar. 3, 1937; BBA, Northwestern U., Evanston, Ill., 1964; JD, John Marshall Law Sch., Chgo., 1969. Asst. state's atty. DuPage County, Ill., 1969-71, dep. pub. defender Ill., 1971-73, assoc. judge Ill., 1973-77, 78-81, cir. judge Ill., 1977-78, 81-84; judge U.S. Dist. Ct. (no. dist.) Ill., Chgo., 1984—2006, Criminal Law Com., Chgo., 2006—. Mem. exec. com. No. Dist. Ill.; mem. 7th Cir. Jud. Coun., 7th Cir. Jud. Conf. planning com., subcom. grant requests Fed. Defender Orgn., Fed. Defender Svcs. Com.; mem. Jud. Conf. Criminal Law Com.; adj. faculty Northwestern U. Sch. Law, John Marshall Law Sch., Chgo.; pres. Atticus Finch Inn Ct. Mem. ABA, Fed. Bar Assn., Fed. Circuit Bar Assn., Ill. Bar Assn., DuPage County (Ill.) Bar Assn., Nat. Attys. Assn., DuPage Assn. Women Attys., Chgo. Legal Club, Northwestern Club. Office: US Dist Ct 219 S Dearborn St Ste 2346 Chicago IL 60604-1802

NORGREN, WILLIAM ANDREW, retired religious denomination administrator; b. Frostburg, Md., May 5, 1927; s. William Andrew and Martha Elizabeth Leona (Richardson) N. BA, Coll. William and Mary, 1948; STB, now STM, Gen. Theol. Sem., NYC, 1953; LittB, Oxford U., Eng., 1959; DD (hon.), Gen. Theol. Sem., NYC, 1984, Berkley Div. Sch., Yale U., New Haven, 1995. Ordained to ministry Episcopal Ch., 1953. Chaplain Christ Ch. Cathedral, Oxford, 1955-59; exec. dir. Commn. on Faith and Order Nat. Coun. Chs. of Christ in U.S.A., NYC, 1959-71, mem. gen. bd., 1979-95; pastoral asst. Trinity Ch., NYC, 1972-74; assoc. ecumenical officer Episcopal Ch., NYC, 1975-79, ecumenical officer, 1979-94, theol. cons., 1995-2000. Observer 2d Vatican Coun., Roman Cath. Ch., Vatican City, 1963-65; mem. assemblies World Co. Chs., various cities, 1961, 68, 83, 91. Editor: Living Room Dialogues, 1965, Implications of the Gospel, 1988, Toward Full Communion and Concordat of Agreement, 1991; author: Commentary on Called to Common Mission, 1999. Fellow, Gen. Theol. Sem., 1953—55. Democrat. Episcopalian. Avocations: art, music, theater, walking.

NORINS, ARTHUR LEONARD, dermatologist, educator; b. Chgo., Dec. 2, 1928; s. Russell Joseph and Elsie (Lindemann) N.; m. Mona Lisa Wetzer, Sept. 12, 1954; children: Catherine, Nan, Jane, Arthur. BS in Chem. Engring, Northwestern U., 1951, MS in Physiology, 1953, MD, 1955. Diplomate: Am. Bd. Dermatology; subcert. in dermatopathology. Intern U. Mich., Ann Arbor, 1955-56; resident in dermatology Northwestern U., Chgo., 1956-59; asst. prof. Stanford U., 1961-64; prof., chmn. dept. dermatology, prof. pathology Ind. U. Sch. Medicine, Indpls., 1964-93, prof. emeritus, 1993—. Mem. staff Riley Children's Hosp., Univ. Hosp., Wishard Hosp.; cons. VA Hosp. Contbr. articles to profl. jours. Capt. M.C. U.S. Army, 1959-61. Recipient Pres.' award Ind. U., 1979 Fellow ACP; mem. Am. Acad. Dermatology (bd. dirs.), Am. Dermatol. Assn., Soc. Pediatric Dermatology (founder, past pres.), Am. Soc. Dermatopathology, Am. Soc. Photobiology (founder), Soc. Investigative Dermatology. Home: 10100 Torre Ave Apt 211 Cupertino CA 95014-2168 Office: 550 University Blvd Ste 3240 Indianapolis IN 46202-5149 E-mail: norinssr@ix.netcom.com.

NORIS, PETER DANA, investment company executive; b. Dec. 5, 1955; BS in Econs., U. Pa., 1978; MBA in Fin., NYU, 1984. CFA. Portfolio mgr. Continental Asset Mgmt., NYC, 1983-84; prin. Morgan Stanley, NYC, 1984-92; v.p. Salomon Bros., NYC, 1992-95; exec. v.p., chief investment officer Axa Fin./Equitable, NYC, 1995—2004; chief investment officer Northstar Fin. Services, NYC, 2005—07, Ivy Asset Mgmt. Corp., NYC, 2007—. Bd. dirs. Alliance Capital Mgmt., NYC; chmn. EQ Advisors Trust, AXA Premier VIP Trust. Office: Ivy Asset Management Corp 1633 Broadway 30th Fl New York NY 10019 *

NORKIN, CYNTHIA CLAIR, retired physical therapist; b. Boston, May 6, 1932; d. Miles Nelson and Carolyn (Green) Clair; m. Stanislav A Norkin, Feb. 19, 1955 (dec. 1970); 1 child, Alexandra. BS in Edn., Tufts U., 1954; cert. phys. therapist, Bouve Boston Coll., 1954; MS, Boston U., 1973, EdD, 1984. Instr. Bouve Boston Coll., 1954—55; staff phys. therapist New Eng. Med. Ctr., Boston, 1954—55, Abington (Pa.) Meml. Hosp., 1965—70, Ea. Montgomery Country Vis. Nurse Assn., 1970—72; asst. prof. phys. therapy Sargent Coll./Boston U., 1973—84; assoc. prof. phys. therapy, dir., founder Ohio U. Sch. Phys. Therapy, Athens, 1984—95, ret., 1995. Consult Boston Ctr Independent Living, Cambridge Vis Nurse Asn, Mass Medicaid Cost Effectiveness Project, 1978; secy Health Planning Coun Greater Boston, 1976—78; book, manuscript reviewer F A Davis Co, 1986—; arthritis adv comt Ohio Dept Health. Author (with P Levangie and C Norkin): Joint Structure and Function: A Comprehensive Analysis, 1983, 4th edit., 2005; author: (with D J White) Joint Measurement: A Guide to Goniometry, 1985; author: 3d edit., 2003. Trustee Brimmer and May Sch, 1980. Mem.: APHA, AAAS, Athens County Vis Nurse Asn (secy adv coun 1984—95), Mass Asn Mental health, Mass Physical Therapy Asn (chair quality assurance comt 1980—83), Am Physical Therapy Asn (on site evaluator comn on accreditation 1986—95). Episcopalian.

NORLAND, DONALD RICHARD, retired foreign service officer; b. Laurens, Iowa, June 14, 1924; s. Norman and Aletta (Brunsvold) N.; m. Patricia Bamman, Dec. 13, 1952; children: Richard Boyce, David, Patricia D. Student, Iowa State Tchrs. Coll., 1941-43, N.W. Mo. State Tchrs. Coll., 1943-44; BA, U. Minn., 1948, MS, 1950; postgrad., U. Mich., 1951-52, Grenoble U., France, 1948-49. Instr. history and polit. sci. U. No. Iowa, 1949-51; teaching fellow U. Mich., 1951-52; with Fgn. Svc., U.S. Dept. State, 1952-81; posts include Rabat, Morocco, 1952-56, Washington, 1956-58, Abidjan, Ivory Coast, 1958-60; mem. NATO del., Paris, 1961-63, NATO delegation, The Hague, The Netherlands, 1964-69; dep. chief mission Conakry, Guinea, 1970-72; U.S. Dept. State fellow Stanford (Calif.) U., 1969-70; dep. dir. Office Mil. Assistance and Sales, Bur. Politico-Mil. Affairs, Dept. State, Washington, 1972-73, chief polit. officers counseling br. Office Pers., 1973-75; dep. dir. Office Mgmt. Ops., 1975-76; amb. to Botswana, Lesotho and Swaziland, 1976-79; amb. to Chad, 1979-81; ret. Fgn. Svc., U.S. Dept. State, 1981; lectr. African affairs; internat. cons., specialist econ. devel. Chmn. African studies Fgn. Svc. Inst. of U.S. Dept. of State, Washington, 1987-89; program dir. Ctr. for Internat. Pvt. Enterprise affiliate U.S. C. of C., Washington, 1990-91; sr. cons. World Space, Inc., 1995, sr. policy advisor, 1996—. Bd. dirs. Calvert New Africa Fund, 1995. Lt. (j.g.) USNR, 1943-46. Mem. Am. Fgn. Svc. Assn. (v.p. for retirees 1993-95, sec. 1995-97, mem. editl. bd. Fgn. Svc. Jour. 1992-95), World Space Found. (pres. 1997-98). Home: 4000 Cathedral Ave NW Apt 636B Washington DC 20016-5286 Home Phone: 202-338-2026; Office Phone: 202-338-2026. E-mail: donnorland@aol.com.

NORMAN, ALBERT GEORGE, JR., lawyer; b. Birmingham, Ala., May 29, 1929; s. Albert G. and Ila Mae (Carroll) N.; m. Catherine Marshall DeShazo, Sept. 3, 1955; children: Catherine Marshall, Albert George III. BA, Auburn U., 1953; LLB, Emory U., 1958; MA, U. NC, 1960. Bar: Ga. 1957. Assoc. Moise, Post & Gardner, Atlanta, 1958-60, ptnr., 1960-62, Hansell & Post, Atlanta, 1962-86, Long, Aldridge & Norman, Atlanta, 1986-2000. Dir. Atlanta Gas Light Co., 1976-2000. Served with USAF, 1946-49. Mem. ABA, Ga. Bar Assn., Atlanta Bar Assn., Lawyers Club Atlanta (pres. 1973-74), Am. Law Inst., Am. Judicature Soc. (dir. 1975-78), Old War Horse Lawyers Club, (pres. 1991-92), Cherokee Town and Country Club. Episcopalian. Office: 134 Peachtree St NW Atlanta GA 30303-1802 Personal E-mail: almarnorman@mindspring.com.

NORMAN, ANNE E. C., state librarian; MLS. With Del. Divsn. Libraries, 1985—, acting dep. dir., 1999—2002, acting dir., 2002, dir., state libr., 2002—. Mem.: Chief Officers of State Libr. Agencies (treas. 2006—08). Office: Del Divsn of Libraries 43 S DuPont Hwy Dover DE 19901 Office Phone: 302-739-4748. Office Fax: 302-739-6787. Business E-Mail: anne.norman@state.de.us. *

NORMAN, ARNOLD MCCALLUM, JR., engineer; b. Little Rock, May 1, 1940; s. Arnold McCallum and Ann Carolyn (Gibson) N.; m. Sylvia Burton, July 1, 1962 (div. 1967); m. Marisha Irene Malin, June 7, 1969; children: Frank Lee, Paul James. BS in Physics, Ga. Inst. Tech., 1962. Test engr. Rocketdyne div. Rockwell Internat., Canoga Park, Calif., 1962-64, engr. in charge of various programs, 1964-75, engr. in charge, project engr. large chem. lasers, 1975-85, project engr. space sta. propulsion system, 1985-87, project engr. nat. launch system health mgmt. systems, 1987-92, project engr. kinetic energy weapons, 1993-94; project engr. advanced propulsion systems Rockwell Internat., Canoga Park, Calif., 1994-95, sr. engring. specialist, 1995-96; health mgmt. sys. team head, x-33 Aerospike rocket engine Boeing-N.Am. Rocketdyne Divsn., Canoga Park, Calif., 1996-97; cons. rocket propulsion sys., ops. and health mgmt., 1997—. Mem. ops. com. health mgmt. ctr. U. Cin., 1988-94; mem. program com. Ann. Internat. Conf. on Engring. Applications of Artificial Intelligence, 1988-90; presenter in field. Mem. editorial bd. Jour. Applied Intelligence, 1990-94; author numerous papers in field. Bd. dirs. Sebastopol Ctr. for Arts, 2000—, treas., 2003—04, pres. 2005-07. Fellow AIAA (assoc., sect. chair sr. adv. com. 1991-93, San Fernando Valley sect., chmn. 1989-90, sys. effectiveness & safety com. 1995-97), Inst. Advancement Engring; mem. Sonoma County Astronomical Soc., Tau Beta Pi. Avocations: astronomy, woodworking, photography. Home: 4053 Bones Rd Sebastopol CA 95472-9756

NORMAN, BOBBY DON, artist, writer, research scientist; b. Dallas, June 5, 1933; s. Reuben Ray Norman and Bessie Mae Norman-Gregory; m. Mae Pearl Delley (dec. July 8, 2001); 1 child, Parette Michelle. Cert. grad. (hon.), S.W. Sch. Bus. Adminstrn., 1959. Mgr. Mile High Club, Dallas, 1955—57; city distbn. clk. U.S. Post Office, Dallas, 1956—66; office mgr., co-dir. So. Christian Leadership Conf., Dallas, 1969—73; cmty. liaison dir. Planned Parenthood N.E. Tex., Dallas, 1974—76; exec. v.p., gen. mgr. Davis Norman & Zanders, Inc., Dallas, 1977—78; house mgr., supr. Fed. Bur. Prisons, Dallas, 1982—83; supr. Halfway House Tex. Dept. Corrections, Dallas, 1983—84; artist, writer, scientist, publ. speaker Dallas, 1955—. Founder, pres. Assn. Advancing Artists and Writers, Inc., Dallas, 1969—76; active Internat. Platform Assn. Pub. Spkrs., Dallas, 1977—78. Author: Artistic Theological Science, 1998, Biblical Geology, 1998, Tectonic Fundamentals of Biblical Geology, 1998, Tectonic Analyses and Notes of Modern Biblical Geology and Earth Science, 1998, Tectonic Verbal Postering and Various Advanced Studies of Earth Science, 1998, Glossary and Cross Reference of Biblical Geology and Tectonics, 1999, Biblical Geology: Events, Writings and Geo-Morality, 2003, Time of Babel: Biblical Geology and Tectonics, 2004; Artistic Theology and Perpendicular Line Compostion, 2005. Commr. Greater Dallas Cmty. Rels. Commn., 1970—72; mem. block partnership com. Greater Dallas Coun. Chs., 1970—71; organizer, tactical negotiator Dallas-Ft. Worth Coalition for the Free Flow of Info., 1970—72. Cpl. USAF, 1951—55, Korea. Recipient Tng. award, So. Christian Leadership Conf., 1969, Svc. award, Greater Dallas Cmty. Rels. Commn., 1972, Art award, Black C. of C., 1973. Mem.: Dallas Black C. of C. Baptist. Achievements include research in in Biblical geology. Avocations: fishing, art. Office: Biblical Geology and Tectonics PO Box 191904 Dallas TX 75219-8509 Office Phone: 214-534-2584.

NORMAN, CHRISTINA, broadcast executive; b. July 30, 1963; m. Charles Hunt; children: Zoe, Asha. BA, Boston U. Freelance prodn. coord MTV, 1986—91, prodn. mgr., 1991—93, supervising prodr., on-air promotions, 1993—94, dir., on-air promotions, 1994—95, v.p., on-air promotions, 1995—97, sr. v.p., on-air promotions, 1997—99, sr. v.p., mktg. & on-air promotion, 1999—2002; exec. v.p., gen. mgr. VH1, 2002—04, pres., 2004—05, MTV, 2005—. Named one of 10 Most Powerful Blacks in TV, Ebony mag., 2002, 100 Most Powerful Women in Entertainment, Hollywood Reporter, 2006; named to 100 Most Powerful Women in Hollywood list, 2003, 40 under 40 list, Crain's NY Bus., 2003; recipient Nat. Pub. Svc. award, Television Acad. Emmy Awards, 2002, Namiq Qasar Vision award, 2003. Office: VH1 20th Fl 1515 Broadway New York NY 10036 *

NORMAN, COLIN ARTHUR, astrophysics educator; b. Melbourne, Australia, May 3, 1948; came to U.S., 1984; s. Howard Arthur Norman and Jean Olice (Macgregor) Downing; m. Wen Shen, June 2, 1988; children: Alexandra Jean, Arthur Shen, Victoria Amelia. BE with honours, U. Melbourne, 1969; DPhil, Oxford U., 1973. Rsch. fellow Magdalen Coll., Oxford U., England, 1973—77, U. Calif., Berkeley, 1975—77; asst. prof. U. Leiden, Netherlands, 1977—84; prof. physics and astronomy Johns Hopkins U., Balt., 1984—; head acad. affairs divsn. Space Telescope Sci. Inst. Johns Hopkins U., 1987—91, head Hubble fellow program, 1991—94. Sr. rsch. fellow Inst. Astronomy, Cambridge, Eng., 1981-84, European So. Obs., Munich, 1983-84, 2000-03; vis. prof. U. Paris, 1983; Sackler lectr. Cambridge, 1995, Astor lectr. Oxford U., 2002; prof. fellow U. Melbourne, 2002—; prin. investigator Hubble Origins Project, 2004-05; Minnaert prof. U. Utrecht, Netherlands, 2005; Blaauw Prof. Groningen U., 2006. Editor: Stellar Populations, 1987, Quasar Absorption Lines, 1988, Massive Stars and Star Formations, 1991; contbr. articles to astrophysics jours. Rhodes scholar, 1970-73; recipient Perelberg prize Scotch Coll., Melbourne, 2002. Fellow Royal Astron. Soc.; mem. Am. Phys. Soc., Am. Astron. Soc., Amnesty Internat., Greenpeace, Johns Hopkins Club. Office: Johns Hopkins U Dept Physics and Astronomy Baltimore MD 21218 Business E-Mail: norman@stsci.edu.

NORMAN, DONALD ARTHUR, psychologist, educator; b. NYC, Dec. 25, 1935; s. Noah N. and Miriam F. N.; m. Martha Karpati (dec.); children: Cynthia, Michael; m. Julie Jacobsen; 1 child, Eric. BSEE, MIT, 1957; MSEE, U. Pa., 1959, PhD in Psychology, 1962; degree in psychology (hon.), U. Padua, Italy, 1995; PhD in Indsl. Design (hon.), Tech. U. Delft, The Netherlands, 2006. Lectr. Harvard U., 1962-66; prof. dept. psychology U. Calif.-San Diego, La Jolla, 1966-92, prof. emeritus, 1992—, prof., chair dept. cognitive sci., 1988-92, chair dept. psychology, 1974-78; Apple fellow Apple Computer Inc., Cupertino, Calif., 1993-97, v.p. advanced tech., 1995-97; exec. info. appliances Hewlett Packard, Palo Alto, Calif., 1997-98; co-founder, prin. Nielsen Norman Group, Fremont, Calif., 1998—; pres. learning sys. UNext, 1999—2001; prof. departments elec. engring., computer sci., psychology and cognitive sci. Northwestern U., 2001—. Cons. to industry on human centered product design. Author: Human Information Processing, 2d edit., 1977, Learning and Memory, 1982, User Centered System Design, 1986, The Psychology of Everyday Things, 1988, The Design of Everyday Things, 1989, 2002, Turn Signals Are the Facial Expressions of Automobiles, 1992, Things That Make Us Smart, 1993, The Invisible Computer, 1998, Emotional Design, 2004, Design of Future Things, 2007; mem. editl. bd. Ency. Brit. Recipient Excellence in Rsch. award, U. Calif., 1983, Benjamin Franklin medal in Computer and Cognitive Sci., Franklin Inst., 2006. Fellow: APA, Am. Psychol. Soc. (charter fellow, Franklin V. Taylor award 2005), Assn. Computing Machines (Lifetime Achievement award (Human-Computer Interaction Group)), Cognitive Sci. Soc. (chmn., founding mem.), Human Factors and Ergonomics Soc., Am. Acad. Arts and Scis.; mem.: Sigma Xi. E-mail: norman@nngroup.com.

NORMAN, ELAINE MITCHELL, information technology executive; Chief info. officer United Way of Met. Atlanta; sr. dir. info. tech. strategy and planning Ga. Pacific; v.p. info. tech. Am. Cancer Soc. Mem.: Women in Tech. (Named Woman of Yr. Tech. (not for profit/public sector) 2005), Tech. Assn. Ga., Ga. Chief Info. Officer Leadership Assn. (chair membership com. 2005, Ga. Chief Info. Officer of Yr. 2002). Office: American Cancer Society 1599 Clifton Rd NE Atlanta GA 30329-4251

NORMAN, GREGORY JOHN, professional golfer; b. Mt. Isa, Australia, Feb. 10, 1955; m. Laura Norman, July 1, 1981; children: Morgan-Leigh, Gregory. Profl. golfer, 1976—; chmn., CEO Gt. White Shark Enterprises Inc., Hobe Sound, Fla. Winner Brit. Open Championship, 1986, 93, 20 PGA Tour titles, 68 additional internat. titles; winner Vardon trophy, 1989, 90, 94; recipient Arnold Palmer award for leading money winner, 1995, Byron Nelson trophy for the lowest scoring average, 1995; ranked #1 in World Golf Ranking for 331 Weeks; named PGA Player of Yr., 1995, PGA Tour Player of Yr., 1995; named to World Golf Hall of Fame, 2001. Achievements include being the leading Money Winner PGA Tour 1986, 90. Office Phone: 561-743-8818.

NORMAN, JESSYE, soprano; b. Augusta, Ga., Sept. 15, 1945; d. Silas Sr. and Janie (King) N. B.M. cum laude, Howard U., 1967; postgrad., Peabody Conservatory, 1967; M.Mus., U. Mich., 1968; MusD (hon.), U. South, 1984, Boston Conservatory, 1984, U. Mich., 1987, U. Edinburgh, 1989, Cambridge U., 1989. Pres. L'Orchidee, Inc., Croton on Hudson, NY.

Debut, Deutsche Oper, Berlin, 1969, Italy, 1970; appeared: in operas Die Walküre, Idomeneo, L'Africaine, Marriage of Figaro, Aida, Don Giovanni, Tannhauser, Gotterdammerung, Ariadne auf Naxos, Les Troyens, Dido and Aeneas, Oedipus Rex, Hérodiade, Les Contes d'Hoffmann; debut in operas, La Scala, Milan, Italy, 1972, Salzburg Festival, 1977, U.S. debut, Hollywood Bowl, 1972, appeared with, Tanglewood Festival, Mass., also Edinburgh (Scotland) Festival, debut, Covent Garden, 1972; appeared in 1st Great Performers recital, Lincoln Center, N.Y.C., 1973—; other guest performances include, L.A. Philharm. Orch., Boston Symphony Orch., Am. Symphony Orch., Chgo. Symphony Orch., San Francisco Symphony Orch., Cleve. Orch., Detroit Symphony, N.Y. Philharm. Orch., London Symphony Orch., London Philharm. Orch., BBC Orch., Israel Philharm. Orch., Orchestre de Paris, Nat. Symphony Orch., English Chamber Orch., Royal Philharm., London Phila. Orch., Milw. Symphony Orch., Stockholm Philharm. Orch., Vienna Philharm. Orch., Berlin Philharm. Orch.; tours, Europe, S. Am., Australia, numerous recs., Columbia, EMI, Philips Records; PBS TV spcls. include Kathleen Battle and Jessye Norman Sing Spirituals, 1991, Concert at Avery Fisher Hall, 1994; recordings include Amazing Grace, Brava, Jessye!, Jessye Norman at Notre Dame (Cable Ace award), Lucky to Be Me, Sacred Songs, With a Song in My Heart, In The Spirit. Nat. spokesperson Partnership for the Homeless, Lupus Found.; bd. mem. Ms. Found., Nat. Music Found., City-Meals-on-Wheels, NYC, N.Y. Bot. Garden, Paine Coll., Augusta, Ga. Recipient 1st prize Bavarian Radio Corp. Internat. Music Competition, 1968, Grand Prix du Disque, Acad. du Disque Francais, 1973, 76, 77, 82, 84, Deutsche Schallplatten, Preis, 1975, 81, Alumni award U. Mich., 1982, Outstanding Musician of Yr. award Musical Am., 1982, Grand Prix du Disque Academie Charles Cros, 1983, Commandeur de l'Ordre des Arts et des Lettres, France, 1984, Grammy awards, 1980, 82, 85, Legion d'Honneur, France, 1989, Radcliffe medal Radcliffe Coll. Alumnae Assn., 1997, numerous other awards; named hon. life mem. Girl Scouts U.S., 1987; inductee Am. Classical Music Hall of Fame, 2002. Fellow Am. Acad. Arts & Scis.; mem. Royal Acad. Music (hon.), Alpha Kappa Alpha, Gamma Sigma Sigma, Sigma Alpha Iota, Pi Kappa Lambda. Clubs: Friday Morning Music (Washington). Office: L'Orchidee W Mount Airy Rd Croton On Hudson NY 10520 *

NORMAN, JOHN BARSTOW, JR., graphics designer, educator; b. Paola, Kans., Feb. 5, 1940; s. John B. and Ruby Maxine (Johnson) N.; m. Roberta Jeanne Martin, June 6, 1967; children: John Barstow III, Elizabeth Jeanne. BFA, U. Kans., 1962, MFA, 1966. Designer and illustrator Advt. Design, Kansas City, Mo., 1962-64; asst. instr. U. Kans., Lawrence, 1964-66; art dir. Hallmark Cards, Inc., Kansas City, 1966-69; instr. dept. art U. Denver, 1969-73, asst. prof., 1973-78, assoc. prof., 1978-93, disting. prof., 1980-93, prof. emeritus, 1993—; sr. designer Mo. Coun. Arts & Humanities, 1966-67; cons. designer Rocky Mt. Bank Note Corp., Denver, 1971—. Cons. designer Signage identity System, U. Denver; bd. dirs. comm. U. Denver; tech. cons. Denver Art Mus., 1974—, designed exhbns, 1974-75; adv. cons. Jefferson County (Colo.) Sch. System, 1976—; chmn. Design and Sculpture Exhbn., Colo. Celebration of the Arts, 1975-76. One-man shows include GalleryCortina, Aspen, Colo., 1983; commd. works include Jedda, Saudi Arabia, Synegistics Corp., Denver; represented in permanent collections Pasadena Ctr. for Arts, N.Y. Arts Dirs. Club, Calif. State U./Fiber Collection, Pasadena Ctr. Arts, N.Y. Art Dirs. Club, Midland Art Coun./Fiber Collection, Geologic Soc. Am.; represented in traveling exhbns. L.A. Art Dirs. Show and N.Y. Art Dirs. Show, U.S., Europe, Japan, 1985; featured in Denver Post, 1984, Post Electric City Mag., 1984, Rocky Mt. News, 1984, Douglas County Press, 1984, Mile High Cable Vision, 1985, Sta. KWGN-TV, 1985, Les Krantz's Am. Artists, 1988; illustrated Survey of Leading Contemporaries, 1988, U.S. Surface Design Jour., 1988; co-work represented in film collectin Mus. Modern Art, N.Y.C.; selected fashion show designs displayed Sister City dels., Denver, 1987. Recipient Silver medal award N.Y. Internat. Film and Video Competition, 1976, Design awards Coun. ADvancement and Support Edn., 1969, 71, 73, 76, Honor Mention award L.A. Art Dirs. Club, 1984, Honor Mention award N.Y. ARt Dirs. Club, 1984, Native Am. Wearable Art Competition, 1985, 5th pl. Nat. Wind Sail Am. Banners Competition, Midland, Mich., 1985, also awards for surface designs in Colo. Ctr. for Arts Wearable ARt Competition, 1984-85, Foothills Art Gallery Nat. Wearable Competition, 1984-85, Fashion Group Denver Competition, 1984-85. Mem. Art Dirs. Club Denver (Gold medals 1974-82, Best of Show Gold medal 1983, Honor Mentin award 1984, 3 gold medals 1989), Univ. Dirs. Assn. Home: PO Box 507 Lake George CO 80827-0507 Office Phone: 719-339-1751. Personal E-mail: normanranch@earthlink.net.

NORMAN, KRISTY WEST, writer; d. Wilber Earl and Janet Applegate West; m. Dustin Michael Norman, June 12, 2004. PhD, U. Conn., Storrs, 2004. Med. writer Custom Learning Designs, Inc., Belmont, Mass., 2004—06, PPD, Inc., Morrisville, NC, 2006—. Mem.: Soc. Exptl. Biology and Medicine, Am. Soc. Nutritional Scis., Am. Diabetes Assn., Drug Info. Assn., Am. Med. Writing Assn., Gamma Sigma Delta.

NORMAN, MARCIA MACY, writer, realtor; b. Newton, Mass. d. Cyrus Stegner and Elizabeth Dewing (Macy) Kaufmann; m. Charles William Norman; children: Melanie Elizabeth Ferreira, Jeffery, Andrew, Steven. BSBA, Northwestern U., 1951; postgrad., Newark State Coll., 1972, Fairfield U., 1982. Investigative reporter, feature writer, Fairfield County, Conn., 1976-97; stringer NY Times, Christian Sci. Monitor; freelance radio broadcaster Sta. WMNR, Westport, Conn., 1976-88; TV broadcaster Conn. Pub. TV Channel 49, 21, 1976-98. Host backstage Westport County Playhouse, 1981; commnetator, guest Pub. TV, 1979—82. Trustee Friends Music Fairfield County, Conn., 1995—, Sarah Coldwell Opera, New Eng.; v.p. comm. Jr. Symphony Guild, Denver, 2004—; broker assoc. Keller Williams Execs. Mem.: New Eng. Press Assn. Home: 10516 Brown Fox Trl Littleton CO 80125-9080 Office Phone: 303-471-6165. Fax: 303-904-0164. Personal E-mail: macynorman@msn.com.

NORMAN, MARY MARSHALL, academic administrator, alcohol/drug abuse services professional, educator; b. Auburn, NY, Jan. 10, 1937; d. Anthony John and Zita Norman. BS cum laude, LeMoyne Coll., 1958; MA, Marquette U., 1960; EdD, Pa. State U., 1971. Cert. alcoholism counselor. Tchr. St. Cecilia's Elem. Sch., Theinsville, Wis., 1959-60; vocat. counselor Marquette U., Milw., 1959-60; dir. testing and counseling U. Rochester (N.Y.), NY, 1960-62; dir. testing and counseling, dean women, assoc. dean coll. Corning (N.Y.) C.C., Corning (NY) C.C., 1962-68, asst. dean students, dir. student activities, asst. prof. ps University Park, 1962-68; rsch. asst. Ctr. for Study Higher Edn. Pa. State U., University Park, Pa., 1969-71; dean faculty South Campus C.C. Allegheny County, West Mifflin, Pa., 1971-72, campus pres., coll. v.p., 1972-82; pres. Orange County C.C., 1982-86; alcohol counselor Sullivan County Alcohol Drug Abuse Svc., 1985-90; sr. counselor Horton Family Program, 1990-96, edni. cons., writer, 1996—. Cons. Boricua Coll., N.Y.C., 1976-77; reader NSF, 1977-78; govtl. commn. com. Am. Assn. Cmty. and Jr. Colls., 1976-79, bd. dirs., 1982—; chmn. middle state accreditation teams; chmn. Ernest Boyer, pres. Carnegie Found., 1987. Contbr. articles to profl. jours. Active Econ. Devel. Seneca County, Seneca County Tourism Bd.; com. to redefine the Liberal Arts degree Carnegie Found., 1982; mem. planning bd. Town of Seneca Falls, 2006—; active St. Patrick's Ch.; bd. dirs. Orange County United Way, Orange County Alcoholism and Drug Abuse Coun., 1993—96, Seneca County Hist. Soc., 1997—, Guild and Altar Soc., 1999. Mem. Nat. Women's Hall of Fame. Mem.: Pa. Coun. on Higher Edn., Nat. Am. Coun. on Edn. (Pa. rep. identification women for adminstrn. 1978—82, pres. 1980—96, bd. dirs.), Pitts. Coun. Women Execs. (charter), Pa. Assn. Acad. Deans, Pa. Assn. Two-Yr. Colls., Am. Assn. Women in Cmty. and Jr. Colls. (charter, Woman of the Yr. 1981), Nat. Assn. Women Deans and Counselors, Am. Assn. Higher Edn., Seneca County C. of C. (bd. dirs., mem. tourism com.), Orange County C. of C. (bd. dirs.), Amnesty Internat. (charter mem. women's coun. 2000—), Concerned Citizens for Good Govt. (charter), Kiwanis (bd. dirs. 2002—05, planning bd. Seneca Falls 2006—), Gamma Pi Epsilon. Home: 9 S Park St Seneca Falls NY 13148-1423

NORMAN, PHILIP SIDNEY, physician; b. Pittsburg, Kans., Aug. 4, 1924; s. P. Sidney and Mildred A. (Lawyer) Norman; m. Marion Birmingham, Apr. 15, 1955 (dec.); children: Margaret Reynolds, Meredith Andrew, Helen Elizabeth. AB, Kans. State Coll., 1947; MD cum laude, Washington U., St. Louis, 1951. Intern Barnes Hosp., St. Louis, 1951-52; resident Vanderbilt U. Hosp., Nashville, 1952-54; fellow Rockefeller Inst., 1954-56; instr. medicine Johns Hopkins U. Sch. Medicine, Balt., 1956-59, asst. prof., 1959-64, assoc. prof., 1964-75, prof., 1975—, chief allergy and immunology div., 1971-91. Editor Jour. of Allergy and Clin. Immunology, 1993-98; contbr. chpt. to books, articles to profl. jours. Served with USAAF, 1943-46; Served with USPHS, 1954-56. Fellow Am. Acad. Allergy (pres. 1975); mem. Am. Fedn. Clin. Research, Am. Assn. Immunologists, Am. Soc. Clin. Investigation, Am. Assn. Physicians, N.Y. Acad. Scis., Soc. Exptl. Biology and Medicine, Am. Thoracic Soc., Am. Clin. and Climatol. Assn., Johns Hopkins Med. Soc., Alpha Omega Alpha. Episcopalian. Office: Johns Hopkins U Asthma and Allergy Ctr 5501 Hopkins Bayview Cir Baltimore MD 21224-6821 Office Phone: 410-550-2300. Business E-Mail: pnorman@jhmi.edu.

NORMAN, PHYLLIS B., volunteer; b. Chgo., Oct. 25, 1924; d. Philip James and Rosemary Benzel Line; m. Lester Ralph Norman, Sept. 8, 1945 (dec. July 2005); children: Elizabeth Anne, Lester Ralph Jr., Mary Sue. With Electrical Rsch. Lab., Evanston, Ill.; film reader, electron microscopist, data analyst, radioactive chemistry technician Los Alamos Sci. Lab., Los Alamos. Cadet nurse in WWII, Hammond, Ind.; adv. bd. Palo Duro Sr. Ctr., vol. Mem.: DAR (hon. state regent 1999—2001, state chaplain, pres. state officers club, regent Valle Grande chpt., state conservation chmn. 1993—95, state organizing sec. 1991—93, state 2d vice regent 1995—97, state vice regent 1997—99, state regent 1999—2001, nat. vice chmn. S.W. dist. for chpt. achievement awards 1998—99, treas. state vice regents club 1998—99, mem. state regents club, fifty yr. club, heritage club, nat. officer club), Los Alamos Hist. Soc. (past pres.), Arlington Heights Hist. Soc. (life), Order of Eastern Star (grand rep.), Los Alamos Garden Club (past pres.). Republican. Methodist. Home: 5007 Kokopelli Dr NE Rio Rancho NM 87144-0549

NORMAN, RALPH LOUIS, retired physicist, consultant; b. Kingston, Tenn., Mar. 25, 1933; s. Walter Hugh and Helen Irene (Smith) N.; m. Agnes Irene Pickel, Sept. 5, 1964; children: Mark Alan, Max Alvin. BS, U. Tenn., 1959; LL.B., Blackstone Sch. Law, 1967, JD, 1971; certificate, Indsl. Coll. Armed Forces, 1969; MA in Pub. Adminstrn, U. Okla., 1971; D.Sci. (hon.), Apollo Research Inst., 1976. Engr. Chrysler Corp. Missile Div., Huntsville, Ala., 1959-60; physicist Army Rocket & Guided Missile Agy., Redstone Arsenal, Ala., 1960-61; asst. project mgr. Army Missile Command, Redstone Arsenal, 1961-62, project mgr., 1962-89, ret., 1989; cons. to several def. contractors, 1989—; faculty Athens (Ala.) Coll., 1970-71, Calhoun Jr. Coll., Decatur, Ala., 1971-74, 85-90, U. Montevallo, Ala., 1973-74, U. Ala. at Huntsville, 1976-77, Columbia (Mo.) Coll., 1977-79. Cons. firm Bishop and Sexton, 1973—, Athens State Coll., Ala.; reviewer NSF, 1974-76; FAA examiner. Contbr. articles profl. jours. Served with USN, 1951-55. Recipient Dept. Def. commendations, 1961, 65, Dept. Army commendation, 1972 Mem. N.Y. Acad. Scis., Assn. U.S. Army. Home: 102 Nobleton Ln NW Huntsville AL 35806-4014 *I strive to make the knowledge gained through my research benefit all mankind.*

NORMAN, STEPHEN PECKHAM, finance company executive; b. Norwich, Conn., May 20, 1942; BA, Yale U., 1964; JD, U. Pa., 1967. Bar: Conn. 1967, N.Y. 1972. Corp. sec. Am. Express Co., NYC, 1982—2003; corp. sec., chief governance officer, 2003—. Mem. Am. Soc. Corp. Secs. (past chmn.). Clubs: Am. Yacht (Rye). Republican. Episcopalian. Home: 6 Highland Park Pl Rye NY 10580-1736 Office: Am Express Co 200 Vesey St New York NY 10285 Office Phone: 212-640-5583. E-mail: stephen.p.norman@aexp.com.

NORMAN, THENA MONTS DURHAM, microbiologist, researcher, health facility administrator; b. Bradenton, Fla., July 10, 1945; d. Turner and Silverrene (Taylor) M.; m. Millard Durham, Aug. 30, 1969 (div. 2001); children: Bryce Vincent-Barnard, Brittanie Yvonne; m. Herman H. Norman, August 6, 2005. BS, Fisk U., 1966; MS, Purdue U., 1968. Rsch. microbiologist Ctrs. for Disease Control, Atlanta, 1968-86, assoc. dir. for programs Nat. Ctr. for Prevention Svcs., 1988-95; program analyst Office Dir. Ctr. for Health Promotion and Edn., 1986-88; dir. exec. secretariat Ctrs. for Dis. Control and Prevention, Atlanta, 1995—2001; dep. dir. for policy Nat. Ctr. for HIV, STD, and TB Prevention for CDC, Atlanta, 2001—05; ret., 2005. Cons. FDA; mem. alumnae adv. com., pres. coun. dept. biol. scis. Purdue U.; bd. dirs. Balm in Gilead, Inc. Contbr. articles to profl. jours. Mem. NAACP, Neighborhood Planning Unit, SCLC/Women Adv. Coun., So. Christian Leadership Council/Women, Atlanta, 2005; bd. dirs. Cmty. Advanced Practices Nurses, Atlanta, 2004. Recipient Sec.'s award for Disting. Svc. Dept. HHS, 2001. Mem. AAAS, Sci. Rsch. Soc., Am. Soc. Microbiologists, CDC Assn. Exec. Women (founder, co-chmn.), Women in Sci. and Engring., Alumni Adv. Com., Nat. Assn. Broaden and Enchance Images (bd. dirs.). Democrat. Office Phone: 404-753-1322, 678-613-6265. Personal E-mail: thena1@bellsouth.net.

NORMAN, WYATT THOMAS, III, landman, consultant; b. Austin, Tex., Dec. 30, 1952; s. Wyatt Thomas Jr. and Frances Claire (Bliss) N. BS in Agronomy, Tex. A&M U., 1975. Cert. profl. landman, environ. site assessor. Mgr. farm and ranch Bennett Bros., Inc., Pearsall, Tex., 1975-78; landman Corpus Christi, Tex., 1978—; pres. Norman & Co. Inc., Corpus Christi, 2005—. Mem. Flour Bluff (Tex.) Vol. Fire Dept., 1984-90. Mem. Am. Assn. Profl. Landmen, Corpus Christi Assn. Profl. Landmen (pres.), Assn. Former Students, Padre Isles Property Owners Assn., Internat. Game Fish Assn., Single Action Shooting Soc., Coastal Conservation Assn., Saltwater Fisheries Enhancement Assn., Tex. State Rifle Assn., Tex. Riviera Pistoleros, Paloma de Arcabus Club (charter, treas.), Safari Club Internat., Century Club. Republican. Presbyterian. Avocations: hunting, fishing, skiing. Home: 13946 Man O'War Ct Corpus Christi TX 78418-6340 Office: 615 Leopard St Ste 434 Corpus Christi TX 78476-2225 Personal E-mail: wtn111@aol.com.

NORMAND, ROBERT, retired lawyer; b. Montreal, Que., Can., Sept. 24, 1936; s. Lucien and Eva (Rochon) N.; m. Madeleine Scott, Sept. 16, 1961; children: Eric, Yves, Genevieve. BA, U. Montreal, 1956; LLL, U. Sherbrooke, Que., 1960; diploma, Inst. d'etudes politiques, Paris, 1962. Bar: Que. 1960. Legal adviser Nat. Assembly, Quebec City, 1962-67, law clk., 1967-71; asst. dep. min. justice Que. Govt., Quebec City, 1970-71, dep. min. justice, 1971-77, dep. min. intergovtl. affairs, 1977-82, dep. min. fin., 1982-87; pres., pub. Le Soleil (Hollinger), Quebec City, 1987-93; v.p. corp. affairs UniMedia Inc., 1993-94, dep. min. internat. affairs, 1994-96; pres., dir. gen. Télé-Québec, 1996-99, ret., 1999. Sec. Study Com. on Expropriation 1965-67; guest prof. legis. law faculty Laval U., Ottawa U., 1971; pres. Que. Police Inst., 1974; chmn. Com. Supervising Olympic Security, 1974-76; chmn. Uniform Law Conf. Can.; dir. Caisse de Dèpot et Placement du Québec, 1982-87; v.p. Can. del. Diplomatic Conf. on travel contracts, Brussels, 1970; pres. Can. del. at convs. Internat. Inst. French Lang. law, 1974, 76. V.p. Hosp. du Saint-Sacrement, Quebec City, 1988-94; vice chmn. Inst. Rsch. on Pub. Policy, Montreal, 1988-94; pres. Que. Symphony Orch., Quebec City, 1989-92; consul gen. Sweden, Quebec City, 1989-94; co-pres. United Way Campaign Greater Quebec Region, 1989, hon. chmn. Telethon for Cerebral Palsy, 1990; mem. Citizens Forum, Spicer Commn., 1990-91; chmn. Ec. Nat. de l'Humour, 1997-99. Capt. Can. Army, 1954-60. Named Queen's Counsel, 1971, Comdr., Royal Order of the Polar Star, Sweden, Chevalier de la Legion d'honneur, France; recipient Pub. Adminstrn. award of excellence Nat. Sch. Pub. Adminstrn. Alumni, Quebec City, 1986. Mem. Investment Dealers Assn. Can. (dir. 1989-94), Que. Garrison Club (dir. 1991-96), Profl. Liability Ins. of Que. Bar (dir. 1991-94), Que. Bar (supervisory com. 1988-93), La Commanderie de Bordeaux. Roman Catholic. Avocations: fishing, hunting. Home: 2750 de L'Anse Sainte-Foy PQ Canada G1W 2G5 E-mail: robenorm@videotron.ca.

NORMANDEAU, ANDRE GABRIEL, criminologist, educator; b. Montreal, May 4, 1942; s. Gabriel E. and Laurette D. (Sauve) N.; m. Pierrette La Pointe, Aug. 14, 1965; children: Alain, Louis, Jean. MA in Criminology, U. Pa., Phila., 1965, PhD in Sociology, 1968. Asst. prof. criminology U. Montreal, 1968-71, assoc. prof., 1971-76, prof., 1976—, chmn. dept. criminology, 1970-80, dir. Internat. Ctr. Comparative Criminology, 1983-89, dir. Rsch. Inst. on Police, 1990—. Author: Public Attitudes and Crime, 1970, The Measurement of Crime, 1975, Patterns of Robbery, 1980, Crimes of Violence, 1985, A Vision of the Police, 1990, Crime Prevention, 1993, Justice and Minorities, 1995, Community Policing, 1998, Death Penalty, 2003, Terrorism, 2006. Woodrow Wilson fellow, 1964-68 Mem. Internat. Soc. Criminology, Am. Soc. Criminology, Am. Sociol. Assn., Can. Criminal Justice Assn. Roman Catholic. Home: 3150 Ave Kent Montreal PQ Canada H3S 1N1 Office: Dept Criminology U Montreal Montreal PQ Canada H3C 3J7 Home Phone: 514-345-0038; Office Phone: 514-343-6111 ext 3999. Business E-Mail: andre.normandeau@umontreal.ca. *Happiness is achieved by working for it, not by waiting for it to come to you.*

NORMILE, ROBERT J., lawyer; b. July 1959; BA in econ. & philosophy, Fordham U.; JD, NYU. Atty. Latham & Watkins, Sullivan & Cromwell; asst. gen. counsel Mattel Inc., El Segundo, Calif., 1992—94, v.p., asst. gen. counsel, 1994—98, v.p., assoc. gen. counsel, sec., 1998—99, sr. v.p., gen. counsel, sec., 1999—. Office: Mattel Inc 333 Continental Blvd El Segundo CA 90245-5012 Office Phone: 310-252-2000. Office Fax: 310-252-2180.

NORQUIST, DAVID L., federal agency administrator; b. 1966; BA, MA, U. Mich., Georgetown U. Staff mem. appropriations com. US Ho. of Reps.; dep. under sec. for fin. mgmt., comptr. US Dept. Def., acting prin. under sec., comptr., dep. under sec. for budget and appropriations affairs, comptr.; CFO US Dept. Homeland Security, 2006—. Office: US Dept Homeland Security Seventh and D Streets SW Washington DC 20528 Office Phone: 202-401-4782. Office Fax: 202-772-9646.

NORQUIST, GROVER GLENN, economist; b. Sharon, Pa., Oct. 19, 1956; s. Warren Elliott and Carol (Lutz) N. BA, Harvard Coll., 1978; MBA, Harvard U., 1981. Exec. dir. Nat. Taxpayers Union, Washington, 1978-79, Coll. Rep. Nat. Com., Washington, 1981-82, Ams. for Reagan Agenda, Washington, 1982-83; chief speechwriter U.S. C. of C., Washington, 1983-85; field dir. Citizens for Am., Washington, 1985; founder, pres. Ams. for Tax Reform, Washington, 1985—. Econs. adviser UNITA, Angola, 1985-88; mem. Small Bus. Survival Com., 1994. Author: Rock the House, 1995; polit. columnist Am. Spectator mag., 1992—. Speechwriter DuPont for Pres. Campaign, Washington, 1987; issues mgr. Bush for Pres. Campaign, Washington, 1988; lectr. Krieble Found., Albania, Romania, 1992; advisor Tory Party Scotland, 1989. Mem.: Am. Society Competitiveness (pres.), Am. Conservative Union (bd. dirs.), NRA (bd. dirs.). Office: Ams for Tax Reform Ste 200 1920 L St NW Washington DC 20036-5036

NORQUIST, JOHN OLAF, former mayor; b. Princeton, NJ, Oct. 22, 1949; s. Ernest O. and Jeannette (Nelson) N.; m. Susan R. Mudd, Dec. 1986; children: Benjamin Edward, Katherine Elisabeth. Student, Augustana Coll., Rock Island, Ill., 1967-69; BS, U. Wis., 1971, MPA, 1988. Assemblyman Wis. State Assembly, Madison, 1974-82, co-chmn. state joint com. fin., 1980-81; mem. Wis. State Senate, 82-88, asst. majority leader, 1984-85, 87; mayor City of Milw., 1988—2004. Adj. assoc. prof. Sch. Arch. U. Wis., Marquette U. Author: The Wealth of Cities, 1998. Bd. dirs. Congress for the New Urbanism. Sgt. USAR, 1971-77. Mem. Wis. Alliance of Cities, Congress for New Urbanism (bd. dirs.). Democrat. Presbyterian. Avocation: map collecting.

NORRBY, KLAS CARL VILHELM, pathology educator; b. Shanghai, Jan. 8, 1937; s. Åke Vilhelm and Ingrid Maria (Wedblad) N.; m. Ulla Margareta Hjort, June 17, 1961; children: Katarina, Cecilia, Jacob. BSc, Uppsala U., Sweden, 1957; MB, Göteborg (Sweden) U., 1959, MD, 1964, PhD, 1970. Asst. prof. pathology Göteborg U., 1967-71; sr. lectr. in pathology Linköping U., 1972-84, chmn. Inst. Med. Microbiology and Pathology, 1980-84; prof. pathology, regal chair Göteborg U., 1985—; vis. prof. in cell biology Harvard Med. Sch., Boston, 1989-90; chmn. Inst. Labor Medicine Sahlgrenska U. Hosp., Göteborg, 1997-2000. Author over 200 articles to profl. jours. Sub.-lt. Royal Swedish Navy Med. Corps, 1972-86. Office: Sahlgrenska U Hosp Dept Pathology SE-41345 Göteborg Sweden

NORRID, HENRY GAIL, osteopathic physician and surgeon, researcher, educator, healthcare facility administrator; b. Amarillo, Tex., June 4, 1940; s. Henry Horatio and Johnnie Belle (Combs, Cummins) N.; m. Andreia Maybeth Hudson, Jan. 29, 1966 (dec. 1988); children: Joshua Andrew, Noah Adam; m. Cheryll Diane Payne, Mar. 19, 1989 (div. Aug. 2000); stepchildren: Kim Sheri Payne, Matthew Dominic Payne; m. Carolyn A. Layton, June 8, 2002; stepchildren: Crissey Ann Elizabeth Bruce, David Randall Marshall Bruce. AA, Amarillo Coll., 1963; BA, U. Tex., 1966; MS, W. Tex. State U., 1967; DO, Kirksville Coll., 1973. Diplomate Bd. Osteo. Physicians and Surgeons, Nat. Bd. Examiners Osteo. Physicians and Surgeons; cert. basic sci. tchr. Iowa, Tex., Colo. Intern Interboro Gen. Hosp., Bklyn., 1973-74; attending physician dept. gen. practice Osteo. Hosp. and Clinic N.Y., NYC, 1974-77; gen. practice medicine specializing in osteo. Amarillo, Tex., 1978—; emergency care physician Amarillo Emergency Receiving Ctr. Amarillo Hosp. Dist., 1978-79, Ready Care Emergency Ctr., Arlington and Bedford, Tex., 1990-92, St. Anthony Hosp., Amarillo, 1992; history cons. Tex. Panhandle Heritage Found., 2004—. Emeritus mem. consulting staff physician dept. family practice Northwest Tex. Hosp., Amarillo, 1995; emergency/trauma physician Tex. EM Care, 1995—; mem. mass casualty nat. disaster response team ARC, 1995; contract staff physician Tex. Tech. Univ. Sch. Medicine and Health Scis. Ctr., med. dept. and infirmary Tex. Dept. Corrections, Tex. Dept. Criminal Justice, 1992-94; med. cons. rehab. medicine vocat rehab. divsn. Tex. Rehab. Commn., Plano, 1992-94; cattleman, ranch owner, Van Zandt County, Tex.; lectr. osteo. prins. and practice, The Osteo. Hosp. and Clinic N.Y., 1974-77, mem. credentials com., 1975-76; mem. exec. com. Southwest Osteo. Hosp., Amarillo, 1983-84, chief of staff, 1984-85; sec. dept. family practice Northwest Tex. Hosp., Amarillo, 1981-82, mem. credentials com., 1984-85, joint practice com. dept. family practice, 1986-87; mem. orgnl. com. for devel. of dept. osteo. prins. and practices, chmn. N.Y.C. group N.Y. Coll. Osteo. Med., 1977; mem. founding com. N.Y. Coll. Osteo. Medicine, N.Y. Inst. Tech., Old Westbury L.I., 1976-77; mem. North Tex. Support Group, Dallas; instr. human anatomy and physiology dept. biol. scis. Amarillo Coll., 1998-2001, fall 2003. Contbr. articles to Tex. Jour. Sci., other publs. Scout physician Llano Estecato coun. Boy Scouts Am., Tex., 1978-85; vol. physician Hurricane Katrina, 2005; active Polk St. Meth. Ch., Amarillo. Served to E-4 U.S. Army, 1956-63. Recipient William M. Giltner Meml. Fund award 1972, Humanitarian award Am. Cath. Conf., 1979, Century award Boy Scouts Am., 1982, Pfizer Sr. Med. Student award, 1973; Maxwell D. Warmer Meml. scholar 1973; scholar Kirksville

Coll. Osteo. Medicine, 1970; Tex. Legislature scholar, 1969-73; named to Eminent Soc. Border Legionaires, 11th Armored Cavalry Regiment, Germany, 1958. Mem. Am. Coll. Gen. Practitioners, Tex. Osteo. Med. Assn. (pres. dist. I, mem. ho. of dels. 1981-82, 95), Tex. C.C. Tchrs. Assn., SAR, The Sons of Republic of Tex., Am. Osteo. Assn., World Future Soc. (profl.), Gen. Soc. War of 1812, N.Y. Acad. Scis., Ex-Student's Assn. of The Univ. Tex. (life), 11th Armored Cavalry Regiment Assn., 36th (Tex.) Inf. Divsn. Assn. (life), Baron of the Magna Charta (Somerset chpt. Magna Charta Barrons 1994—), Masons, Am. Legion, Beta Beta Beta, Sigma Sigma Phi (pres. 1972), Alpha Phi Omega, Psi Sigma Alpha, Theta Psi, Theta Psi Clowns (1969-73). Avocations: astronomy, short wave listening, camping, fishing, history. Office Phone: 806-373-7005. Personal E-mail: hgnorrid@aol.com.

NORRIS, ALAN EUGENE, federal judge; b. Columbus, Ohio, Aug. 15, 1935; s. J. Russell and Dorothy A. (Shrader) N.; m. Nancy Jean Myers, Apr. 15, 1962 (dec. Jan. 1986); children: Tom Edward Jackson, Tracy Elaine; m. Carol Lynn Spohn, Nov. 10, 1990. BA, Otterbein Coll., 1957, HLD (hon.), 1991; cert., U. Paris, 1956; LLB, NYU, 1960; LLM, U. Va., 1986; HLD (hon.), Capital U. Law Sch., 2001. Bar: Ohio 1960, US Dist. Ct. (so. dist) Ohio 1962, US Dist. Ct. (no. dist) Ohio 1964. Law clk. to judge Ohio Supreme Ct., Columbus, 1960-61; assoc. Vorys, Sater, Seymour & Pease, Columbus, 1961-62; ptnr. Metz, Bailey, Norris & Spicer, Westerville, Ohio, 1962-80; judge Ohio Ct. Appeals (10th dist.), Columbus, 1981-86, US Ct. Appeals (6th cir.), Columbus, 1986—. Contbr. articles to profl. jours. Mem. Ohio Ho. of Reps., Columbus, 1967—80. Named Outstanding Young Man, Westerville Jaycees, 1971; recipient Legislator of Yr. award Ohio Acad. Trial Lawyers, Columbus, 1972. Mem. Ohio Bar Assn., Columbus Bar Assn. Lodges: Masons (master 1966-67). Republican. Methodist. Office: US Ct Appeals 328 US Courthouse 85 Marconi Blvd Columbus OH 43215-2823 *

NORRIS, ALBERT STANLEY, psychiatrist, educator; b. Sudbury, Ont., Can., July 14, 1926; s. William and Mary (Zell) N.; m. Dorothy James, Sept. 2, 1950; children: Barbara Ellen, Robert Edward, Kimberly Ann. MD, U. Western Ont., 1951. Intern Ottawa (Ont.) Civic Hosp., 1951-52; resident in psychiatry U. Iowa, Psychopathic Hosp., Iowa City, 1953-55, Boston City Hosp., 1955-56; practice medicine Kingston, Ont., Canada, 1956-57; instr. Queen's U., Kingston, 1956-57; asst. prof. psychiatry U. Iowa, 1957-62, asso. prof., 1962-64, 1965-66, prof., 1966-72; asso. prof. U. Oreg., 1964-65; prof. So. Ill. U. Sch. Medicine, Springfield, 1972-84, chmn. dept. psychiatry, 1972-82; prof. emeritus, 1984—; practice medicine specializing in psychiatry Cedar Rapids, Iowa, 1984—. Vis. prof. U. Auckland, N.Z., U. Otago, New Zealand, U. Liverpool. Contbr. chpts. to books, articles to med. jours. Fellow Am. Psychiat. Soc. (life); mem. AMA, Am. Psychopath. Assn., Soc. Biol. Psychiatry, Can. Psychiat. Soc., Am. Soc. Psychosomatic Ob-Gyn, Royal Soc. Medicine. Republican. Presbyterian. Home: 5 Penfro Dr Iowa City IA 52246-4927 Office: PO Box 1408 Cedar Rapids IA 52406-1408 Personal E-mail: asnorris@msn.com. *A life is only fulfilled by a quest, a vision of the future and a commitment to a greater value than one's self. A flickering candle is poor light, unless there is no other.*

NORRIS, CHARLES HEAD, lawyer, manufacturing executive; b. Boston, Sept. 14, 1940; s. Charles Head and Martha Marie N.; m. Diana D. Strawbridge, July 27, 1974 (div. 1994); children: Margaret Dorrance, Cecilia Walker; m. Ceil T. Walker, Oct. 13, 2001. BA, U. Pa., 1963; JD, 1968; MA, U. Wash., 1965. Mem. Morgan, Lewis & Bockius, Phila., 1968-77; pres., chief exec. Artemis Corp., 1978-79; chmn. bd., chief exec., 1979-91; chmn. exec. com., vice-chmn. bd. Remington Rand Corp., 1979-81; ptnr. Artemis Energy Co., 1980-92; chmn., CEO Norris Investment Co., 1992—. Chmn. Norris Mfg. Co., 1994—, Garret Precision Products, 1996—; chmn., CEO AmTech Engring. Co., 1996—; trustee maj. stockholders' voting trust Campbell Soup Co., 1987-90; bd. dirs. SBSF Funds, Inc., 1988-91, Del. Trust, 1987-91. Mem. Harvard U. Overseas Com. to Visit Libr., 1989—; mem. Pa. Commn. to Crime and Delinquency, 1980-84; mem. Thouron Award Selection Com., 1985-90; mem. Pa. Electoral Coll., 1980; mem. West Pikeland Twp. Suprs., 1969-72; mem. bd. visitors Carnegie Mellon U. Sch. Urban and Pub. Affairs, 1988-90; corp. mem. Belmont Hill Sch., 1990—. Served with USAF, 1960. Mem. ABA, Pa. Bar Assn., Am. Econ. Assn., Phila., Knickerbocker, Vicmead Hunt, Everglades (bd. dirs. 1986-91), Bath and Tennis Club (treas., bd. dirs. 1985-91), Sunningdale Golf Club, The Brookline (Mass.) Country Club, Coral Beach and Tennis Club, Mid Ocean Club, Rolling Rock Club. Office: PO Box 772719 Memphis TN 38177-2719 Address: Clark Tower 5100 Poplar Ave Ste 2700 Memphis TN 38137 Office Phone: 973-808-4905. Business E-Mail: bfoust@amtechengineering.com.

NORRIS, CHUCK (CARLOS RAY), actor; b. Ryan, Okla., Mar. 10, 1940; s. Ray and Wilma Norris; m. Dianne Holochek, Dec., 1958 (div. 1988), children: Mike, Dina, Eric; m. Gena O. Kelly, Nov. 28, 1998; children: Dakota Alan, Danilee; stepchildren: Kelley, Tim. Film appearances include The Wrecking Crew, 1969, Return of the Dragon, 1972, The Student Teachers, 1973, Slaughter in San Francisco, 1974, Breaker!, Breaker!, 1977, Good Guys Wear Black, 1978, Force of One, 1979, The Octagon, 1980, An Eye for an Eye, 1981, Silent Rage, 1982, Forced Vengeance, 1982, Lone Wolf McQuade, 1983, Missing in Action, 1984, Missing in Action II:The Beginning, 1985, Code of Silence, 1985, Delta Force, 1986, Firewalker, 1986, Hero and the Terror, 1988, Delta Force 2: Operation Stranglehold, 1990, The Hitman, 1991, Hellbound, 1994, Top Dog, 1995, Forrest Warrior, 1996, Bells of Innocence, 2003, Dodgeball: A True Underdog Story, 2004 The Cutter, 2006; actor, co-screenwriter (films) Invasion, U.S.A., 1985, Braddock: Missing in Action III, 1987; actor, co-exec. prodr. (films) Sidekicks, 1993; actor, exec. prodr. (TV films) Logan's War: Bound by Honor, 1998, The President's Man, 2000, The President's Man: A Line in the Sand, 2001, Walker, Texas Ranger: Trial By Fire, 2005; actor, (TV series) Walker, Texas Ranger, 1993-2001; actor, exec. prodr. (TV series) Walker, Texas Ranger, 1995-2001, Sons of Thunder, 1999; exec. prodr. (films) Birdie and Bogey, 2004; author: (with Joe Hyams) The Secret of Inner Strength: My Story, 1988, The Secret Power Within: Zen Solutions to Real Problems, 1996, (with K. Abraham) Against All Odds, 2004; (novels) The Justice Riders, 2006, Threat to Justice, 2007; host: The Ultimate Stuntman: A Tribute to Dar Robinson. Founder, chmn. United Fighting Arts Fedn.; founder, chmn. Kick Start Found., Houston, 1992; founder, World Combat League, 2005. Profl. world middleweight karate champion, 1968-74; Named Fighter of the Yr., Black Belt mag., 1969, Veteran of the Yr., Am. Veteran awards, 2000 Address: Kick Start Found Ste 203 427 W 20th St Houston TX 77008

NORRIS, DARELL FOREST, retired insurance company executive; b. Pontiac, Mich., Oct. 19, 1928; s. Forest Ellis and Mabel Marie (Smith) N.; m. Thordis Marie Johansen, Aug. 21, 1955; children: Dara Lee, Jennifer, Lisa, Nancy. BS, U. Kans., 1950. CLU; ChFC. Reporter, mem. sports staff Kansas City (Mo.) Star, 1950-51; pilot TWA, 1955-58; divsn. agy. mgr. Merced (Calif.) region Farmers Group, Inc., 1959-62, sales rep. Colorado Springs (Colo.) region, 1962-64, regional agy. mgr. Aurora, Ill., 1964-66, regional sales mgr. Santa Ana, Calif., 1966-69, mem. mgmt. tng. program staff, dir. agys. LA, 1969—71, regional mgr. Austin, Tex., 1971-73, v.p. sales LA, 1973-76, v.p. field ops. midwestern zone, 1976-79, v.p. field ops. western zone, 1979—. Pres. Farmers New World Mgmt. Co., 1977-81, v.p. staff ops., 1981-85, sr. v.p. life co. ops. and staff support svcs., 1985-90, farmers cons., 1990-93, gen. ins. cons., 1993—, vice chmn., 2. Vice chmn. bd. dirs. Northridge Hosp. Med. Found.; chmn. bd. deacons 1st Bapt. Ch., Granada Hills, Calif., 1977-89, 2003-07; sustaining mem. Rep. Nat. Com. Served with SAC, USAF, 1951-55; capt. Calif. Air N.G., 1958-62. Mem. Am. Soc. CLUs, ChFC, Ins. Edn. Assn. (trustee 1982-84). E-mail: DNorris268@aol.com.

NORRIS, DOLORES JUNE, elementary school educator; b. Belmore, NY, Feb. 10, 1938; d. Abe and Doris Cyril (Stahl) Wanser; m. William Dean Norris, June 11, 1960; children: William Dean II, Ronald Wayne, Darla Cyrille. BS in Elem. Edn., So. Nazarene U., 1959; MS in Computer Edn., Nova U., 1988, EdS in Computer Applications, 1990. Cert. elem. edn. and computer sci. tchr., Fla. Tchr. 4th and 5th grades Ruskin (Fla.) Elem. Sch., 1959-61; tchr. 5th grade Emerson Elem. Sch., Kansas City, Kans., 1961-63; tchr. 1st grade Hickman Mills, Mo., 1964-65; tchr. 3d and 4th grades Lake Mary Elem. Sch., Sanford, Fla., 1968-72; tchr. 1st grade St. Charles Cath. Sch., Port Charlotte, Fla., 1976-77; primary tchr. Meadow Park Elem. Sch., Port Charlotte, 1977-89; computer specialist Vineland Elem. Sch., Rotanda West, Fla., 1989-90, Myakka River Elem. Sch., Port Charlotte, 1990—, tech. trainer, 1995—. Reading coun. Charlotte County Schs., Port Charlotte, 1987—, rep., 1989-90, in-svc. com. 1990-93, 98; program planner Meadow Park Elem. Sch., 1988-89; program planner Myakka River Elem. Sch. 1991-93, 2004-05; tech. facilitator Myakka Tiver Elem. Sch., 1999—; instr. in edn. U. Phoenix, 2002—. Mem. Rotary, Punta Gorda, Fla., 1982-86; co-dir. teens Touring Puppet Group, Punta Gorda, 1982-86; puppet co-dir. NOW Teens, Punta Gorda, 1976-80. Mem. Internat. Tech. in Edn., Fla. Assn. Computers in Edn, pres. Southwest Florida Assn. Computers in Edn. Avocations: piano, swimming, travel. Home: 1171 Richter St Port Charlotte FL 33952-2870 Personal E-mail: norrisdj@gmail.com.

NORRIS, EDWIN L., lawyer; b. Columbus, Ohio, Oct. 6, 1946; BA, Duke U., 1968; JD, Yale U., 1972; LLM in taxation, NYU, 1978. Bar: NY 1973, US Tax Ct. 1979, Calif. 1987, Okla. Ptnr. Sidley Austin LLP, LA. Contbr. articles to profl. jours. Mem. ABA (mem. fgn. activities on U.S. taxpayers com. sect. taxation 1984—), State Bar Calif. (mem. tax sect.), L.A. County Bar Assn. Office: Sidley Austin LLP 555 W 5th St Fl 40 Los Angeles CA 90013-1010 Office Phone: 213-896-6026. Office Fax: 213-896-6600. E-mail: enorris@Sidley.com.

NORRIS, FLOYD HAMILTON, financial journalist; b. LA, Sept. 6, 1947; s. Floyd H. and Martha Leota (Buntin) N.; m. Mary Christine Bockelmann, Oct. 5, 1984; 1 child, John Buntin. Student, U. Calif., Irvine, 1965-68; MBA, Columbia U., 1982. Reporter Coll. Press Svc., Washington, 1969-70; reporter, editor Manchester (N.H.) Am., 1970-72; reporter Concord (N.H.) Monitor, 1972-74, UPI, 1974-77; press sec. Sen. John Durkin, Washington, 1977-78; bus. writer and editor AP, NYC, 1978-81; columnist for The Trader column Barron's Nat. Bus. and Fin. Weekly, NYC, 1982-88; fin. columnist N.Y. Times, NYC, 1988-98, mem. editl. bd., 1998-99, chief fin. corr., 1999—. Compiled and edited with wife The New York Times Century of Business, 1999. Bd. advisor Knight Bagehot Fellowship Program, Columbia U. Named a Walter Bagehot Fellow in Econ. and Bus. Journalism, Columbia U.; Recipient lifetime achievement, Fin. Writers Assn., N.Y., 1998, Gerald Loeb award for fin. journalism commentary, UCLA Anderson Sch. Mgmt., 2001, lifetime achievement award, 2003. Mem.: Soc. Am. Bus. Editors and Writers (dir.). Office: Fin Columnist N Y Times 229 W 43rd St New York NY 10036-3959 E-mail: norris@nytimes.com.

NORRIS, FRANK B., historian; b. LA, June 17, 1950; s. Harold B. and Beryl Z. Norris; m. Candy Dyer, Apr. 2, 1988; 1 child, Alice M. PhD, U. Wash., 1994. Historian Westec Svcs., San Diego, 1977—83, Nat. Pk. Svc., Skagway, Alaska, 1983—88, Anchorage, 1990—. Author: Histories of NPS Units in Alaska; contbr. 20 articles in field. With Alaska Hist. Soc., 1985—; pres. Alaska Assn. Hist. Preservation, 1990—99, Anchorage Hist. Properties, Inc., 2005. Recipient Beaver Log award, Alaska Hist. Soc., 1995. Office: National Park Service 240 W Fifth Ave Anchorage AK 99501 Business E-Mail: frank_norris@nps.gov.

NORRIS, JAMES HAROLD, lawyer; b. New Kensington, Pa., Sept. 18, 1953; s. J. Harold and Eleanore Rose (Arch) N.; m. Ann Marie Annase, Nov. 25, 1988; children: Ryan, Scott, Nicholas. BA, Washington Jefferson Coll., 1975; JD, Duquesne U., 1978. Bar: Pa. 1978, U.S. Dist. Ct. (we. dist.) Pa. 1978, U.S. Ct. Appeals (3d cir.) 1994, U.S. Dist. Ct. (no. dist.) W.Va. 1996, U.S. Supreme Ct., 2003. Assoc. Ruffin Hazlett Snyder Brown & Stabile, Pitts., 1979-83; ptnr. Eckert Seamans Cherin & Mellott, Pitts., 1983—; exec. v.p., gen. counsel Academy System. Adj. prof. U. Pitts. Sch. Law, 2000—04; chief counsel Allegheny Regional Asset Dist. Bd. dirs. Epilepsy Found. Western Pa., Western Pa. Growth Fedn., North Hills YMCA, 2002—06. Mem. Allegheny County Bar Assn., Pa. Bar Assn. (chmn. adminstrv. law sect. 1992-94, spl. achievement award 1993). Home: 3475 Palomino Dr Gibsonia PA 15044 Office: Eckert Seamans Cherin & Mellott 600 Grant St Pittsburgh PA 15219-2702 Office Phone: 412-566-6159. Business E-Mail: jnorris@eckertseamans.com.

NORRIS, JEANNIE, headmaster; m. Peter Norris; 2 children. BA, Pittsburg State U., Kansas; MusM, Temple U. Head of sch. Miss Hall's Sch., Pittsfield, Mass., 1996—. Mem. bd. dirs. Secondary Sch. Admission Test Bd., 2004—05, Assn. Independent Schools in New England. Corporator Berkshire Mus.; bd. trustees South Mountain Assn. Mem.: Nat. Assn. of Principals of Schs. for Girls. Office: Miss Hall's School 492 Holmes Rd PO Box 1166 Pittsfield MA 01202-1166 Office Phone: 413-443-6401. E-mail: jnorris@misshalls.org. *

NORRIS, JO ANNE WAREHAM, school counselor; b. Roaring Spring, Pa., Jan. 31, 1953; d. C. Roscoe and Wilma Irene (Allen) Wareham; m. Raymond H. Norris, June 16, 1973; children: Charles (dec.), Joanna. BSEd in Communicative Disorders, West Chester U., Pa., 1981; MEd in Sch. Counseling, U. Del., Newark, 1992. Cert. sch. counselor, Pa., 1992, Md., 1993, trainer Crisis Prevention Inst., 1998; nat. cert. counselor, 1995, nat. cert. sch. counselor Nat. Bd. Cert. Counselors, 1996; lic. profl. counselor, Pa., 2002. Exec. sec. Keystone Auto Club, Phila., 1973-78; office mgr. Holy Family Ch., Newark, Del., 1985-88; staff asst., dean's office U. Del., Newark, 1988-93; child devel. counselor Cecil County Pub. Schs., Elkton, Md., 1993—2002; intervention specialist Lancaster Sch. Dist., Pa., 2002—06; sch. counselor Columbia Boro Sch. Dist., Pa., 2006—. Mem. NEA, ACA, Am. Sch. Counselors Assn., Pa. Sch. Counselors Assn., Pa. State Edn. Assn., Columbia Edn. Assn, Kappa Delta Pi (Outstanding Mem. of Yr. U. Del. chpt. 1993). Avocations: travel, computers, desktop publishing. Home: 1121 State Rd Lincoln University PA 19352-1005 Office Phone: 717-684-4010 ext. 302. Business E-Mail: jnorris@columbia.k12.pa.us.

NORRIS, JOHN ANTHONY, health products executive, lawyer, educator; b. Buffalo, Dec. 27, 1946; s. Joseph D. and Maria L. (Suite) Norris; m. Kathleen E. Mullen, July 13, 1969; children: Patricia Marie, John Anthony II, Joseph Mullen, Mary Kathleen, Elizabeth Mary. BA, U. Rochester, 1968; JD, MBA with honors, Cornell U., 1973; cert., Harvard U., 1986. Bar: Mass. 1973. Assoc. Peabody, Brown, Boston, 1973-75; from assoc. to ptnr., exec. com., v.p., dir. Powers Hall, Boston, 1975-80; chmn. bd., pres., CEO, founder Norris & Norris, Boston, 1980-85; dep. commr., COO FDA, Washington, 1985-88, chmn. action planning and cap coms., 1985-88, chmn. reye syndrome com., 1985-87, chmn. trade legis. com., 1987-88; corp. officer, exec. v.p. Hill & Knowlton, Inc., NYC, 1988-93; worldwide dir. Health Scis. Cons. Group., 1988-93; chmn. health scis. policy coun. Health Scis. Cons. Group, 1989-93; chmn. bd., pres., CEO, founder John A. Norris, Esq., PC, Boston, 1993—; pres., CEO Nat. Pharm. Coun., Reston, Va., 1995-96. Instr. Tufts Dental Sch., 1974—79, Boston Coll. Law Sch., 1976—80, Boston U. Law Sch., 1979—83, Harvard U. Pub. Health Sch., 1988—; mem. bd. editors FDA Drug Bull., FDA Consumer Report, 1985—88; bd. dirs. Summit Tech., Inc., Cytologics, Inc., Horus Therapeutics, Inc., Nat. Applied Scis., Med. Knowledge Processing, Inc.; trustee Caritas Christi Healthcare Sys. Editor-in-chief: Cornell Internat. Law Jour., 1971—73, founder, faculty editor-in-chief: Am. Jour. Law and Medicine, 1973—81, assoc. editor: Medicolegal News, 1973—75, reviewer: New Eng. Jour. Medicine Law-Medicine Notes, 1980—81. Mem. U.S. Pres. Chernobyl Task Force, 1986, vice-chmn. health affects sub-com.; mem. Fed. Pain Commn.; chmn. Mass. Stuatory Adv. Com. Regulation Clin. Labs., 1977—83; mem. Mass. Gov.'s blue ribbon task force hosp. determination of need DON, 1979—80; chmn. Mass. Clin. Lab. Regulatory Commn.; mem. U.S. Intra-Govtl. AIDS Task Force, 1987; chmn. bd. dirs. Boston Holiday Project, 1981—83; bd. dirs. Mass. 4-H Found., 1982—2002, vice-chmn. bd. dirs., 1996—2002; chmn. U.S. del. Japan, Austria, Saudi Arabia, 1987, Finland, Denmark, Italy, 1986; chmn. Boston alumni and scholarship com. U. Rochester, 1979—85, mem. trustees coun., 1979—85, chmn. reunions; mem. exec. com. Cornell Law Sch. Assn., 1982—85, class pres., chmn. reunions; trustee Jordan Hosp., 1978—80, mem. exec. com., 1979—80, chmn. CEO search com., 1980; chmn. Joseph D. Norris, Esq. Health Law and Pub. Policy Fund, 1979—; mem. IOM Drug Devel. Forum, 1986—88, co-chmn. end points sub-com., 1987—88. With US Army, 1972—73. Named one of Ten Outstanding Young Leaders award, Jaycees, 1982; recipient Kansas City Hon. Key award, 1988, award Merit, FDA, 1987—88, PHS award, 1987, HHS Sec. award, 1988; Comprehensive Health Planning fellow, 1970—73. Mem.: ABA (vice-chmn. medicine and law com. 1977—80), Internat. Coun. Global Health Progress (bd. dirs. 1989—95), Soc. Computer Applications Med. Care Informatics (bd. dirs. 1984—85), Am. Soc. Law and Medicine (1st v.p. 1975—80, chmn. bd. dirs. 1981—84, life mem. award 1981), Nat. Health Lawyers, Am. Soc. Hosp. Attys., Mass. Bar Assn., Phi Kappa Phi. Home: 531 W Washington St Hanson MA 02341-1067 Office Phone: 781-447-3732. E-mail: John_Norris_Sr@NorrisCapital.com.

NORRIS, JOHN HART, lawyer, director; b. New Bedford, Mass., Aug. 4, 1942; s. Edwin Arter and Harriet Joan (Winter) Norris; m. Anne Kiley Monaghan, June 10, 1967; children: Kiley Anne, Amy O'Shea. BA, Ind. U., 1964; JD, U. Mich., 1967. Bar: Mich. 1968, U.S. Ct. Mil. Appeals 1969, U.S. Supreme Ct. 1974, U.S. Ct. Claims 1975, U.S. Tax Ct. 1979. From assoc. to ptnr. Monaghan, Campbell, LoPrete, McDonald and Norris, 1970-83; of counsel Dickinson, Wright, Moon, Van Dusen & Freeman, 1983-84, ptnr., 1985—; dep. asst. atty. gen. State of Mich., 1997—. Natural gas law counsel to claims mediator Columbia Gas Transmission Corp.; chpt. 11 bankruptcy procs. Wilmington (Del.) Bankruptcy Ct., 1992—; dep. asst. atty. gen. State of Mich., 1997—; bd. dirs. Prime Securities Corp., Ray M. Whyte Co., Ward-Williston Drilling Co., One Stop Capital Shop. Contbr. articles to profl. jours. Trustee Boys and Girls Clubs Southeastern Mich., 1979—, Mich. Wildlife Habitat Found.; trustee, bd. dirs. African Wildlife Found.; mem. Rep. State Fin. Com.; founder, co-chmn. Rep. Majority Club; trustee Mercy Coll., Detroit, Detroit Hist. Soc., 1984—; trustee, 1st vice chmn. Salk Inst. Fellow: Mich. State Bar Found.; mem.: ABA (litig. and natural resources sects.), Def. Orientation Conf. Assn., Fin. and Estate Planning Coun. Detroit, Am. Arbitration Assn., Detroit Bar Assn. (mem. pub. adv. com.), Oakland County Bar Assn., State Bar Mich. (chmn. environ. law sect. 1982—83, probate and trust law sect., mem. energy conservation task force, mem. oil and gas com.), Mich. Oil and Gas Assn. (mem. legal and legis. com.), Detroit Zool. Soc., Yondotega Club, Bloomfield Hills Country Club, Turtle Lake Club, Prismatic Club, Hundred Club, Thomas M. Cooley Club, Detroit Athletic Econ. Club (Detroit), Blue Key, Phi Delta Phi. Home: 1325 Buckingham Ave Birmingham MI 48009-5881 Office: Dickinson Wright 38525 Woodward Ave Ste 2000 Bloomfield Hills MI 48304-2971 Home Phone: 248-646-7139; Office Phone: 248-433-7227. Business E-Mail: jnorris@dickinsonwright.com.

NORRIS, JOHN STEVEN, healthcare company executive; b. Chgo., Apr. 25, 1943; s. Norris Dale and Olive (Grissinger) N.; m. Susan Jean Armstrong, May 3, 1975; children: Lindsey Jean, Whitney Ann, John Scott. BA, U. Ariz., Tucson, 1967, MPH, 1995; B in Fgn. Trade, Thunderbird Grad Sch. Internat. Mgmt., Glendale, Ariz., 1968. lic. nursing home adminstr., gen. contractor, real estate broker. Inspection officer Citicorp, Brazil, Colombia, Mex., Peru, Venezuela, 1968—73, asst. cashier NYC, 1973—74; pres., gen. mgr. Phoenix Athletic Club, 1974-76; bus. mgr. Phoenix Pub. Inc., 1976-77; project mgr. Environ. Constn. Co., Phoenix, 1977-79; pres. AGN Devel. Corp., Phoenix, 1979—, Valley View Realty, Inc., Phoenix, 1981-87; exec. v.p., sec., pres. RGW Constrn. Co., Inc.; pres. Norris/Roberts Group, Inc., Phoenix, 1987-90; CEO Christian Care Co., Inc., Phoenix, 1990—. Chmn. Covenant Health Network, 2001—; mem. ASP curriculum devel. expert panel U. North Tex. Ex officio bd. dirs. Christian Care Found.; chmn. bd. dirs. Dove's Transitional Housing, Inc.; bd. dirs., past chmn. region 1 Area Agy. Aging. Recipient award of honor Ariz. Assn. Homes and Svcs. for Aging, 1999, Time and Talent award Am. Assn. Homes and Svcs. for the Aging and U. North Tex., 2004. Fellow: Am. Coll. Healthcare Exec., Am. Assn. Home Svcs. Aging (retirement housing profl.), Am. Coll. Healthcare Adminstrs.; mem.: Rotary Internat. (treas., past pres. Phoenix club, Paul Harris fellow, Service Above Self award 2002), Phi Delta Theta. Republican. Avocations: skiing, racquetball, horsemanship. Home: 6912 East Paradise Dr Scottsdale AZ 85254 Office: Christian Care Cos 2002 W Sunnyside Dr Phoenix AZ 85029-3554 Office Phone: 602-443-5411. Business E-Mail: john.norris@christiancare.org.

NORRIS, LONNIE HAROLD, dean; b. Houston, Nov. 22, 1942; m. Donna M. Farmer, June 18, 1966; children: Marlaina M., Michael A. BA in Chemistry, Fisk U., 1964; DMD, Harvard U., 1976, MPH, 1977. Cert. diplomate Am. Bd. of Oral/Maxillofacial Surgeons. Asst. prof. oral & maxillofacial surgery Tufts U. Sch. Dental Medicine, Boston, 1981-88, assoc. prof., 1988-95, prof., 1995—, interim dean, 1995-96, dean, 1996—. Mem. com. dental accreditation; chmn. coun. deans Am. Dental Edn. Assn., 2005—. Mem. Gov.'s commn. Study Oral Health Staus and Accessibility Dental Care Svcs. Residents Commonwealth Mass. Named Disting. Practitioner, Nat. Acads. Practice, Dentist of the Yr., New Eng. chpt. Pierre Fauchard Acad. Fellow: Pierre Fauchard Acad., Internat. Coll. Dentists, Am. Bd. Oral/Maxillofacial Surgery, Am. Assn. Oral/Maxillofacial Surgeons, Am. Coll. Dentists, Am. Acad. Dental Sci., Phi Beta Kappa, Omicron Kappa Upsilon. Avocation: travel. Office: Tufts U Sch Dental Medicine 1 Kneeland St Boston MA 02111-1527 Office Phone: 617-636-6636. Business E-Mail: lonnie.norris@tufts.edu.

NORRIS, MACKIE LYVONNE HARPER, registered nurse, health care consultant; b. Bivins, Tex., Dec. 10, 1940; d. McNoble and Corine Rosetta (Collins) Harper; m. Alfred L. Norris Sr., Sept. 9, 1961; children: Alfred, Lisa, Tyrone, Angela. BSN, Dillard U., 1960; MN, Emory U., 1971, PhD, 1996. RN, N.Mex., La., Ga. Asst. prof. Dillard U., New Orleans, 1977-84; assoc. prof. Woodruff Sch. Nursing Emory U., Atlanta, 1985-92. Cons. Aftercare, Ltd., Atlanta, 1991-92, United Meth. Ch., N.Y.C., 1996—, Not Even One Project, N.Mex., 1997; mem. faculty U. Phoenix Nursing Dept. Mem. Presbyn. Hosp. IRB, Albuquerque, 1993—; treas. N.Mex. Sickle Cell Coun., Albuguerque, 1994—. Mem. ANA, APHA, Nat. League Nursing, N.Mex. Pub. Health Assn., Omichron Delta Kappa, Sigma Theta Tau.

NORRIS, MEREDITH SOMERVILLE, educator; b. Mass. BS, U. Mass., Amherst; MS, U. Calif., Davis. Rsch. tech. U. Calif., 2003—04; lectr., lab. coord. U. NC, Charlotte, acad. advisor, 2005—. Vol. Therapeutic Horseback Riding Children, Charlotte.

NORRIS, PAUL J., chemicals executive; Grad., Mt. St. Mary's Coll.; MBA, U. Md. With mktg. and bus. devel. divsns. W.R. Grace, 1971—81; v.p., then pres. catalysts & chemicals Engelhard Corp., 1981—89; pres. fluorine products Allied Signal Inc., 1989—94, pres. polymers, 1994—97, sr. v.p., pres. splty. chems. unit, chmn. UOP, 1997-98; pres. W.R. Grace, Columbia, Md., 1998—2003, CEO, 1998—2005, chmn., 1999—2005, non-exec. chmn., 2005—. Office: WR Grace 7500 Grace Dr Columbia MD 21044

NORRIS, PHILIP JOHN, medical educator, researcher; b. Carmichael, Calif., May 25, 1967; s. John Clark Norris and Ann Dorothy Benson; m. Alexandra Margot Burgess, June 24, 2000; children: Katherine Ann, Britannia Campbell children: Cleo Elisabeth. BA, BS, U. Calif., Berkeley, 1989; MD, Columbia U., 1995. Diplomate Internal Medicine Am. Bd. Internal Medicine, 1995, Infectious Diseases Am. Bd. Internal Medicine, 2000. Intern internal medicine The Presbyn. Hosp. in the City N.Y., 1995—96; resident internal medicine Duke U. Med. Ctr., Durham, NC, 1996—98; clin. and rsch. fellow in infectious diseases Mass. Gen. Hosp., Boston, 1998—2001, instr. medicine, 2002—03; dir. immunology and assoc. investigator Blood Systems Rsch. Inst., San Francisco, 2004—. Recipient award, Calif. Scholarship Fedn., 1985, Scholar's award, Bank Am. Corp., 1985, James B. Black award, Pacific Gas and Electric Co., 1985—89, Clin. Scientist Devel. award, Doris Duke Charitable Found., 2000—05; scholar, Chancellor U. Calif., 1985—89, U. Calif. Alumni Assn., 1985—89; Nat. Merit Scholar, Nat. Merit Scholarship Corp., 1985. Mem.: Am. Soc.Microbiology, Am. Assn. Immunologists, Infectious Diseases Soc. Am. Republican. Episcopalian. Office: Blood Sys Rsch Inst 270 Masonic Ave San Francisco CA 94118 Office Phone: 415-923-5769. Business E-Mail: pnorris@bloodsystems.org.

NORRIS, REBECCA SACHS, religious studies educator; d. Robert Green and Jean Woolf Sachs, Carolyn Levin Sachs (Stepmother); m. Harry L. Norris, May 27, 1978; children: Jesse Alexander, Leah Elizabeth. BA, Clark U., Worcester, Mass., 1969—73; PhD, Boston U., 1992—99. Asst. prof. Merrimack Coll., North Andover, Mass., 2002—; lectr. Boston U. Sch. Medicine, 2002—. Contbr. articles to profl. jours. and pubs. Post-Doctoral fellow, Boston U., 2000—01. Mem.: AAUW, Am. Anthropology Assn., Am. Acad. Religion (organizer, co-chair anthropology group 2003—, mem. New Eng. maritimes regional bd.). Office: Merrimack Coll 315 Turnpike St C-2 North Andover MA 01845 Office Phone: 978-837-5000 4521. Business E-Mail: norrisr@merrimack.edu.

NORRIS, RICHARD A., lawyer, mediator; b. NYC, Mar. 9, 1927; s. Herman R. and Rose L. Novros; m. Barbara M. Lavine; children: Robert, Nancy. BS in Chemistry, Lehigh U., Bethlehem, Pa., 1949; JD, Harvard U., Cambridge, Mass., 1952. Bar: DC 1952, NJ 1955. Ptnr. Norris, McLaughlin & Marcus, Bridgewater, NJ, 1955—. Bd. dirs. North Plainfield State Bank, NJ, New Era Bank, Somerset, NJ. Pres. Kiwanis Club, Somerville, NJ; trustee Temple Sholom, Bridgewater, Jewish Fedn., various counties, NJ, Somerset Valley Vis. Nurses Assn. Capt. USAF, 1952—54. Fellow: Am. Acad. Matrimonial Lawyers (bd. mgrs. 1990—); mem.: ABA, Somerset County Bar Assn. (pres. 1969, Lifetime Achievement award 2005). Democrat. Avocations: travel, reading, golf. Home: 1616 Mountain Top Rd Bridgewater NJ 08807 Office: Norris McLaughlin & Marcus PO Box 1018 Somerville NJ 08876

NORRIS, RICHARD ANTHONY, accountant; b. Birmingham, July 6, 1943; s. Albert Edward and Audrey (Rowley) N.; m. Geri M., Jan. 20, 1947; 1 child, Karen Louise. BA, U. Leeds, York, Eng., 1966. Chartered acct., UK, Can. Auditor Price Waterhouse & Co., Bristol, Eng., 1966-70, mgr. Montreal, Que., Can., 1970-78; mgr. corp. acctg., controller Can. Pacific Enterprises, Montreal, Calgary, Alta., Can., 1978-85; v.p. fin. US Ops. Laidlaw Waste Systems Inc., North Richland Hills, Tex., 1986-96; v.p., CFO Nexcycle, Inc., Dallas, 1997-2000; sr. v.p., CFO Casella Waste Systems Inc., Rutland, Vt., 2000—. Mem.: FEI. Home: 448 Curtis Brook Rd Rutland VT 05701 Office: Casella Waste Sys Inc 25 Greens Hill Ln Rutland VT 05701 Office Phone: 802-775-0325. Business E-Mail: Richard.Norris@casella.com.

NORRIS, TRACY HOPKINS, retired public relations executive; b. Ainsworth, Iowa, Nov. 1, 1927; s. Lee E. and Ruth C. (Simpson) N.; m. Emilie Lathrop, Nov. 11, 1956; 1 child, Shawn Tracy. BA, Cornell Coll., 1952; MA, U. Iowa, 1957. Admissions counselor Cornell Coll., Mt. Vernon, Iowa, 1952—54; dir. news bur. Wittenberg U., Springfield, Ohio, 1956—70; exec. dir. rels. and comm. Ball State U., Muncie, Ind., 1970—88; ret., 1988. Active United Way Springfield, Ohio, Muncie, 1965—. Served with USN, 1945-48. Recipient Silver Anvil award, Pub. Rels. Soc. Am., 1967. Mem.: Coun. for Advancement and Support Edn., Exch. Club. Lutheran. Avocations: golf, travel, gardening. Home: 3700 Allen Ct Muncie IN 47304 Personal E-mail: tnorris629@aol.com.

NORRIS, WILLIAM ALBERT, lawyer, mediator, retired judge; b. Turtle Creek, Pa., Aug. 30, 1927; s. George and Florence (Clive) Norris; m. Jane Jelenko, Feb. 17, 1991; children: Barbara, Donald, Kim, Alison, David Jelenko. Student, U. Wis., 1945; BA, Princeton U., 1951; JD, Stanford U., 1954. Bar: Calif. 1955, D.C. 1955. Assoc. Northcutt Ely, Washington, 1954—55; law clk. to Justice William O. Douglas US Supreme Ct., Washington, 1955—56; sr. mem. Tuttle & Taylor, Inc., LA, 1956—80; judge U.S. Ct. Appeals (9th cir.), LA, 1980—97; atty. Folger, Levin & Kahn, LA, 1997—2000, mediator, 1997—; sr. counsel Akin Gump Strauss Hauer & Feld, LLP, 2000—. Spl. counsel Pres.' Kennedy's Com. on Airlines Controversy, 1961; mem. Calif. State Bd. Edn., 1961—67; mem. bd. dir. L.A. Eye Inst., 2001—. Trustee Calif. State Colls., 1967—72, Craft and Folk Art Mus., 1979—87; pres. L.A. Bd. Police Commrs., 1973—74; founding pres., trustee Mus. Contemporary Art, LA, Calif., 1980—92; Dem. nominee for atty. gen. State of Calif., 1974. With USN, 1945—47. Office: Akin Gump Strauss Hauer & Feld LLP Ste 2400 2029 Century Park E Los Angeles CA 90067 Home Phone: 310-472-2238; Office Phone: 310-229-1047. Business E-Mail: wnorris@akingump.com.

NORSTEN, TODD, artist; Attended Norfolk Program, Yale U., 1989; BFA, Minn. Coll. Art and Design, 1990. One-man shows include Paintings and Drawings, Willmar Cmty. Coll., Minn., 1992, Vermillion Gallery, Minn., 1992, Montgomery Glasoe Fine Art, Minn., 1994, New Paintings, 1996, Paintings and Drawings, Jennifer Armetta Fine Art, Chgo., 1997, Sighting, Weinstein Gallery, Minn., 1998, TrueFalse, 2001, Paintings, Stwphen Wirtz Gallery, San Francisco, 1999, Recent Paintings, Finesilver, San Antonio, 1999, Allsomenone, High Point Ctr. Printmaking, Minn., 2003, Happy Happy Happy, Franklin ArtWorks, Minn., 2004, Treasures from the Upper Midwest, Cohan and Leslie, 2006, Safety Club, Midway Contemporary Art, Minn., 2006, exhibited in group shows at Marks and Lines, Montgomery Glasoe Fine Arts, 1993, Brown Whiskey Club, 1995, Composing a Collection, Walker Art Ctr., Minn., 1996, Visitor's Voices: Recomposing the Collection, 1996, Dialogues, 1997, 11/5/98, Elizabeth Dee Gallery, NY, 1998, Five McKnight Artists, MCAD Gallery, Minn., 1999, Summer Show, Margaret Thatcher Gallery, NY, 2000, Uncanny Visions, Plains Art Mus., Fargo, 2004, Abstract Painting in Minnesota, Minn. Mus. Am. Art, 2005, Young Americans, Arario Mus., Seoul, 2006, Whitney Biennial: Day for Night, Whitney Mus. Am. Art, NY, 2006. Mailing: c/o Cohan and Leslie 138 Tenth Ave New York NY 10011

NORSWORTHY, ELIZABETH KRASSOVSKY, lawyer; b. NYC, Feb. 26, 1943; d. Leonid Alexander and Wilma (Hudgens) Krassovsky; m. John Randolph Norsworthy, June 24, 1961 (div. 1962), m. Nov. 26, 1977 (div. 1984); 1 child, Alexander. AB magna cum laude, CUNY, 1965; MA, U. N.C., 1966; JD, Stanford U., 1977. Bar: D.C. 1978, Mass. 1992, Vt. 1998, U.S. Ct. Appeals (D.C. cir.) 1979. Atty. applications, disclosure rev. and investment adviser regulation, divsn. investment mgmt. SEC, Washington, 1978-79, 80-82, atty. operating brs. and disclosure policy divsn. corp. fin., 1979-80, chief, spl. counsel office of regulatory policy divsn. investment mgmt., 1983-86; assoc. Kirkpatrick & Lockhart, Washington, 1986-90; ptnr. Sullivan & Worcester, Boston, 1990-92; pvt. practice Norfolk, Mass., 1992; pvt. practice in juvenile law Concord, Vt., 1996—. Pub. arbitrator, chairperson NASD; mediator, facilitator Cmty. Justice Ctr., St. Johnsbury. Mem. North Country Chorus, Wells River; chair investment com. North Congl. Ch., St. Johnsbury; mem. St. Andrews Episcopal Ch., St. Johnsbury. Mem.: College Club (St. Johnsbury), Athenaeum (St. Johnsbury), Phi Alpha Theta, Phi Beta Kappa. Democrat. Episcopalian. Avocations: farming, swimming, singing, environmental protection. Office: Winterbrook Farm 1342 Woodward Rd Concord VT 05824-9620 Home Phone: 802-695-1408; Office Phone: 802-695-1408. Fax: 602-695-2516. Business E-Mail: ekn@kingcon.com.

NORTELL, BRUCE, lawyer; b. Nov. 19, 1946; s. Joseph and Dorothy Nortell; children: Adam, Daniel, Anthony. AB, Boston U., 1968; JD, U. Chgo., 1971. Bar: Ill. 1971, U.S. Dist. Ct. (no. dist.) Ill. 1971, U.S. Supreme Ct. 1979. Sole practice, Chgo., 1971—74; asst. dir. legal affairs AMA, Chgo., 1974—81, counsel, sec. jud. coun., 1976—81; dir. tax and fin. planning Loyola U., Chgo., 1981—88, North Ctrl. Coll., Naperville, Ill., 1988—. Contbr. articles to profl. jours.;, author two books novels. Mem.: ABA, Chgo. Bar Assn., Ill. Bar Assn. (Lincoln award 1975), Phi Beta Kappa (bd.). Home: 1124 Dickens Ln Naperville IL 60563-4301 Office: 30 N Brainard St Naperville IL 60540-4607 Office Phone: 630-637-5214. Business E-Mail: bnortell@noctrl.edu.

NORTH, A. FREDERICK, physician; b. Milw., July 3, 1931; s. Alexander F. and Florence (Reineking) N.; m. Jane Whittlesey, Dec. 18, 1954; children: Lindsay Elizabeth, Robert Whittlesey, Wendy Katherine. Student, Yale Coll., 1953; MD, Yale U., 1956. Intern Strong Meml. Hosp., Rochester, N.Y., 1956-58, resident pediatrics, 1960-62; instr. pediatrics U. Rochester, 1962-66; sr. pediatrician Project Head Start, Washington, 1966-68; assoc. prof. pediatrics George Washington U., Washington, 1968-72; assoc. med. dir. Children's Hosp. of D.C., Washington, 1968-72; vis. prof. pediatrics, pub. health U. Pitts., 1972-79; physician for retarded persons Govt. of D.C., Washington, 1978-88; pvt. practice in pediat. Rockville, Md., 1988—. Cons. various locations, 1966-88. Author: Infant Care, 1980; contbr. articles to publs. Lt. USNR, 1958-60. Fellow Acad. of Pediatrics, Am. Pub. Health Assn.; mem. Am. Pediatric Soc., Ambulatory Pediatric Assn. (pres. 1966-67), Chevy Chase Club. Republican. Episcopalian. Home: 5703 Overlea Rd Bethesda MD 20816-1918 Office Phone: 301-229-2159. Personal E-mail: afnorth@msn.com.

NORTH, DOUGLAS MCKAY, academic administrator; b. Albany, NY, Oct. 14, 1940; s. Henry Saxe and Elsie (Sewell) N.; m. Ellen Cole, Dec. 10, 1975; children: Jeffrey, Lisa, Anton, Gabriel. BA, Yale U., 1962; MA, Syracuse U., 1964; PhD, U. Va., 1970. Asst. prof. SUNY, New Paltz, 1964-67, Wesleyan U., Middletown, Conn., 1970-71; prof. Goddard Coll., Plainfield, Vt., 1973-81, dir. devel., 1982-89; pres. Prescott (Ariz.) Coll., 1989—94; prof., pres. Alaska Pacific U., 1995—. Contbr. articles to profl. jours. Dept. Edn. grantee, Washington, 1988-91. Mem. Nat. Consortium Single Parent Educators (bd. dirs. 1988—). Office: Office of Pres 4101 University Dr Anchorage AK 99508 E-mail: dnorth@alaskpacific.edu. *

NORTH, DOUGLASS CECIL, economist, educator; b. Cambridge, Mass., Nov. 5, 1920; s. Henry Emerson and Edith (Saitta) North; m. Elisabeth Willard Case, Sept. 28, 1972; children from previous marriage: Douglas Alan, Christopher, Malcolm Peter. BA, U. Calif., Berkeley, 1942, PhD, 1952; D in Natural Scis. (hon.), U. of Cologne, Federal Republic of Germany, 1988, U. Zurich, Switzerland, 1993, Stockholm Sch. of Econs., Sweden, 1994, Prague Sch. Econs., 1995. Asst. prof. econs. U. Wash., 1950—56, assoc. prof., 1957—60, prof., 1960—83, chmn. dept., 1967—79, prof. emeritus, 1983—; dir. Inst. Econ. Research, 1960—66, Nat. Bur. Econ. Research, 1967—87; Spencer T. Olin prof. in arts and scis. Washington U., St. Louis, 1983—. Pitt prof. Am. history and instns. Cambridge U., 1981—82; fellow Ctr. for Advanced Study on Behavioral Scis., 1987—88; co-founder Internat. Soc. for the New Institutional Econ., 1997. Author: The Economic Growth of the U.S. 1790-1860, 1961, Growth and Welfare in the American Past, 1966; author: (with L. Davis) Institutional Change and American Economic Growth, 1971; author: (with R. Miller) The Economics of Public Issues, 1971, 1974, 1976, 1978, 1980; author: (with R. Thomas) The Rise of the Western World, 1973; author: Structure and Change in Economic History, 1981, Institutions, Institutional Change and Economic Performance, 1990. Recipient Nobel Prize in Econ. Sci., Nobel Found., 1993; fellow Guggenheim Found., 1972—73; grantee, Social Sci. Rsch. Coun., 1962, Rockefeller Found., 1960—63, Ford Found., 1961, 1966, NSF, 1967—73, Bradley Found., 1986—. Fellow: Am. Acad. Arts and Scis.; mem.: Econ. History Assn., The Brit. Acad. (corr.), Am. Econ. Assn. Office: Dept Econ Washington Univ Rm 305 Elliot Hall Box 1208 Saint Louis MO 63130 *

NORTH, E(DWARD) LEE, retired writer, former aerospace company professional; b. Englewood, NJ, June 2, 1924; s. Edward Louis North and Genevieve Jean (Smith) North Francais; m. Florence Kirkland Hennen, Aug. 29, 1945; children: Patrick Lee, Diane North Goncalves. BA, Washington and Jefferson Coll., 1946. Sports editor Washington Reporter, Pa., 1947-49; publicity dir. Washington and Jefferson Coll., 1949-51; writer, editor Grumman Aerospace Corp., Bethpage, NY, 1951-78, proposal mgr., 1978-89. Hon. consul Free Polish Govt., London, 1980-95. Author: For This One Hour, 1970, Redcoats, Redskins, and Red-Eyed Monsters: A human-interest history of West Virginia, 1979, Battling the Indians, Panthers, and Nittany Lions, 1991, The Fifty-Five West Virginias, 1998, Mark of the White Wolf, 2000, Snowflakes on the Don, 2002, 2d edit., 2007, Eyes that Haunt, 2005; co-author (with Jane Wyman): Chris, the Rhode Island Wonder Dog, 1993; co-author: (with Arthur Dromerhauser) The History of Bay Shore High School Athletics, 1994. Chmn. Good Govt. Party, Suffolk County, NY, 1956—57; bd. of policy Liberty Lobby, Washington, 1975—2001; chmn. Islip Town (NY) Conservative Party, 1970s; historian Brightwaters Village, 1990—2006. Recipient Gold Cross of Merit Free Poland Govt., 1985. Mem.: The Authors Guild, Football Writers of Am., Am. Edn. Assn. (bd. dirs. 1992—), Rep. Nat. Com., Assn. of Pub. Historians of N.Y. State, Phi Kappa Psi. Episcopalian. Avocations: tennis, golf, bridge, Scrabble, study of wolves. Home: 55 Woodland Dr Brightwaters NY 11718 Personal E-mail: north444@aol.com.

NORTH, GARY L., career military officer; B in Polit. Sci., East Carolina U.; MPA, Golden Gate U., 1984, M in Human Resources Mgmt., 1986; M in Nat. Resource Strategy, Nat. Def. U., 1994. Advanced through grades to lt. gen. USAF, 2006; weapons sys. officer 35th tactical fighter squadron Kunsan AB, Republic of Korea, 1978—79; F-4G Wild Weasel elec. warfare officer 561st and 563rd tactical fighter squadrons George AFB, Calif., 1979—80; fighter lead-in training Holloman AFB, N.Mex., 1981—82, Hill AFB, Utah, 1981—82; squadron scheduler, squadron weapons officer19th tactical squadron Shaw AFB, SC, 1982—85, wings weapons officer, 363rd tactical fighter wing SC, 1985—86; F-16 weapons officer, fligt comdr. 526th tactical fighter squadron Ramstein AB, Germany, 1986—87, aide-de-camp, F-16 instr. pilot to Commander-in-Chief of USAF Europe, 1987—89; asst. ops. officer 19th tactical fighter squadron, wing chief standardization and evaluation Shaw AFB, SC, 1990—93, chief wing weapons and safety Operation Desert Storm, comdr. 33rd fighter squadron SC, 1990—93; comdr. 35th ops. group Misawa AB, Japan, 1994—96; comdr. 8th fighter wing Kunsan AB, Republic of Korea, 1999—2000; chief joint requirements divsn., dep. dir. joint matters USAF Hdqs., Washington, 1996—97, dep. dir. politico-military affairs for Asia-Pacific, joint staff, 2002—04; dir. ops. U.S. Pacific command Camp H.M. Smith, Hawaii, 2004—06; comdr. 9th Air Force, U.S. Ctrl. Command Air Forces Shaw AFB, SC, 2006—. Decorated Df. Superior Svc. Medal with two oak leaf clusters, Legion of Merit with oak leaf cluster, Disting. Flying Cross with "V" device and oak leaf cluster, Meritorious Svc. Medal with oak leaf cluster, Air Medal with four oak leaf clusters, Aerial Achievement Medal with wto oak leaf clusters, Air Force Commendation Medal with two oak leaf clusters, Combat Readiness Medal with four oak leaf clusters; recipient Lance P. Sijan USAF Leadership Award, 1993.

NORTH, HELEN FLORENCE, classicist, educator; b. Utica, NY; d. James H. and Catherine (Debbold) N. AB, Cornell U., 1942, MA, 1943, PhD, 1945; LLD (hon.), Rosary Coll., 1982; DLitt (hon.), Trinity Coll., Dublin, 1984, Fordham U., 1999; LHD (hon.), La Salle U., 1985, Yale U., 1986. Instr. classical lang. Rosary Coll., River Forest, Ill., 1946-48; faculty Swarthmore Coll., 1948—91, prof. classics, 1961-91, chmn. dept., 1959-91, emerita, 1991—, Centennial prof. classics, 1966-73, 78-91, Kenan prof., 1973-78, sr. rsch. scholar, 2003—. Vis. asst. prof. Cornell U., 1952—; vis. assoc. prof. Barnard Coll., 1954—55; vis. prof. LaSalle Coll., Phila., 1965, Am. Sch. Classical Studies, Athens, 1975, Athens, 87; Blegen disting. vis. rsch. prof. Vassar Coll., 1979. Author: Sophrosyne: Self-Knowledge and Self-Restraint in Greek Literature, 1966, From Myth to Icon: Reflections of Greek Ethical Doctrine in Literature and Art, 1979, (with Mary C. North) The West of Ireland: A Megalithic Primer, 1999, Cork and the Rest of Ireland: A Megalithic Primer II, 2003; translator: John Milton's Second Defense of the English People, 1966; editor: Interpretations of Plato: A Swarthmore Symposium, 1977; co-editor: Of Eloquence, 1970; editor Jour. History of Ideas; mem. editl. bd. Catalogus Translationum et Commentariorum, 1979. Bd. dirs. Am. Coun. Learned Socs., 1977-85; trustee LaSalle U., 1972-2003, chmn. bd. trustees, 1991-93; trustee King's Coll., Am. Acad. in Rome; chmn. com. on Classical Sch. Recipient Harbison prize Danforth Found., 1969, Centennial medal Am. Acad. Rome, 1995; named Distinguished Daughter of Pa., 1989, del. of Am. Philological Assn. to Am. Coun. Learned Socs., 1991-95; grantee Am. Coun. Learned Socs., 1943-45, 73, fellow, 1971-72, 87-88; Mary Isabel Sibley fellow Phi Beta Kappa Found., 1945-46, Ford Fund Advancement Edn. fellow, Fulbright fellow Rome, 1953-54, Guggenheim fellow, 1958-59, 75-76, AAUW, 1963-64; grantee Danforth Found., 1962, Lindbach Found., 1966; Sr. fellow NEH, 1967-68; NEH Coll. Tchrs. fellow, 1983-84; Martin classical lectr. Oberlin Coll., 1972. Mem. Am. Philol. Assn. (dir. 1968—, pres. 1976—, Charles J. Goodwin award 1969, Disting. Svc. medal 1996), Classical Assn. Atlantic States, Catholic Commn. Intellectual and Cultural Affairs (chmn. 1968-69), Am. Acad. Arts and Scis., Am. Philos. Soc., Soc. Religion Higher Edn., Phi Beta Kappa (bd. vis. scholars 1975-76, senate 1991—2003), Phi Kappa Phi. Home: 604 Ogden Ave Swarthmore PA 19081-1131 Personal E-mail: hnorth1@swarthmore.edu.

NORTH, JOHN ADNA, JR., accountant, real estate appraiser; b. Atlanta, Oct. 20, 1944; s. John Adna and Julia Osborn (Napier) N.; m. Alexa Ruth Bryans, Mar. 20, 1976; 1 child, William Bryans. BA in Econs., U. Ga., 1966; M of Profl. Accountancy, Ga. State U., 1977, M of Taxation, 1980; JD, Woodrow Wilson Coll. Law, Atlanta, 1980. CPA, Ga.; cert. real estate appraiser. Trust adminstr. Trust Co. Bank, Atlanta, 1968-71; fin. produce sales exec. Dean Witter Reynolds Inc., Atlanta, 1971-73; with acctg. firm and in pvt. practice Atlanta, 1973-80; multi-state tax, staff, gen. tax counsel Texaco Inc., White Plains, N.Y., 1980-87; mgr. multi-state tax Price Waterhouse, Atlanta, 1987-88; dir. various corps. MacMillan Bloedel (USA) Inc., Wilmington, Del., 1988-91; pres. Cobb Svc. Assocs. Inc., Marietta, Ga., 1991—. Chmn. supervisory com. Texaco Fed. Credit Union, Atlanta, 1980-88; bd. dirs., treas. Atlanta Credit Union League, 1986-87; v.p. The Planning Forum, Atlanta, 1984-85. Alumni trustee The Lovett Sch., Atlanta, 1985-89. Capt. U.S. Army, 1966-68. Mem. Nat. Soc. Scabbard and Blade, Mil. Order of Stars and Bars, Beta Alpha Psi. Anglican. Avocations: personal computers, building custom fly fishing rods, genealogy.

NORTH, JULIE A., lawyer; b. Canberra, Australia, Mar. 20, 1962; BA cum laude, Hamilton Coll., NY, 1984; JD magna cum laude, Syracuse Univ., 1989. Bar: NY 1990. Assoc. Cravath Swaine & Moore LLP, NYC, 1989—97, ptnr., litig., 1997—. Notes, comments editor Syracuse Law Rev. Bd. trustees Hamilton Coll., Clinton, NY; bd. visitors Syracuse Univ. Coll. of Law. Office: Cravath Swaine & Moore LLP Worldwide Plz 825 Eighth Ave New York NY 10019-7475 Office Phone: 212-474-1752. Office Fax: 212-474-3700. Business E-Mail: jnorth@cravath.com.

NORTH, MARJORIE MARY, columnist; b. Mt. Clemens, Mich., Oct. 21, 1945; d. Robert Haller and Hilla Beryl (Willard) Wright; m. William B. Hirons; children: Laura, Christina, Angela. Features editor Elizabeth City (N.C.) Daily Advance, 1966-69; news/mng. editor Brandon (Fla.) News, 1977-78; city editor Leesburg (Fla.) Comml., 1978-79; metro editor Sarasota (Fla.) Herald Tribune, 1979-80, Fla. West editor, 1980-85, daily columnist, 1985—. Host Weekly Interview Show, SNN-TV, 1997—. Author: Sarasota: A City For All Seasons, 1994, (plays) With the Best Intentions, 1994, Back in the Game, 1998. Recipient Layout, Creativity and Overall Publ. awards Fla. Press Assn., numerous comty. awards and citations; winner Fla. shorts competition Fla. Studio Theater New Play Festival, 1994, 98; Paul Harris fellow. Avocations: tennis, entertaining, theater. Office: Sarasota Herald-Tribune PO Box 1719 Sarasota FL 34230-1719 E-mail: mnorth10@comcast.net.

NORTH, OLIVER LAURENCE (OLLIE NORTH), syndicated columnist, retired military officer; b. San Antonio, Oct. 7, 1943; m. Betsy Stuart, 1967; children: Tait, Dornin, Sarah, Stuart. Student, SUNY, Brockport; B, US Naval Acad., Annapolis. Commd. lt. USMC, 1966, advanced through ranks to lt. col., ret., 1990; mem. NSC, 1981—83; counter-terrorism coord. The White House, 1983—86; host, War Stories Fox News Channel; founder Freedom Alliance, 1990. Lectr. Oxford, Cambridge, Trinity Colls. Syndicated columnist; author: Under Fire: An American Story, 1991, War Stories: Operation Iraqi Freedom, 2003; co-author (with Joe Musser): War Stories II: Heroism in the Pacific, 2004; co-author: (with Sara Horn) A Greater Freedom: Stories of Faith from Operation Iraqi Freedom, 2004; co-author: (with Joe Musser) (novels) Mission Compromised, 2002, Jericho Sanction, 2003, The Assassins, 2005. Decorated Silver Star, Bronze Star, Purple Hearts (2). Address: Creators Syndicate Ste 700 5777 W Century Blvd Los Angeles CA 90045

NORTH, ROBERT L., computer software executive; b. Topeka, Sept. 19, 1935; BEE, Stanford U., 1953, MEE, 1958; postgrad., UCLA Grad. Bus. Sch., 1977; post grad., Stanford Grad. Bus. Sch., 1981. Tech. staff mem. Aerospace Corp., 1962-65; various positions TRW, 1965-81, v.p., gen. mgr., 1981-86; CEO HNC Software, Inc., San Diego, 1987-2000, chmn., 2000—. Mem. San Diego C. of C., 1983-84; bd. dir. San Diego Econ. Devel. Coun., 1983-84, United Way Pres. Coun., 1984 Office: Fair Isaac Corp 3661 Valley Centre Dr San Diego CA 92130-3317

NORTH, RYAN ELLIOT, geophysicist, researcher; b. Marion, Ohio, Mar. 9, 1975; s. Richard Eugene and Betty Allene North; m. Jessica Leigh Pond; children: Caleb Elliot, Cody James. BS in Engring. Physics, W.Va. Wesleyan Coll., Buckhannon, 1997; MS in Geophys. Engring., Colo. Sch. Mines, Golden, 2002. Geophys. intern Western Geophysics, New Iberia, La., 1997, Spirit Energy, Lafayette, La., 1998, Schlumberger-Doll Rsch., Ridgefield, Conn., 2001; rsch. geophysicist US Army ERDC, Vickburg, Miss., 2002—. Mem.: Environ. and Engring. Geophys. Soc. (assoc.), Am.

Geophys. Union (assoc.), Soc. Exploration Geophysicists (assoc.). Libertarian. Home: 4303 Windsor Point Vicksburg MS 39180 Office: US Army ERDC 3909 Halls Ferry Rd Vicksburg MS 39180 Home Phone: 601-631-8191; Office Phone: 601-634-3486. Office Fax: 601-634-3453. Business E-Mail: ryan.e.north@erdc.usace.army.mil.

NORTH, WILLIAM HAVEN, foreign service officer; b. Summit, NJ, Aug. 17, 1926; s. Eric M. and Gladys (Haven) N.; m. Jeanne Foote, Sept. 2, 1950; children: Jeannette Haven, William Ashby, Charles Eric. BA in History with honors, Wesleyan U., Middletown, Conn., 1949; MA in History, Columbia, 1951. Program officer ICA, Ethiopia, 1953-57; then dep. chief program divsn. ICA (African-European Regional Office), Washington, 1958—61; asst. dir. for program USAID Mission, Nigeria, until 1965; dir. Ctrl. and Western African affairs AID, Washington, 1966-70; mission dir. U.S. AID mission to Ghana, 1970-76; dep. asst. adminstr. Africa Bur. AID, 1976-82, spl. asst. Office of the Adminstr., 1982-83, assoc. asst. adminstr. Ctr. Devel. Info. and Evaluation, 1983-89, ret.; pvt. cons. Internat. Devel. for World Bank, 1989—, UN Devel. Program USAID, 1989—; coord. Evaluation of Global Environ. Facility, 1993, Evaluation Spl. Porgram of Asst. to Africa, 1997-98, Evaluation DAC/OECD Eval. Group, 1998; evaluator UNDP Aid Coordination, 1998—. Evaluator UNDB Global Program for HIV/AIDS, 2000, African Governance Capacity Bldg, UNDP, Danida, Denmark, 2002-03; fellow Ctr. for Internat. Affairs, Harvard U., 1965-66; chmn. experts group on evaluation Devel. Assistance Commn., OECD, 1985-88; vice-chmn. editl. bd. Fgn. Svc. Jour., 1983-86; mem. adv. panel on evaluation Inter-Am. Devel. Bank, 1993-94; prin. evaluator Internat. Fin. Corp.; program dir. U.S. Fgn. Assistance Oral History Program, 1995—; cons. UN Devel. Coop. Policy Branch, 2000-02. Interviewer Iraq, Afghanistan, Sudan for US Inst. Peace and Assn. Diplomatic Studies and Tng., 2005—06. Evaluator USAID Program in Iraq, 2003-04. Served with AUS, 1944-46. Recipient Meritorious Svc. award for exemplary achievement in pub. adminstrn., W.A. Jump Honor cert., Superior Honor award for Nigerian Relief Adminstrn., Equal Employment Opportunity award, Disting. Honor award AID, Presdl. Meritorious Svc. medal, Adminstrs. Career Svc. award. Mem. Soc. for Internat. Devel., African Studies Assn., Assn. Diplomatic Studies and Tng., Am. Evaluation Assn., Applachian Mountain Club. Methodist. Home and Office: Internat Development 6748 Brigadoon Dr Bethesda MD 20817-5436 Office Phone: 301-320-4235. E-mail: willnorth@aol.com.

NORTHCUTT, CLARENCE DEWEY, lawyer; b. Guin, Ala., July 7, 1916; s. Walter G. and Nancy E. (Homer) Northcutt; m. Ruth Eleanor Storms, May 25, 1941. AB, U. Okla., 1939, LL.B., 1938. Bar: Okla. 1938. Pvt. practice, Ponca City, 1938—. Mem. bd. visitors U. Okla. Served with AUS, 1941-46. Decorated Bronze Star, Air medal with oak leaf cluster, Order St. John of Jerusalem; named Outstanding Citizen of Ponca City, 1982; inducted to Okla. Hall of Fame, 2001. Fellow Am. Coll. Trial Lawyers, Am. Coll. Trust and Estate Attys., Am. Bar Found.; mem. Acad. Univ. Fellows, Internat. Soc. Barristers, Am. Bd. Advocacy, Internat. Acad. Trial Lawyers, Okla. Bar Assn. (pres. 1975, bd. govs.), Ponca City C. of C. (past pres.). Clubs: Mason, Kiwanian. Democrat. Baptist. Office: PO Box 1669 Ponca City OK 74602-1669 Office Phone: 580-762-1655. Business E-Mail: cdnorth@northcuttlawfirm.com.

NORTHCUTT, MARIE ROSE, elementary school educator, special education educator; b. White Plains, NY, Feb. 2, 1950; d. Carlo and Marcelline Marie Rose DeMarco; m. Kenneth Walter Northcutt, Mar. 17, 1984; children: James Lee, Thomas Joseph. BA, Lynchburg Coll., 1972; MA, Columbia U., 1977. Cert. elem. and secondary tchr., N.Y. Tchr. Petersburg (Va.) Pub. Schs., 1972-74; asst. relocation mgr. Ticor Co., White Plains, 1974-75; 3rd grade tchr. Resurrection Sch., Rye, 1975-76; 6th grade tchr. Harrison (N.Y.) Cen. Sch. Dist., 1976-78, learning disabilities specialist, 1981—; tchr. of emotionally handicapped N.Y.C. Schs., 1978-80; learning evaluator Empire State Coll., White Plains, 1981-82. Ind. evaluation cons., White Plains, 1981—; chair Mid. States Sub-com. Active Harrison H.S. PTA. Mem. Assn. for Children with Learning Disabilities, Westchester County Assn. for Children with Learning Disabilities, Spl. Edn. Parents Tchrs. Assn., Orton Soc., Phi Delta Kappa. Roman Catholic. Avocations: reading, cooking. Home: 81 Griffin Pl White Plains NY 10603-3609 Office: Harrison Cen Sch Dist Union Ave Harrison NY 10528-2108 Office Phone: 914-835-3300.

NORTHEN, CHARLES SWIFT, III, retired bank executive; b. Birmingham, Ala., Jan. 25, 1937; s. Charles Swift and Jennie Hood (Hunt) S.; m. Margaret Carson Robinson, Dec. 27, 1959 (div. 1972); children: Margaret Allen, Charles Swift IV, Bryce Robinson; m. Betty Jean Taylor, Oct. 3, 1981. BA cum laude, Vanderbilt U., 1959, MA, 1961. Chartered fin. analyst. Mem. staff trust dept. Birmingham Trust Nat. Bank, 1960-64; with First Ala. Bank Birmingham, 1964-80, sr. v.p., trust officer, 1975-80; Central Bank of South, Birmingham, 1981-85; exec. v.p. 1st Ala. Bankshares, 1985-95, corp. investment officer, 1993-95; mng. dir. Sterne, Agee & Leach, Inc., Birmingham, 1995-98, investment cons., 1998—2001; ret. Lectr. So. Trust Sch., Birmingham So. Coll.; pres. First Ala. Investments Inc.; dir. Hubbard Press, Findlay, Ohio. Bd. dirs. United Presbyn. Found., N.Y.C., 1977-86; mem. Birmingham Com. Fgn. Rels., 1970—. Mem. Ala. Security Dealers Assn. (pres.), Ala. Soc. Fin. Analysts (pres.), Inst. Chartered Fin. Analysts, Newcomen Soc., SAR, Kiwanis, Mountain Brook Club, The Club, Soc. Colonial Wars (Ala. gov. 2005-06). Presbyterian. Home: 3024 N Woodridge Rd Birmingham AL 35223-2748

NORTHERN, RICHARD, lawyer; b. Louisville, Dec. 17, 1948; s. James William and Mary Helen (Barry) Northern; m. Mary Lou Grundy, Aug. 28, 1971; children: James Barry, Nancy Hope, Mary Grace. BA in English, U. Louisville, 1970, JD, 1976; MPA, Harvard U., 1977. Bar: Ky. 1976, U.S. Dist. Ct. (we. and ea. dists.) Ky. 1977. Staff writer Courier-Jour., Louisville, 1970-72; dir. planning devel. Jefferson County Govt., Louisville, 1972-76; legis. dir. Office of U.S. Rep. Romano Mazzoli, Washington, 1977-78; spl. asst. U.S. Sec. of Interior, Washington, 1979-80; ptnr., mem. exec. com. Wyatt, Tarrant & Combs, Louisville, 1980—. Bd. dirs. Nugent Sand Co. Chmn. bd. dirs. Cath. Edn. Found., Inc., Louisville, 1998—; treas. Metro Louisville Devel. Authority, 2005—; chair athletic adv. bd. Spalding U., 2005—; chmn.-elect Jewish Hosp. Found., 2006—. White House fellow, 1979, U.S.-Japan Leadership fellow, Japan Soc., Inc., 1988. Democrat. Roman Catholic. Office: Wyatt Tarrant & Combs 2800 Citizens Plz Louisville KY 40202-2898 Office Phone: 502-562-7234. Business E-Mail: rnorthern@wyattfirm.com.

NORTHEY, WILLIAM THOMAS, microbiologist, educator; b. Duluth, Minn., Aug. 10, 1928; s. William Thomas Northey and Mary Ellen Riley; m. Margaret Esparza, July 1, 1972; m. Elizabeth L. Van Laeke, Aug. 12, 1950 (div. June 15, 1970); children: Kathleen, William Northey III, Bruce, Brian, Barry, Brett, Suzanne. BA, U. of Minn., 1950; MA, U. of Kans., 1957, PhD, 1959. Rsch. asst. Abbott Labs., Chgo., 1950—51, Naval Med Rsch. Unit #4, Gt. Lakes, Ill., 1951—55; tchg. and rsch. U. of Kans., Lawrence, Kans., 1955—59; from asst. prof. to prof. emeritus Ariz. State U., Tempe, Ariz., 1959—85, prof. emeritus, 1985—. Cons. Unidynamics Corp., Goodyear, Ariz., 1960—63, AiResearch Corp., Phoenix, 1963—65; pres., dir. Iatric Corp., Tempe, 1960—92. Contbr. articles to profl. jours. Vol. United Fund, Phoenix; grant reviewer Ariz. Heart Assn., Phoenix; bd. dir. Ariz. Br. of Allergy Found. of Ariz., Phoenix. Seaman second USNR, 1946—51. Grantee, NIH, 1960—85, USAF, 1963—68. Fellow: Am. Acad. of Microbiology; mem.: Am. Soc. of Immunology, Am. Soc. of Microbiology (pres. Ariz. chpt. 1963). Achievements include development of scorpion anti-venom; research in aeroallergens in Arizona. Avocations: skiing, swimming, reading. Home: 4818 N 72nd Way Scottsdale AZ 85251-1302

NORTHRIP, ROBERT EARL, lawyer; b. Sleeper, Mo., May 8, 1939; s. Novel and Jessie (Burch) N.; m. Linda Kay Francis, June 15, 1968; children: Robert E. Jr., William F., Darryl F., David F. BA, Southwest Mo. State, 1960; MA, U. N.C., 1965; JD, U. Mo., 1968. Bar: Mo. 1968, U.S. Dist. Ct. (we. dist.) Mo. 1968, U.S. Ct. Appeals (10th cir.) 1976, U.S. Ct. Appeals (8th cir.) 1980, U.S. Ct. Appeals (9th cir.) 1983, U.S. Ct. Appeals (3d cir.) 1987, U.S. Supreme Ct. 1978. Ptnr. Shook, Hardy & Bacon, Kansas City, Mo., 1968—. Active Nelson Art Gallery, Soc. of Fellows, Kans. City, Mo. 1st lt. US Army, 1963-65. Mem. Mo. Bar Assn., Lawyers Assn. Kansas City, Mo. Orgn. Def. Lawyers, Kansas City Met. Bar Assn., U. Mo. Alumni Assn. (past pres. Kansas City chpt.), Nat. Soc. Arts and Letters. Republican. Avocations: baseball, football. Office: Shook Hardy & Bacon 2555 Grand Blvd Kansas City MO 64108-2613 Home: 6439 Wenonga Rd Mission Hills KS 66208 Office Phone: 816-474-6550. Business E-Mail: rnorthrip@shb.com.

NORTHRUP, CHRISTIANE, obstetrician, gynecologist; b. Buffalo, Oct. 4, 1949; d. George Wilbur and Edna (Zwilling) N.; children: Ann Christiane, Kate Northrup. BA, Case Western Res., 1971; MD, Dartmouth Coll., 1975. Diplomate Am. Bd. Ob-Gyn. Intern Tufts New Eng. Med. Ctr. Affiliated Hosps., Boston, 1975; intern then resident Tufts New Eng. Med. Ctr., Boston, 1976-79; assoc. clin. prof. ob-gyn Tufts U. Sch. Medicine, Boston, 1979-80; clin. instr. ob-gyn U. Vt. Coll. Med., Portland, Maine, 1980—82, asst. clin. prof. ob-gyn, 1982—2001; practice medicine specializing in ob-gyn Gynecol. Assocs., South Portland, 1979-85, Women's Health Care Orgn. Women to Women, Yarmouth, Maine, 1985—96; private practice ob-gyn, Yarmouth, Maine, 1979—. Mem. high risk perinatal group Maine Med. Ctr., Portland, 1981-83. Author: Mother-Daughter Wisdom, 2005, The Wisdom of Menopause, 2001, Women's Bodies, Women's Wisdom, 1998; contbr. various articles on women's health to profl. jours. Fellow Am. Coll. Ob-Gyn; mem. Am. Holistic Med. Assn. (sec. 1986-88, pres. 1988-90), Am. Holistic Med. Found. (pres. 1986-88). Avocations: music, harpist, skiing, movies, yoga. Office: PO Box 199 Yarmouth ME 04096

NORTHRUP, HERBERT ROOF, economist; b. Irvington, NJ, Mar. 6, 1918; m. Eleanor Pearson, June 3, 1944; children: James Pearson, Nancy Warren, Jonathan Peter, David Oliver, Philip Wilson. AB, Duke U., 1939; A.M., Harvard U., 1941, PhD, 1942. Instr. econs. Cornell U., 1942-43; sr. hearing officer Nat. War Labor Bd., 1943-45; asst. prof. econs. Columbia U., 1945-49; labor economist Nat. Indsl. Conf. Bd., 1949-52; indsl. relations cons. Ebasco Services, 1952-55; v.p. indsl. relations Penn-Texas Corp., NYC, 1955-58; employee relations mgr. Gen. Electric Co., 1958-61; prof. industry Wharton Sch., U. Pa., Phila., 1961-88, prof. emeritus, 1988—, chmn. dept. industry, 1964-69, dir. indsl. rsch. unit, 1964-88, chmn. Labor Rels. Coun., 1968-85. Cons. and expert witness on manpower, pers. and labor rels. problems for many cos.; arbitrator in labor rels. disputes. Author: Organized Labor and the Negro, 1944, Unionization of Professional Engineers and Chemists, 1946, Economics of Labor Relations, 1950, 9th edit., 1981, Government and Labor, 1963, Readings in Labor Economics, 1963, Boulwarism: Labor Policies of General Electric Company, 1964, Negro and Employment Opportunity, 1965, Hours of Labor, 1965, Compulsory Arbitration and Government Intervention in Labor Disputes, 1966, Restrictive Labor Practices in Supermarket Industry, 1967, Negro in the Automobile Industry, 1968, Negro in the Aerospace Industry, 1968, Negro in the Rubber Tire Industry, 1969, Negro in Paper Industry, 1969, Negro in the Tobacco Industry, 1970, Negro Employment in Basic Industry, 1970, Negro Employment in Southern Industry, 1970, Negro Employment in Land and Air Transport, 1971, Impact of Government Manpower Programs, 1975, Open Shop Construction, 1975, The Impact of OSHA, 1978, Objective Selection of Supervisors, 1978, Black and Other Minority Participation in the All-Volunteer Navy and Marine Corps, 1979, Manpower in the Retail Pharmacy Industry, 1979, The Impact of the ATT-EEO Consent Decree, 1979, Multinational Collective Bargaining Attempts, 1979, Multinational Union Organizations in the Manufacturing Industries, 1980, Employee Relations and Regulations in the 80s, 1982, Internat. Transport Workers' Federation and Flag of Convenience Shipping, 1983, Open Shop Construction Revisited, 1984, Personnel Policies for Engineers and Scientists, 1985, Doublebreasted Operations and Pre-Hire Agreements in Construction: The Facts and the Law, 1987, The Federal Government as Employer: The Federal Labor Relations Authority and the PATCO Challenge, 1988, The Changing Role of Women in Research and Development, 1988, Government Protection of Employees in Mergers and Acquisitions, 1989, The Railway Labor Act, 1990, Union Corporate Campaigns and Inside Games as a Strike Form, 1994, Union Violence: The Record and the Response by Courts, Legislatures, and the NLRB, rev. edit., 1999, Construction Union Tactics to Regain Jobs and Public Policy, 2007, The Impact of Union-Management Relations on Urban Industrial Employment, 2000; contbr. over 300 articles in field. Mem. Am. Econ. Assn., Indsl. Relations Research Assn., Am. Arbitration Assn., Phi Beta Kappa. Clubs: Harvard (N.Y.C.); Harvard-Radcliffe (Phila.); University (Washington), Faculty (U. Pa.). Home and Office: 205 Avon Rd Haverford PA 19041-1612 Office Phone: 610-642-1293.

NORTHUP, ANNE MEAGHER, former congresswoman; b. Louisville, Jan. 22, 1948; d. James L. and Floy Gates (Terstegge) Meagher; m. Robert Wood Northup, Apr. 12, 1969; children: David, Katherine, Joshua, Kevin, Erin, Mark. BA in Econs. and Bus., St. Mary's Coll. Notre Dame, South Bend, Ind., 1970. Mem. Ky. Ho. of Reps., Frankfort, 1987-96, US Congress from 3d Ky. Dist., 1997—2007; mem. house appropriations com.; founder House Reading Caucus, 1998; mem. speaker's drug free task force, 1998; chair speaker's task force on education, 1998; mem. World Trade Org. congl. advisory group, 1999, free trade working group, 2000, comm. on educational accountability, 1993—95, economic development task force, 1991—92, task force to study highway needs, 1990—91, state debt capacity task force. Mem. fin. adv. bd. EPA, 1989-93; mem. home econs. adv. bd. U. Ky. Coll. Agr., 1992— Appeared on Meet the Press, Fox News Sunday, Larry King Live, CNN & Co., Hardball with Chris Matthews. Mem. exec. com. Partnership Ky. Sch. Reform, 1990—; bd. dirs. Greater Louisville Pub. Radio, 1993—, Hospice Louisville, 1994—, Ky. Cancer Consortium, 1992—; mem. cmty. adv. bd. Jr. League Louisville, 1993—; active Holy Spirit Cath. Ch. Named Outstanding Woman of Achievement St. Matthews BPW, 1990; recipient Cath. Schs. Disting. Alumni award, 1991, U. Notre Dame award of the yr. Ky. Alumni Assn., 1991, Clearing the Air award Am. Lung Assn. of Ky., 1991, Svc. Above Self award St. Matthews Rotary Club, 1992, Pub. Svc. award Am. Heart Assn., 1992, Sacred Heart Acad. Alumna award, 1994, Nat. Fedn. of Ind. Bus./Guardian of Small Bus. award, 1996, 97, 98, Legislator of Yr. award Environ. Industry Assn., 1997, Outstanding Freshman Mem. of Congress award Nat. Industries for Blind, 1997, Spirit of Enterprise award U.S. C. of C., 1997, Bulldog award Watchdogs of Treasury, 1998, Jefferson award Citizens for Sound Economy, 1998, Outstanding Support award Am. Printing House for Blind, 1998, Legislator of Yr. award Assn. Equipment Distbrs., 1999, Cmty. Healthcare Champion award Nat. Assn. Cmty. Health Ctrs., Inc., 1999, Spirit of Enterprise award C. of C., 1999, Susan B. Anthony Congl. award, 1999, Pub. Policy Adv. of Yr. award Nat. Assn. Women Bus. Owners, 1999, Honor Roll of Legis. Achievement in Econ. Devel. award So. Econ. Devel. Coun., Inc., 1999, Legislator of Yr. award Nat. Beer Whoesalers Assn., 1999. Mem. Nat. Order Women Legislators, Nat. Conf. State Legislators, Nat. Rep. Legis. Conf., Inst. Rep. Women, So. Legis. Conf. (alternate from Ky. to fiscal affairs and govtl. com.), Nat. Fedn. Ind. Bus. Republican. Roman Catholic.

NORTHUP, NANCY JEAN, lawyer; b. 1959; BA magna cum laude, Brown Univ.; JD, Columbia Univ. Law clk. to Hon. Alvin B. Rubin US Ct. Appeals (fifth cir.); asst. US atty. So. Dist. NY, 1989—96; cons. atty. ACLU Reproductive Freedom Project; dir. Democracy Program Brennan Ctr. Justice, NYU, 1996—2002; pres. Ctr. for Reproductive Rights, NYC, 2003—. Adj. prof. NYU; tchr. Columbia Law Sch. Editor (mng.): Columbia Law Rev. Kent Scholar. Office: Ctr for Reproductive Rights 120 Wall St New York NY 10005 Office Phone: 917-637-3600. Office Fax: 917-637-3666.

NORTON, DAVID K., publishing executive, human resources specialist; married; 5 children. BS, Mich. State U. Dir. human resources Quaker Oats Co., Chgo., PepsiCo, Inc., 1990—94, sr. v.p. food systems, 1994—95, sr. v.p. human resources Frito-Lay N.Am., 1996—2000; exec. v.p. human resources Starwood Hotels & Resorts Worldwide, Inc., White Plains, NY, 2000—06; sr. v.p. human resources NY Times Co., NYC, 2006—. Office: New York Times Co 229 W 43d St New York NY 10036

NORTON, DOUGLAS EVATT, mathematician, educator; b. Danville, Ill., Aug. 2, 1957; s. Luther Hooper and Lucy Evatt N.; m. Kathryn Ann Friggle, Sept. 15, 1979; children: Hannah, Jacob. BS, Wake Forest U., 1979; MA, U. Wis., 1984; PhD, U. Minn., 1989. Asst. prof. math. scis. Villanova (Pa.) U., 1989-96, assoc. prof. math. scis., 1996—, chair dept. math. scis., 2003—. Fulbright lectr., rsch. scholar U. Botswana, 1996-97. Contbr. articles to profl. jours. Co-pres. Haverford H.S. Parent-Tchr. Student Assn., Havertown, Pa., 1999-2000. Rotary fellow 1979-80. Mem. AAAS, AAUP, Am. Math. Soc., Math. Assn. Am., Soc. for Indsl. and Applied Math., Assn. for Women in Math., Nat. Coun. Tchrs. Math., Pa. Acad. Sci., Phi Beta Kappa, Omicron Delta Kappa, Phi Kappa Phi, Sigma Xi. Home: 12 Llandaff Rd Havertown PA 19083 Office: Villanova U Dept Math Scis 800 Lancaster Ave Villanova PA 19085 Office Phone: 610-519-4850. Fax: 610-519-6928. E-mail: douglas.norton@villanova.edu.

NORTON, DOUGLAS RAY, former auditor general; b. Portales, N.Mex., Mar. 23, 1933; s. Clayton G. and Lillian W. Norton; m. Wanda Jones, May 23, 1951 (div. July 1979); children: Debbie Norton Goodman, Vicki Norton Hulet, Denise Norton Jolley; m. Robertta J. Andersen, July 31, 1998. BS, U. Ariz., 1963. CPA, Ariz. Staff acct., audit supr. Ernst & Ernst, Tucson, Ariz., 1963-67; ptnr. Baker, Price & Norton, Prescott, Ariz., 1968-75, Lester Witte & Co., Prescott, Ariz., 1975-76; auditor gen. State of Ariz., Phoenix, 1976-99; ret., 1999. Former mem. Profl. Adv. Bd. Sch. Acctg. Ariz. State U., Tempe; former mem. acctg. bd. advisors U. Ariz. Pres. Prescott Bd. Edn., 1976. Served with U.S. Army, 1953-55. Mem. AICPA, Ariz. Soc. CPAs, Nat. Assn. State Auditors, Comptrollers and Treasurers (pres. 1993-94), Nat. State Auditors Assn. (pres. 1982-83), Lions (pres. Prescott chpt. 1973-74). Home: PO Box 3120 Chino Valley AZ 86323-2707

NORTON, DUNBAR SUTTON, economic developer; b. Hoquiam, Wash., Jan. 30, 1926; s. Percy Dunbar and Anna Fedelia (Sutton) N.; m. Kathleen Margaret Mullarky, Dec. 21, 1948 (dec. Apr. 1994); children: Priscilla K., Rebecca C., Jennifer A., Douglas S.; m. Mary Ethel Wolff, May 25, 1996. Student, U. Oreg., 1946—48; diploma, U.S. Army Command & Gen. Staff, 1964. Enlisted U.S. Army, 1944, commd. 2d lt., 1948, advanced through grades to lt. col., ret., 1974; dir. econ. devel. dept. Yuma County C. of C., Ariz., 1974—83; exec. v.p. Lakin Enterprises, Yuma, 1983—87; owner Norton Cons., Yuma, 1987—. Corp. mem. Greater Yuma Econ. Devel. Corp., 1984-96, vice chmn., 1993-95; dir. Lower Colo. River Rsch. Ctr. Ariz. West Coll./No. Ariz. U., 1996-2000 Active Yuma County Indsl. Devel. Authority, 1984-90, 92-2006, pres., 1992-2006; chmn. fund-raising com. Yuma Cross Park Coun., 1984-88, sec., 1988-90, v.p., 1990-92, bd. dirs., 1982-96; bd. dirs. Yuma Leadership, 1984-93, Yuma Youth Leadership, 1993-96, Ariz. Partnership Air Transp., 1990-96, v.p., 1993-95; chmn. devel. com. Yuma County Airport Authority, 1985-92, v.p., 1992-2002, pres., 2003-04, chmn. mktg. com., 2004, dir., 2007; vice chmn. Yuma Main St. Bd., 1988-90, Yuma County Geog. Info. Sys. Task Force, 1991-95, Yuma Kids Voting, 1990-91; bd. dirs. Yuma County Civic Trusteeship, 1993-95, Ariz. We. Coll. Found. Bd., 2000-02, chmn. scholar awards commn., 2000-02; chmn. The Southwest Inst., 1995-96, What's Best for Our Kids, 1995-96, Yuma Sch. Dist. No. 1 New Elem. Sch. Planning Com., 1996-97, co-chmn. maintain level budget override com., 1999-2001; trustee Yuma County Libr., 1996-02; chmn. Yuma County Complete Count com. U.S. Census, 1990, 95, 2000; com. mem. Yuma County Town Hall, 1999-2005. Decorated Legion of Merit with oak leaf cluster, Bronze Star, Meritorious Svc. and Army Commendation Medal with Oak Leaf Cluster Mem. Ariz. Assn. for Econ. Devel. (bd. dirs. 1975-82, pres. 1982-83, legis. affairs com. 1987-2002, Developer of Yr. 1978, William W. Lampkin award 2001), Yuma Execs. Assn. (sec.-treas., exec. dir. 1987—) Republican. Roman Catholic. Avocations: golf, swimming, singing. Home and Office: 12267 E Del Norte Yuma AZ 85367-7356 Office Phone: 928-342-6217. Personal E-mail: yumexec@msn.com.

NORTON, EDWARD C., economist, educator; PhD, MIT, Boston, 1990. Asst. prof. Harvard Med. Sch., Boston, 1990—93; sr. economist RTI Internat., Research Triangle Park, NC, 1993—96; prof. U. N.C. Chapel Hill, 1996—. Recipient Phillip and Ruth Hettleman prize, U. N.C. Chapel Hill, 2003. Mem.: Am. Soc. Health Economists (bd. trustees 2004—06). Office: Dept Health Policy and Adminstrn Univ North Carolina Chapel Hill NC 27599

NORTON, ELEANOR HOLMES, congresswoman, lawyer, educator; b. Washington, June 13, 1937; d. Coleman and Vela (Lynch) Holmes; m. Edward W. Norton (div.); children: Katherine Felicia, John Holmes. BA, Antioch Coll., 1960; MA in Am. Studies, Yale U., 1963, LLB, 1964. Bar: Pa., 1965, U.S. Supreme Ct., 1968. Law clk. to Judge A. Leon Higginbotham Fed. Dist. Ct., 1964-65; asst. legal dir. ACLU, 1965-70; exec. asst. to mayor City of N.Y., 1971-74; chmn. N.Y.C. Commn. on Human Rights, 1970-77, EEOC, Washington, 1977-81; sr. fellow Urban Inst., Washington, 1981-82; prof. law Georgetown U., Washington, 1982—; del. (at large) US Congress from DC, 1990—, mem. coms. on govt. reform and transp./infrastructure. Named one of 100 Most Influential Black Americans, Ebony mag., 2006. Democrat. Office: US Ho of Reps 2136 RayburnHo Office Bldg Washington DC 20515-0001 Office Phone: 202-225-8050. Office Fax: 202-225-3002. *

NORTON, ELIZABETH WYCHGEL, retired lawyer; b. Cleve., Mar. 25, 1933; d. James Nicolas and Ruth Elizabeth (Cannell) Wychgel; m. Henry Wacks Norton Jr., July 16, 1954 (div. 1971); children: James, Henry, Peter, Fred; m. James Cory Ferguson, Dec. 14, 1985 (div. Apr. 1988). BA in Math., Wellesley Coll., 1954; JD cum laude, U. Minn., 1974. Bar: Minn. 1974. Summer intern Minn. Atty. Gen.'s Office, St. Paul, 1972; with U.S. Dept. Treasury, St. Paul, 1973; assoc. Gray, Plant, Mooty, Mooty & Bennett, P.A., Mpls., 1974-79, prin., 1980-94, of counsel, 1995-96; ret. Mem. Minn. Lawyers Bd. Profl. Responsibility, 1984-89; mem. U. Minn. Law Sch. Bd. Visitors, 1987-92. Trustee YWCA, Mpls., 1979-84, 89-91, co-chmn. deferred giving com., 1980-81, chmn. by-laws com., bd. dirs., 1976-77, lectr.; treas. Minn. Women's Campaign Fund, 1985, guarantor, 1982-83, budget and fin. com. bd. dirs., 1984-87; trustee Ripley Meml. Found., 1980-84; treas. Jones-Harrison Home, 1967, bd. dirs., 1962-69, 2d v.p., chmn. fin., 1968-69; mem. Sen. David Durenberger's Women's Network, 1983-88. Durant scholar. Fellow Am. Bar Found.; mem. ABA (mediation task force family law sect. 1983-84), Minn. Bar Assn. (human rights com. family law sect., task force uniform marital property act 1984-85), Minn. Bar Found. (dir. 1991-94), Hennepin County Bar Assn. (pres. 1987-88, chmn. task force on pub. edn. 1984, chmn., mem. exec. com. family law sect. 1979-94), Minn. Inst. Legal Edn., Minn. Women's Lawyers (exec. com.), Hemlock Soc. of S.W. Fla. (co-chmn. 1999-2001), U. Minn. Law Sch. Alumni Assn. (dir. 1975-81, exec. com. 1981-83), Wellesley Club (Naples, pres. 2002-04), Phi Beta Kappa. Home: 26 Water Oaks Way Naples FL 34105-7157 Personal E-mail: betsynorton@comcast.net.

NORTON, FLOYD LIGON, IV, lawyer; b. Shreveport, La., Oct. 23, 1950; s. Floyd Ligon III and Grace Louise (Julian) N.; m. Kathleen Fair Patterson, Nov. 24, 1979; children: Caroline, Elizabeth. BA with honors, U. Va., 1972, JD, 1975. Bar: Va. 1975, D.C. 1975. Assoc. Reid & Priest, Washington, 1975-83, ptnr., 1983-95, Morgan Lewis & Bockius, 1995—. Mem. ABA, Fed. Energy Bar Assn. Episcopalian. Home: 4107 Bradley Ln Bethesda MD 20815-5236 Office: Morgan Lewis & Bockius 1111 Pennsylvania Ave NW Washington DC 20004-5802 E-mail: fnorton@morganlewis.com.

NORTON, GALE ANN, lawyer, former secretary of the interior; b. Wichita, Mar. 11, 1954; d. Dale Bentsen and Anna Jacqueline (Lansdowne) N.; m. John Goethe Hughes, Mar. 26, 1990. BA, U. Denver, 1975, JD, 1978. Bar: Colo. 1978, U.S. Supreme Ct. 1981. Jud. clk. Colo. Ct. Appeals, Denver, 1978-79; sr. atty. Mountain States Legal Found., Denver, 1979-83; nat. fellow Hoover Instn. Stanford (Calif.) U., 1983-84; asst. to dep. sec. USDA, Washington, 1984-85; assoc. solicitor US Dept. Interior, Washington, 1985-87; pvt. practice law Denver, 1987-90; atty. gen. State of Colo., Denver, 1991—99; sr. counsel Brownstein, Hyatt & Farber, P.C., 1999—2000; sec. US Dept. Interior, Washington, 2001—06; gen. counsel Shell Unconventional Resources, Colo., 2007—. Lectr. U. Denver Law Sch., 1989; transp. law program dir. U. Denver, 1978-79. Contbr. chpts. to books, articles to profl. jours. Past chair Nat. Assn. Attys. Gen. Environ. Com.; co-chair Nat. Policy Forum Environ. Coun.; candidate for 1996 election to U.S. Senate; chair environ. commn. Rep. Nat. Lawyers Assn. Named Young Career Woman Bus. and Profl. Women, 1981, Young Lawyer of Yr., 1991, Mary Lathrop Trailblazer award Colo. Women's Bar Assn., 1999. Mem. Federalist Soc., Colo. Women's Forum, Order of St. Ives. Republican. Methodist. Avocation: skiing.

NORTON, GLYN PETER, literature educator; b. Exeter, Devonshire, England, May 22, 1941; s. Trevor Thomas and Betty (Marshall) N.; m. Victoria Josefina Perez, Oct. 28, 1966; children: Alexandra, Leslie. AB, U. Mich., 1963, AM, 1965, PhD, 1968. Asst. prof. Dartmouth Coll., Hanover, NH, 1968-71; prof. French lit. Pa. State U., University Park, 1971-88; prof. French lit., chmn. dept. romance langs., dir. Ctr. Fgn. Langs., Lits. and Cultures, Williams Coll., Williamstown, Mass., 1988-93, Willcox B. and Harriet M. Adsit prof. internat. studies, 1993—. Author: Montaigne and the Introspective Mind, The Ideology and Language of Translation in Renaissance France, 1984, Improvisation and Inspiration in Quintilan, 2007; editor: The Cambridge History of Literary Criticism, vol. III, 1999; contbr. articles to ednl. jours. Recipient medal City of Melun, France, 1985; NEH fellow, 1973-74, Guggenheim fellow, 1986-87; Am. Coun. Learned Socs. grantee, 1980-81, 85. Fellow Camargo Found.; mem. MLA, Renaissance Soc. Am., Soc. Francaise des Seiziemistes. Avocations: music, gardening, travel. Office: Williams Coll Dept Romance Langs Weston Hall Williamstown MA 01267 Business E-Mail: glyn.p.norton@williams.edu.

NORTON, HUGO WILBERT, JR., journalism educator, dean; b. Karawa, Equatore, Congo, Jan. 13, 1942; came to the U.S., 1949; s. H. Wilbert Norton Sr. and Colene Woodard; m. Susan Kathryn Langdon, Mar. 15, 1980; children: William Kinsey, Elaine Langdon. BA with honors, Wheaton Coll., 1963; MDiv, Garrett Evang. Theol. Sem., 1971; MA, Ind. U., 1971; PhD, U. Iowa, 1974. Sports editor The Daily Jour., Wheaton, Ill., 1963-64; copy editor Chgo. Tribune, 1965-68; mng. editor Christian Life, Inc., Wheaton, 1968-70, The Daily Iowan, Iowa City, 1972-73, pub., 1973-74; prof. U. Miss., Oxford, 1974-90; prof., dean U. Nebr., Lincoln, 1990—. Trustee The First Amendment Ctr., Nashville, 1996—, The Freedom Forum, Arlington, Va., 1998—; bd. mem. Christian Life Missions, Lake Mary, Fla. Mem. Assn. for Edn. in Journalism and Mass Comm. (pres. elect 1999—), Assn. Schs. Journalism and Mass. Comm. (pres. 1989-90), Coun. on Edn. in Journalism and Mass Comm. (accrediting com. 1992-98). Avocation: golf. Home: 3430 Woodshire Pkwy Lincoln NE 68502-4848 Office: Coll Journalism & Mass Comm Univ Nebr Lincoln NE 68588-0127

NORTON, JANE ELLEN BERGMAN (JANE BERGMAN), former lieutenant governor; b. Grand Junction, Colo. d. Walter F. and Elinor (Pitman) Bergman; m. Mike Norton; children: Lacee, Tyler. BS in Health Sci., with distinction, Colo. State U., 1976; MS in Mgmt., Regis U. With Med. Group Mgmt. Assn., Englewood, Colo.; mem. Colo. Ho. Reps., 1986—87; regional dir. US Dept. Health and Human Svcs.; exec. dir. Colo. Dept. Pub. Health Environment, 1999—2002; lt. gov. State of Colo., Denver, 2003—07. Chair Colo. Commn. on Indian Affairs; del. Aerospace State Assn., Edn. Commn. of States; co-chair Colo. Space Coalition; Colo. spokesperson Go Red for Women Campaign Am. Heart Assn.; hon. chair Prematurity Campaign Colo. March of Dimes; hon. chair Colo. Freedom Meml. Bd. dirs. Internat. Found. Electronic Systems, Am. Coun. Young Polit. Leaders; nat. bd. adv. Inst. Sci. and Space Studies; adv. bd. women's health U. Colo.; bd. adv. Colo. History Day; co-chair Colo. Health Disparities Commn. Named Woman of Distinction, Girls Scouts, 2005, Public Servant of Yr., Rocky Mt. Family Coun.; recipient Disting. Veterans Advocate award, United Veterans Com. Colo., Legislator of Yr. award, Persons Living with HIV Action Network of Colo., David M. Clark, S.J. Innovative Leadership award, Regis U., Family Values award, State of Colo., Honor Alumna award, Colo. State U. Coll. Applied Human Sci., US Public Health Svc. award outstanding accomplishment increasing childhood immunization rates, Outstanding Svc. to Seniors award, US Adminstrn. on Aging. Mem.: Nat. Lt. Governors Assn. (chair-elect 2006), Omicron Kappa Upsilon (hon.). Republican. Avocations: hiking, skiing. *

NORTON, KAREN ANN, accountant; b. Nov. 1, 1950; d. Dale Francis and Ruby Grace (Gehlhar) N. BA, U. Minn., 1972; postgrad., U. Md., 1978; MBA, Calif. State Poly. U., Pomona, 1989. CPA Md. Securities transactions analyst Bur. of Pub. Debt, Washington, 1972-79, internal auditor, 1979-81, IRS, Washington, 1981; sr. acct. World Vision Internat., Monrovia, Calif., 1981-83, acctg. supr., 1983-87; sr. sys. liaison coord. Home Savs. Am. (name changed to Washington Mut.), 1987-97, sys. auditor, 1997-2000, sect. mgr., 2000—02, group mgr., v.p., 2003—04, v.p., 2005—; project mgr. II Indy Mac Bank, 2004—05, v.p. to pres., 2005—. Author: (poetry) Ode to Joyce, 1985 (Golden Poet award 1985). 2d v.p. chpt. Nat. Treasury Employees Union, Washington, 1978, editor chpt. newsletter; mem. M-2 Prisoners Sponsorship Program, Chino, Calif., 1984-86. Recipient Spl. Achievement award Dept. Treasury, 1976, Superior Performance award Dept. Treasury, 1977-78; Charles and Ellora Alliss scholar, 1968. Mem. Angel Flight, Flying Samaritans, Habitat for Humanity. Avocations: flying, chess, tennis. E-mail: skypilot@pacbell.net.

NORTON, LARA BROOKS, physical education educator, education educator; d. Marion D. and Kaye Brooks; m. Don A. Norton, Dec. 18, 1993; children: Kayelin, Brooks. EdS in Ednl. Leadership, Ga. So. U., Statesboro. Ednl. leadership Ga. Profl. Stds. Commn., 2006, cert. health and phys. edn. Ga., 1992. Grad. tchg. asst. Ga. So. U., Statesboro; tchr. Toombs County H.S., Lyons, Ga., Washington-Wilkes Mid. Sch., Ga., 1994—98; adj. health prof. Truett McConnell Coll., Washington, 1996—98; tchr. Johnson County Elem., Wrightsville, Ga., 1998—2000; asst. prof. East Ga. Coll., Swasinboro, 2002—. Site coord. Destination Tchg. Program, Swainsboro, 2002—04; advisor Student PA Ga. Educators, Swainsboro, 2002—; group fitness instr. East Ga. Coll., Swainsboro, 2005—; mem. Bd. Regents Area F Resource Team, Ga., 2006—. Mem.: Pa. Ga. Educators (assoc.), Beta Sigma Phi. Home Phone: 478-237-6462; Office Phone: 478-289-2148. Business E-Mail: lnorton@ega.edu.

NORTON, LARRY, oncologist, researcher; b. Bronx, NY, 1947; MD, Columbia U., 1972. Diplomate Am. Bd. Internal Medicine, Am. Bd. Oncology. Intern Bronx Mcpl. Hosp.-Einstein, NYC, 1972-73, resident, 1973-74; mem. staff Meml. Sloan-Kettering Cancer Ctr., NYC, dep. physician-in-chief breast cancer programs, dir. Specialized Program of Rsch. Excellence in Breast Cancer, med. dir. Evelyn H. Lauder Breast Ctr. and Iris Cantor Diagnostic Ctr., Norna S. Sarofim chair clin. oncology, 1995—. Former chair breast com. Cancer and Leukemia Group B, Nat. Cancer Inst.; prin. investigator Program Project Grant, Nat. Cancer Inst.; mem. National Cancer Adv. Bd. Co-recipient NYC Award for Advancement of Cancer Medicine, Gilda's Club, 2006; recipient Sci. Achievement Award, Susan G. Komen Found., 1997. Mem.: Nat. Alliance of Breast Cancer Organs. (pres.), Am. Soc. Clin. Oncology (pres. 2001—02, David A. Karnofsky Meml. Award 2004), Alpha Omega Alpha. Achievements include being the co-developer of the Norton-Simon Hypothesis. Office: Meml Sloan-Kettering Cancer Ctr 1275 York Ave New York NY 10021-6094 Office Phone: 212-639-5325. *

NORTON, MARY BETH, history educator, writer; b. Ann Arbor, Mich., Mar. 25, 1943; d. Clark Frederic and Mary Elizabeth (Lunny) N. BA, U. Mich., 1964; MA, Harvard U., 1965, PhD, 1969; DHL (hon.), Siena Coll., 1983, Marymount Manhattan Coll., 1984, De Pauw U., 1989; DLitt (hon.), Ill. Wesleyan U., 1992. Asst. prof. history U. Conn., Storrs, 1969-71; from asst. prof. to prof. Cornell U., Ithaca, NY, 1971-87, Mary Donlon Alger prof. Am. history, 1987—. Pitt prof. Am. history and instn. U. Cambridge, 2005—06. Author: The British-Americans: The Loyalist Exiles in England, 1774-1789, 1972, Liberty's Daughters: The Revolutionary Experience of American Women, 1750-1800, 1980 (Berkshire prize for Best Book Woman Historian 1980), Founding Mothers and Fathers: Gendered Power and the Forming of American Society, 1996 (finalist Pulitzer prize in history 1997), In the Devil's Snare: The Salem Witchcraft Crisis of 1692, 2002 (Amb. Book award of English-Speaking Union 2003); co-author: A People and A Nation, 1982, 7th rev. edit., 2004; editor: AHA Guide to Hist. Literature, 3d rev. edit., 1995; co-editor: Women of America: A History, 1979, To Toil the Livelong Day: America's Women at Work, 1790-1980, 1987, Major Problems in American Women's History, 1989, 4th rev. edit., 2007; contbr. articles to profl. jours. Trustee Cornell U., 1973-75, 83-88; mem. Nat. Coun. Humanities, Washington, 1979-84. Woodrow Wilson Found. fellow, 1964-65, NEH fellow, 1974-75, Shelby Cullom Davis Ctr. fellow Princeton U., 1977-78, Rockefeller Found. fellow, 1986-87, Soc. for Humanities fellow Cornell U., 1989-90, John Simon Guggenheim Meml. Found. fellow, 1993-94, Starr Found. fellow Lady Margaret Hall, Oxford U., 2000, Mellon postdoctoral fellow Huntington Libr., 2001. Fellow Soc. Am. Hist. (exec. bd. 1974-87, 2003—, v.p. 2007, Allan Nevins prize 1970); mem. Am. Hist. Assn. (v.p. for rsch. 1985-87), Am. Acad. Arts and Sci., Orgn. Am. Hist. (exec. bd. 1983-86), Berkshire Conf. Women Hist. (pres. 1983-85) Democrat. Methodist. Office: Cornell U Dept History 325 Mcgraw Hall Ithaca NY 14853-4601 Home Phone: 607-277-2944. Business E-Mail: mbn1@cornell.edu.

NORTON, NORMAN JAMES, retired exploration geologist, educator; b. Du Quoin, Ill., Apr. 26, 1933; s. James Harlan Norton and Helen Jane (Riley) Norton Rosen; m. Bettie Jean Greer, July 7, 1955; children—Matthew James, Jane Alison BS, So. Ill. U., 1958; MS, U. Minn., 1960, PhD, 1963. From asst. to prof. biology Hope Coll., Holland, Mich., 1964-74; prof., chmn. dept. biology Ball State U., Munice, Ind., 1974-78, acting v.p. acad. affairs, 1978-79; acting dean Ball State U. Coll. Arts and Scis., 1979-81; provost, v.p. acad. affairs Ind. U. Pa., 1981-83; cons. geologist Gulf Oil Corp., Houston, 1970-83; sr. staff geologist Gulf Oil Exploration and Prodn. Co., Houston, 1983-85; biostratigrapher, stratigraphic services, exploration Chevron Overseas Petroleum Inc., San Ramon, Calif., 1985-91; supr. biostratigraphy sect. Chevron U.S.A., Inc., Houston, 1991-93; acting divsn. geologist Chevron U.S.A. Inc., Houston, 1993-95, divsn. geologist, 1995—, geol. cons., 1997-98, ret., 1998. Contbr. articles to profl. jours. Chmn. bd. trustees Kiawah Island Natural Habitat Conservancy, 2002—. With USAF, 1952—56. Recipient Outstanding Tchr. Educator award Sr. Class of Hope Coll., 1969, acad. citation for disting. achievement Mich. Acad. Scis., Art and Letters, 1969, Outstanding Achievement award Chevron Overseas Petroleum Inc., 1990. Mem. Am. Assn. Stratigraphic Palynologists (Disting. Svc. award 1978, chmn. bd. trustees found., archives com. 1970—, constrn. revision com.). Home: 514 Ruddy Turnstone Johns Island SC 29455 E-mail: njnorto@attglobal.net.

NORTON, PETER K., retired computer utilities programmer, writer; b. Aberdenne, Wash., Nov. 14, 1943; m. Eileen Harris Norton, 1983 (div. 2000). Programmer, Norton Utilities (sold bus. to Symantec). Co-author (with David Wild): Peter Norton's Computing Fundamentals, 1995; co-author: (with Arthur Griffith) Peter Norton's Complete Guide to Linux, 1999; co-author: (with Scott Clark) Peter Norton's New Inside the PC, 2002, and several others; contbr. articles to profl. jours. Trustee Mus. Modern Art, NYC. Named one of Top 200 Collectors, Artnews Mag., 2004. Avocation: Collector of Contemporary Art.

NORTON, SALLY PAULINE, lawyer; b. Elkhart, Ind., Jan. 28, 1964; d. Ronald and Peggy Hale; m. Peter Norton, Aug. 28, 1993; children: Alexander, Aileen. BA, Ind. U., 1986, JD, 1989. Bar: Ind. 1991, US Dist. Ct. (no. and so. dists.) Ind. 1991. Law clk. Kalamaros & Assocs., South Bend, Ind., 1990-91, assoc., 1991—2002, Doran-Blackmond LLP, South Bend, 2000—02, prnt., 2002—. Mem. Ind. Bar Assn., St. Joseph County Bar Assn., Def. Trial Counsel Ind., Def. Rsch. Inst. Avocation: martial arts. Home: 10628 N Pheasant Cove Dr Granger IN 46530-7576 Office: Doran Blackmond LLP 211 W Washington South Bend IN 46601

NORTON, WILLIAM ALAN, lawyer; b. Garretsville, Ohio, Apr. 26, 1951; s. Hugh Delbert and Tommie (Leet) N.; m. Denise Ann, May 2, 1991; children: Rachel, Sarah Megan, William Tucker. AA, U. Fla., 1972, BS, 1973, JD, 1976. Bar: Fla. 1977, U.S. Dist. Ct. (so. and mid. dist.) Fla. 1995. Assoc. Law Office of David Paul Horan, Key West, Fla., 1978-79; asst. pub. defender 16th Jud. Cir., Monroe County, Fla., 1979-81, 1st Jud. Cir., Ft. Walton Beach, Fla., 1981-85; assoc. Jones & Foster, P.A., West Palm Beach, Fla., 1985-88, Montgomery Searcy & Denney, West Palm Beach, 1988-89, Searcy Denney Scarola Barnhart & Shipley, P.A., 1989-93, atty./shareholder West Palm Beach, 1989—, shareholder. Lectr. in civil trial and securities litigation. Mem. Fla. Bar Assn. (cert. civil trial litigation), Pub. Investors Arbitration Bar Assn., Palm Beach County Bar Assn., Acad. Fla. Trial Lawyers. Office: Searcy Denney Scarola Barnhart and Shipley PA PO Drawer 1230 Tallahassee FL 32302 Home: 144 Rosehill Dr W Tallahassee FL 32312-9009 Home Phone: 850-668-1802; Office Phone: 850-224-7600. Office Fax: 850-224-7602. Business E-Mail: wan@searcylaw.com.

NORTON-JACKSON, DIANA A., organist, choirmaster; b. Atlanta, July 15, 1944; d. Fred Andrew and Frances M. (Watson) Norton; m. Leland Brooks Jackson, Sept. 29, 1968; 1 child, Anita Norton Jackson Derreza. B of Music Edn., Stetson U., Deland, Fla., 1966; postgrad., Union Theol. Sem., Inst. Sacred Music, NYC, 1966—67; M of Music Edn., U. Ga., Athens, 1968. Choirmaster Grace Episcopal Ch., Nutley, NJ, 1966—67; tchr. music Basking Ridge H.S., NJ, 1969; organist, choirmaster First Bapt. Ch., East Greenwich, RI, St. Mary's Episcopal Ch., Warwick, RI; min. music Kingston Congl. Ch., RI; instr., accompanist U. RI, Kingston; organist, choirmaster Emmanuel Episcopal Ch., Newport, RI, Trinity Episcopal Ch., Newport, 2006—. Mem. Fayerweather Craft Guild, South County Art Assn. Mem.: Am. Guild Organists (past dean). Avocations: kayaking, painting, hiking, reading, travel.

NORVELL, JOHN EDMONDSON, III, retired neuroscientist, educator; b. Charleston, W.Va., Nov. 18, 1929; s. John Edmondson Jr., and Mathilde (Wood) N.; m. Rosemary Justice, June 2, 1962; children: John Edmondson IV, Scott Justice. BS, U. Charleston, W.Va., 1953; MS, W.Va. U., Morgantown, 1956; PhD, Ohio State U., Columbus, 1966. From asst. to assoc. prof. Med. Coll. Va., Richmond, 1966-76; prof., chmn. Oral Roberts U., Tulsa, 1976-87, prof., 1987-89; prof., chmn. Universidad Central del Caribe, Bayamon, P.R., 1990-91; prof. Oral Roberts U., Tulsa, 1992—98, prof. emeritus, 1998. Lectr. dept. surgery US Naval Hosp., Portsmouth, Va., 1968-1971; invited sci. editor New Eng. Jour. Medicine, 1970; vis. lectr. dept. anatomy U. Va., Hebrew U., Hadassah Med. Sch., Jerusalem, 1974, U. Va., Dept. Anatomy; chmn. Okla. State Anatomical Bd., Tulsa, 1978-89; gov.'s mini-cabinet on health and human resources, Okla., 1980-90; vis. prof. Sch. Medicine U. Nairobi, Kenya, 1982, Sch. Med. Scis., U. Benin, Nigeria, 1989; seminar speaker Zhongshan Med. Coll., Guangzhou, People's Republic of China, 1983; presenter in field. Author: Atlas of Neuroanatomy, 1976, Atlas of Cross Sections of Human Body, 1982; contbr. articles to profl. jours. Mem. Am. Assn. Anatomists, Soc. Neurosci., Transplantation Soc. Sigma Xi. Achievements include research in degeneration and regeneration of the intrinsic nerve fibers of hearts and kidneys after transplantation; aorticorenal ganglion. Home: 7018 E 100th St Tulsa OK 74133-6235 Office: Oral Roberts U Dept Biology 7777 S Lewis Ave Tulsa OK 74171-0003 Personal E-mail: jnorvell9@cox.net.

NORVILLE, CRAIG HUBERT, lawyer; b. NYC, June 10, 1944; s. Hubert G. and Harriett (Johnson) N.; 1 child, Margaret Amelia. AB, Harvard U., 1966; LLB, U. Va., 1969. Bar: N.Y. 1971, Pa. 1979, Tenn. 1985, Nev. 2000. Instr. law U. Mich., 1969-70; assoc. Cravath, Swaine & Moore, NYC, 1970-76; sr. atty. Bethlehem (Pa.) Steel Corp., 1976-80; v.p., assoc. gen. counsel Holiday Corp. (name changed to The Promus Cos. Inc.), Memphis, 1980-84, v.p., gen. counsel, 1984-86, sr. v.p., gen. counsel, 1986-93, spl. counsel, 1993-99; of counsel Jones Vargas, Las Vegas, 2000—01, ptnr., stockholder, 2001—. Gen. counsel Diocese of the West, Orthodox Ch. in Am., 2000—. Articles editor U. Va. Law Rev. Mem. Raven Soc., Hasty Pudding Inst. of 1770, Order of Coif, Harvard Varsity Club (Cambridge, Mass.). Avocations: golf, skiing, fishing, tennis, squash. Address: 3773 Howard Hughes Pky Las Vegas NV 89109 Office Phone: 702-862-3396. E-mail: chn@jonesvargas.com.

NORWALK, LESLIE V., federal agency administrator; b. Dayton, Ohio, 1966; B in Economics and Internat. Rels. cum laude, Wellesley Coll.; JD, George Mason U. Atty. Epstein Becker & Green, P.C.; acting dep. adminstr. Ctrs. for Medicare & Medicaid Svcs. (CMS), 2003—04, dep. adminstr., 2004—06, acting adminstr., 2006—. Office: Ctrs Medicare and Medicaid Svcs 200 Independence Ave SW Washington DC 20201 *

NORWARD, JOSEPHINE NORMA, social work educator, consultant; b. Johannesburg, Jan. 8, 1949; arrived in U.S., 1980; d. Henry and Florence Nxumalo; m. Howard Norward, Sept. 22, 1984 (div. June 1996); children: Nontuthuzelo, Mandisa. Diploma in Social Work, U. Zululand, Empangeni, South Africa, 1972; MSW, U. N.C., Chapel Hill, 1982; PhD, Atlanta U., 1989. Social worker City Coun. Johannesburg, 1972—80; asst. prof. Tampa U., Fla., 1987—89; sch. social worker Hillsborough County Bd. Edn., Tampa, 1989—91; assoc. prof. Kean U., Union, NJ, 1991—. Faculty mentor N.J. Undergrad. Minority Academic Career Program; cons. in field. Contbr. chapters to books. Vol. Edn. Law Ctr., Camden, 2005—. Mem.: Nat. Assn. Sch. Social Workers, Coun. Social Work Edn. Episcopalian. Avocations: travel, yoga, theater, pilates. Office: Kean Univ 1000 Morris Ave Union NJ 07083 E-mail: jnorward@aol.com.

NORWITZ, STEVEN BARRY, plastic and reconstructive surgeon, health facility administrator; b. Camden, NJ, July 26, 1941; s. Bernard Benjamin and Ruth Norwitz; m. Anita Rochelle Shrager, Aug. 19, 1967; children: Lisa, Nicole, Suzanne. BA, Rutgers The State U. NJ, New Brunswick, NJ, 1963; MD, Hahnemann Med. Coll. & Hosp., Phila., Pa., 1967. Diplomate Am. Bd. Plastic Surgery.; cert. Nat. Bd. Med. Examiners. Intern, surgery SUNY-Kings County Downstate Med. Ctr., NY, 1967—68, resident, gen. surgery NY, 1968—72, jr. plastic surgery resident NY, 1970—71, chief plastic surgery resident NY, 1972—73; attending physician Monmouth Med. Ctr., Long Branch, NJ, 1973—, Bayshore Cmty. Hosp., Holdmel, NJ, 1973—, Jersey Shore Med. Ctr., Neptune, NJ, CentraState Med. Ctr., Freehold, NJ, Hahnemann Med. Ctr. & Hosp., Phila., Riverview Med. Ctr. Hosp., Red Bank, NJ, chief plastic surgery, 1982—97; dir. The Plastic Surgery Ctr., Shrewsbury, NJ, 1986—. Clin. assoc. prof. Hahnemann Med. Coll. and Hosp., Phila.; dir. Cleft Palete Ctr., Monmouth County, NJ, 2002. Contbr. articles to profl. jours. Recipient State Humanitarian Yr. award, Gov. Whitman, NJ, 1995. Fellow ACS; mem. AMA, Am. Soc. Plastic and Reconstructive Surgeons, Am. Soc. for Aesthetic Plastic Surgery, Am. Soc. Plastic Surgeons, Aesthetic Plastic Surgery Soc., N.J. State Med. Soc., N.J. State Soc. Plastic and Reconstructive Surgeons(pres.), Monmouth County NJ Med. Soc., Doc. Former Residents and Associated of Plastic Surgery Kings County Hosp. Ctr. (pres.), NY, Masons (32 degree). Avocations: photography, motorcycling, Nat. trap shooting Champion-Doubles. Office: Plastic Surgery Ctr 535 Sycamore Ave Shrewsbury NJ 07702-4206 also: Plastic Surgery Ctr 243 Avenel Ct Holmdel NJ 07733 Address: Plastic Surgery Ctr Lion Head Office Par 35 Beaverson Blvd Unit 12 B Brick NJ 08723 Office Phone: 732-275-9004, 732-451-1211. *

NORWOOD, BERNARD, economist; b. Boston, Nov. 21, 1922; s. Hyman and Rose (Fink) N.; m. Janet Lippe, June 25, 1943; children: Stephen Harlan, Peter Carlton. BA, Boston U., 1947; MA, Fletcher Sch. Law and Diplomacy, 1948, PhD, 1957. Internat. economist State Dept., 1949-58; joined U.S. Fgn. Svc., 1955; 1st. sec. U.S. mission to European Communities, Brussels, Belgium, 1958-62; asst. chief comml. policy and treaties divsn. Dept. State, 1962; chmn. trade staff com. Office Spl. Rep. for Trade Negotiations, Exec. Office Pres., 1963-67; assigned The Nat. War Coll., 1967-68; advisor divsn. internat. fin. bd. govs. Fed. Res. Sys., 1968-75; prin. assoc., sr. cons. Nathan Assocs., Inc., 1975-94. Mem. U.S. del. to negotiations and confs. GATT, Geneva, 1953-67. Served with AUS, 1943-46. Home and Office: 5610 Wisconsin Ave # 21D Chevy Chase MD 20815-4415

NORWOOD, BRANDI AISHA, middle school educator; b. Atlanta, Oct. 17, 1978; d. Sara Clements and David A. Norwood. BS, Tenn. State U., Nashville, 2000; MEd in Ednl. Leadership, Troy State U., Augusta, Ga., 2003; cert. in Ednl. Leadership, U. West Ga., Carrollton, 2004; EdS in Ednl. Leadership, Argosy U., Sarasota, Fla., 2006. 7th grade life sci. tchr. Henderson Mid. Sch., Jackson, Ga., 2001—05; 7th grade life sci. and social sci. tchr. Clements Mid. Sch., Covington, Ga., 2005—. Cheerleading coach Clements Mid. Sch., Covington, 2005—; asst. coach girls basketball Henderson Mid. Sch., Jackson, 2001—05, head coach girls track, 2001—05, cheerleading coach, 2001—05. Mem.: Ga. Assn. Educators (assoc.), Profl. Assn. Ga. Educators (assoc.), Pi Lambda Theta (assoc.). Democrat. Baptist. Avocations: reading, travel. Home: 9129 Carr Cir Covington GA 30014 Home Phone: 770-788-7996; Office Phone: 770-784-2934. Personal E-mail: norwoodbrandi@netscape.net.

NORWOOD, BRANDY RAYANA (BRANDY), singer, actress; b. McComb, Miss., Feb. 11, 1979; d. Willie and Sonia Norwood; m. Robert Smith, 2001 (div. 2003); 1 child, Sy'rai. Student, Pepperdine U. Singer: (albums) Brandy, 1994 (NAACP Image Award: Best New Artist, 1996), De Falda Cortita, 1995, Never S-A-Y Never, 1998, Full Moon, 2002, Afrodisiac, 2004, The Best of Brandy, 2005; actor: (TV series) Moesha, 1995—2001 (NAACP Image Award: Best Youth Actor/Actress, 1997), Brandy: Special Delivery, 2002; (TV films) Cinderella, 1997; actor, exec. prodr.: (TV films) Double Platinum, 1999; actor: (films) I Still Know What You Did Last Summer, 1998; voice Osmosis Jones, 2001, judge (TV series) America's Got Talent, 2006, host (TV miniseries) Rhythm & Jam, 1993, guest appearances (TV series) Thea, 1996, The Parkers, 2000, Reba, 2002, Sabrina, the Teenage Witch, 2002, American Dreams, 2004, One on One, 2006. Named Favorite New Artist, Am. Music Awards, 1996; recipient Grammy award (with Monica) Best R&B Performance By A Duo Or Group With Vocal for song "That Boy Is Mine", 1998. Office: 15030 Ventura Blvd 710 Sherman Oaks CA 91403 *

NORWOOD, DEBORAH ANNE, law librarian; b. Honolulu, Nov. 12, 1950; BA, U. Wash., 1972, M in Law Librarianship, 1979; JD, Willamette U., 1974. Bar: Wash., U.S. Dist. Ct. (we. dist.) 1975, U.S. Ct. Appeals (9th cir.) 1980. Ptnr. Evans and Norwood, Seattle, 1975-79; law libr. U.S. Courts Libr., Seattle, 1980-89; state law libr. Wash. State Law Libr., Olympia, 1989—2002, reporter of decisions, 1994-2001; asst. dir. pub. svcs. Jacob Burns Law Libr. George Washington U., Washington, 2002—. Mem. Freedom to Read Found. Mem. Am. Assn. Law Librs. (chmn. state, ct. and county spl. interest sect. 1995-96, chair legal info. svcs. to pub. spl. interest sect. 2001-02). Office: Jacob Burns Law Libr George Washington U 716-20th St NW Washington DC 20052 Office Phone: 202-994-7338. Business E-Mail: dnorwood@law.gwu.edu.

NORWOOD, JAIME GRIFFIS, personal trainer; d. J. Carl and Pamela M. Griffis; m. M. Jason Norwood, Aug. 2, 2002. BS in Health and Fitness, George Mason U., Fairfax, Va., 1999; MS in Athletic Tng., U. Tenn., Chattanooga, 2002. Athletic trainer HS Centre Sport Medicine, Chattanooga, 2001—04, Hutchison Sport Medicine, Fort O, Ga., 2005—. Mem.: Nat. Athletic Trainers Assn.

NORWOOD, JANET LIPPE, economist; b. Newark, Dec. 11, 1923; d. M. Turner and Thelma (Levinson) Lippe; m. Bernard Norwood, June 25, 1943; children: Stephen Harlan, Peter Carlton. BA, Douglass Coll., 1945; MA, Tufts U., Medford, Mass., 1946; PhD, Fletcher Sch. Law and Diplomacy, 1949; LLD (hon.), Fla. Internat. U., 1979, Carnegie Mellon U., Pitts., 1984, Harvard U., Cambridge, Mass., 1997, Rutgers U., 2003. Instr. Wellesley Coll., 1948-49; economist William L. Clayton Ctr., Tufts U., 1953-58; with Bur. Labor Stats., U.S. Dept. Labor, Washington, 1963-91; dep. commr., then acting commr. Bur. Labor Stats. Dept. Labor, Washington, 1975-79, commr. labor stats., 1979-92; sr. fellow The Urban Inst., Washington, 1992-99; counselor, sr. fellow N.Y. Conf. Bd., 2001—. Dir. Nat. Opinion Rsch. Ctr., chair adv. coun. unemployment compensation, 1993—96; pres. COSSA, 2001—02; mem. bd. sci. counselors Nat. Ctr. Health Stats., 1975—77; chair panel on offshoring Nat. Acad. Pub. Adminstrn., 2005—07; chair panel to evaluate Title VI and Fulbright-Hayes programs NAS, 2006—07. Author: Organizing to Count: Change in the Federal Statistical System, 1995; contbr. scientific papers in field. Named Hall Disting. Alumni, Rutgers U., 1987; recipient Disting. Achievement award, Dept. Labor, 1972, Spl. Commendation award, 1977, Philip Arnow award, 1979, Elmer Staats award, 1982, Pub. Svc. award, 1984, Presdl. Disting. Exec. Rank, 1988, Elizabeth Scott award, Com. Pres.'s Statis. Assns., 2002. Fellow: AAAS, Nat. Assn. Bus. Economists, Royal Statis. Soc., Am. Statis. Assn. (pres. 1989, Founder's award 1997); mem.: Nat. Inst. Statis. Sci. (bd. trustees 1991—2000), Nat. Acad. Sci. (assoc.), Nat. Acad. Pub. Adminstrn., Internat. Assn. Ofcls. Stats., Internat. Statis. Inst., Douglass Coll. Soc. Disting. Achievement, Cosmos Club (pres. 1995—96). Home: 5610 Wisconsin Ave Ph 21-d Chevy Chase MD 20815-4444 Personal E-mail: janetnor@aol.com.

NOSAKHERE, AKILAH SHUKURA MONTSHO, librarian, consultant, editor, writer; b. Money, Miss., July 7, 1956; d. David Westbrook and Beatrice Birt. BS, Ball State U., Munice, Ind., 1980—83, MEd, 1983—84; MLS, Atlanta U., 1986—87. Info. mgr. Nuc. Assurance Corp., Norcross, Ga., 1987—89; libr., record analyst EPA, Atlanta, 1989—92; head, circulation dept. Perimeter Coll., Dunwoody, Ga., 1992—95; Africana studies and edn. lilbr. Ga. State U. Libr., Atlanta, 1995—99, head. collection devel., 1999—2002; spl. collections libr. AUC Woodruff Libr., Atlanta, 2002—. Mng. editor Internat. Jour. of Africana Studies, Atlanta, 2003—. Contbr. articles to profl. jours. Co-chair Nat. Coalition of Blacks for Reparations in Am., Atlanta, 2001—; book donations Africa's Children's Fund, Atlanta, 1996—2003. Recipient Outstanding Cmty. Vol., Ga. State U. African Am. Students Services, 1998, Citation for Outstanding Contributions to Africa's Children's Fund, Inc., Ga. Sec. of State, 2003; grantee Whitney-Carnegie Grant, ALA, 1997. Mem.: ALA, Nat. Coun. for Black Studies (mem. editl. bd. 2003—), African Am. Studies Librs. (chair, membership com. 2003—), African Studies Assn. (assoc.; chair, book donations com. 2003—). Office: AUC Woodruff Libr Archives & Spl Coll 111 James P Brawley Dr SW Atlanta GA 30314-4207 Home Phone: 404-758-7115; Office Phone: 404-978-2057. Office Fax: 404-978-2108. Personal E-mail: akilah7@myway.com. E-mail: akilah@auctr.edu.

NOSANOW, BARBARA SHISSLER, museum director, curator; b. Roanoke, Va. d. Willis Morton and Kathryn Sabin (Bradford) Johnson; m. John Lewis Shissler Jr., July 28, 1957 (dec. May 1972); children: John Lewis Shissler III, Ada Holland Shissler; m. Lewis Harold Nosanow, Oct. 15, 1973. AB, Smith Coll., 1957; MA, Case Western Res. U., 1958; ABD, U. Minn., 1972. Asst. mng. editor Jour. Aesthetics and Art Criticism, Cleve. Mus. Art, 1958-63; dir. publs. and rsch. Mpls. Inst. Arts, 1963-72; dir. U. Minn. Art Mus., Mpls., 1972-76; dir. exhbns. and edn. Nat. Archives, Washington, 1976-79; curator Smithsonian Instn., Washington, 1979-82; asst. dir. Nat. Mus. Am. Art, Smithsonian Instn., 1982-88; dir. Portland (Maine) Mus. Art, 1988-93, Art Spaces, 1993—; study leader, lecturer Smithsonian Study Tours of France and Russia, 1997—. Lectr. in field. Past mem. various rev. panels NEH, Washington. Bd. dirs. Md. Com. for Humanities, Balt., 1980-83. Mem. Internat. Women's Forum. Avocation: travel. Office: Art Spaces 7005 Crystalline Dr Carlsbad CA 92011 Office Phone: 760-804-9714. Business E-Mail: lhnosanow@yahoo.com.

NOSBUSCH, KEITH D., multi-industry high-technology company executive; BS in Elec. and Computer Engring., U. Wis., Milw., 1974, MBA, 1976. Joined Allen-Bradley (subs. Rockwell Internat.), Milw., 1974; mktg. devel. specialist, indsl. control div. Rockwell Automation, 1978, sr. market planner, corp. planning, 1980, mgr. bus. planning, motion ctrl. div., 1982, devel. engring. mgr., motion ctrl. div., 1983, dir. prod. planning and devel., motion ctrl. div., 1985, v.p., presence sensing, automation group, 1988, v.p. control logix, automation group, 1994, pres. Automation Control Sys., 1998—2004, pres., CEO, 2004—, chmn., 2005—. Bd. dirs. Manitowoc Co., 2003—, Met. Milw. Assn. of Commerce. Advisory coun. U. Wis., Milw. Sch. Bus.; bd. trustees Boys & Girls Club of Milw. Mem.: Nat. Elec. Mfrs. Assn. (bd. govs.), Mfrs.' Alliance (bd. trustees). Office: Rockwell Automation 1201 2d St Milwaukee WI 53204 *

NOSCO, PETER ERLING, humanities educator, consultant; b. NYC, Mar. 13, 1950; s. John and Beatrice Nosco; m. Margaret Joan Button, June 19, 1976; children: John Alexander, Jean Nosco Wright. BA, Columbia U., 1971; MA (hon.), Cambridge U., Eng., 1973; PhD, Columbia U., 1978. Prof. U. of So. Calif., Los Angeles, Calif., 1986—2003, U. Brit. Columbia, 2003—; asst. prof. St. John's U., Queens, NY, 1979—86. Project dir. Fulbright Group Projects Abroad; dir. NEH Summer Inst. for Coll. Tchrs.; pres. faculty and acad. senate U. So. Calif., 2001—02. Author: (book-length monograph) Remembering Paradise; editor: (scholarly book) Confucianism and Tokugawa Culture; translator: Some Final Words of Advice (Saikaku oritome) (Transl. Ctr. (Nat. Endowment for the Arts Columbia U.), 1980). Recipient Fulbright Sr. Rsch. fellowship, Dept. of Edn., 1986, grant to lead a Fulbright Group Projects Abroad field study of Japan, 1998; grantee grant to direct a summer inst. for coll. tchrs., NEH, 2002. Fellow: L.A. Inst. for the Humanities; mem.: Am. Acad. of Religion, Am. Hist. Assn., Assn. for Asian Studies. Office: UBC-Asian Studies 401-1871 W Mall Vancouver BC Canada V6T 1Z2 Office Phone: 604-822-2835. Personal E-mail: peter.nosco@ubc.ca.

NOSÉ, YUKIHIKO, surgeon, educator; b. Iwamisawa, Hokkaido, Japan, May 7, 1932; came to U.S., 1962; s. Minoru and Haru (Murakami) N.; m. Bonnie Jean MacDonald, Mar. 15, 1965 (div. 1987); children: Kimi Willhelmina, Ken Willem, Kevin Scott; m. Ako Funakoshi, May 5, 1990. MD, U. Hokkaido, Sapporo, Japan, 1957, PhD, 1962. Surgeon in charge sect. artificial organs U. Hokkaido Sch. Medicine, 1961-62; rsch. assoc. Maimonides Hosp., Bklyn., 1962-64; postgrad. fellow dept. artificial organs Cleve. Clinic Found., 1964-66; mem. staff dept. artificial organs Cleve. Clinic, 1966—89, chmn. dept. artificial organs, 1970—90, chmn. emeritus, 1990—; prof. surgery Baylor Coll. Medicine, Houston, 1991—. V.p. Internat. Ctr. Artificial Organs and Transplantation, Cleve., 1979—; cons., mem. surgery and bioengring. study sect. NIH, 1981-87; assoc. dean Asian region Internat. Faculty Artificial Organs, 1992—; prof. Bologna (Italy) U. Sch. Medicine, 1994—. Author: Manual on Artificial Organs: Volume I-The Artificial Kidney, 1969, Volume II-The Oxygenator, 1973, Cardiac Engineering, 1970, Die Kunstliche Niere, 1974, Plasmapheresis, Historical Perspective, Therapeutic Applications and New Frontiers (with Kambic), 1983, Future Perspective for the Development of Artificial Organs (with Kolff), 1988; contbr. to numerous profl. publs. Fellow Am. Inst. Med. and Biol. Engring., N.Y. Acad. Sci.; mem. AMA, AAAS, Internat. Soc. Artificial Organs (trustee, past pres.), Am. Soc. Artificial Internal Organs (past pres., trustee), World Apheresis Assn. (congress pres. 1994), Am. Soc. Testing Materials (chair subcom. on cardiovascular prosthesis in med. and surg. materials and devices, Moses award 1979), Am. Heart Assn., Am. Soc. Apheresis, Am. Soc. Artificial Internal Organs (pres. 1992, congress pres. 1994), Am. Soc. Biomaterials, Assn. Advancement Med. Instrumentation. Achievements include development of various types of artificial organs including cardiac prosthesis, artificial kidney, hepatic assist, respiratory assist, plasmapheresis, biomaterials. Home: 1111 Hermann Dr Houston TX 77004-7142 Office: Baylor Coll Medicine One Baylor Plaza Dept Surgery Houston TX 77030 Office Phone: 713-798-4434. Business E-Mail: ynose@bcm.tmc.edu.

NOSEK, FRANCIS JOHN, lawyer, diplomat; b. Evanston, Ill., Apr. 13, 1934; s. Francis J. and Loretto (Brannan) N.; m. Janet Child, Dec. 30, 1964; children: Francis J. III, Peter C. BA in Polit. Sci., U. Idaho, Moscow, 1956, JD, 1960. Bar: Calif. 1961, US Dist. Ct. (no. dist.) Calif. 1961, US Ct. Appeals (9th cir.) 1961, Alaska 1962, US Dist. Ct. Alaska 1962, D.C. 1978, US Supreme Ct. 2004. Pvt. practice, Anchorage, 1960-67, 75—; assoc. Bell, Sanders & Tallman, Anchorage, 1961-62; sr. ptnr. Nosek, Bradberry, Wolf and Schlossberg, Anchorage, 1967-75; hon. consul Czech Republic. Adj. prof. U. Alaska, Mat-Su C.C., Anchorage, 1976-82; lectr. Anchorage C.C., 1979-83, SBA, 1975-97; editor State of Alaska Real Estate Commn., Anchorage, 1983; presenter in field; bd. of dirs. on real estate and bus. topics. Author: Alaska Mortgage Law, How to Buy and Sell a Business; contbr. articles to law jours. Chmn. Anchorage Parks and Recreation, 1968-83, IIHF World Jr. Championships, Anchorage, 1988; named hon. Consul for Czech Republic, 1999—. Mem. Am. Coll. Real Estate Lawyers, Alaska Bar Assn. (chmn. real estate law 1978, mem. internat. law exec. com. 1991-95), Calif. Bar Assn. (real estate law coms.), DC Bar Assn. (internat. law com.), Anchorage Bar Assn. Avocations: mountain climbing, ice hockey, antique cars. Office: 810 N St Ste 100 Anchorage AK 99501-2041 Office Phone: 907-274-2602. Personal E-mail: franknosek@hotmail.com, fnosek@alaska.net. Business E-Mail: frank@noseklaw.com.

NOSKI, CHARLES H., telecommunications executive; Degree, Calif. State U., Northridge, 1973. Corp. v.p., controller Hughes Elec. Corp., 1990—92, senior v.p., CFO, 1992—99, vice chmn., 1996—99; with Haskins & Sells (known as Deloitte & Touche), 1973-83, ptnr., 1983-90; v.p., CFO At&T Corp., NYC, 1999—2002; vice chmn. of bd. AT&T Corp., 2002; corp. v.p., CFO Northrup Grumman, 2003—05. Sr. advisor Blackstone Group, 2003—; bd. dirs. Air Products and Chemicals Inc., Northrop Grumman Corp., Teledyne Technologies Inc., Microsoft Corp., 2003—. Office: AT&T Corp 32 Ave of the Americas New York NY 10013-2412

NOSKO, MICHAEL GERRIK, neurosurgeon, educator; b. Montreal, Feb. 24, 1957; came to U.S., 1991; s. Joseph John and June Elizabeth (Salter) N.; m. Deborah Anne Branciere, May 23, 1981; children: Douglas Joseph, Denise Elizabeth, Keith Michael. BS, McMaster U., 1978; MD, U. Toronto, 1982; PhD, U. Alberta, 1986. Intern U. Toronto Gen. Hosp., Ont., Canada, 1982—83; resident U. Alberta Hosps., Edmonton, Canada, 1986—91; assoc. prof. neurosurgery Robert Wood Johnson Med. Sch., New Brunswick, NJ, 1991—, chief, neurosurgery divsn., 1991—. Cons. and presenter in field. Contbr. articles to profl. jours., chpts. to books. Rsch. fellow Alberta Heritage Found., 1983-86; Chancellor' scholar McMaster U., 1975, Univ. scholar, 1976, Edwin Marwin Dalley Meml. scholar, 1977; recipient Acad. award Am. Acad. Neurol. Surgery, 1986. Fellow Am. Coll. Surgeons (Resident Rsch. award 1986), Royal Coll. Surgeons Can., Acad. Medicine N.J.; mem. AMA, Am. Assn. Neurol. Surgeons, Can. Neurosurg. Soc., N.J. Neurosurg. Soc., N.Y. Acad. Scis., Middlesex County Med. Soc., Soc. Critical Care Medicine, Congress Neurol. Surgeons, Alpha Omega Alpha. Anglican. Avocations: instructing/flying aircraft and helicopters, fishing. Office: Divsn Neurosurgery 125 Paterson St Ste 2100 New Brunswick NJ 08901-1962 Office Phone: 732-235-7756. Business E-Mail: nosko@umdnj.edu.

NOSLER, PETER COLE, construction company executive; b. Portland, Oreg., May 7, 1940; s. Lyle and Elizabeth (Lewis) Nosler; m. Kay Hanson, Apr. 25, 1971; 1 child, Alexander. BS in Physics and Math., Walla Walla Coll., 1962; postgrad., U. Wash., 1962-63, U. Calif., Berkeley, 1965-70. Physicist GE, Richland, Wash., 1963-65; pvt. practice Portland, 1970-72; project mgr. Stolte Constrn., San Leandro, Calif., 1972-75; v.p. ops. Rudolph & Sletten, Foster City, Calif., 1975-90; founder, pres. DPR Constrn. Inc., Redwood City, Calif., 1990, CEO. Lectr. Stanford U., Palo Alto, Calif., 1988—. Recipient Young Constrn. Profl. of Yr. award, Jour. Bldg. Design and Constrn., 1978. Mem.: Soc. Model Exptl. Engring. Avocations: model engineering and construction, history. Office: DPR Constrn Inc 1450 Veterans Blvd Redwood City CA 94063-2612

NOSTRO, LOUIS, lawyer; b. NYC, Feb. 11, 1956; BSBA with honors, U. Fla., 1978, JD with honors, 1982, LLM in Taxation, 1987. Bar: Fla. 1982, cert.: Fla. Bar Bd. Legal Specialization and Edn. (taxation and estate planning and probate). Ptnr., chair trusts and estates and tax law practice grp. Shutts & Bowen, LLP, Miami, Fla. Adj. prof. grad. prog. in estate planning U. Miami Coll. Law, 2003—06. Contbr. articles to profl. jours. Named one of Top 100 Attys., 2005. Fellow: Am. Coll. Trust and Estate Counsel; mem.: Fla. Bar (mem. estate and trust planning com.), ABA, Miami-Dade County Bar Assn. Office: Shutts & Bowen LLP 1500 Miami Ctr 201 S Biscayne Blvd Miami FL 33131 Office Phone: 305-358-6300. Business E-Mail: lnostro@shutts.com.

NOSTWICH, THEODORE DANIEL, literature educator, researcher; b. Akron, Ohio, Sept. 14, 1925; s. John and Amelia Rose Nostwich; m. Ann Elizabeth Baker, Mar. 21, 1953; children: Mark, Paul, Michael, Elisabeth, Sarah. BA, Ohio State U., 1948, MA, 1950; PhD, U. Tex., 1968. Asst. prof. Ferris State U., Big Rapids, Mich., 1955—58, Purdue U., West Lafayette, Ind., 1962—63, Del Mar Coll., Corpus Christi, Tex., 1963—68; asst. prof. to prof. Iowa State U., Ames, 1968—95; lectr. Am. Lit. U. Glasgow, Scotland, 1996; prof. Iowa State U., 1996—98; ret., 1998. Rschr. in Am. lit. Editor: Dreiser's Heard in Corridors, 1988, Dreiser's Journalism Volume I, 1988, Dreiser's Newspaper Days, 1991, Dreiser's "Fulfillment and Other Tales", 1992, Dreiser's "Dawn", 1998. Grantee Travel grantee, NEH, 1987—89. Mem.: Nat. Assn. Scholars, Am. Studies Assn. Achievements include research in Theodore Dreiser's biography and writings. Avocations: classical music, art galleries, collecting postage stamps. Home: 707 Hodge Ave Ames IA 50010 Office: Iowa State Univ Dept English Ames IA 50012 Office Phone: 515-294-3367.

NOTAROS, BRANISLAV M., electrical engineer, educator; b. Zrenjanin, Serbia-Montenegro, Jan. 2, 1965; s. Milivoj D and Smilja J Notaros; m. Olivera K Micic; children: Jelena, Milica. BSEE, U. Belgrade, 1988, MSEE, 1992, PhD in Elec. Engring., 1995. Tchg. and rsch. asst. dept. elec. engring. U. Belgrade, Serbia, 1989—96, asst. prof. dept. elec. engring., 1996—98; rsch. assoc. U. Colo., Boulder, 1998—99; asst. prof. U. Mass., Dartmouth, 1999—2004, assoc. prof., 2004—06, dir. telecom lab. Advanced Mfg. Ctr., 2001—06; assoc. prof. dept. elec. computer engring. Colo. State U., Ft. Collins, 2006—. Author: Collection of Examination Questions and Problems in Electromagnetics, 1998, Collection of Examination Problems in Fundamentals of Electrical Engineering with Solutions, 1997, Electromagnetic Theory, 2003; contbr. chapters to books, articles to profl. jours. Recipient Marconi Premium, Instn. Elec. Engrs., London, 1999, Young Scientist award, Internat. Union of Radio Sci., Toronto, Can., 1999, IEEE MTT-S Microwave prize, Microwave Theory and Techniques Soc., Inst. IEEE, 2005. Mem.: IEEE (sr. Microwave prize Microwave Theory and Techniques Soc. 2005). Serbian Orthodox. Avocations: swimming, skiing, travel. Office: Colo State U Elec Computer Engring Dept 1373 Campus Delivery Fort Collins CO 80523-1373 Home: 802 Gilgalad Way Fort Collins CO 80526 Office Phone: 970-491-3537. Business E-Mail: notaros@colostate.edu.

NOTEBAERT, RICHARD C., telecommunications industry executive; b. 1947; m. Peggy Notebaert; 2 children. BA, U. Wis., 1969, MBA, 1983; four hon. degrees. With Wis. Bell, 1969-83; v.p. mktg. and ops. Ameritech, Chgo., 1983-86; pres. Ameritech Mobile Comm., 1986-89, Ind. Bell Tel. Co., 1989-92, Ameritech Svcs., 1992-93, pres., COO, 1993-94; chmn., pres., CEO Ameritech Corp., Chicago, 1994—99; pres., CEO Tellabs, 2000—02; chmn., CEO Qwest Comm. Internat., Inc., Denver, 2002—07. Bd. dirs. AON Corp., Cardinal Health, Inc., Qwest Comm. Internat., Inc.; trustee, corp. leadership bd. dirs. U. Notre Dame, mem., bus. coun.; chmn. Reliability and Interoperability Coun. FCC, 2002—; apptd. mem. Nat. Security Telecom. Adv. Com., 2003—. Co-chmn. Alexis de Toqueville Soc. United Way; bd. dirs. Denver Ct. Performing Arts; vice chmn. civic com. The Comml. Club Chgo.; bd. dirs. The Execs. Club, Chgo. Recipient Dist. Alumni award, U. Wis., 1999. Office: Qwest Commn Internat Inc 1801 California St Denver CO 80202 Office Phone: 303-992-1414. Office Fax: 303-896-8515. *

NOTHAFT, FRANK EMILE, economist; b. Jersey City, Apr. 10, 1956; s. Frank Emil and Rita Johanna (Laer) N.; m. Lisa Beth Greenfield, June 13, 1981; children: Frank Austin, Daniel Blake, John Paul. BA, N.Y.U., 1976; MA, Columbia U., 1977, MPhil, 1979, PhD, 1986. Economist Bd. Govs. Fed. Reserve System, Washington, 1983-86; sr. economist Freddie Mac, McLean, Va., 1986-88, dep. chief economist, 1988-90, dir., office of chief economist, 1990—2001, chief economist, 2001—, v.p., 2004—. Contbr. articles to profl. jours. Sec., bd. dirs. Falls Church Housing Corp., Va., 1988-91. Sloan Found. grantee, 1982; Columbia U. fellow, 1976-79; recipient Founders' Day award, N.Y.U., 1976. Mem. Am. Real Estate Urban Econs. Assn. (bd. dirs. 1990-92, 2002-04, 06-), Fin. Mgmt. Assn. (bd. dirs. 2006-), Am. Real Estate Soc. Office: Freddie Mac 8200 Jones Branch Dr Mc Lean VA 22102-3110

NOTKIN, LEONARD SHELDON, architect; b. NYC, Apr. 1, 1931; s. Murry and Evelyn (Mofshatz) N.; m. Ann Mathilda Stefanko, Nov. 24, 1956; children: Jennifer, Mead. BArch, U. Pa., 1954. Registered architect, N.Y., Mass., Ohio, Pa., Nat. Coun. Archtl. Registration Bds. Architect, Percival Goodman (Architect), NYC, 1956-58; Architect Bloch and Hesse (Architects), NYC, 1958-59, Resnick and Green (Architects), NYC, 1959-60; architect, prin., v.p. The Architects Collaborative, Inc., Cambridge, Mass., 1960-95; chief design critic Boston Archtl. Center, 1964-69; mem. Lexington (Mass.) Design Adv. Com., 1970-73, chmn., 1972; profl. studio critic Harvard Grad. Sch. Design, 1974-76; pres. Boston Design Assocs., Inc., Waltham, Mass., 1995—. Major recent works include Intermediate Sch. 137, Bronx, N.Y., 1976, Visual Arts Instructional Facility SUNY, Purchase, 1976, Lahey Clinic Med. Ctr., Burlington, Mass., 1976—, W. Penn Hosp., Pitts., 1977, St. Francis/St. George Hosp., Cin., 1978, Blue Cross/Blue Shield of Conn. Hdqrs., North Haven, Temple U. Hosp., Phila., composite hosp. Loring AFB, Limestone, Maine, Med. Facilities, Fort Drum, N.Y., Health Care Internat. Ltd., Glasgow, Scotland, Intensive Care Hosp. and Hotel, U. Ky. Cancer Rsch. Ctr., Children's Hosp. Med. Ctr. Rsch. Lab., Cin., new main entrance, lobby and admissions facilities Hosp. of U. Pa., Phila., Childrens Hosp., Kuwait, 1996, Health Facilities, Algiers, Algeria, 1996, Nigeria, 2003, Office Building/Auburn, Mass., Greenfield Comty. Coll., Mass. Served with U.S. Army, 1954-56. Recipient Design award for IBM Hdqrs., Gaithersburg, Md. Progressive Architecture mag., 1964; 1st pl. award for Worcester (Mass.) Community Center AIA, 1966; Design award for Worcester Found. Exptl. Biology bldg. Mass. chpt. AIA, 1968; Design award NIH Rsch. Lab., Bethesda, Md. GSA, 1972; Best Bldg. of Yr. award for Norwalk HS Assn. for Better Cmty. Design, Conn., 1972; Honor award Conn. Soc. Architects AIA, 1974. Mem. AIA, Mass. State Assn. Architects, Boston Soc. Architects (dir. 1976-79, spl. design citation 1993). Office: Boston Design Assocs Inc 393 Totten Pond Rd Waltham MA 02451-2003 Office Phone: 781-259-9190. Personal E-mail: leonardnotkin@comcast.net.

NOTOPOULOS, ALEXANDER ANASTASIOS, JR., lawyer; b. Altoona, Pa., Jan. 29, 1953; s. Alexander Anastasios Sr. and Christine (Economou) N.; m. Alexis J. Anderson, Aug. 4, 1984. BA summa cum laude, Amherst Coll., 1974; JD magna cum laude, Harvard U., 1977. Bar: Mass. 1978, U.S. Dist. Ct. Mass. 1979. Law clk. to judge U.S. Ct. Appeals (3d cir.), Phila., 1977-78; assoc. Sullivan & Worcester, Boston, 1978-85, ptnr., 1985—. Mem., bd. dir. Newton Presbyn. Ch. Nursery Sch., 1992—94. Recipient Mass. Super Lawyer, Boston Magazine, 2004—06, Best Lawyers in Am., 2007; grantee Am. Coll. Investment Counsel. Mem.: ABA, coun. Harvard Law Sch. Assn. 1987-1991., Nat. Assn. Bond Lawyers, Comml. Fin. Svcs. & Fed. Regulation Securities Com. Bus. Law Sect. Aba., Uniform Comml. Code, Boston Bar Assn. Home: 96 Shornecliffe Rd Newton MA 02458-2421 Office: Sullivan & Worcester One Post Office Sq Boston MA 02109 Office Phone: 617-338-2810. Office Fax: 617-338-2880. Business E-Mail: anotopoulos@sandw.com.

NOTT, ROBIN K., theater educator, theater director; b. Grand Rapids, Mich. BA, Western Mich. U., Kalamazoo, 1973; MA, Ea. Mich. U., Ypsilanti, 1983. Fine arts specialist City of Kalamazoo, 1973—77; educator, drama specialist The Kazoo Sch., Kalamazoo, 1978—83; theater educator, dir. Gull Lake Cmty. Schs., Richland, Mich., 1987—. Storyteller, folksinger, 1983—. Musician: (bluegrass/gospel band) Hoot Owls. Bd. dirs. Mich. Youth Arts Festival, Kalamazoo, 2004—, Richland Area Cmty.

Ctr., 2001—. Named Mich. Theater Tchr. of Yr., MIFA, 1995. Mem.: Nat. Story Telling Network, Am. Alliance Theater and Edn. (John C. Barner Theater Tchr. of Yr. 1999), Mich. HS Theatre Assn. (com. 1993—). Avocations: camping, model building, classic cars, folk music. Office: Gull Lake HS 9550 E M-89 Richland MI 49083 Office Phone: 269-629-5803 ext 1216. Office Fax: 269-629-3077. Business E-Mail: rnott@gulllakecs.org.

NOTTAGE, JAMES H., museum administrator, curator, historian; b. Laramie, Wyo., 1950; s. Harold J. and Frieda (Oliver) N.; m. Mary Ellen Hennessey, 1976. BA in History, U. Wyo., 1972; MA in Mus. Studies, SUNY, Oneonta, 1976; MA in Am. Studies, U. Wyo., 1978. Curator exhibits Kans. State Hist. Soc., Topeka, 1977-79, asst. mus. dir., 1979-81, supervisory historian, 1981-85; chief curator Autry Mus. Western Heritage, LA, 1985-95, v.p. and chief curator, 1995—. Author: (monograph) Stagecoach!, 1990; (book) Saddlemaker to the Stars, 1996. Certification insp. U.S. Army Mus. Sys., 1983-84. Smithsonian Inst. fellow, 1973; Team Planning fellow Kellogg Seminars, 1982. Mem. Am. Assn. Mus. (mus. assesment cons. 1980-85), Western History Assn. Avocation: saddle making. Office: Autry Mus Western Heritage 4700 Western Heritage Way Los Angeles CA 90027-1462

NOTTENBURG, RICHARD N., electronics executive; BSEE, Polytechnic Inst. NY; MSEE, Colo. State Univ.; PhD elec. engring., Ecole Polytechnique Federale de Lausanne, Switzerland. Mem. tech. staff Bell Laboratories, 1984—90, disting. mem. tech. staff, interim dept. head, 1990—91; assoc. prof. elec. engring. Univ. So. Calif., 1991—98; co-founder, pres., CEO Multilink Tech. Corp., 1995—2003; v.p., gen. mgr. Vitesse Semiconductor Corp., 2003—04; strategic adv. Motorola, Inc., Schaumburg, Ill., 2004, sr. v.p., chief strategy officer, 2004—05, exec. v.p., chief strategy officer, 2005—. Contbr. articles to profl. jours. Achievements include patents in field. Office: Motorola Inc 1303 E Algonquin Rd Schaumburg IL 60196 *

NOTTERMAN, DANIEL A., pediatrician, educator; BA, Cornell U., 1973; MA in Philosophy, Tufts U., 1977; MD, NYU, 1978. Diplomate Am. Bd. Pediatrics. Intern, resident NYU Med. Ctr., NYC, 1978—81, chief resident in pediat., 1981—82; rsch. fellow clin. pharmacology Cornell Med. Ctr., NYC, 1983—84; dir. divsn. pediatric critical care medicine N.Y. Hosp. Cornell Med. Ctr., NYC, 1985—97; postdoctoral rschr., prof. Princeton (N.J.) U., 1992—93; chief pediatric svcs. Bristol-Myers Squibb Children's Hosp. Robert Wood Johnson U. Hosp., 2002—; chair dept. pediat. U. Medicine and Dentistry N.J. - Robert Wood Johnson Med. Sch., 2002—. Office: Robert Wood Johnson Med Sch 1 Robert Wood Johnson Pl MEB 306 New Brunswick NJ 08903 Home: 7 Symmes Ct Cranbury NJ 08512 Home Phone: 609-395-5521; Office Phone: 732-235-7900. Business E-Mail: d.notterman@umdnj.edu.

NOTTI, DONNA BETTS, special education educator; b. Manassas, Va., Sept. 4, 1968; d. William Jackson and Christine Joan (Fant) B.; m. David L. Notti, Oct. 14, 1995. BS in Spl. Edn., Old Dominion U., Norfolk, Va., 1990. Tchr., counselor Southeastern Cooperative Ednl. Programs, Norfolk, Va., 1991—2004; vol. tutor Tonelson Teaching and Learning Ctr., Norfolk, Va., 1989; secondary spl. edn. tchr. Chesapeake City Schs., Va., 2004—. Chair child study com. Oscar Smith HS, Chesapeake, Va., 2006—. Mem. Coun. for Exceptional Children (v.p. 1989-90), Coun. for Children With Behavior Disorders, Coun. for Exceptional Children-Mental Retardation, Am. Re-ED Assn., Va. State Reading Assn., Chesapeake Reading Coun. Lutheran. Office: 1994 Tiger Dr Chesapeake VA 23320 Personal E-mail: dbnotti@yahoo.com.

NOTTINGHAM, EDWARD WILLIS, JR., federal judge; b. Denver, Jan. 9, 1948; s. Edward Willis and Willie Newton (Gullett) N.; m. Cheryl Ann Card, June 6, 1970 (div. Feb. 1981); children: Amelia Charlene, Edward Willis III; m. Janis Ellen Chapman, Aug. 18, 1984 (div. Dec. 1998); 1 child, Spencer Chapman. AB, Cornell U., 1969; JD, U. Colo., 1972. Bar: Colo. 1972, U.S. Dist. Ct. Colo. 1972, U.S. Ct. Appeals (10th cir.) 1973. Law clk. to presiding judge U.S. Dist. Ct. Colo., Denver, 1972-73; assoc. Sherman & Howard, Denver, 1973-76, 78-80, ptnr., 1980-87, Beckner & Nottingham, Grand Junction, Colo., 1987-89; asst. U.S. atty. U.S. Dept. Justice, Denver, 1976-78; U.S. dist. judge Dist. of Colo., Denver, 1989—. Mem. Jud. Conf. of the U.S. Com. on Automation and Tech., 1994-2000, chmn., 1997-2000. Bd. dirs. Beaver Creek Met. Dist., Avon, Colo., 1980-88, Justice Info. Ctr., Denver, 1985-87, 21st Jud. Dist. Victim Compensation Fund, Grand Junction, Colo., 1987-89. Mem. ABA, Colo. Bar Assn. (chmn. criminal law sect. 1983-85, chmn. ethics com. 1988-89), Order of Coif, Denver Athletic Club, Delta Sigma Rho, Tau Kappa Alpha. Episcopalian. Office: US Dist Ct 901 19th St Denver CO 80294 Office Phone: 303-844-5018. E-mail: NottinghamChambers@cod.uscourts.gov.

NOTTINGHAM, ROBINSON KENDALL, insurance company executive; b. Balt., Apr. 4, 1938; s. Robinson Jr. and Juliet (Moore) N.; m. Elizabeth LeViness, Aug. 26, 1960; children: Robinson Kendall Jr. (dec. July 18, 2007), Charles Denmead. BA in Polit. Sci., Johns Hopkins U., 1959; postgrad., Johns Hopkins U., Washington, 1965. With Am. Internat. Group, Inc., Hong Kong and Bangkok, 1968-71; mng. dir. Hanover Ins. Co., Universal Ins. Co., Bangkok, 1971-73, Am. Internat. Ins. Co., Lagos, Nigeria, 1973-75; regional pres. African div. Am. Internat. Underwriters, NYC, 1975-78, Middle Ea. div., 1978-83, European div., 1983-86; chief exec. officer for Japan and Korea Am. Internat. Group, Inc., Tokyo, 1986-89; chmn., bd. dirs., CEO Am. Life Ins. Co., Wilmington, Del., 1989—; exec. v.p., life ins. Am. Internat. Group, 1998—. Bd. dirs. AIG Overseas Fin. (Japan) Inc., Tokyo, Am. Home Assurance Co., N.Y.C., AIU Ins. Co., N.Y.C.; trustee John Hopkins U., 2005 Pres. USO Coun., Tokyo, 1987-89; mem. world bd. govs. USO, Washington, 1987-97; mem. adv. coun. Johns Hopkins U. Sch. Advanced Internat. Studies, Washington, 1984-96. Served to lt. comdr. USNR, 1960-68. Mem. Princeton Club (N.Y.C.), Short Hills Club (N.J.), Bay Head Yacht Club (N.J.), Baltusrol Club (Springfield, N.J.), Chevy Chase (Md.) Club, Met. Club (Washington), Univ. and Artist Club (Washington), Delta Phi. Republican. Episcopalian. Avocation: sailing. Office: Am Life Ins Co 1 Alico Plz Wilmington DE 19899 E-mail: ken.nottingham@aig.com.

NOTTINGHAM, WILLIAM JESSE, retired religious organization administrator, retired minister; b. Sharon, Pa., Nov. 22, 1927; s. Jess William and Alice May (Green) Nottingham; m. Patricia Clutts, Feb. 1, 1949; children: Theodore Jess, Deborah Joan Selke, Nancy Alice, Gregory Philip. BA, Bethany Coll., W.Va., 1949, DD (hon.), 1987; BD, Union Theol. Sem., NYC, 1953; PhD, Columbia U., 1962; DD (hon.), Christian Theol. Sem., Indpls., 1984. Ordained to ministry Christian Ch. (Disciples of Christ), 1945, ministerial standing United Ch. of Christ. Machinist apprentice Westinghouse, 1943—45; pastor Ch. of Christ, Canoe Camp and Covington, Pa., 1949-50; field worker Ch. of the Master, NYC, 1950-53; assoc. min. Nat. City Christian Ch., Washington, 1954-58; fraternal worker Coun. on Christian Unity, France, 1958-65; with CIMADE and Centre de Glay; with youth dept. World Coun. of Chs., Geneva, 1965-68; exec. sec. for Latin Am. and Caribbean Christian Ch. (Disciples of Christ) and United Ch. Christ, Indpls., 1968-76; exec. sec. East Asia and Pacific Divsn. Overseas Ministries, Christian Ch. (Disciples of Christ), 1976-83; pres., exec. sec. Europe Divsn. Overseas Ministries Christian Ch. (Disciples of Christ), Indpls., 1984-94, pres. emeritus, 2004; ret., 1994; affiliate prof. mission Christian Theol. Sem., 1995—2005. Author: Christian Faith and Secular Action: An Introduction to the Life and Thought of Jacques Maritain, 1968, The Practice and Preaching of Liberation, 1986, The Social Ethics of Martin Bucer 1491-1551, 1962; translator: God's Underground, 1970, Prayer at the Heart of Life, 1975, Materialist Approaches to the Bible, 1985, Madeleine Barot, 1991; contbr. articles to theol. jours. Mem. Ind. Faith and Labor Network, Com. To Free Lori Berenson. Chaplain USNR, 1954—65. Recipient Disting. Alumnus award, Union Theol. Sem., 1999, Martin Luther King, Jr. Drum Major for Justice award, 2003; Fulbright scholar, Strasbourg, France, 1953—54. Mem.: Disciples Justice Action Network, United Christian Missionary Soc., Assn. Disciples for Theol. Discussion, Indpls. Peace and Justice Ctr. (bd.). Democrat. Business E-Mail: bnottingham@cts.edu.

NOTZ, JOHN KRANZ, JR., arbitrator, mediator, retired lawyer; b. Chgo., Jan. 5, 1932; s. John Kranz and Elinor (Trostel) N.; m. Janis Wellin, Apr. 23, 1966; children: Jane Elinor Notz, John Wellin. BA, Williams Coll., Williamstown, Mass., 1953; JD, Northwestern U., Chgo., 1956. Bar: Ill. 1956, Fla. 1957, Wis. 1989, U.S. Supreme Ct. 1960. Assoc. 1st Nat. Bank Chgo., 1954, 1956; from assoc. to ptnr. Gardner, Carton & Douglas, Chgo., 1960-95, of counsel, 1990-95; ret., 1996. Arbitrator, mediator Am. Arbitration Assn., Chgo. Internat. Dispute Resolution Assn., NASD Dispute Resolution Inc., Nat. Futures Assn., N.Y. Stock Exch. Contbr. articles to profl. jours. Mem. Sec. of State Corp. Acts Adv. Com., 1982-95, chmn., 1987-89; pres. Chgo. Lit. Club, 1996-97; mem. Ill. Inst. Continuing Legal Edn., 1980-91, chmn., 1990-91; former pres. Black Point Historic Preserve, Inc.; trustee Graceland Cemetery; former treas. Soc. Archl. Historians; bd. dirs. Libr. Am. Landscape History. 1st lt. USAF, 1957-60. Recipient Svc. award Northwestern U., 1978 Fellow Am. Bar Found. (life), Ill. Bar Found. (life), Chgo. Bar Found. (life); mem. Am. Law Inst., Ill. State Bar Assn., Chgo. Bar Assn., Wis. State Bar, Lawyers Club City Chgo., Racquet Club Chgo., Lake Geneva (Wis.) Country Club, Mid-Day Club (Chgo.), Literary Club (Chgo.), Caxton Club (Chgo.), Cliff Dwellers (Chgo.), The Antiquarian Soc., Asian Arts Coun., Art Inst. Chgo. Office: 191 N Wacker Dr 3700 Chicago IL 60606-1698 Home Phone: 773-348-5196; Office Phone: 312-569-1088.

NOUHAN, REGINA MARIE, plastic surgeon; b. St. Louis, July 20, 1961; Grad., U. Va.; MD, Wash U., St Louis, 1987. Cert. Am. Bd. Plastic Surgery. Resident gen. surgery Barnes/Jewish Hosp., 1987—91; fellowship plastic surgery St Louis U. Med. Ctr., 1991—93; fellowship hand and microsurgery Christine M. Kleinert Inst., Louisville, 1993—94; surgeon Monarch Plastic Surgery, Leawood, Kans. Named one of Kansas City Super Dr.'s, Kansas City Mag., 2006. Fellow: ACS; mem.: AMA, Kansas City Plastic Surgery Soc. (past pres.), Am. Soc. Surgery of Hand, Am. Soc. Aesthetic Plastic Surgery, Am. Soc. Plastic Surgeons. Office: 5401 College Blvd Ste 203 Leawood KS 66211 Office Phone: 913-663-3838. Office Fax: 913-663-4434. *

NOUR, BAKR M., surgeon, health facility administrator; s. Mohamed Mahmoud Nour and Fatheya A. Hussein; m. Sohair A. Kheir, Dec. 23, 1976; children: May, Mohamed. MD, U. Alexandria, 1974, M in Surgery, 1978, D in Surgery, 1986. Diplomate Bd. Gen. Surgery, Egypt. Intern U. Alexandria, Egypt, 1975-76, resident in gen. & pediatric surgery, 1976-79, instr. surgery, 1979, asst. lectr. pediatric surgery, 1979-82, sr. asst. lectr. pediatric surgery, 1984-86, asst. prof. pediatric surgery, 1987-89; clin./rsch. fellow, vis. asst. prof. surgery dept. pediatric surgery U. Pitts. Med. Ctr., Children's Hosp. Pitts., 1982-84, 90; clin. fellow U. Pitts. Med. Ctr., Transplantation Inst., 1990-92, asst. prof. surgery, 1992-94; chief pediatric liver transplantation, adult liver transplant surgeon Okla. Transplantation Inst., Bapt. Med. Ctr., Oklahoma City, 1994-97; chief abdominal transplantation Okla. Transplantation Inst., Integris Bapt. Med. Ctr., Oklahoma City, 1997-98, dir. abdominal organ transplant divsn., 1998-99, interim dir., 1999-2000, dir., chmn., 2000—. Past mem. staff Presbyn. U. Hosp. Pitts., Montefiore Hosp., Pitts.; mem. human rights com. Children's Hosp. Pitts., 1993-94; mem. libr. com. Bapt. Med. Ctr. Okla. Contbr. articles to profl. jours. Founding mem. Innocent Childhood Benevolent Charity Assn., Alexandria; mem Islamic Charity Assn. Recipient World Cmty. award Results, 1998. Mem. AMA, ACS, Arab Am. Med. Assn., Am. Coll. Physician Execs., Am. Assn. Study of Liver Disease, Am. Soc. Transplant Surgeons, Egyptian Physician's Syndicate, Egyptian Med. Assn., Egyptian Soc. Surgeons, Egyptian Assn. Pediatric Surgeons, Alexandria Med. Assn., Brit. Assn. Pediatric Surgeons, Okla. State Med. Assn., Okla. County Med. Soc., Internat. Coll. Surgeons, Internat. Gastro-Surg. Club, Internat. Liver Transplantation Soc., Tex. Transplant Soc., Soc. Surgery Alimentary Tract, Alexandria Sporting Club, Oklahoma City Golf and Country Club. Muslim. Achievements include research in cell model to study bacterial translocation in transplanted small bowel, FK506 as immunosuppressive agent, small bowel transplantation, causes of anemia in transplant patients, Alpha interferon therapy, for viral hepatitis. Home: 14409 Rosebay Pl Oklahoma City OK 73142 Office: Okla Transplantation Inst Nazih Zuhdi 3300 NW Expressway Oklahoma City OK 73112-4418 E-mail: NourBM@Integris-Health.com.

NOVA, CRAIG, writer; b. Los Angeles, July 5, 1945; s. Karl and Elizabeth (Sinclair) N.; m. Christina Barnes, July 2, 1977; children: Abigail, Tate. BA, U. Calif.-Berkeley, 1967; M.F.A., Columbia U., 1969. Disting. prof. humanities U. N.C., Greensboro, 2005—. Author: Turkey Hash, 1972, The Geek, 1975, Incandescence, 1978, The Good Son, 1982, The Congressman's Daughter, 1986, Tornado Alley, 1989, Trombone, 1992, The Book of Dreams, 1994, The Universal Door, 1997, Brook Trout and the Writing life, 1999, Wetware, 2001, Cruisers, 2004. Recipient Harper-Saxton prize Harper and Row, Pubs., 1972; recipient award in lit. Am. Acad. and Inst. Arts and Letters; Guggenheim Found. fellow, 1977; fellow Nat. Endowment for Arts, 1973, Nat. Endowment for Arts, 1975, Creative Artists Pub. Service, 1976; NEA fellow, 1985; story included in Best Am. Short Stories, 1987. Office Phone: 919-732-1857. E-mail: nova@sover.net.

NOVACK, ALVIN JOHN, physician; b. Red Lodge, Mont., Mar. 11, 1925; s. John and Anna Geraldine (Maddio) N.; m. Betty P. Novack, Jan. 10, 1952; children— Vance, Deborah, Michelle, Mitchel, Craig, Brad, Mary Ellen, Garth. MD, U. Wash., 1952. Intern Harper Hosp., Detroit, 1952, resident in surgery, 1953; resident in otolaryngology Johns Hopkins U., 1954-57; resident in surgery Columbia-Presbyn. Med. Center, NYC, 1957-60, fellow head and neck surgery, 1957-60; dir. head and neck surgery Swedish Hosp., Seattle, 1960-91; dir. otolaryngology Children's Orthopedic Hosp., Seattle, 1965-78; ret., 1991. Contbr. articles to med. jours. Served to lt. AUS, 1940-43. Nat. Cancer Inst. fellow, 1957-60 Fellow A.C.S.; mem. AMA, Am. Acad. Otolaryngology and Head and Neck Surgery, Soc. Head and Neck Surgeons, North Pacific Surg. Assn., Pacific Coast Surg. Assn., Seattle Surg. Soc.

NOVACK, JULIE RUTH, internet marketing executive; b. 1969; BA Econ., U. Mich.; MBA, Kellog Sch. of Mgmt., Northwestern U. Exec. tng. program First Chgo. Corp.; co-founder, head Internet Grp. within the First Chgo. Corp., 1994—96; exec. mgmt. positions Agency.com, 1996—2006; gen. mgr. Avenue A Razorfish, 2006—. Named a Woman to Watch, Crain's Chgo. Bus., 2007. Office: Avenue A Razorfish 600 W Fulton St 4th Fl Chicago IL 60661 Office Phone: 312-696-5000. Office Fax: 312-876-9866. *

NOVACK, KENNETH JOSEPH, lawyer; b. Boston, Aug. 25, 1941; s. Hyman and Dorothy Ruth N.; m. Marianne Margaret Lefebvre; children: Laura Ann, Sara Elizabeth, Emily Kate, Jeffrey Nicholas. BA (Rufus Choate scholar), Dartmouth Coll., 1963; LL.B., Harvard U., 1966. Bar: Mass. 1966, D.C. 1972. With Mintz, Levin, Cohn, Ferris, Glovsky and Popeo, P.C., Boston, 1996—98, 2004—, named ptnr., 1970, mem. exec. com., 1972—98, mng. ptnr Boston, 1972—78, pres., CEO, 1991-94, sr. counsel, 2004—; vice chmn. AOL Inc. (AOL and Time Warner merge, 2001), 1998—2001, Time Warner Inc. (formerly AOL Time Warner), 2001—04. Bd. dirs. Time Warner Inc., 2001—, Paratek Pharms., 2002—. Vice chmn. Mus. Sci., Boston, Tufts-New England Med. Ctr., Combined Jewish Philanthropies; pres. Teen Action Campaign Inc.; trustee Facing History and Ourselves, Novack Family Found. Mem. ABA, Internat. Bar Assn., Boston Bar Assn. (co-chmn. securities law com. 1970-85), D.C. Bar Assn., Am. Law Inst. Clubs: St. Botolph, Harvard of Boston. Office: Mintz Levin Cohn Ferris Glovsky and Popeo PC 1 Financial Ctr Fl 39 Boston MA 02111

NOVACK, ROBERT, lawyer; b. Jersey City, May 3, 1953; BA, Rutgers U., 1975; JD cum laude, U. Miami, 1978. Bar: N.J. 1978, U.S. Dist. Ct. N.J. 1978, N.Y. 1985, U.S. Ct. of Appeals (2nd and 3rd cirs.). Law clk. to Hon. Harry A. Margolis N.J. Superior Ct., Law Divsn., 1978-79; ptnr. Budd, Larner, Gross, Rosenbaum, Greenberg & Sade, P.C., Short Hills, NJ; ptnr. litig., office ptnr. in charge Edwards & Angell LLP, Short Hills, NJ, 1997—. Adj. prof. Rutgers U. Sch. of Law; mem. Lawyers Adv. Com., US Dist Ct. NJ; past chmn. Supreme Ct. NJ Dist. Ethics Com. Author: (with Harry A. Margolis) Tort Claims Against Public Entities, 1984, 1st rev. edit., 1986, 2nd rev. edit., 1988, 3rd rev. edit., 1990. Mem. ABA, Fed. Bar Assn., N.J. State Bar Assn., Trial Attys. of N.J., Essex County Bar Assn. Office: Edwards & Angell LLP 51 John F Kennedy Pkwy Short Hills NJ 07078 Office Phone: 973-921-5225. Office Fax: 973-376-3380. Business E-Mail: rnovack@edwardsangell.com.

NOVAK, ALAN LEE, retired pharmaceutical company executive; b. Chgo., Oct. 25, 1928; s. Samuel Adolph and Tina Lillian (Oris) N.; m. Delores Jane Tonkel, Dec. 17, 1950; children: Shaya Ray, G. Alexander, Cheryl Lynn. BS, Fla. So. Coll., 1951. Cert. purchasing mgr. Police officer Lakeland (Fla.) Police Dept., 1952-53; sales rep. Sinclair Refining Co., Tampa, Fla., 1954-58; prin. Novak's Texaco s/s and Fuel Co., Tampa, 1958-62; sales rep. Burroughs Wellcome Co., Columbus, Ohio, 1962-70, purchasing agt. Research Triangle Park, NC, 1970-74, dir. purchasing, 1974-94. Bd. dirs. Eastern N.C. Better Bus. Bur., 1989-96. Active N.C. Coun. on the Holocaust, 1996—2002; vol. Friends Helping Friends Vet. Sch., N.C. State U., 1994—2006; records dept. Raleigh Polic Dept., 1994—2006; area contact Am. Israel Polit. Affairs Coun., Raleigh, 1984—86; fin. sec. Temple Beth Or, Raleigh, 1975—77, treas., 1996—97; pres. Raleigh Chpt. B'nai B'rith, 1999—2000. With US Army, 1946—47, Japan. Mem. Am. Legion Jewish War Vets. 1st Cav. Divsn. Assn., Drug, Chem., and Allied Trades Assn. (area rep. 1975-78, bd. dirs. 1978-84, treas. 1985, v.p. 1986, pres. 1987-88), Nat. Assn. Purchasing Mgmt., Purchasing Mgmt. Assn. Carolinas-Va., Triangle Purchasing Assn., Raleigh C. of C., Burroughs Wellcome Retirees Club (pres.), Tau Kappa Epsilon, Omicron Delta Kappa. Lodges: B'nai B'rith (Double Chai award 1985-87), AMRAN Shrine Temple (charter). Republican. Jewish. Avocations: hunting, fishing. Personal E-mail: zayde1928@gmail.com.

NOVAK, BARBARA, art history educator; b. NYC; d. Joseph and Sadie (Kaufman) N.; m. Brian O'Doherty, July 5, 1960. BA, Barnard Coll., 1951; MA, Radcliffe Coll., 1953, PhD, 1957. TV instr. Mus. Fine Arts, Boston, 1957-58; mem. faculty Barnard Coll., Columbia U., NYC, 1958-98, prof. art history, 1970—, Helen G. Altschul prof., 1984-98, prof. emeritus, 1998—. Vis. Mellon prof. U. Pitts., 1971; mem. adv. coun. Archives of Am. Art, NAD Author: American Painting of the 19th Century, 1969, 3d edit., 2007, Nature and Culture, 1980, 3d edit., 2007, Voyages of the Self, 2007, The Thyssen-Bornemisza Collection 19th Century American Painting, 1986, Alice's Neck, 1987, The Margaret-Ghost, 2003, (novels) The Ape and the Whale, 1995, (play) The Ape and the Whale: Darwin and Melville in Their Own Words, 1987 (performed at Symphony Space 1987), Dreams and Shadows: Thomas H. Hotchkiss in 19th Century Italy, 1993; co-editor: Next to Nature, 1980; mem. editl. bd. Am. Art Jour. Commr. Nat. Portrait Gallery. Recipient disting. tchg. award, Coll. Art Assn., 1997, Lawrence Fleishman award for outstanding scholarship, Archives Am. Art, 1999, medal of distinction, Barnard Coll., 2002; Fulbright fellow, Belgium, 1953—54, Guggenheim fellow, 1974, Nat. Book Critics nominee, 1980, L.A. Times Book Award nominee, 1980, Am. Book Award paperback nominee, 1981. Fellow Soc. Am. Historians, Phila. Atheneum; mem. Soc. Am. Historians, Am. Antiquarian Soc., Coll. Art Assn. (dir. 1974-77, Disting. Tchg. of Art History award 1997), PEN. Achievements include honored with Barbara Novak professorship in art history at Barnard Coll. and Columbia U., 2004; Barbara Novak Acquisition Fund at Nat. Portrait Gallery.

NOVAK, DAVID, theology studies educator, rabbi; b. Chgo., Aug. 19, 1941; s. Syd and Sylvia (Wien) N.; m. Melva Ziman, July 3, 1963; children: Marianne, Jacob George. AB in Classics and Ancient History, U. Chgo., 1961; M in Hebrew Lit., Jewish Theol. Sem. Am., 1964; PhD, Georgetown U., 1971. Ordained rabbi, 1966. Rabbi Shaare Tikvah Congregation, 1966—69; dir. Jewish chaplaincy St. Elizabeth's Hosp., 1966—69; rabbi Emanuel Synagogue, Oklahoma City, 1968—72, Beth Tfiloh Congregation, Balt., 1972—77, Congregation Beth El, Norfolk, Va., 1977—81, Congregation Darchay Noam, Far Rockaway, NY, 1981—89; Edgar M. Bronfman prof. modern Judaic studies U. Va., Charlottesville, 1989—97; J. Richard and Dorothy Shiff chair of Jewish studies U. Toronto, 1997—. Lectr. philosophy Oklahoma City U., 1969-72, New Sch. for Social Rsch., 1982-84; lectr. Jewish studies Balt. Hebrew Coll., 1972-77; adj. asst. prof. philosophy Old Dominion U., 1977-81; vis. assoc. prof. Talmud Jewish Theol. Sem. Am., 1986-88; adj. assoc. prof. Baruch Coll., CUNY, 1984-88, adj. prof., 1989; founder, v.p., coord. panel Halakhic Inquiry Union Traditional Judaism/Inst. Traditional Judaism; disting. vis. prof. religion and corp. ethics Drew U., 1995; Yarnton/Lancaster lectr. Oxford U., 1996; Charles E. Test, MD Disting. vis. scholar Princeton U., 2004, vis. prof. religion, 2006. Contbg. editor First Things. Sec.-treas. Inst. on Religion and Pub. Life. Essay winner Hyman G. Enelow prize Jewish Theol. Sem. Am., 1975; recipient Rabbi Jacob B. Augus award Jewish Theol. Sem. Am., 1984, Best Book Constructive Religious Thought award Am. Acad. of Religion, 2000; Woodrow Wilson Internat. Ctr. for Scholars fellow, 1992-93. Fellow Acad. for Jewish Philosophy, Am. Acad. for Jewish Rsch.; mem. Am. Theol. Soc., Assn. for Jewish Studies, Am. Acad. Religion, Assisted Human Reprodn. Office: Univ Coll 15 King's College Cir Toronto ON Canada M5S 3H7 Home Phone: 416-545-0106; Office Phone: 416-946-3229. Business E-Mail: david.novak@utoronto.ca.

NOVAK, DAVID C., restaurant company executive; Sr. v.p., mktg. Pizza Hut, 1986—90; exec. v.p., mktg. and nat. sales Pepsi-Cola Co., 1990—92, COO, N. Am., 1992—94; pres., CEO N. Am. Kentucky Fried Chicken, 1994—97; group pres., CEO, Pizza Hut, KFC Tricon Global Restaurants, Inc. (now Yum! Brands Inc.), Louisville, 1996—97; vice-chmn. Yum! Brands Inc., Louisville, 1996—97, pres., 1997—, CEO, 2000—, chmn., 2001—. Bd. dirs. J.P. Morgan Chase, Yum Brands, Inc., 1997—. Office: Yum Brands Inc 1441 Gardiner Ln Louisville KY 40213-1914 *

NOVAK, DENNIS E., physician; b. East Liverpool, Ohio, Jan. 5, 1946; BA, Bklyn. Coll., 1966; Lic. in Med. Sci., U. Brussels, 1972; MD, Rutgers U., 1974. Diplomate Am. Bd. Family Medicine, Nat. Bd. Med. Examiners. Resident in family practice Monmouth Med. Ctr., Long Branch, NJ, 1974-77; clin. asst. prof. UMDNJ-Robert Wood Johnson Med. Sch., 1977—; chmn. dept. family medicine Cmty. Med. Ctr., 1978—; pvt. practice, 2001—. Physician reviewer, quality assurance HealthSouth Rehab. Hosp. Mem. exec. adv. bd. Ocean County coun. Boy Scouts Am., asst. scoutmaster Ocean Coun., 1997-2002, com. chair Troop 165, 2000—; former trustee United Way Ocean County., Area VII Physician Rev. Org., 1983-86; bd. dir. Interfaith Hospitality Network Ocean County Homeless Program, 2002-04. Named one of Top Docs in NJ, Castle-Connolly NJ Monthly, 2001, 2003, 2005. Fellow Am. Acad. Family Medicine; mem. Ocean County Acad. Family Medicine (v.p. 1983), Ocean County Med.

Soc. (bd. trustees 1983-87). Avocations: photography, scuba, guitar. Address: 1001 Lacey Rd PO Box 780 Forked River NJ 08731-0780 Office Phone: 609-693-8900. Personal E-mail: dennisnovakmd@expressfind.com.

NOVAK, GORDON S., JR., computer scientist, educator; b. Colo., 1947; m. Susan Raye Strawn, May 7, 1977; children: Genevieve, Courtney. BSEE, U. Tex., 1969, MA in Computer Sci., 1971, PhD in Computer Sci., 1976. Mgr. sys. programming Tracor Inc., Austin, Tex., 1966-76; instr. U. Tex., Austin, 1976-77, asst. prof., 1978-81, 83-84, assoc. prof., 1984-98; prof., 1998—; dir. Artificial Intelligence Lab. U. Tex., Austin, 1984-99; computer sci. SRI Internat., Menlo Park, Calif., 1977-78. Vis. asst. prof. Stanford (Calif.) U., 1981-83. Contbr. articles to profl. jours. Office: U Tex Dept Computer Sci Austin TX 78712

NOVAK, GREGORY, marketing professional; b. Johnstown, Pa., Oct. 19, 1949; s. Eugene F. and Joan (Tross) N.; m. Naomi Sosia Wall; children: Rebecca, Jeffrey, Jacqueline. BA, U. Vt., 1971. Project dir. Dun & Bradstreet, NYC, 1973-74; sr. analyst Colgate Palmolive, NYC, 1974-76; mgr. brand rsch. R.J. Reynolds, Winston-Salem, NC, 1976-77, mgr. group new brand rsch., 1977-80, dir. new bus., 1980-81, dir. group mktg., 1981-84; nat. dir. mktg. Deloitte Haskins & Sells, NYC, 1984-90; pres. Novak Mktg. Inc., 1990—. Office: Novak Mktg Inc 29 Brandon Dr Mount Kisco NY 10549-3720 Office Phone: 914-241-1900. Business E-Mail: greg@novakmarketing.com.

NOVAK, JIRI, professional tennis player; b. Zlin, Czech Republic, Mar. 22, 1975; m. Katerina Novak, June 4, 1999; children: Jakub, Jiri Jr., Katerina. Profl. tennis player ATP Tour, 1993—. Achievements include Winner singles titles: Auckland, 1996, Mexico City, 1998, Gstaad, 2001, Munich, 2001, Gstaad, 2003, Tokyo Outdoor, 2004; Winner doubles titles: Bogota, 1995, Santiago, 1995, Casablanca, 1996, Gstaad, 1996, Ostrava, 1997, San Marino, 1998, Mexico City, 1998, Indianapolis, 1998, Split, 1998, Stuttgart Outdoor, 2000; Stuttgart Indoor, 2000, Gstaad, 2000, Dubai, 2000, Montreal/Toronto TMS, 2001, Miami Ericsson Open, 2001, Stuttgart, 2004. Office: ATP Tour Internat Hdqrs 201 ATP Blvd Ponte Vedra Beach FL 32082

NOVAK, JOE, artist; b. Springfield, Mass., Oct. 15, 1930; s. Benjamin D. and Mae (Lavitt) N. BA, Dartmouth Coll., 1952; JD, Harvard U., 1955. One-man shows include Vered Gallery, East Hampton, NY, 1985, 87-88, Milari Ltd., N.Y.C., 1989, Light Emanations, Tesuque, N.Mex., 1992, Bank of Santa Fe, 1996, Davidson & Daughters, Portland, Maine, 1997, McKesson Plz., San Francisco, 1998, Sirius Art Gallery, Santa Fe, 2000, Circle Elephant Art, LA, 2001, 03, Evo Gallery, Santa Fe, 2001, 02, 04, Hood Mus. Art, Dartmouth Coll., 2002, Etherton Gallery, Tucson, 2004, Bert Green Fine Art, LA, 2005, Buschlen Mowatt Gallery, Palm Desert, Calif., 2006; exhibited in group shows at Parrish Art Mus., Southampton, N.Y., Guild Hall Mus., East Hampton, NY, Mus. Fine Arts, Santa Fe, Palm Springs Art Mus., Calif., Tucson Mus. Art, Tucson, Vered Gallery, Milari, Ltd., Olaf Clasen Gallery, Cologne, Germany, Jill George Gallery, London, Eagle Gallery, London, Lewallen Gallery, Santa Fe, Circle Elephant Art, LA, Anderson Contemporary Art, Santa Fe, James Kelly Contemporary, Santa Fe, Evo Gallery, Santa Fe Art Inst., Pharmake Gallery, LA, Farell Fischoff Gallery, Santa Fe, others; works in pub. collections include Boston Mus. Fine Arts, Guild Hall Mus., U. Tex.-Pan Am., Mus. Fine Arts, Santa Fe, Mus. Art, Ft. Lauderdale, Fla., Hood Mus. Art, Dartmouth Coll., U. Calif.-Berkeley Art Mus., Frost Art Mus. Fla. Internat. U., Miami, Cin. Art Mus., Mus. Fine Arts, Springfield, Mass., Tucson Mus. Art, Palm Springs Art Mus.; subject of articles. Lt. USN, 1955-58. Recipient awards for art. Home: PO Box 162 Rancho Mirage CA 92270-0162 Personal E-mail: kiva@dc.rr.com.

NOVAK, JOHN G., construction executive; Ind. residential contractor; pres. Novak Constrn. Co., Chgo., 1980—, CEO. Achievements include leading Novak Construction Company when it was named one of the 50 fastest growing companies in the Chicago area by Crain's Chicago Business, 2007. Office: Novak Constrn Co 3423 N Drake Ave Chicago IL 60618 Office Phone: 773-278-1100. Office Fax: 773-278-1119.

NOVAK, JOSEPH ANTHONY, law librarian; b. Detroit; s. Thomas Paul and Mary Cecilia N. AA, Macomb C.C., Warren, Mich., 1984; BA, Oakland U., 1986; JD, Mich. State U., 1991; M Libr. and Info. Sci., Wayne State U., 1998. Bar: Mich. 2006. Intern Wayne County Pub. Defender's Office, Detroit, 1986; intern Office of Jud. Assistance 3d Jud. Ct. Mich., Detroit, 1993, law clk. to Hon. Diane M. Hathaway, intern, 1996; law libr. St. Louis Correctional Facility, 2000—01, Mid-Mich. Correctional Facility, 2001—03; asst. libr. Mound Correctional Facility, 2003—. Vol., Vol. Income Tax Assistance Program, Detroit, 1995—2001. Recipient Outstanding Vol. Vol. Income Tax Assistance Program, 1995, 96, 98, 99, 2000, The Spirit of Am. Is In the Heart of Its Volunteers IRS, 1995, 96, 97, 99. Mem. FBA (ea. dist. Mich.), Am. Assn. Law Librs., Am. Corrections Assn., Spl. Librs. Assn., Acctg. Aid Soc., Am. Soc. Info. Sci. and Tech., Coun. State Agy. Librs., Mich. Corrections Assn., Oakland County Bar Assn., State Bar Mich., Mich. Libr. Assn., KC. Democrat. Roman Catholic. Avocations: coin and stamp collecting, biking, walking, bowling. Home and Office: 3524 Hamlet Sterling Heights MI 48310-6905

NOVAK, JOSEPH DONALD, science educator; b. Mpls., Dec. 2, 1930; s. Joseph Daniel and Anna (Podany) N.; m. Joan Owen, July 18, 1953; children: Joseph Mark, Barbara Joan, William John BS, U. Minn., 1952, MA, 1954, PhD, 1958; Doctorate (hon.), U. Comanhue, Neuquen, Argentina, 1998, Pub. U. Navarra, 2002, U. Urbino, 2006. Teaching asst. U. Minn., Mpls., 1952-56, instr., 1956-57; asst. prof. Kans. State Tchrs. Coll., 1957-59, Purdue U., West Lafayette, Ind., 1959-62, assoc. prof., 1962-67; prof. Cornell U., Ithaca, NY, 1967-95, prof. emeritus, 1995—; pres. Joseph D. Novak Knowledge Consultants, Inc.; sr. rsch. scientist Inst. for Human and Machine Cogniion, Pensacola, Fla. Knowledge constrn. and orgn. cons. to Procter & Gamble and other cos.; cons. to over 400 schs. and colls., 1975—; vis. fellow Harvard U., 1965-66; disting. vis. prof. U. N.C., Wilmington, 1980, U. West Fla., 1987-88; vis. prof. U. South Fla., 1995; sr. rsch. scientist Fla. Inst. Human and Machine Congition, 1996—. Author: Learning How to Learn, 1984, in 10 langs., 1984—96, Educational Psychology: A Cognitive View, 1978, A Theory of Education, 1977, Aprendizaje Significativo: Techieas y Aplicaciones, 1997, Learning, Creating and Using Knowledge: Concept Maps as Facilitative Tools for Schools and Corporations, 1998, Teaching Science for Understanding, 1998, Assessing Science Understanding, 2000, Una aportacion a la mejora de la calidad de la docentia universitaria: Los mapas Conceptuales, 2000, Errores Conceptuales: Diagnosis, Tratamientoy Reflexiones, 2001, 15 others; contbr. over 40 chpts. to books, over 130 articles to profl. jours. Fellow Tozer Found., Lydia Anderson, 1955-56; research assoc. Harvard U., 1965-66; Fulbright-Hayes Sr. Scholar, Australia, 1980 Fellow: AAAS (sec. sect. Q); mem.: NSTA, Coun. Sci. Soc. Presidents (1st hon. award for rsch. in sci. edn. 1998), Nat. Assn. Rsch. in Sci. Tchr. (pres. 1968, Outstanding Contbns. Sci. Tchg. Through Rsch. award 1990), Nat. Assn. Biology Tchrs. (hon.), Sigma Xi. Avocations: hiking, swimming, dance, music. Office: Cornell U Dept Edn Kennedy Hall Ithaca NY 14853 Personal E-mail: jnovak@ihmc.us. Business E-Mail: jdn2@cornell.edu.

NOVAK, JULIE COWAN, nursing educator, researcher, clinician; b. Peoria, Ill., Oct. 2, 1950; m. Robert E. Novak, 1972; children: Andrew, Christopher, Nicholas. BS in Nursing, U. Iowa, 1972, MA in Nursing of Children, 1976; DNSc, U. San Diego, 1989. RN, Va., Calif.; pediat. nurse practitioner. Charge nurse surg. and med. ICU U. Iowa Hosp. and Clinics, 1972-73; instr. med. sur. nursing St. Luke's Sch. Nursing, Cedar Rapids, Iowa, 1973-74; instr. family and cmty. health U. Iowa Coll. of Nursing, 1974-75; perinatal nurse clinician U. Iowa Hosps., 1976-77; pediatric nurse practitioner Chicano Cmty. Health Ctr., 1978-80; lectr., asst. prof. child health nursing and physical assesstment San Diego State U., 1977-79; child health nurse practitioner program coord. U. Calif., San Diego, 1978-82; pediatric nurse practitioner San Diego City Schs., 1980-82; coord. infant spl. care ctr. follow-up program U. Calif., San Diego, 1982-83, assoc. clin. prof. intercampus grad. studies, 1983-90, dir. health promotion divsn. cmty. and family medicine, 1985-90; assoc. clin. prof. dept. cmty. family medicine U. Calif. Divsn. Health Care Sci., San Diego, 1990-94; assoc. prof. San Diego State U. Sch. Nursing, 1990-94, Calif. Nursing Students Assn. faculty advisor, 1992-94; pediatric nurse practitioner Naval Hosp., 1990-92, Comp. Health Clinic, 1990-94; prof. (Theresa A. Thomas Endowed), dir. Master's in Primary Health Care/Primary Care Nurse Practitioner, Pediatric Nurse Practitioner Progs. U. Va. Schs., Charlottesville, 1994-2000; sch. hlth. coordinator Alb. County Schs. Clin. Prac. U. Va. Dept. Fam. Med.; assoc. head grad. studies, prof. practice and cmty. collaboration Sch. of Nursing Purdue U., 2000—; pvt. practice Family Health Clinic, Carroll County, 2000—. Cons. child health San Diego State U. Child Study Ctr.; mem. accident prevention com. Am. Acad. Pediats.; chair adv. bd. Albemarle County Sch Health, 1995-2000, Camp Holiday Trails, 1995-99; mem. adv. bd. Am. Lung Assn., 1998-99; sch. health coord. Albemarle County Schs.; clin. practice U. Va. Dept. Family Medicine. Contbr. numerous articles to profl. jours. and book chpts. to 12 texts; co-author: Ingall's & Salerno's Maternal Child Nursing, 1995, 99, Mosby Year Book; mem. editl. bd. Jour. Perinatal and Neonatal Nursing, 1986-2001, Children's Nurse, 1982-2001,; mem. editl. bd., reviewer Jour. Pediatric Health Care, 1987-93, Clin. Letters for Nurse Practitioners, 1999-2001—, Advance for Nurse Practitioners, 1998—; speaker in field. Chair Ann. Refugee Clothing Drive, East San Diego, ESL Program, Car Seat Roundup U. Calif., San Diego, 1983-85; mem. telethon March of Dimes; mem. steering com. Healthy Mothers/ Healthy Babies Coalition; chair ways and means com. Benchley-Weinberger Elem. Sch. PTA, 1985-87, pres., 1988-90; v.p., pres. Friends Jamul Schs. Found.; co-chair teen outreach program Jr. League San Diego, 1987-88, chair, 1989-90, bd. dirs., 1990-92; educator presch. health San Carlos Meth. Ch.; mem. Head Start Policy Coun., 1992-94, San Diego County Dropout Prevention Roundtable, 1991-93, Western Albemarle H.S. Planning Team, 1994—; citizen amb./peace educator Mothers Embracing Nuclear Disarmament, Russia and Estonia; project co-dir. San Luis Xochimilco Health Clinic, Mex. Recipient Svc. award Benchley-Weinberger Elem. Sch. PTA, 1988, Hon. Youth Svc. award Calif. Congress Parents and Tchrs., Loretta C. Ford Award for excellence as an nurse practitioner in edn. U. Colo., 1990, March of Dimes Svc. commendation, 1983, Project Hope Svc. commendation, 1983, Hon. Svc. award Calif. Congress of Parents, Tchrs. & Students, 1988, Doctoral Student fellowship U. San Diego, 1986, 2020 Internat. Commn. commendation, 2000, and numerous others. Mem. ANA (mem. ANCC rsch. coalition on credentialing 1997-99, rep. nat. coalition sch. health, AAP com. sch. health), Nat. Certification Bd. Pediatric Nurse Practitioners and Nurses (pres.), Nat. Assn. Pediat. Nurse Practioners Assoc. (chpt. pres., program com., coord. legis. field, nat. cert. chair 1992-98, nat. pres. 2001-2002), Va. Nurse Assn., Rotary Internat., Pi Lambda Theta, Sigma Theta Tau (mem. nominations com. 1990-91, pres. elect Gamma Gamma chpt. 1993-94, Beta Kappa 1995-2000, Delta Omicron 2000—, Media award 1992). Home: 603 Kossuth St Lafayette IN 47905-1444 E-mail: jnovak@nursing.purdue.edu.

NOVAK, LARRY RAY, secondary school educator, music educator, director; b. Mpls., Aug. 3, 1947; d. Raymond Joseph and Jenny Rose Novak; m. Zelda Rae Kurth, June 21, 1997; children: John, David. BS, Concordia Coll., 1969; MA, Mankato State Coll., 1980; postgrad., U. Wis., 1981—. Tchr. Luth. High West, Detroit, 1970—72, Concordia St. Paul HS, 1972—75, Shattuck Sch., Faribault, Minn., 1975—78, Round Lake (Minn.) Pub. Sch., 1978—79, Lakefield (Minn.) Pub. Sch., 1979—90, Redwood Falls (Minn.) Pub. Sch., 1990—94, Park Rapids (Minn.) Pub. Sch., 1994—. Judge Minn. State HS League, Mpls., 1979—; adv. bd. Park Rapids Pub. Sch., 1996—. Assoc. dir. Park Rapids Cmty. Band; coun. mem. Faith Bapt. Ch., Park Rapids, 2000—05. Named Tchr. of Yr., Lakefield Pub. Schs., 1989. Mem.: Minn. Band Dirs. Assn., Music Educators Nat. Conf., Edn. Minn., Lions Club. Baptist. Avocations: reading, camping, auto restoration, music. Home: 212 Henrietta Ave S Park Rapids MN 56470 Office: Park Rapids Pub Sch 401 Huntsinger Ave Park Rapids MN 56470 Office Phone: 218-237-6422. Personal E-mail: zrkn@unitek.com.

NOVAK, LESLIE HOWARD, lawyer; b. Chgo., May 10, 1944; s. Sidney and Sadie (Jensky) N.; m. Nancy Ruth Sherman, July 2, 1967; children: Heidi Ellen, Shani Beth. BS in Bus. with high distinction, U. Minn., 1966, JD cum laude, 1969. Bar: Minn. 1970, U.S. Dist. Ct. Minn. 1970, U.S. Ct. Appeals (8th cir.) 1974, U.S. Supreme Ct. 1995. Assoc. Robins, Kaplan, Miller & Ciresi, Mpls., 1969-77, ptnr., 1977-92, Mackall, Crounse & Moore, PLC., Mpls., 1992—, mng. ptnr., 1997-99. Bd. dirs. Am. Israel C. of C. and Industry of Minn., Mpls., 1981—, founding pres., 1981-91; founding sec., founding bd. dir. Assn. N.Am.-Israel Chambers Commerce, Inc., 1993—; bd. dirs. United Jewish Fund and Coun., St. Paul, 1986-2007; founding dir. Illusion Theater and Sch.; past bd. dirs., past pres. Jewish Family Svc. St. Paul; past bd. dirs. Mt. Zion Temple. Named Leading Am. Atty., Am.'s Registry Outstanding Profls. Mem. Oakridge Country Club, Gopher Golf Boosters Club, Phi Delta Phi, Beta Gamma Sigma. Avocations: biking, golf, tennis, skiing. Office: Mackall Crounse & Moore PLC 1400 AT&T Tower 901 Marquette Ave Minneapolis MN 55402-2859 Home Phone: 952-471-7575; Office Phone: 612-305-1460. Business E-Mail: lhn@mcmlaw.com.

NOVAK, MARK, lawyer; b. Buffalo, Jan. 28, 1952; s. Eugene Francis and Joan (Tross) N.; m. Charlene Mary Ingoglia, Sept. 2, 1972; children: Jason Charles, Jennifer Rose. BA, U. Rochester, 1974; JD, Loyola U., Chgo., 1977. Bar: Ill. 1977, U.S. Dist. Ct. (no. dist.) Ill. 1977, U.S. Ct. Appeals (7th cir.) 1978. Assoc. Anesi, Ozmon & Lewin, Ltd., Chgo., 1977—83; ptnr. Anesi, Ozmon, Rodin, Novak & Kohen, Ltd., Chgo., 1983—, pres., 2006—. Fundraiser Christmas is for Kids Charity, Chgo., 1992—. Mem. ATLA (product liability sect. 1985—), ABA, Ill. Trial Lawyers Assn., Trial Lawyers for Pub. Justice, Chgo. Bar Assn. (jud. evaluation com. 1995—). Home: 1212 N Lake Shore Dr Chicago IL 60610-2371 Office: Anesi Ozmon Rodin Novak & Kohen Ltd 161 N Clark St Fl 21 Chicago IL 60601-3206 Office Phone: 312-372-3822.

NOVAK, MICHELLE ANNE, history professor; d. James Edward and Beverly Jenkins Novak; children: Teresa Marie Dooling, Heather Denise Leal, Kathryn Elizabeth Thorpe. MA, U. Houston, 1992, PhD, 2007. Prof. history Houston C.C., 1992—. Home Phone: 713-718-7143; Office Phone: 713-718-7143.

NOVAK, RANDI RUTH, systems engineer, computer scientist; b. Chgo., July 10, 1954; d. Bernard Richard and Shirley Ann (Fiedorczyk) Novak; children: Rona Rachel Reich, Bonnie Shaina Reich. BS in Math., U. Calif., Santa Cruz, 1976, BA in Econs. with honors, 1976; postgrad., U. Rochester, 1976-78. Rsch. asst. U. Calif., Santa Cruz, 1974-76; Russian translator U. Chgo., 1977—78; intern economist Congl. Budget Office, Washington, 1977; engr. Lockheed MSC, Sunnyvale, Calif., 1978-82; software engr. contractor Silicon Valley Systems, Belmont, Calif., 1982, 83-84, Data Encore (subs. of Verbatim), Sunnyvale, 1982-83; systems programmer CompuPro/Viasyn Corp., Hayward, Calif., 1984-87; mem. tech. staff Network Equipment Techs., Redwood City, Calif., 1987-89; v.p. engring., founder Segue Setups, Burlingame, Calif., 1989-92, ptnr., 1992—; sr. tech. staff NEC Am., San Jose, Calif., 1992—94; sr. systems engr. Hitachi Computer Products, Santa Clara, Calif., 1994-96; prin. engr. Rapid-City Comms./Bay Networks/Nortel Networks, Santa Clara, Calif., 1996—2002, Trapeze Networks, Pleasanton, Calif., 2002—04; prin. engr. tech. staff Foundry Networks, San Jose, 2004—. Fellow Dept. Treasury, 1974-76, NSF, 1977-78, U. Rochester, Rush Rhees fellow. Mem. IEEE Computer Soc., Am. Math. Assn., Computer Profls. for Social Responsibility, Soc. for Computing and Info. Processing, Internat. Platform Assn., Calif. Scholarship Fedn. (life). Avocations: piano, oboe, music, photography, mathematics. Home: 4166 School St Pleasanton CA 94566-6218 Office Phone: 408-207-1528. Personal E-mail: rrnovak@comcast.net.

NOVAK, RAYMOND FRANCIS, environmental services administrator, pharmacology educator; s. Joseph Raymond and Margaret A. (Cerutti) N.; m. Frances C. Holy, Apr. 12, 1969; children: Jennifer, Jessica, Janelle, Joanna. BS in Chemistry, U. Mo., St. Louis, 1968; PhD in Phys. Chemistry, Case Western Res. U., 1973. Assoc. in pharmacology Northwestern U. Med. Sch., Chgo., 1976-77, asst. prof. pharmacology, 1977-81, assoc. prof., 1981-86, prof., 1986-88; prof. pharmacology Wayne State U. Sch. Medicine, Detroit, 1988—; dir. Inst. Environ. Health Scis. Wayne State U., Detroit, 1988—, dir. EHS Ctr. in Molecular and Cellular Toxicology with Human Application, 1994—, dir. interdisciplinary grad. program in Molecular and Cellular Toxicology, 1994—. Mem. toxicology study sect. NIH, Bethesda, Md., 1984-88, mem. and chair numerous grant review com.; adj. sci. Inhalation Toxicology Rsch. Inst., Lovelace Biomed. and Environ. Rsch. Inst., 1991-98; program leader Epidemiology and Environ. Carcinogenesis, Karmanos Cancer Inst. and Comprehensive Cancer Ctr., 1996-98. Assoc. editor Toxicol. Applied Pharmacology, 1992-96, Toxicol. Scis., 2004—; editor Drug Metabolism and Disposition, 1994-2000; mem. editorial bd. Jour. Toxicology and Environ. Health, 19 87-92, In Vivo, 1986—, Toxic Substances Jour., 1993-98; mem. bd. pub. trustees Am. Soc. Pharmacology and Experimental Therapeutics, 1994-2000; publr. over 125 sci. manuscripts, review articles and book chpt. in profl. jour. and books. Co. comdr., field grade officer (Major) USAR, 1968—99. Recipient Disting. Alumni award U. Mo., St. Louis, 1988; grantee Nat. Inst. Environ. Health Sci., 1979—, Gen. Medicine sect. NIH, 1979-82, 89-94. Mem. Am. Soc. for Biochem. and Molecular Biology, Soc. Toxicology (councilor 1996-98, chmn. cont. edn. com. 1995-96), Am. Assn. for Cancer Rsch., Am. Soc. for Pharmacology and Exptl. Therapeutics (bd. publ. trustees 1994-99), Am. Soc. Hematology, Internat. Soc. for Study Xenobiotics. Achievements include patents in field. Office: Wayne State U Inst Environ Health Scis 2727 2nd Ave Rm 4000 Detroit MI 48201-2671 Office Phone: 313-577-0100. Business E-Mail: R.Novak@wayne.edu.

NOVAK, ROBERT DAVID SANDERS, columnist, commentator; b. Joliet, Ill., Feb. 26, 1931; s. Maurice Pall and Jane Anne (Sanders) N.; m. Geraldine Williams, Nov. 10, 1962; children: Zelda, Alexander. AB, U. Ill., 1952; LLD (hon.), Kenyon Coll., 1987; LittD (hon.), U. Ill., 1998; DHL (hon.), U. St. Francis. Reporter Joliet (Ill.) Herald-News, 1947-51, Champaign-Urbana (Ill.) Courier, 1951-52, AP, Omaha, Lincoln, Nebr., Indpls. and Washington, 1954-58, Wall St. Jour., Washington, 1958-63; syndicated columnist N.Y. Herald-Tribune, Washington, 1963-66; commentator Corinthian Broadcasting, Washington, 1963-65, Metromedia, Washington, 1966-76, RKO-Features, Washington, 1976-78; syndicated columnist Chgo. Sun-Times, Washington, 1966—; commentator Cable News Network, Washington, 1980—2005, Am. Voice, 1993—2002, Fox News, 2006—. Pub. Evans-Novak Polit. Report, Washington, 1967—, Evans-Novak Tax Report, Washington, 1985-92, Evans-Novak Japan Report, Washington, 1989-92; contbg. editor Readers Digest, 1979—. Author: The Agony of the GOP, 1965, Lyndon B. Johnson: The Exercise of Power, 1967, Nixon In The White House, 1971, The Reagan Revolution, 1981, Completing the Revolution: A Vision for Victory in 2000, 2000, Prince of Darkness: 50 Years of Reporting in Washington, 2007 Trustee Bullis Sch., Potomac, Md., 1987-98, Phillips Found., 1991—, Children Charities Found., 1994—, Youth Leadership Found., 2003—. 1st lt. U.S. Army, 1952-54. Recipient ACE award Cable Broadcasting Industry, 1990, Laureate Order of Lincoln, Lincoln Acad. Ill., 1999. Mem. Soc. Profl. Journalists, Washington Gridiron Club, Nat. Press Club (Fourth Estate award, 2001), Army and Navy Club. Office: Ste 1203 1750 Pennsylvania Ave NW Washington DC 20006-4501 Office Phone: 202-393-4340. Personal E-mail: evansnovak@aol.com.

NOVAK, ROBERT LOUIS, civil engineer, pavement management consultant; b. Chgo., Feb. 29, 1928; s. Louis and Frances (Kucera) N.; m. Virginia Staas, Jan. 22, 1955 (div. 1962); children: Susan Grace, Nina Louise; m. Joyce Eloise Keen, May 7, 1966; stepchildren: Robert John Moore, William Keen Moore, Marilyn Joyce Moore, James Clifford Moore. BCE, Ga. Inst. Tech., 1948. With Am. Bridge Co., 1948-49; soils engr. Soil Testing Svc., Chgo., 1952-54; chief materials engr. Skidmore Ownings and Merrill USAF Acad., Colorado Springs, 1954, dir. field invest; asst. dir. engring. O'Hare field constrn. Naess & Murphy, Chgo., 1958-60; pres. Novak, Dempsey & Assocs., Palatine, Ill., 1960-85; ptnr. Infrastructure Mgmt. Svcs., Arlington Heights, Ill., 1985-89, cons., 1989—. Contbr. articles to profl. jours. With U.S. Army, 1950-52. Mem. ASTM, Am. Pub. Works Assn. (life; Meritorious Svc. award 1990), Transp. Rsch. Bd. Achievements include a pioneer in field of pavement mgmt. and development of one of the first pavement management computer software programs. Home: 1066 Truman St Nokomis FL 34275-4401

NOVAK, RYNELL STIFF, retired academic administrator; b. Collin County, Tex., May 24, 1929; d. Roy Odus and Wilma (Vermillion) Stiff; m. Joseph Robert Novak, May 11, 1954; children: Robert David, Daniel Allan, Timothy Criswell, Rebekah Novak Proctor, Elisabeth Novak Richards. BA, U. North Tex., Denton, 1949, cert. in libr. studies, 1965, MA, 1973, PhD, 1975, postdoctoral studies, 1975—78, Tex. A&M U., College Station, 1987; MRE, S.W. Bapt. Theol. Sem., 1953. cert. profl. in human resources. Tchr. Plainview (Tex.) Ind. Sch. Dist., 1949-50; draftsman Convair, Ft. Worth, 1951-52; rsch. assoc. U. North Tex., Denton, 1974-79; text editor Home Mission Bd. So. Bapt. Conv., Atlanta, 1979-83; staff assoc. Tex. A&M U. System, College Station, 1984—94. Instr. in speech Blinn Coll., Brenham, Tex., 1988-95. Author: The Novak Connection, 1983. Dist. officer Tex. PTA, 1966—71; v.p. Tex. Bapt. Student Union, 1948—49; mem., dir. Missions Coun. Bapt. Ch.; mem. exec. bd. Bapt. Gen. Conv. Tex., 1974—79. Mem.: Stephen Williams Chpt. US Dau. 1812 (pres.), Stiff Chapel Cemetery Assn. (pres.), Hist. Park Found. of Denton County (pres.), Denton County Hist. Commn., Descs. of Washington's Army at Valley Forge (Tex. brigade comdr. 1991—95, comdr.-in-chief 2004—06), Tex. Brigade, Mensa, United Daus. of the Confederacy, Tex. Soc. DAR (regent La Villita chpt. 1990—92, 1994—95, regent Benjamin Lyon chpt. 2000—01, state chmn. 2006—), Nat. Soc. US Daus. 1812 (nat. treas. 2003—), Tex. Soc. US Daus. 1812 (hon. state pres.). Avocations: genealogy, photography, travel. Home: 2500 Hinkle Dr 27 Denton TX 76201 Personal E-mail: rsnovak@juno.com.

NOVAK, TERRY LEE, dean, educator; b. Chamberlain, SD, Sept. 1, 1940; s. Warren F. and Elaine M. N.; m. Barbara Hosea, Aug. 29, 1981; 1 child, David. B.Sc., S.D. State U., 1962; postgrad. (Rotary fellow), U. Paris, 1962-63; M.P.A., Colo. U., 1965, PhD, 1970. Asst. city mgr. City of Anchorage, 1966-68; city mgr. City of Hopkins, Minn., 1968-74, City of Columbia, Mo., 1974-78, City of Spokane, Wash., 1978-91; v.p. bus. and fin. Ea. Wash. U., Cheney, 1991—94, prof. public adminstrn., 1992—, dir. grad. program pub. administrn., 1994-95; dir. Spokane Joint Ctr. for Higher Edn., 1995-98; bus. mgr. Riverpoint campus Wash. State U., 1998-99; prof pub. adminstrn. Eastern Wash. U., 1999—. Asst. adj. prof. U. Mo., Columbia, 1975, 77; adj. instr. Gonzaga U., Spokane, 1986-88; mem. nat. adv. coun. on environ. policy and tech. EPA. Author: Special Assessment

Financing in American Cities, 1970; contbr. articles to profl. jours. Mem. ASPA, Internat. City Mgrs. Assn. (Acad. Profl. Devel.). Episcopalian. Office: 668 N Riverpoint Blvd Spokane WA 99202-1677 E-mail: tnovak@terrynovak.net.

NOVAK, THEODORE J., lawyer; b. Dec. 8, 1940; BS, U. Ill., Urbana-Champaign, 1962; JD, Chgo.- Kent Coll. of Law, Ill. Inst. Tech., 1968. Bar: Ill. 1967, U.S. Dist. Ct. (no. dist.) Ill. 1967. Ptnr. Rudnick & Wolfe, Chgo.; ptnr., Real Estate, Land Use & Devel. practices, chmn. Land Use & Condemnation practice, mem. policy com. DLA Piper Rudnick Gray Cary, Chgo., 2005—. Adj. prof. Northwestern Univ. Sch. Law, 1998—; lectr. Univ. Chgo. Law Sch., 2000—. Co-author: Ill. Zoning, Eminent Domain & Land Use Manual, 1997; contbr. articles to profl. jours. Mem.: ABA, Am. Coll. Real Estate Lawyers, Ill. State Bar Assn., Chgo. Bar Assn., Lambda Alpha Internat., Ely chpt. Office: DLA Piper Rudnick Gray Cary Suite 1900 203 N La Salle St Chicago IL 60601-1293 Office Phone: 312-368-4037. Office Fax: 312-236-7516. Business E-Mail: theodore.novak@dlapiper.com.

NOVAKOV, GEORGE JOHN, JR., gifted and talented educator, consultant, administrative assistant; b. New Orleans, Apr. 1, 1945; s. George John Novakov Sr. and Gloria (Edwards) Frost; m. Ann Marie Mariano, Dec. 27, 1969; children: Jay, Jaime. BA, U. New Orleans, 1967, MEd, 1970, postgrad., 1985, Tulane U., Loyola U., 1985. Tchr. New Orleans Pub. Schs., 1967—, adminstrv. asst., dir. admission Edna Karr Secondary Sch., 1994—, student data mgr. Edna Karr Secondary Sch., 1994—. Grant writer asst. Edna Karr Secondary Sch., New Orleans Pub. Libr., 1987-99. Author: (play) The Christmas Caper, 1980. Ind. Study Humanities fellow, 1991. Mem. La. Assn. of Computer Using Educators (assoc. editor newsletter, 1992), Greater New Orleans Coun. of Tchrs. of English, Presenter at Nat. Edn. Computer Conf., 1998, 2002. Democrat. Roman Catholic. Avocations: opera, science fiction, computers. Office: Edna Karr Secondary Sch 3332 Huntlee Dr New Orleans LA 70131-7046 Home: 70440 6th St Covington LA 70433 also: 139 Indian Paint Dr Justin TX 76247 Office Phone: 504-398-7115. Business E-Mail: gnovakov@webdei.com.

NOVALES, RONALD RICHARDS, zoologist, educator; b. San Francisco, Apr. 24, 1928; s. William Henry and Dorothy (Richards) N.; m. Barbara Jean Martin, Dec. 19, 1953; children: Nancy Ann, Mary Elizabeth. BA, U. Calif., Berkeley, 1950, MA, 1953, PhD, 1958; postgrad., UCLA, 1951-52. Asst. prof. biol. scis. Northwestern U., Evanston, Ill., 1958-64, assoc. prof., 1964-70, prof., 1970-80, prof. neurobiology and physiology, 1981-93, prof. biology 6 yr. med. program, 1993, emeritus prof. neurobiology and physiology, 1993—. Cons. A.J. Nystrom Co., 1969 Mem. editorial bd.: The American Zoologist, 1969-73; Contbr.: articles to profl. jours. Ency. Brit. Book of Year. Served with U.S. Army, 1953-55. NSF research grantee, 1959-73, 75-78 Fellow AAAS. Unitarian Universalist. Home: 2008 Mcdaniel Ave Evanston IL 60201-2125 *Remember not to "die on the barbed wire" of all the conflicting demands of your work. It is possible for you to cut through the individual strands and to make a successful rush for the enemy's trench.*

NOVELLI, WILLIAM DOMINIC, retirement association executive; b. Pitts., May 21, 1941; s. Dominic M. and Celeste J. (DeFife) Novelli; m. Frances D. Bickell, Aug. 1, 1964; children: Peter M., Alexander G., Sarah J. BA, U. Pa., 1963, MA, 1964; postdoctoral studies, NYU, 1967—69. Mgr. mktg. Lever Bros. Co., NYC, 1964—69; supr. account Wells, Rich, Greene, NYC, 1969—70; dir. advt. and creative services Peace Corps and Action, Washington, 1970—72; pres., co-founder Porter Novelli, 1972—90; exec. v.p. CARE; pres. Campaign for Tobacco-Free Kids; assoc. exec. dir. AARP, Washington, 2000—01, CEO, 2001—. Instr. mktg. mgmt. U. Md., instr. health communication and mass media, Dept. Communication Arts and Theatre. Mem. editl. rev. bd. Jour. Health Care Mktg.; contbr. Mem. adv. coun. population communication services program Johns Hopkins U.; mem. adv. panel US AID; vol. cons. United Way Am.; vice chmn. task force on profl. communications Nat. Coun. on Patient Info. and Edn.; bd. dir. Ctr. for Consumer Health Edn., Reston, Va., Campaign for Tobacco-Free Kids. Named one of 100 Most Influential Pub. Relations Professionals fo 20th Century. Mem.: Am. Mktg. Assn. (chmn. attitude rsch. conf. 1985). Office: AARP 601 E St NW Washington DC 20049 Office Phone: 202-434-2300. Business E-Mail: wnovelli@aarp.org.

NOVELLO, ANTONIA COELLO, pediatric nephrologist, former state health commissioner, United States Surgeon General; b. Fajardo, PR, Aug. 23, 1944; d. Antonio and Ana D. (Flores) Coello; m. Joseph R. Novello, May 30, 1970. BS, U. P.R., Rio Piedras, 1965; MD, U. P.R., San Juan, 1970; MPH, Johns Hopkins Sch. Hygiene, 1982; DrPh, Johns Hopkins U., 2000; DSc (hon.), Med. Coll. Ohio, 1990, U. Ctrl. Caribe, Cayey, PR, 1990, Lehigh U., 1992, Hood Coll., 1992, U. Notre Dame, Ind., 1991, N.Y. Med. Coll., 1992, U. Mass., 1992, Fla. Internat. U., 1992, Cath. U., 1993, Washington Coll., 1993, St. Mary's Coll., 1993, Ea. Va. Med. Sch., 1993, Ctrl. Conn. State U., 1993, Georgetown U., 1993, U. Mich., 1994, Mt. Sinai Sch. Medicine, 1995; LHD (hon.), Alvernia Coll., 1996; HHD (hon.), Kings Coll., 1996; D in Health Sci. (hon.), Ponce Sch. of Medicine, 1996; D in Law (hon.), Gannon U., 1997; LHD (hon.), Loyola U., 1997; DSc (hon.), U. North Tex., Ft. Worth, 2002, Howard U., 2003, NYU, 2003, Pace U., 2003, others. Diplomate Am. Bd. Pediatrics. Intern in pediatrics U. Mich. Med. Ctr., Ann Arbor, 1970-71, resident in pediatrics, 1971-73, pediatric nephrology fellow, 1973-74, Georgetown U. Hosp., Washington, 1974-75; project officer Nat. Inst. Arthritis, Metabolism and Digestive Diseases NIH, Bethesda, Md., 1978-79, staff physician, 1979-80; exec. sec. gen. medicine B study sect., div. of rsch. grants NIH, Bethesda, 1981-86; dep. dir. Nat. Inst. Child Health & Human Devel., NIH, Bethesda, 1986-90; surgeon gen. US Dept. Health & Human Services, Washington, 1990-93; spl. rep. for health and nutrition UNICEF, NYC, 1993—96; vis. prof. health policy and mgmt. Johns Hopkins U. Sch. of Hygiene and Pub. Health, 1996—99; commr. of health State of NY, 1999—2007. Clin. prof. pediatrics Georgetown U. Hosp., Washington, 1986, 89, Uniformed Svcs. U. of Health Scis., 1989; adj. prof. pediatrics and communicable diseases U. Mich. Med. Sch., 1993; adj. prof. internat. health Sch. Hygiene and Pub. Health, Johns Hopkins U., Balt.; prof. dept. health policy mgmt. and behavior SUNY, 1999—; clin. prof. pediats. U. Rochester, N.Y., 1999—; mem. Georgetown Med. Ctr. Interdepartmental Rsch. Group; legis. fellow U.S. Senate Com. on Labor and Human Resources, Washington, 1982-83; mem. Com. on Rsch. in Pediatric Nephrology, Washington; participant grants assoc. program seminars Nat. Inst. Arthritis, Diabetes and Digestive and Kidney Diseases, NIH, Bethesda, 1980-81; pediatric cons. Adolescent Medicine Svc., Psychiat. Inst., Washington, 1979-83; nephrology cons. Met. Washington Renal Dialysis Ctr. affiliate Georgetown U. Hosp., Washington, 1975-78; phys. diagnosis class instr. U. Mich. Med. Ctr., Ann Arbor, 1973-74; chair Sec.'s Work Group on Pediatric HIV Infection and Diseases, DHHS, 1988; cons. WHO, Geneva, 1989; mem. Johns Hopkins Soc. Scholars, 1991. Contbr. numerous articles to profl. jours. and chpts. to books in field; mem. editorial bd. Internat. Jour Artificial Organs, Jour. Mexican Nephrology. Served in USPHS, 1978-99. Recipient Intern of Yr. award U. Mich. Dept. Pediatrics, 1971, Woman of Yr. award Disting. Grads. Pub. Sch. Systems, San Juan, 1980, PHS Commendation medal HHS, 1983, PHS Citation award HHS, 1984, Cert. of Recognition, Divsn. Rsch. Grants, NIH, 1985, PHS Outstanding medal HHS, 1988, PHS Unit Commendation, 1988, PHS Surgeon Gen.'s Exemplary Svc. medal, 1989, PHS Outstanding Unit citation, 1989, DHHS Asst. Sec. for Health Cert. of Commendation, 1989, Surgeon Gen. Medallion award, 1990, Alumni award U. Mich. Med. Ctr., 1991, Elizabeth Blackwell award, 1991, Woodrow Wilson award for disting. govt. svc., 1991, Congl. Hispanic Caucus medal, 1991, Order of Mil. Med. Merit, 1992, Washington Times Freedom award, 1992, Charles C. Shepard Sci. award, 1992, Golden Plate award, 1992, Elizabeth Ann Seton award, 1992, Ellis Island Congl. Medal of Honor, 1993, Legion of Merit medal, 1993, Athena award Alumnae Coun., 1993, Nat. Citation award Mortar Bd., 1993, Disting. Pub. Svc. award, 1993, Healthy Am. Fitness Leaders award, 1994, Pub. Leadership Edn. Network Mentor award, 1994, Disting. Svc. award Nat. Coun. Cath. Women, 1995, James E. Van Zandt Citizenship award, 1995, Ronald McDonald Children's Charities Excellence award, 1995, Hispanic Heritage Leadership award, 1998, Disting. Alumnus award Am. Assn. of State Colls. and Univs., 1997, Humanitarian award Am. Cancer Soc., 2001, James Smithson Bicentenial medal Smithsonian Inst., 2002; named Health Leader of Yr., COA, 1992; inductee Nat. Women's Hall of Fame, 1994, Internat. Pediatric Hall of Fame Miami Children's Hosp., 1996, Am. Med. Women Assn. Hall of Fame, 2002. Fellow Am. Acad. Pediatrics (Excellence Pub. Svc. award 1993); mem. AMA (Nathan Davis award 1993, Meritorious Svc. award 1993, Luther L. Terry award, 2000), Inst. Medicine, Internat. Soc. Nephrology, Am. Soc. Nephrology, Latin Am. Soc. Nephrology, Soc. for Pediatric Rsch., Am. Pediatric Soc., Assn. Mil. Surgeons U.S., Am. Soc. Pediatric Nephrology, Pan Am. Med. and Dental Soc. (pres.-elect, sec. 1984), D.C. Med. Soc. (assoc.), Johns Hopkins U. Soc. Scholars, Alpha Omega Alpha. Avocation: collecting antique furniture.

NOVELLY, PAUL ANTHONY, petrochemical and refining company executive; b. St. Louis, 1943; m. Mary Katherine Novelly; 4 children. B in commerce, St. Louis U., 1965. With Shell Oil Co., St. Louis, 1962-68, Apex Oil Co., Inc., St. Louis, 1968—; pres. Apex Oil Co., Inc., St. Louis, 1980—; chmn., CEO Apex Oil Co., Inc., St. Louis. Dep. chmn. bd. dirs. Liquid Funding, Ltd., 2001—; vice chmn. bd. dirs. Clark Oil & Refining Co., St. Louis; bd. dirs. The Bear Stearns Companies, NYC, 2002—. Recipient Horatio Alger award, 2000. Office: Apex Oil Corp 8235 Forsyth Blvd Ste 400 Clayton MO 63105

NOVICH, BRUCE ERIC, chemicals executive; b. Phila., Mar. 15, 1957; s. Samuel David and Vivian Rose Novich; m. Susan S. Novich, Sept. 5, 1982; children: Scott, Spencer, Corey. BA, Colgate U., 1979; BSChemE, MIT, 1980, MS in Geology, 1982, MSCE, 1982, ScD in Materials Processing, 1984. V.p. R & D and engring. Ceramics Process System, Milford, Mass., 1984-95; global bus. dir. electronics-zebralink PPG Industries, Pitts., 1995-2000; global bus. dir. Fujifilm Electronic Materials, 2000—04, Fuji Film Electronic Materials, Inc., Kingstown, RI, 2004—; sr. v.p. Fujifilm Corp., 2007—. Contbr. articles to profle. jours. Recipient 2 R & D 100 awards. Achievements include 25 patents in ceramics, composites and electronic packaging. Office: Fuji Film Electronic Materials Inc 80 Circuit Dr N North Kingstown RI 02852 Home Phone: 401-996-2333. Business E-Mail: bruce_novich@fujifilm-ffem.com.

NOVICH, NEIL S., metals distribution company executive; BA in Physics summa cum laude, Harvard U., 1974; MS in Nuclear Engring., MIT, 1979, MS in Mgmt., 1981. Former dir. Bain & Co.; COO Ryerson Inc., Chgo., 1994—99, chmn., pres., CEO, 1999—. Dir. W.W. Grainger, Inc. Trustee Field Mus. Natural History, Children's Home & Aid Soc. Ill.; mem. vis. com. Divsn. Phys. Scis., U. Chgo. Nat. Sci. Found. scholar, Ford scholar. Mem. Phi Beta Kappa. Office: Ryerson Inc 2621 W 15th Pl Chicago IL 60608 *

NOVICK, ANDREW CARL, urologist; b. Montreal, Apr. 5, 1948; came to U.S., 1974; s. David and Rose (Ortenberg) N.; m. Thelma Silver, June 29, 1969 (div. Dec. 1983); 1 child, Lorne J.; m. Linda Friedman, May 24, 1992; children: Rachel H., Eric D. BSc, McGill U., 1968, MD, CM, 1972. Diplomate Am. Bd. Urology. Resident in surgery Royal Victoria Hosp., Montreal, 1972—74; resident in urology Cleve. Clinic Found., 1974—77, staff dept. urology, 1977—, head sect. renal transplant, 1977—, chmn. Urol. Inst., 1985—, chmn. Organ Transplant Ctr., 1985—92. Trustee Am. Bd. Urology, 1995—2001, Urology Residence Rev. Com., 1997—2002. Editor: Vascular Problems in Urology, 1982, Stewart's Operative Urology, 1989, Renal Vascular Disease, 1995, Innovations in Urologic Surgery, 1997, Campbell's Urology, 2002, 2007, Operative Urology at the Cleveland Clinic, 2006; contbr. more than 500 articles to profl. jours. Fellow ACS, Med. Coun. Can.; mem. Am. Urol. Assn., Am. Assn. Genito-Urinary Surgeons, Clin. Soc. Genito-Urinary Surgeons. Office: Cleve Clinic Found 9500 Euclid Ave A100 Cleveland OH 44195-0001 Home: 24875 Woodside Ln Beachwood OH 44122 Office Phone: 216-444-5584. Business E-Mail: novicka@ccf.org.

NOVICK, DAVID KANDEL, science educator, department chairman; b. Media, Pa., Sept. 3, 1965; s. Harold and Gladys Novick; m. Joanna Victoria Kandel, Aug. 12, 1997; children: Zachary Kandel, Brandon Kandel, Rachel Kandel. BS, Union Coll., Schenectady, NY, 1988; PhD, Tufts U., Medford, Mass., 1997. Rsch. technician ii Dana Farber Cancer Inst., Reinherz Lab, Dept. Immunobiology, Brookline, Mass., 1988—90; lab instr. dept. biology Tufts U., Medford, Mass., 1990—97; postdoc. assoc. human med. genetics unit U. Vt. Med. Sch. Lab of Bertrand C. Liang, Burlington, Vt., 1998—99; sci. chair West Nottingham Acad., Colora, Md., 1999—2001, Darrow Sch., New Lebanon, 2001—05, Gann Acad., Waltham, Mass., 2005—; adj. faculty Berkshire CC, Pittsfield, Mass., 2004; online adj. faculty Colo. Tech. U. Online, Colo., 2005—. Presenter in field. Mem.: ASCD, AAAS, Assn. for Supervision and Curriculum Devel., Nat. Assn. Biology Tchrs., Nat. Sci. Tchr. Assn., Sigma Xi (assoc.). Jewish. Home: 31 Hampshire Ave Sharon MA 02067 Office: Gann Acad 333 Forest St Waltham MA 02452 Home Phone: 781-784-3894; Office Phone: 781-642-6800 301. Office Fax: 781-642-6805. Personal E-mail: dknovick@verizon.net. E-mail: dnovick@gannacademy.org.

NOVICK, JULIUS LERNER, theater critic, educator; b. NYC, Jan. 31, 1939; s. Solomon Joseph and Ethel (Lerner) N.; m. Phyllis Belle Spaeth, May 27, 1983; 1 child, Ilana BA, Harvard U., 1960; D.F.A., Yale U., 1966. Theatre critic WNDT-TV, Channel 13, NYC, 1968-70; asst. prof. English NYU, NYC, 1969-72; assoc. prof. lit. SUNY-Purchase, 1972-80, prof., 1980—2001, prof. emeritus, 2002—; theatre critic The Village Voice, NYC, 1958-89, The N.Y. Observer, NYC, 1987-91, Newsday, NYC, 1992-94, Kempner Disting. prof., 1997-99. Vis. lectr. drama div. Juilliard Sch., N.Y.C., 1968-71; dramaturg The Acting Co., N.Y.C., 1971-73; vis. critic Dartmouth Summer Repertory Co., Hanover, N.H., 1976, 79, 80, 82, 83, 84; master critic Nat. Critics Inst., Waterford, Conn., 1971— Author: Beyond Broadway, 1968. Fulbright scholar, 1960-61; Woodrow Wilson fellow, 1961-62; Guggenheim fellow, 1977; recipient George Jean Nathan award for dramatic criticism, 1981-82 Mem.: Am. Theatre and Drama Soc., Assn. for Theatre in Higher Edn., Assn. for Jewish Studies, Am. Theatre Critics Assn., Am. Soc. for Theatre Rsch. Jewish. E-mail: Jluddite@aol.com.

NOVICK, NELSON LEE, dermatologist, internist, consultant, cosmetic dermasurgeon, writer; b. Bklyn., June 27, 1949; s. Benjamin and Vivian (Meltzer) N.; m. Meryl Sohnis, June 20, 1971; children: Yonatan, Yoel, Ariel, Daniel, Avraham, Shmuel, Yehudah. BA in Biology magna cum laude, Bklyn. Coll., 1971; MD, Mt. Sinai Sch. Medicine, 1975. Diplomate Am. Bd. Internal Medicine, Am. Bd. Dermatology, Am. Bd. Med. Examiners. Resident internal medicine Mt. Sinai Med. Ctr., NYC, 1975—78, postgrad. preceptee, 1980—83, outpatient dept. clinic chief, dermatology svc., 1983—2003, attending, 2004—; resident Skin and Cancer Unit NYU Med. Ctr., NYC, 1978—80; clin. prof. Mt. Sinai Sch. Medicine, NYC, 2004—. Cons. Westwood-Squibb Skin Care Info. Ctr., Vaseline Intensive Care Rsch., Bausch & Lomb, Schering-Plough, Sandoz Internat., Procter & Gamble, Lever-2000, Novartis, Bradley Pharms., Merz Pharms., Inst. for Med. Info., Collagenesis Corp., PediFix, Biocell Tech. Network, others; skin health and beauty expert, Runner's World Mag., 2000-02; expert cons. Dermatology, Guidelines Expert, Nitron Advisors Healthcare Circle of Experts, 2003-, various med. websites; mem. MSSM spkrs. bureau, 2003-. Author: Saving Face, Skin Care for Teens, Super Skin, Baby Skin, You Can Do Something About Your Allergies, You Can Look Younger at Any Age, Diseases of the Mucus Membranes, (novel) In the Path of the Wolf, (audiotape series) Keeping That Baby Skin Look, Healthier and Younger-Looking Skin, Lunchtime Beauty Fixes for a Prettier Face, Breathing Easier, Fido, Food and Fumes; co-author: The External Ear; reviewer Annals Internal Medicine, Jour. Am. Acad. Dermatology, Jour. Dermatol. Surgery, Internat. Jour. Dermatology; editl. advisor Exec. Health's Good Health Report, Snyder Comm., Your Baby Wallboard Program; former med. editor Current Podiatric Medicine, Jour. Am. Analgesia Soc.; contbr. articles to profl. jours. Regent's Coll. scholar, 1971, Max and Leah Strauss Fund scholar, 1971, Grand St. Found. scholar, 1971; recipient Dept. Dermatology award for contbg. to edn. of residents, 2000-01, Dept. Dermatology award for exceptional svc. in patient care, 2001-02; Dept. Dermatology award for two decades of outstanding svc., 2003. Fellow ACP (direct election), Am. Acad. Dermatology (Leadership Cir. 2006), Am. Soc. Dermatol. Surgery, Am. Acad. Cosmetic Surgery, Skin Cancer Found. (hon.); mem. AMA, AAAS, Soc. Investigative Dermatology, Skin Phototrauma Found., Internat. Soc. for Androgenic Disorders, Skin Cancer Found. (charter), N.Y. Acad. Scis., N.Y. County Med. Soc., Am. Soc. Dermatologic Surgery, Am. Analgesia Soc. (past bd. dirs.), Am. Soc. Cosmetic Dermatology & Aesthetic Surgery (charter), Nature Conservancy, Audubon Soc., Nat. Geog. Found., N.Y. Zool. Soc., Am. Mus. Natural History, Smithsonian Instn., Nat. Wildlife Fedn., The Wilderness Soc., Author's Guild, Author's League Am., Phi Beta Kappa. Jewish. Office: 328 E 75th St New York NY 10021-3317 Office Phone: 212-772-9300. Personal E-mail: nnovickmd@aol.com. *The true measure of a person's success in life is not how much he accomplished, but how much of his God-given potential he has used.*

NOVICK, PETER J., cell biologist, educator; PhD, U. Calif., Berkeley, 1981. Prof. cell biology Yale U., New Haven. Contbr. articles to profl. jours. Fellow: Am. Acad. Arts & Scis. Office: Dept Cell Biology Yale U Sch Medicine 333 Cedar St PO Box 208002 New Haven CT 06520-8002 E-mail: Peter.Novick@yale.edu.

NOVICK, RICHARD PAUL, research scientist, public health institute administrator; b. NYC, Aug. 10, 1932; s. Samuel and Mollie (Foster) N.; m. Barbara Zabin, June 1, 1958; children— Lynn Judith, Dorothy Ruth BA magna cum laude, Yale U., 1954; MD with honors in Microbiol., NYU, 1959. Intern dept. medicine Yale U., New Haven, 1959—60; postdoctoral fellow Nat. Inst. Med. Rsch., London, 1961—62; asst. resident dept. medicine Vanderbilt U. Hosp., Nashville, 1962—63; special postdoctoral fellow Rockefeller U., NYC, 1963-65; assoc. Pub. Health Rsch. Inst. of City of NY, 1965-69, assoc. mem., 1969-75, mem., chmn. dept. plasmid biology, 1975-81, dir., 1981—91; prof. depts. microbiol. and medicine NYU Sch. Medicine, 1993—. Adj. prof. dept. microbiol. Sch. Medicine, NYU, 1966—1993; mem. recombinant DNA adv. com. NIH, Bethesda, Md., 1979-82; head sci. adv. com., applied genetics div. Pub. Health Rsch. Inst., 1983 Editor-in-chief Plasmid Jour., 1977; adv. editor Internat. Rev. Cytology, 1979; editl. cons. biol. abstracts, 1984; Contbr. articles to profl. jours. Bd. dirs. Alliance for Prudent Use of Antibiotics, Boston, 1982, sci. adv. bd.; Com. for Responsible Genetics, Boston, 1983; mem. adv. com. on microbiol. and virology Am. Cancer Soc., NYC, 1983 Named 1st ann. W.A. Altemeier lectr. Surg. Infections Soc., Boston, 1982, Selman A. Waksman hon. lectr. Rutgers U., 1983 Mem. Am. Soc. Microbiol., Am. Genetics Soc., Harvey Soc., Phi Beta Kappa, Alpha Omega Alpha, NAS. Avocations: woodworking, skiing, culinary mycology. Home: 10 W 86th St New York NY 10024-3606 Office: Skirball Inst of Biomolecular Medicine 2nd floor Labs 1 and 2 540 First Ave New York NY 10016

NOVICK, ROBERT T., lawyer; b. Oct. 6, 1958; BA, Bucknell Univ., 1980; JD cum laude, Am. Univ., 1983. Bar: DC 1984, US Ct. Internat. Trade. Assoc. Steptoe & Johnson LLP, Washington, 1983—90, ptnr., 1991—97; counselor Office of U.S. Trade Rep., Washington, 1997—99, gen. counsel, 1999—2001; ptnr., chmn. Trade dept. Wilmer Cutler Pickering Hale & Dorr, Washington, 2001—. Commr. Adv. Commn. on Electronic Commerce, U.S. Congress. Editor (exec.): Am. Univ. Law Rev. Office: Wilmer Cutler Pickering Hale & Dorr 1875 Pennsylvania Ave NW Washington DC 20006 Office Phone: 202-663-6140. Office Fax: 202-663-6363. Business E-Mail: robert.novick@wilmerhale.com.

NOVICK, STEPHEN ALAN, cardiologist; b. Hackensack, NJ, July 25, 1938; m. Rita Lynn Schneider; children: David, Michael, Jonathan. BA in Chemistry magna cum laude, Bklyn. Coll., 1959; MD with honors, SUNY, 1963. Intern L.I. Coll. Hosp., Bklyn., 1963—64, resident, chief resident in internal medicine, 1965—67; fellow cardiology Mt. Sinai Med. Ctr., NYC, 1967—69; dir. prenatal cardiology clinic Mt. Sinai Hosp., NYC, 1969—. Dir. cardiac clinic Mt. Sinai Hosp., NYC, 1970—2000; dir. cardiology, dir. ICU Yonkers (N.Y.) Profl. Hosp., 1972—79; cons. cardiologist St. John's Riverside Hosp., Yonkers, NY; cons., presenter in field. Contbr. articles to profl. jours. Founder, dir. Little TOR Homeowners Assn., New City, NY, 1973—75, Bklyn. Coll. Soc. for Free Discussion of Politics, 1955—59. Recipient cardiology fellowship, NIH, 1967—69. Fellow: N.Y. Cardiol. Soc.; mem.: Phi Beta Kappa. Avocations: history, violin, singing, writing. Office: 984 N Broadway Yonkers NY 10701 also: 1160 Fifth Ave New York NY 10029 Office Phone: 914-423-7267.

NOVIKOV, SERGEI PETROVITCH, mathematician; b. Gorky, Russia, Mar. 20, 1938; s. Peter Sergeevitch and Ludmila (Keldysh) N.; m. Eleonora Vikentievna Tsoi, Oct. 2, 1962; children: Irina, Maria, Peter. B.Math., Moscow State U., 1960; PhD in math., Steklov Math. Inst., Moscow, 1964; PhD (hon.), U. Athens, 1988, U. Tel Aviv, 2000. Rsch. prof. math. Steklov Math. Inst., Moscow, 1964-75; chmn. math. dept. Landau Inst. Theoretical Physics, Moscow, 1975-96; disting. prof. math U Maryland, Coll. Park, 1996—. Chmn. geometry and topology Steklov Math. Ins., 1983—, Moscow State U., 1983—. Contbr. articles to profl. jours. Recipient Moscow Math. Soc. Young Mathematicians prize, 1964, Lenin Prize, 1967, Fields medal Internat. Math. Union, 1970, Lobachevskii Internat. Prize, Acad. of Sci. of the USSR, 1981, Wolf prize in math. Wolf Found., Israel, 2005. Mem. Moscow Math. Soc. (pres. 1985-96), Internat. Assn. of Math. Physicists (v.p. 1986-90), London Math. Soc. (hon. mem.), Serbian Acad. of Sci. and Art (hon. mem.), Acad. of Sci of the USSR (corresponding mem. 1966-81, full mem. 1981—), elected foreign mem. of the Academia de Lincei, Italy, 1991, mem. Academia Europea, 1992, foreign mem. of the NAS, 1994, mem of the Pontifical Acad. of Sci. (Vatican), 1996. Office: Landau Inst Kosygin St 2 Moscow Russia also: Dept of Math Math Bldg U of Maryland College Park MD 20742-4015

NOVITCH, MARK, physician, retired pharmaceutical executive; b. New London, Conn., Apr. 23, 1932; s. Charles Weinger and Mary (Margolick) N.; m. Katherine Louise Henderson, Oct. 9, 1971; 1 dau., Julia Drummond. AB, Yale U., 1954; MD, N.Y. Med. Coll., 1958. Intern, asst. resident in medicine Boston City Hosp., 1958-60; rsch. fellow Harvard Med. Sch., 1960-62, asst. in medicine, 1962-64, instr. medicine, 1964-67; mem. med. staff Peter Bent Brigham Hosp., Boston, 1962-67; asst. physician Univ. Health Svcs., Harvard U., 1961-67; asst. to dep. asst. sec. for health and sci. affairs HEW, Washington, 1967-71; dep. assoc. commr. for med. affairs FDA, Washington, 1971-78, assoc. commr. for health affairs, 1978-81; dep. commr. food and drugs HHS, 1981-85; corp. v.p. The Upjohn Co., Kalamazoo, 1985-86, sr. v.p. sci. adminstrn., 1986-88, exec. v.p., 1989-90, vice-chmn. bd. dirs., 1991-93; prof. health scis. George Washington U., Washington, 1994-97. Adj. prof. George Washington U., 1997—2001; bd. dirs. Nat. Acad. Soc. Ins.; chmn. bd. dirs. Food and Drug Law Inst., 2001—02; pres. U.S. Pharmacopeial Conv. Inc., 1990—95, trustee,

1990—2000. Bd. dirs. Nat. Fund Med. Edn. USPHS fellow, 1960-62; Brookings Instn. fed. exec. fellow, 1970-71 Mem. Mass. Med. Soc. Home: 3558 Albemarle St NW Washington DC 20008-4214

NOVITZ, CHARLES RICHARD, broadcast executive, reporter; b. Chgo., Oct. 25, 1934; m. Eve Krzyzanowski, Feb. 11, 1988; 1 child, Alexandra Maris. BS in Journalism, U. Ill., Champaign-Urbana, 1956; MS, Columbia U., 1960; MPA, NYU, 1971. Reporter, writer, editor City News Bur., Chgo., 1956-57, UPI, Chgo., 1957-59; editor, writer, field producer NBC News, NYC and Chgo., 1959-60; with ABC News, 1960-79; mgr. ABC News (TV network syndication), 1973-79; mng. dir. Ind. TV News Assn., NYC, 1979-81; producer, exec. NBC News, NYC, 1982-85, 87; assoc. Rowan & Blewitt, Inc./Exec. TV Workshop, NYC, 1985-95; pres. NovaNews Comm. Cons., NYC, 1994—. On-air talent Money Call News, 1988; freelance TV producer, cable and pub. TV series, 1985—; adj. instr. LIU, 1967-69, NYU, 1969-70; asst. adj. prof. Lehman Coll., 1970-71; adj. prof., producer interactive televised course CUNY, 1972-75 Mem. Silurians, Broadcast Pioneers, Radio TV News Dirs. Assn., Alumni Assn. Columbia Grad. Sch. Journalism (pres. 1979), Deadline Club N.Y.C. (pres. 1969), Deadline Club Found. (pres. 1999—), Soc. Profl. Journalists-Sigma Delta Chi (pres. 1981-82). Office: 160 West End Ave Apt 29D New York NY 10023-5616 also: 392 Moonstone Beach Rd Wakefield RI 02879-5102 Home Phone: 212-787-6908; Office Phone: 212-787-6908. Personal E-mail: evevideo@earthlink.net.

NOVOGRATZ, MICHAEL E., investment company executive; BA, Princeton U. Pres. Latin Am. Goldman Sachs, 1992—99, head Fixed Income, Currencies and Commodities Risk in Asia, 1992—99, ptnr., 1998; pres., prin., mem. mgmt. com. Fortress Investment Group LLC, 2002—. Bd. dirs. Acumen Fund. Chmn. bd. dirs. Sch. of the Strings, Beat the Streets Wrestling Inc. Helicopter pilot US Army. Office: Fortress Investment Group LLC 1345 Avenue of the Americas New York NY 10105 Office Phone: 212-798-6100.

NOVOGROD, NANCY GERSTEIN, editor; b. NYC, Jan. 30, 1949; d. Max and Hilda (Kirschbaum) Gerstein; m. John Campner Novogrod, Nov. 7, 1976; children: James Campner, Caroline Anne. AB, Mt. Holyoke Coll., 1971. Sec. fiction dept. The New Yorker, NYC, 1971-73, reader, 1973-76; asst. editor Clarkson Potter/Pubs., NYC, 1977-78, assoc. editor, 1978-80, editor, 1980-83, sr. editor, 1984-86, exec. editor, 1987; sr. editor HG (House & Garden mag.), NYC, 1987-88, editor-in-chief, 1988-93, Travel + Leisure, NYC, 1993—; editl. dir. Am. Express Pub., NYC, 2000—. Bd. dirs. Am. Soc. Mag. Editors. Bd. dirs. NY Bot. Garden, 1991—; exec. com., bd. dirs. Mount Holyoke Coll., 1992—97; adv. bd. Breast Cancer Rsch. Found., 1993; bd. dirs. Children's Advocacy Ctr. Manhattan, 2003. Office: Travel + Leisure 1120 Avenue of the Americas New York NY 10036-6700 Personal E-mail: nancy.g.novogrod@aexp.com.

NOVOTNEY, DONALD FRANCIS, superintendent of schools; b. Streator, Ill., July 10, 1947; s. Andrew Stephen and Irene Marie (Lux) Novotney; m. Jane Francis Loeffelholz, June 3, 1972; children: Nicole, Tara, Thomas, Michael, Theresa. BA, Loras Coll., 1969; MS in Tchg., U. Wis., Platteville, 1973; MS, U. Dayton, 1985. Cert. tchr., Wis.; cert. tchr. and adminstr., Ohio. Prin. Holy Ghost Sch., Dickeyville, Wis., 1969-75, St. John Sch., Green Bay, Wis., 1975-76, Beaver Dam (Wis.) Cath. Schs., 1976-83; coord. Jordan Cath. Schs., Rock Island, Wis., 1983-85; supt. schs. Diocese of Fargo, ND, 1985—87, Diocese of La Crosse, Wis., 1987—2001, Diocese of Jefferson City, Mo., 2002—. Mem. Nat. Cath. Edn. Assn. (del. to nat. congress for Cath. schs.). Republican. Roman Catholic. Avocations: athletics, travel. Home: 4000 Terra Bella Jefferson City MO 65109 Office: Diocese of Jefferson City 402 N Clark Ave Jefferson City MO 65102 Personal E-mail: donnjanen@aol.com.

NOVOTNY, DAVID JOSEPH, lawyer; b. Melrose Park, Ill., Oct. 3, 1953; s. Joseph F. and Dorothy E. (Erickson) N.; m. Gladys Ruth Korynecky, May 1, 1982. BSc, DePaul U., 1975, JD, 1978. Bar: Ill. 1978, U.S. Dist. Ct. (no. dist.), Ill. 1978, U.S. Ct. Appeals (7th cir.) 1985, U.S. Dist. Ct. (no. dist.), Ind. 1995, U.S. Dist. Ct. (cen. dist.) Ill. 1999. Law clk. to justice Ill. Appellate Ct., Chgo., 1978-80; assoc. Rooks, Pitts & Poust, Chgo., 1980-83, Peterson, Ross, Schloerb & Seidel (now Peterson & Ross), Chgo., 1983-88, ptnr., 1988—. Arbitrator Am. Arbitration Assn., 1987—. Cir. Ct. Cook County Ct.-Annexed Arbitration, 1990—. Exec. editor DePaul Law Rev., 1978. Mem. ABA, Ill. State Bar Assn., 7th Cir. Bar Assn., Soc. Trial Lawyers, Asia-Pacific Lawyers Assn., Lawyer-Pilots Bar Assn., Legal Club Chgo., Def. Rsch. Inst. Office: Peterson Ross 200 E Randolph St Ste 7200 Chicago IL 60601-7719

NOVOTNY, DEBORAH A., management consultant, director; d. Russell Anthony and Barbara J. Novotny. BA in Econs., Northwestern U., 1986; postgrad., U. Minn., 1988-91; masters cert. in project mgmt., George Washington U., 2000. Series 7 lic., mutual fund mktg. analyst, cert. project mgr., QMS coord., auditor, PowerBuilder developer-profl., instr., PowerSoft divsn. Sybase, Inc. Mgr. lab., cons. Northwestern U., Evanston, Ill., 1983-86; asst. mgr. microcomputer services Sara Lee Corp., Chgo., 1986; sr. cons. Lante Corp., Chgo., 1987-88; fin. exec., Series 7 lic. mutual fund mktg. analyst, nat. non-bank banking sys. coord., credit dept. mgr. IDS Fin. Svcs., Inc., Mpls., 1988-91; fin. sys. coord. Met. Water Reclamation Dist. Greater Chgo., Chgo., 1991-92; mgmt. sys. cons., pres., CEO Deborah A. Novotny, Inc., Chgo., 1992—; various consulting, mgmt. positions Sybase, Inc., 1993—2003, area project mgmt. office mgr., 1999—2003; dir. process and portfolio mgmt. global program office LexisNexis, Dayton, Ohio, 2003—05; project dir. Exelon, Chgo., 2005—06; dir. program mgmt. Gen. Growth Properties, Chgo., 2006—. Invited spkr., instr. Ann. Powersoft User Conf., Comdex Trade Show, homeless and underprivileged families Christmas gift program, 1994—. Vol. Cath. Charities, 1990—, Greater Chgo. Food Repository, 1997—; vice chmn., chair fin. com. Mt. Assisi Acad. Bd. Dirs., 1997—99; active teen retreat team St. Michael's Ch., Orland Park, Ill., 1978—84. Ill. State scholar. Mem.: Macintosh Users Group, Chi Omega Rho (charter, chmn. housing assn. 1986—91). Avocations: piloting aircraft, photography, travel, reading, writing.

NOVOTNY, DONALD WAYNE, electrical engineer, educator; b. Chgo., Dec. 15, 1934; s. Adolph and Margaret Novotny; m. Louise J. Eenigenburg, June 26, 1954; children: Donna Jo Kopp, Cynthia Mason. BEE, Ill. Inst. Tech., 1956, MS, 1957; PhD, U. Wis., 1961. Registered prof. engr., Wis. Instr. Ill. Inst. Tech., 1957-58; mem. faculty U. Wis., Madison, 1958—, prof. elec. engring., 1969-96, Grainger prof. power electronics, 1990—96, prof. emeritus, 1996—, chmn. dept. elec. and computer engring., 1976-80. Vis. prof. Mont. State U., 1966, Eindhoven (The Netherlands) Tech. U., 1974, Tech. U. Louvain, Belgium, 1986; Fulbright lectr. Tech. U. Ghent, Belgium, 1981; diw. Wis. Elec. Machines and Power Electronics Consortium, 1981—96; assoc. dir. Univ.-Industry Rsch. Program, 1982—93; chmn. elec. engring. program Nat. Technol. U., 1989—2003; cons. to industry. Author: Introductory Electromechanics, 1965, Vector Control and Dynamics of AC Drives, 1996; contbr. scientific papers to profl. jours.; assoc. editor: Electric Machines and Power Systems, 1976—99. Named Disting. Lectr., IEEE-IAS, 1995; recipient Outstanding Paper award, Engring. Inst. Can., 1966, Outstanding Achievement award, IEEE-IAS, 1998; fellow, GE, 1956, Ford Found., 1960; grantee, numours industries and govt. agys. Fellow: IEEE (prize paper award 1983, 1984, 1986, 1987, 1990, 1991, 1993, 1994, 3d Millennium medal 2000); mem.: Am. Soc. Engring. Edn., Rotary, Sigma Xi, Eta Kappa Nu, Tau Beta Pi. Congregationalist. Home: 1421 E Skyline Dr Madison WI 53705-1132 Office: U Wis Dept Elec and Computer Engring 1415 Engineering Dr Madison WI 53706-1607 Office Phone: 608-262-6926. Business E-Mail: novotny@engr.wisc.edu.

NOVOTNY, F. DOUGLAS, lawyer; b. Mineola, NY, Mar. 10, 1952; s. Frank Joseph and Eleanor Evans (Rose) N.; m. Norma R. Federici, Sept. 7, 1991; children: Nicholas, Christina, Alexander. BA cum laude, SUNY, Albany, 1974; postgrad., NYU, Hofstra U., Hempstead, NY, C.W. Post U.; JD cum laude, Albany Law Sch., 1979. Bar: NY 1980, US Dist. Ct. (no. dist.) NY 1980. Confidential law asst. Appellate Divsn. 3d Dept., Albany, 1979-80; ptnr. DeGraff, Foy, Conway, Holt-Harris & Mealey, Albany, 1980-91; pvt. practice Saratoga, NY, 1991-93; mng. atty. Law Offices of F. Douglas Novotny, 1993—, Am. Internat. Group, Inc., 1993—2006; ptnr. Wilson, Elser, Moskowitz, Edelman & Dicker, 2006—. Mem. Albany County Arbitration Panel, 1984—. Editor Albany Law Rev., 1978-79; contbr. articles to profl. jours. Mem. ATLA, Justinian Soc., Assn. Trial Lawyers Am., Capital Dist. Trial Lawyers Assn. Presbyterian. Home: 27 Mallard Lndg S Waterford NY 12188-1037 Office Phone: 518-449-8893. Business E-Mail: douglas.novotny@wilsonelser.com.

NOVOTNY, GLENN W., consumer products company executive; Various managerial positions in mfg., acctg., strategic planning, sales, gen. mgmt. and bus. turnarounds Weyerhaeuser Co., pres. Weyerhaeuser Garden Supply Co. subs., 1988—90; pres., COO Ctrl. Garden & Pet Co., 1990—2003, pres., CEO, 2003—. Office: Ctrl Garden & Pet Co 1340 Treat Blvd Ste 600 Walnut Creek CA 94597 Office Phone: 925-948-4000. *

NOVOTNY, ROGER, state agency administrator; s. A. M. and Ida Novotny; m. Nila DeWald; 2 children. Dir. motor fuel tax divsn. SD Dept. Revenue, 1972—76, dir. sales tax divsn., 1976—93, dir. bus. tax divsn., 1993—95; govt. rels. mgr. Aman Collection Svc., Aberdeen, SD, 1995, v.p. contract collections, 1998—2001, sr. v.p., COO; dir. divsn. banking SD Dept. Revenue & Regulation, 2004—. Office: SD Divsn Banking 217 1/2 W Missouri Ave Pierre SD 57501 Office Phone: 605-773-3421. Office Fax: 605-773-5367. E-mail: roger.novotny@state.sd.us.

NOVROCKI, MICHAEL W., secondary school educator; BA, U. Scranton, Scranton, Pa., 1993; MA, Millersville U., Pa., 1996. Cert. tchr. secondary edn. social studies Pa., 2001. Tchr. social studies Abington Heights HS, Clarks Summit, Pa., 2001—03, Lake-Lehman HS, Pa., 2003—. Coord. nat. history day Abington Heights HS, 2001—03, Lake-Lehman HS, 2003—. Mem.: Pa. Coun. Social Studies. Avocation: travel. Office: Lake-Lehman School District Old Route 115 Lehman PA 18627-0038

NOWACKI, JAMES NELSON, lawyer; b. Columbus, Ohio, Sept. 12, 1947; s. Louis James and Betty Jane (Nelson) N.; m. Catherine Ann Holden, Aug. 1, 1970; children: Carrie, Anastasia, Emma. AB, Princeton U., 1969; JD, Yale U., 1973. Bar: Ill. 1973, N.Y. 1982, U.S. dist. Ct. (no. dist.) Ill. 1973, U.S. Ct. Appeals (7th cir.) 1978, U.S. Ct. Appeals (6th cir.) 1987, U.S. Supreme Ct. 1992. Assoc. Isham, Lincoln & Beale, Chgo., 1976-79; ptnr. Kirkland & Ellis, Chgo., 1980—. Mem. Winnetka Sch. Bd. Dist. 36, Ill. 1983-91, bd. pres., 1989-91; mem. New Trier Sch. Bd., 1997-99, pres., 1997-98. Harlan Fiske Stone prize Yale U., 1972. Mem. ABA (forum com. on constrn. industry, litigation sect.), Mid-Am. Club, Skokie Country Club. Home: 708 Prospect Ave Winnetka IL 60093-2320 Office: Kirkland & Ellis LLP 200 E Randolph St Fl 60 Chicago IL 60601-6636 Business E-Mail: jnowacki@kirkland.com.

NOWAK, JOHN E., law educator; b. Chgo., Jan. 2, 1947; s. George Edward and Evelyn (Bucci) N.; m. Judith Johnson, June 1, 1968; children: John Edwin, Jeffrey Edward. AB, Marquette U., 1968; JD, U. Ill., 1971. Law clk. Supreme Ct. of Ill., Chgo., 1971-72; asst. prof. U. Ill., Urbana, 1972-75, assoc. prof., 1975-87, law prof., 1978—, grad. coll. faculty, 1982—, Baum prof. Law, 1993—. Chmn. Constl. Law Sch. Sect.; faculty rep. Big Ten Intercollegiate Conf., Schaumburg, 1981—91; vis. prof. law U. Mich., Ann Arbor, 1985; Lee disting. vis. prof. Coll. William and Mary, 1993; Williams vis. prof. law U. Richmond, 2003. Co-author: Treatise on Constitutional Law, 1986, vols. 1 and 2, 4th edit., 2007, supplement, 2007, Story's Commentaries on the Constitution, 1987, Constitutional Law, 7th edit. 2004, Principles of Constitutional Law, 2004, 3d edit., 2007. Scholar-in-Residence, U. of Ariz., Tucson, 1985, 87. Mem. Assn. of Am. Law Schs. (chmn. constl. law sect., accreditation com. 1980-88), Nat. Collegiate Athletic Assn. (mem. infractions com. 1987—), Am. Law Inst., Am. Bar Assn., Ill. Bar Assn., Order of the Coif (Triennial Book award com.). Roman Catholic. Home: 1701 Mayfair Rd Champaign IL 61821-5522 Office: U Ill Coll Law 504 E Pennsylvania Ave Champaign IL 61820-6909 Office Phone: 217-333-6757. Business E-Mail: jnowak@law.uiuc.edu.

NOWAK (JAROSZ), LINDA THERESE, special education educator, consultant; b. Buffalo, Nov. 25, 1954; d. Joseph John Sr. and Theresa E. Jarosz; m. Raymond John Nowak, Sr., June 18, 1982; 1 child, Raymond John Jr. BS in Edn., Buffalo State Coll., 1988, MEd, 1994, Niagara U., NYC, 1998. Cert. sch. dist. adminstr. N.Y., sch. adminstrn. and supervision N.Y., spl. edn. tchr. N.Y., elem. edn. tchr. N.Y. Spl. edn. cons. tchr. West St. Elem. Sch. Niagara Wheatfield Cen. Sch. Dist., Sanborn, NY, 1989—, prin. summer sch., 1999—2000, head tchr. summer sch., 2001—04. Adj. prof. edn. Niagara U., 2004—. Fundraiser, supporter United Spinal Assn., Milford, NH, 2003—05; vol. Am. Cancer Soc., Amherst, NY, 2001—03; bd. dirs., mem. devel. com. Niagara Frontier Ctr. for Ind. Living, Niagara Falls, 2002—05., Orleans/Niagara Tchr. Ctr. grantee, 2002—04. Mem.: ASCD (assoc.), Am. Fedn. Tchrs., NY State United Tchrs., Coun. for Exceptional Children, Delta Kappa Gamma (assoc.). Democrat. Roman Catholic. Avocation: collecting antiques. Home: 5761 Dunnigan Rd Lockport NY 14094 Office: West St Elem Sch 5700 West St Sanborn NY 14132 Home Phone: 716-625-6321; Office Phone: 716-215-3200. Personal E-mail: ltnowak82@adelphia.net. Business E-Mail: lnowak@nwcsd.org.

NOWAK, ROBERT MICHAEL, chemist; b. South Milwaukee, Wis., Oct. 28, 1930; s. Casimer M. and Anita Marie (Anderson) N.; m. Susan Lora Boyd, Oct. 12, 1957; children: Karen Sue Nowak Sapsford, Janet Lynn Nowak McMorris. Student, U. Wis., Racine, 1949-51; BS, U. Wis., Madison, 1953; PhD, U. Ill., 1956. Rsch. chemist Phys. Rsch. Lab., Dow Chem. Co., Midland, Mich., 1956-64, from group leader to asst. lab dir., 1964-72; dir. rsch. and devel. plastics dept. Dow Chem. Co., Midland, 1972-73, dir. rsch. and devel. Olefin and Styrene plastics depts., 1973-78, dir. rsch. and devel. plastics dept., 1978-83, dir. cen. rsch., 1983-90, chief scientist, dir. cen. rsch. and devel., 1990-94; pres., CEO Mich. Molecular Inst., Midland, 1994—. Contbr. articles to profl. jours.; patentee organic reaction mechanisms and reinforced plastics. Mem. NAE, AIChE, Am. Chem. Soc. Office: MI Molecular Inst 1910 W Saint Andrews Rd Midland MI 48640-2657 E-mail: nowak@mmi.org.

NOWAKOWSKI, NICHOLAS J., lawyer; b. Detroit, Aug. 4, 1979; s. Bernard and Christine M. Nowakowski. BA in Polit. Sci., U. Detroit Mercy, 2000, JD, 2005. Bar: Mich. 2006. Legal dept. Plastipak Packaging, Inc., Plymouth, Mich., 2000—. Sr. rep. alumni bd. U. Detroit Mercy Law Sch., 2005—06. Mem. St. Hyacinth's Mens' Choir, Detroit, 1995—, Wavel Folk Ensemble, Detroit, 1997—. Recipient Eagle Scout, Boy Scouts of Am., 1993. Mem.: Acad. Polit. Sci., Am. Bar Assn. Office: Plastipak Packaging Inc 41605 Ann Arbor Rd Plymouth MI 48170 Business E-Mail: nicholas.nowakowski@gmail.com.

NOWE, RONALD JOHN, state legislator, small business owner; b. Gloucester, Mass., Feb. 7, 1946; children: Ronald Jr., Miguel. Student, Hesser Coll., 1976. Owner, mgr. Now Ins. Agy., Epping, N.H., agy. mgr.; propr., mgr. Kamper Kampania Kampground, 3d Street Grocery; mgr., propr. Oak Grove Golfing; mem. N.H. Ho. of Reps. Mem., chmn. wildlife and marine resources com., com. whip, legis. adminstrn. chmn., chmn. sheriff com., mem. long range planning com. Mem. Pub. Water Access Adv. Bd.; vice chair Epping Planning Bd. Mem. DAV (jr. vice. comdr. 1983-94), VFW, Am. Legion, Masons. Republican. Home: PO Box 327 Epping NH 03042 Office: Legis Office Bldg Rm 308 Concord NH 03301

NOWELL, LINDA GAIL, not-for-profit executive; b. Ft. Worth, Apr. 24, 1949; d. Jesse Wayne and Bennie Dale (Flint) Stallings. BA in English, U. North Tex., 1970. Cert. secondary edn. tchr. Tex. Ind. sales rep. Jostens Printing & Pub. Div., Owatona, Minn., 1980—84; v.p. Nowell Equipment Co., Cranfils Gap, Tex., 1984—89; edn. coord. Tex. Farm Bur., Waco, Tex., 1987—90; account exec. MAC Printing, Las Vegas, Nev., 1991—94; mgr. frontier health outreach program Nev. Rural Health Ctrs., Inc., 1994—97; state coord. Nev. 5-A-Day Coalition, 1995—96; exec. dir. No To Abuse, Pahrump, Nev., 1999—2005; v.p. cmty. devel. United Way So. Nev., Las Vegas, 2005—. Active Landmark Edn., Inc.; bd. dirs. United Way of Pioneer Terr., 1999—2004. Mem.: NAFE. Office Phone: 702-892-2319. Business E-Mail: lindan@uwsn.org.

NOWELL, PETER CAREY, pathologist, educator; b. Phila., Feb. 8, 1928; s. Foster and Margaret (Matlack) Nowell; m. Helen Worst, Sept. 9, 1950; children: Sharon, Timothy, Karen, Kristin, Michael. BA, Wesleyan U., Middletown, Conn., 1948; MD, U. Pa., 1952. Intern Phila. Gen. Hosp., 1952—53; resident pathology Presbyn. Hosp., Phila., 1953—54; med.-teaching, research specializing in cancer Phila., 1956—; from instr. to prof. pathology Sch. Medicine U. Pa., 1956—, chmn. dept. pathology, 1967—73; dir. (Cancer Center), 1973—75. Lt. M.C. USNR, 1954—56. Recipient Rsch. Career award, USPHS, 1964—67, Parke-Davis award, 1965, Lindback Disting. Tchg. award, 1967, Passano award, 1984, Rous-Whipple award, Am. Assn. Pathology, 1986, de Villers award, Leukemia Soc. Am., 1987, Mott prize, GM Cancer Rsch. Found., 1989, 3M award, FASEB, 1993, Lasker Found. award, 1998. Home: 345 Mount Alverno Rd Media PA 19063-5313 Office: U Pa Sch Medicine Dept Pathology & Lab Medicine Philadelphia PA 19104-6082 Office Phone: 215-898-8066. Business E-Mail: nowell@mail.med.upenn.edu.

NOWICK, ARTHUR STANLEY, metallurgy and materials science educator; b. NYC, Aug. 29, 1923; s. Hyman and Clara (Sperling) N.; m. Joan Franzblau, Oct. 30, 1949; children: Jonathan, Steven, Alan, James. AB, Bklyn. Coll., 1943; A.M., Columbia U., 1948, PhD, 1950. Physicist NACA, Cleve., 1944-46; instr. U. Chgo., 1949-51; asst. prof., then assoc. prof. metallurgy Yale U., 1951-57; mgr. metallurgy research IBM Corp Research Center, Yorktown Heights, NY, 1957-66; prof. metallurgy Columbia U., 1966-90, Henry Marion Howe prof. metallurgy and materials sci., 1990-95, prof. emeritus, 1996—. Adj. prof. chem. engring. and materials sci. dept. U. Calif., Irvine, 2001; Frank Golick lectr. U. Mo., 1970; vis. prof. Technion, Haifa, Israel, 1973; co-chmn. Internat. Conf. Internal Friction, 1961, 69; cons. in field. Author: Crystal Properties Via Group Theory, 1995; co-author: Anelastic Relaxation in Crystalline Solids, 1972; co-editor: Diffusion in Solids, 1975, Diffusion in Crystalline Solids, 1984; contbr. articles to profl. jours. Named David Turnbull lecturer Materials Rsch. Soc., 1994; gold medalist Internat. Conf. Internal Friction, 1989. Fellow AIME, Am. Phys. Soc.; mem. Materials Rsch. Soc. (Turnbull lectr. 1994), Sigma Xi (pres. Kappa chpt. 1983-85). Home: 24 Hillsdale Dr Newport Beach CA 92660-4234 Office: U Calif Irvine 916 Engineering Tower Irvine CA 92697-2575 Business E-Mail: anowick@uci.edu.

NOWICKI, STEPHEN, dean, biology professor; b. Johnson City, NY, June 18, 1955; s. Theodore William and Elizabeth (Wilcox) N.; m. Susan Smith Peters, Nov. 1, 1986; 1 child, Schuyler. BS in Biology and Music summa cum laude, Tufts U., 1976, MS in Behavioral Biology, 1978; PhD in Neurobiology and Behavior, Cornell U., 1984. USPHS postdoctoral rsch. fellow Rockefeller U., NYC, 1984-86, asst. prof., 1986-89; asst. prof. zoology and neurobiology Duke U., Durham, NC, 1989—94, assoc. prof., 1994—2002, Anne T. and Robert M. Bass prof., 1999—2004, dean natural scis., Anne T. and Robert M. Bass fellow, prof., 2004—, dean undergraduate edn., 2007—. Asst. adj. prof. Rockefeller U., 1989-90, NYU; instr. Rocky Mountain Biol. Lab., Gothic, Colo., 1983, 84; guest lectr. Isle of Shoals Marine Lab., Portsmouth, N.H., 1985-88, instr., 1990; rsch. lectr. Princeton U., Columbia U., 1986, U. Ariz., Am. Mus. Natural History, Inst. Animal Behavior, Rutgers U., U. Lausanne, U. Pa., U. Wis., Inst. Animal Behavior, Newark, 1988, U. NC, Greensboro, Wake Forest U., 1989, U. Toronto, Tufts U., Queen's U., Kingston, Ont., Can., 1990, Ekologiska Inst., Lund U., Sweden, 1999. Contbr. articles to Condor, Ethology, Animal Behavior, Hormones and Behavior, Bioacoustics, Music Perception, Nature, Jour. Neurosci., Sci., Psyche, Jour. Chem. Ecology, also others. Recipient Irma T. Hirschl Career Scientist award Hirschl Found., 1989; Andrew D. White fellow, 1977-81, Henry Sage fellow, 1982-83, USPHS fellow, 1983-84, fellow Cary Charitable Trust, 1987-89, Alfred P. Sloan fellow, 1990; Harris Fund grantee World Wildlife Fund, 1983, Chapman Fund grantee Am. Mus. Natural History, 1982, Bache Fund grantee NAS, 1983, 90, travel grantee NSF, Tokyo, 1986, grantee Whitehall Found., 1986, rsch. grantee NIH, 1987; fellow John Simon Guggenheim Meml. Found., 1999. Mem. AAAS, Acoustical Soc. Am., Am. Ornithologists Union, Animal Behavior Soc., Cooper Ornithol. Soc., Internat. Soc. for Neuroethology, Soc. for Neurosci., Phi Beta Kappa, Sigma Xi, Phi Kappa Phi. Achievements include research on neuroethology of animal communication, comparative physiology of vocal production, evolution of behavior mechanisms. Office: Dept Biology Duke U Box 90338 Durham NC 27708-0338 Office Phone: 919-668-2728, 919-684-6950. E-mail: snowicki@duke.edu. *

NOWIK, JOHN DAVID, music educator, musician; b. Allentown, Pa., Aug. 26, 1960; s. Stanley John and Helen Mary Nowik; m. Martha Elizabeth Huddleston, Jan. 9, 1982; children: Elizabeth J., Anna M., Krystyna H., Sofia M., Katerina T., Lucia F., Johanna C., Alexander S., Monica R., Clare Magdalena. MusB, Westminster Choir Coll., 1982; MusM, Emory U., 1996. Organist, choir dir. St. Joseph the Worker Ch., Fallsington, Pa., 1980—83; instr., organist St. Joseph's Prep. Sem., Princeton, NJ, 1981—85; cathedral organist, dir. music Cathedral St. Francis of Assisi, Metuchen, NJ, 1983—2001; univ. organist Seton Hall U., South Orange, NJ, 1996—; dir. music, organist Immaculate Conception Sem., South Orange, NJ, 1996—. Dir. concerts, arts Cathedral Concert Series, Metuchen, NJ, 1984—2001; assoc. condr. Brunswick Symphony Orch., New Brunswick, NJ, 1985—2001. Editor (contributor) hymnal. Recipient Excellence in Achievement award, Middlesex County Cultural and Heritage Commn., 1993; scholar, Emory U., 1995—96. Mem.: Conf. Roman Cath. Cathedral Musicians, Am. Guild Organists (dean 1993—95). Roman Catholic. Avocations: composing, music, bicycling, stamp collecting/philately. Office: Seton Hall U 400 South Orange Ave South Orange NJ 07079 Office Phone: 973-761-9069. Business E-Mail: nowikjoh@shu.edu.

NOWITZKI, DIRK WERNER, professional basketball player; b. Würzburg, West Germany, June 19, 1978; s. Joerg and Helen N. Forward Dallas Mavericks, 1998—. Served in German Army, 1997—98. Named NBA MVP, 2007; named to All-NBA Second Team, 2002, NBA Western Conf. All-Star Team, 2002—07, All-NBA First Team, 2006, 2007. Achievements include winning All-Star 3-point Contest, 2006. Avocations: reading, playing saxaphone. Mailing: Dallas Mavericks The Pavilion 2909 Taylor St Dallas TX 75226 Office Phone: 214 747 MAVS. *

NOWLAND, JAMES FERRELL, lawyer; b. Talladega, Ala., Dec. 7, 1942; s. James Franklin and Wilma Delene (Dean) N.; m. Faye Roberts, Aug. 28, 1964; children: Angela Roschelle, James Ferrell II. BS, Jacksonville State U., Ala., 1967; BS in Med. Technology, U. Ark., 1972; grad., U. Ark. Med. Ctr., 1974; JD, Oglethorpe U., 1983. Bar: Ga. 1984, U.S. Dist.

Ct. (no. dist.) Ga. 1984, U.S. Ct. Appeals (11th cir.) 1984, U.S. Supreme Ct. 1988. Chemist U.S. Army C.E., Marietta, Ga., 1972-97; pvt. practice Cobb County, Ga., 1984—. Capt. USAF, 1967-72. Mem. ABA, Ga. Bar Assn., Cobb County Bar Assn. Home: 50 Mt Calvary Rd Marietta GA 30064-1918 Office: PO Box 1847 Marietta GA 30061-1847 Office Phone: 770-425-0601. Personal E-mail: jim1nowland@msn.com.

NOWLIN, CONNIE BLACKWELL, artist; b. Jacksonville, Fla., Oct. 1, 1948; d. Joseph Earl Blackwell and Harryet Hazel Stewart Blackwell; m. Phillip Neil Nowlin, Aug. 22, 1970; children: Stewart Andrew, Erin Blake. BS, East Tenn. State U., 1970; postgrad., Arrowmont Sch. Crafts, 1973—78; EdM, U. N.C., Charlotte, 1979. Art tchr. West Charlotte High, 1970—86, Myers Park H.S., Charlotte, 1986—2006. Mem. tchr. adv. bd. Mint Mus. Craft and Design, Charlotte, 1998—. Contbg. author Arttalk, 4th edit., 2005. Home: 100 Emory Pl Huntersville NC 28078 Personal E-mail: cnowlin421@roadrunner.com.

NOWLIN, JAMES ROBERTSON, federal judge; b. San Antonio, Nov. 21, 1937; s. William Forney and Jeannette (Robertson) N. BA, Trinity U., 1959, MA, 1962; JD, U. Tex., Austin, 1963. Bar: Tex. 1963, Colo. 1993, U.S. Dist. Ct. D.C. 1966, U.S. Ct. Claims 1969, U.S. Supreme Ct. 1969, U.S. Dist. Ct. (we. dist.) Tex. 1971. Assoc. Kelso, Locke, & King, San Antonio, 1963-65; assoc. Kelso, Locke & Lepick, San Antonio, 1966-69; legal counsel U.S. Senate, Washington, 1965-66; propr. Law Offices James R. Nowlin, San Antonio, 1969-81; mem. Tex. Ho. of Reps., Austin, 1967-71, 73-81; judge U.S. Dist. Ct. for Western Dist. Tex., Austin, 1981-99, chief judge, 2000—03, sr. judge, 2003—. Instr. Am. govt. and history San Antonio Coll., 1964-65, 71-73. Capt. U.S. Army, 1959-60, USAR, 1960-68. Fellow State Bar Found (life); mem. San Antonio Bar Assn., Colo. Bar Assn. Republican. Presbyterian. Avocations: pilot, skiing, hiking, jogging. Office: US Courthouse 200 W 8th St Austin TX 78701-2325 Office Phone: 512-916-5675. Business E-Mail: james_r_nowlin@trwd.uscourts.gov.

NOWLIN, WILLIAM B., surgeon; b. Jan. 1, 1955; MD, Okla. U. Health Sci. Ctr., Oklahoma City, 1981. Diplomate Am. Bd. Surgery, Am. Bd. Colon and Rectal Surgery. Resident in gen. surgery Bapt. Health Sys., Birmingham, Ala., 1986; fellow colon and rectal surgery La. State U. Health Sci. Ctr., Shreveport, 1987. Fellow: ACS, Am. Soc. Colon and Rectal Surgeons; mem.: AMA, Ark. Med. Soc., Washington County Med. Soc. Office: 3000 N Market Ave Ste D Fayetteville AR 72703

NOWOCIN, DEBRA TERESE, gifted and talented secondary education educator; b. Chicago Heights, Ill., Aug. 4, 1951; d. Anthony F. and Anita G. (Cioe) N. BS in Edn., Ea. Ill. U., 1973; gifted cert., Nat. Coll. Edn., 1978; MS in Edn., No. Ill. U., 1981. Cert. tchr., gifted tchr., gen. administrv. Tchr., grades 4-6 Sch. Dist. 170, Chicago Heights, 1973-76, tchr. title I summer sch., 1974-76, tchr. summer enrichment program, various yrs., sci. and gifted enrichment tchr., grade 7, 1976—. Tchr. Worlds of Wisdom and Wonder program for gifted and talented children Ctr. for Gifted, Nat.-Louis U., Evanston, Ill., 1990-97; coord. sci. fair Washington Jr. High Sch. (team sponsor); co-sponsor Spartan Explorers Social Studies Club; key leader Bldg. a Presence Sci., 2002-. Appeared in video Team Up With TV: Using Video in the Classroom, 1991. Active various dist. curriculum coms. Recipient Presdl. award for excellence in sci. teaching nominee, 1984, 96. Mem. NSTA, Ill. Coun. for Gifted, Ill. Sci. Tchrs. Assn., Ill. Jr. Acad. Sci. (sec., treas. region 9, asst. to state safety chmn.), South Suburban Sci. Coun., Kappa Delta Pi. Home: 121 E 24th St Chicago Heights IL 60411-4248 Office: Washington Jr High Sch 25 W 16th Pl Chicago Heights IL 60411-3475 Personal E-mail: dnowocin@sbcglobal.net.

NOYALAS, JONATHAN ALEX, history professor, consultant; b. Pottsville, Pa., Mar. 7, 1979; s. Robert John Richard and Arlene Roberta Noyalas; m. Brandy Nicole Helmick, June 19, 2004. BS in History, Shenandoah U., Winchester, Va., 2001; MA in US History, Va. Tech., Blacksburg, 2003. Guide Stonewall Jackson's Hdqrs., Winchester, 1999—2001; instr. asst. Va. Tech., Blacksburg, 2002—03; history prof. Lord Fairfax C.C., Middletown, Va., 2003—, dir. Inst. Culture and History, 2005—. Mem. adv. bd. Civil War Inst. Shenandoah U., Winchester, 1999—. Author: Plagued by War: Winchester, Virginia During Civil War, 2003, My Will Is Absolute Law: A Biography of Gen. R.H. Milroy, 2006; editor: If This Valley is Lost, Virginia is Lost, 2006; contbr. articles to profl. jours. Recipient Young Career Alumni award, Shenandoah U., 2004. Mem.: So. Hist. Assn., Kernstown Battlefield Assn. (bd. dirs. 2004—, mem. adv. bd.), Shenandoah Valley Battlefield's Found. (interpretation and edn. com. 2004—, Vol. of Yr. award 2006), Phi Alpha Theta. Republican. Byzantine Catholic. Avocation: black powder shooting.

NOYES, RICHARD HALL, bookseller; b. Evanston, Ill., Feb. 12, 1930; s. George Frederick and Dorothy (Hall) N.; m. Judith Claire Mitchell, Oct. 10, 1953; children— Catherine, Stephanie, Matthew. BA, Wesleyan U., Middletown, Conn., 1952. Tng. program, elementary-high sch. salesman Rand McNally & Co., Colo., Utah, Idaho, Wyo., 1955-59; founder, owner, mgr. The Chinook Bookshop, Colorado Springs, Colo., 1959—. Contbr. to A Manual on Bookselling, 1974, The Business of Book Publishing, 1984; contbr. articles to newspapers and trade jours. Co-chmn. Colo. Media Coalition, 1974—; bd. dirs. Colorado Springs Fine Arts Ctr., 1977-81, Citizens Goals for Colorado Springs, 1976-88; trustee Fountain Valley Sch., 1979-81; vice chmn. Colorado Springs Charter Rev. Commn., 1991-92; mem. adv. com. U. Colo., Colorado Springs, 1997—, Downtown Partnership, 1998—. Served with AUS, 1952-54. Recipient Intellectual Freedom award Mountain Plains Librs. Assn., 1977, Disting. Svc. award U. Colo., 1980, Recognition award Pikes Peak Arts Coun., 1989, Charles S. Haslam award, 1990), Entrepreneur of Yr. award U. Colo., 1992, Gordon Saull award for outstanding bookseller Mountains and Plains Booksellers Assn., 1996. Mem. Am. Booksellers Assn. (pres., dir.) Home: 1601 Constellation Dr Colorado Springs CO 80906-1609

NOYES, ROBERT EDWIN, publisher, writer; b. NYC, June 22, 1925; s. Clarence A. and Edith (LaDomus) N.; m. Janet Brown, Mar. 24, 1952 (div. June 1963); children— Keith, Steven, Mark, Geoffrey; m. Mariel Jones, July 24, 1964; children— Rebecca, Robert. BSChemE, Northwestern U., 1945. Chem. engr. Am. Cyanamid Co., Pearl River, NY, 1947; sales exec. Titanium Pigment Corp., NYC, 1948-55; market research mgr. U.S. Indsl. Chem. Co., NYC, 1956-58; sales mgr. atomic energy Curtiss Wright Export, NYC, 1958-60; founder, pres., chmn. bd. Noyes Data Corp., Westwood, NJ, 1960-99; pub. Noyes Press, Noyes Publs., Westwood, 1961-99, Noyes Strategic Pubs., Saddle River, NJ, 1999—. Served to lt. (j.g.) USNR, 1945-47. Mem.: AIAA, Am. Inst. Chem. Engrs., Am. Chem. Soc., N.Y. Yacht Club. Episcopalian. Home: 224 W Saddle River Rd Saddle River NJ 07458-2620

NOZKOWSKI, THOMAS, painter; b. Teaneck, NJ, 1944; BFA, Cooper Union, NYC, 1967. Assoc. prof. Mason Gross Sch. of the Arts, Rutgers U., NJ, 2000—. One-man shows include Max Protetch Gallery, NYC, 1990, 1991, 1993, 1995, 1997, 2000, 2001, 2003, exhibited in group shows at From Earth To Archetype, Ledisflam Gallery, NY, 1990, 10 Abstract Painters, Baumgartner Galleries, Washington, 1991, Shades of Difference, Sandra Gering Gallery, NYC, 1992, Return of the Cadavre Exquis, The Drawing Center, NYC, 1993, A Hundred Hearts, The Contemporary, NYC, 1994, Re-Picturing Abstraction, 1708 Gallery, Richmond, Va., 1995, New Narrative Abstraction, Bklyn. Coll., 1996, Purely Painting, Elizabeth Harris Gallery, NYC, 1997, Pertaining to Painting, Contemporary Arts Mus., Houston, 2002, 181st Ann.: An Invitational Exhbn. Contemporary Art, Nat. Acad. Mus., NYC, 2006, exhibitions include Michael Berger Gallery, Pitts., 2003, pub. collections, Whitney Mus., NYC, San Francisco Mus. Modern Art, Orlando Mus. Art, Fla., Mus. Modern Art, NYC, Met. Mus. Art, Hirshhorn Mus. and Sculpture Garden, Washington, High Mus. Art, Atlanta, Corcoran Gallery of Art, Washington, Bklyn. Mus. Art. Recipient Am. Acad. Arts and Letters Purchase prize, 1998, 1999, Am. Acad. Arts and Letters Award in Painting, 1999; grantee Nat. Endowment for the Arts Individual Artist Grant, 1984, NY State Creative Artists Pub. Svc. grant, 1985, NY State Found. for the Arts fellowship, 1989, John Simon Guggenheim Meml. Found. fellowship, 1993. Mailing: c/o Max Protetch Gallery 511 W 22nd St New York NY 10011

NRIAGU, JEROME OKON, environmental geochemist; b. Ora-eri Town, Anambra, Nigeria, Oct. 24, 1942; arrived in U.S., 1993; s. Martin and Helena (Anaekwe) N.; children: Chinedu Delbert, Uzoma Vivian, Osita Jide. BSc with honors, U. Ibadan, Nigeria, 1965, DSc, 1987; MS, U. Wis., 1967; PhD, U. Toronto, Ont., 1970. Rsch. scientist Environment Can., Burlington, Ont., 1970-93; prof. environ. chem. sch. of pub. health U. Mich., Ann Arbor, 1993—; dir. environ. health scis. program, 1996-99; rsch. prof. Ctr. for Human Growth and Devel., U. Mich., 1997—. Adj. prof. U. Waterloo, Ont., 1985—96; vis. scientist NOAA, Ann Arbor, 1992; bd. dirs. Ecology Ctr. Mich., Alliance to End Childhood Lead Poisoning, Washington, 1998—. Author: Lead and Lead Poisoning in Antiquity, 1983; editor: (book series) Advances in Environmental Science and Technology, 1982—, Trace Metals in the Environment, 1996—, 29 books on various environ. topics, 1979—, Sci. of the Total Environment, 1983—; mem. editl. bds.: 9 jours.; contbr. articles to profl. jours. Recipient Rigler medal, Can. Soc. Limnologists, 1988; Fulbright sr. fellow, 2002. Fellow: Royal Soc. Can. (Romanowski medal 1999); mem.: AAAS, Am. Pub. Health Assn. Roman Catholic. Avocations: photography, reading (African authors), travel. Office: Univ Michigan Environ/Indsl Health 109 Observatory St Ann Arbor MI 48109-2029

NSOFOR, LESLIE MONAGOLUM, food scientist, researcher; b. Oguta, Nigeria, July 10, 1955; arrived in U.S.A., 1997; s. Francis Chukwudifu Nsofor and Florence Chinelo Anamaleze; m. Obianuju Nwamaka Ikpeze, Apr. 29, 1983; children: Leslie, Valentine, Stephanie. BS in microbiology, U. Nigeria, 1978; MS in food sci., Utah State U., 1983, PhD in food sci., 1984. Lectr. Kaduna (Nigeria) Poly., 1978—80; grad. rsch. asst. Utah State U., 1981—84, post doctoral rsch. fellow, 1984—85; assoc. prof., assoc. dean Fed. U. Tech., Owerri, Nigeria, 1986—97; adj. assoc. prof. Mich. State U., 1999—; rsch. dir., co-owner, dep. CEO Soy Ultima LLC, East Lansing, Mich., 2000—. Acting head of dept. Abia State U., Uturu, Nigeria, 1990—92; mem. senate Fed. U. Tech., Owerri, Nigeria, 1994—96; founder Lensof Konsult LLC, Lansing, 2006—. Co-author 27 jour. articles, Instrument for Measuring Milk Coagulation in Cheese Vat. Ch. harvest com. St. Joseph Cath. Chaplaincy, Imo State Univ., Owerri, Nigeria, 1996—97. Rsch. grant, Internat. Found. Sci., 1989. Roman Catholic. Achievements include patents for soy beverage mfg. method. Avocations: jogging, jazz, travel. Home: 4436 Wagon Wheel Ln Lansing MI 48917 Home Phone: 517-202-0995; Office Phone: 517-202-0995. Personal E-mail: lensofor@aol.com.

NTAIMO, LEWIS, engineering educator, researcher; b. Kitwe, Zambia, May 21, 1973; s. Laso and Alice Bwalya Ntaimo; m. Chloe Agnes Balfour; children: Joseph Mulenga, Claire Mumba, Ceanah Bwalya. PhD in Systems and Indsl. Engring., U. Ariz., Tucson, 2004. Rsch. asst. dept. mining and geol. engring. U. Ariz., Tucson, 1999—2000, rsch. asst. dept. sys. and indsl. engring., 2001—04; asst. prof. dept. indsl. and sys. engring. Tex. A&M U., College Station, 2004—. Grantee, NSF, 2005—. Mem.: Inst. Indsl. Engrs. (assoc.; faculty advisor student chpt. 2005—06). Office: Tex A&M U 3131 Tamu College Station TX 77843 Home Phone: 979-204-1883; Office Phone: 979-862-4066. Office Fax: 979-847-9005. Business E-Mail: ntaimo@tamu.edu.

NTZIACHRISTOS, VASILIS, radiology, bioengineering educator; Diploma in Elec. Engring., Aristotle U., 1993; postgrad., U. Copenhagen Med. Sch., 1994—95; MS in Bioengring., U. Pa., 1998, PhD in Bioengring., 2000. Asst. prof. Harvard U. Med. Sch.; head lab. for biooptics and molecular imaging Mass. Gen. Hosp. Editor (assoc.): IEEE Transactions on Med. Imaging, 2005—. Named one of Top 100 Innovators, MIT Tech. Review, 2004; recipient Solomon R. Pollack award, U. Penn., 2002; Damon Runyon Cancer Rsch. Found. fellowship, 2001. Mem.: Optical Soc. Am. (chair biomed. optical imagineg group 2004—, chair biomed. topical mtgs. 2006—). Office: Harvard Med Mass Gen Hosp Rm 5406 Radiology 149 13th St Charlestown MA 02129 Business E-Mail: vasilis@helix.mgh.harvard.edu.

NUCCI, ANTONIO, information technology executive; BSEE, MSEE, Politecnico di Torino, Italy; PhD Telecom. Networks and Engring., Politecnico di Torino, 2002. Rsch. scientist to prin. mem. tech. staff Sprint; chief tech. officer Narus, Mountain View, Calif. Author: more than 30 papers for internat. conferences and profl. jours. Named one of Top 25 chief tech. officers, InfoWorld mag., 2007. Office: Narus 500 Logue Ave Mountain View CA 94043 Office Phone: 650-230-9300. Office Fax: 650-230-9400. Business E-Mail: anucci@narus.com.

NUCCIARONE, A. PATRICK, lawyer; b. Denville, NJ, Aug. 29, 1947; s. H. Joseph and Alice Marie (McGuirk) N. BA, U. So. Calif., 1969; JD, George Washington U., 1973. Bar: N.J. 1973, N.Y. 1981, Vt. 1984, U.S. Dist. Ct. N.J. 1973, U.S. Dist. Ct. (no. dist.) Ohio 1986, U.S. Ct. Appeals (3d cir.) 1976, U.S. Supreme Ct. 1995. Com. staff asst. U.S. House of Reps., Washington, 1971-72; staff asst. Exec. Office of Pres. of U.S., Washington, 1972-73; asst. U.S. Atty. Office of U.S. Atty., Newark, 1974-83, chief environ. sect., 1978-83; spl. asst. Atty. Gen. Office of Atty. Gen., Montpelier, Vt., 1984; ptnr. Hannoch Weisman, Roseland, NJ, 1984-91, Dechert, Price & Rhoads, Princeton, NJ, 1991-95; fed. monitor U.S. Dist. Ct., NY, 2001—. Co-chmn. N.J. Hazardous Task Force, Trenton, 1978-83; supr. Rutgers U. Environ. Law Clinic, Newark, 1978-83; mem. Environ. Expn. Adv. Bd., Trenton, 1985-90; chmn. ann. seminar on impacts of environ. law bus. trans. Practicing Law Inst., 1986-92, mem. adv. com. on environ. law, 1986—; mem. faculty NYU Summer Inst. on Environ. Law, 1991-94. Contbr. articles to profl. jours. Recipient Outstanding Service award U.S. Dept. Justice, Washington, 1980, Spl. Achievement awards U.S. Dept. Justice, 1978, 79, Presdl. Citation for Excellent Performance Exec. Office of Pres., Washington, 1973. Mem. ABA (vice chmn. sect. on natural resources, energy and environ. law 1987-93), N.J. State Bar Assn. (bd. dirs. environ. law sect. 1985-89). Office: 1540 Hwy 138 Ste 107 Wall NJ 07719-3766 Office Phone: 732-280-4800.

NUCHI, LIOR O., lawyer; b. Tiberius, Israel, Aug. 8, 1960; BA, Columbia Univ., 1982; JD, NYU, 1987. Bar: Calif. Sr. bus. ptnr. Bingham McCutchen, East Palo Alto, Calif.; ptnr., chmn. Cross-Border Transactions group & Israel practice Pillsbury Winthrop Shaw Pittman, Palo Alto, Calif., 2004—. Mem.: Nat. Assn. of Corp. Directors, Silicon Ventures, Calif.-Israel C. of C. Office: Pillsbury Winthrop Shaw Pittman 2475 Hanover St Palo Alto CA 94304-1114 Office Phone: 650-233-4803. Office Fax: 650-233-4545. Business E-Mail: lior.nuchi@pillsburylaw.com.

NUCKOLLS, JOHN HOPKINS, physicist, researcher; b. Chgo., Nov. 17, 1930; s. Asa Hopkins and Helen (Gates) N.; m. Ruth Munsterman, Apr. 21, 1952 (div. 1983); children: Helen Marie, Robert David; m. Amelia Aphrodite Liaskas, July 29, 1983. BS, Wheaton Coll., 1953; MA, Columbia U., 1955; DSc (hon.), Fla. Inst. Tech., 1977. Physicist U. Calif., Lawrence Livermore Nat. Lab., 1955—, assoc. leader thermonuclear design divsn., 1965-80, assoc. leader laser fusion program, 1975-83, divsn. leader, 1980-83, assoc. dir. physics, 1983-88, dir., 1988-94, assoc. dir. at large, 1994-97, dir. emeritus, 1997—. Mem. emeritus U.S. Strategic Command Strategic adv. group; tech. adv. bd. Network Physics, Inc.; cons. def. sci. bd. Dept. Def.; mem. adv. coms. to dir. CIA, 1989-99. Recipient E.O. Lawrence award Pres. and AEC, 1969, Fusion Leadership award, 1983, Edward Teller medal Internat. Workshop Laser Interaction and Related Plasma Phenomena, 1991, Resolution of Appreciation, U. Calif. Regents, 1994, Sec. of Def. Outstanding Pub. Svc. medal, 1996, Disting. Assoc. award U.S. Dept. Energy, 1996, Career Achievement award Fusion Power Assocs., 1996. Fellow: AAAS (J.C. Maxwell prize 1981), Am. Phys. Soc.; mem.: NAE. Office: Lawrence Livermore Nat Lab PO Box 808 Livermore CA 94551-0808 Home Phone: 925-736-8018; Office Phone: 925-422-5435. Personal E-mail: jhnuckcl@comcast.net.

NUCKOLS, FRANK JOSEPH, psychiatrist; b. Akron, Ohio, Apr. 7, 1926; s. William Alexander, Jr. and Jean (Harrison) Nuckols; m. Jane Fleetwood McIntosh, June 16, 1948; children: Claud Alexander, John Andrew. BA, U. Louisville, Ky., 1946; MD, U. Ala., Birmingham, 1951. Diplomate Am. Bd. Psychiatry and Neurology, 1959, cert. med. profl. Nat. Assn. Disability Examiners, 2005. Intern Holy Name Jesus Hosp., Gadsden, Ala., 1951; ward physician Ala. State Hosp., Tuscaloosa, 1951-52; resident U. Louisville, USPHS Hosp., Lexington, Ky., 1953-56; mem. faculty dept. psychiatry U. Ala. Med. Ctr., Birmingham, 1958-68, dir. tng. psychiat. residents, 1964-68, head div. community psychiatry, 1964-68, head continuing psychiat. edn. for physicians, 1964-68; chief psychiat. staff in-patient svc. U. Hosp., Birmingham, 1966-68; dir. tng. Hill Crest Hosp., Birmingham, 1975-79; pvt. practice Birmingham, 1968-93; cons. Ala. Div. Disability Determinations, Birmingham, 1993—. Staff Med. Ctr. East Hosp., Birmingham, Bapt. Med. Ctr. Montclair, Birmingham; cons. staff St. Vincent's Hosp., Birmingham, Lloyd Noland Hosp., Birmingham, South Highland Hosp., Birmingham; vis. faculty, mem. interuniv. forum cmty. psychiatry Harvard U., Boston, 1963—66; vis. faculty Baylor U. Med. Sch., Houston, 1967—71. Sr. surgeon USPHS, 1956—. Ensign USNR, 1943—45. Fellow: So. Psychiat. Assn., Am. Psychiat. Assn. (life; disting.); mem.: Nat. Assn. Disability Examiners (cert. med. prof. 2005, State Ala. Med. Cons. of Yr. 2005, Commr.'s citation 2005), Mental Health Assn. State Ala. (chmn. profl. adv. com. 1961), Jefferson County Med. Soc., Jefferson County Mental Health Assn. (v.p. 1960), So. Med. Assn., Med. Assn. Ala., Tau Kappa Epsilon, Phi Beta Pi. Home and Office: 300 Royal Towers Dr Apt 720 Vestavia AL 35209 Office Phone: 205-870-7196.

NUCKOLS, OTIS WILLS, lawyer, educator; b. Cumberland, Va., Mar. 25, 1921; s. Marshall Waverly Nuckols and Annie Bowden Camden; m. Dorothy Brown Hale, May 24, 1946; children: Pamela, Patricia, Thomas. BA cum laude, Lincoln Meml. U., 1948; JD, U. Richmond, 1951; CLU, Am. Coll., 1964. Bar: Va. 1951. Legal claims staff Va. Farm Bur. Ins. Cos., Richmond, 1951—64, dir. mktg., 1964—70, exec. v.p., CEO, 1970—86; ptnr. Sinnott, Nuckols & Logan, P.C., Midlothian, Va., 1986—. Adj. prof. Va. Commonwealth U., Richmond, 1986—2002; instr. ins. seminars various ins. cos., Richmond, 1986—2002. Treas. Va. Coun. on Econ. Edn., Richmond, 1970—86; chair ethics bd. Richmond Assn. Life Underwriters, 1990—2002; elder Presbyn. Ch. Sgt. US Army, 1942—46. Recipient Appreciation of Svc. award, Va. Poly. Inst., 1982. Mem.: ABA (life), Am. Legion (life), Willow Oaks Country Club, Commonwealth Club, Alpha Psi Omega, Tau Kappa Alpha. Republican. Avocation: reading. Home: 3119A Stony Point Rd Richmond VA 23235 Office: Sinnott Nuckols & Logan PC 13811 Village Mill Dr Midlothian VA 23114 Office Phone: 804-378-7600 ext. 3303.

NUECHTERLEIN, KEITH H., psychology professor; b. Akron, Ohio, Sept. 23, 1948; s. Harold F. and Frieda D. L. Nuechterlein; m. Nancy Alexander Nuechterlein, Apr. 27, 1981. BA, U. Minn., 1970, PhD, 1978. Cert. psychologist Bd. of Psychology, Calif., 1980. Asst. prof. dept. psychiatry UCLA, 1978—85, assoc. prof. dept. psychiatry and psychology, 1985—89, prof., 1989—. Dir. UCLA Aftercare Rsch. Program, 1980—; co-chair MATRICS Neurocognition Com., LA, 2002—; dir. UCLA Ctr. for Neurocognition and Emotion in Schizophrenia, 2003—. Contbr. articles to profl. jours. Recipient Joseph Zubin Meml. Fund award, N.Y. State Psychiat. Inst., 1995, Disting. Sci. Achievement in Psychology, Calif. Psychol. Assn., 1997; grantee Devel. Processes in Schizophrenic Disorders, NIMH, 1983—, Transmission of Vulnerability Factors in Schizophrenia, 1994—, Ctr. Neurocognition and Emotion in Schizophrenia, 2003—08. Fellow: Am. Psychopathological Assn., Am. Psychol. Soc.; mem.: AAAS, APA, Soc. for Psychophysiological Rsch., Soc. for Rsch. in Psychopathology (pres. 2006—07). Achievements include research in MATRICS Consensus Cognitive Battery for Clinical Trials in Schizophrenia; development of Degraded-Stimulus Continuous Performance Test; 3-7 Continuous Performance Test; research in Cognitive Domains in Schizophrenia; Attentional Deficits in Schizophrenia. Office: UCLA Dept Psychiatry 300 UCLA Medical Plz Rm 2240 Los Angeles CA 90095-6968 Office Phone: 310-825-0036. Office Fax: 310-206-3651. Business E-Mail: keithn@ucla.edu.

NUERNBERG, WILLIAM RICHARD, lawyer; b. Pitts., July 7, 1946; s. William W. and Frances (Hubler) N. BA cum laude, Denison U., 1968; JD cum laude, U. Mich., 1971. Bar: Pa. 1971, U.S. Dist.Ct. (we. dist.) Pa. 1971, Fla. 1995. Mem. Eckert Seamans Cherin & Mellott LLC, 1981-98; ptnr. Duane Morris LLP, Miami, 1999—. Bd. govs. Big Bros. Big Sisters Greater Miami. Pitt fellow U. Pitts. Sch. Bus., 1987-88. Mem. ABA, Pa. Bar Assn., Fla. Bar Assn., Miami City Club. Office: Duane Morris LLP 200 S Biscayne Blvd Ste 3400 Miami FL 33131-2318

NUESSLE, WILLIAM RAYMOND, surgeon; b. Bismarck, ND, Sept. 17, 1951; s. Robert Frederick and Margaret Elizabeth (Bergeson) N.; m. Anna Maria Marlow, June 26, 1982; children: Aaron, Alexa, Matthew. BS, U. N.D., 1973, BS Medicine, 1975; MD, U. Ala., 1977. Diplomate Am. Bd. Surgery and Colon and Rectal Surgery. Resident gen. surgery Ochsner Found., New Orleans, 1977-1982; resident colon and rectal surgery U. La., Shreveport, 1982-83; colon and rectal surgeon Quain and Ramstat Clinic, Bismarck, ND, 1983-90, Clinic for Colon & Rectal Surgery, Huntsville, Ala., 1990—, Huntsville (Ala.) Hosp., 1990—, Crestwood Hosp., Huntsville, 1990—. Fellow ACS, Am. Soc. Colon and Rectal Surgeons; mem. SAGES. Avocations: tennis, fishing, music. Office: Clinic for CRS 115 Manning Dr SW Ste D101 Huntsville AL 35801-4341 Office Phone: 256-533-6070. Personal E-mail: wrn@hiwaay.net.

NUGENT, GARY W., lawyer; b. Shreveport, La. BBA in Fin., So. Methodist U., 1988; JD, Northwestern U., 1991. Bar: Calif. 1991, US Dist. Ct., Calif. (Ninth Circuit Ct. of Appeals). Assoc. Jones Day (formerly Jones, Day, Reavis & Pogue), Los Angeles, Calif., 1996—2002, ptnr., civil litigation, 2002—. Mem.: ABA, Calif. State Bar Assn., Los Angeles County Bar Assn. Office: Jones Day 555 S Flower St # 50 Los Angeles CA 90071-2300 Office Phone: 213-489-3939. Office Fax: 213-243-2539. Business E-Mail: gnugent@jonesday.com.

NUGENT, GRATIAN MACRAE, music educator; BA, Case Western Res. U., Cleve., 1950; MusM, Cleve. State U., 1983. Tchr. music Cleve. Pub. Schs., 1951—59; dir. music Beechwood Presbyn. Ch., 1951—60, Rocky River Meth. Ch., Ohio, 1960—65, Olmsted Cmty. Ch., Olmsted Falls, 1965—2000, St. Barnabas Episc. Ch., Bay Village, 2002—; dir. music emeritus Olmsted Cmty. Ch., 2000—. Mem.: Am. Guild Organists (assoc.; sub-dean Cleve. chpt, dean Cleve. chpt 1994—97).

NUGENT, HELEN JEAN, history professor; b. Indpls., Oct. 14, 1934; d. John Isaac and Ruth Augusta (Mather) McClelland; m. Paul Thomas Nugent, Aug. 19, 1935; children: Paula Jean Nugent Barickman, Thomas J. Nugent II, Ruth E. B. Nugent Simard. BA, Franklin Coll., 1956; MA, U. Ill., 1965, Ind. U., 1971; PhD, Mich. State U., 1983. Lifetime cert. in secondary edn., Ind. Tchr. grades 9-12 Union City H.S., Ind., 1956—57, Seven Mile H.S., Ohio, 1957—58; tchr. history St. Rose Acad., Vincennes, Ind., 1962—64; instr. history Margaret Hall Sch., Versailes, Ky., 1964—66; lectr. history Ind.U./Purdue U., Columbus, 1976—82; vis. lectr. Ind. U./Purdue U., Columbus, 2001; dir. Can. studies Franklin Coll., Ind., 1984—95, chair dept. history, 1996—99, prof. emerita history, dir. emerita Can. studies, 1999—. Contbr. numerous articles, papers to profl. jours., chpts. to books. Mem. Franklin Coll. Alumni Coun., 2002—05; judge consistory ct. Anglican Cath. Ch., 2006—. Recipient Alumni award Franklin Coll., 1997. Mem. Mid West Assn. Can. Studies (v.p. 1990-92, exec. coun. 1992-94), Assn. Can. Studies U.S. (exec. bd. 1993-97), Ind. Hist. Soc., Assn. Can. Studies, Phi Alpha Theta, Theta Alpha Phi, Delta Kappa Gamma, Phi Kappa Phi. Anglican Catholic.

NUGENT, JOHN HILLIARD, communications executive; b. Paterson, NJ, Aug. 20, 1944; s. James Joseph and Jacqueline Ann (Storms) N.; m. Mary Elizabeth Maher, June 3, 1967; 1 child, Jill Frances. BA, Columbia U., NYC, 1970; MSA, Southeastern U., Washington, DC, 1978; DBA, Bus. Sch., Lausanne, Switzerland, 1989. CPA; cert. fraud examiner Nat. Assn. Cert. Fraud Examiners, Austin, info. security mgr. Adminstr. Chase Manhattan Bank, NYC, 1970-71; analyst U.S. Dept. of Army, Washington, 1971-72; chmn. Strategic Planning & Rsch. Corp., Dallas, 1977-95; pres. AT&T Aviation Tech. and Sys., Ltd., Arlington, Va., Hong Kong, Beijing, 1993; exec. CDX, Inc., Dallas, 1995; pres., bd. dirs. SA Telecomm., Inc., Richardson, Tex., 1996-97, also bd. dirs., pres., 1996; mng. dir. Cordoba Capital, Southport, Conn., 1998-99. V.p., fin. acct. AdCon Inc./Internat. Bank, Reston, Va., 1971-79; CFO HDS, Inc., Reston, 1979-82; pres. Group L Corp., Herndon, Va., 1983-85; pres., bd. dirs. AT&T/Datotek, Dallas, 1985-92; assoc. prof. telecomms. Grad. Sch. Mgmt. U. Dallas, 1999—. Author: Corporate Decline: Causes, Symptoms, and Prescriptions for a Turnaround, 1989, Plan to Win: Analytical and Operational Tools-Gaining Competitive Advantage, 2002, 2nd edit., 2003. Cpl. USMC, 1962—66. Mem. AICPAs, Greater Washington Soc. CPAs, Tex. Soc. CPAs, Nat. Assn. Accts., Dallas Com. on Fgn. Rels., Nat. Assn. Cert. Fraud Examiners, Columbia Club of N.Y. Republican. Avocation: reading. Office: Grad Sch Mgmt U Dallas Irving TX 75062-4736 Address: 2469 County Road 855 Mc Kinney TX 75071 Office Phone: 214-682-8025. Personal E-mail: jnugent@texoma.net. Business E-Mail: jnugent@gsm.udallas.edu.

NUGENT, LORI S., lawyer; b. Peoria, Ill., Apr. 24, 1962; d. Walter Leonard and Mary (Frost) Meyer; m. Shane Vincent Nugent, June 14, 1986; children: Justine Nicole, Cole Tyler. BA in Polit. Sci. cum laude, Knox Coll., 1984; JD, Northwestern U., Chgo., 1987. Bar: Ill. 1987, US Dist. Ct. (no. dist.) Ill. 1988, US Ct. Appeals (7th cir.) 1995, US Ct. Appeals (8th cir.) 2003, US Supreme Ct. 2006. Assoc. Peterson & Ross, Chgo., 1987-94; ptnr. Blatt, Hammesfahr & Eaton, Chgo., 1994, Cozen O'Connor, Chgo., 2000—. Chmn. Nat. Punitive Damages Practice Area, 2001—, Nat. Enterprise Risks Practice Group, 2005—. Co-author: Punitive Damages: A Guide to the Insurability of Punitive Damages in the United States and Its Territories, 1988, Punitive Damages: A State-by-State Guide to Law and Practice, 1991, 6th edit., 2006, Japanese edit., West Pub. Co. 1995, @Risk: Internet and E-Commerce Insurance and Reinsurance Legal Issues, 2000, 2d edit., 2002, Reinsurance Claims, 2004; contbr. articles to law jours. Office: Cozen O'Connor Ste 1500 222 S Riverside Plz Chicago IL 60606-6000 Office Phone: 312-382-3103. Business E-Mail: LNugent@cozen.com.

NUGENT, NELLE, theater, film and television producer; b. Jersey City, May 24, 1939; d. John Patrick and Evelyn Adelaide (Stern) N.; m. Donald G. Baker, June 6, 1960 (div. 1962); m. Benjamin Janney, June 22, 1969 (div. Apr., 1980); m. Jolyon Fox Stern, Apr. 7, 1982; 1 child, Alexandra Fox Stern. BS, Skidmore Coll., 1960, DHL (hon.), 1981. Chmn. bd. McCann & Nugent, Prodns. Inc., NYC, 1976-86; pres. Foxboro Prodns., Inc., NYC, 1985-94; pres., CEO Foxboro Entertainment, 1990-94; pres. The Foxboro Co., Inc.; co-prin. Golden Fox Films, Inc. Adj. faculty NYU, NYC, 2003—. Stage mgr. various off-Broadway shows, 1960-64; stage mgr. Broadways plays Any Wednesday, 1963-64, Dylan, 1964, Ben Franklin in Paris, 1964-65; v.p., prodn. supr. Theatre Now, 1966-69; prodn. supr., then gen. mgr., 1969-76, assoc. mng. dir. Nederlander Corp., operating theaters and producing plays in, NYC and on tour, 1970-76; co-founder McCam & Nugent Prodns., Inc., 1976; prodr.: Dracula, 1977 (Tony award), The Gin Game (Tony nomination), The Elephant Man, 1978 (Tony award, Drama Critics award), Morning's at Seven, 1980 (Tony award), Home, 1980 (Tony nomination), Otherwise Engaged, Amadeus, 1981 (Tony award); also produced: Rose and Piaf, 1980, Otherwise Engaged, The Life and Adventures of Nicholas Nickleby, 1981 (Tony award, Drama Critics award), The Dresser (Tony award nominee), 1981, Mass Appeal, 1981; The Lady & The Clarinet, 1982; The Glass Menagerie (revival), 1983; Painting Churches (Obie award), 1983; Total Abandon, 1983; All's Well That End's Well, 1983 (Tony nomination); Pilobolus Dance Company, 1983; Pacific Overtures (revival), 1984; Much Ado about Nothing/Cyrano de Bergerac (repertory) (Tony award nominees), 1984; Leader of the Pack (Tony award nominee), 1985, The Life and Adventures of Nicholas Nickleby (revival) (Tony award nominee), 1986; prodr.: TV spls.; Morning's At Seven, Piaf; Pilobolus; prodr. A Fighting Choice, 1986-88, A Conspiracy of Love, 1987, The Final Verdict, 1990 (Cable Ace award nominee Best Picture); exec. prodr. (TV pilot) Morning Maggie, 1987, Dick Clark Prodns., 1988-90, (feature films) Student Body, 1993, Getting In, 1994, Jane Doe, 1996; (TV films) In the Presence of Mine Enemies, 1995-96 (Houston Festival Silver Star award), A Town Has Turned to Dust, 1997 (World Festival Silver medal 1998), After the Storm (Best Feature Film NY Internat. Independent Film & Video Festival, 2000), Angelciti Festival (Best Feature 2001), Houston Worldfest (Platinum award, Best Film Made for TV 2001), (Broadway prodn.) The Smell of the Kill, 2002, Sly Fox, 2004, A Mother, A Daughter and a Gun, 2005, And Then There Were None, London, West End, 2005. Mem.: Acad. TV Arts and Scis., Prodrs. Guild Am. East (exec. bd., co-founder), League Am. Theaters and Producers. Avocations: sailing, gardening, opera. Office: 222 E 44th St 4th Fl New York NY 10017

NUGENT, PAUL C., lawyer; b. Glen Ridge, NJ, Jan. 21, 1957; BA cum laude, Boston Coll., 1979; JD cum laude, Suffolk U., 1983. Bar: Mass. 1983, Tex. 1985, Supreme Ct. Tex. 1985, Supreme Jud. Ct. Mass., US Dist. Ct. (dist. Mass.), US Dist. Ct. (dist. Ariz.), US Dist. Ct. (so. and ea. dists.) Tex., US Ct. Appeals (5th, 6th and 11th cirs.). Law clk. to Hon. Hugh Gibson US Dist. Ct.; ptnr. Foreman, DeGuerin & Nugent, Houston, 1985—. Editor: Law Review. Recipient Pursuit of Justice award, Tex. Human Rights Found., 2001, Tex. Justice Alliance award, 2003. Fellow: Houston Bar Assn.; mem.: Harris County Criminal Lawyers Assn. (Lawyer of Yr. 1999), Tex. Criminal Def. Lawyers Assn., NACDL, Coll. State Bar Tex. Office: Foreman DeGuerin & Nugent 300 Main St Houston TX 77002 Office Phone: 713-655-9000. Office Fax: 713-655-1812.

NUGENT, ROBERT J., JR., fast food company executive; b. 1942; BBA, U. Cin., 1964. Loan officer Citizens Savs., 1964-67; asst. v.p. Gem City Savs., 1967-69; v.p. Ponderosa System Inc., 1969-78, Ky. Fried Chicken, 1978-79, Foodmaker Inc., San Diego, from 1979, exec. v.p. ops., mktg., 1985-95, CEO, pres., 1995-99, Jack in the Box, Inc., San Diego, 1999—. Office: Jack in the Box Inc 9330 Balboa Ave San Diego CA 92123-1598

NUGENT, S. GEORGIA, academic administrator; m. Thomas J Scherer. B cum laude, Princeton U., 1973; PhD in classics, Cornell U. Instr. Swarthmore Coll.; assoc. prof. Brown U., 1985; asst. prof. Princeton U., 1979, dean, Harold McGraw Jr. Ctr. for tchg. and learning, asst. to pres., 1992—95, assoc. provost, 1995; pres. Kenyon Coll., 2003—. Author books. Recipient Wriston award for excellence in tchg. Office: Office of Pres Ransom Hall Kenyon Coll Gambier OH 43022 Office Phone: 740-427-5111. Office Fax: 740-427-2335. Business E-Mail: nugent@kenyon.edu. *

NUGENT, TED (THEODORE ANTHONY NUGENT), musician, radio personality; b. Detroit, Dec. 13, 1948; s. Warren Henry and Marion (Johnson) Nugent; m. Sandra Janowski, Jan. 30, 1971 (div. Dec. 31, 1979); children: Sasha Emma, Theodore Tobias, Starr; m. Shemane Deziel, Jan. 21, 1989; 1 child, Rocco. Student, Oakland Community Coll., Detroit. Guitarist Amboy Dukes, 1967—75, Damn Yankees, 1989—96; solo artist, 1975—; Mich. County Sheriff dep., 1978—; host, Ted Nugent Morning Show WWBR, Detroit. Pres. Ted Nugent United Sportsmen of Am. Guitarist: (albums with Amboy Dukes) Ted Nugent and the Amboy Dukes, 1968, Migration, 1969, Journey to the Center of the Mind, 1969, Marriage on the Rocks, 1970, Call of the Wild, 1973, Survival of the Fiittest, 1974, Tooth, Fang, and Claw, 1974, Dr. Slingshot, 1975; (solo albums) Ted Nugent, 1975, Free for All, 1976, Cat Scratch Fever, 1977, Double Live Gonzo, 1977, Weekend Warriors, 1978, State of Shock, 1979, Scream Dream, 1980, Great Gonzos/The Best of Ted Nugent, 1981, Intensities in Ten Cities, 1981, Nugent, 1982, Penetrator, 1984, Little Miss Dangerous, 1986, The Ultimate Collection, 1987, If You Can't Lick 'Em...Lick 'Em, 1988, Call of the Wild, 1991, Out of Control, 1993, Spirit of the Wild, 1995, Motor City Madness, 1996, Live at Hammersmith '79, 1997, Super Hits, 1998, Over the Top, 1998, On the Edge, 1998, Loaded for Bear: The Best of Ted Nugent, 1999, Noble Savage, 2001, Full Blontal Nugity, 2001, Take No Prisoners, 2002, The Ultimate Ted Nugent, 2002, Take Two, 2002, Craveman, 2002, The Ultimate Ted Hungent, 2002, Hunt Music, 2003, Love Grenade, 2007; (with Damn Yankees) Damn Yankees, 1990, Don't Tread, 1992; author: Blood Trails: The Truth about Bowhunting, 1991, God, Guns and Rock 'n' Roll, 2000, Blood Trails II: The Truth about Bowhunting, 2004; co-author: (with Shemane Nugent) Kill It and Grill It: A Guide to Preparing and Cooking Wild Game and Fish, 2002; actor: (TV series) Surviving Nugent, 2003-04; editor, publisher Ted Nugent Adventure Outdoors Mag.; creator, prodr. Ted Nugent Spirit of the Wild, PBS; contbr. articles to profl. jours. Sheriff dep. Mich. County, 1978—; founder Ted Nugent Kamp for Kids; appointee Mich. State Parks Found.; bd. dirs. Lyme Alliance. Named Man of Yr., Mich. Recreation and Parks Assn., Mich. Conservationist of Yr., 1999; named to The Native Am. Strongheart Soc.; recipient Nat. Arbor Day Conservation Award, 1999, ATV Image Award, 2004. Mem.: ASCAP, Safari Club Internat., Native Am. Strongheart Soc., Quality Deer Mgmt. Assn. of Mich. (dir.), Ducks Unlimited (life sponsor), Mich. Bowhunters (life), Nat. Trappers Assn. (life), Nat. Rifle Assn. (life; bd. dirs. 1995—). Office: Nugent USA 4008 W Michigan Ave Jackson MI 49202

NUGENT, WALTER TERRY KING, historian; b. Watertown, NY, Jan. 11, 1935; s. Clarence A. and Florence (King) Nugent; m. Suellen Hoy, 1986; children from previous marriage: Katherine, Rachel, David, Douglas, Terry, Mary. AB, St. Benedict's Coll., 1954, DLitt, 1968; MA, Georgetown U., 1956; PhD, U. Chgo., 1961. Instr. history Washburn U., 1957—58; asst. prof. Kans. State U., 1961—63, Ind. U., Bloomington, 1963—64, assoc. prof., 1964—68, prof., 1968—84, assoc. dean Coll. Arts and Scis., 1967—71, dir. overseas study, 1967—76, chmn. history dept., 1974—77; Andrew V. Tackes prof. history U. Notre Dame, 1984—2000, Andrew V. Tackes prof. emeritus, 2000—. Paley lectr., Fulbright vis. prof. Hebrew U., Jerusalem, 1978—79; summer seminar dir. NEH, 1979, 84, 86; vis. prof. U. Hamburg, U. Warsaw, 1982; Mary Ball Washington Fulbright prof. U. Coll., Dublin, 1991—92. Author: (book) The Tolerant Populists, 1963, Creative History, 1967, The Money Question During Reconstruction, 1967, Money and American Society 1865-1880, 1968, Modern America, 1973, From Centennial to World War: American Society 1876-1917, 1977, Structures of American Social History, 1981, Crossings: The Great Transactlantic Migrations 1870-1914, 1992; author: (with Martin Ridge) The American West: The Reader, 1999, Into the West: The Story of Its People, 1999 (Caughey award, 2000); author: Making Our Way: A Family History, 2003. Bd. dirs. U.S.-Israel Ednl. Found., 1985—89. Recipient medal of Merit, Warsaw U., 1992; Newberry Libr. fellow, 1962, Guggenheim fellow, 1964—65, Huntington Libr. fellow, 1979, 1985, Beinecke fellow, Yale U., 1990. Mem.: Soc. Historians the Gilded Age and Progressive Era (pres. 2000—02), Soc. Am. Historians, Western Hist. Assn. (pres. 2005—06, hon. life mem.). Democrat. E-mail: wnugent@nd.edu.

NUGTEREN, CORNELIUS, air force officer; b. Colton, SD, Feb. 7, 1928; s. Adrian Joe and Marie Johanna N.; m. Liane Albrecht, Sept. 22, 1956; children: Cecile, Aneli. BA, Central Coll., Pella, Iowa, 1951. Commd. 2d lt. USAF, 1953, advanced through grades to maj. gen., 1980; advisor Vietnam Air Force, 1970-71; served in Germany, 1971-77; vice comdr. (Air Logistics Center), Utah, 1977-79; comdr. (Aerospace Rescue and Recovery Service), Scott AFB, Ill., 1979-81; chief (Joint U.S. Mil. Aid Group), Greece, 1981-82; comdr. Air Logistics Ctr., Robins AFB, Ga, 1983-88; ret.; cons. for def. industries Warner Robins, Ga., 1988-94; v.p. Chem. Tech. Internat., Warner Robins, Mercer U. Engring. Rsch. Ctr., Warner Robins, 1996—. Decorated D.S.M., Legion of Merit, Bronze Star, Superior Service medal; recipient USAF EEO award, 1979; named to Ga. Aviation Hall of Fame, 2004. Mem. Air Force Assn., Order Daedalians, Internat. Order Hansen, Order of the Sword. Office: 114 Holly Dr Warner Robins GA 31088-6615 Office Phone: 478-953-6810. Personal E-mail: gennewt@aol.com. *Service to one's country is not just a job...it's a calling. Integrity to and within the institution to which you belong is an absolute necessity. Loyalty to peers and subordinates is equally important as loyalty to your superiors. Attitude toward life, humankind and profession is key determinant to success. Goals should be set high enough so as to be unattainable. Standard of conduct must always include duty, honor, country.*

NÜHN, ADRIAAN, food products executive; b. 1953; BA, Eindhoven Hogere Econ. Sch., Netherlands; MBA, U. Puget Sound, Tacoma, Wash. With Xerox Corp., Rochester, NY, Richardson Vicks/Procter & Gamble; mng. dir. Procter & Gamble, Vienna; gen. mgr., household and body care divsn. Sara Lee/DE, Netherlands, 1990—91, pres., Kortman Intradal, 1991—94, regional v.p., Beneleux countries, 1994, regional v.p., continental Europe, 1994—95, corp. v.p., CEO worldwide household and body care divsn., bd. mgmt., 1995—96, chmn., bd. mgmt., 2003—; corp. sr. v.p. Sara Lee Corp., 1996—99, pres., worldwide coffee & tea divsn., 1999—2003, exec. v.p., chmn. bd. mgmt. Sara Lee Internat., 2003—. Office: Sara Lee Corp Three First Nat Plaza Chicago IL 60602-4260 *

NUKALA, SIRISHA SARIPALLI, research scientist, educator; b. Visakhapatnam, Andhra Pradesh, India, Apr. 8, 1980; d. Narayana Rao Yagya and Aruna Saripalli; m. Sirisha Saripalli, May 21, 2003. B in Mech. Engring., Andhra U., India, 2001; MS, Clemson U., SC, 2003, U. Tenn., Knoxville, 2006, PhD, 2007. Rsch. asst. Clemson U., SC, 2001—03; rsch., tchg. asst. U. Tenn., Knoxville, 2003—. Summer rsch. student Oak Ridge Nat. Lab., Tenn., 2005, summer rsch. assoc., 06. Vol. ASHA, Knoxville, Tenn., 2003—; vol Am. Cancer Soc., 2003—, ARC, 2003—. Recipient Roller Skating Champion award, Sr. Women's Nat., Andhra Pradesh, India, 1983—97. Home: 2512 Wild Fern Ln Knoxville TN 37931 Office: Univ Tenn 303 Esh Knoxville TN 37996 Office Phone: 865-898-8457. Business E-Mail: ssaripal@utk.edu.

NULAND, ANTHONY C. J., lawyer; b. NYC, 1943; AB cum laude, Princeton U., 1965; JD, NYU, 1968. Bar: N.Y. 1969, D.C. 1977, Ga. 1978. Asst. dir. divsn. market regulation SEC, 1975-76, assoc. dir. divsn. market regulation, 1976-77; now ptnr. Seward & Kissel, NYC, 1977—. Office: Seward & Kissel 1200 G St NW Ste 350 Washington DC 20005-3881 Office Phone: 202-737-8833.

NULAND, SHERWIN, surgeon, writer; b. NYC, Dec. 8, 1930; s. Meyer and Violet (Lutsky) N.; m. Sarah Peterson, May 29, 1977; children: Victoria Jane, Andrew Meyer, William Peterson, Amelia Rose. BA, NYU, 1951; MD, Yale U., 1955. Surgeon Yale-New Haven Hosp. (Conn.), 1962—92; clin. prof. surgery Yale Sch. Medicine, New Haven, 1962—; rsch. affiliate history sci. and medicine program Yale U. Author: The Origins of Anesthesia, 1983, Doctors: The Biography of Medicine, 1988, Medicine: The Art of Healing, 1991, How We Die: Reflections on Life's Final Chapter, 1994 (Nat. Book award for non-fiction, 1994, Pulitzer prize finalist, 1995), The Wisdom of the Body: How We Live, 1997, The Mysteries Within: A Surgeon Reflects on Medical Myths, 2000, Leonardo da Vinci, 2000, Lost in America, 2003, The Doctors' Plague, 2003, Maimonides, 2005, The Art of Aging, 2007; contbg. editor The New Republic, mem. editl. bd. Perspectives in Biology and Medicine. V.p. Conn. Hospice, New Haven, 1978-80; bd. dirs. Hastings Ctr. Hastings Ctr. fellow. Fellow AAAS, ACS; mem. New Eng. Surg. Soc., Assocs. of Yale Med. Sch. Libr. (chmn. 1982-94), Yale-China Assn. (chmn. med. 1988-93), History of Medicine and Allied Scis. (chmn. bd. jour. 1979-2002). Democrat. Jewish. Avocation: tennis. Home: 29 Old Hartford Tpke Hamden CT 06517-3523 Office: PO Box 6356 Hamden CT 06517-0356 Office Phone: 203-776-5635. Personal E-mail: snuland@comcast.net.

NULAND, VICTORIA, ambassador; m. Robert Kagan. BA, Brown U., RI. Chief of staff to dep. sec. of state US Dept. State, 1993—96, dep. dir. former Soviet Union affairs, 1997—99, US dep. permanent rep. to NATO in Brussels, 2000—03, US permanent rep. to NATO, 2005—; prin. dep. nat. security adv. to US v.p. Cheney Office of the V.P., 2003—05. "Next Generation" fellow Coun. Fgn. Rels., 1999—2000, state dept. fellow, 1996—97; speaks Russian, French and some Chinese. Recipient Disting. Civilian Svc. medal, US Sec. Def. Office: US Mission NATO Blvd Leopold III 1110 Brussels Belgium *

NULL, ELISABETH HIGGINS, librarian, editor; b. Worcester, Mass., Dec. 1, 1942; d. Carter Chapin Higgins and Katharine Huntington (Bigelow) Doman; m. Henry Harrison Null IV, July 13, 1963 (div. 1970); children: John Higgins, Jacob Van Vechten. BA, Sarah Lawrence Coll., Bronxville, NY, 1983; MA, Yale U., 1985, MPhil in Am. History, 1989; MA in Folklore, U. Pa., 1987; M Libr. and Info. Sci., Cath. U. Am., 1995. V.p. Abington Pub. Co., Clark's Summit, Pa., 1966-70; CEO Green Linnet Records, Danbury, Conn., 1971-81; vis. lectr. Am. Musical Life, Georgetown U., 1991-98; libr. and conversion specialist nat. digital libr. program Libr. of Congress, Washington, 1996-98, expert cons., 1995; writer on edn. issues Rural Sch. and Cmty. Trust, 1999—2004; rsch. coord. congl. campaign Janine Selendy (Dem.) N.Y. Dist. 17, 2002, 2004; freelance editor, writer Null Editl. Svcs., 2005—; rsch. assoc. for Journalist John Dickerson, 2005—. Bd. dirs. Maine Folklife Ctr.; program co-chair Washington Folk Festival, 1999-2000; program chair Folklore Soc. Greater Washington, 1993-94; humanities scholar-in-residence Conn. Coun. for Humanities and Conn. Dept. for the Arts, Waterbury, Conn., 1986-87; fieldworker in folklore Waterbury Ethnic Music Project, 1986-87. Singer 2 recordings: The Feathered Malden, 1977, American Primitive, 1981; performance career with guitarist Bill Shute included 6 appearances with Garrison Keillor's A Prairie Home Companion; major venues include Phila. Folk Festival, Bklyn. Mus., Mus. Natural History. Incorporator John Woodman Higgins Armory, Worcester, Mass., 1966—; sec. Stanton Park Neighborhood Assn., Washington, 1990; bd. dirs. John and Clara Higgins Found., 1999—, Horizon Internat., 1980-2006. Folger Shakespeare Libr. Seminar fellow, 1989-91. Mem. ALA, Am. Folklore Soc. Democrat. Episcopalian. Avocations: folk music performer, song writer. Home and Office: 706 Bonifant St Silver Spring MD 20910-5534 Office Phone: 301-587-2286. Personal E-mail: enul@starpower.net.

NULL, PAUL BRYAN, minister; b. Oakland, Calif., May 7, 1944; s. Carleton Elliot and Dorothy Irene (Bryan) N.; m. Renee Yvonne Howell, Aug. 23, 1969; children: Bryan Joseph, Kara Renee. BS, Western Bapt. Coll., 1973; MDiv, Western Conservative Bapt. Sem., 1979; DMin, Trinity Theol. Sem., 1994. Ordained to ministry Bapt. Ch., 1982. Asst. pastor Bethel Bapt. Ch., Aumsville, Oreg., 1972-74, sr. pastor, 1974-87, The Calvary Congregation, Stockton, Calif., 1987-94; pastor Sierra Cmty. Ch., South Lake Tahoe, Calif., 1994—99; exec. pastor Dayspring Fellowship, Salem, Oreg., 1999—2004; gen. dir. Conservative Bapt. Assn. No. Calif. and Nev., 2004—. Trustee Conservative Bapt. Assn. of Oreg., 1982-85, mem. Ch. extension com., 1975-85. Radio show commentator Food for Thought, 1987. Panel mem. Presdl. Anti-Drug Campaign, 1984; bd. dirs. Western Bapt. Coll., Salem, 1998—. Served with U.S. Army, 1965-67. Named Outstanding Young Man Am., 1979. Mem. Conservative Bapt. Assn. of Am., No. Calif. Conservative Bapt. Assn. (pres. 1992-93), Delta Epsilon Chi. Avocations: weight training, aerobics, writing, hiking, cross country skiing. Home: 2922 Lonnie Beck Way Stockton CA 95209 Office: 1545 St Marks Plz Ste 1 Stockton CA 95207 Home Phone: 209-477-2851; Office Phone: 209-954-0499. Personal E-mail: nextgenpbn@sbcglobal.net. Business E-Mail: paul@nextgenchurches.com.

NULL, WILLIAM SETH, lawyer; b. NYC, Apr. 15, 1954; s. Douglas P. Null and Barbara M. (Black) Schacker; m. Lauren E. Thaler, May 10, 1981; children: Danielle, Evan. BA, Hampshire Coll., 1977; JD, Yeshiva U., 1980. Bar: N.Y. 1981, U.S. Dist. Ct. (ea. and so. dists.) N.Y. 1981, U.S. Supreme Ct. 1987. With Null & Null, P.C., Garden City, N.Y., 1980-83, Kraver & Martin, NYC, 1983-85, Cuddy & Feder LLP, White Plains, NY, 1985—, mng. ptnr., 1999—. Dir. The Housing Partnership, Elmsford, NY, 1995—2001, White Plains Bridge of Friendship Found., 1994—; dir. Westchester chpt. Juvenile Diabetes Rsch. Found. Internat., 1998—, pres., 2004—06; dir. Gilda's Club Westchester, 2001—, The Briarcliff Manor Edn. Found., 2001—03, White Plains Hosp. Ctr., 2002—. Office: Cuddy & Feder LLP 445 Hamilton Ave 14th Fl White Plains NY 10601 Office Phone: 914-761-1300. Business E-Mail: wnull@cuddyfeder.com.

NULTON, WILLIAM CLEMENTS, retired lawyer; b. Pittsburg, Kans., Feb. 22, 1931; s. Perley Edgar and Mary Celia (Anderson) N.; m. Vicki Smith, Aug. 20, 1956; children: Carnie, Erica. BA, Kans. U., 1953, LLB with honors, 1958; postgrad., NYU, 1953-54. Bar: Kans. 1958, Mo. 1959. Sr. atty. Great Lakes Pipe Line Co., Kansas City, Mo., 1958-66, asst. sec., 1961-66; assoc. Blackwell, Sanders, Matheny, Weary & Lombardi, Kansas City, 1966-68, ptnr., 1968-81; assoc. Shughart Thomson & Kilroy, Kansas City, 1981-83, ptnr., 1983-94. Contbr. articles to profl. jours. Bd. dirs. Corinth Hills Home Assn., Shawnee Mission, 1974-76, Faith Friends, 1999-2004, Front Porch Alliance, 1999—2006, Ivanhoe Neighborhood Coun., 2003—, Kansas City Civil Rights Consortium, 1993-2005, Marillac Acad., 1994-99; pres. Beta Theta Pi Kansas City Alumni Assn., 1977 (Man of Yr. award 2002); mem., elder Village United Presbyn. Ch., Prairie Village, Kans., 1976—, trustee, 1992-94, endowment bd., 1997-2001; bd. dirs. Prairie Village Mcpl. Found., 1987—, v.p., 2000-05, pres., 2005-; Kans. adv. com. U.S. Civil Rights Commn., 1994-2006, acting chmn., 1998; Shawnee Mission Unified Bd. Edn., 1969-73, v.p., 1973; pres. Corinth Elem. Bd. Edn., Johnson County, Kans., 1969; chmn. Full Employment Task Group on Employment Disabled, Kansas City, 1987. Summerfield scholar, Kans. U., 1949—53, Root-Tilden scholar, NYU, 1953—54. Mem. ABA (mgmt. chmn. labor and employment law sect., com. on arbitration and collective bargaining 1989-92), Am. Acad. Hosp.

Attys. (co-chmn. task group on bylaws for small rural hosps. 1992-93), Mo. Bar Assn. (chmn. labor law com. 1982), Nat. Health Lawyers Assn. (co-chmn. task group on alternative dispute resolution in health care field 1990-91), Phi Beta Kappa, Order of Coif. Republican. Home: 7908 El Monte St Shawnee Mission KS 66208-5047

NUNAMAKER, SUSAN SUN, mathematics professor; d. Chin-tse and Jean Hwei-Lan Sun; m. Michael Edward Nunamaker; 1 child, Marina. BS in Math., U. Ill., Urbana-Champaign, 1982, BS in Civil Engring., 1982, MS in Applied Math., 1984. Rsch. asst. Ill. State Water Survey, 1979—81; tchg. and rsch. asst. U. Ill., 1982—86; math. prof. DeVry U., Addison, Ill., 1997—2006; math instr. Triton Coll., River Grove, Ill., 1997, Waubonsee CC, Sugar Grove, Ill., 2005—, Coll. DuPage, Glen Ellyn, Ill., 2006—; owner Sunflower Bear R & D, Urbana-Champaign, 1993—96, cons., 2006—. Computing analyst Minnow Bear Computers, Urbana-Champaign, 1984—93; engring. technician US Corps Engring. Rsch. Lab, Urbana-Champaign, 1979—80; instr. Waubimsee C.C., Sugar Grove, Ill., 2006—. Recipient Book award, Harvard U., 1976, Lazarus Human Rels. award, Am. Jewish Cmty., 1977; Engring. scholarships, U. Ill., 1977, Math scholarships, 1978. Mem.: Ill. Math. Assn. CC, Math. Assn. Am., Am. Math. Soc. (assoc.). Home: 5 South 370 Vest Naperville IL 60563 Office: Coll DuPage 425 Fawell Blvd Glen Ellyn IL 60137 also: Waubonsee CC Route 47 at Waubonsee Dr Sugar Grove IL 60554 Home Phone: 630-778-6806; Office Phone: 630-942-2800 ext. 51498, 630-466-7900 ext. 3587, 312-671-9340. Personal E-mail: susan@nunamaker.com. Business E-Mail: nunama@cdnet.cod.edu.

NUNES, DEVIN, congressman; b. Tulare, Calif., Oct. 1, 1973; m. Elizabeth Tamariz. BS in Agrl. Bus., Calif. Poly. State U., 1995, MS in Agrl., 1996; BS, Coll. Sequoias. Calif. state dir. USDA; mem. U.S. Congress from 21st Calif. dist., 2003—; mem. Ways and Means com. Mem. Coll. Sequoias Bd. Trustees, 1996—2002; grad. Calif. Agr. Leadership Fellowship Program, 2000. Republican. Roman Catholic. Office: US Ho Reps 1013 Longworth Ho Office Bldg Washington DC 20515-0521 *

NUNES, WINIFRED O., minister, educator; d. Jacob Albert Oliver and Katherine Collis Champion; children: Katherine Taylor, Julius Harper. A, U. Hartford, 1978. Ordained to ministry Pentecostal Assemblies of World, 1977. Paraprofl. Sch. Readiness, Hartford, Conn., 1966—67, tchr. presch., 1967—80; assoc. pastor Zion Apostolic Ch., Hartford, 1970—75; pastor New Testament Tabernacle, Bloomfield, 1988—. Author: Born & Bred in the Apostolic Way, 2004; contbr. articles to profl. jours. Mem.: Internat. Missionary & Christian Women's Aux. (pres. 1998—2004). Avocations: reading, travel, writing. Personal E-mail: pwnunes@aol.com.

NUNEZ, OSCAR, actor; b. Cuba, Nov. 18, 1958; m. Carla Nunez. Attended, F.I.T., Parsons Sch. Design, NYC; grad., Magna Inst. Dental Tech. Cert. Dental Tech. Former mem. Shock of the Funny Comedy Troupe, Groundlings Sunday Co. Actor: (films) The Italian Job, 2003, When Do We Eat?, 2005, The Chipotle Diamonds, 2005, Glory Road, 2006, Reno 911!: Miami, 2007; (TV series) Resurrection Blvd., 24, Arrested Development, The Steve Harvey Show, That's Life, Ally McBeal, Curb Your Enthusiasm, 2000, The Bad Girl's Guide, 2003, Reno 911!, 2004—06, The Office, 2006— (winner Outstanding Performance by an Ensemble in a Comedy Series, SAG awards, 2007). Office: OmniPop Talent Group Ste 201 4605 Lankershim Blvd Toluca Lake CA 91602 *

NUNEZ-LAWTON, MIGUEL G., financial analyst; b. Havana, Cuba, Feb. 8, 1949; came to U.S., 1964; s. Miguel Nunez-Cancio and Silvia Lawton-Alfonso. BSBA, Georgetown U., 1971, postgrad. in Econs., 1973. Asst. treas. Deltec Securities Corp., NYC, 1971; debt specialist internat. econs. dept. World Bank, Washington, 1973-95; internat. cons. Miami, Fla., 1996—; World Bank del. Paris Club Debt Renegotiation for Senegal, 1982. UN Conf. in Trade and Devel. cons. Nat. Bank Angola, Luanda, 2000, Geneva; chief tech. adviser UN Conf. Trade and Devel. Bur. Treasury, Manila, 1989—90. Bd. dirs., treas. Friends of Art Mus. of the Americas, OAS, Washington, 1988-90; bd. dirs. Friends of Peru, 1991-1996, Friends of the Cuban Heritage Collection, U. Miami, 2003—; panel mem. The Lawrenceville Sch., 1992; mem. Presdl. Inaugural Com., Washington, 1997. Roman Catholic. Avocations: art collecting, genealogy. Home: 8860 SW 123rd Ct Apt K106 Miami FL 33186-4152 Office Phone: 305-606-0983. Personal E-mail: mnlawton@hotmail.com.

NUNEZ-PORTUONDO, RICARDO, investment company executive; b. NYC, June 9, 1933; s. Emilio and Maria (Garcia) N-P.; m. Dolores Maldonado, Sept. 7, 1963; children— Ricardo Jose, Emilio Manuel, Eduardo Javier. LL.D., U. Havana, Cuba; postdoctoral in law, U. Fla., 1975. Bar: Cuba, Fla. Editor Latin Am. div. USIA, Miami, Fla., 1961-71, editor Washington, 1961-71; nat. dir. Cuban Refugee Program, Washington, 1975-77; pres. Cultural Pub., Inc., Miami, 1994—, Central Investment Trust, Coral Gables, Fla., 1977—; chmn. bd. Interstate Bank of Commerce, Miami, 1986-88; v.p. Century 21, Coral Gables, 1989—; adv. Miami-Dade County Commr. Jimmy L Morales, 1996—; litigation cons. Cohen & Kandell, P.A. Attorneys at Law, 1998—. Author: A Critique on the Linowitz Report, 1975, Cuba: La Otra Imagen, 1994, Un Procer Cubano, 1994, Cuban Refugee Program, The Early Years, 1995. Dir. Nat. Hispanic Scholarship Fund, San Francisco, 1978—; dir. COSSMHO, Washington, 1980—; trustee emeritus Fla. Internat. U., 1984—; pres. Mercy Hosp. Found., Miami, 1985—; bd. dirs. ARC, Greater Miami. Recipient numerous awards for civic contbns. including day named in honor Ricardo Nunez Day, Miami, 1975. Mem. Cuban Lawyers Assn., Cuban Acad. History, Metro. Club, Lyford Cay Club, Ocean Reef Club, Key Biscayne Yacht Club, Big Five Club, 200 Club. Republican. Roman Catholic. Office: PO Box 141720 Coral Gables FL 33114-1720

NUNN, CHARLES BURGESS, retired religious organization administrator; b. Richmond, Va., May 1, 1931; s. Charles Burgess Sr. and Virginia Atkinson (Goode) N.; m. Helen Agnes Parker, Sept. 1, 1957; children: Patsy Virginia, Catherine Louise, Stephen Charles, Stewart Gavin. BA in Econs., Randolph Macon Coll., 1953; BD, Southwestern Bapt. Theol. Sem., 1959, MDiv, 1969; DMin, Pitts. Theol. Sem., 1979. Ordained to Gospel ministry, 1954. Pastor Warwick Rd. Bapt. Chapel, Richmond, Va., 1952-53, Garrett's Bluff Bapt. Ch., Arthur City, Tex., 1954-56, Plymouth Haven Bapt. Ch., Alexandria, Va., 1959-68, First Bapt. Ch., Bluefield, W.Va., 1968-77; exec. dir. missions Richmond (Va.) Bapt. Assn., 1977-97; adminstr., treas. So. Bapt. Conf./Assoc. Dirs. Missions, 1997—2003, ret., 2003. Trustee Bluefield (Va.) Coll., 1972-82, U. Richmond, Va., 1989-93; first v.p. Va. Bapt. Gen. Bd., Richmond, 1974-75; dir. Home Mission Bd., So. Bapt. Conv., Atlanta, 1976-84. Author: (children's book) Following Jesus, 1968. Commr. Bluefield (W.Va.) Urban Renewal Authority, 1971-74; chmn. Bluefield (W.Va.) Beautification Commn., 1972-73; pres. North Chamberlayne Civic Assn., Richmond, 1989-91. Recipient Disting. Svc. award City of Bluefield, 1970, Disting. Alumnus award Alumni Soc. Randolph Macon, Ashland, Va., 1992, Vol. Missions award Richmond Regional Devel. Coun. of the Fgn. Mission Bd., So. Bapt. Conv., 1995. Mem. Richmond Rotary Club (bd. dirs. 1990-92), Sandston Rotary Club, Pawleys Island Rotary Club, Omicron Delta Kappa. Avocations: travel, fishing, photography, baseball. Personal E-mail: cbunnjr@aol.com.

NUNN, DONALD RAY, plastic surgeon; b. Mt. Airy, NC, Sept. 22, 1953; BS in Biochemistry/Nutrition, Va. Poly. Inst. and State U., Blacksburg; DDS, Med. Coll. Va./Va. Commonwealth U., Richmond, 1979, MD, 1992. Cert. Am. Bd. Oral/Maxillofacial Surgery, 1985, Am. Bd. Otolaryngology, 1998, Am. Bd. Plastic Surgery, 2001. Resident maxillofacial plastic surgery U. NC, Chapel Hill, 1979—82; intern surgery Med. Coll. Va. Hosps., Richmond, 1992—93; resident otolaryngology Ea. Va. Med. Sch., Norfolk, 1993—97; resident plastic surgery UCLA, 1997—99; fellow Manhattan Eye, Ear and Throat Hosp., NYC, 1999—2000; active staff mem. plastic surgery Northside Hosp., Atlanta, 2001. Featured: magazines Atlanta Style & Design, Jezebel. Mem.: Am. Assn. Oral and Maxillofacial Surgeons, Am. Soc. Aesthetic Plastic Surgery, Am. Soc. Plastic Surgeons. Office: 5673 Peachtree Dunwoody Rd NE Ste 870 Atlanta GA 30342 Office Phone: 404-255-2975. Office Fax: 404-255-2276. E-mail: donaldrnunn@aol.com.

NUNN, GRADY HARRISON, retired political science professor; b. Arlington, Tex., Apr. 12, 1918; s. William Roy and Floy Brooke (Dugan) N.; m. Ann Torrey Welsh, June 15, 1951 (dec. 1980); 1 child, Therese von Hohoff.; m. Virginia Cotton Chivington, Dec. 18, 1982. BA, U. Okla., 1939, MA, 1941; PhD (Penfield fellow), N.Y.U., 1961. Instr. N.Y.U., 1946-49; from instr. to asso. prof. U. Ala., Tuscaloosa, 1949-65, prof., chmn. dept. polit. sci. Birmingham, 1969-83, prof. emeritus, 1983—; vis. asst. prof. Ind. U., 1960-61; asst. prof., asso. prof. U. Pitts. at Ahmadu Bello U., Nigeria, 1964-68; assoc. prof. U. Pitts., 1968, Auburn U., 1968-69. Bd. dirs. Unitarian Universalist Service Com., 1978-84, v.p., 1981-82 Assoc. editor: Background on World Politics, 1957-62; Contbr. to: Readings in Government in American Society, 1949, Federalism in the Commonwealth, 1963, The Politics and Administration of Nigerian Government, 1965; editorial bd.: Jour. of Politics, 1971-74. Mem. Birmingham Regional Planning Commn., 1995-2000. Capt. F.A., AUS, 1942-46. Ford Found. Fgn. Area fellow, 1956-57 Mem. Am. Polit. Sci. Assn., So. Polit. Sci. Assn. (exec. council 1974-77), Royal African Soc., AAUP (pres. Ala. conf.), Phi Beta Kappa, Pi Sigma Alpha, Phi Eta Sigma, Alpha Tau Omega, Omicron Delta Kappa. Unitarian Universalist. Home: 805 Rockhurst Ln Birmingham AL 35209 Personal E-mail: ghnunn@aol.com.

NUNN, KEN, lawyer; b. Louisville, Mar. 22, 1940; s. Richard and Grace (Lynch) N.; m. Leah K. Blades, Aug. 19, 1962; children: Vicky A., David L. BS in Bus., Ind. U., 1964, JD, 1967. Bar: Ind. 1967, U.S. Dist. Ct. (so. dist.) Ind. 1967, U.S. Ct. Appeals (7th cir.) 1974, U.S. Supreme Ct. 1974. Pvt. practice, Bloomington, Ind. Office: 104 S Franklin Rd Bloomington IN 47404-5295

NUNN, PATARICA DIAN, poet; b. Arkadelphia, Ark., Aug. 10, 1951; m. Freddie Lee Nunn, Mar. 16, 1979; children: Katarica Lakisha, Roshonda Lanae, Ophelia Lorraine, Opal Laverne. Student, Ouachita Bapt. U., 1971—72. Dir. assistance operator Southwestern Bell Tel. Co., Hot Springs, Ark., 1978—2003; ret., 2003. Songwriter My Moment of Miles, Time, 1998, Mellow Drifting, 2002, Sassy Sassy Lady, 2003; author: (poetry) Sacred Memories, 1996, A True Mother's Love, 1997, A True Father's Love, 1998, Out in Left Field, 1998, A Breathe of Fresh Air, 2002. Bd. dirs., mem. adv. com. Nat. Libr. Poetry. Named to Internat. Poetry Hall of Fame, 1997, Internat. Hall of Fames's Mus. Mem.: Poetry Guild, Nat. Author's Registry. Democrat. Home: 4 Stillman Dr Little Rock AR 72209

NUNN, ROBERT WARNE, lawyer; b. Salem, Oreg., Sept. 20, 1950; s. Warne Harry and Delores Nunn; m. Kandis Brewer; 1 child, Hayley Elisabeth. Student, U. Vienna, Austria, 1971; BS, Willamette U., 1972; MS in Acctg., Northeastern U., Boston, 1973, MBA, 2000; JD, U. Oreg., 1976. Bar: Oreg 1976, U.S. Dist. Ct. Oreg. 1977, U.S. Ct. Appeals (9th cir.) 1977, U.S. Supreme Ct. 1982, Wash. 1986. Ptnr. Schwabe, Williamson &, Wyatt, Portland, Oreg., 1976-92; ptnr., chmn. corp. dept. Preston, Gates & Ellis, Portland, 1992-96; founder, mng. ptnr. Nunn Motschenbacher & Blattner LLP, Portland, 1996—. Dir. Oreg. State Bar Profl. Liability Fund, 1996—2004; ptnr. Sussman Shankman LLP, 2001—. Mem. exec. com. Am. Leadership Forum, 1988-94, sr. fellow, 1988—; bd. mgrs. Multnomah Metro Br. YMCA, Portland, 1983-86, chmn., 1984-85; pres. Oreg. divsn. Am. Cancer Soc., Portland, 1986-87, bd. dirs., 1982-88; trustee Marylhurst Coll., Oreg., 1985-91, Willamette U., 1991—; trustee World Affairs Coun. Oreg., 1991-97, pres., 1995-96; bd. dirs. United Way of Columbia-Willamette, Portland, 1984-87. Named Order of Red Sword, Am. Cancer Soc., 1985; fellow Am. Leadership, 1987. Mem. ABA, Oreg. Bar Assn. (past chmn. CPA joint com., past chmn. legal assts. and legal investigators com., cert. subcom., fee arbitration panel), Univ. Club, Multhnomah Athletic Club (Portland). Republican. Lutheran. Avocations: rowing, skiing, sailing. Office: Sussman Shank LLP 1000 SW Broadway Ste 1400 Portland OR 97205 Office Phone: 503-227-1111.

NUNN, SAM (SAMUEL AUGUSTUS NUNN), former senator, lawyer; b. Perry, Ga., Sept. 8, 1938; s. Samuel Augustus and Elizabeth (Cannon) N.; m. Colleen O'Brien, Sept. 25, 1965; children: Michelle, Brian. Student, Ga. Inst. Tech., 1956-59; AB, LL.B., Emory U., 1962. Bar: Ga. 1962. Legal counsel armed services com. U.S. Ho. Reps., 1963; mem. firm Nunn, Geiger & Rampey, Perry, Ga., 1964-73; mem. Ga. Ho. Reps., 1968-72; U.S. senator from Ga., 1972-96; ranking Dem. mem., chmn. armed svcs. com.; mem. govtl. affairs com., intelligence com., small bus. com.; ptnr. King & Spalding, Atlanta, 1997—2003; disting. prof. Ga. Inst. Tech., 1997—; co-chmn. Nuc. Threat Initiative, Washington, 2003—. Former ranking Dem., former chmn. Permanent Subcom. on Investigations of Govt. Affairs; bd. dirs. Chevron Texaco Corp., Coca-Cola Co., Dell Computer Corp., GE, Internet Security Systems Inc., Scientific-Atlanta; disting. prof. Sam Nunn Sch. Internat Affairs Ga. Tech. Office: Nuc Threat Initiative 1747 Pennsulvania Ave NW Ste 700 Washington DC 20006

NUNN, TODD L., lawyer; b. Seattle, Apr. 7, 1968; BA, Univ. Wash., 1990, JD, 1993. Bar: Wash. 1993, U.S. Dist. Ct., Western Dist. Wash. 1994, U.S. Dist. Ct., Eastern Dist. Wash. 1997, U.S. Ct. Appeals, Ninth Circuit 1997. Assoc. atty., class action, complex litig. Preston Gates & Ellis, LLP, Seattle. Contbr. articles to numerous profl. jours. Named Wash. Rising Star, SuperLawyer Mag., 2006. Mem.: ABA, Wash. Defense Trial Lawyers Assn., Wash. Bar Assn. Office: Preston Gates & Ellis LLP Ste 2900 925 Fourth Ave Seattle WA 98104-1158

NUNNALLY, ALLEN C., lawyer; BA, Amherst Coll., 1999; JD, Boston U., 2002. Bar: Mass. 2003, D.C. 2005, U.S. Dist. Ct. Mass. 2003. Mng. editor Boston U. Jour. Sci. and Tech. Law, 2001—02; litigation assoc. Wilmer Cutler Pickering Hale and Dorr LLP, Boston, 2002—. Vol. tchr. discovering justice Citizen Schs. Mock Trial Legal Apprenticeship Program, 2002—. Contbr. chapters to books, articles to profl. jours. Vol. Friends of Tanzanian Schs., 2005—; bd. trustees Cmty. Charter Sch. Cambridge, 2007—; vol. legal counsel Kerry-Edwards Campaign/Dem. Nat. Com., 2004; bd. dirs. Friends of the Children, Boston, 2006—, treas., 2007—. Edward F. Hennessey scholar, Boston U. Sch. Law, 2002. Mem.: ABA, Mass. Bar Assn., Boston Bar Assn. Avocations: politics, reading, personal fitness, Boston sports enthusiast. Office: Wilmer Cutler Pickering Hale and Dorr 60 State St Boston MA 02109 Office Phone: 617-526-6242.

NUNNELLY, MARK EDWARD, investor; b. Covington, Ky., Nov. 30, 1958; s. Donald Alfred and Lillian Ethel (Black) N.; m. Denise Marcel Dupre, Nov. 18, 1989; 1 child, Cameron. BA in History and Govt., Ctr. Coll. Ky., 1980; MBA, Harvard U., 1984. Legis. asst. U.S. Ho. of Reps., Washington, 1980; mem. brand mgmt. Procter & Gamble, Cin., 1980-82; mgmt. cons. Bain & Co., Boston, 1983-89; equity investor, mng. dir. Bain Capital, Boston, 1989—. Bd. dirs. Environ. Data Resources, Southport, Conn., Strategic Mapping, San Jose, Calif., Corp. Software, Boston, Houghton-Mifflin Co., Warner Music and DoubleClick, Inc., Domino's Pizza, 1998-. Mem. fin. bd. City Year, Boston, 1987; mem. alumni bd. Centre Coll., Danville, Ky., 1989—. Mem. Harvard Club. Office: Bain Capital 111 Huntington Ave Boston MA 02199 *

NUOVO, BETTY A., state representative; b. Englewood, NJ, Dec. 10, 1931; m. Victor L. Nuovo, 1953; two children. BS, Bucknell U., 1953. State rep. Vt. Ho. of Reps., Middleury, 1981-90, 96—; pvt. law practice Middleury, 1974—94. Jud. com. Ho. of Reps., 1981-88, chmn. 1985-88, chmn. jud. rules com. 1985-86, adminstrv. rules com. 1985-88, vice-chmn. 1987-88, ways and means com. 1989-90, Middlebury natural resources and energy com., 1996-2000, jud. com., 2001-02, agr. com., 2003-04, ways and means com., 2005-06, ranking mem. natural resources and energy com., 2007—. Chair Vt. State Dem. Platform Com., Middlebury Charter Comn., Vt., Addison County Dem. Com.; bd. dirs., exec. bd. Addison County Regional Planning Com; bd. selectmen Middlebury; bd. dirs. Vt. YMCA; mem. Middlebury LWV. Office: PO Box 1113 Middlebury VT 05753-0347 E-mail: bnuovo@leg.state.vt.us.

NURENBERG, DAVID, retired oil company executive; b. NYC, Mar. 25, 1939; s. Abraham S. and Katherine G. N.; m. Brenda G. Schwait, Sept. 1963; children— Jill Suzanne, Brian Michael. BS in Marine Engring, U.S. Mcht. Marine Acad., 1960; MS in Indsl. Mgmt, Columbia U., 1963, PhD in Mgmt. Sci, 1965. With Exxon Corp., 1963-67; employee relations mgr. Esso Pappas, Athens, Greece, 1968-72; labor relations and compensation mgr. Esso Europe, London, 1972-77; corp. sec. Esso Eastern Inc., Houston, 1977-82; mgr. exec. compensation Exxon Corp., NYC, 1982-90, mgr. compensation and exec. programs Irving, Tex., 1990-98; ret. Past mem. coun. exec. compensation Conf. Bd., past chmn.; adj. prof. Union Inst. Past mem. exec. edn. adv. bd. Wharton Sch., U. Pa.; past mem. adv. bd. Ctr. for Effective Orgns., U. So. Calif. Mem. Am. Compensation Assn. (bd. dirs., chmn., exec. comp. coun., bd. steering com.), Am. Contract Bridge League (Silver life master).

NURICK, CARL J., writer, consultant, poet; b. Harrisburg, Pa., Mar. 29, 1934; s. Gilbert and Sylvia Nurick; m. Elizabeth Parker Nurick; children: Kim, Scott, Todd, Craig. BA, Pa. State U., 1955; postgrad., Mich. State U., Columbia U. Area v.p. AT&T, Phila., 1982—86; internat. v.p. Internat. Alliance, 1987—93; exec. v.p. Transnet, Huntington Valley, Pa., 1993; v.p. OutSource Internat., 1995—96; pres. and COO Vircom, West Chester, Pa., 1996—97; freelance author Tafton, Pa., 1998—; cons. world religions and military. Mem. MBA adv. bd. Pa. State U. and Bloomsburg U., 1974—86; mktg. adv. bd. Drexel U., Phila., 1974—78. Author: The Truth About Islam, 2003, Living To Die, 2003, The World According to Green Street Boy, 2006, poetry. Bd. dirs. Suburban Gen. Hosp., Norristown, Pa., 1979—80. Lt. USN, 1955—57, surface warfare officer USN, 1958—70. Mem.: Fairview Lake Assn., U.S. Naval Inst., Inlets Assn., US Navy League. Avocations: reading, fitness, boating, music.

NURKIN, SIDNEY J., lawyer; b. Durham, NC, Nov. 12, 1941; BSEE, Duke U., 1963, LLB, 1966. Bar: Ga. 1967. Mem. Powell, Goldstein, Frazer & Murphy; now sr. ptnr., corp. group Alston & Bird LLP, Atlanta. Mem. ABA (mem. com. on corp. laws, 1987—), Atlanta Bar Assn., Omicron Delta Kappa, Tau Beta Pi, Eta Kappa Nu. Office: Alston & Bird LLP One Atlantic Ctr 1201 W Peachtree St NW Atlanta GA 30309-3424 Office Phone: 404-881-7260. Office Fax: 404-881-7777. Business E-Mail: snurkin@alston.com.

NURMIKKO, ARTO VEIKKO, engineering educator; b. Finland; BSEE, MSEE, PhD, Univ. Calif., Berkeley. Engring. faculty Brown Univ., Providence, 1975—, L. Herbert Ballou Univ. prof. engring., physics, 1994—, dir., Ctr. Adv. Advanced Materials Rsch., 1989—2001. Author: more than 300 scientific jour. articles. Grantee Guggenheim Fellowship. Fellow: IEEE, Optical Soc. Am., Am. Phys. Soc., Am. Acad. Arts & Scis.; mem.: AAAS, Phi Beta Kappa. Office: Dept Physics Divsn Engring Brown Univ Providence RI 02912 Office Phone: 401-863-2869. Business E-Mail: Arto_Nurmikko@brown.edu. *

NURNBERG, CHARLES GORDON, publishing executive; b. Newark, Nov. 16, 1947; s. Max and Eleanor (Gordon) N.; m. Barbara Ann Goldstein, Dec. 20, 1970; children: Jeremy, Peter, David. BA, Syracuse U., 1969. Proofreader Frederick Fell Pub., Inc., NYC, 1969, editor, 1970-72, sales, 1972-74, sales mgr., 1974-75, v.p. sales, 1975-77, exec. v.p., 1977-78, pub., 1978; pub. paperbacks Sterling Pub. Co., Inc., NYC, 1978-80, v.p., dir. mktg., 1980-82, sr. v.p., 1982-89, exec. v.p., 1990—2003, pres., 2003—, CEO, 2003—, pub., 2003—. Mem. Book Industry Study Group com., 1992-95. Mem. Assn. Am. Pubs. (mem. mktg. com. 1970-73, chmn. pubs. forum com. 1973-79), Marlboro Soccer Assn. (bd. dirs., coach 1974, boys travel team). Avocations: writing, travel, exercise. Home: 25 Whitman Rd Morganville NJ 07751-1442 Office: 387 Park Ave S New York NY 10016-8810 Office Phone: 212-532-7160. Business E-Mail: cnurnberg@sterlingpub.com.

NURNBERG, ROGER C., county official; b. Creston, Iowa, Jan. 31, 1943; s. Mansel and Harriet J. Nurnberg; m. JoAnn I. Stringham, Aug. 5, 1962; children: Kathryn A., Leah T., Stephani J. Student, Creston C.C., 1961—63. Cert. fire instr. I and II Okla. U., 1982, EMT Iowa, arson investigator Iowa. Salesman S&L Clothing and Farm and Home Supply, Creston, 1961—64; letter carrier USPS, Creston, 1965—66; firefighter Creston Fire Dept., 1966—77, fire lt., 1977—96, fire chief, 1996—2000; emergency coord. Union County Emergency Mgmt., Creston, 2000—, E911 coord., 2000—. Author (editor): How to Install Dry Fire Hydrants, 1991; originator FireHousesoftware.com, 1990. Pres. 10,000 Crestonians, 2003—. Mem.: Union County Geneol. Soc., Creston Pyrotechnic Assn. (safety officer), Iowa Pyrotechnic Assn., Iowa Fireman's Assn., Masons (3d degree, 32d degree). Presbyterian. Avocations: travel, winemaking, geocaching, genealogy. Office: Union County Emergency Management Agency 208 W Taylor St Creston IA 50801 Office Phone: 641-782-1622. E-mail: ucema@mchsi.com.

NURNBERGER, JOHN I., JR., psychiatrist, educator; b. NYC, July 18, 1946; married; 3 children. BS in Psychology magna cum laude, Fordham U., 1968; MD, Ind. U., 1975, PhD, 1983. Diplomate Am. Bd. Psychiatry and Neurology. Resident in psychiatry Columbia Presbyn. Med. Ctr., NYC, 1975-78, med. officer sect. psychogenetics, 1977-78; sr. staff fellow, outpatient clinic adminstr. sect. psychogenetics NIH, Bethesda, Md., 1978-83, staff psychiatrist, chief NIMH Outpatients Clinic, 1983-86, acting chief sect. clin. genetics, 1986; prof. psychiatry, dir. Inst. Psychiatric Rsch., rsch. coord. dept. psychiatry Ind. U. Med. Ctr., Indpls., 1986—; prof. med. psychiatry, neurobiology and med. genetics Ind. U. Grad. Sch., Indpls., 1987—; Joyce and Iver Small prof. psychiatry, dir. Inst. Psychiat. Rsch., Ind. U., Indpls. Clin. cons. Cold Spring VA Hosp., 1986—; cons., lectr. in field. Editor-in-chief: Psychiatric Genetics; field editor: Neuropsychiatric Genetics; contbr. articles to profl. jours. NSF fellow, 1968; recipient NAMI Exemplary Psychiatrist award Nat. Alliance Mentally Ill, 1992, 94. Fellow Am. Psychiatric Assn., Am. Psychpathological Assn.; mem. AAAS, Am. Soc. Human Genetics, Internat. Soc. Psychiatric Genetics (bd. dirs.), Am. Coll. Neuropsychopharmacology, Soc. Light Treatment and Biol. Rhythms, Soc. Neursci., Assn. Rsch. in Nervous and Mental Disease, Soc. Biol. Psychiatry, Sigma Xi. Office: Ind U Sch Medicine Psychiatric Rsch Inst 791 Union Dr Indianapolis IN 46202-2873

NURSE, SIR PAUL M., academic administrator; m. Anne Nurse; children: Sarah, Emily. BSc, U. Birmingham, 1970; PhD, East Anglia, 1973. Dir. rsch. Imperial Cancer Rsch. Fund, 1993—96, dir. gen., 1996—2002; chief exec. Cancer Rsch. U.K., London, 2002—03; pres. Rockefeller U., NYC, 2003—, pres. lab. yeast genetics and cell biology, 2003—, prof., dept. molecular, cellular and develop. biology, 2003—. Chair microbiology U. Oxford, 1988—93. Recipient Gairdner Internat. award, Gairdner Found., 1992, Royal medal Royal Soc., 1995, H. P. Heineken prize for biochemistry and biophysics Royal Netherlands Acad. Arts and Scis., 1996, Dr. Josef Steiner prize, Cancer Found., Bern, Switzerland, 1996, Alfred P. Sloan Jr. prize and medal, GM Cancer Rsch. Found., 1997, Albert Lasker award, basic med. rsch., USA, 1998, Berkan Judd award, 1998, Nobel Prize in Physiology or Med., The Nobel Found., 2001. Fellow: Am. Acad. Arts & Sciences, Royal Soc. (Copley medal 2005); mem.: NAS (foreign assoc.). Avocations: hiking, flying. Office: Rockefeller U 1230 York Ave New York NY 10021-6399 Business E-Mail: nurse@rockefeller.edu.

NUSBACHER, GLORIA WEINBERG, lawyer; b. NYC, July 22, 1951; d. Murray and Doris (Togman) Weinberg; m. Burton Nusbacher, Aug. 4, 1974; 1 child, Shoshana. BA magna cum laude, Barnard Coll., 1972; JD with hons., Columbia U., 1975. Bar: N.Y. 1976. Assoc. Hughes Hubbard & Reed LLP, NYC, 1975-83, counsel, 1983-91, ptnr., 1991—. Lectr. in field. Mem. Columbia Law Rev.; contbr. articles to profl. jours. Troop leader, leader trainer Girl Scouts USA, 1991-97. Fellow Am. Coll. Employee Benefits Counsel; mem. ABA (employee benefits and exec. compensation com. 1987—, fed. regulation securities com., subcom. employee benefits, exec. compensation and sect. 16, 1983—, task force Sect. 16, 1991-97, vice-chair com. employee benefits and exec. compensation 2001-03, chair subcom. fed. and state securities laws of com. employee benefits and exec. compensation 1994-2001, 03-, mem. task force exec. compensation 1992-94). Office: Hughes Hubbard & Reed LLP 1 Battery Park Plz New York NY 10004-1482 Office Phone: 212-837-6719. Business E-Mail: nusbache@hugheshubbard.com.

NUSBAUM, EDWARD E., accounting company executive; BS in Bus. Adminstrn. (summa cum laude), Ohio State U.; MS in Mgmt., Purdue U. CPA. Mem. audit staff Grant Thornton LLP, Chgo., 1978—86, ptnr., 1986, nat. dir. assurance svcs., 1993—97, mng. ptnr., 1997—99, interim exec. ptnr., 2001, CEO, exec. ptnr., 2002—. Mem. Fin. Acctg. Standards Bd.; spkr. in field. Recipient Elijah Watts Sells award. Mem.: AICPA (former mem. exec. com., Securities and Exchange Commn. Practice Sect., former mem. profl. issues task force, former mem. auditing standards bd. & audit issues task force). Office: Grant Thornton 175 W Jackson Blvd 20th Fl Chicago IL 60604 Office Phone: 312-856-0200. Office Fax: 312-602-8099. *

NUSBAUM, JACK HENRY, lawyer; b. Casablanca, Morocco, July 22, 1940; came to U.S., 1941; s. Simon and Regine (Kleefeld) N.; m. Ronni Danciger, June 10, 1962 (div. 1983); children: Lisa B., Gary D.; m. Margie Goldsmith, Feb. 5, 1984 (div. 1997). BS, U. Pa., 1962; JD, Columbia U., 1965. Bar: N.Y. 1965. Assoc. Willkie, Farr & Gallagher LLP, NYC, 1965-70, ptnr., 1971—, co-chmn., 1979-95, chmn., 1995—, leader Corp. and Fin. Svcs. Dept. Bd. dirs. W.R. Berkley Corp., Greenwich, Conn., GEV Corp., Greenwich, Fine Host Corp., Greenwich, Hirschl & Adler Galleries, Inc., N.Y.C., The Topps Co., Inc., N.Y.C., Pioneer Cos. Inc., Greenwich, Prime Hospitality Corp., Fairfield, N.J. Active The Robert Steel Found., N.Y.C., Prep for Prep, N.Y.C., The Joseph Collins Found., N.Y.C., Strategic Distbn. Inc., Greenwich. Mem. ABA, N.Y. State Bar Assn., N.Y. County Lawyers Assn. Home: 250 E 54th St New York NY 10022-4810 Office: Willkie Farr & Gallagher LLP 787 7th Ave New York NY 10019-6018 E-mail: jnusbaum@willkie.com.

NUSBAUM, MARGARET REBECCA HARVEY, physician, educator, military officer; b. Feb. 5, 1959; BS, Albright Coll., 1981; DO, Ohio U., 1985; MPH, U. Wash., 1993. Commd. 2d lt. U.S. Army, 1981, advanced through grades col., 2003; intern in family medicine Dwight D. Eisenhower Army Med. Ctr., Augusta, Ga., 1985-86, resident, 1986-88, chief resident, 1987-88, dir. faculty devel., rsch. dir. asst. residency dir., 1993-95; med. dir. 757th Med. Detachment, Schwabish Gmund, Germany, 1988-91, 762nd Med. Detachment, Gottingen, Germany, 1990-91; clin. asst. prof. Madigan Army Med. Ctr., Tacoma, 1991-93; co-dir. residency program U. N.C., Chapel Hill, 1997—2005, prof., 2005—. Office Phone: 919-966-3711. Business E-Mail: mnusbaum@med.unc.edu.

NUSIM, STANLEY HERBERT, chemical engineer, consultant; b. NYC, Oct. 2, 1935; s. Seymour and Ranna T. (Weiner) Nusim; m. Marcia Anne Borsig, Feb. 21, 1960; children: David Mark, Jill Wendi. BChemE, CCNY, 1957; MChemE, N.Y. U., 1960, PhD, 1967. Rsch. engr. Battelle Meml. Inst., Columbus, Ohio, 1956; researcher, chem. engring. rsch. and devel. Merck Rsch. Labs. Div., Rahway, NJ, 1957-68, sect. mgr., 1968-70; tech. svcs. mgr. Merck Chem. Mfg. Div., Rahway, 1970-73, mfg. mgr., 1973-80; dir. subsidiary projects Merck Internat. Div., Rahway, 1981-82, exec. dir. Latin Am., Far East, Near East ops., 1982-88; exec. dir. licensee, Latin Am., Far East, Asia ops. Merck Pharm. Mfg. Div., Rahway, 1989-92; exec. dir. licensee ops. worldwide Merck Mfg. Divsn. Merck & Co. Inc., Whitehouse Station, NJ, 1992-94; v.p. mfg. and ops. Therics Inc., Princeton, NJ, 1994-97; pres. S.H. Nusim Assocs., Inc., Aventura, Fla., 1994—. Mem. adv. bd. CCNY Sch. Engring., 1982—2004; bd. dirs. AGI Dermatics Inc., Freeport, NY, 1998—. Author: Kinetic Studies on C4 Hydrocarbon Systems, 1967; editor: Active Pharmaceutical Ingredients: Development, Manufacturing and Regulation, 2005. V.p. men's club Temple Beth Shalom, Livingston, N.J., 1975-78; bd. govs. Turnberry Isle Yacht and Racquet Club, Aventura, Fla., 1992-94. Mem. Am. Inst. Chem. Engrs. (bd. dir. N. Jersey sect. 1968-71, scholarship award 1955), Am. Chem. Soc., Tau Beta Pi, Garden State Yacht Club (bd. govs. 1987-88), Otis Woodlands Club (bd. dirs. 2002-2004). Achievements include U.S. and foreign patents on the continuous manufacture of halogenated acetone, development of "clean room" concepts for API manufacturing, development of sophisticated training techniques for sterile pharmaceutical manufacturing. Office Phone: 305-935-7576. E-mail: shn@pipeline.com.

NUSINOVICH, GREGORY SEMEON, physicist, researcher; b. Berdichev, Ukraine, July 18, 1946; arrived in U.S., 1991; s. Semeon and Esther (Burdo) Nusinovich; m. Yelena Naydich, July 2, 1968; children: Maria, Liza, Paulina. MSc, Gorki U., Russia, 1968, PhD, 1975. Rsch. scientist Radiophys. Rsch. Inst., Gorky, 1968-77; sr. rsch. scientist, group leader Inst. Applied Physics, Acad. Scis. of Russia, Gorky, 1977-90; sr. rsch. scientist Inst. for Rsch. Electronics and Applied Physics, U. Md., College Park, 1991—. Mem. sci. coun. phys. electronics Acad. Scis. Russia, 1981—90; cons. Phys. Scis., Inc., Alexandria, Va., 1991—2001, Sci. Applications Internat. Corp., McLean, Va., 1991—93, 2000—, Omega-P, New Haven, 1995—2000, Calabazas Creek Rsch. Inc., Saratoga, 2003—04, Saratoga, 2006—, Stanford U., Menlo Park, 2004—05; sr. editor IEEE-PS, 2007—. Co-editor: Gyrotrons, 1980, Gyrotron, 1981, Gyrotrons, 1989, Modern Microwave and Millimeter-Wave Power Electronics, 2005, IEEE-Press-Wiley-Intersci., High Energy Density and Higher Power RF, AIP Conf. Procs. Vol. 691, 2003, High Energy Density and Higher Power RF, AIP Conf. Procs. Vol. 807, 2006; guest editor (spl. issues) IEEE-PS on high-power microwaves, 1996, IEEE-PS on cyclotron resonance masers and gyrotrons, 1999; author: Introduction to the Physics of Gyrotrons, 2004; contbr. chapters to books. Fellow: IEEE, Am. Phys. Soc. Achievements include development of the theory of multimode gyrotrons; the nonlinear theory of relativistic gyrodevices; theory of gyroamplifiers and the gyrotron producing 100 KW power at the frequency of 500 GHZ as well as numerous contrib. to the theory of various microwave sources. Office: U Md Inst Rsch Electronics and Appli Physics College Park MD 20742-3511 Business E-Mail: gregoryn@umd.edu.

NUSS, BARBARA GOUGH, artist; b. Washington, Apr. 11, 1939; d. Gaines Homer Gough and Edwerta Barbara (Beyer) Barber; m. Frederick A. Johnson, Sept. 30, 1968 (div. 1975); 1 child, Mark Eugene; m. Fred Dean Nuss, Dec. 18, 1982. BFA, Syracuse U., 1960; postgrad., Schuler Sch. Fine Arts, Balt., 1986—87. Art dir. Chappell's Dept. Store, Syracuse, NY, 1960-62, 66; mgr., illustrator Holman Anderson & Moore, Washington, 1967-70; art dir., advt. mgr. Ad-Media & Howard Advt. Assocs., Columbia, Md., 1970-75; acct. exec. Graphic Arts Inc., Alexandria, Va., 1975-77; sales mgr. The Jour. Newspapers, Washington, 1977-82; tchr., adult edn. Montgomery Coll., Rockville, Md., 1984-85; pvt. tchr. fine arts, Woodbine, Md., 1982-96; instr. Plein air painting workshop, 1998—2005. Chmn. Montgomery County Juried Art Exhibit, Rockville, 1988, Mid-Atlantic Regional Watercolor Exhibit, 1998—99; pres. Nuss Fine Arts, Inc., 1992—; judge Am. Landscape Show Art League Torpedo Factory, Alexandria, Va., 2002; judge Mountain State Forest Festival Fine Art Exhibition, Elkins, W.Va., 2002, Potomac Valley Watercolorists Ann. Juried Show, 2004, Mont. County Art Assn. Ann. Show, 2001, 04, 05. One-woman shows include Pa. State U., 1986, NIH, Bethesda, Md., 1989—90, Md. Nat. Capital Pk. and Planning Commn., 1991, Art League Gallery, Alexandria, 1992, Bendann Art Galleries, Towson, Md., 1999—2000, Troika Gallery, Easton, Md., 2004, Strathmore Hall Art Ctr., Bethesda, Md., 2004, Washington County Arts Coun. Gallery, Hagerstown, Md., 2004, Grand Style Gallery, Balt., 2004, Andrei Kushnir / Michele Taylor Gallery, N.Y.C, 2005, American Painting, Washington, DC, 2006, exhibited in group shows at Art League at the Torpedo Factory, 1987—92, 2002, Mid-Atlantic Regional Watercolor Exhbn., 1989 (Holbein award, 2006), Heritage Gallery Classical Realism, 1989—90, Art Barn Gallery, Washington, 1990, Carmen's Gallery, 1991—2000, Art Showcase 100 Md. Artists, 1991—92, Assn. pour la Promotion du Patrimoine Artistique Francais, Galerie Jean Lammelin, Argenteuil, France, 1991, Salmagundi Club 14th Ann. Exhbn., 1991, 18th Annual Exhbn., 1995, Thumb Box Exhbn., 2005, Atrium Gallery Georgetown U., Washington, 1991, 18th Ann. Exhbn., 1995, State House, Annapolis, 1996, World Trade Ctr., Balt., 1996, Bendann's Art Gallery, Towson, 1997—2002, Principle Gallery, Alexandria, 1998—2005, Miniature Painters, Sculptors and Gravers Soc. Washington, 1999, Addison/Ripley Fine Art Gallery, Washington, 1999, Rock Creek Gallery, 1999, 2001, Main St. Gallery, Annapolis, 1999—2000, Miniature Art Soc. Fla., 2000, Oil Painters Am., 2000—01, Troika Gallery, Easton, 2001—05, Washington County Arts Coun. Gallery, Hagerstown, 2001—04, Brazier Fine Art, Richmond, Va., 2002, Grand Style Gallery, Balt., 2002—04, Black Rock Ctr. for the Arts, Germantown, Md., 2003—04, Andrei Kushnir / Michele Taylor Gallery, Ellicott City, Md., and N.Y.C., 2003, MD Hall, Annapolis, Md., 2004, 2005, 2006, Washington County Mus. Fine Arts, Hagerstown, Md., 2006, Mill Atelier Gallery, Santa Fe, N.Mex., 2006, Jackson Lake Lodge, Wyo., 2006, Ratner Mus., Bethesda, Md., 2006, American Painting, Washington, DC, 2006, Illuminaria, Chatham, Mass., 2007, Represented in permanent collections Am. Coun. Edn., NIH, Bell Atlantic, Kiplinger Washington Editors, Fairhaven Retirement Cmty., Md. State Treas.'s Office, NIH; work represented in: Art from the Parks, How Did You Paint That?, 2000; author: 14 Formulas for Painting Fabulous Landscapes, 2004; contbr. chapters to books. Finalist still life competition, Artist's mag., 1996, landscape competition, 2003; recipient 1st prize for watercolor, C&O Canal Show, 1987, 1st prize for oil painting, Rockville Art League, 1987, Montgomery County Art Assn., 1983, 1989, Gaithersburg Fine Arts Assn., 1983, 1989, grand champion award for oil painting, Howard County Fair, 1989, Top 100 award for oil painting, Nat. Arts for Parks, 1989, 1991, 1992, 2001, 2006, Top 200, 1990, 1993, 1996, 2006, award of excellence, Washington Soc. Landscape Painters, 1999, 2005, Best in Show award, Nat. League Am. Pen Women, Md. Biennial Conv., 1999, 2003, 1st Prize Watercolor, 1st Prize Oils award, MAPAPA Paint Annapolis, 2003, Award of Excellence, 2004. Mem. Nat. League Am. Pen Women (sec. Bethesda, Md. 1989, treas. 2000-06, state treas. 2006), Balt. Watercolor Soc. (bd. dirs. 1997-99), Washington Soc. Landscape Painters (sec. 1999, pres. 2000-03, 07—), MidAtlantic Plein Air Painters Assn., Salmagundi Club (NYC), Oil Painters Am. (assoc.). Avocations: crossword puzzles, quilting. Home: 3132 Cabin Run Woodbine MD 21797-7933 E-mail: barbara@barbaranuss.com.

NUSS, JOANNE RUTH, artist; b. Gt. Bend, Kans., May 2, 1951; d. Melvin Oliver and Ruth Helen (Brauer) Nuss. Student, Valparaiso U., Ind., 1969—71, U. Kans., 1972—73, U. Copenhagen, 1974; BA, Ft. Hays State U., 1975; MFA, Santa Fe Inst. Fine Arts, 1991. Lectr. Noon Edition Sta. KCMO-TV, Kansas City, 1981, Menoriah Hosp., Brookridge Elem. Sch., Jill Shurin Show Telecable 10, Kansas City, 1982, Barton County CC, Gt. Bend, Nelson-Atkins Mus., Kansas City, Mo., 1984; artist-in-residence Helen Wurlitzer Found., Taos, N.Mex., 1984, Taos, 90. One-woman shows include Bette Moses Gallery, Great Bend, 1980, Art Expo Ctr., San Francisco, 1981, Univ. Gall., Ft. Hays State U., 1985, Am. Legation Mus., Tangiers, Morocco, 1986, Inma Gallery, Dhahran, Saudi Arabia, 1994, Bab Rouah Gallery, Rabat, Morocco, 1996, Agora Gallery, Soho, New York, 2001, Amsterdam Whitney Internat. Fine Art Gallery, N.Y.C., 2003, others, exhibited in group shows at Second Internat. Sculpture Fair, Boston, 1980, Joan Cooke Gallery, Kansas City, Mo., 1983, Batz Lawrence Gallery, Kansas City, 1984, Galerie de Rond Point des Champs Elyssees, Paris, 1989, Tetouan & La Kabila Gallery, Tetouan, Morocco, 1991, N.Mex. Sculptors Guild, Fuller Lodge Art Gallery, Los Alamos, 1992, Hermosas Fine Arts Gallery, Durango, Colo., 1995, Tanjah Flandria Art Gallery, Tangiers, 1997—99, Shidoni Gallery, Tesuque, N.Mex., 1999—2002, Birger Sandzen Gallery, Lindsborg, Kans., 2000, Nat. Assn. Women Artists, Sarasota Visual Arts Ctr., 2000, U. No. Iowa, Cedar Falls, 2001 (1st pl., 2001, 1st Pl. award Period Gallery, Omaha, Nebr., 2002), Coplan Gallery, Boca Raton, Fla., 2002, Attleboro (Mass.) Mus., 2002, Jeanette Hare Art Gallery, West Palm Beach, Fla., 2002, Attleboro (Mass.) Mus., 2003, Nat. Assn. Women Artists Fifth Ave. Gallery, NYC, 2003, Baker Arts Ctr., 2004, McDowell Arts and Crafts Assn., Shelby Arts, 2004—05, exhibitions include Nat. Assn. Women Artists, 2003, Baker Arts Ctr., 2004, 2005, Nat. Assn. Women Artists Travelling the Carolinas, Ashe County Arts, 2004—05, Pen & Brush 59th Annual Sculpture exhbn., N.Y.C., The Lawrence-Arnott Art Gallery, Marrakech, Morocco, 2005, 2006, Upstream People Gallery, Omaha, 2006, Longview Mus. Fin Arts, Tex., 2007, prin. works include archtl. project, Tangiers, 1988—90; featured artist Artist Spectrum Mag. Named 1st female fgn. artist commd. for archtl. major project, Tangiers, 1988—90; recipient Best 3-D Works award, Wichita Art Assn, 1983, 1st Kans. Artist Purchase award, Ft. Hays State U., 1985, 1st Pl. award, Nat. Exhbn., U. No. Iowa, 2001, Award of Excellence, 7th Annual All Media Internat. Juried Online Exhbn., Lipstream People Gallery, Omaha, 2005, Spl. Recognition award, Upstream People Gallery, 2006. Mem.: Kans. Sculptors Assn., Internat. Sculpture Ctr., Nat. Sculpture Soc., Nat. Assn. Women Artists, Internat. Platform Assn., N.Mex Women in Arts, Nat. Mus. Women in Arts. Avocations: travel, working with other artists, developing private sculpture garden.

NUSS, LAWTON R., state supreme court justice; b. Salina, Kans., Dec. 30, 1952; m. Barbara Nuss; 5 children. BA in English and History, U. Kans., 1975, JD, 1982. Atty. Clark Mize & Linville, 1982—2002; special prosecutor City of Salina, 1994—96; justice Kans. Supreme Ct., Topeka, 2002—. Former mediator U.S. Dist. Ct., Kans. Combat engring. officer USMC. Mem.: Kans. Assn. Def. Counsel (pres.), Kans. Bar Assn. (chmn. bd. editors jour.). Office: Kans Jud Ctr 301 SW 10th Topeka KS 66612-1507 *

NUSSBAUM, BENNETT, food products executive; BS in Econs., U. Pa., 1969; MBA, Columbia U., 1971. With PepsiCola Internat.; CFO Kinko's Inc., Ventura, Calif., Burger King Corp., exec. v.p.; sr. v.p. Winn-Dixie Stores, CFO. Office: Winn Dixie Stores Inc 5050 Edgewood Ct Jacksonville FL 32254 Office Phone: 904-370-6655. Business E-Mail: bennettnussbaum@winn-dixie.com.

NUSSBAUM, BERNARD J., lawyer; b. Berlin, Mar. 11, 1931; came to U.S., 1936; s. William and Lotte (Frankfurther) N.; m. Jean Beverly Enzer, Sept. 4, 1956; children: Charles, Peter, Andrew AB, Knox Coll., 1948-52; JD, U. Chgo., 1955. Assoc. Proskauer Rose Goetz & Mendelsohn, NYC, 1955-56, Sonnenschein Nath & Rosenthal LLP, Chgo., 1959-65; sr. ptnr. Sonnenschein Nath & Rosenthal, Chgo., 1965—. Master bencher Am. Inns of Ct., 1986—; appointed to com. on civility 7th cir. U.S. Ct. Appeals, 1989-92. Editor U. Chgo. Law Rev., 1954-55; mem. nat. adv. bd. BNA Civil Trial Man., 1985—; contbr. articles to profl. jours. Mem. vis. com. U. Chgo. Law Sch., 1977-83. Served to capt. U.S. Army, 1956-59 Fellow Am. Bar Found., Ill. Bar Found. (charter); mem. ABA, Chgo. Bar Assn. (chmn. com. on fed. civil procedure 1968-69, mem. com. on judiciary 1970-76), Ill. Bar Assn. (council Antitrust sect. 1971-73, assembly del. 1972-80), U. Chgo. Law Sch. Nat. Alumni Assn. (pres. 1981-83). Avocations: skiing, bicycling. Office: Sonnenschein Nath & Rosenthal LLP 7800 Sears Tower 233 S Wacker Dr Ste 8000 Chicago IL 60606-6491 Office Phone: 312-876-8039. Business E-Mail: bnussbaum@sonnenschein.com.

NUSSBAUM, BERNARD W., federal official, lawyer; b. NYC, Mar. 23, 1937; m. Toby Nussbaum; 3 children. BA, Columbia U., 1958; LLB, Harvard U., 1961; LLD (hon.), George Washington Univ., 1993. Bar: N.Y. 1962, U.S. Dist. Ct. So. N.Y. 1964, U.S. Dist. Ct. Ea. N.Y. 1973, U.S. Ct. Appeals 2d cir. 1964, U.S. Supreme Ct. 1973. Asst. U.S. atty U.S. Dist. Ct. (so. dist.), N.Y., 1962-66; atty., then sr. ptnr. Wachtell, Lipton, Rosen & Katz, NYC, 1966—; sr. staff atty. Judiciary Com., U.S. Ho. Rep., Washington, 1974; counsel to Pres. Clinton White House, Washington, 1993—94. Lectr. Columbia Law Sch. Note editor Harvard Law Review. Trustee Mt. Sinai Hosp., N.Y.C., Jewish Mus., Jewish Theological Sem. Am., Boys Brotherhood Rep. Recipient Torch of Learning lawyer's divsn. Am. Friends Hebrew U. Jerusalem, 1985; Sheldon travelling fellow Harvard U., 1961; Gould Award, Office of Appellate Def. Fellow Am. Bar Found.; mem. Assn. Bar City N.Y. (exec. com., v.p.), Fed. Bar Coun. (pres. 1991-93); Phi Beta Kappa. Office: Wachtell Lipton Rosen & Katz 51 W 52nd St New York NY 10019 Office Phone: 212-403-1266. Office Fax: 212-403-2266. Business E-Mail: BWNussbaum@wlrk.com.

NUSSBAUM, JEFFREY JOSEPH, musician; b. NYC, July 7, 1952; s. Eli and Dorothy (Wolkowitz) N.; m. Alison Knopf (div. 1984); m. Joan Feigenbaum, April 5, 1990; 1 child, Samuel Leonard Baum. BA in Music, Hunter Coll., NYC, 1977; MA in Edn., Bklyn. Coll., 1987; MFA in Early Music, Sarah Lawrence Coll., Bronxville, Tex., 1989. Cert. N.Y.S., N.Y.C. Freelance musician (trumpet, cornetto, natural trumpet), 1979—; tchr. music Park West H.S., NYC, 1984—. Pres., founder Historic Brass Soc., NY, 1989—; dir. Manhattan Early Wind Ensemble, NY, 1992—, Pan Brass Quintet, NY, 1978—84; organizer Internat. Hist. Brass Symposium, Amherst, Mass., 1995, Early Brass Colloquium, Royal Acad. Music, London, 1997, Internat. Hist. Brass Symposium, co-sponsored by Cité de la Musique, Paris, 1999, Internat. Symposium co-sponsored with Stimu, Utrecht, Germany, 2000, HBS Cometto Symposium, Bate Coll., Oxford U., joint meet with IEGB 2006 and Internat. Symposium on Early Jazz Brass music, Inst. for Jazz Studies, Rutgers U., 2005; co-organizer Toronto 2000: Musical Intersections, 2000. Author: Brass Teaching and Learning: History, Development and Technology of Brass Instruments, 1998; contbr. articles to jours. in field. Mem. Am. Fedn. Musicians, Am. Musicological Soc., Internat. Trumpet Guild, Galpin Soc. Jewish. Home: 148 W 23rd St Apt 5F New York NY 10011-2447 Business E-Mail: president@historicbrass.org.

NUSSBAUM, MICHAEL SCOT, physician, medical educator; b. Cleve., Nov. 4, 1956; s. Fritz S. and Elaine (Sukenik) N.; m. Sue Ellen Weinstein, Aug. 6, 1983; children: Jaclyn, Rachel. BA, Northwestern U., 1977; MD, U. Pa., 1981. Intern dept. surgery U. Cin., 1981-82, resident dept. surgery, 1982-86, chief resident dept. surgery, 1985-86; dir. surg. edn. Jewish Hosp., Cin., 1986-90; asst. prof. surgery U. Cin., 1986-96, assoc. prof. surgery, 1996—, asst. prof. molecular and cellular physiology, 1991—, prof. surgery, 2006—; attending physician dept. parenteral and enteral nutrition U. Cin. Hosp., 1989—, dir. surg. endoscopy and laparoscopy, 1993—2000, chief sect. gen. surgery, 1999—2003, chief of staff, 2000—, vice chmn. clin. affairs, 2003—, asst. dean for hosp. affairs, 2003—. Med. records com. Jewish Hosp. Cin., 1986-88, med. incident rev. com., 1986-92, intensive care com., 1986-2000, CPR com., 1986-92, course dir. ACLS, 1987-92, chmn. nutrition support com., 1988-2000; chmn. adverse drug reaction com. U. Cin. Hosp., 1988-92, edn. coordinating com., 1990-93, oper. rm. adv. com. 1992-2000, patient care rev. com., 1992-2000, chmn. pharmacy and therapeutics com., 1992-2000, med. co-dir. collaborative care unit, 1993—, clin., tech. and support design team, 1994—, others; ACLS subcom. Am. Heart Assn.-Southwestern Ohio Chpt., 1988-95, affiliate faculty ACLS, 1988-95; assoc. examiner The Am. Bd. Surgery, 1990, 94, 96; trauma adv. com. Ohio Emergency Med. Svcs. Bd., 1993-2000; intern chair dept. surgery, U. Cin., 2006-. Editor-in-chief: The Mont Reid Handbook, The University of Cincinnati Surgical Manual, 1987; editl. bd. mem. Current Summaries in the Jour. Parenteral and Enteral Nutrition, 1991-97; contbr. chpts. to books and articles to profl. jours. Bd. mem. Yavneh Day Sch., Cin., 1992-95. Fellow ACS (com. on trauma, instr. advanced trauma life support 1987—, Ohio chpt. chmn. resident essay contest 1994—, sec. Ohio chpt. 1997-2000, chair local arrangements 1996 annual meeting); mem. Am. Soc. for Parenteral and Enteral Nutrition (liaison com. 1993-95), Am. Trauma Soc., Assn. for Acad. Surgery (com. on edn. 1989-91, nominating com. 1992, com. on issues 1992-94, councilor 1994-96), Assn. for Surg. Edn., Ctrl. Surg. Assn. (sec. 2006-2009), Cin. Acad. Medicine, Cin. Surg. Soc. (treas. 1990-92), Collegium Interatn. Chirurgia Digestivae, Mont Reid Surg. Soc. U. Cin., Ohio Soc. for Parenteral and Enteral Nutrition (dir.-at-large 1990, pres.-elect 1991, pres. 1991-92), Ohio State Med. Assn., Pancreas Club, Inc., Soc. Am. Gastrointestinal Endoscopic Surgeons (resident edn. com. 1998—, rsch. com. 2001--, membership com. 2001--), Soc. Critical Care Medicine, Soc. for Parenteral Alimentation, Soc. for Surgery of the Alimentary Tract, Surg. Infection Soc., Soc. Univ. Surgeons (com. on surg. edn. 1998-2002, chair 1999-2002), Am. Surg. Assn., Halsted Soc., Alpha Omega Alpha. Office: Univ Cin Dept Surgery PO Box 670558 231 Albert Sabin Way Cincinnati OH 45267-0558 Office Phone: 513-558-4014. E-mail: michael.nussbaum@uc.edu.

NUSSBAUM, MICHAEL W., military officer, paramedic; b. Buffalo, Oct. 24, 1974; s. George Frederick and Carol Lynn Nussbaum; m. Heathre H. Litz, Sept. 21, 2002; children: James Eldon, Ellina Oslyn. Lic. EMT, paramedic Niagara CC, Sauborn, NY, 2000. Inf. US Army, Bamhelder, Germany, 1993—96; paramedic, dir. EMS Cmty. Ambulance, Sauborn, 1996—2006; paramedic Twin City Ambulance, Tonananda, NY, 1997—2006; EMT instr. Niagara CC, Sauborn, 2001—06; paramedic Lancaster Ambulance, 2001—06; combat medic US Army, Houston, 2006—. Vol. firefighter. Recipient Best Save award, Mt. St. Mary's Hosp., Lewisten, NY, 2002, EMS Achievement award, 2006. Mem.: VFW, Am. Legion. Republican. Avocation: hockey.

NUSSBAUM, MICHEL ERNEST, physician; b. LA, Nov. 7, 1947; s. Schymen and Jeannette Eleanor (Pequignot) N.; m. Joyce Wendy Laudon, Nov. 1, 1981; children: Eleanor, Anna. BA, Cornell U., 1969; MD, Free U. Brussels, 1977. Intern internal medicine NY Hosp. Queens, Flushing, 1977-78, resident, 1978-80, fellow gastroenterology, 1980-82, attending physician, 1982—; physician pvt. practice, Flushing, NY, 1982—; attending physician Flushing Hosp. Med. Ctr., 1987—; clin. instr. medicine Weill Med. Coll. Cornell U., NYC, 1994-98, clin. asst. prof. medicine, 1998—; med. dir. Franklin Ctr. for Nursing and Rehab., Flushing, 1995-99. Dir. endoscopic svcs. N.Y. Hosp. Queens, 1990—, asst. dir. gastroenterology, 1998-2004, assoc. dir. gastroenterology, 2004—, pres. med. staff soc.,

1992-96, chmn. med. bd., 1997-2003, trustee, 1998-2003 Fellow: ACP, Am. Gastroent. Assn., Am. Coll. Gastroenterology. Office: 142-43 Booth Memorial Ave Flushing NY 11355-5343 Home Phone: 212-254-9549; Office Phone: 718-886-1919.

NUSSBAUM, PAUL M., lawyer; b. Bklyn., 1959; BA, Fairleigh Dickinson U., 1980; JD cum laude, Calif. Western Sch. Law, 1984. EIT; bar: NY 1984, NJ 1984, Md. 1988, US Ct. Appeals, US Bankruptcy Ct., US Dist. Ct. (so. and ea. dists. NY), US Dist. Ct. (dist. NJ), US Dist. Ct. (dist. Md.). Law clk. to Hon. Prudence B. Abram US Bankruptcy Ct. (so. dist. NY), 1984—85; ptnr. Whiteford, Taylor & Preston, LLP, head Debtor/Creditor Rights and Bankruptcy Dept. Named one of Best Lawyers in Am., 2000; recipient Am. Jurisprudence Award in Bankruptcy, Contracts and Remedies. Mem.: ABA, Md. Inst. Continuing Profl. Edn. Lawyers, Bankruptcy Bar Assn. Office: Whiteford, Taylor & Preston Seven Saint Paul St Baltimore MD 21202-1626 Office Phone: 410-347-8974. Office Fax: 410-223-4394. E-mail: pnussbaum@wtplaw.com. *

NUSSBAUM, PAUL STOWELL, retired urologist; b. St. Louis, Mo., Sept. 25, 1930; s. Paul Beckman and Claire Stevenson Nussbaum; m. Joyce Lee Linebarger, May 27, 1955; children: Paul Stevenson, John Michael, David Matthew, Barbara Lee. Academic diploma, Castle Heights Mil. Acad., Lebanon, Tenn., 1948; AB in Biol. Scis., S.E. Mo. State Coll., Cape Girardeau, 1952; MD, U. Tenn. Coll. Medicine, Memphis, 1955. Cert. Am. Bd. Urology. Chief urology U.S. Army Hosp., Ft. Leonard Wood, Mo., 1961—64; pvt. practice urology Cape Girardeau, Mo., 1965—67; program dir. urology Scott White Meml. Hosp., Temple, Tex., 1967—77; pvt. practice urology Santa Fe, 1977—87; ret. Cons. urology U.S. Vets. Adminstrn., Marion, Ill., 1965—69, Temple, Tex., 1969—77. Author: (med. jour.) Surgery, Gynecology and Obstetrics. Maj. US Army, 1957—64. Fellow: ACS; mem.: Am. Urol. Assn. (sr.), Masonic, Scottish Rite, Order of Ea. Star (Santa Fe #19, Past Patron). Republican. Methodist. Avocations: flying, hunting, fishing, sailing, golf. Home: 102 Pinehurst Meadowlakes TX 78654-6416

NUSSBAUM, ROBERT L., senior genetics investigator; AB, Harvard Coll., 1971; MD, Harvard Med. Sch., 1975. Intern in internal medicine Washington U. and Barnes Coll., St. Louis, 1975—78; genetics fellow Baylor Coll. Medicine, Houston, 1978—81, asst. prof. medicine, 1981—84; assoc. investigator Howard Hughes Med. Inst., Chevy Chase, Md., 1984—93; with Nat. Human Genome Rsch. Inst., Bethesda, Md., 1993—, sr. investigator, chief, genetic disease rsch. br. Exec. faculty mem. NIH-Johns Hopkins U. Genetic Counseling Training Program. Mem.: Inst. Medicine. Office: Nat Human Genome Rsch Inst MSC 4472 40 Convent Dr Bldg 49 Bethesda MD 20892-4472 Office Phone: 301-402-2039. Office Fax: 301-402-2170. E-mail: rlnuss@nhgri.nih.gov.

NUSSBAUM, SAMUEL R., healthcare insurance company executive, medical educator; MD, Mt. Sinai Sch. Medicine. Prof. Harvard Med. Sch.; sr. v.p. health care delivery Blue Cross Blue Shield Mass.; pres., CEO Physician Partners of New Eng.; CEO health plan, pres. med. grp. BJC Health Sys., 1996—2000, exec. v.p. med. affairs and sys. integration, 1996—2000; exec. v.p., chief med. officer WellPoint, Inc., Indpls., 2001—. Chmn. Nat. Com. Quality Health Care; chair Chief Med. Officer Leadership Coun. Am.'s Health Ins. Plan, bd. mem.; chmn. health care data and quality subcommittee Ind. Commn. on Excellence in Health Care; prof. clin. medicine Washington U. Sch. Medicine; adj. prof. Washington U. Olin Sch. Bus. Recipient Physician Exec. Award of Excellence, Am. Coll. Physician Execs. and Modern Physician mag., 2004. Mem.: Disease Mgmt. Assn. Am. Office: WellPoint Inc 120 Monument Cir Indianapolis IN 46204 *

NUSSENZWEIG, MICHEL CLAUDIO, immunologist, educator; BA, NYU; PhD, Rockefeller Univ., NYC; MD, NYU Med. Sch. Faculty Rockefeller Univ., 1990—. Sherman Fairchild prof. immunology, and head, immunology sect., 2001—; also investigator Howard Hughes Med. Inst., 1990—. Recipient Solomon A. Berson award for basic sci., Huang Found. Meritorious Career award, Am. Assn. Immunologists. Fellow: Am. Acad. Arts & Scis. Office: Rockefeller Univ 1230 York Ave New York NY 10021 Office Phone: 212-327-8000. Business E-Mail: nussen@rockefeller.edu. *

NUSSLE, JIM (JAMES ALLEN NUSSLE), former congressman; b. Des Moines, June 27, 1960; s. Mark S. and Lorna Kay (Fisher) N.; m. Leslie J. Harbison, Aug. 23, 1986 (div. July 2, 1996); children: Sarah, Mark; m. Karen Chiccehitto, 2001 BA, Luther Coll., Decorah, Iowa, 1983; JD, Drake U., 1985. Bar: Iowa 1985. Pvt. practice law, Manchester, Iowa, 1986; states atty. Delaware County Atty., Manchester, 1986-90; mem. US Congress from 2nd Iowa dist., Washington, 1991—2007, mem. house ways & means com., chmn. budget com., 2001—06; adv. Rudolph Guiliani Presdl. Exploratory Com., NYC, 2007—. Republican. Lutheran. Avocation: guitar. Office: Rudolph Guiliani Presdl Exploratory Com 295 Greenwich St #371 New York NY 10007 *

NÜSSLEIN-VOLHARD, CHRISTIANE, medical researcher; b. Magdeburg, Germany, Oct. 20, 1942; d. Rolf Volhard and Brigitte (Haas) Volhard. Diploma in Biochemistry, U. Tübingen, 1968, PhD, 1973; ScD (hon.), Yale U. Rsch. assoc. lab. of Dr. Schaller Max-Planck Inst. for Devel. Biology, Tübingen, 1972-74; postdoctoral fellow lab. of Dr. W. Gehring, Biozentrum, Basel, Switzerland, 1975-76; postdoctoral fellow lab of Dr. K. Sander U. Freiburg, 1977; head rsch. group European Molecular Biology Lab., Heidelberg, 1978-80; rsch. group leader Friedrich-Miescher Lab. Max-Planck-Gesellschaft, Tübingen, 1981-85; sci. mem. Max-Planck Assn., dir. Max-Planck Inst. for Devel. Biology, Tübingen, 1985-90, dir. genetics dept., 1990—. Hon. prof. U. Tübingen. Contbr. numerous articles to profl. jours. Recipient Albert Lasker Basic Med. Rsch. award Albert and Mary Lasker Found., 1991, Louisa Gross Horowitz prize Columbia U., 1992, Forderpreis award Deutschen Forschungsgemeinschaft, 1986, Franz Vogt prize U. Giessen, 1986, Carus medal German Acad. Leopoldine, 1989, Schering prize, Berlin, 1993, Rosenstiel medal Brandeis U., Nobel prize in physiology or medicine, 1995, L'oréal-UNESCO Tribute award (for UNESCO's 60th anniversary), 2006. Mem. European Molecular Biology Orgn., Berlin Brandenburgische Acad., Am. Philosophical Soc. Achievements include rsch. in using embryos, created a series of genetic screens that led to the identification of most of the genes responsible for the organism's body segment development, establishing that genes encode signaling molecules that tell cells where they are in the organism's overall structure and what their function is to be. Office: Max-Planck-Institut fur Entwicklungsbiologie Abt III Genetik D-72076 Tübingen Germany

NUSUM, JOHN BARRY, professional soccer player; b. Mineola, NY, Mar. 18, 1981; s. John (former profl. soccer player, MISL and NASL) and Ellvera (Robinson) N. Grad. in Health and Exercise sci., Furman U., Greenville, SC, 2002. Forward Men's Soccer Team, Furman U., 1998—2002, Bermuda Nat. Team, 1999—. Mem. Umbro Select All-Star Classic, Ft. Lauderale, Fla., 2000—01. Named first team All-American, NSCAA, 1999, 2000, All-Southern Conf. Player of Yr., 2001; recipient first team All-American, NSCAA, 2001, Finalist, Hermann Trophy, MO Athletic Club, 2001, Finalist, Player of Yr. award, 2001. 22nd player in the NCAA history to earn 2 First-team All-American Citations; All-time leader in points (161), Men's Soccer, Furman U., 2001; All-time leader in goals (61), Men's Soccer, Furman U., 2001.

NUTAN, MOHAMMAD TAWHIDUL HAQUE, pharmacy educator, researcher; b. Bangladesh, July 12, 1972; s. Enamul and Fatema Haque; m. Manna Salowa, 2000; 1 child, Mohammad Muhitul Haque (Arnob). B of Pharmacy, U. Dhaka, Bangladesh, 1994, PharmM, 1997; PhD, Tex. Tech U. Health Scis. Ctr., Amarillo, 2004. FPFEC cert. Nat. Assn. of Bds. of Pharmacy, 2004. Lectr. dept. pharmacy U. Asia Pacific, Dhaka, Bangladesh, 1997; lectr. pharmacy discipline Khulna U., Bangladesh, 1997—2000; grad. pharmacy intern Walgreen Co., Miami, Fla., 2004—06; tchr, rsch. asst. sch. pharmacy Tex. Tech U. Health Scis. Ctr., Amarillo, 2000—04; asst. prof. Tex. A&M U. Health Scis. Ctr., Irma Lerma Rangel Coll. Pharmacy, Kingsville, Tex., 2006—. Chair, pharms. faculty search com. Tex. A&M U. Health Scis. Ctr. Coll. Pharmacy, Kingsville, 2006—, mem., acad. credentialing com., 2006—, mem., curriculum affair com., 2006—, advisor PharmD students, 2006—. Contbr. articles to scientific jours. Mem.: Am. Assn. Coll. Pharmacy, Am. Assn. Pharm. Scientists, Bangladesh Pharm. Soc., Pharmacy Grad. Assn. Bangladesh. Achievements include research in developed a controlled release multi-particulate formulation coated with starch acetate; developed a limonene-based coenzyme Q-10 self-nanoemulsified dosage form; developed an enteric dual-controlled gastrointestinal therapeutic system of salmon calcitonin; developed a cellulose acetate butyrate dispersion for controlled release coating; discovery of isolated a new alkaloid, Bismurrayafoline E, from plant source. Avocations: astronomy, geography, reading, travel, movies. Office: Texas A&M Coll Pharmacy 1010 West Ave B MSC 131 Kingsville TX 78363

NUTI, WILLIAM R., computer services company executive; married; 1 child. BS in Fin. and Economics, Long Island U., 1986. Various sales positions to sr. sales staff mem. IBM, 1982—88; sales mgr. Network Equipment Technologies, 1988—90, Netrix Corp., 1990—92; with Cisco Systems, 1992—2002, v.p. then pres. Greater Asia Pacific region, sr. v.p., pres. Europe, Middle East and Africa ops. London, 1999—2001, sr. v.p. worldwide service provider bus. and US theatre ops., 2001—02; pres., COO Symbol Tech., Holtsville, NY, 2002—03, pres., CEO, 2003—05; pres. & CEO NCR Corp., Dayton, Ohio, 2005—. Bd. dirs. Opus 360, 1999—. Bd. dir. Fair Media Council; trustee Long Island U. Office: NCR Corp 1700 S Patterson Blvd Dayton OH 45479 *

NUTILE, DAVID ALBERT, retired information security and systems consultant; b. New Haven, Feb. 3, 1942; s. Albert Joseph Nutile and Helen Josephine Moore. BS in Physics, Fairfield U., Conn., 1964; MS in Engring., Cath. U., Washington, 1977. Rsch. asst. Columbia U., NYC, 1965—68; rsch. physicist Naval Rsch. Lab., Washington, 1968—82, electronic engr., 1983—87; computer specialist U.S. Naval Obs., Washington, 1987—98; sr. info. tech. security cons. Network Resources, Charlotte, NC, 1999—2000; pvt. practice info. sys. cons. part-time Alexandria, Va., 2000—. Sr. info. resource mgmt. ofcl. U.S. Naval Obs., Washington, 1991—98. Contbr. articles to profl. jours. Recipient Rsch. Publ. award, Naval Rsch. Lab., 1974. Mem.: IEEE Computer Soc., Sci. Rsch. Soc. Am., Acoustical Soc. Am. (emeritus 2006), KC. Avocations: computer imaging, golf, bowling, writing. Home: 6300 Hillview Ave Alexandria VA 22310

NUTT, HOUSTON, university football coach; b. Oct. 14, 1957; m. Diana Nutt; children: Houston, Hailey, Hanna, Haven. Grad., Okla. St. Univ., 1981. Former grad. asst. Arkansas Univ., wide receivers coach, 1990—93, head coach, 1998—; former grad. asst. Okla. St. Univ., receivers coach, 1984, offensive coord., 1989; head coach Murray St., 1993—96, Boise State, 1996—98. Office: Univ Arkansas Athletics Fayetteville AR 72701 *

NUTT, ROBERT L., lawyer, educator; b. New Castle, Pa., Mar. 30, 1945; s. James Earl and Dorothy Nutt; children: David, Jonathan. BA, Grove City Coll., 1967; JD, U. Pa., 1970. Bar: N.Y., Mass. Law clerk U.S. Ct. Appeals (2d cir.), NYC, 1970-71; assoc. Ropes & Gray, Boston, 1971-79, ptnr., 1979—. Lectr. in law Boston U., 1989-98. Contbr. articles to profl. jours. Trustee Shore County Day Sch., Beverly, Mass., 1986-2001; moderator First Ch. of Christ, Marblehead, Mass., 1993-2000; trustee Grove City Coll., 1998—. Mem. ABA (bus. law sect. sec. com. on corp. laws), Boston Bar Assn. (bus. law sect. chair 1990-93). Congregationalist. Avocations: skiing, golf, upland bird hunting. Office: Ropes & Gray LLP One International Pl Boston MA 02110-2624 Office Phone: 617-951-7384. Business E-Mail: rnutt@ropesgray.com.

NUTT, SANDRA KAY, elementary school educator; b. Ashland, Wis., Dec. 3, 1955; d. Arthur Arnold and Myra Marie Riemer; m. Rickard Lee Nutt, June 14, 1975; children: Bonnie Lee, Katy Lynn. BA, Northland Coll., 1976; MS in Tchg. Reading, U. Wis., Superior, 1981. Cert. K-8 tchr. Wis., reading tchr. Wis. Kindergarten tchr. Mellen (Wis.) Sch. Dist., 1980—82; tchr. Ashland (Wis.) Sch. Dist., 1977—79; tchr. grades 1-2 South Shore Sch. Dist., Herbster, Wis., 1979—80; tchr. grades kindergarten, 1 and 6 Ondossagon Pub. Schs., Ashland, 1982—90; 1st grade tchr. Washburn (Wis.) Pub. Schools, 1990—, Title 1 and sage tchr., 2003—05. Adj. faculty mem. Northland Coll., Ashland, 1982—83; home trainer United Cerebral Palsy, Superior, 1978—79. Leader Brunswillow Busy Beavers 4-H Club, Marengo, Wis., 1988—; communicator Thrivent Fin. Lutherans, Ashland, 2000—; pres.and ch. rep. Luth. Brotherhood, Ashland, 1984—2000; advisor to youth group Zion Luth. Ch., Ashland, 2002—, sec. ch. coun., mem. evangelism bd., Sunday sch. tchr.,vacation bible sch. tchr. Named Fraser Tchr. of Yr., Washburn Sch. Dist., 1993, Thrivent Fin. Vol. Yr., Thrivent Fin. Lutherans Superior Shores Chpt., 2005; recipient Thrivent Fin. Vol. Yr. award, Thrivent Fin. Lutherans, Wis., 2006. Mem.: Washburn Edn. Assn. (treas. 2002—04), Wis. State Reading Assn., Internat. Reading Assn., Ashland County 4-H Parent Leader Orgn. (4-H Vol. of Yr. 2004, 2005). Lutheran. Avocations: travel, hosting exchange students. Office: Washburn Pub Schs 411 W 8th St Washburn WI 54891

NUTTALL, RICHARD NORRIS, management consultant, physician; b. Hamilton, Ont., Can., Feb. 7, 1940; s. James William and Margaret Gay (Walsh) N.; m. Ethel Jane Pickering, July 9, 1977; children: Andrew Richard, John Patrick. BSA, U. Toronto, 1961; MPA, Harvard U., 1964; MB, BS, U. London, 1974; TM, MPH, James Cook U., 2003; MSc, U. Western Ont., 2005. Cert. mgmt. cons. Zone dir. Health and Welfare Can., Prince Rupert, B.C., 1977-79, regional dir. Edmonton, Alta., 1980-82; pres. Rutland Consulting Group, Ltd., Vancouver, B.C., Canada, 1982-87, Richmond Assocs. Internat., Vancouver, 1988-90; med. health officer Govt. N.W. Ters., Yellowknife, B.C., Canada, 1990-93, Regina (Can.) Health Dist., 1993-97; pres. Anjohn Med. Svcs., Inc., Victoria, Canada, 1997—. Staff physician Royal Jubilee Hosp. Fellow Am. Coll. Preventive Medicine, Am. Coll. Healthcare Execs., Can. Coll. Health Svc. Execs., Coll. Family Physicians Can. Office: 1494 Fairfield Rd Victoria BC Canada V8S 1E8 Office Phone: 250-598-5158.

NUTTER, DAVID GEORGE, city planner; b. Manchester, Conn., Nov. 25, 1939; s. George Huitt and Catherine Lavina (Casey) N.; m. Ellen Marie Manfredonia, Sept. 7, 1968; children: Susan Katherine Bailey, Anne Amelia. Student in Ancient Greek and Modern Drama, Brandeis U., Waltham, Mass., 1960; BA in English cum laude, Tufts U., Medford, Mass., 1961; MS in Urban Planning, Columbia U., NYC, 1967, postgrad., 1974; postgrad. in Real Estate Law and Constrn. Mgmt., Johns Hopkins U., Balt., 1974; cert. in real estate mkt. analysis, Urban Land Inst., 1986. Cert. real estate appraiser Am. Inst. Real Estate Appraisal, 1977. City planner Balt. City Planning Commn., 1967-69; dir. planning Charles Ctr.- Inner Harbor Mgmt., Inc., 1969-72, v.p., 1972-76; pvt. cons., 1976-83; dir. downtown mall mgmt. dist. Denver Partnership, Inc., 1983-85; exec. dir. Rochester Downtown Devel. Corp., NY, 1985-87; prin. Nutter Assocs., 1987-2000; dir. Salisbury-Wicomico Planning and Zoning Commn., Md., 2000—02; prin. Nutter Assocs., 2002—. Author: Selecting a Developer, 1983, Vienna-on-the Nanticoke: The 2003 Greater Vienna Comprehensive Plan, 2003, Laurel of Delaware: The 2004 Greater Laurel Comprehensive Plan, 2004, Ellendale of the Forest:The 2004 Greater Ellendale Comprehensive Plan, 2004, Town of the Railroad: The 2007 Town of Houston Comprehensive Plan, 2007. Bd. dirs. Soc. Preservation of Fed. Hill, Balt., 1969-73, Arts for Greater Rochester, 1986-90, Nabb Rsch. Ctr. Delmarva History and Culture, Salisbury U., Md., 1998-03, Lower Eastern Shore Heritage Com., 2000-02; chmn. Town of Brighton Conservation Bd., NY, 1992-95. Sgt. US Army, 513th Army Intelligence Corps, 1962-65, Germany. William F. Kinne fellow for travel in Europe, Columbia U., 1967. Mem. Am. Inst. Cert. Planners, Am. Planning Assn., Chesapeake Bay Found., Canal Soc. NY State. Avocations: American English and World history, hiking, swimming, travel. Home: 507C South Blvd Salisbury MD 21801 Office Phone: 443-270-2760. Personal E-mail: dnutter@aol.com.

NUTTER, SUSAN K., librarian, academic administrator; b. Boston, Aug. 9, 1944; m. Joe Hewitt, 1982; stepchildren: Kirsten Elizabeth Hewitt(dec.), Stephen A. Hewitt. BS, Colby Coll., 1966; MLIS, Simmons Coll., 1968. Libr. intern to libr. Project INTREX MIT, 1966—73, assoc. head engring. libraries, assoc. dir. libraries collection mgmt. and technol. services, 1980—87; Coun. on Libr. Resources Academic Libr. Mgmt. Intern U. NC, Chapel Hill, 1979—80; dir. libraries NC State U., Raleigh, 1987—, vice provost, 1995—. Mem. steering com. NC Libraries for Virtual Edn. (NC LIVE); mem. exec. com., governing bd. Triangle Rsch. Libraries Network. Named Libr. of Yr., Libr. Jour., 2005; recipient Alumni Achievement Award, Simmons Coll., 1995, Hugh C. Atkinson Meml. Medal, Assn. College & Rsch. Libraries, 1999. Mem.: Assn. Rsch. Libraries (pres. 1993). Office: DH Hill Libr NC State U Campus Box 7111 Raleigh NC 27695-7111 Office Phone: 919-515-7188. Office Fax: 919-515-3628. Business E-Mail: susan_nutter@ncsu.edu. *

NUTTER, ZOE DELL LANTIS, retired public relations executive; b. Yamhill, Oreg., June 14, 1915; d. Arthur Lee Lantis and Olive Adelaide (Reed) Lantis-Hilton; m. Richard S. West, Apr. 30, 1941 (div. Nov. 1964); m. Ervin John Nutter, Dec. 30, 1965. Assoc. in Bus., Santa Ana Jr. Coll., 1944. Cert. spl. emergency secondary tchr., Calif.; FAA cert. lic. commercial, instrument, single/multi engine land airplanes pilot. Promoter World's Fair & Comml. Airlines Golden Gate Internat. Expn., San Francisco, 1937-39; pirate theme girl, official hostess Treasure Island's World Fair, San Francisco, 1939-40; prin. dancer San Francisco Ballet, 1937-41; artist, 1941-45; program dir. Glenn County H.S., Willows, Calif., 1952-58; pub. rels. Monarch Piper Aviation Co., Monterey, Calif., 1963-65; pilot, pub. rels. Elano Corp., Xenia, Ohio, 1968-85. Bd. dirs. Nat. Aviation Hall of Fame, Dayton, Ohio, pres., chmn., 1989-92, bd. trustees, 1976—, chmn. bd. nominations, 1992—; bd. trustees Ford's Theatre, Washington, Treasure Island Mus., San Francisco; charter mem. Friends of First Ladies, Smithsonian, Washington, 1990-93. Assoc. editor KYH mag. of Shikar Safari Internat., 1985-87; contbg. columnist Scripps Howard San Francisco News, 1938. Bd. dirs. Cin. May Festival, 1976-80, San Francisco Aero. Soc., 1997-; cen. com. Glenn County Rep. Party, Willows, 1960-64; state cen. com. Rep. Party, 1962-64; adv. bd. Women's Air & Space Mus., Dayton, 1987-94. Warrant officer, Civil Air Patrol, 1967-69. Recipient Civic Contbn. Honor award Big Brothers/Big Sisters, 1991, John Collier Nat. award Camp Fire Girls & Boys, 1988, Tambourine award Salvation Army, 1982, State of Ohio Gov.'s award for Volunteerism, 1992, Spirit of Innovation award Wright State U., 2001, Amb. award Wright Bros. Heritage Benefit, 2001, East Ann. Zoe Dell Nutter Dayton Air Show award, 2003, In grateful appreciation of contbn. 1909 Wright Flyer Monument award Inventing Flight (orgn. charted by Congress), 2003, Deeds-Kettering award Outstanding Contbn., Engrs. CLub Dayton, 2004; named Most Photographed Girl in World, News Burs. & Clipping Svcs., 1938-39. Mem., founder Dancers Over 40, NYC; Fellow Pres.'s Club U. Ky., Ohio State U., Wright State U.; mem. 99's Internat. Women Pilots Orgn. (life, hospitality chmn. 1968), San Francisco Aeronaut. Soc. (bd. dirs. 1997—), Monterey Bay Chapter 99's (mem. chmn. 1964-65), Walnut Grove Country Club, Rotary (Paul Harris fellow 1987), Shikar Safari Internat. (host com. 1976), Country Club of the North. Achievements include established ann. Zoe Dell Nutter Dayton Air Show award, 2003. Avocations: aviation, flying, horseback riding, hunting, shooting, fashion. Home: 986 Trebein Rd Xenia OH 45385-9534

NUTTING, MAUREEN MURPHY, historian, educator; b. NYC; d. Patrick Joseph and Marie (Clarke) Murphy; m. Theodore Michael Nutting, May 3 1975; children: Teresa, Andrew, Stephen, Eileen. BA in History, Fordham U., 1968; MA in Am. Studies, U. Notre Dame, 1969, PhD in History, 1975. Asst. prof. history Humboldt State U., Arcata, Calif., 1972—75, Chaminade U., Honolulu, 1975—77; asst. dir. minorities & women's scholarly & profl. interests Am. Hist. Assn., Washington, 1979—81; asst. prof. history U. Miami, Coral Gables, Fla., 1987—90, Seattle U., 1990—91; instr. history Seattle Ctrl. C.C., 1992—96; prof. history, chair North Seattle C.C., 1996—. Vol. Seattle Pub. Sch. Dist., 1982—86, 1990—98; chair local draft bd. U.S. Selective Svc., Seattle, 1998—2006, local draft bd., 1992—2006; trustee Nat. History Ctr., 2004—; vol. homeless ministry St. James Cathedral, Seattle, 1994—; bd. dirs. HistoryLink.org, 2005—. Rsch. Travel grant Asian Studies Devel. Program, East-West Ctr., China, 1996, India, 1995, Summer Inst. grant NEH, Hawaii, 1994, Brazil, 1998, Guatemala, Honduras and Mex., 2002, Trustees' Lifetime Learning award Seattle C.C. Dist., 1999; selected rsch. seminar Libr. of Congress, Am. Hist. Assn., C.C. Humanities Assn., Washington, 1999. Mem.: Coordinating Coun. for Women's History, We. Assn. Women Historians, Immigration and Ethnic History Soc. (program com. 1999—2002), C.C. Humanities Assn. (chair nat. conf. program 2001, Disting. Humanities Educator award 2005), Orgn. Am. Historians (com. on cmty.colls. 2006—, chair 2007—), Am. Hist. Assn. (mem. coun. 2001—04, task force on pub. history 2001—, nat. history ctr. bd. 2004—, chair ann. meeting local arrangements com. 2005). Roman Catholic. Office: North Seattle CC 9600 College Way N Seattle WA 98103-3514 Office Phone: 206-526-7010. Business E-Mail: mnutting@sccd.ctc.edu.

NUTZLE, FUTZIE (BRUCE JOHN KLEINSMITH), artist, writer, animator; b. Lakewood, Ohio, Feb. 21, 1942; s. Adrian Ralph and Naomi Irene Kleinsmith; children: Adrian David, Ariel Justine and Tess Alexandra (twins); m. Halina Pochron Kleinsmith. Author: Modern Loafer, Thames and Hudson, 1981, (authobiography) Futzie Nutzle, 1983, Earthquake, 1989, Run the World: 50 Cents Chronicle Books, 1991; illustrator: The Armies Encamped Beyond Unfinished Avenues (Morton Marcus), 1977, Box of Nothing, 1982, The Duke of Chemical Birds (Howard McCord), 1989, Book of Solutions, 1990, Fact and Friction, 1990, Managing for the 90s, 1992, Soundbites for Success, 1994; feature cartoonist Rolling Stone, N.Y.C., 1975-80, The Japan Times, Tokyo and L.A., 1986-98, The Prague Post, Czechoslovakia, 1991-92; contbr. exhbns. include Inaugural, 1966, Cupola, 1967, Rolling Renaissance, San Francisco, 1968, 100 Acres, O.K. Harris 1971, N.Y.C., San Francisco Mus. Art, 1972, Indpls. and Cin. Mus. Art, 1975, Leica, L.A., 1978, Santa Barbara Mus. Annex, Calif., 1978, Swope, Santa Monica, West Beach Cafe, Venice, Calif., 1985, Les Oranges, Santa Monica, Correspondence Sch., NY Correspondence Sch., 1968-75, 1st Ann. Art-A-Thon, N.Y.C., 1985, Am. Epiphany with Phillip Hefferton, 1986, Polit. Cartoon Show, Braunstein, San Francisco, Komsomolskaya Pravda, 1988, retrospective Eloise Packard Smith, 1990, exemplary contemporary, Cowell, U. Calif. Santa Cruz, 1991, Silicon Graphics Inc., Computer Graphics for NAB, Las Vegas, 1993, Prague Eco-Fair, 1991; represented in pvt. and pub. collections (complete archives) Spl. Collections, McHenry Libr., U. Calif., Santa Cruz, Mus. Modern Art, N.Y.C., San Francisco Mus. Modern Art, Oakland Mus., San Francisco

Mus. Cartoon Art, Whitney Mus. Am. Art, N.Y.C., Aromas (Calif.) Libr., San Juan Bautista Libr. Address: Fools Gold 34A Polk St PO Box 1083 San Juan Bautista CA 95045 Office Phone: 831-623-9275. Personal E-mail: fnutzle@aol.com.

NUWER, HENRY JOSEPH (HANK NUWER), journalist, educator; b. Buffalo, Aug. 19, 1946; s. Henry Robert and Teresa (Lysiak) N.; m. Alice May (Cerniglia), Dec. 28, 1968 (div. Mar. 1980); 1 child, Henry Christian; m. Jenine (Howard), Apr. 9, 1982 (div. 2004); 1 child, Adam.;m. Lizabeth Klein, Aug. 9, 2005. BS in English, State U. Coll. NY, Buffalo, 1968, DHL, 2006; MA in English, Highlands U., Las Vegas, 1971; PhD Equivalency, Ball State U., Muncie, Ind., 1988. H.S. tchr., NY, 1968—69, N.Mex., 1970—71; freelance author, journalist, 1969—; asst. prof. Clemson U., SC, 1982—83; assoc. prof. Ball State U., Muncie, Ind., 1985—89; sr. editor Rodale Press, Emmaus, Pa., 1990—91; editor in chief Arts Ind. Mag., Indpls., 1993—95; assoc. prof. journalism U. Richmond, Va., 1995—97. Expert lectr. Hazing, 1990—; hazing cons. NBC Movie-of-the-Week, Moment of Truth: Broken Pledges, Indpls., 1994, U.S. Dept. Edn., 2002—; adj. prof. journalism Ind. U. Sch. Journalism, Indpls., 1995—; Anderson U., 1998-2002; asst. prof. journalism, Franklin (Ind.) Coll., 2002—; nat. advisor NCAA study and survey on hazing in coll. athletic groups Alfred U., 1999. Author: Steroids, 1990; Broken Pledges: The Deadly Rite of Hazing, 1990; How to Write Like an Expert, 1995; The Legend of Jesse Owens, 1998; Wrongs of Passage, 1999, rev. edit., 2002; High School Hazing, 2000, To the Young Writer, 2002, The Hazing Reader, 2003, At the Crest, 2004; mem. editl. staff Reporter Dispatch, 1969-70, Chic Mag., 1976-77; contbr. articles to profl. jour. Grantee: Nat. Endowment for the Arts, 1976; Idaho Humanities Coun., 1985; Gannett Found., 1988; named New Mag. Adviser of Yr., Coll. Media Advisers, 1988; Disting. Alumnus, Buffalo State Coll., 1999. Mem.: SAR, Investigative Reporters and Editors, Soc. Profl. Journalists (3d pl. Best Bus. Article Ind. competition 2002), Sons of Am. Legion, Sigma Tau Rho, Alpha Lambda Delta, Phi Kappa Phi. Democrat. Roman Catholic. Office: Franklin Coll Journalism Dept 101Branigin Blvd Franklin IN 46131-2598 also: Ind Univ Sch Journalism 902 W New York St ES 4104 Indianapolis IN 46202 Business E-Mail: hnuwer@hanknuwer.com.

NUZUM, ROBERT WESTON, lawyer; b. Evanston, Ill., Dec. 11, 1952; s. John Weston and Janet Marie (Talbot) N.; m. Julia Ann Abadie, Sept. 16, 1983. BS in Fin., La. State U., 1974, JD, 1977; LLM in Taxation, N.Y.U., 1978. Bar: La. 1977, D.C. 1979. Assoc. Office Chief Counsel, Washington, 1978-81, Jones, Walker, Waechter, Poitevent, Carrere & Denegre, New Orleans, 1981-85; ptnr. Jones, Walker, Waechter, Potevent, Carrere & Denegre, New Orleans, 1985-88, Deutsch, Kerrigan & Stiles, New Orleans, 1988-89, Phelps Dunbar, L.L.P. and predecessor firm, New Orleans, 1989—2003, Baker, Donelson, Bearman, Caldwell and Berkowitz, 2003—. Prof. law, state and local taxation Tulane U. Sch. Law, New Orleans, 1998—. Editor La. Law Rev., 1977; contbr. articles to profl. jours. Wallace scholar N.Y.U., 1978. Mem.: Tulane Tax Inst. (planning com. 1993—, tax specialization adv. commn.), New Orleans Bar Assn. (chmn. tax sect. 2001—), La. Bar Assn. (program chmn. tax sect. 1992—93, sec.-treas. 1993—94, vice chmn. 1994—95, chmn. 1995—96), Order of Coif. Republican. Roman Catholic. Avocations: golf, reading, fishing. Office: Baker Donelson Ste 3600 201 St Charles Ave New Orleans LA 70170 Business E-Mail: law@robertnuzum.com. E-mail: nuzumr@bellsouth.net.

NUZZO, ANTHONY GERALD, bank executive; b. New Haven, Aug. 9, 1951; s. Michael Anthony and Theresa Mary (Aitro) N.; m. Julie Nuzzo, Mar. 22, 1975; children: Beth, Michael, Cortney. BA, Boston Coll., 1973; MBA, Columbia U., 1975. CLU, cert. in long-term care. Brand asst. Procter & Gamble, Cin., 1975-76, sales rep., 1976, asst. brand mgr., 1976-77; asst. product dir. Johnson & Johnson, New Brunswick, NJ, 1977-78, spl. project dir., 1978-79, product dir. Milltown, NJ, 1979-82, group product dir., 1982-84; v.p. Am. Express Travel Related Svcs., NYC, 1984-87; v.p., exec. com. Am. Express Can., Inc., Markham, Ont., 1987-88; v.p. internat. mktg. Am. Express, NY, 1988; v.p. Chem. Bank, NYC, 1988-90, sr. v.p., 1990-91; pres., CEO Chem. Bank Del., Wilmington, 1991-92; pres., founder Advanced Mktg. Assocs., Inc., East Brunswick, NJ, 1992-93; pres., CEO Fidelity Trust Co., Salt Lake City, 1993-98, chmn., 1998-99; pres., CEO Fidelity TempWorks/TempSource, Boston, 1998-99; chmn., pres., CEO @Bank, Framingham, Mass., 1999-2000; pres., CEO Engage, Andover, Mass., 2000—01; pres., CEO, founder The Nuzzo Group, Inc., Wellesley, Mass., 2001—05; fin. adviser The Commonwealth Fin. Group, Newton, Mass., 2002—05; sr. v.p. Citizens Bank, Norwood, Mass., 2005—06, TD Banknorth, Burlington, Mass., 2007—. Mem. Visa Mktg. Advisors, 1989—92, 1993—98. Editor: Physiology, 1984. Dir., co-chair, co-founder Citizens Against UnSafe Environments, East Brunswick, 1981-93; bd. dirs. Utah Bd. Fin. Instns., 1995-98. Named to PS&D Merchandising Hall of Fame Procter & Gamble, Cin., 1977, named Scholar of the Coll., Boston Coll., 1973; recipient Bus. Sch. Svc. award Columbia U., 1975, Excellence award Package Designer Coun., NYC, 1980, Clio Creative Excellence award Clio Adv. Body, NYC, 1981, Effie award, NYC, 1989. Mem. Boston Coll. Alumni Assn., Columbia Bus. Sch. Alumni Assn. (dir. NY club 1975), Utah Bankers Assn. (bd. dirs. 1996-98), Utah Assn. Fin. Svcs. (bd. dirs. 1993-98, treas. 1995-96). Avocations: golf, skiing, reading. E-mail: agnuzzo@aol.com.

NWACHUKU, LEVI AKALAZU, social sciences and behavioral studies educator; b. Okpala, Nigeria, Aug. 23, 1940; came to U.S., 1963; s. Moses Akalazu and Evangeline (Enwere-Uzo) N.; m. Ugochi Justina Nwachuku, Dec. 19, 1981; children: Uchenna, Nneka, Chimereze, Chinomso, Enyinna. BA, Lincoln U., Pa., 1967; MA, Howard U., 1969; PhD, Mich. State U., 1973. V.p. acad. Shorter Coll., Little Rock, 1977; assoc. prof. U. Mich., Flint, 1977-81, dir. Black studies, 1973-81; reader history U. Maiduguri, Nigeria, 1981-88; coord. African Am. studies Lincoln U., 1989-94, chair dept. history, 1993—2002, chair dept. history, polit. sci., 2003—, dean faculty social scis., 1994-97. Co-author: Exploring the African-American Experience, 1995, Troubled Journey: Nigeria Since the Civil War, 2004; editor: Lincoln Jour. Social and Polit. Thought, 2001—; lead editor: Exploring the African American Experience, 2006. Recipient Christian R. and Mary F. Lindback Tchg. award, 2005; named Outstanding Male Faculty Mem., NAACP, 1995, Prof. of Yr., Lincoln U., 2004. Mem. Phi Alpha Theta, Alpha Phi Alpha. Home: PO Box 153 Lincoln University PA 19352-0153 Office: Lincoln U Lincoln University PA 19352

NWAGBARAOCHA, JOEL ONUKWUGHA, academic administrator, educator; b. Victoria, Cameroons, Nov. 21, 1942; came to U.S., 1964; naturalized, 1974; s. John O. and Christiana (Ihejeihu) N.; m. Patsy Coleman, Aug. 27, 1977; children: Jason, Jonathan, John, Eric. BS in Math., Norfolk State U., 1969, cert. in physics, 1969; EdM, Harvard U., 1970, EdD (Univ. fellow), 1972. Tchr. math. and physics Emmanuel Coll., Owerri, Nigeria, 1960-64; asst. dir. Manpower Rsch. Inst./Norfolk (Va.) State Coll., 1969-70; rsch. assoc. Harvard U. Grad. Sch. Edn., 1969-72; assoc. dir. co-op acad. planning program Inst. for Svcs. to Edn., Washington, 1972-74, dir. instnl. planning and mgmt. program, 1974-76, dir. divsn. acad. planning and faculty devel., 1976-78; assoc. prof. edn., v.p. planning and ops. analysis Morgan State U., Balt., 1978-87; v.p. acad. affairs Voorhees Coll., Denmark, S.C., 1987-80; pres. Barber-Scotia Coll., Concord, N.C., 1990-94; prof. edn., bus. adminstrn. Strayer U., Washington, 1994—, dir. grad. studies, 2000—02, dean grad. sch., 2005—07, interim pres., 2006—07, provost, chief academic officer, 2007—. Dean Tacoma Park Campus, Strayer Coll., Washington; interim pres., Strayer U., 2006-; cons. in higher edn. planning and evaluation system devel., 1972—. Co-author: Operational Manual for ollege Planning Development, 1977, Planning Management and Evaluation System, 1979; mem. editl. bd. Spartan Echo, 1967-69; contbr. articles to profl. jours. Mem. AAAS, Am. Coun. on Edn., Nat. Coun. on Social Studies, Am. Assn. for Higher Edn., Am. Humanist Assn., Soc. for Coll. and Univ. Planning, Am. Assn. Univ. Adminstrs., Am. Mgmt. Assn., Higher Edn. Group of Washington, Smithsonian Nat. Assoc., Alpha Kappa Mu, Phi Beta Sigma, Beta Kappa Chi, Phi Delta Kappa. Home: 10928 Battersea Ln Columbia MD 21044-2701 Office: Strayer Univ Washington DC Campus 1133 15th St NW Washington DC 20005-2601 Business E-Mail: jon@strayer.edu.

NWANGBURUKA, OKECHUKWU NKEM, psychiatrist; b. Aba, Nigeria, Mar. 9, 1965; arrived in US, 1994; s. Joseph and Festa Nwangburuka; m. Iheoma B. Nwangburuka. MD, U. Maiduguri, Nigeria, 1988. Resident physician MCP/Hahnemann U. Hosps., Phila., 1995—98; clin. instr. Ohio State U., Columbus, 1998—2000; sr. psychiatrist Shasta County Mental Health, Redding, Calif., 2000—. Named Physician of the Yr., NRCC, 2005. Mem.: Nigeria Nat. Assn. USA, Central Calif. Acad. Child and Adolescent Psychiatry, Central Calif. Psychiatry Soc., North Valley Med. Assoc., Nigerian Med. Assn., Shasta Psychiat. Soc., Am. Acad. Child and Adolescent Psychiatry, Am. Psychiat. Assn. Office: Shasta County Mental Health 2640 Breslauer Way Redding CA 96001 Mailing: PO Box 493579 Redding CA 96049 Home Phone: 530-355-0655; Office Phone: 530-225-5200. Business E-Mail: onwangburuka@co.shasta.ca.us.

NWOMEH, BENEDICT C., pediatric surgeon; b. Ozara, Enugu State, Nigeria, Mar. 3, 1965; arrived in US, 1994; s. Peter and Margaret Nwomeh; m. Henrietta A. Osodi, Dec. 6, 1999; children: Chiedozie, Chukwuemeka, Chioma. MB, U. Lagos, Nigeria, 1981, MD, 1986. Intern Med. Coll. Va. Commonwealth U., 1994—95, jr. resident, 1995—96, rsch. fellow, 1996—98, sr. resident, 1998—2000, chief resident, 2000—01; asst. prof. surgery Ohio State U., Columbus, 2003—; attending pediat. surgeon Columbus Children's Hosp., Ohio, 2003—. Dir. surg. edn. Columbus Children's Hosp., 2004—, surg. dir. Ctr. for Pediat. and Adolescent Inflammatory Bowel Disease, 2005—. Editor: Paediatric Trauma Care in Africa: A Practical Guide, 2006; contbr. articles to profl. jours. Mem. strategic decision making First Love Inc., Columbus, 2005—06. Named Young Investigator of Yr., Wound Healing Soc., 1997—98; recipient Residents Rsch. prize, Va. Soc. Plastic Surgery, 1997, David Hume Rsch. award, Humera Surg. Soc., Med. Coll. Va., 1999, Outstanding Surgeon award, Children's Hosp. Pitts. Critical Care Staff, 2003, Gold Found. Little Apple Tchg. award, U. Pitts. Sch. Medicine, Class 2004, 2004, Ohio Health Policy Rsch. award, Health Policy Inst. Ohio, 2006. Fellow: ACS, Royal Coll. Surgeons Eng., Royal Coll. Physicians and Surgeons Glasgow, Am. Acad. Pediat., Assn. for Surg. Edn., Royal Coll. Surgeons Edinburgh, West African Coll. Surgeons, Soc. Black Academic Surgeons (mem. publs. com. 2006); mem.: Ctrl. Ohio Pediat. Soc., Internat. Pediat. Endosurgery Group, Brit. Med. Assn., Assn. Pediat. Surgeons Nigeria. Achievements include described the dynamics of the matrix metalloproteinases MMP-1 and MMP-8 in acute open human dermal wounds; research in Contrast extravasation predicts the need for operative intervention in children with blunt splenic trauma; racial and socioeconomic disparity in perforated appendicitis among children; discovery of MMP-8 is the predominant collagenase in healing wounds and nonhealing ulcers. Office: Columbus Childrens Hospital 700 Childrens Drive ED379 Columbus OH 43205 Office Phone: 614-722-3972.

NYBERG, DONALD ARVID, oil industry executive; b. Ridgewood, NJ, Aug. 23, 1951; s. Arvid H. and Rita T. (Tenwick) N.; m. Susan Radis, Feb. 16, 1985; children: Matthew D., Ryan T. BA, St. Lawrence U., 1973; MBA, Harvard U., 1975. Mgr. marine ops. Standard Oil, LA, 1982-83, mgr. ops. planning Cleve., 1984-85, dir. strategic studies, 1986; divsn. mgr. Brit. Petroleum, Ltd., London, 1987-88; v.p., gen. mgr. U.S. gas bus. BP Exploration, Houston, 1989, v.p., gen. mgr. tech., 1990, v.p. comml., 1991-94; pres., CEO BP Pipelines, Anchorage, 1991-94; pres. Marya Resources, Houston, 1994—; v.p. MAPCO, Tulsa, 1996; pres. Tesoro Marine Svcs., Houston, 1996—2003; CEO McDonough Marine, 2004—, bd. dirs., 2004—; CEO Champion Elevators, 2005—, bd. dirs., 2004—. Bd. dirs., exec. com. Boys and Girls Country Houston. Mem. Forest Club, Bentwater Country Club. Avocations: running, weightlifting, reading. Office: McDonough Corp 17500 Market St Channelview TX 77530 Home Phone: 713-463-9712. Personal E-mail: don.nyberg@yahoo.com.

NYBERG, STANLEY ERIC, research scientist; b. Boston, Jan. 30, 1948; s. Leroy Milton and Anna Maria (Olson) N. PhD, SUNY, Stony Brook, 1975; MBA, Yale U., 1984. Postdoctoral fellow U. Calif., Berkeley, 1975-76; asst. prof. North Park Coll., Chgo., 1976-79, Barnard Coll., Columbia U., NYC, 1979-82; sys. mgmt. Interactive Data Corp., Lexington, Mass., 1984-88, Dept. of Revenue, Commonwealth of Mass., Boston, 1988-2000; with Dept. of Environ. Protection, Commonwealth of Mass., 2000—01; registrar vital records and stats. Commonwealth of Mass., 2001—. Co-author: Human Memory: An Introduction to Research and Theory, 1982. Bd. dir. Childrens Home Cromwell, Conn., 1988-94, Decade Fund, Yale U. Sch. Mgmt., 1984-1985; ch. coun. Luth. Ch. of Redeemer, Woburn, Mass., 1991-1997, West Roxbury Rugby Football Club, 1984-1987; v.p., sec. L Street Running Club, South Boston, 1987—; mem. divsn. ecumenism New Eng. Synod, Evang. Luth. Ch. in Am., 1997—2002; bd. dir. Scandinavian Charitable Soc. Greater Boston, 2000—, v.p. 2002-2004, pres., 2004-06. Fellow Assn. Psychol. Sci.; mem. APA, Soc. Applied Rsch. in Memory and Cognition, Ea. Psychol. Assn., Midwestern Psychol. Assn. Personal E-mail: snyberg@aol.com.

NYBORG, WESLEY LEMARS, physics professor; b. Ruthven, Iowa, May 15, 1917; s. Isaac and Leva (Larson) N.; m. Beth Woolsey, Sept. 8, 1945; 1 dau., Elsa Beth. BA, Luther Coll., 1941; MS, Pa. State U., 1944, PhD, 1947. Asst. prof. physics Pa. State U., University Park, 1948-50; asst. prof. Brown U., Providence, 1950-54, asso. prof., 1954-60; prof. U. Vt., Burlington, 1960-86, acting chmn. physics dept., 1978-79, prof. emeritus, 1986—. Vis. scientist Oxford (Eng.) U., 1960-61, Univ. Coll., Cardiff, Wales, 1969, U. of Rochester, 1987; Exec. council Am. Inst. Ultrasound in Medicine, 1972-74, 76-78, chmn. bioeffects com., 1976-78; adv. bd. Bur. Radiol. Health, 1972-75; cons. FDA, 1976—; chmn. sci. com. 66 Nat. Council Radiation Protection and Measurements, 1980—; mem. working group on biol. effects ultrasound, WHO, 1982, 85, 88; mem. study sect. diagnostic radiology NIH, 1982-85; adv. mem. Rochester Ctr. for Biomed. Ultrasound, 1986; Lauriston S. Taylor lectr. Nat. Coun. Radiation Protection and Measurements, Bethesda, Md., 2001. Author: Intermediate Biophysical Mechanics, 1975; co-editor: Biological Effects of Ultrasound, 1985, (with J. Wu) Emerging Therapeutic Ultrasound, 2006; mem. editl. bd.: Ultrasound in Medicine and Biology, Jour. Ultrasound in Medicine; co-editor Proc. Symposium on Safety and Standardization in Med. Ultrasound, 2d World Fedn. Ultrasound in Medicine and Biology, 1989; contbr. to profl. jours. Recipient Presdl. recognition award Am. Inst. Ultrasound in Medicine, 1977, Univ. scholar award in phys. scis. U. Vt., 1984, Disting. Svc. award Luther Coll., 1996, Vt. Acad. Sci. and Engring., 1997, Lauriston S. Taylor Lectr. award 2001, P.P. Lele award, 5th Internat. Symposium, 2005; USPHS fellow MIT, 1956-57; research grantee NIH, 1955—. Fellow AAAS, Acoustical Soc. Am. (exec. coun. 1965-68, Silver medal 1990), Am. Inst. Ultrasound in Medicine (Joseph H. Holmes award 1985, W.J. Fry Lecture award 1990), Ultrasonic Soc. India (hon.); mem. NAS, Nat. Acad. Engrs., Am. Phys. Soc., Biophys. Soc., Am. Assn. Physics Tchrs., Sigma Xi, Sigma Pi Sigma. Home: 2 Stirling Pl Burlington VT 05408-2634 Business E-Mail: wesley.nyborg@uvm.edu.

NYCE, JOHN DANIEL, lawyer; b. York, Pa., Sept. 7, 1947; s. Harry Lincoln and Dorothy (Wagner) Nyce; m. Deborah Dvorak; children: Joshua David, Laura Kimberly. BA, SUNY, Buffalo, 1970; JD, U. Miami, 1973. Bar: Fla. 1973, U.S. District Ct. (so. dist.) Fla. 1973, U.S. Dist. Ct. (middle dist.), Fla. 1973, U.S. Ct. Appeals (5th and 11th cirs.) 1986, U.S. Supreme Ct. 1984. Assoc. Ralph P. Douglas, Pompano Beach, Fla., 1974, Coleman, Leonard & Morrison, Ft. Lauderdale, Fla., 1975-78; ptnr. Nyce and Smith, Ft. Lauderdale, 1979; sole practice Ft. Lauderdale, 1980—. Adj. prof. bus. law, inernat. bus. law Lynn U., Boca Raton, Fla., 2001—. Author: Proof of God's Existence in the Seven C's and Christian Handbook of Lists, 2003. Mem. Social Register Ft. Lauderdale; mem. Broward County Right to Life, Operation Rescue, South Fla., Beach Street Aid to the Homeless of Ft. Lauderdale, Legis. Adv. Coun. on Adoptions, Am. Assn. Adoption Attys., Nat. Right to Life Com., Inc.; founder Broward County Christian Lawyers Assn., past pres., bd. dirs.; founder Am. Assn. Adoption Attys., past pres., bd. dirs.; mem. Christian Legal Soc.; mem. exec. com. Broward County Rep. Party; Broward Citizens bd. U. Miami; mem. Conservative Caucus of Broward County; bd. dirs. Shepherd Care Ministries, Inc.; co-founder Christian Adoption Svcs. of Shepherd Care Ministries, Inc.; cert. trainer Evangelism Explosion III Internat., Inc.; legal counsel and evangelism trainer Coral Ridge Presbybn. Ch., Christ the Rock Cmty. Ch., First Bapt. Ch., West Hollywood, Fla., Calvary Chapel of Ft. Lauderdale Ch.; bd. dirs. Alliance for Responsible Growth, Inc. Mem.: Am. Assn. Adoption Attys., Nat. Acad. Elder Law Attys., Attys. Title Ins. Fund, NRA, Am. Numismatic Assn., U. Miami Alumni Assn., SUNY Buffalo Alumni Assn., S.D. Rifle and Hunting Assn., Holiday Park Tennis Ctr., U.S. Tennis Assn., U. Miami Hurricane Club, Sports Fitness Clin., Palm Aire Golf and Country Club. Republican. Presbyterian. Office: PO Box 11071 Fort Lauderdale FL 33339-1071 Office Phone: 954-567-3305. E-mail: miamijd73@comcast.net.

NYCUM, SUSAN HUBBELL, lawyer; BA, Ohio Wesleyan U., 1956; JD, Duquesne U., 1960; postgrad., Stanford U., Calif. Bar: Pa. 1962, Calif. 1964, U.S. Supreme Ct. 1967. Pvt. practice, Pitts., 1962—65; designer, adminstr. legal rsch. sys. U. Pitts., Aspen Sys. Corp., Pitts., 1965-68; mgr. ops. Computer Ctr., Carnegie Mellon U., Pitts., 1968-69; dir. computer facility Computer Ctr., Stanford U., 1969-72, Stanford Law and Computer fellow, 1972-73; cons. in computers and law, 1973-74; sr. assoc. MacLeod, Fuller, Muir & Godwin, Los Altos, LA and London, 1974-75; ptnr. Chickering & Gregory, San Francisco, 1975-80; ptnr.-in-charge high tech. group Gaston Snow & Ely Bartlett, Boston, NYC, Phoenix, San Francisco, 1980-86; mng. ptnr. Palo Alto office Kadison, Pfaelzer, Woodard, Quinn & Rossi, LA, Washington, Newport Beach, Palo Alto, Calif., 1986-87; sr. ptnr., chmn. U.S. intellectual property/info. tech. practice group Baker & McKenzie, Palo Alto, 1987—2002, mem. U.S. leadership team, 1987-97, mem. Asia Pacific regional coun., 1995—2002; with Tech. Disputes Resolution Svcs. Inc., 2002—. Founder Tech. Disputes Resolution Svcs., Inc., 2002—; trustee EDUCOM, 1978-81; mem. adv. com. for high tech. Ariz. State U. Law Sch., Santa Clara U. Law Sch., Stanford Law Sch., U. So. Calif. Law Ctr., Harvard U. Law Sch., U. Calif.; U.S. State Dept. del. OECD Conf. on Nat. Vulnerabilities, Spain, 1981; invited spkr. Telecom., Geneva, 1983; lectr. N.Y. Law Jour., 1975—, Law & Bus., 1975—, Practicing Law Inst., 1975—; chmn. Office of Tech. Assessment Task Force on Nat. Info. Sys., 1979-80. Author:(with Bigelow) Your Computer and the Law, 1975, (with Bosworth) Legal Protection for Software, 1985, (with Collins and Gilbert) Women Leading, 1987; contbr. monographs, articles to profl. publs. Fellow Am. Bar Found.; mem. Town of Portola Valley Open Space Acquisition Com., Calif., 1977; mem. Jr. League of Palo Alto, chmn. evening div., 1975-76 NSF and Dept. Justice grantee for studies on computer abuse, 1972-. Fellow Am. Bar Found., Assn. Computer Machinery (mem. at large of coun. 1976-80, nat. lectr. 1977—, chmn. standing com. on legal issues 1975—, mem. blue ribbon com. on rationalization of internat. propr. rights protection on info. processing devel. in the '90s 1990—, Hall of Fame 2004), Coll. Law Practice Mgmt. (trustee 2002—), Coll. Comml. Arbitration; mem. ABA (chmn. sect. on sci. and tech. 1979-80), Computer Law Assn. (v.p. 1983-85, pres. 1986—, bd. dirs. 1975—), Calif. State Bar Assn. (founder first chmn. econs. of law sect., vice chmn. law and computers com.), Internat. Bar Assn. (U.S. mem. computer com. of corps. sect.), Nat. Conf. Lawyers and Scientists (rep. ABA), Strategic Forum on Intellectual Property Issues in Software of NAS, Internat. Coun. for Computer Comm. (gov. 1998). Office: 35 Granada Ct Portola Valley CA 94028-7736 Office Phone: 650-851-3304, Business E-Mail: susan@nycum.net.

NYDEGGER, RICK D., lawyer; b. Salt Lake City, Apr. 24, 1949; s. A. Don and Jean Virginia (Hansen) N.; m. Denise Winegar, Oct. 22, 1970; children: Dan L., Chad E., Kurt D., Brittney, Trent R. BSEE cum laude, Brigham Young U., Provo, Utah, 1974, JD cum laude, 1977. Bar: Utah 1977, US Dist Ct. (ctrl. dist.) Utah 1977, US Patent Office 1977, US Ct. Appeals (5th and 10th cirs.) 1980, US Supreme Ct. 1990, US Ct. Appeals (fed. cir.) 1994. Assoc. Fox, Edwards, & Gardiner, 1977-81, shareholder, dir., 1981-84; founding shareholder, dir., officer Workman, Nydegger, Salt Lake City, 1984—. Adj. prof. S.J. Quinney Coll. Law, U. Utah, 1988-99, J. Reuben Clark Law Sch., Brigham Young U., 1998-2002. Contbr. articles to profl. jours. Pres. Nat. Inventors Hall of Fame, 2000-05; bd. dirs. NIHF Found., 1998-2006, pres.; trustee Am. Intellectual Property Law Edn. Found., 2001-03. Named Hon. Alumnus of Yr., U. Utah, 2004, Alumnus of Yr., Brigham Young U., 2005. Fellow Am. Intellectual Property Law Assn. (founding mem., chmn. electronic computer law com. 1990-93, bd. dirs. 1993-96, editl. bd. quar. jour., vice-chmn. ad hoc com. PCT practice, 1994-98, chmn. nominations com. 2005, chmn. mid-winter Inst. 2000 planning com., 2d v.p. 2000-01, 1st v.p. 2001-02, pres-elect 2002-03, pres. 2003-04); mem. ABA, Utah State Bar (chmn. patent, trademark, copyright sect. 1985-87), Fed. Cir. Bar Assn., US Supreme Ct. Hist. Soc. (10th cir. rep. 1993-94, Utah rep. 1992-93, 2005, trustee 2005-), Nat. Coun. Intellectual Property Law Assn. (chmn. 2000-01), Order of Coif. Office: Workman Nydegger 60 E South Temple Ste 1000 Salt Lake City UT 84111-1011 Home Phone: 801-756-4751; Office Phone: 801-533-9800. Business E-Mail: rnydegger@wnlaw.com.

NYE, BETTY ANN, professional society administrator; b. Rockford, Ill., Sept. 27, 1948; d. Thomas Sorrels and Betha Harris; children: Lillian Loftin, Jimmy Skinner Jr. Diploma, Inst. Childrens Lit., 1993; cert. in basic acctg., Rock Valley Coll., Rockford, 1999. Rec. sec. Kishwaukee Genealogist, Rockford, 1999—2000, corr. sec., pres., 2002—04, winnebago co. il. rschr., newsletter editor, 1995—. Owner Memories by Nye. Author: A Mississippi River Adventure, The Adventure of Annabelle; author: (with Lillian Loftin) Frozen Dead - Shasta's Story, Frozen Dead - Continues with Claire's Story, 2007. Recipient Silver Poet, World of Poetry, 1990. Office: Memories by Nye PO Box 1588 Vidor TX 77670 Home Phone: 409-550-7777. E-mail: mbnls@aol.com.

NYE, BILL S., research scientist, engineer, comedian, writer, inventor; b. Washington, Nov. 27, 1955; m. Blair Tindall, Feb. 3, 2006. BS in Mech. Engring., Cornell U., 1977; PhD in Sci. (hon.), Rennselaer Polytechnic Inst., Rochester, NY; PhD (hon.), Goucher Coll., Baltimore, Md. With Boeing Corp., Seattle, 1977—80, Marco, Seattle, 1980—81, Sundstrand Data Control, Redmond, Wash., 1981—86; lic. mech. engr. State of Washington, 1983—; cons. engr. US Dept. Justice, 1987—, Micro Encoder, Inc., 1987—, Avtech, 1987—; Frank H.T. Rhodes Class of '56 Univ. Prof. Cornell U., 2001—04. Established, promoter EarthDial Project; bd. dir. Mars Athena Exploration Team, Cornell U., 1998—2011, Denver Mus. Nature and Sci., 2001—, New Horizons Mission to Pluto, John Hopkins U., 2001—14. Originated Bill Nye-The Science Guy, KJR Radio, Seattle, 1986—92, writer, talent (TV comedy) Almost Live, KING TV, 1986—92, host, writer (video) Fabulous Wetlands, Washington State Dept. Ecology, 1988, writer, prodr., talent Bill Nye-The Science Guy (pilot and subsequent series) (Emmy awards for Best Performer, Best Writing and Producing, and Best Show), spokesperson, cons., on-air host Noggin TV (MTV Networks), 1999—, host (TV series) The 100 Greatest Discoveries (Science Channel),

The Eyes of Nye (PBS); co-author: (book) Big Blast of Science, 1993, Bill Nye the Science Guy's Great Big Dinosaur Dig, 2002, Bill Nye the Science Guy's Great Big Book of Tiny Germs, 2005, Bill Nye the Science Guy's Great Big Book of Science: Featuring Oceans and Dinosaurs, 2005; author: Bill Nye the Science Guy's Big Blue Ocean, 1999, Bill Nye's Consider the Following: A Way Cool Set of Science Questions, Answers, and Ideas to Ponder, Mozart in the Jungle. Recipient Best Children's Live Action Show, Environ. Media Assn., 1994, 1996, 1997, Carl Sagan Candle in the Dark award for the Develop. of Critical Thinking, 1997, Gold Camera award, Internat. Film and Video Festival, 1997, Best Children's Live Action Show, Environ. Media Assn., 1998, Coun. for Elementary Sci. Internat. Sci. Advocate award, 2000, US Forest Svc. Disting. award for conservation. Mem.: Planetary Soc. (bd. dir. 1998—). Achievements include at Boeing Corporation, designed a hydraulic pressure resonance suppressor that is still flying on Boeing 747's; at Marco, designed equipment for oil slick skimming at sea, and for separation of water produced with oil in oil fields; at Sundstrand Data Control, designed oil well logging instruments, and an inertial navigation system for business jets; two patents on educational products-a magnifier made of water and an abacus that does arithmetic like a computer; patent pending on a device to help people learn to throw a baseball better; Won 28 Emmy awards in five years for writing and performing; and other designs as consulting engineer. Avocations: bicycling, baseball, Frisbee, tinkering, especially with bikes. Address: c/o William Morris Agy Attn: Betsy Berg 1325 Avenue of the Americas New York NY 10019

NYE, DAN, Internet company executive; BA in Polit. Sci., Hamilton Coll., 1988; MBA, Harvard Bus. Sch., 1994. Mem. brand mgmt. Proter & Gamble, 1988—92; various positions including, v.p., gen. mgr. internat. divsn., dir. mktg. for small bus. products and svcs., v.p., gen. mgr., small bus. divsn. Intuit, Inc., 1995—2001; exec. v.p., gen. mgr., investment mgmt. Advent Software, 2002—07; CEO LinkedIn Corp., 2007—. Office: LinkedIn Corp 2029 Stierlin Ct Mountain View CA 94043 *

NYE, DOROTHY MAE, freelance journalist, educator; d. Robert Nathan and Marinda Josephine Nye; m. Joseph Arlo Westby, Nov. 20, 1955 (div.); children: Timothy Scott Westby, Pamela Kay Westby, Lisa Maureen Westby Peltier, Thomas Oscar Westby, Theodore Edward Westby, Erik Charles Westby. BA, U. Denver, 1999—2001, Combined Licensure & Master's Program, 2002—03. Administrator's Credential Nat. Assn. Edn. of Young Children (NAEYC) & Red Cross, 1993, Montessori Certification Nat. Ctr. for Montessori Edn., 1992. Asst. to v.p. of sales Morton Buildings, Morton, Ill., 1971—83; assoc. dir. of admissions Parks Coll., Denver, 1984—86; dir. of admissions Denver Tech. Coll., 1986—90; primary tchr. Montessori Inst., Houston, 1991—93; sales team mgr. Time Warner, Denver, 1993—96; counselor Open Door, Valley City, ND, 1996—99; communicatons specialist Theodore Roosevelt Medora Found., Medora, ND, 1999—2000; ednl. specialist for elderly Life Care of Am., Aurora, Colo., 2001—04; h.s. english tchr. Life Skills Charter Sch. of Colo. Springs, 2004—. Coord. for internat. program U. of ND & Mexican Universities, Valley City, ND, 1997—99. Com. monitor Majority Caucus Colo. Ho. of Representatives, Denver, 1993—95. Mem.: Pi Lambda Phi, Sigma Tau Delta. Office Phone: 719-471-0684. Business E-Mail: dorothy.nye@lifeskillscenters.com. E-mail: grand_ma10@msn.com.

NYE, ERIC W., English language and literature educator; b. Omaha, July 31, 1952; s. William Frank and Mary Roberta (Lueder) N.; m. Carol Denison Frost, Dec. 21, 1980; children: Charles William, Ellen Mary. BA, St. Olaf Coll., 1974; MA, U. Chgo., 1976, PhD, 1983; postgrad., Queens' Coll., Cambridge, England, 1979-82. Tutor in coll. writing com. U. Chgo., 1976-79, tchg. intern, 1978; tutor Am. lit. Cambridge (Eng.) U., 1979-82; asst. prof. English and religious studies U. Wyo., Laramie, 1983-89, assoc. prof., 1989—, dir. English honors program, 1985—89, 1992—93, 2002—04. Pres., bd. dirs. Plainview Tel. Co., Nebr.; hon. vis. fellow U. Edinburgh (Scotland) Inst. for Advanced Studies in the Humanities, 1987; guest lectr. NEH summer Inst., Laramie, Wyo., 1985, Carlyle Soc. of Edinburgh, 1987, Wordsworth summer Conf., Grasmere, Eng., 1988, cons. NEH. Contbr. articles and reviews to profl. jours. Elected mem. Wyo. Coun. for Humanities, 1992—96, mem. exec. com., 1993—94; mem. adv. bd. Wyo. Ctr. for the Book, 1995—, chair, 2006—; mem. Peripatetics, 1989—, The Grolier Club, 2007—; leader Boy Scouts Am., 1999—2005. Nat. Merit scholar St. Olaf Coll., 1970-74; Amb. fellow Rotary Found., 1979-80; grantee Am. Coun. Learned Socs., 1988; recipient Disting. Alumnus award Lincoln (Nebr.) East H.S., 1986, Slater Tchg. award 2000, Extraordinary Merit Tchg. award 2006. Mem.: MLA (del. assembly 1991—93), Guild Book Workers, Bibliog. Soc. London (hon. treas. for N.Am. 2002—), Soc. History of Authorship, Reading, and Pub., Assn. Lit. and Linguistic Computing, Am. Acad. Bookbinding, Assn. Literary Scholars and Critics (life), Gen. Soc. Mayflower Descendents, The Victorian Inst., Coleridge Soc. (life), Friends of Dove Cottage (life), Jane Austen Soc. N.Am. (life), Carlyle Soc. (life), Wyo. State Hist. Soc. (life), Tennyson Soc. (life), Friends of Cambridge U. Libr. (life), Charles Lamb Soc., Royal Oak Found., Am. Friends Cambridge U., Am. Trust for the Brit. Libr., Queens' Coll. Club (Cambridge), Pen Club (London), The Grolier Club, Phi Beta Kappa (rep. Triennial Coun. 1988, pres., v.p., sec. Wyo. chpt. 1988—, rep. Triennial Coun. 1994, 2000, 2003, 2006, Dedicated Svc. award 1997). Home: 1495 Apache Dr Laramie WY 82072-6966 Office: U Wyo Dept English 3353 1000 E U Ave Laramie WY 82071 Office Phone: 307-766-6452. Business E-Mail: nye@uwyo.edu.

NYE, ERLE ALLEN, electric power industry executive, lawyer; b. Ft. Worth, June 23, 1937; s. Ira Benjamen N.; m. Alice Ann Grove, June 5, 1959; children: Elizabeth Nye Janzen, Pamela Nye Schneider, Erle Allen Jr., Edward Kyle, Johnson Scott. BEE, Tex. A&M U., 1959; JD, So. Meth. U., 1965. With Dallas Power & Light Co., 1960-75, v.p., 1975-80, Tex. Utilities Co. (dba TXU Corp.), Dallas, 1980, exec. v.p., 1980-87, pres., 1987-95, pres., CEO, 1995-97, chmn., CEO, 1997—2004, chmn., 2004—. TU Svcs., 1982-97, chmn., CEO, 1997—, Tex. Utilities Properties Inc., 1994, Tex. Utilities Commn., Dallas, 1995-97, chmn., CEO, 1997—; pres. Tex. Utilities Fuel Co., 1982-97, chmn., CEO, 1997—; chmn. Tex. Utilities Australia Pty., Ltd., 1996—, chmn. and CEO ENSERCH Corp., Enserch Devel. Corp., Dallas, 1997—, chmn. Enserch Energy Svcs. Inc., 1997—; dir. The Energy Group PLC, London, 1998—; chmn. and CEO Tex. Energy Industries Inc., Dallas, 1997—, Southwestern Electric Svc. Co., 1997—, chmn. Lufkin-Conroe Comm. Co., 1997—, chmn. bd., CEO Tex. Utilities Integrated Solutions Inc., 1997—. Bd. dirs. Dallas Bar Found., 1980-83, Dallas Cen. Bus. Plan Com., 1980-83, Inroads/Dallas-Ft. Worth Inc., 1984-88, trustee Baylor Dental Coll., Dallas, 1985-94; mem. Dallas Together Forum, 1989—, Dallas Com. Fgn. Rels., 1991—, Bd. of Boys & Girls Clubs of Am., 1991—; The Dallas Found., 1994—; The Science Pl., Dallas, 1995-99; The Salvation Army's Dallas County Adv. Bd., 1995-99. Mem. ABA, Dallas Bar Assn., Tex. State Bar Assn., Dallas C. of C. (bd. dirs. 1991-95, vice chmn. 1992-95). Clubs: Engineers (pres. 1982-83), Northwood (Dallas). Methodist. Home: 6924 Desco Dallas TX 75225 Office: TXU Corp 1601 Bryan St Fl 41 Dallas TX 75201-3411

NYE, JOSEPH SAMUEL, JR., political science professor, former dean; b. South Orange, NJ, Jan. 19, 1937; s. Joseph S. and Else (Ashwell) N.; m. Molly Harding, June 10, 1961; children: John Bundy, Joseph Benjamin, Daniel Tupper AB in Pub. Affairs, Princeton U., 1958; BA in Philosophy, Politics and Econs., Oxford U., Eng., 1960; PhD in Polit. Sci., Harvard U., 1964. Prof., govt. Harvard U., Cambridge, Mass., 1964—95, dean Kennedy Sch. Govt., 1995—2004, Disting. Svc. prof., 2004—; dep. undersec. state, security assistance, science & tech. U.S. Dept. State, Washington, 1977-79, cons., 1979; asst. sec. def., internat. security affairs U.S. Dept. Def., Washington, 1994—95; dean Harvard U. JFK Sch. of Govt., 1995—2004, Sultan of Oman prof. internat. relations, 2005—. Cons. Dept. Energy, Washington, 1979; U.S. rep. UN Adv. Bd. on Disarmament; chmn. Nat. Intelligence Coun., 1993-94; vis. prof. Balliol Coll., Oxford, Eng., 2005. Author: Pan Africanism and East African Integration, 1965, Peace in Paris: Integration and Conflict in Regional Organization, 1971 (with Robert O. Keohane) Power and Interdependence: World Politics in Transition, 1977, The Making of America's Soviet Policy, 1984, (with Graham Allison and Albert Carnesale) Hawks, Doves and Owls: An Agenda for Avoiding Nuclear War, 1985, Nuclear Ethics, 1986, Bound to Lead: The Changing Nature of American Power, 1990, (with Kurt Biedenkopf and Motoo Shiina) Global Competition After the Cold War: A Reassessment of Trilateralism, 1991, Understanding International Conflicts: An Introduction to Theory and History, 1993, The Paradox of American Power: Why the World's Only Only Superpower Can't Go It Alone, 2002, Soft Power: The Means to Success in World Politics, 2004, The Power Game: A Washington Novel, 2004; (with Yukio Satoh and Paul Wikinson) Addressing the New International Terrorism: Prevention, Intervention, and Multilateral Cooperation, 2003; co-editor: Canada and the United States: Transnational and Transgovernmental Relations, 1974, Energy and Security, 1980, Global Dilemmas, 1985, Seeking Stability in Space: Anti-Satellite Weapons and the Evolving Space Regime, 1987, On The Defensive? The Future of SDI, 1988, Fateful Visions: avoiding Nuclear Catastrophe, 1988, democracy.com?: Governance in a Networked World, 1999, Governance in a Globalizing World, 2000, For the People: Can We Fix Public Service, 2003. Recipient: US Dept. State Disting. Honor award, 1979; Rhodes scholar Oxford U., 1958-60, Montague Burton Professorship, U. Edinburgh, 1990, Intelligence Cmty. Disting. Service medal, 1994, Dept. Def. Disting. Service medal with Oak Leaf Cluster, 1995, Charles E. Merriam award Am. polit. Sci. Assn., 2003, Woodrow Wilson award Princeton U., 2004; fellow, Woodrow Wilson Internat. Ctr., Smithsonian Inst., 1993, Hon. fellow, Exeter Coll, Oxford, 1996. Fellow Am. Acad. Arts and Scis., Aspen Inst. for Humanistic Study (sr. fellow, 1983-93); mem. Amer. Assoc. for the Advancement of Science: Com. on Science, Arms Control, and Nat. Security, 1984-90, bd. dirs., Amer. Council on Germany, 1985-93, bd. govs., Atlantic Inst. for Internat. Affairs, 1974-77, Internat. Inst. Strategic Studies (council), Coun. Fgn. Rels. (bd. dirs.), Trilateral Commn., Am. Acad. Diplomacy. Office: Harvard U JFK Sch Govt 79 John F Kennedy St Cambridge MA 02138-5801 E-mail: joseph_nye@harvard.edu.

NYE, LINDA PURCELL, secondary school educator; d. George T and Sara Jane Purcell; m. Stephen Christopher Nye, Aug. 5, 2001; children: Levi, Clifton. MusB in Edn., U. of Puget Sound, Tacoma, Wash., 1975; MEd in Counseling, U. of Puget Sound, 1986; Cert. of Vocal Mastery, Austro-Am. Inst. of Edn., Vienna, Austria, 1972—73. Choir/dramateacher White River Sch. Dist., Buckley, Wash.; choir/drama tchr. Clover Pk. Sch. Dist., Lakewood, Wash., 1986—96; choir/drama/English tchr. Evergreen Sch. Dist., Vancouver, Wash., 1996—. Dir.: Best in the Northwest Festival (Best Dir., 1992); (plays) Grease (Outstanding Theatre Prodn. in Pierce County, 1989); choreographer (plays) He's Risen! (Best Artistic Design, 1993). V.p. Adelphian Concert Choir, pres., 1974—75; treas. Puyallup Bus. and Profl. Women, Puyallup, Wash., 1977—78. Named Outstanding Woman in Pierce County, Bus. and Profl. Women, 1979; recipient Inspirational award, Adelphian Concert Choir/ U. of Puget Sound, 1974; scholar Four Yr. Vocal scholar, U. of Puget Sound Sch. of Music, 1971—75. Fellow: NEA (assoc.); mem.: Am. Choral Dirs. Assn. (organizing chmn. women's hon. choir N.W. divsn. 1988), EEA, Wash. Edn. Assn., Music Educator's Nat. Conf. (assoc.; dist. pres. 1979—83, v.p. 1979—83, organizing chmn. all-N.W. choir), Mortar Bd. (life), Sigma Alpha Iota Alumnae Assn. (assoc.; pres. 1974—84, v.p. 1974—84, treas. 1974—84, Ruby Sword of Honor/ Nu Province Leadership Award 1976). Liberal. Avocations: travel, singing. Home Phone: 360-546-1194; Office Phone: 360-604-3200 x7079. Personal E-mail: lnye525@comcast.net. Business E-Mail: lnye@egreen.wednet.edu.

NYE, W. MARCUS W., lawyer; b. NYC, Aug. 3, 1945; s. W.R. and Nora (McLaren) N.; m. Eva Johnson BA, Harvard U., 1967; JD, U. Idaho, 1974. Bar: Idaho 1974, U.S. Dist. Ct. Idaho 1974, U.S. Ct. Appeals (9th cir.) 1980; lic. pilot. Ptnr. Racine, Olson, Nye, Budge & Bailey, Pocatello, Idaho, 1974—. Vis. prof. law U. Idaho, Moscow, 1984; pres. Idaho State U. Found., 2001-03, U. Idaho Coll. Law Found. Commr., Idaho State Centennial Found., 1985-90. Recipient Alumni Svc. award U. Idaho, 1988, Bartz award Idaho State U, 2004; named Dist. Lawyer of Yr., Idaho State Bar, 2005. Fellow ABA (bd. govs. 1997-2000), Am. Bar Found. (stat. chmn. 1992-95); mem. Am. Bd. Trial Advs. (nat. bd. dirs.), Am. Coll. Trial Lawyers, Idaho State Bar Assn. (pres. 1987-88), Idaho Def. Counsel Assn. (pres. 1982), 6th Dist. Bar Assn. (pres. 1982). Avocation: travel. Home: 173 S 15th Ave Pocatello ID 83201-4056 Office: Racine Olson Nye Budge & Bailey PO Box 1391 Pocatello ID 83204-1391

NYE, WILLIAM ROGER, psychologist; b. Haverhill, Mass., Oct. 23, 1940; s. Kenneth Enoch and Virginia Pauline (Cook) N.; children: Michael Shepherd Abowitz Nye; 1 stepson, Christopher J. Wells. BA, Yale U., 1962; MDiv, Union Theol. Sem., NYC, 1965; PhD, Adelphi U., Garden City, NY, 1981. Lic. psychologist, N.Y. Pastor Ch. of the Evangel, Bklyn., 1965-77; asst. minister Plymouth Ch. of the Pilgrims, Bklyn., 1977-82; pastor All Souls Bethlehem Ch., Bklyn., 1983—2003; exec. dir. Blanton-Peale Counseling Ctrs., 1983—2006. Past pres. Met. Assn. N.Y. Conf. United Ch. of Christ, 1969—73. Pres. Bklyn. Cmty. and Housing Svcs., 1983—87, Vinmont Found., NYC, 1988—2006. Mem. Am. Psychol. Assn. Democrat. United Ch. of Christ. Home: 888 E 19th St Brooklyn NY 11230-3108 Home Phone: 718-377-0178; Office Phone: 718-253-9001. E-mail: realbilnye@aol.com.

NYENHUIS, JACOB EUGENE, academic administrator; b. Mille Lacs County, Minn., Mar. 25, 1935; s. Egbert Peter and Rosa (Walburg) N.; m. Leona Mae Van Duyn, June 6, 1956; children: Karen J. Louwsma, Kathy J. Kurtze, Lorna J. Cook, Sarah Van Duyn N. AB in Greek, Calvin Coll., 1956; AM in Classics, Stanford U., 1961, PhD in Classics, 1963; LittD (hon.), Hope Coll., 2001. Asst. in classical langs. Calvin Coll., Grand Rapids, Mich., 1957-59; acting instr. Stanford (Calif.) U., 1962; from asst. prof. to prof. Wayne State U., Detroit, 1962-75, dir. honors program, 1964-75, chmn. Greek and Latin dept., 1965-75; prof. classics, dean for humanities Hope Coll., Holland, Mich., 1975-78, dean for arts and humanities, 1978-84, provost, 1984—2001, prof. and provost emeritus, 2001—; sr. rsch. fellow A.C. Van Raalte Inst., 2001—02, dir., 2002—. Cons. Mich. Dept. Edn., Lansing, 1971-72, Gustavus Adolphus Coll., St. Peter, Minn., 1974, Northwestern Coll., Orange City, Iowa, 1983, Whitworth Coll., Spokane, Wash., 1987, The Daedalus Project, 1988, Albion Coll., 2002-03, Kalamazoo Coll., 2003—04; reviewer NEH, Washington, 1986-87, panelist, 1991; reviewer Lilly Endowment, Indpls., 1987-89, U.S. Dept. Edn., 1993, Mich. Humanities Coun., 1999-2001, 2006; vis. assoc. prof. U. Calif., Santa Barbara, 1967-68, Ohio State U., Columbus, 1972; vis. rsch. prof. Am. Sch. Classical Studies, Athens, Greece, 1973-74, mng. com.; vis. scholar Green Coll. Oxford U., 1989; mem. editl. adv. bd. Christianity and The Arts, 1998-2001, chmn., 1999-2001. Co-author: Latin Via Ovid, 1977, rev. edit., 1982, A Dream Fulfilled: The Van Raalte Sculpture in Centennial Park, 1997; editor: Petronius: Cena Trimalchionis, 1970, Plautus: Amphitruo, 1970, A Goodly Heritage: Essays in Honor of the Reverend Dr. Elton J. Bruins at Eighty, 2007; author: Centennial History of 14th Street Christian Reformed Church, Holland, Michigan, 2002, Myth and the Creative Process: Michael Ayrton and the Myth of Daedalus, the Maze Maker, 2003; contbr. articles to profl. jours. Elder Christian Ref. Ch., Palo Alto, Calif., 1960—62, elder, clk. Grosse Pointe, Mich., 1964—67, Holland, Mich., 1976—85, v.p., 1988—91, exec. com., 1994—95; trustee Calvin Theol. Sem., 2001—07, mem. exec. com., 2002—07, v.p., 2003—07; chmn. human rels. coun. Open Housing Com., Grosse Pointe, 1971—73. Mem. Am. Philol. Assn., Danforth Assocs. (chmn. regional com. 1975-77), Mich. Classical Conf. (1st v.p. 1965-66, pres. 1966-67), Mich. Coun. Humanities (bd. dirs., 1976-84, 88-92, 96-99, chmn. 1980-82, Disting. Svc. award 1984), Nat. Fedn. State Humanities Couns. (bd. dirs. 1979-84, pres. 1981-83), Gt. Lakes Colls. Assn. (bd. dirs. 1991-93), Coun. on Undergrad. Rsch. (councilor-at-large 1993-99), Green Coll. Soc., Mortar Board, Phi Beta Kappa, Eta Sigma Phi. Democrat. Avocations: photography, carpentry. Office: Hope Coll Van Raalte Inst PO Box 9000 Holland MI 49422-9000 Office Phone: 616-395-7171. Business E-Mail: nyenhuis@hope.edu.

NYERGES, ALEXANDER LEE, museum director; b. Rochester, NY, Feb. 27, 1957; s. Sandor Elek and Lena (Angeline) N.; m. Kathryn Gray; 1 child, Robert Angeline. BA, George Washington U., 1979, MA, 1981. Intern The Octagon, Washington, 1976-79; archeol. asst. Smithsonian Instn., Washington, 1977; curatorial intern Nat. Mus. Am. History, 1978-79; adminstrv. asst. George Washington U., Washington, 1979-81; exec. dir. DeLand Mus. Art, Fla., 1981-85, Miss. Mus. Art, Jackson, 1985-92; dir. Dayton Art Inst., 1992—2006, Va. Mus. Fine Arts, Richmond, 2006—. Mem. grants panel Nat. Endowment for the Arts, 1988—; field surveyor Inst. Mus. Svcs., Washington, 1985-88, nat. review panel, 1990-92; treas., bd. dirs. Volusia County Arts Coun., Daytona Beach, Fla., 1983-85. Author: Selections from the Permanent Collection, 1999, In Praise of Nature: Ansel Adams and Photographers of the American West, The Harold W Shaw Collection: Pre Columbian Treasures, 2003, Edward Weston: A Photographer's Love of Life, 2004; contbr. articles to profl. jours. Bd. dirs. West Volusia Hist. Soc., 1984-85; pres. Miss. Inst. Arts and Letters, 1987-88; trustee Cultural Arts Ctr., DeLand, 1984-85, Miami Valley Cultural Alliance, 1993-95, Intermus. Conservation Lab., 1993-99, Montgomery County Arts and Culture Dist., 1994-2001; trustee, chmn. Dayton-Montgomery County Conv. and Visitors Bur.; bd. trustees Assn. Art Mus. Dirs., 2007—. U.S. Dept. Edn. scholar, 1973. Mem. DeLand Area C. of C. (bd. dirs., tourist adv. com. 1984-85), Assn. Art Mus. Dirs., Am. Assn. Mus. (S.E. regional rep. to non-print media com. 1983-85, nat. legis. com. 1986-93), Miss. Mus. Assn., Southeastern Mus. Conf. (bd. dirs. 1991-92), Fla. Mus. Assn., Fla. Art Mus. Dirs. Assn., Cultural Roundtable (pres. 1993-95), Ohio Mus. Assn. (trustee 1993-98), Phi Beta Kappa. Avocations: photography, music, writing, sports, scuba diving. Office: Virginia Mus Fine Arts 200 N Blvd Richmond VA 23220 E-mail: anyerges@aol.com.

NYGAARD, RICHARD LOWELL, federal judge; b. Thief River Falls, MN, 1940; BS cum laude, U. So. Calif., 1969; JD, U. Mich., 1971. Mem. Orton, Nygaard & Dunlevy, 1972—80; judge Ct. Common Pleas, 6th Dist. Pa., Erie, 1981—88, US Ct. Appeals (3d cir.), Erie, Pa., 1988—2005, sr. judge, 2005—; sr. lecturer Penn State Univ., 1999—2003. Councilman Erie County, Pa., 1977—81. With USNR, 1958—64. Mem.: ABA, Erie County Bar Assn., Pa. Bar Assn. Office: James A Byrne Courthouse 601 Market St Rm 2100 Philadelphia PA 19106 also: 17 S Park Row Ste B-230 Erie PA 16501-1164 *

NYGREN, CHRISTIAN THOMAS, lawyer; b. Escunaba, Mich., Oct. 27, 1961; s. Harold Thomas and Patricia Ann Nygren; m. Julia Rebecca Crotler, June 13, 1982; children: Patrick, Mark. BSChemE, Mont. State U., 1983; JD, U. Mont., 1997. Bar: Mont., U.S. Dist. Ct. Mont., U.S. Ct. Appeals (9th cir.). Officer USN, Charleston, SC, 1983—88; environ. engr. Willamette Industries, Albany, Oreg., 1988—94; atty., ptnr. Milodragovich Dale Steinbrener & Bierey, Missoula, Mont., 1997—. Capt. USNR, 1982—. Office: Milodragovich Dale et al 620 High Park Way Missoula MT 59801 Office Phone: 406-728-1455. Business E-Mail: nygren@bigssylawyers.com.

NYGREN, LAN MA, finance educator; d. Zhanhong Ma and Shufeng Tian; m. Kjell Ake Nygren, Jan. 14, 1999; children: Edward Patrick, Alexa Michelle. BS in Stats., JiangSu Inst. Tech., China, 1992; MS in Stats., Renmin U. China, Beijing, 1995; MA in Econs., Ohio State U., Columbus, 1997; PhD in Stats., NYU, NYC, 2003. Tchg. asst. Ohio State U., Columbus, 1997—98; rsch. asst. NYU, NYC, 1998—2001, instr., 2002—02; asst. prof. mgmt. scis. Rider U., Lawrenceville, NJ, 2003—. Contbr. articles to profl. jours. Fellow, Ohio State U., 1996; scholar, Jiangsu Inst. Tech., 1989—92; Guang-Hua scholar, Renmin U. China, 1993—95, W. Edwards Deming fellow, 2002, Summer fellow, Rider U., 2004, Davis fellow, 2006—07. Mem.: Inst. Ops. Rsch. and Mgmt. Scis., Am. Statis. Assn. Office: Rider U 2083 Lawrenceville Rd Lawrenceville NJ 08648 Office Phone: 609-895-5533. Business E-Mail: lnygren@rider.edu.

NYHAN, LAWRENCE J. (LARRY), lawyer; b. Chgo., May 16, 1955; BA, U. Chgo., 1977; JD, Loyola U., Chgo., 1980. Bar: Ill. 1980. Extern to Hon. Robert Eisen US Bankruptcy Judge, no. dist. Ill., 1979—80; now ptnr. bankruptcy law Sidley Austin LLP, Chgo., chmn. nat. and internat. corp. reorgn. and bankruptcy group, mem. exec. com. Office: Sidley Austin LLP 1 S Dearborn St Chicago IL 60603 Office Phone: 312-853-7710. Office Fax: 312-853-7036. Business E-Mail: lnyhan@sidley.com.

NYHAN, WILLIAM LEO, pediatrician, educator; b. Boston, Mar. 13, 1926; s. W. Leo and Mary N.; m. Christine Murphy, Nov. 20, 1948; children: Christopher, Abigail. Student, Harvard U., 1943-45; MD, Columbia U., 1949; MS, U. Ill., 1956, PhD, 1958; doctorate (hon.), Tokushima U., Japan, 1981. Intern Yale U.-Grace-New Haven Hosp., 1949-50, resident, 1950-51, 53-55; asst. prof. pediatrics Johns Hopkins U., 1958-61, assoc. prof., 1961-63; prof. pediatrics, biochemistry U. Miami, 1963-69, chmn. dept. pediatrics, 1963-69; prof. U. Calif., San Diego, 1969—, chmn. dept. pediatrics, 1969-86. Mem. FDA adv. com. on Teratogenic Effects of Certain Drugs, 1964-70; mem. pediatric panel AMA Council on Drugs, 1964-70; mem. Nat. Adv. Child Health and Human Devel. Council, 1967-71; mem. research adv. com. Calif. Dept. Mental Hygiene, 1969-72; mem. med. and sci. adv. com. Leukemia Soc. Am., Inc., 1968-72; mem. basic adv. com. Nat. Found. March of Dimes, 1973-81; mem. Basil O'Connor Starter grants com., 1973-93; mem. clin. cancer program project rev. com. Nat. Cancer Inst., 1977-81; vis. prof. extraordinario U. del Salvador (Argentina), 1982. Author (with E. Edelson): The Heredity Factor, Genes, Chromosomes and You, 1976; author: Genetic & Malformation Syndromes in Clinical Medicine, 1976, Abnormalities in Amino Acid Metabolism in Clinical Medicine, 1984, Diagnostic Recognition of Genetic Diseases, 1987; author: (with P. Ozand) Atlas of Metabolic Diseases, 1998; author: (with B. Barshop and P. Ozand) 2d edit., 2005; author: (with G. Hoffmann, J. Zschocke, S.G. Kahler and E. Mayatepek) Inherited Metabolic Diseases, 2001; editor: Amino Acid Metabolism and Genetic Variation, 1967, Heritable Disorders of Amino Acid Metabolism, 1974; mem. editl. bd.: Jour. Pediat., 1964—78, Western Jour. Medicine, 1974—86, King Faisal Hosp. Med. Jour., 1981—85, Annals of Saudi Medicine, 1985—87, mem. editl. com.: Ann. Rev. Nutrition, 1982—86, mem. editl. staff: Med. and Pediat. Oncology, 1975—83. Served with U.S. Navy, 1944-46; U.S. Army, 1951-53. Nat. Found. Infantile Paralysis fellow, 1955-58; recipient Commemorative medallion Columbia U. Coll. Physicians and Surgeons, 1967, Guthrie award Am. Assn. Mental Retardation, 1998, Pool of Bethesda award Bethesda Luth. Homes and Svcs., 1999. Fellow: Inst. Medicine of Nat. Acad. Scis., Am. Acad. Pediat. (Borden award 1980, Lifetime Achievement award 1999); mem.: AAAS, Biochem. Soc., Am. Coll. Med. Genetics, Am. Assn. Clin. Chemists, Am. Soc. Human Genetics (dir. 1978—81), Am. Soc. Clin. Investigation, Soc. Exptl. Biology and Medicine, Am. Inst. Biol. Scis., Am. Pediatric Soc., South African Human Genetics (hon.), Inst. Investigaciones Citologicas (Spain) (corr.), Soc. Francaise de Pediatrie (corr.), N.Y. Acad. Sci., Western Soc. Pediatric Rsch. (pres. 1976—77), Am. Soc. Pharmacology and Exptl.

Therapeutics, Am. Assn. Cancer Rsch., Soc. Pediatric Rsch. (pres. 1970—71), Am. Chem. Soc., Am. Fedn. Clin. Rsch., Alpha Omega Alpha, Sigma Xi. Office: U Calif San Diego Dept Pediatrics # 0830 9500 Gilman Dr La Jolla CA 92093-0830 Office Phone: 619-543-5237. Business E-Mail: wnyhan@ucsd.edu.

NYHUS, LLOYD MILTON, retired surgeon, educator; b. Mt. Vernon, Wash., June 24, 1923; s. Lewis Guttorm and Mary (Shervem) N.; m. Margaret Goldie Sheldon, Nov. 25, 1949; children: Sheila Margaret, Leif Torger. BS, Pacific Luth. Coll., 1945; MD, Med. Coll. Ala., 1947; Doctor honoris causa, Aristotelian U., Thessalonika, Greece, 1968, Uppsala U., Sweden, 1974, U. Chihuahua, Mex., 1975, Jagallonian U., Cracow, Poland, 1980, U. Gama Filho, Rio de Janeiro, 1983, U. Louis Pasteur, Strasbourg, France, 1984, U. Athens, 1989. Diplomate Am. Bd. Surgery (chmn. 1974-76). Intern King County Hosp., Seattle, 1947-48, resident in surgery, 1948-55; practice medicine specializing in surgery Seattle, 1956-67, Chgo., 1967—; instr. surgery U. Wash., Seattle, 1954-56, asst. prof., 1956-59, assoc. prof., 1959-64, prof., 1964-67; Warren H. Cole prof., head dept. surgery U. Ill. Coll. Medicine, 1967-89, emeritus head, 1989—, prof. emeritus, 1993, established Lloyd M. Nyhus, MD chair of gen. surgery, dept. surgery Chgo., 2007; ret., 1993. Emeritus surgeon-in-chief U. Ill. Hosp.; sr. cons. surgeon Cook County, West Side VA, Hines VA hosps., Ill.; cons. to Surgeon Gen. NIH, 1965-69. Author: Surgery of the Stomach and Duodenum, 1962, 4th edit., 1986, named changed to Surgery of the Esophagus, Stomach and Small Intestine, 5th edit., 1995, Hernia, 1964, (book name change) Nyhus and Condon's Hernia, 5th edit., 2002, Chinese (Mandarin) edit., 2004, Abdominal Pain: A Guide to Rapid Diagnosis, 1969, 95, Spanish edit., 1996, Russian edit., 2001, Manual of Surgical Therapeutics, 1969, latest rev. edit., 1996, Mastery of Surgery, 1984, 3d edit., 1997, Spanish edit., 1999, Surgery Ann., 1970-95, Treatment of Shock, 1970, 2d rev. edit., 1986, Surgery of the Small Intestine, 1987; editor-in-chief Rev. of Surgery, 1967-77, Current Surgery, 1978-90, emeritus editor, 1991—; assoc. editor Quar. Rev. Surgery, 1958-61; editl. bd. Am. Jour. Digestive Diseases, 1961-67, Scandinavian Jour. Gastroenterology, 1966-97, Am. Surgeon, 1967-89, Jour. Surg. Oncology, 1969-99, Archives of Surgery, 1977-86, World Jour. Surgery, 1977-95; contbr. articles to profl. jours. Served to lt. M.C. USNR, 1943-46, 50-52. Decorated Order of Merit (Poland); postdoctoral fellow USPHS, 1952-53; recipient M. Shipley award So. Surg. Assn., 1967, Rovsing medal Danish Surg. Soc., 1973; Disting. Faculty award U. Ill Coll. Medicine, 1983, Disting. Alumnus award Med. Coll. Ala., 1984, Disting. Alumnus award U. Wash., 1993, 99; Guggenheim fellow, 1955-56. Fellow ACS (1st v.p. 1987-88), Assn. Surgeons Gt. Brit. and Ireland (hon.), Royal Coll. Surgeons Eng. (hon.), Royal Coll. Surgeons Ireland (hon.), Royal Coll. Surgeons Edinburgh (hon.), Royal Coll. Physicians and Surgeons Glasgow (hon.), Internat. Soc. Surgery Found. (hon., sec.-treas. 1992-2001); mem. Am. Gastroent. Assn., Am. Physiol. Soc., Pacific Coast Surg. Assn., Am. Surg. Assn. (recorder 1976-81, 1st v.p. 1989-90), Western Surg. Assn., Ctrl. Soc. Clin. Rsch., Chgo. Surg. Soc. (pres. 1974), Ctrl. Surg. Assn. (pres. 1984), Seattle Surg. Soc., St. Paul Surg. Soc. (hon.), Kansas City Surg. Soc. (hon.), Inst. Medicine Chgo., Internat. Soc. Surgery (hon. fellow 2001, pres. U.S. sect. 1986-88, pres. 34th World Congress 1991, internat. pres. 1991-93), Internat. Soc. for Digestive Surgery (pres. III world congress Chgo. 1974, internat. pres. 1978-84), Soc. for Surgery Alimentary Tract (sec. 1969-73, pres. 1974), Soc. Clin. Surgery, Soc. Surg. Chmn., Soc. U. Surgeons (pres. 1967), Duetschen Gesellschaft für Chirurgie (hon.), Polish Assn. Surgeons (hon.), L'Academie de Chirurgie (France) (corr.), Nat. Acad. of Medicine (France, Argentina and Brazil, hon.), Swiss Surg. Soc. (hon.), Brazilian Coll. Surgeons (hon.), Surg. Biology Club, Warren H. Cole Soc. (pres. 1981), Japan Surg. Soc. (hon.), Assn. Gen. Surgeons of Mex. (hon.), Columbian Surg. Soc. (hon.), Costa Rican Coll. Medicine & Surgery (hon.), Assn. Surgeons Costa Rica (hon.), Internat. Fedn. Surg. Colls. (hon. treas. 1992-99), Sigma Xi, Alpha Omega Alpha, Phi Beta Pi. Home: 310 Maple Row Northfield IL 60093-1036 Office: U Ill Coll Medicine Dept Surgery MC 958 840 S Wood St Chicago IL 60612-7322 Personal E-mail: lmn_23@msn.com.

NYIKOS, STACY ANN, publishing executive; d. Michael J. and Martha Nyikos; m. Rainer Kohrs, Dec. 1, 1994; children: Alysia Bella Kohrs, Sophia Johanna Kohrs. BA, U. Notre Dame, 1990; MA, Christian Albrecht U., Germany, 1994; PhD, U. Va., 2000. Gen. mgr. Stonehorse Pub., Tulsa, Okla., 2004—07; stats. lab coord. U. Okla., Tulsa, 2004—06. Author: (children's lit.) Squirt, 2005, Shelby, 2006, Dizzy, 2007. Organizer Okla. involvement Screentime Awareness, Internat. TV Turnoff Week. Finalist Foreword Bk. of Yr. award, 2006; named winner, Ariz. Author's Literacy Contest, 2006; grantee, Fulbright Com., 1998—99; Dissertation Improvement grantee, NSF, 1999—2001, President's fellow, U. Va., 1995—98, Dumas Malone Traveling fellow, 1998—99. Liberal. Roman Catholic. Avocations: running, travel. Office: Stonehorse Pub LLC 10632 S Memorial Ave 245 Tulsa OK 74133 Home Phone: 918-298-2302; Office Phone: 888-867-1927. Office Fax: 888-867-1927. Business E-Mail: snyikos@stonehorsepublishing.com.

NYIRJESY, ISTVAN, obstetrician, gynecologist; b. Budapest, Hungary, Nov. 14, 1929; came to U.S., 1954, naturalized, 1960; s. Sandor D. and Margit (Bertalan) N.; m. Michelle Shoepp, June 16, 1956; children: Francis, Paul, Christine. MD, Catholic U. Louvain, Belgium, 1955. Diplomate: Am. Bd. Ob-Gyn. Intern Cath. U. Louvain and Little Co. Mary Hosp., Evergeen Park, Ill., 1954-55; resident in gynecology obstetrics, 1960-63; chief obstetrical research Nat. Naval Med. Center, Bethesda, Md., 1966-68; ret., 1968; practice medicine specializing in Ob-Gyn Bethesda, 1968—. Clin. prof. Ob-Gyn Georgetown U., 1968—; cons. NIH, 1974—, FDA, 1977-88. Lit. editor Breast Disease: contbr. articles to med. jours.; author: Prevention and Detection of Gynecologic and Breast Cancer, 1994. Pres., Internat. Found. for Gynecol. Cancer Detection and Prevention, 1993—. Officer M.C. USN, 1956-68; advanced through grades to comdr. Recipient Sword of Hope pin Am. Cancer Soc., 1973, Vicennial medal Georgetown U., 1988. Fellow ACOG (Host award 1964), Hungarian Gynecologic Soc. (hon.), Internat. Coll. Surgeons; mem. Montgomery County (Md.) Med. Soc. (chmn. profl. edn. com. 1971-72), Am. Soc. of Breast Disease (past pres.), Assn. Profs. Ob-Gyn., Am. Soc. Reproductive Medicine, Washington Gynecol. Soc. (v.p. 1993-94, 1st v.p. 1994-95, pres. 1996-97). Office: 5301 Westbard Cir Ste 5 Bethesda MD 20816-1429 Home Phone: 301-229-3387; Office Phone: 301-654-0445.

NYKROG, PER, French literature educator; b. Copenhagen, Nov. 1, 1925; came to U.S., 1979; s. Kai S. Nathanson and Karen E. (Olsen) Nykrog; m. Vibeke H. Rasmussen, 1951 (dec. 1977); children: Thomas, Jakob; m. Usha Saksena Nilsson, Jan. 2, 1981. Grad., U. Copenhagen, 1952; PhD, U. Aarhus, Denmark, 1957. Asst. prof. U. Aarhus, 1953-57, prof., 1957-79; prof. French lang. and lit. Harvard U., Cambridge, Mass., 1979-98. Author: Les Fabliaux, 1957, La Pensée de Balzac, 1965, L'Amour et la Rose, 1986, La Recherche du Don perdu, 1987, Chrétien de Troyes romancier discutable, 1995. Mem. Royal Soc. Scis. Denmark. Home: 243 Concord Ave Cambridge MA 02138-1360 Office: Harvard U Dept Romance Langs Boylston Hall Cambridge MA 02138 Business E-Mail: nykrog@fas.harvard.edu.

NYLAND, WILLIAM LEWIS, retired military officer; b. Coronado, Calif., Oct. 2, 1946; m. Brenda Petty; 3 children. BS in Biology, U. N.Mex., 1968; MS in Sys. Mgmt. R & D, U. So. Calif., 1980; student, Amphibious Warfare Sch., 1975, Navy Fighter Weapons Sch. (TopGun), 1977, Naval War Coll., 1981, Air War Coll., 1988. Commd. 2nd lt. USMC, 1968, advanced through grades to gen., 2002; comdr. VMFA-232, 1985—87, Marine Aviation Training Support Group, Pensacola, Fla., 1990—92; chief of staff 2nd Marine Aircraft Wing, 1992—94, asst. wing comdr., 1992—94, 2nd MAW, 1994—95; dep. dir. force structure & resources USMC Joint Staff (J-8), Washington, 1995-97; dep. commdg. gen. II Marine Expeditionary Force, Camp Lejeune, NC, 1997—98; commdg. gen. 2d Marine Aircraft Wing, MCAS, Cherry Point, NC, 1998—2000; dep. comdt. programs & resources USMC, 2000—01, dep. comdt. aviation, 2001—02, asst. comdt. Washington, 2002—05. Decorated Def. Disting.Svc. medal, Legion of Merit, Def. Meritorious Svc. medal, Meritorious Svc. medal, Air medal with 8 Strike/Flight awards, Joint Svc. Commendation medal. Office Phone: 703-966-9750. E-mail: spidernyland@aol.com.

NYLANDER, JANE LOUISE, museum director, educator, writer; b. Cleve., Jan. 27, 1938; d. James Merritt and Jeannette Cayford; m. Daniel Harris Giffen, 1963 (div. 1970); children: Sarah Louise, Thomas Harris; m. Richard Conrad Nylander, 1972: 1 child, Timothy Frost. AB, Brown U., Providence, RI, 1959; MA, U. Del., Newark, 1961; postgrad., Attingham Summer Sch., Eng., 1970; PhD (hon.), New Eng. Coll., Henniker, NH, 1994. Curator Hist. Soc. York County, Pa., 1961-62, N.H. Hist. Soc., Concord, 1962-69; instr. New Eng. Coll., Henniker, 1964-65, Monadnock C.C., Peterborough, NH, 1966-69; curator of textiles and ceramics Old Sturbridge Village, Mass., 1969-85; adj. assoc. prof. Boston U., 1978-85; sr. curator Old Sturbridge Village, 1985-86; dir. Strawbery Banke Mus., Portsmouth, NH, 1986-92, Soc. for Preservation of New Eng. Antiquities, Boston, 1992-93, pres., 1993—2002, pres. emerita, 2002—. Adj. prof. art history and Am. studies Boston U., 1993—96; mem. adv. bd. Concord (Mass.) Mus., 1986—94, Wentworth-Coolidge Commn., 1991—96, mem. adv. com., 1996—2004; mem. adv. bd. John Nicholas Brown Ctr. for Am. Studies, Providence, 1995—2003; mem. adv. bd. dept. Am. decorative arts Mus. Fine Arts, Boston, 1971—99, Art of the Ams., 1999—2000; mem. adv. com. Lakes Region Conservation Trust, 2002—04, Charles S. Parsons Fund, 2004—06; advisor house com. Moffatt Ladd House, 1973—; mem. nat. coun. Strawbery Banke Mus., 2004—, mem. steering com. Ctr. for Study of Cmty., 2004—05; cons. in field. Author: Fabrics for Historic Buildings, 4th edit., 1990, Our Own Snug Fireside: Images of the New England Home 1760-1860, 1993, paperback edit., 1994, Windows on the Past, 2000, The Art of Family, 2002; author: (with Richard C. Nylander) Fabrics and Wallpaper for Historic Buildings, 2005; mem. editl. bd.: Hist. N.H., 1993—, The Dublin Seminar, 1984—; contbr. numerous articles to profl. jours. Trustee Worcester (Mass.) Hist. Mus., 1978—84, Hist. Deerfield (Mass.) Inc., 1981—94, 2003—, chair strategic planning com., 2003—, hon. trustee, 1994—2003, Hist. Mass., Inc., 1991—93, Decorative Arts Trust, 1991—, Portsmouth Athenaeum, 1988—90, Japan Soc. N.H., 1988—92, Fort Ticonderoga, 2000—02; mem. adv. bd. New Eng. Heritage Ctr., 1993—2002; active State Ho. Adv. Com., Boston, 1984—85, Gov.'s Coun. for Wentworth Coolidge Mansion, Concord, 1964—66; mem. Com. for Preservation of N.H. State Flags, 1989—92; mem. H.F. duPont award com. Winterthur Mus., 1993—, mem. Mt. Vernon adv. com. for 1999, 1996—99; designator The Henderson Found., 1992—2004. Recipient Charles F. Montgomery prize, Decorative Arts Soc., 1985, Disting. Sophomore Book prize, Boston U., 1993, (with Richard C. Nylander) The Anne and Roger Webb award, Historic Mass., Inc., 1996, John F. Ayer award, The Bay State League, 2002, Boston History award, Bostonian Soc., 2003, award for outstanding contbn. to decorative arts, Iris Found., 2005, Lifetime Achievement award (with Richard C. Nylander), Victorian Soc. Am., 2005, Roll of Honor, Nat. Soc. Colonial Dames of Am., N.H., 2006. Mem.: N.H. Hist. Soc. (interpretation com. 2003—05, exbns. and pubs. com. 2005—, trustee 2007—, chair 2007—), Costume Soc. Am. (bd. dirs. 1977—83), New Eng. Hist. Geneal. Soc., N.H. Humanities Coun., Soc. Preservation of N.H. Forests, Soc. Winterthur Fellows, Mass. Hist. Soc., Portsmouth Athenaeum, Royal Oak Assn., Nat. Trust for Hist. Preservation, Am. Assn. for State and Local History (Cert. of Commendation 2001), Am. Antiquarian Soc., Castle Preservation Soc. (bd. dirs. 2004—, vice chair 2004—), Colonial Soc. Mass., Nat. Soc. Colonial Dames in N.H. (bd. dirs. 1967—73, program chair 2002—, Roll of Honor 2006), Friends of Hist. Deerfield, Friends of the Moffatt Ladd House, Lakes Region Conservation Trust, Brown Club N.H. (trustee 1988—93). Episcopalian. Home: 17 Franklin St Portsmouth NH 03801-4501

NYOKKA, SUZETTE, artist, natural health educator; b. Meadowbrook, Pa., June 10, 1961; d. Barbara Louise and adopted d. Walter H. Schmitz, Thomas Ziemba; children: Gaelen Ishi Nyokka Morrell, Emily Luna Rose Nyokka Morrell. BA, Calif. Inst. Integral Studies, 2001. Advanced Massage Therapies, Natural Health Educator Inst. of Ednl. Therapy, Heartwood Inst., 1988, cert. in Jin Shin Jyutsu 2005. Founder Heartwood Garden, Garberville, Calif., 1984—89; creator/artist Island Mt. Basketry, Garberville, 1986—; massage therapist/ educator Advanced Massage Therapies, Woodside, Menlo Park, Calif., 1989—2005, massage therapist/educator Garberville/Novato, 2005—; ednl. activist So. Humboldt Cmty. Sch. Dist., Garberville, 1984—; dir. Skyfish Sch. Permaculture Program, Garberville, 1997—2005; artistic dir. Teen's Radio, Redway, Calif., 2005—; instr. permacuture design, adj. advisor Skyfish Sch., Briceland, 1997—. Prodr.: (storytelling festivals) Live Performances; co-creator (cd) All Spirits Sing (Best Native Am. Rec., 1998). Co-coord. Arts and Ecology Ctr., Garberville, Calif., 2005—; developmennt coord. KMUD Teen's Cmty. Radio, Garberville, Calif., 2004—05; vp So. Humboldt Youth and Cmty. Ctr., Garberville, Calif.; pres. Trees Found., Garberville, Calif., 1996—98; participant in a cross cultural sharing Nat. Storytelling Assn., San Francisco, 2002, China, 2002. Grant, Music For Little People Found., 2002, Humboldt Area Found., 2004, Calif. Inst. of Integral Studies, 2000. Mem.: So. Humboldt Cmty. Parks and Garden Club (life). Democrat-Npl. Avocations: reading, photography, language, film, travel. Home: 352 Meadowview Rd Garberville CA 95542 Home Phone: 707-923-2478; Office Phone: 415-250-1733. Personal E-mail: suzette@asis.com.

NYQUIST, CORINNE ELAINE, librarian; b. Minnesota Falls, Minn., Nov. 1, 1935; d. Clair Francis and Ebba Ingeborg Johnson; m. Thomas Eugene Nyquist, Dec. 22, 1956; children: Jonathan Eugene, Lynn Marie. BA (cum laude), Macalester Coll., 1956; MALS, U. Minn., 1971; PhD (hon.), U. Albany, 2004. Asst. librarian U. Minn., Mpls., 1959-60, Evanston (Ill.) Pub. Library, 1962-64, Skokie (Ill.) Pub. Library, 1965-66; asst. librarian, research asst. Rhodes U., Grahamstown, Republic of South Africa, 1967; asst. librarian to librarian SUNY, New Paltz, 1968—, ombudsman, 1983-85. Co-project dir. human rights documentation project Ford Found., 1986-88; cons. N.Y. State Edn. Dept., Albany, 1980-82; chmn. internat. librs. com. SUNY, 1984-86. Contbr. articles to profl. jours. Chmn. Town Dem. Com., New Paltz, 1984-86, 2007—; adv. com. on awards SUNY, 1989-94. Recipient Chancellor's award, 1986; grantee SUNY Rsch. Found., 1975, 84-86, Ford Found., 1986. Mem. ALA (chmn. human rights task force 1989-91, exec. internat. rels. task force 1987-92, interlibr. loan code revision com. 2006—, codes, guidelines and tech. stds. com. 2007—), African Studies Assn., NY African Studies Assn. (co-editor newsletter 1974-99, v.p. 1991-92, pres. 1992-93), Ulster County Librs. Assn. (exec. com. 1984-94), Sojourner Truth Inst. (bd. dirs. 1997-2001), SUNY Librs. Assn., Beta Phi Mu. Avocations: reading, hiking, cross country skiing, travel. Office: SUNY Sojourner Truth Libr New Paltz NY 12561-2493 Home: 140 Huguenot St New Paltz NY 12561-1018 Home Phone: 845-255-0558; Office Phone: 845-257-3681. E-mail: nyquistc@newpaltz.edu.

NYQUIST, JOHN DAVIS, retired radio manufacturing company executive; b. Peoria, Ill., May 28, 1918; s. Eliud and Linnea (Widen) N.; m. Alice Schmidt, June 5, 1942; 1 child, Sarah Lynn. BS in Mech. Engring, U. Ill., 1941. With Collins Radio Co., Cedar Rapids, Iowa, 1941—, v.p., gen. mgr. Iowa region, 1965-69, v.p. operations, 1969-70, sr. v.p., 1970-73, also dir.; ret., 1973; cons. Rockwell-Collins. Dir. Norwest Bank Iowa N.A. (formerly Peoples Bank & Trust Co.), Cedar Rapids. Bd. dirs. Am. Cancer Soc., YMCA, St. Lukes Hosp. Recipient award for outstanding achievement Am. Inst. Indsl. Engrs., 1966, Indsl. Engring. award, 1969, Coll. Engring. Alumni Honor award, 1977; both U. Ill.). Mem. Iowa Mfrs. Assn., Am. Mgmt. Assn., Am. Inst. Indsl. Engrs., IEEE, Cedar Rapids C. of C. (dir.) Clubs: Cedar Rapids Country. Home: 2115 1st Ave SE Cedar Rapids IA 52402

NYQUIST, MAURICE OTTO, retired federal agency administrator, scientist; b. Fairmont, Minn., May 30, 1944; s. Carl Arther and Wilda Yvette (Freitag) N.; m. Mary Maud Magee, Aug. 8, 1977; children: Gretchen, Beth. BS in Biology, Hamline U., St. Paul, Minn., 1966; MA in Biology, Minn. State U., Mankato, 1968; PhD in Zoology, Wash. State U., Pullman, 1973. Asst. prof. zoology Wash. State U., Pullman, 1973-74; scientist Nat. Park Svc., Lakewood, Colo., 1974-76, mgr., 1979-93; mgr., scientist Nat. Biol. Svc., Denver, 1993-96, USGS, Denver, 1996—2004; coord. Aurora Partnership, 1999—2003. Formerly affiliate faculty Sch. Natural Resources, Colo. State U., Ft. Collins; mem. peer rev. coms. for academia, govt. and pvt. industry; agy. rep. Fed. Geographic Data Com., chair biol. data working group, mem. standards working group and coordination group, vegetation subcom. Dir. prodn. interactive computer exhibit on remote sensing for Denver Mus. Nat. History; contbr. sci. articles to profl. jours. Bd. dirs. Nat. Park Service Equal Employment Opportunity Com., Denver, 1981, chmn., 1982. Recipient Mgrs. award Nat. Park Service, Lakewood, 1981, Performance Commendation award, 1988, Excellence of Svc. Team awrd U.S Dept. Interior, 1999; NRA rsch. grantee, 1972. Fellow Am. Soc. Potogrammetry and Remote Sensing (exec. com., bd. dirs. 1988-90, v.p. 1992, pres.-elect 1993, pres. 1994, dir. remote sensing applications divsn. 1987-89); mem. Am. Congress on Surveying and Mapping (joint satellite mapping and remote sensing com.), The Wildlife Soc., ELAS Users Group (co-chmn. 1985-86, chmn. 1986-87), Sigma Xi. *Personal philosophy: We need to view the land as a community to which we all belong, instead of a commodity for individual gain. (adopted from Aldo Leopold's A Sand County Almanac, 1949).*

NYREN, NEIL SEBASTIAN, publishing executive, editor; b. Boston, June 13, 1948; s. Karl Edwin and Dorothy Elizabeth (Smith) N.; m. Lois Miriam Sharfman, Oct. 11, 1970; 1 child, Alexander BA, Brandeis U. V.p. G.P. Putnam's Sons Pub., NYC, 1997—; editor Random House Pubs., NYC, 1974-77, Arbor House Pubs., NYC, 1977-78; exec. editor Atheneum Pubs., NYC, 1978-84; sr. editor G.P. Putnam's Sons Pub., NYC, 1984-86, editor-in-chief, 1986—, pub., 1989—, sr. v.p., 1997—. Democrat. Jewish. Office: GP Putnam's Sons 375 Hudson St New York NY 10014-3658 Business E-Mail: nnyren@penguinputnam.com.

NYROP, DONALD WILLIAM, air transportation executive; b. Elgin, Nebr., Apr. 1, 1912; s. William A. and Nellie (Wylie) N.; m. Grace Cary, Apr. 19, 1941; children: Nancy, William, Karen, Kathryn. AB, Doane Coll., 1934; JD, George Washington U., 1939. Bar: D.C. 1938. Atty. Gen. Counsel's Office, CAA, Washington, 1939-41; exec. officer to chmn. CAB, 1942, chmn., 1952; rep. U.S. airlines; mem. ofcl. U.S. delegations Internat. Civil Aviation Orgn. Assemblies, 1946, 47; dep. adminstr. for ops. CAA, 1948-50, adminstr., 1950-51; chmn. CAB, 1951-52; pres. Northwest Airlines, Inc., 1954-78. Served with Air Transport Command USAAF, 1942-46. Decorated Legion of Merit. Mem.: Mpls. Club. Home: 4505 Golf Ter Minneapolis MN 55424-1510

NYS, JOHN NIKKI, lawyer; b. Duluth, Minn., May 3, 1948; s. Leslie Leo and Kathleen Cecilia (Beaudin) N.; 1 child, John Stephenson. BA, Dartmouth Coll., 1970; JD, Stanford U., 1973. Bar: Minn. 1973, U.S. Dist. Ct. Minn. 1973, U.S. Ct. Appeals (8th cir.) 1984, U.S. Dist. Ct. (we. dist.) Wis. 1985, Wis. 1986. Ptnr. Johnson, Killen & Seiler, Duluth, 1973—. Pres., treas., bd. dirs. Duluth Regional Care Ctr., 1979-85; v.p., bd. dirs. Western Community Coun., 1980-86; cubmaster Lake Superior coun. Boy Scouts Am., 1987-90; mem. state cen. com. Dem. Farmer Labor Party, 1976-78; pres., bd. dirs. Morgan Park Smithville Community Club, 1978-85. Mem. ABA, Duluth Young Lawyers (pres. 1974-75), Minn. State Bar Assn. (chmn. lawyers referral com. 1986-88, bd. govs. 1990-98, pres. 1996-97), 11th Dist. Bar Assn. (pres. 1989-90). Lutheran. Business E-Mail: jnys@duluthlaw.com.

NYWEIDE, JEFFREY O., management and business executive; b. Chgo., Feb. 8, 1956; s. Lysle John and Marion (Ottmuller) N. BS in Econs., Northwestern U., 1978. Product specialist Service Bur. Co., Chgo., 1978-79, account exec., 1980-81, sales and service mgr., 1981-82; cons. Control Data Bus. Ctrs., Atlanta, 1982-84, product sales mgr. Greenwich, Conn., 1984-85, nat. product mgr., 1985-87; mng. ptnr. Quantum Mgmt., Inc., Greenwich, 1987-88; exec. v.p., pres., COO Dataware Technologies, Inc., Boston, 1988-2000, also bd. dirs.; venture ptnr., sr. advisor, entrepreneur in residence Millennium Tech. Ventures LP, NYC, 2001—. Exec. v.p. corp. devel., CFO Global Options Group, 2004—. Contbr. articles to profl. jours. Mem. ADAPSO, Am. Mgmt. Assn., Human Resources System Profls., Am. Payroll Assn., Phi Gamma Delta. Clubs: Norwalk Yacht. Avocations: sailing, swimming, music. Home: PO Box 1426 Manchester Center VT 05255 Office: 75 Rockefeller Plaza New York NY 10019

O, CAO K., cultural organization administrator; b. Vietnam; arrived in US, 1975. BS in Sociology, Cornell U., 1980; MS, Hunter Coll. Sch. of Social Work; attended, Columbia U. Former social worker and case mgr. NYC Dept. for the Aging, Vietnamese Am. Cultural Org.; develop. dir. Hamilton-Madison House, 1983—86; program developer NY State Office of Mental Health, 1986—88; consultant United Way of NYC, 1988—90. Exec. dir. Asian Am. Federation of NY, 1991—; vice chair 9/11 United Services Group; bd. mem. Museum of Chinese in Am., Hamilton-Madison House, Nonprofit Coordinating Com. of NY, Human Svc. Council of NYC; chmn. Coalition for New Philanthropy in NY, 2003—. Office: Asian Am Federation of NY 120 Wall St New York NY 10005

O, KENNETH KYONGYOP, engineering educator; s. Sang-Chol and Yong-Ae O; m. Hyun-Joo Nam, Dec. 28, 1991; children: Stephen Tae-Jin, Daniel Tae-Su, Andrew Tae-Yoon. BS, MS, MIT, 1984, PhD, 1989. Sr. process engr. Analog Devices Inc, Wilmington, Mass., 1989—94; prof. U. Fla., Gainesville, Fla., 1994—, Rsch. Found. Prof., 2004—06. Chief tech. officer Global Communication Device, North Andover, Mass., 2002—03. Recipient Faculty Partnership award, IBM, 1995, 1997, 2000, Copper Design Challenge award, Semiconductor Rsch. Corp., 1999, Career Devel. award, NSF, 1996, Copper Design Challenge award, Semiconductor Rsch. Corp., 1999; Materials Processing Ctr. fellow, MIT, 1985. Mem.: IEEE, Sigma Xi. Achievements include development of RF silicon bipolar process technology; first to show CMOS technology can be used to produce RF integrated circuits for WLAN applications which are competitive to those fabricated using the SiGe technology; development of Aapproaches to improve on-chip inductors and varactors in silicon integrated circuits; first to show on-chip antennas can be used for communication within and between IC's; development of Schottky diodes with cut-off frequency greater than 1 THz in CMOS technology; research in 200-GHz CMOS oscillator. It holds the highest operating frequency silicon based circuits. Office: U Florida Dept ECE 539 New Engineering Building Gainesville FL 32611 Office Phone: 352-392-6618. Office Fax: 352-392-8381. Business E-Mail: kko@tec.ufl.edu.

OAK, CLAIRE MORISSET, artist, educator; b. St. Georges, Quebec, Can., May 31, 1921; came to U.S., 1945; d. Louis and Bernadette (Coulombe) Morisset; m. Alan Ben Oak, July 2, 1947. Student, Ecole des Beaux Arts, 1938—42, Parsons Sch. Design, NYC, 1945, Art Students

League, 1945—46. Staff artist Henry Morgan & R. Simpson, Montreal, 1942-45; artist illustrator W.B. Golovin Advt. Agy., NYC, 1947-49; freelance illustrator Arnold Constable & Advt. Agy., NYC, 1948-50, Le Jardin des Modes, Paris, 1950-51, May & Co., LA, 1956, Katten & Marengo Advt., Stockton, Calif., 1962-84; pvt. practice illustrator, designer San Joaquin Valley, Calif., 1984-92; art instr. San Joaquin Delta Coll., Stockton, 1973—. Owner Fashion Illustrator's Workshop, N.Y.C., 1953-54; instr. Bauder Coll., Sacramento, 1975-76; painting workshop leader Lodi Art Ctr., 1991—; watercolor workshop leader D'Pharr Painting Adventures, Virginia City, Nev., 1992; watercolor workshop Galerie Iona, Stockton, Calif., 1993—. Named S.B. Anthony Woman of Achievement in the Arts, U. Pacific, 1982. Mem. Stockton Art League, Lodi Art Ctr., Ctrl. Calif. Art League, The League of Carmichael Artists, Delta Watercolor Soc. (bd. mem. 1988—). Avocations: painting, drawing. Home: 2140 Waudman Ave Stockton CA 95209-1755 Personal E-mail: oaklair@sbcglobal.net. *You are a success in the visual arts if you teach others how to see.*

OAKAR, MARY ROSE, congresswoman; b. Cleve., Mar. 5, 1940; d. Joseph M. and Margaret Mary (Ellison) O. BA in English, Speech and Drama, Ursuline Coll., Cleve., 1962, LHD (hon.); MA in Fine Arts, John Carroll U., Cleve., 1966; LLD (hon.), Ashland U., 1978, Ursuine Coll., 1984, St. Mary's Notre Dame, 1989, Baldwin Wallace Coll., 1988; LHD (hon.), Trinity Coll., 1987. Instr. English and drama Lourdes Acad., Cleve., 1963-70; asst. prof. English, speech and drama Cuyahoga Community Coll., Cleve., 1968-75; mem. Cleve. City Council from 8th Ward, 1973-76, 95th-102nd Congresses from 20th Dist. Ohio, 1977-92; mem. Pepper Commn. on Long Term Health Care, chair subcom. internat. devel., fin., trade and monetary policy; chair task force on social security, elderly, women; chair subcom. on personnel and police; mem. banking, fin. and urban affairs com., select com. on aging, post office and civil service com., com. on house adminstrn., also numerous subcoms.; ptnr. Mary Rose Oakar and Assocs. Apptd. to Sec. Conf. to Establish Nat. Action Plan on Breast Cancer, 1994, by Pres. Clinton to bd. dirs. Bldrs., For Peace, 1994, to policy to White House Conf. on Aging. Founder, vol.-dir. Near West Side Civic Arts Center, Cleve., 1970; ward leader Cuyahoga County Democratic Party, 1972-76; mem. Ohio Dem. Central Com. from 20th Dist., 1974; trustee Fedn. Community Planning, Cleve., Health and Planning Commn. Cleve., Community Info. Service Cleve., Cleve. Soc. Crippled Children, Public Services Occupational Group Adv. Com., Cuyahoga Community Coll., Cleve. Ballet, Cleve. YWCA. Recipient Outstanding Service awards OEO, 1973-78, Community Service award Am. Indian Center, Cleve., 1973, Community Service award Nationalities Service Center, 1974, Community Service award Club San Lorenzo, Cleve., 1976, Cuyahoga County Dem. Woman of Yr., 1977, Ursuline Coll. Alumna of Yr. award, 1977, awards Irish Nat. Caucus, awards West Side Community Mental Health Center, awards Am. Lebanese League, awards Cleve. Fedn. Am.-Syrian Lebanese Clubs, Breast Cancer Awareness award Nat. Women's Health Resource Ctr., 1989, 1st lay recipient Barbara Bohen-Pfeiffer award Italian-Am. Found. Cancer Rsch., 1989, Disting. Svc. award Am. Cancer Soc., 1989, Myrl H. Shoemaker award Ohio Dem. Party, 1992, Philip Hart award Consumer Fedn. Am., 1987; cert. appreciation City of Cleve.; Woman of Yr. award Cuyahoga County Women's Polit. Caucus, 1983; decorated Knight of Order of St. Ladislaus of Hungary, Women in Aerospace Outstanding Ach. award, Black Focus Woman of the Decade award. Office: 1888 W 30th St Cleveland OH 44113-3447

OAKES, DENNIS, lawyer, insurance company executive; b. 1951; AB, Hamilton Coll., 1973; JD, Cath. U. of Am., 1977. With Wolf, Block Schorr and Solis-Cohen, 1977—80, 1984—87; chief of staff Mayor of Phila., 1980—84; adminstrv. asst. Phila. Congressman William J. Green, 1973—77; spl. counsel Ronald O. Perelman, 1988—93; exec. dir., Acad. Medicine and Managed Care Forum Aetna Inc., 1996—2001, chief investor rels. officer, 2001—03, v.p. pub. policy, 2003—.

OAKES, JAMES L., retired federal judge; b. Springfield, Ill., Feb. 21, 1924; m. Evelena S. Kenworthy, Dec. 29, 1973 (dec. Oct. 1997); m. Mara A. Williams, Jan. 1, 1999; m. Rosalyn Landon, Oct. 2, 1945; 3 children. AB, Harvard Coll., 1945; LLB, Harvard U. Law Sch., 1947; LLD, New Eng. Coll., 1976, Suffolk U., 1980, Vt. Law Sch., 1995. Bar: Calif. 1949, Vt. 1950. Pvt. practice, Brattleboro, Vt.; spl. counsel Vt. Pub. Svc. Commn., 1959—60; counsel Vt. Statutory Revision Commn., 1957—60; mem. Vt. Senate, 1961—65; atty. gen. Vt., 1967—69; US dist. judge, 1970—71; judge US Ct. Appeals (2d cir.), Brattleboro, 1971—2007, chief judge, 1989—92. Adj. faculty Duke U. Law Sch., 1985—96, Iowa U. Coll. Law, 1993—97. *

OAKES, JEANNINE, education educator; BA, San Diego State U., 1964; MA, Calif. State U., 1969; PhD in Edn., UCLA, 1980. Presdl. prof. in ednl. equity UCLA, dir. Inst. for Democracy, Edn. & Access, dir. All Campus Consortium on Rsch. for Diversity. Contbr. articles to profl. jours.; author: Keeping track: How schools structure inequality, 1985; co-author: Teaching to Change the World, 1998, Becoming Good American Schools: The Struggle for Civic Virtue in Education Reform, 1999. Recipient Disting. Achievement Award, Ednl. Press Assn. of Am., Ralph David Abernathy Award for Pub. Svc., So. Christian Leadership Conf., Multicultural Rsch. Award, Nat. Assn. Multicultural Edn., Jose Vasconcelos World Award in Edn., World Cultural Coun., 2002. Office: UCLA Grad Sch Edn Info Studies 1033D Moore Hall Los Angeles CA 90095 Office Phone: 310-825-2494. E-mail: oakes@ucla.edu.

OAKES, LESTER CORNELIUS, retired electrical engineer, consultant; b. Knoxville, Oct. 11, 1923; s. Charles Vaughn and Maude Cornelia (Harrison) O.; m. Kathleen Clark, Dec. 27, 1947; children: Michael, Richard, Cynthia, Melissa. BS in E.E., U. Tenn., 1949, MS, 1962. Registered profl. engr., Tenn. Engr. Fairchild Engring. and Aircraft, Oak Ridge, 1949-51; engr. I&C div. Oak Ridge Nat. Lab., 1951-68, dep. head I&C div., 1968—, asst. dir. I&C div., 1971-90; cons. Oak Ridge Nat. Lab., electric Power Rsch. Inst., Nuclear Regulatory Commn., 1990—. Contbr. articles to profl. jours.; patentee in field. Served with USAF, 1943-46. Martin Marietta Corp. fellow. Fellow IEEE Presbyterian. Home: 710 Pleasant Hill Rd Maryville TN 37803-7337 Personal E-mail: lesoakes@earthlink.net.

OAKES, PAMELA R., retired elementary school educator; d. Frederick O. and Virginia Hoover Abrams; m. F. Michael Oakes, Oct. 4, 1958; children: Michael, Lisa Poole, Gigi Kershner, Gina Korsi. AA, Jefferson C.C., Louisville, 1971; BS in Edn., U. Louisville, 1979, postgrad., 1979—80, U. St. Thomas, Houston, 1992—94. Cert. ESL and gifted and talented tchr. Tchr. spl. edn. Jefferson County Sch. Dist., Louisville, 1979—80; tchr. 5th/6th grade St. Thomas Acad., West Hartford, Conn., 1980—82; tchr. 5th grade Our Lady of Victory, Victoria, Tex., 1982—84, St. Gregory the Great, San Antonio, 1984—85; tchr. 2d grade Houston Ind. Sch. Dist., 1985—89; tchr. 5th grade Cypress-Fairbanks Ind. Sch. Dist., Houston, 1989—2005, ret., 2005. Demonstration tchr. Houston Ind. Sch. Dist., 1988; coord. spelling bee Matzke Elem. Sch., 1995—2005. Mem.: Tex. Edn. Assn., Ky. Cols., Kappa Delta Pi. Roman Catholic. Avocations: sewing, interior decorating. Home: 15027 Rain Shadow Ct Houston TX 77070 Office: Cypress-Fairbanks ISD Matzke Elem 13102 Jones Rd Houston TX 77070 Personal E-mail: pamoakeshouston@aol.com.

OAKES, ROBERT JAMES, physics and astronomy professor; b. Mpls., Jan. 21, 1936; s. Sherman E. and Josephine J. (Olson) O.; children: Cindy L., Lisa A. BS, U. Minn., 1957, MS, 1959, PhD, 1962. NSF fellow Stanford U., 1962-64; asst. prof. physics, 1964-68; assoc. prof. physics Northwestern U., 1968-70, prof. physics, 1970-76, prof. physics and astronomy, 1976—. Vis. staff mem. Los Alamos Sci. Lab., 1971-92; vis. scientist, user Fermi Nat. Accelerator Lab., 1975-2006, CERN, 1966-67; mem. Inst. for Advanced Study, Princeton, 1967-68; vis. scientist DESY, 1971-72; faculty assoc. Argonne Nab. Lab., 1982—2002; U.S. scientist NSF-Yugoslav joint program, 1982-92; panelist Nat. Rsch. Coun., 1990-98. A.P. Sloan fellow 1965-68; Air Force Office Sci. Rsch. grantee, 1969-71, NSF grantee 1971-87, Dept. Energy grantee, 1987—; named Fulbright-Hays Disting. prof. U. Sarajevo, Yugoslavia, 1979-80; recipient Natural Sci. prize China, 1993. Fellow Am. Phys. Soc., AAAS; mem. N.Y. Acad. Sci., Ill. Acad. Sci., Sigma Xi, Tau Beta Pi. Office: Northwestern U Dept Physics 2145 Sheridan Rd Evanston IL 60208-0834

OAKES, TERRY LOUIS, apparel executive; b. Denver, June 12, 1953; s. Robert Walter and Stella Marie (Ray) O.; m. Cynthia Alison Bailey, Jan. 10, 1981; children: Madeleine Bailey, Robert Alan. BBA, So. Meth. U., 1975. Dept. mgr. Woolf Bros., Dallas, 1975-76; buyer I.K.O. Dry Goods, Denver, 1976-79, gen. sales mgr., 1979-81, exec. v.p., mdse. mgr., 1981-86; nat. sales mgr. Fresh Squeeze div. Bayly Corp., Denver, 1986-88; owner, pres. Bolderdash, Denver, 1988—. Tchr., mem. adv. bd. fashion mdse. divsn. Colo. Inst. Art., Denver, 1991-98. Bd. dirs. Cherry Creek North Bus. Improvement Dist., Vail Racquet Club, Vail, Colo. Mem. Vail Racquet Club (bd. dirs.). Democrat. Presbyterian. Home: 5390 S Geneva St Englewood CO 80111-6205 Office: Bolderdash 2721 E 3d Ave Denver CO 80206-4919 Personal E-mail: ctmaokes@aol.com.

OAKES, THOMAS WYATT, environmental engineer, computer engineer; b. Danville, Va., June 14, 1950; s. Wyatt Johnson and Relia (Sceacre) O.; m. Terry Lynn Jenkins, June 15, 1974; 1 child, Travis Wyatt. BS in Nuclear Engring., Va. Polytechnic U., 1973, MS in Nuclear Engring., 1975; MS in Environ. Engring., U. Tenn., 1981. Ordained deacon Bapt. Ch., 1989. Health physics asst. Va. Polytechnic U., Blacksburg, 1972-74; radiation engr. Babcock and Wilcox Co., Lynchburg, Va., 1974-75; dept. mgr. Oak Ridge (Tenn.) Nat. Lab., 1975-78, environ. mgr., 1978-85; corp. environ. coord. Martin Marietta, Oak Ridge, 1985-87; asst. v.p. Sci. Applications Internat. Corp., Oak Ridge, 1987-90; environ. mmgr. Westinghouse Environ. and Geotech. Svcs., Knoxville, Tenn., 1990-91; mgr. S.E. region environ. svcs. ATEC & Assocs., Inc., Marietta, Ga., 1991-93; asst. v.p. environ. svcs. Scitek, Ft. Campbell, Ky., 1993-98; ind. sr. cons., 1998—; pres. T30 Nat. Svc. Inc., 1998—. Safety dir. DSSI/MOEC, 2002—. Contbr. over 107 articles to scholarly and profl. jours. Recipient Spl. Recognition award Union Carbide Corp., 1980, Best Paper award Nat. Safety Coun., 1982, Tech. Publs. award Soc. Tech. Communications, 1987. Mem. AAAS, Am. Indsl. Hygiene Assn., N.Y. Acad. Scis., Health Physics Soc. (sec.-treas. environ. sect. 1984-85), Am. Naval Soc., Am. Soc. for Quality Control. Office: 11130 Kingston Pike Ste 1-328 Knoxville TN 37922-2800 E-mail: t30oakes@inetmail.att.net.

OAKES, WALTER JERRY, pediatric neurosurgeon; b. De Soto, Mo., July 10, 1946; s. Marvin Melton and Mildred Florene (Link) O.; m. Linda Helen Maas (div. Jan. 1985); 1 child, Kathleen Suzanne; m. Jean Evans, Dec. 1988; children: Matthew Marvin, Peter Clifford. BA in Chemistry, U. Mo., 1968; MD, Duke U., 1972. Diplomate Am. Bd. Neurol. Surgeons. Neurosurgery resident Duke U., Durham, NC, 1972-78, asst. prof. neurosurgery, 1979-90, assoc. prof. neurosurgery, 1991—, asst. prof. pediatrics, 1981-92, assoc. prof. pediatrics, 1992; pediatric neurosurgery resident U. Toronto Hosp. for Sick Children, Ont., Canada, July-Dec., 1975; registrar pediatric neurosurgery U. London Hosp. for Sick Children, England, Sept., 1978-Feb., 1979; prof. neurosurgery and pediat. U. Ala., Birmingham, 1992—, Dan Hendley chair pediatric neurosurgery, 2002—. Fellow: ACS. Office: Children's Hosp Ala 1600 7th Ave S Ste 400 Birmingham AL 35233-1785 Office Phone: 205-879-7754. Business E-Mail: wjomd@uab.edu.

OAKLEY, ANDREW ARTHUR, journalist, educator; b. Chgo., Oct. 22, 1958; s. Arthur George and Dolores Margarite (Hernandez) O.; m. Suzanna Pinter, Sept. 7, 1985; children: Glen Matthias, Ryan Arthur. BS in Journalism, Northwestern U., 1980, MS, 1981. Reporter Woodstock (Ill.) Daily Sentinel, 1980-81; police reporter Herald-Palladium, St. Joseph, Mich., 1981-82; city hall reporter Daily Herald, Arlington Heights, Ill., 1982-84; instr. journalism Oakton C.C., Des Plaines, Ill., 1984-85; features editor North Shore Mag., Winnetka, Ill., 1985-86; news editor City and State, Chgo., 1986-93; journalism editor P.O. Publ. Co., Port Murray, NJ, 1993-2000; newsletter editor All Aboard for Hackettstown, NJ, 1996-98. Lectr. Northwestern U., Evanston, Ill., 1990-96; columnist Daily Herald, Arlington Heights, Ill., 1995-96; copy editor Full Time Dads Mag., Clifton, N.J., 1997-2000; corr. Daily Herald, Arlington Heights, 1995—. Author: Eighty-Eight, 1988, Issues Confronting City and State Governments, 1992, Beginning Journalism Packet, 1994; cons. editor P.O. Pub. Co., Skokie, Ill., 1988-92. Lifetime mem. N Club, 1980—; commr. Skokie Human Rels. Commn., 1987-94; advisor Mcpl. Alliance Lit. Club, 1997-98; U.S. Soccer Fedn. coach, referee, 1999—; edn. chmn. Charleston (Ill.) Alliance Ch., 2000-04; v.p. Blairstown Little League, 2005—. Mem. Medill Alumni Assn., Evanston Running Club. E-mail: nwarrenunited@aol.com.

OAKLEY, CAROLYN LE, state legislator, city manager, director; b. Portland, Oreg., June 28, 1942; d. George Thomas and Ruth Alveta Victoria (Engberg) Penketh; children: Christine, Michelle. BS in Edn., Oreg. State U., 1965. Educator Linn County (Oreg.) Schs., 1965-76; owner Linn County Tractor, 1965-90; mem. Oreg. Legis. Assembly, Salem, 1989—, asst. majority leader, 1993—, majority whip, 1994; apptd. regional dir. region 10 Dept. Health and Human Svcs., Seattle, 2002—. Mem. exec. bd. Oreg. Retail Coun., 1987-90. Chmn. Linn County Rep. Ctrl. Com., 1982-84; chmn. bd. dirs. North Albany Svc. Dist., 1988-90; chair Salvation Army, Linn and Benton Counties, 1987—; vice chmn. bd. trustees Linn-Benton C.C. Found., 1987—; pres. Women for Agr., Linn and Benton Counties, 1984-86; mem. STRIDE Leadership Round Table, 1991—; state chair Am. Legis. Exch. Coun., 1991-96; nat. bd. dirs., 199-99, exec. com., 1995, 1st vice chair, 1998; mem. Edn. Commn. of the States, 1991—, com. policies and priorities, 1993—, steering com., 1998—, exec. com., 1998; mem. Leadership Coun. on Higher Edn., 1995—; mem. nat. policy bd. Danforth Found., 1995—; state dir., Women in Govt., 1996—; state dir., Nat. Order Women Legislators, 1993—; hon. mem. Linn-Benton Compact Bd., 1993—; active Linn County Criminal Justice Coun., 1994—; vol. Good Samaritan Hosp. Found., State Land Trust for Affordable Housing, Majestic Theater; bd. trustees Good Samaritan Found., 2006—; pres. Benton County Rep. Women, 2000-02. Named Woman of Yr. Albany chpt. Beta Sigma Phi, 1970. Mem. Nat Conf. State Legislators (chmn. edn. com. 1992—), Albany C. of C. (bd. dirs. 1986-93, 96—), Linn County Rep. Women (legis. chmn. 1982-91, pres. 2006—), Greater Corvallis Rotary Club (bd. dirs.). Republican. Methodist. Avocations: gardening, camping, volunteering. Home: 3197 NW Crest Loop Albany OR 97321-9627 Office Phone: 541-928-7745. Personal E-mail: cloakley@juno.com.

OAKLEY, DEBORAH JANE, public health service officer, nursing educator; b. Jan. 31, 1937; d. George F. and Kathryn (Willson) Hacker; m. Bruce Oakley, June 16, 1958; children: Ingrid Andrea, Brian Benjamin. BA, Swarthmore Coll., 1958; MA, Brown U., 1960; MPH, U. Mich., 1969, PhD, 1977. Dir. teenage and adult programs YWCA, Providence, 1959-63; editl. asst. Stockholm U., 1963-64; rsch. investigator, lectr. dept. population planning U. Mich., 1971-77, asst. prof. cmty. health programs Ann Arbor, 1977-79, asst. prof. nursing rsch., 1979-81, assoc. prof., 1981-89, prof., 1989—2002, interim dir. Ctr. Nursing Rsch., 1988-90, acting dir. Ctr. Nursing Rsch., 1998, prof. emeritus, 2002—, interim dir. Health Asian Ams. program, 2005. Vis. prof. Beijing Med. U., 1996-2002; prin. investigator NIH, CDC and pvt. found. funded rsch. grants and contracts on family planning, women's health and health care in China, nat. adv. com. nursing rsch., 1993-97; adv. workshop on Nat. Survey on Family Growth, 1994-97; co-chair Mich. Initiative for Women's Health, 1993-95. Author: (with Leslie Corsa) Population Planning, 1979; contbr. articles to profl. jours. Bd. dirs. Planned Parenthood Fedn. Am., 1975-80. Recipient Margaret Sanger award Washtenaw County Planned Parenthood, 1975, Outstanding Young Woman of Ann Arbor award Jaycees, 1970, Dist. Faculty award Mich. Assn. Gov. Bds., 1992, Blue Cross Blue Shield Found. of Mich. award for Excellence in Health Policy, 1996. Mem. APHA (chmn. population sect. coun.), Internat. Union Sci. Study Population, Midwest Nursing Rsch. Soc., Population Assn. Am., Delta Omega, Sigma Theta Tau (hon.). Democrat. Home: 5200 S Lake Dr Chelsea MI 48118-9481 Office: U Mich Sch Nursing Ann Arbor MI 48109-0482 Office Phone: 743-763-6730. E-mail: doakley@umich.edu.

OAKLEY, FRANCIS CHRISTOPHER, historian, educator; b. Liverpool, Eng., Oct. 6, 1931; arrived in U.S., 1957, naturalized, 1968; s. Joseph Vincent and Siobean (NiCurean) O.; m. Claire-Ann Lamenzo, Aug. 9, 1958; children: Deirdre, Christopher, Timothy, Brian. BA, Corpus Christi Coll., Oxford U., 1953, MA, 1957; postgrad., Pontifical Inst. Medieval Studies, Toronto, 1953—55; MA, Yale U., 1958, PhD, 1960; LLD, Amherst Coll., 1986, Wesleyan U., 1989, U. Notre Dame, 2006; LHD, Northwestern U., 1990, North Adams State Coll., 1993, Bowdoin Coll., 1993; LittD, Williams Coll., 1994. Mem. faculty Yale U., 1959-61, Williams Coll., Williamstown, Mass., 1961—, prof. history, 1970—2002, dean faculty, 1977-84, Edward Dorr Griffin prof. history of ideas, 1984—85, pres., 1985-94, pres. emeritus, 1994—, Edward Dorr Griffin prof. history of ideas, 1994—2002, prof. emeritus, 2002—; interim pres. Am. Coun. Learned Socs., 2002—03, pres. emeritus, 2003—; hon. fellow Corpus Christi Coll., Oxford U., 1991—; sr. fellow Oakley Ctr. Humanities, Williams Coll., 2002—. Vis. lectr. Bennington (Vt.) Coll., 1967; Sir Isaiah Berlin vis. prof. Oxford U., 1999-2000; Merle Curti lectr. U. Wis., Madison, 2001; Étienne Gilson lectr. Pontifical Inst. Medieval Studies, Toronto, 2002; mem. Inst. Advanced Study Princeton, 1981-82; assoc. Nat. Humanities Ctr., 1991; guest scholar Woodrow Wilson Internat. Ctr. for Scholars, 1994; chair bd. dirs. Am. Coun. Learned Socs., 1993-97; trustee Sterling and Francine Clark Art Inst., 1985—, pres. bd. trustees, 1998-2005; trustee MassMoCA Found., 1995-2004, Willamstown Art Conservation Ctr., 1995-98, Williamstown Theatre Festival, 1985-93; trustee Nat. Humanities Ctr., 1996-02, 2003—, chmn. bd. trustees, 2004—, Lake Forest Coll., 1997-2001; trustee Inst. Advanced Cath. Studies, 1998-2005, vice chair, 2002-05; mem. MassMoCA Cultural Devel. Commn., 1988—; mem. adv. coun. Ctr. for Study of Religion, Princeton U., 1999—. Author: The Political Thought of Pierre d'Ailly: The Voluntarist Tradition, 1964, Kingship and the Gods: The Western Apostasy, 1968, Council over Pope?, Towards a Provisional Ecclesiology, 1969, Medieval Experience: Foundations of Western Cultural Singularity, 1974, rev. England edit., The Crucial Centuries, 1979, Spanish edit., 1980, 95, Medieval Acad. edit., 1988, 93, The Western Church in the Later Middle Ages, 1979, rev. edit., 1985, 88, 91, Natural Law, Conciliarism and Consent in the Late Middle Ages, 1984, Omnipotence, Covenant and Order: An Excursion in the History of Ideas, 1984, Community of Learning: The American College and the Liberal Arts Tradition, 1992, Scholarship and Teaching: A Matter of Mutual Support, 1996, Politics and Eternity: Studies in the History of Medieval and Early Modern Political Thoughts, 1999, The Leadership Challenges of a College Presidency, 2002, The Conciliarist Tradition, 2003 (Roland H. Bainton History prize, 2004), Natural Law, laws of Nature and Natural Rights, 2005, Kingship: The Politics of Enchantment, 2006; editor: (with Daniel O'Connor) Creation: The Impact of an Idea, 1969, (with Bruce Russett) Governance, Accountability and the Future of the Catholic Church, 2003; contbr. articles to profl. jours. Lt. Brit. Army, 1955-57. Goldsmith's Co. London fellow, 1953-55, Social Sci. Rsch. Coun. fellow, 1963, Am. Coun. Learned Socs. fellow, 1965, 69-70, Weil Inst. fellow, 1965, Folger Shakespeare Libr. fellow, 1974, NEH fellow, 1976, 81-82, Mellon emeritus rsch. fellow, 2005, Academic fellow, Carnegie Corp. NY, 2003-05; recipient Wilbur Lucius Cross medal Yale Grad. Sch., 1997. Fellow Medieval Acad. Am. (pres. fellows 1999-2002), Am. Acad. Arts and Scis.; mem. Am. Hist. Assn., Am. Cath. Hist. Assn., Am. Ch. History Soc., New Eng. Medieval Conf. (pres. 1983-84), The Century Assn., Am. Cusanus Soc. (adv. bd. 1997—). Democrat. Roman Catholic. Office: Williams Coll Oakley Ctr Humanities & Soc Sci Williamstown MA 01267 Office Phone: 413-597-2149. Business E-Mail: foakley@williams.edu.

OAKLEY, GERARD JOSEPH, gynecologist; b. Teaneack, NJ, June 14, 1955; s. Gerard J. and Joan P. Oakley; m. Tanyia Kim Tooley, Sept. 2, 1978; children: G. Joseph, Robben M., Kevin C., Colin J. BS, Mich. State, East Lansing, 1977; MD, U. Mich., Ann Arbor, 1983. Cert. OBGYN 1992. Resident gynecol. Wright State U., Dayton, Ohio, 1983—87; fellow, gynecol. U. Minn., Mpls., 1987—90; dir. gynecol. Wright Patt AFB Med. Ctr., Dayton, Ohio, 1990—97, Marshall U. Som, Huntington, W.Va., 1997—2006, Edwards Cancer Ctr., Huntington, W.Va., 2006—. Cancer com. chair Abell Huntington Hosp., Huntington, W.Va., 1997—; chair, mem. Mt. of Hope, Charleston, W.Va., 2000—; principal investigator Ovarian Cancer Awareness, Huntington, 2002—. Vol. raising ovarian cancer awareness, Huntington, 2002—, Ronald MacDonald House, Huntington, 2003—; adv. coun. WVBCCSP, Charleston, W.Va., 2004—. Lt. col. (ret.) USAF, 1979—2003. Named Hometown Hero, WSAZ Huntington; recipient Humanism in Medicine award, Marshall Med., 2004. Fellow: Am. Coll. OB-GYN; mem.: Makers Mark Ambassador Soc., Cabell Co. Med. Soc., Phi Beta Kappa. Avocations: woodworking, knitting, puzzles, music. Office: ECCC Cabell Huntington Hosp 1340 Hal Creek Blvd Huntington WV 25701 Office Phone: 304-399-6666.

OAKLEY, GODFREY PORTER, JR., medical educator; b. Greenville, NC, June 1, 1940; s. Godfrey Porter and Carrie O.; m. Mary Ann Bryant, Sept. 2, 1961; children: Martha Gray, Susan Herndon, Robert Bryant. Student, Duke U., 1958-61; MD, Bowman Gray Sch. of Medicine, 1965; MS in Preventive Medicine, U. Washington, 1972. Diplomate Am. Bd. Pediatrics, Nat. Bd. Med. Examiners, Am. Bd. Preventive Medicine, Am. Bd. Med. Genetics. Intern in straight pediatrics Cleve. Met. Gen. Hosp., 1965-66, resident in pediatrics, 1966-68; sr. fellow in teratology and human embryology U. Washington Sch. of Medicine, Ctrl. Lab. Human Embryology, Dept. of Pediatrics, Seattle, 1970-72; sr. fellow U. Washington Sch. Pub. Health and Community Medicine, Seattle, 1971-72; EIS officer leukemia sect. Ctrs. Disease Control and Prevention (CDC), Atlanta, 1968-70, chief etiology studies sect., bur. epidemiology, cancer and birth defects, 1972-81; chief birth defects br., chronic diseases divisn. Nat. Ctr. Environ. Health, Ctrs. Disease Control and Prevention, Atlanta, 1981-85, dir. divsn. birth defects and devel. disabilities, 1985-94; clin. asst. prof. pediatrics divsn. med. genetics Emory U., Atlanta, 1968-70, 72-85, clin. asst. prof. gynecology-obstetrics divsn. med. genetics, 1981-85; mem. visiting med. staff Grady Meml. Hosp., Atlanta, 1974-84; vis. prof. epedemiology Rollins Sch. Pub. Health, Emory Univ., 1998—. Med. adv. bd. Ctrs. Disease Control & Prevention (CDC); mem. task force on predictors of hereditary desease or congenital defects NIH Consensus Conf., 1979; mem. genetics coordinating com. NIH/CDC; mem. adv. com. biometric and epidemiological methodology FDA/CDC; cons. bur. med. svcs. FDA; mem. Chronic Diseases Surveillance Working Group; mem. patient registry com. Cystic Fibrosis Found., med. adv. coun., 1978—; mem. drug experience coordinating com. Dept. Health, Edn. and Welfare; mem. genetics com. Ga. Dept. Human Resources, 1980—; ex-officio mem. genetic diseases rev. and adv. com. Health Svcs. Adminstrn., 1981; mem. master community health program, interdisciplinary faculty com., curriculum com. Emory U.; mem. working group on heart disease epidemiology Nat. Heart, Lung and Blood Insts., 1978; mem. ad hoc com. on Alphafetoprotein Pub. Health Svc.; mem. profl. adv. coun. Spina Bifida Assn. Am., 1981—; mem. WHO EURO-China Consultation, Beijing, China,

1983; lectr. in field. Mem. editorial bd. Pediatric & Perinatal Epidemiology, 1987-89; contbr. articles to profl. jours., chpts. to books. Nancy Lybrook Lasater scholar 1961-67; recipient Physician's Recognition award AMA, 1973-76, Outstanding Svc. medal Pub. Health Svc., 1981, Meritorious Svc. award, 1988, Spl. Recognition award, 1993, President's Excellence award Spina Bifida Assn. Am., 1988-89, Disting. Alumnus award U. Washington Sch. Pub. Health, 1990, Hebert L. Needleman award Am. Pub. Health Assn., 1996; named Person of Week, World News Tonight, 1996. Mem. Am. Acad. Pediatrics (past com. drugs/CDC liaison, com. genetics 1990, exec. com. 1990—, CDC rep. Ga. chpt. 1993), Am. Soc. Human Genetics, Am. Coll. Epidemiology, Am. Coll. Med. Genetics, Atlanta Genetics Soc., Greater Atlanta Pediatric Soc., Atlanta Obstetrical and Gynecological Soc. (assoc.), Soc. Epidemiologic Rsch., Soc. Pediatric Rsch., Teratology Soc. (pres. elect 1983-84, pres. 1984-85, editorial bd. Teratology 1978-83, edn. com. 1988), Internat. Clearinghouse Birth Defects Monitoring Systems (chmn. 1981-82, vice chmn. 1982-83, chmn. 1983-84), Pub. Health Leadership Inst., Alpha Omega Alpha, Inst. Medicine. Office: Rollins Sch Pub Health Emory U Dept Epedemiology 1510 Clifton Rd NE Atlanta GA 30322-4218

OAKLEY, JOHN BILYEU, law educator; b. San Francisco, June 18, 1947; s. Samuel Heywood and Elsie-Maye (Bilyeu) O.; m. Fredericka Barvitz, May 25, 1969; children: Adélie, Antonia. BA, U. Calif., Berkeley, 1969; JD, Yale U., 1972. Bar: Calif. 1972, U.S. Dist. Ct. (no. dist.) Calif. 1974, U.S. Dist. Ct. (ctrl. and ea. dists.) Calif. 1975, U.S. Supreme Ct. 1977, U.S. Ct. Appeals (5th cir.) 1979, U.S. Ct. Appeals (9th cir.) 1992. Rsch. atty. chief justice Donald R. Wright Supreme Ct. of Calif., 1972-73, sr. rsch. atty. chief justice Donald R. Wright, 1974-75; sr. law clk. chief judge M. Joseph Blumenfeld U.S. Dist. Ct. Conn., Hartford, 1973-74; assoc. U. Calif. (philos.Dept.), Davis, 1996; acting prof. law U. Calif., Davis, 1975-79, prof. law, 1979—; vice-chair U. Calif. (Academic Senate), 2005—06, chair, 2006—. Reporter Speedy Trial Planning Group, U.S. Dist. Ct., Sacramento, 1977-82, Civil Justice Reform Act Adv. Group, 1991-94, U.S. Jud. Conf. Com. on Fed.-State Jurisdiction, 1991-96, Western Regional Conf. on State-Fed. Jud. Relationships, 1992-93, 2000; scholar-in-residence, sr. trial atty. Civil Rights Divsn., U.S. Dept. Justice, Washington, 1979-80; vis. scholar U. Coll., Oxford (Eng.) U., 1982-83; apptd. counsel death penalty appeal Supreme Ct. Calif., 1984-96; cons. Calif. Jud. Coun. Commn. on the Future of the Cts., 1992-93; vis. prof. U. Calif. Berkeley, 2001, U. Tenn., 2001. Co-author: Law Clerks and the Judicial Process, 1980, An Introduction to the Anglo-American Legal System, 1980, 2d edit., 1988, 3d edit., 2001, Civil Procedure, 1991, 2d edit., 1996, 3d edit., 2001, with Charles Alan Wright fed. CT.: CASES AND MATERIALS Found., 9th edit. 1992, 10th 1995,11th 2005, contbr.: Restructuring Justice, 1990, with Rex R. Perschbacher,Civil Prodr. Casenotes Publishing Co. 1st edit. 1991, 2d 1996, 3d 2001, author Fed.Judical Code Revison Project, Am. Law Inst. (2004), contbd. artical to profl. jour. Pub. mem. New Motor Vehicle Bd. Calif., Sacramento, 1976-82, Calif. Jud. Coun. Appellate Process Task Force, 1997-2001; bd. dirs. Fallen Leaf Lake (Calif.) Mutual Water Co., 1980-82, 94—; western regional assoc., field assoc. Duke U. Primate Ctr., 1986-91, bd. visitors, 1997-2000. With U.S. Merchant Marine, 1969, Vietnam, Appellate Process Task Force Calif. Jud. Coun. (by appointment Chief Justice Supreme Ct. Calif.) Nat. Merit scholar, 1964. Mem. Am. Law Inst. (reporter Fed. Jud. Code Revision Project 1995—), Assn. Am. Law Schs. (chair sect. on civil procedure 1979-80, 96-97), Am. Judicature Soc. (bd. dirs. 1996-98), Am. Inns of Ct., 1997-2001, Phi Beta Kappa. Avocations: aviation, photography, railroads, rugby, running. Office: UC Davis Sch Law 400 Mrak Hall Dr Davis CA 95616

OAKLEY, MARY ANN BRYANT, lawyer; b. Buckhannon, W.Va., June 22, 1940; d. Hubert Herndon and Mary F. (Deeds) Bryant; m. Godfrey P. Oakley, Jr., Sept. 2, 1961; children: Martha, Susan, Robert. AB, Duke U., 1962; MA, Emory U., 1970, JD, 1974. Tchr. Winston-Salem/Forsyth County Schs., NC, 1961-65; assoc. Margie Pitts Hames, Atlanta, 1974-80; ptnr. Stagg Hoy & Oakley, Atlanta, 1980-83, Oakley & Bonner, Atlanta, 1984-90; pvt. practice, 1990-96; ptnr. Holland & Knight LLP, Atlanta, 1996—. Adj. prof. trial practice Ga. State U., 1986-95; adj. prof. pretrial Emory U. Law Sch., 1991, 95; bd. dirs. Nat. Employment Lawyers Assn., 1989-94; founding coord. NELA, Ga.; mem. Ga. Supreme Ct. Commn. on Racial and Ethnic Bias, 1994-95; mem. Ga. Bd. Bar Examiners, 1990-94, chmn., 1994. Author: Elizabeth Cady Stanton, 1972; mem. editl. rev. bd.: The Ga. Labor Letter, 1997—2001, notes and comments editor: Emory Law Jour., 1973—74; contbr. articles to law jours. Bd. dirs. Holland & Knight Charitable Found. Bd., 2002—, Atlanta Met. YWCA, 1975—79, 1st v.p., 1978—79; mem. Leadership Atlanta, 1979; bd. dirs. Ga. chpt. ACLU, 1981—83; bd. dirs. Ga. Legal Svcs. Program, 1991—98, Planned Parenthood Ga., 2006—; trustee Unitarian Universalist Congregation Atlanta, 1977—80, pres., 1979—80; mem. Unitarian Universalist Commn. Appraisal, 1980—85; bd. dirs. Unitarian Universalist Svc. Com., 1984—90, v.p., 1986—88, pres., 1988—90. Recipient Lifetime Commitment to Pub. Svc. award, Emory U. Sch. Law, 2005, Shining Star award, Atlanta Women's Found., 2006, Randolph Thrower award, Emory U. Sch. Law, 2005; Nat. Merit scholar, 1958. Fellow: Ga. Bar Found., Am. Bar Found.; mem.: ABA, Atlantic Vol. Lawyers Found. (adv. bd. 2006—), Ga. State Bar Disciplinary Bd. (investigative panel 1985—88, chmn. 1987—88), Ga. Assn. Women Lawyers (Kathleen Kessler award 1998), Atlanta Bar Assn., State Bar Ga. (chmn. individual rights sect. 1979—81, H. Sol Clark Pro Bono award 1996, Disting. Svc. award 1998), Am. Judicature Soc., Order of Coif, Phi Beta Kappa, Bleckley Inn of Ct. (pres. 1996—99). Home: 2224 Kodiak Dr NE Atlanta GA 30345-4152 Office: 1201 W Peachtree St One Atlantic Ctr Ste 2000 Atlanta GA 30309-3400 Office Phone: 404-817-8507. Business E-Mail: maryann.oakley@hklaw.com.

OAKLEY, RICHARD PUTNEY, investment banker; b. White Plains, NY, Apr. 8, 1920; AB, NYU, 1941. Partner Lehman Bros., NYC, 1958-65; v.p., dir. One William St. Fund, NYC, 1962-65; mgr. investment adv. Goldman, Sachs, 1965-66, partner, 1967-72; chmn. bd. Siff, Oakley & Marks, NYC, 1973-77. Trustee No. Westchester Hosp. Center, 1977-82; chmn. bd. Mt. Pleasant Indsl. Devel. Agy., 1980— Chmn. Mt. Pleasant Zoning Bd.; trustee Pleasantville, 1950-52. Fellow Fin. Analysts Fedn.; mem. Nat. Assn. Bus. Economists, N.Y. Soc. Security Analysts, Westchester Assn. Tax Receivers (founder); Lodges: Rotary Internat. Home: 116 Meadow Rd Briarcliff Manor NY 10510-1135 Personal E-mail: rputneyoak@yahoo.com.

OAKLEY, ROBERT LOUIS, law librarian, educator; b. NYC, Nov. 6, 1945; s. Bert Tuttle Oakley and Allese (Duffin) Vestigo; m. Madeleine Cohen, Aug. 13, 1971 (div. 2002); children: Esther Shulamit, Daniel Isaac-Meir; m. Barbara DesRosiers, May 1, 2005 BA, Cornell U., 1968; MLS, Syracuse U., 1972; JD, Cornell U., 1976. Bar: N.Y. 1977, U.S. Dist. Ct. (no. dist.) N.Y. 1977. Assoc. dir. law libr. Cornell U., Ithaca, NY, 1976-79; dir. law libr., assoc. prof. Boston U. Law, 1979-82, Georgetown U., Washington, 1982-87, dir. law libr., prof., 1987—. Contbr. articles to profl. jours. Mem. Libr. of Congress, Network Adv. Com., 1986-92, 1995-99, copyright office study group on sec. 108 of Copyright Act; adv. nat. commn. on Preservation and Access, 1988-94; bd. dirs. Montgomery County (Md.) Pub. Librs., 1988-92. Mem. ABA, ALA, Am. Assn. Law Librs. (Washington Affairs rep. 1989—, mem. exec. bd. 1991-94, v.p. 1999-2000, pres. 2000-01), Assn. Am. Law Schs. Avocations: photography, music, amateur radio. Office: Georgetown U Law Ctr 111 G St NW Washington DC 20001-1417 Office Phone: 202-662-9160. E-mail: oakley@law.georgetown.edu.

OAKS, SUNNY, child and family advocate, consultant, lyricist; b. Cardston, Alta., Can., Aug. 21, 1944; d. Willard Glen Hansen and Priscilla Pearl Hansen-Wallace; m. Guy Eugene Williams (dec.); children: Shelley, Jason; m. Michael Oaks, Jan. 28, 1984; children: Brian, Anna, Bethany, Christen. Grad high sch., Moses Lake, Wash. Bus. leader Shaklee Wholesale Distbn., 1972—92; founder, dir. Adults Supporting Kids, Wenatchee, Wash., 1995—96, CARE for Kids, 1997—99; founder, CEO, dir. trainer. grant writer HOME Connection, 1998—99; pvt. practice East Wenatchee, 1999—2006. Mem. adv. bd. Home Connection, Care for Kids, Adults Supporting Kids. Author: Secrets, 1992; singer, composer: albums Sunny's Song, 1987. Recipient High Volume award, Shaklee; grantee, Cmty. Found., 1997, Cmty. Network, 1997—98, Target Stores, 1997—98, Washington Assn. Prevention of Child Abuse and Neglect, 1998, Alcoa, 2000. Mem.: Shaklee Pres.' Club (Altus award). Avocations: writing, music, sewing, swimming. E-mail: healthyhorizons@verizon.net.

OATES, JOHN ALEXANDER, III, medical educator; b. Fayetteville, NC, Apr. 23, 1932; s. John Alexander and Isabelle (Crowder) O.; m. Meredith Stringfield, June 12, 1956; children: David Alexander, Christine Larkin, James Caldwell. BS magna cum laude, Wake Forest Coll., 1953; MD, Bowman Gray Sch. Medicine, 1956. Intern, asst. resident medicine N.Y. Hosp.-Cornell U. Med. Center, NYC, 1956-58, 61-62; from clin. assoc. to sr. investigator Nat. Heart Inst., 1958-63; faculty Vanderbilt U. Sch. Medicine, Nashville, 1963—, prof. medicine and pharmacology, 1969—, Werthan prof. investigative medicine, 1974-84, chmn. dept. medicine, 1983-97, Thomas F. Frist Sr. prof. medicine, 1984—. Drug rsch. bd. Nat. Acad. Scis.-NRC, 1967-71; chmn. pharmacology and toxicology tng. com. Nat. Inst. Gen. Med. Scis., 1969-70; adv. coun. Nat. Heart, Lung and Blood Inst., 1985-89. Master ACP; fellow Am. Acad. Arts and Scis., Am. Assn. Advancement Sci.; mem. Am. Fedn. Clin. Rsch. (pres. 1970-71), Am. Soc. Clin. Investigation (v.p. 1976-77), Assn. Am. Physicians (pres. 1981-82), Am. Soc. Pharmacology and Exptl. Therapeutics (chmn. exec. com. divsn. clin. pharmacology 1967-69), Inst. of Medicine. Achievements include co-discovery of antihypertensive effect of methyldopa, elucidation of a number of interactions between drugs in humans; research in biochemistry and pathophysiology of eicosanoids. Home: 2032 Sunset Hills Terr Nashville TN 37215 Office: Vanderbilt Med Ctr 536 RRB Nashville TN 37232-6602 Home Phone: 615-665-1976; Office Phone: 615-343-4845. Business E-Mail: john.oates@vanderbilt.edu.

OATES, JOYCE CAROL, writer; b. Lockport, NY, June 16, 1938; d. Frederic James and Caroline (Bush) O.; m. Raymond Joseph Smith, Jan. 23, 1961. BA, Syracuse U., 1960; MA, U. Wis., 1961. Instr. English U. Detroit, 1961-65, asst. prof., 1965-67; prof. English U. Windsor, Ont., Canada, 1967-87; writer-in-residence Princeton (N.J.) U., 1978-81, prof., 1987—. Author: (short story collections) By the North Gate, 1963, Upon the Sweeping Flood, 1966, The Wheel of Love, 1970, Marriages and Infidelities, 1972, The Hungry Ghosts, 1974, The Goddess and Other Women, 1974, Where Are You Going, Where Have You Been?: Stories of Young America, 1974, The Poisoned Kiss and Other Stories From the Portuguese, 1975, The Seduction and Other Stories, 1975, Crossing the Border, 1976, Night-Side, 1977, All the Good People I've Left Behind, 1978, The Lamb of Abyssalia, 1980, A Sentimental Education: Stories, 1981, Last Days: Stories, 1984, Wild Nights, 1985, Raven's Wing: Stories, 1986, The Assignation, 1988, Heat: And Other Stories, 1991, Where is Here?: Stories, 1992, Haunted: Tales of the Grotesque, 1994, Will You Always Love Me? and Other Stories, 1995, The Collector of Hearts: New Tales of the Grotesque, 1996, Faithless: Tales of Transgressions, 2001, Small Avalanches: And Other Stories, 2003, I Am No One You Know, 2004, High Lonesome: Stories 1966-2006, 2006; (novels) With Shuddering Fall, 1964, A Garden of Earthly Delights, 1967 (Nat. Book award nomination 1968), Expensive People, 1967 (Nat. Book award nomination 1969), them, 1969 (Nat. Book award for fiction 1970), Wonderland, 1971, Do With Me What You Will, 1973, The Assassins, 1975, Childwold, 1976, The Triumph of the Spider Monkey, 1976, Son of the Morning, 1978, Unholy Loves, 1979, Cybele, 1979, Bellefleur, 1980 (LA Times Book award nomination 1980), A Sentimental Education, 1981, Angel of Light, 1981, A Bloodsmoor Romance, 1982, Mysteries of Winterthorn, 1984, Solstice, 1985, Marya, 1986, You Must Remember This, 1987, (as Rosamond Smith) The Lives of the Twins, 1987, American Appetites, 1989, (as Rosamond Smith) Soul-Mate, 1989, Because It Is Bitter, and Because It Is My Heart, 1990, (as Rosamond Smith) Nemesis, 1990, I Lock My Door Upon Myself, 1990, The Rise of Life on Earth, 1991, Black Water, 1992, (as Rosamond Smith) Snake Eyes, 1992, Foxfire: Confessions of a Girl Gang, 1993, What I Lived For, 1994 (PEN/Faulkner award nomination 1995), Zombie, 1995, First Love, 1996, We Were the Mulvaneys, 1996, Man Crazy, 1997, Devil's Half Acre, 1997, Come Meet Muffin!, 1998, My Heart Laid Bare, 1998, Broke Heart Blues, 1999, Starr Bright Will Be With You Soon, 1999, Blonde, 2000, The Barrens, 2001, Faithless: Tails of Transgression, 2001, Middle Age: A Romance, 2001, Big Mouth and Ugly Girl, 2002, I'll Take You There, 2002, Freaky Green Eyes, 2003, Rape: A Love Story, 2003, Where Is Little Reynard, 2003, The Tattooed Girl, 2003, Sexy, 2005, Missing Mom, 2005, The Female of the Species: Tales of Mystery and Suspense, 2006, The Gravedigger's Daughter, 2007; (as Lauren Kelly) The Stolen Heart, 2005, Blood Mask, 2006, Black Girl/White Girl, 2006; (non-fiction) The Faith of a Writer: Life, Craft, Art, 2003; (poetry collections) Women in Love, 1968, Expensive People, 1968, Anonymous Sins, 1969, Love and Its Derangements, 1970, Angel Fire, 1973, Dreaming America, 1973, The Fabulous Beasts, 1975, Season of Peril, 1977, Women Whose Lives are Food, Men Whose Lives are Money: Poems, 1978, The Stepfather, 1978, Celestial Timepiece, 1981, Invisible Women: New and Selected Poems, 1970-1972, 1982, Luxury of Sin, 1983, The Time Traveller, 1987; (plays) The Sweet Enemy, 1965, Sunday Dinner, 1970, Ontological Proof of My Existence, 1970, Miracle Play, 1974, Three Plays, 1980, Daisy, 1980, Presque Isle, 1984, Triumph of the Spider Monkey, 1985, In Darkest America, 1990, I Stand Before You Naked, 1990, The Perfectionist and Other Plays, 1995; (essays) The Edge of Impossibility, 1972, The Hostile Sun: The Poetry of D.H. Lawrence, 1973, New Heaven, New Earth, 1974, Contraries: Essays, 1981, The Profane Art, 1984, On Boxing, 1987, (Woman) Writer: Occasions and Opportunities, 1988; editor, compiler: Scenes from American Life: Contemporary Short Fiction, 1973, (with Shannon Ravenel) Best American Short Stories of 1979, 1979, Night Walks, 1982, First Person Singular: Writer's on Their Craft, 1983, (with BoydLitzinger) Story: Fictions Past and Present, 1985, (with Daniel Halpern) Reading and Fights, 1988, The Oxford Book ofAmerican Short Stories, 1992, The Sophisticated Cat: An Anthology, 1992,(editor)The Best American Mystery Stories 2005; editor (with Raymond Smith) Ontario Rev.; contbr. to nat. mags. including NY Times Book Rev., Mich. Quarterly Rev., Mademoiselle, Vogue, North Am. Rev., Hudson Rev., Paris Rev., Grand Street, Atlantic, Poetry, Esquire. Recipient O. Henry award, 1967, 73, Rosenthal award Nat. Inst. Arts and Letters, 1968, O. Henry Spl. award continuing achievement, 1970, 86, Award of Merit Lotos Club, 1975, St. Louis Lit. award, 1988, Rea award for the Short Story, 1990, Alan Swallow award for fiction, 1990, Nobel Prize in Lit. nomination, 1993; Guggenheim fellow, 1967-68, Nat. Endowment for the Arts grantee, 1966, 68. Mem. Am. Acad. and Inst. Arts and Letters. Office: care John Hawkins Agy 71 W 23rd St Ste 1600 New York NY 10010-4102 also: Princeton U Dept Creative Writing 117 185 Nassau St Princeton NJ 08544-0001

OATES, MARY JOSEPHINE, historian, educator; b. Boston, Apr. 18, 1935; d. Thomas Francis and Mary (Folan) Oates. BA summa cum laude, Cath. U. Am., Washington, 1963; MA, Yale U., New Haven, 1964, PhD, 1969. Mem. Congregation of the Sisters of St. Joseph of Boston, 1952—; asst. prof. econs. Regis Coll., Weston, Mass., 1970—74, assoc. prof. econs., 1974—80, prof. econs., 1980—2000, rsch. prof. econs., 2000—. Chair com. on internat. fellowships and awards AAUW, Washington, 1978—80, chair com. on fellowships to Am. women, 1983—85; mem. nat. adv. bd. Project on Religion and Am. Culture, Ind. U., Purdue U., Indpls., 1988—90; mem. com. on rsch. Nat. Fedn. of Congregations of Sisters of St. Joseph, U.S. and Can., St. Louis, 1988—96; cons. religion divsn. program Lilly Endowment, Indpls., 1992; mem. currriculum devel. project Ctr. for the Study of Philanthropy, CUNY, NYC, 1996—99; chair com. on Cath. women U. of Notre Dame - Lilly Endowment Rsch. Initiative in Twentieth Century Studies in Am. Catholicism, Notre Dame, Ind., 1997—2000. Author: The Role of the Cotton Textile Industry in the Economic Development of the American Southeast, 1900-1940, 1975; editor: Higher Education for Catholic Women: An Historical Anthology, 1987; author: The Catholic Philanthropic Tradition in America, 1995 (Hon. Mention, Staley-Robeson-Ryan-St. Lawrence prize, Nat. Soc. of Fund Raising Execs., 1996), Catholic Philanthropy in America, Curriculum Guide, 1999; contbr. chpts. to books and articles to profl. and scholarly jours. Mem. history adv. bd. Mus. of Women's History - The Leadership Ctr., NYC, 2000—; cons. U.S. CSC - Boston Region, 1971; mem. women's strategy group Giving New Eng., Associated Grant Makers, Boston, 2001—03; mem. ad hoc com. on stewardship Nat. Conf. of Cath. Bishops, Washington, 1990; mem. investment com. Congregation of the Sisters of St. Joseph of Boston, 1977—; mem. bd. dirs. Takayasu's Arteritis Assn., Bedford, NH, 1998—2002. Recipient Disting. Historian award, Conf. on the History of Women Religious, 2001; fellow Charlotte Dickson Fisher Fellowship, AAUW, 1966—67, Fellowship in Academic Adminstrn., Am. Coun. on Edn., 1969—70, Faculty Fellowship in Sci., Harvard U., NSF, 1976—77, Rsch. Fellowship, Mary I. Bunting Inst., Radcliffe Coll., 1980—81; grantee Kress Grant, Baker Libr., Harvard U. Grad. Sch. of Bus. Adminstrn., 1972, Rsch. Grant, Am. Philos. Soc., 1976, Curriculum Devel. Grant, Shelby Cullom Davis Found., 1978, Course Devel. Grant, Assn. of Am. Colls., 1986—89, Rsch. Grant, 1988, Lilly Endowment, 1988, 1990—92, Louisville Inst., 1997, Spencer Found., 2002—03. Mem.: Mass. Hist. Soc., Am. Cath. Hist. Assn. (chair, book prize com. 1997—98, 2d v.p. 2005), Econ. History Assn. (program com. 1971—73), Social Sci. History Assn. (program com. 1982, chair, book prize com. 1990—91), Assn. for Rsch. on Nonprofit Orgns. and Voluntary Action (book prize com. 2001), Orgn. of Am. Historians, Am. Hist. Assn., Phi Beta Kappa. Roman Catholic. Office: Regis Coll 235 Wellesley St Weston MA 02493 Office Phone: 781-768-7420. Business E-Mail: mary.oates@regiscollege.edu.

OATES, STEPHEN BAERY, retired historian; b. Pampa, Tex., Jan. 5, 1936; s. Steve Theodore and Florence (Baer) O.; divorced; children: Gregory Allen, Stephanie. BA magna cum laude, U. Tex., 1958, MA, 1960, PhD, 1968; Litt.D. (hon.), Lincoln Coll., 1981. Prof. history U. Mass., Amherst, 1971—98, Paul Murray Kendall prof. biography, 1980—98, adj. prof. English, 1981—98. Author: Confederate Cavalry West of the River, 1961, Rip Ford's Texas, 1963, Republic of Texas, 1968, Visions of Glory, 1970, To Purge This Land With Blood: A Biography of John Brown, 1970, Portrait of America, 2 vols., 1973, rev. edits., 2005, The Fires of Jubilee: Nat Turner's Fierce Rebellion, 1975, With Malice Toward None: The Life of Abraham Lincoln (Christopher award for outstanding lit., Barondess/Lincoln award N.Y. Civil War Round Table 1977), Our Fiery Trial: Abraham Lincoln, John Brown, and the Civil War Era, 1979, Let the Trumpet Sound: The Life of Martin Luther King, Jr., 1982 (Christopher award, Robert F. Kennedy Meml. Book award), Abraham Lincoln, The Man Behind the Myths, 1984, Biography as High Adventure: Life Writers Speak on Their Art, 1986, William Faulkner: The Man and the Artist, 1987, A Woman of Valor: Clara Barton and the Civil War, 1994, The Approaching Fury: Voices of the Storm, 1820-1861, 1997, The Whirlwind of War: Voices of the Storm, 1861-1865, 1998; contbr. articles and essays to periodicals; lectr. Presdl. Writers award, 1985; Master Tchr. award U. Hartford, 1985; Silver Medal award Case Council for Advance and Support of Edn., Prof. of Yr., 1986, 87, Kidger award New Eng. History Tchrs. Assn., Nevins-Freeman award Chgo. Civil War Round Table, 1993; Guggenheim fellow, 1972; sr. summer fellow NEH, 1978. Fellow Tex. State Hist. Assn.; mem. Tex. Inst. Letters, Soc. Am. Historians, Am. Antiquarian Soc., Phi Beta Kappa. Office: U Mass Dept History Amherst MA 01003

OATES, THOMAS R., former university executive; married; 4 children. BA in English and Philosophy, St. Louis U., 1964, MA in English, 1970; postgrad., Am. Film Inst. Ctr., Beverly Hills, Calif., 1971; PhD in Am. Lit., St. Louis U., 1979. Coord., dir. program assts. and counselors upward bound pgm. Webster Coll., 1970-71, dir. media/journalism degree program, 1974-81, coord. MA program in media comms., 1975-81; chair, assoc. prof. dept. journalism St. Michael's Coll., 1981-85; campus dean U. Wis. Ctr., Richland Center, 1985-89; dir. U.S. ops. and acad. programs Coop. Assn. of States for Scholarships, Georgetown U., Washington, 1989-94; pres. Spalding U., Louisville, 1994—2002, Rocky Mountain Coll., Billings, Mont., 2002—06. Mem. media adv. com. Mo. State Coun. of Arts, 1973-77; mem. planning commn. State Dept. of Higher Edn., Baton Rouge, 1979-80; mem., rep. Mo.'s ind. colls. and univs. Cen. Ednl. Network Mo., 1979-81; mem. adv. bd. Tri-State Bilingual Tng. Program, St. Michael's Coll., 1981-83; mem. Vt. Cath. Press Assn. Bd., 1984-85; mem., appointed chair Internat. Edn. Coun., U. Wis. Sys., 1987-88, designer, author Ctr. of Excellence project, 1988; mem. acad. staff adv. bd., U. Wis. Ctr. Sys., 1987-89, chair acad. staff grievance com., 1988; mem. 9-person state commn. to develop criteria for legal evaluations of devel. projects reviewed under Act 250 environ. law, Vt., 1984-85; presenter on internat. ednl. regional and nat. meetings of various orgns. Author, designer: (slide-tape program on history of early French and English explorers in mid-west) Old Land, New Land, 1985; author, designer: (book) Images, Values, and Development in Chittenden County, 1984; prodr.: (documentary photographic study on 5 rural Alaskan comtys.) Images of Continuity, Images of Change, 1977; prodr., dir.: (16mm documentary film) The Faces of British Honduras, 1974. Grantee Mo. Coun. on Arts, 1972, 76, NEH, 1975, U. Alaska, 1978, Mo. Coun. on Humanities, 1979, Vt. Coun. on Humanities, 1981, IBM, 1982, U. Wis. Ext., 1988, Wis. Coun. for Humanities, 1989, Orgn. for Petroleum Exporting Countries, 1992, C.C.'s for Internat. Devel., 1992.

OATES, WILLIAM ARMSTRONG, JR., investment company executive; b. Pitts., July 27, 1942; s. Wiliam Armstrong and Margaret (Nichols) O.; m. Elizabeth Dick Macy, Sept. 7, 1968; children: Elizabeth N., Katherine M., Emily E.A. BA, Colby Coll., 1965; MBA, Harvard U., 1972. Asst. treas. Morgan Guaranty Trust, NYC, 1966—2004; pres. N.E. Investors Growth Fund, Boston, 1980—; ptnr. N.E. Investment Mgmt. Inc., Boston, 1984—. Dir. Horn Corp., Ayer, Mass., Furman Lumber Co., Boston, Clifford Inc., Bethel, Vt. Pres. bd. trustees Groton (Mass.) Sch., 1979; trustee, treas. Roxbury Latin Sch., West Roxbury, Mass., 2005; trustee Colby Coll., Waterville, Maine, 2005. 2d lt. Army N.G., 1966-70. Mem.: Country Club, Somerset Club, Harvard Club. Republican. Episcopalian. Home: 201 Village Ave Dedham MA 02026-4230 Office: NE Investment Mgmt Inc 150 Federal St Ste 1000 Boston MA 02110-1745

OBAFUNWA, JOHN OLADAPO, academic administrator, pathologist, educator; b. Ibadan, Oyo State, Nigeria, Apr. 17, 1958; s. Mathew Taiwo and Sabinah Alice Obafunwa; m. Titilola Folasade Babatunde, Dec. 13, 1986; children: Sylvester Ayodeji, Valentina Olumayowa. MB, BChir, U. Lagos, Nigeria, 1980; LLB, U. Northumbria, Newcastle-upon-Tyne, Eng., 2004. Resident dept. morbid anatomy Lagos U. Tchg. Hosp., 1982—87; cons. pathologist, lectr. I Jos U. Tchg. Hosp. and U. Jos, Nigeria, 1987—90; cons. pathologist Fed. Ministry Health, Lagos, 1990—90; trainee, rsch. fellow forensic med. unit U. Edinburgh, Scotland, 1991—93; govt. pathologist Cayman Islands, George Town, 1993—99, Bermuda Hosps. Bd., Hamilton, 1999—2002; cons. histopathologist South Tyneside

Dist. Hosp., South Shields, England, 2002—04; prof. forensic pathology Lagos State U. Coll. Medicine, 2004—; cons. histopathologist, med. examiner Lagos State U. Tchg. Hosp. and Min. Health, 2004—; provost Lagos State U. Coll. Medicine, 2006—. Mem. adv. bd., tchr., rschr. Nebr. Inst. Forensic Scis., Lincoln, 2003—. Contbr. articles to profl. jours. Scholar, Fed. Govt. Nigeria, 1975—80. Fellow: Royal Soc. Medicine UK, Am. Acad. Legal Medicine; mem.: Brit. Assn. Forensic Medicine, Coll. Am. Pathologists (assoc.), Brit. Acad. Forensic Scis., Am. Acad. Forensic Scis., Sands Rotary Club Bermuda (assoc.), Bermuda Garrison Orgn., Gothic Lodge (assoc.). Home: 5540 S 72nd St Lincoln NE 68516 Home Phone: 402-327-2581; Office Phone: 234-8033966199.

O'BAIRE-KARK, MARIKA, nurse, educator, poet, writer; b. Manila, Oct. 3, 1947; d. Gerald John and Giovanna (BelForti) Barry; m. Pieter Kark, Oct. 3, 2004; children from previous marriage: Matthew Plocharczyk, Alexei Plocharczyk, Rita Higgins, D. Patrick Higgins. Student, U. Conn., 1964—65; diploma, Ellis Hosp. Sch. Nursing, 1977; BSN, Russell Sage Coll., 1980, postgrad., 1983, postgrad., 1994; grad. ontological design, Logonet Inc. ODC-J, 1993; postgrad. humanities, Calif. State U., Dominguez Hills, 1995; postgrad., U. Dundee, 2000; postgrad. in Disaster and Emergency Mgmt., Touro U., 2005—; postgrad. in Writing, Stanford U., 2006—. RN NY, Calif.; lic. avatar master/wizard Star's Edge Internat. Tchr. English Lang. Inst., Taipei, Taiwan, 1971—73; team leader, staff nurse acute psychiatry Samaritan Hosp., Troy, NY, 1978—80; staff nurse pediat. ICU Albany Med. Ctr., NY, 1980—84, 1997—; rsch. nurse Commn. on Quality Care for Mentally Disabled, Albany, 1984; staff nurse Columbia-Greene Med. Ctr., Catskill, NY, 1984—89; night charge nurse Conifer Park, Scotia, NY, 1991—92; nursing educator St. Clare's Hosp., Schenectady, NY, 1992—96; adj clin. educator Albany Med. Ctr. So. Vt. Coll., Bennington, 1997—2001; nurse, specialized surg. pre-ICU, Stanford U. Hosp., 2005—. On-call nurse Cmty. Hospice Saratoga, NY, 1998—2004; founder Future Design: Create What You Prefer, Avatar Tech. and Skills, 1999—, Favorite Nurses, Colonie, NY, 2002—. Author: (novels) Dragon, 2002, Future Joyous, 2002, (short stories) About Love, (screenplays) Syin; contbr. articles to Echo Mag. Past vol. curriculum designer gifted and talented programs; firefighter Cazenovia, NY. Mem.: Ontological Design Cmty., Upstate Ind. Filmakers/Screenwriters, Childreach Plan Internat., Toastmasters Internat. Home Phone: 650-962-9660. Personal E-mail: mobaire@yahoo.com.

OBAMA, BARACK HUSSEIN, JR., senator, former state legislator; b. Honolulu, Hawaii, Aug. 4, 1961; s. Barack Obama Sr. and Shirley Ann (Dunham); m. Michelle Robinson, 1992; children: Malia Ann, Natasha. Student, Occidental Coll., 1979—81; BA in Polit. Sci., Columbia U., 1983; JD magna cum laude, Harvard U., 1991. Editor-in-chief Harvard Law Review; writer, fin. analyst Bus. Internat. Corp., 1984—85; dir. Developing Communities Project, 1985—88; exec. dir. PROJECT VOTE!, Ill., 1992; assoc. Davis, Miner, Barnhill & Galland, P.C., 1993—96, of counsel, 1996—2004; mem. Ill. Senate Dist. 13, Springfield, 1997—2005; mem. judiciary & local govt. com. Ill. Senate, Springfield, chmn., pub. health & human svcs. com.; US Senator from Ill., 2005—. Sr. lecturer U. Chgo. Law Sch., 1993—2004; keynote speaker Dem. Nat. Convention, Boston, 2004; mem. com. environment and public works US Senate, com. fgn. relations, com. veterans affairs. Author: Dreams From My Father: A Story of Race and Inheritance, 1995 (Publishers Weekly paperback besteseller list, 2005, Best Spoken Word or Non-Musical Album The Recording Acad., 2006), Audacity of Hope: Thoughts on Reclaiming the American Dream, 2006 (Best Literary Work in Nonfiction, NAACP Image awards, 2007). Bd. dirs. Chgo. Lawyers Com. for Civil Rights Under the Law and Pub. Allies, Joyce Found., 1994—, Woods Fund Chgo., Ctr. for Neighborhood Tech., Chgo. Annenberg Challenge, Lugenia Burns Hope Ctr.; chmn. Chgo. Lawyers Com. for Civil Rights Under the Law. Named one of The World's Most Influential People, TIME mag., 2005—07, Most Influential Black Americans, Ebony mag., 2006; recipient 40 Under 40 award, Crains Chgo. Bus., 1993, Monarch award for Outstanding Public Service, 1994, "Legal Eagle" award for Litigation, IVI-IPO, 1995, Freshman Legis. award, Ind. Voters of IL Ind. Precint Organizations, 1997, Outstanding Legis. award, Campaign for Better Health Care-IL Primary Health Care Assn., 1998, Legis. award, Associated Firefighters of IL, 2004, Chmn.'s award, NAACP, 2005, Howard Blake Walker award, Christopher House, 2005, Lifetime Achievement award, Detroit, Mich. chapter NAACP, 2005, Congl. Leadership award, Nat. Urban League, 2006. Mem.: vis. com., Irving B. Harris Grad. Sch. Pub. Policy Studies, U. Chgo., IL Bar Assn., Cook County Bar Assn. Democrat. Ch. Christ. Office: US Senate B40B Dirksen Senate Office Bldg Washington DC 20510 also: John C Kluczynski Fed Office Bldg Ste 3900 230 South Dearborn St Chicago IL 60604-1480 Office Phone: 202-224-2854, 312-886-3506. Office Fax: 202-228-4260, 312-886-3514. *

OBAMOGIE, MERCY A., physician; b. Lagos, Nigeria, Jan. 18, 1954; d. Godwin I and Janet E. (Amiolemen) O.; m. Abiodun O. Odunmbaku, June 20, 1980 (div. 1995); children: Abisola, Adenike, Abiodun. BS, Columbia U., 1980; MD, U. Medicine and Dentistry N.J., Piscataway, 1984; MPH, Johns Hopkins U., 1987; MBA, U. Calif., Irvine, 2000. Diplomate Am. Bd. Family Practice, Nat. Bd. Med. Examiners. Intern in internal medicine Muhlenberg Hosp., Plainfield, NJ, 1984-85; resident in gen. preventive medicine Johns Hopkins U., Balt., 1985-86; resident in family practice Georgetown U./Providence Hosp., Washington, 1986-89; pvt. practice Washington, Greenbelt, Md., 1989—; med. dir. Doctors Slim and Fitness Ctr., Greenbelt, 1996-98. Med. adv. bd. Metra Health Ins. Co., 1992-94; utilization com. Aetna Ins. Co., 1993-95, credentialing com., 1996; med. adv. com. United HealthCare, 1997; mem. planning com. Providence Hosp., Washington, 1996-98; with Prince George's Hosp. Ctr., Cheverly, Md., Howard U. Hosp., Washington, Doctors Cmty. Hosp., Lanham, Md., Providence Hosp., Washington; pres., med. dir. Mercy Med. Ctr., Benin City, Nigeria, 1996—; pres., CEO ASAKI Corp., Greenbelt, Md., 2000—. Contbr. articles to profl. jours. Home: 25 Atwood Ct Silver Spring MD 20906-2089 Office: 7323 Hanover Pkwy Ste A Greenbelt MD 20770-3617 Home Phone: 301-871-1084; Office Phone: 301-345-5900. E-mail: aimmercy@aol.com.

OBANA, WILLIAM G., neurosurgeon; s. George and Mary Obana. BS, Stanford U., Calif., 1983; MD, U. Calif., San Francisco, 1987. Chief neurosurgery dept. surgery U. Hawaii John A. Burns Sch. Medicine, Honolulu, 1994—. Mem.: Congress Neurol. Surgeons, Am. Assn. Neurol. Surgeons. Office: William G Obana MD Inc 1380 Lusitana St Ste 410 Honolulu HI 96813 Office Phone: 808-523-8883.

OBARA, ICHIRO, economics professor; b. Tokyo; PhD, U. Pa., Phila., 2001. Asst. prof. U. Calif., LA, 2001—. Office Phone: 310-794-7098.

O'BARR, BOBBY GENE, SR., lawyer; b. Houston, May 5, 1932; s. Walter Morris and Maggie (Whitt) O'B.; children: Morris Clayton, William Clinton, Candace Jean, Bobby G.; m. Jennifer Ryals, Dec. 5, 1984; 1 child, Richard. BA, U. Miss., 1959, JD, 1958. Bar: Miss. 1958, U.S. Dist. Ct. (no. dist.) Miss. 1958, U.S. Dist. Ct. (so. dist.) Miss. 1966, U.S. Ct. Appeals (5th cir.) 1970, U.S. Supreme Ct. 1971. Pvt. practice, Houston, 1958-59; assoc. W.M. O'Barr, Jr., Okolona, Miss., 1959-60; adminstrv. judge Miss. Workmen's Compensation Commn., 1960-65; assoc. Cumbest, Cumbest, O'Barr and Shaddock, Pascagoula, Miss., 1965-68, Hurlbert & O'Barr, O'Barr, Hurlbert and O'Barr, Biloxi, Miss., 1968-80; pvt. practice, owner Bobby G. O'Barr, P.A., Biloxi, 1980—2004; lawyer Denham, Backstrom, O'Barr & Hollingsworth Ltd., 2004—. Mem., pres. Biloxi Port Commn., 1975-90; mem. mgmt. coun. Gulf Mex. Fishery, 1979-82. With USAF, 1951-54. Mem. VFW, State Bar Found., Southeastern Admiralty Law Inst., Am. Trial Lawyers Assn., So. Trial Lawyers Assn., Miss. Trial Lawyers Assn., Am. Legion, Masons, Shriners. Office: Denham Backstrom O'Barr Hollingsworth Ltd PO Box 580 Ocean Springs MS 39566-0580 Office Phone: 228-875-1234.

OBBIE, MARK JOSEPH, communications educator; b. Rochester, NY, May 16, 1959; s. Joseph S. and Patricia R. (O'Brien) O.; m. Nancy E. Lane, Oct. 2, 1982; children: Raema C., Dale M. BA, St. John Fisher Coll., 1980; MA, U. Mo., 1981. Reporter Tribune Chronicle, Warren, Ohio, 1982-83, Houston Post, 1983-86, Tex. Lawyer, Houston, 1987, mng. editor Dallas, 1987-88, editor, 1988-89, former editor, pub., 1989—98; former exec. editor Am. Lawyer, NYC, 1998; assoc. prof., communciations Syracuse Univ., NY. Mem. Freedom of Info. Found. Tex., Soc. Profl. Journalists, Investigative Reporters and Editors. Avocations: reading, camping. Office: Public Communications Syracuse University Syracuse NY 13244 Office Phone: 585-298-1470. Business E-Mail: mjobbie@syr.edu.

OBEAR, FREDERICK WOODS, academic administrator; b. Malden, Mass., June 9, 1935; s. William Fred and Dorothea Louise (Woods) O.; m. Patricia A. Draper, Aug. 30, 1959 (dec. Dec. 1993); children: Jeffrey Allan, Deborah Anne, James Frederick; m. Ruth Crowley Sundell, Feb. 21, 1998. BS with high honors, U. Mass., Lowell, 1956, LHD, 1985; PhD, U. N.H., 1961. Mem. faculty dept. chemistry Oakland U., Rochester, Mich., 1960-81, prof., 1979-81, v.p. for acad. affairs, provost, 1970-81; chancellor U. Tenn., Chattanooga, 1981-97, univ. prof., chancellor emeritus, 1997—. Mem. nat. adv. panel Nat. Commn. on Higher Edn. Issues, 1981; mem. pres. commn. NCAA, 1991-94. Trustee Marygrove Coll., 1973-79. Am. Council Edn. fellow, 1967-68 Mem. AAAS, Am. Assn. State Colls. and Univs. (bd. dirs. 1992-96, chair 1995), Am. Chem. Soc., Am. Assn. Higher Edn., Sigma Xi. Roman Catholic. Office: 417H Fletcher Hall 615 McCallie Ave Chattanooga TN 37403-2504 Home Phone: 423-886-4190; Office Phone: 423-425-5281. Business E-Mail: frederick-obear@utc.edu.

OBED, LEONORA RITA VILLEGAS, writer; b. Manila, Philippines, May 22, 1971; arrived in US, 1973; d. Reynaldo Nera and Josefina Kalaw (Villegas) Obed. BA in English Lit. and Philosophy, St. Joseph's U., 1993; MA in English Lit., U. Toronto, 1994; postgrad. cert. in 18th Century Lit. with honors, Coll. of NJ, Trenton, 1993; postgrad. in English Lit., U. Edinburgh. Tchr. seminar M courses U. Toronto, Canada, 1994—95; pvt. tutor, 1996; lector Our Lady of Good Counsel, 2005—. Spkr., presenter in field; reader various radio broadcasts, 2006, Lib. for Blind and Handicapped, 2006. Author: The Invention of Candles, 2001, I Won't Send Roses, 2001, (plays) Epitome, 2003; contbr. scientific papers, articles to profl. jours. Mem.: Hopkins Soc., Yeats Soc., Oscar Wilde Soc. Avocations: piano, dance, stamp collecting/philately, horseback riding, wine tasting. Home and Office: 10 Michelle Ct Trenton NJ 08628-2924 Office Phone: 609-213-4434. Personal E-mail: leonora.obed@hotmail.com.

OBENHAUS, STEVEN LEE, secondary school educator; b. Dallas, Aug. 30, 1958; s. Robert Edward and Betty Lee Obenhaus; m. Cindy Long Browning, June 12, 1992; children: Benjamin Christopher Long, Ann Elizabeth Long, Andrew David Long. BA, Lubbock Christian U., 1980, U. Mo., Kansas City, 1988, MA, 1995. Cert. secondary edn. Kans. Tchr. Leavenworth (Kans.) Sch. Dist., 1988—94, Olathe (Kans.) Sch. Dist., 1994—. Contbr. articles to profl. jours. Mapping, testing, and statis. analyst Maison de Naissance, Larnage, Torbeck, Haiti, 2004—06; rsch. malaria prevalence in Haiti, water contamination in Dominican Republic, sanitation and hygiene in Haiti. Recipient Presdl. award Excellence in Math and Sci. Tchg., Kans. State. Mem.: Nat. Coun. Tchr. Math., Math. Assn. Am. (assoc.), Engrs. Without Borders. Democrat. Achievements include research in using GIS to site new well locations in Haiti; malaria control in Haiti and Dominican Republic; hygeine and in-home water storage in rural Haiti; design of. Avocations: marathon racing, cheese tasting, winter backpacking, candlepin bowling. Home: 6718 Granada Ln Prairie Village KS 66208 Office: Olathe North HS 600 East Prairie Olathe KS 66061 Home Phone: 913-236-7839; Office Phone: 913-780-7140. Personal E-mail: scobenhaus@kc.rr.com. Business E-Mail: sobenhauson@olatheschools.com.

OBER, RICHARD FRANCIS, JR., lawyer, director, banker; b. Balt., Dec. 12, 1943; s. Richard Francis and Caroline Fisher Ober; m. Carol Laycock Munger, Aug. 25, 1973; children: Julia Keyser Allen, Margaret Delancey. AB cum laude, Princeton U., 1965; LLB, Yale U., 1968. Bar: Md. 1968, Pa. 1970, N.J. 1977. Law clk. to chief judge Md. Ct. Appeals, Annapolis, 1968; assoc. Ballard, Spahr, Andrews & Ingersoll, Phila., 1969-75; gen. counsel Summit Bancorp, Princeton, NJ, 1975—2001; v.p., gen. counsel, sec. TerraCycle, Inc, Trenton, NJ, 2004—. Sec. Summit Bancorp, Princeton, 1978-2001, sr. v.p., 1982-88, exec. v.p., 1988-2001; bd. dirs. sec. Summit Credit Life Ins. Co., Summit Credit Corp.; sec. Summit Bank, Summit Leasing Co., Summit Venture Capital, Inc. Fire commr. South Brunswick Fire Dist. 3, NJ, 1981-85; Republican county committeeman, 1975-04; v.p. Republican Assn. Princeton, 1995-96; trustee Princeton Day Sch., 1986-92, treas., 1988-92, vice-chmn., 1990-92; trustee Yale Law Sch. Assn. N.J.; first vice-chmn., dir NJ. Spl. Olympics; co-facilitator Trinity Jobseekers, 2005—; ombudsman NJ Com. Employer Support Guard and Res., 2005-. Mem. ABA, Bank Corp. Counsel Com. (chmn. 1979-80), NJ Bar Assn. (gen. coun. 1982-85, 93-94, exec. com. banking law sect. 1979-94, sec. sect. 1980-81, vice-chmn. 1981-82, chmn. 1984-85, exec. com. pro bono com. 1982-85, vice-chmn. 1984-85), NJ Corp. Counsel Assn. (exec. com. 1980-91, 2d v.p. 1982-85, pres. 1985-86, chmn. banking and fin. instns. com. 1984-85), Am. Bankers Assn. (exec. com. bank counsel unit 1990-95, vice-chmn. 1993-94, chmn. 1994-95), NJ Bankers Assn. (chmn. bank lawyers coun. 1993-94, chmn. legal and tax com. 1994-95), NJ Bus. and Industry Assn. (legis. affairs com.), Pa. Bankers Assn. (legal affairs com.), Assn. Corp. Counsel (contbr. articles to profl. jours.), Princeton Bar Assn., Fin. Svcs. Roundtable, Lawyers Coun., Bedens Brook Club (Princeton). Episcopalian.

OBER, RUSSELL JOHN, JR., lawyer; b. Pitts., June 26, 1948; s. Russell J. and Marion C. (Hampson) O.; children: Lauren Elizabeth, Russell John III; m. Sandi J. Antill. BA, U. Pitts., 1970, JD, 1973. Bar: Pa. 1973, U.S. Dist. Ct. (we. dist.) Pa. 1973, U.S. Tax Ct. 1982, U.S. Ct. Appeals (4th cir.) 1976, U.S. Ct. Appeals (3d cir.) 1979, U.S. Ct. Appeals (D.C. cir.) 1985, U.S. Ct. Appeals (2d cir.), 1990, U.S. Ct. Appeals (7th cir.) 1993, U.S. Supreme Ct. 1976, U.S. Ct. Appeals (6th cir.) 2000. Asst. dist. atty. Allegheny County, Pitts., 1973-75; ptnr. Wallace Chapas & Ober, Pitts., 1975-80, Rose, Schmidt, Hasley & DiSalle, Pitts., 1980-92, Meyer, Unkovic & Scott, Pitts., 1992—. Bd. dirs. Parent and Child Guidance Ctr., Pitts., 1983-90, treas., 1985-86, pres., 1986-88; bd. mgmt. South Hills Area YMCA, 1989-91; mem. Mt. Lebanon Traffic Commn., 1976-81; bd. dirs. Whale's Tale Youth Family Counseling Ctr., 1990-95. Mem. ABA (discovery com. litigation sect. 1982-88, ho. of dels. young lawyers div. 1982-83), Pa. Bar Assn. (ho. of dels. 1983-2004), Allegheny County Bar Assn. (chmn. young lawyers sect. 1983, bd. govs. 1984, fin. com. 1984-88, mem. coun. civil litigation sect. 1991-93, judiciary com. 2004—), Nat. Bd. Trial Advocacy (diplomate), Acad. Lawyers Allegheny County (fellow 1983—, bd. govs. 1988-90) U. Pitts. Law Alumni Assn. (bd. govs. 1984-89, v.p. 1985-87, pres. 1987-88), Rivers Club Office: Meyer Unkovic & Scott 1300 Oliver Bldg Pittsburgh PA 15222 E-mail: rjo@muslaw.com.

OBER, STUART ALAN, investment advisor, writer; b. NYC, Oct. 2, 1946; s. Paul and Gertrude E. (Stollerman) Ober; m. Allison Craig; children: Erik Kenneth, Alexander Gabriel. BA, Wesleyan U., Middletown, Conn., 1968; postgrad., U. Sorbonne, Paris, 1972, CUNY, 1976—77. Accredited investment fiduciary analyst, cert. fraud examiner. Specialist tax investment Fidelity Mutual Life, NYC, 1972—73; sr. assoc. mktg. ENI Corp., 1973; with mktg. and analysis J.F. Crowley and Co., Inc., 1974; co-mgr. Tax Investment Dept. Moseley, Hallgarten & Estabrook, NYC, 1974; co-dir. mktg. NFC Petroleum, NYC, 1975; specialist tax investment Loeb, Rhoades & Co., NYC, 1976—77; divisional dir. Dept. Tax Investment Josephthal & Co., Inc., NYC, 1977—78; founder, mgr. Dept. Tax Investment Bruns, Nordeman, Rea & Co., NYC, 1978—79; pvt. practice cons. NYC, 1979—81; founder, pres. Securities Investigations, Inc., Woodstock, NY, 1981—. Arbitrator Nat. Futures Assn., 2003—, Am. Arbitration Assn.; chmn. NASD, NYSE; cons. in field; expert witness in field; lectr. in field. Author: Everybody's Guide to Tax Shelters; editor-in-chief: Ober Income Letter, 1983-88; pub.: Tax Shelter Blue Book, 1983—. Bd. dirs., v.p. Woodstock Playhouse Assn., 1985-87; trustee Maverick Concerts, 1986—; chmn. Woodstock Arts and Cultural Com., 1988. Mem.: Inst. Cert. Fin. Planners (fin. products stds. bd. 1986—90, treas. 1988—90). Office: PO Box 888 Woodstock NY 12498-0888 Office Phone: 845-679-2300.

OBERBILLIG, MOLLY CASTLEMAN, utilities executive; b. Gibraltar, Feb. 11, 1934; arrived in U.S., 1935; d. William Ferguson and Mary Castleman (Davis) Cavenaugh; m. Gary Joel Oberbillig, Nov. 8, 1961; children: Andrew Ferguson, Julie Anne. Student, Reed Coll., Portland, Oreg., 1951—53, Antioch Coll., Yellow Springs, Ohio, 1953—54, U. Wash., Seattle, 1954—55, San Jose State Coll., 1963—64. Conservation mgr. Mason County Pub. Utility Dist., 1975—90. Founding trustee Anne Williston Scholarship, Seattle, 1988—; sec. Mason Coun. Fire Dist., Lilliwaup, Wash., 1979—81; founder Youth Diversity award Thurston Coun. Cultural Diversity and Human Rights, 1995; charter mem. Nat. Women's History Mus.; mem. leadership coun. So. Poverty Law Ctr., 1992—; mem. Nordiska Folkdance Exhibition Team; continuing trustee Anne Williston Scholarship; vice chmn. Dem. Ctrl. Com., Shelton, Wash., 1991—92. Mem.: Thurston Coun. Cultural Diversity and Human Rights. Avocations: gardening, ethical investing, environmental concerns. Home: 1907 Parkwood Dr SE Olympia WA 98501

OBERDORFER, JOHN L., lawyer; b. Lewes, Del., Feb. 19, 1944; AB, Dartmouth Coll., 1966; LLB, Yale U., 1969. Bar: Ohio 1969, D.C. 1972, US Ct. Appeals (several dists.), US Supreme Ct. Atty. office gen. counsel U.S. Dept. Trans., 1971-74; ptnr., chmn. Litigation dept. Patton Boggs LLP, Washington. Bd. dirs. Washington Lawyers Com. for Civil Rights Under Law 1981-, Washington Airport Task Force 1988-; mem. Clinton-Gore Transition Team, 1992. Contbr. articles to profl. jours. Reginald Heber Smith Law fellow 1969-71. Mem. D.C. Bar, Ohio State Bar Assn. Office: Patton Boggs LLP 2550 M St NW Washington DC 20037-1301 Office Phone: 202-457-6424. Office Fax: 212-457-6315. Business E-Mail: joberdorfer@pattonboggs.com.

OBERFIELD, RICHARD ALAN, oncologist; b. NYC, July 29, 1932; s. George B. and Frances Oberfield; m. Valerie I. Oberfield, Feb. 14, 1954 (dec. Jan. 1980); children: Elizabeth A., Alice A.; m. Keren G. Oberfield, July 28, 1988. BA cum laude, Alfred U., 1953; MD, NYU, 1957. Lic. physician, Mass., N.Y.; diplomate Am. Bd. Internal Medicine. Intern Greenwich (Conn.) Hosp., 1957-58; USPHS sr. asst. surgeon venereal disease br. Detroit Receiving Hosp., 1958-60; tng. fellow pathology NYU Med. Ctr., NYC, 1960-61; resident in medicine Dartmouth Med. Ctr. Affiliated Hosps., Hanover, NH, 1961-63, fellow in hematology and cancer chemotherapy, 1963-65; staff physician sect. med. oncology dept. internal medicine Lahey Clinic Med. Ctr., Burlington, Mass., 1965—, head sect. med. oncology dept. internal medicine, 1969-85. Hosp. appts. include New Eng. Bapt. Hosp., Boston, 1965—80, New Eng. Deaconess Hosp., Boston, 1965—97, Mary and Arthur R. Clapham Hosp., Lahey Clinic Med. Ctr., Burlington, 1980—97; chmn. emeritus sect. med. oncology dept. internal medicine Lahey Clinic Med. Ctr., Burlington, 1997—; clin. rsch. cons. dept. rsch., 1997—; clin. instr. medicine Harvard Med. Sch., Boston, 1972—; asst. prof. dept. medicine Tufts U. Sch. Medicine, 2000—. Contbr. numerous articles to profl. pubis. Fellow ACP (Meade Johnson postgrad. scholar 1962-63); mem. AMA (Cert. Merit 1966), Internat. Assn. for Study of Lung Cancer (founding mem.), Nat. Bd. Med. Examiners (diplomate), Am. Assn. for Cancer Rsch., Inc., Am. Soc. Clin. Oncology, Am. Assn. for Cancer Edn., Mass. Med. Soc., Mass. Soc. Internal Medicine, New Eng. Cancer Soc., Mass. Soc. Clin. Oncologists. Avocations: piano, writing, running, reading. Office: Lahey Clinic Med Ctr 41 Mall Rd Burlington MA 01805 Home Phone: 617-244-8171.

OBERFIELD, SHARON ELEFANT, pediatric endocrinologist; b. NYC, Aug. 14, 1950; d. Nicholas and Anna (Weiss) Elefant; m. Richard A. Oberfield; 2 children. AB in Biology, Cornell U., 1970, MD, 1974. Diplomate in pediatrics and pediatric endocrinology Am. Bd. Pediatrics. Intern in pediatrics The N.Y. Hosp., 1974-75, resident in pediatrics, 1975-76, fellow in pediatric endocrinology, 1976-79, asst. attending pediatrician, 1979-84; asst. attending pediatrian endocrinology Meml. Sloan Kettering Cancer Ctr., NYC, 1986—2001. Provisional pediatrician to outpatient dept. N.Y. Hosp., 1976-79; assoc. attending pediatrician St. Luke's-Roosevelt Hosp. Ctr., N.Y.C., 1984-91, Presbyn. Hosp., N.Y.C., 1991, Tisch Hosp., Bellevue Hosp., N.Y.C., 1992—; attending pediatrician Children's Hosp. of N.Y.-Presbyn. Hosp., 1998—; asst. attending pediatrician Meml. Sloan Kettering Cancer Ctr., 1979-84; asst. prof. pediatrics Cornell U. Med. Coll., N.Y.C., 1979-84, Columbia U. Coll. Physicians & Surgeons, N.Y.C., 1984-91, assoc. prof. clin. pediatrics, 1991, prof., 1998—, dir. pediat. endocrinology, 2004—. Grantee NIH, 1978-84, 2005-, Hoffman-LaRoche, 1985-89, Eli Lilly, 1986-92. Children's Brain Tumor Found., 1995-98; recipient Mitchell Spivak Meml. prize in pediatrics, 1974. Mem. Am. Med. Women's Assn. (citation 1974), N.Y. Acad. Scis., N.Y. Pediatric Soc., Soc. Pediatric Rsch., Endocrine Soc., Lawson Wilkins Soc., Pediatric Endocrinology, Alpha Omega Alpha. Office: Divsn Pediat Endocrinology 630 W 168th St PH-5E-522 New York NY 10032 Office Phone: 212-305-6559. Business E-Mail: seo8@columbia.edu.

OBERG, LYLE, physician, academic administrator; b. Forestburg, Alberta, Can. m. Evelyn Oberg; children: Jillian, Scott. Pre-med studies, Red Deer Coll.; MD, U. Alberta, Can. Physician Gen. Practice, Alberta; elected to legis. assembly Alberta Parliament, Edmonton, 1993—, appointed minister of learning, 1999—2004, appointed minister infrastructure and transp., 2005—06, minister fin., 2006—. Chmn. standing policy com. on health restructuring Alberta Legis. Assembly, Edmonton, Canada, 1995—97, minister of family and social svcs., 1997—99; Alberta rep. Ministerial Coun. on Social Policy Renewal; mem. treasury bd, and standing com. on learning and employment Alberta Legislative Assembly, 1999—. Avocations: golf, hunting, sailing. Office: 408 Legislative BGldg 10800 97th Ave Edmonton AB T5K 2B6 Canada Office Phone: 780-427-8809.

OBERHAUS, GEOFFREY LUTHER, lawyer; b. Bowling Green, Ohio, Dec. 15, 1969; s. Luther and Cindy Oberhaus. BChemE, U. Detroit, 1992; JD, Rutgers U., 1998. Bar: Ohio 1998. Environ. engr. Occidental Chem. Corp., Burlington, NJ, 1992—98; ptnr. Dinsmore & Shohl LLP, Cin., 1998—. Named one of Ohio's Rising Stars, Super Lawyers, 2006. Mem.: Ohio State Bar Assn., Cin. Intellectual Property Law Assn., Cin. Bar Assn., ABA, Am. Intellectual Property Owners Assn., Am. Intellectual Property Lawyers Assn. Office: Dinsmore & Shohl LLP 255 East 5th St Cincinnati OH 45202 Home Phone: 513-826-0903; Office Phone: 513-977-8623. Office Fax: 513-977-8141. Business E-Mail: geof.oberhaus@dinslaw.com.

OBERHELMAN, DOUGLAS R., tractor company executive; Grad., Millikin Univ. With Caterpillar Inc., Peoria, Ill., 1975—, mng. dir., Shin Caterpillar Mitsubishi Tokyo, 1991—94, v.p., CFO Peoria, Ill., 1995—98, v.p., dir. engine products divsn., 1998—2001, pres., 2001—, bd. dir.,

2003—. Bd. dir. Nat. Assn. Manufacturers, Ameren Corp., South Side Bank. Trustee, past chmn. Millikin Univ.; bd. dir. Ill. chpt., Nature Conservancy, Forest Park Found., Cordell Hull Inst. Office: Caterpillar Inc 100 NE Adams St Peoria IL 61629-0002 *

OBERHELMAN, HARRY ALVIN, JR., surgeon, educator; b. Chgo., Nov. 15, 1923; s. Harry Alvin and Beatrice (Babel) O.; m. Betty Jane Porter, June 12, 1946; children: Harry Alvin III, James I., Robert P., Thomas L., Nancy L. Student, Yale U., 1942-43; BS, U. Chgo., 1946, MD, 1947. Diplomate: Am. Bd. Surgery. Intern U. Chgo. Clinics, 1947—48, resident surgery, 1948—51, 1952—57; asst. prof., assoc. prof. surgery U. Chgo. Sch. Medicine, 1957—60; mem. faculty Stanford Sch. Medicine, Calif., 1960—, prof. surgery, 1964—95, emeritus prof. surgery, 1995—; med. dir. Stanford Internat. Med. Svc., 2006—. Mem. div. licensing Calif. Bd. Med. Quality Assurance, 1970-82 Author papers in field. Served with USAF, 1951-53. Mem. AMA, Calif. Med. Assn., Soc. Univ. Surgeons, Am., Western, Pacific Coast surg. assns., Soc. Alimentary Tract, Halsted Soc., Fedn. State Med. Bds. U.S. (bd. dirs. 1979-82) Home: 668 Cabrillo St Stanford CA 94305-8404 Office Phone: 650-736-7964. Personal E-mail: hoberhelman@hotmail.com.

OBERING, TREY (HENRY A. OBERING II), federal agency administrator, career military officer; BS cum laude, U. Notre Dame, 1973; disting. grad., Squadron Officer Sch., Maxwell Air Force Base, 1977; MS in astronautical engring., Stanford U., 1980; grad., Defense Systems Mgmt. Coll., 1984; disting. grad., Air Command and Staff Coll., 1988, Indsl. Coll. of Armed Forces, 1993. Advanced through the ranks to lt. gen. USAF, 2004; student, undergraduate pilot training Craig Air Force Base, Ala., 1973—75; student pilot, F-4E Replacement Training Unit MacDill Air Force Base, Fla., 1975—76; operational F-4E pilot, chief aircraft maintenance unit, base exec. officer Moody Air Force Base, Ga., 1976—79; design mgr., space shuttle ground support; chief, space shuttle vehicle integration Vandenberg Air Force Base, Calif., 1980—82; engr., NASA Orbiter Project Kennedy Space Ctr., Fla., 1982—84; space shuttle project engr.; dir. shuttle engring. Western Space and Missile Ctr., Vandenberg Air Force Base, 1984—87; chief, spl. projects inspections Norton Air Force Base, Calif., 1988—90; program element monitor, Air Force Medium Space Launch Vehicles Program; dep. chief, Space Systems Div. Office of Sec. of Air Force for Acquisition, Washington, 1990—91; exec. officer to asst. sec. Office of Sec. of Air Force for Acquisition, the Pentagon, 1991—92; mission area dir., information dominance Office of Sec. of Air Force for Acquisition, 1999—2001; dep. dir., Acquisition and Tech. Group Defense Mapping Agency, Washington, 1993—96; prog. dir., spl. projects, Electronic Systems Ctr., Air Force Materiel Command Hanscom Air Force Base, Mass., 1993—96, dir., Expeditionary Forces Experiment System Program Office, 1997—99; dep., Force Structure Integration and Deployment; prog. dir., Battle Mgmt. Command and Control Missile Defense Agency, Washington, 2001—03; dir. Joint Nat. Integration Ctr., 2003—04, Missile Defense Agency, 2004—. Top Gun, Air-to-Air F-4E Replacement Training Unit. 2nd. lt. USAF, 1973, 1st lt., 1975, captain, 1977, major, 1986, lt. col., 1989, col., 1994, brigadier gen., 2000, major gen., 2004. Decorated Defense Superior Service Medal, Def. Disting. Svc. medal, Legion of Merit with oak leaf cluster, Meritorious Service Medal with three oak leaf clusters, Air Force Commendation Medal, Air Force Achievement Medal. Mailing: Military Defense Agency 7100 Defense Pentagon Washington DC 20301-7100

OBERLANDER, MICHAEL I., lawyer, consumer products company executive; AB, U. Chgo.; JD, Vanderbilt U. Bar: Mo. 1993, Ill. 1994. Atty. Bryan Cave LLP, 1993—2000; v.p., gen. counsel Brown Shoe Co., Inc., St. Louis, 2000—01, v.p., gen. counsel, corp. sec., 2001—06, sr. v.p., gen. counsel, corp. sec., 2006—. Office: Brown Shoe Co, Inc 8300 Maryland Ave Saint Louis MO 63105 Office Phone: 314-854-4119. E-mail: moberlander@brownshoe.com.

OBERLIN, EARL CLIFFORD, III, securities brokerage company executive; b. Bryan, Ohio, Dec. 10, 1956; s. Earl Clifford II and Pauline Lois (Weber) O. BS in Acctg. and Fin., Miami U., Oxford, Ohio, 1979; grad., Harvard Bus. Sch., Cambridge, Mass. CFP; CPA, PFS, Ohio; gen. securities prin., mcpl. bond prin., registered options prin. V.p. MFI Investments Corp., Bryan, 1977—80, treas., 1980—84, pres., chief exec. officer, vice chmn. Toledo and Bryan, 1984—; v.p. Merit Co., Bryan, 1979—87, pres., chief exec. officer, 1988—95; v.p. Oberlin-Ford, Inc., Bryan, 1979—87; vice-chmn. Oberlin and Ford, Inc., Bryan, 1979—95, pres., CEO, 1988—95; chmn. Sky Investments Corp., 1996—2000; chmn. bd. R&O Memls., Inc., 2000—; CEO Oberlin Fin. Corp., 2000—, Oberlin Fin. Mortgage Group, LLC, 2000—. Author: Building a High End Financial Services Practice, 2004; bi-weekly columnist Personal Investing for Women, 1987. Bd. dirs. Jr. Achievement N.W. Ohio Inc., 1989—; pres., bd. dirs. Jr. Achievement, Bryan, 1989-91. Jr. Achievement NW Ohio scholar, 1975. Mem. AICPA, Inst. CFP, Internat. Assn. Fin. Planning (broker/dealer coun., chmn.-elect 1991, chmn. 1992), Young Pres.'s Orgn., Nat. Assn. Securities Dealers (dist. 8 bus. conduct com. 1994-96, chmn. dist. 8 nominating com. 1999), Securities Ind. Regulatory Coun. on Continuing Edn. (chmn. firm element com. 2007), Toledo Club, Rotary (Paul Harris fellow), Eagles, Moose. Republican. Methodist. Avocations: sailing, skiing. Home: 127 Country Club Rd Bryan OH 43506-9139 Office: Oberlin Financial Corp PO Box 998 Bryan OH 43506-0998

OBERLIN, RUSSELL, tenor, retired music educator; b. Akron, Ohio, Oct. 11, 1928; s. John Russell Oberlin and Mary Ethel Keys. Diploma in Voice, Julliard Sch., NYC, 1951. Performer: (recordings) NY Philharmonic, NY Pro Musica, Cantata Singers, Robert Shaw Chorale. Named Thomas Hunter Prof. Music, Hunter Coll. CUNY, 1986; recipient Sr. Fulbright Rsch. award, Eng., 1969. Mem.: NY Pro Musica, Am. Acad. Tchrs. of Singing.

OBERLY, KATHRYN ANNE, lawyer, diversified financial services company executive; b. Chgo., May 22, 1950; d. James Richard and Lucille Mary (Kraus) Oberly; 1 child, Michael W. Goelzer; m. Haynes B. Johnson, June 29, 2002. Student, Vassar Coll., 1967—69; BA, U. Wis., 1971, JD, 1973. Bar: Wis. 1973, D.C. 1981, N.Y. 1995. Law clk. U.S. Ct. Appeals, Omaha, 1973-74; trial atty. U.S. Dept. Justice, Washington, 1974-77, spl. asst., 1977-81, spl. litig. counsel, 1981-82, asst. to Solicitor Gen., 1982-86; ptnr. Mayer, Brown & Platt, Washington, 1986-91; assoc. gen. counsel Ernst & Young LLP, Washington, 1991-94, vice-chair, gen. counsel NYC, 1994—. Bd. dirs. Appleseed Found., 2003—04. Named one of 50 Most Influential Women Lawyers in Am., Nat. Law Jour., 1998; recipient Aiming High award, Legal Momentum, 2007. Mem. ABA, Am. Law Inst. (coun. mem.), Am. Acad. Appellate Lawyers, Wis. Bar Assn., D.C. Bar Assn., NY Bar Assn. Democrat. Office: Ernst & Young LLP 5 Times Sq New York NY 10036 Home Phone: 202-387-3901; Office Phone: 212-773-2500. Business E-Mail: kathryn.oberly@ey.com.

OBERMAN, IDA, research and evaluation director, consultant; b. Brummen, Holland, Nov. 22, 1957; arrived in US, 1976; d. Heiko and Gertruida (Reesink) Oberman; m. Lis Cox, Mar. 7, 1999. BA, Swarthmore Coll., 1980; MA, Stanford U., 1983, PhD, 1998. Tchr. H.S. Green Meadow Waldorf Sch., Spring Valley, NY, 1984—87, Trinity Sch., NYC, 1987—92; found. officer Hewlett Found., Menlo Park, Calif., 1998—2001; dir. rsch. and evaluation Springboard Schs., San Francisco, 2002—. Mem. adv. com. Calif. Dept. Edn., 1998—2000, Alameda Unified Sch. Dist., Calif., 2002; mem. adv. bd. Dept. Edn., Calif. Co-author: Teacher Learning, 1996; author: Fidelity & Flexibility, 1998. Co-founder Waldorf-in-the-Mainstream, NYC, 1990, West Side Cmty. Sch., Harlem, NY, 1992. Scheffel grant, Germany. Mem.: Am. Edn. Rsch. Assn. (chair edn. and philanthropy spl. interest group 2001—). Avocations: pottery, swimming. Home: 516 Taylor Ave Alameda CA 94501 Office: Springboard Schs 181 Fremont San Francisco CA 94105

OBERMAN, MICHAEL STEWART, lawyer; b. Bklyn., May 21, 1947; s. Hyman Martin and Gertrude O.; m. Sharon Land, Oct. 8, 1975; 1 child, Abigail Land. AB, Columbia U., 1969; JD, Harvard U., 1972. Bar: N.Y. 1973, U.S. Dist. Ct. (so. and ea. dists.) N.Y. 1973, U.S. Ct. Appeals (2d cir.) 1973, U.S. Supreme Ct. 1976, Calif. 1981, U.S. Dist. Ct. (no. dist.) Calif. 1981, U.S. Ct. Appeals (9th cir.) 1981, U.S. Dist. Ct. (so. and cen. dists.) Calif. 1982, U.S. Ct. Appeals (5th cir.) 1989, D.C. 1992, U.S. Ct. Appeals (7th cir.) 1993. Law clk. to Hon. Milton Pollack, U.S. Dist. Ct. (so. dist.) N.Y., 1972-73; assoc. Kramer Levin Naftalis & Frankel LLP, NYC, 1973-79, ptnr., 1980—. Contbr. articles to profl. jours Recipient Nathan Burkan prize ASCAP, 1973. Mem. N.Y. State Bar Assn. (mem. ho. of dels. 1989-91, exec. com. comml. and fed. litigation sect.). Office: Kramer Levin Naftalis & Frankel LLP 1177 Avenue of the Americas New York NY 10036-1003 Office Phone: 212-715-9294. Business E-Mail: moberman@kramerlevin.com.

OBERMAN, STEVEN, lawyer; b. St. Louis, Sept. 21, 1955; s. Albert and Marian (Kleg) O.; m. Evelyn Ann Simpson, Aug. 28, 1977; children: Rachael Diane, Benjamin Scott. BA in Psychology, Auburn U., 1977; JD, U. Tenn., 1980. Bar: Tenn. 1980, Tenn. Supreme Ct. 1980, Tenn. Criminal Ct. Appeals 1980, U.S. Dist. Ct. (ea. dist.) Tenn. 1980, U.S. Ct. Appeals (4th cir.) 1981, U.S. Ct. Appeals (6th cir.) 1983, U.S. Supreme Ct. 1985; bd. cert. in DUI Defense, 1999. Law clk. Daniel, Duncan & Claiborne, Knoxville, Tenn., 1978-80; assoc. Daniel, Claiborne & Lewallen, Knoxville, Tenn., 1980-82, Daniel, Claiborne, Oberman & Buuck, Knoxville, 1983-85, Daniel & Oberman, Knoxville, 1986—. Pres. Project First Offender, Knoxville, 1983—86; bd. dirs. Fed. Defender Svcs. Ea. Tenn., Inc., 1994—97, pres., 1998—2000; guest instr. U. Tenn., 1988—90, guest instr. legal clinic, trial advocacy program, 1984—; guest lectr. U. Tenn. Law Sch., 1982—88, adj. prof., 1993—, coach nat. trial team, 1991—96; guest instr. U. Tenn. Grad. Sch. Criminal Justice Program, 1983, 84; guest spkr. Ct. Clk.'s Meeting, Cambridge, England, 1984; spl. judge criminal divsn. Knox County Gen. Session Ct.; spkr. in field. Author: D.U.I.: The Crime and Consequences in Tennessee, 1991; co-author: Drunk Driving Defense, 6th edit., 2005, D.W.I. Means Defend With Ingenuity, 1987; contbr. legal articles on drunk driving to profl. jours. Bd. dirs. Knoxville Legal Aid Soc., Inc., 1986-88 (pres. 1990), Arnstein Jewish Community Ctr., 1987-91, pres. 1990; bd. dirs. Knoxville Racquet Club, 1991-93, pres. 1992-93; vice chair Tenn. Gov.'s DUI Task Force, 2006. Named a Super Lawyer, Mid-South Super Lawyers Mag., 2006, 2007; named Col. Aide de Camp, Tenn. Gov.'s Staff, 1983; named one of Top 150 Tenn. Lawyers, Bus. Tenn. Mag., 2004, 2005, 2006, 2007; recipient Forrest W. Lacey award for outstanding faculty contbn. to moot ct. program, U. Tenn. Coll. Law, 1993—94, Outstanding Adj. Prof. award, 2002, Moot Ct. Bd. Spl. Svc. award, 1995—96. Mem.: ATLA, Knoxville Bar Assn., Tenn. Assn. Criminal Def. Lawyers (bd. dirs. 1983—89), Nat. Coll. DUI Def. (bd. regents 1999—, founding), Nat. Assn. Criminal Def. Lawyers (chair/co-chair DUI advocacy com. 1995—, editl. bd. The Champion mag.). Jewish. Office: Daniel & Oberman 550 W Main St Ste 950 Knoxville TN 37902-2536 Home Phone: 854-588-5004; Office Phone: 865-546-4292. Business E-Mail: oberman@daolaw.com.

OBERMANN, RICHARD MICHAEL, governmental technology and policy analyst; b. May 21, 1949; s. Baird J. and Phyllis L. (Weber) Obermann; m. Grace Karaffa; children: Pearl Louise, John Baird. BS of Engring. in Aerospace and Mech. Scis. cum laude, Princeton U., 1971, PhD in Engring., Aerospace and Mech. Scis., 1977; MS of Engring. in Astronautics and Aeros., Stanford U., 1972; postgrad., Va. Poly. Inst. and State U., Am. U., Harvard U., 1993. With MITRE Corp., McLean, Va., 1977-88, engr. transp. systems analysis, transp. energy analysis, telecommunications, project leader, mem. tech. staff in communications and system design; sr. staff officer aeros. and space engring. bd. NRC, Washington, 1988-90, study dir. and analyst technol. and policy issues; mem. profl. staff for space subcom. US Ho. of Reps. Com. on Sci., Space and Tech., Washington, 1990-95; minority staff dir., space and aeronautics subcom. US Ho. of Reps. Com. on Sci., Washington, 1995—2007; staff dir. space and aeronautics subcom. US Ho. of Reps. Com. on Sci. and Tech., Washington, 2007—. Lectr. in field; presenter in field. Contbr. articles to profl. jours.; reviewer for jours.:. Fellow AIAA (internat. activities com., pub. policy com.), Brit. Interplanetary Soc., Am. Astronaut. Soc. (bd. dirs., exec. com., internat. policy com.); mem. IEEE, AAAS, NY Acad. Sci., Asia Soc., Nat. Space Club, Pacific Telecomms. Coun., Women in Aerospace (bd. dirs.), Internat. Acad. Astronautics, World Affairs Coun. Avocations: languages, sports, trumpet. Office Phone: 202-225-7858.

OBERMAYER, HERMAN JOSEPH, newspaper publisher; b. Phila., Sept. 19, 1924; s. Leon J. and Julia (Sinsheimer) O.; m. Betty Nan Levy, June 28, 1955; children: Helen O. Levy-Myers, Veronica O. Atnipp, Adele O. Malpass, Elizabeth O. Weintraub. Student, U. Geneva, Switzerland, 1946; AB cum laude, Dartmouth Coll., Hanover, NH, 1948. Reporter L.I. Daily Press, Jamaica, NY, 1950-53; classified advt. mgr. New Orleans Item, 1953-55; asst. to pub. Standard-Times, New Bedford, Mass., 1955-57; editor, pub. Long Branch Daily Record, NJ, 1957-71, No. Va. Sun, Arlington, 1963-89; adj. prof. journalism U. Md., 1989-93; vis. lectr. U. West Indies, Jamaica, 1994-95; publ. com. Commentary Mag., 1989—. Pulitizer Prize juror, 1983, 84; lectr. publs. mgmt. Hungary, Poland, Lithuania, Latvia, Estonia, Ukraine, Moldova, Slovenia, Macedonia, Russia, Croatia, Serbia, 1990-2002, Internat. Ctr. Journalists, 1992-2002. Author: Jews in the News, 2001, Soldiering for Freedom: A GI's Account of World War II, 2005; contbr. articles to popular mags., local newspapers. Bd. dirs. Monmouth Med. Ctr., 1958-71; exec. coun. Monmouth Boy Scouts Am., 1958-71, exec. com. Nat. Capital coun., 1971-79, v.p., 1974-77; mem. Va. Legis. Alcohol Beverage Control Study Commn., 1972-74; trustee Arlington (Va.) Bicentennial Commn., Am. Jewish Com. Cmty. Svc. award, 1986, nat. bd. govs., 1989-96, nat. coun., 1996—; trustee Jewish Inst. for Nat. Security Affairs, 1996—. With AUS, 1943-46, ETO. Rhineland Campaign Star; Recipient Silver Beaver award Boy Scouts Am., 1977, Knight Internat. Press fellow, 1994-95. Mem. Am. Soc. Newspaper Editors, So. Newspaper Pubs. Assn. (dir. 1981-84), Mont. Pelerin Soc., Nat. Press Club (Washington), Cosmos Club (Washington), Washington Golf and Country Club (Arlington, Va.), Burning Tree Club (NYC), Sigma Chi. Jewish. Rotarian. Personal E-mail: obenews@aol.com.

OBERMEYER, THERESA NANGLE, sociology educator; b. St. Louis, July 25, 1945; d. James Francis and Harriet Clare (Shafer) Nangle; m. Thomas S. Obermeyer, Dec. 23, 1977; children: Thomas Jr., James, Margaret, Matthew. BA, Maryville U., St. Louis, 1967; MEd, St. Louis U., 1970, PhD, 1975. Lic. real estate broker Alaska, 1979, cert. Type A tchr. Alaska, 1979. Dir. student activities Lindenwood U., St. Charles, Mo., 1969—70; asst. dean of students Loyola Coll., Balt., 1972—73; asst. dir. student activities St. Louis C.C., Florissant Valley, 1973—78; dir. student activities U. Alaska, Anchorage, 1978—79; instr. sociology Chapman U., Anchorage, 1981—93; tchr. secondary McLaughlin Youth Ctr. for Juvenile Delinquents, 1984—90. Mem Anchorage Munic Health Commn., 1980—81; elected alt. coun. urban bd edn. Nat Sch. Bds. Assn., 1994; mem. bd. cert. com. Advocacy Fair Alaska Law and Alaska PErmanent Fund; maj. party nominee US Senate Gen. Election, 1996; founder, mem. Alaska Women's Polit. Caucus, 1979—; elected Anchorage Sch. Bd., 1990—94, treas., 1993. Recipient Fed Women's Equity Act, US Dept Educ Univ Alaska, 1978—79; fellow Fulbright, Project India, 1974, Project Jordan, 1977; grantee Title I, Univ Md and Loyola Col, 1972—73; scholar NDEA, 1968—70. Mem.: AAUW (bd. dirs. Anchorage br. 1980—81), DAR (regent col. John Mitchell chpt. 1992—94), Am. Soc. Pub. Adminstrn. (pres., bd. dirs. south ctrl. chpt. 1981). Avocations: sports, swimming, horseback riding, skiing, running. Home and Office: 3000 Dartmouth Dr Anchorage AK 99508-4413 Office Phone: 907-278-9455. Office Fax: 907-278-9455. Personal E-mail: tobermeyer@gci.net.

OBERN, VIVIAN MARIE, volunteer; b. Park Ridge, Ill., May 26, 1921; d. Vaughn Webber and Beatrice Beckwith Hapeman; m. Earl George Obern, Dec. 4, 1942; children: George Vaughn, Dale Marie, Reade Webber. BA, Principia Coll., Elsah, Ill., 1942. Exec. sec. Santa Barbara County Trails Coun., 1966—2007; co-chmn. Am. Revolutionary Bicentennial Com., 1974—77; chmn. County Christopher Columbus Quincentennial, 1992; pres. Santa Barbara Trust for Hist. Preservation, 1989—91; leader Girl Scouts Am., 1960—66; mem. Calif. Recreational Trails Com., Sacramento, 1971—76; vol. Hope House, 1986; mem. adv. com. to suprs. Santa Barbara County Riding and Hiking Trails, Calif., 1967—2006; mem. Santa Barbara Courthouse Docents Coun., 1974—2006. Named Woman of Yr., Santa Barbara Advt. Club, 1989, George and Vie Obern Preservation Stewardship award in her honor, Santa Barbara Trust for Historic Preservation, 2006; recipient Hon. Life Svc. award, PTA, 1968, 1976, Disting. Alumna award, Principia Coll., 1996, Lifetime Achievement award, Calif. Recreational Trails, 1997, Environ. award, Santa Barbara County Trails Coun., 1997, Pearl Chase Hist. Preseravation award, Santa Barbara Trust for Hist. Preservation, 1998, Wildlife Sanctuary award, 2002, Obern Bikeway/Trail named in her honor, 2004, Environ. Studies Cmty. Svc. award, U. Calif., Santa Barbara, 2006. Mem.: Calif. Recreational Trails (com. mem. 1971—76), Daus. of Union Vets. (pres. Calif. dept.). Christian Scientist. Avocations: equestrian activities, baking. Home: 4140 Marina Dr Santa Barbara CA 93110

OBERNAUER, MARNE, JR., technology industry executive; b. Lakehurst, NJ, July 1, 1943; s. Marne and Joan Carolyn (Strassburger) O.; m. Marion Fleck Gislason, Aug. 22, 1976 (dec. Jan. 1996); children: Matthew Gene, Michael Sidney; m. Margaret Anne Culver, Oct. 1, 2005. BA, Yale U., 1965; MBA, Harvard U., 1972. With First Nat. City Bank (Citibank, N.A.), NYC, 1965-70, Donaldson, Lufkin & Jenrette, NYC, 1972-74, Devon Group, Inc., NYC and Stamford, Conn., 1974-98, pres., 1978, CEO, 1980-98, chmn. bd., 1986-98; vice chmn. Applied Graphics Techs., Inc., 1998—2003, also bd. dirs. Chmn. bd. dirs. Beverage Distbrs. Co. Trustee The Trinity Sch., The Obernauer Found., Inc.; bd. dirs. Com. for Responsible Fed. Budget. Mem.: Am. Bus. Conf. Found. for Econ. Growth (chmn.), Am. Bus. Conf., Assn. Yale Alumni (bd. govs. 1999—2003, treas. 2002—03), Maroon Creek Club (Aspen), Century Country Club, Yale Club NYC. Office: Ste 1912 60 E 42d St New York NY 10165

OBERNDORF, MEYERA E., mayor; m. Roger L. Oberndorf; children: Marcie, Heide. BS in Elem. Edn., Old Dominion U., 1964. Broadcaster Sta. WNIS, Norfolk, Va.; chair Pub. Libr. bd., Va.; mem. city coun. City of Virginia Beach, Va., 1976—, vice-mayor Va., 1986—88, mayor Va., 1988—. Mem. exec. bd. Tidewater coun. Boys Scouts Am.; bd. dirs. Va.Beach Pub. Libr., 1966-76, chmn. bd., 1967-76; past pres. Va. Muncipal League; bd. dir. Hampton Roads Partnership; Econ. Develop. Alliance; adv. com. Va. Inst. of Gov. Named 25 Most Dynamic Mayors in the US, Newsweek. Mem. AAUW, U.S. Conf. Mayors (trustee), Va. Mcpl. League (exec. bd.), Nat. League Cities (vice-chmn., mem. adv. bd., past chair Energy, Environ., and Natural Resources Steering Com.), Princess Anne Women's Club; chair Standing Com. on Internat. Affairs. Jewish. Home: 5404 Challedon Dr Virginia Beach VA 23462-4112 Office: 2401 Courthouse Drive City Hall Bldg 1 Municipal Ctr Virginia Beach VA 23456 Office Phone: 757-427-4581. Office Fax: 757-426-5669. E-mail: moberndo@VBgov.com. *

O'BERRY, CARL GERALD, former military officer, electrical engineer; b. Lansing, Mich., Apr. 11, 1936; s. Gerald Ray and Edith Lenore (Watson) O'B.; m. Charlene Marice Bussche, June 21, 1958; children: Brian, Eileen, Kevin, Bradley, Kathleen. BSEE, N.Mex. State U., 1972; MS in Systems Mgmt., Air Force Inst. Tech., 1977. Commd. 2d lt. USAF, 1961, advanced through grades to lt. gen., 1993; comdr. 2019 Communications Squadron, Griffiss AFB, NY, 1974-76; project engr. Rome Air Devel. Ctr., Griffiss AFB, 1979-81; asst. dep. chief of staff requirements Air Force Systems Command, Andrews AFB, Md., 1982-84; comdr. Rome Air Devel. Ctr., Griffiss AFB, 1984-86; joint program mgr. WWMCCS info. system Hdqrs. USAF, Washington, 1986-88; dir. command, control and communications U.S. European Command, Stuttgart, Fed. Republic Germany, 1988-90; dir. command control systems and logistics U.S. Space Command, Peterson AFB, Colo., 1990-92; command control comm. and computers DCS, HQ USAF, Washington, 1992-95; v.p., dir. strategic planning Motorola Space and Sys. Tech. Group, Scottsdale, Ariz., 1995-98; tech. cons. Def. Sci. Bd., Washington, 1998—; v.p., gen. mgr. govt. info. and comms. sys., space group The Boeing Co., Anaheim, Calif., 2000—05; ret. Exec. chair Network Centric Ops. Industry Consortium, 2004—. Mem. Air Force Assn., Armed Forces Communications-Electronics Assn., Soc. Logistics Engrs. Roman Catholic.

O'BERRY, PHILLIP AARON, retired veterinarian; b. Tampa, Fla., Feb. 1, 1933; s. Luther Lee and Marjorie Mae (Mahlum) O'B.; m. Terri Martin, July 31, 1960; children: Kelly, Eric, Holly, Danny, Andy, Toby. BS in Agr., U. Fla., Gainsville, 1955; DVM, Auburn U., Ala., 1960; PhD, Iowa State U., Ames, 1967. With Agrl. Rsch. Svc. USDA, 1956—2003, asst. to dir. vet. scis. rsch. div. Beltsville, Md., 1967-72; asst. dir. Nat. Animal Disease Ctr., Ames, Iowa, 1972-73, dir., 1973-88, tech. transfer coord., 1988—2003; prin. scientist Office Agr. Biotech., USDA, 1988-90; ret., 2003. Adj. prof. Coll. Vet. Medicine, Iowa State U., 1973—; expert panel livestock infertility FAO; sci. adv. com. Pan Am. Zoonosis Ctr., Buenos Aires; mem. Fed. Coun. Sci. and Tech.; com. animal health, world food and nutrition study NRC; cons. Govt. of Italy, Govt. of Mex., USDA, Govt. of Egypt; nat needs grad. fellowship rev. panel USDA, 1989-91, cons. agr. biotech. rsch. adv. com.; sci. adv. bd. Biotech. R&D Corp., 1992-2001, sci. review bd. Am. Jour. Vet. Rsch., 1990-92; mem. USDA Patent Review Com., 1988-2003. Author 27 rsch. publs.; mem. editl. adv. bd. Food Safety mag. Recipient Cert. Merit, Agrl. Rsch. Svc., 1972, 84, 2005, Alumni Merit award Iowa State Club Chgo., 1982, Cert. Appreciation, 1988, Tech. Transfer award 1989, 2004, USDA, Disting. Alumnus award Auburn U., 1991; named Hon. Diplomate Am. Coll. Vet. Microbiologists, 1995, Ames Citizen the Yr., 2000, Iowa Gov.'s Vol. award, 2001, Philanthropy award, 2006. Mem. APHA, AVMA, AAAS, Nat. Assn. Fed. Vets., Iowa Vet. Med. Assn., NY Acad. Scis., Conf. Rsch. Workers Animal Diseases, Am. Soc. Microbiology, Am. Assn. Lab. Animal Sci., US Animal Health Assn., Am. Assn. Bovine Practitioners, Livestock Cons. Inst., Sigma Xi, Phi Zeta, Phi Kappa Phi, Gamma Sigma Delta (Alumni award Merit 1976), Alpha Zeta, Spades, Blue Key. Democrat. Home: 1612 Woodhaven Cir Ames IA 50010-4130 Personal E-mail: terrioberry@mchsi.com.

OBERST, ROBERT JOHN, financial analyst; b. Hackensack, NJ, Aug. 20, 1929; s. Bernard and Elsie (Schneider) O.; m. Ingrid Heilbut, Oct. 6, 1956; children: Jeanne, Robert John, Carl Edward. PhD in Fin. Mgmt., Columbia Pacific U., 1984. Cert. fin. planner, registered health underwriter. Spl. agt., mgr. Prudential Ins. Co. Am., Asbury Park, N.J., 1958-68; pres. Robert J. Oberst, Sr. & Assocs., Red Bank, N.J., 1969-92, chmn. bd., 1993—. Newspaper columnist Fin. Planning, 1986-87; prodr., host TV show Fin. Planning Today, 1983-93; contbr. articles to profl. jours. Author newspaper column Fin. Planning, 1986-87; producer, host TV show Fin. Planning Today, 1983-93; contbr. articles to profl. jours. Pres. Monmouth-Ocean Devel. Coun., Manasquan, N.J., 1981-83; bd. dirs. Monmouth County coun. Boy Scouts Am., 1986-93; trustee Brookdale Coll. Found., Middletown, N.J., 1986-92; founder Palmetto State Shooting Ctr. LLC,

2003; mng.ptnr. of Gun Sch., Range, and Gun Retail Ctr. With USN, 1946-50. Recipient Silver Gull Service award Monmouth/Ocean Devel. Council, 1984. Mem. Inst. Cert. Fin. Planners (Fin. Planner of Yr. award 1979), Internat. Assn. Fin. Planning (bd. dirs. 1986-93, chmn. bd. dirs. 1992-93), Estate Planning Coun. (pres. 1971-72), Million Dollar Round Table (life), Nat. Assn. Life Underwriters, Red Bank C. of C. (bd. dirs.), Registry Fin. Planning Practitioners (chmn. 1987-88), N.J. Assn. Life Underwriters (state pres. 1969-70). Republican. Avocations: civil war history, bicycling, gourmet dining, theater, reading. Home: 2 Cottingham Rd Bluffton SC 29910-4714 Office: Robert J Oberst Sr & Assocs 218 Broad St Red Bank NJ 07701-2002 E-mail: rjo33@aol.com.

OBERSTAR, JAMES L., congressman; b. Chisholm, Minn., Sept. 10, 1934; s. Louis and Mary (Grillo) O.; m. Jo Garlick, Oct. 12, 1963 (dec. July 1991); children: Thomas Edward, Katherine Noelle, Anne-Therese, Monica Rose; m. Jean Kurth, Nov. 1993; stepchildren: Corinne Quinlan Kurth, Charles Burke Kurth, Jr. BA summa cum laude, St. Thomas Coll., 1956; postgrad. in French, Laval U., Que., Can.; MS in Govt. (scholar), Coll. Europe, Bruges, Belgium, 1957; postgrad. in govt, Georgetown U. Adminstrv. asst. Congressman John A. Blatnik, 1963-74; adminstr. Pub. Works Com. US Ho. Reps., 1971-74; mem. US Congress from 8th Minn. Dist., 1975—, ranking minority mem. transp. and infrastructure com. Mem.: Am. Polit. Sci. Assn. Democrat. Office: US Ho Reps 2365 Rayburn Ho Office Bldg Washington DC 20515-2308 *

OBERSTEIN, NORMAN S., lawyer; b. Oskaloosa, Iowa, Nov. 5, 1940; BA magna cum laude, U. Iowa, 1962; JD, U. Calif., Berkeley, 1965. Bar: Calif. 1966, US Supreme Ct. 1996. Mng. mem. and sr. ptnr. Litig. Dept. Kaplan, Livingston, Goodwin, Berkowitz & Selvin, Beverly Hills, Calif.; of counsel Gipson Hoffman & Pancione, Calif., 2006—. Mem.: LA County Bar Assn., Beverly Hills County Bar Assn., State Calif. Bar Assn., Omicron Delta Kappa, Order of Coif, Phi Beta Kappa. Office: Gipson Hoffman & Pancione Floor 11 1901 Avenue of the Stars Los Angeles CA 90067 Office Phone: 310-556-4660. Office Fax: 310-556-8945. E-mail: noberstein@ghplaw.com. *

OBERT, PAUL RICHARD, lawyer, manufacturing executive; b. Pitts. s. Edgar F. and Elizabeth T. Obert. BS, Georgetown U., 1950; JD, U. Pitts., 1953. Bar: Pa. 1954, D.C. 1956, Ohio 1972, Ill. 1974, U.S. Supreme Ct. 1970. Sole practice, Pitts., 1954-60; asst. counsel H.K. Porter Co., Inc., Pitts., 1960—62, sec., gen. counsel, 1962-71, Addressograph-Multigraph Corp., Cleve., 1972-74; v.p. law Marshall Field & Co., Chgo., 1974-82, sec., 1976-82; v.p., gen. counsel, sec. CF Industries, Inc., Long Grove, Ill., 1982—, also officer, dir. various subs. Served to lt. col. USAF. Mem. ABA (corp. gen. counsel com.), Pa. Bar Assn., Allegheny County Bar Assn., Ill. Bar Assn., Chgo. Bar Assn., Am. Soc. Corp. Secs., Am. Retail Fedn. (bd. dirs. 1977-80), Georgetown U. Alumni Assn. (bd. govs.), Pitts. Athletic Assn., Univ. Club (Chgo.), Delta Theta Phi. Office: CF Industries Inc 1 Salem Lake Dr Long Grove IL 60047-8401

OBERTON, WILLARD D., industrial supply company executive; Grad., St. Cloud Tech. Coll. V.p., COO Fastenal Co., Winona, Minn., 1997—2002, bd. dir., 1999—, exec. v.p., COO, 2000—01, pres., COO, 2001—02, pres., CEO, 2002—. Bd. dir. Wincraft Inc., Donaldson Co. Inc. Trustee Coll. St. Benedict. Office: Fastenal Co 2001 Theurer Blvd Winona MN 55987 *

OBEY, DAVID ROSS, congressman; b. Okmulgee, Okla., Oct. 3, 1938; s. Orville John and Mary Jane (Chellis) Obey; m. Joan Therese Lepinski, June 9, 1962; children: Craig David, Douglas David. BS in Polit. Sci., U. Wis., Madison, 1960; MA in Soviet Politics, U. Wis., 1962. Mem. Wis. State Gen. Assembly, 1963-69, asst. minority leader, 1967-69; mem. US Congress from 7th Wis. dist., 1969—, ranking minority mem. appropriations com., ranking minority mem. labor, health and human svcs., edn. and related agencies subcommittee. Mem. adminstrv. com. Wis. Dem. Com., 1960-62 Named Edn. Legislator of Yr., Rural div. NEA, 1968; recipient Legis. Leadership award Eagelton Inst. Politics, 1964, award of merit Nat. Coun. Sr. Citizens, 1976, citation for legis. statesmanship Coun. Exceptional Children, 1976. Democrat. Office: US Ho Reps 2314 Rayburn Ho Office Bldg Washington DC 20515-4907 Office Phone: 202-225-3365. *

OBIOZOR, GEORGE ACHULIKE, ambassador; b. Nigeria, Aug. 15, 1942; married. BA in Polit. Sci. and Hist., U. Puget Sound, Tacoma, Wash.; M in Internat. Affairs, Columbia U., NYC, 1971, M of Philos. in Internat. Affairs, 1974, PhD in Internat. Affairs, 1976. Lectr. Pratt Inst., NYC, 1971—75; asst. prof. polit. sci. CUNY Medgar Evers Coll., 1975—79; Ralph Bunche Rsch. Fellow in UN CUNY Grad. Ctr., 1977—78; spl. asst. Office of Polit. Adv. to Pres., Nigeria, 1980—83; sr. rsch. fellow Nigerian Inst. Internat. Affairs, Lagos, Nigeria, 1984—87; spl. adv. to Min. of Fgn. Affairs Nigeria, 1988—89; spl. asst. to pres. of Nigeria on internat. affairs, 1990; dir. gen. Nigerian Inst. Internat. Affairs, 1991—99; Nigerian amb. to Israel and high commr. to Cyprus, 1999—2003; Nigerian amb. to US Washington, 2004—. Chmn. Commonwealth Tech. Meeting, Abuja, 1996; vis. prof. internat. affairs African Inst., Russian Acad. Sci., Moscow, 1998. Author and editor of numerous profl. books. Recipient Ugwumba 1 of Orlu, 1991; grantee Albert Schweitzer fellowship, 1969—71, Alice Stetten fellowship, Columbia U. Sch. Internat. Affairs, 1969—71. Office: Embassy of Nigeria 3519 International Ct NW Washington DC 20008 Office Phone: 202-986-8400.

OBLINGER, JAMES L., academic administrator; b. Ashland, Ohio, Nov. 3, 1945; s. Richard Bruce and Pauline (Frary) Oblinger; m. Diana G. Oblinger; 4 children. BA in Bacteriology, DePauw U., Greencastle, Ind., 1967; MS in Food Tech., Iowa State U., 1970, PhD in Food Tech., 1972. Asst. prof. to prof. food sci. and human nutrition U. Fla., Gainesville, 1972-84; assoc. dean, dir. resident instrn. Coll. Agr., U. Mo., Columbia, 1984-86; assoc. dean, dir. acad. affairs Coll. Agr. and Life Sci., N.C. State U., Raleigh, 1986—97; dean, exec. dir. for agrl. programs N.C. State U., Raleigh, 1997—2003, provost, exec. vice chancellor for acad. affairs, 2003—04, chancellor, 2005—. Contbr. articles to profl. jours., chpts. to books. Recipient Award of Merit, Inst. of Food and Agrl. Scis., 1981, William V. Cruess Nat. Award, 1983, Disting. Educator Award, Nat. Assn. Colls. and Tchrs. of Agriculture, 1994, Iowa State Disting. Alumni Achievement award, 2006. Mem. Inst. Food Technologists (Wm. V. Cruess Nat. Award Excellence 1983), Coun. for Agrl. Sci. and Tech. (pres. 1990-91), Am. Assn. Higher Edn., Sigma Xi, Phi Kappa Phi, Gamma Sigma Delta, Phi Tau Sigma, Phi Epsilon Phi, Phi Beta Kappa. Episcopalian. Office: NC State U A Holladay Hall Campus Box 7001 Raleigh NC 27695-7101 Office Phone: 919-515-2191. Business E-Mail: james_oblinger@ncsu.edu.

O'BLOCK, ROBERT, association, publishing executive; BS in Sociology, Pitts. State U., Kans., 1972, MS in Sociology, 1973, EdS, 2001; PhD, Kans. State U., 1976; MA in Psychology, Newport U., 1998, PsyD in Psychology, 2000; MDiv, Trinity Coll., 2001, DMin, 2003; STD (hon.), St. Elins Sch. Orthodox Theology, 2003. Ordained deacon So. Episcopal Ch., 1999; ordained priest So. Episcopal Ch., 2002. Patrolman Frontenac (Kans.) Police Dept., 1971-73; probation officer Crawford County Juvenile Ct., 1973-74; supr. Children's Ct. Ctr., 1974; adminstrv. asst. to dean student affairs/cmty. svc. Labette Cmty. Jr. Coll., 1976; dir. night sch. Marymount Coll., 1976; asst. prof. dept. adminstrv. justice Wichita State U., 1977-79; assoc. prof. dept. criminal justice/polit. sci. Appalachian State U., Boone, NC, 1979-89; prof. and chair dept. adminstrn. justice Coll. Ozarks, Point Lookout, Mo., 1989—93; exec. dir. Am. Coll. Forensic Examiners, Springfield, Mo., 1994—. Founder Am. Bd. Forensic Medicine, Am. Bd. Forensic Examiners, Am. Bd. Forensic Psychol.; lectr., cons. in field. Author: Criminal Justice Research Sources, 1983, 4th edit., 1992, (with others) Security and Crime Prevention, 2d edit., 1990, The 7 Steps to the Cure of Souls, 2005; founder, pub. The Forensic Examiner, Annals of the Am. Psychotherapy Assn., contbr. articles to profl. jours., holder 25 U.S. fed. trademarks. Adv. bd. Larnard State Hosp. Named Knight Chevalier, Sovereign Military Order of Temple of Jerusalem, 2001; grantee, Gov.'s Commn. on Criminal Adminstrn., 1976—77. Mem.: Am. Assn. Integrative Medicine (co-founder, CEO), Am. Coll. Forensic Examiners (founder), Am. Psychotherapy Assn. (founder, chmn., CEO). Office: 2750 E Sunshine St Springfield MO 65804-2047 Home: 3686 E Kingswood Dr Springfield MO 65809-4635 Office Phone: 417-881-3818. Personal E-mail: rloblock@aol.com.

O'BLOCK, ROBERT PAUL, management consultant; b. Pitts., Mar. 9, 1943; s. Paul Joseph and Mary Elizabeth (Galicic) O'B.; m. Megan Marie. BSME, Purdue U., 1965; MBA, Harvard U., 1967. Rsch. and tchg. fellow in fin., econs. and urban mgmt. Harvard U., 1967-70; assoc. in real estate mgmt. and fin. McKinsey & Co., Inc., Boston, 1969-78; gen. and mng. ptnr. Freeport Ctr., Clearfield, Utah, 1971—; prin. McKinsey & Co., Inc., Boston, 1979-84, dir., 1984-98, McKinsey Adv. Coun., Boston, 1998—. Vis. lectr. urban econs. Yale Law Sch., Princeton U.; cons. Mass., N.J. housing fin. agys., Rockefeller Assn., HUD, 1968-76; chmn. mgmt. com. Snowbird Lodge (Utah), 1974-86. Contbr. articles to profl. jours. Mem. nat. adv. bd. Snowbird Arts Inst., 1977-83; mem. budget com. N.Y. Pub. Libr., 1977-79; mem. adv. bd. Internat. Tennis Hall of Fame, 1986-89, bd. dirs., 1989-95; mem. bd. overseers Boston Symphony Orch., 1988-2000, vice-chmn. bd. overseers, 1992-95, chmn., 1995-2000, trustee, 2000—, vice chmn. bd. trustees, 2002—; trustee U.S. Ski Ednl. Found., 1989-2001, Park Sch., 1997—2003; bd. dirs. Bankrate, Inc. Mem. Devon Yacht Club, Maidstone Club, Nat. Golf Links Am., The Country Club (Brookline), Univ. Club Boston. Office: 60 Cramond Rd Chestnut Hill MA 02467-2803

OBLOY, LEONARD GERARD, priest; b. Cleve., Sept. 1, 1951; s. Henry Joseph and Ruth Elsie (Walter) Obloy. AB, Borromeo Coll. of Ohio, 1973; MDiv, St. Mary's Sem., 1977; SSL, Pontifical Bibl. Inst., Rome, 1983, postgrad., 1984. Ordained priest Roman Cath. Ch., 1977. Assoc. pastor St. Helen Parish, Newbury, Ohio, 1977-80, St. Rose of Lima Parish, Cleve., 1984-88; vice-rector Mt. St. Mary's Sem., Emmitsburg, Md., 1988-97, asst. prof. sacred scripture and computer sci., 1988-99, dir. aux. svcs., 1997-99; assoc. pastor St. Francis of Assisi Parish, Gates Mills, Ohio, 1999—2002; pastor St. William Parish, Euclid, Ohio, 2002—. Adj. prof. St. Mary's Sem., Cleve., 1984—88, Cleve., 1999—; dean grad. divsn. Cath. Distance U., Hamilton, Va., 1995—2003, dean emeritus, 2003—; guest lectr. Our Lady of Holy Cross Coll., New Orleans, 1998—2003; lectr. in field. Author, narrator pub. TV series And God Said, Witness; author various pamphlets, audio casettes for Cath. Distance U. Mem.: IEEE Computer Soc., Vatican Radio, Sacred Congregation for Doctrine of Faith, Nat. Cath. Edn. Assn., Corp. for Pub. Broadcasting, Cath. Bibl. Fedn., NY Acad. Scis., Assn. Computing Machinery, GTO Assn. Am. Avocations: computers, audio engineering, audio recording, auto mechanics. Office: St William Parish 367 E 260th St Euclid OH 44132 Office Phone: 216-731-1515. Business E-Mail: lgobloy@aol.com, info@saintwilliameuclid.org.

OBNINSKY, VICTOR PETER, lawyer; b. San Rafael, Calif., Oct. 12, 1944; s. Peter Victor and Anne Bartholdi (Donston) Obninsky; m. Clara Alice Bechtel, June 8, 1969 (div. Oct. 30, 2003). BA, Columbia U., NYC, 1966; JD, U. Calif., Hastings, 1969. Bar: Calif. 1970. Sole practice, Novato, Calif., 1970-2001, Tiburon, Calif., 2001—02, Sonoma, Calif., 2003—. Arbitrator Marin County Superior Ct., San Rafael, 1979—; superior ct. judge pro tem, 1979—; lectr. real estate and partnership law. Author: The Russians in Early California, 1966. Bd. dir. Calif. Young Reps., 1968-69, Richardson Bay San. Dist., 1974-75, Marin County Legal Aid Soc., 1976-78; baseball coach Little League, Babe Ruth League, 1970-84; mem. nat. panel consumer arbitrators Better Bus. Bur., 1974-88; leader Boy Scouts Am., 1970-84; permanent sec. Phillips Acad. Class of 1962, 1987—; mem. Phillips Acad. Alumni Coun., 1991-95; bd. cmty. advisors Buck Ctr. Rsch. on Aging, 1990-2001. Recipient Diploma of Honor, City Mus. Obninsk, Russia, 2004. Mem.: ABA, State Bar Calif., Marin County Bar Assn. (bd. dirs. 1985—91, treas. 1987—88, pres.-elect 1989, pres. 1990), Sonoma Bar Assn., Russian Nobility Assn. Am., Inc., Phi Gamma Delta, Phi Delta Phi. Libertarian. Russian Orthodox. Home and Office: 21453 Shainsky Sonoma CA 95476-8412 Office Phone: 707-935-7422. Personal E-mail: vpobninsky@comcast.net. *An all-out intellectual attempt to understand baseball thoroughly may give sufficient insight to understand oneself; the so-called "designated hitter" rule should be abolished immediately.*

OBOGEANU, MADALINA MARIA, reporter; arrived in U.S., 1997; d. Vasile and Calina Obogeanu. BA in polit. sci, German studies (spl. hons.), Hunter Coll., NYC, 2004. Analyst UNICEF, UN, NYC, 2000; rsch. asst. Dept. Econ. Affairs, UN, NYC, 2001; asst. prodr. Clear Channel, NYC, 2003; rsch. analyst Hunter Coll., NYC, 2004; reporter Instl. Investor, NYC, 2004—. Mem.: German Academic Exch. Svc. (Scholarship 2002), The Acad. Polit. Sci. Avocations: tennis, skiing, reading. Office: Instl Investor Inc 225 Park Ave S New York NY 10003

OBOLENSKY, IVAN, investment banker, foundation administrator, writer; b. London, May 15, 1925; s. Serge and Alice (Astor) O. (parents Am. citizens); m. Claire McGinnis, 1949 (div. 1956); children: Marina Ava, Ivan Serge, David; m. Mary Elizabeth Morris, 1959; 1 child, Serge. AB, Yale U., New Haven, Conn., 1947. Pres. Hotel Investments, Inc., NYC, 1950-58; dir. Silver Bear Inc., Atla., 1947—69; v.p., treas. Serge Obolensky Assocs., 1952-75; pres. Ivan Obolensky Inc. and Astor Books, Ivan Obolensky Inc., pubs., 1956-65; ptnr. A.T. Brod & Co., investment bankers, 1960—65, Dominick & Dominick Inc., investment bankers, 1965-70, Middendorf Colgate, investment bankers, 1970-73; v.p. C.B. Richard, Ellis/Moseley Hallgarten, investment bankers, 1974-81, Sterling Grace & Co., investment bankers, NYC, 1982-87; sr. v.p. Jesup, Josephthal & Co., investment bankers, NYC, 1987-90; principal Astor Capital Mgmt. Assocs. LLC, 1980—; v.p. Capital Mgmt. Assocs., NYC, 1990—, Shields & Co., NYC, 1990—. Bd. dirs. Gold Canyon Resources, 1996—, HiEnergy Technologies, 2005-06; cons. and lectr. in field. Author: Rogues' March, 1956; contbr. to Nihon Keizai Shimbun, Tokyo, on precious metals, 1985—, program com. NY Soc. of Security Analysts for pub., aerospace, metals and mining, nuc. power, oil and gas; contbr. articles to profl. publs. Bd. dirs. Police Athletic League, NYC, 1975-85, exec. com., 1980-85, 96—, U.S.O., 1987—2004, Audubon Canyon Ranch, Calif., 1989—, Tolstoy Found., 1994-2000, Soldiers', Sailors', Marines' and Airmen's Club, 1976—, pres., 1987-2000, chmn., ceo, 2000—, Russian Nobility Assn. in Am., 1990—, treas., 1991—, v.p., 1995—, Musicians Emergency Fund, 1985-93, pres.1987-92, Children's Blood Found., NY Hosp., 1952—, pres., 1981-95, pres. emeritus, 1995—; pres., dir. Josephine Lawrence Hopkins Found., 1971-2000, chmn., 2000-; pres. Whitemarsh Found., 1980-90, Masonic Toys for Tots Found., 2003-; bd. dirs. Masonic Brotherhood Found., 1996—. Lt. (j.g.) USNR, 1943-45, ret., 1980. Published works by James Agee: A Death in the Family and Tad Mosel: All the Way Home, which received Pulitzer prizes, 2 Caldecott awards. Mem. Am. Legion, Mil. Order Loyal Legion US (sr. vice-comdr. 1955, comdr. 1967-70), St. Elmo Soc., Met. Mus. Art (life), Knickerbocker Club, NY Yacht Club, New Eng. Soc. NY, St. George's Soc. NY, The Navy League, The Naval Inst., The Naval Order, Army and Navy Club, The Pilgrims, Order of Lafayette, Explorer's Club, Masons (Holland #8 master 1981, dist. dep. grand master 1st Manhattan 1983-84, grand treas. 1994-96), DeMolay (hon. mem.), Masonic Brotherhood Found. (chmn. fin. oversight com. 1999-, chmn. com. endowments, 2004-), Grand Lodge State of NY. Office: Shields & Co 140 Broadway New York NY 10005-1101 Office Phone: 212-320-3000. Personal E-mail: iobolensky@aol.com. Business E-Mail: ivan.obolensky@shieldsandco.com.

OBOLENSKY, MARILYN WALL (MRS. SERGE OBOLENSKY), metals company executive; b. Detroit, Aug. 13, 1929; d. Albert Fraser and Christine (Frischkorn) Wall; m. Serge Obolensky, June 3, 1971. Student, Duschesne Jr. Coll., 1947. Chmn. bd. Wall-Colmondy Corp., Detroit, 1959-61, exec. sec., 1961—. Chmn. bd. Wall-Gases Inc., Morrisville, Pa., 1959-61; pres. Serge Obolensky Assocs. Bd. dirs. Heart and Lung Assn. N.Y.C., 1963—. Mem.: Bathing Corp. (Southampton, N.Y.), Southampton. Republican. Roman Catholic. Address: 45 Preston Pl Grosse Pointe Farms MI 48236-3035

OBOT, ISIDORE SILAS, public health service officer; s. Silas and Jane Obot; m. Theresa Isidore Adadiaha, Dec. 1, 1984; children: Ifiok Isidore, Aniekan Isidore, Ubong Isidore, Tete Isidore. BA, Loyola Coll., Balt., 1976, MA, 1978; PhD, Howard U., Washington, 1982; MPH, Harvard U., 1984. From lectr. to sr. lectr. psychology U. Jos, Nigeria, 1985—2001; rsch. fellow Johns Hopkins U. Sch. Pub. Health, Balt., 1998—2000; scientist substance abuse WHO, Geneva, 2002—06; prof. sch. pub. health and policy Morgan State U., Balt., 2006—, chmn. dept. behavioral health scis., 2006—. Bd. dirs. Centre for Rsch. and Info. on Substance Abuse, Jos, 1990—2002. Editor: African Jour. Drug and Alcohol Studies. Rsch. and Writing grant, John D. and Catherine T. McArthur Found., 2000—01. Mem.: Internat. Soc. Addiction Jour. Editors (bd. dirs. 2004—), Kettil Bruun Soc. for Alcohol Rsch. (steering com. 2003—), Coll. on Problems of Drug Dependence, Beta Kappa Chi, Psi Chi. Roman Catholic. Avocations: travel, reading, music, walking. Home Phone: 410-602-1614. Office Fax: 443-885-8309. Business E-Mail: isobot@mdac.morgan.tdu.

OBRAMS, GUNTA IRIS, clinical research administrator; b. Düsseldorf, Germany, Sept. 2, 1953; came to U.S., 1961; d. Robert and Olga (Baltins) O.; m. Malcolm DeWitt Patterson, Dec. 22, 1975; 1 child, Andrew McDougal Patterson. BS in Biology cum laude, Rensselaer Poly. Inst., 1977; MD, Union U., Albany, NY, 1977; MPH, Johns Hopkins U., 1982, PhD, 1988. Resident in obstetrics and gynecology Ea. Va. Grad. Sch. Medicine, Norfolk, 1977-78; community physician Southampton Meml. Hosp., Franklin, Va., 1978-81; resident in gen. preventive medicine sch. hygiene and pub. health Johns Hopkins U., Balt., 1981-84, project dir., 1983-85, med. dir., 1985-86; med. officer divsn. cancer etiology Nat. Cancer Inst., Bethesda, Md., 1986-89, dep. chief, 1989-90, chief, 1990-96, dir. extramural epidemiology & genetics program, 1996-2001; mgmt. US Coast Guard Health Svcs., 2001—05; med. officer divsn. clin. resources NIH, Bethesda, 2005—. Editor: (with M. Potter): The Epidemiology and Biology of Multiple Myeloma, 1991; contbr. articles to profl. jours. With USPHS, 1987—. Recipient Nat. Cancer Inst. Nat. Rsch. Svc. award, 1981, Rsch. Career award Nat. Inst. Occupational Safety & Health; scholar Am. Med. Women's Assn., 1977. Mem. Phi Beta Kappa, Delta Omega, Alpha Omega Alpha. Office: DCRR NCRR NIH 6701 Democracy Blvd MSC-4874 Bethesda MD 20892 Office Phone: 301-435-0768. Personal E-mail: gowellness@comcast.net.

O'BRIEN, ADRIENNE GRATIA, communications educator; b. NYC, Nov. 19, 1935; d. John Robert and Regina C. (Murphy) O'B.; m. David G. Salten, Dec. 21, 1987 (dec. Oct. 2006). AB, Hunter Coll., NYC; MA, MA, Villanova U., Pa.; PhD, Syracuse U. Faculty Cabrini Coll., Radnor, Pa., 1962-68, dir. R & D, 1971-72; prof., chair MA program NY Inst. Tech., Old Westbury, 1974-78, dean Sch. Media and Arts, 1979-91, prof. comm. arts, 1992—. Pres. AID Assocs., NYC, 1972-74, Creative Cons., Port Washington, NY, 1992—; reviewer Nat. Coun. Humanities, Washington, 1981; pres. Women in Instrnl. Tech., Washington, 1981. Editor: Computer Based Training Today, 1987; prodr., dir. (video) Then and Now, 1995 (Communicator award, 1996), Legacy of Mother Ursula, 1996 (Communicator award, 1997), Maritime Mus. of L.I., founder, exec. prodr. L.I. News tonight, 1984; reviewer: Jour. Staff Devel., 1990. Mem. project steering com. Where Are the Women?, 2002; bd. dirs. Girl Scouts of Nassau County, 2002—. Named one of 90 Women for 90 Yrs., Girl Scouts of Nassau County; recipient Instrnl. Nat. Leadership award, Assn. Ednl. Comm. and Tech., Washington, 1989, Comm. award, Maritime Mus. L.I., 2001, L.I. Top 50 Women award, L.I. Bus. News, 2002, Lifetime Achievement award, Pub. Rels. Profls. L.I., 2005, Cmty. Svc. award, Patron of the Arts, NY, 2005, Women on the Job Achievement in Edn. award, 2005, Adult Recognition award for cmty. svc., Girl Scouts Nassau County, 2007. Mem.: Women on the Job (v.p. 1995—2004), Alpha Epsilon Rho (hon.). Avocation: videography. Office: NY Inst Tech Old Westbury NY 11568

O'BRIEN, BARBARA, lieutenant governor; b. Apr. 18, 1950; m. Rick O'Brien; children: Jared, Connor. BA, U. Calif., LA, 1972; PhD, Columbia U., NYC, 1981. Project asst. Inst. for Urban and Minority Edn., Columbia U., 1977—79; head speechwriter, dep. dir. Policy Office of Gov., Gov. Richard Lamm, 1983—85; dir., Campus Affairs U. Colo. Denver, 1985—88; exec. dir. Inst. Internat. Bus., Colo. U. Denver, 1988—90; pres. Colo. Children's Campaign, 1990—; lt. gov. State of Colo., 2007—. Mem. Mayor's Leadership Team on Early Edn., Governor's Commn. on Children and Families, Nat. Kids County Steering Com., Tony Grampsas Youth Services Fund; founder, co-chair Kids Caucus. Democrat. Office: Lieutenant Governor 130 State Capital Denver CO 80203 Office Phone: 303-866-2087. Office Fax: 303-866-5469. Business E-Mail: Ltgovernor.obrien@state.co.us.

O'BRIEN, BEA JAE, artist; b. Oshkosh, Wis., Dec. 4, 1940; d. Harry A. and Mammie Anna (Smith) Mac Farlane; m. John Walsh O'Brien, July 27, 1965; 1 child, John Christian. BA, U. Wis. Profl. artist B.J.'s Fine Arts, Moraga, Calif. Art included in various art publs., including Collage in All Dimensions and Watercolor By Design, exhibitions include Dennos Mus. Calif. Art & Wine Festival, 2001, Internat. Art Show, 2001, Valley Art Gallery, Calif., 2001—03, Calif. Art (3 awards), Internat. Art Show, Chgo., First Cyberspace Art Exhibit, New Zealand, Internat. Collage Constrn. Mus., Mexico City, one-woman shows include, Moraga, Calif., 1996—2001. Vol. children's art publ. Moraga Sch. Sys.; vol. local sch. projects Calif. Open Art Exhbits, 2003; vol. organizer Cmty. Art Gallery, Moraga Gallery, 2000—01; donated, vol. Outreach Art Funds and Scholarships, Calif. Recipient 1st pl. award, Calif. Art and Wine Festival, 1999, Bay Area Art Festival, 1999, 2000. Mem.: Digital Image Art Career, Intuitive Layering Art Group, Valley Arts Ctr., Collage Artists Am., Nat. Collage Soc. (award 1997—99, 2004, signature), Internat. Soc. Exptl. Artists (Nautilus award 2003, signature), Lamorinda Arts Alliance, Coll. Art Am., Women in Arts Mus. (honor roll). Avocations: reading, volunteering. Office: BJs Fine Arts 34 Sea Pines Moraga CA 94556-1029 Home Phone: 925-376-8018; Office Phone: 925-376-8018. Personal E-mail: dancincollag7@yahoo.com.

O'BRIEN, CATHY, media company executive; b. 1959; m. Steve O'Brien. CPA. Sr. auditor Deloitte & Touche; v.p., gen. mgr. Entertainment Weekly; fin. positions Fortune, Time Internat., Home Box Office; v.p., Bus. Devel. Time Inc., grp. pub., Growth Markets; pres., COO Beliefnet Inc., 2006—. Named a Women to Watch, Advertising Age. *

O'BRIEN, CHARLES HAROLD, writer, priest; s. Erwin Joseph and Margaret Alice O'Brien; m. Elvy Astrid Setterqvist, Dec. 21, 1964. BA, Notre Dame U., 1951, MA, 1952; PhD, Columbia U., 1967. Instr. Ohio State U., Columbus, 1964—65, Skidmore Coll., Saratoga Springs, NY, 1965—66; asst. prof. Wittenberg U., Springfield, Ohio, 1966—72; prof.

Western Ill. U., Macomb, 1972—94; author Williamstown, Mass., 1994—. Author: Ideas of Religious Toleration at the Time of Joseph II, 1969, (novels) Mute Witness, 2001, Black Gold, 2002, Noble Blood, 2004, Lethal Beauty, 2005, Fatal Carnival, 2006, Cruel Choices, 2007. Vicar St. Paul's Episcopal Ch., Warsaw, Ill., 1984—88. With US Army, 1945—47, Korea. Mem.: Am. Hist. Assn. Avocation: reading. Home Phone: 413-458-2811. Personal E-mail: obrien@bcn.net.

O'BRIEN, CLARE, lawyer; b. Ireland, 1961; children: Una, Lucy. BA summa cum laude, Trinity Coll., 1982. Bar: Ireland, NY 1986, U.S. Dist. Ct. NY (so. dist.) 1987. Atty. Eugene F. Collins & Son, Brady & Tarpey, 1987—88, Shearman & Sterling LLP, NYC, 1988—95, mem., mergers & acquisitions group, 1989—, ptnr., 1995—. Bd. dirs. Am. Assn. Internat. Commn. Jurists. Named Dealmaker of Yr., Am. Lawyer mag., 2006. Office: Shearman & Sterling LLP 599 Lexington Ave New York NY 10022-6069 Office Phone: 212-848-8966. Office Fax: 212-848-7179. E-mail: cobrien@shearman.com.

O'BRIEN, CONAN, talk show host, writer, performer; b. Brookline, Mass., Apr. 18, 1963; m. Liza Powel, Jan. 2002; children: Neve, Beckett. BA Am. Hist., Lit., Harvard U., 1985. Staff mem. The Harvard Lampoon, 1981-85 (pres. 1983, 84); head Conaco. Stage appearances with: The Groundlings (L.A.) 1985-87; writer, performer The Happy Happy Good Show (L.A., Chgo.) 1988; writer (TV) Not Necessarily the News (HBO) 1985-87, Saturday Night Live, 1988-91 (NBC, Emmy Outstanding Writing in Comedy series 1989), Lookwell (NBC) 1991; writer, prodr. The Simpsons (Fox) 1991-93, The Wilton North Report (syndicated) 1987, Late Night with Conan O'Brien (NBC) 1993— (Best Writing in Comedy/Variety Show Writer's Guild award 1997, TV award Writers Guild Am. 2000), host, Emmy Awards 2002; film appearances include Tomorrow Night, 1998, Barenaked in America, 1999, Vanilla Sky, 2001, Bewitched, 2005; TV appearances include (voice) The Simpsons, 1994, The Single Guy, 1996, Arli$$, 1996, (voice) Dr. Katz, Professional Therapist, 1997, Veronica's Closet, 1998, Spin City, 1998, LateLine, 1999, Space Ghost Coast to Coast, 1999, (voice) Futurama, 1999, Tomorrow Night, 1998, (voice) Robot Chicken, 2005. Named one of 25 Most Intriguing People, People Mag., 50 Funniest People Alive, Entertainment Weekly. Office: Late Night with Conan O'Brien NBC 30 Rockefeller Plz New York NY 10112-0002

O'BRIEN, DANIEL J., lawyer; b. Los Alamos, N.Mex., Nov. 18, 1951; BS, U. N.Mex., 1975, MBA, 1980, JD, 1983. Bar: N.Mex. 1983, Tex. 1993, U.S. Dist. Ct. N.Mex. 1984, U.S. Ct. Appeals (10th cir.) 1987. Ptnr. O'Brien & Ulibarri, P.C., Albuquerque, shareholder. Mem.: ABA, Albuquerque Bar Assn., N.Mex. Trial Lawyers Assn., N.Mex. Def. Lawyers Assn. (pres. 1999—2000), State Bar N.Mex. (bd. commrs. 1994—2000, v.p. 2002, pres. 2004). Office: O'Brien & Ulibarri PC 6000 Indian Sch NE Ste 200 Albuquerque NM 87110 Office Phone: 505-883-8181. Office Fax: 505-883-3232. Business E-Mail: dobrien@obrienlawoffice.com. *

O'BRIEN, DANIEL ROBERT, lawyer; b. Peoria, Ill., May 7, 1951; s. William Patrick and Irene Cornelia O'Brien; m. Eileen Mary Kahn, Aug. 17, 1974; children: Colleen, Patrick, Bridget. BS, No. Ill. U., 1973; JD, Wash. U., St. Louis, 1976. Bar: U.S. Dist. Ct. (so. dist.) Ill. 1977. Ptnr. Smith Moos Schmitt & O'Brien, Peoria, 1976-82, Moos, Schmitt & O'Brien, Peoria, 1982—. Lectr. Peoria County Bar Assn., Ill. Continuing Legal Edn., Springfield. Dem. precinct committeman Dem. Party, 1986. Named to Greater Peoria Sports Hall of Fame, 2000. Fellow Ill. Bar Found. (charter mem., Leading Ill. Atty. award), Beta Gamma Sigma. Avocation: coaching children's basketball. Office: Moos Schmitt & O'Brien Ste 314 331 Fulton St Peoria IL 61602-1499 Office Phone: 309-673-3600.

O'BRIEN, DANIEL WILLIAM, lawyer, lumber company executive; b. St. Paul, Jan. 6, 1926; s. Daniel W. and Kathryn (Zenk) O'B.; m. Sarah Ward Stoltze, June 20, 1952; children: Bridget Ann, Daniel William, Kevin Charles, Timothy John. Student, U. Dubuque, 1943, Ill. State U., 1944; BSL, U. Minn., 1948, JD, 1949. Bar: Minn. 1949. Practice in, St. Paul, 1950—; partner Randall, Smith & Blomquist, 1955-65; of counsel Doherty, Rumble & Butler, 1965-99; pres., chmn. bd. dirs. F.H. Stoltze Land & Lumber Co., 1964—; pres. Maple Island, Inc., 1968—. Served to ensign USNR, 1943-46. Mem. Minn., Ramsey County bar assns., World Pres's. Orgn., Chief Execs. Orgn. Office: 2497 7th Ave E Ste 105 North Saint Paul MN 55109-2902 Home (Winter): 3951 S Placita de la Moneda Green Valley AZ 85614-5063 Address: 4734 Bouleau Rd White Bear Lake MN 55110-3355 Business E-Mail: dwobrien@maple-island.com.

O'BRIEN, DAVID A., lawyer; b. Sioux City, Iowa, Aug. 30, 1958; s. John T. and Doris K. (Reisch) O'B. BA, George Washington U., 1981; JD with distinction, U. Iowa, 1984. Bar: Iowa 1985, U.S. Dist. Ct. (no. dist.) Iowa 1985, Nebr. 1990, U.S. Dist. Ct. Nebr. 1990, U.S. Ct. Appeals (8th cir.) 2004. Legis. asst. Nat. Transp. Safety Bd., Washington, 1978-81; assoc. O'Brien, Galvin & Kuehl, Sioux City, 1985-88; ptnr. O'Brien, Galvin Moeller & Neary, Sioux City, 1989-94; chair Wage Appeals Bd. & Bd. of Svc. Contract Appeals U.S. Dept. Labor, Washington, 1994-96, acting dir. Office Adminstrv. Appeals, 1995-96, chair adminstrv. review bd., 1996-98; atty. White & Johnson, P.C., Cedar Rapids, Iowa, 1998-2000; ptnr. Willey & O'Brien, PLC, Cedar Rapids, 2000—. Dem. candidate for Congress, 6th dist. of Iowa, Sioux City, 1988; chmn. Woodbury County Dem. Party, Sioux City, 1992-94, chair Iowa campaign Clinton for Pres., Des Moines, 1992; bd. dirs. Mid-Step Svcs. Inc., Sioux City, 1986-91, Mo. River Hist. Devel., Sioux City, 1989-94. Mem.: Iowa Trial Lawyers Assn. (bd. govs. 1991—94, 2002—, chair 2004—), Nat. Assn. Trial Lawyers. Roman Catholic. Avocations: sports, politics. Office: Willey O'Brien 3519 Center Pointe Rd NE Cedar Rapids IA 52402 Home Phone: 319-286-0165; Office Phone: 319-390-5555. Home Fax: 319-378-1413. Business E-Mail: dobrien@willeylaw.com.

O'BRIEN, DAVID MICHAEL, law educator; b. Rock Springs, Wyo., Aug. 30, 1951; s. Ralph Rockwell and Lucile O'Brien; m. Claudine M. Mendelovitz, Dec. 17, 1982; children: Benjamin, Sara, Talia. BA, U. Calif., Santa Barbara, 1973, MA, 1974, PhD, 1977. Fulbright lectr. Oxford (Eng.) U., 1987-88; lectr. U. Calif., Santa Barbara, 1976-77; asst. prof. U. Puget Sound, Tacoma, Wash., 1977-79; Spicer prof. U. Va., Charlottesville, 1979—. Fulbright rschr., Tokyo, Kyoto, Japan, 1993-94, Fulbright chair, Bologna, Italy, 1999; jud. fellow U.S. Supreme Ct., Washington, 1982-83; Fulbriht lectr., Oxford U., England, 1987-1988; vis. postdoctoral fellow Russell Sage Found., NYC, 1981-82; lectr. USIA, Burma, Japan, France, 1994-95. Author: Supreme Court Watch, 1991—, Constitutional Law and Politics, 2 vols., 6th edit., 2005, Storm Center: The Supreme Court in American Politics, 7th edit., 2005, To Dream of Dreams: Constitutional Politics in Postwar Japan, 1996, To Dream of Dreams: Religious Freedom in Postwar Japan, 1996, Animal Sacrifice & Religious Freedom, 2004; editor: Views from the Bench, 1985, Judges on Judging, 1997, Government by the People, 22nd edit., 2005. Rappatour, jud. selection 20th Century Fund Task Force, N.Y., 1986-87. Tom C. Clark Jud. Fellow, Jud. Fellows Commn., Washington, 1983. Mem. ABA (Silver Gavel award 1987), Am. Judicature Soc., Am. Polit. Sci. Assn., Supreme Ct. Hist. Soc. (editl. bd. 1982—), Internat. Polit. Sci. Assn. Democrat. Avocations: painting, travel. Home: 916 Tilman Rd Charlottesville VA 22901-6338 Office: U Va 232 Cabell Hall Charlottesville VA 22901 Office Phone: 434-994-3358.

O'BRIEN, DAVID PETER, corporate director; b. Montreal, Que., Can., Sept. 9, 1941; m. Gail Baxter Cornell, June 1, 1968; children: Tara, Matthew, Shaun. BA in Econs. with honors, Loyola Coll., Montreal, 1962; BCL, McGill U., Montreal, 1965. Assoc. and ptnr. Ogilvy, Renault, Montreal, 1967-77; v.p., gen. counsel Petro-Can., Calgary, Alta., 1977-81, sr. v.p., 1982-85, sr. v.p. fin. and planning, 1982-85, exec. v.p., 1985-89; pres., CEO Noverco Inc., Montreal; 1989; chmn. bd., pres., CEO PanCan. Petroleum Ltd., Calgary, 1990—95; pres., COO Can. Pacific Ltd., Montreal, 1995—96, chmn., pres., CEO Calgary, 1996—2001; chmn., CEO PanCan. Energy Corp., 2001—02; chmn. EnCana Corp., 2002—. Chmn. Royal Bank Can., 2004—; bd. dirs. TransCan. PipeLines Ltd., Molson Coors Brewing Co., Focus Energy Trust. Mem.: Calgary Golf and Country Club, Calgary Petroleum Club, Glencoe Club.

O'BRIEN, DENIS P., utilities executive; m. Carolyn O'Brien; 3 children. B in Indsl. Engring., Rutgers U., NJ; M in Bus., Drexel U., Phila. V.p. ops. Exelon Corp., sr. v.p., pres. PECO Energy. Bd. mem. Energy Assn. Pa., Am. Gas Assn., Pa. Bus. Roundtable, Pa. Economy League, Greater Phila. C. of C., Select Greater Phila., Franklin Inst., WHYY, Inc., Greater Phila. YMCA; bd. trustees Drexel U. Office: PECO Energy 2301 Market St PO Box 8699 Philadelphia PA 19101 Office Phone: 800-494-4000. *

O'BRIEN, DENNIS M., state legislator; b. 1952; m. Bernadette Benson; children: Dennis Jr., Brendan, Joseph. BS, La Salle U. Mem. Pa. Ho. of Reps. from Dist. 169, Harrisburg, 1977—80, 1983—, spkr. of the House, 2007—. Address: Pa Ho of Reps 401 South Office House Box 202020 Harrisburg PA 17120-2020

O'BRIEN, DOUGLAS J., lawyer, educator; Grad. magna cum laude, Loras Coll.; JD with honors, U. Iowa; LLM in Agr. Law, U. Ark. Law clk. to Justice Jerry L. Larson Iowa Supreme Ct.; legal specialist Nat. Hog Office US Dept. of Agr.'s Grain Inspection Packers and Stockyards Adminstrn., Washington; counsel Senate Agr. Com.; staff atty., rsch. asst. prof. law, interim co-dir. Nat. Agrl. Law Ctr., U. Ark., 2006—. Tchr. Drake Law Sch., Des Moines. Office: Nat Agrl Law Ctr U Ark Sch Law 1 University of Arkansas Fayetteville AR 72701 Office Phone: 479-575-7642. Office Fax: 479-575-5830. E-mail: dobrien@uark.edu.

O'BRIEN, EDWARD IGNATIUS, corporate financial executive, director, investor, lawyer; b. NYC, Sept. 15, 1928; s. Edward I. and Marguerite (Malone) O'B.; m. Margaret M. Feeney, June 29, 1957; children: Edward Ignatius III, Margaret Mary, Thomas Gerard, John Joseph. AB, Fordham U., 1950; LLB, St. John's U., 1954; grad., Advanced Mgmt. Program, Cornell U., 1965. Bar: N.Y. 1954. With firm Hale, Kay & Brennan, NYC, 1954-55; with Bache & Co., Inc., NYC, 1955-74, gen. counsel, 1960, gen. ptnr., 1964, sec., 1968, v.p., 1965-68, sr. v.p., mem. exec. com., 1969, exec. v.p., 1969, chmn. exec. com., 1971-74; pres. Securities Industry Assn., 1974-93; retired, 1993. Bd. dirs. 8 corps.; lectr. Am. Law Inst., Practising Law Inst., Am. Mgmt. Assn.; exch. ofcl. Am. Stock Exch., 1972; mem. adv. bd., mem. exec. com. Securities Regulation Inst., U. Calif., 1975—. Mem. Cardinal's com. Laity Cath. Archdiocese N.Y., mem. Cardinal's com. for edn.; chmn. Fordham U. Coun., 1971-73; bd. dirs. 3 non-profit orgns.; chmn. corp. devel. com. Fordham U.; trustee, chmn. bd. trustees Fordham Prep. Sch., 1975-77, Capt. USAR. Mem. N.Y. State Bar Assn., Am. Arbitration Assn., Am. Soc. Internat. Law, Guild Cath. Lawyers, Securites Industry Assn. (chmn. publicly owned firms com. 1972), Nat. Assn. Securities Dealers (dist. com. 1973-74), Shenorock Shore Club (Rye, N.Y.), Town Club (Scarsdale, N.Y.), Met. Club (Washington). Home and Office: 12 Woods Ln Scarsdale NY 10583-6408

O'BRIEN, EDWIN FREDERICK, archbishop; b. Bronx, NY, Apr. 8, 1939; BA, St. Joseph's Sem., Yonkers, NY, 1961, MDiv, 1964, MA, 1965; STD, Algelicum U., Rome, 1976. Ordained priest Roman Cath. Ch., 1965. Parish priest, chaplain U.S. Mil. Acad., West Point, NY, 1965—70; commd. 2d lt. U.S. Army, 1970, advanced through grades to capt., 1973, chaplain, 1970—73, 82nd Airborne Divsn., Ft. Bragg, NC, 1970—71, 173rd Airborne Brigade, 1st Calalry Brigade, Vietnam, 1971—72; post chaplain Ft. Gordon, Ga., 1972—73; assoc. pastor St. Patrick's Cathedral, NYC, 1976—81; vice chancellor Archdiocese NY, 1976—81, dir. comm., 1981—83, sec. Cardinals Terence Cooke, John O'Connor, 1983—85; rector St. Joseph's Sem., Dunwoodie, NY, 1985—89, 1994—97, Pontifical N. Am. Coll., Rome, 1990—94; titular bishop Diocese of Tizica, 1996—99; auxillary bishop Diocese of N.Y., 1996—97; archbishop Archdiocese of Mil. Svcs., Washington, 1997—2007; archbishop of Balt. Md., 2007—. Bd. dirs. Nat. Conf. Cath. Bishops, Basilica Nat. Shrine Immaculate Conception; Trustee St. Joseph's Sem., Pontifical Coll. Josephinum; chmn. bd. trustees Pontifical N. Am. Coll. Mem.: Fellowship Cath. Scholars. Roman Catholic. Office: Archdiocese of Balt 320 Cathedral St Baltimore MD 21201 *

O'BRIEN, EILEEN KATHRYN, art educator; b. Hudson Falls, NY, June 4, 1961; d. James Michael and Lorraine Catherine O'Brien; children: Ashley Gatto, Krista Gatto, Michelle Gatto. AAS in Fine Arts, Jr. Coll. Albany, NY, 1981; BS in Art Edn., SUNY, New Paltz, 1983, MS in Elem. Edn., 1995. Cert. tchr. N.Y., N.C. Tchr. art/recreation McQuade Children's Svcs., New Windsor, NY, 1984—87; tchr. art Goshen Secure Ctr., NY, 1992—95, Jeffersonville-Youngsville C.S., NY, 1989—95; tchr. 3d grade St. Casimir's Cath. Sch., Albany, NY, 1996—97; tchr. visual arts Western Harnett Mid. Sch., Lillington, NC, 1997—. Mgr. Rite-Aid, Monticello, NY, 1993—94; swing shift mgr. McDonalds, Lillington, NC, 2003—. Tchr., leader People to People Orgn., Raleigh, NC, 2006; mem. Boonetrail Elem. PTO, 2001—06. Mem.: Profl. Educators of N.C. Avocations: gardening, painting, sewing, reading. Home: 485 Ray Byrd Rd Lillington NC 27546 Office: Western Harnett Mid Sch 11135 NC Hwy 27 W Lillington NC 27546 Office Phone: 919-499-4497. Office Fax: 919-499-1788. E-mail: eobrien_61@msn.com.

O'BRIEN, ELMER JOHN, librarian, educator; b. Kemmerer, Wyo., Apr. 8, 1932; s. Ernest and Emily Catherine (Reinhart) O'B.; m. Betty Alice Peterson, July 2, 1966. AB, Birmingham So. Coll., 1954; Th.M., Iliff Sch. Theology, 1957; MA, U. Denver, 1961. Ordained to ministry Methodist Ch., 1957; pastor Meth. Ch., Pagosa Springs, Colo., 1957—60; circulation-reference librarian Boston U. Sch. Theology, 1961—65; asst. librarian Garrett-Evang. Theol. Sem., Evanston, Ill., 1965—69; librarian, prof. United Theol. Sem., Dayton, Ohio, 1969—96, prof. emeritus, 1996—; abstractor Am. Bibliog. Center, 1969—73; dir. Ctr. for Evang. United Brethren Heritage, 1979—96; acting libr. Iliff Sch. Theology, 2000—01. Chmn. div. exec. com. Dayton-Miami Valley Libr. Consortium, 1983-84; rsch. assoc. Am. Antiquarian Soc., 1990. Author: Bibliography of Festschriften in Religion Published Since 1960, 1972, Religion Index Two: Festschriften, 1960-69; contbg. author: Communication and Change in American Religious History, 1993, Essays in Celebration of the First Fifty Years, 1996; pub. Meth. Revs. Index, 1818-1985, 1989-91; contbr. articles to profl. jours. Recipient theol. and scholarship award Assn. Theol. Schs. in U.S. and Can., 1990-91; Libr. Staff Devel. grant Assn. Theol. Schs. in U.S. and Can., 1976-77, Rsch. grant United Meth. Ch. Bd. Higher Edn. and Ministry, 1984-85 Mem. ALA, Acad. Libr. Assn. Ohio, Am. Theol. Libr. Assn. (head bur. personnel and placement 1969-73, dir. 1973-76, v.p. 1977-78, pres. 1978-79), Am. Antiquarian Soc. (rsch. assoc. 1990), Delta Sigma Phi, Omicron Delta Kappa, Eta Sigma Phi, Kappa Phi Kappa. Clubs: Torch Internat. (v.p. Dayton club 1981-82, pres. 1982-83). Home: 4840 Thunderbird Dr Apt 281 Boulder CO 80303-3829 Personal E-mail: ejobr@aol.com.

O'BRIEN, GEORGE ALOYSIUS, JR., paper company executive; b. Port Arthur, Tex., Dec. 13, 1948; s. George Aloysius and Avril Colleen (Adkins) O'B.; m. Cynthia Jean McCaa, Aug. 16, 1973; children: Erin Colleen, Meghan Anne, Caitlin Jean. BS in Petroleum Engring., U. Tex., 1971, MBA, 1975. Engr. Tesoro Petroleum Corp., San Antonio, 1972-73; exec. asst. Mesa Petroleum Co., Amarillo, Tex., 1975-79; v.p., treas. Transco Energy Co., Houston, 1979-82; sr. v.p., chief fin. officer Spectrum Energy Co., Houston, 1982-83; v.p. Smith Barney Harris Upham & Co., Houston, 1984-86; 1st v.p. E.F. Hutton & Co., NYC, 1986-88; v.p., dir. corp. devel. Internat. Paper Co., Purchase, NY, 1988-91, v.p. land and timber, sr. v.p. forest resources Savannah, Ga., 1997—2001; CFO Carter Holt Harvey Pulp, Paper & Tissue, Auckland, New Zealand, 1991-94, CEO, 1995-97; sr. v.p. forest products Internat. Paper Co., 1997—. Dir. Nat. Tree Trust, Savannah C. of C., United Way of Savannah, Arbor Gen LLC. Mem.: Savannah Harbour Golf Club. Republican. Roman Catholic. Avocations: golf, tennis, sailing.

O'BRIEN, GEORGE DENNIS, retired academic administrator; b. Chgo., Feb. 21, 1931; s. George Francis and Helen (Fehlandt) O'B.; m. Judith Alyce Johnson, June 21, 1958; children: Elizabeth Belle, Juliana Helen, Victoria Alyce. AB in English, Yale, 1952; PhD in Philosophy, U. Chgo., 1961. Tchr. humanities, Carnegie rsch. fellow U. Chgo., 1956-57; from instr. to asst. prof., asst. dean Princeton (N.J.) U., 1958-65; on leave in Athens, Greece, 1963-64; spl. honors seminars LaSalle Coll., spring 1963, fall 1964, spring 1965; assoc. prof. philosophy Middlebury (Vt.) Coll., 1965-71, prof., 1971-76, dean of men, 1965-67, dean of coll., 1967-74, dean faculty, 1975-76; pres. Bucknell U., 1976-84, U. Rochester, NY, 1984-94; ret., 1994. Author: Hegel on Reason in History, 1975, God and the New Haven Railway, 1986, What to Expect from College, 1991, All the Essential Half-Truths About Higher Education, 1997, The Idea of a Catholic University, 2002; contbr. articles to profl. jours. Trustee LaSalle Coll., Phila., 1965—; bd. dirs. Union Theol. Sem., 1985-90, Rsch. Librs. Group, 1994-96; chair Commonweal Found., 2002—. Fellow Am. Coun. Learned Socs., London, 1971-72; Nat. Phi Beta Kappa scholar, 1996-97. Mem. Am. Philos. Assn., Phi Beta Kappa. Home: 153 Wildflower Ln Middlebury VT 05753-9172 Office Phone: 802-388-1376. Business E-Mail: gdob@middlebury.edu.

O'BRIEN, GERALD JAMES, utilities executive; b. St. Paul, May 1, 1923; s. Dewey Joseph and Henrietta Elizabeth O'B.; m. Patricia Margaret McCorison, Feb. 23, 1946; children: Kathleen, Thomas, John, Andrew. Student, St. Thomas Coll., 1940-41, 45-46; B.C.S., Drake U., 1948. Staff acct. Haskins & Sells, Mpls., 1948-50; with Donovan Cos., Inc., St. Paul, 1950-81, sec., asst. treas., 1977-81; utility rate cons., 1981-84. Dir. Alumbaugh Coal Co., Donovan Constrn. Co., So. Tier Gas Corp., Gas Distbrs. Info. Service. Served with U.S. Army, 1942-45. Decorated Purple Heart. Address: 11111 River Hills Dr Apt 234 Burnsville MN 55337

O'BRIEN, GREG, real estate company executive; m. Lynne O'Brien; 3 children. BS in Electrical Engring., magna cum laude, Tufts U.; MBA, Harvard U. Broker Staubach Co., Washington, 1993, pres. Northeast Region, exec. com., leadership coun., CEO. Bd. dirs. Greater Washington Bd. Trade, Nat. Fedn. Independent Bus., Teach for Am., Washington. Office: Staubach Co 575 7th St NW Ste 400 Washington DC 20004 Office Phone: 202-783-8181. *

O'BRIEN, GREGORY MICHAEL ST. LAWRENCE, academic administrator; b. NYC, Oct. 7, 1944; s. Henry Joseph and Mary Agnes (McGoldrick) O'B.; m. Mary K. McLaughlin, Dec. 28, 1968; children: Jennifer Jane, Meredith Kathleen. BA with honors, Lehigh U., 1966; MA, Boston U., 1968, PhD, 1969. Assoc. in psychology Lab. Community Psychology, Harvard Med. Sch., Boston; dir. Human Svcs. Design Lab., Sch. Applied Social Scis., Case Western Res. U., Cleve., 1970-74; dean, prof. Sch. Social Welfare, U. Wis., Milw., 1974-78; provost, prof. psychology U. Mich.-Flint, 1978-80; prof. social work and psychology, v.p. acad. affairs U. South Fla., Tampa, 1980-83, provost, 1983-87, prof. mgmt., 1986-87; chancellor U. New Orleans, 1987—2003; interim supr. New Orleans Paris Schs., 1999; pres. Argosy U. Sys., 2004—; DeBlois Endowed Chair in Private/Public Initiatives U. New Orleans, 2004—. Evaluation research cons. Cambridge Dept. Health and Hosps. and USPHS, 1968; bd. dirs. WLAE-TV (PBS), Bank One New Orleans Region, Entergy New Orleans, Nat. Coalition for Advanced Mfg., Nat. Assn. State Univs. and Land-Grant Colls. Contbr. chpts. to books, articles to profl. jours. State of La. Econ. Devel. Coun., 1997—; vice chmn. State of La. Film and Video Commn., 1993-94, mem., 1993—; chmn. Metro. Coun. Govts. MetroVision, 1992—; adv. mem. Bus. Coun. New Orleans and the River Region; bd. dirs. The Chamber/New Orleans and the River Region, 1988—; mem. Kellogg Commn. on Future of Land Grant Colls. and State Univs., 1996—. NIMH fellow, 1968-69 Fellow Am. Coll. Mental Health Adminstrs. (founding fellow, pres. 1984-86); mem. NCAA (chair pres. commn. 1992-93), Nat. Assn. Social Workers, Nat. Conf. Social Welfare, Soc. Gen. Systems Research, Am. Psychol. Assn., Am. Public Health Assn., Metrovision Partnership Found. (1992-93), Council Social Work Edn. (presdl. task force on structure of assn.), Indsl. Relations Research Assn. Roman Catholic. Office: Argosy U 2 First National Plz 20 S Clark St 3d Fl Chicago IL 60603 Home: 512 N Mcclurg Ct Apt 5407 Chicago IL 60611-4185 *

O'BRIEN, H. MICHAEL, lawyer; b. Auburn, NY, Feb. 10, 1954; BA cum laude, SUNY, Oswego, 1976; JD, Pace U., 1979. Bar: NY 1980, US Dist. Ct. So., Ea. & No. Districts NY, US Dist. Ct. Dist. NJ, registered: Japanese Ministry of Justice, 1989-92 (fgn. law solicitor). Ptnr. Wilson, Elser, Moskowitz, Edelman & Dicker LLP, White Plains, NYC. Mem.: ABA (tort & ins. sect.), Internat. Assn. Arson Investigators, Nat. Fire Protection Assn., Consumer Electronics Manufacturers Assn. (mfr.'s rep. to R-1 safety com.), Assn. Home Appliance Manufacturers (mfr.'s rep. to product liability task force/govt. rels. com.), Def. Rsch. Inst., Assn. Trial Lawyers of Am., NY State Trial Lawyers Assn., NJ State Bar Assn. Office: Wilson Elser Moskowitz Edelman & Dicker LLP 3 Gannett Dr White Plains NY 10604 Office Phone: 212-490-3000 ext. 4234. Office Fax: 212-490-3038. Business E-Mail: obrienm@wemed.com.

O'BRIEN, J. WILLARD, lawyer, educator; b. NYC, Oct. 19, 1930; s. J. Willard and Anna C. (Carroll) O.'B.; m. Peggy J. O'Brien. BS, Fordham U., 1952, JD, 1957. Bar: N.Y. 1957. Assoc. Cahill, Gordon, Reindel & Ohl, NYC, 1957-62; asst. prof. law Syracuse U. Coll. Law, 1962-65; prof. law Villanova (Pa.) U. Sch. Law, 1965-98, dean, 1972-83, dir. Connelly Inst. Law and Morality, 1983-95, dean and prof. of law emeritus, 1998—. Mem. Pa. Fed. Jud. Nominating Commn., 1977-80, vice chmn., 1978-80; mem. Pa. Law and Justice Inst., 1972-73, chmn. exec. com., 1973-75, pres., 1975-77 Editor-in-chief Fordham Law Rev, 1956-57. Bd. dirs. Nat. Inst. on Holocaust, 1984-85; bd. dirs. Phila. Coordinating Council on the Holocaust, 1983—2003. Served with USAF, 1952-54; Served with N.Y. Air N.G., 1954-58. Mem.: ABA, Pa. Bar Assn. Roman Catholic.

O'BRIEN, JACK GEORGE, artistic director; b. Saginaw, Mich., June 18, 1939; s. J. George and Evelyn (MacArthur Martens) O'B. AB, U. Mich., 1961, MA, 1962. Asst. dir. APA Repertory Theatre, NYC, 1963-67, asso. dir., 1967-69; worked with San Diego Nat. Shakespeare Festival, 1969-82, A.C.T., 1970-80, Loretto Hilton, 1975, Ahmanson, Los Angeles, 1978-80, San Francisco Opera, Houston Grand Opera, Washington Opera Soc.; artistic dir. N.Y.C. Opera, 1982, Old Globe Theatre, San Diego, 1981—. Dir.: (Broadway plays) Cock-A-Doodle Dandy, 1969, The Time of Your Life, 1975, Porgy and Bess, 1976, 1983, The Most Happy Fella, 1979, Two Shakespearean Actors, 1992, Damn Yankees, 1994—95, Getting Away With Murder, 1996, The Little Foxes, 1997, More to Love, 1998, The Full Monty, 2000—02 (Tony nom. best dir. of a musical, 2001), Imaginary Friends, 2003, Hairspray, 2002 (Tony award best dir. of a musical, 2003), Henry IV, 2003—04 (Tony award best dir. of a play, 2004), The Coast of Utopia, 2006 (Outer Critics Cir. award outstanding dir. of a musical, 2007, Tony award best dir. of a play, 2007, Drama Desk award outstanding dir. of a play, 2007); art. dir. (Broadway plays) Into the Woods, 1987—89,

Rumors, 1988—90, The Piano Lesson, 1990—91, Two Trains Running, 1992, Redwood Curtain, 1993, Play On!, 1997, Oldest Living Confederate Widow Tells All, 2003. Mem. Actors' Equity, Am. Soc. Composers and Performers, Soc. Stage Dirs. and Choreographers, Dirs. Guild Am. Office: Old Globe Theatre PO Box 122171 San Diego CA 92112-2171 *

O'BRIEN, JAMES ALOYSIUS, foreign language educator; b. Cin., Apr. 7, 1936; s. James Aloysius and Frieda (Schirmer) O'B.; m. Rumi Matsumoto, Aug. 26,1961. BA, St. Joseph's Coll., 1958; MA, U. Cin., 1960; PhD, Ind. U., 1969. Instr. English, St. Joseph's Coll., Rensselaer, Ind., 1960-62; asst. prof. Japanese, U. Wis., Madison, 1968-74, assoc. prof., 1974-81, prof., 1981—2003, prof. emeritus, 2003—, chmn. East Asian langs and lit., 1979-80, 82-85, 1996—2000. Author: Dazai Osamu, 1975, Akutagawa and Dazai: Instances of Literary Adaptation, 1988; translator: Selected Stories and Sketches (Dazai Osamu), 1983, Three Works (Muro Saisei), 1985, Crackling Mountain and Other Stories (Dazai Osamu), 1989. Mem. MIddleton City Common Coun., 1996-2004. Ford Found fellow, 1965-66; Fulbright-Hays and NDEA fellow, 1966-68; Social Sci. Research Council fellow, 1973-74; Japan Found. fellow, 1977-78 Mem. Assn. Asian Studies, Assn. Tchrs. of Japanese (exec. com. 1981-84, dir. devel. 1981-83, pres. 1984-90) Home: 2533 Branch St Middleton WI 53562-2812 Office Phone: 608-262-2291. Business E-Mail: jaobrie1@wisc.edu.

O'BRIEN, JAMES D., language educator, communications executive; s. Eldon Sanford O'Brien and Catherine O'Briend. BA in Polit. Sci., St. Mary's Coll., Moraga, Calif., 1973; MA in Bilingual Edn., LaVerne Coll., Calif., 1984. Chair fgn. lang. dept. Damien HS, LaVerne, 1984—; pres. O'Brien's Comm., Lake Arrowhead, Calif., 1998—. Author: (books and tapes) Beginning and Intermediate Spanish, 1990, 1992. Vol. Peace Corps, Guatemala, 1973—75. Named to Damien HS Hall of Fame. Roman Catholic. Avocations: soccer, baseball, sailing. Home: 2280 Damien Ave La Verne CA 91750 Office: Damien HS 2280 Damien Ave La Verne CA 91750 Office Phone: 909-596-1946. Office Fax: 909-596-6112. E-mail: obrien@damien-hs.edu.

O'BRIEN, JAMES EDWARD, surgeon; b. Hartford, Conn., June 15, 1963; s. James Edward and Joan O'Brien; m. Lina Maheswata Pattanayak, Jan. 10, 1998; children: Lauren Maya, Connor Rajan, Christine Mira. BS, Rensselaer Polytechnic Inst., Troy, NY, 1985; MD, U. Conn., Farmington, 1989. Resident Thomas Jefferson U. Hosp., 1989—99, Children's Hosp. Phila., 1999—2001; pediatric cardiothoracic surgeon Children's Mercy Hosp., Kans. City, Mo., 2001—. Contbr. articles to profl. jours. Fellow: ACS; mem.: AMA, So. Thoracic Surg. Assn., Am. Heart Assn., Soc. Thoracic Surgeons. Avocations: swimming, golf, travel. Office: Children's Mercy Hosp 2401 Gillham Rd Kansas City MO 64108 Home Phone: 913-906-9948; Office Phone: 816-234-3580. Office Fax: 816-802-1245. Business E-Mail: jobrien@cmh.edu.

O'BRIEN, JAMES F., lawyer; b. Bklyn., Nov. 27, 1960; BS, Manhattan Coll., 1985; JD, Pace U., 1990. Bar: NY 1990, Conn. 1990, US Dist. Ct. No., So., Ea. & We. Districts NY, US Dist. Ct. Dist. DC, US Ct. Appeals 2nd Cir., US Supreme Ct. Ptnr. Wilson, Elser, Moskowitz, Edelman & Dicker LLP, White Plains, NYC. Mem.: ABA, Assn. of the Bar of the City of NY, NY State Bar Assn. Office: Wilson Elser Moskowitz Edelman & Dicker LLP 3 Gannett Dr White Plains NY 10604 Office Phone: 914-323-7000 ext. 4233. Office Fax: 914-323-7001. Business E-Mail: obrienj@wemed.com.

O'BRIEN, JAMES J., manufacturing executive; b. Circleville, Ohio; Degree in Acctg., Fin., Ohio State U., MBA. Exec. asst. to chmn. Ashland Inc., 1992—94; v.p., gen. mgr. branded mktg. Ashland Petroleum Co., 1994; v.p. Ashland Inc.; pres. Valvoline, 1995—2001; with Ashland Inc., 1976—, sr. v.p., 1997, group oper. officer, pres., COO, 2002, chmn., CEO, 2002—. Bd. dir. Humana Inc., 2006—. Nat. bd. dirs. Big Bros. Big Sisters Am.; adv. bd. sch. bus. Ohio State U.; chmn. bd. trustees Midway Coll. Ky. Mem.: Am. Chemistry Coun., Assn. Governing Bds. Univ. Colls. Office: 50 E River Ctr Blvd Covington KY 41012-0391 *

O'BRIEN, JAMES JEROME, construction management consultant; b. Phila., Oct. 20, 1929; s. Sylvester Jerome and Emma Belle Filer (Fulforth) O'B.; m. Carmen Hiester, June 10, 1952 (div. Aug. 1, 1984); children: Jessica Susan, Michael, David; m. Rita F. Gibson, Nov. 1, 1984 BCE, Cornell U., 1952; postgrad., U. Houston, 1957-58. Registered profl. engr., NY, NJ, Pa., Ga., Conn., Maine. Project engr. Rohm & Haas, Phila. and Tex., 1955-59, RCA Corp., Moorestown, NJ, 1959-62; cons. Mauchly Assocs., Fort Washington, Pa., 1962-65; founding ptnr., exec. v.p. Meridian Engring. Co., Phila., 1965-68; pres. MDC Systems, Cherry Hill, 1968-72; ptnr. James J. O'Brien P.E., Cherry Hill, 1972-77; pres. O'Brien-Kreitzberg & Assocs., NYC, Pennsauken, San Francisco, 1977-80, chief exec. officer, 1980-89, chmn. bd. dirs., 1989-93, vice chmn., 1993—2002; cons. in field, 2002; prin. James J. O'Brien P.E., 2003—. Author: CPM in Construction Management-Scheduling by the Critical Path Method, 1965; co-author: CPM in Construction Management-Project Management with CPM, 6th edit., 2005, Management Information Systems-Concepts, Techniques and Applications, 1970, Management with Computers, 1972, Construction Inspection Handbook, 1974, 4th edit., 1997, Value Analysis in Design and Construction, 1976, Construction Delay-Risks, Rsponsibilities and Litigation, 1976, Preconstruction Estimating: Budget to Bid, 1994, Construction Documentation, 3d edit., 1995; co-author: Construction Management: A Professional Approach, 1974; editor: Recollections (L.D. Miles), 1987; author, editor: Scheduling Handbook, 1969, Contractor's Management Handbook, 1971, 2d edit., 1990, Standard Handbook of Heavy Construction, 3d edit., 1996, Construction Change Orders, 1998; contbr. articles to profl. jours. Lt. USN, 1952—55. Recipient Profl. Mgr. award, N.Y. Chpt. Soc. Advancement Mgmt., 1969. Fellow: ASCE (v.p. 1985, pres. South Jersey br. 1985, pres. NJ sect. 1987—89, com. on quality in civil engring. profession 1990—97, Constrn. Mgmt. award 1976, Disting. Engr. South Jersey br. 1986), Cornell Soc. Engrs. (dean's adv. com. sch. civil and environ. engring. 1986—87), Constrn. Mgmt. Assn. Am. (bd. dirs. 1990—92, Fellow award 1993, Constrn. Mgr. of Yr. award NY-NJ chpt. 1994), Project Mgmt. Inst. (sec. 1971, v.p. 1972, pres. 1973, chmn. bd. 1974—75, project mgmt. profl. 1984, v.p. edn. 2002—, editor Time Mgmt. chpt. PMBOK 3d edit. 2004, charter mem. Coll. Scheduling, award for contbn. to project mgmt. 1983, Fellow award 1989, Coll. Scheduling 1st Jim O'Brien Achievement in Life award 2005); mem.: Regional Alliance Small Contractors (bd. dirs. 1989—95), Port Authority NY and NJ, Miles Value Found. (bd. dirs. 1987—90, trustee 1990—99, bd. dirs. 1999), Soc. Am. Value Engrs. (v.p. NE region 1986—87, cert. value specialist, Fallon Value-in-Life award 1993, fellow 2005), Chi Epsilon, Tau Beta Pi. Home and Office: 2 Linden Ave Riverton NJ 08077-1124 Office Phone: 856-786-8287. Personal E-mail: jimobriendd527@aol.com.

O'BRIEN, JAMES PHILLIP, lawyer; b. Monmouth, Ill., Jan. 6, 1949; s. John Matthew and Roberta Helen (Cavanaugh) O'B.; m. Laurene Reason, Aug. 30, 1969 (div. 1980); m. Lynn Florsheim, Sept. 5, 1987 (dec. May 2005). BA, Western Ill. U., 1971; JD, U. Ill., 1974. Bar: Ill. 1974. Asst. atty. gen. State Ill., Springfield, 1974-75; jud. clerk Ill. Appellate Ct., Springfield, 1975-76; assoc. Graham & Graham, Springfield, 1976-81; corp. counsel Am. Hosp. Assn., Chgo., 1981-84; ptnr., chmn. health care dept. Katten, Muchin Rosenman, Chgo., 1984—. Task force med. malpractice reform legislation Am. Hosp. Assn., 1983-84, tax adv. com., 1987-91, tax reporting and compliance com., 1990-91; spkr. in field. Contbr. numerous articles to profl. jours. Recipient cert. recognition Ill. Dept. Children and Family Svcs., 1981; Edward Arthur Mellinger Found. scholar, Western Ill. U. 1971. Mem.: Am. Arbitration Assn. (Task Force Health Care Dispute Resolution 1982—84), Am. Health Lawyers Assn. Office: Katten Muchin Rosenman 525 W Monroe St Ste 1900 Chicago IL 60661-3693 Home Phone: 312-943-9460; Office Phone: 312-902-5630. Business E-Mail: phillip.obrien@kattenlaw.com.

O'BRIEN, JANE MARGARET, academic administrator; b. Washington, Nov. 17, 1953; d. Thomas and Edith (Pedersen) O'B; m. James A. Grube, June 28, 1975; children: William Howard Grube-O'Brien, Harold Thomas Grube O'Brien. BS in Biochemistry, Vassar Coll., 1975; PhD in Chemistry, U. Del., 1981. Rsch. asst. U. Vt., Burlington, 1978-79; asst. prof. chemistry Middlebury (Vt.) Coll., 1980-88, assoc. provost, 1988-89, assoc. prof. chemistry, 1988-91, dean of faculty, 1989-91; pres. Hollins Coll., Roanoke, Va., 1991—96, St. Mary's Coll., Md., 1996—. Ednl. chmn. biology task force New Eng. Consortium Undergraduate Sci., 1988-91; project mgr. H. Hughes Med. Inst. Instl. Awards, 1988-91; mem. steering com. Sloan New Liberal Arts Initiative, 1988-91; bd. dir. Norfolk Southern Corp., So. Md. Navy Alliance, Nat. Outdoor Leadership Sch.; mem. NCAA Div. III Pres. Council. Implementation com. Vermont EPSCoR, 1989-91; bd. dirs. Coun. Ind. Colls. in Va., 1991-96, Va. Found. for Ind. Colls., 1991-96; ednl. adv. com. Rainforest All, 1991—; bd. dir. Md. Citizens for the Arts Found., Univ. Mobility. Grad. fellow U. Del., 1975-76, Kellogg fellow W.K. Kellogg Found., 1989-92, Internat. fellow Assoc. Am. Colls., 1990-91, Regional fellow finalist White House Fellowship, 1991; Eisenhower Fellow, 1999. Mem.: Phi Beta Kappa, Sigma Xi. Office: St Mary's College Office of the President 18952 E Fisher Rd Saint Marys City MD 20686-3001

O'BRIEN, JEANNE H., medical educator; d. William Joseph and Jeanne Marie (Blanche) Sullivan; m. David Michael O'Brien, June 25, 1994; children: Fiona, Quinn, Sylvan. BA, St. Lawrence U., Canton, NY, 1991; MD cum laude, Loyola U., Canton, NY, 1997. Asst. prof. U. Rochester, NY, 1997—; resident in urology U. Rochester Med. Ctr., 1999—2002, chief resident urology, 2002—03, fellow in male infertility, 2003—04. Presenter in field. Buswell Rsch. grant, U. Rochester Med. Ctr., 2004—05. Mem.: Soc. Male Reprodn. (nat. coding rep.), Soc. Women Urologists, Am. Soc. Reproductive Medicine, Am. Soc. Andrology, Am. Urol. Assn. (assoc.). Office: Univ Rochester Dept Urology 601 Elmwood Ave Box 656 Rochester NY 14642-8656 Office Fax: 585-756-5457. Business E-Mail: jeanne_obrien@urmc.rochester.edu.

O'BRIEN, JIM, professional basketball coach; b. Phila., Feb. 11, 1952; m. Sharon O'Brien; children: Jack, Shannon, Caitlyn. B in Mgmt. & Mktg., St. Joseph's U., 1974; MBA, U. Md., 1981. Asst. coach Wheeling Jesuit Coll., 1974—75, Pembroke State Coll., 1975—76, U. Md., 1976—77, St. Joseph's U., 1977—78, U. Oreg., 1978—82, NY Knicks, 1987—88, U. Ky., 1994—97; head coach Wheeling Jesuit Coll., 1982—87, U. Dayton, 1989—94; interim head coach Boston Celtics, 2001, head coach, 2001—04, Phila. 76ers, 2004—05, Ind. Pacers, 2007—. Named to St. Joseph's U. Hall of Fame, 1988, Big Five Hall of Fame, 1989; recipient Markward award, 1970. Office: Ind Pacers 125 S Pennsylvania St Indianapolis IN 46204 *

O'BRIEN, JOAN SUSAN, lawyer, educator; b. NYC, Apr. 14, 1946; d. Edward Vincent O'Brien and Joan Therese (Kramer) Quinn; m. Michael P. Wilpan, May 27, 1979; children: Edward B. Wilpan, Anabel T. Wilpan. BA, NYU, 1967; JD, Georgetown U., 1970. Bar: N.Y. 1971, Mass. 1971, U.S. Dist. Ct. (so. and ea. dist.) N.Y. 1972, U.S. Ct. Appeals (2d cir.) 1971. Law clk. to Hon. Frank J. Murray U.S. Dist. Ct. Mass., Boston, 1970-71; asst. U.S. atty. Office of U.S. Atty. U.S. Dist. Ct. (ea. dist.) N.Y., Bklyn., 1972-76; pvt. practice NYC, 1976-79; trial atty. Mendes & Mount, NYC, 1979-84; asst. prof. St. Johns U., Jamaica, N.Y., 1984-90; adminstrv. law judge N.Y. State Workers Compensation Bd., Hempstead, N.Y., 1990-93; appellate atty. Scheine, Fusco, Brandenstein & Rada, Woodbury, N.Y., 1993-97; trial atty. Grey & Grey, L.L.P., Farmingdale, N.Y., 1997—. Editor: Georgetown Law Jour., 1968-70. Pres. Nassau County Dem. Com. Women's Caucus, Westbury, N.Y., 1988-90; leader Girl Scouts Nassau County, 1990-93. Unitarian-Universalist. Office: Grey & Grey LLP 360 Main St Farmingdale NY 11735-3592 Office Phone: 516-249-1342.

O'BRIEN, JOHN, professional soccer player; b. LA, Calif., Aug. 29, 1977; With youth system Ajax Amsterdam, Netherlands, 1996—98; midfielder FC Utrecht, Netherlands, 1998—99, Ajax Amsterdam, Netherlands, 1999—2005, ADO Den Haag, Netherlands, 2005—06, CD Chivas USA, LA, 2006—. 31 caps, 3 goals U.S. Nat. Soccer Team, 1998—; mem. U.S. World Cup Team, 2002, 06. Office: US Soccer Fedn 1801 S Prairie Ave Chicago IL 60616

O'BRIEN, JOHN FEIGHAN, investment banker; b. Cleve., Aug. 8, 1936; s. Francis John and Ann (Feighan) O'B.; m. Regina Quaid Harahan, June 27, 1959 (div. 1976); children: Regina, Victoria, Julie, John Jr.; m. Marilyn E. Schreiner, 1977. BS, Georgetown U., 1958. Salesman Appliance Mart, Cleve., 1958-59, ptnr., 1960-66; investment broker McDonald & Co. Investments, Cleve., 1966-71, ptnr., 1971-83, exec. v.p., 1983-88, mng. dir., 1988-91, sr. mng. dir., 1993—2007; investment assoc. UBS, 2007—. Bd. dirs. Hitchcock House, Cleve., 1978-89, Recovery Resources; chmn. Alcoholism Svcs. of Cleve., 1989-92, Alcohol and Drug-Addiction Svcs. Bd. of Cuyahoga County, 1992-98; trustee St. Edward H.S., Lakewood, Ohio, Alumnus of Yr., 1997, chmn. capital campaign, 1993-95; grand jury foreman Cuyahoga County, 2000. Named Good Fellow of Yr., Irish Good Fellows Club Cleve., 1996, Benefactor of Yr., St. Edward HS, 2003. Mem. Leadership Cleve., Greater Cleve. Growth Assn., Georgetown U. Alumni Assn. (alumni bd. senator, John Carroll award 1999), Westwood Country Club, Cleve. Yacht Club, Catawba Island Club, Lago Mar Club. Home (Winter): 1800 S Ocean Dr Fort Lauderdale FL 33316-3704 Office: McDonald & Co Investments 18500 Lake Rd Ste 300 Rocky River OH 44116-1744 Personal E-mail: jfeighanob@aol.com.

O'BRIEN, JOHN GRAHAM, lawyer; b. NYC, May 12, 1948; s. John Edward and Marian Helen (FitzGerald) O'B.; m. Phyllis Mary Eyth, Apr. 10, 1976; children: John Graham Jr., Jennifer A. BS cum laude, Mt. St. Mary's Coll., Emmitsburg, Md., 1970; JD, Am. U., 1973. Bar: N.J. 1974, D.C. 1974, N.Y. 1982, U.S. Supreme Ct. 1982. Law clk. to Hon. F.C. Kentz and J.H. Coleman, Superior Ct. of N.J., Elizabeth, N.J., 1973-74; assoc. Carpenter, Bennett & Morrissey, Newark, 1975-81; sr. counsel GAF Corp., Wayne, N.J., 1981-90; assoc. gen. counsel Keene Corp., NYC, 1990-93, ISS Internat. Svc. Sys., NYC, 1994-95; cons. GE, Fairfield, Conn., 1993-94; mng. ptnr. Atkins O'Brien Ekblom LLP, NYC, 1995-2000; of counsel McGivney, Kluger & Gannon, NYC, 2000—01; gen. counsel Brickforce Staffing Inc., Edison, NJ, 2001—03; of counsel Karasik & Einbinder, LLP, 2003. Author: (monograph) Responding to Products Liability Claims, 1986, also supplements; contbg. author: Toxic Torts Practice Guide, 1992. Recipient Disting. Young Alumni award Mt. St. Mary's Coll., 1976. Mem. N.J. Bar Assn., D.C. Bar, Echo Lke Country Club (assoc.), Coll. Mens Club. Roman Catholic. Office: 2 Ethel Rd Ste 204B Edison NJ 08817-2839 E-mail: obriennj2@aol.com.

O'BRIEN, J(OHN) PATRICK, psychiatrist, educator; b. Washington, Aug. 25, 1941; s. John Francis and Gertrude Estelle (Offutt) O'B. BA magna cum laude, Yale U., 1963; MD, Johns Hopkins U., 1968. Diplomate Am. Bd. Psychiatry and Neurology. Intern U. Pa.-Phila. Gen. Hosp., 1970-71; resident Mass. Gen. Hosp., Boston, 1971-74, asst. in psychiatry, 1974-83, asst. psychiatrist, 1983—; clin. fellow psychiatry Harvard U., Boston, 1971-74, clin. instr. psychiatry, 1974-79; asst. clin. prof. psychiatry, 1979—. Lectr. Harvard Ext. Sch., Boston, 1985-88. Author: The Disorganized Mind, 1978, poems; translator: (jour.) Formations, 1987. Fellow Royal Soc. Medicine; Am. Psychiat. Assn., NY Acad. Scis., Mass. Psychiat. Assn., Yale Club Mass., Phi Beta Kappa. Democrat. Office: Mass Gen Hosp ACC 806C 15 Parkman St Boston MA 02114-3117

O'BRIEN, JOHN WILFRID, economist, educator, retired university president; b. Toronto, Ont., Can., Aug. 4, 1931; s. Wilfred Edmond and Audrey (Swain) O'B.; m. Joyce Helen Bennett, Aug. 4, 1956; children: Margaret Anne, Catherine Audrey. BA, McGill U., 1953, MA, 1955, PhD, 1962, LLD, 1976; postgrad., Inst. Polit. Studies, Paris, 1954; DCL, Bishop's U., 1976; LLD, Concordia U., 2004. Lectr. econs. Sir George Williams U., Montreal, 1954-57, asst. prof., 1957-61, assoc. prof., 1961-63, asst. dean U., 1961-63, dean arts, 1963-68, vice-prin. acad., 1968-69, prof., 1965-96, prin., vice chancellor, pres., 1969-74; rector, vice chancellor, pres. Concordia U., Montreal, 1974-84, rector emeritus, 1984—. Provincial ednl. TV com. Dept. Edn. Que., 1962-66, dep. chmn., 1965-66, mem. tchr. tng. planning com., 1964-66; mem. Gauthier Ad Hoc Com., Univ. Operating Budgets, 1965-68, Council Univs., 1969-76; pres. Conf. Rectors and Prins. Que. Univs., 1974-77; mem. council Assn. Commonwealth Univs., 1975-78; bd. dirs. Assn. Univs. and Colls., Can., 1977-79; mem. Conseil Consultatif sur l'Immigration, Que. Gov., 1977-79, Corp. Higher Edn. Forum, 1983-84; bd. govs. YMCA, 1969-89, Vanier Coll., 1975-79, Fraser-Hickson Inst., 1975-00, pres. 1989-92, Que. div. Can. Mental Health Assn., 1977-79, Montreal World Film Festival, 1985-2004; sec., treas., Cinematheque Can., 1988-96, bd. dirs.; sec., treas. World Film Fest. Found., 1989-96; exec. mem. Alliance Que., 1989-96, chmn., 1990-96, bd. dirs.; hon. mem. Corp. Higher Edn. Forum, 1984-00; hon. v.p. Que. Provincial council Boy Scouts Can., 1974-90; hon. councillor Montreal Mus. Fine Arts, 1969-2003. Author: Canadian Money and Banking, 1964, (with G. Lermer) 2d edit., 1969.

O'BRIEN, JOHN WILLIAM, JR., management consultant; b. Bronx, NY, Jan. 1, 1937; BS, MIT, 1958; MS, UCLA, 1964. Sr. assoc. Planning Rsch. Corp., LA, 1962—67; dir. fin. systems group Synergetic Scis., Inc., Tarzana, Calif., 1967—70; dir. analytical svcs. divsn. James H. Oliphant & Co., LA, 1970—72; chmn. bd., CEO, pres. Wilshire Assocs. (formerly O'Brien Assocs. Inc.), Santa Monica, Calif., 1972—75; v.p. A.G. Becker Inc., 1975—81; chmn., CEO Leland O'Brien Rubinstein Assocs., 1981—97; mng. dir. Credit Suisse Asset Mgmt., NYC, 1997—2000; adj. prof. fin. U. Calif. Berkeley Haas Sch. Bus., 2000—. Recipient Graham and Dodd award Fin. Analysts Fedn., 1970, Matthew McArthur award Investment Mgmt. Consultants Assn., 2004; named Businessman of Yr. Fortune Mag., 1987. Mem.: Delta Upsilon. Home: 119 Jasmine Creek Dr Corona Del Mar CA 92625-1418 Office Phone: 510-643-1396. Personal E-mail: obrien@jwobrien.com. Business E-Mail: obrien@haas.berkeley.edu.

O'BRIEN, KATHLEEN L., special education educator; b. Oneida, NY, Aug. 31, 1975; d. Neal Patrick and Teresa Joan O'Brien. BS in Psychology, LeMoyne Coll., Syracuse, NY, 1997; MA of Edn., Cambridge Coll., Mass., 2006. Behavior specialist May Ctr., May Inst., Chatham, NJ, 1997—98; spl. edn. tchr. Albien Pub. Schs., NY, 1999—2000, Barnstable Pub. Schs., Hyanis, Mass., 2000—. Mentor Health Adventures Cape Cod Hosp., Hyannis, 2003—04. Mem. Barnstable Rep. Com., Hyanis, 2001—02. Republican. Roman Catholic. Avocations: tennis, volleyball, softball, music, reading. Home: 415 Cedar St West Barnstable MA 02668 Office: Barnstable Mid Sch 895 Falmouth Rd Hyannis MA 02601

O'BRIEN, KENDRA ALLEN, psychologist, researcher; b. Tachikawa, Japan, July 25, 1959; (parents Am. citizens); d. Jerry Eugene and Beverly Ann Allen; m. Daniel Kehaulani O'Brien, Apr. 19, 2002; 1 child, Pierce Keahi Aualii. BA, Colo. U., 1982; MA, Calif. Sch. Profl. Psychology, 1990, PhD in Clin. Psychology, 1997. Adolescent unit coord. Castle Med. Ctr., Kailua, Hawaii, 1983—88; addiction recovery aftercare coord. Vista Hill Hosp., San Diego, 1991—94; clin. rsch. coord. Damluji Bari Clinic, 1993—95; VA program specialist Nat. Ctr. Post Traumatic Stress, Honolulu, 1997—98; individual, family therapist C.A.R.E. Hawaii Inc., 1998—. With athletics dept. drug edn. San Diego State U., 1993—96; drug edn. addiction cons. Atlantic Richfield Co. Olympic Tng. Ctr., Chula Vista, Calif., 1994; adj. faculty Nat. U., San Diego, 1994—96. Named Most Innovative Intern, Met. Correctional Ctr. Fed. Bur. Prisons, San Diego, 1992. Mem.: APA, Hawaii Psychol. Assn., Gen. Soc. Mayflower Descs. (sec. 2001—03). Democrat. Methodist. Achievements include development of a drug education and consulting program that was used as a national model for effective education and intervention at an athletics conference in 1995. Avocations: photography, reading, scuba diving, running. Home: 485 Wana'ao Rd Kailua HI 96734 Office: CARE Hawaii Inc Ste 1003 677 Ala Moana Blvd Honolulu HI 96813-5417

O'BRIEN, KEVIN D., medical educator; BS summa cum laude, U. Idaho, 1980; MD honors, U. Wash., 1984. Diplomate Am. Bd. Internal Medicine, Cardiovascular Diseases Am. Bd. Internal Medicine. Intern, resident U. Wash., Seattle, 1984—87, chief med. resident, 1987—88; atteding physician U. Wash. Med. Ctr., Seattle, 1988—. Med. student rsch. fellow Fred Hutchinson Cancer rsch. Ctr., Seattle, 1981; assoc. prof. medicine U. Wash., Seattle, 1999—. Contbr. articles to profl. jours. Recipient Sheard-Sanford award, Am. Soc. Clin. Pathologists, 1983. Fellow: Am. Heart Assn.; mem.: Western Soc. Clin. Investigation (pres. 2007—, councilor 2003—06, Outstanding Investigator award 2003), Am. Fedn. Med. Rsch. (pres. 2001—02, found. pres. 2002—03). Office: Univ Wash Med Ctr Campus Box 356422 1959 NE Pacific St Seattle WA 98195-6422 Office Phone: 206-685-3930. Business E-Mail: cardiac@u.washington.edu.

O'BRIEN, KEVIN J., lawyer; b. NYC, Mar. 12, 1934; s. George and Kathleen (Fox) O'B.; m. Winifred Gallagher, Aug. 23, 1958; children: Karen A., Kevin J., Susan M. BS, Fordham U., 1959; LLB, Columbia U., 1962. Bar: N.Y. 1962, U.S. Ct. Appeals (2d cir.) 1971, U.S. Dist. Ct. (so. dist.) N.Y. 1972, U.S. Tax Ct. 1972. Law clk. to presiding justice U.S. Ct. Appeals (2d. cir.), NYC, 1962-63; assoc. Paul, Weiss, Rifkind, Wharton & Garrison, NYC, 1963-70, ptnr., 1970—. Contbr. articles to profl. jours. Served with USN, 1952-55. Mem. N.Y. State Bar Assn. (exec. com. tax sect. 1979-83), Assn. Bar City N.Y. Office: Paul Weiss Rifkind Wharton & Garrison 1285 Ave of the Americas New York NY 10019-6065

O'BRIEN, KRISTIANA, lawyer; b. Chapel Hill, NC, Aug. 12, 1973; BA, Bucknell Univ., Penn., 1995; MA, Columbia Univ., 1996; JD, Univ. Wash., 1999. Bar: Wash. 1999, U.S. Dist. Ct., Western Dist. Wash. 1999, U.S. Ct. Appeals Ninth Circuit 1999. Bus. atty. Montgomery Purdue Blankinship & Austin LLP, Seattle. Contbr. articles to numerous profl. jours. Named Wash. Rising Star, SuperLawyer Mag., 2006. Mem.: ABA, Wash. State Bar Assn. Office: Montgomery Purdue Blankinship and Austin LLP 55th Fl Bank of America Tower 701 Fifth Ave Seattle WA 98104-7096

O'BRIEN, MARK STEPHEN, pediatric neurosurgeon; b. West New York, NJ, Jan. 2, 1933; s. Mark Peter and Hannah (Dempsey) O'B.; m. Mary Morris Johnson, June 3, 1961 (div.); children: David, Derek, Marcia; m. Karen-Marie Sampson, June 1, 1984; children: Blythe, Blake, Lauren-Blair, Connor. AB cum laude, Seton Hall U., 1955; MD, St. Louis U., 1959. Diplomate Am. Bd. Neurol. Surgery, Am. Bd. Pediat. Neurol. Surgery. Intern St. John's Hosp., St. Louis, 1959-60, resident in surgery, 1960; resident in neurology Charity Hosp., New Orleans, 1962-63; resident in neurosurgery St. Vincent's Hosp., NYC, 1963-64, resident in surgery, 1965; sr. resident, chief resident Cin. Children's Hosp., U. Cin., 1965-68, research fellow in neurosurgery, 1966-67, 67-68; NIH spl. fellow in neuroradiology Albert Einstein Coll. Medicine, NYC, 1968-69; mem. faculty dept. surgery Emory U. Sch. Medicine, Atlanta, 1969—2003, prof.

surgery, assoc. prof. pediatrics, 1979—2003; chief neurosurgery Henrietta Egleston Hosp. for Children, Atlanta, 1971—2003; prof. neurosurgery U. Ark. for Med. Scis., Little Rock, 2005—. Trustee Elaine Clark Center for Exceptional Children; mem. med. adv. bd. Nat. Found., March of Dimes; trustee Henrietta Egleston Hosp. for Children; mem. profl. adv. panel Spina Bifida Assn. Am. Editorial bd. Pediatric Neurosurgery; contbr. chpts. to books, articles to med. jours. Served with USNR, 1960-62. Mem. Am. Assn. Neurol. Surgeons, Soc. Neurol. Surgeons, Congress Neurol. Surgeons, Internat. Soc. Pediatric Neurosurgery, Greater Atlanta Pediatric Soc., Med. Soc. Atlanta, AMA, ACS, Ga. Neurosurg. Soc., Am. Acad. Pediatrics, Am. Soc. Pediatric Neurosurgery, Pediatric Oncology Group, Am. Bd. Pediatric Neurol. Surgery (sec.), Acad. Pediatric Neurosurgeons. Home: 5720 Hawthorne Rd Little Rock AR 72207 Office: Ark Childrens Hosp 800 Marshall St Slot 838 Little Rock AR 72202 Office Phone: 501-364-1448. Personal E-mail: mobrien33@aol.com. Business E-Mail: obrienmark@uams.edu.

O'BRIEN, MARY DEVON, communications executive, consultant; b. Buenos Aires, Feb. 13, 1944; came to U.S., 1949, naturalized, 1962; d. George Earle and Margaret Frances (Richards) Owen; m. Gordon Covert O'Brien, Feb. 16, 1962 (div. Aug. 1982); children: Christopher Covert, Devon Elizabeth; m. Christopher Gerard Smith, May 28, 1983 BA, Rutgers U., 1975, MBA, 1976. Project mgmt. cert., 1989. Contr. manpower Def. Comm. divsn. ITT, Nutley, NJ, 1977-80, adminstr. program, 1977-78, mgr. cost, schedule control, 1978-79, voice processing project, 1979-80; mgr. project Avionics divsn. ITT, Nutley, 1980-81, sr. mgr. projects, 1981-93, cons. strategic planning, 1983-95; pres. Anamex, Inc., 1995—. Bd. trustees South Mountain Counseling Ctr., 1987-98, chmn. bd. trustees, 1994—; bd. dir. N.J. Eye Inst.; session leader Internet Conf., Florence, Italy, 1992; session moderator, panel mem. MES Conf., Cairo, Egypt, 1993, spkr., session leader Vancouver, 1994, keynote spkr. New Zealand, 1995; lectr. in field Author: Pace: System Manual, 1979, Voices, 1982; contbr. articles to profl. jours. and Maplewood Community calendar. Chmn. Citizens Budget Adv. Com., Maplewood, N.J., 1984-87, chmn. recreation, libr., pub. svcs., 1982-83, 94-96, chmn. pub. safety, emergency svcs., 1983-84, chmn. schs. and edn., 1984-85, chmn. gen. gov. and fin., 1998-2000; first v.p. Maplewood Civic Assn., 1987-89, pres., 1989-91, 2000—, sec. 1993-94, bd. dirs., officer, 1984—; chmn. Maple Leaf Svc. award Com., 1987-89, 94—, Community Svc. Coun. of Oranges and Maplewood Homelessness, Affordable Housing, Shelter Com., 1988—; chmn. speaker's bur. United Way, 1989-93; bd. trustees United Way Essex and West Hudson Cmty. Svc. Coun., 1988—; v.p. mktg. United Way Community Svc. Coun. of Oranges and Maplewood, 1990-93, v.p. 1994; mem. Maplewood Zoning Bd. of Adjustment, 1983-95; officer, mem. exec. bd. N.J. Project Mgmt. Inst., 1985—, pres., 1987-88, 95-2000, v.p. adminstrn., 1994-95; bd. dirs. Performance Mgmt. Assn.; chmn. Charter Com.; chmn. Internat. Project Mgmt. Inst. Jour. and Membership survey, 1986-87, mktg. com., 1986-89, long range planning and steering com., 1987—; bd. dir., vice chmn. Coun. Chpt. Pres. Interaction Com., 1986-90, chmn., 1991—, pres. Internat. Project Mgmt. Inst., 1991, chmn., 1992, v.p. Region II, 1989-90; adv. bd. Project Mgmt. Jour., 1987-90, N.J. PMI Ednl., 1987—; liaison officer, PMI internat. liaison to Australian Inst. of Project Mgmt. and Western Australia Project Mgmt. Assn.; apptd. fellow Leadership N.J., 1993—, Internat. Project Mgmt. Inst. and Performance Mgmt. Assocs.; mem. MCA/N.J. Blood Bank Drive; chmn. Maplewood Community Calendar, 1990-98; trustee community svc. coun. and edn. program United Way Essex and West Hudson, 1988—, also, chmn. leadership div., chmn. speakers bur., 1991— and mem. communications com.; mem. bd. dirs. Governing Inst. N.J.; chmn. Maplewood Rep. County Com., 1996—; chair, sec. Essex County Rep. County Com. Recipient Spl. commendation for Cmty. Svc. Twp. Maplewood, 1987; First Place award Anti-Shoplifting Program for Distributive Edn. Club Am., 1981, N.J. Fedn. of Women's Clubs, 1981, 82, Retail Mchts. Assn., 1981, 82; Commendation and Merit awards Air Force Inst. Tech., 1981; Pres.'s Safety award ITT, 1983; State award 1st Pl. N.J. Fedn. of Women's Clubs Garden Show, 1982; Cert. Spl. Merit award N.J. Fedn. of Women's Clubs, 1982, Disting. Contbn. award United Way, 1990, Pursuit of Exellence Cost Savs. Achievement award ITT Avionics, 1990, Maple Leaf award outstanding cmty. svc., 1992, Phoebe and Benjamin Shackelford award United Way, 1992, U.S. Ho. Reps. citation, 1992, N.H. Gen. Assembly Senate resolution Cmty. Leadership and Svc., 1992, resolution of Appreciation Township of Maplewood, Maplewood C. of C. Disting. Svc. award, 2005; N.J. Leadership fellow, 1993, awarded fellow of Internat. Project Mgmt. Inst., 1995. Mem. NAFE, Internat. Platform Speakers Assn., Grand Jury Assn., Telecomms. Group and Aerospace Industries Assn., Women's Career Network Assn., Nat. Security Indsl. Assn., Assn. for Info. and Image Mgmt., Internat. Project Mgmt. Inst. (liaison officer pres. 1991—, Outstanding Svc. and Contbrn. award 1986-87, Outstanding Pres. award 1988, Meritorious Svc. Recognition award 1989-1990), Performance Mgmt. Assn, Indsl. Rels. Rsch. Assn., ITT Mgmt. Assn., Rutgers Grad. Sch. Bus. Mgmt. Alumni Assn., Maplewood LWV (chair women and family issues com., voter registration bd. dir.), Maplewood Women's Evening Membership Div. (pres. 1980-82), Lions (Maplewood dir. 1992-95, program chmn. 1991-92, treas. 1994-95, N.J. dist. 16E zone gov., chmn. 1992-93, 95-96, cabinet sec. internat. dist., region chmn. 1993-94, 96-98, trustee Eye Bank N.J., internat. dist. 16-E cabinet sec. 1994-95, dist. 16-E chmn. peace poster contest 1995-99, pres. Newark 1995-97, sec. 1997—, N.J. State chmn. youth outreach and quest 1995-98, internat. dist. 16-E gov., 1999—, dist. MD16 treas., 1999—, youth oppportunities chmn. N.J dist. MD-16, coun. chmn. 2003-2004, state advisor 2004-, trustee Eye Bank of Delaware Valley, sec.-treas. 2003-05, 3d vice chmn. 2005-). Home: 594 Valley St Maplewood NJ 07040-2616 Office: 21 Madison Plz Ste 152 Madison NJ 07940-2354

O'BRIEN, MICHAEL J., lawyer, advertising executive; Ptnr. O'Sullivan LLP, Goodwin Procter LLC, 2002—03; sr. v.p., gen. counsel, sec. Omnicom Group Inc., NYC, 2003—. Office: Omnicom Group Inc 437 Madison Ave New York NY 10022 Office Phone: 212-415-3640. Fax: 212-415-3530. *

O'BRIEN, MORGAN EDWARD, communications executive, lawyer; b. Washington, Dec. 14, 1944; AB Classical with honors, Georgetown U., 1966; JD, Northwestern U., 1969. Bar: Ill. 1969, Washington 1971. Lawyer Mobile Svcs. divsn. Common Carrier Bur. FCC, Washington, 1970-72; asst. bur. chief Spectrum Mgmt. Pvt. Radio Bur. FCC, Washington, 1976-87; co-founder, chmn. bd. Nextel Comm., Inc., Reston, Va., 1987-96, vice chmn., 1996—2005; co-founder, chmn. Cyren Call Comms., McLean, Va., 2006—. Ptnr. Jones, Day, Reavis & Pogue, Washington, 1986-90; pvt. practice, Washington, 1979-90. Office: Cyren Call Comm 7601 Lewinsville Rd Ste 201 Mc Lean VA 22102 Office Phone: 703-760-4830. Business E-Mail: mobrien@cyrencall.com.

O'BRIEN, MURROUGH HALL, lawyer; b. Portland, Maine, July 23, 1945; s. Francis Massey and Constanze Kathryn (McDonnell) O'B. m. Johannah M. Hart, June 11, 1968; children: John David, Ellen Hart AB magna cum laude, Harvard U., 1969; JD, U. Maine, 1975. Bar: Maine 1975. Reporter, asst. city editor Evening Express, Portland, Maine, 1970-71; ptnr. firm Dunlap, Wood & O'Brien, Portland, Maine, 1975-80, Dunlap & O'Brien, Portland, Maine, 1980-85, Murrough H. O'Brien, Esquire, Portland, Maine, 1985—2006; exec. sec. Maine Jud. Coun., Portland, Maine, 1981-97; of counsel Jackson & MacNichol, Portland, 2006—. Pres. Portland Book Co. Mem. Keep Maine Scenic Com., 1974-79, So. Coastal Family Planning, Inc., Portland, 1975-79; mem. steering com. Study of the Future of Maine Legal Profession, 1983-89; mem. steering com. Gov.'s Commn. on Land Use Violation, 1983-84; treas. Coalition for Cruise Missile Referendum, 1989; trustee, v.p. Portland Ministry at Large, 1990-96, pres., 1996-99. Served with USNR, 1969-70. Green Party. Office: 85 India St Portland ME 04101 Office Phone: 207-772-9000.

O'BRIEN, NANCY PATRICIA, librarian, educator; b. Galesburg, Ill., Mar. 17, 1955; d. Leo Frederick O'Brien and Yvonne Blanche (Uhlmann) O'Brien Tabb; 1 child, Nicole Pamela. AB in English, U. Ill., 1976, MS in LS, 1977. Vis. instr. U. Ill., Urbana, 1977-78, asst. prof. libr. adminstrn., 1978-84, assoc. prof., 1984-91, prof., 1991—, serials bibliographer, 1977-78, social sci. bibliographer collection devel. div., 1979-81, project dir. Title II-C grant, 1987-88, acting libr. and info. sci. libr., 1989-90, head Edn. and Social Sci. Libr., 1994—, coord. social scis. divsn., 1996—2003, edn. subject specialist, 1981—. Discussion leader Ill. White House Conf. on Libr. and Info. svcs., 1990; mem. nat. adv. bd. Office Ednl. Rsch. and Improvement, US Dept. Edn., 1989-91; grant proposal reviewer NEH, 1991; mem. adv. bd. Ctr. for Children's Books, 1992-97; cons. Ark. Coll., 1989; chmn. rev. team Instrnl. Materials Ctr., U. Wis., Madison, 1989; chair exec. com. Nat. Edn. Network Nat. Libr. Edn. US Dept. Edn., 1998—2002; mem. ERIC Steering Com., Inst. Edn. Sci., US Dept. Edn., 2007- presenter in field. Author: Test Construction: A Bibliography of Resources, 1988, (with Emily Fabiano) Core List of Books and Journals in Education, 1991; Education: A Guide to Reference and Information Sources, 2d edit., 2000, (with Paul Fehrmann) Directory of Test Collections in Academic, Professional, and Research Libraries, 2001, (with John Collins III) Greenwood Dictionary of Edn., 2003; (with Kate Corby) Education in Resources in College Libraries, 2006; co-editor Media/Microforms column Serials Rev., 1979-82; mem. editl. bd. Bull. Bibliography, 1982-90; asst. editor Libr. Hi Tech., 1983-85; editor EBSS Newsletter, 1990-91; contbr. articles to profl. jours., chpts. to books. Mem. ALA (Whitney-Carnegie grantee 1990-91), Am. Ednl. Rsch. Assn. (mem. spl. interest group libr. resources and info. tech.), Assn. Coll. and Rsch. Librs. (mem. access policy guidelines task force 1990-95, vice chmn., chmn.-elect edn. and behavioral scis. sect. 1993-94, chmn. 1994-95, mem. acad. status com. 1996-2000, Disting. Edn. and Behavioral Scis. Libr. award 1997, mem. new pubs. adv. bd. 2004-07, chair disting. edn. and behavioral sci. libr. award com., 2004-07), Libr. Adminstrn. and Mgmt. Assn. (mem. edn. and tng. com. pub. rels. sect. 1990-95), Resources and Tech. Svcs. Divsn.(mem. micropub. com. 1982-85, chmn. 1983-85, cons. 1985-87). Office: U Ill Edn & Social Sci Libr 100 Main Libr 1408 W Gregory Dr Urbana IL 61801-3607 Office Phone: 217-333-2408. Business E-Mail: npobrien@uiuc.edu.

O'BRIEN, ODESSA LOUISE, protective services official; m. John Daniels O'Brien, May 30, 1964; children: James John, Jeanne Jacqueline, Kevin Raymond. B.Elective Studies, St. Cloud State U., 1975. Lic. pilot. Stewardess Northwest Airlines, St. Paul. Sec. Gen. E.W. Rawlings chpt. 213 Air Force Assn. Area rep. Youth for Understanding, Brainerd, Minn., 1979—82; v.p. Christian Women's Club, Brainerd, 1976—80; chmn. St. Francis Ch. Women's Guild, Brainerd, Minn., 1978—79; chmn. bd. St. Francis Parochial Sch. Bd., Brainerd, Minn., 1979—80; mem. coun. St. Francis Ch., Brainerd, Minn., 1979—80; adv. bd. Pine County Vo-Tech Sch., Pine City, Minn., 1967—71. Lt. col. USAF Aux. CAP. Recipient Outstanding Woman of Collier County, Am. Bus. Women's Assn., 1983—2006, Comdrs. Commendations, Fla. Wing, CAP, 1983, Grover Loening award, CAP, Paul E. Garber award, 2003, Gill Robb Wilson award, 2004. Mem.: AAUW (life; pres. Naples br. 1983—85), Collier Automotive Mus. (sec. of vol. docents), Naples Woman's Club (internat. chmn.), Phi Theta Kappa (life). Roman Catholic. Avocations: bridge (Bronze Life Master), flying, travel, tennis, reading.

O'BRIEN, ORIN YNEZ, musician, educator; b. Hollywood, Calif., June 7, 1935; d. George Joseph and Marguerite Graham (Churchill) O'Brien. Studied with Frederick Zimmermann, Milton Kestenbaum and Herman Reinshagen; diploma, The Juilliard Sch., 1957. Double bassist N.Y.C. Ballet Orch., 1956—66, Saidenberg Little Symphony, Music Aeterna, Am. Symphony (with Stokowski), N.Y. Philharm., NYC, 1966—; faculty Manhattan Sch. Music, NYC, 1969—, Mannes Coll. Music, NYC, 1988—, The Juilliard Sch., NYC, 1990—, co-chair double bass dept., 1992—2002. Participant numerous chamber music festivals, including Marlboro; featured in 1st performances of Gunther Schuller Quartet for 4 double basses; artist for GM, CBS and RCA Recording cos. Mem.: Internat. Soc. Bassists, Am. Fedn. Musicians, The Bohemians. Avocations: reading, writing, cooking.

O'BRIEN, PATRICK MICHAEL, library administrator; b. Newport, RI, Mar. 17, 1943; s. Joseph Xavier and Loretta (DeCotis) O'B.; m. Roberta Luther, Nov. 27, 1977; children: Megan MacRae, Brendan Watters. BA in Eng. Lit., Merrimack Coll., North Andover, Mass., 1964; M.L.S., U. R.I., Kingston, 1965; MBA, Case Western Res. U., Cleve., 1983. Reference libr. Newsweek mag., NYC, 1965-72; asst. dir. rsch. FIND/SVP, NYC, 1972-74; head cen. libr., cultural ctr. Chgo. Pub. Libr., 1974-79; dir. Cuyahoga County Pub. Libr., Cleve., 1979-84; dir. librs. Dallas Pub. Libr., 1984-92; dir. Alexandria (Va.) Libr., 1992—. Mem. editorial bd. Handel's Nat. Directory for Performing Arts; contbr. articles to profl. jours. Participant, alumnus Leadership Dallas Program, 1984-85, Leadership Cleve. Program, 1981; mem. nat. adv. com. to Libr. of Congress; mem. adv. coun. Tex. State Libr., Libr. Svcs. and Constrn. Act, 1986-89; co-chair, del. selection com. Tex. Conf. on Librs. and Info. Svcs.; mem. com. Goals for Dallas, 1985; mem. exec. bd. univ. librs. So. Meth. U., 1985-93; bd. dirs. Urban Community Sch., Cleve., 1982-84, Mus. African-Am. Life and Culture, 1985-86; mem. client data base com. Dallas Assn. Svcs. to Homeless, 1988-90; mem. Latchkey Children's Task Force, 1985-90. Recipient Servant as Leader award City of Dallas, 1989, Disting. Alumnus award U. R.I. Grad. Sch. Libr. and Info. Studies, 1990. Mem. ALA (coun. mem. 1987-95), Am. Libr. Trustee Assn. (bd. dirs.), Pub. Libr. Assn. (pres. 1985-86), Pub. Libr. Systems Sect (pres. 1983), Tex. Libr. Assn. (legis com. 1986-92), Tex. Women's Univ. Sch. Libr. and Info. Studies Vis. Com., Tex. Ctr. for Book Dallas Pub. Libr., Cleve. Area Met. Libr. Systems (pres. bd. 1980), Chgo. Libr. Club (pres. 1978), D.C. Libr. Assn., Va. Pub. Libr. Dirs. Assn. (bd. dirs. 1994-96), Va. Libr. Assn., Online Computer Libr. Ctr. (bd. trustees 1992-98), The White House Conf. on Librs. and Info. Svcs. (del. 1991), Pub. Lib. Adminstrs. N.Tex. (pres. 1990-91), Dallas 40, Rotary of Alexandria (bd. dirs. 1996-97, pres. 2002-03, Rotarian of Yr. 2001), Alexandria Commn. on Info. Tech., Beta Gamma Sigma. Office: Alexandria Libr 5005 Duke St Alexandria VA 22304-2903 E-mail: pobrien@alexandria.lib.va.us.

O'BRIEN, PATRICK MICHAEL, federal agency administrator; BA, U. Notre Dame; JD, U. Minn. Prin. dep. asst. atty. gen. legis. affairs U.S. Dept. Justice, Washington, counsel to dir. FBI, sr. counsel office of dep. atty. gen.; asst. sec. terrorist financing U.S. Dept. Treasury, Washington, 2005—. Office: US Dept of Treasury 1500 Pennsylvania Ave NW Rm 2058 Washington DC 20220 Office Phone: 202-622-0470. Office Fax: 202-622-7154.

O'BRIEN, PATRICK T., lawyer; b. NYC, Nov. 14, 1942; BS, Wheeling Coll., 1964; MA in Criminal Justice, John Jay Coll., 1976; JD cum laude, Univ. Miami, 1990. Bar: Fla. 1990, US Ct. Internat. Trade 1996. Spl. agent US Customs Svc.; now shareholder, tech., media, telecom. Greenberg Traurig LLP, Ft. Lauderdale, Fla. Mem.: ABA (Fla. regional subcom. on white collar crime), Fla. Bar Assn., Assn. Cert. Anti-Money Laundering Specialists, Interactive Gaming Counsel. Office: Greenberg Traurig LLP Ste 2000 401 E Las Olas Blvd Fort Lauderdale FL 33301-2296 Office Phone: 954-768-8221. Office Fax: 954-765-1477. Business E-Mail: obrienp@gtlaw.com.

O'BRIEN, RAYMOND FRANCIS, transportation executive; b. Atchison, Kans., May 31, 1922; s. James C. and Anna M. (Wagner) O'B.; m. Mary Ann Baugher, Sept. 3, 1947; children: James B., William T., Kathleen A., Christopher R. BS in Bus. Adminstrn., U. Mo., 1948; grad., Advanced Mgmt. Program, Harvard, 1966. Accountant-auditor Peat, Marwick, Mitchell & Co., Kansas City, Mo., 1948-52; contr., treas. Riss & Co., Kansas City, Mo., 1952-58; regional contr. Consol. Freightways Corp. of Del., Indpls., also, Akron, Ohio, 1958-61; contr. Consol. Freightways, Inc., San Francisco, 1961—, v.p., treas., 1962-63, bd. dirs., 1966, v.p. fin., 1967-69, exec. v.p., 1969-75, pres., 1975—, chief exec. officer, 1977-88, 90-91, chmn., 1988—; now chmn. emeritus CNF Transportation. Pres. CF Motor Freight subs. Consol. Freightways, Inc., 1973; dir. Transam. Corp., Watkins-Johnson, Inc.; past chmn. WesternHwy. Inst., Champion Road Machinery, Ltd. Former mem. bus. adv. bd. Northwestern U., U. Calif., Berkeley; bd. dirs., regent, former chmn. bd. trustees St. Mary's Coll.; bd. dirs., regent Charles Armstrong Sch., 1991—; mem. Pres.'s Adv. Herbert Hoover Boys and Girls Club; dir. Boy Scouts Am. Bay Area Coun. Served to 1st lt. USAAF, 1942-45. Recipient Disting. Svc. Citation Automotive Hall Fame, 1991; named Outstanding Chief Exec. five times Financial World Mag. Mem. Am. Trucking Assn. (bd. dirs. Found., exec. com.), Pacific Union Club, World Trade Club, Commonwealth Club (San Francisco), Menlo Country Club.

O'BRIEN, RAYMOND VINCENT, JR., banker; b. Bronx, NY, Sept. 23, 1927; s. Raymond Vincent and Blanche (Harper) O'B.; m. Theresa Sweeney, Mar. 29, 1952 (dec. June 1981); children: Susan, Raymond, Christopher, Sean, Carol, Nancy Meisenzahl; m. Ellen Boyle, July 24, 1982. BA, Fordham U., 1951, JD, 1958; postgrad., Harvard U. Advanced Mgmt. Program, 1969. With Chase Manhattan Bank, N.A., NYC, 1953-74; chief exec. officer, chmn. bd. Emigrant Savs. Bank, NYC, 1978—93, pres., 1974-77. Bd. dirs. Internat. Shipholding Corp. Trustee Fordham U., 1979-92; chmn. bd. trustees Regis H.S., 1988-92; past chmn. Cmty. Bankers Assn., N.Y., Nat. Assn. Cmty. Bankers. Served with AUS, 1946-47, 51-53. Mem. Guild Cath. Lawyers, Navesink Country Club (Middletown, N.J.), Plantation Country Club (Ponte Vedra, Fla.), K.M., Friendly Sons St. Patrick. Republican. Roman Catholic. Home: 102 Lands End Ponte Vedra Beach FL 32082-3906

O'BRIEN, RICHARD L(EE), physician, educator, academic administrator; b. Shenandoah, Iowa, Aug. 30, 1934; s. Thomas Lee O'B. and Grace Ellen (Sims) Parish; m. Joan Frances Gurney, June 29, 1957; children: Sheila Marie, Kathleen Therese, Michael James, Patrick Kevin. MS in Physiology, Creighton U., 1958, MD, 1960. Diplomate Nat. Bd. Med. Examiners. Intern and resident Columbia med. divsn. Bellevue Hosp., NYC, 1960-62; postdoctoral fellow in biochemistry Inst. for Enzyme Rsch., U. Wis., 1962-64; asst. prof. to prof. pathology Sch. Medicine, U. So. Calif., LA, 1966-82, dep. dir. Cancer Ctr., 1975-80, dir. rsch. and edn. Cancer Ctr., 1980-81, dir. Cancer Ctr., 1981-82; dean Sch. Medicine Creighton U., Omaha, 1982-92, acting v.p. health scis., 1984-85, v.p. health scis., 1985-99, prof. health policy and ethics, Univ. prof., 2000—, dir. office of interprofl. edn., 2002—05. Vis. prof. molecular biology U. Geneva, 1973-74; mem. cancer control rsch. grants rev. com. NIH, Nat. Cancer Inst.; mem. Cancer Ctr. Support grant rev. com. Nat. Cancer Inst., 1984-88, chmn. 1987-88; co-chmn. United Way/CHAD Pacesetter campaign, 1988, 94; bd. dirs. Health Future Found., 2003—; cons. in field. Contbr. articles to profl. jours.; editor various profl. jours. Bd. dirs. Opera Omaha, 1994-2001, 04—, pres., 1998-2000, Opera Omaha Found., 2000—06, chmn., 2004—06; co-chair Building Bright Futures Adolescent Behavioral Health Task Force, 2007-. Capt. US Army, 1964-66. Recipient Disting. Svc. award Met. Omaha Med. Soc., 1987, Silver Rose Opera Omaha, 2000; Spl. fellow Nat. Cancer Inst., 1967-69; named Citizen of Yr. Combined Health Agys. Drive-Health, 1986. Mem. ACP, Am. Assn. Pathologists, Am. Assn. Cancer Rsch., Am. Assn. Cancer Edn., AAAS, Am. Assn. Cancer Insts. (dir. 1982-83), Assn. Am. Med. Colls. (chmn. MCAT evaluation panel 1987-88, liaison com. on med. edn., 1988-93, co-chmn, 1989-93, adv. panel Strategic Planning Health Care Reform 1992-96), Assn. Acad. Health Ctrs. (long-range planning com. 1986, 2000, nominating com. 1987, 96, Task Force Health Care Delivery 1992, mem. task force on leadership and instl. values 1993-99, bd. dirs. 1998-99), Am. Cancer Soc. (adv. com. Inst. Rsch. Grants 1977-80, Outstanding Leadership award 1981, dir. Calif. divsn. 1980-82, dir. Nebr. divsn. 1992-96), Am. Hosp. Assn. (com. on med. edn. 1986-89), Alpha Omega Alpha. Home: 9927 Essex Dr Omaha NE 68114-3873 Office: Creighton Univ California At 24th Omaha NE 68178-0001 Home Phone: 402-392-0331; Office Phone: 402-280-2017. Business E-Mail: rlo@creighton.edu.

O'BRIEN, RICHARD T., mining executive; BA in Economics, U. Chgo., 1976; JD, Lewis and Clark Coll., Northwestern Sch. Law, 1985. Joined PacificCorp, 1983; CFO, sr. v.p. PacifiCorp, Portland, Oreg., 1995—98, CFO, exec. v.p., 1998; v.p. Mirant (formerly S. Energy, Inc.), 2000—01, pres., Mirant Capital Mgmt., 2000—01; sr. v.p., CFO AGL Resources, 2001, exec. v.p., CFO Atlanta, 2001—05; sr. v.p., CFO Newmont Mining Co., Denver, 2005—06, exec. v.p., CFO, 2006—07, pres., CEO, 2007—. Office: Newmont Mining 1700 Lincoln St Denver CO 80203 *

O'BRIEN, ROBERT BROWNELL, JR., banker, consultant, yacht broker, opera company executive; b. NYC, Sept. 6, 1934; s. Robert Brownell and Eloise (Boles) O'B.; m. Sarah Lager, Nov. 28, 1958; children: Robert Brownell III, William Stuart, Jennifer. BA, Lehigh U., 1957; postgrad., NYU, Am. Inst. Banking. Asst. treas., credit officer, br. locations officer Bankers Trust Co., NYC, 1957-63; v.p., dir. bus. devel. George A. Murray Co., gen. contractors, NYC, 1964; also v.p. Bowery Savs. Bank, 1964-69; dir., chief exec. officer Fed. Savs. & Loan Ins. Corp., Washington, 1969-71; chmn. exec. com. Fed. Home Loan Bank Bd., 1969-71; v.p. Bowery Savs. Bank, NYC, 1972; exec. v.p. First Fed. Savs. & Loan Assn., NYC, 1973-75; chmn., chief exec. officer Carteret Savs. Bank, Morristown, 1975-91, also bd. dirs.; mng. dir. Printon Kane Group Inc., Short Hills, NJ, 1991-94; dir., former chief exec. officer Govs. Bank Corp., West Palm Beach, 1992-94; pres., CEO Hubert Johnson Inc., 1998—. Bd. dirs. Fed. Home Loan Bank N.Y., Govs. Bank Corp., Ocean Med. Ctr. Found., Ocean County Atty. Ethics Com.; vice chmn. 1st Mortgage Capital Corp., Vero Beach, Fla.; chmn. Neighborhood Housing Svcs. Am., 1972-91; vice chmn., bd dirs. U.S. League Savs. Instns., Washington, O'Brien Yacht Sales. Contbr. articles to trade mags. Trustee Trinity Pawling Sch., Palm Beach County Housing Partnership, Lehigh U., Ocean Med. Found., Tuckerton Seaport; devel. cons. Ocean County Coll., Toms River, N.J.; chmn. Housing Opportunities Found.; trustee, pres. Toms River Seaport Soc., N.J. Mus. Boating; trustee, pres., past chmn. Cmty. Found. of N.J., 1987—; trustee, pres. Bay Head Hist. Soc.; vice chmn., bd. dirs. Dalt Found.; chmn. adv. bd. Palm Beach Maritime Mus., Peanut Island, Fla.; active Nat. Commn. on Neighborhoods, The Kemp Commn.; past chmn., exec. dir. N.J. State Opera. Mem. Nat. Coun. Savs. Instns. (past chmn.), Essex County Savs. and Loan League (past chmn.), NJ Savs. League (past chmn.), NJ Hist. Soc. (past chmn.), Greater Newark C. of C. (bd. dirs.), NJ C. of C. (bd. dirs.), Union League Club, Delray Beach Yacht Club (past commodore), NY Yacht Club, Morris County Golf Club, Somerset Hills Golf Club, Palm Beach Yacht Club, Bay Head Yacht Club (past commodore), Bay Head Fire Co. #1. Republican. Episcopalian. Home: 500 Club Dr Bay Head NJ 08742-5016 Home Phone: 732-295-4263. E-mail: bob@woodenboatsnj.com.

O'BRIEN, ROBERT CHARLES, lawyer; s. Robert Charles and Judith Lorie O'Brien; m. Louisa Maria Thuynsma, May 9, 1988; children: Margaret Elizabeth, Robert Christopher, Lauren Marie. BA, UCLA, 1988; JD, U. Calif., Berkeley, 1991. Bar: Calif. 1991. Legal officer UN Compensation Commn., Geneva, Vaud, 1996—98; ptnr. O'Brien Abeles

LLP, LA, 1999—2006; US alt. rep. to UN Gen. Assembly US Dept. State, NYC, 2005—06; ptnr. Arent Fox LLP, LA, 2006—. Co-chmn. Lawyers for Bush Cheney, Calif., 2004; mem. nat. steering com. Lawyers for Mitt Romney, Boston, 2007—. Maj. US Army, 1992—2005. Mem.: State Bar Calif. (exec. com. 1999—2002), J. Reuben Clark Law Soc. (chmn. LA chpt. 2003—05). Mem. Lds Ch. Office: Arent Fox LLP 445 S Figueroa St Ste 3750 Los Angeles CA 90071 Office Fax: 213-629-7401. E-mail: obrien.robert@arentfox.com.

O'BRIEN, ROBERT EMMET, insurance company executive; b. St. Louis, Sept. 13, 1923; s. Algernon Francis Adams and Adeline (von Weisert) O'B.; m. Mary Lou Gallagher, July 20, 1946 (div. 1978); children: Robert Jr., Gardnar, Scott, Derek, Mary Berkeley; m. Marian Strong Achilles, June 30, 1983. BBA, St. Louis U., 1946, MBA, 1947. Prin., ptnr. R. Newman & R. O'Brien, St. Louis, 1946-52; mem. Lloyd's of London, 1952—; dir. Hunter Engring. Co., St. Louis, 1946-72, Atlas Mfg. Co., St. Louis, 1965-80, Narragansett Corp., St. Louis and Moberly, Mo., 1965-80, Mid-America Coffee Co., St. Louis, 1970-75, Golden-Dipt Corp. and DCA (N.Y.), NYC, 1948-1970; cons. internat. ins. The Law Firm of Honorable Wilbur D. Mills and Herman E. Talmadge, Washington, London, 1976—. Pres. North Atlantic Assurance Co. Ltd., London, 1962-75; elected hon. dir. Atlantic Coun. of the U.S. Treas. St. Louis Trust Coun., 1949-65; apptd. to Bd. Life Govs. Royal Hosp. Putney, West Hill, London, 1969; councillor The Athletic Coun. of U.S., Atlantic Coun. of U.S., Carnegie Found.; mem. U.S. Olympics (Ice) Speed Skating Team, 1939; trustee Errol Flynn Estate, Jamaica and London, 1959-64; mem. Hiberian United Svcs. Club, Dublin, Ireland. With AC U.S. Army, 1942-45, ETO, NATOUSA. Decorated DFC (Eng.). Mem. DAV (life), Royal Air Force Soc., Zurich Internat. Insurers (apptd.), Life Underwriters, Million Dollar Round Table (life), Mid-Atlantic Club, Royal Yacht Club Hobart Tasmania, Royal Yacht Club Tasmania, Army and Navy Club Washington (hon.), Devonshire Club (London), Irish Nat. (London), Liberal Club (London), Royal Jamacia Yacht Club (life), Mo. Athletic Club, Royal Yacht of Fiji, Royal Scots Mil. Club (Edinburgh), U.S. SAMOA Soc. So. Pacific, Bridlespur Hunt and Polo Club, Flying Tigers Club (life, China and DC) Home: 117 Old Wharf Rd North Chatham MA 02650-1129

O'BRIEN, ROBERT JOHN, JR., public relations executive, former government official, air force officer; b. Wheeling, W. Va., Apr. 16, 1935; s. Robert John and Martha Virginia (Hunter) O'B.; m. Margaret Eugenia Schultz BS in Journalism, Northwestern U., Evanston, Ill., 1957; MA in Journalism, U. Wis., Madison, 1970; grad., Indsl. Coll. Armed Forces, 1977. Comnd. officer U.S. Air Force, 1957, advanced through grades to col.; dir. pub. affairs N. Am. Air Def. Command, Colorado Springs, Colo., 1977-80, Air Force Systems Command, Camp Springs, Md., 1980-82; dir. def. info. Office Sec. Def., Washington, 1982-83, dep. asst. sec. def., 1983-86; dir. pub. rels., Washington McDonnell Douglas Corp., Arlington, Va., 1986-97; v.p. pub. rels. The Boeing Co., Arlington, Va., 1997-99. Decorated D.S.M., Legion of Merit, Bronze Star, Air medal, Honor medal (Republic Vietnam) Mem. Air Force Assn., Pub. Rels. Soc. Am., Aviation/Space Writers Assn., U.S. Space Found., Ret. Officers Assn., Williamsburg Nat. Golf Club (Williamsburg, Va.), Nat. Press Club. Republican. Methodist. Avocations: golf, stamp collecting/philately, model railroading.

O'BRIEN, SEAN, chef; b. NY, 1968; B in Mktg., Santa Clara U. Chef Ritz-Carlton Dining Room, San Francisco, Fifth Floor, Viognier, San Mateo, Calif.; exec. sous chef Restaurant Gary Danko, San Francisco, 1999—2004; owner, exec. chef Myth, San Francisco, 2004—. Named Myth Best New Restaurant, Esquire mag., 2005, Rising Star Chef, San Francisco Mag., 2005; named one of Best New Chefs, Food and Wine Mag., 2007. Office: Myth 470 Pacific Ave San Francisco CA 94133 Office Phone: 415-677-8986. Office Fax: 415-677-8987. Business E-Mail: seanobrien@mythsf.com.

O'BRIEN, SOLEDAD, news anchor; m. Brad Raymond; children: Sofia, Cecilia, Charlie, Jackson. Degree in English and Am. Lit., Harvard U.; hon. degree, Siena Coll., Mercy Coll. Prodr. Second Opinion, reporter Health Week in Review Sta. KISS-FM, Boston; assoc. prodr., newswriter Sta. WBZ-TV, Boston; prodr. NBC News, 1991—93; co-host The Know Zone Discovery Channel; chief East Bay bur. Sta. KRON-TV, San Francisco, reporter, 1993—96; co-host The Site, Nightly News, Weekend Today MSNBC, 1996—99; anchor, Weekend Today NBC, 1999—2003; co-anchor, American Morning CNN, 2003—07. Named one of 50 Most Beautiful People, People Mag., 2001, PEOPLE Mag. (In Spanish) 50 Most Beautiful People, 2004, Crain's Bus. Reports', Essence Mag. & Black Enterprise, "40 under 40", Top 100 Irish Americans (several times), Irish Am. Mag.; recipient Emmy as a co-host on Discovery Channel's The Know Zone, Women of Power award, Nat. Urban League, 2006, Mickey Leland Humanitarian award, Nat. Assn. Minorities in Cable, 2006, President's award, NAACP Image Awards, 2007. Mem.: Nat. Assn. Hispanic Journalists, Nat. Assn. Black Journalists. *

O'BRIEN, TERRENCE LEO, federal judge; b. Lincoln, Nebr., Aug. 8, 1943; s. Leo James and Luella Mildred (Benting) O'B.; m. Dorothy Marguerite Driskill, Mar. 30, 1966; children: Sean Brendan, Heather Kathleen. BS in Acctg., U. Wyo., 1965, JD with honors, 1972. Bar: Wyo. 1972. Staff atty. Land and Natural Resources-US Dept. Justice, Washington, 1972-74, Omohundro & O'Brien, Buffalo, Wyo., 1974—80; judge 6th Jud. Dist. Wyo., Gillette, 1980—2001; pres. Visionary Communications Inc, 2000—01; private practice Wyo., 2001—02; judge US Ct. Appeals (10th cir.), 2002—. Justice of Peace Johnson County, Buffalo, 1975-80. Mem. Wyo. Community Coll. Commn., 1978-80. Capt. US Army, 1966-69. Mem.: Rotary. Republican. Office: US Courthouse 2120 Capitol Ave Rm 2141 Cheyenne WY 82001 *

O'BRIEN, THOMAS GEORGE, III, lawyer; b. NYC, Aug. 26, 1942; s. Thomas George Jr. and Margaret Patricia (Arctander) O'B.; m. Alison Marie Rich, Aug. 26, 1967; children: Christian Arctander, Kylin Stafford. AB magna cum laude, U. Notre Dame, 1964; LLB, Yale U., 1967; MA in Theology summa cum laude, St. Vincent de Paul Regional Sem., 2003. Bar: N.Y. 1967, Fla. 1988. Assoc. Carter, Ledyard & Milburn, NYC, 1971-78; assoc. gen. counsel Frank B. Hall & Co. Inc., Briarcliff Manor, NY, 1978-79, v.p., sec., gen. counsel, 1979-86; exec. v.p., sec., gen. counsel CenTrust Savs. Bank, Miami, 1986-87; of counsel Steel Hector & Davis, Miami, 1987-88, ptnr. West Palm Beach, Fla., 1988—2001. Author: Florida Law of Corporations and Business Organizations, 1990, 92-98. Trustee Bus. Vols. for Arts, Miami, 1986—88, Fla. Repertory Theatre, West Palm Beach, 1989—91, chmn., 1990—91; vestry mem. Episcopal Ch., Bethesda-by-the-Sea, 1991—94, sr. warden Bethesda-by-the-Sea, 1992—94; bd. dirs. Palm Beach Fellowship Christians and Jews, 1993—97, sec., 1996—97; chmn. Diocesan Sch. Christian Studies Bd., 2003—; lay dep. Episcopal Ch. Gen. Conv., 2004—, mem. program, budget and fin. com., 2005—; mem. exec. bd. Episcopal Diocese of S.E. Fla., 2001—04, sec., 2006—; bd. dirs. Bus. Devel. Bd. Palm Beach County, 1991—98, sec., 1992—93, chmn., 1993—94; bd. dirs. Directions 21st Century, 1995—98, chmn., 1996—98; bd. dirs. Toward a More Perfect Union, 2000—, sec., 2000—01, 2005—06, chair, 2003—05. Mem.: ABA (com. on legal opinions 1992—2001, negotiated acquisitions com. 1998—2001), Am. Soc. Corp. Secs. (sec. N.Y. regional group 1984—86), Fla. Bar Assn. (chmn. com. on opinion stds. 1988—95, mem. corps./securities law com. 1988—2002, vice-chmn. 1989—90, exec. coun. bus. law sect. 1989—93, chmn. 1990—91), PGA Nat. Club. Home: 272 Eagleton Estates Blvd Palm Beach Gardens FL 33418-8423 Personal E-mail: tgobrien@comcast.net.

O'BRIEN, TIM, lawyer; BA, Princeton U.; JD, U. Minn. Assoc. atty. Sheppard, Mullin, Richter & Hampton, LA; asst. gen. counsel NRG Energy, Inc., Princeton, NJ, 1996—2000, dep. gen. counsel, 2000—04, v.p., gen. counsel, corp. sec., 2004—. Office: NRG Energy Inc 211 Carnegie Ctr Princeton NJ 08540-6213

O'BRIEN, TIMOTHY ANDREW, journalist, writer, lawyer, educator; b. NYC, July 11, 1943; s. Timothy Andrew and Hildegarde J. (Schenkel) O'B.; m. Maria de Guadalupe Margarita Moreno, Jan. 15, 1971; children: Theresa Marie, Tim A. BA in Comm., Mich. State U., 1967; MA in Polit. Sci., U. Md., 1972; postgrad., Tulane U., 1974-75; JD, Loyola U., New Orleans, 1976. Bar: La. 1976, D.C. 1977, U.S. Supreme Ct 1981. News writer, reporter, anchor WKBD-TV, Detroit, 1968-69, WTOP-TV, Washington, 1969-72, WDSU-TV, New Orleans, 1972-74, WVUE-TV, New Orleans, 1974-77; law corr. ABC News, 1977-99; corr. Cable News Network (CNN), 2001—. Leo Goodwin Prof. Law Southeastern U., 1997; disting. prof. law Hofstra U., Sch. Law, 2000, St. Thomas Sch. Law, Miami, 2001, Nova U., 2002; disting. vis. prof. law, Nova Southeastern U., 1999, 2001, Loyola Sch. of Law, 2003. Contbr. articles to profl. jours. Bd. govs. Woodward Acad., College Park, Ga.; bd. visitors Loyola U. Sch. Law, 1997—. Recipient AP award for outstanding reporting of extraordinary event, 1976, New Orleans Press Club award for non-spot news reporting, 1976, Emmy award for documentary on D.C., 1969, ABA awards of merit, 1979 (2), 80, 85, Gavel award for documentary, 1980, Nat. award for human rights reporting Women in Comm., 1981, Disting. Alumnus award Mich. State U., 1996. Mem. Am. Law Inst., Radio-TV Corrs. Assn. Washington, Am. Judicature Soc. (bd. dirs. 1991-97). Home Phone: 301-942-1036.

O'BRIEN, TIMOTHY JAMES, lawyer; b. Detroit, Nov. 4, 1945; m. Hyon Baek, Jan. 31, 1970; children: Jean, Jane. AB, Yale U., 1967; JD, Harvard U., 1976. Bar: N.Y. 1977, Hong Kong, 1999. Assoc. Cleary, Gottlieb, Steen & Hamilton, NYC, 1976-80; ptnr. Coudert Bros., NYC and Hong Kong, 1980—2005, mng. ptnr. Hong Kong office, 2002—05; sr. fgn. legal counsel Shin & Kim, Seoul, Republic of Korea, 2005—06; sr. counsel Kim & Chang, Seoul, 2006—. Lectr. symposium on internat. investment Southwestern Law Found., 1995; dir. MetLife Korea, Ltd. Co-author: Corporate Governance in Korea at the Millennium, 2002; mem.: Harvard Law Rev., 1975—76; contbr. articles to profl. jours. Assoc. dir., vol. Peace Corps, Republic of Korea, 1967-73. Mem. ABA (vice-chmn. Aisia Pacific com. internat. section., co-chmn. conf. on Korea-U.S. trade and investment 1990-92), Assn. of Bar City of N.Y. (internat. law com., Asian affairs com. 1989-94), Korea Soc. (N.Y., sec., bd. dir. 1996-99). Office: Kim & Chang Seyang Bldg 223 Naeja-dong Jongno-gu Seoul Republic of Korea Home Phone: 82-2-796-7479.

O'BRIEN, WALTER JOSEPH, II, lawyer; b. Apr. 22, 1939; s. Walter Joseph O'Brien and Lorayne (Stouffer) Steele; children: Kelly A., Patrick W., Kathleen; m. Sharon Ann Curling, July 8, 1978; 1 child, John Joseph. BBA, U. Notre Dame; JD, Northwestern U. Bar: Ill., U.S. Dist. Ct. (no. dist.) Ill., U.S. Supreme Ct. Assoc. Nicholson, Nisen, Elliott & Meier, Chgo., 1966-70; pres. Capstan Co., Chgo., 1970-73, Walter J. O'Brien II, Ltd., Oak Brook, Ill., 1973-78, O'Brien & Assocs., P.C., Oakbrook Terrace, Ill., 1978—. Chmn. emeritus, bd. dirs. Atty. Title Guaranty Fund, Inc., Champaign, Ill., 1979—; arbitrator chairperson 18th Jud. Ct., DuPage County, Ill.; chmn. bd. dirs. ATG Trust Co., Chgo. Contbr. articles to legal jours. Commr. Oak Brook Plan Commn., 1980-85; mem. Oak Brook Zoning Bd. Appeals, 1985-87, Bd. Edn. Elem. Dist. # 53, Oak Brook, 1991-95; commr. Ill. and Mich. Canal, Nat. Heritage Corridor Commn.; v.p. Oak Brook Civic Assn., 1972; trustee St. Isaac Jogues Ch., Hinsdale, Ill., 1975-76. Capt. Q.M.C., U.S. Army, 1964-66. Fellow Ill. Bar Found.; mem. Ill. State Bar Assn. (mem. assembly), DuPage Bar Assn. (bd. dirs. 1987-88, elected Man of Yr. 1988), Am. Inn of Ct. (master DuPage chpt.), Butterfield Country Club (bd. dirs. 1982-88). Roman Catholic. Office: O'Brien & Assocs PC Ste 501 1900 Spring Rd Oak Brook IL 60523 Office Phone: 630-832-6000. Personal E-mail: obrienlaw@msn.com.

O'BRIEN, WILLIAM JEROME, II, lawyer; b. Darby, Pa., Oct. 22, 1954; s. Richard James O'Brien and Margaret (McGill) Hahn. BA in Econ. and Polit. Sci., Merrimack Coll., North Andover, Mass., 1976; JD, Del. Law Sch., 1981. Bar: Pa. 1982, US Dist. Ct. (ea. dist.) Pa. 1983, US Supreme Ct. 1986. Law clk. Commonwealth Ct. of Pa., Harrisburg, 1982-83; assoc. Philips, Curtin and DiGiacomo, Phila., 1983-86, O'Brien & Assocs. PC, Phila., 1986—. Bd. dirs. New Manayunk Corp., Phila. counselor, 1987-98. Bd. dirs. North Light Inc., 1986-94, sec., 1988-90, pres., 1990-92; bd. dirs. Manayunk Cmty. Ctr. for Arts, 1988-90, chmn. Chaminouix Mansion, 1989—, chmn., 1991—; spl. asst. to U.S. Senator H. John Heinz, 1976-78; Rep. candidate for Phila. City Coun., 1991, for Phila. City Contr., 1997; mem. Rep. State Com. Pa., 1998-2000; mem. Phila. Rep. Exec. Com. Mem.: Bus. Assn. Manayunk (bd. dirs. 1987—89), Pa. Bar Assn., Phila. Bar Assn., Del. Law Sch. Alumni Assn. (sec. 1985—87), Racquet Club (mem. com. 1985—87). Roman Catholic. Avocations: bicycling, squash, court tennis, scuba diving, golf. Personal E-mail: taxwatch@aol.com.

OBRIGHT, NEIL ALLEN, computers and displays company executive; b. Burbank, Calif., Aug. 17, 1945; s. Alvin Carl and Laura Margaret (Rich) O.; m. Marie Stilwell, Aug. 7, 1969 (div. 1975); children: Marie Christine, Laura Jean; m. Bonnie Lee George, Aug. 12, 1979. AA, El Camino Jr. Coll., 1972; BS, Pepperdine U., 1974, MBA, 1976. Technician Electronic Memories, Inc., Hawthorne, Calif., 1963-66, TRW, Redondo Beach, Calif., 1966-68; assoc. engr. Xerox Corp., El Segundo, Calif., 1968-75; mgr. bus. devel. Litton Data Sys., Van Nuys, Calif., 1975-84; dir. mktg. Sci. Applications Inc., San Diego, 1984—; prin., pres. NEMAR Assocs., LA, 1970. Contbr. articles to profl. jours. Sgt. at arms Young Republicans, Redondo Beach, 1976-77. Served with US Army, 1966-72, Vietnam. Decorated Purple Heart. Mem. Assn. US Army, Armed Forces Communications and Electronics Assn., Soc. Info. Displays, Nat. Thespian Soc. Office: Sci Applications Inc Tech 4060 Sorrento Valley Blvd San Diego CA 92121-1405

O'BRYAN, JAMES A., communications specialist, political organization administrator; BS, Boston U., 1978. Sen. U.S. V.I., 1985-87; dir. youth prevention program Dept. Human Svcs., V.I., 1987-90; press sec. to gov. of V.I. Office of Gov., 1990-95, asst. to gov. pub. affairs, 1999—2003, dist. dir. comms. for congresswoman Christian Christensen, 1997; adminstr. St. Thomas/Water Island, 2003—; gen. mgr. Ackley Media Group, 2007—. Chmn. Dem. State Party, 1998—. Mem. Assn. State Dem. Chairs. Office: PO Box 501 St Thomas VI 00804-0501 Office Phone: 340-776-1000.

O'BRYAN, MARGARET SUNDBERG, music educator; b. Potsdam, NY, Dec. 18, 1957; d. Randell Llewellyn and Marion Hamlin Sundberg; m. Thomas Henry O'Bryan, Aug. 25, 1984. MusB, Crane Sch. of Music, Potsdam, 1980, MusM, 1986. Cert. tchr. music K-12 NY. Tchr. vocal music Somersworth City Schs., Somersworth, NH, 1980—81, Central Square Ctrl. Sch., NY, 1983—84, Harpursville Ctrl. Sch., NY, 1984—2001, St. Regis Falls Ctrl. Sch., NY, 2001—. Dist. rep. Broome County Music Educators Assn., Harpursville, 1986—2001, county music festival chair; Chenango County vocal adjudicator Assn. Chenango Area Music Tchrs., Harpursville, 1988—2000, county music festival chair; mem. policy bd. St. Regis Falls Ctrl. Sch. Mem. St. Regis Falls Sports Boosters, PTO, St. Regis Falls, 2002—05, Olympic Chorus, Lake Placid, NY, 1980; mem. adv. bd. No. Gateway, 2006—; founder, instr. Harpursville Juggling Club, 1998—2001, St. Regis Falls Juggling Club, 2002—. Regents scholar, NY State, 1976—80. Mem.: Inst. Learning Centered Edn., Franklin County Music Educators Assn. (chair vocal music festival 2006—), NY State United Tchrs., St. Regis Falls United Tchrs. (co-organizer benefit auction 2004), NY State Sch. Music Assn., Music Educators Nat. Conf., Internat. Jugglers Assn. Mem. Lds Ch. Avocations: juggling, genealogy, landscape photography, travel. Home: PO Box 109 Port Kent Rd Nicholville NY 12965 Office: St Regis Falls Ctrl Sch 92 N Main St Saint Regis Falls NY 12980 Home Phone: 315-328-4064; Office Phone: 518-856-9421. Business E-Mail: mobryan@mail.fehb.org.

O'BRYANT, DANIEL R., consumer products company executive; BS in Mgmt. Sci., Calif. State Polytechnic U., Pomona, Calif.; MBA, U. So. Calif. Fin. mgmt. positions Baker Hughes; dir. cap. planning Avery Dennison, Pasadena, Calif., 1990—91, dir. fin. spl. tape div. Belgium, 1991—92, group fin. dir. Netherlands, 1992—94, v.p. fin. European ops., 1994—95, v.p. ops. planning Pasadena, Calif., 1995—96, v.p. ops. audit, 1996—97, v.p. gen. mgr. Fasson Roll div. Painesville, Ohio, 1997—2001, sr. v.p. fin., CFO, 2001—05, exec. v.p. fin., CFO, 2005—. Office: Avery Dennison Corp Ctr 150 North Orange Grove Blvd Pasadena CA 91103-3596 *

O'BRYON, JAMES FREDRICK, defense consultant; b. Schenectady, NY, Oct. 1, 1941; s. Frederick Stanley and Elizabeth Mary O'B.; m. Margaret Adina Bell, Oct 23, 1965; children: Daniel, Douglas, Cris, Kera. BS in Math., King's Coll., Briarcliff, NY, 1964; MSA in Ops. Rsch., George Washington U., 1973; SM in Elec. Engring., MIT, 1975. Mathematician Ballistics Rsch. Lab. Aberdeen Proving Ground, Md., 1966-74, asst. to dir. Ballistics Rsch. Lab., 1975-76, ops. rsch. analyst smart munitions group Ballistics Rsch. Lab., 1976-79, chmn. red-on-blue working group Joint Tech. Coord. Group, 1979-85, chief combat survivability and tech. U.S. Army Materiel Systems Analysis Activity, 1985-86; asst. dep. undersec. def. Office Sec. Def., Washington, 1986-88, dir. live-fire testing, 1988-95, dep. dir. operational test and evaluation, 1995—2001; chmn. O'Bryon Group, 2001—. Dir. Live Fire Test Program, Washington, 1986-2001; mem. Conventional Sys. Com., Washington, 1987—; panel mem. NAS, 2000-05, chmn. com. 2005—; newscaster, radio personality WRBS-FM, Balt., 1965-80; chmn. Mobius Bus. Solutions, 2002-04, Cons. Svc. Engring. Co., 2002-; cons. Inst. Def. Analysis, 2005-, ORSA Corp., 2005-, Scitech Corp., 2006-. Singer (albums) Until Then, 1968, Portrait of a Man, 1972, My Favorite Song, 1977, Celebration of Praise, 1982; author: I Fail to Miss Your Point, 2007; co-author: Red-on-Blue Weapons, Effects, 1983, Lessons Learned From Live Fire Testing, 2006, I Fail to Miss Your Point, 2007; contbr. articles to profl. jours. Active edn. coun. MIT, Cambridge, 1980—; bd. dir. Internat. Bible Soc. Found., Colo., Sch. Ministries, Inc., 2004—; mem. adv. bd. N.Y. Theol. Sem. With U.S. Army, 1964-66. Named Outstanding Young Man in Am., Jaycees, 1970, Disting. Lectr., Def. Aquisition U., 1988; fellow Ctr. Advanced Engring. Study MIT. Mem. AIAA, NAS/NRC (com. mem., chmn.), Nat. Def. Indsl. Assn. (chmn. Test and Evaluation divsn., Walter Hollis award, 2007), Internat. Test and Evaluation Assn., Sigma Xi. Home: 1608 S Tollgate Rd Bel Air MD 21015-5825 Office Phone: 443-528-2711. Business E-Mail: jamesobryon@obryongroup.com.

O'BRYON, LINDA ELIZABETH, broadcast executive; b. Washington, Sept. 1, 1949; d. Walter Mason Ormes and Iva Genevieve (Batrus) Ranney; m. Dennis Michael O'Bryon, Sept. 8, 1973; 1 child, Jennifer Elizabeth BA in Journalism cum laude, U. Miami. News reporter Sta. KCPX (now KTVX), Salt Lake City, 1971-73; documentary and pub. affairs prodr. Sta. WPLG-TV, Miami, Fla., 1974-76; producer, reporter, anchor, news dir. then v.p. for news and pub. affairs, exec. editor, sr. v.p. Nightly Business Report Sta. WPBT (PBS), Miami, 1976—. Recipient award Fla. Bar, Tallahasse, 1977, 2 awards Ohio State U., 1976, 79, award Corp. for Pub. Broadcasting, 1978, Econ. Understanding award Dartmouth Coll., 1980, award Fla. AP, 1981, 1st prize Nat. Assn. Realtors, 1986, Bus. News Luminary award TJFR, 1990, Am. Women in Radio and TV award, 1995, 98, Disting. Achievement award Soc. Am. Bus. Editors and Writers, 2004; named Most Influential Woman Bus. News Exec., TJFR, 2001. Mem. NATAS (past bd. dirs. So. Fla. chpt., regional Emmy award), Radio-TV News Dirs. Assn. (past trustee). Republican. Roman Catholic. Avocations: aerobics, tennis, golf. Office: Sta WPBT 14901 NE 20th Ave Miami FL 33181-1121 Home Phone: 954-557-7676; Office Phone: 305-424-4050.

O'BYRNE, MICHAEL, retired management consultant; b. Butte, Mont., Dec. 26, 1938; s. Michael E. and Margaret F. (Turner) O'B.; m. Penny L. Graham, Nov. 14, 1964; children: Jennifer L. McLellan, Gregory M. O'Byrne, Andrew G. O'Byrne. BSME, U. Wash., 1961. Cert. engr., Wash. V.p. PACCAR, Inc., Bellevue, Wash., 1969-84; pres. Mobi-Dock, Inc., Mercer Island, Wash., 1985-86; ptnr. The Catalyst Group, Mercer Island, 1986-89; pres. Raima Corp., Bellevue, 1988-89, Pacific North Equiptment Co., Kent, Wash., 1990-95; cons. Master Performance, Inc., Bellevue, 1995-2000, Vehicle Monitor Corp., Redmond, Va., 1996—2004; ret. Council mem. Hunts Point, Wash., 1980-97; mem. bd. dirs. Mcpl. League of King County, Seattle, 1994-95; dist. chmn. Boy Scouts Am., Seattle, 1994-98; pres. USO Puget Sound Area, 1997-2004. Lt. comdr. USN, 1961-69. Mem. Soc. Automotive Engrs., Assoc. Equipment Distributors (chpt. pres. 1994-95), Rotary Internat., Seattle Yacht Club. Republican. Avocations: sailing, skiing, fishing. E-mail: michael.obyrne@comcast.net.

OCAL, TARKAN, computer engineer; b. Ankara, Turkey, Dec. 1955; Attended, U. So. Miss., U. Minn.; MS in Mechanical Design Engring., Trinity Coll., London. Junior drafter HAKO Minutemen Corp., St. Paul; designer apprentice Sperry-Univac, Honeywell, Hutchinson Technologies; junior engr. 3M Corp.; sr. engr. Matra-Manurhin Corp., Ft. Lauderdale; project engr. Dept. of Defense, Washington; founder, v.p. G&T TECH, Inc.; contractor Broward County Commn. Info. Techn., Fla.; sys. network analyst Broward County Commn. Info. Tech.

O'CALLAGHAN, BARRY, investment banker; Grad. in Law, Trinity Coll., Dublin. Internat. investment banker Morgan Stanley, Credit Suisse; chmn., CEO Riverdeep Holdings PLC, San Francisco, 1999—.

O'CALLAGHAN, JERRY ALEXANDER, federal agency administrator; b. Klamath Falls, Oreg., Feb. 23, 1922; s. Jeremiah Patrick and Marie Jane (Alexander) O'C.; m. Florence Marie Sheehan, Aug. 6, 1949; children—Jane Mary, Susan Margaret. BS with honors, U. Oreg., 1943, MA with honors, 1947; PhD, Stanford, 1951. Acting instr. history Stanford, 1951-52, U. Wyo., 1952-53; oil editor Tribune-Herald, Casper, Wyo., 1953-55; acting asst. prof. U. Wyo., 1955-56; legis. asst. to Senator Joseph O'Mahoney (Wyo.), 1956-60; exec. asst. to Senator Joseph Hickey(Wyo.), 1961; asst. dir. lands and minerals mgmt. Bur. Land Mgmt., Dept. Interior, 1961-62, asst. dir. plans and legislation, 1962-64, chief legislation and coop. relations, 1964-69, chief div. coop. relations, 1969-80, chief hist. studies, 1980-82, historian emeritus, 1982—. Author: Disposition of the Public Domain in Oregon, 1960, America 200— The Legacy of Our Lands, 1976. Bd. govs. St. Columba's Episc. Nursery Sch., 1959-71; vestryman Episc. Ch., 1964-68, outreach leader, 1985-90; lay ministry St. Columba's, 1990-2004. With AUS, 1943-46. Mem. Soc. of Forest History, Fed. Profl. Assn. (pres. 1972), Fossils, Phi Kappa Psi. Home: 5607 Chesterbrook Rd Bethesda MD 20816-1301

O'CALLAGHAN, MARK CHARLES, physicist; b. San Leandro, Calif., Jan. 21, 1971; s. Thomas Paul and Kathleen Elynor O'Callaghan; m. Guadalupe Elisa Calero, Aug. 30, 2002; 1 child, Elisabeth Charlotte. BA in Math., U. Puget Sound, Tacoma, Wash., 1994, BS in Physics, 1994; BS in Mech. Engring., Wash. U., St. Louis, 1996; MS in Physics, San Diego State U., 2002. Engr. BAE Sys., San Diego, 1996—2003; mem. rsch. staff Arete Assocs., Sherman Oaks, Calif., 2003—05; adj. prof. math. Coll. the

Canyons, Santa Clarita, Calif., 2004—05; rsch. scientist staff Lockheed Martin Aeronautics Co., Palmdale, Calif., 2005—. Mem.: Soc. Physics Students, Am. Mensa, Ltd. Conservative. Roman Catholic. Home Phone: 661-951-9434.

OCAMPO, JOSE ANTONIO, economist, educator, former international organization official, former Colombian government official; b. Cali, Colombia, Dec. 20, 1952; married; 3 children. BA in Econs. and Sociology, U. Notre Dame, 1972; PhD, Yale U., 1976. Rschr. CEDE, Universidad de los Andes, 1976-79; prof. econs. Universidad de los Andes, 1976—84, 1988—93; prof. history Universidad Nacional de Columbia, 1990; dir. Ctr. for Devel. Studies Universidad de los Andes, 1980-82; dep. dir. FEDESARROLLO, 1983-84, nat. dir. employment mission, 1985-86, exec. dir., 1984-88, sr. rschr., 1988-89, bd. dir., 1989; min. agriculture Colombian Govt., 1993-94, dir. Nat. Planning Dept., Ministry of Planning, 1994—96, min. fin. and pub. credit, 1996—97; exec. sec. Econ. Commn. Latin Am. & Caribbean, Santiago, Chile, 1998—2003; under-sec. gen. for econ. and social affairs UN, 2003—07; prof. profl. practice in internat. and pub. affairs Columbia U., NYC. Vis. fellow Yale U., 1977, Oxford U., 1984; mem. Mission on intergovernmental Fins., 1980-82, Adv. Commn. for Fiscal Reform, 1982-83, Pub. Expenditure Commns., 1983, 85, Technical Commn. on Coffee Affairs, 1986; mem. mission to Nicaragua The Swedish Internat. Devel. Authority-World Inst. for Devel. Econ. Rsch., 1989, head, 1989-93; advisor to Colombian Govt. on Coffee Affairs, 1989-90; cons. Inter-Am. Devel. Bank, World Bank, UN; advisor Nat. Coun. Entrepreneurial Assns., 1992, Ministry of Fgn. Trade, 1993; vis. rschr. UN Conf. on Trade and Devel., 1992. Author: Colombia and the World Economy 1830-1910, 1984, 2d edit., 1987, Los capitales extranjeros en las economías latinoamericanas, 1994; co-author, editor Economic Policy at the Crossroads, 1984, Economic History of Colombia, 1987, 2d edit., 1988, 3rd edit., 1991, 4th edit., 1994, The Colombian Labor Problem: Special Reports of the Employment Mission, 1987, Post-Keynesian Economics, 1988; co-author (with Santiago Montenegro) World Depression, Protection and Industrialization: Essays on the Economic History of Colombia, 1984, (with Eduardo Lora) Colombia's Foreign Debt: From the moratoria of the 1930s to the crossroads of the 1980s, 1988; co-editor: (with Eduardo Lora) Introduction to Colombian Macroeconomics, 1989, 2d edit., 1992, (with Eduardo Lora and Roberto Steiner) 3rd edit., 1994; dir. Jour. Desarrollo y Sociedad, 1980-82; co-editor Jour. Coyuntura Economica, 1984; mem. editl. bds. Jour. of L.Am. Studies, 1989-, El Trimestre Economico (Mex.), 1985-, Jour. of Develop. Econ. (North-Holland), 1985-1990, Econ. Forecasts (North-Holland), 1985-1994; contbr. articles to profl. jours. Named Exec. of Yr., Jr. Chamber of Bogotá, 1989; recipient Alejandro Angel Escobar, Nat. Prize for Sci., 1988, Order of Boyaca: Great Cross, Highest Distinction, 1997. Mem. Colombian Acad. Econ. Scis., Colombian Acad. Hist.; Fellow Colombian Acad. Econ. Office: Sch Internat and Pub Affairs Columbia U 420 W 118th St New York NY 10027 Office Phone: 212-854-3239. E-mail: jao2128@columbia.edu. *

OCAMPO, MANUEL, artist; b. Philippines; Exhibitions include Corcoran Biennial, 1993, Kwangju Biennial, 1997, Biennale d'art Contemporain de Lyon, 2000, Berlin Biennale, 2001, Venice Biennale, 2001, Seville Biennale, 2004, Casa Asia, Barcelona, 2005, Lieu d'Art Contemporain, Sigean, France, 2005, exhibited in group shows at Asia Society, NYC, 1994, Setagaya Art Mus., Tokyo, 1997, Aldrich Mus. Art, 1998, LA County Mus. Art, 2000. Recipient Rome Prize, Am. Acad., 1995, award, Nat. Endowment for the Arts, 1996, Pollock-Krasner Found., 1995. Office: c/o Gray Kapernekas Gallery 526 W 26 St Ste 814 New York NY 10001

OCASIO-MELENDEZ, MARCIAL ENRIQUE, history professor; b. San Juan, Aug. 22, 1942; s. Manuel C. and Amparo (Melendez) Ocasio; m. Mimi Rivera, Apr. 15, 1973 (div. 1976). BA, U. PR, 1964, MA, 1977; PhD, Mich. State U., East Lansing, 1988. Tchr. sci. PR Dept. Edn., San Juan, 1966-67; tchr. sci., history Nyack Schs., NY, 1967-71; tchr. sci. Robinson Prep. Sch., Condado, PR, 1971-72; instr. PR Jr. Coll., Rio Piedras, 1972-80; teaching asst. Mich. State U., E. Lansing, 1979-83; instr. history Caribbean U., Bayamon, P.R., 1983-85; instr. Inter Am. U., Bayamon, 1985-87, U. PR, Rio Piedras, 1983-87; vis. asst. prof. Mich. State U., East Lansing, 1987-88; asst. prof. history U. Mich., Flint, 1988-91; prof. history U. PR, Rio Piedras, 1991—, dir. grad. program history, 1991-93, assoc. dean acad. affairs Coll. Humanities, 1993-95, dir. internat. rels., 1995—2001, chair, dept. history, 2004—; prof. Ctr. Advanced Grad. Studies PR and The Caribbean. Vis. prof. U. Zaragoza, Spain, 2001; bd. dirs. Spanish Speaking Info. Ctr., Flint; lectr. Universidad del Valle, Cali, Universidad de Los Andes, Bogota, Universidad Pedagogica Nacional, Tunja, U. del Norte Barranquilla, Colombia, Nat. U. Nicaragua, 2005; dir. Rockefeller Found. Caribbean 2000 Project, U. PR, 1994-95, Urban Preservation Project of Rio Piedras, PR, 1994-95; pres. PR's Bd. Hist. Preservation, 1999—; mem. editl. bd. Caribbean Studies, 1994-99; rev. panel mem. NEH, 2006-. Author: Rio Piedras Notas, 1985, Las Americas, Su Tierra, Su Gente, 1997, Capitalism and Development, Tampico 1876-1924, 1998, Los Pueblos de America, 2006, America, Un Mundo en Próceso, 2007. Mich. State U. scholar 1981, urban affairs grantee, 1982-83; Fulbright scholar (Colombia) 1989, 90, 01-, Fulbright scholar specialist, 2002—, Fulbright scholar NEH, 2006-; NEH fellow, 1973, 78-79, 91, 02-. Mem. Social Sci. Studies Assn., Coun. Latin Am. History, Am. Hist. Assn., L.Am. Studies Assn., Assn. PR Historians (pres. 1995-97), Joint Border Rsch. Inst., Assn. Caribean Historians, Caribbean Studies Assn., Hispanic Coun. on Internat. Rels., Phi Alpha Theta. Office: Univ PR History Dept PO Box 23350 San Juan PR 00931-3350 Office Phone: 787-764-0000 ext. 3777. Personal E-mail: kokoroko9@hotmail.com. Business E-Mail: mocasio@uprrp.edu.

OCCHIATO, MICHAEL ANTHONY, municipal official; b. Pueblo, Colo. s. Joseph Michael and Joan Occhiato; m. Peggy Ann Stefonowicz, June 27, 1964 (div. Sept. 1983); children: Michael, James, Jennifer. BBA, U. Denver, 1961; MBA, U. Colo., 1984; postgrad., U. So. Colo. Grad. Real Estate Inst., 1996, cert. residential specialist 2000. Sales mgr. Tivoli Brewing co., Denver, 1965-67, acting brewmaster, prodn. control mgr., 1967-68, plant mgr., 1968-69; adminstrv. mgr. King Resources Co., Denver, 1969-70; ops. mgr. Canners Inc., Pepsi-Cola Bottling Co., Pueblo, 1970-76; pres. Pepsi-Cola Bottling Co., Pueblo, 1978-82; gen. mgr. Pepsi-Cola Bottling Group div. PepsiCo., Pueblo, 1982, area v.p., 1982-83; ind. cons. Pueblo, 1983—; broker assoc. Sound Venture Realty, Pueblo, 1996-98, Jones Healy Better Homes & Gardens, 1998—. V.p. Colo. Soft Drink Assn., 1978, pres., 1979; regional dir. Pepsi Cola Mgmt. Inst. divsn. Pepsi Co., 1979-82; pres. Ethnic Foods Internat. dba Taco Rancho, Pueblo, Exodus 20, 1996—; chmn. Weifang (China) Sister City Del., 1991—; bd. dirs. Pueblo Diversified Industries, Pueblo Crime Stoppers, Pueblo Regional Bldg; rancher, 1976—; land devel. real estate broker assoc., 1996—. Mem. Pueblo City Coun., 1978—93, 2001—, pres., 1986—87, 1991, 1992, 2003, 2006, 2007; mem. Pueblo Bd. Health, 1978—80, Pueblo Regional Planning Commn., 1980—81, Pueblo Action Inc., 1978—80, Pueblo Planning and Zoning Commn., 1985; chmn. Pueblo Area Coun. Govts., 1980—82, 1984—85; mem. Pueblo Econ. Devel. Corp., 1983—91; chmn. fundraising Pueblo chpt. Am. Heart Assn., 1983—; active Earth Wise Pueblo, 1991; pres. Pueblo City Coun., 2002; active Pueblo Regional Bldg. Bd., 2003—; rep. in signing Sister City Agreement with Bergamo, Italy City of Pueblo, 2004; pres. Pueblo City Coun., 2006—; bd. dirs. Pueblo Urban Renewal Authority, 1993—, Pueblo Crime Stoppers, 2001—, El Pueblo Boys Ranch; v.p. Colo. Soft Drink Assn., 1979—80, pres., 1980—81; del. 1st World Conf. Local Elected Ofcls. to 1st UN Internat. Coun. for Local Environ. Initiative. Lt. USN, 1961—65. Mem. So. Colo. Emergency Med. Technicians Assn. (pres. 1975), Am. Saler Assn., Am. Quarter Horse Assn., Colo. Cattle Assn., Pueblo C. of C., Rotary, Pi Kappa Alpha (v.p. 1960). Home and Office: 11 Harrogate Ter Pueblo CO 81001-1723

OCEAN, ALLYSON JOY, oncologist, educator; b. Jan. 27, 1972; MD with honors, Tufts U. Sch. Medicine, 1998. Cert. Internal Medicine, Hematology, Med. Oncology. Intern NY Presbyn.-Cornell Campus, resident, fellow, hematology and med. oncology; med. oncologist, attending physician gastrointestinal oncology NY Presbyn. Hosp.-Columbia U. Coll. Physicians & Surgeons & Weill Med. Coll. Cornell U.; asst. prof. medicine Weill Med. Coll. Cornell U.; med. oncologist Jay Monahan Ctr. for Gastrointestinal Health. Mem. bd. advisors OralChemo. Contbr. articles to profl. publications. Mem.: Am. Assn. for Cancer Rsch., Am. Soc. Hematology, Am. Soc. Clin. Oncology. Office: 525 E 68th St Payson 3 New York NY 10021 Office Phone: 212-746-2927, 212-746-2844. Office Fax: 212-746-6645. *

OCELLO, CLAUDIA BARBARA, museum program director; b. Passaic, NJ, July 15, 1966; d. Fortunato and Adriana Concetta (Dominianni) Ocello. BA in Classical and Near Ea. Archaeology, Bryn Mawr Coll., 1988; BS in Mus. Edn., Bank St. Coll. Edn., 1993. Intern J. Paul Getty Mus., Malibu, Calif., 1993—94; coord. edn. and vol. Barnum Mus., Bridgeport, Conn., 1994—96; curator edn. NJ Hist. Soc., Newark, 1996—2005, dir. program and exhbns., 2005—06; asst. dir. for edn. and pub. programs Save Ellis Island, Inc., 2006—. Adj. prof. Seton Hall U., South Orange, NJ, 1997—; mem. adv. bd. NJ History Day, 1997—2005. Author: First Steps: A Scrapbook & Guide for Young Parents, 2002. Vol., project mgr. Jersey Cares, 1998—2003. Named Outstanding Educator, NJ History Day, 2004. Mem.: Mid-Atlantic Assn. Mus. (program com. 2006), Am. Assn. Mus. (Edn. Com. Excellence in Programming award 2002). Avocations: cooking, reading, yoga. Office: 500 Internation Dr Ste 350 Budd Lake NJ 07828 E-mail: cocello@saveellisisland.org.

OCHMANEK, DAVID ALAN, defense analyst; b. Oak Park, Ill., Apr. 10, 1951; s. Edwin Joseph and Phyllis Jean (Straass) O.; m. Barbara Jane Larson, June 16, 1973; children: James Edwin, Anne Skaaden. BS in Internat. Affairs, Polit. Sci., USAF Acad., 1973; MPA in Pub. Affairs and Internat. Rels., Princeton U., 1980. Fgn. svc. officer U.S. Dept. State, 1980-85; profl. staff The Rand Corp., 1985-93, 95—; dep. asst. sec. of def. for strategy Washington, 1993-95; sr. def. analyst The RAND Corp., Washington, 1995—. Author: Military Operations Against Terrorist Groups Abroad, 2003, NATO's Future: Implications for U.S. Military Capabilities and Force Posture, 2000; co-author: (with Edward L. Warner III) Next Moves: An Arms Control Agenda for the 1990's, 1989, (with Christopher Bowie et al) The New Calculus, 1993, (with Zalmay Khalilzad) Strategic Appraisal, 1997, (with Edward Harshberger el at) To Find and Not to Yield, 1998, (with Anthony Lake) The Real and the Ideal, 2001; contbr. articles to profl. jours., chpts. to books. Capt. USAF, 1973-78. Lutheran. Office: The RAND Corp 1200 S Hayes St Arlington VA 22202-5050 Home Phone: 202-543-5896; Office Phone: 703-413-1100.

OCHOA, ARTHUR J., lawyer, hospital administrator; b. LA, Calif., Sept. 16, 1968; s. Arthur P. and Josephine E. Ochoa; m. Daniele J. Worth, Jan. 25, 1998; children: Madeleine Worth, Eloise Worth. BA, U. of So. California, 1986—90; JD, Yale Law Sch., 1992—95. Bar: State of Calif. 1995. Policy coord. Youth Svc. Am., Washington, 1990—92; assoc. O'Melveny & Myers LLP, LA, Calif., 1995—98; atty. Irell & Manella LLP, Century City, 1998—2001; dir. planned giving Cedars-Sinai Med. Ctr., LA, 2001—04, sr. v.p. cmty. rels., 2004—. Mem. and sec., bd. of directors Youth Svc. Am., Washington, 1997—98; adj. faculty mem., mba program U. of Judaism, LA, 2001—03; adv. bd. mem. Neopets Found., Glendale, 2001—06. Chmn. tax exempt orgn. com. LA County Bar Assn., 2004; mem., bd. of trustees Mexican Am. Bar Found., LA, 2002—; chair tax expert orgn. com. L.A. County Bar Assn., 2004—05. Mem.: Nat. Eagle Scout Assn., Jonathan Club (L.A.), Yale Club N.Y.C., Phi Beta Kappa. Office: Cedars-Sinai Med Ctr 8700 Beverly Blvd Ste 2416 Los Angeles CA 90048 E-mail: ochoaa@cshs.org.

OCHOA, ELLEN, astronaut; b. LA, May 10, 1958; d. Roseanne Ochoa; m. Coe Fulmer Miles; one son. BS in Physics, San Diego State U., 1980; MSEE, Stanford U., 1981, PhD in EE, 1985. Rsch. engr. Sandia Nat. Labs., Livermore, Calif., 1985—88; chief intelligent systems tech. br. NASA/Ames Rsch. Ctr./Moffet Field Naval Air Sta., Mountain View, Calif.; Astronaut NASA, Houston, 1991—, dep. dir., flight crew ops. Recipient two Space Act Tech Brief Awards, 1992, Space Flight Medals 1993, 1994, 1999, 2002; Outstanding Leadership Medal, 1995, Exceptional Svc. Medal, 1997, Women in Aerospace Outstanding Achievement Award, the Hispanic Engr. Albert Baez Award for Outstanding Tech. Contribution to Humanity, the Hispanic Heritage Leadership Award, San Diego State U. Alumna of the Year. Mem. Optical Soc. Am., Am. Inst. Aeronautics and Astronautics, Phi Beta Kappa, Sigma Xi, Pres. Commn. on the Celebration of Women in Am. History. Achievements include being the first female Hispanic astronaut chosen for Space Shuttle program. Office: NASA Johnson Space Ctr Astronaut Office Houston TX 77058

OCHOA, JUAN A., not-for-profit business association executive; b. 1970; Citizenship coord. United Neighborhood Orgn.; project mgr. Hispanic Am. Constrn. Industry Assn.; pres., CEO Ill. Hispanic C. of C. Bd. dirs. Ill. Sports Facilities Authority, 2001; mem. Congl. Hispanic Caucus Inst., 2005; vice chair Econ. Com., Transition Team. Machine gunner USMC, combat vet., Gulf War. Office: Illinois Hispanic Chamber of Commerce 111 W Washington Ste 1660 Chicago IL 60602 Office Phone: 312-425-9500. Office Fax: 312-425-9510. *

OCHOA, LORENA, professional golfer; b. Guadalajara, Mex., Nov. 15, 1981; d. Javier and Marcela. Student, U. Ariz., 2000—02. Profl. golfer LPGA, 2003—. Five-time U.S. 8-12 Jr. World Championship winner; NCAA Player of Yr., 2001; NCAA Freshman of Yr., 01; finished second NCAA Championships, 2001; finished first place Futures Tour money list, 2002. Named Female Player of Yr., Golf Writers Assn. Am., 2006, Female Athlete of Yr., AP, 2006; recipient Nat. Sports award, Mex., 2001, Nancy Lopez award for Outstanding Amateur Accomplishments, 2002, Louise Suggs Rolex Rookie of Yr. award, LPGA, 2003, Rolex Player of Yr. award, 2006. Achievements include winning LPGA Tour events including the Franklin Am. Mortgage Championship, 2004, Wachovia LPGA Classic, 2004, Wegmans LPGA, 2005, 07, Takefuji Classic, 2006, Sybase Classic Presented by Lincoln Mercury, 2006, Wendy's Championship for Children, 2006; winner, Corona Morelia Championship, 2006, Samsung World Championship, 2006, Tournament of Champions, 2006, Safeway Internat., 2007, Sybase Classic, 2007, Women's British Open, 2007, Can. Women's Open, 2007, Safeway Classic, 2007; topped $1 million in earnings in 2002 and 2005. Avocations: triathalons, marathons, mountain climbing, tennis, basketball, accordion. Office: c/o LPGA 100 International Golf Dr Daytona Beach FL 32124-1092 *

OCHOA, MANUEL, JR., oncologist; b. NYC, Apr. 22, 1930; s. Manuel and Maria (Diaz) O.; m. Suzanne Ellen Recca, Sept. 1, 1956; children: Elizabeth, Suzanne Elise. AB, Columbia Coll., 1951; MD, Columbia U., 1955. Diplomate Am. Bd. Internal Medicine; lic. physician, NY, Mass. Asst. in medicine U. Rochester Med. Sch., NY, 1958-61; instr. medicine, assoc., asst. prof. Columbia U., NYC, 1964-68; attending physician Meml. Sloan-Kettering Cancer Ctr., NYC, 1973—. Investigator Marine Biol. Lab., Woods Hole, Mass., 1965; assoc. prof. clin. medicine Cornell U., NYC, 1982-96, prof., 1996—; cons. Harlem Hosp. Ctr., NYC, 1966-68, Kingston Hosp., NY, 1970-85; vis. prof. U. Hawaii, Honolulu, 1971, U. Mex., Mexico City, 1979. Contbr. articles to profl. jours. Capt. USAF, 1956-58, ETO. Fellow Lalor Found., 1965. Fellow ACP, ACS. Republican. Roman Catholic. Achievements include discovery of genetic code and protein synthesis in cancer cells, cancer chemotherapy. Home: 82 E Middle Patent Rd Bedford NY 10506-2106 Office: Meml Sloan-Kettering Cancer Ctr 1275 York Ave New York NY 10021-6007 Office Phone: 212-639-8245.

OCHOA-BRILLEMBOURG, HILDA MARGARITA, investment banker; b. July 8, 1944; BS in Econs., U. Catolica Andres Bello, Caracas, Venezuela; MPA, Harvard U.; postgrad. in fin., Harvard Bus. Sch. Chief investment officer, pension investment div. World Bank, 1976—87; mng. dir. Emerging Markets Investment Corp.; founder, pres., CEO Strategic Investment Group, 1987—. Bd. dirs. Harvard Mgmt. Co., Bank Fund Staff Fed. Credit Union, Gen. Mills, Inc., McGraw-Hill Inc.; treas. C.A. Luz Electrica de Venezuela, Caracas, 1967—71; lectr. U. Catolica Andres Bello, 1970; ind. cons. in econs. and fin. Published articles in Fin. Analyst Jour. and Pensions & Investments. Bd. dirs. Nat. Symphony Orch., Washington Nat. Opera; chmn. bd. dirs. Youth Orch. of the Americas; mem. investment com. Rockefeller Family Fund; vice chair, Group of 50 Carnegie Endowment for Internat. Peace; mem. adv. com. Rockefeller Ctr. for Latin Am. Studies, The Hauser Ctr. at Harvard U.; bd. dirs. Fulbright Found., Atlantic Coun. US. Fulbright-Hays fellow. Office: 1001 19th St N 16th Fl Arlington VA 22209-1722 Office Phone: 703-243-4433.

OCHS, CAROL REBECCA, theologian, writer, theology studies educator, philosopher; b. NYC, May 7, 1939; d. Herman and Clara Florence (Michaels) Blumenthal; m. Michael Ochs, Sept. 27, 1959; children: Elisabeth Amy, Miriam Adina. BA, CUNY, 1960, MA, 1964; PhD, Brandeis U., 1968. Philosophy lectr. CUNY, 1964-65; from asst. prof. to prof. philosophy Simmons Coll., Boston, 1967-92, prof. emerita, 1992—. Adj. faculty Grad. Sch. Union Inst., Cin., 1992—97, Hebrew Union Coll.-Jewish Inst. Religion, NYC, 1994—97, dir. grad. studies, vis. prof. philosophy, 1997—2001, dir. grad. studies, adj. prof. Jewish Religious Thought, 2001—; cons. Inst. for Svc. to Higher Edn., Chestnut Hill, Mass., 1972, St. Mary's Coll., South Bend, Ind., 1980; scholar-in-residence Hollins Coll., Roanoke, Va., 1987, numerous temples and synagogues; mem. selection com. Kent Postdoctoral Fellowships Bunting Inst., Radcliffe Coll.; lectr. in field. Author: Behind the Sex of God: Toward a New Consciousness Transcending Matriarchy and Patriarchy, 1977, Women and Spirituality, 1983, 2d edit., 1997, An Ascent to Joy: Transforming Deadness of Spirit, 1989, The Noah Paradox: Time as Burden, Time as Blessing, 1991, Song of the Self: Biblical Spirituality and Human Holiness, 1994, Jewish Spiritual Guidance, 1997, Our Lives as Torah: Finding God in Our Own Stories, 2001, Reaching Godward: Voices from Jewish Spiritual Guidance, 2004; contbr. articles to profl. jours. Mem. Jewish-Cath. Dialogue, Boston, 1989-93; mem. Cath.-Jewish com. Archdiocese of Boston, 1989-93. Fellow NEH, 1976, 88, Nat. Humanities Inst., U. Chgo., 1978-79, Danforth Found., 1981-86, Coolidge Rsch., Colloquium, 1985, Resource Theologian, 1995-99. Fellow Soc. for Values in Higher Edn. (bd. dirs. 1982-88, chair ctrl. com. 1985-87, 2003—, v.p. 2004-), Assn. for Religion and Intellectual Life (mem. editl. bd. 1986—). Office: Hebrew Union Coll 1 W 4th St New York NY 10012 Office Phone: 212-824-2267. Personal E-mail: cochs@earthlink.net.

OCHS, MICHAEL, editor, librarian, music educator; b. Cologne, Germany, Feb. 1, 1937; came to U.S., 1939, naturalized, 1945; s. Isaac Julius and Claire (Baum) O.; m. Carol Rebecca Blumenthal, Sept. 27, 1959; children— Elisabeth Amy, Miriam Adina BA, CCNY, 1958; MS, Columbia U., 1963; A.M., NYU, 1964; D.A., Simmons Coll., 1975. Cataloguer CCNY, 1963-65, lectr. in music, 1964; music libr. Brandeis U., Waltham, Mass., 1965-68, creative arts libr., 1968-74; asst. prof. libr. sci. Simmons Coll., Boston, 1974-78; libr. Eda Kuhn Loeb Music Libr., Harvard U., Cambridge, Mass., 1978-88, Richard F. French libr., 1988-92; lectr. music Harvard U., Cambridge, Mass., 1978-81, sr. lectr. music, 1981-92, also libr. cons., 1977-78; music editor W. W. Norton and Co., NYC, 1992-2001; pres. Ochs Editl., 2001—. Libr. cons. Biblioteca Berenson, Florence, Italy, 1983, Columbia U., 1987; project dir. U.S. Répertoire International des Sources Musicales Manuscript Inventory Ctr. at Harvard U., NEH, Cambridge, Mass., 1985-88. Editor Notes, Jour. Music Libr. Assn., 1987-92, Music Librarianship in America, 1991; contbr. articles to profl. jours., 1976—. Mem. Am. Musicol. Soc. (bd. dirs. 2000-02), Internat. Assn. Music Librs. (pres. rsch. librs. br. 1987-90), Music Libr. Assn. (bd. dirs. 1976-78, pres. 1993-95). Office Phone: 212-987-1089. Personal E-mail: mochsed@earthlink.net.

OCHS, SIDNEY, neurophysiology researcher, educator; b. Fall River, Mass., June 30, 1924; s. Nathan and Rose (Kniaz) O.; m. Bess Ratner; children: Rachel F., Raymond S. Susan B. PhD in Physiology, U. Chgo., 1952. Rsch. assoc. Ill. Neuropsychiat. Inst., Chgo., 1952-54; rsch. fellow Calif. Inst. Tech., Pasadena, 1954-56; asst. prof. dept. physiology U. Tex. Med. Br., Galveston, 1956-58; assoc. prof. dept. physiology Ind. U., Indpls., 1958-61, prof., 1961-94, prof. emeritus, 1994—. Author: Elements of Neurophysiology, 1965, Axoplasmic Transport and Its Relation to Other Nerve Functions, 1982, A History of Nerve Functions: From Animal Spirits to Molecular Mechanisms, 2004; founding editor, editor-in-chief: Devel. Neurobiology (formerly Jour. Neurobiology), 1969-76, assoc. editor, 1977-86. With US Army, 1943—45. Mem. Internat. Brain Rsch. Orgn., Internat. Soc. Neurochemistry, Internat. Soc. Hist. Neurosciences, Am. Physiol. Soc., Soc. Neurosci., Am. Soc. Neurochemistry, Peripheral Nerve Soc., Hist. Sci. Soc. Democrat. Jewish. Avocations: amateur radio, history. Office: Ind U Med Ctr Dept Cellular & Integ Physiology 635 Barnhill Dr Indianapolis IN 46202-5126 Office Phone: 317-274-7940. Business E-Mail: sochs@iupui.edu.

OCHS, WALTER J., civil engineer, consultant; b. Springfield, Minn., May 20, 1934; s. Walter Minrod and Cleo (Schultz) O.; m. Connie Mae Strate, Sept. 15, 1956; children: Julie, Brian. BS in Agrl. Engring., South Dakota U., 1957. Registered profl. civil engr., Mich. Engr. in training USDA, Soil Conservation Svc., Watertown, S.D., 1957-58, project engr. Britton, S.D., 1958-61, area engr. Sioux Falls, S.D., 1961-63, asst. state conservation engr. East Lansing, Mich., 1963-66, state conservation engr., 1966-69, asst. state conservationist Saint Paul, Minn., 1969-71, nat. drainage engr. Washington, 1971-86; drainage adviser World Bank, Washington, 1986-96; internat. ind. water mgmt. cons., 1996—. Bd. dirs. Internat. Inst. for Land Reclamation and Improvement Postgrad Land Drainage Course, The Netherlands, 1990-98; particpated in project work over 30 countries; mem. Internat. Commn. Irrigation and Drainage. Contbr. to profl. jours. Named Fed. Engr. of Yr., NSPE, 1982; recipient Outstanding Alumnus award S.D. State U., 1977, Outstanding Contbn. award Corrugated Plastic Tubing Assn., 1981, Svc. to the Profession award U.S. Com. on Irrigation and Drainage, 2004; named to Internat. Drainage Hall of Fame, 1996. Fellow: Am. Soc. Agrl. Engrs.; mem.: ASCE (chmn. drainage com. 1975—76, Royce J. Tipton award 2001). Office: 6731 Fern Ln Annandale VA 22003-1903 E-mail: wochs@hotmail.com.

OCHSNER, JOHN LOCKWOOD, thoracic-cardiovascular surgeon; b. Madison, Wis., Feb. 10, 1927; s. Edward William Alton and Isabel (Lockwood) O.; m. Mary Lou Hannon, Mar. 20, 1954; children: John L., Joby Hannon, Katherine Lockwood, Frank Hannon. MD, Tulane U., 1952; hon. diploma (hon.), U. Delgado, San Salvador, El Salvador, 1999. Diplomate Am. Bd. Thoracic Surgery (chmn. 1993-95), Am. Bd. Surgery, Am. Bd. Vascular Surgery. Intern Univ. Mich. Hosp., Ann Arbor, 1952-53, resident, 1953-54, Baylor U. Affiliated Hosp., Houston, 1956-58, 1958-59; chief surg. resident Tex. Children's Hosp., 1959-60; instr. Baylor U., Houston, 1960-61; mem. staff Ochsner Clinic, New Orleans, 1961—, chmn. dept. surgery, 1966-87, chmn. emeritus dept surgery, 1987—; clin. asst. prof. Tulane U., New Orleans, 1961-65, clin. assoc. prof., 1965-70, clin. prof. surgery, 1970—. Vis. prof. to more then 40 univs. and colls. Author: (with others) Coronary Artery Surgery, 1978. Pres. Tennis Patrons Assn. New Orleans, 1972; image amb. City of New Orleans, 1982; bd. dirs. Internat. Trade Mart, New Orleans, 1983. Capt. USAF, 1954-56. Named Rex, King of Carnival, Mardi Gras, New Orleans, 1990, Grand Marshall, Oktoberfest, 1990, 1992; recipient award, Life Mag., 1961, Golden Plate Acad. Achievement award, 1962, award of distinction, Am. Heart Assn. La., 1976, Svc. award, Cystic Fibrosis Rsch. Found., 1977—78, medal of honor, Ecuador, 1981, Crystal Achievement award, Child's Wish of Greater New Orleans, 1987, Young Leadership Coun. award, 1987, medal of honor, Czechoslovakian Surg. Soc., 1996, Honor of Achievement, Am. Heart Assn., 1997, Internat. Recognition award, Denton A. Cooley Cardiovasc. Surg. Soc., 1998, Outstanding Alumnus award, Tulane Sch. Medicine, 1998, Spirit of Love award, Ronald McDonald House Charities, 1999, DeBakey award, DeBakey Internat. Surg. Soc., 2000, Outstanding Physician award, Orleans Parish Med. Soc., 2002, Weiss Brotherhood award, New Orleans chpt. Nat. Conf. for Cmty. and Justice, 2002, Outstanding Person award, Family Svc. Greater New Orleans, 2004, DeBakey medal, Covenant Heart Inst., 2007, Order of the Plimsoll Mark, World Trade Ctr. Mem. Am. Assn. Thoracic Surgery (sec. 1979-83, pres. 1992-93), New Orleans Surg. Soc. (pres. 1977-78), So. Surg. Assn. (pres. 1991), So. Assn. for Vascular Surgery (pres. 1983), Boston Club, La. Club, New Orleans Country Club, City Club, Alpha Omega Alpha. Republican. Office: Ochsner Clinic Found 1514 Jefferson Hwy BH 231 New Orleans LA 70121-2483 Home: 170 Walnut St 9-H New Orleans LA 70118

OCKERBLOOM, RICHARD C., newspaper executive; b. Medford, Mass., Dec. 19, 1929; s. Carl F. and Helen C. (Haraden) O.; m. Anne Joan Torpey, Sept. 17, 1955; children: Catherine, Carl (dec.), Gail, Mark, John, Peter. BSBA, Northeastern U., 1952; D Pub. Svc. (hon.), Westfield State Coll., 1989; LLD (hon.), Northeastern U., 1995. With Boston Globe, 1948—, salesman, 1955-63, asst. nat. advt. mgr., 1963-70, nat. advt. mgr., 1970-72, asst. advt. dir., 1972-73, advt. dir., 1973-77, v.p. mktg. and sales, 1977-81, exec. v.p., 1981—, gen. mgr., chief operating officer, 1984-86, pres., chief operating officer, 1986-93, vice chmn., 1993-94; ret.; retired; chmn. bd. Met. Sunday Newspapers. Bd. dirs. Greater Boston Conv. and Visitors Bur., Winchester Hosp., United Way Mass. Bay; vice chmn. bd. trustees Northeastern U.; mem. adv. bd. U. Mass., Boston. With U.S. Army, 1952-54. Mem. Algonquin Club (pres.), Winchester Country Club, Phi Kappa Phi. Nat. Honor Soc. Home: 80 Arlington St Winchester MA 01890-3735

OCKERMAN, HERBERT W., agricultural studies educator; b. Chaplin, Ky., Jan. 16, 1932; m. Frances Ockerman (dec.). BS with Distinction, U. Ky., 1954, MS, 1958; PhD, N.C. State U., 1962; postgrad., Air U., 1964-70, Ohio State U., 1974, postgrad., 1983, postgrad., 1987, postgrad., 2001, postgrad., 2003—07; PhD (hon.), Wyzial U., Poland, 2004. Asst. prof. Ohio State U., Columbus, 1961-66, assoc. prof., 1966-71, prof., 1971—. Former mem. Inst. Nutrition and Food Tech.; judge regional and state h.s. sci. fairs, 1965—, Ham Contest, Ky. State Fair, Sausage and Ham Contest, Ohio Meat Processing Groups, 1965; cons. Am. Meat Inst., 1977-88, USDA, 1977-2003, CRC Press., Inc., 1988—; bd. examiners U. Calcutta, 1987-88; examiner U. Mysore, India, 1990-97, U. We. Sydney, Australia, 2005, U. Newcastle, Australia, 2005-07; expert witness, various firms, 1992—, UN expert 95; expert cons. com. FAO/WHO, 2003; hon. mem. vet., med. faculty Assiut U., Egypt; adv. bd. Bull. Vet. Inst. Poland, 2004—; chmn. sci. bd. Egyptian Jour. Meat Sci. and Tech.; presenter, cons. in field. Chmn. sci. bd.: Egyptian Jour. Molecular Sci. and Tech., 2002; contbr. more than 222 articles to profl. jours., more than 126 chpts. to books. Comdr. pilot USAF, 1955-58. Fisher Packing scholar; named Highest Individual in Beef Grading, Kansas City Meat Judging Contest, 1952, Hall of Disting. Alumni, U. Ky., 1995; recipient Am. Soc. Animal Sci. Meat Rsch. award Lilly Rsch. Labs., 1987, Appreciation cert. Ohio Assn. Meat Processors, 1987-2006, Profl. Devel. award Cahill Faculty, commendation Ohio Ho. of Reps., Merit Svc. badge Polish Govt., plaque Argentina Nat. Meat Bd., Animal Sci. award Roussel UCALF, France, U. Assiuit, Egypt, Silver Platter award Nat. Meat Bd., Sec. Agr., Livestock and Fishery, Argentina, Svc. award Coun. Grad. Students, Pomerance Tchg. award, Outstanding Alumni award U. Ky., Outstanding Ednl. Achievements award Argentine Soc. Agr., Coop. award Vet. Faculty. U. Cordoba, Svc. award Panoma Legis. Br., Brazil; Vet. Faculty award U. Cordoba, Spain, 1982, 94, award Nat. Chung-Hsing U., 1982, 95, You Are The Best award INTA Sci., 1997, award Vet. Mus. Ciechanowcu, Poland, Internat. award Assn. Nat. Tech. en Alimentos de Mexico, Can. Indst. Food Sci. and Tech., 1998, Appreciation plaque Republic of Argentina, 1999, Candle Stick of Knowledge award Ludhiana U., Punjab, India, 1999, Internat. award Am. Meat Sci. Assn., 1999, 2000, Appreciation plaque Am. Coll. Commerce, Taiwan, 1999, plaque Selcuk U., Turkey, 1999, Folklore and Cultural memento Sudanese Socs., Sudan U., 1999, Homage and Acknowledgment award Argentine Sec. Agr., 2000, Internat. award Am. Most. Sci. Assn., 2000, Most Honored Guest award Weifang, China, 2001, World History award Jhadong U., China, 2001, plaque Congress of Ham, Cordoba, Spain, 2001, Michal Oczapowski award Polish Acad. Sci., 2002, Sausage Maker award Poland, 2001, Great Educator award China, 2001, Silver Medallion award INTA Argentina, 2001, Pub. award Taiwan, 2002, Animal Sci. plaque, China, 2002, Food award China, 2002, Publ. award Dayeh U., Taiwan, 2003, Coop. award Cath. U., Argentina, 2004, Lifetime Achievement award PAU India, 2005, Sci. award Argentina Nat. Acad., 2006, The World is your Classroom award DaYeh U., 2006, numerous others; co-recipient 2 plaques Al Falat HS, India, 2006; plaque Tangai U., Taiwan; plaque for 36,000 books Da Yeh U., Yunnan U., China, Symobolism award U. Turkey, Predsl. plaque Chkurova, Turkey. Mem. NAS, NCR, ASTM, Am. Meat Sci. Assn., Am. Soc. Animal Sci. (Rsch. award 1987), Reciprocal Meat Conf., European Meeting of Meat Rsch. Workers, Polish Vet. Soc. (hon.), Inst. Food Technologists (nat. and OVS chpts.), Inst. Food Tech. (Internat. award 1998, 2000), Can. Meat Sci. Assn., Internat. Congress Meat Sci. and Tech., Rsch. in Basic Sci., Nat. Acad. Agronomy and Vet. Medicine Argentina(corr. academic), Phi Beta Delta (treas. 1987, pres. 1991, Internat. scholar award 1991, Internat. Faculty award 1991, Presdl. medallion award), Gamma Sigma Delta (Rsch. award 1977, Internat. award of merit 1988), Sigma Xi (outstanding advisor in coll. award 1995), Phi Beta Kappa (Outstanding Tchg. award 1997, Extension Diversity award 1997, Pomerene Tchg. Enhancement award 1997, Outstanding Internat. Faculty award 1997), Internat. Gamma Sigma Delta (Disting. Achievement Nat. award 1998), Phi Kappa Phi. Office: Ohio State U Meat Lab Animal Sci 2029 Fyffe Rd Columbus OH 43210-1007 Office Phone: 614-292-2201. Business E-Mail: ockerman.2@osu.edu.

OCKEY, RONALD J., lawyer; b. Green River, Wyo., June 12, 1934; s. Theron G. and Ruby O. (Sackett) O.; m. Arline M. Hawkins, Nov. 27, 1957; children: Carolyn S. Ockey Baggett, Deborah K. Ockey Christiansen, David, Kathleen M. Ockey Hellewell, Valerie Ockey Sachs, Robert. BA, U. Utah, Salt Lake City, 1959, postgrad., 1959-60; JD with honors, George Wash. U., Washington, DC, 1966. Bar: Colo. 1967, Utah 1968, US Dist. Ct. Colo. 1967, US Dist. Ct. Utah 1968, US Ct. Appeals (10th cir.) 1969, US Ct. Claims 1987. Missionary to France for Mormon Ch., 1954-57; law clk. to judge U.S. Dist. Ct. Colo., 1966-67; assoc. ptnr., shareholder, v.p., treas., dir. Jones, Waldo, Holbrook & McDonough, Salt Lake City, 1967-91; pres. IntelliTrans Internat. Corp., 1992-94; mem. Utah Ho. of Reps., 1988-90, Utah State Senate, 1991-94; of counsel Mackey Price & Williams, Salt Lake City, 1995-98; asst. atty. gen. Utah, 1998—. Trustee SmartUtah, Inc., 1995-2002; trustee Utah Tech. Fin. Corp., 1995-98; lectr. in securities, pub. fin. and bankruptcy law. Mem. editl. bd. Utah Bar Jour., 1973-75; mem. staff and bd. editors George Washington Law Rev., 1964-66; contbr. articles to profl. jours. State govtl. affairs chair Utah Jaycees, 1969; del. state Rep. Convs., 1972-74, 76-78, 80-82, 84-86, 94-96, del. Salt Lake County Rep. Conv., 1978-80, 88-92; sec. Wright for Gov. campaign, 1980; legis. dist. chmn. Utah Rep. Party, 1983-87; trustee Food for Poland, 1981-85, pres., trustee Unity to Assist Humanity Alliance, 1992-95; bd. dirs. Utah Opera Co., 1991-94; trustee Utah Info. Tech. Assn., 1991-2000. Lt. US Army, 1960-66, to capt. JAG, USAR, 1966-81. Mem. ABA, Utah State Bar Assn. (various coms.), Nat. Assn. Bond Lawyers (chmn. con. on state legislation 1982-85), George Washington U. Law Alumni Assn. (bd. dirs. 1981-85), Order of Coif, Phi Delta Phi. Home: 4502 Crest Oak Cir Salt Lake City UT 84124-3825 Home Phone: 801-278-3809; Office Phone: 801-366-0359. Business E-Mail: rockey@utah.gov.

OCKWELL, GARY, electrical engineer, marketing professional; s. Nick Babchuk and Linda Bland; m. Linda Grelle Ockwell, Aug. 11, 1995; children: Tanis L., Tiffany E. Karoly, Matthew Gary, Grant Byrum. BS in Elec. Engring., U. of Sask., Saskatoon, 1973. Mgr. control dept. Sask. Power Corp., Regina, Saskatchewan, Canada, 1973—85; product mgr. Harris Controls Divsn., Melbourne, Fla., 1985—95; dir. mktg. and tech. support Advanced Control Sys., Norcross, Ga., 1995—. Adult bible study tchr. old testament CrossPointe Ch., Duluth, Ga., 2006—. Achievements include first to use smart grid distribution network technologies. Office: Advanced Control Sys 2755 Northwoods Pky Norcross GA 30071 Home Phone: 770-232-1590; Office Phone: 770-446-8854. Office Fax: 770-448-0857. Business E-Mail: gary.ockwell@acsatlanta.com.

O'CLAIR, KATHERINE CLEMENS, library and information scientist; m. Tim O'Clair, 2005. BS in Environ. Sci., Nazarteth Coll., 2001; MS in Libr. and Info. Sci., Fla. State U., 2004. Intern Fletcher Libr. Ariz. State U., asst. libr., sci. reference libr. Life Sciences, Noble Sci. and Engring. Libr., 2005—. Named one of the Movers & Shakers, Libr. Jour., 2007. Mem.: Ariz. Libr. Assn. (co-chair Coll. and Univ. Divsn.), Spl. Libraries Assn. (New Mem. of Yr. 2005). Office: Univ Libraries Ariz State Univ PO Box 871006 Tempe AZ 85287 Office Phone: 480-965-5964. E-mail: katherine.oclair@asu.edu.

O'CONNELL, BRIAN, community organizer, educator, writer; b. Worcester, Mass., Jan. 23, 1930; s. Thomas J. and Mary (Carroll) O'C.; m. Ann C. Brown, July 11, 1953; children: Todd, Tracey, Matthew. BA, Tufts Coll., Medford, Mass., 1953; postgrad., Maxwell Sch. Citizenship and Pub. Adminstrn., 1953-54; also numerous hon. degrees. Field rep. Am. Heart Assn., Pa., 1954-56, Md. exec. dir., 1956—61, Calif. exec. dir., 1961—66; exec. dir. Nat. Assn. Mental Health, 1966-78, dir. emeritus, 1978—; pres. Nat. Council on Philanthropy, 1978-80; exec. dir. Coalition of Nat. Vol. Orgns., 1978-80; pres. Ind. Sector, 1980-95, founding pres., pres. emeritus, 1995—; prof. pub. svc. Tufts U., Medford, Mass., 1995—2006. Mem. U.S. Pres.'s Com. Employment of Handicapped, 1966-68; chmn. Liaison Group Mental Health, 1969-72. Author: Effective Leadership in Voluntary Organizations, 1976, Finding Values That Work: The Search for Fulfillment, 1977, America's Voluntary Spirit, A Book of Readings, 1983, The Board Members Book, 1985, Philanthropy in Action, 1987, Our Organization, 1987, Volunteers in Action, 1989, People Power: Service Advocacy, Empowerment, 1994, Board Overboard, 1995, Powered By Coalition: The Story of Independent Sector, 1997, Voices from the Heart: In Celebration of America's Volunteers, 1999, Civil Society: The Underpinnings of American Democracy, 1999, Fifty Years in Public Causes: Stories From a Road Les Traveled, 2005. Mem. Alumni Coun. Tufts U., 1970-80, trustee, 1988-2000, trustee emeritus, 2000—, chmn. pres. search com., 1992; trustee Points of Light Found., 1989-95; bd. dirs. Hogg Found., 1990-95; chmn. organizing com., 1st chmn. Civicus: World Alliance for Citizen Participation, 1992-96; bd. dirs. E.M. Kauffman Found., 1994—2003, BridgeSpan Group, 1999—, Cape Cod Found., 2003—. Recipient outstanding agy. prof. award United Way Am., 1979, Lincoln Filene Citizenship award, 1985, John W. Gardner Leadership award, 1994, Gold Key award Am. Soc. Assn. Execs., 1994, Chmns. award, NSFRE, 1994, The Tiffany award, 1998. Fellow Am. Pub. Health Assn., Nat. Acad. Pub. Adminstrn. (trustee 1993-2000), Nat. Com. Patients' Rights (chmn. 1975-77). Home: 50 Chase St Chatham MA 02633-2404 Office Phone: 508-945-2250.

O'CONNELL, BRIAN MICHAEL, computer scientist, educator; b. Hartford, Conn., Nov. 2, 1960; s. Robert F. and Elizabeth S. O'Connell; m. Sarah E. Cox, Oct. 31, 2000. BA, Trinity Coll., Hartford, 1983; JD, U. Conn., 1987. Bar: Conn. 1988, U.S. Supreme Ct. 1992. Assoc. prof. ethics law, computing Ctrl. Conn. State U., New Britain, 1997—. Recipient Franklyn S. Haiman, Nat. Commn. Assn., 1999. Mem.: IEEE (pres. social implications tech. 2003, 2005), IEEE Computer Soc. (bd. govs. 2000—). Office: Central Conn State Univ 1615 Stanley St New Britain CT 06050 Office Phone: 860-832-2718. E-mail: oconnellb@ccsu.edu.

O'CONNELL, CARMELA DIGRISTINA, appraisal executive, consultant; b. Johnstown, Pa., Nov. 8, 1925; d. Salvatore and Josephine (Riggio) Digristina; m. Maurice F. O'Connell, Sept. 21, 1974 (dec. Feb. 1984); children: Geraldine, John, Bernard. Diploma, Eastern Secretarial Sch., NYC, Sch. Interior Design. From typist to sec.-treas. Philip P. Masterson Co., NYC, 1942-72; exec. v.p., bd. dirs. Masterson & O'Connell Inc., NYC, 1972-80, cons., 1981—; founder, pres. N.Y. Appraisal Corp., NYC, 1971-80; co-founder, pres. Park Ave. Appraisal, NYC, 1981—. Mem. N.Y. Rep. Com., 1974—, Met. Opera Guild, N.Y.C., 1986; chmn. Ch. of Our Saviour, N.Y.C., 1986; mem. Ladies of Charity, Cath. Charities Archdiocese of N.Y., 1990; bd. dirs. 80 Park Avenue Condominiums, 1997—. Recipient Amita award for Bus. Woman of Yr., 1977, Lena Madesin Phillips award N.Y. League/Fortune 500 Bus. and Profl. Women, 1989. Mem. Nat. Fedn. Bus. and Profl. Women's Clubs Inc. (2d v.p. 1964, 1st v.p. 1966). Roman Catholic. Home: 2421 Old Collier Rd Land O Lakes FL 34639 Office Phone: 813-948-8941.

O'CONNELL, DANIEL CRAIG, retired psychologist, educator; b. Sand Springs, Okla., May 20, 1928; s. John Albert and Letitia Rutherford (McGinnis) O'C. BA, St. Louis U., 1951, Ph.L., 1952, MA, 1953, S.T.L., 1960; PhD, U. Ill., 1963. Joined Soc. of Jesus, 1945; asst. prof. psychology St. Louis U., 1964-66, asso. prof., 1966-72, prof., 1972-80, trustee, 1973-78, pres., 1974-78; prof. psychology Loyola U., Chgo., 1980-89, Georgetown U., Washington, 1990-98, emeritus, 1998—, chmn., 1991-96. Vis. prof. U. Melbourne, Australia, 1972, U. Kans., 1978-79, Georgetown U., 1986, Loyola U., Chgo., 1998-2003; Humboldt fellow Psychol. Inst. Free U. Berlin, 1968; sr. Fulbright lectr. Kassel U., W. Ger., 1979-80. Author: Critical Essays on Language Use and Psychology, 1988; contbr. articles to profl. jours. Recipient Nancy McNeir Ring award for outstanding teaching St. Louis U., 1969; NSF fellow, 1961, 63, 65, 68; Humboldt Found. grantee, 1973; Humboldt fellow Tech. U. of Berlin, 1987. Fellow: APA, Mo. Psychol. Assn.; mem.: AAAS, AAUP, Mo. Acad. Sci., N.Y. Acad. Sci., Psychonomic Soc., Eastern Psychol. Assn., Southwestern Psychol. Assn., Midwestern Psychol. Assn., Soc. Scientific Study of Religion, Psychologists Interested in Religious Issues, Phi Beta Kappa. Home and Office: 4517 W Pine Blvd Saint Louis MO 63108-2109 Office Phone: 314-758-7143. Business E-Mail: doconnell@jesuits-mis.org. *Were it over, it would have been more than my expected share already. The challenge of learning to serve others has moved it along at a quick pace, and I am grateful that I have always received more than I've been able to give in return—from the Lord and from many good people.*

O'CONNELL, DANIEL FRANCIS, lawyer; b. Orange, NJ, May 5, 1943; BS with honors, Villanova U., 1965; JD, Rutgers U., 1968. Bar: NJ 1968, NY 1980, US Supreme Ct. 1980. Ptnr. Lanigan & O'Connell PC, Basking Ridge, NJ, 1969—85; ptnr. mng. ptnr. Shanley & Fisher PC, Morristown, NJ, 1985—99; ptnr., bus. fin. dept., ptnr.-in-charge Drinker Biddle & Reath LLP, Florham Pk., NJ, 1999—, mng. ptnr., mem. mgmt. com., 1999—. Dist. VII ethics com. Supreme Ct. NJ, 1978-83, sec., 1980-83; chmn. NJ Commn. Legal and Ethical Problems in the Delivery of Health Care, 1986-90. Mem. ABA (labor and employment law sect., antitrust law sect., health law sect. 1977—), NJ State Bar Assn. (labor law sect., health and hosp. law sect.), Somerset County Bar Assn. (exec. com. 1977-81, pres. 1979), Am. Health Lawyers Assn., Am. Hosp. Assn. Office: Drinker Biddle & Reath LLP 500 Campus Dr Florham Park NJ 07932-1047 Home Phone: 908-781-7073; Office Phone: 973-549-7160. Office Fax: 973-360-9831. Business E-Mail: daniel.oconnell@dbr.com.

O'CONNELL, DANIEL JAMES, lawyer; b. Evergreen Park, Ill., Aug. 14, 1954; s. Edmund J. and Kathryn J. (Hanna) O'C.; m. Nancy L. Eichler, March 21, 1992; children: Kelly Jacklyn, Kirby Kathryn. BS, Millikin U., 1976; JD, IIT, 1980; postgrad., DePaul U., 1981, U. Mich., 1997—2001; MPH, U. Ill., 2005, postgrad., 2006—. Bar: Ill. 1980, US Dist. Ct. (no. dist.) Ill. 1980, US Dist. Ct. (ctrl. dist.) Ill. 2000, US Dist. Ct. Ariz. 1989. Ins. regulatory counsel Kemper Group, Long Grove, Ill., 1980-81, environ. claims counsel, 1981-82; sr. home office claim counsel Zurich Ins. Cos., Schaumburg, Ill., 1982-83; assoc. Clausen, Miller, Gorman et al, Chgo., 1983-86; ptnr. environ. toxic tort litigation O'Connell & Moroney, P.C., Chgo., 1986-90; ptnr. toxic tort litigation Burditt, Bowles & Radzius, Chgo., 1990-91; ptnr. Daniel J. O'Connell & Assocs., P.C., Elgin, Ill., 1991—2002, O'Connell & O'Sullivan, P.C., Elgin, 2002—03, Daniel J. O'Connell & Assocs., P.C., Elgin, 2003—05, O'Connell, Tivin, Miller & Burns, LLC, 2006—. James S. Kemper Found. scholar, 1972—76. Mem.: ABA, APHA, AAAS, Ill. Bar Assn., Kane County Bar Assn., Def. Rsch. Inst., NY Acad. Scis. Home: 177 Macintosh Ct Glen Ellyn IL 60137-6478 Office Phone: 847-741-4603. E-mail: doconn3@uic.edu.

O'CONNELL, DAVID M., academic administrator, priest; b. Phila., Apr. 21, 1955; BPh magna cum laude, Niagara U., 1978; ThM, Mary Immaculate Seminary, 1981, DivM, 1983; PhD in Canon Law, Cath. U., 1987; Licentiate in Canon Law, Cath. U. Am., 1990; PhD (hon.), Franciscan U. Steubenville, St. Thomas Aquinas Coll., St. Charles Sem., St. John's U. Ordained Cath. priest 1982. Religion tchr., dir. student activities Archbishop Wood H.S. for Boys, Warminster, Pa.; registrar, asst. acad. dean, asst. prof. philosophy, homiletics and canon law Mary Immaculate Seminary, Northampton, Pa., 1987—90; prof. theology St. John's U., Jamaica, NY, 1990—98, acad. dean, dean faculty Coll. Liberal Arts and Scis., 1991—98, assoc. v.p., 1996—98; interim acad. v.p. Niagara U., 1994—95; pres. Cath. U. Am., Washington, 1998—, John Joseph Keane U. prof., 2006—. Canonical cons. and ecclesiastical judge on the tribunals Diocese of Harrisburg, Pa., Diocese of Birmingham, Ala., Diocese of Scranton, Pa.; co-host, commentator during papal visit to U.S. CBS-TV, 1995; trustee Consortium Univs. Washington Met. Area; cons. Vatican Congregation for Cath. Edn., 2005—. Contbr. articles to profl. jours. Trustee Cath. U. Am., St. John's U., Archbishop John Carroll H.S., Washington, Basilica of the Nat. Shrine of the Immaculate Conception; active Greater Washington Bd. Trade; mem. adv. bd. U. St.Thomas, St. Paul. Recipient President's medal, St. John's U., St. Elizabeth Ann Seton award, Nat. Cath. Ednl. Assn., 2006. Mem.: Assn. Cath. Colls. and Univs., Ea. Regional Canon Lawyers Assn., Canon Law Soc. Am. Office: Office Pres Cath Univ Am Nugent Hall 620 Michigan Ave NE Washington DC 20064 Office Phone: 202-319-5100. E-mail: cua-president@cua.edu. *

O'CONNELL, EDWARD JAMES, JR., psychologist, educator, systems administrator, consultant; b. Sterling, Ill., Aug. 15, 1932; s. Edward James and Elizabeth E. (Clapham) O.; m. Pamelia Canon Floyd, Aug. 21, 1959; children— Edward James III, John Matthew BS in Psychology, Ill. Inst. Tech., 1958; MA in Psychology, Northwestern U., 1961, PhD in Psychology, 1962. NSF postdoctoral fellow Carnegie Inst. Tech., Pitts., 1962-63, asst. prof. psychology, 1963-65; psychology faculty Syracuse (N.Y.) U., NY, 1965-93, prof., 1975-93, prof. emeritus, 1993—. Cons. Rand Corp., Santa Monica, Calif., 1962-64, Abt Assocs., Boston, 1970-73, Marcy Psychiat. Hosp., N.Y., 1979-82 Served to cpl. U.S. Army, 1952-54 NSF predoctoral fellow, 1959-62: NSF postdoctoral fellow, 1962-63; Northwestern U. predoctoral fellow, 1958-59 Mem. Sigma Xi. Democrat. Avocations: billiards, computer programming. Address: PO Box 570 Cashiers NC 28717-0570 Office Phone: 828-743-3257. E-mail: ejoconn@dnet.net.

O'CONNELL, HUGH MELLEN, JR., retired architect; b. Oak Park, Ill., Nov. 29, 1929; s. Hugh M. and Helen Mae (Evans) O'C.; m. Frances Ann Small, Apr. 13, 1957; children: Patricia Lynn, Susan Marie, Jeanette Maureen. Student mech. engring., Purdue U., 1948-50; BS in Archtl. Engring, U. Ill., 1953. Registered architect, Ariz., Calif., La., Nev., Nat. Council Archtl. Registration Bds. Designer John Mackel; structural engr. Los Angeles, 1955-57; architect Harnish & Morgan & Causey, Ontario, Calif., 1957-63; pvt. practice Ventura, Calif., 1963—69; architect Andrews/O'Connell, Ventura, 1970-78; dir. engring. div. Naval Constrn. Bn. Center, Port Hueneme, Calif., 1978-91, supervisory architect, 1991-93; ret., 1993. Mem. tech. adv. com. Ventura Coll., 1965-78; sec. Oxnard Citizens' Adv. Com., 1969-79, v.p., 1970-72, pres., 1972—; chmn. Oxnard Beautification Com., 1969, 74, Oxnard Cmty. Block Grant adv. com., 1975-76; mem. Oxnard Planning Commn., 1976-86, vice chmn., 1978-79, chmn., 1980-81. Mem. Oxnard Art-in-Pub. Places Commn., 1988-93, 2003—. Served with AUS, 1953-55. Mem. AIA (emeritus, pres. Ventura chpt. 1973), Am. Concrete Inst., Soc. Am. Registered Architects (Design award 1968, dir. 1970), Am. Legion, Soc. for Preservation and Encouragement of Barbershop Quartet Singing in Am. (chpt. pres. 1979, chpt. sec. 1980-83), Acad. Model Aeros. (#9190 1948—), Channel Islands Condors Club (treas. 1986-99), Sports Flyers Assn., Alpha Rho Chi (Anthemios chpt.). Presbyterian (elder 1963, deacon 1967). Lodges: Kiwanis (pres. 1969, div. sec. 1974-75), Elks. Home and Office: 520 Ivywood Dr Oxnard CA 93030-3527 Personal E-mail: hughoarch@msn.com.

O'CONNELL, JACK, school system administrator; b. Glen Cove, NY, Oct. 8, 1951; m. Doree O'Connell; 1 child, Jennifer Lynn. Student, Ventura Coll.; BA in History, Calif. State U., Fullerton; cert. secondary tchr., Calif. State U., Long Beach, 1975. Tchr. various high schs.; mem. Calif. State Assembly, 1982—94, Calif. State Senate, 1994—2002; state supt. pub. instrn. State of Calif., 2002—. Mem. Santa Barbara County Sch. Bd. Democrat. Office: Calif Dept Edn Ste 5602 1430 N St Sacramento CA 95814 Office Phone: 916-319-0800. *

O'CONNELL, JAMES F., anthropologist, educator; PhD in Anthropology, U. Calif., Berkeley, 1971. Rsch. fellow prehistory Australian Nat. U., 1973—78; faculty to prof. dept. anthropology U. Utah, Salt Lake City, 1978—. Chair dept. anthropology U. Utah, dir. Archaeol. Ctr. Contbr. articles to profl. jours., chapters to books. Fellow: NAS. Office: Dept Anthropology U Utah 270 S 1400 East Salt Lake City UT 84112-0060 E-mail: james.oconnell@anthro.utah.edu.

O'CONNELL, JEANNE, financial planner, insurance broker; b. Stoneham, Mass., Dec. 9, 1951; d. Kenneth Edward and Frances Evelyn (Matulewicz) O'C.; 1 child, Ryan Sulloway. Student, U. Oreg., 1971-72; BFA cum laude, U. Mass.-Amherst, 1974, U. Calif.-Sacramento, summer 1973; postgrad., Northeastern U., 1975; MBA, Suffolk U., 1984. CPCU, CLU; chartered fin. cons.; assoc. in underwriting; enrolled agt. designation. Ins. clk. S.B. Swaim & Co., Boston, 1969-72, Hollis Perrin & Co., Boston, 1972; underwriting asst. Pub. Svc. Mut. Ins. Co., Newton, Mass., 1974-77; personal lines analyst Comml. Union Ins. Co., Boston, 1977-80, sr. personal lines analyst, 1980-83, tech. specialist, 1983-88; pvt. practice fin.

cons., brokerage Boston, 1988—. Instr. ins. and fin. planning Ins. Libr. Boston, 1988—; speaker in field; ind. tax preparer; pub. arbitrator NASD; founder, dir. Red Dragon Arts Coop., Boston, 1983, Ebay Store-Reddragonarts, 2005-; potter, artist Radcliffe Pottery Studio, Boston, 1980-85. Mem. exec. student adv. bd. Suffolk U., 1982—83, student liaison mem. between Exec. MBA Program and regular MBA Program and dean's adv. bd., coord. Exec. MBA Program Policy Seminar Weekend, 1983; v.p., trustee Friends Waltham Pub. Libr., 1998, 1999, asst. treas., 2000, 2000—. Fellow Nat. Tax Practice Inst.; mem. Nat. Soc. Enrolled Agts., Nat. Soc. Accts., Nat. Assn. Tax Preparers, Waltham Garden Club (photographer 1997-), Garden Club Fedn. Mass. (photographer 2007), Delta Mu Delta. Avocations: reading books on tape, photography, rubber stamps, gardening. Studio: 229 School St Waltham MA 02451-4546 Office Phone: 781-891-1721. Personal E-mail: reddragonarts@yahoo.com.

O'CONNELL, JEFFREY, law educator; b. Worcester, Mass., Sept. 28, 1928; s. Thomas Joseph and Mary (Carroll) O'C.; m. Virginia Kearns, Nov. 26, 1960 (dec. 1994); children: Mara, Devin. Grad. cum laude, Phillips Exeter Acad., 1947; AB cum laude, Dartmouth Coll., 1951; JD, Harvard U., 1954. Bar: Mass. 1954, Conn. 1954, Va. 1983, hon. admittance to Ark. and Minn. bar. Instr. speech Tufts U., 1953-54; assoc. Sherburne, Powers & Needham, 1954-57, Hale & Dorr, Boston, 1958-59; asst. prof., then assoc. prof. law U. Iowa Coll. Law, 1959-62; assoc. dir. automobile claims study Harvard Law Sch., 1963-64; assoc. prof. law U. Ill. Coll. Law., 1964-65, prof., 1965-79; prof. law U. Va. Law Sch., 1980-83, John Allan Love prof., 1983-90, Samuel H. McCoy II prof., 1990—, Class of 1948 rsch. prof., 1994-97. Summer vis. prof. Northwestern U., 1963, U. Mich., 1966, 75, So. Meth. U., 1972, U. Tex., 1977, U. Wash., 1979; John Marshall Harlan vis. prof. N.Y. Law Sch., 1991; vis. fellow Centre for Socio-Legal Studies, Wolfson Coll., Oxford (Eng.) U., 1973, 79; Thomas Jefferson vis. fellow Downing Coll. Cambridge U., Eng., 1989; mem. U. Va. Ctr. for Advanced Study, 1980-83. Author: (with R.E. Keeton) Basic Protection for the Traffic Victim, 1965, After Cars Crash: The Need for Legal and Insurance Reform, 1967, (with Arthur Myers) Safety Last: An Indictment of the Auto Industry, 1966, (with R.E. Keeton, John McCord) Crisis in Car Insurance, 1968, (with Wallace Wilson) Car Insurance and Consumer Desires, 1969, The Injury Industry, 1971, (with Rita James Simon) Payment for Pain and Suffering, 1972, Ending Insult to Injury: No-Fault Insurance for Products and Services, 1975, (with Roger Henderson) Tort Law, No-Fault and Beyond, 1975, The Lawsuit Lottery: Only the Lawyers Win, 1979, (with C. Brian Kelly) The Blame Game: Injuries, Insurance and Injustice, 1986, (with Lester Brickman and Michael Horowitz) Rethinking Contingency Fees: A Proposal to Align the Contingency Fee System with its Policy Roots and Ethical Mandates, 1994, (with Peter Bell) Accidental Justice: The Dilemmas of Tort Law, 1997 Mem. Nat. Hwy. Safety Adv. Com., 1967-70; ednl. adv. bd. John Simon Guggenheim Found., 1973-87; bd. dirs. Consumers Union, 1970-76; mem. com. on competitive safeguards and med. aspects of sports NCAA, 1985-87. Served as 1st lt. USAF, 1954-57. Recipient Robert B. McKay award for ins. scholarship Tort and Ins. Practice sect. ABA, 1992; Guggenheim fellow, 1972-73, 79-80. Mem. ABA, Va. Bar Assn., Casque and Gauntlet, Farmington Country Club, Phi Beta Kappa, Psi Upsilon. Democrat. Roman Catholic. Home: 505 Oak Cir Charlottesville VA 22901-3220 Office: U Va Sch Law 580 Massie Rd Charlottesville VA 22903-1738 Home Phone: 434-979-8330; Office Phone: 434-924-7809. Business E-Mail: jo@virginia.edu.

O'CONNELL, KEVIN, lawyer; s. Michael Frederick and Kathryn Agnes (Kelley) O'Connell; m. Mary Adams, July 14, 1990; children: Tiffany W., Elizabeth H., Dana A., Lisel E. AB, Harvard, 1955, JD, 1960. Bar: Calif. 1961. Assoc. firm O'Melveny & Myers, LA, 1960-63; asst. U.S. atty. criminal div. Ctrl. Dist. Calif., LA, 1963-65; staff counsel Gov. Calif. Commn. to Investigate Watts Riot, LA, 1965-66; ptnr. Tuttle & Taylor, LA, 1966-70, Coleman & O'Connell, LA, 1971-75; pvt. practice law LA, 1975-78; of counsel firm Simon & Sheridan, LA, 1978-89; ptnr. Manatt, Phelps & Phillips, LA, 1989—. Adj. prof. law U. So. Calif. Law Sch., 2002—. Bd. editors Harvard Law Rev., 1958—60. Bd. dirs. Calif. Supreme Ct. Hist. Soc.; mem. Los Angeles County Dem. Ctrl. Com., Calif., 1973—74. Lt. USMCR, 1955—57. Recipient Best Lawyers in Am. Mem.: Pacific Coun. on Internat. Policy, Am. Law Inst. Avocation: reading. Home: 426 N Mccadden Pl Los Angeles CA 90004-1026 Office: Manatt Phelps & Phillips Trident Ctr E Tower 11355 W Olympic Blvd Los Angeles CA 90064-1614 Home Phone: 323-935-2116; Office Phone: 310-312-4222. Business E-Mail: koconnell@manatt.com.

O'CONNELL, MARY-KATHLEEN, lawyer; BA cum laude, Yale U., 1977; JD, NYU, 1981. Bar: Mass. 1981. With Goodwin Procter LLP, Boston, 1981—, ptnr., chair, trusts & estate planning practice, mem., investment com. Staff NYU Law Rev. Mem.: ABA, Estate Planning Coun., Women's Bar Assn., Mass Bar Assn., Boston Bar Assn. Office: Goodwin Procter LLP Exchange Pl 53 State St Boston MA 02109 Office Phone: 617-570-1391. Office Fax: 617-523-1231. Business E-Mail: moconnell@goodwinprocter.com.

O'CONNELL, MAUREEN C., county official, former state legislator; m. Donald O'Connell; 1 child, Donald. BS in Health Care Adminstrn., St. Josephs Coll.; JD, St. John's U.; RN, Flushing Hosp. Med. Ctr. Mem. NY State Assembly, Dist. 17, 1998—2006; clk. Nassau Co., NY, 2006—. Mem. adv. bd. Nassau Cmty. Coll., Molloy Coll. Sch. of Nuring. Recipient Am. Jurisprudence award. Mem.: Oncology Nursing Soc., Nassau Co. Bar Assn., Am. Cancer Soc. Republican. Office: Nassau County Clk 1 West St Mineola NY 11501

O'CONNELL, MAUREEN ELIZABETEH, publishing executive; b. NYC, Sept. 18, 1961; d. Patrick Joseph and Theresa C. Dowling; m. Donale Laurance O'Connell, Apr. 16, 1964; children: Tyler, Courtney. BS in Acctg. and Econs., NYU, 1985. CPA, N.Y. Dir. stragetic planning Primedia, NYC, 1990-93, various positions, 1993-98; CFO Newfield Publs., Sheton, Conn., 1993-95, New Bridge Comms., NYC, 1995-97, BMG Direct, NYC, 1997-98, Pubs. Clearing House, Port Washington, 1998—2000, Barnes & Noble, Inc., NYC, 2000—02; CFO, chief adminstrv. officer Gartner, Inc., Stamford, Conn., 2002—03, pres., COO, 2003—06; exec. v.p., CFO Affinion Group, Inc., Norwalk, Conn., 2006—07; exec. v.p., CFO, chief adminstrv. officer Scholastic Corp., NYC, 2007—. Mgr. Equitable, N.Y.C., 1988-90; audit supr. Coopers & Lybrand, N.Y.C., 1984-88; bd. dirs. Beazer Homes USA, 2002- Office: Scholastic Corp 567 Broadway New York NY 10012

O'CONNELL, MAURICE DANIEL, lawyer; b. Ticonderoga, NY, Nov. 9, 1929; s. Maurice Daniel and Leila (Geraghty) O'C.; m. Joan MacLure Landers, Aug. 2, 1952; children: Mark M., David L., Ann M., Leila K., Ellen A. Grad., Phillips Exeter Acad., 1946; AB, Williams Coll., 1950; LLB, Cornell U., 1956. Bar: Ohio 1956. Since practiced in, Toledo; assoc. Williams, Eversman & Black, 1956-60; ptnr. Robison, Curphey & O'Connell, 1961-95, of counsel, 1996—; spl. hearing officer in conscientious objector cases U.S. Dept. Justice, 1966-68. Mem. complaint rev. bd. Bd. Commrs. on Grievance and Discipline of Supreme Ct. Ohio, 1987. Mem. Ottawa Hills Bd. Edn., 1963-66, pres., 1967-69; former trustee Toledo Soc. for Handicapped; past trustee Woodlawn Cemetery; past trustee Toledo Hearing and Speech Center, Easter Seal Soc.; mem. alumni council Phillips Exeter Acad. Served to 1st lt. USMCR, 1950-53. Fellow Ohio State Bar Found.; mem. NW Ohio Alumni Assn. of Williams Coll. (past pres.), Ohio Bar Assn., Toledo Bar Assn. (chmn. grievance com. 1971-74), Kappa Alpha, Phi Delta Phi. Clubs: Toledo. Home: 3922 W Bancroft St Toledo OH 43606-2533 Office: 9th Flr Four SeaGate Toledo OH 43604

O'CONNELL, PHILIP RAYMOND, retired lawyer, paper company executive; b. NYC, June 2, 1928; s. Michael Joseph and Ann (Blaney) O'C.; m. Joyce McCabe, July 6, 1957; children: Michael, Kathleen, Jennifer, David. AB, Manhattan Coll., 1949; JD, Columbia U., 1956; grad., Advanced Mgmt. Program, Harvard U., 1967. Bar: N.Y. 1956, U.S. Supreme Ct. 1961, Conn. 1988. Assoc. Dewey, Ballantine, Bushby, Palmer & Wood, NYC, 1956-61, 62-64; gen. counsel, sec. Laurentide Finance Corp., San Francisco, 1961-62; gen. counsel Wallace-Murray Corp., 1964-66, div. mgr., 1966-70; pres., chief exec. officer, dir. Universal Papertech Corp., Hatfield, Pa., 1970-71; sec. Champion Internat. Corp., Stamford, Conn., 1972-90, v.p., 1979-81, sr. v.p., 1981-90. Mem. legal adv. com. N.Y. Stock Exch., 1985-88, corp. governance subcom., legal adv. com., 1985-94; chmn. lawyers steering com. corp. governance task force The Bus. Roundtable, 1981-87, mem., 1981-94. Mem. Champion Internat. Found., 1979-90; mem. bd. visitors Fairfield Univ. Sch. Bus., 1981-93, chmn., 1983-93; bd. dirs. Kearney-Nat. Corp., 1975-78. With USNR, 1951-54. Mem. Am. Soc. Corp. Secs. (hon.; chmn. 1988-89).

O'CONNELL, RALPH ANTHONY, dean, psychiatrist, educator; b. NYC, Jan. 26, 1938; s. Ralph E. and Agnes H. (O'Connell) O'C.; m. Jane Burke, June 15, 1963; children: Ralph E. III, Ellen C., John B. AB cum laude, Coll. of Holy Cross, Worcester, Mass., 1959; MD, Cornell U., 1963. Diplomate Am. Bd. Psychiatry and Neurology. Intern St. Vincent's Hosp. and Med. Ctr. N.Y., NYC, 1963-64, resident, 1964, 67-69, rsch. psychiatrist, 1969-71, chief inpatient dept. psychiatry, 1971-76, clin. dir. and vice chmn. psychiatry, 1974-95; prof. psychiatry N.Y. Med. Coll., Valhalla, 1984—, dean and provost, 1996—. Editor-in-chief Comprehensive Psychiatry, 1983-96. Served to capt. U.S. Army, 1965-66. Fellow Am. Psychiat. Assn., N.Y. Acad. Medicine (trustee 1989—). Clubs: Univ. (N.Y.C.). Roman Catholic. Office: NY Med Coll Valhalla NY 10595 Office Phone: 914-594-4900.

O'CONNELL, RICHARD (JAMES), English literature educator, poet; b. NYC, Oct. 25, 1928; s. Richard James and Mary Ellen (Fallon) O'C.; BS, Temple U., 1956; MA, Johns Hopkins, 1957. Instr. English Temple U., Phila., 1957-61, asst. prof., 1961-69, assoc. prof., 1969-86, sr. assoc. prof., 1986-93, assoc. prof. emeritus, 1993; guest lectr. poetry dept. writing seminars Johns Hopkins U., 1961-74; participant Poetry in Schs. Program, Pa. Coun. Arts, 1971-73; Fulbright lectr. Am. lit. U. Brazil, Rio de Janeiro, 1960, U. Navarre, Pamplona, Spain, 1962-63. Served with USN, 1948-52. Recipient prize Contemporary Poetry Press, 1972. Mem. PEN, MLA, Assocs. Writing Programs, Walt Whitman Poetry Ctr. (dir. 1975-84), Lit. Fellowship Phila. Author: From an Interior Silence, 1961, Cries of Flesh and Stone, 1962, New Poems and Translations, 1963, Brazilian Happenings, 1966, Terrane, 1967, Thirty Epigrams, 1971, Irish Monastic Poems (transl.), 1975, The Word in Time (selected transl. of Antonio Machado), 1975, Sappho (selected transl.), 1975, Lorca (selected transl.), 1976, Middle English Poems (transl.), 1976, More Irish Poems (transl.), 1976, Epigrams from Martial (transl.), 1976, One Hundred Epigrams from the Greek Anthology (trans.), 1977, Hudson's Fourth Voyage, 1978, The Epigrams of Luxorius (transl.), 1984, Temple Poems, 1985, Hanging Tough, 1986, Battle Poems, 1987, Selected Epigrams, 1990, Lives of The Poets, 1990, New Epigrams From Martial (transl.), 1991, The Caliban Poems, 1992, RetroWorlds, 1993 (transl.) Simulations, 1993, Voyages, 1995, The Bright Tower, 1997, American Obits, 2001, Fractals, 2002, Dawn Crossing, 2003, Waiting for the Terrorists, 2006; editor: Apollo's Day, 17th Century Songs, 1969, Atlantis Edits., 1962—, Poetry Newsletter, 1971-86. Home: 1147 Hillsboro Mile Apt 510 Hillsboro Beach FL 33062-1720 Personal E-mail: rocon100@comcast.net.

O'CONNELL, RICHARD JOHN, geophysicist, educator; b. Helena, Mont., Aug. 27, 1941; BS in Physics, Calif. Inst. Tech., 1963, MS in Geology, 1966, PhD in Geophysics, 1969. Rsch. fellow in geophysics Calif. Inst. Tech., 1969-70; rsch. geophysicist Inst. of Geophysics and Planetary Physics UCLA, 1970-71; asst. prof. dept. geol. scis. Harvard U., 1971-74, assoc. prof., 1974-77, prof. geophysics, 1977—, mem. Ctr. for Earth and Planetary Physics, 1971—86, dir. Ctr. for Earth and Planetary Physics, 1983-86. Cons. Rockwell Internat., 1984-87, AMOCO Tulane Rsch. Ctr., 1984—; vis. staff mem. Los Alamos Nat. Lab., 1980—. Contbr. numerous articles to profl. jours. Fellow Am. Geophys. Union (Inge Lehmann Medal, 2000), AAAS, Am. Acad. Arts & Scis.; mem. Geological Soc. Am. (Arthur L. Day Medal, 2001), Royal Astron. Soc., Sigma Xi. Office: Dept Earth & Planetary Sci Harvard U 20 Oxford St Cambridge MA 02138-2902 Business E-Mail: oconnell@geophysics.harvard.edu. *

O'CONNELL, ROBERT FRANCIS, physics professor; b. Athlone, Ireland, Apr. 22, 1933; came to U.S., 1958; s. William and Catherine (O'Reilly) O'C.; m. Josephine Molly Buckley, Aug. 3, 1963; children: Adrienne Molly, Fiona Catherine, Eimear Kathleen. BSc, Nat. U. Ireland, Galway, 1953, DSc, 1975; PhD, U. Notre Dame, 1962. Telecommunications engr. Dept. Posts and Telegraphs, Dublin, Ireland, 1954-58; scholar Inst. Advanced Studies, Dublin, 1962-63; systems analyst IBM, Dublin, 1963-64; sr. rsch. assoc. Inst. Space Studies, NYC, 1966-68; asst. prof. physics La. State U., Baton Rouge, 1964-66, assoc. prof., 1966-69, prof., 1969-86, Boyd prof., 1986—. Editor for theoretical physics Hadronic Jour.; former bd. mem. Phys. Rev. A; contbr. articles to profl. jours. Named Disting. Rsch. Master, La. State U., 1975; NAS-NRC fellow, 1966-68, Sci. Rsch. Coun. (Eng.) sr. vis. fellow, 1976. Fellow Am. Phys. Soc.; mem. Am. Astron. Soc., Internat. Astronomy Union, Internat. Soc. Gen. Relativity and Gravitation. Republican. Roman Catholic. Avocation: tennis. Home: 522 Bancroft Way Baton Rouge LA 70808-4807 Office: La State Univ Dept Physics And Astronomy Baton Rouge LA 70803-0001

O'CONNELL, VIRGINIA ADAMS, sociologist; m. Stephen Austin O'Connell. MA in Sociology, U. Pa., Phila., 1991, PhD in Sociology. Lectr. dept. sociology and anthropology Swarthmore Coll., Pa., 2001, vis. asst. prof. dept. sociology and anthropology, 2001—. Mem. rsch. ethics com. Swarthmore Coll., 2002—, mem. pub. policy curriculum com., 2002—, mem. health sci. advisory com., 2002—. Author: (book) Getting Cut: Failing to Survive Surgical Residency Training, 2007; contbr. chapters to books, articles to profl. jours. Mentor WoMentoring Program Haverford Coll., Pa., 1997—2001; mem. Host Family A Better Chance, Inc., Strath Haven, Pa., 1998—2001; soccer coach Swarthmore Recreation Assn., 2000—. Grantee Hewlett Rsch. grant, Swarthmore Coll., 2002—03, 2003—04, faculty rsch. grant, 2003, Lang Ctr. for Social Responsibility, 2004; Dissertation fellow, AAUW, 2000—01. Mem.: Ea. Sociol. Soc., Am. Sociol. Assn., Am. Sociol. Soc. (mem. com. profl. ethics 2007—). Office: Swarthmore College 500 College Avenue Swarthmore PA 19081 Office Phone: 610-328-8109.

O'CONNELL, SISTER VIRGINIA M., school librarian; b. Boston, Apr. 26, 1930; d. John Joseph and Katherine Walsh O'Connell. AB, Boston Coll., 1962; postgrad., Framingham State U. Tchr., libr. Marian High Sch., Framingham, Mass., 1969—84; tchr., bus mgr. Newton Cath. High Sch., 1984—88; pastoral assoc. St. Rose Parish, Chelsea, 1988—92; libr. Matignon High Sch., Cambridge, 1993—. Mem. adv. bd. Boston Coll. Advancement Studies, Chestnut Hill, 1993—; mem. adv. group Marian High Sch., 1994—96. Named Woman of Excellence, Mt. St. Joseph Acad., 1999. Mem.: LWV, Sisters St. Joseph Chorus, Mt. St. Joseph Acad. Roman Catholic. Avocations: travel, walking, reading. Home: 106 Waban St Newton MA 02458 Personal E-mail: oconnell2001@hotmail.com.

O'CONNELL, WILLIAM EDWARD, JR., retired finance educator; b. NYC, Sept. 16, 1937; s. William Edward and Helen Margaret (Brazel) O'Connell; m. Janet Elinor Shields, Aug. 15, 1965; children: William Edward III, Cathleen Anne. AB, Manhattan Coll., Riverdale, NY, 1959; MBA, Columbia U., NYC, 1961; DBA with honors, Ind. U., Bloomington, 1967; JD, Coll. William and Mary, Williamsburg, Va., 1974. Fin. analyst Pfizer, Inc., NYC, 1962-64; asst. prof. U. Conn., Storrs, 1967-69; Morris prof. banking U. Va., Charlottesville, 1988; Chessie prof. bus. Coll. William and Mary, Williamsburg, Va., 1969—2005. Mem. faculty Va. Bankers Sch., Charlottesville, 1975—99, Stonier Grad Sch. Banking, Newark, 1977—91, Bank Adminstrn. Inst., Madison, Wis., 1978—97; bd. dirs. C. & F Fin. Corp., Citizens & Farmers Bank. Author: Asset & Liability Management, 1979, Advanced Financial Planning, 1984, Financial Planning for Credit Unions, 1989, Strategic Financial Managment for Commercial Banks, 1993. Mem.: Fin. Mgmt. Assn., Am. Fin. Assn., Fords Colony Country Club, Omicron Delta Epsilon, Beta Gamma Sigma. Roman Catholic. Home: 102 Overlook Dr Williamsburg VA 23185-4434 Office: Coll William & Mary Mason Sch Business PO Box 8795 Williamsburg VA 23187-8795 Office Phone: 757-221-2881. Business E-Mail: william.oconnell@mason.wm.edu.

O'CONNELL, WILLIAM RAYMOND, JR., educational consultant, retired academic administrator; b. Richmond, Va., Jan. 4, 1933; s. William Raymond and Mary Helen (Wenenger) O'C.; m. Peggy Annette Tucker, June 29, 1957; 1 child, William Raymond III. B of Music Edn., Richmond Profl. Inst., 1955; MA, Columbia U., 1962, EdD, 1969; HLD (hon.), New Eng. Coll., 1995. Asst. to provost Richmond Profl. Inst., Va., 1955-57, dean of men, 1957-59, dean of students, dean of men, 1959-61; asst. to provost, dir. student info. ctr. Tchrs. Coll. Columbia U., NYC, 1962-65, rsch. asst. inst. of higher edn. Tchrs. Coll., 1965-66; rsch. assoc. So. Regional Edn. Bd., Atlanta, 1966-69, dir. spl. programs, 1969-73, project dir., undergrad. edn. reform, 1973-79; dir. curriculum and faculty devel. Assn. Am. Colls., Washington, 1979-80, v.p. for programs, 1980-82, v.p., 1982-85; pres. New Eng. Coll., Henniker, NH, 1985-95, pres. emeritus, 1995—; vis. sr. fellow Assn. Am. Colls. and Univs., 1995—97; dir. health edn. and leadership program Nat. Assn. Student Pers. Adminstrs., 1996—2002, 2003—05. Cons. Coun. for Advancement Small Colls., 1975; adv. com. project on instnl. renewal through improvement of tchg. Soc. for Values in Higher Edn., 1975-78; evaluator NH Postsecondary Edn. Commn., 1987-95, vice chmn., 1990-92, chmn., 1992-94; evaluator Nat. Ctr. for Rsch. to Improve Postsecondary Tchg. and Learning, 1987-90, New Eng. Assn. Schs. and Colls., 1988, 91; higher edn. rev. panel awards for pioneering achievements in higher edn. Charles A. Dana Found., 1988, 89. Author, editor: articles to profl. publs. Pres. Richmond Cmty. Amb. Project, 1958-60, bd. dirs., 1960-61; bd. dirs. Alumni Assn. Acad. divsn. Va. Commonwealth U., 1970-73; chmn. fundraising com. Atlanta Boys Choir, Inc., 1976-77, trustee 1978-79; trustee Atlanta Coun. for Internat. Visitors, 1973-76, 78-79; pres. UN Assn., Atlanta, 1976-77; steering com. Nat. Coun. chpt., divsn. pres. UN Assn. US, 1977-79, nat. coun., 1980-90; steering com. Leadership Concord, 1992-95, chmn., 1994-95. Named Cmty. Amb. to Sweden Cmty. Amb. Project of the Experiment in Internat. Living, 1956. Fellow Royal Soc. of the Arts UK (life); mem. NH Coun. on World Affairs (bd. dirs. 1993-95), Williamsburg AIDS Network (bd. dirs., 2006-), Greater Concord C. of C. (bd. dirs. 1989-93), Coordinating Coun. for Internat. Univs. (bd. dirs. 2001-06), Va. Commonwealth U. Alumni Assn. (bd. dirs. 2006-), Phi Delta Kappa. Methodist. Avocations: antiques, travel. E-mail: wroconn@cox.net.

O'CONNOR, ABIGAIL ELIZABETH, mathematician, educator, science educator; b. New Brunswick, NJ, Feb. 18, 1978; d. Samuel Margulies and Jennifer Alman Michaels; m. George O'Connor, Jr., Aug. 18, 2002; 1 stepchild, Nathan Edward. BA in Math., Rutgers U., 1999; MS in Applied Math., Rensselaer Poly. Inst., 2002; postgrad., Albany Law Sch., 2005—. Adj. math. lectr. Rutgers U., New Brunswick, NJ, 1999—2000; comml. pilot, flight instr. O'Connor Aviation, Inc., Albany, NY, 2000—01; owner, flight instr. No. Flight Acad., Inc., Scotia, NY, 2002—; instr. math. and physics Schenectady (N.Y.) County CC, 2002—03; instr. math Albany Coll. Pharmacy, NY, 2003—05. Presenter in field. Fellow, Claire Booth Luce Found., 2001—02. Mem.: Aircraft Owner and Pilot Assn., Am. Math. Soc. Avocations: alpaca farming, geology, home improvement, aviation. Home: 219 Verbeck Ave Schaghticoke NY 12154 Home Phone: 518-753-4211. Personal E-mail: abby@oconnorfarm.com.

O'CONNOR, ANAHAD S., journalist; b. NYC, 1982; B, Yale U., 2003. Intern NY Times, 1999, CAP Advisors, St. Vincent's Hosp., Dublin; staff reporter Yale Daily News; health & fitness columnist NY Times. Writer: published in NY Times, 1999—. Office: NY Times Science & Health Desk 229 W 43rd St New York NY 10036 Office Phone: 212-556-7141. Office Fax: 212-556-7306.

O'CONNOR, BRIAN D.A., music educator, French horn musician; b. Albuquerque, Dec. 6, 1951; s. Joseph Fredrick and Mary Adger (King) O'Connor; m. Coral Lynn Johnson, Sept. 21, 1972 (dec. July 1993); 1 child, Sean Adger. Student, New Eng. Conservatory of Music, Boston, 1970—72; BFA, Calif. Inst. of the Arts, Valencia, 1973. Recording musician French horn L.A. Recording Orch., 1974—; prof. horn UCLA, 1998—. Horn clinician Calif State Music Edn., LA, 2001—; French horn performer Pacific Serenades, LA, 2000—, UCLA Faculty Chamber Group, Westwood, 2001—. Musician (horn, soloist): (more than 1,900 films, including) Flicka, The Notebook, The Rock, Crimson Tide, Contact, Backdraft, Star Trek-First Contact, others, (films) Cinderella Man, (TV series) Star Trek, others, The Pacifier, Star Trek: Enterprise. Mem.: Recording Musicians Assn. of L.A. (pres. 1999—2005). Avocations: soccer, running, flying, bicycling. Office: 20335 Ventura Blvd Ste 400 Woodland Hills CA 91364 Personal E-mail: horn51@aol.com.

O'CONNOR, CHARLES P., lawyer; b. Boston, Sept. 29, 1940; m. Mary Linda Hogan; children: Jennifer, Amy, Austin, Catherine. Bachelors degree, Holy Cross Coll., Worcester, Mass., 1963; LLB, Boston Coll., 1966. Bar: Mass. 1966, D.C. 1968, U.S. Supreme Ct. 1974. Atty., gen. counsel's office NLRB, Washington, 1966-67; assoc. Morgan, Lewis & Bockius, LLP, Washington, 1968-71; ptnr. Morgan, Lewis & Bockius, Washington, 1971—2003, chmn. labor and employment law sect., 1996-99, mng. ptnr. Washington office, 1995-97; v.p., gen. counsel Maersk, Inc., 2003—. Gen. counsel Major League Baseball Player Rels. Com., N.Y.C., 1989-94. Contbr. numerous articles on labor and employment law to law jours. Spl. counsel elections com. U.S. Ho. of Reps., Washington, 1968-69. Fellow Coll. Labor and Employment Lawyers; mem. ABA, D.C. Bar Assn., Met. Club Washington, Belle Haven Country Club, N.Y. Athletic Club, Cape Cod Nat. Golf Club. Office: Maersk Inc 2 Giralda Farms Madison Ave Madison NJ 07940-0880 Home: 6237 Radcliff Rd Alexandria VA 22307-1143 Office Phone: 973-514-5014. Office Fax: 973-514-5003. Business E-Mail: namlawmng@maersk.com.

O'CONNOR, CHRISTOPHER JOHN, information technology manager, consultant; b. Stoughton, Mass., Jan. 29, 1967; s. James Edward and Sally Anne O'Connor; m. Martha Treichel O'Connor, Apr. 6, 2002; children: Brigid Grace, Brendan Padraig. BS, US Mil. Acad., West Point, NY, 1989. Sr. analyst Teledyne Brown Engring., Arlington, Va., 1999—2000; sr. cons. BearingPoint/KPMG Consulting, Alexandria, Va., 2000—04; program mgr. Kepler Rsch., Inc, Arlington, 2004—; founder/pres. Change 1 Person, Alexandria, 2006—. Maj. US Army, 1989—99. Decorated Bronze Star medal US Army; recipient Meritorious Svc. medal, 1999. Mem.: Project Mgmt. Inst. (life cert. project mgmt. profl.). Republican. Roman Catholic. Avocations: soccer, hockey. Home: 8612 Pilgrim Ct Alexandria VA 22308 Office: Kepler Research Inc 1530 Wilson Blvd Ste 600 Arlington VA 22209 Home Phone: 703-780-0167; Office Phone: 703-465-4035. Personal E-mail: chrisoconnor@change1person.org. Business E-Mail: chris.oconnor@keplerresearch.com.

O'CONNOR, CHUCK (CHARLES O'CONNOR), painter; b. Buffalo, 1943; Student, Pratt Inst., Bklyn., 1961—64, NY Studio Sch., 1964—66. Exhibited in group shows at Celebration, Lohin Geduld Gallery, NYC, 2005, 181st Ann.: An Invitational Exhbn. Contemporary Art, Nat. Acad. Mus., NYC, 2006. Fulbright fellow, Caps fellow, Tiffany fellow, MacDowell Colony fellow. Mailing: c/o Lohin Geduld Gallery 531 W 25th St New York NY 10001-5501

O'CONNOR, CLINT HAYNIE, electrical engineer; b. Corpus Christi, Tex., June 23, 1955; s. Robert Barnard Jr. and Edith H. (Haynie) O'C.; m. Christine Ann Schroeder, Mar. 30, 1985. BA, Wabash Coll., Crawfordsville, Ind., 1978. Pres., dir. R&D Analytical Engines, Austin, Tex., 1982-86; sr. project engr. Gould Indsl. Automation, Andover, Mass., 1986-88; mgr. elect. engring. Webtron Corp., Fort Lauderdale, Fla., 1988-93; sr. tech. staff Office Chief Tech. Officer Dell Computer Corp., Austin, 1993—. Chmn. bd. Analytical Engines, 1982-86; cons. Marine Sci. Inst., Galveston, Tex., 1980. Vol. Dolphin Rsch. Ctr., Grassy Key, Fla., 1989-90. Mem. Sigma Xi. Achievements include development of first 68000 co-processor for Apple II, 68010 co-processor for IBM PC; author 68000 Applesoft BASIC compatible interpreter; software development of Gould C986 co-processor, printing press control systems, development of Dell battery gauge, Dell control, Dell PC-card central and utilities for Dell Latitude portables; 18 patents in field. Office: Dell Computer Office Chief Tech Officer One Dell Way Round Rock TX 78682

O'CONNOR, DORIS JULIA, not-for-profit fundraiser, consultant; b. Apr. 30, 1930; 1 child: Kim C. BA cum laude in Econs., U. Houston, 1975. Adminstrv. asst. Shell Cos. Found. Inc., NYC, 1966-71, asst. sec. Houston, 1971-73, sec., 1973-76, sr. v.p., dir., mem. exec. com., 1976-93; prin. Doris O'Connor & Co., 1993—. Corp. assoc. United Way of Am., Washington, 1976-93; corp. advisor Bus. Com. of Arts, N.Y.C., 1976-91, del., 1982-87; dir. Ind. Sector, Washington, 1981-89, vice chmn., 1983-87; mem. contbns. coun. Conf. Bd., N.Y.C., 1976-93; advisor Coun. of Better Bus. Burs., Washington, 1975-94, vice chmn., 1983-87; commr. adv. commn. on work-based learning, Dept. Labor, 1991-93; mem. Houston/Harris County Arts Task Force, 1991-93, Houston Ind. Sch. Dist. Task Force, 1991-93; trustee Houston Grand Opera, 1993-99, Houston Symphony Soc., 1993-99, Soc. Performing Arts, 1993-99, Cultural Arts Coun., 1993-96, Greater Houston Coalition Edn. Excellence, 1993-96; mem. adv. bd. Houston Zool. Soc., 1993-99; mem. Mus. Fine Arts, Houston. Mem. Houston Com. Fgn. Rels., Houston World Affairs Coun., Houston Philos. Soc., Plaza Club (bd. givs. 1987-89), Omicron Delta Epsilon. Office Phone: 713-522-3278.

O'CONNOR, EDWARD GEARING, lawyer; b. Pitts., May 5, 1940; s. Timothy R. and Irene B. (Gearing) O'C.; m. Janet M. Showalter, June 17, 1972; children: Mark G., Susan M. BA, Duquesne U., 1962, JD, 1965. Bar: Pa. 1965, US Dist. Ct. (we. dist.) Pa. 1965, US Ct. Appeals (3d cir.) 1968, US Supreme Ct. 1976. Assoc. Eckert, Seamans, Cherin & Mellott, Pitts., 1965-72, ptnr., 1973-99, sr. counsel, 2000—. Mem. adv. com. on appellate ct. rules Supreme Ct. Pa., 1986—92, mem. procedure rules com., 1998—2004; bd. dirs., mem. audit com., compliance com. Federated Investors, Inc. Editor Duquesne U. Law Rev., 1964-65. Chmn. Hampton Twp. Planning Commn., Pa., 1986—87; mem. Hampton Twp. Zoning Hearing Bd., 1997—; bd. dirs. Duquesne U., 1995—2007. Recipient Disting. Alumni award Duquesne U. Law Rev., 1985, Disting. Law Alumni award Duquesne U. Sch. Law, 1991, Disting. Svc. award Hampton Twp., 1991, McAnurlty Svc. award Duquesne U., 1992; named Century Club Disting. Alumni, Duquesne U., 1985. Fellow: Pa. Bar Found., Am. Bar Found.; mem.: Ally City Bar Found. (chair fellows com. 2000—01), Acad. Trial Lawyers Allegheny County (bd. govs. 1986—89, 1998—), Pa. Bar Assn. (ho. of dels. 1985—90), Pitts. Athletic Assn., Duquesne U. Alumni Assn. (pres. 1980—82, 1988—90, bd. govs. 1982—90, bd. dirs. 1988—89), Duquesne Club. Republican. Roman Catholic. Home: 4288 Green Glade Ct Allison Park PA 15101-1202 Office: Eckert Seamans Cherin & Mellott 600 Grant St Ste 44th Pittsburgh PA 15219-2702 Office Phone: 412-566-6053. Business E-Mail: eoconnor@eckertseamans.com.

O'CONNOR, EDWARD JOSEPH, neurologist; b. LA, Jan. 12, 1944; s. Edward Joseph and Claire Smith O'Connor; m. Laura Davidson Folks, Mar. 6, 1982; children: Charles, Kevin, Andrew. BS, U. Notre Dame, Ind., 1966; MD, UCLA, 1970. Diplomate Am. Bd. Neurology and Psychiatry, Am. Bd. Electrodiagnostic Medicine. Intern U. Calif. Affiliate Hosps., 1970—71; resident internal medicine Wadsworth VA Hosp., LA, 1671—1972; resident neurology U. N.Mex., 1974—76; chief resident UCLA, 1676—1977; chief section neurology White Meml. Hosp., LA, 1979—86; owner Nerol. Assocs. West LA, Santa Monica, Calif., 1986—. Bd. dirs. UCLA Rugby. Fellow: Am. Acad. Neurology. Democrat. Roman Catholic. Office: Neurol Assocs West LA 2811 Wilshire Blvd # 790 Santa Monica CA 90403

O'CONNOR, EDWARD VINCENT, JR., lawyer; b. Yokosuka, Japan, Nov. 9, 1952; s. Edward Vincent and Margaret (Robertson) O'C.; m. Kathy J. Hunt, May 23, 1992. BA, Duke U., 1975; JD, N.Y. Law Sch., 1981. Bar: Va. 1982, D.C. 1983. Assoc. Lewis, Kinsey, Dack & Good, Washington, 1982-87; ptnr. Lewis, Dack, Paradiso & Good, Washington, 1988-89, Lewis, Dack, Paradiso, O'Connor & Good, Washington, 1989-94, The Lewis Law Firm, 1994, Byrd, Mische, Bevis, Bowen, Joseph & O'Connor, Fairfax, Va., 1995—2003; pvt. practice Fairfax, 2003—. Arbitrator DC Superior Ct.; neutral case evaluator and concilliator Fairfax County Cir. Ct.; lectr. in field. Bd. dirs., treas. Potomac Legal Aid Soc., 2001—. Named One of Best 50 Divorce Lawyers Washingtonian mag., 1995, 2000, Va. Super Lawyer, 2007. Mem. Va. State Bar (spl. com. on access to legal svcs. 1994-04, 5th dist. discipline com. 2001-03, sec., 2003-04, vice chair, 2004-06, bar coun. 2005—), DC Bar, Fairfax County Bar Assn. (vice chair family law sect. 1995-96, continuing edn. com. 1988-95, chair 1995, pub. svc. com. 1995, chair 1996-98, cir. ct. com. 1994-96, 99-01, jud. selection com., pro bono com., James Keith award for pub. svc. 1999), Legal Svcs. No. Va. (bd. dirs., chmn. pro bono com., sec.-treas. 1998-02, pres. 2002-03, treas. 2003-06, pro bono award for outstanding svc. 1997), Potomac Legal Aid Soc. (treas. 2003—). Home Phone: 703-437-4414; Office Phone: 571-432-0555. Personal E-mail: eddie52911@hotmail.com. Business E-Mail: evojr@cox.net.

O'CONNOR, EILEEN J., lawyer, former federal agency administrator; Grad., Columbus State U.; JD, Cath. U. Corp. tax law specialist IRS; ptnr. Office Fed. Tax Svcs. Grant Thornton, 1984—99; officer for tax svcs. Aronson, Fetridge and Weigle, 1999—2002; asst. atty. gen. tax divsn. US Dept. Justice, Washington, 2002—07; ptnr. Pillsbury Winthrop Shaw & Pittman LLP, Washington, 2007—. Disting. adj. prof. law George Mason U. Law Sch.; adj. prof. law Georgetown U. Law Sch.; former tax cons. various acctg. firms. Mem.: Am. Inst. Cert. Pub. Accountants (past mem. tax. exec. com.), Fed. Bar Assn., DC Bar Assn. Office: Pillsbury Winthrop Shaw & Pittman LLP 2300 N St NW Washington DC 20037 *

O'CONNOR, FRANCIS PATRICK, former state supreme court justice; b. Boston, Dec. 12, 1927; s. Thomas Lane and Florence Mary (Hagerty) O'C.; m. Ann Elizabeth O'Brien; children: Kathleen, Francis P., Brien T., Maureen T., Ellen M., Ann E., Jane C., Joyce E., Thomas J., Matthew P. AB, Holy Cross Coll., 1950; LLB, Boston Coll., 1953; JD (hon.), Suffolk U., 1983, New Eng. Sch. Law, 1984. Bar: Mass. 1953. Assoc. Friedman, Atherton, Sisson & Kozol, Boston, 1954-57, Mason, Crotty, Dunn & O'Connor, Worcester, Mass., 1957-73, Wolfson, Moynihan, Dodson & O'Connor, Worcester, 1974-75; judge Mass. Superior Ct., 1976-81; assoc. judge Mass. Supreme Ct., 1981-97, ret., 1997. Office: Supreme Judicial Court 1 Pemeberton Sq Ste 2-500 Boston MA 02108-1717

O'CONNOR, FRANCIS X., financial executive; b. Bklyn., May 7, 1929; s. Richard B. and Mary (McCafferty) O'C.; m. Leona A. Windorf, June 30, 1951; children: Francis X., Edward K., Brendan T., Richard B. III, A. Bruce, Marianne, Margaret, Leona. BS, St. Peter's Coll., 1951. CPA, N.Y., N.J. Audit mgr. Coopers & Lybrand, NYC, 1951-65; controller Ward Foods, Inc., NYC, 1965-66, v.p. fin., CFO, 1966-72, also bd. dirs., 1968-73; v.p. fin., CFO UMC Industries, Inc., NYC, 1973-76; v.p. fin. and corp. devel., CFO SKF Industries, Inc., King of Prussia, Pa., 1976-87; v.p. corp. fin. Moore & Schley Securities Corp., Morristown, NJ, 1987-89; mng. dir. Sterling Manhattan Corp. Investment Bankers, NYC, 1989-93. Adv. bd. Boyden Cons. Corp. Mem. AICPA, AIM, N.Y. State Soc. CPAs. Fin. Excs. Inst., Nat. Conf. on Power Transmission (trustee), Machinery and Allied Products Inst. Fin. Coun., St. Peter's Coll. Alumni Assn. (trustee, past pres. Monmouth chpt.), Navy League U.S., Spring Lake Golf Club, (past pres., trustee), Seaview Country Club (N.J.), Green Gables Croquet Club (past pres.), Legacy Golf Club (Ft. Pierce, Fla.), Yacht and Country Club (Stuart, Fla.). Home: 2355 NE Ocean Blvd Stuart FL 34996-2945 Office: 16 St Clair Ave Spring Lake NJ 07762

O'CONNOR, SISTER GEORGE AQUIN (MARGARET M. O'CONNOR), academic administrator, educator; b. Astoria, NY, Mar. 5, 1921; d. George M. and Joana T. (Loughlin) O'C. BA, Hunter Coll., 1943; MA, Catholic U. Am., 1947; PhD (NIMH fellow), NYU, 1964; LL.D. Manhattan Coll., 1983; D of Pedagogy (hon.), Dowling Coll., 1997; DHL, St. Francis Coll., 1997, St. Joseph's Coll., 1997. Mem. faculty St. Joseph's Coll., Bklyn., 1946—, prof. sociology and anthropology, 1966—, chmn. social sci. dept., 1966-69, pres., 1969-97; pres. emeritus. Fellow African Studies Assn., Am. Anthrop. Assn.; Bklyn. C. of C. (dir. 1973-97), Alpha Kappa Delta, Delta Epsilon Sigma. Author: The Status and Role of West African Women: A Study in Cultural Change, 1964. Named one of N.Y. State Senate's Women of Distinction. Office: Saint Joseph's Coll 245 Clinton Ave Brooklyn NY 11205-3602 Office Phone: 718-636-6800. Business E-Mail: goconnor@sjcny.edu.

O'CONNOR, G(EORGE) RICHARD, ophthalmologist; b. Cin., Oct. 8, 1928; s. George Leo and Sylvia Johanna (Voss) O'C. AB, Harvard U., 1950; MD, Columbia U., 1954. Resident in ophthalmology Columbia-Presbyn. Med. Center, NYC, 1957-60; research fellow Inst. Biochemistry, U. Uppsala, Sweden, 1960-61, State Serum Inst., Copenhagen, 1961-62; asst. prof. ophthalmology U. Calif., San Francisco, 1962-68, prof., 1972-84; dir. Francis I. Proctor Found. for Research in Ophthalmology, 1970-84. Nat. adv. eye coun. NIH, 1974—78. Author: (with G. Smolin) Ocular Immunology, 1981; asso. editor: Am. Jour. Ophthalmology, 1976-81. Served with USPHS, 1955-57. Recipient Janeway prize Coll. of Physicians and Surgeons, Columbia U., 1954; Doyne medal Oxford U., 1984; NIH grantee, 1962-84 Mem. Am. Bd. Ophthalmology (sr. examiner), Assn. for Rsch. in Vision and Ophthalmology (trustee 1979-83, pres. 1982-83, Weisenfeld award 1990), Am. Ophthal. Soc., Calif. Med. Assn., Frederic C. Cordes Eye Soc., Pan Am. Ophthal. Assn., Faculty Club. Republican. Presbyterian. Home: 22 Wray Ave Sausalito CA 94965-1831 Office: U Calif Med Ctr 310 S San Francisco CA 94143-0001 Business E-Mail: richard.oconnor@ucsf.edu.

O'CONNOR, JAMES, JR., (JIM O'CONNOR), telecommunications industry executive; b. 1967; m. Julie O'Connor; 2 children. BA, JD, Georgetown Univ.; MBA, Northwestern Univ. Kellogg Sch. Bar: Ill. Mgmt. consultant AT Kearney; fell. White House, 1998; founder Motorola Ventures, Chgo., 1999; v.p., tech. incubation., commercialization Motorola, Chgo., 1999—. Adv. bd. mem. J.L. Kellogg Sch. Mgmt.; co-chmn. Chicagoland Entrepreneurial Ctr.; bd. mem. Chicagoland Chamber Commerce; founder Kellogg Corps, Field Mus. Assoc., Lyric Opera Aux. Bd.; mem. bd. Children's Home & Aid Soc., Chgo. Cities in Schools, Big Shoulders Bd. Recipient East Coast Athletic Conf. All-Star, GTE Academic All-American, CEO Volunteer award, Motorola, 2002, CEO outstanding Achievement award, 2004; grantee Leadership Greater Chgo., 2000, Japan Leadership, 2000, Henry Crown Leadership, Aspen Inst., 2004. Mem.: Econ. Club Chgo., ABA. Office: Motorola Inc 1303 E Algonquin Rd Schaumburg IL 60196 Office Fax: 847-576-5372. *

O'CONNOR, JAMES E., waste management executive; b. May 14, 1949; m. Cathy O'Connor; children: Kerry O'Connor Stiles, James, Kevin. BS, DePaul Univ., 1972. Staff acct. Waste Mgmt., Oakbrook, Ill., 1972-78, with, 1982-87, v.p. southeastern region, 1987-91, sr. v.p. N.Am., 1991-92, area pres., 1992-98; CEO Republic Svcs., Inc., Ft. Lauderdale, Fla., 1998—2003, chmn., CEO, 2003—. Bd. dirs. Broward Workshop, Children's Cardiac Found.; mem. bd. advisors Broward Econ. Devel. Coun., Broward County Make-A-Wish Found.; trustee Fla. Tax Watch, Mus. Art, St. Thomas Aquinas H.S. Found. Recipient Tree of Life award Jewish Nat. Fund, 1995. Office: Republic Svcs Inc 110 SE 6th St 28th Fl Fort Lauderdale FL 33301 *

O'CONNOR, JAMES JOHN, retired utility company executive; b. Chgo., Mar. 15, 1937; s. Fred James and Helen Elizabeth O'Connor; m. Ellen Louise Lawlor, Nov. 24, 1960; children: Fred, John (dec.), James, Helen Elizabeth. BS, Holy Cross Coll., 1958; MBA, Harvard U., 1960; JD, Georgetown U., 1963. Bar: Ill. 1963. With Commonwealth Edison Co., Chgo., 1963-98, asst. to chmn. exec. com., 1964-65, comml. mgr., 1966, asst. v.p., 1967-70, v.p., 1970-73, exec. v.p., 1973-77, pres., 1977-87, chmn., 1980-98, CEO, also bd. dirs., 1998; chmn., CEO Unicom Corp., Chgo., 1994-98, ret., 1998. Bd. dirs. Corning, Inc., United Air Lines, Smurfit-Stone Container Corp., Armstrong World Industries. Bd. dirs. Lyric Opera, Joffrey Ballet, Helen Brach Found.; bd. dirs., trustee Mus. Sci. and Industry, Chgo. Symphony; past chmn. Met. Savs. Bond Campaign; trustee Northwestern U.; bd. dirs., past chmn. Chgo. Urban League, Chicagoland C. of C.; past chmn. bd. trustees Field Mus. Natural History; life trustee Adler Planetarium, Mus. Sci. and Industry; mem. exec. bd. Chgo. Area coun. Boy Scouts Am.; chmn. Cardinal Bernardin's Big Shoulders Fund; exec. v.p. The Hundred Club Cook County; dir., past pres. Cath. Charities; past chmn., hon. dir. Am. Cancer Soc., Chgo. Conv. and Tourism Bur. With USAF, 1960-63.

O'CONNOR, JOHN DENNIS, biology professor; b. Chgo., Mar. 20, 1942; married, 1964; 3 children. BS, Loyola U, Chgo., 1963; MS, DePaul U., 1966; PhD, Northwestern U., 1968. NIH fellow Mich. State U., East Lansing, 1968-70; asst. prof. biology UCLA, 1969-74, assoc. prof., 1974-77, prof. biology, 1977-81, chmn. biology, 1979-81, dean, life scis., 1981-87; vice chancellor for research, dean of grad. sch., prof. biology U. N.C., prof. biology Chapel Hill, 1988-91; chancellor, prof. biology U. Pitts., 1991-95; provost Smithsonian Instn., Washington, 1996-99, under sec. for sci., 2000—02; v.p. rsch., dean grad. studies U. Md., College Park, 2002—04, prof. biology, 2004—. Vis. prof. U. Nijmegen, Netherlands, 1975-76, Monash U., 1977. Fellow AAAS; mem. Am. Soc. Zoology, Soc. Devel. Biology, Am. Soc. Molecular Biology and Biochemistry, Bus. Higher Edn. Forum (vice chair 1994-96, chair 1996-98), Assn. Univs. for Rsch. in Astronomy (bd. dirs.). Office: U Md 2133 Lee Bldg College Park MD 20742-5121

O'CONNOR, JOHN JOSEPH, information technology manager; b. Smyrna, Tenn., June 1, 1959; s. John O'Connor and Dolores Jane (Bell) Brem; m. Lea Ann Bradford, Sept. 6, 1986; 1 child, Colleen Michelle. BS, Tex. A&M U., 1981. Cert. marine engr. 3rd asst. engr. Marine Engrs. Beneficial Assn., Houston, 1981-84; asst. engr. Biehl Ship Mgmt., Houston, 1984; balance technician Hickham Industries, Inc., LaPorte, Tex., 1984-86, prodn. scheduler/Sulzer, 1986-87, project engr./Sulzer, 1987-88, engring. mgr./Sulzer, 1988-89, ops. mgr./Sulzer Huntington Beach, Calif., 1989-93, sr. engr., corp. mergers and acquisitions La Porte, Tex., 1993-94; tech. and field svc. mgr. Sulzer Turbosys. Internat., Houston, 1994-98; engring. projects mgr. Hickham Industries, Inc., LaPorte, Tex., 1998—. Guest speaker Tex. A&M U., Galveston, Tex., College Station, Tex., 1981-89, U. Houston, 1986-89; moderator Power Machinery and Compressor Conf., Houston, 1989. Prin. engr. inventions in field (Achievement awards 1989); author: Steam Turbine Overhaul and Repair Specifications, 1994. Bd. dirs. Cedar Lawn Assn., pres., 1998-2001; bd. dirs. East End Presch., pres., 1998-99; bd. dirs. (pres.) Galveston Alliance of Island Neighborhoods, 1998-2003; adv. bd. Galveston Hist. Found., 1999. Recipient Outstanding Records in Engring., Gulf Oil Corp., Galveston, 1981. Mem. ASME (guest speaker convs.), Pacific Energy Assn. (guest speaker convs. 1990-92), Assn. of Former Students/Tex. A&M. Avocations: hiking, camping, travel, automotive restoration, litigation. Business E-Mail: john.oconnor@sulzerhickham.com.

O'CONNOR, JOHN JOSEPH, oil industry executive; b. Dublin, Mar. 7, 1946; BE, MEngSc, Univ. Coll., Dublin. Various engring. and managerial positions Mobil Oil Corp., N.Y., Libya and Abu Dhabi, 1968-81, Arun field mgr. Indonesia, 1981-83, Gulf Coast producing mgr. New Orleans, 1983-86, gen. mgr. producing Europe/Africa NYC, 1987-88, gen. mgr. internat. negotiations and acquisitions, 1988; pres. Mobil Oil Can., Calgary, Alta., 1988-89, chmn., CEO, 1989-90; v.p. Middle East and marine transp. Mobil Oil Corp., Va., 1990-92, v.p. corp. strategic ventures group Va., 1992-93, exec. v.p. exploration and prodn. Europe/Russia/Africa Va., 1993-94; CEO BHP Petroleum Pty. Ltd., Melbourne, Australia, 1994—97; sr. v.p., pres. worldwide exploration & prod. Texaco, 1997—2001; exec. v.p., pres. worldwide exploration & prod. Hess Corp., NYC, 2001—. Bd. dirs. Broken Hill Pty. Co. Ltd. Avocations: music, theater, reading, skiing, golf. Office: Hess Corp 1185 Ave of the Americas New York NY 10036 *

O'CONNOR, JOHN MORRIS, III, retired humanities educator; b. Evanston, Ill., Sept. 21, 1937; s. John Morris and Clare Evelyn (Merrick) O'Connor; m. Mary Bittner, Dec. 30, 1960 (div.); 1 child, Emily; m. Miranda E. P. Ind, Aug. 14, 1971 (div.); 1 child, Amanda; m. Beate A. Schiwek, July 3, 2006. Student, Georgetown U., 1955—56; BA, Cornell U., 1959; MA, Harvard U., 1962, PhD, 1965. Instr. Vassar Coll., 1964-66, asst. prof. philosophy, 1966-68; asst. prof. Case Western Res. U., Cleve., 1968-70, assoc. prof., 1970-77; exec. sec. Am. Philos. Assn. U. Del., Newark, 1977-84, assoc. prof., 1977-83; asst. dir. programs Nat. Humanities Ctr., Research Triangle Park, NC, 1983-87; dean Sch. Humanities William Paterson Univ., Wayne, NJ, 1987—91, dean Sch. Humanities, Mgmt. and Social Scis., 1991-92, coord. spl. projects Office of Provost, 1992-93, prof. philosophy, 1992-2001; ret., 2001. Editor (with others): Introductory Philosophy, 1967, Modern Materialism, 1969, Moral Problems in Medicine, 1976; contbr. articles to profl. jours. Woodrow Wilson Nat. fellow, 1959—60. Home: 523 Guilford Ave Chambersburg PA 17201

O'CONNOR, JOHN THOMAS, civil engineering educator; b. NYC, Feb. 11, 1933; married, 1966; 2 children. BCE, Cooper Union, NYC, 1955; MSCE, NJ Inst. Tech., Newark, 1958; EngD, Johns Hopkins U., Balt., 1961. Sanitary engr. Elson T. Killam Sanit & Hydraulic Consulting Engrs., 1955-56; civil engr. George A. Fuller Constrn. Co., N.Y., 1956-57; sanitary engr. Parsons, Brinckerhoff, Quade & Douglas, 1957; from asst. prof. to prof. civil engring. U. Ill., Urbana-Champaign, 1961-75; prof. civil engring. U. Mo., Columbia, 1975-92, chmn. dept., 1975-89; chief Ill. State Water Survey, 1992-95; pres. H2O'C Engring., LLC, 1995—. Mem. ASCE, Am. Chem. Soc., Am. Water Works Assn., Am. Soc. Limnology and Oceanography, Water Environment Fedn. Achievements include research on drinking water treatment processes; removal of arsenic, microorganisms, organic substances, iron and manganese, radionuclides; wastewater treatment and disinfection; solid and hazardous waste site remediation. Address: 2401 Tahoe Ct Columbia MO 65203-1444 Home Phone: 573-234-1012; Office Phone: 573-446-5595. Business E-Mail: info@h2oc.com.

O'CONNOR, JOSEPH A., JR., lawyer; b. NYC, Aug. 12, 1937; s. Joseph A. and Louise G. (Lucht) O'C.; children: Joseph A. III, Edward W. BA, Yale U., 1959; LLB, Columbia U., 1962. Bar: N.Y. 1963, U.S. Supreme Ct. 1968, Pa. 1973, Fla. 1978. Assoc. Davis, Polk & Wardwell, NYC, 1963-72; ptnr. Morgan, Lewis & Bockius, Phila., 1972—2002, spl. coun., 2002—; exec. dir. E. Rhodes & Leona B. Carpenter Fedn., 2002—. Mem. ABA, N.Y. State Bar Assn., Pa. Bar Assn., Fla. Bar Assn., Phila. Bar Assn., Assn. of Bar of City of N.Y. Clubs: Racquet (Phila.). Roman Catholic. Office: Morgan Lewis & Bockius LLP 1701 Market St Philadelphia PA 19103-2903

O'CONNOR, KAREN, political science professor, researcher, writer; b. Buffalo, Feb. 15, 1952; d. Robert J. and Norma (Wilton) O'Connor; m. Allen McDonogh, June 7, 1974 (div. 1986); 1 child, Meghan; m. Richard Cupitt, July 31, 1992. BA, SUNY, Buffalo, 1973, JD, 1977, PhD, 1979. Bar: Ga. 1978. Instr. polit. sci. Emory U., Atlanta, 1977—78, asst. prof., 1978—83, assoc. prof., 1983—88, prof., 1988—95, Am. U., Washington, 1995—2006, Jonathan N. Halfat disting. prof., 2006—. Editor Women & Politics, 1999—2004; mem. editl. bd. Law & Policy, 1982—2005; editor Jour. of Politics, 1984—87, Am. Politics Quar., 1987—90; founder and dir. Women& Politics Inst., 1999. Author: Women's Organization's Use of the Courts, 1980; author: (with N.E. McGlen) Women's Rights, 1983; editor: Women and Congress, 2002; co-author (with McGlen): Women, Politics and American Society, 2004; co-author: (with L. Sabato) American Government, 9th edit., 2007; co-editor (with S. Brewer and M. Fisher): Gendering Politics, 2005; mem. editl. bd. Women, Politics & Public Policy; contbr. articles to profl. jours. Mem.: Nat. Capitol Area Polit. Sci. Assn. (pres. 2001—02), So. Polit. Sci. Assn. (pres. 2000—01), Women and Politics (pres. organized sect. 2006—), Am. Polit. Sci. Assn. (exec. coun. 1985—87), Cosmos Club. Home: 4383 Westover Pl NW Washington DC 20016-5555 Office: Dept of Govt American Univ 4400 Massachusetts Ave NW Washington DC 20016 Office Phone: 202-885-6237. Business E-Mail: oconn@american.edu.

O'CONNOR, KARL WILLIAM (GOODYEAR JOHNSON), retired lawyer; b. Washington, Aug. 1, 1931; s. Hector and Lucile (Johnson) O'C.; m. Sylvia Gasbarri, Mar. 23, 1951 (dec.); m. Judith Ann Byers, July 22, 1972 (div. 1983); m. Eleanor Celler, Aug. 3, 1984 (div. 1986); m. Alma Hepner, Jan. 1, 1987 (div. 1996); children: Blair, Frances, Brian, Brendan; m. Allie O'Connor, Jul. 15, 2000. BA, U. Va., 1952, JD, 1958. Bar: Va. 1958, D.C. 1959, Am. Samoa 1976, Calif. 1977, Oreg. 1993. Law clk. U.S. Dist. Ct. Va., Abingdon, 1958-59; practice law Washington, 1959-61; trial atty. U.S. Dept. Justice, Washington, 1961-65; dep. dir. Men's Job Corps OEO, Washington, 1965-67; mem. civil rights div. Dept. of Justice, chief criminal sect., prin. dep. asst. atty. gen., 1967-75, spl. counsel for intelligence coordination, 1975; v.p., counsel Assn. of Motion Picture and Television Producers, Hollywood, Calif., 1975-76; assoc. justice Am. Samoa, 1976; chief justice, 1977-78; sr. trial atty. GSA Task Force, Dept. Justice, 1978-81; insp. gen. CSA, 1981-82; spl. counsel Merit Systems Protection Bd., Washington, 1983-86; U.S. atty. for Guam and the No. Marianas, 1986-89; pvt. practice Medford, Oreg., 1989—; Am. counsel O'Reilly Vernier Ltd., Hong Kong, 1992-93; ptnr. O'Connor & Vernier, Medford, Oreg., 1993-94; emeritus, 1994. Served with USMC, 1952-55. Mem. Oreg. Bar Assn., D.C. Bar Assn., Va. Bar Assn., Calif. Bar Assn., Am. Samoa Bar Assn., Soc. Colonial Wars, Phi Alpha Delta, Sigma Nu. Home: Box 126 6743 Griffin Ln Jacksonville OR 97530

O'CONNOR, KATHLEEN MARY, lawyer; b. Camden, Jan. 14, 1949; d. John A. and Marie V. (Flynn) O'C. BA, U. Fla., 1971, JD, 1981. Bar: Fla. 1981, U.S. Ct. Appeals (11th cir.) 1982, U.S. Supreme Ct. 1987. Atty. Walton, Lantaff, Schroeder & Carson, Miami, Fla., 1981-84, Thornton,

Davis & Murray PA, Miami, 1984-98, Thornton, Davis & Fein, P.A., Miami, 2002—. Exec. editor U. Fla. Law Rev., 1981; contbr. articles to profl. jours. Legal advocate Miami Project to Cure Paralysis, 1992-97. Mem. ABA, Dade County Bar Assn. (chmn. appellate cts. com. 2004—), Def. Rsch. Inst., Fla. Def. Lawyers Assn., Fla. Assn. for Women Lawyers (bd. dirs. Miami-Dade County chpt. 2002—), Fla. Bar (mem. appellate rules com. 2002—, cert. 1995—). Office: Thornton Davis & Fein PA 80 SW 8th St Ste 2900 Miami FL 33130 Home: 7445 SW 147 St Coral Gables FL 33158 Office Phone: 305-446-2646. E-mail: oconnor@tdflaw.com.

O'CONNOR, KEVIN, computer programming executive; BSEE with honors, U. Mich. Co-founder ICC Software Co., Atlanta, 1983—91; chief tech. officer, v.p. rsch. DCA, Atlanta, 1992—95; funded and built ISS Group, Atlanta, 1995, chmn. bd. dirs., 1995—; co-founder, chief exec. officer Internet Advt. Network, 1995—; co-founder, pres., chief exec. officer DoubleClick, NY, 1996—. Office: DoubleClick 111 Eighth Ave 10th Fl New York NY 10011 Office Phone: 212-683-0001, 212-271-2542. Office Fax: 212-287-1203.

O'CONNOR, KEVIN, electronics executive; b. 1958; Degree in Mgmt., Ariz. State U. With Sperry Flight Sys.; with Frito-Lay PepsiCo; various positions Dell Computer; sr. v.p. global human resources Iomega Corp., Axcelis Technologies; exec. v.p. Worldwide Human Resources Solectron Corp., Milpitas, Calif., 2002—. Mem.: Am. Compensation Assn., Asian Human Resource Alliance, Soc. Human Resources Mgmt., Am. Lung Assn., North Shore C. of C., Boys and Girls Clubs Weber County. Office: Solectron Corp 777 Gibraltar Dr Milpitas CA 95035

O'CONNOR, KEVIN, construction materials manufacturing executive; b. 1969; JD, Calif. Western Sch. Law, San Diego, 1996; MBA, U. Chgo. Lic.: (before Supreme Ct.). Copy writer Foote Cone & Belding, Taipei, Taiwan; litigator LA, 1996—2000; corp. atty. Caterpillar Inc., Peoria, Ill., 2000—02, legal counsel Beijing, 2002—06, dir. China bus. devel., 2006—. Named one of 40 Under 40, Crain's Chgo. Bus., 2006. Office Phone: 480-345-7330. Business E-Mail: kevinro@cat.com.

O'CONNOR, KEVIN, professional sports team executive; b. Bronx, NY; m. Linda O'Connor; children: Katie, Adam, Lindsay, Brian(dec.). Grad. in Econs. and Bus., Belmont Abbey Coll., NC, 1969. Asst. coach Va. Poly. Inst. and State U., 1972—74, Va. Mil. Inst., 1974—76, U. Colo., 1976—79, UCLA, 1979—84; scout LA Clippers, Portland Trail Blazers, NJ Nets, 1990—94, Utah Jazz, 1994—97, v.p. basketball ops., 1999—2002, sr. v.p. basketball ops., 2002—; dir. player pers. Phila. 76ers, 1997—99. Mem. Men's Sr. Nat. Team Com. USA Basketball. Served in US Army, 1969—71. Office: Utah Jazz 301 W South Temple Salt Lake City UT 84101 *

O'CONNOR, KEVIN JAMES, prosecutor, lawyer; b. Hartford, Conn., May 3, 1967; s. Dennis Edmund and Mary Theresa (Leahy) O'Connor. BA with honors, U. Notre Dame, 1989; JD with high honors, U. Conn., 1992. Conn. 1992, NY 1993, US Dist. Ct. Conn. (so. and ea. dists.) NY 1994, US Ct. Appeals (2d cir.) 1994. Law clk. to Hon. William H. Timbers US Ct. Appeals (2nd Cir.), NYC, 1992-93; assoc. Cahill, Gordon & Reindel, NYC, 1993-95; sr. counsel Divsn. Enforcement SEC, Washington, 1995-97; ptnr. Day Berry & Howard, Hartford, 1999—2002; corpn. counsel Town of West Hartford, 1999—2001; US atty. Dist. Conn. US Dept. Justice, Hartford, 2002—, assoc. dep. atty. gen. Washington, 2007—. Adj. prof. George Washington U. Law Sch., Washington, 1996-97, U. Conn. Law Sch., 1998—. Republican. Roman Catholic. Office: US Attys Office New Haven Office Conn Fin Ctr 157 Ch St Fl 23 New Haven CT 06510 Office Phone: 203-821-3700. Office Fax: 203-773-5376. *

O'CONNOR, KEVIN JOHN, psychologist, educator; b. Jersey City, July 18, 1954; s. John Lanning and Marilyn (Reynolds) O'C.; m. Ryan Michael, Matthew Benham. BA, U. Mich., 1975; PhD, U. Toledo, 1981. Clin. psychologist Blythedale Children's Hosp., Valhalla, NY, 1980-83; dir. psychol. svcs. Walworth Barbour Am. Internat. Sch., Kfar Shmaryahu, Israel, 1983-84; adj. faculty dept. psychology Iona Coll., New Rochelle, NY, 1984; clin. psychologist No. Westchester Guidance Clinic, Mt. Kisco, NY, 1985; exec. dir., newsletter editor Assn. for Play Therapy, Fresno, Calif., 1982-97; cons. psychologist Fresno (Calif.) Treatment Ctr., 1986-87, Diagnostic Sch. for Neurologically Handicapped Children, Fresno, Calif., 1986-90; adj. faculty Pacific Grad. Sch. of Psychology, Palo Alto, Calif., 1997—2001, Calif. Sch. Profl. Psychology, Berkeley, Calif., 1988-89; prof. Alliant Internat. U., Calif. Sch. Profl. Psychology, Fresno, 1985—, dir. clinical PsyD and PhD programs, 1985—. Contbr. numerous publications and presentations in field. Named Psychologist of Yr. San Joaquin Psychol. Assn., 1994. Fellow APA; mem. Assn. for Play Therapy (dir. emeritus). Democrat. Avocations: travel, art, ceramics. Office: Calif Sch Profl Psych Alliant Internat U 5130 E Clinton Way Fresno CA 93727-2014 Office Phone: 559-253-2273. Business E-Mail: koconnor@alliant.edu.

O'CONNOR, KEVIN THOMAS, religious organization administrator; b. Dubuque, Iowa, Oct. 9, 1950; s. Francis John and Marion Helen (Rhomberg) O'C.; m. Abbie J. O'Connor, July 17, 1993; 1 child, Sean Francis. BS, Regis Coll., Denver, 1973. Spl. agt. Northwestern Mut. Life, Denver, 1973-78; account exec. Blue Cross/Blue Shield of Colo., Denver, 1978-82; pres., owner O'Connor Ins. Cons., Denver, 1982-92; dir. devel. Archdiocese of Denver, 1992-95, mgr. Cath. appeal, 1995-96; dir. devel. Archdiocese of L.A., 1996—2006; exec. dir. devel. Archdiocese of Washington, 2006—. Chmn. Regis Coll. Telefund, Denver, 1987-88, 90-91; treas., 1st vice chmn. Serra Trust Fund for Vocations, 1988-93, chmn., 1993-96; mem. fin. coun. St. James Parish, 1988-95, chmn. autumn bazaar, 1985, 87, mem. choir, 1993-95; sec. Mother Teresa Com., 1989; mem. choir St. Bede The Venerable, La Canada, Calif., 2001-06. Recipient Share Serra Comm. award Serra Internat., 1989, Spl. Project award Dist. 6, 1986, 88, Spl. Recognition award, 1989, Outstanding Serran award, 1995, Jan Berbers award, 1996, Alumni Svc. award Regis Coll., 1990, Disting. Alumnus award Wahlert H.S., 1994. Mem. Serra Internat. (trustee 1997-2003, sec. bd. 1998-2001, chmn. internat. vocation com. 2000-01, v.p. 2001-03, co-founder Pueblo chpt., 1992, Colo. Springs chpt., 1995, Greeley chpt., 1996, pres. Denver chpt., 1991-92, dist. 6 gov., 1995-96). Roman Catholic. Avocations: golf, tennis, mountain climbing, handball, running. Home: 406 Calloway Ct Silver Spring MD 20905 Office: Archdiocese 5001 Eastern Ave Hyattsville MD 20782-3447 Home Phone: 301-421-1172; Office Phone: 301-853-4574. Personal E-mail: oconnorak@verizon.net. Business E-Mail: koconnor@adw.org.

O'CONNOR, MAUREEN, state supreme court justice; b. Washington, Aug. 7, 1951; d. Patrick and Mary E. O'Connor; children: Alex, Ed. BA, Seton Hill Coll., 1973; postgrad., SUNY, 1975-76; JD, Cleve. State U., 1980. Pvt. practice, 1981-85; magistrate Summit County Probate Ct., 1985-93; judge Summit County Ct. of Common Pleas, 1993-95; prosecuting atty. Summit County, 1995-99; lt. gov., dir. Dept. Pub. Safety State of Ohio, 1999—2003; justice Ohio Supreme Ct., Ohio, 2003—. Dir. Summit County Child Support Enforcement Agy.; former chair Ohio Security Task Force, Building Security Review Com.; spkr. in field. Parishioner St. Vincent's Ch.; vol. Comty. Drug Bd., Am. Cancer Soc., bd. dirs.; bd. dirs. Victim Assistance, St. Edward Home, Fairlawn, Furnace St. Mission. Recipient MADD Law Enforcement award, 1997, Cleve. State Disting. Alumnae award for Civic Achievement, 1997. Mem. MADD, Nat. Dist. Attys. Assn., Nat. Child Support Enforcement Assn., Nat. Coll. Dist. Attys. Assn., Ohio Prosecuting Attys. Assn. (exec. com.), Ohio Family Support Assn., Atty. Gen.'s Prosecutor Liaison Com., Summit County Police Chiefs Assn., Summit Forum, Summit County Child Mortality. Republican. Office: Ohio Supreme Ct 65 S Front St Columbus OH 43215 *

O'CONNOR, MICHAEL B., biology professor, researcher; b. Boston, Apr. 28, 1954; s. Thomas Lee and Grace Marie O'Connor; m. MaryJane Shimmel, Sept. 24, 1983; children: Ethan Robert, Kyle Anthony. BS in Biochemistry, Brown U., 1976; PhD, Tufts U., Boston, 1984; postgrad., Harvard U., 1984—88. Prof. molecular biology and biochemistry U. Calif., Irvine, 1988—97; prof. genetics, cell biology and devel. U. Minn./Howard Hughes Med. Inst., Mpls. Investigator Howard Hughes Med. Inst. Home: 564 Owasso Hills Dr Roseville MN 55113 Office: Univ Minn Dept Genetics 6-160 Jackson Hall Minneapolis MN 55455 Home Phone: 612-626-0642; Office Phone: 612-626-0642. Office Fax: 612-625-5402.

O'CONNOR, MICHAEL E., lawyer; b. Syracuse, NY, Sept. 15, 1948; s. Leo T. and Geraldine (Hager) O'Connor; m. Margaret A. Soplop, June 3, 1972. AA, Auburn CC, NY, 1968; BA, SUNY, Buffalo, 1970; JD, Syracuse U., 1974. Bar: N.Y. 1975, U.S. Supreme Ct. 1983. Assoc. Coulter, Fraser, Bolton, Bird & Ventre, Syracuse, 1975-80, ptnr., 1981-90, Hancock & Estabrook, 1990-94, DeLaney & O'Connor LLP, 1994—. Pres. Onondaga Title Assn., 1979, Ctrl. N.Y. Estate Planning Coun., 1981; adj. prof. law U. Syracuse; pres. Most Holy Rosary Home Sch. Assn., 1985—86, Aurora of CNY, Inc., 1988—90. Bd. dirs. Syracuse Symphony Orch.; chmn. bd. CNY Cmty. Found.; pres. Citizens Found., Inc., 1983—85. Fellow: Am. Coll. Trust and Estate Counsel (state chair 1997—2002); mem.: ABA, Onondaga County Bar Assn. (chmn. estate and surrogates ct. com. 1981—87, bd. dirs. 1984—86), N.Y. State Bar Assn. (ho. of dels. 1982—85, chair elder law sect. 1999—2000, chair trusts and estates sect. 2005), Century Club of Syracuse, Lions (pres. 1984—85). Republican. Roman Catholic. Home: 154 Robineau Rd Syracuse NY 13207-1644 Office: DeLaney & O'Connor LLP One Lincoln Ctr Syracuse NY 13202 Office Phone: 315-476-8450. Business E-Mail: oconnor@delaneyoconnor.com.

O'CONNOR, PAMELA JOHNSON, relocation company executive; b. NYC, Nov. 19, 1950; d. Vernon M. and Gloria R. (Banks) Johnson; m. Thomas P. O'Connor, May 8, 1982; 1 child, Molly Patricia. BS in Comm., U. Tenn., 1972. Lic. real estate agt., Ga.; cert. sr. relocation profl. Promotion asst. Sta. WSB-TV, Atlanta, 1972-74; dir. pub. rels. Equity Realty, Atlanta, 1980-83; ptnr. Bryson-O'Connor Pub. Rels., Atlanta, 1983-85; dir. mktg. svcs. All Points Relocation Svc. Inc., Atlanta, 1974-80, exec. v.p., 1985-92, pres., 1992; pres, CEO Leading Real Estate Companies of World, Chicago. Speaker confs. in field, 1987—. Contbr. articles to profl. publs., chpt. to book. Recipient award of excellence Know Atlanta mag., 1989; named one of Real Estaet's 25 Most Influential Thought Leaders Realtor Mag., 2006. Mem. Atlanta Relocation Network (bd. dirs., treas. 1988-91), Employee Relocation Coun. (industry adv. coun. 1990—, various coms. 1985—, Meritorious Svc. award 1990, Disting. Svc. award 1993). Republican. Roman Catholic. Avocations: writing, needlecrafts, reading. Office: All Points Relocation Svc Inc 161 N Clark St Ste 1250 Chicago IL 60601-3294 Address: Leading Real Estate Cos of World 161 N Clark St Ste 1250 Chicago IL 60601-3294 *

O'CONNOR, PATRICK JOHN, education educator; b. Nov. 4, 1937; BA, Assumption Coll., Worcester, Mass., 1960; MA in English, Niagara U., Niagara Falls, NY, 1965; EdD, U. Mass., Amherst, 1978. Cert. tchr. secondary English Mass. English tchr. Worcester Pub. Schs., 1965—95; prof. edn. Worcester State Coll., 1995—. Named Tchr. of Yr., Ctrl. Mass. chpt. Phi Delta Kappa, 1988. Mem.: Mass. Tchrs. Assn., Nat. Assn. Scholars.

O'CONNOR, PATRICK JOSEPH, writer, musician, university educator; b. Wichita, Dec. 27, 1948; s. Rubie Nell Bishop; m. Carolyn Sue Drummond-Hay (div. Apr. 1, 1979); 1 child, Dalton. MA Comm., Wichita State U., 1989; grad., Citizen's Acad., Wichita, 2003. Lectr. Wichita State U., 1994—2000; instr. Embry-Riddle U., Wichita, 1996—98, 2004—06, Friends U., Wichita, 1997—98; artist in residence Wichita Pub. Schs., 1998—99; music reviewer for popular music and soc. Bowling Green State U., Ohio, 1996—98; instr. Newman U., Wichita, 2004. Dir. mus. exhibit Traditions of the Blues in Wichita First Nat. Black Hist. Soc. Kans. and Kans. Interpretive Traveling Exhibit, Kans. State Hist. Soc./Kans. Humanities Coun./NEH, Wichita, 1996—; dir. prodn. for panel and happening Wichita Art Mus., 1999; interviewer/writer Documentary: The Wichita Blues History Project, 1999—; panelist Friends U., Wichita, 2002—. Author: Tales From A Blackout, 1997, Wichita Blues: Discovery, 1998, Moody's Skidrow Beanery, 1999, Delano/ Stories From The Neighborhood, 2001, short stories; musician: (cassette tape) Upscale Blues, 1994, (CD) Blue Heaven: Bill Garrison with Jimmy D. Lane, 2000; actor: (musical revue) Pump Boys and Dinettes, 1998, Old Town Theatre; contbr. articles to profl. jours.; actor: Blues Brothers at Caberet Old Town; musical dir.: Taming of the Shrew, 2007. Mem. Art and Design Bd, Wichita, 2004; bd. dirs. Fisch Haus Gallery; regional judge Internat. Blues Challenge Blues Found. Memphis. Delano Maggard Scholarship grant, Wichita State U., 1989, Profl. Devel. grant, Kans. Arts Commn., 1994, Heritage Program grant, Kans. Humanities Coun./NEH, 1996, Rsch. grant, Wichita Cmty. Found., 1996, Multicultural Activity grant, Kans. Arts Commn./Nat. Endowment for Arts, 1997, Folk Arts Apprenticeship grant, Kans. State Hist. Soc./Nat. Endowment for Arts, 1997. Mem.: Kans. Folklore Soc., Am. Fedn. Musicians (bd. dirs. 2003), Poetic Genius Soc. Personal E-mail: Rowfant@hotmail.com.

O'CONNOR, PAUL DANIEL, lawyer; b. Paterson, NJ, Nov. 24, 1936; s. Paul Daniel and Anne Marie Christopher O'C.; children: Steven Paul, Sheryl Lynn, Laura Ann. BS in Engring, U.S. Naval Acad., 1959; LLB, U. Va., 1965. Bar: N.Y. 1965, Calif. 1995. Assoc. firm Winthrop, Stimson, Putnam & Roberts, NYC, 1965-72, partner, 1972-80; sr. v.p., gen. counsel Singer Co., Stamford, Conn., 1980-86; CEO Citation Builders, 1986—95; trustee Valley Trusts, Oakland, Calif., 1986—; gen. coun. Berg Holdings, Sausalito, Calif., 2007—. 1st lt. USAF, 1959-62. Mem.: Sonoma County Bar Assn., Bar Assn. San Francisco, Assn. Bar City NY, Fairfield County Hunt Club. Office: 2330 Marinship Way Ste 301 Sausalito CA 94965 Personal E-mail: poconnor59@comcast.net.

O'CONNOR, R. D., retired healthcare executive; BS in Psychology and Sociology, U. So. Miss., 1960, MS Adminstrv. Pers., 1961, PhD Mgmt. and Orgnl. Comm., 1983. Asst. dean student affairs Holmes Jr. Coll., Goodman, Miss., 1961-64, Dept. Edn., Jackson, Miss., 1964-65; asst. adminstr. Hinds Gen. Hosp., Jackson, Miss., 1965-68; adminstr. Rankin Gen. Hosp., Brandon, Miss., 1968-76; v.p. Human Resources/ Mktg. Delta Mgmt. Systems, Metairie, La., 1976-79; asst. to pres. Bapt. Med. Ctr., Jacksonville, Fla., 1979-82; pres. RiverGroup Riverside Hosp., Rivercorp Inc., Riverside Found., Jacksonville, Fla., 1982-87; owner O'Connor & Assocs., Jacksonville, Fla., 1987-91; pres. Fla. 1st: Managed Health Care, Winter Haven, Orlando & Tampa, Fla., 1991-94; dir. orgn. devel. Mid Florida Med. Svcs. Inc., Winter Haven, Fla., 1994-97. Instr. U. So. Miss., Hattiesburg, Ms.; tchr., lectr. various univs., C.C.s, military acads.; grad. faculty coord. Webster U.; online instr. for univs. Contbr. articles to profl. jours. and books. Commr. Cleary Heights Sewer Dist., 1978-79; pres'. selective task force Induction Procedures, 1969; chmn. personnel com. San Jose Baptist Ch., 1981-86, strategic planning com., 1986-87; gov's. com. Statewide Planning Vocat. Rehab., 1968; bd. dirs. Rankin County C. of C., 1970-73, exec. com., chmn. health affairs com., 1970-72, chmn. highway com. 1970-74, fin. com. 1971-73), Family Blood Assurance Program, 1972-77, v.p. 1977, Vol. Action Coun., 1973-76, United Givers Fund, 1973-76. With Army Security Agy., Air Nat. Guard, Med. Svc. Corps., ret. Fellow Am. Coll. Healthcare Execs. (life); mem. Fla. Hosp. Assn. (com. chmn. 1984), Greater Jacksonville Area Hosp. Coun. (chmn. 1985), Jackson-Vicksburg Hosp. Coun. (chmn. 1974), Nat. Assn. Mental Health (bd. dirs. 1973-74), Miss. Assn. Mental Health (pres. 1972-74), Miss. Hosp. Assn. (bd. dirs. 1973-76, exec. devel. com. 1972-75, mgmt. engring. adminstrv. bd. 1973, fin. com. 1972-74, chmn. nominating com. 1971, coord. divsn. profl. practice 1970). Home: 12837 Julington Forest Dr E Jacksonville FL 32258-2294

O'CONNOR, RALPH STURGES, investment company executive; b. Pasadena, Calif., Aug. 27, 1926; s. Thomas Ireland and Edith Masury (Sturges) O'Connor; m. Alice Maconda Brown, Apr. 28, 1950; children: George Rufus, Thomas Ireland III, Nancy Isabel, John Herman. BA, Johns Hopkins U., Balt., 1951; postgrad., Harvard U., Cambridge, Mass., 1967. With Highland Resources, Inc., Houston, 1951-87, exec. v.p., 1961-64, pres., 1964-87; pres., CEO Ralph S. O'Connor and Assocs., Houston, 1987—. Chmn. bd. dirs. Arnaud's Restaurant, New Orleans. Pres. Marian and Speros Martel Found., Houston, 1983—2003; trustee emeritus Rice U., Johns Hopkins U., Oldfields Sch., Glencoe, Md. With USAAF, 1943—46. Mem.: NAS, Presdl. Counselors, Houston Landmen's Assn. (past pres.), All Am. Wildcatters, Am. Assn. Petroleum Landmen, Johns Hopkins Instns., Players Club, River Oaks Country Club, Bayou Club. Home: 5627 Indian Cir Houston TX 77056-1006 Office: Ralph S O'Connor & Assocs 10000 Memorial Dr Ste 510 Houston TX 77024-3422 Office Phone: 713-682-3441. Personal E-mail: ralphsoconnor@yahoo.com.

O'CONNOR, ROD, chemist, consultant, inventor; b. Cape Girardeau, Mo., July 4, 1934; s. Jay H. and Flora (Winters) O'C.; m. Shirley Ann Sander, Aug. 7, 1955; children: Mark Alan (dec.), Kara Ann, Shanna Suzanne, Timothy Patrick. BS, S.E. Mo. State Coll., 1955; PhD, U. Calif., Berkeley, 1958. Asst. prof. chemistry U. Omaha, 1958-60, Mont. State Coll., 1960-63; assoc. prof. chemistry Mont. State U., Bozeman, 1963-66; assoc. prof., coordinator gen. chemistry Kent (Ohio) State U., 1966-67; prof., dir. 1st year chemistry U. Ariz., Tucson, 1968-72; staff assoc. Adv. Council on Coll. Chemistry Stanford (Calif.) U., 1967-68; vis. prof. Wash. State U., Pullman, 1972-73; prof. chemistry Tex. A&M, College Station, 1973-86; pres. Texas ROMEC Inc., College Station, 1983-98; prof. environ. studies Baylor U., Waco, Tex., 1996-99. Cons. insect venoms Hollister-Stier Labs., Spokane, Wash., 1963-67; lab. separates editor W.H. Freeman Co., 1968-78; ednl. cons. TUCARA-4 Media Resources, Inc., 1971-74; mem. Coll. Chemistry Cons. Service; vis. scientist, tour lectr. Am. Chem. Soc., 1970-86. Author: (with T. Moeller) Ions in Aqueous Systems, 1972, Fundamentals of Chemistry, 1981, (with C. Mickey and A. Hassell) Solving Problems in Chemistry, 1981, (with L. Peck and K. Irgolic) Fundamentals of Chemistry in The Laboratory, 1981, (with T.E. Taylor and P. Glenn) Toward Success in College, 1981, (with A. Hassell and C. Mickey) Advanced Problems in Applied Chemistry, 2000; films Laboratory Safety, 1971; Contbr. articles to profl. jours.; patentee in field Recipient nat. teaching award Mfg. Chemists Assn., 1978; 4 regional teaching awards. Fellow AAAS, Am. Inst. Chemists, Sigma Xi; mem. Internat. Soc. Toxinology, Am. Chem. Soc. Office: Chem Consulting Svcs 1300 Angelina Cir College Station TX 77840-4855 Office Phone: 979-693-5804. E-mail: docroc34@hotmail.com.

O'CONNOR, SANDRA DAY, retired United States Supreme Court Justice; b. El Paso, Tex., Mar. 26, 1930; d. Harry A. and Ada Mae (Wilkey) Day; m. John Jay O'Connor, III, 1952; children: Scott, Brian, Jay. BA with great distinction, Stanford U., 1950, LLB, 1952. Bar: Calif., Ariz. Dep. county atty., San Mateo, Calif., 1952—53; civilian atty. Q.M. Market Ctr., Frankfurt am Main, Germany, 1954—57; pvt. law practice Maryvale, 1958—60; asst. atty. gen. State of Ariz., 1965—69; mem. Ariz. State Senate, 1969—75, majority leader, 1972—75, chmn. com. on state, county and mcpl. affairs, 1972—73; judge Maricopa County Superior Ct., Phoenix, 1975—79, Ariz. Ct. Appeals, 1979—81; assoc. justice US Supreme Ct., Washington, 1981—2006; chancellor Coll. William & Mary, Williamsburg, Va., 2005—; vis. judge US Ct. Appeals (2nd Cir.), NYC, 2006—. Mem. Maricopa County Bd. Adjustments and Appeals, 1963—64, Ariz. Criminal Code Commn., 1974—76, Nat. Defense Adv. Com. on Women in Svcs., 1974—76; chmn. vis. bd. Maricopa County Juvenile Detention Home, 1963—64; chmn. Ariz. Supreme Ct. Com. to Reorganize Lower Cts., 1974—75, Maricopa County Superior Ct. Judges Tng. and Edn. Com., 1977—79; vice chmn. Ariz. Select Law Enforcement Review Commn., 1979—80; served on Legis. Coun., Probate Code Commn., Ariz. Adv. Coun. on Intergovernmental Relations; mem. Iraq Study Group, 2006. Mem. bd. editors: Stanford (Calif.) U. Law Rev.; co-author (with H. Alan Day): (memoir) Lazy B: Growing Up on a Cattle Ranch in the American Southwest, 2002; author (with Dan Andreasen, illustrator): (children's books) Chico: A True Story from the Childhood of the First Woman Supreme Court Justice, 2005. Trustee Rockefeller Found.; mem. adv. bd. Smithsonian Nat. Mus. Natural History, 2006—; mem., selection com. Okla. City Nat. Meml. and Mus., 2005—; co-chair nat. adv. coun. Campaign for Civic Mission of Schs., 2005—; mem. Cathedral Chpt. Wash. Nat. Cathedral, 1991—99. Named Woman of Yr., Phoenix Advt. Club, 1972, National Women's Hall of Fame, 1995; named one of Most Powerful Women, Forbes mag., 2005; recipient Ann. award, NCCJ, 1975, Disting. Achievement award, Ariz. State U., 1980, Gimble Nat. award, Gimble Phila. awards Com., 1982, Elizabeth Blackwell award, Hobart & William Smith Coll., 1985, award of Merit, Stanford Law Sch., 1990, OH State Law award, OH State U., 1992, Fordham Stein prize, Fordham U., 1992, Sara Lee Frontrunner award, 1997, ABA medal, 1997, Thomas Jefferson award of Law, U. Va., 1987, William Green award for Profl. Excellence, U. Richmond, 1990. Fellow: Am. Acad. Arts & Scis.; mem.: Anglo-Am. Exchange, Ariz. State Personnel Commn., Stanford Ctr. Ethics (adv. bd. 2005—), Am. Soc. Internat. Law (adv. com. 2001—), Ariz. Women Lawyer's Assn., Nat. Assn. Women Judges, Adv. Com. for Judiciary Leadership Devel. Coun. (hon.), Ariz. Judges' Assn., Calif. Bar Assn., Maricopa County Bar Assn. (chmn. Lawyer Referral Svc. 1960—62), Ariz. Bar Assn. (former mem. Com. Legal Aid, former mem. Com. Public Relations, former mem. Com. Lower Ct. Reorganization, former mem. Com. Continuing Legal Edn.), ABA (exec. bd. Ctrl. European and Eurasian Law Initiative 1990—, exec. com. Mus. Law 2000—, adv. commn. Standing Com. on Law Library of Congress 2002—, mem. Commn. on Civic Edn. and Seperation of Powers 2005—). *

O'CONNOR, SHERYL BRODERICK, literature and language educator; b. Macon, Ga., Apr. 14, 1943; d. Charles Robert and Gloria Broderick; children: Kimberly O'Connor Biss, Broderick Jeffrey. BA, Mt. Holyoke Coll., South Hadley, Mass., 1965; MA in Tchg. English, Smith Coll., Northampton, Mass., 1965. Cert. tchr. English Mass., tchr. secondary English N.J. Tchr. Sweeney Meml., Chicopee, Mass., 1966—69; tchr., jr. sch. chair MacDuffie Sch., Springfield, Mass., 1969—72; instr. critical reading Camden County Coll., Blackwood, NJ, 1987—90; tchr. East Camden Mid. Sch., Camden, NJ, 1984—. Mem. curriculum adv. com. Camden Bd. Edn., 1996; mem., v.p. Bd. Edn., Medford, NJ, 1979—89. Contbr. poetry to mags. Fellow: Rotary Found. of Rotary Internat.; mem.: Camden Edn. Assn. (rep. 2000—), Mensa, Cherry Hill Rotary (pres. 2000—). Republican. Anglican. Home: 2 Andover Ct Southampton NJ 08088

O'CONNOR, THOMAS C., energy executive; b. 1955; m. Diane O'Connor; 3 children. BS cum laude in Biology, U. Mass., Lowell, 1977, MS in Environ. Studies, 1980. Dir. mktg. svcs., dir. bus. devel. Tex. Ea. Transmission Corp.; pres. PanEnergy Devel. Co.; supr. environ. compliance to mgr. environ. compliance to mgr. market devel. Algonquin Gas Transmission Duke Energy Corp., Charlotte, NC, 1987—89, sr. v.p. mktg. and capacity mgmt., v.p. mktg., v.p. east coast mktg. NE pipeline group, 1994—2002, pres., CEO Duke Energy Gas Transmission's US ops.,

2002—05, group v.p. corp. strategy, 2005—06, group exec., COO US Franchised Electric and Gas, group exec., pres. comml. businesses, 2006—; pres. Maritimes & NE Mgmt. Co. Mem. sci. devel. bd. U. Mass Lowell Coll. Arts & Scis. Office: Duke Energy Corp 526 S Church St Charlotte NC 28202-1803 *

O'CONNOR, THOMAS EDWARD, petroleum geologist, management consultant; b. Boston, Dec. 16, 1936; s. John Stephen and Lucille (Arnold) O'C.; m. Jeannette Canuel, June 30, 1962 (dec. Mar. 1976); children: Kevin Patrick, David Andrew, Shelley Elizabeth; m. Moufida Banawi, Apr. 28, 1977; children: Tammer Thomas, Amr Adel Hammouda (dec. July 2006). BSc, Stanford U., Calif., 1958; MSc., U. Colo., 1961. Geologist Amoco Prodn. West, Denver, 1963-67, Amoco Netherlands, Utrecht, 1968-69, Amoco Europe, London, 1969-74; chief geologist Gulf of Suez Petroleum Co., Cairo, 1974-79; geol. mgr. Amoco Africa, Mid East, Houston, 1979-80; v.p. Aminoil, Houston, 1980-84; prin. petroleum engr. The World Bank, Washington, 1985-98; internat. petroleum mgmt. cons., 1998—; chmn. bd. dirs. Benchmark Oil & Gas AB, Stockholm, 2003—. Adj. prof. George Washington U. Grad. Sch. Polit. Mgmt., 2003—, Royal Sch. Mines, Imperial Coll., London, 2004—; presenter in field. Lt. USNR, 1960—63. Mem. Am. Assn. Petroleum Geologists (cert.), Houston Geol. Soc. Muslim. Home and Office: 937 5th St Camano Island WA 98282 Personal E-mail: teoconnor@aol.com.

O'CONNOR, TOM, corporate executive, management consultant; b. Boston, June 11, 1942; s. Thomas Henry and Blanche (Cosgrove) O'C.; m. Mary Alice Kelly; 1 child, Michael Kelly O'Connor. BA in econs., U. Mass., 1971; postgrad., U. Wis., Milw., 1971-73, U. Del., 1978, Am. U., 1980. Economist Interstate Commerce Commn., Washington, 1973-74; mgr. planning U.S. Railway Assn., Washington, 1974-75; cons. transp. R.L. Banks & Assocs., Washington, 1975-77; asst. dir. Conrail, Phila., 1977-79; asst. v.p. econs. Assn. Am. R.R.'s, Washington, 1979-82; v.p. DNS Assocs., Inc., Washington, Lexington (Mass.), 1982-88; v.p., ptnr. Snavely, King, Majoros, O'Connor & Lee, Inc., Washington, 1988—. Chmn. surface freight transport regulation com. Transp. Rsch. Bd., 1994—. Pres. Green Briar Civic Assn., Fairfax, Va., 1985, Greenbriar Dem. Club, Fairfax, 1984-89, Greenbriar Community Ctr., Fairfax, 1984; v.p. Greenbriar West PTA, Fairfax, 1986-88. Sgt. U.S. Army, 1963-66. Mem. Am. Econ. Assn., Am. Statis. Assn., Coun. Logistics Mgmt., Transp. Rsch. Forum (pres. Washington chpt. 1987-89), Nat. Def. Assn. (bd. dirs. 1991-94), Air Force Assn., Phi Beta Kappa, Phi Kappa Phi. Democrat. Roman Catholic. Avocations: camping, reading, counseling. Home: 13222 Point Pleasant Dr Fairfax VA 22033-3515 Office: Snavely King Majoros O'Connor & Lee Inc 1111 14th St Ste 300 Washington DC 20005-4050 Office Phone: 202-371-9149. Fax: 202-842-4966. Personal E-mail: skmoltom1@aol.com.

O'CONNOR, WILLIAM MICHAEL, search company executive; b. Chgo., Sept. 28, 1947; s. Maurice Francis and Margaret (Brand) O'C.; m. Karen Jean Gipson, Jan. 30, 1972; children: Sean, Mary, William, David. BA in History, Loyola U., Chgo., 1970. Interviewer Ill. State Employment Svc., Chgo., 1970-73; ins. agt. Equitable Life Assurance Soc., Chgo., 1973-76; recruiting officer U.S. Army, Chgo., 1977-78; profl. employment rep. GTE Network Systems, Northlake, Ill., 1978-81; employment mgr. Molex, Inc., Lisle, Ill., 1981-85, Rand McNally & Co., Skokie, Ill., 1986; v.p. Richards Cons., Ltd., Chgo., 1987-88; v.p., ptnr. Chestnut Hill Ptnrs., Deerfield, Ill., 1988-95; v.p. Kennedy & Co., Chgo., 1995-2001; pres. Edgewood Internat., Woodridge, Ill., 2001—. Mem. Art Inst. Chgo., Smithsonian Inst., Field Mus. Natural History, Rep. Nat. Com., 1984—. Lt. col. USAR, 1971-99. Decorated Chevalier, Sovereign Mil. Order of Temple of Jerusalem, 1998—. Mem. Res. Officers Assn., U.S. Armor Assn. (Order of St. George), Mil. Police Assn., 337th Cavalry Regiment (Order of the Spur), Bus. Mobilized for Loyola U. Roman Catholic. Home: 3018 Edgewood Pky Woodridge IL 60517 Office: Edgewood Internat 3018 Edgewood Pkwy Woodridge IL 60517 Office Phone: 630-985-6067. E-mail: wocatedgewood@aol.com.

O'CONNOR, WILLIAM RIORDAN, lawyer, educator; b. Bronx, NY; s. Charles Samuel O'Connor and Elizabeth Mary Riordan; 1 child, Charles. BA, Fordham Coll., Bronx, 1973; MA, Fordham U., Bronx, 1977, PhD, 1982; JD, Cardozo Sch. Law, NYC. Asst. prof. philosophy Siena Coll., Londonville, NY, 1983—84; law clk. Weg and Myers, PC, NYC, 1987—90, assoc., 1990—91; pvt. practice Bronx, NY, 1996—. Adj. lectr. St. Peter's Coll., Jersey City, 1991—; assoc. Law Offices of Stephen K. Seung, NYC, 1999—; arbitrator small claims NYC Civil Cts., 2004—, guardian ad litem, 2006—. Mem.: Am. Philos. Assn., NY County Lawyers Assn., Assn. Bar NYC. Democrat. Roman Catholic. Home: 5775 Mosholu Ave 1-C Bronx NY 10471 Office Phone: 718-548-8576. Office Fax: 718-548-2306. Personal E-mail: wroc9675@earthlink.net.

OCVIRK, OTTO GEORGE, artist; b. Detroit, Nov. 13, 1922; s. Joseph and Louise (Ekle) O.; m. Betty Josephine Lebie, June 11, 1949; children: Robert Joseph, Thomas Frederick, Carol Louise. B.F.A., State U. Iowa, 1949, M.F.A., 1950. Advt. artist apprentice Bass-Luckoff Advt. Agy., Detroit, 1941; engring. draftsman Curtiss-Wright Aircraft Corp., Buffalo, 1942; faculty Bowling Green (Ohio) State U., 1950—, assoc. prof., 1960-65, prof. art, 1965-85, prof. emeritus, 1985—. Exhibited in group shows at, Denver Mus. Art, 1949, 50, 53, Detroit Inst. Art, 71948, 49, 50, 53, 56, Dayton (Ohio) Art Inst., 1950, 51, 56, Ohio State U., 1953, Walker Art Center, Mpls., 1948, 49, Library of Congress, Washington, 1949, Bklyn. Mus., 1949, Joslyn Mus., Omaha, 1949, Colorado Springs Fine Arts Center, 1949; represented in permanent collections, Detroit Inst. Arts, Dayton Art Inst., Friends of Am. Art, Grand Rapids, Mich., State U. Iowa, Iowa City, Bowling Green State U.; (Recipient 24 nat., regional juried art exhbn. awards 1947-57, others.); Author: (with R. Stinson, P. Wigg, R. Bone and David Cayton) Art Fundamentals— Theory and Practice, 1960-97, 7th edit., 1994, 8th edit., 1997, 9th edit., 2001, 10th edit., 2005. Scoutmaster Toledo Area council Boy Scouts Am., 1960-63, asst. scoutmaster, 1963-74, dist. commr., 1978-80. Served with AUS, 1943-46. Recipient Silver Beaver award Boy Scouts Am., 1976, Magnifico award Medici Circle, Bowling Green State U., 1987. Mem. Delta Phi Delta (hon.) Methodist. Home and Office: 231 Haskins Rd Bowling Green OH 43402-2206 *"Freedom for expression" keys creative thought into a productive whole.*

O'DAY, PAUL THOMAS, trade association executive; b. May 2, 1935; s. James Thomas and Jeannette Irene (Deschenes) O'D.; m. Nancy Frances Eitler, June 16, 1962; children: Kathleen, Maureen, Michael, Ellen. BA, Am. Internat. Coll., Springfield, Mass., 1958; JD, Georgetown U., 1963; MPA, Am. U., 1967; D of Pub. Adminstrn. honoris causa, Am. Internat. Coll., 1997. Bar: D.C. 1964, Va. 2005, U.S. Supreme Ct. 1974. Patent examiner US Patent Office, Washington, 1959-62; exec. sec. panel high-speed ground transp., auto. air poll. Dept. Commerce, Washington, 1965-66, staff asst. to sec., 1967-69, exec. asst. to sec., 1969-71, dep. dir. bur. domestic commerce, 1972-74; dep. dir. Nat. Bus. Coun. for Consumer Affairs, Washington, 1971-72; cons. to Gen. Counsel GE, Fairfield, Conn., 1974-75; asst. trade rep. Exec. Office of the Pres., Washington, 1975-77; dep. asst. sec. US Dept. Commerce, Washington, 1978-84; pres. Am. Fiber Mfrs. Assn., Washington, 1984—. Chmn. Fiber Econs. Bur., 1984—; pres. Eisenhower World Affairs Inst., 1993-99, exec. com., 2000-06. Corporator Am. Internat. Coll., 1974—; mem. governing coun. Shakespeare Theater Guild, 1989-2001. Recipient Constl. Law award Georgetown U. Law Ctr., 1962; Alumni award Am. Internat. Coll., 1970; Pres.'s Meritorious Exec. award., 1984; Nat. Inst. Pub. Affairs fellow Princeton U., 1964 Mem.: AAAS, Nat. Assn. Mfrs. (bd. dirs. 2006—), Am. Chem. Soc., Jussi Bjorling Soc. USA (charter), O'Dea Clan Assn. (Corofin, Ireland), Cosmos Club. Home: 8261 Private Ln Annandale VA 22003-4471 Office: Am Fiber Mfrs Assn 1530 Wilson Blvd Ste 690 Arlington VA 22209 Home Phone: 703-425-7727.

O'DAY, STEPHEN EDWARD, lawyer; b. Indpls., Nov. 8, 1953; s. George R. and M. Kate (Harrington) O'D.; m. Fran Bold, Dec. 16, 1973; children: Jeremy, Kelly, Rory, Curry. Student, Ga. Inst. Tech., 1971-72; BA summa cum laude, Furman U., 1976; JD cum laude, Harvard U., 1979. Bar: Ga. 1979, US Dist. Ct. (no. dist.) Ga. 1979, US. Ct. Appeals (5th cir.) 1979, US Ct. Appeals (11th cir.) 1981, US Claims Ct. 1981, US Supreme Ct. 1986. Assoc. Hurt, Richardson, Garner, Todd & Cadenhead, Atlanta, 1979-85, former ptnr.; now mem. Smith, Gambrell & Russell, Atlanta, ptnr. Trustee Ga. Conservancy, Atlanta, 1981-91, sec. 1984-85, vice chmn. 1986; bd. dirs. Southern Environ. Law Ctr., Charlottesville, Va., 1985—, sr. litig. counsel., chmn. Environ. Adv. Coun. for Ga. Lt. Gov., Solid Waste Task Force, Ga., part-time instr. Ga. Tech. Youth dir. Episcopal Ch. of St. Peter and St. Paul, Marietta, Ga., 1982-84, vestry, 1984-85; bd. trustees Upper Chattahoochee River Keeper, 1996-, mem. Met. Atlanta C. of C. (water quality task froce), Leadership Atlanta. Named Ga. Super Lawyer, Atlanta Mag. and Law & Politics Media, Inc, Am. Leading Lawyers for Bus., Chambers USA, Best Environ. Lawyer, Corp. Counsel; recipient River Guardian award. Mem. ABA (natural resources, energy and environ. sect., litigation, tort trial & ins. practice sects.), Ga. Bar Assn. (chmn. com. on the handicapped, 1980-81, mem. young lawyers sect., vice chmn. environ. sect. 1995), Phi Beta Kappa, Phi Eta Sigma, Pi Gamma Mu. Democrat. Chmn. Harvard Environ. Law Soc. Office: Smith Gambrell & Russell LLP Ste 3100 1230 Peachtree St NE Promenade II Atlanta GA 30309 Office Phone: 404-815-3527. Office Fax: 404-815-6827. Business E-Mail: soday@sgrlaw.com.

ODDEN, ALLAN ROBERT, education educator; b. Duluth, Minn., Sept. 16, 1943; s. Robert Norman and Mabel Eleanor (Bjornnes) Odden; m. Eleanor Ann Rubottom, May 28, 1966; children: Sarina, Robert. BS, Brown U., 1965; MDiv, Union Theol. Sem., 1969; MA, Columbia U., 1971, PhD, 1975. Tchr. N.Y.C. Pub. Schs., 1967-72; rsch. assoc. Teachers' Coll. Columbia U., NYC, 1972-75; dir. policy Edn. Commn. of the States, Denver, 1975-84; prof. U. So. Calif., LA, 1984-93, U. Wis., Madison, 1993—. Rsch. dir. Sch. Fin. Commns., Conn., 1974—75, SD, 1975—76, Mo., 1975—76, Mo., 1993, Mo., 94, NY, 1978—81, NJ, 1991—92, Ark., 2003, Ark., 2005—06, Wyo., 2005, Wyo., 05, Wyo., 06, Wash., 2005—06, Wis., 2005—07; co-dir. Consortium Policy Rsch. Edn.; cons. Nat. Govs. Assn., Nat. Conf. State Legislatures, US Sec. Edn., US Senate, US Dept. Edn., many state legislatures and govs.; mem. task force sch. fin. equity adequacy and productivity NRC, 1996—99; ct. master Superior Ct. NJ in Abbott V. Burke Sch. Fin. Case, 1997—98. Author: (book) Education Leadership for America's Schools, 1995; co-author: (books) Financing Schools for High Performance, 1998, Paying Teachers for What They Know and Do, 1997, 2d edit., 2002, School Finance: A Policy Perspective, 1992, 4th edit., 2007, Reallocating Resources: How to Boost Student Achievement Without Spending More, 2001, How to Create World Class Teacher Compensation, 2007; editor: Education Policy Implementation, 1991, Rethinking School Finance, 1992, School-Based Financing, 1999; contbr. articles to profl. jours., chapters to books. Mem. L.A. Chamber Edn. and Human Resources Commn., 1986, Gov.'s Sch. Fin. Commn., Calif., 1987, Calif. Assessment Policy Com., Gov.'s Edn. Task Force, Wis., 1996, Carnegie Corp. Task Force Edn. in the Early Yrs., 1994—96; mem. nat. rsch. coun. com. sch. fin. equity, adequcy and productivity, 1996—99; mem. Gov.'s Blue Ribbon Commn. State and Local Partnerships 21st Century, Wis., 2000. Grantee, Dept. Edn., Carnegie Corp., Spencer Found., Ford Found., Atlantic Philanthropic Svcs., Mellon Found., Carnegie Corp., Pew Charitable Trusts, Rockefeller Found., Joyce Found. Mem.: Nat. Soc. Study Edn., Politics Edn. Assn., Am. Ednl. Fin. Assn. (pres. 1979—80), Am. Ednl. Rsch. Assn. Avocations: Lionel training collecting, youth soccer, baseball coach. Office: U Wis Sch Edn Wis Ctr Edn Rsch 1025 W Johnson St # 653E Madison WI 53706-1706 Home: 360 W Washington Ave Unit 1002 Madison WI 53703-2766 Home Phone: 608-233-8720. Business E-Mail: arodden@wisc.edu.

ODDIS, JOSEPH ANTHONY, health associations executive; b. Greensburg, Pa., Nov. 5, 1928; s. Giacinto and Felicetta (D'Amico) O.; m. Jeanne Trevena, July 10, 1954; children: Joseph Michael, Marie Theresa/ BS, Duquesne U., 1950; DSc (hon.), Mass. Coll. Pharmacy, 1975, Phila. Coll. Pharmacy and Sci., 1975, Albany Coll. Pharmacy, Union U., 1976, Duquesne U., 1989, Mercer U., 1995; LHD (hon.), L.I. U., 1991. Staff pharmacist Mercy Hosp., Pitts., 1950-51, asst. chief pharmacist, 1953-54; chief pharmacist Western Pa. Hosp., Pitts., 1954-56; staff rep. hosp. pharmacy Am. Hosp. Assn., Chgo., 1956-60; dir. div. hosp. pharmacy Am. Pharm., Washington, 1960-62; exec. v.p. Am. Soc. Health-System Pharmacists, Washington, 1960-98. Pres. Am. Soc. Hosp. Pharmacists Research and Edn. Found., 1986-98. Active Boy Scouts Am., Camp Fire Girls; Sec. Am. Soc. Health-System Pharmacists Research and Edn. Found., 1970-86. Served with AUS, 1951-53. Recipient 1st cert. Honor award Duquesne U. Sch. Pharmacy, 1969, named Outstanding Alumnus, 1978; recipient Harvey A.K. Whitney award Am. Soc. Hosp. Pharmacists, 1970, Julius Sturmer Meml. Lecture award Rho Chi soc. Phila., 1971, Howard C. Newton Lecture award 1977, Samuel Melendy Lecture award, 1978, Hugo H. Schaefer award, 1983, Reed and Alice Henninger Lecture award, 1984, Donald E. Francke medal, 1986, Remington medal award, 1990. Fellow AAAS; mem. Am. Pharm. Assn., Am. Soc. Hosp. Pharmacists, Am. Inst. History Pharmacy, Internat. Pharm. Fedn. (pres. hosp. pharmacy sect. 1977-81, v.p. 1984-86, pres. 1986-90), Drug Info. Assn., Am. Soc. Assn. Execs., Can. Soc. Hosp. Pharmacists (hon.), Soc. Hosp. Pharmacists Australia (hon.), Pharm. Soc. Gt. Britain (hon.), Pharm. Soc. Nigeria (hon.), Nat. Coun. Patient Info. and Edn. (sec. 1982-85), Israel Pharm. Soc. (hon.), Rho Chi, Kappa Psi (hon.), Duquesne U. Century Club (charter). Home: 6509 Rockhurst Rd Bethesda MD 20817-1661 Office: Am Soc Health-System Pharmacists 7272 Wisconsin Ave Bethesda MD 20814-4836

ODDONE, PIERMARIA JORGE, physicist; b. Arequipa, Peru, Mar. 26, 1944; came to US, 1961; s. Pietro Giovanni and Maria Vittoria (Jona) O.; m. Barbara S. Oddone, Aug. 27, 1965; children: Gian Michele, Alessandra. BS in Physics, MIT, 1965; PhD in Physics, Princeton U., 1970. Postdoctoral fellow Calif. Tech. Inst., Pasadena, 1970-72, Lawrence Berkeley Nat. Lab., Calif., 1972-76, staff scientist Calif., 1976-78, sr. staff scientist Calif., 1978-87, dir. physics div. Calif., 1987-91, lab. dep. dir. Calif., 1990—2005; dir. Fermi Nat. Accelerator Lab., Batavia, Ill., 2005—. Head initial positron electron project Accelerator Stanford Linear Accelerator Ctr., 1976—82, leader, sci. coord. Time Project Chamber collaboration, 1984—87. Recipient Panofsky award, Am. Phys. Soc., 2005. Fellow Am. Phys. Soc. Achievements include research in in high energy physics; development of Time Projection Chamber and Asymmetric B-Factory (a particle collider). Office: Fermilab PO Box 500 Batavia IL 60510-0500 Office Phone: 630-840-3211. Business E-Mail: pjoddone@fnal.gov.

O'DEA, THOMAS JOSEPH, clinical engineer, medical physicist; b. NYC, July 7, 1938; s. Patrick Jostph O'Dea and Beatrice Gaffney; m. Kathryn Jean O'Dea, July 11, 1970; children: Christine, Patrick. BA, Cath. U. Am., 1961; MA, SUNY, Buffalo, 1967; PhD, U. Minn., 2001. Registered profl. engr., Minn. Physics tchr. Christian Bros., NYC, 1961—67; dir. med. physics Evanston (Ill.) Hosp., 1968—77; dir. engring. U. Minn. Hosp., Mpls., 1977—97; prin. Tom O'Dea Health Care Engring., St. Paul, 1997—. Ptnr. Hemoxy LLC, Mpls., 1998—; adj. prof. med. physics and elec. engring. U. Minn., 2007; cons. in field. Contbr. articles to profl. jours. Mem. Telecomm. and Tech. Com., Shoreview, Minn., 2000—. Recipient Best Mgmt. article, Biomed. Inst. and Tech., 1997, Best Rsch. Article award, 2001; grantee, NSF, 1967, NIH, 1968. Mem.: Assn. Advanced Med. Physics, Assn. Advanced Med. Inst. (various offices), Am. Coll. Clin. Engrng (chmn. advocacy 1984—, award 2002). Roman Catholic. Achievements include patents for device for measuring O2 diffusion from red blood cells. Avocation: swimming. Home and Office: 925 Arbogast St Shoreview MN 55126 Office Phone: 651-283-8542. Personal E-mail: tomkayjodea@comcast.net.

O'DEAR, CRAIG STEVEN, lawyer; b. Quincy, Ill., June 26, 1957; s. H.C. and Martha Lou (Holbert) O'D.; m. Stephanie Doolin Patterson, Feb. 11, 1995. BS in Engring. Mgmt., U. Mo., Rolla, 1979; JD, Vanderbilt U., 1982. Bar: Mo. 1982, U.S. Dist. Ct. (we. dist.) Mo. 1982, U.S. Ct. Appeals (8th cir.) 1984, U.S. Ct. Appeals (10th cir.) 1988, U.S. Ct. Appeals (11th cir.) 1994. Indsl. engr. IBM Corp., Endicott, N.Y., summer 1979; summer assoc. Bass, Berry & Sims, Nashville, 1980, Stinson, Mag & Fizzell, Kansas City, Mo., 1981, Kirkland & Ellis, Chgo., 1981; assoc. Stinson, Mag & Fizzell, Kansas City, 1982-88, Bryan Cave LLP, Kansas City, 1988-89, ptnr., 1990—, mem. exec. com. Chmn. recruiting com. Bryan Cave, Kansas City, 1988-92, coord. litigation dept., 1994—, group leader product liability client svc., 1996—. Chmn. United Way Pacesetter Camp, Kansas City, 1985; mem. leadership devel. program Kansas City Tomorrow, Kansas City, 1990. Patrick Wilson scholar Vanderbilt U., 1979-82. Mem. Kansas City Club. Republican. Presbyterian. Avocations: flying, golf, running, motorcycling. Office: Bryan Cave LLP 3500 One Kansas City Pl 1200 Main St Kansas City MO 64105-2122 Office Phone: 816-374-3207. E-mail: csodear@bryancave.com.

ODELL, HERBERT, lawyer; b. Phila., Oct. 20, 1937; s. Samuel and Selma (Kramer) O.; m. Valerie Odell; children: Wesley, Jonathan, James, Sarah, Samuel. BS in Econs., U. Pa., 1959; JD magna cum laude, U. Miami, 1962; LLM, Harvard U., 1963. Bar: Fla. 1963, Pa. 1968, D.C. 2002. Trial atty. tax div. U.S. Dept. Justice, Washington, 1963-65; assoc. Walton, Lantaff, Schroeder, Carson & Wahl, Miami, Fla., 1965-67; from assoc. to ptnr. Morgan, Lewis & Bockius, Phila., 1967-89; ptnr. Zapruder & Odell, Phila., 1989-98, Odell & Ptnrs., Phila., 1998-99, Miller & Chevalier, Chartered, Phila., 2000—06, Chamberlain, Hrdlicka, White, Williams & Martin, 2007—. Adj. prof. U. Miami, Villanova U.; lectr. various tax insts. Contbr. articles to profl. jours. Ford fellow, 1962-63. Mem.: ABA, D.C. Bar Assn., Phila. Bar Assn., Pa. Bar Assn., Fla. Bar Assn., Harvard Club, Beta Alpha Psi, Omicron Delta Kappa, Phi Kappa Phi. Avocations: sailing, running, tennis, scuba diving, fishing. Office: Chamberlain Hrdlicka et al Ste 570 300 Conshohocken State Rd West Conshohocken PA 19428 Home Phone: 610-827-0967; Office Phone: 610-772-2310. Business E-Mail: hodell@chamberlainlaw.com.

ODELL, JAMES CALVIN, history professor, theology studies educator; b. Weed, Calif., Nov. 23, 1951; s. Calvin Harry and Bessie Pearl (Matthews) Odell; m. Nancy Louise Everest, June 28, 1975; children: Abigail B. Cook, Rebekah L. Brooking, Rachel L. BS in Sem. Studies, We. Bapt. Coll., Salem, Oreg., 1974; ThM in Hist. Theology, Dallas Theol. Sem., Tex., 1978; PhD in Bibl. Studies, Pensacola Christian Coll., Fla., 2000. Pastor Lafayette Bapt. Ch., Oreg., 1979—81; missionary Bapt. Mid. Missions, Cleve., 1984—99; prof. Crossroads Bible Coll., Indpls., 1987—. Chaplain USAR, 1983—. Author: Odells Offspring and Kinfolk, 2003. Lt. col. USAR, 1983—, Desert Storm, Bosnia, Kuwait. Avocation: genealogy. Office: Crossroads Bible Coll 601 N Shortridge Rd Indianapolis IN 46219

ODELL, PATRICK LOWRY, retired mathematics professor; b. Watonga, Okla., Nov. 29, 1930; s. Max Vernon and Pamela (Massey) Odell; m. Norma Lou Maddox, Aug. 16, 1958 (dec. May 1980); children: James M., David L., Michael R.L., Julie K., Patricia L., Deborah L.; m. Dovalee Dorsett, Aug. 3, 1985. BS, U. Tex., 1952; postgrad., UCLA, 1953-54; MS, Okla. State U., 1958, PhD, 1962. Mathematician White Sands (N.Mex.) Proving Grounds, 1952-53, Kaman Nuclear, Albuquerque, 1958-59, U.S. Naval Nuclear Ordnance Evaluation Unit, 1959-62, Ling-Temco Vought Aeros., 1962; asst. prof. math. U. Tex., Austin, 1962-66; prof., chmn. dept. math. Tex. Technol. U., Lubbock, 1966-71, coordinator insts., dir. rsch., Coll. Arts and Sci., 1971-72; prof math. scis. and environ. scis. U. Tex., Dallas, 1972-88, prof. emeritus, 1988—; prof. emeritus math. sci. Baylor U., Waco, Tex., 1988—2001; exec. dean grad. studies and rsch. U. Tex., Dallas, 1972-75. Assoc. dir. Tex. Ctr. for Rsch., Austin, 1964—66; rsch. scientist Def. Rsch. Lab., 1963—65; cons. math. statistician, 1962—. Capt. USAF, 1953—57. Fellow: Am. Statis. Assn., Tex. Acad. Sci. (Disting. Tex. Scientist award 1994). Home: 1117 Deer Run Rd Valley Mills TX 76689 Personal E-mail: pat_odell@baylor.edu.

ODEN, GLORIA, language educator, poet; b. Yonkers, NY, Oct. 30, 1923; d. Redmond Stanley and Ethel (Kincaid) Oden. *Great Uncle A.G. Oden served in the Civil War from 1863-1866. Grandfather Collins William Oden, at was sole boatmaker in Beaufort, NC. Great Uncle Samuel Jesse Battle was the first black Parole Commissioner in NYC. Grandfatehr George Washington Kincaid was a pioneer builder of black churches across the South. R.S. Oden was the first black member of New Rochelle Housing Authority. Bertha Bea Oden White was a prime mover in Lincoln School Desegregation Case. Ethel Redmond Oden received a four-year scholarship to NYU. R.S. Oden, Jr. received a four-year Avery scholarship to University of Pittsburgh. First cousin Aurelia Whittington, wife to historian John Hope Franklin.* BA in History, Howard U., 1944, JD, 1948. Faculty New Sch. for Social Rsch., NYC, 1966; vis. lectr. dept. English SUNY, Stony Brook, 1969-70; asst. prof. English U. Md., Balt., 1971—75, assoc. prof., 1975—83, prof., 1983—96. Sr. editor IEEE proc. and tech. mags., 1966—67; supr. math./sci. books Appleton-Century-Crofts, 1967—68; project dir. lang. arts books Hold, Rinehart and Winston, 1968—72, sr. editor coll. dept., 1968—71; editor Am. Inst. Physics/Am. Jour. Physics, 1961—66; lectr. in field; condr. numerous poetry readings; juror fiction panel Mass. Cultural Coun., 1994; juror poetry panel N.J. State Coun., 1993, 94; numerous others; cons. Reel Deal Prodns. Co., NEH, 1984, 87. Author: (poems) Resurrections, 1978, The Tie that Binds, 1980, Appearances, 2003; contbr. poetry to mags., newspapers, audio, anthologies, articles to profl. jours. Recipient Disting. Black Women's award, Towson U., 1984; NEH Summer grantee, 1974, Breadloaf Writers scholar, 1960, Creative Writing fellow, John Hay Whitney Found., 1955—56, Yaddo fellow, 1956. Mem.: PEN Am. Ctr., Poetry Soc. Am. (bd. govs. 1981—82, v.p. 1983—84). Home: 707 Maiden Choice Ln Apt 8119 Catonsville MD 21228-4185

ODEN, GREG, professional basketball player; b. Buffalo, Jan. 22, 1988; s. Greg Oden, Sr. and Zoe Oden. Student in Bus. Adminstrn., Ohio State U., Columbus, 2006—07. Draft pick Portland Trail Blazers, Oreg., 2007. Mem. USA Basketball Men's Sr. Nat. Team, 2007—. Named a McDonald's All-Am., 2006; named USA Today Player of Yr., 2005, 2006, Parade Mag. Player of Yr., 2005, 2006, Gatorade Ind. and Nat. Player of Yr., 2005, 2006, Gatorade Nat. HS Male Athlete of Yr., 2006, Player of Yr., Nat. HS Coaches Assn., 2006, Ind. Mr. Basketball, Indpls. Star, 2006, Atlanta Tipoff Club 2006 Naismith Prep Player of Yr.; recipient Arthur L. Trester Mental Attitude award, Ind. Boy's Basketball Class 4A, 2005—06, Morgan Wootten award (McDonald's All-Am. Player of Yr.), 2006. Achievements include being picked first in the 2007 NBA draft. Office: Portland Trail Blazers Rose Quarter One Center Ct Portland OR 97227 *

ODEN, JOHN TINSLEY, engineering educator, mathematician, consultant; b. Alexandria, La., Dec. 25, 1936; s. John James and Sara Elizabeth (Lyles) O.; m. Barbara Clare Smith, Mar. 19, 1965; children: John Walker, Elizabeth Lee. BS, La. State U., 1959; MS, Okla. State U., 1960, PhD, 1962; DSc (hon.), Tech. U. Lisbon, Portugal, 1986; Doctorate (hon.),

Polytechnique de Mons, Belgium, 2000, Tech. U. Krakow, Poland, 2001, Ecole Normale Superior Cachan, 2006. Registered profl. engr., Tex., La. Teaching asst. La. State U., Baton Rouge, 1959; asst. prof. Okla. State U., Stillwater, 1961-63; sr. structures engr. Gen. Dynamics, Fort Worth, 1963-64; prof., head dept. engring. mechanics U. Ala., Huntsville, 1964-73; prof. U. Tex., Austin, 1973—, Carol and Henry Groppe prof. engring., Ernest and Virginia Cockrell chair in engring. Austin, 1987-93, Cockrell Family Regents chair engring., 1993—. Prof. Coope U. Fed., Brazil, 1974; dir. Inst. Computational Engring and Sci., 2003, assoc. v.p. for rsch., 2003—; mem. Sci. Rsch. Coun. vis. scholar Brunel U., Eng., 1981; com. on computational mechanics NRC; chmn. U.S. Nat. Com. on Theoretical and Applied Mechanics, 1992-94; founder, CEO computational Mechanics Co., Inc., 1982-96; Peter O'Donnell Jr. chair in computer sys., 2003. Author, editor 45 books; editor Jour. Computer Methods in Applied Mechanics and Engring., 1980—; contbr. over 500 articles to profl. jours. Decorated Chevalier Ordre des Palms Academique (France); recipient rsch. award Southeastern Conf. on Theoretical and Applied Mechanics, 1978, Lohmann medal Okla. State U., 1991, Hocott Rsch. award, 1992, Computational Mechanics Medal Japan Soc. Mech. Engrs., 1993, Presdl. Citation, U. Tex. Austin, 2004 Fellow ASCE (life; Outstanding Svc. award 1968, Walter Huber rsch. award 1973, Theodore von Karman medal 1992, Joe J. King Prof. Engring. award 1994), ASME (hon. mem., Worcester Reed Warner medal 1990, Timoshenko medal 1996), NAE, Soc. Engring. Sci. (pres. 1978, Eringen medal 1991), Am. Acad. Mechanics (pres. 1990-94, Disting. Svc. medal 1995), Internat. Assn. Computational Mechanics (pres. 1990-94, Congress-Gauss-Newton medal 1994); mem. Soc. Indsl. and Applied Math., U.S. Assn. Computational Mechanics (pres. 1990-92, John Von Neumann medal 1993), Soc. Natural Philosophy, Nat. Acad. Engring. Mex., Nat. Acad. Engring. Brazil, World Innovation Found. (hon. 2004), Polish Assn. Computational Mechanics (Zienkiewicz medal, 2007). Home: 7403 W Rim Dr Austin TX 78731-2044 Office: Univ Tex Austin ICES Campus Code CO200 Austin TX 78712

ODEN, ROBERT A., JR., academic administrator; m. Teresa Oden; children: Robert, Katherine. BA in History and Lit., Harvard Coll.; MA in Religious Studies/Oriental Langs., Cambridge U.; MA in Theology, Harvard Divinity, 1972; PhD in Near Eastern Langs. and Lit., Harvard U., 1975; MA (hon.), Dartmouth Coll., 1987. Faculty Dartmouth Coll., 1975—89, prof., 1985—89, chair dept. of religion, 1983—89; dir., founder Dartmouth's Humanities Inst.; headmaster Hotchkiss Sch., Lakeville, Conn., 1989—95; pres. Kenyon Coll., Gambier, Ohio, 1995—2002, Carleton Coll., Northfield, Minn., 2002—. Chmn. com. on orgn. and policy Dartmouth Coll., com. on admissions and fin. aid; lectr. in field. Author: The Bible Without Theology, 1987. Mem.: Conn. Assn. Ind. Schs. (bd. dirs.). Avocations: fishing, running, religious studies, archaeology. Office: Carleton Coll 1 North College St Northfield MN 55057 Office Phone: 507-646-4305. E-mail: president@acs.carleton.edu. *

ODEN, ROBERT RUDOLPH, surgeon; b. Chgo., Dec. 2, 1922; s. Rudolph J. E. and Olga H. (Wahlquist) Oden; m. Nancy Clow; children: Louise, Boyd, Beach, Lisbeth. BS, U. Ill., 1943; MD, Northwestern U., 1947, MS in Anatomy, 1947. Intern Augustana Hosp., Chgo., 1947-48, resident in surgery, 1948-49; resident in orthopaedics Hines Vets. Hosp., Chgo., 1949-51; resident in children's orthopaedics Shriner's Hosp., 1953-54; pvt. practice Chgo., 1954-57, Aspen, Colo., 1957—. Clin. assoc. prof. orthopedics U. Colo.; orthop. surgeon U.S. Olympic Com., 1960, 72, 76, 80; founder, trustee Pitkin County Bank, 1983—. Assoc. editor: Clin. Orthopedics and Related Rsch. Founder Aspen Inst. Theol. Futures, 1978, Gt. Tchrs. and Preachers Series Episc. Ch., 1989; trustee U.S. Ski Ednl. Found., 1967—82, Aspen Valley Hosp., 1978—86; founder Aspen Orthop. and Sports Medicine Pub. Found., 1985; mem. organizing com. Aspen World Cup, 1976—92; founder Aspen Pitken Employee Housing, 1975. Named to Colo. Ski Hall of Fame, 2002, U.S. Ski Hall of Fame, 2002; recipient Biegan award Most Outstanding Svc. to U.S. Skiing, 1985, Halsted award, U.S. Ski Assn., 1987. Mem.: SICOT, ACS, Internat. Knee Inst., Internat. Soc. Knee, ACL Study Group, Internat. Ski Safety Soc., Am. Orthop. Soc. Sports Medicine (Hall of Fame 2004), Can. Orthop. Assn., Rocky Mountain Traumatologic Soc., Am. Assn. Bone & Joint Surgeons, Western Orthop. Assn., Internat. Coll. Surgeons, Am. Acad. Orthop. Surgeons, Phi Beta Kappa. Home: PO Box 660 Aspen CO 81612-0660 also: PO Box 172 Captiva FL 33924-0172 Office: 100 E Main St Aspen CO 81611-1778 E-mail: capoden@earthlink.net.

ODEN, WILLIAM BRYANT, bishop, educator; b. McAllen, Tex., Aug. 3, 1935; s. Charles Alva and Evea (Bryant) O.; m. Marilyn Brown, July 12, 1957; children: Danna Lee Oden Bowen, William Dirk, Valerie Lyn, Charles Bryant. BA, Okla. State U., 1958; MDiv, Harvard U., 1961, postgrad., 1964; ThD, Boston U., 1964; DD (hon.), Oklahoma City U., 1980; LHD (hon.), Centenary Coll., 1990. Ordained to ministry Meth. Ch., 1961. Pastor Aldersgate United Meth. Ch., Oklahoma City, 1963-69, St. Stephen's United Meth. Ch., Norman, Okla., 1969-76, Crown Heights United Meth. Ch., Oklahoma City, 1976-83; prof. Phillips Grad. Sem., Enid, 1976-88; pastor 1st United Meth. Ch., Enid, 1983-88; bishop United Meth. Ch., La., 1988-96, Dallas area, 1996—2004, Ecumenical del. to Lambeth Conf., 1998. Pres., United Meth. Coun. Bishops, 2000-01; pres. SCJ Coll. of Bishops, 1989-90; del. Gen. Conf., 1976, 80, 84, 88; chmn. Okla. Del. to Gen. and Jurisdictional Confs., 1984, 88; Jackson lectr. Perkins Sch. Theology, So. Meth. U., 1975, Wilson lectr. SCJ Bishop's Week, 1989; co-chair World Meth.-Anglican Dialogue, 1991-95; bd. dirs. Wesley Works Project; pres. Gen. Bd. Higher Edn. & Ministry, 1996-01; pres. comm., United Meth. Comm., 2000-04; Ecumenical officer, head communion, 2004-. Author: Oklahoma Methodism in the Twentieth Century, 1968, Liturgy as Life Journey, 1976, Wordeed: Evangelism in Biblical and Wesleyan Perspective, 1978; contbr.: Send Me: The Iteneracy in Crisis, 1991, Vision and Supervision, 2003. Trustee Oklahoma City U., 1980-88, Southwestern U., Winfield, Kans., 1983-88, Centenary Coll., 1988-96, Dillard U., 1988-96, So. Meth. U., 1996—2004. Named to U. Hall of Fame, Okla. State, 2003; recipient Outstanding Alumni award, Harvard Divinity Sch., 2005; Charles E. Merrill fellow, Harvard U., 2003. Mem. Am. Acad. Homiletics. Methodist. Avocations: writing, reading biographies, mountain climbing, backpacking. Office Phone: 214-768-1200. Personal E-mail: wbo8@earthlink.net.

ODENATH, DAVID R., JR., diversified financial services company executive; married; 3 children. Grad., Susquehanna U. Sr. v.p., dir. sales, Investment Consulting Group Paine Webber; pres. Prudential Investments Prudential Fin., Inc., Newark, 1999—2003, pres. annuities, 2003—. Avocations: ice hockey, water-skiing. Office: Prudential Financial Inc 751 Broad St Newark NJ 07102-3777 *

ODENIGBO, INNOCENT CHUKWUNWIKE, linguist, writer, consultant; b. Nri, Anambra State, Nigeria, Sept. 28, 1941; arrived in U.S., 1998; s. Lazarus Okonkwo and Rosaline Ama Odenigbo; m. Monica Chinwe Akpu, Oct. 6, 1996; m. Felicia Umekwulu Egesi, Sept. 26, 1967 (div. Sept. 16, 1996); children: Uchenna Zephyrina, Ifeanyi Innocent, Chukwuemeka John-Mary, Uzoamaka Assumpta. BA in Languages, U. Grenoble, 1971; postgrad., U. Besancon, 1974—75, U. Aston, Birmingham, Eng., 1981—82, CIRNEA, Paris, 1990—94; PhD in Languages, Am. West U., 2002; MBA, Dowling Coll., 2002. Lang. prof. Inst. Mgmt. and Tech., Enugu, Nigeria, 1971—73; rsch. officer Nigerian Nat. Supply Co., London, 1973—78; sr. news presenter Nigerian TV Authority, Enugu, Nigeria, 1979—81; chief editor, anchorman Anambra Broadcasting Svc., Awka, Nigeria, 1983—98; pres. IMC Info. Svcs., Newark, 2003—. Cons. IMC Info. Services, Newark, 2003—. Author: (poetry) Thank God for America; prodr.: (TV Documentaries) Les Halles de Paris, 1990, Le Louvre du Pouvoir, 1992, L'enfant qui Prolonge La Vie, 1994. Patron French Lang. Students Assn. Nnamdi Azikiwe U., Awka, Nigeria. Recipient Best Broadcaster award, Nigeria Union Journalists, 1984. Mem.: Nigerian Inst. Mgmt., Nigerian Inst. Pub. Rels., Soc. Nigerian Broadcasters, Inst. Linguists London, Soc. Profl. Journalists, Internat. Soc. Poets (Disting. Mem. 2000, 2001). Office Phone: 973-677-2665. E-mail: odenigbo5@aol.com.

ODENWELLER, ROBERT PAUL, philatelist, trade association administrator, retired pilot; b. Sept. 19, 1938; s. Charles Joseph and Robina Katharine (Watson) O.; m. Jane Blackistone Rawlings, June 24, 1965; 1 stepchild, Joy McCorriston; 1 child, Liesl Hasbrouck. BS, US Air Force Acad., 1960. Commd. USAF, 1956, advanced through grades to capt., 1963, resigned, 1956-66. Mem. Collectors Club Inc., NYC, 1964—, gov. 1969—, program chmn., 1970-80, 2004—, mem. editl. bd., 1975—, sec. 1979-82, v.p. 1983-86, pres. 1987-90, trustee, 1992-98; trustee, vice chmn. then chmn. expert com. Philatelic Found., NYC, 1970—. Author: The FIP Guide to Exhibiting and Judging Traditional and Postal History Exhibits, 1993; author, editor: Philatelic Vocabulary in Five Languages, 1978 (Vermeil medal 1979); editor: Opinions VI, 1992 (Gold medal), The Stamps and Postal History of Nineteenth Century Samoa, 2004 (Gold medal, Nat. Grand award, Internat. Gold medal, 2005, Spl. prize, 2005, Best in Show, 2005), The Collectors Club Philatelist, 2005- (3 Gold medals, Vermeil medal 2006, Diane Boehret award Am. Philatelic Congress, 2006); contbr. articles to profl. jours. Recipient Grand Prix d'Honneur, Zeapex Orgn., 1980; selected to sign Roll of Disting. Philatelists, Brit. Philatelic Fedn., 1991, Alfred Lichtenstein Meml. award Collectors Club, NY, 1993, TWA Flight Ops. Meritorious Achievement award 1995, award of Excellence, 1995, 2000. Fellow Royal Philatelic Soc. London (hon., spl. rep. for US 2003—, conduct com. 2004—, Crawford medal, 2005), Royal Philatelic Soc. N.Z. (Collins award 2005); mem. Fedn. Internat. de Philatelie (pres. commn. traditional philately 1978-96; Grand Prix d'Honneur 1980, Svc. medal 1996, Rsch. medal 2006), Am. Philatelic Soc. (bd. dirs. 1981-84, 89-90, named Champion of Champions 1973, Luff award 1996, chmn. 2003-), Assn. Internat. Des Experts Philateliques (expert 1980-, bd. dirs. 1987-), Fedn. New Zealand Philatelic Socs., Grand Prix Club Internat. (sec., treas. 1980-89, bd. dirs. 1989-92, 94-00, v.p. 1994-96, pres. 1996-2000), Soc. Australasian Specialists (pres. 1969-72), US Chess Fedn., European Acad. Philately, Smithsonian Instn. Coun. Philatelists. Republican. Episcopalian. Avocations: stamp collecting/philately, photography, languages, chess, bridge. Home: Chalon Round Top Rd Bernardsville NJ 07924 Office: Collector's Club Inc 22 E 35th St New York NY 10016-3806 Office Phone: 908-766-5460. Business E-Mail: ccpeditor@cs.com.

ODER, BROECK NEWTON, history educator, director; b. Ill. s. Bruce Newton and Mary Louise Oder; m. Jolene Marie Peragine, 1975 (dec. June 1979). BA in History, U. San Diego, 1974, MA in History, 1975; postgrad., U. N.Mex., 1976-79. Life C.C. tchg. credential, Calif. Rsch. asst. to pres. U. San Diego, 1975; grad. asst. U. N.Mex., Albuquerque, 1976-79; tchr. history, chmn. dept. Santa Catalina Sch., Monterey, Calif., 1979—, asst. dean students, 1981-83, dir. ind. study, 1981-95, dean students, 1983-91, dir. emergency planning, 1986—, dean campus affairs, 1991-94, dir. security, 1994—. Disaster preparedness coun. Monterey County Office Edn., 1988-99; chair Diocesan Sch. Emergency Preparedness Coun, 1991-98. Mem. bd. of tchrs. The Concord Rev.; contbr. articles to profl. publs. including American National Biography, Safety and Security Adminstrn. in Sch. Facilities, 2d edit. Participant Jail and Bail, Am. Cancer Soc., Monterey, 1988, 89; reviewer sch. emergency plans, Monterey, 1989—. Recipient award of merit San Diego Hist. Soc., 1975, Outstanding Tchr. award U. Chgo., 1985, Outstanding Young Educator award Monterey Peninsula Jaycees, 1988, resolution of commendation Calif. Senate Rules Com., 1988, cert. of commendation Calif. Gov.'s Office Emergency Svcs., 1991, nat. cert. of achievement Fed. Emergency Mgmt. Agy., 1991, Outstanding High Sch. Tchr. award Tufts U., 1998, High Sch. Tchr. of Excellence, U. Calif. at San Diego, 1998, 05, Outstanding Tchr. of Am. History award Calif. DAR, 2001-02; nominee Disney Tchr. award, 2002, 03. Mem. ACLU, NAACP, NRA (life), Am. Hist. Assn., Orgn. Am. Historians, Nat. Coun. on History Edn., Soc. for History Edn., Second Amendment Found., Law Enforcement Alliance Am., Calif. State Sheriffs Assn., Nat. Assn. Sch. Resource Officers, Phi Alpha Theta. Avocations: reading, sports, target shooting. Office: Santa Catalina Sch 1500 Mark Thomas Dr Monterey CA 93940-5291

ODERMATT, ROBERT ALLEN, architect; b. Oakland, Calif., Jan. 3, 1938; s. Clifford Allen and Margaret Louise (Budge) O.; m. Diana Birtwistle, June 9, 1960; children: Kristin Ann, Kyle David. BArch, U. Calif., Berkeley, 1960. Registered architect, Calif., Oreg., Nev., Colo., Hawaii; cert. Nat. Coun. Archtl. Registration Bds. Draftsman Anderson Simonds Dusel Campini, Oakland, 1960-61; architect James R. Lucas, Orinda, Calif., 1961-62, ROMA Architects, San Francisco, 1962-76, architect, pres., 1976-84; prin. ROMA Design Group, San Francisco, 1962-92; pres. The Odermatt Group, Berkeley, Calif., 1992—. Prin. spkr. Internat. Conf. on Rebuilding Cities, Pitts., 1988; mem. U.S. Design in Am. Program, Sofia, Bulgaria, Armenian Disaster Assn. Team, 1989, NA Collateral Internship Mgmt. Com.; prin. State of Calif. Bay Arera Facilities Plan, 1992, Greece Resort Privatization Program, 1993. Prin. designer U.S. Embassy, Bahrain, Grand Canyon Nat. Park, 1977, Yosemite Nat. Park, 1987; prin. planner hotel complex Westin Hotel, Vail, Colo., 1982, Kaanapali Resort, 1987, Las Montanas Resort, San Diego; master plan U. Calif., Berkeley, 1988, Kohanaiki and Mauna Lani resorts, 1989, Calif. State Strategic Real Estate Plan, 1992, Greek Resort/Marina Privatization Program, 1993, Tektronix Strategic Plan, 1994, United Labs, Manila Master Plan, 1995, State of Calif. Real Estate Orgn. Plan, 1996, Ford Island Pearl Harbor Master Plan, 1996, Pearl Harbor Visitor Ctr. Plan, 1997, Albiano Resort Study, 1998; master plans include Trefethen Vineyards, Bell Garden, Napa Valley Expo. Bd. dirs. Nat. Archtl. Accrediting Bd., 2003—, pres., 2005; mem. Santa Cruz Downtown Assessment, Eisenhower E. Plan, Alexandria, Va., Upper Potomac W. Plan, Alexandria, King St. Revitalization Study, Alexandria, 2004, Oakland Mayor's Com. on High Density Housing, 1982, Oakland Gen. Plan Congress, 1994; mem. waterfront plan adv. com. City of Oakland, 1996, Westpark Town Ctr., 2003, Koa Ridge Cmty., Oahu, Hawaii, King St. Retail Plan, Alexandria; mem. adv. com. Queen Emma Founds. Lands of Waikiki Plan, 2004—05. Recipient Leslie M. Boney Spirit of Fellowship award. Fellow AIA (dir. East Bay chpt. 1969-71, pres. 1980-81, dir. Calif. coun. 1979-81, Disting. Svc. award Calif. chpt., 1991, nat. dir. 1983-86, nat. v.p. 1986-87, chair AIA internat. steering com. 1993-94, graphic stds. adv. com. 1991-92, U. Calif. archtl. review commn. 1992-96, exec. com. Coll. Fellows 1996-98, vice chancellor Coll. Fellows 1999, chancellor 2000, East Bay medal 1997, Edward C. Kemper medal for outstanding svc. 2004), Am. Archtl. Found. (regent, bd. dirs.), Nat. Archt. Accreditation Bd. (pres.). E-mail: raomatt@aol.com.

ODESCALCHI, EDMOND PÉRY, international financial consultant, author; b. Budapest, Hungary, Oct. 11, 1928; came to U.S., 1950; s. Prince Bela and Princess Charlotte (de Bay) O.; m. Esther de Kando, Sept. 30, 1961; children: Daniel, Dominic. Student, Cornell U., 1951, U. Pa., 1956-57; MS in Econs., St. Andrews U., Scotland, 1959. Adminstrv. asst. French Govt., Baden, Fed. Republic Germany, 1948-50; world trade specialist IBM Corp., Poughkeepsie, NY, 1952-60, project mgr., 1960-74, devel. mgr. East Fishkill, NY, 1974; pres. Global Tech., Inc., NYC, 1975-91. Internat. fin. cons., 1975-93. Author: The Global Arena, 1973, Faces of Reality, 1975, The Third Crown, 1997, The Evolution of Behavior, 2002; contbr. articles to profl. jours. Mem. Rep. Nat. Com., 1984—. Mem. Bus. Cons. Assn., Am. Mus. Natural History (assoc.), Internat. Platform Assn. Home and Office: 1020 Freedom Rd Pleasant Valley NY 12569-7636

O'DESKY, ILYSE HOPE, psychologist, educator; b. Newark, Oct. 27, 1964; d. Sheldon O'Desky and Leona Brenner; m. Leonard Brian Garber, June 28, 1992. D of Clin. Psychology, Yeshiva U., Bronx, 1992. Asst. prof. Kean U., Union, NJ, 2001—; pediatric neuropsychologist Neuropsychological Testing Ctr., Springfield, 2003—. Med. staff St. Barnabas Med. Ctr., Livingston, NJ, 1997—. Invited spkr. Nat. NLD Orgn., San Francisco, 2006. Recipient Rschr. Yr. award, NJ Psychol. Assn., 2003; grantee, Kean U., 2001—02, 2005—06. Mem.: APA, NJ Psychol. Assn. (sec. to academic and sci. affairs com. 2003—06), NJ Neuropsychological Soc. (exec. bd. 2002—04), Nat. Acad. Neuropsychology. Achievements include patents for Thinking Board Game Line by Line; Board Game Boxed In; research in Overdiagnosis of Attention Deficit/Hyperactivity Disorder; Misdiagnosis of ADHD and NLD. Office: 26 Linden Avenue Springfield NJ 07081 Home Phone: 908-322-0589; Office Phone: 973-376-5511.

ODGERS, RICHARD WILLIAM, lawyer; b. Detroit, Dec. 31, 1936; s. Richard Stanley and Elsie Maude (Trevarthen) O.; m. Gail C. Bassett, Aug. 29, 1959; children: Thomas R., Andrew B. AB, U. Mich., 1959, JD, 1961. Bar: Calif. 1962. Assoc. Pillsbury, Madison & Sutro, San Francisco, 1961—69, ptnr., 1969—87, 1998—2000; exec. v.p., gen. counsel Pacific Telesis Group, 1987-98; ptnr. Pillsbury Winthrop Shaw Pittman, San Francisco, 2001—. Mem. Calif. Task Force Lawyer Support for Legal Svcs. Exec. vice chmn., bd. dirs. Legal Aid Soc. Employment Law Ctr.; dir. Legal Cmty. Against Violence; dir., sec.-treas. Van Loben Sels/RembeRock Charitable Found.; bd. dirs. Immigrant Legal Resource Ctr., Fed. Dist. Ct. Hist. Soc.; mem. Calif. Legal Svcs. Trust Fund Commn. With USNR. Fellow Am. Bar Found., Am. Judicature Soc., Am. Coll. Trial Lawyers; mem. ABA, Am. Law Inst., Am. Coll. Law Practice Mgmt., Bar Assn. San Francisco (past dir., co-chair task force charitable giving). Office: Pillsbury Winthrop Shaw Pittman 50 Fremont St San Francisco CA 94105 Office Phone: 415-983-1202. Office Fax: 415-983-1200. Business E-Mail: richard.odgers@pillsburylaw.com.

ODIERNO, RAYMOND T., career military officer; b. Rockway, NJ, 1954; s. Raymond J. and Helen Odierno; m. Linda Odierno; children: Anthony, Kathrin, Michael. BS, U.S. Mil. Acad., West Point, NY, 1976; MS in Nuc. Effects Engring., N.C. State U.; MA in Nat. Security and Strategy, U.S. Naval War Coll. Commd. lt. U.S. Army, advanced through grades to lt. gen., 2004, nuc. rsch. officer, chief acquisition support divsn. Def. Nuc. Agy., 1986—87, various positions, commdr. 2d bat., 1992—94, commdr. artillery divsn. Ft. Hood, Tex., 1995—97, dir. requirements and force mgmt. Office Dep. Chief Staff Ops. and Plans Washington, commdg. gen., 4th Infantry Divsn. (Mechanized) Ft. Hood, Tex., 2002—04; asst. to the Chmn. of the Joint Chiefs of Staff US Dept. Def., Washington, 2004—06; commdg. gen. III Corps. & Ft. Hood U.S. Army, Ft. Hood, Tex., 2006; comdr. Multi-Nat. Corps-Operation Iraqi Freedom, Baghdad, Iraq, 2006—. Decorated Army Disting. Svc. medal, Def. Superior Svc. medal, Legion of Merit with 5 oak leaf clusters, Meritorious Svc. medal with 3 oak leaf clusters, Def. Meritorious Svc. medal. Office: Multi-Nat-Forces-Iraq 7115 S Boundary Blvd MacDill AFB Tampa FL 33621

ODLAND, STEVE, consumer products company executive; BBA, U. Notre Dame, Ind., 1980; M in Mgmt., Northwestern U., 1981. Various positions Quaker Oats Co.; sr. v.p., gen. mgr. snacks divsn. Sara Lee, 1996—98, pres. bakery foodservice. divsn., 1997—98; pres., CEO Tops Markets, Inc., 1998—2000; COO Ahold USA, Inc., 2000—01; chmn., pres., CEO AutoZone Inc., Memphis, 2001—05; chmn., CEO Office Depot, Inc., Delray Beach, Fla., 2005—. Chmn. corp. governance task force Bus. Roundtable, 2004; bd. dirs. Gen. Mills, Inc. Named Top New CEO, Bloomberg Markets Mag., 2002. Office: Office Depot Inc 2200 Old Germantown Rd Delray Beach FL 33445

ODLE, ROBERT CHARLES, JR., lawyer; b. Port Huron, Mich., Feb. 15, 1944; s. Robert Charles and Elizabeth Dagmar (Lassen) O.; m. Lydia Ann Karpinol, Aug. 2, 1969. BA, Wayne State U., Detroit, 1966; JD, Detroit Coll. Law, 1969, LLD (hon.), 1992. Staff asst. to pres. of US, 1969-71; dir. adminstrn. Com. Re-election of President, 1971-73; dep. asst. sec. HUD, 1973-76; Washington corp. affairs rep. Internat. Paper Co., 1976-81; asst. sect. Dept. Energy, 1981-85; ptnr. Weil, Gotshal & Manges, 1985—. Mem. Mich. Bar Assn., DC Bar Assn., Delta Theta Phi. Clubs: University (Washington). Republican. Roman Catholic. Home: 476 S Union St Alexandria VA 22314-3826 Office: Weil Gotshal & Manges LLP Ste 900 1300 Eye St NW Washington DC 20005 Office Phone: 202-682-7180.

O'DOHERTY, BRIAN, writer; b. Ballaghadereen, Ireland; came to U.S., 1957; m. Barbara Novak, 1960. MB BCh, Univ. Coll. Dublin, Nat. U. Ireland, 1952, DPH with honors, 1955; MS in Hygiene, Harvard U., 1958. TV host Invitation to Art, Mus. Fine Arts, Boston, 1958-61; art critic N.Y. Times, 1961-64; host Dialogue, WNBC, 1961-64; vis. prof. Berkeley U., 1967; dir. visual arts Nat. Endowment for Arts, 1969-76, dir. media arts, 1976-94; dir. Millennium Projects, 1994-96. Art and architecture critic Today Program, 1971-77; adj. prof. Barnard Coll., 1969-96; editor-in-chief Art in Am., 1971-74; Univ. prof. fine arts and media L.I. U., 1997—2007. Author: (art book) Object and Idea: A New York Art Journal, 1961-67, 1967; editor: (museum study) Museums in Crisis, 1972, (art books) American Masters, The Voice and the Myth, 1973, 2d edit., 1995, Inside the White Cube, 1986, revised edit., 1999, Studio and Cube, 2007, (novels) The Strange Case of Mile P., 1992 (Saggitarius award, 1993), The Deposition of Father McGreevy, 1999 (Booker prize short list, 2000); dir.: (films) Hopper's Silence, 1981; contbr. articles to profl. jours. Recipient Mpls. Citizens award, 1961, Eire Soc. Gold medal for contbns. to culture, 1963, Grand Prix Montreal Internat. Festival of Arts Film award, 1982, Emmy nominations; Smith-Mundt fellow. Fellow Royal Coll. Physicians Ireland (hon.); mem. Am. Irish Hist. Soc. (bd. dirs.), Whitney Mus. Am. Art (bd. dirs. 1996-2000), Coll. Art Assn. (life; Mather award 1964). Office: 15 W 67th St New York NY 10023-6226

O'DOHERTY, SUSAN ANN, psychologist, writer; b. Flushing, NY, Mar. 22, 1952; d. Dorothy and Cahir O'Doherty; m. William Steven Donnenberg, Nov. 27, 1975; 1 child, Benjamin Donnenberg. PhD, Adelphi U., 1994. Lic. psychologist N.Y., 1999, cert. hypnotherapist Bklyn Inst. Psychotherapy and Psychoanalysis, 2000. Pvt. practice, Bklyn., 1999—. Vol. psychologist Doctors of the World, NYC, 2001—. Author: Getting Unstuck Without Coming Unglued: A Woman's Guide to Unblocking Creativity, 2007, (weekly advice column) The Doctor is In, (short stories) Special Needs, 2005, From the Diary of Ethel Muggs, 2005, At Fairlawn, 2005, Spring to Fall, 2005, Land of the Silver Birch, 2006, The Tower, The Velvet Underground, 2005. Clk., peace and social action com. Bklyn. Friends Meeting, 2002—04. Mem.: APA, Authors Guild. Democrat. Avocations: family life, reading, swimming, baking, travel. Office: 120 Remsen St Ste 1A Brooklyn NY 11201 Home Phone: 718-855-1035. Business E-Mail: dr.sue@mindspring.com.

ODOM, FLOYD CLARK, surgeon; b. Cisco, Tex., 1946; MD, U. Tex., San Antonio, 1972. Diplomate Am. Bd. Colon & Rectal Surgery, Am. Bd. Surgery. Intern Bexar County Hosp., San Antonio, 1972-73, resident in gen. surgery, 1973-77; fellow in colon & rectal surgery Baylor Med. Ctr., Dallas, 1977-78; colorectal surgeon Presbyn. Hosp., Dallas, 1997—. Fellow ACS, Am. Soc. Colon and Rectal Surgeons. Office: 8220 Walnut Hill Ln Dallas TX 75231-4406 Home Phone: 214-360-0364; Office Phone: 214-739-5758.

ODOM, LAMAR JOSEPH, professional basketball player; b. Jamaica, NY, Nov. 6, 1979; Student, UNLV; grad., U. Rhode Island, 2001. Player LA Clippers, 1999—2003, Miami Heat, 2003—04, LA Lakers, 2004—. Mem. US Olympics Basketball Team, Athens, Greece, 2004. Named to All-Rookie First Team, 2000. Office: c/o LA Lakers 555 N Nash St El Segundo CA 90245 *

ODOM, WILLIAM ELDRIDGE, retired military officer; b. Cookeville, Tenn., June 23, 1932; s. John Albert and Callie Frances (Everhart) O.; m. Anne Weld Curtis, June 9, 1962; 1 child, Mark Weld. BS, U.S. Mil. Acad., 1954; MA, Columbia U., 1962, PhD, 1970; DSc (hon.), Middlebury Coll., 1987. Commd. 2nd lt. U.S. Army, 1954, advanced through grades to lt. gen., 1984, ret., 1988; mem. U.S. Mil. Liaison Mission to Soviet Forces, Germany, 1964-66; from asst. prof. to assoc. prof. govt. U.S. Mil. Acad., West Point, 1966-69, 74-76; asst. Army attache U.S. Embassy, Moscow, 1972-74; nat. security staff mem. White House, 1977-81; asst. chief of staff for intelligence Dept. Army, US Dept. Def., Washington, 1981-85; dir. Nat. Security Agy., Fort Meade, Md., 1985-88; sr. fellow Hudson Inst., 1988—. Adj. prof. polit. sci. Yale U., 1989—; chmn. bd. dirs. Am. Sci. and Engring. Author: The Soviet Volunteers, 1973, On Internal War, 1992, Trial After Triumph, 1992, America's Military Revolution, 1993, The Collapse of the Soviet Military, 1998, Fixing Intelligence for a More Secure America, 2003; co-author (with Robert Dujarric) Commonwealth or Empire? Russia, Central Asia and The Transcaucasus, 1995(with Robert Dujarric) America's Inadvertent Empire, 2004; contbr. articles to profl. jours. Trustee Middlebury Coll., 1987-97. Decorated Def. D.S.M. with oak leaf cluster, D.S.M. with oak leaf cluster, Legion of Merit, Nat. Security medal, Nat. Intelligence D.S.M.; grand cross Order of Merit with Star (Fed. Republic Germany); Order Nat. Security Merit (Republic of Korea), officer Nat. Order of Merit (France). Mem. Coun. on Fgn. Rels., Am. Philos. Soc., Am. Assn. for Advancement of Slavic Studies, Internat. Inst. for Strategic Studies, Am. Polit. Sci. Assn., Acad. Polit. Sci., Am. Philos. Soc., Am. Legion. Office: Hudson Inst 1015 15th St NW Ste 600 Washington DC 20005 Office Phone: 202-974-2401.

ODONER, ELLEN J., lawyer; b. NYC, Jan. 23, 1952; BA magna cum laude, Yale U., 1973; JD, Harvard U., 1977. Bar: N.Y. 1978. Mem. Weil, Gotshal & Manges, NYC. Mem.: Assn. Bar City NY. Office: Weil Gotshal & Manges LLP 767 Fifth Ave New York NY 10153-0119 Office Phone: 212-310-8438. E-mail: ellen.odoner@weil.com.

O'DONNELL, BERNARD JOSEPH, JR., lawyer; b. Cleve., Oct. 31, 1969; s. Bernard Joseph and Afkam O'Donnell. BA in English, Mary Washington Coll., Fredericksburg, Va., 1993; MA in English, Loyola U. Chgo., 1996; JD summa cum laude, Fla. State U., 2000. Bar: Fla. 2000, US Dist. Ct. (mid. dist.) Fla. 2003, US Ct. Appeals (9th cir.) 2006. Adj. prof. English Palm Beach Atlantic Coll., West Palm Beach, Fla., 1997—98, Fla. State U., Tallahassee, 1998—2000, U. Fla., Gainesville, 2000—03; pvt. practice law Gainesville, 2000—03; assoc. Henderson, Franklin, P.A., Ft. Myers, Fla., 2003—06; sr. assoc. Newmeyer & Dillion, LLP, Newport Beach, Calif., 2006—. Pro-bono atty. Guardian Ad Litem, Ctrl. Fla., 2001—03; vis. prof. English U. Fla., 2006. Contbr. articles to profl. jours. Bd. dirs. S.W. Fla. Symphony, 2003—06. Recipient Excellence in Tchr. award, U. Fla., 2002, Excellence in Tchg. award, U. Fla. Anderson Scholars, 2002, 2003; Lester Crow scholar in edn., 1993, Dean's scholar in law, 1998, Katzentine-Simon scholar in law, 1999, Grinter fellow in English, 2000—03. Mem.: ABA, MLA, Fla. Bar Assn., Order of the Coif. Roman Catholic. Avocations: reading, basketball, guitar. Office: Newmeyer & Dillion 895 Dove St 5th Fl Newport Beach CA 92660 Office Phone: 201-488-1200. Business E-Mail: bernard.odonnell@ndlf.com.

O'DONNELL, CATHERINE ROSE, lawyer; b. South Charleston, W.Va., Feb. 15, 1964; d. Philip John and Madeline Marie Ripepi; m. Neil Taney O'Donnell, May 6, 1989; children: Neil Philip, Renata Marie. BA in Bus. and Econs., U. Pitts., 1984, JD, MBA, U. Pitts., 1987. Bar: D.C. 1988, Pa. 1988, U.S. Dist. Ct. (ea. dist.) Pa. 1988, U.S. Dist. Ct. (ctrl. dist.) Pa. 1990. Assoc. Drinker Biddle & Reath, Phila., 1988—90; assoc. to shareholder Elliott Reihner Siedzikowski & Egan, Scranton, Pa., 1990—2000; dist. justice Wilkes-Barre, Pa., 2000—02; assoc. O'Donnell Law Offices, Wilkes-Barre, 2002—. Mem. parish coun. St. Therese Ch., Wilkes-Barre, 1990—93, mem. fin. coun., 2000—, cantor, 2001—; bd. dirs. Wyoming Valley Montessori Sch., Kingston, Pa., 1997—2000; pres. Wyoming Valley Montessori Sch. PTA, Kingston, Pa.; bd. dirs. Osterhout Libr., Wilkes-Barre, 1999—2000, Cath. Youth Ctr., Wilkes-Barre, 1996—99, Wyoming Valley Habitat for Humanity, Kingston, 1991—93, Luzerne County LWV, Kingston, 1999—2000, Wyo. Sem. Lower Sch. Parents Assn., 2003—. Mem.: ATLA (social security disability sect. 2004—, bd. dir.), ABA (bd. dir. Pa. chpt.), Nat. Orgn. of Social Security Rep., Soical Security Disability Section, Northeast Trial Lawyers Assn., Lackawanna County Bar Assn., Wilkes-Barre Law and Libr. Assn., Pa. Trial Lawyers Assn., Pa. Bar Assn. Office: O'Donnell Law Offices 22 E Union St Wilkes Barre PA 18701 Home Phone: 570-826-0674; Office Phone: 570-821-5717. Business E-Mail: cro@odonnell-law.com.

O'DONNELL, CHRIS, actor; b. Winnetka, Ill., June 26, 1970; m. Caroline Fentress, Apr. 19, 1997; children Lilly Ann, Christopher Jr., Charles, Finley BA in Mktg., Boston Coll., 1995. Actor: (films) Men Don't Leave, 1990, Fried Green Tomatoes, 1991, Scent of a Woman, 1992 (Golden Globe award nomination best supporting actor 1992), School Ties, 1992, The Three Musketeers, 1993, Blue Sky, 1994, Circle of Friends, 1995, Mad Love, 1995, Batman Forever, 1995, In Love and War, 1996, The Chamber, 1996, Batman & Robin, 1997, Cookie's Fortune, 1999, Vertical Limit, 2000, 29 Palms, 2002, Kinsey, 2004, The Sisters, 2005; actor, prodr. (films) The Bachelor, 1999; actor: (TV films) The Amazing Westermans, 2004; actor:(TV appearances) The Practice, 2003, Two and a Half Men, 2004, Head Cases, 2005, Grey's Anatomy, 2005; prodr. (TV films) The Triangle, 2001, Miracle on the 17th Green, 1999 Office: Creative Artists Agy care Josh Lieberman 9830 Wilshire Blvd Beverly Hills CA 90212-1804

O'DONNELL, DENISE ELLEN, state official, former prosecutor; m. John F. O'Donnell; children: Maura, Jack. BS in Polit. Sci., Canisius Coll., 1968; MSW, SUNY, Buffalo, 1973, JD summa cum laude, 1982. Bar: NY 1983, U.S. Dist. Ct. (we., no., ea. and so. dists.) NY, U.S. Ct. Appeals (2d cir.), U.S. Supreme Ct. Law clk. to Hon. M. Dolores Denman NY Appellate Divsn. 4th Dept., Buffalo, 1982-85; asst. U.S. atty. (we. dist.) NY, US Dept Justice, Buffalo, 1985-90, appellate chief, 1990-93, 1st asst. US atty., 1993—97, US atty., 1997-2001; ptnr. Hodgson, Russ LLP, Buffalo, 2001—07; sr. adv. on criminal justice & domestic security Eliot Spitzer Election Campaign, 2006; commr. Divsn. Criminal Justice Services State of NY, Albany, 2007—. Part-time instr. trial technique program SUNY, 1990—2002; lectr. ethics, evidence and trial practice Office Legal Edn.U.S. Dept. Justice, 1988—2000; lectr. NITA seminar Western NY Trial Acad., 1994, 98; mem. Atty. Gen.'s Adv. Com., 1999—2001, vice-chair, 2000—01; trustee SUNY Buffalo Found.; sr. adv. on criminal justice & domestic security Eliot Spitzer Election Campaign, 2006. Mem. Vol. Lawyers Program, 1997—2001; bd. dirs. NCCJ, 2000—; trustee SUNY Buffalo Found., 2004—; sec. Nat. Women's Hall of Fame, 2001—04, bd. dirs., 2001—. Named to The We. NY Women's Hall of Fame; recipient Ruth G. Shapiro award, NY State Bar Assn. Fellow: N.Y. State Bar Found.; mem.: ABA, Nat. Assn. Former U.S. Attys. (bd. dirs.), Western NY Trial Lawyers Assn., Women's Bar Assn. State NY (founding mem. Western NY chpt. 1985), Bar Assn. Erie County (dep. treas. 1992—93, treas. 1993—94), West Side Rowing Club. Office: NY State Divsn Criminal Justice Services 4 Tower Pl 10th Fl Albany NY 12203 *

O'DONNELL, EDWARD FRANCIS, JR., lawyer; b. Waterbury, Conn., May 13, 1950; s. Edward Francis and Dorothy Patricia (Breheny) O'D.; m. Jayne Ann DeSantis, Dec. 29, 1972; children: Ryan Anderson, Brooke Stires. BA, St. Anselm Coll., Manchester, NH, 1972; JD, U. Conn., 1977. Bar: S.C. 1978, Conn. 1977, U.S. Dist. Ct. S.C. 1978, U.S. Dist. Ct. Conn. 1980, U.S. Ct. Appeals (1st and 2d cirs.) 1980. Assoc. Ogeltree, Deakins, Nash, Smoak & Stewart, Greenville, S.C., 1977-79; ptnr. Siegel, O'Connor, Zagari, O'Donnell & Beck, P.C., Hartford, Conn., 1979—. Contbr. articles to profl. jours. Mem. ABA, Conn. Bar Assn., S.C. Bar Assn., Hartford Bar Assn., Hartford Club, Phi Alpha Theta. Roman Catholic. Office: Siegel O'Connor O'Donnell & Beck PC 150 Trumbull St Fl 5 Hartford CT 06103-2400

O'DONNELL, EDWARD JOSEPH, bishop, retired editor; b. St. Louis, July 4, 1931; s. Edward Joseph and Ruth Mary (Carr) O'Donnell. Student, Cardinal Glennon Coll., 1949-53; postgrad., Kenrick Sem., 1953-57. Ordained priest Roman Cath. Ch., 1957, consecrated bishop, 1984; assoc. pastor in 5 St. Louis parishes, 1957-77; pastor St. Peter's Ch., Kirkwood, Mo., 1977-81; assoc. dir. Archdiocesan Commn. on Human Rights, 1962-70; dir. Archdiocesan Radio-TV Office, 1966-68, Archdiocesan Vocation Council, 1965; editor St. Louis Rev., 1968-81; vicar-gen. Archdiocese of St. Louis, 1981-84, aux. bishop, 1984-94; bishop emeritus Diocese of Lafayette, Lafayette, La., 1994—. Bd dirs Nat Cath Conf Interracial Justice, 1980—85; chmn Interfaith Clergy Coun Greater St Louis, 1963—67; NAACP, 1964—66; bd dirs Urban League St Louis, 1962—68. Named to Golden Dozen, Int Soc Weekly Newspaper Eds, 1970, 1977. Mem.: Nat Asn TV Arts and Scis, Cath Press Asn. Roman Catholic. Home: 6825 Natural Bridge Rd Saint Louis MO 63121-5314

O'DONNELL, JAMES FRANCIS, retired health scientist administrator; b. Cleve., July 22, 1928; s. John Michael and Mary Louise (Hayes) O'D.; m. Winifred Locke, Sept. 10, 1955; children— Anne Catherine, Patrick John, Mary Elizabeth BS in Biology, St. Louis U., 1949; PhD in Biochemistry, U. Chgo., 1957. Asst., then. assoc. prof. biol. chemistry and exptl. medicine Coll. Medicine, U. Cin., 1957—68; grants assoc., divsn. rsch. grants NIH, Bethesda, Md., 1968—69; program dir. population and reprodn. grants br. Ctr. for Population Research, Nat. Inst. Child Health and Human Devel., NIH, 1969—71; asst. dir. divsn. rsch. resources NIH, Bethesda, 1971—76, dir. divsn. rsch. resources, 1976—90, acting dir. divsn. rsch. resources, 1981—82, dir. Office of Extramural Programs, Office of the Dir., 1990-99; ret., 1999. Sci. cons. Commonwealth Health Rsch. Bd., Richmond, Va., 1999—. Served with U.S. Army, 1950-52 Home: 11601 Bunnell Ct S Rockville MD 20854-3603 Personal E-mail: jfwlodonnell@erols.com.

O'DONNELL, JAMES V., apparel executive; Mgmt. positions The Gap Inc., 1980—87, exec. v.p., bd. dir., 1987—92, COO, 1989—92; CEO Computer Aided Systems Inc., 1992—97; project cons. C. Everett Koop Found., 1997—2000; dir. merchant banking Colmen Capital Adv. Inc., 1997—2002; pres., COO Lyte Inc., 1999—2000; COO Am. Eagle Outfitters, Warrendale, Pa., 2000—03, bd. dir., 2000—, co-CEO, 2002—03, CEO, 2003—. Mem. adv. bd. Coll. Commerce & Fin. Villanova Univ. Office: American Eagle Outfitters 150 Thorn Hill Dr Warrendale PA 15086 *

O'DONNELL, JOHN LOGAN, retired lawyer; b. Chgo., Mar. 6, 1914; s. William Joseph and Elizabeth (McLogan) O'D.; m. Mary Ellen Sipe, Sept. 2, 1939 (dec. Dec. 29, 1979); 1 son, John Logan; m. Michele G. Fischer, May 9, 1981. BA, Williams Coll., 1934; JD, Northwestern U., 1937. Bar: Ill. 1937, N.Y. 1943, D.C. 1977. Asso. firm Defrees, Buckingham, Jones and Hoffman, Chgo., 1937-38; staff atty. Office Gen. Counsel, SEC, 1938-41; instr. Cath. U. Law Sch., 1938-41; assoc. Cravath, Swaine & Moore, NYC, 1941-52; ptnr. Olwine, Connelly, Chase, O'Donnell & Weyher, NYC, 1952-91, of counsel, 1991, Twomey, Hoppe & Gallanty, NYC, 1991—2003; ret., 2003. Bd. dirs. Near East Found., 1968-84. Fellow Am. Coll. Trial Lawyers; mem. Assn. Bar City N.Y., Am., Fed., bar assns., Beta Theta Pi, Phi Delta Phi. Clubs: Union, Univ., Williams, (N.Y.C.). Roman Catholic. Avocations: piano, sports. Home: 181 E 73rd St New York NY 10021-3549

O'DONNELL, JOHN MICHAEL, lawyer; b. Washington, Aug. 27, 1958; s. John M. and Mildred B. O'Donnell; m. Bonnie Humphrey, June 30, 1984; childraen Jack and Kate (twins). BA, U. Chgo., 1980; JD, U. Pa., 1983. Bar: Ill. 1983. Ptnr. Sonnenschein Nath & Rosenthal, Chgo., 1984-95; assoc. gen. counsel The Interlake Corp., Lisle, Ill., 1995-98; v.p., secretary, and general counsel Interlake Material Handling, Inc., Lisle, Ill., 1998—2004; dep. gen. counsel GKN, 2005—.

O'DONNELL, KATHLEEN C., artist; b. Clifton, NJ, Nov. 15, 1919; d. George Francis and Alvina Rose (Munzell) Denzel; m. John Joseph O'Donnell, Feb. 17, 1942; children: John Joseph, Sharon Rose. BA cum laude, Montclair State U., NJ, 1983. Designer Denzell Mfg. Co., Passaic, NJ, 1937—38, clk., 1939—41; sec. Marschalk Ins., Clifton, NJ, 1941—42; clk. The Fair, Passaic, 1968—69; designer Arise Ministry, Lakewood, NJ, 1983—91; assoc. NJ Bell, Clifton & Totowa, 1969—85. Represented in numerous pvt. collections, group and one-woman shows. Mem.: Roxbury Assn. Art, Clifton Assn. Artists, Bell Atlantic Pioneers. Roman Catholic.

O'DONNELL, KATHLEEN MARIE, lawyer; b. Methuen, Mass., Dec. 16, 1955; d. John Joseph and Helen Miriam (McCormack) O'D. BA magna cum laude, Wheaton Coll., Norton, Mass., 1977; JD cum laude, Suffolk U., 1980. Bar: Mass. 1981, U.S. Dist. Ct. Mass. 1982, U.S. Ct. Appeals (1st cir.) 1982. Instr. Suffolk U., Boston, 1980-82; assoc. Law Office Albert J. Marcotte, Lowell, Mass., 1982—. Bd. dirs. Greater Lowell Pastoral Gounseling Ctr., 1987—, Greater Lowell Rape Crisis Ctr., Sohier Park Com., York, Maine, 1989—, co-chair, 1991—; bd. govs. Mass. Acad. Trial Attys. Mem. ATLA, ABA, Mass. Bar Assn. (v.p. 2001, treas. 2002, pres.-elect 2003, pres. 2004), Mass. Acad. Trial Attys.(treas. 1995, pres. 1996), Greater Lowell Bar Assn. (treas. 1987, sec. 1988, v.p. 1989, pres. 1990), Am. Bd. Trial Advocates, Phi Delta Phi. Democrat. Roman Catholic. Office: Law Office Albert Marcotte 45 Merrimack St Lowell MA 01852-1729 Home Phone: 978-458-2724; Office Phone: 978-458-1229. E-mail: mlfko@aol.com.

O'DONNELL, KEVIN, retired metal products executive; b. Cleve., June 9, 1925; s. Charles Richard and Ella (Kilbane) O'Donnell; m. Ellen Blydenburgh, Aug. 16, 1965; children: Kevin, Susan, Michael, John, Maura, Neil, Megan, Hugh. AB, Kenyon Coll., Gambier, Ohio, 1947, PhD (hon.) in Law, 1980; MBA, Harvard U., 1947; PhD in Econs. (hon.), Pusan Nat. U., Korea, 1970; PhD in Humanities (hon.), Ohio Wesleyan U., 1972. Gen. sales mgr. Steel Improvement & Forge Co., Cleve., 1947-60; mgmt. cons. Booz, Allen and Hamilton, Cleve., 1960-62; gen. mgr., dir. Atlas Alloys-Rio Algom Corp., Cleve., 1963-66; dir. Peace Corps, Seoul, Republic of Korea, 1966-70, dir. administrn. and fin., then acting dep. dir., 1970-71; assoc. dir. internat. ops. ACTION, 1971-72; exec. v.p. SIFCO Industries, Inc., Cleve., 1972-75, pres., chief oper. officer, 1976-83, pres., chief exec. officer, 1983-89, chief exec. officer, 1989-90, chmn., exec. comm., 1990-94; ret., 1994. Bd. dirs. Ctrl. Pk. Media Corp., NYC, Doyle Pacific Industries, Ltd., Hong Kong; adv. dir. Capital Strategies, Inc., Cleve. Mem. Washington Inst. Fgn. Affairs, Cleve. Com. Fgn. Rels., chmn., 1979—82, CCWA, 1982—89; pres. Guest Ho., Inc., 1990—92; trustee Alcohol Svcs., Cleve., 1993—, Cleve. Coun. World Affairs, Nat. Peace Corps. Assn. Decorated Order Civil Merit Republic of Korea; recipient Disting. Internationalist award, Cleve. Coun. World Affairs, 2007. Mem.: Harvard Bus. Sch. Alumni Assn. (dir. Boston 1991—94), Army-Navy Club (Washington), Westwood Country Club, Union Club, 50 Club, First Friday Club, Harvard Bus. Sch. Club Cleve., Knights of Malta (master knight). Republican. Roman Catholic. Avocations: golf, reading. Office Phone: 216-226-3505. Personal E-mail: kevodoncle@aol.com.

O'DONNELL, LAURENCE GERARD, retired managing editor; b. Bklyn., June 30, 1935; s. Thomas Edward and Dorothy (Clark) O'D.; m. Joan M. Coniglio, Jan. 9, 1960; children: Christopher, Carolyn, Jeffrey, Anthony. AB, Holy Cross Coll., Worcester, Mass., 1957. Reporter Wall Street Jour., NYC, 1958-66, chief Detroit Bur., 1966-74, asst. mng. editor, 1974-77, mng. editor, 1977-83; assoc. editor Dow Jones & Co., Inc., NYC, 1983-90, cons., 1991-99. Pres. Dow Jones Newspaper Fund, 1988-93, bd. dirs.; vis. lectr. Queens Coll./CUNY, 1992-99. Trustee Holy Cross Coll., 1982-90, adv. bd. 2006; journalism adv. bd. Queens Coll./CUNY, 1989-2003; juror Pulitzer Prize, 1982, 83; bd. dirs. Interam. Press Assn., 1986-2001. Mem. Am. Soc. Newspaper Editors. Mem. Natl. adv. com., Robert Wood Johnson Found., 2002-. Office: Dow Jones Newspaper Fund PO Box 300 Princeton NJ 08543-0300

O'DONNELL, LAWRENCE, III, waste management executive; b. Houston, Dec. 14, 1957; s. Lawrence Jr. and Annell O'D.; m. Dare Boswell, May 22, 1981; children: Linley, Lawrence IV. BS in Archtl. Engring., U. Tex., 1980; JD cum laude, U. Houston, 1983. Bar: Tex. 1983. Assoc. Wood, Campbell, Moody & Gibbs, Houston, 1983-84; ptnr. Campbell & Riggs, Houston, 1984-91; dep. gen. counsel Baker Hughes Inc., Houston, 1991-94, corp. sec., 1991-96, v.p., gen. counsel, 1995-2000, Baker Hughes Oilfield Ops., Houston, 1993-95; sr. v.p., gen. counsel, sec. Waste Mgmt., Inc., Houston, 2000—01, exec. v.p., gen. counsel, corp. sec., 2001, exec. v.p. western ops., 2001—03, exec. v.p. ops. support, chief adminstrv. officer, 2003—04, pres., COO, 2004—. Bd. dirs., mem. exec. com. Spring Br. Edn. Found.; bd. dirs. Am. Arbitration Assn., U. Tex. Med. Br.; mem. energy planning coun. State of Tex., 2004. Trustee Houston Police Activities League; mem. adv. bd. Brookwood. Mem.: ASCE, ABA, Houston Bar Assn., Tex. State Bar, Order of Barons, Phi Delta Phi. Avocations: golf, sailing, skiing. Office: Waste Mgmt Inc 1001 Fannin St Ste 4000 Houston TX 77002-6711 Office Phone: 713-512-6325. *

O'DONNELL, MICHAEL E., microbiologist, educator; b. Vancouver, Wash., Sept. 4, 1953; s. Ken and Rosemary O'D.; m. Sharon Deep; children: Brogan, Mason, Ian. BS in Biochemistry magna cum laude, U. Portland, 1971-75; MD in Biochemistry, Johns Hopkins U., 1975-76; PhD in Biochemistry, U. Mich., 1976-82. Postdoctr. fellow dept. biochemistry Stanford U. Sch. Medicine, Calif., 1982-84, 84-86; asst. prof. dept. microbiol. Cornell U. Med. Coll., NYC, 1986-91, assoc. prof., 1991-93, prof., 1993, Rockefeller U., NYC. Asst. investigator Howard Hughes Med. Inst., 1990-97, investigator, 1997-. Ad hoc reviewer: NIH Biochemistry Study Sect., 1993, Journ. Biol. Chemistry, Nucleic Acids Rsch., Biochemistry, NSF, 1983—; contbr. chpts. to books, articles to profl. jours. Grantee NIH, 1987-96, 88-93, 93-98, NSF, 1987-88, 93-96, Howard Hughes Med. Inst., 1990—; recipient Irma T. Hirschl award 1989; Merrill-Lynch Found. scholar 1972, Jackson-White Found. scholar 1972, Steinbach Founs. scholar, 1973; Wash. State U. Undergrad. Rsch. fellow NSF, 1974, Helen Hay Whiteny Postdoct. fellow 1983. Mem. AAAS, Fed. Am. Socs. for Exptl. Biology, Am. Soc. Biochemistry and Molecular Biology, NAS. Office: The Rockefeller Univ 1230 York Ave New York NY 10021

O'DONNELL, PATRICK EMMETT, lawyer; b. NYC, Mar. 17, 1937; s. Emmett and Lorraine Antoinette (Muller) O'D.; m. Janet Eve Mottershead, Sept. 21, 1968; children: Patrick Justin, Hollace Tobin, Darcy Tanner. Student, Georgetown U., 1955-58; LLB, Am. Univ., 1962. Bar: D.C. 1962. Asst. corp. counsel City of Washington, 1962-69; spl. asst. to the pres. The White House, Washington, 1971-76; legal counsel to chmn. FCC, Washington, 1969-71; Washington counsel Gen. Electric Co., Washington, 1976-78, J.C. Penney Co., Inc., Washington, 1978-80; regional polit. dir. Howard Baker for Pres., Washington, 1980; asst. dir. legis. affairs Ronald Reagan for Pres., Washington, 1980-81; ptnr. O'Connor & Hannan, Washington, 1981; ptnr., legislative, govtl. affairs Venable LLP, Washington, 2001—. Vice chmn. fin. George Bush Com., Washington, 1988; economic affairs counsel Rep. Nat. Com., Washington, 1976-80; bd. dirs. Radio Marti (Presdl. Commn.), Washington, 1981-84. Mem. USO (bd. dirs. 1978-91). Republican. Roman Catholic. Office: Venable LLP 575 Seventh St NW Washington DC 20004 Office Phone: 202-344-4702. Office Fax: 202-344-8300. Business E-Mail: peodonnell@venable.com.

O'DONNELL, PIERCE HENRY, lawyer; b. Troy, NY, Mar. 5, 1947; s. Harry J. and Mary (Kane) O'Donnell; m. Dawn Donley, Mar. 17, 1995; children: Meghan Maureen, Brendan Casey, Courtney Dawn, Pierce Dublin, Aidan Yeats. BA, Georgetown U., 1969, JD, 1972; LLM, Yale U., 1975. Bar: D.C. 1973, US Supreme Ct. 1975, Calif. 1978. Law clk. to Justice Byron R. White U.S. Supreme Ct.; law clk. to Judge Shirley M. Hutstedler U.S. Ct. Appeals (9th cir.); assoc. Williams & Connolly, Washington, 1975-78; ptnr. Beardsley, Hufstedler & Kemble, LA, 1978-81, Hufstedler, Miller, Carlson & Beardsley, LA, 1981-82, O'Donnell & Gordon, LA, 1982-87, Kaye, Scholer, Fierman, Hays & Handler, LA, 1988-95, O'Donnell Shaeffer & Mortimer, L.L.P., LA, 1996—. Exec. asst. U.S. Sec. Edn., 1979; spl. counsel Commn. Jud. Performance, San Francisco, 1979; chmn. Nat. Media, Inc., 1984—92. Co-author: (book) Fatal Subtraction: The Inside Story of Buchwald v Paramount, 1992, Toward A Just and Effective Sentencing System: Agenda for Legislative Reform, 1976; author: Dawn's Early Light, 2001, Funny You Asked About That, 2005, In Time of War, 2005; contbr. articles to profl. jours. Chmn. Friends Cal Tech YMCA, 1983—84, Verdugo-San Rafael Urban Mountain Park Fund, 1980—84; bd. dirs. Foothill Family Svc., 1979—85, chmn., 1984—85; bd. dirs. Interfaith Ctr. To Reverse Arms Race, 1984—90, pres., 1987—88; mem. Econ. Round Table of L.A., 1979—, pres., 2000—01; chmn. Calif. Coast Baseball Acad., 2001—; mem. Santa Barbara Sheriff's Coun., 2003—; bd. dirs. Friends of Altadena Libr., 1979—81, Pasadena-Foothill Urban League, E. Altadena Little League, 1993—97. Fellow: Internat. Acad. Trial Lawyers; mem.: NAACP, PEN, Am. Coll. Trial Lawyers, Cal Tech Assocs., Am. Law Inst., Am. Bd. Trial Advocates, Sierra Club, Calif. Club, Gridiron Club (Georgetown U.), Bel Air Country Club. Episcopalian. Office: O'Donnell & Shaeffer LLP 550 S Hope 20th fl Los Angeles CA 90071-2027 Home: 735 Picacho Ln Santa Barbara CA 93108-1226 Home Phone: 805-565-2226; Office Phone: 213-532-2000. Business E-Mail: pod@oslaw.com.

O'DONNELL, ROSIE, television personality, actress, comedienne; b. Commack, NY, Mar. 21, 1962; m. Kelli Carpenter, Feb. 26, 2004; children: Parker Jaren, Chelsea Belle, Blake Christopher, Vivienne Rose. Attended, Dickinson Coll., Boston Univ. Appearances include (TV series) Gimme A Break, 1986-87, Stand By Your Man, 1992, Women Aloud, 1992, Stand-up Spotlight, VH-1 (American Comedy award nomination best female performer in a TV special 1994, Cable ACE award nomination best entertainment host 1994); (TV) host The Rosie O'Donnell Show, 1995-2002 (Daytime Emmy awards 1997, 98, 99, 2000, 2001); (TV) co-host The View, 2006-2007; (TV films) The Twilight of the Golds, 1997; (films) A League of Their Own, 1992, Sleepless in Seattle, 1993 (American Comedy award nomination best supporting female in a motion picture 1994), Another Stakeout, 1993 (American Comedy award nomination best actress in a motion picture 1994), Car 54, Where Are You?, 1994, I'll Do Anything, 1994, The Flintstones, 1994, Exit to Eden, 1994, Now and Then, 1995, Beautiful Girls, 1996, Harriet the Spy, 1996, A Very Brady Sequel, 1996 (uncredited), Wide Awake, 1996, Get Bruce, 1999, Jackie's Back, 1999, Tarzan, 1999 (voice), Flintstones in Viva Rock Vegas, 2000; Broadway shows include Grease, 1994, Seussical the Musical, 2001, Fiddler on the Roof, 2005; author: Find Me, 2002; editor: Rosie mag., 2000-2002; prodr.:

Taboo (Broadway) 2003-2004; exec. prodr. (TV films) Kids are Punny, 1998, (films) Mina & the Family Treasure, 2004; actor, exec. prodr. (TV films) Riding the Bus with My Sister, 2005; guest appearances Ally McBeal, 1999, Third Watch, 2000, The Practice, 2000, Will & Grace, 2002, Judging Amy, 2003, Queer as Folk, 2005, Nip Tuck, 2006. Named one of 100 Most Influential People, Artists and Entertainers, Time Magazine, 2007.

O'DONNELL, TERRENCE, lawyer, multi-industry company executive; b. NYC, Mar. 3, 1944; s. Emmett and Lorraine (Muller) O'Donnell; m. Margaret Lynne Kidder; children: Stephanie T., Erin K., Victoria L. BS, USAF Acad., Colo., 1966; JD, Georgetown Law Sch., 1971. Bar: DC 1971, US Ct. Appeals (DC cir.) 1978, US Ct. Appeals (4th cir.) 1987, US Dist. Ct. Md. 1986, US Ct. Mil. Appeals 1990, US Ct. Fed. Claims, US Supreme Ct., others. Commd. 2nd lt. USAF, 1966, advanced through grades to capt., various positions Washington and Republic of Vietnam, 1966-72, resigned, 1972; spl. asst. Pres. of US, The White House, Washington, 1972-77; appointments sec. Pres. Ford, Washington, 1974-77; assoc. Williams & Connolly, Washington, 1977-82, ptnr., 1982-89, 1992—; gen. counsel Dept. Def., Washington, 1989-92; exec. v.p., gen. counsel Textron Inc., 2000—. Presdl. appointee to bd. visitors US Air Force Acad., Colorado Springs, 1982-87, chmn., 1985-86; US corr. and rep. UN Prog. to Prevent Crime, Washington and NYC, 1977-81; bd. dirs. IGI Inc., ePlus, Inc. Trustee Gerald R. Ford Found., Grand Rapids, Mich., 1987—; mem. Adminstrv. Conf. US, 1991-92; mem. adv. com. US Ct. Fed. Claims; mem. code com. US Ct. Mil. Appeals for the Armed Forces, 1993-95; bd. dirs. Falcon Found., 1988—. Decorated Bronze star; recipient Disting. Pub. Svc. medal Dept. Def., 1992, Disting. Svc. award US Atty. Gen., 1992. Mem. ABA, DC Bar Assn., Bar of US Supreme Ct., and others. Office: Textron Inc 40 Westminster St Providence RI 02903 Office Phone: 202-434-5678. Personal E-mail: todonnell@wc.com. Business E-Mail: todonnell@textron.com. *

O'DONNELL, TERRENCE, state supreme court justice; b. Cleve., Feb. 11, 1946; m. Mary Beth O'Donnell; children: Terrence, Michael, Colleen, Nora. BA in Polit. Sci., Kent State U., 1968; JD, Cleve. State U., 1971. Bar: Ohio 1971. Instr. speech and debate Cuyahoga Cmty. Coll., 1968—70; instr. grades 7 & 8 St. Brendan Sch., North Olmstead, 1970; law clerk to Judge Justice J.J.P. Corrigan Supreme Ct. Ohio, 1971—72; law clerk to Judge John M. Manos and Judge V. Corrigan 8th Dist. Ct. Appeals, 1972—74; dir. program paralegal edn. David M. Myers Coll., 1974—76; atty. Marshman, Snyder & Corrigan, 1976—80; judge Cuyahoga County Ct. Common Pleas, 1980—95, 8th Dist. Ct. Appeals, 1995—2003; justice Ohio Supreme Ct., 2003—. Vis. judge counties throughout Ohio, 2003—; chmn. Ohio Legal Rights Svc. Commn.; instr. CPA bus. law rev. Cleve. State U.; instr. several continuing legal edn. programs; mem. Ohio Supreme Ct. Commn. on Professionalism. Past pres. Legal Eagles; former mem. bd. trustees Magnificat HS, Rocky River, past pres. Father's Club; exec. dir. emeritus St. Patrick's Day Parade, Cleve.; coach Little League Baseball, Rocky River; instr. pub. sch. religion program St. Bernadette Ch., Westlake; mem. St. Bernadette Parish, Westlake, Ohio; mem. bd. dirs. Our Lady Wayside. Mem.: Ohio Supreme Ct., Ohio State Bar Assn. (mem. pub. understanding law sect.), Cleve. Bar Assn. (chmn. law related edn. com., Pres.'s award 1989—99), Cath. Lawyer's Guild Cleve. (officer). Office: Ohio Supreme Ct 65 S Front St Columbus OH 43215-3431

O'DONNELL, THOMAS LAWRENCE PATRICK, lawyer; b. Taunton, Mass., Aug. 12, 1926; s. Patrick Francis and Ellen Balfe (Brady) O'D.; m. Carol Hodgdon, Feb. 16, 1952; children: Ellen, Thomas, Janet Gael, Christopher Hodgdon AB magna cum laude, Harvard U., 1947, LL.B., 1949. Bar: Mass. 1950. Assoc. Ropes & Gray, Boston, 1949-52, 54-61, ptnr., 1962-97, chmn., 1984-90, of counsel, 1998—. Dir. Rath & Strong, Inc., 1985-96. Trustee, Trustees of Reservations, 1970—, chmn. bd., 1975-76; bd. dirs. Mass. Land Conservation Trust, 1975-2002, chmn. bd., 1986-2002; bd. dirs. Mass. Taxpayers Found., 1972—, chmn. bd., 1977-79, 93-95, mem. exec. com., 1976—; bd. dirs. Boston Mcpl. Rsch. Bur., 1965—, chmn. bd., 1967-72; mem. pub. pension task force Mass. Bus. Roundtable, 1983-86; bd. dirs., sec. Jobs for Mass., Inc., 1981-83; moderator Town of Hingham, 1967—; del. Rep. Nat. Conv., 1972, all Rep. State convs., 1960-94; overseer Harvard U., 1986-92; bd. dirs. United Way Mass. Bay, 1987—, mem. exec. com. 1993—, chmn. bd. 1997-2000. Lt. USNR, 1944-45, 52-54. Recipient Cushing award Labor Guild of Archdiocese Boston, 1973, Humanitarian award The Nat. Conf. Greater Boston, 1997, The Harvard medal, 1997; mem. Knights of Malta, 1983— Fellow Am. Bar Found.; mem. ABA, Mass. Bar Assn., Boston Bar Assn., Indsl. Rels. Rsch. Assn. (pres. Boston chpt. 1980), Harvard Alumni Assn. (bd. dirs. 1978-81, 1st marshal class of 1947), Harvard Club Boston (bd. govs. 1985-91), Union of Boston Club, Hingham Yacht Club, Comml. Club. Roman Catholic. Home: 7 South Ln Hingham MA 02043-2446 Office: Ropes & Gray LLP 1 International Pl Boston MA 02110-2624 Office Phone: 617-951-7455. Business E-Mail: todonnell@ropesgray.com.

O'DONNELL, WILLIAM DAVID, retired construction firm executive; b. Brockton, Mass., Aug. 21, 1926; s. John Frank and Agnes Teresa (Flanagan) O'D.; m. Dixie Lou Anderson, Jan. 31, 1951; children— Craig Patrick, Ginger Lynn BS, U. N.Mex., 1953. Registered profl. engr., Ill., 1958. Engr. State of Ill., 1953-59; with Gregory-Anderson Co., Rockford, Ill., 1959—, gen. mgr., 1960-61, sec., 1961-81, pres., 1981-94; ret. Bd. dirs. Growth Enterprise, Davis Meml. Park, BankOne, Rockford. Dir. St. Anthony Med. Ctr., Youth Svcs. Network, Cath. Conf. of Ill.; bd. dirs. Rockford YMCA, pres., 1984. Served with USN, 1943-47 Recipient Friend of the Boy award Optimist Club, 1966, Excalibur award for cmty. svc. Rockford Register Star, 1971; named Titan of Yr., Boylan H.S., 1974, Papal Knight Order of St. Gregory the Great; fellow Wisdom Hall of Fame. Fellow: NSPE, ASCE, Soc. Am. Mil. Engrs.; mem.: VFW (life), No. Ill. Bldg. Contractors, Amateur Trapshooting Assn., World Future Soc., Aircraft Owners & Pilots Assn., Balloon Fedn. Am., Am. Polar Soc., Nat. Sporting Clays Assn., Old Antarctic Explorers Assn., Forest Hills Country (Rockford), Metropolitan Club (Chgo.); Adventurers (Chgo.), Adventurers Club, Metropolitan Club, Forest Hills Country Club, Rotary (Service Above Self award 1972; v.p. Rockford chpt. 1983, pres. 1984), Rotary (v.p. Rockford chpt. 1983, pres. 1984, Svc. Above Self award 1972), Am. Legion (life), Tau Beta Pi, Chi Epsilon, Sigma Tau. Home: 2004 Bradley Rd Rockford IL 61107-1258 Office: PO Box 900 Rockford IL 61105-0900 Personal E-mail: odonnellbill@hotmail.com.

O'DONNELL, WILLIAM JAMES, engineering executive; b. Pitts., June 19, 1935; s. William James and Elizabeth (Rau) O'D.; m. Joanne Mary Kusen, Jan. 31, 1959; children: Suzanne, Janice, William, Thomas, Kerry, Amy. BSME, Carnegie Inst. Tech., 1957; MSME, U. Pitts., 1959, PhD, 1962. Jr. engr. Westinghouse Research Lab., 1957-58, asso. engr., 1958; with Westinghouse Bettis Atomic Power Lab., West Mifflin, Pa., 1961-70, adv. engr., 1966-70; pres., chmn. bd. O'Donnell & Assos., Inc., Pitts., 1970—. Contbr. numerous articles on engring. and mechanics to profl. jours.; holder patents on processes and devices. Served with C.E. AUS, 1963-64. Recipient Machinery's Achievement award as outstanding mech. designer, 1957, Pi Tau Sigma Gold medal for achievements in engring., 1967, Pressure Vessel and Piping award ASME, 1994, Disting. Alumni award U. Pitts. Sch. Mech. Engring., 1996, Disting. Achievement award, Carnegie Mellon U., 2004. Fellow ASME (nat. award for outstanding contbn. to engring. profession 1973, internat. award for best publ. in pressure vessels and piping 1988, Engr. of Yr. award 1988, Pressure Vessel and Piping medal 1994); mem. NSPE, AAAS, ASTM, Soc. Exptl. Mechanics, Am. Nuclear Soc., Am. Soc. Metals Internat., The Minerals, Metals and Materials Soc., Sigma Xi. Home: 121 Sunrise Ln Venetia PA 15367 Office: O'Donnell Consulting Engrs 2940 S Park Rd Pittsburgh PA 15102 Office Phone: 412-835-5007. Business E-Mail: wjo@odonnellconsulting.com.

O'DONOVAN, CORMAC A., neurologist, educator; children: Katherine, Maura. BS, U. Coll. Galway, Ireland, 1982, MD, 1985. Assoc. prof. neurology Wake Forest U. Sch. Medicine, Winston-Salem, NC, 1995—. Med. dir. meg lab., dir. eeg and evoked potential labs., assoc. prof. internal medicine-cardiology Wake Forest U. Sch. Medicine. Fellow: Am. Clin. Neurophysiology; mem.: AMA, Am. Acad. Sleep Medicine, Irish Neurol. Assn., So. Epilepsy and Ctrl. EEG Soc., Am. EEG Soc., Am. Epilepsy Soc., Am. Acad. Neurology. Office: Wake Forest Univ Sch of Medicine Medical Center Blvd Winston Salem NC 27157 Office Phone: 336-716-2357. Business E-Mail: odonovan@wfubmc.edu.

O'DONOVAN, LEO JEREMIAH, former academic administrator, priest, theologian; b. NYC, Apr. 24, 1934; s. Leo J. O'Donovan Jr. AB, Georgetown U., 1956; Licentiate in Philosophy, Fordham U., 1961; STB, Woodstock Coll., 1966, Licentiate in Sacred Theology, 1967; ThD, U. Münster, Fed. Republic Germany, 1971; LittD (hon.), Sogang U., Seoul, 1993; DHL, Loyola Coll., 1991, Coll. St. Rose, 2000; MD (hon.), Georgetown U., 2001. Ordained to ministry Cath. Ch., 1966. Instr. philosophy Loyola Coll., Balt., 1961—63; asst. prof. Woodstock Coll., Woodstock, 1971—74; assoc. prof. Weston Sch. Theology, Cambridge, Mass., 1974—81, prof., 1981—89; pres. Georgetown U., Washington, 1989—2001, prof., 2001—. Provincial asst. formation Md. Province S.J., Balt., 1985—88; cons. Nat. Conf. Cath. Bishops, Washington, 1986—89; bd. dirs. The Riggs Nat. Bank, Walt Disney Co., 2001—, MedStar Health, Inc. Bd. dirs. U. Detroit Mercy, 1986—95; mem. Consortium of Univs. Washington Met. Area, 1989—2001, chair, 1994—96; mem. Fed. Cuty Coun., 1993—2001, Bus.-Higher Edn. Forum, 1989—2001, Nat. Coun. Arts, 1994—98, Consortium Fin. Higher Edn., 1990—98, chmn., 1995—97; mem. Am. Reads Stery Com., 1997—. Recipient Knight Comdr.'s Crodd, Germany; fellow, Danforth Found., 1956—71, vis. fellow, Woodstock Theol. Ctr.; grantee teaching grantee, Assn. Theol. Schs., 1978—79; scholar, Fulbright Found., U. Lyon, France, 1956—57. Fellow: Soc. Values in Higher Edn. (bd. dirs. 1989—); mem.: Boston Theol. Soc., Assn. Cath. Colls. and Univs. (bd. dirs. 1994—2000), Assn. Jesuit Colls. and Univs., Univ. Club. Office: Georgetown U 37th and O St NW Washington DC 20057-1789

ODOR, RICHARD LANE, mental health administrator, psychologist; b. Oberlin, Ohio, Aug. 11, 1954; s. Frank and Marjorie O. Student, Moody Bible Inst., 1972-74; BA, Ohio State U., 1977, MA, 1978, PhD, 1986. Counselor children's groups Gladden Community House, Columbus, Ohio, 1978-79; partial hospitalization counselor Columbus Area Cmty. Mental Health Ctr., 1979-81, residential counselor, 1978-82; grad. rsch. assoc. dept. family rels. and human devel. Ohio State U., 1983-85; emergency svcs. counselor S.E. Cmty. Mental Health Ctr., Columbus, 1983-86, dir. emergency svcs., 1986-87; program dir., psychologist Southeast Counseling Svcs., Columbus, 1987-92; psychologist Psychol. and Counseling Svcs., Reynoldsburg, Ohio, 1989-98, Richard L. Odor, PhD, Inc., Reynoldsburg, Ohio, 1998—; pres. Achieve Performance Cons., Inc., Reynoldsburg, 2002—; sr. cons. The Global Cons. Partnership, Inc., Wayne, Pa., 2003—. Psychologist, clin. supr. New Source Counseling Ctrs., Twinsburg, Ohio, 1990-97; psychologist, owner Psychol. and Recovery Svcs., Columbus, 1991-94; employee assistance program affiliate McDonnell Douglas Corp., Columbus, 1992-95; staff Grant Med. Ctr., Columbus, 1995—; profl. adv. com. Mt. Carmel Behavioral Healthcare, 1998-99. Profl. adv. bd. Ctrl. Ohio chpt. Nat. Multiple Sclerosis Soc., 1995-97. Recipient Silver medal IWF Pan Am. Master's Weightlifting Championships, 1999, Bronze medal, 2000, Gold medal, 2003, 04, Gold medal Nat. Masters Championships, 2005. Mem. APA, Interact Behavioral Healthcare (credentialling com. 1996-98), Ohio Psychol. Assn., U.S.A. Weightlifting, Ohio State U. Weightlifting Club (coach 1982-85, faculty advisor 1984-85), Rotary (bd. dirs. Reynoldsburg-Pickerington chpt. 1992-94, Paul Harris fellow), Phi Kappa Phi, Omicron Nu, Phi Upsilon Omicron. Republican. Avocations: competitive weightlifting, internat. travel. Office: 7664 Slate Ridge Blvd Reynoldsburg OH 43068-8158

O'DOR, RONALD KEITH, dean, biology professor, research scientist; b. Kansas City, Mo., Sept. 20, 1944; s. Claude Marvin O'Dor and Opal LaMoyne (Sears) Mathes; m. Janet Ruth Spiller, Dec. 30, 1967; children: Matthew Arnold, Stephen Roderick. AA, El Camino Coll., 1965; AB, U. Calif., Berkeley, 1967; PhD, U. BC, Can., 1971. From asst. prof. to prof. Dalhousie U., Halifax, NS, Canada, 1973—, chmn. dept. biology, 1997—2000, assoc. dean R & D, 2004—; dir. Aquatron Lab., Halifax, 1986-93; sr. scientist Census Marine Life, Consortium for Oceanographic Rsch. and Edn., Washington, 2000—. Summer scientist Laboratoire Arago, Banyuls-sur-Mer, France, 1979-85; vis. scientist Pacific Biol. Sta., Nanaimo, BC, 1980, U. Papua New Guinea, Motupore Island, 1989-91, Port Elizabeth Mus., South Africa, 1994; vis. prof. U. BC, Vancouver, 1986-87; sessional prof. Bamfield (BC) Marine Sta., 1987; cons. UN, Rome, 1987—; adv. space stas. Can. Space Agy., Ottawa, 1992-04; mem. mgmt. com. Ocean Prodn. Enhancement Network, Halifax, 1993-95; mem. adv. bd., Strange Days, Ocen, Sea Studios Found. Author, editor: Cephalopod Fishery Biology, 1993, Physiology of Cephalopod Molluscs, 1994, Squid Recruitment Dynamics, 1998, Baseline Report of the Census of Marine Life, 2003; contbg. author Cephalopod Life Cycles, Vol. I, 1983, Vol. II, 1987; contbr. articles and revs. to profl. jours. Scholar Med. Rsch. Coun. Can., 1968; fellow MRC, Cambridge U., Eng., 1971-73, Stazione Zoologica, Naples, Italy, 1971-73; recipient Hon. Mention Rolex Awards Enterprise, 1987, Natural Scis. and Engring. Rsch. Coun. (Can.) Univ.-Industry Synergy awards, 1997. Mem. Can. Soc. Zoologists (councillor 1989-92), Can. Fedn. Biological Socs., Soc. Integrative and Comparative Biology, Am. Soc. Gravitational and Space Biology, Cephalopod Internat. Adv. coun. (councillor, pres. 1988-91), Phi Beta Kappa. Achievements include isolation salmon calcitonin; co-development of acoustic pressure transducer/transmitters and radio-linked tracking systems for monitoring cephalopod bioenergetics in nature; co-organization of projects in the Azores, South Africa, Australia, and Papua New Guinea to monitor squid, cuttlefish and nautilus, first international cephalopod research conference in Japan, experiment with Aquatic Research Facility Space Shuttle STS-77, 1996. Home: 109 E St SE Washington DC 20003 Office: Consortium Oceanographic Rsch 1201 New York Ave Ste 420 Washington DC 20003 Office Phone: 202-448-1233. Business E-Mail: rodor@coreocean.org. *

O'DOWD, CHARLES EDWYN, physician; b. Nyack, NY, Oct. 12, 1962; s. Michael William and Helene Marie (Albert) O'D.; m. Barbara Ann Finan, May 18, 1991; children: Matthew, Patrick, Maureen, Caitlin. BS in Biology, Fordham U., 1984; MD, N.Y. Med. Coll., 1988. Diplomate Am. Bd. Internal Medicine. Resident physician Westchester County Med. Ctr., Valhalla, N.Y., 1988-91; attending physician Clarkstown Med. Assocs., New City, N.Y., 1991—. Mem. ACP, AMA, Med. Soc. State N.Y. Roman Catholic. Office: Clarkstown Med Assocs 200 E Eckerson Rd New City NY 10956-7153

O'DOWD, DONALD DAVY, retired university president; b. Manchester, NH, Jan. 23, 1927; s. Hugh Davy and Laura (Morin) O'D.; m. Janet Louise Fithian, Aug. 23, 1953; children: Daniel D., Diane K., James E., John M. BA summa cum laude, Dartmouth Coll., 1951; postgrad. (Fulbright fellow), U. Edinburgh, Scotland, 1951-52; MA, Harvard U., 1955, PhD, 1957. Instr., asst. prof. psychology, dean freshmen Wesleyan U., Middletown, Conn., 1955-60; assoc. prof., prof. of psychology, dean Univ. Oakland Univ., Rochester, Mich., 1960-65, provost, 1965-70; pres. Oakland U., Rochester, Mich., 1970-80; exec. vice chancellor SUNY, Albany, 1980-84; pres. U. of Alaska Statewide System, 1984-90. Carnegie Corp. fellow, 1965—66. Mem. APA, AAAS, Phi Beta Kappa, Sigma Xi. Home and Office: 801 A Senda Verde Santa Barbara CA 93105

O'DRISCOLL, MARGARET MILLAR (PEGGY O'DRISCOLL), real estate broker; b. Hollywood, Calif., Aug. 2, 1925; d. Russell Hartney and Marion Scott (Macarthur) Millar; m. William Harrington Walker, Jan. 10, 1949 (dec. Dec. 22, 1968); children: William Russell Walker, Elizabeth Howland, Hiram Scott Walker; m. James O'Driscoll, Oct. 17, 1970. Student UCLA, 1942-44. Lic. ins. solicitor, real estate broker, Calif. Salesman, Carol Smart Real Estate, Del Mar, Calif., 1966-68, Bernard & Assocs., Solana Beach, Calif., 1968-70; owner Town and Country Real Estate, Rancho Santa Fe, Calif., 1970—; pres. Peggy O'Driscoll Enterprises, Inc. Mem. publicity com. Rancho Santa Fe Republican Women, 1950-58; mem. San Dieguito Citizens Planning Group, 1977-78; mem. vestry St. Peter's Episcopal Ch., Del Mar, 1976-78; bd. dirs. Rancho Santa Fe Cmty. Svcs. Dist., 1982-85, chmn., 1985, mem., 1986—. Mem. San Dieguito Bd Realtors (v.p. 1980-82, pres. 1983-84), Calif. Assn. Realtors (hon. life mem., bd. dirs. 1981-86, ins. trustee 1982-86, regional v.p. dist. 29 1986), Rancho Santa Fe Cmty. Ctr., Rancho Santa Fe Hist. Soc. (bd. dirs. 1985-86), San Diego County Coun. Real Estate Bds., Rancho Santa Fe Club, The Country Friends, The Gold Diggers (San Diego, Gifts of Loving Donors), Garden Club (publicity chmn. 1965-74), Rancho Santa Fe Women's Golf Club (founding mem.). Home: PO Box 457 Rancho Santa Fe CA 92067-0457 Home Phone: 858-756-1528; Office Phone: 858-756-1422.

ODUM, JEFFERY NEAL, mechanical engineer; b. Bristol, Tenn., Sept. 11, 1956; s. Herschel S. and Minnie Lee (Carrier) O.; m. Stacy Elaine Ferrell, mar. 18, 1989; 1 child, Charles Wesley Ferrell. BSME, Tenn. Technol. U., 1978; MS in Engring., U. Tenn., 1983. Sr. project engr. TVA, Knoxville, 1978-81; sr. constrn. engr. Stone & Webster Engring. Corp., Boston, 1981-84; div. engr. E.I. DuPont de Nemours & Co., Aiken, S.C., 1984-89; engring. mgr. Flour Daniel, Greenville, S.C., 1989-92; mgr. of projects, Pharmaceutical Bus. Group CRS Sirrine Engrs., Inc., Raleigh, N.C., 1992-93; sr. project mgr. Gilbane Bldg. Co., Raleigh, 1993-95; dir. engring. Gilbane Process Group, Vacaville, Calif., 1995-98; biopharm. office leader Clark, Richardson and Biskup, Cons. Engrs., Cary, NC, 1998—2005; prin. NC Biosource, 2005—; dir. validation acad. NC Cmty. Coll. Sys. Author: Sterile Product Facility Design and Project Management, 1996, 2d edit., 2004, Large Scale Biomanufacturing, 2004, Advances in Large Scale Biomanufacturing-Capital Projects, 2004, 07, Advanced Technologies For Biopharmaceutical Processing, 2005; contbr. articles to profl. jours Vol. Spl. Olympics, Habitat for Humanity; mem. bd. govs. U. Tenn., 2002—06. Recipient DuPont Engring. Achievement award 1986, 88, 89, Nat. Svc. Alumni award Univ. Tenn. Mem. Parenteral Drug Assn., Internat. Soc. Pharm. Engrs. (bd. dirs., pres. Carolina chpt. 1996-97, chair N.Am. Chpt. Coun. 1998, chair publs. com. 2000-01, chair chpt. excellence 2000-01, chair tng. 2002, Svc. award 1999, 2001, 2003, 2005, chmn. N. Am. edn. com. 2004, Richard Purdy Outstanding Achievement award 2002, edn advisor N. Am.), ISPE Tng. Faculty (N.Am. edn. advisor 2006—), U. Tenn. Nat. Alumni Assn. (pres. Augusta chpt. 1987-89, bd. govs.), Order Engr., Kappa Sigma Republican. Presbyterian. Avocations: sports, biking, cooking, writing, skiing. Office: NCBiosource 1213 Enoerbury Dr Raleigh NC 27614 Office Phone: 919-341-3565. E-mail: jodum@ncbiosource.com.

O'DWYER, MARY ANN, automotive executive; BS, DePaul U.; MS, Benedictine U. CPA. With Ernst and Young, McDonald's Corp.; various positions CC Industries (a Henry Crown Co.); sr. v.p. fin. ops., CFO Wheels, 1991—; sr. v.p. fin & ops., CFO Frank Consol. Enterprises. Office: Frank Consol Enterprises 666 Garland Pl Des Plaines IL 60016

ODYA, GREGORY MATTHEW, music educator, musician; b. Bloomington, Ind., Apr. 22, 1980; s. Charles Ervin and Martha Fortenberry Odya; m. Erin Catherine Stapleton, June 23, 2001. Degree in instrumental music edn., Ind. U., 2004. Lic. tchr. Ind. Weekend coord., program asst. Christole, Inc., Bloomington, Ind., 2000—02; asst. program coord. Edgewood H.S. Marching Band, Ellettsville, Ind., 2000—03; instr. Bloomington H.S. North Marching Band, 2002; instrumental music arranger, instr. and performer Edgewood H.S. Show Choirs, 2002—04; assoc. instr. The PA Inst., MSD Lawrence Twp., Indpls., 2004; assoc. dir. of bands Decatur Ctrl. H.S. MSD Decatur Twp., Indpls., 2004—. Adjudicator Edgewood H.S. Contest of Champions, 2004. Music performer St. John the Apostle Cath. Ch., Bloomington, 2003—04. Mem.: Ind. State Tchrs. Assn., Music Educators Nat. Conf., Phi Lambda Theta, Golden Key, Nat. Soc. Collegiate Scholars. Avocations: running, swimming, music composition, music performance. Home Phone: 812-320-6563; Office Phone: 317-856-5288. Personal E-mail: gmodya@gmail.com.

ODZA, RANDALL M., lawyer; b. Schnectady, May 6, 1942; s. Mitchell and Grace (Mannes) O.; m. Rita Ginness, June 19, 1966; children: Kenneth, Keith. BS in Indsl. and Labor Rels., Cornell U., 1964, LLB, 1967. Bar: N.Y. 1967, U.S. Ct. Appeals (2d cir.) 1970, U.S. Dist. Ct. (so. and ea. dists.) N.Y. 1969, U.S. Dist. Ct. (we. dist.) N.Y. 1970. Assoc. Proskauer, Rose, Goetz & Mandelsohn, NYC, 1967-69, Jaeckle, Fleischmann & Mugel, Buffalo, 1969-72, ptnr., 1972—. Sec. bd. trustees Buffalo Philharm. Orch. Soc.; past trustee, legal counsel, treas. Temple Beth Am; bd. trustees Buffalo Philharm. Orch. Soc., sec. bd. trustees. Recipient Honow award Western NY Retail Mchts. Assn., 1980. Fellow Coll. Labor and Employment Lawyers; mem. ABA, Labor and Employment Relations Assn. Western NY, Erie County Bar Assn., NY State Bar Assn. Office: Jaeckle Fleischmann & Mugel 12 Fountain Plz Rm 700 Buffalo NY 14202-2292 Home Phone: 716-636-8893; Office Phone: 716-843-3877. Business E-Mail: rodza@jaeckle.com.

ODZE, ROBERT D., pathologist; s. Walter Karl Odze and Helen Natasha Menkes. BSc, McGill U., Montreal, 1980, MDCM, 1984. Cert. anatomic pathology. Staff pathologist Mount Sinai Hosp., Toronto, Canada; instr. pathology U. Toronto Med. Sch., Canada, 1991—93; cons. GI pathology New Eng. Deaconess Med. Ctr., Boston, 1994—99, Beth Israel Deaconess Med. Ctr., Boston, 1996—99; dir. GI pathology svc. Brigham and Women's Hosp., Boston, 1997—; assoc. prof. pathology Harvard Med. Sch., Boston, 1999—; cons. pathologist Dana Farber Cancer Inst., Boston, 2004—. Author, editor: Surgical Pathology GI Tract, Liver, Bilary Tract and Pancreas, 2003, assoc. editor: Am. Jour. Gastroenterology, 2003—, mem. editl. bd.: Human Pathology, 2001—, Gastrointestinal Endoscopy, 2001. Recipient MRC award, McGill U. Dept. Sci., 1980, CIBA prize for anatomy, McGill U. Med. Sch., 1981, MRC award, 1981, Joseph Morley Drake prize for pathology, 1982, Outstanding Surgery Student award, ACP and McGill U. Med. Sch., 1983, Pathology Finlayson Rsch. award, McGill U., 1988; grantee, Am. Coll. Gastroenterology, 1994—95, 1998—99, Stanley Robbins Rsch. Award, 1996—97; Univ. scholar, McGill U. Dept. Sci., 1981, Faculty scholar, McGill U. Med. Sch., 1982. Mem.: Arthur Purdy Stout Soc. Surg. Pathologists, U.S. and Can. Acad. Pathology Gastrointestinal Pathology Soc., U.S. and Can. Acad. Pathology, Am. Gastroenterol. Assn., Am. Coll. Gastroenterology, Crohn's Colitis Found. Am. Home: 1175 Chestnut St Unit 3 Newton MA 02464 Office: Brigham & Womens Hosp 75 Francis St Boston MA 02115

OECHLER, HENRY JOHN, JR., lawyer; b. Charlotte, NC, Apr. 9, 1946; s. Henry J. and Convere Jones (McAden) O. AB, Princeton U., 1968; JD, Duke U., 1971. Bar: N.Y. 1972, U.S. Ct. Appeals (2d cir.) 1974, U.S. Ct. Appeals (D.C. cir.) 1975, U.S. Ct. Appeals (8th cir.) 1986, U.S. Ct. Appeals (9th cir.) 1995. Assoc. Chadbourne & Parke, NYC, 1971-80, ptnr.,

1980—2006, of counsel, 2006—. Avocation: studying airline schedules. Office: Chadbourne & Parke 30 Rockefeller Plz Fl 31 New York NY 10112-0129

OEFELEIN, WILLIAM A., astronaut, military officer; b. Ft. Belvoir, Va., Mar. 29, 1965; s. Randall W. and Billye N. Oefelein; m. Michaella Davis; 2 children. BS in Elec. Engring., Oreg. State U., Corvallis, 1988; MS in Aviation Systems, U. Tenn. Space Inst., 1998. Commd. ensign USN, Pensacola, Fla., 1988, advanced in grades to lt. cmmdr.; student pilot USN Marine Fighter/Attack Tng. Squadron, El Toro, Calif., 1990—91; fighter pilot USN Strike Fighter Squadron, Naval Air Sta., Lemoore, Calif., 1991—95; student test pilot Naval Air Sta., Patuxent River, Md., 1995; test pilot Strike Air Force Test Squadron, 1995—97; test pilot instr. Test Pilot Sch., Patuxent River, 1997—2008; pilor,strike ops. officer Carrier Air Wing 8 Naval Air Sta., Oceana, Va., 1998; astronaut NASA Johnson Space Ctr., Houston, 1998—. Pilot STS-116 Mission (Discovery), 2006. Recipient Strike/Flight Air medal, Navy Commendation medal, Navy Achievement medal. Mem.: Aircraft Owners and Pilots Assn., Seaplane Owners Assn. Achievements include 3000 flight hours in more than 50 different aircraft, 200 carrier landings. Avocations: fishing, hiking, skiing, weightlifting, wake boarding, snowboarding. Office: Astronaut Office/CB Johnson Space Ctr Houston TX 77058 *

OEHLER, JUDITH JANE MOODY, retired counselor; b. Farner, Tenn., Mar. 5, 1942; d. William Henry and Peggy (Lindsey) Moody; m. Carl Bailey Oehler, June 1, 1963; children: David W., Paul E. BS in Elem. Edn., U. Tex., 1964; MEd, Tex. Christian U., 1976. Lic. profl. counselor. Elem. tchr. Arlington (Tex.) Ind. Sch. Dist., 1965-78, elem. counselor, 1979—96, ret., 1996. Mem. Arlington Women's Club. Fellow AACD; mem. DAR (regent 2000-04), Tex. Assn. Counseling and Devel., North Ctrl. Tex. Assn. Counseling and Devel. (sec. 1995-96, Caring award 1995), Tex. State Tchrs. Assn., Arlington Assn. Tex. Profl. Educators (sec. 1994—95), Aux. Tex. Soc. Profl. Engrs. (pres. Mid-Cities chpt. 1992-94, state sec. 1993-94, v.p. Region V 1994-95, state pres. 1997-98), Encore Club (1st v.p. 2004-05), Arlington Woman's Club (antique dept. chmn. 2003-05, club photographer 2005—), Nat. Soc. US Daus 1812, Daus. Am. Colonists (sec. 2007-), Nat. Soc. Tex. Colonial Dames XVII Century, Nat. Huguenot Soc., Arlington Women Rotary, Phi Delta Kappa. Methodist. Avocations: travel, reading, swimming, gardening, walking. Home: 2408 Westwood Dr Arlington TX 76012-2905

OEHLER, RICHARD WILLIAM, lawyer; b. NYC, Nov. 24, 1950; s. John Montgomery and Florence Mae (Jahn) O.; m. Linda Tyson. BA, Dartmouth Coll., 1972; JD, Harvard U., 1976. Bar: Calif. 1976, Wash. 1987, D.C. 1988, U.S. Dist. Ct. (no. dist.) Calif. 1976, U.S. Dist. Ct. Wash. 1987, U.S. Claims Ct. 1979, U.S. Ct. Appeals (fed. cir.) 1982. Assoc. Pillsbury, Madison & Sutro, San Francisco, 1976-78; trial atty. U.S. Dept. Justice, Washington, 1978-87; of counsel Perkins Coie, Seattle, 1987-90, ptnr., 1990—. Mem. ABA, Nat. Contract Mgmt. Assn. (Spl. Achievement award 1990-92), Wash. State Bar Assn. Office: Perkins Coie 1201 3rd Ave Fl 40 Seattle WA 98101-3029 Office Phone: 206-359-8419. Business E-Mail: roehler@perkinscoie.com.

OEHME, FREDERICK WOLFGANG, medical researcher, educator; b. Leipzig, Germany, Oct. 14, 1933; arrived in U.S., 1934; s. Friedrich Oswald and Frieda Betha (Wohlgamuth) Oehme; m. Nancy Beth McAdam, Aug. 6, 1960 (div. June 1981); children: Stephen Frederick, Susan Lynn, Deborah Ann, Heidi Beth; m. Pamela Sheryl Ford, Oct. 2, 1981; 1 child, April Virginia. BS in Biol. Sci., Cornell U., 1957, DVM, 1958; MS in Toxicology and Medicine, Kans. State U., 1962; DMV in Pathology, Justus Liebig U., Giessen, Germany, 1964; PhD in Toxicology, U. Mo., 1969. Diplomate Am. Bd. Toxicology, Am. Bd. Vet. Toxicology, Acad. Toxicol. Scis. Resident intern, Large Animal and Ambulatory Clinic Cornell U., 1957-58; gen. practice vet. medicine, 1958-59; from asst. to assoc. prof. medicine Coll. Vet. Medicine Kans. State U., 1959-66, 69-73, dir. comparative toxicology labs., 1969—, prof. toxicology, medicine and physiology Coll. Vet. Medicine, 1974-96, prof. toxicology, pathobiology, medicine and physiology, 1996—; postdoctoral research fellow in toxicology, NIH U. Mo., 1966-69. Cons. FDA, Washington, Ctr. for Vet. Medicine, Rockville, Md.; cons. animal care com. U. Kans., Lawrence, 1969—76, Syntex Corp., Palo Alto, Calif., 1976—77; mem. sci. adv. panel on PBB Gov.'s Office, State of MIch., 1976—77; mem. Coun. for Agrl. Sci. and Tech. Task Force on Toxicity, Toxicology and Environ. Hazard, 1976—83; cons., mem. adv. group on pesticides EPA, Cin., 1977—; expert state and fed. witness; advisor WHO, Geneva; presenter numerous papers to profl. meetings. Reviewer: Toxicology and Applied Pharmacology, Spectroscopy, numerous others. Mem. adv. coun. Cub Scouts Am., Eagle Scouts; mgr., coach Little League Baseball; active PTA; mem. Manhattan Civic Theatre; trustee Manhattan Marlin Swim Team; dir. meet Little Apple Invitational Swim Meet, 1984; mem. coun. Luth. Ch. Am., mem. sr. choir, numerous coms. Recipient Disting. Grad. Faculty award, Kans. State U., 1977—79, Dir.'s Letter of Commendation, FDA, 1983, Kenneth P. DuBois award, Midwest Soc. Toxicology, 1991, Kenneth F. Lampe award, Am. Acad. Toxicology, 1993, John Doull award, Ctrl. States Soc. Toxicology, 1994, medal, Azabu U., 1994, Silver award, Aristotelian U., 1995, others; fellow, Morris Animal Found., 1967—69. Fellow: Am. Acad. Vet. and Comparative Toxicology (past sec.-treas., numerous coms.), Am. Acad. Toxicology (past pres., numerous coms.); mem.: NRC (subcom. on organic contaminants in drinking water, safe drinking water com., adv. ctr. on toxicology assembly life scis. 1976—77, panel on toxicology marine bd., assembly of engring. 1976—79), AVMA (com. on environmentology 1971—73, adv. com. coun. on biol. and therapeuric agts. 1971—74, Samuel Shiedy award 1999), Nat. Ctr. Toxicol. Rsch. (vet. toxicology rep. sci. adv. bd., sci. adv. bd. 1974—77), N.Y. Acad. Scis., Soc. Toxicologic Pathologists, World Fedn. Clin. Toxicology Ctrs. and Poison Control Ctrs. (past pres.), Soc. Toxicology (past pres., numerous coms., Edn. award 2003), Cornell U. Athletic Assn., Manhattan Square Dance Club, Cornell U. Crew Club, Sigma Xi, Phi Zeta, Omega Tau Sigma. Republican. Avocations: reading, writing, walking, travel. Home: 148 S Dartmouth Dr Manhattan KS 66503-3079 Office: Kans State Univ Comparative Toxicology Labs 1800 Denison Ave Manhattan KS 66506-5660 Office Phone: 785-532-4334. E-mail: oehme@vet.ksu.edu.

OEHME, REINHARD, physicist, researcher; b. Wiesbaden, Germany, Jan. 26, 1928; arrived in U.S., 1956; s. Reinhold and Katharina (Kraus) O.; m. Mafalda Pisani, Nov. 5, 1952. Dr. rer. nat., U. Goettingen, Germany, 1951; Diplom Physiker, U. Frankfurt am Main, Germany, 1948. Asst. Max Planck Inst. Physics, Goettingen, 1949-53; research asso. Fermi Inst. Nuclear Studies, U. Chgo., 1954-56; mem. faculty dept. physics and Fermi Inst., 1958—, prof. physics, 1964—; mem. Inst. Advanced Studies, Princeton, 1956-58. Vis. prof. Inst. de Física Teórica, São Paulo, Brazil, 1952-53, U. Md., 1957, U. Vienna, Austria, 1961, Imperial Coll., London, Eng., 1963-64, U. Karlsruhe, Fed. Republic Germany, 1974, 75, 77, U. Tokyo, 1976, 88; vis. scientist Internat. Centre Theoretical Physics, Miramare-Trieste, Italy, Brookhaven Nat. Lab., Lawrence Radiation Lab., U. Calif., Berkeley, CERN, Geneva, Switzerland, Max Planck Inst., Munich, Fed. Republic Germany, Rsch. Inst. for Fundamental Physics, Kyoto (Japan) U. Author articles in field, chpts. in books. Guggenheim fellow, 1963-64; recipient Humboldt award, 1974, Japan Soc. for Promotion of Sci. Fellowship awards, 1976, 88. Fellow: Am. Phys. Soc. Achievements include discovery of chargeconjugation non-invariance; formulation and proof of Edge of the Wedge theorem, and of hadronic dispersion relations. Office: U Chgo Enrico Fermi Inst 5640 S Ellis Ave Chicago IL 60637-1433 Home Phone: 773-684-7983; Office Phone: 773-702-7299. Business E-Mail: oehme@theory.uchicago.edu.

OEHME, WOLFGANG WALTER, landscape architect; b. Chemnitz, Germany, May 18, 1930; came to the U.S., 1957; s. Walter Gustav and Elisabeth Elsa (Neumann) O.; 1 child, Roland. Degree in horticulture, Bitterfeld Trade Sch., 1950; degree in landscape architecture, U. Berlin, 1954. Exch. student Waterer & Sons Nurseries, Bagshot, United Kingdom, 1954-56; landscape architect Baltimore County Planning, Towson, Md., 1958-65, The Rouse Co., Columbia, Md., 1965-66; asst. prof. U. Pa., Phila., 1962-64, U. Ga., Athens, 1965; pvt. practice Balt., 1965-74; CEO Oehme, Van Sweden and Assocs., Inc., Washington, 1974—. Co-author: Bold Romantic Gardens, 1990, Gardening with Water, 1995, Process Architecture, 1996, Gardening with Nature, 1997. Recipient Spl. Resolution for Disting. and dedicated vol. svc. Baltimore County Coun., 2003; mamed to Hall of Fame, Towson Devel. Corp., 1995; named Man of Yr., German Soc. Md., 1996. Fellow Am. Soc. Landscape Architects; mem. Perennial Plant Assn. (Disting. Svc. 1988), Garden Writers Assn. (Quill and Trowel award 1991). Mass. Hort. Soc. (George Robert White medal of honor 2002). Home: 511A W Joppa Rd Baltimore MD 21204-3819 Office: 800 G St SE Washington DC 20003-2816 Office Phone: 202-546-7575. Business E-Mail: oehme@ovsla.com.

OEI, LOK S., digital communications systems and DSP engineer, researcher; BSEE, U. Mich., 1973, MA in Math., 1973; DSc, Washington U., 1977. Mem. tech. staff Mitre Corp., McLean, Va., 1977—81; staff engr. Hughes Aircraft Co., Fullerton, Calif., 1981—86; prin. sys. engr. Lockheed Martin, Sunnyvale, Calif., 1986—94; sr. prin. engr. Boeing/Raytheon/Hughes Electronics Sys., El Segundo, Calif., 1994—2006. Mem.: IEEE, AIAA, Sigma Xi, Phi Kappa Phi, Eta Kappa Nu, Tau Beta Pi. Home: PO Box 1186 Mountain View CA 94042 Office: PO Box70191 Sunnyvale CA 94087 Office Phone: 408-431-7854. Personal E-mail: lsoei@ieee.org.

OELBERG, DAVID GEORGE, neonatologist educator, researcher; b. Waukon, Iowa, May 26, 1952; s. George Robert and Elizabeth Abigail (Kepler) O.; m. Debra Penuel, Aug. 4, 1979; children: Anna Elizabeth, Benjamin George. BS with highest honors, Coll. William and Mary, 1974; MD, U. Md., 1978. Diplomate in pediat. and in neonatal-perinatal medicine Am. Bd. Pediat. Intern U. Tex. Med. Br., Galveston, 1978-79, resident, 1979-81, house pediat. staff, 1978-81; postdoctoral fellow in neonatal medicine U. Tex. Med. Sch., Houston, 1981-84, asst. prof. dept. pediat., 1984-90, assoc. prof., 1990-93; assoc. prof. pediat., head perinatal rsch. Ctr. Pediat. Rsch. Ea. Va. Med. Sch., 1993-2001, prof., interim chmn. dept. pediat. Ctr. Pediat. Rsch., 2001—, dir. divsn. neonatal-perinatal medicine. Mem. hosp. staff Hermann Hosp., Houston, 1983-93; physician Crippled Children's Svcs. Program, Houston, 1985-93; mem. hosp. staff Lyndon B. Johnson County Hosp., 1990-93; vis. prof. Wyeth-Ayerst Labs., 1992; med. dir. Office Rsch., Children's Hosp. of King's Daus., 1993—, v.p. for acad. devel., 2001—; med. dirs. Office of Rsch., Sentara-Norfolk Gen. Hosp., 1993—, pres. med. staff. Mem. editl. adv. bd. jour. Neonatal Intensive Care; contbr. articles to profl. jours.; ad hoc reviewer profl. jours.; patentee in field. Physician cons. Parents of Victims of Sudden Infant Death Syndrome, Houston, 1984; chmn. Instl. Animal Care and Use Com. Recipient award in analytical chemistry Am. Chem. Soc., 1974, NIH Clin. Investigator award NHLBI, 1989-94; rsch. grantee Am. Lung Assn., 1989-90, NIH, 1989-94. Fellow Am. Acad. Pediat. NY Acad. Scis.; mem. AMA, NAS, Soc. Exptl. Biology and Medicine, So. Soc. Pediatric Rsch. (councilor, pres., sec.-treas.), Soc. Pediatric Rsch. Achievements include development of a method for optical measurement of bilirubin in tissue and ion channel proteins in pulmonary surfactant. Home: 1624 W Little Neck Rd Virginia Beach VA 23452-4720 Office: Ea Va Med Sch Ctr Pediatric Rsch 855 W Brambleton Ave Norfolk VA 23510-1005 Office Phone: 757-668-7456. Business E-Mail: doelberg@chkd.org.

OELBERG, ROBERT NATHAN, landscape architect; b. Washington, May 7, 1956; s. George Robert and Elizabeth Abigail (Kepler) Oelberg; m. Katherine Jane Shoffner, Nov. 9, 2002; stepchildren: Forrest Dungan, Katelyn Dungan. BA in Art magna cum laude, Maharishi Internat. U., Fairfield, Iowa, 1981; M.Landscape Arch., U. Va., Charlottesville, 1985. Registered landscape architect NC. Landscape architect, sr. project mgr. Land Design Inc., Alexandria, Va., 1985-93; owner Robert N. Oelberg ASLA PA, Boone, NC, 1994—97, 1999—2005; dir. HMR Land Planning and Landscape Arch., Boone, 1997-99, v.p. planning Ginn NC region, 2005—. Chmn. Boone Country Dancers; bd. dir. Wilkes Vocational Svcs. With USMC, 1974—76. DuPont fellow, 1984. Mem.: Am. Soc. Landscape Architects. Democrat. Episcopalian. Mailing: 432 Fawn Dr Boone NC 28607 Office: 389 Little Laurel Rd Ext Boone NC 28607 Home Phone: 828-264-4297; Office Phone: 828-263-5904. E-mail: boelberg@ginncompany.com.

OELER, ROBERT P., bank executive; b. Pa., Dec. 6, 1949; Grad., U. Pitts. With Dollar Bank FSB, Pitts., 1973—, v.p., 1978—84, sr. v.p., 1984—92, exec. v.p., 1992—2007, pres., COO, 2007, pres., CEO, 2007—. Office: Dollar Bank FSB 3 Gateway Ctr Pittsburgh PA 15222 Office Phone: 412-261-4900. Office Fax: 412-261-8535. *

OELSCHLAGER, BRANT KURT, surgeon, researcher; b. Lenoir, NC, Aug. 10, 1969; s. Kurt Worth and Sandra Lee Oelschlager; m. Anne-Marie Amies, Oct. 28, 2000; 1 child, Kurt Edward. MD, U. NC, Chapel Hill, 1995. Cert. Am. Bd. Surgery, 2000. Resident U. Wash., Seattle, 2000—01, fellow, advanced laparoscopic surgery, 2000—01, dir., swallowing ctr., dir., Ctr. for Videoendoscopic Surgery, dir., bariatric surgery program, acting asst. prof. surgery, 2001—02, asst. prof. surgery, 2002—06, assoc. prof. surgery, 2006—. Dir. of the swallowing ctr. U. Wash., Seattle, 2001. Contbr. several articles to profl. jour. Office: Univ Wash Dept Surgery 1959 NE Pacific St Box 356410 Seattle WA 98195-6410 Office Phone: 206-543-3518. Office Fax: 206-543-8136. E-mail: brant@u.washington.edu. *

OELSNER, RICHARD S., lawyer; b. NYC, Jan. 23, 1951; BA, NYU, 1973, MA, 1976; JD, Fordham U., 1980. Bar: NY 1981, US Dist. Ct. Ea. Dist. NY, US Dist. Ct. So. Dist. NY. Ptnr. Wilson, Elser, Moskowitz, Edelman & Dicker LLP, NYC. Mem.: NY State Bar Assn. Office: Wilson Elser Moskowitz Edelman & Dicker LLP 23rd Fl 150 E 42nd St New York NY 10017-5639 Office Phone: 212-490-3000 ext. 2483. Office Fax: 212-490-3038. Business E-Mail: oelsnerr@wemed.com.

OEMLER, AUGUSTUS, JR., astronomer, educator; b. Savannah, Ga., Aug. 15, 1945; s. Augustus and Isabelle Redding (Clarke) O.; children: W. Clarke, Bryan S. AB, Princeton U., 1969; MS, Calif. Inst. Tech., 1970, PhD, 1974. Postdoctoral assoc. Kitt Peak Nat. Obs., Tucson, 1974-75; instr. astronomy Yale U., New Haven, 1975-77, asst. prof., 1977-79, assoc. prof., 1979-83, prof., 1983-96, chmn. dept., 1988-96; dir. Carnegie Obs., Pasadena, Calif., 1996—2003, staff astronomer, dir. emeritus, 2003—. Contbr. articles to profl. jours. Alfred P. Sloan fellow, 1978-80 Mem. Am. Astronom. Soc., Internat. Astronom. Union Republican. Roman Catholic. Office: Carnegie Obs 813 Santa Barbara St Pasadena CA 91101-1232

OERTEL, GOETZ KUNO HEINRICH, physicist, professional society administrator; b. Stuhm, Germany, Aug. 24, 1934; arrived in US, 1957; s. Egon F.K. and Margarete W. (Wittek) O.; m. Brigitte Beckmann, June 17, 1960; children: Ines M.H. Oertel Downing, Carsten K.R. Abitur, Robert Mayer, Heilbronn, Fed. Republic Germany, 1953; vordiplom, U. Kiel, Fed. Republic Germany, 1956; PhD, U. Md., College Park, 1963. Aerospace engr. Langley Ctr. NASA, Hampton, Va., 1963-68, chief solar physics Washington, 1968-75, policy analyst for sci. advisor to Pres. and Office Mgmt. and Budget, 1974-75; head astronomy divsn. NSF, Washington, 1975; dir. def. and civilian nuc. waste programs US Dept. Energy, Washington, 1975-83; acting mgr. sav. river ops. office Aiken, SC, 1983-84; dep. mgr. ops. office Albuquerque, 1984-85; dep. asst. sec. of energy for EH, Washington, 1985-86; pres., CEO Assn. Univs. for Rsch. in Astronomy, Inc., Washington, 1986-99; also bd. dirs. Assn. Univs. for Rsch. in Astronomy, Inc. (AURA, Inc.), Washington, disting. advisor, 2000—. Cons. Los Alamos Lab., N.Mex., 1987-92, Westinghouse Electric, 1988-99, Lampadia Found., Fundacion Andes of Santiago de Chile, Vitae Found. Sao Paulo, Brazil; bd. dirs. Inst. for Sci. and Soc., Ellensburg, Wash., IUE Corp.; mem. bd. internat. sci. orgns. NAS, 2001—; bd. mem. Sch. of Computational Sci., George Mason U., 1995—, chair, 2002-03, bd. mem. Coll. Sci., 2006—; mem. US Com. for CODATA, 1993-03, chmn. 1997-2000; US nat. del. CODATA ICSU, 1999-03; mem. peer rev. com. ASME, 1996-2000; cons. conicyt, Govt. of Chile, 2000-04, VITAE Found., Brazil, 2001-04, Fundacion Andes, Chile, 2000-03; chmn., bd. dirs. Ctr. of Excellence for Hazardous Materials Mgmt., Carlsbad, N.Mex., 2003-04; lifetime nat. assoc. Nat. Acads. Washington, 2003—; trustee FLF Trust, 2006—. Contbr. articles to profl. jours. Recipient ASME Dixy Lee Ray prize, 2005; Fulbright grantee, 1957; Exceptional Svc. medal NASA, 1973, Bronze medal Dept. Energy, 1983, Silver medal, 1985, Disting. Svcs. award NSF, 1999; asteroid named in his honor, Internat. Astronomical Union, 2006. Fellow AAAS; mem. Am. Phys. Soc., Am. Astron. Soc., Internat. Astron. Union (named minor planet Goetzoertel in honor), NY Acad. Scis., Philos. Soc. Washington, Internat. U. Exch., Inc. (bd. dirs.), Cosmos Club (admissions com. 2004-07, awards com. 2007—), Sigma Xi. Lutheran. Achievements include patents in field. Avocations: exercise, chess, computing, genealogy. Address: 8833 Watts Mine Terr Potomac MD 20854-5439 Office Phone: 301-365-1061. Business E-Mail: goetz@oertel.org.

OERTEL, MICHAEL, researcher, medical educator; b. Berlin, May 6, 1971; arrived in U.S., 2001; s. Dieter and Heiderose Oertel. Diploma in Biology, U. Leipzig, 1995, PhD, 2000. Postdoctoral fellow Inst. Clin. Immunology U. Leipzig, Germany, 2000—01; rsch. assoc. Albert Einstein Coll. Medicine Yeshiva U., Bronx, NY, 2001—03, instr. medicine Marion Bessin Liver Rsch. Ctr., 2004—. Contbr. articles to profl. jours. Mem.: German Assn. for the Study of the Liver, Am. Assn. for Study of Liver Diseases, German Transplantation Soc. Avocations: reading, music, chess, horseback riding, travel. Office: Albert Einstein Coll Medicine Yeshiva U Marion Bessin Liver Rsch Ctr 1300 Morris Park Ave Ullm 605 Bronx NY 10461 Office Phone: 718-430-3310. Business E-Mail: moertel@aecom.yu.edu.

OERTEL, YOLANDA CASTILLO, pathologist, educator; b. Lima, Peru, Dec. 14, 1938; came to U.S., 1966; d. Leonardo A. and Dalila (Ramirez) C.; m. James E. Oertel, Sept. 24, 1969. MD, Cayetano Heredia, Lima, 1964; Dr. honoris causa, U. Peruana Cayetano Heredia, 1999. Diplomate Am. Bd. Pathology (mem. test com. for cytopathology 1988-94). Internat. postdoctoral fellowship NIH, Bethesda, Md., 1966-68; asst. prof. pathology Sch. Medicine George Washington U., Washington, 1975-78, assoc. prof., 1978-84, prof., 1984-98, prof. emerita, 1998—. Adj. prof. pathology and lab. medicine MCP Hahnemann U. Sch. Medicine; cons. Registry Cytology Armed Forces Inst. Pathology, Washington, 1981—. Author: Fine Needle Aspiration of the Breast, 1987; contbr. chpts. to books, articles to profl. jours. Decorated comendador de la Orden Cayetano Heredia, 1999; recipient Francisco A. Camino prize Peruvian Med. Assn., 1965, cert. Meritorious Svc. Armed Forces Inst. Pathology, 1974; named Disting. Alumna Cayetano Heredia Med. Sch., 1989. Mem. Assn. Mil. Surgeons (hon.), Colombian Soc. Pathology (hon.), Argentinian Soc. Pathology (hon.), Peruvian Soc. Pathologists (hon.), Argentinian Soc. Cytopathology, (hon.), Am. Soc. Cytopathology, Internat. Acad. Pathology, Soc. Latinoamericana Patologia, Am. Soc. Clin. Pathologists (coun. on cytopathology 1982-88), Coll. Am. Pathologists, Arthur Purdy Stout Soc. Surg. Pathologists, Am. Thyroid Assn., L.Am. Thyroid Soc. Avocations: reading, opera. Office: Washington Hosp Ctr Pathology Dept Washington Cancer Inst 110 Irving St NW Washington DC 20010-2975 Home Phone: 703-836-0639; Office Phone: 202-877-2740. Office Fax: 202-877-0197. Business E-Mail: Yolanda.C.Oertel@medstar.net.

OERTER, CYNTHIA LYNN, medical technologist; b. Waupaca, Wis., Mar. 8, 1948; d. Lavern Charles and Geraldine Mae (Huffcutt) Trinrud; m. Gregory Van Oerter, June 8, 1968; children: Nathan, Justin. BS, U. Wis., Oshkosh, 1971; MS, Cardinal Stritch Coll., 1993. Cert. Am. Soc. Clin. Pathologists. Med. technologist Mercy Med. Ctr., Oshkosh, Wis., 1970-76, Iola (Wis.) Hosp., 1978-86, wellness cons., 1985-86, Riverside Med. Ctr., Waupaca, Wis., 1986—95, med. technologist, hematology supr., insvc. coord., cons., 1987-95; pres. Pro Health Consul, Inc., Waupaca, Wis., 1994—; bus. ptnr., adminstr. Garden Park House, 1994—2000, owner, adminstr., 2000—; owner Back Door Bakery, 2003—, Secret Garden Cafe, 2003—. Tchr. Fox Valley Coll., Appleton, Wis., 1986, 87; organizer Overeaters Anonymous, Iola, 1985-89; owner Green Fountain Inn, 1995—. Mem. parent's com. gifted and talented Waupaca Sch. Sys., 1984, charter mem. edn. employment coun., 1989-92, mem. adv. com. guidance program K-12, 1992; vol. Nat. Wellness Inst., 1986-97, Am. Lung Assn., 1986-87; tchr. smokeless program Am. Inst. Preventative Medicine, 1988-93; com. mem. Main St. Design, 1999-01. Mem. NAFE, Nat. Platform Assn., Am. Sch. Health Assn. (com. mem.), Waupaca C. of C. (tourism com. 2002—, Athena award 2003), Rotary (sec. 1996-98, bd. dirs. 1995-04, 2006—, pres. 2000-01). Republican. Lutheran. Avocations: gardening, gourmet cooking, sailing, Bible study. Business E-Mail: greenfountaininn@yahoo.com.

OESTERLE, ERIC ADAM, lawyer; b. Lafayette, Ind., Dec. 2, 1948; s. Eric Clark and Germaine Dora (Seelye) O.; m. Carolyn Anne Scherer, Sept. 16, 1973; children: Adam Clark, Allison Margaret. BS, U. Mich., 1970, JD, 1973. Bar: Ill. 1973, U.S. Dist. Ct. (no. dist.) Ill. 1973, U.S. Ct. Appeals (7th cir.) 1987, U.S. Supreme Ct. 1986. Assoc. Sonnenschein, Carlin, Nath & Rosenthal, Chgo., 1973—80; ptnr. Sonnenschein Nath & Rosenthal, Chgo., 1980—. Major gifts com. U. Mich. Law Sch., 2002—. Fellow Am. Bar Found.; mem. ABA, Ill. Bar Assn., Chgo. Bar Assn Home: 645 Lake Rd Glen Ellyn IL 60137-4249 Office: Sonnenschein Nath & Rosenthal 7800 Sears Tower 233 S Wacker Dr Ste 8000 Chicago IL 60606-6491 Business E-Mail: eoesterle@sonnenschein.com.

OESTERLE, STEPHEN N., medical products executive, cardiologist, educator; b. LaGrande, Oreg., Mar. 3, 1951; BA summa cum laude, Harvard Univ., 1973; MD, Yale Univ., 1977. Intern & resident Mass. Gen. Hosp., 1977—80; fellowship in cardiology Stanford Univ., 1981—83; cardiologist Good Samaritan Hosp., LA, 1986—91; cardiologist, med. educator Georgetown Univ., 1991—92; assoc. prof. med. & dir. cardiac catheterization & coronary intervention labs Stanford Univ. Med. Ctr., 1992—98; assoc. prof. med. Harvard Med. Sch., 1998—2002; dir. invasive cardiology svc. Mass. Gen. Hosp., 1998—2002; sr. v.p. medicine & tech. Medtronic Inc., Mpls., 2002—. Office: Medtronic Inc 710 Medtronic Pkwy Minneapolis MN 55432-5604 *

OESTERLIN, LOVYE GWENDOLYN, retired chemist, educator, retired educational consultant; b. Cheraw, SC, Aug. 26, 1932; d. John Eliot Davis and Lucile Monica (Davis) McIver; m. Rudolf Oesterlin, Dec. 29, 1956; children: Monika Oesterlin Wiltshire, Barbara Oesterlin Heath, Michael, Margrete Oesterlin Jean-Louis. BS, Bennett Coll., Greensboro, NC, 1953; MS, N.Mex. Highlands U., Las Vegas, 1966. Chem. technician Sloan-Kettering Inst., NYC, 1953; rsch. chemist sanitary engring. U. Calif., Berkeley, 1955—59; phys. sci. tchr. Hamilton Jr. H.S., Oakland, Calif., 1960—63; tchr. chemistry Columbia H.S., East Greenbush, NY, 1967—93, SUNY, Albany, 1988—93, ret., 1993; field supr. of student tchrs. Cabrini Coll., Radner, Pa., 1994—2001. Cons. State Edn. Dept., N.Y. State,

Albany, NY, 1973—93. Recipient Belle Tobias award, Bennett Coll., 1949; grantee, NSF, 1960, 1962, 1981; Fulbright grant, State Dept., Washington, 1953. Mem.: NSTA (evaluator), Am. Chem. Soc., East Greenbush Tchrs. Assn., State Tchrs. Assn. N.Y. State (Sci. Fair dir.), Nat. Assn. Biology Tchrs. (dir.), Sci. Tchrs. Assn. N.Y. (rep. to bd. regents, Svc. award), The Links, Inc., Delta Sigma Theta. Democrat. United Methodist. Avocations: reading, piano, quilting, travel, opera. Home Fax: 610-469-1047. E-mail: loveBBS@aol.com.

OESTERMAN, PAUL JOSEPH, pharmacist, educator; b. London, Eng., July 7, 1953; s. Richard J. Oesterman and Helen R. Utley; m. Melinda A. Olson, June 28, 2002; m. Susan J. Sweat, Sept. 28, 1978 (div. Oct. 1, 2001); children: Gigi Nicoson, Todd R., Joe P. AS, Marin Jr. Coll., Kentfield, Calif., 1972; Pharm.D., U. Pacfic, Stockton, Calif., 1976. Cert. Am. Diabetes Assn., 2000, pharmacy based immunization delivery Am. Pharmacists Assn., 2005, healthcare BLS instr. Am. Heart Assn. (scholar, 2006, 2007), 2006, osteoporosis care NIPCO, 2006. Dir. ancillary svcs. Lodi Cmty. Hosp., Lodi, Calif., 1977—88; chief pharmacist, drug edn. coord. Kaiser Permanente, Calif., 1988—2000; clin. pharmacist cons. Medco Health, Henderson, Nev., 2001—05; asst. prof. pharmacy practice U. So. Nev., Henderson, 2005—. Ind. pharmacist cons., Stockton, Calif., 1992—, Lodi, Calif., 1992—; drug utiliazation rev. bd. State Nev., Carson City, 2006—. Vol. Med. Res. Corps, Las Vegas, 2004—, Habitat for Humanity, Las Vegas, 1998—. Mem.: Calif. Pharmacists Assn. (Preceptor Yr. 1983), Nat. Cmty. Pharmacists Assn. (faculty liaison 2006—), Am. Soc. Health Sys. Pharmacists, Am. Pharmacists Assn., Am. Assn. Colls. Pharmacy, Kappa Psi Profl. Pharmacy Frat. (corr. sec. 1972—). Avocations: travel, sports. Office: Univ So Nev 11 Sunset Way Henderson NV 89114 Home Phone: 702-361-4805; Office Phone: 702-968-2089. Office Fax: 702-990-4435. Business E-Mail: poesterman@usn.edu.

OESTING, DAVID W., lawyer; b. Chgo., Aug. 6, 1944; AB, Earlham Coll., 1967; JD, Wash. U., 1970. Bar: Wash. 1970, Alaska 1981. Ptnr. in charge of Anchorage Office Davis Wright Tremaine, Anchorage, 1980—. Editor-in-chief Wash. U. Law Quarterly, 1969-70. Mem. ABA, Am. Coll. Trial Lawyers, Wash. State Bar Assn., Alaska Bar Assn., Anchorage Bar Assn., Order of Coif. Office: Davis Wright Tremaine 701 W 8th Ave Ste 800 Anchorage AK 99501-3467 Home Phone: 907-248-3146; Office Phone: 907-257-5300. Business E-Mail: daveoesting@dwt.com.

OESTREICH, CHARLES HENRY, retired university president; b. Columbus, Ohio, June 8, 1932; s. Henry F. and Martha (Schwartz) O.; m. Rhoda J. Haseley, Aug. 26, 1957; children: Martha, Mary, David. BS, Capital U., 1954; MS, Ohio U., 1956, PhD, 1961; LLD, Capital U., 1986. Instr. chemistry Va. Mil. Inst., 1956-57, Capital U., Columbus, 1960-62, asst. prof., 1962-64, assoc. prof., 1965-69; acad. dean Tex. Luth. U., Seguin, 1969-76, interim pres., 1976-77, pres., 1977-94, pres. emeritus Seguin, 1995—. Postdoctoral rsch. fellow Vanderbilt U., 1965-66 Bd. dirs., past pres. Mid-Tex. Symphony; bd. dirs. St. Luke's Health Ministries, Eden Home, Inc. Mem. Rotary (past pres. Seguin). Home and Office: 2269 S Abbey Loop New Braunfels TX 78130-8965 E-mail: charleso@satx.rr.com.

OESTREICH, JAMES R., editor; Founder Opus magazine; editor High Fidelity; classical music & dance editor, critic NY Times, 1989—. Office: NY Times 229 W 43rd St New York NY 10036 Office Phone: 212-556-5825.

OETJEN, DAVID L. (JON DAVID DOUGLAS), writer, film producer; b. Washington, Iowa, May 23, 1938; s. Walter Theodor Oetjen and Alyce Marie Peterson. BA, U. of Iowa, 1960. Prodr. Home Shopping Network, Clearwater, Fla.; broadcast prodn. dir. Barlow/Johnson Advt., Syracuse, Albany, Buffalo, Springfield, N.Y. and Mass., 1969—73; dir. of promotion, advt. mgr. Sta. WTVH-TV, Meredith Corp., Syracuse, NY, 1977—91. Prodr.: (TV series, television) Dari-Lean "Magic", 1971 (Chgo. Film Festival, 1971); author: (novels) Cody, A Boy's Odyssey, 2002, Place Out of Time, 2003, The American Boy, 2005, Deadly High School, 2007. Citizen's adv. Bayfront Med. Ctr., St. Petersburg, 1997—99; advisor Office of the Mayor, Syracuse, 1988—91, Syracuse (N.Y.) Symphony, 1988—90; prodr. Bring Them Home Alive-Missing Childrens' Clearing House, Tampa Bay. Recipient Silver Shaker award for Winterfest, CNY-Pub. Rels. Soc. Am., 1989, 1st Pl. TV Promotion award for Gimmie Five!, Syracuse Advt. Club, 1988, 1st Pl. TV Promotion award for Tell 'Em, 1989, Media award, CNY Parks and Recreation Soc., 1985, Award of Appreciation for svc. as dir. of broadcast promotion and publicity, AAU/USA Jr. Olympics, 1987. Mem.: Fiction Writers Roundtable, Broadcast Promotion Assn., Village Writers' Group. Home: 1617 Duran Dr The Villages FL 32162 Personal E-mail: dleeo@earthlink.net.

OETTGEN, HERBERT FRIEDRICH, physician; b. Cologne, Germany, Nov. 22, 1923; came to U.S., 1958; s. Peter and Minna (Kaul) O.; m. Trudi Hesberg, Feb. 16, 1957; children: Hans Christoph, Joerg Peter, Anne Barbara. MD, U. Cologne, 1951. Diplomate Bd. Internal Medicine, Fed. Republic of Germany. Resident in pathology City Hosp., Cologne, 1952-54, resident in medicine, 1955-58; fellow Meml. Sloan-Kettering Cancer Ctr., NYC, 1958-62, assoc. to assoc. mem., 1963-69, mem., 1972—, attending physician, 1971—; prof. medicine Cornell U. Med. Coll., NYC, 1972—. Assoc. dir. Cancer Rsch. Inst., N.Y.C., 1985—. Author over 350 publs. in hematology, cancer rsch., immunology and clin. oncology. Recipient award for cancer rsch. Wilhelm Warner Found., Hamburg, Fed. Republic Germany, 1970, Lisec-Artz award Friedrich Wilhelm U., Bonn, Fed. Republic of Germany, 1982. Presbyterian. Avocations: violin, woodworking. Home: 48 Overlook Dr New Canaan CT 06840-6825 Office: Meml Sloan-Kettering Cancer Ctr 1275 York Ave New York NY 10021-6094 Home Phone: 203-966-5709; Office Phone: 212-639-7505. Business E-Mail: oettgenh@mskcc.org, hoettgen@licr.org.

OETTING, ROGER H., lawyer; b. Ft. Wayne, Ind., Dec. 17, 1931; s. Martin W. and Valetta E. (Holman) O.; m. Marcia J. Highlands, Aug. 10, 1957; children: Richard H., Susan E., Catherine R. BBA, U. Mich., 1953, MBA, JD, U. Mich., 1956; LLM in Taxation, Georgetown U., 1958. Ptnr. Touche Ross & Co., Detroit, 1960-80, Warner Norcross & Judd LLP, Grand Rapids, Mich., 1980—. Adj. prof. taxation Grand Valley State U., 1984-99. Past pres., dir. treas. Chamber Music Soc. Grand Rapids, 1980-89; past dir., treas. Opera Grand Rapids, 1980-87; dir. Porter Hills Presbyn. Village, 1989—, treas., 1990—; dir., chair fin. Aquinas Emeritus Coll. Fellow Am. Coll. Tax Lawyers; mem. State Bar Mich. (coun. fed. tax sect. 1991—), Grand Rapids Bar Assn. (chair fin. com. 1983—), Econ. Club (past treas., bd. dirs. 1982-91), Sugar Bush Assn. (dir., sec., treas. 1985—), Kent Country Club (fin. com.), Leland Country Club, Leland Yacht Club, Univ. Club (bd. dirs., treas.), Rotary (bd. dirs. 1989-93), Delta Kappa Epsilon. Office: Warner Norcross & Judd LLP 900 Fifth Third Ctr 111 Lyon St NW Grand Rapids MI 49503-2487 Home Phone: 616-949-8182; Office Phone: 616-752-2122. E-mail: roetting@wnj.com.

OETTINGER, ANTHONY GERVIN, mathematician, educator; b. Nuremberg, Germany, Mar. 29, 1929; came to U.S., 1941, naturalized, 1947; s. Albert and Marguerite (Bing) O.; m. Marilyn Tanner, June 20, 1954; children: Douglas, Marjorie. AB, Harvard U., 1951, PhD, 1954; Henry fellow, U. Cambridge, Eng., 1951-52; Litt.D. (hon.), U. Pitts., 1984. Mem. faculty Harvard, 1955—, asso. prof. applied math., 1960-63, prof. linguistics, 1963-75, Gordon McKay prof. applied math., 1963—, chmn. program on info. resources policy, 1972—, mem. faculty of govt., 1973—2004, prof. info. resources policy, 1975—. Mem. command control comm. and intelligence bd. Dept. Navy, 1978-83; mem. sci. adv. group Def. Comm. Agy., 1979-90; chmn. bd. visitors Nat. Def. Intelligence Coll., 1986—; chmn., dir. Nat. Intelligence Sci. Adv. Bd., 1994—; cons. Arthur D. Little, Inc., 1956-80, Office Sci. and Tech., Exec. Office of Pres., 1960-73, Bellcomm, Inc., 1963-68, Sys. Devel. Corp., 1965-68, Nat. Security Coun., Exec. Office of Pres., 1975-81, Pres.'s Fgn. Intelligence Adv. Bd., 1981-90; chmn. Computer Sci. and Engring. Bd., Nat. Acad. Scis., 1968-73; mem. Mass. Cmty. Antenna TV Commn., 1972-79, chmn., 1975-79; mem. rsch. adv. bd. Com. for Econ. Devel., 1975-79; trustee Babbage Inst., 1991—; panel mem. Naval Studies Bd. NAS/NRC, 1993-95; mem. banking and fin. team Pres.' Commn. on Critical Infrastructure Protection, 1998; mem. Def. Sci. Bd., 2003—. Author: A Study for the Design of an Automatic Dictionary, 1954, Automatic Language Translation: Lexical and Technical Aspects, 1960, Run Computer Run: The Mythology of Educational Innovation, 1969, High and Low Politics: Information Resources for the 80s, 1977, Behind the Telephone Debates, 1988, Mastering the Changing Information World, 1993; editor: Proc. of a Symposium on Digital Computers and Their Applications, 1962; contbr. chpts. to The Information Resources Policy Handbook: Research for the Information Age, 1999. Fellow Am. Acad. Arts and Scis., AAAS, IEEE, Assn. Computing Machinery (mem. coun. 1961-68, chmn. com. U.S. Govt. Rels. 1964-66, editor computational linguistics sect. Commn. 1964-66, pres. 1966-68); mem. Soc. Indsl. and Applied Math. (mem. coun. 1963-67), Coun. on Fgn. Rels., Phi Beta Kappa, Sigma Xi. Clubs: Cosmos (Washington); Harvard (N.Y.C.). Home: 65 Elizabeth Rd Belmont MA 02478-3819 Office: Harvard U Maxwell Dworkin 125 33 Oxford St Cambridge MA 02138-2901 Business E-Mail: anthony@seas.harvard.edu.

OETTINGER, JULIAN ALAN, lawyer, pharmaceutical executive; b. Jan. 1939; BS, U. Ill., 1961; JD, Northwestern U., 1964. Bar: Ill. 1964. Atty. SEC, 1964-67, Walgreen Co., Deerfield, Ill., 1967-72, sr. atty., 1972-78, dir. law, 1978-89, v.p., gen. counsel, corp. sec., 1989-2000, sr. v.p., gen. counsel, corp. sec., 2000—05. *

O'FARRELL, MARK THEODORE, religious organization administrator; b. Milw., Apr. 13, 1948; s. Theodore Wolfred and Ernestine (Shelhammer) O.; m. Phillis Gilley, Sept. 18, 1948; children: Gwen, Kevin. BA, Columbia Bible Coll., 1970; DD, Toccan Falls Coll., 1996. Asst. pastor 1st Alliance Ch., Macon, Ga., 1970-71, sr. pastor Port Charlotte, Fla., 1981-86, Belle Glade (Fla.) Alliance Ch., 1971-81; asst. to dist. supt., ext. dir. Southeastern Dist. of Christian and Missionary Alliance, Orlando, Fla., 1986-93, dist. supt., 1993—2005; pres. Trinity Coll. Fla., New Port Richey, 2005—. Recipient Spiritual Aims award Kiwanis, Antioch award Ch. Planting Nat. Office: Trinity Coll Fla 2430 Welbilt Blvd New Port Richey FL 34655 Office Phone: 727-376-6911.

OFFEN, RONALD CHARLES, retired school librarian; b. Chgo., Oct. 2, 1930; s. Charles Henry and Ellen (Shirreffs) O.; m. Sharon Rae Nealy, Mar. 17, 1951 (div.); children: Deirdre, Eric; m. Rosine J. Franke, Aug. 20, 1966 (dec. Apr. 21, 2000); children: Michele, Darren P.; m. Beverly Kahling Drick, April 27, 2003. AA, Wright Jr. Coll., Chgo., 1950; MA, U. Chgo., 1967. Ins. investigator various ins. cos., Chgo., 1952-68; mng. editor Chicagoland Mag., Chgo., 1968-70; editor Automotive Fleet, Glenview, Ill., 1970-71; freelance editor, writer, author Chgo., 1971-78; sch. libr. Capistrano Unified Sch. Dist., Laguna Niguel, Calif., 1983-98; ret., 1998. Adminstr. theater co. The Peripatetic Task Force, Chgo., 1975-78. Co-editor Odyssey: Explorations in Poetry, 1956-58; exec. editor Lit. Times, 1975-78; co-author: (non-fiction) Dillinger: Dead or Alive?, 1970; author: (biographies) Cagney, 1973, Brando, 1974; (poetry) Poet as Bad Guy, 1963, Instead of Gifts, 1995, Questions, Answers, 1996, God's Haircut (And Other Remembered Dreams), 1999, Off-Target, 2006; editor: The Starving Poet's Cookbook, 1994; editor Free Lunch, 1989—. Chair James T. Farrell Centenary Com. Mem. Acad. Am. Poets (1st prize 1958), Authors Guild.

OFFENBERGER, ALLAN ANTHONY, retired electrical engineering educator; b. Wadena, Sask., Can., Aug. 11, 1938; s. Ivy Viola (Hagglund) O.; m. Margaret Elizabeth Patterson, Apr. 12, 1963; children: Brian, Gary. BS, U. B.C., 1962, MS, 1963; PhD, MIT, 1968. Asst. prof. U. Alta., Edmonton, Canada, 1968—70, assoc. prof., 1970—75, prof., 1975—95, prof. emeritus, 1996—. Vis. prof. UK Atomic Energy Agy., Abingdon, Oxon, 1975-76, U. Oxford, UK, 1992, U. Osaka, Japan, 2000; project dir. Laser Fusion Project, Edmonton, 1984-91; mem. strategic adv. com. Nat. Fusion Program, Atomic Energy Can. Ltd., Chalk River, Ont., 1987-96; Cons. Lawrence Livermore Nat. Lab., Calif., 1996-2007; served on several execs. bds., sci. adv. and rsch. grant committees; hosted internat. scholars; invited lectr., cons. in field. Mem. editorial bd. Laser and Particle Beams, 1987-2004; contbr. over 150 sci. articles on lasers and plasma physics Killam Rsch. fellow Can. Coun., 1980-82. SERC rsch. fellow, Eng., 1992. Mem. Can. Assn. Physicists (exec. officer, v.p. elect 1987-88, pres. 1989-90), Am. Phys. Soc., Sigma Xi. Achievements include establishing a major center for high power laser research and development (particularly krypton fluoride lasers) for fusion energy and other applications. Home: 412 Lessard Dr Edmonton AB Canada T6M 1A7 Office: U Alta Dept Elec Computer Engring Edmonton AB Canada T6G 2V4 Office Phone: 780-492-3939. Business E-Mail: aao@ece.ualberta.ca.

OFFER, STUART JAY, lawyer; b. Seattle, June 2, 1943; m. Judith Spitzer, Aug. 29, 1970; children: Rebecca, Kathryn. BA, U. Wash., 1964; LLB, Columbia U., 1967. Bar: D.C. 1968, U.S. Tax Ct. 1968, Calif. 1972. Atty., advisor U.S. Tax Ct., Washington, 1967-68; assoc. Morrison & Foerster, LLP, San Francisco, 1972-76, ptnr., 1976—. Trustee Am. Tax Policy Inst. Served as capt. U.S. Army, 1968-72. Mem. ABA (chmn. taxation sect., corp. tax com. 1991-92, coun. dir. 1995-98, vice chmn. adminstrn. 1998-2000), Internat. Fiscal Assn. (regent), Am. Coll. Tax Counsel. Office: Morrison & Foerster LLP 425 Market St San Francisco CA 94105-2482 Office Phone: 415-268-7052. Business E-Mail: soffer@mofo.com.

OFFEREINS, DIANE M., finance company executive; BBA, Loyola Univ., New Orleans. Positions through v.p., dir. application devel. Southeast Bank, Miami, Fla.; v.p. retail delivery systems Bank of Am., San Francisco; sr. exec. v.p. MBNA Am.; exec. v.p., CIO Discover Fin. Services, Riverwoods, Ill., 1999—2005, exec. v.p., chief adminstrv. & tech. officer, 2005—. Bd. mem. Loretto Hosp. Found. Office: Discover Fin Services 2500 Lake Cook Rd Riverwoods IL 60015 *

OFFIT, MORRIS WOLF, investment company executive; b. Balt., Jan. 22, 1937; s. Michael and Rhea (Wolf) O.; m. Nancy Silverman, Nov. 26, 1959; children: Ned S., Daniel W. BA in History, Johns Hopkins U., 1957, LHD (hon.), 1996; MBA in Fin., U. Pa., 1959. V.p. investment dept. Mercantile Safe Deposit and Trust, Balt., 1960—68; gen. ptnr. Salomon Bros. Inc., NYC, 1968-80; pres. Julius Baer Securities, NYC, 1980-82; now CEO Offit Hall Capital Mgmt. LLC, 2002—; CEO Offit Assoc. Inc., NYC, 1983—2001. Trustee, former chmn. bd. trustees Johns Hopkins U.; chmn. adv. coun. Nitze Sch. Advanced Internat. Studies; trustee Jewish Mus., former chmn.; trustee Jewish Theol. Sem., Thirteen-WNET, United Jewish Appeal Fedn. N.Y., Am. Jewish Com. Mem. Coun. on Fgn. Rels. Office: Offit Hall Capital Mgmt LLC 65 E 55th St New York NY 10022

OFFIT, SIDNEY, writer, educator; b. Balt., Oct. 13, 1928; s. Barney and Lillian (Cohen) O.; m. Avodah Crindell Komito, Aug. 8, 1952; children: Kenneth, Michael Robert. BA, Johns Hopkins U., Balt., 1950; DHL (hon.), LI U., 1999. Editorial staff Mercury Publs., NYC, 1952-53, Macfadden Publs., NYC, 1953-54; contbg. editor Baseball mag., Washington, 1955-58; faculty NYU, 1964—2002; assoc. editor Intellectual Digest, 1970-72, sr. editor, 1972-74; adj. prof. creative writing NYU, 1977—2003. Lectr. creative writing New Sch. U., 1965—; curator George Polk Awards for Journalism, 1977—; commentator Channel 5 TV, NYC, 1975-85, Channel 11 TV, 1992. Author: He Had it Made, 1959, The Other Side of the Street, 1962, Soupbone, 1963, Topsy Turvey, 1965, The Adventure of Homer Fink, 1966, The Boy Who Made a Million, 1968; short stories Not All the Girls Have Million Dollar Smiles, 1971; Only a Girl Like You, 1972, What Kind of Guy Do You Think I Am?, 1977, Memoir of the Bookie's Son, 1995; book editor: Politics Today, 1978-80. Selection com. Dist. Sch. Bd., NYC, 1968; exec. bd. Lexington Democratic Club, 1957-60, NY Dem. County Com., 1966-; chmn. 19th Precinct Cmty. Coun. NYC, 1964-80. Recipient Disting. Alumni award Valley Forge Mil. Acad., 1961, Otty Cmty. Svc. award, 1975, Tchg. Excellence award NYU, 1981, commendation for achievment as teacher, scholar, communicator NY State Legislature, 1983, proclamation for contbns. to city, NYC Coun., 1983, Police Athletic League citation for svc. to children of NYC, 1991, 96, 2002, 04, Honors Convocation award Marymount Manhattan Coll., 1994, Detlev W. Bronk award Johns Hopkins Alumni Assn., 1994, Disting. Univ. Tchg. award New Sch. U., 2000, Poets and Writers award Writers for Writers, 2005 Mem. Tudor and Stuart Club, Authors Guild Found. (pres. 1993—), Authors Guild (coun. 1970-77, 79—, v.p. 1993-95), Authors League (nat. coun. 1976-), Authors League Fund (v.p. 1998—, acting pres. 2004-05), Am. Ctr. PEN (exec. com. 1969, 2003—, v.p. 1970-74, internat. del. 1971-72, 74), Century Assn. Club (NYC), Coffee House Club (NYC). Home: 23 E 69th St New York NY 10021-4919 *I have been guided by a strong devotion to my family and friends and moderate ambition. In both these priorities I have been influenced by my parents. With my writing I have tried to fulfill my own needs, and for the most I have been satisfied by the reception. I do not aspire to fame or great fortune, and this leaves me free to enjoy the sharing of experiences with my friends and family. I consider myself a lucky man and this keeps me grateful to whatever forces there are that contrive man's fortune.*

OFFNER, ERIC DELMONTE, lawyer; b. Vienna, June 23, 1928; came to U.S., 1941, naturalized, 1949; s. Sigmund J. and Kathe (Delmonte) O.; m. Julie Cousins, 1955 (dec. 1959); m. Barbara Ann Shotton, July 2, 1961; 1 son, Gary Douglas; m. Carol Sue Marcus, Jan. 12, 1980 (dec. 1983) BBA, CCNY, 1949; JD in Internat. Affairs, Cornell U., 1952. Bar: NY 1952. Assoc. Langner, Parry, Card & Langner, NYC, 1952-57; ptnr. Haseltine, Lake, Waters & Offner, NYC, 1957-77; sr. ptnr. Offner & Kuhn, 1978-83; pvt. practice NYC, 1965—. Instr. George Washington U. Law Sch., Cornell U. Law Sch.; spl. prof. law Hofstra Law Sch., 1974-92; jazz disc jockey ProgressiveRadioNetwork.org.; jazz record prodr. Author: International Trademark Protection, 1964, Japanese edit., 1977, International Trademark Service, Vols. I-III 1970, Vol. IV, 1972, Vol. V., 1973, Vol. VI, 1976, Vol. VII, 1981, Vols. I-VII, 2d edit., 1981, Legal Training Course on Trademarks, 1982; editor in chief: Cornell Law Forum, 1950-51; mem. editorial bd.: Trademark Reporter, 1961-64, 69-72; book reviewer Jour. Humanism and Ethical Religion; contbr. articles to profl. jours.; prodr. jazz concerts N.Y.C., 1996—, jazz video and jazz CDs. V.p. Riverdale Mental Health Clinic, N.Y.C., 1966-67; pres. Riverdale Mental Health Assn., 1967-69, Ethical Culture Soc., Riverdale-Yonkers, 1964-67, Ethical Cultural Retirement Ctr., 1975-94; trustee Am. Ethical Union, 1967-73, Internat. Alliance of Holistic Lawyers; bd. dirs. Fit Kids; pres. The Sidney Bechet Soc., Ltd., 1997—. Mem. N.Y. Patent Law Assn. (assoc. editor Bull. 1961-66, gov. 1973-76), ABA, City N.Y. Bar Assn. (sec. 1962-64), U.S. Trademark Assn., World Peace Through Law (charter), Trademark Soc. Washington (charter), Inst. Trade Mark Agts. (London), Sidney Bechet Soc. Ltd. (pres. 1997—), Australian Patent Inst., Internat. Assn. Protection Indsl. Property, Nat. Coun. Patent Law Assn., Internat. Patent, Trademark Assn., Phi Alpha Delta. Home: 20 Joy Dr New Hyde Park NY 11040-1109 Office Phone: 516-627-4468. E-mail: eoffner@optonline.net. *Do unto others so as to elicit the best in them and thereby the best in yourself.*

OFFUTT, BRIAN, broadcast executive; BA, MBA, Harvard U. Investment banking analyst JP Morgan; exec. recruiter Spencer Stuart; pres., COO Interdimensions; COO Broadway Video Entertainment; sr. v.p. entertainment products Nickelodeon & Viacom Consumer Products, NYC, 2005—. Office: Nickelodeon Networks 1515 Broadway 42d Fl New York NY 10036 *

OFFUTT, GERALD M., lawyer; b. New Haven, Sept. 20, 1950; AB, Harvard U., 1973, JD, 1976. Bar: Ill. 1976. Ptnr. McDermott, Will & Emery, Chgo. Contbr. articles to profl. journs. Mem. ABA, Chgo. Bar Assn., Cook County Bar Assn., Nat. Bar Assn. Office: McDermott Will & Emery 227 W Monroe St Fl 31 Chicago IL 60606-5096 Office Phone: 312-984-7662. Office Fax: 312-984-7700. Business E-Mail: goffutt@mwe.com.

O'FLYNN, THOMAS M., utilities executive; m. Cheryl O'Flynn; 1 child. BA in Econ., Northwestern U., 1982; MBA, U. Chgo., 1986. Fin. adv. to PSEG Morgan Stanley, mng. dir. global power and utility group, head North Am. region, 1986—2000; exec. v.p., CFO Pub. Svc. Enterprise Group Inc., Newark, 2001—; pres., COO PSEG Energy Holdings. Chmn. fin. exec. adv. com. Edison Electric Inst.; bd. dirs. Nuc. Electric Ins. Ltd. Bd. dirs. NJ Performing Arts Ctr., Newark Mus. Office: Pub Svc Enterprise Group Inc PO Box 570 Newark NJ 07101 Office Phone: 973-430-7000. Office Fax: 973-430-5845. *

OFNER, WILLIAM BERNARD, investor, lawyer; b. LA, Aug. 24, 1929; s. Harry D. and Gertrude (Skoss) Ofner; m. Florence Ila Maxwell, Apr. 13, 1953 (div. 1956). AA, LA City Coll., 1949; BA, Calif. State U., LA, 1953; LLB, Loyola U., LA, 1965; postgrad., Sorbonne, 1951, U. So. Calif., 1966, Glendale CC, 1986-92; cert. de Langue Francaise, 1987. Bar: Calif. 1966, U.S. Dist. Ct. Calif. 1966, U.S. Supreme Ct. 1972. Assoc. Thomas Moore and Assoc., LA, 1967-69; pvt. practice LA, 1969-70, 74—; assoc. Peter Lam, LA, 1981-94, mng. atty., 1993—99. Assoc. C. M. Coronel, 1986—87, Jack D. Janofsky, 1987—89, Mario P. Gonzalez, 1990—92, Genaro Legorreta, Jr., 1997—98; lectr. Van Norman U., 1975; property mgr., 1982—2004; investor, 1984—. Electronics instr. USNR, 1949—54. Mem.: LA Fitness Athletic Club, Inst. Gen. Semantics, Toastmasters. Democrat. Avocations: photography, linguistics, tutoring, painting, walking. Office: PO Box 163 Chino Hills CA 91709 Home Phone: 909-851-5670; Office Phone: 909-590-4484.

OFRI, DANIELLE, internist; b. NYC, Aug. 22, 1965; d. Zacharia and Marcia Kashdan Ofri; m. Benjamin Akman, Nov. 7, 1999; children: Naava Ofri-Akman, Noah Ofri-Akman, Ariel Ofri-Akman. BSc, McGill U., Montreal, Que., Can., 1986; MS, NYU, 1990, PhD, 1992, MD, 1993. Lic. physician N.Y. State. Resident physician Bellevue Hosp., NYC, 1993—96; attending physician Bellevue Hosp./NYU Sch. Medicine, NYC, 1998—. Dir. Anticoagulation Clinic Bellevue Hosp., NYC, 2002—. Editor-in-chief, co-founder: lit. mag. Bellevue Lit. Rev., 2000—; author: (memoir) Singular Intimacies, 2003, (songs) (non-fiction) Incidental Findings: Lessons from My Patients in the Art of Medicine, 2005; assoc. chief editor: med. textbook Bellevue Guide to Outpatient Medicine, 2001 (AMWA Best Med. Textbook, 2002). Recipient Editors Prize for nonfiction, Mo. Rev., 2001, award, Best Am. Essays, 2001, 2005, Pushcart Prize nomination, 2002, award, Best Am. Sci. Writing, 2003, McGovern award, Am. Med. Writers Assn., 2005. Jewish. Avocations: writing, music, piano, literature. Office: Bellevue Hosp Md Clinic 462 1st Ave New York NY 10016 E-mail: danielle.ofri@nyu.edu.

OFSTAD, EVELYN LARSEN BOYL, retired primary school educator, radio personality, film producer; b. Laurel, Oreg., Sept. 11, 1918; d. Walter

Winfred and Nellie Lyle (Gellatly) Larsen; m. Robert Morris Boyl (dec.); children: Kathleen Roberta Boyl, Robert Morris Boyl Jr., Shannon Gae Boyl, Brian Larsen Boyl; m. Olaf Ofstad, Nov. 15, 1988. BS, Oreg. State U., 1940; MS in Tchg., Portland State U., 1968. Cert. learning specialist. Radio announcer Sta. KOAC, Corvallis, Oreg., 1939-40; announcer, script writer Sta. KWIL, Albany, Oreg., 1940-42, operator, announcer, 1941-42; sec. Higgins Ship Bldg., New Orleans, 1943-44; elem. tchr. Portland Pub. Schs., 1968-71; learning specialist North Clackamas Schs., Milw., Ore., 1972-85, home instr. Milwaukie, Oreg., 1985-86. Prodr., actor (video travelogues) Portland Cable Access, 1987—; actor: Oreg. Sr. Theater, 1987—95, Plz. Players, 1999—. Co-leader Girl Scouts Am., Oak Grove, Oreg., 1954—55, Webelos Boy Scouts Am., 1956—57, 1970—71; videographer Ptnrs. Ams., Oreg., Costa Rica, 1990—91; head video prodn. Channel 29 In-House TV Ret., 1999—2004; prodr. biweekly travel show, 1999—; mem. synchronized swim team Holladay Park Plz., 2003—04. Mem.: AAUW (pres. Albany chpt.). Avocations: painting, video production, travel, narration, script writing.

OFTE, DONALD, retired nuclear energy industry executive; b. NYC, Aug. 23, 1929; s. Sverre and Ingeborg Ofte; m. Margaret Mae McHenney, July 23, 1955; children: Marc Christian, Nancy Carolyn Appleby, Kirk Donald Jr. BA in Chemistry, Dana Coll., 1952; postgrad. study metall. engring., Ohio State U., 1958-60. Jr. chemist Inst. Atomic Rsch., Ames, Iowa, 1952-53; sr. rsch. chemist Monsanto Rsch. Corp., Miamisburg, Ohio, 1958-66; ops. engr. AEC, Miamisburg, 1966-69, br. chief, div. dir. ops. office Albuquerque, 1969-73, mgr. Pinellas area office Largo, Fla., 1973-79; mgr. Rocky Flats area office Dept. Energy, Golden, Colo., 1979-82, asst. mgr. devel. and prodn. Albuquerque, 1982-83, dep. mgr. ops. office, 1983-84; prin. dep. asst. sec. Dept. Energy Defense Programs, Washington, 1984-87; mgr. ops. office Dept. Energy, Idaho Falls, Idaho, 1987-89; mgmt. cons. Idaho Falls, 1990—92; v.p. govt. ops. United Engrs. & Constructors (Raytheon Engrs. & Constrn.), Denver, 1992-93; v.p. Adv. Scis., Inc., Albuquerque, 1993-94; pres. FERMCO (also known as Fluor Daniel, Fernald), Cin., 1994-96; chmn., bd. mgrs. Washington Group BWXT Oper. Svcs., LLC, 2004—05; ret. V.p. Fluor-Daniel, Inc., 1994—96; affiliate prof. Idaho State U., 1990—92; cons. in field. Author: (with others) Plutonium 1960, 1965, Physicochemical Methods in Metals Research; contbr. articles to profl. jours. on metallurgy and ceramics. Campaign chmn. United Way Pinellas, St. Petersburg, Fla., 1978; bd. dirs. Bonneville County United Way, Idaho Rsch. Found.; mem. adv. bd. Teton Peaks Council Boy Scouts of Am., 1987-92, Eastern Idaho Tech. Coll.; chmn. Excellence in Edn. Fund Com., 1990-92; vice chmn., bd. dirs. Rio Grande Ch. ARC, Albuquerque, 1982-84; trustee, bd. dirs. Nat. Atomic Mus., 1999—2003. Served to lt. (j.g.) USN, 1953-57. Recipient citation AEC for Apollo 12 SNAP 27 Radioisotope Generator, 1969, High Quality Performance award AEC, 1968, Group Achievement award NASA, 1972; Meritorious Svc. award Dept. Energy, 1985, Disting. Career Svc. award, 1989. Mem. Am. Chem. Soc. (emeritus), Am. Nuclear Soc., Am. Soc. Metals, Nat. Contract Mgmt. Assn., Am. Soc. Pub. Adminstrs., Suncoast Archeol. Soc., Idaho Falls C. of C. (bd. dirs., cmty. svc. award 1990), Rotary Internat. (Paul Harris fellow). Avocations: reading, bridge, gardening, golf. Home: 1129 Salamanca St NW Albuquerque NM 87107-5643 Personal E-mail: dofte@aol.com.

OFTENESS, OVE (O.V. MICHAELSEN), writer, musician; b. Bergen, Norway, Mar. 2, 1954; came to U.S., 1954; s. Michael and Betsy Lydia (Vik) O.; m. Lois Marin Fischer, July 11, 1989 (div. Jan., 2002) Pvt. practice, 1973—. Author: Words at Play: Quips, Quirks and Oddities, 1998, The Word Play Almanac, 2002, Never Odd or Even: Palindromes, Anagrams & Other Tricks Words Can Do, 2005; musician (albums) Suzy Fischer and the Dinosaurs, 2005. Democrat. Avocation: collecting and preserving rare folk and rock recordings. Home: 2870 Adeline St Apt 406 Berkeley CA 94703 Personal E-mail: wordplayauthor@yahoo.com.

OGAN, RUSSELL GRIFFITH, real estate broker; b. Reading, Pa., Nov. 20, 1923; s. Russell John and Edna Gwendlyn (Griffith) O.; m. Gloria Mae Withers, Oct. 30, 1943; children: Susan Ann (Mrs. Greg Gunn), Russell Lee. Student, Wyomissing Polytech. Inst., 1942, Air Command Staff Coll., 1948; grad., Nat. War Coll., 1963. Enlisted as pvt. U.S. Army, 1942; advanced through grades to brig. gen. USAF, 1970; fighter squadron comdr. Dover AFB, Del., 1951; dir. combat operations (11th Air Div.), Ladd AFB, Alaska, 1951-53; dir. (Combat Operations Center), Hamilton AFB, Calif., 1953-56; with (Hdqrs. Air Def. Command), Ent AFB, Colo., 1956-60; dir. (Aerospace Def. Systems Office, Air Force Ballistic Missile Div.), 1960-62; from dep. dir. plans to comdr. Sector Operation Ctr. NATO, Germany, 1963-66; dep. dir. personnel data and records (USAF Mil. Personnel Center), Randolph AFB, Tex., 1966-68; comdr. 71st Missile Warning Wing, then vice comdr. (14th Aerospace Force), Ent AFB, Colo., 1968-71; dep. dir. personnel programs Hdqrs. USAF, Washington, 1971-72; dir. Prisoner of War and Missing in Action Affairs, Office Sec. Def., Washington, 1972-74; former pres. Vacation Interval Mktg.; real estate broker Fishermen's Village, Punta Gorda, Fla. Decorated D.S.M., Legion of Merit with bronze oak leaf cluster, Air medal with 1 silver and 1 bronze oak leaf cluster. Mem. Daedalians, T.R.O.A., Kingsway Country Club. Flew 62 missions as fighter pilot over France and Germany, 1944-45. Home (Winter): 12413 SW Kingsway Cir Lake Suzy FL 34269 Personal E-mail: ogan43@aol.com.

OGATA, KATSUHIKO, engineering educator; b. Tokyo, Jan. 6, 1925; came to U.S., 1952; s. Fukuhei and Teruko (Yasaki) O.; m. Asako Nakamura, Sept. 6, 1961; 1 son, Takahiko. BS, U. Tokyo, 1947; MS, U. Ill., 1953; PhD, U. Calif., Berkeley, 1956. Research asst. Sci. Research Inst., Tokyo, 1948-51; fuel engr. Nippon Steel Tube Co., Tokyo, 1951-52; mem. faculty U. Minn., 1956—, prof. mech. engring., 1961—; prof. elec. engring. Yokohama Nat. U., 1960-61, 64-65, 68-69. Author: State Space Analysis of Control Systems, 1967, Modern Control Engineering, 1970, 2002, Dynamic Programming, 1973, Ingenieria de Control Moderna, 1974, 1998, Metody Przestrzeni Stanow w Teorii Sterowania, 1974, System Dynamics, 1978, 2003, Engenharia de Controle Moderno, 1982, 2003, Teknik Kontrol Automatik, 1985, Discrete-Time Control Systems, 1986, 1995, Gendai Seigyo Riron, 1986, Dinamica de Sistemas, 1987, Solving Control Engineering Problems with MATLAB, 1994, Gendai Seigyo Kogaku, 1994, Designing Linear Control Systems with MATLAB, 1994, Kejuruteraan Kawalan Moden, 1996, Sistemas de Control en Tiempo Discreto, 1996, Projeto de Sistemas Lineares de Controle com MATLAB, 1996, Solucao de Problemas de Engenharia de Controle com MATLAB, 1997, MATLAB for Control Engineers, 2007. Recipient Outstanding Adv. award Inst. of Tech., U. Minn., 1981, John R. Ragazzini Edn. award Am. Automatic Control Coun., 1999. Fellow ASME; mem. Sigma Xi, Pi Tau Sigma. Personal E-mail: kogata02@aol.com.

OGAWA, JOICHI RAPHAEL, director, consultant; b. Tokyo, July 2, 1958; arrived in U.S., 2002; s. Isamu and Yoshiko Ogawa. BA in Econs., Keio U., Tokyo, 1982, BA in Psychology, 1986, MA in Sociology, 1989, PhD in Human Rels., 1993. Tchr. Jogakukau Girls' HS, Tokyo, 1988—90; rschr. Inst. Behavioral Sci. Uchido Yoko Co. Ltd., Tokyo, 1989—90; lectr. Fukuoka Prefecture U., Tagawa-shi, Japan, 1992—93; mgr. info. planning divsn. Nippon Kouatsu Electric Co. Ltd., Obu-shi, Japan, 1993—97; gen. mgr. cons. Shinjuku Gen. Acctg. Firm, Tokyo, 1997—98; liaison mgr. O'Hara Coll. Bus. San Jose (Calif.) State U., 1997—2002; program coord. Palo Alto (Calif.) Ctr. Devel. Studies, Inc., 2002—. Rschr. human sensory Ministry of Internat. Trade and Industry, Tokyo, 1990—92; cons. Long Term Credit Bank, Tokyo, 1991—93; family psychologist Nagoya (Japan) Nat. Hosp., 1991—92; clin. psychologist Azabu HS, Tokyo, 1997—2000. Mem.: APA, Acad. Mgmt., Internat. Soc. Psychodynamic Studies Orgn. Office: Bay Process Cons Ctr Inc 322 S Abel St Milpitas CA 95035 Home Phone: 408-920-2593; Office Phone: 408-262-0306. Office Fax: 408-205-7517. E-mail: info@bayprocessconsultingctr.com.

OGBONNAYA, CHUKS ALFRED, entomologist, agronomist, environmentalist; b. Akoli-Imenyi, Abia, Nigeria, June 30, 1953; came to U.S., 1975; s. Alfred Agbaeze and Christy (Agubuche) Ogbonnaya; m. Joyce Elizabeth Belgrave, Mar. 30, 1985; children: Latoya, Oluchi, Kelechi, Chioma. BS, U. Nebr., 1979, PhD, 1985; MS, N.W. Mo. State U., 1981. Cert. profl. crop scientist, profl. agronomist. Lab. asst. U. Nebr., Lincoln, 1976-78, rsch. asst., 1978-80, 82-85, postdoctoral fellow, 1985; asst. prof., fellow Mountain Empire Coll., Big Stone Gap, Va., 1985-90, prof., 1990—, coord., prof. environ. sci. dept., 1986—, asst. dean, 1996—99. Disting. scholar-in-residence Pa. State U., summer 1990, vis. prof., 1990. Soccer coach Parks and Recreation, Big Stone Gap, 1989; mem. Va. Water Resources Statewide Adv. Bd., govt.-mined land reclamation adv. bd. Recipient Times Teaching award, 1990, Chancellor's Profs. award Va., 1990; Fulbright sr. scholar, 1993-94. Mem. Am. Soc. Agronomy, Crop Sci. Soc. Am., Entomol. Soc., Va. Acad. Sci., Va. Mining Assn. (Outstanding Contbn. to Comty. award 1993), Internat. Platform Assn., Phi Beta Kappa. Methodist. Avocations: tennis, soccer. Home: 520 Bays View Rd Kingsport TN 37660-3202

OGBURN, HUGH BELL, chemical engineer, consultant; b. Lexington, Va., July 13, 1923; s. Sihon Cicero Jr. and Bettie Mae (Bell) O.; m. Anne Wotherspoon, Mar. 2, 1946 (div.); children: Margaret Mathews Berenson, Scott A.; m. Nancy Wrenn Petersen, Sept. 5, 1974. BS, Princeton U., 1944, MS, 1947, PhD, 1954. Sect. dir. R&D dept. Atlantic Refining Co., Phila., 1950—61; mgr. process engring. M.W. Kellogg Co., NYC, London, 1961—67; dir. rsch. and engring. Union Carbide Corp., NYC, 1967—69; dir. new bus. devel. Weyerhaeuser Co., Tacoma, 1969—72; pres. H.B. Ogburn Assoc., Greenwich, Conn. and Honolulu, 1971—; v.p., dir. Incontrade Inc., Stamford, Conn., 1973—78; v.p. Pacific Resources Inc., Honolulu, 1978—83; chmn. Pacific Oasis, LA, 1983—85. Dir. Danmore Corp., Planning Research Corp.; cons. AEC; prof. chem. engring. Drexel U., Phila., 1951-61 Contbr. articles to profl. jours.; patentee in field. Pres. bd. trustees Woman's Hosp., Phila., 1954-62, Kapiolani Women's and Children's Med. Ctr., 1980-90; mem. adv. bd. Princeton U., 1960-70. Served to lt. j.g. USNR, 1942-46, PTO. Mem. AIChE, Am. Chem. Soc., Research Engrs. Soc., Pacific (Honolulu) Club, Greenwich Field (Conn.) Club, Princeton (N.Y.C.) Club, Phi Beta Kappa, Sigma Xi, Tau Beta Pi. Republican. Presbyterian. Home and Office: 4340 Pahoa Ave Apt 16 A Honolulu HI 96816-5032 Office Phone: 808-732-6503. Business E-Mail: hbogburn@hawaii.rr.com.

OGBURN, JOYCE L., library director; B in Athropology, U. NC, Greensboro; MS in Libr. Sci., U. NC, Chapel Hill; MA in Anthropology, Ind. U. Libr. Pa. State U.; chief acquisitions libr. Yale U.; assoc. univ. libr. info. resources and systems Old Dominion U.; assoc. dir. librs., resources and collection mgmt. svcs. U. Wash., 1999—2005; dir. J. Willard Marriott Libr. U. Utah, Salt Lake City, 2005—. Mem.: ALA, Ctr. Rsch. Librs., Assn. Rsch. Librs., Am. Anthrop. Assn. Office: J Willard Marriott Libr 295 S 1500 E Salt Lake City UT 84112-0860 Office Phone: 801-585-9521. E-mail: joyce.ogburn@utah.edu. *

OGDEN, DANIEL MILLER, JR., public official, educator; b. Clarksburg, W.Va., Apr. 28, 1922; s. Daniel Miller and Mary (Maphis) O.; m. Valeria Juan Munson, Dec. 28, 1946; children: Janeth Lee Martin, Patricia Jo Hunter, Daniel Munson. BA in Polit. Sci., Wash. State U., 1944; MA, U. Chgo., 1947, PhD, 1949. From instr. to assoc. prof. Wash. State U., Pullman, 1949-61; staff asst. resources program U.S. Dept. Interior, 1961-64; asst. dir. U.S. Bur. Outdoor Recreation, 1964-67; dir. budget U.S. Dept. Interior, Washington, 1967-68; dean Coll. Humanities and Social Scis. Colo. State U., Ft. Collins, 1968-76; disting. vis. prof. Lewis and Clark Coll. and Portland (Oreg.) State U., 1977-78; dir. Office of Power Mktg. Coordination U.S. Dept. Energy, 1978-84; mgr. Pub. Power Coun., Portland, Oreg., 1984-88, ret., 1988. Mem. profl. staff com. interstate and fgn. commerce U.S. Senate, 1956-57; spll. asst. to chmn. Dem. Nat. Com., 1960-61; lectr. Mgmt. Devel. Ctrs., U.S. Office Pers. Mgmt., 1966-2004. Co-author: Electing the President, rev. edit., 1968, American National Government, 7th edit., 1970, American State and Local Government, 5th edit., 1972, Washington Politics, 1960, How National Policy is Made, 5th edit., 2004. Committeeman Wash. Dem. Ctrl. Com., 1952-56; chmn. Whitman County Dem. Ctrl. Com., 1958-60; chmn. 49th Legis. Dist. Dem. Com., 1990-94; chmn. Clark County Dem. Ctrl. com., 1994-98, 1999-2000, vice chair, 1998-99. With inf. U.S. Army, 1943-46. Mem. Phi Beta Kappa, Phi Kappa Phi, Pi Sigma Alpha, Sigma Delta Chi. Mem. Unitarian Ch. Home: 3118 NE Royal Oak Dr Vancouver WA 98662-7435 Office Phone: 360-254-8886.

OGDEN, JAMES RUSSELL, marketing educator, consultant, lecturer, writer; b. Paris, Ill., Nov. 4, 1954; s. Russell Lee and Marianne (Johnson) O.; children: David James, Anne Marie, Kari Kristine; m. Denise T. Alarid, 1989. B of Bus. Edn., Ea. Mich. U., 1978; MS, Colo. State U., 1981; PhD, U. No. Colo., 1986. With acctg. and fin. dept. Hydra-Matic Divsn. GM Motors, 1978; dir. mktg. Mich. Tech. Inst., 1979; grad. fellow Colo. State U., Ft. Collins, 1979—81, asst. mgr. family housing, 1979—81; placement counselor U. No. Colo., Greeley, 1981—83, instr. mktg., 1982—83; CEO, prin. The Doctors Ogden Group, LLC, Allentown, Pa., 1982—; chair advt. and mktg. dept., assoc. prof. Adams State Coll., Alamosa, Colo., 1983—89; dept. chair, prof. mktg. Coll. Bus. Kutztown U., Pa., 1989—, bd. bus. advisors Students in Free Enterprise Coll. Bus., 1996—. Interim dir. Small Bus. Devel. Ctr., Adams State Coll., 1988-89; adj. prof. Ctrl. Mich. U., Mt. Pleasant, 1987—, Cedar Crest Coll., Allentown, 1989—, Pa. State U., 1994-95, Nova Southeastern U., doctoral com. chair, Ft. Lauderdale, Fla., 1995—; spkr. in field; mktg. and advt. cons.; corp. trainer; textbook reviewer, editl. cons. Merrill Pub. Co., Allyn & Bacon, Inc., Richard Irwin, Inc., Macmillan Pub., John Wiley & Sons, Inc., Prentice-Hall, Houghton & Mifflin Co., Austen Press, Simon & Schuster; textbook reviewer Fairchild Books and Visuals, Inc.; tech. editor Rsch. and Edn. Assn.; doctoral com. mem. Nova Southeastern U., Drexel U., Phila., Pace U., NYC, Temple U., Phila.; bd. dir. Z-Coil, Inc., Albuquerque; CEO Group 8 Think Tank Bus. and Edn., 2006—. Author: Developing a Creative and Innovative Integrated Marketing Communication Plan, 1998, The Power of Point-of-Purchase Advertising: Marketing at Retail, 2004, Retailing: Integrated Retail Management, 2005; co-author: The Best Test Preparation for the CLEP College-Level Examination Program Principles of Marketing, 1996, Retailing: Integrated Retail Management, 2005; contbg. author, editor: Principles of Business, 1991, Essentials of Advertising, 1992, rev. edit., 1994, Marketing's Powerful Weapon: Point-of-Purchase Advertising, 2001; editor: Essentials of Marketing, 1994; contbr. over 40 articles to profl. jours Treas. Com. to Elect Jorge Amaya County Commr., Colo., 1985, Bob Pastore for Senate Com.; senator Assoc. Student and Faculty Senate, Adams State Coll., 1984-85; bd. dirs. Am. Advt. Fedn. Acad. Com., 1991-97, Alamosa Personnel Bd., 1986-88, Alamosa County Devel. Corp., 1987-89, Alamosa Tourism Com., 1988-89, trustee bd. dirs. Creede Repertory Theatre, 1987-89; expert witness in tourism and mktg. State of Colo.; advisor team entries into Nat. Student Advt. Competition, Coll. World Series of Advt., 1989-90, 93—; trustee Dr. R.L. Ogden Meml. Scholarship, Colo. State U. Found., 1992—; faculty advisor Students in Free Enterprise Nat. Competition, 1997—, faculty advisor, bus. adv. bd. Kutztown U. chpt. Recipient award for Excellence in Econ. Edn., Freedoms Found. Valley Forge, 1986, Capital award for contbn. to edn., Nat. Leadership Coun., 1991-92; named Outstanding Educator of Sch. Bus., Adams State Coll., 1987-88; Sam Walton fellow Students in Free Enterprise, 1997, 98, Outstanding Educator award, 1998. Fellow Direct Mktg. Assn.; mem. Am. Advt. Fedn. (faculty advisor 1987—, bd. dirs. acad. com. 1991-97), Western Mktg. Educators Assn. (paper reviewer), Nat. Guild Hypnotists (cert.), Acad. Mktg. Sci., Advt. Club N.Y., Point of Purchase Advt. Inst., Am. Collegiate Retailing Assn., Assn. Nat. Advertisers, Nat. Assn. Hispanic Profs. of Bus. Adminstrn. and Econs., New Eng. Bus. Adminstrn. Assn., Ctrl. Pa. Advt. Club, Phi Kappa Phi, Alpha Sigma Alpha (fin. advisor 1992—), Alpha Kappa Psi (dist. dir.). Democrat. Avocations: scuba, music, travel. Office: Kutztown U Coll Bus Dept Mktg Kutztown PA 19530 Office Phone: 610-434-6252. Business E-Mail: ogden@kutztown.edu.

OGDEN, JOHN CLIFTON, III, environmental scientist, director; b. Nashville, Tenn., Nov. 18, 1938; s. John Clifton Ogden, Jr. and Mary Ruth McKay; m. Maryanne Biggar, Sept. 12, 1975; m. Mary Ann Hollingsworth (div.); children: Laura Ann, Nicholas Alan. BA, George Peabody Coll., Nashville, 1961. Rsch. biologist Nat. Pk. Svc., Homestead, Fla., 1965—74, chair ecology working team, Man & the Biosphere Everglades team, 1993—94, coord. Fish & Wildlife Svc. wood stork recovery group, 1988—90, sr. rsch. scientist, 1988—95; mem. Fish & Wildlife Svc. crocodile recovery team Nat. Audubon Soc., Tavernier, Fla., 1974—78, sr. rsch. biologist, 1974—88, pres., Colonial Waterbird Soc., 1976—79, co-dir. Calif. condor recovery program Ventura, 1980—85, mem. Fish & Wildlife Svc. condor recovery team, 1980—88, dir. ornithol. rsch. unit Tavernier, Fla., 1986—88; adj. prof. U. Miami, Rosensteil Sch. Marine & Atmospheric Sci., 1996—2001; lead environ. scientist South Fla. Water Mgmt. Dist., West Palm Beach, 1995—2003; co-chair sci. coordination team South Fla. Ecosystem Restoration Task Force, West Palm Beach, 2003—04; chief environ. scientist South Fla. Water Mgmt. Dist., West Palm Beach, 2003—. Co-editor: (Everglades sci. rev.) Everglades. The Ecosystem and its Restoration, 1994; author: (two book chapts.) Monitoring Systems: Interdisciplinary Approaches, 2003; author: (lead coord.) 13 papers in Wetlands Jour., 2005; author: (and co-editor) (conf. proceedings) Wading Birds, National Audubon Society Report 7, 1972; author: (and sr. editor) Transactions North American Osprey Conference, 1978; author: (and co-editor) White Stork. Status and Conservation, 1980. Mem. Fla. Ornithol. Soc., 1986—88. Recipient Ann. Conservationist of Yr., Everglades Coalition, 1994, Disting. Svc. award, Colonial Waterbird Soc., 1996, Palladium medal, Am. Assn. Civil Engrs. & Nat. Audubon Soc., 1999, Charles Brookfield award for Exceptional Contbn. to South Fla. Conservation, Tropical Audubon Soc., 2004; fellow, Fla. State U., 1962—64, Am. Ornithologists Union, 1992. Mem.: Waterbird Soc. (life; pres. 1976—79). Democrat. Avocations: canoeing, hiking, birdwatching, collecting Florida landscape art, collecting orchids & palms. Home: 17390 Avocado Dr Homestead FL 33030 Office: S Florida Water Mgmt Dist 3301 Gun Club Rd West Palm Beach FL 33406 Home Phone: 305-248-0340; Office Phone: 561-682-6173. Personal E-mail: palmlodge@aol.com. Business E-Mail: jogden@sfwmd.gov.

OGDEN, JONATHAN, professional football player; b. Washington, July 31, 1974; BA in History, UCLA, 1996. Tackle Balt. Ravens, 1996—. Founder Jonathan Ogden Found.; bd. trustee's Urban League. Named First Team All-American, 1995, NFL First Team All-Pro, 2000; named to NFL Pro-Bowl, 1997—2005. Achievements include being a member of Super Bowl XXV Champion Baltimore Ravens, 2001; having his jersey number retired by UCLA, 1997. Office: c/o Baltimore Ravens 1101 Russel St Baltimore MD 21230

OGDEN, MAUREEN BLACK, retired state legislator; b. Vancouver, BC, Nov. 1, 1928; came to U.S., 1930; d. William Moore and Margaret Hunter (Leitch) Black; m. Robert Moore Ogden, June 23, 1956; children: Thomas, Henry, Peter. BA, Smith Coll., 1950; MA, Columbia U., 1963; M in City and Regional Planning, Rutgers U., 1977. Researcher, staff asst. Ford Found., NYC, 1951-56; staff assoc. Fgn. Policy Assn., NYC, 1956-58; mem. Millburn (N.J.) Twp. Com., 1976-81; mayor Twp. of Millburn, N.J., 1979-81; mem. N.J. Gen. Assembly, Trenton, 1982-96. Chmn. Assembly Environment Com., N.J. Gen. Assembly; chmn. Energy and Pub. Utilities Com., Coun. State Govts., 1991-92; mem. adv. bd. Sch. Policy and Planning, Rutgers Univ., New Brunswick, N.J., 1992-96, vice chair Nat. Affairs and Legis. Com. Energy Sources. Author: Natural Resources Inventory, Township of Millburn, 1974. Bd. govs. N.J. Hist. Soc., Newark, 1992-2000; trustee NJ chpt. The Nature Conservancy, 1994-99; hon. trustee Paper Mill Playhouse, Millburn, 1990—; former trustee St. Barnabas Med. Ctr., Livingston, NJ; former pres. NJ Drug Abuse Adv. Coun.; chair Gov.'s Coun. on NJ Outdoors, 1996-99; mem. Palisades Interstate Park Commn., 1996-99; chair Garden State Preservation Trust, 1999—; co-chair policy com. NJ Conservation Found., 2000-, trustee, 2006-; mem. steering com. Highlands Coalition of NJ-NY-Conn. Recipient citation Nat. Assn. State Outdoors Recreation Liaison Officers, 1987, cert. appreciation John F. Kennedy Ctr. for the Performing Arts, The Alliance for Art Edn., 1987, disting. svc. award Art Educators N.J., 1987, ann. environ. quality award EPA Region II, 1988, citation Humane Soc. U.S., 1989, award N.J. Hist. Sites Coun., 1989, N.J. Sch. Conservation, 1990, pres.'s award The Nature Conservancy, 1995, pub. policy award Nat. Trust for Hist. Preservation, 1995. Mem.: Garden Club Am. (vice chair, energy sources, nat. affairs and legislation com. 2005—). Republican. Episcopalian. Home: 59 Lakeview Ave Short Hills NJ 07078-2240 Personal E-mail: mrogden@worldnet.att.net.

OGDEN, VALERIA MUNSON, management consultant, state representative; b. Okanogan, Wash., Feb. 11, 1924; d. Ivan Bodwell and Pearle (Wilson) Munson; m. Daniel Miller Ogden Jr., Dec. 28, 1946; children: Janeth Lee Ogden Martin, Patricia Jo Ogden Hunter, Daniel Munson Ogden. BA magna cum laude, Wash. State U., 1946. Exec. dir. Potomac Coun. Camp Fire, Washington, 1964-68, Ft. Collins (Colo.) United Way, 1969-73, Designing Tomorrow Today, Ft. Collins, 1973-74, Poudre Valley Community Edn. Assn., Ft. Collins, 1977-78; pres. Valeria M. Ogden, Inc., Kensington, Md., 1978-81; nat. field cons. Camp Fire, Inc., Kansas City, Mo., 1980-81; exec. dir. Nat. Capital Area YWCA, Washington, 1981-84, Clark County YWCA, Vancouver, Wash., 1985-89; pvt. practice mgmt. cons. Vancouver, 1989—; mem. Wash. Ho. of Reps., 1990—2002, spkr. pro tempore, 1999—2002. Mem. adj. faculty pub. adminstrn. program Lewis and Clark Coll., Portland (Oreg.) State U., 1979-94; mem. Pvt. Industry Coun., Vancouver, 1986-95; mem. regional Svcs. Network Bd. Mental Health, 1993-03. Author: Camp Fire Membership, 1980. Mem. Wash. State Coun. Vol. Action, Olympia, 1986—90; county vice-chair Larimer County Dems., Ft. Collins, 1974—75; spkr. pro tem Wash. Ho. of Reps., 1999—2002; rep. Gov. Chris Gregoire S.W. Wash., 2005; mem. precinct com. Clark County Dems., Vancouver, 1986—88; treas. Mortar Bd. Nat. Found., Vancouver, 1987—96; bd. dirs. Clark County Coun. for Homeless, Vancouver, 1989—2004, chmn., 1994; bd. dirs. Wash. Wild Life and Recreation Coalition, 1995—2002, Human Svcs. Coun., 1996—2002, Wash. State Hist. Soc., 1996—2006, State Legis. Leaders Found., 2001—02, Columbia Springs Environ. Edn. Ctr. Found., 2003—06, Clark County Skill Ctr. Found., 2003—06, S.W. Wash. Child Care Consortium, 2003—; chair arts and tourism com. Nat. Conf. State Legis., 1996—97; chair Affordable Cmty. Environments, 1998—, Wash. State Interagy. Com. for Outdoor Recreation, 2003—, Wash. State Historic Preservation Fund, 2003—06, S.W. Wash. Ctr. for the Arts, 2003—; pres. Nat. Order of Women Legislators, 1999—2001; mem. exec. com. Nat. Conf. State Legis., 2000—02; mem. adv. bd. Wash. State U., Vancouver, 2002—. Named Citizen of Yr. Ft. Collins Bd. of Realtors, 1975, State Legislator of Yr., Wash. State Labor Coun., 2000, Citizen of Yr., Vancouver, Wash., 2002, First Citizen, Clark County, 2006; recipient Gulick award Camp Fire Inc., 1956, Alumna Achievement award Wash. State U. Alumni Assn., 1988; named YWCA Woman of Achievement, 1991, 100 Most Powerful Women, Clark County, 2007. Mem. AAUW, Internat. Assn. Vol. Adminstrs. (pres.

Boulder 1989-90), Nat. Assn. YWCA Exec. Dirs. (nat. bd. nominating com. 1988-90), Sci. and Soc. Assn. (bd. dirs. 1993-97), Women in Action, Philanthropic and Ednl. Orgn., Soroptimists, Phi Beta Kappa. Democrat. Avocations: hiking, travel. Home and Office: 3118 NE Royal Oak Dr Vancouver WA 98662-7435 Office Phone: 360-254-8886. Personal E-mail: repval@comcast.net.

O'GEARY, DENNIS TRAYLOR, retired engineering company executive; b. Waverly, Va., Feb. 20, 1925; s. King William and Mary Virginia (Traylor) O'G.; m. Alice Stuart Baum, Aug. 3, 1947; children: Dennis Patrick, Mary Alice O'Geary Eisenbarth, Elizabeth Christina O'Geary Bernstorf. Surveying degree, Tri-State U., 1943; BS in Civil Engring., Ill. Inst. Tech., 1947. Resident engring trainee Va. Hwy. Dept., Richmond, 1947-50; civil engring. supt. Wiley Jackson Co., Roanoke, Va., 1950-57; engr., asst. estimator, project mgr., v.p. and asst. to area mgr. S.J. Groves & Sons Co., Mpls. and Springfield, Ill., 1957-77, v.p., area mgr., 1978-82, v.p., asst. divsn. mgr., divsn. estimator Atlanta, 1982-84; pres. Peabody S.W., Inc., Houston, 1984-85; v.p. Houston ops. J.D. Abrams, Inc., Austin, Tex., 1985-99; ret., 1999. Cons. J.D. Abrams, Inc. With USNR, 1943—46. Mem. ASCE (life), Am. Concrete Inst. (50 yr. mem.), Soc. Am. Mil. Engrs. (50 yr. mem.), Nat. Maritime Hist. Soc. Christian (Disciples Of Christ). Home: 15402 Cresent Oaks Ct Houston TX 77068-2079 Personal E-mail: dennisalice@gmail.com.

OGG, WILSON REID, lawyer, retired judge, poet, curator, publishing executive; b. Alhambra, Calif., Feb. 26, 1928; s. James Brooks and Mary (Wilson) Ogg. Student, Pasadena Jr. Coll., 1946; AB, U. Calif., Berkeley, 1949; JD, U. Calif., 1952; Cultural D in Philosophy of Law, World U. Roundtable, 1983. Bar: Calif. 1955. Assoc. trust dept. Wells Fargo Bank, San Francisco, 1954-55; pvt. practice Berkeley, 1955—. Instr. Taegu English Lang. Inst., 1954, 25th Sta. Hosp., Taegu, Republic of Korea, 1954; rsch. atty., legal editor dept. of continuing edn. bar U. Calif., 1958—63; curator-in-residence, Pinebrook, 1964—; adminstv. law judge, 1974—93; real estate broker, cons., 1974—; trustee World U., 1976—80; dir. admissions internat. Soc. Phil. Enquiry, 1981—84; dep. dir. gen. Internat. Biog. Ctr., England, 1986—; dep. gov. Am. Biog. Inst. Rsch. Assn., 1986—; owner Pinebrook Press, Berkeley, Calif., 1988—; sci. faculty Cambridge U., 2000—. Author: The Enfolding Universe, 1995, Constitutional Law. Constitutional Crisis Facing American Democracy, 2005, Collective Essays of Wilson Ogg, 2005, numerous poems; contbr. articles to profl. jours. With AUS, 1952—54. Named to Internat. Poetry Hall of Fame, Nat. Libr. Poetry, 1997; recipient Internat. Peace prize, Auth. of United Cultural Conv., U.S., 2002, Auth. of United Culture Conv., U.S., 2005, 50 Yr. Commemorative medal, Albert Schweitzer Assn., 2003, World medal Freedom, 2006. Mem.: ACLU, ASCAP, ABA, VFW, AAAS, London Diplomatic Acad., Inst. Noetic Scis., Intertel, Calif. Soc. Psychical Study (pres., chmn. bd. 1963—65), Am. Arbitration Assn. (nat. panel arbitrators), San Francisco Bar Assn., State Bar Calif., Internat. Soc. Individual Liberty, Internat. Platform Assn., Faculty Club of the U. Calif. at Berkeley (emeritus), Men's Inner Cir. Achievement, Amnesty Internat., Marines Meml. Club, Elks, Shriners, Masons, Am. Legion. Unitarian Universalist. Home Fax: 510-540-6052. Business E-Mail: wilsonogg@cal.berkeley.edu.

OGIER, WALTER THOMAS, retired physics educator; b. Pasadena, Calif., June 18, 1925; s. Walter Williams and Aileen Vera (Polhamus) O.; m. Mayrene Miriam Gorton, June 27, 1954; children: Walter Charles, Margaret Miriam, Thomas Earl, Kathryn Aileen. BS, Calif. Inst. Tech., 1947, PhD in Physics, 1953. Research fellow Calif. Inst. Tech., 1953; instr. U. Calif. at Riverside, 1954-55, asst. prof. physics, 1955-60, Pomona Coll., Claremont, Calif., 1960-62, assoc. prof., 1962-67, prof. physics, 1967-89, prof. emeritus, 1989—, chmn. dept., 1972-89. Contbr. articles on metals, liquid helium, X-rays and proton produced X-rays to profl. jours. Served with USNR, 1944-46. NSF Sci. Faculty fellow, 1966-67 Mem. Am. Phys. Soc., Am. Assn. Physics Tchrs. (pres. So. Calif. sect. 1967-69), Tau Beta Pi. Home: 8555 San Gabriel Rd Atascadero CA 93422-4928 Business E-Mail: wogier@pomona.edu. E-mail: ogierwt@charter.net.

OGILVIE, KELVIN KENNETH, academic administrator, chemist, educator; m. Emma Roleen; children: Kristine, Kevin. BS with honors, Acadia U., 1964, DSc (hon.), 1983; PhD, Northwestern U., 1968; DSc (hon.), U. N.B., Can., 1991, McGill U., 1998. Assoc. prof. U. Man., Winnipeg, 1968-74; prof. chemistry McGill U., Montreal, 1974-88, Can. Pacific prof. biotech., 1984-87; bd. dirs. Sci. Adv. Bd., Biologicals, Toronto, Ont., 1979-84; dir. Office of Biotech. McGill U., 1984-87; prof. chemistry Acadia U., Wolfville, N.S., 1987—, v.p. acad. affairs, 1987—93, pres., vice-chancellor, 1993—2003. Invited lectr. on biotech. Tianjin, People's Republic of China, 1985; Snider lectr. U. Toronto, 1991; Gwen Leslie Meml. lectr., 1991; Centennial Mossman lectr. McGill U., 1998; mem. Nat. Adv. Bd. Sci. and Tech., 1994-95; chair selection com. Indsl. Postgrad. Scholarship program NSERCC, 1994; mem. Coun. N.S. Univ. Pres. 1993-2003; mem. Coun. of Applied Sci. and Tech. for N.S., 1988-93; mem. Nat. Biotech. Adv. Com., 1988-99; mem. Fisher Biotech. Adv. Ctr., Can., 1989-92; mem. sci. adv. bd. Allelix Biopharms., 1991-93, 2007—; chair adv. bd. NRC Inst. for Marine Bioscis., 1990-93, 2007; mem. steering com. on biotech. labor Can., 1990-92; mem. Atlantic regional com. Prime Min.'s Awards for Tchg. Excellence in Sci., Tech. and Math., 1993-2004; chair regional planning forum for a pharm. industry, Atlantic, Can., 1993; mem. Atomic Energy Control Bd., Can., 1997-99; chair sci. adv. bd. Quanta Nova Can., 1998-2001; mem. Can. Electronic Bus. Roundtable, 1999-2002, Can. Global Bus. Dialogue on Electronic Commerce, 1999, Coun. of Ministers Com. on Online Learning, 2000-01; mem. IBM Global Edn. Policy Coun., 2000-03, The Can. e-Bus. Initiative, 2002-04; chair Premier's Coun. on Innovation, N.S., 2003-06, AIMS Sr. fellow on Postsecondary Edn., 2004—; mem. adv. bd. Atlantic Innovation Fund, 2007—; bd. dirs. Gerome Can., 2005—; mem. adv. bd. NRC Atlantic Inst. for Marine Bioscience, 2006—. Mem. editl. bd. Nucleosides and Nucleotides, 1981-92; contbr. over 150 articles to profl. jours.; holder 14 patents. Decorated Knight of Malta, 1985, Order of Can., 1991; named Hon. Col. 14th Air Maintenance Squadron, RCAF, 1995-2000; recipient Commemorative medal for 125th Anniversary of Confedn. Can., 1992, Buck-Whitney medal, 1983, Manning Prin. award, 1992, Queen Elizabeth Golden Jubilee medal, 2002; named to McLean's Honor Roll of Canadians Who Made a Difference, 1988; E.W.R. Steacie Meml. fellow, 1982-84; inducted into Discovery Ctr. Sci. and Tech. Hall of Fame, 2002. Fellow Chem. Inst. Can.; mem. Am. Chem. Soc., Assn. Univs. and Colls. Can. (standing com. on rsch. 1993-2000), Atlantic Univ. Athletic Assn. (pres. 1995-97). Achievements include inventing of BIOLF-62 (ganciclovir), antiviral drug used worldwide; developer general synthesis of RNA; developer original 'gene machine'; developer complete chemical synthesis of large RNA molecules; developer Acadia Advantage Program. Home: PO Box 307 Canning NS Canada B0P 1HO Office: Acadia U Dept Chemistry Wolfville NS Canada B4P 2R6 E-mail: kelvin.ogilvie@acadiau.ca.

OGILVIE, LLOYD JOHN, clergyman; b. Kenosha, Wis., Sept. 2, 1930; s. Vard Spencer and Katherine (Jacobson) O.; m. Mary Jane Jenkins, Mar. 25, 1951. BA, Lake Forest Coll., 1952, Garrett Theol. Sem., 1956; postgrad., New Coll., U. Edinburgh, Scotland, 1955-56; D.D., Whitworth Coll., 1973; L.H.D., U. Redlands, 1974; D.Humanities, Moravian Coll., 1975; LLD, Ea. U., 1988. Ordained to ministry Presbyn. Ch., 1956; student pastor Gurnee, Ill., 1952-56; first pastor Winnetka (Ill.) Presbyn. Ch., 1956-62; pastor 1st. Presbyn. Ch., Bethlehem, Pa., 1962-72, 1st Presbyn. Ch., Hollywood, Calif., 1972—95. Preacher Chgo. Sunday Evening Club, 1963—1989, also frequent radio and TV personality weekly syndicated TV program Let God Love You. Chaplain US Senate, 1995-2003, ret. 2003. Author: A Life Full of Surprises, 1969, Let God Love You, 1974, If I Should Wake Before I Die, 1973, Lord of the Ups and Downs, 1974, You've Got Charisma, 1975, Cup of Wonder, 1976, Life Without Limits, 1976, Drumbeat of Love, 1977, When God First Thought of You, 1978, The Autobiography of God, 1979, The Bush Is Still Burning, 1980, The Radiance of the Inner Splendor, 1980, Congratulations, God Believes in You, 1981, Life as it Was Meant to Be, 1981, The Beauty of Love, The Beauty of Friendship, 1981, The Beauty of Caring, The Beauty of Sharing, 1981, God's Best for My Life, 1981, God's Will in Your Life, 1982, Ask Him Anything, 1982, Commentary on Book of Acts, 1983, Praying with Power, 1983, Falling into Greatness, 1983, Freedom in the Spirit, 1984, Making Stress Work For You, 1984, The Lord of the Impossible, 1984, Why Not Accept Christ's Healing and Wholeness, 1984, If God Cares, Why Do I Still Have Problems?, 1985, Understanding the Hard Sayings of Jesus, 1986, 12 Steps to Living Without Fear, 1987, A Future and a Hope, 1988, Enjoying God, 1990, Silent Strength, 1990, The Lord of the Loose Ends, 1991; gen. editor: Communicator's Commentary of the Bible, 1982; host: (TV and radio program) Let God Love You. Office: 1760 N Gower St Los Angeles CA 90028-5422

OGILVIE, RICHARD IAN, clinical pharmacologist; b. Sudbury, Ont., Can., Oct. 9, 1936; s. Patrick Ian and Gena Hilda (Olson) O.; m. Ernestine Tahedl, Oct. 9, 1965; children— Degen Elisabeth, Lars Ian. MD, U. Toronto, 1960. Intern Toronto (Ont.) Gen. Hosp., 1960-61; resident Montreal Gen. and Univ. Alta. hosps., 1962-66; fellow in clin. pharmacology McGill U., Montreal, 1966-68, asst. prof. medicine, pharmacology and therapeutics, 1968-73, assoc. prof., 1973-78, prof., 1978-83, chmn. dept. pharmacology and therapeutics, 1978-83. Prof. emeritus, U. Toronto, 2002-, clin. pharmacologist Montreal Gen. Hosp., 1968-83, dir. div. clin. pharmacology, 1976-83; prof. medicine and pharmacology U. Toronto, 1983—2002; dir. div. cardiology Toronto Western Hosp., 1983-88, div. clin. pharmacology, 1983-91; mem. pharm. grants com. Med. Research Coun. Can., 1977-82, chmn. 1980-82; mem. med. adv. com. Que. Heart Found., 1976-82, chmn. 1977-81. Editor Hypertension Canada, 1989—. Bd. dirs. PMAC Health Care Found., 1986-92; hon. sec.-treas. Banting Research Found., 1984-87, chmn. grant rev. com., 1985-86 Decorated knight comdr. Sovereign Mil. Order St. John of Jerusalem, Knights of Malta, 1987, nat. chmn., recipient prize in med. ethics, 1988-98, sci. advisor to the prior, 1987—, Knight Grand Cross, 1990; jury mem. Can. Prix Galien, 1994-99; grantee Can. Kidney Found., J.C. Edwards Found., Med. Rsch. Coun., Que. Heart Found., Can. Found. Advancement Therapeutics, Conseil de la recherche en sante du Que. Fellow ACP, Royal Coll. Physicians of Can.; mem. Can. Soc. Clin. Investigation (coun. 1977-80), Can. Hypertension Soc. (bd. dirs. 1979-81, 89-94, 96—, v.p. 1991-92, pres. 1992-93, Disting. Svc. award, 2002), Can. Found. Advancement Clin. Pharmacology (dir. 1978-86), Canadian Soc. for Clin. Pharmacology (pres. 1979-82, Sr. Investigator award 1993), Internat. Union Pharmacology (coun. mem. clin. pharmacology sect. 1981-84, chmn. 1984-87), Pharm. Soc. Can., Can. Cardiovascular Soc., Am. Soc. Pharmacology and Exptl. Therapeutics, Am. Soc. Clin. Pharm., Toronto Hypertension Soc. (pres. 1988-98). Home: 79 Collard Dr King City ON Canada L7B 1E4 Office: Toronto Western Hosp 399 Bathurst St Toronto ON Canada M5T 2S8 Home Phone: 905-833-0686; Office Phone: 416-603-5176. Business E-Mail: ri.ogilvie@utoronto.ca.

OGILVIE, T(HOMAS) FRANCIS, marine engineering educator; b. Atlantic City, Sept. 26, 1929; s. Thomas Fleisher and Frances Augusta (Wilson) O.; m. Joan Husselton, Sept. 11, 1950; children: Nancy Louise, Mary Beth, Kenneth Stuart. BA in Physics, Cornell U., 1950; M.Sc. in Aero. Engring., U. Md., 1957; PhD in Engring. Sci., U. Calif., Berkeley, 1960; D in Naval Arch./Marine Engring. (hon.), Nat. Tech. U. Athens, 1996. Physicist, David Taylor Model Basin, Dept. Navy, Bethesda, Md., 1951-62, 64-67; liaison scientist Office of Naval Research, London, 1962-63; asso. prof. naval architecture and marine engring. U. Mich., Ann Arbor, 1967-70, prof. fluid mechanics, 1970-81, chmn. dept. naval architecture and marine engring., 1973-81; prof. ocean engring. MIT, Cambridge, 1982-96, prof. emeritus, 1996—, head dept., 1982-94. Vis. prof. naval architecture Osaka (Japan) U., 1976; vis. prof. math. U. Manchester, Eng., 1976; founding mem. Ariz. Sr. Acad., Tucson, 1997. Contbr. articles to profl. jours. Recipient Meritorious Pub. Svc. award U.S. Dept. of Transp., 1982. Fellow Soc. of Naval Architects and Marine Engrs. (coun. 1977-82, exec. com. 1978-80, 83-84, William H. Webb medal 1989); mem. Sigma Xi, Phi Beta Kappa. Home: 7559 S Eliot Ln Tucson AZ 85747-9627

OGILVY, GEOFF, professional golfer; b. Adelaide, Australia, June 11, 1977; m. Juli Ogilvy. Profl. golfer Profl. Golf Assn., 2001—. Achievements include winning Tasmanian Open, 1998; runner-up five PGA events, winner 3 PGA events including the Chrysler Classic of Tucson, 2005, US Open, Winged Foot, 2006, WGC Accenture Match Play Championship at La Costa, 2006. Office: Pro Sports Mgmt 7373 E Doubletree Ranch Rd #170 Scottsdale AZ 85258 Office Fax: 61 3 9592 5633.

OGLE, D. CLARK, textiles executive; b. 1947; Buyer and numerous positions Super Valu, Eden Prairie, Minn., 1968-74; pres. W.Va. div. Fox Grocery Co., 1974-78; pres., COO, bd. dirs. Scrivner, Inc., 1978-87; pres., CEO Affiliated Food Stores, Keller, Tex., 1987-90; industry cons. Hoover, Ala.; CEO Peter J. Schmitt; pres., CEO various pvt. cos., 1987-96; mng. dir. KPMG Peat Marwick, LLP; pres., CEO Johnston Industries, Inc., 1998—. Office: Johnston Textile Industries 3101 23rd Dr Valley AL 36854-3042 Fax: 706-641-3159.

OGLE, EDWARD PROCTOR, JR., investment advisor; b. Inglewood, Calif., Dec. 20, 1935; s. Edward Proctor and Allene Emma (Blumenthal) O.; m. Elizabeth Lovejoy Myers, Mar. 28, 1958; children: Kathryn Ogle Nava, Terry Ogle Nelson, Wendy Ogle Reeves. BA, U. So. Calif., 1964; MA, Claremont Grad. Sch., 1980. Cert. fin. planning practitioner. Zone mgr. Investors Diversified Svcs., Pasadena, Calif., 1964-66; asst. mgr. Merrill Lynch Pierce Fenner Smith, Pasadena, 1966-72; mgr. Clark Dodge & Co-Capital Place Dept., LA, 1972-74; sr. v.p. Security Pacific Bank - Pacific Century Group, LA, 1974-86; sr. v.p., registered prin. Brown Bros. Harriman & Co., LA, 1986—2003; prin., cert. sr. advisor Philip V. Swan Assocs., 2003—. Author: (booklet) Role of Bank Trust Department, 1981; editor (booklet) Parade Operations Manual, 1992, 93. Com. sec. Tournament of Roses Assn., Pasadena, 1976—; mem. Town Hall of Calif., LA, 1977—, Orange County World Trade Assn.; mem. exec. com. U. S.C. Alumni Assn., 2003—; chmn. bd. councilors U. So. Calif., 1998—, bd. govs., 2003—; mem. Rep. Presdl. Task Force, Orange County, Calif., 1984—; elder Presbyn. Ch. Recipient Corp. Fund Raising Cert. United Way, L.A., 1978-80, Exec. Mgmt. Cert. Claremont Grad. Sch., 1979, Mgmt. and Exec. Cert. Security Pacific Bank, L.A., 1981. Mem. Fin. Planning Assn., Drucker Ctr. Mgmt. Assn., Claremont Grad. Sch. Alumni Assn. (pres. 1984-86), Pasadena Bond Club, Bond Club L.A., Jonathan Club, City Club. Republican. Avocations: photography, golf, basketball, music, travel. Home Phone: 714-974-1088; Office Phone: 626-793-0377. E-mail: eogle@philipswan.com.

OGLE, JAMES DAVID, lawyer; b. Kirksville, Mo., Mar. 23, 1968; s. John Charles and Elizabeth Ann Ogle; m. Laura Kerr Ogle, Aug. 14, 1993; children: Taylor, Jackson. BSc Okla. State U., Stillwater; JD, Okla. City U., Okla. Bar: Okla. 1997, US Dist. Ct. (no., ea., and we. dists.) 1997, US Ct. Appeals (10th cir.) 1998, US Supreme Ct. 2004. Various sales, mktg. positions G.D. Searle, Skokie, Ill., 1990—93, Carter Healthcare, Okla. City, 1993—95; atty. Martin Law Office, Okla. City, 1995—2003, Ogle & Welch, P.C., Okla. City, 2003—. Spkr. in field. Mem., assoc. Okla. City Art Mus., Okla., 1997—2002; trustee Okla. County Law Libr. Named one of Top 100 Okla. Lawyers, 2006. Mem.: Okla. County Bar Assn. (pres.), Okla. Criminal Def. Assn., Nat. Assn. Criminal Def. Lawyers (life). Office: Ogle & Welch PC 117 Park Ave 3d Fl Oklahoma City OK 73102 Office Phone: 405-232-9800. Office Fax: 405-232-1608.

OGLE, JAMES WORKMAN, aerospace engineer; s. Richard Norman Ogle and Susan Ruth Workman, Gail Anne Drahos (Stepmother); m. Julie Marie Glazer; 1 child, Jared Joseph. BS, Ohio State U., Columbus, 1992—95, MS, 1998—2000. Performance analyst Allied Signal, Greenbelt, Md., 1996—98; cons. Robert Half, Internat., Cleve., 1998—2002; sr. engr. ITT Space Sys. Divsn., Fort Wayne, Ind., 2002—. Contbr. scientific papers. Mem.: Am. Mensa (assoc.). Office: ITT Space Sys Divsn 1919 W Cook Rd M/S 630 Fort Wayne IN 46818 Home Phone: 260-483-1392. Office Fax: 260-451-6033. Personal E-mail: james.ogle@gmail.com. Business E-Mail: james.ogle@itt.com.

OGLE, ROBBIN SUE, criminal justice educator; b. North Kansas City, Mo., Aug. 28, 1960; d. Robert Lee and Carol Sue (Gray) O. BS, Ctrl. Mo. State U., 1982; MS, U. Mo., 1990; PhD, Pa. State U., 1995. State probation and parole officer Mo. Dept. Corrections, Kansas City, 1982-92; collector J.C. Penney Co., Mission, Kans., 1990-92; instr. U. Mo., Kansas City, 1990-92; grad. lectr. Pa. State U., University Park, 1992-95; prof. criminal justice dept. U. Nebr., Omaha, 1995—. Author: Battered Women Who Kill: A New Framework, 2002, The Wienie Dog Adventure Series: The Great Ham Heist, 2005; contbr. articles to profl. jours. Athletic scholar Ctrl. Mo. State U., Warrensburg, 1978-82. Mem. AAUW, ACLU, NOW, Am. Soc. Criminology, Acad. Criminal Justice Scis., Am. Correctional Assn., Phi Kappa Phi. Avocations: reading, watching basketball, walking dog. Office: U Nebr Dept Criminal Justice 1100 Neihardt Lincoln NE 68588-0630 Home: 2410 N 99th St Omaha NE 68134-5642 Office Phone: 402-472-3677. Personal E-mail: rsogle@cox.net. Business E-Mail: rogle@mail.unomaka.edu.

OGLESBY, CHARLES R., automotive executive; BBA in Mktg., U. Ga. COO First Am. Automotive, Inc., San Francisco; pres., North Point Automotive Group. Asbury Automotive Group., Inc., Little Rock, 2002—06, pres., Nalley Automotive Group. Atlanta, 2004—06, sr. v.p., COO NYC, 2006—07, pres., CEO, 2007—. Bd. dirs. Asbury Automotive Group., Inc., 2006—. Office: Asbury Automotive Group Inc 622 Third Ave 37th Fl New York NY 10017 Office Phone: 212-885-2500. *

OGLESBY, ELAINE SUE, elementary school educator; b. Rensselaer, Ind., Dec. 11, 1958; d. Richard E. and Lois I. Oglesby. BS in Natural Resources and Environ. Sci., Purdue U., 1981; MEd, Ind. U., 1988, MLS, 2005. Tchr. Indpls. Pub. Schs., 1986—2004, digital coach, 2004—. Recipient Shining Star, Indpls. Pub. Schs., 1993—94, Spirit of Harshman, Harshman Mid. Sch., 1998, Tchr. of the Yr. award, 2003, Top Ten Tchr. award, Indpls. Pub. Schs., 2003; grantee, Eli Lily Found., 1993. Mem.: Ind. Mid. Level Educators (assoc.), Nat. Mid. Sch. Assn. (assoc.), Ind. Libr. Fedn. (assoc.), Assn. Curriculum and Devel. (assoc.). Home Phone: 317-345-2081; Office Phone: 317-226-4030.

OGLESBY, JOSEPH WOODSON (MIKE ENGLISH), writer, publishing executive; b. Louisville, Aug. 14, 1931; s. Joseph Woodson Oglesby, Sr. and Mary Lee (Wigginton) Oglesby; m. Marianna Bachmann, Sept. 4, 1971; 1 child, Shane Woodson. BA, U. Louisville, 1953. Staff writer Louisville Times, 1954—56, asst. editor, 1954—56; city editor New Albany Tribune, Ind., 1956—59; editor Frankfort Crusader, Ky., 1960, pub., 1960; investigative reporter Tonawanda News, North Tonawanda, NY, 1961—63; exec. editor Voice Newspapers, Louisville, 1964—70; pub., CEO Lucky Publs., Louisville, 1988—2000; freelance writer, 1970—. Founding mem. Ky. Thoroughbred Media, Lexington, Ky., 1990; pub. rels. adv. Nat. Kitchen Cabinet Assn., Louisville, 1970—72, Contact Lens Soc. of Am., Louisville, 1972. Author: (novels) The Devil's Disciple, 1977, Ghost Riders of the Staked Plains, (play) The Dodge, 1998 (nominee Pulitzer prize, 1999), (memoir) Dinner with D.W. Griffith and Other Memories, 2005, (children's book) The Marvelous Kingdom of Wee, 1976, monographs on Ky. history; contbr. articles to newspapers and magazines. Vice chmn. bd. dir. YMCA, St. Matthews, Ky., 1970; mem. bd. dir. Talbot Ho., Louisville, 1962; pub. rels. adv. Recovery, Inc., Louisville, 1960—62. Nominee Eclipse award, 1998; recipient Best Feature award, Ky. Press Assn., 1967, Short Story award, Writer's Digest, 1982, 1985; grantee, P.E.N. Internat. Ctr., NYC, 1983. Mem.: Nat. Turf Writers Assn., Mystery Writers Am., Authors Guild, Authors Legacy Soc., Hon. Order Ky. Cols., Omicron Delta Kappa. Democrat. Avocations: travel, history, thoroughbred handicapping, coin collecting/numismatics. Personal E-mail: novelistjosephoglesby@msn.com.

OGLETREE, CHARLES J., JR., law educator; b. Calif., Dec. 31, 1952; m. Pamela Barnes, 1975; children: Charles III, Rashida. BA in Polit. Sci., Stanford U., 1974, MA in Polit. Sci., 1975; JD, Harvard U., 1978; LLD (hon.), NC Ctrl. U., New Eng. Sch. Law, Tougaloo Coll., Amherst Coll., 2002, U. Miami Sch. Law, 2003, Wilberforce U., 2003. Bar: DC 1979, US Supreme Ct. 1983. Staff atty. DC Pub. Defender Svc., tng. dir., 1982—83, trial chief, 1983—84, dep. dir., 1984—85; joined Jessamy, Fort & Ogletree, 1985; of counsel Jordan, Keys & Jessamy, Washington; lectr. law Harvard Law Sch., Cambridge, Mass., 1984, vis. prof. law from practice, 1985—89, Edward R. Johnston Lectr. Law, 1989, asst. prof. law, 1989—93, dir. Criminal Justice Inst., 1990, prof. law., 1993—, faculty dir. clin. progs., 1996, Jesse Climenko Prof. Law, 1998—, assoc. dean clin. progs., 2002—03, vice dean clin. progs., 2003, dir. Charles Hamilton Houston Inst. Race and Justice, 2004—. Adj. prof. Am. U., Washington, 1983—85; moderator various nationally televised forums; guest commentator various nat. and local TV and radio progs. Co-author: Beyond the Rodney King Story: An Investigation of Police Conduct in Minority Communities, 1995; author: All Deliberate Speed: Reflections on the First Half-Century of Brown v. Board of Education, 2004; co-editor: Brown at 50: The Unfinished Legacy, 2004; contbr. articles to profl. jours., chapters to books. Chmn. bd. trustees U. DC; chmn. bd. dirs. B.E.L.L. Found.; mem. bd. trustees Stanford U., chmn. Stanford Fund. Named one of 100 Most Influential Lawyers in Am., Nat. Law Jour., 2000, 100 Most Influential Blacks in Am., Black Enterprise mag., 2003, Savoy mag., 2003; named to The Ebony Power 150, Ebony mag., 2007; recipient Charles Hamilton Houston Medallion of Merit, Washington Bar Assn., 2001, Equal Justice award, Nat. Bar Assn., 2002, Tribune Soc. Justice award, Courts of NY State, 2003, Universal Humanitarian award, NAACP, 2003. Office: Harvard Law Sch 1563 Massachusetts Ave Cambridge MA 02138 Office Phone: 617-495-5097. Office Fax: 617-496-3936. E-mail: ogletree@law.harvard.edu. *

OGLIARUSO, MICHAEL ANTHONY, retired chemist, educator, actor; b. Bklyn., Aug. 10, 1938; s. Andrea and Anna (Bianco) O.; m. Basila Gallo, Apr. 2, 1961; 1 child, Michael Dana. BS, Poly. Inst. Bklyn., 1960, PhD, 1965. Postdoctoral rsch. assoc. UCLA, 1965-67; asst. prof. chemistry Va. Poly. Inst. and State U., Blacksburg, 1967-72, assoc. prof., 1972-78, prof., 1978-95, assoc. dean Coll. Arts and Scis., 1984-95; ret. Coll. Arts and Scis.; profl. actor. Contbr. articles to profl. jours. Served with C.E. U.S. Army, 1960-61. Mem. Am. Chem. Soc., Va. Acad. Sci., Sigma Xi, Phi Lambda Upsilon. *I have been fortunate to be associated with the most personally rewarding profession available today, the professional education of young men and women. This career is best suited to persons who wish to remain young in spirit, since regardless of your age you are always surrounded with students who are between 18 and 22 years old. This is the best way I know to remain spiritually young.*

OGNIBENE, ANDRE JOHN, internist, educator, retired military officer; b. NYC, Nov. 18, 1931; s. Morris S. and Josephine C. (Macaluso) O.; m. Margaret A. Haug, Apr. 21, 1957; children: Judy, Andrea, Adrienne, Marc, Eric. BA cum laude, Columbia U., 1952; MD, NYU, 1956. Diplomate Am. Bd. Internal Medicine, Am. Bd. Geriatrics, Am. Bd. Med. Mgmt. Intern in medicine Bellevue Hosp., NYC, 1956-57, resident in medicine, 1957-59; commd. capt. US Army M.C., 1957, advanced through grades to brig. gen., 1978; resident in medicine Manhattan VA Hosp., NYC and chief resident in medicine, 1959-60; chief med. service US Army Hosp., Nurnburg, Germany, 1961-62, chief dept. medicine, 1962-64; fellow in cardiology Walter Reed Gen. Hosp., Washington, 1964-65, asst. in cardiology, 1965-66, asst. chief dept. medicine, 1969-72; chief dept. medicine, chief profl. services US Army Hosp., Ft. Meade, Md., 1966-68; cons. in medicine Hdqrs. US Army, Vietnam, 1969; asst. chief dept. medicine Walter Reed Army Med. Ctr., 1970-72; from chief dept. medicine to dir. med. edn. Brooke Army Med. Ctr., Ft. Sam Houston, Tex., 1972-78, dir. med. edn., 1976-78, dep. comdr. and chief profl. services, 1976-78, comdr., commanding gen., 1978-81; hosp. dir. San Antonio State Chest Hosp., 1981-85; program dir. internal medicine Canton, Ohio, 1985-95; prof. medicine NE Ohio U., Rootstown, 1985-98, prof. emeritus, 1998—, chmn. dept. medicine, 1989-98, assoc. dean for med. edn., 1989—98; med. dir. Mercy Med. Ctr., 1995—98; v.p., treas. Majomed Corp., San Antonio, 1999—. Instr. medicine NYU, 1960; assoc. clin. prof. Georgetown U., 1970-72; clin. prof. U. Tex. Health Sci. Ctr., San Antonio, 1973-85, mem. postgrad. adv. com., 1977-78; mem. Instl. Rev. Bd., 1981-85; pres. Bexar Met. unit Am. Cancer Soc., 1984; dir. Eisenhower Nat. Bank; bd. dirs. Cancer Therapy and Rsch. Ctr.; chmn. South Tex. Epilepsy Found., 1985. Contbr. articles to med. publs. and chpts. to books; editor, prin. author Internal Medicine in Vietnam, Vol. II, 1982; editor-in-chief: Internal Medicine in Vietnam, vol. I, 1977. Trustee Regina Health Ctr., 1992-97; mem. med. adv. bd. Access Health Inc., 1998-2000. Decorated DSM, Legion of Merit; named among Am. Top Physicians, Consumer Rsch. Coun., 2003-05. Master ACP (laureate, master tchr.); fellow Am. Coll. Physician Execs. (cert.), Am. Coll. Angiology; mem. NY Acad. Scis., Am. Fedn. Clin. Rsch., Bexar County Med. Soc., Stark County Med. Soc., Assn. Profs. Medicine, Tex. Med. Found., Alpha Omega Alpha. Home and Office: 27671 Ramblewood St San Antonio TX 78261-2013 Personal E-mail: aognibene@satx.rr.com. *Compassion must remain the universal prescription in medical practice. Technology can provide no solutions in the absence of humanity.*

OGNIBENE, FREDERICK PETER, internist; b. Jamestown, NY, Aug. 30, 1953; s. Vincent Larry and Alma Linda (Martinelli) O. BA, U. Rochester, 1975; MD, Cornell U., 1979. Diplomate Am. Bd. Internal Medicine, Am. Bd. Internal Medicine-Critical Care. From intern to resident N.Y. Hosp./Cornell Med. Ctr., 1979-82; from med. to sr. staff fellow Critical Care Medicine Dept. NIH, Bethesda, Md., 1982-87, sr. investigator, 1987—, fellowship dir., 1998—2003. Assoc. clin. prof. George Washington U., Washington, 1996—; adj. assoc. prof. U. Md., 2000—; dir. clin. rsch. tng. program NIH, 2000—, dir. office clin. rsch. tng. and med. edn., 2003—. Manuscript reviewer; contbr. articles to profl. jours., chpts. to books. Mem. adv. bd. Washington Project of the Arts/ Corcoran; bd. dirs. Cultural Devel. Corp. D.C., 2003—06, Curator's Cir. Hirshhorn Mus. and Sculpture Garden, 2004-. Capt. USPHS, 1985-2007. Fellow ACP, Am. Coll. Critical Care Medicine (chair credentials com. 1992-94, bd. regents 1994-2000); mem. Cornell U. Med. Coll. Alumni Assn. (bd. dirs.), Am. Fedn. Clin. Rschs. (nat. coun. 1987-95, sec.-treas. ea. sect. 1987-91, chair-elect 1991-92, chair 1992-93), Am. Fedn. Clin. Rsch. Found. (trustee), Soc. Critical Care Medicine (co-chair symposium 1998, governing coun. 2000-04, sec. 2004-05, pres. 2007), Alpha Omega Alpha. Democrat. Roman Catholic. Avocations: travel, studying Italian language, collecting contemporary American art. Home: 1661 Crescent Pl NW Apt 308 Washington DC 20009 Office: NIH Rm BIL 403 9000 Rockville Pike Bldg 10 Bethesda MD 20892 Office Phone: 301-496-9425, 301-402-0563. Business E-Mail: fognibene@cc.nih.gov.

OGNIBENE, PETER JOHN, writer; b. Washington, Dec. 9, 1941; s. Peter Joseph and Dorothea Vita (D'Amico) Ognibene; m. Brigid Ann Selz, Apr. 7, 1984 (dissolved 2006); 1 child, Matthew. BS, U.S. Air Force Acad., 1963; MSE in Aerospace Engring., U. Mich., 1965; MA in Govt. and Politics, U. Md., 1967. V.p. Applied Sys. Inst., Washington, 1986-93, Synex Inc., Columbia, Md., 1993-95; pres. Smart Card Devel. Svcs., Silver Spring, Md., 1995—. Author: (book) Scoop: The Life and Politics of Henry M. Jackson, 1975, The Big Byte, 1984. Capt. USAF, 1963—70. Recipient Excellence in Consumer Journalism, Nat. Press Club, 1979, Award of Merit, Soc. Tech. Comm., 1988. Mem.: Washington Ind. Writers (adv. bd. 1981—). Democrat. Roman Catholic. Avocations: skiing, running.

O'GORMAN, GERALD JOSEPH, language educator; b. Richmond Heights, Mo., Jan. 6, 1934; s. Florent Edmond and Veronica Catherine (Kelly) O'Gorman; m. Julia Lee Finn, Aug. 27, 1960; children: Brian Thomas, Gregory Paul. BA in English, St. Louis U., Mo., 1958, MA in Latin, 1965, PhD in English, 1973. Cert. computer programming St. Louis C.C., 1989. English, Latin tchr. Corpus Christi High Sch., Jennings, Mo., 1958—60, Park Country Day Sch., Indpls., 1960—62, St. Louis Preparatory Seminary, Shrewsbury, Mo., 1962—64; English instr. U. Mo. - St. Louis, Normandy, 1964—67; asst. prof. St. Louis Coll. Pharm., 1967—75, assoc. prof., 1967—75; lectr. Am. Lit. U. Gar-Yonis, Benghazi, Libya, 1975—77; assoc. prof. Southern Ill. U., Edwardsville, 1977—89, 1989—99; ret. Dir., freshman English Southern Ill. U., 1979—80, 1994—95, coord. undergrad. program review, 1984—85, coord. humanities honors, 1988—93. Editor: Marcus Tullius Ciceroes thre bokes of duties, to Marcus his sonne, turned oute of latine into English, 1990; contbr. articles various profl. jours. Asst. dir., drug abuse edn. program St. Louis Coll. Pharm., 1969—74; chair, citizen faculty Lindbergh Sch. Dist., St. Louis, 1973—74; exec. dir. So. Ctrl. CYC Soccer Dist., St. Louis, 1974—75. With US Army, 1953—55, Korea, Hawaii. Rsch. fellowship, NEH, 1983—84, Rsch. grant, Am. Philosophical Soc., 1973, Rsch. fellowship, Folger Shakespeare Libr., 1970. Mem.: St. Louis Mercantile Libr., MENSA, Mo. Athletic Club. Avocations: languages, computers, golf, exercise. Home: 622 Acorn Dr Saint Louis MO 63126

O'GORMAN, JAMES FRANCIS, art educator, writer; b. St. Louis, Sept. 19, 1933; s. Paul Joseph and Dorothy Frances (Hogan) O'G.; m. Jean Baer, Feb. 9, 1957 (div. 1987); children: Christopher, Harold, Michael (dec.), Samuel; m. Susan Danly, Aug. 1, 1998. BArch, Washington U., St. Louis, 1956; MArch, U. Ill., 1961; PhD, Harvard U., 1966. Grace Slack McNeil prof. Am. art Wellesley Coll., Mass., 1975—2004, prof. emeritus, 2004—. Author: H.H. Richardson and His Office: Selected Drawings, 1973, This Other Gloucester, 1976, H.H. Richardson, Architectural Forms for an American Society, 1987; Three American Architects: Richardson, Sullivan and Wright, 1865-1915, 1991, Living Architecture: A Biography of H.H. Richardson, 1997, Accomplished in All Departments of Art: Hammatt Billings of Boston, 1818-1874, 1998, ABC of Architecture, 1998, Connecticut Valley Vernacular: The Vanishing Landscape and Architecture of the New England Tobacco Fields, 2002; co-author: Principles of Architectural History, 1968, The Architecture of Frank Furness, 1973, American Architects and Their Books to 1848, 2001, The Makers of Trinity Church in the City of Boston, 2004, The Main Perspective: Architectural Drawings, 1800-1980, 2006. Phila. Athenaeum fellow, 1985. Mem.: Am. Antiquarian Soc. Office Phone: 207-892-6273. Business E-Mail: jogorman@wellesley.edu.

OGRA, PEARAY L., pediatrician, educator; b. Srinagar, Kashmir, India, Mar. 19, 1937; came to U.S., 1961, naturalized, 1969; s. Govinda Kaul and Gunvati (Daftari) O.; children: Sanjay, Monica. MB, Christian Med. Coll., Ludhiana, India, 1961. Intern Binghamton (N.Y.) Gen. Hosp., 1962-63; resident U. Chgo., 1963-64, N.Y. U.-Bellevue Med Center, 1964-66, fellow in infectious diseases, 1966-68; asst. prof. pediatrics SUNY, Buffalo, 1968-71, assoc. prof. pediatrics and microbiology, 1972-74, prof., 1974-91; John Sealy disting. chair, prof. U. Tex. Med. Br., Galveston, 1991-2000, chmn. dept. pediatrics, 1991-99; prof. pediatrics Children's Hosp., Buffalo, 2000—. Dir. divsn. virology Children's Hosp. Buffalo, 1969-81, chief dept. infectious diseases, 1970-91; dir. Clin. Labs. Children's Hosp., 1985-90; mem. study sect. NIH, 1979-85, maternal child health com., 1987-91; mem., chmn. bd. Internat. Pediat. Rsch. Found., Inc., 1984-89; mem. com. on vaccines for 21st century Inst. of Medicine NAS, 1997-2000, com. in infant formula, 2002; adv. bd. Internat. Vaccine Inst., Seoul, Rep. Korea, 2003—, Merck scholar-in-residence, 2006—; chmn. external rev. group Program on Mucosal Vaccines, European Commn., 2005—. Recipient E. Mead Johnson award for Pediatric Research Am. Acad. Pediatrics, 1978; Kalhana award Kashmir Sci. Culture and Soc., 1984; Stockton Kimball award SUNY, 1985; Buswell fellow, 1968-71. Fellow Royal Soc. Medicine, Assn. Am. Physicians, Am. Acad. Pediatrics, Am. Acad. Microbiology; mem. Am. Soc. Clin. Investigation, Soc. Pediatric Rsch., Infectious Disease Soc. Am., Soc. Exptl. Biology and Medicine, Am. Assn. Immunologists, Am. Soc. Microbiology, AAAS, Am. Fedn. Clin. Rsch., Am. Soc. Virology, Pediatric Infectious Disease Soc. (chmn. com. internatl health 2006—). Home: 163 Troy Del Way Williamsville NY 14221-4505 Office Phone: 716-878-7407. Business E-Mail: pogra@upa.chob.edu. E-mail: plogra@buffalo.edu.

O'GRADY, DENNIS JOSEPH, lawyer; b. Hoboken, NJ, Nov. 16, 1943; s. Joseph A. and Eileen O'Grady; m. Mary Anne Amoruso, Sept. 9, 1966 (div. Apr. 1984); 1 child, Kara Anne. AB, Seton Hall Coll., 1965; MA, U. So. Calif., 1969; JD, Rutgers U., 1973. Bar: N.J. 1973, U.S. Ct. Appeals (3d cir.) 1975, U.S. Dist. Ct. N.J., U.S. Supreme Ct. 2000. Ptnr. Riker, Danzig, Scherer, Hyland & Perretti, Newark, Trenton and Morristown, NJ, 1974—. Adj. asst. prof. of bus. law St. Peter's Coll., Jersey City, 1973—; adj. prof. law Rutgers U. Law Sch., 1997—. Named to, Best Lawyers in Am., 2003—. Fellow: Am. Coll. Bankruptcy Lawyers; mem.: ABA (bus./bankruptcy sect.), NJ Turnaround Assn. (bd. dirs.), Am. Bd. Cert. (faculty subcom.), Am. Bankruptcy Inst. (health career subcom., bd. profl. cert.), Fed. Bar Assn., N.J. State Bar Assn. (debtor/creditor sect.). Democrat. Roman Catholic. Office: Riker Danzig Scherer Hyland & Perretti 1 Speedwell Ave Morristown NJ 07960-6823 Office Phone: 973-538-0800. Business E-Mail: dogrady@riker.com.

O'GRADY, JOHN JOSEPH, III, lawyer; b. NYC, Mar. 21, 1933; s. John Joseph and Terese (O'Rourke) O'G.; m. Mary E. McHugh, June 28, 1958; children: Glennon, Ellen, Carol, Paul. AB, Holy Cross Coll., 1954; JD, Harvard U., 1957. Bar: N.Y. 1958. Assoc. Cadwalader, Wickersham & Taft, NYC, 1958-66, ptnr., 1966-96, counsel, 1997—. Office: Cadwalader Wickersham & Taft One World Fin Ctr New York NY 10281 Office Phone: 212-504-6000.

O'GRADY, MICHAEL J., lawyer; b. Cin., 1970; BA, U. Mich., 1992; MBA, U. Cin., 1996, JD, 1995. Bar: Ohio 1995, US Dist. Ct. Southern Dist. Ohio 1996, US Ct. of Appeals Sixth Cir. 2002. Jud. clerk Hon. Burton Perlman, Southern Dist. Ohio, 1995—97; atty. Frost Brown Todd, LLC, Cin. Named one of Ohio's Rising Stars, Super Lawyers, 2006. Mem.: Am. Bankruptcy Inst., ABA, Ohio State Bar Assn., Cin. Bar Assn. Office: Frost Brown Todd LLC 2200 PNC Ctr 201 E Fifth St Cincinnati OH 45202-4182 Office Phone: 513-651-6800. Office Fax: 513-651-6981.

OGREAN, DAVID WILLIAM, sports association executive; b. New Haven, Feb. 7, 1953; s. Richard Berton and Dorothy (Nystrom) O.; m. Maryellen Harvey, Aug. 10 1974; children: Matthew David, Tracy Erin, Dana Marie. BA in English cum laude, U Conn., 1974; MS in Film, Boston U., 1978. Asa S. Bushnell intern Ea. Coll. Athletic Conf., Centerville, Mass., 1977—78; dir. pub. rels. Amateur Hockey Assn. U.S., Colorado Springs, Colo., 1978—80; mng. editor Am. Hockey and Arena mag., 1979—80; comm. rep. ESPN, Inc., Bristol, Conn., 1980—83, program mgr., 1983—88; asst. exec. dir. for TV Coll. Football Assn., Boulder, Colo., 1988—90; dir. broadcasting US Olympic Com., Colorado Springs, 1990—93, dep. exec. dir. mktg., 1999—2000; exec. dir. USA Hockey, Colorado Springs, 1993—99, 2005—; chmn. Colorado Springs Sports Corp., 1996—97, pres., CEO, 2000—02; exec. dir. USA Football, 2002—05. Chmn. legis. com. US Olympic Com., 1997-99, 2000-04; chmn. Colo. Springs Sports Corp., 1996-97; bd. dirs. Colo. Springs World Arena, 1998-2002, 05-, Colo. Springs Conv. and Visitors Bur., 2000-02. Home: 4110 San Felice Pointe Colorado Springs CO 80906 Office: USA Hockey 1775 Bob Johnson Dr Colorado Springs CO 80906 Business E-Mail: daveo@usahockey.org.

OGRETMEN, BESIM, science educator, molecular biologist, researcher; b. Ankara, Turkey, Jan. 5, 1966; s. Necati and Ayse Ogretmen; m. Sarita Ogretmen, Nov. 6, 1993; children: Ari Cem, Talia Bahar. PhD, Ill. Inst. of Tech., 1989—94. Post-doctoral fellow The U. of Chgo., 1994—96; rsch. assoc. Med. U. of SC., 1996—2000, asst. prof., 2000—. Contbr. articles to profl. jours. Rsch. grant, Nat. Cancer Inst., 2002. Mem.: Am. Soc. for Biochemistry and Molecular Biology, Am. Assn. for Cancer Rsch. Office: Med U of South Carolina 173 Ashley Ave Dept of Biochemistry Charleston SC 29425

O'GUINN, M. DAVE, III, lawyer; b. Dec. 29, 1969; BS, DePauw U., 1992; MS in Polit. Sci., Ind. U., 1994; JD, Notre Dame Law Sch., 2001. Bar: Ohio 2001, US Dist. Ct. Southern Dist. Ohio 2002, US Dist. Ct. Northern Dist. Ohio, US Dist. Ct. Southern Dist. Ind., Ct. of Appeals Sixth Dist. Assoc. Dinsmore & Shohl LLP, Cin. Chair, Young Professionals Com. Am. Red Cross, Cin., mem., Personnel Com., mem., Ops. Com. Named one of Ohio's Rising Stars, Super Lawyers, 2006. Mem.: Ohio State Bar Assn., ABA, Cin. Bar Assn. Office: Dinsmore & Shohl LLP 255 E Fifth St Ste 1900 Cincinnati OH 45202-4700 Office Phone: 513-977-8200. Office Fax: 513-977-8141.

OGUL, MORRIS SAMUEL, political science professor, consultant; b. Detroit, Apr. 15, 1931; s. Jack and Sarah (Zimmerman) O.; m. Eleanor Simon, Aug. 26, 1954. BA, Wayne State U., 1952; MA, U. Mich., 1953, PhD, 1958. Instr. polit. sci. U. Pitts., 1957-59, asst. prof., 1959-64, assoc. prof., 1964-67, prof., 1967-98, prof. emeritus, 1998—. Cons. U.S. Ho. of Reps., 1973, 83, U.S. Office Personnel Mgmt., Washington, 1975—, U.S. Senate, 1977 Author: (with William J. Keefe) American Legislative Process, 1964, 7th edit., 1989, 8th edit., 1993, 9th edit., 1997, 10th edit., 2001, Congress Oversees the Bureaucracy, 1976. Carnegie Corp. research grantee, 1965-68 Mem. Am. Polit. Sci. Assn., Midwest Polit. Sci. Assn. (council 1982-84), Pa. Polit. Sci. Assn. Democrat. Home: 1500 Cochran Rd Apt 814 Pittsburgh PA 15243-1068 Office: U Pitts Dept Polit Sci 4614 Posvar Hall Pittsburgh PA 15260-7454 Home Phone: 412-561-6552. E-mail: morrissogul@comcast.net.

OGUNKOYA, ANDREA, marketing executive; BA in Law, Thames Valley Univ., Ealing, London. Retail, wholesale, sales, mktg. AT&T Wireless, Mount Vernon, NY, 1993—96; sr. mktg. specialist Nortel Networks, Tarrytown, NY, 1996—99; dir. mktg. Technotel Data Svcs., NYC, 1999—2001; sr. acct. dir. MSCO Mktg., NYC, 2001—05; v.p. ops., sales, mktg. Storage Deluxe, NYC, 2005—. Vol. Arthritis Found., Child Abuse Prevention Ctr. Office: Storage Deluxe 2887 Atlantic Ave Brooklyn NY 11207

OH, ALICE, art educator; b. Seoul, Republic of Korea, Aug. 10, 1967; d. Seayoung Oh and Ockja Jang; m. Christifer F. Portner; 1 child, Isabel J. Portner. BFA, Temple U., 1991; MFA, Yale U., 1994. Assoc. prof. Moore Coll. Art &Design, Phila., 1997—. Fellow, Pew Found., Phila., 2000, Pa. Coun. Arts, 2004; grantee, The Ludwig Found., Phila., 2000. Mem.: Phila. Inst. Contemporary Art, Coll. Art Assn. Office: Moore Coll Art & Design 20th and the Pky Philadelphia PA 19103 Office Phone: 215-568-4515 4096. Business E-Mail: aoh@moore.edu.

OH, ALLEN JAMES, lawyer; b. Warren, Mich., Feb. 5, 1973; s. Kong Ping and Soo Khuan Oh; m. Tiffany Ann Millay, June 16, 2001; children: Madison Rose Kathleen, Mikyla Renee. BS in Elec. Engring., U. Mich., 1993; JD, U. Pa., 1996. Bar: Minn. 1996, Mich. 1998, U.S. Patent and Trademark Office 1998. Assoc. Merchant & Gould PC, Mpls., 1996—98, Rader, Fishman & Grauer PLLC, Bloomfield Hills, Maine, 1998—99, Schwegman, Lundberg, Woessner & Kluth, P.A., Mpls., 1999—2001, Shumaker Sieffert, Woodbury, Minn., 2001—02; patent atty. Law Office of Allen J. Oh, Rogers, Minn., 2002—03, Moore & Hansen, PLLP, Mpls., 2003—. Bd. dirs. EECS Alumni Soc. U. Mich., Ann Arbor, Mich.; presenter in field. Mem.: IEEE, Minn. State Bar Assn. (mem. assembly 2005—), Tau Beta Pi, Eta Kappa Nu (v.p. 1992—93). Libertarian. Episcopalian. Office: Moore & Hansen PLLP 225 South Sixth Street Suite 4850 Minneapolis MN 55402 Home Phone: 763-428-6360; Office Phone: 612-332-8200. Business E-Mail: ajoh@mhsiplaw.com.

OH, ANGELA E., lawyer; b. LA, Sept. 8, 1955; BA, UCLA, 1977, MPH, 1981; JD, U. Calif., Davis, 1986. Bar: Calif. 1986. Lawyer, 1987—. Lawyer del. 9th Cir. Jud. Conf., 1995-96, lawyer rep.; mem. Senator Boxer's Jud. Noms. Com. for Ctrl. Dist. Calif., 1994-95; bd. dirs. Calif. Women's Law Ctr., Lawyers Mut. Ins. Co.; mem. cmty. adv. bd. First Interstate Bank Calif.; spkr. in field. Contbr. articles to profl. jours. and newspapers. Spl. counsel to the Assembly Spl. Com. on the L.A. Crisis. Mem. ABA, State Bar Calif., Korean-Am. Bar Assn. So. Calif. (pres.), L.A. County Bar Assn. Office: 8th Fl 601 W Fifth St Los Angeles CA 90071 Office Phone: 213-225-5825.

OH, JOHN KIE-CHIANG, political science professor, academic administrator; b. Seoul, Nov. 1, 1930; came to U.S., 1954, naturalized, 1971; s. Sung-Jun and Duk-Cho (Kim) O.; m. Bonnie Cho, Sept. 5, 1959; children: Jane J., Marie J., James J. BS, Marquette U., 1957; postgrad., Columbia U., 1957-58; PhD, Georgetown U., 1962. Asst. prof. St. Thomas Coll., St. Paul, 1962-66; assoc. prof. polit. sci. Marquette U., Milw., 1967-71, prof., chmn., 1971-77, dean grad. sch., 1977-85; acad. v.p. Cath. U. Am., Washington, 1985-89, Banigan scholar, prof. dept. politics, 1990-2001, prof. emeritus, 2001—. Adviser Republic of Korea Embassy, 2001—03; nat. chmn. Asian Sect. Fulbright Hays Program. Author: Korea: Democracy on Trial, 1968, (with Peter Cheng et al) Emerging Roles of Asian Nations in the 1980's, 1979, Democratization and Economic Development in Korea, 1990, Korean Politics: The Quest for Democratization and Economic Development, 1999, Thai transl., 2004, The Korean Embassy in America, 2003; contbr. articles to profl. jours. Chmn. scholarship com. World Affairs Coun., 1976-78; mem. Wis. Gov.'s Commn. for UN, Madison, 1971-74; chmn. Korean Studies com., Assn. Asian Studies, 1975-76. Grantee Hill Found., 1963, Relm Found., 1968, Social Sci. Rsch Coun., 1973, Am. Coun. Learned Socs., 1973. Mem. Am. Polit. Sci. Assn., Assn. Asian Studies, Internat. Polit. Sci. Assn., Midwest Conf. Asian Affairs (pres. 1970-71), Assn. Cath. Colls. and Univs. (bd. dirs. 1983-87), Indian Spring Country Club (bd. govs. 2000). Roman Catholic. Home: 807 Davis St 1506 Evanston IL 60201 Personal E-mail: jnboh@aol.com.

OH, JUNG HUN, computer engineer; b. Jeonnam, Korea (South), Dec. 25, 1971; s. Seung Ok Oh and Dong Jin Choi; m. Young Bun Kim, Dec. 1, 1972; 1 child, Yu Na. BS, Soongsil U., Seoul, 1995, MS, 1997; postgrad., U. Tex., Arlington, 2003—06. Sys. engr. Jinro Industries, Seoul, Republic of Korea, 1997—98; sr. software engr. Willtech, Seoul, 1997—2002, Sk C&C, Seoul, Republic of Korea, 2002—03; rsch. scholar U. Tex., Arlington, 2004—. Software engring. tng. Satyam, Hyderabad, India, 2003; product edn. Willtech, Seoul, Korea (South), 1998—2002. Contbr. articles to profl. jours. Fellow Hermann fellow, U. Tex. at Arlington, 2003; scholar Grad. Study Abroad scholar, Korea Sci. and Engring. Found., 2003. Mem.: IEEE (assoc.), Internat. Assn. Engring. (assoc.). Democrat-Npl. Christian. Avocations: travel, golf, basketball. Home Phone: 817-795-0846; Office Phone: 817-272-7526.

OH, JUNGHWAN, biomedical scientist, researcher; b. Busan, Feb. 19, 1969; s. Hyungen Oh and Jungja Kim; m. Jiyoung Hur; children: Grace, Christine. BS in Mech. Engring., MS in Mech. Engring., Pukyung Nat. U.; MS in Biomed. Engring., U. Tex., Austin, PhD, 2006. Sr. rschr. Rsch. Ctr. Ocean Indsl. Devel., Pusan, Republic of Korea; lectr. U. Ulsan, Republic of Korea; rsch. asst. U. Tex., Austin, 2001—06, tchg. asst., 2005, postdoctoral fellow Anderson Cancer Ctr. Houston, 2006—. Contbr. articles to profl. jours. Recipient Young Investigator award in ultrasound in medicine and biology, 2006; Presenter grant, Ultrasound Medicine & Biology, 2006. Pacific. Achievements include patents for catheter imaging probe and method; catheter imaging probe and method in Mexico, Europe, Australia; patents pending for multichannel catheter imaging probe and method; the use of iron oxide nanoparticles with optical coherence tomography; hemoglobin contrast in magneto-motive optical doppler tomography; method for detection of nanoparticles by an externally applied magnetic field using ultrasound imaging; hemoglobin contrast in magneto-motive ultrasound; pulsed laser to both identify and kill macrophages causing tissue pathology including vulnerable plaque; molecular-specific imaging using magnetically actuated hybrid plasmonic nanoparticles; observation method of cell or tissue sample by detection of nanoparticles using confocal microscope and system theory. Avocations: travel, swimming. Home: 9955 Buffalo Speedway #4107 Houston TX 77054 Office: UT MD Anderson Cancer Ctr 1515 Holcombe Blvd Unit 66 Houston TX 77030 Home Phone: 832-512-9250; Office Phone: 832-512-9250. Business E-Mail: jung.oh@mdanderson.org.

OH, MARK EDWARD, minister; s. Kap Soo and Boonhak Oh; m. Rosemary McGuire, Aug. 20, 1965; children: Christopher Douglas, Jonathan David. BA, Keimyung U., 1958; MA, San Francisco Theol. Sem., 1963; MRE, New Orleans Bapt. Theol. Sem., 1964; MDiv, We. Sem. Portland, 1968; PhD, Calif. Grad. Sch. Theology, 1971; D of Ministry, Fuller Theol. Sem., 1988. Ordination Crescent-Bay Bapt. Assn., CA, 1968. Pastor Internat. Bible Ch., LA, 1972—. Pres. Christ Bible Coll., LA, 2001—. Mem.: Am. Assn. Christian Counselors (charter). Office Phone: 213-382-7925.

OH, MYOUNGHO, computer scientist, educator; b. Pusan, South Korea, Dec. 11, 1960; s. Suntae Oh and Bokcheol Baek; m. Kyungyoon Shim, Aug. 27, 1989; children: Hyunju, Hyunwoo. BS, Korea Mil. Acad., Seoul, 1984; MS, Oreg. State U., Corvallis, 1988; PhD, KAIST, Taejon, 1996. Chmn. dept. comp sci Korea Mil. Acad., 2000—04, assoc. prof. computer sci., prof. info. sci. Asst. mgr. acad. bd. Korea Mil. Acad., Seoul, 1990—91, asst. dir. computer ctr., 1997—98, dir. ednl. development, 2005—06; planning mgr. Hwarangdae Rsch. Inst., 2006—07. Author: (books) Introduction to Computer Science, Improvement of Computer Efficiency, Differential Equation, Computer Network, C Language, Practical Use of Computers, Computer Science; contbr. articles to profl. jours. Lt. col. South Korea Mil. Decorated True Soldier of Yr. Korean Army; recipient Honor Prize, Prime Min. of Korea, 1984, Edn. award, Korea Mil. Acad., 2001, Best Achievement Prof. award, 2002, 2003, 2006. Mem.: Korea Info. Soc., Korea Inst. of Mil. Sci. and Tech., Korea Math. Soc. Buddhism. Avocations: running, swimming. Office: Korea Mil Acad Dept Electronics & Info

Nowon Gu PO Box 77 Gongneung Dong Seoul 139-799 Republic of Korea Office Phone: 02 2197 2877. Business E-Mail: mhoh@kma.ac.kr.

OH, ROBERT, physician; BA, Boston U., 1993; MD, 1998; MPH, U. Wash., 2004. Commd. 2d. lt. US Army, 1998, advanced through grades to maj.; faculty devel. fellow Madigan Army Med. Ctr., Tacoma, 2003—05; asst. program dir. family medicine Tripler Army Med. Ctr., Honolulu. Maj. US Army, 1998—2007. Mem.: Am. Acad. Family Physicians.

OH, SANDRA, actress; b. Nepean, Ont., Can., July 20, 1971; m. Alexander Payne, Jan. 1, 2003 (div. Dec. 21, 2006). Actor: (films) Double Happiness, 1994, Bean, 1997, The Princess Diaries, 2001, Big Fat Liar, 2002, Full Frontal, 2002, Long Life, Happiness & Prosperity, 2002, Rick, 2003, Under the Tuscan Sun, 2003, Break a Leg, 2003, Wilby Wonderful, 2004, Sideways, 2004 (Screen Actors Guild Award, outstanding performance by cast in motion picture, 2005), 8 Minutes to Love, 2004, Hard Candy, 2005, Break a Leg, 2005, Cake, 2005, 3 Needles, 2005, Sorry, Haters, 2005, The Night Listener, 2006, For Your Consideration, 2006; (TV series) Arli$$, 1996—2002 (CableACE Award, 1997), Grey's Anatomy, 2005— (Best Performance by an Actress in a Supporting Role in a Series, Mini-Series or Motion Picture Made for TV, Hollywood Fgn. Press Assn. (Golden Globe), 2006, Outstanding Performance by a Female Actor in a Drama Series, Screen Actors Guild award, 2006, Outstanding Performance by an Ensemble in a Drama Series, SAG, 2007); (TV miniseries) Further Tales of the City, 2001. *

OH, SANGYOON, research scientist; b. Seoul, Republic of Korea, July 7, 1971; s. Choonjae Oh and Sunmin Park. BS in Engring., Sungkyunkwan U., Seoul, Republic of Korea, 1994; MS, Syracuse U., NY, 1999; PhD, Ind. U., Bloomington, 2006. Project engr. Hansol Paper Co., Seoul, Republic of Korea, 1995—96; rsch. asst. NE Parallel Archs. Ctr. Syracuse U., 1999—2000; rsch. asst. computational sci. and info. tech. Fla. State U., Tallahassee, 2000—01; rsch. asst. cmty. grids lab. Ind. U., Bloomington, 2001—06; rsch. scientist SK Telecom, Seoul, Republic of Korea, 2006—. Contbr. articles to profl. jours. V.p. young adult group Korean United Meth. Ch., Bloomington, 2003—04, youth min., 2005—06. Pvt., 1991, Republic of Korea Mil. Grad. Rsch. scholar, Syracuse U., 1999—2000, Fla. State U., 2000—01, Ind. U., 2001—06. Mem.: IEEE. Achievements include design of handheld flexible representation architecture for web service on mobile devices; development of handheld message service for light weight messaging on mobile devices; tango interactive collaboration system; research in collaboration framework for universal accessibility. Avocations: golf, tennis, history. Office: SK Telecom SK T-Tower 11 Euljiro2-ga, Jung-gu Seoul Republic of Korea 100-999 Business E-Mail: oh_sangyoon@nate.com.

OH, SEONGSHIK, physicist, researcher; b. Republic of Korea, May 31, 1970; BS with honors, Seoul Nat. U., Korea, 1992, MS, 1994; PhD, U. Ill., Urbana, 2003. Rsch. assoc. NIST, Boulder, Colo., U. Ill., 2003—04. 1st lt. Korean Air Force, 1994—97, Korea. Recipient Outstanding Poster Presentation award, Dept. of Commerce, 2006; Academic Excellence scholarship, Bosung-Oh Scholarship Found., 1988-1990, Seoul Nat. U., 1990-1992, Ambassadorial scholarship, Rotary Internat. Found., 1997-2000. Achievements include development of first epitaxial qubit with a single-crystal tunnel barrier; invention of first microfabricated doping control scheme for mixed-valent metal oxides; discovery of unconventional superconductor-insulator transition in cuprates. Office: NIST Quantum Devices Group 81703 325 Broadway Boulder CO 80305 Home Phone: 303-261-5584; Office Phone: 303-497-4655. Office Fax: 303-497-4311. Business E-Mail: seongshik@gmail.com.

OH, SOOJIN SUSAN, elementary school educator; b. Seoul, July 7, 1980; d. Hyun Kyung and Eunsim Oh. BA summa cum laude, U. Pa., Phila., 2003, MS in Edn., 2004; doctoral candidate in Edn., Harvard Grad. Sch. Edn., Cambridge, Mass., 2007—. Cert. tchr. elem. edn. Pa. Info. tech. asst. mgr. Coll. Ho. Computing, U. Pa., Phila., 1999—2003; acad. and career advisor U. Pa., Phila., 2000—03; product mgmt. intern Chubb Group of Ins. Cos., Washington, 2001; pub. svc. intern Korean Am. Coalition, Washington, 2001; tchg. asst. Wharton Sch., U. Pa., Phila., 2002—03; strategic mktg. intern Toyota Motor Corp., Torrance, Calif., 2002; rsch. analyst U. Pa. Grad. Sch. Edn., Phila., 2004; head tchr. grade 1 Abington Friends Sch., Jenkintown, Pa., 2004—; ednl. cons. Laurus Enterprise, Seoul, 2005. Mem. math curriculum planning and devel. com. Abington Friends Sch., Jenkintown, Pa., 2004—, mem. acad. planning com., 2004—, internat. intern liaison; ethnographer Hist. Soc. Pa., Phila., 2004; transl., interpreter interviews, press confs., articles; fellow Klingenstein Summer Inst., Columbia U., 2006; presenter in field. Editor rev. bd.: Urban Edn. Jour.; editl. bd. Dear Theopilus Newsletter; contbr. articles to profl. jours. Local area coord. Habitat for Humanity, Reseda, Calif., 1995—99; liaison Tree People, Beverly Hills, 1995—99; chpt. mem. UNICEF, Phila., 2003—; curriculum developer Quo Vadis West Philly Edn. Outreach Program, Phila., 2004—; vol. nursery, maternity, oncology, pediat., newborn ICU Valley Presbyn. Hosp., Van Nuys, Calif., 1993—99; liaison Salvation Army, Canoga Park, Calif., 1995—99; pub. svc. intern Korean Am. Coaltion, Washington, 2001—; women's ministry, small group ministry leader Emmanuel Ch. in Phila., 1999—; pianist, ministry dir., youth group pres. Calvary Presbyn. Ch., Granada Hills, Calif., 1992—99. Recipient Korean Am. Student Leader of the Yr. award, Korean Heritage Found., Nat. Leadership and Svc. award, USAA Ednl. Found., 1997, Nat. Math. award, U.S. Acade. Achievement, 1997, Nat. Prudential Leadership award, Prudential Fin., 1998, Leadership award, Korean Sr. Citizens Mut. Club, 2001; fellow, Columbia U. Tchrs. Coll., 2000, Roothbert Fund, 2007; grantee, Samuel S. Fels Fund, 2004, U. Pa. Grad. Sch. of Edn., 2004; scholar, Boston U., 1999, UCLA Chancellor, 1999, UCLA Alumni Assn., 1999, U. Calif. Berkeley Regents, 1999, Korean Am. Scholarship Found., 2000, 2001, 2002, 2003, 2004, Korea Times, 2000, 2002, Central Daily News, 2001, Ca. Golden State; All Am. scholarship, USAA Ednl. Found., 1996, Toyota Cmty. scholarship, Toyota Motor U.S.A., 1999—2003, Tylenol Cmty. scholarship, Johnson & Johnson, 1999, Nat. AP scholar, Edn. Testing Svcs., 1999, Penn Alumni scholarship, U. Pa., 1999—2003, Nat. Merit Commended scholar, Edn. Testing Svcs., 1999, Korean Ambassadorial scholarship, Embassy of Republic of Korea, 2003, Scott Kyungmo Kim Scholarship, 2004. Mem.: North Am. Reggio Emilia Alliance (assoc.), Nat. Assn. for Edn. of Young Children (assoc.), Key Club Internat. (life; pres., v.p., dist. rep. 1995—99, Kiwanis Internat. Cmty. Leadership award 1999, Disting. Leader of the Yr. award 1995), Kiwanis (pres. local chpt. Key Club 1995—99), Pi Gamma Mu (life), Ephebian Honor Soc. (life), Golden Key Internat. Honor Soc. (life; pres. 2002—03), Psi Chi (life; pres., v.p., fin. dir. 2000—03). Achievements include research in educational policy, research and practice across K-12 schools and higher education institutions in China; key factors that facilitate effortless recall, accuracy and memory retention for simple multiplication; historical, cultural, and sociopolitical forces that have shaped the West Philadelphia neighborhood; featured in various newspapers such as: LA Times, Korea Times, Dong-A Daily News, Central Daily News. Avocations: photography, travel, interior design, literature, classical concerts. Office: Abington Friends Sch 575 Washington Ln Jenkintown PA 19046 Office Phone: 215-886-4350.

OH, SO-RYEOK, research scientist; b. Pusan, Republic of Korea, Nov. 20, 1970; arrived in U.S., 2001; s. Kum-Soon Jeon; m. Hyun-Ju Kim, Jan. 9, 1999; children: Hyoung-In, Joseph Soo-in. BS, Pusan Nat. U., 1997, MS, 1999; PhD, U. of Del., Newark, 2006. Rsch. assoc. Samsung, Changwon, Republic of Korea, 2000—01; rsch. asst. U. Del., Newark, 2001—06; rsch. fellow real time and advanced control engring. lab., dept. naval archtl. and marine engring. U. Mich., Ann Arbor, 2006—. Vis. scholar Australian Def. Force Acad., Canberra, Australia, 2004. Contbr. articles to profl. jours. Univ. campus leadership The Navigators, Pusan, 1990—93. Recipient Competitive Grad. fellowship, U. of Del., 2005—06, Rsch. Assistantship, 2002—05, Tchg. Assistantship, 2001—02, NSF Travel Award for IEEE Internat. Conf. on Robotics and Automation, Barcelona, Spain, 2005; grantee NSF Exch. Rsch. Grant, U. of NSW, ADFA, Australia, 2004. Mem.: ASME (Student Travel award for Am. Control Conf. 2005, ASME-DSCD Student Travel grants for 2004 ASME Internat. Mech. Engring. Congress and R&D Expo 2004), IEEE. Achievements include design of in-house 6DOF Cable Suspended Robot; flapping wing flying robots; research in dynamic modeling and robust controller design of a two-stage parallel cable robot; cable suspended planar robots with redundant cables: controllers with positive tensions; dual stage planar cable robot: dynamic modeling and design of a robust Controller with positive inputs; Feasible Workspace of a Set Point Controller for a Cable Suspended Robot with Input Constraints and Disturbances; computationally efficient feasible set points generation and control of a cable robot; optimum vessel performance in evolving wave fields: path following and motion control. Office: U Mich Marine Sys Lab 131 NAME Bldg 2600 Draper Rd Ann Arbor MI 48109-2145 Home: 1221 McIntyre St Ann Arbor MI 48105 Office Phone: 302-384-3929. Office Fax: 734-936-8820. Personal E-mail: soryeok@yahoo.com.

OH, TAI KEUN, business educator, consultant; b. Seoul, Korea; came to U.S., 1958, naturalized, 1969; BA, Seijo U., 1957; MA, No. Ill. U., 1961; MLS, U. Wis., 1965, PhD, 1970; m. Gretchen Brenneke, Dec. 26, 1964; children: Erica, Elizabeth, Emily. Asst. prof. mgmt. Roosevelt U., Chgo., 1969-73; assoc. prof. Calif. State U., Fullerton, 1973-76, prof. mgmt., 1976—2001; prof. mgmt. emeritus, 2001—; vis. prof. U. Hawaii, 1983-84, 86, U. Nuertingen, Germany, 1996-97, 99; advisor Pacific Asian Mgmt. Inst., U. Hawaii; internat. referee Asia-Pacific Jour. Mgmt., 1990—; cons. Calty Design Rsch., Inc. subs. Toyota Motor Corp.; guest lectr. Chiba U. Commerce, Japan; cons., spkr. in field. Named Outstanding Prof., Sch. Bus. Adminstrn. and Econs., Calif. State U., Fullerton, 1976, 78. Tai Keun Oh received early tenure and jump promotion to full professor in 1976 before completing the regular probationary period at California State University Fullerton, which is regarded as one of the more rapid promotions in the California State University system. He helped over 100 organizations solve complex human resource and management problems over the course of his career and has served as consultant to Calty Design Research, one of Toyota Motor Corporation's think tanks, for over 25 years. Grandfather, Cung Sun Oh, was the first Western trained medical doctor in Korea; he came to the United States in 1902 to begin his education at Center College of Kentucky and completed his medical training at the University of Louisville in 1909. In Korea, he founded a Presbyterian church and high school in Kunsan and then pioneered in the area of social services by establishing Kyungsan orphanage in 1919 and a home for the elderly. In Seoul, he became associated with Severance Hospital and Yonsei University Medical School and eventually became its Korean president. He died at 85 as one of the most respected men in Korea. NSF grantee, 1968-69, recipient Exceptional Merit Svc. award Calif. State U., 1984, Meritorious Performance and Profl. Promise award Calif. State U., 1987. Editl. bd. Acad. Mgmt. Rev., 1978-81; contbg. author: Ency. Profl. Mgmt., 1978, Handbook of Management 1985; contbr. articles to profl. jours.; Mem. Acad. Mgmt Home: 2044 E Eucalyptus Ln Brea CA 92821-5911 E-mail: toh@fullerton.edu.

OH, WILLIAM, physician; b. The Philippines, May 22, 1931; came to U.S., 1958, naturalized, 1970; s. Bun Kun and Chay Suat (Lim) Oh; m. Mary Oh, June 4, 1960; children: Kenneth Albert, Kerstin Amy. MD, U. Santo Tomas, Phillipines, 1958; MA (hon.), Brown U., 1974; DSc (hon.), R.I. Coll., 1985. Diplomate Am. Bd. Pediatrics, Am. Bd. Neonatal Perinatal Medicine. Intern Deaconess Hosp., Milw., 1958-59; resident in pediatrics Michael Reese Hosp., Chgo., 1959-63; fellow in neonatology Kavolinska Inst., Stockholm, 1963-65; dir. neonatology Michael Reese Hosp., Chgo., 1965-69; dir. neonatology, assoc. prof. pediatrics UCLA, 1969-73, prof., 1973-74; prof. pediatrics and obstetrics Brown U., Providence, 1974-88, Sylvia Kay Hassenfeld prof. pediatrics, chmn. dept., 1989—2003; pediatrician-in-chief Women and Infants Hosp. of R.I., Providence, 1974—89, R.I. Hosp.; prof., chmn. dept. pediatrics Brown U., 1989—2003; prof. pediat. Women and Infants' Hosp., Brown U., 2003—. Mem. NIH study sect. on human embryology and devel., chmn., 1985-93; mem. pediatric test com. Bd. Med. Exam., 1985-89; mem. sub-bd. of neonatal-perinatal medicine Am. Bd. Pediatrics, 1982-88; chair com. on Fetus and Newborn, Am. Acad. Pediatrics; mem. Nat. Adv. Coun. for Child Health, 1995-99. Author book in field; contbr. chpts. to books, numerous articles to profl. jours.; editor profl. jour. Adv. com. Nat. Found. of March of Dimes. NIH grantee. Mem. Am. Pediatric Soc., Am. Acad. Pediatrics (fetus and newborn com. 1986-90), Soc. Pediatric Research, Perinatal Research Soc. (pres. 1981), Am. Inst. Nutrition, Fedn. Am. Socs. Exptl. Biology. Roman Catholic. Home: 24 Robbins Dr Barrington RI 02806-2612 Office: Dudley Providence RI 02905-4923 Office Phone: 401-274-1100. Business E-Mail: woh@wihri.org.

O'HAGAN, JAMES JOSEPH, lawyer; b. Chgo., Dec. 29, 1936; s. Francis James and Florence Agnes (Dowgialo) O'H.; m. Suzanne Elizabeth Wiegand, June 28, 1958; children: Timothy, Karen, Peggy, Kevin. B in Commerce, De Paul U., 1958, JD, 1962. Sr. ptnr. O'Hagan Spencer, Chgo., 2006—. Mem. Cook County Pres.'s Com. on the Cts. for the 21st Century, chmn. suburban subcom., 1998—2000; lawyer Chgo. Claim Mgrs. Assn., 1992—2006; chmn. USLaw Network, Inc., 2001—03, mem. exec. com., 2001—06; founding mem. Profl. Lines Atty. Network. Mem. ABA, Ill. Bar Assn. Chgo. Bar Assn., Am. Bd. Trial Advocates, Internat. Assn. Def. Coun., Def. Rsch. Inst., Profl. Liability Underwriters Soc. Roman Catholic. Avocations: golf, tennis, physical conditioning, painting, reading. Office: O'Hagan Spencer 55 W Wacker Dr Ste 1400 Chicago IL 60601 Home Phone: 847-292-1266; Office Phone: 312-422-6121. Business E-Mail: johagan@ohaganspencer.com.

O'HAGAN, WILLIAM D., metal products manufacturing executive; Grad., Rutgers U., Harvard U. V.p., gen. mgr. NIBCO Inc.; with Cambridge-Lee Industries, Phelps Dodge Copper Products Co.; pres., COO Mueller Industries, Memphis, 1992—94, pres., CEO, 1994—. Office: Mueller Industries Inc 8285 Tournament Dr Ste 150 Memphis TN 38125 *

O'HALLORAN, THOMAS ALPHONSUS, JR., retired physicist, retired researcher; b. Bklyn., Apr. 13, 1931; s. Thomas Alphonsus Sr. and Nora (Sheehan) O'H.; m. Barbara Joyce Hug, June 4, 1954; children: Theresa Joyce, Maureen Ann, Kevin Thomas, Patrick Joseph. Student, San Jose State U., 1948-50; BS in Physics & Math., Oreg. State U., 1953, MS in Physics, 1954; PhD, U. Calif., Berkeley, 1963. Rsch. asst. Lawrence Berkeley Lab., U. Calif., 1963-64; rsch. fellow Harvard U., Cambridge, Mass., 1964-66; asst. prof. physics U. Ill., Urbana, 1966-68, assoc. prof., 1968-70, prof., 1970-93, prof. emeritus, 1993—; vis. scholar U. Utah, Salt Lake City, 1990-93, rsch. prof. physics, 1993-97; ret., 1997. Vis. scientist Lawrence Berkeley Lab., U. Calif., 1979-80. Contbr. numerous articles on elem. particle physics to profl. jours. Lt. USNR, 1954-58. Guggenheim fellow, 1979-80. Fellow Am. Phys. Soc. Home: 4614 Ledgemont Dr Holladay UT 84124-4735 Personal E-mail: tomohal@comcast.net.

OHAMA, GARY LOUIS, dental ceramist; b. Abington, Pa., Dec. 9, 1948; s. Benjamin Saburo and Kuniko Hirokawa Ohama; 1 child from previous marriage, Jennifer Suzanne. BS, Pa. State U., 1971. Owner, ceramist Ohama Dental Studio, Inc., Abington, 1973—91; finisher Nakashima Woodworkers, New Hope, Pa., 2000—02; dental ceramist Ft. Washington (Pa.) Dental Lab., 2002—. Cons., lectr. on dental ceramics N.Y. Dental Lab. Congress, Dentsply Internat., Ney Co., Sterngold, Colo., others. Aikido instr. Served with USAR, 1971—77. Recipient Outstanding Alumni award, Pa. State U., 1982. Methodist. Achievements include development of internal translucency and effects of refractive index in dental ceramics; of special oil, and oil/polyurethane wood finishing processes; research in breath dynamics and biomechanical movements and body functions; effects of breathing and spinal cord alignment on bio-mechanical performance. Avocation: Aikido instructor. Home: 207 Quigley Ave Willow Grove PA 19090 Office Phone: 215-628-4944.

OHANIAN, BERNARD JAY, writer, editor; b. Tokyo, Apr. 22, 1956; came to U.S., 1956; s. Abraham Sam and Bernadine Jeanette (Preis) O.; m. Catharine Greta Vollmer, July 2, 1983 (div. 1990); m. Kathleen Karen Kelly, Aug. 14, 1994; children: Rafael Kelly, Sofia Kelly. Student, U. Degli Studi, Pisa, Italy, 1977-78; BA, U. Calif., Berkeley, 1980. Editor Newsfront Internat., Oakland, Calif., 1978-81; editor-in-chief Mediafile, San Francisco, 1981-83; corr. RKO Radio, Rome, 1983-84; English lang. editor Inter Press Svc., Rome, 1983-84; sr. editor Rip N Read News Svc., San Francisco, 1984-85, Mother Jones mag., San Francisco, 1985-88; sr. editor, features MacWeek mag., San Francisco, 1988-89; editl. dir. RX Media Publs., Sausalito, Calif., 1989-90; mem. editl. staff Nat. Geographic mag., Washington, 1992-95, editl. dir. internat. edits. to assoc. editor, 1995—2006; editl. dir. AARP Publications. Freelance editl. cons., 1990—; vis. faculty mem. Sch. of Journalism U. Calif., Berkeley, 1990. Author (books) Baseball in America, 1991, A Day in the Life of Italy, 1990; editor (books) The Power to Heal, 1990, A Day in the Life of Ireland, 1991; caption writer (book) In Pursuit of Ideas, 1992; editorial cons., caption writer: The Face of Mercy, 1993. Bd. dirs. Media Alliance, San Francisco, 1986-93, pres., 1988-92. Recipient Best Feature Article award Western Publs. Assn., 1990. Mem. Am. Soc. Mag. Editors, U. Calif. Berkeley Alumni Assn. (life). Avocations: travel, basketball, photography, current affairs, opera. Office: AARP Publications 601 E St NW Washington DC 20049 Office Phone: 202-434-6804. Personal E-mail: bernardohanian@aol.com.

OHANIAN, MIHRAN JACOB, nuclear engineer, educator, dean, researcher; b. Istanbul, Turkey, Aug. 7, 1933; came to U.S., 1956, naturalized, 1967; s. Mark and Mary Catherine (Sayabalian) O.; m. Sandra Jean Blair, Apr. 22, 1962; children: Heather Jean Allen, Holly Lynn Welty. BSE.E. with high honors, Robert Coll. Engring. Sch., Istanbul, 1956; M.E.E., Rensselaer Poly. Inst., 1960, PhD in Nuclear Engring. and Sci., 1963. Lectr. nuclear engring. Rensselaer Poly. Inst., 1963, instr., 1958-62; asst. prof. nuclear engring. U. Fla., Gainesville, 1964-67, assoc. prof., 1967-70, prof., 1970-2001, prof. emeritus, 2001—, chmn. dept., 1969-79, assoc. dir. Engring. and Indsl. Expt. Sta., 1977-99, assoc. dean for rsch., 1979-90, assoc. dean for adminstrn. and planning, 1990-91, assoc. dean for rsch. and adminstrn., 1991-98, interim v.p. rsch., dean of grad. sch., 1998-99, pres. Rsch. Found., 1998-99, interim dean Coll. of Engr., assoc. v.p. Engring. and Indsl. Experiment Station, 1999-2001; sabbatical leave Inst. Energy Analysis, Oak Ridge, 1976-77, on assignment, 1977-78. Cons. Fla. Power Corp., Batelle Meml. Inst., Fla. Nuc. Assocs., Oak Ridge Nat. Lab., Inst. Energy Analysis, Argonne Nat. Lab., Savannah River Lab., U. Va., Tex. Higher Edn. Bd., NSF; U. Fla. rep. U.S. Nuc. Energy Inst., 1972-2001, mem. adv. coun., 1972-80; U. Fla. rep. to Oak Ridge Assoc. Univs., 1972-76; mem. engring. accreditation commn. Accreditation Bd. Engring. and Tech., 1984-88; mem. rev. com. reactor analysis and safety divsn. Argonne Nat. Lab, 1982-88, chmn. 1986-87, mem. rev. com. reactor engring. divsn., 1992-2001; mem. adv. com. Consol. Fuel Reprocessing Program Oak Ridge Nat. Lab., 1982-88; mem. com. on univ. rsch. reactors Energy Engring. Bd., NRC, 1986-88; mem. U.S. Dept. Energy's Adv. Com. on Nuc. Facility Safety (ACNFS), 1988-90; bd. dirs., chmn. Fla. Inst. Phosphate Rsch., 1990-2001. Contbr. articles to profl. jours. Trustee Fla. Defenders of the Environment, 1969-71, treas., 1969-70, mem., 1969—80. Recipient valor medal Am. Legion, 1966, Disting. Faculty award Fla. Blue Key, 1984; Alumnus fellow Rensselaer Poly. Inst., 1994. Fellow AAAS, Am. Nuclear Soc. (v.p., pres.-elect 1989-90, pres. 1990-91, bd. dirs. 1974-77, 84-93, vice chmn., chmn. edn. divsn. 1975-76, exec. com. nuc. fuel cycle divsn. 1978-81, mem. profl. devel. and accreditation com., chmn. tech. program internat. conf. Washington, 1980, mem. nominating com., 1980-81, 87-88, chmn., 1991-92, exec. com., 1986-92, honors and awards com. 1997—, chmn. 2004—07, Exceptional Svc. award 1980, adv. editor Nuclear Sci. and Engring. Jour. 1989— hon. chmn. ann. conf. 1997, hon. chmn. 10th Internat. Conf. on Robotics, 2004), Engr. Coun. Profl. Devel. (dir. 1976-78), Am. Assn. Engring. Soc. (awards com. 1985-86, bd. dir. 1990-91, exec. com. 1990-95, sec.-treas., 1992, chair-elect 1993, chair 1994, chair nominating com. 1995, chair awards com. 1996), Am. Soc. Engring. Edn. (adv. com. Ford Found. Resident Fellow Program 1971-79, sec.-treas. nuc. engring. divsn. 1981-82, vice chmn. 1982-83, chmn. 1983-84, projects bd. 1981-87, chmn. awards com. 1985-87); mem. Nat. Audubon Soc. (pres. 1965-66), Ret. Faculty U. Fla. Inc. (pres. 2004—05), Rotary (Paul Harris fellow), Sigma Xi, Tau Beta Pi (eminent engr.), Alpha Nu Sigma (pres. 1981-83), Eta Kappa Nu, Phi Kappa Phi, Epsilon Lambda Chi. Presbyterian. Home: 6095 Twin Lakes Rd Keystone Heights FL 32656-9728 Business E-Mail: johanian@ufl.edu.

OHANJANIAN, RUZANNA, clinical psychologist; d. Vladimir and Nina Ohanjanian; 1 child, Irene Gyulnazarian. BA in Linguistics & Lit. with honors, Leninakan Ednl. Inst., 1977; MA in Psychology, Yerevan P. State U., 1981; PhD, Moscow Acad. Scis., 1985; postdoctoral, U. San Francisco Med. Ctr., 1996. Cert. trauma specialist, Traumatic Incident Reduction Calif., 1991, lic. clin. psychologist Bd. Psychology, Calif., 1999. Clin. psychologist Dept. Pub. Health, San Francisco, 1998—2002, Family Svcs., Palo Alto, Calif., 1998—2002, Multilingual Psychology Cons., Mountain View, Calif., 1996—98, UCSF Med. Ctr., Mt. Zion Hosp., San Francisco. Nat. disaster team mem. Min. Health, Armenia, 1989—91; assoc. prof. Yerevan State U., Armenia, 1990—92, vis. prof., 1992; presenter State of World Forum, San Francisco, 1997; crisis mgmt. team mem. Family Enterprise Internat. Behavioral Health, 1999—. Contbr. over 30 publs. and presentations in field. Chmn. Irene Gyulnazarian Ednl. Fund for Armenia, Los Gatos, Calif., 2003—. Named Hon. Dr., Yerevay State U., 2005; recipient Appreciation award, FEI Behavioral Health, 2000, Alaska Airlines, 2000, Make a Difference award, Total Employee Assistance and Mgmt. Inc., 2002, Employee Assistance Program Appreciation award, Pacific Care Behavioral Health. Mem.: APA, Armenian Profl. Soc. Avocations: painting, piano. Office: Ohanjanian Ruzanna POBox 320652 Los Gatos CA 95032 Home Phone: 408-379-6565. Personal E-mail: irachka2@hotmail.com.

O'HANLON, NANCYANNE, school librarian, educator; b. Chgo., Apr. 8, 1947; d. Irvin Walter and Edith Mary Nielsen; m. Timothy Patrick O'Hanlon, Aug. 24, 1968; 1 child, Matthew Aron. BA, So. Meth. U., 1968; MS in Libr. and Info. Sci., U. of Ill., 1983. Reference libr. Ohio State U. Librs., Columbus, Ohio, 1983—92; assoc. dir. Eisenhower Nat. Clearinghouse for Math. and Sci. Edn., Columbus, 1992—95; prof. Ohio State U. Librs., 1996—, instrn. libr., 1996—. Owner FoolProof Solutions Digital Pub., Columbus, 1995—2005. Recipient Web Access award, Ohio State U. Partnership Grant, 2001. Mem.: ALA (ref. adult svcs. divsn. 1989—90). Achievements include development of net.TUTOR (Online Instructional Program). Office: Ohio State University Libraries 1858 Neil Avenue Mall Columbus OH 43210 Home Phone: 614-299-0177. Business E-Mail: ohanlon.1@osu.edu.

OHANNESSIAN, HARRY HAROUTUNE, travel agency executive; b. Jerusalem, Jan. 5, 1919; s. Ohannes and Heripsimeh (Soultanian) C.; m. Eva Hamparsoumian, July 7, 1946 (div. Mar. 1978); children: John, Robert; m. Beatriz Araujo, Dec. 19, 1984. Matriculation, Brit. Govt., 1938; grad., London Sch. of Maths., 1940, London Sch. of Econ. Scis., 1942. Pres.

Cedars Travel, Inc., NYC, 1963—; chmn. Wataniyah Corp., NYC, 1973-88; v.p. U.S.-Arab C. of C., NYC, 1973-88; internat. commerce and bus. cons. to the middle east Stony Brook, N.Y., 1989—. Cons. in field. Decorated Knight (Order of St. John). Mem. St. George's Golf and Country Club, Stony Brook Club. Republican. Mem. Christian Ch. Avocations: tennis, swimming, gardening, music. Home: 9 Hillside Rd Stony Brook NY 11790-1002 Office: PO Box 120 Stony Brook NY 11790-0120 Office Phone: 718-446-4152.

O'HARA, CATHERINE, actress, comedienne; b. Toronto, Mar. 4, 1954; m. Bo Welch, 1992; children: Dylan, Matthew. Actress: films include After Hours, 1985, Heartburn, 1986, Beetlejuice, 1988, Dick Tracy, 1990, Betsy's Wedding, 1990, Home Alone, 1990, Little Vegas, 1990, There Goes The Neighborhood, 1992, Home Alone II: Lost In New York, 1992, (voice) The Nightmare Before Christmas, 1993, The Paper, 1994, Wyatt Earp, 1994, A Simple Twist of Fate, 1994, Tall Tale, 1995, Waiting for Guffman, 1996, The Last of the high Kings, 1996, (voice) Pippi Longstocking, 1997, Home Fries, 1998, The Life Before This, 1999, Surviving Christmas, 2004, Lemony Snicket's A Series of Unfortunate Events, 2004, Game 6, 2005, (voice) Chicken Little, 2005, (voice) Over the Hedge, 2006, Monster House, 2006, Penelope, 2006, For Your Consideration, 2006 (Best Supporting Actress Nat. Bd. Review, 2006); (TV films) The Last Polka, 1985, Hope, 1997, Late Last Night, 1999, The Wool Cap, 2004, (TV series) SCTV, 1976-1979 (Emmy award), Coming Up Rosie, 1976-77, The Steve Allen Comedy Hour, 1980, SCTV Network 90, 1981-82, (voice) Committed, 2001; dir.: (TV series) Dream On, 1990-96; writer Really Weird Tales, 1987; TV guest appearances The Simpsons Show, The Larry Sanders Show, 1992, The Outer Limits, 1995. *

O'HARA, JOHN PATRICK, lawyer, consultant; b. NYC, Jan. 11, 1930; s. Thomas James and Anne (Henry) O'H.; m. Mary Ann Leavey, Oct. 15, 1955; children: Ann O'Hara Carroll, Kathleen O'Hara Geary, Maureen O'Hara-Padden. BBA in Acctg., St. John's U., NYC, 1952; JD, U. Balt., 1960. Bar: Md. 1960. Acct. Am. Cyanamid Corp., 1954—55; spl. agt. FBI, 1955-62; chief counsel, staff dir. emeritus subcom. on investigations and oversight Com. on Pub. Works and Transp., Ho. of Reps., Washington, 1962-86; dir. corp. security Flying Tiger Ln., LA, 1986-89; ptnr. Burgess & O'Hara, Upper Marlboro, Md., 1990-91; cons. Legal Svcs. Corp., Washington, 1990-91, pres., 1991-94; cons., 1994—. 1st lt. USMC, 1952-1960. Decorated Nat. Def. Svc. medal, UN medal, Korean Svc. medal. Mem. Md. Bar Assn., Bolling AFB Officers Club, Marines Meml. Assn., Am. Legion. Home: 5904 Mount Eagle Dr Apt 911 Alexandria VA 22303-2539 also: 4490 Vincitor St Las Vegas NV 89135 E-mail: johnpohara@aol.com.

O'HARA, JOHN PAUL, III, orthopedic surgeon; b. Detroit, June 10, 1946; m. Randy Baird, Mar. 11, 1987; children: Riley Anne, Nolan Baird, Evan John. BA, U. Mich., Ann Arbor, 1968, MD, 1972. Resident U. Va. Med. Ctr., Charlottesville, 1973-77; fellow Nuffield Orthopaedic Ctr., Oxford, Eng., 1977; practice medicine specializing in orthopaedic surgery Southfield, 1978—; staff Providence Hosp., Southfield, Mich., 1978—, pres. elect med. staff, 1990, pres. med. staff, 1991; sect. chief orthopedics; pres. Porretta Orthopedic Ctr., 1996—, med. dir., 2001—; pres. Providence Med. Group. Pres. Providence Hosp. Med. Staff Research Found., 1984-85, bd. dirs., 1982—; bd. dirs. Mich. Master Health Plan, Southfield, 1982. Contbr. articles to profl. jours. Pres. Birmingham (Mich.) Little League Baseball. Recipient Disting. Alumni award Brother Rice High Sch., 1986. Fellow Am. Acad. Orthopaedic Surgery, Mid Am. Orthopaedic Soc.; mem. Detroit Orthopaedic Soc., Mich. Orthopaedic Soc., Detroit Acad. Orthopaedic Surgeons (past pres.), Oakland Hills Country Club (Birmingham, Mich.), Beverly Hills (Mich.) Club. Avocations: earthwatch vol., travel, sports. Home: 627 Waddington St Bloomfield Hills MI 48301-2346

O'HARA, KEVIN J., information technology executive; Grad., Drexel U., 1983. Mgmt. staff Peter Kiewit Sons', Inc.; area mgr. Kiewit Network Tech., Inc.; v.p. network svcs. MFS Telecom.; pres. MFS Devel.; pres., CEO MFS Global Network Svcs.; COO Level 3 Comm., Inc., Broomfield, Colo., 1998—, pres., 2000—. Recipient Alumni Achievement award, Drexel U. Coll. Engring., 2001. Office: Level 3 Comm 1025 Eldorado Blvd Broomfield CO 80021 *

O'HARA, PATRICIA ANNE, dean, law educator; BA summa cum laude, Santa Clara U., 1971; JD summa cum laude, Notre Dame, 1974. Bar: Calif. 1974. Assoc. Brobeck, Phleger & Harrison, 1974—79, 1980—81; assoc. prof. law Notre Dame Law Sch., 1981, prof., 1990, v.p. student affairs, 1990—99, Joseph A. Matson dean, law educator, 1999—. Chair nominating com. Am. Assn. Law Schools, 2005—06, chair, sect. law sch. deans, 2007—. Contbr. chapters to books, articles to law jours. Mem.: Law Sch. Admissions Coun. (bd. trustees). Office: U Notre Dame 203 Law Sch PO Box 780 Notre Dame IN 46556-0780 Office Phone: 574-631-6789. Office Fax: 574-631-8400. E-mail: Patricia.A.O'Hara.3@nd.edu.

O'HARA, ROBERT SYDNEY, JR., lawyer; b. Englewood, NJ, Apr. 26, 1939; s. Robert Sydney and Katharine (Drayton) O'Hara; m. Elizabeth Crocker, June 17, 1961 (div.); children: Jennifer, Isabelle; m. Bonnie Durkin, July 19, 1975. AB, Princeton U., 1960; JD, U. Pa., 1963. Bar: N.Y. 1964. Ptnr. Milbank, Tweed, Hadley & McCloy, NYC, 1965—. Served to capt. AUS, 1963—65. Office: Milbank Tweed Hadley & McCloy 1 Chase Manhattan Plz Fl 47 New York NY 10005-1413

O'HARA, SARA MARIE, radiologist; d. John Francis and Claire Annastasia O'Hara; m. Jeffrey Brian Betts, Sept. 6, 1997; children: Sailor Delaney Betts, Sanibel Star Betts. BS, Georgetown U., Washington, 1984, MD, 1988. Diplomate Am. Bd. Radiology, 1993, CAQ pediat. radiology Am. Bd. Radiology, cert. spl. competance in nuc. medicine Am. Bd. Radiology. Chief ultrasound divsn. Cin. Children's Hosp., 2000—. Avocation: travel. Office: Cincinnati Childrens Hosp Radiology 3333 Burnet Ave MLC 5031 Cincinnati OH 45229 Office Phone: 513-636-2164.

O'HARA, THOMAS J., priest, academic administrator, educator; b. Hazleton, Pa., Mar. 16, 1949; s. Thomas John and Bridget Helen O'Hara. BA, King's Coll., Wilkes-Barre, Pa., 1971; MTh, U. Notre Dame, Ind., 1977; PhD, Am. U., Washington, 1988. Ordained priest Congregation of the Holy Cross, 1978. Relief work Missionary Sisters of Charity, Dacca, Bangladesh, 1975; prof. English Notre Dame Coll., Bangladesh, 1975; assoc. pastor Our Lady of Good Counsel, Bklyn., 1977—82; chaplain Holy Cross Hosp., Silver Springs, Md., 1982—84; adj. prof. Am. U., 1987; prof. polit. sci. Philosophical Ctr. Jinja, Uganda, 1994—96, King's Coll., 1998—, assoc. v.p. academic affairs, 1996—99, pres., 1999—. Bd. dirs. St. Mary's Day Care Ctr., Wilkes-Barre, 1999—, Pa. Campus Compact, 2001; bd. trustees Stonehill Coll., North Easton, Mass., 1998—; mem. Geisinger South Wilkes-Barre Adv. Coun., 2006—. Contbr. articles to profl. jour. Bd. dirs. Greater Wilkes-Barre Chamber of Bus. and Industry, 2001—; adv. coun. Jewish Family Svc., Wilkes-Barre, 2004; bd. dirs. Diamond City Partnership, 2002—, St. Vincent de Paul Kitchen, 1999—, Healthy NEPA Initiative, Scranton, 2004; exec. leadership coun. PreK Counts in Pa., 2006. Recipient Northeast Pa. award, Ethics Inst., 2003, Ny State award, NY State Dept. Juvenile Affairs, 1982, Ezamper award, U. Notre Dame Alumni Assn., 1997. Mem.: Pa. Soc., Delta Epsilon Sigma. Roman Catholic. Office: King s Coll 133 N River St Wilkes Barre PA 18711 Office Phone: 570-208-5899.

O'HARA, THOMAS PATRICK, managing editor; b. Phila., July 15, 1947; s. Hugh James and Agatha Mary (Gilroy) O'H.; m. Juliet Munro, 1970 (div. 1974); m. Pamela Smith, Oct. 8, 1977; children: Rachel Kathleen, Patrick Graham. BA in English, Rutgers U., 1972; MA in Communications, U. Fla., 1974. Sports reporter Gainesville SUN, 1972-74; reporter Orlando (Fla.) Sentinel, 1974-76, Daytona Beach (Fla.) News Jour., 1976-78; various editing and reporting positions Miami (Fla.) Herald, 1978-86, city editor Palm Beach ed., 1985-86; asst. met. editor Palm Beach Post, West Palm Beach, Fla., 1986-87, met. editor, 1987-88, asst. mng. editor, 1988-89, mng. editor, 1989—2000, The Plain Dealer, Cleve., 2000—. Sgt. USAF, 1969-71. Home: 8890 Spring Valley Dr Broadview Heights OH 44147-2573 Office: The Plain Dealer 1801 Superior Ave Cleveland OH 44114 E-mail: tohara@plaind.com.

O'HARE, DEAN RAYMOND, retired insurance company executive, director; b. Jersey City, June 21, 1942; s. Francis and Ann O'H.; m. Kathleen T. Walliser, Dec. 2, 1967; 2 sons, Dean, Jason. BS in Fin. Mgmt., NYU, 1963; MBA, Pace U., 1968. Underwriter trainee Chubb Corp., NYC, 1963-64, tax advisor, 1964-67, asst. v.p., mgr. corp. fin. devel., 1968-72, sr. v.p., mgr. corp. fin. devel. dept., from 1979, CFO, 1979-94, pres., 1986-88, chmn., CEO, 1988—2002, ret. Warren, 2002. Dir., chmn., audit com. Fluor Corp.; chmn. US Coun. Internat. Bus.; chmn. bd. SeaPass Solutions, HJ Heinz Corp., DFA Capital Mgmt., Proudfoot Consulting. The NJ Partnership; co-chmn. Hosp. Spl. Surgery, NYC; chmn., trustee fin. com. St. Benedict's Prep. Sch., Newark; trustee U. Dublin, Ireland, Intrepid Mus., NYC. Mem. The Links Club (N.Y.C.). Office Phone: 908-903-3565. Business E-Mail: dohare@chubb.com.

O'HARE, DENIS, actor; b. Kansas City, Mo., Jan. 17, 1962; BA, Northwestern U. Actor: (Broadway plays) Racing Demon, 1995, Cabaret, 1998, Major Barbara, 2001, Take Me Out, 2003 (Drama Desk award outstanding featured actor in a play, 2003, Tony award best featured actor in a play, 2003, Clarence Derwent award, 2003, Outer Critics Circle award, OBIE award, Village Voice, Lucille Lortel award), Assassins, 2004, Sweet Charity, 2005 (Drama Desk award outstanding featured actor in a musical, 2005), Inherit the Wind, 2007; (films) St. Patrick's Day, 1997, River Red, 1998, Sweet and Lowdown, 1999, The Anniversary Party, 2001, 21 Grams, 2003, Garden State, 2004, Heights, 2004, Derailed, 2005, Stephanie Daley, 2006, Half Nelson, 2006, The Babysitters, 2007, Michael Clayton, 2007; (TV films) St. Maybe, 1998, Hamlet, 2000, Angel, 2005, Once Upon a Mattress, 2000; (TV series) The Young Indiana Jones Chronicles, 1993, Law & Order: Special Victims Unit, 2000, 100 Centre Street, 2001, Law & Order, 1993, 1996, 1997, 2003, Justice, 2006. *

O'HARE, JAMES RAYMOND, energy executive; b. Evergreen Park, Ill., July 20, 1938; s. Raymond Clarence and Helen (Nickel) O'H.; m. Nan Jane Raleigh, Sept. 18, 1965; children: Joan, Daniel, Colleen, Patrick. BS, Marquette U., 1960; MBA, U. Calif. at Los Angeles, 1961. C.P.A., Ind., Ill., Ky., Calif., Tex. Mgr. Peat, Marwick, Mitchell & Co., Chgo., 1961-68, South Bend, Ind., 1968-69; controller Essex Internat., Inc., Fort Wayne, Ind., 1969-76, Am. Air Filter Co., Inc., Louisville, 1976-80; fin. v.p. and treas. Petrolane Inc., Long Beach, Calif., 1980-85; treas. Tex. Eastern Corp., Houston, 1985-87, v.p., treas., 1987-88; sr. v.p. fin. and adminstrn. Tex. Ea. Gas Transmission Co., Houston, 1988—89; v.p., CFO Enclean Inc., Houston, 1991—93; fin. cons., 1993—97; v.p., CFO Ascendant Healthcare Group, Inc., Houston, 1997, John March Ptnrs., Inc., Houston, 1998—2004, Sensor Microsystems, Inc., San Antonio, 2004; gen. ptnr. Connemara Ventures, LLC, The Woodlands, 2004. Controller Afras USA, Inc., 2005. Served with USNR, 1962-68. Mem. Evans Scholars, Fin. Execs. Inst., The Woodlands Country Club, Beta Gamma Sigma. Personal E-mail: johare@swbell.net.

O'HARE, JOHN MITCHELL, lawyer; b. Oak Park, Ill., Apr. 9, 1946; s. John Mitchell Jr. and Doris Margaret (Lundblad) O'h.; m. Carole Beth Silver, Jan. 6, 1985; children: Rachele Olia, Suzanna Dee. AB, U. Ill., 1967, MS in Fin., 1969; JD cum laude (hon.), Harvard U., 1971. Bar: Ill. 1971, US Dist. Ct. (no. dist.) Ill. 1971. Assoc. Sidley & Austin, Chgo., 1971-76, ptnr., 1977-85, 88—, resident ptnr. Singapore, 1985-88, ptnr. Chgo. Guest lectr. Northwestern U Law Sch. Mem. ABA, Chgo. Bar Assn., Phi Beta Kappa. Office: Sidley & Austin 1 S Dearborn Chicago IL 60603 Office Phone: 312-853-7454. Office Fax: 312-853-7036. Business E-Mail: johare@Sidley.com.

O'HARE, JOSEPH ALOYSIUS, priest, editor-in-chief, former academic administrator; b. NYC, Feb. 12, 1931; s. Joseph Aloysius and Marie Angela (Enright) O'H. AB, Berchmans Coll, Cebu City, Philippines, 1954, MA, 1955; STL, Woodstock Coll., Md., 1962; PhD, Fordham U., 1968; DHL (hon.), Fairfield U., 1980, Rockhurst Coll., Kansas City, Mo., 1984, Ateneo de Manila U., 1990, CUNY, 1991, Coll. of St. Rose, Albany, NY, 1995, St. Francis Coll., Bklyn., 1996, St. Peter's Coll., 1997, Albertus Magnus Coll., 2004; DLitt (hon.), Coll. New Rochelle, 1984; D.D. (hon.), Muhlenberg Coll., 1998; DLitt (hon.), Fordham U., 2003. Joined S.J., 1948, ordained priest Roman Cath. Ch., 1961. Instr. Ateneo de Manila U., 1955-58, prof. philosophy, 1968-72; assoc. editor Am. Mag., NYC, 1972-75, 2003—, editor-in-chief, 1975-84; pres. Fordham U., Bronx, NY, 1984—2003, Regis HS, NYC, 2004—05. Author weekly column Of Many Things (Best Original Column award Cath. Press Assn. 1976, 78, 81, 84) Office Phone: 212-581-4640. Business E-Mail: johare@fordham.edu.

O'HARE, SANDRA FERNANDEZ, education educator; b. NYC, Mar. 19, 1941; d. Ricardo Enrique and Rosario de Los Angeles (Arenas) Fernandez; m. S. James O'Hare, Oct. 12, 1963; children: James, Richard, Michael, Christopher. BA, Marymount Coll., 1962; MA, U. San Francisco, 1980. Cert. elem. and coll. tchr.; bilingual and lang. devel. specialist. Instr. adult edn., Guam, 1964-66, Spanish Speaking Ctr., Harrisburg, Pa., 1977-79; tchr. Colegio Salesiano, Rota, Spain, 1973-74, 84, Alisal Sch. Dist., Salinas, Calif., 1979—81, Liberty Sch., Petaluma, Calif., 1981-85, Cinnabar Sch., Petaluma, 1985—2005; instr. Chapman U., 1994-98; also summer migrant edn. programs, 1990-91; ret., 2005. Instr. Santa Rosa (Calif.) Jr. Coll., 1982-83; mem. math. curriculum com. Sonoma County Office Edn., Santa Rosa, 1988; mem. Summer Sci. Connections Inst., Sonoma State U., 1994, Redwood Empire Math. Acad., summer 1995; mem. Sonoma County Math Project, 1995-96; summer '96 NEH stipend to Harvard U. Translator: Isabel la Catolica, 1961. Mem. Asian relief com. ARC, Harrisburg, 1975, Boy Scouts Am., Petaluma, 1983, Mechanicsburg, Pa., 1974, Monterey, Calif., 1971, Sonoma County Adult Literacy League, 1996—. Sarah D. Barder fellow Johns Hopkins U., 1990. Mem. NEA, AAUW (chair edn. founds. com. 1985-86, 06-07), Club Hispano-Americano Petaluma (pres. 1987-89), Delta Kappa Gamma. Roman Catholic. Avocation: travel. Home: 1289 Glenwood Dr Petaluma CA 94954-4326 Personal E-mail: funsohare@yahoo.com.

OHBERG, PAMELA ANDERSON, retired high school drama educator; d. Franklin Bruce and Helen O'Neal Anderson; m. Robert Nils Ohberg, Sept. 5, 1981; children: Gunnar Franklin, Johanna Helen. Masters, Vanderbilt U., Nashville, 1974. Dancer Tenn. Dance Repertory Theatre, Nashville, 1973—76; tchr. Walton HS, Marietta, Ga., 1977—81, Lassiter HS, Marietta, 1981—2007; ret., 2007. Drama dir. Mem.: Ga. Assn. Educators, Ednl. Theatre Assn. (life), Kappa Delta Pi (life). Liberal. Methodist. Avocations: hiking, travel, reading, theater. Home Phone: 770-977-4707; Office Phone: 678-494-7863.

O'HEARN, MICHAEL JOHN, lawyer; b. Akron, Ohio, Jan. 29, 1952; s. Leo Ambrose and Margaret Elizabeth (Clark) O'H. BA in Econs., UCLA, 1975; postgrad., U. San Diego, 1977; JD, San Fernando Valley Coll. Law, 1979; postgrad., Holy Apostles Sem., 1993-94. Bar: Calif. 1979, U.S. Dist. Ct. (ctrl. dist.) Calif. 1979. Document analyst Mellonics Info. Ctr., Litton Industries, Canoga Park, Calif., 1977-79; pvt. practice Encino, Calif., 1979-80; atty. VISTA/Grey Law Inc., LA, 1980-81; assoc. Donald E. Chadwick & Assocs., Woodland Hills, Calif., 1981-84, Law Offices Laurence Ring, Beverly Hills, 1984-85; atty., in-house counsel Coastal Ins. Co., Van Nuys, Calif., 1985-89; atty. Citrus Glen Apts., Ventura, Calif., 1989-92; pvt. practice Ventura County, 1992-2000; arbitrator, 1995—; property mgr. Channel Islands Village Mgmt. Co., 1998-2000. Instr. religious edn. Santa Clara Sch., Oxnard, Calif., 2000—01. Life mem. Rep. Nat. Com. Recipient Cert. of Appreciation, Agy. for Vol. Svc., 1981, San Fernando Valley Walk for Life, 1988, Cert. of Appreciation, Arbitrator for the Superior and Mcpl. Cts., Ventura County Jud. Dist., 1996. Mem. KC, Ventura County Bar Assn., Ventura County Trial Lawyers Assn., Secular Franciscan Order., Ahern Clan/Family Assn., Irish Geneal. Soc. Internat., German-Bohemian/Heritage Soc., Calix Soc. Republican. Roman Catholic. Avocations: golf, yachting, fishing. Home: 1941 Fisher Dr Apt B Oxnard CA 93035-3022 Office: 3650 Ketch Ave Oxnard CA 93035-3029 Personal E-mail: mohearn_brightstar@yahoo.com.

O'HEARN, ROBERT RAYMOND, stage designer; b. Elkhart, Ind., July 19, 1921; s. Robert Raymond, Sr. and Ella May (Stoldt) O'H. BA, Ind. U., 1939-43; student, Art Students League, 1943-45. Designer Brattle Theatre, Cambridge, Mass., 1948-52; prof. stage design, chmn. design dept. Sch. Music Ind. U., 1989—. Instr. Studio and Forum Scenic Design, 1968-88. Stage designer: Broadway shows The Relapse, 1950, Loves Labor's Lost, 1953, Othello, Festival, 1955, The Apple Cart, Child of Fortune, 1956; asst. designer: Broadway shows Kismet, 1953, Pajama Game, 1955, My Fair Lady, 1956, West Side Story, 1958; designer: for film A Clerical Error, 1955; designer prodns. Central City Opera House, 1959-63, Opera Soc. Washington, 1958-61, L'Elisir D'Amore at Met. Opera House, 1960, Die Meistersinger, 1962, Aida, 1963; stage designer: As You Like It, Stratford, Conn., 1961, Troilus and Cressida, Stratford, 1961, Kiss Me Kate, Los Angles Civic Light Opera, 1964, N.Y.C. Center, 1965, Samson and Delila, Met. Opera, 1964, La Sylphide, Am. Ballet Theatre, 1964, Italian Symphony, 1971, Adam Cochrane, Broadway, 1964, Pique Dame, Met. Opera, 1965, La Ventana, 1966, Die Frau Ohne Schatten, 1966, Porgy and Bess, Vienna Volksoper, 1965, Bregenzer Festspiele, 1971, Otello, Boston Opera, also Hamburg State Opera, 1967, Hansel and Gretel, Met. Opera, 1967, Nutcracker Ballet, San Francisco Ballet, 1967, L.A. Ballet, 1979, La Traviata, Santa Fe Opera, 1968, Rosalinda, L.A. Civic Light Opera, 1968, Der Rosenkavalier, Met. Opera, 1969, Tallis Fantasia, N.Y.C. Ballet, 1969, Boris Godunov (unproduced), Met. Opera, 1970, Parsifal, Met. Opera, 1970, Porgy and Bess, Bregenz Festspiel, Austria, 1971, Falstaff, Marriage of Figaro, Gianni Schicci, Central City Opera House, 1972, Barber of Seville, 1973, The Enchanted, Kennedy Center, 1973, The Mind with the Dirty Man, Los Angeles, 1973, Midsummer Night's Dream, Central City Opera, 1974, Coppelia, Ballet West, 1974, Carmen, Strasbourg, 1974, The Pearl Fishers, Miami Opera, 1974, N.Y.C. Opera, 1980, Don Pasquale, Miami Opera, 1976, Scipio Africanus, Central City Opera, 1975, Swan Lake, Strasbourg, 1975, Marriage of Figaro, Met. Opera, 1975, Die Meistersinger, Karlsruhe, Germany, 1975, Girl of the Golden West, Houston Opera, 1976, N.Y.C. Opera, 1977, Vienna Staatsoper, 1976, Boris Godunov, Strasbourg, 1976, Der Rosenkavelier, Karlsruhe, 1976, Don Quixote, Ballet West, 1977, Die Meistersinger, Chgo. Lyric Opera, 1977, Adriana Lecouvreur, Miami Opera, 1978, La Boheme, 1978, Coppelia, Pacific N.W. Dance, Seattle, 1978, Andrea Chenier, N.Y.C. Opera, 1978, Der Rosenkavelier, Can. Opera Co., Toronto, 1978, Taming of the Shrew, Pa. State U., 1980, Die Fledermaus, Miami Opera, 1980, Tosca, Miami Opera, 1981, West Side Story, Bregenz Festspiel, Austria, 1981, Mich. Opera Theatre, 1985; Pique Dame, San Francisco Opera, 1982, La Traviata, Miami Opera, 1982, Of Mice and Men, Miami Opera, 1982, Carousel, Annie Get Your Gun, Miami Opera, 1984, Lucia di Lammermoor, 1984, L'Italiana in Algeri, 1985, Porgy and Bess, Met. Opera, 1985, West Side Story, Mich. Opera Theatre, 1985, Aida, Don Giovanni, Opera Colo., 1986, My Fair Lady, Mich. Opera Theatre, 1986, Samson and Delilah, Manon Lescaut Opera Colo., 1987, Annie Get Your Gun, Paper Mill Playhouse, 1987, Peter Grimes, Ind. U., 1987, Madama Butterfly, N.J. State Opera, 1990. Mem. vis. com. Costume Inst., Met. Museum. Recipient Robert L. B. Tobin award for lifetime achievement in theatrical design, 2005. Mem. United Scenic Artists. Home: 2604 E 2nd St Bloomington IN 47401-5351

O'HERN, JANE SUSAN, psychologist, educator; b. Winthrop, Mass., Mar. 21, 1933; d. Joseph Francis and Mona (Garvey) O'H. BS, Boston U., 1954, EdD, 1962; MA, Mich. State U., 1956. Instr. Mercyhurst Coll., 1954-55, Hofstra Coll., 1956-57, State Coll., Salem and Boston, 1957-60; asst. prof. Boston U., 1962-67, assoc. prof., 1967-75, prof. edn. and psychiat. (psychology), 1975-95, prof. emeritus, 1995—, chmn. dept. counseling psychology, 1972-75, 88-89, dir. mental health edn. program, 1975-81, dir. internat. edn., 1978-81, asst. v.p. internat. edn., 1981; prof. emeritus mental health and behavioral medicine program Boston U. Sch. Medicine, 2001—. Pres. ASSIST Internat., Inc., 1989—98; adv. bd, Internat. Study Cons., 1994—98; founder BettyBoston LLC, 2002—. Contbr. articles to profl. jours. Trustee Boston Ctr. Modern Psychoanalytic Studies, 1980-92. Recipient grants U.S. Office Edn., NIMH, Dept. of Def. Mem. Assn. Counselor Edn. and Suprs., Am. Counseling Assn., North Atlantic Assn. Counselor Edn. and Supervision (past pres.), Mass. Psychol. Assn., Am. Psychol. Assn., Mortar Bd., Pi Lamda Theta, Sigma Kappa, Phi Delta Kappa, Phi Beta Delta. Home: 111 Perkins St Apt 287 Boston MA 02130-4324 Office Phone: 617-414-2325. Personal E-mail: assistint@aol.com. E-mail: johern@bu.edu.

OHGA, NORIO, retired electronics executive; b. Numazu, Shizuoka, Japan, Jan. 29, 1930; s. Shoichi Ohga and Toshi Mizuno; m. Midori Matsubara, 1957. Grad., Tokyo Nat. U. Fine Arts and Music, 1953, Kunst U., Berlin, 1957; Dr hc music (hon.), Rochester U., 1996, McGill U., 1999. Cons., advisor Tokyo Tsushin Kogyo (later Sony Corp.), 1953-59; gen. mgr. tape recorder divsn., product planning divsn., indsl. design divsn. Sony Corp., Tokyo, 1959; originally trained as an opera singer; bd. dirs. Sony Corp., Tokyo, 1964-72, mng. dir., 1972-74, sr. mng. dir., 1974-76, dep. pres., 1976-82, pres., chief oper. officer, 1982-89, pres. and CEO, 1989-95, chmn. and CEO, 1995-99, chmn., rep. dir., 1999-2000, chmn. bd., 2000—03, hon. chmn., 2003—; CEO Nobuyuki Idei. Sr. mng. dir. CBS/Sony Group, Inc., 1968-70, pres., 1970-80, chmn., 1980-91; chmn. Sony Corp. Am., 1988-98; vice chmn. Keidanren, 1998. Decorated Cmdr. Cross First Class of the Order of Merit of the Rep. of Austria, 1987, Medal of Honor with Blue Ribbon by J.M. the Emperor of Japan, 1988, Comdr.'s Cross Order of Merit of Germany, 1994, Officier de l'Ordre Nat. de la Legion d'Honneur France, 1996, Grande Ufficiale dell'Ordine Al Merito della Repubblica Italiana award Pres. Italian Republic, 1998, Grand Decoration of Honour in Silver with Star of the Rep. of Austria, 1999, Order of Panglima Jasa Negara of Malaysia, 1999, Knight Comdr.'s Cross (Badge and Star, FRG, 2001, First Class Order of the Sacred Treasure of Japan, 2001. Mem. Japan Fedn. Econ. Orgn. (vice-chmn. 1998), Tokyo C. of C. and Industry (vice chmn.). Avocations: yachting, flying. Office: Sony Corp 6-7-35 Kitashinagawa 6-chome Shinagawa-ku Tokyo 141 Japan also: Sony Corp Am 550 Madison Ave New York NY 10022-3211

OHIWEREI, GODWIN OISEOZOJE, sociologist, educator; b. Ibadan, Oyo, Nigeria, July 15, 1956; arrived in U.S., 1976; s. Joel Wellington and Lyne Ohiwerei; children: A.J., Oise. BA, Dillard U., 1980; MA, So. U., Baton Rouge, 1980; PhD, La. State U., 1998. Assoc. prof. N.J. City U., Jersey City, 1990—, chmn. dept. sociology, 1996—. Author: The Effect of International Trade on Economic Development in Nigeria, 1988; editor: Developing Strategies for Excellence, 1996. Fellow, Nat. Coun. Black Studies, 1989, NEH, 1990. Mem.: Nat. Assn. Multicultural Edn., Am. Sociol. Assn., Ora-Ekpea Assn., Eghosa Alumni Assn. Episcopalian. Avocations: travel, reading. Office: NJ City Univ 2039 Kennedy Blvd Jersey City NJ 07305

OHL, JOAN ESCHENBACH, federal agency administrator; b. Harrisburg, Pa. m. Ronald E. Ohl. Grad., U. Del., 1967; EdM, SUNY, Buffalo, 1969; post grad., Pa. State U. Dir. women's housing Colo. Coll., Colo. Springs, 1969; positions at U. Ark., Pa. State U.; asst. to v.p. Fairleigh Dickinson U., Rutherford, NJ, 1975—82; v.p. Independent Coll. Fund of NJ; cons. to C.E. "Jim" Compton of FIVE-J Energy Inc. & Grafton Coal Co., 1984—93; sec. Dept. Health and Human Resources, W.Va., 1997—2001; commr. Adminstrn. Children, Youth and Families Adminstrn. Children and Families, HHS, Washington, 2002—. Bd. mem. W.Va. Health Care Cost Rev. Authority, 1993—97. Recipient Disting. West Virginian award, 2000, Joan E. Ohl Rural Health Leadership award, W.Va. Rural Health Assn., 2000, Leadership award, Multi-CAP, Inc., 2000, Bateman award, W.Va. Hosp. Assn., 2000, Leadership award, W.Va. Pub. Health Assn., 2000, James Hansen Humanitarian award, U. Buffalo, 2004. Office: HHS Adminstrn Children and Families 370 L'Enfant Promenade SW Washington DC 20447

OH-LEE, JUSTIN DOHOON, psychology professor; b. Seoul, Republic of Korea, May 23, 1963; arrived in US, 1979; s. Myung Suck and Bong Sun Oh; m. Connie Chong Lee, Mar. 31, 1996; 1 child, Grace Nara. Degree in chemistry with distinction, Colo. Coll., 1986; PhD in Psychology, UCLA, 1995. Postdoctoral fellow Nat. Inst. Neurol. Disorders and Stroke, NIH, Bethesda, Md., 1995—99, rsch. fellow clin. pharmacology, 1999—2001; faculty psychiatry and psychology Found. for Advanced Edn. in the Scis., NIH, Bethesda, 1999—2001; assoc. prof. psychology Ctrl. Mich. U., Mount Pleasant, 2001—. Spl. vol., cons. Nat. Inst. Neurol. Disorders and Stroke, NIH, Bethesda, Md., 2001—03. Contbr. chapters to books, articles to profl. jours. Faculty advisor Adventist Students for Christ, Mount Pleasant, 2003—05; sci. advisor Parkinson's Support Group, Mount Pleasant, 2002—05. Named Hon. Recognition for Outstanding Rsch., Nat. Inst. Neurol. Disorders and Stroke; recipient Outstanding Rsch. award, Assn. Korean Neuroscientist Assn., Grad. Divsn. award, UCLA, Grad. Divsn. Travel Grant Rsch. award, 1990—91, Pres. AA Fellowship award, 1993, Coll. Letters and Sci. Grad. Student award, 1993, Disting. Svc. award, NINDS ACUC, NIH, 1999, Spl. Act/Svc. award, U.S. Dept. Health and HUman Svcs., 2000, Rsch. Professorship award, Ctrl. Mich. U., 2003; fellow, Nat. Parkinson Found. Ctr. Excellence, 2003; grantee, NIH, 2001, 2005, Pres. Rsch. Investment Fund grantee, Ctrl. Mich. U., 2002; Rsch. Enhancement Award grantee, NIH, NINDS, Summer Faculty scholar, CHSBS, Ctrl. Mich. U., 2003. Mem.: APA, NIH, Asian and Pacific Islanders Am. Orgn., Soc. for Neuroscience, Am. Psychol. Soc. (faculty advisor Student Caucus, Ctrl. Mich. U. 2002—05). Home: 1412 Abbey Ln Mount Pleasant MI 48858 Office: Central Michigan Univ Psychology 1280 E Campus Dr HP 2181 Mount Pleasant MI 48859 Home Phone: 989-775-6275; Office Phone: 989-774-6492. Office Fax: 989-774-2553; Home Fax: 989-774-2253. Business E-Mail: oh1jd@cmich.edu.

OHLMEYER, DONALD WINFRED, JR., film and television producer; b. New Orleans, Feb. 3, 1945; s. Donald W. and Eva Clare (Bivens) O.; m. Linda Jonsson, 2003; children by previous marriage: Justin Drew, Christopher Brett, Todd Bivens, Kemper Perry. BA in Comms., U. Notre Dame, 1967. Pres. Roadblock Prodns., 1977—; chmn. bd., CEO, Ohlmeyer Comms., LA, 1982—92; pres. NBC West Coast, Burbank, Calif., 1993—2000. Adj. prof. Pepperdine U., 2002—. Assoc. dir. ABC Sports, N.Y.C., 1967-70, dir., 1971-72, prodr., 1972-77; dir. Olympic Games, 1972; prodr., dir. Summer and Winter Olympics, 1976; prodr. ABC Monday Night Football, 1972-76; exec. prodr. NBC Sports, N.Y.C., 1977-82; exec. prodr.: 1980 Olympic Games, Crime of Innocence, 1985, Under Siege, Bluffing It, 1987, Right to Die, 1987, Special Bulletin, The Golden Moment: An Olympic Love Story (also writer) 1980, Crazy in Love, 1992, Cold Sassy Tree, The Heroes of Desert Storm (also dir.) 1991; prodr.: The Emmy Awards Show, Fast Copy, Crimes of the Century, Lifestories; creator, dir.: MTV Awards Show, 1983-86, The Skins Game. Recipient 15 Emmy awards 1975-99, Cine Golden Eagle award, 1979, Miami Film Festival award 1979, award Nat. Film Bd., 1980, award Glaad Media, 1991, Humanities prize, 1983, 96. Mem. Dirs. Guild Am., Writers Guild Am., Acad. TV Arts and Scis., Bel-Air Club (Calif.), The Reserve (Indian Wells). Office: DWOCO Inc 10880 Wilshire Blvd Ste 920 Los Angeles CA 90024-4101

OHLSON, DOUGLAS DEAN, artist, educator; b. Cherokee, Iowa, Nov. 18, 1936; s. Lloyd E. and Effie O. (Johnson) O. BA, U. Minn., 1961. Prof. art Hunter Coll., NYC, 1964—2001; ret., 2001. One man shows include Fischbach Gallery, N.Y.C., 1964, 66-70, 72, Susan Caldwell Gallery, N.Y.C., 1974, 76, 77, 79, 81, 82, 83, Portland (Oreg.) Ctr. for Visual Arts, 1977, Ruth Siegel Gallery, N.Y.C., 1985, 87, Andre Zarre Gallery, N.Y.C., 1985, 90, 92, 93, 95, 2000, Andre Zarre Gallery, N.Y.C., 2004, Gallery 99, Nina Freudenheim Gallery, Buffalo, 1986, Jaffe Gallery, Miami, 1989, Elaine Baker Gallery, Boca Raton, 1986, 2003, Doug Ohlson 20 Years of Painting: 1982-2002; group shows include Mus. Modern Art, N.Y.C., 1968, Tate Gallery, London, 1969, Whitney Mus., N.Y.C., 1969, 71, Corcoran Gallery, Washington, 1972, 73, UCLA, 1975, Born in Iowa: The Homecoming, 1986-87, Hunter Coll./Times Sq. Gallery, N.Y.C.; invitational Am. Acad. Arts and Letters, 1992, 94, 97, 2002; represented in permanent collections Met. Mus. Art, N.Y.C., Nat. Gallery Art, Washington, Am. Fedn. Art, Mus. Modern Art, Frankfurt, Fed. Republic Germany, Lowe Art Mus., Miami, Fla., Karl Ernst Osthaus Mus., Hagen, Germany, Mus. Contemporary Art, Helsinki, Mpls. Inst. Art, Dallas Mus., Bklyn. Mus., Whitney Mus., N.Y.C., Harvard Art Mus., Cambridge, Mass. Served with USMC, 1955-58. Guggenheim fellow, 1968; Creative Artists Public Service grantee, 1974; Nat. Endowment for Arts grantee, 1976 Home: 35 Bond St New York NY 10012-2426

OHLY, D. CHRISTOPHER, lawyer; b. NYC, Nov. 7, 1950; s. Bodo Charles and Ellen Charlotte (Nekolla) O.; m. Karen Vanacek; 1 child, Sara Rebecca. AB, Johns Hopkins U., 1972; JD, U. Va., 1975. Bar: Md. 1975, US Dist. Ct. Md. 1975, DC 2004, US Dist. Ct. DC 2006, US Ct. Appeals (1st, 2d and 4th cirs.), US Tax Ct., US Supreme Ct. Asst. U.S. Atty. U.S. Atty.'s Office, Balt., 1978-81; ptnr. Schiff Hardio, LLP, Washington, 2006—. Contbr. articles to profl. jours. Mem. ABA, Md. Bar Assn., Phi Beta Kappa, Omicron Delta Kappa, Pi Sigma Alpha. Avocations: skiing, computers, amateur radio. Home: 5714 Saint Albans Way Baltimore MD 21212-2454 also: Village Chalet 5 Middle Ridge Rd South Londonderry VT 05155-9747 Office Phone: 202-778-6458. Business E-Mail: dcohly@schiffhardin.com.

OHM, HERBERT WILLIS, agronomy educator, agriculturist; b. Albert Lea, Minn., Jan. 28, 1945; s. Wilhelm Carl and Lena Ann (Finkbeiner) O.; m. Judy Ann Chrisinger, Aug. 8, 1964; children: Cari Lynn, David William. BS in Agrl. Edn., U. Minn., St. Paul, 1967; MS in Plant Breeding, N.D. State U., 1969; PhD in Plant Genetics and Breeding, Purdue U., 1972. Cert. agronomist. Asst. prof. Purdue U., West Lafayette, Ind., 1972-77, assoc. prof. agronomy, 1977-83, prof., 1983—2004, disting. prof., 2004—. Team leader Interdisciplinary Wheat and Oat Genetics and Breeding Program, West Lafayette, 1980—, Interdisciplinary Purdue/AID Devel. Program, Burkina Faso, West Africa, 1983-85; mgr. hard red winter wheat rsch. Pioneer Hi-Bred Internat., Inc., Hutchinson, Kans., 1980. Contbr. book chpts. Recipient Soils and Crops Merit award Ind. Crop Improvement Assn., 1988, Merit award Orgn. of African Unity, 1989, Meritorious Svc. award Sci., Tech. and Rsch. Commn., 1989, Agronomic Achievement award American Soc. of Agronomy, 1994, Sch. of Agr. Team award, 2000, Distinction cert. Purdue Agr. Alumni Assn., 2005. Fellow: AAAS, Crop Sci. Soc. Am. (chmn. divsn. 1991), Am. Soc. Agronomy; mem.: Am. Registry Cert. Profls. in Agrl. Crops and Soils (cert.), Coun. Agrl. Sci. and Tech., Nat. Oat Improvement Coun. (chmn.), Am. Oat Workers Conf. (chmn.). Avocations: woodworking, music. Office: Purdue U Dept Agronomy Lilly Hall Life Scis West Lafayette IN 47907-1150 Office Phone: 765-494-8072. Business E-Mail: hohm@purdue.edu.

OHMAN, E. MAGNUS, cardiologist, educator; s. Karl-Erik Ohman and Maj-Britt Borjeson; m. Elspeth O'Reilly-Hyland, June 12, 1987; children: Edward, Elsa-Maria, Henry, Henry Kenneth. MB, BCh, MD, Royal Coll. of Surgeons in Ireland, Dublin, 1981. Fellow in cardiology Duke U. Med. Ctr., Durham, NC, 1987—91, asst. prof. medicine, 1991—96, assoc. prof. medicine, 1996—2001, prof. medicine, 2005—, U. NC, Chapel Hill, NC, 2001—05. Dir. Heart Ctr. U. of N.C., Chapel Hill, 2001—05. Recipient Edith Walsh award, Brit. Med. Assn., 1985. Fellow: Am. Coll. Cardiology, European Soc. Cardiology, Royal Coll. Physicians of Ireland, Soc. of Cardiac Aniography and Intervention. Achievements include patents for Methods patent for assessing reperfusion in heart attacks. Office: Duke Univ Med Ctr DUMC 3126 Erwin Rd Durham NC 27710 Home Phone: 919-572-0680; Office Phone: 919-681-2069. Office Fax: 919-681-4454.

OHMAN, FRANKLIN ERIC, ballet educator, choreographer; b. LA, Jan. 7, 1939; s. Eric Ohman and Irene Iris Harsen; m. Gloria Isaksen, June 24, 1978 (div. Aug. 1984); 1 child, Johan Eric. Grad. h.s., Ontario, Calif., 1957. Dancer San Francisco Ballet, 1959—62, N.Y.C. Ballet, 1962—84; dir. N.Y. Dance Theatre, 1974—. Artistic dir. N.Y. Dance Theatre, 1974—; choreographer, tchr. Ohman Sch. Ballet, LI, NY, 1980—; choreographer Boston Ballet, Am. Movie Classics (divsn. Rainbow Cablevision), Broadhollow Players, LI; tchr., choreographer Long Lake Performing Arts Camp, NY; ballet master Ballet Philippines, Manila, 2004; lectr.-demonstrations covering life of George Balanchine at pub. librs. and museums throughout N.Y. and Conn. Century of Balanchine 1904-2004; ballet tchr. St. Louis Ballet, 2004—06; completed 25th season Nutcracker, Hofstra U. Exhibitions include Nat. Mus. Dance, Saratoga Spa, 2007, Artist of Week, WLIW21 Pub. TV, 2007. Pvt. US Army, 1961—67. Grantee, NY State Coun. on Arts, Suffolk County Office of Cultural Affairs. Avocations: painting, choreography, writing. Office Phone: 631-462-6266. Fax: 631-462-6361. Personal E-mail: frankohman@yahoo.com.

OHNO, APOLO ANTON, Olympic athlete; b. Seattle, May 22, 1982; Mem. US Elite Short Track Speedskating Team. Performer: Dancing with the Stars, 2007 (Named Champion, 2007). Named US Champion, 1997, World Jr. Short Track Champion, 1999, World Cup Overall Champion, 2001, 500 meter champion, 2001, 1000 meter champion, 2001, 1500 meter champion, 2001; named to Asian-Am. Hall of Fame, 2007; recipient US Champion, 1999, 2001, 2002, 1500 meter Gold medal, 2002 Olympic Games, 1000 meter Silver medal, 1000 meter Bronze Medal, 2006 Winter Olympic Games, Men's Short Track Relay Bronze Medal, Gold Medal 500 meter Speed Skating, 2006 Winter Olympics. Achievements include was a national champion and record holder in indoor inline skating, earned a state championship as a swimmer in the breaststroke. Avocations: music, badminton, basketball, break dancing. Address: US Speedskating PO Box 450639 Westlake OH 44145 *

OHRENSTEIN, ROMAN ABRAHAM, economist, educator, rabbi; b. Slomniki, Poland, June 12, 1920; arrived in U.S., 1951, naturalized, 1957; s. Joseph Barukh and Gena (Fiefkopf) O.; m. Ruth Silberstein, Aug. 30, 1953; children: Gena Ann, Ilana Rose. MA in Econs., U. Munich, 1948, PhD in Econs. cum laude, 1949, postgrad. in medicine, 1949—51; MHL, Jewish Theol. Sem. Am., 1955; postgrad., Columbia U., 1963—64. Ordained rabbi, 1955. Rabbi, Auburn, NY, 1955—57, Pittsfield, Mass., 1957—60, Atlanta, 1960—62, NYC, 1962—66; prof. econs. Nassau Coll., SUNY, Garden City, 1964-99, chmn. econs. dept., 1976-78, 82-84, prof. emeritus, 1999—, campus chaplain, 1970—; chaplain Nassau County Civic Preparedness, NY, 1965—; mem. Coll. Coun. Am. Coll. Jerusalem, 1967-73, prof. econs., 1968-73. Vis. prof. U. Newcastle, Australia, 1985, vis. rsch. prof., 1989; past chaplain Kiwanis, Police Dept. Cayuga County, NY, 1955-57, Mt. Sinai Hosp., NYC, 1963-64; mem. Coun. of Orgns., U.S.A., 1978-85; mem. spl. com. on Jewish law Rabbinical Assembly, 1971; condr. seminars U. Queensland, Sydney U., Nat. U., Australia, 1989, Sorbonne, Paris, 1990; lectr., guest spkr. Jewish civic and profl. orgns. Author: (series) Economic Thought in Talmudic Literature, 1968, 70, 83, 86, 87, 89, 91-93, 96, 2003 (citation Am. Biog. Inst. 1985), Inventories During Business Fluctuations, 1973, Inventory Control as an Economic Shock Absorber, 1975, Economic Analysis in Talmudic Literature, 1992, ed edit., rev. and enlarged, 2003; contbr. chpt. to anthology: Ancient and Medieval Economic Ideas, 1998; mem. editl. adv. bd. Internat. Rev. Econs. and Ethics; columnist Algemeiner Jour., NYC; contbr. articles to profl. jours. Mem. nat. exec. comm. Am. Profs. for Peace in the Mid. East, 1971-73; mem. adv. bd. Am. Acad. Alliance for Israel, 1995—. Recipient 1st Faculty Disting. Achievement award Nassau Coll., SUNY, 1992, 95, Citation of Excellence, Anbar Electronic Intelligence, Eng., 1996, Poineering Rsch. in Talmudic Economics, 1968; SUNY fellow, 1968, 70. Mem. Nat. Assn. Jewish Chaplains, Rabbinical Assembly NY Bd. Rabbis, Am. Econ. Assn., History of Econs. Soc., Assn. Social Econs., Learned Soc., NY Acad. Scis., Internat. Soc. for Intercommunication New Ideas, Literati Club (Eng.). Home: 28-74 208th St Bayside NY 11360-2421 Personal E-mail: ohrenste@aol.com. *I kept my faith in God coupled with loyalty to tradition, sharpened my mind while maintaining discipline of the heart; tenacity in the face of adversity, turning stumbling blocks into stepping stones while never losing sight of life's supreme purpose: to leave the world a little better than I found it.*

OHRI, SANGEETA JEAN MARY, social studies educator; b. Mumbai, India, Sept. 12, 1943; d. Joseph Marshall and Hilda Mary (Varel) D'Aguiar; m. N. Ohri, Nov. 20, 1961 (div. May 1999); children: Sanjay, Sandeep. BA part I, Shrimati Nathibai Damodar Thackersey, 1980. Organiser day sch. Soc. for Edn. of Crippled, Mumbai, 1978—82, acting prin., 1979—81; resource person Indian Assn. Presch. Edn., Mumbai, 1979—, Indian Nat. chpt. Orgn. Mondiale Edn. Prescolaire (World Body Presch.), Mumbai, 1987—95. Jt. sec. Poona Womens Coun., 2002—; com. mem. Nat. Coun. Women, India, 2002—; chair Rural Project, Pune, India, 1993-96; adv. panel Ctrl. Bd. Film Certification, Govt. of India, 2000-03 Joint hon. sec. Local Gen. Hosp., Santa Cruz, Mumbai, 1987-89; active State Commn. for Handicapped, Pune, India, 1996; v.p. All India Balkanji-Bari (Pioneer Child Welfare Assn.), Mumbai, 1996—; exec. v.p. Indian Assn. Presch. Edn., Mumbai, 1997; exec. Bombay Vigilance Assn., 1990—; cons. Save the Children, India; hon. treas. Indian Assn. Pre-sch. Edn., Mumbai, 1979-81, hon. sec., 1981-86; adminstr. Soc. for Edn. Crippled, Mumbai, 1979-93. Recipient Sahyog award for women's welfare and social work, 1999. Mem.: Nat. Coun. for Women in India (convenor twinning com. 2005—07), U. Womens Assn., Pers. Mgmt. and Tng. Assn. Indian Women (v.p.), Spectrum, Soroptimist Internat. Avocations: creative dramatics, writing, travel, organising welfare activities. Home: A-14 Hill View Residency Baner Road Baner Pune 411045 India Personal E-mail: sohri@yahoo.com.

OHRN, NILS YNGVE, chemistry and physics educator; b. Avesta, Sweden, June 11, 1934; came to U.S., 1966; s. Nils E. and Gerda M. (Akerlund) O.; m. Ann M.M. Thorsell, Aug. 24, 1957; children: Elisabeth, Maria. MS, Uppsala U., 1958, PhD, 1963, F.D., 1966. Research assoc. Uppsala (Sweden) U., 1963-66; assoc. prof. U. Fla., Gainesville, 1966-70, prof. chemistry and physics, 1971—, assoc. dir. Quantum Theory Project, 1976-77, dir. Quantum Theory Project, 1983-98, chmn. dept. chemistry, 1977-83. Editor: Internat. Jour. Quantum Chemistry, 1970—. Fulbright grantee Com. for Internat. Exchange of Scholars, Washington, 1961-63; recipient Bicentennial Gold medal King of Sweden, 1980; Fla. Acad. Scis. medal, 1984; named Tchr./Scholar of Yr., U. Fla., 2003-04. Fellow Am. Phys. Soc., Chaire Francqui Interuniversitaires Belgium; mem. Am. Chem. Soc. (Fla. award 1997), Royal Acad. Scis. Uppsala Sweden (fgn.), Finnish Acad. Scis. (fgn.), Royal Danish Acad. Scis. (fgn.), Sigma Xi, Phi Beta Kappa. Home: 1823 NW 11th Rd Gainesville FL 32605-5323 Office: U Fla Quantum Theory Project 2301 NPB Bldg # 92 Gainesville FL 32611-8435 Business E-Mail: ohrn@qtp.ufl.edu.

O'HURLEY, JOHN, actor; b. Kittery, Maine, Oct. 9, 1956; m. Eva LaRue Callahan, 1992 (div. 1994); m. Lisa Mesloh, Aug. 14, 2004; 1 child, William Dylan. BA, Providence Coll., 1976. Owner Era Aviation, Alaska; part owner J. Peterman Co., bd. dirs.; principal ptnr. Heritage Capitol Advisors, Atlanta, Round One Investments, Los Angeles; investor Piccadilly Restaurants. Actor: (TV series) The Edge of Night, 1983—84, Loving, 1984—86, As the World Turns, 1988, The Young & the Restless, 1989—91, Santa Barbara, 1990—91, Scorch, 1992, General Hospital, 1992, Valley of the Dolls, 1994, A Whole New Ballgame, 1995, Seinfeld, 1995—98, Lost on Earth, 1997, Over the Top, 1997, Cursed, 2000—01, The Mullets, 2003—04; (TV films) Something is Out There, 1988, Billy the Kid, 1989, White Hot: The Mysterious Murder of Thelma Todd, 1991, Seduction: 3 Tales from the "Inner Sanctum", 1992, My Son is Innocent, 1996, The Secret, 1997, Murder Live!, 1997, Blood on Her Hands, 1998, Tempting Fate, 1998, Life of the Party: The Pamela Harriman Story, 1998, Wild Grizzly, 1999, Three Secrets, 1999; (films) Night Eyes II, 1992, Mirror Images, 1992, The Power Within, 1995, Love Stinks, 1999, Slammed, 2001, Firetrap, 2001, Race to Space, 2001, Teddy Bears' Picnic, 2002, Buying the Cow, 2002, Knuckle Sandwich, 2004; voice actor: (TV series) Mickey Mouse Works, 1999—2000; Buzz Lightyear of Star Command, 2000; House of Mouse, 2001—02; Duck Dodgers, 2003—; Father of the Pride, 2004; (films) Tarzan & Jane, 2002; host: (TV series) Extraordinary World of Animals, 1999; Get Golf with the PGA Tour!, 2000; contestant Dancing with the Stars, 2005; composer: (albums) Peace of Our Minds, 2005. Named one of sexiest men alive, People mag., 2005. Avocations: golf, tennis, carpentry, interior design, wine collection. Office: The J Peterman Company 1001 Primrose Ct Lexington KY 40511

OJAKLI, ZIAD S., automotive executive; b. Brooklyn, NY; BA, Georgetown Univ.; MA, Johns Hopkins Univ. Legis. asst. U.S. Senator Dan Coats, Washington, 1988—94; chief of staff U.S. Rep. Mark Souder, Washington, 1995—98; policy dir. & chief of staff U.S. Senator Paul Coverdell, Washington, 1998—2000; Senate liason Bush-Cheney Transition Team, Washington, 2000; dep. asst. to the Pres. for legis. affairs The White House, Washington, 2001—04; group v.p. corp. affairs Ford Motor Co., Dearborn, Mich., 2004—. Bd. mem. Alliance of Automobile Manufacturers, Arab-Am. Mus. Adv. Bd., Arab-Am. Ctr. for Econ. & Social Services, Fabretto Children's Found., Henry Ford Learning Inst., NAM; del. World Econ. Forum's Young Global Leaders; bd. mem. Mich. Manufacturers Assn., Washington Ctr. for Internships. Office: Ford Motor Co 1 American Rd Dearborn MI 48126 *

OJALVO, MORRIS, civil engineer, educator; b. NYC, Mar. 4, 1924; s. Nissim and (Fanny) O.; m. Anita Bedein, Dec. 26, 1948; children: Lynne, Joseph, Howard, Isobel. B.C.E., Rensselear Poly. Inst., Troy, NY, 1944, M.C.E., 1952; PhD, Lehigh U., Bethlehem, Pa., 1960; JD, Ohio State U., Columbus, 1978. Bar: Ohio 1979. Draftsman Am. Bridge Co., Elmira, N.Y., 1946-47; tutor civil engrng. CCNY, 1947-49; instr. Rensselaer Poly. Inst., 1949-51; asst. prof. Princeton U., 1951-58; research instr. Lehigh U., 1958-60; mem. faculty Ohio State U., 1960—, prof. civil engrng., 1964-82, prof. emeritus, 1982—; vis. prof. U. Tex.-Austin, 1982-83. Author: Thin-Walled Bars With Open Profiles, 1990; contbr. papers in field; patentee warp restraining device. With USN, 1943—46. Mem.: ASCE, Structural Stability Rsch. Coun. Home and Office: 1024 Fairway Ln Estes Park CO 80517-7156 Home Phone: 970-577-0237; Office Phone: 970-577-0237. E-mail: morris_ojalvo@yahoo.com.

OJEDA, ANA MARIA, therapist, clinical caseworker; b. Miami, Feb. 1, 1980; d. Juan Bruno and Daisy Irene Ojeda. BSc in Psychology and Elem. Edn., U. Miami, Coral Gables, Fla., 2002, MSc in Mental Health Counseling, 2004; MA in Clin. Psychology, Regent U., 2006. Milieu therapist Miami Children's Hosp., 2001—03; therapist Psychsolutions, Miami, 2002; psychotherapist Miami Children's Hosp., 2003—04; residential counselor The Pines Residential Treatment Ctr., Portsmouth, Va., 2004—05, therapist/clin. caseworker, 2005—06. Assoc. tchr. U. Miami, Hialeati, 2002, rsch. asst., Coral Gables, 03. Nominee Excellence award, Miami Children's Hosp., 2003; named to Provost's Honor Roll, U. Miami, 2001—02, Dean's List, 2001—02; recipient academic merit, 2004, certificate of appreciation, Miami Children's Hosp., 2003. Mem.: APA, Pi Lambda Theta. Republican. Catholic. Avocations: travel, bicycling, running, reading. Office: The Pines Residential Treament Ctr 825 Crawford Pkwy Portsmouth VA 23704 Personal E-mail: anamojeda@aol.com.

OJEDA, JOSEPH A., psychotherapist; b. NYC, Mar. 25, 1950; s. Benigno Ojeda and Maria Luisa Ayala; children: Kenneth, Lorraine. D of Naturopathy, Westbrook U., Weirton, W.Va., 2004; PhD in Hypnotherapy, LaSalle U., Mandeville, La., 2002; DD, U. of Universal Life, Modesto, Calif., 1975; M in Holistic Healing, Westbrook U., 1996. Diplomate Am. Coll. Forensic Examiners, 1997, Am. Psychotherapy Assn., 1998, bd. cert. Am. Acad. of Experts in Traumatic Stress. Psychotherapist/clergy Counseling Ch. of the Universal Living God, Jamaica, NY, 1972—97; psychotherapist Holistic Healing, Hypnotherapy & Psychotherapy Family, Middletown, 1998—. Marriage officiant Counseling Ch. of the Universal Living God, 1976—, pastoral counseling, 1976—; free counseling walk-in clinic, Counseling Ch. of the Universal Living God, 1972—97. Author: (book) Re-education & Reprogramming with Hypnotherapy..., 2001, Integration of Behavioral & Relaxation Approaches..., 2002, Application of Self-Hypnosis Reprogramming Procedure..., 2002, Secrets of Clairvoyance, Explanation & Instructions, 2007. Recipient award for poem Mysterious Woman, Nat. Libr. of Poetry, 1997, Medal of Merit for cmty. involvement, Pres. Ronald Reagan, 1986, award letter for emergency control ctr. assistance, Commr. Joseph V. Terrenzio, Dept. of Hosp. Bur., 1970. Fellow: Am. Acad. of Experts in Traumatic Stresss. Home and Office: 27 Sproat Street Middletown NY 10940 Personal E-mail: hypnotex@juno.com.

OJEDA, NELSON A., II, musician; b. LA, May 27, 1972; s. Nelson A. Ojeda Sr. and Martha E. Ojeda. MusB, Calif. State U., Fullerton, 1997, MusM, 1999; Diploma profl. studies, Manhattan Sch. of Music, 2004. Collaborative pianist Calif. State U., Long Beach, 1998—2001; prof. piano Mt. San Antonio Coll., Walnut, Calif., 2002—03; choir accompanist Via Magna, Madrid, 2005—, Univ. Politecnica, Madrid, 2004—; concert artist Vivace Concert Agy., Madrid, 2005—. State adjudicator Music Tchrs. Assn. Calif., 1997; nat. adjudicator Am. Coll. Musicians, 1999—; pianist Madrid Chamber Music Internat., 2005—. Translator (piano method book) Alfred Basic Piano Course, 2004. Finalist Ft. Collins (Colo.) Concerto Competition, 1998; recipient Grand prize, Music Assocs. Competition, Orange County, Calif., 1997, Spl. Recognitioin, La Peña Cubana, L.A., 2005. Achievements include Guest artist at David Dubal's World of Piano, Juilliard Sch., Lincoln Ctr. N.Y.C; concert tours in Asia and Europe; soloist with Pacific Symphony Orch. and Southwest Symphony. Avocation: Spanish, Italian, French. Home: 32464 Bergamo Ct Temecula CA 92592 E-mail: pianonelson@yahoo.com.

OJEDA EISELEY, JAIME DE, former Spanish ambassador, educator; b. Aug. 5, 1933; BL maxima cum laude in Law, U. Madrid, Spain, 1957; grad., Internat. Acad. of The Hague, The Netherlands; student, Naval War Coll. and Sr. Ctr. for Nat. Def. Studies, Madrid, Spain. Prof. polit. law Complutense U. Madrid, Spain, 1958; joined diplomatic svcs., 1958; served Embassy of Spain, Washington, 1962—69; min. counselor Peking,

China, 1973—76; consul-gen. of Spain Hong Kong and Macao, 1976-79; fellow Ctr. Internat. Rels., Harvard U., Cambridge, Mass., 1979-80; dep. permanent rep. NATO, 1982-83, permanent rep., 1983-90; amb. to U.S.A., Spanish Embassy, Washington, 1990-97; pres. high level coun. fgn. affairs Min. F.A. Madrid, 1997; amb.-in-residence Shenandoah U., Winchester, Va., 1997—. Vis. scholar Johns Hopkins U., Washington, 1997; disting. adj. fellow CSIS, Washington, 1997. Translator: Alice in Wonderland and Through the Looking Glass, by Lewis Carroll, 1971—74, Spain and America: The Past and Future, 1994, El 98 en el Congreso y en la Prensa de los Estados Unidos, 1999. Lt. Reserve Marine Corps. Spanish Navy, 1957. Decorated Great Cross Mil. Merit, Great Cross of Civil Merit, Order of Charles III. Home: PO Box 57 3770 Leeds Manor Rd Markham VA 22643-1817 Office: Shenandoah U 1460 University Dr Winchester VA 22601-5195

OJEMANN, JEFFREY G., neurosurgeon; b. Seattle; MD, Washington U., St. Louis, 1992. Diplomate Am. Bd. Neurol. Surgeons, 2002, Am. Bd. Pediatric Neurosurgeons, 2004. Neurosurgeon Children's Hosp., St. Louis, 2000—03, Seattle, 2003—. Office: U Washington - Children's Hosp 4800 Sand Point Way Seattle WA 98105 Office Phone: 206-987-4240.

OJI, PAULINE E., secondary school educator; b. Ozuitem, Nigeria; arrived in U.S., 1995; d. Shedrack N. and Mercy O. Udah; m. Madumere Oji, June 1, 1995; children: Mercy A., Victoria O. BS in Chemistry, Univ. Port Harcourt, 1987; MEd Spl. Edn., Coppin State Coll., 1999. Cert. spl. educator. Sub. tchr. Balt. City Pub. Sch., Balt., 1997—99; math. tchr. Woodbourne Ctr. Inc., Balt., 1997; sci. tchr. Strawbridge Sch., Balt., 2001—04, Woodlawn H.S., Balt., 2004—. Dept. chair Strawbridge Sch., Balt., 2001—02; mem. adv. com. John Hopkins Univ., 2003—. Facilitator (presentation) Picoturbine Windmills, 2001. Vol. Girl Scouts of Am. Troop 1536, Balt., 2003—; presenter Md. Assn. of Non Pub. Spl. Edn. Facilities, 2002, Md. Assn. of Non Pub. Spl. Edn. Facilitier, 2003; supporter Spl. Olympics, 2000—. Nominee Educator of the Yr., Ten Conf., 2001; recipient Gov. Citation, Md. Gov., 2000. Mem.: NEA, ASCD, Nat. Sci. Tchrs. Assn., Internat. Reading Assn., Coun. Exceptional Children (vol.), Md. State Tchrs. Assn. (vol.), Nat. Coun. for Tchrs. of Math., Md. State Coun. for Tchrs. of Math. Achievements include participated in Md. Educators Summer Rsch. Program. Avocations: reading, travel, dance, basketball, tennis. Home: 12 Hickory Nut Ct Baltimore MD 21236 Office: Balt County Pub Sch Woodlawn H S 1801 Woodlawn Dr Baltimore MD 21207 Office Phone: 410-887-1309. Personal E-mail: mvpeo@juno.com.

OJIMA, IWAO, chemistry professor; b. Yokohama, Japan, June 5, 1945; came to U.S., 1983; s. Masaharu and Sumiko (Takatsuki) O.; m. Yoko Ogino, Apr. 24, 1971. BS, U. Tokyo, 1968, MS, 1970, PhD in Organic Chemistry, 1973. Rsch. fellow Sagami Inst. for Chem. Rsch., Japan, 1970-76, sr. rsch. fellow, group leader, 1976-83; assoc. prof. chemistry SUNY, Stony Brook, 1983-84, prof., 1984-91, leading prof., 1991-95, disting. prof., 1995—, chmn., 1997—2003; dir. Inst. Chem. Biology and Drug Discovery, 2003—. Editor: Catalytic Asymmetric Synthesis, 1993, 2d edit., 2000, Taxane Anticancer Agents, 1994, Biomedical Frontiers of Fluorine Chemistry, 1996, Anticancer Agents-Frontiers in Cancer Chemotherapy, 2001, Comprehensive Organometallic Chemistry III, vol. 10, 2006; contbr. numerous articles to profl. jours.; numerous patents in fieldl 630 publications. Fellow J.S. Guggenheim Meml. Found. Fellow AAAS, NY Acad. Scis.; mem. Am. Chem. Soc. (A.C. Cope Scholar award 1994, E.B. Hershberg award 2001), Chem. Soc. Japan (Nat. Young Investigator award 1976, Disting. Achievement award 1999), Soc. Synthetic Organic Chemistry Japan, Sigma Xi. Achievements include research in homogenous catalysis of transition metal complexes; asymmetric synthesis; organic synthesis by means of organometallic reagents; peptides and peptide mimetics; beta-lactam chemistry; organofluorine chemistry, medicinal chemistry especially in regard to taxane anticancer agents and enzyme inhibitors. Home: 41 Roslyn Ct Port Jefferson NY 11777-1462 Office: State U New York Dept Chemistry Stony Brook NY 11794-3400 Home Phone: 631-476-8582; Office Phone: 631-632-7947. Business E-Mail: iojima@notes.cc.sunysb.edu.

OKA, MASAYORI See OKA, MASI

OKA, MASI (MASAYORI OKA), actor; b. Tokyo, Dec. 27, 1974; BS in Math. and Computer Sci., Brown U., 1997. Visual effects artist Indsl. Light & Magic, 1998—. Actor: (films) Austin Powers: Goldmember, 2002, Uh Oh!, 2003, Legally Blonde 2: Red, White & Blonde, 2003, Along Came Polly, 2004, Chester's Big Night, 2004, (voice) God Wears My Underwear, 2005, One Sung Hero, 2006, Balls of Fury, 2007; (TV films) House of the Dead 2, 2005, (voice) The Proud Family Movie, 2005,: (TV series) Scrubs, 2002—04, Heroes, 2006— (Saturn award, Acad. Sci. Fiction, Fantasy & Horror Films, 2007); appearances on (TV series) Dharma & Greg, 2001, Citizen Baines, 2001, Gilmore Girls, 2001, Yes, Dear, 2002, Sabrina, the Teenage Witch, 2002, She Spies, 2002, On the Spot, 2003, Luis, 2003, Still Standing, 2004, All of Us, 2004, Less Than Perfect, 2005, Reno 911, 2005, Reba, 2006, Without a Trace, 2006, The Loop, 2006, Joey, 2006, Sarah Silverman Program, 2007, featured on Time mag. cover, 1987. Avocations: Kendo, video games, piano, singing. Office: c/o Paulo Andres LINK Talent Grp 4741 Laurel Canyon Blvd #106 Valley Village CA 91607 *

OKA, TAKASHI, journalist, consultant, educator; b. Tokyo, Oct. 21, 1924; s. William Masakazu and Fumiko Mary Oka; m. Hiroko Imai, Sept. 8, 1956; children: Megumi, Sakuya. B in Econs., Rikkyo U., 1947; BA, Principa Coll., 1950; MA, Harvard U., 1954. Asst. to fgn. editor Christian Sci. Monitor, Boston, 1954-59, fgn. corr. Hong Kong, Saigon, Moscow, 1959-68, Paris, London, Beijing, Tokyo, 1971-92; bur. chief Tokyo office NY Times, 1968-71; staff dir. internat. dept. New Frontier Party, Tokyo, 1994-98; Washington rep. Liberal Party of Japan, 1999—2002; vis. scholar Sigur Ctr. George Washington U., Washington, 1998-99, 2003—04. Rsch. assoc. Internat. Inst. of Strategic Studies, London, 1976-78; rsch. fellow Carnegie Endowment for Internat. Peace, 1992-95. Author: Prying Open the Door: Foreign Workers in Japan, 1995. Avocation: tennis. Home and Office: 800 25th St NW Washington DC 20037-2207

OKA, TAKESHI, physicist, physical chemist, astronomer, educator; b. Tokyo, June 10, 1932; arrived in U.S., 1981, naturalized, 2004; s. Shumpei and Chiyoko O.; m. Keiko Nukui, Oct. 24, 1960; children: Ritsuko, Noriko, Kentaro, Yujiro. B.Sc., U. Tokyo, 1955, PhD, 1960; DSc (hon.), U. Waterloo, 2001, Univ. Coll., London, 2004. Rsch. assoc. U. Tokyo, 1960-63; fellow NRC Can., Ottawa, Ont., 1963-65, asst., 1965-68, assoc., 1968-71, sr. rsch. physicist, 1971-80; prof. U. Chgo., 1981—, Robert A. Millikan disting. prof., 1989—; prof. Enrico Fermi Inst., 1993—2004, emeritus, 2004—. Mem. editorial bd. Chem. Physics, 1972-92, Jour. Molecular Spectroscopy, 1973—, Jour. Chem. Physics, 1975-77. Recipient Steacie prize, 1972; Earle K. Plyler prize, 1982, Norman McLean award U. Chgo., 2004. Fellow Royal Soc. Can., Royal Soc. London (Davy medal 2004), Am. Phys. Soc., Optical Soc. Am. (William F. Meggers award 1997, Ellis R. Lippincott award 1998), Am. Acad. Scis. and Arts; mem. Am. Astron. Soc; Am. Chem. Soc. (E. Bright Wilson award, 2002). Home Phone: 773-753-5263; Office Phone: 773-702-7070. Business E-Mail: t-oka@uchicago.edu.

OKADA, RONALD SHIG, lawyer; b. Cleve., June 11, 1960; s. Shig and Mary Mariko (Machida) O.; m. Ann (Haugan) Aug. 18, 1984; children: Lauren Mariko, David Ryon, Julia Elise. BA, Carleton Coll., 1982; JD, U. Mich., 1985. Bar: Ohio 1985, U.S. Dist. Ct. (no. dist.) Ohio 1985, U.S. Ct. Appeals (6th cir.) 1988, (11th cir.), 1998, U.S. Supreme Ct., 1999. Assoc. Baker & Hostetler LLP, Cleve., 1985-92, ptnr., litigation dept., 1993—, mem. policy com., 2002—. Mem. ABA, Ohio Bar Assn., Cleve. Bar Assn., Carleton Coll. Alumni Club (no. Ohio). Office: Baker & Hostetler LLP 3200 National City Ctr Cleveland OH 44114-3485 Home Phone: 440-572-6514; Office Phone: 216-861-7645. Office Fax: 216-696-0740. Business E-Mail: rokada@bakerlaw.com.

OKADA, RYOZO, medical educator, researcher; b. Kiryu, Japan, July 20, 1931; s. Kenji and Sachi (Ishihara) O.; m. Shigeko Shindo, May 25, 1958; children: Kyoko, Taro. MD, Tokyo U., 1956, PhD, 1961. Intern then resident; asst. Tokyo U. Sch. Medicine, 1962-63; rsch. fellow Hektoen Inst. Cook County Hosp., Chgo., 1963-66; attending physician Yoikuin Hosp., Tokyo, 1966-68; assoc. prof. Sch. Med. Juntendo U., Tokyo, 1968-83, prof., 1983—97, prof. emeritus, 1997—; rector Gumma Paz Coll., 1998—2005, emeritus prof., 2005—; dir. Gumma Paz Rsch. Inst., 2005—; sr. advisor PAS Coll., 2005—. Councilor Cardiovasc. Inst. Roppongi, Tokyo, 1990—; cons. in field. Contbr. chapters to books, articles to profl. jours. Bd. dirs. Shirane Kaizen Sch. Fellow: Japanese Geriat. Soc., Japanese Angiology Soc., Japanese Circulation Soc., Coun. Prevention Heart Disease, Am. Heart Assn., Internat. Cardiovasc. Pathology, Am. Geriat. Soc., Internat. Electrocardiology, Internat. Union Angiology; mem.: Sports Medicine Occupl. Medicine, Japanese Soc. Medicine. Avocation: travel. Office: Gumma Paz Rsch Inst 5-4 Iwaoshicho Takasaki Gunma 370-0044 Japan Home: 25-9 Asahigaoka Kanagawaku Yokohama 221-0814 Japan Office Phone: 027 310 7766.

OKADA, SHIGERU, medical educator; b. Okayama, Japan, Feb. 15, 1940; s. Keizo and Moyoko (Nishigaki) O.; m. Naoko Kobashi, Nov. 7, 1965; children: Satoru, Rie, Mari. MD, Okayama U., Japan, 1964, PhD, 1969. Chief pathologist Kyoto City Hosp., Japan, 1977-80; lectr. Sch. Medicine Kyoto U., 1980-90; asst. Med. Sch. Okayama U., 1969-71, lectr., 1971-77; prof. Okayama U. Med. Sch., Japan, 1990—2001; dir. Isotope Ctr. Okayama U., Japan, 1995—2001, advisor to the pres., 1999—2001, prof., dean Sch. of Medicine, 2003—05, prof. emeritus, 2005—; prin. Tamano Inst. Med. Tech. and Nursing, 2005—. Head radiation protection com. Okayama U., 1991-2001; trustee Kake Ednl. Inst., 2005-; vis. prof. Okayama U., 2005-. Contbr. articles to profl. jours. Mem. Japan Pathol. Soc. Tokyo, Japan Haematological Soc. Kyoto, Internat. Soc. Hematology, Japanese Cancer Assn. Tokyo, NY Acad. Sci. Office: Okayama U Grad Sch Medicine Dentistry and Pharm Scis 2-5-1 Shikata Okayama 700-8558 Japan Office Phone: 81-86-235-7491. Personal E-mail: dragon40@beach.ocn.ne.jp. Business E-Mail: okadas@cc.okayama-u.ac.jp.

OKAFOR, EMEKA, professional basketball player; b. Houston, Tex., Sept. 28, 1982; BA in Finance, U. Conn., 2004. Player Charlotte Bobcats, 2004—. Mem. US Olympics Basketball Team, Athens, Greece, 2004. Named Most Outstanding Player, NCAA Final Four, 2004, Co-Nat. Player of the year, NABC, 2004, Big East Player of the Year, 2004, Defensive Player of the Year, 2004, Academic All-American first team, 2003—04, NBA Rookie of the Yr., 2005; named to All-American First Team, AP, 2004. Achievements include Mem.of NCAA Nat.Championship Team U. Conn Huskies, 2004; First ever draft pick (second overall) of expansion Charlotte Bobcats, 2004.

OKAMOTO, ALLEN M., real estate company executive; m. Patricia Okamoto; children: Scott, Kara. BA in Fin., San Francisco State U., 1965. Chartered Property and Casualty Underwriter, Grad. Realtor Inst., Sr. Residential Specialist, cert. Real Estate Broker. Owner-broker T. Okamoto & Co., San Francisco, 1973—. Bd. dirs. Chinese Real Estate Assn., Nat. Assn. Realtors, Calif. Assn. Realtors; pres. Sakura Matsuri Inc.; v.p. Nihonmachi Parking Corp.; chmn. Asian Real Estate Assn. of Am. Pres. bd. Japanese Cultural & Cmty. Ctr.; chmn. Cherry Blossom Festival of Northern Calif.; bd. trustees Calif. Historical Soc.; bd. dirs. Japanese Am. Citizens League; chmn. 100th Anniversary of Japantown Com., San Francisco-Osaka Sister City Assn. Named a Local Hero, PBS TV Station KQED, 2001; named one of Real Estate's 25 Most Influential Thought Leaders, Realtor Mag., 2006; recipient Silver Spur, San Francisco Planning and Urban Rsch. Orgn., 2000, Cert. of Commendation, US Senator Dianne Feinstein, 2001, Cert. of Honor, San Francisco Mayor Gavin Newsom, 2006. Mem.: San Francisco Assn. Realtors (pres. 1990, Realtor of Yr.), Calif. Assn. Realtors (Dir. for Life 2003, President's award). Office: Asian Real Estate Assn America 5740 Fleet St Ste 155 Carlsbad CA 92008 Office Phone: 760-918-9162. Office Fax: 760-918-6924. *

OKAMURA, ARTHUR SHINJI, artist, educator; b. Long Beach, Calif., Feb. 24, 1932; s. Frank Akira and Yuki O.; m. Elizabeth Tuomi, Aug. 7, 1953 (div.); children: Beth, Jonathan, Jane, Ethan; m. Kitty Wong, 1991. Student, Art Inst. Chgo., 1950-54, U. Chgo., 1951, 52, 57. Faculty Ctrl. YMCA Coll., Chgo., 1956, 57, Evanston (Ill.) Art Center, 1956-57, Art Inst. Chgo., North Shore Art League, Winnetka, Ill., Acad. Art, San Francisco, 1957, Calif. Sch. Fine Arts, 1958, Ox Bow Summer Art Sch., Saugatuck, Mich., 1963, Calif. Coll. Arts and Crafts, Oakland, 1958-59, prof. arts, 1966-97, prof. emeritus, 1997—. Instr. watercolor painting, 1987; dir. San Francisco Studio Art, 1958; tchr. watercolor workshops, Bali, Indonesia, 1989, 92; lectr. in field. Author (with Robert Creeley): 1, 2, 3, 4, 5, 6, 7, 8, 9, 0, 1971; author: (with Joel Weishaus) Ox-Herding, 1971; author: (with Robert Bly) Basho, 1972, Ten Poems by Issa, 1992; author: (with Steve Kowit) Passionate Journey, 1984; author: (with David Rosen and Joel Weishaus) The Healing Spirit of Haiku; author: Magic Rabbit, 1995, The Paper Propeller, 2000; one-man shows include Charles Feingarten Galleries, Chgo., 1956, 1958, 1959, San Francisco, 1957, Santa Barbara Mus. Art, 1958, Oakland Mus. Art, 1959, Legion Honor, San Francisco, 1961, Dallas, 1962, La Jolla (Calif.) Mus., 1963, U. Utah, 1964, San Francisco Mus. Art, 1968, Hanssen Gallery, 1968, 1971, Ruth Braunstein, San Francisco, 1981, 1982, 1984, 1986—88, 1990, 1994, 1997, 2000, 2003, 2006, Commonweal Gallery, Bolinas, Calif., 2001, exhibited in group shows at Pa. Acad. Fine Art, U. Chgo., U. Wash., U. Ill., Art Inst. Chgo., L.A. County Mus., Am. Fedn. Art, Denver Mus., NAD, De Young Mus., San Francisco, Knoedler Gallery, N.Y.C., Feingarten Galleries, Whitney Mus. Art, others; retrospective at Bolinas Mus., 2002, Claudia Chapline Galleries, Stinson Beach, Calif., 1995; Represented in permanent collections Art Inst. Chgo., Borg-Warner Collections, Chgo., Whitney Mus. Art, Santa Barbara Mus. Art, San Francisco Mus. Art, Ill. State Normal, Corcoran Mus., Nat. Collection Fine Arts, Smithsonian Instn., many others. Served as pvt. AUS, 1955-56. Recipient 1st prize religious art U. Chgo., 1953; Ryerson travelling fellow, 1954; Martin Cahn award contemporary Am. paintings Art Inst. Chgo., 1957; purchase award U. Ill., 1959; purchase award Nat. Soc. Arts and Letters, N.Y.C., 1960; Neysa McMein purchase award Whitney Mus. Art, 1960; Schwabacher-Frey award 79th Ann. of San Francisco Mus. Art, 1960 Mem.: Commonweal (bd. dirs. 1993—2002). Home: 210 Kale Rd Bolinas CA 94924 E-mail: arthurokamura@earthlink.net.

O'KANE, BARBARA LYNN, research psychologist; b. Jersey City, Sept. 7, 1950; d. Herbert and Pearl Clair Sandick; m. David Dean O'Kane, June 25, 1988; 1 child, Nathan Sean. BS, Suffolk U., 1976; PhD, Brandeis U., 1982. Rsch. psychologist U.S. Army Natick R&D Ctr., Natick, Mass., 1979-85; R&D insp. U.S. Army Material Command, Alexandria, Va., 1985-89; engring. rsch. psychologist U.S. Army Night Vision and Electronic Sensors Directorate, Ft. Belvoir, Va., 1985—. Author: (chpt.) Vision Models for Target Detection and Recognition, 1995; contbr. articles to profl. jours. Avocations: music, public speaking, creation science, skiing. Home: 6117 Burnett St Alexandria VA 22310-2662 Office: US Army Night Vision Lab Burbeck Rd Fort Belvoir VA 22060 Business E-Mail: okane@nvl.army.mil.

OKANO, TAKESHI, thoracic surgeon; b. Kona, Hawaii, May 22, 1921; s. Waichi Okano and Kame Tanaka; married, Aug. 22, 1967. BS, U. Hawaii, Honolulu, 1943; MD, Tulane U., New Orleans, 1947. Thoracic surgeon VA Med. Ctr., Bay Pines, Fla., 1960—. Fellow: ACS, So. Thoracic Surg. Assn.; mem.: Alpha Omega Alpha. Home: 2313 Lanai Ave Belleair Bluffs FL 33770 Office: VA Med Ctr Bay Pines FL

OKARMA, JEROME D., lawyer, manufacturing executive; m. Pam Okarma; 2 children. BA, Western Ill. U., 1974; JD, Northwestern U., 1977. Bar: Ill. 1977, Wis. 1989. Atty. Inland Steel Co., 1977—82; sr. atty. Borg-Warner Corp., 1982—89; joined Johnson Controls, Inc., Milw., 1989, asst. sec., 1990—2004, dep. gen. counsel, 2000—04, corp. v.p., 2003—, gen. counsel, sec., 2004—. Office: Johnson Controls, Inc 5757 N Green Bay Ave Milwaukee WI 53209 Office Phone: 414-524-1200. E-mail: jerome.d.okarma@jci.com. *

OKAY, JOHN LOUIS, management consultant; b. Emmett, Mich., Mar. 27, 1942; s. Stanley John and Mildred Isabell (Little) O.; m. Judith Ann Gerlach, Aug. 22, 1964; children: Stephen, Christopher, Douglas. BS in Agr., Mich. State U., 1964, MS in Agrl. Econs., 1967, PhD in Resource Econs., 1974. Agrl. economist U.S. Soil Conservation Svc., East Lansing, Mich., 1967-73, program analyst Washington, Mich., 1974-83, dir. info. systems, 1983-85; assoc. dir. info. systems USDA, Washington, 1985-91, dir. info. systems, 1991-95; dep. commr. Fed. Technology Svc., GSA, Falls Church, Va., 1995-97; sr. v.p. Fed. Sources Inc., McLean, Va., 1997-99; pres. J.L. Okay Cons., Oak Hill, Va., 1999—2003; ptnr. Topside Cons. Group, 2003—. Recipient Meritorious Exec. award Pres. of U.S., 1989, 97, Fed. Computer Week's Fed. 100 award, 1992, 1994, 1997, 2004. Mem. Armed Forces Comm. and Electronics Assn. (bd. dirs. 1994-98), Sr. Execs. Assn. (bd. dirs. 1989-98). Office: 2857 Fox Mill Rd Oak Hill VA 20171-1829 Personal E-mail: john.okay@verizon.net.

O'KEEFE, EDWARD FRANKLIN, lawyer; b. SI, NY, June 9, 1937; s. Francis Franklin and Bertha (Hall) O'K.; m. Toni Lynne McGohan; children: Kira Kathleen, Douglas Franklin, Andrew Franklin, Alison Elizabeth, Theadore William, Nigel Francis. AB, U. N.C., 1959; JD, U. Denver, 1961. Bar: Colo. 1962, N.C. 2000. Law clk. Colo. Supreme Ct., Denver, 1962-63; assoc. gen. counsel Hamilton Mgmt. Corp., Denver, 1966-69, sec., 1968-76, v.p. legal, gen. counsel, 1969-76; ptnr. Moye White, Denver, 1976—2006; pvt. practice Southport, NC, 2006—. Assoc. gen. counsel, sec. ITT Variable Annuity Ins. Co., Denver, 1969, v.p. legal, gen. counsel, 1969-70; sec. Hamilton Funds Inc., Denver, 1968-76 With USNR, 1963—66. Mem. Nat. Assn. Security Dealers (dist. conduct com., chmn. 1976), Colo. Assn. Corporate Counsel (pres. 1974-75) Office Phone: 910-253-5040.

O'KEEFE, FRANCIS RONALD, lawyer; b. Oct. 7, 1950; AB, Georgetown U., 1972; JD, Cleve.-Marshall Coll., 1977. Bar: Ohio 1977, U.S. Dist. Ct. (no. dist.) Ohio 1978, U.S. Supreme Ct. 2002. Pvt. practice, 1977—86; sec. and gen. counsel Broadview Fin. Corp., 1986—89; ptnr. Hahn, Loeser & Parks LLP, 1989—. Named Ohio Super Lawyer, Cin. mag., 2004, 2005; named to Best Lawyers in Am. in corp. law, 2001—; recipient Sindell Tort Competition prize, Cleve.-Marshall Law Sch., 1977, Most Useful to Practicing Attys. Law Rev. Article award, 1977. Mem.: ABA, Soc. Corp. Governance Profls., Greater Cleve. Bar Assn., Ohio State Bar Assn. Office: Hahn Loeser & Parks LLP 200 Public Sq Ste 3300 Cleveland OH 44114-2301 Office Phone: 216-274-2396. E-mail: frokeefe@hahnlaw.com.

O'KEEFE, GARY RAYMOND, actor; b. Riverside, Calif., Oct. 3, 1940; s. Harold Clarence and Geraldine Amelia (Richardson) O'K.; m. Annette Barbara Dimeo, June 2, 1967. Grad. high sch., Santa Monica, Calif. Actor, LA, 1969—. Appeared in over 200 movies, TV shows and on stage. Chmn. Gower Gulch Neighbor Assn., Hollywood, Calif., 1978-79. Sgt. U.S. Army, 1960-66, Europe, Korea, Vietnam. Decorated Purple Heart with oak leaf cluster. Mem. SAG, AFTRA, VFW (life), 28th Inf. Assn. Democrat. Avocation: ironman triathlons (finished 5 times). E-mail: rayclb@sbcglobal.net.

O'KEEFE, JOHN DAVID, brokerage house executive; b. NYC, Nov. 16, 1941; s. Timothy J. and Agnes V. (Timlin) O.; m. Stefanie Carreau Keegan, Jan. 28, 1978; children: Douglas G., Hillary C., John M., Meredith B. BBA, Iona Coll., 1963; MBA, L.I. U., 1968. Analyst L.I. Lighting Co., Mineola, NY, 1965-69, Pershing and Co., NYC, 1969-72; mng. dir. Kidder, Peabody and Co., Inc., NYC, 1972-89; v.p. Smith Barney, NYC, 1989—. Bd. dirs. Heisman Found. Sgt. USMC, 1963-65. Mem.: Marine Corps. League, Union Club NYC, Downtown Athletic Club (gov. 1986, chmn. Heisman Trophy com. 1987—88, gov. 1988). Republican. Home: 31 Linden Tree Rd Wilton CT 06897-1613 Office: Smith Barney 200 Nyala Farms Rd Westport CT 06880-6267 Office Phone: 203-221-6082. Business E-Mail: john.d.okeefe@smithbarney.com.

O'KEEFE, KATHLEEN MARY, state official; b. Butte, Mont., Mar. 25, 1933; d. Hugh I. and Kathleen Mary (Harris) O'Keefe; m. Nick M. Baker, Sept. 18, 1954 (div. 1970); children: Patrick, Susan, Michael, Cynthia, Hugh, Mardeen. BA in Comm., St. Mary Coll., Xavier, Kans., 1954. Profl. singer, mem. Kathie Baker Quartet, 1962-72; rsch. cons. Wash. Ho. of Reps., Olympia, 1972-73; info. officer Wash. Employment Security Commn., Seattle, 1973-81, dir. pub. affairs, 1981-90, video dir., 1990-95, ret., 1995. Freelance writer, composer, producer, 1973—. Author: Job Finding In the Nineties, The Third Alternative, handbook on TV prodn., (children: So You Want to be President, 1995; composer numerous songs, also writer, dir., prodr. numerous spots. Founder, pres. bd. Eden, Inc., visual and performing arts, 1975—; pub. rels. chmn. Nat. Women's Dem. Conv., Seattle, 1979, Wash. Dem. Women, 1976-85; bd. dirs., composer, prodr., dir. N.Y. Film Festival, 1979; Dem. candidate Wash. State Senate, 1968. Recipient Silver medal Seattle Creative Awards Show for composing, directing and producing Rent A Kid, TV Pub. Svc. spot, 1979. Mem. Wash. Press Women. Roman Catholic. Home: 11225 19th Ave SE C104 Everett WA 98208 Office Phone: 425-337-0356. E-mail: kathie@nwrain.com.

O'KEEFE, LINDA LEE, physical education educator; b. Mojave, Calif., Apr. 28, 1947; d. Edward and Betty June O'Keefe. BS in Phys. Edn., U. Dayton, Ohio, 1971, MS in Phys. Edn., 1976. Tchr. Bellehaven Elem. Sch., Dayton, 1971—72, Meadowdale HS, Dayton, 1972—78; prof. Sinclair CC, Dayton, 1979—, coach, 1979—2003. Spkr., event organizer Am. Cancer Soc., Dayton, 2000—. Named Coach of Yr., Sinclair CC, 1979—2003; named one of Ohio's Top Educators, Ohio Mag., 2003; named to Hall of Fame, Dayton Tennis Commn., 1987, Nat. Jr. Coll. Athletic Assn., 1996; recipient Excellence in Tchg. award, Nat. Inst. Staff Devel., 2003, Faculty Excellence and Innovation award, Southwestern Ohio Coun. Higher Edn., 2003. Mem.: AAHPERD, Am. Assn. Health Educators, Ohio Assn. Health, Phys. Edn., Recreation and Dance. Avocations: reading, bicycling, tennis, hiking, gardening. Home: 1100 Stanwick Beavercreek OH 45430 Office: Sinclair CC 444 W 3d St Dayton OH 45430 Office Phone: 937-512-2287. Fax: 937-512-3056. Business E-Mail: linda.okeefe@sinclair.edu.

O'KEEFE, MARY A., marketing executive; Grad., No. Ill. U., 1978. Media rels. mgr. Prin. Fin. Group, Inc., Des Moines, 1990—93, dir. corp. rels, 1993—99, sr. v.p. Prin. Life, 1998, sr. v.p., 2001—04, sr. v.p., chief mktg. officer, 2004—. Bd. mem. Greater Des Moines Partnership Exec. Com.; bd. dirs. Greater Des Moines Cmty. Found., Dowling HS Found., Kum & Go, Nat. PRSA Audit Com. Named a Woman to Watch, Advt. Age, 2007. Office: Prin Fin Group 711 High St Des Moines IA 50392 Office Phone: 515-247-5111. Office Fax: 515-248-8469. *

O'KEEFE, MICHAEL, academic administrator, physicist; b. Mc Cloud, Minn. BS in Physics, Mathematics & Philosophy, Marquette U.; MS in Nuclear Physics & Mathematics, U. Pitts.; LittD (hon.), Hamline U. Pres. Consortium for Advancement of Pvt. Higher Edn., Washington, 1983—89; exec. v.p. & CEO McKnight Found., Mpls.; asst. sec. Fed. Dept. Health, Edn. & Welfare; human svcs. commr. State of Minn., 1999—2002; pres. Mpls. Coll. Art & Design, 2002—. Co-chmn. - edn. program Aspen Inst., 1987—; bd. regents U. Minn., 1996—2002; bd. dirs. Minn. Pub. Radio. Office: Office of President Minneapolis College Art & Design 2501 Stevens Ave Minneapolis MN 55404 Office Phone: 612-874-3785. *

O'KEEFE, MICHAEL DANIEL, lawyer; b. St. Louis, Jan. 3, 1938; s. Daniel Michael and Hanoria (Moriarty) O'K.; m. Bonnie Bowdern, July 11, 1964; children: Collen Coyne, Daniel Michael. AB, LLB, St. Louis U., 1961; postgrad., George Washington U., 1963. Bar: Mo. 1961, U.S. Ct. Appeals (8th cir.) 1961, U.S. Dist. Ct. (ea. dist.) Mo. 1961, Ill. 1975, U.S. Dist. Ct. (so. dist.) Ill. 1975, U.S. Ct. Appeals (5th and 7th cirs.) 1983, (10th cir.) 1995. Asst. cir. atty., St. Louis, 1961—62, 1964—65; pvt. practice, 1964-67; ptnr. Lucas, Murphy & O'Keefe, St. Louis, 1967-74, Thompson & Mitchell, St. Louis, 1974-96, Thompson Coburn, St. Louis, 1996—. Adj. prof. trial practice Sch. of Law, St. Louis U., 1992—. Editor: American Maritime Cases, 1985—. Trustee St. Louis U. Capt. USAF, 1962-64. Fellow Am. Coll. Trial Lawyers; mem. Internat. Assn. Def. Counsel, Fedn. Ins. and Corp. Counsel, Maritime Law Assn., Nat. Assn. Railroad Trial Counsel, Am. Law Inst. Democrat. Roman Catholic. Avocations: reading, tennis, fencing, archaeology, microbiology. Home: 372 Walton Row Saint Louis MO 63108-1909 Office: Thompson Coburn One US Bank Plz Saint Louis MO 63101-1643 Home Phone: 314-361-6048; Office Phone: 314-552-6092. Business E-Mail: mokeefe@thompsoncoburn.com.

O'KEEFE, SEAN CHARLES, academic administrator, former federal agency administrator; b. Monterey, Calif., Jan. 27, 1956; s. Patrick Gordon and Patricia Carlin O'Keefe; m. Laura Jean McCarthy, Oct. 7, 1978; children: Lindsey, Jonathan, Kevin. BA, Loyola U., New Orleans, 1977; MPA, Syracuse U., 1978. Budget analyst U.S. Dept. Def., Washington, comtr., CFO, 1989—92, apptd. sec. of the Navy, 1992; profl. staff U.S. Senate Appropriations Com., Washington; staff dir. U.S. Def. Appropriations Subcommittee, Washington; asst. to sr. v.p. for rsch., dean grad. sch. Pa. State U., prof., bus. adminstrn. University Park; Louis A. Bantle Prof., business and govt. policy Maxwell Sch. Citizenship and Pub. Affairs, Syracuse U., 1996, endowed chair, 1996; dir., Nat. Security Studies Partnership, Syracuse U. and John Hopkins U., 1996; dep. dir. Office of Mgmt. & Budget, Washington, 2000—01; adminstr. NASA, Washington, 2001—05; chancellor La. State U. and A&M Coll., Baton Rouge, 2005—. Bd. dirs. DuPont, Battele, Sensis Corp.; vis. scholar Wolfson Coll. U. Cambridge. Co-author: The Defense Industry in Post Cold War Era: Corporate Strategies and Public Policy Perspectives, 1998; contbr. articles to profl. jours.; chpts. to books. Staff rep. platform com. Rep. Nat. Com., New Orleans, 1988, advisor, Washington, 1994-97, mem. bd. adv. Naval Postgraduate Sch. Named Honorary Engr., Engrs. Coun., 2005; named one of Top 100 Irish Americans, Irish Am. Mag., 2003—04, the Stars of the South, 2006; named to, La. Polit. Hall of Fame, 2007; recipient Disting. Pub. Svc. award, 1993, Navigator award, Potomac Inst. for Policy Studies, 2005. Fellow Nat. Acad. Pub. Adminstrn., Internat. Acad. Astronautics; mem. Ft. Ticonderoga Assn., Cavalry Club. Republican. Roman Catholic. Avocations: golf, fishing. Office: La State U Chancellor's Office 156 Thomas Boyd Hall Baton Rouge LA 70803 Office Phone: 225-578-6977. Fax: 225-578-5982. Business E-Mail: chan@lsu.edu.

O'KEEFE, THOMAS MICHAEL, academic administrator; b. St. Cloud, Minn., Mar. 25, 1940; s. Thomas William and Genevieve B. (McCormick) O'K.; m. Kathleen Marie Gnifkowski, Aug. 20, 1966; children: Steven Michael, Ann Catherine. Student, Marquette U., 1961-65, BS, 1965; MS in Nuclear Physics, U. Pitts., 1968; DHL, Hamline U., 1989. Dir. edn. planning HEW, Washington, 1969-70, dep. asst. sec., 1977-80; v.p. Carnegie Found. for Advancement of Teaching, Washington, 1980-83; pres. Consortium for Advancement Pvt. Higher Edn., Washington, 1983-89; exec. v.p. McKnight Found., Mpls., 1989-99; commr. Dept. Human Svcs., State Minn., St. Paul, 1999—2002; pres. Mpls. Coll. Art and Design, 2002—. Dir. Washington internships in edn. George Washington U., 1970-73; dir. policy analysis and evaluation U. Ill., Chgo., 1973-74, assoc. v.p. acad. affairs, 1974-77; head U.S. del. to Orgn. Econ. Coop. and Devel., 1979, 80; mem. Carnegie Forum on Edn. and the Economy, 1985-88; mem. N.J. Commn. on Ind. Higher Edn., 1986-88; mem. task force on ind. higher edn. Edn. Commn. States, 1987-89; co-chair Edn. Program, The Aspen Inst., 1987—. Contbr. articles to profl. jours.; contbg. editor: Change mag., 1985—2001; bd. dirs.: Editl. Project in Edn., 1984—93. Bd. dirs. The Edn. Resources Inst., Boston, 1987-94, Minn. Coun. on Founds., 1994-99, Minn. Pub. Radio, 1999—, Alliance Excellent Edn., 2004-; trustee Buena Vista Coll., Storm Lake, Iowa, 1984-90; mem. Coun. on Fgn. Rels., 1995-99; bd. regents U. Minn., 1996-02. Mem.: Mpls. Club. Democrat. Office: Mpls Coll Art and Design 2501 Stevens Ave S Minneapolis MN 55404 Home Phone: 612-617-0285. Business E-Mail: michael_okeefe@mcad.edu.

O'KEEFE, VINCENT THOMAS, clergyman, educational association administrator; b. Jersey City, Jan. 10, 1920; s. James and Sarah (Allen) O'K. AB, Georgetown U., 1943; MA, Woodstock Coll., 1945, Ph.L., 1944; Th.L., St. Albert de Louvain, Belgium, 1951; student, Muenster U., Germany, 1951-52; S.T.D., Gregorian U., Rome, 1954. Ordained priest Roman Cath. Ch., 1950. Instr. Latin and math. Regis High Sch., NYC, 1944-47; assoc. prof. fundamental theology Woodstock Coll., 1954-60; acad. v.p. Fordham U., Bronx, NY, 1960-62, exec. v.p., 1962-63, pres., 1963-65, rector Jesuit community, 1984-88; gen. asst. to superior gen. Soc. of Jesus, Rome, 1965-83, v.p. spl. projects Jesuit Conf., 1988-90, superior, writer provincial residence, Bronx, 1990-94; superior Am. House, NYC, 1994-2000. Mem. regents exams. and scholarship center N.Y. State Dept. Edn.; pres., dir., mem. exec. com. Council Higher Ednl. Instns. of N.Y.C. Author: The History and Meaning of Ex Attrito Fit Contritus, 1957; Contbr. articles to religious publs., also book reviews. Dir. N.Y. World's Fair, 1964-65; Corp. Bd. mgrs. New York Bot. Garden; dir., mem. bd. Center Intercultural Formation, Cuernavaca, Mexico; trustee Fordham U. Fellow Royal Soc. Encouragement Arts Mfrs. and Commerce (London); mem. Council Higher Edn. City N.Y., Religion Council Cath. Secondary Schs. Archdiocese of N.Y., Cath. Bibl. Assn., Cath. Theol. Assn. Am., Religion Edn. Assn., NEA, Jesuit Ednl. Assn., Nat. Cath. Edn. Assn., Internat. Assn. Univs., Soc. Cath. Coll. Tchrs. Sacred Doctrine, Phi Beta Kappa. Roman Catholic. Office: 106 W 56th St New York NY 10019-3803 Office Phone: 212-581-4640.

OKEKE, CHRISTIAN NWACHUKWU, law educator; b. Obinofia, Enugu, Nigeria, June 8, 1941; s. Stephen Agueze and Sussana Nwaduvu Okeke; m. Justina Nwanagu Okeke. LLM Summa Cum Laude, Kiev State U., Ukraine, 1969; PhD, Free U., Holland, 1973. Lic. Nigerian Coun. Legal Edn. Sr. Lectr. U. Nigeria, Enugu, Nigeria, 1974—85; pioneer dean emeritus Nnamdi Azikiwe U., Awka, Nigeria, 1985—91; dep. vice chancellor, dean of law emeritus Enugu State U. of Sci. Tech., Enugu, Nigeria, 1991—95; fellow MaxPlanck Inst., Heidelberg, Germany, 1994—95; law prof. Golden Gate U., San Francisco, 1996—. Ptr. ILegbune, Okeke & Co., Enugu, Nigeria, 1980—94; cons. African Network for Prevention of Child Abuse and Neglect, Enugu, 1974—; trustee mem. Internat. First Aid Soc., Enugu, 1974—. Author: Expansion of New Subjects of International Law, 1973, Controversial Subject of Contemporary International Law, 1974, Theory & Practice of International Law in Nigeria, 1986. Exec. dir. Internat. First Aid Soc., Inc., Antioch, Calif., 1994—. Rsch. fellowship, Hague Acad. of Internat. Law, 1970, fellowship, Cambridge U., England, 1971. Mem.: Nigerian Bar Assn., Nigerian Soc. of Internat. Law. Home: 4320 Mink Ct Antioch CA 94531 Office: Golden Gate U Sch of Law 536 Mission St San Francisco CA 94105 Office Phone: 415-442-6695. Office Fax: 415-442-6756. E-mail: cokeke@ggu.edu.

O'KELLEY, WILLIAM CLARK, federal judge; b. Atlanta, Jan. 2, 1930; s. Ezra Clark and Theo (Johnson) O'K.; m. Ernestine Allen, Mar. 28, 1953; children: Virginia Leigh O'Kelley Wood, William Clark Jr. AB, Emory U., 1951, LLB, 1953. Bar: Ga. 1952. Pvt. practice, Atlanta, 1957-59; asst. U.S. atty. No. Dist. Ga., 1959-61; partner O'Kelley, Hopkins & Van Gerpen, Atlanta, 1961-70; U.S. dist. judge No. Dist. Ga., Atlanta, 1970—, chief judge, 1988-94. Mem. com. on adminstrn. of criminal law Jud. Conf. U.S., 1979-82, exec. com., 1983-84, subcom. on jury trials in complex criminal cases, 1981-82, dist. judge rep. 11th cir., 1981-84, mem. adv. com. of fed. rules of criminal procedure, 1984-87; bd. dirs. Fed. Jud. Ctr., 1987-91, adv. com. history program, 1989-91, com. on orientation of newly appointed dist. judges, 1985-88; mem. Com. Jud. Resources, 1989-94; mem. Jud. Coun. 11th Cir., 1990-96, exec. com., 1990-96; mem. Fgn. Intelligence Surveillance Ct., 1980-87; mem. Alien Terrorist Removal Ct., 1996—; corp. sec., dir. Gwinnett Bank & Trust Co., Norcross, Ga., 1967-70. Mem. exec. com., gen. counsel Ga. Republican Com., 1968-70; mem. fin. com. Northwest Ga. Girl Scout Coun., 1958-70; trustee Emory U., 1991-97. Served as 1st lt. USAF, 1953-57; capt. USAFR. Mem. Fed. Bar Assn., Ga. State Bar, Atlanta Bar Assn., Dist. Judges Assn. 5th Cir. (sec.-treas. 1976-77, v.p. 1977-78, pres. 1978-80), Lawyers Club Atlanta, Kiwanis (past pres.), Atlanta Athletic Club, Sigma Chi (named Significant Sig 1983), Phi Delta Phi, Omicron Delta Kappa. Baptist. Home: 550 Ridgecrest Dr Norcross GA 30071-2158 Office: US Dist Ct 1942 US Courthouse 75 Spring St SW Atlanta GA 30303-3309 Office Phone: 404-215-1530.

O'KELLEY, WINNIE, editor; m. Patrick McGeehan; 2 children. Grad., Northwestern U., 1984. Asst. copy desk chief Adv. Age, 1985; with Am. Banker, 1988; mng. editor Banking Week; dep. bus. editor, enterprise editor NY Times, NYC, 1993—. Recipient Best in Bus. for Overall Excellence Cert. Merit, Am. Bus. Editors and Writers, 2003. Office: New York Times 229 W 43rd St New York NY 10036 Office Phone: 212-556-7356. Office Fax: 212-556-7614.

OKEN, MARC D., retired bank executive; m. Celene Oken; 5 children. BSBA, Loyola Coll., Balt., Md., 1968; MBA, U. of West Fla., 1973. With Price Waterhouse, 1974—81, 1983—89; fellow Securities and Exchange Commn., 1981—83; principal fin. exec. Bank Am. Corp., Charlotte, NC, 1989—98, CFO, 1998—2005. Bd. dirs. Sonoco Products Co., Star Scientific, Inc., 2005—, Marsh & McLennan Cos. Inc., 2006—. Aviator USN, 1968—73, Vietnam. Office: 100 N Tryon St Ste 5120 Charlotte NC 28202

OKEN, ROBERT, retired neuroscientist, consultant; b. NYC, Oct. 15, 1929; s. Milton and Etta (Weiner) Oken. BA, NYU, 1949, PhD, 1958. V.p., dir. Oken Fabrics Inc., NYC, 1959-68, 71-73; rschr., cons. U.S. Army, USN, Washington, Frederick, Md., 1955-56, Teller Environ. Sys., NYC, 1969-70; businessman R.A. Siegel Galleries, NYC, 1978-87; cons. to dir. N.Y. State Inst. Basic Rsch., SI, 1991-93; cons. Gerex Biotech. P.L. McGeer, Vancouver, BC, Canada, 1994—98; ret., 1998. Editl. advisor NIMH, 2001—, Neurosci. Rsch., 1998—. Contbr. articles to profl. jours. Sci. advisor Lifer Environ. Group, Roxbury, NJ, 1984—87; vol. Dover Gen. Hosp., NJ, 1989—90. With US Army, 1955—56. Recipient medal of achievement, Dover Gen. Hosp., 1990. Mem.: AAAS, Internat. Assn. Improvement Mental Health (advisor 2006), N.Y. Neuropsychology Group, N.Y. Acad. Scis., Am. Chem. Soc., Intertel, Mensa Internat., Am. Philatelic Soc., Phi Beta Kappa. Home and Office: PO Box 412 Hopatcong NJ 07843-0412 Office Phone: 973-770-0006. Personal E-mail: robertoken@nac.net.

OKERE, CHUMA ONYEAGHALA, neuroscientist; b. Enugu, Nigeria, Mar. 20, 1964; s. Geoffrey Chukwuma and Marian Nnenna (Ike) O.; m. Maria Anayo Iwuoha, Jan. 17, 1993; children: Chukwumerije Uzoma, Tochukwu Eziihe, Enyichukwu Nneoma. BSc, U. Ibadan, Nigeria, 1987, MSc, 1990; PhD, Kochi Med. Sch., Japan, 1997. Lectr. U. Maiduguri, Nigeria, 1990-93; rsch. assoc. Kochi Med. Sch., 1999-2000, postdoctoral rsch. fellow, 1997-99; rsch. fellow Med. Coll. Pa. Drexel U., Phila., 2000—. Adj. prof. C.C. of Phila. Fgn. Rsch. fellow Ministry Sci. Culture and Sports, Japan, 1993. Mem. AAAS, Internat. Behavioral Neurosci. Soc., Japan Neuroendocrine Soc. Avocations: reading, nature viewing. Office: Drexel U Coll Medicine 2900 Queen Dr Philadelphia PA 19129 Home: 48 Melrose Ave Lansdowne PA 19050-2528 Home Phone: 610-410-7111; Office Phone: 215-991-8428. Business E-Mail: cokere@drexelmed.edu.

OKERLUND, ARLENE NAYLOR, academic administrator, writer; b. Emmitsburg, Md., Oct. 13, 1938; d. George Wilbur and Ruth Opal (Sensenbaugh) Naylor; m. Michael Dennis Okerlund, June 6, 1959 (div. Apr. 1983); 1 dau., Linda Susan. BA, U. Md., 1960; PhD, U. Calif.-San Diego, 1969. Instr. sci. Mercy Hosp. Nursing Sch., Balt., 1959-63; prof. English San Jose (Calif.) State U., 1969—2005, dean humanities and arts, 1980-86, acad. v.p., 1986-93. Cons. Ednl. Testing Svc., Berkeley, Calif., 1976—80. Author: Elizabeth Wydeville: The Slandered Queen, 2005; editor San Jose Studies, 1975—80; contbr. articles on the humanities to profl. jours. Bd. dirs. World Forum Silicon Valley, Peninsula Banjo Band. Grantee NEH, 1979; grantee San Jose State U., 1971-72. Mem.: MLA (del. to assembly, west coast rep. 1976—77), Am. Beethoven Soc. (v.p. bd. dirs. 1983—2006), Calif. Coun. Fine Arts Deans (pres. 1984—86), Internat. Coun. Fine Arts Deans, Philol. Assn. Pacific Coast (sec.-treas. 1975—78). Democrat. Office: San Jose State U Dept English Washington Sq San Jose CA 95192-0090 Office Phone: 408-924-4425. Business E-Mail: okerlund@email.sjsu.edu.

OKERSON, ANN SHUMELDA LILLIAN, librarian; d. Jacob and Alexandra Tereshtshenko Shumelda. MLS, U. Calif. Libr. Simon Fraser U., Vancouver, B.C., Canada, 1970—85; dir. libr. svcs. Jerry Alper Inc., Eastchester, N.Y., 1985-90; sr. program officer Assn. of Rsch. Libraries., Washington, 1990-95; assoc. univ. libr., collection develop and mgmt. Yale U., New Haven, 1995—, assoc. univ. libr., collections and technical services, 1999—, assoc. univ. libr., collections and internat. programs, 2003—. Adj. faculty mem., grad. sch. info. U. Mich., 1995; private investigator, project coord. Liblicense, 1997—; worked over the years on numerous projects, adv. boards, and speaking engagements. Author (synopsia chpt.) Andrew W. Mellon study University Libraries and Scholarly Communications, 1992; creator, pub., Directory of Electronic Journals, Newsletters and Academic Discussions Lists, 1991-95; co-editor (with James O'Donnell) Scholarly Journals at the Crossroads: a Subversive Proposal for Electronic Journal Publishing, 1995; co-owner, co-moderator, NewJour, 1993-; Editor numerous books; contbr. articles to profl. publs. Named Alumni of Yr., Mt. View Acad., 1995, Serials Libr. Yr., ALA, 1993; recipient Best Article in the area of serials, acquisitions, and/or collections award, ALA, 1988, 93, Libr. Info. Tech. Assn.(LITA)/High Tech award, 1999; numerous grants. Avocations: chocolate, travel, reading. Office: Yale U Libr PO Box 208240 New Haven CT 06520-8240 Office Phone: 203-432-1764. Business E-Mail: ann.okerson@yale.edu.

OKIISHI, THEODORE HISAO, mechanical engineering educator; b. Honolulu, Jan. 15, 1939; s. Clifford Muneo and Dorothy Asako (Tokushima) O.; m. Rae Wiemers, May 28, 1963; children: Christopher Gene, John Clifford, Mark William, Kenneth Edward. Student, U. Hawaii, 1956-57; BS, Iowa State U., 1960, MS, 1963, PhD, 1965. Registered profl. engr., Iowa, Ohio. From asst. prof. to prof., assoc. dean coll. engring. Iowa State U., Ames, 1967—. Cons. on fluid dynamics Contbr. articles to profl. jours. Served to capt. C.E., U.S. Army, 1965-67 Decorated Joint Services Commendation award; named Outstanding Prof., Iowa State U. student sect. ASME, 1983, Mech. Engring. Dept. Prof. of Yr., Iowa State U., 1977, 86, 90; recipient award for research NASA, 1975; Ralph R. Teetor award Soc. Automotive Engrs., 1976, Engring. Coll. Superior Teaching award Iowa State U., 1987, Cardinal Key Iowa State U., 1991. Fellow ASME (Melville medal 1989, 98); mem. AIAA, Sigma Xi. Republican. Mem. Ch. of Jesus Christ of Latter-day Saints. Club: Osborn Research Home: 2940 Monroe Dr Ames IA 50010-4362 Office: Iowa State U 104 Marston Hl Ames IA 50011-0001 Office Phone: 515-294-4395. Business E-Mail: tedo@iastate.edu.

OKINAGA, LAWRENCE SHOJI, lawyer; m. Carolyn Hisako Uesugi, Nov. 26, 1966; children: Carrie, Caryn, Laurie. BA, U. Hawaii, 1963; JD, Georgetown U., 1972. Bar: Hawaii 1972, U.S. Dist. Ct. Hawaii 1972, U.S. Ct. Appeals (9th cir.) 1976. Adminstrv. asst. to Congressman Spark Matsunaga, Honolulu, 1964, 65-69; law clk. to chief judge U.S. Dist. Ct. Hawaii, Honolulu, 1972-73; assoc. Carlsmith Ball, Honolulu, 1973-76, ptnr., 1976—. Mem. Gov.'s Citizens Adv. Com. Coastal Zone Mgmt., 1974—79; sec. Hawaii Bicentennial Corp., 1975—77, vice chmn., 1983—85, chmn., 1985—87; mem. Jud. Selection Commn., State of Hawaii, 1979—87, vice chmn., 1986; mem. consumer adv. coun. Fed. Res. Bd., 1984—86; chmn. Jud. Conduct Commn., State of Hawaii, 1991—94; apptd. mem. Fed. Savs. and Loan Adv. Coun., Washington, 1988—89; mem. nat. adv. coun. U.S. SBA, 1994—2000; mem. adv. coun. Fed. Res. Bank, San Francisco, 1995—2002. Pres., bd. dirs. Moiliili Cmty. Ctr., Honolulu, 1965—68, 1973—86, trustee, 1993—; bd. dirs. Pub. Sch. Hawaii Found., 2004—; bd. visitors Georgetown U. Law Ctr., 1993—; trustee Kuakini Med. Ctr., 1984—88, 1989—96. Capt. USAFR, 1964—72, capt. USAFR, 1974—76. Mem.: ABA (ho. of dels. 1991—94, mem. standing com. jud. selection tenure and compensation 1993—96, mem. standing com. jud. independence 1999—2002), Am. Judicature Soc. (bd. dirs. 1986, treas. 1995—97, pres. 1997—99), Hawaii Bar Assn. (sec., bd. dirs. 1981), Georgetown U. Law Alumni Assn. (bd. dirs. 1986—91), Omicron Delta Kappa. Office: Carlsmith Ball PO Box 656 Honolulu HI 96809-0656 E-mail: lso@carlsmith.com.

OKITA, GEORGE TORAO, retired pharmacologist; b. Seattle, Jan. 18, 1922; s. Kazuo and Fusao (Muguruma) O.; m. Fujiko Shimizu, Nov. 29, 1958; children: Ronald Hajime, Sharon Mariko, Glenn Torao. Student, U. Cin., 1943-44; BA, Ohio State U., 1948; PhD, U. Chgo., 1951. Rsch. asst., rsch. assoc., instr., then asst. prof. U. Chgo., 1949-63; assoc. prof. Northwestern U. Med. Sch., 1963-66, prof. pharmacology, 1966—90, acting chmn. pharmacology, 1968—70, 1976—77; prof. emeritus molecular pharmacology and biol. chemistry, 1990—. Contbr. articles to profl. jours.; Asst. editor: Jour. Pharmacology and Exptl. Therapeutics, 1965-68. Served with AUS, 1944-46. NIH Postdoctoral fellow, 1952 Mem. AAAS, AAUP, Am. Soc. Pharmacology and Exptl. Therapeutics, Internat. Soc. Biochem. Pharmacology, Am. Heart Assn., Cardiac Muscle Soc., Sigma Xi. Achievements include research in med. field. Home: 95-1058 Kihene St Mililani HI 96789 Personal E-mail: gtoki@aol.com.

OKOAMPA-AHOOFE, KWAME, language educator, historian; arrived in US, 1985; s. Kwame and Adwoa Aninwaa Okoampa-Ahoofe; m. Dolly D. Mensah, June 24, 2004; children: Abena Aninwaa, Kwame III. BA with honors, CCNY, 1990; MA, Temple U., Phila., 1993, PhD, 1998. Instr. English Tech. Career Inst., NYC, 1991—93; instr. history Ind. State U., Terre Haute, 1994—95; asst. prof. English SUNY-Nassau CC, Garden City, 1997—2007, assoc. prof., 2007—. Curator-at-large Okyeman Archives, Kibi, Ghana, 2006—. Author: Atumpan, 2004, The New Scape Goats, 2005, Dr. J.B. Danquah, 2005; reporter, book critic/editor: NY Amsterdam News, 1987—2002, asst. editor, spl. corr./columnist: African Profiles Internat., 1991—95, dep. editor: Terra Haute Vanguard, 1994—95, columnist: NY Beacon, 2003—05, Harlem Times, 2003—04, Accra Mail, 2005—; contbr. articles to profl. jous. Mem. Okyeman Coun., Ghana, 2006—. Recipient John J. Reyne Artistic Achievement award for English poetry, CCNY, 1988, Best Essay award, Nassau Rev., Nassau C.C., SUNY, 1999; Ford Found. undergrad. fellow, City Coll. CUNY, 1987—90. Mem.: MLA, Nat. Coun. Tchrs. English. Independent. Presbyterian. Avocations: journalism, debating political and social issues. Office: Nassau CC SUNY One Education Dr Garden City NY 11530 Office Phone: 516-572-8121.

O'KONSKI, MARJORIE KATHERINE, music educator; d. Robert Thomas and Katherine Josephine Kilbride; m. James Edward O'Konski, July 15, 1972; children: Mary Elizabeth, Katherine Helena, Robert Michael, Brian James, Richard Joseph. MusB in Piano Performance, U. Mo., Kansas City, 1968; MusM in Piano Performance, U. Mich., Ann Arbor, 1970; MusM in Edn. and Music Therapy, U. Kans., Lawrence, 1996. Tchg. asst. U. Mich., Ann Arbor, 1968—70; instr. piano Wash. State U., Pullman, 1970—71, Southwestern Coll., Winfield, Kans., 1971—72, O'Konski Piano Studio, Bradenton, Fla., 1973—79, Olathe, Kans., 1979—89, Lawrence, 1990—97; music therapist Wichita Falls State Hosp., Tex., 1996—97; instr. piano O'Konski Piano Studio, Topeka, 1997—2003; dir. music therapy clin. tng. and activities Midwest Health Svcs., 1997—2003; music therapist O'Konski Music Therapy Contract Svcs., 2002—03; dir. music therapy program Wartburg Coll., Waverly, Iowa. Advisor music therapy majors Wartburg Coll. Music Therapy Program, Waverly, Iowa, 2003—; mem. Wartburg Coll. Human and Animal Rsch. Com., 2004—06, Wartburg Coll. Faculty Interest Group, 2006—, Wartburg Coll. Instrnl. Resources Com., 2006—; advisor Southwestern Coll. Female Athletes, Winfield, Kans., 1971—72; coord. quality assurance Lexington Pk. Nursing and Post-Acute Care Facility, Topeka, 2001—03; mem. practice analysis com. Certification Bd. Music Therapists, Kansas City, Mo., 2003—03; advisor Wartburg Coll. Cath. Knights, 2003—, Wartburg Music Therapy Student Assn., 2003—; adj. faculty Washburn U., Tokepa, 1998—2003; presenter, spkr. in field. Performer: (soloist) Kansas City Philharmonic, Bach Concerto for Four Harpsichords, (piano accompanist) Washburn U. Faculty Recital, Saxophone, Graduate Recital, Saxophone, Washburn U. Student Recital, voice, Washburn U. Studio Recital, Violin, Violin Music for Memorial Service, Washburn University Faculty Recital, Voice, Senior Recital, Violincello, Senior Recital, Trumpet, Senior Recital, Percussion, Auditions for Washburn Univ.Honors Recital, (soloist) Kansas City Youth Symphony, Symphonic Variations, C. Frank, (piano accompanist) Honors Recital, Washburn University, Studio Recital, Trumpet, Student Recital, Washburn University, Washburn University Senior Recital, Voice, Washburn University Faculty Recital, Voice, Senior Recital, Violincello, Student Recital, Washburn University, Regional Voice Competition, NATS, Washburn University Joint Faculty Recital, Opera Selections, (soloist) Concerto in A Minor, R. Schumann, (piano accompanist) Studio Recital, Violin, Washburn University Student Recital, Opera Selections, Topeka Opera Society (KS), Masterclass, Violincello, Student Recital, Washburn University, Senior Recital, Viola, Wartburg College Faculty Recital, Voice, Benefit Concert, Violincello, (piano soloist) Fundraiser (Dinner), Wartburg Symphony, (piano accompanist) Wartburg College Scholarship Auditions, (soloist) Southwestern Coll. Orch., Concerto in A Major, W. A. Mozart, (piano accompanist) Wartburg College Senior Recital, Bassoon, Wartburg College Junior Recital, Voice, Student Recitals, Wartburg College, Voice Audition, Wartburg Faculty Position, (symphony pianist) Topeka Symphony Orchestra Concerts, Wartburg Community Symphony Concerts; piano adjudicator (performance evaluation) Student Day Auditions, FSMTA (Florida), Student Day Auditions, KMTA (Kansas); performer: (piano) Chorale Fantasy, L. van Beethoven, (piano soloist) Salon Music at Lexington Park, (piano accompanist) University of Kansas Faculty Recital, Trombone, Violin Studio Recital (KS), University of Kansas Senior Recital, Student Compositions. Mem. Lawrence Civic

Choir, Kans., 1991—94; sec., mem. Wartburg Cmty. Symphony, Waverly, 2003—06. Recipient Activity Dir. Yr., Kans. Health Care Assn., 1999, Aging Rsch. Devel. Support award, Wartburg Coll., 2005; fellow, Robert F. Unkefer Acad. Neurologic Music Therapy, Colo. State U., 2005; grantee, Midwest Health Svcs., Kans., 2000, 2002, Wartburg Coll., 2005. Mem.: AAUW (assoc.), AAUP (assoc.), Topeka Activity Dirs. Assn. (sec. 1999—2000, pres. 2000—01, sec., treas. 2001—03), Am. Music Therapy Assn. (assoc.; mem. rep. midwestern region 2003—06), Pi Kappa Lambda, Mu Phi Epsilon (life; pres., Alpha Kappa chpt. 1966—68, Outstanding Sr. 1968). Conservative. Roman Catholic. Achievements include development of comprehensive music therapy program for long-term care, Midwest Health Services (Kansas); six-month national roster music therapy internship program at Midwest Health Services (KS); Tone Bar Chimes Performing Ensemble For Long-Term Care Residents; Performances Within Facility, Local Community, And Adjoining Communities; Uniform Concert Attire; Compact Discs And Videos Produced; intergenerational performing ensemble; choreography, singing, playing instrument, spoken dialogue included; costumes, set designs, original scripts; music arranged by Marjorie O'Konski. Avocations: reading, travel, hiking, cryptography, solving sudoku puzzles. Home: 1209 Charlene Street Waverly IA 50677-9631 Office: Wartburg College 100 Wartburg Boulevard Waverly IA 50677-0903 Home Phone: 319-230-5179; Office Phone: 319-352-8401. Office Fax: 319-352-8501. E-mail: marj.okonski@wartburg.edu.

OKOSHI-MUKAI, SUMIYE, artist; b. Seattle; One-woman shows include Gallery Internat., N.Y.C., 1970, Miami Mus. Modern Art, 1972, Galerie Saison, Tokyo, 1982, St. Peter's Ch., Living Room Gallery, N.Y.C., 1987, Viridian Gallery, 1987, 1992, 1996, 1999, Port Washington (N.Y.) Pub. Libr., 1985, NAS, Washington, 1991—92, exhibited in group shows at Bergen Mus. Art and Scis., 1983, Am. Acad. Arts and Scis., 1984, Port Washington Pub. Libr., 1985, Hudson River Mus., 1985, Sao Paulo and N.Y. Culture Exch., 1988, Hyundai Gallery, Pusan, Korea, 1988, Gary Snyder Fine Art, N.Y.C., 2002, Represented in permanent collections The Mitsui & Co., N.Y., Hotel Nikko, Atlanta, Bank of Nagoya, N.Y., Palace Hotel, Guam Island, Port Washington Pub. Libr., Lowe Gallery-U. Miami, Miami Mus. Modern Art, Nat. Women's Edn. Ctr., Saitama-ken, Japan, NAS, Hammond Mus., North Salem, N.Y., The Jane Voorhees Zimmerli Art Mus., N.J., Asian Traditions Modern Expressions; included in Collage-Techniques, 1994. Mem. Nat. Women Artists Assn. (Belle Cramer award Zluta and Joseph Fund award, Ralph Mayer Meml. award, Doris Kreindler Meml. award 2002), Nat. Mus. Women in the Arts (charter mem. 1994).

OKOUNKOV, ANDREI, mathematics professor; b. Moscow, 1969; 2 children. BA in Math., PhD in Math., Moscow State U. Rsch. fellow, Dobrushin Math. Lab. Inst. for Problems of Info. Transmission, Russian Acad. Sciences; instructor U. Chgo.; asst. prof. U. Calif., Berkeley; prof., math. dept. representation theory Princeton U, 2002—. Mem. Inst. for Advanced Study, Math. Sciences Rsch. Inst., Berkeley. Recipient Sloan Research Fellowship, 2000, Fields medal, Internat. Math. Union, 2006. Office: Princeton U Dept Math 701 Fine Hall Washington Rd Princeton NJ 08544-1000

OKRENT, DAVID, engineering educator; b. Passaic, NJ, Apr. 19, 1922; s. Abram and Gussie (Pearlman) O.; m. Rita Gilda Holtzman, Feb. 1, 1948 (dec. June 2005); children: Nina, Jocelyne. ME, Stevens Inst. Tech., 1943; MA, Harvard, 1948, PhD in Physics, 1951. Mech. engr. NACA, Cleve., 1943-46; sr. physicist Argonne (Ill.) Nat. Lab., 1951-71; regents lectr. UCLA, 1968, prof. engring., 1971-91, prof. emeritus, rsch. prof., 1991—. Vis. prof. U. Wash., Seattle, 1963, U. Ariz., Tucson, 1970-71; Isaac Taylor chair Technion, 1977-78 Author: Fast Reactor Cross Sections, 1960, Computing Methods in Reactor Physics, 1968, Reactivity Coefficients in Large Fast Power Reactors, 1970, Nuclear Reactor Safety, 1981; contbr. articles to profl. jours. Mem. adv. com. on reactor safeguards AEC, 1963-87, also chmn., 1966; sci. sec. to sec. gen. of Geneva Conf., 1958; mem. U.S. del. to all Geneva Atoms for Peace Confs. Guggenheim fellow, 1961-62, 77-78; recipient Disting. Appointment award Argonne Univs. Assn., 1970, Disting. Service award U.S. Nuclear Regulatory Commn., 1985. Fellow Soc. for Risk Analysis, Am. Phys. Soc., Am. Nuclear Soc. (Tommy Thompson award 1980, Glenn Seaborg medal 1987, George C. Lawrence Pioneering award 2007), Nat. Acad. Engring. Home: 439 Veteran Ave Los Angeles CA 90024-1956 Business E-Mail: okrent@ucla.edu.

OKTAVEC, EILEEN M., anthropologist, artist; b. Apr. 9, 1942; d. Albert W. and Margaret (O'Reilley) O. Student, Cooper Union, NYC, 1960-61; BA in Anthropology, SUNY, Stony Brook, 1973; MA in Anthropology, U. Ariz., 1975. Instr. anthropology White Pines Coll., Chester, NH, 1975-76; art dir. Great Walks, Inc., Goffstown, NH, 1989—. Author: Answered Prayers: Miracles and Milagros Along the Border, 1995; photographs in: Great Walks of Acadia National Park and Mount Desert, 1990, Great Walks of Southern Arizona, 1991, Great Walks of Big Bend National Park, 1991, Great Walks of the Great Smokies, 1992, Great Walks of Yosemite National Park, 1993, Great Walks of Sequoia and Kings Canyon National Parks, 1994, Great Walks of Acadia National Park and Mount Desert Island, 1994, Great Walks of the Olympic Peninsula, 1999, The Woodland Garden, 1996; exhibited in group shows at Rockport (Mass.) Art Festival, 1977, 78, Berkshire Art Assn., Pittsfield, Mass., 1979, The Ogunquit (Maine) Art Ctr., 1982, 83, N.H. Art Assn., Manchester, 1985, Concord (Mass.) Art Assn., 1988, 91, 92, 96-98, Sharon (N.H.) Art Ctr., 1998. Winner Southwest Book award for Answered Prayers, 1997. Mem. Concord Art Assn., Sharon Arts Ctr. Home: 3151 Hazens Notch Rd Montgomery Center VT 05471-4408 Office Phone: 603-497-8020.

OKTAY, MAJA HRZENJAK, medical educator; b. Zagreb, Croatia, May 20, 1965; arrived in US, 1972; d. Vjekoslav and Terezija Hrženjak; m. Kutluk Han Oktay, Aug. 5, 1995; children: Isabelle, Kenan, Lara. MD, U. Zagreb, 1989; MSc, U. Natural Scis., Zagreb, 1992; PhD, U. Zagreb and U. Tex., San Antonio, 1995. Bd. cert. anatomical pathology, bd. cert. cytopathology. Intern U. Hosp. Petrova, Zagreb, 1989—90; postdoctoral fellow Meml. Sloan-Kettering Cancer Ctr., NYC, 1996—97, clin. scholar biomed. rsch. training, 1997—98; anatomical pathology resident Yale New Haven Hosp., 1998—2001; cytopathology fellow Montefiore Med. Ctr., Bronx, NY, 2001—02; asst. prof. Albert Einstein Coll. Medicine, Montefiore Med. Ctr., Bronx, 2002—. Contbr. chapters to books, articles to profl. jours. Recipient Outstanding Achievement in Autopsy Pathology award, Dr. Halina Goldstein Fund, 1999; Charles A. Dana fellow, Sloan-Kettering, NY, 1997—98, Clin. scholar, Biomed. Rsch. fellow, grantee, Nat. Cancer Inst., 1997—98. Mem.: US and Can. Acad. Pathology, Coll. Am. Pathologists. Avocations: swimming, jogging, tennis, skiing. Home: 152 Florence Ave Rye NY 10580 Office: Montefiore Med Ctr 111 E 210th St Bronx NY 10467

OKTEM, OZGUR, medical doctor, researcher; b. Kars, Turkey, Aug. 1, 1971; s. Lutfi and Fatma Oktem. MD, Erciyes U. Sch. of Medicine, Turkey, 1996. Cert. obstetrics and gynecology Marmara U. Hosp., 2001. Residency obstetrics and gynecology Marmara U. Hosp., Istanbul, Turkey, 1997—2001; rsch. fellow in reproductive medicine Ctr. For Reproductive Medicine and Infertility, Weill Med. Coll. of Cornell U., New York, NY. Dir., chief attending clinician of obgyn Pendik Sifa Hosp., Istanbul, Turkey, 2001—03. Mem.: Postdoctoral Assn. NY, Nat. Geographic Soc., NY Acad. Sci., Soc. Gynecologic Investigations, Am. Soc. Reproductive Medicine (Best Rsch. Study award 2005). Achievements include research in three dimention follicle culture, xenografting human ovary, ovarian transplantation. Avocations: guitar, astronomy. Office Phone: 212-746-1086. Office Fax: 212-746-8848. Personal E-mail: ozo2001@med.cornell.edu.

OKUHARA, TETSU, artist, photographer; b. LA, Mar. 3, 1940; Student, U. Chgo., 1958-61, The Cooper Union, 1970-71. Lectr., workshop leader Otis Coll., L.A., Hartwick Coll., Oneonta, N.Y., NYU, Rutgers U., New Brunswick, N.J., Sch. Visual Arts, N.Y.C., New Sch., N.Y.C., Wesleyan U., Middletown, Conn, Cornish Inst., Seattle. Exhibited in one person and group shows at L.A. County Mus., 2002, Small Works, NYU, 1999, Fotomassan, Goteborg, Sweden, Chgo. Cultural Ctr., 1997, Gotland Konst Mus., Sweden, 1995, San Francisco Camera Work, 1994, Art Inst. Boston, 1994, Artist Space, N.Y.C., 1992, Chgo. Art Inst., 1991-92, Art in General, N.Y.C., 1990, Cleve. Mus. Art, 1978, San Francisco Mus. Modern Art, 1979, 2003, Tokyo Met. Mus. Photography, 2005, numerous others; represented in permanent collections Mus. Modern Art, N.Y.C., Met. Mus. Art, N.Y.C., Hasselad Collection, Goteborg, Sweden, Tokyo Met. Mus. Photography, Art Inst., Chgo., San Francisco Mus. Modern Art, L.A. County Mus., numerous others. Grantee Creative Artist Pub. Svc., 1973-74, 75-76, N.Y. Found. for the Arts, 1988-89, Nat. Endowment for the Arts, 1988-89, La Napoule Found./Nat. Endowment for the Arts, France, 1989, Intercambio, San Juan, P.R., 1991, James P. Phelan Art Award, San Francisco, 1993-94; Guggenheim fellow, 1975-76, N.Y. Found. for Arts fellow, 2000. Home: 202 E 42nd St New York NY 10017-5808 Office Phone: 212-986-0356. Personal E-mail: tetsuokuhara@yahoo.com.

OKUN, DANIEL ALEXANDER, environmental engineering educator; b. NYC, June 19, 1917; s. William Howard and Leah (Seligman) O.; m. Elizabeth Griffin, Jan. 14, 1946; children: Michael Griffin, Tema Jon. BS, Cooper Union, 1937; MS, Calif. Inst. Tech., 1938; ScD, Harvard U., 1948; ScD (hon.), U. NC, 2000. Registered profl. engr., NC, NY. With USPHS, 1940-42; tchg. fellow Harvard U., 1946-48; with Malcolm Pirnie, NYC, 1948-52; from assoc. prof. dept. environ. scis. and engring. to prof. U. NC, Chapel Hill, 1952-73, Kenan prof., 1973-82, Kenan prof. emeritus, 1982—, head dept. environ. scis. and engring., 1955-73. Vis. prof. Tech. U. Delft, 1960-61, U. Coll., London, 1966-67, 73-75, Tianjin U., 1981; editor environ. scis. series Acad. Press, 1968-75; cons. to industry, cons. engrs., govtl. agys. World Bank, WHO, UNDP, with spl. svc. in Switzerland, Israel, Jordan, Peru, Egypt, Colombia, Brazil, Venezuela, Thailand, Indonesia, Kenya, Singapore, Lesotho, Zambia, Tunisia, Australia, Taiwan, Bangladesh, Argentina, Chile, New Zealand, Jamaica, Guatemala, Turkey, Finland, Eng., Morocco, China, The Philippines, India, Singapore, Israel, Lesotho; environ. coun. Rohm & Haas Co., Inc., 1985-92; chmn. expert panel on NYC water supply EPA, 1992-93. Author: (with Gordon M. Fair and John C. Geyer) Water and Wastewater Engineering, 2 vols., 1966-68, Elements of Water Supply and Wastewater Disposal, 1971; (with George Ponghis) Community Wastewater Collection and Disposal, 1975; Regionalization of Water Management—A Revolution in England and Wales, 1977; editor: (with M.B. Pescod) Water Supply and Wastewater Disposal in Developing Countries, 1971; (with C.R. Schulz) Surface Water Treatment for Communities in Developing Countries, 1984; contbr. articles to profl. jours. Chmn. Chapel Hill Fellowship for Sch. Integration, 1961-63; adv. bd. Ackland Meml. Art Mus., 1973-78; bd. dirs. Warren Regional Planning Corp., 1971-77, Inter-Faith Coun. Housing Corp., 1975-83, NC Water Quality Coun., 1975-77; mem. adv. com. for med. rsch. Pan Am. Health Orgn., 1976-79; chmn. Washington Met. Area Water Supply Study Com., 1976-80, NAS-NRC; bd. sci. and tech. for internat. devel. NRC, 1978-81, vice chmn. environ. studies bd., 1980-83, chmn. water sci. and tech. bd., 1991-94; com. on human rights NAS, 1988-94; pres. Chapel Hill chpt. NC Civil Liberties Union, 1991-93. Maj. AUS, 1942-46, PTO. Decorated Philippine Liberation medal; recipient Harrison Prescott Eddy medal for rsch. Water Pollution Control Fedn., 1950, Gordon Maskew Fair award Am. Acad. Environ. Engrs., 1973, Thomas Jefferson award U. NC at Chapel Hill, 1973, Gordon Y. Billard award NY Acad. Scis., 1975, 1st Thomas R. Camp Meml. lectr. Boston Soc. Environ. Engrs., Gordon Maskew Fair medal Water Pollution Control Fedn., 1978, First Allen Hazen lectr. New Eng. Water Works Assn., 1990, Donald R. Boyd award Assn. Met. Water Agys., 1993, Jones award Chapel Hill chpt. ACLU NC, 1998, Gano Dunn award for profl. achievement in sci. and engring. The Cooper Union, 2002; Friendship medal Inst. Water Engrs. and Scientists (Gt. Britain), 1984; NSF fellow, 1960-61; Fed. Water Pollution Control Adminstrn. fellow, 1966-67; Fulbright-Hayes lectr., Eng., 1973-74; Daniel A. Okun Disting. Professorship in Environ. Engring. established by U. NC, 1999. Mem. NAE, AAUP (pres. U. NC chpt. 1963-64), ASCE (hon., chmn. environ. engring. divsn. 1967-68, 1st Simon W. Freese award 1977, Lifetime Achievement award Environ. and Water Resources Inst. 2006), Am. Water Works Assn. (hon., NC Fuller award 1983, Best Paper award edn1. divsn. 1985, Abel Wolman award of Excellence 1991, Best Paper Water Resources Divsn. 1999), Inst. Medicine, Water Environ. Fedn. (hon., chmn. rsch. com. 1961-66, dir.-at-large 1969-72), Am. Acad. Environ. Engring. (pres. 1969-70, hon. diplomate, Kappe lectr. 1995), Assn. Environ. Engring. Profs. (Founders' award 1994), NC Pub. Health Assn. (Jarrett award 1994), Internat. Water Assn. (Grand award 2006), U. NC Order of Golden Fleece, Sigma Xi (pres. U. NC chpt. 1968-69). Home: 750 Weaver Dairy Rd Apt 204 Chapel Hill NC 27514-1466 Office: ESE U NC CB 7431 Chapel Hill NC 27599-7431 Office Phone: 919-918-3500. Business E-Mail: dokun@unc.edu.

OKUN, DEANNA TANNER, federal official; m. Bob Okun; children: Rachel, Kelsi. BA in Polit. Sci., Utah State U.; JD, Duke U. Sch. of Law. Research assoc. Competitive Enterprise Inst., Washington; assoc. attorney and mem. of Internat. Trade Group Hogan & Hartson law firm, Washington; legis. asst. to Senator Frank Murkowski US Senate, counsel for internat. affairs to Sen. Frank Murkowski, 1993—99; commr. U.S. Internat. Trade Comm., 1999—, vice chmn., 2000—02, 2004—06, chmn, 2002—04. Office: US Internat Trade Commission 500 E Street SW Washington DC 20436

OKUN, HERBERT STUART, diplomat, educator; b. NYC, Nov. 27, 1930; s. Irving and Ida Muriel (Levine) O.; m. Lorraine Joan Price, Dec. 5, 1954 (div. 1985); children: Jennifer, Elizabeth, Alexandra; m. Enid Curtis Bok, Dec. 27, 1990. AB with great distinction, Stanford U., 1951; postgrad., Syracuse U., 1951—52, Princeton U., 1952; Hochschule fuer Politische Wissenschaft, Munich, 1956—57; MPA, Harvard U., 1959; M Naval Warfare, Naval War Coll., 1969. Mem. US Fgn. Svc., 1955—91, Munich vice consul, 1955—57; with Bur. Intelligence and Rsch., Dept. State Office Soviet Union Affairs, Washington, 1959-61, alt. dir., 1971-73; 2d sec. Am. Embassy, Moscow, 1961-63; consul, prin. officer Am. Consulate, Belo Horizonte, Brazil, 1964-65; 1st sec., prin. officer Am. Embassy, Brasilia, Brazil, 1965-66, counsellor embassy, prin. officer, 1967-68; assigned to Naval War Coll., 1968-69; spl. asst. to sec. of state Dept. State, Washington, 1969-71, dep. chmn. U.S. Del., U.S.-USSR Talks on Prevention Incidents at Sea, 1971-72; polit. advisor and spl. asst. for internat. affairs to comdr.-in-chief NATO So. Command, Naples, Italy, 1973-74; min.-counsellor, dep. chief mission Am. Embassy, Lisbon, Portugal, 1975-78; dep. chmn. U.S. del. Strategic Arms Limitation Talks with Soviet Union, Geneva, 1978-79; vice chmn. U.S. del. to trilateral U.S.-U.K.-USSR Talks on comprehensive test ban treaty, Geneva, 1979-80; amb. to German Dem. Rep. Berlin, 1980—83; amb.-in-residence Aspen Inst., Washington, 1983-85; amb., dep. permanent rep. of U.S. to the UN NYC, 1985-89. Rep. of US to Gen. Assembly UN, to UN Security Coun., 1985-89, to Com. on Peaceful Uses of Outer Space, 1986-87, to Disarmament Commn. UN, 1985-89, to Commn. Human Rights, 1985-89, to com. on program and coordination of Econ. and Social Coun., 1987, 89; amb. in residence Carnegie Corp. NY, 1989-90; US mem. UN Sec. Gen's. Expert Group on Enhancing UN Structure for Drug Abuse Control, 1990, UN Internat. Narcotics Control Bd., Vienna, Austria, 1992-2002; founding exec. dir. Fin. Svcs. Vol. Corps, NYC, 1990-97; vis. lectr. Yale Law Sch., New Haven, 1991-2002; professorial lectr. in internat. rels., internat. law and instns. Johns Hopkins. U. Sch. Advanced Internat. Studies, Washington, 2002—; spl. adviser, dep. personal envoy of the sec. gen. UN, Former Yugoslavia and Nagorno-Karabakh, 1991-92; spl. adv., dep. co-chmn. Internat. Conf. on former Yugoslavia, 1992-93; UN mediator Dispute between Greece and Former Yugoslav Republic of Macedonia, 1993-97; bd. dirs. World Rehab. Fund; adv. bd. Minority Rights Group USA; spl. advisor Carnegie Commn. on Preventing Deadly Conflict. Commr. U.S.-Poland Action Commn; mem. Internat. Coun., Found. Inter-Ethnic Rels., The Hague, Netherlands, 1995—, mem. Adv. Com., Human Rights Watch, N.Y., 1995—; mem. group internat. advisors Internat. Com. Red Cross, Geneva, 1996-2000; bd. overseers Curtis Inst. Music, Phila.; adv. bd. internat. security studies Yale U., New Haven; mem. adv. bd. Portuguese-Am. Leadership Coun.; bd. dirs. Internat. Ctr. N.Y., 2004-. Served with AUS, 1952-54. Recipient Meritorious Honor award Dept. of State, 1972, Superior Honor award Dept. of State, 1980, Presdl. Meritorious Svc. award, 1983. Mem. Am. Fgn. Policy (nat. com.), Am. Acad. Diplomacy, Lawyers Alliance World Security (nat. bd. dirs.), Washington Inst. Fgn. Affairs, Phi Beta Kappa. Home: 970 Park Ave 6-N New York NY 10028-0324

OKUN, NEIL JEFFREY, vitreoretinal surgeon; b. St. Louis, Nov. 21, 1957; s. Edward and Barbara J. (Braham) O.; m. Joan A. Sosnoff, May 19, 1984; children: David E., Sarah E. AB, Dartmouth Coll., 1980; MD, Washington U., 1984. Diplomate Am. Bd. Ophthalmology. Intern internal medicine Jewish Hosp. at Washington U., St. Louis, 1984-85; resident ophthalmology Washington U. Med. Ctr., St. Louis, 1985-88; fellow vitreoretinal Retina Cons., Ltd., Washington U., St. Louis, 1988-89; vitreoretinal surgeon Fla. Retina Inst., Jacksonville, Fla., 1990-91, Retina Assocs. Ctrl. Fla., Orlando, 1991—2004, Ctrl. Fla. Retina, Orlando, 2004—. Instr. dept. ophthalmology Washington U. Sch. Medicine, St. Louis, 1988-89; clin. asst. prof. dept. ophthalmology U. South Fla., Tampa, 1992—; chmn. dept. ophthalmology Fla. Hosp. Orlando, 1996-97 Recipient Upjohn Achievement award for endocrinology and metabolism Washington U. Sch. Medicine, St. Louis, 1984. Fellow ACS, Am. Acad. Ophthalmology; mem. AMA (Physicians's Recognition award for continuing med. edn. 1992—), Am. Soc. Retina Specialists, Assn. for Rsch. in Vision and Ophthalmology, Fla. Med. Assn., Fla. Soc. Ophthalmology, Ctrl. Fla. Soc. Ophthalmology, Orange County Med. Soc., Vitreous Soc., Paul Cibis Club. Avocations: music, art. Office: Ctrl Florida Retina 2501 N Orange Ave Ste 401 Orlando FL 32804-4644 Office Phone: 407-896-1224.

OKUR, MEHMET, professional basketball player; b. Yalova, Turkey, May 26, 1979; s. Abdullah and Nimet Okur; m. Yeliz Caliska, 2004. Profl. basketball player Turkish League Oyak Renault, Turkey, 1997—98, Turkish League Tofas Bursa, Turkey, 1998—2000, Turkish League Efes Pilsen, Turkey, 2000—02; draft pick NBA Detroit Pistons, 2001, ctr./power forward, 2002—04, NBA Utah Jazz, 2004—. Named to Western Conf. All-Star Team, NBA, 2007. Achievements include winning an NBA Championship as a member of the Detroit Pistons in 2004; winner, Turkish National Cup as a member of Tofas Bursa in 1999. Mailing: Utah Jazz 301 W South Temple Salt Lake City UT 84101 *

OKURA-MARSZYCKI, MINDY EMI, editor; b. Honolulu, July 15, 1976; d. Gary and Gail Okura; m. Brian Marszycki, Mar. 27, 2004. BA in English and Psychology, Boston Coll., Chestnut Hill, Mass., 1998; MA in Pub., NYU, NYC, 2003; attending, St. John's U., Queens, NY, 2005—. Web content editor/mktg. assoc. PhysicianEd, Boston, 1998—2001; lit. agt. asst. Liza Dawson & Assocs., NYC, 2002; editl. asst. Columbia U. Press, NYC, 2002, Taylor and Francis, NYC, 2002; book editor Other Press, NYC, 2003—. Grad. Student Dean's fellow, NYU, 2001. Mem.: Young to Pub. Group, NYU Pub. Alumni Steering Com., Sigma Tau Delta. Office: Other Press 2 Park Ave New York NY 10016 Home Phone: 917-757-6479; Office Phone: 212-414-0054.

OKUWA, MAKOTO, chef; b. Japan; Chef Sushi Tarp, Washington; head sushi chef Morimoto, Phila., 2006, NYC, 2006—. Named one of NYC's Rising Stars, StarChefs.com, 2006. Office: Morimoto 88 10th Ave New York NY 10011 Office Phone: 888-354-8842. *

OLADI, REZA, education educator; PhD, McGill U., Montreal. Asst. prof. Utah State U., Logan, 2004—. Home: 351 W 1600 N C102 North Logan UT 84341 Office: Utah State Univ 3530 Old Main Hill Logan UT 84322 Office Phone: 435-797-8196.

OLAFSON, FREDERICK ARLAN, philosophy educator; b. Winnipeg, Man., Can., Sept. 1, 1924; s. Kristinn K. and Fredericka (Björnson) O.; m. Allie Lewis, June 20, 1952 (dec.); children— Peter Niel, Christopher Arlan, Thomas Andrew. AB, Harvard U., 1947, MA, 1948, PhD, 1951. Instr. philosophy and gen. edn. Harvard U., 1952-54; asst. prof. philosophy, then assoc. prof. Vassar Coll., 1954-60; assoc. prof. Johns Hopkins U., 1960-64; prof. edn. and philosophy Harvard Grad. Sch. Edn., 1964-71; prof. philosophy U. Calif., San Diego, 1971-91, chmn. dept., 1973-76, assoc. dean grad. studies and research, 1980-85. Author: Principles and Persons, 1967, Ethics and Twentieth Century Thought, 1973, The Dialectic of Action, 1979, Heidegger and the Philosophy of the Mind, 1987, What Is A Human Being?, 1995, Heidegger and the Ground of Ethics, 1998, Naturalism and the Human Condition, 2001. Served to lt. (j.g.) USNR, 1943-46. Mem. Nat. Acad. Edn. Home: 6081 Avenida Chamnez La Jolla CA 92037-7404 Business E-Mail: folafson@ucsd.edu.

OLAFSSON, OLAF, communications executive; b. Reykjavik, Iceland, 1962; Grad. in Physics, Brandeis U. With Sony Corp., 1985—97, founder, pres., CEO Sony Interactive Entertainment, Inc., 1991; bd. dirs. Advanta Corp., 1997, pres., 1998; vice chmn. Time Warner Digital Media Time Warner Inc., exec. v.p. NYC. Author: Absolution, 1994, The Journey Home, 2000, Walking Into the Night, 2003. Office: Time Warner Inc 1 Time Warner Ctr New York NY 10019-8016 *

OLAH, GEORGE ANDREW, chemist, educator; b. Budapest, Hungary, May 22, 1927; arrived in U.S., 1964, naturalized, 1970; s. Julius and Magda (Krasznai) Olah; m. Judith Agnes Lengyel, July 9, 1949; children: George John, Ronald Peter. PhD, Tech. U. Budapest, 1949, D (hon.), 1989; DSc (hon.), U. Durham, 1988, U. Munich, 1990, U. Crete, Greece, 1994, U. Szeged, Hungary, 1995, U. Veszprem, 1995, Case Western Res. U., Cleve., 1995, U. So. Calif., 1995, U. Montpellier, 1996, SUNY, 1998, U. Pecs, Hungary, 2001, U. Debrecen, 2003. Mem. faculty Tech. U. Budapest, 1949—54; assoc. dir. Ctrl. Chem. Rsch. Inst., Hungarian Acad. Scis., 1954—56; rsch. scientist Dow Chem. Can. Ltd., 1957—64, Dow Chem. Co., Framingham, Mass., 1964—65; prof. chemistry Case Western Res. U., Cleve., 1965—69, C.F. Mabery prof. rsch., 1969—77; Donald P. and Katherine B. Loker disting. prof. chemistry, dir. Hydrocarbon Rsch. Inst., U. So. Calif., LA, 1977—. Vis. prof. chemistry Ohio State U., 1963, U. Heidelberg, Germany, U. Colo., 1969, Swiss Fed. Inst. Tech., 1972, U. Munich, 1973, U. London, 1973—79, Louis Pasteur U., Strasbourg, France, 1974, U. Paris, 1981; hon. vis. lectr. U. London, 1981—95; cons. to industry. Author: Friedel-Crafts Reactions, Vols. I-IV, 1963—64; author: (with P. Schleyer) Carbonium Ions, Vols. I-V, 1969—76; author: Friedel-Crafts Chemistry, 1973, Carbocations and Electrophilic Reactions, 1973, Halonium Ions, 1975; author: (with Goeppertau Prakash and J. Somer) Superacids, 1984; author: (with G. Prakash, R.E. Williams, L.D. Field and K. Wade) Hypercarbon Chemistry, 1987; author: (with R. Malthotra and S.C. Narang) Nitration, 1989; author: Cage Hydrocarbons, 1990; author: (with Wade and Williams) Electron Deficient Boron and Carbon Clusters, 1991; author: (with Chambers and Prakash) Synthetic Fluorine Chemistry, 1992; author: (with Molnar) Hydrocarbon Chemistry, 1995; author: (with Laali, Wang, Prakash) Onium Ions, 1998; author: A Life of Magic

Chemistry, 2001; author: (with Prakash) Across Conventional Lines, 2003; author: (with Goeppertau and Prakash) Beyond Oil and Gas: The Methanol Economy, 2006; contbr. chapters to books, articles to profl. jours. Recipient Alexander von Humboldt Sr. US Scientist award, 1979, Calif. Scientist of Yr. award, 1989, Pioneer of Chemistry award, Am. Inst. Chemists, 1993, Mendeleev medal, Russian Acad. Scis., 1992, Nobel prize in Chemistry, 1994, Kapitsa medal, Russian Acad. Natural Scis., 1995, Order of the Hungarian Corvin-Chain, 2001, Albert Einstein medal, Russian Acad. Natural Scis., 2002, Bolyai prize, Hungarian Acad. Sci., 2002, Order of Merit with Cross of Star, Republic of Hungary, 2006; Guggenheim fellow, 1972, 1988. Fellow: AAAS, Chem. Inst. Can., Brit. Chem. Soc. (hon.; hon./centenary lectr. 1978, Centenary lectr. 1978); mem.: NAS, Indian Nat. Acad. Sci. (fgn.), Can. Royal Soc., Royal Soc. Sci. Arts Barcelona, Royal Acad. Sci. and Arts, Am. Acad. Arts and Sci., Chem. Soc. Japan (hon.), Italy Chem. Soc. (hon.), Royal Chem. Soc. (hon.), Hungarian Acad. Sci. (hon.), Am. Philos. Soc., Am. Chem. Soc. (award petroleum chemistry 1964, Leo Hendrik Baekeland award N.J. sect. 1966, Morley medal Cleve. sect. 1970, award Synthetic Organic Chemistry 1979, Roger Adams award in organic chemistry 1989, Arthur C. Cope award 2001, Priestley medal 2005), European Acad. Arts, Sci. and Humanities, Royal Soc. London (fgn. mem.), Italian Nat. Acad. Sci. Lincei, Grand Cordon of the Order of the Rising Sun (Japan). Achievements include patents in field. Office: U So Calif Loker Hydrocarbon Rsch Inst Los Angeles CA 90007 Business E-Mail: olah@usc.edu. *America still is offering a new home and nearly unlimited possibilities to the newcomer who is willing to work hard for it. It is also where the "main action" in science and technology remains.*

OLALDE, JOSE ANGEL, entrepreneur, consultant; b. Maturín, Venezuela, Nov. 12, 1956; s. José Olalde and Yolanda Rangel; m. Fabiola Pérez, May 21, 1969; children: Diego, Aitor. Diploma, Wimbledon Coll., Eng., 1972. Cert. Engr., Ctrl. U. Venezuela, 1983. Pres. Adaptogenic Med. Ctrs., Caracas, Venezuela, 1994—, Medicina Sistémica Integrativa, San Juan, 2004—. Cons. Nulab Inc. Corp., Clearwater, Fla., 1994—. Pres. Adaptogenic Found., Caracas, Venezuela, 2002—06. Recipient Engring. award, Ctrl. U. Venezuela, 1983. Achievements include patents pending for 20 Patents Pending; first to A treatment for Renal Failure; A treatment for Immune defficiency; A treatment for Irritable colon syndrome; A treatment for Artherosclerosis; development of A cure for Diabetic Foot; A cure for Multiple Sclerosis; discovery of A cure for liver disease; development of A cure for Varicose ulcers; A cure for Psoriasis; An effective treatment for Prostate Cancer; A cure for ovarian & uterine cysts; A cure for Heart Insufficiency. Home Phone: 727-385-6574; Office Phone: 727-214-1334. Personal E-mail: jolalde@tampabay.rr.com. Business E-Mail: adaptogen@cantv.net.

OLANSKY, SIDNEY, retired dermatologist; b. Boston, Jan. 11, 1914; s. Samuel and Anna Olansky; m. Marian Elizabeth Freehafer, June 30, 1945; children: Leann, Alan, David, Sidney. BS, NYU, 1934; MD, Glasgow U., Scotland, 1940. Diplomate Am. Bd. Dermatology. Intern Met. Hosp., NYC, 1940-42; commd. officer USPHS, 1942, advanced through grades to med. dir., 1950; med. officer in charge Rapid Treatment Ctr., Washington, 1943-46; resident dept. dermatology Duke U. Hosp., 1946-48; pvt. practice dermatology Washington, 1948-50; dir. V.D. Rsch. Lab., Chamblee, Ga., 1950-55; assoc. prof. dermatology Duke U. Med. Ctr., 1955-59; prof. medicine, chief divsn. dermatology Emory U. Sch. Medicine, Atlanta, 1959-81, emeritus prof., 1981—; ret., 2006. Rschr. USPHS, Gallinger Meml. Hosp., 1948-50; mem. nat. serology adv. com. to Surgeon Gen. of Pub. Health Svc.; cons. 3rd Army Hdqs.; mem. med. sci. com. Dermatology Found. Contbr. articles to profl. jours. Fellow ACP; mem. AMA, Am. Acad. Dermatology and Syphilology (bd. dirs.), Am. Dermatol. Assn., Am. Venereal Disease Assn. (pres. 1971-72), Am. Fedn. Clin. Rsch., Med. Assn. Ga., Med. Assn. Atlanta, Southeastern Dermatol. Assn. (sec., pres. 1971-73), Atlanta Dermatology Assn. (pres. 1971-72). Avocations: reading, sports. Office: Sidney Olansky Md 3379 Peachtree Rd NE Ste 500 Atlanta GA 30326-1418

OLATUNJI, THABITI SHAWKI, executive director, marketing executive; b. Mt. Holly, NJ, Aug. 22, 1958; s. Marquette Alexander Williams Jr. and Virginia Mae Chavis; 1 child, Tabatha Josephine. Student in Bus. Adminstrn., U. Iowa, Iowa City, 1982—85; student in Physics, Maharishi Internat. U., Fairfield, Iowa, 1981—82; student in Electronics Engring., Camden County Coll., Blackwood, NJ, 1980—81; DD (hon.), U. Magi, Golden, Colo., 1992; D in Metasymbology (hon.), U. of Magi, Golden, Colo., 1995. Ordained min. Order of Magi, 1992. Owner, founder Supreme Oracle, Superior, 1992—; pres., founder U. Of Magi, Golden, 1995—; owner, v.p. LoveTheName.com, Superior, Colo., 2005—; owner, exec. dir. ThePower.org, Superior, 2005—. Prodr. radio show host Empowerment Hour, Denver, 2003—; founder Divine Sci. Supreme Oracle, 1990. Chief min. all possibilities r&d World Congress Assn., Fairfield, Iowa, 1981—. E-4 US Army, 1976—80. Named Grand Mastsesr, Order of Magi, 1992. Mem.: Capitols For Age Enlightenment. Avocations: meditation, yoga.

OLAYAN, LUBNA S., finance company executive; b. Saudi Arabia; d. Suliman S. Olayan. BS in Agr., Cornell U.; MBA, Ind. U. With Morgan Guaranty, NYC, 1979—81; joined Olayan Grp., Riyadh, Saudi Arabia, 1983—; CEO Olayan Financing Co., Riyadh, Saudi Arabia. Bd. dirs. Olayan Investments Co. Establishment, Egyptian Fin. Co., Capitol Union, Dubai, United Arab Emirates; non-exec. dir. Chelsfield, UK, WPP, UK; bd. trustees Arab Thought Found.; pres. Suliman S. Olayan Found. Named one of 100 Most Influential People, Time mag., 2005, 50 Most Powerful Women, Fortune mag., 2005, 100 Most Powerful Women, Forbes mag., 2006; recipient Achievement award, Arab Bankers Assn. of N.Am., 2004. Mem.: World Econ. Forum (Women Leadership Initiative, Arab Bus. Coun. Exec. Com.), World Bank (World Links Adv. Coun.), INSEAD Internat. Coun. Office: Olayan Financing Co PO Box 8772 Riyadh 11492 Saudi Arabia

OLBERMANN, KEITH, news analyst, former sportscaster; b. NYC, Jan. 27, 1959; BS in Comm. Arts, Cornell U., 1979. Sports reporter UPI Radio, NYC, 1979-80, RKO Radio, NYC, 1980-82, WNEW-AM, NYC, 1980-83; nat. sports reporter, anchor CNN, NYC, 1981-84, WCVB-TV, Boston, 1984; weeknight sports anchor, reporter KTLA-TV, LA, 1985-88; sports commentator KNX-AM, LA, 1986-91; sports anchor, host The Keith Olbermann Show KCBS-TV, LA, 1988-91; weekend co-host ESPN Sports Radio, 1992-93; co-anchor, co-host SportsCenter ESPN, Bristol, Conn., 1992-97; co-anchor SportsNight ESPN2, 1993-94; anchor, exec. prodr. Fox Sports Net, 1998—2001; columnist Salon.com, 2002—03; host, Countdown with Keith Olbermann MSNBC, 2003—; co-host ESPN Radio, 2005—. Co-author (with Dan Patrick): The Big Show: Inside ESPN's Sport Center, 1997; author: The Worst Person in the World: And 119 More Strong Contenders, 2006. Recipient 11 Golden Mike awards Best Sportscaster, 1985, 86, 87, 88, 89, 90, Best Sportscast Calif. Radio and TV News Assn., 1985-91, Cable Ace award Best Sportscaster Nat. Acad. Cable Programming, 1995, Edward R. Murrow award, 2002; voted Calif. A.P. Sportscaster of Yr., 1985, 87, 89. Office: MSNBC Cable LLC 1 MSNBC Plz Secaucus NJ 07094

OLBETER, ERIK R., financial analyst, investment advisor; BA, Rutgers Univ.; MPP, Georgetown Univ. Rsch. analyst Economic Strategy Inst.; securities analyst, technology sector, aerospace & defense industries Stanford Group Co., Washington. Named one of Best Securities Analysts, Forbes Mag. Office: Stanford Group Ste 450 1055 Thomas Jefferson St NW Washington DC 20007 *

OLBRICHT, WILLIAM LEE, engineering educator; s. Benjamin H. and Elaine Olbricht. BS, Stanford U., Calif., 1973; PhD, Calif. Inst. Tech., Pasadena, 1980. Asst. prof. chem. engring. Cornell U., Ithaca, NY, 1980—86, assoc. prof. chem. engring., 1986—92, dir., sch. chem. engring., 1993—98, prof., sch. chem. & biomolecular engring., 1993—. Contbr. articles to profl. jours. Recipient Faculty Devel. award, IBM, 1986, Excellence in Tchg. award, Cornell Engring., 1999, 2002, 2005. Mem.: AIChE, Fed. Demonstration Partnership (faculty chair 2000—02), Biomedical Engring. Soc. Office: Cornell Univ Olin Hall Ithaca NY 14850

OLCER, NURI YELMAN, engineering researcher, educator; b. Gaziantep, Turkey, July 22, 1932; arrived in U.S., 1958; s. Samet and Besire Olcer. MS, Tech. U. Istanbul, 1956; PhD, Northwestern U., 1964. Rsch. engr. Ordnance Engring. Assocs., Chgo., 1960—66; assoc. prof. Ill. Inst. Tech., Chgo., 1966—69; mgr. engring. mechanics OEA, Inc., Des Plaines, Ill., 1970—84, v.p. engring. mechanics, 1984—97; cons., 1998—. Resident rsch. fellow Argonne Nat. Lab., Ill., 1962—64. Author: Recoilless Rifle Weapon Systems, 1976; contbr. articles to profl. jours., Fulbright Scholar, 1958—59, Walter P. Murphy Rsch. fellow, Northwestern U. Tech. Inst., 1960—62. Mem.: AIAA, ASME (Calvin Rice Meml. scholar 1959), Soc. Engring. Sci., Am. Soc. Engring. Edn., Can. Math. Soc., N.Y. Acad. Scis., Soc. Nat. Philosophy, Math. Assn. Am., Am. Math. Soc., Am. Acad. Mech., Sigma Xi, Pi Tau Sigma. Avocations: rare book collecting, stamp collecting/philately, hiking, travel. Home: 9756 East Maplewood Cir Englewood CO 80111 Office Phone: 303-773-3659.

OLCHYK, SAMUEL, lawyer; b. Havana, Cuba, Feb. 26, 1960; married; 2 children. BBA, Univ. Tex., 1982, JD, 1985; LLM in Taxation, NYI, 1987. CPA Tex., 1985; bar: Tex. 1985, DC 1989. Tax counsel US Congress Joint Com. on Taxation, 1995—2003; ptnr., taxation, bus. transactions Venable LLP, Washington, 2003—. Contbr. articles to profl journals. Mem.: DC Bar Assn., State Bar Tex. Office: Venable LLP 575 Seventh St NW Washington DC 20004 Office Phone: 202-344-4034. Office Fax: 202-344-8300. Business E-Mail: solchyk@venable.com.

OLCOTT, CORNELIUS, IV, surgeon; b. Harlingen, Tex., 1942; s. Cornelius III and Margaret Ella (Dole) O.; m. Phoebe Swan Allen, Aug. 1, 1964; children: Cornelius V, Jocelyn Harrison. AB magna cum laude, Princeton U., 1963; MD, Columbia P&S, 1967. Diplomate Am. Bd. Surgery. Intern U. Calif. San Francisco, 1967-68, resident in surgery, 1968-74, fellow in vascular surgery, 1974-75; surgeon Stanford U. Hosp., Palo Alto, Calif., 1977—; prof. surgery Stanford U., 1993—; attending surgeon Lucille Packard Children's Hosp., Palo Alto, Calif., 1991—. Numerous clin. and faculty appointments, including attending surgeon Palo Alto VA Hosp., 1978—, Washington Hosp., Fremont, Calif., 1980-90, others. Contbr. articles to profl. jours., chpts. to books; presenter in field. Mem. Am. Coll. Surgeons (pres. No. Calif. chpt. 1984-85), Am. Trauma Soc., Naffziger Surg. Soc., Assn. Acad. Surgery, San Francisco and Calif. Med. Assn., Internat. Cardiovascular Soc., No. Calif. Vascular Soc., San Francisco Surg. Soc., Santa Clara County Med. Soc., Pacific Coast Surg. Assn. (pres. 2005-06), Soc. for Vascular Surgery, Soc. Clin. Vascular Surgery, Western Vascular Soc. (pres. 2002). Office: Stanford U Med Ctr Divsn Vascular Surgery Ret 2 No H-3630 Stanford CA 94305 Office Phone: 650-725-5227. Business E-Mail: olcott@stanford.edu.

OLCOTT, JOHN WHITING, air transportation executive; b. Orange, NJ, Oct. 20, 1936; s. Egbert Whiting and Marion Richmond (Braillard) Olcott; m. Hope Bennett Phillips, May 14, 1966 (div. Feb. 1987); children: David Whiting, Bradley Philips, Carter Howell; m. Isobel Waxman Ritter, Nov. 25, 1989. BS in Aero. Engring., Princeton U., 1960, MS in Aero. Engring., 1964; MBA in Gen. Mgmt., Rutgers U., 1970. Cert. Internat. Std. Bus. Aircraft Ops. Auditor Accreditation 2003, 2005. V.p. Linden Flight Svc., NJ, 1960-66; flight rsch. specialist Princeton U., NJ, 1966-68; v.p. corp. devel., sr. cons. Aero. Rsch. Assocs. Princeton, Inc., 1968-74; v.p., group pub., editorial dir. McGraw-Hill Aviation Week Group, Rye Brook, NY, 1973-92; pres. Nat. Bus. Aviation Assn., Inc., 1992—2003, Gen. Aero Co., Inc., 2003—. Rsch. engring. and devel. adv. com. FAA, 1990—2003; mem. bd. govs. Flight Safety Found., 1992—2000; bd. dirs. aerospace tech. adv. com. NASA, 1998—2003, mem. small aircraft transp. sys. coun., 2002—06; co-chair safer skies program FAA, 1999—2003; chmn. Be a Pilot, 2003—05; bd. dirs. Nat. Coalition Aviation Mobility, 2004—06; chmn. bus. aviation adv. bd. Airbus, 2005—; auditor Internat. Std. Bus. Aircraft Ops., 2003—. Chmn. panel gen. aviation and commuter tech. NASA, Washington, 1974—86; chmn. panel gen. aviation safety FAA, Washington, 1983—88; crew chief, mem. New Vernon Vol. First Aid Squad, NJ, 1974—92; bd. dirs. Aviation Rsch. and Edn. Found., Washington, 1988—92; mem. bd. visitors Aircraft Owner and Pilots Assn. Air Safety Found., Frederick, Md., 1988—93; mem. New Vernon Bd. Adjustment, 2003—; mem. integrated devel. team Joint Program and Devel. Office; mem. airports and integrated product team Agile ATC Sys., 2005—; trustee Embry-Riddle Aero. U., Daytona Beach, Fla., 1988—93, 1995—97. Named to NJ Aviation Hall of Fame, 2001; recipient Meritorious Svc. award, Flight Safety Found., 1983, 2003, Dir.'s award, FAA Ctrl. Region, 1984, Am. Spirit award, Nat. Bus. Aviation Assn., 2003, Commendation cert., FAA, 1984, Gill Robb Wilson award, Embry-Riddle Aero. U., 1986, Journalism award, Helicopter Assn. Internat., 1990, William F. Shea award for Disting. Contbn. to Aviation, 2004, Turning Goals into Reality award, NASA, 2005, Langley Rsch. Ctr. Team award, 2005, Elder Statesman award, Nat. Aeronautics Assn., 2006. Mem.: Nat. Air Transp. Assn., Aircraft Owners and Pilots Assn., Soc. Exptl. Test Pilots, Nat. Bus. Aviation Assn., NJ Aviation Assn. (pres. 2005—06). Republican. Presbyterian. Office: Gen Aero Co Hangar One 1 Airport Rd Morristown NJ 07960 Home Phone: 973-540-9862; Office Phone: 973-734-9994. Business E-Mail: jack@generalaerocompany.com.

OLCYZK, ED, professional athletics coach; Hockey player Chgo. (Ill.) Blackhawks, 1983—87, 1998—2000, Toronto (Can.) Maple Leafs, 1987—90, Winnipeg Jets, 1990—92, 1995—96, N.Y. Rangers, 1992—95, LA (Calif.) Kings, 1996—97, Pitts. (Pa.) Penguins, 1997—98, head coach, 2003—05. Mem. Team USA Olympic Hockey Team, 1984, World Championships Tournament, 1985—87, 1989, Can. Cup Tournament, 1987, 91.

OLCZAK, PAUL VINCENT, psychologist, educator; b. Buffalo, May 25, 1943; s. Vincent Henry and Helen (Babula) O.; m. Marie Rose Oliveri, Oct. 20, 1973; children: Paul V. II, Patrick J., Drew M. MA, No. Ill. U., 1969, PhD, 1972. Clin. psychologist Family Ct. Psychiat. Clinic, Buffalo, 1975-77, cons. supervisory psychologist, 1977—; supr. psychol. svcs. Hopevale, Inc., Hamburg, NY, 1977-89; clin. psychologist Amherst (N.Y.) Police Dept., 1989—; asst. prof. psychology SUNY, Geneseo, 1977-83, assoc. prof. psychology, 1983-90, prof. psychology, 1990—, chairperson, 1999—; clin. psychologist child and adolescent psychiatry Niagara Falls Meml. Hosp., 1996—, clin. psychologist bariatric medicine program, 2002—; cons. psychologist Batavia (N.Y.) Sch. Dist. Co-editor: Community Mediation, 1991; contbg. author: The POI in Clinical Situations: A Review, 1991, Self-actualization-Polemics Surrounding Its Use, 1991; contbr. articles to profl. jours./publs. Mem. APA, Ea. Psychol. Assn., Midwestern Psychol. Assn., Psychonomic Soc., Soc. Exptl. Social Psychology, Internat. Assn. for Conflict Mgmt., Psi Chi, Sigma Xi. Home: 278 Troy Del Way Buffalo NY 14221-3358 Office: SUNY Dept Psychology Geneseo NY 14454 E-mail: olczak@geneseo.edu.

OLD, HUGHES OLIPHANT, theologian, minister; b. Redondo Beach, Calif., Apr. 13, 1933; s. Shadburne Edward and Emma Coulter (Oliphant) O.; m. Mary Chase McCaw, June 12, 1982; children: Hannah Chase, Isaac Houghton Chambers. BA, Centre Coll., Danville, Ky., 1955; BD, Princeton Theol. Sem., 1958; postgrad., U. Tubingen, 1964-66; ThD, U. Neuchatel, 1971. Ordained to ministry Presbyn. Ch., 1959. Minister Presbyn. Ch., Atglen, Pa., 1959-64, Faith Presbyn. Ch., West Lafayette, Ind., 1972-85; mem. Ctr. for Theol. Inquiry, Princeton, NJ, 1985—; prof. Erskine Theol. Sem., 2004—; dean Inst. Reformed Worship, 2004—. Lectr. Princeton Theol. Sem., 1998-2004. Author: Patristic Roots of Reformed Worship, 1975, Worship, 1984, enlarged edit. 2002, Shaping of the Reformed Baptismal Rite, 1992, Leading in Prayer, 1995, Themes and Variations for A Christian Doxology, 1992, The Reading and Preaching of Scripture in the Worship of the Christian Church, Vols. I and II, 1998, Vol. III, 1999, vol. IV, 2002, vol. V, 2004, vol. VI, 2007; contbr. numerous articles to scholarly jours. Fellow N.Am. Acad. Liturgy; mem. Union League Phila. Republican. Avocations: painting, music. Home: 818 Lower Ferry Rd Trenton NJ 08628-3501

OLDAKER, GUY BROOKLYN, III, lawyer; b. Washington, June 18, 1950; s. Guy B. and Elisabeth H. Oldaker; m. Cynthia L. Keiser, Aug. 3, 1980; children: Guy B. IV, Mary Elisabeth. BA in Chemistry, U. Va., 1972; PhD in Chemistry, Va. Polytech. Inst. & State U., 1978; JD, W.Va. U., 1995. Bar: N.C. 1996, U.S. Dist. Ct. (mid. dist.) N.C. 1996. Tchr. Albemarle H.S., Charlottesville, Va., 1972—75; instr. Va. Polytech. Inst. and State U., Blacksburg, Va., 1977—78; sr. project mgr. Entropy Environmentalists, Inc., Raleigh, NC, 1978—85; sr. staff R&D chemist R.J. Reynolds Tobacco Co., Winston-Salem, 1985—92, cons., 1992—95; exec. dir. Ctr. for Indoor Air Rsch., Winston-Salem, NC, 1987—88; assoc. Gordon & Nesbit, PLLC, 1996—97; pvt. practice Winston-Salem, 1997—. Asst. coach cross country and track Albemarle H.S., Charlottesville, Va., 1972—75; sci. illustrator pvt. practice, Blacksburg, 1978; environ. cons., Morgantown, NC, 1993—95; vocalist Piedmont Opera Theater, Winston-Salem, 2001—; expert witness. Contbr. articles to profl. jours. Pres. Winston-Salem Youth Symphony, 1997—99. Mem.: Forsyth County Criminal Def. Trial Lawyers Assn. (v.p. 2005), N.C. Acad. Trial Lawyers, Winston-Salem Symphony Chorale (treas.), Alpha Chi Sigma. Republican. Episcopalian. Achievements include patents for device for sampling indoor air. Avocations: running, reading, music, calligraphy, pen and ink drawing. Office: Ste 115 3410 Healy Dr Winston Salem NC 27103 Home Phone: 336-945-9681; Office Phone: 336-725-2346. Personal E-mail: oldakerg@bellsouth.net.

OLDEN, KEVIN WILLIAM, medical researcher; b. NYC, Aug. 18, 1948; s. William and Josephine Olden; m. Sylvia Suikam Hom, Apr. 23, 1983; 1 child, Kimberly Jane. AB, NYU, 1971; MD, SUNY Downstate Med. Sch., 1976. Diplomate Am. Bd. of Internal Medicine with subspecialties in gastroenterology and addiction medicine, Am. Bd. of Psychiatry and Neurology. Intern categorical medicine UCLA-San Fernando Valley Med. Program, Sepulveda, Calif., 1976—77, resident internal medicine, 1977—79; resident psychiatry Mass. Gen. Hosp., Boston, 1979—81; postdoctoral fellow substance abuse and gastroenterology DVA Med. Ctr., Palo Alto, Calif., 1981—83; dir. alcohol rehab. unit Calif. Pacific Med. Ctr., San Francisco, 1983—86; asst. prof. medicine and psychiatry U. Calif., Davis, 1986—91, assoc. prof. medicine and psychiatry San Francisco, 1991—98, Mayo Med. Sch., Scottsdale, Ariz., 1998—2005; Levy prof. medicine, chair divsn. gastroenterology U. Ark., Little Rock, 2006—. Cons. Rome Internat. Working Teams on Functional GI Disorders, Rome, 1994—; fellow gastroenterology DVA Med. Ctr., Martinez, Calif., 1988—89; assoc. prof. medicine and psychiatry U. South Ala. Sch. Medicine, Mobile, 2005—06. Editor: (book) Handbook of the Functional Gastrointestinal Disorders, Chronic Abdominal Pain: A Comprehensive Approach; guest editor (med. jour.) Psychiat. Annals, Seminars in Gastroenterology, Jour. Psychosomatic Rsch., editl. bd. Am. Jour. Drug and Alcohol Abuse, Medicine and Psychiatry, Am. Jour. Gastroenterology. Med. advisor Internat. Found. for Functional Gastrointestinal Disorders, Milw., 1997—2003, Cyclic Vomiting Assn., Scottsdale, Ariz., 1998—2003; med. cons. Med. Bd. of Calif., San Francisco, 1986—98; med. advisor Physician Diversion Program State of Calif., 1986—97. Capt. USNR, 1978—2003. Recipient Harvard Macy scholar in Med. Edn., Harvard Med. Sch., 2000, Clin. Scholar award, Am. Coll. of Gastroenterology, 1999, Outstanding Physician Educator (Rsch.), Mayo Clinic Scottsdale, 2000, Outstanding Physician and Educator, St. Mary's Med. Ctr., 1992—93, Clinician Engaged in Edn., Mayo Clinic Scottsdale, 1999—2000. Fellow: Acad. of Psychosomatic Medicine, ACP, Am. Coll. of Gastroenterology, Am. Psychiat. Assn.; mem.: Calif. Soc. Addiction Medicine (pres. 1990—92), Calif. Med. Assn. (chair chem. dependency 1986—98), Am. Gastroent. Assn. (pres. functional brain-gut rsch. group 2001—03). Avocations: fishing, scuba diving. Office: Univ Ark Sch Medicine Mail Slot 567 4301 W Markham Little Rock AR 72205-7199 Office Phone: 501-686-5126. Office Fax: 501-686-6871. Business E-Mail: kwolden@uams.edu.

OLDENBURG, CLAES THURE, artist; b. Stockholm, Jan. 28, 1929; arrived in US, 1936, naturalized, 1953; s. Gosta and Sigrid (Lindforss) O.; m. Patricia Joan Muschinski, Apr. 13, 1960 (div. Apr. 1970); m. Coosje van Bruggen, July 22, 1977. BA, Yale, 1951; student, Art Inst., Chgo., 1953—54; degree (hon.), Oberlin Coll., 1970, Art Inst. Chgo., 1979, Bard Coll., 1995, Royal Coll. Art, London, 1996, NSCAD, 2005. One-man shows include Judson Gallery, NYC, 1959, Reuben Gallery, 1960, Green Gallery, 1962, Sidney Janis Gallery, 1964—70, Galerie Ileana Sonnabend, Paris, 1964, Robert Fraser Gallery, London, 1966, Moderna Museet, Stockholm, 1966, 1977, Mus. Contemporary Art, Chgo., 1966, 1977, Irving Blum Gallery, L.A., 1968, Mus. Modern Art, NYC, 1969, Stedelijk Mus., Amsterdam, 1970, 1977, Tate Gallery, London, 1970, Pasadena (Calif.) Art Mus., 1971, Nelson-Atkins Mus., Kansas City, Mo., 1972, Art Inst. Chgo., 1973, Leo Castelli Gallery, NYC, 1974, 1976, 1980, 1990, Margo Leavin Gallery, LA, 1975—76, 1978, 1988—89, Walker Art Ctr., Mpls., 1975, 1992, Art Gallery Ont., Toronto, 1976, Ctr. Georges Pompidou, Paris, 1977, Rijksmus. Kröller-Muller Otterlo, 1979, Mus. Ludwig, Cologne, 1979, Wave Hill, Bronx, N.Y., 1984, Solomon R. Guggenheim Mus., NYC, 1986, 1995, Mus. Haus Esters Krefeld, Germany, 1987, Kunstmus., Basel, 1992, Pace Gallery, 1992, 1994, Nat. Gallery Art, Washington, 1995, Mus. Contemporary Art, LA, 1995, Kunst und Ausstellungshalle der Bundersrepublik Deutschland, Bonn, 1996, Hayward Gallery, London, 1996, Whitney Mus. Am. Art, NYC, 2002, two person show with Coosje van Bruggen, No. Ctr. Contemporary Art, Sunderland, 1988, Leeds City Art Gallery, 1988, Palais des Beaux-Arts, Brussels, 1988, IVAM Ctr. Julio González, Valencia, 1988, Galleria Christian Stein, Milan, 1990, Leo Castelli Gallery, NYC, 1986, 1990, Pace Gallery, 1994, Mus. Correr, Venice, 1999, Mus. Serralves, Porto, Portugal, 2001, Met. Mus. Art, NYC, 2002, two person show, Paula Cooper Gallery, 2004, two person show with Coosje van Bruggen, PaceWildenstein, NYC, 2002, 2005, Frederick Meijer Gardens and Scupture Park, Grand Rapids, Mich., 2002, exhibited in group shows at Martha Jackson Gallery, NYC, 1960—61, Dallas Mus. Contemporary Art, 1962, Sidney Janis Gallery, NYC, 1962, 1964, Inst. Contemporary Arts, Lndon, 1963, Art Inst. Chgo., 1962—63, Mus. Modern Art, NYC, 1963, 1988, 1990—91, Washington Gallery Modern Art, 1963, Am. Pavilion, Venice, 1964, 1968, Moderna Museet, Stockholm, 1964, Whitney Mus. Am. Art, N.Y.C., 1964—66, NYC, 1968, 1970, 1974, 1981, 1984, 1999, Solomon R. Guggenheim Mus., 1965, Inst. Contemporary Art, Boston, 1966, Mus. Fridericianum, Kassel, 1968, 1972, 1977, 1982, Richard Feigen Gallery, Chgo., 1968—69, Minami Gallery, Tokyo, 1975, Mus. Contemporary Art, Chgo., 1980, Westfalisches Landesmus. Kunst und Kulturegeschichte, Munster, 1987, 1997, exhibited in group shows, Venice Biennale, 1997, Mus. Nat. Modern Art, Ctr. Georges Pompidou, 1989, La Grande Halle-La Villette, Paris, 1989, exhibited in group shows, Royal Acad. Arts, London, 1991, Mus. Contemporary Art, L.A., 1992, exhibited in group shows, Guggenheim Mus., NYC, 1993, Nat. Gallery, London, 2000, exhibited in group shows at others, Represented in permanent collections Solomon R. Guggenheim Mus., NYC, Mus. Modern Art, Albright-Knox Art Gallery, Buffalo, Ctr. Georges Pompidou, Stedelijk Mus., Tate Gallery, Mus. Ludwig, Moderna Museet, Rose Art Mus.

Brandeis U., Waltham, Mass., Oberlin Coll., Nat. Gallery Art, Canberra, Art Gallery Ont., Art Inst. Chgo., Hirshorn Gallery and Sculpture Garden, Whitney Mus. Am. Art, Mus. Contemporary Art, LA, others, exhibitions include public exhibitions and sculptures with Coosje van Bruggen Rijksmus. Kröller-Muller, Otterlo, The Netherlands, 1979, Nollen Plz. Civic Ctr., Greater Des Moines, Iowa, 1984, Vitra Internat. AG, Weil am Rhein, 1988, Mpls. Sculpture Garden, Walker Art Ctr., Mpls., 1990, Parc de la Villette, Paris, 1993, Ctrl. Gardens, Middlesbrough, Eng., 1994, Nelson-Atkins Mus. Art, Kansas City, Mo., 1996, Tokyo Internat. Exhbn. Ctr., 1996, Guggenheim Found., 2000, Piazzale Cadorna, Milan, 2000, Eindhoven, The Netherlands, 2001, Neumarkt Galerie, Cologne, Germany, 2001, exhibitions include Rincon Bank, San Francisco, 2002, exhibitions include public exhibitions and sculptures with Coosje van Bruggen High Mus., Atlanta, 2005, exhibitions include Stream, Seoul, South Korea, 2006; author: Store Days, 1967, Notes in Hand, 1971, Raw Notes, 1973, Multiples in Retrospect, 1991; author: (with Coosje van Bruggen) Claes Oldenburg: Sketches and Blottings Toward the European Desktop; Large-Scale Project, 1994, Claes Oldenburg Coosje van Bruggen, 1999, Down Liquidambar Lane: Sculpture in the Park, 2001, Images á la Carte, 2004. Recipient Sculpture award, Brandeis U., 1971, Skowhegan Sculpture medal, 1972, Am. Ann., Chgo. Art Inst., 1976, medal, AIA, 1977, Wilhelm-Lehmbruck prize, Germany, 1981, Wolf prize in arts (sculpture), Wolf Found., Israel, 1989, Creative Arts award, Brandeis U., Jack I. and Lillian Poses medal, 1993, Lifetime Achievement award, Internat. Sculpture Ctr., 1994, award, Rolf Schock Found., Stockholm, 1995, Nathaniel S. Saltonstall award, ICA, Boston, 1996, Nat. Medal Arts, Washington, 2000. Mem.: Am. Acad. Arts and Scis., Am. Acad. Inst. Arts & Letters.

OLDENBURG, RICHARD ERIK, auction company executive; b. Stockholm, Sept. 21, 1933; came to U.S., 1936, naturalized, 1959; s. Gösta and Sigrid Elisabeth (Lindforss) O.; m. Harriet Lisa Turnure, Dec. 17, 1960 (dec. Apr. 1998); m. Mary Ellen Meehan, June 11, 2003. AB, Harvard U., 1954. Mgr. design dept. Doubleday & Co., Inc., NYC, 1958-61; mng. editor trade div. Macmillan Co., Inc., NYC, 1961-69; dir. publs. Mus. Modern Art, NYC, 1969-72, dir., 1972-94, dir. emeritus, hon. trustee, 1995—; chmn. Sotheby's North and South America, NYC, 1995-2000, hon. chmn., 2000—06, cons., 2006—. Served with AUS, 1956-58. Home: 447 E 57th St New York NY 10022-3064 Office: Sotheby's Inc 1134 York Ave New York NY 10021-8300

OLDENBURG, RONALD TROY, lawyer; b. Eldora, Iowa, June 2, 1935; s. Lorenz Frank and Bess Louise (Lewis) O.; m. Vickie Yu; children: John, Keith, Mark. BA, U. N.C., 1957; postgrad., Brunnsvik Folkhogskola, Sorvik, Sweden, 1957-58; JD, U. Miss., 1961. Bar: Miss. 1961, Hawaii 1975. Mgr. Continental Travel Svc., Chapel Hill, N.C., 1956-57, Meridian Travel Svc., Raleigh, N.C., 1961, Linmark Internat. Devel., Seoul, 1972-74; fgn. atty. Li Chun Law Office, Taipei, Taiwan, 1965-67; pvt. practice, Taipei, 1967-72, Honolulu, 1975—. Adj. prof. immigration law U. Hawaii Sch. Law, 1985—97. Contbr. articles on immigration law to legal jours. Capt. JAGC, USAF, 1962-65. Mem. Am. Immigration Lawyers Assn. Office: 700 Bishop St Ste 2100 Honolulu HI 96813-3215 Also: 94-229 Waipahu Depot Rd Ste 204 Waipahu HI 96797 E-mail: ronaldt.oldenburg@hawaiiantel.net.

OLDER, JAY JUSTIN, ophthalmic plastic surgeon; b. Jersey City, Feb. 7, 1940; m. Lois Rosner; children: Benjamin, Jessica. AB, Rutgers U., 1961; MD, Stanford U., 1966. Diplomate Am. Bd. Ophthalmology. Intern, resident in internal medicine Cornell U./Bellevue Hosp. Ctr., NYC, 1968; resident in ophthalmology Stanford (Calif.) U., 1973; fellow in ophthalmic plastic and reconstructive surgery Stanford U., San Francisco, 1974; pvt. practice Tampa, Fla., 1974—. Clin. prof. ophthalmology U. South Fla. Coll. Medicine, Tampa, 1975—, dir. oculoplastic svc., 1974—99. Author: Eyelid Tumors: Clinical Diagnosis and Surgical Treatment, 1987, 2d edit., 2003. Fellow Am. Acad. Ophthalmology (Sr. Honor award 1995), Am. Soc. Ophthalmic Plastic and Reconstructive Surgery (pres. 1987, sec. 1983-84), ACS; mem. Phi Beta Kappa (v.p. Greater Tampa Bay Assn. 1995-96). Office: Older & Slonim Eyelid Inst 4444 E Fletcher Ave Ste D Tampa FL 33613-4937

OLDERMAN, GERALD, retired medical device company executive; b. NYC, July 16, 1933; s. Cass and Hilda (Klein) O.; m. Myrna Ruth Schwartz, Aug. 3, 1958; children: Sharon, Neil, Lisa. BS in Chemistry, Rensselaer Poly Inst., Troy, NY, 1958; MS Phys. Chemistry, Seton Hall U., South Orange, NJ, 1971, PhD, 1972. Rsch. chemist Nat. Cash Register, Dayton, Ohio, 1958-61; tech. mgmt. positions Johnson & Johnson, New Brunswick, NJ, 1961-75, dir. R & D, bd. dirs. surg. products hosp. divsn., 1972-75, v.p. R & D, Surgikos divsn., 1975-78; v.p. R & D, bd. dirs. Am. Convertors divsn. Am. Hosp. Supply corp., Evanston, Ill., 1978-85; v.p. internat. R & D Pharmaseal divsn. Baxter Healthcare Corp., Valencia, Calif., 1985-91; v.p. R & D, bd. dirs. cardiopulmonary divsn. C.R. Bard, 1991-96; cons. R.F. Caffrey & Assoc., Inc., Brownsville, Vt., 1996—; exec. v.p. R&D tech. and commercialization, bd. dirs. Quick-Med Techs., Inc., Wilmington, Del., 1998—. With USMC, 1954-56. Recipient Robert Wood Johnson medal, Johnson & Johnson, 1969. Fellow Am. Inst. Chemists; mem. Assn. Advancement Med. Instrumentation, INDA, Assn. Nonwovens Industry (bd. dirs., corp. rep. 1986, 87), Nat. Fire Protection Assn. (industry rep.), Am. Soc. Artificial Internat. Organs. Home: 17 Pickman Dr Bedford MA 01730-1009 Office: RF Caffrey & Assoc Inc PO Box 319 Brownsville VT 05037-0319 also: Quick Med Techs Inc 401 NE 25th Terr Boca Raton FL 33431 Office Phone: 781-271-9893. Personal E-mail: jolderman@aol.com.

OLDERSHAW, LOUIS FREDERICK, retired lawyer; b. New Britain, Conn., Aug. 30, 1917; s. Louis A. and Annie Louise (Bold) O.; m. Virginia Wakelin, Nov. 30, 1940; children: Peter W., Robert L., David L. AB, Dartmouth Coll., 1939; LLB, Yale U., 1942. Bar: Mass. 1946, Fed. 1947. Mem. legal staff Army Ordnance Dist., Springfield, Mass., 1942-43; with firm Lyon, Green, Whitmore, Doran & Brooks, Holyoke, Mass., 1947-49; ptnr. firm Davenport, Millane & Oldershaw, Holyoke, 1949-64; treas. Nat. Blank Book Co., Inc., Holyoke, 1964-65, pres., 1965-78, chmn. bd., 1978-83; group v.p., dir. Dennison Mfg. Co., Framingham, Mass., 1967-82; counsel Bulkley, Richardson & Gelinas, Springfield, Mass., 1983—2003, ret., 2002. Mem. editl. bd.: Yale Law Jour, 1941-42. Trustee Mt. Holyoke Coll., 1966-76, Greater Holyoke YMCA; bd. dirs. emeritus Holyoke C.C. Found., Sta. WGBY-TV. Lt. USNR, 1943-47. Mem.: Abenakee Club, Orchards Golf Club, Rotary, Colony Club, Longmeadow (Mass.) Country Club. Republican. Mem. United Congl. Ch. Home: 30 Bayon Dr South Hadley MA 01075 Office: Baybank Tower 1500 Main St Ste 2700 Springfield MA 01115-0001 Personal E-mail: louolder@aol.com.

OLDFIELD, BARNEY, entertainment executive; b. Boston, June 28, 1956; s. Wilbur Joseph and Thelma Florence (Coombs) O. AB, Harvard U., 1979, Cert. Advanced Studies, 1981; Cert. Bus. Entertainment, NYU, 1996. Editor Musicians, 1979-83; copy editor Social Register Assocs., NYC, 1983-87; advt. dir. Local Listings, NYC, 1987-89; mkt. rep. Societa Italiana Lavor Oro, NYC, 1989-90; bus. mgr. Al-Bab Internat., NYC, 1990-92, McKenzie Internat., NYC, 1992-96; gen. mgr. Angelika Entertainment, NYC, 1996—; CEO Angelika Releasing, 1999—, Angelika.Com, 1999—; pres. Angelika TV.com, 2000—; gen. mgr. Prophet Pictures, 2005. Bd. dirs. Anthology Film Archives, N.Y.C., 1995—, Havana Film Festival in N.Y., Howl Arts Festival, SX Mobile Media, 2005; chair bd., coord. Harvard Ind. Film Group; mem. adv. com. Internat. Film and TV Exch., exec. prodr. New Filmmakers Series; exec. prodr. Metro Angelika Film Festival. Prodr.: Too Much Sleep, Zero Day, Another Deep Breath, All Ivy, Maniac 2; columnist: So. Voice newspaper, 1976—79; editor: Harvard Today, 1997—; prodr.: Maniac 2. Mem. Soc. Calif. Pioneers, San Francisco, 1981—. Mem. Friars Club of Calif., Harvard Club of N.Y., Harvard Club of Boston, Harvard Club of So. Calif., Harvard Faculty Club, Union League Club N.Y. Republican. Anglican. Avocations: squash, tennis. Office: PO Box 4956 New York NY 10185-4956 Office Phone: 212-410-9404, 213-840-6224. Office Fax: 213-477-2004. Business E-Mail: barney@angelikafilm.com.

OLDFIELD, E. LAWRENCE, lawyer; b. Lake Forest, Ill., Dec. 21, 1944; s. W. Ernest and Evelyn Charlotte (Gyllenberg) O.; m. Kaaren Elaine Sabey, Aug. 24, 1974; 1 stepchild, Kimberly Jo; 1 child, Lauren Elizabeth. Student, L.I. U., 1961-62, Wheaton Coll., 1962-64, Near East Sch. Archeology, Jordan, 1964; BA in Polit. Sci., No. Ill. U., 1969; JD, DePaul U., 1973. Bar: Ill. 1973, U.S. Dist. Ct. (no. dist.) Ill. 1973, U.S. Ct. Appeals (7th cir.) 1974, U.S. Supreme Ct. 1979, U.S. Ct. Appeals (3d cir.) 1985, U.S. Ct. Appeals (10th cir.) 1986, U.S. Ct. Appeals (8th cir.) 1990. Fed. agt. Dept. HUD, 1969-70; assoc. Ruff & Grotefeld Ltd., Chgo., 1973-77; gen. counsel livestock dept. Hartford Fire Ins. Co., Chgo., 1977-87; prin. E. Lawrence Oldfield & Assocs., Oak Brook, 1987-2000, Oldfield & Fox, P.C., Oak Brook, 2000—. Mediator, arbitrator U.S. Arbitration and Mediation, 1994-97, Resolute Systems, Inc., 1997-2001; ind. arbitrator, 2002—. Dir. Edgewater Cmty. Coun., 1973-74; precinct capt. 50th Ward Dems., 1974-77; trustee North Shore Bapt. Ch., 1974-77, chmn. constn. com., 1976-77; dir. Chgo. Bapt. Assn., 1974-77, treas., 1976-77; dir. Ctrl. Bapt. Children's Home, 1978-81, chmn. pers. com., 1980-81; deacon, 1981-83, chmn. bd. deacons, 1983, First Presbyn. Ch. Glen Ellyn, 1983-84; dir. Chgo. Bible Soc., 1980-84; v.p., 1983-84; trustee Village of Glen Ellyn, 1981-85; committeeman Milton Twp., DuPage County Reps., Wheaton, Ill., 1985-88; publicity chmn. Milton Twp. Reps., Wheaton, 1986-88; mem. Dist. 41 Sch. Bd., 1991-95; elder Christ Ch. of Oak Brook, 1993-2000; bd. govs. Execs. Breakfast Club of Oak Brook 1993—2005, 1st v.p., 1997-99, pres., 1999-2001. Served in U.S. Army, 1964-67. Mem. ABA, AAJ, Ill. State Bar Assn., Chgo. Bar Assn., DuPage County Bar Assn., Ill. Trial Lawyers' Assn., Fed. Trial Bar, U.S. Golf Assn., Safari Club Internat., Wheaton Comty. Radio Amateurs, Am. Legion, VFW, Kiwanis, Moose, Masons, Shriners (mem. sec. 1998-2001), Elks, Tau Kappa Epsilon. Avocations: fishing, hunting, golf, amateur radio, chess. Home: 1050 Crescent Blvd Glen Ellyn IL 60137-4276 Office: Oldfield & Fox PC 2021 Midwest Rd Ste 201 Oak Brook IL 60523-1367 also: 30 N Lasalle St Ste 1524 Chicago IL 60602-2502 also: 1622 W Colonial Pkwy Palatine IL 60067-4795 Home Phone: 630-858-8699; Office Phone: 630-495-3377. Business E-Mail: eloesq@oldfieldfox.com.

OLDFIELD, JAMES EDMUND, retired nutrition educator; b. Victoria, BC, Can., Aug. 30, 1921; came to U.S., 1949; s. Henry Clarence and Doris O. Oldfield; m. Mildred E. Atkinson, Sept. 4, 1942; children: Nancy E. Oldfield McLaren, Kathleen E. Oldfield Sansone, David J., Jane E. Oldfield, Richard A. BSA, U. B.C., 1941, MSA, 1949; PhD, Oreg. State U., 1951. Faculty Oreg. State U., Corvallis, 1951-90, head dept. animal sci., 1967-83, dir. Nutrition Rsch. Inst., 1986-90; ret., 1990. Mem. nat. tech. adv. com. on water supply U.S. Dept. Interior, Washington, 1967-68; bd. dirs. Coun. for Agrl. Sci. and Tech., Ames, Iowa, 1978-84; mem. nutrition study sect. NIH, Bethesda, Md., 1975-80, 85-87; cons. Selenium Tellurium Devel. Assn., Grimbergen, Belgium, 1990-2002. Editor: Selenium in Biomedicine, 1967, Sulphur in Nutrition, 1970, Selenium in Biology and Medicine, 1987; author: Selenium in Nutrition, 1971, Selenium World Atlas, 1999. Served to maj. Can. Army, 1942-46, ETO. Decorated Mil. Cross Can.; Fulbright Rsch. scholar U.S. Dept. State, 1974, Massey U., New Zealand; recipient Klaus Schwarz medal Internat. Assn. Bioinorganic Scientists, 1998. Fellow Am. Soc. Animal Sci. (pres. 1966-67, Morrison award 1972), Am. Inst. Nutrition; mem. Am. Chem. Soc., Am. Registry Profl. Animal Scientists (pres. 1990, editor: Profl. Animal Scientist 1993-96), Fedn. Am. Socs. Exptl. Biol., Pacific Fisheries Technologists (pres. 1966), Kiwanis (pres. 1964, lt. gov. 1986). Republican. Episcopalian. Office: Oreg State Univ Dept Animal Sci Corvallis OR 97331 Home: 4766 SW Birdsong Dr Corvallis OR 97333 Office Phone: 541-737-1894. Office Fax: 541-737-4174. Business E-Mail: james.e.oldfield@oregonstate.edu.

OLDHAM, CHERYL, federal agency administrator; BA, Tex. Christian U.; JD, St. Mary's U. Dir. Office of White House Liaison, Washington; exec. dir. Sec. Edn.'s Commn. on Future of Higher Edn. US Dept. Edn., Washington, 2003—, chief of staff to under sec. edn. Office: US Dept Edn Sec's Commn on Future of Edn 400 Maryland Avenue, SW, Rm 7E317 Washington DC 20202-0160 Office Phone: 202-205-8741. E-mail: Cheryl.Oldham@ed.gov. *

OLDHAM, DARIUS DUDLEY, lawyer; b. Beaumont, Tex., July 6, 1941; s. Darius Saran and Mary Francis (Carraway) O.; m. Judy J. White, Jan. 23, 1965; children: Steven, Michael BA, U. Tex., Austin, 1964; JD, U. Tex., 1966. Bar: Tex. 1966, U.S. Dist. Ct. (so., no., ea. and we. dists.) Tex. 1966, U.S. Supreme Ct. 1974, U.S. Ct. Appeals (3rd, 5th and 11th cirs.) 1968; cert. arbitrator and mediator. Assoc. Fulbright & Jaworski, Houston, 1966—74, ptnr., 1974—2006, of counsel/ret. ptnr., 2007—, mem. policy com., 1980—97, 2001—04, mem. exec. com., 1997—2000, mem. litigation mgmt. com., 1998—2004, chair, 2001—02. Mem. faculty grad. litigation program U. Houston; adv. com. Nat. Ctr. State Cts.; mem. chancellors coun. exec. com. U. Tex.; lectr. in field. Former mem. bd. editors Aviation Litigation Reporter, Personal Injury Def. Reporter, Inter-nat. Ins. Law Rev.; contbr. articles to profl. jours. Adv. coun. Nat. Jud. Coll.; past liberal arts adv. coun. U. Tex.; past bd. dirs. FDCC Found., Houston Pops Orch. Fellow Am. Coll. Trial Lawyers (chair complex litigation and jud. com.), Tex. Bar Found. (life), Am. Bar Found. (life), Houston Bar Found. (life), Am. Bd. Trial Advs. (pres. Houston chpt. 1999); mem. ABA (mem. ho. of dels. 1996-98, chair tort and ins. practice sect. 1988-98, presdl. emissary 1994-95, mem. coun. tort and ins. practice sect. 1988-98, presdl. emissary 1993-95, chmn. Standing Com. on Independence of the Judiciary 2001-04, chmn. Select Commn. on Jud. Campaign Fin. 2000-01, standing com. fed. jud. improvements, chmn. John Marshall award selection com. 2004-05), U. Tex. Law Sch. Alumni Assn. Exec. Com., 2003—, Tex. Bar Assn. (chmn. liaison fed. jud. com. 1989-90, pattern jury charges Vol. IV com. 1988-92), Tex. Young Lawyers Assn. (bd. dirs., chmn.), Fed. Def. and Corp. Counsel (pres. 1989-90, chmn. bd. 1990-91, exec. com. 1988-91), Tex. Assn. Def. Counsel, Maritime Law Assn. U.S., Am. Counsel Assn. (bd. dirs. 1982-83, 89-94), Def. Rsch. Inst. (chmn. aerospace com. 1984-87, Presdl. Achievement award 1987, bd. dirs. 1989-92, exec. com. 1991-92), Lawyers for Civil Justice (bd. dirs. 1988-98, chmn. 1998, exec. com. 1990-98, pres. 1997), Nat. Ctr. for State Cts. Lawyers Commn., U. Tex, Chancellors Coun. Exec. Com., River Oaks Country Club, Houston Ctr. Club, Sigma Chi (Significant Sig), Phi Delta Phi. Office: Fulbright & Jaworski 1301 Mckinney St 51st Fl Houston TX 77010-3031 Home Phone: 713-465-5804; Office Phone: 713-651-5397. Personal E-mail: doldham@fulbright.com.

OLDHAM, JOHN MICHAEL, physician, psychiatrist, educator; b. Muskogee, Okla., Sept. 6, 1940; s. Henry Newland and Alice Gray (Ewton) O.; m. Karen Joan Pacella, Apr. 24, 1971; children: Madeleine Marie, Michael Clark. BS in Engring., Duke U., 1962; MS in Neuroendocrinology, Baylor U., 1966, MD, 1967. Licensed physician NY, NJ, SC, Tex.; diplomate in psychiat. and forensic psychiatry Am. Bd. Psychiatry and Neurology; cert. Am. Psychoanalytic Assn. Intern pediatrics St. Luke's Hosp., NYC, 1967-68; resident psychiat. Columbia U. Dept. Psychiat., N.Y.S. Psychiatric Inst., NYC, 1968-70; chief resident in psychiatry Columbia U., NY State Psychiat. Inst., 1970-71; grad. Columbia Psychoanalytic Ctr., NYC, 1977; dir. psychiatric emergency svcs. Roosevelt Hosp., NYC, 1973-74, dir. residency tng. dept. psychiat., 1974-77; dir. short term diagnostic and treatment unit NY Hosp. Westchester Divsn., White Plains, NY, 1977-80, dir. divsn. acute treatment svcs., 1980-84; deputy dir. NY State Psychiatric Inst., NYC, 1984-89, acting dir., 1989-90, dir., 1990—2002; assoc. chmn. dept. psychiatry Columbia U. Coll. Physicians & Surgeons, NYC, 1986-96, vice chmn., 1996-2000, acting chmn., 2000—02; chief med. officer NY State Office Mental Health, Albany, 1989—2002; prof. psychiatry Med. U. SC, 2002—07, chmn. dept. psychiatry and behavioral sci., 2002—07, exec. dir. Inst. Psychiatry, 2002—07; sr. v.p., chief of staff The Menninger Clinic, 2007—; prof., exec. vice chmn. clin. affairs and devel., Menninger Dept. of Psychiatry and Behavioral Scis. Baylor Coll., 2007. From instr. clin. psychiatry to prof. clin. psychiatry Columbia U. Coll. P&S, 1974-96, 1988-96, Elizabeth K. Dollard profl clin. psychiatry medicine and law, 1996-2002; asst. prof. psychiatry Cornell U. Med. Coll., NYC, 1977-83, assoc. prof. clin. psychiatry, 1983-84; attending staff dept. psychiatry Roosevelt Hosp., NYC, 1973-77; assoc. attending in psychiatry, NY Hosp., 1977-84, Presbyn Hosp., NYC, 1984-88, attending in psychiatry, 1988-2002; tng. and supervising psychoanalyst Columbia Psychoanalytic Ctr., NYC, 1983-2002; coord. med. student edn., dept. psychiatry Cornell U. Med. Coll., Westchester Divsn., White Plains, NY, 1977-84; coord. clin. clerkships in psychiatry Roosevelt Hosp., Columbia U. Coll. P&S, NYC, 1974-77; spl. adv. bd. Freedom From Fear, Inc.; examiner Am. Bd. Psychiatry and Neurology; chmn. acute divsn. rsch. group, Westchester Divsn., NY Hosp., 1981-84, co-project dir. borderline rsch. group, 1982-84, co-prin. investigator familial transmission DSM III personality disorders, 1982-84; prin. investigator personality disorders in bulimia, NYS. Psychiat. Inst., 1985-90, structured DSM III assessment psychoanalytic patients, Columbia Psychoanalytic Ctr., 1986-91; co-prin. investigator validity DSM III R personality disorders, NY State Psychiat. Inst., 1987-94; co-investigator NIMH, 1996-2002; Hall-Mercer vis. scholar, dept. psychiatry, U. Pa., 2004; Judge Bernard Thompson Meml. Lectr., dept. psychiatry, North Shore U. Hosp., 2004; Albert M. Biele MD vis. prof. in psychiatry, Jefferson Med. Coll., 2005; Wolfe-Adler Lectr., SHeppard Pratt Health Sys., 2006; Ferald R. Klerman MD Meml. Lectr., Payne Whitney Clinic, NYC, 2007. Author: (with L.B. Morris) The Personality Self-Portrait, 1990; editor Jour. Psychia. Practice; editor bd. Jour. Personality Disorders; dep. editor Am. Psychiat. Pub., Inc.; mem. exec. editl. bd. Psychiat. Quar.; reviewer Arch Gen. Psychiatry, Am. Jour. Psychiatry, Psychiat. Svcs., Jour. of Neuropsychiatry; contbr. numerous articles to profl. jours.; presentations in field. Major USAF, 1971—73. Recipient John J. Weber prize Excellence in Psychoanalytic Rsch. Columbia Psychoanalytic Ctr., 1990, Dorothea Dix Award Mental Illness Found., 1996, Spl. Comm.'s award NY State Office Mental Health, 1997, Spl. Presdl. commendation Am. Psychiat. Assn., 1999, 2005, Payne Whitney Clin. award for Extraordinary Pub. Svc., 2002; Spl. Citation conferred by Governor George E. Pataki, State of NY, 2002; Paul Hoch award for Disting. Leadership, NY State Office Mental Health, 2002. Fellow Am. Coll. Psychiatrists (treas. 2004-; Bowis award 2007), Am. Psychiat. Assn. (pres. NY County dist. br., 1989-90, com. rsch. psychiat. treatment 1987-93, coun. rsch., steering com. practice guidelines, chmn. sci. program com. 1992-95, chmn. com. quality indicators 1999-2003, chmn. coun. quality care 2003—06), Am. Psychopath. Assn., NY Acad. Medicine; mem. AMA, Am. Psychoanalytic Assn. (cert.), Assn. Psychoanalytic Medicine (pres. 1989-91), Internat. Psychoanalytical Assn., NY Acad. Sci., NY State Med. Soc., Assn. Rsch. Personality Disorders (bd. dirs.), Internat. Soc. for Study of Personality Disorders (pres. 2000—03), SC Psychiat. Assn. (pres. 2006-07), Houston Psychiatric Soc. Office: Menninger Clinic PO Box 809045 Houston TX 77280-9045 Office Phone: 713-275-5016. Office Fax: 713-275-5117. Business E-Mail: joldham@menninger.edu.

OLDHAM, KIMBERLY ELISE See ELISE, KIMBERLY

OLDHAM, MAXINE JERNIGAN, real estate broker; b. Whittier, Calif., Oct. 13, 1923; d. John K. and Lela Hessie (Mears) Jernigan; m. Laurance Montgomery Oldham, Oct. 28, 1941; 1 child, John Laurence. AA, San Diego City Coll., 1973; student Western State U. Law, San Diego, 1976-77, LaSalle U., 1977-78; grad. Realtors Inst., Sacramento, 1978. Mgr. Edin Harig Realty, LaMesa, Calif., 1966-70; tchr. Bd. Edn., San Diego, 1959-66; mgr. Julia Cave Real Estate, San Diego, 1970-73; salesman Computer Realty, San Diego, 1973-74; owner Shelter Island Realty, San Diego, 1974—. Author: Jernigan History, 1982, Mears Geneology, 1985, Fustons of Colonial America, 1988, Sissoms. Mem. Civil Svc. Commn., San Diego, 1957-58. Recipient Outstanding Speaker award Dale Carnegie. Mem. Nat. Assn. Realtors, Calif. Assn. Realtors, San Diego Bd. Realtors, San Diego Apt. Assn., Internationale des Professions Immobilieres (internat. platform speaker), DAR (vice regent Linares chpt.), Colonial Dames 17th Century, Internat. Fedn. Univ. Women. Republican. Roman Catholic. Avocations: music, theater, painting, genealogy, continuing edn. Home: 3348 Lowell St San Diego CA 92106-1713 E-mail: lilyham@coxs.com.

OLDHAM, STEVE ANTHONY, lawyer; b. Madisonville, Ky., Dec. 8, 1951; s. Maurice Eugene and Peggy Sue (Nance) O.; m. Sharon Leigh Pavach, June 24, 1974; children: Douglas, Patrick, Ashley. BA with high distinction, Ind. U., 1973; JD, Harvard U., 1976. Bar: Ind. 1976, U.S. Dist. Ct. (so. dist.) Ind. 1976, U.S. Ct. Appeals (7th cir.) 1978. Assoc. Barnes, Hickam, Pantzer & Boyd, Indpls., 1976-79; atty. Hillenbrand Industries Inc., Batesville, Ind., 1979-82, sr. atty., asst. sec., 1982-86, former assoc. gen. counsel, asst. sec., 1986; sec., gen. counsel Boehringer Mannheim Pharms., Indpls.; v.p., gen. counsel and sec. Roche Diagnostics Corp. Mem. ABA, Ind. Bar Assn., Phi Beta Kappa. Office: Roche Diagnostics Corp 9115 Hague Rd PO Box 50457 Indianapolis IN 46250-0457 Office Phone: 317-845-2000. Office Fax: 317-576-3082.

OLDHAM, TODD, fashion designer; b. Corpus Christi, Tex., 1960; s. Jack and Linda Oldham. Founder Times 7, Dallas; founder, designer Todd Oldham, NYC, 1989; design dir. Escada, Munich, 1994; dorm room furniture designer Target Corp., 2001—03; furniture designer La-Z-Boy Inc., 2002—. Host, dir. Todd Time MTV House of Style, 1993-96; host Top Design, Bravo TV, 2007-;guest Tracy Takes On with Tracy Ullman, 1994, The Nanny, 1996, Roseanne, 1996; designer spl. collection for Batman Forever, 1995, MTV's Choose or Lose bus, 1996, GM Bravada to raise money for cancer rsch., 1997; music video co-dir. (with Hype Williams) Maxi Priest's That Kind of Girl, 1996; music video dir. Us3's Come on Everybody, 1997. Active Design Industries Found. for AIDS, People for the Ethical Treatment of Animals, POWARS, Pet Pals. Recipient Rising Star award Internat. Apparel Mart, Dallas, 1991, Fashion Execellence award Internat. Apparel Mart, Dallas, 1993; named Designer of Yr. Calif. Fashion Industry Friends of AIDS Project, 1996. Mem. Coun. Fashion Designers Am. (Perry Ellis award for new fashion talent 1991). Office: Todd Oldham Store NY 120 Wooster St Frnt 3 New York NY 10012-5200

OLDING, MICHAEL, plastic and reconstructive surgeon; b. Celina, Ohio, July 4, 1950; s. Paul Robert and Virginia Lee (Hierholzer) O. BS, U. Dayton, 1972; MD, U. Ky., 1980. Diplomate Am. Bd. Plastic Surgery. Intern N.Y. Hosp./Cornell Med. Ctr., NYC, 1980-81, resident in surgery, 1981-82, McGill U., Montreal, Canada, 1982-83, fellow, plastic and reconstructive surgery, 1983-85; assoc. prof. surgery divsn. plastic/reconstructive surgery George Washington U., Washington, 1985—; chief divsn. plastic and reconstructive surgery, dir. Cosmetic Surgery & Laser Ctr., George Washington Univ. Med. Faculty Assoc., Washington. Staff privileges George Washington U. Med. Ctr., Sibley Hosp., Children's Hosp., Washington; served on numerous FDA adv. panels; lectr. in field; presenter King Fisal Hosp., Riyadh, Royal Coll. Surgeons Traveling Fellowship and Plastic Surgery Rsch. Coun., London. Author: Clinicians Pocket reference, 1986; contbr. articles to profl. jours. Annals of Plastic Surgery, Plastic Reconstructive Surgery; featured on Discovery Channel, interviewed by CBS, ABC, FOX, WUSA, Washington Post, Washington Times, NY Times Style mag., Boston Globe; quoted in online articles at

ABCnews.com, Forbes.com, CNN.com and participated in an online forum with Washingtonpost.com Bd. dirs. D.C. Ballet Co., 1995—. Named a Top Doc, Washingtonian mag., 1989-, Washington Consumers' Checkbook. Fellow ACS; mem. Northeastern Soc. Plastic Surgery (bd. dirs.), Nat. Capitol Soc. Plastic Surgeons, McGill Plastic Surgery Soc. (bd. dirs.), Am. Soc. Plastic Surgeons, Am. Soc. Aesthetic Plastic Surgeons. Office: George Washington Univ Hosp 2150 Pennsylvania Ave NW Washington DC 20037-3201 Office Phone: 202-741-3241. Office Fax: 202-741-3183. *

OLDMAN, GARY, actor; b. London, Mar. 21, 1958; m. Lesley Manville (div.); 1 child, Alfie; m. Uma Thurman, 1990 (div. 1992); m. Donya Fiorentino, Feb. 16, 1997 (div. Apr. 13, 2001); children: Gulliver Flynn, Charlie John. BA, Rose Buford Coll. Speech and Drama, 1979. Appearances include (TV movies) Meantime, 1984, Honest, Decent and True, 1985, Fallen Angels: Dead End for Delia, 1993 (Cable Ace award, Actor in a Dramatic Series), The Firm, 1988, Heading Home, 1991, Jesus, 1999; (TV miniseries) Who Was Lee Harvey Oswald, 1992; (video) Since I Don't Have You by Guns n' Roses, 1994; (films) Remembrance, 1982, Sid and Nancy, 1986, Prick Up Your Ears, 1987 (Brit. Acad. Film and TV Arts nomination 1988), Track 29, 1988, We Think the World of You, 1988, Criminal Law, 1988, Paris by Night, 1989, Chattahoochee, 1989, Henry & June, 1990, State of Grace, 1990, Rosencrantz and Guildenstern Are Dead, 1990, JFK, 1991, Bram Stoker's Dracula, 1992, True Romance, 1993, Romeo is Bleeding, 1993, The Professional, 1994, Immortal Beloved, 1994, Murder in the First, 1995, The Scarlet Letter, 1995, Basquiat, 1996, The Fifth Element, 1997, Air Force One, 1997, Lost in Space, 1998, Quest for Camelot (aka Magic Sword), 1998, The Contender (also exec. prodr.), 2000, Nobody's Baby, 2001, Hannibal, 2001, Interstate 60, 2002, The Hire: Beat the Devil, 2002, Sin, 2003, Harry Potter and the Prisoner of Azkaban, 2004, Who's Kyle, 2004, Batman Begins, 2005, Harry Potter and the Goblet of Fire, 2005; dir., author, prodr. Nil By Mouth, 1998; (theatre) Massacre at Paris, 1980, Chinchilla, 1980, Desperado Corner, 1980, A Waste of Time, 1980, Summit Conference, 1982, Rat in the Skull, 1984, The Pope's Wedding, 1984 (Drama Mag. Best Actor award 1985, Fringe Best Newcomer award 1985-86), The War Plays, 1985, The Desert Air, 1985, Women Beware Women, 1986, Real Dreams, 1986, Serious Money, 1987. Recipient Outstanding Brit. Film award Brit. Acad., Best Screenplay award Brit. Acad., Dirs. prize Edinburgh Festival Channel Four, Best Dir. prize Cannes Film Festival, Best Actor and Best Newcomer, Brit. Ind. Film Awards Best Actors. Office: c/o Douglas J Urbanski Douglas Mgmt Inc 5o5 N Robertson Blvd Los Angeles CA 90048-1730

OLDS, DAVID ANDREW, food scientist, educator; b. San Francisco, Nov. 20, 1967; s. John Ward Olds, M.D. and Rosemary Burns Olds, D.A. Culinary Arts Degree, Des Moines Area C.C., Ankeny, Iowa, 1993; BS in Hotel, Restaurant and Instn. Mgmt., Iowa State U., Ames, 2002; MS in Foodsvc. and Lodging Mgmt., Iowa State U., 2004; postgrad., Kans. State U., Manhattan, 2004—. Cert. Hazard Analysis and Critical Control Point Kans. State U., 2004, ServSafe® food protection mgr. Nat. Restaurant Assn. Edn. Found., 2002. Cook Sheffield's Restaurant, Des Moines, 1984—86, Des Moines Art Ctr. Restaurant, Des Moines, 1986—91; sauté cook Embassy Club, Des Moines, 1988—90, French Quarter Bar and Restaurant, Des Moines, 1990—92, Met. Club, Des Moines, 1992—93; gen. mgr. Sheffield's West, Clive, Iowa, 1994—96; catering asst. Mary Miller Catering, Des Moines, 1993—97; sales assoc. A-Okay Antiques, West Des Moines, Iowa, 1997—2000; smokehouse cook Hickory Pk. Restaurant Co., Ames, 1997—2000; tchg. asst. Iowa State U., Ames, 2001—04; instr. Kans. State U., Manhattan, 2004—. Pres. Grad. Student Coun. - Kans. State U., Manhattan, 2006—. Contbr. articles to profl. jours. Participant Men's Conf. To End Violence Against Women, Ames, 2000; cook - vol. Ames Homeless Shelter, 2000—03; contbr. - grant writer Beyond Welfare, Ames, 2001; com. mem. All-University Theme Com. Mem., "Challenging Students to Become Their Best, " Iowa State U., 2001—02. Recipient Outstanding Grad. Asst. award, Golden Key, 2006, Top 2% of Graduating Class, Iowa State U., 2002; scholar Timothy R. Donoghue Grad. scholar, Kans. State U., 2004—05, Dr. Carol Shanklin scholar, Kans. State U. - Coll. of Human Ecology, 2005, L.M. & C.H. Beasley scholar, 2004, McKinley scholar, Iowa State U., 2003—04, Alice M. Ford scholar, 2002, NRAEF Undergraduate scholar, Nat. Restaurant Assn. Ednl. Found., 2001, Adult Student scholar, Iowa State U., 2001, Matthew Spencer Meml. scholar, 2001, Edalene Stohr Brown Meml. scholar, 2001. Mem.: Hotel, Restaurant and Instn. Mgmt. Club (treas. 2000—02), Grad. Foodsvc. and Hospitality Mgmt. Orgn. (chpt. v.p. 2004—05), Nat. Restaurant Assn. (assoc.), Internat. Assn. For Food Protection (assoc.), Inst. of Food Technologists (assoc.), Food Systems Mgmt. Ednl. Coun. (assoc.), Coun. on Hotel, Restaurant, and Instn. Edn. (assoc.), Club Mgrs. Assn. of Am. (assoc.; chpt. treas. 2002—03), Iowa State U. Alumni Assn. (life), Eta Sigma Delta, Kappa Omicron Nu (assoc.), Golden Key (assoc.), Phi Theta Kappa (assoc.), Phi Kappa Phi (life). D-Conservative. Episcopalian. Office: Kansas State U 110 Justin Hall Manhattan KS 66506-1404 Office Phone: 785-532-5513. Personal E-mail: mrdavidolds@hotmail.com. E-mail: daveolds@ksu.edu.

OLDS, JACQUELINE, psychiatrist, educator; b. Springfield, Mass., Jan. 4, 1947; d. James and Marianne (Ejier) O.; m. Richard Stanton Schwartz, Aug. 26, 1978; children: Nathaniel Leland, Sarah Elizabeth. BA, Radcliffe Coll., 1967; MD, Tufts U., 1971. Diplomate Am. Bd. Psychiatry and Neurology. Resident in adult psychiatry Mass. Mental Health Ctr., Boston, 1974; resident in child psychiatry McLean Hosp., Belmont, Mass., 1976, assoc. attending child psychiatrist, 1979—; psychiatrist-in-charge inpatient unit McLean Hall-Mercer Children's Ctr., Belmont, 1976-79; assoc. child psychiatry Beth Israel Hosp., Boston, 1979—; cons. in child psychiatry Mass. Gen. Hosp., Boston, 1994—. Instr. psychiatry Harvard U. Med. Sch, Boston, 1976-86; asst. prof. clin. psychiatry, 1986-2000, assoc. clin. prof. psychiatry, 2000—; cons. North Shore Mental Health Ctr., Salem, 1981-82; bd. dirs. Guidance Ctr., Inc. Author: Overcoming Loneliness in Every Day Life, 1996, Marriage in Motion, 2000, editor Clin. Challenges column in Harvard Rev. of Psychiatry; contbr. articles to profl. jours.; author (translator into Spanish): Matrimonio in Moviemento. Recipient Mentoring award Mass. Gen. Hosp. Dept. Child Psychiatry, 1998. Disting. fellow, Am. Psychiat. Assn.; mem. Mass. Psychiat. Soc. (ethics com. 1988-93, mem. pub. affairs com. 1992—), Am. Acad. Child Psychiatry, Am. Psychoanalytic Assn., New England Coun. Child and Adolescent Psychiatry (bd. dirs.). Democrat. Avocations: piano, writing, cooking, watercolors. Office Phone: 617-547-5920. Business E-Mail: jolds@partners.org.

OLDS, JOHN WARD, internist; b. Apr. 25, 1935; s. Thayer Stevens and Dorris (La Venture) O.; m. Rosemary Burns, July 10, 1957; children: David, James, Miriam. BS, Iowa State U., 1956; MD, U. Tenn., 1967. Diplomate Am. Bd. Internal Medicine, Am. Bd. Infectious Diseases, cert. physician exec. Intern San Francisco Gen. Hosp., 1967—68; resident, fellow U. N.Mex., 1968—72; practice internal medicine Des Moines, 1972—2002; dir. continuing med. edn. Iowa Meth. Med. Ctr., 1983—93, cons. infectious diseases, 1972—2002, attending physician, 1972—2002; asst. clin. prof. U. Iowa, Iowa City, 1978—95; co-dir. infectious disease and epidemiology Iowa Meth. Med. Ctr., 1985—93, dir. med. affairs, 1989—93; Medicare med. dir. for Iowa, 1993—97; Part A Medicare med. dir. for Iowa and S.D., 1997—2004; med. dir. Medicare RHHI, 1997—2007. Mem. Iowa Bd. Med. Examiners, 1987—93, vice chmn., 1991—93, med. advisor, 2005—. Contbr. articles to med. jour. Lt. USNR, 1956—61. Recipient Roche award, U. Tenn., 1966. Fellow: ACP, Infectious Diseases Soc. Am., Am. Coll. Physician Execs.; mem.: AMA, Iowa Found. Med. Care (dist. chmn. 1981—83, bd. dirs. 1985—), Iowa Med. Soc. (councilor 1980—84), Med. Libr. Club (pres. 1985—86). Avocation: squash. Office: 400 E Court Ave Des Moines IA 50309 Business E-Mail: john.olds@iowa.gov.

OLEARCHYK, ANDREW, cardiothoracic surgeon, educator; b. Peremyshl, Ukraine, Dec. 3, 1935; s. Symon and Anna (Kravéts) O.; m. Renata M. (Sharan), June 26, 1971; children: Christina N., Roman A., and Adrian S. Grad., Med. Acad., Warsaw, Poland, 1961, U. Pa., Phila., 1970. Diplomate Am. Bd. Surgery, Am. Bd. Thoracic Surgery. Chief divsn. anesthesiology, asst. dept. surgery Provincial Hosp., Kielce, Poland, 1963-66; resident in gen. surgery Geisinger Med. Ctr., Danville, Pa., 1968-73; resident in thoracic, cardiac and vascular surgery Allegheny Gen. Hosp., Pitts., 1980-82; pvt. practice medicine splty. in cardiac, thoracic and vascular surgery Phila. and Camden, NJ, 1982—. Author: A Surgeon's Universe, 2003, 2d edit., 2006; contbr. articles to profl. jours. Achievements include description of mimicking of the subclavian steal syndrome (2004); application of the ultrasonic Doppler flow detector to localize an intramyocardial coronary artery to perform coronary artery bypass surgery on a beating heart in the presence of neoplastic pericarditis aiming to preserve cellular immunity (2003); recognition of a triad of the severe atherosclerosis of the aortic valve, a low incidence of coronary artery disease and rheumatic fever in patients with a congenital bicuspid aortic valve (2002); modification of a vertical reduction aortoplasty by a distal external synthetic grafting for surgical treatment of aneurysms of the ascending aorta (2002); treatment of a bullous emphysema of the lung by a conservative resection of bullae and a local application of a biological glue (2001); noted association between congenital diaphragmatic defect with peritoneopericardial communication and congenital bicuspid aortic valve (2000); applied a staged treatment of the left subclavian steal syndrome and coronary artery disease by the left carotid-subclavian and coronary artery bypasses (1999); establishing that in patients with coronary artery disease, the causes of congestive heart failure in those with a mild to moderate reduction of the left ventricular ejection fraction were hypertension, myocardial infarction or ishemic insufficiency of the mitral valve, and in those with severe reduction of the left ventricular ejection fraction were left ventricular dysfunction alone, or in combination with ischemic mitral regurgitation (1999); repair of a pseudoaneurysm of the ascending aorta on a beating heart (1997); ligation of bilateral coronary-pulmonary artery fistulas on a beating heart (1996); internal repair of the coronary sinus (Valsalva) aneurysm (1996); grafting of the internal thoracic to coronary arteries without touching the atherosclerotic ascending aorta, on cardiopulmonary bypass with a beating, warm and vented heart and bradycardia induced by beta-blockers (1994); design of Olearchyk R Triple Ringed Cannula Spring Clip to secure vein grafts over blunted cannulas in coronary artery bypass surgery (1989); combined right femoral and iliac retroperitoneal surgical approach to remove retained intraaortic balloon device (1989); technique a side graft during replacement of the ascending aorta in proximal aortic dissection (1989); intro. of endarterectomy and external prosthetic grafting of ascending and transverse aorta under hypothermic circulatory arrest (1987); first to combine insertion of the inferior vena cava filter with a protected iliofemoral venous thrombectomy (Olearchyk's operation, 1986); pioneering promotion of grafting of diffusely diseased coronary arteries with the internal thoracic artery (1980-82) and of the left anterior descending coronary artery sys. during resection of cardiac aneurysms (1979-80); used an inflated Foley balloon catheter to control hemorrhage from cardiac wounds and to infuse fluids through it to replace blood loss before and during suture repair (1978); description of a combined treatment of advanced gastric carcinoma by resection and chemotherapy (1975); recognized that alcoholism and smoking were common habits of patients with stomach cancer (1975); demonstration of safety of simultaneous use of fluothane and curare as gen. anesthesia (1966); description of combined treatment of advanced testicular seminoma with chemotherapy, resection and radiotherapy (1961). Address: 129 Walt Whitman Blvd Cherry Hill NJ 08003-3746 Office Phone: 856-428-0505. Personal E-mail: asolearchyk@yahoo.com.

O'LEARY, DEANNA KAY, benefits compensation analyst, consultant; b. Corcoran, Calif., Feb. 14, 1967; d. Harold Devoe and Glenda Lea Hoppert; m. Michael Patrick O'Leary, Nov. 16, 1996. BA, U. Fresno, 2000. Cert. six sigma green belt 2003. Benefit analyst CIGNA HealthCare, Visalia, Calif., 1991—96, project specialist, 1996—99, sr. claims examiner, 1999—2000, process and orgn. evaluation analyst, 2000—02, sr. process and orgn. evaluation analyst, 2002—04, resource planner, 2004—. Author: inspirational short book, poems (Featured in Sparrowgrass Poetry Forum, 1996, featured in Famous Poets Soc., 2004), Don't Miss It - Reflections on the Journey of Life, 2003, The Cadence Of My Soul, 2005; composer, musician, singer (inspirational music) Beyond the Clouds. Trainer of ergonomics and time/motion economy City of Visalia, Visalia, 2002—02; asst. to vols. Youth Vision, Visalia, Calif., 2002—03; v.p. Children's Mus. of the Sequoias, Visalia, 2002—; music dir., min. Tulare (Calif.) Missionary Bapt. Ch., 1998—, ins. com., 2001—03; ladies choir dir. Visalia Missionary Bapt. Ch., 1993—96; bd. mem. Imagineli Children's Mus., 2005—; vol. Gift of Life Found., Visalia, 2002—03, v.p., 2003—05; promoter and vol. Calif. Transplant Donor Network, Central Valley, Calif., 1996—2001. Recipient U. Merit award, Fresno Pacific U., 1999. Republican. Baptist. Avocations: writing inspirational and motivational works, songwriting and performing, enrichment of others, volunteer work, motion and time study. Home: 2602 S Silvervale St Visalia CA 93277 Office: CIGNA HealthCare 5300 W Tulare Ave Visalia CA 93277 Office Phone: 559-738-2153. Business E-Mail: kismet01@sbcglobal.net.

O'LEARY, DENNIS SOPHIAN, accrediting body executive; b. Kansas City, Mo., Jan. 28, 1938; s. Theodore Morgan and Emily (Sophian) O'L.; m. Margaret Rose Wiedman, Mar. 29, 1980; children: Margaret Rose, Theodore Morgan. BA, Harvard U., 1960; MD, Cornell U., 1964. Diplomate Am. Bd. Internal Medicine, Am. Bd. Hematology. Intern U. Minn. Hosp., Mpls., 1964-65, resident, 1965-66, Strong Meml. Hosp., Rochester, NY, 1966—67, chief resident and hematology fellow, 1967—68; asst. prof. medicine and pathology George Washington U. Med. Ctr., Washington, 1971-73, assoc. prof., 1973-80, prof. medicine, 1980-86, assoc. dean grad. med. edn., 1973-77, dean clin. affairs, 1977-86; pres. Joint Commn., Oakbrook Terrace, Ill., 1986—. Med. dir. George Washington U. Hosp., 1974-85, v.p. Univ. Health Plan, 1977-85; pres. D.C. Med. Soc., 1983. Chmn. editl. bd. Med. Staff News, 1985-86; contbr. articles to profl. jours. Founding mem. Nat. Capital Area Health Care Coalition, Washington, 1982; trustee James S. Brady Found., Washington, 1982-87; bd. dirs. Nat. Quality Forum, 2001-07, Nat. Adv. Coun. Agy. for Healthcare Rsch. and Quality, 2002-04. Maj. U.S. Army, 1968-71. Recipient Community Service award D.C. Med. Soc., 1981, Key to the City, Mayor of Kansas City, Mo., 1982. Master ACP; fellow Am. Coll. Physician Execs.; mem. AMA (Resolution commendation 1981, Disting. Svc. award 2005), Am. Hosp. Assn. (del. 1984-86, Resolution commendation 1981), Internat. Club (Chgo.). Avocation: tennis.

O'LEARY, ELIZABETH LOKEY, curator; d. James S. and Ruth L. Lokey; m. John W. Martin, 1992. BA in Art, U. Tenn., Knoxville, 1976; MA in History of Art, U. Va., Charlottesville, 1988, PhD in History of Art, 1992. Collections asst. Hunter Mus. Am. Art, Chattanooga, 1982—86; rsch. asst. Monticello Thomas Jefferson Found., Charlottesville, Va., 1988; coord. acad. affairs Reynolda Ho. Mus. Am. Art, Winston-Salem, NC, 1993—94; rsch. assoc. Va. Mus. of Fine Arts, Richmond, 1995—98; adj. asst. prof. art history U. Richmond, 1998—2001; assoc. curator Am. art Va. Mus. Find Arts, Richmond, 2002—. Guest curator Maymont Ho., Maymont Found., Richmond, Va., 1998—2005. Author: (books) At Beck and Call: The Representation of Domestic Servants in Nineteenth-Century American Painting, 1996, From Morning to Night: Domestic Service in Maymont House and the Gilded Age South, 2003; co-author (book) American Dreams: Painting and Decorative Arts from the Warner Collection. Rev. panelist Nat. Endowment for Humanities, DC, 2004. Grantee Pre-doctoral fellowship, Smithsonian Instn., 1990—91. Mem.: Tenn. Assn. Mus. (at-large dir. 1984—86), Am. Heart Assn. (bd. dirs. 1982—84), Va. Assn. Mus., Am. Studies Assn., Assn. Historians Am. Art, Am. Assn. Mus. Episc. Office: Va Mus Fine Arts 200 North Blvd Richmond VA 23220 Home Phone: 804-359-5494. Business E-Mail: beth.oleary@vmfa.mus.

O'LEARY, JOSEPH EVANS, lawyer; b. Newton, Mass., Sept. 17, 1945; s. Cornelius Joseph and Dorothy Mary (Evans) O'L.; m. Carolyn Brady, Aug. 16, 1969; children: Caryn, Kevin, David, Catherine. AB, Boston Coll., 1967, JD, 1970; LLM, Georgetown U., Washington, DC, 1974. Bar: Mass. 1970, Ill. 1974, NY 1979. Assoc. Seyfarth, Shaw, Fairweather & Geraldson, Chgo., 1974-78, ptnr. NYC, 1978-82; of counsel Choate, Hall & Stewart, Boston, 1982-83, a ptnr., 1983-99; ptnr. McDermott, Will, Emery, Boston, 1999—. Lt. USN, 1971-74. Mem. ABA, Mass. Bar Assn., Boston Bar Assn. Home: 23 Freeman St Harwich Port MA 02646 Office: McDermott Will Emery 28 State St Boston MA 02109-1775 Home Phone: 508-432-9015; Office Phone: 617-535-4000. Business E-Mail: joleary@mwe.com.

O'LEARY, MARION HUGH, retired dean, chemist; b. Quincy, Ill., Mar. 24, 1941; s. J. Gilbert and Ruth Elizabeth (Kerr) O'L.; m. Sandra E. Eisemann, Sept. 5, 1964 (div. 1979); children— Catherine, Randall, Jessica; m. Elizabeth M. Kean, Jan. 24, 1981. BS, U. Ill., 1963; PhD, MIT, 1966. Asst. prof. chemistry U. Wis., Madison, 1967-73, assoc. prof., 1973-78, prof. chemistry and biochemistry, 1978-89; prof. and head dept. biochemistry U. Nebr., Lincoln, 1989-96; dean Coll. Natural Scis. and Math., Calif. State U., Sacramento, 1996—2006. Cons. Institut Pertanian Bogor, Indonesia, 1983-84; vis. prof. Universitas Andalas, Padang, Indonesia, 1984-85, Australian Nat. U., 1982-83. Author: Contemporary Organic Chemistry, 1976. Editor: Isotope Effects on Enzyme-Catalyzed Reactions, 1977. Contbr. articles to sci. publs. Grantee, NSF, U.S. Dept. Agr., Dept. Energy, NIH; Guggenheim Found. fellow, 1982-83; Sloan Found. fellow, 1972-74. Fellow AAAS; mem. Am. Chem. Soc., Am. Soc. Biochemistry and Molecular Biology. Home: 6428 Orange Hill Ln Carmichael CA 95608-4580 E-mail: moleary@csus.edu.

O'LEARY, PAUL GERARD, retired insurance company executive; b. Boston, June 22, 1935; s. Gerard Paul and Marie Agnes (Hennessey) O'Leary; m. Elizabeth Jane Pollins, Oct. 14, 1961; children: Paul Hennessey, William Gerard, Mary Elizabeth Conroy, James Daniel. AB cum laude, Harvard U., 1956; MBA, U. Pa., 1958. Alumni dir. Wharton Grad. Sch., U. Pa., Phila., 1958-60; asst. to pres. Colonial Trust Co., NYC, 1960; asst. sec. Empire Trust Co., NYC, 1960-65; sr. investment analyst Blyth & Co., Inc., NYC, 1965-70; v.p. William D. Witter, Inc., NYC, 1970-76, also bd. dirs.; investment sr. v.p. Prudential Ins. Co. Am., Newark, 1977—2002. Instr fin Univ Pa, 1957—60. V.p. Prudential Found., Newark, 1986—96. 1st lt. artillery US Army Nat. Guard, 1953—60. Mem.: Ireland House NYU, NY Hist. Soc., Boston Latin Sch. Alumni Assn., NY Property Ins. Underwriting Assn. (mem. investment com. 1994—2002), Ins. Inst. Hwy. Safety (mem. investment com. 1983—2002), Assn. Ins. and Fin. Analysts (pres. 1973—74), Am. Nuc. Insurers (chmn. investment com. West Hartford, Conn. 1989—96), Inst. Chartered Fin. Analysts, Am. Irish Hist. Soc. (NYC), Hobbyists Unltd. (Ridgewood, NJ), Harvard Club (NYC), Upper Ridgewood Tennis Club, Harvard Club (NJ) (pres. 1983—84). Roman Catholic. Avocations: tennis, philately, cartography, history. Home: 719 Belmont Rd Ridgewood NJ 07450-1300 Personal E-mail: ploleary@yahoo.com.

O'LEARY, PRENTICE LEE, retired lawyer; b. LA, May 6, 1942; BA, UCLA, 1965, JD, 1968. Bar: Calif. 1969. Of counsel Sheppard, Mullin, Richter & Hampton, LA, 1974—2005; ret., 2005. Bd. dirs. Legal Aid Found. LA, 1987—93, Legal Aid Found. L.A., 2000—06. Mem. ABA (bus. bankruptcy com.), State Bar Calif., Los Angles County Bar Assn. (chmn. bankruptcy com., chmn. comml. law and bankrupt sect. 1985-86), Am. Coll. Bankruptcy Profls., Order of Coif. Office: Sheppard Mullin Richter & Hampton 333 S Hope St Fl 48 Los Angeles CA 90071-1406 Home Phone: 310-458-1357; Office Phone: 213-359-9094.

O'LEARY, ROBERT C., publishing and media executive; BA magna cum laude, Boston Coll., MBA. Fin. & mgmt. positions GE; v.p. fin. Cox Cable Comm., 1982, sr. v.p. fin., 1982—86, sr. v.p. fin. & adminstrn., 1986—89, sr. v.p. ops., 1989—96; sr. v.p., CFO Cox Enterprises Inc., Atlanta, 1996—99, exec. v.p., CFO, 1999—. Vice-chmn. Ga. Chpt. Nat. Multiple Sclerosis Soc.; trustee Woodruff Arts Ctr., Atlanta. Named to Boston Coll. Athletic Hall of Fame. Office: Cox Enterprises Inc PO Box 105357 Atlanta GA 30348-5357 *

O'LEARY, THOMAS MICHAEL, lawyer; b. NYC, Aug. 16, 1948; s. James and Julia Ann (Connolly) O'L.; m. Luise Ann Williams, Jan. 13, 1978; 1 child, Richard Meridith. BA, CUNY, 1974; JD, Seattle U., 1977. Bar: Wash. 1977, U.S. Ct. Mil. Appeals 1978, U.S. Ct. Appeals (9th cir.), U.S. Supreme Ct. 1983. Dep. pros. atty. Pierce County, Tacoma, 1978; commd. 1st lt. U.S. Army, 1978, advanced through grades to capt., 1978; chief trial counsel Office of Staff Judge Adv., Ft. Polk, La., 1978-79, trial def. counsel, trial def. svc., 1979-81; chief legal advisor Office Insp. Gen., Heidelberg, Fed. Republic of Germany, 1981-82; sr. def. counsel Trial Def. Svc., Giessen, Fed. Republic of Germany, 1982-84; asst. chief adminstrv. law U.S. Army Armor Ctr., Ft. Knox, Ky., 1984-85, chief adminstrv. law, 1985, chief legal asst., 1985-86; ret. U.S. Army, 1996; sr. trial atty. Immigration and naturalization Svc., Phoenix, 1987; sector counsel, spl. asst. U.S. atty., U.S. Border Patrol, Tucson, 1987-90; enforcement counsel U.S. Immigration and Naturalization Svc., Tucson, 1990-95, asst. dist. counsel Phoenix litigation, 1995-97. Apptd. U.S. Immigration Judge, U.S. Immigration Ct., Imperial, Calif., 1997-2000, apptd. sr. U.S. Immigration Judge, Tucson, 2000—; adj. prof. Embry-Riddle Aero. U., Tucson, 2002-Decorated Purple Heart, Cross of Gallantry (Vietnam). Mem. Judge Advs Assn., Wash. State Bar Assn., Order Ky. Cols. (commd. col. 1985). Home: 9080 E 25th St Tucson AZ 85710-8675 Office: US Immigration Ct 1705 E Hanna Rd Ste 366 Eloy AZ 85231-9612 Office Phone: 520-466-3671.

OLEJNICZAK, BERNARD CHARLES, education educator; b. Green Bay, Wis., Aug. 23, 1930; s. Bernard Clement and Helen Josephine (LeClair) Olejniczak; m. Mary Jean Barrett-Terry, Oct. 13, 1956 (div. Dec. 1979); children: Ann Marie, Mary Rose, Patrick James, Thomas Bernard; m. Margaret Jean Olson, Sept. 19, 1980. BA in Philosophy, St. Norbert Coll., 1953; MA in Counseling, U. Wis., 1966. Tchr. in Latin, French and journalism Pulaski H.S., Wis., 1957—71; adminstr. Pulaski Elem. Schs., 1971—92; ednl. cons., 1993—96; tech. lectr. U. Wis., Oshkosh, 1996—2007. Chmn. curriculum U. Wis. Learning in Retirement, 1997, 2004—06. Editor (newsletter): Polish Heritage, 1993—2006, Wisconsin Counselor, 1995—2005. Pres. Village Bd., Pulaski, 1965—70; v.p. Bd. Edn., Pulaski, 1992—96; sec. Pulaski C. of C., 1958—64; pres. Brown County Libr. Bd., Green Bay, Wis., 1985—96, Nicolet Fed. Libr., Green Bay, Wis., 1987—92. Named Trustee of Yr., Wis. Libr. Assn., 1997; recipient Profl. Writing award, Wis. Counselors Assn., 1999. Mem.: Lions Club (newsetter editor, sec. 1993—2004), Phi Delta Kappa. Democrat. Roman Catholic. Avocations: reading, computers. Home: 1625 Graber St Oshkosh WI 54901 Office: Univ Wis Coll Edn 800 Algoma Blvd Oshkosh WI 54901 Business E-Mail: olejnicz@uwosh.edu.

OLENDER, JACK HARVEY, lawyer; b. McKeesport, Pa., Sept. 8, 1935; m. Lovell Olender. BA summa cum laude, U. Pitts., 1957, JD, 1960; LLM, George Washington U., 1961. Bar: DC 1961, US Supreme Ct. 1965, Md. 1966, Pa. 1985; diplomate Am. Bd. Trial Advocates, Inner Cir. Advocates. Pvt. practice, Washington, 1961-79; prin. Jack H. Olender & Assocs., P.C., Washington, 1979—. Contbr. articles to profl. jours. Active World Peace through Law, Washington. Named to Hall of Fame Nat. Assn. Black

Women Attys., 1987, DC Hall of Fame, 2000, Washington Bar Assn. Hall of Fame, 2000, Nat. Bar. Assn. Hall of Fame, 2005; recipient Presdl. award Nat. Bar Assn., 1996, 2000, 02, 04, Advocate for Justice award Nat. Bar Assn., 2000, Internat. B'nai B'rith Pursuit of Justice award, 2001, named one of 30 Best Lawyers in Washington, Washingtonian survey mag., 2005, Champion Justice award Trial Lawyers Assn., DC, 2004, Charles Hamilton Houston medallian award Washington Bar Assn., 2005. Fellow Am. Coll. Trial Lawyers, Internat. Acad. Trial Lawyers and Inner Cir. Advs.; mem. Trial Lawyers Assn. Met. Washington (pres. 1969-1970); Am. Coll. Legal Medicine; ATLA, Nat. Bar Assn. (adv. for justice 2000), Am. Bd. Profl. Liability Attys. (sec. 1989—), Trial Lawyers Pub. Justice (bd. dirs.), Internat. Assn. Jewish Lawyers and Jurists (bd. dirs.), Bar Assn. DC (pres. 1999-2000). Office: Jack H Olender & Assocs PC 888 17th St NW Fl 4 Washington DC 20006-3939 Office Phone: 202-879-7777. Business E-Mail: jhop.c@olender.com.

OLENDORF, WILLIAM CARR, JR., small business owner; b. Albany, NY, Oct. 3, 1945; s. William Carr Sr. and Mary Zilpha (Gillies) O.; m. Barbara Kay Cowan, Aug. 14, 1966; children: Mark, Julie, Jennifer. Student, Columbia Coll., 1964—65, So. Ill. U., 1965—66. Prodn. asst. Sta. WTTW-TV, Chgo., 1962-64; radio announcer Sta. WERX, Wyoming, Mich., 1967-68; sales rep. Sta. WCFL, Chgo., 1968-70, Sta. WJJD-AM & FM, Chgo., 1970-72; v.p. Promotion Network, Chgo., 1972-74; account exec. AVCO-TV, Chgo., 1974-76, Peters, Griffin & Woodward, Chgo., 1976-82, Petry TV, Chgo., 1982-83; owner, pres. Point South KOA Resort, Yemassee, S.C., 1983—. Commr. Point South Pub. Svc. Dist., 1987-88, Lowcountry & Resort Island Tourism Commn., 1994—; mem. tourism tax adv. bd. Jasper County, S.C., 1985—; chmn. Jasper County Hist. Preservation Commn., S.C., 1994-99; trustee S.C. Battleground Preservation Trust, Inc., 1994-98, 2003-2004; mem. Low Country Revolutionary War Trail Commn. Recipient S.C. Honor award for Historic Preservation, Palmetto Trust for Historic Preservation, S.C. Dept. Archives and History, 1997. Mem. Nat. Campground Owners Assn. (campground nat. adv. bd. 1989-93, Take Pride in Am. award 1992), Kampground Owners Assn. (S.C. regiona pres. 1994-97, Award of Merit 1990), S.C. Campground Assn. (pres. 1987-88), Point South Mchts. Assn. (pres. 1990—), Jasper County Hist. Soc., Jasper County C. of C. (bd. dirs. 2001-2003), Beaufort Yacht and Sailing Club. Republican. Episcopalian. Avocations: amateur radio operator, sailing. Home and Office: 14 Campground Rd Yemassee SC 29945-1760

OLENICOFF, IGOR, real estate company executive; b. Russia, 1942; married; children: Andrei(dec.), Natalia. B in Corp. Fin., U. So. Calif., MBA, M in Statistics and Quantitative Analysis. Cons., corp. exec.; founder, pres. Olen Properties Corp., Newport Beach, Calif., 1973—. Named one of Forbes' Richest Americans, 2006. Office: Olen Properties Corp 7 Corporate Plaza Dr Newport Beach CA 92660 Office Phone: 949-644-6536.

OLERUD, JOHN GARRETT, professional baseball player; b. Seattle, Aug. 5, 1968; s. John E. Olerud. Student, Washington State U. Player Toronto Blue Jays, 1989-96, NY Mets, 1997-99, Seattle Mariners, 2000—04, New York Yankees, 2004—, Boston Red Sox. Named to Am. League All-Star Team, 1993, 2001; recipient Am. League Gold Glove Award, 2000, 2002, 2003. winner A.L batting title, 1993. Office: c/o NY Yankees E 161st St and River ave Bronx NY 10452

OLES, PAUL STEVENSON (STEVE OLES), architect, educator; b. San Antonio, Sept. 26, 1936; s. Paul Stevenson Sr. and Suda (Willis) O.; m. Carole Simmons, Oct. 11, 1963 (div. 1991); children: Brian Thomas, Julia Oles Carr; m. Susan Thompson, Sept. 26, 1992. BArch, Tex. Tech U., 1960; MArch, Yale U., 1963. Registered architect, Mass. Draftsman The Architects Collaborative, Cambridge, Mass., 1963-65, Cambridge Seven Assocs., Cambridge, 1965-67; architect MIT, Cambridge, 1968-70; prin. architect Interface Architects, Newton, Mass., 1971—. Vis. faculty RISD, Providence, 1974-79; lectr. architecture Harvard Grad. Sch. Design, Cambridge, 1984-88, vis. scholar, 1989-91. Author: Architectural Illustration, 1979, Drawing the Future, 1988. Mem. vestry Episcopalian Ch., 1995-98. Named Loeb fellow Harvard Grad. Sch. Design, 1982. Fellow AIA (inst. honor 1983, fellow 1989), Boston Soc. Architects, Am. Soc. Archtl. Perspectivists (founder, pres. 1986-90, bd. dirs. 1993-97, Hugh Ferriss Meml. prize 1996). Democrat. Avocations: music, painting, photography. Office Phone: 857-636-0881. Personal E-mail: steveoles@gmail.com.

OLES, STUART GREGORY, lawyer; b. Seattle, Dec. 15, 1924; s. Floyd and Helen Louise (La Violette) O.; m. Ilse Hanewald, Feb. 12, 1954; children: Douglas, Karl, Stephen. BS magna cum laude, U. Wash., 1947, JD, 1948. Bar: Wash., 1949, US Supreme Ct. 1960. Dep. pros. atty. King County, Wash., 1949, chief civil dept., 1949—50; gen. practice law Seattle, 1950—95; sr. ptnr. firm Oles, Morrison & Rinker and predecessor, 1955—90, of counsel, 1991—95. Author: A View From the Rock, 1994, On Behalf of My Clients--A Lawyer's Life, 1998. Chmn. Seattle Cmty. Concert Assn., 1955; pres. Friends Seattle Pub. Libr., 1956; mem. Wash. pub. Disclosure Commn., 1973-75; trustee Ch. Divinity Sch. of Pacific, Berkeley, Calif., 1974-75; mem. bd. curators Wash. State Hist. Soc., 1983; former mem. Seattle Symphony Bd.; pres. King County Ct. House Rep. Club, 1950, U. Wash. Young Rep. Club, 1947; Wash. conv. floor leader Taft, 1952, Goldwater, 1964; Wash. chmn. Citizens for Goldwater, 1964; chmn. King County Rep. convs., 1966, 68, 76, 84, 88, 90, 92, 96, Wash. State Rep. Conv., 1980. Served with USMCR, 1943-45. Mem. ABA (past regional vice-chmn. pub. contract law sect.), Wash. Bar Assn., Order of Coif, Scabbard and Blade, Am. Legion, Kapoho Bay Club (pres.), Am. Highland Cattle Assn. (v.p. and dir.), Phi Beta Kappa, Phi Alpha Delta. Home: 22715 SE 43rd Ct Issaquah WA 98029-5200 also: Cape St Mary Rnch Lopez Island WA 98261 also: RR 2 Pahoa HI 96778-9802

OLESEN, ERIK L., psychotherapist, writer; b. Feb. 27, 1954; BA in Psychology and Music, Antioch U., San Francisco, 1981; MS in Counseling Psychology, San Francisco State U., 1984. Lic. marriage and family therapist Calif. Prin. Olesen & Assocs., Auburn, Calif., 1983—. Author: Mastering the Winds of Change, 1993, The Little Sailboat and the Big Storm, 1994; contbr. stories to 7 different Chicken Soup books. Named Best Spkr., Nat. Spkrs. Assn. and Meeting Planners Internat., 1995; recipient Young Artist award, Milw. Symphony, 1970, winner Young Artist Competition, Green Bay Symphony, Wis., 1971. Mem.: Internat. Soc. Neuronal Regulation. Office: 3288 Bell Rd Auburn CA 95603 Office Phone: 530-885-2673. Business E-Mail: strongu@strongu.com.

OLESEN, ROBERT LIND OLE, electrical engineer; s. Henning Lind and Birte Olesen; m. Janet Marie Reilly, Nov. 5, 1994; children: Peter Abner, Hannah Marie. BSEE, U. Mass., Amherst, Mass., 1980; MSEE, Poly. U., Bklyn., 1988; MBA with honors, Hofstra U., Hempstead, NY, 2006. Lic. ham radio operator FCC, 2003. Engr. Charles Stark Draper Lab., Boston, 1980—82, TRW Corp., San Jose, Calif., 1982—84; project engr. Eaton AIL Corp., Commack, NY, 1984—88; prin. engr. Mission Scis., Commack, NY, 1988—90, APS Corp., Commack, NY, 1990—91; staff scientist Target Sys. Tech. Corp., Stony Brook, NY, 1991—99; sr. mgr. InterDigital Comm. Corp., King of Prussia, Pa., 1999—. Adj. prof. Suffolk C.C., Selden, NY, 1995—96. Contbr. articles to profl. jours. Recipient CTO Patent award, InterDigital Comm. Corp., 2005. Mem.: IEEE, Am. Soc. Engring. Mgmt., Internat. Soc. Photographers (award 2006). Achievements include patents for wireless communications support for development of training programs. Avocations: photography, sailing, web site development. Home: 3 Country Club Dr Huntington NY 11743 Office: InterDigital Communications Corporation 2 Huntington Quadrangle Melville NY 11747 Home Phone: 631-427-3101; Office Phone: 631-622-4344. Personal E-mail: rolesen@mac.com.

OLESON, JOHN ROY, retired US foreign services officer, consultant; b. Waukesha, Wis., Oct. 12, 1930; s. Emil Oleson and Arline Caroline Wittig; m. Mary-Elizabeth Russell, Sept. 28, 1957; children: Lisa, Neil, Eric. BA, Harvard Coll., Camibridge, Mass., 1952; JD, Harvard Law Sch., Cambridge, Mass., 1956. Legal advisor Agy. Internat. Devel., Washington, 1965—67, asst. mission dir., 1967—70, mission dir. Paraguay, 1971—73, Bolivia, 1973—76, dep. mission dir., 1976—79, mission dir. Honduras, 1979—81; asst. adminstr. LAB Bur., 1982—85; internat. cons. various orgns., 1986—2000; ret. Mem.: Am. Fgn. Source Assn.

OLGAARD, ANDERS, economics educator; b. Aabenraa, Denmark, Sept. 5, 1926; s. Axel O. and Anna Lebeck; m. Alice Christiansen, 1951; three children. Dr. Polit., Univ. Copenhagen, 1966. Civil servant Econ. Sec., 1953-60; prof. econs., Univ. Copenhagen, 1962-96; adviser in Malaysia, Harvard U. Devel. Adv. Service, 1968-69; mem. Econ. Council, 1966-68, chmn., 1970-76. Author: Growth, Productivity and Relative Prices, 1966; The Danish Economy, EEC Economic and Financial Series, 1980. Mem. Danish Econ. Assn. (pres. 1983-88). Home: 12 Lerbaekvej DK-2830 Virum Denmark Office: U Copenhagen Inst Econs Studiestraede 6 DK-1455 Copenhagen Denmark

OLIAN, JOANNE CONSTANCE, curator, art historian; b. NYC; d. Richard Edward and Dorothy (Singer) Wahrman; m. Howard Olian; children: Jane Wendy, Patricia Ann; m. Gerald Weintraub; 1 child, Amy Rose Olian Weintraub. Student, Syracuse U.; BA, Hofstra U., 1969; MA, NYU Inst. Fine Arts, 1972. Grad. internship Met. Mus., NYC, 1973; asst. curator Mus. City of N.Y., 1974, curator costume collection, 1975—91; cons. curator Costume Collection, 1992—95, curator emeritus, 1995—. Lectr. Parsons Sch. Design; vis. lectr. Musée des Arts Decoratifs, Paris, summers, 1983—85; co-curator Art and Fashion Nassau County Mus. Art, 2006, assoc. trustee. Author: The House of Worth: The Gilded Age, 1860-1918, 1982; editor: Authentic French Fashions of the Twenties, 1990, Everyday Fashions of the Forties, 1992, Children's Fashions from Mode Illustrée 1860-1914, 1994, Wedding Fashions, 1862-1912, 1994, Everyday Fashions, 1909-1920, 1995, La Mode Illustrée, 1997, Victorian and Edwardian Fashions, 1998, 80 Godey's Full-Color Fashions Plates, 1838-1880, 1998, Full-Color Victorian Fashion, 1870-1893, 1999, Everyday Fashions of the Sixties, 1999, Parisian Fashions of the Teens, 2002, Everyday Fashions of the Fifties, 2002, Children's Fashions, 1900-1950, 2003; contbr. articles to profl. jours., chpts. to books Assoc. trustee Nassau County Mus. Art, 2007—; mem. Landmarks Commn. Village of Sands Pt., NY, 1990—2002. Mem. Internat. Coun. Mus. (costume com.), Costume Soc. Am. (dir. 1976-79, 83-86), Fashion Group (bd. dirs. 1985-86), Centre Internat. d'Etude des Textiles Anciens, Cosmopolitan Club N.Y.C Home and Office: 2 Shepherds Ln Sands Point NY 11050 Personal E-mail: joanneolian1@aol.com.

OLIAN, JUDY D., dean; b. Australia; BS in Psychology, Hebrew U., 1974; MS in Indsl. Rels., U. Wis., 1977, PhD in Indsl. Rels., 1980. Lectr. to full prof. mgmt. and orgn. Robert H. Smith Sch. Bus., U. Md., 1979—2000, sr. assoc. dean, 1999—2000; fellow Am. Coun. Edn. Fellow to pres. U. Md., 1990—91, special asst. to pres., 1991—92, founder, dir. IBM-TQ Project, 1991—92; dean, prof. mgmt. Smeal Coll. Bus., Pa. State U., 2000—; dean UCLA Anderson Sch. Mgmt., 2006—. Exec. com. Personnel and Human Resources divsn. Acad. Mgmt., 1984—87, 1991—94; exec. com. bd. dirs. Assn. to Advance Collegiate Sch. Bus., 2000—01. Author: (syndicated weekly column) About Business; past mem. editl. bd.: Jour. Quality and Mgmt., Acad. Mgmt. Review. Bd. dirs. The Second Mile, Penn State Found. Recipient award for curriculum innovation, Md. Assn. for Higher Edn., 1996. Office: Office of Dean UCLA School Mgmt F 407 Box 951481 Los Angeles CA 90095 Office Phone: 814-863-0448. Office Fax: 814-865-7064. Business E-Mail: jdo10@psu.edu. *

OLIAN, ROBERT MARTIN, lawyer; b. Cleve., June 14, 1953; s. Robert Meade and Doris Isa (Hessing) Olian; m. Terri Ellen Ruther, Aug. 10, 1980; children: Andrew Zachary, Alix Michelle, Joshua Brett. AB, Harvard U., 1973, JD, 1977, M in Pub. Policy, 1977. Bar: Ill. 1977, U.S. Dist. Ct. (no. dist.) Ill., U.S. Ct. Appeals (7th cir.) 1983, U.S. Dist. Ct. (no. dist. trial bar) Ill. 1992, U.S. Dist. Ct. (we. dist.) Mich. 1994, U.S. Dist. Ct. (cen. dist.) Ill. 2004. Assoc. Sidley & Austin, Chgo., 1977-84; ptnr. Sidley Austin LLP, Chgo., 1985—. Editor: (book) Illinois Environmental Law Handbook, 1988, 1997. Panel atty. Chgo. Vol. Legal Svcs., 1983—; bd. dirs. Friends IDF, 2003—07; trustee North Shore Congregation Israel, 1990—, sec., 1995—96, v.p., 1996—2003, first v.p., 2004—05, pres., 2005—; mem. regional strategic/mktg. com. Alexian Bros. Ill., Inc., Elk Grove, 1985—88; mem. dean's alumni leadership coun. JFK Sch. Govt. Harvard U., 2003—. Mem.: ABA, Chgo. Bar Assn., Harvard Club (Chgo.), Std. Club. Jewish. Home: 85 Oakmont Rd Highland Park IL 60035-4111 Office: Sidley Austin LLP One S Dearborn # 2800 Chicago IL 60603-2302 Home Phone: 847-432-5662; Office Phone: 312-853-7208. Business E-Mail: rolian@sidley.com.

OLICK, PHILIP STEWART, lawyer; b. NYC, Oct. 2, 1936; s. Jack and Anita (Babsky) O.; m. Alice D. Chait, Mar. 25, 1961; children: Jonathan A., Jeffrey K., Diana M. BA, Columbia U., 1957; LLB, NYU, 1960. Bar: N.Y. 1961, Mo. 1966. Ptnr. Benjamin, Galton, Robbins & Flato, NYC, 1961-65; gen. counsel, v.p., sec. Nat. Bellas Hess, Inc., Kansas City, Mo., 1965-69, dir., 1970-76; ptnr. Burke & Burke, NYC, 1970-73, Townley & Updike, 1973-89, Moses & Singer, 1989—. Bd. arbitrators N.Y. Stock Exch. Bd. dirs. Univ. Glee Club NYC, pres.; bd. dirs. Young Peoples Chorus NYC. With AUS, 1960-61. Mem. Assn. of Bar of City of N.Y., Univ. Club (N.Y.C.), Columbia Club. Home: 860 5th Ave # 19J New York NY 10021-5856 also: 4 Rosebud Ln East Quogue NY 11942-3627 Office: The Chrysler Bldg 405 Lexington Ave New York NY 10174-1299 Office Phone: 212-554-7891. E-mail: polick@mosessinger.com.

OLIFF, MICHAEL D., finance educator; b. Washington, Mar. 3, 1955; s. Julian Lawrence Oliff and Dorothy Pearson. BA, Appalaachian State U., Boon, NC, 1977; PhD, Clemson U., SC, 1982. Corp. mgr. rsch. Milliken & Co., Spartanburg, SC, 1982—84; prof. Inernational Mgmt. Inst., Lausanne, Switzerland, 1988—93; founder, pres. The Phoenix Performance Group, Dallas, 1993—. Adv. Accenture, Chgo., 1991—99; dir. enterprise 2020 U. Tex., Richardson, 2002—, prof., 2002—. Author: (book) Intelligent Manufacturing, Restructuring for Tomorrows Market, Navigating the Enterprise in Turbulent Times. Recipient Outstanding Bus. Case award, European Found. Mgmt. Devel., 1994, Outstanding Prof. award, Master Bus. Program; fellow, World Productivity Coun., 1991; scholar, So. Mgmt. Assn., 1987. Office: The Univ Texas at Dallas 2601 Floyd Richardson TX 78080 Home Phone: 972-998-7536; Office Phone: 972-883-4118. Business E-Mail: michael.oliff@utdallas.edu.

OLIKER, DAVID WILLIAM, healthcare management administrator; b. Elkins, W.Va., Mar. 29, 1948; married; 3 children. BA in Sociology and Anthropology, East Carolina U., 1970; MA in Social Anthropology, Am. U., 1973; Cert. in Healthcare Adminstrn., George Washington U., 1977. Health svcs. specialist United Mine Workers Am. Health and Retirement Funds, 1976-78; health planner Health Sys. Agy. Western Md., Cumberland, 1978-79; ops. mgr. Md.-Individual Practice Assn., Inc., Rockville, 1979-81; project dir. N.Y. Health Maintenance Plan, Inc., NYC, 1981-82; pres., CEO MVP Health Plan, Schenectady, NY, 1982—, Preferred Care (merger with MVP Health Plan), Rochester, NY, 2005—. Mem. bd. dir. Schenectady 2000, Albany Colonie Regional C. of C., Twin Rivers Boy Scout Coun. Mem. APHA, Am. Assn. Health Plans, N.Y. State HMO Conf. (bd. dirs.), Nat. Managed Care Inc. (chmn.). Office: MVP Health Plan PO Box 2207 Schenectady NY 12301-2207 also: Preferred Care 259 Monroe Ave Rochester NY 14607

OLIKER, VLADIMIR, mathematician, educator; b. Ulianovsk, Russia, Oct. 7, 1945; came to U.S. 1975, naturalized 1980; s. Yosef and Sonia (Bakelman) Oliker; m. Elena Matis, Mar. 20, 1969; children: Olga, Aviva, Yosef Matis. MS, Leningrad U., Russia, 1967; PhD, Leningrad U., 1971. Sr. researcher Hydrometeorological Inst., Leningrad, Russia, 1970-72; group leader Dept. Transportation, 1972-74; vis. prof. Temple U., Phila., 1975-77; assoc. prof. to prof. U. Iowa, Iowa City, 1977-80, 80-84; prof. math. Emory U., Atlanta, 1984—. Vis. mem. Math Scis. Research Inst., Berkeley, Calif., 1983; vis. prof. U. Florence, Italy, 1983, Technische U., Berlin, 1982, U. Heidelberg, Fed. Republic Germany, 1981 Contbr. articles to profl. jours. Jewish. Home: 1565 Adelia Pl NE Atlanta GA 30329-3805 Office: Emory U Dept Math And Computer Sci Atlanta GA 30322-0001 Business E-Mail: oliker@mathcs.emory.edu.

OLIN, LAURIE DEWAR, landscape architect, educator; BArch U. Wash., 1961. Lectr. to practice prof. landscape arch., regional planning Univ. Pa., 1976—; chair, landscape arch. dept., grad. sch. design Harvard Univ., 1982—86; prin. Hanna/Olin Ltd. landscape architects, Phila., 1976—96, Olin Partnership, Phila., 1996—. Prin. works include ARCO Hdqs., Newtown Sq., Pa., 1976, Johnson & Johnson Hdqs., Denver, 1977, Canary Wharf, London, 1985, LA County Mus. Art, 1987, Vila Olimpica, Barcelona, Spain, 1991, Nat. Gallery Sculpture Garden, Washington, DC, 1993, Toledo Mus. Art, 1995, Independence Nat. Historic Park, Phila., 1997, site design, Washington Monument, 2002. Recipient Bradford Williams medal for writing on landscape architecture, 1991. Fellow: Am. Acad. Arts and Sciences, Am. Soc. Landscape Architects; mem.: AAAL, Am. Inst. Architects (hon. Design medal 2005). Office: Olin Partnership Public Ledger Bldg Ste 1123 150 S Independence Mall W Philadelphia PA 19106 Office Phone: 215-440-0030. Office Fax: 215-440-0041.

OLIN, MARILYN, secondary school educator; b. Rochester, NY; BA in English, Nazareth Coll. Rochester, 1965; MS in English Edn., SUNY, Brockport, 1971. Nat. bd. cert. tchr. 1999. Tchr. Rochester Diocese Cath. Schs., 1965—68, Rochester Pub. Schs., 1968—71, Duval County (Fla.) Pub. Schs., 1972—, Paxon Sch. for Advanced Studies, Jacksonville, Fla., 1996—. Mem.: Nat. Forensic League, Nat. Bd. for Profl. Tchg. Stds. Office: Paxon Sch for Advanced Studies 3239 Norman E Thagard Blvd Jacksonville FL 32254 Office Phone: 904-693-7583 ext 161.

OLIN, WILLIAM HAROLD, orthodontist, educator; b. Menominee, Mich., Mar. 7, 1924; s. Harold H. and Lillian (Hallgren) Olin; m. Bertha Spitters, May 6, 1950; children: William Harold, Paul Scott, Jon Edward. DDS, Marquette U., 1947; MS, U. Iowa, 1948. Asst. prof. orthodontics Univ. Hosps., U. Iowa, Iowa City, 1948, assoc. prof., 1963-70, prof., 1970-93, prof. emeritus, 1995—. Chmn. bd. dirs. Hills Bank. Author: (book) Cleft Lip and Palate Rehabilitation, 1960; contbr. articles to profl. jours. Fund raiser, participant Ops. Smile. Served to capt. US Army, 1952—54. Mem.: Am. Acad. Sports Dentistry (bd. dirs., sec./treas. 1989—95), Am. Cleft Palate Assn. (pres. 1970), Iowa Orthodontic Soc. (pres. 1959), Midwest Orthodontic Soc. (pres. 1968—69), Angle Orthodontic Soc. Midwest (pres. 1982), Univ. Athletic Club (bd. dirs.), Rotary (pres. Iowa City). Republican. Methodist. Avocations: collecting political memorabilia, music box collecting, sports, travel, politics, coin collecting/numismatics. Home: 426 Mahaska Dr Iowa City IA 52246-1610 Personal E-mail: w.olin@mchsi.com.

OLINGER, CARLA D(RAGAN), medical advertising executive; b. Cin., Oct. 8, 1947; d. Carl Edward and Selene Ethel (Neal) Dragan; m. Chauncey Greene Olinger, Jr., May 30, 1981. BA, Douglass Coll., 1975. Mgr. info. retrieval services Frank J. Corbett, Inc., NYC, 1976—77; editor, proofreader, prodn. asst. Rolf W. Rosenthal, Inc., NYC, 1977—78, copywriter, 1978—80, copy supr., 1980—82, v.p. copy dept., 1982—83; v.p., group copy supr., adminstrv. copy supr. Rolf W. Rosenthal, Inc., divsn. Ogilvy & Mather, 1984—89; v.p., assoc. creative dir. RWR Advt., 1989; v.p., copy supr. Barnum & Souza, NYC, 1990—92, Botto, Roessner, Horne & Messinger, Ketchum Comm., NYC, 1992—95, Lyons Lavey Nickel Swift, NYC, 1995—. Editor: Antimicrobial Prescribing (Harold Neu), 1979. Mem.: Nat. Inst. Social Scis., St. George's Soc. N.Y., Church Club N.Y. Office: Lyons Lavey Nickel Swift 220 E 42nd St New York NY 10017-5806

OLINGER, CHAUNCEY GREENE, JR., investment company executive, editorial consultant; b. Long Beach, Calif., Jan. 16, 1933; s. Chauncey Greene and Cora Blount (Urquhart) O.; m. Carla R. Dragan, May 30, 1981. BA in Philosophy with honors, U. Va., Charlottesville, 1955; MA, Columbia U., NY, 1971. Cert. fin. planner Cert. Fin. Planning Bd. Standards. Coadjutant in philosophy Rutgers U., New Brunswick, NJ, 1968—72; rep. NY World Federalists, USA, NYC, 1970; dir. subcom. U.S. sec. of state adv. com. Dept. of State, Washington, 1972; editl. cons. Columbia U., NYC, 1973—82; editor, pres. Met. Rsch. Co., NYC, 1982—91; investment exec. First Albany, NYC, 1991—92, Janney Montgomery Scott LLC, NYC, 1992—. Sec. univ. seminar Columbia U., NYC, 1968—72, mem. increase corp. philanthrophic giving com., 1980—83, founder, co-chmn. u. seminar, 1998—2004, chmn. u. seminar, 2005—. Editor: World Enough, (Margaret Mead and Ken Heyman), 1975, A Celebration of Thanksgiving For the Life of I. I. Rabi, 1991, Columbia and the City: The University's Commitment to New York City, 1993, Courtney C. Brown: In Memory, 1995; author: New York City: An Economic Resource Profile, 1989, The I.I. Rabi Memorial Room, 1996. Pres. Fellowship of Young Churchmen, Episcopal Diocese of So. Va., 1950-52; trustee Cathedral Ch. St. John the Divine, 1988; nat. chmn. Coalition to Stop SST Environmental Damage, NY, 1975-78; NGO rep. Friends of Earth at UN, 1977-1986; pub. mem. human rights in rsch. com. NY Hosp.-Cornell Med. Ctr., 1975-80; pres. grad. faculty alumni Columbia U., NY, 1977-81, pres. student coun.Columbia U., NY 1963-64; bd. dirs. Bar Harbor (Maine) Festival, 1969-74, Bloomingdale House of Music, NYC, 1976-81. Lt. (j.g.) USN, 1955—58. Recipient Conspicuous Alumni Svc. medal Columbia U., 1980, Svc., Loyalty and Dedication award Grad. Faculty Alumni of Columbia U., 1988. Mem. Am. Philos. Assn., Nat. Inst. Social Scis. (dir. 1988-92, 2005—, pres. 2006-), Fin. Planning Assn., Pilgrims of the US, Am. Soc. Most Venerable Order of Hosp. of St. John of Jerusalem, St. Andrew's Soc. of the State of NY (sec. 1991-95), St. George's Soc. NY, Century Assn., Emeritus Profs. in Columbia (assoc.), The Ch. Club of NY (v.p. 1985-86, 88-89, 96-97, pres. 1997-2000, trustee 1983-89, 93-2000, 2001-24), Laymen's Club of the Cathedral of St. John the Divine (pres. 1988, gov. 1982—, 1st v.p. 2004—06), Ft. Ticonderoga Assn. Episcopalian. Avocations: reading, writing, walking, theater, ballet, sculpture. Office: Janney Montgomery Scott LLC 575 Lexington Ave New York NY 10022-6102

O'LINGER, JOANN C., astronomer; b. Palo Alto, Calif., Nov. 23, 1955; d. Robert Daniel and Jeanette Ann O'Linger; m. Douglas Morris, Feb. 14, 1974 (div. Apr. 4, 1995); m. Paul C. Luscusk, Feb. 7, 2004; children: Karen Elizabeth Morris, Matthew Isaiah Luscusk, Emma Clarissa Luscusk, Robin Michelle Betcher (nee Morris), Cheryl Renee Morris, Stephen William Morris. BS in Physics, U. Calif., Riverside, 1990; MS in Physics, U. Calif.,

1997, PhD in Soil Sci., 1998. Postdoctoral fellow Jet Propulsion Lab., Pasadena, Calif., 1998—2000; staff scientist Calif. Inst. Tech., Pasadena, 2000—. Mem.: Am. Astron. Soc. Office: Calif Inst Tech Mail Stop 314-6 Pasadena CA 91125

OLINS, ROBERT ABBOT, communications research executive; b. Cambridge, Mass., Sept. 25, 1942; s. Harry and Janice Olins; m. Irma Westrich, June 16, 1967; 1 son, Matthew Abbot. Student, Hobart Coll., 1961-62, San Francisco Art Inst., 1962; BA, U. Mass., 1967; postgrad., U. Tampa, 1968; MA, U. Mo., 1969, PhD, 1972. With Marsteller, 1972, N.W. Ayer, 1972, Post, Keys & Gardner, Chgo., 1973, Young & Rubicam, Chgo., 1973-76, mng. dir. comm. rsch. divsn., 1976-77; pres., CEO, subs. Comm. Rsch. Inc., Chgo., 1978—, owner, chmn., 1979—. Pres., CEO Insights, Chgo., 1976—; assoc. prof. Howard Univ., 2004— Contbr. articles to profl. jours. Recipient Chgo./4 award for creative excellence, 1974; winner Chgo. Mackinac race, 1981; Am. Assn. Advt. Agys. grantee, 1968-71 Mem.: Mid North Assn. (bd. dirs., chmn. planning), Am. Mktg. Assn., Chgo. Yacht Club, Lake Mich. Yachting Assn., U.S. Sailing Club, Skyline Club. Avocations: skiing, sailing, power boating.

OLIPHANT, CHARLES FREDERICK, III, lawyer; b. Chattanooga, Sept. 25, 1949; s. Charles Frederick and Jayne (Shutting) O.; m. Nancy Ann Stewart, May 15, 1976; children: James Andrew, Alexander Stewart. BA in Econs., U. N.C., 1971; JD, U. Mich., 1975. Bar: D.C. 1975. Assoc. Miller & Chevalier, Chartered, Washington, 1975-81, mem. firm, 1982—. Bd. adv. Jour. of Pension Planning and Compliance. Fellow Am. Coll. Employee Benefits Counsel; mem. ABA, Bar Assn. D.C. Episcopalian. Avocations: music, reading. Office: Miller & Chevalier Chartered 655 15th St NW Ste 900 Washington DC 20005-5799 Office Phone: 202-626-5834. E-mail: foliphant@milchev.com.

OLIPHANT, CHARLES ROMIG, retired physician; b. Waukegan, Ill., Sept. 10, 1917; s. Charles L. and Mary (Goss) R.; m. Claire E. Canavan, Nov. 7, 1942; children: James R., Cathy Rose, Mary G., William D. Student, St. Louis U., 1936-40, MD, 1943; postgrad., Naval Med. Sch., 1946. Intern Nat. Naval Med. Ctr., Bethesda, Md., 1943; pvt. practice medicine and surgery San Diego, 1947-99; ret., 1999. Bd. dirs. Midway Med. Enterprises; former chief staff Balboa Hosp., Doctors Hosp., Cabrillo Med. Ctr.; chief staff emeritus Sharp Cabrillo Hosp.; mem. staff Mercy Hosp., Children's Hosp., Paradise Valley Hosp., Sharp Meml. Hosp.; sec. Sharp Sr. Health Care, S.D., 1985-98; mem. exec. bd., program chmn. San Diego Power Squadron, 1985-93, 95; charter mem. Am. Bd. Family Practice. Served with M.C., USN, 1943-47. Recipient Golden Staff award Sharp Cabrillo Hosp. Med. Staff, 1990; inducted into Wisdom Hall of Fame, 2003. Fellow Am. Geriatric Soc. (emeritus), Am. Acad. Family Practice, Am. Assn. Abdominal Surgeons; mem. AMA, Calif. Med. Assn., Am. Acad. Family Physicians (past pres. San Diego chpt., del. Calif. chpt.), San Diego Med. Soc., Pub. Health League, Navy League, San Diego Power Squadron (past comdr.), SAR, San Diego Yacht Club, Douglas County Scottish Soc. Home: Riverview Terr Unit # 109 1970 W Harvard Ave Roseburg OR 97470-2746

OLIPHANT, MARTHA CARMICHAEL, civic worker; b. Providence, Sept. 17, 1935; d. Leonard and Pearl (Kidston) Carmichael; m. S. Parker Oliphant, June 2, 1962 (dec. Jan. 2001); children: Leonard Carmichael, Samuel Duncan. BA, Wellesley Coll., 1957. Lab. asst. NIMH, Bethesda, Md., 1957-63; chmn. DC Com. for Stratford Hall, Robert E. Meml. Assn., 2004—06. Bd. govs. Washington Home and Hospice, 1976—. Bd. dirs., past pres. All Hallows Guild, Washington Cathedral, 1971-93; mem. bd. lady visitors Childrens Nat. Med. Ctr., 1971-93, Children's Hosp. Found., 1974-90; mem. Com. of 100 of Fed. City, 1977-86; bd. dirs. Washington Home and Hospice, 1976—, also past pres.; past bd. dirs., v.p. Jr. League Washington; mem. Smithsonian Women's Com., Washington, 1993—. Recipient voluntarism award Jr. League Washington, 1988. Mem. Sulgrave Club (bd. dirs. 1985-88), Evergreen Garden Club (pres. 1989-91). Republican. Episcopalian. Home: 4977 Glenbrook Rd NW Washington DC 20016-3222

OLIPHANT, URETZ JOHN, physician, surgeon; b. Chgo., May 9, 1953; s. John and Letha (Fryson) O.; m. Mercidita DeJesus, Jan. 11, 1985; children: Michael, Jonathan, Kathryn. AB, Boston U., 1976; MD, U. Minn., 1983. Diplomate Am. Bd. Surgery. Fellow in trauma/critical care Ill. Masonic Hosp./U. Ill., Chgo., 1991-92; attending surgeon Carle Found. Hosp., Urbana, Ill., 1992—, head divsn. trauma, 1995—; clin. assoc. prof. dept. surgery U. Ill. Coll. Medicine, Urbana, 1994—, head dept. surgery, 1996—. Chmn. bd. dirs. Frances Nelson Cmty. Health Ctr., urbana, 1994—; chmn. Region 6 Trauma Com., Urbana, 1995-97. Founding mem. Nat. Safe Kids, Champaign, Ill., 1995—. Recipient Golden Apple Tchg. award U. Ill. Coll. Medicine, 1994, 95, 97, 99, 2006, 07. Fellow ACS, Internat. Coll. Surgeons. Avocations: chess, basketball. Office: Carle Found Hosp 602 W University Ave Urbana IL 61801-2530 Office Phone: 217-383-3204. Business E-Mail: uretz.oliphant@carle.com.

OLISA, NZEDEGWU ROBERT, III, information technology executive, manufacturing executive; b. Onitsha, Nigeria, Aug. 5, 1967; arrived in US, 1971; s. Emeka Geoffrey and Ifey Stella Olisa. BSc, U. Jos, Nigeria, 1990; MS, U. Tex., 1996, MPA, 2006. Bd. cert. Am. Soc. Clin. Pathologists, 1996, Am. Acad. Microbiologists, 1999. Founder, CEO Biol. Agts. Corp., El Paso, Tex., 1998—. Guest scholar U. Tuebingen, Germany, 2002—04. Lt. comdr. USN, 2005. NIH Minority Biomed. Rsch. scholar, Howard U., 1998—2002. Conservative. Roman Catholic. Achievements include copyrights from US library of congress for electronic mail evaluation system for infectious disease surveillance and the biological agents index; patents for braunmycin (olisferol), a broad spectrum antimicrobial vaccine. Avocations: software development, jogging, travel. Office: 7362 RemconCir #36 El Paso TX 79912 Office Phone: 915-526-4595.

OLITZKY, KERRY MARC, rabbi; b. Pitts., Dec. 22, 1954; s. Abraham Nathan and Frances (Reznick) O.; m. Sheryl Mandy Rosenblatt, Aug. 28, 1977; children: Avi Samuel, Jesse Michael. BA, U. South Fla., 1974, MA, 1975; MA in Hebrew Lit., Hebrew Union Coll., 1980, D in Hebrew Letters, 1985. Ordained rabbi, 1981. Asst rabbi, dir. religious edn. Congregation Beth Israel, West Hartford, Conn., 1981-84; dir. sch. edn. Hebrew Union Coll., NYC, 1984; dir. Jewish Life Network/Steinhardt Found. Author, editor: We Are Leaving Mother Russia, Glossary of Jewish Life, A Jewish Mourner's Handbook, The Safe Deposit and Other Stories about Old Lovers, Grandparents and Crazy Old Men, Twelve Jewish Steps to Recovery, Renewad Each Day. Named one of The Top 50 Rabbis in America, Newsweek Mag., 2007. Mem. Religious Edn. Assn., Assn. Reform Zionists of Am., Nat. Assn. Temple Educators, Cen. Conf. Am. Rabbis, Coalition for the Advancement of Jewish Edn., Gerontology Soc. Am., Joint Commn. on Jewish Edn., Assn. for Supervision and Curriculum Devel., Nat. Interfaith Coalition on Aging. Democrat. Office: Hebrew Union Coll Jewish Inst Religion 1 W 4th St New York NY 10012-1105 *

OLIVA, LAWRENCE JAY, retired academic administrator, history professor; b. Walden, NY, Sept. 23, 1933; s. Lawrence Joseph and Catherine (Mooney) Oliva; m. Mary Ellen Nolan, June 3, 1961; children: Lawrence Jay, Edward Nolan. BA, Manhattan Coll., 1955; MA, Syracuse U., 1957, PhD, 1960; postgrad., U. Paris, 1959; DHL (hon.), Manhattan Coll., 1987; LLD (hon.), St. Thomas Aquinas Coll., 1988; DHL (hon.), Hebrew Union Coll., 1992; DLitt, Univ. Coll., Dublin, 1993; PhD, Tel Aviv U., 1994. Prof. history NYU, 1969—, assoc. dean, 1969—70, vice dean, 1970—71, dean faculty, 1971—72, dep. vice chancellor, 1970—75, v.p. acad. planning and services, 1975—77, v.p. acad. affairs, 1977—80, provost, exec. v.p. acad. affairs, 1980—83, chancellor, exec. v.p., 1983—91, pres., 1991—2002, pres. emeritus, 2002—. Author: Misalliance: A Study of French Policy in Russia during the Seven Years' War, 1964, Russia in the Era of Peter the Great, 1969; editor: Russia and the West from Peter to Kruschev, 1965, Peter the Great, 1970, Catherine the Great, 1971; contbr. articles to profl. jours. Trustee Inst. Internat. Edn.; active Onassis Found., UN Assn. of N.Y. Adv. Coun., N.Y.C. Partnership, Assn. for Better N.Y., Am. Mus. Immigration; adv. bd. U. Athletic Assn.; bd. dirs. Chatham House, Royal Inst. Internat. Affairs, Am. Bd. Dirs. Coun. for U.S. and Italy Nat. Collegiate Athletic Assn., Pres.'s Commn.; adv. bd. Pres.'s Coun.; bd. dirs. N.Y. State Commn. on Nat. and Cmty. Svc. Recipient Medal of Sorbonne, U. Paris, 1992, Man. in Edn. award, Italian Welfare League, medal of honor, Ellis Island; fellow Fribourg fellow, 1959. Mem.: Irish-Am. Cultural Inst., Assn. Colls. and Univs. of State of N.Y, Am. Coun. Edn., Soc. Fellows NYU, Phi Gamma Delta, Phi Beta Kappa. Home: 33 Washington Sq W New York NY 10011-9154 Office: 60 Wash Square S 503 New York NY 10012

OLIVAS, DANIEL ANTHONY, lawyer; b. LA, Apr. 8, 1959; s. Michael A. and Elizabeth M. (Velasco) O.; m. Susan L. Formaker, Oct. 19, 1986; 1 child, Benjamin Formaker-Olivas. BA in English Lit., Stanford U., 1981; JD with honors, UCLA, 1984. Bar: Calif. 1987, U.S. Dist. Ct. (cen. dist.) Calif. 1988, U.S. Ct. Appeals (9th cir.) 1988, U.S. Supreme Ct. 1995. Law clk., atty. Hunt & Cochran-Bond, LA, 1984-88; atty. Heller, Ehrman, White & McAuliffe, LA, 1988-90; dep. atty. gen. dept. of justice antitrust div. State of Calif., LA, 1990-91, dep. atty. gen. dept. of justice land law sect., 1991—. State apptd. bd. dirs. Western Ctr. Law and Poverty, L.A., 1988-94; mem. Hispanic employees adv. com. Calif. Dept. Justice, 1990—; mem. exec. com. eviron. law sect. State Bar Calif., 2002-04. Contbr. articles to L.A. Daily Jour., and others; writer fiction and poetry. Recipient Atty. Gen.'s award for outstanding achievement in litigation, 1994; named one of Outstanding Young Men of Am., 1984. Mem. Mex.-Am. Bar Assn., Mex.-Am. Bar Found. (bd. dirs. 1993-94), L.A. County Bar Assn. (Jud. Appointments Com 1993-97), Stanford Chicano/Latino Alumni Assn. (pres.-elect 1992-93, pres. 1993-94). Democrat. Jewish. Office: State of Calif Ste 1702 300 S Spring St Los Angeles CA 90013-1230 Office Phone: 213-897-2705. Personal E-mail: olivasdan@aol.com. Business E-Mail: dan.olivas@doj.ca.gov.

OLIVAS, JOHN D. (DANNY), astronaut; b. North Hollywood, Calif. married; 5 children. BSME, U. Tex., El Paso; MSME, U. Houston; PhDME and Materials Sci., Rice U. Mech., materials engr. Dow Chem. Co., Freeport, Tex.; mem. support team Kelly AFB; mem. support team crew and thermal sys. directorate NASA, Johnson Space Ctr., Houston; sr. rsch. engr. Jet Propulsion Lab., program mgr. advanced interconnect and mfg. assurance program; astronaut, mission specialist candidate NASA, Johnson Space Ctr., Houston, 1998—. Lead, spl. purpose dexterous manipulator robot and the mobile transporter, robotics br., 1999—2002; assigned to EVA Br. and supported rsch. effort focused on developing materials, tools and techniques to perform on-orbit shuttle repair, 2002—05; lead, hardware integration sect., Space Shuttle Br., 2006; crew mem., space electrician, spacewalker STS-117 Mission (Atlantis), 2007. Contbr. articles to profl. jours. tech. confs. Named Most Promising Engr., HENAAC, U. Tex.-El Paso Disting. Alumnus; recipient McDonald's Hispanos Triunfadores award, NASA Class One Tech Brief awards (4), JPL-Calif. Inst. Tech. Novel Tech. Recognitions, NASA ASEE Summer Faculty Fellowship award, Dow Life Saving award. Mem.: Tex. Registered Profl. Engrs., Am. Soc. Materials Internat. Achievements include principal developer of seven inventions. Avocations: mountain biking, weightlifting, hunting, fishing, surfing. Office: Astronaut Office/CB NASA Johnson Space Ctr Houston TX 77058 *

OLIVE, DAVID MICHAEL, journalist, editor; b. Toronto, Ont., Can., Nov. 9, 1957; s. Harold Leslie and Alison Linton (Black) O.; m. Margaret Anne O'Reilly, Feb. 13, 1982 (div. June 1992). B of Applied Arts in Journalism, Ryerson Polytech. U., 1979. Copy editor Toronto Life Mag., 1979-81; assoc. editor Can. Bus. Mag., Toronto, 1981-84; sr. writer Report on Bus. Mag., Toronto, 1984-87, Toronto Life Mag., 1988-90; editorial writer The Globe and Mail, Toronto, 1990-91, current affairs columnist, 1991-92, bus. ethics columnist, 1996-98; editor Report on Bus. Mag., 1991-97, sr. writer, 1997-98, Fin. Post, 1998, Nat. Post, Toronto, 1998—2001; bus. columnist Toronto Star, 2001—. Dir. Can. Ctr. for Ethics and Corp. Policy, 1988-91, Jessie's Ctr. for Teenagers, 1994—; pres. Jessie's Ctr. Non-Profit Homes Corp., 1994—; pres. Nat. Mag. Awards Found., 1988-90. Author: Just Rewards: The Case for Ethical Reform in Business, 1987, White Knights and Poison Pills: A Cynic's Dictionary of Business Jargon, 1990, Political Babble: The 1,000 Dumbest Things Ever Said by Politicians, 1992, Gender Babble: The Dumbest Things Men Ever Said About Women, 1993, Canadian Political Babble: A Cynic's Dictionary of Political Jargon, 1993, More Political Babble: The Dumbest Things Ever Said by Politicians, 1996, Canada Inside Out: How We See Ourselves, How Others See Us, 1996, No Guts, No Glory: How Canada's Greatest CEOs Built Their Empires, 2000, A Devil's Dictionary of Business Jargon, 2001, The Quotable Tycoon: A Treasury of Business Quotations, 2002. Recipient Silver, Nat. Mag. awards, 1987, Gold, 1988, hon. mention, 1983, 1985, 1987, 1989, 1996, Nat. Bus. Book awards, 2001, Nat. Newspaper awards, 2005. Mem. Can. Soc. Mag. Editors, Ethics Practitioners Assn. Can.

OLIVER, ANN BREEDING, secondary school educator, art dealer; b. Hollywood, Fla., Sept. 21, 1945; d. Harvey James and Ruth (Lige) Breeding; 1 child, Anna Liege; m. Ted J. Oliver, June 29, 1996. BA in Fgn. Lang., U. Ky., 1967; MA in History of Art, Ohio State U., 1971. Curatorial intern Lowe Art Mus., Coral Gables, Fla., 1972; adj. faculty Fla. Atlantic U., Boca Raton, Fla., 1972-73, 78; lectr. Miami (Fla.) Dade C.C., 1974, with art-music workshop, 1980-81, lectr.-cons., 1972—, adj. faculty music dept., 1991; curator of edn. Ctr. for the Fine Arts, Miami, 1987-92, High Mus. of Art, Atlanta, Ga., 1992-96; Spanish tchr. Sprayberry H.S., Cobb County Bd. Edn., Marietta, Ga., 1997—. Mem. Artists in Edn. Panel, Ga. Coun. for Arts, 1994; field reviewer Inst. Mus. Svcs., 1994; adj. faculty in art history Kennesaw State U., Marietta, Ga., 1996—; Spanish tchr. Cobb County Bd. Edn., Atlanta, Spray H.S., Marietta, Ga; collector, dealer, historial so. folk art & outsider culture. Contbg. editor African Art: An Essay for Teachers, 1993; project mgr. and contbg. author: Rings: Five Passions in World Art: Multicultural Curriculum Handbook, 1996. Mem. Cobb County Com. for Fgn. Lang. Curriculum Alignment. Recipient Nat. award for graphics Mead Paper Co., 1989, Gold Medal of Honor publication design S.E. Mus. Educators Publ. Design, 1994. Mem. Am. Assn. of Mus., Inst. Mus. Svcs., Nat. Art Edn. Assn., Am. Coun. Tchrs. Fgn. Langs., Fla. Art Edn. Assn. (dir. mus. divsn.), Ga. Art Edn. Assn. (dir. mus. divsn., Mus. Educator of Yr. 1993), Fgn. Lang. Assn. of Ga. Home: PO Box 1032 Flat Rock NC 28731 Personal E-mail: oliverta@bellsouth.net.

OLIVER, BRUCE LAWRENCE, retired information systems educator; b. Westfield, Mass., Nov. 20, 1951; s. Ernest Lawrence and Elizabeth (Welchek) O. AS, Greater Hartford C.C., 1972; BS, U. Mass., 1974; MBA, U. Hartford, 1989. Cert. tchr. sec. and vocat. edn., Mass., Conn.; cert. asset protection and fin. privacy cons. Comml. sales Gordon Realty, Enfield, Conn., 1972—75; forestry tech. rsch. Dept. Environ. Protection State of Conn., Hartford, 1973—74; res. sales Forsman Realty, Enfield, 1975—77; substitute secondary tchr. Enfield Sch. Sys., 1975—78; collections mgr. New Eng. Bank & Trust, Enfield, 1978—79; ops. CCEC/McCullahg Leasing, Inc., S. Windsor, Conn., 1979—81; pres. Ollie & Ike's, Inc., Enfield, 1985—86; MBA Adj. U. Hartford, West Hartford, Conn., 1988—89; workstation engr. Travelers, Hartford, 1982—89; ret., 1989. V.p. 1st Class Expert Sys., Inc., Wayland, Mass., 1989—90, Microsoft Corp., Boston, 1991—94; cons., pres. Profl. Office Solutions, Enfield, 1981—2003; pres. New Venture Inc., Enfield, 1994—2004; owner nvi:Ednl. Multimedia Group, nvi: Webmaster Internet Devel.; del. leader Comparative Studies Assn., Internat. Cultural Exch. with China, Washington; pub. spkr. Spkrs. Bur., U. Hartford; vis. mem. faculty mgmt. info. sci. U. Hartford, 1989—91; realtor Sentry Real Estate Svcs., Inc., Enfield, Conn., 2003—. Author: A Novice's Guide to Personal Computer Buying, New Ventures to Egypt, New Ventures to China, Faith, Hope and Love: Coping With Life and Death. Gubernatorial appointee Conn. bd. trustees Reg. C.C.s, 1985-89; vice chmn. Student Affairs and Acad. Policies Com. Hartford, 1987; chmn., trustee Conn. Data Processing Curriculum Com., Hartford, 1989; elected com. mem. Enfield Dem. Com., 1975; chmn. regional adv. coun. Asnuntuck C.C.; notary pub. Conn., 1972—; gubernatorial appointee Conn. bd. trustees Cmty. Tech. Colls., 1990-93. Recipient CTM degree Toastmaster Internat., Hartford, 1987, State Farmer degree Conn. Future Farmers Am., DeKalb Agrl. Accomplishment award, cert. of recognition Bicentennial (USA) Commn., Enfield, 1976, Vigil Hon. BSA Order of the Arrow, Hartford, 1972, Merit award State of Conn. Cmty.-Tech. Colls. Bd. Trustees, 1994. Mem. World Affairs Coun. of Hartford, Computer Soc. of IEEE, Am. Assn. for Artificial Intelligence, Assn. C.C. Trustees, Am. Assn. Cmty. and Tech. Colls., Microsoft AlumNet Assn., Internat. Platform Assn., Oldefield Farms Homeowners' Assn. (residence com. sec. 1990-91), Hartford County Soil and Water Conservation Dist., Nat. Press Club Found., Robert Schueller's Eagles Club, Masons, Hartford Club. Republican. Roman Catholic. Avocations: travel, refinishing antiques, tennis, hiking, real estate investment, photography. Home: 102 N Maple # 8A Enfield CT 06082 Office Phone: 877-257-0525. Personal E-mail: bruce@bruceloliver.com.

OLIVER, DALE HUGH, lawyer; b. Lansing, Mich., June 26, 1947; s. Alvin Earl and Jean Elizabeth (Stanton) Oliver; m. Sarah Elyse Sanders, Mar. 18, 2001; children: Nathan Corey, John Franklin. BA, Mich. State U., 1969; JD cum laude, Harvard U., 1972. Bar: DC 1973, Calif. 1991, US Dist. Ct. (DC dist.) 1973, US Ct. Appeals (DC cir.) 1976, US Supreme Ct. 1980, US Ct. Appeals (fed. cir.) 1983, US Ct. Claims 1983. Assoc., ptnr. Jones, Day, Reavis & Pogue, Washington, 1975—79; ptnr. Crowell & Moring, Washington, 1979—84, Gibson, Dunn & Crutcher, Washington, 1984—87, Jones, Day, Reavis & Pogue, Washington, 1987—92, Quinn Emanuel Urquhart & Oliver, LA, 1992—. Editor: (jour.) Pub. Contracts Law, 1980—86; contbr. articles to profl. jours. Spl. counsel 1980 Presdl. Inaugural Com., Washington, 1980; bd. dirs. LA coun. Boy Scouts Am., 1991—; bd. dirs. Armory Ctr. for Arts, 2006—. Capt. USAF, 1973—75. Mem.: ABA (com. chmn. pub. contract sect. 1979—), Pasadena Arts and Cultural Commn. (commr. 2006—), Nat. Security Indsl. Assn., Nat. Contract Mgmt. Assn., Harvard Law Sch. Assn., Mich. State U. Alumni Club of Washington (pres., dir. 1984—88). Office: Quinn Emanuel Urquhart & Oliver & Hedges 865 S Figueroa St 10 Fl Los Angeles CA 90017-2543 Office Phone: 213-443-3154. E-mail: daleoliver@quinnemanuel.com.

OLIVER, DANIEL T., military education administrator, career officer, retired; b. Camden, SC, Apr. 22, 1945; BA, MA, U. Va.; student, Harvard U. Commd. ensign U.S. Navy, advanced through grades to vice admiral, 1996-2000, ret., 2000; pres. Naval Postgraduate Sch., Monterey, Calif., 2007—. Office: Naval Postgrad Sch Office of the President 1 University Cir Monterey CA 93943 Office Phone: 831-656-2023. Office Fax: 831-656-3238. *

OLIVER, DEAN S., petroleum engineer, educator; b. Bremerton, Wash., July 14, 1953; s. Donald H. and Shirley I. Oliver; m. Mary Alice Oliver; children: Sarah Aileen, Elizabeth Suzanne Burgess. BS in Physics, Harvey Mudd Coll., Claremont, Calif., 1970—75; PhD, U. Wash., Seattle, 1976—80. Sr. reservoir engr. Chevron USA, San Ramon, Calif., 1983—87; lead petroleum engr. Arabian Chevron, Dhahran, Saudi Arabia, 1987—91; staff rsch. scientist Chevron Petroleum Tech. Co., La Habra, Calif., 1991—97; prof. petroleum engring. U. Tulsa, 1997—2002; academic dir. Mewbourne Sch. Petroleum Engring. U. Okla., Norman, 2002—. Mem.: Soc. Indsl. & Applied Math., Am. Geophys. Union, Soc. Petroleum Engrs. (Reservoir Description & Dynamics award 2004). Office: Univ Okla 100 E Boyd Rm T301 Norman OK 73019 Business E-Mail: dsoliver@ou.edu.

OLIVER, DIANE FRANCES, publisher, writer; b. NYC, Feb. 7, 1935; m. Ben Martin Oliver, Sept. 3, 1960 (div. 1973). BA, Syracuse U., 1955. Reporter Millinery Rsch. mag., NYC, 1956-58; with NYC Bur., London Daily Mail and London Daily Sketch, 1964-69; editor The Celebrity Bull., Celebrity Svc. Inc., NYC, 1971-78; pub. The Celebrity Bull., pres., owner Celebrity Svc. Ltd., London, 1978—. Former publicist Lake Lucerne (NY) Playhouse, Bklyn. Acad. Music, Statler Hilton Hotel, NYC. Author: Older Woman/Younger Man, 1975; columnist Palm Beach Social Pictorial mag., 1981-85. Avocations: music, ballet, films, theater, travel. Home: 44 Lennox Gardens London SW1X 0DJ England Office: Celebrity Service Ltd 4th Fl Kingsland House 122 124 Regent St London England W1B 5SA Office Phone: (020) 7439-9840. E-mail: celebritylondon@aol.com.

OLIVER, DONNA H., academic administrator, former secondary school educator; AB, Elon Coll., 1972; MEd, U. NC, Greensboro, 1978; MS, NC Agrl. and Tech. State U., 1987; PhD, U. NC, 1995. Tchr. biology Hugh M. Cummings High Sch., Burlington, NC; v.p. academic affairs Bennett Coll., Greensboro, NC, 1989—. Named Nat. Tchr. Yr., 1987. Office: Bennett College 900 E Washington St Greensboro NC 27401 *

OLIVER, EDWARD CARL, retired state legislator, insurance company executive, small business owner; b. St. Paul, May 31, 1930; s. Charles Edmund and Esther Marie (Bjugstad) O.; m. Charlotte Severson, Sept. 15, 1956; children: Charles E., Andrew T., Peter A. BA, U. Minn., 1955. Sales rep. Armstrong Cork Co., NYC, 1955; registered rep. Piper, Jaffray & Hopwood, Mpls., 1958; mgr. Mut. Funds Inc., subs. Dayton's, Mpls., 1964, NWNL Mgmt. Corp. subs. Northwestern Nat. Life Ins. Co., Mpls., 1968-72, v.p., 1972-81, pres., dir., 1981-90; mem. Minn. State Senate, 1992—2003, asst. minority leader, 1998—2003; owner Oliver Fin., 2003—. Arbitrator/mediator, Nat. Assn. Securities Dealers Dispute Resolution, Inc., 1988—; bd. dir. 1st Minn. Bank, N.A. Mem. Gt. Lakes Commn., 1993—; bd. dirs. Minn. State Arts Bd., 2003—. Mem. Internat. Assn. Fin. Planners (past pres. Twin City chpt., nat. governing com.), Psi Upsilon, Mpls. Athletic Club. Home: 20230 Cottagewood Rd Excelsior MN 55331-9300 Office: 464 2d St Ste 203 Excelsior MN 55331 Office Phone: 952-380-0107. E-mail: oliverfinancial@earthlink.net.

OLIVER, HARRY MAYNARD, JR., retired brokerage house executive; b. Kansas City, Mo., Jan. 21, 1921; s. Harry Maynard and Marie (Curtin) O. BA, Williams Coll., 1943. Pres. M.A. Gesner & Co., Marsh & McLennan Co., Chgo., 1947-88. Chmn. Chgo. Commn. for Sr. Citizens, 1960-69; mem. Chgo. Bd. Edn., 1966-69; pres. Vol. Agys. Chgo., 1956-86; mem. vis. com. Sch. Edn. and div. of social scis., U. Chgo.; pres., bd. dirs. Benton House Settlement, 1953-58; bd. dirs. Adult Edn. Council Greater Chgo., Nat. Fedn. Settlements and Community Centers, 1961-67; trustee Old Peoples Home Chgo., Pub. Sch. Tchrs. Pension and Retirement Fund Chgo., 1966-69, George M. Pullman Ednl. Found., Field Mus. Natural History, 1971-75. Served to lt. (j.g.) USNR, World War II. Mem. Chgo. Club, Racquet Club, Commonwealth Club, Tavern Club, Onwentsia Club (Lake Forest, Ill.), Chi Psi. Home: 1948 N Lincoln Ave Chicago IL 60614-5476 also: PO Box 1319 Big Pine Key FL 33043 also: New Richmond PO Box 100 Fennville MI 49408-0100

OLIVER, JACK ERTLE, geophysicist, educator; b. Massillon, Ohio, Sept. 26, 1923; s. Chester L. and Marie (Ertle) O.; m. Gertrude van der Hoeven, Apr. 16, 1964; children: Cornelia Oliver, Amy Oliver. AB, Columbia U., 1947, MA, 1950, PhD, 1953; DSci (hon.), Hamilton Coll., 1988. Rsch. asst., then rsch. assoc. Columbia, 1947-55, mem. faculty, 1955-73, prof. geology, 1961-71, chmn. dept., 1969-71, adj. prof., 1971-73; Irving Porter Church prof. engring. dept. geol. scis. Cornell U., 1971-93, prof. emeritus, 1993—, chmn. dept., 1971-81; chmn. exec. com. COCORP. Terrestrial physicist USAF Cambridge (Mass.) Rsch. Labs., 1951; dir. Inst. for Study of the Continents, 1981-88; cons. AEC, 1969-72, ACDA, 1962-74, USAF Tech. Applications Ctr., 1959-65; mem. Polar Rsch. Com., 1959-71, also nat. commn. uppermantle program, 1963-71; mem. panel solid earth problems NAS, 1962; mem. adv. com. U.S. Coast and Geodetic Survey, 1962-66, on seismology, 1960-72, chmn., 1966-70; mem. Geophysics Rsch. Bd., 1969-70; U.S. coord. 2d U.S.-Japan Earthquake Prediction Conf., Palisades, 1966; earth sci. panel NSF, 1962-65; mem. USAF Sci. Adv. Bd., 1960-63, 64-69; mem. geophysics adv. panel Office Sci. Rsch., USAF, 1961-74, chmn., 1966-68; U.S. del. Test Ban Conf., Geneva, Switzerland, 1958-59; intergovtl. meeting seismology and earthquake engring., mem. exec. com. IASPEI, 1968-71; mem. governing com. Internat. Seismol. Summary Commn., 1963-67, 75-76; mem. exec. com. UNESCO, Paris, France, 1964, U.S.-Japan Earthquake Prediction Conf., Tokyo, 1964; mem. UNESCO Joint Com. on Seismology and Earthquake Engring., 1965-71; chmn. exec. com. Office Earth Scis., NRC, 1976-79, Internat. Seismol. Centre, 1976-78; mem. U.S. Geodynamics Com., 1979-87, chmn., 1984-87; mem. Geol. Scis. Bd., Assembly of Math. and Phys. Scis., NRC, 1981-84; Cabot Disting. vis. scholar U. Houston, 1985-86; commn. on phys. scis., math. and resources NRC, 1987-90, commn. on geoscis., environ. and resources, 1990—. Served with USNR, 1943-46. Recipient Hedberg award Inst. for Study of Earth and Man, So. Meth. U., 1990. Fellow Am. Geophys. Union (pres. seismology sect. 1964-68, Walter H. Bucher medal 1981), Geol. Soc. Am. (coun. 1970-73, v.p. 1986, pres. 1987, Woollard medal 1990, Penrose medal 1998), Geol. Soc. London (hon.); mem. AAAS (chmn. geol. geog. sect. 1993), NAS, Seismol. Soc. Am. (pres. 1964-65, bd. dirs. 1961-70, 72-76, Eighth medal 1984), Soc. Exploration Geophysicists (Virgil Kauffman Gold medal 1983), European Union Geoscis. (hon. fgn. fellow), Sigma Xi. Home: 340 Savage Farm Dr Ithaca NY 14850 Home Phone: 607-257-7554; Office Phone: 607-255-2377. Business E-Mail: oliver@geology.cornell.edu.

OLIVER, JAMIE, chef, television personality; b. Essex, England, May 1, 1975; s. Trevor and Sally Oliver; m. Juliette Norton; children: Poppy, Daisy. Grad., Westminster Catering Coll., London. Head pastry chef Neal Street Restaurant, London, 1991—97; chef River Cafe, London, 1997—99; consulting chef Monte's, London, 2000; founder, owner Fifteen Restaurant, London, 2002—. Former columnist GQ mag.; former feature writer The Times Mag., London; designer cookware & tableware line Royal Worcester. Host, chef (TV series) The Naked Chef, 1999-2001 (BAFTA award 2001), Jamie's Kitchen, 2002-04, Oliver's Twist, 2004-, Jamie's School Dinners, 2006- (Best Factual Series award, Outstanding Presenter award, BAFTA 2006); author (cookbooks) The Naked Chef, 1999, The Return of The Naked Chef, 2000, Happy Days with The Naked Chef, 2001, Jamie's Kitchen, 2003, Jamie's Dinners, 2004, Jamie's Italy, 2005. Founder Fifteen Found., 2002. Decorated MBE; named GQ Man of the Yr., 2000; recipient GQ Best Chef award, 2000, Tatler Best Restaurant award (for Fifteen Restaurant), 2003, Excellence award, Tio Pepe Carlton London Restaurant Awards, 2003, Time Out special award for outstanding achievement, 2003, Glenfiddich Food and Drink award, 2003. Office: Fifteen Restaurant & Fifteen Found Westland Place London N1 7LP England also: c/o Penguin Publicity 80 Strand WC2R 0RL London England

OLIVER, JEFFREY MICHAEL, protective services official; b. Shelby, NC, Feb. 6, 1972; s. Harold Dean and Janette Mullinax Oliver; m. Kimberly Curtis, Dec. 23, 2003; children: Cade Michael, Patrick Christopher Rucker, McKenzie Raye Rucker. Cert.: NC Criminal Justice Tng. & Standards (law enforcement officer) 1995, S. Piedmont Region Criminal Justice Program, NC (advanced tactics) 1997, US Dept. Justice (basic narcotic investigator) 2003, NC Criminal Justice Tng. & Standards (advanced law enforcement) 2005; healthcare security officer Internat. Assn. Healthcare Safety & Security, 2005, advanced healthcare safety & security officer Internat. Assn. Healthcare Safety & Security, 2005. Police sgt. Shelby Police Dept., NC, 1995—2004, detective sgt., 2001—04; police officer, investigator Cleve. County Healthcare Sys., Shelby, 2004—. Founder Healthcare Identity Fraud Prevention Program, Shelby; team leader/coord. Am. Cancer Soc./Relay For Life, Shelby, 2002; bd. mem. Cleve. County Safe Kids Coalition, Shelby, 2004, child safety seat check coord., 2006—. Mem.: NC Law Enforcement Officers Assn. (assoc.). R-Consevative. Bapt. Avocation: travel. Office: Cleve County Healthcare Sys 201 E Grover St Shelby NC 28150 Home Phone: 704-473-2474. Personal E-mail: jeff.oliver@yahoo.com. Business E-Mail: crmcpolice@carolinas.org.

OLIVER, JERRY ALTON, former police chief; 5 children. BS in Criminal Justice, Ariz. State U., MS in Pub. Adminstrn., 1988; postgrad., Police Exec. Rsch. Forum, Washington. From patrolman to supr. Phoenix Police Dept., from supr. to asst. chief of police, 1971-90; dir. drug policy Memphis Mayors Office; chief of police Pasadena (Calif.) Police Dept., 1991—94, Richmond (Va.) Police Dept., 1995—2002, Detroit, Mich., 2002—03; spl. policy advisor Ariz. Atty. Gen., 2004—05; dep. dir. Ariz. Dept. Admin., 2005—. Founder Spl. Friends Project, Richmond, 1988—. Inductee Ariz. State U. Coll. Pub. Programs Hall of Fame, 1989; recipient Phoenix chpt. Image award NAACP, 1990, People of Yr. award Law Enforcement News, 1999, Richmonder of Yr. award Richmond Style Mag., 1999, U.S. Atty. Gen.'s award for outstanding contbns. to cmty. partnership for pub. safety, 2000, othrs. Home Phone: 480-840-1313; Office Phone: 602-542-0878. E-mail: jaoxfive@hotmail.com.

OLIVER, JOHN WILLIAM POSEGATE, minister; b. Vincennes, Ind., Apr. 9, 1935; s. Dwight L and Elizabeth (Posegate) Oliver; m. Cristina Shepard Hope, Oct. 19, 1968; children: John William Posegate Jr, Sloan Christian Shepard. BA, Wheaton Coll., 1956; BD, Fuller Theol. Sem., 1959; ThM, So. Bapt. Theol. Sem., 1963; DD, Western Conservative Bapt. Sem, 1996. Ordained to ministry Presby Ch, 1962. Asst. pastor Covenant Presbyn. Ch., Hammond, Ind., 1964-66, Trinity Presbyn. Ch., Montgomery, Ala., 1966-69; pastor 1st Presbyn. Ch., Augusta, Ga., 1969-97, Trinity Presbyn. Ch., Montgomery, Ala., 1997-99; Robert Strong prof. of homiletics and practical theol. Reformed Theol. Sem., Charlotte, NC, 1999—. Bd dirs Equip, Inc; moderator Cent Ga Presby, Presby Ch Am, 1976. Founder, trustee Westminster Schs, Augusta, 1972—97; bd. commrs. Augusta Housing Authority, vice chmn., 1976—93; trustee, chmn. bd. Columbia Internat. U., 1978—; dir. Bailey Manor Retirement Ctr., Clinton, SC, 1992—97; chmn. clergy Augusta United Way Campaign, 1974; exec. bd. clergy staff Univ. Hosp., Augusta, 1975—76; bd. dirs. Mission to the World, Presbyn. Ch. Am, 1984—89, bd dirs, 1992—96; ministerial adv. bd. Ref. Theol. Sem., Jackson, Miss., 1978—85, 1989—93, Charlotte, 1996—99. Mem.: Evang Theological Soc, Wynlakes Country Club, Nassau Club, Kappa Sigma. Office: 2101 Carmel Rd Charlotte NC 28226-6318 Home: 731 Stanhope Ln Matthews NC 28105

OLIVER, KERRYN HINRICHS, music educator, religious studies educator; b. Webster City, Iowa, Dec. 1, 1954; d. Lowell K and Kathryn Rosa Hinrichs; m. Michael L. Oliver, Dec. 16, 1978; children: Erin Michelle Bandow, Mark Michael. AA, Ellsworth Coll., Iowa Falls, 1985; MusB, U. No. Iowa, Cedar Falls, 1997. Lic. pastor NE Assn. UCC/Iowa, 2005, NW Assn. UCC/Iowa, 2005; cert. Level I in Kodaly Drake U., Iowa, 2003. Pvt. piano/vocal tchr., Alden, Iowa, 1980—; music dir. Immanuel Meml. United Ch. of Christ, Alden, Iowa, 1985—, parish assoc./christian educator/pastor, 2005—; vocal music tchr. Alden Elem., Alden, 1999—, Iowa Falls-Alden Schs., Iowa, 1999—; adj. vocal instr. Ellsworth Coll., Iowa Falls, 2003—05; parish assoc./christian educator/pastor Jewell United Ch. of Christ, 2005—. Workshop leader/cons. Nebr. Conf. United Ch. of Christ, Lincoln, 2003—05, Iowa Conf. United Ch. of Christ, Des Moines, 2005—; ptnr. in edn. United Ch. of Christ, Cleve. and Des Moines, 1997—. Contbr. article/workshop. Vol. music tchr. Alden Cmty. Presch., Iowa, 2001. Mem.: Iowa State Edn. Assn., NEA, Iowa Choral Dirs. Assn., Am. Choral Dirs. Assn., Alden Edn. Assn. (membership chair 2003—04), Phi Theta Kappa, Pi Kappa Lambda Music, Kappa Delta Pi Edn., Golden Key, Omicron Delta Kappa, Sigma Alpha Iota. United Church Of Christ. Avocations: reading, perennial gardens, backyard bird watching/feeding, travel. Home: P O Box 63 712 Hardin St Alden IA 50006-0063 Home Phone: 515-859-7016; Office Phone: 515-859-7259. Personal E-mail: olivers@iowatelecom.net.

OLIVER, KIMBERLY, primary school educator; b. Wilmington, Del. BA in English Arts, Hampton U.; MEd in elem. edn., Wilmington Coll. Cert. Nat. Bd. Profl. Teaching Standards, 2004. Kindergarten teacher Broad Acres Elem., Silver Spring, Md., 2000—. Named Md. Tchr. of Yr., 2006, Nat. Tchr. of the Yr., Coun. Chief State Sch. Officers, 2006; recipient Greenblatt Excellence Teaching award, Greenblatt Edn. Fund, award for tchg. excellence, Concerned Black Men Nat. caucus, 2006. Office: Broad Acres Elem Sch 13313 Old Columbia Pike Silver Spring MD 20903 *

OLIVER, LEANN MICHELLE, government official; b. Eureka, Calif., Nov. 15, 1955; d. George L. and Laura Maxine (Jennings) O. BS, Willamette U., 1977; MPA, SUNY, Albany, 1980; cert., Nat. Comml. Lending Sch. of Am. Bankers Assn., Norman, Okla., 1982. Mgmt. trainee U.S. GAO, Albany, 1979-80; presdl. mgmt. intern U.S. SBA, Washington, 1980-83, fin. analyst, policy program devel., 1983-89, acting dir. Office Rural Affairs Econ. Devel., 1995, dir. divsn. Program Devel., 1995-2000, dep. assoc. adminstr. fin. assistance, 2000—05; dep. dir. program devel. Office Econ. Devel., 1989-92; dep. dir. Office Rural Affairs Econ. Devel., 1992-94; acting dir. One Stop Office, Capital Shop Project, 1994; acting dep., assoc. dep. adminstr. Entrepreneurial Devel., 2006; dep. adminstr., coop. programs USDA Rural Devel., 2006—. Bd. dirs. Lafayette Fed. Credit Union, Washington, 1986-2007, treas., 1997-2000, asst. treas., 2000-04, treas., 2004-07. Roman Catholic. Office: USDA Rural Development 1400 Independence Ave SW Mail Stop 3250 Rm 4016 Washington DC 20250 Home Phone: 703-525-3275; Office Phone: 202-720-7558. Personal E-mail: lmoliver@verizon.net. Business E-Mail: le.oliver@sba.gov, leann.oliver@wdc.usda.gov.

OLIVER, LOUISE V., ambassador; m. Daniel Oliver; 5 children. BA with distinction, Smith Coll. Apptd. commr. Nat. Commn. on Children, 1989; pres. Oliver Mgmt. Consultants; permanent US rep. UNESCO, Paris, 2004—. Chmn. Philanthropy Roundtable, Washington, Intercollegiate Studies Inst.; co-founder New Atlantic Initiative; bd. dirs. Independent Women's Forum. Office: 2 Avenue Gabriel 75382 Cedex 08 Paris France Office Phone: 33-1-4524-7416. E-mail: parisunesco@state.gov.

OLIVER, MARY, poet; b. Maple Heights, Ohio, Sept. 10, 1935; d. Edward William and Helen Mary (Vlasak) O. Student, Ohio State U., 1955—56, Vassar Coll., 1956—57. Chmn. writing dept. Fine Arts Work Ctr., Provincetown, Mass., 1972-73, mem. writing com., 1984; Banister poet-in-residence Sweet Briar Coll., 1991-95. William Blackburn vis. prof. creative writing Duke U., 1995; Catharine Osgood Foster prof. Bennington Coll., 1996-2001. Author: No Voyage and Other Poems, 1963, enlarged edit., 1965, The River Styx, Ohio, 1972, The Night Traveler, 1978, Twelve Moons, 1979, American Primitive, 1983, Dream Work, 1986, House of Light, 1990, New and Selected Poems, 1992, Vol. 2, 2005, A Poetry Handbook, 1994, White Pine, 1994, Blue Pastures, 1995, West Wind, 1997, Rules for the Dance, 1998, Winter Hours, 1999, The Leaf and the Cloud, 2000, What Do We Know, 2002, Owls and Other Fantasies, 2003, Why I Wake Early, 2004, Long Life, 2004, Blue Iris, 2004, New and Selected Poems, Vol. 2, 2005, Thirst, 2006; contbr. to Yale U. Rev., Kenyon Rev., Poetry, Atlantic, Harvard mag., others. Recipient Shelley Meml. award, 1970, Alice Fay di Castagnola award, 1973, Cleve. Arts prize for lits., 1979, Achievement award Am. Acad. and Inst. Arts and Letters, 1983, Pulitzer prize for poetry, 1984, Christopher award, 1991, L.L. Winship award, 1991, Nat. Book award, 1992, Lannan award, 1998; Nat. Endowment fellow, 1972-73; Guggenheim fellow, 1980-81. Mem. PEN. Home: PO Box 619 Provincetown MA 02657-0619

OLIVER, MILTON MCKINNON, lawyer, translator; b. Columbia, SC, 1951; s. Caldwell Hardy and Eleanor (McKinnon) Oliver; m. Joan Nichols, July 12, 1981; children: John, James, Lindsay. BA, Harvard U., 1972; JD, Golden Gate U., 1975. Bar: Calif. 1975, Mass. 1975, Patent and Trademark Office 1976, Fla. 1978, D.C. 1983, N.Y. 1984, U.S. Supreme Ct. 1979, U.S. Ct. Appeals (fed. cir.) 1982. Assoc. Wolf, Greenfield & Sacks, P.C., Boston, 1977—83; assoc., then ptnr. Frishauf, Holtz, Goodman & Woodward, P.C., NYC, 1983—94; of counsel Dike, Bronstein, Roberts & Cushman, Boston, 1994—97; ptnr. Ware, Fressola, Van Der Sluys & Adolphson, LLP, Monroe, Conn., 1997—. Mem.: Am. Intellectual Property Law Assn., IEEE, Am. Translators Assn., Calif. State Bar, Boston Patent Law Assn., Conn. and NY Intellectual Property Law Assns., Aircraft Owners and Pilots Assn. Episcopalian. Home: 72 Green St Canton MA 02021-1020 Office: Ware Fressola Van Der Sluys & Adolphson LLP 755 Main St Monroe CT 06468-0224 Home Phone: 781-910-9664; Office Phone: 203-261-1234. E-mail: miltonoliver@ieee.org.

OLIVER, NANCY LEBKICHER, artist, retired elementary school educator; b. Stockton, Calif., 1939; d. John B. and Marjorie Lebkicher; m. Douglas C. Oliver, 1963; children: Charles, Elaine. BA with honors, San Jose State U., 1961. Summer playground dir. Recreation Dept., Redwood City, Calif., 1956-61; 1st grade tchr. Redwood City (Calif.) Elem. Sch. Dist., 1961-63; kindergarten tchr. Ukiah (Calif.) Unified Sch. Dist., 1963-67; assoc. tchr. kindergarten San Carlos (Calif.) Elem. Sch. Dist., 1976-81. Dept. store shopper Macy's, San Francisco, 1975-82; asst. hist. rsch., 2000—. Active White Oaks PTA, San Carlos, 1973-81, newsletter editor, 1978-81; leader Girl Scouts U.S.A., San Carlos, 1978-81; bd. dirs. Sequoia H.S. Ednl. Found., co-chmn., 2002-05, sec., 2005-; bd. dirs. San Mateo County Hist. Resources Adv. Bd., 2000-; Sunday sch. dir. St. Peter's Episcopal Ch., Redwood City, 1973-78; mem. San Mateo County Sesquicentennial Com., 2005-06. Mem.: AAUW (pres. Willits br. 1966—67, San Carlos br. newsletter editor 1972—74, chmn. historic preservation sect. 1979—, editor historic tour booklet 1981, editor historic resources booklet 1989, co-pres. San Carlos br. 2002—04, dir.-at-large 2004—06, parliamentarian 2004—, Gift honoree 1976), SeriPrinters (serigrapher 1986—), San Carlos Heritage Assn. (founder and dir. 1995—), Sequoia H.S. Alumni Assn. (founding sec. and membership chmn 1985—, centennial coord. 1992—95, pres. 1996—98, sec. 2002—, newsletter editor 2003—, Unsung Hero award 1998), Internat. Order Rainbow Girls (grand officer Calif. 1957—58, mother advisor Redwood City 1987—89, quilt com. 1989—). Democrat. Episcopalian. Avocations: needlecrafts, historic preservation activities, walking, calligraphy, classical music. Home: 147 Belvedere Ave San Carlos CA 94070-4818

OLIVER, NURIA MARIA, computer science researcher; b. Alicante, Spain; BS, Tech. U. Madrid, 1992, MS, 1994; PhD in Media Arts & Scis., MIT, 2000. Rsch. asst. engr. Siemens F&E, 1992—93; software engr. Telefonica R&D, Spain, 1994—95; rsch. asst. Media Lab, MIT, 1995—2000; rschr. adaptive systems & interaction group Microsoft Rsch., 2000—. Named one of 40 Most Promising Young Spanish Persons, El Pais, 1999, Top 100 Young Innovators, MIT Tech. Review, 2004; fellow, La Caixa Found., 1995; Motorola fellow, 1997. Mem.: ACM, IEEE. Avocations: ballet, dance, yoga, swimming, art. Office: Microsoft Rsch One Microsoft Way Redmond WA 98052-6399

OLIVER, PATRICIA, lawyer; b. Erie, Pa. m. Jim Oliver; 3 children. BA magna cum laude in Polit. sci., Allegheny Collge; JD, Case Western Reserve U. Sch. Law, Cleve. Atty. Squire, Sanders & Dempsey, Cleve.; gen. counsel BB&T Corp, Winston-Salem, NC, 2004—. Founder Women in Family Bus. Seminar Series, Cleve. Pres. Children's Aid Soc. Recipient Rainmaker (community svc.), No. Ohio Live Magazine, 2003, Profl. Woman of Excellence, Cleve. YMCA. Office: BB&T Corp 200 W 2nd St Winston Salem NC 27101 *

OLIVER, ROBERT BRUCE, retired investment company executive; b. Brockton, Mass., Aug. 1, 1931; s. Stanley Thomas and Helen (Sabine) O.; m. Sylvia E. Bell, Feb. 17, 1954; children: Susan Pamela, Robert Bruce. AB, Harvard U., 1953; postgrad., Bus. Sch., 1971, Boston U. Law Sch., 1955-57; MA, Mich. State U., 1958. Ret. chmn., pres., chief exec. officer John Hancock Income Securities Trust, Boston, 1989. Ret. chmn., pres. chief exec. officer John Hancock Investors Trust, John Hancock Bond Trust, John Hancock Growth Trust, John Hancock Tax Exempt Cash Mgmt. Trust, John Hancock Govt. Securities Trust, John Hancock Tax Exempt Income Trust, John Hancock Cash Mgmt. Trust, John Hancock Spl. Equities Trust, John Hancock Global Trust, John Hancock World Trust, John Hancock High Income Trust, John Hancock Tax Exempt Series Trust; chmn., dir. John Hancock Distbrs.; vice chmn., chief exec. officer John Hancock Advisers, Inc.; chmn., mng. dir. John Hancock Advisers Internat. Ltd. 1st lt. USMCR, 1953-55. Mem. Marine Corps League, Haile Plantation Country Club. Home: 9271 SW 29th Ave Gainesville FL 32608 Personal E-mail: rboliver72@aol.com.

OLIVER, ROBERT M., engineer; PhD in Physics, MIT, 1957; grad., U. London. Dir. Mgmt. Sci. Div. Broadview Rsch. Corp., 1958; prof. U. Calif., Berkeley, chmn. Dept. Industrial Engring. and Ops. Rsch., 1964—69, dir. Ops. Rsch. Ctr., 1972—75, assoc. dean rsch. Coll. Engring., prof. emeritus, 1993—. Bd. dirs. Fair Isaac Corp., 1983; chmn. Fair Isaac Cos., 1995; mem. bd. trustees ANSER Corp., Arlington, Va., 1959, chmn. bd., 1989—. Trustee Math. Scis. Rsch. Inst.; bd. mem. Berkeley Repertory and Aurora Theatres. Co-recipient Lanchester Prize, Ops. Rsch. Soc. Am., 1963. Mem.: NAE. Office: ANSER Corp Ste 800 2900 S Quincy St Arlington VA 22206 Office Phone: 703-416-2000.

OLIVER, SANDRA, art dealer, painter; b. Bronxville, NY, Apr. 2, 1941; d. Clarence Charles and Mary Bell E. (McTeique) Simoni; m. Paul Alan Williams, May 2, 1982; children: John Mortimer Wilson, Melissa Anne Wilson, PHilip Keith Wilson. BA, BFA, Marymount Coll., Tarrytown, NY, 1963. Art and art history tchr. N.Y.C. Sch. System, 1963-65; art tchr. Diocese Cath. Sch., Westchester, N.Y., 1963-65; comml. artist rep. Weston, Conn., 1979-84; pres. Sandi Oliver, Weston, 1984—. Author catalog: American Impressionist Paul Williams: His Garden and His Oil Paintings, 1994. Recipient 1st prize Christmas Show, Pelham (N.Y.) C. of C., 1960, Bravo award, Revlon Corp., 1980, 1st prize, Braswell Galleries, 1998, honors, Westport Art Show, 2001, award, The Westport Downtown Merchants Assn., 2002, auction record (paintings), 1988—2001. Mem. New Eng. Appraisers Assn., Allied Arts Am. Inc., Am. Fedn. Artists, Nat. Mus. Women in Arts (charter mem.). Avocations: painting, antiques, gardening, walking, dog breeding. Home: 11 Tubbs Spring Dr PO Box 1203 Weston CT 06883-0203 Office: Sandi Oliver PO Box 1203 Weston CT 06883-0203 E-mail: sandioliver@aol.com.

OLIVER, TERRY JAMES, retired electronics engineer, communications engineer; b. Greensboro, NC, Sept. 5, 1949; s. William Alfred and Elizabeth Ellen (Baker) O.; m. Janice Marie Jones, Mar. 16, 1974 (div. May 1989); 1 child, Shonn Aaron; m. Janice Marie Meris, Nov. 25, 1990; children Jennifer G. Meris, Kelly Cervero. MS, St. John's U., 1981; PhD, Pacific Western U., 1985; AA, Thomas A. Edison State Coll., 1986, AS, 1987; BS, SUNY, Albany, 1988, SUNY, 2006. Cert. tchr., N.C., sr. electronics technician, sr. biomed. electronics technician, video photographer, open water diver; lic. trainer NC Dept. Pub. Instrn. Pub. edn. officer Civil Affairs and Signal Corps USAR, Greensboro, NC, 1975—79; comms.-electronic technician U.S. Army, 1968-75; sound systems engr. Soundak Engineered Systems, Greensboro, 1975-76; electronics tchr. Guilford County Sch. System, Greensboro, 1976-79; commn. electronics engr. U.S. Army, Washington, 1979-86; dir., prof. photoelectronics Randolph C.C., Asheboro, NC, 1986—99; prof. electronics, computers and telecomms. ECPI Coll. Tech., Greensboro, NC, 1999—2004; ret., 2004. Faculty rep. N.C. Assn. Educators, Guilford County, N.C., 1976-79; cons. Guilford Tech. CC New Industry Tng., Greensboro, 1988-90. Mem. Guilford County PACE, 1977-79; party nominee N.C. Ho. of Reps., 1992, N.C. State Senate, 1996; candidate Guilford County Bd. Edn., 1993, N.C. State Senate, 1994; appt. ad large mem. Guilford County Bd. Environ. Quality, 1999-2004. With USAR, 1975-79. Mem. Nat. Soc. Profl. Engrs., Internat. Soc. for Optical Engrs., Soc. Am. Mil. Engrs., Photo Mktg. Assn. Democrat. Moravian. Avocations: scuba diving, tennis, bicycling, walking. Home: 7310 Shellford St Greensboro NC 27406-9165 Personal E-mail: t_oliver5@bellsouth.net.

OLIVER, THORNAL GOODLOE, retired health care executive; b. Memphis, Aug. 26, 1934; s. John Oliver and Evelyn Doris (Goodloe) Mitchell; m. Pauline Reid, Oct. 1, 1959. B.S., Tenn. State U., Nashville, 1956; M.H.A., Washington U., St. Louis, 1973. Cert. nursing home adminstr., Mo. Asst. dir., King Meml. Hosp., Kansas City, Mo., 1973-75; evening mgr. Truman Med. Ctr., Kansas City, Mo., 1975-77; asst. adminstr. Mid-Am. Radiation Ctr. U. Kans. Coll. Health Sci., Kansas City, Kans., 1977-81; dir. CHS, Inc., Leawood, Kans., 1981-82; adminstr. Poplar Bluff Hosp., Mo., 1982-83; adminstr. The Benjamin F. Lee Health Ctr., Wilberforce, Ohio, 1983-86; asst. clin. prof. Dept. Community Medicine, Wright State U., Dayton, 1986-89; asst. patent adminstr. Munson Army Hosp., Ft. Leavenworth, Kans., 1987-2004, ret., 2004; cons. Urban Health Assocs., Nashville, 1986-87, others. Contbr. articles to profl. jours. Served with U.S. Army, 1957-59, USAR, 1959-63. Fellow Am. Coll. Hosp. Adminstrs.; mem. Am. Hosp. Assn., Nat. Assn. Health Services Execs., Am. Med. Record Assn., Mo. League of Nursing Home Adminstrs. Home: 10641 N Grand Ave Kansas City MO 64155-1655

OLIVER, WALTER M., human resources specialist; b. Decatur, Ill. B in Psychology, Whitworth Coll.; M in Human Resources Mgmt., Gonzaga U. Corp. personnel mgr., personnel rels. superintendent, labor rels. rep. Kaiser Aluminum and Chem. Corp., 1973—80; v.p. human resources Hoover Universal, Inc., 1980—85; v.p. orgnl. devel. to v.p. adminstrn. Johnson Controls, Inc., 1985—89, corp. v.p. human resources, 1989—94; sr. v.p. human resources Ameritech, 1994—2001; v.p. human resources and adminstrn. General Dynamics Corp., Falls Church, Va., 2001—02, sr. v.p. human resources and adminstrn., 2002—. Dir. Am. Family Ins. Co., Telect, Inc. Bd. trustees Nat. Pension Fund; trustee Whitworth Coll. Office: General Dynamics Corp 2941 Fairview Park Dr Ste 100 Falls Church VA 22042-4513 Office Phone: 703-876-3000. Office Fax: 703-876-3125.

OLIVER, WILLIAM DONALD, orthodontist; b. Montreal, Ont., Can., Dec. 14, 1946; s. Austen William and Margaret Kay (Donald) O. BS in Physics, Mt. Allison U., 1964; DDS, McGill U., 1968; MSD in Orthodontics, U. Pa., 1970. Pres. Orthodontic Enterprises Internat., Geneva, 1973—78; orthodontist Barrington, RI, 1979—94; pvt. practice Everett, Wash., 1993—. Instr. Frankfurt Carolinium, 1972-74; witness Senate

Armed Svcs. Com., 1975. Inventor Piezo Electric Bone Healing; contbr. articles to profl. jours. Mem. Olympic Ski Team, Squaw Valley, 1960. Served with USAF, 1970-73. Recipient Carter Meml. award, 1964, M.T. Dohan prize, 1966. Mem. ADA, Can. Assn. Orthodontists, Am. Assn. Orthodontists, European Orthodontic Soc., Can. Dental Assn., Fedn. Internat. d'Automobile, Wash. State Soc. Orthodontists, Royal Ocean Racing Club. Republican. Office: 10812 19th Ave SE Everett WA 98208-5153 Office Phone: 425-338-5414. Business E-Mail: braces@seanet.com.

OLIVER, WILLIAM JOHN, pediatrician, educator; b. Blackshear, Ga., Mar. 30, 1925; s. John Wesley and Katherine (Schalwig) O.; m. Marguerite Bertoni, May 28, 1949; children: Ralph Scott, Catherine, Susan. Student, Ga. Southwestern Coll., 1942-43, Mercer U., 1943-44; MD cum laude, U. Mich., 1948. Diplomate Am. Bd. Pediatrics (examiner), Subsplty. Bd. Pediatric Nephrology. Intern, resident U. Mich. Med. Center, 1948-53, dir. pediatric labs., 1959-67; pvt. practice medicine specializing in pediatrics Ann Arbor, Mich., 1953—; instr. dept. pediatrics U. Mich., 1953-56, asst. prof., 1956-61, assoc. prof., 1961-65, prof., 1965, chmn. dept. pediatrics, 1967-79; chief pediatric service Wayne County Hosp., 1958-61. Co-chmn. task force on recent advances of coordinating com. on continuing edn. and recertification Am. Bd. Pediats. and Am. Acad. Pediats., 1977-80; mem. task force for pediatric rev. edn. program, 1980-88; mem. com. program for renewal certification in pediat. Am. Bd. Pediat., 1989-91, mem. exam writing com. for cert. pediatric nephrology, 1989-93, PRCP pilot test com., 1993-96; mem. rev. and question writing com. for Pediat. in Rev. Am. Acad. Pediat., 1991-97; cons. U. Riyadh, Saudi Arabia, 1980, Rsch. Rev. Com. on Pediat., 1989; ednl. cons. dept. pediat. Stanford U. Hosps., 1991-98; mem. self-assessment program for Pediat. in Rev., 1990-98; investigator adaptation primitive So. Ams. Indians, 1976—, African Pygmies, 1987—, worldwide primitive socs., 1997. Author: Primitive Peoples Without Salt, 1998, Amerindian Children: Mortality Study--Human Behavior and Evolution Society, 2005, child abuse study, 2006; mem. editl. bd. IRCS Jour. Med. Sci., 1975-90. Pres. Mich. Kidney Disease Found., 1969, Washtenaw County br. Mich. Childrens Aid Soc., 1964; trustee Ann Arbor Hands-On Mus., 1983-88; pres. bd. trustees Perry Nursery Sch., Ann Arbor, 1989-90. With USNR, 1950-52. Fellow Am. Acad. Pediatrics (chmn. com. med. edn. 1974-80, chmn. coun. on pediatric edn. 1975-80, chmn. task force oversight of pediatric rev. and edn. program 1984-88, Clifford G. Grulee award 1979); mem. Soc. Pediatric Rsch., Midwest Soc. Pediatric Rsch. (pres. 1968), Am. Soc. Nephrology, Assn. Med. Sch. Pediatric Dept. Chairmen (mem. coun. 1977-79), Soc. for Exptl. Biology and Medicine, Am. Pediatric Soc., Alpha Omega Alpha, Gamma Sigma Epsilon. Home: 2892 Bay Ridge Dr Ann Arbor MI 48103-1704 Personal E-mail: wjoandmbo@aol.com.

OLIVERA, BALDOMERO M., biology professor; BS summa cum laude, Univ. Philippines, 1960; PhD, Calif. Inst. Tech., 1966; postdoctoral study, Stanford Univ., 1966—68. Rsch. assoc. prof. biochemistry Univ. Philippines Coll. Medicine; vis. rsch. prof. Univ. Kans.; assoc. prof. Univ. Utah, 1970—73, prof., 1973—92, disting. prof. biology, 1992—. Fellow: Am. Acad. Arts & Scis. Office: Molecular Biology Program EIHG 533 Rm 1400 15 N 2030 E Salt Lake City UT 84112-5330 Office Phone: 801-581-5207. Business E-Mail: olivera@biology.utah.edu. *

OLIVERI, EUGENE ALFRED, gastroenterologist; b. NYC, Apr. 30, 1937; children: Gregory, Lisa, Michelle. Student, Bklyn. Coll., 1954-56, 58-60; DO summa cum laude, Kansas City Coll., 1964; LHD, U. Health Scis., 2000; MSc, Trinity So. U., 2003; D of Osteopathic Edn., U. New Eng., Biddeford, Maine, 2007. Diplomate Am. Bd. Internal Medicine, Am. Bd. Gastroenterology. Intern Detroit Osteo. Hosp., 1964-65; resident in internal medicine Botsford/Ziegler Hosps., 1965-67; fellowship in gastroenterology VA Hosp., East Orange, NJ, 1967-68; asst. dean Coll. Osteo. Medicine Mich. State U. Prof. dept. internal medicine sect. of gastroenterology Botsford Gen. Hosp., assoc. program dir. gastroenterology residency emeritus; mem., courtesy staff emeritus dept. of internal medicine Huron Valley Hosp. Trustee Pikeville (Ky.) Coll., 1998—, U. New Eng., Biddeford, Maine, 2001—. With US Army, 1956—58. Recipient Highest Acad. Achievement award Mead-Johnson, 1964, Outstanding Alumni Achievement award U. for Health Scis., Coll. Osteo. Medicine, 1991, Dr. J.O. Watson Disting. Lecr. Ohio Osteo. Assn., 1991, Walter Patenge medal for humanitarian svc. MSU, 1999, Phillips medal Pub Svc., Ohio U., 2002; named Physician of Yr. Mich. chpt. Ileitis and Colitis Found., 1985, Botsford Prof. Staff, 1994. Fellow Am. Coll. Osteo. Internists (pres. 1982-83, Disting. Svc. award 1982, Disting. Lectr. award 1983); fellow Am. Coll. Internists (master); mem. Am. Osteo. Assn. (pres. 1999-2000, trustee mem. bd., Disting. Svc. certificat 2005), Mich. Assn. Osteo. Physician and Surgeons (pres. 1991-92), Oakland County Osteo. Assn., Am. Coll. Gastroenterology, Am. Soc. Gastrointestinal Endoscopy, Am. Soc. Addiction Medicine, Am. Osteo. Found. (bd. dirs., past pres. bd. dirs., com. on awards), Mich. Osteo. Coll. Found. (chair, trustee, bd. dirs.), Crohn's and Colitis Found. Am. (Physician of Yr. 1991), Psi Sigma Alpha, Sigma Sigma Phi. Avocations: cooking, health policy. Home: 844 Old Milford Farms Milford MI 48381-3363 Personal E-mail: docoli@aol.com.

OLIVERI, PAUL FRANCIS, lawyer; b. Far Rockaway, NY, Feb. 27, 1954; s. Alphonse J. and Rita (Gregorace) O.; m. Debra Lynn Malkin, Aug. 7, 1977; children: Jason, Evan, Rebecca. BA, NYU, 1976; JD, St. John's U., Queens, NY, 1978. Bar: N.Y. 1979, U.S. Dist. Ct. (ea. and so. dists.) N.Y. 1980. Assoc. Fuchsberg & Fuchsberg, NYC, 1979-83; ptnr. Oliveri & Schwartz, NYC, 1983—. Mem. N.Y. State Bar Assn., Am. Trial Lawyers Assn., N.Y. State Trial Lawyers Assn. (dir. emeritus). Avocations: music, coin collecting/numismatics. Office: Oliveri & Schwartz 30 Vesey St New York NY 10007-4208 Office Phone: 212-608-7080. E-mail: poliveri@oliveriandschwartz.com.

OLIVERIO, PONZIO, protective services official, educator; b. San Diego, Calif., June 14, 1958; s. Ponzio and Harriet Jean Oliverio; m. Amy Amber Edsall, Nov. 19, 1983; children: Giulia Marie, Giana. BA in Humanities, Thomas Edison Coll., Trenton, NJ, 1992; JD, U. San Diego Sch. Law, 1996. Bar: Calif. 1997; cert. in hostage negotiations FBI, 2004. Dep. sheriff San Diego County Sheriff, 1985—; prof. Nat. U., San Diego, 1999—; adj. faculty San Diego Regional Police Acad., 2000—; prof. U. Phoenix, San Diego, 2003—, faculty advisor; guest lectr., criminal procedure U. San Diego Sch. Law; instr. USN, Master-at-Arms Sch., San Diego. Uniform com. mem. San Diego Sheriff, 1993—95, process improvement team mem., 2003—, tng. officer. Columnist The Silver Star Holding Court, San Diego County Herald Cuff Links; co-author: (training manual) Crime-Free Mobile Housing Man., (anthology publ. in True Blue) Jimmy, 2004. Moot ct. judge U. San Diego Sch. Law, 2002—04; com. mem. State Bar Domestic Violence Com., Santa Ana, Calif.; facilitator Domestic Violence Restraining Order Clinic, San Diego, 1995—96. Recipient Letter of Appreciation, Calif. Dept. Corrections, 2000, Chula Vista, Calif. Police Dept., 2000, U.S. Border Patrol, 2001, Award of Exemplary Performance, San Diego Sheriff, 2000, Medal of Valor, 2001. Mem.: Statewide Calif. Coalition for Battered Women (assoc.), Dep. Sheriff's Assn. (assoc.), Fraternal Order of Police (assoc.). Conservative. Avocations: hunting, fishing. Home: 2208 Boulders Ct Alpine CA 91901 Personal E-mail: ponzio2@cox.net.

OLIVER LEAHY TINEN KAEHLER, JEANNETTE See LEAHY, JEANNETTE

OLIVER-WARREN, MARY ELIZABETH, retired library science educator, library and information scientist; b. Hamlet, NC, Feb. 23, 1924; d. Washington and Carolyn Belle (Middlebrooks) Terry; m. David Oliver, 1947 (div. 1971); children: Donald D., Carolyn L.; m. Arthur Warren, Sept. 14, 1990 (dec. Feb. 1995). BS, Bluefield State U., 1948; MS, South Conn. State U., 1958; student, U. Conn., 1977. Cert. tchr., adminstr. and supr., Conn.; cert. pub. sch. substitute tchr., K-12, NJ. Media specialist Hartford Pub. Schs., Conn., 1952—86; with So. Conn. State U., New Haven, 1972—, asst. prof. Sch. Libr. Sci. and Instructional Tech., 1987—95, ret., 1995; substitute tchr. K-12 Windsor, Conn., 1999—2004, Grady County Pub. Schs., Cairo, Ga., 2004—. Mem. dept. curriculum com. So. Conn. State U., 1987-95, adj. prof., 1995—; cert. substitute tchr. Somerset County Pub. Schs., 1997—; cert. substitute tchr. Windsor, Conn. Sch. Sys., 1999-. Author: My Golden Moments, 1988, The Elementary School Media Center, 1990, Text Book Elementary School Media Center, 1991, I Must Fight Alone, 1991, (textbook) I Must Fight Alone, 1994. Mem. ALA, Conn. Ednl. Media Assn., Black Librs. Network NJ Inc., Assn. Ret. Tchrs. Conn., Black and Hispanic Consortium, So. Conn. State U. Women's Assn., Cicuso Club (v.p.), Friends Club (v.p.), Delta Kappa Gamma, Alpha Kappa Alpha. Avocations: reading, music, piano, walking. Home: 3085 Creel Rd Atlanta GA 30349

OLIVIER, KATHY RICKS, college basketball coach; b. Placentia, Calif. 1 child, Alexis. Student, Calif. State U., Fullerton; grad., U. Nev., 1982. Various coaching positions U. Nev., U. Calif.-Irvine, U. So. Calif., 1981-86; asst. coach UCLA Bruins, 1986; reached NCAA Sweet 16, 1991-92; head coach UCLA Bruins, 1993—. Achievements include finished 2nd in conf. (sch. record), 1997-98. Office: c/o Athletic Dept UCLA Women's Basketball PO Box 951361 Los Angeles CA 90095-1361

OLIVIER, LEON J., utilities executive; m. Bernadette Olivier. MBA, Northeastern Univ.; D in pub. svc. (hon.), Bridgewater State Coll. Mgmt. positions through v.p. nuclear Boston Edison; sr. v.p., chief nuclear officer Northeast Nuclear Energy Co., 1998—2001; sr. v.p. Entergy Nuclear Northeast, 2001; pres., COO Conn. Light & Power Co., 2001—05; pres. transmission group Northeast Utilities Sys., Hartford, Conn., 2005, exec. v.p. ops., 2005—. CEO Conn. Light & Power Co., Pub. Svc. Co. NH, We. Mass. Elec. Co., Yankee Gas Services Co. Bd. mem. Lawrence & Meml. Hosp., New London, Ea. Conn. C. of C., Spl. Olympics Conn., World Affairs Council Conn. Mailing: Northeast Utilities Sys PO Box 270 Hartford CT 06141-0270 *

OLK, FREDERICK JAMES, county official, legal assistant; b. Clintonville, Wis., Apr. 30, 1952; s. James Howard and Bernice Helen (Durben) O. Student, Inst. Comp. Polit.& Econ. Sys., 1973; BS in Liberal Arts, U. Wis. River Falls, 1976; cert., Wis. Sch. Real Estate, 1980. Notary pub., Ill. Libr. asst. U. Wis., Stevens Point and Oshkosh, 1977—80; contract libr. U.S. Dept. Justice, Oxford, Wis., 1980; editl. libr. The Chgo. Cath. newspaper Archdiocese Chgo., 1980—89; tax. examiner Cook County, Chgo., 1990—. Congl. intern U.S. Ho. of Rep., Washington, 1973; sales rep. Waupaca (Wis.) Pub. Co., 1978-79; freelance paralegal, Chgo., 1988—; security guard, account mgr. Glenbrook Security Svcs., Wheeling, Ill., 1988—; asst. reference libr. Cicero (Ill.) Pub. Libr., 1989; genealogy rschr. Lineage Search Assocs., Mechanicsville, Va., 1980-99; v.p. New World Credit Union, Chgo., 1981-86 Columnist Looking back Chgo. Cath., 1985-89. Tutor Mercy Home for Boys, Chgo., 1987—88; coord. Friends of Vatican Libr., Chgo., 1995—; mem. exec. bd. customer adv. coun. U.S. Postal Svc., Cicero, 1997—; Cicero rep. for Ill. 43d dist. Anti-Crime Adv. Bd., 1999—2001; precinct capt. Wis. and Ill. Rep. coms., 1973—; Rep. judge of election Cook County, 1980—; mem. Rome tour St. John Cantius Parish Resurrection Choir, 2001, sang at St. Peter's Basilica, 2001. Named adm. Nebr. Navy, State of Nebr., 1982, col. State of Ala., 1988, Internat. Citizen of Yr., Hutt River Province, Australia, 1995; recipient Legion of Merit Rep. Nat. Com., 1997, Order of the Arrow, Boy Scouts Am., 1971. Mem. Am. Soc. Notaries (life, chmn. govt. rels. 1984-85), Nat. Assn. Investigative Specialists, Am. Legion (life), Amtrak Hist. Soc. (asst. archivist 1996—), Chgo. Geneal. Soc. (life, bd. dirs. 1988-90), 20th Century R.R. Club (sec. 1994-98, 2006—, Century Club 1996, dir. 1998-2000), KC (del. archdiocesan pastoral coun. 1996—, grand knight cardinal coun. 2001-03) Avocations: rail travel, genealogy, reading, music, stamp collecting/philately. Office: Cook County Clk 118 N Clark St Ste 434 Chicago IL 60602-1382 Home: 1347 S 61st Ave Cicero IL 60804-1012 Office Phone: 847-452-3595.

OLKINETZKY, SAM, artist, educator, retired museum director; b. NYC, Nov. 22, 1919; s. Isidor and Jennie Olkinetzky; m. Sammie Lee Sturdevant, Dec. 20, 1959; children: Jov Shan, Tova Shana. BA, Bklyn. Coll., 1942; postgrad., Inst. Fine Arts, N.Y. U., 1946-47. Asst. prof. art and humanities Okla. A&M U., Stillwater, 1947-57; vis. asst. prof. art U. Okla., Norman, 1957-58; assoc. prof. art Mus. of Art, 1959—; dir. Mus. Art U. Okla., Norman, 1959-83. Vis. prof. art and humanities U. Ark., Fayetteville, 1962—63, Fayetteville, 1967—68, Langston U., Okla., 1969—70; art cons. Kerr-McGee Industries, Inc.; advisor State of Okla. Visual Arts; mem. State Art Collection Com., Norman Arts and Humanities Coun. One-man shows include Arts Pl. II, Okla. Art Ctr., Firehouse Art Ctr., Norman, 1989, exhibitions include Mus. Non-Objective Art, NYC, Mus. Modern Art, 50-Yr. Retrospective Exhbn., 1942—92, Norick Art Ctr., Oklahoma City, 1992, Represented in permanent collections Mus. Art U. Okla., Philbrook Art Mus., Tulsa, Oklahoma City Mus. Art. With USAAF, 1942—45. Recipient Gov.'s Art award, 1981. Mem.: Art Mus. Assn., Am. Assn. Mus., Mountain-Plains Mus. Assn., Internat. Coun. Mus., Okla. Mus. Assn. (pres. 1978—79).

OLLER, WILLIAM MAXWELL, retired energy executive, retired military officer; b. Lancaster, Pa., Apr. 7, 1924; s. John Secrist and Mabel Margaret (Coffman) O.; m. Doris Seitz Greenleaf, June 15, 1946; children: Arthur G., J. Richard. BS, U.S. Naval Acad., 1946; MBA, George Washington U., 1960. Commd. ensign USN, 1946, advanced through grades to rear adm., 1972; svc. in Samoa, Philippines and Italy; exec. officer Naval Supply Ctr., Newport, R.I., 1966-67, Ships Parts Control Ctr., Mechanicsberg, Pa., 1970-72; comdr. Def. Fuel Supply Ctr., Alexandria, Va., 1972-76; comdg. officer Naval Supply Ctr., Norfolk, Va., 1976-77; gen. mgr. corp. supply and distbn. Champlin Petroleum Co., Houston, 1977-79, Ft. Worth, 1979-81; sr. v.p. Petroleum Ops. and Support Svcs., Inc., New Orleans, 1981-82, pres., 1982-84; spl. asst. to pres., CEO Kaneb Svcs., Inc., Houston, 1984-85; exec. v.p. Tex. Ea. Products Pipeline Co., Houston, 1986-90. Pres. Am. Leadership Forum, Houston, 1986. Decorated Legion of Merit with gold star, Meritorious Svc. medal with gold star, Joint Svc. Commendation medal. Home: 20510 Falcons Landing Circle # 1205 Sterling VA 20165

OLLEY, ROBERT EDWARD, economist, educator; b. Vendun, Que., Can., Apr. 16, 1933; s. Edwin Henry and Elizabeth (Reed) O.; m. Shirley Ann Dahl, Jan. 19, 1957; children— Elizabeth Anne, George Steven, Susan Catherine, Maureen Carolyn BA, Carleton U., Can., 1960; MA, Queen's U., Can., 1961, PhD in Econs., 1969. Vis. asst. prof. Queen's U., Kingston, Canada, 1967-68; asst. prof. econs. U. Sask., Saskatoon, Canada, 1963-67, 68-69, assoc. prof., 1969-71, 73-75, prof., 1975-93, prof. emeritus, 1993—; pres. Gen. Econs. Ltd., 1993—. Dir. rsch. Royal Commn. on Consumer Problems and Inflation, 1967-68; econ. advisor Bell Can., Montreal, Que., 1971-73, 78-79, Can. Telecom. Carriers Assn., 1978-85, Sask. Power Corp., 1980-83; econ. advisor AT&T, 1980-90, Waste Mgmt., Inc., 1990-92, SaskTel, 1989-93; chmn. adv. com. on consumer stds. Stds. Coun. Can., 1992-93; Can. rep. to ISO/COPOLCO, Geneva, 1992-93. Author, editor: Consumer Product Testing, 1979; Consumer Product Testing II, 1981; Consumer Credit in Canada, 1966; Economics of the Public Firm: Regulation, Rates, Costs, Productivity Analysis, 1983, Total Factor Productivity of Canadian Telecommunications, 1984; Consumer Reps. Conf. Procs., 1st-4th, 1982-91. Bd. dirs. Can. Found. for Econ. Edn., 1974-82, Can. Gen. Stds. Bd., 1977-81; v.p. Niagara-on-the-Lake Hosp. Found., 2000-03, bd. dirs., 1998-. Recipient Silver Jubilee medal Her Majesty The Queen, 1977, Can.'s Jean P. Carriere Exptl. Contbr. Vol. Standardization award, 1995. Mem. Royal Econ. History Soc., Royal Econs. Assn., Econ. History Assn., Am. Econ. Assn., Can. Econ. Assn., Consumers Assn. Can. (v.p. 1967-75, chmn. 1975-77), Can. Stds. Assn. (dir., exec. com. 1971-93, vice chmn. 1985-87, chmn. 1987-89, Award of Merit 1995), Consumer's Assn. Found. Can. (v.p. 1989-95), Can. Comm. Rsch. Ctr. (dir. 1992-97), Internat. Telecom. Soc. (bd. dirs. 1986-2004), Shaw Guild, Niagara Hist. Soc. (bd. dirs. 1997-99), Niagara-on-the-Lake Golf Club (bd. dirs. 2001-05, v.p. 2002-05) Home and Office: PO Box 1040 374 Queen St Niagara-on-the-Lake ON Canada L0S 1J0 Office Phone: 909-468-0530. Personal E-mail: olley@niagara.com.

OLLINGER, W. JAMES, lawyer; b. Kittanning, Pa., Apr. 5, 1943; s. William James and Margaret Elizabeth (Reid) Ollinger; m. Susan Louise Gerspacher, Oct. 20, 1979; children: Mary Rebecca, David James. BA, Capital U., Columbus, Ohio, 1966; JD, Case Western Res. U., 1968. Bar: Ohio 1968, US Dist Ct (no dist) Ohio 1971. Ptnr. Baker & Hostetler, Cleve., 1968—. Mem. Bentleyville Village Coun., Ohio, 1990—93; mayor Bentleyville, 1997—99. Mem.: Order of Coif, Phi Delta Phi. Office: Baker & Hostetler 3200 Nat City Ctr 1900 E 9th St Ste 3200 Cleveland OH 44114-3475 Office Phone: 216-861-7473. Business E-Mail: jollinger@bakerlaw.com.

OLMOS, EDWARD JAMES, actor; b. LA, Feb. 24, 1947; m. Kaija Keel, Dec. 29, 1972 (div. 1992); children: Mico, Bodie; m. Lorraine Bracco, Jan. 28, 1994 (div. Mar. 4, 2002). AA in Sociology, East Los Angeles City Coll.; postgrad., Calif. State U., LA; degree (hon.), U. Colo., Whittier Coll., Calif. State U., Fresno, Occidental Coll., Film Inst., Hollywood, Calif. Exec. dir. Lives in Hazard Ednl. Project, nat. gang prevention program. Performed in exptl. theater, L.A.; actor (play) Zoot Suit (Tony nominee, Los Angeles Drama Critics Circle award, Theatre World award), Broadway and Los Angeles, 1978-80; actor, producer film The Ballad of Gregorio Cortez, 1982, Triumph of the Spirit, 1989; actor, co-producer film Stand and Deliver, 1988 (nominee best actor Acad. Awards 1988); actor films Wolfen, 1981, Zoot Suit, 1981, Blade Runner, 1982, (also assoc. prodr., composer, music adapter) The Ballad of Gregorio Cortez, 1983, Saving Grace, 1986 (also prodr.) Stand and Deliver, 1988, Triumph of the Spirit, 1989, Talent for the Game, 1991, (also dir., prodr.) American Me, 1992, A Million to Juan, 1994, My Family, 1995, Caught, 1996, Selena, 1997, Death in Granada, 1997, The Wonderful Ice Cream Suit, 1998, The Wall, 1998, Gossip, 1999, (voice) The Road to El Dorado, 2000, Gossip, 2000, Jack and Marilyn, 2002; (TV series) Miami Vice, 1984-89 (Emmy award for best supporting actor in drama series 1985, Golden Globe award 1986); Battlestar Galactica, 2004-; (TV miniseries) The Fortunate Pilgrim, 1988, Menendez: A Killing in Beverly Hills, 1994, The Burning Season, 1995 (Golden Globe award for Best Supporting Actor in a TV Movie, Miniseries or Series 1994), Mirage, 1995, Slave of Dreams, 1995, Roosters, 1995, American Family, 2002, Battlestar Galactica, 2003, The Batman, 2004; (TV movies) The Pricess and the Barrio Boy, 2000, The Judge, 2001, In the Time of the Butterflies, 2001; star ABC miniseries Dead Man's Walk (prequel to Lonesome Dove), 1996; co-star TV movie 12 Angry Men, 1997; prodr., dir. (TV documentary) Lives in Hazard, 1994, The Limbic Region, 1995. U.S. goodwill amb. UNICEF; nat. spokesman for voter registration, Juvenile Diabetes Found., AIDS Awareness Found.; bd. dirs. Heal L.A., Recruiting New Tchrs., 20th Century Fund, UCLA Sch. Film and Theater, Miami Children's Hosp., L.A. Children's Hosp., Nat. Coun. on Adoption, Children's Action Netowrk, Hollywood Supports, Nat. Hispanic U., Plaza del Raza, Whittier Coll.; spkr. at numerous chs., charities and juvenile instns. throughout U.S. Address: Olmos Productions 18034 Ventura Blvd Ste 288 Encino CA 91316-3516 Office: AA Creative Artists Agency 830 Wilshire Blvd Beverly Hills CA 90210 *

OLMSTEAD, CECIL JAY, lawyer; b. Jacksonville, Fla., Oct. 15, 1920; s. Cecil Jay Sr. and Bessie (Irby) O.; m. Frances Hughes (dec. 2006); children: Cecil Jay III, Frank Hughes, Jane Olmstead Murphy, Amy Olmstead Vanecek. BA, U. Ga., 1950, LLB, 1951; Sterling Grad. fellow, Yale Law Sch., 1951-52; LLD (hon.), U. Hull, Eng., 1978. Bar: Ga. 1950, U.S. Supreme Ct 1964, D.C. 1978. Asst. to legal adviser Dept. State, counsel Mut. Security Agy., counsel Hoover Commn. on Orgn. Exec. Br. of Govt., 1952-55; prof. N.Y. U. Sch. Law, 1953-61; dir. Inter-Am. Law Inst., 1958-61, adj. prof. law, 1961-69; atty. Texaco, Inc., NYC, 1961-62, asst. to chmn. bd., 1962-70, v.p., asst. to chmn. bd., 1970, v.p., asst. to pres., 1970-71, v.p., asst. to chief exec. officer, 1971-73, exec. dept., v.p., 1973-80; mem. firm Steptoe & Johnson, Washington, 1980—. Vis. prof. Columbia U. Sch. Law, 1959; Wang Disting. vis. prof. St. Johns U., 1987-90; mem. adv. panel on internat. law to sec. state; adv. com. law of sea State Dept.; also adv. com. transnat. enterprise; U.S. del. UN Com. on Law of Sea, 1972-73; U.S. del. UN Conf. on Law of Sea, 1974-76; Eisenhower lectr. Nat. War Coll., 1973; mem. U.S. del. UN Conf. on Code of Conduct for Transnat. Corps., ann. 1984-90; mem. World Bank's panel of conciliations of the Internat. Ctr. for Settlement of Investment Disputes, 1988-95; vis. fellow All Souls Coll., Oxford U., 1988; vis. scholar Yale Law Sch., 1990-91. With USAF, 1943-46, 8th and 20th Air Forces. ETO, PTO. Recipient Gold medal City of Brussels (Belgium, 1973, Gold medal City of Paris (France), 1984; named Commdr. Brit. Empire (hon.), 1990. Mem. Internat. Law Assn. (pres. and chmn. Am. br. 1966-73, vice chmn. exec. coun. 1975-86, chmn. exec. coun. 1986-88, 1st Disting. Svc. award London br. 2004), Am. Law Inst. (assoc. reporter Restatement of the Fgn. Rels. Law of the U.S., 1st edit. 1964, advisor 3d edit.), Coun. on Fgn. Rels., Washington Inst. Fgn. Affairs, Nat. Fgn. Trade Coun. (dir. 2004), Am. Coun. on Germany (hon. dir.), Coun. on Ocean Law (dir.), Knickerbocker Club, Yale Club, Fairfield County Hunt Club (Westport), Cosmos Club (Washington), Order of Coif, Phi Beta Kappa. Home: 4 Sprucewood Ln Westport CT 06880-4021 Office: 1330 Connecticut Ave NW Washington DC 20036-1704 Office Phone: 202-429-6483.

OLMSTEAD, CLARENCE WALTER, JR., lawyer; b. Alexandria, Va., Jan. 24, 1943; s. Clarence Walter and Rhea Nancy (Donnelly) O.; m. Kathleen Frances Heenan, Sept. 7, 1973; children: Nicholas Heenan, Jonathan Heenan, Caitlin Heenan. AB, Stanford U., 1965; LLB, Columbia U., 1968. Bar: N.Y. 1970, U.S. Dist. Ct. (so. and ea. dists.) N.Y. 1970, U.S. Ct. Appeals (2d cir.) 1970, U.S. Supreme Ct. 1986. Law clk. to presiding judge U.S. Dist. Ct. (we. dist.) Wis., 1968-69; assoc. Shearman & Sterling, NYC, 1969-76, ptnr., 1976, of counsel. Bd. dirs. West Side Montessori Sch., N.Y.C., 1983-89, pres., 1985-87; mem. sch. com. Cathedral Sch., N.Y.C., 1992-95; trustee North Country Sch. Camp Treetops, 1992-95. Mem. ABA, N.Y. State Bar Assn., Assn. Bar City of N.Y., Phi Beta Kappa.

OLMSTEAD, MARJORIE ANN, physics professor; b. Glen Ridge, NJ, Aug. 18, 1958; d. Blair E. and Elizabeth (Dempwolf) Olmstead. BA in Physics, Swarthmore Coll., 1979; MA in Physics, U. Calif., Berkeley, 1982, PhD, 1985. Rsch. staff Palo Alto (Calif.) Rsch. Ctr. Xerox Corp., 1985-86; asst. prof. physics U. Calif., Berkeley, 1986-90, U. Wash., Seattle, 1991-93, assoc. prof., 1993-97, prof., 1997—, dir. nanotech. PhD program, 2004—. Prin. investigator sci. materials divsn. Lawrence Berkeley Lab., 1988—93. Contbr. articles to profl. jours. Named Presdl. Young Investigator, NSF, 1987; recipient Devel. award, IBM, 1986, 1987, Rsch. award, A. von Humboldt Found., 2000. Fellow: Am. Phys. Soc. (chair com. on status of women in physics 1999, Maria Goeppart-Mayer award 1996), Am. Vacuum Soc. (Peter Mark Meml. award 1994). Office: U Washington Dept Physics PO Box 351560 Seattle WA 98195-1560 Office Phone: 206-685-3031. E-mail: olmstd@u.washington.edu.

OLMSTEAD, WILLIAM EDWARD, mathematics professor; b. San Antonio, June 2, 1936; s. William Harold and Gwendolyn (Littlefield) Olmstead; m. Adele Cross, Aug. 14, 1957 (div. 1967); children: William Harold, Randell Edward. BS, Rice U., 1959; MS, Northwestern U., 1962, PhD, 1963. Mem. rsch. staff S.W. Rsch. Inst., San Antonio, 1959—60; Sloan Found. postdoctoral fellow Johns Hopkins, 1963—64; prof. applied math. Northwestern U., Evanston, Ill., 1964—, chmn. dept. engring. scis. and applied math., 1991—93. Vis. mem. Courant Inst. Math. Scis. NYU, 1967—68; faculty visitor U. Coll. London, 1973, Calif. Inst. Tech., 1987, 90; editor Options Prof. Newsletter, Spear Capital Mgmt., 2003—. Contbr. articles to profl. jours. Named Technol. Inst. Tchr. of Yr., 1980, Charles Deering McCormick prof., 1994—97; recipient Award for Tchg. Excellence, Northwestern Alumni Assn., 1993. Mem.: Am. Contract Bridge League (silver life master), Soc. Indsl. and Applied Math. (editl. bd. jour. 1998—), Am. Phys. Soc., Am. Math. Soc., Am. Acad. Mechanics, Soc. Engring. Sci. (bd. dirs. 1998—2000), John Evans Club, Sigma Tau, Tau Beta Pi, Sigma Xi. Episcopalian. Home: 153 E Laurel Ave #203 Lake Forest IL 60045 Office: Northwestern U Dept Engring Scis And Applie Evanston IL 60208-0001

OLMSTED, JENNIFER, medical transcriptionist; BS, East Tenn. State U., Johnson City, 1998, grad. cert. bus. adminstrn., 1999; cert. med. transcription, Edn. Direct, Scranton, Pa., 2003. Grad. assisant East Tenn. State U., 1998; agy. mgr. Farmer's Ins., Patrick Becker Agy., Boulder, Colo., 2000; ins. sec. Boulder Orthopedics, LLC, Colo., 2001—03; med. transcriptionist Idle Hands, San Marcos, Calif., 2004—, Healthcare Employee Services, LLC, Carlsbad, Calif., 2004—05, Lab. Corp. Am., San Diego, 2005—06. Scholar, So. Adventist U., 1994, East Tenn. State U., 1996—98. Mem.: Am. Assn. Med. Transcription (assoc.), Eta Sigma Gamma, Gamma Beta Phi, Phi Kappa Phi, Alpha Xi Delta Alumni.

OLMSTED, JERAULD LOCKWOOD, telephone company executive; b. Des Moines, Aug. 26, 1938; s. George Hamden and Virginia (Camp) O.; m. Mary Karen Autenrieth, June 20, 1962 (div. Dec. 1986); children: Scott H., Victoria L., Jerauld; m. Gisele A. Child, June 17, 1988. BS, Iowa State U., 1961; MBA, George Washington U., 1979; Cert. mgmt. accountant. Vice-pres. First Nat. Bank of Washington, 1969; v.p., dir. Intermediate Credit Corp., 1969-73, Internat. Gen. Industries, Inc., 1974-79, pres., dir., 1980-82, IB Credit Corp., 1982-85, N.Am. Communications, Inc., Bethesda, Md., 1985—. Sr. v.p., dir. Internat. Bank, 1978-85. Bd. govs. Iowa State U. Found., 1980—; chmn. corporate adv. bd. div. arts and humanities U. Md., 1982—86; sec.-treas. George Olmsted Found., 1970—85. Served with US Army, 1961-63. Decorated Knight of Malta, Order of St. John Mem. Fin. Execs. Inst., Mensa, Soc. Cincinnati, Met. Club, Georgetown Club, Bethesda Country Club, Beta Alpha Psi., Beta Gamma Sigma. Republican. Episcopalian. Home and Office: 7735 Arrowood Ct Bethesda MD 20817-2821 Office Phone: 301-365-7225.

OLNESS, KAREN NORMA, medical educator; b. Rushford, Minn., Aug. 28, 1936; d. Norman Theodore and Karen Agnes (Gunderson) O.; m. Hakon Daniel Torjesen, 1962. BA, U. Minn., 1958, BS, MD, 1961. Diplomate Am. Bd. Pediat., Am. Bd. Med. Hypnosis, Develop. & Behavioral Pediatrics. Intern Harbor Gen. Hosp., Torrance, Calif.; resident Nat. Children's Hosp. Med. Ctr., Washington; asst. prof. George Washington U., Washington, 1970-74; assoc. prof. U. Minn., Mpls., 1974-87; prof. pediat., family medicine and internat. health Case Western Res. U., Cleve., 1987—. Named Outstanding Woman Physician, Minn. Assn. Women Physicians, 1987; recipient Christopherson award Am. Acad. Pediat., 1998, Aldrich award, Am. Acad. Pediat., 1999, Ann. award Soc. Devel. and Behavioral Pediat., 2003, Outstanding Alumni award U. Minn., 2007; named to Cleve. Med. Hall of Fame, 2000. Fellow: Soc. Clin. and Exptl. Hypnosis (pres. 1991—93), Am. Soc. Clin. Hypnosis (pres. 1984—86), Am. Acad. Pediat. (chair internat. health sect. 2001), Am. Acad. Family Physicians; mem.: Internat. Hypnosis Soc. (pres. 2003—06), Northwestern Pediat. Soc. (pres. 1977), Soc. Devel. and Behavioral Pediat. Office: Case Western Res U 11100 Euclid Ave Cleveland OH 44106-6038 Office Phone: 216-368-4368. Business E-Mail: karen.olness@case.edu.

OLNEY, JOHN WILLIAM, psychiatry professor; b. Marathon, Iowa, Oct. 23, 1931; married, 1957; 3 children. BA, U. Iowa, 1957, MD, 1963. Diplomate Am. Bd. Psychiatry, Am. Bd. Neurology. Intern Kaiser Permanente Found., San Francisco, 1963-64; resident, 1964-68; from instr. to assoc. prof. psychiatry Washington U., St. Louis, 1968-77, prof. psychiatry and neuropathology Sch. Medicine, 1977—. NIMH biol. sci. trainee Washington U., 1966-68; asst. psychiatrist Barnes Hosp., 1968—; cons. psychiatrist Malcolm Bliss Mental Health Ctr., 1968—; elected to Inst. Medicine/NAS, 1996. Recipient Wakeman award Rsch. Neurosci., 1992; co-recipient Charles A. Dana award for Pioneering Achievements in Health, 1994. Mem. APA, Am. Assn Neuropathology, Soc. Neurosci. Assn. Rsch. Nervous & Mental Disorders, Psychiatric Rsch. Soc. Achievements include research in role of excitatory neurotoxins in disorders of the nervous system. Office: Washington U Dept Psychiatry Sch Med Saint Louis MO 63110

OLNEY, ROBERT STANBURY, III, sportswriter and baseball analyst; BA in Jour., Vanderbilt Univ. Former sports feature writer, lead sports editor NY Times, NYC, 1998—2003; columnist ESPN The Mag., 2003—, ESPN.com; baseball analyst ESPN's Baseball Tonight, 2003—. Author: (sports books) The Last Night of the Yankee Dynasty, 2004. Office: ESPN ESPN Plz 935 Middle St Bristol CT 06010

OLOFSON, TOM WILLIAM, technology company executive; b. Oak Park, Ill., Oct. 10, 1941; s. Ragnar V. and Ingrid E. Olofson; m. Jeanne Hamilton, Aug. 20, 1960; children: Christopher, Scott. Various mgmt. positions Bell Telephone Co. of Pa., Pitts., 1963-67; sales mgr. Xerox Corp., Detroit, 1967-68, nat. account mgr. Rochester, NY, 1968, mgr. govt. planning, 1969, mgr. Kansas City (Mo.) br., 1969-74; corp. v.p. health products group Marion Labs., Inc., Kansas City, 1974-78, sr. v.p., mem. Office Pres., 1978-80; exec. v.p., dir. Electronic Realty Assocs., Inc., 1980-83; chmn. bd., CEO Emblem Graphic Sys., Inc., 1983-88, EPIQ Sys., Inc., 1988—. Dir. DemoGraFX, Elinco Internat., Access Industries, Inc., Saztec Internat., Capital Ptnrs. Bd. visitors U. Pitts., Joseph M. Katz Grad. Sch. Bus.; past trustee Barstow Sch.; past chmn. bd. trustees Village United Presbyn. Ch.; chmn. Tom. W. and Jeanne H. Olofson Found., 2001-. Mem. Carlton Club (Chgo.), Kansas City Club, Omicron Delta Kappa, Sigma Chi. Republican. Presbyterian. Office: EPIQ Sys Inc 501 Kansas Ave Kansas City KS 66105-1309

OLOFSSON, DANIEL JOEL, lawyer; b. Chgo., Sept. 29, 1954; s. Joel Gustav and Patricia Marie (Casey) O.; children: Nicole Lynn, Gustave Daniel, Jonathan Leonard; m. Catherine Elaine Baehler, July 24, 1999; AA, Thornton C.C., 1974; BA, U. Ill., 1976; JD with honors, Chgo.-Kent Coll. Law, Ill. Inst. Tech., 1979. Bar: Ill. 1979, U.S. Dist. Ct. (no. dist.) Ill. 1979, U.S. Ct. Appeals (7th cir.) 1979, U.S. Tax Ct. 1980. Assoc. Jerry L. Lambert, Flossmoor, Ill., 1979-80, John P. Block, Chgo., 1980-82; pvt. practice, Dolton, Ill., 1982-94; mgr. ops Signature Mortgage, Inc., 1994-2003; sales mgr. Wells Fargo Mortgage, 2003—. Elected trustee Village of Dolton, 1985. James scholar U. Ill., Champaign, 1976. Mem. Chgo. Bar Assn., South Suburban Bar Assn., Ill. State Bar Assn., ABA, Phi Theta Kappa. Democrat. Roman Catholic. Lodges: Rotary, Elks. Home: 18521 S Marshfield Homewood IL 60430 Home Phone: 708-922-3437; Office Phone: 708-226-7413. Business E-Mail: daniel.j.olofsson@wellsfargo.com.

OLONI, ANTHONY OLUSHEGUN, medical association administrator, director; s. James Bolaji and Deborah Funmi Oloni. MBBS, U. Ilorin, Nigeria, 1987; grad. cert. in Pub. Health Informatics, U. Ill., 2006, MPH in Informatics, 2004. Med. intern Mil. Hosp., Yaba, Lagos, Nigeria, 1988—89; med. rsch. assoc. Coll. of Medicine, U. Lagos, 1989—90; med. dir. Mc'Lonie Indsl. Clin., Lagos, 1990—92; pub. health cons. Phila. Dept. Pub. Health, 1994—99; pres., CEO, med. dir. Pub. Health Informatics Cons., Atlanta, 2000—; med. dir. Preventive Medicine Assoc., Atlanta, 2000—03. Directorship Nat. Black Leadership Initiative on Cancer, Phila., 1997—99; chaiman Metro-Atlanta Coalition for Cancer Awareness, Atlanta, 2001—02; dir., health adminstr. Project Flow, Mayors Office Cmty. Svcs.; chief health coord. Your Health. Recipient Ujama award for Cmty. Economics. Mem.: Am. Med. Informatics Assn. (assoc.). Achievements include design of patient electronic health record sys. Home: 1862 Hickory Creek Ct Acworth GA 30102 Office: Public Health Informatics Cons PO Box 2822 Acworth GA 30102 Home Phone: 678-886-7992; Office Phone: 678-354-6144. Home Fax: 678-355-0462. Business E-Mail: anthony.oloni.md@phicon.org.

OLOPADE, OLUFUNMILAYO FALUSI (FUNMI OLOPADE), geneticist, educator, oncologist, hematologist; b. Nigeria, Apr. 29, 1957; m. Christopher Sola Olopade; 3 children. MD with distinction, U. Ibadan, Nigeria, 1980. Diplomate Am. Bd. Internal Medicine, Am. Bd. Med. Oncology, Am. Bd. Hematology; lic. MD Ill., Ind. Med. officer Nigerian Navy Hosp.; intern in medicine, surgery, pediatrics, ob-gyn. Univ. Coll. Hosp., Ibadan, 1980—81; intern in internal medicine Cook County Hosp., Chgo., 1983—84, resident in internal medicine, 1984—86, chief resident in medicine, 1986; clin. instr. U. Ill. Abraham Lincoln Sch. Medicine, Chgo., 1986—87; postdoctoral fellow jt. sect. hematology/oncology U. Chgo., 1987—91, asst. prof. hematology/oncology, Pritzker Sch. Medicine, 1991—2002, mem. Cancer Rsch. Ctr., 1991—, mem. Cancer Biology com., 1994—, mem. Genetics com., 1996—, assoc. prof. medicine, prof. medicine and human genetics Ill., 2002—, dir. Ctr. for Clinical Cancer Genetics, Cancer Risk Clinic Ill., 1992—, dir. Hematology/Oncology Fellowship Program Ill., 1998—. Attending physician Cook County Hosp., Chgo., 1987; mem. steering com., cooperative family registry for breast cancer studies, Nat. Cancer Inst., also mem. adv. com. Cancer Genetics Network and bd. scientific counselors; mem. adv. bd. Cancerandcareers.org; lectr. in field. Ad hoc reviewer Jour. AMA, Genes, Chromosomes and Cancer, Genomics, Human Molecular Genetics, Cancer Rsch., Blood, Molecular Carcinogenesis, Jour. Clin. Oncology, New Eng. Jour. Medicine; contbr. articles to profl. jours.; contbr. to book chpts. and abstracts on topics including genetics of cancer. Mem. med. adv. bd. Young Survival Coalition. Named a Top Doctor, Chicago Mag., 1997; recipient Sir Samuel Manuwa Gold medal for Excellence in Clin. Sciences, 1980, Scholar award, James S. McDonnell Found., 1992, Doris Duke Disting. Clin. Scientist award, 2000, Phenomenal Women award, 2003, People Are Today's Heroes (PATH), Gov. Rod R. Blagojevich, presented by First Lady Patti Blagojevich, State Ill., 2005, Heroes In Healthcare award, Access Cmty. Network, 2005, Am. Assn. Cancer Rsch. (AACR)-Minorities in Cancer Rsch. Jane Cooke Wright Lectureship, 2006; Ellen Ruth Lebow Fellowship, Assn. for Brain Tumor Rsch., 1990, MacArthur "Genius Grant" Fellow, John D. and Catherine T. MacArthur Found., 2005. Mem. AAAS, Am. Assn. Cancer Rsch. (membership credentialing com. 1994-95, program com. carcinogenesis subcom. 1993), Am. Soc. Clin. Oncology (mem. program com. subcom. tumor biology and genetics 1997, Young Investigator award, 1991), Am. Assn. Preventive Oncology, Women in Cancer Rsch., Am. Soc. Hematology, Am. Coll. Physicians, Am. Soc. Breast Disease, Am. Soc. Hematology, Assn. Am. Professors, Nigerian Med. Assn., Am. Cancer Soc. (adv. com. cancer control investigations, epidemiology, diagnosis, therapy 1994-97). Office: U Chgo Med Ctr 5841 S Maryland Ave # MC2115 Chicago IL 60637-1463 Office Phone: 773-702-1632, 773-702-6149. Office Fax: 773-702-0963. Business E-Mail: folopade@medicine.bsd.uchicago.edu.

O'LOUGHLIN, SANDRA S., lawyer; b. Buffalo, Jan. 15, 1942; BA summa cum laude, Rosary Hill Coll., 1973; JD cum laude, U. Buffalo, 1978. Bar: N.Y. 1979. Atty. Hiscock & Barclay, LLP, Buffalo, 1978-79, ptnr., 1990—. Chmn. character and fitness com. appellate divsn. 4th dept. 8th jud. dist. N.Y. Supreme Ct., 1986—2006; adj. prof. SUNY Law Sch., Buffalo. Note editor Buffalo Law Rev., 1977-78. Mem. Erie County Legis. Task Force Mental Health, 1979-81; mem. adv. bd. Congregation of Sisters of St. Joseph, 1987—. Mem. ABA (bus. law com. on securities), Nat. Assn. Bond Lawyers, N.Y. State Bar Assn. (ethics com. 1984-94, 2000-03, vice chmn. 1987-92, unauthorized practice of law com. 1998-2002, mem. com. on securities regulation 1999—, com. standards atty. conduct 2004—), Erie County Bar Assn. (ethics com. 1984-87, chmn. 1987-89, corp. law com. 1984, grievance com. 1993—). Office: Hiscock & Barclay LLP 1100 M&T Ctr 3 Fountain Plaza Buffalo NY 14203-1414 Business E-Mail: soloughlin@hiscockbarclay.com.

O'LOUGHLIN, VALERIE DEAN, medical educator; m. Robert O'Loughlin; 1 child, Erin. BS, Coll. William & Mary, Williamsburg, Va., 1985—89; MA, Ind. U., Bloomington, 1992, PhD, 1989—95. Assoc. prof., anatomy Med. Scis., Ind. U., Bloomington, 1995—, dir., undergraduate human anatomy, 1998—. Author: (textbook) Human Anatomy. Mem.: Am. Assn. Phys. Anthropologists, Human Anatomy and Physiology Soc., Am. Assn. Anatomists (Basmajian award 2007), Sigma Xi. Office: Med Sci Ind Univ 1001 E 3rd St Bloomington IN 47405 Office Phone: 812-855-7723.

O'LOUGHLIN-BROOKS, JENNIFER L., psychology professor; married; children: Jon, Trenton. BA in Psychology and Speech/Comm., Tex. Christian U., 1991; MS in Exptl. Psychology, Emporia State U., 1994. Assoc. prof. Collin County CC, Tex., 1995—2002, prof. psychology Tex., 2002—. Assoc. editor: Jour. Psychol. Inquiry. Recipient US Prof. of Yr. award, Carnegie Found. for Advancement of Tchg. and Coun. for Advancement and Support of Edn., 2006. Mem.: Tex. Jr. Coll. Tchr.'s Assn., Southwestern Tchrs. of Psychology Assn., Southwestern Psychol. Assn., APA, Psi Beta. Office: Collin County CC 4800 Preston Park Blvd Plano TX 75093 E-mail: jbrooks@ccccd.edu. *

OLSCHAN, JACQUELINE NICOLA, lawyer; b. Bridgeport, Conn., Oct. 26, 1978; d. Andrew H. and Kathryn N. Olschan. BA, Frankling & Marshall Coll., Lancaster, Pa., 2000; JD, NYU, 2003. Bar: Conn. 2003, NY 2004, NJ 2004. Atty. Sandak Hennessey & Greco LLP, Stamford, Conn., 2003—. Mem.: Fed. Bar Assn., NJ Bar Assn., NY Bar Assn., Conn. Bar Assn. Democrat. Avocations: golf, travel, cooking. Office: Sandak Hennessey & Greco LLP 707 Summer St Stamford CT 06901 Office Phone: 203-425-4200. Office Fax: 203-325-8608. Business E-Mail: jolschan@shglaw.com.

OLSCHWANG, ALAN PAUL, lawyer, crossword and variety puzzle author; b. Chgo., Jan. 30, 1942; s. Morton James and Ida (Ginsberg) O.; m. Barbara Claire Miller, Aug. 22, 1965; children: Elliot, Deborah, Jeffrey. BS, U. Ill., Champaign Urbana, 1963, JD, 1966. Bar: Ill. 1966, NY 1984, Calif. 1992. Law clk. Ill. Supreme Ct., Bloomington, 1966-67; assoc. Sidley & Austin and predecessor firm, Chgo., 1967-73; with Montgomery Ward & Co., Inc., Chgo., 1973-81, assoc. gen. counsel, asst. sec., 1979-81; ptnr. Seki, Jarvis & Lynch, Chgo., 1981-84, dir., mem. exec. com.; dir., exec. v.p., gen. counsel Mitsubishi Electric & Electronics USA, Inc. and predecessors, NYC, 1983-91, Cypress, Calif., 1991—. Mem. ABA, Am. Corp. Counsel Assn., Calif. Bar Assn., Ill. Bar Assn., Chgo. Bar Assn., NY State Bar Assn., Am. Arbitration Assn. (panel arbitrators). Office: Mitsubishi Elec & Electronics USA Inc PO Box 6007 5665 Plaza Dr Cypress CA 90630-0007 Business E-Mail: alan.olschwang@meus.mea.com.

OLSCHWANG, DAN, telecommunications industry executive, entrepreneur; Head of products & svcs. Orange, Israel; gen. mgr. Fun divsn. Comverse Tech. Inc., 2001—05; pres. & CEO JumpTap, Inc., Cambridge, Mass., 2005—. Capt. Israeli Air Force. Office: JumpTap Inc Ste 1100 245 First St Cambridge MA 02142 Office Phone: 617-301-4550. E-mail: info@jumptap.com.

OLSEN, ALFRED JON, lawyer; b. Phoenix, Oct. 5, 1940; s. William Hans and Vera (Bearden) O.; m. Susan K. Smith, Apr. 15, 1979. BA in History, U. Ariz., 1962; MS in Acctg., Ariz. State U., 1964; JD, Northwestern U., 1966. Bar: Ariz. 1966, Ill. 1966, U.S. Tax Ct. 1970, U.S. Supreme Ct. 1970; C.P.A., Ariz., Ill. cert. tax specialist. Acct. Arthur Young & Co., C.P.A.s, Chgo., 1966-68; dir. firm Ehmann, Olsen & Lane (P.C.), Phoenix, 1969-76; dir. Streich, Lang, Weeks & Cardon (P.C.), Phoenix, 1977-78; mgr. Olsen-Smith, Ltd., Phoenix, 1978—. Chmn. tax adv. commn. Bd. Legal Specialization, 1990-92. Bd. editors: Jour. Agrl. Law and Taxation, 1978-82, Practical Real Estate Lawyer, 1983-95. Mem. Phoenix adv. bd. Salvation Army., 1973-81. Fellow: Am. Coll. Tax Counsel, Am. Coll. Trust and Estate Counsel (state chair 2002—03, regent 2005—); mem.: ABA (chmn. com. on agr., sect. taxation 1976—78, chmn. CLE com. sect. taxation 1982—84), AICPA, Internat. Acad. Estate and Trust Law (exec. coun. 1994—99), Nat. Cattlemen's Assn. (tax com. 1979—88), Am. Law Inst. (life; chmn. tax planning for agr. 1971—82), Ctrl. Ariz. Estate Planning Coun. (pres. 1972—73), State Bar Ariz., Ariz. Soc. CPAs, Phi Beta Kappa, Phi Kappa Phi, Beta Gamma Sigma, Sigma Nu Internat. (pres. 1986—88). Office: 3300 Virginia Fin Pla 301 E Virginia Ave Phoenix AZ 85004-1218

OLSEN, BEN, professional soccer player; b. Harrisburg, Pa., May 3, 1977; Attended, Univ. Va. Midfielder DC United, 1998—. 34 caps, 6 goals U.S. Nat. Soccer Team, 1998—; mem. U.S. World Cup Team, 2006. Named Player of the Yr., Soccer Am. mag., 1997, Humanitarian of the Yr., U.S. Soccer Found., 2003. Mailing: US Soccer Fedn 1801 S Prairie Ave Chicago IL 60616

OLSEN, DAVID ALEXANDER, insurance executive; b. Bklyn., Nov. 29, 1937; s. Alexander and Meile (Anderson) O.; m. Roberta Ruth Garverick, May 11, 1963; children: Bradford, Amy. With marine dept. Gt. Am. Ins. Co., NYC and Chgo., 1959-62; acct. exec. Johnson & Higgins, San Francisco, 1966-71, v.p., mgr. marine dept. Chgo., 1971-78, exec. v.p. Ill. br., 1978-79, br. mgr., exec. v.p. Houston, 1979-80, chmn., bd. dirs. Tex. br., 1980-85, exec. v.p. NYC, 1985-87, pres., COO, 1987-93, CEO, 1990-97, chmn., 1991—97; dir. Marsh & McLennan, NYC, 1997—. Bd. dirs. U.S. Trust Corp. Trustee Bowdoin Coll., South St. Seaport Mus., Salisbury (Conn.) Congl. Ch., Vis. Nurse Assn., Landmark Vols. 1st lt. U.S. Army, 1960-62. Mem. India House, Sharon Country Club, Psi Upsilon. Avocations: art, photography, antiques, scuba diving, tennis, skiing.

OLSEN, DOROTHY S., music educator; d. J. F. and Ebba V. Anderson Swenson; children: Donald Bruce, Linda Christine. BS, NYU, NYC, 1940, MA, 1946. Dir. music, Piermont, NY, 1941—43, Ft. Edward, NY, 1943—44; music tchr. Pub. Sch. 39, NY, 1946—52, Herricks Pub. Schs., New Hyde Park, NY, 1966—79; music coord. NYC Boro Richmond, 1952—53; adj. prof. music Queens Coll., NY, 1990—96; music dir. organ & choir St. Paul's Episcopal Ch., Great Neck, NY, 1990—. Mem.: Am. Guild Organists, NY State Ret. Tchrs. Home: 427 Wilson Blvd Mineola NY 11501-1027

OLSEN, EDWARD JOHN, geologist, educator, curator; b. Chgo., Nov. 23, 1927; s. Edward John and Elizabeth (Bornemann) O.; children—Andrea, Ericka. AB, U. Chgo., 1951, MS, 1955, PhD, 1959. Geologist Geol. Survey Can., 1953, U.S. Geol. Survey, 1954—, Canadian Johns-Manville Co., Ltd., 1956, 57, 59; asst. prof. Case Inst. Tech., also Western Res. U., 1959-60; curator mineralogy Field Mus. Natural History, 1960-91, chmn. dept. geology, 1974-78; research assoc. prof. dept. geophys. scis. U. Chgo., 1977—. Adj. prof. U. Ill., Chgo. Circle, 1970-91. Assoc. editor Geochim. et Cosmochim. Acta., 1985-91. Fellow Mineral. Soc. Am.; mem. Mineral. Assn. Can., Geochem. Soc., Meteoritical Soc. Achievements include spl. research stability relations of minerals in earth's mantle and meteorites. Home: 437 Wild Indigo Ln Madison WI 53717-2148 Office: U Chgo Dept Geophys Sci Chicago IL 60637

OLSEN, ELISE, dermatologist, researcher; BA, U. Tex., 1974; MD, Baylor U., 1978. Diplomate Am. Bd. Dermatology, N.C. Med. Bd. Asst. prof. Duke U., Durham, NC, 1985—91, assoc. prof., 1991—99, prof., 1999—. Cons. in field; mem. sci. adv. bd. NAAF, Calif.; mem. com. misconduct rsch. Duke U., Durham. Editor: Hair Disorders: Diagnosis & Treatment, 1984, 2003; assoc. editor: Derm Therapy, 1995—, asst. editor: Jour. Am. Acad. Dermatology, 1998—. Mem.: So. Consortium Dermatology (chmn. steering com. 1991—, pres.), Internat. Soc. Cutaneous Lymphomas (past pres.), N.Am. Hair Rsch. Soc., N.C. Dermatologic Assn., Am. Dermatologic Assn. Office: Duke U Med Ctr Box 3294 DUMC Durham NC 27710

OLSEN, FRANCES ELISABETH, law educator, theorist; b. Chgo., Feb. 4, 1945; d. Holger and Ruth Mathilda (Pfeifer) O.; m. Harold Irving Porter, June 8, 1984. Cert., Roskilde (Denmark) Højskole, 1967; BA, Goddard Coll., 1968; JD, U. Colo., 1971; SJD, Harvard U., 1984. Bar: Colo. 1972, U.S. Dist. Ct. Colo. 1972. Law clk. hon. Arraj U.S. Dist. Ct. Colo., Denver, 1972; lawyer Am. Indian Movement, Wounded Knee, S.D., 1973; pvt. practice Denver, 1973-74; law prof. U. Puget Sound, Tacoma, Wash., 1975-79, St. John's U., Jamaica, N.Y., 1982-83, UCLA, 1984—. Vis. fellow New Coll., Oxford (Eng.) U., 1987; vis. prof. U. Mich., Ann Arbor, 1988, Harvard U., Cambridge, Mass., 1990-91, U. Berlin, Germany, 1995, Ochanomizu U., Tokyo, 1997, U. Tokyo, 1997, Cornell U., 1997, French U. Reunion, 2000, Hebrew U. Jerusalem, 2001, Haifa U., 2001, Tel Aviv U., 2001, 2002, Addis Ababa U., 2002, Bar Ilan U., 2002, Alberto Hurtado U., Santiago, Chile, 2004; sr. Fulbright prof. U. Frankfurt, Germany, 1991-92; overseas fellow Churchill Coll., Cambridge, Eng., 1997-99; mem. faculty law Cambridge U., 1997-99; del. UN 4th World Conf. on Women, Beijing, China, 1995, NGO Forum, Huairou, China, 1995. Co-author: Cases and Materials on Family Law: Legal Concepts and Changing Human Relationships, 1994; editor: Feminist Legal Theory I: Foundations and Outlooks, 1995, Feminist Legal Theory II: Positioning Feminist Theory Within the Law, 1995; contbr. articles to law revs. Named Outstanding Alumnus U. Colo., 1989. Mem. Assn. Am. Law Schs. (chair jurisprudence sect. 1987-88, chair women in law tchg. sect. 1995-96), Conf. on Critical Legal Studies, European Conf. Critical Legal Studies, Internat. Bar Assn. Avocations: scuba diving, kayaking, hiking. Office: UCLA Sch Law 405 Hilgard Ave Los Angeles CA 90095-1476 Home Phone: 310-475-6225; Office Phone: 310-825-6083. E-mail: olsen@law.ucla.edu.

OLSEN, GREGORY H., fiber optic manufacturing executive, researcher; b. Bklyn., 1945; 2 children. BS in physics; BSEE in physics, Fairleigh Dickinson U., MS in physics magna cum laude; PhD in materials sci., U. Va., 1971. Tech. staff RCA Lab. (now Sarnoff Corp.), Princeton, NJ, 1972—83; founder, pres., CEO EPITAXX Inc. (acquired by Nippon Sheet Glass, 1990 and by JDS Uniphase, 1999), 1984; co-founder Sensors Unlimited, Inc. (acquired by Finisar Corp., 2000, bought back 2002), Princeton, 1991; pres., CEO Sensors Unlimited, Inc., Princeton, 1991—2000, 2002—, pres., 2000—02; chmn. bd. dirs. Sensors Unlimited Inc.; officer, dir. Finisar Corp., 2000—02. Vis. scientist physics dept. U. Port Elizabeth, South Africa; lectr. in field; bd. dir. Princeton Power Sys., Achieve 3000, Eye Response Tech. Author over 100 papers, co-author several books on crystal growth and semiconductor devices; contbr. articles for trade jour. Investor NJ Tech. Coun. Venture Fund; adv. com. Princeton U., U. So. Calif. Photonics Ctr., U. Fla. Microelectronics Ctr., U. Va., City Coll. NY. Named Inventor Yr., NJ Inst. Tech., NJ Small Bus. Person Yr., US Small Bus. Adminstrn., Entrepreneur Yr., Arthur Young/Inc. Mag.; recipient Young Authors award, Am. Assn. Crystal Growth. Mem.: NJ Crystal Growth Assn., IEEE Laser & Electro-Optics Soc. (LEOS) (bd. gov., Aron Kressel award, named disting. leader), IEEE (fellow, named disting. leader), IEEE Electro, Electrochemical Soc., Internat. Soc. Optical Engring. (SPIE). Achievements include 12 US patents; named next Pvt. Space Explorer in 2003. Third civilian in history to visit the International Space Station (Soyuz TMA-7 spacecraft, Baikonur Cosmodrome, Kazakhstan) in 2005. Office: Sensors Unlimited Inc 3490 Rt 1 Bldg 12 Princeton NJ 08540-5914 Office Phone: 609-520-0610. Office Fax: 609-520-1663. Business E-Mail: golsen@sensorinc.com.

OLSEN, HANS PETER, lawyer; b. Detroit, May 21, 1940; s. Hans Peter and Paula M. (Olsen) O.; m. Elizabeth Ann Gayton, Sept. 14, 1968; children: Hans Peter, Heidi Susanne, Stephanie Elizabeth BA, Mich. State U., 1961; JD, Georgetown U., 1965; LLM, NYU, 1966. Bar: Mich. 1967, Pa. 1969, R.I. 1974. Law clk. Monaghan, McCrone, Campbell & Crawmer, Detroit, 1964, U.S. Ct. of Claims, Fed. Appellate Ct., Washington, 1966—68; assoc. Pepper, Hamilton & Scheetz, Phila., 1968—72; ptnr. Hinckley, Allen, & Snyder, Providence, 1974—. Adv. planning com. U. R.I. Fed. Taxation Inst.; continuing legal edn. adv. bd., tax symposium adv. bd. Bryant Coll.; mem. Gov.'s State Task Force, R.I. Pub. Expenditure Coun.; cons. Bur. Nat. Affairs; liaison Bar Assn. and North Atlantic region IRS; tax adminstrs. adv. com. R.I.; lectr. tax insts. and other profl. groups N.Y., L.A., Phila., Boston, R.I.; advisor R.I. Econ. Policy com. Contbr. articles to profl. jours. Fellow Am. Bar Found.; mem. ABA (sect. taxation, exempt orgns. com., subcom. healthcare, corp.-shareholders rels. com., partnerships com.), R.I. Bar Assn. (sect. taxation, sec.-treas. 1977-80, liaison with CPAs, specialization com., mem. various coms.), Providence C. of C., R.I. C. of C. (chmn. com. on bus. taxes and public spending, mem., past chmn. legis. action council), Mich. State Bar, Pa. State Bar, RI Bar Assn. Home: 274 Olney St Providence RI 02906-2305 Office: 28 State St Boston MA 02109-1775 also: 43 N Main St Concord NH 03301-4934 also: 50 Kennedy Plz Ste 1500 Providence RI 02903 Office Phone: 401-274-2000. Personal E-mail: hpeterolsen@cox.net. Business E-Mail: holsen@haslaw.com.

OLSEN, HAROLD FREMONT, lawyer; b. Davenport, Wash., Oct. 17, 1920; s. Oscar E. and Dorothy (Sprowls) O.; m. Jeanne L. Rounds, Aug. 30, 1942; children: Eric O., Ronald R., Margaret Ruth. BA, Wash. State U., 1942; LLB, Harvard U., 1948. Bar: Wash. 1948, U.S. Ct. Claims 1970, U.S. Supreme Ct. 1982; CPA, Wash. Instr. Oxford Bus. Sch., Cambridge, Mass., 1946-47; examiner Wash. State Dept. Pub. Utilities, 1948; with firm Perkins Coie (and predecessors), Seattle, 1949—, ptnr., 1954-88, of counsel, 1989—. Trustee Exec. Svcs. Corp. Wash., 1990-96. Bd. dirs. Northwest Hosp. Found., Northwest Hosp., 1980-90; trustee Wash. State U. Found., chmn. 1986-88; mem. adv. coun. Wash. State U. Sch. Bus. and Econs., 1978-90; trustee, mem. exec. com., pres. Mus. of Flight, 1991-92, chmn., 1993; trustee Horizon House, 1994-97. Maj. USAAF, 1942-45, NATOUSA, Mid. East, ETO. Decorated Silver Star. Mem. ABA, Wash. Bar Assn., Seattle Bar Assn., Aircraft Industry Assn. (chmn. legal com. 1957), Phi Beta Kappa, Phi Kappa Phi, Tau Kappa Epsilon, Rainier Club, Queenstown (New Zealand) Golf Club, Seattle Golf Club (pres. 1986-87), Sr. N.W. Golf Assn. Congregationalist. Home: 8875 Overlake Dr W Medina WA 98039-5347 Office: 1201 3rd Ave Ste 4500 Seattle WA 98101-3029 Office Phone: 206-359-8503. Personal E-mail: holsen@seanet.com. Business E-Mail: holsen@perkinscoie.com.

OLSEN, HARRIS LELAND, diplomat, writer, real estate company executive, educator; b. Rochester, NH, Dec. 8, 1947; s. Harries Edwin and Eva Alma (Turmelle) O.; m. Mimi Kwi Sun Yi, Mar. 15, 1953; children: Garin Lee, Gavin Yi, Sook Ja. AS, SUNY, Albany, 1983, BS, 1988; MA in Polit. Sci., U. Hawaii, 1990; PhD in Internat. Bus. Adminstrn., Kennedy Western U., Idaho, 1993. Enlisted USN, 1967, advanced through grades to, served in various nuclear power capacities Conn., 1971-76, Hawaii, 1976-87, ret., 1987; v.p. Waiono Land Corp., Honolulu, 1981-92, dir., 1993-95; v.p. Asian Pacific Electricity, Honolulu, 1988-89, Kapano Land Assocs., Honolulu, 1988-92, 94-95, MLY Networks, Inc., Honolulu, 1989-99, THO Consultants Corp., 1991—2002, Clarix Internat. Corp., 1994; consulate gen. Papua New Guinea, 1996—2002. Staff cons. Mariner-Icemakers, Honolulu, 1982-84, Transpacific Energy Corp., Honolulu, 1982-84; dir. Asian Pacific Devel. Bank, 1983; sr. cons. Western Rsch. Assocs., Honolulu, 1984-87, 94-95; quality assurance cons. Asian Pacific, Inc., Honolulu, 1987-88; instr., lectr. Asian history and culture U. Chaminade in Honolulu, 1991; nuclear reactor plant specialist Pearl Harbor Emergency Recall Team, 1991-95; instr. nuclear reactor theory Pearl Harbor, Hawaii, 1992-95; v.p. Schwartz, Inc., 1992-98, dir. Schwartz Jewelry Sch., 1996-98; cons. Waiono/Kapano Devel. Co., 1993; bd. dirs., sec. Pacific Internat. Engring. Corp., 1994-95; Keiretsu sec. Global Ocean Cons., Inc. and Assocs., 1994-95; joint venture Premier Fisheries Pty. Ltd., Papua New Guinea, 1995-98; cons. BFD Devel. Group, 1995-96; co-drafter Nat. Tuna Industry Devel. Plan for Papua New Guinea, 1995; quality analyst, Pearl Harbor, 1995; rep. for Min. for Fisheries, Papua New Guinea, Bi-lateral Fisheries Access Rights Japan and Papua New Guinea, 1996-97, drafter Bi-Lateral Fishing Treaty Japan and Papua New Guinea, 1996; U.S. del. to 4th World Tuna Conf., Manila, 1995, U.S. del. to 5th Aquatic Coninent Conf., Maui, Hawaii, 1995, 6th, 1996; apptd. rep. Abau Electorate, Papua New Guinea Timber Sales, 1995-98; apptd. hon. consul gen. and trade rep., dep. trade min. for Govt. of Papua New Guinea in Honolulu, 1996-2001; bd. dirs. Island Art; cons. Pew Global Devel. Corp., 1998-99, Niugini Enterprises LLC, 1999-2001, Niugini Millenium Co., Ltd., 1999-2001. Author: The Price for Gold, 2002, Candi, 2003, Sialon, 2003, Small Prices, 2004, Silent, 2004, Emergence, 2005, Dark Water August, 2005, Emergence 2, 2007; co-host: Hyscience Blog, 2005—; contbr. articles to profl. jours. Head coach USN Men's Softball, Honolulu, 1978-79; pres. Pearl Harbor (Hawaii) Welfare and Recreation Com., 1983-84; mem. Rep. Senatorial Inner Cir.; commd. hon. consul gen. Ind. State Papua New Guinea, 1996; mem. Consular Corps of Hawaii, 1997-2001. Named Alumnus of Yr., Kennedy Western U., 1993; recipient Citation of Leadership, Rep. Nat. Com., 1996, Letter of Commendation for Svc. During Aitape Tidal Wave Disaster in Papua New Guinea, 1998; selected to represent Hawaii at Presdl. Inauguration, Rep. Leadership U.S. Senate, 2001. Mem.: Nat. Assn. Scholars, Navy League, Delta Epsilon Sigma. Republican. Roman Catholic and Buddhist. Achievements include invention of alternate power supply sys. Avocations: chess, philosophy, japanese haiku poetry, native american cultures. Home and Office: 94 1025 Anania Cir Apt 56 Mililani HI 96789-2045 Personal E-mail: HarryTho@aol.com.

OLSEN, INGER ANNA, retired psychologist; b. Copper Mountain, BC, Can., Dec. 25, 1926; BS, Wash. State U., 1954, MS, 1956, PhD, 1962. Psychiat. nurse Provincial Mental Health Svcs. B.C., 1947-51, psychologist, 1956-58, Vancouver (B.C.) City Met. Health Svcs., 1958-60; psychologist Student Counseling Ctr., Wash. State U., Pullman, 1960—62; sr. psychologist Met. Health Svcs., Vancouver, 1962-66; instr. psychology Langara Coll., Vancouver, B.C., 1966—87; ret., 1987. Contbr. articles to profl. jours. Docent Vancouver Aquarium Assn.; bd. dirs. Second Mile Soc., 1975—89. Mem. APA, Gerontol. Soc. Am., Can. Assn. Gerontology, Phi Beta Kappa, Sigma Xi, Alpha Kappa Delta. Home: 1255 Bidwell St Apt 1910 Vancouver BC Canada V6G 2K8

OLSEN, JODY (JOSEPHINE K. OLSEN), federal agency administrator; B, U. Utah; MSW, PhD, U. Md. Vol. Peace Corps, Tunisia, 1966—68, various positions incuding chief of staff, regional dir. North Africa, Near East, Asia and the Pscific, country dir. Togo, 1979—84, 1989—92; exed. dirs. Coun. Internat. Exch. of Scholars, 1992—97; sr. v.p., dir. Peace Corps, Washington, 1997—2002, dep. dir., 2002—, acting dir., 2006. Office: Peace Corps 1111 20th St NW Washington DC 20526-0001

OLSEN, KATHIE LYNN, science foundation director; b. Portland, Oreg., Aug. 3, 1952; d. Roland Berg and Gladys Elizabeth (Eldreth) O. BS, Chatham Coll., 1974; PhD, U. Calif., Irvine, 1979. Postdoct. fellow Harvard Med. Sch., Boston, 1979-80; rsch. scientist Long Island Rsch. Inst., Stony Brook, N.Y., 1980-83; rsch. asst. prof. SUNY, Stony Brook, 1982-85, asst. prof., 1985-89; assoc. program dir. NSF, Washington, 1984-86, program dir., 1988, leader neurosci., 1991; legis. fellow Brookings Instn., Washington, 1996—97; chief scientist NASA, 1999—2002; acting assoc. adminstr. Enterprise in Biological and Physical Research, 2000—02; assoc. director, tech. Off. Science & Tech. Policy, Washington, 2002—05; dep. dir. NSF, Washington, 2005—. Adj. assoc. prof. George Washington U., Washington, 1989—; cons. editor Hormones and Behavior, 1988—. Contbr. articles to profl. jours, chapters to books. Recipient Dir. Superior Accomplishmentaward, NSF, Barry M. Goldwater Educator award, Am. Inst. of Aeronautics & Astronautics -Nat. Capital Section, Outstanding Leadership medal, NASA, Internat. Behavioral Neuroscience Soc. award, Soc. for Behavioral Endocrinology award, Barnard medal of Distinction. Mem. Soc. Neurosci., Endocrine Soc., Women in Neurosci., Sod. Study of Reproduction, Internat. Acad. Sex Rsch. Office: NSF 4201 Wilson Blvd Arlington VA 22230

OLSEN, KENNETH HAROLD, geophysicist, astrophysicist, historian; b. Ogden, Utah, Feb. 20, 1930; s. Harold Reuben and Rose (Hill) O.; m. Barbara Ann Parson, June 15, 1955; children: Susan L., Steven K., Christopher P., Richard S. BS, Idaho State Coll., 1952; MS, Calif. Inst. Tech., 1954, PhD, 1957. Grad. rsch. asst. Calif. Inst. Tech., Mt. Wilson and Palomar Obs., Pasadena, 1952-57; staff mem., group leader Los Alamos (N.Mex.) Nat. Lab., 1957-89, lab. assoc., 1989-95; geophys. cons. Lynnwood, Wash., 1989—. Vis. rsch. fellow Applied Seismol. Group, Swedish Nat. Def. Inst., Stockholm, Sweden, 1983; sr. vis. scientist fellow Norwegian Seismic Array, Oslo, Norway, 1983; vis. scholar Geophysics Program, U. Wash., Seattle, 1989-91. Author, editor: Continental Rifts: Evolution, Structure, Tectonics, 1995; contbr. articles to profl. jours. Mem. Am. Geophys. Union, Geol. Soc. Am., Seismol. Soc. Am., Am. Astron. Soc., Royal Astron. Soc. Home: 1029 187th Pl SW Lynnwood WA 98036-4986 Personal E-mail: barbolsen@verizon.net.

OLSEN, M. KENT, lawyer, educator; b. Denver, Mar. 10, 1948; s. Marvin and F. Winona (Wilker) O.; m. Shauna L. Casement; children: Kristofor Anders, Alexander Lee, Nikolaus Alrik, Amanda Elizabeth. BS, Colo. State U., 1970; JD, U. Denver, 1975. Bar: Colo. 1982, U.S. Dist. Ct. Colo. 1982, U.S. Tax Ct. Law clk. Denver Probate Ct., 1973-75; assoc. ptnr. Johnson & McLachlan, Lamar, Colo., 1975-80; assoc. Buchanan, Thomas and Johnson, Lakewood, Colo., 1981-82, William E. Myrick, P.C., Denver, 1982-83; referee Denver Probate Ct., Denver, 1983-89; ptnr. Haines & Olsen, P.C., Denver, 1989-95; pvt. practice Denver, 1995—2001; ptnr. Olsen & Traeger, LLP, 2001—. Adv. bd. Denver Career Coll., 1993—2004, Elder Law Inst., 1994—. Active Gov.'s Commn. on Life and the Law, Denver, 1991-2000; bd. dirs. Adult Care Mgmt., Inc., Denver, 1985-95, Colo. Guardianship Alliance, Denver, 1990-91, Arc of Denver, Inc., 1990—, pres., 1995-97, 2004-06; bd. dirs. Colo. Fund for People with Disabilities, 1994—, pres., 1994-2000. Recipient Outstanding Vol. Svc. award Adult Care Mgmt., 1990, Outstanding Svc. award The Arc of Denver, 1991, Vol. Svc. award Colo. Gerontol. Soc., 1997, Pres.'s award Arc of Denver, 1998, 2002; named one of Colo. Super Lawyers, Law and Politics, 2006, 07. Mem. ABA, Colo. Bar Assn. (past chair probate sect.), First Jud. Dist. Bar Assn., Nat. Acad. Elder Law Attys., Colo. Assn. Homes and Svcs. to the Aging, Denver Bar Assn., Denver Estate Planning Coun., Denver C. of C. Avocations: running, skiing, racquetball, art, hiking. Home: 3030 S Roslyn St Denver CO 80231-4153 Office: 650 S Cherry St Ste 850 Denver CO 80246-1805 Home Phone: 303-306-6185; Office Phone: 303-329-4670. Business E-Mail: mkolsen@olsentraeger.com.

OLSEN, MARTIN E., obstetrician, educator; b. Morgantown, W.Va., 1959; m. Natalie Ann Maschmann, June 25, 1985; 1 child, Karen Rebeca. BS, Muskingum Coll., New Concord, 1981; MD, Med. Coll. Ohio, Toledo, 1981. Diplomate Am. Bd. Ob-Gyn., Am. Bd. Family Practice. Resident in family practice Akron (Ohio) Gen. Med. Ctr., 1985-88; resident in ob-gyn. U. Tenn., Chattanooga, 1989-91; mem. faculty E. Tenn. State U., Johnson City, 1992—, chmn. dept. ob-byn., 1999—; dir. residency program Johnson City Med. Ctr., 1994—. Contbr. articles to profl. jours. Office: PO Box 70569 Johnson City TN 37614-1707 Office Phone: 423-439-8097. Business E-Mail: olsen@etsu.edu.

OLSEN, PATRICE ELIZABETH, history professor, photographer; d. Albert R. and Mary Elizabeth Olsen. AB, U. Ill., Urbana, 1980; MA, Pa. State U., Univ. Pk., 1991, PhD, 1998. Asst. prof. Stephen F. Austin U., Nagadoches, Tex., 1998—2000, Ill. State U., Normal, 2000—06, assoc. prof., 2006—. Dir. Cuban study tours Dept. History Ill. State U., Normal, 2002—, dir. grad. studies, 2004—. Author: Artifacts of Revolution, 2006 (Lewis Hanke prize, 1999, Meyer prize, 2003). Named Outstanding Coll. Tchr., Coll. Arts and Scis. Ill. State U., 2004—05; recipient Faculty Tchg. Initiative award, Ill. State U., 2002—03. Mem.: L.Am. Studies Assn., Conf. L.Am. History, Southwest Conf. L.Am. Studies. Office: Ill State U Dept History 301 Schroeder Hall Normal IL 61790

OLSEN, R. NILLS, dean, law educator; BA, U. Wis., 1969; JD, Columbia U. Sch. Law, 1974. Law clerk to Chief Justice Thomas E. Fairchild Seventh Cir. U.S. Ct. Appeals, Chgo.; law lectr. and clin. fellow U. Chgo. Sch. Law; assoc. prof. U. Buffalo Law Sch., SUNY, 1978, vice dean, 1994—98, dean, 1998—, dir. clin. edn. Mem. Lewiston-Porter sch. bd.; bd. dirs. N.Y. State Environmental Activists, Youngstown Free Libr., Great Lakes United. Office: U Buffalo Law Sch SUNY 319 O'Brian Hall, N Campus Buffalo NY 14260-1100 E-mail: nolsen@buffalo.edu.

OLSEN, RANDY J., university librarian; b. Logan, Utah; BA, Utah State U.; MLS, Brigham Young U., 1973, MPA, 1981. German cataloguer Harold B. Lee Libr. Brigham Young U., Provo, 1972, asst. univ. libr. collection devel. and pub. svcs., asst. univ. libr. budget and adminstrv. svcs., dep. univ. libr., univ. libr., 2002—. Mem.: Utah Academic Libr. Coun., Mountain Plains Libr. Assn., Am. Libr. Assn., Utah Libr. Assn. (past pres.). Office: Brigham Young U Harold B Lee Libr PO Box 26800 Provo UT 84602-6800 Office Phone: 801-422-2905. E-mail: randy_olsen@byu.edu. *

OLSEN, REX NORMAN, trade association executive; b. Hazeltown, Idaho, Apr. 9, 1925; s. Adolph Lars and Pearl (Robbins) O. B.J., BA in English, U. Mo., 1950. Editor Clissold Pub. Co., Chgo., 1950-54; copy editor Am. Peoples Ency., Chgo., 1955; asst. editor Am. Hosp. Assn., Chgo., 1956-59, mng. editor, 1959-64, dir. jours. div., 1964-69, dir. publs. bur., 1969-75, exec. editor, asso. pub., 1975-79; v.p., treas. Am. Hosp. Pub., Inc., 1980-85; pres. Words Ltd., 1985—. Dir. publs. ETNA Comms., Chgo., 1997—. Served with USNR, 1943-46. Mem. Soc. Nat. Assn. Pubs (sec. 1975-76, 2d v.p. 1976-77, 1st v.p. 1977-78, pres. 1978-79), Chgo. Bus. Publs. Assn. (dir. 1974-78, 4th v.p. 1978-79), Sigma Delta Chi. Home and Office: 5510 N Sheridan Rd Unit 12-A Chicago IL 60640-1630 Personal E-mail: rexorudy@aol.com.

OLSEN, RICHARD JAMES, artist, educator; b. Milw., Nov. 15, 1935; s. Edward Marinus and Ann Frances (Keymar) Olsen; m. Nina Marsh Civilette-Olsen, July 25, 1969; children: Dayna Kim, Dawn Beth(dec.), Josh Keymar. BS, U. Wis., 1958, MFA in Painting and Printmaking, 1966. Tchg. asst. U. Wis., 1965-66; art tchr. grade 8 Winnequah Grade Sch., Monona, Wis., 1966-67; instr. printmaking Oper. Area Arts, Green Bay, Wis., 1967-69; from instr. painting and drawing to prof. emeritus U. Ga., Athens, 1969—2000, Gen. Sandy Beaver tchg. prof., 1998—2000, emeritus prof., 2001—; represented by Berman Gallery, Atlanta, 1986-97, Novus Inc., Atlanta, 1990—, Maurine Littleton Gallery, Washington, 1990, Miriam Perlman Gallery, Chgo., 1991, EDL & Assocs., Atlanta, 1994, Elements of Art, Columbus, Ohio, 1995, Ellen Wallace-Paushter, Art Cons., Chgo., 1999, Mercury Art Works, Athens, Ga., 2001—. Wrestling coach Monona Grove (Wis.) H.S., 1966-67; panelist Steinham Arts Festival St. Lawrence U., N.Y., 1987, Crossroads in Cultural Studies, Tampere, Finland, 1996; head praparator Reflexes and Reflections Russell Rotunda Capitol Hill, Washington, 1983, Lincoln Ctr., N.Y.C., 1984. One-man shows include Claywork Gallery, Atlanta, 1986, H. Smith Gallery U. SC, Spartanburg, 1991, Nat. Vietnam Vets. Art Mus., Chgo., 1999, Mercury Art Works, Athens, Ga., 2003, Floataway Complex, Atlanta, 2005, Augusta State U., Ga., 2007, numerous group shows including most recently, exhibited in group shows at Peace Mus., Chgo., 2002, Aurora (Ill.) Hist. Ctr., 2003, U. N.Mex., 2004, Children of War, Nat. Vietnam Vets. Art Mus., 2005, Wis. Vets. Mus., Madison, 2006, Athens Acad., Ga., 2007, Represented in permanent collections Nat. Vietnam Vets. Art Mus., Chgo., Nat. Mus. Fine Art, Hanoi, Vietnam., Ga. Mus. of Art, Athens, Ga., Ga. World Congress Ctr., Atlanta, U. Ga. Complex Carbohydrate Rsch. Ctr., Bank South Ga., Tifton, Ga., Western Carolina U., Oullowhee, NC; featured (in over 150 mags.). With U.S. Army, 1959-63, Vietnam. Decorated Purple heart, 1963; Visual Arts fellow So. Arts Fdn./NEA, 1988; Sr. Faculty grantee U. Ga. Rsch. Found., Inc., 1991-93, 96-98, Individual Artist grantee Ga. Coun. Arts, 1993-94; recipient Purchase award 8th Annual Maine/Maritime Internat. Flatworks Exhibn., 1990, Merit award Three Works 29th Juried Exbhn., Lyndon House Arts Center, Athens, Ga., 2004. Mem. VFW, Mil. Order of the Purple Heart (comdr. 1999-2000), Vietnam Helicopter Pilots Assn. Home: 165 Springdale St Athens GA 30605-1237 Office Phone: 706-540-2937. Personal E-mail: richard.j.olsen@att.net.

OLSEN, ROBERT C., JR., academic administrator, military officer; b. Bklyn. m. Maureen Olsen; 2 children. BS, USCG Acad., 1969; MS in Adminstrn., U.S. Naval Postgrad. Sch., Monterey, Calif., 1979; MA in Nat. Security and Strategic Studies, Naval War Coll., 1990. Commd. USCG, advanced through grades to rear admiral; exec. officer USCGC Madrona; comdg. officer various cutters USCG; comdt. of cadets USCG Acad., asst. supt., maritime law enforcement and intelligence br. chief for 3d Coast Guard Dist. NY; mgr. surface forces Coast Guard Atlantic Area; detailer for officer assignments USCG Hdqrs., mem. tng. and edn. staff, dir. pers. mgmr.; supt., pres. USCG Acad., New London, Conn., ret., 2005; pres. Webb Inst., Glen Cove, NY, 2005—. Decorated Legion of Merit (3), Meritorious Svc. medal, Coast Guard Commendation medal (4), Humanitarian Svc. medal (2). Office: Webb Inst 298 Crescent Beach Rd Glen Cove NY 11542-1398 Office Phone: 860-444-8285.

OLSEN, STEVEN KENT, dentist; b. Spanish Fork, Utah, Nov. 20, 1944; s. Earl Clarence and Adela (Faux) O.; children: Curt, Christopher, Sara Kate, Vanessa BS, Brigham Young U., 1969; DDS, U. Pacific, 1974. Ptrn. practice dentistry in surg. and endodontics Brooks & Olsen, Salt Lake City, 1974—; gen. practice dentistry Steven K. Olsen, D.D.S., San Francisco, 1974-75; pres. S.K. Olsen, P.C., San Francisco, 1975—; ptnr. Olsen, H. & P., San Francisco, 1977-83; instr. U. Pacific, San Francisco, 1978—, Baylor U., 1978—. Chmn. bd. Am. Dentists Ins. Corp., Grand Cayman, W.I., 1978-81; instr. Stanford (Calif.) Inst., Chabot Coll. Inst., 1979-82; med. staff Latter-day Saints Hosp.; cons. Calif. Inst., San Francisco, 1981—; ptnr. J.B. Devel. Co., Russell Harris Restorations, Ryan Bott Restorations, Jason Herget Restorations, D.W. Mmgt. Co., Bob Steck Mgmt. Co., Dave Olsen & Co.; chmn. bd., pres. R.O.R., 1977-80; bd. dirs. Wilks & Topper, Inc., San Francisco, Curt Facchino Ltd., Woodside. Author: Accolade, 1963, (play) Lancer Ballade, 1963, (acad. course) World Religions, 1979; editor corr. course Calif. Inst., 1981. Recipient Good Citizenship medal SAR, 1963, Golden State award, 1988, others. Mem. Assn. Coll. of Physicians and Surgeons, ADA, Calif. Dental Assn., Utah Dental Assn., Physicians and Surgeons Club (San Francisco), Alpha Epsilon Delta. Home: 385 Old La Honda Rd Woodside CA 94062-2617 Office: 2 Embarcadero Ctr Promenade San Francisco CA 94111

OLSEN, THOMAS RICHARD, SR., air force officer; b. Houston, June 28, 1934; s. Oscar Leonard and Catherine (Byers) O.; children: Thomas Richard Jr., Lisa Kendrick Olsen Wesolick; m. Jacquelyn Beasley Keels, June 28, 1998. BSME, Tex. A&M U., 1956; MS in Internat. Affairs, George Washington U., 1968. Mech. engr. Tex. Gas Corp., Houston, 1956; commd. 2d lt. USAF, 1957, advanced through grades to maj. gen., 1986; pilot trainee Greenville AFB, Miss., 1957-58; fighter pilot 326 FIS/526 FIS, U.S. and Fed. Republic Germany, 1958-65, 614 TFS/615 TFS, England AFB, La., 615 TFS, Phan Rang AB, Vietnam, 1966-67; instr. U.S. Naval Amphibious Sch., Coronado, Calif., 1968-71; fighter pilot 391 TFS, Mt. Home AFB, Idaho, 1971-72, squadron ops. officer, squadron comdr., 1972-74; chief rated officer Mgmt. Hdqrs. AFMPC, Randolph AFB, Tex., 1975-78; chief of staff Hdqrs. 9th Air Force, Shaw AFB, SC, 1978-79; dep. comdr. Hdqrs. 314th Air Div., Seoul, Republic of Korea, 1979-81; dir. ops. Hdqrs. 5th Air Force, Yokota AFB, Japan, 1981-82; wing comdr. 51 TFW, Osan AB, Republic of Korea, 1982-83; dep. dir. ops. Hdqrs. Pacific Command, Camp Smith, Hawaii, 1983-85; asst. chief of staff ops. Hdqrs. AFCENT, NATO, Brunsuum, The Netherlands, 1985-87; dep. comdr., chief of staff Hdqrs. 4 ATAF, NATO, Heidelberg, Fed. Republic Germany, 1987-89; vice comdr. Hdqrs. 9th Air Force, Shaw AFB, SC, 1989-91; dep. comdr. U.S. Cen. Command Air Forces (Desert Shield/Desert Storm), Riyadh, Saudi Arabia, 1990-91; ret., 1991. Exec. dir. Sumter Base Defense Com., 1994—. Mem. Optimist Club, Coronado, 1969-71. Mem. Air Force Assn., Ret. Officers Assn., Daedalians, Kiwanis, Rotary. Baptist. Home: 3030 Lowfalls Ln Sumter SC 29150-2337 Business E-Mail: tolsen@ftc-i.net.

OLSHAKER, MARK BRUCE, scriptwriter, filmmaker; b. Washington, Feb. 28, 1951; s. Bennett and Thelma A. (Abramson) O.; m. Carolyn M. Clemente, Aug. 28, 1977. BA, George Washington U., Washington, 1972. Spl. correspondent St. Louis Post Dispatch, Washington Bur., 1974-75; writer, author, film maker Washington Area, 1972—. V.p. Unicorn Projects, Inc., Washington, 1983—, Mindhunters, Inc. Vienna, Va., 1995—; bd. dirs. Shakespeare Guild, Washington. Author: (novels) Einstein's Brain, 1981, Unnatural Causes, 1986, Blood Race, 1989, The Edge, 1994, Mindhunters: Broken Wings, 1999; (anthology) Unusual Suspects, 1996; (non-fiction) The Instant Image, 1978; co-author (with John Douglas), Mindhunter, 1995 (Anthony award nomination, Brit. Gold Dagger nomination, Edgar nomination, Mystery Writers of Am.), Unabomber: On the Trail of America's Most-Wanted Serial Killer, 1996, Journey into Darkness, 1997, Obsession, 1998, The Anatomy of Motive, 1999, The Cases That Haunt Us, 2000; (with C.J. Peters) Virus Hunter, 1997; contbr. (textbook) Forensic Emergency Medicine; (screen writing) Stormchasers, 1995, (CINE Golden Eagle), The Edge, 1996 (TV Writing and Prodn.) We All Came to America, 1974, A Moment in Time, 1975, Patent Pending, 1975 (silver medal Inst. Film & TV Festival N.Y.), Lewis Mumford: Toward Human Architecture, 1979, Castle, 1983 (Am. Film Festival Red Ribbon), Cathedral, 1985 (Am. Film Festival Blue Ribbon, Cine Golden Eagle) Pyramid, 1988 (CINE Golden Eagle, Nat. Ednl. Film and Video Festival Gold Apple), What's Killing the Children?, 1990, Discovering Hamlet, 1990 (Am. Film Festival Red Ribbon, Bronze medal Inst. Film & TV Festival N.Y.), Mind of a

Serial Killer, 1992 (Emmy nomination news and documentary 1993), Roman City, 1994 (Emmy award), Bridge, 1998, Mill Times, 2001, Bioterror: Dealing with a New Reality, 2001, Avoiding Armageddon, 2003, Flashpoints USA: God and Country, 2004; contbr. articles to newspapers, mags., wrote exhibition films for Nat. Park Svc., and Nat. Bicentennial Grand Parade, 1976. Media advisor, NEH, Corp. Pub. Broadcasting, Washington, 1984, 89, 91, 98, DC Comm. Arts and Humanities; hearing com. DC Ct. of Appeal Bd. on Profl. Responsibility, 1988-91; judge Helen Hays Theater Awards, 2007-. Mem. Am. Coll. Forensic Examiners, Writers Guild of Am. East, The Authors Guild, The Cosmos Club, Cosmos Club Found. (chmn.), English-Speaking Union. Office: PO Box 1957 Vienna VA 22183-1957

OLSHAN, BERNARD, artist; b. NYC, Jan. 31, 1921; Student, Am. Artists Sch., NYC, 1937—40, Ozenfant Sch. Fine Arts, 1945—47, Academie de la Grand Chaumiere, Paris, 1948—51. Cultural arts dir. Mosholu Montefiore YMCA/YWCA, NY; instr. Crafts Students League, 1953, NYC CC, 1965—69; teacher, dir., cultural arts dept. Mosholu Montefiore Cmty. Ctr., NYC, 1966—79; chmn., visual arts com. Amalgamated Houses, NYC, 1980—; faculty Nat. Acad., NYC, 1998—. One-man shows include Ward Eggelston Galleries, 1952, 1954, 1958, Grace Coll. Gallery, NY CC, 1969, exhibitions include Pearl St. Gallery, 1965, Whitney Mus., Dallas Mus. of Art. Served in US Army, 1941—45. Recipient Emily Lowe award, 1950, Ralph Mayer Meml. award, 1984, 1987, Andrew Carnegie award, Nat. Acad. Design, 1999. Mem.: Fedn. Modern Painters & Sculptors, Nat. Acad. of Design (Academician), Am. Soc. Contemporary Artists. Office: National Academy Sch 5 E 89th St New York NY 10128 Office Phone: 212-996-1908. Office Fax: 212-426-1711.

OLSHAN, JUDD DAVID, ecologist; s. Marc Allen and Toni Peckham Olshan; m. Hannah Joy Spencer, Sept. 14, 2002. BA in Human Ecology, Coll. of the Atlantic, Bar Harbor, Maine, 1992; MA in Resource Mgmt., Ctrl. Wash. U., 1997; BA in History, SUNY Cortland, 2005. Lic. real estate salesperson Mass., 2001. Tour leader Trek Am., Gardena, Calif., 1994—2000; tchr. Nature's Classroom, Charlton, Mass., 1993—2004; program dir. Regional Environ. Coun., Worcester, Mass., 2000—02; program mgr. Cornell Coop. Ext., Ithaca, NY, 2002—03. Ranger Greater Worcester Land Trust, Worcester, Mass., 2001—02; chair Youth Environ. Svc. Corps Adv. Bd., Worcester, Mass., 2001—02. Contbr. articles to encys. Mem., vol. Greater Worcester Land Trust, 2001—06, Lime Hollow Nature Ctr., Cortland, NY, 2002—06. Recipient Alumni Acheivment awards, SUNY Cortland Alumni Assn., 2004—05, All Coll. Writing award, 2005; fellow Univ. fellow, Syracuse U., 2005—; scholar Adult Learner scholar, SUNY Cortland, 2004. Mem.: Am. Hist. Assn. (assoc.), Alpha Sigma Lambda, Tau Sigma, Phi Alpha Phi, Phi Kappa Phi. Green Party. Avocation: back country canoeing. Home Phone: 607-753-9404; Office Phone: 315-223-2210. E-mail: jolshan@syr.edu.

OLSHEVSKY, GEORGE, editor; b. Karlsruhe, Germany, June 12, 1946; arrived in U.S., 1947; s. George Eugene and Catherine Sergeyevna Olshevsky; m. Andrea Marie Matyas, Aug. 25, 1982. BSc, MIT, Cambridge, Mass., 1967; MSc, U. Toronto, Ontario, Can., 1970. Computer programmer U. Toronto Computer Ctr., Canada, 1967—77; freelance writer, publisher Official Marvel Comics Index, Toronto, San Diego, Calif., 1976—84; freelance writer The Official Index to Marvel Comics, NYC, 1984—88, Dino Frontline Mag., Tokyo, 1992—96, Dino Press Mag., Tokyo, 2000—02; indexer self employed, 1989—. Author: (book) Mesozoic Meanderings #3, 2000; co-author (cons. with Howard Zimmerman): (children's book) Dinosaurs! The Biggest, Baddest, Strangest, Fastest, 2000; author: Encyclopedia of Dinosaurs, 2001; co-author (cons.): (childrens books series) Discovering Dinosaurs, 2002; contbr. articles to books and mags. on dinosaurs. Office: Publs Requiring Rsch PO Box 161015 San Diego CA 92176-1015 Home Phone: 619-283-5320. Personal E-mail: dinogeorge@aol.com.

OLSON, ALLISON W., social studies educator; b. Provo, Utah, Mar. 4, 1965; d. Donald Jex and Kelly (Duke) Woolley; m. Steven W. Olson, Dec. 15, 1986; children: Christopher, Cameron, Rylee, Paige. BS Elem. Edn. and Spl. Edn., Brigham Young U., Provo, 1988; postgrad., U. Phoenix. Cert. Social Studies Endorsement Colo. Dept. Edn., type D endorsement administr., prin. lic. Resource specialist Highlands Elem. Sch. Salt Lake City Sch. Dist., 1988—89; resource specialist, tchr. 4th grade Bancroft Elem. Sch. LaMesa/Spring Valley Sch. Dist., San Diego, 1991—94; tchr. 5th grade Stafford Elem. Sch. Stafford County Schs., Va., 2000—03; tchr. 6th grade Heritage Elem. Sch. Douglas County Sch. Dist., Highlands Ranch, Colo., 2003—04; tchr. 8th grade AP Social Studies Liberty Mid. Sch. Cherry Creek Sch. Dist., Aurora, Colo., 2004—. Pvt. tutor, Salt Lake City, 1989—90; tutor Sylvan Learning Ctr., Spring Valley, Calif., 1994—96; mem. Excellence in Equity com. Liberty Mid. Sch., Aurora, 2005—06, coord. Social Studies Dept., 2005—06. Mem.: ASCD, Nat. Coun. Social Studies. Republican. Mem. Lds Ch. Avocations: boating, gardening, volleyball, basketball. Office: Liberty Mid Sch 2500 Dry Creek Rd Aurora CO 80016

OLSON, BARBARA FORD, physician; b. Iowa City, June 15, 1935; d. Leonard A. and Anne (Swanson) Ford; m. Robert Eric Olson, 1959 (div. 1973); children: Katherine Gee, Eric Ford, Julie Marie. BA, Gustavus Adolphus Coll., 1956; MD, U. Minn., 1960. Diplomate Am. Bd. Family Medicine, Am. Bd. Geriat. Medicine, added qualification geriat. medicine. Intern St. Paul-Ramsy Med. Ctr., 1960-61; resident in anesthesiology U. Hosp. Cleve., 1961-62, U. Minn. Hosp., Mpls., 1962-63; pvt. practice anesthesiology St. Johns Hosp. and Devine Redeemer Hosp., St. Paul, 1963-67, Mercy Hosp., Coon Rapids, Minn., 1967-74; staff physician Oak Terrace Nursing Home, Minnetonka, Minn., 1974-88; staff physician, med. dir. geriatric evaluation clinic VA Med. Ctr., St. Cloud, Minn., 1988—. Pres. Alpha Epsilon Iota Med. Found., Mpls., 1980—86, bd.dirs., 1980—86, 2003—. Mem. Minn. Med. Assn., Minn. Women Physicians (pres. 1981-82, bd. dirs. 2003—). Office: VA Med Ctr 4801 8th St N Saint Cloud MN 56303-2015 Home: P O Box 27187 Minneapolis MN 55427 Business E-Mail: Barbara.Olson@va.gov.

OLSON, BYRON LOUIS, biochemist, educator; s. Louis Nels and Mary Virginia Olson; m. Patricia Ann Thomas, June 28, 1969; children: Ann Marie, Michael David. BS, U. of Akron, 1964; PhD, Case Western Res. U., Cleve., 1970. Asst. prof. of preventive dentistry and biochemistry Ind. U. Schools of Dentistry and Medicine, Indpls., 1972—79, assoc. prof. of preventive and cmty. dentistry and biochemistry and molecular biology, 1979—92, prof. of oral biology, biochemistry and molecular biology, 1992—. Pres. faculty coun. Ind. U. Sch. Dentistry, 2000—01; chair faculty coun. campus planning com. Ind. U.-Purdue U., Indpls., 1997—99. Contbr. articles to profl. jours. Mem. and bd. chair Ind. Fedn. of Communities for Drug-Free Youth, Inc., Zionsville, 1991—95. 1st lt. US Army, 1964—66. Recipient Tchg. Excellence awards, Ind. U. Sch. of Dentistry, 1997—99; grantee numerous grants. Mem.: Am. Assn. for Dental Rsch. (assoc.; pres. Ind. sect. 1991—92), Internat. Assn. for Dental Rsch. (assoc.), Royal Soc. of Chemistry (assoc.), Am. Dental Edn. Assn. (assoc.; chair biochemistry and nutrition sect. 1992—93, chair, oral biology sect. 1997—99), Am. Chem. Soc. (assoc.; chair, Ind. sect. 1996), Omicron Kappa Upsilon (hon.; chpt. pres. 1998). Roman Catholic. Avocations: swimming, travel, reading, music, fishing. Home: 4994 Tudor Pl Carmel IN 46033 Office: Indiana Unviersity School of Dentistry 1121 W Michigan St Indianapolis IN 46202 Home Phone: 317-844-3408. Personal E-mail: byrols@iquest.net. Business E-Mail: bolson@iupui.edu.

OLSON, CHARLES ERIC, economist; b. Wausau, Wis., June 2, 1942; s. Roland Anthony and Lois (Erickson) O.; m. Pamela Ann Templin, July 1, 1967 (div. Oct. 1973); children: Sonja Anne, Erika Christine; m. Carole Emily Collesian, Dec. 1, 1973 (div. Oct. 1990); children: Cora Elizabeth, Sarah Emily; m. Jeanne Esther Katz, Apr. 14, 1991. Student, U. Wis., Marathon County, 1960-62; BBA with honors, U. Wis., Madison, 1964, MS, 1966—67; PhD, U. Wis., 1968. Instr. U. Wis., Madison, 1966-68; asst. prof. U. Md., College Park, 1968-71, assoc. prof. bus., 1971-76; sr. economist H. Zinder & Assocs., Washington, 1976-77, v.p., 1977-79, sr. v.p., 1979—80, pres., 1986-2000, Olson & Co., Inc., 1980-86; Tyser tchg. fellow R.H. Smith Sch. Bus. U. Md., College Park, 2000—06, prof. practice, 2007—. Cons. Devel. Adv. Service, atty. gens. N.C., Minn., Ky., Mass., Va. U.S. Postal Rate Commn., Dept. Def., numerous electric and gas utlities in U.S. and Can. Testified numerous pub. utility rate cases, before Senate Subcom. on Inter-govtl. Relations; mem. advisory com. research and devel. and energy conservation Fed. Power Commn., 1973-74, vice chmn. rate design task force, 1976—. Author: Cost Considerations for Efficient Electricity Supply, 1970; contbr. chpts. to books, articles to profl. jours. Mem. Prince Georges County (Md.) Citizens Airpark Advisory Com., 1970-71. Grantee Inst. Pub. Utilities, 1967-68; U. Md. 1970, 76. Mem. Transp. and Pub. Utilities Group. Home: 10822 Alloway Dr Rockville MD 20854-1503 Office: RH Smith Sch Bus Univ Md College Park MD 20742 Business E-Mail: colson@rhsmith.umd.edu.

OLSON, DALE C., public relations executive; b. Fargo, ND, Feb. 20, 1934; s. Arthur Edwin and Edith (Weight) Olson Neubauer. Sr. v.p., prin., pres. motion picture divsn. Rogers and Cowan, Inc., Beverly Hills, Calif., 1967-85; prin. Dale C. Olson & Assocs., Beverly Hills, 1985—; mktg. dir. Hollywood History Mus., 2003. Cons. Filmex, L.A., 1972-83; U.S. del. Manila Film Festival, 1982-83. Editor L.A. edit. Theatre ann. Best Plays, 1963-67. V.p. Diamond Cir. City of Hope, Duarte, Calif., 1980-83; mem. adv. bd. Calif. Mus. Sci. and Industry, L.A., 1975-81; mem. bd. govs. Film Industry Workshops, Inc., 1965-80; pres. Hollywood Press Club, 1963-66; assoc. Los Angeles County Art Mus., 1981-83; bd. trustees Hollywood Arts Coun.; chair 1999 jury USA Film Festival, Dallas; cons. L.A. 2000. Recipient Golden Key, Pub. Rels. News, 1982, Les Mason and pub. svc. awards Publicists Guild, Golden Satellite award for lifetime achievement Internat. Press Acad., 1999, Prism award for pub. svc. Entertainment Industries Coun., 2000, Named in his honor, Dale Olson Lobby, Actors' Fund L.A. Office, 2005. Mem. NATAS, Acad. Motion Picture Arts and Scis. (chmn. pub. rels. coordinating com. 1982—), Actors Fund Am. (chmn. Western coun. 1991, trustee 1992, exec. com. 1998), Hollywood Arts Coun. (bd. dirs.), Pres.'s Club, Thalians. Lutheran. Office Phone: 323-876-9331. Personal E-mail: dolson2000@earthlink.net.

OLSON, DAVID CARL, physician; b. Sparta, Wis., Jan. 22, 1950; s. Oral Clifton and Ramona LaBelle Olson; m. Barbara Anne Roeming (div.); children: Emily Sullivan, Paul, Alexander. BA, U. Wis., Madison, 1972; MD, Med. Coll. Wis., Milw., 1986. Cert. AAFP, 2001. Physician Family Health Plan, Elm Grove, Wis., 1989—2002, Pro-Health, Brookfield, Wis., 2002—. Assoc. clin. prof. family and cmty. medicine Med. Coll. Wis. Pres. Med. Soc. Milw. County, 2004, mem. bd., 2005. Named Wis. Family Physician of Yr., 1995; named one of Best Drs. in Am., 2002, 2006, Am. Top Family Doctors, 2004—05. Mem.: Wis. Acad. Family Physicians (alternate del., pres., Family Physician of Yr. 1995). Unitarian Universalist. Avocations: jogging, movies. Office: 2085 N Calhoun Rd Brookfield WI 53005 Business E-Mail: dcolson@phci.org.

OLSON, DAVID JOHN, political science professor; b. Brantford, ND, May 18, 1941; s. Lloyd and Alice Ingrid (Black) O.; m. Sandra Jean Crabb, June 11, 1966; 1 dau., Maia Kari. BA, Concordia Coll., Moorhead, Minn., 1963; Rockefeller fellow fellow, Union Theol. Sem, NYC, 1963-64; MA (Brookings Instn. predoctoral rsch. fellow 1968-69), U. Wis., Madison, 1966, PhD (univ. fellow 1967), 1971. Cmty. planner Madison Redvel. Authority, 1965-66; lectr. U. Wis., 1966-67; from lectr. to asso. prof. polit. sci. Ind. U., Bloomington, 1969-76; prof. polit. sci. U. Wash., Seattle, 1976—2005, chmn. dept., 1983-88, Harry Bridges endowed chairlabor studies, 1992-94; bd. dirs. Harry Bridges Inst.; Disting. lectr. in labor studies San Francisco State U., 1994; dir. Ctr. Labor Studies U. Wash., Seattle, 1992-94, prof. emeritus polit. sci., 2005—. Vis. prof. U. Bergen, 1987, Harvard U., 1988-89, U. Hawaii, 1989, U. Calif., Berkeley, 1996, U. Wales, 2006. Co-author: Governing the United States, 1978, Commission Politics, 1977, To Keep the Republic, 1975, Black Politics, 1971; co-editor: Theft of the City, 1974. Named faculty fellow, Ind. U., 1973; recipient Disting. Tchg. award, 1973, Alumni Achievement award, Concordia Coll., 1998, S. Sterling Munro Disting. Tchg. award, 2005, Disting. Tchg. award, U. Wash., 2005, knight, Harold V of Norway, 2006, Outstanding Civic Educator award, Wash. State Senate, 2007. Mem. Am. Polit. Sci. Assn., Western Polit. Sci. Assn. (v.p. 1984, pres. 1985), Midwest Polit. Sci. Assn., So. Polit. Sci. Assn. Democrat. Lutheran. Home: 6512 E Green Lake Way N Seattle WA 98103-5418 Office: U Wash Dept Polit Sci Seattle WA 98195-0001 Office Phone: 206-543-7948. Business E-Mail: davidols@u.washington.edu.

OLSON, DAVID W., health and medical products executive; BA in English, Washington and Lee U., Lexington, Va. Dir. corp. comm. and investor rels. FCS Labs., Inc.; v.p. Rifkind, Pondel & Parsons; dir. shareholder comm. to v.p. corp. comm. Nat. Med. Enterprises, Inc., 1989—94; with Health Systems Internat., Inc., 1994, v.p. investor and pub. rels.; sr. v.p. corp. comm. Health Net, Inc., Woodland Hills, Calif. Mem. Nat. Investor Rels. Inst. Sr. Roundtable. Bd. trustees Rolling Hills Prep. Sch. Office: Health Net Inc 21650 Oxnard St Woodland Hills CA 91367 Office Phone: 818-676-6000. *

OLSON, DEAN A., lawyer; BA in Psychology, Bethel U., St. Paul, 1953; BD in Ministry, Bethel Sem., St. Paul, 1956; D Ministry, San Francisco Theol. Sem., San Anselma, Calif., 1974; JD, U. Tulsa, 1977. Sr. min. Am. Bapt. Chs., various locations, including Des Moines, 1956—74; pvt. practice law Georgetown, Tex., 2003—. Part-time mcpl. judge, Gun Barrel City and Seven Points, Tex., 1993—2000. Mem.: Kiwanis (past pres., bd. dirs. 1969—2006). Office: 404 W 9th St Ste 101B Georgetown TX 78626-5559

OLSON, DENNIS OLIVER, lawyer; b. Seminole, Tex., Oct. 19, 1947; s. Edwin and Beulah Matilda (Strang) O.; m. Leonee Lynn Claud, Jan. 30, 1971; children: James Edwin, Stacy Rae. BA in English, U. Tex., 1969; JD, Tex. Tech U., 1974. Bar: Tex. 1974, U.S. Ct. Mil. Appeals 1974, U.S. Dist. Ct. (no. dist.) Tex. 1978, U.S. Dist. Ct. (we. dist.) Tex. 1978, U.S. Ct. Appeals (5th cir.) 1984, U.S. Supreme Ct. 1985, U.S. Dist. Ct. (ea. dist.) Tex. 2002. Commd. USMC, 1969, advanced through grades to capt., 1973, infantry officer various locations including Vietnam, 1969—74, judge advocate various locations, 1974—78, resigned, 1978; assoc. Carr, Evans, Fouts & Hunt, and predecessor, Lubbock, Tex., 1978—81, ptnr., 1981—85; pvt. practice Dallas, 1985—88; shareholder, co-chmn. bankruptcy sect. Godwin & Carlton, P.C., Dallas, 1989—94; ptnr. Olson Nicoud & Gueck, LLP and predecessor, Dallas, 1994—. Bd. dirs. Presbyn. Ctr. Doctors Clinic, Lubbock, 1983-85, United Campus Ministry, Tex. Tech U., Lubbock, 1984-85, Discovery Sch.of Canyon Creek, Richardson, 1999-2002; elder Preston Hollow Presbyn. Ch., Dallas; treas., bd. dirs. Lubbock chpt. ARC, 1981-83; vol. Lubbock United Way, 1978-80. Decorated Bronze Star; named Outstanding Young Man of Am., 1983. Fellow Tex. Bar Found. (sustaining life); Dallas Bar Assn., Lubbock County Bar Assn. (bd. dirs. 1983-85), Tex. Young Lawyers Assn. (bd. dirs. 1981-83), Judge Advocates Assn. (bd. dirs. 1976-78), Lubbock C. of C. (grad. Leadership Lubbock program 1981), U. Tex. NROTC Alumni Found., (bd. dirs. 2001-), Phi Delta Phi. Home: 313 Forest Grove Dr Richardson TX 75080-1937 Office Phone: 214-979-7302. Business E-Mail: denniso@dallas-law.com.

OLSON, DONALD RICHARD, mechanical engineering educator; b. Sargent, Nebr., Dec. 26, 1917; s. Harry T. and Gyneth E. (Wittemyer) O.; m. Nancy Walker Benton, June 17, 1944; children: Walter H., Sally, Timothy W. BS, Oreg. State U., 1942; M.Engring., Yale U., 1944, D.Engring., 1951. Profl. engr., Conn. Asst. prof., asso. prof. mech. engring. Yale U., New Haven, 1951-62; prof. mech. engring. Pa. State U., University Park, 1962-83, prof. emeritus, 1983—; head underwater power plants Applied Research Lab., 1962-72, head dept. mech. engring., 1972-83; mem. engring. accreditation commn., 1979-82. Contbr. tech. papers in field to publs. Mem. ASME, Soc. Automotive Engrs. (dir. 1968-71), Sigma Xi. Home: 1930 Cliffside Dr State College PA 16801 E-mail: dro@psu.edu.

OLSON, EDWARD CHARLES, entrepreneur, conservationist, foundation administrator, consultant, ecologist, writer; b. Jacksonville, Fla., July 6, 1956; s. Edward Charles and Marcine Era (Hall) O.; m. Krista Lynn Neuberger, Aug. 5, 1978; children: Laura Ellen, Edward Charles, Natalie Rose. BS, Miami U., Oxford, Ohio, 1978; MS, Wash. State U., 1980; PhD, Ohio State U., 1983. State dir. Nature Conservancy, Columbus, Ohio, 1983-86; pres., CEO Florida Keys Land & Sea Trust, 1986-93, Catalina Island Conservancy, Avalon, Calif., 1993-96; chmn., CEO E.C. Olson & Assocs., 1996—; ptnr. Oceanwatch Prodn. Group, 1996—. Cons. non-profit orgns., 1987—; chmn., CEO Man-O-War Clothing, Co., 1996—; pres., CEO St. Lucie Wetland Solutions, Inc., 1997-99, Fla. Wetlands Stewardship Group, Inc., 1998-99; dir. Reef Relief, 1997-2000; chmn., CEO Fregata Publ. Co., 1998—; pres., CEO MitBank-USA, 1999—; pres., CEO Bluefield Ranch Metigation Bank, 1998—; mng. ptnr. Lemon Grove Mitigation Bank, 2003—. Editor: Guide to the Florida Keys, 1989; author: Winds of the Marquesas, 1996, Hardball, 1998, After Matthias, 1999. Bd. dirs. Catalina Cmty. Pub. Radio, 1993-96, Fla. Nat. Parks and Monuments Assn., Homestead, 1988-93, Fla. Keys Meml. Hosp., Key West, 1989-91, Fla. Keys Guidance Clinic, Marathon, 1990-92. Recipient Leadership Fla. Grad. award Fla. C. of C., 1990, Outstanding Young Floridian, Fla. Jaycees, 1991, Chevron Conservation award, 1994; named Man of Yr., Marathon Jaycees, 1990. Avocations: fishing, travel, reading, writing, civil war study. Office: 205 Olive Ave Port Saint Lucie FL 34952-1347 E-mail: ecolson@inetw.net.

OLSON, ERIC THOR, career military officer; b. Tacoma, 1952; married; 2 children. Grad., USN Acad., 1973; MA in Nat. Security Affairs, Naval Postgraduate Sch. Advanced through grades to adm. USN, 2007, asst. dep. chief naval ops. (plans, policy & ops.), comdr. Naval Spl. Warfare Command San Diego, dir. strategy & policy divsn., N51, Office Chief Naval Ops.; dep. comdr. US Spl. Ops. Command (USSOCOM), MacDill AFB, Fla., 2003—07, comdr., 2007—. Decorated Disting. Svc. medal, Silver Star, Bronze Star with V device. Achievements include participating in Operation Restore Hope in Mogadishu, Somalis where he led a recue team to the crash site of two downed Black Hawk helicopters. Office: US Spl Ops Command 7701 Tampa Point Blvd MacDill AFB Tampa FL 33621 *

OLSON, FERRON ALLRED, metallurgist, educator; b. Tooele, Utah, July 2, 1921; s. John Ernest and Harriet Cynthia (Allred) O.; m. Donna Lee Jefferies, Feb. 1, 1944; children: Kandace, Randall, Paul, Jeffery, Richard. BS, U. Utah, 1953, PhD, 1956. Ordained bishop LDS Ch., 1962. Research chemist Shell Devel. Co., Emeryville, Calif., 1956-61; assoc. research prof. U. Utah, Salt Lake City, 1961-63, assoc. prof., 1963-68, chmn. dept mining, metall. and fuels engring., 1966-74, prof. dept. metallurgy and metall. engring., 1968-96, prof. emeritus, 1996—. Cons. U.S. Bur. Mines, Salt Lake City, 1973-77, Ctr. for Investigation Mining and Metallurgy, Santiago, Chile, 1978; dir. U. Utah Minerals Inst., 1980-91. Author: Collection of Short Stories, 1985, (hist. book) Seymour Brunson: Defender of the Faith, 1998, (novel) Harriet Cynthia Allred Olson, 1995; contbr. articles to profl. jours. Del. State Rep. Conv., Salt Lake City, 1964; bishop, 1962-68, 76-82, missionary, 1988. With U.S. Army, 1943-46, PTO. Named Fulbright-Hayes lectr., Yugoslavia, 1974-75, Disting. prof. Fulbright-Hayes, Yugoslavia, 1980, Outstanding Metallurgy Instr., U. Utah, 1979-80, 88-89, Disting. Speaker U. Belgrade-Bor, Yugoslavia, 1974. Mem. Am. Inst. Mining, Metall. and Petroleum Engrs. (chmn. Utah chpt. 1978-79), Am. Soc. Engring. Edn. (chmn. Minerals div. 1972-73), Fulbright Alumni Assn., Am. Bd. Engring. and Tech. (bd. dirs. 1975-82). Republican. Achievements include research on explosives ignition and decomposition; surface properties of thoria, silica gels, silicon monoxide in ultra high vacuum; kinetics of leaching of Chrysocolla, Malachite and Bornite; electrowinning of gold; nodulation of copper during electrodeposition. Home: 1862 Herbert Ave Salt Lake City UT 84108-1832 E-mail: donnaolson1@mailstation.com.

OLSON, GARY ROBERT, banker; b. Milw., May 9, 1946; s. Ward Louis and Mary Jane (Brown) O.; m. Mia Kristina Sohn, Feb. 26, 1972; children: Kristin Anne, Brian Ward. Student, Loyola U., Rome, 1966-67; AB, Marquette U., 1968; M Internat. Mgmt., Am. Grad. Sch. Internat. Mgmt., Glendale, Ariz., 1973. Instr. Sogang Jesuit U., Seoul, 1968-70, Hankuk U. Fgn. Studies, Seoul, 1971-72; grad. asst. Am. Grad. Sch. Internat. Mgmt., 1972; credit analyst Chase Manhattan Bank, N.A., NYC and Tokyo, 1973-75, asst. treas. NYC, 1975-77, 2d v.p. Madrid, 1977, Paris, 1977-80, v.p., mgr. Regional Banking Office Chgo., 1980-83; v.p., regional mgr. Case Nat. Corp. Svcs., San Francisco, 1983-87; sr. v.p. Chase Bank Ariz., Phoenix, 1987-90; v.p. Bklyn. and S.I. commercial mgr. Chase Manhattan Bank, N.A., Bklyn., 1990-93, v.p., team leader Nassau mid. mkt. mgr. Melville, L.I., 1993-97; mgr. corp. banking L.I. Dime Savs. Bank, Huntington Station, NY, 1997-99; sr. v.p. comml. banking Dime Savings Bank, 2000—. Advisor English program USIS, Seoul, 1969; alumni domestic counselor Am. Grad. Sch. Internat. Mgmt., 1990—, Marquette U., 1990—; vol. Spl. Olympics, Phoenix, 1988-89; fund drive capt. Phoenix Econ. Growth Corp., 1988; trustee, bd. dirs. Variety Pre-schooler's workshop, 1994—; bd. dirs. L.I. chpt. Robert Morris Assocs., 1994—, chmn., 1995—; trustee, bd. dirs., mktg. com., chmn.'s coun. Hecksher Mus., Huntington, N.Y., 1995—. Mem. Robert Morris Assocs. (assoc.), Econ. Club Phoenix, World Trade Club. Republican. Roman Catholic. Avocations: reading, skiing, swimming, golf. Office: Washington Mutual Commercial Banking 3929 W John Carpenter Fwy Irving TX 75063-2909 E-mail: garyolson281@hotmail.com.

OLSON, HERBERT THEODORE, trade association executive; b. Bridgeport, Conn., Feb. 9, 1929; s. Herbert Theodore and Inez Evelyn (Lindahl) O.; children: Christina, Victoria; m. Kathleen A. Harrison, Dec. 27, 1988. Student, Heidelberg Coll., 1947-49; AB, Ohio U., 1951, postgrad., 1951-52. Asst. to dean of men Ohio U., Athens, 1951-52; with Union Carbide Corp., 1952-71, mgr. employee rels., coord. pub. affairs NYC, 1969-71; exec. v.p. Am. Assn. for Aging, Washington, 1971-75; dir. spl. projects Am. Healthcare Assn., Washington, 1975-79; pres. Promotional Products Assn. Internat., Irving, Tex., 1979-96, pres. emeritus, 1996—. Event coord.-supplier Stars Showcase, 1998-2000; mem. adv. bd. Allied Bank. Mem. nat. exploring com., vice chmn. nat. events com., ann. meetings com., mem.-at-large nat. coun. Boy Scouts Am., 1980—; treas. U.S. Found. for Internat. Scouting, 1988—99, chmn. audit com., 1984—87, mem. internat. com., 1998—2003, mem. direct svc. coun. bd., 1997—2002; mem. long-term care for elderly rsch. rev. and adv. com. Dept. Health, 1972—77; mem. Longterm Care grant rev. com. HEW, 1972—77; mem. planning commn. City of Torrance, Calif., 1962—64, city councilman, 1964—67; chmn. Gov.'s Operation Leegit; mem. adv. bd. Irving Hosp.; chmn. bd. dirs. Irving Cancer Soc., 1997—2002; exec. bd. cir. 10 coun. Boy Scouts Am., 1979—; bd. mem. Irving chpt. Salvation Army, 2005—, adv. coun. Irving, 2005—; mem. exec. bd. Circle 10 Coun., 1979—; mem. Irving Vistors and Cmty Bur., 2004—05; chmn. Irving

Sister Cities, 2006—; bd. dirs. Irving Conv. and Visitors Bur., 2001—, chmn., 2004—; bd. dirs. DFW Humane Soc., 2001—. Lord Baden Powell fellow, 1986; recipient Disting. Eagle award Boy Scouts Am., 1974, Silver Beaver award, 1968, Silver Buffalo award, 1998; named person of Yr. in Promotional Products in Counselor Mag., 1995, Hall of Fame Promotional Products Assn. Internat., 1997, Hall of Fame Can. Promo Prod. Assn., 1996. Mem. Meeting Planners Internat. (charter), Am. Soc. Assn., Execs., U.S. C. of C., Washington Soc. Assn. Execs., Nat. Assn. Exhibit Mgrs., Small Bus. Legis. Coun. (chmn. bd. 1993-95), Dallas Ft. Worth Soc. Assn. Execs. (v.p. 1985-87), Irving C. of C. (bd. dirs. 1999-2004), Am. Advt. Fedn., Am. Cancer Soc. (Irving chpt.), Tex. Soc. Assn. Execs., Las Colinas Country Club, Rotary (bd. dirs. 2004—), Internat. Fellowship Scouting Rotarians (world chmn. 2005-06, internat. commr. 06—), Masons, Shriners, Kiwanis (lt. gov.), DFW Humane Soc. Irving (bd. dirs. 2000-). Baptist. Home: 2910 Pacific Ct Irving TX 75062-4624 Office: 807 W Pioneer Dr Irving TX 75061

OLSON, JACK CONRAD, JR., geriatrician; b. Muskegon, Mich., 1955; BS in Chemistry, Mich. State U., 1977, BA in English, 1977; MD, U. Mich., 1984. Bd. cert. internal medicine, bd. cert. geriatric medicine. Intern U. Wis. Hosps. and Clinics, Madison, 1984—85, resident internal medicine, 1985—87, fellow geriatrics, 1987—89; assoc. med. dir. Mendota Mental Health, U. Wis., 1989—92; dir. Windermere Sr. Health Ctr., U. Chgo., 1992—99; asst. clin. prof., fellowship dir. Rush U. Med. Ctr., Chgo., 1999—. Office: 1725 W Harrison St Ste 955 Chicago IL 60612 Office Phone: 312-942-7030. Business E-Mail: jolson@rush.edu.

OLSON, JAMES (JIM OLSON), telecommunications industry executive; BS in Elec. Engring., Univ. Calif., Davis; MS in Elec. Engring, Santa Clara Univ., MBA. Sr. mgmt., engring. mfg., mktg. Hewlett-Packard Co.; gen. mgr., Stanford Park Divsn. Hewlett-Packard, 1992; sr. v.p., gen. mgr., Wide Area Network Ops. 3Com Corp.; pres., CEO SkyStream Networks, 1997—. Spkr. in field. Office: SkyStream Networks 455 DeGuigne Dr Sunnyvale CA 94085-3890 Office Fax: 408-616-3404.

OLSON, JAMES RICHARD, retired transportation executive; b. Alexandria, Minn., Mar. 11, 1941; s. Orie D. and Theresa Marie (Erickson) O.; m. Ronna Lee, Feb. 1, 1969 (dec.); 1 child, Trevor James. BS, N.D. State U., 1963; LLD, U. Minn., 1966; MBA, Harvard U., 1968. Asst. to v.p. finance Cargill Inc., Mpls., 1968-69; with Graco Inc., Mpls., 1969-75, v.p. finance, 1972-75; exec. v.p. finance Ponderosa System, Inc., Dayton, Ohio, 1975-77; v.p. planning Pillsbury Co., Mpls., 1977-79, v.p. restaurant group, 1979-80; group v.p.-restaurants The Carlson Cos., Inc., Mpls., 1981-83; exec. v.p., chief fin. and adminstrv. officer Schneider Nat., Inc., 1983-87, pres. van group, 1987-92, pres. transp. sector, 1992-98. Bd. dirs., chair compensation com. Meritex Enterprises, Inc. Mem. Harvard Bus. Sch. Club Minn. (past pres.) Lutheran. Home: 1103 Winslow House 100 2d St SE Minneapolis MN 55414-2157 Office Phone: 612-617-8869. Personal E-mail: jrolson1@att.net.

OLSON, JAMES WILLIAM PARK, architect; b. St. Louis, Oct. 6, 1940; s. James William Park; s. Louis Garfield and Gladys Helen (Schuh) O.; m. Katherine Fovargue, June 11, 1971; children: Park, Reed. BArch, U. Wash., 1963. Registered arch., Wash., Oreg., Calif., Ill., Colo., Hawaii, Ga., Fla. Ptnr. Olson Sundberg Kundig Allen Archs., Seattle, 1985—. Assoc. arch. New Seattle Art Mus., 1991. Prin. works include Pike and Virginia Bldg. (AIA Honor award 1980), Seattle's Best Coffee Retail Locations (AIA Honor award 1984), Hauberg Residence (AIA Honor award 1997), Mayer Lodo residence, Denver (AIA Honor award 1998, AIA NW and Pacific Regional Merit award 1999, AIA We. Internat. Design award 2000), St. Mark's Cathedral Renovation (AIA Commendation award), Seattle (IFFRA award 1998, AIA citation 1998, AIA and Pacific Regional Merit award 2000), numerous residences nationwide; (subject of monologue) Monacelli Press: Architecture, Art and Craft. Bd. dirs. Ctr. Contemporary Art, Seattle, 1982-86, Artist Trust, Seattle, 1986-90, U. Wash. Henry Art Gallery, Seattle, 1986-92, Seattle Art Mus., 1996—. Recipient Best Arch. award Seattle Mag., 1985. Fellow AIA; mem. NEA (juror). Avocation: art. Office: Olson Sundberg Kundig Allen Architects 159 South Jackson St Ste 600 Seattle WA 98104-2557 Office Phone: 206-624-5670. E-mail: jim@olsonsundberg.com. *

OLSON, JEANNINE EVELYN, history professor; b. Caledonia, Minn. d. Aloysius and Evelyn Hazel (Ellingson) Fahsl; children: Karen, Daniel, Rebecca. BA, St. Olaf Coll., Northfield, Minn., 1961; MA, Stanford U., 1962, PhD, 1980. Teaching asst. U. Minn., Mpls., 1972-76; asst. prof. San Francisco Theol. Sem., San Anselmo, Calif., 1979-86; mem. doctoral faculty Grad. Theol. Union, Berkeley, Calif., 1979-86; asst. prof. history R.I. Coll., Providence, 1986-90, assoc. prof., 1990—99, prof., 1999—. Mem. Internat. Congress for Luther Rsch., Erfurt, Germany, Norway, Mpls., 1983, 88, 93, Heidelberg, 1997, Copenhagen, 2002, Brazil, 2007; mem. Task Force on the Confessional Nature of the Ch., Presbyn. Ch., 1983-86, com. Theol. edn., 1991-93; mem. Internat. Congress for Calvin Rsch., 1990, 1994, 2002, 06. Author: Histoire de L'Eglise, 1972, Calvin and Social Welfare, 1989, Deacons and Deaconesses Through the Centuries, 1992, 2d edit., 2005; contbr. articles to profl. jours. Woodrow Wilson fellow, Danforth Found. fellow, 1976-81; grantee Govt. of France rsch., 1978-79, Am. Coun. Learned Socs., 1982, 95, NEH, 1985, 88-92, 96, 99, 2001, 2004-05, Am. Acad. Religion, 1990-92, 94-95, 2003, Am. Philosophical Soc., 1994-95. Mem. Renaissance Soc. Am., 16th Century Studies Soc., Calvin Studies Soc. (exec. com. 1995-99), Am. Soc. Reformatin Rsch., Am. Soc. Ch. History (instl. liaison com.), Hoguenot Soc. of Great Britain and Ireland, Reformation Soc. of Am., Ski Wheelers Ski Club, Rinconada Master Swim Club, Phi Beta Kappa. Avocation: swimming. Office: RI Coll Dept History Providence RI 02908 Home: 1654 Portola Ave Palo Alto CA 94306

OLSON, JOHN KARL, judge; b. Springfield, Mass., Aug. 14, 1949; s. Harold Gunnar and Louise Theodora (Shukis) Olson; m. Ann Catherine Sullivan, June 16, 1973; children: Elizabeth Ann, Katherine Louise. AB, Harvard Coll., 1971; JD, Boston Coll., 1975. Bar: Fla. 1975, U.S. Dist. Ct. (mid. and so. dists.) Fla. 1976, U.S. Ct. Appeals (5th cir.) 1979, U.S. Supreme Ct. 1979, U.S. Ct. Appeals (11th cir.) 1981. From assoc. to ptnr. Carlton, Fields, Ward et al., Tampa, Fla., 1975-86; exec. v.p., gen. counsel, dir. Jet Fla., Inc., Miami, 1986-88; ptnr. Stearns Weaver Miller Weissler Alhadeff & Sitterson P.A., Tampa, 1988—2006; US bankruptcy judge So. Dist. Fla., 2006—. Author: Creditors and Debtors Rights in Florida, 1979, 2d edit., 1989, Collier Bankruptcy Practice Guide, 1986. Trustee Tampa Mus. Art, 1992—98; mem. parent bd. U. Del., 1998—2002, co-pres., 2000—02. Fellow, U. Tampa, 1986—2006. Mem.: ABA (vice chmn. bankruptcy com. 2005—, 2006—), Fla. Bar Assn. (chmn. bus. law sect. 1988—89), Am. Bankruptcy Inst., Harvard Club (pres. 1982—84). Office: So Dist Fla US Courthouse Rm 403 299 E Broward Blvd Fort Lauderdale FL 33301 Home Phone: 813-259-1487; Office Phone: 954-769-5770. Business E-Mail: john_k_olson@flsb.uscourts.gov.

OLSON, JOHN MARSHALL, lawyer; b. Milw., Feb. 16, 1949; s. John Robert and Helen (Linder) O.; m. Lynde Bradley Uihlein, Jan. 6, 1973 (div. Dec. 1986); children: Sarah Lynde, John Uihlein. BA summa cum laude, Princeton U., 1971; postgrad., Oxford U., Eng., 1971-72; JD, Yale U., 1976. Bar: Wis. 1976, U.S. Dist. Ct. (ea. dist.) Wis. 1981, U.S. Ct. Appeals (7th cir.) 1981. Assoc. Whyte & Hirschboeck, S.C., Milw., 1976-82, ptnr., 1982-89, Foley & Lardner, Milw., 1989—. Bd. dirs. Banner Welder, Inc., Germantown, Wis., Phoenix Products Co., Inc., Milw., Schroeder-Manatee Ranch, Inc., Sarasota, Fla. Contbr. articles to profl. jours. Trustee David Uihlein Racing Mus. Found., Cedarburg, Wis., 1978, Univ. Sch. Milw., 1979-85, Lakeland Coll., Sheboygan, Wis., 1984-86; bd. dirs. AWARE Inc., Ft. Atkinson, Wis., 1991—, Tympanuchus Soc., Milw., 1992—. Mem. State Bar Wis. (chmn. bus. law sect. 1992-93), Univ. Club. Milw., Coleman Lake Club (bd. dirs., Goodman, Wis.), Milw. Club., Milw. Country Club. Avocations: grouse hunting, fly fishing, tennis. Office: Foley & Lardner 777 E Wisconsin Ave Ste 3800 Milwaukee WI 53202-5367 Office Phone: 414-297-5640. Office Fax: 414-297-4900. Business E-Mail: jolson@foley.com.

OLSON, KARL, lawyer; b. San Francisco, Nov. 6, 1952; s. Leon and Reeva (Pearlstein) O.; m. Caroline M. Grannan, July 1, 1979 (div. Dec. 1982); m. Carolyn Ann Johnston, Jan. 1, 1990; children: Mark Johnston Olson, Jack Johnston Olson. BA, Sonoma State U., Rohnert Park, Calif., 1975; JD magna cum laude, U. Calif., San Francisco, 1982. Bar: Calif. 1982, U.S. Dist. Ct. (no. dist.) Calif. 1982, U.S. Ct. Appeals (9th cir.) 1983, U.S. Supreme Ct. 1990. Rsch. atty. to Justice Joseph Grodin Calif. Supreme Ct., San Francisco, 1982-83; assoc. Morrison & Foerster, San Francisco, 1983-86, Cooper, White & Cooper, San Francisco, 1986-89, ptnr., 1990-97, Levy, Ram & Olson, San Francisco, 1997. Contbr. articles to profl. jours. Precinct leader Dem. Party, San Francisco, 1988, 92, 96, 2000. Recipient James Madison award outstanding legal counsel, No. Calif. Soc. Profl. Journalists, 2005. Mem. State Bar Calif., Bar Assn. San Francisco (co-chmn. bench bar-media com. 1990—), Order of Coif, Thurston Honor Soc. Avocations: politics, journalism, sports. Office: Levy Ram & Olson 639 Front St 4th fl San Francisco CA 94111 Office Phone: 415-433-4949. Business E-Mail: KO@lrolaw.com.

OLSON, KEITH WALDEMAR, historian, educator; b. Poughkeepsie, NY, Aug. 4, 1931; s. Ernest Waldemar and Elin Ingeborg (Rehnstrom) O.; m. Marilyn Joyce Wittschen, Sept. 10, 1955; children: Paula, Judy. BA, SUNY, Albany, 1957, MA, 1959; PhD, U. Wis., 1964; PhD (hon.), U. Tampere, Finland, 2000. Mem. history faculty Syracuse U., NY, 1963-66; mem. history faculty U. Md., College Park, 1966—, prof. history. Fulbright prof. U. Tampere, 1986-87, 2004, U. Oulu, Finland, 1993, U. Jyväskylä, Finland, 1994. Author: The G.I. Bill, the Veterans and the Colleges, 1974; Biography of a Progressive: Franklin K. Lane, 1979, Watergate: The Presidential Scandal That Shook America, 2003. Pres. Am. Scandinavian Found., Washington, 1977-79. Served with U.S. Army, 1952-54. U.S. Office Edn. grantee, 1965-66; U. Md. grantee, 1971, 76, 78. Mem. Am. Hist. Assn., Orgn. Am. Historians, Wis. Hist. Soc., Swedish Am. Hist. Soc., Finnish Hist. Soc. (hon.), Soc. Historians of Am. Fgn. Rels., Cen. Study of Presidency, Am. Scandinavian Assn. (pres. 1998-99). Unitarian Universalist. Home: 10746 Kinloch Rd Silver Spring MD 20903-1226 Office: U Md Dept History College Park MD 20742-0001 Office Phone: 301-405-4286. Business E-Mail: kwolson@umd.edu.

OLSON, LEROY CALVIN, retired educational administration educator; b. Kane, Pa., Mar. 7, 1926; s. Vernon Reinhold and Gertrude Viola Olson; m. Miriam Marie Vogler, June 19, 1954; children— David Lee, Thomas Edward, Steven Andrew. BS, Clarion State Coll., 1949; M.Ed., Pa. State Coll., 1950; Ed.D., Pa. State U., 1962; postgrad., U. Del., Newark, 1964-65. Tchr.-counselor Boiling Springs H.S., Pa., 1950-52, Gordon Jr. H.S., Coatesville, Pa., 1952-54; guidance dir. Ctrl. Dauphin Sch. Dist., Harrisburg, Pa., 1954-57; coordinator pupil personnel services, asst. supt. for instrn. and personnel, acting supt. Alfred I. duPont Sch. Dist., Wilmington, Del., 1957-65; prof. ednl. adminstrn. Temple U., Phila., 1965-92, prof. emeritus, 1992—. Cons. to schs. bds. and dists., also Nat., Wis., Pa. sch. bds. assns. Contbr. articles to profl. jours. Trustee Luth. Ch., 1963-66, chmn. bd., 1976-78, chmn. various coms., discussion groups. Served with USNR, 1944-46, PTO. Recipient Disting. Alumni award, Clarion State Coll., 1972. Mem. Am. Personnel and Guidance Assn., AAUP, Am. Assn. Sch. Personnel Adminstrs., Assn. Supervision and Curriculum Devel., Council Profs. Instrn. Supervision, Nat. Staff Devel. Council, Am. Legion, Phi Delta Kappa, Phi Kappa Phi. Republican. Home: 211 Azalea Lane West Grove PA 19390 *God's gift of life is a marvelous thing. My attempt to make the best use of that gift is to try to live an integrated and balanced life. This means that active attention must be paid to the physical, social, spiritual, psychological, mental, and recreational aspects as well as to the work or career dimension. It also means we must share that gift through loving and caring about others.*

OLSON, LYNN, sculptor, painter, writer; b. Chgo., Mar. 23, 1952; s. Ellen (Nelson) Olson. Instr. direct cement sculpture workshops Montoya Art Studios, West Palm Beach, Fla., 1988—89, Alta. Sculptors Assn., Edmonton, Canada, 1990, Mendocino Art Ctr., Calif., 1992—93, Sierra Nev. Coll. Lake Tahoe, Incline Village, 1993, Lighthouse Art Ctr., Crescent City, Calif., 1990—96, Elisabet Ney Sculpture Conservatory, Austin, 1995, Tarrant County Jr. Coll., Ft. Worth, 1995, Art Students League Denver, 2000, Indpls. Art Ctr., 2002. Artist-in-residence St. Joseph Coll., 2000. Prin. works include Good Shepherd, Chy. Good Shepherd, Albion, Ind., Kneeling Figure, Manta Ray. World Concrete, Addison, Ill., Rose, Carter Meml., Chesterton, Ind., Redwood Tree, Lighthouse Art Ctr., Crescent City, Calif., George Bartholomew Meml., Bellefontaine, Ohio, Color Concerto, Purdue U., Hammond, Ind., Continuity III, Tower East, Shaker Heights, Ohio, Aluma Beam, Aluma Corp., Toronto, Amobius, St. Joseph Coll., Rensselaer, Ind., Flying Fish, Lake Sara, Effingham, Ill., Kim (stone sculpture), Irene Newhard portrait sculpture (cement), one-man shows include U. Ill., Chgo., 2001, 2006, No. Ind. Arts Assn., 1999, Munster, CCT Gallery, Evanston Hall, Northwestern U. Settlement, Chgo., 2000—, 18 Artists Gallery, Chesterton, Ind., Block Fine Arts, Inc., New Buffalo, Mich., Marion Coll., Indpls., 2003, Ill. Ctrl. Coll., East Peoria, 2003, U. Ill., Chgo., 2006, 2006, exhibited in group shows at Danada Sculpture Show, Cantigny Park, Wheaton, Ill., 1999—2001, Prairie Arts Coun., Rensselaer, Ind., 2000, Ind. U. N.W., 2001, Effingham's 3d Ann. Sculpture on Ave. Exhbn., Ill., 2001, McHenry CC, Crystal Lake, Ill., 2002, 4th Ann. Sculpture on Aves. Exhibit, Effingham, 2002, 5th Ann., 2003, 6th Ann., 2004, 7th Ann., 2005, 8th Ann., 2006, 9th Ann., 2007, 15th Ann. Outdoor Sculpture Exhibit, Lawrence, Kans., 2002, Art Pub. Places, Cedar Rapids, Iowa, 2002, 2003, 2004, Torso, Delta State U., Cleveland, Miss., 2002, 5th Ann. Sculpture in Pk., White River State Pk., Indpls., 2003, Barrington (Ill.) Area Libr. Sculpture Garden, 2003, Tall Grass Arts Assn., Park Forest, Ill., 2004, Davlan Park, Mass. Ave. Urban Art Gallery, Indpls., 2004, U. Indpls., 2005—06, exhibitions include Effingham Cmty Com. Arts, Ill., 2005—07; author, pub.: Sculpting with Cement, 1981—2007; contbr. articles to profl. jours. Mem.: Am. Concrete Inst. (mem. com. 124 concrete aesthetics). Home and Office: Steelstone 4607 Claussen Ln Valparaiso IN 46383-1526 Office Phone: 219-464-1792.

OLSON, LYNN, editor; m. Steve Olson; 2 children. Grad., Yale U. Sr. editor Edn. Week, 1990—. Author: The School to Work Revolution: How Employers and Educators Are Joining Forces to Prepare Tomorrow's Skilled Workforce, 1997. Recipient award, Edn. Writers Assn., Nat. Assn. Secondary Sch. Prins., Internat. Reading Assn.; grantee, Alfred P. Sloan Found., N.Y., 1995. Mem.: Carnegie Found. for Advancement Tchg. (bd. mem.). Office: Editl Projects in Edn Inc Ste 100 6935 Arlington Rd Bethesda MD 20814-5233

OLSON, MARIAN KATHERINE, management consultant; b. Tulsa, Okla., Oct. 15, 1933; d. Sherwood Joseph and Katherine M. (Miller) Lahman; m. Ronald Keith Olson, Oct. 27, 1956 (dec. May 1991). BA in Polit. Sci., U. Colo., 1954, MA in Elem. Edn., 1962; EdD in Ednl. Adminstrn., U. Tulsa, 1969. Tchr. pub. schs., Wyo., Colo., Mont., 1956-67; tchg. fellow, adj. instr. edn. U. Tulsa, 1968-69; asst. prof. edn. Eastern Mont. State Coll., 1970; program assoc. rsch. adminstrn. Mont. State U., 1970-75; on leave with Energy Policy Office of White House then with Fed. Energy Adminstrn., 1973-74; with Dept. Energy and predecessor, 1975—, program analyst, 1975-79, chief planning and environ. compliance br., 1979-83; regional dir. Region VIII Fed. Emergency Mgmt. Agy., 1987-93; exec. dir. Search and Rescue Dogs of the U.S., 1993—. Pres. Marian Olson Assocs., Bannack Pub. Co Contbr. articles in field. Bd. dirs. Disaster Preparedness and Emergency Response Assn. Internat.; incorporator Jeffco Citizens League. Grantee Okla. Consortium Higher Edn., 1969, NIMH, 1974. Mem. Internat. Assn. Emergency Mgrs., Am. Soc. for Info. Sci., Am. Assn. Budget and Program Analysis, Assn. of Contingency Planners, Nat. Inst. Urban Search and Rescue (bd. dirs.), Nat. Assn. for Search and Rescue, Colo. Search and Rescue, Search and Rescue Dogs of U.S., Colo. Emergency Mgmt. Assn., Front Range Rescue Dogs, Kappa Delta Pi, Phi Alpha Theta, Kappa Alpha Theta. Republican. Home: 203 Iowa Dr Golden CO 80403-1337 Office: Marian Olson Assocs 203 Iowa Dr Ste B Golden CO 80403-1337 Personal E-mail: mlolson@ix.netcom.com.

OLSON, MARK WALTER, non-profit corporation administrator, former federal official; b. Fergus Falls, Minn., Mar. 17, 1943; s. Walter Roland and Agnes Marie (Peterson) Olson; m. Renee Irene Korda, July 5, 1980; children: Benjamin, Stephanie. BA in economics, St. Olaf Coll., 1965. Joined First Bank Sys., St. Paul, 1966, named officer, 1969; legis. asst. banking issues Congressman Bill Frenzel, Washington, 1971—72, dir. Minn. dist. office, 1974—76; with Andrews Allen Co., St. Paul, 1972—74; pres., CEO Security State Bank, Fergus Falls, Minn., 1976—88; ptnr. Ernst & Young LLP (formerly Arthur Young & Co.), 1988—99, nat. dir. regulatory consulting practice; staff dir. Securities Subcom., Banking, Housing and Urban Affairs com. US Senate, 2000—01; mem. bd. govs. Fed. Res. Sys., 2001—06, adminstrv. gov., 2002—06; chmn. Pub. Co. Acctg. Oversight Bd., 2006—. Bd. dirs. Pioneer Home, Fergus Falls, 1977—86, Lake Region Hosp., Fergus Falls, 1978—88, Fergus Falls Area YMCA, 1977—83. Named a Disting. Alumni, St. Olaf Coll., 2003. Mem.: Am. Bankers Assn. (chmn. govt. rels. coun., bd. dirs. 1982—84, pres. 1986—87), C. of C. (bd. dirs. 1980—84). Republican. Lutheran. Office: Pub Co Acctg Oversight Bd 1666 K St NW Washington DC 20006 Office Phone: 202-207-9100.

OLSON, NORMAN FREDRICK, not-for-profit developer, retired food science educator; b. Edmund, Wis., Feb. 8, 1931; s. Irving M. and Elva B. (Rhinerson) O.; m. Darlene Mary Thorson, Dec. 28, 1957; children: Kristin A., Eric R. BS, U. Wis., 1953, MS, 1957, PhD, 1959. Asst. prof. U. Wis.-Madison, 1959-63, assoc. prof., 1963-69, prof., 1969-93, dir. Walter V. Price Cheese Research Inst., 1976-93; dir. Ctr. Dairy Research, 1986-93; disting. prof. U. Wis.-Madison, 1993-97, prof. emeritus, 1997—; dir. outreach Shama, Inc., 2007—. Cons. to cheese industry, 1997—. Author: Semi-soft Cheeses; inventor enzyme microencapsulation; sr. editor Jour. Dairy Sci., 1996-2000. Lt. U.S. Army, 1953-55. Recipient Laureate award Nat. Cheese Inst., 1998, Disting. Svc. award Coll. Agrl. Life. Sci., U. Wis., 2002; named Highly Cited Rschr. ISI, 2002. Fellow Inst. Food Technologists (Macy award 1986), Am. Dairy Sci. Assn. (v.p. 1984-85, pres. 1985-86, Pfizer award 1971, Dairy Rsch. Inc. award 1978, Borden Found. award 1988, Hon. award 1997); mem. Inst. Food Technologists. Democrat. Lutheran. Avocation: cross country skiing. Home: 114 Green Lake Pass Madison WI 53705-4755 Office: U Wis Dept Food Sci Babcock Hall Madison WI 53706 Business E-Mail: nfolson@wisc.edu.

OLSON, PAMELA FAITH, lawyer, former federal agency administrator; b. Fargo, ND, July 6, 1954; d. Norman Clifford and Inga (Larson) O.; m. Grant Douglas Aldonas, Apr. 12, 1980; children: Nicole Helen, Kirsten Inga, Noah Grant. BA magna cum laude, U. Minn., 1976, JD, 1980, MBA, 1984. Bar: DC 1981. Instr. U. Minn., Coll. Bus. Adminstrn., Mpls., 1979; atty., Office of Chief Counsel, IRS US Dept. Treasury, Washington, 1981—86; assoc. Skadden, Arps, Slate, Meagher & Flom, LLP, Washington, 1986-90, ptnr., 1990—2001, 2004—; dep. asst. sec. for tax policy US Dept. Treasury, Washington, 2001—02, asst. sec. for tax policy, 2002—04. Bd. dirs. Tax Analysts, 2004-, So. Fed. Tax Inst., 2005-. Coun. mem. Resurrection Luth. Ch., Va., 2002-05; trustee Millenium Inst., 1993-99. Fellow Am. Bar Found., Am. Coll. Tax Counsel; mem. ABA (vice chmn. employment taxes com. 1988-90, chair employment tax com. 1990-92, com. on govt. rels. 1992—, com. on coms. 1992—, com. on women and minorities 1993—, com. on membership and mktg. 1993—, coun. dir. sect. on taxation 1993-95, vice chair sect. taxation 1995-98, chair-elect sect. on taxation 1999-00, chair sect. on taxation 2000-01, bd. dirs. retirement funds 2004-), Equipment Leasing Assn., DC Bar Assn. (chmn. legis. and regulations com.), U. Minn. Law Sch. Alumni Assn. (bd. dirs. 1992-97), Phi Beta Kappa. Avocations: children, volunteering, cooking, softball, skiing. Office: Skadden Arps Slate Meagher & Flom LLP 1440 New York Ave NW Ste 600 Washington DC 20005-6000

OLSON, PATRICIA HAGEY, retired elementary school educator; b. South Bend, Ind., Mar. 16, 1926; d. George Lee and Catherine Blakeman Hagey; m. Robert Anderson Olson; children: Cathy Lee, Keith Alan. BS, Purdue U., West Lafayette, Ind., 1947; MA, Loyola U., Chgo., 1955; MEd, U. Ariz., Tucson, 1972, PhD, 1975. Substitute tchr. Chgo. Bd. Edn., 1949—55; tchr. 6th grade Deerfield Pub. Schs., Ill., 1955—59, Palatine Pub. Schs., Ill., 1959—63; tchr. Spanish Lake Geneva HS, Wis., 1963—66; tchr. 3d grade LA Pub. Schs., 1968—71; tchr. 6th grade Tucson Pub. Schs., 1972—75; ret. Home: 324 Linden Apt 105 Wilmette IL 60091

OLSON, PETER, publishing executive; b. Chgo., May 1, 1950; m. Candice Carpenter, Sept. 8, 2001. AB in History magna cum laude (hon.), Harvard Coll., 1972; JD cum laude, Harvard Law Sch.; MBA, Harvard Bus. Sch. Assoc. Baker & Botts, Wash., DC, 1976—77, Hamada & Matsumoto, Tokyo, 1977—79; officer, internat. group Dresdner Bank, Frankfurt, 1979—81, deputy mgr., corp. bus. dept. Tokyo, 1981—84, mgr., credit dept., 1984—87, v.p. planning dept., treasury div. Frankfurt, Germany, 1987—88; mgr. Bertelsmann AG, 1988, sr. v.p., Doubleday Book and Music Clubs Garden City, NY, 1989—90, pres., Bertelsmann, Inc., 1990—92, exec. v.p., CFO, Bantam Doubleday Dell Pub. Group, 1992—94; exec. v.p., chief admin. officer, Bantam Doubleday Dell Pub. Group, 1992—94; chmn, CEO Bertelsmann book group N. Am. Bertelsmann AG, 1994—98, mem. exec. bd., Bertelsmann Book AG, 1994—98, chmn., CEO, Random House Inc. NYC, 1998—, exec. bd. mem., trade book pub. worldwide, 2001—. Exec. com. The Quills. Mem.: Phi Beta Kappa. Office: Random House Inc 1540 Broadway New York NY 10036-4039

OLSON, PETER L., geophysicist, educator; B in Geology, U. Colo., Boulder, 1972; M in Geophysics, U. Calif., Berkeley, 1974, PhD in Geophysics, 1977. Prof. geophys. fluid dynamics Morton K. Blaustein Dept. Earth and Planetary Scis. Johns Hopkins U., Balt. Contbr. articles to sci. jours. Fellow: Am. Acad. Arts & Scis.; mem.: NAS. Office: Dept Earth and Planetary Scis Johns Hopkins U 3400 N Charles St Baltimore MD 21218 Office Phone: 410-546-7707. Office Fax: 410-516-7933. E-mail: olson@jhu.edu.

OLSON, PHILLIP DAVID LEROY, agriculturist, chemist; b. Anchorage, Feb. 3, 1940; s. Marvin Willard and Bernadette (McName) O.; m. Deborah Andreé Butler, Apr. 10, 1982; children from a previous marriage: Jamie Kay, Samuel Phillip, Jill Andre. BS, U. Idaho, 1963; MS, Oreg. State U., 1972. Technician U. Calif., Riverside, 1963—65; rsch. staff Oreg. State U., Corvallis, 1965—75; mgr. R & D Hoechst-Roussel Agri-Vet Co., Somerville, NJ, 1975—91; owner, pres. Profl. Agrl. Cons., Palm Desert, Calif., 1991—. R & D cons. and quality assurance rsch. contractor, ret., 2000. Mem. Am. Mus. Natural History. Mem. Nat. Space Soc., Soc. Quality Assurance, Pacific Regional Quality Assurance Soc., Oreg. State U. Found. (hon.), Smithsonian Instn., Archaeol. Soc. Am., Acad. Model Aeronautics, Elks, Am. Mus. Natural History, Planetary Soc., Scale Ship Modelers Assn., Sun City Shadow Hills Country Club, Sun City Golf Assn.

Avocations: reading, fishing, rc model building, scale boat modeling, ho train modeling. Home and Office: 80-536 Avenida Santa Carmen Indio CA 92203 Personal E-mail: pdolson100@verizon.net.

OLSON, RAY ALAN, librarian; b. Yankton, SD, Mar. 26, 1946; s. Oliver Bernard Olson and Mabel Highland; m. Carol Ann Nygaard; children: Eric Robert, Peter Alan. BA in History and Philosophy, Augustana Coll., 1968; MDiv, Luther Theol. Sem., St. Paul, 1972; MA in Libr. Sci., U. Minn., 1974; ThM, Luther Northwestern Sem., St. Paul, 1985. Reference and pub. svcs. supr. Luther Theol. Sem., St. Paul, 1972-74; reference libr. Luther Northwestern Sem., St. Paul, 1974-89; acting libr. Luther Sem., St. Paul, 1975-76, 81-82, 88-89, pub. svcs. libr., 1989-96, interim libr., 1996; dir. Hamma Libr. Trinity Luth. Sem., Columbus, Ohio, 1996—. Co-editor: (with others) Landings Across the Ocean, 1997. Publicity chair Luth. Brotherhood Br. Bd., St. Paul, 1994-96. Mem.: Totenlag, Valdres Samband, Landings Laget (editor newsletter 1984—94, chair publs. com. 1994—2001), Am. Theol. Libr. Assn., Vesterheim Norwegian Am. Mus. (life), Ohio Theol. Libr. Assn. (life; pres. 1999—2001), Scandinavian Club Columbus. Avocations: reading, walking, genealogy, local history. Office: Hamma Libr Trinity Luth Sem 2199 E Main St Columbus OH 43209-2334 Office Phone: 614-384-4640.

OLSON, RICHARD DAVID, psychology professor; b. Reading, Pa., Oct. 10, 1944; s. Milton Stuart and Sarah Ellen (Moyer) O.; m. M. Gayle Augustine, Aug. 26, 1967. BA, U. Redlands, 1966; MS, St. Louis U., 1968, PhD, 1970. Lic. psychologist, La. Asst. prof. psychology U. New Orleans, 1970-74, assoc. prof., chmn. dept. psychology, 1974-79, prof., chmn. dept., 1979-81, assoc. dean Grad. Sch., 1981-82, dean, 1982-88, vice chancellor, 1984-88, rsch. prof., 1988—2000, prof. emeritus, 2000—; chmn. dept. psychology, 1995—2000. Cons. psychologist, New Orleans, 1973—2002; pres. Statis. Cons. of New Orleans, 1977-82 Editor: Learning in the Classroom, 1971, The Comma After Love, The Selected Poems of Raeburn Miller, 1994, The Collected Poems of Raeburn Miller, 1997; contbr. articles to profl. jours. Grantee HEW, 1976-81 Fellow APA, Am. Psychol. Soc.; mem. Soc. for Neuroscis., Am. Statis. Assn. Home: 40 Infinity Dr Poplarville MS 39470 Office: U New Orleans Dept Psychology Lake Front New Orleans LA 70148 Office Phone: 601-795-4838. E-mail: rolsonredoak@bellsouth.net.

OLSON, ROBERT EUGENE, physician, biochemist, educator; b. Minn., Jan. 23, 1919; s. Ralph William and Minnie (Holtin) O.; m. Catherine Silvoso, Oct. 21, 1944; children: Barbara Lynn, Robert E., Mark Alan, Mary Ellen, Carol Louise. AB, Gustavus Adolphus Coll., 1938; PhD, St. Louis U., 1944; MD, Harvard, 1951; MD (hon.), Chiang Mai U., Thailand, 1983. Diplomate: Nat. Bd. Med. Examiners, Am. Bd. Nutrition (pres. 1962-63). Postgrad. research asst. biochemistry St. Louis U. Sch. Medicine, 1938-43, asst. biochemistry, 1943-44, Alice A. Doisy prof. biochemistry, chmn. dept. biochemistry, 1965-82, asso. prof. medicine, 1966-72, prof. medicine, 1972-82; vis. prof. (sabbatical) dept. biochemistry U. Freiburg, Breisgau, West Germany, 1970-71; also Hoffman-La Roche Co., Basel, Switzerland, 1970-71; instr. biochemistry and nutrition Harvard Sch. Pub. Health, 1946-47; research fellow Nutrition Found., 1947-49, Am. Heart Assn., 1949-51, established investigator, 1951-52; house officer Peter Bent Brigham Hosp., Boston, 1951-52; prof., head dept. biochemistry and nutrition Grad. Sch. Pub. Health U. Pitts.; lectr. medicine Sch. Medicine, 1952-65; mem. panel malnutrition Japan-U.S. Med. Scis. Program, 1965-69; dir. Nutrition Clinic, Falk Clinic, 1953-65; mem. sr. staff Presbyn. Hosp., dir. metabolic unit, 1960-65; mem. staff St. Louis U. Hosp., 1965-81; prof. biochemistry, prof. medicine, assoc. dean acad. affairs U. Pitts. Sch. Medicine, 1982-84; prof. medicine, prof. pharm. scis. SUNY-Stony Brook, 1984-90, prof. emeritus, 1990—; prof. pediatrics U. South Fla., Tampa, 1994—. Cons. Mercy Hosp., U. Pitts. Med. Center; assoc. in medicine St. Margaret's Meml. Hosp., Pitts., dir. metabolic unit, 1954-60; cons. divsn. rsch. grants USPHS, 1954-69, 72-76; dir. Anemia and Malnutrition Center, Chiang Mai, Thailand, 1967-77; vis. scholar dept. biochemistry Oxford (Eng.) U., 1961-62; vis. prof. dept. biochemistry U. Freiburg, West Germany, 1970-71; food and nutrition bd. NRC, 1977-83; adv. council Nat. Inst. Arthritis, Diabetes, Digestive and Kidney Diseases, 1981-85; William A. Noyes lectr. U. Ill., Urbana, 1980. Author: Perspectives in Biological Chemistry, 1970, Methods in Medical Research, 1970, Protein-Calorie Malnutrition, 1975, Balanced Nutrition, 1989; assoc. editor Nutrition Revs., 1954-56, editor, 1978-88; assoc. editor Am. Jour. Medicine, 1956-65, Circulation Rsch., 1956-76, Am. Heart Jour., 1958-65, Am. Jour. Clin. Nutrition, 1960-66, Methods in Med. Rsch., 1963-70, Biochem. Medicine, 1967-90, Molecular and Cellular Cardiology, 1967-78, Ann. Rev. Nutrition, 1979-84, editor, 1984-94; co-editor: Vitamins and Hormones, 1975-81; author 236 original sci. papers in peer-reviewed jours.; contbr. 114 chpts. in books and major reviews to profl. jours. Bd. dirs. Nat. Nutrition Consortium, 1977-81, Am. Council on Sci. and Health, 1984-91. Lt. (j.g.) USNR, 1944-46. Recipient Fulbright award, 1961-62, Guggenheim Found. award, 1961-62, 70-71, McCollum award, 1965, Joseph Goldberger award, 1974; named Atwater Meml. lectr., 1978; Geiger Meml. lectr., 1979, William A. Noyes lectr. U. Ill., 1980, H. Brooks James lectr. N.C. State U., 1981, Virginia Beal lectr. U. Mass., 1990. Fellow ACP, Internat. Acad. Cardiovasc. Scis., Am. Pub. Health Assn. (chmn. food and nutrition sect. 1960-61); Am. Inst. Nutrition (pres. 1981-82, Conrad Elvehjem award 1998), Assn. Am. Physicians; mem. AAAS (sec. med. scis. N. sect. 1965-67), Am. Assn. Cancer Research, Am. Heart Assn., AMA (mem. council food and nutrition 1959-67, vice chmn. 1962-67), Royal Soc. Health (London), N.Y. Acad. Scis., Am. Fedn. Clin. Research, Am. Soc. Clin. Investigation, Boyleston Med. Soc., Am. Chem. Soc. (pres. biochemistry group Pitts. sect. 1960-61), Am. Soc. Biol. Chemists, Soc. Exptl. Biology and Medicine, Am. Soc. Clin. Nutrition (pres. 1961-62, McCollum award 1965, Herman award 2002), Assn. Med. Sch. Depts. Biochemistry (pres. 1979-80), Pa., St. Louis, Allegheny County med. socs., Am. Soc. Study Liver Diseases, Phi Beta Kappa, Sigma Xi, Phi Lambda Upsilon, Alpha Omega Alpha, Alpha Sigma Nu. Clubs: Cosmos (Washington), Countryside Country Club (Clearwater, Fla.). Home: 2673 Camille Dr Palm Harbor FL 34684-2217 Office: U South Fla Dept Pediatrics 17 Davis Blvd Ste 200 Tampa FL 33606-3438 Office Phone: 813-259-8700. Personal E-mail: roberteolsonr@cs.com. Business E-Mail: rolson@hsc.usf.edu.

OLSON, ROBERT GRANT, lawyer; b. Ft. Dodge, Iowa, Mar. 29, 1952; s. Grant L. and R. June (Pohlmann) Olson; m. Cynthia Lynn Murray, Sept. 7, 1978; children: Brendon, Elisabeth, Jeffrey, Daniel. BS, Iowa State U., 1973; JD, U. Iowa, 1976. Bar: Mo. 1976, Ill. 1977. Ptnr. Thompson & Mitchell, St. Louis, 1976-92, Riezman & Blitz, P.C., St. Louis, 1992-2000, Stone, Leyton & Gershman, P.C., St. Louis, 2000—. Editor: Jour. Corp. Law, 1975—76. Vol. Habitat for Humanity, Gephardt for Pres. Campaign, 1988, Carnahan for Lt. Gov. Campaign, 1988, Carnahan for Gov. Campaign, 1992; arbitrator Better Bus. Bur., Taxpayer Assistance Program. Mem.: ABA, Met. St. Louis Bar Assn., Ill. Bar Assn., Mo. Bar Assn., Downtown St. Louis Lions Club (pres. 1990—91). Home: 424 E Jackson Rd Saint Louis MO 63119-4128 Office: Stone Leyton & Gershman 7733 Forsyth Blvd Ste 500 Saint Louis MO 63105-1817 Home Phone: 314-968-0570; Office Phone: 314-721-7011.

OLSON, ROBERT HOWARD, lawyer; b. July 6, 1944; s. Robert Howard and Jacquiline (Wells) O.; m. Diane Carol Thorsen, Aug. 13, 1966; children: Jeffrey, Christopher. BA in Govt. summa cum laude, Ind. U., 1966; JD cum laude, Harvard U., 1969. Bar: Ohio 1969, Fla. 1980, Ariz. 1985, Calif. 2001, U.S. Supreme Ct. 1973. Assoc. Squire, Sanders & Dempsey, L.L.P., Cleve., 1969, 70-71, 76-81, ptnr., 1981—, Phoenix, 1985—2002, Squire, Sanders & Dempsey, San Francisco, 2002—; sr. law clk. U.S. Dist. Ct., No. Dist., Ind., 1969-70; chief civil rights divsn. Ohio Atty. Gen.'s Office, Columbus, 1971-73, chief consumer protection, 1973-75, chief counsel, 1975, 1st asst. (chief of staff), 1975-76. Instr. Ohio State U. Law Sch., Columbus, 1974; Cen. Phoenix com. to advise city council and mayor City of Phoenix, 1987—89; bd. dirs. Orpheum Theater Found., 1989—2002, sec., 1989—90, pres., 1990—97, exec. com., 1997—99, The Ariz. Ctr. for Law in the Pub. Interest, 1989—2001, treas., 1992—93, 1997—2001, v.p., 1993—94; mem. Ariz. Ctr. for Disability Law, 1994—96, treas., 1994—95; mem. Valley Leadership Class XIV; rsch. com. Ariz. Town Hall, 1998—2002; mem. fin. com. Pub. Advs., Inc.; co-chair Calif. Pub. Fin. Conf., 2006. Contbr. articles to profl. jours. Bd. dirs. 1st Unitarian Ch. Phoenix, 1987-89, 98-2001, v.p., 1987-89, 2000-2001, pres. 1998-99; bd. dirs. 1st Unitarian Ch. Found., 1987-93, pres., 1990-93; exec. com. San Francisco (Calif.) Heartwalk, Am. Heart Assn., 2005. Named Arts Advocate of Yr. Bus. Vols. Arts/Phoenix, 1997. Mem. Ariz. State Bar Assn., Calif. Bar Assn., Phi Beta Kappa. Office: Squire Sanders & Dempsey LLP One Maritime Plaza Suite 300 San Francisco CA 94111-3492

OLSON, ROBERT MARTIN, plastic surgeon; b. Abington, Pa., Dec. 15, 1949; s. Carl Martin Olson and Jacqueline Mary O'Neill; m. Megan Evans Thomas, Dec. 30, 1982; children: Robert, Gwyneth, Nevin, Sonja. MD, U. Pa., 1974; ThM, New Brunswick Theol. Sem., 2004. Cert. Am. Bd. Plastic Surgery, Am. Bd. Surgery. Tng., plastic surgery Mayo Clinic Grad. Sch. Medicine; tng., gen. surgery Harvard U., Peter Bent Brigham Hosp. & Children's Hosp. Med. Ctr., Boston; plastic surgeon Plastic Surgery Arts, New Brunswick, NJ, 1983—; clin. assoc. prof. surgery and biomedical engrng. U. Medicine and Dentistry NJ-Robert Wood Johnson Med. Sch., New Brunswick, NJ, 1983—; chief plastic surgery St. Peters U. Hosp., New Brunswick, NJ. Travels worldwide Operation Smile. Lt. col. USAR, 1988—96. Named one of Top Plastic Surgeons, NJ Mag.; recipient Humanitarian award, Friends Health Connection, 2002, Middlesex County Med. Soc., 2003, Svc. award, USAR, 1991. Fellow: ACS. Episcopalian. Office: 78 Easton Ave New Brunswick NJ 08901 Office Phone: 732-418-0700. Business E-Mail: rolson@psanj.com. *

OLSON, ROBERT WILLIAM, writer, retired counselor; b. Chgo., Feb. 5, 1930; s. Milton Olaf Olson and Leonore Stillman; m. Seiko Itoyama, Jan. 16, 1955. BA, George Williams Coll., 1952; MA, U. Chgo., 1959; 7th yr. cert. counselor-cons., Oreg. State U., 1967. Tchr. 6th grade Matteson Elem. Sch., Ill., 1956—59; cons., sch. counselor elem. schs., jr. and sr. h.s., various cities Ill., Wash., 1959—91; instr. counseling U. Wash., Seattle, 1979—81; family counselor Seattle, 1980—91. Behavioral rschr., U. Wash., 1979-81. Author: Memories with a Christmas Attitude, 1994, Rich Memories with a Christmas Spirit, 2005; editor FOKUS Newsletter, 1998—; contbr. numerous articles to profl. counseling jours. Vol. Love and Forgiveness Seminar, Monroe Penitentiary, 1996—; pres. King County Guidance Assn., Wash., 1978—79; bd. mem. Children Around the World Resource Ctr. With US Army, 1952—56, Korea and Japan. Mem. NEA (life), Wash. Edn. Assn., Internat. Assn. Near-Death Studies, Full Gospel Businessmen Internat. (vol. King County Jail 1998—), Eastside Writers Assn. (hospitality chmn. 1999—), Northwest Christian Writers Assn. Avocations: ceramics, storytelling, swimming. Home and Office: 252 168th Ave SE Bellevue WA 98008 Office Phone: 425-747-3879. E-mail: membob@aol.com.

OLSON, ROBERT WYRICK, lawyer; b. Madison, Wis., Dec. 19, 1945; s. John Arthur and Mary Katherine (Wyrick) O.; m. Carol Jean Duane, June 12, 1971; children: John Hagan, Mary Catherine Duane. BA, Williams Coll., 1967; JD, U. Va., 1970. Assoc. Cravath, Swaine & Moore, NYC, 1970-79; asst. gen. counsel Penn Cen. Corp., Cin., 1979-80, assoc. gen. counsel, 1980-82, v.p., dep. gen. counsel, 1982-87; sr. v.p., gen. counsel, sec. Am. Premier Underwriters, Inc. (formerly Penn Cen. Corp.), Cin., 1987-95; sr. v.p., gen. counsel and sec. Chiquita Brands Internat., Inc., Cin., 1995—2006; ret., 2006. Mem. ABA.

OLSON, RONALD LEROY, lawyer; b. Carroll, Iowa, July 9, 1941; s. Clyde L. and Delpha C. (Boyens) Olson; m. Jane Tenhulzen, June 21, 1964; children: Kristin, Steven, Amy. BS, Drake U., 1963; JD, U. Mich., 1966; Diploma Law, Oxford U., Eng., 1967. Bar: Wis. 1966, Calif. 1969, US Dist. Ct. (cen. dist.), Calif. 1969, US Dist. Ct. (so. dist.),Calif. 1973, US Ct. Appeals (9th cir.) 1974, US Ct. Appeals (10th cir.) 1980, US Ct. Appeals (5th cir.) 1982, US Supreme Ct. 1976, US Dist. Ct., Alaska 1983. Atty. civil rights divsn. US Dept. Justice, 1967; law clk. to chief judge David L. Bazelon US Ct. Appeals (DC cir.), Washington, 1967—68; ptnr. Munger, Tolles & Olson LLP, Los Angeles, Calif., 1968—; lawyer del. Am. 9th Cir. Conf., 1984—89; lectr. in field; mem. editorial bd. Alternatives, 1983—. Mem. bd. dirs. The Wash. Post Co., 2003—. Contbr. articles legal jour. Named one of 100 Most Influential Lawyers, Nat. Law Jour., 2006; recipient Burton scholar, U. Mich.; fellow Am. Coll Trial Lawyers. Fellow: Am. Bar Found., Ford Found. Oxford U.; mem.: 9th Cir. Jud. Conf. (exec. com. 1984—89), Chancery, LA County Barristers (pres. 1976), Assn. Bus. Trial Lawyers (mem. adv. com. trial ct. improvement fund for Calif. jud. coun. 1988—), State Bar Calif. (bd. dir. 1985, v.p. 1986—87), LA County Bar Assn., Am. Arbitration Assn. (bd. dir. 1983, comml. panel 1983), LA Bar Found. (bd. dir. 1977), Am. Judicature Soc., Human Rights (editorial bd., publ. sect. ind. rights and responsibilities 1986—), Soviet Exchange Program (litig. sect. com. 1983—), ABA (litig. sect. council 1976, chmn. sp. com. on dispute resolution 1976—86, chmn. litig. section 1981—82, chmn. standing com. on fed. judiciary 1991—92), Skid Row Housing Trust of LA (mem. 1986—), U. Mich. Law Sch. (com. visitors 1986—), Salzburg Seminar (bd. dir.), Legal Aid Found. LA (bd. dir. 1975—86, pres. 1984—85), Claremont U. Ctr. and Grad. Sch. (chmn. bd. fellows 1984—94), Sequoia Nat. Pk. Natural History Assn., Drake U. (trustee 1977), Alternatives (mem. editorial bd. 1983—88), LA Arts Festival (sec. 1985), Lawyers Alliance for Nuclear Arms Control (adv. com. Los Angeles and Orange Counties chpt.), Frat. of Friends of Music Ctr. (bd. dir., pres. 1978), Omicron Delta Kappa, Phi Eta Sigma, Beta Gamma Sigma. Democrat. Episcopalian. Office: Munger Tolles & Olson 355 S Grand Ave Fl 35 Los Angeles CA 90071-1560 E-mail: Ron.Olson@mto.com. *

OLSON, ROY ARTHUR, retired government official; b. Dec. 8, 1938; s. Elof Herman and Beatrice Lorraine (Dolezal) O.; m. Elisabeth Rigge Behrens, June 24, 1967; children: Heather Elisabeth, Peter Roy. BS, Northwestern U., 1960. Writer, editor Chgo. Am., 1956-68; pres. Roy Olson Pub. Rels. Co., Oak Park, Ill., 1968-70; asst. regional adminstr. SBA, Chgo., 1970-95; Chgo. spokesman Ill. Dept. Transp., 1995—2003. Bd. dirs. Am. Food Industries, Chgo., Covenant Village Retirement Ctr., Northbrook, Ill., Brandel Care Ctr., Northbrook. Author: From Bistros to Bible Study, 2006. Chmn. Northbrook Covenant Ch., 1980-81, 97-2000. Mem. Soc. Profl. Journalists, Art Inst. Chgo., City Club (media com.), Execs. Club, Chgo. Press Club, Chgo. Headline Club (past dir. 1964-66), Northwestern Club. Home: 2015 Prairie St Glenview IL 60025-2824 E-mail: olsons2015@yahoo.com.

OLSON, STEPHEN M(ICHAEL), lawyer; b. Jamestown, NY, May 4, 1948; s. Charles R. and Marilyn (Dietzel) O.; m. Linda C. Hanson, Aug. 24, 1968; children: Kevin, Darren. AB cum laude, Princeton U., 1970; JD, U. Chgo., 1973. Bar: Pa. 1973, U.S. Dist. Ct. (we. dist.) Pa. 1973, U.S. Ct. Appeals (3d cir.) 1975, U.S. Ct. Appeals (1st and D.C. cirs.) 1986, U.S. Ct. Appeals (7th cir. and 8th cir. 1988), U.S. Supreme Ct. 1986. Assoc. Kirkpatrick & Lockhart Preston Gates Ellis LLC, Pitts., 1973-81, ptnr., 1981—. Mem.: ABA (rlwy./airline labor law com.), Allegheny County Bar Assn., Pa. Bar Assn., Princeton Alumni Assn. West Pa., Duquesne Club. Avocations: photography, bicycling. Office: Kirkpatrick & Lockhart Preston Gates Ellis LLC Henry W Oliver Bldg 535 Smithfield St Pittsburgh PA 15222-2312 Office Phone: 412-355-6496. Business E-Mail: stephen.olson@klgates.com.

OLSON, STEVEN R., lawyer; b. Baraboo, Wis., July 10, 1955; BS, Andrews U., 1978; JD, John Marshall Law Sch., 1982. Bar: Ill. 1982. Ptnr., chmn. Health Care Practice, mem. exec. com. Katten Muchin Zavis Rosenman, Chgo. Mem.: Am. Health Lawyers Assn. Office: Katten Muchin Rosenman LLP 525 W Monroe St Chicago IL 60661 Office Phone: 312-902-5640. Office Fax: 312-577-8954. E-mail: steven.olson@kattenlaw.com.

OLSON, THEODORE BEVRY, lawyer, former federal agency administrator; b. Chgo., Sept. 11, 1940; m. Barbara Kay Bracher, May 1996 (dec. Sept. 11, 2001); 2 children; m. Lady Booth, Oct. 21, 2006 BA cum laude, U. Pacific, 1962; LL.B., U. Calif.-Berkeley, 1965. Bar: Calif. 1965, DC 1982. Assoc. Gibson, Dunn & Crutcher LLP, Los Angeles, 1965—71, ptnr., 1972—81, 1984—2001, 2004—, co-chair, appellate & constitutional law practice group, 2004—; asst. atty. gen. US Dept. Justice, Washington, 1981—84, solicitor gen., 2001—04. Panelist Gen. Counsel Leadership Series, 2007; vis. scholar Nat. Constn. Ctr. and U. Pa. Sch. Law, 2007. Mem. Calif. Law Review, 1964-1965, Calif. Commn. on Uniform State Laws, 1972-74, Privacy and Civil Liberties Oversight Bd, 2005-; del. Republican Nat. Conv., 1976, 80. Named one of 100 Most Influential Lawyers, Nat. Law Jour., 2006; recipient Edmund J. Randolph award, US Dept. Justice, 1984, 2004, Disting. Pub. Svc. medal, US Dept. Def., 2004. Fellow Am. Acad. Appellate Lawyers, Am. Coll. Trial Lawyers; mem. ABA, Order of the Coif. Republican. Office: Gibson Dunn & Crutcher LLP 1050 Connecticut Ave NW Washington DC 20036 Personal E-mail: tolson@gibsondunn.com.

OLSON, WALTER GILBERT, lawyer; b. Stanton, Nebr., Feb. 2, 1924; s. O.E. Olson and Mabel A. Asplin; m. Gloria Helen Bennett, June 26, 1949; children: Clifford Warner, Karen Rae Olson. BS, U. Calif., Berkeley, 1947, JD, 1949. Bar: Calif. 1950, U.S. Dist. Ct. (no. dist.) Calif. 1950, U.S. Tax Ct. 1950, U.S. Ct. Appeals (9th cir.) 1950. Assoc. Orrick, Herrington and Sutcliffe (formerly Orrick, Dahlquist, Herrington and Sutcliffe), San Francisco, 1949-54, ptnr., 1954-88. Bd. dirs. Alltel Corp., Little Rock, 1988-94; mem. Commn. to Revise Calif. Corp. Securities Law, 1967-69, Securities Regulatory Reform Panel, 1978-80; mem. corp. security adv. com. Calif. Commr. of Corps, 1975-88. Editor-in-chief Calif. Law Review, 1948-49. Bd. dirs. Internat. Ho., Berkeley, 1981-86. With U.S. Army, 1943-46, ETO. Fellow Am. Bar Found.; mem. ABA (trust divsn. nat. conf. of lawyers and reps. of Am. Bankers Assn.), Calif. Bar Assn. (chmn. corps com. 1975-76, exec. com. bus. law sect. 1977-78), San Francisco Bar Assn., U. Calif. Alumni Assn., Boalt Hall Alumni Assn. (bd. dirs. 1982-90, sec. 1985, v.p. 1987, pres. 1988), Order of Coif, Menlo Country Club (Woodside, Calif.), Pacific-Union Club. Home: 501 Portola Rd #8162 Portola Valley CA 94028-8616

OLSON, WALTER JUSTUS, JR., management consultant; b. Paterson, NJ, July 27, 1941; s. Walter Justus and Viola Patricia (Trautvetter) O. BS, BA, Brown U., 1964; MBA, Columbia U., 1967. CPA Va. Design engr. Rockwell Internat., Inc., Downey, Calif., 1964-65; mgmt. officer CIA, Washington, 1969-73; sr. cons. Booz, Allen and Hamilton, Inc., Washington, 1973-78; corp. planning coordinator Washington Gas Light Co., Washington, 1978-82; prin. Walter J. Olson & Assoc., McLean, Va., 1982-83; dep. asst. sec. for export adminstrn. U.S. Dept. Commerce, Washington, 1983-86; prin. Walter J. Olson & Assoc., Washington, 1986—; sr. rsch. analyst U.S. House Select Com. Technology Transfer to PRC, Washington, 1998-99. Vice-chmn. fin. com. Fairfax County Reps., Va., 1982-83. Served to 1st lt. USAF, 1967—69. Mem. AICPA, Greater Wash. Soc. CPAs, Strategic Leadership Forum (pres. Washington chpt. 1990-91). Republican. Episcopalian. Home: 7348 Dartford Dr Mc Lean VA 22102-7348 Office: 8180 Greensboro Dr Ste 1070 Mc Lean VA 22102-3860 Office Phone: 703-356-6919. Personal E-mail: walterolson@mindspring.com.

OLSON, WILLIAM JEFFREY, lawyer; b. Paterson, NJ, Oct. 23, 1949; s. Walter Justus and Viola Patricia (Trautvetter) O.; m. Janet Elaine Bollen, May 22, 1976; children: Robert J., Joanne C. AB, Brown U., 1971; JD, U. Richmond, 1976. Bar: Va. 1976, D.C. 1976, U.S. Ct. Claims 1976, U.S. Ct. Appeals (4th, 6th, 10th,11th and D.C. cirs.) 1976, U.S. Supreme Ct. 1982. Assoc. Jackson & Campbell, Washington, 1976-79; ptnr. Gilman, Olson & Pangia, Washington, 1980-92; prin. William J. Olson PC, McLean, Va. and Washington, 1992—. Sec., treas. bd. dirs. Victims Assistance Legal Orgn., McLean, Va., 1979—; presdl. transition team leader Legal Svcs. Corp., Washington, 1980; chmn. and bd. dirs. nat. Legal Svcs. Corp., 1981-82; mem. Pres.'s Export Coun. Subcom. on Export Adminstrn., Washington, 1982-84; spl. counsel bd. govs. U.S. Postal Svc., Washington, 1984-86. Author: Tuition Tax Credits and Alternatives, 1978; co-author: Debating National Health Policy, 1977, Executive Orders and National Emergencies, 1999, An Evaluation of Postal Service Worksharing, 2003, Enhancing Competition By Unbundling the Postal Adminstration, 2005. Trustee Davis Meml. Goodwill Industries, Washington, 1980-86, 88-93; chmn. Fairfax County Rep. Com., Fairfax, Va., 1980-82; mem. Rep. State Ctrl. Com., Richmond, Va., 1982-86. Republican. Avocation: gardening. Office: 8180 Greensboro Dr Ste 1070 Mc Lean VA 22102-3860 Home Phone: 540-868-2890; Office Phone: 703-356-5070. Personal E-mail: wjo@mindspring.com.

OLSON-HELLERUD, LINDA KATHRYN, elementary school educator; b. Wisconsin Rapids, Wis., Aug. 26, 1947; d. Samuel Ellsworth and Lillian (Dvorak) Olson; m. H. A. Hellerud, 1979; 1 child, Sarah Kathryn Hellerud. BS, U. Wis., Stevens Point, 1969, tchg. cert., 1970, MST, 1972; MS, U. Wis., Whitewater, 1975; EdS, U. Wis., Stout, 1978. Cert. reading specialist, technology tng. Clk. U. Counseling Ctr. U. Wis., Stevens Point, 1965—69; elem. sch. tchr. Wisconsin Rapids, 1970—76; sch. counselor, 1976—79; dist. dir. elem. guidance, 1979—82; tchr. elem. and reading, 1982—. Instr. Summer Remedial Reading Program; cons. in field. Advocate Literacy Mentoring Program; active St. Luke's Luth Ch. Mem.: NEA, Ctrl. Wis. Reading Assn., Internat. Reading Assn., Wood County Lit. Coun. (cons.), Wis. Reading Assn. Avocations: literacy activities and research, piano, aerobics, Spanish. Home: 120 11th St N Wisconsin Rapids WI 54494-5371 Office: Howe Elem Sch Wisconsin Rapids WI 54494

OLSSON, ANN-MARGRET See ANN-MARGRET

OLSSON, BJÖRN ESKIL, railroad supply company executive; b. Kristianstad, Sweden, Oct. 7, 1945; came to U.S., 1990; m. Cecilia Lindblad, July 6, 1968; children: Fredrik, Karin, Eva. M Bus. and Adminstrn., U. Lund, Sweden, 1968. Internal auditor Kockums Mek. Verkstad, Malmö, Sweden, 1969-71, mgr. acctg., 1971-74; v.p. fin. and adminstrn. Kockums Industri, Söderhamn, Sweden, 1974-76, Linden Alimak, Skellefteå, Sweden, 1976-81, Sonessons, Malmö, 1981-82; pres. Sab-Nife, Malmö, 1982-87; v.p. corp. devel. Investment AB Cardo, Malmö, 1987-90; pres., CEO Harmon Industries Inc., Blue Springs, Mo., 1990—. Bd. dirs. BJ Papperats, Malmo, Green & Co., Malmö; mem. adv. bd. Ctrl. Mo. State U. Bus. Sch., Warrensburg, 1991—. Staff sgt. Swedish Army, 1964-65. Avocations: golf, skiing. Office: Harmon Industries Inc PO Box 600 Grain Valley MO 64029-0600

OLSSON, CARL ALFRED, urologist, department chairman; b. Boston, Nov. 29, 1938; s. Charles Rudolph and Ruth Marion (Bostrom) O.; m. Mary DeVore, Nov. 4, 1962; children: Ingrid, Leif Eric. Grad., Bowdoin Coll., 1959; MD, Boston U., 1963. Diplomate Am. Bd. Urology (trustee 1988-94, pres. 1993-94). Asst. prof. urology Boston U. Sch. Medicine, 1971-72, assoc. prof., 1972-74, prof., chmn. dept., 1974-80; dir. urology dept. Boston City Hosp., 1974-77; chief urology dept. Boston VA Med. Ctr., 1971—75; urologist-in-chief Univ. Hosp., Boston, 1971-80; John K. Lattimer prof., chmn. dept. urology Coll. Phys. and Surgs., Columbia U., NYC, 1980—2005, chmn. emeritus, 2005—. Dir. Squier Urol. Clinic, urology service Presbyn. Hosp., NYC; lectr. surgery Tufts U. Sch. Medicine. Boston Interhosp. Organ Bank, 1976-79; mem. working cadre Nat. Prostate Cancer Project, Nat. Cancer Inst., 1979-84; mem. adv. coun. Nat. Inst. Diabetes, Digestive Disease and Kidney; mem. integration panel for prostate cancer rsch. Dept. of Def., 1998-2002, chmn., 2000-01. Editl. bd. Jour. Prostate, World Jour. Urology, Jour. Urodynamics and Neurourology, Jour. Urology; asst. editor Jour. Urology, 1978-2004; contbr. chpts. to books, articles to med. jours. Recipient Disting. Alumnus award Boston U., 1985, Boston U. Alumni award, 2007. Fellow ACS; mem. Am. Urol. Assn. (coord. continuing med. edn. New Eng. sect. 1977-80, del. rsch. com., bd. dirs. 2001-06, exec. com. 2002-06, sec. 2000-06, found. operating bd. 2005-06, Gold Cystoscope award 1979, Grayson-Carroll award 1971, 73, Hugh Hampton Young award 2001), Boston Surg. Soc. (exec. com. 1976-80), Am. Assn. Clin. Urologists, Am. Surg. Assn., Am. Assn. Genitourinary Surgeons (pres. elect 2006), Clin. Soc. Genitourinary Surgeons (pres.-elect 2006-), Transplantation Soc., Soc. Urologic Oncology (pres. 1993), Soc. Pelvic Surgeons, Soc. Univ. Urologists (pres. 1990), N.Y. Sect. Am. Urol. Assn. (pres. 2002), AMA, Assn. Acad. Surgery, Am. Soc. Artificial Internal Organs, Am. Soc. Transplant Surgeons, Assn. Med. Colls., Can. Urol. Assn., Societe Internationale d'Urologie, Internat. Urodynamics Soc., Mass. Med. Soc., Soc. Govt. Urologists, Australasian Urol. Soc. (hon.), New Eng. Handicapped Sportsmen's Assn. (exec. com. 1977-81), U.S. Yacht Racing Union, Yacht Racing Union L.I. Sound, N.Y. Yacht Club, Cottage Park Yacht Club, Larchmont Yacht Club, Storm Trysail Club, Alpha Omega Alpha, Am. Found. Urol. Diseases (bd. dirs. 2002-05, exec. coun. 2002-05), NY Acad. Scis. (Valentine award medal 2006). Episcopalian. Office: Columbia-Presbyn Hosp Irving Pavilion 161 Ft Washington Av New York NY 10032-3702 Home Phone: 914-834-9442; Office Phone: 212-305-0100. Office Fax: 212-305-0106. Business E-Mail: cao2@columbia.edu.

OLSTAD, ROGER GALE, science educator; b. Mpls., Jan. 16, 1934; s. Arnold William and Myra (Stroschein) O.; m. Constance Elizabeth Jackson, Aug. 20, 1955; children: Karen Louise, Kenneth Bradley. BS, U. Minn., 1955, MA, 1959, PhD, 1963. Instr. U. Minn., Mpls., 1956-63; asst. prof. U. Ill., Urbana, 1963-64; mem. faculty U. Wash., Seattle, 1964—, asso. prof. sci. edn., 1967-71, prof., 1971-95, asso. dean grad. studies Coll. Edn., 1971-85; prof. emeritus, 1995—. Bd. trustees Shoreline C.C., 2006—. Chair environ. quality commn. City of Lake Forest Park, Wash., 1997-2000, city coun., 2000—, mayor pro tempore, 2006—. Fellow AAAS; mem. NSTA (bd. dirs.) Wash. Sci. Tchrs. Assn. (pres. 1973-74), Nat. Assn. Rsch. Sci. Teaching (pres. 1977-78, bd. dirs.), N.W. Sci. Assn. (chmn. 1966-68), Assn. Edn. Tchrs. in Sci. (regional pres. 1966-68, pres. 1991-92), Nat. Assn. Biology Tchrs., Biol. Scis. Curriculum Study (chmn., bd. dirs. 1989-94), U. Wash. Faculty Club, Phi Delta Kappa. Home: 20143 53rd Ave NE Seattle WA 98155-1801 Office: U Wash Coll Edn Seattle WA 98195-0001 Personal E-mail: rolstad@earthlink.net. Business E-Mail: rolstad@u.washington.edu.

OLSZEWSKI, WOJCIECH, economist, mathematician; m. Anna Krystyna Kucharska; children: Maciej Wojciech, Adam Ignacy. Doktor Matematyki, Uniwersytet Warszawski, Warsaw, Poland, 1992; PhD in Econs., Princeton U., NJ, 2001. Asst. prof. Nortwestern U., Evanston, Ill., 2001—. Contbr. articles to profl. jours. NSF grantee. Home: 2742 Garrison Ave Evanston IL 60201 Office: Northwestern U 2003 Sheridan Rd Evanston IL 60208 Home Phone: 847-733-1409; Office Phone: 847-491-8482. Office Fax: 847-491-7001. Business E-Mail: wo@northwestern.edu.

OLTMAN, JOHN HAROLD, patent lawyer; b. Nov. 18, 1929; s. Peter Harold and Hazel Evelyn (Kelly) O.; m. Lita Marilyn Hagen, Aug. 16, 1952; children: David K., Laura G., John K. BS in Chem. Engring., U. Mich., 1952, JD, 1957. Bar: Ill. 1957, Ariz. 1964, Mich. 1965, Fla. 1968. Mem. firms Mueller & Aichele (Attys.), Chgo. and Phoenix, 1957—64, Barnes, Kisselle, Rasich & Choate (Attys.), Detroit, 1964—65, Settle, Batchelder & Oltman (Attys.), Detroit, 1965—67, Settle & Oltman (Attys.), Detroit and Ft. Lauderdale, 1967—72, Oltman and Flynn (Attys.), Ft. Lauderdale, 1972—90, Oltman, Flynn & Kublev, Ft. Lauderdale, 1990—. With USMC Res., 1952—54. Mem.: IEEE, ABA, Fla. Engring. Soc., Intellectual Property Law Assn. So. Fla., Am. Intellectual Property, Broward County Bar Assn., Fla. Bar Assn., Kiwanian (dir. Ft. Lauderdale Club 1972—74, 1977—78, pres. 1983—, chmn. Key Club com. 1970—78), Tau Beta Pi, Phi Eta Sigma. Office: 915 Middle River Dr Ste 415 Fort Lauderdale FL 33304-3561 Home: 168 Marion Oaks Golf Way Ocala FL 34473 E-mail: oltman@bellsouth.net.

OLUBODUN, JOEL OLADAPO, medical researcher, physician; b. Ipoti, Ekiti, Nigeria, July 12, 1950; came to U.S., 1996; s. Samson Folayan and Alice Olawande O.; m. Margaret Olufunke, Feb. 21, 1981; children: David Oluwaseun, Israel Olaoluwa, Elizabeth Ifejesu. BS, MB, U. Ibadan, Nigeria, 1977. Houseman Adeoyo Specialist Hosp., Ibadan, Nigeria, 1977-78; resident in internal medicine U. Coll. Hosp., Ibadan, 1979-85; rsch. fellow cardiology Freeman Hosp., Newcastle Upon Tyne, U.K., 1985-86; physician, cardiologist, sr. lectr. Ogun State U. Tchg. Hosp., Shagamu, Nigeria, 1988-91; sr. rschr. fellow U. Newcastle & Freeman Hosp., Newcastle Upon Tyne, 1991-96; resident U. Pa. Health Sys., Presbyn. Med. Ctr., Phila., 1996-2000; rschr. drug devel. Tufts U. Pfizer Global Rsch. and Devel., Boston, 2000—. Chmn. cardiovas. svcs. bd. Ogun State U. Tchg. Hosp., 1989-91, disciplinary bd., 1990-91, acting head medicine dept., 1990-91, dept. rep. U. senate, 1989-91; cons. in field. Contbr. numerous articles to profl. jours.; editl. bd. Jour Ethnicity & Disease, 1999—. Active vol. African Christian Fellowship, 1996—. Med. officer 22d. armoured bridage, Ilorin, Nigeria, 1978-79. Recipient Elizabeth Wherry award, 1995, Searle Dist. Rsch. award 1996, med. degree (MRCP), Royal Coll. Physicians of Ireland, 1995, award Am. Coll. Clin. Pharmacology, 2001, 02, award Am. Soc. Clin. Pharmacology and Therapeutics, 2002, James A. Bain Young Scientist award World Congress Pharmacologists, 2002; fellow Assn. Commonwealth Univs., London, 1991, Pfizer, 1991. Fellow Postgrad. Med. Coll. Physicians Nigeria; mem. Royal Coll. Physicians Ireland, Royal Coll. Physicians Nigeria, Am. Coll. Physicians (bd. cert.), Internat. Soc. Hypertension in Blacks (editl. bd. 1990—, manuscript reviewer). Avocations: chess, travel, writing. Office: Tufts Univ Med Sch 136 Harrison Ave Boston MA 02111 Home: 20 Ponte Ln North Kingstown RI 02852-4755 E-mail: olubodun@yahoo.com.

OLUYITAN, EMMANUEL FUNSO, communications educator; b. Efon-Alaye, Nigeria, July 25, 1940; BA cum laude in Polit. Sci., Bowie State U., Md., 1972; MPA in Policy Analysis and Journalism, Ind. U., 1975, EdD in Instructional Tech., 1980. News reporter Nigerian Nat. Press, Lagos, 1964-65; music libr., news translator, news reporter Nigerian Broadcasting Corp., 1965-69; pub. info. coord. Aerospace Rsch. Ctr., Sch. Pub./Environ. Affairs, Ind. U., Bloomington, 1973-75; victim assistance officer Indpls. Police Dept., 1975-76; prin. lectr. Nigerian TV Authority, Lagos, 1978-81; assoc. prof. dept. edn. Ahmadu Bello U., Zaria, Nigeria, 1981-88, asst. dean postgrad. studies, 1985-88, head instructional tech. divsn., 1983-88; program officer Nat. Assn. for Equal Opportunity in Higher Edn., Washington, 1988-93; dir. Office of Pub. Rels. and Pubs. Lincoln University, Pa., 1993-96; dir. integrated info. tech. Bennett Coll., Greensboro, N.C., 1996-97; prof. comm. Wilberforce U., Ohio, 1997—2006. Staff writer Office of Pub. Info., Bowie State U., 1973; vice chmn. bd. Adventures in Health, Edn. and Agrl. Devel., Inc., Rockville, Md., 1993—; bd. dirs. Anthony J. Cebrun Journalism Ctr., Nashville; CEO, ASE African Ctr., Dayton, Ohio. Author: Africa Yesterday & Today; photographer, fgn. news editor: Ebony Tree, 1970-72; editor: African Insight, 1973, Nigeria Audio-Visual Newsletter, 1982-86, Nigeria Audio-Visual Jour., 1982-86, Global Vision, 1988-93, Update, 1988-93; assoc. editor: Black Excellence, 1988-93; editor-in-chief: Weekly Calendar, 1993-96, LU Newsletter, 1993-96, The Lincoln Lion, 1993-96, The Lincoln-Jour., 1993-96; contbr. articles to profl. jours., newspapers; contbr. photographs to books, jours.; prodr. numerous ednl. materials (videos, slides, pictures). Recipient Dir. Gen.'s Commendation, Nigerian TV Authority, 1987, Fed. Govt. of Nigeria's Postgrad. award, 1977-80, Award of Accomplishment and Worthiness, Indpls. Police Dept., 1976, Contr.'s Citation, Nigerian Broadcasting Corp., 1967. Mem. Assn. of Nigerians Against Corruption (founder), Nigerian Assn. for Ednl. Media and Tech., Internat. Assn. Black Profls. in Internat. Affairs, Assn. of Ednl. Comm. and Tech., Oxford Rotary Club (v.p. 1995-96). Avocations: tennis, ping-pong, photography, travel. Office: ASE African Ctr 4550-A Salem Ave Trotwood OH 45416 Personal E-mail: iyaboase@aol.com.

OLVER, JOHN WALTER, congressman; b. Honesdale, Pa., Sept. 3, 1936; s. Helen Fulleborn Olver; m. Rose Alice Richardson, Sept. 12, 1959; 1 child, Martha. BS, Rensselaer Poly. Inst., 1955; MS, Tufts U., 1956; PhD, MIT, 1961. Asst. prof. chemistry U. Mass., Amherst, 1962-67; mem. Mass. Ho. of Reps., Boston, 1969-72, Mass. Senate, 1973-91, U.S. Congress from 1st Mass. dist., 1991—, mem. com. on appropriations, mem. subcoms. on transp. and mil. constrn., mil. appropriations, asst. whip, 1991—. Contbr. articles to profl. jours. Democrat. Avocations: hiking, gardening, tennis. Office: US Ho Reps 1111 Longworth Ho Office Bldg Washington DC 20515-2101 Office Phone: 202-225-5335. Office Fax: 202-226-1224. *

OLVEY, STEPHEN EARL, internist; b. Indpls., Mar. 24, 1943; s. Ottis Niel Olvey and Ruth Ridgeway Nair; m. Lynne Vittorio Olvey, Oct. 8, 1985; children: Nicole, Dawn, Kyle. BS, Hanover Coll., Ind., 1965; MD, Ind. U., Indpls., 1969. Diplomate Am. Bd. Internal Medicine. Intern Meth. Hosp. Ind., 1969, resident internal medicine, 1970—72; pvt. practice, 1972—77; assoc. dir. Meth. Hosp., Indpls., 1977—91; dir. neurol. intensive care Jackson Meml. Hosp., Miami, Fla., 1991—. Clin. asst. prof. Ind. U., Sch. Medicine, Indpls., 1977—91; assoc. prof. U. Miami, Sch. Medicine, Miami, 1991—. Author: Rapid Response, 2006. Recipient Mario Andretti High Performance award in medicine for motorsports, Detroit Med. Ctr., Wayne State U., Detroit, 1998. Fellow: FIA Inst. Motorsport Safety; mem.: ACP, Internat. Coun. Motorsport Sci. (bd. dirs. 1988—), Soc. Critical Care Medicine. Avocations: water-skiing, sailing, motorcycling. Office: Univ Miami Sch Medicine 1095 NW 14th Ter Miami FL 33136

OLYPHANT, TIMOTHY, actor; b. Honolulu, Hawaii, May 20, 1968; m. Alexis Knief; 3 children. Student, U. So. Calif. Actor: (films) The First Wives Club, 1996, A Life Less Ordinary, 1997, Scream 2, 1997, Nineteen Ninety-Nine, 1998, Go, 1999, No Vacancy, 1999, Advice From a Caterpillar, 1999, The Broken Hearts Club: A Romantic Comedy, 2000, Gone in Sixty Seconds, 2000, Auggie Rose, 2000, Head Over Heels, 2001, Doppelganger, 2001, The Safety of Objects, 2001, Rock Star, 2001, Coastlines, 2002, Dreamcatcher, 2003, A Man Apart, 2003, The Girl Next Door, 2004, Catch and Release, 2006; (TV films) Ellen Foster, 1997, When Trumpets Fade, 1998, Shadow Realm, 2002; (TV series) Deadwood, 2004—, (TV appearances) Mr. & Mrs. Smith, 1996, High Incident, 1997, Sex in the City, 1998, Night Visions, 2002, My Name Is Earl, 2006. *

O'MALLEY, BERT WILLIAM, JR., head and neck surgeon, educator, researcher; b. Pitts., Sept. 7, 1962; s. Bert. W. and Sally A. (Johnson) O'M.; m. Cheryl Anne Moore, Jan. 17, 1987; children: Bartley, Annette, Michael. Student, U. Notre Dame, 1980-81; BA in Biochemistry, U. Tex., 1984; MD, U. Tex., Dallas, 1988. Gen. surgery resident U. Tex. Southwestern, Parkland Meml. Hosp., Dallas, 1984-88; otolaryngology and head and neck surgery resident Baylor Coll. Medicine, Houston, 1988-90, clin. instr. dept. otorhinolaryngology, 1993-94; head and neck oncology and cranial base surgery fellow U. Pitts., 1994-95, clin. instr. dept. otolaryngology and head and neck surgery, 1994-95; asst. prof. dept. otolaryngology—head and neck surgery Johns Hopkins U. Sch. Medicine, Balt., 1995, dir. gene therapy divsn., dept. otolaryngology-HNS, 1995—99, asst. prof. dept. oncology, 1996; chief otolaryngology U. Maryland, 1999—2003; prof., chmn. Dept. Otorhinolaryngology Sch. Medicine U. Pa., 2003—. Cons. head and neck gene therapy project GeneMedicine, Inc. The Woodlands, Tex.; lectr. dept. otolaryngology—head and neck surgery Grand Rounds, Greater Balt. Med. Ctr., 1995, U. Pitts., 1995, Johns Hopkins U., Balt., 1996, others; presenter in field. Contbr. book chpts.: Fundamentals of Molecular Biology and Gene Therapy, 1997, Surgery of the Anterior and Middle Cranial Base, 1997; contbr. articles to Transplantation Procs., Archives of Otolaryngology—Head and Neck Surgery, Human Gene Therapy, Seminars in Surg. Oncology, Cancer Rsch., others; reviewer: Otolaryngology—Head and Neck Surgery, Head and Neck, Cancer Rsch., Archives of Otolaryngology—Head and Neck Surgery, Clin. Cancer Rsch. Mem. AAAS, Am. Assn. for Cancer Rsch., Am. Soc. Gravitational and Space Biology, Am. Acad. Otolaryngology Head and Neck Surgery, Cell Transplant Soc. (founding mem.), Md. Soc. Otolaryngology. Roman Catholic. Achievements include patents pending for gene therapy to thyroid, somatic gene therapy. Office: U Penn Sch Medicine Otorhinolaryngology Dept 3400 Spruce St 5 Ravdin Bldg Philadelphia PA 19104

O'MALLEY, CARLON MARTIN, judge; b. Phila., Sept. 7, 1929; s. Carlon Martin and Lucy (Bol) O'M.; m. Mary Catherine Lyons, Aug. 17, 1957; children: Carlon Martin III, Kathleen B. O'Malley Aikman, Harry Tighe, John Todd, Cara M. O'Malley Colombo. BA, Pa. State U., 1951; LLB, Temple U., 1954. Bar: Pa. 1955, Fla. 1973, U.S. Supreme Ct. 1973. Practiced law, 1957-61; asst. U.S. atty. for Middle Dist. Pa., Dept. Justice, 1961-69, U.S. atty., 1979-82; ptnr. O'Malley & Teets, 1970-72, O'Malley, Jordan & Mullaney (and predecessor firms), 1976-79; pvt. practice Pa. and Fla., 1972-79, 82-87; judge Ct. Common Pleas of Lackawanna County (45th Judicial Dist.), 1987-97, sr. judge, 1998—. Dir. pub. safety City of Scranton, 1983-86; lectr. Lackawanna Coll., 1982-86. Editorial bd.: Temple Law Rev, 1952-53. Pres. Lackawanna County (Pa.) unit Am. Cancer Soc., 1966-67; bd. dirs. Pa. Cancer Soc., 1967-68, Lackawanna county chpt. ARC, 1967-69; mem. solicitation team, govtl. divsn. Lackawanna United Fund, 1963-68; chmn. profl. divsn. Greater Scranton (Pa.) YMCA Membership Drives; trustee Everhart Mus., Scranton, 1987—. Pilot USAF, 1955-57, Pa. N.G., 1957-59. Mem. Am. Judges Assn., Nat. Assn. Former U.S. Attys., Pa. Bar Assn., Lackawanna County Bar Assn. (bd. dirs., fin. sec.), Fla. Bar Assn., Country Club of Scranton, Elks (pres. Pa. chpt. 1978-79, judiciary com. 1985-89, justice Grand Forum 1991, 1995-97, chief justice 1992-93, nat. pres. 1997-98), K.C., Phi Kappa (pres.), Delta Theta Phi (pres.). Democrat. Office: Judges Chambers Lackawanna County Courthouse Scranton PA 18503

O'MALLEY, JAMES TERENCE (TERRY), lawyer; b. Omaha, Nov. 24, 1950; s. John Austin and Mayme Bernice (Zentner) O'M.; m. Colleen L. Kizer, May 22, 1972; children: Erin C., Michael B., Patrick J. BA magna cum laude, U. Notre Dame, 1972; JD, Stanford U., 1975. Bar: Calif. 1975, Tex. 1998. Ptnr. Gray, Cary, Ames & Frye, San Diego, 1975-87, of counsel, 1987-91, ptnr., 1991—94; vice chmn., exec. v.p., gen. counsel Noble Broadcast Group, Inc., San Diego, 1987-91; ptnr. Gray Cary Ware & Freidenrich LLP, San Diego, 1994—2004, chmn., CEO, 1996—2004; mng. ptnr. US DLA Piper Rudnick Gray Cary US LLP, San Diego, 2005—. Pres. San Diego Taxpayers Assn., 1986—87; co-chmn. Mayor's City of the Future Health Care Task Force, San Diego, 1994—95; mem. C. of C. CEO Roundtable, San Diego, 1997—2002; adv. bd. Hildebrandt Internat., Inc., 2001; bd. dirs. San Diego Regional Econ. Devel. Corp., 1997—2002. Mem. Order of Coif, Sorin Soc. Avocations: jogging, music. Office: DLA Piper Rudnick Ste 1700 401 B St San Diego CA 92101-4297 Office Fax: 858-677-1401. Business E-Mail: terry.omalley@dlapiper.com.

O'MALLEY, JOHN DANIEL, lawyer, educator, banker; b. Chgo., Dec. 18, 1926; s. William D. and Paula A. (Skaugh) O'M.; m. Caroline Tyler Taylor, July 12, 1958; children: John Daniel, Taylor John. Grad., St. Thomas Mil. Acad., 1945; BS, Loyola U., Chgo., 1950, MA, 1952, JD, 1953; grad., U.S. Army Intelligence Sch., 1962, Command & Gen. Staff Coll., 1965. Bar: Ill. 1953, Mich. 1954, U.S. Supreme Ct. 1962. Asst. prof. law Loyola U., 1953-59, asso. prof., 1959-65; formerly spl. counsel and bond claims mgr. Fed. Ins. Co.; prof. law Loyola U. Grad. Sch. Bus., 1965—, chmn. dept. law, 1968-86. Trust officer, v.p. First Nat. Bank Highland Park (Ill.), Marina City Bank, Chgo., Hyde Park Bank & Trust Co., 1970-75; exec. v.p. Harris Bank Winnetka, Ill., 1975-95. Author: Subrogation Against Banks on Forged Checks, 1967, Common Check Frauds and the Uniform Commercial Code, 1969; contbr. articles to profl. jours. and law revs. Served to maj. AUS, 1945-47, 61-62. Decorated Knight Grand Cross Papal Order of Holy Sepulchre, Knight Comdr. with star Constantinian Order of St. George (Italy), Knight of Malta. Mem. ABA, Chgo., Ill., Mich. bar assns., Chgo. Crime Commn., French Nat. Hon. Soc., Am., Chgo. bus. law assns., Mil. Govt. Assn., Order of St. Maurice and St. Lazarus (Italy, officer). Home: 1630 Sheridan Rd 6-L Wilmette IL 60091-1830 Office: Loyola U Ste 530 820 N Michigan Ave Chicago IL 60611-2147

O'MALLEY, KEVIN FRANCIS, lawyer, educator, writer; b. St. Louis, May 12, 1947; s. Peter Francis and Dorothy Margaret (Cradick) O'M.; m. Dena Hengen, Apr.2, 1971; children: Kevin Brendan, Ryan Michael. AB, St. Louis U., 1970, JD, 1973. Bar: Mo. 1973, U.S. Ct. Appeals D.C. 1974, U.S. Ct. Appeals (8th cir.) 1979, Ill. 1993. Trial lawyer U.S. Dept. Justice, Washington, 1973-74, Los Angeles, 1974-77, Phoenix, 1977-78, asst. U.S. atty. St. Louis, 1978-83. Adj. prof. law St. Louis U., 1979—85; lectr. Ctrl. and Ea. European Law Initiative, Russian Fedn., 1996, Poland, 99. Author: (with Devitt, Blackmar, O'Malley) Federal Jury Practice and Instruction, 1990, 92, (with O'Malley, Grenig & Lee), 1999, 2000, 01; contbr. articles to law books and jours. Cmty. amb. Expt. in Internat. Living, Prague, Czechoslovakia, 1968; bd. dirs. St. Louis-Galway (Ireland) Sister Cities. Capt. U.S. Army, 1973. Named one of Best Lawyers in Am., 2005—; recipient Atty. Gen.'s Disting. Svc. award, US Dept. Justice, 1977, John J. Dwyer Meml. Scholarship award, 1967—70, Best Lawyers in Am., 2006, 2007. Fellow Am. Coll. Trial Lawyers; mem. ABA (chmn. govt. litigation counsel com. 1982-86, chmn. jud. com. 1986-87, chmn. com. on ind. and small firms, chmn. trial practice com. 1991-94, health care litigation 1994-98, mem. task force on fed. practice 2005-06), Am. Law Inst., Met. Bar Assn. St. Louis (chmn. criminal law sect.), Nat. Inst. Trial Advocacy, Mo. Athletic Club. Roman Catholic. Office: Greensfelder Hemker & Gale PC 10 S Broadway Ste 2000 Saint Louis MO 63102-1747 Business E-Mail: kom@greensfelder.com.

O'MALLEY, MARTIN JOSEPH, governor, former mayor, lawyer; b. Washington, Jan. 18, 1963; m. Catherine (Katie) Curran, 1990; children: Grace, Tara, William, Jack. BA, Cath. U., 1985; JD, U. Md. Sch. Law, Balt., 1988; D (hon.), Strayer U. Legis. fellow, state field dir. Staff of US Senator Barbara Mikulski, 1987—88; asst. state's atty. City of Balt., 1988-90, mem. city coun., 1991—99, mayor, 1999—2007; gov. State of Md., Annapolis, 2007—. Co-chmn. task force on fed.-local law enforcement US Conf. Mayors. Former state coord. Senator Bob Kerrey Dem. Primary. chmn. Com. Taxation and Fin., chmn. Legis. Investment. Recipient Svc. to Humanity award Md. Jaycees, 1994. Mem.: Md. Bar Assn., Friendly Sons St. Patricks. Democrat. Roman Catholic. Office: Office of Gov 101 State Cir Annapolis MD 21401-1925 *

O'MALLEY, SEAN PATRICK CARDINAL, Archbishop of Boston, cardinal; b. Lakewood, Ohio, June 29, 1944; s. Theodore and Mary Louise O'Malley. Student, St. Fidelis Sem., Herman, Pa., Capuchin Coll., Washington; MA in Religious Edn., Catholic U., Ph.D in Spanish & Portuguese, 1978. Ordained priest Roman Cath. Ch., 1970. Prof. Catholic U., Washington, 1969—73; exec. dir., Centro Catolico Hispano Archdiocese of Washington DC, Washington, 1973—78, episcopal vicar of priests serving Portuguese, Haitian & Hispanic communities, 1978-84; coadjutor bishop Diocese of St. Thomas, VI, 1984—85, bishop VI, 1985—92, Diocese of Fall River, Mass., 1992—2002, Diocese of Palm Beach, Fla., 2002—03; archbishop Archdiocese of Boston, Brighton, 2003—; elevated to Cardinal by Pope Benedict XVI, 2006—. Mem.: US Catholic Conf. of Catholic Bishops (chmn., Com. on Consecrated Life). Office: Archbishop of Boston 2121 Commonwealth Ave Brighton MA 02135-3192

O'MALLEY, SUSAN, former professional sports team executive; d. Peter and Jan O'Malley. BS in Bus. and Fin., Mt. St. Mary's Coll., 1983; law degree, Georgetown U., 2007. With Earl Palmer Brown Advt., 1983—86; dir. advt. Washington Bullets, 1986—87, dir. mktg., 1987—88, exec. v.p., 1988—91, pres., 1991—96, Washington Wizards, 1996—2007, Washington Sports and Entertainment, 1991—2007. Recipient Americanism award, Alexandria-Olympic Boys and Girls Club, 1997, Adj. Prof. of Yr. award, Georgetown U., 2002. Achievements include becoming first female president of an NBA franchise. Avocations: tennis, travel. *

O'MALLEY, THOMAS ANTHONY, gastroenterologist, internist; b. St. Helens, Lancashire, Eng., Jan. 21, 1932; s. Michael and Margaret (Melia) O'M.; m. Margaret Mary O'Kane, Apr. 7, 1958 (dec. Apr. 1985); m. Marianne Rapier, Jan. 23, 1988; children: Anne, Patricia, Katherine, Jane, Margaret. MBChB, U. Liverpool, Eng., 1956; Lic. Medicine, U. State N.Y., 1964. Diplomate Am. Bd. Internal Medicine, State Bd. Med. Examiners Fla. House physician Royal Infirmary, Liverpool, 1956-57; house surgeon Royal Liverpool Children's Hosp., 1957; resident in medicine C.S. Wilson Meml. Hosp., Johnson City, NY, 1957-58; fellow internal medicine Lahey Clinic, Boston, 1958-59; USPHS trainee in gastroenterology U. Rochester (N.Y.), Strong Meml. Hosp., 1959-60; chief resident medicine/Segal Watson fellow gastroenterology Genesee Hosp., Rochester, 1960-61; gastroenterologist Cancer Clinic, Regina, Sask., Canada, 1963; asst. dir. med. edn. Genesee Hosp., U. Rochester, 1964—66; pvt. practice Rochester, NY, 1967—72; clin. asst. prof. medicine U. Rochester, 1967—72; clin. assoc. prof. medicine U. South Fla., Tampa, 1972—. Chief medicine Sarasota (Fla.) Meml. Hosp., 1973, Doctors Hosp., Sarasota, 1985. With RAF, 1961-62. Recipient Physician of Yr. award Doctors Hosp. Sarasota, 1985; listed among Best Dr.'s of Am., 1998. Fellow: ACP, Am. Coll. Gastroenterology; mem.: Cavalieri del Vini Nobili (amb. 1989—, pres. 1997—), Chevalier du Tastevin (comdr. 1985—, officieur comdr. 2001—). Office: O'Malley & Hall MD PA 2650 Bahia Vista St Sarasota FL 34239-2635 Office Phone: 941-366-8960. Personal E-mail: t.omalley10@comcast.net.

OMAN, HENRY, retired electrical engineer, engineering executive; b. Portland, Oreg., Aug. 29, 1918; s. Paul L. and Mary (Levonen) O.; m. Winifred Eleanor Potter, June 17, 1944 (dec. Nov. 1950); m. Earlene Mary Boot, Sept. 11, 1954; children: Mary Janet, Eleanor Eva, Eric Paul. BSEE, Oreg. State U., 1940, MSEE, 1951. Registered profl. engr., Wash. Application engr. Allis Chalmers Mfg. Co., Milw., 1940—48; rsch. engr. Boeing Co., Seattle, 1948—63, engring. mgr., 1963—91; ret., 1991. Author: Energy Systems Engineering Handbook, 1986; co-author: Electric Bicycles, a Guide to design and Use, 2005; contbr. numerous articles to profl.

jours. Mem. team that restarted amateur radio communication to the outside world from the People's Republic of China, 1981. Recipient prize paper award Am. Inst. Elec. Engrs., 1964. Fellow IEEE (founder power electronics sys. confs., 1970—, v.p. Aerospace and Electronics Sys. Soc. 1984-88, Harry Mimno award 1989, Third Millenium medal 2000, editor-in-chief Aerospace and Electronic Sys. mag. 1995-99/rated in top two by Inst. for Sci. Info.), AIAA (assoc. fellow); mem. AAAS (bd. dir. Pacific divsn.). Republican. Methodist. Achievements include development of concepts for solar power satellite which generates power in geo-synchronous orbit 24 hours per day and beams it to the Earth surface with a microwave beam; research in simple battery-powered electric bicycles for low-cost, pollution-free transportation in developing nations. Home and Office: 19221 Normandy Park Dr SW Seattle WA 98166-4129 Office Phone: 206-878-4458. Personal E-mail: h.oman@ieee.org.

OMAN, MARK C., bank executive; b. Cedar Falls, Iowa; B, U. No. Iowa. CPA. With Delooitte, Haskins & Sells, Des Moines, Norwest Corp., 1979; CEO Wells Fargo Home Mortgage, Inc., 1989—97, chmn., 1997—; exec. v.p. mortgage svcs. Norwest, 1997—98; group exec. v.p. home and consumer fin. Wells Fargo & Co., 2002—. *

OMAN, RALPH, lawyer; b. Huntington, NY, July 1, 1940; s. Henry Ferdinand and Annamarie (Retelsdorf) O.; m. Anne K. Henehan, Oct. 21, 1967; children: Tabitha Russell, Caroline Adams, Charlotte Ericsson. Diploma, Sorbonne U., Paris, 1961; BA, Hamilton Coll., 1962; LLD, Georgetown U., 1973. Bar: D.C. 1973, U.S. Dist. Ct. Md. 1973, U.S. Ct. Appeals (4th cir.) 1974, U.S. Supreme Ct. 1977. Law clk. to U.S. Dist. Ct. judge U.S. Dist. Ct. Md., Balt., 1973-74; trial atty U.S. Dept. Justice, Washington, 1974-75; chief minority counsel patents, trademarks and copyrights subcom. U.S. Senate, Washington, 1975-77; legis. dir. Senator Charles Mathias, Washington, 1977-78; minority counsel judiciary com. U.S. Senate, Washington, 1978-81, chief counsel, staff dir. criminal law subcom., 1981-82, chief counsel patents, copyrights and trademarks subcom., 1982-85; register of copyrights U.S. Copyright Office, Washington, 1985-94; counsel Dechert Price and Rhoads, Washington, 1996—. Adj. prof. copyright law George Washington U.; speaker in field. Contbr. numerous articles to profl. jours. Served to lt. USN, 1965-70, Vietnam. Mem. ABA (chair authors com.), Fed. Bar Assn. (past pres. Capitol Hill chpt.). Episcopalian. Home: 1110 E Capitol St NE Washington DC 20002-6225 Office: Dechert Price and Rhoads 1775 Eye St NW Ste 1100 Washington DC 20006-2424 E-mail: ralph.oman@dechert.com.

OMAN, RICHARD HEER, retired lawyer; b. Columbus, Ohio, Jan. 4, 1926; s. B. R. Oman and Marguerite H. (Oman) Andrews; m. Jane Ellen Wert, Oct. 5, 1963; children: Sarah M., David W. BA, Ohio State U., 1948, JD, 1951; D in Cmty. Leadership (hon.), Franklin U., 2005. Bar: Ohio 1951. Atty. Ohio Nat. Bank, Columbus, 1951-55; ptnr. Isaac, Postlewaite, O'Brien & Oman, Columbus, 1955-71; dir. Columbus Found., 1955-77, counsel, 1955—2005; ptnr. Porter, Wright, Morris and Arthur (and predecessor firm), Columbus, 1972-89; of counsel Vorys, Sater, Seymour and Pease, Columbus, 1990, ptnr., 1991-96, of counsel, 1997—2004, ret., 2005. Mem. Columbus Airport Commn., 1960-64; trustee Reinberger Found., Cleve., 1980—, Columbus Acad., 1981-87, Grant Hosp., 1978-86, Harding Hosp., 1978-86; sr. warden Trinity Episc. Ch., 1985-88; counsel Columbus Jewish Found., 1985-2005, Wexner Ctr. Found., 1990-2005, Found. Cath. Diocese, Columbus, 2000-2005. Fellow Ohio State Bar Found.; mem. ABA, Am. Coll. Trust and Estate Counsel, Ohio State Bar Assn. (past mem. bd. govs. probate and trust law sect.), Columbus Bar Assn., Columbus Club, Rocky Fork Hunt and Country Club, Nantucket (Mass.) Yacht Club, Kit Kat Club. Republican. Episcopalian. Office: Vorys Sater Seymour & Pease LLP PO Box 1008 52 E Gay St Columbus OH 43215-3161 Home Phone: 614-755-4843; Office Phone: 614-464-6453. Fax: 614-714-4731. Business E-Mail: rhoman@vssp.com.

O'MARA, CHARLES SNOW, surgeon; b. Jackson, Miss., Sept. 23, 1948; s. Junior and Mary Jane (Wright) O'Mara; m. Jane Cleland O'Mara (div.); 1 child, Kate Cleland; m. Susan Holder O'Mara, Apr. 4, 1999. BS, U. Miss., Oxford, 1970; MD, Tulane U., New Orleans, 1973. Cert. Am. Bd. Surgery, vascular surgery Am. Bd. Surgery. Intern, surg. resident Johns Hopkins Hosp., Balt., 1973—79; vascular surgery fellow Northwestern Med. Ctr., Chgo., 1979—80; acad. surg. staff Johns Hopkins Hosp., Balt., 1980—82; ptnr. Cardiovasc. Surg. Clinic, P.A., Jackson, Miss., 1982—. Bd. mem. Miss. Bapt. Health Systems, Jackson; staff Miss. Bapt. Med. Ctr., Jackson, St. Dominic-Jackson Meml. Hosp., Ctrl. Miss. Med. Ctr., Jackson, U. Miss. Med. Ctr., Jackson. Contbr. chapters to books, articles to profl. jours. Bd. mem. Leukemia Soc., Jackson, 1993—94. Named Critical Care Physician of Yr., Miss. Bapt. Med. Ctr., 1990; recipient Arthur Priest award, Phi Delta Theta, 1969, Taylor medal, U. Miss., 1969, Roche award, Tulane Med. Sch., 1972, Dr. Walter G. Unglaub Meml. award, 1973, Oscar Creech award, 1973, Isador Dyer Meml. prize, 1973, Richard M. Nowell award, Callender Soc. Ann. Meeting, 1990, 1992, 1996, 2000; grantee, So. Med. Assn., 1981; Carrier scholar, U. Miss., 1966—69. Fellow: ACS (pres. Miss. chpt. 1993—94, Young Surgeon of Yr. Miss. chpt. 1988), Soc. for Vascular Surgery (disting.); mem.: Internat. Soc. for Endovascular Surgery, So. Surg. Assn., So. Assn. for Vascular Surgery, Alpha Omega Alpha (pres. 1972—73). Episcopalian. Avocations: bicycling, hiking, photography, golf. Office: Cardiovascular Surg Clinic PA 501 Marshall St Ste 100 Jackson MS 39202 Office Phone: 601-948-1416.

O'MARA, JOHN ALOYSIUS, retired bishop; b. Buffalo, Nov. 17, 1924; arrived in Can., 1940; s. John Aloysius and Anna Theresa (Schenck) O'Mara. Student, St. Augustine's Sem., Toronto, Ont., Can., 1944-51; JCL, St. Thomas U., Rome, 1953. Ordained priest Roman Cath. Ch., 1951. Mem. chancery Archdiocese of Toronto, Canada, 1953-69; pres., rector St. Augustine's Sem., Toronto, 1969-75; pastor St. Lawrence Parish, Scarboro, Ont., Canada, 1975-76; bishop Diocese of Thunder Bay, Ont., 1976-94, Diocese of St. Catharines, Ont., 1994—2002; ret., 2002. Pres. Ont. Conf. Cath. Bishops, 1986—92. Mem. Ont. Hosp. Svcs. Commn., 1964—69; bd. dirs. Ont. Hosp. Assn., 1961—65. Named Hon. Prelate of Papal Household with title Monsignor, 1954; Hon. fellow, U. St. Michael's Coll., Toronto, 1997. Mem.: Cath. Health Assn. Ont. (bd. dirs. 1982—86, 1988—92, 1996—), Cath. Ch. Ext. Soc. (bd. dirs. 1992—96). Home: Holy Rosary Rectory 21 Queen St S Thorold ON Canada L2V 3M7 E-mail: h-rosary@computan.on.ca.

O'MARA, THOMAS PATRICK, manufacturing executive; b. St. Catharine's, Ont., Can., Jan. 17, 1937; s. Joseph Thomas and Rosanna Patricia (Riordan) O'M.; m. Nancy Irene Rosevear, Aug. 10, 1968; children: Patricia Catharine, Tracy Irene, Sara Megan. BS, Allegheny Coll., 1958; MS, Carnegie Inst. Tech., 1960. Mktg. analyst U.S. Steel Corp., Pitts., 1960-65; dir. info. systems AMPCO Pitts. (formerly Screw & Bolt Corp.), Pitts., 1965-68; v.p., gen. mgr. Toy div. Samsonite Corp., Denver, 1968-73; regional mgr. Mountain Zone, Hertz Corp., Denver, 1973-75; asst. to chmn. Allen Group, Melville, NY, 1975-76; group exec. v.p. fin. and adminstrn. Bell & Howell Co., Chgo., 1976-77, corp. controller, 1977-78, corp. v.p., 1978-85, pres. visual communications, 1978-85; pres., chief operating officer, dir. Bridge Product Inc., Northbrook, Ill., 1985-87; chmn., chief exec. officer Micro Metl Corp., Indpls., 1987-91; chmn. Omara Ptnrs., 1992—; CEO Engineered Materials Corp., 2002—. Bd. dirs. Loyola U. Press; chmn. Plastics Group, ABC Windows. Mem. Lake Forest H.S. Bd., 1989-96, pres. 1993-96. With USAR, 1961-66. Mem. Econs. Club Chgo., Newcomen Soc. U.S., Sigma Alpha Epsilon, Knollwood Club. Home: 1350 Inverleith Rd Lake Forest IL 60045-1540 Business E-Mail: tomara@omarapartners.com.

OMARI, BASSAM O., cardiothoracic surgeon; s. Omar and Munawwar Omari; m. Rana Azhari, Sept. 30, 2004. MD, Am. U. Beirut, 1984. Cert. Am. Bd. Thoracic Surgery, 1996, Am. Bd. Surgery, 1992. Chief divsn. cardiothoracic surgery Harbor-UCLA Med. Ctr., Torrance, Calif., 1994—. Contbr. scientific papers to profl. jours. Fellow: ACS; mem.: Western Thoracic Surg. Assn., Soc. Thoracic Surgery. Office: Harbor-UCLA Med Ctr 1000 W Carson St Torrance CA 90509 Office Phone: 310-222-2747. Office Fax: 310-320-2129. E-mail: bomari@ucla.edu.

OMASS, GEORGE A., federal agency administrator; b. Biloxi, Miss. Grad., U. Miss. Exec. v.p. Nat. Apt. Assn.; dir. Action Agy. Speakers Bur.; mem. com. on Post Office and Civil Svc. U.S. Ho. of Reps.; postal rate commr. U.S. Postal Rate Commn., 1997—2006, vice chmn., 1999—2001, chmn., 2006—. Mem. bd. govs. Nat. Rep. Club Capitol Hill; chmn. pastoral coun. Ch. of the Annunciation. Office: US Postal Commn 901 New York Ave NW Ste 200 Washington DC 20268-0001

OMATSU, GLENN, Asian American studies professor; b. Cleve., 1947; Grad., East Los Angeles Coll., U. Calif., Santa Cruz. Assoc. editor Amerasia Jour., 1985—2002; editor CrossCurrents, 1985—2002; prof. Asian Am. studies UCLA, Calif. State U., Northridge, Pasadena City Coll. Co-editor: Asian Americans: The Movement and the Moment, 2001. Mem. New Otani Workers Support Com., Koreatown Restaurant Workers Support Com. Recipient Cmty. Svc. award, Japanese Am. Hist. Soc. of So. Calif., Cmty. Activism award, Korean Immigrant Workers Advocates of L.A. Office: CSUN EOP 18111 Nordhoff St Northridge CA 91330-8366 Business E-Mail: glenn.omatus@csun.edu.

O'MEALLIE, KITTY, artist; b. Bennettsville, SC, Oct. 24, 1916; d. Earle and Rosa Estelle (Bethea) Chamness; m. John Ryan O'Meallie, June 27, 1939 (dec. Apr. 26, 1974); children: Sue Ryan, Kathryn Bethea; m. Lee Harnie Johnson, Aug. 21, 1976. BFA, Tulane U., New Orleans, 1937; postgrad., Tulane U., 1954—59. One-woman shows include Masur Mus., Monroe, La., 1979, Marlboro County Mus. of S.C., 1975, Meridian Mus. ARt, Miss., 1981, 85; exhibited in group shows at New Orleans Mus. Art, Contemporary Art Ctr., Meadows Mus. Cushing Gallery, SE Ctr. for Contemporary Art, Art 80, Art Expo West, Art Expo 81; represented in permanent collections New Orleans Mus. Art, Ogden Mus. So. Art, Tulane U. Pan-Am. Life Ctr., Masur Mus. Art, Meridian Mus. Art. Nat. officer Newcomb Coll. Alumnae Assn., 1964-66; lectr. exhibitor for many charitable orgns. Recipient award WYES-TV, 1979, Hon. Invitational New Orleans Women's Caucus, 1986; winner NC cover art contest Continuing Care Ref. Guide, 2003; numerous awards and prizes in competitive exhibitions; grantee St. Charles Ave. Presbyn. Ch., New Orleans, 1995-96. Mem. Arts Coun. New Orleans, Fine Arts League Cary, Chi Omega Alumnae Assn. (pres. mothers' club 1964). Avocations: bird-watching, bridge. Home and Office: 1202 Fernglen Pl Cary NC 27511 Office Phone: 919-481-9904.

O'MEARA, CHRISTOPHER M., investment company executive; BA business administration, Georgetown U. CPA. Finance div. Lehman Bros. Holdings, 1994—95, asst. controller, 1995—2001, v.p., 2001—, financial controller, 2001—02, global controller, 2002—, CFO, 2004—. Office: c/o Lehman Bros 745 Seventh Avenue New York NY 10019 *

O'MEARA, JOHN CORBETT, federal judge; b. Hillsdale, Mich., Nov. 4, 1933; s. John Richard and Karolyn Louise (Corbett) O'M.; m. Penelope Reingier Appel, June 9, 1962 (div. Feb. 1975); children: Meghan Appel, John Richard, Corbett Edge, Patrick Fitzpatrick, Tighe Roberts; m. Julia Donovan Darlow, Sept. 20, 1975; 1 child, Gillian Darlow. AB, U. Notre Dame, 1955; LLB, Harvard U., 1962. Bar: Mich. 1962. Assoc. Dickinson, Wright, Moon, Van Dusen & Freeman, Detroit, 1962-70; mem. faculty U. Detroit, 1965-70; ptnr. Dickinson, Wright, Moon, Van Dusen & Freeman, Detroit, 1970-94, head of labor group, 1985-94; judge U.S. Dist. Ct., Detroit, 1994—. Bd. dirs. Mich. Opera Theatre, Detroit. Contr. articles to profl. jours. Fin. chmn. Dem. Party Mich., 1968-70; chmn. U.S. Cts. Com. State Bar Mich., 1984-94. Lt. USN, 1955-59. Fellow Am. Coll. Trial Lawyers, Am. Bar Found.; mem. ABA, U.S. Supreme Court Bar, Am. Judicature Soc., Mich. State Bar Assn., 6th Cir. Court Appeals Bar (life mem., 6th Cir. Jud. Conf. 1986). Office: US Dist Ct 200 E Liberty St Ann Arbor MI 48104 Office Phone: 734-741-2106. Personal E-mail: omearajomeara@sbcglobal.net.

O'MEARA, JOHN FRANCIS, lawyer; b. Chgo., Apr. 14, 1936; s. John J. and Mary (Joyce) O'M.; children: Marcia A. Hiehle, John A., Timothy D. BS, Loyola U., 1959; JD, Northwestern U., 1960. Bar: Ill. 1961, U.S. Dist. Ct. (no. dist.) Ill. 1964, U.S. Ct. Appeals (7th cir.) 1992. Assoc., ptnr. Lord, Bissell & Brook, Chgo., 1961-74; atty. pvt. practice, Chgo. and Park Ridge, Ill, 1975—. Instr. John Marshall Sch. Law, Chgo., 1966-71. Author: Tort Liability of Illinois Land Occupiers, 1968. Bd. dirs. St. Mary of Angels, 1987—; founder, officer Ind. Precinct Orgn., Chgo., 1969-71. With U.S. Army Res., 1960-66. Mem. Holy Name Soc. Roman Catholic.

O'MEARA, ONORATO TIMOTHY, academic administrator, mathematician; b. Cape Town, Republic of South Africa, Jan. 29, 1928; arrived in U.S., 1957; s. Daniel and Fiorina (Allorto) O'M.; m. Jean T. Fadden, Sept. 12, 1953; children: Maria, Timothy, Jean, Kathleen, Eileen. B.Sc., U. Cape Town, 1947, M.Sc., 1948; PhD, Princeton U., 1953; LLD (hon.), U. Notre Dame, 1987. Asst. lectr. U. Natal, Republic South Africa, 1949; lectr. U. Otago, New Zealand, 1954-56; mem. Inst. for Advanced Study, Princeton, NJ, 1957-58, 62; asst. prof. Princeton U., 1958-62; prof. math. U. Notre Dame, Ind., 1962-76, chmn. dept., 1965-66, 68-72, Kenna prof. math., 1976-98, provost, 1978-96, provost emeritus, 1996—, Kenna prof. emeritus, 1998—. Vis. prof. Calif. Inst. Tech., 1968; Gauss prof. Göttingen Acad. Sci., 1978; mem. adv. panel math. scis. NSF, 1974-77, cons., 1960—. Author: Introduction to Quadratic Forms, 1963, 71, 73, 2000, Lectures on Linear Groups, 1974, 2d edit., 1977, 3d edit., 1988, Russian translation, 1976, Symplectic Groups, 1978, 82, Russian translation, 1979, The Classical Groups and K-Theory (with A.J. Hahn), 1989; contbr. articles on arithmetic theory of quadratic forms and isomorphism theory of linear groups to Am. and European profl. jours. Mem. Cath. Commn. Intellectual and Cultural Affairs, 1962—, Commn. on Cath. Scholarship, 1997-99; life trustee U. of Notre Dame, 1996—. Recipient Marianist award U. Dayton, 1988; Alfred P. Sloan fellow, 1960-63. Mem. Am. Math. Soc., Am. Acad. Arts and Sci., Collegium (bd. dirs. 1992-96). Roman Catholic. Home: 1227 E Irvington Ave South Bend IN 46614-1417 Office: U Notre Dame Office of Provost Emeritus 255B Hurley Hall Notre Dame IN 46556 Personal E-mail: omeara1227@sbcglobal.net.

O'MEARA, PATRICK O., political science professor; b. Cape Town, South Africa, Jan. 7, 1938; came to U.S., 1964. s. Daniel and Fiorina (Allorto) O'M. BA, U. Capetown, 1960; MA, Ind. U., 1966, PhD, 1970; D (hon.), Nat. Inst. Devel. Adminstrn., Bangkok, 2005. Dep. dir. African studies program, asst. prof. polit. sci. Ind. U., Bloomington, 1970-72, dir. African studies program, 1972—, assoc. prof. polit. sci. and pub. and environ. affairs, 1972-81, prof. polit. sci. and pub. and environ. affairs, 1981—, dean office of internat. programs, 1993—. Mem. Ind. Gov.'s Asia Delegation, 2005; cons. in field. Author: Rhodesia: Racial Conflict or Coexistence?, 1975; editor (with Gwendolen M. Carter): Southern Africa in Crisis, 1977; editor: African Independence: The First Twenty-Five Years, 1985, Southern Africa: The Continuing Crisis, 1979, International Politics in Southern Africa, 1982; editor: (with Phyllis M. Martin) Africa, 1977, 3d edit., 1995; editor: (with C.R. Halisi and Brian Winchester) Revolutions of the Late Twentieth Century, 1991; editor: (with Howard D. Mehlinger and Matthew Krain) Globalization and the Challenges of a New Century, 2000; editor: (with Howard D. Mehlinger and Roxanna Ma Newman) Changing Perspectives on International Education, 2001; contbr. articles to profl. jours., chapters to books. Decorated Cross of St. George (Catalonia, Spain); recipient John D. Ryan award Ind. U., 1993, Thomas Hart Benton medallion Ind. U., 1994, Medal of Warsaw U., 2001, Amicus Poloniae, Embassy of Poland, 2003, Founders award Soc. Coll. and Univ. Planning, 2005, Gold Cross of Merit, Republic of Hungary, 2007. Mem. African Studies Assn., Pi Alpha Alpha. Roman Catholic. Office: Ind U Bryan Hall 205 Bloomington IN 47405 Business E-Mail: omeara@indiana.edu.

O'MEARA, STEPHEN CHARLES, lawyer; b. Milw., Feb. 13, 1950; s. Stephen Mayer and Virginia Claire (Coffey) O'M.; m. Karen Virginia Karstedt, Aug. 23, 1980. AB, U. Notre Dame, 1972; JD, Marquette U., 1975. Bar: Wis. 1975, U.S. Dist. Ct. (ea., we. dist. Wis. 1975), U.S. Supreme Ct. 1985. From assoc. to ptnr. O'Meara Eckert Powos and Gonring, West Bend, Wis., 1975-92; sr. v.p., gen. counsel, sec. The Ziegler and Cos., Milw., 1993, sr. mng. dir. pvt. equity. Rsch. editor, Marquette Law Rev. Bd. dirs. The Threshhold, Inc., West Bend, 1985—. Mem. ABA, Am. Corp. Counsel Assn., Am. Soc. Corp. Secretaries, Securities Industry Assn., State Bar Wis., Wash. County Bar Assn. (pres. 1985-86), Order of Barristers. Office: The Ziegler Cos Ste 2000 250 E Wisconsin Ave Milwaukee WI 53202 Office Phone: 414-978-6400. Office Fax: 414-978-6401.

O'MEARA, THOMAS FRANKLIN, priest, educator; b. Des Moines, May 15, 1935; s. Joseph Matthew and Frances Claire (Rock) O'M. MA, Aquinas Inst, Dubuque, Iowa, 1963; PhD, U. Munich, Germany, 1967. Ordained priest Roman Cath. Ch., 1962. Assoc. prof. Aquinas Inst. of Theology, Dubuque, Iowa, 1967-79; prof. U. Notre Dame, South Bend, Ind., 1981-84, William K. Warren prof. of theology, 1985—. Author 14 books, including: Romantic Idealism and Roman Catholicism, 1983, Theology of Ministry, 1985, revised edit., 1999, Church and Culture, 1991, Thomas Aquinas: Theologian, 1997, Erich Przywara, S.J., His Theology and His World, 2002, A Theologian's Journey, 2002, God in the World: Harl Rahnen's Theology. Mem. Catholic Theol. Soc. Am. (pres. 1980). Roman Catholic. Office: St Thomas Aquinas Priory 7200 Division St River Forest IL 60305 Office Phone: 708-714-9155. Personal E-mail: tomeara@nd.edu.

O'MEARA, VICKI A., lawyer; b. Mpls., May 13, 1957; d. James Michael and Joan Kathleen (Shepers) O'M.; children: Joseph O'Meara Masterman, Nicolas James Reisinger O'Meara. BA in Polit. Sci. cum laude, Cornell U., 1979; JD, Northwestern U., Chgo., 1982; MA in Environment & Natural Resource, George Washington U., Washington, 1987. Bar: Minn. 1982, D.C. 1983, Ill. 1989. Asst. to Army gen. counsel U.S. Army-Pentagon, Washington, 1982-86; spl. asst. to White House Counsel The White House Fellows Program, Washington, 1986-87; dep. exec. sec., domestic policy counsel, cabinent affairs The White House, Washington, 1987; dep. gen. counsel litigation and regional ops. U.S. EPA, Washington, 1987; ptnr. Jones, Day, Reavis & Pogue, Chgo., 1988-92, 93—; asst. atty. gen. U.S. Dept. Justice, 1992; exec. vice-pres., chief corp. ops., gen. counsel Ryder Systems Inc., Miami, Fla., pres. US Supply Chain Sol. Faculty mem. Army Logistics Management Inst., Ft. Lee, Va., 1982—86; guest lctr. Nat. ALI ABA progs., 1984—97; adj. prof. Union Inst., Cin., 1994—95. Author rev. Nat. Wetlands Newsletter, 1990; contbr. articles to profl. jours. Bd. dirs. Northwestern U. Alumni Assn., Chgo., 1988-90, Laidla Inc., 2003-04, Health Management Assn.; dir. Defenders of Property Rights, Zoological Soc. S.Fla.; mem. com. Chgo. Coun. Fgn. Rels, Cornell Pres. Coun. Women, Fla. Coun. Econ. Edn. Mem. Chgo. Econ. Club Chgo. (com. fgn. affairs). Office: Ryder System Inc 11690 NW 105th St Medley FL 33178-1103

O'MEILIA, DAVID E., prosecutor, lawyer; b. July 1951; Grad. Okla. State U.; grad. in Law, Tulsa Coll. Atty. Tulsa County Dist. Atty.'s Office, 1980—84; asst. US atty. US Atty.'s Office, Tulsa, Okla., 1986—96; atty. Nichols, Wolfe, Stamper, Nally, Fallis & Robertson, 1996—99; ptnr. Lyons, Clark, Danielson & O'Meilia, Tulsa, Okla., 1999—2001; US atty. (no. dist.) Okla. US Dept. Justice, 2001—. Office: US Attys Office 110 W 7th St Ste 300 Tulsa OK 74119

OMEL, JUNE M., elementary school educator; b. Spring Grove, Minn., June 4, 1945; d. Ernest W. Jameson and Norma L. Wiste; m. Alexander A. Omel, July 13, 1968 (dec.); children: Andrei A., Peter E. BA, Luther Coll., Decorah, Iowa, 1967; postgrad., South Conn. State U., New Haven, 1968—95, Cen. Wash. U., Ellensburg, 1968—95, Ea. Wash. U., Cheney, 1968—95, Antioch U., Seattle, 1968—95, Fresno U., Calif., 1968—95, Portland State U., Oreg., 1968—95. Tchr. 2d grade Turkey Hill Sch., Orange, Conn., 1967—69; tchr. 4th grade Kiona-Benton Elem. Sch., Benton City, Wash., 1979—81, tchr. 2d grade, 1981—91, tchr. 3d grade, 1991—. Chmn. Young Aus. Com., Benton City; mem. Safe and Civil Schs. Com., Benton City. Contbr. articles to newspapers. Mem. Yale-New Haven (Conn.) Chorale, 1968, Redeemer Oratorio Choir, New Haven, 1968, Chancel Choir, Richland, Wash., 1996—2000. Mem.: ASCD, NEA, Wash. Tchrs. Assn. Republican. Avocations: music, art, writing, reading, gardening. Office: Kiona-Benton Elem Sch 1107 Grace Ave Benton City WA 99320

OMELL, GARY H., radiologist; b. Memphis, Tenn., Nov. 1, 1942; Student, Memphis State U., 1960—63; MD, U. Tenn., Memphis, 1967. Diplomate Am. Bd. Radiology, 1973. Staff radiologist St. Luke's Hospital, Chesterfield, Mo., 1975—99, chmn. radiology dept., 1999—. Pres. Citizens for Responsible Devel., St. Louis, 1980—82; bd. mem. Planning & Zoning Com., Town & Country, Mo., 1996—, chmn., 2004—. Maj. MC Diagnostic Radiology USAF, 1973—75, Scott AFB, Ill. Named one of Best Doctors, St. Louis Mag., 2005, 2006, Best Doctors in Am., 2005—06. Mem.: Greater St. Louis Soc. Raiologists (breast screen com. chmn. 1986, sec., treas. 1989—90, v.p. 1990—91, pres. 1991—92), Mo. State Radiological Soc. (bd. dirs. 1982—87). Avocation: golf. Home: 467 Killearn Ln Saint Louis MO 63141 Office: St Lukes Hosp 232 S Woods Mill Rd Chesterfield MO 63017 Office Phone: 314-205-6887. E-mail: omelgh@aol.com.

OMENN, GILBERT STANLEY, academic administrator, internist; b. Chester, Pa., Aug. 30, 1941; s. Leonard and Leah (Miller) O.; m. Martha Darling; children: Rachel Andrea, Jason Montgomery, David Matthew. AB, Princeton U., 1961; MD, Harvard U., 1965; PhD in Genetics, U. Wash., 1972. Lic. Mass., Washington, Bd. Internal Medicine Part 1(1970), Part 2, (1972), Specialty Bd. Med. Genetics-Clin. Genetics, 1982. Intern Mass. Gen. Hosp., Boston, 1965-66; tchg. fellow in medicine Harvard U., 1966-67; rsch. assoc., Nat. Inst. Arthritis and Metabol Diseases NIH, Bethesda, Md., 1967-69; fellow, divsn. med. genetics U. Wash., 1969-71, asst. prof. medicine Seattle, 1971—74, assoc. prof. medicine, 1974—79, dir., Robert Wood Johnson Clin. Scholars Program, 1975—77, investigator Howard Hughes Med. Inst., 1976-77, prof. medicine, 1979-97, prof. environ. health, 1981—, chmn. dept environ. health, 1981-83; dean U. Wash. Sch. Pub. Health and Cmty. Medicine, 1982-97, dean emeritus, 1997—; CEO health sys. U. Mich. Health Sys., Ann Arbor, 1997—2002; exec. v.p. med. affairs U. Mich., 1997—2002, prof. internal medicine, human genetics and pub. health, 1997—, dir. ctr. biomedical proteomics, 2002—, dir. ctr. computational medicine and biology, 2005—. Bd. dirs. Amgen, Rohm & Haas Co., CNAC, Population Svcs. Internat.; sci. adv. bd. 3M, Motorola, Divergence, Pac N.W. Nat. Lab.; attending staff, U. Hosp., Harborview Med. Ctr., VA Hosp, Providence Hosp., cons. staff, Children's Hosp. and Med. Ctr., Seattle, 1971-97; White House fellow/spl. asst. to chmn. AEC, 1973-74; asst. dir., 1977-78, assoc. dir., for Human Resources and Social and Economic Svcs, Office Sci. and Tech. Policy, The White House, 1977-80; assoc. dir. human resources Office Mgmt. and Budget,

1980-81; vis. sr. fellow Woodrow Wilson Sch. Pub. and Internat. Affairs, Princeton U., 1981; sci. and pub. policy fellow Brookings Instn., Washington, 1981-82; joint mem. Fed Hutchinson Cancer Rsch. Ctr., Seattle, 1983-; cons. govt. agys., Lifetime Cable Network; mem. Nat. Commn. on the Environment, Rene Dubos Ctr. for Human Environments, AFL-CIO Workplace Health Fund., Electric Power Rsch. Inst., Carnegie Commn. Task Force on Sci. and Tech. in Jud. and Regulatory Decision Making, adv. com. to dir., Ctrs. Disease Control, 1992-95, adv. com. Critical Technologies Inst., RAND; mem. Pres.'s Coun., U. Calif., 1992-97; chair, Pres. Congrl. Commn. on Risk Assessment and Risk Mgmt.; mem. Nat. Enterprise for the Environment. Co-author: Clearing the Air, Reforming the Clean Air Act, 1981. Editor: (with others) Genetics, Environment and Behavior: Implications for Educational Policy, 1972; Genetic Control of Environmental Pollutants, 1984; Genetic Variability in Responses to Chemical Exposure, 1984, Environmental Biotechnology: Reducing Risks from Environmental Chemicals through Biotechnology, 1988, Biotechnology in Biodegradation, 1990, Biotechnology and Human Genetic Predisposition to Disease, 1990, Annual Review of Public Health, 1991-97, Clinics in Geriatric Medicine, 1992, Xoford Textbook of Public Health, 1997; editor: Exploring the Human Plasma Proteome, 2006; mem. editl. bd. Jour. Protesme Research, Environ. Health Perspective; contbr. articles on cancer prevention, human biochem. genetics, prenatal diagnosis of inherited disorders, susceptibility to environ. agts., clin. medicine and health policy to profl. publs. Mem. Pres.'s Coun. on Spinal Cord Injury; mem. Nat. Cancer Adv. Bd., Nat. Heart, Lung and Blood Adv. Coun., Wash. State Gov.'s Commn. on Social and Health Svcs., Ctr. for Excellence in Govt.; chmn. awards panel Gen. Motors Cancer Rsch. Found., 1985-86; chmn. bd. Environ. Studies and Toxicology, Nat. Rsch. Coun., 1988-91; mem. Bd. Health Promotion and Disease Prevention, Inst. Medicine; mem. adv. com. Woodrow Wilson Sch., Princeton U., 1978-84; trustee Pacific Sci. Ctr., Fred Hutchinson Cancer Rsch. Ctr., Seattle Symphony Orch., Seattle Youth Symphony Orch., Seattle Chamber Music Festival, Santa Fe Chamber Music Festival, Univ. Mus. Soc., Ann Arbor, United Way Washtenaw County, Mich.; chmn. rules com. Dem. Conv., King County, Wash., 1972. Served with USPHS, 1967-69. U.S. Pub. Health Svc. Spl. Fellow, 1969-71, Nat. Genetics Found. Fellow, 1971-72, White House fellow, 1973-74; recipient Research Career Devel. award USPHS, 1972-76. Fellow ACP, AAAS (pres.-elect, pres., chmn. bd. dirs. 2004-07), Hastings Ctr. Inst. Soc., Ethics and Life Sciences, Collegium Ramazzini; mem. Nat. Acad. Social Ins., Western Assn. Physicians, Inst. Medicine of NAS, White House Fellows Assn., Am. Soc. Human Genetics, Western Soc. Clin. Rsch., Assn. Am. Physicians, Am. Acad. Arts and Scis., Am. Assn. for Advancement of Humanities, Am. Occupational Medicine Assn., Phi Beta Kappa, Sigma XiAlpha Omega Alpha. Jewish. Home: 3340 E Dobson Ann Arbor MI 48105-2583 Office: Univ Mich Med Sch 2057 F Palmer Commons 100 Washtenaw Ave Ann Arbor MI 48109-2218 E-mail: gomenn@umich.edu.

OMER, GEORGE ELBERT, JR., orthopaedic surgeon, educator; b. Kansas City, Kans., Dec. 23, 1922; s. George Elbert and Edith May (Hines) O.; m. Wendie Vilven, Nov. 6, 1949; children: George Eric, Michael Lee. BA, Ft. Hays Kans. State U., 1944; MD, Kans. U., 1950; MSc in Orthopaedic Surgery, Baylor U., Waco, Tex., 1955. Diplomate Am. Bd. Orthopaedic Surgery, 1959, (bd. dirs. 1983-92, pres. 1987-88), re-cert. orthopaedics and hand surgery, 1983, cert. surgery of the hand, 1989. 2nd lt. US Army, 1945, advanced through grades to col., 1967, ret., 1970; rotating intern Bethany Hosp., Kansas City, 1950-51; resident in orthopaedic surgery Brooke Army Hosp., San Antonio, 1952-55, William Beaumont Army Hosp., El Paso, Tex., 1955-56; chief surgery Irwin Army Hosp., Ft. Riley, Kans., 1957-59; cons. in orthopaedic surgery 8th Army, chief orthop. surgery 121st Evacuation Hosp. Republic of Korea, 1959-60; asst. chief orthopaedic surgery, chief hand surgeon Fitzsimons Army Med. Center, Denver, 1960-63; dir. orthopaedic residency tng. Armed Forces Inst. Pathology at Walter Reed Army Med. Ctr., Washington, 1963-65; chief orthopaedic surgery and chief Army Hand Surg. Center, Brooke Army Med. Center, 1965-70; cons. in orthopaedic and hand surgery Surgeon Gen. Army, 1967-70; prof. orthopaedics, surgery, and anatomy, chmn. dept. orthopaedic surgery, chief div. hand surgery U. N.Mex., 1970-90, med. dir. phys. therapy, 1972-90, acting asst. dean grad. edn. Sch. Medicine, 1980-81. Mem. active staff U. N.Mex. Hosp., Albuquerque, 1970—2005, chief of med. staff, 1984-86; cons. staff other Albuquerque hosps.; cons. orthopedic surgery USPHS, 1966-85, US Army, 1970-92, USAF, 1970-78, VA, 1970-2000; cons. Carrie Tingley Hosp. for Crippled Children, 1970-99, interim med. dir., 1970-72, 86-87, mem. bd. advisor 1972-76, chair, 1994-96. Mem. bd. editors Clin. Orthopaedics, 1973-90, Jour. AMA, 1973-74, Jour. Hand Surgery, 1976-81; trustee Jour. Bone and Joint Surgery, 1993-99, sec., 1993-96, chmn., 1997-99; contbr. more than 300 articles to profl. jours., numerous chpts. to books. Decorated Legion of Merit, Army Commendation medal with oak leaf cluster; recipient Alumni Achievement award Ft. Hays State U., 1973, Recognition plaque Am. Soc. Surgery Hand, 1989, Recognition plaque N.Mex. Orthopaedic Assn., 1991, Recognition award for hand surgery Am. Osteo. Acad. Orthopaedics, 1982, Pioneer award Internat. Socs. for Surgery Hand, 1995, Rodey award U. N.Mex. Alumni Assn., 1997, Cornerstone award U. N.Mex. Health Scis. Ctr., 1997; recognized with Endowed Professorship U. N.Mex. Sch. Medicine, 1995; recognized with named Annual Orthop. Seminar and Alumni Day Brooke Army Med. Ctr., 1999. Fellow ACS, Am. Orthopaedic Assn. (pres. 1988-89, exec. dir. 1989-93), Am. Acad. Orthopaedic Surgeons, Assn. Orthopaedic Chmn., N.Mex. Orthopaedic Assn. (pres. 1979-81, 1999-2000), La. Orthopaedic Assn. (hon.), Korean Orthopaedic Assn. (hon.), Peru Orthopaedic Soc. (hon.), Caribbean Hand Soc., Am. Soc. Surgery Hand (pres. 1978-79), Am. Assn. Surgery of Trauma, Assn. Bone and Joint Surgeons, Assn. Mil. Surgeons US, Riordan Hand Soc. (pres. 1967-68), Sunderland Soc. (pres. 1981-83), Soc. Mil. Orthopaedic Surgeons, Brazilian Hand Soc. (hon.), S.Am. Hand Soc. (hon.), Groupe D'Etude de la Main, Brit. Hand Soc. (hon.), Venezuela Hand Soc. (hon.), South African Hand Soc. (hon.), Western Orthopaedic Assn. (pres. 1981-82), AAAS, Russell A. Hibbs Soc. (pres. 1977-78), 38th Parallel Med. Soc. (Korea) (sec. 1959-60); mem. AMA, Phi Kappa Phi, Phi Sigma, Alpha Omega Alpha, Phi Beta Pi. Achievements include pioneer work in hand surgery. Home: 316 Big Horn Ridge Rd NE Sandia Heights Albuquerque NM 87122 Office: U N Mex HSC Dept Orthop and Rehab MSC 10-5600 Albuquerque NM 87131 Office Fax: 505-856-6793. Personal E-mail: geoomer@juno.com.

OMER, ROBERT WENDELL, hospital administrator; b. Salt Lake City, Feb. 10, 1948; s. Wayne Albert and Melva Bernice (Thunell) O.; m. Deborah Jackson, May 4, 1972;children: Melinda, Carmen, Creighton, Preston, Allison. BS in Biology, U. Utah, 1972; MHA, Washington U., St. Louis, 1975. V.p. St. Luke's Hosp., Cedar Rapids, Iowa, 1974-80; asst. adminstr. Franciscan Med. Ctr., Rock Island, Ill., 1980-82, Latter Day Saints Hosp., Salt Lake City, 1982-85, Clarkson Hosp., Omaha, 1985-93, v.p., COO, 1993-97; CEO Creighton St. Joseph's Clinics, Omaha, 1998-99; pres., CEO MCH Health Sys., Blair, Nebr., 1999—2001; CEO Cooper County Hosp., Boonville, Mo., 2002—03; rural health advisor U. Mo. Health Care, 2003—; CEO Pioneers Hosp., Meeker, Colo., 2003—. Bd. dirs. ARC, Heartland chpt. Omaha; bd. dirs. Nebr. Scanning Svcs. Lt. col. USAR, 1972. Fellow Am. Coll. Healthcare Execs. (regent); mem. Nebr. Hosp. Assn., Omaha C. of C. (Leadership Omaha award 1978), Omaha Healthcare Execs. Group (pres. 1989-90), Rotary (bd. dirs. 1990). Republican. Mem. Lds Ch. Avocations: jogging, history, bicycling, backpacking, racquetball. Home: PO Box 333 Meeker CO 81641

OMHOLT, BRUCE DONALD, product designer, mechanical engineer, consultant; b. Salem, Oreg., Mar. 27, 1943; s. Donald Carl and Violet Mae (Buck) Omholt; m. Mavis Aronow, Aug. 18, 1963 (div. July 1972); children: Madison, Natalie; m. Darla Kay Faber, Oct. 27, 1972; 1 child, Cassidy. BSME, Heald Coll. Engring., San Francisco, 1964. Real estate salesman R. Lea Ward and Assocs., San Francisco, 1962—64; sales engr. Repco Engring., Montebello, Calif., 1964; various mfg., engring. and mgmt. positions Ford Motor Co., Rawsonville, Saline, Owosso, Ypsilanti, Mich., 1964—75; chief engr. E.F. Hauserman Co., Cleve., 1975—77; dir. design and engring. Am. Seating Co., Grand Rapids, Mich., 1977—80; pres. Trinity Engring., Grand Rapids, 1980—81, Rohnert Park, Calif., 1981—. Cons. in mfg., carrier rack apparatus, motorcycle improvements. Achievements include patents for a vertical mitre machine; a merchandise display unit; underwater breathing apparatus. E-mail: omholt@pacbell.ne.

OMIDYAR, PIERRE M., Internet company executive; b. Paris, June 21, 1967; arrived in U.S., 1973; m. Pam Kerr; 3 children. BS in Computer Sci., Tufts U., 1988. With developer rels. Gen. Magic, Inc.; software developer Claris (subsidiary of Apple Computer), 1988—91; co-founder Ink Devel. Corp., 1991; founder, chmn. eBay, Inc., 1995—. Trustee Tufts U., mem. adminstrn. and finance com., mem., com. on trusteeship.; trustee Santa Fe Inst. Co-founder, chair bd. dirs. Omidyar Found., 1998—; co-founder, CEO Omidyar Network; bd. dir. Meetup.com. Named one of World's Richest People, Forbes, 1999—2007, 50 Most Generous Philanthropists, Fortune Mag., 2005, Forbes Richest Americans, 2006; recipient Light on the Hill award (with Pam Omidyar), Tufts U. Office: eBay Inc 2125 Hamilton Ave San Jose CA 95125-5905 *

OMINSKY, HARRIS, lawyer; b. Phila., Sept. 14, 1932; s. Joseph and Lillian (Herman) O.; m. Rosalyn Rita Rutenberg; children— Michelle, David. BS in Econs., U. Pa., 1953, LLB cum laude, 1956. Bar: Pa. 1956. Ptnr. Ominsky & Ominsky, Phila., 1958-64; ptnr. Blank, Rome, Comisky & McCauley, Phila., 1964—2003, Blank Rome LLP, 1964—2003; co-chmn. real estate dept. Blank, Rome, Comisky & McCauley, Phila., 1988-93. Lectr. Law Sch., Temple U., Phila., 1969-71, lectr. Real Estate Inst., 1996—. Author: Real Estate Practice: New Perspectives, 1996, Real Estate Practice: Breaking New Ground, 2001, If I'm Still Around, I Can't Be Dead, 2002, Real Estate Lore, 2006; contbr. columns to newspapers and mags.; contbr. numerous articles to profl. jours. Pres. bd. Phila. Singing City Choir, 1984-88; chmn. zoning com. Merion Civic Assn., Pa., 1984-91. Fellow Am. Bar Found.; mem. ABA (Harrison Tweed Spl. Merit award 1988), Pa. Bar Assn. (ho. of dels. 1984—2004), Pa. Bar Inst. (bd. dirs. 1981—, exec. com. 1986-93, v.p. 1988-89, pres. 1989-90, lectr., planner 1969—), Phila. Bar Assn. (chmn. real estate taxes subcom. 1984-85, real property sect. 1991-92, Leon J. Obermayer Edn. award 1989, Good Deed award real property sect. 1999), Am. Coll. Real Estate Lawyers (bd. govs. 1993-95), Order of Coif. Home: 526 Baird Rd Merion Station PA 19066-1302 Office: Blank Rome LLP One Logan Sq Philadelphia PA 19103-6998 Home Phone: 610-664-8063; Office Phone: 215-569-5668. Business E-Mail: ominsky@blankrome.com.

OMIROS, GEORGE JAMES, medical foundation executive; b. Uniontown, Pa., Oct. 26, 1956; s. Chris George and Alice (Zervoudi) O.; m. Sophia Florent, June 28, 1980; children: Christopher George, Alicia Helene. BS in Politics and Philosophy, U. Pitts., 1978; M, Ctrl. Mich. U., Mount Pleasant, 1982. Campaign coord., program assoc. S.W. Pa. chpt. Am. Heart Assn., Greensburg, 1979, fundraising dir., 1979-80, dir. devel., 1980-84, v.p. devel., ops. We Pa. chpt. Pitts., 1984-85, dep. exec. v.p., 1985-87, exec. v.p., 1987-88; exec. dir. Leukemia Soc. Am., The Leukemia and Lymphoma Soc., Pitts., 1988—, nat. mktg. rep., 1988—, asst. v.p. nat. office, 1991-93; sr. exec. dir., nat. dir. Don Devel., Pitts., 1993-95, sr. exec. dir., group dir., nat. dir. comm. campaign, 1995—. Mem. coun., rev. com. Health Sys. Agy. S.W. Pa., Pitts., 1983—87; mem. com. Fayette County Rep. Party; mem. Order St. Andrew-Ecumenical Patriarchate Istanbul, 2001—; cons. devel. Greek Orthodox Archdiocese, Pitts., 1982—, v.p., 1987—, fin. chmn., 1999—; chair Pitts. met. com. Pitts. Metro Com.Internat. Orthodox Christian Charities, Balt., 1993—; mem. parish coun. St. Spyridon Greek Orthodox Ch., Monessen, Pa., 1982—2000; met. chmn. Internat. Orthodox Christian Charities. Decorated Order of St. Andrew, 2001. Mem. Nat. Soc. Fundraising Execs. (cert., founder 1980, pres. 1985-87, Outstanding Fundraising Exec. 1990), Oncology Nursing Soc. (chmn. Camp Raising Spirits 2000—), Pitts. Planned Giving Coun. (founding com. 1983—), Friends of George C. Marshall (steering com. 1990-92), Uniontown Country Club, Uniontown Rotary (local treas. 1985, sec. 1986, v.p. 1987, pres. 1988), Chestnut Ridge Rotary, Pitts. Rotary (dist. gov. Rotary dist. 2003-2004), Masons, Order St. Andrew, Order Jesters, Syria Shrine (pres. Uniontown chpt. 2005). Republican. Greek Orthodox. Avocations: stained glass work, art collections, gardening, antiques. Office: Leukemia and Lymphoma Soc 333 E CarsonSt Ste 441 Pittsburgh PA 15219 Office Phone: 412-395-2873. Business E-Mail: omirosg@lls.org.

OMMAYA, AYUB KHAN, neurosurgeon, educator; b. Pakistan, Apr. 14, 1930; came to US, 1961, naturalized, 1968; s. Sultan Nadir and Ida (Counil) Khan; m. Ghalazala Nangiana, 1984; children: David, Alexander, Shana, Aisha, Iman, Sinan. MD, U. Punjab, Pakistan, 1953; MA, Oxford U., Eng., 1956; DSc (hon.), Tulane U. Diplomate Am. Bd. Neurol. Surgery. Intern Mayo Hosp., Lahore, Pakistan, 1953-54; resident in neurosurgery Radcliffe Infirmary, Oxford, Eng., 1954-61; vis. scientist NIH, Bethesda, Md., 1961-63, assoc. neurosurgeon, 1963-68, head sect. applied rsch., 1968-74, chief neurosurgery, 1974-79; clin. prof. George Washington U. Med. Sch., 1970—. Cons. VA, Armed Forces Radiobiology Rsch. Inst.; chmn. Inter-Agy. Com. for Protection Human Rsch. Subjects of Fed. Coordinating Coun. for Sci., Engring. and Tech., NAS; chmn. biomechanics adv. com. com. Nat. Hwy. Traffic Safety Adminstrn.; mem. adv. com. Nat. Ctr. Injury Control & Prevention, Atlanta; inaugural Lewin Meml. lectr. U. Cambridge, Eng., 1983; mem. adv. coun. CDC; Snively lectr. Am. Assn. Auto. Medicine, 1988; Ibn-Sina lectr. Islamic Med. Assn. N.Am. Contbr. articles to profl. jours.; inventor, patentee spinal fluid flow driven artificial organs for diabetes and degenerative diseases of the nervous system. Pres. Ctr. Integrative Neuroscience, Bethesda; v.p., dir. rsch. Cyborgan, Inc., Bethesda. Recipient J.W. Kirkdaldy prize Oxford U., 1956, Lifetime Achievement award Internat. Coll. Surgeons, 1996; recipient Sitara-i-Imtiaz for Achievements in Neurosurgery Govt. Pakistan, 1981; Hunterian prof. Royal Coll. Surgeons, 1968; Rhodes scholar, 1954-60 Fellow ACS, Third World Acad. Scis. (assoc., med. scis. com.), Royal Coll. Surgeons Eng.; mem. ASME (exec. affiliate), Soc. for Neurosci., Am. Assn. Neurol. Surgeons, Rsch. Soc. Neurosurgeons, Brit. Soc. Neurol. Surgeons, Am. Assn. Pakistani Physicians (pres.), Internat. Brain Rsch. Orgn. (life), Pan-Am. Med. Assn. Home: 8901 Burning Tree Rd Bethesda MD 20817-3007

O'MORCHOE, CHARLES CHRISTOPHER CREAGH, anatomist, surgeon, educator; b. Quetta, India, May 7, 1931; came to U.S., 1968; s. Nial Francis C. and Jessie Elizabeth (Joly) O'M.; m. Patricia Jean Richardson, Sept. 15, 1955; children: Charles Eric Creagh, David James Creagh. BA, Trinity Coll., Dublin U., Ireland, 1953, MB, BCh, BAO, 1955, MA, 1959, MD, 1961, PhD, 1969, DSc, 1981. Resident Halifax Gen. Hosp., England, 1955-57; lectr. in anatomy Sch. Medicine Trinity Coll., Dublin (Ireland) U., 1957-61, 63-65, lectr. in physiology, 1966-67, assoc. prof. in physiology, 1967-68; instr. in anatomy Harvard Med. Sch., Boston, 1962-63; vis. prof. physiology U. Md. Sch. Medicine, Balt., 1961-62, assoc. prof. anatomy, 1968-71, prof. anatomy, 1971-74; chmn. anatomy bd. State of Md., 1971-73; prof., chmn. dept. anatomy Stritch Sch. Medicine Loyola U., Maywood, Ill., 1974-84; dean Coll. Medicine, U. Ill., Urbana-Champaign, 1984-98, prof. anat. scis. and surgery, 1984-98, emeritus dean and prof., 1998—. WHO cons., vis. prof. physiology Jaipur, India, 1967, S.M.S. Med. Coll., U. Rajasthan, vis. prof. anatomy, 1971; vis. scholar U. Wash. Sch. Medicine, 2003—. Assoc. editor: Anatomical Record, 1978-98, Am. Jour. Anatomy, 1987-91, Lymphology, 2004—; contbr. articles to profl. jours. Elected fellow Trinity Coll., Dublin U., 1966; named faculty mem. of yr. Loyola U., Chgo., 1982. Mem. N.Am. Soc. Lymphology (v.p. 1982-84, pres. 1984-86, sec. 1993-98, Cecil K. Drinker award 1992), Am. Assn. Anatomy Chairmen (emeritus), Am. Assn. Anatomists (dir. placement svc. 1981-91), Internat. Soc. Lymphology (exec. com. 1987-97, pres. 1993-95, Presdl. award 2001), Alpha Omega Alpha. Mem. Church of Ireland. Home: 5645 NE Lincoln Rd East Poulsbo WA 98370-7756 Office: U Ill Coll Medicine 190 Med Sci Bldg 506 S Mathews Ave Urbana IL 61801-3618 Business E-Mail: cccom@uiuc.edu.

OMOTOSO, EDWARD, diplomat, journalist; s. Joseph Ojo Omotoso and Omotoso Adesiyan; m. Florence Ayo Ogunyemi, May 28, 1966; children: Michael Olu, Abimbola Yetunde, Kemi Ayotunde. LLB with honors, London Sch. Econs. and Polit. Sci., U. London, 1966; MS, Columbia U., NYC, 1967; postgrad., Kennedy Sch. Govt. Exec. Edn., Harvard U., Cambridge, Mass., 2004. Exec. sec., conf. establishing internat. fund agrl. devel. UN, Rome, 1974—77, sec. world food coun., 1975—80, resident coord., resident rep. Maseru, Lesotho, 1998—2001; head, external rels. Orgn. Petroleum Exporting Countries, Vienna, 1980—85; dir. divsn. external rels. UN Devel. Program, NYC, 1992—98, sr. spl. advisor, 2003—. Mem.: Assn. Former Internat. Civil Servants (1st v.p. 2006—). Home: 214-46 Whitehall Ter Queens Village NY 11427 Office: UN Devel Program United Nations Plz New York NY 10017 Home Phone: 718-740-2322. Personal E-mail: edomotoso@post.harvard.edu. Business E-Mail: edward.omotoso@undp.org. E-mail: edomotoso@gmail.com.

OMS, LUIS J., physician; b. Ponce, PR, Nov. 26, 1942; s. Javior Oms and Isabel Loyola; m. Magali Maldonado, May 21, 1977; children: Ingrid, Michelle, Nicole, Lara, Luis J. BS, U. PR, Ponce, 1963; MD, U. PR, San Juan, 1967. Intern Mercy Hosp., Buffalo, 1967—68; resident U. PR, 1970—73; fellow Wills Edge Hosp., Phila., 1973—74. Lt. comdr. med. corps. USN, 1968—70. Office: Ctrl Asst Med Optics 1250 J Tpsneiro San Juan PR 00921

OMTVEDT, CRAIG P., consumer products executive; m. Jane Omtvedt. Degree, U. Minn. Dir. of audit Fortune Brands, Inc., Lincolnshire, Ill., 1989-92, dep. contr., 1992-97, v.p., chief acctg. officer, 1997-99, sr. v.p., CFO Deerfield, Ill., 1999—. Bd. dir. Gen. Cable. Mem. Fin. Exec. Inst., Inst. of Mgmt. Accts., Tax Exec. Inst. Office: Fortune Brands Inc 520 Lake Cook Rd Deerfield IL 60015 *

OMTVEDT, IRVIN THOMAS, academic administrator, educator; b. Rice Lake, Wis., June 12, 1935; s. Thomas and Irene M. (Nelson) O.; m. Wanda Ruth Rank, Aug. 15, 1959; children: Mark, Penny. BS in Agr., U. Wis., Madison, 1957; MS in Animal Science, Okla. State U., Stillwater, 1959, PhD in Genetics and Animal Breeding, 1961. Fieldman livestock program, Meat and Animal Science Dept. U. Wis., 1956-57; grad. rsch. asst., Animal Science Dept. Okla. State U., 1958-61; extension livestock specialist U. Minn., 1962-64; assoc. prof. animal science Okla. State U., 1964-70, prof. animal science, 1970-73; asst. dean agr., assoc. dir. Ala. Agrl. Experiment Sta. Auburn U., 1973-75; grad. faculty fellow U. Nebr., Lincoln, 1975—, prof. animal science, 1975-2000, head animal science dept., 1975-82, dean agrl. rsch., dir. Nebr. Agrl. Experiment Sta., 1982-88, interim vice chancellor for agr. and natural resources, 1987-88, vice chancellor Inst. Agr. and Natural Resources, 1988-2000, v.p. agr. and natural resources, 1992-2000, interim sr. vice chancellor for acad. affairs, 1996-97, vice chancellor for extended edn., 1997-99; prof. emeritus animal sci., 2000—. Commr. Nebr. Rural Devel. Commn., 2000—03; sec. Agr. Builders of Nebr., 2000—; mem. task force NASULGC Food & Soc. Project, 2000—05; bd. dirs. UNL Emeriti Assn., 2001—, Nebr. Cmty. Found., 2003—05. Author: 1 textbook; contbr. numerous articles to profl. jours. Bd. dirs. St. Mark's United Meth. Ch. Found., 1989-95, 2006—, adminstrv. bd., 2000-05; bd. dirs. Nebr. Human Resources Found., 1990-91, ADEC Distance Ed Consortium, 1989-95; mem. staff parish com. St. Mark's Ch., 2000-05. Named to NE Hall Agr. Achievement, 1982; recipient Appreciation award, Nebr. SPF, 1981, Booster award, Nebr. Pork Producers, 1983, Agrl. Achievement award, Ak-Sar-Ben, 1989, ADEC Leadership award, 1995, NE Rural Radio Assn. Svc. to Agr. award, 1999, Pound-Howard Disting. Career award, U. Nebr., Lincoln, 2000, NE Agribus. Club Svc. to Agr. award, 2001, NE Farm Bur. Silver Eagle award, 2001, NE Hall Agr. Achievement honoree, 1997. Fellow AAAS, Am. Soc. Animal Sci. (editl. bd. Jour. Animal Sci. 1970-73, intersociety coun. rep. 1984-86, mem. bd. dirs. 1980-86, sec.-treas. 1980-83, pres. 1984-85); mem. Nat. Assn. State Univ. and Land Grant Colls. (bd. dirs. bd. on agr. 1992-97), Am. Registry of Profl. Animal Scientists (gov. bd. 1985-88, pres. 1986-87), Coun. for Agrl. Sci. and Tech. (bd. dirs. 1986-89, chair nat. concerns com. 1986-89), Kiwanis (life, bd. dirs. Lincoln-Capital-City, 1980-83, 2002-06, pres. 1982, 2005, lt. gov. dist., 2006-07, dist. found. star, Hixon fellow 2006), Innocents Soc. U. Nebr.-Lincoln (hon.), Lincoln Agribusiness Club, Sigma Xi, Alpha Zeta, Gamma Sigma Delta (Merit award 1993), Phi Beta Delta. Avocations: travel, gardening. Office Phone: 402-472-0272, 402-472-0272. E-mail: iomtvedt1@unl.edu.

OMURA, EMILY FOWLER, retired dermatologist; b. Oklahoma City, Okla., Oct. 19, 1938; d. Richard William and Emma (Fraiser) Fowler; m. George A. Omura, Dec. 27, 1962; children: June, Susan, Ann, George F. BA cum laude, Barnard Coll., NYC, 1960; MD, Cornell U. Med. Coll., NYC, 1964. Cert. Am. Bd. Dermatology, Am. Bd. Dermatopathology. Intern mixed-medicine Roosevelt Hosp., NYC, 1965—66; resident dermatology Cornell/N.Y. Hosp., NYC, 1966—69, clin. instr. dermatology, 1969—70; asst. prof. dermatology U. Ala., Birmingham, 1970—75; assoc. prof. U. Ala. Med. Ctr., Birmingham, 1975—83, prof. dermatology, dir. dermatopathology, 1983—99, emeritus prof. dermatology, 1999—2006; with dermatopathology Skin Path Assocs., Birmingham, 1999—2006, ret., 2006. Dir. dermatopathology fellowship training program U. Ala., Birmingham, 1983-99. Med. Student award for Outstanding Performance in Dermatology established by U. Ala. Birmingham, named for Emily F. Omura, 1999— Fellow Am. Acad. Dermatology, Am. Soc. Dermatopathology (pres. 2000-01). Methodist. Avocations: dance, reading, museum docent.

OMURA, GEORGE ADOLF, medical oncologist; b. NYC, Apr. 30, 1938; s. Bunji K. and Martha (Pilger) O.; m. Emily Fowler, Dec. 27, 1962; children: June Ellen, Susan, Ann, George Fowler. BA magna cum laude, Columbia U., 1958; MD, Cornell U., 1962. Intern Bellevue Hosp., NYC, resident, 1965-67; fellow Meml. Sloan Kettering Cancer Ctr., NYC, 1967-70; asst. prof. medicine U. Ala., Birmingham, 1970-73, assoc. prof. medicine, 1973-78, prof. medicine, 1978-95, prof. emeritus, medicine, 1995—, prof. ob-gyn., 1991-95; v.p. clin. devel. BioCryst Pharms., Inc., Birmingham, 1995-99, med. dir., 1996-99; prof. emeritus, ob-gyn U. Ala., Birmingham, 1996—. Cons. Nat. Cancer Inst., 1975-97; chmn. Southeastern Cancer Study Group, 1983-87; cons. to FDA, 1994-95; cons. to pharm. industry, 2000—; prin. investigator cancer and leukemia Group B for Ala., 1986-95. Contbr. articles to profl. jours. Served with USNR, 1963-65. Am. Cancer Soc. jr. faculty clin. fellow, 1971-74. Fellow: ACP; mem.: Am. Assn. Cancer Rsch., Am. Soc. Hematology, Am. Soc. Clin. Oncology, Gynecol. Oncology Group (co-prin. investigator Ala. 1988—2003, bd. dirs. 2003—07), Soc. Gynecologic Oncologists (hon.), Alpha Omega Alpha, Phi Beta Kappa. Home: 3621 Crestside Rd Birmingham AL 35223-1514 Office: University Sta Birmingham AL 35294-0001 E-mail: geoaomura@aol.com.

OMURA, YOSHIAKI, medical educator; b. Tomari, Toyama-ken, Japan, Mar. 28, 1934; arrived in U.S., 1959, naturalized, 1979; s. Tsunejiro and Minako (Uozu) Omura; m. Rose Ninon Alexander, Sept. 8, 1962 (separated 1983); children: Alexander Kenji, Vivienne Midori, Richard Itsuma. A degree, Nihon U., 1952—54; BSc in Applied Physics, Waseda U., 1957;

MD, Yokohama City U., 1958; postgrad. exptl. physics, Columbia U., 1960—63; ScD (Med.), Coll. Physicians and Surgeons, Columbia U., 1965. Diplomate Internat. Coll. Acupuncture and Electro-Therapeutics, Am. Acad. Pain Mgmt., Am. Bd. Forensic Medicine, Am. Acad. Experts in Traumatic Stress. Rotating intern Tokyo U. Hosp., 1958, Norwalk (Conn.) Hosp., 1959; rsch. fellow cardiovasc. surgery Columbia U., NYC, 1960; resident physician in surgery Francis Delafield Hosp., Cancer Inst., Columbia U., 1961—65; asst. prof. pharmacology and instr. surgery N.Y. Med. Coll., 1966—72; vis. prof. (summers) U. Paris, 1973—77; Maitre de recherche, Disting. Fgn. Scientist program of INSERM Govt. of France, 1977. Rsch. cons. orthop. surgery Columbia U., 1965—66; part-time emergency rm. physician Englewood Hosp., 1965—66; rsch. cons. pharmacology dept. NY Downstate Med. Ctr., SUNY, 1966; co-founder, cons. Lincoln Hosp. Acupuncture Drug Detoxification Program, 1974—75; chmn. Columbia U. Affiliation and Cmty. Medicine com., Cmty. Bd. Francis Delafield Hosp., 1974—75; vis. rsch. prof. dept. elec. engring. Manhattan Coll., 1960—99; chmn. Sci. Divsn. Children's Art & Sci. Workshops, NYC, 1971—92; dir. med. rsch. Heart Disease Rsch. Found., Bklyn., 1972—; adj. prof. dept. pharmacology Chgo. Med. Sch., 1982—93; vis. prof. physiology Sch. Med. Showa U., Tokyo, 1988—96; adj. prof. preventive medicine NY Med. Coll., 1997—; vis. prof. Inst. Anesthesiology and Reanimation U. Padua, Italy, 1999; prof. dept. non-orthodox medicine Ukrainian Nat. Med. U., Kiev, 1993—; attending physician dept. neurosci. LI Coll. Hosp., 1980—88; cons. NY Pain Ctr., 1988—92, NIH Rsch. Grant Evaluation, 1994—96; v.p. Internat. Kirlian Rsch. Assn., 1981—94; mem. NY State Bd. Medicine, 1984—94; mem. alumni coun. Coll. Phys. and Surg. Columbia U., 1986—; vice chair Am. Bd. Forensic Medicine, 2002—07. Author: 7 books; mem. editl. bd. Alternative Medicine, 1985—93, Scandinavian Jour. Acupuncture and Electrotherapy, 1987—, Functional Neurology, 1988—2002; founder, editor-in-chief: Acupuncture & Electro-Therapeutics Rsch. Internat. Jour., 1974—; editl. cons. Jour. Electrocardiology, 1980—86, Am. Jour. Traditional Chinese Medicine, 2006—; contbr. chapters to books, over 220 articles to profl. jours. Recipient Acupuncture Scientist of Yr. award, Internat. Congress of Chinese Medicine, 1989, World 1st Qi Gong Scientist of Yr. award, Internat. Congress of Chinese Medicine & Qi Gong, 1990; fellow, Columbia U., 1960; grantee, Am. Cancer Soc. Inst., 1961—63, John Polacek Found., 1966—72, NIH, 1967—72, Heart Disease Rsch. Found., 1972—. Fellow: Internat. Coll. Angiology, NY Cardiol. Soc., Am. Coll. Angiology, Am. Assn. Integrative Medicine (diplomate) (life; vice chair 2002—07), Am. Coll. Forensic Examiners (life; vice chair sect. forensic medicine 2002—07), Royal Soc. Medicine (life), Internat. Coll. Acupuncture and Electro-Therapeutics (pres. 1980—), Am. Coll. Acupunture (life); mem.: NY Japanese Med. Soc. (pres. 1963—73), Am. Soc. Artificial Internal Organs, Japan Bi-Digital O-Ring Test Med. Soc. (pres. 1990—), Japan Bi-Digital O-Ring Test Assn. (pres. 1986—), NY Acad. Sci., Internat. Assn. for Study of Pain (founding mem. 1975—). Achievements include 7 US and 7 Japanese patents in medical field; originator of Bi-Digital O-Ring test. Home and Office: 800 Riverside Dr Ste 8I New York NY 10032-7400 Office Phone: 212-781-6262. Business E-Mail: icaet@yahoo.com.

ONAH, EJEMBI JOHN, chemist, researcher; b. Aobidah, Benue, Nigeria, Apr. 4, 1963; s. Onah Isaac Ogbeh and Onyelu Oyijewu; m. Onyemowo Joy Okoh, Dec. 10, 1993; children: Owoicho-Oche children: Ihotu, Ijeyikowoicho, Ehikowoicho. BSc in Chemistry, U. Jos, Nigeria, 1985, MSc in Applied Organic Chemistry, 1992; PhD summa cum luade, U. Tech., Dresden, Germany, 2001. Asst. lectr. Benue State U., Makurdi, Nigeria, 1993—96; vis. scientist Max Planck Inst., Golm, Germany, 1996—97; scientist/ph.d. student Inst. Polymer Rsch., U. Tech., Dresden, 1998—2001; rsch. assoc., post-doc Va. Poly. Inst. and State U., Blacksburg, 2001—02; vis. scientist Cornell U., Ithaca, NY, 2002—05; rsch. tech. dir. N.Am. Nanonige Corp., 2005—; pres., CEO Focus Nanotechnology Africa, 2005—. Vis. scientist NSF, 2002. Author: Questions and Answers in Chemistry; contbr. articles to profl. publs. Recipient USA Presdl. recognition, White Ho., 2004; scholar, KAAD, 1996; postdoctral fellow, Va. Poly. Inst. and State U., 2001. Mem.: AAAS, Am. Chem. Soc. Achievements include first to fabrication of film with the lowest dielectric constant of 1.5. Home Phone: 607-869-9755. Personal E-mail: eo42@cornell.edu.

ONAT, BORA M., research and development company executive, electrical engineer; Exec. MBA, Temple U., Phila., 2007; PhD in Elec. Engring., Boston U., 1998. Characterization mgr. Celight Inc., Iselin, NJ, 2001—02; mem. of tech. staff Lucent Tech., Breinigsville, Pa., 1998—2001; sr. device designer Infinera Corp, Sunnyvale, Calif., 2002—04; r&d progam mgr. Goodrich Corp., Princeton, NJ, 2004—. Recipient Photonics award, Melles Griot, 1996; fellow, EG&G, 1997; Rsch. fellow, Boston U., 1993—98, GAANN scholar, Dept. Edn., 1996—97. Mem.: IEEE Lasers and Electro-Optics Soc. (mem. 1990—2007). Achievements include 2 US patents in field. Office: 3490 Route 1 S Bldg 12 Princeton NJ 08540 Home Phone: 610-390-9114; Office Phone: 609-524-0256.

O'NEAL, C. DUANE, lawyer; b. Indpls., Mar. 10, 1950; s. Chlois D. and A. Rosalie (Lawrence) O'Neal; m. Roberta R. Halvorson, Aug. 17, 1974; children: Amy E., Christopher D. BA in History, Ind. U., Bloomington, 1973; MBA in Fin., Ind. U., Indpls., 1979, JD summa cum laude, 1985. Bar: Ind. 1985, Appelate Ct. (7th cir.) 1986, US. Supreme Ct. 1986, US Tax Ct. 1986. Dir. purchasing Brookside Corp., McCordsville, Ind., 1973—75; materials mgr. Inland Container Corp., Indpls., 1975—76; v.p. O. O. McKinley Co., Indpls., 1976—79; sales mgr. Price Bros. Co., Dayton, Ohio, 1979—84; atty. Bose, McKinney and Evans, Indpls., 1984—96; ptnr. Lewis and Kappes P.C., Indpls., 1986—. Lectr. in field. Founding mem. Greenwood Cmty. Concert Band, Ind., 1993—; commr. Greenwood Plan Commn., 1997—; lobbyist Ind. Gen. Assembly, Indpls., 1999—; elder Southport Presbyn. Ch., Indpls., 2003—. Recipient Leadership award, WRTV, Indpls., 1997—. Mem.: Ind. U. Alumni Assn., Mensa, Ind. Law Rev. (bd. mem. 1983—84), Indpls. Bar Assn. (section chmn. 2003—05), Am. Arbitration Assn. (panel arbitrator and mediator 1990, arbitrator, mediator 1994—). Presbyterian. Avocations: bicycling, travel, gardening. Office: Lewis and Kappes PC 2500 One America Sq Indianapolis IN 46282

O'NEAL, CYNTHIA ANN, lawyer; b. Smithfield, NC, Apr. 24, 1974; d. Jasper and Azzie O'Neal. BA, Duke U., Durham, NC, 1992; JD, Duke U. Law Sch., Durham, NC, 1999. Cert. constrn. industry technician Nat. Assn. Women in Constrn. and Clemson U., 2005. Law clk. NC Supreme Ct., Raleigh, 1999—2000; assoc. Smith Helms Mulliss & Moore, LLP, Raleigh, 2000—02, Taylor Penry Rash & Riemann, PLLC, Raleigh, 2003—07; ptnr., gen. counsel GCS Constrn. Co., Durham, 2007—. Co-author: Broker Dealer Liability: Investment Adviser Misconduct, North Carolina Law for The Law of Motor Vehicle Dealer Bond Claims; author: (book rev.) Fidelity & Surety Law Committee Newsletter. Vol. Habitat for Humanity, Raleigh, 2005—06, N.C. Bar Assn. Lawyers in the Schools Com., Raleigh, 2005—, Wake County Bar Assn. Lunch with a Lawyer Program, Raleigh, 2005—06, Duke Connect, Durham, 2006; legal dir. PLM Families Together, Inc., Raleigh, 2006—. Recipient Under 40 Leadership award, Triangle Bus. Jour., 2006, Young Careerist award, Bus. and Profl. Women, Raleigh, 2006, Bus. and Profl. Women, USA Dist. IV, 2006. Mem.: ABA, NC Assn. Women Attys., Bus. and Profl. Women (chair N.C. dist. IV young careerist 2006—), Triangle Urban League, Associated Gen. Contractors Am., United Minority Contractors NC, Triangle Comml. Real Estate Women, Nat. Assn. Women in Constrn. (corr. sec. 2006—, Pres. award 2005—06), NC Bar Assn. Achievements include First African-American woman elected to the Council of the North Carolina Bar Association Construction Section. Office: GCS Constrn Co 1111 Fayetteville St Ste B Durham NC 27701 Home Phone: 919-272-7735; Office Phone: 919-682-0260. Office Fax: 919-682-0257. Personal E-mail: cynoneal@yahoo.com. Business E-Mail: gcs_nc@yahoo.com.

O'NEAL, E. STANLEY (STANLEY O'NEAL), investment company executive; b. Roanoke, Ala., Oct. 7, 1951; m. Nancy A. Garvey; 2 children. BS, Kettering U., 1974; MBA, Harvard U., 1978. Analyst GM Corp., 1978—80, dir., 1980—82, treas. Spanish divsn. Madrid, 1982—84, asst. treas., 1984—87; dir. investment banking Merrill Lynch & Co., Inc., 1986, mng. dir. investment banking, head global capital markets group, 1997, exec. v.p., co-head corp. and instl. client group, 1998, exec. v.p., CFO, 1998—2000, pres. U.S. pvt. client group, 2000—01, COO NYC, 2001—02, pres., 2001—, CEO, 2002—, chmn., 2003—. Bd. dirs. Merrill Lynch & Co., Inc., 2001—, GM Corp., 2001—06, Financial Svcs. Roundtable. Bd. dirs. Nat. Urban League, Catalyst; trustee Ctr. Strategic & Internat. Studies, Washington DC; bd. dirs. NYC Partnership, Lower Manhattan Devel. Corp., Ronald McDonald House, NY; mem., adv. bd. The Bronx Prep. Sch.; trustee Buckley Sch.; overseer Meml. Sloan-Kettering Cancer Ctr. Recipient Corp. Exec. of the Yr., Black Enterprise, 2000, Achievement award, Exec. Leadership Coun., 2000, Most Influential Black Americans, Ebony mag., 2006. Office: Merrill Lynch & Co Inc 4 World Financial Ctr 250 Vesey St New York NY 10080 *

O'NEAL, EDGAR CARL, psychology professor; b. St. Louis, Apr. 30, 1939; s. Clarence Edgar O'Neal and Alyce (Mullins) Redwine; m. Ellen Rose Luther, Aug. 31, 1963; children: Colleen Ruth, Patrick Blaine BA, Duke U., 1961; M.Div., Drew U., 1964; MA, U. Mo., 1968, PhD, 1969. Ordained to ministry United Meth. Ch., 1964. Minister Community Meth. Ch., Cold Spring Harbor, NY, 1962-65; NIMH fellow U. Mo., Columbia, 1966-69; asst. prof., assoc. prof. psychology Tulane U., New Orleans, 1969-76, chmn. dept. psychology, 1978-84, prof. psychology, 1977—99, John Madison Fletcher prof. psychology, 1999—. Editor: Perspectives on Aggression, 1976; mem. editl. bd. Jour. Personality and Social Psychology, 1991-97, Jour. Non-verbal Behaviour, 1991-94, Aggressive Behavior, 1995-2004; contbr. articles to profl. jours. Fellow APA (coun. 1982-85); mem. Sigma Xi, Sigma Chi. Democrat. Methodist. Home: 7219 O'Neil Dr Harahan LA 70123-4844 E-mail: edgar.oneal@cox.net, edgar.oneal@tulane.edu.

O'NEAL, HANK, entertainment producer, small business owner; b. Kilgore, Tex., June 5, 1940; s. Harold Lee and Sarah (Christian) O'N.; m. Shelley M. Shier, May 14, 1985. BA, Syracuse U., 1962. With CIA, Washington and NYC, 1963-76; exec. v.p. Hammond Music Enterprises, NYC, 1980-83; pres., owner Chiaroscuro Records Co./Downtown Sound recording studio, NYC, 1970-80, 85—; exec. v.p. HOSS, Inc., NYC, 1983—, Broadway Bound, Inc., 1998—; v.p. Festival Network, Inc., NYC, 2007—. Instr., dept. head New Sch. for Social Rsch., N.Y.C., 1970-92; bd. dirs. The Jazz Found. Am., N.Y.C., The Jazz Gallery, N.Y.C.; chair bd. govs. Jazz and Contemporary Music, New Sch. U.; pres. SOS Prodns., Wilkes Barre, Pa., 1987—. Author: Eddie Condon Scrapbook of Jazz, 1973, A Vision Shared, 1976, Berenice Abbott-American Photographer, 1982, Djuna Barnes 1978-81, 1990, Charlie Parker/The Funky Blues Date, 1995; author/photographer: The Floating Jazz Festival, 1985, The Ghosts of Harlem, 1997, Hank O'Neal, 2000, Gay Day, 2006; photographer: (books) Allegra Kent's Water Beauty Book, 1976, All the King's Men, 1990; prodr., cover photographer/designer numerous record albums, 1967—. Capt. U.S. Army, 1963-67. Recipient various awards and prizes for books. Mem. Phi Gamma Delta. Home: Glenside PO Box 101 Thornhurst PA 18424-0101 Office: Chiaroscuro Records 830 Broadway New York NY 10003-4827 Home Phone: 212-598-4325; Office Phone: 212-674-0265. Personal E-mail: chiarohank@aol.com.

O'NEAL, JERMAINE, professional basketball player; b. Columbia, SC, Oct. 13, 1978; s. Angela Ocean. Basketball player Portland Trail Blazers, 1997—2000; forward ctr. Ind. Pacers, 2000—. Named to All-NBA 2nd Team, 2002—04, Ea. Conf. All-Star Team, NBA, 2002—04, 2007. Achievements include being the youngest person to play in an NBA game, 1996. Office: Ind Pacers 125 S Pennsylvania Ave Indianapolis IN 46204 *

O'NEAL, LYMAN HENRY, biology educator; b. Princeton, Ind., Jan. 18, 1942; s. Henry and Eleanor Anne (Reibold) O'N.; m. Cynthia Sue Woods, June 13, 1964; children: Michael Lyman, Cheri Sue. BA, Oakland City U., 1963; MS, U. Minn., 1970, PhD, 1973. Secondary sch. tchr. Francisco HS, Ind., 1963-66; prof. biology Oakland City U., 1973-89, Edison Coll., Punta Gorda, Fla., 1989—. Rsch. asst. U. Minn., St. Paul, 1967-73; adj. prof. Henderson CC, Ky. 1982, Fla. So. Coll., Port Charlotte, 1989, Fla. Gulf Coast U., 1998—; bd. dirs. Ecol. Consortium Mid Am. Hancock Biol. Sta. Murray State U., 1982-89; mem. validation study panel Ind. State Dept. Edn., 1986; mem. Mote Marine Lab. Charlotte Harbor Adv. Coun., 1994—; mem. curriculum task force Fla. Gulf Coast U., 1994—. Contbr. articles to profl. jours. Mem. cmty. adv. bd. Fawcett Meml. Hosp. Mem. Am. Inst. Biol. Sci., Fla. Acad. Scis., Nat. Sci. Tchrs. Assn., Nat. Assn. Biology Tchrs. Avocations: bass guitar, painting, multimedia, cartooning. Home: 23 Amazon Dr Punta Gorda FL 33983-5208 Office: Edison Coll 26300 Airport Rd Punta Gorda FL 33950 Office Phone: 941-637-5614. Business E-Mail: loneal@edison.edu.

O'NEAL, MICHAEL RALPH, state legislator, lawyer; b. Kansas City, Mo., Jan. 16, 1951; s. Ralph D. and Margaret E. (McEuen) O'N.; children from a previous marriage: children: Haley Anne, Austin Michael; m. Cindy Wulfkuhle, Apr. 9, 1999. BA in English, U. Kans., 1973, JD, 1976. Bar: Kans. 1976, U.S. Dist. Ct. Kans. 1976, U.S. Ct. Appeals (10th cir.) 1979. Intern Legis. Counsel State of Kans., Topeka, 1975-76; assoc. Hodge, Reynolds, Smith, Peirce & Forker, Hutchinson, Kans., 1976-77; ptnr. Reynolds, Peirce, Forker, Suter, O'Neal & Myers, Hutchinson, 1980-88; shareholder Gilliland & Hayes, P.A., Hutchinson, 1988—, mng. ptnr., 1999—2000; mem. Kans. Ho. of Reps., 1984, minority whip, 1991-92, majority whip, 1995-96; pres. Gilliland & Hayes, P.C., 1999-2000. Instr. Hutchinson CC, 1977-88; com. mem., chmn. jud. com. Kans. Ho. Reps., 1997—, fiscal oversight com., 1997-2001, tax, commerce, transp. and jud. budget com., 2003-06, vice-chmn. ho. select com. sch. fin., 2005-06, vice-chmn. ho. rules com., 2005-, vice chmn. ho. edn. budget sub-com., 2007-; vice-chmn. Kans. Jud. Performance Commn., 2006-. Vice chmn. Rep. Ctrl. Com., Reno County, Kans., 1982-86; bd. dirs. Reno County Mental Health Assn., Hutchinson, 1984-89, YMCA, 1984-86, Crime Stoppers (ex-officio), Hutchinson; chmn. adv. bd. dirs. Wesley Towers Retirement Cmty., 1984-96; mem. Kans. Travel and Tourism Commn., 1990-94; bd. govs. U. Kans. Law Sch., 1991-94; mem. Kans. Sentencing Commn., 1997-2000, Tax Transp. Jud. Budget subcom., 2003-06. Recipient Leadership award Kans. C. of C. and Industry, 1985; named one of Outstanding Young Men Am., 1986. Mem. ABA, Nat. Conf. State Legislatures (criminal justice com.), Kans. Assn. Def. Counsel, Def. Rsch. Inst., Kans. Bar Assn. (prospective legis. com., Outstanding Svc. award), Hutchinson C. of C. (ex-officio bd. dirs., Leadership award 1984), Am. Coun. Young Polit. Leaders (del. Atlantic conf. biennial assembly), Kans. Jud. Coun., Commn. Uniform State Laws. Avocations: basketball, tennis, golf. Home: 8 Windemere Ct Hutchinson KS 67502-2020 Office: Gilliland & Hayes PA 2d Flr Box 2977 20 W 2nd Ave Hutchinson KS 67504-2977 Home Phone: 620-663-9181; Office Phone: 620-662-0537. Business E-Mail: mike@gh-hutch.com.

O'NEAL, MICHAEL SCOTT, SR., lawyer; b. Jacksonville, Fla., Dec. 22, 1948; s. Jack Edwin and Lucille (Colvin) O'N.; m. Barbara Louise Hardie, Jan. 30, 1971 (div. Sept. 1974); 1 child, Jennifer Erin; m. Helen Margaret Joost, Mar. 18, 1985; children: Mary Helen, Angela Marie, Michael Scott O'Neal Jr. AA, Fla. Jr. Coll., 1975; BA in Econs. summa cum laude, U. No. Fla., 1977; JD cum laude, U. Fla., 1979. Bar: Fla. 1980, U.S. Dist. Ct. (mid. dist.) Fla. 1980, U.S. Dist. Ct. (no. dist.) Fla. 1981, U.S. Ct. Appeals (11th cirs.) 1981, U.S. Supreme Ct. 1986. Assoc. Howell, Liles, Braddock & Milton, Jacksonville, Fla., 1980-83; ptnr. Commander, Legler, Werber, Dawes, Sadler & Howell, Jacksonville, 1983-91, Foley & Lardner, Jacksonville, 1991-93, Howell O'Neal & Johnson, Jacksonville, 1993-96, Howell & O'Neal, Jacksonville, 1996—. Pro bono atty. Legal Aid Soc., Jacksonville, 1980—; practicing atty. Lawyers Reference, Jacksonville, 1980—. Pres. Julington Landing Homeowners Assn., Jacksonville, 1980-83. Served to staff sgt. USAF, 1968-74. Mem. ATLA, ABA, Jacksonville Bar Assn., Fed. Bar Assn., Am. Bd. Trial Advs. (Jacksonville treas. 2007), Jacksonville Am. Bd. Trial Advocates (treas. 2007), Fla. Def. Lawyers Assn., Northeast Fla. Med. Malpractice Claims Coun. (pres. 1996), Jacksonville Assn. Def. Counsel (pres. 1999), Internat. Assn. Def. Counsel, Def. Rsch. Inst., San Jose Country Club (Jacksonville). Republican. Methodist. Avocations: golf, music. Home: 1299 Norwich Rd Jacksonville FL 32207-7525 Office: Howell O'Neal One Independent Dr Ste 2902 Jacksonville FL 32202-3500 Office Phone: 904-353-0024. E-mail: msoneal@hotmail.com.

O'NEAL, RODNEY, automotive company executive; b. Dayton, OH, Aug. 27, 1953; s. James H. and Ida B. O'Neal; m. Pamela Estell O'Neal, Aug. 20, 1983; children: Heather Marie, Damien Cain. B Indsl. Adminstrn., GM Inst., 1976; MBA (Sloan fellow), Stanford U., 1991. Various engring. and mfg. pos. GM Inland Divsn., Dayton, Portugal, and Can., 1976—91; dir. indsl. engring. Chevrolet-Pontiac-GM of Can. Group, 1991—92; dir. mfg. GM Automotive Components Group Worldwide, Troy, Mich., 1992—94; gen. dir. warehousing and distbn. GM Svc. Parts Ops., 1994—97; v.p. GM, 1997—98; pres. Delphi Interior Systems, Troy, Mich., 1998—2000, exec. v.p. Safety, Thermal and Elec. Arch. sector, 2000—03; pres. dynamics, propulsion and thermal Delphi Corp., Troy, Mich., 2003—05, pres., COO, 2005—06, pres., CEO, 2007—. Bd. dir. Goodyear Tire & Rubber Co., 2004—, Delphi Corp., 2005—, Sprint Nextel Corp., 2007—; mem. Exec. Leadership Coun. Adv. bd. Focus: HOPE. Recipient Lifetime Achievement in Industry award, Nat. Soc. Black Engineers, 2002. Office: World Hdqrs Delphi Corp 5725 Delphi Dr Troy MI 48098-2815 *

O'NEAL, SHAQUILLE RASHAUN, professional basketball player; b. Newark, Mar. 6, 1972; s. Philip A. Harrison and Lucille O'Neal; m. Shaunie Nelson, Dec. 26, 2002; children: Shareef Rashaun, Amira Sanaa, Shaquir Rashaun, Me'arah Sanaa. BS, La. State U., Baton Rouge, 2000; MBA, U. Phoenix, 2005. Ctr. Orlando Magic, Fla., 1992—96, LA Lakers, 1996—2004, Miami Heat, Fla., 2004—. Mem. Dream Team II, 1994; Owner (Clothing line and Record label) TWIsM. Actor: (films) Blue Chips, 1994, Kazaam, 1996, Steel, 1997, The Wash, 2001, After the Sunset, 2004, The Year of the Yao, 2004, Scary Movie 4, 2006; performer: (albums) Shaq Diesel, 1993, Shaq Fu: Da Return, 1994, You Can't Stop the Reign, 1995, The Best of Shaquille O'Neal, 1996, Shaquille O'Neal Presents his Superfriends, Vol. 1, 2002. Named Co-MVP of NBA All-Star game, 2000, MVP of NBA All-Star game, 2004, Regular Season MVP (by media), 2000, NBA Finals MVP, 2000—02; named one of 50 Greatest Players in NBA Hist., 1996; named to All-Am. 1st Team, Sporting News, 1990—91, Ea. Conf. All-Star Team, NBA, 1993—96, 2004—05, 2007, Western Conf. All-Star Team, 1997—98, 2000—02, All-NBA 1st Team, 1998, 2000—02, 2006, All-NBA 2nd Team, 1995, 1999; recipient Rookie of Yr. award, NBA, 1993, Gold Medal, US Olympic Team (Atlanta), 1996. Achievements include being first pick overall in draft, 1992, mem. of 3 consecutive championship teams, 2000-2002, NBA Scoring Champion, 1995, 2000; signed a five-year contract which gives Li Ning the right to produce and market a "Li Ning Shaq" line of professional basketball shoes and apparel only in China, 2006. Office: c/o Miami Heat American Airlines Arena 601 Biscayne Blvd Miami FL 33132 *

O'NEAL, STEPHEN V., lawyer; b. Bloomington, Ill., Mar. 23, 1953; AB, UCLA, 1975; JD, U. Calif. Boalt Hall Sch. Law, 1980. Bar: Calif. 1980, US Dist. Ct. (No. Dist.) Calif., US Dist. Ct. (Ea. Dist.) Calif. Ptnr., Construction & Govt. Contracts Practice Group Thelen Reid & Priest LLP, San Francisco, chmn. of firm, mem. exec. com. & partnership coun.; mng. ptnr. Mason Thelen Reid LLP. Assoc. editor Calif. Law Rev., 1979—80. Mem.: Calif. Bar Assn. (Real Property Law Sect.), Am Arbitration Assn., Bar Assn. San Francisco, ABA (Litig. Sect., Construction Industry Forum Com.). Office: Thelen Reid & Priest LLP 101 Second St Ste 1800 San Francisco CA 94105-3601 Office Phone: 415-369-7222. Office Fax: 415-371-1211. Business E-Mail: svoneal@thelenreid.com.

ONEAL-COBLE, LESLIE, lawyer; d. Lawrence Donald and Lilyan England King; m. Richard J. Coble, June 2, 2001; 1 child, Lacey N. Harris. Student, Furman U., Greenville, SC, 1970—72, U. Fla., Gainesville, 1972—74, JD, 1977. Shareholder McDonough, Oneal & O'dell, Orlando, Fla., 1978—2004, Greenberg Traurig PA, Orlando, 2004—; ptnr. Holland & Knight LLP, Orlando, 2004—. Co-author: Construction Damages and Remedies, 2004. Dir. Orlando-UCF Shakespeare Festival, 2004—. Named one of Outstanding Young Women of Orlando, PACE, 2003; recipient Myoshi Smith Meml. award, Fla. Rural Legal Svcs., 2003, award of excellence for legal aid, Orange County Bar Assn., 2004. Fellow: Am. Coll. Constrn. Lawyers (bd. govs. 1999—2001); mem.: ABA (mem. governing com. forum on constrn. 1993—99, chmn. forum on constrn. 1997—98), Am. Bd. Trial Advocates (assoc.). Office: Greenberg Traurig 450 S Orange Ave Ste 650 Orlando FL 32801 Office Phone: 407-420-1000. Business E-Mail: coble1@gtlaw.com.

O'NEAL-SERALATHAN, CRESCENTIA, advocate; d. Andrew and Mary Patricia O'Neal; m. Muthiah Seralathan, Aug. 18, 1984; children: Ashanthi Meena Seralathan, Chithra Andasi Seralathan. JD, CWRU, Cleve., 1983. Sr. rschr. Roosevelt Ctr. Am. Policy Studies, Ill. Sch. Reform Project, Chgo., 1984; allocations mgr. United Way of Buffalo and Erie County, 1985—86; we. regional dir. N.Y. Civil Liberties Union, Buffalo, 1986—90; owner, fundraising and program devel. cons. Meendasi, Potomac, Md., 1990—. Planning com. UN 1985 Internat. Youth Yr., Washington, 1981—85; mem. task force women's issues NY State Assembly, Albany, 1986—91; adv. bd. Erie County Task Force on Women, Buffalo, 1986—91, Erie County Task Force on Homeless, Buffalo, 1987—91, NY State Divsn. Human Rights, Buffalo, 1987—90; founder, chmn. We. NY Coalition Against the Death Penalty, Buffalo, 1989—91; del. UN Internat. Conf. on Population and Devel., Cairo, 1994; planning com. UN 4th Internat. Conf. on Women, NYC, 1994—95; del. UN 4th Internat. Conf. On Women, Beijing, China, 1995; fed. grant reviewer LCG, Washington, 2002—; e-commerce exec. Distinctly Yours, Potomac, Md., 2005—, My Kidz Got Syle. Bd. dirs. Ams. for Dem. Action, 1996—97, Nat. Student Christian Leadership Consultation, Atlanta, 1981—85. Recipient Vol. Clearinghouse Vol. Activist award, Govt. of D.C., 1983, Congl. Cert. of Appreciation, U.S. Congress, Ho. Spkr. Thomas P. O'Neal, 1981, Cmty. Leader award, SCLC, 1989; L.B.J. Internship fellow, Congressman Walter E. Fauntroy, 1980. Mem.: UN Assn. (bd. dirs., resource and devel. com. chair 1994—2001). Avocations: jazz, reading, politics, movies, travel. Office Phone: 301-646-4989. Business E-Mail: crescentia@mykidzgotstyle.com.

O'NEIL, HAROLD FRANCIS, psychologist, educator; b. Columbia, SC, Jan. 26, 1943; s. Harold Francis Sr. and Margaret Mary O'Neil; m. Eva L. Baker, Sept. 15, 1984; children: Tristan, Christopher. PhD, Fla. State U., 1969; MS, Hollins Coll., 1970. Asst., assoc. prof. U. Tex., Austin, 1971-75; program mgr. Def. Advanced Rsch. Projects Agy., Arlington, Va., 1975-78; from team chief to dir. tng. rsch. lab. sr. exec. svc. Army Rsch. Inst., Alexandria, Va., 1978—85; prof. U. So. Calif., LA, 1985—. Cons. Army Rsch., 1985—, Inst. Def. Analyses, Alexandria, 1985—, Amry Sci. Bd.,

Washington, 1994—2001, Def. Sci. Bd. Task Force on Tng., Washington, 1999—2002. Editor: (book) Academic Press Education and Technology Series, 1977—92; editl. adviser Lawrence Erlbaum Assocs., Inc., Pubs., 1992—; contbr. chapters to books, articles to profl. jours.; founding editor Japanese Jour. Edn. Fellow: APA, Am. Psychol. Soc. Achievements include research in role of cognition and affect in computer-based instruction, role of motivation in testing, cross-cultural rsch. in Japan on the role of test anxiety and performance; Taiwan and Korea on the role of self-regulation anc achievement, games for tng; development of measures for metacognition, effort, and anxiety. Office: Univ So Calif 600 Wph University Park Los Angeles CA 90089-0001 Business E-Mail: honeil@usc.edu.

O'NEIL, J. PETER (JAMES PETER O'NEIL), elementary school educator, computer scientist; b. Rockville Center, NY, Apr. 2, 1946; s. Clement Lee and Frances Rita (Theis) O'N.; m. Carol Ann Sypniewski, June 8, 1968; children: Kelly Ann, Thomas Joseph. BA in Psychology, Loyola U., Chgo., 1968; MA in Sci. Edn., Webster Coll., St. Louis, 1972. Cert. elem. tchr. K-8, Mo., elem. tchr. K-8, Wis., dir. instruction, Wis. Tchr., student tchr. Sacred Heart Sch., Florissant, Mo., 1968-73; tchr. sci. Waunakee (Wis.) Mid. Sch., 1973-96, chmn. K-8 sci. dept., chmn. K-12 dept., 1984-92; learning coord. Deforest (Wis.) Area Sch. Dist., 1992—2000. Dir. Waunakee Summer Sci. Program, 1975-91; dir. instrn./tech. Brodhead Wis., 1996-99; designer sci. curriculum computer CD-ROM programs Sci. Curriculum Assistance Program and Elem. Sci. Curriculum Assistance Program, 1990—; dir. instrn. DeForest (Wis.) Area Sch. Dist., 2000—; adj. prof. Viterbo U., 2003—; rsch. cons. IDEAS Wis., 2002—. Feature editor: Science Scope, 1989-96; contbr. over 30 activities and articles to profl. jours. Group worker settlement houses Chgo., St. Louis; mem. Parish Coun.; dir. Waunakee Area Edn. Found. Named Master Tchr. NSF, Waunakee, 1986-96; recipient Tchr. of Yr. award Waunakee, 1984, 90, 92, Kohl Found. award, 1992, Mid. Sch. Tchr. of Yr. award Wis., 1992-93. Mem.: Wis. Soc. Curriculum Designers, Am. Soc. Curriculum Designers. Roman Catholic. Avocations: computers, sports, writing, walking. Home: 119 Simon Crestway Waunakee WI 53597-1721 Office: Deforest Area Sch Dist 520 E Holum St De Forest WI 53532-1316 Office Phone: 608-842-6531. Business E-Mail: jponeil@deforest.k12.wi.us.

O'NEIL, JOHN JOSEPH, lawyer; b. Detroit, July 20, 1943; s. John J. and Dora J. (Collins) O'N.; children: Meghan, Kathryn. BA, Trinity Coll., 1965; LLB, U. Va., 1968. Bar: N.Y. 1969, U.S. Ct. Appeals (2d cir.) 1969, Fla. 1979, D.C. 1982. Assoc. Jackson & Nash, NYC, 1968-71, Paul, Weiss, Rifkind, Wharton & Garrison, NYC, 1971-77, ptnr., 1977—. Fellow Am. Coll. Trusts and Estates Counsel; mem. ABA (com. on spl. problems of aged), N.Y. State Bar Assn. (com. on taxation, trusts and estates sect.), Assn. Bar City N.Y. (com. on trusts and estates), Pi Gamma Mu. Office: Paul Weiss Rifkind Wharton & Garrison Ste 3221 1285 Avenue Of The Americas Fl 21 New York NY 10019-6064 Fax: 212-373-3379. E-mail: joneil@paulweiss.com.

O'NEIL, KELLY LYNN, pharmacist; b. Pittsfield, Mass., Sept. 16, 1979; d. John Thomas and Hulda Teresa O'Neil. D of Pharmacy, Northeastern U., Boston, 2003. Lic. pharmacist Mass., Ga., cert. ACLS 2003, basic cardiac life support 1999. Pharmacy practice resident Grady Health Sys., Atlanta, 2003—04, infectious diseases pharmacotherapy resident, 2004—05; med. liaison Astra Zeneca Pharms., Atlanta, 2005—06; med. liaison-virology Abbot Labs., Atlanta, 2006—. Avocations: running, scuba diving, hiking. Home: 2050 Ridgestone Landing SW Marietta GA 30008 Personal E-mail: kel.oneil@gmail.com.

O'NEIL, MICHAEL C., lawyer; b. Pitts., Nov. 21, 1961; BA with high honors, Bklyn. Coll., 1986; JD with honors, DePaul Univ., 1989. Bar: Ill. 1989. Ptnr., chmn. Privacy Litigation practice group DLA Piper Rudnick Gray Cary, Chgo. Editor (articles & notes): DePaul Law Rev., 1988—89. Office: DLA Piper Rudnick Gray Cary Suite 1900 203 N LaSalle St Chicago IL 60601-1293 Office Phone: 312-368-4098. Office Fax: 312-236-7516. Business E-Mail: michael.oneil@dlapiper.com.

O'NEIL, SCOTT M., sports association executive; m. Lisa O'Neil; 2 children. Grad. in Mktg., Villanova U.; MBA, Harvard Bus. Sch. V.p. sales Phila. Eagles; corp. mktg. mgr. NJ Nets; pres. HoopsTV.com; v.p. bus. ops. and team consulting NBA, 2001—04, sr. v.p. team mktg. and bus. ops., 2004—. Author: Fantasy Land to the Rat Race, 2000. Named one of 40 Under 40, Street and Smith's Sports Bus. Jour., 2004, 2005, Advt. Age, 2006. Office: NBA Olympic Tower 645 5th Ave Fl 10 New York NY 10022-5986 *

O'NEIL, THOMAS FRANCIS, III, lawyer; b. Fairfield, Conn., Apr. 8, 1957; s. Thomas F. Jr. and Carmen A. (Therrien) O'N.; m. Nancy D., Aug. 14, 1982; children: Caley Elizabeth, Patrick McGee. AB magna cum laude, Dartmouth Coll., 1975-79; JD, Georgetown U., 1979-82. Bar: Md. 1982, U.S. Dist. Ct. Md. 1983, U.S. Ct. Appeals (4th cir.) 1983, D.C. 1992, NY. Legis. asst. Congressman Stewart B. McKinney, Washington, 1980-82; law clk. Hon. Alexander Harvey II U.S. Dist. Ct. Md.; assoc. Venable, Baetjer & Howard, Balt., 1984-86; asst. U.S. atty. U.S. Dept. Justice, Balt., 1986-89; assoc. Hogan & Hartson, Balt., 1990-91, ptnr., 1992-95; chief litig. counsel MCI Comms. Corp., Washington, 1995-98; sr. v.p., chief legal counsel MCI, 1999—2001; sr. v.p., gen. counsel MCI Group, 2001—02; sr. ptnr. Piper Rudnick LLP, 2002—04; joint global leader legis. and regulatory group, chmn. govt. affairs practice group, co-chmn. govt. controversies practice group DLA Piper, Washington, 2005—. Bd. regents mem. Georgetown Univ., 2005—; mem., bd. visitors Georgetown Univ. Law Ctr., 1999—; mem. adv. bd. Georgetown Corp. Counsel Inst.; bd. govs. Fed. Bar Assn., Balt., 1992; ex officio trustee Walters Art Mus., 1995—96, trustee, 1997—2002; mem. adv. bd. Marbury Inst., 2000—02; pres. bd. trustees The Contemporary Mus., Balt., 2005. Contbr. articles to profl. jours. Recipient Chief Postal Insps. Spl. award U.S. Postal Svc., Washington, 1988, Letter of Commendation award Bur. of Investigation, Washington, 1989, Spl. Achievement award U.S. Dept. Justice, 1989. Mem. Internat. Bar Assn., Serjeants Inn Law Club. Republican. Roman Catholic. Office: DLA Piper 1200 19th St NW Washington DC 20036-2412 Office Phone: 202-861-6685. Office Fax: 202-689-7436. Business E-Mail: thomas.oneil@dlapiper.com.

O'NEIL, WAYNE, linguist, educator; b. Kenosha, Wis., Dec. 22, 1931; s. L.J. and Kathryn (Obermeyer) O'N.; married; children: Scott Leslie, Patrick Sean, Elizabeth Erla. AB, U. Wis., 1955, AM, 1956, PhD, 1960; AM (hon.), Harvard U., 1965. Asst. prof. linguistics and lit. U. Oreg., 1961-65; prof. linguistics and edn. Harvard U., 1965-68, lectr. edn., 1968-72, vis. prof. edn., 1978-86; prof. linguistics MIT, 1968—, chmn. lit. faculty, 1969-75, chmn. linguistics program, 1986-97, head dept. linguistics and philosophy, 1989-97. Lectr. human devel. Wheelock Coll., Boston, 1991—; lectr. Beijing Normal U., 1980, Beijing and Shanghai Fgn. Lang. Insts., 1981; lectr. linguistics Shandong (China) U., 1982-83, prof., 1984—; prof. Summer Inst. on Lang. Change, NEH, 1978; vis. prof. Tsuda Coll., Tokyo, 1983, Kanda U. Internat. Studies, Makuhari, Japan, 1997, Am. Indian Lang. Devel. Inst., 2000—, Kanazawa Inst. of Tech., Japan, 2001—; co-dir. MIT-Japan Sci. and Tech. mind articulation project, 1996—. Author: (in Chinese) English Transformational Grammar, 1981, Linguistics and Applied Linguistics, 1983, (with S.J. Keyser) Rule Generalization and Optionality in Language Change, 1985, (with S. Flynn) Linguistic Theory in Second Language Acquisition, 1988, (with S. Flynn and G. Martohardjono) The Generative Study of Second Language Acquisition, 1998, (with A. Marantz and Y. Miyashita) Image, Language, Brain, 2000, (with M. Honda) Understanding First and Second Language Acquisition, 2004, (with M. Honda) Thinking Linguistically, 2007; mem. editl. group Radical Tchr., 1975—. Mem. steering com. Resist, 1967—, Peoples Coalition for Peace and Justice, 1970-72; co-founder, mem. Linguistics for Nicaragua, 1985—. With U.S. Army, 1952-54. Fulbright fellow in Iceland, 1961; Am. Council Learned Socs. study fellow M.I.T., 1964-65; George Watson fellow U. Queensland, Brisbane, Australia, 1998. Mem. AAAS, Linguistic Soc. Am., Nat. Coun. Tchrs. English, Am. Assn. Applied Linguistics, Assembly for the Tchg. English Grammar. Office: MIT Dept Linguistics and Philosophy Cambridge MA 02139-4307 Business E-Mail: waoneil@mit.edu.

O'NEIL, WILLIAM FRANCIS, academic administrator; b. Worcester, Mass., Mar. 26, 1936; s. John J. and Mary A. (Trahant) O'N.; m. Mary Elizabeth Dillon, Aug. 22, 1959; children: Kathleen, Mary Elizabeth. BS, Boston U., 1960; MEd, Worcester State Coll., 1963; diploma, U. Conn., 1970; EdD, Wayne State U., 1972; PhD in Pub. Edn. (hon.), Bridgewater State Coll., 2002; BFA (hon.), Montserrat Coll. Art, 1994. Tchr. Worcester Pub. Schs., 1960—68, cmty. sch. dir., 1968—73; assoc. prof., dir. community edn. devel. ctr. Worcester State Coll., 1973-75, dir. community svc., 1975—77, dean grad. and continuing edn., 1977—83, exec. v.p., 1983—85, Mass. Coll. Art, Boston, 1985—86, acting pres., 1986—87, pres., 1987—96; exec. officer Mass. State Coll. Coun. Pres., 1996—2002. Contbr. articles to profl. jours. Mem. Worcester Dem. City Com., Ward I Dem. Com., 1980-2005; pres., trustee Worcester Pub. Libr., 1977-82; mem. Mass. Bd. Libr. Commrs., 1984-89; bd. dirs. Worcester State Coll. Found., 2001—, Worcester Pub. Libr. Found., 2003—. Recipient Outstanding Alumni award field of edn. Worcester State Coll., 1996, citation Mass. Ho. of Reps., 1977, key City of Worcester, 1982; Mott fellow Charles Stewart Mott Found., 1971; Godine Cmty. Svc. medal, Mass. Coll. Art, 2002. Mem. Mass. Pub. Colls. and Univs. Pres. and Chancellors Assn. (chair 1991-92), Assn. Ind. Colls. Art and Design (bd. dirs. 1988-96), Mass. Cmty. Edn. Assn. (life; bd. dirs. 1972-77), Mass. State Colls. Pres. Assn. (chair 1992-93), Profl. Arts Consortium (v.p. Boston 1986-96, pres. 1993-94). Roman Catholic. Home: 47 Harvest Cir Holden MA 01520-3401 Personal E-mail: westwoods1@charter.net.

O'NEILL, ALBERT CLARENCE, JR., lawyer; b. Gainesville, Fla., Nov. 25, 1939; s. Albert Clarence and Sue Virginia (Henry) O'N.; m. Vanda Marie Nigels, Apr. 26, 1969; 1 child, Heather Marie. BA with high honors, U. Fla., 1962; LL.B. magna cum laude, Harvard U., 1965. Bar: Fla. 1965. Law clk. to judge U.S. Dist. Ct. (mid. dist.) Fla., Jacksonville, 1965-66; assoc. Fowler, White, Collins, Gillen, Humkey & Trenam, Tampa, Fla., 1966-69; ptnr. Trenam, Simmons, Kemker, Scharf & Barkin, Tampa, 1970-77; mem. firm Trenam, Kemker, Scharf, Barkin, Frye, O'Neill & Mullis (P.A.), Tampa, 1977—, also bd. dirs. Vis. lectr. law Stetson Law Sch., 1970-73; mem. adv. coun. IRS, 2001-03. Exec. editor Harvard Law Rev., 1964-65; contbr. articles to profl. jours. Bd. dirs. Fla. Gulf Coast Symphony, Inc., 1975-86, U. Fla. Found., Inc., 1976-84, 97-2001, 03-, Fla. Orch., 1988-2005, Gator Boosters, Inc., 2002—. Mem. ABA (chmn. tax sect. 1992-93), Am. Law Inst., Am. Coll. Tax Counsel, Fla. Bar (chmn. tax sect. 1975-76), Am. Bar Retirement Assn. (pres. 2000-01, bd. dirs. 1995-04), Phi Beta Kappa. Office: Trenam Kemker Scharf Barkin Frye O'Neill & Mullis 101 E Kennedy Blvd Ste 2700 Tampa FL 33602-5150 Office Phone: 813-227-7437. Business E-Mail: aconeill@trenam.com.

O'NEILL, BEVERLY LEWIS, former mayor, former college president; b. Long Beach, Calif., Sept. 8, 1930; d. Clarence John and Flossie Rachel (Nicholson) Lewis; m. William F. O'Neill, Dec. 21, 1952 AA, Long Beach City Coll., 1950; BA, Calif. State U., Long Beach, 1952, MA, 1956; EdD, U. So. Calif., 1977. Elem. tchr. Long Beach Unified Sch. Dist., 1952-57; instr., counsellor Compton (Calif.) Coll., 1957-60; curriculum supr. Little Lake Sch. Dist., Santa Fe Springs, Calif., 1960-62; women's advisor, campus dean Long Beach City Coll., 1962-71, dir. Continuing Edn. Ctr. for Women, 1969-75, dean student affairs, 1971-77, v.p. student svcs., 1977-88, supt.-pres., 1988—93, exec. dir. LBCC, 1983—; mayor City of Long Beach, Calif., 1994—2006. Mem. New Commn. Skills Am. Workforce; bd. dirs. Internat. City Bank, 2007-. Advisor Jr. League, Long Beach, 1976—, Nat. Coun. on Alcoholism, Long Beach, 1979—, Assistance League, Long Beach, 1982—; bd. dirs. NCCJ, Long Beach, 1976—, Meml. Hosp. Found., Long Beach, 1984-92, Met. YMCA, Long Beach, 1986-92, United Way, Long Beach, 1986-92. Named Woman of Yr., Long Beach Human Rels. Commn., 1976, to Hall of Fame, Long Beach City Coll., 1977, Disting. Alumni of Yr., Calif. State U., Long Beach, 1985, Long Beach Woman of Yr. Rick Rackers, 1987, Assistance League Aux., 1987, Woman of Yr., Calif. Legislature 54th Dist., 1995; recipient Hannah Solomon award Nat. Coun. Jewish Women, 1984, Outstanding Colleague award Long Beach City Coll., 1985, NCCJ Humanitarian award, 1991, Woman of Excellence award YWCA, 1990, Community Svc. award Community Svcs. Devel. Corp., 1991, Citizen of Yr. award Exch. Club, 1992, Pacific Regional CEO award Assn. Community Coll. Trustees, 1992, EDDY award, 1999, Long Beach Excellence in Leadership, 1999. Mem. Assn. Calif. Community Coll. Adminstrs. (pres. 1988-90, Harry Buttimer award 1991), Calif. Community Colls. Chief Exec. Officers Assn., Rotary, Soroptomists (Women Helping Women award 1981, Hall of Fame award 1984), U.S. Conf. Mayors (trustee, 2001-), League Calif. Cities (pres. 2002-). Democrat. *

O'NEILL, BRIAN, science administrator; b. Bristol, Eng., Sept. 20, 1940; s. Raymond and Phyllis Mary (Marshall) O'N.; m. Alayne O'Neill, Aug. 31, 1969 (div. Sept. 1987); children: Allison Sarah, Stuart Douglas, Lesley Alexandra; m. Karen O'Neill, Feb. 20, 1988. BSc in Math. and Stats., Bath. U. Tech., 1965. Cons. in stats. and ops. research Unilever Ltd., London, 1965-66; research assoc. Tech. Ops. Inc., Ft. Belvoir, Va., 1966-67; mgr. applied math. dept. Wolf Research & Devel. Corp., Riverdale, Md., 1967-69; v.p., sr. v.p., exec. v.p. Ins. Inst. for Hwy. Safety, Washington, 1969-85, pres., 1985—; v.p., sr. v.p., exec. v.p. Hwy. Loss Data Inst., Washington, 1969-85, pres., 1985—. Witness at numerous fed. and state hearings on hwy. safety and transp. Contbr. numerous articles to profl. jours.; also presentations at profl. confs. Mem. Am. Pub. Health Internat. Com. on Alcohol Drugs and Traffic Safety, Royal Statis. Soc., Soc. Automotive Engrs. Office: Ins Inst for Hwy Safety 1005 N Glebe Rd Ste 800 Arlington VA 22201-5759 Office Phone: 703-247-1500. Business E-Mail: boneill@iihs.org.

O'NEILL, BRIAN, national recreation area administrator; b. Washington, 1942; s. John and Virgina O'Neill; m. Marti Hendricks; 2 children. Student, U. Md., 1964. Joined Bur. Outdoor Recreation, Dept. Interior, 1965, mgr. Heritage Conservation and Recreation Svc. Albuquerque, 1973—81, San Francisco, 1973—81; asst. supt. Golden Gate Nat. Recreation Area, San Francisco, 1981—86, supt., 1986—; acting assoc. dir. Nat. Pk. Svc. Bd. mem. San Francisco Planning and Urban Rsch. Assn.; instr. Dale Carnegie & Assocs., 1975—77. Recipient Exec. Leadership award, Dept. of the Interior, 2004. Avocations: gardening, glasswork, sailboarding, body surfing, hiking. Office: Golden Gate Nat Rec Area Fort Mason Bldg 201 San Francisco CA 94123

O'NEILL, BRIAN BORU, lawyer; b. Hancock, Mich., June 7, 1947; s. Brian Boru and Jean Anette (Rimpela) O'N.; m. Ruth Bohan, Sept. 18, 1991; children: Dru Groves, Brian Boru, Maggie Byrne, Phelan Boru, Ariel Margaret. BS, U.S. Mil. Acad., 1969; JD magna cum laude, U. Mich., 1974; D in Pub. Svc. (hon.), Northland Coll., 1999. Bar: Mich. 1974, U.S. Dist. Ct. Minn. 1977, U.S. Ct. Mil. Appeals 1975, U.S. Ct. Appeals (6th cir.) 1975, U.S. Ct. Appeals (8th cir.) 1977, U.S. Ct. Appeals (Fed. cir.) 1983, U.S. Ct. Appeals (7th cir.) 1985, U.S. Ct. Appeals (10th cir.) 1986, U.S. Ct. Appeals (9th cir.) 1990, U.S. Ct. Appeals (D.C. cir.) 2005, U.S. Ct. Claims 1981, U.S. Supreme Ct. 1981. Asst. to gen. counsel Dept. Army, Washington, 1974-77; assoc., ptnr. Faegre & Benson, Mpls., 1977—. Mem. com. vis. Mich. Law Sch., 1994—; counsel Defenders of Wildlife, Washington, 1977—, also bd. dirs; counsel Sierra Club, Audubon Soc. Mng. editor: Mich. Law Rev., 1973—74. Advocate Am. Bd. Trial Advocates, 2004—. Capt. US Army, 1969—77. Decorated Meritorious Svc. medal; named Environmentalist of Yr. Sierra Club North Star, 1982, 96, 97, 98; recipient William Douglas award Sierra Club, 1985, Trial Lawyer of Yr. award Trial Lawyers for Pub. Justice, 1995. Fellow Am. Coll. Trial Lawyers (regent 2003—), Internat. Acad. Trial Lawyers, Order of the Coif; mem. Am. Bd. Trial Advs. (adv. 2005—), Mpls. Golf Club, Mpls. Athletic Club (pres.) Office: Faegre & Benson 2200 Wells Fargo Tower 90 S 7th St Ste 2200 Minneapolis MN 55402-3901 Office Phone: 612-766-8318. E-mail: boneill@faegre.com.

O'NEILL, BRIAN DENNIS, lawyer; b. Phila., Feb. 21, 1946; s. Harry William and Margaret Elizabeth (Miller) O'N.; m. Bonnie Anne Ryan, Aug. 17, 1968; children: Aimee Kathleen Fulchino, Catherine Margaret O'Sullivan. BA, Fla. State U., 1968, JD, 1971. Bar: Fla. 1971, D.C. 1975, U.S. Ct. Appeals (D.C. cir.) 1978, U.S. Ct. Appeals (5th and 11th cirs.) 1981, U.S. Ct. Appeals (10th cir.) 1985, U.S. Supreme Ct. 2003. Trial atty. Fed. Power Commn., Washington, 1972-75; assoc. Farmer, Shibley, McGuinn & Flood, Washington, 1975-80; ptnr. LeBoeuf, Lamb, Greene & MacRae LLP, 1980—, mng. ptnr. DC office, 1998—2003, chmn. energy/utilities dept., co-chmn. Natural Gas Practice Group. Lectr. in field. Editorial bd. Energy Law Jour., Washington, 1983-84; contbr. articles to profl. jours. Bd. dirs. Immaculata Coll., Rockville, Md., 1989-91; bd. trustees Acad. of Holy Cross, Kensington, Md., 1994-2005, chmn. 2001-02; bd. visitors Fla. State U. Coll. of Law, 1994-; 2d lt. USAF, 1971-72. Mem.: ABA (chmn. coun., pub. utilities, comm. and transp. law sect.), Energy Bar Assn. (chmn. coms. 1983—84), Fla. Bar, Congl. Country Club (Bethesda, Md. bd. govs. 2002—), Phi Alpha Delta. Democrat. Roman Catholic. Office: LeBoeuf Lamb Greene & MacRae LLP 1101 New York Ave NW Washington DC 20005-4213 Home Phone: 301-365-3554; Office Phone: 202-986-8012. Office Fax: 202-986-8102. Business E-Mail: boneill@llgm.com.

O'NEILL, CHARLES K., lawyer; b. Mineola, NY, June 12, 1947; BA, U. Pa., 1969; JD, Fordham U., 1972. Bar: NY 1973, US Dist. Ct. (So. Dist.) NY 1974, US Dist. Ct. (Ea. Dist.) NY 1974, US Ct. Appeals (2nd Cir.) 1977, US Supreme Ct. 1979, US Ct. Appeals (DC Cir.) 1979, US Ct. Appeals (9th Cir.) 1980. Ptnr. Chadbourne & Parke LLP, NYC, mng. ptnr., mgmt. com., 1998—. Dir. Chadbourne & Parke Found. Lectr. in field; editor: Fordham Law Rev. Bd. dirs. CAMBA Legal Svcs., NYC; trustee NY Meth. Hosp., NYC. Mem.: Assn. Bar City NY, Fed. Bar Coun., NY State Bar Assn., ABA. Office: Chadbourne & Parke LLP 30 Rockefeller Plz Fl 31 New York NY 10112-0129 Office Phone: 212-408-5365. Office Fax: 212-541-5369. Business E-Mail: co'neill@chadbourne.com.

O'NEILL, CHARLES KELLY, marketing professional, retired advertising executive; b. Springfield, Mo., Apr. 2, 1933; s. Charles Chester and Frances (Kelly) O'N.; m. Kyoko Hirano, June 2, 1981. B.J., U. Mo., 1955. With Galvin-Farris-Alvine, Kansas City, Mo., 1957-58, copy chief, 1958; with Potts-Woodbury, Inc., Kansas City, 1958-61, chief time buyer, 1960-61; with Gardner Advt. Co., St. Louis, 1962-88, assoc. media dir., 1964-65, media dir., 1965-69, v.p., 1966-76, corp. media dir., dir. co., 1969-88, sr. v.p., 1976-78, pres., 1978-88; gen. mgr. Advanswers div., 1971-72; pres. Advanswers Media/Programming, Inc., 1973-78, chmn., 1978-88; v.p. Wells, Rich, Greene, NYC, 1974-88, exec. v.p., 1979-88, dir., 1978-88; vice chmn. WRG-USA, 1981-88; chmn. O'Neill Mktg., Honolulu, 1988—; exec. v.p. Kyoko O'Neill, Inc., 1993—; dir. Colony Surf Ltd., Honolulu, 1990-94, chmn., bd. dirs., 1994. Bd. dirs. Waialae Iki Ridge Cmty. Assn., Honolulu, 1991—, 1st v.p., 1993-94. Lt. (j.g.) USN, 1955-57. Mem. St. Louis Advt. Club (gov. 1981-83), Outrigger Canoe Club (Honolulu), N.Y. Athletic Club, St. Louis Club, St. Louis Racquet Club, The Bridge (Navy League of the U.S.-Honolulu), Labrador Retriever Club of Hawaii, Sigma Chi, Alpha Delta Sigma. Episcopalian. Home: 1594 Hoaaina St Honolulu HI 96821-1345

O'NEILL, HARRIET, state supreme court justice; married, 2 children. BA, Converse Coll.; studied, U. Coll., Oxford, England; JD, U. S.C., 1982; PhD (hon.), Converse Coll., 2001. Practice law, Houston; atty. Porter & Clements, Morris & Campbell; pvt. practice, 1982-92; judge 152d Dist. Ct., Houston, 1992—95; justice 14th Ct. Appeals, Houston, 1995—98, Tex. Supreme Ct., Austin, 1998—. Lectr. continuing edn. courses; adv. bd. CLE Inst., 1996; panelist Tex. Ctr. Advanced Jud. Studies., Austin, 1993. Contbr. articles to profl. publs. Mem. U. S.C. academic honors soc.; founder Jud. Outreach for Literacy Training. Named Appellate Justice of Yr., Tex. Assn. of Civil Trial & Appellate Specialists, 2002, 2006. Mem.: Harris County Bar Assn., ABA. Office: Supreme Ct PO Box 12248 Austin TX 78711-2248 *

O'NEILL, HARRY WILLIAM, retired research market and opinion company executive; b. Atlantic City, Jan. 30, 1929; s. Harry William and Marian Elizabeth (Kuhl) O'N.; m. Carmel Gullo, Sept. 21, 1952; children: Sharon Ruth, Randal Bruce. BA, Colgate U., 1950; MS, Pa. State U., 1951. Lic. practicing psychologist, N.J. Research analyst Prudential Ins. Co., Newark, 1957-62; with Opinion Research Corp., Princeton, NJ, 1962-87, sr. v.p., 1970-73, exec. v.p., 1973-80, pres., 1980-85, vice chmn., 1985-87, NOP World, Princeton, NJ, 1988—2005. Mem. co-adj. faculty Rutgers U., 1959-64; vis. lectr. Woodrow Wilson Sch., Princeton U., 1980-82; mem. part-time faculty Rutgers U., 1999—2005. Editor Marketing Research: A Magazine of Management & Applications, 1988-93. Pres. Nat. Coun. Pub. Polls, 1984-94, trustee, 1994—; bd. dirs. Roper Ctr. for Pub. Opinion Rsch., 1984—, chmn., 1994—2004; bd. dirs. Coun. Am. Survey Rsch. Orgns., 1981-83, chmn., 1982-83; vice chmn. Rsch. Industry Coalition, 1993-94, chmn., 1994-95; bd. dirs. Market Rsch. Inst. Internat., 1999—2005; mem. Highland Park (N.J.) Human Rights Commn., 1973-77; bd. dirs. Del-Raritan Lung Assn., 1974-88, v.p., 1977-82, chmn., 1982-84; fin. chmn. Highland Park Rep. Orgn., 1977-89. With USAF, 1951-54. Recipient Maroon citation, Colgate U., 1975, induction into Market Rsch. Coun. Hall of Fame, 1997, Lifetime Achievement award, Coun. Am. Survey Rsch. Orgns., 2001. Mem. Am. Psychol. Assn., Ea. Psychol. Assn., Am. Assn. Pub. Opinion Rsch. (Exceptionally Disting. Achievement 2007, Outstanding Achievement award NY chpt. 1997, Exceptionally Disting. Nat. Achievement award, 2007), Assn. Consumer Rsch., Am. Mktg. Assn., Market Rsch. Coun., Highland Park Rep. Club, Masons, Elks. Presbyterian. Personal E-mail: honeill536@aol.com.

O'NEILL, JAMES ANTHONY, JR., pediatric surgeon, educator; b. NYC, Dec. 7, 1933; m. Susan Pokorny; childen: James Anthony III, Elizabeth, Kathryn S. BS, Georgetown U., 1955; MD, Yale U., 1959. Diplomate Am. Bd. Surgery (bd. dirs. 1981-87, sr. 1988—), Am. Bd. Thoracic Surgery; lic. surgeon, Ohio, La., Tenn., Pa.; cert. instr. advanced trauma life support. Intern Vanderbilt U. Hosp., 1959-60, asst. resident, 1960-64, resident, instr. surgery, 1964-65; chief burn study divsn. U.S.A. Surgl Rsch. Unit Brooke Army Med. Ctr., 1965-67; resident, USPHS fellow in pediatric oncology Columbus Children's Hosp., 1967-69; instr. pediatric surgery Coll. Medicine Ohio State U., 1967-69; asst. prof. surgery and pediatrics, chief pediatric surg. svc. Sch. Medicine La. State U., 1969-70, assoc. prof. surgery, chief sect. pediatric surgery, 1970-71; prof. surgery, chmn. dept. pediatric surgery Sch. Medicine Vanderbilt U., 1971-81, chief med. staff Med. Ctr., 1976-77; prof. pediatric surgery Sch. Medicine U. Pa., Phila., 1981-95, C.E. Koop prof. pediatric surgery, 1988-95; surgeon-in-chief Children's Hosp. Phila., 1981-95; chmn. of surgery, J.C. Foshee Disting. prof. surgery Vanderbilt U. Med. Ctr., Nashville, 1995—. Site visitor residency rev. com. for surgery AMA; mem. trauma care subcom. med. adv. com. Phila. Emergency Med. Svcs. Coun.; surg. cons. U.S. Army Inst. Surg. Rsch., Ft. Sam Houston, Tex. Mem.

editorial bd. Jour. Burn Care and Rehab., Jour. Enteral and Parenteral Nutrition, Jour. Surg. Rsch., Pediatrics, 1984—, Pediatric Emergency Care, 1984—, Pediatric Surgery, Pediatric Surgery Internat., 1988; mem. assoc. editorial bd. Jour. Pediatric Surgery; sect. editor Jour. Trauma, 1983—, Jour Vascular Surgery, 1992; contbr. 350 articles to med. jours. Mem. med. adv. bd. Hope Found.; mem. adv. bd. James Whitcomb Riley Rsch. Found., 1986-89; mem. standards com. State Pa. Found. for Trauma Care. Fellow Am. Acad. Pediatrics (surg., pediatric trauma care coord. Pa. chpt., sect. on oncology-hematology chmn. surg. sect. program com. 1975-77, adv. com. postgrad. edn. 1979-81, exec. com. surg. sect. 1977-80, chmn. 1980-81); mem. ACS (founding, cancer liason physician, Met. Phila. chpt., exec. com. trauma com. 1975-77, adv. coun. pediatric surgery 1977-83, 86-88, 90—, postgrad. edn. com. 1979-82, continuing edn. com. 1981-88, nominating com. 1986, regental ad hoc com. on legis issues in trauma in emergency med. svcs. 1987—, bd. govs. 1990—, com. to study fiscal affairs coll. 1992-93, subcom. on burns, spl. soc. gov. from. AM. Pediatric Surg. Assn. 1992—, coun. on acad. surgery 1993—, v.p. Phila chpt. 1993-94), Am. Assn. for Surgery Trauma, Am. Trauma Soc. (bd. dirs. 1974-78), Am. Burn Assn., Am. Pediatric Surg. Assn. (sec. 1976-79, chmn. edn. com. 1984-87, pres.-elect 1987-88, pres. 1988-89, manpower, trauma and issues and ethics coms.), Am. Surg. Assn. (1st v.p. 1997-98), Assn. for Acad. Surgery (membership com. 1973-74), Soc. for Surgery Alimentary Tract, Soc. Univ. Surgeons (edn. com. 1974-75), Assn. Program Dirs. in Surgery (steering com. 1990-94), Internat. Soc. for Burn Injuries, Internat. Soc. Parenatal Nutrition, Brit. Assn. Pediatric Surgeons, S.E. Surg. Congress (program com. 1979-82, 1st v.p. 1998-99, pres. 1999-2000), So. Gut Club, So. Soc. for Pediatric Rsch., So. Surg. Assn., Tenn. Med. Assn. (del. 1976, 77), Tenn. Pediatric Soc., New Orleans Surg. Soc., Phila. Acad. Surgery, Phila Pediatric Soc., Coll. Physicians Phila. (coun. 1988-91), Portland Surg. Soc. (hon.), Nashville Surg. Soc., Davidson County Med. Assn., James D. Rives Surg. Soc., Halsted Soc. (bd. govs. 1986-89), Alpha Omega Alpha. Office: Vanderbilt Univ Med Ctr Dept Surgery 1001 Oxford House Nashville TN 37232-0001 Office Phone: 615-936-1290. Business E-Mail: james.oneill@vanderbilt.edu.

O'NEILL, JAMES H., psychotherapist, educator; s. Eugene J. and Celeste R. O'Neill; m. Vera M. Woods, Dec. 10, 1977; 1 child, Lisa M. STB, Gregorian U., Rome, 1968; MDiv, Notre Dame U., New Orleans, 1970; EdD, New Orleans Bapt. Theol., 1982. Lic. La. Lic. Profl. Counselors Bd., 1983. Dir. Pastoral Counseling Ctr., New Orleans, 1981—92; pvt. practice profl. counselor Metairie, La., 1983—. Adj. prof. Loyola U. Inst. for Ministry, New Orleans, 1991—. Retreat facilitator, elder Men's Soul Work New Orleans Men's Ctr. Recipient Disting. Svc. ward, La. Assn. for Marriage and Family Therapy, 1992. Fellow: Am. Assn. Pastoral Counselors. Achievements include development of models of marriage and family. Avocations: golf, gardening, poetry, tennis, photography. Office: 3330 W Esplanade Ave S Ste 512 Metairie LA 70002 Office Phone: 504-835-4340.

O'NEILL, JAMES PAUL, psychiatrist; b. Elizabeth, NJ, Sept. 3, 1958; s. Paul James and Dorothy (Semansky) O'Neill; m. Patricia Anne Scott, Aug. 1989. BS in Biology, Niagara U., 1980; MD, U. N.E., Mex., 1984, U. Medicine & Dentistry NJ, 1985. Diplomate Am. Bd. Psychiatry and Neurology (added qualifications in addiction). Intern Jersey Shore Med. Ctr., Neptune, NJ, 1985-86; resident in psychiatry U. Medicine & Dentistry, Robert Wood Johnson Med. Sch., Piscataway, NJ, 1986-89, chief resident in psychiatry, 1988-89; pvt. practice Avon By The Sea, NJ, 1989—2003, Wall, NJ, 2003—. Attending psychiatrist Monmouth Med. Ctr., Long Branch, NJ; clin. asst. prof. psychiatry U. Medicine & Dentistry N.J., Robert Wood Johnson Med. Sch., Med. Coll. Pa., Drexel U. Coll. Medicine; profl. supporter Nat. Assn. Mental Illness. Contbr. articles to profl. jours. Mem. com. Gov.'s coun. Addictions Managed Care Round Table, 1992—93; adv. bd. Cath. Charities, Monmouth County, NJ; mem. Rep. Nat. Com. Named one of Am. Top Psychiatrists, Consumers Rsch. Coun. Am., 2003, 2004; NIMH fellow, 1988. Fellow: Am. Psychiatrist Assn. (disting. fellow); mem.: AMA (N.J. del. to resident physician sect. 1987—89, Physician Recognition award 1991, 1994, 1997, 2000, 2003, 2006), Monmouth County Med. Soc., Am. Coll. Psychiatry, Med. Soc. N.J. (del. Monmouth County 1990—), U.S. Life Saving Assn. (lifeguard), Am. Soc. Addiction Medicine (cert.), Am. Acad. Addiction Psychiatry (past N.J. chmn.), Monmouth Ocean County Psychiat. Assn. (pres.-elect 1998—99, pres. 1999—2000), N.J. Psychiat. Assn. (founding pres. resident physician sect. 1987—88, treas. 2000—01, sr. v.p. 2001—02, pres.-elect 2002, pres. 2003—04, chmn. addictive disorders treatment com., counselor, officer governing coun., chmn. strategic orgnl. long term planning com., personel commn.), US Golf Assn., Manasquan River Golf Club. Avocations: sports, travel. Office: 1540 Rt 138 Suite 307 Wall NJ 07719 Office Phone: 732-280-7555.

O'NEILL, JOAN, editor; Internat. bus. editor New York Times. Office: New York Times 229 W 43d St New York NY 10036 Office Phone: 212-556-5994. Office Fax: 212-556-1448.

O'NEILL, JOHN H., JR., lawyer; b. Bainbridge, Md., Oct. 20, 1946; s. John Hardin and Lois May (Schnepfe) O'N.; m. Vivian Lidwina Gemelli, Nov. 29, 1969; children: Eric Michael, David Christopher, Sean Timothy, Daniel Ryan. BS with distinction in Naval Engring., U.S. Naval Acad., 1968, grad. in Nuclear Power, 1969; JD, Yale U., 1976. Bar: Md. 1976, D.C. 1977, U.S. Supreme Ct., U.S. Dist. Ct. D.C.; lic. to supervise operation, maintenance naval nuclear propulsion power plants AEC. Commd. ensign USN, 1968; advanced through grades to lt. comdr., 1975; officer on nuclear submarines USN, 1968-73; resigned, 1973; ptnr., chmn. nuclear energy practice group Shaw Pittman LLP, Washington, 1976—2005; ptnr., leader regulatory dept., mng. bd. Pillsbury Winthrop Shaw Pittman LLP, Washington, 2005—. Counsel various nuclear industry cos.; cons. in field to fgn. govs. Trustee U.S. Naval Academy Found. Mem. ABA, Internat. Bar Assn., Internat. Nuclear Law Assn. Republican. Roman Catholic. Avocations: squash, tennis, skiing. Office: Pillsbury Winthrop Shaw Pittman 2300 N St NW Washington DC 20037-1128 Office Phone: 202-663-8148. Office Fax: 202-663-8007. Business E-Mail: john.o'neill@pillsburylaw.com.

O'NEILL, JOHN JOSEPH, JR., retired chemicals executive; b. NYC, Sept. 13, 1919; s. John Joseph and Margaret (Patterson) O'N.; m. Irene Ray, Apr. 18, 1940; children— Anne, Mary (Mrs. George Schuler). BS in Chem. Engring, Mo. Sch. Mines, 1940, Chem. Engr., 1951. Research engr. Western Cartridge Co., 1940-49; with Olin Industries, Inc., 1949-60, dir. prodn. explosives operations, energy div., 1959-60; with Olin Mathieson Chem. Corp., 1960-71, asst. to pres., 1963-64, staff v.p. planning, 1964-65, v.p. comml. devel., chems. group, 1965-67, corporate v.p. plastics, 1967-70, corporate v.p. product diverification, 1970-71; cons., 1971-72; exec. v.p., chief operating officer Kleer-Vu Inc., NYC, 1972-76; v.p. planning and devel. Vertac Consol., 1976-77; pres., chief exec. officer Vertac, Inc., 1977-78, cons., 1979-80, vice chmn. bd., chief oper. officer, 1980-81; cons., 1981—; pres. Jonco, Inc., 1986-89. Mem. bd. advisors Am. Express Sr. Card, 2001-2003. Contbr. articles to profl. jours.; patentee explosives, chemicals, ordnance items. Emeritus trustee St. Mary-of-Woods Coll., Terre Haute, Ind. Fellow Am. Inst. Chemists; mem. Am. Inst. Chem. Engring., Chemists Club (N.Y.C.). Clubs: Chemists (N.Y.C.). Home and Office: 7 Castlewood Ln PO Box 429 Pinehurst NC 28370-0429

O'NEILL, JUDITH D., lawyer; b. NYC, Dec. 9, 1945; BA in Romance Lang., Am. Univ. and Univ. Madrid, 1966; MA magna cum laude, Am. Univ., 1972; JD summa cum laude, Univ. Balt., 1975. Bar: Md. 1975, DC 1979, NY 2001, US Supreme Ct. 1976. Shareholder tech. media, telecom. Greenberg Traurig LLP, NYC. Founder, dir. Pan Am. Tech. Policy Forum. Contbr. articles to profl. journals. Mem.: ABA, Fed. Comm. Bar Assn., InterAm. Bar Assn. Office: Greenberg Traurig LLP MetLife Bldg 200 Park Ave New York NY 10166-1400 Office Phone: 212-801-9387. Office Fax: 212-801-6400. Business E-Mail: oneillj@gtlaw.com.

O'NEILL, JUNE ELLENOFF, economist; b. NYC, June 14, 1934; d. Louis and Matilda (Liebstein) Ellenoff; m. Sam Cohn, 1955 (div. 1961); 1 child, Peter; m. David Michael O'Neill, Dec. 24, 1964; 1 child, Amy. BA, Sarah Lawrence Coll., Bronxville, NY, 1955; PhD, Columbia U., 1970. Econs. instr. Temple U., Phila., 1965-68; rsch. assoc. Brookings Instn., Washington, 1968-71; sr. economist Pres.'s Coun. Econ. Advisors, Washington, 1971-76; chief human resources budget Congl. Budget Office, Washington, 1976-79; sr. rsch. assoc. The Urban Inst., Washington, 1979-86; dir. Office Policy and Rsch. U.S. Commn. Civil Rights, Washington, 1986-87; prof. econs. and fin., dir. Ctr. for Study Bus. and Govt. Baruch Coll., CUNY, 1987—; Morton Wollman Prof. Econs. Zicklin Sch. Bus. Baruch Coll., 1999—; dir. Congl. Budget Office U.S. Congress, Washington, 1995-99. Adj. scholar Am. Enterprise Inst., 1994-95, 99—; mem. Nat. Adv. Com., The Poverty Inst., U. Wis., 1988-95; chair bd. sci. counselors Nat. Ctr. for Health Stats., 2003—; mem. Nat. Bur. Econ. Rsch., 2004—. Contbr. articles to profl. jours. Mem. Am. Econs. Assn. (v.p. 1998-99), Nat. Acad. Social Ins. Republican. Jewish. Home: 420 Riverside Dr New York NY 10025-7773 Office: CUNY Baruch Coll Ctr Study of Bus and Govt 17 Lexington Ave New York NY 10010-5518 Home Phone: 212-662-1784; Office Phone: 646-312-3540. E-mail: june_oneill@baruch.cuny.edu.

O'NEILL, LAWRENCE JOSEPH, federal judge; b. Oakland, Calif., 1952; BA, U. Calif. Berkeley, 1973; MPA, Golden Gate U., 1976; JD, U. Calif. Hastings Coll. Law, 1979. Bar: Calif. 1979. Police officer, San Leandro, Calif., 1973—76; law clk. Alameda County Dist. Atty.'s Office, 1976—78, Hon. Robert Francis Kane, Calif Ct. Appeal, 1st dist., 1978—79; assoc. McCormick, Barstow, Sheppard, Wayte & Caruth, Fresno, 1979—84, ptnr., 1984—90; judge Superior Ct. (Fresno County) Calif., 1990—98, presiding judge juvenile divsn., 1992—93, presiding judge, 1996—98; magistrate judge US Dist. Ct. (Ea. dist.) Calif., 1999—2007, dist. judge, 2007—. Adj. prof. San Joaquin Coll. Law, 1986—92. Mem. adv. bd. Fresno County Sch. Dist., 1983—; life mem. Calif. Scholarship Fedn., 1970; mem. adv. bd. United Way, 1992—; exec. mem. Fresno County Suspected Child Abuse & Neglect Com., 1992—93; mem. adv. bd. YWCA, 1993—, Drug Abuse Resistance Edn. Program (D.A.R.E.), 1993—, pres., 1993—. Recipient Outstanding Young Men in Am. award, Nat. Jr. C. of C., 1979, Prof. of Yr. award, San Joaquin Coll. Law, 1992, Ann. Mentor's award, Fresno County Bar Assn. Young Lawyers, 1992, Judy Andreen-Nilson award, 1993, Achievement in Juvenile Justice award, Fresno County Juvenile Justice Commn., 1993. Mem.: Assn. Bd. Trial Advocates, State Bar Calif., Calif. Judges' Assn. (state chmn. Com. Pub. Info & Edn. 1993—94, Com. Benchguide Pub. Rev. 1993—, Bench Bar Media 1992—93). Office: US Dist Ct Ea Calif 2500 Tulane St Fresno CA 93721 Office Phone: 559-499-5682. Office Fax: 559-494-3961. *

O'NEILL, MALCOLM R., aerospace executive; b. Chgo. m. Judy O'Neill. BS in Physics, DePaul U., 1962; MA in Physics, Rice U., 1970, PhD in Physics, 1975. Commd. US Army, advanced through grades 2nd lt. to lt. gen., 1993, ret., 1996, dir. Ballistic Missile Def. Orgn., dep. dir. Strategic Def. Initiative Orgn., dir. Army Acquisition Corps, comdr. Army Lab. Command; dep. for program assessment and internat. coop. Office of the Asst. Sec. of the Army; project mgr. multiple launched rocket system US Army, dep. project mgr. NATO patriot systems; program mgr. strategic fire control systems Def. Advanced Rsch. Projects Agy.; v.p. mission success, ops. and best practices in space systems Lockheed Martin, Bethesda, Md., 1996—99, v.p., chief tech. officer, 1999—. Mem. Aero. and Space Engring. Bd., NAS, Bd. Army Sci. and Tech., Air Force Sci. Adv. Bd., Space Dept. Adv. Bd. Named US Army Ordinance Hall of Fame. Fellow: AIAA (hon.); mem.: NAE, BOD Sandia Corp. Office: Lockheed Martin Corp 6801 Rockledge Dr Bethesda MD 20817 *

O'NEILL, MARK E., military officer; b. St. Louis; married; 2 children. BS, US Mil. Acad., 1978; MA, Naval Postgrad. Sch.; grad., Def. Lang. Inst., Armed Forces Staff Coll., US Army War Coll. Commd. inf. officer US Army, 1978, advanced through grades to brig. gen.; asst. Army attaché Am. Embassy, Beijing; served in Operation Uphold Democracy, Haiti, Operation Enduring Freedom, Afghanistan, Operation Iraqi Freedom, Baghdad; dep. divsn. comdr. Multinational Divsn., Baghdad; dep. dir. US Army Dept. Strategy, Plans & Policy; dep. comdt. US Army Command & Gen. Staff Coll., Ft. Leavenworth, Kans.; acting comdt. Combined Arms Ctr., Ft. Leavenworth, Kans. Mem. Coun. Fgn. Rels. Decorated Legion of Merit with four oak leaf clusters, Bronze Star medal, Def. Meritorious Svc. medal, Meritorious Svc. medal with four oak leaf clusters, Army Commendation medal with oak leaf cluster, Army Achievement medal, Iraq Campaign medal, War on Terrorism Svc. medal, Nat. Def. Svc. medal with star, Armed Forces Expeditionary medal, Humanitarian Svc. medal, Army Svc. ribbon, Four Overseas Svc. ribbons. Office: US Army Command & Gen Staff Coll 100 Stimson Ave Fort Leavenworth KS 66027

O'NEILL, MARY JANE, not-for-profit administrator, consultant; b. Detroit, Feb. 24, 1923; d. Frank Roger and Kathryn (Rice) Kilcoyne; m. Michael James O'Neill, May 31, 1948; children: Michael, Maureen, Kevin, John(dec.), Kathryn. PhB summa cum laude, U. Detroit, 1944; postgrad., U. Wis., Madison, 1949—50. Editor East Side Shopper, Detroit, 1939—45; club editor Detroit Free Press, 1945—48; reporter UP, Milw. and Madison, 1949; dir. pub. rels. Fairfax-Falls Church Cmty. Chest, Va., 1955—60; copy editor Falls Church Sun-Echo, 1958—60; freelance writer Washington, 1960—63; assoc. editor Med. World News, Washington, 1963—66; dir. publ. rels. Westchester Lighthouse N.Y. Assn. for Blind, 1967—71; dir. pub. edn. The Lighthouse, NYC, 1971—73, dir. pub. rels., 1973—80; exec. dir., CEO Eye-Bank for Sight Restoration, Inc., 1980—2000; ret., 2000. Mem. N.Y. State Transplant Coun., 1991—2002; mem. instl. rsch. rev. bd. Manhattan Eye, Ear and Throat Hosp., 1981—; bd. dirs. N.Y. Organ Donor Network, 1997—2003, Pro Mujer, 1997—2003, mem. adv. coun., 2004—. Named to Top 100 Irish Ams., Irish Am. Mag., 1999. Mem.: Pan Am. Eye Bank Assn. (bd. dir.), Women Execs. in Pub. Rels. (dir. 1982—88, pres. 1986—87, found. bd. dir. 2002—, treas. 2004—), Eye Bank Assn. Am. (lay adv. bd. 1981—83, dir. 1983—86, pres. N.E. Region 1993—96, exec. com. 1994—96, EBAA Heise award 1997), Women in Comm. (pres. NY chpt. 1980—81), Cosmopolitan Club. E-mail: maryjaneoneill@aol.com.

O'NEILL, MATTHEW, film producer; Grad., Yale U. With Downtown Cmty. TV, NYC, 1997—, prodr. & dir., 2001—. Prodr.: (TV episodes) Wide Angle, 2002—06; prodr., dir., cinematographer (documentaries) Speak Up New York!, 2002, Venezuala: Revolution in Progress, 2005, Baghdad ER, 2006 (3 Emmy awards, including Outstanding Cinematography, Outstanding Direction, and Exceptional Merit in Nonfiction Filmmaking, 2006, Alfred I. duPont-Columbia U. award, 2007). Recipient Sigma Delta Chi award for Pub. Svc. TV Journalism, Soc. Profl. Journalists, 2003, Carl Spielvogel award, Overseas Press Club Am., 2007. Office: DCTV 87 Lafayette St New York NY 10013 Office Phone: 212-966-4510 ext. 236. Office Fax: 212-226-3053. E-mail: info@dctvny.org. *

O'NEILL, MICHAEL JAMES, editor, author; b. Detroit, Nov. 19, 1922; s. Michael J. and Ellen Mary (Dacey) O'Neill; m. Mary Jane Kilcoyne, May 31, 1948; children: Michael, Maureen, Kevin, Kathryn. BA, U. Detroit, 1946, LHD (hon.), 1977; postgrad., Fordham U., 1946—47. Writer Standard News Assn., NYC, 1946—47; with UPI, 1947—56; Washington corr. N.Y. Daily News, 1956—66, asst. mng. editor, 1966—68, mng. editor, 1968—74, v.p., 1971—79, exec. editor, 1974—75, editor, 1975—82, exec. v.p., 1979—82, dir. Freelance writer; lectr., 1983—. Author (with L. Tanzer): The Kennedy Circle, 1961; author: (with K.M. Cahill) Preventive Diplomacy, 1996; author: China Today, 1976, Terrorist Spectaculars: Should TV Coverage Be Curbed, 1986, The Roar of the Crowd, How TV and People Power are Changing the World, 1993. Mem. Nat. Adv. Coun. Health Professions Edn., 1967—71; chmn. Fund of City of N.Y., 2003—06. With US Army, 1943—45, ETO. Decorated Bronze Star; recipient Nat. Affairs Reporting award, Nat. Headliner's, 1956. Mem.: Coun. Fgn. Rels., Am. Soc. Newspaper Editors (pres. 1981—82), Overseas Writers (pres. 1965), Century Club (N.Y.C. chpt.). Address: 23 Cayuga Rd Scarsdale NY 10583-6941

O'NEILL, MOLLY ANN, federal agency administrator; d. Vincent and Pam O'Neill. BS in Biology, Va. Tech. Environ. biologist; environ. cons. to exec. mgmt. of state environ. depts.; with Environ. Coun. of the States, 2002—06, exec. coord. for exchange network leadership coun.; asst. adminstr. for environ. info. EPA, 2007—. *

O'NEILL, PATRICIA TYDINGS, performing arts educator, language educator; b. Prince Frederick, Md., Dec. 16, 1953; d. James Martin and Mary Evelyn O'Neill, Edward Joseph Pineault (Stepfather); children: Lauren Ann Veneziani, Scott Martin Veneziani. M in English, Pa. State U., State College, 1976; M in Edn., Shenandoah U., Winchester, Va., 2004. Cert. Nat. Bd. Profl. Tchg. Stds., 2005. Theatre/English tchr. No. H.S., Owings, Md., 1976—. Theatre dir. No. High. Dir. Parks and Recreation Summer Theatre for Children, Owings, 1999—2005. Named Outstanding Theatre Educator, Md. HS Theatre Assn., 2007; recipient Tchr. of Yr., No. H.S., 1996, Shakespeare Tchr. of Yr., English Speaking Union Wash. DC Area Br., 2004, Outstanding Sch. in Theatre, Md. HS Theatre Assn., 1996, 2000, 2006. Mem.: NEA/CEA (assoc.), Delta Kappa Gamma (life). Avocations: travel, directing plays. Office: Northern HS 2950 Chaneyville Rd Owings MD 20736 Office Phone: 410-257-1519. Office Fax: 410-257-1530.

O'NEILL, PAUL HENRY, former secretary of the treasury; b. St. Louis, Dec. 4, 1935; s. John Paul and Gaynald Elsie (Irvin) O'N.; m. Nancy Jo Wolfe, Sept. 4, 1955; children: Patricia, Margaret, Julie, Paul Henry. BA, Fresno State Coll., 1960; Haynes Found. fellow, Claremont Grad. Sch., 1960-61; postgrad., George Washington U., 1962-65; MPA, Ind. U., 1966; DSc (hon.), Clarkson U., 1993, Georgetown U., 2005; D Pub. Svc. (hon.), Edinboro U., 1997, California U. Pa., 1998; D Bus. Leadership (hon.), Duquesne U., 1999; LHD (hon.), Calif. State U., 1999; D Pub. Svc. (hon.), U. Pitts., 2003; D Pub. Policy (hon.), Carnegie-Mellon U., 2003; PhD in Pub. Policy (hon.), Pardee RAND, 2004. Site engr. Morrison-Knudsen, Inc., Anchorage, 1955-57; systems analyst VA, Washington, 1961-66; budget examiner Bur. of Budget, Washington, 1967-69; chief human resources program divsn. Office Mgmt. & Budget, Exec. Office of the Pres., Washington, 1969-70, asst. dir., 1971-72, assoc. dir., 1973-74, dep. dir., 1974-77; v.p. Internat. Paper Co., NYC, 1977-81, sr. v.p., 1981-85, pres., dir., 1985-87; CEO Alcoa Inc., Pitts., 1987-99, chmn., 1987-2000; founding co-chair Pittsburgh Regional Healthcare Initiative, 1997—2005; sec. US Dept. Treasury, Washington, 2001—02; sr. advisor The Blackstone Group, L.P., NYC, 2003—. Chmn. Pres.'s Edn. Policy Adv. Com., 1989—92; bd. dirs. Eastman Kodak, 2003—06, Ctr. for Global Devel., 2004—, Celanese Corp., 2004—, Nalco Co., Qcept, TRW Automotive Holdings, RAND, 2003—, mem. bd. of health, 2003—, bd. adv., 2003—, former chmn.; sr. advisor Blackstone Group, 2003—; mem. nat. bd. visitors Calif. State U., Fresno; mem. Nat. Quality Forum, 2003—. Trustee Coun. for Excellence in Govt., 2003—; bd. visitors Heinz Sch., 2004—; active Riverlife Task Force, Pitts., 2003—; bd. dirs. Gerald R. Ford Found., 1981—, chmn. fin. com. Recipient Nat. Inst. Pub. Affairs Career Edn. award, 1965, William A. Jump Meritorious award, 1971, Health Quality award, Nat. Com. Quality Assurance, 2003; Fellow Nat. Inst. Pub. Affairs, 1966. Fellow Nat. Acad. Pub. Adminstrn.; mem. Am. Acad. Arts and Sci., Nat. Acad. Social Ins. (founding mem., hon. advisor), Peterson Inst. (bd. dirs. 2003—). Republican. Methodist. Office: Ste 100 One North Shore Ctr Pittsburgh PA 15212 Home Phone: 412-683-6867; Office Phone: 412-553-1238. Personal E-mail: jceledoniapa@aol.com.

O'NEILL, PHILIP DANIEL, JR., lawyer, educator; b. Boston, Sept. 19, 1951; s. Philip Daniel Sr. and Alice Maureen (Driscoll) O'N.; m. Lisa G. Arrowood, June 25, 1983; children: Alexander Edwin, Sean Matthew, Madeleine Clarice. BA, Hamilton Coll., 1973; JD cum laude, Boston Coll., 1977. Bar: Mass. 1977, N.Y. 1985, R.I. 1988. Assoc. Hale and Dorr, Boston, 1977—83, ptnr., 1983—87, Edwards Angell Palmer & Dodge LLP, Boston, 1987—. Cons. Arms Control and Disarmament Agy. U.S. Dept. Def., 1983—84; adj. rsch. fellow John F. Kennedy Sch. Govt., Ctr. for Sci. and Internat. Affairs Harvard U., Cambridge, Mass., 1983—86; adj. prof. law Boston U., 1992, 2001—, Boston Coll., 1988—, Fletcher Sch. Law and Diplomacy, Boston, 2007; Nomura lectr. Harvard U. Law Sch., Cambridge, 2005; panelist in internat. and domestic legal programs; lectr. in field; arbitrator in field. Contbr. articles to profl. jours., chapters to books. Fellow Chartered Inst. Arbitrators (Eng.), Am. Bar Found.; mem. ABA (vice-chmn. nat. security and arms control com. 2002-05), Internat. Law Assn. (chmn. Am. br. arbitration com. 1985-89, rep. internat. arbitration com. 1989—), Boston Bar Assn. (chmn. internat. law sect. 1994-96, past chmn. internat. litig. and arbitration com.), Am. Soc. Internat. Law, Nat. Security Network. Home: 11 Blackburnian Rd Lincoln MA 01773-4317 Office: Edwards Angell Palmer & Dodge LLP 111 Huntington Ave Boston MA 02199-7613

O'NEILL, ROBERT CHARLES, inventor, consultant; b. Buffalo, Dec. 3, 1923; s. Albert T. and Helen (Lynch) O'N.; m. Agnes Balischak; 1 dau., Eileen Anne. BS in Chemistry, Rensselaer Poly. Inst., 1945; PhD in Organic Chemistry, MIT, 1950. Sr. chemist Merck & Co., Inc., Rahway, NJ, 1950-56, marketing devel. specialist, 1956-58; v.p. Stauffer Pharms. div. Stauffer Chem. Co., NYC, 1958-61; v.p., dir. R & D Cooper Labs., Inc., 1961-70, exec. v.p., 1970-76, gen. mgr., 1975-76, pres., 1976-77, also dir. Cons. in field. Contbr. articles to profl. jours. Served with USNR, 1943-46. Mem. Am. Chem. Soc., Chemists Club N.Y. Achievements include patents in field. Home: 10 Whitlaw Close Chappaqua NY 10514-1008

O'NEILL, RUSSELL RICHARD, engineering educator; b. Chgo., June 6, 1916; s. Dennis Alysious and Florence Agnes (Mathurin) O'N.; m. Margaret Bock, Dec. 15, 1939; children: Richard A., John R.; m. Sallie Boyd, June 30, 1967. BSME, U. Calif., Berkeley, MSME, 1940; PhD, UCLA, 1956. Registered profl. engr., Calif. Design engr. Dowell, Inc., Midland, Mich., 1940-41; design engr. Dow Chem. Co., Midland, 1941-44, Airesearch Mfg. Co., Los Angeles, 1944-46; lectr. engring. UCLA, 1946-56, prof. engring., 1956, asst. dean engring., 1956-61, assoc. dean, 1961-73, acting dean, 1965-66, dean, 1974-83, dean emeritus, 1983—; staff engr. NAS-NRC, 1954; dir. Data Design Labs., 1977-86, dir. emeritus, 1986—. Mem. engring. task force Space Era Edn. Study Fla. Bd. Control, 1963; mem. regional Export Expansion Coun. Dept. Commerce, 1960-66, Los Angeles Mayor's Space Adv. Com., 1964-69; mem. Maritime Transp. Rsch. Bd., 1974-81; bd. advisers Naval Postgrad. Sch., 1976-84; mem. Nat. Nuclear Accreditation Bd., 1983-88; mem. accrediting bd. Dept. Energy, 1992—. Trustee West Coast U., 1981-90; bd. dirs. Western region United Way, 1982-90. Mem. NAE, Am. Soc. Engring. Edn., Sigma Xi, Tau Beta Pi. Home: 15430 Longbow Dr Sherman Oaks CA 91403-4910 Office: UCLA HSSEAS Box 951600 Los Angeles CA 90095-1600 Business E-Mail: russ@ea.ucla.edu.

O'NEILL, THOMAS J. (TOM O' NEILL), engineering company executive; b. Buffalo, July 22, 1952; AB, Dartmouth Coll., 1973, BE, 1974.

With Parsons Brinckerhoff/Tudor, Atlanta, 1974-77, Tudor Engring. Co., Atlanta, 1978-92; pres., COO, CEO Parsons, Brinckerhoff, Quade, NYC, 1992—. Mem. Chief Executive Group, L.P., Montvale, NJ. Office: Parsons Brinckerhoff 1 Penn Plz Fl 2 New York NY 10119-0021 Office Phone: 212-465-5000. Office Fax: 212-465-5096.

O'NEILL, THOMAS NEWMAN, JR., federal judge; b. Hanover, Pa., July 6, 1928; s. Thomas Newman and Emma (Cornpropst) O'N.; m. Jeanne M. Corr., Feb. 4, 1961; children: Caroline Jeanne, Thomas Newman, III, Ellen Gitt. AB magna cum laude, Catholic U. Am., 1950; LL.B. magna cum laude, U. Pa., 1953; postgrad. (Fulbright grantee), London Sch. Econs., 1955-56. Bar: Pa. 1954, U.S. Supreme Ct. 1959. Law clk. to Judge Herbert F. Goodrich U.S. Ct. Appeals (3d cir.), 1953-54; law clk. to Justice Harold H. Burton U.S. Supreme Ct., 1954-55; assoc. Montgomery, McCracken, Walker & Rhoads, Phila., 1956-63, ptnr., 1963-83; judge U.S. Dist. Ct. (ea. dist.) Pa., 1983—; counsel 1st and 2d Pa. Legis. Reapportionment Commns., 1971, 81. Lectr. U. Pa. Law Sch., 1973 Articles editor: U. Pa. Law Rev, 1952-53. Former trustee Lawyers Com. for Civil Rights Under Law; former mem. Gov.'s Trial Ct. Nominating Commn. for Phila. County; former mem. bd. overseers U. Pa. Mus.; mem. adv. bd. Civil War and Underground R.R. Mus. Phila. Fellow Am. Coll. Trial Lawyers; mem. Am. Law Inst. (life), Phila. Bar Assn. (chancellor 1976), Pa. Bar Assn. (gov. 1978-81), U. Pa. Law Alumni Soc. (pres. 1976-77), Pa. Conf. County Bar Officers (pres. 1981-82), Pa. Soc. of SAR, Am. Inn of Ct. (founding chmn. U. Pa.), Order of Coif (pres. U. Pa. chpt. 1971-73), Merion Cricket Club, Edgemere Club, Broadacres Trouting Assn., Phi Beta Kappa, Phi Eta Sigma. Office: US Dist Ct 4007 US Courthouse 601 Market St Philadelphia PA 19106-1713 Office Phone: 215-597-2750.

O'NEILL, WILLIAM LAWRENCE, retired history professor; b. Big Rapids, Mich., Apr. 18, 1935; s. John Patrick and Helen Elizabeth (Marsh) O'N.; m. Elizabeth Carol Knollmueller, Aug. 20, 1960; children: Cassandra Leigh, Catherine Lorraine. AB, U. Mich., 1957; MA, U. Calif., Berkeley, 1958, PhD, 1963. Asst. prof. history U. Colo., 1964—66; asst. prof. U. Wis., 1966—69, assoc. prof., 1969—71; prof. Rutgers U., New Brunswick, NJ, 1971—2006; ret., 2006. Vis. asst. prof. U. Pitts., 1963-64; vis. asso. prof. U. Pa., 1969-70 Author: Divorce in the Progressive Era, 1967, Everyone Was Brave: The Rise and Fall of Feminism in America, 1969, rev. and repub. as: Feminism in America: A History, 1989, Coming Apart: An Informal History of America in the 1960's, 1971, 2005, The Last Romantic: A Life of Max Eastman, 1978, 2d edit., 1991, A Better World: The Great Schism: Stalinism and the American Intellectuals, 1982, repub. as: A Better World: Stalinism and the American Intellectuals, 1989, American High: The Years of Confidence, 1945-60, 1986, A Democracy at War: America's Fight at Home and Abroad in World War II, 1993. Nat. Endowment Humanities fellow, 1979-80 Mem.: Hist. Soc. Office: Rutgers U Dept History New Brunswick NJ 08903 Personal E-mail: wlohp@aol.com.

O'NEILL, WILLIAM PATRICK, lawyer; b. Joplin, Mo., Sept. 14, 1951; s. Fred Charles and Dorothy Isabel (Snyder) O'N.; m. Mary Louise Richardson, June 17, 1989. BA, U. Kans., 1973; JD, U. Mich., 1976. Bar: Ill. 1976, U.S. Dist. Ct. (no. dist.) Ill. 1976, U.S. Dist. Ct. D.C. 1982. Assoc. Kirkland & Ellis, Chgo., 1976-81, Sidley & Austin, Chgo., 1982-85, Skadden, Arps, Slate, Meagher & Flom, NYC, 1986-87, Crowell & Moring, Washington, 1987-88, ptnr., 1988—2000, Latham & Watkins, 2001—. Gen. counsel Ill. Common Cause, Chgo., 1979-81. Editor, author: (with others) Successfully Acquiring A U.S. Business, 1990; editorial chmn. Antitrust Law Jour., 1984-89. Mem. University Club of Chgo. Office: Latham & Watkins 555 11th St NW Washington DC 20004-2595 Business E-Mail: williamoneill@lw.com.

O'NEILL, WILLIAM WALTER, physician, educator; b. Nov. 24, 1951; BS, U. Mich., 1972; MD, Wayne State U., 1977. Diplomate Am. Bd. Internal Medicine, Am. Bd. Cardiology. Intern in internal medicine U. Wis., Madison, 1977-78; resident in internal medicine Wayne State U., Detroit, 1978-80; fellow U. Mich., Ann Arbor, 1980-82, instr. internal medicine, 1982-83, asst. prof., 1983-86, assoc. prof., 1986-87; dir. cardiac catheterization lab. U. Mich. Hosp., Ann Arbor, 1984-87; corp. chief cardiology William Beaumont Hosp., Royal Oak, Troy, Mich., 1987—. Attending cardiologist VA Hosp., Ann Arbor, 1982-90; chmn. govt. rels. subcom. Nat. Cardiovasc. Network; rsch. peer rev. com. Am. Heart Assn. Mich., 1988-89; chmn. publs. com. Mansfield Scientific Balloon Valvuloplasty Registry; bd. govs. William Beaumont Hosp. Rsch. Inst.; presenter in field. Author: Myocardial Revascularization by Coronary Angioplasty or Bypass Surgery During MI in Acute Myocardial Infarction: New Approaches to Evaluation and Therapy, 1986, (chpt.) Acute Coronary Intervention, 1987, Current Perspective in Coronary Care, 1987, Interventional Cardiovascular Medicine, 1994, Acute Coronary Care, 2d edit., 1995; co-author: (chpts.) Cardiovascular Review, 6th edit., 1985, 8th edit., 1987, Tissue Plasminogen Activator in Thrombolytic Therapy, 1987, Techniques and Applications in Interventional Cardiology, 1991, Atherectomy, 1992, Emergency Medicine: A Comprehensive Study Guide, 3d edit., 1992, Adjunctive Therapy for Acute Myocardial Infarction, 1992, Manual of Interventional CArdiology, 1992, Cura Intensiva Cardiologica, Primary Coronary Angioplasty in Acute Myocardial Infarction; author, co-author: (chpt.) Interventional Cardiovascular Medicine, 1994; editl. cons. Jour. Intervention Cardiology; mem. editl. bd. Catheterization Cardiovasc. Diagnosis; contbr. over 400 articles to profl. publs. Grantee Smith/Kline Beecham, 1989-90, 90—, Advanced Cardiovasc. Sys., Inc., 1988-90, 90—, Midwest Heart Rsch. Found., Abbott Labs., 1990—, Duke U., 1990—, William Beaumont Hosp. Rsch. Inst., 1990—. Fellow Am. Coll. Cardiology (chpt. sec.-treas. 1993-94, reimbursement com.), Am. Coll. Chest Physicians, Coun. Clin. Cardiology; mem. AMA, ACP, Internat. Andreas Gruentzig Soc. Office: William Beaumont Hosp 3601 W 13 Mile Rd Royal Oak MI 48073-6712

O'NEILL MORELAND, TAMARA, lawyer; b. 1972; BA in Polit. Sci. summa cum laude, Centenary Coll., Shreveport, La., 1994; JD cum laude, Hamline U. Sch. Law, St. Paul, 1997. Bar: Minn. 1997, US Dist. Ct. (dist. Minn.) 2001, US Ct. Appeals (7th cir.) 2002. Law clk. to Judge John J. Sommerville Hennepin County Dist. Ct., 1997—98; shareholder, mem. real estate litig. dept. Larkin, Hoffman, Daly & Lindgren, Ltd., Mpls., 1998—. Named a Rising Star, Minn. Super Lawyers mag., 2006. Mem.: Minn. State Bar Assn., Minn. Women Lawyers, Minn. Comml. Real Estate Women, Phi Alpha Delta. Office: Larkin Hoffman Daly & Lindgren Ltd 1500 Wells Fargo Plz 7900 Xerxes Ave S Minneapolis MN 55431 Office Phone: 952-896-6711. E-mail: toneill@larkinhoffman.com. *

ONEL, SUZAN, lawyer; b. NYC, Sept. 29, 1964; d. Joseph and Miriam (Spitzer) O.; m. Keith B. Bickel, Sept. 8, 1990. BA with hons., U. Pa., 1986; JD, U. Va., 1990. Bar: Pa. 1990, D.C. 1991. Assoc. Arent, Fox, Kintner, Plotkin & Kahn, Washington, 1990-92, Hyman, Phelps & McNamara, Washington, 1992-94, McKenna & Cuneo, Washington; ptnr. Kirkpatrick & Lockhart Nicholson Graham LLP, Washington. Mem. Food and Drug Law Inst. Notes editor Va. Environ. Law Jour.; contbr. articles to profl. jours. Mem. facilities com. Williamsburg Condominium, 1994—; legal clk./investigator D.C. Pub. Defenders Svcs./Mental Health Divsn., D.C., 1988. Mem. ABA (past co-chmn. tech. assessment com.), Regulatory Affairs Profl. Soc., D.C. Bar Assn. Avocations: travel, photography, aerobics, bicycling, reading. Office: Kirkpatrick & Lockhart Nicholson Graham LLP 2d Fl 1800 Massachusetts Ave Washington DC 20036-1221 Office Phone: 202-778-9134. Office Fax: 202-778-9100. Business E-Mail: sonel@klng.com.

ONES, DENIZ S., psychologist, educator; b. Istanbul, Turkey, Aug. 12, 1965; d. Somer and Ulker (Saime) Ones; m. Ates Haner, July 5, 1993; 1 child, Daria M. Haner. BA, Augustana Coll., 1988; PhD, U. Iowa, 1993. Asst. prof. U. Houston, 1993—96; Hellervik Prof. indsl. psychology U. Minn., Mpls., 1996—; founder Thetametrics LLP, Maple Grove, Minn., 2004—. Author: Handbook of Industrial, Work and Organizational Psychology. Recipient Cattell Award for Outstanding Early Career Contbns., Soc. of Multivariate Exptl. Psychology, 2003, Ernest J. McCormick Award for Disting. Early Career Contbns., Soc. for Indsl. and Orgnl. Psychology, 1998; Fellow of Divsn. 14 (Indsl. and Orgnl. Psychology), APA, 1999, Fellow of Divsn. 5 (Measurement, Stats., and Evaluation), 1998. Achievements include research in meta-analyses of integrity tests, managerial selection, police selection, employment testing. Office: Thetametrics LLP 6427 Ranchview Ln N Maple Grove MN 55311 E-mail: ones@thetametrics.com.

ONESTI, SILVIO JOSEPH, psychiatrist; b. San Francisco, Jan. 3, 1926; s. Silvio Joseph and Johanna (Kristoffy) Onesti; m. Jean Thomas, May 12, 1956; children: Sally Joanna, Stephen Thomas. BS, Stanford U., 1947; MD, McGill U., 1951. Diplomate Am. Bd. Psychiatry and Neurology. Instr. pediatrics Yale Med. Sch., New Haven, 1956-58; career tchr. psychiatry NIMH, Harvard Med. Sch., Beth Israel Hosp., Boston, 1963-65; head child psychiatry unit Beth Israel Hosp., Boston, 1965-73; dir. child and adolescent psychiatry McLean Hosp., Belmont, Mass., 1973-91, dir. Hall-Mercer Ctr. for children and adolescents, 1973-91; dir. child and adolescent psychiat. tng., 1973-92; dir. clin. svcs. McLean Hosp., Belmont, 1981-83; asst. prof. psychiatry Harvard Med. Sch., Boston, 1969—. Contbr. articles to profl. jours. With USN, 1944—46. Fellow: Am. Coll. Psychiatrists, Am. Acad. Child and Adolescent Psychiatry, Am. Psychiat. Assn.; mem.: Mass. Med. Soc., Boston Psychoanalytic Soc. and Inst. (faculty 1971—81), Group Advancement Psychiatry (bd. dirs. 1987—89, fellow 1959—61), Alpha Omega Alpha. Home: 4 Gray Gdns W Cambridge MA 02138-2312 Office: McLean Hosp 115 Mill St Belmont MA 02478-1048 Home Phone: 617-354-3704; Office Phone: 617-855-2801.

ONG, CHEE-MUN, engineering educator; b. Ipoh, Perak, Malaysia, Nov. 23, 1944; came to U.S., 1978; s. Chin-Kok Ong and Say-Choo Yeoh; m. Penelope Li-Lok, July 17, 1971; children: Yi-Ping, Yi-Ching, Chiew-Jen. BE with honors, U. Malaya, 1967; MS, Purdue U., 1968, PhD, 1974. Registered profl. engr. Ind., Eng. Plant engr. Guinness Brewery, Malaysia, 1967; asst. lectr. U. Malaysia, 1968-73, lectr., 1976-78; rsch. asst. Purdue U., West Lafayette, Ind., 1973-74, vis. asst. prof., 1975-76, asst. prof., 1978-81, assoc. prof., 1981-85, prof., 1985—. Cons. SIMTECH, West Lafayette, 1978-85, L.A. Water and Power Co., 1986-88, Caterpillar, 1993-94, Franklin Electric, 1997-98, P Plus Corp., 1999-, PPlus, 1999-, Unibus, 2002. Author: Dynamic Simulation of Electric Machinery, 1998; contbr. articles to profl. jours. Fulbright-Hayes scholar, 1967-68; UNESCO fellow, 1969-70. Avocations: gardening, fishing, reading. Office: Purdue U Dept Elec/Computer Engring West Lafayette IN 47907-1285 Business E-Mail: ong@purdue.edu.

ONG, JOHN DOYLE, former ambassador, retired manufacturing executive; b. Uhrichsville, Ohio, Sept. 29, 1933; s. Louis Brosee and Mary Ellen (Liggett) O.; m. Mary Lee Schupp, July 20, 1957; children: John Francis Harlan, Richard Penn Blackburn, Mary Katherine Caine. BA, MA, Ohio State U., 1954; LLB, Harvard, 1957; LHD, Kent State U., 1982; HHD (hon.), Ohio State U., 1996; LHD (hon.), U. Akron, 1996; D in pub. svc. (hon.), SD State U., 2002. Bar: Ohio 1958. Asst. counsel B.F. Goodrich Co., Akron, 1961-66, group v.p., 1972-73, exec. v.p., 1973-74, vice chmn., 1974-75, pres., dir., 1975-77, pres., COO, 1978-79, chmn. bd., pres., CEO, 1979-84, chmn. bd., CEO, 1984-96, chmn. bd., 1996-97, chmn. emeritus, 1997—; US amb. to Norway Oslo, 2002—05. V.p. exploring Great Trail coun. Boy Scouts Am., 1974-77; bd. dirs. Nat. Alliance of Bus., 1981-94, chmn., 1984-86, 91; trustee Mus. Arts Assn., Cleve., 1975-, chmn., 1995-2002; Bexley Hall Sem., 1974-81, Case Western Res. U., 1980-92, Ft. Ligonier Assn., 1997-, Kenyon Coll., 1983-85, Hudson Libr. and Hist. Soc., Ohio, trustee, 1967-80, pres., 1971-72, Western Res. Acad., Hudson, 1975-95, pres. bd. trustees, 1977-95; nat. trustee Nat. Symphony Orch., 1975-83, John S. and James L. Knight Found., 1995-2002; mem. bus. adv. com. Transp. Ctr. Northwestern U., 1975-78, Carnegie-Mellon U. Grad. Sch. Indsl. Adminstrn., 1978-83; life trustee U. Chgo., 1991—; chmn. Ohio Bus. Roundtable, 1994-97; trustee Ohio Hist. Soc., 1998-2002; dir. New Amn. Schs., 1991, chmn., 1998-2002. Mem. Ohio Bar Assn. (bd. govs. corp. counsel sect. 1962-74, chmn. 1970), Rubber Mfrs. Assn. (bd. dirs. 1974-84), Chem. Mfrs. Assn. (bd. dirs. 1988-91, 94-97), Conf. Bd., Coun. Ret, Chief Execs., Coun. Am. Ambs., RTI Internat. (sr. vis. fellow 2006-), Bohemian Club, Chagrin Valley Hunt Club, Portage Country Club, Rowfant Club, Union Club, Links, Union League, Ottawa Shooting Club, Met. Club, Rolling Rock Club, Castalia Trout Club, Phi Beta Kappa, Phi Alpha Theta. Episcopalian. Home Phone: 330-650-1649; Office Phone: 330-665-3830.

ONG, MICHAEL KING, mathematician, educator, bank executive; b. Manila, Philippines, Dec. 16, 1955; s. Sanchez and Remedios (King) Ong. BS in Physics cum laude, U. Philippines, 1978; MA in Physics, SUNY Stony Brook, 1979, MS in Applied Math., 1981, PhD in Applied Math., 1984. Asst. prof. Bowdoin Coll., Brunswick, Maine, 1984—91; sr. mathematician, fin. analyst Chgo. Rsch. & Trading Group Ltd., 1990—92; v.p., sr. rsch. analyst First Chgo. NBD, 1993—94; head market risk analysis unit First Chgo. Corp., 1994—, 1st v.p., head corp. rsch. unit, 1996—97; sr. v.p., head treasury bus. rsch. ABN-AMRO Bank, Chgo., 1997—, head of enterprise risk mgmt., 1999—2000; exec. v.p., chief risk officer Credit Agricole Indosuez, 2000—03; prof. fin. Stuart Grad. Sch. Bus. Ill. Inst. Tech., 2003—, dir. fin. program, exec. dir. Ctr. for Fin. Markets, Stuart Grad. Sch. Bus., 2003—. Adj. prof. fin. markets and trading program Stuart Sch. Bus. Ill. Inst. Tech., 1990—, bd. dirs. Carr Global Advs., 2000—. Author: Internal Credit Risk Models-Performance Measurement and Capital Allocation, 1999, Credit Ratings-Methodologies, Rationale and Default Risk, 2002, The Basel Handbook-A Guide for Financial Practitioners, 2004, 2d edit., 2006, Risk Management-A Modern Perspective, 2006; editor-in-chief Jour. Credit Risk, assoc. editor The RMA Jour., mem. editl. bd. Jour. Fin. Regulation & Compliance, Jour. of RISK; mem. editl. bd.: Jour Risk Mgmt. for Fin. Instns.; editor Jour. of Global Fin. Markets; contbr. articles to profl. jours. Mem. Am. Fin. Assn., Am. Math. Soc., Math. Assn. Am., Soc. Indsl. and Applied Math., Consortium for Math. and Its Applications, Am. Phys. Soc., Phi Kappa Phi. Avocations: writing, singing, travel, painting. Home: 2650 N Lakeview Ave Apt 4106 Chicago IL 60614-1833 Office: Ill Inst Tech Stuart Grad Sch Bus 565 W Adams St Chicago IL 60661-3691 Office Phone: 312-906-6568. Personal E-mail: michaelong123@aol.com. Business E-Mail: ong@stuart.iit.edu.

ONG, NAI-PHUAN, physicist, educator; came to U.S., 1967; s. Chin-Seng and H. Kean O.; m. Delicia Lai, Aug. 1982 BA, Columbia Coll., 1971; PhD Physics, U. Calif., Berkeley, 1976. Asst. prof. U. So. Calif., LA, 1976—82, assoc. prof., 1982—84; prof. Princeton U., NJ, 1985—2003, Eugene Higgins prof. physics, 2003—. Cons. David Sarnoff Labs., Princeton, 1987-89. Co-discoverer (with Pierre Monceau) of Charge-Density-Wave conduction in metals; patentee in superconductivity, 1991; contbr. numerous articles to profl. jours Alfred P. Sloan fellow, 1982-84; recipient Kamerlingh Onnes prize for superconductivity experiments, 2006. Fellow Am. Phys. Soc., Am. Acad. Arts & Sciences; mem. AAAS Office: Princeton Univ Dept Physics PO Box 708 Princeton NJ 08544-0708 Office Phone: 609-258-4347. Business E-Mail: npo@princeton.edu.

ONISHI, YASUO, environmental researcher; b. Osaka, Japan, Jan. 25, 1943; came to U.S., 1969; s. Osamu and Tokiko (Domukai) O.; m. Esther Anna Stronczek, Jan 22, 1972; children: Anna Tokiko and Lisa Michiyo. BS, U. Osaka Prefecture, 1967, MS, 1969; PhD, U. Iowa, 1972. Rsch. engr. U. Iowa, Iowa City, 1972—74; sr. rsch. engr. Pacific NW Nat. Lab., Richland, Wash., 1974—77, staff engr., 1977—2001, mgr. rsch. program office, 1984—92, chief scientist, 2001—05; mem. Yasuo Onishi Cons., LLC, 2006—. Adj. grad. faculty Wash. State U., Tri-Cities, 1993-2004, adj. prof. 2005—. Co-author: Principles of Health Risk Assessment, 1985, others; editor: Chernobyl--What Have We Learned?, 2007; contbr. articles to profl. jours.; featured on TV program NOVA. Recipient Best Platform Presentation award ASTM, 1979. Mem.: IAEA (advisor on environ. issues), NAS (com. mem. "Understanding Oil Spill Disgersants: Efficacy and Effects" 2004—05), ASCE (chmn. task com. 1986—96), Nat. Coun. Radiation Protection and Measurements (adj. mem. 1983—), Sigma Xi. Lutheran. Achievements include rsch. in bilateral USA/former USSR joint soil and environmental assessment of Chernobyl accident. Home and Office: 144 Spengler St Richland WA 99354-1971 Office Phone: 509-375-0454. Personal E-mail: yasuo.onishi@yahoo.com.

ONKST, WAYNE, state librarian; b. London, Ky., 1956; m. Deborah Onkst; children: David, Noah. B in Hist., U. Ky., 1978, MLS, 1979. Reference libr. Kenton County Pub. Libr., 1979, head adult services, assoc. dir. libr. system, dir., 1999—2006; state libr., commr. Ky. Dept. Libraries and Archives, 2006—. Founder Ky. County Pub. Libr. Found. Recipient Children Inc. award, 2001, Sullivan award, ALA, 2005. Mem.: Ky. Pub. Libr. Assn. (pres.), Greater Cin. Libr. Consortium (pres. 2002—03), Leadership Northern Ky. Baptist. Avocations: genealogy, history. Office: Ky State Dept for Libraries PO Box 537 Frankfort KY 40602-0537 Office Phone: 502-564-8300. Business E-Mail: wayne.onkst@ky.gov. *

ONLEY, SISTER FRANCESCA, academic administrator; Prin. Nazareth Acad. H.S.; asst. to pres. Holy Family U., Phila., 1980—81, pres., 1981—. Chair Internat. Assn. of U. Pres., UN Commn. on Disarmament Edn., Conflict Resolution and Peace. Office: Holy Family U Office of Pres 9801 Frankford Ave Philadelphia PA 19114 Office Phone: 215-637-7700 3220. E-mail: fonley@holyfamily.edu. *

ONN, AMIR, medical educator, researcher; b. Rehovot, Israel, Nov. 19, 1959; arrived in U.S., 2000; s. Itzhak and Nitza Onn; m. Elizabeth E. Half, July 18, 1989; children: Lior, Dana, Alon, Yuval. BA, Hebrew U., Jersalem, MD, 1990. Intern Tel-Aviv Med. Ctr., Tel Aviv Sch. Medicine, resident internal medicine, fellow pulmonary medicine; postdoctoral fellow U. Tex. MD Anderson Cancer Ctr., Houston, fellow interventional pulmonary oncology; asst. prof. medicine and cancer biology U. Tex. M.D. Anderson Cancer Ctr., Houston, 2000—. Recipient Physician Scientist award, U. Tex. MD Anderson Cancer Ctr., 2004—. Home: 5422 Valkeith Dr Houston TX 77096 Home Phone: 713-729-8345; Office Phone: 713-563-6707. Office Fax: 713-794-4922; Home Fax: 713-729-8700. Business E-Mail: amironn@mdanderson.org.

ONO, EIICHI, engineering educator, researcher; BS in Agriculture, Meiji U., Kanagawa, Japan, 1990; MS in Agriculture and Biosystems Engring., U. Ariz., 1997, PhD, 2001. Rsch. assoc. U. Ariz., Tucson, 2002—05; rsch. fellow Tamagawa U. Rsch. Inst., Tokyo, 2005—. Mem.: ASAE. Office: Tamagawa Univ Research Inst 6-1-1 Tamagawagakuen Machida-shi Tokyo 194-8610 Japan

ONO, KENT ALAN, communications educator; b. Casper, Wyo., 1964; BA in English, DePauw U., 1987; MA in Comm., Miami U., 1988; PhD in Rhetoric, U. Iowa, 1992. Founder, Asian Am. cultural politics rsch. cluster U. Calif.-Davis, 1997, interim dir. MURALS undergrad. rsch. program, 1999—2000, co-founder & dir. cultural studies grad. program, 1999—2002; dir. & prof. Asian Am. studies and prof. comm. U. Ill., Urbana-Champaign, 2003—. Founder Comm. and Critical/Cultural Studies Jour.; former chair, critical and cultural studies Div. NCA, chair, Asian Pacific Am. Caucus, 1996—97, co-founder, Asian Am. studies, latino studies, and gay and lesbian studies div.; chair Asian Pacific Am. Caucus of Soc. for Cinema Studies, 1999—2001. Co-author: Shifting Borders: Rhetoric, Immigration, and California's Proposition 187, 2002; co-editor: Enterprise Zones: Critical Positions on Star Trek, 1996. Grantee Ford Found. Diversity of Edu. Grant, 1990—91. Office: U Ill Inst Comm Rsch 228 Gregory Hall 810 S Wright St Urbana IL 61801

ONOCHIE, FLORENCE N., accountant; b. Lagos, Nigeria, Apr. 27, 1961; arrived in U.S., 1987; d. Francis Wilcock E. and Mary Nwamaka E. Okolo; m. Henry Chuks Onochie; children: Chuks, Chizo, Kosi, Ndo's, Kenn. Degree in Fin., U. Tech. Enugu, Nigeria, 1985; BS in Acctg., U. Indpls., 1991. Reconciler Peoples Bank and Trust Co., Indpls., 1988—92; field examiner Ind. State Bd. Accounts, Indpls., 1992—94; acct., pres. HCO, Inc., Indpls., 1992—2001; auditor RGIS, Indpls., 1993—94; reconciler Bank One, Indpls., 1994; acct., pres. FNO, Inc., Indpls., 2001—. Mem. Inst. Bus. Fin. and Estate Planning. Former v.p. Rotary Club Nigeria; bd. mem. Profl. Womens Adv. Bd., Indpls., 2000. Named Woman of Yr., 2000, 2004. Mem.: NAFE, Greater Indpls. C. of C., Ind. Assn. Black Accts., Nat. Assn. Black Accts. (v.p. 2005—), Ind. Soc. Pub. Accts., Nat. Assn. Pub. Accts. Home: 8836 Worthington Cir Indianapolis IN 46278 Office: FNO Profl Svcs Inc Ste 130 3921 N Meridian St Indianapolis IN 46278 Office Phone: 317-872-3437.

ONORATO, NICHOLAS LOUIS, retired program director, economist; b. South Barre, Mass., Feb. 24, 1925; s. Charles and Amalia (Tartaglia) O.; m. Elizabeth Louise Settergren, July 19, 1947; children: Gary, Deborah, Nicholas, Jeffrey, Glenn, Charles (dec.), Lisa. Assoc., Becker Jr. Coll., 1949; BS in Pub. Rels., Boston U., 1951; MA in Econs, Clark U., 1952, PhD, 1959. Mem. faculty Becker Jr. Coll., Worcester, Mass., 1952-54; prof. econs. Worcester Poly. Inst., 1955-68, chmn. dept. econs., govt., bus., 1968-74, dir. Sch. Indsl. Mgmt., 1972-99; prof. emeritus Worcester (Mass.) Poly Inst., 1994. Vis. prof. Clark U., Worcester, 1964-66; fin. cons. Coz Chem. Co., Northbridge, Mass., 1959-95. Contbr. to newspapers and mags. Trustee Bay State Savs. Bank, Worcester. Served with USNR, 1943-46. Mem. Torch Club (pres. Worcester 1967, 87, 95). Home: 39 Knollwood Dr Shrewsbury MA 01545-3329

ONSTOTT, TULLIS, microgeologist, geology professor; b. Carlsbad, NM, Jan. 12, 1955; BS in Geophysics, Calif. Inst. of Tech., 1976; MA, PhD in Geology, Princeton U., 1980. Rsch. asst. U.S.G.S. Flagstaff, Ariz., 1974—76; post-doctoral fellow Princeton U., 1980—83; rsch., study Physics Dept., U. of Toronto, 1980—82; rsch. assoc. Princeton U., 1983—85, asst. prof., 1985—91, assoc. prof., 1991—2001, prof., 2001—. Mem. multiple NASA Workshops on Mars Drilling/Sampling. Named one of The World's Most Influential People, TIME Mag., 2007; recipient Presidential Young Investigator Award, Nat. Sci. Found., 1985—89, Jubilee Medal, Geological Soc. of South Africa, 1988, Meritorious Accomplishments in the field of Subsurface Microbiology, U.S. Dept. of Energy, 1996, Meritorious Achievements, 1998, Appreciation Award for Rsch. Excellence Office of Sci., 2002. Office: Princeton Univ Dept of Geosciences B79 Guyot Hall Princeton NJ 08544 Office Phone: 609-258-7678. E-mail: tullis@princeton.edu. *

ONTON, ANN LOUISE REUTHER, chemist; b. Bridgeport, Conn., Sept. 29, 1943; m. Aare Onton, 1965; children: Alan David, Daryl John, Julie Ann. BS in Chemistry, Purdue U., 1965. Lab. chemist Great Lakes Chem. Corp., 1965-67; rsch. asst. Geigy Chem. Corp., 1967-70; abstractor Chem. Abstracts Svc., 1970-72; rschr. Cancer Prevention II Study, 1980-

90; chemist Prototek Enzyme Sys. Products, 1992-93; rsch. assoc. Applied Biotech Concepts, Inc., 1995-98, Genaissance Pharms., 1999-2000; mgr. rsch. devel. and prodn. AllExcel, Inc., 2000—03; lab. asst. U. San Diego, 2003—05; lab. mgr. TheraCour Pharma, Inc., 2005—06; sr. scientist NanoViricides Inc., 2006—. NIH grantee, 1996, 97. Mem. NAFE, AAUW, Am. Chem. Soc., Assn. for Women in Sci. Achievements include co-inventor on patent pending for solubilization and targeted delivery of drugs with amphilphilic polymers; first to isolate, sequence and clone A Nidulans ahr asparaginase gene; development of novel materials and methods for improved electrophoresis and DNA sequencing technologies, development of methodologies for purification and testing of enzymes, U.S.A. Nat. and world medalist in Masters and Senior Olympic Swimming. Office: NanoViricides Inc 135 Wood St Ste 205 West Haven CT 06516-3700 Office Phone: 203-937-6137. Business E-Mail: annonton@snet.net.

ONUCHIC, JOSÉ NELSON, biophysics educator, electrical engineer; came to U.S., 1990; BS in Elec. Engring., U. Sao Paulo, Brazil, 1980, BS in Physics, 1981, MS in Applied Physics, 1982; PhD in Chemistry, Calif. Inst. Tech., 1987. Asst. prof. physics Inst. Physics and Chemistry Sao Carlos U. Sao Paulo, Brazil, 1987-90, U. Calif. San Diego, 1990-92, assoc. prof. physics, 1992-95, prof. of physics, 1995—. Co-dir. Ctr. for Theoretical Biol. Physics U. Calif., San Diego. Contbr. articles to profl. jours. Sr. fellow San Diego Supercomputer Ctr., 1997—; recipient Engring. Inst. prize Sao Paulo, 1980, Internat. Ctr. for theoretical Physics Prof. Werner Heisenberg prize, Trieste, Italy, 1988; elected assoc. mem. Acad. Scis. Estado de Sao Paulo, 1991; named Beckman Young Investigator, 1992. Fellow Am. Phys. Soc.; mem. NAS. Office: Univ Calif at San Diego Dept Physics La Jolla CA 92093-0319

ONUFRIEV, ALEXEY, science educator; s. Vlad and Irina Onufriev. PhD, Brown U., Providence, RI, 1997. Asst. prof. Va. Tech., Blacksburg, 2003—. E-mail: alexey@vt.edu.

ONUFROCK, RICHARD SHADE, retired pharmacist; b. Colorado Springs, Colo., July 5, 1934; s. Frank and Mildred Joy (Overstreet) O.; m. Karen Faye Larson, June 15, 1958 (div. 1980); children: Richard Alan (dec.), Amy Mildred. BS in Pharmacy, U. Colo., 1961; diploma, Famous Artists Schs., 1963. Registered pharmacist, Colo., Ariz., South Africa. Pharmacist Aley Drug Co., Colorado Springs, 1961-75, St. Joseph Hosp., Denver, 1976-77, Navajo Nation Health Found., Ganado, Ariz., 1977-81, Kearny (Ariz.) Kennecott-Samaritan Hosp., 1984-85, NIH, Warren G. Magnuson Clin. Ctr., Bethesda, Md., 1988—2003; dir. pharmacy, chief pharmacist Tintswalo Hosp., South Africa, 1981-84; pharmacist, chief pharmacist Miami (Ariz.)-Inspiration Hosp., 1985-88; ret., 2004. Instr. Coll. of Ganado, 1979-80; asst. in textbook revision and illustration U. Colo., 1961; cons. Heritage Health Care Ctr., Globe, Ariz., 1988, Gerson Lehrman Groups Coun. of Healthcare Advisors, 2004—. Illustrator Pharmacy for Nurses, 1961, Colo. Jour. of Pharmacy, 1962-64; illustrations exhibited Colo. Springs Fine Art Ctr., 1964-66, Gilpin County Art Assn., Central City, Colo., 1968-74, 1st Nat. Space Art Show, Denver, 1969. Dem. precinct committeeman, 1974-76; den leader Boy Scouts Am., com. mem., 1975-76; fireman, lt. Ganado Vol. Fire Dept., 1977-81; compassionate med. missionary Nazarene Ch., Tintswalo Hosp. Gazankulu, South Africa, 1981-84; bd. dirs. Friends of Libr., Kearny, 1985-87; active Grace Episcopal Ch. Mem.: Pharm. Soc. of S. Africa, Washington Met. Soc. Hosp. Pharmacists, Am. Soc. Health Sys. Pharmacists, Am. Pharm. Assn., Delta Sigma Phi, Phi Delta Chi. Avocations: travel, bicycling, hiking, skiing, computers. Personal E-mail: pasquache@aol.com.

ONUKWULI, FRANCIS OSITA, computer scientist, secondary school educator, mathematician; b. Warri, Nigeria, Aug. 5, 1955; arrived in U.S., 1977; s. Chief Mathias Nwafor and Mercy (Okonkwo) O.; m. Sandra Anthonia Mgbemena, Oct. 12, 1986; children: Francis Osita, Victor Chinedu, Anthony Tochukwu, Precious Chinenye. BS in Math. and Physics, Philander Smith Coll., Little Rock, 1981; MS in Computer Sci., Atlanta U., 1983; EdD in Ednl. Leadership Higher Edn., Clark Atlanta U., 1990. Billing and credit supr. Standard Bank Nigeria Ltd., Benin, 1975-77; tutor, counselor Philander Smith Coll., 1978-81; math. rsch. asst. Atlanta U., 1982-83; instr. computer sci. Spelman Coll., Atlanta, 1983-86; asst. prof. computer sci., mgr. computer and info. sci. lab. Morris Brown Coll., Atlanta, 1986-96, assoc. prof, chmn. computer sci. dept., 1991-92; gifted math. tchr. Lovejoy (Ga.) H.S., 1998—. Cons. PBT Engring. Co., Atlanta, 1985-86; judge Ga. Sci. Fair, 1989, 90, 93, 94, 95, 99, 2001. Co-author: Computer Applications for the Twenty-First Century; author microcomputer materials for calculus students. Named Man of Yr., Atlanta Met. Coll., 2002, Prof. of Yr., 2002, Coca Cola Tchr. of Yr., 2004—05, Tchr. of Yr., Lovejoy H.S., 2004—05; recipient Tchr. of the Yr. award, Parent-Tchr.-Student Assn., 2005—06. Mem. NSF (co-chair proposal review panelist 1989-90), Math. Assn. Am., Assn. Computing Machinery, Am. Math. Soc., Internat. Devel. Edn. Coun. (sec. 1987), Igbo Union (pres. Atlanta chpt. 1986-91), Umuoji Improvement Union (nat. v.p. U.S. and Can. 2000—04, pres. Atlanta chpt. 2001-07), Anambra State Assn. (nat. edn. com. chmn.), Knights of Columbus (adv. Jonesboro coun. 2005-). Democrat. Roman Catholic. Home: 7544 Sedona Dr Jonesboro GA 30236-2740 Office: Lovejoy HS 1587 McDonough Rd Lovejoy GA 30250 Home Phone: 678-230-8864; Office Phone: 770-473-2920. Personal E-mail: Dronukwuli@aol.com. E-mail: fonukwuli@clayton.k12.ga.us.

ONYEWU, OGUCHI, professional soccer player; b. Washington, May 13, 1982; Attended, Clemson Univ. Defender FC Metz, France, 2002—03, La Louviere, Belgium, 2003, Standard de Liege, Belgium, 2004—. 14 caps, 1 goal U.S. Nat. Soccer team, 2004—; mem. U.S. World Cup team, 2006. Mailing: US Soccer Fedn 1801 S Prairie Ave Chicago IL 60616

ONYIDO, JOHN CHIKE, lawyer; b. Ihiala, Anambra State, Nigeria, Feb. 14, 1969; s. John Paul and Clara Chibuogu Onyido; m. Bertha Fountain-Onyido. LLB, U. Benin, Nigeria, 1989; BL, U. Lagos, Nigeria, 1990; LLM, U. Lagos, 1998; MS in Internat. Law and Diplomacy, U. Lagos, Nigeria, 1998. Bar: Nigerian Supreme Ct. 1990, N.Y. 2005; cert. notary pub. Nassau County, 2005. Assoc. ptnr. Allan * Ogunkeye, 1992—99; sr. assoc. counsel The Law Union, 1999—2001, head Dept. Intellectual Property Law and Litig., 1999—2001; ptnr. R.U. Metu and Assocs., 2001—05, Jones, Lewis & Simpson Ptnrs., 2001—. Author: (poems) www.Poetry.com, Collection of Poems (Pub. Poet Editor's Choice award, 2005); contbr. articles to profl. jours. Named Resource Person on Fgn. Investment and Nigerian Intellectual Property Laws, South Africa, 2000. Mem.: ABA, Nigerian Bar Assn., Internat. Bar Assn., Am. Soc. Internat. Law, N.Y. County Lawyers Assn., N.Y. State Bar Assn., Human Rights Inst. (mem. African forum). Office Phone: 646-957-0204. Personal E-mail: johnchike@msn.com. Business E-Mail: johnonyido@optonline.net.

OOI, TENG KEONG, aerospace and mechanical engineer, educator; b. Penang, Malaysia, June 6, 1958; s. Leong Kee Ooi and Siew Poh Tan; m. Vivian Kcont-Salirrosas, Aug. 1, 1997. BS in aero. engring., Queen Mary Coll., U. London, England, 1981; MS in mech. engring., Okla. State U., 1983; MS in aviation mgmt., Embry-Riddle Aero. U., Fla., 1989; MS in indsl. engring., U. Ark., 1997; PhD in mech. engring., U. Ala. in Huntsville, 2002. Instr. Credential, Calif. CC, 1986. Adj. assoc. prof. dept. mech. and aerospace engring. U. Ala., 2004—. Adj. assoc. prof. dept. civil and environ. engring. U. Ala., 2004—06, 2006—; vis. scholar dept. mech. and aerospace and elec. engring. UCLA, 2005—; vis. asst. prof. dept. aeros. and astronautics Stanford U., Calif., 2005—; adj. prof. dept. materials sci. and engring. Va. Polytech. Inst. and State U., Blacksburg, 2006—. Contbr. articles various profl. jours. With USAF, 1986—90, with USAFR, 1993—2005, lt. (jr. grade) USNR, 2005—. Decorated Achievement medal for Civilian Svc. US Army, Outstanding Unit award with Valor USAF, Achievement medal, Commendation medal; recipient Group Achievement awards, NASA, Def. Recognition cert., Under Sec. Def. Mem.: Structural Engring. Inst., ASCE, Soc. of Exptl. Mechanics, Am. Acad. of Mechanics, Order of the Engr., Phi Kappa Phi. Achievements include research in modal testing of a lightweight cementitious structure and structural health monitoring of composite structure, and nano-sensor technology. Home: 4416 Kiger St Huntsville AL 35805 Office: UAH Dept of MAE Huntsville AL 35899 Home Phone: 256-512-9692.

OOLIE, SAM, manufacturing and investment company executive; b. NYC, Aug. 11, 1936; s. Bernadt S. and Rose (Moyel) O.; m. Marjorie R. Oolie, Dec. 3, 1961; children: Janis Oolie, Caroline Gross, Tara. BS in Metallurgy, MIT, 1958; MBA, Harvard U., 1961. Chmn. Food Concepts, Inc., Rutherford, NJ, 1962-85; pres. CFC Venture Capital Corp., Fairfield, NJ, 1984-90; chmn. Oolie Enterprises, Upper Saddle River, NJ, 1985—; vice chmn. Am. Mobile, Inc., Secaucus, NJ, 1986-89; chmn. The Nostalgia Network, NYC, 1987-90, New Thermal Corp., Keasbey, NJ, 1991-95, NoFire Tech., Inc., Upper Saddle River, NJ, 1995—. Mem. exec. com. State of N.J.-Israel Commn., 1989-93; commr. Essex County Improvement Authority, 1987-88; trustee Coun. Jewish Fedns., 1986—; bd. govs. Haifa U., 1986-90, 93-95; trustee Garden State Cancer Ctr., 1989-96, Beth Israel Med. Ctr., 1990-96, Assn. Reform Zionists Am., 1990-97, Am. Joint Distbn. Com., 1990-98; pres. United Jewish Fedn. Met. West N.J., 1988-90; vice chmn. United Jewish Appeal, 1986-96; chmn. Beth Israel Health Care Found., 1993-96. Recipient Gates of Jerusalem award Boys Town of Jerusalem, 1990, Israel 40th Ann. medal State of Israel Bonds, 1988. Mem. Harvard Club. Avocations: golf, coin collecting/numismatics. Office: 21 Industrial Ave Upper Saddle River NJ 07458 Home Phone: 201-224-3114; Office Phone: 201-818-1291. E-mail: samoolie@cs.com.

OORT, ABRAHAM HANS, meteorologist, researcher, educator; b. Leiden, The Netherlands, Sept. 2, 1934; came to U.S., 1961; s. Jan Hendrik and Johanna Maria (Graadt Van Roggen) O.; m. Bineke Pel, May 20, 1961; children: Pieter Jan, Michiel, Sonya. MS, MIT, 1963; PhD in Meteorology, U. Utrecht, The Netherlands, 1964. Rsch. meteorologist Koninklyk Nederlands Meteorologisch Instituut, De Bilt, Netherlands, 1964-66, Geophys. Fluid Dynamics Lab/NOAA, Washington, 1966-68, Princeton, NJ, 1968-77, sr. rsch. meteorologist, 1977-96, ret., 1996. Prof. dept. geol. and geophys. scis. Princeton U., 1971-96; Shiatsu tchr. Kushi Inst. for Macrobiotic Studies, Becket, Mass., 1999–. Author: Physics of Climate, 1992; contbr. monographs in field. 2nd lt. Netherlands Air Force, 1959-61. NATO sci. fellow MIT, Cambridge, 1961-63; 10th Victor P. Starr Meml. lectr. MIT, 1988; recipient Gold medal U.S. Dept. Commerce, Washington, 1979. Fellow N.Y. Acad. Scis., Am. Meteorol. Soc. (Jule G. Charney award 1993), Royal Meteorol. Soc.; mem. Am. Geophys. Union. Democrat. Avocations: sculpture, shiatsu, meditation.

OOSTERHUIS, PAUL WILLIAM, lawyer; b. Webster, Iowa, Nov. 5, 1946; m. Bronson Clayton, Jan. 21, 1978; children: Elizabeth, Christopher. BA magna cum laude, Brown U., 1969; JD cum laude, Harvard U., 1973. Bar: D.C. 1973, U.S. Tax Ct. 1989. Legislation staff atty. joint com. on tax. U.S. Congress, Washington, 1973-76, legislation counsel, 1977—78; assoc. Hogan & Hartson, Washington, 1979-80, ptnr., 1981-88; ptnr., internat. and corp. tax law Skaddon, Arps, Slate, Meagher & Flom, LLP, Washington, 1988—. Adj. prof. lae Georgetown U. Law Ctr., 1977—83. Contbr. articles to profl. publs.; author and co-author (books and articles). Office: Skadden Arps Slate Meagher & Flom LLP 1440 New York Ave NW Ste 600 Washington DC 20005 Office Phone: 202-371-7130. Office Fax: 202-661-8232. Business E-Mail: poosterh@skadden.com.

OOSTWOUDER, PETER HENRY, physician; b. Sioux City, Iowa, June 27, 1956; s. Cornelius and Alice Theresa (Roghair) O.; m. Joanna Ruth Field, June 7, 1997; children: Christina Elaine, Cornelius Wayne, Emily Theresa, Andrew Jacob. BA cum laude, Washington U., St. Louis, 1978; MD, St. Louis U., 1982. Diplomate in family practice and geriatrics Am. Bd. Family Practice. Resident in family practice United Hosp., Clarksburg, W.Va., 1982-85; family physician Jasper Med. Svcs., Heidelberg, Miss., 1985-88, Ormond Family Physicians, Ormond Beach, Fla., 1989, Ctrl. Fla. Cmty. Clinic, Sanford, Fla., 1990—. Clin. assoc. prof. Nova Southeastern Sch. Osteo. Medicine, Ft. Lauderdale, Fla., 1997—. Contbr. articles to profl. jours. Mem. Am. Acad. Family Physicians, Mensa, Sigma Xi. Republican. Mem. St. Andrews Chapel. Avocations: photography, travel, scuba diving, stamp collection. Office: Ctrl Fla Family Health Ctr 2400 State Rd 415 Sanford FL 32771-6012 Home: 33 Woodall Rd Debary FL 32713 Office Phone: 407-322-8645. Personal E-mail: oostwouder@pol.net.

OPACICH, MILAN, protective services official, musician; b. Gary, Ind., Apr. 12, 1928; s. Mile and Roza (Perpic) O.; m. Rosalyn Helen Nicolich, Oct. 20, 1951; 1 child, Karin Joann. Grad. h.s., Gary, Ind. Tool and die maker Gary Screw and Bolt Co., 1947-58; lt. Gary Fire Dept., 1958-78; instr. Purdue U. NW, Hammond, Ind., 1978-80; luthier Schererville, Ind., 1950—. Rev. panelist Ind. Arts Commn. Music, 2003; co-founder, N.W. Ind. Youth Tamburita Orch., 2004; lectr. in field; guest on numerous radio and TV shows; instr. guitar building, repair Joblink/Inland-ispat-Mittel, 2005—. Author Tamburitza America, 2005; writer Serb World, USA, 1984-; exhbns. include Mall, Washington, 1976, Remwick Gallery, Washington, 1978, 79-80, Smithsonian Inst., Washington, 1981, Bailey Ctr., 1982, Balzekas Lithuanian Culture Mus., Chgo., 1988, Arie Crown Theater, Chgo., 1990, Old Town Sch. Music, 1998; represented in permanent collection Roy Acuff Mus., Nashville; recordings include Bleda Djeva, Kreni Kreni, Jamin with Julius, Drina and Mel Dokich, Vintage 59 and Patriotic Songs of the Serbs; featured in books, magazines and newspaper articles. Founder, co-dir. Tamburitza Orch. St. Sava Orthodox Ch., 1964-70; founder First Tamburitza Extravanganza, 1971—. Recipient Pres.'s award for 50 yrs. of beautiful Tamburitza music, 1999, Am. Slavic Assn. honoree, 2000, Nat. Heritage Fellowship award, 2004; Ind. Arts Commn. grant, 2000, Master Artist grant Traditional Arts Ind., 2003, Northwest Ind. Lifetime Achievement award, 2005, Ivy Tech. Cmty. Linkage award, 2005; inductee Tamburitza Assn. Am. Hall of Fame. Mem.: Assn. Stringed Instrument Artisans. Ea. Orthodox. Avocations: collecting 78-rpm records, rare vintage instruments, documenting historical data, photographs, memorabilia tamburitza orchs. Home and Office: 2255 Robinhood Blvd Schererville IN 46375-1847 Personal E-mail: bgla_ruza@comcast.net.

OPALA, MARIAN PETER, state supreme court justice; b. Lódz, Poland, Jan. 20, 1921; JD, Oklahoma City U., 1953, BSB in Econs., 1957, LLD (hon.), 1981; LLM, NYU, 1968; HHD, Okla. Christian U. Sci. & Arts, 1981. Bar: Okla. 1953, U.S. Supreme Ct. 1970. Asst. county atty., Oklahoma County, 1953—56; practiced law Oklahoma City, 1956—60, 1965—67; referee Okla. Supreme Ct., Oklahoma City, 1960—65; prof. law Oklahoma City U. Sch. Law, 1965—69; asst. to presiding justice Supreme Ct. Okla., 1967—68; administrv. dir. Cts. Okla., 1968—77; presiding judge Okla. State Indsl. Ct., 1977—78; judge Workers Compensation Ct., 1978; justice Okla. Supreme Ct., 1978—, chief justice, 1991—92. Adj. prof. law Okla. City U., 1962—, U. Okla. Coll. Law, 1969—; prof. law U. Tulsa Law Sch., 1982—; mem. permanent faculty Am. Acad. Jud. Edn., 1970—; mem. NYU Inst. Jud. Adminstrn.; mem. faculty Nat. Jud. Coll., U. Nev., 1975—; chmn. Nat. Conf. State Ct. Adminstrs., 1976-77; mem. Nat. Conf. Commrs. on Uniform State Laws, 1982—. Co-author: Oklahoma Court Rules for Perfecting a Civil Appeal, 1969 Mem. Adminstrn. Conf. U.S., 1993-95. Recipient Herbert Harley award Am. Judicature Soc., 1977, Disting. Alumni award Oklahoma City U., 1979, Americanism medal Nat. Soc. DAR, 1984, ABA/Am. Law Inst. Harrison Tweed Spl. Merit award, 1987, Humanitarian award NCCJ, 1991, Jour. Record award, 1995, Constn. award Rogers State U., 1996, Jud. Excellence award Okla. Bar Assn., 1997, Leo H. Whinery Disting. Svc. award, 1999, Lifetime Achievement award Oklahoma City Univ. Sch. Law, 2000, First Amendment award FOI Okla., Inc., 2002; inductee Okla. Hall of Fame, 2000. Mem. ABA (edn. com. appellate judges conf. 1984-93), Okla. Bar Assn. (Earl Sneed Continuing Legal Edn. award 1988, Jud. Excellence award 1997), Okla. County Bar Assn., Am. Soc. Legal History, Oklahoma City Title Lawyers Assn., Am. Judicature Soc. (bd. dirs. 1988-92), Am. Law Inst. (elected), Order of Coif, Phi Delta Phi (Oklahoma City Alumni award). Office: Okla Supreme Ct State Capitol Rm 238 Oklahoma City OK 73105 Office Phone: 405-521-3839.

OPARIL, SUZANNE, cardiologist, educator, researcher; b. Elmira, NY, Apr. 10, 1941; d. Stanley and Anna (Penkova) Oparil. AB, Cornell U., 1961; MD, Columbia U., 1965. Diplomate Am. Bd. Internal Medicine. Intern in medicine Presbyn. Hosp., NYC, 1965—66; sr. asst. resident in medicine Mass. Gen. Hosp., Boston, 1967—68, clin. and rsch. fellow in medicine, cardiac unit, 1968—71; asst. prof. medicine Med. Sch., U. Chgo., 1971—75, assoc. prof., 1975—77; assoc. prof. dept. medicine U. Ala., Birmingham, 1977—81, asst. prof. physiology and biophysics, 1980—81, assoc. prof., 1981—, prof. medicine, 1981—, dir. vascular biology and hypertension program, 1985—, prof. med. physiology and biophysics, 1993—. Mem. vis. faculty Nat. High Blood Pressure Edn. Program, 1974—, Joint Nat. Com. on Detection, Evaluation and Treatment High Blood Pressure, 1991; mem. bd. sci. advisors Sterling Drug, Inc., 1988—91; lectr. in field; Selkurt lectr. Ind. U. Sch. Medicine, 1994; hon. prof. Peking Union Med. Coll., 1994; Louis Gross-Harold Segall lectr. Jewish Gen. Hosp., Montreal, Que., 1995; Joy Goodwin Disting. lectr. Auburn U., 1996; A Ross McIntyre award U. Nebr., 1996. Author books on hypertension; editor: Am. Jour. Med. Scis., 1984—94; assoc. editor: Hpertension, 1979—83, mem. editl. bd.:, 1984—, assoc. editor: Am. Jour. Physiology-Renal, 1989—91, mem. editl. bd.: Jour. Hypertension, 1989—98; contbr. over 450 articles to profl. jours., chapters to books. Recipient Young Investigator award, Internat. Soc. Hypertension, 1979, ann. award, Med. Coll. Pa., 1984; fellow, Am. Coll. Cardiology, 1992. Fellow: Am. Coll. Cardiology; mem.: AAAS, Am. Fedn. for Clin. Rsch. (midwest councillor 1974—75, nat. councillor 1975—78, sec.-treas. 1978—80, pres. 1981—82), Assn. Am. Physicians, So. Soc. for Clin. Investigation (Founder's award 1995), Soc. Exptl. Biology and Medicine (councillor 1993—), Am. Soc. for Clin. Investigation (sec.-treas. 1983—86), Am. Physiol. Soc. (clin. physiology advd. com. 1992—, Carl Ludwig disting. lectr. 2002), Am. Heart Assn. (coun. for high blood pressure rsch. 1973—, coun. on basic scis. 1978—, mem.-at-large, exec. com. 1979—81, chmn. Louis B. Katz Prize com. 1984—86, exec. com. 1985—90, vice chmn. 1986, v.p. Ala. affiliate 1986—87, pres.-elect Ala. affiliate 1987—88, pres. Ala. affiliate 1988—89, chmn. 1988—90, chmn. budget com. 1990—91, mem.-at-large bd. dirs. 1992, Lewis K. Dahl Meml. lectr. 1993, pres.-elect Ala. affiliate 1993—94, nat. pres.-elect 1993—94, nat. pres. 1994—, Arthur C. Corcoran Meml. lectr. 1998, Irving Page-Alva Bradley Lifetime Achievement award 2002), Assn. for Women in Sci., Am. Soc. Hypertension (sci. program com. 1990—92, pub. policy com. 1990—), Inter-Am. Soc. Hypertension, Endocrine Soc., Inst. Medicine of NAS (corr. com. on human rights 1992, chmn. com. adviser Dept. Def. 1993 Breast Cancer Rsch. Program), Phi Kappa Phi, Alpha Omega Alpha (mem. nat. bd. dirs., dir.-at-large 1991, treas. 1993), Sigma Xi, Phi Beta Kappa. Avocations: horseback riding, tennis, hiking, travel. Office: U Ala 703 S 19th St ZRB 1034 Birmingham AL 35294-0007 E-mail: soparil@uab.edu.

OPAT, MATTHEW JOHN, lawyer; b. Riceville, Iowa, Nov. 5, 1952; s. Wesley John and Dolores Genevieve (Ludwig) O.; m. Therese Ann Dusheck, Aug. 13, 1977; children: Michael, Kristin, Steven. BA in History, U. Iowa, 1974; JD, Hamline U., 1977. Bar: Iowa 1977, Minn. 1977. Prin. Opat Law Office, Chatfield, Minn., 1977—. Atty. Fillmore County, 1997-2003. Mem. Fillmore County Bar Assn. (pres. 1984-85), Minn. State Bar Assn. (bd. dirs. 1985-87), Tenth Dist. Bar Assn. (chmn. ethics com. 1989-96, pres. 2001-2002, 2004-2005) Office: 22 2nd St SE PO Box 455 Chatfield MN 55923-1203 Office Phone: 507-867-4080.

OPDAHL, VIOLA ELIZABETH, secondary school educator; b. Watervliet, NY, Jan. 6, 1925; d. Leslie Rouse and Violetta Frances (O'Bryon) Woodruff; m. Robert Clarence Opdahl, Aug. 4, 1956. BA, Skidmore Coll., 1945; MS in Edn., Cornell U., 1951; postgrad., SUNY, Albany, 1959-61. Cert. tchr. social studies, guidance. Tchr. social studies New Lebanon Ctrl. Sch., Lebanon Springs, NY, 1945-50, Patchogue HS, 1951-55, Selkirk (NY) Sch. Dist., 1955-56, Kingston (NY) City Schs., 1956-58, secondary guidance, 1958-62, tchr. social studies, 1962-86; ret., 1986; coll. student tech. supr. SUNY, New Paltz, 1989-94; ret., 1994. Ad hoc syllabi and testing coms. NY State Edn. Dept., Albany, 1967—82; adj. instr. psychology Marist Coll., 1972—86. Author (with Robert Opdahl): A Shaker Musical Legacy, 2004. Spl. activities organizer Town of Hurley Spl. Events Com., 1988—. Named Outstanding Social Studies Tchr., Mid Hudson Soc. State Coun. NY, 1986; recipient Pres. award, Marist Coll., 1986, Dean's award, SUNY, New Paltz, 1989. Mem.: LWV, AAUW, Hurley Heritage Soc., Friends of Senate House. Avocations: reading, writing. Home: PO Box 218 431 Wynkoop Rd Hurley NY 12443-5108 E-mail: vewo431@hvc.rr.com.

OPDYCKE, LEONARD EMERSON, retired elementary school educator, publishing executive, writer; b. Boston, May 22, 1929; s. Leonard and Frances (Prescott) O.; m. Susan Wolcott, 1951 (div.); children: Susan, Deborah, Margot; m. Jeanne Bernhard, 1963 (div.); children: Sarah, Frances; m. Sandra S. Auchincloss, 1976. BA, Harvard U., 1951; MA, U. Rochester, 1965. Tchr. Southfield Sch., Shreveport, La., 1952-53, Dedham (Mass.) Country Day, Harley Sch., Rochester, NY, 1956-64; dir. Poughkeepsie (NY) Day Sch., 1965-72; chair English dept. Rhinebeck (NY) HS, 1974-77; adj. prof. Marist Coll., Poughkeepsie, 1977-84, 93-95. Co-chair citizen's adv. com. Poughkeepsie Sch. Dist., 1994—2002. Author: French Aeroplanes before the Great War, 1999; editor, pub. WWI Aero, 1961—; pub. Skyways, 1987—. Bd. dirs. Cmty. Family Devel. Day Care Ctr., 1984—, Hudson River Housing, 2003—05. Mem. Phi Beta Kappa. Avocations: aviation history, linguistics, education. Home and Office: 15 Crescent Rd Poughkeepsie NY 12601-4405 Home Phone: 845-473-3679; Office Phone: 845-473-3679.

OPDYKE, NEIL DONALD, geology educator; b. Frenchtown, NJ, Feb. 7, 1933; BA, Columbia U., 1955; PhD, Durham U., Eng., 1958; DSc, U. Newcastle-upon-Tyne, 1982. Postdoctoral fellow Rice U., Houston, 1958-59, Australian Nat. U., 1959-60, U. Coll. Rhodesia and Nyasaland, Salisbury, Southern Rhodesia, 1960-63; rsch. assoc. Lamont-Doherty Geol. Observatory, 1964-66, sr. rsch. assoc., 1966-81; geology lectr. Columbia U., NYC, 1967-69, adj. prof. geology, 1974-81; prof., chmn. geology U. Fla., 1981-88, prof. geology, 1994—. Vis. prof. U. Paris, 1989. Mem. editl. bd. Quaternary Rsch., 1982. Fulbright grantee, 1959, 77-78, 89. Fellow AAAS, Am. Geophys. Union (John Adam Fleming medal 1996, com. on pub. affairs 1990-91, geomagnetism and paleomagnetism sect. 1984-86, pres.); mem. NAS (geodynamics com. 1984-86), Am. Acad. Arts. and Scis., Geol. Soc. Am. (George P. Woollard award 1987, assoc. editor bull. 1983, day medal com. 1982), Geol. Soc. Australia (Stillwell award 1982). Office: U Fla Dept Geology PO Box B137 1112 Turlington Hall Gainesville FL 32611-7340

OPEL, DOUG, composer, arranger; b. Richmond, Ind., Mar. 5, 1967; s. Richard and Alice Opel. BS, Ball State U., Muncie, Ind., 1990; MusM, U. Mich., Ann Arbor, 1993; MusD, Ind. U., Bloomington, 2002. Pvt. tchr., Ft. Wayne, Ind., 2006; music arranger WFWA PBS39, Ft. Wayne, 2001, ESPN, Bloomington, Ind., 1996. Composer: (orchestral music) Drive! for chamber orchestra (Commd. by the Ft. Wayne Alumnae Chpt. of Sigma Alpha Iota, 2005), (electronic music) Carving Lorien for amplified violin and tape, (chamber music) NeoCons & Libertines for voice, mixed ensemble and live electronics (Commd. by MATA, 2005), (piano music) 3 Preludes to Missing the Point for piano (Commd. by Nicola Melville, Underwritten by the Am. Composers Forum with funds provided by the Jerome Found., 2006), (orchestral music) Episodica for full orchestra, (chamber music) Patchwork for large chamber ensemble, Ferlinghetti for speaker and mixed chamber ensemble, (piano music) Dilukkenjon for two pianos, (chamber music) Pentableaux for wind quintet, Faces for baritone and piano quartet (Commd. by Bass-Baritone Timothy Jones, 1993), (electronic music) Our God For Tape. Recipient Aaron Copland award, Copland Ho., Inc., 2003—04; fellow, Ball State U., Dept. Music History, 1989—90; Evelyn Marin scholar, U. Mich., 1992—2003. Mem.: Coll. Music Soc., Broadcast Music, Inc., Am. Music Ctr., Am. Composers Forum, Phi Mu Alpha. Personal E-mail: dougopel@yahoo.com.

OPEL, PAMELA LYNN, elementary school educator; d. Richard Gene and Virginia Beaty Opel; 1 child, Thomas Wendolin. BA, U. So. Miss., Hattiesburg, 1977, MEd, 1997. Cert. Nat. Bd. Profl. Tchg. Stds. Educator Biloxi Pub. Sch., Miss., 1986—87, Vernon Parish Sch., Ft. Polk, La., 1987—90; tech. editor XMCO, Sterling Heights, Mich., 1991—94; educator Gulfport Sch. Dist., Miss., 1994—2007, specialist, 2007—. Substitute tchr. Northside Ind. Sch. Dist., San Antonio, 1994—95; adj. faculty U. So. Miss., Long Beach, 1997—2004, chair 504 com., 2005—06; assessor Nat. Bd. Profl. Tchg. Stds., San Antonio, 2004, San Antonio, 05, Mobile, Ala., 2004—; editor, manuscript evaluator Corwin Press, 2006. Grantee, Miss. Dept. Edn., 2003. Mem.: Miss. Profl. Educators Assn., Assn. Edn. Therapists, Phi Kappa Phi, Pi Lamba Theta, Phi Delta Kappa. Avocations: reading, sketching, travel, spelunking. Office: Gulfport Sch Dist 37 Pass Rd Gulfport MS 39507 Office Phone: 228-865-4619. Business E-Mail: popel@gulfportk12.ms.us, pam.opel@gulfportschools.org.

OPEL, WILLIAM, medical research administrator; BA, Pepperdine U., 1968; MBA, U. So. Calif., 1993; PhD, Claremont Grad. U., 1998. Mem. staff Pasadena (Calif.) Found. Med. Rsch., Pasadena, Calif., 1961-63, rsch. assoc., 1964-70, asst. to dir., 1970-72, adminstr., 1972-76, exec. dir., 1976-82; acting exec. dir. Huntington Inst. Applied Med. Rsch., 1978-82; exec. dir. Huntington Med. Rsch. Inst., Pasadena, Calif., 1982—. Lectr. in technology, mgmt., Pepperdine U.; adj. prof. tech. mgmt. Claremont Grad. U. Mem. Beta Gamma Sigma, Phi Kappa Phi. Office: Huntington Med Rsch Insts 734 Fairmount Ave Pasadena CA 91105-3104

OPFER, GEORGE J., federal agency administrator; b. NYC, May 12, 1947; m. Elizabeth Opfer; 3 children. BS in Mgmt., St. John's U., 1969. With U.S. Secret Svc., spl. agt., treasury agt., asst. dir. Office of Investigations Washington; inspector gen. FEMA, Washington, 1994—2005, US Dept. Vet. Affairs, Washington, Del., 2005—. Recipient Presdl. Rank of Meritorious Exec. award Sr. Exec. Svc., 1992. Office: US Dept Veterans Affairs 810 Vermont Ave NW Rm 1114 Washington DC 20420

OPHORI, DUKE URHOBO, environmental scientist, educator, research scientist, consultant; b. Ughelli, Delta, Nigeria; s. Samuel Atua and London Ophori; m. Grace Aroghene Ekperuoh, Aug. 9, 1980; children: Ejovwoke, Oghenevwogaga, Emueje, Eta. BSc in Geology, U. Ibadan, Nigeria, 1976; MSc in Hydrogeology, U. Waterloo, Ont., Can., 1982; PhD in Hydrogeology, U. Alta., Edmonton, Can., 1986. Geol. cons. Minstry of Works, Kano, Nigeria, 1976—77; geologist Geol. Survey Nigeria, Kano, 1977; lectr. U. Ilorin, Ilorin, Nigeria, 1977—79, U. Pt. Harcourt, Nigeria, 1979—87; post doctoral fellow U. Alta., Edmonton, Canada, 1987—89; rsch. scientist Atomic Energy Can. Ltd., Pinawa, Manitoba, Canada, 1989—95; prof. Montclair State U., Upper Montclair, NJ, 1995—. Contbr. articles to profl. jours. Mem.: Am. Assn. Ground Water Scientists, Internat. Assn. Hydrogeologists, Am. Geophys. Union. Avocations: soccer, tennis. Office: Montclair State Univ 1 Normal Ave Upper Montclair NJ 07043

OPIE, JOHN D., retired electric power industry executive; BSMetE, Mic. Coll. Mining & Tech., 1961. With magnetic materials bus. GE, 1961-64, various carboloy sys., 1964-73, nat. sales mgr. carboloy sys., 1973-74, gen. mgr. mining bus., 1974-75, gen. mgr. battery bus., 1975-77; gen. mgr. Lexan products divsn. GE Plastics, 1977-80, v.p. Lexan products divsn., 1980-82, pres. specialty plastics divsn., 1982-83; v.p. distbn. equipment bus. GE, 1983-86, sr. v.p., 1986; pres., CEO GE Lighting, 1986-95; vice chmn., exec. officer GE, 1995—2000; interim non-exec. chmn. The Stanley Works, New Britain, Conn., 2004. Bd. dirs. Delphi Corp., 1999—, The Stanley Works, 2000, Wal-Mart Stores Inc., 2003—06. Life Trustee Mich. Tech. U. Office: Delphi Corp 5725 Delphi Drive Troy MI 48098-2815

OPITZ, DONALD L., science historian; b. Chgo., June 25, 1969; s. Donald O. Opitz and Angeline L. Rispoli, Antoinette I. Opitz (Stepmother); life ptnr. Gregg J. Albrecht. BS, DePaul U., 1991; MA, U. Minn., 1998, PhD, 2004. Dir. Women's Ctr. U. Minn., Mpls., 2001—02, dir. Gen. Coll. Math. Ctr., 2002—06; asst. prof. DePaul U., Sch. New Learning, 2006—. Author: (pamphlet) Three Generations in the Life of the Minnesota Women's Center: A History, 1960-2000; contbr. chapters to books, articles to profl. jours. Bd. dirs. Calhoun-Isles Cmty. Band, Mpls., 2002—06, Ladd Arboretum, Evanston, Ill. Recipient vis. studentship, U. Cambridge, 2001; fellow, U. of Minn., 1991—92; grantee, NSF, 2001; scholar, DePaul U., 1987—91. Mem.: Brit. Soc. for History of Sci., Am. Hist. Assn., History of Sci. Soc. Roman Catholic. Avocations: bicycling, French horn performance. Home: 134 Clyde Ave Apt 2W Evanston IL 60202 Office: DePaul U 25 East Jackson Blvd Chicago IL 60604

OPOLKA, JAYME LYN, medical writer, researcher; b. Iron Mountain, Mich., Nov. 8, 1977; d. Frank David and Suzan Ann Opolka. BS in Biol. Scis. summa cum laude, Mich. Technol. U., 1999; MS in Pharmacy Adminstrn. summa cum laude, U. Tex., 2001. Cert. pharmacy technician. Global outcomes profl. intern Pharmacia Corp., Kalamazoo, 2001—02; health outcomes vis. scientist Eli Lilly and Co., Indpls., 2002—03; med. writer Takeda Pharms. N.Am., Lincolnshire, Ill., 2003—04; brand sci. copywriter Corbett Accel Healthcare Group, Chgo., 2004; freelance copywriter, med. writer, med. educator, 2005—. Health outcomes cons. Eli Lilly and Co., Indpls., 1999—2003; adj. faculty Butler U., Indpls., 2003; grad. rsch. asst., cons. Office Quality Assurance for Tex. Long-Term Care Facilities, Tex. Dept. Human Svcs., 2000—03; presenter in field. Contbr. articles to profl. jours. Recipient numerous scholarships. Mem.: Am. Coll. Clin. Pharmacy, Internat. Soc. Pharmacoecons. and Outcomes Rsch. Democrat. Roman Catholic. Achievements include research in neuroscience, diabetes, women's health, ophthalmology. Avocations: travel, outdoor activities, crafts, photography. Home: 4630 River St Quinnesec MI 49876 E-mail: jlopolka@yahoo.com.

OPPEDAHL, JOHN FREDERICK, newspaper publisher, executive; b. Duluth, Minn., Nov. 9, 1944; s. Walter H. and Lucille (Hole) Oppedahl; m. Alison Owen, 1975 (div. 1983); m. Gillian Coyro, Feb. 14, 1987 (div. 2002); 1 child, Max. BA, U. Calif., Berkeley, 1967; MS, Columbia U., 1968. Reporter San Francisco Examiner, 1967; reporter, asst. city editor Detroit Free Press, 1968-75, city editor, 1975-80, exec. city editor, 1981, exec. news editor, 1981-82, asst. mng. editor, 1983; nat. and fgn. editor Dallas Times Herald, 1983-85, asst. mng. editor, 1985-87; mng. editor/news L.A. Herald Examiner, 1987-89; mng. editor Ariz. Republic, Phoenix, 1989-93; exec. editor Phoenix Newspapers, Inc., 1993-95; pub., CEO The Republic, 1996—2000; chmn., pub., CEO San Francisco Chronicle, 2000—03. Chmn. bd. The Daily Californian. Mem.: Am. Soc. Newspaper Editors. Personal E-mail: joppedahl@yahoo.com.

OPPEDAHL, PHILLIP EDWARD, computer company executive; b. Renwick, Iowa, Sept. 17, 1935; s. Edward and Isadore Hannah (Gangstead) O.; m. Sharon Elaine Ree, Aug. 3, 1957 (dec. Aug. 1989), m. Karen Suzanne Ungar, July, 4, 2004; children: Gary Lynn, Tamra Sue, Sue Ann, Lisa Kay. BS in Naval Sci., Navy Postgrad. Sch., 1963, MS in Nuclear Physics, 1971; MS in Sys. Mgmt., U. S.C., 1978. Commd. ensign U.S. Navy, 1956, advanced through grades to capt., 1977; with Airborne Early Warning Squadron, 1957-59, Anti-Submarine Squadron, 1959-65; asst. navigator USS Coral Sea, 1965-67; basic jet flight instr., 1967-69; test group dir. Def. Nuclear Agy., 1972-74; weapons officer USS Oriskany, 1974-76; program mgt. for armament Naval Air Sys. Command, Washington, 1977-79; test dir. Def. Nuclear Agy., Kirtland AFB, N.Mex., 1979-82, dep. comdr., 1982-83; pres., CEO Am. Systems, Albuquerque, 1983—. Bd. dirs. BASIS Internat., 1991—; command pilot Angel Flight, N.Mex. Author: Energy Loss of High Energy Electrons in Beryllium, 1971, Understanding Contractor Motivation and Incentive Contracts. Decorated Def. Superior Svc. medal; recipient Alumni Disting. Svc. award Waldorf Coll., 2006. Mem. Naval Inst., Aircraft Owners and Pilots Assn., Assn. Naval Aviation, Navy League. Lutheran.

OPPENHEIM, ALAN VICTOR, electrical engineering educator; b. NYC, Nov. 11, 1937; s. Sydney and Dorothy (Arenz) Oppenheim; m. Phyllis Arnold, June 20, 1964; children: Justine Ruth, Jason Philip. SB, SM, MIT, 1961, ScD, 1964; D (hon.), Tel Aviv U., 1995. Asst. prof. dept. elec. engring. MIT, 1964-69, assoc. prof. dept. elec. engring. and computer scis., 1969-76, prof., 1976-90, Disting. prof. elec. engring., 1990-96, Ford prof. engring., 1996—, MacVicar faculty fellow, 1997—; staff scientist Lincoln Lab., 1967-69, assoc. head data systems divsn., 1978-80. Cons. Lincoln Lab., Atlantic Aerospace Inc., Sanders Assocs., Inc. Co-author: Digital Signal Processing, 1975, Signals and Systems, 1983, 2d edit. 1997, Discrete-Time Signal Processing, 1989, others; editor: Applications of Digital Signal Processing, 1978, (with others) Advanced Topics in Signal Processing, 1988; contbr. articles to profl. jours. Guggenheim fellow, 1972-73 Fellow IEEE (Edn. medal 1988, Jack S. Kilby Signal Processing Medal 2007); mem. NAE, Sigma Xi, Eta Kappa Nu, Tau Beta Pi.

OPPENHEIM, ANTONI KAZIMIERZ, mechanical engineer; b. Warsaw, Aug. 11, 1915; came to U.S., 1948, naturalized, 1954; s. Tadeusz and Zuzanna (Zuckerwar) O.; m. Lavinia Stephens, July 18, 1945; 1 dau., Terry Ann. Diploma in Engring., Warsaw Inst. Tech., London, 1943; PhD in Engring., U. London, 1945; Diploma of Imperial Coll., 1945; DSc, U. London, 1976; Dr. Honoris Causa, U. Poitiers, France, 1981, Tech. U., Warsaw, 1989, Imperial Coll., 1995. Registered profl. engr., Calif. Research asst. City and Guilds Coll., 1942-48, lectr., 1946-48; asst. prof. mech. engring. Stanford U., 1948-50; faculty U. Calif. at Berkeley, 1950—, prof. mech. engring., 1958-86, Miller prof., 1961-62, prof. emeritus, 1986—. Prof. assoc. Sorbonne, Paris, 1960-61, U. Poitiers, France, 1973, 80; staff cons. Shell Devel. Co., 1952-60. Editor-in-chief: Acta Astronautica, 1974-79; contbr. articles to profl. jours., also monographs. Chmn. Heat Transfer and Fluid Mechanics Inst., 1958; IAA Com. on Gasdynamics of Explosions, 1968—; organizer Internat. Colloquia on Gas Dynamics of Explosions and Reactive Systems, 1967, 69, 71, 73, 75, 77, 79, 81, 83; mem. NASA, adv. com. fluid mechanics, 1963-69. Recipient Water Arbitration prize Inst. Mech. Engrs., 1948, Numa Manson medal Inst. for Dynamics of Explosions and Reactive Sys., 1981, Dionizy Smolenski medal Polish Acad. Scis., 1987, Alfred C. Egerton medal The Combustion Inst., 1988, Berkeley citation U. Calif., Berkeley, 1988; fellow Imperial Coll. Fellow Imperial Coll.; mem. U.S. Nat. Acad. Engring, Polish Acad. Scis. Achievements include contributions to compressible fluid flow, gas turbines and internal combustion engines, heat transfer, combustion, detonation and blast waves. Home: 54 Norwood Ave Kensington CA 94707-1119 Office Phone: 510-642-0211. Business E-Mail: ako@me.berkeley.edu.

OPPENHEIM, CHARLES B., lawyer; b. NYC, Oct. 18, 1962; s. Barry J. and Jean Elizabeth (Reeve) O.; m. Lydia Vitlacil, July 25, 1992; children: Calvin, Dean. BA, Cornell U., 1984; JD, Fordham U., 1988. Bar: Calif. 1988. Assoc. Skadden Arps et al., San Francisco, 1988-90, McDermott & Trayner, Pasadena, Calif., 1991-93, Weissburg and Aronson, LA, 1993-95; ptnr. Weissburg & Aronson, LA, 1996, Foley, Lardner, Weissburg & Aronson, LA, 1996, Foley & Lardner LLP, LA, 1996—. Co-editor: Health Care Law Sourcebook, 1995-2000; contbr. articles to profl. jours. Bd. trustees The Accelerated Sch., LA, 2000—. Recipient Nat. Philanthropy Day medallion, L.A., 2001. Mem. Am. Health Lawyers Assn., Calif. Soc. Healthcare Attys. Office: Foley & Lardner LLP 2029 Century Park E Ste 3500 Los Angeles CA 90067-3021 Office Phone: 310-975-7790. Business E-Mail: coppenheim@foley.com.

OPPENHEIM, IRWIN, chemical physicist, educator; b. Boston, June 30, 1929; s. James L. and Rose (Rosenberg) O.; m. Bernice Buresh, May 18, 1974; 1 child, Joshua Buresh. AB summa cum laude, Harvard U., 1949; postgrad., Calif. Inst. Tech., 1949-51; PhD, Yale, 1956. Physicist Nat. Bur. Standards, Washington, 1953-60; chief theoretical physics Gen. Dynamics/Convair, San Diego, 1960-61; assoc. prof. chemistry MIT, Cambridge, 1961-65, prof., 1965—. Lectr. physics U. Md., 1953-60; vis. assoc. prof. physics U. Leiden, 1955-56, Lorentz prof., 1983; vis. prof. Weizmann Inst. Sci., 1958-59, U. Calif., San Diego, 1966-67; Van der Waals prof. U. Amsterdam, 1966-67. Author: (with J.G. Kirkwood) Chemical Thermodynamics, 1961; editor: Phys. Rev. E, 1992-2001. Recipient Hildebrand award, 1998. Fellow Am. Phys. Soc., Am. Acad. Arts and Scis., Washington Acad. Sci.; mem. Phi Beta Kappa, Sigma Xi. Achievements include research in quantum statis. mechanics, statis. mechanics of transport processes, thermodynamics. Home: 140 Upland Rd Cambridge MA 02140-3623 Office: MIT 77 Massachusetts Ave #6-223 Cambridge MA 02139-4307 Office Phone: 617-253-1478. Business E-Mail: irwin@mit.edu.

OPPENHEIM, MARTHA KUNKEL, pianist, educator; b. Port Arthur, Tex., June 25, 1935; d. Samuel Adam and Grace (Moncure) Kunkel; m. Russell Edward Oppenheim, June 18, 1960; children: Lauren Susan, Kristin Lee Oppenheim Mortenson. MusB with honors, U. Tex., 1957, MusM, 1959; diploma in piano, Juilliard Sch. Music, 1960; student, Am. Conservatory, Fontainebleau, France, 1956, student, 1958. Soloist Amarillo (Tex.) Symphony, Austin (Tex.) Symphony, U. Tex. Orch., San Antonio Symphony, Dallas Symphony, Heilbronner Kammer Orch., Heilbron, Germany. Solo and chamber music recitals in Tex., N.Y., France; mem. Halcyon Trio, 1974—77; tchg. asst. U. Tex., 1957—59, 1968—69; pvt. piano tchr., San Antonio, 1962—; pianist in duo with cellist Dan Zollars, 1991—. Recipient 1st place award, Internat. Piano Rec. Festival, Nat. Guild Piano Tchrs., 1956, 1956, Tuesday Mus. Club Young Artist Competition, 1956, 1st place award Young Artist Competition, Amarillo Symphony, 1959, 1st place award G.B. Dealey competition, Dallas Symphony and Dallas Morning News, 1959; scholar, U. Tex., Juilliard Sch. Music. Mem.: San Antonio Music Tchrs. Assn., Tex. Music Tchrs. Assn., Music Tchrs. Nat. Assn., Tuesday Musical Club (San Antonio, bd. dirs.), Pi Kappa Lambda, Sigma Alpha Iota. Presbyterian. Home and Office: 9118 E Valley View Ln San Antonio TX 78217-5160 E-mail: moppenheim@satx.rr.com.

OPPENHEIM, ROBERT, beauty industry executive; b. NYC, May 21, 1925; s. Hyman and Hannah (Lieberman) O.; m. Ruth Wigler, Feb. 7, 1954; children: Nancy Ellen, David Paul, Howard P. BS cum laude, Syracuse U., 1950. Product sales specialist McKesson & Robbins, Yonkers, NY, 1950-55; asst. sales mgr. Clairol, Inc., NYC, 1955-60, pres. Salon div., 1976-83, chmn. Profl. Products div., 1983-87; dir. mktg. Haircolor div. Revlon, Inc., NYC, 1960-68, dir. mktg. and sales Salon div., 1968-70; exec. v.p. Milton R. Barrie Co., Inc., 1970-71; pres. Oppenheim Communications, NYC, 1987—. Pub. Beauty Salon Newsletter, NYC, 1971—83, Salon Update, 1988—95, The Oppenheim Letter, 1988—95; mgmt. cons., 1988—; contbg. commentator Beauty Store Bus., 1998—2004, Profl. Beauty Mfr., 1998—99; bd. dirs. Cosmetology Advancement Found., 1995—98, Internat. Haircolor Exch., 1995—96. Author: 101 Salon Promotions, 1999. With AUS, 1942-44, ETO. Decorated Purple Heart; recipient Spirit of Life award City of Hope, 1989, Showman Wall of Fame award Internat. Beauty Show, 1994; inducted into Nat. Cosmetology Assn. Hall of Fame, 1994, Barber & Beauty Supply Inst. Hall of Leaders, 1998. Mem. Nat. Beauty and Barber Mfrs. Assn. (pres. 1984-85), Am. Beauty Assn. (pres. 1985-86), Masons. Address: 1755 York Ave # 22C New York NY 10128-6871 Office Phone: 212-600-1324.

OPPENHEIMER, BONNIE LOU, mathematics professor; b. Canton, Ohio, Dec. 2, 1955; d. Robert Earl and Elsie Marie (Rock) Sprankle; m. Seth F. Oppenheimer, Jan. 3, 1983; children: Albert Clark, Kathryn Rose. MusB and BS, Baldwin-Wallace Coll., Berea, Ohio, 1978; MA in Teaching, U. Chgo., 1979; MA, Miss. State U., 1991; PhD, U. Tex., 1992. Dept. chmn., tchr. math. Zion Benton Twp. HS, Ill., 1979-81; computer operator Interiors by Bruce, Park Ridge, Ill., 1981-82; tchr. Round Rock Ind. Sch. Dist., Tex., 1982-88; part-time faculty Austin C. C., Tex., 1985-88; tchr. Starkville HS, Miss., 1988—89, 1994—98; part-time faculty E. Miss. C. C., Mayhew, 1989, 1995—98; instr. math. Miss. State U., 1991, grad. teaching asst. in math., 1990-91; asst. prof. Delta State U., Cleveland, Miss., 1992-94; cons. Miss. State U. Tchr. Networking and Design Ctr., 1995—96; asst. prof. Miss. U. Women, Columbus, 1998—2003, assoc. prof., 2003—06, prof., 2006—. Prin. oboist Starkville Symphony Orch. Mem. AAUW (Woman of Achievement award, Miss. chpt., 2007), Nat. Coun. Tchrs. Math., Math. Assn. Am., Kappa Delta Pi, Pi Lambda Theta, Kappa Mu Epsilon, Phi Kappa Phi. Democrat. Jewish. Avocations: science fiction, needlecrafts. Home: 214 Hiwassee Dr Starkville MS 39759-2118 Office Phone: 662-329-7239. Business E-Mail: boppen@muw.edu.

OPPENHEIMER, DAVID GRAY, botanist, educator; s. Glen E. and Betty A. Oppenheimer; m. Paris Hannah Grey. BS, U. Minn., Twin Cities, 1982, PhD, 1987. Assoc. prof. biol. sciences U. Ala., Tuscaloosa, 1994—2003; assoc. prof. botany U. Fla., Gainesville, 2003—. Mem.: Japanese Soc. Plant Physiologists, Soc. for Devel. Biology, Genetics Soc. Am., Am. Soc. Plant Biologists, Am. Soc. for Cell Biology. Office: Univ Fla 1376 Mowry Rd Gainesville FL 32610 Office Phone: 352-273-8105.

OPPENHEIMER, FRANZ MARTIN, lawyer; b. Mainz, Germany, Sept. 7, 1919; s. Arnold and Johanna (Mayer) O.; m. Margaret Spencer Foote, June 17, 1944; children: Martin Foote, Roxana Foote, Edward Arnold. BS, U. Chgo., 1942; student, U. Grenoble, France, 1938-39; LL.B. cum laude (note editor Law Jour. 1945), Yale U., 1945. Bar: N.Y. 1946, D.C. 1955. Rsch. asst. com. human devel. U. Chgo., 1942-43; law clk. to Judge Swan, U.S. Circuit Ct. of Appeals, NY, 1945-46; assoc. atty. Chadbourne, Wallace, Parke & Whiteside, NYC, 1946-47; atty. IBRD, Washington, 1947-57; individual practice law, 1958-59; ptnr. firm Leva, Hawes, Symington, Martin & Oppenheimer, 1959-83, Fort & Schlefer, Washington, 1984-94; pvt. practice Washington, 1995—2001; sr. of counsel Swidler Berlin Shereff Friedman (formerly Swidler & Berlin), Washington, 1996—2001; individual consulting and law practice, 2001—; atty. Internat. legal Inst., 2004—. Contbr. articles to profl. and other jours, chpts. to books. Bd. dirs. Internat. Student House; founding mem. Company of Christian Jews. Decorated officer's cross Order of Merit (Fed. Republic Germany), chevalier Nat. Order of Merit (France). Mem. ABA, Am. Soc. Internat. Law (hon. v.p., treas. 1964-76), Coun. Fgn. Rels., Yale Club, Century Assn. (N.Y.), City Tavern, Met. Club (Washington). Anglican. Home: 3248 O St NW Washington DC 20007-2847 Personal E-mail: franzmfmo@aol.com.

OPPENHEIMER, MAX, JR., foreign language educator, consultant; b. NYC, July 27, 1917; s. Max and Louise (Pourfuerst) O.; m. Christine Backus, Oct. 14, 1942; children: Edmund Max, Carolyn Christine Oppenheimer Burns. Bachelier ès Lettres, U. Paris, 1935; BA cum laude, NYU, 1941; MA, UCLA, 1942; PhD, U. So. Calif., 1947. Instr. fgn. langs. San Diego State Coll., 1947-49; asst. prof. Romance langs. Washington U., St. Louis, 1949-51; assoc. prof. modern langs. Fla. State U., Tallahassee, 1958-61; prof., chmn. dept. Russian U. Iowa, Iowa City, 1961-67; prof. SUNY, Fredonia, 1967-76, prof. emeritus, 1976—, chmn. dept. fgn. langs., 1967-74; prof. English Yunnan Normal U., Kunming, Peoples Republic of China, 1985-86. Intelligence officer CIA, 1956—58. Author: Outline of Russian Grammar, 1962; translator: Theory of Molecular Excitons (Davydov), 1962, Theory of Ship Waves and Wave Resistance (Kostyukov), 1968, The Fake Astrologer (Calderón de la Barca), 1976, 94, The Lady Simpleton (Lope de Vega), 1976, Don Juan (Tirso de Molina), 1976, Swim First and Last, 1981, An Innocent Yank at Home Abroad, 2000, Is That What It Means?, 2004, Is That What It Means? II, 2007; contbr. articles to scholarly and profl. jours. Active YMCA, 1936—. Served to lt. col. M.I., AUS, 1942-46, 51-56, lt. col. Res. ret. Decorated Bronze Star; Fla. State U. grantee, 1961, Office Naval Rsch. grantee, 1965, SUNY grantee, 1973. Mem.: MLA, Am. Soc. Geolinguistics (pres. 1975—76), Nat. Order Battlefield Commns., Dobro Slovo, Am. Mensa Ltd., Mil. Officers Assn. Am., Am. Soc. Dowsers, Elks, Phi Beta Kappa, Alpha Mu Gamma, Pi Delta Phi (nat. pres. 1946—51), Sigma Delta Pi. Avocation: swimming. Home: 10963 W Coggins Dr Sun City AZ 85351-3346 Personal E-mail: maxojr@earthlink.net. *When you speak, always say what you think, not what you think you should say for the sake of expediency. Steadfastly, stubbornly, cling to your ideals, principles and beliefs, but be flexible enough to change whenever changing them reflects wisdom, not weakness or compromise. Avoid ego trips or being awed by your own alleged accomplishments.*

OPPENHEIMER, MICHAEL, physicist; b. Bklyn., Feb. 28, 1946; s. Harry and Shirley Oppenheimer; m. Leonie Haimson, Dec. 31, 1986; children: Chloe, Nathaniel. S.B., MIT, 1966; PhD, U. Chgo., 1970. Research fellow Harvard Coll., 1971-73; lectr. astronomy Harvard U., 1973-81; physicist Harvard-Smithsonian Center for Astrophysics, Harvard U., 1973-81, Environ. Def., NYC, 1981—2001, chief scientist, 1996-2001; Albert G. Milbank prof. geoscis. and internat. affairs Princeton U., 2002—, dir. program on sci. tech. and environ. Mem. panel on atmospheric effects of aviation NRC, 1995—99, mem. panel on climate variability and change, 2005—06; lead author Intergovernmental panel on climate change. Author: Dead Heat: The Race Against the Greenhouse Effect, 1990; contbr. articles to profl. jours. Fellow, Union Carbide, 1969—70, A.F. Morrison, 1979, Guggenheim, 1978—79; vis. scholar, Russell Sage Found., 2005—06. Mem.: AAAS, Internat. Glaciological Soc., Am. Meteorol. Soc., Am. Geophys. Union, Am. Phys. Soc. Office: Princeton U Robertson Hall 448 Princeton NJ 08544 Business E-Mail: michael@princeton.edu.

OPPENHEIMER, PAUL, literature educator, poet; b. NYC, May 1, 1939; s. Fred R. Oppenheimer and Gertrude Samuels; children: Julie Sarah, Ben. BA, Princeton U., 1961; MA, Columbia U., 1963, PhD, 1970. Lectr. Hunter Coll. CUNY, NYC, 1964-67, lectr., poet-in-residence City Coll., 1967-70, from asst. prof. to assoc. prof. City Coll., 1970-84, prof. City Coll., 1984—; prof. comparative lit. The Grad. Ctr./CUNY, 2001—. Exch. prof., dir. CUNY student exch. program Sorbonne nouvelle, Paris, 1984-85; exch. prof. U. North London, Eng., 1989-90, Univ. Coll. London German Dept., 1993, 95, 97, 99; Fulbright prof. U. Osnabrück, Germany, 1993-94. Author: Before a Battle and Other Poems, 1967, Beyond the Furies, 1985, The Birth of the Modern Mind: Self, Consciousness, and the Invention of the Sonnet, 1989, Evil and the Demonic: A New Theory of Monstrous Behavior, 1996, An Intelligent Person's Guide to Modern Guilt, 1997, Rubens: A Portrait, 1999, 2002, Blood Memoir, or the First Three

Days of Creation, 1999, Infinite Desire: A Guide to Modern Guilt, 2000, The Flame Charts, new poems, 2002; translator: Till Eulenspiegel: His Adventures, 1972, 4th edit., 2001. Woodrow Wilson fellow, 1961-62, Alfred Hodder fellow, 1969-70, Fulbright sr. fellow, Germany, 1993-94; recipient Eisner Scholars award Rifkind Ctr. for the Humanities, 1998. Mem. Dante Soc. Am. Home: 50 W 67th St New York NY 10023-6227 Office: CCNY Dept English and Comparative Lit NAC 138 St and Convent Ave New York NY 10031 Also: The Graduate Ctr CUNY Dept Comparative Lit 365 Fifth Ave New York NY 10016 Office Phone: 212-650-6322. Personal E-mail: pauloppenheimer@hotmail.com.

OPPENHEIMER, PETER, computer company executive; BA with honors, Calif. Polytechnic U.; MBA with honors, U. Santa Clara. Former mgr. info. tech. cons. practice Coopers and Lybrand; former CFO automatic data processing Apple Computer Inc., controller Americas, 1996—97, v.p. worldwide sales controller to corp. controller, 1997—2004; sr. v.p. fin., CFO Apple Inc. (formerly Apple Computer Inc.), 2004—. Office: Apple Inc 1 Infinite Loop Cupertino CA 95014 Office Phone: 408-996-1010. *

OPPENHEIMER, RANDOLPH CARL, lawyer; b. NYC, Feb. 5, 1954; s. Bennett and Sandra (Haber) O.; m. Cynthia Ellen Shatkin, June 19, 1976; children: Benjamin David, Adam Jeremy, Jacob Aaron, Jordan Michael, Daniel Corey. BA, U. Vt., 1976; JD, Case Western Res. U., 1979. Bar: N.Y. 1980, U.S. Dist. Ct. (we. dist.) N.Y. 1980, U.S. Dist. Ct. (no. dist.) N.y. 1995, U.S. Bankruptcy Ct. 1980, U.S. Ct. Appeals (2d cir.) 1981. Assoc. Kavinoky & Cook, Buffalo, 1979-84, ptnr., 1984—. Instr. legal research, writing and adv., Case Western Res. U., 1978-79. Assoc. editor Case Western Reserve Law Rev., 1977-79. Mem. ABA, N.Y. Bar Assn., Erie County Bar Assn. Home: 195 Greenaway Rd Buffalo NY 14226-4165 Office: Kavinoky Cook LLP 726 Exchange St Buffalo NY 14210 Office Phone: 716-845-6000. Business E-Mail: roppenheimer@kavinokycook.com.

OPPENHEIMER, RANDY (MARK RANDALL OPPENHEIMER), lawyer; b. Balt., 1952; AB summa cum laude, Harvard U., 1974; JD, U. Chgo., 1977. Bar: Calif. 1977. Ptnr., co-chair Entertainment, Sports, and Media practice O'Melveny & Myers LLP, LA. Mem.: ABA. Office: O'Melveny & Myers LLP 1999 Ave of Stars, 7th Fl Los Angeles CA 90067-6035 Office Phone: 310-246-6722. Office Fax: 310-246-6779. E-mail: roppenheimer@omm.com. *

OPPER, BARBARA NEGRI, financial economist; b. Torrington, Conn., Sept. 8, 1939; d. Albert Frederick and Anna (LaRocco) Negri; m. Franz Frederick Opper, Dec. 2, 1967 (dec. Mar. 1991); children: Gretchen Elizabeth, Stephen Frederick. BA, Conn. Coll., 1961; MA in Econs., U. Mich., 1965. Analyst Conn. Gen. Ins., Hartford, 1961-63; econ. rsch. assoc. Life Ins. Assn. Am., NYC, 1965-66; corp. sec., dir. Krambo Corp., NYC, 1966-67; from economist to sr. economist Fed. Res. Bd., Washington, 1967—76, sr. economist, 1976—83; fin. economist Travelers Ins. Cos., Hartford, 1972-76; lectr. Mt. Holyoke Coll., South Hadley, Mass., 1975-76; chief officer, sr. mgr., sr. advisor The World Bank, Washington, 1983—98; pres. ConFirm, Chevy Chase, Md., 1998—. Bd. dirs. Bank Fund Staff Fed. Credit Union, Washington, sec., 1999-2006; advisor sovereign debt mgmt. U.S. Treasury, Office of Tech. Assistance, Washington, 2000—. Contbr. articles to Fed. Res. Bull. Bd. dirs. Washington Bach Consort, 1998—2004, pres., 2002-04. Mem.: Cosmos Club, Phi Beta Kappa. Home: 7004 Meadow Ln Chevy Chase MD 20815

OPPERMAN, JOHN R., lawyer; b. Charles City, Iowa, May 31, 1953; s. H. Herschel and LaVora M. (Fick) O.; m. Julianne Elizabeth Radkowski, June 12, 1976; children: Paul D., Lucas J. BS in Govt., U. S.D., 1975; JD, Harvard U., 1978. Bar: Maine 1978, U.S. Dist. Ct. Maine 1978, U.S. Supreme Ct. 1981. Assoc. to ptnr. Perkins, Thompson, Hinckley & Keddy, Portland, 1978-83; sr. v.p., legal dept. mgr. Banknorth Group, Inc., Portland, Maine, 1998—2000, exec. v.p., dep. gen. counsel, legal dept. mgr., 2000—. Lectr., panelist legal and fin. seminars; instr. paralegal program U. So. Maine, Portland, 1986-87. Contbr. articles to profl. publs. Mem. Organizational com. Parkside Neighborhood Assn., Portland, 1979; del. Maine State Rep. Conv., Bangor, 1980; mem. adv. bd. Maine Alliance Arts Edn., Augusta, 1980-81; mem. govt. rels. com. Greater Portland United Way, 1980-83; trustee Ram Island Dance Ctr., Portland, 1980-81; trustee, advisor Portland Stage Co., 1981-91; mem. coun. 1st Luth. Ch., Portland, 1980-81, 88, pres., 1989-90; mem. City Mgrs.' Policy Adv. Com., Portland, 1987-94; trustee Portland Pub. Libr., 1997—; bd. dirs. Downtown Portland Corp., 1991—. Mem. ABA, Nat. Assn. Coll. and Univ. Attys., Maine State Bar Assn. (chmn. comml. law sect. 1992—), Maine Assn. Community Banks, Cumberland Club. Home: 25 Woodmont St Portland ME 04102-2708 Office: Banknorth Group Inc PO Box 9540 Portland ME 04112-9540 Office Phone: 207-761-8500. E-mail: jopperman@banknorth.com.

OPPERMAN, ROSANNA RESENDEZ, vice principal; b. LA, Apr. 06; d. Victor Thomas and Dolores Resendez Mendez; m. Daniel Charles Opperman, Aug. 3, 1974; children: Joshua Mendez, Timothy Mendez, Laura Mendez. BA in Exptl. Psychology, U. Calif., Santa Barbara, Calif., 1976; degree in Multiple Subject Tchg., Azusa Pacific Coll., 1979; MA in Ednl. Leadership, Calif. State U., Sacramento, 2005. Admin. Svcs. Credential Calif. State U., Sacramento, 2003. From instr. to coord. ABE Program Fremont Sch. for Adults, Sacramento, 1989—2002, coord. ESL Program, 2002—04, Wasc accreditation co-chair, 2002—03; from coord. to vice prin. Winterstein & Bella Vista Adult Ctrs., Sacramento, 2004—; chair Wasc, 2000. Awards chmn. no. sect. Calif. Coun. Adult Edn., Sacramento, 1997—99, pres. no. sect., 1999—2000, v.p. no. sect., 1999—2000. Cmty. adv. co-chair Fremont Sch. for Adults, Sacramento, 1999—2000; caravans dir. Nazarene Ch., Sacramento, 1988—94. Recipient Outstanding Leadership award, Calif. Coun. Adult Edn., 1997—2001, Excellence in Tchg. award, 1998. Mem.: Adult Basic Educators (assoc.), Calif. Assn. Tchrs. English to Spkrs. Other Langs. (assoc.). Office: Winterstein Adult Ctr 900 Morse Ave Sacramento CA 95864 Office Phone: 916-979-8521.

OPPERWALL, STEPHEN GABRIEL, lawyer; s. Raymond and Helen Bertha Opperwall; m. Kathleen O'Neill, Oct. 27, 1990; children: Christopher Stephen, Scott O'Neill. BA, Calvin Coll., 1975; JD, U. Santa Clara, 1981. Bar: Calif. 1981, U.S. Dist. Ct. (no., ea., ctrl. and so. dists.) Calif. 1981, U.S. Tax Ct. 1994, U.S. Ct. Appeals (9th cir.) 1984; cert. in creditor's rights, Am. Bd. Cert. Tchg. asst. U. Santa Clara (Calif.) Sch. Law, 1979; judge's law clk. U.S. Ct. Appeals, 9th Cir., San Francisco, 1980; assoc. Pitto & Ubhaus, San Jose, Calif., 1980-82, Germino, Layne & Brodie, Palo Alto, Calif., 1982-87, Tarkington, O'Connor & O'Neill, San Jose, 1988-90, Smith & Smith, San Jose, 1990-92; pvt. practice Law Offices of Stephen G. Opperwall, Pleasanton, Calif., 1992—. Judge pro tem Santa Clara County Cts., 1986—, Alameda County (Calif.) Cts., 1992-. Editor Santa Clara Law Review, 1980. Mem. bd. dirs. Fremont Symphony, 1994; meme. adv. bd. Fremont Bank, Calif., 1996. Mem. Coml. Law League Am., Pleasanton C. of C., Am. Bankruptcy Inst. Avocations: golf, tennis, computers, gardening, music. Office: 4900 Hopyard Rd Ste 100 Pleasanton CA 94588-3149 Office Phone: 925-417-0300. Office Fax: 925-417-0301. Business E-Mail: steve.opperwall@comcast.net. E-mail: lawofcsgo@aol.com.

OPRE, THOMAS EDWARD, retired editor, film company executive; b. Evansville, Ind., Nov. 6, 1943; s. William Jennings and Ruth (Strouss) O.; children: Thomas Andrew, William Hartley. AB in Journalism, Ind. U., 1965. Writer sports and outdoors Decatur (Ill.) Herald and Rev., 1965-66; outdoor editor Detroit Free Press, 1966—91; field editor Midwest div. Field and Stream mag., 1971-81; editorial dir. Gt. Lakes Sportsman mag., 1972-75; editor-at-large and sports vehicles editor Outdoor Life mag., 1981-93; pres. Tom Opre Prodns., 1967—2004. Pres. TOP Safaris, Inc., 1986—2004. Author numerous articles in outdoor and travel fields. Recipient James Henshall award Am. Fish Tackle Mfrs. Assn., 1969, Teddy award Internat. Outdoor Travel Film Festival, 1973, Environ. award EPA, 1977, Nat. Writer's award Safari Club Internat., 1977, Deep Woods Writing award OWAA, 1977, Conservation Service award Ducks Unltd., 1977; World Wildlife Found. award, 1981; named to Internat. Fishing Hall of Fame, 1968, Conservation Communicator of Yr., 1985. Mem. Outdoor Writers Assn. Am. (past dir., pres., v.p., chmn. bd.), Assn. Gt. Lakes Outdoor Writers (past dir., chmn. bd., pres., v.p.), Mich. Outdoor Writers Assn. (v.p., pres., chmn. bd. dirs.), Alpha Tau Omega. Home and Office: 255 Powers Cv NE Marietta GA 30067-1503 Personal E-mail: topsafaris@aol.com.

OPREA, DRAGOS, mathematician, educator; s. Decebal and Maria Oprea. AB, Harvard U., Cambridge, Mass., 1996—2000; PhD, MIT, Cambridge, 2000—05. Samuelson fellow Stanford U., Palo Alto, Calif., 2005—06, szego asst. prof., 2006—.

OPRIESSNIG, TANJA, veterinary pathologist; d. Gerd and Ilse Opriessnig. M in Vet. Medicine, U. Vet. M in Vet. Medicine, D in Vet. Medicine, U. Vet. Medicine, Vienna; PhD, Iowa State U., Ames. Post doctoral rsch. assoc. Iowa State U., Ames, asst. prof., 2006—. Office: Iowa State University 1600 S 16th St Ames IA 50011-1250

OPRSAL, NANCY UPSHAW, retired elementary school educator; b. Dallas, Tex., July 10, 1931; d. Banks and Catherine Richards (Butler) Upshaw; m. George Oprsal, Apr. 23, 1957 (dec.); 1 child, Paul Oprsal (dec.). BS in elem. edn., No. Tex. State U., 1952; MA in edn., George Peabody Coll. for Teachers, 1953. Pre-sch. music tchr. Greenhill Sch., Dallas, 1948—53; tchr. Denver Pub. Schools, 1953—55; music tchr. Ft. Worth Pub. Schools, Tex., 1955—57; tchr. Dallas Ind. Sch. Dist., 1957—60, Del Paso Heights Sch. Dist., Sacramento, 1960—62, San Juan Sch. Dist., Sacramento, 1966—96; ret. Server Loaves and Fishes; ch. sch. tchr. Unitarian Universalist Soc. of Sacramento, 1960—; receptionist and docent Effie Yeaw Nature Ctr., Carmichael, Calif., 1980—; sec. Carmichael Garden Club, 1962—66; coord. Family Promise Interfaith Hospitality Network, 2004—. Democrat. Unitarian. Avocations: gardening, hiking. Home: 6235 Vernon Way Carmichael CA 95608 Personal E-mail: noprsal@aol.com.

O'QUINN, APRIL GALE, obstetrician, gynecologist, educator; b. Columbia, Miss., Apr. 21, 1936; d. R.V. and Anna Pauline (Cook) O'Q. Diploma, Scott and White Sch. Nursing, 1965; AA, Temple Jr. Coll., 1965; BS with honors, Baylor U., 1968; MD, U. Tex. Med. Br., 1971. Diplomate Am. Bd. Ob-Gyn. Intern U. Tex. Med. Br., Galveston, 1971-72, resident ob-gyn., 1972-75; fellow in oncology M.D. Anderson Hosp., Houston, 1976-78; practice medicine specializing in ob-gyn. Galveston, 1978-81, New Orleans, 1981—. Asst. prof. dept. ob-gyn. U. Tex. Med. Br., Galveston, 1975—81; mem. staff John Sealy Hosp., St. Mary's Hosp., Galveston, Tulane Med. Ctr., New Orleans Charity Hosp., Touro Infirmary, New Orleans; assoc. prof., dir. div. gynecol. oncology dept. ob-gyn. Tulane U. Sch. Medicine, New Orleans, 1981—85, prof., 1985—89, prof., chair dept. ob-gyn., 1989—. Fellow: ACOG, Willard R. Cooke Obstet. and Gynecol. Soc.; mem.: AMA, La. Med. Assn., Assn. Profs. in Ob-Gyn., Coun. Univ. Chmn. in Ob-Gyn., Soc. Gynecologic Oncologists, Felix Rutledge Soc. Orleans Parish. Republican. Baptist. Office: Tulane U Sch Medicine Dept Ob Gyn New Orleans LA 70112 E-mail: aoquinn@tulane.edu.

O'QUINN, JOHN M., lawyer; b. 1941; BS, U. Houston, 1965, JD magna cum laude, 1967. Bar: Tex. 1967, US Supreme Ct. 1972, US Ct. Appeals (5th cir.) 1984, US Dist. Ct. (so. and ea. dists. Tex.) 1986. Founding ptnr. O'Quinn, Kerensky, McAninch & Laminack, Houston, 1981—. Mem. adv. com. Tex. State Supreme Ct., 1984-94; trustee U. Houston Law Found., 1985—; adj prof. law, U. Houston, So. Tex. Coll. Law, Tex. So. Coll. Law. Regent U. Houston, 1993-99. Named one of Top 10 Trial Lawyers in Am., Nat. Law Jour., 1993, 2004, 100 Most Influential Lawyers in US, 1994, 100 Legal Legends of Tex., Tex. Lawyer, 5 Best Tex. Trial Lawyers of the Century, Houston Chronicle. Am. Trial Lawyers Assn., Tex. Trial Lawyers Assn. (dir.), Houston Trial Lawyers Assn. (dir.), Houston Bar Assn., State Bar Tex., U. Houston Law Alumni Assn. (pres. 1978). Office: O'Quinn Law Firm 2300 Lyric Ctr Bldg 440 Louisiana St Houston TX 77002-1639 Office Phone: 713-223-1000. Office Fax: 713-222-6903. *

O'QUINN, TERRY (TERRANCE QUINN), actor; b. Newberry, Mich., July 15, 1952; m. Laurie O'Quinn; 2 children. Grad., Iowa Univ., Ctrl. Mich. Univ. Actor: (TV films) FDR: The Last Year, 1980, Right to Kill, 1985, An Early Frost, 1985, Women of Valor, 1986, Between Two Women, 1986, A Mother's Request, 1987, When the Time Comes, 1987, Stranger on My Land, 1988, Guts and Glory, 1989, Roe vs. Wade, 1989, Kaleidoscope, 1990, Perry Mason: The Case of the Desperate Deception, 1990, The Last to Go, 1991, Son of the Morning Star 1991, Shoot First, 1991, Deliver Them from Evil, 1992, Trial, 1992, Sexual Advances, 1992, Wild Car, 1992, The Good Fight, 1992, Born Too Soon, 1993, Visions of Murder, 1993, MacShayne: Winner Takes All, 1994, Heart of a Child, 1994, Don't Talk to Strangers, 1994, Justice in a Small Town, 1994, A Friend to Die For, 1994, Ray Alexander: A Menu for Murder, 1995, On the Edge of Innocence, 1997, My Stepson, My Lover, 1997, Murder in a Small Town, 1999, Harsh Realm, 1999, Semper Fi, 2001, WW3, 2001, Hometown Legend, 2002, The Locket, 2002, Phenomenon II, 2003; (films) Heaven's Gate, 1980, Without a Trace, 1983, All the Right Moves, 1983, Places in the Heart, 1984, Mrs. Soffel, 1984, Mischief, 1985, Silver Bullet, 1985, Space Camp, 1986, The Stepfather, 1987, Black Widow, 1987, Pin, 1988, Jogger, 1988, Young Guns, 1988, Blind Fury, 1989, Stepfather II, 1989, The Forgotten One, 1990, Prisoners of the Sun, 1990, The Rocketeer, 1991, Company Business, 1991, My Samurai, 1992, The Cutting Edge, 1992, Tombstone, 1993, Lipstick Camera, 1994, Shadow Warriors, 1996, Primal Fear, 1996, Ghosts of Mississippi, 1996, Shadow Conspiracy, 1997, Breast Men, 1997, Rated X, 2000; (TV series) The Doctors, 1981, The X Files, 1998, JAG, 2000-2002, Alias, 2003-2004, The West Wing, 2004, Lost, 2004- (Outstanding Performance by an Ensemble in a Drama Series, Screen Actors Guild award, 2006); numerous TV series guest appearances. Mailing: care Touchstone TV Prodn Bldg #343 500 S Buena Vista Burbank CA 91521

ORAM, FERN AMY, editor-in-chief, director; b. Phila., May 19, 1965; d. Linda Shirley and Stuart Jerome Oram; m. David Adam Riegelhaupt, Oct. 5, 2002. Listings editor TVSM, Horsham, Pa., 1986—87, listings mgr., 1987—97, listings dir., 1997—99; prodn. mgr. Thomson Peterson's, Lawrenceville, Pa., 1999—2003, editl. dir., 2003—. Mem.: So. Poverty Law Ctr., Eta Theta Chpt. of Kappa Delta at Villanova U. (chair 2004—06, chpt. adv. bd.), Phila. Suburban West Alumna Assn. of Kappa Delta (pres. 1997—2004), Kappa Delta. Office: Thomson Petersons 2000 Lenox Dr Lawrenceville NJ 08648 Home: 707 Manton St Philadelphia PA 19147-5117 Home Phone: 215-784-9315; Office Phone: 800-338-3282. Personal E-mail: thinkpink@zdial.com. Business E-Mail: fern.oram@petersons.com.

ORAM, ROBERT W., library administrator; b. Warsaw, Ind., June 11, 1922; s. George Harry and Lottie Mae (Gresso) O.; m. Virginia White, June 16, 1949; 1 child, Richard W. BA, U. Toledo, 1949; MS in Library Adminstrn., U. Ill., 1950. Asst. to librarian U. Mo.-Columbia, 1950-56; circulation librarian U. Ill.-Urbana, 1956-67, dir. pub. service, 1968-71, assoc. univ. librarian, 1971-79, acting univ. librarian, 1975-76; dir. Central Univ. Libraries So. Meth. U., Dallas, 1979-89, dir. emeritus, 1989. Mem. adv. com. Ill. State Library, Springfield, 1975-79 Contbr. articles to profl. jours. Exec. sec. Friends of So. Meth. U. Librs., 1980-89; former mem. bd. dirs. Urbana Free Libr., Lincoln Trails Libr. Sys., Champaign, Ill.; trustee Friends Austin (Tex.) Pub. Libr., 1994-99. Mem. ALA (life, pub. com. 1975-79), Friends of Libraries U.S.A. (exec. bd. 1980-86), Ill. Library Assn. (treas. 1972-73), Democrat. Avocations: reading, music. Home: The Heritage 4409 Gaines Ranch Loop # 252 Austin TX 78735 E-mail: Roam1@austin.rr.com.

ORAN, ELAINE SURICK, physicist; b. Rome, Ga., Apr. 16, 1946; d. Herman E. and Bessye R. (Kolker) Surick; m. Daniel Hirsh Oran, Feb. 1, 1969. AB in Physics and Chemistry, Bryn Mawr Coll., 1966; MPh in Physics, Yale U., 1968, PhD in Solid State Physics and Statistical Mechanics, 1972; Doctorate (hon.), Ecole Ctrl. Lyon, France, 2006. Rsch. physicist Naval Rsch. Lab., Washington, 1972-76, supervisory rsch. physicist, 1976-88, sr. scientist reactive flow physics, 1988—. Head Ctr. for Reactive Flow and Dynamical Systems, 1985-87; mem. adv. bd. NSF; cons. to U.S. govt., agys., NATO.; mem. Aero. Adv. Coun. NASA, 1995-97; adj. prof. dept. aerospace engring. U. Mich., 2005—. Author: Numerical Simulation of Reactive Flow, 1987, 2d edit., 2001, Numerical Approaches to Combustion Modeling, 1991; assoc. editor Jour. Computational Physics, 1992-2002; mem. editl. bd. Prog. Ener. Comb. Sci., 1990-2005; mng. editor Shock Waves, 1998-2002; editor-in-chief AIAA Jour., 2003-; contbr. numerous articles to profl. jours., chpts. to books. Named hon. prof., U. Wales, 2001—05; named to Hall of Fame, Women in Tech. Internat., 2002; recipient Arthur S. Flemming award, 1979, Women in Sci. and Engring. award, 1988, Oppenheim prize, 1999, Zeldovich Gold medal, 2000; grantee, USN, NASA, USAF, Def. Advanced Rsch. Projects Agy. Fellow AIAA (publs. com. 1986-2002, v.p. publs. 1993-97, Dryden Disting. lectr. 2002, editor-in-chief AIAA Jour.), Am. Phys. Soc. (exec. com. fluid dynamics divsn. 1986, 96, exec. com. computational physics 1989-97, chair 1991-92); mem. NAE, Am. Geophys. Union, Combustion Inst. (bd. dirs. 1990-2002), Inst. Dynamics of Energetic Sys. (bd. dirs. 1989—, pres.), Soc. Indsl. and Applied Math., Soc. Women Engrs.(Achievement award 2006), Sigma Xi. Office: Naval Rsch Lab Code 6404 6004 Washington DC 20375 Office Phone: 202-767-2960. Business E-Mail: oran@lcp.nrl.navy.mil.

O'RANGERS, ELEANOR ANN, medical education company executive; d. John Joseph and Eleanor Mary O'Rangers. PharmD, U. Md., Balt., 1990. Cardiovasc. pharmacology rsch. fellow U. Conn., Hartford Hosp., Conn., 1990—92; cardiovasc. pharmacotherapeutic specialist Veterans Affairs Med. Ctr., Balt., 1992—94; med. svcs. mgr. Bristol-Myers Squibb, Princeton, NJ, 1995—97, Parke-Davis, Morris Plains, NJ, 1997—2000; dir. med. affairs AstraZeneca LP, Wilmington, Del., 2000—05; v.p. cardiovasc. & metabolic brand strategist Phase Five Comm., Inc., NYC, 2005—. Docent Nat. Air & Space Museum, DC, 1995—.

ORANSKY, IVAN, writer, editor; b. Nyack, NY, Aug. 20, 1972; s. Stanley Howard and Lesley Marsha Oransky. BA, Harvard U., 1994; MD, NYU, 1998. Editor-in-chief Praxis Post, NYC, 2000—02; web editl. dir. The Scientist, Phila., 2002—04, dep. editor, 2004—. Adj. asst. prof. journalism NYU, NYC, 2002—, clin. asst. prof. medicine, 2005—; adj. asst. prof. journalism CUNY, 2007—. Author: Insider's Guide to Medical Schools, 1999, Appleton & Lange's Review of Psychiatry, 6th edit., 2001, 9th edit., 2007, Common Symptom Answer Guide, 2005; contbr. The Lancet. Mem.: Online News Assn., Assn. for Health Care Journalists (bd. dirs. 2002—), Am. Soc. Bioethics and Humanities, Nat. Assn. Sci. Writers. Personal E-mail: ivan-oransky@erols.com.

ORATZ, RUTH, physician; d. Murray and Rosalyn Oratz; m. Hank B. Ridless, Nov. 1, 1993. AB in History and Philosophy of Sci., Harvard U., 1977; MD, Albert Einstein Coll. Medicine, 1982. Diplomate in internal medicine and med. oncology Am. Bd. Internal Medicine. Assoc. prof. clin. medicine NYU Sch. Medicine, NYC, 1997—. Mem. adv. bd. breastcancer.org, cancerandcareers, sharsheret. Named Physician of Yr., Cancer Care, 2005. Fellow: ACP; mem.: Am. Assn. for Cancer Rsch., Am. Soc. Clin. Oncologists. Office: Womens Oncology and Wellness Practice Ste 202 345 E 37th St New York NY 10016 Office Phone: 212-400-4904. E-mail: contact@thewomenspractice.org.

ORBACH, RAYMOND LEE, federal agency administrator, physicist, researcher; b. LA, July 12, 1934; s. Morris Albert and Mary Ruth (Miller) O.; m. Eva Hannah Spiegler, Aug. 26, 1956; children: David Miller, Deborah Hedwig, Thomas Randolph. BS, Calif. Inst. Tech., Pasadena, 1956; PhD, U. Calif., Berkeley, 1960; PhD in Policy Analysis (hon.), The Rand Grad. Sch., Santa Monica, Calif., 2002; PhD in Engring. (hon.), Colo. Sch. Mines, Goldon, 2005. NSF postdoctoral fellow Oxford U., 1960-61; asst. prof. applied physics Harvard U., 1961-63; prof. physics UCLA, 1963-92, asst. vice chancellor acad. change and curriculum devel., 1970-72, chmn. acad. senate L.A. divsn., 1976-77, provost Coll. Letters and Sci., 1982-92; chancellor U. Calif., Riverside, 1992—2002, chancellor emeritus, Disting. prof. physics emeritus, 2002—; dir. Office Sci. US Dept. Energy, Washington, 2002—, under sec. for sci., 2006—. Mem. physics adv. panel NSF, 1970-73; mem. vis. com. Brookhaven Nat. Lab., 1970-74; mem. materials rsch. lab. adv. panel NSF, 1974-77; mem. Nat. Commn. on Rsch., 1978-80; chmn. 16th Internat. Conf. on Low Temperature Physics, 1981; Joliot Curie prof. Ecole Superieure de la Physique et Chimie Industrielle de la Ville de Paris, 1982, chmn. Gordon Rsch. Conf. on Fractals, 1986; Lorentz prof. U. Leiden, Netherlands, 1987; Raymond and Beverly Sackler lectr. Tel Aviv U., 1989; faculty rsch. lectr. UCLA, 1990; Andrew Lawson lectr. U. Calif., Riverside, 1992; mem. external rev. com. Nat. High Magnetic Fields Lab., 1994-01. Author: (with A.A. Manenkov) SpinLattice Relaxation in Ionic Solids, 1966; divsn. assoc. editor Phys. Rev. Letters, 1980-83, Jour. Low Temperature Physics, 1980-90, Phys. Rev., 1983-87; contbr. articles to profl. jours. Recipient Whitney M. Young Humanitarian award Urban League of Riverside and San Bernardino, 1998, El Sol Azteca award La Prensa Hispana, 2000, Disting. Alumni award Calif. Inst. Tech., 2005; Alfred P. Sloan Found. fellow, 1963-67; NSF sr. postdoctoral fellow Imperial Coll., 1967-68; Guggenheim fellow Tel Aviv U., 1973-74. Fellow AAAS (chairperson steering group physics sect.), Am. Phys. Soc. (chmn. nominations com. 1981-82, counselor-at-large 1987-91, chmn. divsn. condensed matter 1990-91); mem. NSF (mem. rsch. adv. com. divsn. materials 1992-93), Phys. Soc. (London), Univ. Rsch. Assn. (chair coun. pres. 1993), Sigma Xi, Phi Beta Kappa, Tau Beta Pi. Office: US Dept Energy 1000 Independence Ave SW Washington DC 20585 Office Phone: 202-586-0505. Personal E-mail: rorbach@earthlink.net. Business E-Mail: ray.orbach@hq.doe.gov.

ORBEN, JACK RICHARD, investment company executive, director; b. Bklyn., June 16, 1938; s. Stanley Souza and Helena Emily (Hall) O.; m. Patricia Wells, Dec. 17, 1960; children: Stacey Souza, Stephanie Anne, Bradford Richard. AA, Valley Forge, Pa., 1956; BA, Tufts U., Medford, Mass., 1960. Sales mgr. nat. accts. NY Tel. Co., 1960—66; founder, exec. v.p. Facts, Inc., 1966—69; chmn., CEO Fiduciary Alliance, Inc., NYC, 1970—; chmn. Oaktree Asset Mgmt., LLC, NYC, 2004—05. Chmn., CEO, pres. Fiduciary Counsel, Inc., 1979-04; chmn. White Plains Charter Revision Commn.; fin. com. City of White Plains; past pres. White Plains Child Day Care Assn., Thomas Slater Ctr.; past chmn., bd. dirs. YMCA Ctrl. and No. Westchester Sec., treas., bd. dirs., Indsl. Devel. Agy. Town of Riverhead, NY. With USNG, 1960-66. Mem. Investment Advisors Assn., Am. Inst. Econ. Rsch., Larchmont Yacht Club, NY Yacht Club, Union League Club, Windemere Island Club, Univ. Club, Down Town Assn., The

Econ. Club of NY, Inst. for Pvt. Investors, Fgn. Policy Rsch. Inst., The Pilgrims. Home: 61 Harbor Rd Riverhead NY 11901 Office Phone: 631-722-5649. Personal E-mail: jrorben@aol.com.

ORBEN, ROBERT, scriptwriter, writer; b. NYC, Mar. 4, 1927; s. Walter August and Marie O.; m. Jean Louise Connelly, July 25, 1945. Humor and speech writer for entertainment personalities, bus. execs., politicians, 1946—; writer Jack Paar Show, NYC, 1962-63, Red Skelton Hour, Hollywood, Calif., 1964-70; editor Orben's Current Comedy, Wilmington, Del., 1971-89; cons. to Vice Pres. Gerald R. Ford, Washington, 1974; speechwriter Pres. Gerald R. Ford, Washington, 1974-75; spl. asst. to pres., dir. White House speechwriting dept., Washington, 1976-77; speaker on uses of humor in communication, 1977—. Author: 2500 Jokes to Start 'Em Laughing, 1979, 2100 Laughs for All Occasions, 1983, 2400 Jokes to Brighten Your Speeches, 1984, 2000 Sure-Fire Jokes for Speakers, 1986, Speechwriter's Handbook of Humor, 2007, others. Recipient World Humor award Workshop Libr. on World Humor, 1992, Humor award Gliner Humor Ctr., U. Md., 2005; Literary fellow Acad. Magical Arts, 1996. Mem. Writers Guild Am. Clubs: Nat. Press (Washington). Unitarian Universalist. Avocations: travel, theater. Home: 3709 S George Mason Dr Apt 205E Falls Church VA 22041-3700 *I have spent most of my lifetime creating laughter and consider it a lifetime well spent. Laughter is one of the glories of the human experience. It warms, amuses, instructs, and opens emotional doors. For me, laughter has been a living and a loving as well.*

ORBISON, JAMES ARCHER, JR., cardiologist, surgeon; b. Dryden, Mich., Aug. 22, 1914; s. James Archer Sr. and Florence (Thomas) Orbison; m. Pil-Sook Lee Orbison, Nov. 7, 1988; m. Helen Alice Bentley (dec.); children: Carole Ann Seeley, James Archer Obison III. Student, U. Denver, 1933—34; BA, U. Mich., 1937, MD, 1940. Diplomate Am. Bd. Internal Medicine, Am. Bd. Cardiovascular Disease, lic. physician Hawaii, Mich. Intern Harper Hosp., 1940—41; commd. 2d lt. US Army, 1941, advanced through grades to col., 1968; resident in internal medicine Oliver Gen. Hosp., Augusta, Ga., 1947—49; asst. prof. clinical medicine Med. Coll. Ga., Augusta, 1949—50; fellow in cardiovascular disease Walter Reed Gen. Hosp., Washington, 1951—52; asst. clin. prof. medicine U. Colo. Sch. Medicine, Denver, 1960—64; cons. tchg. internal medicine Queen's Med. Ctr., Honolulu, 1964—67, attending staff, 1970—88; assoc. clin. prof. medicine U. Hawaii Sch. Medicine, 1967—; assoc. clin. prof. John Burns Sch. Medicine, Honolulu, 1967—88. Presenter in field. Contbr. articles to profl. jours. Decorated Commendation medal US Army, Legion of Merit, Am. Def. medal; recipient Cardiology Laureate award, Hawaii Heart Assn., 1988; grantee, US Army R & D Command, 1959. Fellow: Am. Coll. Cardiology (program com. annual meeting 1962, Hawaii gov. 1971—74); mem.: ACP (life; program com. Colo. regional meeting 1960—64, program com. annual meeting 1963, program com. Hawaii regional meeting 1964), Hawaii Med. Soc. (med. edn. com. 1971—, chronic illness com. 1972—), Assn. for Hosp. Med. Edn., Am. Soc. Clinical Pharmacology and Therapeutics, Am. Fedn. Clin. Rsch. (sr.), Honolulu County Med. Soc. (postgrad. com. 1970—), Hawaii Heart Assn. (bd. dirs. 1964—, 2d v.p. 1972—73, exec. com. 1972—, pres.-elect 1973—). Republican. Presbyterian. Avocations: fishing, tennis, golf, photography, football.

ORBIT, WILLIAM (WILLIAM WAINWRIGHT), record producer; b. Eng., 1959; Hit records include Torch Song Wish Thing, 1984, Ecstasy, 1985, Exhibit A, 1987, Toward the Unknown Region, 1995, William Orbit, Orbit, 1987, Strange Cargo, 1984-87, Strange Cargo 2, 1990, Strange Cargo 3, 1993, Strange Cargo Hinterland, 1995, William Orbit The Best of Strange Cargos, 1996, The Electric Chamber Places in a Modern Style, 1995, Beth Orton Superpinkymandy, 1993, Caroline Lavelle Spirit, 1995, Bassomatic Set the Controls for the Heart of the Bass, 1990, and Science and Melody, 1997, Belinda Carlisle Belinda, 1986, Madonna Ray of Light (album, 1999 Grammy winner for best prodn.), 1998, Wishbone Ash Nouveau Calls, 1998, various Guerrilla Grooves Volume 1, 1991. TV and movie appearances include Rebellious Jukebox, 1983-84, Bachelor Party, 1984, Youngblood, 1986, Texas Chainsaw Massacre 2, 1986, Hot Shot, 1987, Heat, 1996, and Harald, 1997, Pieces in a Modern Style, 2000.

ORCE, KENNETH W., lawyer; b. Yonkers, NY, Apr. 3, 1943; s. Edmund John and Helen (Mulcahy) Orce; m. Helene Mary Sparti, Aug. 20, 1966; children: Kenneth W., Kimberley J., Brian C. BS with honors, Manhattan Coll., 1965; LLB cum laude, Harvard U., 1968. Bar: NY 1969. Assoc. Cahill Gordon & Reindel LLP, NYC, 1968—76, ptnr., 1976—91, mem. exec. com., 1991—. Editor: Harvard Law Rev., 1966—68. Mem.: Down Town Assn., Hudson Nat. Golf Club, Met. Opera Club, Scarsdale Golf Club. Office: Cahill Gordon & Reindel LLP 80 Pine St Fl 17 New York NY 10005-1702 Office Phone: 212-701-3215. Office Fax: 212-378-2324. Business E-Mail: korce@cahill.com.

ORCHARD, ROBERT JOHN, theater producer, educator; b. Maplewood, NJ, Dec. 3, 1946; s. Robert Orchard and Beatrice (Gould) Todd; m. Pamela Marcy Pritchard, Sept. 6, 1969; children: Christopher, Katherine. Student, The Lawrence Acad., 1965; BA, Middlebury Coll., 1969; MFA, Yale U., 1972. Gen. mgr. Peterborough (N.H.) Players, 1967-70; asst. mng. dir. Yale Repertory Theatre, 1971-72, artistic admistr., 1972-73; instr. Yale Sch. Drama, 1972-73; mng. dir. Yale Repertory Theatre and Sch. Drama, 1973-79, Am. Repertory Theatre, Cambridge, Mass., 1979—2002, exec. dir., 2002—. Assoc. prof., co-chmn. theatre adminstrn. tng. program Yale Sch. Drama, 1975-79; mng. dir. Loeb Drama Ctr., Harvard U., 1979-2000, dir., 2000—, mng. dir. Inst. for Advanced Theatre Tng., 1979-2002, exec. dir., 2002—; orgn. ptnr. Inst. Arts and Civic Dialogue at Harvard U. Former mem. bd. dirs. Theatre Comms. Group; pres. bd. Mass. Cultural Edn. Collaborative, Am. Arts Alliance, Peterborough Players, Cambridge Multi-Cultural Arts Ctrs.; former exec. com. League of Residents Theatres; chmn. NEA, Profl. Theatre Cos., Opera/Mus. Theatre Panels. Office: Am Repertory Theatre 64 Brattle St Cambridge MA 02138-3443

ORCUTT, BEN AVIS, retired social work educator; b. Falco, Ala., Oct. 17, 1914; d. Benjamin A. and Emily Olive Adams; m. Harry P. Orcutt, 1946 (dec.). AB, U. Ala., 1936; MA, Tulane U., 1939, MSW, 1942; DSW, Columbia U., 1962. Social worker ARC, Lagarde Gen. Hosp., New Orleans; social worker, acting field dir. Fort Benning (Ga.) Regional Hosp., 1942-46; chief social work svc. VA Regional Office, Phoenix, 1946—51; chief social work svc. unit outpatient office VA, Birmingham, Ala., 1954-57, 58; rsch. asst. Rsch. Ctr. Sch. Social Work, Columbia U., NYC, 1960-62, field advisor social work, 1962, assoc. prof. social work, 1965-76, La. State U., Baton Rouge, 1962-65; prof. social work, dir. doctoral program U. Ala., University, 1976-84; ret. Rsch. cons. Tavistock Centre, London, 1972; cons. sch. social work U. Houston, 1990, Troy State System, 1992. Author: Science and Inquiry in Social Work Practice, 1990, (with Harry P. Orcutt) America's Riding Horses, 1958, (with Elizabeth R. Prichard, Jean Collard, Austin H. Kutscher, Irene Seeland, Nathan Lefkowitz) Social Work with the Dying Patient and the Family, 1977, (with others) Social Work and Thanatology, 1980; editor: Poverty and Social Casework Services, 1974; mem. editl. bd. Jour. Social Work, 1982-84; contbr. articles to profl. books and jours. Mem. alumni bd. Sch. Social Work Columbia U., 1985—88, 1991—94. Recipient Centennial award for edn. Columbia U. Sch. Social Work, 1998; named to Ala. Social Work Hall of Fame, 1999; NIMH fellow, 1957-60; Ben Avis Adams Orcutt doctoral scholar in social work named in her honor, U. Ala. Mem. Group for Advancement Doctoral Edn. (steering com., editor newsletter 1980-83). Episcopalian. Office: PO Box 870314 Tuscaloosa AL 35487-0314 Home: 1199 Valley View Dr Andalusia AL 36424

ORDAL, CASPAR REUBEN, retired executive; b. Martell, Wis., May 5, 1922; s. Zakarias John and Sina Carlovna (Wulfsberg) O.; m. Ann Elizabeth Brady, June 7, 1947; Christopher Rolf, Peter Stuart. BS, Harvard Coll., 1946; M.P.A., Harvard U., 1947. Supr. central indsl. relations staff Ford Motor Co., Dearborn, Mich., 1947-53; dir. orgn. planning and mgmt. devel. Colgate-Palmolive Co., NYC, 1953-65; v.p., gen. mgr. New Holland div. Sperry Rand Corp., (Pa.), 1965-76; corp. v.p. personnel Norton Simon Inc., NYC, 1976-78; sr. v.p. adminstrn. Max Factor & Co., Hollywood, Calif., 1978-85. Served to 1st lt. USAAF, 1943-46. Mem. Personnel Round Table (chmn. 1983-84), Am. Mgmt. Assn. (adv. coun. 1977-82), Lancaster (Pa.) Country Club, Phi Beta Kappa. Lutheran.

ORDEN, STEWART L., lawyer; b. NYC, Jan. 13, 1953; s. Charles Quigley and Esther (Ash) O.; m. Bonnie Lynn Raymond, Nov. 12, 1988; children: Molly, Justin, Tyler. BA, Clark U., 1975; JD, Bklyn. Law Sch. Biology, 1979. Bar: N.Y. 1979. Sr. trial atty. Kings Dist. Atty., Bklyn., 1979-87; ptnr. Orden & Cohen, NYC, 1987-91; pvt. practice, NYC, 1991—. Expert witness on trial techniques, complex personal injury, med. malpractice, comml. and white collar cases; won largest pub. settlement against NYC in discrimination case; profiled on 60 Minutes. Mem. N.Y. Coun. Def. Lawyers, Assn. Bar City N.Y., N.Y. Criminal Bar Assn., Nat. Assn. Def. Lawyers. Avocations: skiing, windsurfing, swimming, roller-blading, biking.

ORDIN, ANDREA SHERIDAN, lawyer; m. Robert Ordin; 1 child, M. Victoria; stepchildren: Allison, Richard. AB, UCLA, 1962, LLB, 1965. Bar: Calif. 1966. Dep. atty. gen. Calif., 1965-72; So. Calif. legal counsel Fair Employment Practices Commn., 1972-73; asst. dist. atty. L.A. County, 1975-77; U.S. atty. Central Dist. Calif. LA, 1977-81; adj. prof. UCLA Law Sch., 1982; chief asst. atty. gen. Calif. LA, 1983-90; sr. counsel Morgan, Lewis & Bockius, LA, 1993—. Mem. L.A. County Bar Assn. (past pres., past exec. dir.). Office: Morgan Lewis & Bockius 300 S Grand Ave Ste 2200 Los Angeles CA 90071-3109 Office Phone: 213-612-1090. Business E-Mail: aordin@morganlewis.com.

ORDOG, TAMAS, research scientist, educator; b. Nagykanizsa, Hungary, Feb. 8, 1964; arrived in U.S., 1992; s. Ferenc Ordog and Julianna Domjan; m. Katalin Malek; 1 child, Norbert. MD, U. Pecs, Hungary, 1988. Rsch. fellow neurophysiology rsch. group Hungarian Acad. Scis., Pecs, 1989—92; rsch. fellow U. Tex.-Houston Health Sci. Ctr., 1992—95, sr. rsch. fellow, 1995—97; rsch. asst. prof. U. Nev. Reno Sch. Medicine, 1997—2003, asst. prof., 2003—06; assoc. prof. Mayo Clinic Coll. Medicine, Rochester, Minn., 2006—. Contbr. articles to profl. jours. Recipient Young Investigator award, Am. Motility Soc., 2000, 2002, Alvarez award, Internat. Electrogastrography Soc., 2005; grantee, Am. Motility Soc. and Janssen Pharmaceutica, 2002—03, NIH, 2002—; scholar, Republic of Hungary, 1984—88; Rsch. fellow, Hungarian Acad. Scis., 1989—91. Mem.: AAAS, Am. Neurogastroenterology and Motility Soc., Am. Gastroenterol. Assn., The Endocrine Soc. Achievements include research in neuroendocrine regulation of reproduction; gastrointestinal pacemaking; Diabetic gastroenteropathy. Office: Stabile 7 Mayo Clinic 200 1st St SW Rochester MN 55905 Business E-Mail: ordog.tamas@mayo.edu.

ORDONEZ, MAGGLIO JOSE, professional baseball player; b. Caracas, Venezuela, Jan. 28, 1974; m. Dagly Ordonez; children: Magglio Jr., Maggliana, Sophia. Player Chgo. White Sox, 1997—2004; baseball player Detroit Tigers, 2005—. Mem. Venezuela Team World Baseball Classic, 2006. Named MVP, Venezuelan Winter League, 1996; named to Winter League All-Star Team, Baseball Am., 1997, Am. League All-Star Team, 1999—2001, 2003, 2006—07; recipient Silver Slugger award, 2000, 2002. Mailing: Detroit Tigers Comerica Pk 2100 Woodward Ave Detroit MI 48201 *

ORDORICA, STEVEN ANTHONY, obstetrician, gynecologist, educator; b. NYC, Jan. 4, 1957; s. Vincent and Rose (Goiricelaya) O. BA magna cum laude, NYU, 1979; MD, Stony Brook U., 1983. Diplomate Am. Coll. Obstetrics and Gynecology, speciality cert. maternal-fetal medicine; lic. Nat. Bd. Med. Examiners. Resident obstetrics and gynecology NYU-Bellevue Hosp. Ctr., 1983-87, fellow maternal-fetal medicine, 1987-89, instr. obstetrics-gynecology, 1989-91; clin. instr. obstetrics-gynecology NYU, 1986-89, asst. prof. ob/gyn., 1989—2001, clin. assoc. prof. ob/gyn., 2001—; dir. perinatal clinics and prenatal diagnostic unit Gouverneur Hosp., NYC, 1989-94. Perinatal cons. Bellevue Hosp. Ctr., N.Y.C., 1989—; faculty mem. perinatal div. NYU Med. Ctr., 1989—; presenter in field. Contbr. articles to Surgery, Am. Jour. Obstetrics and Gynecology, Am. Jour. Perinatal, Surgery, Obstetrics and Gynecology, Jour. Reproductive Medicine, Acta Geneticae Medicae et Gemellologiae, Jour. Rheumatology. Named NYU scholar; recipient Founder's Day award, NYU, Wash. Sq. Alumni award. Mem. Am. Coll. Obstetrics and Gynecology, Soc. Perinatal Obstetricians, N.Y. Acad. Scis., N.Y. State Perinatal Soc., AMA, Phi Beta Kappa, Beta Lambda Sigma. Achievements include research in investigating aspects of maternal-fetal physiology. Office: NYU Med Ctr 530 1st Ave Ste 10Q New York NY 10016-6402

ORDWAY, ELLEN, biologist, educator, entomologist, researcher; b. NYC, Nov. 8, 1927; d. Samuel Hanson and Anna (Wheatland) Ordway. BA, Wheaton Coll., Mass., 1950; MS, Cornell U., 1955; PhD, U. Kans., 1965. Field asst. N.Y. Zool. Soc., NYC, 1950-52; rsch. asst. Am. Mus. Natural History, NYC, 1955-57; tchg. asst. U. Kans., Lawrence, 1957-61, rsch. asst., 1959-65; asst. prof. U. Minn., Morris, 1965-70, assoc. prof. biology, 1970-85, prof., 1986-97, prof. emeritus, 1997, acad. advisor, 1997—. Cooperator, cons. USDA Bee Rsch. Lab., Tucson, 1971, Tucson, 83. Contbr. articles to profl. jours. Lectr. Morris area svc. clubs, 1972—2004; mgr. preserves Nature Conservancy, Mpls., 1975—; bd. dirs. county chpt. ARC, 1998—2003; vol. Stevens County Hist. Mus., 2005—; bd. dirs. U. Minn. Morris Retirees Assn., 1997—2003, sec., treas., 1998—2003. Mem.: AAAS, Ecol. Soc. Am., Internat. Bee Rsch. Assn., Kans. Entomol. Soc., Sigma Xi. Episcopalian. Avocations: travel, photography. Office: U Minn Div Sci And Math Morris MN 56267

ORDWAY, FREDERICK IRA, III, science educator, consultant, researcher, writer; b. NYC, Apr. 4, 1927; s. Frederick Ira and Frances Antoinette (Wright) O.; m. Maria Victoria Arenas, Apr. 13, 1950; children: Frederick Ira IV, Albert James, Aliette Marisol. SB, Harvard U., Cambridge, Mass., 1949; postgrad., U. Alger, 1950, U. Paris, France, 1950-51, 53-54, U. Barcelona, Spain, 1953, U. Innsbruck, Austria, 1954, Air U., 1952-63, Alexander Hamilton Bus. Inst., 1952-58, Indsl. Coll. Armed Forces, 1953-63; DSc (hon.), U. Ala., 1992. Various geol., engrng. positions Mene Grande Oil Co., San Tome, Venezuela, 1949-50, Orinoco Mining Co., Cerro Bolivar, Venezuela, 1950, Reaction Motors, Inc., Lake Denmark, NJ, 1951-53; with guided missiles divsn. Republic Aviation Corp., 1954-55; pres. Gen. Astronautics Rsch. Corp., Huntsville, Ala., 1955-59, 65-66; v.p. Nat. R & D Corp., Atlanta, 1957-59; asst. to dir. Saturn Systems Office, Army Ballistic Missile Agy., Huntsville, 1959-60; chief space info. systems br. George C. Marshall Space Flight Ctr. NASA, 1960-64; prof. sci. and tech. applications Sch. Grad. Studies and Rsch., U. Ala. Rsch. Inst., 1967-73; cons. Sci. and Tech. Policy Office, NSF, 1974-75; cons. ops. analysis divsn. Gen. Rsch. Corp., 1974-75; asst. to adminstr. ERDA, 1975-77, Dept. Energy, 1977-94, policy/internat. affairs dir. spl. projects office, cons., 1994—; also participant internat. energy devel. program Office of Asst. Sec. Internat. Affairs, Dept. Energy, 1978-79. Cons. to industry, Ency. Britannica, Am. Coll. Dictionary of English Lang., M.G.M. film 2001: A Space Odyssey, 1965-66, Paramount Picture Corp., The Adventurers, 1968-69; internat. lectr. space flight and energy programs. Author: (with C.C. Adams) Space Flight, 1958, (with Ronald C. Wakeford) International Missile and Spacecraft Guide, 1960, Annotated Bibliography of Space Science and Technology, 1962, (with J.P. Gardner, M.R. Sharpe, Jr.) Basic Astronautics: An Introduction to Space Science, Engineering and Medicine, 1962, (with Adams, Wernher von Braun) Careers in Astronautics and Rocketry, 1962, (with Gardner, Sharpe, R.C. Wakeford) Applied Astronautics: An Introduction to Space Flight, 1963, (with Wakeford) Conquering the Sun's Empire, 1963, Life in Other Solar Systems, 1965, (with Roger A. MacGowan) Intelligence in the Universe, 1966, (with W. von Braun) History of Rocketry and Space Travel, 1966, 1969, 1975, L'Histoire Mondiale de l'Astronautique, 1968, 70, (with W. von Braun) Rockets' Red Glare, 1976, (with C.C. Adams, M.R. Sharpe) Dividends from Space, 1972, Pictorial Guide to Planet Earth, 1975, (with W. von Braun) New Worlds, 1979, (with M.R. Sharpe) The Rocket Team, 1979, 2d edit., 2003, (with F.C. Durant and R.C. Seamans) Between Sputnik and the Shuttle, 1981, (with E.M. Emme) Science Fiction and Space Futures, 1982, (with von Braun, Dave Dooling) Space Travel: A History, 1985, (with Ernst Stuhlinger) Wernher von Braun: Aufbrach in den Weltraum, 1992, Wernher von Braun: Crusader for Space (2 vols.), 1994, rev. 1996, single vol. edit., 1996, (with Randy Liebermann) Blueprint for Space, 1992, Visions of Spaceflight, 2001; editor: Advances in Space Science and Technology, vols. I-XII, 2 supplements, 1959-72, (with R.M.L. Baker, N.W. Makemson) Introduction to Astrodynamics, 1960, (with others) From Peenemünde to Outer Space, 1962, Astronautical Engineering and Science, 1963; mem. editl. bd.: IX Internat. Astronautical Congress procs., 2 vols, 1959, Xth Congress procs., 2 vols, 1960; guest editor: Acta Astronautica, 1985, 94, History of Rocketry and Astronautics, Vol. IX, 1989, Digital book Mars: Target for Tomorrow Microsoft Network & Internet, 1996; Co-developer of biographical film He Conquered Space, 1996, History of Astronautics Video, 1996, inter-active CD Rom, 1997, rev., 2001, interactive CD ROM and video versions) Mars: Past, Present, Future, 1998; contbr. articles to profl. jours., chpts. to books; organizer Blueprint for Space exhbn., 1991-95, US Space and Rocket Ctr., IBM Gallery of Sci. and Art, NASA Vis. Ctr., Houston, Spaceport USA, Cape Canaveral, Fla., Nat. Air and Space Mus., Washington, Va. Air and Space Ctr., Hampton exhibit Shaping The Vision exhibit Art Inst. Chgo., 2001, Bruce Mus. Art and Scis., Greenwich, Conn., 2001, Mus. Flight, Seattle, 2002, others. Served with USNR, 1945. Co-recipient diplome d'honneur French Commn. d'Histoire, Arts et Letters, Paris, 1969, citation Arthur C. Clarke Found., 2005; commended for contbns. to US Space and Rocket Ctr., Ala. Space Sci. Exhibit, US Space Walk of Fame Found. Fellow: AAAS, AIAA (assoc.; history com. 1975—, internat. activities com. 1980—89, sel. com. hons. and awards 1996—, 2003 Centennial of Flight Ctr. 1998, Hermann Oberth award 1977, K.E. Tsiolkowski award 1988), Brit. Interplanetary Soc. (guest editor 1992—96); mem.: US Space and Rocket Ctr. (Saturn V rocket restoration com., mus. com., sci. adv. coun.), Acta Astronautica (guest editor 1994, 1997), Eurasian Acad. Scis., Nat. Space Soc. (bd. dirs. 1986—95, publs. com. 1987—88, nominating com. 1990—92, bd. govs. 1997—, Ctr. for Lunar Rsch. com. 1998—, awards com. 1992—), Am. Astron. Soc. (Emme award 1994, Nat. Space Club award 1997), Internat. Acad. Astronautics (history of astronautics com. 1983—, space activities and soc. com. 1986—, peer rev. com. 1995—, Luigi Napolitano Lit. award 1992), Arthur C. Clarke Found. (bd. dirs. 2000—, commendation 2005), Washington Golf and Country Club, Harvard Club NY, Cosmos Club (bd. mgmt. 1986—91, v.p. 1988—90, award 2001). Home and Office: 2401 N Taylor St Arlington VA 22207-4021 also: 3423 Lookout Dr SE Huntsville AL 35801 Personal E-mail: ordmars@aol.com.

ORDWAY, JOHN DANTON, retired pension fund administrator, lawyer, accountant; b. Mpls., Mar. 19, 1928; s. John Dunreath Ordway and Inez Adelaide (Stahl) Larson; m. Mary E. Bateman, June 16, 1951 (div. 1978); 1 child, David; m. Patricia A. Nagle, Dec. 27, 1996. BBA, Am. U., 1963, JD, 1965. CPA Minn.; bar: US Dist. Ct. DC 1966. Dir. ins. Nat. Automobile Dealers Assn., Washington, 1957—69; v.p. Edward H. Friend and Co., Washington, 1969—74; exec. v.p., CEO pension bd. United Ch. of Christ, NYC, 1974—96; ret., 1996. Mem. Planning Bd., Stamford, Conn., 1982—86. With US Army, 1946—47. Mem.: AICPA, Black Hall Club (Old Lyme, Conn.), Quail Run Golf Club (Naples, Fla.), Westwood Country Club (Vienna, Va.), Kena Temple. Republican. Mem. United Ch. Of Christ. Home: 7520 Citrus Hill Ln Naples FL 34109 Personal E-mail: wocph@yahoo.com.

O'REAR, DENNIS JOHN, chemical engineer, consultant; b. Harrisburg, Pa., Nov. 21, 1950; s. John Dennis and Charlotte Virginia O'Rear; m. Virginia Helen Vilnis; 1 child, Katherine Lindsey. BS in Chem. Engring., Pa. State U., State College, 1972; PhD in Chem. Engring., Stanford U., Calif., 1977. Rsch. engr. Chevron Rsch. Co., Richmond, Calif., 1977—82, rsch. program area leader, 1982—85, rsch. team leader, 1985—2000, intellectual property cons., 2000—. Contbr. articles to profl. jours. Achievements include 70 patents in field. Office: Chevron Corp Law Dept 100 Chevron Way Richmond CA 94802-0627 Home Phone: 707-664-8351; Office Phone: 510-242-4908. Office Fax: 510-242-5540. Business E-Mail: dennisorear@chevron.com.

O'REILLY, SIR ANTHONY JOHN FRANCIS, media company executive, former food products company executive; b. Dublin, May 7, 1936; s. John Patrick and Aileen (O'Connor) O'Reilly; m. Susan Cameron, May 5, 1962 (div.); children: Susan, Cameron, Justine, Gavin, Caroline, Tony; m. Chryss Goulandris, Sept. 14, 1991. Student, Belvedere Coll., Dublin, Univ. Coll., Dublin, Wharton Bus. Sch. Overseas, 1965; BCL DCL (hon.), Ind. State U.; PhD in Agrl. Mktg, U. Bradford, Eng.; LLD (hon.), Wheeling Coll., 1974, Trinity Coll., Dublin, 1978; LL.D. (hon.), Allegheny Coll., 1983, De Paul U., Chgo., 1988; D in Bus. Studies (hon.), Rollins Coll., 1978; DHC in Civil Law (hon.), Ind. State U., 1980; DBA (hon.), Boston Coll., 1985; D in Econ. Sci. (hon.), Nat. U. Ireland, 1989. Indsl. cons. Weston Evans, 1958—62; personal asst. to chmn. Suttons Ltd., Cork, Ireland, 1960—62; lectr. dept. applied psychology Univ. Coll., Cork, 1960—62; dir. Robert McCowen & Sons Ltd., Tralee, Ireland, 1961—62; mng. dir. An Bord Bainne/Irish Dairy Bd., 1962—66; dir. Agrl. Credit Corp. Ltd., 1965—66, Nitrigin Eireann Teoranta, 1965—66; mng. dir., CEO Comhlucht Siuicre Eireann Teo. (Irish Sugar Co.) and Erin Foods Ltd., Dublin, 1966—69; joint mng. dir. Heinz-Erin Ltd., 1967—70; mng. dir. H.J. Heinz Co. Ltd., England, 1969—72; sr. v.p. N.Am. and Pacific H.J. Heinz Co., 1971—72, exec. v.p., COO Pitts., 1972—73, pres., COO, 1973—79, pres., 1979—96, CEO, 1979—98, chmn., 1987—2000, Waterford Wedgwood plc, 1994—; exec. chmn. Independent News & Media PLC, 2000—04, chief exec., 2004—. Chmn. Fitzwilliam Securities Ltd., 1971—77, Ind. Newspapers Plc, Atlantic Resources, Dublin, Am. Ireland Fund; ptnr. Cawley Sheerin Wynne and Co., solicitors, Dublin; bd. dirs. Bankers Trust N.Y. Corp., 1980—90, Washington Post Co., 1987—94, London Tablet Found., Inc., Starkist Foods Inc., Ore-Ida Foods, Inc.; founder O'Reilly Found., 1998—. Author: Prospect, 1962, Developing Creative Management, 1970, The Conservative Consumer, 1971, Food for Thought, 1972. Mem. Nat. Com. Whitney Mus. Art; bd. govs. Hugh O'Brian Found., LA; mem. coun. Rockefeller U., NYC; trustee U. Pitts., Com. for Econ. Devel.; bd. dirs. Assocs. Grad. Sch. Bus. Adminstrn. of Harvard U., Cambridge, Mass.; sr. bd. dirs. The Conf. Bd. Named Hon. Officer, Order of Australia, 1988. Fellow: Royal Soc. Arts, Brit. Inst. Mgmt.; mem.: Marks Club London, Exec. Coun. Fgn. Diplomats (bd. dirs.), Irish Mgmt. Inst. (coun.), Internat. Life Scis. Inst. Nutrition Found. (chmn., CEO coun.), Am. Irish Found., Grocery Mfrs. Am. (sec., bd. dirs.), Law Soc. Ireland (treas.), Inst. Dirs., Inc., Lyford Cay Club (Bahamas), Rolling Rock Club (Ligonier), Pitts. Golf Club, Allegheny Club, Duquesne Club, The Bd. Rm. (N.Y.C.), The Links, Union League, Les Ambassadeurs, Annabels, Univ. Club Dublin, Kildare St. Club, St. Stephens Green Club. Office: Independent News & Media PLC Independent House 2023 Bianconi Ave Naas Rd Dublin 24 Ireland

O'REILLY, BILL (WILLIAM O'REILLY JR.), commentator, writer; b. NYC, Sept. 10, 1949; s. William and Angela O'Reilly; m. Maureen McPhilmy; children: Madeline, Spencer. BA in History, Marist Coll., Poughkeepsie, NY, 1971; MA in Broadcast Journalism, Boston U., 1976; MA in Pub. Policy, Harvard U., 1996. Tchr. H.S., Miami, Fla.; reporter WNEP-TV, Scranton, Pa., WFAA-TV, Dallas, KMGH-TV, Denver, WFSB-TV, Hartford, WCBS-TV, NYC, 1980; fgn. correspondent CBS News; anchor CBS, Boston, ABC, Boston, KATU-TV, Portland; correspondent, The World News Tonight ABC, 1986—88; sr. correspondent Inside Edition, 1988, anchor, 1989—95; host, exec. prodr. FOX News Channel The O'Reilly Factor, 1996—; host Radio Factor, 2002—. Author: Those Who Trespass: A Novel of Television and Murder, 1998, The O'Reilly Factor: The Good, the Bad and the Completely Ridiculous in American Life, 2000, The No Spin Zone: Confrontations with the Powerful and Famous in America, 2001, Who's Looking Out for You?, 2003, The O'Reilly Factor for Kids: A Survival Guide for America's Families, 2004, Culture Warrior, 2006. Recipient Disting. Alumni award, Boston U., 2001. Office: FOX News Channel 1211 Avenue of the Americas New York NY 10036

O'REILLY, CHARLES TERRANCE, university dean; b. Chgo., May 30, 1921; s. William Patrick and Ann Elizabeth (Madden) O'R.; m. Rosella Catherine Neilland, June 4, 1955; children: Terrance, Gregory, Kevin, Joan Bridget, Kathleen Ann. BA, Loyola U., Chgo., 1942, MSW., 1948; postgrad., U. Cattolica, Milan, Italy, 1949-50; PhD, U. Notre Dame, 1954. Instr. DePaul U., Chgo., 1948-49; asst. in psychology U. Cattolica, 1949-50; caseworker Cath. Charities, NYC, 1953-54; exec. dir. Family Service, Long Branch, N.J., 1954-55; asst. prof. Loyola U., 1955-59; vis. lectr. Ensiss Sch. Social Work, Milan, 1959-60; asso. prof. U. Wis.-Milw., 1961-64; prof., asso. dir. U. Wis. Sch. Social Work, Madison, 1965-68; dean social welfare, v.p. acad. affairs SUNY-Albany, 1969-76; dean social work Loyola U., Chgo., 1976-92, dean emeritus, sr. prof., 1994—; vis. prof. sch. social work SS Maria Asunta, Rome, 1992-93. Author: OAA Profile, 1961, People of Inner Core North, 1965, Men in Jail, 1968, Italian Social Work Education 1946-1997, 1998, Italy's War of Liberation, 1998, The Enola Gay Controversy and the Smithsonian, 2004; contbr. articles to profl. jours. Pres. Community Action Commn. Dane County, Wis., 1967-68; bd. dirs. Council Community Services, Albany, Family and Children's Service, Albany; mem. adv. bd. Safer Found.; vice chmn. Ill. Pub. Aid Citizens Council. Served with AUS, 1942-46, 51-52. Fulbright scholar, 1949-50; fellow, 1959-60 Mem. AAUP, Nat. Assn. Social Workers. Roman Catholic. Home: 4073 Bunker Ln Wilmette IL 60091-1001 Office: Sch Social Work Loyola Univ Chicago IL 60611 E-mail: coreill@luc.edu.

O'REILLY, DAVID E., auto parts company executive; s. Charles Chub O'Reilly; 3 children. Grad., Drury Coll., 1971. With Southwestern Bell; joined O'Reilly Automotive, Springfield, Mo., 1972—, now co-chmn., CEO. Bd. dir. O'Reilly Automotive, 1993—; past chair Auto Value Inc. Mem. Springfield Catholic Schs. Devel. bd.; past pres. Drury Univ. Alumni Assn., Springfield YMCA. Mem.: Automotive Warehouse Distributors Assn. (past chmn.). Office: O'Reilly Automotive 233 S Patterson Springfield MO 65802 Office Phone: 417-862-6708.

O'REILLY, DAVID J., oil industry executive; b. Dublin, Jan. 1947; BS ChemE, University Coll., Dublin, 1968, D (hon.) of Sci., 2002. Process engineer Chevron Corp., 1968—71, process engineer, operating assist., 1971—75, adviser, foreign operations, 1976—78, planning mgr., chemical div., 1979, mgr. agricultural chem., 1980—82, mgr. Salt Lake Refinery, 1983—85; mgr. manufacturing Chevron Chemical Co., 1985; gen. mgr. El Segundo Refinery, 1986—88; sr. v.p. Chevron Chemical Corp., 1989—90; v.p. Chevron Corp., 1991—94; pres. Chevron Products Co., San Francisco, 1994—98; dir., vice-chmn. Chevron Corp., San Francisco, 1998—2000, chmn. bd. dirs., CEO, 2000—01; CEO, chmn. ChevronTexaco Corp. (now Chevron Corp.), San Francisco, 2001—. Bd. govs. San Francisco Symphony, Bay Area Coun. Mem.: Am. Soc. Corp. Execs., Bus. Coun., Nat. Petroleum Coun., Am. Petroleum Inst. (treas., bd. dirs.). Office: Chevron Corp 6001 Bollinger Canyon Rd San Ramon CA 94583-2324 *

O'REILLY, HEATHER ANN, Olympic athlete; b. East Brunswick, NJ, Jan. 2, 1985; Student, U.N.C. Mem. U.S. Women's Nat. Soccer Team, 2002—, U.S. Women's Olympic Soccer Team, Athens, 2004. Named National High School Player of the Yr., 2002; named to NCAA All-Tournament Team, 2003. Achievements include being a member of NCAA Champion University of North Carolina Tar Heels Women's Soccer Team, 2003; being a member of gold medal US Women's Soccer Team, Athens Olympic Games, 2004. Office: c/o US Soccer Federation 1801 S Prairie Ave Chicago IL 60616

O'REILLY, JAMES, marketing executive; b. Collingwood, Ont., Can., Sept. 29, 1966; s. Gerrard and Linda O'Reilly; m. Marie Christine Paraninfo, Nov. 14, 1992; children: Justin, Jordan. BSc, McMaster U., Hamilton Ont., 1989; MBA, York U., Toronto, Ont., 1991. Brand mgr. Procter & Gamble Inc., Toronto, 1990—96; mktg. dir. KFC Can., Toronto, 1996—99, YUM L.Am., Deerfield Beach, Fla., 1999—2001; sr. dir. mktg. Pizza Hut UK, Borhamwood, England, 2001—03; v.p. mktg. KFC Corp., Louisville, 2004—06, chief mktg. officer, 2006—. Dir. bd. trustees Walden Sch., Louisville, 2006—.

O'REILLY, JAMES THOMAS, lawyer, educator, writer; b. NYC, Nov. 15, 1947; s. Matthew Richard and Regina (Casey) O'R.; children: Jean, Ann. BA cum laude, Boston Coll., 1969; JD, U. Va., 1974. Bar: Va. 1974, Ohio 1974, U.S. Supreme Ct. 1979, U.S. Ct. Appeals (6th cir.) 1980. Atty. Procter & Gamble Co., Cin., 1974-76, counsel, 1976-79, sr. counsel for food, drug and product safety, 1979-85, corp. counsel, 1985-93, assoc. gen. counsel, 1993-98; adj. prof. in adminstrv. law U. Cin., 1980-97, vis. prof. law, 1998—. Cons. Adminstrv. Conf. U.S., 1981-82, 89-90, Congl. Office of Compliance, 1995-96; arbitrator State Employee Rels. Bd.; mem. Ohio Bishops Adv. Coun., Mayor's Infrastructure Commn., Cin. Environ. Adv. Coun.; city coun. Wyo., Ohio. Author: Federal Information Disclosure, 1977, Food and Drug Administration Regulatory Manual, 1979, Unions' Rights to Company Information, 1980, Federal Regulation of the Chemical Industry, 1980, Administrative Rulemaking, 1983, Ohio Public Employee Collective Bargaining, 1984, Protecting Workplace Secrets, 1985, Emergency Response to Chemical Accidents, 1986, Product Defects and Hazards, 1987, Protecting Trade Secrets Under SARA, 1988, Toxic Torts Strategy Deskbook, 1989, Complying With Canada's New Labeling Law, 1989, Solid Waste Management, 1991, Ohio Products Liability Handbook, 1991, Toxic Torts Guide, 1991, ABA Product Liability Resource Manual, 1993, RCRA and Superfund Practice Guide, 1993, Clean Air Permits Manual, 1994, United States Environmental Liabilities, 1994, Elder Safety, 1995, Environmental and Workplace Safety for University and Hospital Managers, 1996, Indoor Environmental Health, 1997, Product Warnings, Defects & Hazards, 1999, Accident Prevention Manual, 2000, Food Crisis Management Manual, 2002, Police Racial Profiling, 2002, Homeland Security Deskbook, 2004, Ohio Tort Reform, 2005, Ohio Personal Injury Practice, 2006, Gangs and Law Enforcement, 2007; mem. editl. bd. Food and Drug Cosmetic Law Jour.; contbr. articles to profl. jours. Trustee Regional Coun. of Govts.; mem. Hamilton County Dem. Ctrl. Com. With US Army, 1970—72. Mem. ABA (chmn. AD law sect.), FBA, Food and Drug Law Inst. (chair program com.), Leadership Cin. Democrat. Roman Catholic. Office: 24 Jewett Dr Cincinnati OH 45215-2648 Office Phone: 513-556-0062. Personal E-mail: joreilly@fuse.net. Business E-Mail: james.oreilly@uc.edu.

O'REILLY, KENNETH WILLIAM, retired military officer; b. NYC, July 17, 1953; s. Thomas Michael and Dorothy Marie (Garvin) O'R.; m. Ginger Lee Jacobs, Apr. 22, 1978; children: Ryan, Erin. AAS, SUNY, Farmingdale, 1973; BS, Dowling Coll., 1975; MA, Webster U., 1982; cert., Harvard U., 2006. Sales rep. N.W. Airlines, NYC, 1976-78; commd. 2d lt. USAF, 1978—, advanced through grades to lt. col.; student navigator 452 Flight Tng. Squadron, Mather AFB, Calif., 1979-80; KC135 unit navigator 11th Air Refueling Squadron, Altus AFB, Okla., 1980-83, instr. navigator, 1984-85; wing exec. officer 340 Air Refueling Wing, Altus AFB, 1984-85; chief of navigation 34 Strategic Squadron, Zaragoza AB, Spain, 1985-88; strategic plans advisor 2 Airborne Command and Control Squadron, Offutt AFB, Nebr., 1988-91; action officer Hdqrs. SAC/Directorate of Strategic Plans, Offutt AFB, 1991-92; chief of tanker plans Hdqrs. Air Mobility Command/Dir. Ops. and Transp., 1992-93; chief pers. mgmt. br., dir. ops. and transp. Hdqrs. Air Mobility Command, 1993-96; chief ops. watch divsn., headqrs., dir. ops. and plans The Pentagon, Washington, 1996-97, chief command control and comms. divsn., dir. ops. and tng., 1997-2000, chief global command and ctrl. sys. br., dep. dir. global ops., 2000—03, chief nuc. plans and programs, 2004—05; chem., biol. radiol. nuc., high yield explosives program mgr. Def. Threat Reduction Agy., Ft. Belvoir, Va., 2005; dep. dir. security svcs. directorate Pentagon Force Protection Agy., Washington, 2005—. Committeeman Levittown South-North Wantagh, Rep. Club, N.Y.C., 1971-78; mem. Nat. Rep. Com., 1993-. Decorated 3 Meritorious Svc. medal, 2 Commendation medals, 2 Defense Meritorious Svc. medals, others. Mem. Air Force Assn., Ops. Security Soc. Roman Catholic. Home: 6907 Atkins Way Gainesville VA 20155 Office: Security svcs Directorate Pentagon Force Protection Agy Washington DC 20301-9000 Office Phone: 703-697-2157. E-mail: koreilly@pfpa.mil.

O'REILLY, MARY, environmental scientist, educator; b. NYC, Aug. 3, 1948; d. Luke Edward and Regina (Mahoney) O'Reilly; m. Jonathan Haney; children: Robert Brophy, Sara Brophy, Lena Reid. Student, Fordham U., 1966—68; BS, U. Mich., 1970, MS, 1972, PhD, 1979. Rsch. asst. prof. Health Sci. Ctr., Syracuse, NY, 1979-84; environ. toxicologist Syracuse Rsch. Corp., 1984-86; pres. ARLS Cons., Inc., Syracuse, 1993—; sr. indsl. hygienist N.Y. State Dept. Labor, Syracuse, 1987—2000; environ. specialist N.Y. State Dept. Transp., Binghamton, 2000—. Adj. asst. prof. SUNY Sch. Pub. Health, Albany, 1990—; dir. Am. Bd. Indsl. Hygiene, Lansing, Mich., 1995—2001; adj. prof. chemistry LeMoyne Coll., 2000; mem. Z10 com. Am. Nat. Stds. Inst., 2001—05; mem. adv. bd. N.Y. State Inst. Health and Environment, 2001—; bd. dirs. Am. Conf. Govt. Indsl. Hygienists, 2006—. Author: An Ergonomics Guide to VDTs, 1994; author: (with others) Occupational Ergonomics, 1996; co-author: ILO's Encyclopedia of Occupational Health and Safety, 1998, Implications of Hormesis for Industrial Hygienists, 2003, Health Risk Assessment at Brownfield Redevelopment Sites, 2003, Groundwater Effects from Highway Tire Shreds, 2004, An Ergonomics Guide to Computer Workstations, 2007, Canasawacta Creek Watershed Initiative, 2007, others; contbr. articles to profl. jours. Mem. Syracuse Peace Coun. Mem.: Hormesis Soc., N.Y. State Assn. Transp. Engrs., Human Factors and Ergonomics Soc., Am. Assn. Govtl. Indsl. Hygienists, Am. Indsl. Hygiene Assn. Avocations: Karate, fly fishing, dance, folk harp. Home: 7705 Farley Ln Manlius NY 13104-9571 Home Phone: 315-682-3064; Office Phone: 607-721-8138. Personal E-mail: Mary_O'Reilly@sln.suny.edu. Business E-Mail: moreilly@dot.state.ny.us.

O'REILLY, MICHAEL, insurance company executive; BS, NYU; MBA, Pace U. Securities analyst investment dept. The Chubb Corp., 1969, chief investment officer, 1986, interim CFO, 2002—03, vice chmn., 2002—, CFO, 2003—. Served in US Army, 1966—67, capt. USAR, 1968—71. Office: The Chubb Corp 15 Mountain View Rd Warren NJ 07059 Office Phone: 908-903-3764. Office Fax: 908-903-2027. E-mail: moreilly@chubb.com. *

O'REILLY, RICHARD JOHN, pediatrician; b. Bklyn., Apr. 29, 1943; s. John Russell and Margaret (Cronin) O'R.; m. E. Jean Capitano, Nov. 1984; children from previous marriage: John, Steven. BS, Coll. Holy Cross, 1964; MD, U. Rochester, 1968. Diplomate Am. Bd. Pediatrics. Intern U. Minn. Hosp., Mpls., 1968-69; resident in pediatrics Children's Hosp. Med. Ctr. and Beth Israel Hosp., Boston, 1971-72; with dept. pediatrics Meml. Sloan Kettering Cancer Ctr., NYC, 1973—; attending pediatrician, chmn. dept. pediatrics Meml. Hosp., NYC, 1986—; mem. dept. immunology Sloan-Kettering Inst. Cancer Research; prof. pediatrics Cornell U. Med. Coll., 1980, Lila Acheson Wallace prof. pediatric research, 1980, Claire L. Tow, chair in pediat. oncology rsch., 2004; chief marrow transplantation svc. Meml. Sloan-Kettering Cancer Ctr., 1981—. Pres. Damon Runyon-Walter Winchell Cancer Fund, 1991-96. Editor-in-chief BBMT, 1995-2001; assoc. editor Cancer Rsch., Clin. Cancer Rsch., 1994-2002. Served with USPHS, 1969-71. Recipient Louise and Allston Boyer-Young Investigator award for clin. research, 1980, Boarhaave medal Leiden U., Pediat. Oncology award ASCO, Lifetime Achievement award ASEMT. Mem. AAAS, Am. Pediatric Soc., Am. Assn. Immunologists, Am. Acad. Pediatrics, Am. Assn. Pathologists, Soc. Pediatric Rsch., N.Y. Transplantation Soc., N.Y. Acad. Scis., Am. Assn. Clin. Radiology, Am. Soc. Hematology, Am. Soc. Blood and Marrow Transplantation (sec. 1993-95, v.p.-elect 1999, pres. 2001). Democrat. Roman Catholic. Achievements include first successful application of marrow transplantation from unrelated donors and from genetically mismatched donors, 1973. Office: Meml Sloan-Kettering Cancer Ctr 1275 York Ave New York NY 10021-6094

O'REILLY, TERENCE JOHN, lawyer; b. Farnborough, Eng., Apr. 12, 1945; came to U.S., 1960, naturalized, 1965; s. Arthur Francis and Doris Eileen (Burden) O'R.; m. Katharine Van Dyke Wallace, Sept. 26, 1970; children: Tobin Cooper, Matthew Wallace. BA, Loyola U., 1966; JD, U. Calif., Berkeley, 1969. Bar: Calif. 1970. Assoc. Voegelin, Barton, LA, 1969-70, Walkup, Downing & Sterns, San Francisco, 1970-75; mem. Walkup, Shelby, Bastian, Melodia, Kelly & O'Reilly, San Francisco, 1975-87; prin. O'Reilly, Danko & Yamane, San Mateo, Calif., 1987—. Lectr. Kennedy Law Sch., Moraga, Calif., 1975-76, Inner Cir. of Advocates, 1998—; bd. govs. Consumer Attys. of Calif., 1995— bd. govs., diplomate Am. Bd. Profl. Liability Lawyers, 1989—. V.p. No. Calif. Rugby Football, San Francisco, 1975-80, bd. dirs., 1975—; trustee U.S. Rugby Football Found., 1987—; trustee The Philip Brooks Sch., 1986-89, Coun. of Bancroft Libr., U. Calif.; bd. dirs. San Francisco Traditional Jazz Found., 2002— Mem. Boalt Hall Alumni (bd. dirs. 1982-85), Assn. San Francisco Trial Lawyers (bd. dirs. 1985—), Assn. San Mateo Trial Lawyers (dir. 1992—, pres. 2003), Bohemian Club, Burlingame Country Club, Menlo Circus Club, Pacific Union Club. Roman Catholic. Office: 1900 O'Farrell St Ste 360 San Mateo CA 94403 E-mail: toreilly@oreillylaw.com.

O'REILLY, TIM, computer book publishing company executive, open sourcer advocate; b. Cork, Ireland, 1954; BA in Classics (cum laude, Harvard Coll., 1975. Founder, pres. O'Reilly & Associates (now called O'Reilly Media, Inc.), Sebastopol, Calif., 1978—. Former bd. dir. Macromedia; bd. dir. CollabNet; spkr. in field. Co-author UNIX Text Processing (with Dale Dougherty and Howard Sams), 1987, (with Grace Todino) Managing UUCP and USENET, (with Valerie Quercia) The X Window System Users' Guide, (with Adrian Nye) The X Toolkit Intrinsics Programming Manual, (with Jerry Peek and Mike Loukides) UNIX Power Tools, (with Troy Mott) Windows 98 in a Nutshell; editor, (with O'Reilly & Associates) major contbr. in the development of many of other titles, including UNIX in a Nutshell, Programming Perl, Sendmail, Essential System Administration, and The Cathedral and the Bazaar; O'Reilly Media Inc. published The Whole Internet User's Guide & Catalog (First popular book about the internet, selected by NY Pub. Libr. as one of the most signicant books of the 20th Century), 1992; introduced Safari Books Online (first web-native svc. for online book content), 2000; writer (web blog) radar.oreilly.com Named one of 50 Who Matter Now, CNNMoney-.com Bus. 2.0, 2006, 2007; recipient Industry Achievement award for advocacy on behalf of the open source community, InfoWorld, 1998. Mem.: Electronic Frontier Found. (bd. trustee), Internet Soc. (bd. trustee). Achievements include O'Reilly's Global Network Navigator site (GNN, sold to American Online in 1995) was the first web portal and the first true commerical site on the World Wide Web in 1993. Office: O Reilly Media Inc 1005 Gravenstein Hwy N Sebastopol CA 95472-2811 Office Phone: 707-827-7000. Office Fax: 707-829-0104. *

O'REILLY, TIMOTHY PATRICK, lawyer; b. San Lorenzo, Calif., Sept. 12, 1945; s. Thomas Marvin and Florence Ann (Ohlman) O'R.; m. Susan Ann Marshall, July 18, 1969; children: T. Patrick Jr., Sean M., Colleen K. BS, Ohio State U., 1967; JD, NYU, 1971. Bar: Pa. 1971, U.S. Dist. Ct. (ea. dist.) Pa. 1971, U.S. Dist. Ct. (mid. dist.) Pa. 1972, U.S. Ct. Appeals (3d cir.) 1977, U.S. Supreme Ct. 1988. Ptnr. Morgan, Lewis & Bockius, Phila., 1978—. Editor: Developing Labor Law, 1989; contbr. articles to profl. jours. Bd. dirs. Notre Dame Acad. and Devon Preparatory Sch.; bd. govs. Aronimink Golf Club, J. Wood Platt Caddie Scholarship Trust, Applebrook Golf Club. Elected to Coll. of Labor and Employment Lawyers. Mem. ABA (chmn. com. on devel. of the law under the Nat. Labor Rels. Act., editor-in-chief The Developing Labor Law jour., elected mem. coun. labor and employment sect.), Pa. Bar Assn., Phila. Bar Assn., Ohio State U. Alumni Assn., Aronimink Golf Club (bd. govs.). Avocation: golf. Home: 1127 Cymry Dr Berwyn PA 19312-2056 Office: Morgan Lewis & Bockius 1701 Market St Philadelphia PA 19103-2903 Office Phone: 215-963-5470. Business E-Mail: toreilly@morganlewis.com, roreilly@morganlaw.com. E-mail: tpoirish@comcast.net.

O'REILLY, WILLIAM M., lawyer, insurance company executive; BA, U. Ill., 1977; JD, Loyola U., 1980. Bar: Ill. 1980, Wis. 1987. Law clk. & assoc. William B. Handley & Assocs., 1979—80; assoc. Bell, Boyd & Lloyd, 1981—84, Ross & Hardies, 1984—86; assoc. counsel Sentry Insurance Group, Stevens Point, Wis., 1986—92, assoc. gen. counsel, corp. sec., 1992—94, v.p., gen. counsel, corp. sec., 1994—. Office: Sentry Insurance 1800 N Point Dr Stevens Point WI 54481 Office Phone: 715-346-6000. Fax: 715-346-7516. *

O'REILLY, WILLIAM R., JR., lawyer; b. 1955; m. Elizabeth Ross; children: Alex, Sam. BA summa cum laude with spl. honors, Tufts U., 1977; JD magna cum laude, Georgetown U., 1980. Bar: Mass. 1980. Assoc. to ptnr. Hale & Dorr, Boston, 1980—2004; ptnr., vice chmn. Real Estate dept. Wilmer Cutler Pickering Hale & Dorr, Boston, 2004—. Mem. editl. bd. Georgetown Law Jour.; contbr. articles to profl. jours. Trustee Tufts Univ., 2004—. Named a Mass. Super Lawyer, Boston Mag., 2004. Mem.: ABA, Mass. Bar Assn., Boston Bar Assn., Am. Coll. Real Estate Lawyers, Pension Real Estate Assn., Urban Land Inst., Real Estate Fin. Assn., Tufts Alumni Assn. (pres. 2000—02, Disting. Svc. award 2004), Tufts Alumni Council. Office: Wilmer Cutler Pickering Hale & Dorr 60 State St Boston MA 02109-1816 Office Phone: 617-526-6210. Office Fax: 617-526-5000. Business E-Mail: william.o'reilly@wilmerhale.com.

OREMUS, STEPHEN, composer; Grad., Berklee Coll. Music. Music dir.: Andrew Lippa's The Wild Party, Rent, regionally Into the Woods (Ordway), Dorian (World Premiere, Goodspeed), A Little Night Music, Jesus Christ Superstar (with Billy Porter and Emily Skinner), Nite Club Confidential (with Barbara Eden), The Radio City Music Hall Christmas Spectacular, vocal arranger, music supr.: Signed, Sealed, Delivered - The Music of Stevie Wonder, music supr., vocal arranger, orchestrator: Broadway plays Avenue Q, 2003; music supr., vocal arranger, orchestrator (Broadway plays) All Shook Up; music supr., arranger, orchestrator: Broadway plays tick.tick.BOOM!, musical dir.: Broadway plays Wicked, 2003. Office: Gershwin Theatre 222 W 51st St New York NY 10019 E-mail: storemus@earthlink.net.

OREN, BRUCE CLIFFORD, editor, artist; b. Mineola, NY, Aug. 31, 1952; s. Ralph and Bernice (Lands) O.; 1 child, Adam Nathaniel; m. Angela Malone Williams, Mar. 4, 1990. Student, U. Md., College Park, 1970-74. Archtl. sculptor Universal Restoration Inc., Washington, 1974-76; tech. illustrator Tex. Instruments, Stafford, Tex., 1976-77; graphic artist Houston Chronicle, 1977-79, photo editor, 1979-86, artist, 1986—, L.A. Times Syndicate, 1987-91. Named Best Art/Graphic, Hearst Newspapers, 1998, 2000; recipient Bronze medal, Soc. Newspaper Design, 1992, 1st Pl. Graphics award, Tex. Associated Press Mng. Editors, 2002. Jewish. Office: 801 Texas Ave Houston TX 77002-2904 Business E-Mail: bruce.oren@chron.com.

ORENDER, DONNA, sports association executive; m. M.G. Orender; children: Jacob, Zachary stepchildren: Morgan, Colleen. Grad., Queens Coll., NY, 1978; postgraduate student in Social Work, Adelphi U. Player (Women's Profl. Basketball League) NY Stars, 1978—79, NJ Gems, 1979—80, Chgo. Hustle, 1980—81; with ABC Sports, SportsChannel; owner Primo Donna Prodns.; with NBA Entertainment, PGA Tour, 1988—2001, sr. v.p. strategic devel., 2001—05; pres. WNBA, NYC, 2005—. Prodr.: Insided the PGA Tour. Bd. mem. Beth El - The Beaches Synagogue, Monique Burr Found. for Children, Inc., Jacksonville Film & TV Adv. Coun., Maccabi USA/Sports for Israel. Mem.: Women's Basketball Coaches Assn. (bd. dirs.). Office: WNBA Olympic Tower 645 Fifth Ave New York NY 10022 Office Phone: 212-688-9622, 212-750-9622. E-mail: dorender@wnba.com. *

ORENGO-NANIA, SILVIA, ophthalmologist; b. Detroit, June 24, 1961; d. Antonio and Christina Orengo; m. Jay Nania, Aug. 8, 1992; children: Christina Nania, Jason Nania, Julia Nania. Med. degree, Baylor Coll. of Medicine, Houston, 1983. Exec. eye care line Michael E. DeBakey Vets. Affair Med. Ctr., Houston, 1998—2006; prof. Baylor Coll. of Medicine, Houston, 2006—. Achievements include research in Central Corneal Thickness and Intraocular Pressure. Office: Cullen Eye Inst 6565 Fannin NC205 Houston TX 77030 Office Phone: 713-798-6100.

ORENSTEIN, DAVID M., medical educator; b. Plainfield, NJ, Nov. 3, 1945; s. Jacob and Florence J. Orenstein; m. Alexandra Kast, Nov. 2, 2000; 1 child, Jacob Atticus An Toan. BA, Amherst Coll., Mass., 1967; MD, Case Western Res. U., Cleve., 1973. Cert. pediat. pulmonology Am. Bd. Pediat., 1989. Dir. Antonio J. and Janet Palumbo Cystic Fibrosis Ctr. Children's Hosp. Pitts., 1984—, Antonio J. and Janet Palumbo prof. cystic fibrosis, 2000—, chair ethics com., 2004—; prof. pediat. U. Pitts. Sch. Medicine, 1993—; prof. health and phys. activity U. Pitts. Sch. Edn. Author: (textbook) Cystic Fibrosis: A Guide for Patient and Family, Cystic Fibrosis: Medical Care; editor: Treatment of the Hospitalized Cystic Fibrosis Patient. Named Man of Yr., Sci. and Medicine, Vectors, Pitts., 2003. Fellow: Am. Acad. Pediat.; mem.: Am. Pediat. Soc., Soc. for Pediat. Rsch. Office: Childrens Hospital of Pittsburgh 3705 Fifth Ave Pittsburgh PA 15213 Home Phone: 412-692-8736; Office Phone: 412-692-8736.

ORENSTEIN, FRAN M., small business owner, writer; b. Bklyn., Oct. 31, 1939; s. Nathan Gitterman and Gertrude Celia Chall-Gitterman; m. Walter Orenstein, Dec. 21, 1958 (div. Jan. 1977); children: James, Susannah, Peter. BA, Bklyn. Coll., 1960; MEd, Coll. NJ, 1976; EdD, Nova Southeastern U., Ft. Lauderdale, Fla., 1993. Lic. tchr. NY, NJ, guidance NJ, Calif., cert. pub. mgr. NJ. Tchr. Pub. Sch. 256-NYC Bd. Edn., Bklyn., 1960—63, Hilltop Acad., Morganville, NJ, 1973—74; editor, writer Univ. Comms., Rahway, NJ, 1975—79; tchr., content specialist East Windsor Regional Schs., NJ, 1979—80; sr. rehab. counselor NJ Divsn. Vocat. Rehab., Trenton, 1980—88; disability officer Americorps NJ Dept. Edn., Trenton, 1998—2002; program devel. specialist NJ Dept. Cmty. Affairs,

Trenton, 1988—98, 2002—; Reiki master, founder Sunshine Healing Arts, LLC. Presenter local, nat., and internat. confs. on gender equity in schs., violence prevention in schs., sexual harassment in schs and the workplace, and; cons., presenter Ednl. Visions Group, East Windsor, NJ, 1990—98. Author, editor: Bus. World for Women / Men mag., 1975—78 (Navy citation, 1977), SACC Talk, 1991—92. Campaign worker NJ Dem. Party, 1992; founding bd. dirs. Ctrl. NJ Breast Cancer Coalition, 2000—02, Am. Cancer Soc. Chpt. N.J. Breast Cancer Coalition, Manalapan, 1973—77, Am. Cancer Soc. Chpt. NJ Breast Cancer Coalition, Freehold, 2000—; bd. dirs., newsletter editor Women's Agenda/NJ Law, 1993—96; vol. bd. dirs. Susan B. Komen Race for the Cure, Princeton, NJ, 1995—99. Mem.: Soc. Children's Book Writers and Illustrators, Mensa (Ariz. proctor coord., S.C., Ga., Tampa, Fla. proctor), Phi Delta Kappa, Kappa Delta Pi. Avocations: reading, gardening, writing, poetry. Personal E-mail: franoren2@yahoo.com.

ORENSTEIN, MICHAEL (IAN ORENSTEIN), philatelic dealer, columnist; b. Bklyn., Jan. 6, 1939; s. Harry and Myra (Klein) Orenstein; m. Linda Turner, June 28, 1964; 1 child, Paul David. BS, Clemson U., 1960; postgrad., U. Calif., Berkeley, 1960-61. Career regional mgr. Minkus Stamp & Pub. Co., Calif., 1964-70; mgr. stamp div. Superior Stamp & Coin Co., Inc., Beverly Hills, Calif., 1970-90; dir. stamp divsn. Superior Galleries, Beverly Hills, Calif., 1991-94; dir. space memorabelia Superior Stamp and Coin. Co., Inc., Beverly Hills, Calif., 1992-94; dir. stamp and space divsn. Superior Stamp & Coin an A-Mark Co., Beverly Hills, Calif., 1994-97; sr. buyer, appraiser Superior Stamp & Coin, Beverly Hills, Calif., 1997-2000; v.p., COO Superior Galleries, 2001; co-founder, ptnr., prin., pres. AuroraGalleries Internat., 2002—04; pres. The Right Stuff Inc., 2001—. Cons. Office Insp. Gen. NASA, Nassau County Dist. Atty., NY, Regency Superior Auction Co. Columnist: L.A. Times, 1965—93; philatelic advisor/creator The Video Guide to Stamp Collecting, 1988; author: Stamp Collecting is Fun, 1990; contbr. articles to publs. With US Army, 1962—64. Recipient medal of Yuri Gagarin, Fedn. Supporting Russian Cosmonauts, 2002. Mem.: AIAA, Internat. Soc. Appraisers: Stamps, Space Memorabilia, Internat. Fedn. Stamp Dealers, Am. Philatelic Soc. (writers unit 1975—80, 1989—93), Confederate Stamp Alliance, German Philatelic Soc., C. Z. Study Group, Am. Stamp Dealers Assn. Republican. Avocation: fishing. Address: 19546 Minnehaha Northridge CA 91326 Home Phone: 818-368-6888; Office Phone: 818-368-6888. Personal E-mail: rightstuf@verizon.net.

ORENTLICHER, JOHN, video research educator, artist; b. Roanoke, Va., June 7, 1943; s. Herman and Jeanette (Levin) O. BA, Goddard Coll., 1968; MFA, Sch. Art Inst. Chgo., 1970. Asst. prof. Ea. Mich. U., Ypsilanti, 1970-76; assoc. prof. Syracuse U., NY, 1976—, chmn. exptl. studios, 1978-81, chmn., prof. art media studies Coll. of Visual and Performing Arts, 1981-85, 87-89, chair dept. transmedia, 2005—. U.S. curator, 1st Internat. Video Festival Invitational, 1986, 2nd Internat. Video Festival, Mus. de Arte Medellin, Colombia, 1988; Fulbright Hays sr. lectr., Colombia, 1985; exec. producer WHAT-TV, Syracuse, 1983; video artist. Vol. Peace Corps, Aisen Province, Chile, 1964-66; curator 2d bi-ann. Internat. Video Festival, Medellin, Colombia. Exhibitions include Recontre's Paris/Berlin, 2006—07, Athens Internat. Film Video Festival, 2007. N.Y. State Coun. grantee, 1984, grantee Rockefeller Found., Nat. Endowment Arts; recipient ACE award. Avocation: music. Home: 6074 Sewickley Dr Jamesville NY 13078-9464 Office: Syracuse U Dept Transmedia 102 Sheffer Bldg Syracuse NY 13244 Office Phone: 315-443-1033. E-mail: jorentli@syr.edu.

ORESKES, IRWIN, biochemistry educator; b. Chgo., June 30, 1926; s. Herman and Clara (Rubenstein) O.; m. Susan E. Nagin, June 18, 1949; children: Michael, Daniel, Naomi, Rebecca. BS in Chemistry, CCNY, 1949; MA in Phys. Chemistry, Bklyn. Coll., 1956; PhD in Biochemistry, CUNY, 1969. Cert. clin. lab. dir. NYC, NY State. Chemist Tech. Tape Co., Bronx, NY, 1949; technician NYU Sch. Medicine, 1950-51; phys. chemist Kingsbrook Jewish Med. Ctr., 1951-56; rsch. fellow Poly. Inst., NY, 1957-58; rsch. assoc. Mt. Sinai Hosp., NYC, 1959-68, dir. arthritis lab., 1961-90; rsch. asst. prof. Mt. Sinai Sch. Medicine, NYC, 1969-74, rsch. assoc. prof., 1974-91; assoc. prof. Hunter Coll. Sch. Health Scis., CUNY, 1969—74, prof., 1974—2002, prof. emeritus, 2002—, dean, 1977-80; mem. doctoral faculty in biochemistry Grad. Ctr., CUNY, 1970—2002, emeritus, 2002—. Vis. prof. Johns Hopkins U. Sch. Health Svcs., 1976-77; cons. to diagnostic reagent and instrument mfrs., 1953-; mem. Internat. Sci. Coun., Albert Einstein Rsch. Inst., Buenos Aires, 1969-79; mem. bd. examiners for clin. labs. NYC Dept. Health, 1973-75; sr. cons. Biotech. Rev. Assocs., 1983-92. Co-editor: Rheumatology for the Health Care Professional, 1991; contbr. numerous articles to profl. jours. Served with U.S. Army, 1944-46. Nat. Inst. Arthritis and Metabolic Diseases grantee, 1961-69; Arthritis Found. grantee, 1961-65, 69, 72; Lupus Found. grantee, 1975-76; CUNY Found. grantee, 1982-83. Mem. Am. Chem. Soc., Am. Coll. Rheumatology, AAAS, NY Acad. Scis., Am. Assn. Immunologists, Am. Assn. Clin. Chemistry, Harvey Soc., Nat. Acad. Clin. Biochemistry, Acad. Clin. Lab. Physicians and Scientists, Clin. Immunology Soc., Sigma Xi, Phi Lambda Upsilon. Home: 670 West End Ave New York NY 10025-7313 Office: Hunter Coll Sch Health Sci 425 E 25th St New York NY 10010-2547 Office Phone: 212-481-5115. *I have always tried to live and work by the idea that strength is not harshness, caring is not sentimentality, and honesty is not vulnerability.*

ORESKES, NAOMI, science historian; b. NYC, Nov. 25, 1958; d. Irwin Oreskes and Susan Eileen Nagin Oreskes; m. Kenneth Belitz, Sept. 28, 1986; children: Hannah Oreskes Belitz, Clara Oreskes Belitz. BSc with honors, Imperial Coll., London, 1981; PhD, Stanford U., 1990. Geologist We. Mining Corp., Adelaide, Australia, 1981—84; rsch. and tng. asst. Stanford U., Calif., 1984—89; vis. asst. prof. Dartmouth Coll., Hanover, NH, 1990—91; asst. prof., 1991—96; assoc. prof. Gallatin Sch. NYU, 1996—98, U. Calif., San Diego, 1998—2005, prof., 2005—. Consulting geologist Western Mining Corp., 1984-90; consulting historian Am. Inst. Physics, N.Y.C., 1990-96. Author: The Rejection of Continental Drift, 1999, Theory and Method in American Earth Science, 1999; editor: Plate Tectonics: An Insider's History of the Modern Theory of the Earth, 2001; contbr. articles to profl. jours. Recipient Lindgren prize Soc. Econ. Geologists, 1993, Young Investigator award NSF, 1994-99, George Sarton Lectr. award AAAS, 2004; fellow NEH, 1993. Mem. Geol. Soc. Am., History Sci. Soc., History Earth Scis. Soc. (pres.). Jewish. Office: U Calif San Diego 9500 Gilman Dr La Jolla CA 92093-0104 Office Phone: 858-534-4695. Business E-Mail: noreskes@ucsd.edu.

OREY, DANIEL CLARK, mathematics professor; b. San Jose, Calif., June 30, 1955; s. Robert Lee and Dorothy Jean Washington Orey; life ptnr. Milton Rosa, Mar. 0, 2000; 1 child, Spencer Dwight. BS, Oreg. State U., Corvallis, 1977; MA, N.Mex State U., Las Cruces, 1983; PhD, U. N.Mex, Albuquerque, 1988. Instr. Monitor Elem. Sch., Mount Angel, Oreg., 1977—78; instr. math. Riverdale Elem. Sch., Portland, 1978—80, Colegio Americano de Guatemala, Ciudade de Guatemala, 1980—81; instr. Escuela Americana de Bananera, Bananera, Guatemala, 1981—82; instr., grad. tchg. asst. U. N.Mex, Albuquerque, 1984—87; asst. prof. Calif. State U., Sacramento, 1988—92, assoc. prof., 1993—97, math. instr. dept. learning skills, 1996—, prof. math. and multicultural edn., 1997—, organizer Luso-Brazilian studies, 2007—. Overseas dir. interchange programs and internat. rsch., programas intercâmbio pesquisas internacionais Academia Brasileira Ciências Matemática, Sacramento, 2000—01; adj. vis. prof. Programa Educação Matemática: Modelação Etnomatemática. Instituto Ciências Exatas. Pontifícia Universidade Católica Campinas, Campinas, Brazil, 1998—98; vis. prof. Instituto Ciências Exatas Biológicas, Universidade Fed. Ouro Preto, Brazil, 2005—06; adv. Brazil-Calif. partnership Calif. State Senate. Author: (text) Trigonometria: Linguagem e Instrumento. Escolas Associadas Pueri Domus: co-author (with M. Rosa): Modelação Algébrica. Escolas Associadas Pueri Domus, (book) Etnomatemática como Ação Pedagógica; contbr. chapters to books. Comite internacional, iv festival internacional de matemática Centro Nacional de Alta Tecnología, San Jose, Costa Rica, 2004; bd. mem., treas. Calif. Math Coun., No. Sect., 1992—94; bd. mem. human dignity cmty. commn. office supt. San Juan Unified Sch. Dist., Carmichael, Calif., 2002—05; csus rep. to the internat. assn. of universities 12th gen. conf. Unesco - Iau, Sao Paulo, 2004. Fellow, Comissão Fulbright Brasil, 1998, CNPq: Conselho Nacional de Desenvolvimento Científico e Tecnológico., 2005—06; grantee, Fulbright Found., 2007. Mem.: Sociedade Brasileira de Educação Matemática, Nat. Coun. Tchrs. Math., Calif. Math. Coun., Sociedade Internacional para Estudas da Criança, Internat. Study Group Ethnomathematics. Office: California State University Sacramento 6000 J St Sacramento CA 95819-6079 Home Phone: 916-359-3061.

ORFIELD, ANTONIA MARIE, optometrist, researcher; d. Alfred Anthony and Eva Swenson Stoll; m. Gary Allan Orfield, May 24, 1963 (div. 2005); children: Amy Elizabeth, Sonia Marie, Rosanna Antonia. BA in History, Smith Coll., 1963; MAT in History/Social Studies, U. Chgo., 1966; BS in Visual Sci., Ill. Coll. Optometry, 1987, OD, 1989. Lic. Mass. Bd. Optometry. Optometrist Michael Reese HMO, Chgo., 1989—91, Eye Exam 2000, Chgo., 1989—91; behavioral optometrist Harvard U. Health, Cambridge, Mass., 1991—. Asst. prof. New Eng. Coll. Optometry, Boston, 1991—2000, dir., chief investigator, clin. preceptor Mather Sch. Vision and Learning Rsch./Svc. Clinic, 1993—99; pvt. practice behavioral optometrist, Cambridge, 1996—; spkr. in field. Author: Eyes for Learning: Preventing and Curing Vision Related Learning Problems, 2007; contbr. articles to profl. jours. Parent rep. Kenwood Acad. Sch. Coun., Chgo., 1989—91. Grantee, State Street Bank, N.E. Congress Optometry, Mass. Soc. Optometrists, Am. Found. Vision Awareness, Friends of the Sensorily Deprived. Fellow: Coll. Optometrists in Vision Devel., Am. Acad. Optometry; mem.: Neurooptometric Rehab. Assn. (charter), Internat. Coll. Applied Kinesiology. Democrat. Achievements include research in children in poverty have a great number of vision problems that interefere with learning; near poiint glasses can raise test scores; tracking problems are correlated with reading failures; vision therapy is correlated with improvement in grades. Avocations: study of homeopathic medicine, sports vision training, study of educational kinesiology, study of nutrition and vision, swimming. Office: Harvard Univ Health Svc 75 Mt Auburn St Cambridge MA 02138 also: Ste 205 678 Massachussetts Ave Cambridge MA 02139 Personal E-mail: antoniaorfield@yahoo.com.

ORFORD, ROBERT RAYMOND, physician, consultant; b. Winnipeg, Manitoba, Can., Apr. 18, 1948; came to U.S., 1988; s. Robert Raymond and Sarah Gloria L. (Gullden) O.; m. Dale Laura Stuart, June 2, 1972; children: Carolyn Tiffany, Andrew Craig, Loren Brent. BS, McGill U., 1969, MD, 1971; MS, U. Minn., 1975; MPH, U. Wash., 1976. Assoc. prof. cmty. medicine U. Alberta, Edmonton, Can., 1978-88; dir. med. svcs. Govt. of Alberta, Edmonton, Can., 1979-81, exec. dir. occupational health svcs., 1981-85, deputy min. cmty. occupational health, 1985-88; med. dir. employee health U. Alberta Hosp., Edmonton, Can., 1988; sr. assoc. cons. Mayo Clinic, Rochester, Minn., 1988-91; cons. preventive medicine, 1991-96, Scottsdale, Ariz., 1996—. Asst. prof. Mayo Med. Sch., Rochester, 1988—; mem. Alberta Energy Resource Conservation Bd., 1988-89; chmn. divsn. preventive and occupl. medicine, dir. exec. health program, Mayo Clinic, Scottsdale, 1999—. Contbr. articles to profl. jours. Mem. Olmsted County Environ. Commn., Rochester, 1991-96, chair, 1994. Govt. of Can. Nat. Health fellow, 1975-76. Fellow Royal Coll. Physicians and Surgeons Can., Am. Coll. Occupational and Environ. Medicine (pres.-elect 2007-), Am. Coll. Preventive Medicine, Aerospace Med. Assn.; mem. Internat. Commn. Occupational Health Medicine (nat. sec. 2001—). Presbyterian. Avocations: languages, fitness, travel. Home: 15516 E Acacia Way Fountain Hills AZ 85268-3158 Office: Mayo Clinic Scottsdale Divsn Preventive Medicine 13400 E Shea Blvd Scottsdale AZ 85259-5499 Office Phone: 480-301-7379. Office Fax: 480-301-7569. Business E-Mail: rorford@mayo.edu.

ORGAN, RITA C., museum administrator, consultant; b. Omaha, Aug. 7, 1965; d. Claude Harold and Elizabeth Lucille Organ. BFA, Calif. Coll. Arts & Crafts, 1987; attended, Ind. U., 1987—90. Curator African-Am. materials Children's Mus., Indpls., 1990—96; dir. exhibits & collections CHW Mus. African-Am. History, Detroit, 1996—2000, Nat. Underground Railroad Freedom Ctr., Cin., 2000—04; exec. dir. Ind. Mus. African-Am. History, Indpls.; 2004—06. Bd. pres. Assn. African-Am. Mus., Detroit, 1999—2002; bd. mem. Assn. Study of African Am. Life and History, Washington, 2000—02; mem. nat. adv. bd. The Freedom Ctr., Cin., 2005—. Author: (preface) Black History Resource Guide, 1998. Mem.: Nat. Coun. Negro Women, Assn. Midwest Mus., Assn. African Am. Mus. Avocations: hiking, bicycling, cooking.

ORGEBIN-CRIST, MARIE-CLAIRE, retired biology professor, department chairman; b. Vannes, France, Mar. 20, 1936; License Natural Scis., License Biology, Sorbonne, U. Paris, 1957; D. Scis., Lyons U., France, 1961. Stagiaire dept. biochemistry faculty medicine, Paris, 1957—58; stagiaire Centre Nat. de la Recherche Scientifique, Paris, 1958—60, attachee de recherche, 1960—62; research assoc. Population Council (Med. Div.), NYC, 1962—63; research assoc. dept. ob/gyn Vanderbilt Sch. Medicine, 1963—64, research instr., 1964—66, asst. prof., 1966—70, assoc. prof., 1970—73, Lucius E. Burch prof. reproductive biology, 1973—2005, prof. dept. anatomy, 1975—2005; dir. Vanderbilt Sch. Medicine (Center Reproductive Biology Research.), 1973—2005, prof. emeritus, 2005—. Editor-in-Chief Jour. Andrology, 1983-89 Recipient Career Devel. award NIH, 1968-73, NIH Merit award, 1986,; Fogarty Internat. sr. fellow, 1977; Disting. Scientist award Am. Soc. Reproductive Medicine, 1996. Mem. Am. Assn. Anatomists, Am. Soc. Cell Biology, Am. Soc. Andrology (v.p. 1994-95, pres. 1995-96, Disting. Svc. award 1997, Disting. Andrologist award 1990), Internat. Com. on Andrology, Endocrine Soc., Soc. for Study Fertility (Eng.), Soc. for Study Reprodn., N.Y. Acad. Scis. Office: Vanderbilt U Sch Med Ctr Reproductive Biology Rsch Rm C-3306 MCN Nashville TN 37232-0001 E-mail: m-c.orgebin-crist@vanderbilt.edu.

ORGEGA, GREGORY LUIS, hematologist, oncologist; b. NY, Dec. 23, 1954; s. Luis and Dolores B. Ortega; m. Glennys Orteg; children: Glennys, Ramon. MD cum laude, Nat. U. Pedro, Santo Domingo, Domincian Republic, 1979. Diplomate internal medicine and hematology, medical oncology. Resident family practice Peninsula Gen. Hosp., Far Rockaway, NY, 1981; resident internal medicine East Tenn. State U., Johnson City, 1984; fellow hematology Mt. Sinai Sch. Medicine, NYC, 1986; fellow oncology Albert Einstein Coll. Mecidine, Bronx, NY, 1987; prin. investigator Mid. Fla. Hematology and Oncology Ctrs., PA, 1989—. Prin. investigator Sarah Cannon Ctr., 1997—2004, Viccan, 2006—; mem.-at-large Fla. Hosp., Fla., 2000—02; chife staff, med. exec. com. CFRH, 2007—. Contbr. articles to profl. jours. Mem.: AMA, FMA, ASW, ASH. Avocations: golf, travel. Office: Mid Fla Hematology and Oncology Ctrs PA 1061 Medical Center Dr Ste 100 Orange City FL 32763

ORIANI, RICHARD ANTHONY, metallurgical engineer, educator; b. El Salvador, July 19, 1920; arrived in U.S., 1929, naturalized, 1943; s. Americo and Berta (Siguenza) Oriani; m. Constance Amelia Gordon, June 26, 1949; children: Margaret, Steven, Julia, Amelia. B in Chem. Engring, CCNY, 1943; MS, Stevens Inst. Tech., 1946; MA, Princeton U., 1948, PhD, 1949. Lab. asst. CCNY, 1943; chemist Bakelite Corp., Bloomfield, NJ, 1943-46; instr. physics Miss Fine's Finishing Sch., Princeton, NJ, 1946-47; rsch. assoc. GE Rsch. Lab., Schenectady, 1949-59; asst. dir. U.S. Steel Corp. Rsch. Lab., Monroeville, Pa., 1959-80; prof. U. Minn., Mpls., 1980-89, dir. Corrosion Rsch. Ctr., 1980-87, prof. emeritus, dir. emeritus, 1989—. Cons. in field. Contbr. articles to profl. jours., chapters to books. Founder, mem. Foxwood Civic Assn., Monroeville, 1959—80; founder, v.p. Monroeville Pub. Libr., 1960—80. Recipient Alexander von Humboldt Sr. Scientist award, 1984, W. R. Whitney award, 1987. Fellow: Electrochemical Soc., Nat. Assn. Corrosion Engrs., N.Y. Acad. Scis., Am. Inst. Chemists, Am. Soc. Metals; mem.: AAAS, Am. Inst. Metall. Engrs., Am. Phys. Soc. Republican. Home: 4623 Humboldt Ave S Minneapolis MN 55409-2264 Office: U Minn 112 Amundson Hall 221 Church St SE Minneapolis MN 55455-0113 Office Phone: 612-625-5862. E-mail: orian001@umn.edu.

ORICCHIO, MICHAEL, editor; m. Renee Oricchio. Writer Washington Post, 1984; staff writer, editor San Jose Mercury News, 1987—2002; mng. editor NY Times Syndication Sales Corp, 2002—. Office: NY Times Syndication Sales Corp 14th Fl 122 E 42nd St New York NY 10168 Office Phone: 212-499-3314. Office Fax: 212-499-3382. E-mail: oricchio@nytimes.com.

ORIGITANO, THOMAS CHARLES, neurological surgeon; BS in Chemistry and Biology, MacMurray Coll., 1976; MD, Loyola-Stritch U., Maywood, Ill., 1984; PhD, Loyola U., Chgo., 1984. Diplomate Am. Bd. Neurol. Surgery, 1995. Intern gen. surgery Loyola U. Med. Ctr., Maywood, 1984—85, resident neurol. surgery, 1985—90, asst. prof., 1990—96, assoc. prof., 1996—98, prof., 1998—, chmn. neurol. surgery med. ctr., 1998—. Home and Office: Loyola Univ Med Ctr 2160 South First Ave Maywood IL 60153 Home Phone: 708-216-8920.

ORING, STUART AUGUST, audio-visual specialist, writer, photographer, researcher; b. Bronx, NY, Aug. 28, 1932; s. Irving and Helen Flora (Greenhut) O.; m. Mary Carolyn Barth, Aug. 22, 1957; children: Carlene Marie Oring, Sheri Alyce Oring. AAS, Rochester Inst. Tech., 1957; BFA, R.I. Tech., 1959; MA, Am. U., 1970. Photo lab asst. Nat. Geographic, Washington, summer 1957; photography asst. IJBecker, Nepo-Nuss Advt Photo, Studio Assocs. & Art Green Inc., NYC, 1959-61; freelance photographer pvt. practice, Washington, 1961; indsl. photographer Vitro Corp., Rockville, Md., 1962-64; health photographer Nat. Ctr. Radiol. Health, Rockville, Md., 1964-67; visual info. specialist ARS Info. div. USDA, Washington, 1967-69; audio visual specialist Nat. AV Ctr., Washington, 1969-71; photojournalist Office of Econ. Opportunity, Washington, 1971-74; visual info. specialist ASCS, U.S. Dept. Agr., Washington, 1974-94; ret., 1994. Mgr., owner ISIS Visual Comms.; photography tchr. Prince George's C.C., Largo, Md., 1975-96; guest lectr. U. Md. Balt. County, Catonsville, Corcoran Gallery of Art, Washington; spkr. in field. Author, editor and pub.: (textbook/gallery text) Understanding Pictures-A Teacher's Planning Guide, 1994, Understanding Pictures-Theories, Exercises and Procedures, 1990, rev. 1992, rev. 1995, A Beginner's Guide to Looking at Pictures, 1997; contbr. numerous articles to profl. jours.; photos published in books, mags., brochures, pamphlets. Photographer with U.S. Army, 1952-55. Recipient Cert. Recognition award Eastman Kodak Co., 1973, Nat. Ctr. Radiol. Health, Rockville, Md., 1965. Mem.: APA (divsn. 10 psychology and the arts, program spkr. 105th ann. conf., 108th ann. conf.), Inst. for Psychol. Study of Arts (program spkr.), Am. Soc. Psychopathology of Expression (bd. dirs.). Achievements include research and development of new approaches for analyzing and interpreting art and photographs. Home and Office: 2570 Redbud Ln Owings MD 20736-4308 Office Phone: 410-257-5709. Personal E-mail: stuartoring@comcast.net.

ORINGER, KENNETH, chef, restaurant owner; Degree, Bryant Coll.; grad., Culinary Inst. Am. Cook River Cafe, NYC; pastry chef Al Forno, Providence; chef de partie, sous chef Le Marquis de Lafayette, Boston; owner, chef Terra; chef de cuisine Silks, San Francisco; chef, ptnr. Tosca, Hingham, Mass.; exec. chef, owner Clio, Boston, 2000—, Toro, Boston, 2005—. Named Best New Chef, San Francisco Chronicle, Rising Star Chef, Restaurant Hospitality, Best Chef in Boston, Boston Mag., 2000, Best Chef in N.E., James Beard Found., 2001. Office: Restaurant Clio 370 Commonwealth Ave Boston MA 02215 *

ORKAND, DONALD SAUL, management consultant; b. NYC, Mar. 2, 1936; s. Harold and Sylvia (Wagner) O.; children: Dara Sue, Katarina Day; m. Kim Lim Sang, July 22, 2001; 1 child, Aaron J. BS summa cum laude, NYU, 1956, MBA, 1957, PhD, 1963. Statistician Western Electric Co., NYC, 1956-58; group v.p. Ops. Rsch., Inc., Silver Spring, Md., 1960-69; pres. Ops. Rsch. Industries, Ltd., Ottawa, Ont., Canada, 1968-69; CEO Orkand Corp., Tysons Corner, Va., 1970—2004; ptnr. DC Ventures and Assocs. LLC, Mc Lean, Va., 2004—. Bd. dirs. U. Md. Found., Inc., College Park, 1993-2002. Bd. vis. Univ. Coll., 2002—; trustee Suburban Hosp., 1994-2000. 1st lt. Ordnance Corps, USAR, 1958-60. Mem. Am. Econs. Assn., Am. Statis. Assn. Republican. Jewish. Avocations: reading, theater, travel, exercise. Office: Dc Ventures Associates PO Box 10625 Mc Lean VA 22102-8625

ORKIN, JENNA, writer; b. NYC; d. Harvey Orkin; 1 child, One. BA, Hunter Coll., NYC; JD, NY Law Sch., NY; BA/MA, Oxford U., England. Interviewer Exploring Post One, New York, NY, 1984—86; educator Juilliard, New York, NY, 1978—83; press chairperson 911 Environ. Action, NYC, 2002—04; founder World Trade Ctr. Environ. Orgn., 2002—. Moderator 1st Peak Oil Conf., NYC, 2005. Author: (poem) Dubya's Lament (Best of 2005).

ORKIN, LOUIS RICHARD, physician, educator; b. NYC, Dec. 23, 1915; s. Samuel David and Rebecca (Rish) O.; m. Florence Fine, Mar. 5, 1938; 1 dau., Rita. BA, U. Wis., 1937; MD, NYU, 1941; AAS in Marine Tech., Kingsborough Coll., 1992. Intern Bellevue Hosp., NYC, 1942, resident anesthesiology, 1946-48; practice medicine specializing in anesthesiology Bronx, NY, 1946—48; dir. anesthesiology Backus Hosp., Norwich, Conn., 1948-50; asst. prof. anesthesiology NYU Coll. Medicine, 1950-55; prof., chmn. dept. anesthesiology Albert Einstein Coll. Medicine, 1955-82, Disting. univ. prof., 1982-86, dist. univ. prof. emeritus, 1986—. Vis. prof. depts. bioengring., anesthesiology U. Calif., San Diego, 1971; Cons. VA, USPHS, USN; mem. com. anesthesiology Nat. Acad. Scis., 1964-69; mem. com. anesthetic drugs FDA, Dept. Health, Edn. and Welfare, 1970— Author: Patient in Shock, 1965, Physiology of Obstetrical Anesthesia, 1969; Contbr. articles to profl. jours. V.p. and trustee Wood Library Mus. Served to capt. M.C. AUS, 1942-45. Decorated Bronze Star; honoree Albert Einstein Coll. Medicine, 2005. Fellow Am. Coll. Chest Physicians, NY Acad. Sci., NY Acad. Medicine, Am. Coll. Anesthesiology (past chmn. bd. govs.); mem. NY State Soc. Anesthesiologists (past pres.; Disting. Svc. award 2000). Home: 11 Stuyvesant Oval Apt 11F New York NY 10009-2001 Personal E-mail: Louis_Orkin@hotmail.com.

ORLANDO, LORI ANN, medical researcher, educator; d. Geraldine Sainthill and Roy Charles Orlando; m. Bradley F. Mann, May 19, 1995. BS, U. N.C., 1990—2001; MD, Tulane Med. Ctr., 1998; M in health sci., Duke U. Med. Sch., 2004. Diplomate Am. Bd. Internal Medicine. Resident in internal medicine Tulane Med. Ctr., New Orleans, 1998—2001, chief resident in internal medicine, 2001—02; internal medicine fellow Duke U. Med. Ctr., Durham, NC, 2002—04, assoc. in medicine, 2004—06, asst. prof. in medicine, 2006—; rsch. assoc. Durham VA Med. Ctr., NC, 2002—. Contbr. articles to profl. jours. Recipient Rsch. internship, Harvard U., Brigham and Women's Hosp., Dept. of Pathology, 1987, Med. Student Achievement award, Endocrine Soc., 1998, Owl Club award for Outstanding Med. Resident, 2000, 2001, Outstanding Trainee award, so. sect. Am.

Fedn. Med. Rsch., 2002, Milton W. Hamuisky award outstanding jr. faculty presentation, 2005, Best Sci. Abstract award, 2005. Mem.: Soc. of Gen. Internal Medicine (assoc.; chair planning com.). Achievements include research in describing chronic kidney disease in Virginia and evaluating interface between generalist and specialist care. Home Phone: 919-730-2055; Office Phone: 919-286-3399 ext. 240.

ORLEBEKE, WILLIAM RONALD, retired lawyer, writer; b. El Paso, Tex., Jan. 5, 1934; s. William Ronald and Frances Claire (Cook) O.; children: Michelle, Julene, David; m. Susan K. Nash, 2000. BA, Willamette U., Salem, Oreg., 1956, JD, 1966; MA, U. Kans., Lawrence, 1957. Bar: Calif. 1966, US Dist. Ct. (no. dist.) Calif. 1967, US Ct. Appeals (9th cir.) 1967, US Ct. Appeals (7th cir.) 1989, US Dist. Ct. (no. dist.) Ill. 1989, US Dist. Ct. (cen. dist.) Calif. 1989. Mem. staff Travelers Ins. Co., Sacramento, 1957-61; br. claim mgr. NY Life Ins. Co., 1961-62; branch claim mgr. Transamerica Ins. Co., San Francisco, 1962-63; assoc. Eliassen & Postel, San Francisco, 1966-69; ptnr. Coll, Levy & Orlebeke, Concord, Calif., 1969-77, Orlebeke & Hutchings, Concord, Calif., 1977-89; prin. Law Offices W. Ronald Orlebeke, 1989-98; hearing officer Contra Costa County, Calif., 1981-98; arbitrator Contra Costa County Superior Ct., 1977-98, US Dist. Ct. No. Calif., 1978-98, Mt. Diablo Mcpl. Ct., 1987-89; ret., 1998. Judge pro tem Mt. Diablo Mcpl. Ct., 1973-75; criminology prof. Pioneer-Pacific Coll., 2002-03. Author: Orlebeke Family in Europe and America, 1570-1990, 1988, Don't Tell Me I Can't, 2003, (novels) Code Jeremiah, 2004, Lightning, 2004. Alumni bd. dir. Willamette U., 1978-81, trustee, 1980-81 scholar chmn. Concord Elks, 1977-79; del. Joint US/China Internat. Trade Law Conf., Beijing, 1987. With USMCR, 1952-59. Sr. scholar Willamette U., 1955-56; Woodrow Wilson fellow Kans. U., 1956-57, US Bur. Nat. Affairs fellow, 1966, others. Mem. SAR, Sons of Confederate Vets. (Merit award 1989), Sons of Union Vets. Civil War, First Marine Divsn. Assn., Order Ea. Star (worthy patron 1980), Masons (sec. Capitol Masonic Ctr., 2001-04, corp. sec. Oreg. Masonic Low Twelve Club, Inc 2005-07, spl. trustee Oreg. chpt. 2006-07), Elks, Rotary (charter pres. Clayton Valley/Concord Sunrise club 1987-88, chmn. dist. 5160 Calif. membership devel. 1989-90, dist. gov. liaison dist. 5160 1990-92, dist. Rotarian of Yr. 1989-90, Paul Harris fellow 1988, 1992 dist. conf. chmn. benefactor 1990, Merit award 1990), Shriners (v.p. Salem Shrine Club 2004-07). Republican.

ORLIN, KAREN J., lawyer; b. Washington, Apr. 2, 1948; d. Hyman and Lenore O.; 1 child. AB Summa Cum Laude, in math., U. Pa., 1969; JD, Harvard U., 1972. Bar: N.Y. 1973, U.S. Dist. Ct. (so. and ea. dists.) N.Y. 1973, U.S. Ct. Appeals (2d cir.) 1973, Fla. 1982. Assoc. Kronish, Lieb, Weiner & Hellman, NYC, 1972-81; sr. assoc. Valdes-Fauli, Bischoff, Kriss and Mandler, Miami, 1981-82, ptnr., 1982-83; sr. assoc. Ruden, Barnett, McClosky, Smith, Schuster & Russell, P.A., Ft. Lauderdale, Fla., 1983-85, Shea & Gould, NYC and Miami, 1985-87; of counsel Thomson, Muraro, Razook and Hart P.A., Miami, 1987-88; sr. v.p.-assoc. counsel, asst. sec. Am. Savs. of Fla., F.S.B., Miami, 1988—95; pvt. practice Miami, Fla., 1995—. Mem. Trustee's Coun. Penn Women, U. Pa., 1987—, Harvard Club Miami, parents coun., Wash. U. St. Louis, Friends U. Miami Sch. Music, Leukemia & Lymphoma Soc. (marathons). Mem. Fla. Bar (corps. and securities com. 1983—), Am. Mensa, Nat. Auctioneers Assn., U. Pa. Dade Alumni Club (pres. 1993—), Greater Miami C. of C. (lawyers com. bus. revitalization group), Zonta Internat. (Downtown Miami chpt. bd. dirs.), Mortar Bd., Sphinx Soc., Nat. Auctioneers Assn., Phi Beta Kappa, ABA (bus. law sect.) NYC Bar Assn. Office: PO Box 430620 Miami FL 33243 Office Phone: 305-794-6387. Office Fax: 305-668-7072. Business E-Mail: karen@orlinlaw.com, kjorlin@bellsouth.net.

ORLOFF, BARBARA-LEE MARGUERITE HEWITT, retired social worker; b. NYC, Feb. 18, 1944; d. Richard Elliott Hewitt and Elise Harriet (Hofer) DeMeritt; m. Jonathan Harris Orloff, Apr. 22, 1967 (div. May 1985); children: Aleksandr Monford, Piotr Richard. BA, Chatham Coll., Pitts., 1966; postgrad., Portland State U., 1988—90. Info. and referral specialist Info. and Vol. Svcs., Pitts., 1967—70; vol. coord. Friends of Tryon Creek State Park, Portland, Oreg., 1975—81, Oreg. State Parks, Salem, 1978, Portland Dept. Parks and Recreation, 1979; exec. dir. Friend of Tryon Creek State Park, Portland, 1985—88; social svc. coord. Lake Oswego Adult Ctr., Oreg., 1985—90; program dir. N.W. Housing Alternatives, Milwaukie, Oreg., 1990—2007; ret. Vol. coord. book Guide to Urban Wilderness, 1978. Watercolor artist, photographer Monday Studio. Docent Portland Art Mus., 1970—74; opera evening vol. host Lake Oswego Adult Ctr., 1985—2001; mem. Clackamas County Cmty. Action Bd., 2007; mgr.bookstall Friends of Ledding Libr., 2007. Named Merit Mother of Oreg., Am. Assn. Mothers, Portland, 1991. Democrat. Episcopalian. Avocations: sailing, hiking, needlepoint, opera, literature. Home: 1400 SE Lava Dr # 14 Milwaukie OR 97222 Personal E-mail: barbaraleeorloff@yahoo.com.

ORLOFF, CHET, historian; b. Bellingham, Wash., Feb. 22, 1949; s. Monford A. and Janice (Diamond) O.; m. Wendy Lynn Lee, Sept. 20, 1970; children: Callman Labe, Hannah Katya, Michele Alison. BS, Boston U., 1971; BA, U. Oreg., 1971; MA, Portland State U., 1978. Tchr. Peace Corps, Afghanistan, 1972-75; asst. dir. Oreg. Hist. Soc., Portland, 1975-86, exec. dir., 1991-2000, Ninth Cir. Hist. Soc., Pasadena, Calif., 1987-91. Adj. prof. Portland State U.; prin. Oreg. History Works. Editor: Western Legal History, 1987-91, Law for the Elephant, 1992; sr. editor: Oreg. Hist. Quar. Commr. Met. Arts Commn., Portland, 1981-84, Portland Planning Commn., 1989-92; pres. Nat. Lewis and Clark Bicentennial Coun., 1996—; v.p. Portland Parks Bd. Mem. Phi Alpha Theta. Avocations: reading, tennis. Office: Oreg Hist Works 3332 NW Savier St Portland OR 97210

ORLOVSKY, DONALD ALBERT, lawyer; b. Essex County, NJ, 1951; AB, Cornell U., 1973; JD, Rutgers U. Sch. Law, 1976. Bar: Fla. 1976, US Dist. Ct. NJ 1977, US Ct. Appeals (5th cir.) 1976, US Ct. Appeals (11th cir.) 1981, US Ct. Appeals (8th cir.) 2003, US Ct. Appeals (2d cir.) 2005, US Supreme Ct. 1980. Assoc. Smathers & Thompson, Miami, 1976—77; ptnr. McCune, Hiaasen, Crum, Ferris & Gardner, P.A., Ft. Lauderdale, Fla., 1978—86, Kamen & Orlovsky PA, West Palm Beach, 1988—. Sec., bd. dirs. Fla. Lawyers Assistance, Inc., bd. dirs., supervising monitor and counselor, 1993—; pres., bd. dirs. Comprehensive Alcoholism Treatment Program, Inc., 2000—01. Author: Nova U. Law Review, 1977, U. Miami Law Review, 1978. Recipient All-Am. recognition in springboard diving, 1966-69; inducted Hall of Fame Newark Acad., Livingston, N.J., 1997. Mem. ABA, ATLA, Fla. Bar (civil procedure rules com. 1981), Acad. Fla. Trial Lawyers Episcopalian. Office: 1601 Belvedere Rd Ste 402 West Palm Beach FL 33406-1541 Office Phone: 561-687-8500. Personal E-mail: dao4law@aol.com.

ORLOWSKA, REY ELAINE, plastic surgeon; b. Zion, Ill., Feb. 20, 1965; d. Michael Peter and Betty Ann (Franklin) Wells; m. Jack Lewis Orlowska, Apr. 1, 1990; children: Bianca May, David Michael. BS in Biology, U. Chgo., 1987; MD, U. Pitts., 1992. Diplomate Am. Bd. Surgery, 1996, Am. Bd. Plastic Surgery, 2001. Intern surgery U. Pitts. Med. Ctr., 1992—93, resident surgery, 1993—96, chief resident, 1996—99; staff surgeon U. Ill. Hosp., 1999—2001; plastic surgeon Meriks Med. Ctr., Evanston, Ill., 2002—. Mem.: Am. Soc. Plastic Surgeons. Green Party. Lutheran. Avocations: history, exercise, travel.

ORM, SALLY S., music educator, consultant; d. Harvey Jacob and Lucille Mae Seyler; children: Jennifer E. Orm Seager, Andrea S., Jonathan D. Gilbert. Student, Eastman Sch. Music. With FBI, Washington, 1970—75; owner All Things Music, LLC. Founder keyboard donations Orm Music Studios, Neenah, Wis., 2001—. Treas. Regional Domestic Abuse, Oshkosh, Wis., 1984—86, pres., 1986—88; treas. Audubon Soc., Appleton, 1985—86; Gold award coord. Fox Valley Area Girl Scouts, Appleton, Wis., 1995—99. Named Mem. of the Yr. award, Fox Valley Area Girl Scouts, 1999. Mem.: Wis. Music Tchrs. Assn. (found. chair 2006—), Music Tchrs. Nat. Assn., Fox Valley Keyboard Tchrs. (v.p., program dir. 1999—2003, Mem. of the Yr. award 2002), World Piano Pedagogy Conf., Keyboard Music Educators Assn. (adjudicator keyboard competition 2002—). Presbyterian. Avocations: gardening, travel. Office: Orm Music Studios 749 S Commercial St Neenah WI 54956 Business E-Mail: sormusic@aol.com.

ORMAN, LEONARD ARNOLD, lawyer; b. Balt., June 15, 1930; s. Samuel and Bertie (Adler) O.; m. Barbara Gold, June 9, 1978; children: Richard Harold, Robert Barton. AB summa cum laude, U. Md., 1952, JD, 1955. Bar: Md. 1955, U.S. Ct. Appeals (4th cir.) 1956, U.S. Dist. Ct. Md. 1955, Ct. Appeals Md. 1955, U.S. Supreme Ct. 1977, U.S. Ct. Claims 1990, D.C. Ct. Appeals 1987. Law clk. Hon. Frederick W. Brune, Chief Judge Md. Ct. of Appeals, 1955-56; mem. dept. legis. reference Md. Legislature, 1957-58; mem. Gov.'s Commn. to Revise Criminal Code, 1958-59; pvt. practice law Balt., 1956—. Lectr. in trial tactics. Mem. editl. bd. Md. Law Rev., 1953-55; contbr. articles to profl. jours. Pres. Young Dems. 2d Dist., Balt., 1960-63. With AUS, 1948-49; lt. col. USAF Res. ret. Rosco Pound Inst. fellow, trustee. Mem. Nat. Bd. Trial Advocacy (cert. civil trial adv.), Am. Bd. Trial Advs., Md. State Bar Assn., Balt. City Bar Assn., Nat. Coll. Trial Advocacy (trustee), AAJ (nat. committeeman 1976-80, bd. govs. 1985—2006, exec. com. 1988-90, chmn. orgn. rev. com., home office and budget com., orgn. and home office com., election com., key man com., past steering com., past publ. com., past ednl. adv. group 1989-90, chmn. Stalwarts Hall of Fame com., past vice-chair ABA-ATLA liaison com., M Club, co-chair conv. site planning com., co-chair polit. insight com., long-range planning com., auth-hwy. adv. com., toy safety conf., med. malpractice adv. com., product liability adv. com., co-chair home office capital improvements adv. com., co-chmn. conv. planning com. Washington, Wiedmann/Wysocki award 1989-90, 1996, 2002), Acad. Catastrophic Injury Attys., Trial Lawyers for Pub. Justice, Md. Trial Lawyers Assn. (bd. govs., pres. 1984-85, Lifetime Achievement award 2002), Order of Coif, Masons. Home: 2 Celadon Rd Owings Mills MD 21117-3010 Office: 26 South St Baltimore MD 21202-3215 Office Phone: 410-962-0400. Business E-Mail: lorman@triallaw.com.

ORMAN, NANETTE HECTOR, psychiatrist; b. Highland Park, Ill., Feb. 1, 1943; d. William Joseph and Agnes (Daly) Hector; m. John Christopher Orman, July 2, 1964; children: Laurel Anne, Nathaniel William. BA in Journalism, U. Calif., Berkeley, 1964; postgrad., Stanford U., 1978-81; MPH in Epidemiology, U. Calif., Berkeley, 1984, MS in Health and Med. Scis., 1985; MD, U. Calif., San Francisco, 1987. Diplomate Am. Bd. Psychiatry and Neurology; lic. physician, Calif. Residency in psychiatry McAuley Neuro-Psychiatric Inst., St. Mary's Hosp., San Francisco; psychiatrist San Jose State U., Calif., 1989-93; pvt. practice Los Altos, Calif., 1991—; staff El Camino Hosp., 1991-94, Stanford U. Hosp. and Med. Ctr., Calif., 1998—2006. Asst. clin. prof. Stanford (Calif.) U. Sch. Medicine, 1995—; oral bd. examiner Am. Bd. Psychiatry & Neurology, Deerfield, Ill., 1995-2006, chief resident in psychiatry, 1991; spkr. and cons. in field. Editor San Mateo County Planned Parenthood Assn. Newsletter, 1968-69. Bd. dirs. Mid-Peninsula Task Force for Integrated Edn., 1972-82, Psychiat. Found. No. Calif., 2001—; consumer mem. San Mateo County Mental Health Adv. Bd., 1987. Fellow Am. Psychiat. Assn. (disting., 2004; pub. info. com. 1989—); mem. No. Calif. Psychiat. Soc. (chair membership com. 1996-2002, pub. info. com., media spokesperson, moderator ann. meetings 1993-94), Psychiat. Found. No. Calif. (mem. bd. dirs.). Office: 851 Fremont Ave Ste 98 Los Altos CA 94024-5602

ORMAN, SUZE, news correspondent, writer; b. Chgo., June 5, 1951; Cert. fin. planner. Account exec. Merrill Lynch, 1980—83; v.p. investments Prudential Bache Securities, 1983—87; dir. Suze Orman Fin. Group, 1987—97. Former fin. contbr. NBC News' Today; host QVC Fin. Freedom hour. Contbr. to Self mag.; author: (PBS spl.) The Road to Wealth; co-prodr.: (PBS spl.) The Road to Wealth; host (PBS spl.) The Road to Wealth; author: (PBS spl.) The Courage to Be Rich; co-prodr.: (PBS spl.) The Courage to Be Rich; host (PBS spl.) The Courage to Be Rich; author: (PBS spl.) The 9 Steps to Financial Freedom; co-prodr.: (PBS spl.) The 9 Steps to Financial Freedom; host (PBS spl.) The 9 Steps to Financial Freedom; contbg. editor: O: The Oprah Mag.; host (nat. syndicated radio talk show) The Suze Orman Show; author: The 9 Steps to Financial Freedom: Practical & Spiritual Steps so You Can Stop Worrying, 1997 (NY Times bestsellers), The Courage to Be Rich: Creating a Life of Material and Spiritual Abundance, 1999 (NY Times bestsellers, Motivational book award Books for a Better Life, 1999), The Road to Wealth: Suze Orman's Complete Guide to Your Money, 2001 (NY Times bestsellers), The Laws of Money, the Lessons of Life: Keep What You Have and Create What You Deserve, 2003, The Money Book for the Young, Fabulous & Broke, 2005 (Publishers Weekly Bestseller), Women and Money: Owning the Power to Control Your Destiny, 2007; co-author (with Linda Mead): You've Earned It, Don't Lose It: Mistakes You Can't Afford to Make When You Retire, 1995. Named Top 30 Power Brokers Who Most Influenced Mutual Fund Industry and Affected Money, Smart Money mag., 1999, Outstanding Svc. Show Host for Suze Orman: For the Young, Fabulous & Broke, Nat. Acad. TV Arts and Sciences, Daytime Emmy award, 2006; named to 100th issue as those "who have revolutionized the way Am. thinks about money", Worth mag., 2001. Office: CNBC 2200 Fletcher Ave Ste 5 Fort Lee NJ 07024 Mailing: c/o Amanda Urban ICM 40 W 57th St New York NY 10019 Office Phone: 201-585-2183. *

ORMASA, JOHN, retired utilities executive; b. Richmond, Calif., May 30, 1925; s. Juan Hormaza and Maria Inocencia Olondo; m. Dorothy Helen Trmble, Feb. 17, 1952; children: Newton Lee, John Trumble, Nancy Jean Davies. BA, U. Calif., Berkeley, 1948; JD, Harvard U., Cambridge, Mass., 1951. Bar: Calif. 1952, US Supreme Ct. 1959. Assoc. Clifford C. Anglim, 1951—52, Richmond, Carlson, Collins, Gordon & Bold, 1952—56, ptnr., 1956—59; v.p. sys. gen. counsel Pacific Lighting Svc. Co., LA, 1966—72; gen. atty., v.p., gen. counsel So. Calif. Gas Co., LA, 1959—66; v.p. gen. counsel Pacific Lighting Corp., LA, 1973—75, v.p., sec., gen. counsel, 1975; ret., 1975. Acting city atty. El Cerrito, Calif., 1952. With USN, 1943—46. Mem.: ABA, Richmond Bar Assn. (pres. 1959), Calif. State Bar Assn., Kiwanis (v.p. 1959). Republican. Roman Catholic.

ORME, ANTONY RONALD, geography educator; b. Weston-Super-Mare, Somerset, Eng., May 28, 1936; came to U.S., 1968; s. Ronald Albert and Anne (Parry) O.; m. Amalie Jo Brown, Nov. 18, 1984; children: Mark Antony, Kevin Ronald, Devon Anne. BA with 1st class honors, U. Birmingham, 1957, PhD, 1961. Lectr. Univ. Coll., Dublin, Ireland, 1960-68; mem. faculty UCLA, 1968—, prof. geography, 1973—, dean social scis., 1977-83. Cons. in field. Editor-in-chief Phys. Geography. Recipient Award of Merit Am. Inst. Planners, 1975, Outstanding Svc. award USAF, 1977-80, Founders' medal Brit. Soc. for Geomorphology Mem. Geol. Soc. Am., Assn. Am. Geographers (Disting. Career award), Assn. Geography Tchrs. Ireland (pres. 1964-68), Inst. Brit. Geographers, Internat. Geog. Union. Home: 5128 Del Moreno Dr Woodland Hills CA 91364-2426 Office: UCLA Dept Geography Los Angeles CA 90095-1524 Business E-Mail: orme@geog.ucla.edu.

ORMES, JONATHAN FAIRFIELD, astrophysicist, researcher, educator; b. Colorado Springs, Colo., July 18, 1939; s. Robert Manly and Suzanne (Viertel) O.; m. Karen Lee Minnick, Dec. 26, 1960 (div.); 1 child, Laurie Kylee; m. Janet Carolyn Dahl, Sept. 12, 1964; children: Marina, Nicholas. BS, Stanford U., 1961; PhD, U. Minn., 1967. NRC assoc. Goddard Space Flight Ctr., NASA, Greenbelt, Md., 1967-69, astrophysicist, 1969, head cosmic radiations br., 1981-82, head nuclear astrophysics br., 1983-87, assoc. chief lab. for high energy astrophysics, 1987-90, chief lab. for high energy astrophysics, 1990-2000, project sci. for gamma ray astronomy obs., 1998—2004, dir. space scis., 2000—04; rsch. prof. U. Denver, 2004—; dir. Denver Rsch. Inst., 2005—. Acting head high energy astrophysics NASA hdqrs., Washington, 1982-83, mem. high energy astrophysics mgmt. ops. working group, 1975-83, cosmic ray program working group, 1984-91; com. on space and solar physics, com. on cosmic ray physics Nat. Acad. Sci., Washington, 1991-94; adj. prof. U. Md. Balt., 2000-, U. Utah, 2001—. Editor: Essays in Space Science, 1987; assoc. editor astrophysics Phys. Rev. Letters, 1991-93; contbr. Astrophysics Jour., Phys. Rev. Letters, Astronomy and Astrophysics. Trustee Paint Br. Unitarian Universalist Ch., Adelphi, Md., 1987-88, chair bd. trustees, 1989, numerous positions, 1972—. Recipient Meritorious Exec. Award (presdl. rank), 2001. Fellow: Am. Phys. Soc. (various divsn. offices); mem.: Am. Geophys. Union, Am. Astron. Soc. (sec.-treas. High Energy Astrophysics divsn. 1985—87), Internat. Astron. Union. Achievements include discovery of unusual isotopic abundance of Ne in galactic cosmic rays; research on composition and energy spectra of cosmic rays, antiprotons and gamma rays from the Milky Way galaxy. Office: U Denver Dept Physics & Astronomy Denver CO 80208-0001 Office Phone: 303-871-3552. Business E-Mail: jonathan.ormes@du.edu.

ORMOND, JULIA, actress; b. Surrey, Eng., Jan. 4, 1965; m. Rory Edwards, Apr. 1989 (div. 1994); m. Jon Rubin, 1999; 1 child. Grad., Webber Douglas Acad. Drama Art, 1988; attended, West Surrey Coll. Art and Design. Founder prodn. co. Indican. Appeared in films The Baby of Macon, 1992, Legends of the Fall, 1994, Nostradamus, 1994, Captives, 1994, First Knight, 1995, Sabrina, 1995, The Prime Gig, 2000, Resistance, 2003, Inland Empire, 2006; TV appearances include Traffik, 1990, Young Catherine, 1991, Stalin, 1992, The 67th Annual Academy Awards, 1995, Smilla's Sense of Snow, 1997, Sibirsky Tsiryulnik, 1998, (voice) Animal Farm, 1999, Varian's War, 2001, Iron Jawed Angels, 2004, Beach Girls, 2005, The Way, 2006, I Know Who Killed Me, 2007; stage appearances include Faith, Hope and Charity, 1989 (London Critics best newcomer award); prodr.: Calling the Ghosts, 1996. Recipient Female Star of Tomorrow award Sho West Awards, 1995. *

ORMOND, PAUL A., healthcare company executive; b. Aurora, Ill. B in economics with honors, Stanford U., 1971, MBA, 1973. Mem. corp. staff, positions with glass container divsn. Owens-Ill., Inc., 1973-77, nat. mktg. mgr. soft drinks, glass container divsn., 1977-78; mgr. Atlanta sales dist., glass container divsn. Owens-Ill. Inc., 1978-80, asst. gen. mgr. Gerresheimer Glas (internat. affiliate Owens-Ill. Inc.) Germany, 1980-82, v.p. glass container group, 1982-84, v.p. packaging ops., dir. market strategy and devel., 1984-91, corp. v.p., 1986-91; pres., CEO Health Care and Retirement Corp. (HCR) (subs. Owens-Ill. Inc.), Toledo, 1986-91; chmn., pres., CEO Health Care and Retirement Corp. (HCR) (now ind. co.), Toledo, 1991—98; pres., CEO HCR Manor Care Inc., Toledo, 1998—99, Manor Care, Inc., Toledo, 1999—2001, chmn., pres., CEO, 2001—. Office: Manor Care 333 N Summit St Toledo OH 43604-2617 *

ORMSBY, ERIC LINN, writer, educator; b. Atlanta, Oct. 16, 1941; s. Robert and Virginia (Haire) O.; m. Dorothy Louise Hoffmann, July 22, 1967; children: Daniel Paul, Charles Martin. BA summa cum laude, U. Pa., 1971; MA, Princeton U., 1973, PhD, 1981; MLS, Rutgers U., 1978. Near East bibliographer libr. Princeton (NJ) U., 1975-77, Near East curator libr., 1977-83; libr. dir. Cath. U. Am., Washington, 1983-86, McGill U., Montreal, Canada, 1986-96, assoc. prof. Inst. Islamic Studies, 1986-96, prof., 1996—2005; prof., chief libr. Inst. Ismaili Studies, London, 2005—. Cons. NYU, 1981-82; mem. libr. com. Mid. East Inst., Washington, 1985-87, Al Akhawayn U., Morocco, 1994-95, Saudi Arabian Monetary Agy., Riyadh, 1995-96; chmn. continuing edn. com. Washington Consortium, 1983-86; mem. bd. Ctr. Rsch. Librs., 1989-95. Author: Theodicy in Islamic Thought, 1984 (Choice Mag. award 1984), Bavarian Shrine and Other Poems, 1990 (QSPELL award for poetry 1991), (poems) Coastlines, 1992, (with others) Handlist of Arabic Manuscripts, 1986, For a Modest God: New and Selected Poems, 1997, (poems) Araby, 2001, (poems) Daybreak at the Straits, 2004, Time's Covenant: Selected Poems, 2007, (essays) Facsimiles of Time, 2001, Ghazali: The Revival of Islam, 2007; editor: Moses Maimonides and His Time, 1989; contbr. articles and book revs. to profl. jours., poetry and essays to various mags., including New Republic, New Yorker, Grand St., Shenandoah, The New Criterion, The Yale Rev., The Times Lit. Supplement, So. Rev. and Chelsea; weekly columnist N.Y. Sun, 2004—. Instr. Princeton Adult Sch., 1978-80. DAAD fellow German Acad. Exch., 1973-74; recipient Ingram Merrill award, 1993. Mem. Mid. East Librs. Assn. (v.p. 1981-82, pres. 1982-83), Societe des Amis de Jean de la Fontaine, Can. Assn. Rsch. Librs. (v.p. 1988-89), Can. Libr. Assn., Assn. pour l'Avancement des Scis. et des Techniques de la Documentation, Conseil des recteurs et des principaux des univs. du Québec, Sous-Comité des Bibliotheques (pres. 1989-91). Roman Catholic. Address: 22 Belsize Park Gardens Flat 2 London NW3 4LH England Office: Libr Inst Ismaili Studies 42-44 Grosvenor Gardens London SW1W 0EB England Office Phone: 44 207 881 6045. E-mail: eric.ormsby@btinternet.com.

ORNE, EMILY CAROTA, psychologist, researcher; b. Boston, Sept. 7, 1938; d. Emil and Ruth (Farrell) Carota; m. Martin T. Orne, Feb. 3, 1962; children: Franklin Theodore, Tracy Meredith. BA, Bennington Coll., 1959. Rsch. assoc. Mass. Mental Health Ctr., Boston, 1963-64; rsch. psychologist Unit for Exptl. Psychiatry, Phila., 1964-79, sr. rsch. psychologist, 1979-83, co-dir., 1982—; rsch. assoc. psychology U. Pa. Sch. Medicine, Phila., 1983—. Trustee Inst. Exptl. Psychiatry Rsch. Found., Mass., 1964—, assoc. co-dir., 1987-97, exec. dir., 1998—; bd. dirs. False Memory Syndrome Found., 1995- Contbr. articles to profl. jours.; assoc. editor Internat. Jour. Clin. and Exptl. Hypnosis, 1977- Recipient Benjamin Franklin Gold medal Internat. Soc. Hypnosis, 1982, Roy M. Dorcus award Soc. Clin. and Exptl. Hypnosis, 1985, Bernard B. Raginsky award, 1993, Morton Prince award Soc. Clin. and Exptl. Hypnosis and APA, 1994 Avocations: fishing, swimming, reading. Office: U Pa Sch Medicine 1013 Blockley Hall 423 Guardian Dr Philadelphia PA 19104-6021

ORNELLAS, MAILE LOUISE, filmmaker, educator; b. Stockton, Calif., Nov. 18, 1948; d. Henry Alexander and Janet Evelyn Ornellas; 1 child, Maia An. BA in Psychology, U. Calif., Berkeley, 1971, M Journalism, 1977; MA in Psychology, San Jose State U., Calif., 1972. Prodn. asst. KPLX TV, San Francisco, 1975, prodr. pub. affairs programming, 1978; freelance reporter A Closer Look, KQED, San Francisco, 1977—77; prof. film/TV dept. Solano CC, Fairfield, Calif., 1979—; documentary prodr./reporter -capital news bur. PBS, Sacramento, 1979—79; prodr., audio visual cons. Burdick Group, San Francisco, 1980—83; lectr. ethnic studies U. Calif., Berkeley, 1995; lectr. Am. studies coll. fogn. langs. Hue U., Hue City, Vietnam, 2007—. Co-dir., writer, editor: (documentary film) Like Any Child, Only More So, 1977 (Student Acad. award for documentary, selected for permanent collection Libr. of Congress, LA Regional Emmy nominee); dir., writer, editor (public affairs program) All Together Now, 1978 (San Francisco Regional Emmy nominee). Mem. MoveOn.org, Berkeley, 2005—; pres. bd. dirs. G.R.O.U.P., Berkeley, 1973—76. Fulbright scholar, Ctr. Internat. Exch. of Scholars/J. William Fulbright Scholarship Bd., 2007. Mem.: Solano Coll. Calif. Tchrs. Assn (life; pres. 1988—89, W.H.O. award 1989). Avocations: travel, dance, cross country skiing. Office: Solano CC 4000 Suisun City Fairfield CA 94585 Business E-Mail: maile.ornellas@solano.edu.

ORNISH, DEAN, medical association administrator, medical educator; MD, Baylor Coll. Medicine. Resident in internal medicine Mass. Gen. Hosp., Boston, 1981-84; clin. fellow in medicine Harvard Med. Sch., 1981-84; clin. prof. medicine U. Calif., San Francisco, 1984—; founder, pres. Preventive Medicine Rsch. Inst., Sausalito, Calif., 1984—; also bd. dirs. Physician cons. to Pres. Bill Clinton, U.S. Congress, others; U.S. bd. dirs. UN High Commn. on Refugees. Author: 5 books including Dr. Dean Ornish's Program for Reversing Heart Disease, 1990, Eat More, Weigh Less, 1993, Love & Survival: The Scientific Basis for the Healing Power of Intimacy, 1998; contbr. numerous articles to profl. jours. Bd. dirs. Quincy Jones Listen Up Found. Recipient Outstanding Young Alumnus award U. Tex., 1994, U.S. Army Surgeon Gen. medal, Beckmann medal German Soc. Prevention and Rehab. Cardiovascular Diseases, 1996. Mem. Calif. Acad. Medicine. Office: Preventive Med Rsch Inst 900 Bridgeway Sausalito CA 94965-2100 Office Phone: 415-332-2525. Fax: 415-332-5730. Business E-Mail: info@pmri.org.

ORNT, DANIEL B., physician; b. Jan. 21, 1951; m. Jeanine Arden-Ornt. BA, Colgate U., 1973; MD, U. Rochester, 1976. Diplomate in internal medicine and nephrology Am. Bd. Internal Medicine, lic. physician N.Y., Ohio. Intern then resident U. Vt., 1976—79; fellow in nephrology U. Mich., 1979—81; from sr. instr. medicine to assoc. prof. U. Rochester (N.Y.) Sch. Medicine and Dentistry, 1981—97, prof. medicine and pediat., 1997—; assoc. dean for clin. affairs Sch. Medicine, Case Western Res. U., Cleve., 2003—. Assoc. chmn. clin. svcs. dept. medicine U. Rochester, 1998—2000, vice-chmn. dept. medicine, 2000—03, acting chief divsn. gastroenterology, 2000, assoc. program dir. gen. clin. rsch., 2002—03. Contbr. articles to profl. jours. Recipient Disting. Svc. award, Nat. Kidney Found., Inc., 1998. Fellow: ACP; mem.: Soc. for Clin. Trials, Am. Physiol. Soc., Am. Soc. Nephrology. Office: Case Western Res U Sch Medicine BRB 110 10900 Euclid Ave Cleveland OH 44106-4993 E-mail: dbo@case.edu.

ORONA, JOSEPH RYAN, information technology executive; b. Albuquerque, N.Mex., Aug. 10, 1967; s. Jose Ramon Jorge Orona and Maria Melinda Sanchez. BS in Aero. Studies, Embry-Riddle Aero. U., 1989. Pres. Retis Techs., Inc., Albuquerque, 1993—. Presdl. scholar, U. N.Mex, 1985. Mem.: Aircraft Owners and Pilots Assn. (life). Independent. Roman Catholic. Achievements include design of Scientific collaborative networks and data visualization. Avocations: flight, global travel, mountain biking, wine making, photography. Office: Retis Techs Inc PO Box 40305 Albuquerque NM 87196 Home Phone: 505-270-8129; Office Phone: 505-247-8129 202. Office Fax: 505-247-2473.

OROPEZA, DAWN MARTINEZ, art association administrator, artist, curator; d. Vincent Joseph Martinez and Helen Marie Feinberg Waitter; m. Juan Carlos Romero, Oct. 6, 2001; children: Juan Carlos, Agustin Cruz. BFA, Sch. Art Inst. Chgo., 1992; MFA, U. Calif. San Diego, La Jolla, 1998. Gallery mgr. Mexican Heritage Plz., San Jose, Calif., 2000—01; curator, cons. Cesar E. Chavez Found., LA, 2001, Wesley Images, San Jose, 2001—05; arts edn. and cmty. programs coord. Iowa Arts Coun., Des Moines, 2006—. Grad. student rep. affirmative action com. U. Calif. San Diego, La Jolla, 1996—97, grad. student rep., 1996—98. Exhibitions include Familia, installation, Abuelita, cmty. mural project, Corn Goddess, exhibitions include Mexihcahs: Keepers of the Fire. Recipient Kodak Medallion award, Ctrl. Iowa Regional Exhbn., 1985, Reconocimiento, Huey Tlahtokan, 2006; grantee Neighborhood Arts Program Partnership, Commn. Arts and Culture, San Diego, 1998; James Nelson Raymond fellow, Sch. Art Inst. Chgo., 1992, Russell Found. fellow, U. Calif. San Diego, 1996, Rsch. grantee, 1997. Mem.: Works San Jose (assoc.; programming chair 2002—04), Assn. Latino Artists (assoc.; founder 2006), Art Inst. Artists of Color United (assoc.; latino gov. 1989—92). Office: Iowa Arts Council 600 E Locust Des Moines IA 50319-0290 Home Phone: 515-480-0904; Office Phone: 515-281-5773. Business E-Mail: dawn.oropeza@iowa.gov.

OROPEZA, JENNY, state official; b. Montebello, Calif., Sept. 27, 1957; m. Tom Mullins. Mem. Long Beach Unified Sch. Dist. Bd. Edn., 1988—94; coun. mem. Long Beach City Coun., 1994—2000; state assembly mem. Dist. 55 Calif. State Assembly, 2000—. Mem. Latino Caucus. Democrat. Mailing: PO Box 942849 Rm 2148 Sacramento CA 94249 Office: One Civic Plaza Dr Ste 460 Carson CA 90745 Office Phone: 916-319-2055. Business E-Mail: assemblymember.oropeza@assembly.ca.gov.

O'RORKE, JAMES FRANCIS, JR., lawyer; b. NYC, Dec. 4, 1936; s. James Francis and Helen (Weber) O'R.; m. Carla Phelps, Aug. 6, 1964. AB, Princeton U., 1958; JD, Yale U., 1961. Bar: N.Y. 1962. Assoc. Davies, Hardy & Schenck, 1962-69; ptnr. Davies, Hardy, Ives & Lawther, 1969-72, Skadden, Arps, Slate, Meagher & Flom, NYC, 1972—2006, of counsel, 2007—. Dir. Clinipad Corp.; mem. adv. bd. Chgo. Title Ins. Co. N.Y. Trustee Mus. Am. Indian-Heye Found., 1977-80; dir. James Lenox House Assn., Inc., 1998-02. Mem. ABA, N.Y. State Bar Assn., Assn. Bar City N.Y., Am. Coll. Real Estate Lawyers, Princeton Club N.Y.C. Office: Skadden Arps Slate Meagher & Flom 4 Times Sq Fl 24 New York NY 10036-6595 Address: C/O Skadden Arps 4 Times Sq Rm 44200 New York NY 10036-6522 Home Phone: 212-262-0362; Office Phone: 212-735-2620. Business E-Mail: jororke@skadden.com.

O'ROURKE, C. LARRY, lawyer; b. Colusa, Calif., Dec. 10, 1937; s. James Harold and Elizabeth Janice (Jenkins) O'R.; m. Joy Marie Phillips, May 22, 1965; children: Ryan, Paula, Alina. BSEE, Stanford U., 1959, MBA, 1961; JD, George Washington U., 1972. Bar: Va. 1971, D.C. 1974, Calif. 2002, U.S. Ct. Appeals (fed. cir.) 1973, U.S. Patent and Trademark Office 1971, U.S. Supreme Ct. Patent atty. Westinghouse Elec., Washington, 1969-70, Pitts., 1970-73; assoc. Finnegan, Henderson, Farabow, Garrett & Dunner, Washington, 1974-79, ptnr., 1979—, mng. ptnr. Palo Alto, Calif. Dir. Zest Inc., Md., 1988, chmn. bd. dirs., 1990-95; mem. George Washington Law Sch. I.P. adv. coun., mem. bd. dirs. Stanford Bus. Sch. Alumni and mem. devel. coun. Stanford GSB. Mem. ABA, Am. Intellectual Property Law Assn., Inter-Pacific Bar Assn. Democrat. Presbyterian. Home Phone: 650-462-1889; Office Phone: 650-849-6640.

O'ROURKE, KATHLEEN ANN, education educator; b. Chgo., Ill., Aug. 1, 1972; BS, Ea. Ill. U., Charleston, 1994, MS, 1995; PhD, U. Tenn., 1999. Geriatric cons. St. Mary's Health Sys., Inc., Knoxville, Tenn., 1996—99; instr. Carson-Newman Coll., Jefferson City, Tenn., 1998—2001; asst. prof. U. Tenn., Knoxville, 1999—2001; assoc. prof. Ea. Ill. Univ. Sch. of Family and Consumer Sci., Charleston, 2001—. Vol. Am. Cancer Soc.-Relay for Life, Charleston, Ill., 2005—07. Mem.: Kappa Omicron Nu (advisor 2002—07). Office: Ea Ill Univ 600 Lincoln Ave Klehm Hall Charleston IL 61920 Office Phone: 217-581-6350. Office Fax: 217-581-6090. Business E-Mail: kaorourke@eiu.edu.

O'ROURKE, MAUREEN A., dean, law educator; BS summa cum laude, Marist Coll.; JD, Yale Law Sch. With IBM, 1985—93; assoc. prof. Boston U. Sch. Law, 1993—98, prof., 1998—, assoc. dean adminstrn., 2001—03, assoc. dean academic affairs, 2003—04, interim dean, 2004—06, dean, 2006—. Vis. prof. U. Victoria Law Sch., British Columbia, British Virgin Islands, 1999, Columbia U. Sch. Law, 1999, La Trobe U., Australia, 2002. Co-author: Copyright in a Global Economy; contbr. articles to law jours. Recipient Metcalf Award, 2002. Mem.: Marist Coll. Pre-Law Adv. Bd., Inst. for Study of Info. Techn. and Soc., Am. Law Inst., Alpha Chi. Mailing: Boston U Sch Law 765 Commenwealth Ave Boston MA 02215 Office Phone: 617-353-3123. Office Fax: 617-353-3077. Business E-Mail: morourke@bu.edu. *

O'ROURKE, ROBERT A., cardiologist, educator; b. San Francisco, Calif., June 12, 1936; m. Suzann Reiter, June 8, 1963; children: Michael, Kevin, Sean, Kathleen, Ryan. Student, Santa Clara U., 1954-55; BS, Creighton U., 1957, MD, 1961. Diplomate Am. Bd. Internal Medicine, Am. Bd. Cardiology. Straight med. internship Georgetown U. Hosp., Washington, 1961-62, jr. asst. resident internal medicine, 1962-63, sr. asst. resident internal medicine, 1963-64, med. houseofficer internal medicine, 1961-65, fellow cardiology dept., 1964-65, instr. in medicine cardiology, 1968-69; fellow U. Calif Cardiovasc. Rsch. Inst., Washington, 1965-66; staff cardiologist Madagan Army Hosp., Washington, 1966-68; asst. prof. medicine cardiology coll. medicine U. Ariz., Tucson, 1969-70; asst. prof. medicine cardiology, dir. clin. cardiology section, dir. heart station U. Calif., San Diego, 1970-73, assoc. prof. medicine cardiology, dir. clin. cardiology section, dir. coronary care unit, assoc. dir. myocardial infarction rsch. unit, 1973-76; acting chief medicine Audie L. Murphy Vets. Adminstrn. Hosp., 1977-78; Charles Conrad Brown disting. prof. cardiovasc. disease, dir. cardiovasc. divsn. U. Tex. Health Sci. Ctr., San Antonio, 1976—. Cons. in field for various hosps.; vis. professorships to various med. ctrs./univs. Mem. editl. bd.: Jour. Am. Coll. Cardiology, 1983-87, Am. Jour. Cardiology, 1976-81, 83—, Am. Heart Jour., 1980—, Clin. Cardiology, 1985—, Jour. Intensive Care Medicine, 1985—, Internat. Jour. Cardiology, 1981—, Annals of Internal Medicine, 1979-82, Med. Month, 1983—, Weekly Update: Cardiology, 1978-80, Cardiovasc. Medicine, 1976-80, Cardiologic Consultation, 1980—, Cardiovasc. Drugs and Therapy, 1989-90, Coronary Artery Disease, 1990—, Cardiology, 1990—, Jour. Heart Valve Disease, 1992, Current Problems in Cardiology, 1975—, assoc. editor, 1980-83, editor-in-chief, 1984—, Circulation, 1977-80, 81-83, 83-86, 86—, consulting editor, 1993, Yr. Book Cardiology, 1986-92, assoc. editor, 1986-92; assoc. editor: Jour. Applied Cardiology, 1985-90, Am. Jour. Cardiovasc. Pathology, 1985—. Recipient Sinsheimer award for Cardiovasc. Rsch., 1969-70; grantee from various sponsors. Fellow Am. Coll. Physicians, Am. Coll. Cardiology; mem. Am. Soc. Clin. Investigation, Am. Fedn. Clin. Rsch., Am. Heart Assn., Am. Physiological Soc., Assn. Army Cardiologists, Southern Soc. Clin. Rsch., Am. Soc. Echocardiography, Assn. U. Cardiologists, Alpha Omega Alpha, others. Office: The Univ Tex Health Sci Ctr VAH Rm C644 7703 Floyd Curl Drive San Antonio TX 78229-3900

O'ROURKE, THOMAS DENIS, civil engineer, educator; b. Pitts., July 31, 1948; s. Lawrence Robert and Adele Mildred (Moloski) O'R.; m. Patricia Ann Lane, Aug. 12, 1978; 1 child, Adele Christina. BSCE, Cornell U., Ithaca, NY, 1970; MSCE, U. Ill., 1973, PhD, 1975. Geotech. engr. Dames & Moore, NYC, 1970; rsch. asst. U. Ill., Urbana, 1970-75, asst. prof., 1975-78, Cornell U., Ithaca, NY, 1978-80, assoc. prof., 1981-87, prof., 1987-98, Thomas R. Briggs prof. engring., 1999—. Recipient Trevithick prize, Brit. Instn. Civil Engrs., 2002, Outstanding Paper award, Japan Gas Assn., 2003, Engr. Dist. Svc. award, U. Ill., 2005. Fellow: AAAS; mem.: ASTM (C.A. Hogentogler award 1976), ASME, NAE, ASCE (pres. Ithaca sect. 1981—82, chair exec. com. tech. coun. lifeline earthquake engr. 1998—99, Collingwood prize 1983, Huber prize 1988, C. Martin Duke award 1995, Stephen D. Bechtel pipeline engrng. award 1997, Ralph B. Peck award 2005), U.S. Com. on Tunnelling Tech. (chmn. 1987—88), Internat. Soc. Rock Mechanics, Internat. Soc. Engrng. Geology, Earthquake Engrng. Rsch. Inst. (bd. dirs. 1998—2000, v.p. 2000, pres. 2003—04, Outstanding Paper award 1996). Home: 10 Twin Glens Rd Ithaca NY 14850-1041 Office: Cornell U Sch Civil Environ Engring 273 Hollister Hall Ithaca NY 14853-3501 Office Phone: 607-255-6470. Business E-Mail: tdo1@cornell.edu.

O'ROURKE, WILLIAM ANDREW, literature and language professor, writer; b. Chgo., Dec. 4, 1945; s. William Andrew and Elizabeth (Kompare) O'R.; m. Marion Teresa Ghilarducci, July 9, 1986; 1 child, Joseph Ghilarducci. BA, U. Mo. at Kansas City, 1968; M.F.A., Columbia U., 1970. Instr. journalism Kean Coll., Union, NJ, 1973; asst. prof. English Rutgers U., 1975-78, Mount Holyoke Coll., 1978-81, U. Notre Dame, Ind., 1981-87, assoc. prof. Ind., 1987-94, prof. Ind., 1994—. Writer-in-residence Thurber House, Columbus, Ohio, fall 1984 Author: The Harrisburg 7 and the New Catholic Left, 1972, The Meekness of Isaac, 1974, Idle Hands, 1981, Criminal Tendencies, 1987, Signs of the Literary Times: Essays, Reviews, Profiles 1970-92, 1993, Notts, 1996,Campaign America '96: The View From the Couch, 1997, Campaign America 2000: The View From the Couch, 2001, On Having a Heart Attack: A Medical Memoir, 2006; editor: On the Job, 1977. Fine Arts Work Ctr. fellow, Provincetown, Mass., 1970-72; recipient Creative Artists Pub. Svc. award N.Y. State Coun. on Arts, 1975; Nat. Endowment for Arts creative writing fellow, 1981-82, 90-91. Mem. Authors Guild, PEN Am. Ctr., Nat. Book Critics Cir. Office: U Notre Dame Dept English 356 O'Shag Notre Dame IN 46556 Office Phone: 574-631-7377.

OROZCO, GABRIEL, artist; b. Jalapa, Veracruz, Mex., 1962; Student, Escuela Nat. Arte Plasticas, 1981—84, Circulo de Bellas Artes, Madrid, 1986—87. Artist-in-residence DAAD, 1995. One-woman shows include Kanaal Art Found., Kortrijk, 1993, Galerie Crousel Robelin BAMA, Paris, 1993, Mus. Modern Art, N.Y.C., 1993, Mus. Contemporary Art, Chgo., 1994, Marian Goodman Gallery, N.Y.C., 1994, 1996, 1998, Musée d'Art Moderne de la Ville de Paris, 1995, 1998, De Cardenas, Milan, 1995, Galerie Micheline Szwajcer, Antwerp, 1995, DAAD Gallery, Berlin, 1995, Art Gallery Ont., Toronto, 1996, Staalichen Mus. am Kulturforum, Berlin, 1997, Stedelijk Mus., Amsterdam, 1997, Anthony d'Offay Gallery, London, 1997, Centro Fotográfico Alvarez Bravo, Oaxaca, Mex., 1998, St. Louis Mus. Art, 1998, exhibited in group shows at Ill. Encuentro Nacional de Arte joven, Inst. Nacional de Bellas Artes, Aguascalientes, 1983 (hon. mention), Museo U. del Chopo, Mexico City, 1984, Museo Carrillo Gil, 1985, Museo de Art Moderno, 1987, Am. de Arte y Cultura, Brasilia, 1989, Bronx Mus. Art, 1990, Pasadena Art Ctr., 1991, New Mus. Contemporary Art, N.Y.C., 1993, Marian Goodman Gallery, 1993, 1994, 1998, 2000—03, 2005, Margo Leavin Gallery, L.A., 1994, Zacheta Nat. Gallery Contemporary Art, Warsaw, 1996, Whitney Biennial, N.Y., 1997, Berlin Biennial, 1998, Phila. Mus. Art, 1999, Yokohama Triennale, Tokyo, 2001, Moving Pictures, Guggenheim Mus., 2002, Venice Biennial, 2003, Taipei Biennial, 2004, Guangzhou Triennial, 2005, Speaking with Hands, Mus Folkwang Essen, 2006. Office: care Marian Goodman Gallery 24 W 57th St New York NY 10019-3918 Fax: 212-581-5187.

ORPHANIDES, GUS GEORGE, licensing executive; b. NYC, Jan. 27, 1947; s. Gus G. and Savesta (Agapetus) O.; m. Jeanne Wood, Feb. 3, 1968; children: Alyson, Paul, Lindsay. BS with honors, Hobart Coll., 1967; PhD, Ohio State U., 1972. Chemist E.I. Du Pont de Nemours & Co., Wilmington, Del., 1974—79, Beaumont, Tex., 1979—81, Air Products, Allentown, Pa., 1981—84, applications mgr., 1984—85, comml. mgr., 1985—88, rsch. mgr., 1988—91, sr. comml. devel. mgr., 1991—94, comml. devel. mgr., 1995—96, mgr. R&D, 1996—98, mgr. global tech. svc., 1998—2000, dir. applications devel., tech. svc., chem. tech., 2000—02, dir. intellectual asset mgmt. and licensing, 2002—. Contbr. articles to profl. publs.; patentee in field; developed new polymers for adhesives, non-wovens, paper coatings, polyurethane elastomers, rubber cross-linking. Phys. rehab. hosp. vol. in occupl. therapy. 1st lt. U.S. Army, 1972-74. Decorated Army Commendation medal; recipient Army Cert. of Achievment, Raker Meml. award Good Shepherd Hosp.; N.Y. State Regents scholar, 1963-67. Mem. Am. Chem. Soc., Licensing Exec. Soc. Roman Catholic. Achievements include development of novel emulsion polymers and polymer intermediates, international technology transfer, new business creation technology licensing, contract negotiation, work process devel. and instituionalism, R&D project management, acquisition due diligence, lab-to-plant technology transfer, plant start-up, new products commercialization, new bus. start-up, work process devel., deal closure, acquisitions/divestments. Home: 4046 Providence Ct Schnecksville PA 18078-3524 Office: Air Products 7201 Hamilton Blvd Allentown PA 18195-1526 Home Phone: 610-398-8966; Office Phone: 610-481-6142. E-mail: orphangg@airproducts.com, g.orphanides@att.net.

ORPHANIDES, NORA CHARLOTTE, ballet educator; b. NYC, June 4, 1951; d. M.T. and Mary Elsie (Tilly) Feffer; m. James Mark Orphanides, July 1, 1972; children: Mark, Elaine Orphanides Mastrosimone, Jennine. BA, CUNY, 1973; student, Joffrey Ballet Sch., NYC, 1970-75; postgrad., Princeton Ballet Sch., 1976-86. Cert. speech and hearing handicapped tchr. With membership dept. M.M.A., NYC, 1987—2002; mem. faculty Princeton (N.J.) Ballet Sch., 1983—, trustee emeritus, 1992—. Master tchr. ballroom dance. Mem. cast Princeton Ballet ann. Nutcracker, 1985-90, now Am. Repertory Ballet Co., 1993—; appeared in Romeo & Juliet, 1995-96, 2000. Fundraising gala chmn. Princeton Ballet, 1985, 86, 91-92, chmn. spl. events, 1987—, trustee, 1986—, chmn. Nutcracker benefit, 1990—, Dracula benefit, 1991, honoree, 1999; dept. chmn. June Fete to benefit Princeton Hosp., 1988, 90-92, 96, 2000, trustee, 1995-99; vol. Nat. Hdqrs. Recording for the Blind, 1991-93; dinner chmn. Nassau Ch. Music Festival, 1992, Handel Festival, Nassau Ch., 1993, Princeton Chamber Symphony, 1993; hon. chmn. Princeton Ballet Gala, 1993, Art First to benefit U. Med. Ctr., 2006; chmn. Christmas Boutique, Princeton Med. Ctr., 1993; trustee, Princeton Med. Ctr. Aux. Bd., 1992-2002, trustee 1995—, pres., 1997-99, past pres., 2000-2002; found. bd. dirs. U. Med. Ctr. Princeton, 2004—; choreographer Stuart Country Day Sch., Princeton, 1996-99, 2001; chmn. benefit dinner Eden Inst., 2000; sponsor, co-chair Am. Ballet Theatre Spring Gala, NYC, 2007. Named honoree Princeton Ballet, 1999, recipient Edward R. and Irene D. Farley Cmty. Stewardship award Eden Inst. Found., 2003. Democrat. Avocations: piano, skiing, tennis. Office: 301 N Harrison St Princeton NJ 08540-3512

ORR, A. SUMMEY, III, lawyer; b. Monroe, NC, 1960; AB, U. NC, Chapel Hill, 1983, JD, 1986. Bar: Ga. 1986, Ga. Ct. Appeals 1987, Ga. Supreme Ct. 1987, US Dist. Ct. (No. Dist. Ga.). Ptnr. Holland & Knight LLP, Atlanta, mem. dir. com. Mem.: State Bar Ga. (mem. real estate sect.), ABA (mem. real property, probate and trust sect.), Atlanta Bar Assn. (mem. real estate sect.), Internat. Coun. Shopping Ctrs., Nat. Assn. of Indsl. and Office Parks, Phi Delta Phi (magister 1985—86). Office: Holland & Knight LLP 1 Atlantic Ctr Ste 2000 1201 W Peachtree St NE Atlanta GA 30309 Office Phone: 404-898-8102. Business E-Mail: summey.orr@hklaw.com.

ORR, BOBETTE KAY, diplomat; b. Oak Park, Ill., Oct. 28, 1941; d. Robert Jay and Neta (Hoobler) Pottle; m. William Rucker Orr, Oct. 11, 1974; step children: Bridgette, Brietta, Alyson, William Jr. BA in Econs., Conn. Coll. for Women, 1963; student auditor Internat. Econs., London Sch. of Econs., 1964; postgrad. studies in Internat. Econs., George Washington U., 1964-65. Rsch. asst. C. of C. USA. Washington, 1965—66; country desk officer for Scandanavia U.S. Dept. Commerce, Washington, 1966—69, country desk officer for France, 1970—72, 1979—81, country desk officer for Belgium, Netherlands, Luxembourg, 1974—77, country desk officer for Japan, 1981—82; mkt. rsch. officer United States Trade Ctr., Stockholm, 1973, trade promotion officer London, 1977—78; asst. comml. attache Am. Embassy, Paris, 1982—87; comml. attache Am. Consulate Gen., Auckland, New Zealand, 1988—92, consul gen. Edinburgh, Scotland, 1992—95; comml. counselor Am. Embassy, London, 1995—99, Cairo, 1999—2002; regional dir. Africa, Near East, South Asia U.S. Dept. Commerce, Washington, 2002—04, 2006, regional dir. for Europe, 2005, regional dir. for Africa, Near East, South Asia, 2006—. Mem. bd. dirs. U.S. Dept. Commerce Fed. Credit Union, Washington, D.C., 1972-77, pres., 1976-77, mem. supervisory com., 1979-81; equal employment opportunity counselor for Greater Washington Met. Area, 1972-75; mission dir. for USDOC's Concrete Constrn. Techniques Seminar Mission to Hong Kong, Singapore, Malaysia, 1980; detailed to Office of Dir. Fgn. Comml. Svc. as evaluator of candidates for Fgn. Comml. Svc., 1981. Author: (with others) 10 pamphlet series, on free enterprise, The Power of Choice, 1966; contbr. to Bus. Am., 1966-81, Overseas Bus. Reports 1966-76 (Dept. Commerce publs.). Mem. Am. Women's Club of Edinburgh, (hon. pres.), The English Speaking Union. Avocations: skiing, bicycle riding. Home: PO Box 63 Great Falls VA 22066-0063 Office: USFCS/ITA Dept Commerce 14th and Constitution Ave NW Rm 2013 Washington DC 20230 Home Phone: 703-759-5555; Office Phone: 202-482-0368. Business E-Mail: Bobette.Orr@mail.doc.gov.

ORR, CAROLE, artist; b. Alexandria, Ind., June 10, 1933; d. Carl Victor and Marian Martha (Long) Coonse; m. Larry D. Ribble (dec. July 1953); m. Thomas LeRoy Orr, Nov. 10, 1950 (div. Oct. 1979); children: Karen Sue, Terri Ribble, David Thomas; m. Lev C. Hamblet Jr., Feb. 5, 1982 (div. Oct. 1998); stepchildren: James, Jean, Laura, Anne. Cert., Famous Artist Sch., Westport, Conn., 1956, Art Instrn. Schs., Mpls., 1962. Asst. art dir. La Gallerie du Mall, Houston, 1975—78; freelance fine artist Lantern Ln. Gallery, Houston, 1968—81, asst. mgr., design cons., 1979—81; artist Artist Showroom, Houston, 1982—. Participating artist Assistance Guild, Houston, 1968, Beaux Arts, Houston, 1968-70, Houston Gamma Phi Gallery, 1971-72, Houston Delta Gamma Found., 1978-81, Glassell Sch. of Art Houston, 1983; art instr. children's art Houston Park and Recreational Programs, 1964-68. One-woman shows include Nobler Gallery, Houston, 1967, Art Gallery, Pasadena, Tex., 1968, Gallarie La Rue, Austin, Tex., 1971, Gallery 12, Houston, 1972, Main St., Houston, 1974, La Galerie de Mall, Houston, 1976-78, Triumvirate Gallery, Santa Fe, N.Mex., 1980, Houshang's Gallery, Dallas, 1980-82, Battle Horn Galleries Ltd., Santa Fe, 1984, New Trends Inc., Santa Fe, 1985-88, Horizons Galleries, Houston, 1990-93, Houston C.C., 1992, Heinen Theatre, 1992, Windsor Gallery, Ft. Lauderdale, Fla., 1994; exhibited in group shows at Motorola Invitational, Houston, 1964, Assistance Guild Houston, 1968, Am. Gen. Bldg., Houston, 1968, Beaux Arts, Houston, 1968-70, Gamma Phi Gallery, Houston, 1971-72, Lantern Ln. Gallery, Houston, 1971-72, Delta Gamma Found., Houston, 1978-81, Glassell Sch. Art, Houston, 1983, New Trends Gallery Inc., Santa Fe, 1985-88, Pasadena (Tex.) Art Invitational, 1988, Double Tree Hotel, Houston, 1990, Horizons Gallery, Houston, 1990-93, Windsors Gallery, Dania, Fla., 1993, 2003, Magnolias Art Gallery, Town and Country Ctr., Houston, 2003-06, Bakery of the Poets, 2005—; T. Symington & Co. Interiors, Brenham, Tex., 2006. Art instr. adults Ch. of the Advent, Houston, 1968-70; adult edn. instr. arts Ch. Sch. Conf., Dept. Christian Edn., Trinity Ch., Diocese of Tex., Houston, 1969. Recipient Profl. Best Ann. Competition Art Instrn. Schs., Mpls., 1965; named Best-Selling Artist of Yr., 2001, Paintings DIRECT, N.Y.C., 2001, 03, Art on 5th, Austin, 2005, Diamond Domani Galleria, Houston, 2005, T. Sumington & Co. Interiors, Tex., 2006. Avocations: self-study in psychology, music, dance. Home and Office: Artist Showroom DBA 880 Tully Rd Apt 29 Houston TX 77079-5418

ORR, DENNIS PATRICK, lawyer; b. NYC, Dec. 29, 1952; s. Gerard Samuel and Mary Ellen (Dowd) O.; m. Laurie Louise Lawless, Jan. 15, 1977; children: Kathryn, Kristen, Megan, Matthew. BA, Boston Coll., 1975; JD, St. John's U., 1978. Bar: NY 1979, US Dist. Ct. (so. and ea. dists. NY) 1979, US Ct. Appeals (2nd cir.) 1986. Assoc. Shearman & Sterling, NYC, 1978-86, ptnr., 1987-97, Mayer, Brown & Platt, NYC, 1997—2006, Morrison & Foerster, NYC, 2006—. St. Thomas More scholar St. John's

Law Sch., Jamaica, NY, 1975. Mem. ABA, NY State Bar Assn. Roman Catholic. Office: Morrison & Foerster 1290 Avenue of the Americas New York NY 10104-0050 Office Phone: 212-468-8161. Business E-Mail: dorr@mofo.com. *

ORR, ETHAN, non-profit organization executive; b. 1974; BA in Hist., U. Ariz., BA in Polit. Sci., MPA. Empowerment Zone adminstr. Office of Econ. Devel., Tucson; coun. aid City of Tucson City Coun.; exec. dir. Linkages Inc. Adj. faculty Polit. Sci. dept., U. Ariz., Bus. dept., Pima Cmty. Coll.; faculty mentor Flinn Found. of Ariz. Mem. Faith Christian Ch. Make A Difference Day projects; mem Ariz. Joint Legis. Com. on Homelessness; mem. Fred G. Acosta Cmty. Rels. Coun. Named one of 40 Under 40, Tucson Bus. Edge, 2006. Mem.: Southern Ariz. Job Developers Assn. (co-chair). Office: Linkages Inc Goodwill Bldg Ste 201 1920 E Silverlake Rd Tucson AZ 85710 Office Phone: 520-571-8600.

ORR, FRANK HOWARD, III, architect; b. Jasper, Ala., Sept. 4, 1932; s. Frank Howard Jr. and Lola Ruth (Lynch) O.; m. Nancy Gayle Gentry, Apr. 13, 1957; children: Mark Daniel, Steven Gentry, Karen Diann, Amy Ruth. B in Applied Art, Auburn U., Ala., 1961. Registered Tenn. Assoc. architect Edwin A. Keeble Assocs., Nashville, 1962-70, Bianculli & Tyler, Inc., Chattanooga, 1970; prin. Frank Orr Architects, Nashville, 1970-76; pres., prin. Orr/Houk & Assocs. Architects, Inc., Nashville, 1976-2001; v.p. Hart Freeland Roberts, Inc. (merged with Orr/Houk), Brentwood, Tenn., 2001—04; prin. Frank Orr, AIA, Cons. Arch., 2004—. V.p. Hart Freeland Roberts, Inc., Brentwood, Tenn.; adj. faculty O'More Sch. Design, Franklin, Tenn., 1972—77, Nashville State Tech. Inst., 1978—79; guest lectr. Sch. Arch., Victoria U., Wellington, New Zealand, 1987; exam grader Nat. Coun. Archtl. Registration Bds., Ft. Lauderdale, Fla., 1985; guest lectr. Coll. Arch., Auburn U., 2001. Author: Professional Practice in Architecture, 1982, Scale in Architecture, 1985, Alabama Boy, An Architect's Memoir, 2006; author (column) Urban Life, Nashville Bus. Jour., 1995; editor, co-author: Notable Nashville Architecture 1930-1980; contbr. articles to profl. jours.; prin. works include Woodmont Bapt. Ch. (design commendation 1979, Design award of Merit 1990), Appalachian Ctr. for Crafts, Two Rivers Bapt. Ch. (design commendation 1979), 1st Bapt. Ch., Hendersonville, Tenn. (design award of merit 1992), First Bapt. Ch., Athens, Ala., First Bapt. Ch., Pasadena, Tex., Tenn. Bapt. Conf. Ctrs., Carson and Linden, First Baptist Ch., Joelton, Tenn., Lake Providence Missionary Bapt. Ch., Nashville. Active Citizens com. Met. Nashville Gen. Plan, 1994; mem. Plan of Nashville Project, 2002—03; co-team leader Project Plan of Nashville, Nashville Civic Design Ctr., 2004—05; missionary trips, Guatemala, 1977, 1982, Mexico, 1980, Sierra Leone, 1985, 88, Poland, 1998, Brazil, 2000, Portugal, 2004. Mem.: AIA (dir. Mid. Tenn. chpt. 1971—78, chmn. Gulf States design awards com. 1985, com. environ. edn. 1972—76), Tenn. Soc. Architects (sec.-treas. 1977), Nashville C. of C. (regional transp. com. 1993—94), Scarab Archtl. Honor Soc., Auburn U. Baptist. Avocations: drawing, writing. Personal E-mail: forr1@comcast.net.

ORR, FRANKLIN MATTES, JR., petroleum engineering educator; b. Baytown, Tex., Dec. 27, 1946; s. Franklin Mattes and Selwyn Sage (Huddleston) O.; m. Susan Packard, Aug. 30, 1970; children: David, Katherine. BSChemE, Stanford U., Calif., 1969; PhD in Chem. Engring., U. Minn., 1976; DEng (hon.), Heriot-Watt U., Edinburgh, Scotland, 2005. Asst. to dir. Office Fed. Activities EPA, Washington, 1970-72; rsch. engr. Bellaire Rsch. Ctr. Shell Devel. Co., Houston, 1976—77; head miscible flooding and gas injection N.Mex Petroleum Recovery Rsch. Ctr. N.Mex Inst. Mining and Tech., Socorro, 1978-84; assoc. prof. petroleum engring. Stanford U., Calif., 1985-87, prof., 1987—, prof. chem. engring., 1994—, Keleen and Carlton Beal prof. petroleum engring., 1994—; dir. Global Climate and Energy Project, 2002—. Bd. dirs. Monterey Bay Aquarium Rsch. Inst., 1987—, Am. Geol. Inst. Found., 1997—2002, David and Lucile Packard Found., 1999—; interim dean Stanford U. Sch. Earth Scis., 1994—95, dean, 1995—2002; mem. adv. bd. Princeton U. Carbon Mitigation Initiative, 2004—; sr. fellow Ctr. Environ. Sci. and Policy Stanford U. Inst. Internat. Studies, 2005—; mem. com. to visit Earth and planetary scis. Harvard U., 2006—. Contbr. articles to profl. jours. Bd. dirs. Wolf Trap Found. for Performing Arts, 1988-94 Recipient Robert Earll McConnell award, AIME, 2001. Mem.: Soc. Indsl. and Applied Math., Soc. Petroleum Engrs. (Disting. Lectr. award 1988—89, Disting. Achievement award, Petroleum Engring. Faculty 1993), AAAS, AIChE, NAE. Office: Stanford U Dept Petroleum Engring 074 Green Earth Scis Bldg 367 Panama Str Stanford CA 94305-2220 Home Phone: 650-853-3066. E-mail: fmorr@pangea.stanford.edu.

ORR, JAMES F., III, foundation administrator; b. Mpls., 1943; BA, Villanova U., 1962; MA, Boston U., 1969. With New Eng. Mchts. Bank, Boston, 1965-67, Bache & Co., NYC, 1967-69; ptnr. Cardinal Mgmt. Co., Boston, 1969-75; exec. v.p., treas. Conn. Bank and Trust Corp., 1975-86; with UNUM, 1986-98, COO, pres.; chmn. bd., CEO UNUM Corp., 1987—99; also pres., chmn., CEO UNUM Life Ins. Co. (subs.), to 1999; pres., CEO United Asset Mgmt. Corp., Boston, 2000—01; chmn. bd. trustees Rockefeller Found., NYC, 2000—. Bd. dir. Mellon Fin. Corp., 2003—. Bd. trustees Bates Coll., Villanova Univ.; bd. overseers Harvard Sch. Pub. Health. Office: Rockefeller Found 420 Fifth Ave New York NY 10018-2702

ORR, JAMES FRANCIS, business process outsourcing executive; b. Phila., Oct. 10, 1945; s. James F. Jr. and Dorothy (Gallagher) O.; m. Catherine Marie Reinholt; children: Kristin Leah, Lauren Beth, James Desmond. Student, Pa. State U., 1963-64, Rutgers U., Camden and New Brunswick, NJ, 1964-67. Various sales mgmt. positions Procter & Gamble, 1967-73, dist. mgr. White Plains, N.Y., 1973-76, nat. accounts mgr. Cin., 1976-78, sales div. mgr., 1978-81, sales merchandising mgr., 1981-82; sales dir. Procter & Gamble Ltd., Newcastle upon Tyne, Eng., 1982-85; v.p. sales Crush Internat. Inc., Cin., 1985-88; v.p. mkt. devel. Matrixx Mktg. Inc. subs. Cin. Bell Inc., Cin., 1989-92, pres., CEO, 1993; COO Cincinnati Bell Inc.; pres Convergys Corp., Cin., 2000—05, CEO, 2000—07, chmn., 2000—. Mem. parents adv. coun. Hamilton Coll., Clinton, N.Y., 1989-91, vice chmn. Parents Fund, 1989-90, chmn., 1990-91; active Grad. Leadership Cin., class XVI, 1992-93. Mem. Direct Mktg. Assn., Soc. Consumer Affairs Profls., Greater Cin. C. of C., Coldstream Country Club (trustee), Melrose Club (Daufuskie Island, S.C.). Avocations: golf, theater, antiques, travel. Office: Convergys Corp PO Box 1638 Cincinnati OH 45201-1638 *

ORR, JENNIE MARIE (JENNIE THOMAS), family physician; b. Sioux City, Iowa, Feb. 16, 1952; d. J. Allen and Ione B. (Gronlund) O.; m. Daniel Joel Thomas, Aug. 23, 1980; children: Lorraine Marie, Joel Allen. BS in Computer Sci., Mich. State U., 1973, MD, 1976. Diplomate Am. Bd. Family Practice. Sub-intern pediatrics Grad. Med. Edn., Inc., Lansing, Mich., 1977; intern, resident family practice Cedar Rapids (Iowa) Med. Edn. Program, 1977-80; staff Allina Med. Clinic, Hastings, Minn., 1980—, corp. sec., 1984—88. Chmn. dept. obstetrics Regina Meml. Hosp., Hastings, 1986-90. Fellow Am. Acad. Family Practice. Lutheran. Office: Allina Med Clinic 1210 1st St W Hastings MN 55033-1085

ORR, JIM (JAMES D. ORR), editor, writer, publishing executive; b. Buffalo, Feb. 7, 1960; s. David James and Doris Kathleen (Wolos) O.; m. JoEllen Black, June 4, 1994. B in Journalism, Ind. U. of Pa., 1982, M in Comm., 1987. Station mgr. Sta. WIUP-TV, Ind., Pa., 1983-84; sports writer, news writer Ind. (Pa.) Gazette, 1984-88; reporter Stuart (Fla.) News, 1988-89; staff writer, columnist Gannett Rochester (N.Y.) Newspapers, 1989-96; staff writer The Bus. Jour., Fresno, Calif., 1997; sr. writer The Fresno Bee, 1998-99; features, spl. projects and weekend editor, page designer The Westerly (R.I.) Sun, 2000—03; editor, pub. Heartland Pub. Newspapers, Halstead, Kans., 2004—06; pub. Sidney Sun-Telegraph, Nebr., 2007—. Columnist Orrdinary People, 1994—95, 2007—. Moderator polit. debate Edu-Cable Corp., Greece, N.Y., 1993; panelist conf. New England Soc. Newspaper Editors, 2002. Recipient Agrl. Writing 1st Place award Penn-Ag Industries, 1985, 2d Pl. Keystone State Press award Pa. Newspaper Pub. Assn., 1987, 2 Writing awards Scripps Howard, 1989, award Gannett Enterprise Project, 1994, Cmty. Svc. award N.Y. Newspaper Pubs. Assn., 1994-95, 4 awards R.I. Press Assn., 2000-03, Cmty. Svc. editing awards Kans. Press Assn., 2004, 05. Home: PO Box 943 Chappell NE 69129 Office Phone: 308-254-2818. Business E-Mail: jorr@suntelegraph.com. E-mail: jorr777@hotmail.com.

ORR, JOSEPH NEWTON, recreational guide, outdoor educator; b. San Francisco, Oct. 25, 1954; s. James Neewah and Verna Louise (Butler) O. BA in Spanish, Sul Ross State U., 1981. Cert. swiftwater rescue technician, wilderness first responder, open water scuba diver, Grand Canyon river guide, Tex. master naturalist. Instr. astronomy lab. Sul Ross State U., Alpine, Tex., 1972-75; svc. sta. attendent, store clerk Nat. Park Concessions, Big Bend Nat. Park, 1975-78; surveyor's aide Gila Nat. Forest U.S. Dept. Agriculture, N. Mex., 1979; instr. ESL Centro Universitario de Idiomas, Mexico City, 1981; English and Spanish tutor Ctr. Student Devel. Sul Ross State U., 1980-83, instr. ESL, Intensive Summer Lang. Tng. Inst. Alpine, Tex., 1980-83; ednl. cons. Chihuahuan Desert Rsch. Inst., Alpine, Tex., 1983; editor The Skyline (student newspaper) Sul Ross State U., 1984; interpreter, translator, guide Dr. John M. Miller, Mexico, 1980-85; guide in U.S., Mex., Belize, Guatemala and Honduras for Far Flung Adventures, Terlingua, Tex., 1986-94, Remarkable Journeys, Houston, 1994-98; with Ceiba Adventures, Flagstaff, 1998—, Mountain Travel Sobek, 2005—. Active Grand Canyon River Guides. Mem. Internat. Dark Sky Assn., Grand Canyon Assn., Planetary Soc., Tex. Ornithol. Soc., Audubon Soc., Tex. Wildlife Assn., Astron. Soc. of Pacific, San Antonio Astron. Assn., Night Sky Network. Democrat. Avocations: astronomy, archaeology, birding, camping, hiking. Home and Office: 13235 Trentwood San Antonio TX 78231 E-mail: josephorr@aol.com.

ORR, KENNETH BRADLEY, academic administrator; b. Charlotte, NC, Mar. 15, 1933; s. Frank Wylie and Kate Harriett O.; m. Ruth Douglas Currie; children: Kevin, Jeffrey, Jonathan. BA, Duke U., 1954; MDiv, Union Theol. Sem., 1960, ThM, 1961; PhD, U. Mich., 1978; LittD, Carroll Coll., 1990; DD, Presbyn. Coll., 1997. Ordained to ministry, Presbyn. Ch., 1961. Minister West End Presbyn. Ch., Roanoke, Va., 1961-64; asst. to pres. Union Theol. Sem., Richmond, Va., 1964-68, v.p., 1968-74; pres. Presbyn. Sch. Christian Edn., Richmond, 1974-79, Presbyn. Coll., Clinton, S.C., 1979-97, pres. emeritus, 1997—; sr. v.p. John McRae & Assocs., Atlanta, 1997—. Past mem. coun. presidents Nat. Assn. Intercollegiate Athletics, Kansas City, Mo., chmn. S. Atlantic Conf., 1989—91; mem. nat. adv. com. on instnl. quality and integrity U.S. Dept. Edn., 1995—2001. Contbr. to religious and ednl. publs. Mem. Assn. Presbyn. Colls. and Univs. (pres. 1994, exec. com.), Coun. Ind. Colls. (bd. dirs. 1993-96), Laurens County C. of C. (past pres.), Kiwanis. Democrat. Avocations: reading, travel, classical music.

ORR, MARCIA, primary school educator, consultant, director; b. Anamosa, Iowa, Mar. 2, 1949; d. Harold Edward Eiben and Clara Elizabeth (Hubbard) E.; m. Robert J. Orr, Sept. 6, 1969; 1 child, Jennifer. Student, U. Iowa, 1977; BS, St. Xavier U., Chgo., 1981; MEd in Early Childhood Leadership, Nat. Louis U., 1996. Bookkeeper Monticello State Bank, 1967-69; exec. sec. Davenport Bank and Trust, 1969-73; asst. educator Elisabeth Ludeman Devel. Ctr., Park Forest, Ill., 1979; tchr. Flossmoor Hills (Ill.) Elem. Sch., 1980-1984; exec. dir. Co-Care, Inc., Park Forest, 1984-89; child devel. rschr., Flossmoor, Ill., 1989—; tchr. Nazarene Nursery Sch. and Kindergarten, Chicago Heights, Ill., 1991; child care ctr. cons. Matteson Sch. Dist. 162, Park Forest, 1991—, adv. mem. project early start, 1991—, home-sch. coord., 1992—; founder, pres., exec. dir. Before and After Sch. Enrichment, Park Forest, 1991—. Grant writer Matteson Sch. Dist. 162 and Before and After Sch. Enrichment, Inc., founder, pres., exec. dir. Child Care Enrichment Ctr. and pre-sch.; officer Boleo Childcare Ctr., Iowa City, 1975-77; mentor to dirs. child care programs early childhood edn. dept. Nat.-Louis U., Ill, 1994—; co-founder Reaching New Horizons, Inc., 1996—; mem. oversight and coord. com. Ill. State Bd. Edn. Early Learning Coun., 2007-. Contbr. articles pub. to profl. jour. Tchr. religion Infant Jesus of Prague Ch., Flossmoor, Ill., 1982—; mem. Flossmoor PTO, 1987-89; music chmn. Dist. 161 PTO, 1980-90; exec. dir. Before and After Sch. Enrichment, Inc.; parent resource coord. Matteson Sch. Dist. 162. McCormick fellow, 1995—; recipient Golden Achievement award Nat. Sch. Pub. Rels. Assn., 2001; named Best Practices and Rsch. honoree Louis U., Evanston, Ill., 2001. Mem. NAFE, Nat. Assn. for Edn. Young Children (validator), Women Employed Orgn., Internat. Platform Assn., Parent Inst., South Suburban Small Bus. Assn. (charter). Democrat. Roman Catholic. Avocations: piano, classical music, travel. Home: 9411 Fox Run Ct Frankfort IL 60423-1380 Office: Before and After Sch Enrichment 210 Illinois St Park Forest IL 60466-1100 Office Phone: 708-606-5426. Business E-Mail: base@base-inc.net.

ORR, RICHARD CLAYTON, mathematician, retired securities trader; b. Oakland, Calif., Mar. 28, 1941; s. James Clayton and Helen (Kittle) Orr; children: Robert Clayton, Debra Orr Kostoff. AB in Math., Humboldt State Coll., Arcata, Calif., 1964; MA in Math., Syracuse U., 1966, PhD in Math., 1969. From asst. prof. to assoc. prof. SUNY, Oswego, 1969—81, chmn. dept. math.; pres. Contratrend, Inc., Lexington, Mass., 1981—84; v.p. rsch. John Gutman Investments Corp., New Britain, Conn., 1984—90; pres. Chronos Corp., Lexington, Mass., 1990—95; gen. ptnr. ROME Ptnrs., Marblehead, Mass., 1995—2003; mng. dir. Calibar, LLC, Glastonbury, Conn., 2000—04. Reference Market Technicians Assn., NYC, 1989—2002, assoc. editor, 1985—89. Contbr. articles to profl. jours. Avocations: meteorology, hiking, sailing. Home Phone: 510-524-4586. Personal E-mail: rco.calibar@comcast.net.

ORR, ROBERT F., not-for-profit administrator, retired state supreme court justice; b. Norfolk, Va., Oct. 11, 1946; married; 4 children. AB, U. N.C., 1971, JD, 1975. Bar: N.C. 1975. Pvt. practice, Asheville, NC, 1975—86; judge N.C. Ct. Appeals, 1986—94; assoc. justice N.C. Supreme Ct., Raleigh, 1994—2004; exec. dir., sr. counsel N.C. Inst. of Constitutional Law, 2004—. Mem. N.C. Alcoholic Beverage Control Commn., 1985—86; adj. prof. appellate advocacy N.C. Ctrl. U. Sch. Law, 1989—2003, adj. prof. N.C. State constl. law, 2004. Mem. Asheville-Revitalization Commn., 1977—81, Asheville-Buncombe Hist. Resources Commn., 1980—81; bd. trustees Hist. Preservation Found. NC, 1982—85; mem. Nat. Park Sys. Adv. Bd., 1990—95, chmn., 1992—93; bd. visitors U. NC-Chapel Hill, 1993—97; mem. NCBAs Adminstrn. Justice Comm., 2004—, Gov.'s Crime Commn. With US Army, 1968—71. Mem.: N.C. Bar Assn., 28th Jud. Dist., N.C. State Bar. Republican.

ORR, SAN WATTERSON, JR., lawyer; b. Madison, Wis., Sept. 22, 1941; s. San Watterson and Eleanor Augusta (Schalk) Orr; m. Joanne Marie Ruby, June 26, 1965; children: San Watterson III, Nancy Chapman. BBA, U. Wis., 1963, JD, 1966. CPA Wis.; bar: Wis. 1966. Sec., treas., bd. dirs. Yawkey Lumber Co., Wausau, Wis., 1971—; pres. Forewood, Inc., Wausau, 1979—, also bd. dirs.; dir. Marshall & Ilsley Bank, Wausau, 1988—, Marshall & Ilsley Corp., 1994—; chmn. bd. dirs. Wausau Paper Corp., 1997—. Editor: U. Wis. Law Rev., 1962—63. Bd. dirs. Aytchmonde Woodson Found., Inc., Wausau, 1966—2006, Leigh Yawkey Woodson Art Mus., Inc., Wausau, 1981—; pres. Woodson YMCA Found., Wausau, 2002, Nancy Woodson Spire Found., Inc., 2002, Aspirus Health Found., Inc., Wausau, 1998—; chmn. U. Wis. Found., Madison, 2003—05, chmn. emeritus; bd. dirs. Wis. Taxpayers Alliance, Madison, 1983—2006, Wis. Mfrs. and Commerce, 2001—04, Woodson YMCA Found., Wausau, 1979—, Nancy Woodson Spire Found., Inc., 1980—, Aspirus Health Found., Inc., Wausau, 1981—, U. Wis. Found., Madison, 1991—, Wis. Policy Rsch. Inst., Milw., 1995—2006; bd. regents U. Wis. Sys., Madison, 1993—2000, pres., 1998—2000; bd. dirs. Lynde and Harry Bradley Found., 2006—. Mem.: Am. Law Inst., Wis. Bar Assn., Ocean Club Fla., Country Club Fla., Minocqua Country Club. Office: Yawkey Lumber Co 500 3rd St Ste 602 Wausau WI 54403-4857

ORR, TERRENCE S., dancer, ballet master, artistic director; b. Berkeley, Calif., Mar. 12, 1943; m. Cynthia Gregory (div.); m. Marianna Tcherkassky. Student, San Francisco Ballet Sch. With San Francisco Ballet, 1959-65; with Am. Ballet Theatre, NYC, 1965-97, soloist, 1967-72, rehearsal asst., 1970-73, prin. dancer, 1972-78, assoc. ballet master, 1973-78, ballet master, 1978-97; artistic dir. Pitts. Ballet Theatre, 1997—. Prodr. Royal Winnipeg Ballet, Nat. Ballet of Mexico, Teatro alla Scala in Millan, Nat. Ballet de Nancy in France, Teatro Colon in Buenos Aires, Pitts. Ballet Theatre, Boston Ballet, Ballet West, Dance Theatre of Harlem, N.Y.C. Ballet, Cleve./San Jose Ballet, San Francisco Ballet, Ballet Ariz., Sadler's Wells Royal Ballet, Paris Opera Ballet, Australian Ballet. Dancer (ballets) The Nutcracker, San Francisco Ballet, Fantasma, Divertissement d'Auber, Jeu des Cartes, Con Amore, Billy the Kid, Am. Ballet Theatre, Coppelia, La Fille Mal Gardee, Petrouchka, The River, Rodeo, Don Quixote, At Midnight, Dark Elegies, Fancy Free, Graduation Ball, Harbinger, Variations for Four, Pulcinella Variations, Brahms Quintet, Schubertiade, Mendelssohn Symphony, Polyandrion, Giselle, Swan Lake, La Sylphide, Gartenfest, Ontogeny; prodr., dir. Gala Performance, 1984; prodr.: La Sylphide, Rodeo; performer: Fancy Free; prodr.: Graduation Ball, Etudes, Billy the Kid, Fall River Legend, Giselle, Coppelia, Don Quixote, Swan Lake. Office: Pitts Ballet Theatre 2900 Liberty Ave Pittsburgh PA 15201-1511 *

ORR, ZELLIE, entrepreneur, educator, writer, researcher; b. Holly Ridge, Miss., May 12, 1951; d. Leonard and Lucille Rainey; m. Foster G. Orr Jr., Feb. 28, 1976 (div. July 14, 1998); children: Kai A., Nia Haley. Student, L.A. City Coll., 1970—71, U. Calif., Northridge, 1971—73; cert., Airline Schs. Pacific, 1974, CMLS Inst., 1979; MA in Human Letters, U. Metaphysics, 1983. Cert. real estate salesperson, Ga., 1979, pub. notary, Ga, 1985. Personal lines underwriter Kemper Ins. Co., LA, 1976—78, Comml. Union Ins. Co., Atlanta, 1980—82, Moore Group ins. Co., Atlanta, 1982—85; lic. real estate agent Wofford Realty, Riverdale, Ga., 1979—81; owner Traffic Jam Lounge and Restaurant, Sunflower, 1986—89; documentation specialist Windsor Group, Atlanta, 1989—2001, mem. billing and collection mgmt. sys., 1991; pres., founder Comm. Unltd., Austell, Ga., 1995—. Mem. rsch. bd. advisors Am. Biog. Inst., Raleigh, NC, 1992—93. Co-author: Treasured Poems of America, 1989 (Editor's Choice award, 1989), The Best Poems & Poets of the 20th Century, 2000 (Editor's Choice award, 2000), Theatre of The Mind, 2003; author: numerous poems. Co-organizer Sunflower County Civil Rights and Cmty. Reunion, Indianola, 1999; founder Charles E. Scattergood Meml. Found., Marietta, Ga., 2000; mem. So. Poverty Law Ctr., Habitat for Humanity, Feed the Children. Named 1967 Pioneer of Sch. Desegregation, Mayor of Indianola, Miss., 2007; recipient Cert. Appreciation, Superior Ct., Calif., 1976, Cert. Recognition, CME Ch., Indianola, 1999, Disting. Svc. award, Nat. Mus. of Tuskegee Airmen, 2004, Disting. Svc. and Dedication award, Alva N. Temple chpt. Tuskegee Airmen Inc., 2005, Presdl. award, Tuskegee Airmen, Inc., 2006, Pioneers of Indianola Sch. Desegregation Cert. of Recognition, Martin Luther King Jr. Steering Com., 2007. Mem.: NAACP, NAFE, Am. Metaphys. Drs. Assn., Nat. Trust Hist. Preservation, Nat. Mus. Women in Arts, Internat. Soc. Poets, Nat. Black MBA Assn. Avocations: stamp collecting/philately, reading, coin collecting/numismatics, antiques, chess. Home: 3285 Doyle Ln Marietta GA 30060 Office: Comm Unltd 3999 Austell Rd Ste 303 #158 Austell GA 30106 Personal E-mail: orrs@artsonwheels.com. E-mail: orrz@bellsouth.net.

ORRAJ, CRAIG ALLEN, lawyer; BS, Ariz. State U., 1985; JD, U. Ariz., 1988. Bar: N.Mex., Tex. Ptnr. Acosta & Associates, Albuquerque; mng. ptnr. Law Offices of Craig A. Orraj, Albuquerque; staff counsel Farmer's Ins. Exch. & Affiliates. Mem.: ABA Tort Trial & Ins. Practice Sect. (vice chair staff counsel com.), N.Mex State Bar (commr. 2002—, pres.-elect 2006—08). Office: Ste 525 500 Marquette Ave NW Albuquerque NM 87102-5301 Office Phone: 505-242-8654, 505-246-2924. E-mail: craig.orraj@farmersinsurance.com.

ORRINGER, JEFFREY S., dermatologist, educator; b. Balt., Dec. 7, 1967; s. Mark B. and Susan M. Orringer; m. Kelly A. Orringer, May 1, 1994; children: Matthew J., Kate A. BA with honors, Brown U., 1990; MD, Harvard Med. Sch., 1994. Diplomate Am. Bd. Dermatology. Resident U. Mich., Ann Arbor, 1994—2000, fellowship in Mohs surgery and cosmetic dentistry, 2000—02, asst. to assoc. prof. dept. dermatology, 2002—; dir. Cosmetic Dermatology and Laser Ctr., Ann Arbor, 2002—. Contbr. articles to profl. jours. Patient-Directed Investigation grantee, Dermatology Found., 2001—02, Clin. Career Devel. grantee, 2002—05. Fellow: Am. Acad. Dermatology, Am. Soc. Dermatologic Surgery, Am. Coll. Mohs Micrographic Surgery and Cutaneous Oncology, Am. Soc. Laser Medicine and Surgery; mem.: Assn. Acad. Dermatologic Surgeons. Achievements include research in laser therapy and cosmetic dermatology. Office: U Mich Dept Dermatology 1500 E Medical Center Dr Ann Arbor MI 48109 Office Phone: 734-615-0682.

ORROCK, ROBERT DICKSON, agricultural educator, state legislator; b. Fredericksburg, Va., Nov. 13, 1955; s. Welford and Cornelia (Houck) O.; m. Betsy Malinda Massey, Mar. 18, 1978; children: Robby, Lila, Welford. Student, Va. Poly. Inst. & State U., 1974-75, BS in Agrl. Edn., 1978; MS in Agrl. Edn., Va. State U., 1984-87; student, Germanna C.C., Locust Grove, Va., 1975-76. Agrl. edn. instr. Hanover County, Va., 1978, 86-91; vocat. edn. instr. Spotsylvania County, Va., 1978-85, 91—; sales rep. New Holland, Gordonsville, Va., 1985-86; announcer WFLS-Radio, Fredericksburg, 1988—. Vol. instr. Va. Game Commn.; past adv. bd. Rappahannock Electric Coop.; bd. mem. Rappahannock Emergency Med. Svcs. Coun., 1986—; mem. Ladysmith Vol. Rescue Squad, 1973—; deacon Bethany Bapt. Ch., Spotsylvania; treas. Caroline County (Va.) Rep Com., 1987-89; del. Va. Ho. Dels., Richmond, 1990—; bd. mem. Rappahannock Area Assn. Retarded Citizens, 1991—. Named Outstanding Educator, Tri-County Soil and Water Conservation, 1980-83, Va. State Dairyman's Assn., 1983, Va. Farm and Home Electrification Coun., 1987, named Outstanding Young Virginian, Va. Jaycees, 1994, Legislator of Yr., Va. Vocat. Assn., 1992; recipient Community Svc. award Fredericksburg Area Builders Assn., 1994. Mem. Va. Vocat. Agrl. Tchrs. Assn. (state pres. 1991-92). Republican. Baptist. Avocations: gardening, hunting, woodworking. Home: 12387 Nancy Wrights Dr Woodford VA 22580-2307

ORR-WEAVER, TERRY L., cell biologist, educator; PhD in Biol. Chemistry, Harvard U., 1984. Mem. Whitehead Inst. Biomedical Rsch., Cambridge, Mass., 1987—; prof. biology MIT, Cambridge, 1987—. Chair sci. adv. com. Damon Runyon Cancer Rsch. Found.; co-grad. officer dept. biology MIT, 1998—2004. Contbr. articles to sci. jours. Named a Searle Scholar, 1988; grantee Jane Coffin Child Meml. Fund fellowship, 1984. Fellow: NAS; mem.: Genetics Soc. Am. (v.p. 2004, pres. 2005). Achievements include discovery of two proteins crucial for proper partitioning of chromosomes during meiosis. Office: Dept Biology MIT 31 Ames St 68-132 Cambridge MA 02139 E-mail: weaver@wi.mit.edu.

ORSATTI, ERNEST BENJAMIN, lawyer; b. Pitts., Nov. 14, 1949; s. Ernest Ubaldo and Dorothy Minerva (Pfeiffer) O.; m. Ingrid Zalman, May 3, 1975; 1 child, Benjamin E. BA, Marquette U., 1971; JD, Duquesne U.,

1974; postgrad., Army Command and Gen. Staff Coll., 1984. Bar: Pa. 1974, U.S. Dist. Ct. (we. dist.) Pa. 1974, U.S. Ct. Appeals (3d cir.) 1977, U.S. Ct. Appeals (6th cir.) 1992, U.S. Ct. Appeals (4th cir.) 2006, U.S. Supreme Ct. 1978. Assoc. Jubelirer, Pass & Intrieri, Pitts., 1974-81, ptnr., 1981—. Contbg. editor: The Developing Labor Law, 4th edit., 1992—2002; chpt. editor The Developing Labor Law, 4th edit., 2002—; contbg. editor: Elkouri and Elkouri, How Arbitration Works, BNA, 2001—. Bd. dirs. Am. Italian Cultural Inst., Pitts., 1999—2004. Served to capt. US Army, 1975, lt. col. USAR, ret. Mem. ABA, ACLU (legal com. 1996-2005), Am. Arbitration Assn., Pa. Bar Assn., Allegheny County Bar Assn. (profl. ethics com. 2000—), Am. Legion. Democrat. Roman Catholic. Home: 9343 N Florence Rd Pittsburgh PA 15237-4815 Office: Jubelirer Pass & Intrieri 219 Fort Pitt Blvd Pittsburgh PA 15222-1576 Office Phone: 412-281-3850. Personal E-mail: eborsatti@aol.com. Business E-Mail: ebo@jpilaw.com.

ORSILLO, JAMES EDWARD, computer engineer, information technology executive; b. Elmira, NY, Oct. 30, 1939; s. Giacomo and Irene (Heppy) O.; 1 child, June Lynne. BEE, RCA Insts., 1962; BS in Elec. Engring. and Math., Ind. Inst. Tech., 1964; MS, Rensselear Poly., 1968; BS in Nuclear Engring., Capital Radio Electronic Inst., 1974. Communications engr. Bell Telephone Labs., Holmdel, N.J., 1962-63; video engr. Westinghouse, Elmira, N.Y., 1965-66; computer engr. GE, Pittsfield, Mass., 1966-67; systems specialist Control Data Corp., Mpls., 1968-70; software specialist Computer Sci. Corp., Morristown, N.Y., 1970-72; prin. cons. Computer Cons. Assocs., Elmira, 1972-78; CEO ORTHSTAR, Inc., Elmira, 1974—; acquired Hughes Tng., Inc. Rail Simulation Bus., 1996—. Owner, pres. Shadowstand Properties, Inc. (FKA O-K Properties), Elmira, 1984—, Thundering Hooves Stables, Elmira, 1985—. Author: Mindstorm, 2004. Mem. IEEE, Am. Nuclear Soc., Soc. Indsl. and Applied Math., Am. Helicopter Soc., Army Aviation Assn. Am., Internat. Flying Engrs., USAF Assn., U.S. Naval League, U.S. Polo Assn. Republican. Achievements include invention of Integrated Data Acquisition System (IDAS), of Thread Algebra used in simulation development, of Extended Sentient Non-linear Ensemble (ESNE). Office: ORTHSTAR Inc Airport Corp Park PO Box 459 Big Flats NY 14814-0459 Home Phone: 607-562-8737; Office Phone: 607-562-2100. Business E-Mail: orsillo@orthstar.com.

ORSON, BARBARA TUSCHNER, actress; b. NYC, May 19, 1929; d. Jonah Tuschner and Rebecca Traceman; m. Jay M. Orson, June 24, 1956; children: Beth-Diane, Theodore. Student, Dramatic Workshop, NYC, 1948-50. Leading soubrette Am. Savoyards, NYC, 1950-51, 53-55; actress Trinity Repertory, Providence, 1964—2002. Founding mem. Trinity Sq. Repertory Co., Providence, 1964—2001. Actress Edinburgh Festival, Scotland, 1968, Am. Repertory Theatre, Cambridge, Mass., 1981-85, Williamstown (Mass.) Theatre, 1985-89, Dallas Theatre Ctr., 1985, Yale Repertory Co., New Haven, Conn., 1991; appeared in: (films) Mission Hill, Code of Ethics, My One and Only, Swimming Upstream, Mr. North, Strangers in Transit (TV) Theatre in America, Feasting with Panthers, Life Among the Lowly, House of Mirth, Camera Three, RI Demon Murder, Miller's Court, Conflict of Interest (Am. premiere) The Suicide, 1980, (world premiere) Grown Ups, 1981, God's Heart, 1995; founding mem., appeared in over 100 prodns. Trinity Sq. Repertory Co., Providence, 1964—; (radio) House of Mirth, Masterpiece Radio Theatre with Jane Alexander; guest artist (Lady Macbeth), Brown U. Recipient Adrian Hall award, Trinity Repertory Co., RI, 2002. Mem. Am. Fedn. Radio and TV Artists, Screen Actors Guild, Actor's Equity Assn., Trinity Rep. Co. (founder). Home: 281 Hillside Ave Pawtucket RI 02860-6119

ORSZAG, JONATHAN MARC, economist, consultant; b. Boston, Apr. 15, 1973; s. Steven Alan and Reba Karp O.; m. Rica Rodman, June 17, 2000. AB, Princeton U., 1995; MSc, Oxford U., Eng., 1997. Econ. policy advisor The White House Nat. Econ. Coun., Washington, 1996-99; dir. policy and strategic planning U.S. Dept. Commerce, Washington, 1999—2000; mng. dir. Sebago Assocs., Washington, 2000—06, Competition Policy Assocs., Inc. a subs. of FTI Cons., Inc., Washington, 2003—. Mem. Calif. Workforce Investment Bd., Sacramento, 2000-03; mem. Calif. Tech. Adv. Group, Sacramento, 2000-03; adj. lectr. U. So. Calif., 2002-03; fellow U. So. Calif. Ctr. for Comm. Law and Policy; bd. dirs. Ibrix, Inc. Recipient Leadership award, Corp. Enterprise Devel., 1999; Marshall scholar, 1996. Mem. Pacific Coun. on Internat. Policy, L.A. World Affairs Coun., Asia Soc., Am. Econ. Assn., Am. Polit. Sci. Assn. Avocation: golf. Office: 1919 Pennsylvania Ave NW Washington DC 20006 Home: 101 Loring Ave Los Angeles CA 90024 Home Phone: 310-441-0160; Office Phone: 202-263-1444. E-mail: jorszag@competitionpolicy.com.

ORSZAG, PETER RICHARD, economist; b. Boston, Dec. 16, 1968; s. Steven Alan and Reba (Karp) O.; children: Leila Madeleine, Joshua Nathaniel AB summa cum laude, Princeton U., 1991; MS, London Sch. Econs., 1992, PhD, 1997. Econ. advisor Ministry of Fin., Moscow, 1992-93; staff economist Coun. Econ. Advisers, Washington, 1993-94; prof. rsch. staff London Sch. Econs., 1994-95; sr. economist Coun. Econ. Advisers, Washington, 1995-96, sr. adviser, 1996; sr. econ. advisor Nat. Econ. Coun., 1997, spl. asst. to pres for econ. policy, 1998; pres. Sebago Assocs., 1998—2007; dir. Congressional Budget Office, Washington, 2007—. Lectr. in econs. U. Calif., Berkeley, 1999—2000; rsch. assoc. Ctr. Retirement Rsch., Boston Coll., 2000—07. Marshall scholar, 1991-92. Mem. Nat. Acad. Social Ins., Phi Beta Kappa. Office: Congrl Budget Office Ford Ho Office Blg 2d & D St SW Washington DC 20515 Office Phone: 202-226-2700. Business E-Mail: peter.orszag@cbo.gov.

ORSZAG, STEVEN ALAN, applied mathematician, educator; b. NYC, Feb. 27, 1943; s. Joseph and Rose (Siegel) O.; m. Reba Karp, June 21, 1964; children: J. Michael, Peter Richard, Jonathan Marc. BS, M.I.T., 1962; postgrad. (Henry fellow), St. John's Coll., Cambridge U., Eng., 1962-63; PhD, Princeton U., 1966. Mem. Inst. Advanced Study, Princeton, NJ, 1966—67; prof. applied math. MIT, 1967—84; prof. applied and computational math. Princeton U., 1984—98, dir., 1990—92, Hamrick prof. engring., 1989—98; Smith prof. math. Yale U., New Haven, 1998—, chmn. applied math., 1999—2003. Founder Flow, CHI, Ibrix, Inc., Vectek, Inc.; cons. in field. Author: Studies in Applied Mathematics, 1976, Numerical Analysis of Spectral Methods, 1977, Advanced Mathematical Methods for Scientists and Engineers, 1978; contbr. numerous rsch. publs. in field. A.P. Sloan Found. fellow, 1970-74, Guggenheim fellow, 1989-90. Fellow Am. Inst. Physics (Otto Laporte award 1991), AIAA (Fluid and Plasmadynamics award, 1986), Soc. Indsl. and Applied Math., Soc. Engring. Sci. (G.I. Taylor medal, 1995). Business E-Mail: orszag@math.yale.edu.

ORT, SHANNON, lawyer; b. Appleton, Wis. BA magna cum laude in Criminal Justice and Legal Studies, Hamline U., 1998; JD magna cum laude, William Mitchell Coll. Law, 2001. Bar: Minn. 2001, Wis. 2002. Assoc. Steffens & Rasmussen; assoc. atty. litig. dept. Rider Bennett, LLP, Mpls.; founder, ptnr. Terzich & Ort, LLP, Mpls., 2007—. Named a Rising Star, Minn. Super Lawyers mag., 2006; recipient, 2007. Mem.: Hennepin County Bar Assn., Minn. State Bar Assn., Edina C. of C. Office: Terzich and Ort LLP Ste # 5 8525 Edinbrook Crossing Minneapolis MN 55443 Office Phone: 763-391-7412. Business E-Mail: sort@tolawoffice.com.

ORTEGA, GREGORY LUIS, hematologist, oncologist; b. NY, Dec. 23, 1954; s. Luis and Dolores B. Ortega; m. Glennys Ortega; children: Glennys, Ramon. MD cum laude, Nat. U. Pedro Henriquez Urena, Santo Domingo, Dominican Republic, 1979. Diplomate in internal medicine, hematology, subspecialty med. oncology, lic. NY, Tenn., Fla., Va., Ind. Family practice resident Peninsula Gen. Hosp., Far Rockaway, NY, 1980—81; internal medicine resident E. Tenn. State U., Johnson City, 1981—84, asst. prof. internal medicine, 1987—89; hematology fellowship Mount Sinai Sch. Medicine, NYC, 1984—86; oncology fellowship Albert Einstein Coll. Medicine, Bronx, NY, 1986—87; v.p. Mid-Fla. Hematology & Oncology Ctrs., P.A., 1989—. Attending staff N. Side Hosp., Johnson City, 1987—89, Johnson City Med. Ctr., 1987—89, Ctrl. Fla. Regional Hosp., Sanford, 1989—, S. Seminole Cmty. Hosp., Londwood, Fla., 1990—93, courtesy staff, 1993—; chief hematology, oncology Vets. Adminstrn. Med. Ctr., Mt. Home, Tenn., 1988—89; staff affiliation Mid-Fla. Hematology & Oncology Ctrs., P.A., 1989—; attending staff Fla. Hosp. Deland (formerly Meml. Hosp.), 1993—, Fla. Hosp. Fish Meml. (formerly Fish Meml. Hosp.), Orange City, 1993—; prin. investigator Sarah Cannon Cancer Ctr., 1997—2004, Vanderbilt-Ingram Cancer Ctr. Affiliate Network, 2006—; mem. numerous coms. in field. Contbr. scientific papers to profl. jours. Recipient Resident's Clin. Excellence award, E. Tenn. State U., 1983. Mem.: AMA. Avocations: golf, travel. Office: Mid Fla Hematology and Oncology Ctrs PA 1061 Med Ctr Dr Ste 100 Orange City FL 32763

ORTEGA, KENNY, television director, choreographer; b. Palo Alto, Calif., Apr. 18, 1950; Dir.: (films) Newsies, 1992, Hocus Pocus, 1993; (TV films) High School Musical, 2006 (Outstandnig Directorial Achievement in Children's Programs, Dir. Guild Am., 2007), The Cheetah Girls 2, 2006; (TV series) Fame LA, 1997, Chicago Hope, 1998—99, Ally McBeal, 2001, Gilmore Girls, 2002—06; choreographer (films) Xanadu, 1980, One From the Heart, 1982, St. Elmo's Fire, 1985, Pretty in Pink, 1986, Ferris Bueller's Day Off, 1986, Dirty Dancing, 1987, Salsa, 1988, Shag, 1989, To Wong Foo Thanks for Everything, Julie Newmar, 1995, (TV films) The Way She Moves, 2001; supervising choreographer, artistic dir. co-prodr. Salt Lake Winter Olympic Games 2002 Opening Ceremony (Emmy award outstanding dir. for a variety, music or comedy spl., Emmy award outstanding choreography). Recipient Golden Eagle award lifetime achievement, Nosotros. *

ORTEGA, MARIA A., security firm executive, educator; b. NYC, Apr. 28, 1967; d. Humberto and Delia Margarita Ortega. BS, U. Chgo., 1992. Cert. Homeland Sec. Am. Coll. Forensic Examiners, 2003. Police officer N.Y.C. Police Dept., 1985—88; human resources mgr. Burns Internat. Security, NYC, 1988—93; human resources mgr., dir. tng. Initial Security, NYC, 1994—96; dir. human resources and tng. Command Security Svcs., NYC, 1996—98; sr. program mgr. Opportunity Am., NYC, 1998; pres., CEO Security Works Inc., NYC, 1999—. Bd. dirs. N.Y. State Divsn. Criminal Justice Svc.; chmn. N.Y. State Divsn. Labor Latino JSEC, NYC, 2001—. Named to Winner Circle, Burns Internat., 1989; recipient Rising Star award, N.Y. State Dept. Labor, 2000. Mem.: Nat. Assn. Chiefs of Police, ASIS Internat., Bklyn. C. of C. Avocations: basketball, music, reading, cooking. Office: Security Works Inc 41 Belknap Ave Yonkers NY 10710-5403 Office Phone: 718-780-4496.

ORTEGA, TONY, editor-in-chief; b. 1964; Grad., Calif. State U., Fullerton. Staff writer New Times, Phoenix, 1995—99, LA, 1999—2001, assoc. editor Phoenix, 2001—03; mng. editor The Pitch, Kansas City, 2003—05; editor New Times, Broward-Palm Beach, Fla., 2005—07; editor-in-chief Village Voice, NYC, 2007—. Recipient Virg Hill award, Ariz. Press Club, 1996, Best Column award, Assn. Alternative Newsweeklies, 2005. Office: Village Voice LLC 36 Cooper Sq New York NY 10003 *

ORTEGO, GILDA BAEZA, library director, educator; b. El Paso, Tex., Mar. 29, 1952; d. Efren and Bertha (Singh) Baeza; m. Felipe de Ortego y Gasca, Dec. 21, 1986. BA, Tex. Woman's U., 1974, PhD, 2001; MLS, U. Tex., 1976, postgrad., 1990-93; cert., Hispanic Leadership Inst., 1988. Stack maintenance supr. El Paso Libr. U. Tex., 1974-75; pub. svcs. libr. El Paso Community Coll., 1976-77; ethnic studies libr. U. N.Mex., Albuquerque, 1977-81; br. head El Paso Pub. Libr., 1981-82; dep. head Mex.-Am. Svcs., El Paso Pub. Libr., 1982-84; libr. Mex.-Am. Studies U. Tex. Libr., Austin, 1984—86; libr. Phoenix Pub. Libr., 1987-89; assoc. libr., west campus Ariz. State U., Phoenix, 1989-90; Proyecto Leer libr. Tex. Woman's U., Denton, 1991-92; dean divsn. learning resources Sul Ross State U., Alpine, Tex., 1992—99; dir. univ. libr., Tex. A&M U., Kingsville, 1999—. Speaker and cons. in field. Founding editor jour. La Lista, 1983-84; founding indexer Chicano Periodical Index, 1981-86; reviewer jour. Voices of Youth Advocates, 1988-90; contbr. poetry and articles to books and jours. Recipient Silver award, Nat. Commn. Library and Info. Sci., 1996. Mem. ALA (com. on standing of women in profession, com. on profl. edn.), MLA, Assn. for Libr. and Info. Sci. Edn., Tex. Libr. Assn., Ariz. State Libr. Assn. (pres. svcs. Spanish speaking Roundtable 1988-90), Reforma (pres. El Paso chpt. 1983, pres. Ariz. chpt. 1989-90, nat. v.p. 1993-94, natpres. 1994-95), Unltd. Potential, Inc. (treas. 1988-89), Hispanic Leadership Inst. Alumni Assn.

ORTEL, THOMAS LEE, oncologist, hematologist, educator; b. Greenfield, Ind., Aug. 27, 1957; s. Donald William and Shirley Radine (Abbott) O. BS with high distinction, Ind. U., 1979, PhD in Chemistry, 1983; MD, Ind. U. Sch. Medicine, 1985. Diplomate Am. Bd. Internal Medicine, Hematology Subspeciality. Intern Duke U. Med. Ctr., Durham, NC, 1985-86, resident, internal medicine, 1985—88, fellow in hematology and oncology, 1988-91, assoc. in medicine, 1991-93, asst. prof. medicine, 1993-98, med. dir. Clin. Coagulation Lab. and Platelet Immunology Lab., dir. Anticoagulation mgmt. svc., 1994—, assoc. prof. medicine, 1999—, asst. prof. pathology, 1994—2004, assoc. prof. pathology, 2004—. Med. dir. Platelet Antibody Lab., 1999— Mem. editl. bd.: Blood, Thrombosis Rsch.; contbr. articles to profl. jours. Recipient Am. Heart Assn. Clinician Scientist award, 1991-96, Pew Scholar award, 1995-2000, Medforte Innovation award Am. Soc. of Artificial Internal Organs, 2000. Office: Duke U Med Ctr Div Hematology-Oncology DUMC 3422 Durham NC 27702-3422 Office Phone: 919-684-5350. Business E-Mail: ortel001@mc.duke.edu. *

ORTENZIO, ROBERT A., health and medical products executive; V.p. Rehab Hosp. Svcs. Corp.; sr. v.p. Continetal Med. Systems, Inc., Mechanicsburg, Pa., 1986—88, COO, 1988—95, pres., 1995—96; exec. v.p., dir. Horizon/CMS Healthcare Corp.; co-founder, pres., COO Select Medical, Mechanicsburg, Pa., 1997—2001, pres., 2001—04, CEO, 2001—. Bd. dir. US Oncology, Inc. Office: Select Medical 4716 Old Gettysburg Rd Mechanicsburg PA 17055 Office Phone: 717-972-1100. *

ORTENZIO, ROCCO ANTHONY, health facility administrator; b. Steelton, Pa., Nov. 28, 1932; s. Rocco and Minnie Ortenzio; m. Nancy Miller, Jan. 29, 1955; children: John, Robert, Martin. BS, West Chester U., 1955; postgrad., U. Pa., 1955—56. Pvt. practice phys. therapy, Harrisburg, Pa., 1957—69; founder, pres., CEO Rehab. Corp., Harrisburg, 1969—77, Pa. Health Corp., Mechanicsburg, Pa., 1977—79, Rehab. Hosp. Svc. Corp., Mechanicsburg, 1979—85; co-founder, chmn, CEO Continental Med. Sys., Inc. (merged with Horizon Healthcare Corp.), Mechanicsburg, 1986—95, Select Medical, Mechanicsburg, Pa., 1997—2001, exec. chmn., 2001—. Bd. dirs. Continental Med. Sys., Inc., PNC, N.A., AMSCO Internat., Quorum Health Group, Inc. Mem.: World Pres. Orgn. Republican. Roman Catholic. Office: Select Material 4716 Old Gettysburg Rd Mechanicsburg PA 17055 Office Phone: 717-972-1100. *

ORTH, ANDREA, lawyer; b. Oct. 27, 1967; BA, Univ. Wash., 1990; JD cum laude, Univ. Puget Sound Sch. Law, 1994. Bar: Wash. 1994. Former judicial clerk Wash. State Ct. Appeals, Div. II, 1994—95; of counsel Bucknell Stehlik Sato & Stubner, LLP, Seattle. Contbr. articles to numerous profl. jours. Named Wash. Rising Star, SuperLawyer Mag., 2006. Mem.: ABA, Wash. State Assn. Trial Lawyers, Wash. State Bar Assn. Office: Bucknell Stehlik Sato and Stubner LLP Ste 400 2003 Western Ave Seattle WA 98121

ORTH, DAVID NELSON, endocrinologist, educator, sculptor, potter; b. East Orange, NJ, Mar. 5, 1933; s. John Joseph and Marjorie Adelaide (Wauters) O.; m. Linda Diana D'Errico, June 9, 1979; children by previous marriage: John Randall (dec.), Jennifer Stewart, Julie Thomas. ScB in Chemistry, Brown U., 1954; MD, Vanderbilt U., 1962. Intern, Osler med. service Johns Hopkins Hosp., Balt., 1962-63, fellow in medicine, 1962-65; asst. resident John Hopkins Hosp., Balt., 1963-65; mem. faculty dept. medicine Vanderbilt U. Sch. Medicine, Nashville, 1965—, prof., 1975-98, prof. emeritus, 1998—, joint dir. endocrinology div. dept. medicine, 1968-81, dir. cancer research and treatment ctr., 1972-77, dir. div. endocrinology, 1984-96; sculptor and potter, 1998—. Scholar-in-residence Rockefeller Found. Bellagio Study and Conf. Ctr., Italy, 1989; vis. scientist Vollum Inst. for Advanced Biomed. Rsch., Oreg. Health Scis. U., Portland, 1993-94. Contbr. numerous articles in field of endocrinology to med. jours. Served with U.S. Navy, 1954-57. John and Mary R. Markle scholar, 1968-73; Howard Hughes Med. Inst. investigator, 1969-75 Mem. AAUP, AAAS, ACP, Assn. Am. Physicians, Am. Soc. Clin. Investigation, Endocrine Soc. (sec.-treas. 1989-94, pres. 1997-98), N.Y. Acad. Scis., Am. Fedn. Clin. Rsch., So. Soc. Clin. Investigation. Personal E-mail: orth@comcast.net.

ORTH, PAUL WILLIAM, retired lawyer; b. Balt., May 7, 1930; s. Paul W. and Naomi (Howard Bevard) O.; m. Isle Haertle, June 15, 1956; children: Ingrid, Ilse Christine. AB, Dartmouth Coll., 1951; JD, Harvard U., 1954. Bar: Mass. 1954, Conn. 1957, U.S. Dist. Ct. Conn. 1958, U.S. Ct. Appeals (2d cir.) 1960, U.S. Ct. Appeals (1st cir.) 1983, U.S. Supreme Ct. 1960. Assoc. Hoppin, Carey & Powell, Hartford, Conn., 1957-62, ptnr., 1962-86, Shipman & Goodwin, Hartford, 1987-2000, MacDermid, Reynolds & Glissman P.C., Hartford, 2000—. Instr. Sch. Law U. Conn., 1959-81. Editor: Every Employee's Guide to the Law, 1993, 96. Chmn. Farmington Conservation Commn., 1982-83; mem. town com. Town of Farmington, 1973-81; dir. Conn. Opera Assn., 2000-02. With AUS, 1954-56. Fellow Am. Bar Found., Conn. Bar Found.; mem. ABA, Hartford County Bar Assn. (pres. 1983-84), Conn. Bar Assn. (chmn. coms.). Democrat. Office: MacDermid Reynolds & Glissman PC 86 Farmington Ave Hartford CT 06105 Home Phone: 860-677-1559; Office Phone: 860-278-1900. Business E-Mail: porth@mrglaw.com.

ORTH, SUSAN LYNN, judge; b. Evansville, Ind., Nov. 15, 1958; d. Orville William and A. Margaret Orth; m. Terrance D. Becker; 1 child, Brandy L. Orth Becker. BSc, Ind. State U., Terre Haute, 1981; MSc, U. Louisville, Ky., 1982; JD, Salman P. Chase Coll. Law, Ky., 1985. Cert.: (mediator advanced family and civil tng.). Chief dep. prosecutor Floyd County Prosecutor's Office, New Albany, Ind., 1987—2002; sr. prosecutor So. Dist. Ind., 2002—04; judge Floyd County Superior Ct., New Albany, 2004—. Instr. Nat. Dist. Attys. Assn., Columbia, SC, 1998—2002; mem. faculty Ind. Prosecuting Attys. Coun., Indpls., 1998—2002, Ind. Jud. Ctr., Indpls., 2005—; mem. state bd. law examiners com. on character and fitness, local com. on race and gender fairness Ind. Supreme Ct. Atty. New Albany City Coun., 1992—95; mem. judiciary and media com. Ind. Supreme Ct., 2004—; vol. Success by Six Metro United Way, New Albany, 2006; mem. bd. So. Christian Leadership Conf., 1998—, Metro United Way, 2004—; mem. Leadership So. Ind. Class of 2006. Named Citizen of Yr., New Albany Mayor's Office, 2002; recipient Drum Major award, So. Christian Leadership Conf., 1999. Mem.: Sherman Minton Inns of Ct. (pres. exec. bd. 2006—07), Am. Justice Inst. (mem. exec. bd. 2004—), Bus. and Profl. Women. Office: Floyd Superior Ct Room 200 City/G Bldg New Albany IN 47150

ORTIQUE, REVIUS OLIVER, JR., retired judge; b. New Orleans, June 14, 1924; s. Revius Oliver and Lillie Edith (Long) O.; m. Miriam Marie Victorianne, Dec. 29, 1947; 1 child: Rhesa Marie (Mrs. Alden J. McDonald). AB, Dillard U., 1947; MA, Ind. U., 1949; JD, So. U., 1956; LLD (hon.), Campbell Coll., 1960; LHD (hon.), Ithaca Coll., 1971; LLD (hon.), Ind. U., 1983, Morris Brown Coll., 1992, Loyola U. South, 1993, Dillard U., 1996, So. U. Law Ctr., 2005. Bar: La. 1956, U.S. Dist. Ct 1956, Eastern Dist. La 1956, U.S. Fifth Circuit Ct. of Appeals 1956, U.S. Supreme Ct 1964. Practiced in, New Orleans, 1956-78; judge Civil Dist. Ct. for Orleans Parish, 1978-92; assoc. justice La. Supreme Ct., 1993—94, ret., 1994; chmn. New Orleans Aviation Bd., 1994—2002. Lectr. labor law Dillard U., 1950-52, U. West Indies, 1986; formerly assoc. gen. counsel Cmty. Improvement Agy.; former gen. counsel 8th Dist. A.M.E. Ch.; former mem. Fed. Hosp. Coun., 1966, Pres.'s Commn. on Campus Unrest, 1970, Bd. Legal Svcs. Corp., 1975-83; chief judge civil cts. Orleans Parish, 1986-87; spkr. in field; U.S. alt. rep. to 54th Gen. Assembly UN, 1999-2000. Contbr. articles to profl. jours. Former pres. Met. Area Com.; former mem. Bd. City Trusts, New Orleans, New Orleans Legal Assistance Corp. Bd., Ad Hoc Com. for Devel. of Ctrl. Bus. Dist. City of New Orleans; bd. dirs. Cmty. Rels. Coun., Am. Lung Assn.; trustee Antioch Coll. Law, New Orleans chpt. Operation PUSH, 1981-84; pres. Louis A. Martinet Soc., 1959; active World's Fair, New Orleans, 1984, Civil Rights Movement, 1960-79; bd. dirs., exec. com. Nat. Sr. Citizens Law Ctr., L.A., 1970-76, Criminal Justice Coordinating Com., UN Assn. New Orleans, 1980—; former mem. exec. bd. Nat. Bar Found.; mem. exec. com. Econ. Devel. Coun. Greater New Orleans; past chmn. Health Edn. Authority of La.; trustee, exec. com. Dillard U., 1965—; former mem. bd. mgmt. Flint Goodridge Hosp.; former adv. bd. League Women Voters Greater New Orleans; former men's adv. bd. YWCA; trustee AME Ch., former connectional trustee; former chancellor New Orleans Fedn. Chs.; bd. trustees Crimestoppers of New Orleans; mem. Com. for a Better New Orleans; bd. dirs. Nat. Legal Aid and Defender Assn.; trustee Civil Justice Found. 1st lt. AUS, 1943-47, PTO. Recipient Arthur von Briesen medal Disting. Svcs. Disadvantaged Ams. NLADA, 1971, Weiss award NCCJ, 1975, Brotherhood award NCCJ, 1976, Nat. Black Achievement award, 1979, Poor People's Banner award, 1979, His Personal Flag presented by 6 nat. poor people's groups at Nat. Client's Coun. Ann. Conv., San Diego, 1979, William H. Hastie award, 1983, Outstanding Citizen award Kiwanis of Pontchartrain, 1986, Civil Justice award, 1989, Daniel E. Byrd award NAACP, 1991, A.P. Tureaud Meml. medal La. State NAACP, 1993; Revius O. Ortique Jr. Law Libr. named in his honor, Lafayette, La., 1988; named Outstanding Young Man Nat. Urban League, 1958, Outstanding Person in La. Inst. Human Understanding, 1976, Citizen of Yr. Shreveport, 1993; named one of 100 Internat. Leaders as World Opinion Maker The Imperial Govt. of Japan, 1995. Mem. ABA (del., Legal Svcs. program, Nat. adv. coun., 1964-71, jud. divsn., Thurgood Marshal award 2000), Nat. Bar Assn. (pres. 1965-66, exec. bd., Raymond Pace Alexander award, jud. coun. 1987, William Hastie award 1982, Gertrude E. Rush award 1991, Thurgood Marshall award 2000), La. State Bar Assn. (former mem. ho. of dels., Lifetime Achievement award 1986, WTC award for Exceptional Internat. Distinction, 2001), Nat. Legal Aid and Defender Assn. (past pres., mem. exec. bd.), La. District Judges Assn., Am. Judicature Soc. (bd. dirs. 1975-79), Civil Justice Found. (trustee 1989-93), Louis A. Martinet Legal Soc., World Peace Through Law (charter mem.), Blue Key Honor Soc., Phi Delta Kappa, Alpha Kappa Delta. *In 1989 the National Black Law Journal in cooperation with the UCLA Law Center published: Struggle: A Power Reserved to the People, which was distributed nationwide in commemoration of Black History month, the State of Louisiana thru the office of the Secretary of State has installed a life size portrait of Justice Ortique in the gallery of the State Archives, 1986-1994, 99. Appointed U.S. Alternate Representative to the 54th General Assembly of the United Nations, 2000. Delivered U.S. position on Taliban and terrorism before General Assembly.*

"With little or no effort on our part, life unfolds with opportunities and rewards, except that we permit our frailties to enslave our ambitions. I am grateful that there are only horizons.".

ORTIZ, ANGEL VICENTE, church administrator; b. LA, Nov. 9, 1956; s. Benjamin and Petra (Santiago) O.; m. Michele Annette Gaunt, May 5, 1979; children: Angela Nicole, Michael David. BS in Bibl. Studies, Ft. Wayne (Ind.) Bible Coll., 1982. Ordained to ministry Christian and Missionary Alliance, 1987. Pastor, ch. planter Christian and Missionary Alliance, Chula Vista, Calif., 1983-90, supt. Spanish western dist. Escondido, Calif., 1991-96, also nat. conf. spkr., evangelist; asst. to the pres. for program devel. Nyack (N.Y.) Coll., 1996-97, v.p. student devel., dean students, 1997—2002; sr. pastor First Ch. Christian and Missionary Alliance, NYC, 2002—. Republican. Mem. Christian And Missionary Alliance Ch. Avocations: camping, woodworking, refinishing, travel, teaching. Office Phone: 212-604-0300. Business E-Mail: angelortiz@firstchurchnyc.org.

ORTIZ, ANTONIO IGNACIO, public relations executive; b. Mexico City, N. Mex., Feb. 22, 1961; came to U.S., 1988; s. Antonio and Sylvia (Vega) O.; m. Socorro Chinolla, June 12, 1982. B of Bus., Autonoma U. Baja Calif., Tijuana, 1984. With acctg. dept. Bank of Atlantic, Tijuana, 1979-83; mgr. Aldaco, Tijuana, 1983-84; dir. pub. rels. Oh! Laser Club, Tijuana, 1984-88, Iguanas, Tijuana, 1988-90, Euebe, S.A., Tijuana, 1990-2000, R. Noble Enterprises, La Jolla, Calif., AAP, Inc., Chula Vista, Calif., SPD Transport Inc., Chula Vista. Cons. R.P. Noble Enterprises, La Jolla, Ca.; dir. pub. rels. R. Noble Enterprises, AAP, Inc., Chula Vista, Calif., 2000-; gen. ptnr. SPD Transport, Inc., Chula Vista, Calif., 2001-. Avocation: swimming. Home: PO Box 431859 San Diego CA 92143-1859 Office: 482 W San Ysidro Blvd #642 San Ysidro CA 92173

ORTIZ, DAVID (DAVID AMERICO ORTIZ ARIAS), professional baseball player; b. Santo Domingo, Dominican Republic, Nov. 18, 1975; Player Minn. Twins, 1997—2002, Boston Red Sox, 2003—. Mem. Dominican Republic Team World Baseball Classic, 2006. Co-author (with Tony Massaroti): Big Papi: The Story of How My Baseball Dreams Came True, 2007. Named Am. League Championship Series MVP, 2004; named to Am. League All-Star Team, 2004—07; recipient Silver Slugger award, 2004—06, Hank Aaron award, 2005. Achievements include being a member of World Series Champion Boston Red Sox, 2004. Office: Boston Red Sox 4 Yawkey Way Boston MA 02215-3496 *

ORTIZ, FELIX W., state legislator; b. La Playa de Salinas, PR; m. Elba Ortiz; children: Felix, Daniel, Alberto. Student, U. P.R.; BS in Bus. Adminstrn., Boricua Coll., 1983; M in Pub. Adminstrn., NYU, 1986. Sr. budget analyst Office of Mgmt. and Budget, Adminstrn. of Criminal Justice, NYC, 1988-90; adminstrv. mgr. Office of Mgmt. and Budget, Office of Bronx Borough Pres., 1990-95; assemblyman dist. 51 N.Y. State Assembly, Albany, 1995—. Mem. Cmty. Bd. 7, Bklyn., chair pub. safety com.; pres. 33d St. Block Assn., Nat. Hispanic Caucus State Legis.; mem. 72d Precinct Cmty. Coun.; mem. parish coun. Our Lady of Perpetual Help; mem. parent edn. task force Diocese of Bklyn.; mem. Sunset Park Health coun. Luth. Med. Ctr; bd. mem. Nat. Assn. Latino Elected and Appointed Officials. Served with U.S. Army, 1986-88. Mem.: Nat. Conference of State Legis. (NCSL), Council State Gov. (CSG). Office Phone: 518-455-3821.

ORTIZ, FERNANDO, JR., commissioner; b. Havana, Cuba, Dec. 2, 1951; came to the U.S., 1961; m. Frances K. Ortiz; children: William, Fernando III. Attended, Miami-Dade C.C., 1972—74, U. Miami, Coral Gables, Fla., 1974—75, Fla. Internat. U., Miami, 1975—76; MD, U. Centro Estudios Technicos, Santo Domingo, Dominican Republic, 1981; postgrad, Syracuse U., postgrad., 1998—. Mgr. Ortiz Transp., Miami, 1981-84; ptnr. Astrum, Syracuse, NY, 1984-91; bus. developer Rebuild Syracuse, Inc., 1991-92; coord. Urban Bus. Opportunity Ctr. City of Syracuse, 1992-96, sr. econ. devel. officer, 1996-2000, budget dir., 2000-01, commr. cmty. devel., 2001—. Mem. adv. bd. Greater Syracuse Small Bus. Loan Program, 1993-99; bd. dirs. Consol. Industries, Inc., Child Care Coun. Onondago County; mem. educare com. Success By Six, 2000. Sec. bd. dirs. Onondaga Spanish Action League, Syracuse, 1994-95, 2003, pres., 1996-2000; Cultural Resources Coun., 1997-2000; active Onondaga Citizens League, Syracuse, 1995; bd. dirs. Syracuse Neighborhood Housing Svcs., 1997-2000, Met. Water Bd., 1998—, Leadership Greater Syracuse, 2000—, Jubilee Homes, 2001—; corp. mem. United Way Ctrl. N.Y.; mem. bus. and industry adv. bd. Onondaga C.C.; mem. Leadership Greater Syracuse Class of '93, alumni bd. dirs., bd. mem., 2001—; active F.O.C.U.S. Greater Syracuse, 1997—; sec. Syracuse Urban Renewal Agy.; bd. dirs. Syracuse Econ. Devel. Corp.; sec. Spanish Action League Onondaga County, Inc., 2006-. Recipient Syracuse YWCA Acad. Diversity Achievers award, 2006, Sustainable Assessment Design Team award, 2006; named Min. Small Bus. Adv. of Yr., U.S. SBA, Syracuse, 1995, Outstanding Bd. Mem., Spanish Action League Onondaga County, 2006; named to Syracuse Northside Hall of Fame, 2006. Mem. Thursday Morning Roundtable. Avocations: reading, gardening, music. Home: 1412 Lemoyne Ave Syracuse NY 13208-1339 Office: City of Syracuse Dept Cmty Devel 201 E Washington St Rm 612 Syracuse NY 13202 Office Phone: 315-448-8620. Personal E-mail: fortiz@twcny.rr.com. Business E-Mail: fortiz@ci.syracuse.ny.us.

ORTIZ, FRANCIS ROBERT, lawyer; b. Johnstown, Pa., Jan. 8, 1955; s. Ronald A. and Nancy (Rosella) O. AA, Henry Ford C.C., Dearborn, Mich., 1975; BA in polit. sci. (with high distinction), U. Mich., 1977; JD cum laude, Harvard U., 1980. Bar: Mich. 1980, US Dist. Ct. (ea. dist.) Mich. 1980, US Ct. Appeals (6th cir.) 1984, US Dist. Ct. (we. dist.) Mich. 1994, US Supreme Ct. 2004. Assoc. Dickinson Wright, Detroit, 1980-86, ptnr., 1986—. Adj. prof. law sch. U. Detroit, 1989-95, spkr. in field Mem.: Detroit Met. Bar Assn., Fed. Bar Assn., Life Ins. Assn. Mich., State Bar Mich. (appellate practice sect., US Cts. com.), Hispanic Bar Assn. Mich. (bd mem.). Office: Dickinson Wright PLLC 500 Woodward Ave Ste 4000 Detroit MI 48226-3425 Office Phone: 313-223-3690. Office Fax: 313-223-3598. Business E-Mail: fortiz@dickinsonwright.com.

ORTIZ, GUILLERMO, banker; BA, Universidad Nacional Autonoma de Mexico; PhD Economics, Stanford U. Economist Ministry of the Presidency of Mex., 1971—72; mgr. & deputy mgr. Econ. Rsch. Bureau of Bank of Mex., 1977—84; exec. dir. IMF, 1984—88; undersecretary of finance and public credit, 1988—94; sec. telecommunications and transportation Zedillo Adminstrn.; sec. finance and public credit Mexican Fed. Govt., 1994—97; gov. Bank of Mex., 1998—. Instr. Univ. in Mex. and U.S. Author: books and papers on econ. and finance in specialized jour. and mag. Mem.: G-30. Office: Governor Banco de Mexico Avda 5 de Mayo 2 Centro 06059 Mexico City Mexico Office Phone: 5-237-2030. E-mail: gortiz@banxico.org.mx.

ORTIZ, JAIME, business educator; b. Santiago, Chile, Jan. 20, 1958; s. Sergio Ortiz and Pilar Arizabalo; m. Pamela Caballero, June 20, 1987; children: Maria Pamela, Maria Alejandra. BSc, U. Chile, Santiago, 1980, Diploma, 1981; MA, Inst. Social Studies, The Hague, The Netherlands, 1988; PhD, Va. Poly. Inst. and State U., 1993. Freelance bus. and econ. cons., Santiago, 1980—82; econ. analyst Inter-Am. Inst. Cooperation on Agriculture, Ecuador, 1983—85; mgmt. advisor Ecumenical Ch. Loan Fund, Quito, 1985—87; rsch. asst. dept. applied econ. Va. Tech. U., 1989—93; team leader Euroconsult B.V., Quito, Ecuador, 1994—95; sr. advisor COASER, Quito, 1995—96; internat. coord. Pre-investment Orgn. OPALC, Quito, 1996—97; gen. coord. Intern Am. Devel. Bank, Quito, 1997; faculty, dir. internat. programs Fla. Atlantic U. Coll. Bus., Boca Raton, 1998—; prof., exec. dir. internat. edn. William Paterson U., 2004—; assoc. v.p. internat. programs, prof. Tex. A&M Internat. U. Sr. mgmt. cons. Abastefrut S.A., Santiago, 1994, World Bank, Quito, 1995, GTZ gmbH, Quito, 1995, Inter Am. Devel. Bank, Caracas, Venezuela, 1996 Author: Small-scale Agriculture: Its Evolution in Ecuador, 1988, Small and Medium Enterprises as an Alternative to Macroeconomic Adjustments, 1997; contbr. articles to profl. jours., including Jour. Internat. Devel., Econ. Devel., Microfin., Am. Acad. Bus., Food Policy. Roman Catholic. Office: Tex A&M 5201 University Blvd Laredo TX 78041 Office Phone: 956-326-3068. Business E-Mail: jortiz@tnmiu.edu.

ORTIZ, JOHN MICHAEL, provost; BS, U. N.Mex., 1970, MA, 1971; PhD, U. N.C., 1981. Spl. edn. tchr., Albuquerque, 1969-72; instr. Appalachian State U., Boone, N.C., 1972, asst. prof. dept. spl. edn., 1972-75, assoc. prof. grad. faculty dept. spl. edn., 1976-81, interim dept. chair, prof. grad. faculty, 1982-83, dept. chair, prof. grad. faculty, 1983-85, dir. Office Extension Instrn., prof. lang., 1985-90; prof. spl. edn., dean continuing edn., dir. summer sch. U. Southern Colo., 1990-93, assoc. provost, prof. spl. edn., 1993-95, interim provost, prof. spl. edn., 1995-96; assoc. provost, prof. spl. edn. Calif. State U., Fresno, 1996-97, provost, v.p. acad. affairs ad interim, prof. spl. edn., 1997-99, provost, v.p. acad. affairs, 1999—2003; pres. Calif. State Poly. U., Pomona, 2003—. Cons., evaluator North Ctrl. Assn. of Colls. and Schs., 1995-97; pres. N.C. Fedn. of the Coun. for Exceptional Children, 1984-85, state advisor 1979-80; spl. advisor Pres. Com. on Mental Retardation; presenter in field. Contbr. articles to profl. publs. Recipient numerous grants. Mem. ASCD, Am. Assn. of Higher Edn., Nat. U. Continuing Edn. Assn., Am. Assn. for Adult and Continuing Edn., Assn. of the Severely Handicapped, Coun. for Exceptional Children. Office: Calif State U 5241 N Maple Ave MSTA 54 Fresno CA 93740-0001 Fax: 559-278-7987.

ORTIZ, MICHAEL, engineering educator; BS in Civil Engring., Univ. Madrid, 1977; MS, Univ. Calif., Berkeley, 1978, PhD, 1981. Rsch. asst. Univ. Calif., Berkeley, 1979—82; postdoctoral fellow Ministry of Public Works Rsch. and Experimentation Ctr., Madrid, 1982—83; rsch. sci. Dept. Coasts and Harbors, Ministry of Public Works, Madrid, 1983—84; asst. prof. engring Brown Univ., Providence, 1984—87, assoc. prof., 1987—90, prof., 1990—95; prof., aeronautics Calif. Inst. Tech., 1995—2004, Dotty and Dick Hayman prof. aeronautics, mech. engring., 2004—. Recipient Humboldt Rsch. award for Senior US Scientists, 2002; Fulbright Scholarship, 1977—78. Fellow: Internat. Assn. Computational Mechanics (Awards for Rsch. 2002), US Assn. Computational Mechanics, Am. Acad. Arts & Sciences; mem.: Am. Soc. Mech.Engrs., Am. Acad. Mechanics. Office: 115 Firestone MC 105-50 Calif Inst Tech Pasadena CA 91125 Office Phone: 626-395-4530. Business E-Mail: ortiz@aero.caltech.edu. *

ORTIZ, PATRICK T., lawyer; b. 1950; BA, Coll. Santa Fe; JD, Georgetown U. Bar: N.Mex. 1976. Dep. gen. counsel ins. dept. N.Mex. State Corp. Commn., gen. counsel; asst. atty. gen. energy and utilities sect. Atty. Gen.'s Office, N.Mex.; staff counsel N.Mex. Public Svc. Commn., chief commn. counsel, commr.; atty. Mountain States Telephone & Telegraph Co.; chief counsel US West Comm.; sr. v.p., gen. counsel, sec. PNM Resources, Albuquerque, 1991—. Bd. dirs. N.Mex. Bar Bus. Law Sect.; corp. exec. bd. Gen. Counsel Roundtable. Bd. trustees PNM Found.; pro bono counsel Challenge N.Mex.; bd. dirs. Archdiocese Santa Fe Catholic Found., Nat. Hispanic Cultural Ctr. Found.; mem. bd. visitors Coll. Santa Fe. Named one of Most Influential Hispanics, Hispanic Bus. Mag., Corp. Elite, 2007. Mem.: Chief Legal Officers Assn. (mem. exec. com.), Am. Law Inst., N.Mex Hispanic Bar Assn., Oliver Seth Am. Inn of Ct. (master of bench), Edison Elec. Inst. (mem. legal com.), Am. Gas Assn. (mem. legal com.). Office: PNM Resources Inc Alvarado Sq MS2822 Albuquerque NM 87158-0001 *

ORTIZ, SOLOMON PORFIRIO, congressman; b. Robstown, Tex., June 3, 1938; children: Yvette, Solomon P. Cert., Inst. Applied Sci., Chgo., 1962; student, Del Mar Coll., Corpus Christi, Tex., 1965—67, Nat. Sheriff's Tng. Inst., LA, 1977. Constable Neuces County, Tex., 1965—68, commr. Tex., 1969-76, sheriff Tex., 1977—83; mem. US Congress from 27th Tex. dist., 1983—, mem. resources com., mem. armed svcs. com., ranking minority mem. readiness subcommittee, dean Congl. Hispanic Caucus. Served in 61st Mil. Police Co. US Army, 1960—62. Named Man of Yr., Internat. Order Foresters, 1981, one of Hispanic Bus. 100 Most Influential Hispanics in US, Hispanic Bus. Mag., 1999. Mem. Nat. Sheriff's Assn., Sheriff's Assn. Tex. Democrat. Office: US Ho Reps 2470 Rayburn Ho Office Bldg Washington DC 20515-4327 Office Phone: 202-225-7742. *

ORTIZ, VÍCTOR RAÚL, parochial school educator; b. Barranquitas, PR, Feb. 25, 1959; s. Wilfredo and Gladys (Ortiz) O. ThM summa cum laude, MDiv summa cum laude, St. Vicente de Paul Seminary, Fla.; MEd summa cum laude, U. Pheonix, Ariz, PR; Lic. Fil., U. Católica Madre y Maestra, Santo Domingo, Dominican Republic. Tchr. theology, history Colegio Valvanera, Coamo, P.R., 1980-83, asst. prin., 1981-83, tchr. Spanish, 1982-83; supt. catholic schs. Diócesis de Caguas, 1986-89; vicario cooperador-párroco San Andrés Apóstol, Barranquitas, 1986-89; vicario episcopal de educaciÓn Diócesis de Caguas, 1989—. Author (with P. Victor) Concepto del Pecado, 1987, Desarrollo de la Conciencia Moral, 1992. Mem. Alianza Pro-Ley de Cierre, San Juan, P.R., 1991; v.p. Grupo Cívico Contra El Crimen Naranjito, P.R., 1992. Recipient Primer Alto Honor Escuela Superior Dr. Jose N Gandara, 1977, Cuadro Alto Honor del Decano Univ. Pontificia Catholica, 1982. Mem. Assn. Tchrs. of P.R. Office: Superintendencia de Escuelas Catolicas PO Box 8699 Caguas PR 00726-8699

ORTIZ, WILLIAM, composer, music educator; b. Salinas, PR, Mar. 30, 1947; s. William and Guillermina (Alvarado) O.; m. Candida, Mar. 26, 1988; children: Aleyda Enid, Nicole Samara, Amaya E. MusB, PR Conservatory of Music, 1976; MA in Composition, SUNY, Stony Brook, 1978; PhD in Composition, SUNY, Buffalo, 1983. Cons./auditor NY State Arts Coun., NYC, 1976-86; asst. dir. Black Mountain Coll. II, Buffalo, 1982-86; music advisor PR Symphony Orch., San Juan, 1988-90; prof. music U. PR, Bayamon, 1986—, dir. humanities dept., 1997—. Dir./conductor, U. P.R. Band, Bayamon, 1986—, Grammy award nomination, 2001; music critic San Juan Star, 1993-94; composer-in-residence for Music-in-Motion program Atlantic Ctr. for the Arts, 1996-97, pres. music sect. Ateneo Puertorriqueno, 2006—; artist-in-residence René Marquez Mid. Sch., 1999-2000. Composer: 124 E. 107th St., 1979 (Felipe Gutierrez Internat. Composition prize 1980), Llego la Banda, 1984 (Composers Guild Internat. Composition prize 1985), Dos Gritos y una Cancion, 1986 (Composition award Ateneo Puertorriqueno 1989), Tropicalizacion, 1999 (Grammy nomination 2001), others. Assoc. mem. Hispanic Womens League, Buffalo, 1982-86. Recipient commns. P.R. Symphony, San Juan, 1990, Camerata Caribe, San Juan, 1990, grants Inst. of Puerto Rican Culture, San Juan, 1990, P.R. Community Found., San Juan, 1990, Casals Festival, 1995, Orquesta Baja California, Mex., 1999, 2001; guest composer Festival Musica Nova, Sao Paulo, Brazil, 1988, Festival Latinoamericano de Musica, Caracas, Venezuela, 1991, 92, 94, 98, Am. Composers Orch. "Sonidos de las Americas," 1997, VIII Tribuna Musical para América Latina, Mex., 1997, Festival Iberoamericano de las Artes, 2004, 06. Mem. Am. Composers Alliance, Am. Music Ctr., Coll. Music Soc., Composers Alliance of Buffalo (pres. 1984), Assn. de Compositores Puertorriqueno. Home: Plaza de La Fuente 1275 Calle España Toa Alta PR 00953 Office: U PR Bayamon Gardens Sta Bayamon PR 00959 Office Phone: 787-993-0000. Personal E-mail: williamortizupr@yahoo.com.

ORTIZ-BUTTON, OLGA, social worker; b. Chgo., July 12, 1953; d. Luis Antonio and Pura (Acevedo) Ortiz; m. Dennis Vesley, Aug. 11, 1973 (div. 1976); m. Randall Russell Button, Nov. 3, 1984 (div. Oct. 1993); children: Josh, Jordan, Eli. BA, U. Ill., Champaign-Urbana, 1975; MSW, Western Mich. U., Kalamazoo, 1981. Diplomate Am. Bd. Clin. Social Workers, 2006; cert. social worker, sch. social worker, lic. master social worker. Social svcs. dir. Champaign County Nursing Home, Urbana, Ill., 1976; social svcs. and activity dir. Lawton Nursing Home, Mich., 1977; job developer Southwestern Mich. Indian Ctr., Watervliet, 1977-78; staff asst. New Directions Alcohol Treatment Ctr., Kalamazoo, 1978; counselor, instr. Alcohol Hwy. Safety, Kalamazoo, 1978-79; clin. social worker Mecosta County Community Mental Health, Big Rapids, Mich., 1981-84; program dir. substance abuse Sr. Svcs., Inc., Kalamazoo, 1984-85; sch. social worker Martin Pub. Schs., Mich., 1985-96, J.C. Huizenga Charter Schs., Grand Rapids, Mich., 1996—; owner, therapist Plainwell Counseling Ctr., Mich., 1989-98; co-dir. Everlasting Covenant Ministry, Kalamazoo, 1997—2003; owner Christian Counseling Ctr. PLC, 2004—. S.W. cons. Med. Pers. Pool, 1993-94; founder, owner Christian Coun. Ctr., 2003—. Vol. social worker Hospice-Wings of Hope, Plainwell, 1984-85; mem. Hospice Quality Rev. Bd., 1993-96; supporter Students Against Aparteid South Africa, Kalamazoo, 1979-81; mem. World Vision and Countertop Ptnr., 1984-90; mem., vol. Christian Life Ctr., Kalamazoo, 1996; sponsor, vol. People for Ethical Treatment of Animals, 1986-91; vol. helper Sparkies for Awana Club Ch., 1989-95; consortium mem. Mich. Post Adoption Svc. System, 1994-97; co-founder Everlasting Covenant Ministry, Kalamazoo, 1997; sch. social worker Nat. Heritage Acads., 1997-2004; founder Christian Counseling Ctr., 2002. Rural Mental Health grantee, NIMH, 1979—81. Mem.: NASW, ACSW, Nat. Assn. Christian Social Workers, Am. Assn. Christian Counselors, Mich. Assn. Sch. Social Workers. Avocations: walking, gardening, cross country skiing. Home: 1339 Cadet Ln Kalamazoo MI 49009-1838 Office Phone: 269-343-2117. Personal E-mail: obutton@stealthpost.com. E-mail: 14.obutton@heritageacademies.com.

ORTIZ-WALTERS, ROWENA, management educator; d. Ortiz and Rivera; m. Carl Allan Walters, May 14, 1999; children: Ethan Andrew Walters, Noah Daniel Walters. BS Chemistry, U. Conn., 1996; MBA, U. New Haven, 1999; PhD Mgmt., U. Conn., 2005. Chemist Uniroyal Chem. Corp., Middlebury, Conn., 1996—99; instr. bus. mgmt. U. Conn., Storrs, 2000—; asst. prof. entrepreneurship Quinnipiac U., 2004—. Asst. dir. Wolff Family Program in Entrepreneurship, Storrs, 2000—; pres. Mgmt. Doctoral Student Assn., 2001—02; advisor Quinnipiac U. Entrepreneurial Success team; presenter in field. Contbr. articles to profl. jours. Named Best Teaching Asst. of Yr., U. Conn., 2002, Best Student Tchr. of Yr., 2003; recipient 40 Under 40 award, Bus. Times, 2006; grantee, Quinnipiac U., 2005. Mem.: Mgmt. Doctoral Student Assn., Ea. Acad. Mgmt., Acad. Mgmt. Assn. (chair mentoring com., Best Symposium award 2004). Avocations: hiking, snowshoeing, reading, travel.

ORTLEPP, BRUNO, marine navigation educator, master mariner; b. Nortorf, Germany, Apr. 3, 1935; s. Carl and Emilie (Strambovski) O; 1 child: Ann-Marie French. 1 mate fgn. going, Fachhochschule Hamburg, 1958; master fgn. going, N.S. Nautical Inst., Halifax, Can., 1976; teacher diploma, N.S. Tchrs. Coll., Truro, 1984. O.s., a.b. various cos., Germany, 1951-56; 3rd officer German East Africa Line, Hamburg, 1958-60; from 2d officer to chief officer to master Irving Oil Ltd., Saint John, N.B., Can., 1960-76; chief officer Sanko Marine, Tokyo, Japan, 1976-81; marine educator, dept. edn. N.S. Nautical Inst., Halifax, 1982-92; pres. PELTRO Ltd., 1983-94. Author: Canadian Maritimes Sailing Aids, Vol. I, Tidal Streams for Bay of Fundy, 1965, 89, Vol. II, Tidal Streams for the River St. Lawrence, 1966, Vol. III, Distance Tables, 1966, 88, Vol. IV, Natural Squat, 1983, 89, Vol. V, The Deviascope, 1990; contbr. articles to profl. jours. Recipient 20th Century award, 1995. Mem. Nautical Inst. London. Office: care Capt Walter S Franke 12 Sycamore Ct Lower Sackville NS Canada B4C 1G1

ORTLIP, PAUL DANIEL, artist; b. Englewood, NJ, May 21, 1926; s. Henry Willard and Aimee (Eschner) O.; m. Mary Louise Krueger, June 1981 (dec. May 2001); children from previous marriage: Carol, Kathleen, Sharon (dec.), Danielle (dec.), Michele. Diploma, Houghton Acad., NY, 1944; student, Art Students League, 1947—49; diploma, Acad. la Grande Chaumiere, Paris, 1950; DFA (hon.), Houghton Coll., NY, 1988. Tchr. Fairleigh Dickinson U., Teaneck, NJ, 1956-68, artist in residence, curator Rutherford, NJ, 1968-72. Official USN artist on assignment, Cuban missile crisis, Fla., 1963, Gemini 5 Recovery, Atlantic Ocean, 1965, Vietnam, 1967, Apollo 12 recovery, Pacific Ocean, 1969, Apollo 17 recovery, Pacific Ocean, 1972, Internat. Naval Rev., NY harbor, 1976, USCG Sta., Key West, Fla., 1985; mem. USN Art Coop. and Liason Com. Exhbns. include Salonde L'Art Libre, Paris, 1950, Nat. Acad. Design, 1952, Allied Artists of Am., NYC, Acad. Sci., Rundell Gallery, Rochester, NY, Montclair Art Mus., Hist. Mus, Lima, Ohio, Butler Art Inst., Youngstown, Ohio, Fine Arts Gallery, San Diego, State Capitol Bldg., Sacramento, Capitol Mus., Olympia, Wash., Mus. Gt. Plains, Lawton, Okla., Witte Meml. Mus., San Antonio, Nimitz Meml. Mus., Fredericksberg, Tex., Pentagon Collection of Fine Arts, James Hunt Barker Galleries, Palm Beach, Fla., Nantucket, Mass., NYC, Smithsonian Inst., Gallerie Vollem Breuse, Biarritz, France, Galerie Mouffe, Paris, Guggenheim Gallery, London, Wickersham Gallery, NYC, Soc. Illustrators, NYC; retrospective exhbn. Bergen Cmty. Mus., Paramus, NJ 1970, The Curzon Gallery, 1987, 88, 89, 93, 2003, Ardennes et de l'Eifel, Charleville Mézières, France, June-Sept. 1990; represented permanent collections including Salmagundi Club NYC, Houghton Coll., NY, Portrait Meml. J.F. Kennedy Libr., Fairleigh-Dickinson U., Nat. Air and Space Mus., Smithsonian Inst., Intrepid Sea-Air Space Mus., NYC, Hist. Mural Visitors Ctr., Palisades Interstate Pk., Ft. Lee, NJ, Vets. Med. Ctr., East Orange, NJ, USN Exhbn. Ctr., Washington Navy Yard, Am. Coll. Clin. Pharmacology, NYC, NJ U. Dentistry & Medicine, Newark, Bergen County Ct. House, Hackensack, NJ, Dickinson Coll., Carlisle, Pa., George Washingtogn Meml. Pk., Paramus, Marietta Coll., Ohio, Mcpl. Bldg., Ft. Lee, Navy League US, Arlington, Va., Nat. Archives and Records Adminstrn., Washington, (mural) Pub. Libr., Fort Lee, Bush Presdl. Libr., College Station, Tex., Underwater Demolition Team Seal Mus., Fort Pierce, Fla., Lynn U., Boaca Raton, Fla. Served to sgt. US Army, 1944-47, ETO, PTO, 1946-47. Recipient 1st prize Am. Artists Profl. League State Exhibit NJ chpt., Paramus, 1960, 1st prize U.S. Armed Forces Exhibit Far East, Seoul, Korea, Tokyo, 1946, Franklin Williams award, Salmagundi Club, NY, 1967, Outstanding Achievement award for oil painting, USN, 1968, Artist of Yr. award, Hudson Artists, Jersey City Mus., 1970, Statue of Victory World Culture prize, Academia Italia, Parma, 1982, Men of Achievement medal Cambridge, Eng., 1990, Connaissance de Notre Europe Gold medal Charleville-Mézières, France, 1990. Mem. Allied Artists Am. (art coop. and liaison com. with USN), Nat. Soc. Mural Painters, Nat. Soc. Arts and Letters, Bergen County Artists Guild (pres. 1960-62), Portrait Soc. Am., Inc., Artists Fellowship, Inc., USCG Art Program, Art Students League NY (life), Navy League U.S., VFW (life), Am. Legion, Salmagundi Club (NYC, art chmn. 1979-81), Gov.'s of the Palm Beaches Club (Fla.). Office: Four Generations Art Gallery Paul D Ortlip Studio PO Box 4150 Vineyard Haven MA 02568 Office Phone: 508-693-5501. Business E-Mail: paulortlip@fourgenerationsart.com.

ORTLOFF, GEORGE CHRISTIAN, SR., (CHRIS ORTLOFF), commissioner, journalist; b. Lake Placid, NY, Sept. 20, 1947; s. Carl Jacob and Lillian Grace (Travis) O.; m. Ruth Mary Hart, Jan. 28, 1978; children: George Christian Jr., Jonathan Hart. BS, Rensselaer Poly. Inst., 1969; MA, U. Mich., 1975. Reporter, producer Sta. WUOM-FM, Ann Arbor, Mich., 1973-75; reporter Nat. Pub. Radio, 1973-75, Adirondack Daily Enterprise, Saranac Lake, NY, 1976-77, Sta. WNBZ-Am, Saranac Lake, 1975-77; pub. rels. dir. Ctr. for Music, Drama and Art, Lake Placid, 1975-76; pres. Macromedia, Inc., Lake Placid, 1976-82; anchor, mng. editor Sta. WPTZ-

TV, Plattsburgh, NY, 1981-85; mem. N.Y. State Assembly, Albany, 1986—2006, ranking minority mem. Legis. Commn. on Sci. and Tech., 1987—2006, chmn. Rep. program com., 1993-98, vice-chair Rep. conf., 1999—2002, ranking minority mem. legis. task force redistricting, 1998—2006, mem. higher edn. budget com., 1998—2006, dep. minority whip, 2002, asst. minority leader, 2002—06; commr. bd. parole NY State, 2006—. Mem. health and human svcs. task force Am. Legis. Exch. Coun., 1994-97; N.Y. state chmn., 1997. Author: Lake Placid, The Olympic Years: 1932-80, 1976, A Lady in the Lake, 1985; reporter, producer (TV news series) "Special Segment", 1981-85 (N.Y. State Broadcasters Best Series award 1982, 83, 84, 85), (TV documentary) "A Time to Choose", 1985 (N.Y. State Broadcasters Best award 1986). Chief ceremonies 1980 Olympic Winter Games, Lake Placid, 1978-80; field asst. to congressman David O'B. Martin, Plattsburgh, 1981; chmn. Clinton County Rep. Com., 1995-2002; committeeman Essex County Rep. Com., 1980-81, NY Rep. State Com., 2003-06; district com. mem. Plattsburgh City Repub. Com., 2003-06; trustee Lake Placid Village, 1977-81, Olympic & Winter Sports Mus., 1980-84, Battle of Plattsburgh Assn., 1998-2001, St. Lawrence Aquarium and Ecol. Ctr., 1997-2001, Adirondack Mus., 2001—; lay reader Episcopal Ch., Lake Placid and Plattsburgh, 1976-92. Mem. VFW, AM-VETS, Am. Legion, North Country Vietnam Vets. Assn., Elks, Kiwanis (pres. Lake Placid 1980-81). Avocations: skiing, piano, trumpet, painting, woodworking. Home: 23 Morrison Ave Plattsburgh NY 12901-1417 Office: NY State Parole Bd 97 Ctrl Ave Albany NY 12206 Office Phone: 518-473-5424. Business E-Mail: cortloff@parole.state.ny.us.

ORTLUND, ANNE (ELIZABETH ANNE ORTLUND), writer, musician; b. Wichita, Kans., Dec. 3, 1923; d. Joseph Burton and Mary Elizabeth (Weible) Sweet; m. Raymond Carl Ortlund, Apr. 27, 1946; children: Sherrill Anne, Margot Jeanne, Raymond Carl, Nels Robert. Student, Am. U., 1941—43; AA, Am. Guild Organists, 1944; MusB, U. Redlands, Calif., 1945. Organist Old-Fashioned Revival Hour and Joyful Sound, Radio World-Wide, 1960—75; spkr. Orgn. Renewal Ministries, Newport Beach, Calif., 1980—; composer hymns, anthems NYC, 1963—77. Composer: Macedonia, 1966, 250 hymns; author: Up with Worship, 1975, Disciplines of the Beautiful Woman, 1977, The Gentle Ways of the Beautiful Woman, 1998, How Great Our Joy, 2001, Up With Worship, rev. and updated, 2001, A Fresh Start for Your Friendships, 2001; author: (with Raymond Carl Ortlund) The Best Half of Life, 1976, Discipling One Another, 1979, Children Are Wet Cement, 1981 (Christie award Christian Booksellers Assn., 1982), Joanna: A Story of Renewal, 1982, Building a Great Marriage, 1984; author: (with Raymond C. Ortlund) Staying Power, 1986, Disciplines of the Heart, 1987, Renewal, 1989, Confident in Christ, Disciplines of the Home, 1990, Fix Your Eyes on Jesus, 1991, My Sacrifice His Fire, 1993, In His Presence, 1995, Lord, Make My Life a Miracle, rev. and updated, 2002. Named Profl. Woman of Yr., Pasadena Bus. and Profl. Women, 1975; recipient SESAC award, Gospel Musicians, 1978. Home: 601 Lido Park Dr Apt 6E Newport Beach CA 92663-4403 Office: Renewal Ministries 151 Kalmus Dr Ste E160 Costa Mesa CA 92626-8828 Office Phone: 714-668-0818. E-mail: anne@ortlund.org.

ORTMAN, DON L., principal; b. Battle Creek, Iowa, June 12, 1968; s. Lee Ortman and Peggy Fick. BA, Buena Vista U., Storm Lake, Iowa, 1991; MEd, N.W. Mo. State U., 1995. Tchr. Griswold CSD, Iowa, 1991—97; prin. Rock Valley CSD, Iowa, 1997—. Choir dir. Pioneer Meth. Ch., Rock Valley, Iowa. Recipient Outstanding Tchr. award, Aksarben, 1995, Prin. of Yr., Iowa, 2003, Adminstr. of Yr., Iowa Character Counts, 2005. Mem.: Sch. Adminstrs. Iowa, Iowa Reading Assn. (pres.). Home: 1222 Tenth Ave Rock Valley IA 51247 E-mail: dortman@rvcsd.org.

ORTMAN, GEORGE EARL, artist; b. Oakland, Calif., Oct. 17, 1926; s. William Thomas and Anna Katherine (Noll) O.; m. Conni Whidden, Aug. 5, 1960 (dec.); 1 stepson, Roger Graham Whidden. Student, Calif. Coll. Arts and Crafts, 1947-49, Atelier Stanley William Hayter, 1949, Acad. Andre L'Hote, Paris, 1949-50, Hans Hoffman Sch. Art, 1949-50. Co-founder Tempo Playhouse, NYC, 1954; instr. painting and drawing NYU, 1962-65; co-chmn. fine arts Sch. Visual Arts NYC, 1963-65; artist-in-residence Princeton U., 1966-69, Honolulu Acad. Art, 1969; head painting dept. Cranbrook Acad. Art, Bloomfield Hills, Mich., 1970-92. One-man exhbns. include Tanager Gallery, 1954, Wittenborn Gallery, 1955, Stable Gallery, 1957, 60, Howard Wise Gallery, 1962, 63, 64, 66, 69, Gimpel-Weitzenhoffer Gallery, 1972 (all N.Y.C.), Swetzoff Gallery, Boston, 1961-62, Fairleigh Dickinson U., 1962, Mirvish Gallery, Toronto, Can., 1964, Walker Art Center, Mpls., 1965, Milw. Art Center, 1966, Dallas Mus. Art, 1966, Portland Mus. Art, 1966, Akron Inst. Art, 1966, U. Chgo., 1967, Princeton U. Art Mus., 1967, Honolulu Acad. Art, 1969, Reed Coll., 1970, Cranbrook Acad. Art, 1970, 92, Indpls. Mus. Art, 1971, J.L. Hudson Gallery, Detroit, 1971, Gimpel-Weitzenhoffer, N.Y.C., 1972, 73, Gertrude Kasle Gallery, Detroit, 1976, Lee Hoffman Gallery, Detroit, 1977, Flint (Mich.) Mus. Art, 1977; other one-man exhbns. include Cranbrook Mus. Art, 1982; exhibited numerous group shows including Whitney Mus. Am. Art Annual, 1962, 63, 64, 65, 67, 73, Carnegie Internat., Pitts., 1964, 67, 70, Jewish Mus., N.Y.C., 1964, Corcoran Mus., Washington, 1964, Mitchell Algos Gallery, N.Y.C., 2002, 07, others; represented permanent collections, Walker Art Center, Mpls., Mus. Modern Art, Whitney Mus. Am. Art, (both N.Y.C.), Guggenheim Mus., N.Y.C., Albright-Knox Mus., Buffalo, NYU, Christian Theol. Sem., Indpls., Indpls. Mus. Art, Cleve. Mus. Art, Mus. Am. Art, Washington, Honolulu Acad. Art, Newark Mus. Art, Container Corp. Am., Chgo. Ind. U. Music Bldg., Wausau (Wis.) Hosp. Center, Unitarian Ch., Princeton, Mfr. Hanover Trust Bldg., Albert Kahn & Assos., Detroit, Renaissance Center, Detroit, Mich. State Univ. Performing Arts Ctr., East Lansing, Detroit Inst. Arts. Guggenheim fellow, 1965-66; Ford Found. grantee, 1966, Lee Krasner Found. grantee; One of five Am. artists selected for 1965 Japanese Bi-ann.; recipient Gov. NJ's Purchase award 2d ann. exhbn. art, 1967, Krasner Found. award, 2003, Lifetime Achievement award; Best of Show Religion in Art Exhbn., Birmingham, Ala., 1966. Mem. Nat. Acad. of Design. Office Phone: 212-794-6551.

ORTNER, DONALD J., biological anthropologist, educator; b. Stoneham, Mass., Aug. 23, 1938; s. A. W. and Marie B. (Schweizer) Ortner; m. Joyce E. Walker, Sept. 4, 1960; children: Donald J. Jr., Allison A. May, Karen L. BA, Columbia Union Coll., 1960; MA, Syracuse U., 1967; PhD, U. Kans., 1970; DSc (hon.), U. Bradford, England, 1995. Asst. curator Smithsonian Instn., Washington, 1969-71, assoc. curator, 1971-76, curator, 1976—, chmn. anthropology, 1988-92; acting dir. Nat. Mus. Natural History, Washington, 1994-96. Vis. prof. U. Bradford, 1988—; pres. Paleopathology Assn., 1999—2001. Author: Identification of Pathological Conditions in Human Skeletal Remains, 1981, 2d edit., 2003; editor: How Humans Adapt, 1983; co-editor: Human Paleopathology, 1991; mem. editl. bd. Jour. Paleopathology, 1988—, Internat. Jour. Osteoarch, 1990—. Mem.: Paleopathology Assn., Internat. Skeletal Soc., Am. Assn. Phys. Anthropology (mem. exec. com. 1987—90). Office: Smithsonian Inst Nat Mus Natural History 10th & Constitution Ave NW Washington DC 20560-0112 Personal E-mail: ortnerdj@verizon.net. Business E-Mail: ortner@si.edu.

ORTNER, EVERETT HOWARD, magazine editor, writer; b. Lowell, Mass., Aug. 25, 1919; s. Herman and Anne (Ehrenhaus) O.; m. Evelyn Frances Gelbman, Jan. 1, 1953. BA, U. Ark., 1939. Editor Popular Publs., NYC, 1946-52; assoc. editor Popular Sci., NYC, 1953-56, copy chief, 1956-70, group editor, 1970-76, mng. editor, 1976-80, editor, 1980-85. Pres. Brownstone Revival Coalition N.Y., 1968-76, chmn., 1986-2002, chmn. emeritus, 2002; founder, pres. Back to the City, Inc., N.Y.C., 1974-83, chmn. bd., 1983—; v.p. L.I. Hist. Soc., Bklyn., 1979-83; chmn. bd Preservation Vols. Inc., 2000—. Lt. U.S. Army, 1942-46, ETO. Recipient Cinderella award Bklyn. Union Gas Co., 1978, Honor citation Borough Pres. Bklyn., 1983, Disting. Citizen award City Louisville, 1979, Quality of Life award Kings County Hosp. Ctr., Bklyn., 1976, Spirit of Life award N.Y. Congl. Home, 1994, Excellence in Hist. Preservation award Preservation League NY State, 2002, Grassroots Preservation award Hist. Dists. Coun., 2002, Lifetime Achievement award Victorian Soc. in Am., 2005, Disting. Alumni award U. Ark., 2006, Lucy G. Moses Preservation award N.Y. Landmarks Conservancy, 2006. Mem. Overseas Press Club, Montauk Club, Ft. Hamilton Officers Club. Home: 272 Berkeley Pl Brooklyn NY 11217-3904

ORTOLANO, RALPH J., engineering consultant; b. Phila., Apr. 12, 1931; BS in Marine Engring., U.S. Mcht. Marine Acad., 1954; MBA, Santa Clara U., 1969. Registered profl. engr., Calif. Engring. watch officer USN, 1954-56; sr. design engr. marine divsn. Westinghouse, Lester, Pa., 1956-64, Sunnyvale, Calif., 1964-69; mgr. project engring. corp. cost recovery dept. Litton Ship Systems, Inc., LA, 1969-72; consulting engr., scientist So. Calif. Edison Co., Rosemead, Calif., 1972-92, chief cons., 1993—. Formed Turbine RESCUE, 1984; cons. more than 100 power cos., numerous others, U.S. and abroad; presenter seminars in the field. Contbr. more than 100 articles to profl. jours.; holder 22 U.S. patents in field. Recipient William R. Gould award SCE, 1992, Meritorious Alumni Svc. award USMMAAA, 1989, Outstanding Profl. Achievement award USMMAAA, 1994; named to USMMA Athletic Hall of Fame, 1990; USMMA rifle range named Ortolano Rifle and Pistol Range in honor of being selected to 1952 and 1953 All-Am. Rifle Teams, and 1952-54 All-Am. Pistol Teams, 1999. Fellow ASME (life, past dir. ASME-SCAC power chpt., past chmn. steam turbine com., past chmn. power divsn., mem. exec. com., co-chmn. steam turbine course 1984-99, George Westinghouse Gold medal 1991, past chmn. EEI steam turbine crack prevention task force). E-mail: turbinerescue@msn.com.

ORTON, COLIN GEORGE, medical physicist; b. London, June 4, 1938; came to U.S., 1966; s. Frederick G. and Audrey V. (Sewell) O.; m. Barbara G. Scholes, July 25, 1964; children: Nigel, Susanne, Philip. BS in Physics with honors, Bristol U., 1959; MS in Radiation Physics, London U., 1961, PhD in Radiation Physics, 1965; MA (hon.), Brown U., 1976. Diplomate Am. Bd. Radiology, Am. Bd. Med. Physics. Instr. London U. St. Barts' Hosp., 1961-66; assoc. prof. NYU Med. Ctr., 1966-75, Brown U., RI, 1975-81; prof., chief physicist Wayne State U., Harper Hosp., Detroit, 1981—2003. Dir. grad. program Wayne State U., 1981-2003. Author: Radiation Physics Review Books I, 1971, II, 1978; editor: Electron Treatment Planning, 1978, Progress in Medical Physics I, 1982, II, 1985, Radiation Dosimetry, 1986; editor Medical Physics, 1997-2004. Recipient Marie Curie Gold medal Health Physics Soc., 1987. Fellow Am. Assn. Physicists in Am. (pres. 1981, William D. Coolidge award 1993), Am. Coll. Med. Physics (chmn. 1985, Marvin M. D. Williams award, 1997), Inst. Physics London, Am. Coll. Radiology; mem. Internat. Orgn. for Med. Physics (sec. gen. 1988-94, pres. 1997-2000), Am. Brachytherapy Soc. (pres. 2001-02), Internat. Union Physics and Engring. Sci. in Medicine (pres. 2003-06, Merit award 2003). Avocations: golf, badminton, tennis, running, squash. Home: 15810 Lakeview Ct Grosse Pointe Park MI 48230-1806 Office Phone: 313-823-8079. E-mail: ortonc@comcast.net.

ORTON, GERALDINE LEITL, psychologist, mental health therapist, educator, author; b. Pitts., May 16, 1939; d. Meinrad M. and Virginia (Traska) Leitl; m. Guy M. Orton, June 16, 1962; children: Alisa, Guy Christopher. BS, Ind. U. Pa., 1961; postgrad., Scandinavian Sem. for Cultural Study, Valla Folkhogskola, Linkoping, Sweden, 1961-62; MS, Edinboro U. Pa., 1970; PhD, U. Buffalo, 1978. Cert. in counseling psychology and ednl. adminstrn. Elem. sch. tchr. Ripley (N.Y.) Ctrl. Sch., 1962—70, elem. sch. counselor, 1970—74; program dir. SUNY, Fredonia, 1974—76; asst. prof. Gannon U., Erie, Pa., 1977—81, assoc. prof., 1981—97, prof., 1997—99, mem. grad. faculty, 1990—98, dir. mental health counseling, 1991—98, dir. gen. studies program, 1991—93, chair dept. human svcs., 1992—95; pvt. practice, 1984—; prof. emerita Gannon U., Erie, 2001—. Bd. dirs. mental health counseling program Warren State Hosp., 1984-88, supr. of placements in Warren County, 1984-88; bd. dirs. Home Instrn. Tutorial Program Rsch. Found. SUNY, Fredonia, 1975-76, Learn, Experience and Develop Program, 1974-75; cons. Bur. of Guidance N.Y. State Dept. Edn., Albany, 1983, mental health program Chautauqua County Bd. Cooperative Ednl. Svcs., Fredonia, 1974, career edn. program Westfield (N.Y.) Acad. and Cen. Sch., 1974, Hamot Behavioral Health, Erie, Pa., 1999, Cath. Charities of Pa., 1999; therapist Parents Supporting Other Parents in Sorrow, Erie, 1978; mem. numerous Gannon U. coms. and task forces; presenter in field. Author: (book) Strategies for Counseling with Children and Their Parents, 1997; contbr. articles to profl. jours. Mem. adv. bd. Perspective on Women Series: Pub. Com. on the Humanities in Pa.; mem. Primary Prevention Task Force-Youth Svcs. Coordination Coun. Erie County; numerous presentations Pa. schs. Mem. APA, ACA, NASW, Pi Gamma Mu, Lambda Sigma. Office: Gannon Univ Dept Psychology University Square Erie PA 16541

ORTON, KYLE, professional football player; b. Nov. 14, 1982; s. Byron. BA in History, Purdue Univ., 2005. Quarterback Chgo. Bears, 2005—. Recipient Big Ten Offensive Player Yr, Sporting News, 2004. Office: Chgo Bears 1000 Football Dr Lake Forest IL 60045 Office Fax: 847-295-6600.

ORTON, SHARYN, epidemiologist, government agency administrator; BS, Northeastern U., Boston, 1978; MSPH, PhD, U. South Fla., Tampa, 2000. Cert. specialist in blood banking Am. Soc. Clin. Pathologists, 1983, med. technologist Am. Soc. Clin. Pathologists, 1978. Epidemiologist ARC Holland Lab., Rockville, 1996—2001; dep. dir. and acting chief blood and plasma br. divsn. blood applications Ctr. Biologics Evaluation and Rsch. FDA, Rockville, Md., 2001—07; dir. regulatory affairs Fenwal, Inc., Lake Zurich, Ill., 2007—. Mem.: AABB. Achievements include patents in field. Home Phone: 301-620-0107; Office Phone: 301-827-3524.

ORTTUNG, WILLIAM HERBERT, chemistry professor; b. Phila., June 16, 1934; s. Elmer Herbert and Rosalind Orttung; married; children: Robert W., Mark. H. SB, MIT, 1956; PhD, U. Calif., Berkeley, 1961. Asst. prof. chemistry Stanford (Calif.) U., 1960-63, U. Calif., Riverside, 1963-69, assoc. prof., 1969-79, prof., 1979-94; emeritus prof., 1994—. Mem. AAAS, Am. Chem. Soc., Am. Phys. Soc. E-mail: worttung@att.net.

ORUGUNTA, RAVEENDRA BABU, pediatrician; s. Penchalaiah and Kamakshmamma Orugunta; m. Ramadevi Nanga, Mar. 30, 1994; children: Pranay, Abhinay. MB, BS, Sri Venkateswara U., Tirupati, India, 1991; MD in Pediat., U. of Health Scis., Andhra Pradesh, India, 1995; MD, Bklyn. Hosp. Ctr., 2005. Sr. resident physician in neurology Sri Venkateswara Inst. of Med. Scis., Tirupati, Andhra Pradesh, India, 1995—96; locum intern med. officer in pediatric emergency rm. Bustamante Hosp. for Children, Kingston, Jamaica, 1996—96; sr. resident med. officer in pediat. Savanna-La-Mar Pub. Gen. Hosp., Westmoreland, Jamaica, 1996—2002; house staff in pediat. (resident) The Bklyn Hosp. Ctr., 2002—04, chief resident in pediat., 2004—05; staff physician in pediat. Wyckoff Heights Med. Ctr., Bklyn., 2005—, attending pediatrician in pediatric emergency rm., 2005—. Mem.: Am. Acad. of Pediat. (assoc.). Home: 190 72nd St Apt 182 Brooklyn NY 11209 Office: Wyckoff Heights Med Ctr 374 Stockholm St Brooklyn NY 11237 Home Phone: 718-238-7431; Office Phone: 718-963-7272. Personal E-mail: orugunta@yahoo.com.

ORULLIAN, B. LARAE, retired bank executive; b. Salt Lake City, May 15, 1933; d. Alma and Bessie (Bacon) O. Cert., Am. Inst. Banking, 1961, 63, 67; grad. Nat. Mortgage Sch., Ohio State U., 1969-71; DHL (hon.), Whittier Coll., Calif., 2004. With Tracy Collins Trust Co., Salt Lake City, 1951-54, Union Nat. Bank, Denver, 1954-57; exec. sec. Guaranty Bank, Denver, 1957-64, asst. cashier, 1964-67, asst. v.p., 1967-70, v.p., 1970-75, exec. v.p., 1975-77, also bd. dirs.; chair, CEO, pres. The Women's Bank N.A., Denver, 1977-97, Colo. Bus. Bankshares, Inc., 1980-97; pres. Guaranty Corp., Denver, 1998—2007; ret. Pres., bd. dirs. Lange Golf Co., Holladay Bank, Utah; vice-chmn. bd. dirs. Frontier Airlines; bd. dirs. KBDI Channel 12TV; trustee Delta Dental Colo., 2005—. Treas. Girl Scouts U.S., 1981-87, 1st nat. v.p., chair exec. com., 1987-90, nat. pres., 1990-96; 1st vice chair world bd. World Assn. Girl Guides Girl Scouts, London. Recipient Woman Who Made a Difference award Internat. Women's Forum, 1994, Ultimate Woman of Colo. award, 2005, Women Enterprise award U. Denver, 2005; named to Colo. Women Hall of Fame, 1988; named Colo. Entrepreneur of Yr., Inc. Mag. and Arthyr Young and Co., 1989, Woman of Yr., YWCA, 1989, Citizen of Yr., EMC Lions Club, 1995, laureate Colo. Bus. Hall of Fame, 1999. Mem. Bus. and Profl. Women Colo. (3d Century award 1977, Unique Woman of Colo. 2005, Colo. Woman of Enterprise 2005), Internat. Women's Forum, Com. of 200. Independent. Mem. Lds Ch. Home: 6650 W 10th Pl Denver CO 80214

ORVICK, GEORGE MYRON, religious organization administrator, minister; b. Hanlontown, Iowa, Jan. 9, 1929; s. George and Mabel Olina (Mandsager) O.; m. Ruth Elaine Hoel, Aug. 25, 1951; children: Daniel, Emily, Mark, Kirsten. AA, Bethany Luth. Coll., Mankato, Minn., 1948, candidate of theology, 1953; BA, Northwestern Coll., Watertown, Wis., 1950; postgrad., U. Wis. Ordained to ministry Evang. Luth. Synod, 1953. Pastor Our Saviour Luth. Ch., Amherst Junction, Wis., 1953-54, Holy Cross Luth. Ch., Madison, Wis., 1954-86; cir. visitor Evang. Luth. Synod, Mankato, 1964-69, v.p., 1969—70, pres., 1970—76, 1980—2002, dir. dept. archives and history, 2002—; bd. regents Bethany Luth. Coll., 1957—69. Author: Our Great Heritage, 1966, Forget Not All His Benefits, 2003; columnist: The Luth. Sentinel, 1982-2002. Lutheran. Home: 224 Terrace Dr Mankato MN 56001-4728 Office: Evang Luth Synod 6 Browns Ct Mankato MN 56001-6121 Home Phone: 507-387-1498; Office Phone: 507-344-7308. Business E-Mail: gorvick@blc.edu.

ORWIG, MATTHEW DANE, lawyer, former prosecutor; b. Ardmore, Okla., Jan. 2, 1959; s. Richard R. and Mary E. (Pyle) O.; m. Melissa L. Vaughan, July 11, 1981; children: Joshua Matthew, Rachel Elizabeth, Jacob Andrew. BS, Tex. Tech. U., 1981, JD, 1984. Bar: Tex. 1985, US Dist. Ct. (no. dist.) Tex. 1985, US Ct. Appeals (5th cir.) 1985. Legal intern for no. dist. Tex. US Dept. Justice, Dallas, 1983; briefing atty. for judge US Dist. Ct., Lubbock, Tex., 1984-86; ptnr. Jones, Flygare, Galey, Moody and Brown, Lubbock, Tex., 1986-89; asst. US atty. (ea. dist.) Tex. US Dept. Justice, Dallas, 1989—2001, US atty., 2001—07; mng. ptnr., nat. chair govt. litig. & investigations group Sonnenschein Nath & Rosenthal LLP, Dallas, 2007—. Adj. prof. So. Meth. U. Law Sch, 1990—, Tex. Wesleyan U. Sch. Law, 1990—; legal advisor Exec. Office of U.S. Atty., Office of Legal Counsel, 1997—. Mem. ABA, State Bar Tex., Lubbock County Bar Assn., Lubbock County Young Lawyers Assn. (bd. dirs. 1987-89), Tex. Trial Lawyers Assn. Methodist. Office: Sonnenschein Nath & Rosenthal LLP 1717 Main St 34th Fl Dallas TX 75201 *

ORWOLL, GREGG S.K., lawyer; b. Austin, Minn., Mar. 23, 1926; s. Gilbert M. and Kleonora (Kleven) O.; m. Laverne M. Flentie, Sept. 15, 1951; children: Kimball G., Kent A., Vikki A., Tristen A., Erik G. BS, Northwestern U., Evanston, Ill., 1950; JD, U. Minn., Mpls., 1953. Bar: Minn. 1953, US Supreme Ct. 1973. Assoc. Dorsey & Whitney, Mpls., 1953-59, ptnr., 1959-60; assoc. counsel Mayo Clinic, Rochester, Minn., 1960-63, gen. counsel, 1963-87, sr. legal counsel, 1987-91, sr. counsel, 1991-92. Gen. counsel, dir. Rochester Airport Co., 1962-84, v.p., 1981-84; gen. counsel Mayo Med. Svcs., Ltd., 1972-90; bd. dirs., sec. and gen. counsel Mayo Found. for Med. Edn. and Rsch., 1984-90; gen. counsel Mid-Am. Orthop. Assn., 1984—, Minn. Orthop. Soc., 1985-95; counsel Norwegian Am. Orthopaedic Soc., 1999—, Intl. Soc. of Amyloidosis 2002—; asst. sec./sec. Mayo Found., Rochester, 1972-91; sec. Mayo Emeritus Staff, 1998-99, vice chair, 1999-2000, chair, 2000-2001; bd. dirs. Charter House, 1986-90; dir., officer Travelure Motel Corp., 1968-86; dir., v.p. Echo Too Ent., Inc.; dir., v.p. Oberhamer Inc., 1989-99; bd. dirs. Am. Decal and Mfg. Co., 1989-93, sec., 1992-93; adj. prof. William Mitchell Coll. Law, 1978-84. Contbr. articles to profl. jours., chpts. to books; mem. editl. bd. Minn. Law Rev., 1952-53, HealthSpan, 1984-93 Trustee Minn. Coun. on Founds., 1977-82, Mayo Found., 1982-86; trustee William Mitchell Coll. Law, 1982-88, 89-98, mem. exec. com. 1990-98; bd. visitors U. Minn. Law Sch., 1974-76, 85-91; mem. U. Minn. Regent Candidate Adv. Coun., 1988-99, Minn. State Compensation Coun., 1991-97. With USAF, 1944-45. Recipient Outstanding Svc. medal, US Govt., 1991. Mem. ABA, AMA (affiliate), Am. Corp. Counsel Assn., Minn. Soc. Hosp. Attys. (bd. dirs. 1981-86), Minn. State Bar Assn. (chmn. legal/med. com. 1977-81), Olmsted County Bar Assn. (v.p., pres. 1977-79), Rochester C. of C., U. Minn. Law Alumni Assn. (bd. dirs. 1973-76, 85-91), Rochester U. Club (pres. 1977), The Doctors Mayo Soc., Mid Am. Orthop. Assn. (hon.), Mayo Alumni Assn. (hon.), Phi Delta Phi, Phi Delta Theta. Republican. Home: 2233 5th Ave NE Rochester MN 55906-4017 Office: Mayo Clinic 200 1st St SW Rochester MN 55905-0002 Office Phone: 507-284-2691.

ORY, MARCIA GAIL, social science researcher; b. Dallas, Feb. 8, 1950; d. Marvin Gilbert and Esther (Levine) O.; m. Raymond James Carroll, Aug. 13, 1972. BA magna cum laude, U. Tex., 1971; MA, Ind. U., 1972; PhD, Purdue U., 1976; MPH, Johns Hopkins U., 1981. Rsch. asst. prof. U. N.C., Chapel Hill, 1976-77, from adj. asst. prof. to assoc. prof. sch. pub. health, 1978-88; rsch. fellow U. Minn., Mpls., 1977-78; asst. prof. Sch. Pub. Health U. Ala., Birmingham, 1978-80; program dir. biosocial aging and health Nat. Inst. on Aging, Bethesda, Md., 1981-86, chief social sci. rsch. on aging, 1987—2001; prof. Sch. Rural Pub. Health Tex A&M U. Sys., College Station, 2001—. Dir. RWJF Nat. Program Office on Increasing Phys. Activity in the 50 Plus, 2001—, Program on Health Promotion and Aging. Contbr. articles, editor vols. to profl. jours. Mem. several nat. task forces on aging and health issues; bd. dirs. Ctr. for Health Improvement. Named Disting. Alumna, Purdue U.; named one of 5 Industry Innovators in Active Aging, Internat. Coun. on Active Aging, 2003; named to McKnights Long Term Care News 100, 1997; recipient Dept. HHS award, 1984, 1985, 1988, Dir.'s award, NIH, 1995, Merit award, 1999, 2001, Dir's Lifetime Achievement award, 2000, Polisher award, Gerontol. Soc. Am., 2001, award for excellence in rsch., Sch. Rural Pub. Health, 2006, Excellence in Program Innovation award, Archstone Found., 2005, Excellence in Rsch. award, Sch. Rural Pub. Health, 2005; fellow, Inst. for Advanced Study, LaTrobe U.,vMelbourne, Australia, 2004. Fellow: Soc. Behavioral Medicine (program chmn. pub. health track 1988—89, program com. 1991—92, program chair lifespan/devel. track 2001—02), Acad. for Behavioral Medicine Rsch., Gerontol. Soc. Am.; mem.: APHA (program chmn. 1986, gov. coun. 1986—88, chmn.-elect 1989—91, chmn. 1992—93, leadership group 1996—, chair older women's interest group), Am. Acad. Health Behavior, Am. Sociol. Assn. (regional reporter 1984—94, program com. 1986, nominations com. 1987, councilor-at-large 1992—93), Omicron Nu, Phi Kappa Phi. Avocations: walking, birding, travel. Office: Sch Rural Pub Health 1266 TAMU College Station TX 77843-1266 Office Phone: 979-458-1373. Business E-Mail: mory@srph.tamhsc.edu.

ORY, STEVEN JAY, physician, educator; b. Houston, Aug. 4, 1950; s. Edwin Marvin and Norma Gertrude O.; m. Kathleen Higgins, Jan. 10, 1981; children: Eleanor Claire, Edward Michael. BA, Washington and Lee U., 1972; MD, Baylor Coll., 1976. Diplomate Am. Bd. Obstetrics and Gynecology, subsplty. cert. in Reproductive Endocrinolgy and Infertility. Asst. prof. Duke U., Durham, NC, 1981-82, Northwestern U., Chgo., 1982-85; assoc. prof., cons. Mayo Clinic, Rochester, Minn., 1985-95, chmn. sect. reproductive endocrinology and infertility, 1985-95; pvt. practice reproductive endocrinology and infertility; mem. ob-gyn. staff Internat. U., Margate, Fla., 1995—; assoc. clin. prof. obstets. and gyn. U. Miami, Fla., 1999—. Assoc. dir. Am. Fertility Soc., Birmingham, Ala., 1986-87; bd. trustees Northwest Med. Ctr., Margate, Fla., 2003—. Asst. editor: Fertility and Sterility, 1988-96; contbr. articles to profl. jours. Mem.: Ft. Lauderdale Ob-Gyn. Soc. (pres. 1998—2000), Soc. Reproductive Endocrinologists (sec.-treas., pres. 2001—02), Am. Soc. Reproductive Medicine (chmn. practice com. 1998—2000, bd. dirs. 1999—2002, v.p. 2004—05, pres.-elect 2005—06, pres. 2006—), Soc. for Humanism in Medicine (bd. dirs. 1999—2002, v.p. 2004—05, pres.-elect 2005—06, pres. 2006—07). Office Phone: 954-247-6200.

OSADCHUK, MARGO, publishing executive; BS cum laude, Univ. SD; MA, Univ. St. Thomas, Mpls. Positions with Control Data Corp., Washington Sq. Capital; cons. York & Associates, Mpls.; v.p., leader nat. bus. trans. practice Ciber Inc.; nat. v.p. Nuvolution LLC, Mpls.; v.p. edn. resources Sagebrush Corp.; sr. v.p. ops. Sagebrush Books, now Tandem Library Group, Mpls., Miss., 2006—. Office: Tandem Library Group Ste 600 7900 Xerxes Ave S Minneapolis MN 55431

OSAKI, MARK STEPHEN, foundation administrator, writer; b. Sacramento, Oct. 7, 1952; s. Tadashi Melvin and Haruye (Murata) O. BA, U. Calif., Berkeley, 1974; PhD, Georgetown U., 1984. Assoc. dir. RAND Corp., Santa Monica, Calif., 1992-97, cons., 1997-2001; dir. devel. Disabled Sports USA Far West, Citrus Heights, Calif., 2000—. Comm. dir. U. Calif., 1984-90; dir. devel. Coro Found., San Francisco, 1996-97, Second Harvest Food Bank, San Jose, Calif., 1997-2000, Toigo Found., Sacramento, 1997-98. Author: Poetry of the Vietnam War, 1989, Men of Our Time: An Anthology of Male Poetry in Contemporary America, 1992. Nat. Endowment for Arts fellow, 1981, Alumni Scholar, Univ. Calif. Home: 6615 Fordham Way Sacramento CA 95831 Office: c/o Disabled Sports USA Ste 2540 6060 Sunrise Vista Dr Citrus Heights CA 95610 Personal E-mail: osakimark@comcast.net. Business E-Mail: mark@dsusafw.org.

OSAKWE, CHRISTOPHER, lawyer, educator; b. Lagos, Nigeria, May 8, 1942; arrived in U.S., 1970, naturalized, 1979; s. Simon and Hannah (Morgan) Osakwe; m. Maria Elena Amador, Aug. 19, 1982; 1 child, Rebecca E. LLB, Moscow State U., Lomonosov, 1967; PhD, Moscow State U., 1970; JSD, U. Ill., 1974. Bar: Moscow 1967, Kazakhstan 1997. Prof. sch. law Tulane U., New Orleans, 1972-81, 86-88; Eason-Weinmann prof. comparative law, dir. Tulane U., Eason-Weinmann Ctr. Comparative Law, New Orleans, 1981-86; ptnr. Riddle and Brown, New Orleans, 1989—. Vis. prof. U. Pa., 1978, U. Mich., 1981, Washington and Lee U., 1986, Lomonosov Moscow State U., 1999—2006; vis. fellow St. Anthony's Coll. Oxford (Eng.) U., 1980, vis. fellow Christ Ch. Coll., 1988—89; cons. U.S. Dept. Commerce, 1980—85. Author: The Participation of the Soviet Union in Universal International Organizations, 1972, The Foundations of Soviet Law, 1981, Joint Ventures with the Soviet Union: Law and Practice, 1990, Soviet Business Law, 2 vols., 1991, The Russian Civil Code Annotated: Translation and Commentary, 2000, Comparative Law in Diagrams: General and Special Parts, 2000, 2d edit., 2002, Comparative Law: Diagrammatic Commentary, 2007; author: (with others) Comparative Legal Traditions in a Nutshell, 1982, Comparative Legal Traditions - Text, Materials and Cases, 1985, 2d edit., 1994; editor: Am. Jour. Comparative Law, 1978—86, Jour. Fgn. Legis. and Comparative Law, 2006—; mem. editl. bd.: Am. Jour. Legal Edn., 1983—85. Carnegie fellow, Hague Acad. Internat. Law, 1969, Russian Rsch. fellow, Harvard U., 1972, USSR Sr. Rsch. Exch. fellow, 1982, Rsch. fellow, Kennan Inst. Advanced Russian Studies, 1988. Mem.: ABA, Soc. de Legis. Comparée, Supreme Ct. Hist. Soc., Am. Soc. Internat. Law, Am. Law Inst., Order of Coif. Republican. Roman Catholic. Home: 339 Audubon Blvd New Orleans LA 70125-4124 Office: 201 S Charles Ave Ste 3100 New Orleans LA 70170 Office Phone: 504-861-1272. Personal E-mail: osakwec@aol.com.

OSAN, ANA M., language educator; BA, Ind. U. NW, Gary, 1989; MA, U. Chgo., 1994, PhD, 2000. Asst. prof. Spanish Ind. U. NW, 2000—06, assoc. prof. Spanish, 2006—. Translator: Ithaca, 2004; author: Nuevas Historias de la Tribu, 2007. Office: Ind U NW 3400 Broadway Gary IN 46408

OSBALDESTON, GORDON FRANCIS, finance educator, retired federal agency administrator; b. Hamilton, Ont., Can., Apr. 29, 1930; s. John Edward and Margaret (Hanley) O.; m. Geraldine Keller, Oct. 3, 1953; children: Stephen, David, Robert, Catherine B.Commerce, U. Toronto, Ont., Can., 1952; MBA, U. Western Ont., London, 1953, LL.D., 1984, York U., Toronto, 1984, Dalhousie U., Halifax, NS, 1985, Carleton U., Ottawa, Ont., Can., 1987. Fgn. service officer Dept. Trade and Commerce, Ottawa, 1953-54, vice consul, asst. trade commr. Sao Paula, Brazil, 1954-57, Chgo., 1957-60, consul, trade commr. Los Angeles, 1960-64, asst. dir., personnel trade commr. service Ottawa, 1964-66, asst. dir. ops. trade commr. service, 1966-67, exec. dir. trade commr. service, 1967-68; asst. dep. minister Dept. Consumer and Corp. Affairs, Ottawa, 1968-70, dep. minister, 1972-73; dep. sec. Treasury Bd. Secretariat, Ottawa, 1970-72, sec., 1973-76; dep. minister Dept. Industry, Trade and Commerce, Ottawa, 1976-78; sec. Ministry of State for Econ. Devel., Ottawa, 1978-82; undersec. of state Dept. External Affairs, Ottawa, 1982; clk. privy council, sec. to cabinet Privy Council Office, Ottawa, 1982-86; mem. Queen's Privy Coun. for Can., 1986; prof. emeritus Western Bus. Sch. U. Western Ont., 1986—. Mem. Robarts Rsch. Coun., 2004. Author: Keeping Deputy Ministers Accountable, 1989, Organizing to Govern, 1990. Decorated officer Order of Can., companion, 1997; recipient Outstanding Achievment award Can. Govt., 1981, Vanier medal Inst. Pub. Adminstrn., 1990. Mem. London Hunt and Country Club, Psi Upsilon Roman Catholic. Avocations: stamp collecting/philately, golf. Home: 1353 Corley Dr N London ON Canada N6G 4L4 Personal E-mail: gordon5304@aol.com.

OSBERG, GREGORY JOHN, publishing company executive; b. Jamestown, NY, June 12, 1957; s. John Raymond and Nancy (Jones) O.; m. Linda Burton, Aug. 22, 1981; children: Eric Burton, Alexander Gregory. BS in Mktg., Colo. State U., 1979. Regional mgr. Chilton Pub., Radnor, Pa., 1979-81; account mgr. U.S. News & World Report, NYC, 1981-84, Fortune, NYC, 1984-85; v.p. advt. sales U.S. News & World Report, NYC, 1985-90; from advt. sales dir. to v.p. Newsweek, 1992—94, v.p., 1994—97; pres. sales and mktg. CNET, Inc., 1997—99; pres. Brass Ring, Inc., 1999—2000; exec. v.p. Newsweek, 2000—, worldwide pub., 2000—. Chmn. Careers in Communications, Pitts., 1980-81. Mem. Advt. Club N.Y., Lincoln Ctr. Ctr. Circle (exec. com.), Bedens Brook Club. Avocations: golf, tennis, squash, jogging, skiing. Office: Newsweek 251 W 57th St New York NY 10019-1802 Office Phone: 212-445-5979. Office Fax: 212-350-4987. Business E-Mail: greg.osberg@newsweek.com. *

OSBERG, TIMOTHY MICHAEL, psychologist, educator, researcher; b. Buffalo, Aug. 11, 1955; s. John Carlton and Adeline Rose (Weichsel) O.; m. Debra A. Morreale, July 14, 1990; children: John Peter, Erika Evelyn. BA, SUNY, Buffalo, 1977, MA, 1980, PhD, 1982. Lic. psychologist NY. Intern VA Med. Ctr., Buffalo, 1981-82; asst. prof. Niagara U., NY, 1982-86; assoc. prof., 1986-90; prof., 1990—; pvt. practice Niagara U., Niagara Falls, NY, 1985—. Psychologist Optifast Weight Loss Program, Niagara Falls, 1989-92; editorial bd. Jour. Personality and Social Psychology, 1988-92, Teaching of Psychology, 1991-99, Jour. Correctional Edn., 1993-97, Jour. Clin. Psychology, 1999-2001; instr. Attica Correctional Facility, 1980-93; presenter in field. Contbr. articles to profl. jours. Vol. group leader pre-release program Attica (N.Y.) Correctional Facility, 1984-90, exec. com. Psychol. Assn. Western N.Y., Buffalo, 1982-87. Recipient Feldman-Cohen Meml. award SUNY, Buffalo, 1977, Disting. Faculty award Consortium of Niagara Frontier, 1993, Cmty. Svc. award Niagara County Mental Health Assn., 2000, Professionalism in Mental Health award Niagara County Mental Health Assn., 2004. Fellow APA; mem. Am. Psychol. Soc., Eastern Psychol. Assn., Soc. for Personality Assessment, Phi Beta Kappa. Democrat. Roman Catholic. Avocations: spectator sports, running, golf, bicycling, hockey. Home: 109 Hidden Oaks Ct Grand Island NY 14072-2575 Office: Niagara U Dept Psychology Niagara University NY 14109 Home Phone: 716-773-6167; Office Phone: 716-286-8524. Business E-Mail: tosberg@niagara.edu.

OSBORN, DEVERLE ROSS, insurance company executive; b. Leesburg, Ind., Sept. 29, 1925; s. Leland John and Beth (Bunnell) O.; m. Edith Helaine Germann, June 27, 1948 (dec. Mar. 1990); children: Bradford, Pamela, Andrea, Randall; m. Lillian C. Fellwock, Aug. 1990. Student, U. Notre Dame, 1944; BS in Air Transp. Engrng., Purdue U., 1947. Spl. agt. FBI, Louisville, 1948, NYC, 1948—53; agt. life ins. Conn. Mut. Life, NYC, 1953—56, life ins. exec. Hartford, 1956—65, Allentown, Pa., 1965—70, Aid Assn. Luths., Appleton, Wis., 1970—78, Evansville, Ind., 1978—91; ret., 1991. Liaison State Legislators Justice Fellowship, Washington, 1982-85, chmn., 1989-92; fin. dir. Prescott, Ariz. Spl. Olympics, 1996-98; bd. dirs. Atlantic dist. Luth. Ch.-Mo. Synod, 1961-65, Habitat for Humanity, Evansville, 1991-92, Meals on Wheels, Prescott, 1997-2000, Prayer Family Internat., 1999-2002. Naval Aviation cadet, 1943-45, lt. (j.g.) res., 1950-60. Named Nat. Vol. Yr. Justice Fellowship, 1989. Mem. Soc. CLU (v.p., pres. local chpts. 1968,70), Gen. Agt. Mgr. Assn. (treas., v.p., pres. local chpts. 1966-68), Nat. Assn. Life Underwriters. Republican. Lutheran. Avocation: flying. Home: 5223 East Harvard Ct Columbus IN 47203 Personal E-mail: nrobso@sbcglobal.net.

OSBORN, DONALD ROBERT, lawyer; b. NYC, Oct. 9, 1929; s. Robert W. and Ruth C. (Compton) Osborn; m. Marcia Lontz, June 4, 1955 (div.); children: David, Judith, Robert; m. Marie A. Johnson, Sept. 11, 1986. BA, Cornell U., 1951; LLB, Columbia U., 1957. Bar: NY 1957, US Tax Ct. 1958, US Ct. Claims 1961, US Ct. Appeals (2d cir.) 1974, US Ct. Appeals (8th cir.) 1974, US Dist. Ct. (so. and ea. dists.) NY 1975, US Supreme Ct. 1975. Assoc. Sullivan and Cromwell, NYC, 1957—64, ptnr., 1964—96, sr. counsel, 1997—. Mem. coun. White Burkett Miller Ctr. Pub. Affairs, 1976—82; bd. dirs., pres. Stevens Kingsley Found., 1967—2005; sec., treas. Dunlevy Milbank Found., 1974—; bd. dirs. Spanel Found., 1978—88; trustee Hamilton Coll., 1978—88, Mus. Broadcasting, 1975—80; trustee, treas. Kirkland Coll., 1969—78. With USN, 1951—54. Mem.: ABA, NY State Bar Assn., Assn. Bar City of NY, Am. Bar Found., Scarsdale Golf Club, India House, Regency Whist Club, Country Club of the Rockies. Presbyterian. Home: 1049 Park Ave New York NY 10028-1061 Office: Sullivan and Cromwell 125 Broad St Fl 32 New York NY 10004-2498 Office Phone: 212-558-3724. Personal E-mail: dromao@aol.com.

OSBORN, JOHN EDWARD, lawyer, pharmaceutical industry executive, former government official; b. Davenport, Iowa, Sept. 4, 1957; s. Edward Richard and Patricia Anne (O'Donovan) O.; m. Deborah Lynn Powell, Aug. 11, 1984; children: Delaney Powell, Keeley Rush. Student, Coll. William and Mary, 1975—76; BA, U. Iowa, 1979; cert., Georgetown U., 1980; JD, U. Va., 1983; cert., Wadham Coll., Oxford U., 1987; M in Internat. Pub. Policy, Johns Hopkins U., 1992; cert., Wharton Sch., U. Pa., 1994—95; postgrad., Princeton U., 1997—99. Bar: Mass. 1985, U.S. Supreme Ct. 2001. Staff US Rep. Jim Leach, 1978, Congl. Budget Office, 1979—80, US Senator John Heinz, 1981; law clk. to Hon. Albert V. Bryan US Ct. Appeals (4th cir.), Alexandria, Va., 1983-84; assoc. McDermott, Will & Emery, Chgo., Washington, 1981, Sidley & Austin, Chgo., 1982, Hale and Dorr, Boston, Washington, 1983—88, Dechert Price & Rhoads, Phila., 1988-89; spl. asst. to legal adviser US Dept. State, Washington, 1989-92; sr. counsel DuPont Merck Pharm. Co., Wilmington, Del., 1992-94, assoc. gen. counsel, 1994-96, v.p., assoc. gen. counsel, asst. sec., 1996—97; v.p. legal affairs Cephalon, Inc., Frazer and West Chester, Pa., 1997—98, sr. v.p., 1998—2005, gen. counsel, 1998—, sec., 1998—, exec. v.p., 2006—. Mem. No. Ireland adv. group US Dept. State, Washington, 2005—; mem. intellectual property adv. com. US Dist. Ct., Del., 2005—; mem. adv. coun. Nat. Legal Ctr. for Public Interest, Washington, 2007—; vis. lectr., exec. in residence Ross Sch. Bus. U. Mich., 1997—; mem. leadership coun. U. Mich. Life Sci. Inst., 2005—; vis. scholar East European studies Woodrow Wilson Internat. Ctr. for Scholars, Washington, 1991; bd. advisors Inst. Law Econ. U. Pa., 1999—; Wharton fellow, U. Pa., 2004—; vis. lectr. U. Pa. Law Sch., 2004—; vis. fellow politics, rsch. collaborator Princeton U., 2002—06; mem. bd. dirs. Incept BioSys., Inc., Ann Arbor, Mich., 2005—; nominated mem. US Adv. Commn. on Public Diplomacy, Washington, 2007—. Contbr. articles to numerous profl. jours. and newspapers; articles editor Va. Jour. Internat. Law, 1982—83; contbg. editor: Jour. BioLaw and Bus., 2007—. Trustee Siasconset Beach Preservation Fund, 2004—, Tower Hill Sch., Wilmington, Del., 1997—, Del. Art Mus., 1999—2006; corp. exec. bd. Phila. Mus. Art, 2003—; bd. govs. East-West Ctr., Honolulu, 2004—; mem. parents fund com. Hotchkiss Sch., Lakeville, Conn., 2006—; mem. Del. steering com. Bush-Cheney, 2000, 2004; del. Rep. Nat. Conv., San Diego, 1996; rsch. aide, speechwriter George Bush for Pres. Com., 1979—80, 1988. Fellow, U. Iowa Alumni, 2007; Eisenhower fellow, Ireland and No. Ireland, 1998, study grant, Andrew W. Mellon Found., 1999. Fellow Am. Bar Found.; mem. Am. Law Inst., Atlantic Coun. of US, Brookings Coun., Coun. Fgn. Rels., Princeton Club NY, Congl. Country Club, Cosmos Club, Met. Club Washington, Capitol Hill Club, Sankaty Head Golf and Beach Club, Siasconset Casino Assn., Bidermann Golf Club, Vicmead Hunt Club, Greenville Country Club, Mortar Bd., Phi Beta Kappa, Phi Delta Phi, Omicron Delta Kappa, Omicron Delta Epsilon. Republican. Roman Catholic. Avocations: golf, tennis, skiing. Office: 41 Moores Rd Frazer PA 19355 Home: 75 Baxter Rd Siasconset MA 02564 Office Phone: 610-738-6337. Business E-Mail: josborn@cephalon.com.

OSBORN, JOHN ROBERT, retired engineering educator; b. Kansas City, Mo., Aug. 11, 1924; married, 1945; 3 children. BS, Purdue U., 1950, MS, 1953, PhD in Mech. Engrng., 1957. Jr. engr. Thiokol Chem. Corp., 1950-51; asst. Purdue U., West Lafayette, Ind., 1951-57, from asst. prof. to assoc. prof. mechanical engrng., 1957-61, prof., 1961-70, 71-79, prof. aero. astronautical engrng., 1980—89, prof. emeritus aero. astronautical engrng., 1989—2006; br. chief Ballistics Rsch. Lab. Aberdeen Proving Ground, 1970-71. Mem.: AIAA (assoc. fellow, Wyld Propulsion award 1995), Soc. Automotive Engrs. Achievements include research in combustion instability in rockets; high frequency response instrumentation; combustion in solid rockets and interior ballistics. Home: 40 Stayman Ct Lafayette IN 47905-4446 Personal E-mail: josborn@purdue.edu.

OSBORN, JOHN SIMCOE, JR., lawyer; b. Louisville, Jan. 14, 1926; s. John S. and Ruby (Pinnell) O.; m. Mary Jo Fishback, Sept. 6, 1947; children— Robert, John, Donna LLB, U. Louisville, 1949. Bar: Ky. 1949, U.S. Dist. Ut. (ea. and we. dists.) Ky. 1952. Exec. v.p., gen. counsel Louisville Title Ins. Co., 1954-72; ptnr. Tarrant Combs & Bullitt (name changed to Wyatt Tarrant & Combs 1980), Louisville, 1972—. Chmn. bd. Beargrass Corp. Capt. JAGC, U.S. Army, 1952-54. Fellow Am. Bar Found.; mem. Ky. Bar Assn., Louisville Bar Assn., ABA, Am. Land Title Assn., Am. Coll. Real Estate Lawyers, Rotary. Democrat. Lutheran. Office: Wyatt Tarrant & Combs 2800 Citizens Plz Louisville KY 40202 Office Phone: 502-562-7584. Business E-Mail: josborn@wyattfirm.com.

OSBORN, JOHN W., lawyer; b. Prescott, Ariz., 1951; BA magna cum laude, Mich. State U., 1972; JD, U. Pa., 1975. Bar: Ariz. 1975, NY 1980. Staff atty. divsn. of market regulation SEC, Washington, 1975-78, br. chief divsn. of market regulation, 1978-79; ptnr., head derivatives fin. products Skadden, Arps, Slate, Meagher & Flom LLP, NYC. Chmn. and spkr. Practicing Law Inst.; spkr. in field; primary and documentation contact for Skadden, Arps, Slate, Meagher & Flom, LLP Internat. Swap and Derivatives Assn. Mem.: Bar Assn. City NY (former mem. securities regulation com.). Office: Skadden Arps Slate Meagher & Flom 4 Times Sq New York NY 10036 Office Phone: 212-735-3270. Office Fax: 917-777-3270. Business E-Mail: josborn@skadden.com.

OSBORN, JUNE ELAINE, pediatrician, microbiologist, educator, foundation administrator; b. Endicott, NY, May 28, 1937; d. Leslie A. and Dora W. (Wright) Osborn; children: Philip I. Levy, Ellen D. Levy, Laura A. Jana. BA, Oberlin Coll., Ohio, 1957; MD, Western Res. U., 1961; DSc (hon.), U. Med. Dental Sch. N.J., 1990, Emory U., 1993, Oberlin Coll., 1993, Rutgers U., 1994, Case Western Res. U., 1997, SUNY, Stony Brook, 1999, U. Wis., 2004; DMS (hon.), Yale U., 1992; LHD (hon.), Med. Coll. Pa., 1994. Intern, resident in pediatrics Harvard U. Hosp., 1961—64; fellow Johns Hopkins, 1964—65, U. Pitts., 1965—66; prof. med. microbiology and pediat. U. Wis. Med. Sch., Madison, Wis., 1966—84, prof. pediat. and microbiology, 1974—84, assoc. dean Grad. Sch., 1975—84; dean Sch. Pub. Health U. Mich. Sch. Pub. Health, 1984—93; prof. epidemiology, pediat. and communicable diseases U. Mich. Sch. Pub. Health and Med. Sch., 1984—96, prof. emeritus, 1997—. Pres. Josiah Macy, Jr. Found., 1997—; mem. rev. panel viral vaccine efficacy FDA, 1973—79, mem. vaccines and related biol. products adv. com., 1981—85; mem. exptl. virology study sect. Divsn. Rsch. Grants, NIH, 1975—79; mem. med. affairs com. Yale U. Coun., 1981—86; chmn. life scis. associateships rev. panel NRC, 1981—84; mem. U.S. Army Med. R&D Adv. Com., 1983—85; chmn. working group on AIDS and the Nation's Blood Supply NHLBI, 1984—89; chmn. WHO Planning Group on AIDS and the Internat. Blood Supply, 1985—86. Contbr. articles to profl. jours.; mem. editl. bd.: Jour. AMA, 2002—. Active task force in AIDS, Inst. of Medicine, 1986; adv. com. Robert Wood Johnson Found. AIDS Health Svcs. Program, 1986—91; nat. adv. com. on health of pub. program Pew and Rockefeller Founds.; active Global Commn. on AIDS, WHO, 1988—92; chmn. Nat. Commn. on AIDS, 1989—93; trustee Kaiser Found., 1990—98, Case Western Reserve U., Cleve., 1993—97; nat. vaccine adv. com. HHS, 1995—98; adv. coun. Nat. Inst. on Drug Abuse, 1995—98; internat adv. bd. Nat. Acads., 2002—05; bd. dirs. Legal Action Ctr., 1994—2001, Ctr. for Health Care Strategies, 1998—2003, The Mind Inst., 2003—05, US Pharmacoperia Bd., 2005—. Recipient NIH Pub. Svc. award, 2000, Scientific Freedom and Responsibility award, AAAS, 1994; grantee NIH, 1969, 1972, 1974—75, Nat. Multiple Sclerosis Soc., 1971. Fellow: Infectious Diseases Soc. Am., Am. Acad. Microbiology, Am. Acad. Arts and Scis., Am. Acad. Pediat.; mem.: Inst. Medicine (health promotion and disease prevention bd. 1987—90, coun. mem. 1995—2000), Soc. Pediat. Rsch., Am. Assn. Immunologists. Office: Josiah Macy Jr Found 44 E 64th St New York NY 10021-7306 Home Phone: 212-829-8186; Office Phone: 212-486-2424.

OSBORN, KENNETH LOUIS, financial executive; b. Belleville, Ill., Jan. 9, 1946; s. William Arthur and Louise Mary (Brueggemann) Osborn; m. Roberta Marie Vodicka, Oct. 23, 1971; 1 child, David Anthony. BBA, U. N. Mex., 1968. Auditor Ernst & Ernst, Albuquerque, 1968; budget mgr. Rockwell Internat., Chgo, 1970—74; mgr. internat. acctg. Allied Van Lines, 1974—76; fin. mgr. Sealy, Inc., 1976—79; sr. fin. analyst Newark Electronics, 1979—80, internat. dir. credit, 1980—82; bus. mgr. Prime Computer, Ill., 1982—90; acctg. mgr. and CFO Flexonics, Inc., 1990—96; contr. and CFO Jackson Industries, Ill., 1996—. Fin. cons. Am. European Express. Rep. Nat. Com.; presdl. task force. With US Army, 1968—70. Decorated Air medal. Mem.: Inst. Mgmt. Accts., Soc. Am. Baseball Rsch., Mensa Soc.

OSBORN, LA DONNA CAROL, clergywoman; b. Portland, Oreg., Mar. 13, 1947; d. T.L. and Daisy (Washburn) O.; m. Cory A. Nickerson, Dec. 11, 1981; children: Tommy O'Dell, LaVona Thomas, Daneesa Dolan, Donald O'Dell. Student, Assemblies of God Coll., 1963; BA, Okla. City U., 1994; DD, Bethel Coll., 1995; Doctor of Humane Letters (hon.), Wesley Synod, 1998; MA, Oral Roberts U., 2000; D in Ministry, Am. Christian Coll. and Sem., 2001; DD, Zoe Univ., 2001. Fgn. mission corr., purchaser, personnel agt. Osborn Found., Tulsa, 1969-75, exec. asst., 1975-76, internat. gen. mgr., 1976-81, internat. editor-in-chief, 1981-86, corp. pres., 1986-93; assoc. pastor Internat. Gospel Ctr., Tulsa, 1986-89, sr. pastor, 1989-94, sr. pastor, overseer, 1994-97; founder, presiding bishop Internat. Gospel Fellowship, Tulsa, Okla., 1997—; v.p., CEO OSFO Internat., 1998—. Internat. minister, religious tchr., and motivational spkr. Nigeria, Kenya, Uganda, Colombia, Papua New Guinea, France, Russia, Belarus, Kazakhstan, Kyrgyzstan, Ukraine, Russia, Sweden, Eng., Brazil, Holland, Can., India, Zambia, Guatemala, Ecuador, China, Brazil, Mizoram, Guatemala, Mexico, Myanmar, Indonesia, US; internat. spiritual advisor Christian Women's Fellowship Internat. Nigeria; founder Believers' Network Internat., Women's Internat. Network. Author: Jesus & Women, 2000, God's Big Picture, 2001, Cross-Cultural Communication in a Multicultural Church, 2002, New Miracle Life Now, 2004, Peace is a Lifestyle, 2005; author: (and editor) Bible tng. courses. Republican. Home: 3111 E 89th St Tulsa OK 74137-3362 Home Phone: 918-299-8045; Office Phone: 918-743-0872. Personal E-mail: revldo@aol.com.

OSBORN, MALCOLM EVERETT, lawyer; b. Bangor, Maine, Apr. 29, 1928; s. Lester Everett and Helen (Clark) O.; m. Claire Anne Franks, Aug. 30, 1953; children: Beverly, Lester, Malcolm, Ernest. BA, U. Maine, 1952; postgrad., Harvard U., 1952-54; JD, Boston U., 1956, LLM, 1961. Bar: Maine 1956, Mass. 1956, U.S. Dist. Ct. Mass. 1961, U.S. Tax Ct. 1961, U.S. Claims Ct. 1961, N.C. 1965, U.S. Supreme Ct. 1979, U.S. Ct. Appeals (4th cir.) 1980, Va. 1991. Tax counsel State Mut. Life Assurance Co., Worcester, Mass., 1956-64; v.p., gen. tax counsel Integon Corp. and other group cos., Winston-Salem, NC, 1964-81; ptnr. House, Blanco & Osborn, P.A., Winston-Salem, NC, 1981-88; v.p., gen. counsel, dir. Settlers Life Ins. Co., Bristol, Va., 1984-89; prin. Malcolm E. Osborn, P.A., Winston-Salem, 1988—. Lectr. The Booke Seminars, Life Ins. Co., 1985-87; adj. prof. Wake Forest U. Sch. Law, Winston-Salem, N.C., 1974-82; disting. guest lectr. Ga. State U., 1965; guest lectr. NYU Ann. Inst. Fed. Taxation, 1966, 68, 75, 80; gen. counsel Blue Ridge Mutual Assn., Inc., Galax, Va., 1989—; adj. instr. bus. law Forsyth Tech. C.C., Winston-Salem, N.C., 2004—. Com. editor The Tax Lawyer, ABA, 1974-76; author numerous articles in field. Trustee N.C. Coun. Econ. Edn., 1968-76; bd. dirs. Christian Fellowship Home, 1972-80; co-founder Bereaved Parents Group Winston-Salem, 1978—. Mem. ABA (chmn. com. ins. cos. of taxation sect. 1980-82, chmn. subcom. on continuing legal edn. and publs. 1982-88), Am. Bus. Law Assn. (mem. com. fed. taxation 1968—, chmn. 1972-75), Assn. Life Ins. Counsel (com. on co. tax, tax sect. 1965—), N.C. Bar Assn. (com. taxation 1973—), Fed. Bar Assn. (taxation com. 1973—), Maine State Bar Assn., Va. State Bar Assn., Internat. Bar Assn. (com. on taxes of bus. law sect. 1973—), AAUP, Southeastern Acad. Legal Studies in Bus., Masons (Lincoln, Maine). Office: PO Box 5192 Winston Salem NC 27113-5192 Home Phone: 336-765-5749; Office Phone: 336-659-0613.

OSBORN, MARVIN GRIFFING, JR., educational consultant; b. Baton Rouge, Sept. 7, 1922; s. Marvin Griffing and Marnie (Hester) Osborn; m. Sarah Fleming Osborn, Aug. 3, 1945; children: Jane Fleming, Charles Porter. BA, La. State U., 1942, MA, 1946; LLD, St. Xavier U., 1971; DHum, Phillips U., 1977. Pub. relations counsel La. State U., 1945-47, acting dir. bur. pub. service, 1947; assoc. prof., chmn. dept. journalism and dir. pub. relations Howard Coll. (now Frank Samford U.), 1947-49; dir. pub. relations, lectr. journalism Miss. State Coll. (now Miss. State U.), 1949-53; dir. information Washington U., 1953-58, pub. relations adviser, 1955-58, dir. Devel. Funds, 1958-61; cons. coll. and univ. adminstrn., 1961—, Drake U., Phillips U., Tampa U., Tex. Christian U., others,

Christian Ch. Found., Nat. Meth. Found. Christian Higher Edn., Lexington Theol. Sem., Memphis Theol. Sem., Nat. Benevolent Assn. Christian Ch., Sisters of Loretto; interim pres. St. Xavier Coll. (now St. Xavier U.), 1968—69; pres. Marvin Osborn, Inc., 1979—94. Mem. planning com. Conf. Advancement Understanding and Support Higher Edn., White Sulphur Springs, W.Va., 1958. Mem., co-chair Cypress Village Devel. Coun., Jacksonville, 1992—98; chair first trustee ballot com. Cypress Village Residents Coun., 2005; mem. Fiers-Brown Soc. Christian Ch. Found., 1991; mem. nat. fundraising com. Disciples World, 2002—04; mem. exec. com. program and arrangements com. Gen. Assembly Christian Ch., 1977, 1987—89; trustee National City Christian Ch. Corp., 1981—85; bd. dirs., mem. exec. com., sec. divsn. higher edn. Christian Ch., 1973—77; mem. panel study fin. procedures Disciples of Christ, 1987—89; bd. dirs. St. Louis Heart Assn., 1969—75, Fla. Christian Ctr., 1986—88. Capt. US Army, 1942—45, ETO. Recipient Harry T. Ice Disting. Svc. award for Excellence in Philanthropy, Christian Ch. Found., 1991. Mem.: Soc. Profl. Journalists, Nat. Benevolent Assn. (amb. 1992—98), Am. Coll. Pub. Rels. Assn. (v.p. dists. 1951—52, v.p. membership 1952—53, sec.-treas. 1953—55, pres. 1959—60), Sigma Chi, Omicron Delta Kappa. Home: 13655 Myrica Ct Jacksonville FL 32224-6626

OSBORN, MARY JANE MERTEN, biochemist, educator; b. Colorado Springs, Colo., Sept. 24, 1927; d. Arthur John and Vivien Naomi (Morgan) Merten; m. Ralph Kenneth Osborn, Oct. 26, 1950. BA, U. Calif., Berkeley, 1948; PhD, U. Wash., 1958. Postdoctoral fellow, dept. microbiology NYU Sch. Medicine, NYC, 1959-61, instr., 1961-62, asst. prof., 1962-63; asst. prof. dept. molecular biology Albert Einstein Coll. Medicine, Bronx, NY, 1963-66, assoc. prof., 1966-68; prof. dept. microbiology U. Conn. Health Ctr., Farmington, 1968—, dept. head, 1980—2002, prof. dept. molecular, microbial and structural biology, 2003—. Mem. bd. sci. counselors Nat. Heart, Lung and Blood Inst., 1975-79; mem. Nat. Sci. Bd., 1980-86; adv. coun. Nat. Inst. Gen. Med. Sci., 1983-86, divsn. rsch. grants NIH, 1989-94, chair, 1992-94; trustee Biosci. Info. Systems, 1986-91, chair, 1990-91; mem. German Am. Acad. Coun., 1994-97; mem. space scis. bd. NRC, 1994-2000, chair com. space biology and medicine, 1994-2000; cochair com. on indications for waterborne pathogens, 2002-03. Assoc. editor Jour. Biol. Chemistry, 1978-80; contbr. articles in field of biochemistry and molecular biology to profl. jours. Mem. rsch. com. Am. Heart Assn., 1972-77, chair, 1976-77. NIH fellow, 1959-61; NIH grantee, 1962-95; NSF grantee, 1965-68; Am. Heart Assn. grantee, 1968-71 Fellow Am. Acad. Arts and Scis. (coun. 1988-91), NAS (coun. 1990-93, com. sci. engring. and pub. policy 1993-96); mem. Am. Acad. Microbiology (bd. govs. 1994-2000), Am. Fedn. Soc. Exptl. Biology (pres. 1982-83), Am. Soc. Biol. Chemists (pres. 1981-82), Am. Soc. Microbiology. Democrat. Office: U Conn Health Ctr Dept Molec Micro and Struct Biology MC3205 Farmington CT 06030-0001 Office Phone: 860-679-4206.

OSBORN, SHANE, state official; b. SD, 1974; m. Teri Osborn, 2003; 2 children. BS in Math., Statistics, Univ. Nebr., 1996. State treas. State of Nebr., 2007—. Pilot, World Watchers Fleet Air Reconnaissance Squadron One USN, 1996—2005, Iraq, Iran, Afghanistan, S. Am., Asian Pacific. Decorated Disting. Flying Cross for heroism and extraordinary achievement in flight. Mem.: CAP. Office: State Treas Rm 2005 State Capitol Bldg PO Box 94788 Lincoln NE 68509-4788 Office Phone: 402-471-2455. Office Fax: 402-471-4390. Business E-Mail: info@treasurer.org. *

OSBORN, WILLIAM A., investment company executive; b. Culver, Ind., Oct. 14, 1947; married; 2 children. BA, Northwestern U., 1969, MBA, 1973. Joined No. Trust Corp., 1970, sr. exec. v.p., commercial banking Chgo., COO, 1993—95, pres., 1993—, chmn., CEO, 1995—. Bd. dirs. Caterpillar Inc., 2000—, Nicor, Inc., Tribune Co., 2001—; Class A dir. Fed. Reserve Bank Chgo. Bd. trustees Mus. Sci. and Industry, Chgo., Northwestern U., Chgo.; bd. dirs. Chgo. Symphony Orch., Northwestern Meml. HealthCare, Chgo. Urban League, Chgo. Horticultural Society, Lyric Opera Chgo., United Way Metropolitan Chgo.; bd. mgrs. YMCA Metropolitan Chgo.; advisory bd. J.L. Kellogg Grad. Sch. Mgmt., Northwestern. Mem.: Commercial Club of Chgo. (chmn., vice chmn. civic com.), Chgo. United (bd. dirs.), Chgo. Coun. Foreign Relations (bd. dirs.), Financial Services Roundtable, Chgo. Club, Executives' Club (bd. dirs.), Economic Club (bd. dirs.). Office: No Trust Co 50 S Lasalle St Chicago IL 60675-0001 *

OSBORN, WILLIAM GEORGE, savings and loan association executive; b. Alton, Ill., Dec. 9, 1925; s. Ralph A. and Pauline J. (Horn) O.; m. Hilda M. Alexander, Aug. 12, 1950 (dec.); children: Barbara K., David A., Robert W., James A. BS in Math., Shurtleff Coll., 1947; certificate, Grad. Sch. Savs. and Loan, Ind. U., 1946-48; A.M. in Econs., St. Louis U., 1962. With Germania Fed. Savs. and Loan Assn., Alton, 1946-90, exec. officer, 1955-86, pres., 1964-86, chmn., 1981-86, chmn. trust com., 1982-86; pres. Fin. Service Assocs., Ft. Lauderdale, Fla., 1986—. Pres. Germania Fin. Corp., 1970-86; owner Fin. Guidance, Alton, 1951—; mem. Opportunities Unltd., 1954-58; instr. Am. Savs. and Loan Inst.; bd. dirs. Nat. Coun. Savs. Instns., Washington, 1984-86. Author: Savings and Loan Operating Policies Manual, 1960, Economic Factors Influencing Savings and Loan Interest Rates, 1962. Pres. Alton Wood River Community Chest, 1959; bd. dirs. Piasa Bird coun. Boy Scouts Am., 1961-88, Mississippi Valley Jr. Achievement, Alton Area United Fund, 1961-63; founder, bd. dirs., treas. New Piasa Chautauqua Ch. Assembly, 1982-86; treas. Lewis and Clark Community Coll. Found., 1976-86; bd. dirs., sec. Riverbend Civic Progress, 1984-86; elder Presbyn. Ch. Served to lt. (j.g.) USNR, 1943-46, 50-52. Mem. Nat. Assn. Bus. Economists, Nat. Economists Club, St. Louis Economists Club, Am. Inst. Mgmt., Masons, Shriners, Chautauqua (Ill.) Yacht Club. E-mail: Olazydaze@aol.com.

OSBORNE, BARTLEY PORTER, JR., aeronautical engineer; b. Akron, Ohio, Sept. 1, 1934; s. Bartley P. and Cordelia Inez (Sims) O.; m. Carol Ann Eubanks, Jan. 15, 1966; children: Roxane Elizabeth, Ashley Hamilton. BSME, Carnegie Mellon U., Pitts., 1956; MS in Aerospace Engring., U. So. Calif., 1962. Sr. stress analyst N. Am. Aviation, Columbus, Ohio, 1956-66; sr. design engr. Lockheed Aircraft, Burbank, Calif., 1966-70, project engr., 1970-74; staff specialist aeronautics and ocean vehicles Office Sec. of Def., Washington, 1974-78; engring. prog. mgr. Lockheed Aircraft, 1978-82, chief adv. design engr., 1982-85, chief engr. YF-22, 1985-87, dep. chief adv. design engr., 1987-89; prog. mgr. Lockheed Aero. Sys. Co., Burbank, 1989-90; v.p., engr. Lockheed Aero. Systems Co., Marietta, Ga., 1990-96, v.p. advanced concepts, 1996-97; retired; cons. Aerotec Solutions, 1998—. Chmn. NASA Aeronautics Adv. Com., 1994-97; chmn. Aerospace Coun. SAE, 1997-2002; chmn. program planning com. Quiet Supersonic, 2001-02; bd. dirs. Aerofon Corp., San Diego; guest lectr. Carnegie Mellon U., 2001, Calif. Inst. Tech., 2003. Pres. Chesterfield Mews Homeowners Assn., Fairfax, Va., 1977-78. 1st lt. U.S. Army, 1956-58. Pa. State scholar, 1952; recipient Disting. Pub. Svc. medal U.S. Govt., 1997. Fellow Royal Aero. Soc., AIAA (assoc.); mem. L.A. Violin Cello Soc. Democrat. Avocation: cellist. Home: 405 White Horse Trl Palm Desert CA 92211-8947 Office Phone: 760-772-0582. Personal E-mail: aero21st@aol.com, spdfrk@aol.com.

OSBORNE, BURL, publishing executive, editor; b. Jenkins, Ky., June 25, 1937; s. Oliver and Juanita (Smallwood) O.; m. Betty S. Wilder, Feb. 14, 1974; 1 son, Burl Jonathan. Student, U. Ky., 1955-57; BA in Journalism, Marshall U., 1960; MBA, L.I. U. Sch. Bus., 1984; A.M.P., Harvard Bus. Sch., 1984. Reporter Ashland (Ky.) Daily Ind., 1957-58; reporter, editor Sta. WHTN-TV, Huntington, W.Va., 1958-60; corr. AP, Bluefield, W.Va., 1960-62, statehouse corr. Charleston, W.Va., 1963-64, corr. Spokane, Wash., 1964-67, news editor Denver, 1967-70; chief of bur. AP, Ky., 1970-72, AP, Ohio, 1972-74; asst. chief of bur. AP, Washington, Washington, 1974-76; mng. editor world hdqs. AP, NYC, 1977-80; exec. editor Dallas Morning News, 1980-83, v.p., 1981, sr. v.p., editor, 1983-84, pres., editor, 1985-90, pub., editor, 1991—2001, pub. emeritus, 2001—07. Bd. dirs. AP, 1993—2007, chmn., 2002—07; bd. dirs. J.C. Penney Co.; pres. publ. divsn. Belo Corp., 1995—2002; journalism adv. com. Knight Found., 2001—07; bd. dirs. Nat. Kidney Found., S.W. Transplant Alliance, 2001—07, chmn., 2007; bd. dirs. Freedom Comms., Inc. Bd. dirs. Pulitzer Prize, 1986—95, co-chmn. bd. dir., 1994—95. Named Newspaper Exec. of Yr., Nat. Press Found., 1992; inducted to Ky. Journalism Hall of Fame, 1994; recipient Disting. Alumnus award Marshall U., 1997, Freedoms Found. Next Millinium award, 1999. Mem.: Newspaper Assn. Am. (bd. dirs. 1996—2004), World Assn. Newspapers (mem. exec. com. 1998—2001, bd. dirs.), So. Newspaper Pub. Assn. (bd. dirs. 1995—2003, pres. 2000—01), Tex. Daily Newspaper Assn. (bd. dirs. 1982—92, pres. 1993), Am. Press Inst. (chmn. 1988—93), Am. Soc. Newspaper Editors (bd. dirs. 1982—91, pres. 1990—91), Orgn. Profl. Journalists. Home: 3901 Turtle Creek Blvd Dallas TX 75219 Office: Dallas Morning News PO Box 655237 Dallas TX 75265-5237 Personal E-mail: burlosborne@gmail.com.

OSBORNE, CHARLES DAVID, singer, composer, conductor; b. Suffern, NY, Aug. 14, 1949; s. Harold Clinton and Rosa Maria (Morales) Osborne; m. Kathryn Arden Stokes, Sept. 11, 1971; 1 child, Paul David. Attended in Bach Music, Voice, Hartt Coll. of Music, 1972; post grad. studies in opera, Juilliard Sch., 1974; diploma of Hazzanut with honors in musical composition and conducting, Jewish Theol. Sem., 1987, grad. studies in Jewish lit., 1988. Undergrad. asst. Hartt Coll. of Music, U. Hartford, 1970—71; faculty Jewish Theological Seminary of Am., 1987—88; staff N. Am. Jewish Choral Festival, 1990—, IMUN Program, United Synagogue of Conservative Judaism, 1991; faculty Northeastern U., 1991—94; staff, Hazamir Nat. Jewish HS Chorus, 1993—; faculty, Prozdor Hebrew Coll. of Boston, HS Divsn., 1994—; faculty, Cantor Educator program Hebrew Coll. of Boston, 2003—; founder, dir. Kol Rinah - The Jewish HS Chorus of Greater Boston, 1990—. Singer: (Operas) Avery Fisher Hall, Carnegie Hall, Alice Tully Hall, Merkin Hall, The Jerusalem Theater; singer: (solo) (concerts and recordings) Zamir Chorale of Boston, The Zamir Chorale of NY, Selah and Jubal's Lyre; singer: (recordings with the Western Wind Vocal Ensemble) Birthday of the World (Parts I and II), (recordings) To Heal The Earth, various television and radio appearances; contbr. articles various profl. jours. Mem. bd. dirs. Mazon - The Jewish Response to Hunger, 1994—2002; chmn. long-range planning and recruitment coms. Cantors Assembly, 1991—94, 1996—98; chmn. Boy Scouts of Am. Viking Dist., 1998—; chaplain Philmont Scout Ranch, Boy Scouts of Am., 1991—95, 1998—; bd. dirs. Zamir Chorale of Boston, 1988—, Zamir Chorale Found., 1994—. Recipient Off-Off Broadway Theater award. Mem.: ASCAP, Assn. for Jewish Studies, Am. Soc. of Jewish Music, New England Holocaust Meml. Assn. (adv. bd. 1998—), Jewish Min. Contors Assn. of New England (pres. 1990—94), Cantors Inst. Alumni Assn. (sec. 1990—92, pres. 1992—94), Newton Clergy Assn. Republican. Jewish. Achievements include first student to conduct svcs. at the Nat. Con. of the Cantors Assembly; first student to conduct Selichot svcs. at Jewish Theological Seminary. Avocations: astronomy, civil war, fire engine buff. Office: Congregation Adath Shir Rinah 321 Walnut St Box 263 Newton MA 02460 Office Phone: 617-395-5809. Office Fax: 617-558-8150.

OSBORNE, DONALD EUGENE, performing company executive; b. San Francisco, Feb. 28, 1950; s. Cletus Eugene and Anne Osborne. MusB, San Francisco State U., MA, 1972. V.p. Mariedi Anders Artists Mgmt., San Francisco, 1972—75; dir. Calif. Artists Mgmt., San Francisco, 1976—. Mem.: Nat. Assn. Performing Arts Mgrs. & Agents (pres. 1995—96). Democrat-Npl. Office: Calif Artists Mgmt 564 Market St Ste 420 San Francisco CA 94104-5412 Home Phone: 415-221-6746; Office Phone: 415-362-2787. Business E-Mail: don@calartists.com.

OSBORNE, DUNCAN ELLIOTT, lawyer; b. Orange, NJ, May 24, 1944; s. Walter Dodd Osborne and Anne (Boaz) Treanor; m. Elizabeth May Bachman, Dec. 29, 1965; children: Ellen Osborne Ray, Mark Elliott, Michael Cleveland. BA, Stanford U., 1966; MA, U. Tex., 1968, JD with honors, 1971. Bar: Tex. (cert. estate planning and probate law) 1971, U.S. Supreme Ct. 1975, U.S. Tax Ct. 1975, U.S. Fed. Ct. Claims 1997. Atty. Graves Dougherty, Austin, Tex., 1971-93, Osborne, Lowe, Helman & Smith L.L.P., Austin, 1993-2000, Osborne & Helman L.L.P., Austin, 2001—06, Osborne, Helman, Knebel & Deleery, Austin, 2006—. Bd. dirs. Boatmen's Nat. Bank Austin, 1995-97, Hill Country Bank, Austin, 1998. Co-author, co-editor: Asset Protection: Domestic and International Law and Tactics; contbr. articles to profl. jours. Trustee Susan Vaughan Found., Houston, Still Water Found., Austin, Crail Found., Austin; chair bd. trustees St. Stephens Episcopal Sch., Austin, 1985-91, St. Andrews Episcopal Sch., Austin, 1975-78; dir. Touchstones Discussion Project, Annapolis, Md.; mem. Tex. Law Rev. Fellow Am. Coll. Trust and Estate Counsel (chair internat. estate planning com., bd. regents), Coll. of State Bar of Tex.; mem. ABA, Internat. Bar Assn., Offshore Inst., Internat. Acad. Estate and Trust Law (v.p., exec. com.), Soc. Trusts and Estates Practioners, Tex. Bar Found., Asset Protection Planning Commn. (chair 1996-98)), Order of Coif Avocation: scuba diving. Office: Osborne Helman Knebel & Deleery LLP 301 Congress Ave Ste 1910 Austin TX 78701-2959 Office Phone: 512-542-2010.

OSBORNE, FRANK R., lawyer, educator, lecturer; b. Cleve., Dec. 7, 1946; s. Thomas L. and Doris E. O.; m. Charlotte A. Caston, July 8, 1972; children: James, Thomas, Patricia, Janet, Karen, Kathleen, Linda, Jennifer. AB in Polit. Sci., John Carroll U., 1969; JD, Cleve. State U., 1973. Bar: Ohio 1973, U.S. Dist. Ct. (no. dist.) 1975, U.S. Supreme Ct. 1979, U.S. Ct. Appeals (6th cir.) 1979, U.S. Tax Ct. 1980, U.S. Ct. Appeals (7th cir.) 1982. Law clk. to Hon. John V. Corrigan Ohio Ct. Appeals (8th appellate dist.), Cleve., 1973-76; atty. Roudebush, Brown & Ulrich, LPA, Cleve., 1976-86, Arter & Hadden, LLP, Cleve., 1986—2003, Tucker Ellis & West, LLP, Cleve., 2003—. Adj. faculty mem. Ohio civil procedure Cleve. Marshall Coll. Law, Cleve. State U., 1994-2005; alternative dispute resolution neutral U.S. Dist. Ct. (no. dist.), Cleve., 1990—; lectr. civil procedure Rossen Bar Rev., 2001-2003, DVD Bar Rev., 2003-2004, Supreme Bar Rev., 2004—. Co-author: Civil Discovery Practice in Ohio, 1995. Mem. ABA, Ohio State Bar Assn., Cleve. Bar Assn. Office: Tucker Ellis & West LLP 1150 Huntington Bldg 925 Euclid Ave Cleveland OH 44115 Home: 1278 Croyden Rd Lyndhurst OH 44124-1413 Office Phone: 216-696-3536. E-mail: fosborne@tuckerellis.com.

OSBORNE, JAMES ALFRED, religious organization administrator; b. Toledo, July 3, 1927; s. Alfred James and Gladys Irene (Gaugh) O.; m. Ruth Glenrose Campbell, Nov. 26, 1945; 1 child, Constance Jean (Mrs. Donald William Canning). Grad., Salvation Army Coll., 1947; student, U. Chattanooga, 1954-55; D of Pub. Svc. (hon.), Gordon Coll., 1991. Corps officer Salvation Army, Magness, Nashville, 1947, Southside, Memphis, 1948, Owensboro, Ky., 1949-54, comdg. officer Chattanooga, 1954-61, city comdr. Miami, Fla., 1961-65, divisional sec. Ky.-Tenn. Div., 1965-68, gen. sec. N.C. and S.C. Div., 1968-70, pub. rels. sec. 15 so. states, D.C. and Mex., 1970-71, divisional comdr. Md. and No. W.Va. Div., 1971-73, divisional comdr. Nat. Capital and Virginias Div. Washington, 1973-78, divisional comdr. Fla. Div., 1978-80, chief sec. Western Ter., 1980-84, nat. chief sec. Verona, NJ, 1984-86, territorial comdr. so. states Atlanta, 1986-89; nat. comdr., Republic of Marshall Islands, Guam, P.R., Virgin Islands Salvation Army USA, 1989-93. Chmn. Salvation Army Nat. Planning and Devel. Commn., 1974-76, 84-86; exec. bd. Vision Interfaith Satellite Network, Nat. Assn. Evangelicals, Christian Children's Fund Inc.; chmn. bd. Christian Mgmt. Assn., 1993-94; exec. com. religious alliance Against Pornography; rep. Salvation Army to numerous orgns. Bd. dirs. Nat. Law Ctr. for Children and Families; sec. Tenn. Conf. on Social Welfare, 1959, v.p., 1960; pres. Fla. Conf. on Social Welfare, 1965; pres. Ky. Welfare Assn., 1970. Mem. Chattanooga Pastors Assn. (pres. 1958), Va. and W. Va. Welfare Confs., Rotary. Personal E-mail: jim@jarvosborne.com.

OSBORNE, JOAN ELIZABETH, singer, songwriter; b. Anchorage, Ky., July 8, 1962; d. Jerry and Ruth (Yunker) O.; 1 child. Student, NYU. Singer various blues clubs, NYC. Albums include Soul Show, 1991, Blue Million Miles, 1993, Relish (includes One of Us), 1995 (7 Grammy nominations 1996, named No. 1 album Entertainment Weekly), Early Recordings, 1996, Righteous Love, 2000, How Sweet It Is, 2002, Christmas Means Love, 2005, Pretty Little Stranger, 2006, Breakfast in Bed, 2007. Office: c/o DAS Communications 83 Riverside Dr New York NY 10024 *

OSBORNE, JOHN EDWARDS, lawyer; b. Tucson, Feb. 10, 1953; s. Earle Dean and Helen Edwards Osborne; m. Diana Kuhel, Apr. 10, 1976; children: Monica, Valerie. AB with honors, Stanford U., 1975; JD, U. Tex., 1981. Bar: Ariz. Supreme Ct. 1981, U.S. Dist. Ct. Ariz. 1981, U.S. Ct. Appeals (9th cir.) 1990, U.S. Supreme Ct. 1994, White Mountain Apache Tribal Ct. Assoc. Chandler, Tullar, Udall & Redhair, Tucson, 1981-85; mng. atty. Tucson br. personal injury dept. Jacoby & Meyers Law Offices, Tucson, 1985-89; mng. ptnr. Goldberg & Osborne, Tucson, 1989—. Referee adminstr. Am. Youth Soccer Orgn., Tucson, 1997—. Fellow Ariz. Bar Found.; mem. ATLA, ABA, Am. Bd. Trial Advs. (assoc. mem., Tucson chpt.), Ariz. Trial Lawyers Assn. (sustaining mem., bd. govs.), State Bar Ariz. (cert. specialist in personal injury and wrongful death, pub. rels. com. 1985-89, trial practice sect. 1988—), Pima County Bar Assn. (pro bono com. 1982-95, v.p. young lawyers divsn. 1987-88). Avocations: private pilot, scuba diving, skiing, hunting, soccer referee. Office: Goldberg Osborne 33 N Stone Ave Ste 900 Tucson AZ 85701-1426

OSBORNE, JOHN WALTER, historian, educator, author; b. Bklyn., Aug. 19, 1927; s. Douglas Walter and Gertrude Ann (Purcell) O.; m. Frances Patricia Hannon, Aug. 2, 1958; 1 son, David. BA, Rutgers U., 1957, MA (Louis Bevier fellow), 1959, PhD, 1961. Asst. prof. history Kean Coll. of N.J., 1961-63, N.J. Inst. Tech., 1963-64; asst. prof. Rutgers U., New Brunswick, NJ, 1964-66, assoc. prof., 1966-69, prof., 1969-93, prof. emeritus, 1993—. Author: William Cobbett-His Thought and His Times, 1966, The Silent Revolution: The Industrial Revolution in England as a Source of Cultural Change, 1970, John Cartwright, 1972; co-author: Cobbett in His Times, 1990; editor: Jour. of Rutgers U. Libraries, 1975-80; co-editor: A Grammar of the English Language, 1983; contbr. articles to profl. jours. Recipient Henry Browne award for disting. teaching Rutgers U., 1988; Am. Philos. Soc. grantee, 1966, 75 Home: PO Box 426 Ivoryton CT 06442-0426

OSBORNE, JUDITH BARBOUR, artist; b. Winnipeg, Man., Can., Oct. 14, 1950; came to U.S., 1952; d. John Anderson and Laura May (Jones) Barbour; m. Frederick Spring Osborne Jr., Feb. 15, 1986; children: Sheila, Thomas, Sophia, Jessica. BFA, Univ. of Arts, Phila., 1974; student, Vt. Studio Ctr., 1984-89; MFA, Pa. Acad. Fine Arts, Phila., 1997. Prin. Barbour CalliGraphics, Phila., 1976—2002; dir. publs. and publicity Phila. Conf. on Calligraphic Arts, Phila., 1982; mem. faculty Phila. Coll. Art (now U. of Arts), 1982-85, 92, 00, Drexel U., Phila., 1991—2002; faculty Innovations Internat. Calligraphy Conf., NYC, 1987; exhbns. coord. Calleidoscope Internat. Calligraphy Conf., Trenton, NJ, 1993; guest lectr., workshop instr. Nantucket Island Sch. of Design and Arts, 2004. Guest curator Kamin Gallery, U. Pa., Phila., 1993, 95; exhbn. juror Phila. Calligraphers' Soc., 1989, 91, 94-95, 98, Phila. Sketch Club, 2002; spkr. 19th Internat. Calligraphy Conf., Guilford, Conn., 1999; lectr. in field. One-woman shows include Rourke Art Gallery, Moorhead, Minn., 1999, Phila. Art Alliance, 1999, Artists' House, 1998, 2000, 2002, Living Arts, Tulsa, Okla., 2000, Shipley Sch., Bryn Mawr, Pa., 2000, Delaware Ctr. for Contemporary Arts, 2004, Gallery Siano, Phila., 2004, Alexey von Schlippe Gallery, U. Conn, Avery Point, 2005, DeLong Gallery, Toronto, Can., 2005, West Liberty State Coll., W.Va., 2006, So. Vt. Arts Ctr., Manchester, 2006, Chester Gallery, Conn., 2006; exhibited in group shows at Nat. Arts Club, NYC, 1990, Pa. State Mus., Harrisburg, 1994, 2000-01, Am. Coll., Bryn Mawr, Pa., 1996, Nexus Found. for Today's Art, Phila., 1997, Del. Ctr. for Contemporary Art, 2002, Parallels Gallery, Phila., 2002, Tenri Cultural Inst., NYC, 2002, Shaanxi Mus., Xian, China, 2003, Ice House Gallery, Berkeley Springs, W.Va., 2004, Berman Mus. Art, Collegeville, Pa., 2004, Mobile Mus. Art, Ala., 2004, Calligrammes Gallery, Ottawa, Can., 2004-06, NY Hall Sci., Queens, 2005, Gallery One, Old Saybrook, Conn., 2005-06, Calif. State Polytechnic U., Pomona, Calif., 2006, Tenri Gallery, Paris, 2007; represented in permanent collections Scripps Coll., Claremont, Calif., Mobile Mus. Art, Ala., Brown U., Providence, Bryn Mawr Coll., Pa., Fed. Res. Bank Phila., Blue Cross, Rourke Art Gallery Mus., Moorhead, Barbour/Ladouceur Archs., Mpls.; also pvt. collections; collaborator Sophia Osborne Dance Assocs., 1999-2001, poet Jena Osman, 2001-04; contbr. articles to mags. and newspapers including Art Matters, 1997-2001, Letter Arts Rev., 2003. Recipient Best of Show Abington (Pa.) Art Ctr., 1990; Pa. Acad. Fine Arts fellow, Phila., 1997, Independence Found. fellow, 2001. Mem. Coll. Art Assn., Phila. Calligraphers' Soc. (bd. mem., publs. editor 1980-85), Inst. Noetic Scis. Avocation: metaphysics. Address: PO Box 4023 Old Lyme CT 06371-4023

OSBORNE, LOUISE, publishing executive; Pres. Osborne/Jenks Prodns., Inc., Wethersfield, Conn., 1979—. Office: Osborne/Jenks Prodns Inc 936 Silas Deane Hwy Wethersfield CT 06109-4273

OSBORNE, MARIE-ANGELA, journalist; b. Detroit, Jan. 20, 1957; d. Angelo Guerino and Domenica Mazzocco; m. John Hampton Osborne, Dec. 10, 1945; children: John Taylor children: Domenique Nicole, Robert Hampton. BA, U. Detroit, 1979. Anchor, reporter WJR Radio- ABC Radio, Detroit, 1994—2004; reporter, anchor WWJ Newsradio 950- CBS Radio, Southfield, Mich., 2004—. Adj. instr. Wayne State U., Detroit, 2000—03. Chmn. Lighthouse Oakland County, Pontiac, Mich., 1992. Recipient Edward R. Murrow award, Radio TV News Dirs. Assn., 1997, 1998, 2000, Clarion award, Women in Comm., 1997, 1998, Headliner award, Atlantic City Press Club, 1998. Mem.: Soc. Profl. Journalists. Office: CBS Radio-WWJ Newsradio 950 26495 American Dr Southfield MI 48034 Home Phone: 248-642-5174; Office Phone: 248-945-9950.

OSBORNE, RICHARD DE JONGH, mining and metals company executive; b. Bronxville, NY, Mar. 19, 1934; s. Stanley de Jongh and M. Elizabeth (Ide) O.; m. Cheryl Anne Archibald, Dec. 14, 1957; children: Leslie Coleman, Lindsay Vogel, Nicholas de J., Stanley de J. AB in Econs., Princeton U., 1956. With Cuno Engring. Corp., Meriden, Conn., 1956-60; fin., planning and mktg. exec. IBM Corp., Armonk, NY, 1960-69; investment adviser Sherman M. Fairchild, NYC, 1969-70; exec. v.p. fin. and bus. devel., dir. Fairchild Camera & Instrument Corp., Mountain View, Calif., 1970-74; v.p. fin. ASARCO Inc. (formerly Am. Smelting & Refining Co.), NYC, 1975-77, exec. v.p., 1977-82, pres., 1982-85, chmn., pres., CEO, 1985-99. Bd. dirs. NACCO Industries, Inc., Tinker Found.; bd. dirs., non-exec. chmn., bd. dirs. Datawatch Corp.; treas., mem. bd. dirs. Ams. Soc. Mem.: Nat. Mining Assn. (hon. dir.), Coun. Fgn. Rels., Econs. Club NY, River Club, Brook Club, Sakonnet Golf Club, John's Island Club. Home and Office: 40 E 94th St Apt 32B New York NY 10128-0759 Personal E-mail: rdejo@att.net.

OSBORNE, ROBERT STEPHEN, automotive executive, lawyer; b. Montreal, Que., Can., Oct. 21, 1954; m. Martha Osborne; children: Tom, Sarah. AB magna cum laude, Harvard U., 1976, JD magna cum laude, 1979. Bar: Ill., 1979. Assoc. Kirkland & Ellis LLP, Chgo., 1979-85, ptnr.,

1985—2002, Jenner & Block LLP, Chgo., 2002—, chair corp. practice; group v.p., gen. counsel Gen. Motors Corp., 2006—. Gen. counsel, Lands' End, Inc., Dodgeville, Wis., 1986-95, corp. sec., spl. asst. to bd. dirs., 1995-2002; adj. prof., U. Chgo. Law Sch., 2002-. Bd. dirs. Chgo. Shakespeare Theater, The Nature Conservancy of Alaska. Mem. ABA, Am. Soc. Corp. Secs., Internat. Bar Assn. Avocations: fly fishing, hiking. Office: Jenner & Block LLP One IBM Plz Chicago IL 60611 E-mail: rosbourne@jenner.com. *

OSBORNE, ROBIN, library and information scientist; BA in Philosophy, U. Calif., Berkeley, 1974; MLS with honors, Columbia U., NYC, 1992. Various positions NY Pub. Libr., 1992—97; adult and outreach svcs. cons. Westchester Libr. Sys., Tarrytown, NY, 1997—. Mem. documentary heritage prog. adv. coun. Met. NY Libr. Coun., 1999—2005. Editor: From Outreach to Equity: Innovative Models of Library Policy and Practice, 2004. Founder Westchester Literacy and Learning Alliance; bd. dirs. Literacy Vols. Westchester County, 1999—2005, Literacy Vols. NY State, 2000—03. Recipient Joseph Lewis Wheeler and Joseph Towne Wheeler award for Leadership, Columbia U. Sch. Libr. Svc., NY Times Libr. award, 2006. Mem.: ALA (chair adv. com. Office Literacy and Outreach Svcs. 2004—, mem. literacy com. 2003—05, chair literacy assembly 2002—05), REFORMA, Beta Phi Mu (life). Office: Westchester Libr Sys 540 White Plains Rd Ste 200 Tarrytown NY 10591-5110 Office Phone: 914-231-3237. Office Fax: 914-674-4185. E-mail: rosborne@wlsmail.org.

OSBORNE, SEWARD RUSSELL, writer; b. Catskill, NY, June 28, 1946; s. Seward Russell and Doris Virginia (Tompkins) O.; m. Jean Marie Shaver, June 22, 1968; children: Dean, Sarah. Historic site technician Senate House State Historic Site, Kingston, N.Y., 1976-77; contbg. editor Mil. Images, 1980—; contbg. author Mil. Collector & Historian, 1984—; historian Ulster County Civil War Round Table, 1994—; photographic cons. Arts and Entertainment Network, 1996. Cons. in field. Author: Holding the Left, The 20th New York State Militia at Gettysburg, July 1, 1863, 1990, The Saga of the Mountain Legion (156th N.Y. Vols.) in the Civil War and the Modest Hero Who Saved Our Flag, 1994, The Ninety Days Service of the 20th New York State Militia, 1998; editor: The Civil War Diaries of Col. Theodore B. Gates, 20th New York State Militia, 1991; contbr. articles to North South Trader's Civil War, 1970s, 1980s, Ulster County Gazette, 1970s, 1980s; photographic cons. Legacy TV Prodn. Three Days at Gettysburg, 1994. Active Friends of the Ulysses S. Grant Cottage; founder, dir. 120th Monument Restoration Fund, 1996-97; charter mem. Nat. WWII Meml., 2002—. Cited for erection 20th NY State Militia monument on the Gettysburg Battlefield, 1981, on the Battlefield of 2d Bull Run, Manassas, 1986, Rondout, NY, 2003. Fellow The Co. of Mil. Historians; mem. DAV (life), NRA, Ulster County Com. to Save the Grant Cottage (founder, chmn. 1990), NY State Mil. Heritage Inst., 1997, Ulster County Geneal. Soc. (Civil War history cons.), Zadock Pratt Mus (hon. life), Kingston Area Libr. (Civil War history cons.), Friends of Nat. Parks at Gettysburg, Inc., Surratt Soc. (life), Gettysburg Battlefield Preservation Assn., Lexington Hist. Soc. (hon. life), Friends of Albany Rural Cemetery, Am. Legion, Sons of Union Vets., Mil. Order Loyal Legion of US, Ulster County Hist. Soc. (hon. life). Born Again Christian. Avocations: historical sites, collecting Civil War artifacts, writing Civil War history. Home: 1329 County Road 2 Olivebridge NY 12461-5417 E-mail: info@ulsterguard.us.

OSBORNE, TOM (THOMAS WILLIAM OSBORNE), former congressman, former college football coach; b. Hastings, Nebr., Feb. 22, 1937; m. Nancy Tederman; children: Mike, Ann, Susie. BA in Hist., Hastings Coll., Nebr., 1959; MA in Ednl. Psych., U. Nebr., 1963, PhD in Ednl. Psych., 1965. Flanker NFL Washington Redskins, 1959-61, NFL San Francisco 49ers, 1961-62; asst. football coach U. Nebr., 1962—67, receivers coach, 1967—71, asst. head coach, 1972, head football coach, 1973-97, prof. emeritus, 1998-2000; mem. US Congress from 3rd Nebr. dist., 2001—07, mem. agr. com., mem. edn. and the workforce com., mem. transp. and infrastructure com. Co-founder Osborne Endowment for Youth. Sgt. in US Army Nat. Guard and USAR, 1960—66. Named Big Eight Coach of Yr., 1975, 1978, 1980, Bobby Dodds Nat. Coach of Yr., 1978; recipient Policy Maker of Yr., Assn. Career and Tech. Edn., 2005. Mem.: Fellowship Christian Athletes. Republican. Meth. Achievements include coaching the U. Nebr. football team in several bowl games including the Sugar Bowl, 1971, Cotton Bowl, 1974, Astro-Bluebonnet Bowl, 1976, Liberty Bowl, 1977, Orange Bowl, 1979, 83, 84,89, 92-95, Sun Bowl, 1980; coached team to NCAA Divsn. IA Nat. Championship, 1994, 1995, 1997.

OSBOURNE, OZZY (JOHN OSBOURNE), singer; b. Birmingham, Eng., Dec. 3, 1948; m. Thelma Mayfair, 1971 (div. 1981); children: Jessica Starshine, Louis Jon; m. Sharon Arden, 1982; children: Aimee Rachel, Kelly, Jack. Singer Black Sabbath, 1969—79, solo career, 1980—. Singer: (albums with Black Sabbath) Black Sabbath, 1969, Paranoid, 1970, Master of Reality, 1971, Volume 4, 1972, Sabbath, Bloody Sabbath, 1975, Sabotage, 1975, Technical Ecstasy, 1976, We Sold Our Soul For Rock and Roll, 1976, Never Say Die, 1978, Reunion, 1998, Past Lives, 2002, (solo albums) Blizzard of Ozz, 1980, Diary of a Madman, 1981, Speak of the Devil, 1982, Bark at the Moon, 1983, The Ultimate Sin, 1986, Tribute, 1987, No Rest for the Wicked, 1988, Just Say Ozzy, 1990, No More Tears, 1991, Live & Loud, 1993, Ozzmosis, 1995, Ozzman Cometh, 1997, Down to Earth, 2001, Live at Budokhan, 2002, Essential Ozzy Osbourne, 2003, Under Cover, 2005, Black Rain, 2007; performer: (films) Black Sabbath: Live, 1978, Ozzy Osbourne: Bark at the Moon, 1986, The Decline of Western Civilization Part II: The Metal Years, 1988, Ozzy Osbourne: Don't Blame Me, 1992, Ozzy Osbourne: Live and Loud, 1993, Black Sabbath: The Last Supper, 1999; actor: (films) Trick or Treat, 1986, The Jerky Boys, 1995, Private Parts, 1997, Little Nicky, 2000, (voice only) Moulin Rouge!, 2001,: (TV films) Billy's Shout, 1991; (TV series) The Frank Skinner Show, 1996, The Osbournes, 2002—05, Battle for Ozzfest, 2004—; voice only (TV series) South Park, 1997. Named to Rock and Roll Hall of Fame (as mem. of Black Sabbath), 2006; recipient Grammy award, Best Heavy Metal Performance for I Don't Want to Change the World, 1994. *

OSBURN, CHARLES BENJAMIN, retired librarian, dean; b. Pitts., May 25, 1939; s. C. Benjamin and Lydia (Harmon) O.; divorced; 1 child, Christopher Bart; m. Sharon Tuffendsam, June 12, 1987; 1 stepchild, Bradley Alan Tuffendsam. BA, Grove City Coll., 1961; MA, Pa. State U., 1963; MS, U. N.C., 1971; PhD, U. Mich., 1978. Instr. French Pa. State U., University Park, 1963-66; asst. prof. U. Wis.-Whitewater, 1966-69; humanities bibliographer U. N.C., Chapel Hill, 1969-74; asst. dir. libraries SUNY-Buffalo, 1974-76; asst. univ. librarian Northwestern U., Evanston, 1976-80; dean, univ. librarian U. Cin., 1980-86; dean libraries U. Ala., Tuscaloosa, 1986—2001, prof. library sci., 1986—2001, dean, prof. emeritus univ. libraries, 2001—. Bd. dirs. Ctr. for Research Libraries, Chgo., SOLINET, Atlanta, Assn. Rsch. Librs., 1987-93; mem. rsch. libr. adv. counc. to Online Computer Library Ctr., Dublin, Ohio; adj. prof. Sch. Libr. and Info. Studies, U. Ala., Tuscaloosa, 2001-. Author: Academic Research and Library Resources: Changing Patterns in America, 1979 (award ALA 1980); compiler: Research and Reference Guide to French Studies, 2d edit., 1981; mem. editorial bd. Literary Research: A Journal of Scholarly Method and Technique, 1986—; co-editor: (with R. W. Atkinson) Collection Management: A New Treatise, 2 vols., 1991. Mem. ALA, MLA, Assn. Rsch. Librs., Phi Sigma Iota, Beta Phi Mu. Office: Univ Ala Sch Library and Info Studies Tuscaloosa AL 35487-0252 Office Phone: 205-348-1519. Business E-Mail: cosburn@bama.ua.edu.

OSBURNE, ROBERT CARL, endocrinologist, educator; s. Leonard Kaye and Ida Fitzpatrick Osburne; m. Mary Jacquelin Kitchings, May 20, 1972; children: Kelly Jean, Stephen Howard, Kathryn Osburne Pope. MD, MS, U. Ala., Birmingham, 1974; MBA, U. Ala., Tuscaloosa, 1996. Cert. internal medicine Am. Bd. Internal Medicine, 1977, endocrinology and metabolism Am. Bd. Internal Medicine, 1979, clin. nutrition Am. Bd. Nutrition, 1979. Med. dir. Ga. Med. Care Found., Atlanta, 2000—; chief endocrine sect. Atlanta Med. Ctr., 2004—. Instr. Rollins Sch. Pub. Health, Emory U., Atlanta, 2004—. Lt. comdr. USNR, 1973—82. Mem.: ACP, Am. Assn. Clin. Endocrinologists, Endocrine Soc. Office: Atlanta Medical Center 303 Parkway NE Suite 423 Atlanta GA 30312 Home Phone: 404-367-0204; Office Phone: 404-265-4058. Office Fax: 404-265-4989. Business E-Mail: robert.osburne@tenethealth.com.

O'SCANNLAIN, DIARMUID FIONNTAIN, federal judge; b. NYC, Mar. 28, 1937; s. Sean Leo and Moira (Hegarty); m. Maura Nolan, Sept. 7, 1963; children: Sean, Jane, Brendan, Kevin, Megan, Christopher, Anne, Kate. BA, St. John's U., 1957; JD, Harvard U., 1963; LLM, U. Va., 1992; LLD (hon.), U. Notre Dame, 2002, Lewis & Clark Coll., 2003. Bar: Oreg. 1965, NY 1964. Tax atty. Standard Oil Co. (NJ), NYC, 1963—65; oassoc. Davies, Biggs, Strayer, Sotel & Boley, Portland, Oreg., 1965—69; dep. atty. gen. State of Oreg., 1969—71, pub. utility commr., 1971—73; dir. Oreg. Dept. Environ. Quality, 1973—74; sr. ptnr. Ragen, Roberts, O'Scannlain, Robertson & Neill, Portland, 1978—86; judge US Ct. Appeals (9th cir.), San Francisco, 1986—, mem. exec. com., 1988—89, 1993—94; mem. Jud. Coun. 9th Cir., 1991—93. Mem. US Jud. Conf. Com. on Automation and Tech., 1990—; cons. Office of Pres.-elect and mem. Dept. Energy Transition Team (Reagan Transition), Washington, 1980—81; chmn. com. adminstrv. law Oreg. State Bar, 1980—81; chmn. fed. jud. ctrs. adv. com. appellate edn., 2003. Bd. trustees James Madison Meml. Fellowship Found.; mem. coun. of legal advisors Rep. Nat. Com., 1981—83, mem., 1983—86; chmn. Oreg. Rep. Party, 1983—86; del. Rep. Nat. convs., 1976, 1980, chmn. Oreg. del., 1984; nominee US Ho. of Reps., 1st Congl. Dist., 1974; team leader energy task force Pres.'s Pvt. Sector Survey on Cost Control, 1982—83; trustee Jesuit H.S.; bd. visitors U. Oreg. Law Sch., 1988—; mem. citizens adv. bd. Providence Hosp., 1986—92. Maj. USAR, 1955—78. Mem.: ABA (sec. Appellate Judges Conf. 1989—90, exec. com. 1990—, chmn. 1994—95, chmn. jud. divsn. 2001—02), Fed. Judges Assn., Fed. Bar Assn., Multnomah Club. Roman Catholic. Office: US Ct Appeals Pioneer Courthouse 700 SW 6th Ave Ste 313 Portland OR 97204-1396 Home: 700 SW 6th Ave # 313 Portland OR 97204-1396 Office Phone: 503-833-5380. E-mail: Judge_O'Scannlain@ca9.uscourts.gov. *

OSE, DOUGLAS, former congressman; b. Sacramento, June 27, 1955; m. Lynnda Ose; children: Erika, Emily. BS, U. Calif., Berkeley, 1977. Project mgr. Ose Properties, Sacramento, 1977-85; owner real estate devel. and investment co., 1986—; mem. U.S. Congress from 3d Calif. dist., 1999—2005; mem. agr., fin. svcs., and govt. reform coms., joint com. on printing. Former bd. dirs. Citrus Heights C. of C., Sacramento Housing and Redevel. Commn.; mem. Citrus Heights Incorporation Project. Republican.

OSEGUERA, PALMA MARIE, retired career officer; b. Kansas City, Mo., Dec. 29, 1946; d. Joseph Edmund and Palma Louise (Utke) O'Donnell; m. Alfonso Oseguera, Jan. 1, 1977; stepchildren: Kristie M. Daniels, Michelle L. Nielson, Lori A. Kelley. BA in Phys. Edn., Marycrest Coll., 1969. Commd. 2d lt. USMC, 1969, advanced through grades to col., 1991; asst. Marine Corps exch. officer Hdqs. and Hdqs. Squadron, Marine Corps Air Sta., Beaufort, SC, 1969; classified material control officer Hdqs. and Svcs. Battalion, Camp S.D. Butler, Okinawa, 1971—73; adminstrv. officer, asst. Marine Corps exch. officer Marine Corps Air Sta., El, Toro, Santa Ana, Calif., 1973—76, Marine Corps exch. officer Yuma, Ariz., 1976—77; asst. Marine Corps exch. officer Hdqrs. and Support Bn., Marine Corps Devel. and Edn. Command, Quantico, Va., 1977—79; Marine Corps exch. officer Hqrs. Marine Corps, Washington, 1979—80; adminstrv. officer Marine Air Base Squadon 46, Marine Air Group 46, Marine Corps Air Sta., El Toro, Santa Ana, 1981—83, Hdqs. and Maintanence Squadron 46, Marine Air Group 46, Marine Corps Air Sta., El Toro, Santa Ana, 1983—85, Mobilization Tng. Unit Calif. 53, Landing Force Tng. Command, Pacific, San Diego, 1985—89, 3d Civil Affairs Group, LA, 1989; dep. asst. chief of staff G-1 I Marine Expeditionary Force, Individual Mobilization Augumentee Detachment, Camp Pendleton, Calif., 1990—91; assoc. mem. Mobilization Tng. Unit Del. 01, Del., 1992—94; adminstrn. officer Mobilization Tng. Unit, CA-53, EWTG Pac, NAB, Coronado, San Diego, 1994—96; exch. officer MWRSPT ACT IMA Det MCB, Camp Pendleton, Calif., 1996—99; ret. from 30 yrs. commissioned svc. USMCR, 1999. Choir St. Elizabeth Seaton, Woodbridge, Va., 1978-80, St. Patricks, Arroyo Grande, Calif., 1990-94; vol. Hospice, San Luis Obispo, 1995-2000; active Los Osos (Calif.) Veteran's Events Com., 1994-2000; lector, Eucharistic min., Martha Min. St. Patrick's Cath. Ch., Arroyo Grande, 2004—. Mem. AAUW (past libr.), Marine Corps Assn., Marine Corps Res. Officer Assn., Marine Corps Aviation Assn. (12 dist. dir. 1987), Women in Mil. Svc. for Am., Woman Marine Assn., Marine Corps League. Republican. Roman Catholic. Avocations: gardening, reading, horseback riding, genealogy, photography. Home: 728 Scenic Cir Arroyo Grande CA 93420-1617

OSER, CARRIE B., sociologist, educator; d. Robert J. and Judith A. Oser. BA, U. Ky., Lexington, 1998; MA, U. Ga., Athens, 2001, PhD, 2004. From pre-doctoral trainee asst. prof. sociology U. Ky., 1999—2003, prof. behavioral sci., 2004—06, asst. prof. sociology, 2006—. Cons. in field. Author: (book) The Sociology of Alcohol and Drugs: Syllabi and Teaching Materials, 2005; contbr. articles to profl. jours. Editor Am. Sociol. Assn. Alcohol, Drugs, & Tobacco sect. newsletter, Washinton, DC, 2000—07. Named Sociology Outstanding Undergraduate Sr., U. Ky., 1998; recipient Cert. Excellence award, U. Ga., 2004; fellow, NIH, 1999—2003; grantee, U. Ky. Rsch. Found., 1998, NIH, 2000—07, 2002—, 2003—04, 2004, 2006—, 2006, 2006, Mar. of Dimes, 2005—06; scholar, Seagram's, 1994—98. Mem.: Am. Sociol. Assn. (mem. coun. alcohol, drugs, and tobacco sect. 2005—07, editor newsletter alcohol, drugs, and tobacco sect.), Coll. Problems of Drug Dependence, Am. Soc. Criminology, Alpha Kappa Delta, Psi Chi, Golden Key. Office: Univ Kentucky 1531 Patterson Office Tower Lexington KY 40506 Office Phone: 859-257-6890. Office Fax: 859-323-0272. Business E-Mail: cboser0@uky.edu.

OSETSKY, YURI NICOLAI, physicist, researcher; b. Lvov, Ukraine, May 3, 1959; s. Nicolai Boleslav and Alla Nicolai Osetsky; m. Alla Vladimir Souvorova; children: Nicolai, Tatiana. BSc, MSc with honors, Moscow Engring. Physics Inst., 1982; PhD in Physics and Math., I. V. Kurchatov Atomic Energy Inst., Moscow, 1991. Rsch. scientist Atomic Energy Inst., Moscow, 1982-90; sr. rsch. scientist Russian Rsch. Ctr. "Kurchatov Inst.", Moscow, 1991-93; expert investigator CIEMAT Nuc. Tech. Inst., Madrid, 1993-94; vis. rschr. Poly. U. Catalunya, Barcelona, 1994-95, vis. prof., 1995-97; univ. rsch. fellow U. Liverpool, Eng., 1997—. Contbr. articles to profl. jours. Recipient II Kurchatov prize, 1986, awards Atomic Energy Ministry of Russia, 1989, 94, III Kurchatov prize, 1991. Avocations: informatics, alpine skiing. Office: U Liverpool Dept Materials Sci-Engring Liverpool L69 3GH England E-mail: osetsky@liv.ac.uk.

OSGOOD, CHARLES, news broadcaster, journalist; b. NYC, Jan. 8, 1933; s. Charles Osgood and Mary F. (Wilson) Wood; m. Jean Crafton, Dec. 5, 1973; children: Kathleen, Winston, Anne Elizabeth, Emily Jean, James Edward. BS, Fordham U., 1954; L.H.D. (hon.), St. Bonaventure U., 1977; PhD (hon.), Fordham U.; LLD, St. John's U. Program dir. Sta. WGMS, Washington, 1955—63; gen. mgr. Sta. WHCT, Hartford, Conn., 1963—64; reporter ABC Radio News, 1964—67; anchorman Sta. WCBS, 1967—71; corr. television and radio CBS, NYC, 1971—; anchor CBS News Sunday Morning, 1994—. Author: Nothing Could be Finer Than A Crisis That Is Minor in the Morning, 1979, There's Nothing That I Wouldn't Do If You Would Be My POSSLQ, 1981, Osgood on Speaking, 1988, The Osgood Files, 1991, See You on the Radio, 1999. Recipient Sol Taishoff award for broadcasting excellence, Nat. Press Found., 2005. Mem.: AFTRA. Office: CBS News 524 W 57th St New York NY 10019-2924

OSGOOD, CHRIS, professional hockey player; b. Peace River, Alta., Canada, Nov. 26, 1972; Goalie Detroit Red Wings, 1991—2001, 2005—, NY Islanders, 2001—05. Player NHL All-Star Game, 1996. Co-recipient William M. Jennings Trophy, NHL, 1996; named to WHL East All-Star 2d Team, 1990—91, Sporting News All-Star Team, 1996, Second All-Star Team, NHL, 1996. Achievements include being a member of Stanely Cup Champion Detroit Red Wings, 1997, 98. Office: c/o Detroit Red Wings Joe Louis Arena 600 Civic Center Dr Detroit MI 48226-4408 *

OSGOOD, CHRISTOPHER MYKEL, radio sales manager; b. Northampton, Mass., Nov. 8, 1963; s. Robert Mansfield and Susanne (Mykel) Osgood; m. Angela Baxter; 1 child, Robert Marley. BS, Cornell U., 1989. Media rsch. mktg. analyst Vitt Media Internat., NYC, 1988-89; acct. exec. KAOI AM/FM Radio, Maui, Hawaii, 1989-91, KTXH-TV, Houston, 1991-92; dir. advt. Oilers News, Browns News Illustrated, 49ers Report, Cleve., 1992-93; acct. exec. KRBE-FM, Houston, 1993-96, KLOL-FM, Houston, 1996-99; local sales mgr. KUCD-FM, Honolulu, 1999-2001; gen. sales mgr. KLOL-FM, Houston, 2001—03; local sales mgr. WSB-AM, Atlanta, 2003—05, gen. sales mgr., 2005—. Mem. sales adv. com. Radio Advt. Bur.; advanced competitive tng. coord. Radio Divsn. Cox Enterprises. Coach Bear Creek Basketball League, Houston, 1993—94. Mem.: Cornell Alumni Assn. Gtr. Atlanta, Cornell Soc. Hotelmen. Home: 3333 Sulky Cir Se Marietta GA 30067-5074 Office: News Talk 750 WSB 1601 W Peachtree St NE Atlanta GA 30309 Office Phone: 404-897-7562.

OSGOOD, NANCY JEAN, medical educator, writer; b. July 6, 1951; d. Jack Kent and Lois Emma (Stober) Luttrell; m. Raymond Clifford Jordan, Jr., Oct. 13, 1984. BA in Sociology and Spanish, Yankton Coll., 1972; MA in Sociology, Drake U., 1974; cert. in gerontology, Syracuse U., 1979; PhD in Sociology, 1979. Rsch. assoc. Syracuse Rsch. Corp., NY, 1975—78; asst. prof. SUNY, Cortland, 1979—80, Med. Coll. Va., Richmond, 1980—92, prof., 1992—. Mem. Nat. Com. on Vital and Health Stats., Washington, 1982—84. Author: Senior Settlers: Social Integration in Retirement Communities, 1982, Suicide in the Elderly: A Practitioner's Guide to Diagnosis and Mental Health Intervention, 1985, Suicide Among the Elderly in Long-Term Care Facilities, 1991; editor: Life after Work: Retirement, Leisure, Recreation and the Elderly, 1982; co-author: Seniors on Stage: The Impact of Applied Theatre on the Elderly, 1985, Suicide and the Elderly: An Annotated Bibliography and Review, 1986; co-editor: Dynamic Leisure Programming with Older Adults, 1987, The Science and Practice of Gerontology: A Multi-disciplinary Guide, 1989, Alcoholism and Aging: An Annotated Bibliography and Review, 1995, Treating Alcohol and Drug Abuse in the Elderly, 2002. Selection com. King William HS, Va., 1985; active Va. State Rehab. Bd., Am. Cancer Soc. Recipient acad. scholarship, Yankton Coll., 1969—72, N.Y. State Dept. Mental Hygiene Rsch. fellowship, 1974—75, Nat. Inst. Edn. award, 1975—78, NIMH award, 1977—79, Presdl. Invitation to White House, 1984, 1991; grantee Va. Commonwealth U., 1981—82. Fellow: Gerontol. Soc. Am.; mem.: Internat. Platform Assn., So. Gerontol. Soc., Am. Sociol. Assn., Am. Assn. Suicidology. Avocations: playing piano and clarinet, gourmet cooking, parrots. Home: PO Box 245 Manquin VA 23106-0245 Office Phone: 804-828-6077. Personal E-mail: nosgood@vlu.edu. Business E-Mail: nosgood@mail2.vcu.edu.

OSGOOD, RICHARD MAGEE, JR., electrical engineering professor, researcher; b. Kansas City, Mo., Dec. 28, 1943; s. Richard Magee and Mary Neff (Russell) O.; m. Alice Rose Dyson, June 25, 1966; children— Richard Magee, III, Nathaniel David, Jennifer Anne BS in Engring., U.S. Mil. Acad., 1965; MS in Physics, Ohio State U., 1968; PhD, MIT, 1973. Rsch. assoc. dept. physics MIT, Cambridge, Mass., 1969-72, rsch. staff Lincoln Lab., 1973-80, project leader Lincoln Lab., 1980-81; assoc. prof. applied physics and elec. engring. Columbia U., NYC, 1981-82, prof., 1982-91, Higgins prof., 1989—. Assoc. dir. Brookhaven Nat. Lab., Upton, NY, 2000—03; dir. Microelectronics Sci. Labs., 1984—90; mem. Army Sci. and Tech. Basic Energy Scis. Adv. Com., Def. Scis.-Advanced Rsch. Projects Agy.; cons. Los Alamos Nat. Lab.; mem. ad hoc com. Air Force Sci. Adv. Bd. Editor: Laser Diagnostics and Photochemical Processing of Semiconductor Devices, 1983; contbr. articles to profl. jours.; patentee in field Served to capt. USAF, 1965-69 Recipient Samuel Burka award USAF Avionics Lab., 1968, Leos Travelling Lectr. award, 1986-87, Disting. Travelling Lectr. APS, R.W. Wood Prize, 1991, Optical Soc. Am.; John Simon Guggenheim fellowship, 1989. Fellow IEEE, Am. Phys. Soc., Optical Soc. Am. (R.W. Wood award, 1991); mem. Am. Chem. Soc., Materials Rsch. Soc. (councillor 1983-86), Optical Device Assn. (Japanese hon. lectr. 1990), Am. Phys. Soc. (travelling lectureship 1992). Office: Columbia U Radiation Lab New York NY 10027

OSGOOD, ROBERT MANSFIELD, lawyer; b. Elmira, NY, Jan. 27, 1942; s. Roland Lorenzo and Isabelle (Mansfield) O.; m. Janice Deakin, 1992; children: Christopher, Elisabeth, Abigail, Antonia. BA, Syracuse U., 1963, JD, 1968; postgrad. diploma in EC law, Kings Coll., London, 1994. Bar: N.Y. 1968, U.S. Dist. Ct. (no. dist.) N.Y. 1969, U.S. Dist. Ct. (so. dist.) N.Y. 1970, U.S. Ct. Appeals (2d cir.) 1971, U.S. Dist. Ct. (ea. dist.) N.Y. 1974, U.S. Ct. Appeals (D.C. cir.) 1976, U.S. Supreme Ct. 1977. Ptnr. Sullivan & Cormwell, NYC and London, 1968—. Fellow Am. Coll. Trial Lawyers; mem. Am. Law Inst. Office: Sullivan & Cromwell LLP 125 Broad St Fl 28 New York NY 10004-2489 also: 1 New Fetter Ln London E4A 1AN England Office Phone: 212-558-3710. Business E-Mail: osgoodr@sullcrom.com.

OSGOOD, ROBERT T., JR., architect, strategic planner; b. St. Louis, Sept. 25, 1958; s. Robert T. and Gale Farris (Brandau) Osgood; m. Cheryl Lenor Denler, June 26, 1982; children: Robbie, Chelsea. B cum laude in environ. design, SUNY, Buffalo, 1981; M in Architecture, Ga. Instit. Tech., 1984. Planner Stevens & Wilkinson, Atlanta, 1983—84; sr. rsch. assoc. BOSTI, Buffalo, 1984—86; sr. v.p. HOK, St. Louis, 1986—94; v.p. FLAD, Madison, Wis., 1994—98; sr. v.p. VOA, Columbus, 1999—. Lectr. Washington U., St. Louis, 1989—90, St. Louis, 1992; dir. HOK, 1986—94, FLAD, 1994—98, NBBJ, 1998—99, VOA, 1999—. Contbr. numerous articles to profl. jours. Mem. Downtown St. Louis, Mo., 1993; coach Waunakee Youth Soccer, Madison, 1995—98, BWSA Crew, Columbus, 2000—; vol. Columbus Crew, Columbus, 2000—. Recipient Planning & Design award Famous Footwear HQ, Madison Mag., 1997, Environ. Sustainability award, SC Johnson, 1997, Planning & Design award, SC Johnson HQ Bldg., AIA, 1998, Rsch. and Design awards, Progressive Architecture Jour. Mem.: Internat. Facility Mgmt. Assn., CoreNet Global, Alpha Lambda Delta, Tau Sigma Delta. Avocations: soccer, skiing, running, art, music. Office: VOA Assoc 4449 Easton Way 2nd Fl Columbus OH 43219 Office Phone: 614-934-1117. E-mail: bosgood@voa.com.

OSGOOD, RUSSELL KING, academic administrator; b. Fairborn, Ohio, Oct. 25, 1947; s. Richard M. and Mary Russell Osgood; m. Paula Haley, June 6, 1970; children: Mary, Josiah, Micah, Iain. BA, Yale U., 1969, JD, 1974. Bar: Mass. 1974, U.S. Dist. Ct. Mass. (admitted to) 1976. Assoc. Hill & Barlow, Boston, 1974—78; assoc. prof. Boston U., 1978—80; prof. Cornell U., Ithaca, NY, 1980—88, dean law sch., 1988—98; pres. Grinnell Coll., Iowa, 1998—. Lt. USNR, 1969—71. Mem.: Selden Soc., Stair Soc., Mass. Hist. Soc. Office: Grinnell Coll 1121 Park St Grinnell IA 50112-1640 Office Phone: 641-269-3000. E-mail: osgood@grinnell.edu.

OSGUTHORPE, JOHN DAVID, otolaryngologist, educator; b. Fairbanks, Alaska, 1948; MD, U. Utah, 1973; grad., Med. Ed. in Otolaryngology. Intern UCLA, 1973-74, resident surgery, 1974-75, resident otolaryngology, 1975-78; prof. Med. U. SC, Charleston, SC, 1979—, surg. dir.; otolaryngologist Med. U. Hosp., Charleston, SC. Accreditation coun. Skull Base fellowship U. Zurich. Mem.: HNS, AMA (del. 1998—2005), ACGME (residence rev. comm. 1998—2004, chair, residence rev. comm. 2002—04, bd. mem. 2004—06), Sinus Allergy Health Partnership (bd. dir. 1998—, pres. 2004), Am. Rhinologic Soc. (bd. dir. 1998—2001, editor 1998—2001), Am. Laryngological Assn., Am. Acad. Otolarynologic Allergy (pres. 1995), Am. Acad. Otolaryngology, Head and Neck Surgery (bd. dirs. 1997—, coord. continuing edn. 2000—, Disting. Svc. award 1995, 2004, Pres. award 2004). Office: Med Univ SC Dept Otolaryngology 150 Ashley Ave Charleston SC 29401-5803 Office Phone: 843-792-3533.

O'SHAUGHNESSY, EDWARD JOSEPH, urologist, retired medical educator; b. Bklyn., Jan. 18, 1922; s. Edward Joseph O'Shaughnessy and Lillian Daus; m. Virginia Mary Koch; children: Edward, Margaret, Kathleen, Mary. BSc, Holy Cross Coll., Worcester, Mass., 1944; MD, St. Louis U., 1945; MSc in Urology, U. Minn., Mpls., 1952; MSc in Internat. Affairs, George Washington U., Washington; MSc in Phys. Medicine and Rehab., U. Wash., Seattle, 1974; grad., Nat. War Coll., 1968. Diplomate Am. Bd. Urology. Intern Hackensack Gen. Hosp., NJ, 1945—46; resident urology Mayo Clinic, Rochester, Minn., 1949—52; resident U. Wash., Seattle, 1972—74, asst. prof., 1974—78, assoc. prof., 1978—, ret. Coauthor: Burn Management, 1981; translator: Treatments des las Quenaduro, 1983. Co-founder U.S. Armed Forces Blood Bank. Col. med. corps. US Army, Vietnam. Roman Cath. Avocations: travel, swimming. Home: 1434 Punahou St 617 Honolulu HI 96822 Personal E-mail: lupasmo3@hawaiitel.net.

O'SHAUGHNESSY, JAMES PATRICK, lawyer, consultant; b. Rochester, NY, Mar. 3, 1947; s. John Andrew and Margaret May (Yaxley) O'S.; m. Terry Lee Wood. BS cum laude, Rensselaer Poly. Inst., 1972; JD, Georgetown U., 1977. Bar: Va. 1977, Ohio 1979, Wis. 1987. Assoc. Squire, Sanders & Dempsey, Cleve., 1978-81; ptnr. Hughes & Cassidy, Sumas, Wash., 1981-84; patent counsel Kimberly-Clark Corp., Neenah, Wis., 1984-85; ptnr. Foley & Lardner, Milw., 1986-96; v.p., chief intellectual property counsel Rockwell Automation, Inc., Milw., 1996—2004; ind. cons. Mequon, Wis., 2004—. Founder Innovatech Co., 1996-2000, Lake Street Holdings, LLC 2006-, Donges Bay Group, LLC 2007-; mem. tech. adv. coun. Ideation Internat., Inc., 1999-2004; mem. adv. bd. Licensing Econs. Rev., Intellectual Property Bus. Internat., 2002-04; mem. bd. visitors Georgetown U. Sch. Nursing, 1996-2000; bd. dir. Gemstar TV Guide Internat. Inc., comp. com., 2004—; mem. coun. of advisors Nat. Inst. Play, 2006-; lectr. in field. Contbg. author: Technology Licensing: Corporate Strategies for Maximizing Value, 1996, Profiting From Intellectual Capital: Extracting Value From Innovation, 1998; mem. editl. bd. Am. Criminal Law Rev., 1976-77; contbr. articles to profl. jours. Bd. dirs. Skylight Opera Theatre, 1991-92, Milw. Florentine Opera Co., 1999—, pres., 2002-03. With USN, 1964-68. Recipient Matthew Albert Hunter prize, Rensselaer Poly. Inst., 1972. Mem. CPR Inst. for Dispute Resolution (mediation/arbitration panel), Lic. Execs. Soc., Am. Intellectual Property Law Assn., Assn. Chief Patent Coun. (emeritus); Disabled Am. Vets., Tau Beta Pi, Alpha Sigma Mu. Home and Office: 3207 W Donges Bay Rd Mequon WI 53092-5119 Office Phone: 262-512-9883.

O'SHAUGHNESSY, ROBERT T., automotive executive; Sr. mgr. Ernst & Young LLP, 1987—97; asst. controller United Auto Group, Bloomfield Hills, Mich., 1997—99, v.p., controller, 1999—2005, sr. v.p. fin., 2005—07, exec. v.p., CFO, 2007—. Office: United Auto Group 2555 Telegraph Rd Bloomfield Hills MI 48302-0954 *

O'SHEA, ANNA BELLE MARIE, music educator, liturgy administrator; b. Evergreen Park, Ill., Apr. 9, 1956; d. Joseph Bernard and Anna Belle Marie O'Shea. MusB, De Paul U., 1978; diploma in Pastoral Liturgy, St. Joseph's Coll., 2003, MA in Ch. Music and Liturgy, 2004. Pvt. flut instr., Chgo., 1976—; prin. flutist N.W. Ind. Symphony, Munster, Ind., 1977—88; freelance flutist Chgo., 1978—; founder, pres, dir. music Flutes Unlimited, Chgo., 1997—. Mem. music staff Archdiocese Chgo., 2000—. Co-author: The Liturgical Flutist: A Method Book and More, 2005. Mem.: Nat. Flute Assn. (performer), Nat. Assn. Pastoral Musicians (clinician, bd. dirs. ensemble sect. 1999—). Roman Catholic.

O'SHEA, CATHERINE LARGE, marketing and public relations consultant; b. Asheville, NC, Feb. 27, 1944; d. Edwin Kirk Jr. and Mary Mitchell (Westall) Large; m. Roger Dean Lower, Dec. 19, 1970 (dec. Sept. 1977); children: Thaddeus Kirk Lower and David Alexander Lower (twins, dec.); m. Michael Joseph O'Shea, Dec. 29, 1980 (div. 2001); m. Arthur I. Wetstein, Mar. 28, 2007. BA in History magna cum laude, Emory U., 1966. Mktg. staff mem. Time Inc., NYC, 1966-69; mktg. adminstr. Collier-Macmillan Internat., NYC, 1970-71; circulation mgr. Coll. Entrance Exam. Bd., NYC, 1971-73; spl. asst. to pres. Wayne Dressel Assocs. Exec. Search, NYC, 1973-75; freelance writer, editor, pub. rels. Princeton, N.J., 1975-78; dir. constituency rels. Emory U., Atlanta, 1978-80; devel. assoc. U. Del., Newark, 1981-83; asst. to pres. Elizabethtown (Pa.) Coll., 1983-85; assoc. v.p. Beaver Coll., Glenside, Pa., 1985; cons. mktg. and pub. rels. Phila., S.C., Ga., 1985—. Lectr. in field. Co-author: 50 Secrets of Highly Successful Cats, 1994 (trans. German edit. Schnurrende Tyrannen by Manfred Sommer, 1996); editor Elizabethtown mag., 1983-85; contbr. articles to nat. mags. and profl. jours. Founder Helping Hands Internat.; founding trustee Newberry Opera House Found.; mem. founding com. Rachel Longstreet Found., Jessye Norman Sch. of Arts. Mem. Mortar Bd., Phi Beta Kappa, Phi Mu.

O'SHEA, ELIZABETH THERESE, counselor; d. Richard J. and Kathleen M. O'Shea. BA, Southampton Coll., NY, 1985; MA in Psychol. Counseling, Columbia U., NYC, 2004, EdM, 2004. Cert. provisional sch. counselor NY, 2003, limitied permit mental health counselor NY, 2006. Guidance counselor Pub. Sch. 166, NYC, 2003—04; tchg. asst. childhood and adolescence devel. psychology Tchrs. Coll., Columbia U., 2003—05; mental health counselor intern Psychotechnologies, Patchogue, NY, 2005—06; applied behavioral specialist IGHL, Southampton, NY, 2006—. Treas. World Wings Internat., NYC, 2004—05. Active Oxonian Soc., NYC, 2004—05; active mem., past bd. mem. Women's Nat. Rep. Club, NYC, 1992—2006; active, homeless vol. CRC, NYC, 2003—04; active Young Friends Guggenheim Mus., NYC, 2002—03, NY Hist. Soc., NYC, 1996—97. Mem.: ACA (assoc.). Roman Catholic. Avocation: travel. Home: 225 Central Park West New York NY 10024 Home Phone: 212-579-1004. E-mail: eto18@columbia.edu.

O'SHEA, ERIN K., biomedical researcher; m. Doug Jeffery O'Shea. AB in biochemistry, Smith Coll., 1988; PhD in chemistry, MIT, 1992. Asst. prof. biochemistry and biophysics U. Calif., San Francisco, 1993—97, assoc. prof. biochemistry and biophysics, 1997—2001, prof., vice chair biochemistry and biophysics, 2001—; asst. investigator Howard Hughes Med. Inst., 2000—. Chair sci. adv. bd. Boston U. Sch. Medicine, Dept. Genetics and Genomics, 2002—; mem. sci. adv. com. Helen Hay Whitney Found., 2002—; chair external review com. Bauer Ctr. Genomics Harvard U., 2004. Pub. Libr. Sci., 2003—. Recipient Promega Early Career Life Sci. award, Am. Soc. Cell Biology, 2000, Irving Sigal Young Investigator award, Protein Soc., 2004; fellow, David and Lucile Packard Found., 1994. Fellow: Am. Acad. Arts and Scis.; mem.: NAS (mem. NTC com. on standards and principles in biol. rsch. 2002—, award in molecular biology 2001). Office: Howard Hughes Med Inst Harvard U Dept Molecular & Cellular Biology Bauer 307 7 Divinity Ave Cambridge MA 02138 Office Phone: 617-495-4328. Office Fax: 617-496-5425. Business E-Mail: Erin_OShea@harvard.edu.

O'SHEA, JAMES E., editor-in-chief; b. St. Louis, 1944; BA, MA, U. Mo. Reporter US Army; fin. editor The Des Moines Register, 1973—76, Washington corr., 1976—79; reporter The Chgo. Tribune, 1979—90, assoc. mng. editor for fgn. & nat. news, 1990—95, dep. mng. editor for news, 1995—2001, mng. editor, 2001—06; exec. v.p., editor L.A. Times, 2006—. Bd. gov. Oversea Press Club Am. Author: The Daisy Chain, 1991; co-author (with Charles Madigan): Dangerous Company, 1997. Recipient Disting. Svc. award for Washington Correspondence, Sigma Delta Chi, 1985, 1989, Peter Lisagor award, Pub. Svc. award, AP Mng. Editors, Nat. Edn. Writers award, William Jones award, Chgo. Tribune, 1989. Mem.: Sigma Delta Chi. Office: LA Times 202 W First St Los Angeles CA 90012 also: Tribune Co 435 N Michigan Ave Chicago IL 60611 *

O'SHEA, PATRICK ALAN, elementary school educator; s. Timothy and Elizabeth O'Shea; m. Michelle Rayne Varner; children: Patrick, Keegan, Finnegan, Shealin, Delaney, McGinnis. BS, Clarion U., Pa., 1992. Tchr. Northgate Sch. Dist., Pitts., 1992—93, Seneca Valley Sch. Dist., Harmony, Pa., 1993—. Coach varsity football Laurel Sch. Dist., Newcastle, Pa., 2003—. Office: Seneca Valley Sch Dist 122 Seneca School Rd Harmony PA 16037 Business E-Mail: osheapa@svsd.net.

O'SHEA, PATRICK JOSEPH, lawyer, electrical engineer; b. Chgo., Apr. 10, 1950; s. John Raymond and Alta M. (Bauert) O'S.; m. Patricia Ann Dalaker, Aug. 11, 1980; children: Erin, Tarah, Brian, Meghan. BSEE, U. Ill., 1972; JD, John Marshall Law Sch., 1979. Bar: Ill. 1979, U.S. Dist. Ct. (no. dist.) Ill. 1979, U.S. Patent Office 1982. Elec. engr. elec. div. City of Chgo. Police Dept., 1976-79; elec. engr. Commonwealth Edison, Chgo., 1972-76; atty. Patricik Mazza & Assocs., Chgo., 1979-80, Richard E. Alexander & Assocs., Chgo., 1980-81; sole pratice Chgo. and Lombard, Ill., 1981—; spl. asst. states atty. Du. Page County, Ill., 1988. Spl. appellate prosecutor, 1989. Elected Rep. committeeman, York Twp., Ill., 1982, chmn. rep. committeeman's orgn., 1996; mem. exec. com. York Twp. Rep. Committeeman's Orgn., vice-chmn., 1992, chmn., 1996; mem. exec. com. DuPage County Bd., 1989—, chmn. landfill com., 1989, 94, vice chmn. legis. com., 1994, chmn. jud. and pub. safety com., 2000—; commr. Forest Preserve, 1992; gen. counsel Ill. Rep. Party; gen. counsel Ill. Rep. Party. Mem. Ill. Bar Assn., DuPage Bar Assn., Chgo. Bar Assn., Lombard C. of C., Lombard Rotary. Roman Catholic. Avocations: politics, golf, chess. Business E-Mail: poshea@dupage-co.org.

OSHEFSKY, CAROL ANN, retired elementary school educator; b. Kewaunee County, Wis., Apr. 28, 1931; d. William Edward and Mayme (Hostak) Lazansky; m. Norman Earl Oshefsky, June 20, 1953; children: Quin, Norman II, Cathleen. BS, U. Wis., Oshkosh, 1964; MS, U. Wis., Green Bay, 1980. Cert. tchr., Wis. Tchr. West Klondike Sch., Mountain, Wis., 1950-53, St. Mary Cath. Sch., De Pere, Wis., 1956-57, Howard-Suamico Sch. Dist., Green Bay, Wis., 1962-64, Ashwaubenon Sch. Dist., Green Bay, 1966-90; ret., 1990. Author: The Bohemian/Czech Cultural Landscape of Kewaunee and Manitowoc Counties, Wisconsin, 1980, Lazansky, Machacek, and Opicka Genealogy with Related Families 1742-1992, 1992, Hostak and Plohar/Plouhar Genealogy, 1996. Choralier Czech Choraliers, Wis., 1978—; bd. dirs. Wis. Czechs, Inc., charter mem., 1977—; bd. dirs. Kewaunee County, 1987-89, Kewaunee County Hist. Soc., 1994—; former mem. Brown County Tchrs. Assn., Bay Area Geneal. Soc. Mem. Wis. Ret. Tchrs. Assn., Czechoslovak Geneal. Soc. Internat Roman Catholic. Avocations: doll collecting, sewing, gardening, music, travel. Home: 2253 Barberry Lane Green Bay WI 54304

OSHER, BERNARD, philanthropist, former investment company executive; m. Barbro Osher. Ed., Bowdoin Coll. Mgr. family hardware and plumbing supplies store, Maine; with Oppenheimer & Co., NY; founding dir. World Savings, Calif.; cofounder Golden West Fin.; owner Butterfield & Butterfield, 1970—99. Founder The Bernard Osher Found., 1977. Avocations: hiking, fly fishing. Office: The Bernard Osher Foundation Ste 255 One Ferry Bldg San Francisco CA 94111 *

OSHER, STANLEY JOEL, mathematician, researcher; b. Bklyn., Apr. 24, 1942; s. Irving and Molly Esther (Levy) O.; m. Susan Priscilla Manning, July 5, 1979 (div. Apr. 1984); m. May Renee Stein, June 26, 1987; 1 child, Kathryn Deborah. BS, Bklyn. Coll., 1962; MS, NYU, 1964, PhD, 1966. From asst. to assoc. mathematician Brookhaven Nat. Lab., Upton, N.Y., 1966-68; asst. prof. U. Calif., Berkeley, 1968-70; assoc. prof. SUNY, Stony Brook, 1970-75, prof., 1975-76, UCLA, LA, 1976—; co-founder, chief exec. officer Cognitech, Inc., Santa Monica, Calif., 1987—. Cons. Rockwell Sci. Ctr., Thousand Oaks, Calif., 1981—, NASA/ICASE, Hampton, Va., 1982—, Chevron Oil, La Habra, Calif., 1987—. Contbr. articles to profl. jours. Fulbright Found. fellow, 1971, Alfred P. Sloan Found. fellow, 1972-74, SERC fellow Govt. of Eng., 1982, U.S.-Israel fellow, 1986, SIAM Kleinman prize. Mem. AIAA, Am. Math. Soc., Soc. Indsl. Applied Math., NAS. Achievements include patent pending for nonlinear partial differential equations based aproach to image processing; development of shock and front capturing algorithms widely used by the community. Home: 1058 Embury St Pacific Palisades CA 90272-2501 Office: UCLA Mathematics Dept Los Angeles CA 90024

OSHEROFF, DOUGLAS DEAN, physics professor, researcher; b. Aberdeen, Wash., Aug. 1, 1945; s. William and Bessie Anne (Ondov) Osheroff; m. Phyllis S.K. Liu, Aug. 14, 1970. BS in Physics, Calif. Inst. Tech., 1967; MS, Cornell U., 1969, PhD in Physics, 1973. Mem. tech. staff Bell Labs., Murray Hill, NJ, 1972—82, head solid state and low temperature physics research dept., 1982—87; prof. Stanford (Calif.) U., 1987—, J.G. Jackson and C.J. Wood prof. physics, 1992—, chair physics, 1993—96, 2001—. Mem. Columbia Accident Investigation Bd., 2003. Co-recipient Simon Meml. prize, Brit. Inst. Physics, 1976; recipient Oliver E. Buckley Solid State Physics prize, 1981, Walter J. Gores award, 1991, Nobel prize in Physics, 1996; fellow John D. and Catherine T. MacArthur prize, 1981. Fellow: Am. Acad. Arts and Scis., Am. Phys. Soc.; mem.: NAS. Achievements include research in properties of matter near absolute zero of temperature; co-discovery of nuclear antiferromagnetic resonance in solid 3He, superfluidity in helium-3. Office: Stanford U Rm 150 Varian Physics Bldg 382 Via Pueblo Mall Stanford CA 94305-4060 Fax: 650-725-6544. E-mail: osheroff@stanford.edu.

OSHEROW, JACQUELINE SUE, poet, English language educator; b. Phila., Aug. 15, 1956; d. Aaron and Evelyn (Victor) Osherow; m. Saul Korewa, June 16, 1965 (div. 2003); children: Magda, Dora, Mollie. AB Magna cum laude, Radcliffe Coll., Harvard U., 1978; postgrad., Trinity Coll., Cambridge U., 1978-79; PhD in English and Am. Lit., Princeton U., 1990. Prof. English C. Utah, Salt Lake City, 1989—. Author: (poetry) Looking for Angels in New York, 1988, Conversations with Survivors, 1994, With a Moon in Transit, 1996, Dead Men's Praise, 1999. Recipient Witter Bynner prize Am. Acad. and Inst. Arts and Letters, 1990; Ingram Merrill Found. grantee, 1990; Guggenheim fellow, 1997-98, Nat. Endowment for the Arts fellow, 1999—. Mem. Poetry Soc. Am. (John Masefield Meml. award 1993, Lucille Medwick Meml. award 1995, Cecil Hemley Meml. award 1997). Jewish. Office: U Utah Dept English 255 S Central Campus Dr Rm 3500 Salt Lake City UT 84112-0494 Home Phone: 801-355-7006; Office Phone: 801-581-7947, 801-581-6168. Business E-Mail: j.osherow@english.utah.edu.

OSHIMA, MICHAEL W., lawyer; b. Big Rapids, Mich., Apr. 4, 1957; s. Walter W. and Mitsue Oshima; m. Chiaki Tanaka, July 19, 2003. AB magna cum laude, Brown U., 1979; MA, Harvard U., 1984; JD, NYU, 1987. Bar: NY 1988, DC 1989. Sr. rsch. asst. Harvard U. John F. Kennedy Sch. Govt., Cambridge, Mass., 1981-84; assoc. Davis Polk & Wardwell, NYC, 1987-90, Arnold & Porter LLP, NYC, 1990-96, ptnr., 1997—2006, adminstrv. ptnr. NY office, 1999—2005; dep. gen. counsel Safe Horizon, NYC, 2007—. Contbr. articles, reports to profl. publs. Bd. govs. Japanese Am. Nat. Mus., 2005—; bd. dirs. Asian Am. Arts Alliance, Inc., 2005—. Mem. Am. Sociol. Assn., Law and Soc. Assn., NY State Bar Assn., Assn. Bar City NY (chair, com. on minorities in the profession, 2006-). Business E-Mail: moshima@safehorizon.org.

OSHINS, STEVEN JEFFREY, lawyer; b. Washington, Oct. 21, 1969; BS in Actuarial Stats., U. Calif., Santa Barbara, 1991; JD, U. of the Pacific, 1994. Bar: Calif. 1994, Nev. 1995. Assoc. Law Offices of Oshins & Assocs., Las Vegas, Nev., 1994-98, lawyer, shareholder, 1998—; mem. CEO Law Offices of Oshins & Assocs. LLC, Las Vegas; co-founder Entertainment Direct TV Inc.; pres. Nev. Entity Svcs. LLC; mem. Trust Cons. LLC; owner, CEO The Lockett Oshins Collection; mem., pres. Steven J. Oshin Enterprises LLC; former shareholder Premier Trust of Nev. Inc. Tech. cons. Leimberg & LeChair, 2000-, mem. estate planning & Taxation Com. Trusts & Estates mag. 2001-02. Contbr. articles to profl. jours. and mags., and lectr. at various seminars, co-author: various legis. bills. Named Spl. Tax Counsel for Estates above $10 Million, Paleveda & Fantini LLC, 2000—, Super Lawyer in Nev., Nev. Bus. Jour., 2002; named one of Top 100 Attys., Worth mag., 2006; named to List of Best Lawyers in Am., 2005—06; recipient EPIC award for Best Young Author, Trusts & Estates mag., 1998, Rated AV, Martindale-Hubbell Law Dir., 1999—. Mem. So. Nev. Estate Planning Coun. (pres. 1998-99). designed software prog. Sale to Defective Trust Megaanalyzer. Office: Law Offices Oshins & Assocs LLC 1645 Village Center Cir Ste 170 Las Vegas NV 89134-6371 Office Phone: 702-341-6000. Office Fax: 702-341-6001. E-mail: soshins@oshins.com. *

OSHINSKY, DAVID M., history professor, writer; PhD, Brandeis Univ., 1971. Prof. polit., cultural history Rutgers U., New Brunswick, NJ, 1971—2002; George Littlefield Prof. Am. History U. Tex., Austin, 2002—. Co-editor The Oxford Companion to United States History; co-author: American Passages: A History of the United States; author: A Conspiracy So Immense: The World of Joe McCarthy, 1983 (Hardeman Prize as best book about US Congress, NY Times Notable Book), Worse Than Slavery: Parchman Farm and the Ordeal of Jim Crow Justice, 1996 (Robert Kennedy Prize for contbn. to human rights, NY Times Notable Book), Polio: An American Story, 2005 (Pulitzer Prize for History, 2006). Office: Univ Tex Austin David M Oshinsky--GAR 206 1 Univ Station Austin TX 78712 Office Phone: 512-475-7230. Business E-Mail: oshinsky@mail.utexas.edu.

OSHINSKY, JEROLD, lawyer; b. Jersey City, July 12, 1942; BA cum laude, Bklyn. Coll., 1964; LLB cum laude (Stone scholar), Columbia U., 1967. Bar: NY 1968, US Dist. Ct. (ea. dist.) NY 1968, US Ct. Appeals (2nd cir.) 1968, US Dist. Ct. (so. dist.) NY 1968, US Supreme Ct. 1971, US Dist. Ct. DC 1980, US Ct. Appeals DC Cir. 1980, US Ct. Appeals (5th cir.) 1975, DC 1980. Assoc. Chadbourne, Parke, Whiteside & Wolff, NYC, 1962—72; ptnr. Anderson Kill Olick & Oshinsky, 1972—96, Dickstein Shapiro Morin & Oshinsky, Washington, 1996—, mem. exec. com. Lectr. in field. Co-author: Practitioner's Guide to Litigating Ins. Coverage Actions; contbr. articles to profl. jours. Mem.: DC Bar Assn., NYC Bar Assn. (sec. adminstrv. law com 1972—74, chmn. adminstrv. law com. 1975—77), NY State Bar Assn., ABA. Office: Dickstein Shapiro Morin & Oshinsky 2101 L St NW Washington DC 20037-1526 Office Phone: 202-828-2251. Office Fax: 202-887-0689. Business E-Mail: oshinskyj@dsmo.com.

OSICKA, TERESA D., health economist, consultant; arrived in US, 1998; d. Antoni Osicki and Apolonia Osicka; m. Andrzej Delegacz, Aug. 17, 2003. MA in Econs., U. Warsaw, Warsaw, Poland, 1990, diploma in Health Econs., 1991, U. Tromso, Norway, 1993; MS in Computer Sci., The Cath. U. Am., DC, 2002. Sr. specialist health care Nat. Ctr. Health Sys. Mgmt., Warsaw, 1990—94; coord. health reform project Ministry Health and Social Welfare, Warsaw, 1991—93; chief specialist health care fin. Ministry Fin., Warsaw, 1994—99; database mgr. The Georgetown U., Washington, 1999—, rsch. asst. Med. Ctr., 1999—. Cons. UNESCO, Paris, 2005—, The World Bank, Washington, 2002—; fellow George Wash. U., 1998, Johns Hopkins U., Balt., 1999; lectr. in field. Contbr. articles to profl. jours. Recipient Cum Laude Poster award, Internat. Soc. Optical Engring. Med. Imaging, 2002, Hon. Poster award, 2003. Mem.: Assn. Health Care Mgrs. (v.p. 1991—93). Achievements include research in discrete wavelets transform application to the pulmonary nodules characterization on computer tomography (CT) scans with regard to their ability to discriminate benign and malignant nodules signals. Office: Georgetown U Medical Center 2115 Wisconsin Ave NW Washington DC 20007 Home Phone: 703-243-5722; Office Phone: 202-687-1572. Office Fax: 202-784-3479. Business E-Mail: osicka@isis.imac.georgetown.edu.

OSINSKI, MARTIN HENRY, healthcare consultant; s. Stanley and Shirley (Bobick) Osinski; m. Margie Osinski; children: Ashley, Brett. BBA in Acctg., U. Miami, Coral Gables, Fla., 1975, MBA, 1977. Cert. Accredited Valuation Analyst Nat. Assn. Cert. Valuation Analysts. Grad. asst. U. Miami, Fla., 1975-77; staff acct. Ernst & Ernst, CPA, Miami, 1977-78; asst. buyer, dept. mgr. Burdines Dept. Stores, Miami, 1978-80; buyer menswear Jefferson Ward Dept. Stores, Miami, 1980-82, Richway Dept. Stores, Atlanta, 1982-84; pres. Nat. Health Search, Inc., Miami, 1984-95; chief oper. officer MD Resources, Inc., Miami, 1989-95; prin. Am. Med. Consultants, Inc., Miami, 1996—. Mem. editl. adv. bd. Nephrology News and Issues, 2004—. Bd. dirs. Congregation Bet Breira, 1994-98, 2002-. Mem.: Am. Soc. Nephrology, Nat. Assn. Physician Recruiters (bd. dirs. 1989—96, v.p. 1990—91, pres. 1991—, ethics com. 2001—, bd. dirs. 2004—, v.p. 2006—, Presdl. award 1991, 2006), Iron Arrow Soc. U. Miami, Mens Club (pres. 1992—94). Office: Am Med Consultants Inc 11625 SW 110th Rd Miami FL 33176-3152 Home Phone: 305-274-9910; Office Phone: 305-271-9225. Personal E-mail: amcmo@bellsouth.net.

OSIS, DAIGA GUNTRA, lawyer; b. Riga, Latvia, July 24, 1943; d. Voldemars and Sandra (Seja) Amatnieks; m. Aivars Osis, Dec. 2, 1967; 1 child, Andre. BA cum laude, CUNY, Bklyn., 1971; JD, U. Conn., Bridgeport, 1980. Bar: Conn. 1980, U.S. Dist. Ct. Conn. 1981, U.S Ct. Appeals (2d cir.) 1982, U.S. Supreme Ct. 1984. Assoc. DePiano & Palmesi, Bridgeport, 1980-85; ptnr. Gans, Leo & Osis, Bridgeport, 1985-88, Gans, Osis, Reynolds & Riccio, Bridgeport, 1989-90, Gans, Osis & Reynolds, 1990-94; pvt. practice Bridgeport, 1994—. Asst. prof. law U. Bridgeport, 1982-83. Rsch. editor U. Bridgeport Law Rev., 1979-80. Mem. Bd. Edn., Trumbull, Conn., 1982-84; bd. dirs. Conn. Inst. Vocal Arts, Southport, 1984-87. Mem.: Conn. Bar Assn. Democrat. Lutheran. Home: 175 Middlebrooks Ave Trumbull CT 06611-3016 Office: 325 Reef Rd Ste 212 Fairfield CT 06824 Office Phone: 203-254-1215. Personal E-mail: osisatty@optonline.net.

OSLER, GORDON PETER, retired utilities executive; b. Winnipeg, Man., Can., June 19, 1922; s. Hugh Farquarson and Kathleen (Harty) O.; m. Nancy A. Riley, Aug. 20, 1948; children: Sanford L., Susan Osler Matthews, Gillian Osler Fortier. Student, Queen's U., Kingston, Ont., Can., 1940-41. Pres. Osler, Hammond & Nanton Ltd., Winnipeg, 1952-64, UNAS Investments Ltd., Toronto, Ont., Canada, 1964-72; chmn. Slater Steel Industries, Hamilton, Ont., Canada, 1972-86, N.Am. Life Assurance

Co., Toronto, 1986-95, TransCan. Pipelines, Toronto, 1983-89, ret., 1993. Lt. Can. Army, 1942-45, ETO. Mem. York Club (Toronto), Everglades Club (Palm Beach, Fla.), Manitoba Club (hon. life), Bath and Tennis Club (Palm Beach), Toronto Golf Club. Avocation: golf. Home: 17 Lamport Ave Toronto ON Canada M4W 1S7 Personal E-mail: gosler8660@aol.com.

OSMAN, EDITH GABRIELLA, lawyer; b. NYC, Mar. 18, 1949; d. Arthur Abraham and Judith (Goldman) Udem; children: Jacqueline, Daniel. BA in Spanish, SUNY, Stony Brook, 1970; JD cum laude, U. Miami, 1983. Bar: Fla. 1983, U.S. Dist. Ct. (so. dist.) Fla. 1984, US Dist. Ct. (mid. dist.) Fla. 1988, US Ct. Appeals (11th cir.) 1985, Fla. Supreme Ct. 1987, US Ct. Mil. Appeals 1990; cert. family law mediator Fla. Supreme Ct., civil mediator, Fla. Assoc. Kimbrell & Hamann, PA, Miami, 1984-90, Dunn & Lodish, PA, Miami, 1990-93; pvt. practice Miami, 1993-98; shareholder Carlton Fields, Miami, 1998—, practice group leader, family law divsn. Bd. dirs. Miami City Club, Supreme Ct. Historic Soc., So. Legal Coun., Fla. Women of Achievement (bd. dirs. leading atty). Mem. adv. com. for Implementation of the Victor Posner Judgement to Aid the Homeless, 1986-89. Recipient Breaking the Glass Ceiling award Ziff Mus., 2000, In the Company of Women award Dade County, 2000, Judge Mattie Belle Davis award, 2000, FAWL's Rosemary Barkett Achievement award, 1997, Outstanding Past Vol. Bar Pres.'s award, 1996, Women's Park Founders and Wall of Honor award, 2001; selected for photographic exhibit Florida Women of Achievement, 2000, South Fla.'s Top 250 Lawyers South Fla. Legal Guide, 2001, 02, 03, 04, 05, 06, 07; Women of Impact award Women's History Coalition Miami-Dade County, 2007, named 100 Women to Watch MIA Metro Mag., Fla. Trend, 2000, Women's Park Hall of Fame, 2001, Super Lawyers 2006, 07. Fellow Am. Bar Found., Fla. Bar Found.; mem. ABA (family law, alternate dispute resolution, Ho. of Dels. 1998—, standing com. on independence of judiciary 2000-03, standing com. bar svs. 2003-, house select com., 2004-), The Fla. Bar (budget com. 1989-92, 97-98, voluntary bar liaison com. 1989-90, spl. com. on formation of All-Bar Conf. 1988-89, chair mid-yr. conv. 1989, long range planning com. 1988-90, bd. govs. 1991-98, spl. commn. on delivery of legal svcs. to the indigent 1990-92, bus. law cert. com. 1995-96, practice law mgmt. com. 1995-96, chair program evaluation com., 1993-94, exec. com. 1992-93, 96-2000, rules and bylaws com., 1993-94, vice-chair disciplinary rev. com. 1994-95, investment com. 1994-95, vice-chair rules com. 1994-95, All-Bar Conf. chair 1997, chair grievance mediation com. 1997-99, pres.-elect 1998-99, pres. 1999-2000, exec. coun. family law sect. 2001—, vice-chair legis. 2001-2002, co-chair alternative dispute resolution com. 2003—, chair commn. legal needs of children, 2003-04, spl. commn. on disciplinary rev., 2003—, family law rules procedure com. 2003—,spl. com. succession planning), Dade County Bar Assn. (fed. ct. rules com. 1985-86, chmn. program com. 1988-91, bd. dirs., 1988—, 96-97, exec. com. 1987-88), Fla. Assn. Women's Lawyers Assn. (Dade County chpt. bd. dirs. 1984-85, treas. 1985-86, v.p. 1986-87, pres. 1987-88), Fla. Assn. Women Lawyers (v.p. 1988-89, pres. 1989-90), Fla. Bar Found. (dir. 1998-2001), Nat. Conf. Women's Bar Assn. (dir. nat. conf. 1990-91), Cuban Am. Bar Assn., Fla. Acad. Trial Lawyers, Dade County Trial Lawyers Assn., Nat. Conf. Bar Pres., So. Conf. Bar Pres., Leading Attys. (bd. dirs. 2000—), Iron Arrow Honor Soc., First Family Inns of Ct. Office: Carlton Fields PA 100 SE 2nd St Ste 4000 Miami FL 33131-2148 Home Phone: 305-371-8455; Office Phone: 305-530-0050. E-mail: eosman@carltonfields.com.

OSMAN, LEE R., lawyer; b. 1965; BS in Mech. Engring., Colo. State U., 1988; JD, U. Denver, 1993. Bar: Colo. 1993, registered: US Patent and Trademark Office. Engr. Honeywell, ATMEL Corp.; atty., intellectual property group Holland & Hart, Denver; ptnr. Dorsey & Whitney LLP, Denver, 2000—, and chair, worldwide patent group, 2003—06, head, intellectual property group, 2004—07, chair worldwide patent group, 2007—. Named one of 40 Under 40, Denver Bus. Jour., 2004. Mem.: Pi Tau Sigma. Office: Dorsey & Whitney LLP Ste 4700 Republic Plz Bldg 370 Seventeenth St Denver CO 80202-5647 Office Phone: 303-629-3434. Office Fax: 303-629-3450. Business E-Mail: osman.lee@dorsey.com.

OSMER-MCQUADE, MARGARET, media consultant; b. NYC; d. Herbert Bernard and Margaret Normann (Brunjes) O.; m. Lawrence Carroll McQuade, Mar. 15, 1980; 1 son, Andrew. BA, Cornell U., 1960. Assoc. producer UN Bur., CBS News, NYC, 1962-69; producer 60 Minutes, NYC, 1969-72; reporter, producer Bill Moyer's Jour., Pub. Broadcasting Service, NYC, 1972-73, Reasoner Report, ABC News, NYC, 1973-75; corr., anchor person Good Morning Am., ABC Morning News, Washington, 1975-77; corr. ABC TV News, Washington, 1977-79; v.p., dir. programs Council on Fgn. Relations, 1979-93; pres., CEO Qualitas Internat., NYC, 1994—. Dir. Dime Savs. Bank, Washington Mutual Bank; cons. PBS. Producer, reporter: TV news shows Come Fly A Kite (Nat. Press Photographer's award 1974), Kissinger, 1970, No Tears for Rachel, 1972, Calder: Master of Mobiles, 1975; moderator, producer World in Focus, publ. TV series Coun. Fgn. Relations/Sta. WNYC, PBS, Worldnet, 1988-93. Mem. U.S. delegation World Conf. on Cambodian Refugees, Geneva, 1980; mem. Def. Adv. Com. on Women in the Svc., 1978-82; trustee Cornell U.; mem. bd. overseers Cornell U. Med. Coll., pres.'s coun. Cornell Women; mem. program com. The Ditchley Found., 1994—, task force N.Y. Sch. Vols., 1994—; vol. Nat. Svc. Learning, 1994—. Recipient Peabody award Staff of 60 Minutes, 1970 Mem.: Nat. Assn. Radio and TV Analysts, Nat. Press Club, Coun. Fgn. Rels, Century Club, Cosmopolitan Club.

OSMOND, DENNIS GORDON, anatomist, researcher, medical educator; b. NYC, Jan. 31, 1930; s. Ernest Gordon and Marjorie Bertha (Milton) O.; m. Anne Welsh, July 30, 1955; children: Roger Gordon, Martin Henry, David Richard. BSc with first class honors, U. Bristol, Eng., 1951, MB, ChB, 1954, DSc, 1975. House surgeon Royal Gwent Hosp., Newport, England, 1954-55; house physician Bristol Royal Infirmary, 1955; demonstrator, lectr. anatomy U. Bristol, 1957-60, 61-64; instr. anatomy U. Wash., Seattle, 1960-61; assoc. prof. anatomy McGill U., Montreal, Que., Canada, 1965-67, prof., 1967-74, Robert Reford prof. anatomy, 1974-00, chmn. dept. anatomy and cell biology, 1985-95, Robert Reford emeritus prof. anatomy, 2000—. Vis. scientist Walter and Eliza Hall Inst. Med. Research, Melbourne, Australia, 1972-73; hon. sr. research fellow U. Birmingham, Eng., 1979; vis. scientist Basel Inst. Immunology, Switzerland, 1980, 96; Gaylord scholar Okla. Med. Rsch. Found., 1995. Contbr. numerous articles to profl. jours. Served with Royal Army Med. Corps, 1955-57. Fellow Royal Soc. Can.; mem. Am. Assn. Anatomists, Can. Assn. Anatomists, Anat. Soc. Gt. Britain and Ireland, Am., Can. assns. for immunology, Am. Assn. Immunology, Internat. Soc. for Exptl. Hematology, Order of Can. Home: 1380 Revell Dr Manotick ON Canada K4M 1K8 Personal E-mail: dennisosmond@rogers.com.

OSMOND, DONALD CLARK (DONNY OSMOND), singer; b. Ogden, Utah, Dec. 9, 1957; s. George and Olive Osmond; m. Debra Glenn, May 8, 1978; 1 child, Donald Clark. Student, Brigham Young U. Performer (with): The Osmonds family singing group from age 4; performer: solo act, 1971—; co-star (TV series) Donny & Marie, 1976—79, 1998—, numerous TV guest appearances, appeared in (films) Goin' Coconuts, 1978, rec. artist: (with Marie) (albums) including Songs from Their TV Show, Donny Osmond Album, To You With Love, Donny, Portrait of Donny, Too Young, Alone Together, Disco Train, Donald Clark Osmond, (with Marie) I'm Leaving It All Up to You, Make The World Go Away, solo recordings include Donald Osmond (Soldier of Love), 1988, Eyes Don't Lie, 1990, Christmas at Home, Four (EP), 1997; performer: (Broadway plays) Little Johnny Jones, Joseph and the Amazing Technicolor Dreamcoat, 1995—98, Beauty and the Beast, 2006. Recipient (with Marie Osmond) Georgie award for best vocal team, Am. Guild Variety Artists, 1978. Mem. Lds Ch. Office: care The Osmonds Network 15 S 180 W Lindon UT 84042-1942

OSMOND, MARIE, singer; b. Ogden, Utah, Oct. 13, 1959; d. George and Olive O.; m. Stephen Craig, June 26, 1982 (div. 1985); m. Brian Blosil, Oct. 28, 1986 (separated); children: Stephen James, Jessica Marie, Rachel, Michael, Brandon, Brianna, Matthew, Abigail. Student pub. schs., pvt. tutors. Appeared with The Osmond family singing group from age 7, solo act, 1973;(TV co-star): Donny & Marie TV show, 1976-79, Donny & Marie Christmas Spl, 1979, Osmond Family Show, 1979, Osmond Family Christmas Show, 1980, Donny & Marie, 1998; (star TV spl.) Marie, 1981; appeared in TV series Maybe This Time, 1995, video Buster & Chauncey's Silent Night, 1998; (record albums) include (with Donny Osmond): Make the World Go Away, I'm Leaving It All Up To You; songs from their TV Show Goin Coconuts; (solo albums) include: Paper Roses, In My Little Corner of the World, Who's Sorry Now?, This Is The Way That I Feel, There's No Stopping Your Heart, 1985, I Only Wanted You, 1987, All In Love, 1988, Steppin' Stone, 1989, Twenty Five Hits-Special Collection, 1995; (#1 singles) include Meet Me in Montana (Best Country Duo of Yr. award with Dan Seals), 1986, You're Still New to Me, 1986, There's No Stoppin' Your Heart, 1986, I Only Wanted You, 1987, The Best Of, 1990; toured with Bob Hope, Persian Gulf, 1991; (co-author): Fun, Fame, and Family, 1973; Marie Osmond's Guide to Beauty, Health, and Style, 1980; performer Dancing With the Stars, 2007. Recipient (with Donny Osmond) Georgie award for best vocal team Am. Guild Variety Artists, 1978. Mem. Lds Ch. *

OSNES, LAURA, actress; b. Eagan, Minn., 1985; Ed., U. Wis. Actress (plays) Madeline's Rescue, 1997, The Music Man, 2002, The Wizard of Oz, 2003, Fiddler on the Roof, Seussical the Musical, Working, Aladdin Jr., Prom, Pippi Longstocking, Peter Pan, 2006, Grease, 2006, (Broadway plays), 2007. Achievements include winning the role of Sandy in Broadway production of Grease through competition on NBC Grease: You're the One That I Want. *

OSNOS, DAVID MARVIN, lawyer, director; b. Detroit, Jan. 10, 1932; s. Max and Florence (Pollock) O.; m. Glenna DeWitt, Aug. 10, 1956; children: Matthew, Alison AB summa cum laude, Harvard U., 1953, JD cum laude, 1956. Bar: D.C. 1956. Assoc. Arent, Fox LLP (formerly Arent, Fox, Kintner, Plotkin & Kahn), Washington, 1956—61, ptnr., 1962—2002, chmn. exec. com., 1978—97, of counsel, 2003—. Bd. dirs. EastGroup Properties, Jackson, Miss., VSE Corp., Alexandria, Va., Washington Real Estate Investment Trust, Rockville, Md., Washington Wizards Basketball Club, Washington. Trustee Mt. St. Mary's Coll., Emmitsburg, Md., 1981-90; bd. dirs. Greater Washington Jewish Cmty. Found., Rockville, Md., Jewish Cmty. Ctr. Greater Washington, 1964-75. Avocations: tennis, music, enology. Office: Arent Fox 1050 Connecticut Ave NW Ste 600 Washington DC 20036-5339 Business E-Mail: osnosd@arentfox.com.

OSNOS, GILBERT CHARLES, management consultant; b. Detroit, Nov. 23, 1929; s. Herman Sol and Helen (Yudkoff) O.; m. Margaret N. Paysner, Aug. 18, 1957; children: Steven, Elisabeth. BA, U. Mich., 1951; MBA, Harvard U., 1953. Dept. mgr. Sams, Inc., Detroit, 1956-57, asst. buyer, 1957-58, dir. store ops., 1958, buyer, 1958-59, mdse. buyer, 1959-62; buyer Topps Divsn. Interstate Dept. Stores, NYC, 1962-65; mdse. mgr. Arlans Dept. Stores, NYC, 1965-68; pres. Nazareth Mills divsn. Kayser Roth, NYC, 1968-73, Rosenau Bros., Phila., 1973-75, Warnaco Men's Sportswear, 1975-78; with Grisanti and Galef, 1979-81, ptnr., 1981—; pres. Grisanti, Galef & Osnos, NYC, 1983—. Chmn. RKG Osnos Ptnrs., LLC, 1986-2005; mng. ptnr. Corp. Revitalization Ptnrs., LLC; bd. dirs. Mrs. Fields Famous Brands, Turnaround Mgmt. Assn., chmn., 1990-91. Lt. j.g. USNR, 1953-56. Recipient Disting. Alumnus award, Navy Supply Corps, 2006. Mem. Am. Apparel Assn. (consumer affairs com.), Am. Bankruptcy Inst., Bus. Execs. for Nat. Security, Harvard Club, Halloween Yacht Club, Harvard Bus. Sch. Club of N.Y.C., Corinthians. Avocations: sailing, opera, classical music, photography, reading. Office: CRP LLC Ste 1200 20 W 22d St New York NY 10010-5804 E-mail: gosnos@crpllc.net.

OSNOS, PETER LIONEL WINSTON, publishing executive; b. Bombay, Oct. 13, 1943; s. Joseph Lionel and Marta (Bychowski) O.; m. Susan R. Sherer, Aug. 18, 1973; children: Katherine Mason, Evan L.R. BA, Brandeis U., Waltham, Mass., 1964; MS in Journalism with honors, Columbia U., 1965. Editorial asst. I.F. Stone's Weekly, Washington, 1964-65; corr., editor Washington Post, 1966-84; v.p, assoc. pub. Random House Trade Books and pub. Times Books, Random House, Inc., NYC, 1984-96; cons. 20th Century Fund, 1996-97; founder, pub., chief exec. Public Affairs, 1997—2005, editor-at-large, 2005—. Exec. dir. Caravan Project, 2005—; vice chmn. Columbia Journalism Review, 2006. Contbr. articles to profl. publs. Bd. dirs. Human Rights Watch, U. Mich. Fellowship Journalists, 2000; chmn. Europe and Ctrl. Asia divsns., 1992-2005, emeritus, 2005-; co-chair Inst. for War and Peace Reporting, 2004-06. Fellow NEH, 1973-74. Mem. Assn. Am. Pubs. (vice chmn. gen. pub. divsn. 1993-96), Coun. on Fgn. Rels., Century Club. Office: Pub Affairs 250 W 57th St New York NY 10107 Home Phone: 203-622-0472; Office Phone: 212-397-6666. Business E-Mail: peter.osnos@perseusbooks.com.

OSOFF, JEFFREY ARLIN, media company executive; b. Everett, Mass., June 5, 1936; s. Meyer and Minerva (Cogan) O. (dec.); m. Arlene Shuman, Sept. 23, 1962 (div. Jan. 1988); children: Judith Robin (dec.), David Eric; m. Donna M. Peyre-Ferry, May 26, 1997. BA, Bowling Green State U., 1958; MS, Columbia U., 1959. Reporter Boston Post, 1954-55, Boston Globe, 1955-64, rewriteman, 1962-63, acting asst. city editor, 1963-64; dir. News Bur. Brandeis U., Waltham, Mass., 1964-67, asst. dir. pub. affairs, 1967-69, dir. pub. affairs, 1969-76; chmn. bd. Jansson, Inc., Waltham, 1976-87; pres., chief exec. officer JAO Enterprises, Ltd., Lexington, Mass., 1987—; chmn. Dorian Enterprises, Ltd., 1992—, D & J Enterprises, Ltd., Lexington, Mass., 1995—; chmn. bd. Concannon's Inc., Marlborough and Wellesley, Mass., 1990—98. Lectr. in journalism and pub. rels. cons. First v.p. Dysautonomia Found., NY, 1965-66, bd. dirs., 1965-76, pres., 1973-74; bd. dirs. New Eng. region Anti-Defamation League. Served with USAF, 1961-62. Recipient citation for outstanding journalistic reporting Mass. N.G., 1961; several awards for high achievement in graphics. Mem. New Eng. Press Assn., Internat. Thermographic Assn., Printing Industries Am., Printing Industries New Eng., Am. Coll. Pub. Rels. Assn., Jewish Pub. Relations Soc. Am., Pub. Rels. Soc. Am., Publicity Club Boston, Sigma Delta Chi, Zeta Beta Tau. Jewish. Home and Office: 3E Autumn Dr Hudson MA 01749-2855 Personal E-mail: josoff@comcast.net.

OSORIO, CLAUDIO E., computer company executive; Chmn., pres., CEO CHS Electronics, Miami. Office: Price Waterhouse Coopers 10 10th St NE #1400 Atlanta GA 30309-3906

OSORIO, PEPON, artist; b. Santurce, PR, 1955; Student, U. Inter-Am., Rio Piedras, Puerto Rico, 1974; BS, Herbert H. Lehman Coll., 1978; MA, Columbia U., 1985. Artist-in-residence El Museo del Barrio, NYC, 1989—91, The Fabric Workshop and Mus., Phila., Park Ave. Shelter Homeless Women, Artist/Homless Shelter, NYC, 1993, Mus. Contemporary Art, LA, 1993, Walker Art Ctr., Mpls., 1994, Ctr. Arts at Yerba Buena Gardens, San Francisco, 1996, Manchester Craftsmen's Guild, Pitts.; artist in residence dept. visual arts Rutgers U., Ctr. Innovative Print and Paper, New Brunswick, NJ, 1998; vis. artist dept. visual arts Skidmore Coll., Saratoga Springs, NY, 1995, Temple U., Tyler Sch. Arts, Phila., 1996; vis. artist Skowhegan (Maine) Sch. Painting and Sculpture, 1998, U. Hawaii, Honolulu, 1998; vis. artist dept. fine and pub. art Calif. State U. at Monterey, 1996; vis. faculty R.I. Sch. Design, Providence, 1993, Cleve. Art Inst., 1993; mem. adv. bd. Performance Space 122, NYC, 1989—93; The New Mus., NYC, 1996—98, Centro de Estudios Puertorriqueños at Hunter Coll., NYC, 1996—98; lectr. in field. One-man shows include Hostos Ctr. Arts and Culture, Hostos C.C., Bronx, 1985, CU Art Galleries, U. Colo., Boulder, 1991, El Museo del Barrio, N.Y.C., 1991, U. Arts, Samuel S. Fleisher Art Meml., Phila., 1992, Mus. Am. Art, Acad. Fine Arts, 1992, Cleve. Inst. Art, 1993, Real Art Ways, Hartford, 1994, Storefront, 33 Broadway, Newark, 1995, Museo de Pedro Albizu, Campos, Chgo., 1996, Galerie OZ, Paris, 1996, Ronald Feldman Fine Art, N.Y.C., 1996, Otis Gallery, Otis Coll. Art and Design, Westchester, Calif., 1997, Ctr. Arts at Yerba Buena Gardens, San Francisco, 1997, South Bronx and Manhattan, N.Y., 1997, Museo Nacional Centro de Arte Reina Sofia, Madrid, 1998, Museo Alejandro Otero, Caracas, Venezuela, 1998, Hostos Art Gallery, Bronx, 1998, exhibited in group shows at Mus. Am. Art, Smithsoniann Instn., Washington, 1996, Whitney Mus. Am. Art at Champion, Stamford, Conn., 1997, Setagaya Art Mus., Tokyo, 1997, Africus Inst. Contemporary Art, Johannesburg, South Africa, 1997, The Bertha and Karl Leubsdorf Art Gallery, Hunter Coll., N.Y.C., 1998, Internat. Ctr. Photography Midtown, 1999, Galerie Jean-Luc & Takako Richard, Paris, 2000, Oakland Mus of Calif., 2002, Inst. Contemporary Art, Phila., 2004, Miami Art Mus., 2005, performances include, No Regrets, 1989, Broken Hearts, 1991, Historias, 1992, Familias, 1995, others, commns. include, Cafe Am., N.Y.C., 1990, Bklyn. Acad. Music, 1991, Represented in permanent collections El Museo del Barrio, N.Y.C., Nat. Mus. Am. Art, Phila., Newark Mus., Walker Ctr. Arts, Mpls., Wadsworth Atheneum, Hartford, Whitney Mus. Am. Art, N.Y.C. Recipient N.Y. Dance and Performance award, 1985, Louis Tiffany Comfort award, 1993, Mid-Atlantic Arts Found. Residency award, The Fabric Workshop, 1996, Internat. Assn. of Art Critics award, 1996; fellow Sculpture fellow, Nat. Endowment Arts, 1988, Artist fellow in sculpture, N.Y. Found. Arts, 1988, 1995, Intercultural Film/Video fellow, Rockefeller Found., 1993, Artist's fellow, Joan Mitchell Found., 1996—97, MacArthur fellow, John D. and Catherine T. MacArthur Found., 1999; Krasner Pollack Found. fellow, Theater Comm. Group and Nat. Endowment Arts fellow, 1990. Office: care Ronald Feldman Fine Arts 31 Mercer St New York NY 10013-2541

OSOWIEC, DARLENE ANN, clinical psychologist, educator, consultant; b. Chgo., Feb. 16, 1951; d. Stephen Raymond and Estelle Marie Osowiec; m. Barry A. Leska. BS, Loyola U., Chgo., 1973; MA with honors, Roosevelt U., 1980; postgrad. in psychology, Saybrook Inst., San Francisco, 1985—88; PhD in Clin. Psychology, Calif. Inst. Integral Studies, 1992. Lic. clin. psychologist, Mo., Ill., Calif. Mental health therapist Ridgeway Hosp., Chgo., 1978; mem. faculty psychology dept. Coll. Lake County, Grayslake, Ill., 1981; counselor, supr. MA-level interns, chmn. pub. rels. com. Integral Counseling Ctr., San Francisco, 1983—84; clin. psychology intern Chgo.-Read Mental Health Ctr. Ill. Dept. Mental Health, 1985—86; mem. faculty dept. psychology Moraine Valley C.C., Palos Hills, Ill., 1988—89; lectr. psychology Daley Coll., Chgo., 1988-90; cons. Gordon & Assocs., Oak Lawn, Ill., 1989; adolescent, child and family therapist Orland Twp. Youth Svcs., Orland Park, Ill., 1993; psychology fellow Sch. Medicine, St. Louis U., 1994-95; pvt. practice Chgo., Geneva and St. Charles, Ill., 1996—; founder Maximum Potential, Chgo., 1996—. Contbr., author: Transpersonal Hypnosis, 1999. Ill. State scholar, 1969-73; Calif. Inst. Integral Studies scholar, 1983. Mem. APA (chair edn. and tng. com. divsn. 30 1998-2000, chair mem. svcs. 2001-05), Am. Psychol. Soc., Ill. Psychol. Assn., Calif. Psychol. Assn., Mo. Psychol. Assn., Am. Soc. Clin. Hypnosis, Chgo. Soc. Clin. Hypnosis, Internat. Soc. Hypnosis, Soc. Clin. and Exptl. Hypnosis, NOW (chair legal adv. corps, Chgo. 1974-76), Lincoln Park Bus. Devel. Inst. (chair program com. 2003—). Avocations: playing piano, gardening, reading, backpacking, writing. Office Phone: 630-845-8740. Business E-Mail: maximumpotential@comcast.net.

OSSELLO, KRISTIE, music educator; d. Carmen Holmes; m. John Ossello, Dec. 11, 1991; children: Bailey, Kiley, Jack. BA, U. St. Mary, Leavenworth, Kans., 1992; postgrad., Emporia State U., 2005—. Band dir. Most Pure Heart of Mary Sch., Topeka, 1996—, Hayden H.S., Topeka, 2003—. Musician: (performance) Coleman Hawkins Jazz Festival; composer: (drum line, handbells) Drum Line Features, Handbell Scores. Educator nominator Nat. Youth Leadership Coun., Washington, 2004—07; judge 4-H, Topeka, 1996—98; band mem. Marshall's Civic Band, Topeka, 1997—2006; summer camp tchr. Camp Polycarp, Topeka, 1998—99, Lion's Band, Baldwin City, Kans., 2000—00; dir. parade band St. Patrick's Day Parade, Topeka, 2002—07; judge Battle of the Bands, Topeka, 2004—06; music dir. Most Pure Heart of Mary Ch., Topeka, 1997—2002. Named Educator of Distinction, Nat. Soc. H.S. Scholars, 2005; recipient Teachers Make a Difference award, Channel 49 TV Sta., 2001. Mem.: Cath. Band Dirs. Assn., Am. Guild English Handbell Ringers, Internat. Assn. Jazz Educators, Nat. Assn. Music Educators, Kappa Gamma Pi. Avocations: range shooting, travel, reading, walking, hiking. Home Phone: 785-286-0304; Office Phone: 785-272-5210. Personal E-mail: ossellok@haydenhigh.org.

OSSEO-ASARE, KWADWO, engineering educator; Disting. prof. metals sci. and engring. and geo-environ. engring. U. Pa.; Kwadwo Osseo-Asare disting. prof. material sci. and engring. and geo-environ. engring. Pa. State U., University Park. Contbr. articles to profl. jours. Mem.: NAE. Office: Pa State U 208 Steidle Bldg University Park PA 16802-5000 Office Phone: 814-865-4882. Office Fax: 814-863-4718. E-mail: asare@ems.psu.edu.

OSSER, DAVID NEAL, psychiatrist, educator; b. NYC, Aug. 30, 1946; s. Abe A. and Edna (Meisel) Osser; m. Stephanie D. Fleischer; children: Roselin Emily, Daniel Alexander. BA, Amherst Coll., 1968; MD, SUNY, Syracuse, 1972. Intern in psychiatry U. So. Calif., LA, 1972-73; resident in psychiatry Mass. Mental Health Ctr. Harvard U., Boston, 1973-76; pvt. practice Needham, Mass., 1976—; assoc. prof. psychiatry Harvard U. Med. Sch., Boston, 1999—. Lectr. Tufts U. Med. Sch., 1978—, Taunton State Hosp., 1976—, Faulkner Hosp., 1976—, Brockton VA Med. Ctr., 1995—. Author: internet decision support software for psychopharmacology (www.mhc.com/Algorithms); editor: schizophrenia: www.cogentmedicine.com; contbr. to pharmacol. websites, internat. psychopharmacology algorithm project www.ipap.org, articles to profl. jours.; co-author: drug interaction website www.genelex.com. Recipient Lundbeck Internat. Neuroscience Found. prize, 2004, Journalism award, Kantar Found., 2001, award of excellence in edn., Internat. Psychopharm. Algorithm Project, 2006. Fellow: Am. Psychiat. Assn. (Disting.); mem.: Internat. Coll. Neuro-psychopharmacologicum, Mass. Psychiat. Soc. (pres. 2001—02), Am. Soc. Clin. Psychopharmacology. Democrat. Jewish. Avocations: classical music, opera, piano, canoeing, hiking. Office: 150 Winding River Rd Needham MA 02492-1025 Office Phone: 781-237-7444.

OSSERMAN, ROBERT, mathematician, educator, writer; b. NYC, Dec. 19, 1926; s. Herman Aaron and Charlotte (Adler) O.; m. Maria Anderson, June 15, 1952; 1 son, Paul; m. Janet Adelman, July 21, 1976; children—Brian, Stephen. BA, NYU, 1946; postgrad., U. Zurich, U. Paris; MA, Harvard U., 1948, PhD, 1955. Tchg. fellow Harvard U., 1949-52, vis. lectr., rsch. assoc., 1961-62; instr. U. Colo., 1952-53; mem. faculty Stanford U., 1955-94, prof. emeritus, 1994—, prof. math., 1966—, chmn. dept. math., 1973-79, Mellon Prof. Interdisciplinary Studies, 1987-90; dep. dir. Math. Scis. Rsch. Inst., Berkeley, Calif., 1990-95, dir. spl. projects, 1995—. Mem. NYU Inst. Math. Scis., 1957-58, Math. Scis. Rsch. Inst., Berkeley,, 1983-84, head math. br. Office Naval Rsch., 1960-61; researcher and author publs. on differential geometry, complex variables, differential equations, astronomy, cosmology, especially minimal surfaces, isoperimetric inequalities. Author: Two-Dimensional Calculus, 1968, A Survey of Minimal Surfaces, 1969, 1986, Poetry of the Universe, 1995; author: (videos) Fermat's Last Theorem, 1994, Mathematics in Arcadia, 1999, Galileo: A Dialog, 2000; co-author (with Steve Martin): Funny Numbers, 2003; co-author: (with Michael Fayer) (DVD) The Right Spin, 2005. Fulbright lectr. U. Paris, 1965-66; Guggenheim fellow, 1976-77; vis. fellow U. Warwick, Imperial Coll., U. London; recipient Comms. award Joint Policy

Bd. for Math., 2003, Support of Sci. award Coun. Sci. Soc. Presidents, 2004. Fellow AAAS; mem. Am. Math. Soc. (Comm. award, 2003), Math. Assn. Am., Astron. Soc. Pacific. Office: Math Sci Rsch Inst 17 Gauss Way Berkeley CA 94720 Office Phone: 510-642-0143.

OSSEWAARDE, ANNE WINKLER, real estate company executive; b. Dallas, June 2, 1957; d. Lowell Graves and Ruth Lenore (Lind) Winkler; m. Kirk L Ossewaarde, Apr. 27, 1991. BBA in Fin. with honors, Emory U., 1979; MBA in Acctg. and Fin. with honors, U. Tex., 1983; MS in Real Estate Devel., MIT, 1988. Cert. comml. investment mem., Comml. Investment Real Estate Inst. Mgmt. trainee Citizens & So. Nat. Bank, Atlanta, 1979-81; banking assoc. Continental Ill. Nat. Bank, Chgo. and Dallas, 1983-85; asst. v.p., devel. assoc. Trammell Crow Residential, Dallas, 1985-87, Seattle, 1988-91; devel. mgr. Blackhawk Port Blakeley Cmtys., Seattle, 1991-93; v.p., real estate portfolio mgr. Aegon U.S.A. Realty, Atlanta, 1994-98; dir. UBS Brinson Realty Investors (formerly Allegis Realty Investors), Dallas, 1998—2000; exec. dir. asset mgmt. Morgan Stanley (formerly Lend Lease Real Estate Investments, Inc.), Atlanta, 2000—. Charles Harritt Jr. Presdl. scholar U. Tex., 1982, Alexander Grant scholar, 1982. Mem. Comml. Real Estate Women, MIT Ctr. for Real Estate Alumni Assn., Alpha Epsilon Upsilon. Methodist. Avocations: singing, photography, bicycling, reading. Home: 3170 Windsor Lake Dr Atlanta GA 30319

OSSOFF, ROBERT HENRY, otolaryngologist, surgeon; b. Beverly, Mass., Mar. 25, 1947; s. Michael Max and Eve Joan (Kladky) G.; m. Lynn Spilman, 1984; 2 children: Leslin, Jacob. BA, Bowdoin Coll., Brunswick, Maine, 1969; DMD, Tufts U., Medford, Mass., 1973, MD, 1975; MS in Otolaryngology, Northwestern U., Evanston, Ill., 1981. Diplomate Am. Bd. Otolaryngology. Intern Northwestern Meml. Hosp., Chgo., 1975-76; resident in otolaryngology and and maxillofacial surgery Northwestern U. Med. Sch., Chgo., 1976-80, NIH rsch. fellow dept. otolaryngology and maxillofacial surgery, 1977-78, clin. fellow in head and neck surgery, 1980-81; jr. faculty clin. fellow Am. Cancer Soc. Northwestern Med. Sch., Chgo., 1981-84; faculty practice, otolaryngology, head and neck surgery, laryngology and care of profl. voice Northwestern Med. Sch., Chgo., 1981—86, Vanderbilt U. Med. Ctr., Nashville, 1986—, prof., chmn. dept. otolaryngology, 1986—; exec. med. dir. Vanderbilt Voice Ctr., 1991—. Attending physician Cook County Hosp., Chgo., 1981—83, cons. physician, 1983—86; attending physician Northwestern Meml. Hosp, Chgo., 1981—86, Children's Meml. Hosp., Chgo., 1981—86; attending physician, chief otolaryngology svc. VA Lakeside Hosp., Chgo., 1982—85; attending physician, head divsn. otolaryngology head and neck surgery Evanston Hosp., 1983—86, chief divsn. otolaryngology, 1983—86; asst. prof. Northwestern U. Dental Sch., Chgo., 1980—86, Northwestern U. Med. Sch., Chgo., 1981—85, assoc. prof., 1985—86; attending surgeon, otolaryngologist-in-chief Vanderbilt U. Hosp., Nashville, 1986—, chief staff, 1995—97; attending surgeon VA Hosp., Nashville, 1986—; Guy M. Manness prof., chmn. dept. otolaryngology Vanderbilt U. Med. Ctr., Nashville, 1986—, assoc. vice chancellor health affairs, 1995—2005; assoc. dir. Vanderbilt Free-Electron Laser Ctr. Med. and Materials Rsch., Nashville, 1992—95; dir. Vanderbilt Bill Wilkerson Ctr. Otolaryngology Communication Scis., Nashville, 1997—. Sr. editor Lasers in Surgery and Medicine, 1987—94, editor-in-chief, 1995—2005, laryngology sect. editor Otolaryngology-Head and Neck Surgery, 2005—, mem. editl. bd. Clin. Laser Monthly, 1984—, Jour. Voice, 1987—, The Laryngoscope, 1988—2003, Jour. of Laser Applications, 1988—2004, Otolaryngology-Head and Neck Surgery, 1988—, mem. editl. adv. bd. Gen. Surgery News, 1990—97, assoc. editor Diagnostic and Therapeutic Endoscopy, 1992—2000; co-editor: Complications in Head and Neck Surgery, W.B. Saunders Co., 1993, The Larynx, Lippincott Williams and Wilkins, 2002; contbr. over 160 articles to profl. jours., 60 chpts. in books; editor, co-editor (8 books in field). Bd. dirs. Laser Inst. Am., 1984—90; dir. Am. Bd. Otolaryngology, 1995—; trustee Midwest Biolaser Inst., Chgo., 1981—86, Leadership Nashville, 1988—89. Recipient Nat. Rsch. Svc. award, NIH, 1977-78; Francis L. Lederer-Norval H. Pierce award, Chgo. Laryngol. and Otol. Soc., 1978, Hon. mem., 1986; Guest of Honor, First European Carbon Dioxide Laser Surgery Coruse and Workshop in Otolaryngology Head and Neck Surgery, Roskilde, Denmark, 1984; named a Prin. Investigator, NIH, 1977-78; Am. Cancer Soc., Ill. Divsn., 1981-82; VA Merit Rev., 1884-85; Nat. Cancer Inst., 1985-88; Office Naval Rsch., 1987-90, 91-94; A. Ward Ford Found., 1989-90. Fellow: ACS (bd. govs. 1996—2002, adv. coun. Otorhinolarygology 1996—2003), Am. Laryngol. Assn. (chmn. rsch. support task force 1994—96, coun. mem. 1996—98, sec. 1998—2003, Daniel C. Baker Jr. lectr. 2001, v.p., pres. elect 2003—04, pres. 2004—05, Baker lectr. 2001, Guest of Honor 2002, Presdl. citation 2003, DeRoaldes medal 2004, James Newcomb award 2007), The Triological Soc. (nat. nominating com. 1993, coun. mem. 1996—99, thesis adv. com. 1998—99, v.p. so. sect. 2002—03, coun. mem. 2002—03, 2005—, dir., CME 2005—, Presdl. Citation 2006), Am. Soc. Head and Neck Surgery (coun. mem. 1991—94); mem.: AMA, Soc. Univ. Otolaryngologists Head and Neck Surgeons (coun. mem. 2002—05, pres.-elect 2004—05, pres. 2005—06), Assn. Academic Depts. Otolaryngology Head Neck Surgery (sec.-treas. 1996—98, pres. elect 1998—2000, pres. 2000—02, coun. mem. 2002—04), Am. Laryngol. Voice Rsch. Edn. Found. (bd. dirs. 1996—, sec. 1998—2003), Am. Bd. Otolaryngology (task force for new materials mem. 1985—89, assoc. examiner 1994—97, dir. 1995—2007), Cartesian Soc., Am. Broncho-Esophagological Assn. (coun. mem. 1987—90, treas. 1990—94, pres.-elect 1994—95, pres. 1995—96, Chevalier Jackson award 1997, Guest of Honor 2000), Soc. Head and Neck Surgeons, Am. Soc. Laser Medicine and Surgery (bd. dirs. 1985—88, chmn. program com. 1986—87, pres.-elect 1988—89, pres. 1989—90, nominating com. 1990—91, William B. Mark award 1992, Presdl. citation 2003), Am. Acad. Otolaryngology-Head and Neck Surgery (chmn. laser surgery com. 1983—89, chmn. self instl. package com. 1990—96, bd. dirs. 1992—95, coord. for devel. 2001—, Cert. of Honor 1984, Disting. Svc. award 1995, Presdl. citation 1999, Disting. Svc. award 2004, Presdl. citation 2005), Am. Acad. Oral Pathology, Am. Acad. Oral Medicine, Sigma Xi, Omicron Kappa Upsilon. Achievements include reestablishment of department of otolaryngology at Vanderbilt University Medical Center in 1986; establishment of the Vanderbilt Voice Center in 1991; establishment of an advanced training laryngology fellowship program at Vanderbilt University Medical Center in 1992. Avocations: boating, skiing, fly fishing, golf, photography. Office: Vanderbilt U Med Ctr Dept Otolaryngology 7302 Med Ctr E Nashville TN 37232-8783 Home Phone: 615-352-8150; Office Phone: 615-322-6326. Business E-Mail: robert.ossoff@vanderbilt.edu.

OSTAR, ALLAN WILLIAM, educational consultant; b. East Orange, NJ, Sept. 4, 1924; s. William and Rose O.; m. Roberta Hutchison, Sept. 10, 1949; children: Cert. engring., U. Denver, 1943; BA, Pa. State U., 1948; postgrad., U. Wis., 1949-55; LL.D., U. No. Colo., 1968, Eastern Ky. U., 1972, Whittier Coll., 1973; L.H.D., U. Maine, 1975; D.Letters, Central Mich. U., 1975; D.P.S., Bowling Green State U., 1975, R.I. Coll., 1983; D.Higher Edn., Morehead State U., 1977; L.H.D., Appalachian State U., 1977, No. Mich. U., 1978, Dickinson State Coll., ND, 1979, Towson State U., 1980, Salem State Coll., 1980, Mont. Coll. Mineral Sci. and Tech., 1983, Ball State U., 1984; LL.D., U. Alaska, 1978, Ill. State U., 1983, Western Mich. U., 1984; D. Polit. Sci., Kyung Hee U., Korea, 1984; L.H.D., Fitchburg State Coll., 1986, Bridgewater State Coll., 1988, No. State Coll., 1988, Harris-Stowe State Coll., 1986; LLD, Edinboro U. Pa., 1987, Loch Haven U., Pa., 1989; LHD, No. Ariz. U., 1990, Shepherd Coll., W.Va., 1992, SUNY, 1993, Lincoln U., Mo., 1995. Dir. nat. pub. relations U.S. Nat. Student Assn., 1948-49; exec. asst. Commonwealth Fund, NYC, 1952-53; asst. to dean extension div. U. Wis., 1949-52, dir. office communications services, 1954-58; dir. Joint Office Instnl. Research, Nat. Assn. State Univs. and Land Grant Colls., Washington, 1958-65; pres. Am. Assn. State Colls. and Univs., Washington, 1965-91, pres. emeritus, 1991—; sr. adv. Acad. Search Consultation Svc., 1991—. Adj. prof. edn. Pa. State U., 1990—. Co-author: Colleges and Universities for Change, 1987; contbr. chpts. in books. Mem. 42d (Rainbow) div. U.S. Army, 1943-46. Decorated 2 Bronze Stars with V, Combat Infantryman's badge; recipient Centennial award U. Akron, 1970, Fogelsanger award Shippensburg (Pa.) State Coll., 1974, World Peace Through Edn. medal Internat. Assn. U. Pres., 1975, Disting. Achievement award, U. So. Colo., 1979, Chancellor's award U. Wis., 1985, Chancellor's medal CUNY, 1986, Disting. Alumnus award Pa. State U., 1989, svc. award Coun. on Internat. Ednl. Exch., 1990, Chancellor's medal Internat. Svc. U. Ark., Little Rock, 1990, Disting. Pub. Svc. medal Dept. of Def., 1991; Alumni fellow Pa. State U., 1975. Unitarian-Universalist. Home: 404 Sandy Cove Tinton Falls NJ 07753-7745

OSTBERG, HENRY DEAN, marketing executive; b. Bocholt, Germany, July 21, 1928; came to U.S., 1939, naturalized, 1945. s. Fred and Lotte (Hertz) O.; m. Sydelle Burns, Dec. 13, 1987; 1 child, Neal; stepchildren: Elysa Bari, Brent Adam, Ross Jay. LLB, N.Y. Law Sch., 1950; MBA, Ohio State U., 1953, PhD, 1957. Pres. H.D. Ostberg Assocs., NYC, 1950—; assoc. prof. mktg. NYU, 1954—63. Chmn. bd. Admar Group,Inc., 1960; dir. Self-Instructional Devel. Corp., Amherst Group, Porter Industries, Inc.; pres. Eastman Enterprises, Inc. Contbr. articles to profl. jours. Trustee Ostberg Found.; chmn. Givat Haviva Edn. Found. Capt. USAF, 1950—53. Jewish. Office Phone: 201-767-8000. Personal E-mail: hdousa@earthlink.net.

OSTBY, FREDERICK PAUL, JR., meteorologist, retired government official, science administrator; b. New Haven, Jan. 20, 1930; s. Frederick Paul and Edna Maria (Kruckenberg) O.; m. Joanne Bernice Sorvig, Jan. 1, 1955 (div. 1989); children: Paul, Neil, Karen, Lynn; m. Barbara Richards, Mar. 17, 1989. BS in Meteorology, NYU, 1951, MS in Meteorology, 1960. Cert. Consulting Meteorlogist. Meteorologist TWA, NYC, 1953-54, Kansas City, Mo., 1955-56, N.E. Weather Service, Lexington, Mass., 1955, Travelers Weather Service, Hartford, Conn., 1956-60; research scientist Travelers Research Center, Hartford, 1960-70; meteorologist Nat. Weather Service, Silver Spring, Md., 1970-72; dep. dir. Nat. Severe Storms Forecast Center, Dept. Commerce, Kansas City, Mo., 1972-80; dir. Nat. Severe Storms Forecast Center, 1980-96; assoc. Climatological Cons. Corp., 1997—. Severe weather cons. The Weather Channel, 1997—98. Contbr. papers to profl. lit. Air weather officer USAF, 1951—53. Fellow Am. Meteorol. Soc. (council 1977-80, 84-87). Republican. Methodist. Home: 12537 Broadmoor St Overland Park KS 66209-3234 Home Phone: 913-338-4222; Office Phone: 913-338-4222. Personal E-mail: fostby@sbcglobal.net.

OSTBYE, TRULS, medical researcher, educator; b. Norway, Dec. 15, 1954; arrived in U.S., 1999; m. Hemali Kulatilaka, 1984; children: Trevor, Adrian. MD, U. Bergen, 1979; MPH, Harvard U., 1983; PhD, U. Bergen, 2000; MBA, Edinburgh Bus. Sch., 2000. Exec. officer Directorate of Orgn. and Mgmt., Norway, 1981—84; spl. med. officer Nat. Inst. Pub. Health, Norway, 1984—85; lectr. U. Otago, New Zealand, 1985—86; Lalia B. Chase rsch. fellow Dalhousie U., Halifax, N.S., Canada, 1986—88; asst. prof. to prof. U. We. Ont., London, Canada, 1988—99; prof., vice chair rsch. Dept. Cmty. and Family Medicine Duke U., Durham, NC, 2000—. Contbr. more than 200 articles to profl. jours. Office: Duke U Dept Cmty and Family Medicine DUMC 2914 Durham NC 27710 E-mail: truls.ostbye@duke.edu.

OSTEEN, JOEL, minister; b. Houston; s. John and Dodie Osteen; m. Victoria Iloff, 1987; children: Jonathan, Alexandria. Student, Oral Roberts U., 1981—82. Prodr., creator John Osteen Televison program, 1982—99; ordained, 1992; pres. and co-owner KTBU Channel 55, Houston, 1998—; sr. pastor Lakewood Church, Houston, 1999—. Author: Your Best Life Now: 7 Steps to Living at Your Full Potential, 2004. Named one of Barbara Walters-10 Most Fascinating People of 2006. Achievements include ministering to the one of the largest and most diverse congregations in America; weekly television program appears on six cable networks and internationally in over 100 nations; aquired lease for the Compaq Center in Houston to accommodate growing congregation. Office: Lakewood Church PO Box 23297 Houston TX 77228 Office Phone: 713-635-4154. Office Fax: 713-635-4753. *

O'STEEN, VAN, lawyer; b. Sweetwater, Tenn., Jan. 10, 1946; s. Bernard Van and Laura Emelyne (Robinson) O'Steen; m. Deborah Ann Elias, May 18, 1974; children: Jonathan Van, Laura Ann. BA, Calif. Western U., 1968; JD cum laude, Ariz. State U., 1972. Bar: Ariz. 1972, cert.: US Dist. Ct. Ariz. 1972, US Ct. Appeals (9th cir.) 1973, US Supreme Ct. 1975. Staff atty. Maricopa Legal Aid Soc., Phoenix, 1972—74; atty. Bates & O'Steen Legal Clinic, Phoenix, 1974—77, O'Steen Legal Clinic, Phoenix, 1977—80; ptnr. Van O'Steen Mktg. Group, Inc., Phoenix, 1985—; mng. ptnr. Van O'Steen and Ptnrs., Phoenix and Tucson, 1980—2004; ptnr. O'Steen & Harrison, Phoenix and Tucson, 2004—. Author: numerous self-help legal books. Founding dir. Ariz. Ctr. for Law in the Pub. Interest, 1974—80. With USNR, 1963—69. Mem.: ABA (chmn. spl. com. delivery legal svcs. 1982—85), Assn. Trial Lawyers Am., Am. Legal Clinic Assn. (pres. 1979). Democrat. Office: Ste 400 300 W Clarendon Ave Phoenix AZ 85013-3424 Office Phone: 602-252-8888. Business E-Mail: vosteen@vanosteen.com.

O'STEEN, WENDALL KEITH, anatomist, neurologist, educator; b. Meigs, Ga., July 3, 1928; s. Wellna Hubert and Lillian (Powell) O'S.; m. Sandra Lynn Kraeer, July 30, 1983; children: Lisa Diane, Kerry Keith, Buckley Powell. BA, Emory U., 1948, MS, 1950; PhD, Duke U., 1958. Asst. prof. Emory U. Jr. Coll., Valdosta, Ga., 1948-49; instr. Emory U., Atlanta, 1950-51; prof. Emory U. Sch. Medicine, Atlanta, 1968-77; from asst. prof. to prof. med. br. U. Tex., 1958-67; asst. prof. Wofford Coll., Spartanburg, SC, 1951-53; prof., chmn. dept. neurobiology and anatomy, Bowman Gray Sch. Med. Wake Forest U., Winston-Salem, NC, 1977-93, prof. emeritus, 1993—. Mem. anatomy com. Nat. Bd. Med. Examiners, Phila., 1982-87. Contbr. over 150 articles to books, nat. and internat. jours. Lt. col. USAR. Recipient Golden Apple teaching award Med. Br. U. Tex., Galveston, 1967, Outstanding Tchr. award Emory U., 1973, Williams Disting. Teaching award Emory U., 1974, award for teaching excellence Bowman Gray Sch. Medicine, Wake Forest U. Mem. Am. Assn. Anatomists (exec. com. 1980-84, v.p. 1990-92), Assn. Anatomy Chairmen (exec. com. 1982-84, pres. 1990-91), So. Soc. Anatomists (pres. 1975-76), Soc. for Neurosci., N.C. Soc. Neurosci. (pres. 1980-81), Western N.C. Soc. Neurosci. (pres. 1987-88), Assn. Rsch. in Vision and Ophthalmology, Alpha Omega Alpha. Republican. Methodist. Avocations: gardening, music. Office: Wake Forest U Bowman Gray Sch Medicine Dept Neurobiology and Anatomy Winston Salem NC 27157-0001

OSTEEN, WILLIAM L., federal judge; b. 1930; BA, Guilford Coll., 1953; LLB, U. N.C., 1956. With Law Office of W.H. McElwee, Jr., North Wilkesboro, N.C., 1956-58; pvt. practive Greensboro, N.C., 1958-59; with Booth & Osteen, Greensboro, 1959-69; U.S. atty. U.S. Attys. Office, Greensboro, 1969-74; ptnr. Osteen, Adams & Osteen, Greensboro, 1974-91; fed. judge U.S. Dist. Ct. (mid. dist.) N.C., Greensboro, 1991—. With USAR, 1958-51. Fellow Am. Coll. Trial Lawyers; mem. ABA, N.C. State Bar, N.C. Bar Assn. (mem. and chair subcom. N.C. sentencing commn.), U. N.C. Law Alumni Assn. Office: US Dist Ct PO Box 3485 Greensboro NC 27402-3485

OSTENDORF, LANCE STEPHEN, lawyer, financial consultant, educator; b. New Orleans, Aug. 16, 1958; 1 child, Christine Marie Ostendorf. BBA in Acctg. and Fin., Loyola U., 1976, JD, 1980. Bar: La. 1980, U.S. Dist. Ct. (ea. dist.) La. 1981, U.S. Dist. Ct. La., U.S. Supreme Ct. 1980, U.S. Dist. Ct. (we. and mid. dists.) La. 1983. Founder GO Entertainment, Inc. L.A., New Orleans,Balt./Washington, L.A./Orange County, San Diego/Riverside, Ostendorf, Tate, Barnett & Wells, PLC, L.A./Orange County, San Diego/Riverside, Houston, Balt., New Orleans. Treas., CFO La. State U. Med. Ctr. Found., New Orleans, 1992—; lectr. Lorman Ednl. Seminars; bd. dirs. La. State U. Med. Ctr. Found., New Orleans, tech. transfer com.; speaker and tchr. Lorman Ednl. Svcs., Inc. Author: Insurance Law; contbr. articles to profl. jours. Mem. ABA, Fed. Bar Assn., Internat. Bar Assn., La. Bar Assn., Metairie Bar Assn., Maritime Law Assn., Comite Maritime Internat., Assn. for Transp. Law, Trucking Industry Def. Assn., Logistics and Policy, Assn. Average Adjusters of U.S., Jefferson Bar Assn., New Orleans Bar Assn., La. Restaurant Assn., Am. Trial Lawyers Assn., La. Bar Assn., Jefferson Bar Assn., Fifth Cir. Bar Assn., Def. Rsch. Inst., La. Trial Lawyers Assn., Law Def. Lawyers Assn., Houston Mariners Club, Southeastern Adm. Law Inst., St. Thomas Moore Club, La. Notary Soc., New Orleans South African Connection, Blue Key Honor Soc. Office: 440 Louisiana 1650 Houston TX 77002 Home: P O Box 88 Houston TX 70001 Office Phone: 504-527-0700. Personal E-mail: lanceostendorf@yahoo.com. Business E-Mail: lance.ostendorf@otbw-law.com.

OSTENDORFF, WILLIAM CHARLES, federal agency administrator, career military officer; b. Shreveport, La., Oct. 22, 1954; s. Thomas Julian and Emilie Anne (Connell) O.; m. Christina Lee Miller, July 16, 1977; children: Rebecca, Chuck, Jeff. BS in Systems Engring., U.S. Naval Acad., 1976; JD with honors, U. Tex., 1984; LLM with distinction, Georgetown U., 1992. Bar: Tex. 1984. Commd. USN, 1976, advanced through grades to comdr., 1991, nuclear submarine officer; nuclear power prog. mgr. Office of Chief Naval Ops., Washington; mem. rsch. staff Inst. for Def. Analyses, 2002—03; counsel House Armed Services Com., 2003—07; prin. dep. adminstr., Nat. Nuclear Security Adminstrn. US Dept. Energy, Washington, 2007—. Mem. ABA, State Bar Assn. Tex., U.S. Naval Acad. Alumni Assn., Order of the Coif. Episcopalian. Avocation: running. Office: US Dept Energy Forrestal Bldg 1000 Independence Ave SW Rm 7A-199 Washington DC 20585

OSTER, GEORGE F., molecular biologist, environmental scientist; BS, US Merchant Marine Acad., 1961; PhD, Columbia U., 1967. Asst. prof. dept. mech. engring. U. Calif., Berkeley, 1972—73, prof. cell & devel. biology, dept. molecular & cellular biology, 1973—, prof. environ. sci., policy & mgmt., coll. natural resources, 1973—; prof. Miller Found., 1983—84, 2003; Oppenheimer prof. Los Alamos Nat. Lab., 1985. Mem. sci. adv. bd. Santa Fe Inst. Recipient Levy medal, Franklin Inst., 1971, 1974, Weldon Meml. prize, Oxford U., 1992—94; Postdoctoral Fellow, NIH, 1967—70, U. Calif. Berkeley & Weitzmann Inst. Sci., 1969—71, Guggenheim Fellow, 1975—76, MacArthur Found. Fellow, 1985—90. Fellow: Am. Acad. Arts & Sciences; mem.: NAS. Office: U Calif Berkeley Dept Molecular & Cellular Biology 201 Wellman Hall Berkeley CA 94720-3112 Office Phone: 510-642-5277. Office Fax: 510-642-7428. Business E-Mail: goster@nature.berkeley.edu.

OSTER, LEWIS HENRY, manufacturing executive, industrial engineer, consultant; b. Mitchell, SD, Jan. 18, 1923; s. Peter W. and Lucy (Goetsch) Oster; m. Mary Mills, Aug. 17, 1948; children: David, Lewis, Nancy, Susan. BS in Engring., Iowa State U., 1948; MBA, Syracuse U., 1968. Registered profl. engr., Iowa. Mgr. Maytag Co., Newton, Iowa, 1953—59; sr. staff engr., mgr. Philco-Ford Corp., Phila., 1959—62; mgr. mech. and indsl. engring. Carrier Corp., Syracuse, NY, 1962—75; v.p. Superior Industries Internat., Van Nuys, Calif., 1981—. V.p., gen. mgr. Superior/Ideal, Inc., Oskaloosa, Iowa, 1975—; cons. in field. Author: MTM Application Manual, 1957. Leader Boy Scouts Am., Syracuse, NY, 1965—73; fund chmn. United Fund, Syracuse, 1965—73. Lt. col. USAFR, ETO. Decorated Purple Heart, DFC, Air medal with four oak leaf clusters. Mem.: Am. Inst. Indsl. Engrs. (pres. 1951—53), Ret. Officers Assn., Oskaloosa Country Club, Am. Legion, Elks.

OSTER, ROSE MARIE GUNHILD, foreign language professional, educator; b. Stockholm, Feb. 26, 1934; came to US, 1958; d. Herbert Jonas and Emma Wilhelmina (Johnson) Hagetorn; m. Ludwig F. Oster, May 17, 1956; children: Ulrika, Mattias. Fil. mag., U. Stockholm, 1956; PhD, Kiel U., Germany, 1958. Postdoctoral rsch. fellow linguistics Yale U., 1958-60, rsch. fellow Germanic langs., 1960-64, lectr. Swedish, 1964-66; mem. faculty U. Colo., Boulder, 1966-80, assoc. prof. Germanic langs. and lits., 1970-77, prof., 1977-80, chmn. dept., 1972-75, assoc. dean Grad. Sch., 1975-79, assoc. vice chancellor for grad. affairs Grad. Sch., 1979-80; dean for grad. studies and rsch. U. Md., College Park, 1980-83, prof. Germanic langs. and lits., 1980—, acting chair dept., 1997—2001. Mem. Fulbright Nat. Screening Com., Scandinavia, 1973, 83-87, chair, 1986-87; mem. selection com. Scandinavia Internat. Exch. of Scholars, 1982-86; cons. panelist Nat. Endowment for Humanities, 1975—, mem. bd. cons., 1980—; state coord. Am. Coun. on Edn., Colo., 1978-80, Md., 1981-83, dir. dept. leadership program, 1986-91; mem. exec. com. Assn. Grad. Schs., 1980-83; mem. dean's exec. com. African-Am. Inst., 1981-85; interim dir. Washington Sch. Psychiatry, 1994-95; cons. in field. Contbr. articles and revs. to profl. publs. Bd. dirs. Washington Sch. Psychiatry, Am.-Swedish Hist. Mus., Phila., Open Theatre, Washington; mem. nat. fellowship com. Am.-Scandinavian Found., 1997—, bd. trustees, 2001—. Carnegie fellow, 1974; grantee Swedish Govt., 1977, Am. Scandinavian Found., 1997, German Acad. Exch. Svc., 1983; recipient Translation prize Am.-Scandinavian Found., 1997. Mem. NOW, MLA (mem. Del. Assembly 1995—), AAUP, Soc. Advancement Scandinavian Studies (pres. 1979-80), Am. Scandinavian Assn. of Nat. Capital Area (pres. 1983-86, 96—), Am.-Scandinavian Found., Am. Assn. Higher Edn. Home: 4977 Battery Ln Bethesda MD 20814-4931 Office: U Md Dept Germanic Studies College Park MD 20742-0001 Home Phone: 301-657-4186; Office Phone: 301-405-4096. Business E-Mail: rmoster@umd.edu.

OSTERBERG, EDWARD CHARLES, JR., lawyer; b. Honolulu, Jan. 1, 1942; s. Edward Charles and Emily Julia (Preston) O.; m. Susan Rhea Snider, Aug. 26, 1967; 1 child, Edward Charles III. BA, Northwestern U., Evanston, Ill., 1963, JD cum laude, 1966; LLM in Taxation, So. Meth. U., Dallas, 1972. Bar: Tex. 1966, Ill. 1966. Assoc. Vinson & Elkins, Houston, 1967-73, ptnr., 1974—. Reporter Internat. Fiscal Assn., Sydney, Australia, 1978, Barcelona, Spain, 1991. Contbr. articles to profl. publs. Mem. ABA (chmn. taxation com.), Houston Bar Assn. (chmn. taxation sect. 1987), Petroleum Club, Houston Racquet Club. Methodist. Home: 11222 Wilding Ln Houston TX 77024-5308 Office: Vinson & Elkins LLP 1001 Fannin St Ste 3300 Houston TX 77002-6760 Office Phone: 713-758-2192. Business E-Mail: eosterberg@velaw.com.

OSTERGAARD, JONI HAMMERSLA, lawyer; b. Seattle, May 26, 1950; d. William Dudley and Carol Mae (Gillett) Hammersla; m. Gregory Lance Ostergaard, May 22, 1976 (div. 1985); 1 child, Bennett Gillett; m. William Howard Patton, Jan. 1, 1988; 1 child, Morgan Hollis; stepchildren: Colin W., Benjamin C. BS, U. Wash., 1972; MS, Purdue U., 1974; JD, U. Wash., 1980. Bar: Wash. 1980, U.S. Dist. Ct. (we. dist.) Wash. 1980, U.S. Ct. Appeals (9th cir.) 1981, U. S. Ct. Claims 1983. Clin. psychol. intern Yale Med. Sch., 1976-77; law clk. U.S. Ct. Appeals (9th cir.), Seattle, 1980-81; assoc. Roberts & Shefelman, Seattle, 1982-86, ptnr., 1987, Foster Pepper & Shefelman, Seattle, 1988-92; sole practitioner Seattle, 1996—2003; dep. pros. atty. Snohomish County Prosecuting Attys. Office Civil Divsn., Everett, Wash., 2004—. Contbr. articles to profl. jours.; notes and comments editor Wash. Law Rev., 1979-80. Recipient Sophia and Wilbur Albright scholarship U. Wash. Law Sch., 1979-80, law sch. alumni scholarship U. Wash. Law Sch., 1978-79; fellow NIMH. Avocations: gardening, reading. Office: Snohomish County Prosecuting Attys Office Civil Divsn 3000 Rockefeller Ave M/S 504 Everett WA 98201-4046 Home Phone: 425-697-3050; Office Phone: 425-388-6370. Office Fax: 425-388-6333. Business E-Mail: jostergaard@co.snohomish.wa.us.

OSTERGARD, PAUL MICHAEL, not-for-profit executive; b. Akron, Ohio, Apr. 1, 1939; s. Paul and Janette Beryl (Laube) O.; m. Elizabeth K. McCombs, Jan. 1965 (div. Nov. 1971). AB magna cum laude, Case-Western Res. U., 1961; JD, U. Mich., 1964; MPA, Harvard U., 1969; diploma in hispanic studies, U. Madrid, Spain, 1960. Bar: Ohio 1964. Atty. US Steel Corp., Pitts., 1967—69; gen. atty. TWA Inc., NYC, 1969—71; v.p. adminstrn., sec., counsel Pa. Co. (now Penn Ctrl. Corp.), 1971—74, and subs. Buckeye Pipe Line Co., NYC, 1972—74; pub. affairs exec. GE, Fairfield, Conn., 1974—84; pres. GE Found., Fairfield, 1984—90; chmn., CEO, bd. dirs. Citigroup Found., NYC, 1990—99; pres. Com. to Encourage Corp. Philanthropy, NYC, 1999—2001; pres., CEO Jr. Achievement Internat., 2001—04; pres. Hispanic Scholarship Fund, San Francisco, 2006—. Bd. dirs. Master Card Found., Bond Market Found., Scholarship Am.; trustee Case Western Res. U. Decorated Bronze Star, Legion of Merit (Vietnam); Univ. scholar, 1957-61; Littauer fellow, 1968-69 Mem. Harvard Club, Wexford Plantation Club, Phi Beta Kappa, Omicron Delta Kappa. Episcopalian. Home: 29 Oxford Dr Hilton Head Island SC 29928

OSTERHOLM, MICHAEL T., epidemiologist, public health service officer; Dir. Ctr. Infectious Disease Rsch. & Policy U. Minn., Mpls.; prof. U. Minn. Sch. Pub. Health, Mpls. Author: Living Terrors: What America Needs to Know to Survive the Coming Bioterrorist Catastrophe, 2001; editorial bd. Infection Control & Hosp. Epidemiology, Microbial Drug Resistance; contbr. articles, chapters to books, columns in newspapers, scientific papers. Spl. advisor to sec. HHS, 2001—05, mem. nat. sci. adv. bd. on biosecurity, 2005—; mem. interim mgmt. team CDC, 2002—03; assoc. dir. Nat. Ctr. Food Protection & Def. Dept. Homeland Security; with Minn. Dept. Health, 1975—99, state epidemiologist & chief of acute epidemiology sect., 1984—99. Fellow: Infectious Diseases Soc. America, Am. Coll. Epidemiology; mem.: Am. Soc. Microbiology (mem. pub. & scientific affairs bd., chmn. pub. health com., mem. task force on biological weapons, mem. task force on antibiotic resistance), Coun. State & Territorial Epidemiologists (past pres.), Inst. Medicine. Office: Ctr Infectious Disease Rsch & Policy MMC 263 Mayo 8263 420 Delaware St SE Minneapolis MN 55455 Office Phone: 612-626-6770, 612-625-3908. Office Fax: 612-626-6783. E-mail: mto@umn.edu.

OSTERHOUT, RICHARD CADWALLADER, lawyer; b. Abington, Pa., Nov. 16, 1945; s. Robert Edward and Charlotte Leedom (Cadwallader) O.; m. Diane Renee Higgins, Sept. 15, 1982; children: Steven M., Schuyler C., Cody R. BA in History magna cum laude, Pa. State U., U. Pk., 1967; JD, Temple U., Phila., 1974. Bar: Pa. 1974, U.S. Dist. Ct. (ea. dist.) Pa. 1974, U.S. Ct. Appeals (3d cir.) 1984. Assoc. Wood & Floge, Bensalem, Pa., 1974—77; pvt. practice Trevose, Pa., 1978—85, Feasterville, Pa., 1985—. Solicitor Zoning Hearing Bd., Hulmeville, Pa., 1983—. Contbr. articles to publs. of various hist. socs. Mem. Langhorne Borough Planning Commn. (Pa.), 1974; candidate Rep. Nat. Conv., 1984. With U.S. Army, 1968-70. Mem. Pa. Bar Assn., Bucks County Bar Assn., Feasterville Business Assn. (treas. 1985, 86, v.p. 1987), Phi Beta Kappa. Home: 309 Hemlock Ave Bensalem PA 19020-7331 Office: 1744 Bridgetown Pike Feasterville Trevose PA 19053-2362

OSTERKAMP, DALENE MAY, psychology educator, artist; b. Davenport, Iowa, Dec. 1, 1932; d. James Hiram and Bernice Grace Simmons; m. Donald Edwin Osterkamp, Feb. 11, 1951 (dec. Sept. 1951). BA, San Jose State U., 1959, MA, 1962; PhD, Saybrook Inst., 1989. Lectr. San Jose (Calif.) State U., 1960—65, U. Santa Barbara (Calif.) Ext., 1970-76; prof. Bakersfield (Calif.) Coll., 1961-87, prof. emerita, 1987—; adj. faculty, counselor Calif. State U., Bakersfield, 1990—95. Gallery dir. Bakersfield Coll., 1964-72. Juried group shows include Berkeley (Calif.) Art, Ctr., 1975, Libr. of Congress, 1961, Seattle Art Mus., 1962. Founder Kern Art Edn. Assn., Bakersfield, 1962, Bakersfield Printmakers, 1976. Staff sgt. USAF, 1952-55. Recipient 1st Ann. Svc. to Women award Am. Assn. Women in C.C., 1989. Mem. APA, Assn. for Women in Psychology, Assn. for Humanistic Psychology, Calif. Soc. Printmakers. Home: PO Box 387 Glennville CA 93226-0387 Office: Calif State Univ Stockdale Ave Bakersfield CA 93309

OSTERMANN, CURT, lighting designer, educator; b. Detroit, July 20, 1952; s. G. William and Barbara Ostermann; life ptnr. Ralph W. Hanes, Nov. 19, 1977. BA with honors, U. Mich., Ann Arbor, Mich., 1974; MFA, NYU, NYC, 1977. Cert. lighting designer United Scenic Artists Am., NY, 1976. Freelance lighting designer, NYC, 1977—; lighting dir. The Maury Povich Show, NYC, 1995—. Adj. prof. Tisch Sch. Arts NYU, NYC, 1984—. Lighting designer: (plays) A Streetcar Named Desire; (Operas) X-The Life and Times of Malcolm X; Where the Wild Things Are; From the House of the Dead; lighting designer, scenic designer: (ballets) The Planets. Nominee Emmy award, 1997, 1998. Mem.: United Scenic Artists Am. Democrat. Episcopalian. Avocations: landscape design, gardening, computers. Office: Curt Ostermann Lighting Design 17 W 73rd St 7B New York NY 10023-3008 Home Phone: 518-329-0629; Office Phone: 212-362-3965. Business E-Mail: gco1@nyu.edu.

OSTERTAG, ROBERT LOUIS, lawyer; b. NYC, June 21, 1931; s. Frederick C. and Lillian (Bishop) O.; children: Thomas J., Daniel V., Debra A. BA, Fordham U., 1953; LL.B., St. John's U., Bklyn., 1956; LL.M., Georgetown U., 1960. Bar: NY 1957, US Ct. Mil. Appeals 1959, US Supreme Ct. 1960, US Dist. Ct. (so. dist.) NY 1969, US Tax Ct. 1965, US Dist. Ct. (no. dist.) NY 1988. Atty. office chief counsel IRS, Washington, 1958-60; ptnr. Guernsey, Butts & Walsh, Poughkeepsie, NY, 1963-90, Guernsey, Butts, Ostertag & O'Leary, Poughkeepsie, NY, 1991-95, Ostertag, O'Leary & Barrett, Poughkeepsie, 1995—; adj. prof. paralegal studies Marist Coll., Poughkeepsie, 1975-91; adj. prof. Fordham U. Sch. of Law, NYC, 1993—. Counsel Agr. Com., NY State Assembly, 1967-68; mem. Gov.'s Jud. Screening Com., 1987-93; counsel to cons. and draftsman of proposed county charters and adminstrv. codes for Dutchess, Sullivan, Fulton, Orange and Onondaga Counties, NY, City of Poughkeepsie, NY, City of Beacon, NY; mem. 9th Jud. Dist. Grievance Com., 1975-79, 9th Jud. Dist. Med. Malpractice Panel, 1975-91, mem. 9th Jud. Dist. Arbitration Panel, 1980—90; mem. Chief Judges Com. on Pro Bono Legal Svc., 1992-93. Trustee Joseph F. Barnard Meml. Law Libr., Poughkeepsie, 1979—; dir. Hudson Valley Philharm. Soc., 1973—76; v.p., dir. High Tor Opera Co., 1967—70; dir. United Fund of Dutchess County, 1973—78; dir. Dutchess County chpt. Am. Heart Assn., 1975—81, 1984—89; trustee Sports Mus. Dutchess County, 1989—93, chmn., 1989—90; dir. Hudson Valley Stadium Corp., 1995—, chair, 1998—; cons. Charter Revision Commn., Beacon, 2002—03, Poughkeepsie Charter Rev. Commn., 1994; mem. Dutchess County (N.Y.) Charter Commn., 1966—67, Dutchess County Bd. Health, 1964—70, pres., 1966—70; chmn. Dutchess County Charter Revision Task Force, 1979—88; dep. supr. Town of Poughkeepsie, 1976; bd. dirs. Com. for Modern Cts., 1975—99; dir. Std. Gage Co., 1972—88; mem. adv. coun. Pace U. Sch. Law, 1975—84; paralegal adv. coun. Marist Coll., 1975—. Served to capt. JAGC USAF, 1956—58. Recipient Recognition award Cen. Poughkeepsie Exch. Club, 1967, Marist Coll. Pres.'s award, 1991. Mem.: ABA (chmn. conf. of state bar gen. practice leaders of gen. practice sect. 1980—87, mem. coun. 1982—86, ho. of dels. 1985—2003, Gavel awards com. 1989—, standing com. on solo and small firm practitioners 1992—95, standing com. on profl. discipline 2002—05, ho. of dels. 2006—, Lifetime Achievement award Gen. Practice sect. 2004), Dutchess County Bar Assn. (sec. 1969—79, pres. 1984—85), NY State Bar Assn. (ho. of dels. 1973—79, chmn. unlawful practice of law com. 1977—81, chmn. sect. on gen. practice of law 1980—82, ho. of dels. 1980—, chmn. com. on law office econs. and mgmt. 1982, exec. com. 1983—85, com. profl. ethics 1986—90, exec. com. 1986—93, pres. 1991—92, com. profl. ethics 1996—99, chmn. comm. on future of profession 1998, spl. com. on law governing firm structure and operation 1999—, com. profl. ethics 2000—), NY Bar Found., Am. Bar Found., Hudson Valley Estate Planning Coun. (pres. 1965—66, dir. 1969—74), Delta Theta Phi. Home: 8 High Ridge Rd Poughkeepsie NY 12603 Office: 17 Collegeview Ave Poughkeepsie NY 12603-2406 Office Phone: 845-486-4300. Personal E-mail: r.ostertag@verizon.net.

OSTERYOUNG, JANET GRETCHEN, chemistry professor; b. Pitts., Mar. 1, 1939; d. Arthur Roberts and Elizabeth Jane (Peebles) Jones; m. Bruce Ulrich, Aug. 16, 1967 (div. 1968); m. Robert Allen Osteryoung, Aug. 17, 1969; children: Anne Elizabeth, Adam Armstrong. BA, Swarthmore Coll., 1961; PhD, Calif. Inst. Tech., 1967. Asst. prof. chemistry Mont. State U., Bozeman, 1967-68; fellow Colo. State U., Ft. Collins, 1968-73, asst. prof. civil engring., 1969-73, asst. prof. civil engring., microbiology, 1972-73, assoc. prof., 1973-78, assoc. prof. civil engring., rsch. chemist, 1978-79; assoc. prof. chemistry SUNY, Buffalo, 1979-82, prof., 1982-92, faculty exch. scholar, 1987-92; head dept. chemistry N.C. State U., 1992-94; prof. NSF, 1992—, dir. chemistry divsn., 1994—. Vis. prof. Colo. Coll., 1972, Calif. Inst. Tech., 1985; Guggenheim fellow, vis. prof. U. Southampton (Eng.), 1985-86; cons. Colo. State U., Ft. Collins, 1970-72, EG&G Princeton (N.J.) Applied, 1983—; dir. program chem. analysis NSF, Washington, 1977-78, mem. ad hoc rev. panel 1988. Co-author: Models in Chemical Science, 1971; assoc. editor Electrochemica Acta, 1986—; contbr. over 180 articles to profl. jours.; patentee controlled-growth mercury drop electrode. Hon. Fulbright fellow, 1986; recipient Anachem award Soc. Analytical Chemists of Detroit, 1990, Schoellkopf medalist WNY-Am. Chem. Soc., 1992, ACS award in Electrochemistry-Electrochem. Soc., 1996. Fellow AAAS; mem., Internat. Soc. Electrochemistry (mem. divsn. 3 1985-88), Soc. Electroanalytical Chemistry (founding mem., pres. 1986-87, chmn. 1987-88), Am. Chem. Soc. (Garvan medal 1987, western N.Y. chpt., chmn. exec. com. 1981-89, Disting. Svc. award 1988), Soc. Applied Spectroscopy (Disting. Svc. award Niagara Frontier chpt. 1988), N.Y. Acad. Scis., Electrochem. Soc. (pres. Rocky Mountain sect. 1976-77), Fedn. Am. Scientists, Phi Beta Kappa, Sigma Xi, Iota Sigma Pi (Triennial Hon. mem.). Democrat. Episcopalian. Home: 4201 Wilson Blvd Ste 110 Arlington VA 22203-1859 Office: NC State U Dept of Chemistry PO Box 8204 Raleigh NC 27695-0001

OSTFELD, GREGORY EDWARD, lawyer; b. Houston, July 5, 1973; s. David Martin and Deedee Kessler Ostfeld. BA, George Wash. U., DC, 1991—95; JD, U. Chgo. Law Sch., Ill., 1995—98. Bar: Ill. 1998. Clk. Judge W. Eugene Davis, Lafayette, La., 1998—99; atty. Althimer & Gray, Chgo., 1999—2003, Perkins Coie LLP, Chgo., 2003—05, Greenberg Traurig, LLP, Chgo., 2005—. Pro bono counsel Lambda Legal Def. Fund, Chgo., 2000—06; trustee Congregation Kol Ami, Chgo., 2001—04, pres., 2004—06. Mem.: Chgo. Bar Assn., Lesbian and Gay Bar Assn. of Chgo. Independent. Jewish. Avocations: cooking, flag football. Home: 1201 W Adams St #612 Chicago IL 60607 Office: Greenberg Traurig LLP 77 W Wacker Dr Ste 3000 Chicago IL 60601 Home Phone: 312-666-8180; Office Phone: 312-456-8400. Business E-Mail: ostfeldg@gtlaw.com.

OSTFIELD, ALAN, professional sports team executive; m. Jennifer Ostfield; children: Benjamin, Hannah. B in Econs., U. Pa.; JD magna cum laude, Boston U., MBA. Atty. Wilmer, Cutler & Pickering, Washington; sr. v.p., gen. counsel San Diego Padres Baseball Club; sr. v.p. bus. & legal affairs Palace Sports & Entertainment/Detroit Pistons, 2000—02, COO, asst. gen. mgr., 2002—. Tchr. sport mgmt. masters prog. U. Mich.; tchr. U. San Diego Sch. Law; bd. dirs. Mich. Sports Hall of Fame; bd. advs. Nat. Sports Law Inst. Contbr. articles to profl. publs. Named one of Forty Under 40, St. & Smith SportsBusiness Jour., 2000, 2001, 2002; named to Forty Under 40 Hall of Fame, St. & Smith, 2002. Office: Detroit Pistons 5 Championship Dr Auburn Hills MI 48326 *

OSTLER, CLYDE W., banker; b. 1947; BA, U. Calif. San Diego, 1968; MBA, U. Chgo., 1976. With Touche Ross & Co., San Diego, 1970-71; with Wells Fargo Bank NA, San Francisco, 1971, v.p., 1977-81, sr. v.p., 1981-83, gen. auditor, 1983-85, exec. v.p, 1985-86, CFO, from 1986; with Wells Fargo & Co., San Francisco, 1971—, exec. v.p., CFO, from 1986, vice chmn., now group exec. v.p. internet svcs. Office: Wells Fargo & Co 420 Montgomery St San Francisco CA 94104-1205

OSTLIND, DAN A., retired parasitologist; b. McPherson, Kans., June 19, 1936; s. Harry Dewey and Laura (Bartles) O.; m. Eleanor Ruth Ahlstedt, Oct. 5, 1958; 1 child, Dyanne Dee. MS, Kans. State U., 1962, PhD, 1966. Parasitologist Moorman Mfg. Co., Quincy, Ill., 1966-67; sr. rsch. parasitologist Merck & Co., Rahway, NJ, 1967-69, rsch. fellow, 1969-77, sr. rsch. fellow, 1977-86, sr. investigator, 1986-96. Office Phone: 908-236-9238. E-mail: stanton94@earthlink.net.

OSTLING, PAUL JAMES, corporate financial executive; b. Jamaica, NY, Sept. 22, 1948; s. John Carl and Margaret Ruth (Reilly) O.; m. Jane B. Mahler, June 1, 1974 (div. 1980); m. Julie Eileen Boyum, Feb. 20, 1982 (div. 1988); m. Danita Kay Hoover, May 3, 1991. BS in Math. and Philosophy, Fordham U., 1969, JD, 1973. Bar: NY 1974, US Dist. Ct. (so. and ea. dists.) NY 1974, US Ct. Appeals (2d cir.) 1974, US Ct. Appeals (4th, 5th, 9th, 10th, 11th cirs.) 1978. Assoc. Chadbourne Parke, NYC, 1973-77; asst. gen. counsel Authur Young & Co., NYC, 1977-79, assoc. gen. counsel, 1979-82, ptnr., assoc. gen. counsel, 1982, nat. dir. human resources, 1985-90; vice chmn. human resources Ernst & Young, NYC, 1990-94, assoc. gen. counsel, 1994-95; exec. ptnr. Ernst & Young Internat., NYC, 1995—2003, global COO, 2003—. Office: Ernst & Young 5 Times Sq New York NY 10036

OSTLING, RICHARD NEIL, journalist; b. Endicott, NY, July 14, 1940; s. Acton Eric Sr. and Christine Cathryn (Cumins) O.; m. Joan Elaine Kerns, July 8, 1967; children: Margaret Anne, Elizabeth Anne. BA, U. Mich., 1962; MS in Journalism, Northwestern U., 1963; MA in Religion, George Washington U., 1970; LittD (hon.), Gordon Coll., Mass., 1989. Reporter, copyreader Morning News and Evening Jour., Wilmington, Del., 1963-64; asst. news editor Christianity Today mag., Washington, 1965-67, news editor, 1967-69; staff corr. Time mag., NYC, 1969-74, religion writer, 1975-94, sr. corr., 1994-98; broadcaster Report on Religion, CBS Radio, 1979-98; religion corr. Newshour with Jim Lehrer formerly MacNeil/Lehrer Newshour, 1991-98; religion writer, bible columnist AP, NYC, 1998—2006; freelance, 2006—. Author: Secrecy in the Church, 1974; co-author: Aborting America, 1979, Mormon America, 1999, rev. edit., 2007. Served with USNG, 1964-70. McCormick Found. fellow, 1962-63; recipient Supple, Templeton, Am. Acad. Religion and Wilbur awards for religion writing. Mem. Religion Newswriters Assn. (pres. 1974-76, Lifetime Achievement award 2006), Northwestern U. Alumni Hall of Achievement (charter), Phi Beta Kappa. Mem. Christian Reformed Ch. Home and Office: 280 Hillcrest Rd Ridgewood NJ 07450-2400 Office Phone: 201-445-4795. Personal E-mail: ostlingrn@aol.com.

OSTNER, STEVEN MARK, lawyer; b. Bklyn., June 5, 1952; s. Frederick August and Dorothy (Mittel) O. BA, Amherst Coll., 1974; JD, Yale U., 1978. Bar: NY 1979. Assoc. Debevoise & Plimpton, NYC, 1978-87, ptnr., 1987—. Contbr. Mem. ABA (bus. law sect.), Assn. Bar NYC. Office: Debevoise & Plimpton 919 3rd Ave New York NY 10022-6225 Office Phone: 212-909-6619. Office Fax: 212-909-6836. Business E-Mail: sostner@debevoise.com.

OSTRAGER, BARRY ROBERT, lawyer; b. NYC, July 14, 1947; m. Pamela Goodman, Apr. 8, 1972; children: Anne Elizabeth, Katie, Jane, Betty, Michael. BA, City Coll. of CUNY, 1968, MA, 1973; JD, NYU Sch. Law, 1972. Bar: NY 1973, Calif. 1996, US Dist. Ct. (ea. dist.) NY, 1973, US Dist. Ct. (so. dist.) NY, 1973, US Dist. Ct. Conn., 1978, US Dist. Dist. Tex. 1986, US Dist. Ct. (no. dist.) NY 1993, US Ct. Appeals (2nd cir.) 1974, US Ct. Appeals (7th cir.) 1977, US Dist. Ct. (no. dist.) Calif. 1983, US Ct. Appeals (3rd cir.) 1984, US Ct. Appeals (9th cir.) 1985, US Ct. Appeals (4th cir.) 1989, US Ct. Appeals (6th cir.) 1993, US Supreme Ct. 1982, US Dist. Ct. (ctrl. dist.) Calif. 1997, U.S. Ct. Appeals (D.C. cir.) 1997. Judicial clk. to Hon. Arnold Bauman US Dist. Ct. (So. dist.) NY, 1972—73; sr. litig. ptnr., co-head, litig. dept., mem. exec. com. Simpson Thacher & Bartlett, NYC, 1980—. Lectr. on fed. securities and insurance law. Co-author: Modern Reinsurance Law and Practice, 2nd edit., 2000, Handbook on Insurance Coverage Disputes, 13th edit., 2006; contbr. articles to profl. jours. Named one of Top 10 Litigators, Nat. Law Jour., 2003. Mem. Am. Law Inst., Assn. of Bar of City of NY, ABA. Office: Simpson Thacher & Bartlett 26th Fl 425 Lexington Ave New York NY 10017-3954 Address: Simpson Thacher & Bartlett LLP 1999 Avenue of the Stars 29th Fl Los Angeles CA 90067 Office Phone: 212-455-2655. Office Fax: 212-455-2502. Business E-Mail: bostrager@stblaw.com.

OSTRANDER, ELAINE A., federal agency administrator, geneticist; b. Syracuse, NY; BS, U. Washington, 1981; PhD in Microbiology & Immunology, Oregon Health Sciences U., 1987. With Lawrence Berkeley Nat. Lab., Berkeley, Calif., 1991—93, Fred Hutchinson Cancer Rsch. Ctr., Seattle, 1993—2004; sr. investigator, chief, cancer genetics branch Nat. Human Genome Rsch. Inst., NIH, Bethesda, Md., 2004—, head, comparative genetics sect., 2004—. Affiliate prof., dept. of genome sci., sch. medicine and dept. biology, coll. arts and scis. U. Wash., Seattle; spkr. in field. Co-author more than 100 peer-reviewed publs. Office: Nat Human Genome Rsch Inst NIH Bldg 50 Rm 5351 50 S Dr MSC 8000 Bethesda MD 20892-8000 Office Phone: 301-594-5284. Office Fax: 301-594-0023. E-mail: eostrand@mail.nih.gov. *

OSTRANDER, ROBERT EDWIN, retired United Nations interregional advisor, petroleum company executive; b. Pitts., June 30, 1931; s. Robert Jesse and Elizabeth Raymond (Comstock) O.; m. Margaret Valentina Servello, Dec. 21, 1958; children: Robert Glen, Roseanne. BA, Cornell U., 1953. Cert. petroleum geologist; registered geol. scientist. Area reservoir engr. Mene Grande Oil Co., San Tome, Venezuela, 1956-61; dist. engr. Oasis Oil Co. of Libya, Tripoli, 1962-67; reservoir/petroleum chief engr. Occidental Oil of Libya, Tripoli, 1967-71; divsn. head Iranian Oil Consortium, Ahwaz, Iran, 1972-75; mgr. ops. Ultramar Co. Ltd., Mt. Kisco, NY, 1975-81; v.p. engring. Weeks Petroleum Ltd., Westport, Conn., 1982-85; mng. dir. Reomag Inc., South Salem, NY, 1980—. Cons. World Bank, Washington, 1981—; cons. UN Secretariat, 1994—; advisor to govts. of China, India, others in Asia, Africa, Middle East; lectr. in field. Contbr. articles to profl. jours. Sec. Rep. Com., Town of Lewisboro; chair conservation adv. coun. Town of Lewisboro; pres. Ostrander Family Assn.; mem. Rep. Com. Westchester County; past. bd. dirs. Oakridge Condominium Assn., Vista, NY; fellow Herbert F. Johnson Mus. Art, Cornell U., 1999—. 1st lt. US Army, 1953-55. Mem. Am. Assn. Petroleum Geologists, Soc. Petroleum Engrs., Soc. Mil. Engrs., Holland Soc. NY, Phi Kappa Tau. Address: 5715 State Route 89 Romulus NY 14541-9546 Personal E-mail: reomag@rochester.rr.com. E-mail: reomag@fltg.net.

OSTRANDER, THOMAS WILLIAM, investment banker; b. Detroit, July 20, 1950; s. Roland J. and Sybil (Swartout) O.; m. Kelli Turner, Aug. 28, 2004; children: John Charles, Elizabeth Ann, Brian Thomas, Evan Jacob. BA, U. Mich., 1972; MBA, Harvard Bus. Sch., 1976. CPA., Mich. Staff acct. Ernst & and Whinney, Detroit, 1972-74; sr. acct. Ernst and Whinney, Detroit, 1974, Cleve., 1975; assoc. Kidder, Peabody and Co., NYC, 1976-78, asst. v.p., 1978-80; v.p. Kidder, Peabody and Co., NYC, 1980-86; mng. dir. Kidder, Peabody and Co., NYC, 1986-89, Salomon Bros., Inc., NYC, 1989-97, Salomon Smith Barney, NYC, 1997—2003, Citigroup Global Markets, Inc., NYC, 2003—06, Banc of Am. Securities, NYC, 2006—. Bd. dirs., Westmoreland Coal Co.; mem. adv. bd. Paton Sch. Accountancy U. Mich., 1984-87,; mem. vis. com. Lit., Sci., and Arts Sch., 1988-90, 95- Pres. Ballet Hispanico, 1996- Mem. AICPA, Met. Club, Harvard Club, Hasty Pudding Club, Bond Club, Beaver Dam Winter Sports Club, and Theta Delta Chi Home: 18 Pheasant Run Old Westbury NY 11568 Office: Banc of America Securities 9 W 57th St 24th Fl New York NY 10019

OSTRANDER, WILLIS FREDERICK, retired real estate appraiser; b. Berkeley, Calif., Apr. 23, 1926; s. Willis Frederick and Grace Jackson Ostrander; m. Nancy Majors Ostrander, Jan. 2, 1950; children: Margaret Jaffee, Frederick Adam, Daphne Grace Miller, John Ellery. BA, U Calif., 1948. Cert. MAI, SRA Appraisal Inst., 1994, State Certification Real Estate Appraisal State of Calif., 1996. Sales rep. Signal Oil Co. (Chevron), Alemeda, Calif., 1951—62; exec. v.p. Twin Pines Fed., Berkeley, 1962—84; pres. W.F. Ostrander & Assoc., Inc., Berkeley, 1984—2006; ret., 2006. Dir. East Bay chpt. Soc. Real Estate Appraisers, Calif., 1975—76. Contbr. articles to poetry mag.; author: The Hunchback and the Swan, 1978; editor: Blue Unicorn Mag., 1990—. Sec. Fair Housing and Fair Employment, Berkeley, 1965—. With US Merchant Marines, 1944—45. Mem.: Berkeley Breakfast Club, Appraisal Inst. Democrat. Roman Catholic. Home and Office: 2630 Saklan Indian Dr 3 Walnut Creek CA 94595 Office Phone: 925-930-9524. Personal E-mail: ostrand7@pacbell.net.

OSTREA, ENRIQUE MAPUA, JR., pediatrician, medical educator; b. Manila, Philippines, June 23, 1941; s. Enrique O. Ostrea and Elena Mapua. BS cum laude, U. Philippines, Manila, 1961, MD, 1965. Cert. pediats., neontology Am. Acad. Pediats., 1975. Asst. prof. pediats. Wayne State U., Detroit, 1972—76, assoc. prof. pediats., 1976—87, prof. pediats., 1987—. Dir. Hutzel Hosp., Detroit, 1972—2002, chief pediats., 1972—2002. Contbr. chapters to books. Mem.: Soc. Pediat. Rsch., Am. Pediat. Soc. Office: Hutzel Womens Hosp 3980 Hohn R Detroit MI 48201

OSTRIKER, ALICIA SUSKIN, poet; b. NYC, Nov. 11, 1937; d. David and Beatrice (Linnick) Suskin; m. Jeremiah P. Ostriker, 1958; children: Rebecca, Eve, Gabriel. BA, Brandeis U., 1959; MA, U. Wis., 1961, PhD, 1964. Asst. prof. Rutgers U., New Brunswick, NJ, 1965—68, assoc. prof., 1968—72, prof. English, 1972—2004; mem. faculty MFA program New Eng. Coll. Poetry, Henniker, NH, 2004—. Author: Vision and Verse in William Blake, 1965, Songs, 1969, Once More Out of Darkness, and Other Poems, 1974, A Dream of Springtime, 1979, The Mother/Child Papers, 1980, A Woman Under the Surface: Poems and Prose Poems, 1982, Writing Like a Woman, 1983, The Imaginary Lover, 1986 (William Carlos Williams prize Poetry Soc. Am. 1986), Stealing the Language: The Emergence of Women's Poetry in America, 1986, Green Age, 1989, Feminist Revision and the Bible, 1993, The Nakedness of the Fathers: Biblical Vision and Revisions, 1994, The Crack in Everything, 1996 (Nat. Book award finalist 1996, Paterson Poetry prize 1996, San Francisco State Poetry Ctr. award 1997), The Little Space: Selected and New Poems, 1998 (Nat. Book award finalist 1998), Dancing at the Devil's Party: Essays on Poetry, Politics, and the Erotic, 2000, The Volcano Sequence, 2002, No Heaven, 2005; editor: William Blake: Complete Poems, 1977. Nat. Coun. on Humanities grantee, 1968; NEA fellow, 1976-77, N.J. Arts Coun. fellow, 1982, Guggenheim Found. fellow, 1984-85, faculty fellow Rutgers

Ctr. for Hist. Analysis, 1995-96, Rockefeller Found. fellow, 1982; recipient Strousse Poetry prize Prairie Schooner, 1986, Edward Stanley award Prairie Schooner, 1994, Anna David Rosenberg Poetry award, 1994, Best American Poetry award, 1996, Paterson prize, 1997, San Francisco State Poetry Ctr. award, 1997, Pushcart prize, 1999, Larry Levis prize 2001. E-mail: ostriker@rci.rutgers.edu.

OSTRIKER, JEREMIAH PAUL, astrophysicist, educator; b. NYC, Apr. 13, 1937; s. Martin and Jeanne (Sumpf) Ostriker; m. Alicia Suskin, Dec. 1, 1958; children: Rebecca, Eve; 1 child, Gabriel. AB, Harvard U., 1959; PhD, U. Chgo., 1964, degree (hon.), 1992; postgrad., U. Cambridge, Eng., 1964—65. Rsch. assoc., lectr. astrophysics Princeton U., Princeton, 1965—66, asst. prof., 1966—68, assoc. prof., 1968—71, prof., 1971—, chmn. dept. astronomy, dir. obs., 1979—95, Charles A. Young prof. astronomy, 1982—2002, provost, 1995—2001; Plumian prof. astronomy and exptl. philosophy U. Cambridge, England, 2001—04; dir. Princeton Inst. Computational Sci. and Engring., 2005—. Author: Development of Large-Scale Structure in the Universe, 1991; editl. bd., trustee Princeton U. Press; contbr. articles to profl. jours. Recipient Vainu Bappu Meml. award, Indian Nat. Sci. Acad., 1993, Karl Schwarzschild medal, Astronomische Gesellschaft, 1999, U.S. Nat. medal of Sci., 2000; fellow Alfred P. Sloan, 1970—72; NSF fellow, U. Chgo., 1960—64. Fellow: AAAS; mem.: NAS (counselor 1992—95, bd. govs. 1993—95), Royal Soc. UK (fgn.), Royal Netherlands Acad. Arts and Scis. (fgn.), Am. Acad. Arts and Scis., Am. Philos. Soc., Internat. Astron. Union, Am. Astron. Soc. (councilor 1978—80, Warner prize 1972, Russel prize 1980), Royal Astron. Soc. (assoc. Gold medal 2004), Am. Mus. Natural History (trustee 1997—2006, hon. trustee 2007—). Home: 33 Philip Dr Princeton NJ 08540-5409 Office Phone: 609-258-4267. Business E-Mail: ostriker@princeton.edu. *

OSTROFF, DAWN T., broadcast executive; b. Miami, Mar. 31, 1960; m. Mark Ostroff; children: Lane, Michael, Justin, Jonathan. BS, Fla. Internat. U. V.p. devel. Kushner-Locke Co., 1984—89; pres. Michael Jacobs Prodns.; sr. v.p. creative affairs 20th Century Fox; sr. v.p. programming & prodn. Lifetime TV, 1996—99, exec. v.p. entertainment, 1999—2002; pres. entertainment UPN, 2002—05, pres., 2005—06; pres. entertainment The CW, 2006—. Named one of Top 100 in the Cable Industry, Cablefax mag., 2001, Wonder Women of Cable, Ny ch. Women in Cable & Telecommunication/Cablevision mag., 2001, Most Powerful Women in TV, TV Week, 2002, 12 to Watch, 2003, 100 Most Powerful Women in Entertainment, Hollywood Reporter, 2002—06, 2006; recipient Star award, Am. Women in Radio & TV, 1999. Office: The CW 3300 W Olive Ave Burbank CA 91505 Office Phone: 818-977-2500. *

OSTROFF, PETER I., lawyer; b. Washington, Dec. 15, 1942; BA, Washington U., 1964; JD, U. Chgo., 1967. Bar: Ill. 1967, Calif. 1970. Teaching fellow in law Monash U., Melbourne, Australia, 1968—69; law clk. to Hon. Shirley M. Hufstedler US Ct. Appeals (9th cir.), 1969-70; ptnr. comml. trial and litig. practice Sidley Austin Brown & Wood LLP, LA, mem. exec. com. Named one of Best Lawyers in Am. for Bus. Litig., supplement to Am. Lawyer mag., 2003, LA's pit bull lawyers, LA mag. Mem. ABA (dir. divsn. substantive law 1982-83, chmn. comml. transations litigation com. 1976-80, coun. mem. 1980-83, chmn. computer litigation com. 1985—, dir. programs divsn. 1990—), State Bar Calif. (mem. exec. com. intellectual property sect. 1988-89, litig. sect. 1990—), LA County Bar Assn. (bd. trustees 1974-76, chair human rights sect. 1975-76, mem. ethics com. 1982-84), Assn. Bus. Trial Lawyers (pres. 1988-89, mem. exec. com. litig. sect. 1990—). Office: Sidley Austin Brown & Wood LLP Fl 40 555 W 5th St Los Angeles CA 90013-1010 Office Phone: 213-896-6612. Office Fax: 213-896-6600. Business E-Mail: postroff@sidley.com.

OSTROM, DON, political science professor; b. Chgo., Mar. 9, 1939; s. Irving and Margaret (Hedberg) O.; m. Florence Horan, Jan. 13, 1972; children: Erik, Rebecca, Katherine. BA, St. Olaf Coll., Northfield, Minn., 1960; MA, Washington U., 1970, PhD, 1972. Prof. polit. sci. Gustavus Adolphus Coll., St. Peter, Minn., 1972—2004; state rep. Minn. Ho. of Reps., St. Paul, 1988-96; vis. prof. polit. sci. St. Olaf Coll., Northfield, 2004—. Co-editor: Perspectives on Minnesota Government and Politics, 1998. Democrat. Home: 2737 Ewing Ave S Minneapolis MN 55416 E-mail: dostrom@gac.edu.

OSTROM, ELINOR, political science professor, researcher; b. LA, Aug. 7, 1933; d. Adrian and Leah (Hopkins) Awan; m. Charles Scott, Aug. 8, 1954 (div. 1961); m. Vincent Ostrom, Nov. 23, 1963. AB with honors, UCLA, 1954, MA, 1962, PhD, 1965; D in Econs. (hon.), U. Zurich, 1999; D (hon.), Inst. Social Studies, The Hague, 2002, Luleå U. Tech., Sweden, 2005, Uppsala U., 2007, Humboldt U., Berlin, 2007; DHL (hon.), U. Mich., Ann Arbor, 2006. Vis. asst. prof. dept. gov. Ind. U., Bloomington, 1965-66, asst. prof., grad. advisor, dept. gov., 1966-69, assoc. prof. dept. polit. sci., 1969-74, prof. polit. sci., 1974-91, Arthur F. Bentley prof. polit. sci., 1991—, prof., chmn. dept. polit. sci., 1980—84, acting chair dept. polit. sci., 1989—90, co-dir. workshop in polit. theory and policy analysis, 1973—, co-dir. Ctr. Study Instns., Population and Environ. Change, 1996—2006, prof. part-time Sch. Pub. and Environ. Affairs; founding dir. Ctr. for Study Instl. Diversity, Ariz. State U., 2007—. Employment interviewer, asst. employee relations mgr., Godfrey L. Cabot, Inc., Boston, 1955-57; personnel analyst III, U. Calif., LA, 1957-61; bd. cons., Internat. Assn. Chiefs Police: Police Discipline Project, 1974-75; adv. bd. Nat. Evaluation Program Law Enforcement Assistance (Adminstrn.), Washington, 1975-76; mem. Nat. Adv. Panel, Nat. Acad. Pub, Adminstrn.; Neighborhood-Oriented Metropolitan Gov., 1975-76, task force on criminal justice rsch. and devel. Nat. Adv. Com. on Criminal Justice Standards and Goals, 1975-76, Nat. Sheriffs Assn.: Study of Contract Law Enforcement, 1975-76; adv. panel Div. Policy Rsch. and Analysis, NSF, Washington, 1977-78, panel on Instl. Develop., 1985; rev. panel Polit. Sci. div. NSF, 1983-84; Interuniversity Consortium for Polit. and Social Rsch. Coun., 1983-85; adv. com. nat. urban policy NAS/NRC, 1985-88, panel on Common Property Resources Mgmt., 1985-86, Scientific Com. on Problems of the Environ., 1995-98; rsch. adv. com. U.S. AID, 1989-91; local gov. rsch. adv. bd., US Adv. Commn. on Intergovernmental Rels., 1985-88; adv. bd., Inst. for Policy Reform, 1993-96; bd. dirs., Beijer Internat. Inst. Ecol. Econs., Royal Swedish Acad. Scis., 1997-; academic adv. bd., Max-Planck-Inst. für Gesellschaftsforschung, 2000-; cons. in field. Co-author: Policing Metropolitan America, 1978, Local Government in the United States, 1988, Institutional Incentives and Sustainable Development: Infrastructure Policies in Perspective, 1993, Rules, Games, and Common-Pool Resources, 1994, The Samaritan's Dilemma, 2005, Seeing the Forest and the Trees, 2005; author: Governing the Commons, 1990, Crafting Institutions for Self-Governing Irrigation Systems, 1992, Understanding Institutional Diversity, 2005; editor: Strategies of Political Inquiry, 1982; co-editor: The Commons in the New Millennium: Challenges and Adaptations, 2003, Trust and Reciprocity: Interdisciplinary Lessons from Experimental Research, 2003, Jour. Theoretical Politics, 1987-95, People and Forests: Communities, Institutions, and Governance, 2000, Protecting the Commons: A Framework for Resource Management in the Americas, 2001, Foundations of Social Capital, 2003; mem. editl. bd. Am. Jour. Polit. Sci., Am. Polit. Sci. Review, Criminal Justice Review, Pub. Productivity Review, Publius, Quarterly Jour. Adminstrn., Sage Urban Affairs Ann. Review, Social Sci. Quarterly, Urban Affairs Quarterly, Ecol. Economics; contbr. articles to profl. jours. Grantee NSF, 1974-85, 87—, NIMH, 1977-81, U.S. Dept. Justice, 1978-82, AID, 1984-94, U.S. Geol. Survey, 1987-89, Ford Found., 1991—, FAO, 1992—, MacArthur Found., 1996-; recipient Frank E. Seidman Disting. award in Polit. Economy, 1997, Johan Skytte prize in Polit. Sci., Upsala University, 1999, Aaron Wildavsky Enduring Contbn. award for Governing the Commons, APSA, Pub. Policy Sect., 2000, John J. Carty award for the Advancement Sci., NAS, 2004, Sustainability Sci. award Ecol. Soc. Am., 2005, James Madison award Am. Polit. Sci. Assn., 2005, Cozzarelli prize Proceeding Nat. Acad. Scis., NAS, 2006. Fellow AAAS, Am. Acad. Arts and Scis. (lifetime achievement award Atlas Econ. Rsch. Found. 2003); mem. NAS, Am. Philos. Soc., Assn. for Politics and the Life Scis., Pub. Choice Soc. (pres. 1982-84, co-chair Duncan Black award com. 1986-87, chair Duncan Black award com. 1990, exec. coun. 1982-), Am. Polit. Sci. Assn. (v.p. 1975-76, pres.-elect 1995-96, pres. 1996-97, chmn. several coms. 1978-88, mem. several coms. 1970-2002), Midwest Polit. Sci. Assn. (pres. 1984-85), Internat. Polit. Sci. Assn., Am. Econ. Assn., Internat. Assn. for Study Common Property (pres. 1990-91, program co-chair 2000), Policy Studies Orgn., (nominating com. 1986-87, Miriam Mills award 1996, Thomas R. Dye Svc. award 1997). Democrat. Home: 5883 E Lampkins Ridge Rd Bloomington IN 47401-9726 Office: Ind Univ Workshop in Polit Theory & Policy Analys 513 N Park Ave Bloomington IN 47408-3895 Home Phone: 812-332-9821; Office Phone: 812-855-0441. Office Fax: 812-855-3150. Business E-Mail: ostrom@indiana.edu.

OSTROM, KATHERINE (KATE) ELMA, retired secondary school educator; b. LA, Dec. 30, 1928; d. Charles W. and Mabel M. (Christensen) Shults; m. Carl R. Ostrom, Jan. 29, 1949 (dec.); children: Margaret K. Larson, Carl R. Jr. BA cum laude, U. Wash., 1966, MA in Tchg. English, 1973, EdD, 1994. Std. tchg. cert. grades K-12, Wash.; continuing prin. cert.-secondary, Wash. Substitute tchr. Renton, Kent and South Ctrl. Sch. Dist., 1966; tchr. Foster HS, Tukwila, Wash., 1966-67, 75-76, Showalter Mid.Sch., Tukwila, 1967-79; dept. chair Showalter Mid. Sch., Tukwila, 1968-87, vice prin., 1979-87; tchr., supr. student tchr. U. Wash., Seattle, 1989-91; substitute tchr. Tukwila Sch. Dist., 1999—2005. Tchr. Western Wash. State Coll., Bellingham, 1967-68; liaison, supr. Jr. Achievement, Seattle, 1988-89; cons., trainer Nat. Assn. Elem. Sch. Prins., 1992-98; vol. tchr. Immigrant and Refugee Resources Ctr., Seattle, 1996-2003; dir. Forum on Edn., PDK, Seattle, 1997; mem. Citizen Adv. Com. in Curriculum, Renton, S.D., 2001-06, chair, 2002-03. Host del., mem. Tukwila-Ikawa (Japan) Sister Cities, 1980—88, 1997—, chair, 1999—2002; block-watch organizer King County, Wash., 1994—2001; key communicator Renton (Wash.) Sch. Dist., 1996—2003; mem. Friends of Skyway Libr., King County Libr. Sys., 2006—; emeritus bd. dirs. Friends Alexander Hamilton; tutor Skyway Meth. Ch., Seattle, 1997—2000, staff parish com., 1996—2003. Named Vol. of Yr., BPW, Tukwila, Wash., 1990; Coll. scholar U. Puget Sound, Tacoma, Wash., 1946; PBK Pathfinder award, 1997; honored City of Ikawa, 1999, honored by Mayor Ikawa, Japan, 2000, 2005. Mem.: Wash. Physicians Social Responsibility (del. to Mid. East 1994), Assn. Wash. Sch. Prin. (chair state vice prin. conf. 1986, regional dir. 1986—88), Puget Sound Theatre Organ Soc., Key Players Prosser Piano and Organ, Phi Beta Kappa (bd. trustees Puget Sound Assn. 2000—, pres. Puget Sound Assn. 2003—), Phi Delta Kappa (editor newsletter 1988—90, pres. chpt. 1991—95, area coord. 1995—2001, editor newsletter 1995—2003). Democrat. Home: 12817 80th Ave S Seattle WA 98178-4911 E-mail: kateostrom@aol.com.

OSTROM, VINCENT A(LFRED), political science professor; b. Nooksack, Wash., Sept. 25, 1919; s. Alfred and Alma (Knudson) Ostrom; m. Isabell Bender, May 20, 1942 (div. 1963); m. Elinor Awan, Nov. 23, 1963. BA in Polit. Sci., UCLA, 1942, MA in Polit. Sci., 1945, PhD in Polit. Sci., 1950. Tchr. Chaffey Union H.S., Ontario, Calif., 1943-45; asst. prof. polit. sci. U. Wyo., Laramie, 1945-48, U. Oreg., Eugene, 1949-54, assoc. prof. polit. sci., 1954-58, UCLA, 1958-64; prof. polit. sci. Ind. U., Bloomington, 1964-90, Arthur F. Bentley prof emeritus polit. sci., 1990—. Hooker disting. vis. scholar McMaster U., 1984-85; rsch. assoc. Bur. Mcpl. Rsch., 1950, Resources for Future, Inc., 1962-64; assoc. dir. Pacific NW Coop. Program in Ednl. Adminstrn., 1951-58; founding dir. Workshop in Polit. Theory and Policy Analysis, Ind. U., Bloomington, 1973—; cons. and lectr. in field. Author: Water and Politics, 1953, The Political Theory of a Compound Republic, 1971, 2nd rev. edit., 1987, The Intellectual Crisis in American Public Administration, 1974, 2nd edit., 1989, The Meaning of American Federalism, 1991, The Meaning of Democracy and the Vulnerability of Democracies, 1997; co-author: Understanding Urban Government, 1973, Local Government in the United States, 1988; co-editor: Comparing Urban Service Delivery Systems, 1977, Guidance, Control and Evaluation in the Public Sector, 1986, Rethinking Institutional Analysis and Development, 1988, 2d. edit. 1993; mem. bd. editors Publius, 1972—; mem. editl. bd. Constnl. Polit. Economy, 1989—, Nigerian Jour. Fin. and Human Resources Mgmt., 1996—, Internat. Jour. Orgn. Theory and Behavior, 1997—; contbr. articles to profl. jours. Program coord. Wyo. Assessors' Sch., 1946-48, Budget Officer's Sch., 1947-48; exec. sec. Wyo. League of Municipalities, 1947-48; cons. Wyo. Legis. Interim Com., 1947-48, Nat. Resources, Alaska Constitutional Convention, 1955-56, Tenn. Water Policy Commn., 1956; mem. founding bd. Com. on Polit. Economy of the Good Soc., 1990—. Grantee and fellowships Social Sci. Rsch. Coun., 1954-55, Ctr. Advanced Study in Behavioral Scis., 1955-56, Ctr. Interdisciplinary Rsch., 1981-82; co-recipient (with Elinor Ostrom) Lifetime Achievement award Atlas Economic Rsch. Found. Fund, 2003, Robert O. Anderson Sustainable Arctic award Inst. of the North 2003. Mem. AAAS, Am. Polit. Sci. Assn. (Spl. Achievement award for Significant Contbns. to Study of Federalism, 1991, Best Book on Federalism and Intergovtl. Rels. award 1999, John Gaus Disting. lecturer award 2005), Am. Econ. Assn., Am. Soc. Pub. Adminstrn., Pub. Choice Soc., Internat. Polit. Sci. Assn. Home: 5883 E Lampkins Ridge Rd Bloomington IN 47401-9726 Office: Ind U Workshop in Polit Theory 513 N Park Ave Bloomington IN 47408-3895 Home Phone: 812-332-9821; Office Phone: 812-855-0441. Business E-Mail: ghiggins@indiana.edu, workshop@indiana.edu.

OSTROVSKY, LAWRENCE ZELIG, lawyer; b. Cleve., June 1, 1956; s. Peter and Yetta Ostrovsky. BA, St. John's Coll., Annapolis, Md., 1978; JD, Lewis and Clark Coll., 1982. Bar: Ohio 1982, Alaska 1983. Assoc. Berger & Kirschenbaum, Cleve., 1982, Birch, Horton, Bittner, Pestinger & Anderson, Anchorage, 1983—87; spl. asst. to the commr. of natural resources Alaska Dept. Natural Resources, Anchorage, 1987—91; assoc. dir. for energy and public lands Alaska Gov. Office, Washington, 1991—94; asst. atty. gen. oil, gas, and mining sect., Alaska Dept. Law, Anchorage, 1994—. Mem. Commonwealth North, Anchorage, 1986, Alaska Bar Assn.(bd. of governors, 1998—, pres. elect, 2003, pres. 2004). Office: Alaska Dept Law 1031 W 4th Ave Ste 200 Anchorage AK 99501-1994 Business E-Mail: larry_ostrovsky@law.state.ak.us.

OSTROVSKY, LEV ARONOVICH, physicist, oceanographer, educator; b. Vologda, USSR, Dec. 10, 1934; s. Aaron L. Ostrovsky and Lidiya A. Khvilivitskaya; children: Svetlana, Alexander. Cert. rsch. physicist in radiophysics, U. Gorky, USSR, 1957; PhD, U. Gorky, 1964; Dr Sci, Acoust. Inst., Moscow, 1973. Lead engr. Design Bureau, Gorky, 1957-59; asst. prof., then assoc. prof. physics Poly. Inst., Gorky, 1962-65; sr. rschr. Radiophys. Rsch. Inst., Gorky, 1965-77; chief scientist and head lab. Inst. Applied Physics Russian Acad. Sci., Nizhni Novgorod (formerly Gorky), 1977—94; assoc. prof to prof. U. Nizhni Novgorod, 1966-94; prof. sr. rsch. scientist U. Colo., NOAA Environ. Tech. Lab., Boulder, 1994—2001; Orson Andersen fellow Inst. Geophys. and Planet. Physics Los Alamos Nat. Lab., 1998-99; sr. scientist Zel Tech., NOAA Earth Sci. Rsch. Lab., 2001—. Co-author: Nonlinear Wave Processes in Acoustics, 1990, English edit., 1998, Modulated Waves, 1999, Introduction to the Theory of Modulated Waves, 2003; author or co-author 3 lectr. notes; editor 4 book translations from English to Russian, 3 paper collection books, a topical dictionary; mem. editl. and adv. bds. including Chaos; contbr. sci. papers; patentee in field. Recipient State Prize of USSR, 1985, USSR State Discovery Cert., 1982. Fellow Acoustical Soc. Am.; mem. Acoustical Soc. Russia, European Geophys. Union, Am. Geophys. Union. Office: Zel Tech NOAA Earth Sys Rsch Lab Phys Sci Divsn 325 Broadway Boulder CO 80305

OSTROW, JAY DONALD, gastroenterology educator, researcher; b. NYC, Jan. 1, 1930; s. Herman and Anne Sylvia (Epstein) O.; m. Judith Fargo, Sept. 9, 1956; children: George Herman, Bruce Donald, Margaret Anne. BS in Chemistry, Yale U., 1950; MD, Harvard U., 1954; M.Sc. in Biochemistry, Univ. Coll., London, 1970. Diplomate Am. Bd. Internal Medicine, Am. Bd. Gastroenterology. Intern Johns Hopkins Hosp., Balt., 1954—55; resident Peter Bent Brigham Hosp., Boston, 1957—58; NIH trainee in gastroenterology, 1958—59; NIH trainee in liver disease Thorndike Meml. Lab. Boston City Hosp., 1959—62; instr. in medicine Harvard U., Boston, 1959—62; asst. prof. medicine Case-Western Res. U., Cleve., 1962—70; assoc. prof. U. Pa., Phila., 1970—76, prof., 1977—78; Sprague prof. medicine Northwestern U., Chgo., 1978—89, prof. medicine, 1989—95, prof. emeritus, 1995—, chief gastroenterology sect., 1978—87; vis. prof. gastroenterology and hepatology dept. Acad. Med. Ctr., U. Amsterdam, Netherlands, 1995—98; affiliated prof. medicine GI/Hepatology divsn. U. Wash., Seattle, 1999—. Med. investigator VA Hosp., Phila., 1973-78, VA Med. Ctr. Lakeside, Chgo., 1990-95. Editor, contbg. author: Bile Pigments and Jaundice, 1986. Asst. scoutmaster Valley Forge coun. Boy Scouts Am., Merion, Pa., 1972-78, asst. scoutmaster N.E. Ill. coun., 1978-81; vestryman St. Matthew's Episcopal Ch., Evanston, Ill., 1979-82, Christ Episcopal Ch., Seattle, 2004-07; treas. Classical Children's Chorale, Evanston, 1982; mem. Sacred Music Chorale, Seattle, 1999-, bd. dirs., sec. and editor, 2002-05, mng. dir., 2005—. Advanced from lt. j.g. to lt. comdr. med. corps. USN, 1955—57, with USNR, 1957—63. Recipient Gastroenterology Rsch. award Beaumont Soc., El Paso, 1979, Sr. Disting. Scientist award Alexander von Humboldt Found., Germany, 1989-90; NIH fellow, 1958-62, grantee, 1962-92; VA grantee, 1970-95. Mem. Am. Assn. Study Liver Diseases (councillor 1983-85, v.p. 1985-86, pres. 1987), Am. Gastroent. Assn. (chmn. exhibit com. 1969-72, mem. undergrad. tchg. project 1972-88), Am. Soc. Clin. Investigation, Am. Physiol. Soc. (asst. editor 1979-84), Internat. Assn. Study Liver, Seattle Audubon Soc. (co-chair membership com. 1999-2004). Avocations: birdwatching, singing. Office: GI/Hepatology Divsn HSB AA 103-F Box 356424 Univ Wash Sch Medicine 1959 NE Pacific St Seattle WA 98195-6424 Office Phone: 206-221-6147. Business E-Mail: jdostrow@medicine.washington.edu.

OSTROW, MICHAEL JAY, lawyer; b. Baldwin, NY, Apr. 25, 1934; s. Oscar I. and Ethel M. (Morganstern) O.; m. Judith L. Loewenthal, Aug. 25, 1957; children: Thomas L., Kenneth A., Nancy M. BA, Alfred U., 1955; JD, Cornell U., 1958. Bar: N.Y. 1958, U.S. Supreme Ct. 1964, U.S. Dist. Ct. (so. and ea. dists.) N.Y. 1970; diplomate Am. Coll. Family Trial Lawyers. Ptnr. Taylor & Ostrow, Mineola, N.Y., 1961-69, Taylor Atkins & Ostrow, Garden City, N.Y., 1969-96, Ostrow and Taub, Garden City, 1996-2000. Bd. dirs., lectr Advanced Practice Inst. Hofstra Law Sch., Hempstead; lectr. Practicing Law Inst., N.Y.C. Mem. ABA, Acad. Matrimonial Lawyers (pres. N.Y. chpt. 1980-81, sec. nat. acad. 1988-90, nat. v.p. 1990-94, pres.-elect 1995-96, pres. 1996-97), Internat. Acad. Matrimonial Lawyers (bd. govs. 1990-92), Am. Coll. Family Trial Lawyers (diplomate), N.Y. State Bar Assn. (chmn. family law sect. 1976-78, mem. exec. com.), Nassau County Bar Assn. (pres. 1984-85, chmn. judiciary com. 1992-93), Order of Coif, Zeta Beta Tau, Phi Delta Phi. Home: 712 Balfour Pl Melville NY 11747 Office: Schlissel Ostrow Karabatos & Poepplein PLLC 200 Garden City Plz Suite 301 Garden City NY 11530 Home Phone: 631-367-7373; Office Phone: 516-877-1800. Personal E-mail: mjodix@aol.com. Business E-Mail: mostrow@soklaw.com.

OSTROW, STUART, theatrical producer, educator, author; b. NYC; m. Ann Elizabeth Gilbert; children: Julie Elizabeth, Katherine Ann, John Stuart. Disting. univ. prof. theater U. Houston. Pres. Stuart Ostrow Found., Inc., Mus. Theater Lab.; founding mem. opera-mus. theatre panel NEA; mem. bd. overseers com. to visit Loeb Drama Ctr. Harvard U. Prodr.: We Take the Town, 1961, The Apple Tree, 1966, 1776, 1969, Scratch, 1971, Pippin, 1972, The Moony Shapiro Songbook, 1981, American Passion, 1983, M. Butterfly, 1988, La Bête, 1991, Face Value, 1993; prodr., dir.: Here's Love, 1963, Swing, 1980; author, producer: Stages, 1978; assoc. dir.; Chicago, 1975; author: A Producer's Broadway Journey, 1999, Thank You Very Much, 2002, Present At the Creation, Leaping in the Dark and Going Against the Grain, 2005 Mem. Pulitzer Prize Drama Jury; chmn. bd. trustees Inst. for Advanced Study in Musical Theatre. With USAF, 1952—55.

OSTROWSKI, STACEY, athletic trainer, educator; b. Detroit, Dec. 2, 1973; d. Harry and Betty Ostrowski. AAS, Henry Ford C.C., Dearborn, Mich., 1995; BSc in Sports Medicine/Athletic Tng., Ea. Mich. U., Ypsilanti, 1998; M in Kinesiology/Biomechanics, U. Tenn., Knoxville, 2000. Grad. asst. athletic trainer U. Tenn., Knoxville, 1998—2000; asst. athletic trainer/lectr. Lander U., Greenwood, SC, 2000—02; cert. athletic trainer No. Mich. Sports Medicine Ctr., Petoskey, Mich., 2002—. Guest lectr. anatomy and physiology U. Tenn., 1999—2001; guest spkr. sports medicine No. Mich. Sports Medicine, 2002—. Author: (case studies, articles) Jour. Athletic Tng., Am. Coll. Sports Medicine. Mem. Am. Red Cross, 1998—; lectr. cmty. edn. on knee injuries Bay St. Orthop., Cheboygan, Mich., 2003; lectr. cmty. soccer injury prevention Mich. Dept. Cmty. Health, Indian River, 2004; facilitator phys. therapy/sports medicine involvement Spl. Riders Program, Cheboygan, 2004—; lectr. H.S./cmty. on sports medicine and athletic tng., 2005—. Recipient academic excellence citation, Ea. Mich. U., 1997, Dr. Youman Academic scholarship, Knoxville, 2000. Mem.: Mich. Athletic Trainers Soc., Nat. Athletic Trainers Assn. Catholic. Avocations: hiking, bicycling, kayaking, ice hockey. Office: No Mich Sports Medicine 11153 N Straits Hwy Cheboygan MI 49721 Personal E-mail: michiganatc@aol.com.

OSTRUM, ROBERT F., orthopaedic surgeon; b. Phila., Pa., 1955; MD, Temple U., 1980. Cert. Orthopaedic Surgery. Resident, gen. surgery Albert Einstein Med. Ctr., Phila., 1980—81, resident, orthopaedics, 1981—85; fellow, trauma AONA/ Assn. for the Study of Internal Fixation, 1985; assoc. dir. orthopaedic trauma, dir. trauma rsch. Ohio State Univ., Columbus, asst. prof. orthopedic surgery; dir., orthopaedic trauma Cooper Bone & Joint Inst., Camden; assoc. prof. Cooper Univ. Hosp., Camden, NJ. Lectr. in field. Contbr. articles to profl. jours. Named Top Doctor, Columbus Mag. Mem.: Orthopaedic Trauma Assn., Am. Acad. Orthopaedic Surgery, Am. Bd. Orthopaedic Surgery. Office: Three Cooper Plz Ste 403 Sells AZ 85634 Address: 401 S Kings Hwy Ste 3A Cherry Hill NJ 08034 Office Phone: 856-342-3159. *

OSTRY, SYLVIA, academic administrator, economist; b. Winnipeg, Man., Can. d. Morris J. and B. (Stoller) Knelman; m. Bernard Ostry; children: Adam, Jonathan. BA in Econs., McGill U., 1948, MA, 1950; PhD in Econs., Cambridge U. and McGill U., 1954; also 19 hon. degrees. Lectr., asst. prof. econs. McGill U.; rsch. officer Inst. Stats., U. Oxford, Eng.; assoc. prof. U. Montreal, Can.; with dept. stats. Econ. Coun. Can., Ottawa, 1964-72, chmn., 1978-79; chief statistician Stats. Can., Ottawa, 1972-75; dep. minister consumer and corp. affairs Govt. Can., Ottawa, 1975-78, dep. minister internat. trade, coordinator internat. econ. relations, 1984-85, ambassador for multilateral trade negotiations, personal rep. of Prime Minister for Econ. Summit, 1985-88; chancellor U. Waterloo, 1991-96; head dept. econs. and stats. OECD, Paris, 1979-83; chmn. Ctr. for Internat. Studies U. Toronto, Ont., Can., 1990-97, disting. rsch. fellow Munk Ctr. for Internat. Studies, 1997—. Lectr. Per Jacobssen Found., 1987; chmn. nat. coun. Can. Inst. Internat. Affairs, 1990-95; western co-chmn. Blue Ribbon Commn. for Hungary's Econ. Recovery, 1990-94; mem. adv. bd. Inst.

Internat. Econs., Washington; founding mem. Pacific Coun. on Internat. Policy; Volvo Disting. vis. fellow Coun. on Fgn. Rels., N.Y.C., 1989. Author: Governments and Corporations in a Shrinking World: The Search for Stability, 1990, The Threat of Managed Trade to Transforming Economies, 1993; co-author: (with Richard Nelson) Technonationalism and Technoglobalism: Conflict and Cooperation, 1995; co-editor: (with Karen Knop, Richard Simeon, Katherine Swinton) Rethinking Federalism: Citizens, Markets and Governments in a Changing World, 1995; New Dimensions of Market Access, 1995, (with Gilbert R. Winham) The Halifax G-7 Summit: Issues on the Table, 1995, Who's on First: The Post-Cold War Trading System, 1997, APEC and Regime Creation in the Asia-Pacific: The OECD Model?, 1998, Technology, Productivity and Multinational Enterprise, 1998, Intellectual Property Protection in the World Trade Organization: Major Issues in the Millennium Round, 1999, Globalization Implications for Industrial Relations, 1999, The Future of the World Trading System, 1999, Convergence and Sovereignty: Policy Scope for Compromise?, 2000, Regional Versus Multilateral Trade Strategies, 2000, Making Sense of it All: A Post Mortem on the Meaning of Seattle, 2000; The Uruguay Round North-South Grand Bargain: Implications for Future Negotiations, 2000, Regional Dominos and the WTO: Building Blocks or Boomerang?, 2000, Business, Trade and the Environment, 2000, The Changing Scenario in International Governance, 2000, Looking Back to Look Forward: The Multilateral Trading System after 50 Years, 2000, The WTO: Post Seattle and Chinese Accession, 2001, The WTO and International Governance, 2001, Dominos and the WTO: Building Blocks or Boomerang?, 2000, Business, Trade and the Environment, 2000, The Changing Scenario in International Governance, 2000, Looking Back to Look Forward: The Multilateral Trading System after 50 Years, 2000, The WTO: Post Seattle and Chinese Accession, 2001, The WTO and International Governance, 2001, Global Integration: Currents and Counter Currents, 2003, What are the Necessary Ingredients for the World Trading Order?, 2003, External Transparency in Trade Policy, 2004, The World Trading System: In the Fog of Uncertainty, 2004, Summitry and Trade: What Could Sea Island Do for Doha?, 2004, External Transparency: The Policy Process at the National Level of the Two-level game, 2004; contbg. author: China and the Long March to Global Trade, 2003, Between Feast and Famine: Fixing Global Trade, 2004, The Future of the World Trading System: Beyond Doha, 2004, Global Integration: Currents and Counter-Currents, 2005, A Global Perspective on the Multilateral System, 2006, What Are the Necessary Ingredients for the World Trading Order?, 2006, The World Trade System: In A Fog of Uncertainity, 2006, others; contbr. articles on empirical and policy-analytic subjects to more than 90 profl. publs. Decorated companion Order of Can., 1990; recipient Outstanding Achievement award Govt. of Can., 1987, Hon. Assoc. award Conf. Bd. of Can., 1992; Disting. vis. fellow Volvo, 1989-90. Fellow Royal Soc. Can., mem. Group of Thirty, Inst. for Internat. Econs. (adv. bd.). Avocations: films, theater, contemporary reading. Office: Munk Ctr Internat Studies U Toronto 1 Devonshire Pl Toronto ON Canada M5S 3K7 Home Phone: 416-924-5005; Office Phone: 416-946-8927. Business E-Mail: sylvia.ostry@utoronto.ca.

OSTWALD, DAVID F., theater director, educator; b. San Francisco, Calif., Jan. 20, 1943; s. Hans John and Rosemarie Ostwald; m. Jane Mills; 1 child, Cialin Diedra Mills-Ostwald; m. Ora Ann Lerman, May 21, 1994 (dec. Apr. 1998); m. Birgitte Moyer-Vinding, Nov. 9, 2002. BA, Reed Coll., Portland, Oreg., 1965; MFA, Carnegie Mellon U., Pitts., 1969, PhD, 1973. Stage dir. Western Opera Theater, San Francisco, 1971—76; faculty The Juillard Sch. Music, NYC, 1977—80; vis. faculty U. Calif., Berkeley, Calif., 1981; head opera program SUNY, Purchase, 1983—94, faculty, 1994—99. Freelance stage dir. Author: Acting for Singers, 2005. Bd. sec. Xoregos Performing Co., San Francisco, 1980—; trustee Ora Lerman Charitable Trust, NYC, 1999—; chmn. bd. Bay Area Summer Opera Theater Inst., San Francisco, 2002—. Grantee, Nat. Opera Inst., 1974. Avocations: travel, hiking. Home: 473 West St #1013A New York NY 10014-2040

OSTWALD, MARTIN, retired classicist; b. Dortmund, Germany, Jan. 15, 1922; arrived in U.S., 1946, naturalized, 1956; s. Max and Hedwig (Strauss) Ostwald; m. Lore Ursula Weinberg, Dec. 27, 1948; children: Mark F., David H. BA, U. Toronto, 1946; AM, U. Chgo., 1948; PhD, Columbia U., 1952; D (hon.), Fribourg U., Switzerland, 1995, Dortmund U., Germany, 2001. Instr. classics and humanities Wesleyan U., Middletown, Conn., 1950-51; from lectr. to asst. prof. Greek and Latin Columbia U., 1951-58; mem. faculty Swarthmore Coll., 1958—, prof. classics, 1966-92, prof. emeritus, 1992—; prof. classical studies U. Pa., 1968-92, prof. emeritus, 1992—. Vis. assoc. prof. Princeton (N.J.) U., 1964, mem. Inst. Advanced Study, 1974—75, 1981—82, 1990—91; vis. prof. U. Calif., Berkeley, 1969, Tel-Aviv U., 1996—; vis. fellow Balliol Coll. Oxford (Eng.) U., 1970—71, vis. fellow Wolfson Coll., 1987, 91; dir. fellowships-in-residence classics NEH, 1976—77; dir. d'etudes EHESS, Paris, 1991; mem. Inst. Advanced Studies, Tel Aviv, 1994, 2003. Translator: Nicomachean Ethics (Aristotle), 1962; author: (book) Nomos and the Beginnings of the Athenian Democracy, 1969, Autonomia, Its Genesis and Early History, 1982, From Popular Sovereignty to the Sovereignty of Law, 1987, Anake in Thucydides, 1988, Oligarchia, 2000; author: (with T. G. Rosenmeyer and J. W. Halporn) The Meters of Greek and Latin Poetry, 2d edit., 1980; mem. editl. bd. Cambridge Ancient History, 1976—94; contbr. articles to profl. jours. Fellow, Am. Coun. Learned Socs., 1965—66, NEH, 1970—71, 1990—91; Fulbright Rsch. fellow, Greece, 1961—62, Guggenheim fellow, 1977—78, Lang. fellow, Swarthmore Coll., 1986—87. Fellow: AAAS; mem.: Soc. Ancient Philosophy, Classical Assn. Atlantic States, Classical Assn. Can., Am. Philol. Assn. (pres. 1986—87), Am. Philos. Soc., Soc. Promotion Hellenic Studies (hon.). Home: 408 Walnut Ln Swarthmore PA 19081-1137 Business E-Mail: mostwal1@swarthmore.edu.

OSTWALD, VENICE ELOISE VARNER, librarian, educator, minister, writer; b. Denver, July 19, 1928; d. Earl Robert and Madeline (Shoemaker) Varner; m. Leonard F. Ostwald (div.). BA, U. Colo.-Boulder, 1946; MS, U. So. Calif., 1954. Librarian, tchr. Long Beach Pub. Schs., Calif., 1954-61; asst. prof. U. Oreg., Eugene, 1961-63; dir. libr. and audio-visual Hillsborough Pub. Schs., Calif., 1963-65; adminstrv. asst. to libr. dir. San Jose State U., 1965-67; instrn. specialist/librarian DeAnza Coll., Cupertino, Calif., 1967-87, emeritus, 1987—. Founder, bd. dirs. Singles in Service, Santa Clara, Calif., 1972; co-founder Casa Serena Hospice, San Jose, 1981; pres. Spiritual Edn. Endeavors Publ. Co., 1985-; chmn. bd. SHARE Found., 1985—. Co-author 9 books under pseudonym Virginia Essene; lyricist songs include Part of Me, Oasis, Peru, Caliente, Hyano Cucarumba, Esclava. Mem. Beta Phi Mu, Kappa Delta. Office: SHARE Found 1556 Halford Ave # 288 Santa Clara CA 95051-2661 Home Phone: 408-248-8244; Office Phone: 408-248-8244. Business E-Mail: lovecorps@sharefoundationnetwork.com.

OSUCH, DEBRA K., materials engineer; b. 1969; married; 3 children. BS in Med. Physics, Oakland U.; MS in Hazardous Waste Mgmt., Wayne State U. Mgr., Devel. Services Soil and Materials Engineers Inc., Shelby Twp. Named one of 40 Under 40, Crain's Detroit Bus., 2006. Mem.: Comml. Real Estate Women (pres., Detroit Chpt.). Office: Soil and Materials Engineers Inc 13019 Pauline Dr Shelby Township MI 48315 Office Phone: 586-731-3100. Office Fax: 586-731-3582.

O'SULLIVAN, CINDY MARIE, mathematics professor; b. Blue Island, Ill., Dec. 22, 1956; d. Donald Edward and Frances Gloria Crawford; children: Michael, Ryan, Shannon. BS, No. Ill. U., 1979; M in Math. Edn., Olgethorpe U., Ga., 2000; M in Leadership, Kennesaw U., Ga., 2004. Cert. gifted edn. High sch. math tchr. Bremen High Sch., Midlothian, Ill., 1979—80, Elida High Sch., Ohio, 1980—81; substitute tchr. Grandville Sch. Dist., Mich., 1981; math tutor Huntington Learning Ctr., Mpls., 1987—88; substitute tchr. South Forsyth High Sch., Cumming, Ga., 1995—96; math tchr. South Forsyth Mid. Sch., 1996—99, Vickery Creed Mid. Sch., 1999—. State trainer Ga. Dept. Edn., Atlanta, 2004—05; math dept. chair Vickery Creek Mid. Sch., Cumming, 2000—; math curriculum trainer Forsyth County Schs., 2000—; featured participant Statewide Ednl. Video by Ga. Dept. Edn., Nat. Video by Phil Schlechty Group. Participant, money raiser Relay for Life, Cumming, 2003—05. Recipient Disney Am. Tchr. award, 2001, Honor Tchr., Atlanta Jour. Constitution, 2002, Tchr. of Year, Forsyth County Middle Sch., 2003. Mem.: Ga. Assn. Ednl. Leaders, Assn. Supervision and Curriculum Devel., Nat. Coun. Tchrs. Math. Avocations: reading, travel, exercise, fundraising, embroidery. Home: 4819 S Victor Ave Tulsa OK 74105

O'SULLIVAN, EUGENE HENRY, retired advertising executive, management consultant; b. Plainfield, NJ, June 8, 1942; s. Patrick J. and Helen (Callahan) O'S.; m. Tracy O'Sullivan; children: Meredith Heather, Charlie Hiromichi. BBA, U. Notre Dame, 1964. Media buyer Foote Cone Belding, NYC, 1967-68; account exec., mgmt. supr. Group Dtr, NYC; exec. v.p., dir. client svcs. Young & Rubicam, NYC, 1968-84; sr. v.p., group dir. Ogilvy & Mather, NYC, 1984-86, 87; exec. v.p. Hill, Holliday, Boston, 1986-87; exec. v.p., gen. mgr. McCann Erickson, NYC, 1988-90; ret., 1990. Served to lt. (j.g.) USN, 1964-66. Mem. Lotos Club. Democrat. Home: 21 E 10th St New York NY 10003-5923 Office Phone: 212-614-9570. E-mail: eugeneo@earthlink.net.

O'SULLIVAN, JUDITH ROBERTA, lawyer, writer, artist; b. Pitts., Jan. 6, 1942; d. Robert Howard and Mary Olive (O'Donnell) Gallick; m. James Paul O'Sullivan, Feb. 1, 1964; children: Kathryn, James. BA, Carlow Coll., 1963; MA, U. Md., 1969, PhD, 1976; JD, Georgetown U., 1996. Editor Am. Film Inst., Washington, 1974—77; assoc. program coord. Smithsonian Resident Assocs., Washington, 1977—78; dir. instl. devel. Nat. Archives, Washington, 1978—79; exec. dir. Md. State Humanities Coun., Balt., 1979—81, 1982—84, Ctr. for the Book, Libr. of Congress, Washington, 1981—82; dep. asst. dir. Nat. Mus. Am. Art, Washington, 1984—87, acting asst. dir., 1987—89; pres., CEO The Mus. at Stony Brook, NY, 1989—92; exec. dir. Nat. Assn. Women Judges, Washington, 1993; clk. Office Legal Adviser US Dept. State, Washington, 1994—96; trial atty. Atty. Gen.'s honors program US Dept. Justice, 1996—, sr. trial atty. Criminal divsn., Domestic Security sect., 2002—; spl. asst. US atty. US Dist. (ea. dist.) Va., 1998—2002; asst. US atty. US Dist. Ariz., Tucson, 1999—2000. Summer assoc. Piper & Marbury, Balt., 1995; chair Smithsonian Women's Coun., Washington, 1988-89. Author: The Art of the Comic Strip, 1971 (Gen. Excellence award Printing Industry Am.); Workers and Allies, 1975; (with Alan Fern) The Complete Prints of Leonard Baskin, 1984, The Great American Comic Strip, 1991; editor Am. Film Inst. Catalogue: Feature Films, 1961-70, 1974-77; mem. editl. bd. Am. Film Inst. Catalog, 1979-1990. Trustee Child Life Ctr., U. Md., College Pk., 1971-74; chair Smithsonian Women's Coun., 1988-89. Univ. fellow, U. Md., 1967—70, Mus. fellow, 1970—71, Smithsonian fellow, Nat. Collection Fine Arts, Washington, 1972—73. Mem.: Mystery Writers of Am. (exec. bd. Mid-Atlantic br. 2003—), D.C. Bar Assn., Md. Bar Assn. Avocations: landscape painting, mystery writing.

O'SULLIVAN, LYNDA TROUTMAN, lawyer; b. Oil City, Pa., Aug. 30, 1952; d. Perry John and Vivian Dorothy (Schreffler) Troutman; m. P. Kevin O'Sullivan, Dec. 15, 1979; children: John Perry, Michael Patrick. BA, Am. U., 1974; JD, Georgetown U., 1978, postgrad., 1982-83. Bar: D.C. 1978. Ptnr. Perkins Coie, Washington, 1985-92, Fried, Frank, Harris, Shriver & Jacobson, Washington, 1993-97, Miller & Chevalier, Washington, 1997—2004; asst. dep. gen. counsel dispute resolution USAF, 2004—. Mem. adv. bd. Fed. Contracts Report, 1991-97, Govt. Contract Costs, Pricing & Acctg. Report, 1997-99; mem. faculty govt. contracts program George Washington U., 1993-99; lectr. in field. Contbg. author: Cost Reimbursement Contracting, 3d edit., 2005. Fellow Am. Bar Found.; mem. ABA (chair truth in negotiations com. 1991-94, chair acctg., cost and pricing com. 1996-2000, coun. sect. pub. contract law 1993-95). Office: 1777 N Kent St Arlington VA 22209 Business E-Mail: lynda.osullivan@pentagon.af.mil.

O'SULLIVAN, MEGHAN L., former federal official; b. Sept. 13, 1969; BA in Economics & Govt., Georgetown U., 1991; MA, PhD, Oxford U. Fgn. policy rsch. asst. to Sen. Daniel Patrick Moynihan US Senate; fellow, rsch. assoc. fgn. policy Brookings Inst., 2001; asst. to dir. policy planning Richard N. Haass US Dept. State, 2001—03; adv. to adminstr. Coalition Provisional Authority, Baghdad, Iraq, 2003—04; sr. dir. for strategic planning & SW Asia Nat. Security Coun., Washington, 2004—05, dep. nat. security adv. for Iraq & Afghanistan, 2005—07; spl. asst. to pres. The White House, 2005—07. Co-editor (with Richard N. Haass): Honey and Vinegar; author: Shrewd Sanctions: Statecraft and State Sponsors of Terrorism, 2003. *

O'SULLIVAN, PATRICIA ANN, principal, writer; b. Boston, Apr. 8, 1952; d. Robert Charles and Irene Emily Ritchie; m. Paul Francis O'Sullivan, Jr., June 16, 1974; 1 child, Paul Francis O'Sullivan, III. AS in Early Childhood Edn., Lasell Coll., 1972; BS in Behavioral and Social Scis., U. Md., 1992; postgrad., Bridgewater State Coll., 1994—95; MEd, Framingham State U., 1997. Cert. profl. educator Fla. Dept. Edn., 2001, tchr. Mass. Dept. Edn., 1995, ednl. leadership U. Ctrl. Fla., 2004. Instrnl. asst. Hayfield Elem. Sch., Alexandria, Va., 1988—91; resource tchr. Am. Sch. Bolivia, La Paz, 1992—94; elem. tchr. Internat. Am. Sch. Guatemala, Guatemala City, 1995—99, Sculptor Charter Sch., Titusville, Fla., 1999—2002, asst. prin., 2002—06, prin., 2006—. Internat. Sch. Guatemala rep. Basic Sch., Harrisonburg, Va., 1997—99; mentor tchr. Brevard County Sch. Bd., Viera, Fla., 2000—; Sculptor Sch. rep. Core Knowledge Found., Charlottesville, Va., 2002—; elem. rep. to dirs. adv. coun. Internat. Am. Sch. Guatemala, Guatemala City. Advisor Sculptor Charter Sch. Student Coun., Titusville; adminstrv. team rep. and program director's designee Brevard Innovative Charter Sch., Titusville, 2002. Named Tchr. of Yr., Brevard Innovative Charter, 2000. Mem.: ASCD, Fla. Consortium Charter Schs., Fla. Assn. Sch. Administrs., Nat. Assn. Elem. and Mid. Sch. Administrs., Kapp Delta Pi. Avocations: reading, travel, walking, gardening. Office: Sculptor Charter School 1301 Armstrong Dr Titusville FL 32780 Home Phone: 321-757-8939. Office Fax: 321-264-9995. Personal E-mail: posullivan1@cfl.rr.com. Business E-Mail: o'sullivanp@brevard.k12.fl.us.

O'SULLIVAN, PAUL KEVIN, business executive, management and instructional systems consultant; b. Syracuse, N.Y., May 10, 1938; s. John Hugh and Helen Troy (Smith) O'S.; m. Lynda Troutman; children: Mary Kathleen and Karin Jennifer (twins), John Perry, Michael Patrick. A.B., Dartmouth Coll., 1960. Comm. specialist Gen. Electric Co., Schenectady, N.Y., 1963-66; nat. inst. dir. Gen. Learning Corp., Washington, 1966-67; sr. con. ednl. sys. Aries Corp., McLean, Va., 1967-69; dir. profl. devel. Nat. Audio-Visual Assn., Fairfax, Va., 1969-74; exec. dir. Am. Soc. Tng. and Devel., Madison, Wis., 1974-80; sr. v.p. Sterling Inst., Washington, 1980-87, nat. account mgr. Orgnl. Dynamics, Inc., 1987-94; account exec. Zenger Miller, 1995-96, pres. The O'Sullivan Group, Inc., 1996—; staff dir. Nat. Audio-Visual Inst. for Effective Comm. Ind. U., 1969-74; chief adminstr. Internat. Fedn. Tng. and Devel. Orgns., 1974-80; dir. Internat. Symposia for Tng. Comm. in Switzerland, Australia and Middle East. Producer and dir. films and multi-media presentations; author, editor comm. and tng. courses, textbooks; contbr. articles to profl. jours.; spkr. various profl events. Served to lt. (j.g.), USNR, 1956-63. Recipient Honor medal for Lit. Freedoms Found., 1963; Writers Gold Cup award Gen. Electric, 1966; Resolution for Outstanding Achievement Nat. Audio-Visual Assn., 1974, Pres.'s award for bus. achievement, 1989, 90, 91, 92, 93. Mem. Nat. Soc. for Performance and Instrn. (Presdl. citation 1977), Am. Soc. Assn. Execs. (Grand award for mgmt. achievement 1978), Am. Soc. Tng. and Devel. (hon. life, Spencer Logan Lifetime Outstanding Contbns. award 2007).

O'SULLIVAN, STEPHANIE L., federal agency administrator; With Office of Naval Intelligence, CIA, 1995—, assoc. dep. dir. sci. & tech., 2003—05, dep. dir. sci. & tech., 2005—. Office: Directorate of Science & Technology CIA Office Dir of National Intelligence Washington DC 20505

O'SULLIVAN, TERENCE M., labor union administrator; b. San Francisco; HS tchr.; mem. local 1353 Laborers Internat. Union of No. Am., Charleston, W.Va., 1974—, adminstr. W.Va. Laborers' Tng. Ctr., asst. to gen. pres., mid-atlantic regional mgr., v.p., gen. pres., 2000—; chmn., CEO Union Labor Life Insurance Co., 2003—. V.p. exec. coun. AFL-CIO, v.p. metal trades dept., v.p. bldg. and constrn. trades; chair pension fund of ctrl. and eastern Can. Laborers Internat. Union of No. Am., chair nat. (indsl.) pension fund, chair local union-dist. coun. pension fund, chair staff pension fund, chair death benefit fund, chair polit. league. Office: The Laborers' Union 905 16th St NW Washington DC 20006 Office Phone: 202-737-8320. *

O'SULLIVAN, THOMAS J., lawyer; b. New Haven, Apr. 7, 1940; s. Thomas J. and Marjorie (Hession) O'S.; m. Anita Brady, Aug. 10, 1968; children: Kathleen, Margaret, Mary Tess, Anne Elizabeth. BA in History, Yale U., 1961; LLB, Harvard U., 1966. Bar: Conn. 1966, U.S. Dist. Ct. Conn. 1967, N.Y. 1967, U.S. Dist. Ct. (so. and ea. dists.) N.Y. 1967, U.S. Ct. Appeals (2d cir.) 1971, U.S. Supreme Ct. 1971, U.S. Dist. Ct. (no. dist.) N.Y. 1976, U.S. Ct. Appeals (11th cir.). 2004. Assoc. White & Case, NYC, 1966-74, ptnr., 1974—. 1st lt. U.S. Army, 1961-63. Mem. ABA, N.Y. State Bar Assn., Assn. of Bar of City of N.Y., Internat. Bar Assn. Clubs: Milbrook (Greenwich, Conn.); Yale (N.Y.C.). Home: 56 Hillside Rd Greenwich CT 06830-4835 Office: White & Case Bldg Ll 1155 Avenue of The Americas New York NY 10036-2787

OSVATH, LUDOVIC LAJOS, minister; b. Lupoaia, Romania, July 22, 1938; arrived in US, 1980; s. Lajos and Anna (Feher) O.; m. Jolan Pacso, May 4, 1963; 1 child, Judith. Grad., Inst. Tech., Romania, 1954, Inst. Bus., 1957, Ady Endre Coll., 1978; student, Heritage Bapt. Inst., Cleve., 1986. Ordained to ministry Bapt.Ch., 1955. Preacher Bapt. Ch., Romania, 1955—, mem. coms. Egrespatak, Romania, 1955-65, treas., mem. com. Zalau, Romania, 1965-73; pres. Hungarian Missionary Soc. Inc., Cleve., 1989—. Del. Romanian Bapt. Congress, Bucharest, Romania, 1978; maintenance exec. Sponge, Inc., Cleve., 1985—. Underground rep. Amnesty Internat., Romania, 1977-80; founding mem. Defenders of Religious Freedom and Ideas, Romania, 1978, persecuted and excluded from the country; mem. Internat. Christian Solidarity, Zurich, Switzerland. Mem. Christian Mgmt. Assn., Bocskai Cultural Soc. (sec. 1988—). Office Phone: 440-234-4329.

OSWALD, JAMES MARLIN, education educator, researcher; b. Plainview, Tex., Aug. 17, 1935; s. James Buchanan and Eula Bea (Marlin) O.; m. Dorothy Anne Veigel, Dec. 27, 1956; children: Richard, Ramona, Roberta. BS, West Tex. State Coll., 1957, MA, 1958; EdD, Stanford U., 1970. Tchr., supr. Salt Lake City Pub. Schs., 1958-66; curriculum specialist Am. Insts. Rsch., 1966-68; staff assoc. Nat. Coun. Social Studies, 1968-69; asst. prof. social studies and social sci. edn. Syracuse U., NY, 1969-72; rschr.writer, dir. global cultural studies edn. projects Am. Univs. Field Staff, 1972-75; asst. supt. instrn. East Penn Sch. Dist., Emmaus, Pa., 1975-78; field coord. Pa., Del. and N.J. citizen edn. Rsch. for Better Schs., Phila., 1978-80; instrnl. devel. specialist Cmty. Coll. Phila., 1980-96; energy conservation cons., 1959—. Propr. Energy Cons. and Main Line Stoves, 1972—, Fin. and Retirement Planning Cons., 1980—, Macro/Micro Agro, 1992—, DudeSpa, 2002—; pres. N.Y. State Coun. Social Studies, 1971-72; co-founder, pres. Inst. Plant Based Nutrition, 1996—; nutrition educator, 1997—; career mentor, life coach, 2002—; phys. fitness trainer, martial arts self def. coach, and model, 2002—; cons. in field. Author: The Monroe Doctrine: Does It Survive?, 1969; Research in Social Studies and Social Science Education, 1972; co-author: Earthship, 1974, Planet Earth, 1976, Our Home, the Earth, 1980, Marco Polo Vegan Cuisine, 1998, Christopher Columbus Vegan Cuisine, 1999, Criteria for Nutritional Guidelines for Century 21, 1999, Ferdinand Magellan Vegan Cuisine, 2000, Commemoration of Heroic Produce Grower Sacrifices, Death and Survival on September 11, 2001, 2001, Garden of Eden Vegan Cuisine, 2003, Astronaut Vegan Cuisine, 2003, New York City Vegan Cuisine, 2003, Philadelphia Vegan Cuisine, 2003; introduced concepts of the snaggle-toothed curriculum, 1959, global cultural studies, 1972, humanself, 1972, zero runoff landscaping, 1959, veganomics, 1998, veganocracy, 1998, veganagro, 1998, microagro, 2003, Plant Kingdom Gourmet, 2003, Green Gourmet, 2006; editor quar. newsletter Plant Based Nutrition, 1997—; contbr. articles to profl. jours. With U.S. Army, 1957-58, USAR, 1958-68. Recipient Sertoma Svc. to Mankind award, Salt Lake City, 1966; grantee Stanford U., NSF, U.S. Office Edn., Inst. Internat. Studies; Henry Newell fellow Stanford U., 1966-68; Fulbright-Hays SEAsia U. Singapore Study Program fellow, 1967. Mem. Am. Vegan Soc. (life), Internat. Oak Soc., Vegan Organic Network Horticulture-Agr. (U.K.), Hastings-Halliburton Vegetarian Assn. (Can.), Inst. Nutrition Edn. and Rsch. (bd. advisor), Inst. Plant Based Nutrition, N.Am. Vegetarian Soc. (life), Toronto Vegetarian Assn., Main Line Vegan Soc. (founding pres.), Ctr. for Cancer Edn., Hindu Temple Soc. Am., Internat. Soc. Kirsna Consciousness, Food for Life Internat., Social Sci. Edn. Consortium (emeritus), Tex. Panhandle-Plains Hist. Soc. (life), Utah Hist. Soc. (life), Desc. Founders of Ancient Windsor (life), Windsor Hist. Soc. (life), Internat. Oak Soc., Pa. Forestry Assn., Pa. Vegetable Growers Assn., Pa. Nut Growers Assn., Pa. Assn. Sustainable Agr., Vegetable Growers Assn. N.J., Stanford Club Phila., Keystone Trails Assn., Phi Delta Kappa (emeritus). Avocation: gardening. Home and Office: 333 Bryn Mawr Ave Bala Cynwyd PA 19004-2606 Office Phone: 610-667-6876.

OSWALD, RUDOLPH A., economist; b. Milw., Aug. 4, 1932; s. Carl J. and Anne O.; m. Mary Louise Hurney BA, Holy Cross Coll., 1954; postgrad. (Fulbright scholar), U. Munich, W. Ger., 1954-55; MS, U. Wis., Madison, 1958; PhD in Econs., Georgetown U., 1965. Research and edn. dir. Internat. Assn. Fire Fighters, Washington, 1959-63; economist research dept. AFL-CIO, Washington, 1963-72, asst. dir. edn. dept., 1975-76, dir. research dept., 1976-96, economist-in-residence George Meany Ctr for Labor Studies, 1996—. Vis. prof. Cornell U., 1997, 99, 2000; rsch. dir. Svc. Employees Internat. Union, Washington, 1972-75, instr. GM-UAW Paid Ednl. Leave program, 2001-02; adj. prof. econs. George Washington U., 1966-75; mem. Fed. Employees Pay Coun., 1970-72, Sec. Navy's Adv. Bd. Edn. and Tng., 1975-78, Nat. Commn. Employment and Unemployment Stats., Fgn. Investment Adv. Com.; mem. adv. coun. Indsl. Labor Rels. Sch., Cornell U., 1981-85, 95-99, Sch. Bus. U. S.C. 1992-98; mem. consumer adv. com. SEC, 1994-98mem. labor rsch. adv. coun. Bur. Labor Stats.; mem. Pres.'s Adv. Com. on Trade, 1984-98; mem adv. com. Ex-Im Bank, 1989-92; cons. Alliance for Ret. Ams., 2004-05. Bd. dirs. Nat. Industries for the Blind, 1965-71, Montgomery County United Way, 2006. With US Army, 1956-57. Mem. Indsl. Rels. Rsch. Assn. (past pres.), Nat. Bur. Econ. Rsch. (dir.), Nat. Policy Assn. (dir. 1988-2003), Nat. Coun. on Econ. Edn. (dir. 1976-96). Home: 11804 Devilwood Dr Rockville MD 20854-3407 Office: George Meany Labor Studies Ctr 10000 New Hampshire Ave Silver Spring MD 20903-1706 Personal E-mail: rudyo6@aol.com.

OSWALT, ROY E., professional baseball player; b. Kosciusko, Miss., Aug. 29, 1977; m. Nichol Oswalt. Baseball player Houston Astros, 2001—. Named Rookie of Yr., Baseball Writers Assn. Am. (BBWAA) Houston chpt., Nat. League Championship Series MVP, MLB, 2005; named to TOPPS All-Rookie team, Nat. League All-Star Team, MLB, 2005; recipient Sporting News NL Rookie Pitcher of Yr. honors. Achievements include led Nat. League in wins (20), 2004. Office: Houston Astros Po Box 288 Houston TX 77001-0288

OTAL, MONICA D., music educator; d. Frank N and Amapola Otal. MusB, Oberlin Coll. Conservatory of Music, 1975; MusM, Johns Hopkins U., 1977. Music faculty Duke Ellington Sch. of the Arts, Washington, 1977—93; dir. of music Glenmont United Meth. Ch., Silver Spring, Md., 1988—; lectr. in music Morgan State U., Balt., 1993—99; assoc. prof. of music C.C. of Balt. County, Balt., 1999—; artistic dir. Ctrl. Md. Chorale, Laurel, Md., 2001—. Singer washington opera chorus, baltimore opera chorus. Artistic dir. Ctrl. Md. Chorale, Laurel, Md., 2001. Named Outstanding CC Educator of Yr., Essex, Md., 2006; ECISL grantee, C.C. of Balt. County, 2001. Mem.: Coll. Music Soc. (campus rep. 2001), Nat. Assn. of Teachers of Singing, Am. Choral Directors Assn. (chairperson repertoire and stds. com. for 2-yr. colls. 2000). Office: C C Balt County 7201 Rossville Blvd Baltimore MD 21237 Home Phone: 410-243-8643; Office Phone: 410-780-6726. Personal E-mail: divacoach1@comcast.com. E-mail: motal@ccbcmd.edu.

OTELLINI, PAUL S., electronics company executive; b. San Francisco, Oct. 12, 1950; s. David Otellini; m. Sandy Otellini; 2 children. BA in Econs., U. San Francisco, 1972; MBA, U. Calif., Berkeley, 1974. Joined Intel Corp., Santa Clara, Calif., 1974, managed Intel's bus. with IBM Corp., 1980—85, gen. mgr. peripheral components ops., 1985—87, gen. mgr., Folsom Microcomputer Divsn., 1987—89, v.p. operating group, 1988, asst. to pres. (Andrew S. Grove), 1989, gen. mgr., microprocessor products group, 1990, corp. officer, 1991, exec. v.p., sales and mktg., 1992—98, sr. v.p., 1993—96, exec. v.p., 1996—2002, exec. v.p., gen. mgr., architecture group, 1998—2002, pres., COO, 2002—05, pres., CEO, 2005—. Bd. dirs. Intel Corp., 2002—. Named one of 50 Who Matter Now, CNNMoney.com Bus. 2.0, 2006. Office: Intel Corp 2200 Mission College Blvd Santa Clara CA 95052-8119 Office Phone: 408-765-8080. Office Fax: 408-765-9904. *

OTHERSEN, HENRY BIEMANN, JR., surgeon, physician, educator; b. Charleston, SC, Aug. 26, 1930; s. Henry and Lydia Albertine (Smith) Othersen; m. Janelle Lester, Apr. 4, 1959; children: Megan, Mandy, Margaret, Henry Biemann III. BS, Coll. Charleston, 1950; MD, Med. Coll. S.C., 1953. Diplomate Am. Bd. Surgery, Am. Bd. Thoracic Surgery, Am. Bd. Pediatric Surgery. Intern Phila. Gen. Hosp., 1953-54; postgrad. U. Pa., 1956-57; resident in gen. surgery Med. Coll. S.C., Charleston, 1957-62; resident in pediatric surgery Ohio State U. and Columbus Children's Hosp., 1962-64; research fellow Harvard U., Mass. Gen. Hosp., Boston, 1964-65; from asst. prof. to assoc. prof. pediatric surgery Med. U. S.C., Charleston, 1962—72, prof., 1972—, chief pediatric surgery, 1972-98; med. dir. Med. U. S.C. Hosp., 1981-85, Children's Hosp., 1985—2001, med. dir. profl. staff, 1996—2001, physician liaison documentation, 2002—03; acting chief surgery VA Hosp., 2002—04. Editor: The Pediatric Airway; mem. editl. bd. Jour. Pediatric Surgery, Jour. Parenteral and Enteral Nutrition; contbr. articles to profl. jours. Bd. Children's Hosp. Fund; bd. dirs., pres. S.C. divsn. Am. Cancer Soc., 1977—79; bd. dir. SC Safe Kids. With USN, 1954—56, Korea. Fellow: ACS, Am. Acad. Pediat. (chair); mem.: Charleston County Med. Soc. (pres. 1981—83), Am. Trauma Soc., SC Surg. Assn. (pres. 1991—92), Am. Surg. Assn., Brit. Assn. Pediatric Surgeons (overseas coun. 1995—99), Am. Pediatric Surg. Assn. (pres. 1998—99), Alpha Omega Alpha (councilor 1978—93). Republican. Lutheran. Achievements include first academic pediat. surgeon in SC; first to Established divsn. pediat. surgery and children's hosp. Med. U. SC. Avocation: water sports. Office: Pediatric Surgery PO Box 250613 96 Jonathan Lucas St Ste 418 CSB Charleston SC 29425 Home Phone: 843-722-5939; Office Phone: 843-792-3853. Business E-Mail: othershb@musc.edu. *A man ought to do what he thinks is right.*

OTHMER, DAVID ARTMAN, television and radio consultant; b. West Medford, Mass., Mar. 18, 1941; s. Murray Eade and Mary (Artman) O.; m. Nancy Trumbull, Sept. 12, 1965 (div. Dec. 1982); 1 child, Rachel; m. Maureen Barden, June 4, 1983; 1 child, Matthew. BA, Harvard Coll., 1963; MBA, Harvard U., 1966. Asst. to pres. Sta. WNET, NYC, 1974-75, dir. broadcasting, 1975-82, dir. telecommunications, 1982-83; v.p., sta. mgr. Sta. WHYY, Phila., 1983-2000; cons., 2000—. Exec. producer (TV show) Science Spots, 1985 (Ohio State award 1985); producer (TV show) Who is Red Grooms?, 1986 (Emmy 1986). Recipient Emmy awards, 1980—2000. Avocation: growing grapes and making wine. Home and Office: 4220 Spruce St Philadelphia PA 19104-4040 E-mail: davidothmer@aol.com.

OTIS, CLARENCE, JR., restaurant executive; BA magna cum laude, Williams Coll., 1977; JD, Stanford Univ., 1980. Atty., NY; investment banker First Boston, Kidder Peabody; mng. dir., co-head Mcpl. Securities group Chem. Securities; v.p., treas. Darden Restaurants Inc., Orlando, Fla., 1995-97, sr. v.p. investor rels., treas., 1997-98, sr. v.p. fin., 1998-99, sr. v.p., CFO, 1999—2002, exec. v.p., CFO, 2002, exec. v.p., pres. Smokey Bones div., 2002—04, CEO, 2004—05, chmn., CEO, 2005—. Bd. dir. St. Paul Travelers Ins., VF Corp., Verizon Communications Inc.; mem. Exec. Leadership Council. Trustee Williams Coll.; bd. mem. Enterprise Fla. Inc., Preserve Eatonville Inc. Mem.: Phi Beta Kappa. Office: Darden Restaurants Inc 5900 Lake Ellenor Dr Orlando FL 32809 *

OTIS, JACK, social work educator; b. NYC, Feb. 13, 1923; s. Abraham Osipowitz and Esther (Goldberg) O.; children: Elisabeth H., Erich R., Greta M., Marcus H., Alicia. AB, Bklyn. Coll., 1946; MS in Social Work, U. Ill., 1948, MEd, 1955, PhD, 1957. Social worker Jewish Social Svc. Bur. Dade County, 1948-49; Psychiat. social worker Free Synagogue Social Service, NYU, 1949-50; asso. prof. U. Ill., 1950-61; dep. dir. Office Juvenile Delinquency and Youth Devel., Dept. Health, Edn. and Welfare, 1961-65; dean Grad. Sch. Social Work U. Tex., 1965-77, prof. emeritus, 1993—. Cons. to govt., 1961—; presenter Internat. Coun. on Social Welfare, Inter-Univ. Consortium for Internat. Social Devel., Internat. Assn. Schs. Social Work, 1994; dep. dir. Pres.'s Com. Juvenile Delinquency and Youth Crime, 1961-65; spl. cons. for Am. social work edn. and rsch. European Ctr. for Social Welfare Tng. and Rsch., Vienna, Austria, 1976—; Dean Dan Sanders Meml. lectr. U. Ill., 1999. Author: (with George Barnett) Corporate Society and Education, 1961; contbr. article on child labor to Ency. Social Work, 1995. Bd. overseers Ctr. for Study Violence, Brandeis U., 1966-70; commencement spkr. U. Tex. Sch. Social Work, 2001. With AUS, 1943-46, PTO. Fulbright-Hays rsch.fellow Austria, 1977-78; established Dean Jack Otis Ann. Social Policy awards U. Tex., 2002. Mem. AAUP, Coun. on Social Work Edn. (commn. on accreditation), Philosophy of Edn. Soc., Nat. Assn. Social Workers (chair Calif. Task Force on Child Labor 2001-03), Am. Acad. Polit. and Social Sci., N.Y. Acad. Sci., Johannesburg Child Welfare Soc. (rsch. cons. South Africa chpt. 1990-91), Phi Kappa Phi (pres.). Office Phone: 949-240-9490. *The meaning of my life is whether I have added to the meaning of another's.*

OTIS, JAMES, JR., architect; b. Chgo., July 8, 1931; s. James and Edwina (Love) O.; m. Diane Cleveland, Apr. 9, 1955; children: James III, Julie C., David C. BArch cum laude, Princeton U., 1953; postgrad., U. Chgo., 1955-57. Registered architect, Ill., Ariz., Colo., Ind., Iowa, Wis., N.Mex., Mo. Designer Irvin A. Blietz Co., Wilmette, Ill., 1955-57; pres. Homefinders Constrn. Corp., Wilmette, 1957-59, O & F Constrn. Co., Northbrook, Ill., 1959-61; chmn. bd., chief exec. officer Otis Assocs., Inc., Northbrook, Ill., 1960-89; chmn., CEO Otis Co., 1981—. Bd. dirs. Banco Popular, Chgo., Trout & Grouse, Inc., OCO, Inc., Ranch Ptnrs., LLC. Prin. works include GBC Corp. Hdqrs., Northbrook, Ill., AON Ins. Co. Corp. Hdqrs., Performing Arts Ctr., Northbrook, All State Regional Hdqrs., Skokie, Ill., Zurich Nat. Hdqrs.-Zurich Towers, Schaumburg, Ill. Trustee Evanston (Ill.) Hosp., 1971-93, Better Govt. Assn., Chgo., Graham Found., 1984-86, Ill. Nature Conservancy; chmn. bd. trustees North Suburban YMCA, Northbrook, 1990-97; governing mem. Shedd Aquarium; bd. govs. Chgo. Zool. Soc.; mem. adv. bd. Cook County Forest Preserve Dist.; mem. founder's coun. Field Mus., Chgo. Lt. USNR, 1953-55. Mem. AIA, Nat. Coun. Archtl. Registration Bds., Urban Land Inst., Northwestern U. Assocs., Princeton Club (pres. 1971-72), Econ. Club, Commonwealth Club, Chgo. Club, Comml. Club, Glen View Golf Club, Old Elm Club, Coleman Lake Club, Angler's Club. Republican. Episcopalian. Office: Otisco 1450 American Ln Ste 1750 Schaumburg IL 60173-6010 Office Phone: 847-969-9000. Business E-Mail: jotisjr@otiscompany.com.

OTIS, JOHN JAMES, civil engineer; b. Syracuse, NY, Aug. 5, 1922; s. John Joseph and Anna (Dey) O.; m. Dorothy Fuller Otis, June 21, 1958; children: Mary Eileen Dawn, John Leon. B in Chem. Engring., Syracuse U., 1943, MBA, 1950, postgrad., 1951—55. Registered profl. engr., Ala., Tex. Jr. process engr. GM, Syracuse, 1951-53, prodn. engr., 1954-58, process control engr., 1958-59, process engr., 1960-61; engr., writer GE, Syracuse, 1961-63, configuration control engr. Phila., 1969; assoc. rsch. engr. Boeing Co., Huntsville, Ala., 1963-65; assoc. Planning Rsch. Corp., Huntsville, 1965-67; prin. engr. Brown Engring. Co. subs. Teledyne Co., Huntsville, 1967-69; mech. designer Drever Co., Beth Ayres, Pa., 1970-71; civil engr. U.S. Army Corps Engrs., Mobile, Ala., 1971-74, Galveston, Tex., 1974—2006, supervisory civil engr., 2006—. Lector, lay minister Roman Cath. Ch. Served with USNR, 1944-50. Mem. Am. Inst. Indsl. Engrs. (past v.p. Syracuse and Huntsville chpts.), Tex. Soc. Profl. Engrs. (dir. Galveston County chpt. 1976-79, sec.-treas. 1979-80, v.p. 1980-81, pres. 1982-83), Am. Legion, Tau Beta Pi, Phi Kappa Tau, Alpha Chi Sigma, Chi Eta Sigma. Office: US Army Corps Engrs Jadwin Bldg 2000 Fort Point Rd Galveston TX 77550-3038 Office Phone: 409-766-3157. Business E-Mail: john.j.otis@usace.army.mil.

OTIS, LEE (SARAH) LIBERMAN, lawyer, educator; b. NYC, Aug. 19, 1956; d. James Benjamin and Deen (Freed) L.; m. William Graham Otis, Oct. 24, 1993. BA, Yale U., 1979; JD, U. Chgo., 1983. Bar: N.Y. 1985, D.C. 1994. Law clk. US Ct. Appeals (DC cir.), Washington, 1983-84; spl. asst. to asst. atty. gen., civil div. US Dept. Justice, Washington, 1984-86, dep. assoc. atty. gen., 1986, assoc. dep. atty. gen., 1986; law clk. to Justice Antonin Scalia US Supreme Ct., Washington, 1986-87; asst. prof. law George Mason U., Arlington, Va., 1987-89; assoc. counsel to the Pres. Exec. Office of the Pres., Washington, 1989-92; assoc. Jones, Day, Reavis & Pogue, Washington, 1993-94; chief judiciary coun. US Sen. Spence Abraham, 1995-96; chief counsel subcom. on immigration Com. on the Judiciary, US Senate, 1997-2000; gen. counsel US Dept. Energy, 2001—05; assoc. dep. atty. gen., 2005—07; sr. v.p., dir. Federalist Soc. Law and Pub. Policy, 2007—. Adj. prof. law Georgetown Law Sch., 1995, 96. Mem. Federalist Soc. for Law and Pub. Policy (founder). Republican. Jewish. Avocations: sailing, computers. Office Phone: 202-822-8138.

OTIS, ROY JAMES, lawyer; BA, Stanford U., Calif., 1968; JD, Golden Gate U., 1980. Bar: Calif. 1980, U.S. Dist. Ct. (no. dist.) Calif. 1980; cert. specialist in workman's compensation. Ptnr. Gearheart & Otis, Pleasant Hill, 1996—. Mem. Calif. Applications Atty. Assn. (pres. no. Calif. chpt., 1994-96, bd. govs. 1997—), Assn. of Trial Lawyers of Am. (workplace injury litigation group sect. 1996—). Democrat. Office: Gearheart & Otis 367 Civic Dr Ste 17 Pleasant Hill CA 94523-1935 Office Phone: 925-671-9777.

O'TOOLE, AUSTIN MARTIN, lawyer, mediator; b. New Bedford, Mass., Oct. 5, 1935; s. John Brian, Jr. and Helen Veronica O'T.; m. Valerie Sherlock O'Toole; children: Erin Ann, Austin Martin Jr. BBA, Coll. Holy Cross, 1957; JD, Georgetown U., 1963. Bar: NY 1965, DC 1963, Tex. 1975; cert. disting. mediator, Tex. Mediator Credentialing Assn. Law clk. to judge U.S. Ct. Appeals, Washington, 1962-63; assoc. White & Case, NYC, 1963-74; sr. v.p., sr. counsel, sec. Coastal Corp., Houston, 1974—2001. Bd. editors Georgetown Law Jour., 1962-63. Bd. dirs. Nat. Coun. on Alcoholism and Drug Dependency, Inc., 2001—; charter mem., certificated mediator Inst. for Responsible Dispute Resolution, Houston, 2000—; bd. dirs. Houston Marathon Com., 1973—2002, Houston Dispute Resolution Ctr., 2007—. Officer USMC, 1957—60. Mem. ABA, Am. Soc. Corp. Secs. (bd. dirs. 1982-85), State Bar of Tex., Houston Bar Assn. (past chmn. corp. counsel sect. 1979-80, chair ADR sect. 2007-), Assn. Atty.-Mediators, Tex. Assn. Mediators (bd. dirs. 2007-). Home: 2200 Willowick (10-H) Houston TX 77027 Office: 509 Nineteenth St Galveston TX 77550 Office Phone: 409-763-3130. Personal E-mail: austinotoole@msn.com.

O'TOOLE, FRANCIS J., lawyer; b. Dublin, Feb. 10, 1944; came to U.S., 1960; s. Francis Herbert and Josephine (McCarthy) O'T.; m. Carole Ann Leland, Apr. 11, 1977; children: Kathleen, Kirra. AB, Harvard U., 1967; JD, U. Maine, 1970. Bar: Maine 1970, U.S. Supreme Ct. 1977, U.S. Dist. Ct. D.C., U.S. Dist. Ct. (ea. dist.) Va., U.S. Ct. Appeals (1st, 2d, 4th, 5th, 7th, 8th, 9th and 10th cirs.). Assoc. Fried, Frank, Harris, Shriver & Jacobsen, Washington, 1971-78, ptnr., 1978-92, Sidley & Austin, Washington, 1992—. Editor-in-chief U. Maine Law Rev., 1969-70; contbr. articles to profl. jours. Reginald Heber Smith fellow Calif. Indian Legal Services, 1970-71. Mem. ABA. Avocation: horse breeding and racing. Home: 7700 Burford Dr Mc Lean VA 22102-2105 Office: Sidley Austin Brown & Wood 1501 K St NW #LL Washington DC 20005-1401

O'TOOLE, GEORGE A., JR., judge; b. 1947; AB magna cum laude, Boston Coll., 1969; JD, Harvard U., 1972. Law clerk Arent, Fox, Kintner, Plotkin & Kahn, 1971-72; assoc., jr. ptnr. Hale and Dorr, 1972-82; assoc. justice Boston Mcpl. Ct. Dept., 1982-90, Trial Ct. of Mass., 1990-95; dist. judge US Dist. Ct., Mass., 1995—, judge. Faculty Suffolk U. Law Sch. Bd. dirs. Boston Coll. Alumni Assn., 1984-86, Winchester Boat Club, 1988-93. Mem. Mass. Bar Assn., Boston Bar Assn. Office: US Dist Ct 1 Courthouse Way Boston MA 02210-3002 Office Phone: 617-748-9152.

O'TOOLE, JAMES JOSEPH, business educator; b. San Francisco, Apr. 15, 1945; s. James Joseph and Irene (Nagy) O'T.; m. Marilyn Louise Burrill, June 17, 1967; children: Erin Kathleen, Kerry Louise. BA, U. So. Calif., LA, 1966; DPhil, Oxford U., Eng., 1970. Corr. Time-Life News Service, LA, 1967-68, Nairobi, Kenya, 1967-68; mgmt. cons. McKinsey & Co., San Francisco, 1969-70; coordinator field investigations Pres.'s Comm. on Campus Unrest, Washington, 1970; spl. asst. to sec. HEW, Washington, 1970-73; prof. mgmt. U. So. Calif., LA, 1973-93, Univ. Assocs. Chair of Bus., 1982-93; v.p. Aspen Inst., 1994-97; mng. dir. Booz-Allen & Hamilton Leadership Ctr., San Francisco, 1997—2005; rsch. prof. Ctr. for Effective Orgn., U. So. Calif., 1999—2007; Daniels disting. prof. bus. ethics Denver U., 2007—. Chmn. sec.'s com. work in Am. HEW, Washington, 1971-72; exec. dir. The Leadership Inst., 1990-93. Prin. author: Work in America, 1973, Energy and Social Change, 1976; author: Work, Learning and the American Future, 1977, Making America Work, 1982 (Phi Kappa Phi prize 1982), Vanguard Management, 1985, The Executive's Compass, 1993, Leading Change, 1995, Leadership A to Z, 1999, Creating the Good Life, 2005, The New American Workplace, 2006; bd. editors: Ency. Britannica, 1981-87; editor: New Management, 1983-89, The American Oxonian, 1996-98. Active Project Paideia, Chgo., 1981-83. Rhodes scholar, 1966; recipient Mitchell prize Woodlands Conf., 1979. Mem. Phi Beta Kappa. Office: Daniels Sch Bus Denver Univ 2101 S University Blvd Denver CO 80208 Business E-Mail: jim@jamesotoole.com.

O'TOOLE, JAMES MICHAEL, history educator; b. Worcester, Mass., Feb. 25, 1950; s. George Augustine and Mildred Bercher (O'Grady) O'Toole. AB, Boston Coll., 1972; MA, Coll. William and Mary, 1973; MS, Simmons Coll., Boston, 1975; PhD, Boston Coll., 1987. Dep. archivist Commonwealth of Mass., Boston, 1974—77; archivist Roman Cath. Archdiocese Boston, 1978—86; asst. prof. history U. Mass., Boston, 1986—98; prof. history Boston Coll., Chestnut Hill, Mass., 1998—. Author: Guide to Archives of the Archdiocese of Boston, 1982, Understanding Archives and Manuscripts, 1990, Passing for White, 2002, Habits of Devotion, 2004; author/editor; Catholic Boston, 1985. Fellow Mass. Hist. Soc.; mem. Soc. Am. Archivists (exec. council 1988—, Lane award 1986), Am. Cath. Hist. Assn., Am. Hist. Assn., Orgn. Am. Historians, New Eng. Archivists (pres. 1981-82), New Eng. Hist. Assn. (pres. 2002-03). Democrat. Roman Catholic. Office: Boston Coll History Dept 140 Commonwealth Ave Chestnut Hill MA 02467 Office Phone: 617-552-8456. Business E-Mail: james.otoole@bc.edu.

O'TOOLE, MICHAEL ANTHONY, academic administrator; b. Phila., Feb. 20, 1950; s. John Joseph O'Toole, Jr. and Louise Mary Kopka; m. Mary Louise Castaldi, Jan. 8, 1977; children: Lara Nicole Castaldi, Daniel Peter Castaldi, Colin Peter Castaldi(dec.). AB magna cum laude, U. of Pa., 1972, MA, 1978; EdM, Columbia U., 1997. Info. specialist US FDA, Rockville, Md., 1974; lectr. Abington Coll., Pa. State U., 1987—; tchr. La Salle Coll. HS, Wyndmoor, Pa., 1974—2000, chmn. Dept. English, 1980—88, dir., curriculum and summer sessions, 1989—2000, v.p., 2000—05; prin. Holy Ghost Prep. Sch., Bensalem, Pa., 2005—. Founder NW Cmty. Scholars Program; reader Ednl. Testing Svc., Princeton, NJ, 1987—94; svc. bd. mem. La Salle Coll. HS, 2000—05; team editor NAIS Leading Edge Award, 2005; v.p. Bicentennial Athletic League, 2007—. Editor: (alumni jour.) Explorer Mag., (profl. newsletter) Klingenstein Newsletter. Lay min. music St. Vincent De Paul Ch., Germantown, Pa., 1995—2001; lay mem. Lasallian Soc. Justice Inst., El Paso, Tex., 2004; bd. dirs. Face to Face, Inc., Phila., 2003—. Recipient President's medal, La Salle Coll. HS, 2005, Klingenstein Ctr. fellowship, Tchrs. Coll., Columbia U., 1994—95, fellowship in Am. Civilization, U. of Pa., 1978—79, Ford Fund scholarship, Ford Motor Co. Fund, 1968—72. Mem.: Nat. Coun. Tchrs. of English, Nat. Assn. Secondary Sch. Prins., Nat. Cath. Edn. Assn., Am. Studies Assn., Penn Club of NY. Independent. Roman Catholic. Avocations: bicycling, piano, music, swimming, writing. Home: 810 Elkins Ave Elkins Park PA 19027 Office: Holy Ghost Prep Sch 2429 Bristol Pike Bensalem PA 19020 Office Phone: 215-639-2102.

O'TOOLE, PATRICIA ELLEN, writer, educator; b. Alpena, Mich., Oct. 10, 1946; d. Gordon Roy and Gertrude (McKenna) O'T. BA, U. Mich., 1968. Adj. asst. prof. Columbia U. Sch. Arts, NYC, 1995—2002, lectr., 2002—03, asst. prof., 2004—05, assoc. prof., 2005—, vice chair, 2006. Author: The Five of Hearts: An Intimate Portrait of Henry Adams and His Friends, 1880-1918, 1990 (finalist, Pulitzer Prize and Nat. Book Critics Circle award), Money & Morals in America, 1998, When Trumpets Call: Theodore Roosevelt After the White House, 2005. MacDowell Colony fellow, 1988, Public Policy Scholar Woodrow Wilson Internat. Ctr. for Scholars, 2006. Mem. AAUP, PEN, Am. Hist. Assn., Orgn. Am. Historians. Democrat. Office: Dept Arts Columbia Univ 404 Dodge MC 1804 2960 Broadway New York NY 10027-6902

O'TOOLE, ROBERT JOSEPH, retired manufacturing executive; b. Chgo., Feb. 22, 1941; s. Francis John O'Toole; children: William, Patricia, Timothy, Kathleen, John. BS in Acctg., Loyola U., Chgo., 1961. Fin. analyst A.O. Smith Corp., Milw., 1963-66, mgr. corp. fin. analysis and planning, 1966-68, contr. electric motor div. Tipp City, Ohio, 1968-71; mng. dir. Bull Motors, Ipswich, England, 1971-74; gen. plant mgr. electric motor div. A.O. Smith Corp., Tipp City, 1974-79, v.p., gen. mgr., 1979-83, sr. v.p. Milw., 1984-85, pres., chief oper. officer, 1986-89, pres., 1989—2004, CEO, 1989—2005, also bd. dirs. Milw., and chmn. bd. dirs., 1992—2005. Bd. dirs. Briggs & Stratton Corp., Factory Mutual Ins. Co., Marshall & Ilsley Corp., Manufacturers Alliance/MAPI Inc.; mem. exec. com. TEC XIV, Milw., Mfrs. Alliance for Productivity and Innovation, Bus. Roundtable, Greater Milw. Com., Competitive Wis., Inc. Mem. Wis. Mgrs. and Commerce Assn. (exec. com.), Met. Milw. Assn. Commerce (bd. dirs.), Milw. Country Club, Univ. Club. Office: A O Smith Corp Ste 1001 11270 W Park Pl Milwaukee WI 53224-3690

O'TOOLE, TARA JEANNE, medical educator, former federal agency administrator; b. Newton, Mass., May 3, 1951; d. Harold J. and Jeanne (Whalen) O'T. BA, Vassar Coll., 1974; MD, George Washington U., 1981; MPH, Johns Hopkins U., 1988. Diplomate Am. Bd. Internal Medicine, Am. Bd. Preventive/Occupational Medicine. Rsch. asst. Sloan-Kettering Cancer Inst., NYC, 1974-77; resident in internal medicine Yale New Haven (Conn.) Hosp., 1981-84; physician Balt. Cmty. Health Ctrs., 1984-87; fellow in occupational medicine Johns Hopkins U., Balt., 1987-89; sr. analyst Office Tech. Assessment, Washington, 1989-93; asst. sec. energy for environ., safety and health US Dept. Energy, Washington, 1993-97; dep. dir. Johns Hopkins U. Ctr. Civilian Biodefense Studies, 1998—2001, dir., 2001—03; prof. medicine U. Pitts., 2003—; CEO Ctr. for Bio Security, U. Pitts. Medical Ctr., 2003—. Chmn. Bd. Fedn. Am. Scientists, 2004—. Democrat. Office: Ctr for Biosecurity The Pier IV Bldg 621 E Pratt St Ste 210 Baltimore MD 21202 Business E-Mail: Totoole@upmc-biosecurity.org.

O'TOOLE, WILLIAM EDWARD, III, retired computer science and mathematics professor; b. Waynesboro, Pa., May 27, 1942; s. William Edward Jr. and Dora Alberta O'Toole; m. Annette Marie Smith, June 25, 1966 (div. July 15, 1977); m. Catherine Claire Bodin, Dec. 16, 1989; 1 child, Wendy Elizabeth Garilli. BS in Math. Edn., Mt. St. Mary's Coll., 1966; MA in Math., U. Md., 1975. Prof. math. and computer sci. Mt. St. Mary's U., Emmitsburg, Md., 1966—2007; sci. editor and prognosticator Gruber Almanack Co., Hagerstown, Md., 1969—. Computer cons. Nat. Inst. Stds. and Tech., Gaithersburg, 1969—91. Author: (textbook and software) GRASP: A Generic, Realistic Assembler Simulation Program, 1991—. Mem. Balt. Symphony Orch., Frederick, 1970—90. King Ferdinand III Sci. scholar, Diocese of Harrisburg, Pa., 1960—62. Mem.: Math. Assn. Am. Democrat. Roman Catholic. Avocations: travel, classical music, photography, computers and electronics. Personal E-mail: billotoole@hotmail.com.

O'TOOLE, WILLIAM GEORGE, lawyer; b. Chgo., Oct. 25, 1934; s. George P. and Margaret (Battenhouse) O'T.; m. Gail M. McGregor, Aug. 13, 1960; children: Joyce M. Masterton, Paul G., Katherine A. Gorski. BS, U. Detroit, 1956; JD, DePaul U., Chgo., 1961. Bar: Ill. 1961, US Dist. Ct. (no. dist.) Ill. 1962. Assoc. Jaros, Tittle & O'Toole (and predecessor firm), Chgo., 1961-74, ptnr., 1974-90, pres., 1990—. Pres. Ill. State Title Corp. Bd. dirs. De Paul U. Law Sch.; mem. bd. advisors Mercy Hosp.; bd. dirs. Mortgage Bankers of Ill.; bd adv. De Paul U. Law Sch., Mercy Hosp. Mem. ABA, Ill. Bar Assn., Ill. Mortgage Bankers Assn. (bd. dirs.), Chgo. Bar Assn., Southwest Bar Assn. (past pres.), Chgo. Athletic Assn., Abbey Springs Country Club, Ridge Country Club, Union League Club Chgo., Univ. Club Chgo., Elks, K.C., Beta Alpha Psi. Roman Catholic. Office: Jaros Tittle & O'Toole 20 N Clark St Ste 510 Chicago IL 60602-4188 Home: 127 Acacia Cir Unit 407 Indian Head Park IL 60525 Office Phone: 312-750-1000.

OTREMBA, GERALDINE MARIE, congressional and international relations executive; b. NYC, Apr. 13, 1946; d. Frank Stanley and Beatrice Gloria (O'Malley) O.; m. Stanley F. Turesky, Oct. 26, 1975; children: Sarah, Catherine. BA, St. John's U., 1967; MA, U. N.C., 1969, PhD, 1979. Dep. dir. ops. John F. Kennedy Ctr. for the Performing Arts, Washington, 1984-87, dir. planning, 1987-90, dir. ops., 1990-91, dir. govt. liaison, 1991-92, assoc. mng. dir., 1991-94; dir. congrl. rels. Libr. Congress, Washington, 1994—; exec. dir. Open World Leadership Ctr., Washington, 1999—2002; CEO Ctr. Russian Leadership Devel. (former Russian Leadership Program), Libr. of Congress, Washington, 2002. Chmn. Nat. Conf. Performing Arts Ctrs., 1990-93. Mem.: Cosmos Club. Roman Catholic. Office: Congl Rels Office Libr Congress James Madison Meml Bldg 101 Independence Ave SW Washington DC 20540-4000 Office Phone: 202-707-7720.

OTT, ANDREW EDUARD, lawyer; b. Vancouver, BC, Can., Sept. 23, 1962; s. Eduard Karl and Elfriede Marie (Petryc) O. BA in English, Seattle U., 1986, JD, 1989; D (hon.), U. Graz, Austria, 1986. Bar: Wash. 1990, US Dist. Ct. (we. dist.) Wash. 1992, Alaska 2003, US Ct. Alaska, 2003. Contract atty. Keller Rohrback, Seattle, Lieff Cabraser Heimann & Bernstein, San Francisco, Jamin, Ebell, Schmitt & Mason, Kodiak, Alaska, 1989—. Cons. OMNI Tech. Engring., Bothell, Wash., 1986-2000. Actor musicals and theater, 1992, 93, 95, 96, 98, 99, 2000; musician Cmty. Orch. and Jazz, 1990-2000. Trustee Kodiak Arts Coun. Mem.: ABA. Avocations: skiing, soccer, bike riding, running, acting. Office: Jamin Schmitt St John 323 Carolyn Ave Kodiak AK 99615-6348 E-mail: Andrew@jesmkod.com.

OTT, ATTIAT FARAG, economist, educator; b. Cairo, June 18, 1935; m. David J. Ott (dec.); 1 child, Dana. BA in Econ. with highest honors, Cairo U., 1956; PhD, U. Mich., Ann Arbor, 1962. Assoc. prof., econ. So. Meth. U., 1965—68; vis. assoc. prof. U. Md., College Park, 1968—69; fiscal economist, office tax analysis U.S. Dept. Treasury, 1969; assoc. prof., econ. Clark U., Worcester, Mass., 1969—71, prof., 1971—; dir. Inst. Econ. Studies, 1980—. Vis. scholar Hoover Instn., Stanford U., 1977—78; adj. scholar Am. Enterprise Inst.; prin. investigator Fund for Pub. Policy Rsch.; mem. nat. com. and tax policy bd. Taxation with Representation, Washington. Author: Macroeconomic Theory, 1975, Federal Budget Policy, 1977, The Public Sector in the Global Economy, 2003, The Elgar Companion To Public Economics: Emprica Public Economics, 2006; co-author: The Massachusetts Health Plan, 1988, Privatization and Economic Effiency, 1991, Public Sector Budgets: A Competitive Study, 1993; guest columnist Worcester Telegram and Gazette, mem. editl. bd. Jour. Econ. Devel., mem. editl. bd., guest editor Atlantic Econ. Jour.; contbr. articles to numerous profl. jours. Fellow, Olin Found., 1980—92; grantee, Am. Bar Found., 1969—72, Hoover Instn., 1978—79; H.B. Earhart fellow, 1982. Home: 262 Salisbury St Worcester MA 01609-1641 Office: Clark U Dept Econs Worcester MA 01610 Home Phone: 508-753-2630; Office Phone: 508-793-7447. Business E-Mail: aott@clarku.edu.

OTT, C(LARENCE) H(ENRY), ambassador, retired accounting professor; b. Richmond, Mich., Jan. 20, 1918; s. Ferdinand and Wilhelmina (Radkte) Ott; m. Helen Louise McKay, Oct. 29, 1942 (dec. Apr. 1994); children: James Richard, Dennis McKay, Richard Darrel, Delene Michelle. BA, Valparaiso U., 1940; MBA, Northwestern U., 1970; PhD, Southeastern U., 1980. CPA N.Y., cert. mgmt. acct., N.Y. Chief acct. G.E. X-Ray Corp., Chgo., 1940—41; pub. auditor Arthur Andersen & Co., Chgo., 1941—43; renegotiator contracts U.S. Army Air Corps, Chgo., 1943—45; internal auditor David Bradley Mfg. (Sears), Bradley, Ill., 1945—48; contr., treas. Manco Mfg. Co., Bradley, 1948—59; owner, operator Yellow-Checker Cab Co., Kankakee, Ill., 1959—70; chmn. acctg., prof. Rochester Inst. Tech., NY, 1970—73, Southwestern Mich. Coll., Dowagiac, 1973—; citizen amb. People to People Internat., Kansas City, Mo., 1992—. Curriculum advisor Southwestern Mich. Coll., Dowagiac, 1992—. Citizen amb. People to People Internat., Bora Bora, Que., Canada, Cuba, China, Egypt, England, France, Galapagos Island, Greece, Greenland, Iceland, India, Israel, Italy, Japan, Moorea, Morocco, Portugal, Singapore, Tahiti, Turkey, Russia, Spain, Ecuador, Greek Islands, Hong Kong, Jordan; del. to Russia to facilitate their transition to Dem. form of govt.; del. leader Wharton Sch. Fin. U. Pa., Phila., 1992. Mem.: Planning Execs. Inst. (spkr., chmn.), Inst. Cert. Mgmt. Accts., Nat. Assn. Accts., Pi Gamma Mu, Pi Kappa Alpha, Alpha Kappa Psi. Republican. Avocations: travel, golf, bowling, reading, exercise. Home: 30992 Middle Crossing Rd Dowagiac MI 49047-9268

OTT, DAVID MICHAEL, engineering company executive; b. Glendale, Calif., Feb. 24, 1952; s. Frank Michael and Roberta (Michie) O.; m. Cynthia Dianne Bunce. BSEE, U. Calif., Berkeley, 1974. Electronic engr. Teknekron Inc., Berkeley, 1974-79; chief engr. TCI, Berkeley, 1979-83; div. mgr. Integrated Automation Inc., Alameda, Calif., 1983-87, Litton Indsl. Automation, Alameda, 1987-92; founder, chmn. Picture Elements Inc., Berkeley, 1992—. Inventor method for verifying denomination of currency, method for processing digited images, automatic document image revision. Mem. IEEE, AAAS, Assn. Computing Machinery, Union of Concerned Scientists. Office: Picture Elements Inc 777 Panoramic Way Berkeley CA 94704-2538

OTT, DORIS ANN, librarian; b. Elgin, ND, Sept. 24, 1942; d. Oscar Edward Hirning and Lorraine Wilhelmina Gruebele; m. Richard Donald Ott, Nov. 21, 1998; m. Bernnett Gordon Reinke, Sept. 1961 (div.); 1 child, Scott Bernnett Reinke; m. James Lee Daugherty, June 1974 (div.). BS, Dickinson State U., 1964; MLS, George Peabody Coll., 1965. Lic. Ind. life tchr. Elem. tchr. Mott Pub. Schs., ND, 1963-64; asst. prof. Dickinson State U., ND, 1965-73; media specialist Minot Pub. Schs., ND, 1973-74; head tech. svcs. Bartholomew County Libr., Columbus, Ind., 1974-75; media specialist Rushville Pub. Schs., Ind., 1975-86; head interlibr. loan ND State Libr., Bismarck, 1986-87, asst. state libr., 1987—2001, state libr., 2001—. Image cons. Beauty For All Seasons, 1984—. Mem. Humane Soc. Mem.: ALA, Mountain Plains Libr. Assn., ND Libr. Assn. Avocation: image consulting. Office: ND State Libr 604 E Boulevard Ave Dept 250 Bismarck ND 58505-0800 Office Phone: 701-328-2492. Business E-Mail: dott@nd.gov.

OTT, GILBERT RUSSELL, JR., lawyer; b. Bklyn., Apr. 15, 1943; s. Gilbert Russell Sr. and Bettina Rose (Ferrel) O.; m. Lisa S. Weatherford, Apr. 12, 1986; children: Gilbert R. III, Laura Elisabeth. BA, Yale U., 1965; JD, MBA, Columbia U., 1969. Bar: N.Y. 1970. Assoc. Chadbourne, Parke, Whiteside & Wolff, NYC, 1969-72, LeBoeuf, Lamb, Leiby & MacRae, NYC, 1972-78; assoc. gen. counsel Kidder, Peabody & Co., Inc., NYC, 1978-96, asst. sec., 1978-91, asst. v.p., 1978-79, v.p., 1979-86, mng. dir., 1986-91, sr. v.p., sec., 1992-96; v.p. Kidder, Peabody Group Inc., NYC, 1989-96, asst. sec., 1986-96; exec. v.p., gen. counsel, sec. Rodman & Renshaw Capital Group, Inc., Chgo. and NYC, 1996-98; counsel Cadwalader, Wickersham & Taft, NYC, 1998-99; dep. gen. counsel Datek Online Holdings Corp., Jersey City, 1999—2002; chief legal officer instl. divsn. Ameritrade Holding Corp., Jersey City, 2002—05; dep. gen. counsel TD Ameritrade Holding Corp., Jersey City, 2006—. Mem.: Assn. Bar City of N.Y., Univ. Club, Piping Rock Club. Home: 260 Highwood Cir Oyster Bay NY 11771-3205 Office: Harborside Financial Ctr Plz 4A Jersey City NJ 07310 Home Phone: 516-922-4241; Office Phone: 201-369-8559. Business E-Mail: gott@ameritrade.com.

OTT, JOHN HARLOW, museum administrator; b. Ottawa, Ont., Can., Jan. 29, 1944; s. Thomas Gordon and Lois Elizabeth (Wright) O.; m. Lili Reineck, May 20, 1972; children— Jennie Elizabeth, Michael James Hutchins BA, Eastern Bapt. Coll., St. David's, Pa., 1966; MA, SUNY-Oneonta, 1975; postgrad. Mus. Mgmt. Inst., U. Calif., Berkeley, 1987. Curator Hancock Shaker Village, Inc., Pittsfield, Mass., 1970-72, dir., 1972-83; exec. dir. Atlanta Hist. Soc., 1983-91, B&O R.R. Mus., Inc., Balt., 1991-99, The Nat. Heritage Mus., Lexington, Mass., 1999—. Curator Ga. Hist. Soc., Savannah, 1983-87; mem. adv. bd. Concord (Mass.) Mus. Author: Hancock Shaker Village, 1976 Mem. Lexington Tourism Com., 2002—; bd. dirs. Devens Hist. Mus., 2001—03, bd. govs., 2003—; bd. dirs. Merimack Valley Conv. and Visitors Bur., N.E. Document Conservation Ctr., 2005—; pres. Cooperstown Grad. Program Alumni Assn., 2005—. Decorated Bronze Star; named mus. profl. of yr. in Ga., 1991, profl. of yr. Acad. for Travel, Hospitality and Tourism, 1996. Mem. Am. Assn. Mus. (accrediting officer 1982—), Am. Assn. for State and Local History, Mid-Atlantic Mus. Assn., Ga. Soc. Assn. Execs., Nat. Hist. Communal Socs. Assn. (pres. 1983-84), Nat. Soc. Fund Raising Execs. (bd. dirs. Ga. chpt. 1985-91, bd. dirs. Md. chpt. 1993), Am. Antiquarian Soc., Balt. City C. of C. (bd. dirs., past chmn.), Md. Assn. History Mus. (bd. dirs. 1996), Freedom's Way Heritage Assn. (bd. dirs. 2000—, pres. 2007), Lexington C. of C. (chmn. 2002-2004). Republican. Episcopalian. Office: The Nat Heritage Mus 33 Marrett Rd Lexington MA 02421-5703 Office Phone: 781-457-4102. E-mail: jott@monh.org.

OTT, KARL OTTO, nuclear engineer, consultant; b. Hanau, Germany, Dec. 24, 1925; arrived in U.S., 1967, naturalized, 1987; s. Johann Josef and Eva (Bergmann) Ott; m. Gunhild G. Göring, Sept. 18, 1958 (div. 1986); children: Martina, Monika; m. Birgit Fehse, May 1, 1995. BS, J. W. von Goethe U., Frankfurt, Germany, 1948; MS, G. August U., Göttingen, Fed. Republic Germany, 1953, PhD, 1958. Physicist Nuc. Rsch. Ctr., Karlsruhe, Germany, 1958-67, sect. head, 1962-67; prof. Sch. Nuc. Engring. Purdue U., West Lafayette, Ind., 1967-2001, prof. emeritus, 2000—. Cons. Argonne Nat. Lab., 1967—2001. Author: (book) Nuclear Reactor Statics, 1983, 2d edit., 1989, Nuclear Reactor Dynamics, 1985, Chinese edit., 1991. Recipient Disting. Appointment award, Argonne Universities Assn., 1973. Fellow: Am. Nuc. Soc. (Arthur Holly Compton award 1993). Office Phone: 765-494-5739. E-mail: kobott@sbcglobal.net.

OTT, WALTER RICHARD, information technology executive, writer; b. Bklyn., Jan. 20, 1943; s. Harold Vincent and Mary Elizabeth (Butler) Ott; m. Carla M. Narrett, May 27, 2002; children: Regina Winter Burrell, Christina W. Chiappetta, Walter R. Jr. BS in Ceramic Engring., Va. Poly. Inst. and State U., 1965; MS in Ceramic Engring., U. Ill., 1967; PhD in Ceramic Engring., Rutgers U., 1969; DSc (hon.), Alfred U., 2001. Registered profl. engr., Pa. Process engr. Corning Inc., Buckhannon, W.Va., 1965-66; staff rsch. engr. Champion Spark Plug Co., Detroit, 1969-70; prof. engring. Rutgers U., New Brunswick, NJ, 1970-80; dean, assoc. provost N.Y. State Coll. Ceramics, Alfred, 1980-88; provost, chief acad. officer Alfred U., Alfred, 1988-2000; pres. Predictive Edge, Inc., West Orange, NJ, 1999—; v.p. enrollment mgmt. Caldwell (N.J.) Coll., 2002—04. Rsch. assoc. Atomic Energy Commn.-E.I. duPont de Nemours, Aiken, S.C., 1971; cons. Haight & Hofeldt Inc., Chgo., 1984-88, Pillsbury, Mpls., 1977-79, Ctr. for Profl. Advancement, New Brunswick, 1971-79, Hammond (Ind.) Lead Products, 1970-80; bd. dirs. Victor (N.Y.) Insulator Inc., UNIPEG, 1987-88; treas. Alfred Tech. Resources N.Y.; bd. dirs. Grads Found., N.Y.C. Contbr. articles to profl. jours.; patentee in field. Recipient Ralph Teetor award Soc. Automotive Engrs., 1973, PACE award Nat. Inst. Ceramic Engrs., 1975, Ann. award Ceramic Assn. N.J., 1980; named to Greaves Walker Roll, Keramos, 1991. Fellow Am. Ceramic Soc. (trustee 1980-83, v.p. 1988-89); mem. Ceramic Ednl. Coun. (pres. 1976-77), Ceramic Assn. N.Y. (treas. 1980-88, bd. dirs.), Ceramic Assn. N.J. (bd. dirs. 1974-80), Keramos (pres. 1982-84, Greaves-Walker Roll of Honor 1991), Tau Beta Pi. Avocations: tennis, sailing, reading. Home: 2156 Charlotte Amalie Ct Punta Gorda FL 33950 Business E-Mail: ott@predictiveedge.com.

OTT, WAYNE ROBERT, environmental engineer; b. San Mateo, Calif., Feb. 2, 1940; s. Florian Funstan and Evelyn Virginia (Smith) Ott; m. Patricia Faustina Bertuzzi, June 28, 1967 (div. 1983). BA in Econs., Claremont McKenna Coll., Calif., 1962; BSEE, Stanford U., Calif., 1963, MS in Engring., 1965, MA in Comm., 1966, PhD in Environ. Engring., 1971. Commd. lt. USPHS, 1966, advanced through grades to capt., 1986; chief lab. ops. br. U.S. EPA, Washington, 1971—73, sr. systems analyst, 1973—79, sr. rsch. engr., 1981—84, chief air toxics and radiation monitoring rsch. staff, 1984—90; vis. scientist dept. stats. Stanford U., 1979—81, 1990—. Vis. scholar Ctr. for Risk Analysis and dept. stats., civil engring., Stanford U., 1990—93; sr. environ. engr. EPA Atmospheric Rsch. and Exposure Assessment Lab., 1993—95; cons. prof. civil engring. Stanford U., 1995—; dir. field studies Calif. Environ. Tobacco Smoke Study, 1993—95. Author: Environmental Indices: Theory and Practice, 1976, Environmental Statistics and Data Analysis, 1995, Exposure Analysis, 2006; contbr. articles to profl. jours. Decorated Commendation medal USPHS; recipient Nat. Statistician award, EPA, 1995. Mem.: Internat. Soc. Indoor Air Quality and Climate, Air and Waste Mgmt. Assn., Am. Soc. for Quality Control, Am. Statis. Assn., Internat. Soc. Exposure Analysis (v.p. 1989—90, Jerome J. Weselowski Internat. award for career achievement in exposure assessment 1995), Sierra Club, Theater Club, Jazz Club, Kappa Mu Epsilon, Tau Beta Pi, Sigma Xi, Phi Beta Kappa. Democrat. Achievements include development of nationally uniform air pollution index, first total human exposure activity pattern models; research in indoor air pollution, total human exposure to chems., stochastic models of indoor exposure to chems., stochastic models of indoor exposure, motor vehicle exposures, pers monitoring instruments and environ tobacco smoke. Avocations: hiking, photography, model trains, jazz. Home: 1008 Cardiff Ln Redwood City CA 94061-3678 Office: Stanford U Dept Stats Sequoia Hall Stanford CA 94305 Office Phone: 650-906-8442. Personal E-mail: wott@mac.com. Business E-Mail: wott1@stanford.edu.

OTTAVI, MARCO, computer engineer, researcher; s. Cesare Maria Ottavi and Clara Selva. BSEE, U. Rome La Sapienza, Italy; PhD in Microelectronics and Telecommunication Engring., U. Rome Tor Vergata, Italy. Vis. rsch. assoc. Northeastern U., Boston, 2004—06; vis. rsch. scholar Sandia Nat. Labs., Albuquerque, 2006; sr. design engr. AMD, Boxborough, Mass., 2007—. Contbr. articles to profl. jours. Mem.: IEEE. Achievements include research in solid state mass memory for space applications; circuit design for quantum-dot cellular automata.

OTTE, PAUL JOHN, academic administrator, consultant; b. Detroit, July 10, 1943; s. Melvin John Otte and Anne Marie (Meyers) Hirsch; children: Deanna Kropf, John. BS, Wayne State U., 1968, MBA, 1969; EdD, Western Mich. U., 1983. With Detroit Bank and Trust Co., 1965-68; teaching fellow Wayne State U., Detroit, 1968-69; auditor, mgr. Arthur Young & Co., Detroit, 1969-75; contr., dir. Macomb Community Coll., Warren, Mich., 1975-79, v.p. bus., 1979-86; pres. Franklin U., Columbus, Ohio, 1986—, prof. undergrad. and grad. programs, 1986—. Author various tng. manuals, 1982. Cpl. USMC, 1961-65. Teaching fellow Wayne State U., 1968-69. Mem. AICPA, Mich. Assn. CPAs (chmn. continuing profl. edn. com. 1980-82, leadership com. 1981-83), Nat. Assn. Coll. and Univ. Bus. Officers (acctg. prins. com. 1986), Assn. Ind. Colls. and Univs. Ohio (bd. dirs.), Greater Detroit C. of C. (leadership award 1983), Columbus C. of C. (info. svc. com.). Roman Catholic. Avocation: travel. Office: Franklin U 201 S Grant Ave Columbus OH 43215-5399

OTTEN, ARTHUR EDWARD, JR., lawyer; b. Buffalo, Oct. 11, 1930; s. Arthur Edward Sr. and Margaret (Ambrusko) O.; m. Mary Therese Torri, Oct. 1, 1960; children: Margaret, Michael, Maureen Staley, Suzanne Hoodecheck, Jennifer Shankle. BA, Hamilton Coll., 1952; JD, Yale U., 1955. Bar: N.Y. 1955, Colo. 1959. Assoc. Hodges, Silverstein, Hodges & Harrington, Denver, 1959-64; ptnr. Hodges, Kerwin, Otten & Weeks (predecessor firms), Denver, 1964-73, Davis, Graham & Stubbs, Denver, 1973-86; gen. counsel Colo. Nat. Bankshares, Inc., 1973-93; mem. Otten, Johnson, Robinson, Neff & Ragonetti, P.C., Denver, 1986—. Rec. sec. Colo. Nat. Bankshares, Inc., Denver, 1983-93; gen. counsel Regis U., Denver, 1994-99; mediator Denver Dist. Ct., 1997-99; com. bd. Centura Health, Denver, St. Anthony Hosps., Denver. Bd. dirs. Cath. Charities Archdiocese of Denver, 1998-2004. Lt. USN, 1955-59. Mem. ABA, Colo. Bar Assn., Denver Bar Assn., Am. Arbitration Assn. (panel arbitrators, large complex case panel, mediator panel), Nat. Assn. Securities Dealers (bd. arbitrators), Law club, Univ. Club, Denver Mile High Rotary (pres. 1992-93), Phi Delta Phi. Republican. Roman Catholic. Avocations: hiking, biking, church activities. Home: 4505 S Yosemite St Unit 432 Denver CO 80237-2540 Office: Otten Johnson Robinson Neff & Ragonetti PC 950 17th St Ste 1600 Denver CO 80202-2828 Office Phone: 303-825-8400. Personal E-mail: aotten@ottenjohnson.com.

OTTER, BUTCH (C. L. OTTER, CLEMENT LEROY OTTER), governor, former congressman; b. Caldwell, Idaho, May 3, 1942; s. Joseph Bernard and Regina Mary (Buser) O.; m. Gay Corinne Simplot, 1964 (div. 1992); children: John Simplot, Carolyn Lee, Kimberly Dawn, Corinne Marie; m. Lori Easley, Aug. 18, 2006 BA in Polit. Sci., Coll. Idaho, 1967; PhD (hon.), Mindanao State U., 1980. Mgr. J.R. Simplot Co., Caldwell, Idaho, 1971-76, asst. to v.p. adminstrn., 1976-78, v.p. adminstrn., 1978-82, internat. pres., 1982—93; mem. Idaho Ho. Reps., 1973—77; lt. gov. State of Idaho, Boise, 1987—2001, gov., 2007—; mem. US Congress from 1st Idaho Dist., 2001—07; mem. transp. and infrastructure, resources and govt. reform, energy and commerce coms. Mem. Presdl. Task Force-AID, Washington, 1982—84, U.S. C. of C., Washington, 1983—84; com. mem. invest tech. devel. State Adv. Council, Washington, 1983—84; mem. exec. council Bretton Woods Com., 1984—. With Nat. Guard, 1968—73. Mem. Young Pres.' Orgn., Sales and Mktg. Execs., Idaho Assn. Commerce and Industry, Idaho Agrl. Leadership Council, Idaho Ctr. for Arts, Idaho Internat. Trade Council, Pacific N.W. Waterways Assn., N.W. Food Producers, Ducks Unltd, Safari Club Internat. (life). Clubs: Arid, Hillcrest Country. Lodges: Moose, Elks. Republican. Roman Catholic. Avocations: jogging, music, art collecting, horse training, fishing. Office: Office of Gov PO Box 83720 Boise ID 83720 *

OTTER, JOHN MARTIN, III, retired television advertising consultant; b. Pottsville, Pa., Nov. 26, 1930; s. John Martin and Ruth A. (Knipe) O.; m. Susan Morgan Eaves, May 21, 1960; children— John Martin, IV, Robert Marshal. BA, Cornell U., 1953. Comml. producer Arlene Frances Home Show, 1953-55; producer Dave Garroway Today Show, 1956-59; dir. spl. programs sales NBC-TV, 1959-61, v.p. nat. sales, 1962-64, v.p. charge sales, 1965-73; cons. sta. WNET-TV, Practising Law Inst., also Dragonwk Prodns., 1973-75; v.p., dir. network programming SSC&B Inc., 1975-78; sr. v.p., dir. network programming SSC&B Lintas Worldwide, NYC, 1978-84; sr. v.p. dir. nat. broadcast McCann-Erickson U.S.A., NYC, 1984-88; sr. v.p. spl. projects McCann-Erickson Worldwide, NYC, 1988; pres. RETTO Internat. Inc., NYC, 1989-94; retired, 1994. Mem.: The Chatham Club, The Landings Yacht Club, The Landings Club. Republican. Episcopalian. Home: Four Seafarer's Cir Savannah GA 31411

OTTERBOURG, ROBERT KENNETH, public relations consultant, writer; b. NYC, Jan. 26, 1930; s. Albert Marcus and Frances (Roset) O.; m. Susan Delman, Apr. 14, 1957; children— Laura Ann, Kenneth Douglas. BA, Colgate U., 1951; MS, Columbia U., 1954. Reporter, editor Fairchild Publs., NYC, 1953-57; editor McGraw-Hill Pub. Co., 1957-59; v.p. pub. rels. Charles Mathieu & Co., 1959-61; pres. pub. rels. Otterbourg & Co., NYC, 1962-69, 71—. Sr. v.p. Daniel J. Edelman, 1970. Author: It's Never Too Late, 1993, Retire and Thrive, 1995, 4th edit., 2006, Switching Careers, 2001; contbr. articles to profl. and consumer jours. Legis. asst. N.Y. State Senate, 1962-64; mem. exec. com. Columbia U. Sch. Journalism, N.Y.C., 1980-93, pres. exec. com., 1985-87; trustee Flat Rock Nature Ctr., pres., 1991-92; trustee Planned Parenthood Bergen County, 1985-88, v.p., 1986-88; trustee Urban League for Bergen County, 1988-93; chmn. Durham County Libr., 1997-99, Exec. Svc. Corps of the Greater Triangle; bd. dirs. Colgate U. Alumni Corp., 1969-73; bd. dirs., pres. Threshold, 2003; pres. Triangle Radio Reading Svc., 2004. 1st lt. USAF, 1951-53. Mem. Columbia U. Grad. Sch. Journalism Alumni Assn. (pres. 1985-87). Democrat. Jewish. Home and Office: 68 Beverly Dr Durham NC 27707-2224 Personal E-mail: rkotter@aol.com.

OTTERSON, GREGORY ALAN, oncologist, educator; b. Feb. 8, 1959; MD, Georgetown U. Sch. Medicine, 1986. Cert. Internal Medicine, Med. Oncology. Resident, internal medicine Rush Presbyn.-St. Lukes Med. Ctr., Chgo., Ind., 1986—89; fellow, med. oncology Nat. Cancer Inst., Bethesda, Md., 1989; asst. prof., dept. internal medicine Uniformed Svcs. U., Health Sciences, Bethesda, Md., 1989—98; assoc. prof. internal medicine, divsn. hematology/oncology Ohio State U., Coll. Medicine and Pub. Health, 1998—, dir., solid tumor oncology. Contbr. articles to profl. jours. Office: Ohio State U Coll Medicine and Pub Health 320 W 10th Ave B415 Starling Loving Hall Columbus OH 43210 Office Phone: 614-293-6786. Office Fax: 614-293-4372. Business E-Mail: greg.otterson@osumc.edu. *

OTTINGER, DAVID, art educator, artist; b. St. Louis, July 6, 1951; s. Robert P. Ottinger and Dorothy Ann Menetre; m. Mary Beth Chalovich, Jan. 2, 2005; children from previous marriage: Christopher, Aaron, Todd Behum, Michael Behum. BFA, Kans. City Art Inst., Mo., 1974; MFA, Washington U., St. Louis, 1978. Instr. St. Louis CC, 1975—78, 1979—85; prof. art McKendree Coll., Lebanon, Ill., 1978—. Adv. bd. mem. Art St. Louis, 1993—95. Represented in permanent collections St. Louis C.C., Forest Park, Mo., McKindree Coll. Office: McKendree Coll 701 College Dr Lebanon IL 62254 Office Phone: 800-232-7228.

OTTINGER, RICHARD LAWRENCE, dean emeritus; b. NYC, Jan. 27, 1929; s. Lawrence and Louise (Lowenstein) O.; children from previous marriage: Ronald, Randall, Lawrence, Jenny Louise; m. June Godfrey. BA, Cornell U., 1950; LLB, Harvard U., 1953. Assoc. Cleary, Gottlieb, Friendly & Hamilton, NYC, 1955-56; ptnr. William J. Kridel, Law Firm, NYC, 1956-60; second staff mem., dir. programs Peace Corps, L.Am., 1961-64; mem. 89th-91st Congresses, 1965-71, 94th-98th Congresses, 1975-85; prof. Pace U. Sch. Law, White Plains, NY, 1985—, dean, 1994—99, dean emeritus, 1999—. Chmn. bd. dirs. Environ. and Energy Study Inst., Washington, Legal Environl. Assistance Found., Tallahasse, Fla.; mem. Congress Westchester County, NY, 1965—71, 1976—85; Dem. candidate US Senate, 1970. Author: Environmental Costs of Electricity, 1990; co-author: Energy Law and Sustainable Development, 2003; co-author and co-editor The Law of Energy for Sustainable Development, 2005; co-editor Compendium of Laws on Energy for Sustainable Development, 2005; contbr. articles to profl. jours. Contract mgr. Internat. Coop. Adminstrn., 1960-61; organizer Grassroots to Action, 1971-73. Office: Pace U Sch Law 78 N Broadway White Plains NY 10603-3710 Office Phone: 914-422-4121. Business E-Mail: rottinger@law.pace.edu.

OTTINO, JULIO MARIO, engineering company executive, educator; b. La Plata, Buenos Aires, Argentina, May 22, 1951; came to U.S., 1976; naturalized, 1990; s. Julio Francisco and Nydia Judit (Zufriategui) O.; m. Alicia I. Löffler, Aug. 20, 1976; children: Jules Alessandro, Bertrand Julien. Diploma in Chem. Engring., U. La Plata, 1974; PhD in Chem. Engring., U. Minn., 1979; exec. program Kellogg Sch. Mgmt., Northwestern U., 1995. Instr. in chem. engring. U. Minn., Mpls., 1978-79; asst. prof. U. Mass., Amherst, 1979-83, adj. prof. polymer sci., 1979-91, assoc. prof. chem. engring., 1983-86, prof., 1986-91; Chevron vis. prof. chem. engring. Calif. Inst. Tech., Pasadena, 1985-86; sr. rsch. fellow Ctr. for Turbulence Rsch. Stanford (Calif.) U., 1989-90; Walter P. Murphy prof. chem. engring. Northwestern U., Evanston, Ill., 1991-2000, chmn. dept. chem. engring., 1992-2000; McCormick Inst. prof., 2000—; George T. Piercy Disting. prof.

U. Minn., 1998, adj. prof. mech. engring., 2001—; dir. Northwestern Inst. Complex Sys., 2004—, dean Sch. Engring. and Applied Sci. Cons. to U.S. and European corps.; mem. tech. adv. bd. Dow Chem.; mem. bd. dirs. Coun. Chem. Rsch.; prof. U. Minn.; Reily lectr. Notre Dame U., 2006; lectr. in field. Author: The Kinematics of Mixing: Stretching, Chaos and Transport, 1989; contbr. articles to profl. jours.; assoc. editor Physics Fluids A, 1991—; mem. editl. bd. Internat. Jour. Bifurc. Chaos, 1991—; assoc. editor Am. Inst. Chem. Engring. Jour., 1991-95, assoc. editor., 1995—; one man art exhibit, La Plata, 1974. Recipient Presdl. Young Investigator award NSF, 1984, Alpha Chi Sigma award AIChE, 1994, W.H. Walker award AIChE, 2001, E.W. Thiele award AIChE, Chgo., 2002; Univ. fellow U. Mass., 1988, J.S. Guggenheim fellow, 2001; Lacey lectureship, Calif. Inst. Tech., 1994, Danckwerts lectureship Royal Instn., 1999, Robb lectr. Pa. State U., 2002, Reily lectr., U. Notre Dame, 2006. Fellow Am. Phys. Soc.; mem. AAAS, NAE, Am. Acad. Arts and Scis., Am. Chem. Soc., Am. Phys. Soc., Am. Soc. Engring. Edn., Sigma Xi (disting. lectr. 1997-99), Coun. for Chem. Rsch.(gov. bd. coun. 1999-2001). Achievements include research in granular dynamics, chaos, complex systems and mixing. Avocations: visual arts, painting. Home: 1092 Crescent Ln Winnetka IL 60093-1501 Office: Northwestern U Dept Chem Engring 2145 Sheridan Rd Evanston IL 60208-0834 Office Phone: 847-491-5220. Business E-Mail: jm-ottino@northwestern.edu.

OTTMAN, BOB, insurance company executive; B, Ea. Conn. State U., Willimantic. Cert. flexible compensation instrn. Employers Coun. Flexible Compensation. V.p. Frank Gates USA (formerly Acordia of Dallas); mgmt. position AFLAC Inc., Columbus, Ga., 1999, various leadership positions including v.p. adminstrv. svcs., new bus. & underwriting and new account set-up, sr. v.p. account implementation and mgmt. Office: AFLAC Inc 1932 Wynnton Rd Columbus GA 31999 Office Phone: 706-323-3431. *

OTTO, BYRON LEONARD, retired lawyer, state agency administrator; b. Battle Creek, Mich., Oct. 4, 1940; s. Henry John and Mildred Alice (Wagner) O. BBA, St. Edward's U., 1964, MBA, 1979; JD, U. Tex., 1968. Bar: U.S. Dist. Ct. (we. dist.) 1976. Staff atty. State Welfare Dept., Austin, Tex., 1968-75; sole practice Austin, Tex., 1975-77; assoc. James R. Sloan, Austin, Tex., 1978-79; adminstr. State Comptroller, Austin, Tex., 1980—; ret., 2000. Author articles and monographs. St. Edward's U. scholar, Austin, 1978. Mem. ABA, Tex. Bar. Democrat. Roman Catholic. Home: 4604 S Lamar Blvd Apt C202 Austin TX 78745-1358 Personal E-mail: byron3@austin.rr.com.

OTTO, ELIZABETH HALL, education educator; b. Florence, SC, Aug. 5, 1939; d. William Everette and Elizabeth Hines Hall; m. Willmer Jerome Otto, Nov. 26, 1971; children: Teresa, Michael, John. BA, Winthrop Coll., Rock Hill, SC, 1961; MA, U. N.C., Chapel Hill, 1964. Tchr. Lancaster H.S., SC, 1961—62; instr. Mitchell Coll., Statesville, NC, 1963—65; tchr. Myers Park H.S., Charlotte, 1967—68; instr. Bee County Coll., Beeville, Tex., 1968—72; prof. Fla. C.C., Jacksonville, 1979—. Dept. chair Fla. C.C., 1999—2003. Co-author: (article) Jour. Social Sci., 1990; project dir. (coll. course) Cmty. Econ. Devel., 1983 (2d pl. Joint Coun. Econ. Edn.). Named Outstanding Faculty, Fla. C.C., 1994. Mem.: So. Hist. Assn. Avocations: reading, travel. Home: 3665 Manor Oaks Dr Jacksonville FL 32277 E-mail: eotto@fccj.edu.

OTTO, FRED DOUGLAS, chemical engineering professor; b. Hardisty, Alta., Can., Jan. 12, 1935; BSc, U. Alta., 1957, MSc, 1959; PhD in Chem. Engring., U. Mich., Ann Arbor, 1963. From asst. prof. to assoc. prof. U. Alta., Edmonton, 1962-70, chmn., 1975-84, prof. chem. engring., 1970-96, dean engring., 1985-94, prof. emeritus, 1996—; pres., CEO DB Robinson & Assocs. Ltd., 1998—2002. Mem. governing coun. NRC, 1991-94. Recipient Donald L. Katz award, Gas Processors Assn., 1998. Fellow: Can. Acad. Engring.; mem.: AIChE, Can. Coun. Profl. Engrs. (bd. dirs. 1997—2003), Assn. Profl. Engrs., Geologists and Geophysicists of Alta. (1st v.p. 1995—96, pres. 1996—97, Centennial award 1993), Can. Soc. Chem. Engrs. (pres. 1986—87). Office: 12319 52d Ave Edmonton AB Canada T6H 0P5 Personal E-mail: fotto@interbaun.com.

OTTO, JEAN HAMMOND, journalist; b. Kenosha, Wis., Aug. 27, 1925; d. Laurence Cyril and Beatrice Jane (Slater) Hammond; m. John A. Otto, Aug. 22, 1946; children: Jane L. Rahman, Mary Ellen Takayama, Peter J.; m. Lee W. Baker, Nov. 23, 1973. Student, Ripon Coll., 1944-46. Women's editor Appleton (Wis.) Post-Crescent, 1960-68; reporter Milw. Jour., 1968-72, editorial writer, 1972-77, editor Op Ed page, 1977-83; editorial page editor Rocky Mountain News, Denver, 1983-89, assoc. editor, 1989-92, reader rep., 1992-99; endowed chair U. Denver, 1992-97. Founder, chmn. bd. trustees First Amendment Congress, 1979-85, chmn. exec. com., 1985-88, 89-91, pres. 1991-96, mem. bd. trustees, 1979-96; founding mem. Wis. Freedom of Info. Council. Recipient Headliner award Wis. Women in Communications, 1974; Outstanding Woman in Journalism award YWCA, Milw., 1977; Knight of Golden Quill Milw. Press Club, 1979; spl. citation in Journalism Ball State U., 1980; James Madison award Nat. Broadcast Editorial Assn., 1981; spl. citation for contbn. to journalism Nat. Press Photographers Assn., 1981; Ralph D. Casey award U. Minn., 1984; U. Colo. Regents award, 1985; John Peter Zenger award U. Ariz., 1988; Paul Miller Medallion award Okla. State U., 1990; Colo. SPJ Lowell Thomas award, 1990, Disting. Alumna award Ripon Coll., 1992, Hugh M. Hefner First Amendment Lifetime Achievement award Playboy Found., 1994; named to Milw. Press Club Hall of Fame, 1993, Freedom of Info. Hall of Fame, 1996. Mem.: Soc. Profl. Journalists (nat. treas. 1975, nat. sec. 1977, pres.-elect 1978, pres. 1979—80, pres. Sigma Delta Chi Found. 1989—92, chair Found. 1992—94, First Amendment award 1981, Wells Key 1984), Am. Soc. Newspaper Editors (bd. dirs. 1987—92), Colo. Press Assn. (chmn. freedom of info. com. 1983—89), Assn. Edn. in Journalism and Mass Communications (Disting. Svc. award 1984), Milw. Press Club (Hall of Fame 1993). Home: 2462 N Prospect #311 Milwaukee WI 53211 Personal E-mail: jottofirst@aol.com.

OTTO, MARIE (BERTHA OTTO), educational administrator, educational consulting company executive; b. Houston, July 11, 1930; d. Robert Lillard and Bertha Irene (Allen) Davis; m. Robert Lee Otto, Jan. 7, 1950; children: Lois Ann Otto Buschmann, Barbara Jeane Otto Hunt, Robert Lee Jr. Student, Tex. Christian U., 1947-49, Hardin-Simmons U., summers 1947, 49, 54; BA in Speech, Drama and Edn., Sul-Ross State U., 1954; postgrad., U. Wyo., 1961, U. Calif., Santa Barbara, 1962, Calif. State U., Northridge, 1964; MA, Calif. State U., Long Beach, 1969, postgrad., 1980-82. Lic. tchr., Tex., secondary tchr., Wyo., Calif.; lic. psychologist; lic. marriage and family counselor. Tchr. high schs., Tex., Wyo. and Calif., 1956-64; tchr., counselor Excelsior High Sch., Norwalk, Calif., 1964-66; counselor Neff High Sch., La Mirada, Calif., 1966-69; psychologist Huntington Beach (Calif.) Union High Sch. Dist., 1969-74, project mgr., dir. pupil pers., 1974-80, asst. supt., 1980-84, supt., 1984-88, supt. emeritus, 1988—. V.p. Poole-Young-Koehler Assocs., Inc., Long Beach, 1964-79; pvt. practice marriage and family counselor, Fountain Valley, Calif., 1970—; pres. Marie Otto Assocs., Fountain Valley, 1979—; supr. student tchrs. Chapman Univ. Orange, Calif., 1988—; sec.-treas., Ctr. for Teaching Thinking, Huntington Beach, 1991—. Mem. Fountain Valley Human Svcs. Com., Huntington Beach Human Resources Commn., state planning com. Girl Scouts U.S., Worland, Wyo., 1959-61; pres. Spl. Edn. Local Plan Orgn., 1983-84; bd. dirs. Humana Hosp. Huntington Beach, Golden West Coll. Found., Huntington Beach, Huntington Beach Community Clinic, Orange County chpt. ARC, Santa Ana, Calif, No on Drugs, 1988—; sec., treas. Ctr. for Teaching of Thinking, Huntington Beach, 1992—. Recipient numerous plaques including Fountain Valley Human Svcs. Com., 1979, City of Fountain Valley, 1975, 79, 88, City of Huntington Beach, 1988, Fountain Valley C. of C., 1988, City of Westminster, 1988, Orange Coast Coll., 1988, Golden West Coll., 1988, Ocean View Sch. Dist., 1988, Spl. Edn. Local Plan Orgn., 1984; named Woman of Yr., Soroptimist Club, Westminster, 1984, Disting. Alumnus, Grad. Sch. Edn. Calif. State U., Long Beach, 1988. Home and Office: 16689 Mount Hoffman Cir Fountain Valley CA 92708-2435

OTTO, ROBERT L., information technology executive; Joined US Postal Svc., Washington, 1980, v.p. fin., v.p. info. tech., chief info. officer, chief tech. officer, 2003—. Mailing: US Postal Service Rm 2017 475 L'Enfant Plaza SW Washington DC 20260-4100 Office Phone: 202-268-6900. E-mail: robert.l.otto@usps.gov.

OTUNNU, OLARA A., childrens organization official; b. Mucwini (Chua), Northern Uganda, Sept. 1950; Attended, Makerere U., Kampala; exch. student, Oxford U.; Fulbright Scholar, Harvard U. Assoc. atty. Chadbourne and Parke, NY; asst. prof. law Albany Law Sch.; mem. Uganda Nat. Consultative Coun., 1979—80; permanent rep. of Uganda UN, 1980—85; pres. Security Coun., 1981; chmn. African Group, 1981; vice pres. Gen. Assembly, 1982—83; chmn. Contact Group on Global Negotiations, 1982—93, Commn. on Human Rights, 1983—84, Gen. Assembly Credientials Com., 1983—84, Drafting Com. of the Ministerial Mtg. of Non-Aligned Countries, 1983; min. Fgn. Affairs of Uganda, 1985—86; vis. fellow Inst. Francais des Relations Internat., 1987—89; vis. prof. Am. U., Paris, 1987—89; pres. Internat. Peace Acad., 1990—97; special rep., sec. gen. for Children and Armed Conflict United Nations, 1997—2006; pres. LBL Found. for Children, NYC. Mem. Internat. Task Force on Security Coun. Peace Enforcement; pres. Internat. Peace Acad.; mem. UN Group of Experts on New Concepts of Internat. Security, 1984—85, Commonwealth Group of Experts Study Group on the Security of Small States, 1984—85, Internat. Panel on Mgmt. and Decision-Making in the UN, 1986—87, Group on Rethinking Internat. Governance, 1986—90, Commn. on Global Governance, 1992—95, Carnegie Commn. on Preventing Deadly Conflict, 1994—. Bd. mem. Aspen Inst., Internat. Selection Commn. of the Philadelphia Liberty Medal, Carnegie Endowment for Internat. Peace, Aspen France, Coun. of African Advisors to the World Bank, Internat. Patrons of the Refugee Studies Programme, Oxford U., Aspen Italia; advisory com. Stockholm Internat. Peace Rsch. Inst.; bd. mem. Carnegie Corp. of NY, Hampshire Coll. Recipient Sydney Peace Prize, 2005. Office: LBL Foundation for Children Carnegie Corporation of New York 437 Madison Ave New York NY 10022

OTWELL, RALPH MAURICE, retired newspaper editor; b. Hot Springs, Ark., June 17, 1926; s. Walter Clement and Pearl Oda (Tisdale) O.; m. Janet Barbara Smith, July 18, 1953; children— Brian Thornton, Douglas Keith, David Smith. Student, U. Ark., 1947-48; BS, Northwestern U., 1951; postgrad. (Nieman fellow), Harvard, 1959-60. Reporter, telegraph editor So. Newspapers, Inc., Hot Springs, 1943-44, 47; asst. city editor Chgo. Sun-Times, 1953-59, news editor, 1959-63, asst. mng. editor, 1963-65, asst. to editor, 1965-68, mng. editor, 1968-76, editor, 1976-80, exec. v.p., editor, 1980-84. Mgmt. bd. newspaper div. Field Enterprises, Inc., 1967-84; lectr. Medill Sch. Journalism, Northwestern U., 1955—; charter mem. Nat. News Council, 1973-80; coord. Northwestern Inst. Learning in Retirement, 1992—. Trustee Garrett-Evang. Theol. Sem., 1965-79; mem. nat. bd. Christian Social Concerns, United Meth. Ch., 1968-72; mem. bd. Community Renewal Soc., 1987-90, Chgo. Reporter, 1987-90, student publs. Northwestern U., 1968-72. Served to 1st lt. AUS, 1944-47, 51-53. Recipient Page One award Chgo. Newspaper Guild, 1964; named Ill. Journalist of Year No. Ill. U., 1974 Mem. Am. Soc. Newspaper Editors (chmn. ethics com. 1976-77), AP Mng. Editors Assn., Soc. Profl. Journalists (dir. 1966-71, sec. 1971-72, v.p. 1972-73, pres. 1973-74), Northwestern U. Alumni Assn. (dir. 1965-68, 91-93, sec. 1993-94, Merit award 1969, Svc. award 1995, chair seminar day com. 2001-2002), Sigma Delta Chi (pres. 1987-89), Kappa Tau Alpha, Econ. Club, Headline Club (pres. Chgo. chpt. 1965-66), Harvard Club Chgo., Chgo. Press Club (dir. 1968-77), Northwestern Club. Home: 34 Knox Cir Evanston IL 60201-1912 Personal E-mail: ralph@otwell.com.

OUALLINE, VIOLA JACKSON, psychologist, consultant; b. Edna, Tex., Oct. 17, 1927; d. S.R. Jackson and Myrtle Mae Wood; m. Charles M. Oualline Jr., Sept. 3, 1949; children: Stephen, Susan, Shari. BS, U. Houston, 1949; MS, North Tex. State U., 1962, PhD, 1975. Phys. therapist Hermann Hosp., Houston, 1948-49; pvt. practice Austin, Tex., 1949-54; Miller Orthopedic Clinic, Charlotte, N.C., 1956-57; psychologist Dallas Easter Seal Soc., 1963-81, dir. psychology dept., 1981-93; pvt. practice, 1993—. Psychol. cons. Mesquite Ind. Sch. Dist., Tex., 1974—, Duncanville Sch. Dist., Tex., 1974-76, Grand Prarie Ind. Sch. Dist., Tex., 1976-79. Mem. Am. Psychol. Assn., Tex. Psychol. Assn., Dallas Psychol. Assn., Am. Assn. Counseling Devel., Coun. for Exceptional Children, Chi Omega Mother's Club. Baptist. Avocations: reading, bicycle riding. Office: Ste 208 11311 N Central Expy Dallas TX 75243-6729 Office Phone: 214-696-1079.

OUDERKIRK, ANDREW J., corporate scientist; BS, No. Ill. U., 1978; PhD in Physical Chemistry, Northwestern U., 1983. With Universal Oil Products, DuPont; joined 3M Film and Light Mgmt., St. Paul, 1985, 3M corp. scientist. Mem.: NAE, Am. Chem. Soc. (Creative Invention Award 2004, Industrial Innovation Award 2003). Achievements include invention of 3M Multilayer Optical Film (MOF) technology. Office: 3M Corp Hdqs 3M Ctr Saint Paul MN 55144-1000

OUDERKIRK, MASON JAMES, lawyer; b. Des Moines, Feb. 1, 1953; s. Mason George and Florence Astor (Lowe) O.; m. Kari Aune Hormel, May 28, 1983; 1 child, Mason Christopher. BA, Drake U., 1975, JD, 1978. Bar: Iowa 1978, US Dist. Ct. (so. dist.) Iowa 1978, US Dist. Ct. (no. dist.) Iowa 2006, US Ct. Appeals (8th cir.). Assoc. M.G. Ouderkirk Law Office, Indianola, Iowa, 1978-79; ptnr. Ouderkirk Law Firm, Indianola, 1979-96; sr. mem. Ouderkirk, Ouderkirk & Dougherty, P.L.C., Indianola, 1996-98; proprietor Ouderkirk Law Firm, Indianola, Iowa, 1998—; pres. Avanti Realty Co. (formerly Landmark Real Estate, Ltd.), Indianola, 1978—2002, Avanti Builders Co., Indianola, 1991—2002. Mem. Vol. Lawyers Project of Iowa, 1987-93. Mem. Indianola Police Retirement Bd., 1983-88; instr. Eric Heintz Black Belt Acad., 1988-93, Indianola Parks and Recreation Dept., 1988-93; mem. Nominating Commn., Warren County Assoc. Dist. Ct., 1999-05; mem. Jud. Nominating Commn. for 5A Jud. Dist. of Iowa, 2002-. Mem. ABA, Iowa Bar Assn. (pub. rels. com. 1989-94, family law com. 1989-90), Warren County Bar Assn. (sec., treas. 1985-89, v.p. 1989-90, pres. 1990-92), 5th Jud. Dist. Bar Assn. (sec., treas. 1995), Assn. Trial Lawyers Am., Iowa Trial Lawyers Assn. Episcopalian. Avocations: fishing, fitness and weight training, gardening. Home and Office: 108 S Howard St PO Box 156 Indianola IA 50125-0156 Office Phone: 515-961-5315. Office Fax: 515-961-0304. Business E-Mail: olfirm@qwest.net.

OUDIZ, RONALD, cardiologist; BA, U. Calif., San Diego, 1985; MD, U. So.Calif., LA, 1987—89. Diplomate Calif., 1989. Academic physician dept. med. edn. St. Mary Med. Ctr., Long Beach, Calif., 1996—2002; clin. instr. UCLA Sch. Medicine, 1995—96, asst. prof., 1996—2002; co-dir. Liu Ctr. for Pulmonary Hypertension Harbor-UCLA Med. Ctr., Torrance, 1998—99, dir. Liu Ctr. for Pulmonary Hypertension, 1999—; assoc. prof. divsn. cardiology David Geffen Sch. Medicine, UCLA, 2003—. Office: LA Biomed Rsch Inst UCLA Med Ctr 1124 W Carson St Torrance CA 90502 Office Phone: 310-222-2515. Office Fax: 310-787-0448. Business E-Mail: oudiz@humc.edu.

OUELLETTE, DANIEL RONALD, pulmonary and critical care medicine specialist; b. Detroit, Sept. 9, 1956; s. Lois Emma Schramm Ouellette; m. Christine Fuller, Nov. 16, 2004. BS, Pa. State U., 1977; MS, U. Pitts., 1980, MD, 1984. Diplomate Am. Bd. Internal Medicine, Am. Bd. Pulmonary Medicine, Am. Bd. Critical Care Medicine. Commd. 2d lt. U.S. Army, 1984, advanced through grades to col., 2000; intern William Beaumont Army Med. Ctr., El Paso, Tex., 1984-85, resident in medicine, 1985-87, chief med. resident, 1987-88; pulmonary fellow Brooke Army Med. Ctr., San Antonio, 1988-90, critical care fellow, 1990-91, staff physician, 1994—2005, Fitzsimons Army Med. Ctr., Denver, 1991-94; assoc. dir. med. critical care Henry Ford Health Sys., Detroit, 2005—; assoc. prof. medicine Wayne State U., Sch. Medicine, 2006—. Cons. US Army Surgeon Gen. Pulmonary Disease, 2000—04. Contbr. articles to profl. jours. Decorated Army Commendation medal. Fellow Am. Coll. Chest Physicians; mem. Am. Thoracic Soc. Office: Henry Ford Hosp K17 2799 W Grand Blvd Detroit MI 48202 Home Phone: 248-693-0976; Office Phone: 313-916-2439. Business E-Mail: douelle1@hfhs.org.

OUNDJIAN, PETER, conductor, music director; b. Toronto, Canada; m. Nadine Oundjian; children: Lara, Peter. Grad, Royal Coll. Music, London; studied violin, Julliard Sch., NYC. First violinist Tokyo String Quartet, 1981—95; music dir. Nieuw Sinfonietta Amsterdam, 1998—2003; artistic dir., prin. condr. Caramoor Internat. Music Festival, Katonah, NY, 1995—; music dir. Toronto Symphony, 2004—. Vis. prof. Yale Sch. of Music; prin. guest condr. Colo. Symphony, 2003—; guest condr. San Francisco Symphony, Pitts. Symphony, Detroit Symphony, Houston Symphony, St. Louis Symphony, Nat. Symphony Orch., Cin. Symphony Orch., Konzerthaus, Berlin, City of Birmingham Symphony, NDR Hanover Symphony, Saarbrucken Radio Symphony, Zurich Tonhalle, Chgo. Symphony, LA Philharm.; guest artistic dir., condr. Mozart Festival; guest condr. Grand Teton Festival, 2005, Aspen Festival, 2005, Tanglewood Festivals, 2005. Recipient Gold medal for Most Disting. Student, Royal Coll. of Music, London, Stoutzker prize, First prize, Internat. Violin Competition in Vina Del Mar, Chile, 1980. Office: Toronto Symphony Orch 212 King St W, Ste 550 Toronto ON Canada M5H 1K5 *

OURISMAN, MANDELL JACK, automotive executive; b. Nov. 10, 1926; m. Mary Martin Stiles, June 1993. Student, U.S. Naval Acad., 1944, Georgetown U., 1947. Chmn., CEO Ourisman Automotive Enterprises, Marlow Heights, Md. Office: Ourisman Automotive Enterprises 4400 Branch Ave Temple Hills MD 20748-1802 Home Phone: 202-667-6696; Office Phone: 301-423-4028. Personal E-mail: mjo@ourismanchevrolet.com.

OUROUSSOFF, NICOLAI, architecture critic; Architecture critic LA Times, Calif., 1996—2004, NY Times, 2004—. Finalist 45th Ann. S. Cali. Journalism awards, 2003, Pulitzer Prize, 2003, 2004; recipient 46th Ann. S. Cali. Journalism awards, 2004. Office: NY Times Culture Desk 229 W 43rd St New York NY 10036 Office Phone: 212-556-1702. Office Fax: 212-556-1516.

OURSLER, FULTON, JR., editor, writer; b. West Falmouth, Mass., June 27, 1932; s. Fulton and Grace (Perkins) O.; m. Anne Noel Nevill, Nov. 29, 1954; children: Theresa Noel, Fulton III, Mark Nevill, James Randall, Carroll Grace. BA, Georgetown U., 1954. With Reader's Digest, Pleasantville, NY, 1956-87, book editor, 1968-70, sr. staff editor, 1970-72, asst. mng. editor, 1973, mng. editor, 1974-82, exec. editor, 1982-85, dep. editor-in-chief, 1986-87; editor-in-chief Guideposts mag., 1992—99; editor-in-chief, founding editor Angels on Earth mag., 1995-98, editl. dir., 1998-99; roving editor Guideposts mag., 2001—. Established: Fulton Oursler Meml. Collection, Georgetown U. Library.; editor: (commentary) Behold This Dreamer, 1964. Bd. dirs. Georgetown U. Library Assocs. Mem.: Friends of the Nyacks, Univ. Club. Home: 2 Laveta Pl Nyack NY 10960-1604 E-mail: tedlit1@verizon.net. *Man makes two journeys in life: one in matter, the other in spirit. The first journey is outward and manifest; it leads to family, society, and career. The second journey is inward and invisible; it leads to the kingdom of God. The first journey is limited by logic, flesh, and time. The second is infinite, and its pathway is paradox. Self-preservation is the strongest instinct on the first journey; freedom, maturity, self-knowledge, power, and abundance seem to be important goals. But on the second journey, one learns that to find our truest selves, we must lose the sense of self; that to grow we must become as a child; that freedom is won by surrender, that the one counts for more than the many, that the meek are powerful, and the poor are rich. On both journeys, to gain life one must lose it, and be reborn.*

OUSSANI, JAMES JOHN, manufacturing executive; b. Bklyn., Jan. 3, 1920; s. John Thomas and Clara (Tager) Oussani; m. Lorraine G. Tutundgy, Apr. 25, 1954; children: James J., Gregory P., Rita C. BMechE, Pratt Inst., NYC, 1942; JD (hon.), Lynn U., Boca Raton. Dir. rsch., mfg. Supertronic Co., NYC, 1943—46; sr. ptnr. Perl-Oussani Machine Mfg. Co., NYC, 1946—49; founder Staplex Co., Bklyn., 1949, pres., 1949—. Exec. dir. Lourdes Realty Corp.; bd. dirs. Junios Corp.; prodr. air sampling equipment for radioactive fallout AEC, 1951—. Active Bur. Rsch. Air Pollution Control, Pres.'s Coun. on Youth Opportunity, Cardinal's Com. for Edn., Lumen Christi Found.; founder, bd. dirs. Oussani Found.; founder James J. & Lorraine G. Oussani Scholarship Fund Coll. Boca Raton, Boca Raton; bd. overseers Lynn U., Boca Raton; trustee Ch. of Virgin Mary; founding mem. Lumen Christi-Palm Beach Diocese; cardinal's com. of laity, bishop's com. of laity; bd. dirs. St. Joan Arc Found., Boca Raton, Fla. Decorated knight of Jerusalem; recipient Blue Ribbon Mining award, Sch. Mgmt. award, Aerospace Pride Achievement award. Mem.: Office Equipment Assn., Nat. Stationery and Office Equipment Assn., Office Adminstrn. Assn., Adminstrv. Mgmt. Soc., Nat. Office Products Assn., Nat. Office Machine Dealers Assn., Nat. Office Machine Mfg. Assn., Office Execs. Assn., Bus. Equipment Mfrs. Assn., Our Lady Perpetual Help Holy Name Soc., Salaam Club, Mahopac Golf Club (Lake Mahopac, NY), Boca Raton Hotel and Resort Club, Internat. Club of Boca Raton, Knights of Holy Sepulchre, Knights of St. Gregory, Rotary, Knights of Malta. Achievements include invention of automatic electric stapling machine; patents in field. Home: 875 E Camino Real Boca Raton FL 33432

OUSTERHOUT, DOUGLAS KENNETH, plastic surgeon; b. Bellaire, Mich., Aug. 30, 1935; s. Kenneth and Naomi Ousterhout; children from previous marriage: Donald, Susan, Oliver, Thomas. Student, U. Colo., 1953—55; DDS, U. Mich., 1961, MD, 1965. Resident gen. surgery U. Med.; resident in plastic surgery Stanford U., Palo Alto, Calif., 1969—72; craniofacial tng. Dr. Tessier, Paris, 1972—73; clin. instr. U. Calif., San Francisco, 1973—86, clin. prof., 1986—. Editor: Aesthetic Contouring of the Craniofacial Skeleton, 1991; author: Cocktails for Two (AKA: Death Gets a Facelift), 1993. Capt. US Army, 1966—68. Mem.: French Soc. Maxillofacial Surgeons, French Soc. Plastic, Reconstructive and Aesthetic Surgeons, Pan Pacific Surg. Assn. (pres. 1998—2000), Am. Soc. Maxillofacial Surgeons (pres. 1994—95), Internat. Soc. Craniofacial Surgeons, Am. Assn. Plastic Surgeons, Am. Soc. Plastic Surgeons, Equadorian Soc. Craniofacial Surgery (hon.), Japan Soc. Craniofacial Surgery (hon.). Avocations: piano, sculpting, gardening, travel. Home: 2640 Steiner St San Francisco CA 94115 Office: Ste 150 45 Castro St San Francisco CA 94114 Office Phone: 415-626-2888. E-mail: ousterht@cris.com.

OUTCALT, DAVID LEWIS, academic administrator, mathematics professor, consultant, musician; b. L.A., Jan. 30, 1935; s. Earl Kinyon and Alberta Estes (Ferguson) Outcalt; m. Marcia Lee Beach, July 1, 1956 (dec.); children: Jeffrey David, Kevin Douglas, Gregory Mark, Eric Matthew. BA in Math., Pomona Coll., Claremont, Calif., 1956; MA in Math., Claremont Grad. U., 1958; PhD in Math., Ohio State U., Columbus, 1963; DPub Adminstrn. (hon.), Kyung Hee U., Korea, 1984. Asst. prof. math. Claremont McKenna Coll., 1962-64; from asst. prof. to prof. U. Calif., Santa Barbara, 1964-80, chmn. dept. math., 1969-72, dean instrnl.

devel., 1977-80; vice chancellor acad. affairs U. Alaska, Anchorage, 1980-81, prof. math., 1980-86, chancellor, 1981-86; prof. natural and applied sci. U. Wis., Green Bay, 1986-93, Hendrickson prof. econ. devel., 1994-98, chancellor, 1986—93, chancellor emeritus, 1998—. Pres. Mid-Continent Athletic Conf., 1990—91. Author: math. textbooks; contbr. articles to profl. jours. Mem. exec. bd. western Alaska coun. Boy Scouts Am., 1982—86, mem. exec. bd. Bay-Lakes Coun., 1987—97, v.p. exploring, 1988—92, v.p. ops., 1992—93, pres., 1993—94; mem. Anchorage Symphony Bd., 1986, Green Bay Symphony Bd., 1988—97, Weidner Ctr. Presents Bd., 1994—98; peer reviewer NCAA, 1994—99; trustee, v.p., treas. Kauai Internat. Theatre, 1998—2000; trustee Kauai CC Fund, 2000—05, trustee emeritus, 2005—; moderator bd. trustees Humana Hosp., Anchorage, 1982—83. Grantee, USAF Office Sci. Rsch., 1964—71, U. Calif., 1975—78, NSF, 1976—79. Mem.: Brown County Indsl. Devel. (pres. bd. dirs. 1994—97), Internat. Assn. Univ. Pres.'s (mem. exec. com. 1988—96, mem. N.Am. coun. exec. com. 1988—2002, newsletter editor 1994—95, mem. internat. com. tech. higher edn. 1996—2002), Math. Assn. Am., Greater Green Bay C. of C. (advance bd. 1987—97, bd. dirs. 1991—94, 1995—97), Rotary (bd. dirs. Kapaa club 1999—2004, pres. 2002—03, chair 2003—05, bd. dirs. Kapaa Found. 2003—05), Sigma Xi. Presbyterian. Home: 1606 Palisades Dr Pacific Palisades CA 90272 Personal E-mail: outcaltd@verizon.net.

OUTIN, MARY LOUISE, business, multi-cultural history and geneology educator; b. Peak, SC, July 18, 1948; d. Ralph T. Williams and Mary Frances Wicker-Outin, Theopolis Outin (Stepfather). BA in Bus. Adminstrn., Columbia Coll., Columbia, South Carolina, 1987; MEd, Lesley U., 1999; grad., S.C. Sch. Real Estate, 1986. Owner MO Businesses, Inc., Columbia, 2000—. N/A. Mem.: S.C. Afro-Am. Hist. and Geneal. Soc., Inc. (co-pub. rels. dir. 1998—2000), Am. Legion Aux. (Unit 219 2000). Avocations: family history research, genealogy, cooking, reading. Office: MO Businesses Inc P O Box 3393 Columbia SC 29230

OUTLAW, WANDA CECELIA, priest; b. Washington, Oct. 17, 1954; d. Augustus King and Mary Lena (Booze) Brown; 1 child, Stephen Thomas Jr. Ordained priest 2002. Tng. mgr. Bur. ATF, Washington, 1989—; leadership, women's retreat leader African-Am. Cath. Congregation, Washington, 1993—, priest, 2002—. Preacher Women Uplifting Women Ministries, Washington, 2003—; designer, trainer LJR Group, Inc., Dallas, 2005—. Author: Woven Baskets on the Baobab Tree, In The Fulfillment. Active socks and sandwiches for the homeless Dynamic Crossroads, Washington, 2005; motivational spkr. Execs. of FEW, Balt., 2003—04. Mem.: NAACP (assoc.), NAFE (assoc.). Office: Imani Temple on Capitol Hill 609-611 Maryland Ave NE Washington DC 20002 Home Phone: 202-489-3752; Office Phone: 202-388-8155. Personal E-mail: wanda.outlaw@atf.gov. Business E-Mail: noni.crowmother@verizon.net.

OUTMAN, WILLIAM DELL, II, lawyer; b. St. Petersburg, Fla., Nov. 10, 1940; s. Boyd Johnson and Marion Lucetta (Banks) O.; m. Sally Rockwell, June 29, 1963 (dec. Sept. 1998); children: William Dell III, Stephanie O. Kiker, Sarah O. Brophy; m. Deborah A. Ripoli, Sept. 14, 2002. BS in Bus. Adminstrn., Washington and Lee U., 1962; JD, Georgetown U., 1965, LLM in Taxation, 1968. Bar: DC 1966, NY 1999. Assoc. atty. Baker & McKenzie, Washington, 1965-70, ptnr., 1970-97, mng. ptnr. NYC, 1997-2000, ptnr. Washington, 2000—. Mem. adv. bd. Georgetown U. Internat. Trade Update; sec. bd. trustees Hist. Soc. of US Ct. Internat. Trade, 2006—. Staff sgt. US Army, 1965—71. Mem. Customs and Internat. Trade Bar Assn. (past pres., bd. dirs. 1992-06), Ct. Internat. Trade Adv. Com. (current chmn. 1990—), Congl. Country Club, Met. Club, Omicron Delta Kappa. Office: Baker & McKenzie 815 Connecticut Ave NW Ste 900 Washington DC 20006-4004 Office Phone: 202-452-7010. Business E-Mail: william.d.outman@bakernet.com.

OUTT, HELEN MAY, retired elementary school educator, psychologist; d. Spurgeon Eugene Weir and Edna May Kling; m. Terry Franklin Outt, May 25, 1960; children: Daina, Holly. BS, West Chester U., Pa., 1964, MEd, 1971. Cert. tchr. Ind., 1987, sch. counselor Ind., 1988, psychologist Assn. Masters in Psychology, 1999, lic. mental health counselor Ind., 2000, psychologist Ind., 2002. Tchr. Interboro Sch. Dist., Prospect Pk., Pa., 1966—69; counselor mid. sch. Chester (Pa.) Sch. Dist., 1969—70; tchr. elem. sch. Cin. (Ohio) Sch. Dist., 1974—85; tchr., counselor Indpls. (Ind.) Sch. Dist., 1986—2005, ret., 2005. Actor: (plays) Little Theater. Vol. food and clothing drive Indpls. (Ind.) Pub. Schs., 1986—2005; vol. polls Cin. (Ohio) Rep., 1975. Recipient Above and Beyond Call of Duty award, Indpls. (Ind.) Pub. Schs., 1993. Mem.: NEA (lic. adminstrn. and supr. 1987), Ind. Mental Health Counselors Assn., N.Am. Masters Psychology, Ind. Sch. Counseling Assn., Ind. Counseling Assn., Ind. State Tchrs. Assn., Indpls. (Ind.) Edn. Assn. (dir. region 1986—2000, dir. dist. 1986—2000, bldg. rep. 1986—2005, chmn. profl. devel. com. 1990—98, nat. rep.), Phi Delta Kappa. Republican. Meth. Avocations: photography, making greeting cards.

OUTTEN, KRISTINA MARIE, secondary school educator; b. Ogden, Utah, Dec. 6, 1973; d. Burrett William and June J. Clay; m. Todd Edgar Outten, Nov. 16, 1996; 1 child, Nastassia Jade. BA in English Edn., U. Ariz., 1996, MA in Ednl. Psychology, 2000; postgrad., U. Phoenix. Bar mgr. Bushwacker, Tucson, 1995-96; student tchr. Tucson H.S. Tucson Unified Sch. Dist., 1996, tchr. Alice Vail Mid. Sch., 1996—. Com. mem. 504 rev. team, awards and site-based decision making team Vail Mid. Sch., 1998—; adj. prof. U. Phoenix Online. Author: And So It Begins..., 1999, Snakebite, 2003, In The Spider's Web, 2005; contbr. poetry to Nat. Libr. of Poetry-Libr. of Congress, A View from Afar, The Peace We Knew, A Muse to Follow, Blossom in the Dawning, The Colors of Thought, Serenity at Daybreak; author poems (Editor's Choice awards 1996, 97, 98) Regents scholar U. Ariz., 1991; Vocal Talent scholar Am. Legend, 1991. Mem. Tucson Edn. Assn., Internat. Soc. Poets. Avocations: writing, singing, reading, travel. E-mail: doc@kmoutten.com.

OUTWATER, JOHN OGDEN, mechanical engineering educator; b. London, Jan. 2, 1923; came to U.S., 1924; s. John Ogden and Nenny (Boe) O.; m. Alice Hooker Davidson, Dec. 13, 1952; children— Anne Hooker, Catherine Boe (Mrs. Carl B. Colby), Alice Brookfield (Mrs. Robert B. Lang), John Ogden III. BA, Cambridge U., Eng., 1943, MA, 1948; ScD, MIT, 1950; PhD, Cambridge, Eng., 1976. Registered profl. engr. Research engr. DuPont Co., 1950-52; project engr. Universal Moulded Products, 1952-53; indsl. liaison officer Mass. Inst. Tech., 1954-55; prof. mech. engring. U. Vt., Burlington, 1955—71, chmn., 1955-93, prof. emeritus, 1993—. Leader archaeol. expdns. Wenner-Gren Found., Central Mexico, 1954, Yucatan, 1955, Peru-Bolivia, 1957, Haiti, 1959; cons. non-metallic materials Naval Ordnance Lab., Nat. Acad. Scis., Monsanto Rsch. Corp., Smithsonian Instn., pres. Vt. Inst. Co., Inc. Author: (with others) Engineering Materials, 1959, Esplendor del Mexico Antigua; papers on metal cutting, plastics, archaeology, bones, ski safety, botany. Chmn. Vt. Instrument Co., Inc.; Mem. Vt. Conf. Econ. Growth; vestryman St. Paul's Cathedral, Burlington. Served as officer Brit. Army, 1943-47. Named Vt. Engr. of Year, 1970; grantee USPHS; Timken fellow MIT, 1950 Fellow ASME; mem. ASTM, Holland Soc., Vt. Soc. Engrs., Delta Psi, Tau Beta Pi. Achievements include patents for ski boot tension. Home: 62 Overlake Park Burlington VT 05401-4012 Office: 131 St Pauls St Burlington VT 05401-4595 Office Phone: 802-862-2089. Personal E-mail: jooutwater@aol.com.

OUWELEEN, MICHAEL, communications executive; b. 1968; BA in Eng., Georgetown U., Washington, DC, BA in Theology. V.p. J. Walter Thompson, NY; copywriter Korey, Kay & Partners, NY; co-creator, writer, exec. prodr. Harvey Birdman, Attorney as Law, Cartoon Network; sr. v.p., Programming and Devel. Cartoon Network. Named one of 40 Executives Under 40, Multichannel News, 2006. Office: Cartoon Network Lp LLLP 1050 Techwood Dr Atlanta GA 30303 Office Phone: 404-827-1700. Office Fax: 404-827-2559.

OUYANG, HAO, research scientist; m. Ying Zhang, Dec. 22, 2003. PhD, Rutgers U., NJ, 1996—2001. Mem.: Asp, Sid. Achievements include research in vivo measurement of skin. Office: Unilever 40 Merritt Blvd Trumbull CT 06611 Home Phone: 203-288-7640.

OUYANG, NORMA M., psychologist; arrived in U.S., 1985; m. Steve C. Ouyang, Jan. 1, 1970; children: Francis, Luke. BA, Nat. Taiwan Normal U., 1970; MBA, Pacific State U., 1988; MA, Azusa Pacific U., 1998, D of Psychology, 2003. Clin. psychologist Calif. Bd. Psychology. Founder, cons. Family Enrichment, Irvine, Calif., 1988—; with Orange County Health Care Agy., Westminster, 1999; intern U. Calif., Riverside, 2002—03; clin. psychologist Calif. State U., Fullerton, 2004—. Sr. group coord. Orange County Chimes Cath. Assn., Anaheim, Calif., 1989—93; asst. gen. mgr. Valone Computer Co., Irvine, 1988—93. Fellow, Calif. State U., Fullerton, 2003—04. Mem.: APA, Asian Faculty/Staff Assn., Am. Coll. Personnel Assn. Democrat. Roman Catholic. Avocations: reading, music, writing, travel.

OUZTS, DAVID PERRY, church music director, organist; b. Greenville, SC, Nov. 30, 1962; s. Perry Cooper and Sara Owens Ouzts; life ptnr. Joseph Lee Middleton, Oct. 8, 1995. MusB, Furman U., Greenville, SC, 1985; MusM, diploma in Sacred Music, diploma in Anglican studies, Yale U., 1987. Organist, choirmaster Trinity Episcopal Ch., Huntington, W.Va., 1987—90; dir. of music Congregation B'nai Sholom, Huntington, W.Va., 1988—90; assoc. dir. of music and fine arts St. Luke's United Meth. Ch., Houston, 1990—96; canon musician, liturgist Grace Episcopal Cathedral, Topeka, 1996—2001; dir. of music Ch. of Holy Communion, Memphis, 2001—. Liturgy and music cons. Episcopal Diocese of W.Va., Charleston, 1988—90; commn. on liturgy and music Episcopal Diocese of Kans., Topeka, 1997—2001; music dir. Memphis Girls Choir, 2002—. Mem. Rotary Club, Huntington, W.Va., 1987—89. Named to Order of Ky. Colonels, Commonwealth of Ky., 1989; Homozel Mickel Daniel Music scholarship, Furman U., 1981-85, Grad. Assistantship in Sacred Music, Yale Inst. of Sacred Music, 1985-87, Grad. Assistantship in Organ, Ind. U., 1990. Mem.: Hymn Soc. in the US and Can., Choristers Guild, Assn. of Diocesan Liturgy and Music Commns., Am. Recorder Soc., Am. Guild of English Handbell Ringers, Am. Choral Dirs. Assn., Royal Sch. of Ch. Music, Assn. of Anglican Musicians, Organ Hist. Soc., Am. Guild of Organists (dean 1988—90). Episcopalian. Avocations: walking, history, computers. Office: Church of Holy Communion 4645 Walnut Grove Rd Memphis TN 38117-2597 Home Phone: 901-553-1289. Business E-Mail: douzts@holycommunion.org.

OUZTS, EUGENE THOMAS, minister, secondary education educator; b. Thomasville, Ga., June 7, 1930; s. John Travis and Livie Mae (Strickland) O.; m. Mary Olive Vineyard, May 31, 1956. BA, Harding U., Searcy, AR, 1956, MA, 1957; postgrad., Murray State U., KY, U. Ark., U. Ariz., Ariz. State U., No. Ariz. U. Cert. secondary tchr., Ark., Mo., Ariz.; cert. c.c. tchr., Ariz.; ordained minister Church of Christ, 1956. Min. various chs., Ark., Tex., Mo., 1957—65; tchr. various pub. schs., 1959—92; min. Ch. of Christ, Ariz., 1965—; 1st lt. CAP/USAF, 1980, advanced through grades to lt. col., 1989, chaplain Ariz., 1982—, asst. wing chaplain, 1985—. Adviser student activities Clifton (Ariz.) Pub. Schs., 1965-92; bd. dirs. Ariz. Ch. of Christ Bible Camp, Tucson, 1966-2005. Mem. airport adv. bd. Greenlee County, Clifton, Ariz., 1992—. Recipient Meritorious Svc. award, 1994, Exceptional Svc. award, 1997, Civil Air Patrol; named Ariz. Wing Chaplain of Yr, 1984, Thomas C. Casaday Unit Chaplain of Yr., 1985, Ariz. Wing Safety Officer of Yr., 1989, Ariz. Wing Sr. Mem. of Yr., 1994, Southwest Region Sr. Mem. of Yr., 1995, Civil Air Patrol. Mem. Mil. Chaplains Assn., Air Force Assn., Disabled Am. Vets., Am. Legion, Elks. Democrat. Avocations: flying, building and flying model aircraft, reading. Home and Office: 739 E Cottonwood Rd Duncan AZ 85534-8108

OVAERT, TIMOTHY CHRISTOPHER, mechanical engineering educator; b. Chgo., Apr. 30, 1959; s. Walter Allen and Joyce Ann (Collins) O.; m. Valerie Mora, July 16, 1988; children: Teresa Noel, Christina Lynn. BSME, U. Ill., 1981; MEM, Northwestern U., 1985, PhD, 1989. Plant engr. Wells Mfg. Co.-Dura Bar Div., Woodstock, Ill., 1981-85; mech. engr. Nat. Inst. of Standards and Tech., Gaithersburg, Md., 1986; asst. prof. Penn State U., 1989-95; assoc. prof. Pa. State U., 1995-2000, prof., 2000, U. Notre Dame, Ind., 2000—. Assoc. editor ASME Trans., Jour. Tribology, 1998—2003. Traffic safety com. Borough of State College, Pa., 1992. Named Nat. Young Investigator, NSF, 1992. Office: U Notre Dame 374 Fitzpatrick Hall Notre Dame IN 46556 Office Phone: 574-631-9371.

OVECHKIN, ALEXANDER, professional hockey player; b. Moscow, Sept. 17, 1985; s. Tatiana and Mikhail. Left wing Dynamo Moscow (Russian Super League), Moscow, 2001—05, Wash. Capitals, 2005—. Left wing Team Russia, World Junior Championships, 2003—05, Team Russia, World Championships, 2004, 05, Team Russia, World Cup of Hockey, 2004; mem. Team Russia, Olympic Games, Torino, Italy, 2006. Named to First All-Star Team, NHL, 2006, 2007; recipient Calder Meml. Trophy, 2006. Achievements include being a member of gold medal Team Russia, World Junior Championships, 2003; being the first overall draft pick in NHL entry draft, 2004. Office: c/o Washington Capitals MCI Center 601 F Street NW Washington DC 20004

OVELMEN, RICHARD J., lawyer; b. LaPorte, Ind., July 26, 1952; BA cum laude, Butler U., 1974; JD, Yale U., 1979. Bar: Fla., US Ct. of Appeals (11th Cir.), US Dist. Ct. (so. and mid. Dists.) Fla., US Supreme Ct. Adj. prof. law U. Miami, 1986-87; lectr. U of Miami Coll. of Liberal Arts; mem. Baker & McKenzie, Miami; ptnr. Jorden Burt LPP, Miami, Fla. Judge moot court finals; spkr. in field. Contbr. articles to profl. jour. Named Fla. Legal Elite, Fla. Trend mag., 2005—06, Fla. Super Lawyer, Super Lawyer, 2005—06, Best Lawyer in Am., 1993—2006. Mem. ABA (chmn. media law and defamation com., sect. tort and ins. practice 1989-90), Fla. Bar Assn. Office: Jorden Burt LPP 777 Brickell Ave Ste 500 Miami FL 33131 Office Phone: 305-347-6805. Office Fax: 305-372-9928. Business E-Mail: rjo@jordenusa.com.

OVERALL, THERESA LYNNE, computer professor; d. Edsel and Patricia Overall. AB Divisional Scis., Math. and Stats., Hollins U., Roanoke, Va., 1978; MS Computer Edn. and Cognitive Sys., U. North Tex., Denton, 2000, PhD in Ednl. Computing, 2007. Cert. provisional elem. gen. tchr. Tex. Edn. Assn., 1978, provisional tchr. young children Tex. Edn. Assn., 1978, NK-3 endorsement - gen. Commonwealth Va. State Bd. Edn., 1978. Classroom tchr., tech. coord. The Lamplighter Sch., Dallas, 1978—99; rsch. asst. Inst. Integration Tech. into Tchg. and Learning, Denton, Tex., 1999—2006; vis. asst. prof. U. Maine, Farmington, 2007—. Founder, pres. The Logo Opportunity, Richardson, Tex., 1980—. Author: (curriculum guide) TI Logo Curriculum Guide, (manual) On the Road to Silver and Gold-A Leader's Guide to Helping Girls Earn Preliminary Silver and Gold Award Recognitions: Studio 2B Edition; contbr. articles to profl. jours. Vol. Girl Scouts of the USA, Dallas, 1974—. Named Outstanding Young Women of Am., 1981, 1984, 1985, Outstanding Student of Yr., Computer Edn. and Cognitive Systems Dept., U. North Tex., 2001; recipient Presdl. award for Excellence in Math. Tchg., The Lamplighter Sch., Dallas, 1990, 1991, Outstanding Vol. award, Girl Scouts Tejas Coun., 1995, Green Angel, 1996, Appreciation Pin, 1998, Honor Pin, 2000, Heart of Gold Award, 2005, Tejas award, 2006; Toulouse Sch. Grad. Studies scholar, U. North Tex., Denton, 1999, Alumnae Dau. scholar, Hollins Coll. Alumnae Assn., 1974, 1975, 1976, 1977. Mem.: Am. Ednl. Rsch. Assn., Internat. Soc. for Tech. in Edn., Nat. Coun. Tchrs. Math., Leadership Richardson, Kaligrafos, The Dallas Calligraphy Soc. Home: 423 Marilu Richardson TX 75080-4533

OVERBY, OSMUND RUDOLF, art historian, educator; b. Mpls., Nov. 8, 1931; s. Oscar Rudolph and Gertrude Christine (Boe) O.; m. Barbara Ruth Spande, Mar. 20, 1954; children: Paul, Katherine, Charlotte. BA, St. Olaf Coll., 1953; B.Arch., U. Wash., 1958; MA, Yale U., 1960, PhD, 1963. Asst. in instruction dept. of history of art Yale U., 1959-60, 61-62; architect Hist. Am. Bldgs. Survey, U.S. Nat. Park Service, 1960-61, summers 1959, 62, 63, 65, 68, 69, 70, 73, 85; lectr. dept. fine arts U. Toronto, Ont., Canada, 1963-64; faculty dept. art history and archaeology U. Mo., Columbia, 1964—, dept. chmn., 1967-70, 75-77, prof. art history, 1979-98, prof. emeritus, 1998—, dir. Mus. of Art and Archaeology, 1977-83. Vis. prof. dept. architecture U. Calif., Berkeley, 1980; Morgan prof. U. Louisville, 1989; vis. prof. dept. art history and archaeology Washington U., St. Louis, 1996; bd. advisors Nat. Trust for Hist. Preservation, 1974-83; cons., panelist Nat. Endowment for Humanities, 1974—; bd. Mo. Mansion Preservation Commn., 1974-87; advisor Heritage/St. Louis Survey, 1974-76; counsellor to St. Louis Landmarks Assn., 1977—; chmn. Task Force on Hist. Preservation City of Columbia, 1977-78; cons. on hist. preservation; active Mo. Adv. Council on Hist. Preservation, 1967-82; lectr., exhibitor profl. confs. in field Author: Historic American Buildings Survey, Rhode Island Catalog, 1972, William Adair Bernoudy, Architect, Bringing the Legacy of Frank Lloyd Wright to St. Louis, 1999; co-author: Laclede's Landing, a History and Architectural Guide, 1977, The Saint Louis Old Post Office, A History and Architectural Guide to the Building and Its Neighborhood, 1979; co-author, editor: Illustrated Museum Handbook, A Guide to the Collections in the Museum of Art and Archaeology, University of Missouri-Columbia, 1982; editor in chief Buildings of the United States series, 1990-96; contbr. sects. to books, articles to profl. publs. in field. Served with U.S. Army, 1953-55. Recipient various fellowships and grants in field. Fellow Soc. Arctl. Historians (bd. dirs. 1968-73, 78-81, Jour. editor 1968-73, dir. Mo. Valley chpt., session chmn. ann. meeting 1976, v.p. 1982-86, pres. 1986-88, chmn. coms.), Historic Am. Bldgs. Survey; mem. Mid-Continent Am. Studies Assn. (editorial bd. American Studies 1965-70), Midwest Art History Soc. (bd. 1975-78, gen. chmn. annual meeting 1977), Mid-Am. Coll. Art Assn. (session chmn. annual meeting 1975), Mo. Heritage Trust (pres. 1976-79, 81-83, bd. dirs. 1979—), Coll. Art Assn., Landmarks Assn. St. Louis. Lutheran. Home: 1118 W Rollins Rd Columbia MO 65203-2221 Office: U Mo Dept Art History & Archaeolo Columbia MO 65211-0001 Office Phone: 573-442-7882. Business E-Mail: overbyo@missouri.edu.

OVERGAARD, CORDELL JERSILD, lawyer, rancher, director; b. Chgo., June 1, 1934; s. Kristin and Rose Marie (Jersild) Overgaard; m. Gail A. Gill, Sept. 5, 1959; children: Diane, Karen, Susan. BS with honors, U. Ill., 1957; LLB magna cum laude, Harvard U., 1960. CPA Ill.; bar: Ill. 1960. Assoc. Hopkins & Sutter, Chgo., 1960—67, ptnr., 1967—96, chmn. bus. fin. sect.; chmn., CEO SNG Internet Innovations LLC, 2005—. Dir. mem. exec. com. UPI, Inc., 1982—83; pres. Cmty. Cablevision, Inc., 1980—86, Gore-Overgaard Broadcasting, Inc., 1986—; pres. bd. trustees NorthCare, 1979—81; sec. Family Weekly, Inc., 1976—80; dir. Prudential Health Care Plan, Inc., 1980—89, Cahners Pub. Co., 1970—74; dir., v.p. Small Newspaper Group, Inc., 1981—; prin. mem. Rancho Paso Grande LLC (RanchoPasoGrande.com); exec. com. mem. Paso Fino Horse Assn., 2005—07. Editor: Harvard Law Rev., 1960. Mem. Ill. Bd. Ethics, 1973—76, chmn., 1976—80. Mem.: Chgo. Bar Assn. (chmn. corp. law com. 1972—73), February Group, Alpha Delta Phi, Beta Alpha Psi, Beta Gamma Sigma. Home: 11310 E Arabian Park Dr Scottsdale AZ 85259-4913

OVERGAARD, WILLARD MICHELE, retired political scientist; b. Montpelier, Idaho, Oct. 16, 1925; s. Elias Nielsen and Myrtle LaVerne (Humphrey) O.; m. Lucia Clare Cochrane, June 14, 1946; children: Eric Willard, Mark Fredrik, Alisa Claire. BA, U. Oreg., 1949; MA, U. Wis., 1955; PhD in Polit. Sci., U. Minn., 1969. Instr., Soviet and internat. affairs Intelligence Sch., U.S. Army, Europe, 1956-62, dir. intelligence rsch. tng. program, 1958-61; asst. prof. internat. affairs George Washington U., 1964-67; sr. staff polit. scientist Ops. Rsch. Inst., U.S. Army Inst. Advanced Studies, Carlisle, Pa., 1967-70; assoc. prof. polit. sci., chmn. dept., dir. Internat. Studies Inst., Westminster Coll., New Wilmington, Pa., 1970-72; prof. polit. sci. and pub. law Boise (Idaho) State U., 1972-94, chmn. dept., 1972-87, acad. dir. M.P.A. degree program, pers. adminstr., mem. humanities coun. interdisciplinary studies in humanities, 1976-87, prof. of pub. law emeritus, 1994—, dir. Taft Inst. Seminars for Pub. Sch. Tchrs., 1985-87, coord. Legal Asst. Program, 1990-95. Mem. comml. panel Am. Arbitration Assn., 1974—; mem. Consortium for Idaho's Future, 1974-75; adv. com. Idaho Statewide Tng. Program Local Govt. Ofcls., 1974-78; adv. group Gov. Idaho Task Force Local Govt., 1977; co-dir. Idaho State Exec. Inst., Office of Gov., 1979-83; grievance hearing officer City of Boise, 1981-85; arbitrator U.S. Postal Svc., 1988-90; cons. in field. Author: The Schematic System of Soviet Totalitarianism, 3 vols, 1961, Legal Norms and Normative Bases for the Progressive Development of International Law as Defined in Soviet Treaty Relations, 1945-64, 1969; co-author: The Communist Bloc in Europe, 1959; editor: Continuity and Change in International Politics, 1972; chief editor: Idaho Jour. Politics, 1974-76. Served with USAAF, 1943-45; with AUS, 1951-54; ret. maj. USAR. Named Disting. Citizen of Idaho, Idaho Statesman, 1979; Fulbright scholar, U. Oslo, 1949—50, Non-resident scholar, U. Wis., 1954—55, Adminstrv. fellow, U. Minn., 1955—56, Rsch. fellow, 1962—64. Mem. ABA (assoc.), Res. Officers Assn. (life), Am. Legion. Home: 2023 S Five Mile Rd Boise ID 83709-2316 Personal E-mail: wgaard@velocitus.net.

OVERHAUSER, ALBERT WARNER, physicist; b. San Diego, Aug. 17, 1925; s. Clarence Albert and Gertrude Irene (Pehrson) Overhauser; m. Margaret Mary Casey, Aug. 25, 1951; children: Teresa, Catherine, Joan, Paul, John, David, Susan, Steven. AB, U. Calif., Berkeley, 1948, PhD, 1951; DSc (hon.), U. Chgo., 1979; LLD (hon.), Simon Fraser U., 1998; DSc (hon.), Purdue U., 2005. Rsch. assoc. U. Ill., 1951—53; asst. prof. physics Cornell U., 1953—56, assoc. prof., 1956—58; supr. solid state physics Ford Motor Co., Dearborn, Mich., 1958—62, mgr. theoret. scis., 1962—69, asst. dir. phys. scis., 1969—72, dir. phys. scis., 1972—73; prof. physics Purdue U., West Lafayette, Ind., 1973—74, Stuart disting. prof. physics, 1974—2004, Stuart disting. prof. emeritus, 2004—. With USNR, 1944—46. Recipient Alexander von Humboldt sr. U.S. scientist award, 1979, Nat. medal of Sci., Pres. of U.S., 1994. Fellow: Am. Acad. Arts and Scis., Am. Phys. Soc. (Oliver E. Buckley Solid State Physics prize 1975); mem.: NAS. Home: 236 Pawnee Dr West Lafayette IN 47906-2115 Office: Purdue U Dept Of Physics West Lafayette IN 47907 Home Phone: 765-463-4662; Office Phone: 765-494-3037. Business E-Mail: awo@physics.purdue.edu.

OVERHOLT, HUGH ROBERT, lawyer, retired military officer; b. Beebe, Ark., Oct. 29, 1933; s. Harold R. and Cuma E. (Hall) O.; m. Laura Annell Arnold, May 5, 1961; children: Sharon, Scott. Student, Coll. of Ozarks, 1951-53; BA, U. Ark., 1955, LL.B., 1957. Bar: Ark. 1957. Commd. 1st lt. U.S. Army, 1957, advanced through grades to maj. gen., 1981; chief Criminal Law Div., JAG Sch., Charlottesville, Va., 1971-73; chief personnel, plans and tng. Office of JAG, U.S. Army, Washington, 1973-75; staff judge adv. XVIII Airborne Corps, Ft. Bragg, NC, 1976-78; spl. asst. for legal and selected policy matters Office of Dep. Asst., 1978-79; asst. judge adv. gen. for mil. law Office of JAG, Washington, 1979-81, asst. judge adv. gen., 1981-85, judge adv. gen., 1985-89; atty.

Ward & Smith, New Bern, NC, 1989—. Notes and comment editor Ark. Law Rev, 1956-57. Decorated Army Meritorious Service medal with oak leaf cluster, Army Commendation medal with 2 oak leaf clusters., Legion of Merit, Def. Meritorious Service medal, D.S.M. Mem. ABA, N.C. Bar Assn., Ark. Bar Assn., Assn. U.S. Army, Delta Theta Phi, Omicron Delta Kappa, Sigma Pi. Presbyterian. Office: Ward and Smith 1001 College Ct New Bern NC 28562-4972 Office Phone: 252-672-5462. Business E-Mail: hro@wardandsmith.com.

OVERMAN, DEAN LEE, lawyer, investor, writer; b. Cook County, Ill., Oct. 9, 1943; s. Harold Levon and Violet Elsa (True) O.; m. Linda Jane Olsen, Sept. 6, 1969; children: Elisabeth True, Christiana Hart. BA, Hope Coll., 1965; student, Princeton Sem. and U., 1965-66; JD, U. Calif., Berkeley, 1969; postgrad. in bus., U. Chgo., 1974, U. Calif. Bar: Ill. 1969, D.C. 1977. Assoc. to ptnr. D'Ancona, Pflaum et al., Chgo., 1970-75; White House fellow, asst. to v.p. Nelson Rockefeller, Washington, 1975-76; assoc. dir. Domestic Council The White House, Washington, 1976-77; sr. ptnr., ptnr.-in-charge Winston & Strawn, Washington, 1977—. Cons. White House; spl. counsel to Gov. James Thompson, Springfield, Ill.; faculty in secured financing U. Va. Law Sch., Charlottesville; vice chmn. J.F. Forstmann Co.; chmn. Holland Investment Co.; adj. fellow Ctr. for Strategic and Internat. Studies, 1993-95; vis. scholar, officer Harvard U., 1994-95; Templeton scholar Oxford U., 1999—2005, chmn. adv. bd. First Trust Portfolios, LP Author: Toward a National Policy on State and Local Government Finance, 1976, Effective Writing Techniques, 1980, (with others) Financing Equipment, 1973, Sales and Financing Under the Revised UCC, 1975, A Case Against Accident and Self Organization, 1997, Valuation of a Business, 2000; monthly newspaper column Chgo. Daily Law Bull.; contbr. articles to profl. jours. Commencement spkr. Hope Coll., Holland, Mich., 1978; bd. dirs. Internat. Bus. Inst., White House Fellows Assn., Cmtys. in Schs., Inc.; adv. bd. The Beacon Group; former bd. dirs. U.S. Decathlon Assn. Reginald Heber Smith fellow U. Pa., 1969-70. Mme. Mensa, Intertel, ABA, Ill. Bar Assn., DC Bar Assn., Chgo. Bar Assn., Met. Club (DC), Internat. Philos. Enquiry, Triple Nine Soc., Burning Tree Club (Bethesda, Md.), Congl. Country Club (Bethesda), Harvard Club of NYC, Macatawa (Mich.) Bay Yacht Club. Office: 4900 Glenbrook Rd NW Washington DC 20016

OVERMIER, J. BRUCE, psychology professor; s. James J. Wheelwright and Emma Annette (Carlton) Overmier Jacobson; m. Judith Ann Smith, Aug. 19, 1962; 1 child, Larisa Nicole. BA, Kenyon Coll., 1960; MA, Bowling Green State U., 1962; PhD, U. Pa., 1965; DSc (hon.), Kenyon Coll., 1990. Prof. psychology U. Minn., Mpls., 1965—. Mem. adv. bd. NSF, Washington, 1976-79, 86, USPHS, Washington, 1988-92. Co-author: (with others) Animal Learning: Survey and Analysis, 1979; editor: Learning and Motivation, 1973-76, Affect, Conditioning and Cognition, 1985, Animal Research and Human Health, 2001; cons. editor: Jour. Exptl. Psychology, 1971-74, 88-2004; mem. editl. bd. Behavioral Brain Rsch., 1979-84; contbr. chpts. to books and articles to jours. Grantee NIMH/NICHD, 1966-2003, NSF, 1966-83, 87-93; Fulbright Hays scholar, 1980, Scholar of the Coll., U. Minn., 1989-92; Fogarty Ctr. USPHS fellow, 1984, James McKeen Cattell Found. fellow, 1985, Joseph P. Kennedy found. fellow, 1989; recipient W. Horsely Gantt medal Pavlovian Soc., 2003, Outstanding Contributions award Minn. Psychol. Assn., 2004 Fellow APA (council 1987-97, 2006-pres. divsn. comparative psychology 1991, pres. divsn. experimental psychology 1993, bd. dirs. 1999-2004 pres. divsn. gen. psychology 2003, Disting Svc. award in Begavioral Neurosci. 2002, Neal E. Miller award 2004, Disting. Svc. to Psychol. Sci. award 2005); mem. AAUP (local pres. 1981), Midwestern Psychol. Assn. (council 1984-87, pres. 1987), Psychonomics Soc. (sec.-treas. 1981-83, bd. govs. 1983-88), Internat. Union Psychological Sci. (exec. 1993-2004, pres. 2004—), Pavlovian Soc. (pres. 1996-97), Delta Kappa Epsilon, Sigma Xi (Disting. Lectr. 1999-2001) Avocation: skiing. Office: Psychology Dept Univ Minn 75 East River Terr Minneapolis MN 55455 Home Phone: 612-333-9123; Office Phone: 612-625-1835. Office Fax: 612-626-2079. Business E-Mail: psyjbo@umn.edu.

OVERMYER, DANIEL LEE, humanities educator; b. Columbus, Ohio, Aug. 20, 1935; s. Elmer Earl and Bernice Alma (Hesselbart) O.; m. Estella Velazquez, June 19, 1965; children: Rebecca Lynn, Mark Edward. BA, Westmar Coll., LeMars, Iowa, 1957; BD, Evang. Theol. Sem., Naperville, Ill., 1960; MA, U. Chgo., 1966, PhD, 1971. Pastor Evangel. United Brethren Ch., Chgo., 1960-64; asst. prof. dept. religion Oberlin (Ohio) Coll., 1970-73; prof. Asian studies U. B.C., Vancouver, Canada, 1973—2000, acting head religious studies, 1984-85, head Asian studies, 1986-91, prof. emeritus, 2000—. Vis. prof. Princeton (N.J.) U., 1983, U. Heidelberg, Heidelberg, Germany, 1993, Nat. Chengchi U., Taiwan, 2002; prof. Chinese U., Hong Kong, 1996—98; hon. prof. Shanghai Normal U., China, 1997—. Author: Folk Buddhist Religion, 1976, 2005, Religions of China, 1986; author: (with David Jordan) The Flying Phoenix, 1986, 2005; author: Precious Volumes: An Introduction to Chinese Sectarian Scriptures From the Sixteenth and Seventeenth Centuries, 1999; editor: Ethnography in China Today: A Critical Assessment of Methods and Results, 2002, Religion in China Today, 2003; editor spl. issue: The China Quar.; contbr. articles to encys. and profl. jours. Chmn. Sch. Consultative Com., Vancouver, 1976-77; coord. Vancouver Boys Soccer League, 1979-81; adult edn. coord. United Ch. Can., Vancouver, 1981-84; co-chmn. Endowment Lands Regional Park Com., 1987-90; co-chair China and Inner Asia Coun., Assn. Asian Studies, 1992—. With USNR, 1953-61. Recipient Killam faculty rsch. prize U. B.C., 1986, Killiam faculty tchg. prize, 2000; named Alumnus of Yr., U. Chgo. Divinity Sch., 2001; NEH fellow, 1978, 79, China Rsch. fellow, 1981, sr. fellow coun. humanities Princeton U., 1983, Wang Inst. Grad. Studies fellow, 1985-86. Fellow Royal Soc. Can.; mem. Am. Soc. Study Religion, Soc. Study Chinese Religions (pres. 1985-88), Assn. Asian Studies. Democrat. Avocations: photography, swimming, hiking, gardening, birdwatching. Home: 3393 W 26th Ave Vancouver BC Canada V6S 1N4 Office: UBC Ctr Chinese Rsch Vancouver BC Canada V6T 1Z2 E-mail: eodano@shaw.ca.

OVERSTREET, KAREN A., federal bankruptcy judge; BA cum laude, Univ. of Wash., 1977; JD, Univ. of Oregon, 1982. Assoc. Duane, Morris & Heckscher, Phila., 1983-86; ptnr. Davis Wright Tremaine, Seattle, 1986-93; bankruptcy judge U.S. Bankruptcy Ct. (we. dist.) Wash., Seattle, 1994—. Assoc. editor Oregon Law Review; dir. People's Law Sch.; mem. advisory com. U.S. Bankruptcy Ct. (we. dist.) Wash. Mem. Nat. Conf. of Bankruptcy Judges, Wash. State Bar Assn. (creditor-debtor sec.), Seattle-King County Bar Assn. (bankruptcy sec.), Am. Bar Assn., Wash. Women Lawyers Assn. Office: US Bankruptcy Ct 700 Stewart St Rm 7216 Seattle WA 98101 Office Phone: 206-370-5330.

OVERSTREET, REGINA NIX, mathematics educator; b. Dawsonville, Ga., Feb. 13, 1946; d. Vernon Stancel and Jewell Fouts Nix; m. James Edward Overstreet, Sr., June 27, 1970; children: Jennifer Overstreet Flacke, James Edward Jr. BS in Edn., U. of Ga., Athens, 1968; MEd, Ga. State U., Atlanta, 1979. Math. tchr. Clayton County Schs., Jonesboro, Ga., 1968—70, Marietta City Schs., Ga., 1970—71, Cobb County Schs., Marietta, 1971—81; adj. math instr. Kennesaw State U., Ga., 1986—99; math. instr. Chattahoochee Tech. Coll., Marietta, 2004—. Pres. bd. of edn. Transfiguration Cath. Ch., Marietta, 1983—84. Named Tchr. of the Yr., Sprayberry H.S. Key Club, 1979. Mem.: Am. Math. Assn. of 2-Yr. Colls., Ga. Assn. for Devel. Edn., Nat. Assn. for Devel. Edn. Roman Catholic. Avocation: tennis. Office: Chattahoochee Tech Coll 980 S Cobb Dr Marietta GA 30060 Home Phone: 770-641-0245; Office Phone: 770-528-4566. Office Fax: 770-528-4584; Home Fax: 770-528-4584. Business E-Mail: roverstreet@chattcollege.com.

OVERTON, BO, professional basketball coach; b. Ada, Okla., July 9, 1960; s. Claudell and Sue Overton. BS in Comm., U. Okla., 1983; BA in Phys. Edn., Southwestern Okla. State U., 1987. Draft pick Phoenix Suns, 1983; grad. asst. men's basketball U. Okla., Norman, 1983—84; asst. coach women's basketball U. Okla, 1998—2004; basketball player Continental Basketball Assn. Pensacola Tornadoes, Fla., 1984—85; asst. coach Continental Basketball Assn. Pensacola Tornados, Fla., 1985-86, Oral Roberts U., Tulsa, Okla., 1986—87, 1991—93, S.W. Tex. State U., 1993—94, La. Tech U., 1994—98; head coach, athletic dir. Murray State Jr. Coll., Tishomingo, Okla., 1989—91; head coach women's basketball U. Mo., Kans. City, 2004—06; head coach WNBA Chgo. Sky, 2006—. Office: Chgo Sky 20 W Kinzie St Ste 1010 Chicago IL 60610 *

OVERTON, EDWIN DEAN, retired campus minister, educator; b. Dec. 2, 1939; s. William Edward and Georgia Beryl (Fronk) O. BTh, Midwest Christian Coll., 1963; MA in Religion, Ea. N.Mex. U., 1969, EdS, 1978; postgrad., Fuller Theol. Sem., 1980. Ordained to ministry Christian Ch., 1978. Min. Christian Ch., Englewood, Kans., 1962-63; youth min. 1st Christian Ch., Beaver, Okla., 1963-67; campus min. Cen. Christian Ch., Portales, N.Mex., 1967-68, Christian Campus House, Portales, 1968—2005; acting chmn. religion dept. Ea. N.Mex. U., Portales, 2000, tchr. religion, philosophy, counseling, 1970—2005; ret. Dir. Campus Christian House, 1980-2005; farm and ranch partner, Beaver, Okla., 1963—. State dir. Beaver Jr. C. of C., 1964-65; pres. Beaver H.S. Alumni Assn., 1964-65; elder Cen. Christian Ch., Portales, 1985-88, 90-93; chmn. Beaver County March of Dimes, 1966; neighborhood chmn. Portales March of Dimes, 1997; pres. Portales Tennis Assn., 1977-78. Mem. U.S. Tennis Assn., Am. Assn. Christian Counselors, Ea. N.Mex. U. Faith in Life Com., Lions Club. Republican. Home: 1129 Libra Dr Portales NM 88130-6123 Home Phone: 505-359-0608. E-mail: campusmin@juno.com.

OVERTON, MARCUS LEE, performing arts association administrator, actor, writer; b. Calhoun, Ga., Aug. 13, 1943; s. Marcus Burl, Jr. and Eva Mae (Greene) Overton. BS in Speech and Theatre, Northwestern U., 1965. Actor, tchr. Southeastern Shakespeare Festival, Atlanta, 1965; actor, co. mgr. Eagles Mere Assocs. Repertory Co., Chgo., 1966; prodn. stage mgr. Lyric Opera Chgo., 1966-72; mgr. Ravinia Festival, Highland Park, Ill., 1973-77; performing arts program mgr. Smithsonian Instn., Washington, 1983-92; exec. dir., prod. dir. Spoleto Festival U.S.A., Charleston, SC, 1992-94; program prodr., host Who Do You Know S.C. Pub. Radio, Charleston, 1994-97; instr. theatre and arts mgmt. Coll. Charleston, 1995-97. Adv. panelist Nat. Endowments Arts, 1977—79, DC Commn. Arts and Humanities, 1989, 90, 92; narrator talking books Libr. Congress, Washington, 1982—83; bd. dirs. Performing Arts Assistance Corp., 1992—97; con. in field. Prodr.: Falstaff (LA Philharm.), 1981—82; prodr., host Spoleto Today, S.C. Pub. Radio, 1996—, Supertitles, San Diego Opera, 1999—2003; prodr.: Inside Spoleto, 2001— (Emmy award, 2004). Scholar, Northwestern U., 1961—65. Mem.: La Jolla Music Soc. (artistic adminstr. 2006—), Actors Alliance San Diego (bd. pres. 2001—02, chmn. 2003—06, announcer, program host XLNC1-FM 2004—). Avocations: travel, prehistoric cave art, motorcycle touring, linguistics, French culture. Address: 5581-A Adobe Falls Rd San Diego CA 92120 Home Phone: 619-286-5581. Personal E-mail: smoketree13@juno.com.

OVITSKY, STEVEN ALAN, musician, classical music executive; b. Chgo., Oct. 12, 1947; s. Martin N. and Ruth (Katz) O.; m. Camille Levy; 1 child, David Isaac. MusB, U. Mich., 1968; MusM, No. Ill. U., 1975. Fine arts dir. Sta. WNIU-FM Pub. Radio, Dekalb, Ill., 1972-76; program mgr. Sta. WMHT-FM Pub. Radio, Schenectady, NY, 1976-79; gen. mgr., artistic dir. Grant Park Concerts, Chgo., 1979-90; v.p., gen. mgr. Minn. Orch., Mpls., 1990-95; v.p., exec. dir. Milw. Symphony Orch., 1995-99, pres., exec. dir., 1999—2003; exec. dir. Santa Fe Chamber Music Festival, 2004—; owner Sotone Hist. Recordings. Panelist Ill. Arts Coun., Chgo. Artists Abroad, Nat. Endowment for the Arts; bd. dirs. Ill. Arts Alliance, Chamber Music Chgo.; hon. dir. Chgo. Sinfonietta. With U.S. Army, 1968-71, Korea. Mem. NARAS, Am. Symphony Orch. League. Jewish. Avocations: audio, record collecting, softball, scuba diving. Office: Santa Fe Chamber Music Festival PO Box 2227 Santa Fe NM 87504-2227 Office Phone: 505-231-8212.

OVITZ, MICHAEL S., communications executive; b. Chgo., Dec. 14, 1946; m. Judy Reich, 1969; children Christopher, Kimberly, Eric. Grad., UCLA, 1968. With William Morris Agy., 1969—75; pres., bd. dir. Walt Disney Co., Burbank, Calif., 1995-97; co-founder, chmn. Creative Artists Agy., LA, 1975-95; principal Artists Mgmt. Group, 1998—2002; owner, principal CKE Assocs., Beverly Hills, Calif., 1998—. Chmn. exec. bd. dirs. UCLA Hosp. and Med. Ctr.; bd. advisors Sch. Theater, Film and TV UCLA; bd. dirs. Livent, Inc., Gulfstream Aero. Corp., J. Crew Group, Inc., Opsware, Inc., Yankee Candle Corp. Exec. prodr.: Gangs of NY, 2002; exec. prodr.: Timeline, 2003. Trustee Mus. Modern Art, N.Y.C.; bd. govs. Cedars-Sinai Hosp., L.A.; mem. exec. adv. bd. Pediatric AIDS Found.; bd. dir. D.A.R.E. America; nat. bd. advisors, Children's Scholarship Fund. Named one of Top 200 Collectors, ARTnews Mag., 2004. Mem. Coun. Fgn. Rels., Zeta Beta Tau. Avocation: art collector. Office: 2601 Colorado Ave Santa Monica CA 90404-3518

OWADA, HISASHI, judge; b. Niigata, Japan, Sept. 18, 1932; s. Takeo and Shizuka (Tamura) O.; m. Yumiko Egashira, Oct. 7, 1962; children: Masako, Reiko, Setsuko. BA, U. Tokyo, 1955; LLB, Cambridge U., Eng., 1956. Pvt. sec. to Fgn. Min. of Japan, 1971; dir. UN polit. affairs div., 1972-74; dir. treaties div., 1974-76; pvt. sec. to Prime Min. of Japan, Tokyo, 1976-78; min. Japanese Embassy, Washington, 1979-81, Moscow, 1981-84; dir.-gen. treaties bur. and for law of sea Ministry Fgn. Affairs, 1984-87, dep. vice minister, 1987-88; amb., permanent rep. of Japan to OECD, Paris, 1988-89; dep. min. Ministry Fgn. Affairs, Tokyo, 1989-91; vice min. Fgn. Affairs of Japan, Tokyo, 1991-93; advisor Ministry Fgn. Affairs Japan, Tokyo, 1993-94; amb., permanent rep. of Japan to UN, 1994-98; prof. Waseda U., 1999—2003; advisor to Ministry Fgn. Affairs, Tokyo, 1999—2003; pres. Japan Inst. of Internat. Affairs, 1999—2003; sr. advisor to pres. of World Bank, 1999—2003; judge Permanent Ct. Arbitration, 2001—, Internat. Ct. of Justice, The Hague, Netherlands, 2003—. Adj. prof. U. Tokyo, 1963-88; vis. prof. Harvard U., Cambridge, Mass., 1979-81, 87, 89, 99-02; adj. prof. internat. law Columbia U., 1994-1998; Inge Rennert disting. vis. prof. NYU Global Law Sch., 1994—; acad. prop. advisor Hiroshima U., 2002—; hon. prof. Leiden U., 2006—. Author: Japanese Practice in the Field of International Law, 1984, From Involvement to Engagement, 1994, Diplomacy, 1996, A Treatise on International Relations, 2002. Bd. hon. trust U.N. Found., Ditchley Found.; mem. Inst. de Droit Internat. Named hon. prof., Leiden U., 2006—. Mem. Japanese Assn. Internat. Law, Am. Soc. Internat. Law, l'Institut de Droit Internat., Internat. Law Assn. (exec. coun.) Avocations: skiing, mountain walking, music. Office: Internat Court of Justice Peace Palace 2517 KJ The Hague Netherlands Office Phone: 31 70302 23 23. Fax: 31 70 302 2409. E-mail: h.owada@icj-cij.org. *

OWEISS, IBRAHIM MOHAMED, economist, educator; b. Egypt, Sept. 25, 1931; came to U.S., 1960; s. Mohamed Zaki and Warda (Zeiden) O.; m. Celine M. J. Lesuisse, July 19, 1975; children: Yasmeen, Kareem. B.Com., Alexandria U., Egypt, 1952; MA, U. Minn., 1961, PhD, 1969. Tchr., 1953-55; econ. dir. indsl. projects Cairo, 1958-60; mem. faculty U. Minn., Mpls., 1961-67, Georgetown U., Washington, 1967—, prof. econs., 1973-75; mem. faculty Johns Hopkins U., 1971-74; first undersec. state econ. affairs Govt. Egypt, Cairo, 1977; ambassador, 1977-79; chief Egyptian Econ. Mission to U.S., 1977-79; prof. econs. Harvard U., 1997-98. Cons. econs., 1971—; mem. Pres. Coun. on Egyptian-Am. Rels., 1999—; mem. bd. regents Georgetown U., 2003—. Author: Pricing of Oil in World Trade, 1974, The Israeli Economy, 1974; editor: The Dynamics of U.S.-Arab Economic Relations, 1980, Economic Development of Egypt, 1982, Arab Civilization, Challenges and Responses, 1988, Political Economy of Contemporary Egypt, 1990, The Arab Gulf Economies: Challenges and Prospects, 2000, Economics: New Horizons, Shifting the Paradigm, 2001, A View on Islamic Economic Thought, 2003. Pres. Assn. Egyptian-Am. Scholars, 1984-88; chmn. bd. dirs. Arab-Am. Bus. and Profl. Assn., Howard and Georgeanna Jones Inst. for Reproductive Medicine, 1984-90, Egyptian Am. Cultural Assn., 1975-77, Faith and Hope Project, 1975-77. Officer Egyptian Army, 1955-58. Decorated Egyptian Merit decoration 1st Order, Order of St. John, knight Order of Queen of Sheba, grand cordon Order Mohammed Ali Pasha; Ford Found. fellow, 1979-80. Mem.: Univ. Club (N.Y.C.), Cosmos Club (Washington). Muslim. Home: 4017 Glenridge St Kensington MD 20895-3708 Home Phone: 301-933-7667.

OWEN, AMY, library director; b. Brigham City, Utah, June 26, 1944; d. John Wallace and Bertha (Jensen) Owen. BA, Brigham Young U., 1966, MLS, 1968. Sys. libr. Utah State Libr., Salt Lake City, 1968—72, dir. reference svcs., 1972—74, dir. tech. svcs., 1974—81, dep. dir., 1981—87, dir., 1987—2003. Serials com. chmn. Utah Coll. Libr. Coun., Salt Lake City, 1975—77, exec. sec., 1978—84, mem. coun., 1987—2003; mem. staff Gov.'s Utah Sys. Planning Task Force, Salt Lake City, 1982; staff liaison Utah Gov.'s Conf. on Libr. and Info. Svcs., 1977—79, chmn. exec. planning com., 1990—91; mem. pres.'s adv. panel Baker & Taylor Co., Somerville, NJ, 1977—78; panelist U.S. Dept. Edn., 1992; mem. rsch. project adv. com. U. Wis. Sch. Libr. and Info., Madison, 1992—94; mem. adv. panel Nat. Commn. Libr. & Info. Svcs., 1985, bd. dirs.; Alumni Honor lectr. Coll. Humanities Brigham Young U., 1990; cons., trainer in field. Contbr. chpts. to books; contbg. author: various manuals. Presdl. apptd. mem. Nat. Mus. and Libr. Svcs. Bd., 2004; mem. coun. Utah Endowment for Humanities, 1986—91, vice chmn., 1987—88, chmn., 1988—90; trustee Bibliographic Ctr. for Rsch., 1987—2003, mem. pers. com., 1988—89, chmn. person com., 1989—90, mem. nominating com., 1984, v.p. bd. trustees, 1989—91, pres., 1991—93; active Chief Officers of State Libr. Agys., 1987—2003, mem. stats. com., 1988—93, mem. network com., 1993—97, mem. state info. policy workshop com., 1988, bd. dirs., 1992—96; mem. conf. program com. Fedn. of State Humanities Couns., 1988; mem. coop. pub. libr. data sys. task force Nat. Commn. on Libr. and Info. Svcs., 1988—90; grant rev. panelist NEH, 1988, 1992, panel mem. reading and discussion groups, 1988; regional project mgmt. bd. mem. Intermountain Cmty. Learning and Info. Ctr. Project, 1987—90; mem. midcontinental regional adv. com. Nat. Libr. Medicine, 1991—94; mem. adv. com. Brigham Young U. Sch. Libr. and Info. Svcs., 1989—92. Named Libr. of Yr., Libr. Jour., 1990. Mem.: ALA (planning, orgn. and bylaws com. 1981—85, LITA divsn. Satellite Conf. Task Force mem. 1982, bd. dirs. ASCLA divsn. 1984—86, clene roundtable mem. com. 1984—86, fin. com. 1984—86, SLAS program com. 1984—86, ALA Office for Rsch. coop. pub. libr. data sys. adv. com. 1985—89, pres. program com. 1986, nominations com. 1986—87, PLA divsn. editor column 1987—89, PLA divsn. goals, guidelines and stds. com. 1987—90, nat. adv. bd. office comms. svcs., voices and visions project 1988—89, exec. bd. mem. 1988—90, PLA pub. libr. data svc. adv. com. 1988—91, fin. com. 1989—92, chair 1990—91, PLA non MLS involvement com. 1990—91, PLA Kellogg Phase III EIC project adv. com. chmn. 1990—92, PLA strategic issues and directions com. 1991—92, exec. bd. mem. 1993—94, bd. dirs. ASCLA divsn. 1993—96, fin. com. 1993—96, pres. ASCLA divsn. 1994—95, ASCLA Divsn. Profl. Achievement award 2004), Utah Partnership Edn. and Econ. Devel. (rsch. com. 1995—95), Utah Edn. Network (steering com. 1996—2003), Dynix Snowbird Leadership Inst. (nat. adv. bd. 1990—2002), Mountain Plains Libr. Assn. (rec. sec. 1979—80, fin. com. 1982—84, Disting. Svc. award 1989), Utah Libr. Assn. (exec. bd. 1976—80, pres. 1978—79, Disting. Svc. award 2003, Spl. Svc. award 1989), Alpha Lambda Alpha, Phi Kappa Phi. *

OWEN, BRADLEY SCOTT, lieutenant governor; b. Tacoma, May 23, 1950; s. Laural Willis; m. Linda Knoll, Jan. 20, 1983; children: Shanie, Dana, Mark, Sherrie, Adam, Royce. Student pub. sch., Germany. Rep. Wash. Ho. Rep., Olympia, 1976-82; senator Wash. State Senate, Olympia, 1983-96; lt. gov. State of Wash., Olympia, 1997—. Chmn. Legis. Com. on Economic Devel.; founder, pres. Strategies for Youth. Mem. Wash. State substance abuse coun., 1997—. Mem. Elks. Democrat. Office: Office Lt Governor 220 Legislative Bldg PO Box 40400 Olympia WA 98504-0400 Office Fax: 360-786-7749. Business E-Mail: ltgov@leg.wa.gov.

OWEN, CATHY HESSE, science administrator; d. Albert and Margaret Hesse; m. Ronald Owen; children: Michelle, Christine. BSBA, San Jose State U., Calif., 1977. Programmer IBM, San Jose, Calif., 1978—80, tech. writing mgr., 1984—87, sr. programming mgr., 1987—95, sr. mktg. manger, 1995—99, programmer Tucson, 1980—84; dir., product mgmt. Cardonet, Inc., Santa Clara, Calif., 1999—2000; pres. hotU, Inc., Honolulu, 2000—04, Nanopoint, Inc., Honolulu, 2004—. Bd. dirs. Nanopoint, Inc., Honolulu, 2005—, hotU, Inc., Honolulu, 2002—04. Recipient Outstanding Tech. Achievement award, IBM, 1984, Outstanding Co. award, World Tech. Network, 2005; Rsch. grant, Hawaii Tech. Devel. Venture, 2005—06. Mem.: Women In Tech. (assoc.), NanoBioNexus (assoc.). Office: Nanopoint Inc 900 Fort Street Mall Ste A20 Honolulu HI 96813 Home Phone: 808-529-1084; Office Phone: 808-457-1150. Office Fax: 808-537-4245.

OWEN, CLIVE, actor; b. Keresley, Warwickshire, Eng., Oct. 3, 1964; m. Sarah-Jane Fenton, Mar. 6, 1995; children: Hannah, Eve. Various stage roles including: Design for the Living, The Day in the Death of Joe Egg; actor: (films) Vroom, 1988, Close My Eyes, 1991, Century, 1993, The Turnaround, 1994, The Rich Man's Wife, 1996, Bent, 1997, Croupier, 1998, Greenfingers, 2000, The Hire: Ambush, Chosen, The Follow, Star, Powder Keg, 2001, Godsford Park, 2001, The Bourne Identity, 2002, The Hire: Hostage, Beat the Devil, Ticker, 2002, I'll Sleep When I'm Dead, 2003, Beyond Borders, 2003, King Arthur, 2004, Closer, 2004 (Golden Globe award for best supporting actor, 2005), Sin City, 2005, Derailed, 2005, The Pink Panther, 2006, Inside Man, 2006; (TV films) Precious Bane, 1989, Lorna Doone, 1990, Class of '61, 1993, The Magician, 1993, An Evening with Gary Lineker, 1994, Nobody's Children, 1994, Doomsday Gun, 1994, The Echo, 1998, Second Sight, 1999, Second Sight: Parasomnia, 2000, Second Sight: Kingdom of the Blind, 2000, Second Sight: Hide and Seek, 2000; (TV series) Capital City, 1989—90, Chancer, 1990, Sharman, 1996. Office: Creative Artists Agency c/o Kevin Huvane 9830 Wilshire Blvd Beverly Hills CA 90212-1815

OWEN, CYNTHIA CAROL, sales executive; b. Ft. Worth, Oct. 16, 1943; d. Charlie Bounds and Bernice Vera (Nunley) Rhoads; m. Franklin Earl Owen, Oct. 20, 1961 (div. Jan. 1987); children: Jeffrey Wayne, Valeria Ann, Carol Darlena, Pamela Kay; m. John Edward White, Jan. 1, 1988 (div. Sept. 1991). Cert. Keypuncher, Comml. Coll., 1963; student, Tarrant County Jr. Coll., 1974-77; BBA in Mgmt., U. Tex., Arlington, 1981. Keypunch operator Can-Tex. Industries, Mineral-Wells, 1966-67; sec. Electro-Midland Corp., Mineral-Wells, 1967-68; exec. sec. to v.p. sales Pangburn Co., Inc., Ft. Worth, 1972-78; bookkeeper, sec. CB Svc., Ft. Worth, 1978-82; project mgr. Square D Co., Coppell, Tex., 1982—. Mem.: NAFE, NOW, AAUW. Baptist. Home: 1221 Pine Ridge Rd Roanoke TX 76262 Office: Square D Co 204 Airline Dr Ste 300 Coppell TX 75019-4663 Home Phone: 817-854-0515. Business E-Mail: cindy.owen@us.schneider-electric.com.

OWEN, DANIEL THOMAS, entrepreneur, venture capitalist; b. Dec. 6, 1947; s. Jesse Taylor and Loretta (Kirchner) O.; m. Margaret Wynne Chilton, Jan. 12, 1980; stepchildren: Margaret Anne Worsham Oden, Joseph Irion Worsham II. BA, U. Dayton, 1969. Dir. fundraising KERA-

TV, Dallas, 1972-75; v.p. mktg. and programming Spectradyne, Inc., Dallas, 1975-87, exec. v.p., COO, 1987-89, internat. pres., 1989-90; founder, chmn. Focus Networks, Dallas, 1991-95; co-found. and gen. ptnr. HO2 Ptnr., Dallas, 1997—. Bd. dirs. Ignite Technologies, Inc. Mem. World Pres.'s Orgn. Episcopalian. Home: 3925 Potomac Ave Dallas TX 75205-2116 Office: HO2 Ptnrs Galleria Tower Two 13455 Noel Rd Ste 1670 Dallas TX 75240 E-mail: dan@ho2.com.

OWEN, DUNCAN SHAW, JR., internist, retired educator; b. Fayetteville, NC, Oct. 24, 1935; s. Duncan S. and Mary Gwyn (Hickerson) O.; m. Irene Lacy Rose, Oct. 22, 1966; children: Duncan Shaw III, Robert Burwell, Frances Gwyn. BS in Medicine, U. N.C., 1957, MD, 1960. Diplomate Am. Bd. Internal Medicine (proctor 1977-97). Intern Med. Coll. Va., Richmond, 1960-61; jr. asst. resident in medicine N.C. Meml. Hosp., Chapel Hill, 1961-62; asst. resident in medicine Med. Coll. Va., Richmond, 1964-65, fellow in rheumatic diseases, 1965-66; internal medicine and rheumatology physician Richmond, Va., 1966—; from instr. in medicine to assoc. prof. Med. Coll. Va., Richmond, 1966-78, prof. dept. internal medicine, 1978—; Taliaferro/Scott Disting. prof. internal medicine Med. Coll. Va., Va. Commonwealth U., 1989-2000, emeritus prof., 2000—; dir. residency tng. Med. Coll. Va. Hosp.; dir. rheumatology clinics. Dir. clin. tng. divsn. rheumatology, allergy, immunology, 1975-98, chmn. clin. activities comm., dept. internal medicine, 1970-90; chmn. med. adv. com. Richmond br. Arthritis Found., 1966-75, nat. patient edn. com., 1979-80; med. advisor Social Security Adminstrn., HHS, 1967-2004; co-chmn. arthritis project Va. Regional Med. Program, 1975-76; prodr. Your Health TV series Va. Ednl. TV, 1978-79; prodr. Update in Medicine, Good Morning Virginia TV show, 1980; cons. McGuire VA. Contbr. articles to profl. jours.; assoc. editor: Va. Med., 1978-98; editl. reviewer Jour. AMA, 1979—, Arthritis Rheumatism, 1981-2004, Jour. Rheumatology, 1984—. Mem. usher's guild First Presbyn. Ch., Richmond, Va., 1966-70, deacon, 1974-77, chmn. of diaconate, 1976-77, elder, 1978—, chmn. witness com., 1978-80; co-chmn. physicians statewide capital funds campaign Va. Commn. U., 1986-87; bd. dirs. Mooreland Farms Assn., 1971-73, 77-81, Va. chpt. Arthitis Found., 1970-85; mem. Va. Mus., Richmond Symphony; bd. dirs. Richmond Area Health Care Coalition, 1980-84. Med. officer US Army, 1962—63, Womack Army Hosp., Fort Bragg, NC, post surgeon, asst. divsn. surgeon US Army, 1963—64, Camp Kaiser, Korea. Decorated Army Commendation medal; recipient Gerard B. Lambert award, 1974-75, Disting. Svc. award Arthritis Found., 1971, U. N.C., Chapel Hill, 1999; Nat. Inst. Arthritis and Metabolic Diseases fellow, 1965-66 Fellow ACP (Laureate award 1997), Am. Coll. Rheumatology; mem. AMA (expert on diagnostic and therapeutic tech. assessment program 1990-99), Am. Rheumatism Assn. (exec. com. 1979-80), Richmond Acad. Medicine (pres. 1982, chmn. bd. 1983, parliamentarian 1988-99), Med. Soc. Va. (com. on aging 1980-89, v.p. 1973, 75, del. 1972-99, scholarship com. 1980-89), Richmond Soc. Internal Medicine (bd. dirs. 1971-73), Met. Richmond C. of C. (bd. dirs. 1981-84), Jr. Clin. Club (emeritus), Custis Hunting and Fishing Club, Alpha Omega Alpha Honor Med. Soc. Presbyn. Achievements include development of techniques for arthrocenteses; cellophane tape polarizing microscopic compensator for identifying crystals in joint fluid. Avocations: hunting, fishing, photography, amateur radio. Home: 8910 Brieryle Rd Richmond VA 23229-7704 Personal E-mail: dowen75089@aol.com.

OWEN, EDWARD ROGER JOHN (E. ROGER OWEN), Middle Eastern studies professor, writer; MA, Oxford U., Eng., DPhil, 1964. Dir. Mid. East Ctr. St. Antony's Coll., Oxford U., England, emeritus fellow; A.J. Meyer Prof. Mid. Ea. History Harvard U., Cambridge, Mass., 1993—, dir. Ctr. Mid. Ea. Studies, 1996—99, dir. Contemporary Arab Studies Program, 1995—. Co-author (with Sevket Pamuk): (books) A History of the Middle East Economics in the 20th Century, 1998; author: Cotton and the Egyptian Economy, 1820-1914: A Study in Trade and Development, 1969, The Middle East in the World Economy 1800-1914, 1981, State, Power and Politics in the Making of the Modern Middle East, 1992, 2000, 2004, Lord Cromer: Victorian Imperialist: Edwardian Proconsul, 2004. Fellow: Am. Acad. Arts & Scis. Office: Harvard U Ctr Mid Ea Studies 1430 Massachusetts Ave Cambridge MA 02138 *

OWEN, ELIZABETH MARIE, art historian, educator; d. James E. and Frances R. Owen. BA, Bryn Mawr Coll., Pa., 1985; MA, MPhil, PhD, Yale U., New Haven, 2005. Instr. East Asian art history U. Colo., Boulder, 2002—05; asst. prof., Asian art history U. Denver, 2005—. Part-time acting instr., head tchg. asst. dept. art history Yale U., New Haven, 1994—2001, rsch. asst. Silk Rd. project, 1997—98; adj. prof. art history So. Conn. State U., New Haven, 1995—2002, U. Conn., Storrs, 2000—02, Waterbury, 2000—01, Stamford, 2000—01; adj. prof., art history St. Joseph U., Hartford, Conn., 2001—01, Ctrl. Conn. State U., New Britain, 2000—01; curatorial asst. Asian art dept. Yale U. Art Gallery, New Haven, 1997—98, Andrew W. Mellon curatorial asst. Asian art dept., 1994—95. Exhibition organizer Across Cultures: Foreign Influences in Asian Art, Yale U. Art Gallery, Selections of Chinese and Japanese Art; contbg. author: Three Thousand Years of Chinese Painting. Mem. alumni schs. com. Yale U.; chmn. alumnae admissions rep. com. Colo., Bryn Mawr Coll., 2006—. Recipient Outstanding Tchg. award, Tchr. of Yr., So. Conn. State U., 2001; fellow Lehman Grant for pre-dissertation rsch., Yale U., 1994, Mellon pre-doctoral fellow, 1996; U. fellow, 1993—97, Fgn. Lang. and Area Studies fellow, U. Pa., 1992—93, Andrew W. Mellon pre-dissertation fellowship, Yale U., 1994, 1995, 1997—98, Summer Travel and Rsch. grantee, 1997, Mellon pre-doctoral fellow, 1998—99, Louise Wallace Hackney fellow, Am. Oriental Soc., 1999—2000, Dissertation Rsch. Supplementary grantee, Yale U., 1998—2000. Mem.: Assn. Asian Studies (Svc. award 2005), Coll. Art Assn., AAUP. Office: U Denver 2121 E Asbury Ave Denver CO 80208 Office Phone: 303-871-4138. Office Fax: 303-871-4112. Business E-Mail: elizabeth.owen@aya.yale.edu.

OWEN, H. MARTYN, retired lawyer; b. Decatur, Ill., Oct. 23, 1929; s. Honore Martyn and Virginia (Hunt) O.; m. Candace Catlin Benjamin, June 21, 1952; children: Leslie W., Peter H., Douglas P. AB, Princeton U., NJ, 1951; LLB, Harvard U., 1954. Bar: Conn. 1954, U.S. Ct. Appeals (2d cir.) 1961, U.S. Dist. Ct. Conn. 1962, U.S. Supreme Ct. 1963, U.S. Dist. Ct. Vt. 1975. Assoc. Shipman & Goodwin, Hartford, Conn., 1958-61, ptnr., 1961-94, of counsel, 1995-96; ret. Mem. Simsbury (Conn.) Zoning Bd. Appeals, 1961-67, Simsbury Zoning Commn., 1967-79; sec. Capitol Region Planning Agy., 1965-66; bd. dirs. Symphony Soc. Greater Hartford, 1967-73; trustee Renbrook Sch., West Hartford, Conn., 1963-72, treas. 1964-68, pres., 1968-72, hon. life trustee, 1972—; trustee Simsbury Free Libr., 1970-84; pres. Hartford Grammar Sch., 1987-98, trustee; corporator Hartford Hosp., 1984-96; vestry St. Alban's Ch., Simsbury, 1988-94; warden, vestry St. Paul's Ch., Brunswick, Maine, 1999-2001. Lt. USNR, 1954-62. Mem. ABA, Conn. Bar Assn., Hartford County Bar Assn., Am. Law Inst., Princeton (NYC) Club, Ivy Club (Princeton, NJ). Democrat. Episcopalian. Home: 80 Matthew Dr Brunswick ME 04011-3275 Personal E-mail: hmowen@gwi.net.

OWEN, HENRY, former ambassador, consultant; b. NYC, Aug. 26, 1920; AB, Harvard U., 1941. Economist Dept. State, Washington, 1946-55, mem. policy planning staff, 1955-62, dep. counselor, vice chmn. policy planning coun., 1962-66, chmn. coun., 1966-69; dir. fgn. policy studies Brookings Instn., 1969-77; personal rep. of Pres. U.S. with rank of ambassador to participate in preparations for summit meetings, 1977-81; sr. adviser Salomon Bros., 1981—2002; co-chmn. Capitol Ptnrs. for Edn., Washington, 2002—. Spl. adv. Pan-European Oil Pipeline Romania-Serbian-Croatia-Slovenia- Italy. Editor: Next Phase of U.S. Foreign Policy, 1971, (with Charles Schultze) Setting National Priorities, 1976. Served to lt. USN, 1942-46. Office: 2946 University Ter NW Washington DC 20016 Office Phone: 202-363-8370. Office Fax: 202-363-3492.

OWEN, JOHN, retired newspaper editor; b. Helena, Mont., June 10, 1929; s. John Earl and Ella Jean (McMillian) O.; m. Alice Winnifred Kesler, June 9, 1951; children— David Scott, Kathy Lynn. BA in Journalism, U. Mont., 1951. Sports editor Bismarck (N.D.) Tribune, 1953-55; wire editor Yakima (Wash.) Herald, 1956; with Seattle Post-Intelligencer, 1956-94, sports editor, 1968-80, assoc. editor, 1980-94, columnist, 1968-94. Author: Intermediate Eater Cookbook, 1974, Gourmand Gutbusters Cookbook, 1980, Seattle Cookbook, 1983, Great Grub Hunt Cookbook, 1989, Press Pass, 1994, Gluttony Without Guilt, 1997, Seattle Walks, 2000; also short stories. Served with AUS, 1951-52. Named Top Sports Writer in Wash. Nat. Sportswriters Orgn., 1966, 68, 69, 71, 74, 85, 88. Home: 611 Bell St Apt 4 Edmonds WA 98020-3065 E-mail: ieater@verizon.net.

OWEN, JOHN ATKINSON, JR., internist, educator; b. South Boston, Va., Sept. 24, 1924; s. John Atkinson and Mary Helen (Carrington) O.; m. Wanda Earle Reamy, Nov. 29, 1952; children— John Atkinson III, Ryland R. BS, Hampden-Sydney Coll., 1944; MD, U. Va., 1948. Intern Cin. Gen. Hosp., 1948-49; resident, fellow U. Va. Hosp., 1950-52; rsch. fellow Duke Med. Center, 1954-56; asst. prof. medicine Med. Coll. Ga., 1956-58, George Washington U. Med. Sch., 1958-60; mem. faculty U. Va. Sch. Medicine, 1960-96, prof., 1970-96, vice chmn. dept. internal medicine, 1972-74, James M. Moss prof. diabetes, sr. assoc. dean, 1995-96, prof. emeritus, 1997—. Mem. Va. Vol. Formulary Bd.; mem. exec. com. U.S. Pharmacopeia, 1970-75, pres., 1975-80, trustee, 1975-85. Mem. editorial bd.: Jour. Clin. Pharmacology, 1971-84; editor-in-chief: Hosp. Formulary, 1974-83. Served with USNR, 1942-45, 48-50, 52-53; capt. M.C. Res. Recipient Raven award U. Va., 1948; co-recipient Horsley Research prize, 1962, Walter Reed Disting. Achievement award, 1998; laureate ACP, 1998. Mem. AMA, ACP, Am. Fedn. Clin. Rsch., So. Soc. Clin. Investigation, Med. Soc. Va. (pres. 1990-91), Am. Diabetes Assn., Endocrine Soc. Presbyterian. (elder 1965—). Home: 106 Tally Ho Dr Charlottesville VA 22901-2034

OWEN, LAURI J., lawyer; b. Camp Pendleton, Calif., May 23, 1967; d. Larry H. Owen and Lois L. Allen. BS in Social Scis. summa cum laude, Boise State U., 1998, MA in Comm. summa cum laude, 2001; JD, U. Calif. Boalt Sch. Law, Berkeley, 2006. Cert. peace officers stds. and tng. level III Idaho. Sr. commd. dep. sheriff Ada County Sheriff's Office, Boise, 1990—2003; law clk. Bay Area Legal Aid, San Mateo, Calif., 2005; advocate Internat. Inst. of the East Bay, Oakland, Calif., 2005—06. Presenter workshops on domestic violence; cmty. activist. Contbr. scientific papers to profl. confs. Pres. STOP Domestic Violence U. Calif. Berkeley, Calif., 2004—06; mem. VAWA Task Force, Bay Area, Calif., 2004—06, human Trafficking Task Force, Bay Area, 2006—. Recipient Team award, Ada County Sheriff's Office. Mem.: Alaska Bar Assn., Phi Kappa Phi. Democrat. Office: PO Box 924 Bethel AK 99559

OWEN, LINDSAY ALEXANDER, music director; b. Montgomery, Ala., May 26, 1975; d. David Earl and Charla Davis Alexander; m. Allan Lee Owen III, Oct. 28, 2000; 1 child, Langley Davis. MusB, Vanderbilt U., 1997; MusM, Belmont U., 2000. Music, drama dir. Camp Robindel, Centre Harbor, NH, 1996—97; tchg. asst. Vanderbilt U., Nashville, 1997—99; choir dir. First Presbyn. Ch., Nashville, 1997—99; piano, voice instr. Melody Music Studios, Franklin, Tenn., 1999—2001; music asst. First Presbyn. Ch., 1999—2001, assoc. dir. music Greensboro, NC, 2001—06; adj. prof. voice Mercersburg Acad., Pa., 2006—. Mezzo-soprano Vanderbilt Opera Theatre, Nashville, 1994—96, Vanderbilt Chamber Singers, 1996—97; pres. Vanderbilt U. Concert Choir, 1996—97; mezzo-soprano Bella Voci, Nashville, 1997—2001, Sanctuary Choir First Presbyn. Ch., Nashville, 1997—2001; actress High Point (NC) Cmty. Theatre, 2002—05; mezzo-soprano Chancel Choir First Presbyn. Ch., Nashville, 2004—06. Mem.: Presbyn. Assn. Musicians (assoc.), Choristers Guild (assoc.), Am. Choral Director's Assn. (assoc.), Pi Kappa Lambda (assoc.), Alpha Omicron Pi (assoc.). Independent. Avocation: musical theatre. Office: Mercersburg Acad 300 E Seminary St Mercersburg PA 17236 Personal E-mail: vandygrad97@hotmail.com.

OWEN, MARC, health products executive; b. Wales; Grad., Oxford U.; MBA, Stanford U., Calif. Sr. ptnr. McKinsey and Co., 1988—2000; pres., CEO MindCrossing, 2000—01; sr. v.p. corp. strategy and bus. devel. McKesson Corp., San Francisco, 2001, exec. v.p. corp. strategy and bus. devel. Office: McKesson Corpn One Post St San Francisco CA 94104 *

OWEN, MICHAEL LEE, lawyer; b. LA, Aug. 17, 1942; s. Richard M. Owen and Betty Hamilton; m. Espy Bolivar-Owen. AB in Econ. with distinction, Stanford U., Calif., 1964; LLB, Harvard U., Cambridge, Mass., 1967. Bar: Calif., 1968, NY 1968. Assoc. Reid & Priest, NYC, 1967—69; mem. legal dept. Bank of Am. NT&SA, San Francisco, 1969—81; corp. sec. BRE Properties, San Francisco, 1970—75; v.p., assoc. gen. counsel Bank of Am. NT&SA, LA, 1979—81; ptnr., past co-chair L.Am. practice group Paul, Hastings, Janofsky & Walker, LLP, LA, 1981—. Founder, vice chmn. adv. bd. Inst. for Internat. and Comparative Law Ctr. Am. and Internat. Law (formerly Southwestern Legal Found.). Contbr. articles to profl. jours. regarding legal issues affecting financing and investment in Latin Amer. Bd. dirs. Constnl. Rights Found. Mem. US-Mex. Law Inst. (mem. adv. bd.). Office: Paul Hastings Janofsky & Walker LLP 515 S Flower St 25th Fl Los Angeles CA 90071-2228 Office Phone: 213-683-6214. Office Fax: 213-627-0705. Business E-Mail: michaelowen@paulhastings.com.

OWEN, PRISCILLA RICHMAN, federal judge, former state supreme court justice; b. Palacios, Tex., Oct. 4, 1954; BA, Baylor U., 1975; JD, Baylor U. Sch. of Law, 1977. Bar: Tex. 1978, US Ct. Appeals (4th, 5th, 8th and 11th cirs.). Law clerk Sheehy, Lovelace & Mayfield, 1976—77; assoc. Andrews, Kurth, Campbell & Jones, 1978—85, ptnr., 1985—94; justice Supreme Ct. Tex., Austin, 1995—2005; judge US Ct. Appeals (5th cir.), New Orleans, 2005—. Liaison to Tex. Legal Svcs. for Poor Spl. Supreme Ct. Tex., Supreme Ct. Adv. Com. on Ct.-Annexed Mediations. Bd. mem. Tex. Hearing & Service Dogs, A.A. White Dispute Resolution Inst.; advisory bd. mem. Federalist Soc. (Houston & Austin Chapter). Named Young Lawyer of Yr., Baylor U., Outstanding Young Alumna. Mem.: ABA, Am. Judicature Soc., Am. Law Inst. Office: US Courthouse 903 San Jacinto Blvd Rm 310 Austin TX 78701-2450 *

OWEN, RICHARD, federal judge; b. NYC, Dec. 11, 1922; s. Carl Maynard and Shirley (Barnes) O.; m. Lynn Rasmussen, June 6, 1960; children: Carl R., David R., Richard. AB, Dartmouth Coll., 1947; LLB, Harvard U., 1950; MusD (hon.), Manhattan Sch. Music, 1989. Bar: N.Y. 1950. Practiced in, NYC, 1950-74; assoc. Willkie Owen Farr Gallagher & Walton, 1950-53, Willkie Farr Gallagher Walton & Fitzgibbon, 1958-60; pvt. practice, 1960-65; ptnr. Owen & Aarons, 1965-66, Owen & Turchin, 1966-74; asst. U.S. atty. So. Dist. N.Y., 1953-55; trial atty. antitrust divsn. U.S. Dept. Justice, 1955-58; judge U.S. Dist. Ct. (So. Dist.), 1974-89, sr. judge, 1989—. Asst. prof. N.Y. Law Sch., 1951-53; adj. prof. law Fordham U. Sch. Law, 1996—. Composer, librettist operas Dismissed with Prejudice, 1956, A Moment of War, 1958, A Fisherman Called Peter, 1965, Mary Dyer, 1976, The Death of the Virgin, 1980, Abigail Adams, 1987, Tom Sawyer, 1989, Rain, 1997. Trustee Manhattan Sch. Music, N.Y.C.; founder, bd. dirs. Maine Opera Assn., 1975-85; pres., bd. dirs. N.Y. Lyric Opera Co. 1st lt. USAAC, 1942-45. Decorated D.F.C. with oak leaf cluster, Air medal with 3 oak leaf clusters. Mem. ASCAP, Century Assn., Chelsea Yacht Club. Republican. Mem. Soc. Of Friends. Office: US Dist Ct US Courthouse 40 Centre St Room 2903 New York NY 10007-1501 Office Phone: 212-805-6155. E-mail: operaowen@aol.com.

OWEN, ROBERT FREDERICK, internist, rheumatologist; b. Poplar Bluff, Mo., Oct. 19, 1927; s. John Clarence and Lydia Anna (Laverty) O.; m. Edith Suzanna Trugly, June 11, 1960; 1 child, Suzanne Marie. AB summa cum laude, Princeton U., 1948; MD, Yale U., 1952. Diplomate Am. Bd. Internal Medicine, Nat. Bd. Med. Examiners. Med. intern Barnes Hosp. (Washington U.), St. Louis, 1952-53; asst. resident in internal medicine St. Louis City Hosp. (Washington U. Med. Svc.), 1953-54, 56-57, med. resident, 1957-58; pvt. practice in internal medicine and rheumatology St. Louis, 1958—98. Instr. clin. medicine Washington U. Sch. Medicine, St. Louis, 1958-98, emeritus, 1998—; cons. Arthritis Clinic Washington U. Clinics, St. Louis, 1958-78; attending physician inpatient and outpatient tchg. svcs. at Washington U. and Mo. Baptist, St. Luke's, and Deaconess Hosps., St. Louis, 1958-79. Chmn. Instnl. Rev. Bd. Mo. Baptist Hosp. (monitoring biomed. and behavioral rsch.), 1977-96; mem. St. Louis Cmty. Clin. Oncology Program Human Subjects Rsch. Instnl. Rev. Bd., 1983-96. Capt. U.S. Army Med. Corps, 1954-56, Korea. Commendation by surgeon, Eighth U.S. Army, Far East, 1955. Fellow ACP; mem. AMA (Physician's Recognition award annually 1977—), Sigma Xi, Phi Beta Kappa. Avocations: piano, organ, photography. Office: St Francois Med Ctr 1224 Graham Rd Ste 3008 Florissant MO 63031-8028

OWEN, ROBERT HUBERT, lawyer, real estate broker; b. Birmingham, Ala., Aug. 3, 1928; s. Robert Clay and Mattie Lou (Hubert) O.; m. Mary Dane Hicks, Mar. 14, 1954; children: Mary Kathryn, Robert Hubert. BS, U. Ala., 1950; JD, Birmingham Sch. Law, 1956. Bar: Ala. 1957, Ga. 1965. Methods and procedures analyst, supr. Ala. Power Co., Birmingham, 1952-58; assoc. Martin, Vogtle, Balch & Bingham, Birmingham, 1958-63; asst. sec. So. Services, Atlanta, 1963-69; sec. Southern Co., Atlanta, 1969-71, sec., asst. treas., 1971-77; exec. v.p., sec., gen. counsel, dir. Proverbs 31 Corp., Atlanta, 1978-81, 90-97; broker Bob Owen Realty, Atlanta, 1990-97; pvt. practice law Marietta, 1978-85; v.p., gen. counsel Hubert Properties, 1985-86. Atlanta area rep. Inst. Basic Life Principles, 1970-80; elder Calvary Bapt. Ch., 1997—. Served to maj. USAF, 1951-52, 61-62. Mem.: Meteoritical Soc., Jasons, Phi Eta Sigma, Beta Gamma Sigma, Omicron Delta Kappa, Delta Chi, Delta Sigma Pi. Home and Office: 6590 Bridgewood Valley Rd NW Sandy Springs GA 30328-2906 Personal E-mail: roberthowen@bellsouth.net.

OWEN, ROBERTS BISHOP, lawyer, arbitrator; b. Boston, Feb. 11, 1926; s. Roberts Bishop and Monica Benedict (Burrell) O.; m. Kathleen Comstock von Schrader, Aug. 27, 1966; children— David Roberts, Lucy Leffingwell, William Atreus. Student, Dartmouth Coll., 1943-44; AB cum laude, Harvard U., 1948, LL.B. cum laude, 1951; Dip.C.L.S., Cambridge U., Eng., 1952. Bar: D.C. 1952, U.S. Ct. Appeals (D.C. cir.) 1953, U.S. Supreme Ct. 1958. Assoc. Covington & Burling, Washington, 1952-60, ptnr., 1960-79, 81—; the legal advisor U.S. Dept. State, Washington, 1979-81. Sr. advisor Sec. of State former Yugoslavia, 1995; arbitrator Fedn. Bosnia and Herzegovina, 1995; mem. Permanent Ct. Arbitration, The Hague, The Netherlands, 1980—86, 1993—98; mem. arbitration panel Internat. Ctr. for Settlement of Investment Disputes, 1995—; chair bd. dirs. Internat. Human Rights Law Group, 1996—99; mem. Claims Resolution Tribunal for Dormant Accounts in Switzerland, 1998—2000; sr. U.S. negotiator U.S.-Can. Pacific Salmon Treaty dispute, 1998; vice chair, sr. claims judge Claims Resolution Tribunal, 2001—02. Served to ensign USN, 1943-46. Fulbright scholar, 1951-52; recipient Disting Honor award Dept. of State, 1981, Sec. of State Disting. Svc. award, 1996, Sec. of Defense's medal for outstanding pub. svc., 1996. Fellow Am. Coll. Trial Lawyers; mem. ABA, Council Fgn. Relations, Am. Soc. Internat. Law (exec. council 1981-85). Clubs: Royal Ocean Racing (London); Metropolitan (Washington). Office: Covington & Burling PO Box 7566 1201 Pennsylvania Ave NW Washington DC 20004 Home Phone: 202-363-1134; Office Phone: 202-662-5254. Business E-Mail: rowen@cov.com.

OWEN, STEPHEN LEE, lawyer; b. Danville, Va., Mar. 25, 1952; s. L. Davis and Ann (Brodie) O.; m. Catherine Bryan Mabry; children: Hillary Brodie, Stephen Grayson, Mary Bryan, Davis Hammond, Edward Bloxton. BA, Hampden-Sydney Coll., Va., 1974; JD, Coll. of William and Mary, Williamsburg, Va., 1977. Bar: Va. 1977, Md. 1977, U.S. Tax Ct. 1978, U.S. Dist. Ct. Md., D.C. 1990. Assoc. Venable, Baetjer & Howard, Balt., 1977-84, ptnr., 1985-93, Piper & Marbury Rudnick & Wolfe, LLP, Balt., 1993-99; ptnr., chmn. Tax practice group DLA Piper Rudnick Gray Cary, Washington. Co-author: Federal Taxation of Estates, Gifts & Trusts, 1988; co-author newsletter Real Estate Tax Ideas, 1985—2001; contbr. articles to profl. jours.; editorial bd. Jour. Partnership Taxation, 1984-99, The Practical Tax Lawyer, 1985—, The Jour. Pass Through Entities, 1998—, Jour. of Real Estate Taxation. Bd. dirs. Balt. City Found., 1979-89, Balt. Zoo. Fellow Am. Coll. Tax Coun.; mem. ABA (v. chair ptnrships. com. taxation sect.), Am. Law Inst., Md. Bar Assn. (chmn. sect. of taxation 1989-90), Va. State Bar Assn., DC Bar Assn., Bar Assn. Balt. City, Real Estate Roundtable, Nat. Assn. Real Estate Investment Trusts, Balt. Country Club, Caves Valley Golf Club (bd. mem., Caddie Scholarship Found. bd. mem.). Avocation: golf. Office: DLA Piper Rudnick Gray Cary 1200 19th St NW Washington DC 20036-2412 Office Phone: 410-580-4230, 202-861-6240. Office Fax: 202-223-2085. Business E-Mail: stephen.owen@dlapiper.com.

OWEN, THOMAS LLEWELLYN, investment company executive; b. Patchogue, NY, June 24, 1928; s. Griffith Robert and Jeanette Roberts (Hatfield) O. AB in Econs., Coll. William and Mary, 1951; postgrad., Columbia U., 1952, N.Y. Inst. Fin., 1960—62; MBA, NYU, 1966. Exec. trainee Shell Oil Co., NYC and Indpls., 1951-59, supr., 1958-59; petroleum and chem. investment analyst Paine, Webber, Jackson & Curtis, NYC, 1959-62; sr. oil investment analyst DuPont Investment Interests, Wilmington, Del., NYC, 1962-66, dir. rsch., 1964-66; v.p., sr. investment officer, mem. policy, investment coms. Nat. Securities and Rsch. Corp., NYC, 1966-75, mutual fund portfolio mgr., 1972—75; sr. investment exec., v.p., portfolio mgr F. Eberstadt & Co. and Eberstadt Asset Mgmt., Inc., NYC, 1975-85, mem. policy com., 1979-85, also dir. portfolio rev. com.; sr. investment exec., portfolio mgr. Brown Brothers Harriman, NYC, 1985-89; pres., CEO Owen Capital Mgmt., NYC, 1989—. Contbr. chapters to books. Past chmn. bd. trustees Congl. Ch. Patchogue, NY. Mem.: Investment Assn. NY, Assn. Investment Mgmt. and Rsch., Internat. Assn. Energy Economists, Nat. Assn. Petroleum Investment Analysts, Am. Petroleum Inst., Am. Econ. Assn., Oil Analysts Luncheon Group NY, NY Soc. Security Analysts, Phi Kappa Tau. Home and Office: 109 Namkee Rd Blue Point NY 11715

OWEN, THOMAS WALKER, banker, portfolio manager; b. Everett, Wash., June 7, 1925; s. Thomas Walker and Frances (Yantis) O.; m. Barbara May Neils, Oct. 20, 1951; children: Thomas W., Gerhard, Caroline, Jeffrey; m. Ingrid Lundgren, June 7, 1975. BA, U. Wash., 1949, MA in Finance, 1953; postgrad., Pacific Coast Banking Sch., 1956. Adminstrv. trainee Seattle Trust & Savs. Bank, 1949-54, asst. br. mgr., 1954-56, trust investment officer, 1956-57, mgr. investment dept., chmn. investment com., 1957-59; v.p., mgr. investment dept. Nat. Bank Wash., Tacoma, 1959-66, vice chmn., 1967-71; exec. v.p. bank adminstrn. Pacific Nat. Bank Wash., 1971-73; v.p. Reeder, Owen & Co., Inc., 1975-92; pres., chmn. Owen, Reeder, Inc., Merrill Lynch, 1991-92; bd. dirs. West One Bank Wash., Tacoma, 1981-93. Served with AUS, 1943-45. Decorated Bronze Star, Purple Heart. Mem. N.W. Forum, Tacoma Club (past pres.), Tacoma Country and Golf Club, Phi Gamma Delta. Home: 11204 Tower Rd SW Lakewood WA 98498 Office Fax: 253-588-7483.

OWEN, TONY QUINN, investment company executive, horse trainer; b. Oklahoma City, Mar. 19, 1974; s. John Blair Owen and Margaret Ruth Wolford; 1 child, Danielle Kaye. AA in Architecture & Bus. Mhmt., Harrisburg C.C.; BA in Bus. and Fin. Mgmt., Northwestern U.; BA in Bus. Law, Villanova U., 1995. Cert. horse trainer. Gen. ptnr. Real Estate Lease Cons., Harrisburg, Pa., 1991—2002; architect Stonewall Golf Links, Elverson, 1992—94; pres., CEO Aztec Security Group, Carlisle, 1998—, Mystical Hannah Studios, 2005—, Stone Mountain Concrete, 2004—. Fin. advisor Loda Investment Group, Harrisburg, 2000—; equine instr. One Trick Pony, New Cumberland, 2000—02. Author: 26 Week Equitation Classes, 2003, OCD-Pieces of String, 2005, Tranquility Spirit Guides and Angel Guardians. Asst. master counselor/chevalier Order of DeMolay, Carlisle, 1987—; sec.youth aide panel Office Dist. Atty., Cumberland, 2004. Fellow: Am. Gemological Soc.; mem.: Pa. Guild of Craftsmen, Golf Soc. U.S., PGA Tour Ptnrs. Club. Avocations: horse training, skiing, cliff diving, hot air ballooning, golf. Home Phone: 717-421-6347; Office Phone: 717-557-1293. Personal E-mail: mysticalhannastudios@wildfun.com.

OWEN, WILLIAM FRANKLIN, JR., academic administrator, former research and development company executive; b. Memphis, Nov. 11, 1955; m. Alice Crosby Owen; children: Lauren Leslie, William Franklin III. MD, Tufts U., 1980. Cert. nephrology Am. Bd. Internal Medicine, 1985, internal medicine Am. Bd. Internal Medicine, 1984. Dir. dialysis svcs. Brigham and Women's Hosp., Boston, 1996—99; dir. Duke Inst. Renal Outcomes Rsch. Duke U. Med. Ctr., Durham, NC, 1999—2001; tenured prof. medicine Duke U. Sch. Medicine, Durham, 2001—01, adj. prof. medicine, 2002—; chief scientist Baxter Healthcare Corp., Renal, Deerfield, Ill., 2002—05; chancellor, v.p, health affairs U. Tenn. Health Sci. Ctr., Memphis, 2005—07; pres. U. Medicine and Dentistry NJ, Newark, 2007—. Chmn. internat. med. adv. bd. Nat. Kidney Found. Singapore, 1998; bd. sci. counsilors NIH, Bethesda, Md., 1998—2001; sci. adv. bd. U.S. Renal Data Sys., Bethesda, 2000—01; pres. Renal Physicians Assn., Bethesda, 2001—03; mem. medicare coverage adv. com. Ctrs. for Medicare and Medicaid Svcs., Balt., 2003—. Contbr. articles to profl. jours. Mem. site based com. Hillandale Elem. Sch., Durham, 1999—2000. Fellow, Robert Wood Johnson Found., 1985—89; grantee, NIH, 1984—. Avocation: astronomy. Office: U Medicine and Dentistry NJ Office of Pres 65 Bergen St Newark NJ 07103 Office Phone: 901-448-4796. *

OWENDOFF, STEPHEN PETER, lawyer; b. Morristown, NJ, Aug. 1, 1943; m.; 4 children. Student, Bowdoin Coll., 1966; BA, Kent State U., 1966; JD, Georgetown U., 1969. Bar: Ohio 1969. Assoc. Hahn Loeser & Parks and predecessor firms, Cleve., 1969-77; ptnr. Hahn Loeser & Parks (formerly Hahn, Loeser, Freedheim, Dean and Wellman), 1977—; mgmt. com. Hahn Loeser & Parks (formerly Hahn, Loeser, Freedheim Dean). Lectr. in field. Active Gesu Ch., University Heights, Ohio; mem. adv. bd. Learning About Bus., Inc.; past pres. Parmadale (Ohio) Adv. Bd.; bd. trustees, cmty. svcs. panel Fedn. Cath. Cmty. Svcs.; rep. United Way Assembly, Parmadale; bd. trustees LeBlond Housing Corp., Health Hill Hosp. Mem. Nat. Assn. Bond Lawyers, Nat. Assn. Coll. and Univ. Attys., Shaker Heights (Ohio) Country Club. Office: 3300 Bp Tower 200 Public Sq Cleveland OH 44114-2316

OWEN-LEINERT, SUSAN HUFF, voice educator, vocalist; b. Salisbury, NC, Sept. 6, 1958; d. James Bobby Huff and Mildred Clark Huff Simerson; m. Michael Leinert, Mar. 19, 1999. MusB, East Carolina U., 1980; MusM, U. Tex., 1983. Opera singer Freelance, NYC, 1985—95, Staatstheater Kassel, Germany, 1995—99, Staatstheater Darmstadt, Germany, 2000—02, Freelance, Duesseldorf, Germany, 2003—05; asst. prof. voice U. Memphis, 2005—; classical singer opera and concert Memphis, 2005—. Dir. Carolina Opera & Song Acad., Salisbury, NC, 2005—, Met. Opera Nat. Coun. Auditions, Memphis, 2005—, Memphis Opera & Song Acad., 2007—. Singer: Der Ring des Nibelungen, Elektra, Tristan und Isolde, Der Fliegende Hollaender; author: Discography: Wagner-Die Walkuere, Siegfried, Goetterdaemmerung, (Highwater Classics) Treasure Chest of German Lied; composer: Wagner, Strauss, Wagner. Recipient First Pl. award, Met. Opera Nat. Coun., 1990, Opera Am., 1991, Sullivan Grant award, 1991. Mem.: Nat. Assn. of Tchrs. Singing (life). Office: U Memphis Rudi E Scheidt Sch Music Memphis TN 38152 Home: PO Box 22098 Memphis TN 38122 Office Phone: 901-678-4082. Business E-Mail: susan.owen-leinert@memphis.edu.

OWENS, BETTY RUTH, lawyer; b. Texas City, Dec. 21, 1951; d. Marvin Lee Jr. and Ellen Frances (Nunnally) O.; m. Robert Foster Geary, Oct. 1, 1994. BS, La. State U., 1973, MA, 1975; JD with high honors, U. Tex., 1988. Bar: Tex., U.S. Dist. Ct. (so. dist.) Tex. 1989, U.S. Ct. Appeals (5th cir.) 1989, U.S. Dist. Ct. (we. dist.) Tex. 1999. Ptnr. Vinson & Elkins LLP, Houston, 1988—, dir. atty. devel., 2002—. Author: (with others) ABA Antitrust Law Developments, 4th edit., ABA Annual Review of Antitrust Law Developments, 1992-95; editor ABA Antitrust Summary Judgment Newsletter, 1996-98. Mem. adv. com. Seniors Place, 1994—98, mem. pers. com., 1999—2001; trustee St. Luke's United Meth. Ch., 1998-00, Houston, 2002—04; chair com. on women's ministry St. Luke's United Meth. Ch., Houston, 2002—03; dir. St. Luke's United Meth. Ch. Found., 2002—04, pres. bd. trustees, 2004. Recipient U. Tex. Sch. Law Faculty Service Award, 2001. Mem. ABA (vice chair civil practice and procedure com., antitrust sect. 1993-98, v. chair books and treatises com. 2000-2001), Am. Law Inst., Tex. Bar Found., Houston Bar Found. Avocations: reading, cooking, travel. Office: Vinson & Elkins LLP 1001 Fannin St Ste 2300 Houston TX 77002-6760 E-mail: bowens@velaw.com.

OWENS, BILL (WILLIAM FORRESTER OWENS), investment company executive, former governor; b. Ft. Worth, Tex., Oct. 22, 1950; s. Arthur and June Owens; m. Frances Westbrook, 1975; children: Monica, Mark, Brett. BA, Stephen F. Austin State U., 1973; MPA, U. Tex., 1975. Staff asst. to Senator John Tower US Senate, 1974—75; mgmt. cons. Touche Ross & Co., 1975—77; project mgr. Gates Rubber Co., 1977—79; chmn. Aurora Planning Commn., 1979—81; mem. Colo. Ho. Reps. from Dist. 49, 1983-89, Colo. State Senate from Dist. 27, 1989-94; treas. State of Colo., 1994-98, gov., 1999—2007; vice chmn. Greenwich Capital Markets, Inc., Greenwich, Conn., 2007—. Chmn. Aurora County Reagan for Pres., 1979-80; guest host Mike Rosen, Ken Hamblin and Chuck Baker talk shows; lectr. Russia; part-time fellow, Inst. for Pub. Policy Studies U. Denver, 2007- Contbr. more than 50 articles to profl. jours. Named One of Country's Ten Up-and-Coming leaders Robert Novak. Republican. Catholic. Office: Greenwich Capital Markets Inc 600 Steamboat Rd Greenwich CT 06830 *

OWENS, CHARLES VINCENT, JR., pharmaceutical executive, consultant; b. Kansas City, Mo., May 15, 1927; s. Charles Vincent and Helen (Barrett) O.; m. Cheryl Kreighbaum, Feb. 12, 1955; children: Melody, Kevin, Michael, John, Barbara. BS, U. Notre Dame, 1948; MS (Univ. fellow), U. N.C., 1949. Public health educator Richmond County (N.C.) Health Dept., 1949-51; with Miles Labs., Inc., Elkhart, Ind., 1951-82, pres. Ames Co. div., 1967-71, group v.p. profl. products group, 1971-77, exec. v.p. internat. ops., 1977-82; chmn., CEO Kyoto Diagnostics, Inc., 1982—85. Bd. dirs. Chronimed Inc.; CEO Genesis Inc., 1982—91. Bd. dirs. Elkhart YWCA, 1972-76, St. Jude Med. Inc., 1982-94; vice-chmn. Elkhart County Bd. Health, 1973-77, 2007—; chmn. Child Abuse Task Force, Elkhart County, Ind., 1977-78; pres. Blue Crab Key Condo Assn., 1995-99, dir., 2003-04. With M.C., USAAF, 1945-47. Mem. Am. Public Health Assn., Health Industry Mfg. Assn. (dir.), Pharm. Mfrs. Assn., Nat. Pharm. Council (pres. 1970-71, dir. 1965-73), Am. Mgmt. Assn., Am. Diabetes Assn., Am. Assn. Diabetes Educators, Internat. Diabetes Fedn., Am. Soc. Med. Tech., Elcona Country Club (bd. dirs.), Nat. Notre Dame Monogram Club (bd. dirs.). Republican. Roman Catholic. Office Phone: 574-264-9720.

OWENS, CHRISTINE M., delivery service executive; BS, Shippensburg Univ. Joined UPS, Atlanta, 1979, dist. mgr. NE Tex, Metro Chgo., region mgr., 1997—2004, v.p. transp., 2004—05, sr. v.p. comm. & brand mgmt., mem. mgmt. com., 2005—. Mem. Ill. Gov.'s Commn. on Status of Women. Office: UPS 55 Glendale Pky Atlanta GA 30328 *

OWENS, DANA ELAINE See QUEEN LATIFAH

OWENS, DOUGLAS K., physician, researcher; s. Richard C. and Dorothy D. Owens; m. Sara H. Cody. BS, Stanford U., Stanford, California, 1978; MS, Stanford U., Stanford, Calif., 1991; MD, U. Calif., San Francisco, 1982. Diplomate Am. Bd. of Internal Medicine, 1985. Prof. medicine Stanford U., 2006—, assoc. prof. medicine, 1997—2006, asst. prof. medicine, 1991—97. Trustee Soc. for Med. Decision Making, Phila., 1995—97, pres., 1998—99; chair, clin. efficacy assessment com. ACP, Phila., 2005—. Recipient Rsch. Assoc. Career Devel. Award, Dept. Vet. Affairs, 1992-1995, Sr. Rsch. Assoc. Career Devel. Award, 1995 to 1999, Under Secs. award for outstanding achievement in health svcs. rsch., Dept. Vet. Affairs, 2007; Fellowship Health Care Rsch. and Health Policy, Stanford U., 1998-1991. Mem.: Soc. for Med. Decision Making (pres. 1998—99, Lee Lusted Prize 1991), ACP (chair, clin. efficacy assessment com. 2005), Phi Beta Kappa. Office: Stanford U 117 Encina Commons Stanford CA 94305-6019 Office Phone: 650-723-0933.

OWENS, FREDRIC NEWELL, animal nutritionist, educator; b. Hammond, Wis., Sept. 1, 1941; s. Fred Newell and Stella Elvera Owens; m. Christa F. Hanson, Dec. 1983; children: Gwen, Eric, Crystal. Student, Wis. State U., River Falls, 1959-61; BS, U. Minn., 1964, PhD, 1968. Asst. prof. animal sci. U. Ill., Urbana, 1968-74; prof. animal sci. Okla. State U., Stillwater, 1974-86, Regents prof., 1986-90, Regents prof., Sarkeys Disting. prof., 1990—; sr. rschr. Pioneer Hi-Bred Internat., Johnston, Iowa, 1998—. Lectr. Sigma Xi, 1990, numerous other invted lectures; mem. com. on animal nutrition NRC, 1985-88. Contbr. chpts. to 13 books, more than 180 articles to profl. jours.; sect. editor Jour. Animal Sci., 1975-78, editor-in-chief, 1987-90. Recipient Tyler award Okla. State U., 1980, Am. Feed Industry Nutrition Rsch. award, 1986, Elmo Baumann Prof. award Okla. State U., 1990; NSF fellow, 1966-68. Mem. Am. Soc. Animal Soc. (pres. 1992, Morrison award 1996), Am. Inst. Nutrition, Am. Dairy Sci. Asns., Nutrition Soc. Lutheran. Home: 5004 Brookview Dr West Des Moines IA 50265-2733 Office Phone: 515-334-6416. Business E-Mail: fred.owens@pioneer.com.

OWENS, GAIL FRANCES, pharmaceutical executive; d. Frank Charles and Mary Helen McClain; m. George Edward Owens, Sept. 16, 1967; children: Cara Leanne, Megan Gail, Darren McClain. MS, Temple U., Phila., 2000. Sr. rsch. technologist Hershey Med. Ctr., Pa., 1982—92; dir. regulatory cmc Sanofi Aventis, Bridgewater, NJ, 1992—. Office Phone: 908-231-4005. Business E-Mail: gail.owens@sanofi-aventis.com.

OWENS, GUY, retired neurosurgeon; b. Amarillo, Tex., Jan. 25, 1926; s. Guy Fitzhugh Owens and Mary Helen Virgin; m. Lillian Janet Parkinson, June 20, 1949; children: Victoria Ann, Guy Parkinson. BS, Tufts U., 1946; MD, Harvard U., 1950. Diplomate Am. Bd. Neurol. Surgery. Intern Vanderbilt U. Hosp., Nashville, 1950—51, resident in gen. surgery, 1954—57; asst. prof. Vanderbilt U., Nashville, 1958—62; assoc. prof. SUNY, Buffalo, 1963—68; prof. surgery, head dept. U. Conn. Med. Sch., Farmington, Conn., 1968—75; pvt. practice New Britain, Conn., 1975—2003; ret., 2003. Author: Neurologic and Neurosurgical Nursing, 1975; contbr. over 130 articles to profl. jours. Home: 41 Main St Farmington CT 06032-2229

OWENS, HAROLD B., former state agency consultant; b. Knapp, Wis., Oct. 1, 1926; s. John Donald and Mabel Evelyn (Dunn) O.; m. Hazel Marie Allison, Feb. 18, 1956; children: Robert Bruce, Patrick Brian (dec.), Michael Shawn. Student, U. Mont., 1944, Rollins Coll., 1961—62, U. Hawaii, 1964—65. Airline transport pilot rating, FAA. Field rep. Puget Sound Power & Light, Kirkland, Wash., 1946—48; machinist Boeing Co., Seattle, 1948; commd. officer and pilot USAF, 1949, advanced through grades to col., 1979, ret., 1979; exec. dir. Tex. Soc. Energy Auditors, College Station, 1979—80; v.p. ops. Entek Assocs., Inc., College Station, 1979—88; aviation cons. Tex. Aeronautics Commn., Austin, 1983—89; rsch. assoc. Ctr. for Strategic Tech. Tex. A&M U. Sys., College Station, 1979—82; ret., 1992. Aviation instr. Bryan, Tex., 1979—; ind. energy cons., 1988—. Contbr. articles to profl. jours. Commr. Bryan Hist. Landmark Commn., 1993-96; mem. SCV, 2000—. With U.S. Army, 1944-46, ETO, with USAF, 1947-79, Korea, S.E. Asia. Decorated Legion of Merit, Bronze Star, Air Medal (7). Mem. Nat. Soc. Historic Preservation, Tex. Hist. Found., Nat. R.R. Hist. Soc. (nat. dir. 1988—), Air Force Assn. (charter; chpt. pres. 1980-82, v.p. S.E. region Tex. chpt. 1998-2000), Nat. Assn. Flight Instrs., Order of Daedalians, Tex. A&M Assn. Former Students, Century Club, Faculty Club, Coll. Station Noon Lion's Club, The Ret. Officers Assn., Aircraft Owner's and Pilots Assn., Quiet Birdmen, Sons of Confederate Vets. Republican. Avocations: flying, music, sports, travel. Home: 3207 Wilderness Rd Bryan TX 77807-3222 Office Phone: 979-777-3740. E-mail: tex@txcyber.com.

OWENS, JAMES W., manufacturing executive; b. Elizabeth City, NC; PhD in Econs., NC State U., 1973. Corp. economist Caterpillar Inc., Peoria, Ill., 1972—75; chief economist Caterpillar Overseas S.A., Geneva, 1975—80; mgmt. positions, Acctg., Product Source Planning Depts. Caterpillar Inc., Peoria, 1980—87, mng. dir., P.T. Natra Raya Indonesia, 1987—90, pres., Solar Turbines Inc., 1990—93, v.p. group svcs. divsn. Peoria, Ill., 1993-94, group pres., 1995—2003, vice chmn., 2003—04, chmn., CEO, 2004—. Bd. dir. Inst. Internat. Econ., Washington, Alcoa Inc., IBM. Mem.: Mfg. Council, Council on Fgn. Rels. Office: Caterpillar Inc 100 NE Adams St Peoria IL 61629 *

OWENS, JANA JAE, entertainer; b. Great Falls, Mont., Aug. 30, 1943; d. Jacob G. Meyer and Bette P. (Sprague) Hopper; m. Sidney Greif (div.); children: Matthew N., Sydni C.; m. Buck Owens. Student, Interlochen Music Camp, 1959, Internat. String Congress, 1960, Vienna Acad. Music, 1963—64; BA magna cum laude, MusB magna cum laude, Colo. Womens Coll., 1965. Tchr. music Ontario Pub. Schs., Oreg., 1965—67, Redding Pub. Schs., Calif., 1969—74; entertainer Buck Owens Enterprises, Bakersfield, Calif., 1974—78, Tulsa, 1979—. Concertmistress Boise Philharm., Idaho, 1965—67, Shasta Symphony, Redding, 1969—74; founder Grand Lake Festivals, Inc., Tulsa, 1996—. Rec. artist (violinist, vocalist) Lark Records, 1978—. Avocations: skiing, tennis, swimming. Office: Jana Jae Enterprises Lark Record Prodns Inc PO Box 35726 Tulsa OK 74153-0726 Business E-Mail: janajae@janajae.com.

OWENS, KATHLEEN C., academic administrator; married; 2 children. BS in Biology, Loyola U., Chgo.; MS in Edn. Biol. Scis., DePaul U., Chgo.; EdD in Curriculum and Instr., Loyola U., Chgo. Dean Lewis U., Romeoville, Ill., 1986—92; v.p. academic affairs St. Francis U., Loretta, Pa., 1992—2002; pres. Gwynedd-Mercy Coll., Gwynedd Valley, Pa., 2002—. Office: Gwynedd-Mercy Coll PO Box 901 1325 Sumneytown Pike Gwynedd Valley PA 19437-0901

OWENS, LAURA LEWIS, lawyer; b. Atlanta, Sept. 27, 1960; BA cum laude, Furman U., 1982; JD cum laude, U. Ga., 1985. Bar: Ga. 1985. Ptnr., leader, product liability group Alston & Bird L.L.P., Atlanta. Mem. editl. bd. Ga. Jour. Internat. and Comparative Law, 1983-85, editor-in-chief, 1984-85; author: Annual Survey of Developments in International Trade Law, 1983. Mem. Atlanta Bar Assn., State Bar of Ga. Office: Alston & Bird 1 Atlantic Ctr 1201 W Peachtree St NW Atlanta GA 30309-3424 Office Phone: 404-881-7363. Office Fax: 404-881-7777. Business E-Mail: lowens@alston.com.

OWENS, MAJOR ROBERT ODELL, former congressman; b. Memphis, June 28, 1936; m. Marie Cuprill; children: Christopher, Geoffrey, Millard, Carlos, Cecilia. BA with high honors in Math., Morehouse Coll., Atlanta, 1956; MLS, Atlanta U., 1957; grad. student, Columbia U. V.p. Met. Coun. Housing, 1964; chair Bklyn. Congress Racial Equality, 1964—66; cmty. coord. Bklyn. Pub. Libr., 1964—66; exec. dir. Brownsville Cmty. Coun., 1966—68; commr. NYC Cmty. Devel. Agy., 1968—73; dir. cmty. media libr. prog. Columbia U., 1973—75; mem. NY State Senate, 1975—82, US Congress from 11th NY dist., 1983—2007, mem. edn. and the workforce com., mem. govt. reform com., ranking minority mem. workforce protections subcommittee, chmn. select edn. and civil rights subcommittee, mem. progressive caucus. Mem. Internat. Commn. on Ways of Implementing Social Policy to Ensure Maximum Pub. Participation and Social Justice for Minorities, The Hague, Netherlands, 1972; keynote speaker White House Conf. on Librs., 1979. Pub. author and lectr. on libr. sci. Chmn. Dem. Ops. Com. Major R. Owens Day named in his honor, City Bklyn., 1971; named one of Most Influential Black Americans, Ebony mag., 2006. Mem.: ALA, NAACP. Democrat. Baptist.

OWENS, MARVIN FRANKLIN, JR., oil industry executive, director; b. Oklahoma City, Feb. 20, 1916; s. Marvin Franklin and Levis (Coley) O.; m. Jessie Ruth Hay, June 15, 1941 (dec.); children: Marvin Franklin III, William Earl, Jack Hay. BS, U. Okla., 1937; postgrad., Rutgers U., 1960-62. Petroleum engr. Brit. Am. Oil Producing Co., Oklahoma City, 1937-41; chief petroleum engr. Bay Petroleum Corp., Denver, 1946-54; sr. v.p. Cen. Bank of Denver, 1954-81. Elder Presbyn. Ch., Denver. With U.S. Army, 1941-46; col. Res. ret. Home: 6513 S Glencoe St Centennial CO 80121

OWENS, RICHARD D., lawyer; b. 1962; AB, U. NC, 1984; JD, Harvard U., 1988. Bar: NY 1991. Chief Securities and Commodities Fraud Task Force, 2002—06; asst. US Atty. US Atty. (so. dist.) NY; ptnr. Latham & Watkins, NYC, 2006—. Recipient Disting. Svc. award, US Atty. Gen., 1996, 2000. Mem.: NY Bar Assn. Office: Latham & Watkins 885 Third Ave New York NY 10022-4834 Office Phone: 212-908-1396. Office Fax: 212-751-4864. *

OWENS, ROBERT PATRICK, lawyer; b. Spokane, Wash., Feb. 17, 1954; s. Walter Patrick and Cecile (Phillippay) O.; children: Ryan Barry, Meghan Jane. BA, Wash. State U., 1976; JD, Gonzaga U., 1981; LLM in Admiralty Law, Tulane U., 1983. Bar: Wash. 1982, Alaska 1984, US Dist. Ct. (ea. dist.) Wash. 1982, US Dist. Ct. Alaska 1984, US Ct. Appeals (5th cir.) 1983, US Ct. Appeals (9th cir.) 2006, US Supreme Ct. 2006. Assoc. Groh, Eggers & Price, Anchorage, 1983-88; mng. atty. Taylor & Hintze, Anchorage, 1988-90; Anchorage office mgr. Copeland, Landye, Bennett and Wolf, Anchorage, 1990-99; prin. Law Offices of Robert P. Owens, PC, Anchorage, 2000—05; asst. mcpl. atty. Municipality of Anchorage, 2005—. V.p. bd. dirs. Hope Cmty. Resources, Inc., bd. dirs., 1999-, pres., 2001-03. Coord. supplies Insight Seminars, Anchorage, 1985-86. Mem. ABA (dist. 27 rep. young lawyers div. 1988-90), Alaska Bar Assn., Wash. State Bar Assn., Anchorage Bar Assn. (pres. 1991-92, v.p. 1990-91, pres. young lawyers sect. 1986-88, chair budget com. 1995-, budget com. chair 1995-), Alaska Fly Fishers, Phi Alpha Delta. Roman Catholic. Avocations: fishing, photography, skiing, softball. Office: Municipality of Anchorage Dept Law 632 W 6th Ave Ste 730 Anchorage AK 99501 Office Phone: 907-343-4545. Personal E-mail: rpowens@alaska.com.

OWENS, ROBERT W., gas industry executive; Bus. Degree, Calif. Poly. State U., 1976; MBA, Northwestern U. From mktg. trainee to dist. mgr. Mobil Oil Corp., 1976—88; corp. planner Amerada Hess, 1988—89, mgr. East Coast Branded mktg. ops., 1989—94; v.p. mktg. and svcs. Ultramar Diamond Shamrock, 1994—97; joined Sunoco, Inc., Phila., 1997, v.p. East Coast mktg., 1997—2000, sr. v.p. mktg., 2000—, v.p. Midwest mktg., 2001—. Office: Sunoco Inc Ten Penn Ctr 1801 Market St Philadelphia PA 19103-1699

OWENS, RONALD STEPHEN (RONN OWENS), radio talk show host; b. NYC, Oct. 17, 1945; s. Stanley S. Lowenstein and Monica (Frank) Owens; m. Jan Black; children: Sarah, Laura. BA with honors, Temple U., 1967, MA, 1969. Talk show host Sta. WCAU, Phila., 1968-70, Sta. WKAT, Miami Beach, Fla., 1970-71, Sta. WERE, Cleve., 1971-74, Sta. WRNG, Atlanta, 1974-75, KGO/ABC, San Francisco, 1975—. Hosted live radio call-in from S. Africa, 1985; author: Voice of Reason: Why The Left & Right Are Wrong, 2004. Bd. dirs. Am. Lung Assn., San Francisco. Named Top Radio Personality in San Francisco Bay Area, Oakland Tribune, 1986, One of top three Radio Talk Show Hosts in USA Radio and Records, 1985, one of Top 25 Greatest Radio Talk Show Hosts of All Time, Talkers Mag., 2002; recipient Marconi Radio award for Major Market Personality of Yr., Nat. Assn. Broadcasters, 2003. Mem.: Concordia-Argonaut (San Francisco). Avocation: thoroughbred racing. Office: KGO-AM 3rd Fl 900 Front St San Francisco CA 94111-1427

OWENS, SANDRA NELL, nurse; b. Birmingham, Ala., Aug. 6, 1948; d. Willie Toney Jr. and Eleanor Johnson; children: Zondra Newson, Cassondra Bess, Kendra Owens, Marlon Riley II. BS in Chemistry and Math., Paine Coll., 1969; A in Bus. IBM/Clerical, So. Jr. Coll., Birmingham, 1971; AS in Nursing, Grayson County Jr. Coll., Denison, Tex., 1977; PhD in Healthcare Svc. Mgmt., LaSalle U., 1996. RN, Ala.; ordained to ministry Bapt. Ch., 1992, World Christian Ch., 1995. Tchr. Boggs Acad., Keysville, Ga., 1971-72; packaging engr. Johnson and Johnson, Sherman, Tex., 1972-74; teletype operator, train mover SLSF R.R., Sherman, 1974-75; tchr. Sch. of Open Learning, Sherman, 1975-76; insp. Oscar Mayer Corp., Sherman, 1976-77; nurse St. Vincent's Hosp., Birmingham, 1990—. Worship team singer Internat. Nurses Conv., Birmingham, 1994; del. conf. on cancer prevention and detection in Black Ams., Oncology Nursing, Atlanta, 1991. Author (pamphlet) Let's Talk PMS, 1993, Talking PMS from Philosophical and Theological Point of View, 1997; contbr. poems to lit. publs. (Internat. Soc. Poets awards 1994, 95). Mem. care of the poor com. St. Vincent's Hosp., 1992-93; instr. ARC, 1993—, Birmingham AIDS Outreach, 1994. Recipient Ala. Quality award Examiner, 1999—. Mem. Birmingham City C. of C. (active corp. leadership 1995—). Avocations: singing, cooking, writing, painting, sewing. Office: Saint Vincent's Hosp 833 Saint Vincents Dr Birmingham AL 35205-1606 Home: PO Box 5804 Birmingham AL 35207-0804

OWENS, SUSAN, state supreme court justice; b. Kinston, NC, Aug. 19, 1949; d. Frank and Hazel Owens; children: Sunny Roloff, Owen Golden. BA, Duke U., 1971; JD, U. N.C., Chapel Hill, 1975. Bar: Oreg. 1975, Wash. 1976. Judge Dist. Ct., Western Clallam County, 1981—2001; chief judge Quileute Tribe, Lower Elwha S'Klallam Tribe; justice Wash. Supreme Ct., 2001—. Co-founder, chair Rural Courts Com., 1990; lecturer Jud. Coll., Nat. Coll. of Prosecuting Attorneys' Domestic Violence Conference. Co-author: Northwest Tribal Judges Domestic Violence Manual. Mem.: Dist. and Mcpl. Ct. Judges' Assn. (bd. dirs., sec.-treas., v.p., pres.-elect). Avocation: baseball. Office: Wash Supreme Ct PO Box 40929 Olympia WA 98504-0929

OWENS, SUSAN ELIZABETH, realtor; b. Providence, Nov. 22, 1957; d. Lee Edward and Nancy Elizabeth Norton; m. George Ray Bunch Jr., Aug. 15, 1980 (div. Jan. 1986); children: Michael, Melissa, George Ray III; m. Joseph Craig Owens, Oct. 16, 1987. Cert. ct. reporter, Reporting Acad. Va., 1993; study real estate, Tidewater CC, Chesapeake, Va., 2001. Sec. capital campaign United Way, Norfolk, Va., 1985—86; med. transcriptionist Humana Hosp. Bayside, Virginia Beach, Va., 1986—90; property mgr. Kamla Condominium Assn., Virginia Beach, 1990—93; ct. reporter Adams, Harris & Martin, Norfolk, 1993—94; office mgr. Slone Chiropractic Clinic, Norfolk, 1994—99, Riddle Assoc. Inc., Chesapeake, Va., 1999—2003, comml. real estate agt., 2001—. Pres. So. Bass'n Gal, 1998—2006, Hunter's Creek Property Owners Assn., 2006—, Va. Bassmasters, Inc., 2007—, sec., 1997—2006; youth coord. Va. Region 7 Bass Fedn. Avocations: bass fishing, bowling, writing children's stories. Office: Riddle Assoc Inc Ste 100 530 Woodlake Cir Chesapeake VA 23320 Home Phone: 757-548-8080; Office Phone: 757-523-1900. E-mail: sowens@riddleassociates.com.

OWENS, TERRELL ELDORAD, professional football player; b. Alexander City, Ala., Dec. 7, 1973; s. Marilyn Heard; 1 child, Terique. BA in Merchandising, U. Tenn. Chattanooga, 1996. Wide receiver San Francisco 49ers, 1996—2003, Phila. Eagles, 2004—06, Dallas Cowboys, 2006—. Co-author (with Steven Singular): Catch This: Going Deep With the NFL's Sharpest Weapon, 2004; co-author: (with Jason Rosenhaus) T.O., 2006; co-author: (with Courtney Parker) (children's books) Little T Learns to Share, 2006. Named All-Pro, 2001—02, 2004; named to Pro-Bowl team, 2000—04. Achievements include set NFL record for most receptions in one game (20), 2000. Office: Dallas Cowboys One Cowboys Pkwy Irving TX 75063 *

OWENS, WILLIAM ARTHUR (BILL OWENS), telecommunications industry executive, retired military officer; b. Bismarck, ND, May 8, 1940; s. Earl and Ruth (Arthur) O.; m. Monika Bastian, Sept. 30, 1967; 1 child, Todd. BS in Math., US Naval Acad., 1962; BA, MA in Politics, Philosophy and Econ., U. Oxford, Eng., 1974; MBA, George Washington U., 1976. Registered profl. engr. Commd. ensign USN, 1962, advanced through ranks to admiral, 1996, multiple assignments in nuclear submarines, 1962-77; comdg. officer USS Sam Houston (SSBN609), Honolulu, 1977-80, USS Corpus Christi (SSN705), New London, Conn., 1980-81, Submarine Squadron 4, Charleston, SC, 1984-85, Submarine Group 6, Charleston, SC, 1987-88; dir. office of program appraisal for the Sect. of the Navy Washington, 1988; sr. mil. asst. to Sec. Def., 1988—91; comdr. US 6th Fleet, Gaeta, Italy, 1990—91; dep. chief naval ops. for resources, warfare requirements and assessments Resources, Warfare Requirements & Assessments N-8, Washington, 1991—93; vice-chmn. Joint Chiefs of Staff The Pentagon, Washington, 1993—96; vice chmn., pres., COO Sci. Applications Internat. Corp., 1996-98; joined Teledesic LLC, 1998, vice-chmn., co-CEO, 1999—2003, chmn., CEO, 2003—04; CEO Nortel Networks Corp., Brampton, Ont., Canada, 2004—05, vice-chmn., 2005—. Founder Extend America; bd. dirs. Daimler Chrysler AG, Nortel Networks Corp., 2002—05, Polycom, Inc.; chmn. Intelius LLC; lead dir. EMBARQ. Author: Future of the Maritime Strategy, 1988, High Seas, 1994, Lifting the Fog of War, 2000; contr. articles on national security. Bd. dirs. Carnegie Corp., Carnegie Found.; mem. Brookings Instn., Fred Hutchinson Cancer Rsch. Ctr., Can. Coun. Chief Execs. Decorated 4 Stars; named 50 Most Powerful People in Networking, Network World, 2004; recipient Intrepid Salute award, Intrepid Foundation, 2004. Mem. Oxford Soc., Coun. Fgn. Rels. Episcopalian. Avocations: golf, skiing.

OWENS, WILLIAM DON, anesthesiology educator; b. St. Louis, Dec. 12, 1939; s. Don and Caroline Wilhemena (Raaf) Owens; m. Patricia Gail Brown, Dec. 12, 1964; children: Pamela, David, Susan. AB, Westminster Coll., 1961; MD, U. Mich., 1965. Diplomate Am. Bd. Anesthesiology. Resident and fellow Mass. Gen. Hosp. and Harvard Med. Sch., Boston, 1969—72; instr. Harvard Med. Sch., Boston, 1972—73; asst. prof. anesthesiology Washington U. Sch. Medicine, St. Louis, 1973—76, assoc. prof., 1976—82, prof., 1982—2004, prof. emeritus, 2004—, chmn. dept., 1982—92. Trustee Barnes Hosp., St. Louis, 1987—89; bd. dirs. Anesthesia Found., 1994—, pres., 1999—; sec.-treas. Am. Bd. Anesthesiology, 1991—94, pres., 1995—96, bd. dirs., 1984—96, Found. Anesthesia Edn. and Rsch., 1990—95, pres., 1994—95; mem. Mo. State Bd. Healing Arts, 2003—04. Assoc. editor Survey of Anesthesiology, 1977—92; contbr. numerous articles to profl. jours. and chpts. to books. Served to lt. comdr. USN, 1966—69. Fellow: Am. Coll. Anesthesiology; mem.: Assn. Univ. Anesthesiologists, Acad. Anesthesiology, Internat. Anesthesia Rsch. Soc., Am. Soc. Anesthesiologists (bd. dirs. 1989—99, 1st v.p. 1995—96, pres. 1997—98). Office: Washington U Sch Med Dept Anesthesiology 660 S Euclid Ave Saint Louis MO 63110-1010

OWEN-TOWLE, CAROLYN SHEETS, clergywoman; b. Upland, Calif., July 27, 1935; d. Millard Owen and Mary (Baskerville) Sheets; m. Charles Russell Chapman, June 29, 1957 (div. 1973); children: Christopher Charles, Jennifer Anne, Russell Owen; m. Thomas Allan Owen-Towle, Nov. 16, 1973. BS in Art and Art History, Scripps Coll., 1957; postgrad. in religion, U. Iowa, 1977; DD, Meadville/Lombard Theol. Sch., Chgo., 1994. Ordained to ministry Unitarian-Universalist Ch., 1978. Minister Ist Unitarian Universalist Ch., San Diego, 1978—2004. Pres. Ministerial Sisterhood, Unitarian Universalist Ch., 1980-82; mem. Unitarian Universalist Svc. Com., 1979-85, pres., 1983-85. Bd. dirs. Planned Parenthood, San Diego, 1980-86; mem. clergy adv. com. to Hospice, San Diego, 1980-83; mem. U.S. Rep. Jim Bates Hunger Adv. Com., San Diego, 1983-87; chaplain Interfaith AIDS Task Force, San Diego, 1988—. Mem. Unitarian Universalist Ministers Assn. (exec. com. 1988, pres. 1989-91, African Am. minister's action com. 1995-98). Avocations: reading, walking, promoting human rights.

OWES, JAUNITA, library director; Grad., Ala. State U., 1972. Dir. Montgomery City-County Pub. Libr., Ala. Mem.: Ala. Libr. Assn. (past pres., nominating chair, named Beta Phi Mu Libr. of Yr. 2005). Office: Montgomery City County Pub Libr PO Box 1950 Montgomery AL 36102 Office Phone: 334-240-4300. Office Fax: 334-240-4977. E-mail: jowes@mccpl.lib.al.us.

OWINGS, DONALD HENRY, psychologist, educator; b. Atlanta, Dec. 7, 1943; s. Markley James and Loyce Erin (White) O.; m. Sharon Elizabeth Calhoun, Jan. 29, 1966; children: Ragon Matthew, Anna Rebekah. BA in Psychology, U. Tex., 1965; PhD, U. Wash., 1972. Asst. prof. psychology U. Calif., Davis, 1971—78, assoc. prof., 1978—83, prof., 1983—, chair dept., 1989—93. Editor: (with M.D. Beecher & N.S. Thompson) Perspectives in Ethology, Vol. 12: Communication, 1997, (with R.G. Coss & K.R. Henry) Introduction to Psychobiol., 1998, 99 (2nd edit.), 2003 (3rd edit.), (with C.M. Greene, L.A. Hart and A.P. Klimley) Jour. Comparative Psychology, Special Issue: Revisiting the Unwelt: Environments of Animal Communication, 2002; author: (with E.P. Morton) Animal Vocal Communication: A New Approach, 1998; contbr. articles to profl. jours., book chpts. NSF rsch. grantee, 1978-80, 82-84. Fellow Animal Behavior Soc.; mem. Internat. Soc. for Comparative Psychology, Internat. Soc. for Behavioral Ecology. Democrat. Avocations: hiking, wildlife, travel, reading. Home: 815 Oeste Dr Davis CA 95616-1856 Office: U Calif Dept Psychology 1 Shields Ave Davis CA 95616-8686 Home Phone: 530-753-2839; Office Phone: 530-752-1673. Business E-Mail: dhowings@ucdavis.edu.

OWINGS, MALCOLM WILLIAM, retired management consultant; b. Cin., Feb. 5, 1925; s. William Malcolm and Margaret (Benvie) O.; m. Margie M. Gehiker, Sept. 4, 1948 (dec. June 2000); children: Lynn A., Sandra S., Wendy K., Cheryl M; m. Doris Marie Gorman, Aug. 23, 2002. BS in Bus. Adminstrn., Miami U., Oxford, Ohio, 1950, LL.D., 1976; A.M.P., Harvard U., 1975. With Continental Can Co., 1950-83, corp. v.p., from 1971; v.p., gen. mgr. pub. affairs Continental Packaging Co (Continental Group, Inc.), 1982-83; owner, pres. Owings Assocs., Inc., Pinehurst, NC, 1983-92; ret., 1992. Dir. First Bank, Pinehurst, N.C.; adviser to Am. del. Internat. Tin Coun., 1978-82 Columnist The Pilot, Southern Pines, N.C., 1997-2004. Dean's assoc. exec. in residence Sch. Bus., Miami U., 1973, mem. alumni coun., 1958-65, mem. pres.'s devel. coun., 1965-69, meem. resource devel. bd., 1982; trustee Village of Thiensville, Wis., 1956-59; mem. N.C. Clean, 1985-94, chmn., 1986-93; bd. dirs. Barrington Area Devel. Coun., 1974-79, Sales Mgmt. Execs. Grad. Sch., Am. Soc. Environment, 1976, Keep Am. Beautiful, 1980-81, also chmn., 1990; chmn. Keep N.C. Beautiful Coun., Raleigh, 1988-92, Moore Meml. Hosp. Found., Pinehurst, N.C., 1986-89; mem. Moore Regional Hosp. Scroll Soc., 1991-94, chmn., 1992-93; chmn. Moore County (N.C.) Rep. Party, 1986-88; co-founder Rep. Presdl. Task Force; mem. U.S. Senate Bus. Adv. Bd., 1981-91; commr. Moore County, 1988-96, Youth Svcs., 1993-95; apptd. to N.C. Watershed Protection Adv. Com. by N.C. Environ. Mgmt. Commn., 1990-92; bd. dirs. Pub. Edn. Found., 1994-99, Ptnrs. for Children and Family, 1994-97, Drug-Free Moore County Inc., 1995-98, Dispute Settlement Ctr. of Moore County, 1995-97, Keep Moore County Beautiful, 1997—; mem. Moore County Bd. of Health, 1994-97; pres. Belle Meade Residents Assn., 2000. Recipient Cert. of Meritorious Svc. Miami U., 1967, Meritorious Svc. award Keep Moore County Beautiful, Inc., 1993-94; named Alumnus of Yr. Miami U., 1970; 1st Am. recipient Order of Apteryx Earth Awareness Found., 1971, Order of Long Leaf Pine. Mem. Ill. C. of C. (bd. dirs. 1976-78), Miami U. Alumni Assn. (nat. pres. 1964-65), Omicron Delta Kappa, Sigma Chi, Delta Sigma Pi Clubs: Pinehurst Country, Country of N.C. (Pinehurst). Home and Office: Belle Mead Retirement Resort 107 Caritas Ct Southern Pines NC 28387-2242 Personal E-mail: mal_owings@earthlink.net. *The Golden Rule - "treating others as thyself" is not only a cornerstone for success, it is the foundation of personal happiness. However, it is well to remember that none of this is possible without political freedom and the contingent responsibilities that freedom requires.*

OWINGS, THALIA KELLEY, elementary school educator; b. Franklin, NH, Apr. 11, 1948; d. James Warren and Elizabeth Louise (Chadwick) Kelley; m. Alan Morritt, June 25, 1966 (div. June 25, 1990); children: Manderlee, Tiffany, Brooke; m. Frederick Richard Owings, Dec. 31, 1994; children: Jennifer, Lisa. AA, Harvard U. Ext., Cambridge, Mass., 1982, BA, 1989; student, Calif. State U., San Bernardino, 1996—2000. Cert. tchr., Calif., emergency tchr. Instr. CEA Internat., Providence, 1971-77; adminstrv. asst. Gulf Oil/Cumberland Farms, Norwood, Mass., 1989-91, So. Calif. Edison Co., Rosemead, Calif., 1991-96; substitute tchr. Palm Springs (Calif.) Unified Sch. Dist., 1996—2000. Tutor Calif. for Literacy!, Pasadena, Chino, and Palm Springs, Calif., 1991-96; applicant interviewer Harvard U.; mem. edn. com. Shelter From the Storm, 2000-03, tutor com. chair, 2000-03, vol. coord., 2002-03; cadet troop leader Girl Scouts Am., 2003—, jr. troop leader, 2004-; bd. mem. The Girl Friend Factor, 2007, ednl. inst. liason, mem. grants com. Mem. So. Calif. Harvard/Radcliff Club, Toastmasters Internat. (v.p. pub. rels. 1995-96), Edison's Roundtable. Avocations: screenplay writing, photography, bicycling, golf, dance. Home: 78075 Ravencrest Cir Palm Desert CA 92211 Personal E-mail: fred.thalia@verizon.net.

OWNBY, DENNIS RANDALL, pediatrician, allergist, educator, researcher; b. Athens, Ohio, July 14, 1948; s. Dillard Ralph and Miriam (Lee) Ownby; m. Helen Louise Engelbrecht, May 24, 1970; children: David Randall, Kathryn Louise. BS, Ohio U., 1969; MD, Med. Coll. Ohio, 1972. Diplomate Am. Bd. Allergy and Immunology (bd. dirs. 1993-98, chair 1998, residency rev. com. 1995-2000), Am. Bd. Pediat., Nat. Bd. Med. Examiners. Intern and resident Duke U. Sch. Medicine, Durham, NC, 1972—74, asst. prof., 1977—80; staff physician Henry Ford Hosp., Detroit, 1980—97, dir. Allergy Rsch. Lab., 1986—97; prof. pediat. Case Western Res. U., Cleve., 1997; prof. pediat. and medicine Med. Coll. Ga., Augusta, 1998—. Clin. asst. prof. pediat. U. Mich., Ann Arbor, 1980—86, clin. assoc. prof. pediat., 1986—95. Contbr. articles to med. jours., chpts. to books. Fellow: Am. Acad. Allergy, Am. Acad. Pediat. Office: Med Coll of Georgia Sect Allergy & Immunology BG-1019 Augusta GA 30912-3790 Home Phone: 706-651-9229; Office Phone: 706-721-3531. Business E-Mail: downby@mcg.edu.

OWNBY, JERRY STEVE, landscape architect, educator; b. Shawnee, Okla., Jan. 25, 1939; s. Hugh H. and N. Lorraine (Hopkins) O.; children by previous marriage: Gregory Steve, Mitchell Hugh; m. Arnola Colson, Dec. 19, 1971; 1 child Steven Cory. BS, Okla. State U., 1961; MS in Landscape Architecture, Kans. State U., 1964, M in Landscape Architecture, 1970. Coun. Landscape Archtl. Registration Bds. cert. and registered landscape architect, Ariz., Kans., Mo. Extension landscape architect Kans. State U., Manhattan, 1963-64, instr., 1969-70; landscape architect Beardsley & Talley, Seattle, 1964-65; extension specialist Okla. State U., Stillwater, 1965-69, from asst. prof. to prof. landscape architecture and coordinator landscape architecture, 1970-85; pvt. practice, 1985—. Chmn. Okla. Landscape Architect Registration Bd., 1980-85; mem. 1985 Expert Panel for Uniform Nat. Exam., 1984-85; gov.'s appointee Mo. Coun. Landscape Architects, 1991-97 Designs include Las Laderas residence, 1978 (Merit award 1981), Student Union courtyard Okla. State U., 1981 (Honor award 1983). Chmn. Oklahomans for Landscape Architecture, 1979-80; chmn., vice chmn. Stillwater Park and Recreation Adv. Bd., Okla., 1971-79. Recipient Outstanding Prof. award, Okla. State U. chpt. Alpha Zeta, 1975, Svc. award, Stillwater City Commn., 1980, design awards, Springfield Planning and Zoning Commn., 1988, 1989, 1990, 1999, design award, Springfield Environ. Adv. Bd., 1990, Gov.'s Landscape Design award for Andy Williams's Moon River Theatre, Branson, Mo., 1992, for Charley Pride Theater, Branson, 1995, design award, Watershed Com., 1993, Disting. Alumnus award, dept. horticulture and landscape architecture Okla. State U., 2005; alumni fellow, Kans. State U., 1995, Paul Harris fellow, Rotary Internat., 2006. Fellow Am. Soc. Landscape Architects (v.p. 1983-85, Okla. chpt. Svc. award 1980); mem. Nat. Coun. State Garden Clubs (accredited instr. 1964—), Nat. Coun. of Educators in Landscape Architecture, Mo. Assn. of Landscape Architects, Coun. Landscape Archtl. Registration Bds. (cert.), Phi Kappa Phi, Sigma Lambda Alpha. Republican. Baptist. Avocations: travel, photography, fishing. Home: 234 Sunset Cove # 108 Branson MO 65616-3604 Home Phone: 417-338-8432. E-mail: jsownby@aol.com.

OWSLEY, DOUGLAS W., forensic osteologist, researcher, anthropologist; BS in Zoology, U. Wyoming, 1973; MS, U. Tenn., PhD in Anthropology, 1978. Assistantship, dept. anthropology U. Tenn., faculty mem. anthropology; faculty mem., dept. geography and anthropology La. State U.; assoc. curator, dept. anthropology Nat. Mus. of Natural History, Smithsonian Institution, 1987, divsn. head, divsn. physical anthropology Washington, curator, N.Am. forensics. Lectr. in field assists law enforcement agencies in identifying human remains and in establishing cause of death. Office: Nat Mus Natural History Smithsonian Institution 10th St and Constitution Ave NW Washington DC 20560

OXENHANDLER, NEAL, literature educator, writer; b. St. Louis, Feb. 3, 1926; s. Joseph and Billie (Lutsky) O.; m. Jean Romano (div. May 1976); children: Noelle, Daniel, Alicia; m. Judith I. Josel, Dec. 12, 1979; stepchildren: Rebecca, Marjorie Menza. AB, U. Chgo., 1948; MA, Columbia U., 1951; PhD, Yale U., 1955; MA (hon.), Dartmouth Coll., 1973. Lectr. French St. Louis U., 1951-52; asst. instr. Yale U., New Haven, 1952-54, instr., 1954-57; asst. prof. UCLA, 1957-60, assoc. prof., 1960-65, U. Calif., Santa Cruz, 1965-66, prof., 1966-69, Dartmouth Coll., Hanover, NH, 1969—, Edward Tuck prof., 1987—, chmn. dept. comparative lit., 1980—85, chmn. dept. French and Italian, 1987-91. Dir. NEH Summer Seminar in Comparative Lit., 1981. Author: Scandal and Parade: Theater of Jean Cocteau, 1957, Aspects of French Literature, 1961, French Literary Criticism: The Basis of Judgment, 1966, Max Jacob and Les Feux de Paris, 1964, (novel) A Change of Gods, 1962, Looking for Heroes in Post-War France, 1996, adv. editor Film Quar., Berkeley, 1958-91; mem. editl. com. U. Calif. Press, Berkeley, 1966-69; asst. editor French Rev., 1969-73; contbr. articles, revs., poetry and translations to profl. jours. With U.S. Army, 1941-43, ETO, PTO. Decorated Combat Inf. badge; Fulbright scholar, Italy, 1953; Cross-Disciplinary fellow Soc. for Values in Higher Edn., France, 1966, Guggenheim fellow, France, 1962, Inst. for Shipboard Edn., 1995. Mem. MLA (adv. editor proc. 1977-80), Assn. Literary Scholars and Critics, Assn. Hebrew Caths. Democrat. Roman Catholic. Home: # 502 97 Sunset Dr Sarasota FL 34236 Office: Dartmouth Coll Dept French Hanover NH 03755 Office Phone: 941-330-2086. Personal E-mail: nealoxen@aol.com.

OXFORD, VAYL, federal agency administrator; Asst. prof. aeronautics USAF Acad., 1982—86; dir. counterproliferation Def. Nuc. Agy., Def. Spl. Weapons Agy., 1993—98; dep. dir. tech. devel. Def. Threat Reduction Agy.; dir. counter proliferation NSC; dir. Office Domestic Nuc. Detection US Dept. Homeland Security, 2005—. With USAF. Office: US Dept Homeland Security 3801 Nebraska Ave NW Washington DC 20528 *

OXLEY, JAMES GRIEVE, mathematics professor; b. Sale, Victoria, Australia, Feb. 4, 1953; s. William A. and Dilys C. (Grieve) O.; m. Judith Danute Surkevicius; children: Margaret Catherine, David Grieve (dec.). BSc, U. Tasmania, 1974; MSc, Australian Nat. U., 1975; PhD, U. Oxford, 1978. Lectr., rsch. fellow Australian Nat. U., 1978—82; asst. prof. La. State U., Baton Rouge, 1982—85, assoc. prof., 1985—90, prof., 1990—99, alumni prof., 1999—. Vis. instr. U. N.C., Chapel Hill, 1978; vis. rsch. fellow Merton Coll., Oxford, England, 2005. Author: Matroid Theory, 1992.; mem. editl. bd. Combinatorics, Probability and Computing, Soc. Indsl. and Applied Math. Jour. on Discrete Math., Jour. Combinatorial Theory Series B; reviewer Mathematical Reviews, Zentralblatt für Mathematik; contbr. chpts. to books, articles to profl. jours. Grantee NSF, 1985-87, 89-91, La. Edn. Quality Support Fund, 1987-94, Nat. Security Agy., 1994—, others; Fulbright fellow U. N.C., 1980; named Disting. Rsch. Master of Engring, Sci. and Tech., La. State U., 1999. Mem. Am. Math. Soc., London Math. Soc. Office: La State U Math Dept Baton Rouge LA 70803-4918 Home Phone: 225-769-9106; Office Phone: 225-578-1577. Business E-Mail: oxley@math.lsu.edu.

OXLEY, MICHAEL GARVER, lawyer, former congressman; b. Findlay, Ohio, Feb. 11, 1944; s. George Garver and Marilyn Maxine (Wolfe) Oxley; m. Patricia Ann Pluguez, Nov. 27, 1971; 1 child, Michael Chadd. BA in Govt., Miami U., Oxford, Ohio, 1966; JD, Ohio State U. Coll. Law, 1969. Bar: Ohio 1969, US Supreme Ct. 1986. Agt. FBI, 1969—71; atty. Oxley, Mallone, Fitzgerald & Hollister, 1971—81; mem. Ohio State Ho. Reps., 1973-81, US Congress from 4th Ohio dist., 1981—2007; of counsel Baker & Hostetler LLP, Washington, 2007—; non exec. vice-chmn. Nasdaq Stock Market Inc., NYC, 2007—. Recipient Taxpayer's Friend award, Nat. Taxpayers Union, Guardian of Small Bus. award, Nat. Fedn. Ind. Bus., Spirit of Enterprise award, US C. of C., Award for Mfg. Legis. Excellence, Nat. Assn. Mfrs., Jefferson award, Citizens for Sound Economy, Friend of the Farm Bur. award, Nat. Security award, Am. Security Coun. Mem. ABA, Ohio Bar Assn., Findlay Bar Assn., Soc. Former Spl. Agts. FBI, Ohio Farm Bur., Sigma Chi., Rotary, Elks. Republican. Lutheran. Office: Baker & Hostetler LLP Washington Sq Ste 1100 1050 Connecticut Ave NW Washington DC 20036 *

OXMAN, STEPHEN A., federal official; b. Summit, NJ, 1945; m. Patricia Jo Hedlund; children: Stephen, Gavin, Matthew. BA magna cum laude, Princeton U., 1967; DPhil, Oxford U., Eng., 1973; JD, Yale U., 1972. Assoc. Cravath, Swaine & Moore, 1973-77; spl. asst. to dep. sec. of state, 1977-78; exec. asst. to dep. sec. state, 1978-79; ptnr. Shearman & Sterling, 1980-88; mng. dir., dep. chmn. Wasserstein Perella & Co., 1988-93; asst. sec. state for European and Can. affairs Dept. State, Washington, 1993; chair exec. com. Princeton U., 2002—. Trustee Robertson Found.; mem. adv. coun. Woodrow Wilson Sch. of Pub. and Internat. Affairs. Rhodes scholar, 1967-69. Bd. editors: Yale Law Jour. Office: Princeton U 22 Chambers St Ste 201 Princeton NJ 08542 Office Phone: 609-258-3601. Office Fax: 609-258-1301.

OXMAN, THOMAS ELLIOT, psychiatrist; b. Denver, May 15, 1949; s. Albert Charles and Leah (Hurwitz) O.; m. Judy Ann Heldman, May 27, 1971; children: Elliot Warren, Robert Charles, Annaleah H. AB in Philosophy, Dartmouth Coll., 1971; MD, U. Colo., 1975. Diplomate in psychiatry and geriatric psychiatry Am. Bd. Psychiatry and Neurology (mem. test com. 1987-95). Intern Mt. Zion Med. Ctr., San Francisco, 1976; resident in psychiatry Dartmouth Med. Sch., Hanover, N.H., 1979, fellow in consultation/liaison and cancer psychiatry, 1979-80; asst. prof. psychiatry and family medicine U. Cin. Med. Ctr., 1980-83; asst. prof. Dartmouth Med. Sch., Hanover, 1983-87, assoc. prof. psychiatry and family and cmty. medicine, attending, 1987-95, prof., 1995—2007, prof. emeritus, 2007—. Assoc. dir. consultation liaison psychiatry svc. Dartmouth Hitchcock Med. Ctr., Hanover, 1983-90, dir. geriatric psychiatry, 1988—, mem. sci. rev. com. Hitchcock Found., 1988-95; mem. Mental Disorders of Aging rev. group NIMH, 1995-99; med. dir. glencliff Home for the Elderly, NH, 1996-; assoc. chair MacArthur Found. Initiative on Depression in Primary Care, 2000-2007; ptnr. 3CM, LLC, 2006—. Editor Internat. Jour. Psychiatry in Medicine, 1996-2000, Online Abstract Svc. Am. Assoc. Geriatric Psychiatry, 2005-07; contbr. articles to profl. jours Recipient Merrell Resident Rsch. award Dartmouth Med. Sch., 1978; Rufus Choate scholar Dartmouth Coll., 1971; Mental Health Acad. awardee NIMH, 1987-90, Aging, Social Support and Phys. and Emotional Disability grantee, 1990-95; MacArthur Found. and Hartford Found. Depression in Primary Care grantee, 1995—. Dist. fellow Am. Psychiat. Assn. (liaison com. on consultation/liaison psychiatry 1982-88,)bd. dirs. Am. Assn. Geriatric Psychiatry, 2002-2006; mem. Phi Beta Kappa. Avocations: running, conservation. Office: Dartmouth Med Sch Dept Psychiatry Lebanon NH 03756 Office Phone: 603-650-2887.

OXNAM, PHILIP LINTON, small business owner; b. Pomona, Calif., Nov. 5, 1945; s. Robert Fisher Oxnam and Dalys Oxnam Jaecker; m. JoAnne Buck, Sept. 30, 1989. BA, Norwich U., 1967; grad. Am. Acad. Dramatic Arts, 1972; student various acting schs., NY, LA, 1972—82; grad., NYU, 1979. Lic. theatre arts tchr. Vt. Actor various orgns., NY and LA, 1972—86; ind. casting dir. NY, 1985—88; owner Acting Lab., NY, 1987—89; tchr. theatre arts Lamoille Union HS, Morrisville, Vt., 1990—2000; co-owner TRIXonSTIX skis, Warren, Vt., 2002—03; owner On the Edge Skis, Monument, Colo., 2002—04. Author: novels, plays and screenplays, 1990—99; co-creator (ski sports) TRIXonSTIX, 2002; dir.: (TV commercials), 2006. Figure skating performance coach, 1998—2003. 1st. lt. US Army, 1968—70, U.S., Thailand. Named Ath. Hall of Fame soccer and swimming, Norwich U., Northfield, Vt., 2002; named to All New Eng. Soccer Team, Vt. All State Swimming Team. Mem.: Norwich U. Ath. Assn., Nat. Rifle Assn., Norwich U. Golden Goal Club, Norwich U. Blue Line Club, Tucson Nat. Country Club. Achievements include design of On the Edge Skis. Avocations: skiing, golf, figure skating, tennis.

OXNAM, ROBERT BROMLEY, trust company advisor; b. LA, Dec. 14, 1942; s. Robert Fisher and Dalys Elita (Houts) O.; children: Geoffrey Fisher, Deborah Elizabeth. BA, Williams Coll., 1964; MA, Yale U., 1966, PhD, 1969; LLD (hon.), Trinity Coll., 1994. Asst. prof. Trinity Coll., Hartford, Conn., 1969-74, assoc. prof., 1974-75, spl. asst. to pres., 1971-73; dir. China Coun. The Asia Soc., Washington, 1975-81, dir. Washington Ctr., 1979-81, v.p. NYC, 1979-81, pres., 1981—92; spl. corr. MacNeil/Lehrer NewsHour; sr. adv. Bessemer Trust Co., 1992—. Host and moderator 30-part series Asia: Half the Human Race, Sta. WCBS-TV, summer, 1979; mem. U.S. Nat. Com. for Pacific Econ. Coop.; bd. dirs. Clemente Global Growth Fund, Inc., First Philippine Fund Inc.; trustee, Rockefeller Brothers Fund, Armand Erpf Fund; vis. prof., Beijing Univ., global scholar, Ga. State Univ., Atlanta; chmn., US Trust for Chinese Sci. and Civilization at Needham Rsch. Inst., Cambridge Univ. Author: History and Simulation: Ch'ing Game, 1972, Ruling from Horseback, 1975; co-editor: Dragon and Eagle: U.S.-China Relations, 1978, China Briefing, 1979-82, (novel) Cinnabar, 1990, A Fractured Mind: My Life with Multiple Personality Disorder, 2005. Bd. dirs. Inst. for Shipboard Edn., Semester at Sea, U. Pitts. NDEA fellow, 1964-69, Ford Found. fellow, 1980, Williams Coll. Bicentennial Medal, 1993. Mem. Coun. Fgn. Rels., Am. Assembly, Century Assn., Cosmos Club (Washington), Assn. Asian Studies, Nat. Com. on US-China Rels. Office: Rockefeller Brothers Fund 437 Madison Ave New York NY 10022 also: Sr Advisor Bessemer Securities 630 Fifth Ave New York NY 10111

OXNARD, CHARLES ERNEST, anatomist, anthropologist, biologist, educator; b. Durham, Eng., Sept. 9, 1933; arrived in Australia, 1987; s. Charles and Frances Ann (Golightly) O.; m. Eleanor Mary Arthur, Feb. 2, 1959; children: Hugh, David. BSc with 1st class honors, U. Birmingham, Eng., 1955, MB, BChir in Medicine, 1958, PhD, 1962, DSc, 1975. Med. intern Queen Elizabeth Hosp., Birmingham, 1958-59; rsch. fellow U. Birmingham, 1959-62, lectr., 1962-65, sr. lectr., 1965-66, court govs., 1958-66; assoc. prof. anatomy, anthropology and evolutionary biology U. Chgo., 1966—78, prof., 1970-78, gov. biology collegiate div., 1970-78, dean coll., 1973-77; dean grad. sch. U. So. Calif., Los Angeles, 1978-83, univ. rsch. prof. biology and anatomy, 1978-83, univ. prof., prof. anatomy and cell biology, prof. biol. scis., 1983-87; prof. anatomy and human biology U. Western Australia, 1987-98, dir. ctr. for human biology, 1989-99, head div. agr. and sci., 1990-92, prof. emeritus, 1998—, sr. rsch. fellow, 1998—; Leverhulme prof. U. Liverpool (U.K.), Univ. Coll., London, 2000—03; hon. prof. U. Hull, England, 2004—, Hull York Med. Sch., 2004—. Rsch. assoc. Field Mus. Natural History, Chgo., 1967; overseas assoc. U. Birmingham, 1968—; Lo Yuk Tong lectr. U. Hong Kong, 1973, 94, 97, 2003, hon. prof., 1978, Chan Shu Tzu lectr., 80, vis. scholar, 95, 96; Octagon lectr. U. Western Australia, 1987; Latta lectr. U. Nebr., Omaha, 1987; Stanley Wilkinson orator, 91; rsch. assoc. L.A. County Natural History Mus., 1984—, George C. Page Mus., LA, 1986; vis. scholar Shaw Coll. Chinese U. of Hong Kong, 1995; bd. dirs. U. Western Australia Press, 1993—95; advisor on human biology World Sci. Pub. Co., 1993—; vis. prof. Northwestern U., Xian, China, 1999, U. York, England, 2003, hon. prof., 2004—, Hull York Med. Sch., 2004—; hon. prof. bioengring. U. Hull, 2004—. Author: Form and Pattern in Human Evolution, 1973, Uniqueness and Diversity in Human Evolution, 1973, Human Fossils: The New Revolution, 1977, The Order of Man, 1983, Humans, Apes, and Chinese Fossils, 1985, Fossils, Teeth and Sex, 1987, Anatomies and Lifestyles, 1990; series editor Recent Advances in Human Biology Series World Sci. Pub., Vol. I, The Origin and Past of Modern Humans, 1995, Vol. 2, Bone Structure and Remodeling, 1995, Vol. 3 The Origins and Past of Modern Humans: Towards Reconciliation, 1998, Vol. 4 The Natural History of the Doucs and Snub-nosed Langurs, 1998, Vol. 7 Morphometrics for the Life Sciences, 2000, Perspectives in Human Biology, Vol. 1 Genes, Ethnicity and Aging, 1995, Vol. 2 Humans in the Australasian Region, 1996, Vol. 3 Human Adaptability: Future Trends and Lessons from Past, 1998, Vol. 4, Is Human Evolution a Closed Chaptr, 1999, Vol. 4, Child Growth, Secular Trends and Continuing Human Evolution, Vol. 4, Dento-Facial Variation in Perspective, 1999, Vol. 5 Towards Consilience, 2000, Dedicatee, Shaping Primate Evolution, 2004; mem. editl. bd. Annals of Human Biology; cons. editor: Am. Jour. Primatology, Jour. Human Biology, Jour. Human Evolution: Australia com. mem. Ency. Britannica, 1991-99; bibliographic referee Britannica On-Line, 1994-99; contbr articles to anat. and anthrop. jours. Mem. Pasteur Found., 1988; bd. dirs. West Australian Inst. for Child Health, 1991-98; mem. electoral bd. Freemantle Hosp., 1991-94. Recipient Book award, Hong Kong Coun., 1984, S.T. Chan Silver medal, U. Hong Kong, 1980, Charles Darwin Lifetime Achievement award, Am. Assn. Phys. Anthropology, 2001; grantee, USPHS, 1960—71, NIH, 1974—87, NSF, 1971—87, Raine Found., 1988—91, Viertel Found., 1993—94, Australian Acad. Sci., 1995, Leverhulme Trust, Eng., 2003—06; Marie Curie Evan Rsch. Tng. grantee, 2005—, Marie Curie Palaeo Rsch. Tng. grantee, 2005—. Fellow N.Y. Acad. Sci., AAAS, So. Calif. Acad. Sci. (bd. dirs. 1985); mem. Chgo. Acad. Soc. (hon. life), Australasian Soc. for Human Biology (pres. 1987-90), Australia and New Zealand Anat. Soc. (pres. 1989-90), Anat. Soc. Gt. Britain and Ireland (councillor 1992-94), Nat. Health and Med. Rsch. Coun. (grantee 1994-97), Australian Rsch. Coun. (grantee 1988—), Med. and Health Infrastructure Fund, Western Australia (grantee 2001-03), Leverhulme Trust Rsch. Grant, 2003-06, Marie Curie awards 2005-), Soc. Study Human Biology (treas. 1962-66), Sigma Xi (pres., nat. lectr. 1990), Phi Beta Kappa (pres. chpt.), Phi Kappa Phi (pres., Book award 1984). Office: U Western Australia Nedlands WA 6009 Australia Business E-Mail: coxnard@cyllene.uwa.edu.au.

OXNER, GEORGE DEWEY, JR., lawyer; b. Greenville, SC, Dec. 31, 1933; s. George Dewey and Frances (Ruckman) O.; m. Louise Earle, Sept. 16, 1960; children: Frances, Dewey, Earle. BA, Washington & Lee U., 1956; LLB, U. S.C., 1959. Bar: S.C. 1959, U.S. Dist. Ct. S.C. 1959, U.S. Ct. Appeals (4th cir.) 1959. From assoc. to mng. ptnr. Haynsworth, Marion, McKay & Guerard, Greenville, 1959-98, ptnr., 1998—. Co-chair Chief Justice's Commn. on the Profession. Fellow Am. Coll. Trial Lawyers (state chair 1994), SC Def. Trial Attys. Assn. (pres. 1976), SC Bar Assn. (sec. 1997-98, treas. 1998—), Assn. (sec. 1997-98, treas. 1998-99, pres. elect, 1999-00, pres. 2000-01), Am. Bd. Trial Advs. (pres. 1990-91). Home: 10 Parkins Lake Rd Greenville SC 29607-3668 Office: Haynsworth Sinkler Boyd PA 75 Beattie Pl Greenville SC 29601-2130 Office Phone: 864-240-3208. Business E-Mail: doxner@hsblawfirm.com.

OXNER, GLENN RUCKMAN, financial executive; b. Greenville, SC, July 10, 1938; s. G. Dewey and Frances O.; m. Kathleen Gallagher, 1992. Student, Duke U., 1956-57; BS, U.S.C., 1961. Trainee stock bd. broker Alester G. Furman Co., Greenville, S.C., 1961, v.p., 1964-67, exec. v.p., 1967-75; pres. S.C. Securities Co., 1975-77; sr. v.p. Interstate Securities, Charlotte, N.C., 1977-82, exec. v.p., 1982-85; chmn. First Tryon Securities, Charlotte, 1986-89; mng. dir. Nations Bank Investment Banking Co., Charlotte, 1989-92; chmn. Edgar M. Norris & Co., Charlotte, 1992-2001; exec. v.p. Scott & Stringfellow, Greenville, SC, 2001—04; pres. Belmont Corp., Greenville, SC, 2005—. Served with U.S. Army, 1957. Mem. Nat. Assn. Security Dealers (com. chmn. dist. 7 1974, gov. 1981-84), Security Industry Assn. (gov. 1974), Security Dealers Carolinas (pres. 1977). Home: 18 Woodland Way Cir Greenville SC 29601-3824 Office: Belmont Corp PO Box 313 Greenville SC 29602

OXTOBY, DAVID WILLIAM, academic administrator, chemistry professor; b. Bryn Mawr, Pa., Oct. 17, 1951; s. John Corning and Jean (Shaffer) O., m. Claire Bennett, Dec. 17, 1977; children: Mary-Christina, John, Laura. BA, Harvard U., Cambridge, Mass., 1972; PhD, U. Calif., Berkeley, 1975; DHL (hon.), Occidental Coll., LA, 2005. Asst. prof. U. Chgo., 1977-82, assoc. prof., 1982-86, prof., 1986—2003, Mellon prof., 1987-92, dir. James Franck Inst., 1992-95, dean phys. scis. divsn., 1995—2003, William Rainey Harper prof., 1996—2003; pres., prof. chemistry Pomona Coll., Claremont, Calif., 2003—. Co-author: Principles of Modern Chemistry, 1986, Chemistry: Science of Change, 1990. Trustee Bryn Mawr Coll., 1989—, Tchrs. Acad. Math. and Sci., 1999-03, Toyota Technol. Inst., Chgo., 2002—, The Webb Schs., 2005-; mem. bd. govs. Argonne Nat. Lab., 1996-02, Astrophys. Rsch. Consortium, 1998-03; mem. bd. overseers Claremont Univ. Consortium, 2003-. Recipient Quantrell award U. Chgo., 1986, Alumni award of merit William Penn Charter Sch., 2003; Alfred P. Sloan Found. fellow, 1979, John Simon Guggenheim Found. fellow, 1987; Camille and Henry Dreyfus Found. tchr.-scholar, 1980. Fellow AAAS, Am. Phys. Soc.; mem. Am. Chem. Soc., Am. Assn. Colls. and Univs. (bd. dirs. 2006—), Royal Soc. Chemistry (Marlow medal 1983), Phi Beta Kappa. Office: Office of the Pres Pomona Coll 550 N College Ave Claremont CA 91711 Home Phone: 909-624-0931; Office Phone: 909-621-8131.

OYANA, TONNY J., geoscientist, educator; b. Kampala, Uganda, Apr. 20, 1968; arrived in U.S., 2000; s. Jerry Oyana Odongo and Mary Phoebe Oyana; m. Damalie M. Oyana, Feb. 4, 1992; children: Owen Kiredi-Jean, Phoebe Makimoth-Fayola. BS in Biology and Geography, U. Dar-Es-Salam, Tanzania, 1993; MS in Geog. Info. Sys., Environ. Planning, Nat. U. Ireland, Cork, 1996; PhD in Geog. Info. Sys., Geog. Info. Sci., SUNY, Buffalo, 2003. Biology and geography tchr. Jangwani Secondary Sch., Dar-es-Salaam, 1990—91, Kisitu Girls' Sch., Dar-es-Salaam, 1992; tchr., cons. SNV Netherlands Devel. Orgn., Tanzania and Uganda, 1993—94; tchg. asst. dept. geography Makerere U., Kampala, Uganda, 1993—95, lectr. dept. geography, 1996—98; child advocacy officer Nat. Coun. Children, Redd Barna, Norway, 1994; grad. tutor dept. geography U. Coll. Cork, 1995—96; rsch. fellow, project cons. Internat. Ctr. Tropical Agr., Colombia, 1997—98; tchg. asst. dept. geography U. BC, Vancouver, Canada, 1998—99; rsch. asst. dept. geography SUNY, Buffalo, 2000—02, postdoctoral fellow Ctr. Asthma and Environ. Exposure, 2003; asst. prof. geography info. sys. So. Ill. U., Carbondale, 2003—. Rsch./grad. asst. Nat. Ctr. Geog. Info. and Analysis, Sch. Medicine and Biomed. Scis., Ctr. Asthma and Environ. Exposure, SUNY, 2000—02; dir. rsch. lab. geographic medicine and broad band mapping project; cons. in field. Reviewer: various jours. in field; contbr. articles to profl. publs., chpts. to books. Recipient U. Nairobi Collaborative Rsch. award, Ctr. Devel. Rsch., Denmark, 1995—97, Cross-Border Activities Rsch. award, UN Ctr. Regional Devel., 1995; postgrad. fellow, Dept. Fgn. Affairs, Dublin, Ireland, 1995—96. Mem.: Am. Assn. Geographers, Am. Acad. Sleep Medicine. Office: So Ill U 1000 Farner Carbondale IL 62901

OYER, PAUL, economist; b. Newark, Aug. 10, 1963; s. Calvin E. and Alice Cinader Oyer; m. Amy Friedman, July 25, 1992; children: David Friedman, Lucienne Friedman. BA, Middlebury Coll., Vt., 1985; MBA, Yale U., New Haven, Conn., 1989; PhD, Princeton U., NJ, 1996. Asst. prof. mgmt. and strategy Northwestern U., Kellogg Sch. Mgmt., Evanston, Ill., 1996—2000; assoc. prof. econs. Stanford U., Grad. Sch. Bus., Calif., 2000. Office: Stanford University Grad School of Bus 518 Memorial Way Stanford CA 94305 Office Phone: 650-723-2300.

OYEYIPO, BOLANLE T., geriatrician; b. LA, Sept. 15, 1976; d. Tunde S. and Adeline O. Oyeyipo; m. Adewale B. Ajumobi, Sept. 19, 2002. MD, U. Ilorin, Nigeria, 2000. Diplomate Am. Bd. Family Medicine, 2006. Resident in family medicine Pomona Valley Hosp., Calif., 2003—06; fellow in geriatrics UCLA, 2006—. Mem.: Am. Med. Dirs. Assn., Am. Geriatrics Soc., Am. Acad. Family Physicians. Office: UCLA Dept Geriatrics 10945 Le Conte Ave Los Angeles CA 90095-3000

OYLER, GREGORY KENNETH, lawyer; b. Moses Lake, Wash., Sept. 16, 1953; s. Eugene Milton and Annetta Diane (Williams) O.; m. Evelyn Hartwell Wright, Oct. 18, 1986; 1 child, Elizabeth Atwood. AB, Princeton U., 1975; JD, Georgetown U., 1978; LLM, NYU, 1981. Bar: Pa. 1978, U.S. Tax Ct. 1978, U.S. Ct. Appeals (D.C. cir.) 1979, D.C. 1981, U.S. Supreme Ct. 1982, U.S. Ct. Fed. Claims 1983, U.S. Ct. Appeals (fed. cir.) 1987. Law clk. to judges U.S. Tax Ct., Washington, 1978-80; assoc. Hamel & Park, Washington, Washington, 1981-85; ptnr. Hopkins & Sutter, Washington, 1985-95, Scribner, Hall & Thompson LLP, Washington, 1995—. Mem. adv. com. IRS Info. Reporting Program, 1993—94. Mem. ABA (tax sect., ins. com.), D.C. Bar Assn. (tax sect.), Fed. Bar Assn., Soc. Preservation Md. Antiquities (bd. dirs. 1991-97), Clark-Winchcole Found. (trustee 1999—). Office: Scribner Hall & Thompson LLP 1875 Eye St NW Ste 1050 Washington DC 20006-5441

OZ, FRANK (FRANK RICHARD OZNOWICZ), entertainer, film director; b. Hereford, Eng., May 25, 1944; s. Isidore and Frances Oznowicz. m. Robin Garsen, 1979; 2 children. Student, Oakland City Coll., 1962. Puppeteer with the Muppets, N.Y.C., 1963—; characters performed include The Mighty Favag (Saturday Night Live 1975-76), Miss Piggy, Fozzie Bear, Animal, Sam the Eagle for TV series The Muppet Show, Muppets Tonight!, 1996, films Muppet Treasure Island, 1996, Muppets From Space, 1999; voice of Bert, Grover, Cookie Monster for TV series Sesame Street, video Elmo Saves Christmas, 1996, film Adventures of Elmo in Grouchland, 1999, TV film Cinderelmo, 1999, TV series Play with Me Sesame, 2002; voice for CDROM: The Muppets Inside, 1996; voice film Monsters, Inc., 2001; now v.p. Jim Henson Prodns., N.Y.C.; creative cons. feature film The Great Muppet Caper; appeared in films The Blues Brothers, 1980, Trading Places, 1983, Labyrinth, 1986, Innocent Blood, 1992, Blues Brothers, 2000; voice of Yoda in films The Empire Strikes Back, 1980, Return of the Jedi, 1983, Star Wars: Episode I-The Phantom Menace, 1999, Star Wars: Episode II-Attack of the Clones, 2002, Star Wars III-Revenge of the Sith, 2005, Zathura, 2005; dir. films The Dark Crystal (with Jim Henson), 1982, The Muppets Take Manhattan, 1984, Little Shop of Horrors, 1986, Dirty Rotten Scoundrels, 1988, What About Bob?, 1991, Housesitter, 1992, The Indian in the Cupboard, 1995, In & Out, 1997, Bowfinger, 1999, The Score, 2001, The Stepford Wives, 2004, Death at a Funeral, 2007. Co-recipient Emmy award for outstanding comedy-variety or music program for The Muppet Show, 1978. Mem. AFTRA, Dirs. Guild Am., Writers Guild Am., Screen Actors Guild, Acad. TV Arts and Scis. Office: The Jim Henson Company 627 Broadway Fl 9 New York NY 10012-2612 *

OZ, MEHMET CENGIZ, cardiac surgeon, writer; b. Cleve., June 11, 1960; s. Mustafa and Suna (Atabay) Oz; m. Lisa Oz; children: Daphne, Arabella, Zoe, Oliver. BA magna cum laude, Harvard U., 1982; MD, U. Pa. Sch. Medicine, 1986; MBA, Wharton Bus. Sch., Harvard U., Phila., 1986; doctorate (hon.), Istanbul U. Cert. Am. Bd. Surgery, 1992, Am. Bd. Thoracic Surgery, 2004. Intern/resident, gen. surgery Columbia-Presbyn. Med. Ctr., NYC, 1986—90, chief resident, gen. surgery, 1990—91, resident, cardiothoracic surgery, 1991—93; attending surgeon NY Presbyn. Hosp./Columbia U. Med. Ctr., 1993—; Irving asst. prof., surgery Columbia U. Coll. Physicians and Surgeons, NYC, 1994—2000, assoc. prof., surgery, 2000—01, prof., surgery, 2001—; dir. Cardiovasc. Inst., Dept. Surgery Columbia U. Med. Ctr., 2001—, vice-chmn., cardiovascular svcs., dept. surgery, 2001—. Bd. dirs. Siga Corp.; med. class chmn. U. Pa. Med. Sch., 1982—83, med. sch. pres., 1984—85; dir., Cardiac Assist Device Program Columbia-Presbyn. Med. Ctr., 1994—2001, founder, Complementary Medicine Program; mem. Thoracic Surgical Workforce Com., 1998. Author: Healing from the Heart: A Leading Surgeon Combines Eastern and Western Traditions to Create the Medicine of the Future, 1998 (Books for a Better Am. award, 1999); co-editor (with Daniel J. Goldstein): Minimally Invasive Cardiac Surgery, 1998 (Voted the best health sci. book, Doody, 2000), Minimally Invasive Cardiac Surgery, 2nd edit., 2004, Cardiac Assist Devices, 2000; co-author (with Michael F. Roizen): YOU: The Owner's Manual: An Insider's Guide to the Body That Will Make You Healthier and Younger, 2005 (NY Times Bestseller List, #1 Publishers Weekly Hardcover Bestseller list), YOU: The Smart Patient: An Insider's Handbook for Getting the Best Treatment, 2006, YOU: On a Diet- The Owner's Manual for Waist Management, 2006, (compact disc) YOU: on a Walk, 2007; forward by Eat to Live: The Revolutionary Formula for Fast and Sustained Weight Loss, 2003, The Dorm Room Diet: The 8-Step Program for Creating a Healthy Lifestyle Plan That Really Works, 2006; contbr. chapters to books, articles to profl. jours., to Newsweek. O Mag., Esquire Mag. and New England Journal of Medicine; numerous network news appearances, guest host The Charlie Rose Show, host Second Opinion with Dr. Oz, Discovery Health Channel, YOU: On a Diet, Discovery Health Channel, guest appearances, Ask Dr. Oz Oprah Winfrey Show, guest appearances Life Line, Discovery Channel, Daily Rounds, Discovery Health Channel, Live Transplant, Discovery Health Channel, National Body Challenge, Discovery Health Channel, Accent Health Channel, regular contbr. Oprah & Friends, XM Satellite Radio, 2006—. Mem. trustee adv. coun. One Voice Movement. Named Turkish-Am. of Yr., Assembly Turkish-Am. Assns., 1996; named one of The Best and Brightest, Esquire mag., Doctors of Yr., Hippocrates mag., The Healers of the Millenium, Healthy Living mag., Best Doctors of Yr., NY Mag.; named to Global Leaders of Tomorrow, World Econ. Forum, 1999; recipient Blakemore Rsch. Prize, Columbia U. Coll. Physician and Surgeon, 1988—91, P & S Club Outstanding, House Officer award, 1991, Prize Essay Award, Soc. Clin. Vascular Surgery, 1989, 25th Anniversary Silver award, Bastyr U., 2004. Fellow: ACS, Am. Coll. Cardiology; mem.: Am. Coll. Angiology (mem. scientific coun.), Am. Soc. for Laser Medicine and Surgery (Rsch. award 1991), Internat. Soc. for Optical Engring., Assn. Turkish-Am. Scientists, NY Soc. Thoracic Surgery, NY State Soc. Surgeons, 21st Century Cardiac Surgical Soc., Found. Advancement of Cardiac Therapies (bd. dirs.), Am. Turkish Soc. (bd. dirs.), Global Leader Tomorrow, World Econ. Forums, Am. Soc. Artificial Internal Organs, Am. Heart Assn. (mem. scientific coun.), Turkish-Am. Physicians Assn., Assn. Acad. Surgery, Internat. Soc. for Heart and Lung Transplantation, Am. Bd. Surgery, Am. Bd. Thoracic Surgery, Am. Assn. Thoracic Surgeons. Achievements include patents in field. Office: NY Presbyterian Hosp Columbia Milstein Hosp Bldg Rm 7 GN 435 177 Fort Washington Ave MHB 7 435 New York NY 10032 Office Phone: 212-305-4434. Office Fax: 212-305-2439. E-mail: mco2@columbia.edu. *

OZA, ROHAN, beverage company executive; b. 1972; MBA, U. Mich. Bus. Sch., 1997. Sprite brand mgr. Coca-Cola Co., Powerade sr. brand mgr.; sr. v.p. mktg. Glacéau, 2002—. Named one of Marketers of the Next Generation, Brandweek mag., 2002, 40 Under 40, Crain's NY Bus., 2007. Office: Glacéau 17-20 Whitestone Expy Whitestone NY 11357 *

ÖZALP, NESRIN, mechanical engineer, research scientist; d. Mehmet Orhan and Aysel Özalp. MS, Ege U., Izmir, Turkey, 1998, Stanford U., San Francisco, 2002; PhD, U. of Wash., Seattle, 2005. Rsch. asst. Stanford U., Mech. Engring. Dept., San Francisco, U. Wash., Mech. Engring. Dept., Seattle. Bd. mem. pres. rsch. adv. bd. U. Wash., Seattle, 2004—05; bd. mem. a Wash. State EPA, 2004; com. mem. provost's fund for innovation and redesign U. Wash.; sen. mech. engring. dept. Grad. and Profl. Students Senate, 2003—05; rep. grad. student Stanford U., San Francisco, 2001—02. Contbr. articles to profl. jours. Fellow, Pacific NW Nat. Lab. Mem.: ASME. Home Phone: 90 (546) 439 8880; Office Phone: 90 (546) 439 8880. Office Fax: 90 (232) 388 8562. E-mail: nesrin.ozalp@ege.edu.tr.

OZAWA, MARTHA NAOKO, social work educator; b. Ashikaga, Tochigi, Japan, Sept. 30, 1933; arrived in US, 1963; d. Tokuichi and Fumi (Kawashima) O.; m. May 1959 (div. May 1966). BA in Econs., Aoyama Gakuin U., 1956; MS in Social Work, U. Wis., 1966, PhD in Social Welfare, 1969. Asst. prof. social work Portland (Oreg.) State U., 1969-70, assoc. prof. social work, 1970-72; assoc. rsch. prof. social work NYU, 1972-75; assoc. prof. social work Portland State U., 1975-76; prof. social work Washington U., St. Louis, 1976-85, Bettie Bofinger Brown prof. social policy, 1985—2003, Bettie Bofinger Brown Disting. prof. social policy, 2003—; dir. Martha N. Ozawa Ctr. Social Policy Studies, 2005—. Author: Income Maintenance and Work Incentives, 1982; editor: Women's Life Cycle: Japan-U.S. Comparison in Income Maintenance, 1989, Women's Life Cycle and Economic Insecurity: Problems and Proposals, 1989; editl. bd. Social Work, Silver Spring, Md., 1972-75, 85-88, New Eng. Jour. Human Svcs., Boston, 1987-95, Ency. of Social Work, Silver Spring, 1974-77, 91-95, 99-2003, Jour. Social Svc. Rsch., 1977-97, Children and Youth Svcs. Rev., 1991—, Social Work Rsch., 1994-97, Jour. Poverty, 1997-2004; co-editor-in-chief Asian Social Work and Policy Rev., 2005—. Grantee Adminstrn. on Aging, Washington, 1979, 84, NIMH, 1990-93. Mem. Nat. Assn. Social Workers (presdl. award 1999), Nat. Acad. Social Ins., Nat. Conf. on Social Welfare (bd. dirs. 1981-87), The Gerontol. Soc. Am., Soc. for Social Work and Rsch., Washington U. Faculty Club (bd. dirs. 1986-91). Avocations: photography, tennis, swimming, gardening. Home: 13018 Tiger Lily Ct Saint Louis MO 63146-4339 Office: PO Box 1196 Saint Louis MO 63130-4899 Office Phone: 314-935-6615. Business E-Mail: ozawa@wustl.edu.

OZAWA, SEIJI, conductor, music director; b. Shenyang, China, Sept. 1, 1935; s. Kaisaku and Sakura Ozawa; m. Kyoko Edo; m. Vera Motoki-Ilyin Ozawa; children: Seira, Yukiyoshi. Student, Toho Sch. Music, Tokyo, Japan, 1953-59; studies with, Hideo Saito, Eugene Bigot, Herbert Von Karajan, Leonard Bernstein; student at the invitation of Charles Munch, Tanglewood, 1959; DMus (hon.), U. Mass., New England Conserv. Music, Wheaton Coll. Music dir. Boston Symphony Orch., 1973—2002, music dir. laureate, 2002—; music dir. Vienna State Opera, 2002—. One of three asst. condrs. N.Y. Philharm., 1961—62; music dir., season Ravinia Festival, 1964—68; music dir. Toronto Symphony Orch., 1965—69, San Francisco Symphony Orch., 1970—76; apptd. artistic advisor Tanglewood Festival, 1970; condr. Evening at Symphony Boston Symphony Orch., music advisor, 1972—73, Vienna State Opera, 1988, Saito Kinen Festival, Matsumoto, Japan, 1992; mem. internat. tour Dvorak Gala, Prague, 1993, Vienna Philharm. Asia, 1993, 96, 2000, Vienna Philharm. Europe, 1997, 98, 2000; mem. concert tour Berlin Philharm. Salzburg Festival; co-founder, artistic dir. Tokyo Opera Nomori, 2005—; opened music acad., Geneva, 2005—. Named a Chevalier de la Legion d'Honneur, Pres. France Jacques Chirac; named Laureate, Found. du Japan, 1988, Seiji Ozawa Hall for him, Tanglewood Music Ctr., 1994, Music Dir. Laureate, Boston Symphony Orch., 2002, Musician of the Yr., Musical America; recipient 1st prize, Internat. Competition Orch. Condrs., 1959, Koussevitzky prize, Tanglewood Music Ctr., 1960, Inouye award for Lifetime Achievement, 1964; conducting fellow, Tanglewood Music Ctr., 1959. Avocations: golf, tennis, skiing. Office: Veroza Japan Co Ltd 2F 6-13-21 Seijo Setagaya-ku Tokyo 157-0066 Japan Office Phone: +81-(0)3-5490-6805. Office Fax: +81-(0)3-5490-6985. *

OZCAN, AYDOGAN, electrical engineer, educator; b. Sinop, Turkey, Sept. 24, 1978; BS in Elec. Engring., Bilkent U., Turkey, 2000; MS in Elec. Engring., Stanford U., Calif., 2002, PhD in Elec. Engring., 2005. Postdoctoral fellow Stanford U., 2005—06; instr. Med. Sch. Harvard U., Boston, 2006—; prof. elec. engring. dept. UCLA. Contbr. articles to profl. jours. Mem.: IEEE, OSA. Achievements include patents pending in field; patents in field. Office: Elec Engring Dept UCLA Los Angeles CA 90095 Business E-Mail: ozcan@ee.ucla.edu.

OZELLI, TUNCH, economics professor; b. Ankara, Turkey, May 18, 1938; came to U.S., 1962; s. Sufyan and Saziye (Ozmorali) O.; m. Lale A. Baymur, Dec. 30, 1960 (div. Mar. 1972); children: Selva, Kerem; m. Nancy Ann Goldschlager, Feb. 3, 1974 (div. Dec. 1984); m. Meral Ozdemir, May

9, 1992. MBA, Fla. State U., 1963; PhD, Columbia U., 1968. Rsch. fellow Harvard U., Cambridge, Mass., 1969-70; econ. advisor Office Prime Minister, Ankara, 1970-72; prof. mgmt. N.Y. Inst. Tech., NYC, 1972—. Spl. advisor State Planning Orgn., Ankara, 1989-92. Contbr. articles to profl. jour. Ford Found. scholar, 1963-64, Found. for Econ. Edn. fellow, 1968. Mem. Am. Econ. Assn., Middle East Studies Assn., Turkish Mgmt. Assn., Delta Mu Delta. Avocation: equestrian activities. Office: Dept of Economics NY Inst Tech Old Westbury NY 11568

OZERDEN, HALIL SULEYMAN (SUL), federal judge; b. Hattiesburg, Miss., Dec. 5, 1966; m. Denise Dunaway; 1 child, Vivian. BS in Fgn. Svc. magna cum laude, Georgetown U.Sch. Fgn. Svc., 1989; Grad., Navy Flight Sch., Pensacola, Fla., 1989—90; JD, Stanford Law Sch., 1998. Bar: Miss., Fla., La., Ala., US Ct. Appeals (5th Cir.), US Dist. Ct. (no. & so. dist.) Miss., US Dist. Ct. (ea. dist.) La., US Dist. Ct. (no. dist.) Fla. 1988. Law clk. to Hon. Eldon E. Fallon US Dist. Ct. (ea. dist.) La., 1998—99; ptnr. Dukes, Dukes, Keating & Faneca, P.A., Gulfport, Miss., 1999—2003, shareholder, 2003—07; judge US Dist. Ct. (so. dist.) Miss., Jackson, 2007—. Mem. Rotary Club Gulfport, 1999—; mentor Gulfport Pub. Schools, 1999—; exec. com., v.p. pub. affairs Gulfport C. of C., 2000—03, chmn.-elect, 2005; v.p. Gulfport Bus. Club, 2004—05; vestry mem. St. Peter's By-the-Sea Episcopal Church, 2002—04. Served in USN, 1989—95. Named one of Top Ten South Miss. Bus. Leaders Under 40, 2004; recipient Johnson & Gibbs Law Review award, Outstandsing Contribution as an Assoc. Editor, 1998, Volunteer of Yr., Gulfport C. of C., 2003. Mem.: Am. Inns of Ct., Harrison County Young Lawyers Assn., Harrison County Bar Assn., Ala. Bar Assn., Fla. Bar Assn., Miss. Bar Assn. Office: US Dist Ct PO Box 23552 Jackson MS 39225

OZICK, CYNTHIA, writer; b. NYC, Apr. 17, 1928; d. William and Celia (Regelson) O.; m. Bernard Hallote, Sept. 7, 1952; 1 dau., Rachel Sarah. BA cum laude with honors in English, NYU, 1949; MA, Ohio State U., 1950; LHD (hon.), Yeshiva U., 1984, Hebrew Union Coll., 1984, Williams Coll., 1986, Hunter Coll., 1987, Jewish Theol. Sem. Am., 1988, Adelphi U., 1988, SUNY, 1989, Brandeis U., 1990, Bard Coll., 1991, Spertus Coll., 1991, Skidmore Coll., 1992, Seton Hall U., 1999, Rutgers U., 1999, U. N.C., Asheville, 2000, NYU, 2001, Bar-Ilan U., Israel, 2002, Balt Hebrew U., 2004; LHD (hon.), Georgetown U., 2007. Author: Trust, 1966, reissued, 2004, The Pagan Rabbi and Other Stories, 1971, Bloodshed and Three Novellas, 1976, Levitation: Five Fictions, 1982, Art and Ardor: Essays, 1983, The Cannibal Galaxy, 1983, The Messiah of Stockholm, 1987, Metaphor & Memory: Essays, 1989, The Shawl, 1989, Epodes: First Poems, 1992, What Henry James Knew, and Other Essays on Writers, 1994, Portrait of the Artist as a Bad Character, 1996, The Cynthia Ozick Reader, 1996, Fame & Folly, 1996, The Puttermesser Papers, 1997, (novel) Heir to the Glimmering World, 2004, The Din the Head: Essays, 2006; (plays) Blue Light, 1994, The Shawl, 1996; guest editor Best Am. Essays, 1998, Quarrel & Quandary: Essays, 2000, Collected Stories, 2006; also poetry, criticism, revs., translations, essays and fictions in numerous periodicals and anthologies. Phi Beta Kappa orator, Harvard U., 1985. Recipient Mildred and Harold Strauss Living award Am. Acad. Arts and Letters, 1983, Rea award for short story, 1986, PEN/Spiegel-Diamonstein award for the Art of the Essay, 1997, Harold Washington Literary award City of Chgo., 1997, John Cheever award, 1999, Lannan Found. award for fiction, 2000, Koret Found. award for lit. studies, 2001, Nat. Book Critics Circle award for nonfiction, 2001, Mary McCarthy award Bard Coll., 2007; Lucy Martin Donnelly fellow, Bryn Mawr Coll., 1992, Guggenheim fellow, 1982. Mem. PEN, Authors League, Am. Acad. of Arts and Scis., Am. Acad. of Arts and Letters, Dramatists Guild, Académie Universelle des Cultures (Paris), Phi Beta Kappa.

OZKAN, UMIT SIVRIOGLU, chemical engineering professor; b. Manisa, Turkey, Apr. 11, 1954; came to U.S., 1980; d. Alim and Emine (Ilgaz) Sivrioglu; m. H. Erdal Ozkan, Aug. 13, 1983. BS, Mid. East Tech. U., Ankara, Turkey, 1978, MS, 1980; PhD, Iowa State U., 1984. Registered profl. engr., Ohio. Grad. rsch. assoc. Ames Lab. U.S. Dept. Energy, 1980-84; asst. prof. Ohio State U., Columbus, 1985-90, assoc. prof. chem. engring., 1990-94, prof., 1994—, assoc. dean for rsch. Coll. Engring., 2000—05. Contbr. articles to profl. jours. French Ctr. NAt. Rsch. Sci. fellow, 1994-95; recipient Women of Achievement award YWCA, Columbus, 1991, Outstanding Engring. Educator Ohio award Soc. Profl. Engrs., 1991, Union Carbide Innovation Recognition award, 1991-92, NSF Woman Faculty award in sci. and engring., 1991, Engring. Tchg. Excellence award Keck Found., 1994, Ctrl. Ohio Outstanding Woman in Sci. & Tech., 1996, Pitts.-Cleve. Catalysis Soc. Outstanding Rsch. award, 1998, Achievement award Soc. Women Engring., 2002, Columbus Outstanding Rsch. award ACS, 2002, Fulbright award, 2006. Fellow Am. Inst. Chemists; mem. NSPE, N.Am. Catalysis Soc., Am. Inst. Chem. Engring., Am. Soc. Engring. Edn., Am. Chem. Soc., Combustion Inst., Sigma Xi. Achievements include research in selective oxidation; electrocatalysis; in-situ spectroscopy; fuel reformulation; hydrodenitrogenation; hydrodeoxygenation; hydrodesulfurization; NO reduction; hydrogenation. Office: Ohio State U Chem Engring 140 W 19th Ave Columbus OH 43210-1110 Office Phone: 614-292-6623. E-mail: ozkan.1@usa.edu.

OZOLINSH, SANDIS, professional hockey player; b. Riga, Latvia, Aug. 13, 1972; Defenseman San Jose Sharks, 1992—96, Colo. Avalanche, 1995—2000, Carolina Hurricanes, 2000—01, Fla. Panthers, 2001—03, Anaheim Mighty Ducks, 2002—06, NY Rangers, 2006—. Player NHL All-Star Game, 1994, 1997—98, 2000—03. Achievements include mem. Stanley Cup Champion Colo. Avalanche, 1995. Office: c/o NY Rangers 2 Pennsylvania Plaza New York NY 10121

OZONIAN, STEVE, real estate company executive; BS, Northeastern U.; MBA in Fin., Loyola U. Mng. dir. Employee Transfer Corp., regional pres.; exec. Coldwell Banker; chmn. and CEO Prudential Real Estate and Relocation Solutions; pres. and CEO Realtor.com; sr. exec. RE/MAX Internat.; nat. home ownership exec. Bank of Am.; chmn. Global Mobility Solutions; bd. dirs. Help-U-Sell (Realty Info. Systems Inc.), Irvine, Calif., chmn. and CEO. Sr. leaders group Grad. Inst. Leadership Develop., Cambridge, Mass.; bd. dirs. Spinnaker Capital. Named one of Real Estate's 25 Most Influential Thought Leaders, Realtor Mag., 2006. Office: Help-U-Sell 3333 Michelson Dr Irvine CA 92612 *

OZTURK, MEHMET CEVDET, engineering educator; b. Ankara, Turkey, June 12, 1957; s. Necati Tevfik Ozturk and Fikret Kircali; m. Hatice Orun, Apr. 11, 1960; 1 child, Berk Orun. BSEE, Bosphorus U., Istanbul, Turkey, 1980; PhD, NC State U., Raleigh, 1988. Physics instr. English HS, Istanbul, Turkey, 1980—81; tchg. asst. Mich. Technol. U., Houghton, 1981—83; tchg. & rsch. asst. N.C. State U., 1983—88, prof., 1988—. Contbr. papers to profl. jours. and pubs. Presdl. Faculty fellow, NSF, 1995—2000. Achievements include first to propose the use of SiGe alloys in source/drain regions of nanoscale metal oxide field effect transistors; propose the recessed and in-situ doped SiGe source/drain junction technology as a replacement for ion-implantation. Office: NC State Univ Elec & Computer Engring Dept Raleigh NC 27695 Office Phone: 919-515-5245. Business E-Mail: mco@ncsu.edu.

OZUMBA, BENJAMIN CHUKWUMA, obstetrician, gynecologist, educator; b. Onitsha, Anambra, Nigeria, Mar. 21, 1954; s. Arthur Nwabunwanne and Alice chiebonam (Igebuike) O.; m. Chinelo Obianuju Udokwu, Jan. 29, 1994; children: Benjamin Chukwumdindu, Sarah Onyinyechukwu, Elizabeth Chimfumnanya, Rachel Chidinma. MB, BChir, U. Lagos, Nigeria, 1979; FMCOG, Post Grad. Med. Coll., Nigeria, 1987; MRCOG, Royal Coll. Ob.-Gyn., London, 1993; FICS, Internat. Coll. Surgeons, U.S., 1991; FWACS, W. African Coll. Surgeons, Lagos, Nigeria, 1993. Intern Lagos U. Tchg. Hosp., 1979—80; med. officer Coll. of Edn., Minna, Nigeria, 1980—81; sr. house officer Univ. Nigeria Tchg. Hosp., Enusu, 1981—82, registrar, 1982—83, sr. registrar, 1983—88, sr. lectr./ cons., 1988—93; prof. ob./gyn. U. Nigeria, Nsukka, 1993—, dean faculty med. scis. and dentistry, 2002—04, provost Coll. Medicine, 2004. Chmn. Enugu Med. Soc., 1993-95; coord. Tutorial System Internat., Nigeria, 1993-95; dean medicine U. Nigeria. Editor: Tropical Pediatrics and Child Health, 1999; assoc. editor Orient Jour. Medicine, 1988—, Nigerian Jour. Surgical Scis., 1991—; contbr. articles to profl. jours. V.p. Enugu chpt. Full Gospel Businessmen's Fellowship Internat., 1994-95, chpt. pres., 1997—; chmn. Harvest and Love Feast Com., Chapel of Redemption, Enugu, Nigeria, 1994-95. Takemi fellow Internat. Health Harvard U., 1995-96. Fellow Internat. Coll. Surgeons, W. African Coll. of Surgeons, Nigerian Postgrad. Med. Coll.; mem. AAAS (internat. mem.), Royal Coll. Obstetricians and Gynecologists. Born Again Christian. Achievements include measuring: serum concentrations of alphafetoprotein in mormal pregnancy and in pregnancy induced hypertensions; ivermectin levels in human breast milk. Office: Univ Nigeria Teaching Hosp Dept Ob-gyn Enugu Anambra Nigeria Mailing: 45 Duffield Dr South Orange NJ 07079 Home Phone: 236 42 253496. Personal E-mail: BenOzumba@hotmail.com.

OZZIE, RAY (RAYMOND E. OZZIE), computer software company executive; b. Nov. 20, 1955; B in Computer Sci., U. Ill., Urbana-Champaign, 1979. Sys. programmer Protection Mut. Ins. Co., 1972—73; technician dept. nuc. engring. U. Ill., 1974, sys. programmer PLATO project, 1974—79; co-founder Urbana Software Enterprises, 1978—79; with Data Gen. Corp., 1979—81; co-founder Microcosm Corp., 1981; with Software Arts, 1981—82, Lotus Devel., 1983—84; founder, pres. Iris Assocs., 1984—97; founder, chmn., CEO Groove Networks, Inc. (acquired by Microsoft Corp.), Beverly, Mass., 1997—2005; chief tech. officer Microsoft Corp., Redmond, Wash., 2005—06, chief software architect, 2006—. Adv. bd. mem., Live Labs (rsch. partnership between MSN and Microsoft Rsch.) Microsoft Corp., 2006—. Named Person of Yr., PC Mag., 1995, Disting. Alumnus, U. Ill., Urbana-Champaign; named one of Seven "Windows Pioneers", Microsoft Corp., Top Five Developers of the Century, Computer Reseller News, 50 Who Matter Now, CNNMoney.com Bus. 2.0, 2006; named to Computer Mus. Industry Hall of Fame, InfoWorld Hall of Fame; recipient W. Wallace McDowell award, IEEE Computer Soc., 2000. Mem.: NRC (mem. computer sci. and telecom. bd.), World Econ. Forum (gov. IT and telecom., honored as technology pioneer 2001), NAE. Achievements include first to field of collaboration technology; creator, developer Lotus Notes, 1984; instrumental in development of Lotus Symphony, TK!Solver and VisiCalc. Office: Microsoft Corp 1 Microsoft Way Redmond WA 98052-6399 *

PÄÄBO, SVANTE, molecular biologist, biochemist; b. Stockholm, 1955; PhD in Molecular Immunology, Uppsala U., 1986; PhD (hon.), U. Zurich, 1994, U. Helsinki, 2000. Postdoctoral rsch. Inst. Molecular Biology, U. Zurich., 1986—87, U. Calif., Berkeley, 1987—90; rsch. scientist U. California; prof. biology U. Munich, 1990—98; dir. Max Planck Inst. for Evolutionary Anthropology, Leipzig, Germany, 1997—; hon. prof. genetics and evolutionary biology U. Leipzig, 1999—. Guest prof. comparative genomics Uppsala U., Sweden, 2003. Recipient Leibniz Prize, Deutsche Forschungsgemeinschaft, 1992, Max Delbruck medal, 1998, Carus medal & prize, 1999, Rudbeck prize, Uppsala, 2000, Leipzig Science prize, 2003, Ernst Schering prize, 2003, Louis Jeantet prize medicine, 2005, Virchow medal, Univ. Würzburg, Germany, 2005; Named one of the World's Most Influential People, TIME Mag., 2007 Mem.: Finnish Soc. Arts and Letters, Saxonian Acad. Scis., Deutsche Akademie der Naturforscher Leopoldina, Berlin-Brandenburg Acad. Scis., Royal Swedish Acad. Scis., Academia Europaea, NAS (fgn. assoc.). Achievements include pioneering ancient DNA extraction studies. Office: Max Planck Inst for Evolutionary Anthropology Deutscher Platz 6 04103 Leipzig Germany *

PAANANEN, VICTOR NILES, language educator; b. Ashtabula, Ohio, Jan. 31, 1938; s. Niles Henry and Anni Margaret (Iloranta) P.; m. Donna Mae Jones, Aug. 15, 1964; children: Karl, Neil. AB magna cum laude, Harvard U., 1960; MA, U. Wis., 1964, PhD, 1967. Instr. English Wofford Coll., Spartanburg, SC, 1962-63; asst. prof. Williams Coll., Williamstown, Mass., 1966-68, Mich. State U., East Lansing, 1968-73, assoc. prof., 1973—82, prof., 1982—2002, asst. dean Grad. Sch., 1977-82, chmn. dept. English, 1986-94, prof. emeritus, 2002—. Vis. prof. Roehampton U., London, 1982, 96, hon. fellow, 92; mem. Harvard Inst. Learning Ret., 2006. Author: William Blake, 1977, 2d edit., 1996, British Marxist Criticism, 2000; contbr. articles to profl. and scholarly jours. Univ. fellow U. Wis., 1962, 63-64, Roehampton Inst. hon. fellow, London, 1992—; Harvard Nat. scholar, 1956-60. Home: 350 Revere Beach Blvd 5-5W Revere MA 02151-4851 E-mail: paananen@msu.edu.

PAAR, CHRISTOPHER R., lawyer; b. 1971; m. Martha Paar; 2 children. BA, JD, U. Iowa. Bar: Minn. 1997. Atty. Zelle, Hofmann, Voelbel, Mason & Gette, L.L.P., Mpls. Named a Rising Star, Minn. Super Lawyers mag., 2006. Mem.: ABA, Minn. Bar Assn., Iowa Bar Assn. Office: Zelle Hofmann Voelbel Mason & Gette LLP 500 Washington Ave S Ste 4000 Minneapolis MN 55415 Office Phone: 612-336-9113. E-mail: cpaar@zelle.com. *

PAAS, JOHN ROGER, language educator; b. Chgo., Mar. 14, 1945; s. Walter V. and Doris (Marinoff) P.; m. Martha Clem White, Aug. 24, 1968; children: Emily, Anne. BA summa cum laude, Hamilton Coll., Clinton, NY, 1967; PhD, Bryn Mawr Coll., 1973. Part-time asst. prof. Bryn Mawr (Pa.) Coll., 1973-74; prof. German Carleton Coll., Northfield, Minn., 1974—, dept chair, 1985-88. Author: The German Political Broadsheet 1600-1700, 8 vols., 1985—, Effigies et Poesis: An Illustrated Catalogue of Printed Portaits with Laudatory Verses by German Baroque Poets, 2 vols., 1988; editor: Unbekannte Gedichte und Lieder des Sigmund von Birken, 1990, Hollstein's German Engravings, Etchings and Woodcuts, 1400-1700, vols. 38-41, 1994-95, Der Franken Rom: Nürnburgs Blütezeit in der zweiten Hälfte des 17 Jhts., 1995, Augsburg, die Bilderfabrik Europas, 2001, (with Wolfgang Harms, Michael Schilling and Andreas Wang) Illustrierte Flugblätter des Barock: Eine Auswahl, 1983; contbr. articles to profl. jours. Sgt. US Army, 1969—71. Summer grantee German Acad. Exch. Svc., 1975, 78, 83, Andrew W. Mellon Found., 1976, Faculty Devel. grantee Bush Found., 1978, Carleton Coll., 1985, NEH grantee, 1990, 92-93; vis. fellow Beinecke Libr., Yale U., 1991, IREX fellow, 1978, Fulbright sr. rsch. fellow, 1988-89, Humboldt Rsch. fellow, 2000-01. Mem. Gutenberg Soc., Soc. German Renaissance and Baroque Lit., Internationaler Arbeitskreis für Barockliteratur, Frühe Neuzeit Interdisziplinär. Home: 107 College St Northfield MN 55057-2222 Office: Carleton College 1 N College St Northfield MN 55057-4044

PAASWELL, ROBERT EMIL, civil engineer, educator; b. Red Wing, Minn., Jan. 15, 1937; s. George and Evelyn (Cohen) P.; m. Rosalind Snyder, May 31, 1958; children: Judith Marjorie, George Harold. BA (Ford Found. fellow), Columbia U., 1956, BS, 1957, MS, 1961; PhD, Rutgers U., 1965. Field engring. asst. Spencer White & Prentis, Washington, 1954-56, engr. NYC, 1957-59; rsch. scientist Davidson Lab., NJ, 1964; rsch. fellow Greater London Council, 1971-72; rsch. and teaching asst. Columbia U., 1959-62; asst. prof. civil engring. SUNY, Buffalo, 1964-68; chmn. bd. govs. Urban Studies Coll., 1973-76, assoc. prof., 1968-76, prof. civil engring., 1976-82; dir. Center for Transp. Studies and Research, 1979-82, chmn. dept. environ. design and planning, 1980-82; prof. transp. engring. U. Ill., Chgo., 1982-86, 89-90, dir. Urban Transp. Ctr., 1982-86; exec. dir. Chgo. Transit Authority, 1986—89; dir. Univ. Transp. Rsch. Ctr. CCNY, 1990—, disting. prof., 1991—; dir. CUNY Inst. Urban Systems, 2000—. Faculty-on-leave Dept. Transp., 1976-77, cons., 1981—; v.p. Faculty Tech. Cons., Inc., Midwest Sys. Scis., Inc., 1982-86; dir. Urban Mass Transp. Adminstrn. Summer Faculty Workshop, 1980, 81; cons. transp. planning, energy and soil mechanics; spl. cons. to Congressman T. Dulski, 1973; vis. expert lectr. Jilin U. Tech., Changchun, Peoples Republic of China, 1985, hon. prof. transp., 1986—; bd. dirs. E'Escuto Archs. and Engrs., Chig, Hickling Co., Ottawa, Can., Transic Devel. Corp.; chmn. transp. steering adv. bd. Office of Tech. Assessment for Infrastructure and the Urban Core Project, 1994—; faculty Lincoln Inst. of Land Policy, 1994-95; vis. scholar Tel Aviv U., Israel, 1995—; arbitrator in productivity Met. Transp. Authority, N.Y.C., 1996—; mem. exec. com. Coun. on Transp., 1996—, NSF Ctr. for Infrastructure Sys.; cons. Coun. of North East Govs., 1997—; faculty "Conflict Resolution," NYU, 1998—; mem. exec. com. Inst. for Civil Infrastructure Sys. (NSF), 1998—; chair panel new paradigms in transit Transp. Rsch. Bd., chair panel on risk analysis for informatics, 2006—; bd. dirs. Transit Stds. Consortium, chmn., 2000—; bd. dir. CUNY Sch. Profl. Studies, 2005—, Urban Sustainability Inst. Author: Problems of the Carless, 1977; contbg. author: Transport and Urban Development, 1995, Panels for Transportation Planning, 1997, Studies in Israel Planning, 1996, Dynamic Networks and Spatial Change, 1999, After the World Trade Center, 2002; editor: Site Traffic Impact Assessment, 1992; contbg. author: Decisions for the Great Lakes, 1982, World Book Encyclopedia, 1992, 93, 94, Transport and Urban Development, 1995, Israel Planning Studies, 1996, 97, Panels for Transportation Planning, 1997, New Contributions to Transportation Analysis in Europe, 1999, Intelligent Transportation Systems in "Moving People, Goods and Information", 2002, Policy Analysis of Transport Networks, 2005; mem. bd. editors Jour. Environ. Systems, 1974—, Transp., 1978—, Jour. Urban Tech., 1992—; contbr. articles to profl. jours. Mem. Buffalo Environ. Mgmt. Commn., 1972-74; mem. Area Com. for Transit, Mayor's Energy Adv. Bd., 1974, Block Grant Rev. Com., City of Buffalo; chmn. com. on transp., mem. rev. adv. bd. Rsch. and Planning Coun. Western N.Y.; mem. transp. com. Chgo. 1992 Worlds Fair; mem. citizens' adv. bd. Chgo. Transit Authority, 1985—; mem. strategic planning com. Regional Transp. Authority, 1985; mem. steering com. Nat. Transit Coop. Rsch. Program, 1991—, Borough pres. (Manhattan) Trans. Adv. Bd., Bronx Ctr. Devel. Project; bd. dirs. Transit Devel. Corp., 1992—; exec. bd. Transp. Coun., 1996—; mem. exec. com. Colin Powell Ctr.; bd. dirs. York Aviation Inst., 2003—; chmn. adv. bd. Cmty. Transp. Devel. Ctr., 2003—; mem. MTA Blue Ribbon Commn. 0n Constrn., 2007—, MTA Blue Ribbon Commn. on Workforce Devel., 2007—, NY State Commn. on Higher Edn., 2007-. Recipient Dept. Transp. award, 1977, Outstanding Alumnus award, Rutgers U., 2003; SUNY faculty fellow, 1965-66 Fellow ASCE (past pres. Buffalo sect., chmn. steering com. 1992 splty. conf. traffic impact analysis, chair com. on peer rev. of pub. agys.); mem. AAAS, Transp. Rsch. Bd. (chmn. com. on transp. disadvantaged, mem. exec. com., peer rev. com. nat. transp. ctrs. 1988—), Inst. Transp. Engrs. (transit coun., exec. com., chmn. legis. policy com., rsch. com. surface transp. policy project 1995—), Coun. on Transp. (bd. dirs. 1996—), N.Y. Acad. Scis., Sigma Xi. Avocation: astronomy. Office: CCNY Marshak 917 135th St and Convent Ave New York NY 10031 Business E-Mail: paaswell@utrc2.org.

PAAU, ALAN SHIUKEE, academic administrator, biotechnologist, educator; b. Macau, Dec. 16, 1951; arrived in US, 1971, naturalized, 1985; s. Lokfu and Ping (Li) Paau; m. Florence Hau, Aug. 14, 1978; 1 child. PhD, U. Houston, 1978; MBA, Cardinal Stritch Coll., 1990. Tchg. coord. U. Houston, 1974—78; rsch. assoc U. Wis., Madison, 1978—79, project scientist, 1979—81; scientist, project leader Cetus Madison Corp., Middleton, Wis., 1982—84; sr. scientist, project mgr. Agracetus Corp., Middleton, Wis., 1984—90; project mgr., assoc. W.R. Grace & Co., Columbia, 1991—92; assoc. dir. Biotech. Ctr. Ohio State U., Columbus, 1992—94; exec. dir. Iowa State U. Rsch. Found. Inc., Ames, 1994—98; dir. tech. transfer U. Calif., San Diego, 1998—2006, asst. vice chancellor Tech. Transfer & Intellectual Property Svcs.; vice provost tech. transfer and econ. devel. Cornell U., Ithaca, NY, 2007—, exec. dir. Cornell Ctr. Tech., Enterprise and Commercialization (CCTEC), 2007—. Tech. advisor Chimertech Devel. Corp., 1990—; sci. adv. bd. Human Gene Therapy Rsch. Inst., 1995—97; bd. dirs. PreComp, Inc.; cons. in field. Contbr. articles to prof. jours. Recipient Outstanding Grad. Student award, Am. Soc. Plant Physiologists, 1974. Mem.: AAAS, Assn. Univ. Tech. Mgrs., Licensing Execs. Soc., Am. Soc. Microbiology, Sigma Xi. Roman Catholic. Office: Cornell Ctr Tech, Enterprise, and Commercializa 20 Thornwood Dr, Ste 105 Ithaca NY 14850 Office Phone: 607-257-1081. Office Fax: 607-257-1015. E-mail: ap364@cornell.edu. *

PAAVOLA, FRED G., pharmacist; s. George W. and Eleanor M. Paavola; m. Linda M. Kane, June 25, 1977; children: Nicholas, Chad, Heather. BS, Mont. State U., Bozeman, 1967, ND State U., Fargo, 1970, DSc, 2002. Chief pharmacy officer Indian Health Svc., Eagle Butte, SD, 1981—88, area pharmacy officer, 1987—88; pharmacy manpower analyst Bur. Health Professions, Rockville, Md., 1988—90, chief allied and assn. health professions, 1990—95, chief peer rev., 1995—2000; chief pharmacist officer USPHS, Rockville, Md., 1996—2000; team comdr. Ariz. One Disaster Med. Assistance Team, Tucson, 2003—06. Chair nat. adv. bd. ND State U. Coll. Pharmacy, Fargo, 2005—06. Author: Remington, 2000; contbr. articles to profl. jours. Swim ofcl. Ariz. Swimming, Tucson, 2000—06; v.p. Monument Vista Homeowners Assn., Tucson, 2001—04; dir. emergency svcs. El Tour de Tucson, 2003. With US Army, 1970—80, with USPHS, 1980—2000. Named Pharmacist of Yr., Drug Topics, 2000; named to Wall of Fame, ROTC ND State U., 2003; recipient Exemplary Svc. award, Surgeon Gen., 1993, 1997, 2000. Fellow: Am. Pharmacists Assn.; mem.: Assn. Mil. Surgeons US (life), ND State U. Alumni Assn., George F. Archambault Found., Commd. Officers Assn. (life).

PACALA, LEON, retired professional society administrator; b. Indpls., May 3, 1926; s. John and Anna (Ferician) P.; m. Janet Lefforge, Dec. 28, 1947 (dec. July 1987); children: Mark, Stephen, James; m. Virginia Strasenburgh, Mar. 10, 1990. AB, Franklin Coll., Ind., 1949; BD, Colgate Rochester Div. Sch., 1952; PhD, Yale U., 1960; LLD (hon.), Nazareth Coll., 1980; LHD (hon.), Franklin Coll., 1987. Ordained to ministry Baptist Ch., 1952. Asst. prof. philosophy and religion DePauw U., 1956-61; participant study religion undergrad. coll. Lilly Found., 1957-59; assoc. prof. religion Bucknell U., 1961-68, prof., 1968-73, chmn. dept., 1961-64, dean, 1962-73; pres. Colgate Rochester (N.Y.) Div. Sch., pres. emeritus, 1995—; also Bexley Hall, Crozer Theol. Sem., 1973-80; exec. dir. Assn. Theol. Schs. in U.S. and Can., 1980-91. Chair, founding mem. World Coun. Theol. Instns., 1986-2002; cons. acad. adminstrn. Beirut Coll. Women, 1972. Author: The Role of ATS in Theological Education, 1980-90, 1998; contbr. articles to profl. jours. Exec. com. Christian Faith in Higher Edn. Projects, 1965-68; trustee Franklin Coll., 1967-73, 98-2002; bd. dirs. Rohesters Jobs, Inc., 1973-80, Union Theol. Sem., N.Y.C., 1999—; trustee Rochester Area Colls., 1973-80; dir. Nat. Housing Ministries, Am. Bapt. Chs., 1976-80; mem. adv. bd. Colgate Rochester Div. Sch., 1997—. With USAAF, 1944-45. Internat. Rotary scholar, Louvain U., Belgium, 1952-53. Mem. Am. Conf. Acad. Deans (exec. com., treas., chmn., presiding officer 1973-74), Am. Assn. Higher Edn., Assn. Am. Colls. (commn. religion higher edn.), Assn. Theol. Schs. (com. accreditation), World Conf. Assns. Theol. Instns. (v.p. 1988-93), Am. Bapt. Assn. Sem. Adminstrs. (chmn 1975-80). Home: 56 Woodbury Pl Rochester NY 14618

PACALA, STEPHEN W., ecology educator; b. Greencastle, Ind., Jan. 9, 1957; s. Leon Pacala; m. Katherine Elizabeth Kauzmann, Dec. 29, 1981; children: Katherine, Charles, Connor. BA, Dartmouth Coll., 1978; PhD, Stanford U., 1982. Rsch. asst. Dartmouth Coll., Hanover, NH, 1975-78, tchg. asst., 1978, Stanford U., Calif., 1979-81; assoc. prof. ecology sect. biol. sci. group U. Conn., Storrs, 1982-87, assoc. prof. dept. ecology and evolution biology, 1987-92; prof. dept. ecology and evolutionary biology Princeton U., NJ, 1992—, dir. grad. studies, ecology and evolutionary biology, 1993—2006, assoc. prof. Princeton Environmental Inst., 1994—, co-dir., NOAA Carbon Modeling Ctr., 1995—2003, co-dir., Carbon Mitigation Initiative, 2000—, acting dir., Princeton Environmental Inst., 2005—06, dir., Princeton Environmental Inst., 2006. Cmty. ecology panel NSF, 1992—; adv. bd. mem. NASA, Washington, 1992—, Inter-Am. Inst. for Global Change Rsch., 1994—; mem. ecosystem panel Dept. Energy, 1994—. Assoc. editor Theoretical Population Biology, 1987—90, 93-, The Am. Naturalist, 1990—93; contbr. articles to profl. jours. Fellow NIH, 1993, The Seaver Inst., 1993—; grantee The Seaver Inst., 1993—, NSF Ecology Program, 1993—, NASA Ecosystem Dynamics and Biogeochemical Cycles Br., 1993—, Andrew W. Mellon Found., 1994—, Dept. Energy and Program for Ecosystem Rsch., 1994—; recipient George Mercer award, 1997; named Witherspoon Disting. Lecturer, Lawrence Berkeley Nat. Lab., 2002. Fellow AAAS; mem. Am. Soc. Naturalists, Ecol. Soc., NAS. Office: Princeton Univ Dept Ecology & Evol Biology Guyot Hall Washington Rd Princeton NJ 08544-1003 *

PACE, ANDREW K., information technology library director; BA in Rhetoric and Communication Studies, U. Va., 1991; MSLS, Cath. U. of Am., 1996. Libr. asst. Cath. U. of Am. Libraries, 1994—96; systems libr. Innovative Interfaces, Inc., 1996—99; systems libr. digital projects NC State U. Libraries, 1999, asst. head systems, 1999—2001, head info. tech., 2001—. Named Libr. of Yr., DRA Users' Group, 2002; Frye fellowship, 2006. Mem.: Nat. Info. Standards Orgn. (co-chair metasearch initiative 2003—05), Assn. Coll. & Rsch. Libraries, Libr. and Info. Tech. Assn. (dir.-at-large 2004—07, pres.-elect 2007—). Office: NC State U DH Hill Libr Raleigh NC 27695-7111 Office Phone: 919-515-3087. Office Fax: 919-513-3330. Business E-Mail: andrew_pace@ncsu.edu. *

PACE, CAROL REBECCA, elementary school educator; b. Tokyo, Mar. 9, 1960; d. John Lawrence and Melba Johnson Greene; m. George Swanson Pace, Mar. 12, 1988. AA, Jones County Jr. Coll., Ellisville, Miss., 1980; BA in Edn., U. Miss., Oxford, 1982; MEd, Miss. Coll., Clinton, 1998. Lic. educator Miss. Tchr. 1st, 4th, 5th and 6th grades Pine Hills Acad., Gloster, Miss., 1983—85; 4th grade tchr. St. Patrick's Episcopal Day Sch., Zachary, Miss., 1985—86; 5th grade tchr. Vicksburg (Miss.) Mid. Sch., 1986—89; tchr. 1st, 2d and 5th grades Grove St. Elem., Vicksburg, 1989—99; 1st grade tchr. Sherman Ave. Elem., Vicksburg, 1999—2003; instnl. lead tchr. Dana Rd. Elem., Vicksburg, 2003—, AmeriCorps site supr., 2004—. Named Tchr. of yr., Sherman Ave. Elem., 2000—01. Mem.: NEA, Internat. Reading Assn., Nat. Coun. Tchrs. English, Miss. Assn. Educators, Ole Miss Alumni Assn. Republican. Methodist. Avocations: reading, arts and crafts, metal detecting, antiques, jogging. Home: 8023 Oak Ridge Rd Vicksburg MS 39183 Office: Dana Rd Elem 1247 Dana Rd Vicksburg MS 39180 Office Phone: 601-619-2340. Office Fax: 601-619-2343. Personal E-mail: countrygirlorange@yahoo.com. Business E-Mail: bpace@vwsd.k12.ms.us.

PACE, CAROLINA JOLLIFF, communications executive, investor; b. Dallas, Apr. 12, 1938; d. Lindsay Gafford and Carolina (Juden) Jolliff; m. John McIver Pace, Jr., Oct. 7, 1961. Student, Holton-Arms Jr. Coll., 1956—57; BA in Comparative Lit., So. Meth. U., 1960. Promotional advisor, dir. season ticket sales Dallas Theatre Ctr., 1960—61; exec. sec. Dallas Book and Author Luncheon, 1959—63; promotional and instl. cons. Henry Regnery-Reilly & Lee Pub. Co., Chgo., 1962—65; pub. trade rep. various cos.; instl. rep. Don R. Phillips Co., Southea. area, 1965—67; Southwestern rep. Ednl Reading Svc., Inc.-Troll Assocs., Mahwah, NJ, 1967—72; v.p., dir. multimedia divsn. Melton Book Co., Dallas, 1972—79; v.p. mktg. Webster's Internat., Inc., Nashville, 1980—82; pres. Carolina Pace, Inc., 1982—. Mem. adv. bd. Nat. Info. Ctr. of Spl. Edn. Materials; mem. materials rev. panel Nat. Media Ctr. for Materials of Severely-Profoundly Handicapped, 1981; mem. mktg. product rev. bd. LINC Resources, 1982, 83, 84, mktg. task force, 83, adv. bd., 87; reviewer spl. edn. U.S. Dept. Edn., 1975—79, 1985; rev. cons. HHS, 1982, 83, 84, 86; product rev. task force CEC, 1984, 85, 86; cons. Ednl. Cable Consortium, Summit, NJ, 1982—87. Prodr. ednl. videos; contbr. articles to profl. jours. Mem. adv. coun. Grad. Sys. Sch. Libr. and Info. Sci. Found., U. Tex., 1987—; co-vice chair Friends Highland Park Libr., 1989; mem. focus group City Dallas Growth Policy Plan; mem. art and design com. Downtown Ctrs.; active Dallas City Wide Parking Task Force, Ctrl. Transp. Forum Ctrl. Bus. Dist., Union Sta. Art & Design Com., Downtown Transfer Ctrs., Art and Design Com., West End Task Force, Ctrl. Bus. Dist. Task Force, Tex. Parking Assn.; co-founder Operation TexRec, 1990—91; bd. dirs. Transp. Mgmt. Assn., 1995—; chair Vanpool Use Study, 1995; budget chmn. Dallas County Sesquicentennial com., 1996; mem. adv. bd. Friends of Old Red Courthouse, 1997—, Trinity River Econ. Devel. Bd., 1998—; active Downtown Dallas: Vision 2020, 2001—02; mem. com. Trinity Commons Found., 2002—; active Downtown Dallas Task Force, Ctrl. Bus. Dist., West End, Individual Site Task Force, Dallas. Mem.: DAR (Jane Douglas chpt.), Coun. Exceptional Children (conf. spkr. 1981, dir. exhibitors com., chmn. publ. com. 1979 conf.), Pub. Rels. Soc. Am., Women in Comm., Assn. Spl. Edn. Tech. (nat. dir., v.p. publicity 1980—82), Assn. Ednl. and Comm. Tech., Internat. Comm. Industries Assn., Nat. Audio Visual Assn. (conf. panelist 1979), Downtown Dallas, Ctrl. Dallas Assn. (transp. com. 1996—, planning and greenspace com. 1998—), Dallas Plan (focus com.), Women's Nat. Book Assn., Dallas Founders, Friends of the West End (pres. 1988—), West End Assn. Dallas (chmn. subcom. on traffic and parking 1986—87, com. demographic study 1987—88), Downtown Transp. Mgmt. Assn. (adv. bd., chmn. vanpools subcom. 1995—, econ. devel. com. Trinity project 2000—, citizens adv. com. 2003—), Kimball Art Mus., Dallas So. Meml., Dallas Mus. Art, Dallas Zool. Soc., Dallas West End Hist. Dist. Assn., Tex. Parking Assn., Alpha Delta Pi. Presbyterian. Home: 4524 Lorraine Ave Dallas TX 75205-3613

PACE, CHARLES, library director; m. Wendy Pace; children: David, Emily. BA, U. North Tex., Denton, MLS, 1990. Reference libr. Bklyn. Pub. Libr., Dallas Pub. Libr.; br. mgr. Houston Pub. Libr., Chgo. Pub. Libr.; dir. Fargo Pub. Libr., ND, 2001—06, St. Louis County Libr., 2006—. Named one of the Movers & Shakers, Libr. Jour., 2006. Mem.: ALA, Pub. Libr. Assn. Office: St Louis County Libr 1640 S Lindbergh Blvd Saint Louis MO 63131-3598 *

PACE, CHARLES ROBERT, psychologist, educator; b. St. Paul, Sept. 7, 1912; s. Charles N. and Lenore (Lee) P.; m. Rosella Gaarder, Dec. 18, 1937; children: Rosalind, Jenifer. BA, De Pauw U., 1933; MA, U. Minn., 1935, PhD, 1937. Instr. in gen. coll. U. Minn., 1937-40; research asso. Am. Council Edn., 1941-42; research psychologist Bur. Naval Personnel, Navy Dept., 1943-47; mem. faculty Syracuse U., 1947-61, asso. dir., then dir. evaluation service center, 1947-52, asst. to chancellor, 1948-52, prof. psychology, chmn. dept., dir. psychol. research center, 1952-61; prof. higher edn. UCLA, 1961-82, prof. emeritus, 1982—. Mem. adv. coms. Am. Council Edn., Coll. Entrance Exam. Bd., Social Sci. Research Council. Author: They Went to College, 1941, (with M. E. Troyer) Evaluation in Teacher Education, 1944, The Junior Year in France, 1959, (with F.H. Bowles and J.C. Stone) How to Get Into College, 1968, College and University Environment Scales, 2d edit, 1969, Education and Evangelism, 1972, The Demise of Diversity?, 1974, Measuring Outcomes of College, 1979, Measuring the Quality of College Student Experiences, 1984, CSEQ: Test Manual and Norms, 1987, The Undergraduates, 1990. Post-doctoral fellow Rockefeller Found., 1940-41; fellow Center Advanced Study Behavioral Scis., 1959-60; recipient citation for meritorious civilian service Navy Dept., 1946, E.F. Lindquist award Am. Ednl. Research Assn. and Am. Coll. Testing Program, 1984, Suslow award for outstanding svc. Assn. for Instl. Rsch., 1989. Mem. APA, Am. Ednl. Rsch. Assn. (Disting. Rsch. award divsn. postsecondary edn. 1992), Assn. for Study Higher Edn. (Disting. Career award 1989), Am. Assn. Pub. Opinion Rsch. Office Phone: 707-822-1204. Business E-Mail: crp7001@axe.humboldt.edu.

PACE, DAVID A., human resources specialist, retail executive; BS, Cornell U., 1981. Various positions PepsiCo, Inc. and Tricon Global, 1981—99; sr. v.p. HomeGrocer.com, Seattle; exec. v.p., chief people officer i2 Technologies, Dallas, 2000—02; exec. v.p. ptnr. resources Starbucks Corp., Seattle, 2002—. Office: Starbucks Corp 2401 Utah Ave S Seattle WA 98134 Office Phone: 206-447-1575. Office Fax: 206-447-0828.

PACE, ELIZABETH BARBER, elementary school educator; b. Lexington, NC, Dec. 31, 1971; d. John Luther Barber and Sara Philpott Lang; m. John James Pace III, July 20, 1996; children: Charles Harrison, Sara Margaret. BA in French, Salem Coll., Winston-Salem, NC, 1994; M in Elem. Edn., East Carolina U., Greenville, NC, 1998. Tchr. West Marin Elem. Sch., Oak City, NC, 1995—98, Chowan Mid. Sch., Edenton, NC, 1998—2001, River Rd. Mid. Sch., Elizabeth City, NC, 2001—02, Tate's Sch. Discovery, Knoxville, 2003—. Coord. regional sci. fair Tate's Sch. Discovery, 2006—, chair sch. libr., 2006—, mentor, 2005—. Tchr. Sunday sch., kids. worship Episcopal Ch. Assension, Knoxville, 2003. Mem.: Nat. Assn. Educators Young Children, Nat. Coun. Tchrs. English, Internat. Reading Assn. Democrat. Episcopalian. Avocations: scrapbooks, boating, hiking, gardening, reading. Home: 5316 Buckhead Trail Knoxville TN 37919 Office: Tates Sch Discovery 9215 Bob Gray Rd Knoxville TN 37932

PACE, ERIC DWIGHT, retired journalist; b. NYC, Oct. 13, 1936; s. Eric and Eleanor Robertson (Jones) Paepcke; m. Suzanne Monique Wiedel, June 12, 1976 (div. Jan. 1987); children: Christine, Lydia. Grad., Phillips Exeter Acad., 1953; student, U. Heidelberg, Germany, 1955-56; BA magna cum laude, Yale, 1957; MA, Johns Hopkins, 1959. Reporter San Angelo Standard Times and Evening Standard, Tex., 1957—58; mem. staff Life mag., NYC, 1959-61, assigned to Bonn, 1961, Paris, 1961-62; corr. Time mag., Bonn., 1962-63, Hong Kong, 1963-65; mem. staff New York Times, NYC, 1965-66, assigned to Saigon, 1966, Cairo, 1966-69, Paris, 1969-70, Beirut, 1970-71, NYC, 1971-74, Teheran, 1974-77, NYC, 1977—2004. Author: (novels) Saberlegs, 1970, Any War Will Do, 1973, Nightingale, 1979; contbr. articles to Fgn. Affairs, also others. Served with AUS, 1957. Recipient George Polk Meml. award Overseas Press Club, 1968, Page One award NYC Newspaper Guild, 1968 Mem. Mystery Writers Am., Crime Writers Assn. (Gt. Britain), Am. P.E.N. Clubs: Century (NYC), Squadron A (NYC). Home: 697 West End Ave Apt 11 E New York NY 10025

PACE, G. MICHAEL, JR., lawyer; b. Roanoke, Va., Mar. 11, 1957; BA, Hampden-Sydney Coll., 1979; JD, Washington & Lee U., 1984. Bar: Va. 1984. Ptnr. Gentry Locke Rakes & Moore, Roanoke, Va. Mem. adv. bd. SunTrust, Roanoke, Va.; bd. mem., chmn. Roanoke Regional C. of C., 2002—04; pres. Roanoke Valley Econ. Devel. Partnership, 2002—04; exec. com. Roanoke Valley Bus. Coun.; chmn. Bus. Leadership Fund; bd. mem. Fifth Planning Dist. Regional Alliance, Va. Western Cmty. Coll. Found.; mem. Roanoke Regional Airport Alliance; bd. trustees Hampden-Sydney Coll.; pres. Hampden-Sydney Coll. Alumni Assn. Named one of Legal Elite in field of corp. law, Va. Bus. Mag., 2000—02, Legal Elite in field of real estate/construction, 2003—04, Legal Elite in field of bus., 2005—06; recipient Gold Best Local Lawyer award, The Roanoker Mag., 2004. Mem.: Va. State Bar (past chmn. real property sect.), Va. Bar Assn. (pres.-elect 2006—07, chmn. bd. gov.), Roanoke Bar Assn. (pres. 2000—01). Mailing: Gentry Locke Rakes & Moore PO box 40013 Roanoke VA 24022-0013 Office: Gentry Locke Rakes & Moore 10 Franklin Rd SE Roanoke VA 24011 Office Phone: 540-983-9312. Office Fax: 540-983-9400. E-mail: mike_pace@gentrylocke.com.

PACE, OLE BLY, III, lawyer; b. 1939; AB, Ill. Wesleyan Univ., 1963; JD, Univ. Ill. Coll. of Law, 1966. Bar: 1966, US Dist. Ct., No. and Ctrl. Dist. Ill. Law clerk Appellate Ct. Justice A. J. Scheineman; spl. asst. atty. gen., 1968—80; ptnr. Ward, Murray, Pace & Johnson. Bd. dir. Northwestern Steel & Wire Co., First Nat. Bank, Sterling-Rock Falls, Ill., Mercantile Bank, Sterling-Rock Falls, Ill. Past pres. Sterling C. of C., Sinnissippi Mental Health Ctr. US Army, 1958—60. Named Illinois Super Lawyer, 2005—07; named one of the Best Lawyers in Am., 2003—07. Fellow: Ill. Bar Found.; mem.: ABA, Ill. Cmty. Coll. Attorneys Assn. (bd. mem., vice chair), Ill. Acad. of Lawyers (bd. regents, chancellor), Nat. Assn. of Coll. and Univ. Attorneys, Whiteside County Bar Assn. (past pres.), Ill. State Bar Assn. (bd. gov. 1995—2001, third v.p. 2001, pres. 2004, Bd. of Gov. award 1989), Order of Coif, Phi Delta Phi. Office: Ward Murray Pace & Johnson PC PO Box 400 202 E Fifth St Sterling IL 61081 Office Phone: 812-625-8200. Office Fax: 815-625-8363. Business E-Mail: pace@wmpj.com.

PACE, ORLANDO LAMAR, professional football player; b. Sandusky, Ohio, Nov. 4, 1975; Attended, Ohio State Univ. Lineman St. Louis Rams, 1997—. Donater Disadvantaged Kids; participant Spearheads Annual Offensive Line Thanksgiving Project, Chesterfield, Mo. Named to NFL Pro-Bowl, 1999—2005. Achievements include first to being the first player in college history to win two consecutive Lombardi awards, 1995, 1996; being the overall first pick in NFL Draft, 1997; being a member of Super Bowl XXXIV Champion St. Louis Rams, 2000. Office: 1 Rams Way Saint Louis MO 63045

PACE, PETER, Chairman of the Joint Chiefs of Staff; b. Bklyn., Nov. 5, 1945; m. Lynne Ann Holden; children: Peter Jr., Tiffany Marie. BS, U.S. Naval Acad., 1967; MBA, George Washington U., 1972; student, USMC Command and Staff Coll., 1979-80; grad., Nat. War Coll., 1986; postgrad. in Nat. and Internat. Security, Harvard U. Commd. lt. USMC, 1967, advanced through grades to gen., 2000; served in 2d Bn., 5th Marines, 1st Marine Divsn., Vietnam, 1968-69; ops. officer, Security Element Marine Aircraft Group 15, 1st Marine Aircraft Wing, Nam Phong, Thailand, 1972, exec. officer, 1972; asst. majors' monitor Hdqs. Marine Corps, Washington, 1973-76; ops. officer, 2nd Bn., 5th Marines, exec. officer, 3rd Bn., & divsn. staff sec. 1st Marine Divsn., Camp Pendleton, Calif., 1976—79; commdg. officer Marine Corps Recruiting Sta., Buffalo, 1980-83, 2nd Bn, 1st Marine Divsn., Pendleton, Calif., 1983—85; chief, ground forces branch Combined/Joint Staff, Seoul, Republic of Korea, 1986-87, exec. officer to asst. chief of staff, 1987—88; commdg. officer Marine Barracks, Washington, 1988—91; chief of staff, 2nd Marine Divsn. USMC, Camp Lejeune, NC, 1991—92, pres. Marine Corps. U., commdg. gen. Marine Corps. Combat Devel. Command Quantico, Va., 1992—94, dep. comdr. Marine forces Somalia, 1992—93, dep. comdr. Joint Task Force, 1993—94; dep. comdr., chief of staff US Forces Japan, 1994—96; dir. ops. (J-3) Joint Staff, Washington, 1996—97; comdt. USMC, Washington, 1997—2000; comdr. US So. Command, Miami, 2000—01; vice chmn. Joint Chiefs of Staff, US Dept. Def., Washington, 2001—05, chmn., 2005—. Decorated Def. D.S.M., Def. Legion of Merit, Bronze Star with Combat V., Def. Superior Service medal, Def. Meritorious Service medal, Navy Commendation medal, Navy Achievement medal, Combat Action medal; recipient Tongil Medal of Nat. Security, Govt. of South Korea, 2007 Office: Chmn of Joint Chiefs US Dept Def Pentagon Rm 2E873 Washington DC 20318 *

PACE, STEPHEN SHELL, artist, educator; b. Charleston, Mo., Dec. 12, 1918; s. John C. and Ora K. (Reeves) P.; m. Palmina Natalini, Feb. 26, 1949. Student, Inst. Fine Arts, San Miguel, 1945-46, Art Students League, NYC, 1948-49, Grande Chaumiere, Paris, 1950, Inst. D'Arte Statale, Florence, Italy, 1951, Hans Hofmann Sch., NYC, 1951-52; ArtsD (hon.), U. So. Ind., Evansville, 2002, Maine Coll. Art, Portland, 2003. Artist in residence Washington U., 1959; instr. painting Pratt Inst., NYC, 1961-69; artist in residence Des Moines Art Ctr., 1970; vis. artist U. Calif., 1968; asso. prof. Bard Coll., 1969-71, Am. U., 1975-83; artist in residence U. So. Ind., Evansville, 2005. Artist in residence U. So. Ind., Evansville, 2005. One-man shows include Hendler Gallery, 1953, Artists Gallery, 1954, Poindexter Gallery, 1956, 57, Washington U., St. Louis, 1959, Holland-Goldowsky Gallery, Chgo., 1960, Howard Wise Gallery, Cleve., 1960, N.Y., 1960, 61, 63, 64, Dilexi Gallery, San Francisco, 1960, HCE Gallery, 1956-59, 61-63, 66, Dwan Gallery, L.A., 1961, Hayden Gallery, Cambridge, Mass., 1961, Ridley Gallery, Evansville, Ind., 1966, U. Calif., Berkeley, 1968, Graham Gallery, N.Y.C., 1969, Des Moines Art Ctr., 1970, U. Tex., Austin, 1970, Kansas City Art Inst., 1973, A.M. Sachs Gallery, N.Y.C., 1974, 76, 77, 78, 79, 81, 83, 85, Drew U., 1975, Bard Coll., 1975, Am. U., 1976, Roberto Polo Gallery, Washington, 1976, New Harmony (Ind.) Gallery, 1977, Farm Gallery, Far Hill, N.J., 1978, Barbara Fiedler Gallery, Washington, 1980, Chastenet Gallery, Washington, 1981, Katharina Rich Perlow Gallery, N.Y.C., 1987, 89, 91, 94, 97, 98, 00, 02, 04, 06, Vanderwoude-Tananbaum Gallery, N.Y.C., 1991, U. N.C., Greensboro, 1991, Evansville Mus., 1992, Maine Coast Artists, Rockport, 1994-2006, Bates Coll. Mus., Lewiston, Maine, 1994, Union Coll., Schenectady, NY, 1999, A.J. Buecke Gallery, Northeast Harbor, Maine, 2001, Portland (Maine) Mus. Art, 2004, Farnsworth Mus., 2004; exhibited in group shows in U.S., Europe, Japan, Mid. East, India, Burma, Australia, New Zealand, Hawaii, Ctrl. and S.Am.; represented in permanent collections, Whitney Mus., Chrysler Mus., Norfolk, Va., Provincetown (Mass.) Mus., Evansville Mus., U. So. Ill., Carbondale, Michener Found., Walker Art Ctr., U. Calif., CIBA-Geigy Collection, Hallmark Collection, Bundy Art Gallery, U. N.C., Greensboro, Chase Manhattan Bank, Munson-Williams-Procter Inst., Utica, N.Y., Des Moines Art Ctr., Boston Mus. Fine Arts, Met. Mus., N.Y.C., Phillips Collection, Washington, Am. U., Washington, Corcoran Gallery, Washington, Curie Inst., Paris, Hirshhorn Mus., Washington, Bristol Myers Collection, Indpls. Mus., Portland (Maine) Mus., Bowdoin Coll. Mus., Brown U., Providence, Oberlin (Ohio) Coll. Mus, Farnsworth Art Mus., Rockland, Maine, Bates Coll. Mus., Lewiston, Maine, Nat. Mus. Am. Art, Washington, Columbus Mus. Art, Yale U., New Haven, U. of S. Indiana, Evansville, Union Coll., Schenectady, Newark Art Mus., N.J., U. No. Iowa, Cedar Falls, Colby Coll. Mus., Waterville, Maine, Rutgers U. Mus., NB, NJ, New Orleans Mus. Art, NAD, Baruch Coll., N.Y., U. Maine, Orono, U. Denver, Ogunquit (Maine) Mus., Fryeburg (Maine) Acad., Sweet Briar (Va.) Mus., Yeshiva U., NYC Served with AUS, 1941-45, ETO. Recipient Dolian Lorian award for promising Am. painters, 1954, Hallmark award, 1961, Am. Acad. Arts and Letters prize, 2004; grantee Creative Artists Pub. Svc. Program, 1973; Guggenheim fellow, 1980. Mem.: NAD (Benjamin Altman prize 1993, Edwin Palmer Marine prize 2001, William A. Paton prize 2005).

PACE, THOMAS M., lawyer; b. Mesa, Ariz., Feb. 5, 1952; s. Lemuel Max and Ann (Green) P.; m. Vi Garrett Pace, Jan. 24, 1981; children: Melanie, Brittany. BA, Stanford U., 1973; JD, U. Ariz., 1976. Bar: Ariz.; cert. real estate specialist. Assoc. Martin, Feldhacker & Freidl, Phoenix, 1976-77, Trew & Woodford, Phoenix, 1977-78; ptnr. Hecker, Phillips & Hooker, Tucson, 1978-88; sr. ptnr. O'Connor Cavanagh, Tucson, 1988-95; pvt. practice Law Office of Thomas M. Pace, Tucson, 1995—. Mem. Mayor's Housing Task Force, Tucson, 1993; bd. dirs. Tucson Urban League, 1986-96; chmn. So. Ariz. Homebuilders Polit. Action Com., 1995, 96. Mem. So. Ariz. Homebuilders (tech. com), Stanford Club So. Ariz. Democrat. Office: 1670 E River Rd Ste 124 Tucson AZ 85718-8900 Office Phone: 520-322-5511. Business E-Mail: tom@pacelawaz.com.

PACE, WAYNE H., communications executive; B in Acctg. and Econs., Austin Peay State U.; M in Acctg., U. Ga. J.M. Tull Sch. Accountancy. Joined Price Waterhouse, 1970; exec. v.p. fin., adminstrv. officer Turner Broadcasting Sys., Atlanta, 1993—2001; vice chmn., CFO Turner Broadcasting Sys. (now Time Warner), Atlanta, 2001; exec. v.p., CFO Time Warner Inc, NYC, 2001—. Bd. dirs. Spl. Olympics of Ga. Recipient Disting. Alumnus award, U. Ga., 1988. Office: Time Warner Inc 75 Rockefeller Plaza New York NY 10019 *

PACH, PETER BARNARD, columnist, editor; b. Bklyn., Aug. 3, 1951; s. Stewart Warner and Constance (Barnard) P.; m. Kathleen Ann Megan, Sept. 7, 1985; children: Nell, Samuel. BA in English, Union Coll., 1973. Reporter Record Jour., Meriden, Conn., 1974-78, Wallingford bur. chief, 1978-83; Middletown bur. chief Hartford Courant, Conn., 1983-84, columnist Conn., 1984-95; mem. editorial bd. Hartford (Conn.) Courant, 1992—, town editls. editor, 2001—06, assoc. editor, 2006—. Vis. instr. Wesleyan U., Middletown, Conn., 1985—2003. Recipient First Bus. and Econ. Reporting award New England Press Ass., 1977. Mem. Dedham County and Polo Club. Avocations: running, skiing, golf, squash, gardening. Home: PO Box 46 Middle Haddam CT 06456-0046 Office: Hartford Courant 285 Broad St Hartford CT 06115-2510

PACHECO, BRYAN E., lawyer; b. Akron, Ohio, Mar. 21, 1969; BA, U. Akron, 1992; JD, U. Cin., 1997. Bar: Ohio 1997, US Dist. Ct. Southern Dist. Ohio 1998, US Ct. of Appeals Sixth Cir. 2001. Ptnr. Dinsmore & Shohl LLP, Cin. Dep. solicitor City of Blue Ash, Ohio; city solicitor City of Silverton, Ohio; mem. Hope Evang. Free Ch. Named one of Ohio's Rising Stars, Super Lawyers, 2006. Mem.: ABA, Ohio State Bar Assn., Cin. Bar Assn., Order of Coif. Office: Dinsmore & Shohl LLP 255 E Fifth St Ste 1900 Cincinnati OH 45202-4700 Office Phone: 513-977-8200. Office Fax: 513-977-8141.

PACHECO, MANUEL TRINIDAD, retired academic administrator; b. Rocky Ford, Colo., May 30, 1941; s. Manuel J. and Elizabeth (Lopez) Pacheco; m. Karen M. King, Aug. 27, 1966; children: Daniel Mark, Andrew Charles, Sylvia Lois Elizabeth. BA, N.Mex. Highlands U., 1962; MA, Ohio State U., 1966, PhD, 1969. Mem. faculty Fla. State U., 1968—71, U. Colo., 1971; prof. edn., univ. dean Tex. A&I U., Laredo, 1972—77; prof. multicultural edn., chmn. dept. San Diego State U., 1977—78; prof. Spanish and edn. Laredo State U., 1978—80; exec. dir. Bilingual Edn. Ctr., Kingsville Tex. A&I U., 1980—82; assoc. dean Coll. Edn. U. Tex., El Paso, 1982—86, exec. dir. for planning, 1984; pres. Laredo State U., 1984—88, U. Houston-Downtown, 1986—97, U. Ariz., Tucson, 1991—97, U. Mo. Sys., Columbia, 1997—2002; ret., 2002. Cons. lang. divsn. Ency. Britannica, 1965—72; bd. dirs. Valley Nat. Bank Corp., Nat. Security Edn. Program, ASARCO, PNM Resources, Inc.; mem. exec. com. Bus.-Higher Edn. Forum. Co-editor: Handbook for Planning and Managing Instruction in Basic Skills for Limited English Proficient Students, 1983; prodr.: (videotapes) Teacher Training, 1976. Named, Most Prominent Am.-Hispanics Spanish Tchr. Mag., 1984, one of 100 Outstanding Hispanics Hispanis Bus., 1988, Man of Yr., Hispanic Profl. Action Com., 1991; recipient Disting. Alumnus award, Ohio State U., Columbus, 1984, Disting. Leadership in Higher Edn. award, Sec. of Edn. Richard Riley, 1997; Fulbright fellow, U. de Montepellier, France, 1962. Mem.: Tex. Assn. Chicanos in Higher Edn., Hispanic Assn. Colls. and Univs., Nat. Acad. Pub. Adminstrn., Am. Assn. State Colls. and Univs., Rotary, Phi Delta Kappa.

PACHECO-RANSANZ, ARSENIO, language educator, historian, educator; b. Barcelona, Feb. 8, 1932; s. Arsenio Pacheco and Jacoba Ransanz-Alvarez; m. Mercedes Olivella-Sole, Sept. 1, 1956; children: Arsenio-Andrew, David-George. MA, U. Barcelona, 1954, PhD, 1958. Tutor Colegio Mayor Hispanoamericano Fray Junipero Serra, Barcelona, 1954-56; lectr. Hochschüle für Wirtschaft und Sozialwissenschaften, Nurnberg, Germany, 1956; asst. lectr. U. Glasgow, Scotland, 1957-59; lectr. U. St. Andrews, Scotland, 1960-70; vis. prof. U. Pitts., 1966; prof. Hispanic and Italian studies U. B.C., Vancouver, Canada, 1970-97, prof. emeritus, 1997—. Editor: Historia de Xacob Xalabin, 1964, Testament de Bernat

Serradell, 1971, Varia fortuna del soldado Pindaro, 1975, Obres de Francesc de la Via, 1997; contbr. articles to profl. jours. Bd. dirs. Can. Fedn. Humanities, 1981-84. Fellow Royal Soc. Can.; mem. Can. Assn. Hispanists (pres. 1978-81), Asociacion Internacional de Hispanists, MLA, Assn. Hispanists Gt. Britain and Ireland, N.Am. Catalan Soc. (v.p. 1984-87, pres. 1987-90), Anglo Catalan Soc., Associacio Internacional de Llengua i Literatura Catalana. Roman Catholic. Office: U BC Dept French Hispanic Ital Vancouver BC Canada V6T 1Z1 Home Phone: 604-263-8106. Business E-Mail: arp@interchange.ubc.ca.

PACHER, PÁL, pharmacologist, educator, researcher; b. Budapest, Hungary, Aug. 7, 1969; s. Pál and Irén (Bolfert) P. Diploma in medicine, Semmelweis U., Budapest, 1993; diploma in holistic medicine, UK, 2000; PhD, Hungarian Acad. of Sci., 2001. Lectr. asst. dept. pharmacology Semmelweis U. Medicine, 1994—; postdoctoral rsch. fellow Thomas Jefferson U., Phila., 1999-2001; pharmacologist Inotek Corp., Beverly, Mass., 2001—, dir. cardiovasc. pharmacology, 2002—; sr. rsch. scientist NIAAA, NIH, Bethesda, Md., 2002—04, sect. chief, 2005—. Mem.: Am. Physiol. Soc., Inst. of Holistic Medicine (U.K.), Am. Heart Assn., Am. Diabetes Assn., Juvenile Diabetes Assn., Biophys. Soc., NY Acad. Scis., Internat. Soc. for Heart Rsch., Worldwide Hungarian Med. Acad., Hungarian Cardiol. Soc., Hungarian Chamber Physicians, Hungarian Pharmacol. Soc. Achievements include research in cardiovascular pharmacology and physiology. Avocations: computers, chess, excursions, swimming. Office: NIAAA 5625 Fishers Ln Bethesda MD 20892-9413 Home: 124 Elmcroft Blvd Rockville MD 20850 Business E-Mail: ppacher@gmail.com, pacher@mail.nih.gov.

PACHINO, BARTON P., lawyer; BA in Pol. Sci. magna cum laude, Duke U.; JD cum laude, Northwestern U. Law Sch. Assoc. corp. counsel KB Home, 1987-89, corp. counsel, 1989-91, v.p., 1991-93, sr. v.p., gen. counsel, 1993—. Bd. dirs. Bet Tzecek Legal Svcs., former chmn. corp. law dept. section Century City Bar Assn. Mem. Am. Bar Assoc., Ca. Bar Assoc., L.A. County Bar Assoc. Office: KB Home 10990 Wilshire Blvd Fl 7 Los Angeles CA 90024-3913 E-mail: bpachino@kbhome.com.

PACHMAN, FREDERIC CHARLES, library director; b. Paterson, NJ, Apr. 16, 1952; s. Morris J. and Barbara M. (Haagen) P.; m. Donna Kearns, May 2, 1982; children: Rick, Kristina. BA, Syracuse U., 1973; MLS, Columbia U., 1976; cert., Rutgers U., New Brunswick, NJ, 1996. Libr. dir. Hamilton Twp. Pub. Libr., NJ, 1981-83, Middletown Twp. Pub. Libr., NJ, 1983-85, Monmouth Med. Ctr., Long Branch, NJ, 1985—. Mem. exec. bd. Hist. Soc. Ocean Grove, NJ, 1985-2003, Interagy. Coun. on Info. Resources for Nursing, NYC, 1985-2003; cons. Caucus Archival Program Evaluation Svc., NJ, 1990—; mem. adv. com. on preservation and access NJ State Libr., 1992-95. Contbr. articles to profl. jours. Asst. scoutmaster troop 32 Boy Scouts Am., River Plaza, NJ, 1993—. Mem. ALA, NJ Libr. Assn., Med. Libr. Assn., League Hist. Socs. NJ, Mid Atlantic Regional Archives Conf., Acad. Health Info. Profls. (disting.), Monmouth Librs. Assn. (pres. 1985-86, 1999-2000), NJ Scout Mus., Order of the Arrow (brotherhood mem.). Avocations: backpacking, reading, historic preservation, archives, kayaking. Office: Monmouth Med Ctr 300 2d Ave Long Branch NJ 07740-6300 Office Phone: 732-923-6645. Personal E-mail: fpachman@sbhcs.com.

PACHOLSKI, RICHARD FRANCIS, securities trader, financial consultant; b. Seattle, June 18, 1947; s. Theodore Francis and Nellie (Tarabochia) P.; m. Dorothy Irene Nelson, May 25, 1974; children: Nicolas, Tara. BA cum laude, U. Wash., 1969, MBA summa cum laude, 1970. CPA Wash. Mgr. Arthur Andersen & Co., Seattle, 1970-76; v.p., contr. SNW Enterprises, Seattle, 1976-82; sr. v.p., treas., sec., dir. Seattle N.W. Securities, 1982-93; cons. Carl & Co., Portland, Oreg., 1984-88, Ellis & Carl Inc., Portland, Oreg., 1979-83; pres. R. Pacholski, P.C., Redmond, Wash., 1979—. Adj. prof. U. Wash., Seattle, 1976-80. Mem. AICPA, Nat. Assn. Securities Dealers (past bd. dirs. local dist.), Wash. Athletic Club (life), PacWest Club (Redmond, Wash.). Roman Catholic. Personal E-mail: pacholski@prodigy.net.

PACHTER, IRWIN JACOB, pharmaceutical consultant; b. NYC, July 15, 1925; s. Nathan and Ethel Lillian (Thomases) P.; m. Elaine Anna White, Aug. 23, 1953; children: Wendy, Jonathan. BS, UCLA, 1947; MS, U. N.Mex., 1949; PhD, U. So. Calif., 1951; postgrad., U. Ill., 1951-52, Harvard U., 1952-53. Research chemist Ethyl Corp., 1953-55; asso. research chemist Smith Kline & French, 1955-62, asst. sec. head, 1962; dir. medicinal chemistry Endo Labs., 1962-66; dir. research Endo div. du Pont Co., 1967-70; v.p. research and devel. Bristol Labs. div. Bristol-Myers Co., 1970-82; lectr. Adelphi U., 1963-69. Contbr. articles to profl. jours.; patentee in field Trustee Gordon Research Conf., 1972-75; chmn. medicinal chemistry study group Walter Reed Inst. Research, 1975-77. Served with USN, 1944-46. Mem. Am. Chem. Soc. (chmn. div. medicinal chemistry 1974-76), Pharm. Mfrs. Assn. (chmn. research and devel. sect. 1975-76) Home: 101 Woodberry Ln Fayetteville NY 13066-1745 Personal E-mail: ijpac@aol.com.

PACHTER, LEE M., pediatrician; b. Bklyn., Mar. 12, 1957; s. Harvey Leonard and Rosalind Blau Pachter; married Diedre Reynolds-Pachter; 1 child, Lauren. BA, Franklin and Marshal Coll., 1979; DO, Phila. Coll. Osteo. Medicine, 1983. Diplomate Am. Bd. Osteo. Physicians. Intern Metro. Hosp., Springfield, Pa., 1983-84; resident in pediatrics St. Christopher's Hosp. Children, Phila., 1984-87; fellow in pediatrics Children's Hosp. Phila., 1987-89; from asst. prof. to prof. pediats. and anthropology U. Conn. Sch. Medicine, Farmington, 1989—, head divsn. gen. pediat., 1998—. Trustee The Artists Collective, Hartford, Conn., 1989—. Fellow Am. Acad. Pediatrics, Soc. Applied Anthropology; mem. Am. Anthropol. Assn., Ambulatory Pediat. Assn., Soc. Rsch. and Child Devel., Soc. Applied Anthropology, Soc. for Pediat. Rsch. Personal E-mail: lpachter@comcast.net.

PACHTER, MARC, museum director; B summa cum laude, Univ. Calif., Berkeley; postgrad, Harvard Univ. Faculty Harvard Univ.; chief historian Smithsonian's Nat. Portrait Gallery, 1974—90, asst. dir., 1974—90, dep. asst. sec., external affairs, 1990—94, NPG dir., 2000—; acting dir. Smithsonian's Nat. Mus. of Am. History, 2001—02; former counselor to sec. Smithsonian Instn., 1995—2000. Chair Smithsonian's 150th Anniversary; sr. cons. various history documentaries; cons. Internat. Broadcasting; commentator CBS, Voice of Am., C-SPAN. Author/editor (books) Abroad in America: Visitors to the New Nation, Champions of American Sport, Documentary History of the Supreme Court, Telling Lives: The Biographer's Art, A Gallery of Presidents. Fellow Woodrow Wilson, Harvard Univ., five-yr. prize. Office: Nat Portrait Gallery Victor Bldg-Ste 8300 MRC PO Box 37012 Washington DC 20013-7012 Office Phone: 202-275-1740. Office Fax: 202-275-1887. Business E-Mail: pachterm@si.edu.

PACI, RUTH A., freelance/self-employed writer; b. West New York, NJ, Mar. 7, 1928; d. Joseph Frederick and Theresa Becker Paci. BA in History and Polit. Sci., Fordham U., Bronx, NY, 1984; MA in Journalism, NYU, 1987. Adminstrv. officer, press officer U.S. Info. Agy., Washington and NYC, 1951—86; exec. dir. Fgn. Press Ctr. NYC, 1985—86; ret., 1986; freelance writer. Author: Down By the River and Under the Cliff, 1994, Dearest Friends, 2004, short stories and essays. V.p., trustee Edgewater Pub. Libr., 1995—; mem., founder Cultural and Hist. Commn. Edgewater, 2000—; hist. preservation advisory bd. Bergen County, 2004. Recipient Cert. of Commendation, Bergen County Bd. Chosen Freeholders, 2003, Hist. Preservation resolution, NJ Gen. Assembly, 2003, Career Achievement award, US Info. Agy., 1986. Roman Catholic. Avocations: travel, gardening, reading. Personal E-mail: ruthwrite123@aol.com.

PACIFICO, ALBERT DOMINICK, cardiovascular surgeon; b. Bklyn., Sept. 24, 1940; s. Dominick Vincent and Amelia Catherine (Jannelli) P.; m. Vicki Lynne Overton, May 16, 1980; children: Albert D., Nicole M., Paul V. BS, St. Johns U., 1960; MD, N.J. Coll. Medicine, 1964. Diplomate Am. Bd. Surgery, Am. Bd. Thoracic Surgery. Med. intern Jersey City Med. Ctr., Seton Gall Coll. Medicine, 1964-65; asst. resident in surgery Mayo Clinic, Rochester, Minn., 1965-67; research fellow in surgery U. Ala., Birmingham, 1967-69, sr. resident, then chief resident surgery, resident in thoracic and cardiovascular surgery, 1968-72, mem. faculty dept. surgery, 1970—2006, prof. surgery, 1978-83, John W. Kirklin prof. cardiovascular surgery, 1983—2006, vice chmn. dept. surgery, 1990, dir. divsn. cardiothoracic surgery, 1984—2006, dir. Congenital Heart Disease Diagnosis and Treatment Ctr., 1985—2006; ret., 2006. Mem. staff gen., thoracic and cardiovascular surgery Univ. Hosp., Birmingham, 1972-2006, VA Hosp., Birmingham, 1972-2006; mem. staff Children's Hosp., Birmingham, 1971-2006, chief gen., thoracic and cardiovascular surgery, 1984-2006. Author: (with others) Pediatric Cardiac Surgery, 1985, Cardiology, 1985, Textbook of Surgery, 13th edit., 1986, The Treatment of Congenital Cardiac Anomalies, 1986, Perspectives in Pediatric Cardiology, 1988, Current Therapy in Cardiothoracic Surgery, 1989, Decision Making in Surgery of the Chest, 1989, Cardiac Surgery: Cyanotic Congential Heart Disease, 1989, Reoperation in Cardiac Surgery, 1989, others; mem. editorial bd. Am. Jour. Cardiology, 1983-2006, Heart and Vessel, 1985-2006, Jour. Cardiac Surgery, 1985-2006; cons. editorial referee Ala. Jour. Med. Scis., 1974-75; contbr. articles to med. jours. Fellow ACS, Am. Coll. Cardiology, Am. Surg. Assn.; mem. AMA, Ala. State Med. Soc., Jefferson County Med. Soc., Am. Heart Assn. (Paul Dudley White Internat. Svc. Citation 1977), Am. Assn. Thoracic Surgery, Soc. Thoracic Surgeons, Am. Surg. Soc., Internat. Coll. Pediatrics, John Kirklin Soc., Congentital Heart Surgeons Soc., Assn. Acad. Surgery, Ala. chpt. Mayo Clinic Alumni Assn., Panamanian Soc. Cardiology (hon.), Peruvian Soc. Thoracic and Cardiovascular Surgery (hon.), Soc. Nat. Inst. Cardiology Mex. (hon.), Cardiac Soc. Australia and New Zealand (corr.), Peruvian Soc. Cardiology (corr.), Alpha Omega Alpha. Republican. Roman Catholic.

PACIFICO, JOSEPH CARL, counselor; b. Grosse Ile, Mich., June 10, 1950; s. Carl Richard Pacifico and Mary Milano Campbell; m. Claire Lee Schlauch, Aug. 12, 1972; children: Mark Joseph, David Joseph. BS in Psychology, U. Md., 1972, MBA in Mktg., 1975; MS in Counseling Psychology, Loyola Coll., Balt., 1998. Lic. clin. profl. counselor Md., 2002. Acct. rep. Wallace Computer Svcs., Inc., Rockville, Md., 1975—99; master's level therapist Family and Marriage Therapy Ctr., Burtonsville, Md., 1998—2002, Christian Counseling Assocs., Inc., Columbia, Md., 1999—2002, clin. profl. counselor, 2002—. Leader, anger mgmt. group Christian Counseling Assocs., Inc., 2001—. Worship asst. Our Shepherd Luth. Ch., Columbia, Md., 1998—. Mem.: Christian Assocs. for Psychol. Studies. Avocations: photography, racquetball, tennis, ping pong/table tennis. Office: Christian Counseling Assocs Inc 9650 Santiago Rd # 101 Columbia MD 21045

PACINO, AL (ALFREDO JAMES PACINO), actor, film director, film producer; b. NYC, Apr. 25, 1940; s. Salvatore and Rose Pacino; children: Julie Marie, Anton, Olivia. Student, High Sch. of Performing Arts, Actors Studio. Formerly mail deliverer editorial offices Commentary Mag.; formerly messenger, movie theatre usher, bldg. supt.; co-artistic dir. The Actors Studio, Inc., NYC, 1982-84. Served apprenticeship as actor, dir. and comedy writer in Off-Off Broadway theatres, Elaine Stewart's Cafe La Mama, Julian Beck & Judith Malina's Living Theatre; appeared in New Theatre Workshop prodn. of The Peace Creeps, Dec., 1966; joined Charles Playhouse, Boston, fall, 1967, and performed in New Theatre Workshop prodn. of America Hurrah and Awake and Sing; appeared in a one-act play Off Broadway The Indian Wants the Bronx, opened Astor Pl. Theater on Jan. 17, 1968 (Obie as best actor in Off-Broadway prodn. 1967-68); made Broadway debut in Does A Tiger Wear A Necktie?, 1969 (Tony award as best dramatic actor in a supporting role, named most promising new Broadway actor in a Variety poll of metropolitan drama critics); appeared in The Local Stigmatic at Actors Playhouse, N.Y.C., opening 1969; joined Repertory Theater of Lincoln Center, N.Y.C.; other plays include The Basic Training of Pavlo Hummel, Boston Repertory Theater, 1972, Camino Real, Richard III, 1973, 79, Jungle of Cities, 1979, The Connection, Hello Out There, Tiger at the Gates, American Buffalo, Julius Caesar, 1988, Salome, Chinese Coffee (also dir.) 2000, Circle in the Square, 1992, Dir. and Performer, Hughie, 1996; (films) Me, Natalie, 1969, Panic in Needle Park, 1971, The Godfather, 1972 (Best Actor award Nat. Soc. Film Critics, Acad. award nominee), Scarecrow, 1973, Serpico, 1973 (Golden Globe for best actor, Acad. award nominee), The Godfather, Part II, 1974 (BAFTA award for best actor, Acad. award nominee), Dog Day Afternoon (BAFTA award for best actor, Acad. award nominee), 1975, Bobby Deerfield, 1977, And Justice for All, 1979 (Acad. Award nomination), Cruising, 1980, Author! Author!, 1982, Scarface, 1983, Revolution, 1985, Sea of Love, 1989, Dick Tracy, 1990 (American Comedy award, Acad. award nominee), The Godfather Part III, 1990, Frankie and Johnny, 1991, Glengarry Glen Ross, 1992 (Acad. award nominee), Scent of a Woman, 1992 (Acad. award for best actor, Golden Globe for best actor), Carlito's Way, 1993, Two Bits, 1995, Heat, 1995, City Hall, 1996, (also prodr., dir., writer) Looking for Richard, 1996 (Dir. Guild of Amer. award for best dir. documentary), Donnie Brasco, 1997, Devil's Advocate, 1997, Chinese Coffee, 1999, The Insider, 1999, Any Given Sunday, 1999, People I Know, 2002, Simone, 2002, Insomnia, 2002, The Recruit, 2003, Gigli, 2003, The Merchant of Venice, 2004, Two for the Money, 2005, 88 Minutes, 2007, Ocean's Thirteen, 2007; (TV miniseries) Angels in America, 2003 (Golden Globe for best actor, Screen Actors Guild Award for best actor, 2004, Emmy award Outstanding Lead Actor in a Miniseries or a Movie, 2004). Recipient Lifetime Achievement award Ind. Feature Project Gotham awards, 1996, Cecil B. DeMille Award Hollywood Fgn. Press. Assn., 2001, Am. Cinematheque Lifetime Achievement award, 2006, Lifetime Achievement award, Am. Film Inst., 2007. Office: Creative Artists Agy care Rick Nicita 9830 Wilshire Blvd Beverly Hills CA 90212-1804 *

PACINO, MARIA ANTONIETA, education educator, department chairman; d. Antonio Augusto Osorio de Carvalho and Maria da Conceicao Ponte (de Carvalho); m. Joe Louis Pacino, Dec. 2, 1974; children: Monique Caroline Morelli, Vanessa Paula Morelli. BA, Ball State U., 1977, MLS, 1981, EdD, 1988. Tchg. credential Ind., 1977. Tchr., libr. Muncie Cmty. Schools, Ind., 1978—90; asst. prof. sec. edn. Ball State U., Muncie, 1990—93; assoc. prof. edn. Azusa Pacific U., Calif., 1993—97, prof., dept. chair, 1997—. Spkr. in field. Contbr. articles to profl. jours., chapters to books. Mem. Human Rels. Commn., Azusa, 1999—2000, Pub. Libr. Commn., Azusa, 2000—03; chair U. Diversity Coun., Azusa, 2004—. Mem.: ASCD, Nat. Assn. Multicultural Edn., Am. Ednl. Rsch. Assn. Roman Catholic. Avocations: reading, opera, music, travel, theater. Office: Azusa Pacific U P O Box 7000 Azusa CA 91702 Office Phone: 626-815-5367. Office Fax: 626-815-5416. Business E-Mail: mpacino@apu.edu.

PACK, MICHAEL, television producer, writer, director; b. NYC, May 16, 1954; s. Harvey and Joy P.; m. Gina Cappo, Sept. 20, 1986. Student, Yale U., 1972-74, U. Calif., Berkeley, 1974-75, NYU, 1976. Staff editor R.A.I. (Italian TV Network), NYC, 1976, Pathe News, NYC, 1977; pres. Manifold Prodns., NYC and L.A., 1977—2003; sr. v.p. Corp. Pub. Broadcasting, 2003—06, co-chair internat. TV coun., 2003; independent film prodr., 2006—. Dir. Worldnet U.S. Info. Agy., 1992—93; mem. Nat. Coun. on Humanities. Assoc. producer (feature film) Never Pick Up A Stranger, N.Y.C., 1977; dir., writer (short drama) Hard Bargain, 1979 (CINE Eagle award); exec. producer, dir., writer (TV spl.) Hollywood's Favorite Heavy, 1987 (CINE Gold Eagle award 1987, Bronze award Houston Internat. Film Festival 1988); exec. producer (documentary) American Political Parties: The Republicans (part 2), 1988 (CINE Gold Eagle award 1989); producer, dir., writer (documentary) America's Political Parties: The Democrats, 1988 (Silver award Houston Internat. Film Festival 1989, 90, CINE Gold Eagle award 1989); producer, dir., writer (documentary) Fire From The Sun: The Search for Fusion Energy, 1989 (CINE Gold Eagle award 1990, Bronze award Houston Internat. Film Festival 1990, Red Ribbon award Am. Film and Video Festival 1991). Mem. Internat. Feature Projects, Internat. Documentary Assn., Internat. TV Assn.

PACK, RUSSELL T., theoretical chemist; b. Grace, Idaho, Nov. 20, 1937; s. John Terrell and Mardean (Izatt) P.; m. Marion Myrth Hassell, Aug. 21, 1962; children: John R., Nathan H., Allen H., Miriam, Elizabeth, Quinn R., Howard H. BS, Brigham Young U., 1962; PhD, U. Wis., 1967. Postdoctoral fellow U. Minn., Mpls., 1966-67; asst. prof. Brigham Young U., Provo, 1967-71, assoc. prof., 1971-75, adj. prof., 1975-88; staff scientist Los Alamos (N.Mex.) Nat. Lab., 1975-83, fellow, 1983—, assoc. grp. leader, 1979-81. Vis. prof. Max Planck Institut, Gottingen, 1981; chmn. Gordon Rsch. Conf., 1982; lectr. in field. Contbr. articles to profl. jours. Named Sr. U.S. Scientist, Alexander Vol Humboldt Found., 1981. Fellow Am. Phys. Soc. (sec.-treas. div. Chem. Physics 1990-93); mem. Am. Chem. Soc., Sigma Xi. Mem. Ch. of Jesus Christ of Latter Day Saints. Home: 240 Kimberly Ln Los Alamos NM 87544-3526 Office: Los Alamos Nat Lab T 12 Ms # B268 Los Alamos NM 87545-0001 Business E-Mail: rtpack@lanl.gov.

PACK, SANDY (SANDRA LEE PACK), former federal agency administrator; BS, Coll. Notre Dame, 1991. CPA. Dir. treasury Phil Gramm for Pres., Inc., Washington, 1995; dep. dir. treasury Bob Dole for Pres., Inc., Washington, 1996; dir. planning and ops. MicroProse divsn. Spectrum Holobyte, Inc., Hunt Valley, Md., 1994—95; dir. small bus. cons. and acctg. svcs. Ernst & Young, Balt., dir. microcomputer consulting and acctg. svcs. Atlanta; dir. of treasury Bush for Pres., Inc., Bush-Cheney 2000, Inc.; asst. sec. for fin. mgmt., comptr., Dept. Army US Dept. Def., Washington, 2001—04; CFO Bush-Cheney Re-Election Campaign, 2004; asst. sec. for mgmt. US Dept. Treasury, Washington, 2005—06; CFO Rudolph Guiliani Presdl. Exploratory Com., NYC, 2007—. Office: Rudy Giuliani Presdl Com Inc 295 Greenwich St #371 New York NY 10007 *

PACK, SUSAN JOAN, writer; b. NYC, June 15, 1951; d. Howard Meade and Nancy (Buckley) P. BA summa cum laude, Princeton U., 1973. Copywriter Laurence Charles & Free, NYC, 1978-83, Warwick Advt., NYC, 1983-85; sr. copywriter Saatchi & Saatchi Compton, NYC, 1985-88; pres. The Pack Collection, 1989—. Author: Film Posters of the Russian Avant-Garde, 1995. Mem. Princeton (N.J.) U. Libr. Coun., 1985-93; trustee Pack Found. for Med. Rsch., N.Y., 1983—; bd. dirs. The Poster Soc., N.Y., 1985-87. Recipient 4 Clio awards, 1981, 1 Clio award, 1982, Kitchen of Yr. award San Diego mag., 2003, Bathroom of Yr. award San Diego Home and Garden mag., 2003; named one of top art collectors under 40 Art and Antiques Mag., 1985, one of top 100 collectors in U.S., 1996. Mem. Phi Beta Kappa. E-mail: puredesign100@gmail.com.

PACKARD, JOHN MALLORY, physician, researcher; b. Saranac Lake, NY, Sept. 25, 1920; s. Edward Newman and Mary Bissell (Betts) P.; m. Ann Maurine Schoonover, June 15, 1944; children: Michael David, John Mallory, Ann Maurine, Mary Betts, Charles Edward, Kris Asvananda, Frank Schoonover, Charlotte Mellen. BA, Yale U., 1942; MD, Harvard U., 1945. Diplomate Am. Bd. Internal Medicine. Intern Presbyn. Hosp., NYC, 1945-46; resident in internal medicine Peter Bent Brigham Hosp., Boston, 1948-49; practice medicine specializing in internal medicine and cardiology Pensacola, Fla., 1954-68; prof. medicine, asso. dean Med. Sch. U. Ala., Birmingham, 1968-76; exec. dir. Ala. Regional Med. Program, Birmingham, 1968-73; corp. v.p. med. edn. Bapt. Med. Centers, Birmingham, 1976-92; ret., 1992. Contbr. articles to med. jours. Served with USN, 1946-54. Fellow ACP, Am. Coll. Cardiology, AHA; mem. Jefferson County Med. Soc., Med. Assn. Ala., AMA, Am. Soc. Internal Medicine, Ala. Soc. Internal Medicine (pres. 1981-82), Alpha Omega Alpha. Republican. Episcopalian. Personal E-mail: jmpackard@juno.com.

PACKARD, JOYCE HORNADAY, retired counselor; b. Fordyce, Ark., June 21, 1925; d. John Wesley and Nora (Wright) Hornaday; m. Robert G. Packard, Apr. 15, 1954. BA, Baylor U., 1952, MS, 1957; postgrad., Columbia U., 1966, Baylor U., 1980. Lic. counselor Tex. Office mgr./tchr. Western Union Telegraph Co., Crossett, Ark., 1944-48; asst. dean of women Baylor U., Wace, 1952-54, 57-61; tchr. Edison High Sch., Stockton, Calif., 1954-55, Clinton (Miss.) High Sch., 1955-56; tchr. Am. history/govt. Richfield High Sch., Waco, 1963-66, counselor, 1966—81, 1982—86; lectr. Baylor U., Waco, 1981-82, supr. practice tchrs., 1986—90. Tchr. English, U. Calif. Team Arlangga U., Sarabaja, Indonesia, 1961-62; tchr. cons. U. Sci., Penang, Malaysia, summer 1976; mem. Internat. Del. Citizen Ambassador, China, 1990. Mem. team Greater Asian Evangelism Team, Taiwan, 1970; bd. dirs. Brazos Forum, Waco, 1989—, pres., 1997; bd. dirs. Waco Historic Found., 1988—, pres., 1995-96; reg. facilitator Tex. Hospitality Course, 1987—; mem., chair Waco Conv. and Visitors Adv. Bd., 1987-2006; mem. Ind. Sch. Dist. Ednl. Bd., 1996—; bd. dirs. Brazos Higher Edn., Brazos Performing Arts; pres. Baptist Southern Deans, 1958-59; mem. Baylor U. Student Life. Adv. Bd., 2006—. Recipient Woman of Achievement award, 1972, Waco Hospitality award Convention and Tourism Adv. Bd., 1990, Pathfinder award Waco YWCA, 1990, Cert. award Vol. Svcs. Waco City Coun., 1991, Leadership Waco C. of C. Alumnus award, 1994, Athena award, 1995, DAR Cmty. Svc. award Elizabeth Gordon Bardley Chpt., 1997, Madison Cooper award cmty. leadership Madison Cooper Found. Trustees, 1999, Woman of Distinction award Bluebonnet Girl Scouts, 2003, Disting. Faculty award Waco Ind. Sch. Dist., 2004. Mem. Greater Waco Beautification Assn., Baylor Round Table (pres. 1988-89), Baylor Alumni Assn., Leadership Waco Alumni Assn., Epsilon Chi (achievement award 1984, pres. 1976-78), Delta Kappa Gamma (achievement award 1984, corres. sec. 1987-89). Baptist. Avocations: cooking, travel. Home: 69 Sugar Creek Pl Woodway TX 76712-3407

PACKARD, JULIE, aquarium administrator; b. Los Altos Hills; d. David and Lucile Packard. Co-founder & exec. dir. Monterey Bay Aquarium, Monterey, Calif., 1984—, vice chair, bd of trustees, 1984—. Mem. Pew Oceans Commn. Bd. dirs. David and Lucile Packard Found., Monterey Bay Aquarium Rsch. Inst., Calif. Nature Conservancy. Recipient Audubon Medal for Conservation, 1998, Ted Danson Ocean Hero award, 2004. Office: Monterey Bay Aquarium 886 Cannery Row Monterey CA 93940-1023

PACKARD, PETER, retired internal medical educator; b. Evanston, Ill., Mar. 14, 1927; s. George and Marianna (Dickinson) P.; m. Jenifer Carr, Aug. 28, 1951 (div. 1969); m. Mary Jane P., Nov. 8, 1969; children: Patricia Ann Langlais, Charles Barklay Langlais, Georgia Packard, Caroline L. Gregger, Louise Moskowitz-Packard, Victoria P. Aase, Adam L. Packard. BA, U. Calif., Berkeley, 1945; MD, U. Calif., San Francisco, 1948. Diplomate Am. Bd. Internal Medicine. Intern San Francisco Gen. Hosp., 1948-49; vol. arzt fellow infectious diseases Children's Hosp., Zurich, 1949-50; asst. res. in medicine Franklin Hosp., U. Calif., San Francisco, 1950-51; capt., med. corps USAF, Riverside, Calif., 1951-53; asst. res. medicine Ft. Miley VA Hosp., San Francisco, 1953-54, U. Calif. Hosp., San Francisco, 1954-55; pvt. practice Mills Hosp., Peninsula Med. Lab., San Mateo, Burlingame, Calif., 1955-91. Med. dir., vice chmn. bd. dirs.,

Peninsula Med. Lab., Menlo Park, Calif., 1980-94; chief of medicine, chief of staff Mills Hosp., San Mateo, 1967-74; assoc. clin. prof. medicine, U. Calif. San Francisco, 1955-2006, ret., 2006. Founding trustee, v.p. Mills-Peninsula Found., 1974-90, trustee emeritus, 1990—; pres., mem. bd. San Mateo County Heart Assn., 1964-74. Capt. M.C., USAFR, 1951-53, Korea. Mem. AMA, Calif. Med. Assn., San Mateo County Med. Assn. (various coms., bd. dirs., 1959-91), Am. Soc. Internal Medicine, Calif. Soc. Internal Medicine (del. off and on 1960-93), Calif. Soc. Medicine, U. Calif. San Francisco Assn. Clin. Faculty, Am. Legion. Avocations: tennis, golf, teaching, history, politics. Home and Office: 720 Seabury Rd Hillsborough CA 94010-6532

PACKARD, ROBERT GOODALE, III, urban planner; b. Denver, Apr. 12, 1951; s. Robert and Mary Ann (Woodward) P.; m. Jane Ann Collins, Aug. 25, 1973; children: Jessica Nelson, Robert Gregg. BA, Willamette U., 1973; M in Urban and Regional Planning/Community Devel., U. Colo., 1976. Project mgr. Environ. Disciplines, Inc., Portland, Oreg., 1973-75; asst. dir. planning Portland Pub. Schs., 1976-78; dir. planning Bur. of Parks, Portland, 1978-79; dir. planning and urban design Zimmer Gunsul Frasca, Portland, 1979-81, dir. project devel., 1981-84, mng. ptnr., 1984—. Co-author: The Baker Neighborhood/Denver, 1976. Contbr. articles to profl. jours. Trustee Willamette U., 1994; mem. City of Portland Waterfront Commn., 1982-83; mem. Mayor's Task Force for Joint Use of Schs., Portland, 1979-80; mem. Washington Park Master Plan Steering com., Portland, 1980-81; bd. dirs. Washington Park Zoo, 1983-86, pres. Arts Celebration Inc./Artquake, 1986—, New Rose Theatre, 1981-83; dir., pres. Grant Park Neighborhood Assn., Portland, 1981-83; pres. Pioneer Square Bd., 1997-98; bd. mem. Regional Arts and Cultural Coun.; mem. Archtl. Found. Oreg., 1992; mem. crafts bd. Oreg. Sch. Arts. Recipient Spl. Citation, Nat. Sch. Bds. Assn., 1978; Meritorious Planning Project award Am. Planning Assn., 1980, Nat. Am. Planning Assn., 1981; Meritorious Design award Am. Soc. Landscape Architects, 1981; Honor award Progressive Arch., 1983. Mem. AIA (Architecture Firm award 1991, assoc.), Am. Planning Assn., Young Pres. Assn., Racquet Club, Arlington Club, City Club, Racquet Club. Home: 3313 SW Fairmount Blvd Portland OR 97201-1478 Office: Zimmer Gunsul Frasca Partnership 320 SW Oak St Ste 500 Portland OR 97204-2737

PACKARD, ROCHELLE SYBIL, retired elementary school educator; b. June 25, 1951; d. Dave Wallace and Jeanette (Goddy) P. BA in Early Childhood Edn., Point Park Coll., 1973; MEd in Elem. Edn., U. Pitts., 1975. Instrnl. II permanent tchg. cert., Pa. Substitute tchr. Pitts. Pub. Bd. Edn., 1973-77, tchr. kindergarten, 1st grade, 2d grade, 1977—92, tchr. kindergarten, 1992—. Chair Israel Day Parade, Pitts., 1981; mem. Hadassah, Pitts., 1983—, Pioneer Women, Pitts., 1982—, ORT, Pitts., 1975—. Mem. Pitts. Fedn. Tchrs., Pitts. State Edn. Agy. Democrat. Jewish. Home: 4100 Lydia St Pittsburgh PA 15207-1135

PACKARD, SANDRA PODOLIN, education educator, consultant; b. Buffalo, Sept. 13, 1942; d. Mathew and Ethel (Zolte) P.; m. Martin Packard, Aug. 2, 1964; children: Dawn Esther, Shana Fanny BFA, Syracuse U., 1964; MSEd, Ind. U., 1966, EdD, 1973. Cert. tchr. art K-12, N.Y. Asst. prof. art SUNY-Buffalo, 1972-74; assoc. prof. art Miami U., Oxford, Ohio, 1974-81, spl. asst. to provost, 1979-80, assoc. provost, spl. programs, 1980-81; dean Coll. Edn. Bowling Green State U., Ohio, 1981-85; provost and vice chancellor for acad. affairs U. Tenn., Chattanooga, 1985-92; pres. Oakland U., Rochester, Mich., 1992-95, prof. edn., 1995—, dir. higher edn. doc. cognate; sr. fellow, dir. tech. in edn. Am. Assn. State Colls. and Univs., 1995; acting dir. PhD program in ednl. leadership Oakland U., 2003—04. Cons. Butler County Health Ctr., Hamilton, Ohio, 1976-78, Univ. of the North, South Africa Project of the Am. Coun. on Edn., 1995; vis. prof. art therapy Simmons Coll., 1979, Mary Mount Coll., Milw., 1981; corp. adv. com. Corp. Detroit Mag., 1994-95. Sr. editor Studies in Art Edn. jour., 1979-81; mem. editl. adv. bd. Jour. Aesthetic Edn., 1984-90; editor: The Leading Edge, 1986; contbr. articles to profl. jours., chpts. to conf. papers Chmn. com. Commn. on Edn. Excellence, Ohio, 1982-83, Tenn. State Peformance Funding Task Force, 1988, Tenn. State Task Force on Minority Tchrs., 1988; reviewer art curriculum NY Bd. Edn., 1985; supt. search com. Chattanooga Pub. Schs., 1987-88; mem. Chattanooga Met. Coun., 1987-88, Chattanooga Ballet Bd., 1986-88, Fund for Excellence in Pub. Edn., 1986-90, Tenn. Aquarium Bd. Advisors, 1989-92, Team Evaluation Ctr. Bd., 1988-90; strategic planning action team Chattanooga City Schs., 1987-88, Siskin Hosp. Bd., 1989-92, Blue Ribbon Task Force Pontiac 2010: A New Reality, City of Pontiac Planning Divsn., 1992—; steering com., cultural action bd. Chattanooga, planning com United Way, 1987; Jewish Fedn. Bd., 1986-91; mem. coun. for policy studies Art Edn. Adv. Bd., 1982-91; ex-officio mem. Meadow Brook Theatre Guild, 1992-95; bd. chair Meadow Brook Performing Arts Co., 1992-95; chair World Cup Soccer Edn. Com./Mich. Host Com. 1993-95; bd. dirs. Ptnrs. for Preferred Future, Rochester Cmty. Schs., 1992-95, Traffic Improvement Assn. Oakland County, 1992-95, Oakland County Bus. Roundtable, 1993-95; Rochester C. of C. host com. chair on edn. World Cup, 1992-95; fin. adv. com. Jewish Fedn. Detroit, 1995-97; bd. dirs. United Way Southeastern Mich., 1992-95: bd. dirs. United Way Oakland County, 1992-95, Pontiac 2010: A New Reality, mayor's transition team city/sch. rels. task force: team evaluation leader Dept. of State Am. U. Bulgaria, 1995; bd. trustees Cohn's & Colitis Found., 1996-97; trustee Nat. Art Edn. Found., 2004—, chair fin. com.; steering com. Nat. Forum Access to Democracy Project, 2004. Am. Coun. on Edn. and Mellon fellow Miami U., 1978-79; recipient Cracking the Glass Ceiling award Pontiac Area Urban League, 1992. Fellow Nat. Art Edn. Assn. (disting.); mem. Nat. Coun. Profs. of Ednl. Adminstrn. (technology com., 2000-03), Am. Assn. Colls. for Tchr. Edn. (com. chair 1982-85), Am. Art Therapy Assn. (registered), Nat. Art Edn. Assn. Women's Caucus (founder, pres. 1976-78, McFee award 1986), Am. Assn. State Colls. and Univs. (com. profl. devel. 1993-95, state rep. 1994-95), Econ. Club Detroit (bd. dirs. 1992-95), Rotary Club, Great Lakes Yacht Club (social chmn. 1996-97, ground chmn., bd. dirs. 1997-98), Phi Delta Kappa (Leadership award 1985), Nat. Assn. Profs. of Edn. Adminstrn. (com. chair 1998-), Great Lakes Yacht Club, 1995 (bd. dir. 1996-1998). Avocation: sailing. Home: 10471 Scout Trail White Lake MI 48386 Office: Oakland U 475 Education Bldg Rochester MI 48309-4423 Home Phone: 248-366-3088. Business E-Mail: packard@oakland.edu.

PACKARD, STEPHEN MICHAEL, legal association administrator, lawyer; b. Hartford, Conn., Nov. 26, 1953; s. Charles David and Anne (Moriarty) P.; m. Eileen Mary Joyce, May 23, 1981; children: Stephen Michael Jr., Sheila Marie, James Charles, Brian Joseph. BS, Fairfield U., 1975; JD magna cum laude, N.Y. Law Sch., 1981. Bar: N.Y. 1981, U.S. Dist. Ct. (ea. and so. dists.) N.Y. 1981, U.S. Dist. Ct. Conn. 1983, Conn. 1984. Assoc. Mudge, Rose, Guthrie, Alexander & Ferdon, NYC, 1981-83, Wiggin & Dana, New Haven, 1983-87; atty. Aetna Life & Casualty, Hartford, Conn., 1987-96; ptnr. Accenture, NYC, 1996—2003; v.p. The Hartford Ins. Group, 2003—05; dir. Deloitte Consulting LLP, Hartford, 2005—. Adj. prof. law U. Bridgeport Law Sch., Conn., 1987. Bd. dirs. New Haven Literacy vols., 1985-87; mem. bd. trustees adv. coun., Fairfield U., 2002--. Mem. Deloitte Touche Tohmatsu, Conn. Bar Assn., NYC Bar Assn., Fed. Bar Coun., Conn. Def. Lawyers Assn. Roman Catholic. Business E-Mail: stpackard@deloitte.com.

PACKER, BILLY, sports announcer (broadcast); b. Wellsville, NY, Feb. 25, 1940; m. Barbara Packer; 3 children. Graduated, Wake Forest Univ., 1962. Asst. basketball coach Wake Forest Univ., 1965; basketball announcer, ACC conference games Jefferson Pilot Sports, 1972, NBC Sports, 1974—81; basketball announcer, final four announcer CBS Sports, 1981—. Co-founder Tour DuPont, Buckler Challenge. Author: (sports books) Hoops, College Basketball's 25 Greatest Teams, History of the Final Four, Why We Win. Named to NC Hall of Fame, Wake Forest Hall of Fame, Nat. Basketball Hall of Fame, Nat. Polish Hall of Fame; recipient NC Sportscaster Yr. award. Office: CBS Sports 2200 W Cypress Creek Fort Lauderdale FL 33309 *

PACKER, GEORGE, writer; Grad., Yale U., 1982. Staff writer The New Yorker, 2003—. Tchr. Harvard U., Columbia U., Sarah Lawrence Coll. Author: The Village of Waiting, 1988, 2001, Blood of the Liberals, 2000 (Robert F. Kennedy Book Award, 2001), The Fight Is for Democracy: Winning the War of Ideas in America and the World, 2003, The Assassins' Gate: America in Iraq, 2005 (Cornelius Ryan award for best nonfiction book, Overseas Press Club, 2006), (novels) The Half Man, 1991, Central Square, 1998; contbr. NY Times Mag., Dissent, Mother Jones, Harper's. Mem. Peace Corps, Togo. Recipient Overseas Press Club awards, 2003, Ed Cunningham award, Overseas Press Club Am., 2007; Guggenheim Fellow, 2001—02. Office: New Yorker 4 Times Sq New York NY 10036 *

PACKER, JAMES INNELL, priest, professor of theology; b. Gloucester, Eng., July 22, 1926; Grad., Oxford U.; grad. Theology, Church of England Theol. Ordained Priest Church of England. Greek language teacher Oak Hill Theological Coll., London; assoc. principal Trinity Coll., Bristol, 1971—79; priest, professor Regent Coll., Vancouver; sangwoo youtong chee professor Theology, Regent Coll., Vancouver; exec. ed. Christianity Today. Author: (novels) Fundamentalism and the Word of God, 1958, Knowing God, 1973, Keep In Step With The Spirit: Finding Fullness In Our Walk With God, 1984; co-author Christianity: The True Humanism, 1985; author Evangelism and the Sovereignty of God, 1961, A Quest for Godliness: The Puritan Vision of the Christian Life, 1994, Concise Theology: A Guide to Historic Christian Beliefs, 2001, The Redemption and Restoration of Man in the Thought of Richard Baxter, 2003, One Faith: The Evangelical Consensus, 2004, Praying, 2006. Named one of 25 Most Influential Evangelicals, Time Magazine, 2005. Christian. Office: Regent College 5800 University Blvd Vancouver V6T 2E4 Canada Office Phone: (604) 224-3245. Office Fax: (604) 224-3097. *

PACKER, LINDA S., psychotherapist; b. NYC, July 30, 1941; d. Joseph Wolf Stark and Jean Carson; children: William Joseph, Andrew Landes. BA in English and Psychology with honors, NYU, 1972; CSW, NYU Sch. Social Work, 1987. Fellow Am. Psychotherapy Assn.; LCSW Nat. Assn. Social Workers and SUNY Edn. Dept.; cert. Nat. Acad. Cert. Care Mgrs. Rsch. asst. alcoholic rsch. unit Silver Hill Found., 1972—75; intern clin. social worker Program for Devel. Human Potential, Bishop Ford H.S., 1985—86; intern clin. social worker outpatient psychiat. clinic Met. Hosp., 1986—87; psych. social worker NY Svc. Program for Older People, 1987—88; sr. cons. Helena Internat., Morristown, NJ, 1988—89; psychiat. social worker Geriatric Psychiat. Inpatient Unit, 1989—92; psychiat. social worker adult psychiat. inpatient unit Mt. Sinai Hosp., NYC, 1992—95; sr. assoc. Fine & Newcombie Assocs., NYC, 1995—99; founder, dir. Prime Life Network, NYC, 2000—. Cons., founder Care Mgrs. Consortium, NYC, 2000—; pvt. practice, 1987—. Author: (article) Diseases of Nervous System, Am. Jour. Geriatric Psychiatry. Mem.: NY State Soc. Clin. Social Work Psychotherapists, Nat. Assn. Social Workers, Nat. Assn. Profl. Geriatric Care Mgrs., East Side Coun. on Aging, Am. Soc. on Aging, Am. Psychotherapy Assn., Am. Geriatric Soc. Avocations: gardening, reading, interior decorating. Office: PrimeLife Network 200 E End Ave #10-I New York NY 10128 Business E-Mail: plncsw@att.net.

PACKER, MARK BARRY, lawyer, financial consultant, foundation official; b. Phila., Sept. 18, 1944; s. Samuel and Eve (Devine) P.; m. Donna Elizabeth Ferguson (div. 1994); children: Daniel Joshua, Benjamin Dov, David Johannes; m. Helen Margaret (Jones) Klinedinst, July, 1995. AB magna cum laude, Harvard U., 1965, LLB, 1968. Bar: Wash. 1969, Mass. 1971. Assoc. Ziontz, Pirtle & Fulle, Seattle, 1968-70; pvt. practice Bellingham, Wash., 1972—. Bd. dirs., corp. sec. BMJ Holdings (formerly No. Sales Co., Inc.), 1977—; trustee No. Sales Profit Sharing Plan, 1977—; bd. dirs. Whatcom State Bank, 1995-98. Mem. Bellingham Planning and Devel. Commn., 1975—84, chmn., 1977—81, mem. shoreline subcom., 1976—82, capital improvements adv. com., 1999—2001; mem. Bellingham Mcpl. Arts Commn., 1986—91, landmark rev. bd., 1987—91; chmn. Bellingham campaign United Jewish Appeal, 1979—90; trustee, chmn. program com. Bellingham Pub. Sch. Found., 1991—96, Heavy Culture classic lit. group, 1991—, Jewish studies group, 1993—; trustee Kenneth L. Kellar Found., 1995—; mng. trustee Bernard M. & Audrey Jaffe Found.; Torah reader, trustee Frederick S. & Emma Gartner Charitable Trust, 1996—2007; instr. Acad. Lifelong Learning, 2004—; pres. Congregation Eytz Chaim, Bellingham, 1998—2000; bd. dirs. Whatcom Cmty. Coll. Found., 1989—92. Recipient Blood Donor award ARC, 1979, 8-Gallon Pin, 1988, Mayor's Arts award City of Bellingham, 1993. Mem. Wash. State Bar Assn. (sec. real property, probate and trust, com. law examiners 1992-94). Office: PO Box 1151 Bellingham WA 98227-1151 Home Phone: 360-738-9788; Office Phone: 360-671-7500. Business E-Mail: Packer@nas.com.

PACKER, MATTHEW JAMES, musician, educator, advertising executive; b. Ann Arbor, Mich., Sept. 24, 1965; s. James Dale and Mary Leila Packer; 1 child, Janelle Nichole. B of Music Edn., Ctrl. Mich. U., 1987, MusM, 1995; D of Worship Studies, Inst. Worship Studies, 2004. Tchr. elem. music Lake Ville Cmty. Schs., Otisville, Mich., 1988—89; dir. music & Christian edn. Clare United Meth. Ch., 1990—99; dir. worship and music Fenton United Meth. Ch., 1999—2005; music lectr. U. Mich., Flint; advertising mgr. Natzel Pubs. Inc.; choir dir. Flushing United Methodist Ch. Mem. worship planning team Detroit Ann. Conf., 2000—. Ch. coord. Forgotton Man Mins., Flint, Mich., 2003—. Mem.: Am. Choral Dirs. Assn., Fellowship of United Methodists in Music and Worship Arts. Methodist. Avocations: music, bicycling, stained glass, reading, weightlifting. Office: Natzel Publications Inc 9001 Miller Rd Ste 8 PO Box 417 Swartz Creek MI 48473 E-mail: mpack65@yahoo.com.

PACKER, STUART HOWARD, medical educator; b. Bklyn., May 26, 1948; s. Archie and Rhoda Packer; m. Barbara Rose Lutzky, June 13, 1971; children: Mitchell, Rachel. BA, Case Western Res. U., Cleve., 1970; MD, SUNY, Bklyn., 1974. Cert. Am. Bd. Internal Medicine, diplomate Am. Bd. Hematology and Med. Oncology. Intern Duke U. Med. Ctr., Durham, NC, 1974—75; resident Duke Med. Ctr., 1975—77, fellow in hematology and oncology, 1977—80; attending physician St. Francis Med. Ctr., Trenton, NJ, 1980—85; chief of hematology-oncology St. Mary Med. Ctr., Langhorne, Pa., 1985—2002; assoc. attending physician Meml. Sloan Kettering Med. Ctr., NYC, 2002—04; assoc. prof. Mt. Sinai Sch. Medicine, NYC, 2004—. Mem.: Am. Soc. Clin. Oncology. Office: Mt Sinai Med Ctr 1 Gustave Levy Pl New York NY 10029 Office Phone: 212-241-7637. Office Fax: 212-423-9458. Business E-Mail: stuart.packer@mssm.edu.

PACKERT, G(AYLA) BETH, retired lawyer; b. Corpus Christi, Tex., Sept. 25, 1953; d. Gilbert Norris and Virginia Elizabeth (Pearce) P.; m. James Michael Hall, Jan. 1, 1974 (div. 1985); m. Richard Christopher Burke, July 18, 1987; children: Christopher Geoffrey Makepeace Burke Packert, Jeremy Eliot Marvell Packert Burke. BA, La. Tech. U., 1973; postgrad., U. Ill., 1975—81, JD, 1985; MA, U. Ark., 1976. Bar: Ill. 1985, U.S. Dist. Ct. (no. dist.) Ill. 1985, U.S. Ct. Appeals (7th cir.) 1987, Va. 1988, U.S. Dist. Ct. (we. dist.) Va. 1989. Assoc. Jenner & Block, Chgo., 1985—88; law clk. U.S. Dist. Ct. Va. (we. dist.), Danville, 1988—89; asst. commonwealth atty. Commonwealth of Va., Lynchburg, 1989—95; pvt. practice Lynchburg, 1995—2002; English tchr. Paul Laurence Dunbar Middle Sch. for Innovation, Lynchburg, 2004—06. Notes and comments editor U. Ill. Law Rev., 1984-85. Mem. Phi Beta Kappa. Home: 3900 Faculty Dr Lynchburg VA 24501-3110 Personal E-mail: burkepackert@verizon.net.

PACTER, PAUL ALLAN, accounting standards researcher; b. NYC, Jan. 26, 1943; s. Bernard David and Hilda Libby (Margolies) P. BS, Syracuse U., 1964; PhD, Mich. State U., 1967. C.P.A., N.Y. Asst. prof. N.Y.U., 1967-69; rsch. mgr. KPMG, NYC, 1969-73; exec. dir. Fin. Acctg. Standards Bd., Stamford, Conn., 1973-84; commr. fin. City of Stamford, 1984-90; prof. acctg., MBA program U. Conn., Stamford, 1990-96, adj. prof., 1982-84. Adj. prof. NYU, 1982-84; project cons. Fin. Acctg. Standards Bd., 1990-96; fellow Internat. Acctg. Standards Com., London, 1993-2000, dir., 2003—; bd. dirs. Deloitte Touche Tohmatsu, Hong Kong, 2000—. Consulting editor The Jour. of Accountancy, 1968-73 Chmn. Stamford Commn. on Human Rights, 1977-84, Stamford Film Commn., 1984-90; mem. Charter Revision Commn., Stamford, 1979-80, Gov.'s Tourism Coun., Conn., 1984-90, acctg. adv. coun. U. Conn., 1984-90; pres. N. Stamford Dem. Club, 1983-84, treas., 1987-95; dir. Stamford Coliseum Authority, 1984-90; vice chmn. govtl. acctg. stds. adv. coun., 1984-91; vice chmn. China Beijing Ctr. for Asia-Pacific Fin. and Acctg. Rsch., 2000—; treas. Conn. Tourism Assn., 1987-90, North Stamford Assn., 1993-94; bd. dirs. Stamford Ctr. for the Arts, United Way Stamford, Stamford Theatre Works, Stamford Cmty. Fund, Housing Devel. Fund of Fairfield County. Earhart Found. fellow Mich. State U., 1966-67; U.S. Office of Edn. grantee, 1967 Mem. AICPA, Am. Acctg. Assn. (coun.), N.Y. State Soc. CPA's, Beta Gamma Sigma, Beta Alpha Psi. Jewish. Office: Deloitte Touche Tohmatsu 35/F One Pacific Pl 88 Queensway Hong Kong China Home Phone: +852 2829 7129. Business E-Mail: ppacter@iasb.org.

PADALKA, GENNADY IVANOVICH, cosmonaut; b. Krasnodar, Russia, July 21, 1958; s. Ivan Vasilievich and Valentina Meforievna Padalka; m. Irina Anatiolievna Ponomareva; children: Yulia, Ekaterina, Sonya. Grad., Eisk Mil. Aviation Coll., 1979. Commd., pilot and sr. pilot Russian Air Force, 1979, advanced through grades to col.; cosmonaut candidate Y.A. Gagarin Cosmonaut Tng. Ctr., Russia, 1989—91, test cosmonaut, 1991—, tng. for comdr. back-up crew for Mir 24/NASA-5, Russian-Am. program of 24th primary expdn., Pegasus Russian-French program/Euro-Mir program, 1996—97, tng. for primary crew comdr for the space flight aboard the Soyuz-TM/Mir orbital complex (Expedition 26 Program), 1997—98, crew comdr. Soyuz-TM-28/Mir orbital complex Expedition 26 Russia, 1998—99, tng. for space flight Soyuz-TM transport as ISS contingency crew comdr., 1999—2000, tng. for space flight as ISS-4 back-up crew comdr., 2000—01; station commdr. ISS Expedition-9 crew, 2002; living and working aboard the ISS, Expedition-9 crew aboard Soyuz TMA-4 Baikonur Cosmodrome, Kazakhstan, 2004—. First class pilot; instr. of gen. parachute tng. Named title of Russian Fedn. Test-Cosmonaut; recipient Star of Russian Fedn. Hero. Avocations: theater, diving, parachute sport. Office: Russian Space Agency 42 Shchepkinst 129857 Moscow Russia

PADBERG, HELEN SWAN, violinist; b. Shawnee, Okla. d. Frank P. and Birdie B. (Rudell) Swan; m. Frank Padberg, Feb. 6, 1943; children: Frank, Kristen. AA, Stephens Coll., 1938; MusB, U. Okla., 1940; MusM, Northwestern U., 1941; student, Jacques Gordon. Solo performances and concerts, 1932—; mem. faculty string quartet and symphony soloist Stephens Coll., 1937-38; violinist Oklahoma City Symphony Summer Concerts, 1940; soloist Northwestern U. Symphony, 1941; violinist USO Tours World War II, 1941-43; mem. Nat. Orchestral Assn. and Am. Youth Orch., NYC, 1944-46; asst. concertmaster West Suburban Symphony, Chgo., 1947-48; mem. Chgo. Women's Symphony, Chgo. Civic Orch. and chamber music groups, 1947-51; violinist Ark. Piano Trio, 1952-58; concertmaster Ark. Symphony and Little Rock Philharm., 1953-57, Marjorie Lawrence TV Series, 1953-54; pvt. tchr. violin Little Rock, 1953-66; accompanist and performer on piano, harp. Pres. Ark. Med. Soc. Alliance, 1962-63, historian, 1963-94. Co-founder Little Rock Chamber Music Soc., 1954; pres. bd. dirs. Vis. Nurse Assn. of Pulaski County, Ark., 1967-69; bd. dirs. Internat. Visitors Ctr., Chgo., 1988—, Stephens Coll. Alumna Assn. Bd.; elder, trustee Presbyn. Ch.; docent Newberry Libr., Chgo., 1998—. Mem.: Mu Phi Epsilon, Internat. Women Assocs. (pres. 1988—91), Am. Opera Soc. Chgo. (v.p. and program chmn. 1981—82, pres. 1984—87), Am. Opera Soc. (historian 1987—), Am. Fedn. Musicians, Chgo. Harp Soc. (sec. 1979—84), Am. Harp Soc., English Spkg. Union (Chgo. br., bd. govs. 1997—), Musicians' Club of Women (Chgo., bd. dirs.), Women's Athletic Club of Chgo., Aesthetic Club (pres. Little Rock), Pi Beta Phi (pres. Little Rock Alumnae Club), Pi Kappa Lambda. Home: 175 E Delaware Pl Chicago IL 60611-1756

PADDEN, ANTHONY ALOYSIUS, JR., retired federal government official; b. Kearny, NJ, Apr. 3, 1949; s. Anthony Aloysius and Harriet Margaret Padden. PBA, Fairleigh Dickinson U., 1970, MA in Pub. Adminstrn., 1980; postgrad., U. Tenn. Sch. Law, 1970. Employment interviewer N.J. Dept. Labor, Trenton, 1970—76, prin. procedure analyst, 1976—79; nat. procedure coord. Interstate Compendium Employment Svc. Activities Project, Trenton, 1979—80; mgmt. analyst Dept. Justice, Washington, 1980—83; chief clk. ct. U.S. Immigration Ct., Falls Church, Va., 1983—. Adj. faculty Nat. Judicial Coll., Reno, 1998—2003; cons., Dumfries, Va., 1978—. Author: Dept. Labor tech. report, 1980; contbr. and editor: other profl. studies. Presdl. mgmt. intern, 1980. Logan Chambers grantee, Internat. Assn. Pers. in Employment Security, 1979. Mem.: Pi Alpha Alpha (Adminstr. of Yr. 1991).

PADDEN, PRESTON, broadcast executive; b. Washington, Nov. 26, 1948; m. Barbara Padden; 3 children. Grad., U. Md.; JD, George Washington U. Asst. gen. counsel Metromedia Inc.; pres. Assn. of Ind. TV Sta. Inc.; with News Corp.; chmn., CEO Am. Sky Broadcasting, 1996; pres. ABC TV Network, NYC, 1997-98; exec. v.p. govt. rels. The Walt Disney Co., Washington, 1998—. Bd. dirs. The Advt. Coun., Inc. Mem. Fed. Comm. Bar Assn., Internat. Radio TV Soc. (bd. dirs.). Office: The Walt Disney Co 1150 17th St NW Ste 400 Washington DC 20036-4622

PADDISON, DAVID ROBERT, lawyer; b. Savannah, Ga., May 15, 1949; s. Richard Milton and Josephine Butler (Bowles) P.; m. Frances M. Phares (div. Mar. 1995); children: Hunt, Brian, Margery; m. Jane Ingrid Caddell, Mar. 30, 1996; 1 child, Ethan David. BSBA, La. State U., 1971; JD, Tulane U., 1976. Bar: La. 1976; U.S. Dist. Ct. (ea. dist.) 1976; U.S. Ct. Appeals (5th cir.) 1976; bd. cert. specialist in family law La. State Bar Assn., 1995; U.S. Tax. Ct. 2001. Asst. dist. atty. Dist. Atty.'s Office, Covington, La., 1983-86, New Orleans, La., 1978-83; pvt. practice Covington, La., 1986—. Advisor Contemporary Arts Ctr., New Orleans, 1978-79; clin. advisor Tulane U. Sch. Law, New Orleans, 1980-81; spl. cons. Dist. Atty.'s Office, New Orleans, 1983. Legal advisor Christ Episcopal Church (sch. planning com., lector, usher). Mem. Covington Bar Assn Republican. Episcopalian. Avocations: golf, sailing, skiing. Office: PO Box 1830 Covington LA 70434-1830 Office Phone: 985-893-2280.

PADDOCK, ANTHONY CONAWAY, financial consultant; b. Paris, July 9, 1935; came to U.S., 1940; s. H. Watson and Mildred V. (Decker) P.; m. Wendy E. Brewer, Apr. 24, 1971. AB, Harvard U., 1957, JD, 1960; MBA, Columbia U., 1961. Bar: N.Y. 1961. Assoc. investment bank Merrill Lynch & Co., NYC, 1961-69; v.p. Chase Manhattan Bank, NYC, 1970-78, Standard Rsch. Cons., NYC, 1978-84; mng. dir. Benchmark Valuation Cons., NYC, 1978-84; prin. KPMG Peat Marwick, NYC, 1984-96; mng. dir. Empire Valuation Cons., NYC, 1997—. Adj. prof. NYU, 1979-90. Trustee Sun Capital Advisors Trust, 1998—. Mem. Assoc. for Corp. Growth, Inst. Mgmt. Cons. (cert.). Episcopalian. Home: 14 N Chatsworth

Ave Larchmont NY 10538-2142 Office: Empire Valuation Cons 350 5th Ave Ste 5513 New York NY 10118-5513 Office Phone: 212-714-0122. Business E-Mail: acpaddock@empireval.com.

PADDOCK, JOHN (ALVIN JOHN PADDOCK), professional hockey coach; b. Oak River, Man., Can., June 9, 1954; m. Jill Paddock; children: Jenny, Sally, Anna, Alyssa. Head coach Maine Mariners, 1983—84, asst. coach, 1984—85; head coach Hershey Bears, 1985—89; asst. gen. mgr. Phila. Flyers, 1989-90; head coach Binghamton Rangers, 1990—91, Winnipeg Jets, 1991—95; gen. mgr. Phoenix Coyotes, 1996-97; head coach Hartford Wolf Pack, 1999—2002, Binghamton Senators, 2002—04, co-head coach, 2004—05; asst. coach Ottawa Senators, 2005—07, head coach, 2007—. Recipient Louis A.R. Pieri Meml. Award. Office: Ottawa Senators Scotiabank Place 1000 Palladium Dr Kanata K2V 1A5 Canada *

PADDOCK, LORI ANN, military officer; b. Connellsville, Pa., Apr. 25, 1966; d. William Joseph and Jeannine Wagner; m. Claude Westbrook Paddock, July 27, 2006; stepchildren: Hayley, Jacob; m. Gregory Allen Pickard, Sept. 28, 1985 (div. Mar. 6, 2003); 1 child, Timothy Paul Pickard. AAS in Comm., CC of the Air Force, Maxwell, Ala., 2000. Enlisted USAF, 1984, advanced through grades to sr. master sgt.; intelligence collection mgr. Joint Intelligence Ctr. Pacific, Pearl Harbor Naval Station, Hawaii, 1996—99; chief, test and evaluation 497th intelligence group USAF, Bolling AFB, DC, 1999—2001; supt., XOIRY USAF hdqr. Pentagon, Washington, 2001—04; chief ISR ops. flight 607th air intelligence squadron USAF, Osan AFB, Republic of Korea, 2004—05, supt., intelligence flight 595th ops. support squadron Schriever AFB, Colo., 2005—06. Pres. 607th Air Intelligence Squadron Top Three, Osan AFB, 2005. Decorated Meritorious Svc. medal USAF, Commendation medal, Jt. Svc. Commendation medal US Govt. Avocations: reading, crafts, needlecrafts, walking. Home: 90 McChord St Unit 5000 Hickam Afb HI 96853 Personal E-mail: hazel_44@hotmail.com.

PADDY, DAVID, literature and language professor; BA, Miami U.; MA, American U.; PhD, U. Md., College Park. Assoc. prof., Dept. English Whittier Coll., Calif. Lectr. in field. Recipient U.S. Professor Yr. State of Calif., Carnegie Found. Advancement Tchg., 2006. Office: Whittier Coll 13406 E Phladelphia St PO Box 634 Whittier CA 90608

PADEGS, ANDRIS, electrical engineer, company executive; b. Riga, Latvia, Mar. 27, 1929; s. Arturs and Vera Padegs; m. Mara Berzins, Aug. 28, 1954; children: Anita Batarags, Gints, Sandra Slokenbergs. BA magna cum laude, Dartmouth Coll., Hanover, NH, 1953, MS with highest distinction, 1954; PhD in Elec. Engring., Carnegie Inst. Tech., Pitts., 1958. Engring. positions Internat. Bus. Machines, Poughkeepsie, NY, 1958—68, mgr. processor architecture, 1968—69, mgr., architecture design & control, 1969—71, program mgr., sys. architecture, 1971—87, program mgr., enterprise systems ctrl. architecture, 1987—92; pres. Infologistik Inc., Poughkeepsie, 1992—2006. Cons. Padegs Consulting, Poughkeepsie, NY, 1992—2002; vice chmn. SWH-Technology, Riga, Latvia, 1994—2000; adv. bd. on computers Republic of Latvia, Riga, Latvia, 1991—. Contbr. more than 25 articles to profl. jours.; author: four U.S. patents. Pres. Latvian Found., Inc., Kalamazoo, 1980—82, Mid-Hudson Latvian Assn., Poughkeepsie, NY, 1972—75; exec. vice chmn. Latvian Cultural Assn. TILTS, Poughkeepsie, NY, 1976—. Recipient Three Star Medal (highest civilian medal granted by Republic of Latvia), Republic of Latvia, 2001. Mem.: IEEE (life), Latvian Acad. Scis. (elected fgn. mem., Grand medal 2004), Assn. Latvian Engrs. (v.p. 1986—92), Sigma Xi. Achievements include one of two authors of original IBM System/360 Principles of Operation; patents in field. Avocations: photography, singing, history. Home: 2 Merry Hill Rd Poughkeepsie NY 12603-3214 Home Fax: 845-462-8751. Personal E-mail: apadegs@optonline.net.

PADEN, HARRY, municipal official; children: Shahara, Angela. Student, Am. U., 1971-73, Essex County (N.J.) Coll., 1981-83. Dir. social svcs. Unity Freedom Bapt. Ch., Newark, 1989-92; aide to freeholder pres. Essex County, 1992-96; code enforcement officer Township of Irvington, N.J., 1992-94, chief field rep. Office Neighborhood Preservation, 1994-98. Host, prodr. (cable T.V. program) Parent to Parent; contbg. writer Jersey Girl mag.; columnist Irvington Herald. Chmn. Irvington juvenile conf. com. Superior Ct.; v.p., former pres. PTA Irvington H.S.; program coord. Neighborhood Preservation, 1998—; parent coord. Essex County PTA; ednl. liaison mayor of Irvington; aide Irvington West Ward Council; celebrity reader Essex and Hudson County chpts. United Way; deacon, adminstrv. asst. to pastor Unity Freedom Bapt. Ch., Newark; former mem. Irvington Bd. Edn. Named Irvington African Am. Male of Yr., 1994, One of 100 Most Influential in State, City News, 1997; recipient Pinnacle award Being Single mag., 1995, Spl. Civil award Irvington C. of C. Home: 31 Civic Sq W Apt 14 Irvington NJ 07111-2425 Office Phone: 973-580-2496. Personal E-mail: harry_paden@hotmail.com.

PADEREWSKI, SIR CLARENCE JOSEPH, architect; b. Cleve., July 23, 1908; BArch, U. Calif., 1932. Chief draftsman Sam W. Hamill, 1939-44; with Heitschmidt-Matcham-Blanchard-Gill & Hamill, 1943; prin. C.J. Paderewski, 1944-48; pres. Paderewski, Mitchell, Dean & Assoc., Inc. (and predecessor), San Diego, 1948-78. Instr. adult edn. San Diego city schs., 1939-44, U. Calif. extension div., 1945, 56; lectr. in field. Prin. works include Charactron Labs, Gen. Dynamics Corp., Convair, S.D., 1954, South Bay Elem. Schs., S.D., 1948-74; additions to El Cortez Hotel; including first exterior passenger glass elevator in the world and New Travolator Motor Hotel, S.D., 1959, Palomar Coll., San Marcos, 1951-80, San Diego County U. Gen. Hosp., San Diego Internat. Airport Terminal Bldgs., Fallbrook Elem. Schs., 1948-74, Silver Strand Elem. Sch., Coronado, Tourmaline Terrace Apt. Bldg., San Diego Salvation Army Office Bldg. Mem. adv. bd. Bayside Social Service Center, 1953-75, San Diego Polonia Newspaper, 1994—; mem. San Diego Urban Design Com.; adv. bd. Camp Oliver, 1963—, pres., 1975-76; bd. dirs. San Diego Symphony Orch. Assn., 1954-62, San Diego chpt. ARC, 1971-74; bd. dirs., chmn. coms., pres. San Diego Downtown Assn., 1963—; bd. dirs. Nat. Council Archtl. Registration Bds., 1958-66, bd. dirs. other offices, 1961-64, pres., 1965-66, chmn. internat. relations com., 1967-68, Salvation Army, vice-chmn., 1989, life mem. adv. bd., 1993—, Copernicus Found., 1994—; mem. Calif. Bd. Archtl. Examiners, 1949-61, past pres., commr., 1961—; mem. Nat. Panel Arbitrators, 1953—, Nat. Council on Schoolhouse Constrn.; hon. chmn. Ignacy Jan Paderewski Meml. Com., 1991; adv. bd. S.D. Balboa Park Cmty. Endowment Fund, 1995—. Decorated Knight Order Polonia Restituta, Polish govt. in exile, 1982, recipient Commodore cross, 2002; recipient Award of Merit for San Diego County Gen. Hosp., San Diego chpt., AIA, 1961, Honor award for San Diego Internat. Airport Terminal, Honor award Portland Cement Co., Golden Trowel award Plastering Inst., 1958-60, 4 awards Masonry Inst., 1961, award Prestressed Concrete Inst., 1976, Outstanding Community Leadership award San Diego Downtown Assn., 1963-65, 80, Polish Engring. award for outstanding arch. and achievement, 2000, Gold award Engring. Soc., 2000, Outstanding INdividual Polish Am. award Polish Ctr. of L.A., 2001. Fellow AIA (pres. San Diego chpt. 1948, 49, bd. dirs. 1947-53, chmn. several coms., spl. award 1977, Calif. Coun. Spl. award 1979, Calif. Coun. Disting. Svc. award 1982, Lifetime Achievement award 2000); mem. San Diego C. of C. (bd. dirs. 1959-62, 64-67), Am. Arbitration Assn. (San Diego adv. coun. 1969—), Sister City Soc. (bd. dirs.), Lions (past pres. Hillcrest Club, Lion of Yr. 1990, fellow internat. found. 1991), Father Serra Club (charter, past pres.), Outboard Boating Club San Diego, Chi Alpha Kappa, Delta Sigma Chi.

PADGET, BARBARA JOHNSON, elementary school educator; b. Greenwood, SC, Nov. 14, 1954; d. Charles Rush and Mildred (Faulkner) Johnson; m. Richard Edward Padget, July 15, 1977; children: William Richard, Benjamin Rush, Susan Elizabeth. BA, Clemson U., SC, 1975. Cert. tchr. SC. Tchr. Emerald Jr. HS, Greenwood, SC, 1976—77, Ashwood-Ctrl. HS, Bishopville, SC, 1977—78, Lugoff-Elgin Mid. Sch., Lugoff, SC, 1978—80, Gilbert HS, SC, 1980—93, Gilbert Mid. Sch., 1993—. Co-author: Curriculum for Methods of Teaching Cosmetologists, 1999. Vol. Ho. of Reps. campaign, Lexington, SC, 1988. Named Tchr. of Yr., Ashwood Ctrl. HS, 1978, Gilbert Mid. Sch., 1993; recipient Acheivement award, Gilbert Town Coun., 2004. Mem.: Nat. Coun. Social Studies, SC Coun. Social Studies. Avocations: reading, gardening, travel. Home: 1347 Beechcreek Rd Lexington SC 29072 Office: Gilbert Mid Sch 120 RiKard Cir Gilbert SC 29054 Personal E-mail: bpadgettooz@sc.rr.com.

PADGETT, DOUGLAS EDMUND, orthopedist, surgeon, educator; b. Seaford, NY, July 21, 1956; BA, St. Michael's Coll., 1978; MD, NY Med. Coll., 1982. Lic. NY, cert. Am. Bd. Orthop. Surgery, 1992. Intern, orthop. surgery Roosevelt Hosp., NYC, 1982—83, 1984—85; resident, orthop. surgery Hosp. Spl. Surgery, NYC, 1985—89, assoc. attending orthop. surgeon hip and knee svc., 1993—, chief, hip svc.; postdoctoral fellowship, adult reconstructive surgery of the hip and knee Rush Presbyn. Med. Ctr., Chgo., 1989—90; dir. adult reconstructive svcs. Naval Hosp., San Diego, 1990—93; co-chief orthop. Veterans Hosp., Bronx, NY, 1996—; assoc. attending orthop. surgeon NY-Presbyn. Hosp., NYC. Assoc. prof. orthop. surgery Weill Med. Coll., Cornell U., NYC; field test examiner Am. Bd. Orthop. Surgeons. Editl. bd. mem. Jour. Arthroplasty, cons. reviewer Am. Jour. of Bone and Joint Surgery; contbr. articles to med. jours. Battalion surgeon, 2nd Battalion, 8th Marine Regiment USMC, 1983—84, Ops. in Grenada, West Indies and in Beirut, Lebanon, deployed to Persian Gulf with Fleet Hosp. #6 in support of military operation during Ops. Desert Shield and Desert Storm, 1991. Decorated Naval Achievement medal for meritorious svc.; recipient Philip D. Wilson Rsch. Award. Mem.: Am. Acad. Orthop. Surgeons (mem. program com.). Office: Hosp Spl Surgery 535 E 70th St New York NY 10021 Office Phone: 212-606-1642. Office Fax: 212-606-1917. *

PADGETT, GAIL BLANCHARD, lawyer; b. Douglasville, Ga., Aug. 20, 1949; d. William David and Dorothy Rose (Bennett) P. BA, Ga. State U., 1971, MEd, 1974; JD, Georgetown U., 1981. Bar: Va., Ga., D.C., U.S. Supreme Ct. Tchr. Clayton Co. Bd. Edn., Jonesboro, Ga., 1971-77; spl. asst. to dir. Community Rels Svc., Chevy Chase, Md., 1977-81, gen. counsel, 1981-89, assoc. dir., 1989-96; asst. chief immigration judge U.S. Dept. Justice, Falls Church, Va., 1996—2004, U.S. Immigration Ct., Bradentun, Fla., 2004—. Recipient Disting. Svc. award Atty. Gen. of the U.S., 1992. Home: 9448 Discovery Terrace 102 Bradenton FL 34212 Office: US Immigration Ct 515 11th St West Ste 300 Bradenton FL 34205

PADGETT, GREGORY LEE, lawyer; b. Greenfield, Ind., May 9, 1959; s. William Joseph and Anna Katherine (Hyre) Padgett; m. Ruth Anne Dorworth, June 5, 1982; children: Joshua David, William Joel, Emily Xiao Lei. BA summa cum laude, DePauw U., 1981; JD, Northwestern U., 1984. Bar: Ill., U.S. Dist. Ct. (no. dist.) Ill. 1984, U.S. Ct. Appeals (7th cir.) 1986, Ind. 1988, U.S. Dist. Ct. (no. & so. dists.) Ind. 1988. Assoc. Kirkland & Ellis, Chgo., 1984-88, Baker & Daniels, Indpls., 1988-92; ptnr. Johnson, Lawhead, Buth & Pope, P.C., Indpls., 1992-2000; of counsel Barnes & Thornburg, Indpls., 2000—04; prin. Padgett Law, Indpls., 2004—. Adj. prof. Butler U., 1989—90. Pres., bd. dirs. Theatre on the Square, Indpls., 1994-95; mem. coun. Hope Evang. Covenant Ch., 1992-96; bd. dirs. Meridian St. Found., 1994-96, Ind. Arts Chorale, 2003-06, Oaks Acad., 2006-. Mem. Ind. State Bar Assn., Indpls. Bar Assn., Christian Legal Soc., Phi Beta Kappa. Avocations: theatre arts, vocal music, hiking, writing. Office: Padgett Law Ste 230 9000 Keystone Crossing Indianapolis IN 46240 Office Phone: 317-218-0316. Business E-Mail: gp@indianaestatelaw.com.

PADGETT, JOHN DAVID, lawyer; b. Norfolk, Va., July 8, 1958; s. Royal Claytor and Phyllis (Hunt) Padgett; m. Lee Ann Hagy. BA with distinction, U. Va., 1980; JD, Washington & Lee U., 1983. Bar: Va. 1983, US Bankruptcy Ct. Ea. Dist. 1983, US Dist. Ct. Ea. Dist. Va. 1983, US Ct. Appeals 4th Cir. 1983. Ptnr. Jett, Berkley, Furr & Padgett (merged with McGuireWoods LLP), Norfolk, Va., 1983—93, McGuireWoods LLP, Norfolk, Va., 1993—, mng. ptnr. Norfolk office. Escheator City of Norfolk, Va., 1994—2003; gen. counsel Rep. Party of Va. Sec. Hampton Rd. YMCA, 2005—; chmn. State Coun. of Higher Edn., Va., 1998—2001. Mem. Maritime Law Assn., Southeastern Admiralty Law Inst., Hampton Roads C. of C.(chmn. 2003), Phi Delta Phi., Hampton Roads Fgn. Commerce Club (pres.), Norfolk Rotary Club. Presbyterian. Avocations: baseball, golf, squash, book collecting, politics. Office: McGuireWoods LLP World Trade Ctr Ste 9000 101 W Main St Norfolk VA 23510-1655 Office Phone: 757-640-3779. Office Fax: 757-640-3968. Business E-Mail: jpadgett@mcguirewoods.com.

PADGETT, NANCY WEEKS, retired law librarian, lawyer, consultant; b. Newberry, SC, June 3, 1932; d. Price John and Caroline (Weeks) P.; m. David Lazar, Aug. 6, 1953 (dec. May 19, 2002). BS, Northwestern U., 1953; MLS, U. Md., 1972; JD, Georgetown U., 1977. Bar: D.C. 1977. Asst. law libr. U.S. Ct. Appeals for D.C., Washington, 1972—74, supervisory law libr., 1974—84, circuit libr., 1984—. Mem. ALA, D.C. Bar Assn., Am. Assn. Law Librs. Home: 5301 Duvall Dr Bethesda MD 20816-1873 Office Phone: 202-216-7400.

PADIAN, NANCY, medical educator, epidemiologist; BA cum laude, Colgate U., 1974; MS in Reading Edn., Syracuse U., 1974; MPH, U. Calif., Berkeley, 1983, PhD in Epidemiology, 1987. Co-founder UZ-U. Calif. San Francisco Collaborative Rsch. Programme Women's Health, Zimbabwe, 1994; founder Women's Global Health Imperative, 2001; assoc. dir. rsch. U. Calif. San Francisco Global Health Scis., 2004; dir. AIDS Rsch. Inst. U. Calif. San Francisco; with Ob.-gyn. dept. U. Calif. San Francisco, co-dir. Ctr. Reproductive Health Rsch. and Policy, internat. expert heterosexual transmission HIV and other sexually transmitted infections, prof. dept. Ob.gyn. and reproductive scis., 2005—; with epidemiology dept. U. Calif. Berkeley. Mem.: Inst. Medicine. Achievements include research in developing and evaluating female-controlled methods for disease prevention, such as the diaphram and microbicides, along with alternative strategies for fostering young women's economic independence; thus reducing their susceptibility to HIV, STIs, and unwanted pregnancies.

PADILLA, ALFREDO, state agency administrator; Commr. PR Bur. Fin. Insts., San Juan, 2002—. Office: Office of Commr Financial Instns Fernandez Juncos Sta PO Box 11855 San Juan PR 00910-3855 Office Phone: 787-723-8004. Office Fax: 787-723-4042. E-mail: comisionado@ocif.gobierno.pr.

PADILLA, CHRISTOPHER ALAN, federal agency administrator; b. Kans. City, Mo. BA, Johns Hopkins U., 1986, MA, 1987. Various positions network systems divsn. AT&T, 1987—90, fed. govt. affairs dir. Washington, 1990—96; v.p. internat. pub. affairs Lucent Technologies, 1996—97; dir. internat. trade rels. Eastman Kodak Co., 1997—2002; asst. US trade rep. for intergovernmental affairs, pub. liaison Exec. Office of Pres., Washington, 2002—05; sr. advisor and deputy chief of staff US Dept. State, Washington, 2005—06; asst. sec. for export adminstrn. US Dept. Commerce, Washington, 2006—. Chmn. Bus. Coalition Export Reform, 1993—94; comm. dir., spokesman Bus. Coalition for U.S.-China Trade, 2000, USTrade, 2001—02. Office: US Dept Commerce Herbert Clark Hoover Bldg 14th St and Constitution Ave NW Rm 3888C Washington DC 20230 Office Phone: 202-482-5491. Office Fax: 202-482-3911.

PADILLA, IRENE, library director; b. Md. MPA, George Mason; MLS, Western Mich. U. Circulation supr. Prince William County Pub. Libr., Va., br. mgr. Va., pub. svc. adminstr, Va.; dep. dir. Hartford County Pub. Libr., Md., 1990—94, dir. Md., 1994; asst. state supt. Libr. Devel. and Services, Md. State Dept. Edn., Balt., 2002—. Chair Sailor Governance Bd., State Libr. Network Coordinating Coun. Mem.: Md. Libr. Assn. (pres. 1998—99), Chief Officers of State Libr. Agencies. Office: Md State Dept Edn 200 W Baltimore St Baltimore MD 21207 *

PADILLA, JAMES JEROME (JIM PADILLA), retired automotive executive; b. Detroit, June 13, 1946; s. David J. and Irene C. (Clos) P.; m. Alice M., Dec. 27, 1968; children: James Jr., Kathryn, Daniel. BSChemE, MS in Engring., U. Detroit, 1969, MA in Econ., 1970. Fuel econ. planning mgr. Ford Motor Co., Dearborn, Mich., 1977-78, engine planning engring. mgr. Detroit, 1979-80, engine controls dept. mgr., 1980-83, exec. engr., powertrain-electronics, 1983-85, chief engr., trim-chassis-elect-emissions, 1985, programs operations mgr., 1990, dir., small cars unit, 1991, exec. dir., engring. and mfg., Jaguar Cars, Ltd., 1992—94, dir., performance luxury vehicle lines, 1994—96, pres., Argentina and Brazil operations, 1996—98, pres. S. Am. operations, group v.p., mfg. and quality, 1999—2001, group v.p., N. Am., 2001—02, exec. v.p. Detroit, 2002, pres. Americas, 2002—04, pres., COO, 2004—06, chmn. worldwide automotive operations, 2004—06. Spl. asst to sec., US Dept. Commerce, 1978-79; bd. dirs. Am. Supplier Inst., Dearborn. Pres. Civic Assn., Canton, Mich., 1972-74, Plymouth (Mich.) Sch. Bd., 1981-84; mem. Plymouth Parish Council, 1980-84, Plymouth Edn. Commn., 1980-85. Served to 2d Lt. USNG, 1970-76. White House fellow U.S. Govt., Washington, 1978-79, fellow, Nat. Acad. Engring., 2001-; rsch. grantee Dow Chem. Co., Detroit, 1968-69; recipient Engr. of the Year, Hispanic Engr. Nat. Achievement Awards Conf., 2000, Ohtli medal from Mexican President Vincente Fox, 2004; named one of 50 Most Important Hispanics in Tech. & Bus., Hispanic Engr. & Info. Tech. mag., 2005. Mem. Soc. Automotive Engrs., Engring. Soc. Detroit. (selection com. U.S. Senate fellows 1982-84, named Outstanding Young Engr. 1980). Roman Catholic.

PADILLA, MARIO RENÉ, literature educator, writer; b. Detroit, Oct. 4, 1949; s. Marcelino Ramos and Nina Consolata (Macioce) P.; children: Francesca, Miguel, Marcello, Gabriella; m. Christine Jasiorkowski; stepchildren: Trevor, Laura. BS, Ohio State U., 1971; MA, Loyola Marymount U., 1987; PhD, U. So. Calif., 1993. Prodn. supr. CBS TV, LA, 1972-78; actor LA, 1980—; prof. English lit. and creative writing, Latin Am. lit. Santa Monica (Calif.) Coll., 1994—. Author: Reaching Back for the Neverendings, 1993, Borges, Faulkner, Hemingway: Young Poets of Prose, 1993 (Fulbright award 1993); composer (ballet) The Harbinger of Evolution, 1980 (ASCAP award 1981), (song) I Found Love, (musical) Hercules on Normandie, 2006, and numerous other songs and ballets; actor including Mario on Falcon Crest, 1981-83, Jimmy Rivera on Hunter, 1991-92, officer Lopez in General Hosp., 2000, Dragnet, 2003 (films) Losin' It, 1983, Star Trek III, 1984. Capt. U.S. Army, 1971-72. Mem. ASCAP, MLA, Screen Actors Guild, Am. Fedn. TV Radio Artists, Actor's Equity. Avocations: Karate, soccer, basketball, coaching children's sports, yoga. Home: 1211 Vienna Way Venice CA 90291-4026 Office Phone: 310-434-4064. Personal E-mail: Padilla_mario@smc.edu.

PADLAN, EDUARDO AGUSTIN, retired immunologist; b. Manila, Philippines, Aug. 31, 1940; s. Feliciano Macaraeg Padlan and Aida Almeda Agustin; m. Rosemarie Dino, Dec. 10, 1960; children: Josefina Padlan Simpson, Ramon Eduardo, Cristina Padlan Packard, Anna Maria, Cecilia Padlan Mikita. BS, U. of the Philippines, Diliman, Quezon City, 1960; PhD, Johns Hopkins U., Balt., 1968. Asst. prof. U. The Philippines, Quezon City, Philippines, 1968—69, adj. prof., 2002—; rsch. scientist Johns Hopkins U., Balt., 1978—83, rsch. assoc., 1969—71; vis. scientist NIH, Bethesda, Md., 1971—78, rsch. physicist, 1983—2000. Editor: ImmunoMethods vol. 1 no. 2, 1992; co-editor: Current Opinion in Biotechnology vol. 8, 1997; mem. editl. bd.: Molecular Immunology, 1980—99, Receptor, 1990—96, Macromolecular Structures, 1993—97; author: (book) Antibody-Antigen Complexes, 1994, more than 130 sci. pubs. Mem.: Am. Soc. for Biochemistry and Molecular Biology, Am. Assn. Immunologists, Philippine Am. Acad. Sci. and Engring., Nat. Acad. Sci. and Tech. Philippines (corr.). Achievements include patents in field; patents pending in field. Home: 4006 Simms Dr Kensington MD 20895 Office: Univ of the Philippines Velasquez St Diliman Quezon City 1101 Philippines Home Phone: 301-933-2660. Personal E-mail: edpadlan@aol.com. Business E-Mail: epadlan@upmsi.ph.

PADMANABHAN, ANAND, information technology executive; BS in Engring., Madras U., India, 1989; MS, La. State U., 2002. Ednl. technologist, programmer Ctr. Ednl. Techs. NASA, Wheeling, W.Va., 1992—96; exec. dir. info. techs. Seton Hill U., Greensburg, 1996—98; chief info. officer, dir. Tenn. State U., Nashville, 1998—2000; chief info. officer Hunter Coll. CUNY, NYC, 2000—, v.p. Hunter Coll., 2000—06; chief info. officer NYU Stern Sch. Bus., NYC, 2006—. Contbr. articles to profl. jours. Mem.: IEEE, Soc. for Info. Mgmt., Assn. for Computing Machinery. Avocations: tennis, photography. Office: NYU Stern Sch Bus 44 W 4th St New York NY 10012 Business E-Mail: anand@stern.nyu.edu.

PADNICK, JENNIFER C., lawyer; b. NYC, Jan. 29, 1972; BA in Polit. Sci., U. Ill., 1994; JD, Bklyn. Law Sch., 1997. Bar: NY 1998. Assoc. J.P. Morgan; assoc. atty. Cohen & Perfetto, L.L.P., NYC, founding ptnr. Office: Cohen & Perfetto LLP 444 Madison Ave 5th Fl New York NY 10022 Office Phone: 212-488-1303. Office Fax: 212-813-0767. E-mail: jpadnick@cpllplaw.com. *

PADOS, DIMITRIS A., electrical engineer, educator; b. Athens, Greece, Oct. 22, 1966; arrived in US, 1990, naturalized, 2006; s. Alexandros D. Pados and Anna E. Androvitsanea; m. Stella N. Batalama, Dec. 28, 1994; 1 child, Artemis Anna. BSc in Computer Sci. and Engring., U. Patras, Greece, 1989; PhD in Elec. Engring., U. Va., 1994. Asst. prof. U. La., Laffayette, 1994—97; prof. SUNY, Buffalo, 1997—. Rschr. Rsch. Found. SUNY, Buffalo. Contbr. articles to profl. jours. Recipient Internat. Conf. Telecom. Best Paper award, IEEE, 2001, Transactions Neural Networks Outstanding Paper award, 2003. Achievements include patents for circuitry and method for demodulating code division multiple access (CDMA) signals. Office: SUNY Dept Elec Engring 332 Bonner Hall Buffalo NY 14260 Home Phone: 716-741-4329; Office Phone: 716-645-3115 ext. 2134. Office Fax: 716-645-3656. Personal E-mail: dimitrisapados@aol.com. Business E-Mail: pados@eng.buffalo.edu.

PADOVANI, ROBERTO, communications executive; Degree, U. Padova, Italy; MS in Elec. and Computer Engring., PhD in Elec. and Computer Engring., U. Mass. With M/A-COM Linkabit, 1984—86; from mem. staff to exec. v.p., chief tech. officer QUALCOMM Inc., San Diego, 1986—2002, exec. v.p., 2002—, chief tech. officer, 2002—. Contbr. articles to profl. jours. Mem.: NAE, IEEE (Best Paper award 1991). Achievements include holds over 50 patents on wireless CDMA systems. Office: QUALCOMM Inc 5775 Morehouse Dr San Diego CA 92121

PADOVANO, ANTHONY JOHN, fine arts educator, artist; b. Bklyn., July 19, 1933; s. Pasquale Anthony and Teresa (Pignataro) P.; m. Margaret Padovano, June 6, 1973 (div. 1981); children: Lea, Nicole, Roberto; m. Gerarda Santina Declement, Sept. 15, 1986; children: Francesca, Gina. BFA, Columbia U., 1957; MA, CUNY, 1980. Instr. U. Conn., Storrs, 1962-64; asst. prof. Columbia U., NYC, 1964-71, Sarah Lawrence Coll., Bronxville, 1972-79; assoc. prof. Kingsborough Community Coll., Bklyn., 1983—. Tchr. U. Conn., Storrs, 1962-64, Columbia U., N.Y.C., 1964-70,

Queens Coll., N.Y., 1971-73, Sarah Lawrence Coll., 1974-78, Lacoste, France, summers 1976-78, Kingsborough Coll., 1978-, Parsons Sch. Design, 1978-82, Art Students League, summers 1983, 84; Fulbright fellowship judge UN, N.Y.C., 2001, 02, 03. One-man shows include Lincoln Meml. Gallery, 1954, Columbia U., 1957, Sculptors Studio, 1958, George Lester Gallery, 1962, Ruth White Gallery, 1962, Richard Feigen Gallery, 1964, U. Conn., 1964, Columbia U., 1965, Bertha Schaefer Gallery, 1968, Galerie Simmons Stern, 1968, Graham Gallery, 1972, 75, 79, 81, 82, I.F.A. Gallery, 1976, Alwin Gallery, 1978, Vorpal Gallery, 1986, 88, 90; exhbns. in group shows at Herron Mus. of Art, 1966, Newark Mus., 1969, Inst. Arts and Letters, 1976, Bard Coll, 1979; permanent collections, Newark Mus., Herron Gallery (Ind.), Storm King Art Ctr., Whitney Mus. Am. Art; author: The Process of Sculpture, 1981. Mem.: Audubon Artists (pres. 2002—). Office: Kingsborough CC 2001 Oriental Blvd Brooklyn NY 11235-2333

PADOVANO, ANTHONY THOMAS, theologian, literature educator; b. Harrison, NJ, Sept. 18, 1934; s. Thomas Henry and Mary Rose (Cierzo) P.; m. Theresa Lackamp, 1974; children— Mark, Andrew, Paul, Rosemarie BA magna cum laude, Seton Hall U., 1956; S.T.B. magna cum laude, Pontifical Gregorian U., Rome, Italy, 1958, S.T.L. magna cum laude, 1960, S.T.D. magna cum laude, 1962; Ph.L. magna cum laude, St. Thomas Pontifical Internat. U., Rome, 1962; MA, NYU, 1971; PhD, Fordham U., 1980. Ordained priest Roman Cath. Ch., 1959. Asst. chaplain Med. Center, Jersey City, 1960; asst. St. Paul of the Cross Ch., Jersey City, 1962, St. Catharine Ch., Glen Rock, NJ, 1963; prof. systematic theology Darlington Sem., Mahwah, NJ, 1962-74; founding faculty mem., prof. lit. and philosophy Ramapo Coll., NJ, 1971—; prof. theology, religious studies Fordham U., 1973-93. Mem. Archdiocesan Commn. Ecumenical and Interreligious Affairs, 1965, Commn. Instrn. Clergy in Documents Vatican II, 1966; del. dialogue group Luth.-Roman Cath. Theol. Conversations, 1969; del.-at-large senate of priests Archdiocese of Newark; Danforth assoc., 1975—; Cath. pastor Inclusive Cmty. World Coun. Chs., 1986—; lectr. in field, also appearances on radio and TV; parish min. St. Margaret of Scotland, Morristown, NJ. Author: The Cross of Christ, the Measure of the World, 1962, The Estranged God, 1966, Who is Christ, 1967, Belief in Human Life, 1969, American Culture and the Quest for Christ, 1970, Dawn Without Darkness, 1971, Free to be Faithful, 1972, Eden and Easter, 1974, A Case for Worship, 1975, America: Its People, Its Promise, 1975, Presence and Structure, 1975, The Human Journey, 1982, Trilogy, 1982, Contemplation and Compassion, 1984, Winter Rain: A Play, 1985, His Name is John: A Play, 1986, Christmas to Calvary, 1987, Love and Destiny, 1987, Summer Lightening: A Play, 1988, Conscience and Conflict, 1989, Reform and Renewal, 1990, A Celebration of Life, 1990, The Church Today: Belonging and Believing, 1990, Scripture in the Streets, 1992, A Retreat with Thomas Merton, 1996, Hope is a Dialogue, 1998, Resistance and Renewal, 2002, Life Choices, 2004; editor: Centenary Issue Roman Echoes, 1959; editl. bd. The Advocate, 1966-73; contbr. articles to mags., Padovano Papers, personal and profl. papers, Archives, U. Notre Dame. With Diocese Paterson Ecumenical Commn.; founding pres. Justice and Peace Commn., Diocese of Paterson, active Resigned Priests Com. Mem. Cath. Theol. Soc. Am., Mariological Soc. Am., Nat. Fedn. Priests Couns. (ofcl. rep. to Constl. Conv., Chgo. 1968), Corpus (pres.), Fedn. Christian Ministries, Internat. Fedn. of Married Cath. Priests (v.p. for N.Am.), North Atlantic Fedn. for Renewal Cath. Priesthood (bd. dirs.). Home: 9 Millstone Dr Morris Plains NJ 07950-1536 Office: Sch of Am Internat Studies Ramapo Coll NJ Mahwah NJ 07430 Personal E-mail: tpadovan@optonline.net. *People rather than ideas have been most formative in my life. More accurately, people, as they embodied certain ideas have proved most decisive. There is nothing more persuasive than an idea which becomes so vital that it transforms the person who proclaims it.*

PADRNOS, DIANE E., language arts educator; b. Britton, SD, July 9, 1942; d. Harry L. and Helen J. Nelson; m. Dennis R. Padrnos, Sept. 2, 1967; children: Michael, Beth, Lara. BS in Edn., No. State U., Aberdeen, SD, 1964. Cert. S.D. Dept. Edn. Instr. bus./drama Sisseton (S.D.) Sch. Dist., 1964—65; press aide Sen. George McGovern, Washington, 1965—67, field rep. Mitchell, SD, 1967—69; counselor adult edn. Dakota Wesleyan U., Mitchell, 1977—80, dir. career planning/placement, 1980—88; real estate salesperson Century 21, Mitchell, 1988—95; instr. lang. arts Mitchell Sr. HS, 1993—. Comty. vol. Mitchell C. of C.; active Heart Dr., MD Dr., Cancer Dr.; chair bd. dirs. Enchanted World Doll Mus., Mitchell; chair Corn Palace Devel. Com., Mitchell; mem. steering com. Mitchell Area Comty. Theatre; chairperson Oscar Howe Adv. Bd., Mitchell. Recipient S.D. Jr. C. of C. Person of Yr. award, 1973, Person of Yr. award, Beta Sigma Phi, 1973. Republican. Roman Catholic. Avocations: reading, travel. Home: 340 W McCabe Mitchell SD 57301

PADRON, D. LORENZO, state agency administrator; B in Mgmt., U. Ill., Chgo. Positions in comml. and internat. divsns. First Nat. Bank Chgo.; asst. v.p. Banco Popular; sr. v.p. Met. Bank, Chgo.; owner Nat. Facility and Supply Co./Chgo. Contract Cleaning and Supply Co., 1998—2001; dir. divsn. banking Ill. Office Fin. and Profl. Regulation, 2003—. Bd. dirs. Latin Am. C. of C., chmn. emeritus. Office: Ill Office Fin and Profl Regulation Divsn Banking 122 S Michigan Ave Ste 1900 Chicago IL 60603 Office Phone: 312-793-3000.

PADRÓN, LUIJE, writer; b. Caracas, Venezuela, Sept. 7, 1978; s. Luis Esteban Padrón and Simonette Sánchez, Peter Cherepanov (Stepfather); life ptnr. Alfonso Bustillo. Grad. Info. Sys. Engring., Ctrl. Technol. U., Valencia, Venezuela, 2001, MBA in Bus. Adminstrn. and Mktg., 2001. Project mgr. GM, Valencia, 1999—2000; crm mktg. cons. Procter and Gamble, Caracas, 2000—01; art dir. Grey Worldwide, WING Latino Group, NYC, 2001—03; creative dir. Ogilvy Puerto Rico, DLC, San Juan, 2003—05; assoc. creative dir. JMD Comm., San Juan, 2005—; pres., CEO Luije Creative Svcs., San Juan, 2006—. Author: (comic books) Patriot Factor, Vinculum: The Ties That Bind, (short story) Cuentos Más Allá de la Oscura Realidad; editor: (annual editl.) Sunrise (Editor Yr., 1995); author: (novel) Gatitos (Young Writers award, 2000); contbr. advertising campaign. Hon. mem. Rotary Club, Miami Lakes, Fla., 1994—96; mem. Young Republicans Am., Miami, 1993—95; capt. NY Spirit Project, NYC, 2001—02; pres. Interact, Miami, Fla., 1995—96. Recipient All-Am., Nat. Cheerleaders Am., 1995, 1996. R-Liberal. Christian. Avocations: swimming, water polo, competitive cheerleading, running. Office: Luije Creative Svcs PO Box 29005 San Juan PR 00929-0005 Home Phone: 939-717-1177; Office Phone: 939-717-1177. Personal E-mail: luije10@gmail.com.

PADULA, FRED DAVID, filmmaker; b. Santa Barbara, Calif., Oct. 25, 1937; s. Fred and Mary (Adams) P.; married; 1 child. BA in Music, San Francisco State U., MA in Art, 1965. Adj. faculty U. Calif., San Francisco Art Inst., San Francisco State U.; artist-in-residence U. Minn., Mpls. Filmmaker: Ephesus, 1965 (1st pl. award San Francisco Internat. Film Festival, awards N.Y. Film Festival, Chgo. Internat. Film Festival, others), The Artist Speaks, Two Photographers: Wynn Bullock and Imogen Cunningham, Little Jesus (Hippy Hill), Anthology of Boats, David and My Porch, Salmon River Run, El Capitan (awards: Grand Prize Festival Internat. de Film D'Aventure Uecue, La Plagne, France, Grand Prize Film Festival Internat. Montagna Esplorazione, Trento, Italy, Grand Prize Banff Festival of Mountain Films, Can., Grand Prize Mountain Film, Telluride, Colo., Gold medal Festival Internat. du Film Alpine, Les Diablerets, Switzerland; electronic music compositions include: Barking Dogs, Charnet Loops, others; one-man shows (photography) include San Francisco Internat. Airport, San Francisco Mus. Modern Art, Kalamazoo Inst. Arts, DeYoung Mus., San Francisco, San Fernando Valley State Coll., Bakersfield Coll., Wash. State U., West Chester Coll., Valhalla, NY, George Eastman House; represented in permanent collections, Kalamazoo Inst. Arts, State of Calif., George Eastman House, San Francisco Internat. Airport, Crocker Art Mus., Oakland Mus. Art, 1004 Gallery, Port Towsend, Wash., New Horizons Nat. Bank Hdqs., San Rafael, Calif., SUNY/Westchester CC, Valhalla, NY, Grace Mus., Abilene, Tex. Address: PO Box 254 Mill Valley CA 94941-1551

PADULA, STEPHEN JOSEPH, lawyer; b. Chgo., June 20, 1970; m. Alexandra Ocampo, Aug. 1, 1998; children: Anthony, William. JD, U. Miami, Coral Gables, Fla., 1999. Atty. The Hodkin Kopelowitz Ostrow Firm, PA, Ft. Lauderdale, Fla., 1993—. Office: The Hodkin Kopelowitz Ostrow Firm PA 350 E Las Olas Blvd Ste 980 Fort Lauderdale FL 33301 Home Phone: 561-998-0829; Office Phone: 954-525-4100. Office Fax: 954-525-4300. Business E-Mail: padula@thkolaw.com.

PADULO, LOUIS, university administrator; b. Athens, Ala., Dec. 14, 1936; s. Louis and Helen (Yarbrough) P.; m. Katharine Seamans, Jan. 28, 1963; children: Robert, Joseph. BSEE, Fairleigh Dickinson U., 1959; MSEE, Stanford U., 1962; PhD, Ga. Inst. Tech., 1966. Engr. design and devel. Radio Corp. Am., 1959-60; asst. prof. elec. engring. San Jose State Coll., 1962-63; asst. prof. math. Ga. State U., 1966-67; assoc. prof. Columbia U., summer 1969, Harvard U., summer 1970; asst. prof. Morehouse Coll., 1967-68, assoc. prof., chmn. dept. math., 1968-71; dir. exchange student program Stanford U., 1969-71, assoc. prof. elec. engring., 1971-75, assoc. prof. math., summers 1971-75, dir. MITE program, 1975; prof. elec. engring. and math., dean Coll. Engring. Boston U., 1975-88, assoc. v.p., 1986-87; pres. U. Ala., Huntsville, 1988-90; pres., chief exec. officer Univ. City Sci. Ctr., Phila., 1991-96, pres. emeritus, 1997—; chmn. Invictus, Phila., 1997—. Vis. assoc. prof. Stanford U., 1969-71; vis. prof. U. Tokyo, 1986-88, MIT, 1987-88, 90-91; vis. prof. mgmt. ENPC, France, 2002-, Reims Mgmt. Sch., 2001-, Fairleigh Dickinson U., 2002—, U. Pa., 2004-, Drexel U., 2005-; adj. prof. Wharton, U. Pa., 2005—; program dir. Inst. on Computers, Logic and Automata Theory, NSF, 1969; founder, dir. dual degree program Atlanta U. Ctr. and Ga. Inst. Tech., 1968-70; numerical analyst Airesearch Corp., L.A., 1969; vis. scientist MIT, 1990-91; bd. dirs. Nemawashi, Inc., Carver Fund, Tapelicator, Inc., Ovation Products, Inc., Knite, Inc., Atlantis Components, Inc., Light Media, Inc., Nucycle, Inc., Genpathways, Inc., Workwell, Inc., Art Insts. Internat. Author: System Theory, 1973, Minorities in Engineering, 1974; mem. editl. adv. bd. the Scientist, DiSyCom-Digital Sys. and Comm.; contbr. chpts. to books. Pres. Valley Found., Huntsville, Ala., 1988-89, Ala. Engring. Found., Huntsville, 1989, Consortium Advancement Affordable Distance Edn., 1997—; mem. task force Vision 2000, Huntsville, 1989; bd. dirs. North Ala. Intenat. Trade Assn., 1989, Ala. Supercomputer Network, 1989, Vision 2000, Am. Poetry ctr., 1992, Benjamin Franklin Tech. Ctr., 1991-97; pres. Higher Edn. Congress, 1992-2000; bd. dirs. U.S. Japan Soc., 1990—; adv. com. United Negro Coll. Fund; trustee Fairleigh Dickinson U., 1989—, Presbyn. Found. Phila., 1993-2002, Phila. Fund for Edn., 1995-2001, Internat. House; vis. com. sch. engring. Tuskegee U., Coll. Engring. Drexel U., 1993-2004; mem. Huntsville Army Cmty. Rels. Com.; bd. vis. sch. bus. Temple U., 1993-. Recipient Excellence in Sci. and Engring. Edn. award Nat. Consortium for Black Profl. Devel., 1977, Reginald H. Jones Disting. Svc. award GE Found. and Nat. Action Coun. Minorities in Engring., 1983. Fellow IEEE, Am. Soc. Engring. Edn. (Western Electric Fund Excellence in Tchg. award 1973, Vincent Bendix award 1984, U.S. Interactive fellow 1997); mem. AAAS, ACM, Mass. Engrs. Coun., Math. Assn. Am., Union League of Phila. (life), NAACP (life), Penn Club (life). Office: Invictus 2020 Walnut St Apt 32A Philadelphia PA 19103-5645 Fax: 215-243-8345. E-mail: padulo@verizon.net.

PAESLER, MICHAEL, physics professor, department chairman; PhD, U. Chgo., 1975. Guest scientist Max-Planck-Inst. Festkörperforschung, Stuttgart, Germany, 1975—76; postdoctoral rsch. fellow Harvard U., Cambridge, Mass., 1977—80; asst. prof. dept. physics NC State U., Raleigh, 1980—85, assoc. prof., 1985—90, prof., 1997—, head dept. physics, 2005—. Guest prof. Philipps U., Marburg, Germany, 1985, U. Franche Comté, Besançon, France, 1993, Tech. U. Dresden, Germany, 1996. Fellow, Am. Phys. Soc., 1997. Office: Physics Dept NC State U Raleigh NC 27695-8202 Office Phone: 919-515-2522. Business E-Mail: paesler@ncsu.edu.

PAEZ, RICHARD A., federal judge; b. 1947; BA, Brigham Young U., 1969; JD, U. Calif., Berkeley, 1972. Staff atty. Calif. Rural Legal Assistance, Delano, Calif., 1972—74, Western Ctr. on Law and Poverty, 1974—76; sr. counsel Legal Aid Found. of LA, 1976—78, dir. litigation, 1978—79, act. exec. dir., 1980—81; judge LA Mcpl. Ct., 1981—94, superior ct, Los Angeles, 1993—94, US Dist. Ct. (ctrl. dist.) Calif., LA, 1994—2000, US Dist. Ct. (9th cir.), Pasadena, Calif., 2000—. Active Hollywood-Los Feliz Jewish Cmty. Ctr. Mem.: Calif. Jud. Coun., Mex.-Am. Bar Assn. LA County, LA County Bar Assn., Calif. State Bar Assn. Office: US Ct Appeals Richard H Chambers US Courthouse 125 S Grand Ave Rm 204 Pasadena CA 91105-1652 *

PAGÁN, GILBERTO, JR., psychologist; b. San Juan, Dec. 30, 1950; Exch. student, SUNY, Albany, 1969-70; BA in Psychology magna cum laude, U. P.R., 1972; MS in Devel. Psychology, Rutgers U., 1974, PhD in Clin. Psychology, 1984. Lic. psychologist, N.J.; cert. sch. psychology. Psychometrician Well Baby Clinic of New Brunswick, N.J., 1972-73; staff psychologist Community Orgn. for Mental Health and Retardation, Inc., Phila., 1976-77; intern in clin. psychology Multimodal Therapy Inst., Kingston, NJ, 1979-80; sch. psychologist New Brunswick Pub. Sch. System, 1980-83; mental health clinician Community Mental Health Ctr. U. Medicine and Dentistry N.J., Piscataway, 1983-93; sch. psychologist Perth Amboy Pub. Sch. Sys., 1993-95; pvt. practice clin. psychology Newark, 1988—; sch. psychologist Jersey City Pub. Sch. Sys., 1995-98, Elizabeth (N.J.) Pub. Sch. Sys., 1998—. Assoc. in psychiatry Univ. of Medicine and Dentistry of N.J., Piscataway, 1988-98; field supr. Rutgers U., New Brunswick, N.J., 1988—; cons. in field to clients including Bloomfield Pub. Sch. System, Div. of Youth and Family Svcs. of State of N.J., Project Head Start, Plainfield, N.J. Columnist San Juan Star, 1990-93, 97-98, El Hispano, Phila., 1977-78; contbr. profl. publs.; presenter in field. Pres. N.J. chpt. Nat. Com. for Puerto Rican Statehood, 1990-95; mem. U.S. Coun. for Puerto Rico Statehood, 2004-. NIMH fellow, 1978-79; predoctoral rsch. fellow Inst. for Rsch. in Human Devel., Divsn. Psychol. Studies of Ednl. Testing Svc., Princeton, N.J., 1974-75; recipient P.R. Psychol. Assn. award, 1972, Puerto Rican Action Bds. Parents Assn. award 1985; inducted into Nat. Honor Soc. in Psychology, 1973. Mem. APA, NEA, N.J. Edn. Assn., N.J. Psychol. Assn., Elizabeth Edn. Assn. Democrat. Roman Catholic. Avocation: swimming. Office: 467 Mount Prospect Ave Newark NJ 07104-2907 Home Phone: 732-324-2322; Office Phone: 973-483-0448.

PAGAN, JOHN RUSTON, law educator; b. Little Rock, Aug. 4, 1951; s. John Frank and Betty (Hardin) P. BA, Coll. of William and Mary, 1973; MLitt, Oxford U., 1975; JD, Harvard U., 1978; DPhil, Oxford U., 1997. Bar: Ark. 1979, Va. 1982, D.C. 1984, N.Y. 1996. Clk. hon. Ozell M. Trask US Ct. of Appeals (9th cir.), Phoenix & San Francisco, 1978—79; from asst. to assoc. prof. Marshall-Whyte Sch. of Law Coll. of William and Mary, Williamsburg, Va., 1979-84; assoc. prof. Sch. of Law U. Ark., Little Rock, 1984-86, prof. Sch. of Law, 1986-95; global prof., dir. (global law sch. prog.) NYU, 1996—97; dean, prof. of law U. Richmond Sch Law, Richmond, Va., 1997—2003, prof., 2003—. Contbr. articles to profl. jours. Ark. state senator, Little Rock, 1991-92; legislator Pulaski County Quorum Ct., Little Rock, 1987-90. Mem. Assn. of Marshall Scholars, Phi Beta Kappa. Democrat. Avocation: historical research. Office: U Richmond Sch Law 28 Westhampton Way Rm 216 Richmond VA 23173 Office Phone: 804-289-8188. Office Fax: 804-289-8683.

PAGAN, KEITH AREATUS, music educator, academic administrator; b. Beggs, Okla., June 7, 1931; s. Areatus and Opal Gail (Facker) P.; m. Betty Lois Wallace; children: Melva Joy, Lisa Lynne, Beryl Kay. B in Music Edn., Bethany Nazarene Coll., 1952; M in Music Edn., Okla. U., 1953; D in Music Edn. with honors, Ind. U., 1970. Asst. prof. music Bethany (Okla.) Nazarene Coll., 1952-53, 55-58; prof. music Pasadena (Calif.) Coll., 1961-76; acad. dean, v.p. acad. affairs Point Loma Nazarene Coll., San Diego, 1976-88, prof. music, chair dept. music., 1989—98. Cons. Sch. for Creative and Performing Arts, San Diego, 1990-99, Chula Vista, Calif., 1992-94; dir. S.W. Music Symposium, San Diego, 1991-; mem. vis. team Western Coll. Assn., Calif., 1977-82. Arranger (choral) To God be the Glory, (brass) Keith A. Pagan Brass Quintet Series, The King Shall Come; mem. editl. bd. Christian Scholars Rev., 1986-2006, EverGreen Morning Music Press. Trustee Christian Scholars Rev., 1994-2006; dir. music Village Ch., Rancho Santa Fe, Calif.; v.p. Calif. Higher Edn. Assn., 1970-71. With U.S. Army, 1953-55. Recipient WHO award Calif. Higher Edn. Assn., 1971, Lawrence Vredevoe Disting. Leadership award 1986, Spl. Svc. to Music award Calif. Music Educators Assn., 1991; winner 4th ann. anthem contest Choral Condrs. Guild; grantee Danforth Found., 1960. Mem. Calif. Coll. and Univ. Faculty Assn. (state pres. 1969-70), Music Tchrs. Assn. Calif. (parliamentarian 1971-73), Western Assn. Schs. and Coll. (accreditation liaison 1976-88). Avocations: travel, photography. Home: 5875 Friars Rd #4316 San Diego CA 92110 Personal E-mail: keithapagan@earthlink.net.

PAGANELLI, CHARLES VICTOR, physiologist, educator; b. NYC, Feb. 13, 1929; s. Charles Victor and Mary Paganelli; m. Barbara Harriet Slauson, Sept. 18, 1954; children: William, Kathryn, Peter, Robert, John. AB, Hamilton Coll., Clinton, NY, 1950; MA, Harvard U., Cambridge, Mass., 1952, PhD, 1957. Instr. physiology U. Buffalo, 1958-60, asst. prof., 1960-63; assoc. prof. SUNY, Buffalo, 1963-71, prof. physiology, 1971-97, disting. svc. prof., 1997—. Interim chair SUNY, Buffalo, 1991-98, emeritus, 1998. Editor: Physiological Function in Special Environments, 1990; contbr. articles to profl. jours. Recipient Elliott Coues award Am. Ornithologists Union, 1981, Newman award 1998. Mem.: Am. Physiol. Soc., Gold Humanism Honor Soc., Phi Beta Kappa, Sigma Xi, Alpha Omega Alpha. Business E-Mail: cvp@buffalo.edu.

PAGANI, ALBERT LOUIS, aerospace system engineer; b. Jersey City, Feb. 19, 1936; s. Alexander C. and Anne (Salvati) P.; m. Beverly Cameron, Feb. 23, 1971; children: Penelope, Deborah, Michael. BSEE, U.S. Naval Acad., 1957; MBA, So. Ill. U., 1971. Commd. 2d lt. USAF, 1957, advanced through grades to col., 1978, navigator Lake Charles, La., 1957-63, pilot McGuire AFB, NJ, 1963-65, command pilot Anchorage, 1965-68, mgr. airlift Saigon, Vietnam, 1968-69, chief spl. missions Scott AFB, Ill., 1969-74; commd. tactical airlift group USAF Europe, Mildenhall, England, 1974-76, dep. comdr. Rhein Main Air Base Frankfurt, Germany, 1976-78; chief airlift mgmt. USAF Mil. Airlift Command, Scott AFB, Ill., 1978-81, dir. tech. plans and concepts, 1981, dir. command and control, 1982-85; ret., 1985; program mgr. Lockheed Missile and Space Co., Sunnyvale, Calif., 1985-94; dir. data applications, dir. adv. programs PAR Govt. Sys. Corp., New Hartford, NY, 1994-97; pres. Computer Solutions Group, NY, 1997—; prin. Beval Assocs., Inc., 1997—; CEO CSG, Canada, 1999—; dir. B-Net, NY, 1999—; prin., dir. Asset Trax, Inc., 2000—. V.p. Cath. Ch. Coun., Mildenhall, 1974, pres., 1975. Decorated Legion of Merit, Bronze Star, Air medal, Vietnam Cross of Gallantry. Mem. Nat. Def. Transp. Assn. (sr.), Soc. Logistics Engrs., Air Force Assn., Armed Forces Comm. and Electronics Assn., Air Lift Assn., Inst. Noetic Scis., Daedalions, Mensa. Avocations: woodworking, neurolinguistics, volunteer senior executive consulting. Home: 8592 Red Hill Rd Clinton NY 13323-4210 Business E-Mail: abpagani@bevalinc.com.

PAGANI, MARK, education educator, researcher; b. New York, NY, Mar. 29, 1960; s. Waldo and Bernice Pagani; life ptnr. Teresa Fields; children: Kyla Maria, Ruben Abraham. PhD, Pa. State U., 1998. Assoc. prof. Yale U., New Haven, Conn., 2002—. Achievements include research in paleoclimate. Office: Yale U 210 Whitney Ave New Haven CT 06520 Office Phone: 203-432-6275. E-mail: mark.pagani@yale.edu.

PAGANO, JO ANNE, education educator; b. Rochester, NY, Dec. 30, 1946; d. John Richard and Marlyn Margaret (Mull) P.; m. William Arnold Gietz, Sept. 30, 1977 (div. May 1983); m. Bruce Peter Berlind, Jan. 17, 1985. BA, U. Rochester, 1973, MS, 1980, PhD, 1982. Prof. edn. Colgate U., Hamilton, NY, 1981—. Co-author: Preparing Teachers as Professionals, 1989; author: Exiles and Communities, 1990; mem. editl. bd. Ednl. Theory, 1988-93; editor-in-chief JCT: Interdisciplinary Jour. Curriculum Studies, 1990—; contbr. articles to profl. jours., chpts. to books. Grantee Ford Found., 1986. Mem. Am. Ednl. Rsch. Assn., Philosophy of edn. Soc., Am. Ednl. Studies Assn. (exec. bd. dirs. 1994, exec. coun. 1993—), Profs. of Curriculum, Nat. Women's Studies Assn. Home: PO Box 237 Hamilton NY 13346-0237 Office: Colgate U Edn Dept 13 Oak Dr Hamilton NY 13346-1383 Home Phone: 315-894-7078; Office Phone: 315-228-7253. Business E-Mail: jpagano@mail.colgate.edu.

PAGANO, JOSEPH STEPHEN, internist, educator, researcher; b. Rochester, NY, Dec. 29, 1931; s. Angelo Pagano and Marian (Vinci) Signorino; children: Stephen Reynolds, Christopher Joseph. AB with honors, U. Rochester, 1953; MD, Yale U., 1957. Resident Peter Bent Brigham Hosp. Harvard U., Boston, 1960-61; fellow Karolinska Inst., Stockholm, 1961-62; mem. Wistar Inst., Phila., 1962-65; from asst. to assoc. prof. medicine & microbiology U. N.C., Chapel Hill, 1965-73, prof., 1974—, dir. divsn. infectious diseases, 1972-75; founder, dir. U. N.C. Lineberger Comprehensive Cancer Ctr., Chapel Hill, 1974-97, dir. emeritus, 1997—. Attending physician U. Hosps., Chapel Hill; vis. prof. Swiss Inst. Cancer Rsch., Lausanne, 1970-71, Lineberger prof. cancer rsch., 1986—; mem. virology study sect. NIH, Bethesda, Md., 1973-79; recombinant DNA adv. com. USPHS, 1986-90; bd. dirs. Burroughs Wellcome Fund, 1993-2001, Wachovia Bank, Chapel Hill/Durham/Cary; chmn., adv. com. N.C. Cancer Coord. and Control, 1993—2004; Mclaughlin vis. prof. U. Tex. Med. Br., 1996; Norma Berryhill Disting. lectr. U. N.C., 1997; Harry Eagle lectr. Albert Einstein Coll. Medicine, 1997; Harry F. Dowling lectr. U. Ill. Sch. Med., 1991; Gertrude & Werner Henle lectr. in viral oncology, 1990, Joseph and Ruth McCartney Hauck lectr. Mayo Clinic, 2002; Japan Soc. for Head and Neck Cancer lectr. Kanazawa U., 2003; cons. Franklin St. Ptnrs., Chapel Hill, 1998. Mem. editorial bd. Jour. Virology, Jour. Immunology, Cancer Rsch., Jour. Gen. Virology, Antimicrobial Agts. and Chemotherapy, 1974-93; contbr. articles to profl. jours., chpts. to books. Mem. awards assembly GM Cancer Rsch. Found., 1997-2001. Recipient USPHS Rsch. Career award NIH, 1968-73, N.C. award in sci., 1996. Mem. Inst. of Medicine, Am. Assn. Cancer Rsch., Am. Assn. Cancer Insts. (bd. dirs. 1992-99, pres., chmn.), Internat. Assn. for Rsch. in Epstein-Barr Virus (pres. 1990-94), Chapel Hill Tennis Club (pres. 1980-82), Carolina Club (bd. dirs. 2002—), Baldhead Island and Shoals Club. Episcopalian. Avocations: tennis, squash. Home: 114 Laurel Hill Rd Chapel Hill NC 27514-4323 Office: U NC CB7295 Lineberger Comp Cancer Ctr Chapel Hill NC 27599-0001

PAGE, ALAN C., state supreme court justice; b. Canton, Ohio, Aug. 7, 1945; s. Howard F. and Georgianna (Umbles) P.; m. Diane Sims, June 5, 1973; children: Nina, Georgianna, Justin, Khamsin. BA, U. Notre Dame, 1967; JD, U. Minn., 1978; LLD (hon), U. Notre Dame, 1993, St. John's U., 1994, Westfield State Coll., 1994, Luther Coll., 1995, U. New Haven, 1999; LHD (hon), Winston-Salem State U., 2000, Gustavus Adolphus Coll., 2003, U. Notre Dame, 2004. Bar: Minn. 1979, U.S. Dist. Ct. Minn. 1979, U.S. Supreme Ct. 1988. Profl. football player Minn. Vikings, Mpls., 1967-78, Chgo. Bears, 1978-81; assoc. Lindquist & Vennum, Mpls., 1979-85; special asst. atty. gen. employment law Minn. Atty. Gen.'s Office,

St. Paul, 1985—87, asst. atty. gen., 1987—93; assoc. justice Minn. Supreme Ct., St. Paul, 1993—. Cons. NFL Players Assn., Washington, 1979-84. Commentator Nat. Pub. Radio, 1982-83. Founder Page Edn. Found., 1988. Named NFL's Most Valuable Player, 1971, one of 10 Outstanding Young Men Am., U.S. Jaycees, 1981; named to NFL Hall of Fame, 1988, Coll. Football Hall of Fame, 1993, Internat. Scholar-Athlete Hall of Fame, 2002; named one of 50 Greatest Sports Figures from Ohio Sports Illustrated, 1999; recipient NCAA Theodore Roosevelt award, 2004, Disting. Am. award Nat. Football Found. and Coll. Hall Fame, 2005, Honoree Trumpet awards Found., 2007. Mem. ABA, Minn. Bar Assn., Nat. Bar Assn., Hennepin County Bar Assn., Minn. Assn. Black Lawyers, Am. Law Inst. Avocations: running, biking. Office: 423 Minnesota Judicial Ctr 25 Rev Dr Martin Luther King Jr Blvd Saint Paul MN 55155-1500

PAGE, ALBERT LEE, soil science educator, researcher; b. New Lenox, Ill., Mar. 19, 1927; m. Shirley L. Jessmore, Sept. 14, 1952; children: Nancy, Thomas. BA in Chemistry, U. Calif.-Riverside, 1956; PhD in Soil Sci., U. Calif.-Davis, 1960. Prof. soil sci. U. Calif.-Riverside, 1960—. Dir. Kearney Found., Univ. Calif.-Riverside, program of excellence in energy research Editor: Methods of Soil Analysis, 1983, Utilization of Municipal Wastewater and Sludge on Land, 1983, Heavy Metals in the Environment, 1977 With USN, 1944—52. Recipient Environ. Quality Research award Am. Soc. Agronomy, 1984, Disting. Teaching award U. Calif., Riverside, 1976, Disting. Svc. award USDA, 1991; Fullbright scholar, 1966-67; Guggenheim Meml. Found. fellow, 1966-67 Fellow AAAS, Am. Soc. Agronomy, Soil Sci. Soc. Am.; mem. Internat. Soil Sci. Soc., Western Soil Sci. Soc., Soc. Environ. Geochemistry and Health, Sigma Xi. Home: 5555 Canyon Crest Dr Apt 1F Riverside CA 92507-6443 Office: U Calif Dept Soil & Environ Sci Riverside CA 92521-0001 Home Phone: 951-682-1913; Office Phone: 951-827-3433. Business E-Mail: albert.page@ucr.edu.

PAGE, AMANDA LEE, secondary school educator; b. Jacksonville, Fla., June 13, 1979; d. Clark Neal and Ellen W. Page. BS, Fla. State U., Tallahassee, 2001. Cert. tchr. Fla., 2005. Biology tchr. Sandalwood HS, Jacksonville, 2003—, head coach varsity girls tennis, 2004—. Mem.: Duval Tchrs. United, Mensa.

PAGE, BARBARA ROSE, primary school educator; b. Piney River, Va., Sept. 21, 1940; d. Samuel C. and Tessie Morse Rose; m. Joseph Roland Sr. Page, Dec. 28, 1957 (dec.); children: Joseph Jr., Donna Gail, Janet Lee, Peyton Arthur, Jonathan Edwin. BA, Sweet Briar Coll., 1983. Cert. elem. tchr. Va. Sunday sch. tchr. St. James Bapt. Ch., Roseland, Va., 1958—95; tchr. Bethune Nursery Sch., Lynchburg, Va., 1983—84, Nelson County Pub. Schs., Lovingston, 1984—2000, tutor, 2000—. Vol. PTA, Nelson County, 1966—2000; musician Oak-Hill Bapt. Ch., Massie Mill, Va., 1958—72, Mt. Pleasant Sunday Sch. Conv., 1966—80, Mt. Olive Bapt. Ch., Amherst, Va., 1969—83; tchr. Sunday sch. and vacation Bible sch. Recipient Tchr. award, Monticello Area Cmty. Action Agy., 1989, Svc. award, Mahogany, Inc., 1990, St. James Bapt. Ch., 1998. Mem.: NAACP, Nelson County Hist. Soc., Habitat (bd. dir. 2003—05). Baptist. Avocations: piano, reading, writing, gardening.

PAGE, CHERYL MILLER, elementary school educator; BS in Social Sciences, Calif. Polytechnic State Univ., San Luis Obispo, Calif., 1975; MS in Ednl. Policy, Found. and Adminstrn., Portland State U., 2006. Cert. health edn. specialist Nat. Commn. for Health Edn. Credentialing, 1993, Edn. Certification Program Calif. Polytechnic State Univ., San Luis Obispo, Calif., 1976. Elem. educator The Dalles Pub. Schs., The Dalles, Oreg., 1980—86, Salem-Keizer Pub. Schs., Salem, Oreg., 1986—95, middle sch. health educator, 1995—2002, health educator; prevention curriculum resource specialist Salem-Keizer Pub. Schs. Mid Valley Partnership, prevention program assoc., 2006—. Named Oreg. Outstanding Elementary Health Educator, 1991, Oreg. Outstanding Secondary Health Educator of Yr., 1996, Vol. of Yr., Am. Cancer Soc., 1996; recipient Tambrands award, Am. Assn. Health Edn., 1996, Health and Safety Educator of Year, NW Divsn. AAHPERD, 1996. Mem.: Oreg. Alliance Health, Phys. Edn., Recreation and Dance (treas. 1992—96, pres. 2001—02), Oreg. Assn. for the Advancement of Health Edn. (sec./treas. 1990—92), Nat. Bd. for Profl. Tchg. Stds. (bd. mem.). Avocations: running, reading. Office: Salem-Keizer Sch Dist PO Box 12024 Salem OR 97309 Office Phone: 503-399-3101. E-mail: page_cheryl@salkerz.k12.or.us.

PAGE, CURTIS MATTHEWSON, minister; b. Columbus, Ohio, Oct. 24, 1946; s. Charles N. and Alice Matthewson P.; m. Martha Poitevin, Feb. 12, 1977; children: Allison, Charles, Abigail. BS, Ariz. State U., 1968; MDiv, San Francisco Theol. Sem., 1971, D Ministry, 1985. Ordained Presbyn. Ch., 1971. Pastor Ketchum (Idaho) Presbyn. Ch., 1972-80, Kirk O'The Valley Presbyn. Ch., Reseda, Calif., 1980-90; campaign dir. Kids 1st Edn. Reform Partnership, LA, 1990-91; sr. pastor Orangewood Presbyn. Ch., Phoenix, 1991-93, First Meridian Heights Presbyn. Ch., Indpls., 1993—. Mem. com. Ch. Devel., Ind., 1995—; bd. dirs. Express Pub., Ketchum. Chmn. com. on preparation for the ministry, San Fernando, Calif., 1988-90; chmn. Ketchum City Zoning Commn., 1979-80; L.A. Mayor's Citizen's Adv. Task Force on Ethics, 1990; co-chmn. Voice Cmty. Orgn. L.A., 1988-90; chair Family CARES, Indpls., 1995—; founding pastor AliveTime, 1995; leading innovator in mainline Protestant worship and urban ministry. Avocations: tennis, skiing, coaching softball. Office: First Meridian Heights Pres 4701 Central Ave Indianapolis IN 46205-1828 E-mail: FMHPC@aol.com.

PAGE, DAVID C., biologist, educator; MD magna cum laude, Harvard Med. Sch. Dir. Whitehead Inst.; prof. biology MIT; investigator Howard Hughes Med. Inst. Editor Current Opinion in Genetics and Develop.; assoc. editor Ann. Rev. Human Genetics and Genomics. Recipient Searle Scholar's award, 1989, Amory prize, Am. Acad. Arts and Sciences, 1997, Curt Stern award, Am. Soc. Human Genetics, 2003; MacArthur Found. prize fellowship, 1986. Mem.: NAS. Achievements include mapping and cloning the Y chromosome; publishing the complete sequence of Y chromosome. Office: Whitehead Institute 9 Cambridge Ctr Cambridge MA 02142-1479 Office Phone: 617-258-5203. E-mail: page_admin@wi.mit.edu.

PAGE, ERNEST, retired medical educator; b. Cologne, Germany, May 30, 1927; came to US, 1936, naturalized, 1942. s. Max Ernest and Eleanor (Kohn) P.; m. Eva Veronica Gross, June 5, 1967; 1 son, Thomas J. AB, U. Calif., Berkeley, 1949; MD, U. Calif., San Francisco, 1952. Intern Peter Bent Brigham Hosp., Boston, 1952-53, resident, 1953-54, 57-58; rsch. assoc. Harvard Med. Sch., 1957-65; assoc. prof. medicine and physiology U. Chgo. Med. Sch., 1965-69, prof. physiology, 1969-98, prof. emeritus, 1998—. Editor: (jour.) Am, Jour. Physiology: Heart and Circulatory Physiology, 1981—86; editor: (sects.) Handbook of Physiology Vol. I The Heart, 2002. Served with AUS, 1945-46. Established investigator Am. Heart Assn., 1959-65. Mem. Am. Physiol. Soc., Biophys. Soc., Am. Soc. Cell Biology, Soc. Gen. Physiologists, Assn. Am. Physicians. Home: 5606 S Harper Ave Chicago IL 60637-1832

PAGE, FRANK S., head of religious order; b. Greensboro, NC, 1952; m. Dayle Page; children: Melissa, Lauren, Allison. BS in Psychology, Gardner Webb Univ.; MDiv., PhD, Southwestern Baptist Theological Seminary. Former pastor Southern Baptist Convention Church (SBC Church) Tex., SBC Church No. Carolina, Warren Baptist SBC Church Ga., Taylor's First SBC Church So. Carolina; pres. So. Baptist Church, 2006—. Office: Southern Baptist Convention 1 Lifeway Plz MSN 146 Nashville TN 37234-1001

PAGE, FREDERICK WEST, business consultant; b. East Orange, NJ, Oct. 19, 1932; s. Frederick West and Dorothy (Donham) P.; m. Miriam Lowell Jones, Feb. 14, 1959; children: William, Janet, Thomas, James. AB, Dartmouth Coll., 1954; postgrad., Wharton Grad. Sch. Bus., U. Pa., 1956-57; MBA, NYU, 1960. With Schering Corp. (now Schering-Plough), 1957-91, various mktg. positions, 1957-73, gen. mgr. animal health products, 1973-80, pres. U.S. Animal Health Products Div., 1980-83, v.p. pharm. ops., 1983-91; pres. Bus. Cons. Svcs., 1991—; dir. Immune Tech. Inc., 1996-98. With US Army, 1954—56. Mem. Animal Health Inst. (exec. com. 1978-81, chmn. 1979-80) Clubs: Phi Kappa Psi. Republican. Home and Office: 22 Martin Rd West Caldwell NJ 07006-7419

PAGE, GEORGE ALFRED, JR., lawyer; b. Evanston, Ill., June 30, 1932; AB, Princeton U., NJ, 1954; JD, Harvard U., Cambridge, Mass., 1959; LLM in Taxation, Boston U., 1964. Bar: Mass 1959. From assoc. to ptnr. Peabody & Arnold, Boston, 1959—79; sr. ptnr. Csaplar & Bok, Boston, 1979—90; pvt. practice Boston, 1990—. Lectr grad tax program Boston Univ Sch Law, 1974—77; gen counsel to bd dirs and sr mgmt Woodside Mgmt Sys Inc, Boston, 1978—87. 1st lt USAR, 1954—56. Mem.: ABA (mem. real property, probate and trust law sect.), Boston Bar Assn. (chmn. state tax com. 1971—74, sect. taxation 1974—75, fed. tax com. 1980—82, sr. sect. 1994—96, mem. trusts and estates law sect., mem. estate planning com.). Home and Office: 1 Risley Rd Marblehead MA 01945-3720 Office Phone: 781-631-7243.

PAGE, GREGORY R., agricultural products and diversified services company executive; b. Bottineau, ND, 1951; m. Cynthia M. Page. BA in Economics, U. ND, 1973. Joined as trainee in Feed divsn., various positions in the US animal nutrition bus. in merchandising, prod. services and admin. Cargill, Inc., Kansas City, Kan.; Fort Worth, Texas; Stockton, Calif.; Minneapolis, 1974—85, head animal nutrition operations in Asia, Cargill Southeast Asia Ltd Singapore, 1985, head poultry processing bus., Sun Valley Thailand Saraburi Province, Thailand, 1989—92, returned to US to work with the U.S. beef operations of Cargills Excel subs. Mpls., 1992, pres. red meat group, 1995—98, corp. v.p., sect. pres., 1998—2000, exec. v.p., 1999—2000, pres., COO, 2000—. Bd. dirs. Eaton Corp. Mem.: Am. Meat Inst. (chmn. 2000). Office: Cargill Inc PO Box 9300 Minneapolis MN 55440 *

PAGE, HARRY ROBERT, business administration educator; b. Milw., Mar. 22, 1915; s. Harry Allen and Lydia (Rosendahl) P.; m. Jeanne Tompkins, Apr. 1, 1945; children: Patricia Jeanne, Margaret Berenice. AB, Mich. State U., 1941; postgrad., U.S. Army Command and Staff Coll., 1945-46, Indsl. Coll. Armed Forces, 1958-59; MBA, Harvard, 1950; PhD, Am. U., 1966. Served from 2d lt. to lt. col. U.S. Army, 1941-46; from lt. col. to col. USAF, 1947-61; exec. officer logistics directorate U.S. Joint Chiefs of Staff, Washington, 1959-61; asst. prof. bus. adminstrn. George Washington U., Washington, 1961-65, assoc. prof., chmn. dept., 1965-69, prof., chmn. dept. bus. adminstrn., 1970-74, assoc. dean, 1975-80, prof. emeritus, 1981—. Cons. advanced study program Brookings Instn., Washington, 1966-70, Ednl. Svcs. Inst., US Postal Svc., 1985-92. Author: Church Budget Development, 1964, An Analysis of the Defense Procurement Program Decision-Making Process, 1966, Public Purchasing and Materials Management, 1980, rev. edit., 1989; co-author: Federal Contributions to Management, 1972. Chmn. task force edn. and tng. Commn. Govt. Procurement, 1972-73; bd. dirs., treas. Coun. Chs., Greater Washington, 1963-68; bd. dirs. Hunter Assocs. Lab., Inc.; deacon Rock Spring Congregational Ch., 1994-97. Decorated Air medal USAF, Purple Heart, Legion of Merit, Commendation medal USAF, U.S. Army. Fellow Nat. Contract Mgmt. Assn.; mem. Acad. mgmt., Nat. Assn. Purchasing Mgmt., Internat. Fedn. Purchasing and Materials Mgmt., Harvard Bus. Sch. Assn., Air Force Assn., Nat. Parks and Conservation Assn. (trustee), Air Force Sgts. Assn. (trustee, chmn. scholarship bd. 1971—), Harvard Bus. Club, Sch. of Wash. Club (dir., pres. 1980-81), Alpha Phi Omega, Lambda Chi Alpha Alpha Kappa Psi, Pi Sigma Alpha, Beta Gamma Sigma. Home: 3612 N Glebe Rd Arlington VA 22207-4317

PAGE, HELEN (LYN) BARD WARD, literature educator; b. Evanston, Ill., Oct. 30, 1947; d. Herschel Wayne and Helen Doris (Davies) Ward; m. Joseph Leon Page, 1986; 1 child, Julia Helen. BA in English magna cum laude, Cornell Coll., Mount Vernon, Iowa, 1968; MA in English Lit., Northwestern U., Evanston, 1971; postgrad., Nat. Louis U., Evanston, 1972—82, U. Ill., Chgo., 1983—87. English tchr. Niles West H.S., Skokie, 1969—70, Niles Off-Campus Learning Ctr., Skokie, 1971—76; instrnl. supr. Glenbrook North H.S., Northbrook, Ill., 1976—80; prof. English Oakton C.C., DesPlaines, Ill., 1980—. Part-time instr. English Northwestern U., Evanston, 1987—93, Kendall Coll., 1987—93; coord. Great Books Program Oakton CC, DesPlaines, 2005—; cons. in field; presenter in field. Contbr. articles to profl. jours. Bd. mem., mem.-at-large Experiment in Internat. Living, Chgo., 1969—; active mem., leader, trainer, nat. del. Girl Scouts USA, 1995—; mem., choir mem., com. mem. First Congl. Ch. Evanston, 2003—. Finalist Hartstein Tchg. award, Oakton CC, 1987, 2004, Coll. Tchg. award, Northwestern U., 1989; nominee Hartstein Tchg. award, Oakton CC, 2002, 2007; recipient Outstanding Tchg. Effectiveness award, 1982, Presdl. citation, 1986, 1987, award, Nat. Inst. Staff and Orgnl. Devel., 1996, Beamon-Denoyer award, Girl Scouts USA, 2004. Mem.: Nat. Coun. Tchrs. English, Phi Beta Kappa. Avocations: volunteer work, music, theater. Office: Oakton CC 1600 E Golf Rd Des Plaines IL 60016 Office Phone: 847-376-7669.

PAGE, JACK RANDALL, lawyer; b. Waco, Tex., Aug. 1, 1956; s. Jack Bennett and Mary Elizabeth (Cobbs) P.; m. Shirley Jean Hull, Aug. 5, 1978; children: Anna Christine, Sara Elaine BBA magna cum laude, Baylor U., 1977, JD, 1980. Bar: Tex. 1980, U.S. Tax Ct. 1985, U.S. Dist. Ct. (we. dist.) Tex. 1987, U.S. Ct. Appeals (5th cir.) 1989; cert. in tax law Tex. Bd. Legal Specialization; CPA, Tex. Acct. Allie B. Gates Jr., CPA, Waco, 1975—78; assoc. Pakis, Giotes, Page & Burleson, P.C., Waco, 1980—86, ptnr., 1986—. Chmn. exploring sales team Heart O' Tex. coun. Boy Scouts Am., 1983, dist. chmn., 1984—85, v.p., 1986—88, coun. commr., 1989—91, coun. pres., 1991—94, asst. coun. commr., 1994—95, v.p., 1995—96, mem. adv. coun. Longhorn Coun., 2000—02, dist. chmn., 2002—04; mem. adv. coun. dept. acctg. Baylor U., 1993—2002; co-chmn. Food for Families, 1995—2005. Recipient Dist. Award of Merit Heart O' Tex. coun. Boy Scouts Am., 1985, Silver Beaver award 1993, Commrs. Key, 1994 Life Fellow Tex. Bar Found.; mem. AICPA, Tex. Bar Assn., Coll. of State Bar of Tex., Waco-McLennan County Bar Assn., Tex. Soc. CPA, Waco Estate Planning Coun. (pres. 1983), Order of Demolay (chevalier 1975) Roman Catholic. Avocations: fly fishing, wildlife management. Office: Pakis Giotes Page & Burleson PC PO Box 58 Waco TX 76703-0058 Business E-Mail: page@pakislaw.com.

PAGE, JUTTA ANNETTE, curator; m. Philip Sothern Page, Aug. 16, 1954. MAE, RI State U., Providence, 1986; MA, Brown U., Providence, 1989, PhD, 1991. Curator European glass Corning Mus. of Glass, NY, 1993—2003; curator glass Toledo Mus. Art, 2003—. Chair ICOM Glass Com., Paris, 1999—. Mem.: Glass Art Soc. (bd. dirs. 2004—07). Office: Toledo Museum of Art 2445 Monroe St at Scottwood Ave Toledo OH 43620 Office Phone: 419-255-8000 7468. Office Fax: 419-254-5773. E-mail: jpage@toledomuseum.org.

PAGE, KENNETH R., lawyer; b. Rockville Centre, NY, May 20, 1946; s. Charles Herbert and Dorothy Emma (Koster) P.; m. Nancy McNeer Cummings, Oct. 27, 1973; children: Katherine Spessard Page, Taylor Benton Page; m. Deborah Ann Donovan, Feb. 14, 1998 AB cum laude, with distinction in Govt., Dartmouth Coll., 1968; JD, Cornell U., 1971. Bar: N.Y. 1972, U.S. Dist. Ct. (so. dist.) N.Y., U.S. Ct. Appeals (2d cir.) 1975, U.S. Tax Ct. 2000. Assoc. Cadwalader, Wickersham & Taft, NYC, 1971-80; ptnr. Cole & Deitz, NYC, 1980-83, Coudert Bros., NYC, 1983—2005, head Trusts & Estates practice; ptnr. Baker & McKenzie, NYC, 2005—06, Hughes Hubbard & Reed LLP, NYC, 2006—. Trustee Family Dynamics, N.Y.C., 1976-86, Mus. Am. Folk Art, N.Y.C., 1976-86, Isaac H. Tuttle Fund., N.Y.C., 1980—; bd. trustees Estate and Property of Diocesan Conv., N.Y.C., 1987-93, 94-2000, 01—. Mem. ABA, N.Y. State Bar. Assn., Order St. John, Pilgrims US, Union Club. Avocations: skiing, tennis, fishing, art. Office: Hughes Hubbard and Reed LLP 1114 Ave of the Americas New York NY 10036-7710 Office Phone: 212-837-6440. Business E-Mail: pagek@hugheshubbard.com.

PAGE, LARRY (LAWRENCE E. PAGE), information technology executive; b. Ann Arbor, Mich., Mar. 26, 1973; s. Carl Victor and Gloria Page. BS in Computer Engring., U. Mich., 1995; postgrad., Stanford U. Co-founder Google, Inc., Mountain View, Calif., 1998, CEO, 1998—2001, pres. products, 2001—. Spkr. in field; spkr. World Econ. Forum; bd. dirs. Google, Inc., 1998—. Mem. nat. adv. com. U. Mich. Coll. Engring., Ann Arbor, Mich.; bd. trustee X Prize, 2005—. Co-recipient (with Sergey Brin) Marconi prize, 2004; named Global Leader for Tomorrow, World Econ. Forum, 2002, Young Innovator Who Will Create the Future, MIT Tech. Rev. Mag., Innovator of Yr., R&D Mag., 2002, Persons of Week (with Sergey Brin), ABC World News Tonight, 2004; named one of World's 100 Most Influential People, Time Mag., 2005, Forbes Richest Ams., 2006, 50 Who Matter Now, CNNMoney.com Bus. 2.0, 2006, 2007, World's Richest People, Forbes Mag., 2006, 2007; recipient Engring. Grad. award, U. Mich. Alumni Soc., Bus. Leader of Yr. for Google, Inc., Sci. Am. 50, 2005, Golden Plate award, Acad. Achievement, 2004. Mem.: NAE, Eta Kappa Nu. Office: 1600 Amphitheatre PKWY #41 Mountain View CA 94043-1351 Office Phone: 650-623-4000. Office Fax: 650-618-1499. *

PAGE, LARRY KEITH, neurosurgeon, educator; b. Rayville, La., July 7, 1933; s. Ardie Lee and Edris Estelle (Chaney) P.; m. Joan Marie Doherty, Aug. 27, 1960; children: Matthew, Elizabeth, Jennifer. BS, La. State U., 1955, MD, 1958. Diplomate: Am. Bd. Neurol. Surgery. Intern Grad. Hosp., U. Pa., Phila., 1958-59; resident Children's Hosp. and Peter Bent Brigham Hosp., Boston, 1962-66; assoc. neurosurgeon Children's Hosp., assoc. surgeon Peter Bent Brigham Hosp., 1966-71; cons. Beverly Hosp., Mass., Robert Breck Brigham Hosp., Boston, Pondville Hosp., Boston, West Roxbury VA Hosp., Boston VA Hosp.; clin. instr. neurosurgery Harvard U., Boston, 1966-71; prof., vice chmn. dept. neurosurgery U. Miami, Fla., 1971-95, prof. emeritus Fla., 1995—, chief div. pediatric neurosurgery Fla., 1971-95; neurosurgeon VA Hosp., Miami, 1971-88, Jackson Meml. Hosp., Miami, 1971-95, dir. neurosurgery, 1994-95; chief neurosurgery Mt. Sinai Hosp., Miami, 1990-94. Cons. neurosurg. FDA, 1976-79, NASA, 1979-80 Mem. editorial bds., contbr. articles to profl. jours. Served to lt. USN, 1959-62. Mem. ACS, Am. Acad. Pediatrics, Am. Assn. Neurol. Surgeons, Internat. Soc. Pediatric Neurosurgery, Am. Soc. Pediatric Neurosurgery, Congress Neurol. Surgeons, Fellowship of Acad. Neurosurgeons, Internat. Neurosurg. Forum, Royal Soc. Medicine, Soc. for Rsch. in Hydrocephalus and Spina Bifida, New Eng. Neurosurg. Soc., Fla. Neurosurg. Soc. (pres. 1989-90), Mass. Med. Soc., Dade County Med. Assn., Internat. Palm Soc., Alpha Omega Alpha. Roman Catholic. Home and Office: 13845 SW 73rd Ct Miami FL 33158-1213

PAGE, LESLIE ANDREW, retired consumer products company executive; b. Mpls., June 5, 1924; s. Henry R. and Amelia Kathryn (Steinmetz) Page; m. DeEtte Abernethy Griswold, July 6, 1952 (div. Sept. 1975); children: Randolph, Michael, Kathryn, Caroline; m. Mary Ellen Decker, Nov. 26, 1976. BA, U. Minn., 1949; MA, U. Calif., Berkeley, 1953, PhD, 1956. Asst. microbiologist, lectr. U. Calif., Davis, 1956-61; cons. San Diego Zoological Soc. Zoo Hosp., 1957-60; microbiologist, research leader Nat. Animal Disease Ctr., USDA, Ames, Iowa, 1961-79; specialist in Chlamydial nomenclature and disease; med. text cons. Bay St. Louis, Miss., 1979-85; founder, pres., chmn. bd. Steri-Derm Corp., San Marcos, Calif., 1987—2005. Cons. McCormick Distilling Co., Weston, Mo., 1994—95. Editor: Jour. Wildlife Diseases, 1965—68, Wildlife Diseases, 1976; contbr. chpts. to textbooks, articles to profl. jours. Pres. Garden Island Cmty. Assn., Bay St. Louis, Miss., 1980—81; chief commr. East Hancock Fire Protection Dist., Bay St. Louis, 1982—83; treas. Woodridge Escondido Property Owners Assn., 1986—88; pres. Westminster Men's Group, Westminster Presbyn. Ch., Escondido, Calif., 2002. With 89th divsn US Army, 1943—46, US. Fellow: Am. Acad. Microbiology; mem.: Am. Soc. Microbiology, Wildlife Disease Assn. (life; pres. 1972—73, Disting. Svc. award 1980), Les Familles Pagé d'Amérique, Sigma Xi, Phi Zeta (hon.). Achievements include patent for Liquid Antiseptic Composition. Home: 2209 SE Pine Gate Cir Blue Springs MO 64014 Personal E-mail: lapage1234@hotmail.com.

PAGE, LINDA KAY, bank executive; b. Wadsworth, Ohio, Oct. 4, 1943; d. Frederick Meredith and Martha Irene (Vance) P. Student, Ohio U., 1976-77; grad. banking program, U. Wis., 1982-84; BA, Capital U. Asst. v.p., gen. mgr. Bancohio Corp., Columbus, 1975-78, v.p., dist. mgr., 1979-80, v.p., mgr. employee rels., 1980-81, v.p., divsn. mgr., 1982-83; commr. of banks State of Ohio, Columbus, 1983-87, dir. Dept. Commerce, 1988-90; pres., CEO Star Bank Ctrl. Ohio, Columbus, 1990—92; state dir. Rural Devel/USDA, 1993-2000; pub. svc. dir. City of Columbus, 2000—04; mgr. Nationwide Fed. Credit Union, 2004—. Bd. dirs. Clark County Mental Health Bd., Springfield, Ohio, 1982-83, Springfield Met. Housing, 1982-83, Pvt. Industry Coun. Franklin County, 1990-2000—, Ohio Higher Edn. Facilities Commn., 1990-93, Ohio Devel. Corp., 1995—; bd. advisers Orgn. Indsl. Standards, Springfield, 1982-83; trustee League Against Child Abuse, 1986-90; treas. Ohio Housing Fin. Agy., 1980-90; vice chair Fed. Res. Bd. Consumer Adv. Coun., 1989-91; trustee, treas. Columbus State C.C. Found., 1990-00, pres., 1997-99; bd. dirs. Columbus Urban League, 1992-98; mem. CompDrug Bd., 1998-00; mem. Mid Ohio Regional Planning Commn., 2000-04; devel. chair Ohio Coun. Econ. Edn., 2003-. Recipient Leadership Columbus award Sta. WTVN and Columbus Leadership Program, 1975, 82, Outstanding Svc. award Clark County Mental Health Bd., 1983, Giles Mitchell Housing award, 1996. Mem.: LWV (treas. edn. fund 1992—2000), Ohio Coun. Econ. Edn. (devel. chair 2004—), Womens Fund Ctrl. Ohio (grant reader 2003—05), Risk Mgmt. Assn., Women in Transp. (bd. trustees Ohio chpt. 2000, bd. dirs. 2002), Internat. Womens Forum, Am. Pub. Works Assn. (treas. Ohio chpt. 2000—04, govt. affairs com. 2002—03, treas. 2002—04), Ohio Mortgage Bankers Assn. (legis. commn. 1998), Ohio Devel. Assn., Ohio Bankers Assn. (bd. dirs. 1982—83, 1991—92), Conf. State Bank Suprs. (dist. chmn. 1984—85, sec.-treas. 1985—90, bd. dirs.), Women Execs. in State Govt., Am. Bankers Assn. (govt. rels. coun. 1990—92, cert.), Nat. Assn. Bank Women (pres. 1980—81), Rotary. Democrat. Avocations: reading, cultural arts, travel. Home: 1477 Sedgefield Dr New Albany OH 43054-9431 Personal E-mail: lpage@insight.rr.com.

PAGE, LYMAN ALEXANDER, JR., physicist; b. San Francisco, Sept. 24, 1957; s. Lyman Alexander and Gillet (Thomas) P.; m. Elizabeth Olson, Feb. 12, 1990; children: William, James, Brent. BA with high honors in Physics, Bowdoin Coll., 1978; PhD in Physics, MIT, 1989. Rsch. technician Bartol Rsch. Found., Newark, Del., 1978-80; postdoctoral rsch. fellow MIT, 1989-90; instr. physics Princeton U., NJ, 1990-91, asst. prof. NJ, 1991-95, assoc. prof. NJ, 1995-98, prof. NJ, 1998—2005, Henry DeWolf Smyth prof., 2005—. Contbr. articles to sci. jours. Surdna fellow Bowdoin Coll., 1978, NASA grad. student rschrs. prog. fellow MIT, 1987-89, David and Lucile Packard fellow Princeton U., 1994; Rsch. Corp. Cottrell scholar Princeton U., 1994. Fellow: Am. Acad. Arts & Sci. Mem. Am. Phys. Soc.,

Am. Astron. Soc., NAS. Achievements include measurement of tiny spatial variations in the temperature of the radiation thought to be the afterglow of the big-bang. Office: Princeton U Dept Physics Jadwin Hall PO Box 708 Princeton NJ 08544-0708

PAGE, OSCAR C., academic administrator; b. Bowling Green, Ky., Dec. 22, 1939; s. Elizabeth Page; m. Anna Laura Hood, June 12, 1965; children: Kristen, Matt. BA in Social Sci., Western Ky. U., 1962; MA in History, U. Ky., 1963, PhD in Early Modern European History, 1967. Instr. history Western Ky. U., Bowling Green, 1964; asst. prof., asst. chair history dept. U. Ga., Athens, 1967-71; dean Wesleyan Coll., Macon, Ga., 1971-78; v.p. acad. affairs Lander Coll., Greenwood, S.C., 1978-86, acting pres., 1985, provost, v.p. acad. affairs, 1986-88; pres. Austin Peay State U., Clarksville, Tenn., 1988-94, Austin Coll., Sherman, Tex., 1994—. Bd. dirs.Clarksville Nations Bank. Bd. dirs. United Way, Sherman, 1994—98; mem. pres.'s commn. NCAA, 1990—94, mem. mgmt. coun., 1998—2002; bd. dirs. Meml. Hosp., Clarksville; pres. Assn. Tex. Colls. and Univs., 1998—99. Mem.: Sherman C. of C., Rotary Club. Office: Austin Coll 900 N Grand Ave Sherman TX 75090-4440 *

PAGE, PATRICIA (PATTY) NEWTON, real estate broker, real estate company executive; b. Nashville, Tenn., May 16, 1963; d. James Kelton and Alice (Clement) Cuff; m. James T. Baxter. Grad., Realtor Inst., 1999. Cert. affiliate broker North Ctrl. Inst., 1993, accredited credit buyer rep. Nat. Assn. Realtors, 2001, lic. real estate broker, cert. residential specialist. Sr. customer svc. rep. Comdata Corp., Brentwood, Tenn., 1981—92; realtor Century 21 ABC, Clarksville, Tenn., 1993—94, Lakeland Properties, Dover, Tenn., 1994—96; designated realtor Cherry Properties, Dover, Tenn., 1996—2003; owner, broker Patty Page Properties, LLC, 2004—. Mem.: Nat. Assn. Realtors (coun. residential specialist 2002). Methodist. Avocations: continued education, travel. Office Phone: 931-232-5082. Personal E-mail: PattyPage2000@aol.com.

PAGE, RANDALL, state official; b. Mt. Vernon, Ohio, Feb. 18, 1967; s. James and Nancy Page; m. Melissa Rohrman, Feb. 16, 1991; children: Julie Anne, Jason Ryan. BS, Bob Jones U., Greenville, 1990. Dir. of pub. events Office of the Gov., Columbia, SC, 1995—99; exec. v.p. Jordan and McCallum Co., Greenville, SC, 1999—2001; legislative affairs dir. Office of the Lt. Gov., Columbia, SC, 2001—03, chief of staff, 2003—04; campaign mgr. Beasley for Senate, Columbia, SC, 2004; pres. South Carolinians for Responsible Govt., Columbia, 2005—; sr. assoc. Richard Quinn & Assocs., Columbia, SC, 2004—05. Bd. dirs. Insights, Greenville, SC, 1994—2001; adv. bd. LifeEd, Greenville, SC, 2000—, Eagle Mil. Acad., Summerville, SC, 2006—; exec. bd. SC Citizens for Life, Columbia, 2001—. Cons. George W. Bush for Pres., Columbia, SC, 2000; fourth dist. chmn. SC Rep. Party, Columbia, 2001—03; mem. Lexington County Rep. Exec. Com., 2007—; bd. dirs. Kennerly Rd. Bapt. Ch., Irmo, SC, 2003—06, chmn., 2004—06; mem. exec. bd. Greenville County Libr. Sys., SC, 1999—2001; bd. dirs. Palmetto Family Coun., 2006—. Recipient Order of the Palmetto, Gov. David M. Beasley, SC., 1998, Hon. Order of Ky. Colonels, Gov. Paul Patton, Ky., 2003, Disting. Svc. award, Bob Jones U. Alumni Assn., 2006. Republican. Baptist. Avocation: swimming. Office: South Carolinians for Responsible Govt 3020 Devine St Columbia SC 29205 Office Phone: 803-212-1051. Office Fax: 803-212-1052. Personal E-mail: govpage@sc.rr.com. Business E-Mail: randy@scrgov.org.

PAGE, ROBERT EUGENE, JR., biology professor; b. Bakersfield, Calif., Nov. 12, 1949; PhD in Entomology, U. Calif., Davis, 1980. Mem. faculty dept. entomology Ohio State U., 1986—89, U. Calif., Davis, 1989—91, prof., 1991—2004, prof. emeritus, 2004; found. prof., founding dir. Ariz. State U. Sch. Life Scis., 2004—. Chair dept. entomology U. Calif., Davis, 1999—2004. Contbr. articles to profl. jours., chapters to books; co-editor: Genetics of Social Evolution, 1988; co-author: Queen Rearing and Bee Breeding, 1998. 1st lt. US Army, 1969—72, capt. USAR, 1973—76. Named highest cited rschr., ISI; recipient Alexander von Humboldt Sr. Scientist award, German Govt. Fellow: AAAS, Am. Acad. Arts & Scis.; mem.: Genetics Soc. Am., Soc. for Study of Evolution, Animal Behavioral Soc., Internat. Union for Study of Social Insects, Brazilian Acad. Sci. (fgn. mem.), Sigma Xi. Office: Ariz State U Sch Life Sci PO Box 874501 Tempe AZ 85287 Business E-Mail: Robert.Page@asu.edu.

PAGE, ROBERT HENRY, retired engineering educator, researcher; b. Phila., Nov. 5, 1927; s. Ernest Fraser and Marguerite (MacFarl) P.; m. Lola Marie Griffin, Nov. 12, 1948; children: Lola Linda, Patricia Jean, William Ernest, Nancy Lee, Martin Fraser. BS in Mech. Engring, Ohio U., 1949; MS, U. Ill., 1951, PhD, 1955. Instr., research assoc. U. Ill., 1949-55; research engr. fluid dynamics Esso Research & Engring. Co., 1955-57; vis. lectr. Stevens Inst. Tech., 1956-57, dir. fluid dynamics lab., prof. mech. engring., 1957-61; prof. mech. engring., chmn. dept. mech., indsl. and aerospace engring. Rutgers-The State U., 1961-76, prof., research cons., 1976-79; dean engring. Tex. A&M U., 1979-83, Forsyth prof., 1983-93, prof. emeritus mech. engring., 1994—; ret., 1994. Spl. research base pressure and heat transfer, wake flow and flow separation. Contbr. over 250 articles to profl. publs.; inventor impingement nozzles. Served with AUS, 1945-47, Pacific Theatre of Operations. Recipient Western Electric Fund award Am. Soc. Engring Edn., 1968, Lindback Found. award, 1969, Disting. Alumnus award U. Ill., 1971; Disting. Svc. award, 1973, Life Quality Engring. award, 1974, James Harry Potter Gold medal, 1983, Ohio U. medal, 1983, Ruhr medal, Ruhr U., Germany, 2006; named hon. prof. Ruhr U., Buchum, Fed. Republic Germany, 1984; named to Acad. Disting. Grads., Ohio U., 2001, Hall of Fame, Ctrl. H.S., Phila., 2002. Fellow AAAS, AIAA, ABET, Am. Astron. Soc. (chmn. nat. space engring. com. 1969-70, 72-76), Am. Soc. Engring. Edn. (Centennial medal 1993); mem. ASME (hon. mem. award 1988), Am. Phys. Soc., Pan Am. Acad. Engring. (charter). Home: 1905 Comal Cir College Station TX 77840-4818

PAGE, RODNEY FRED, lawyer; b. Pueblo, Colo., Oct. 27, 1946; s. Franklin H. and Ruth M. (Fetters) P.; m. Deborah Wolfe, Sept. 27, 1986; children: Allison, Tyler, Erin. BA, U. Ky., 1968; JD, Harvard Coll., 1971. Bar: D.C. 1971, Va. 1972. Assoc. Arent Fox Kintner Plotkin & Kahn, Washington, DC, 1971-79, ptnr., 1979-89, mng. ptnr., 1989-93; ptnr., mem. oper. group Bryan Cave LLP, Washington, DC. Corp. sec. Fairfax (Va.) Corp., 1988-92. Chmn. Fairfax County Sch. Bd., Fairfax, 1976-80; bd. dirs. Fairfax Dem. Bus. Adv. Com., 1987-90; trustee Greater Washington Bd. Trade VA-PAC, 1988—. Mem. ABA, D.C. Bar ASsn., Va. State Bar Assn., Tower Club (mem. bd. govs. 1989-90). Episcopalian. Office Phone: 202-508-6002. E-mail: wfbavinger@bryancave.com.

PAGE, ROY CHRISTOPHER, periodontist, scientist, educator; b. Campobello, SC, Feb. 7, 1932; s. Milton and Anny Mae (Eubanks) P. BA, Berea Coll., 1953; DDS, U. Md., 1957; PhD, U. Wash., 1967; ScD (hon.), Loyola U., Chgo., 1983. Cert. in periodontics. Pvt. practice periodontics, Seattle, 1963-98; asst. prof. U. Wash. Schs. Medicine and Dentistry, Seattle, 1967-70, prof., 1974—2002, Disting. prof. dentistry, 1996-98, dir. Ctr. Research in Oral Biology, 1976-96; dir. grad. edn. U. Wash. Sch. Dentistry, 1976-80, dir. rsch. Seattle, 1976-94, dir. Regional Clin. Dental Rsch. Ctr., 1990—, assoc. dean rsch., 1994-2000, prof. emeritus, 2003—. Vis. scientist MRC Labs., London, 1971-72; cons., lectr. in field; fellow Pierre Fauchard Acad. Author: Periodontal Disease, 1977, 2d edit., 1990, Periodontitis in Man and Other Animals, 1982. Recipient Gold Medal award U. Md., 1957; recipient Career Devel. award NIH, 1967-72, Disting. Alumnus award U. Wash. Sch. Dentistry, 2000. Fellow Internat. Coll. Dentists, Am. Coll. Dentists, Am. Acad. Periodontology (Gies award 1982, fellowship award 1989, spl. citation 1998); mem. ADA (Norton Rose award for clin. rsch. 1998), Am. Assn. Dental Rsch. (pres. 1982-83, disting. scientist award 2001), Am. Soc. Exptl. Pathology, Internat. Assn. Dental Rsch. (pres. 1987, basic periodontal rsch. award 1977). Home: 5583 171st Ave SE Bellevue WA 98006-5503 Office Phone: 206-543-5599. E-mail: roypage@u.washington.edu.

PAGE, SALLY JACQUELYN, university official, management educator; b. Saginaw, Mich., 1943; d. William Henry and Doris Effie (Knippel) P. BA, U. Iowa, 1965; MBA, So. Ill. U., 1973. Copy editor C.V. Mosby Co., St. Louis, 1965-69; editl. cons. Editl. Assocs., Edwardsville, Ill., 1969-70; rsch. adminstr. So. Ill. U., 1970-74, asst. to pres., affirmative action officer, 1974-77; officer of instn. U. ND, Grand Forks, 1977—, lectr. mgmt., 1978—. Polit. comentator Sta. KFJM, Nat. Public Radio affiliate, 1981-90; mem. mayor's com. Employment of People With Disabilities, 1980-97. Contbr. articles to profl. jours. Chmn. ND Equal Opportunity Affirmative Action Officers, 1987-2003; chmn. NDUS Diversity Coun.; pres. Pine to Prairie coun. Girl Scouts US, 1980-85; mem. employment com. Ill. Commn. on Status of Women, 1976-77; mem. Bicentennial Com., Edwardsville, 1976, Bikeway Task Force, Edwardsville, 1975-77, Greater Grand Forks Bus. Leadership Network, ND; bd. dirs. Grand Forks Homes, 1985—2003, pres., 1996-2001; mem. found. bd. Valley Meml. Homes, 2005-, vice chair, 2007; mem. Civil Svc. Rev. Task Force, Grand Forks, 1982, civil svc. commr., 1983-98, chmn., 1984, 86, 88, 92, 96; ruling elder 1st Presbyn.; mem. Grand Forks Mayor's Adv. Cabinet, 1998-2000. Mem. AAUW (dir. Ill. 1975-77), PEO, Coll. and Univ. Pers. Assn. (rsch. and publs. bd. 1982-84), Soc. Human Resource Mgmt., Am. Assn. Affirmative Action, ADA Coords. Democrat. Presbyterian. Home: 3121 Cherry St Grand Forks ND 58201-7461 Office: U ND Grand Forks ND 58202 Business E-Mail: SallyPage@mail.und.nodak.edu.

PAGE, STEPHEN FRANKLIN, aerospace transportation executive; b. LA, Jan. 21, 1940; s. Steve and Milla Theresa (Raditich) Page; m. Judith Kelly; children: Stephen D., Mark C., Kathryn K. BBA, Loyola U., LA, 1962, JD, 1968. Bar: Calif. 1969; CPA, Calif. Prin. Deloitte, Haskins & Sells, LA, 1962-72; v.p. sec., gen. counsel McCulloch Corp., LA, 1972-76; pres. McCulloch Mite-E-Lite, LA, 1976-79; v.p., contr., treas. Pacific Internat. Group (div. Black & Decker), LA, 1979-81; v.p., treas. Ams. Internat. Group (div. Black & Decker), LA, 1981-82, Black & Decker Mfg. Co., Towson, Md., 1982-85; v.p. fin., treas. Black & Decker Corp., Towson, 1985-90, exec. v.p., CFO, 1990-92; exec. v.p. United Techs. Corp., Hartford, Conn., 1993—97, CFO, 1993—97, 2002—, dir., vice chmn., 2002—; pres., CEO Otis Elevator Co., Farmington, Conn., 1997—2002. Bd. dirs. Augat, Inc., Mansfield, Mass, Lowe's Corp.; trustee, Loyola Marymount U. Pres. Associated Cath. Charities, Balt., 1987—, The Kennedy Inst., Balt., 1988—, chmn., INROADS for Greater Hartford and Springfield Inc. Mem. ABA, AICPA, Fin. Execs. Inst. (chmn. com. on internat. bus. 1987-89, vice chair 1990). Office: United Techs Corp United Techs Bldg Hartford CT 06101

PAGE, TIM, music critic, writer, producer; b. San Diego, Oct. 11, 1954; s. Ellis Batten and Elizabeth Latimer (Thaxton) Page; m. Vanessa Weeks, Mar. 3, 1984 (div.); children: William Dean, Robert Leonard, John Sherman; m. Julieta Stack, Oct. 12, 2002. Student, Tanglewood Music Ctr., 1970, 74, 75, Mannes Coll. Music, 1975-77; BA, Columbia U., 1979. Music critic Soho News, NYC, 1979-82; music writer N.Y. Times, NYC, 1982-87; music critic Newsday, NYC, 1987-95; writer, music critic Washington Post, 1995—. Artistic advisor St. Louis Symphony, 1999—2000; lectr. in field. Author: Music From the Road, 1992, William Kapell, 1992, Dawn Powell: A Biography, 1998, Tim Page on Music, 2001; editor: The Glenn Gould Reader, 1984; editor: (with Vanessa Weeks Page) Selected Letters of Virgil Thomson, 1988; editor: Dawn Powell at Her Best, 1994, The Diaries of Dawn Powell, 1995, Selected Letters of Dawn Powell, 1999, The Unknown Sigrid Undset, 2001; radio host WNYC-FM, 1981—92. Recipient Pulitzer prize for criticism, N.Y., 1997. Mem.: The Century Assn. Office: Washington Post 1150 15th St NW Washington DC 20071-0002

PAGE, WILLIAM MARION, lawyer; b. Columbus, Ga., July 31, 1917; s. Roger McKeene and Louise Olivia (Seals) P.; m. Lucy Quillian Page, Feb. 8, 1941 (dec. 1982); children: John Roger, Jane Quillian Page McCamy, William Franklin (dec.); m. Barbara Brown Waddell, May 10, 1985 LLB, U. Ga., Athens, 1939, JD. Bar: Ga. 1938, U.S. Supreme Ct. 1955. Ptnr. Page Scrantom Sprouse Tucker & Ford P.C., Columbus, Ga., 1939—. Bd. visitors U. Ga. Law Sch., 1969-74. With U.S. Army, 1941-46 Fellow: Lawyers Found. Ga., Am. Coll. Trial Lawyers; mem.: ABA, Columbus Bar Assn. (pres. 1946—47), Chattahoochee Circuit Bar Assn. (pres. 1948—49), State Bar Ga. (bd. govs. 1964—71), Chattahoochee River Club, Kiwanis. Home: 916 Overlook Dr Columbus GA 31906-3029 Office: PO Box 1199 Columbus GA 31902-1199

PAGE, WILLIS, conductor; b. Rochester, NY, Sept. 18, 1918; Grad. with distinction, Eastman Sch. Music, Rochester., 1939. Mem. Rochester Philharm., 1937-40, Rochester Civic, 1939-40; prof. conducting Eastman Sch. Music, 1967-69; prof. conducting, dir. orchestral activities Drake U., Des Moines, 1969-71. Guest condr. Sony concerts, Chiba, Japan, 1992. Mem. Boston Symphony Orch., 1940-55; prin. bass Boston Pops, 1947-55; condr. Cecilia Soc. Boston, 1952-54, New Orchestral Soc. Boston; assoc. condr. Buffalo Philharm., 1955-59; music dir./condr. Nashville Symphony Orch., 1959-67; music dir. Linwood Music Sch., 1955-59; 1st condr. Yomiuri Nippon Symphony, Tokyo, 1962-63; condr. Des Moines Symphony, 1969-71, Jacksonville (Fla.) Symphony Orch., 1971-83; founder, condr. St. John's River City Band, 1985-86; guest condr. Boston Pops, Toronto, Rochester Civic, Eastman-Rochester, Denver, Muncie, Jerusalem, St. Louis, Colorado Springs, Memphis, Hartford orchs., Yomiuri Nippon Symphony, 1988, 92; founding condr., exec. dir. First Coast Pops Orch., 1989; condr. all-state orchs. of N.Y., Iowa, Ky., Tenn., Fla., also regional festivals; condr. 13 L.P. recordings including Symphony of the Air (Roger Williams soloist), Boston Festival Orch., Cook Labs., Nashville Symphony. Sgt. 95th inf. divsn. U.S. Army, 1943-45. Decorated Bronze Star; recipient Ford Found. European travel award, 1967. Address: 1567 Flanders Rd 302 Jacksonville FL 32207 Personal E-mail: wpage11@comcast.net.

PAGEL, PAUL STANLEY, anesthesiologist; b. Madison, Wis., Dec. 6, 1957; s. Gerald Gordon and Mary Ellen (Young) P.; m. Judith A. May, Sept. 13, 1996. BS, Carroll Coll., 1979; MD, Med. Coll. Wis., 1986, MS, 1991, PhD, 1994. Intern St. Josephs Hosp., Milw., 1986-87; resident Med. Coll. Wis., Milw., 1987-90, instr. cardiac anesthesiology, 1990—93, asst. prof., 1994—96, assoc. prof., 1996—99, prof. and dir. cardiac anesthesia, 1999—. Assoc. examiner Am. Bd. Anesthesiology. Contbr. articles to profl. jours.; editl. bd. Anesthesiology, Jour. of Cardiothoracic and Vascular Anesthesia. Rsch. Anesthesiology fellow Med. Coll. Wis., 1992-93, Rsch. fellow NIH, 1990-92. Office: Zablocki VA Med Ctr 5000 W National Ave Milwaukee WI 53295 Office Phone: 414-384-2000 Ext. 42417. Office Fax: 414-384-2939. Business E-Mail: pspagel@mcw.edu.

PAGEL, SCOTT B., law librarian, educator, dean; BA, Mich. State U.; MA in Libr. Sci., U. Mich.; JD, U. Calif., Berkeley. Pub. svcs. libr. Golden Gate U.; assoc. law libr. Columbia Law Sch.; dir. law libr., assoc. prof. U. Okla.; prof. law, assoc. dean info. svcs., dir. Jacob Burns Law Libr. George Washington U. Law Sch., 1993—. Contbr. articles to profl. jours. Mem.: Am. Assn. Law Librs. Office: Jacob Burns Law Libr George Washington U 716 20th St, NW Washington DC 20052 Office Phone: 202-994-7337. Office Fax: 202-994-1430. E-mail: spagel@law.gwu.edu.

PAGELS, ELAINE HIESEY, theology studies educator, writer; b. Palo Alto, Calif. d. William McKinley and Louise Sophia (van Druten) Hiesey; m. Heinz R. Pagels, June 7, 1969 (dec. July 1988); children: Sarah Marie, David van Druten. BA, Stanford U., 1964, MA, 1965; PhD, Harvard U., 1970. Asst. prof. history religion Barnard Coll., Columbia, 1970—74, from assoc. prof. to prof., chair dept. religion, 1974—82; Harrington Spear Paine prof. religion Princeton U., 1982—. Author: The Johannine Gospel in Gnostic Exegesis, 1973, The Gnostic Paul, 1975, The Gnostic Gospels, 1979 (Nat. Book award and Nat. Book Critics Cir. award), Adam, Eve and The Serpent, 1988, Beyond Belief: The Secret Gospel of Thomas, 2003, Reading Judas: The Gospel of Judas and the Shaping of Christianity, 2007. Grantee, NEH, 1973; Mellon fellow, Aspen Inst. Humanistic Studies, 1974, Hazen fellow, 1975, Rockefeller fellow, 1978—79, Guggenheim fellow, 1979—80, MacArthur prize fellow, 1981—87. Mem.: Am. Acad. Religion., Soc. Bibl. Lit., Bibl. Theologians Club. Episcopalian.

PAGET, JOEL HATHAWAY, lawyer; b. Seattle, Mar. 21, 1945; s. John Bucher and Ruth (Hathaway) P.; children: Dene' Marie, Jeremy Hathaway. BA, Seattle Pacific U., 1967; JD, U. Wash., 1970. Bar: Wash. 1970, U.S. Dist. Ct. (we. dist.) Wash. 1971, U.S. Ct. Appeals (9th cir.) 1971, U.S. Supreme Ct. 1973, U.S. Tax Ct. 1972. Law clk. Wash. Ct. Appeals, Seattle, 1970-71; ptnr. Ryan, Swanson & Cleveland PLLC, Seattle, 1971—. Lectr. bus. law Seattle Pacific U., 1972-81. Contbr. articles to profl. jours. Trustee Seattle Pacific U., 1972-2005, mem. alumni exec. bd., 1969—; sec.-treas. Christian Legal Soc. Puget Sound, Seattle, 1969-90; chmn. Seattle-King County Drug Commn., 1972-78; dir. Seattle Pacific Found., 1979—; bd. dirs. Seattle Pacific Credit Union, 1975-79; mem. Adv. Com. for Drug Abuse, Seattle, 1976-79; bd. dirs. Sammamish Bible Camp Assn., Seattle, 1974-77. Mem. Wash. State Bar Assn. (chmn. sect. taxation 1986-87, mem. bd. bar examiners 1982-84), Am. Immigration Lawyers Assn. (chmn. Wash. chpt. 1984-85, mem. bd. govs. 1984-85), Harbor Club. Republican. Avocations: golf, swimming. Office: Ryan Swanson & Cleveland PLLC 1201 3rd Ave Ste 3400 Seattle WA 98101-3034 Home: 1301 First Ave Seattle WA 98101 Office Phone: 206-464-4224. Business E-Mail: paget@ryanlaw.com.

PAGET, RUTH PENNINGTON, librarian, educator, writer; b. Detroit, Dec. 12, 1963; d. Clarence and Beatrice May Pennington; m. Laurent Albert Paget, July 16, 1988; 1 child, Florence Isabelle Winifred. BA in East Asian Studies, U. Chgo., 1986; M Libr. and Info. Sci., San Jose State U., Calif., 2006. Mktg. mgr. T.L.I. Internat., Chgo., 1985—87; Japanese svcs. sec. Ernst & Young, Chgo., 1987—88; Japanese svc. coord. Deloitte & Touche, Paris, 1989—91; bilingual mkt. rschr. Chamberlain Rsch., Madison, Wis., 1996—97; focus group recruiter Martin Focus Groups, Va. Beach, Va., 1997—99; freelance reviewer Calif., 2000—; adminstrv. asst. Calif. State U., Monterey, Calif., 2002—06; supervising libr. youth svcs. Monterey County Free Librs., Marina, Calif., 2006—. Author: The Edible Tao: Munching My Way Toward Enlightenment, 2003, Eating Soup with Chopsticks: Sweet Sixteen in Japan, 2003, Edible Alchemy: Making Life Magic, 2004, More Leisure than Money: Tales of a Military Wife in Virginia, 2005, China Hand: From the Great Wall to Olive Bull and Beyond, 2005; contbr. articles to publs., to local newspapers; author: (global libr. column) Spl. Librs. Assn. San Francisco Bay Region. V.p. young execs. Am. C. of C., Paris, 1989—91; family group sec. USS Austin USN, Norfolk, Va., 1997—99; cross-cultural trainer Youth for Understanding, Paris, 1986—94, Chgo., 1986—94; v.p. Friends of Seaside Pub. Libr., 2004—05. Grantee, U.S.-China Peoples' Friendship Assn., 1979; Chrysler scholar, Youth for Understanding, 1980, U. Chgo. scholar, 1982—86. Mem.: Monterey Mus. Art, Oriental Art Soc. Avocations: math, foreign languages, comparative religion, cooking, technology. Office: Monterey County Free Librs 188 Seaside Cir Marina CA 93933 Office Phone: 831-796-6022.

PAGHDIWALA, ABID F, dentist; m. Seema Paghdiwala; 3 children. Grad., NJ Dental Sch., 1979. Pvt. practice dentist, 1979—. Mem.: Acad. Gen. Dentistry, Phila. County Dental Soc., Pa. Dental Assn., ADA. Office: Newtown Family Dentistry Tudor Sq 660 Newtown-Yardley Rd Newtown PA 18940 Home Phone: 215-244-0882; Office Phone: 215-504-4070. Office Fax: 215-504-4220. Business E-Mail: drafp@newtownfamilydentistry.com.

PAGLIA, CAMILLE, writer, humanities educator; b. Endicott, NY, 1947; d. Pasquale John and Lydia (Colapietro) P. BA in English summa cum laude with highest honors, SUNY, Binghamton, 1968; MPhil, Yale U., 1971, PhD in English, 1974. Mem. faculty Bennington (Vt.) Coll., 1972-80; vis. lectr. Wesleyan U., 1980, Yale U., New Haven, 1980-84; asst. prof. humanities Phila. Coll. Performing Arts U. Arts, 1984—86, assoc. prof. humanities, 1987—91, prof. humanities, 1991—2000; Univ. prof. humanities and media studies U. Arts, Phila., 2000—. Spkr. in field. Author: Sexual Personae: Art and Decadence from Nefertiti to Emily Dickinson, 1990, Sex, Art, and American Culture, 1992, Vamps and Tramps: New Essays, 1994, Alfred Hitchcock's "The Birds", 1998, Break, Blow, Burn: Camille Paglia Reads Forty-Three of the World's Best Poems, 2005; columnist: Salon.com, 1995—2001; contbg. editor: Interview Magazine, 2001—. Mailing: Univ of the Arts 320 S Broad St Philadelphia PA 19102-4994 Office Phone: 215-717-6265.

PAGLIARO, JAMES DOMENIC, lawyer; b. Phila., Aug. 18, 1951; s. Domenic A. and Nancy I. (D'Amore) P.; m. Susan B. Boag, Aug. 25, 1973; children: Jamie C., Justin A. BA cum laude, LaSalle U., 1973; JD, Dickinson Law Sch., 1976. Bar: Pa. 1976, U.S. Dist. Ct. (ea. dist.) Pa. 1977, U.S. Ct. Appeals (3d, 4th, 8th, 9th and 10th cirs.) 1989, U.S. Supreme Ct. 1989. Regional atty. Gov. of Pa., Phila., 1976-79; sr. trial atty. office regional solicitor U.S. Dept. Labor, Phila., 1979-85; assoc. Morgan, Lewis & Bockius, LLP, Phila., 1985-88, ptnr. litigation, 1988—, mng. ptnr. litigation sect., 1999—. Chmn. Home & Sch. Bd. Norwood Acad., Chestnut Hill, Pa., 1983-87; guide, Phila. Mus. Art, 2003-. Fellow Am. Coll. Trial Lawyers; mem. ABA, Pa. Bar Assn. (speaker continuing legal edn. 1987—), Phila. Bar Assn., Woolsach Honors Soc. Office: Morgan Lewis & Bockius LLP 1701 Market St Philadelphia PA 19103-2903 Home Phone: 215-517-6747; Office Phone: 215-963-5668. Business E-Mail: jpagliaro@morganlewis.com.

PAGLIUCA, STEPHEN, professional sports team owner, investment company officer; m. Judy Pagliuca; 4 children. BA, Duke U.; MBA, Harvard Bus. Sch. CPA. Sr. acct., internat. tax specialist Peat Marwick Mitchell & Co., Netherlands; v.p. Bain & Co.; mng. dir. Bain Capital, 1989—; mng. ptnr., mem. exec. com. Boston Celtics, 2002—. Bd. dirs. Gartner Grp., 1990—, Burger King, 2002—; mem. supervisory bd. ProSiebenSat.1 Media AG; bd. govs. NBA, mem. competition com. Chmn. Mass. Soc. Prevention of Cruelty to Children, Boston Celtics Shamrock Found.; trustee Bain Capital Children's Charity; internat. bd. dirs. The Right to Play, 2004—. Office: Bain Capital 111 Huntington Ave Boston MA 02199 *

PAGNANI, KEITH A., lawyer; b. NYC, 1964; BA, Dickinson Coll., 1986; JD, Cath. Univ. Law Sch., 1989. Bar: NY 1990, Conn. 1990. Joined Sullivan & Cromwell, NYC, 1989—, now ptnr., mergers & acquisitions and hiring ptnr. Office: Sullivan & Cromwell LLP 125 Broad St New York NY 10004-2498 Office Phone: 212-558-4000. Office Fax: 212-558-3588. Business E-Mail: pagnanik@sullcrom.com.

PAGNANI, MICHAEL JOSEPH, orthopaedic surgeon; b. Endicott, NY, Apr. 23, 1961; s. Bruno and Patricia Ann Connors P.; m. Kelly Jackson, May 14, 1988; children: Sarah, Connor. MD, Vanderbilt U., 1987.

Diplomate Am. Bd. Orthopaedic Surgery. Intern Baylor U., Dallas, 1987-88; resident in orthop. surgery The Hosp. for Spl. Surgery-Cornell U., NYC, 1988-92, fellow in sports medicine, 1992-93; pvt. practice The Lipscomb Clinic, Nashville, 1993, Nashville Knee & Shoulder, Nashville; attending orthop. surgeon Centennial Med. Ctr., Nashville, 1993—, St. Thomas Hosp., Nashville, 1993—; clin. asst. prof., orthop., rehabilitation Vanderbilt U., Nashville, 1993—. Bd. dir. Nashville Sports Coun., 1997-2002; asst. orthop. cons. St. John's U., 1992-93; orthop. cons. Tenn. Technological U., 1993-94, Nashville Xpress Baseball Team, 1994, Chgo. White Sox Baseball Orgn., 1995-97, Pitts. Pirates Baseball Orgn., 1998-2003, Miami Dolphins, 2001-; team physician NY Pub. Sch. Athletic League, 1988-92, numerous Nashville area high schools, 1993-, Elite Runner, Country Music Marathon, 2000-2003; orthop. team physician, Nashville Sounds Baseball team, 1994-2003; asst. team physician, NY Giants Football team, 1992-93, NY Mets, 1992-93; med. cons. Ohio Valley Conf. Basketball Tournament, 1994-2000, NCAA Sectional Basketball Tournament, 2000; med. staff mem. US Open Tennis Championships, 1989-92; US Figure Skating Championships, 1997; head team physician, Nashville Kats arena football team, 1997-2002, Tenn. State Univ., 1993-, Nashville Predators Hockey team, 1998-. Cons. Am. Journal of Sports Medicine, Journal of Bone and Joint Surgery. Named Tenn. Sports Medicine Person of Yr., Tenn. Athletic Trainers' Soc., 2004. Fellow, Am. Acad. Orthop. Surgeons, mem. Am. Orthop. Soc. Sports Medicine (rsch. com., 1997-), Nat. Hockey League Team Physicians' Soc., Arthroscopy Assn. N. Am., Nashville Acad. Medicine, Tenn. Med. Assn., Am. Shoulder and Elbow Surgeons. Office: Nashville Knee & Shoulder 2011 Church St Ste 505 Nashville TN 37203 Office Phone: 615-329-2520. Office Fax: 615-329-3530. *

PAGNI, ALBERT FRANK, lawyer; b. Reno, Jan. 28, 1935; s. Bruno and Daisy Rose (Recami) Pagni; m. Nancy Lynne Thomas, Aug. 12, 1961; children: Elisa, Michelle, Melissa, Michael. AB, U. Nev., 1961; JD, U. Calif., 1964. Bar: Nev. 1964. Assoc. Vargas, Dillon, Bartlett & Dixon, Reno, 1965—70; ptnr. Vargas & Bartlett and Jones Vargas, Reno, 1970—. Adv. bd. 9th Cir. Ct., chmn. adv. bd., 2006—; ct.-apptd. arbitrator; dist. ct. judge pro tem. Mem. Nev. Dist. Appeal Bd.; mem. hospice coun. St. Mary's Hosp.; mem. adminstrv. coun. U. Nev., 1974—81; treas. U. Nev. Legis. Commn., 1973—74, pres., 1975; bd. dirs. Better Bus. Bur. With US Army, 1955—57. Named Mountain States Super Lawyer; named one of Best Lawyers in Am.; recipient Outstanding Alumni award, U. Nev., 1978. Master: Am. Inns Ct.; fellow: Am. Bd. Trial Advocates (nat. bd.), Nev. Law Found. (trustee, vice chair), Am. Coll. Barristers, Am. Coll. Trial Lawyers (state chair); mem.: ATLA, ABA, State Bar Nev. (bd. govs. 1976—87, v.p. 1984—85, pres.-elect 1985—86, pres. 1986—87, mediator, arbitrator 1990), Am. Judicature Assn. (mediator, arbitrator 1990), Assn. Def. Counsel Calif. and Nev. (state chmn. 1983—85), Def. Rsch. Inst., Nev. Trial Lawyers Assn., Washoe County Bar Assn., Am. Softball Found. (bd. dirs.), Wolf Club, Order of the Coif. Office: 12th Fl 100 W Liberty St Fl 12 Reno NV 89501-1962 Office Phone: 775-786-5000.

PAGNI, PATRICK JOHN, mechanical engineering science educator, safety engineer, researcher; b. Chgo., Nov. 28, 1942; s. Frank and Helen P.; m. Carol DeSantis, Dec. 26, 1970 (div. Jan. 2000); children: Christina Marie, Catherine Ann, Patrick John Jr; m. Feriel Palmer, Mar. 21, 2003. B in Aeronautical Engring. magna cum laude, U. Detroit, 1965; SM, MIT, 1967, ME, 1969, PhD, 1970. Registered profl. mechanical engr., Calif., fire protection engr., Calif. Rsch. asst. MIT, Cambridge, 1965-70; asst. prof. dept. mech. engring. U. Calif., Berkeley, 1970-76, assoc. prof., 1976-81, prof., 1981—2003, prof. emeritus, 2003—, vice chmn. grad. study, 1986-89; acting assoc. dean Coll. Engring. U. Calif., 1990; assoc. faculty scientist Lawrence Berkeley Lab., 1976—. Vis. scientist Factory Mut. Research Corp., Norwood, Mass., 1980; cons. on fire safety sci. various orgns., 1972—; affiliate prof. fire protection engring. dept. Worcester Poly. Inst., 2000-03; vis. rsch. scholar U. Ulster, No. Ireland, 2000-03. Editor: Fire Science for Fire Safety, 1984, Fire Safety Science--Procs. of the First Internat. Symposium, 1986, Procs. of the Second Internat. Symposium, 1989; contbr. articles to profl. jours. Grantee NSF, NASA, Nat. Bur. Standards, Nat. Inst. Standards and Tech., U.S. Forest Svc., 1971—; Applied Mechanics fellow Harvard U., 1974, 77; Pullman Found. scholar, 1960. Mem. ASME (life), Am. Phys. Soc. (life), Combustion Inst., Soc. Fire Protection Engrs. (hon., Bono award for best paper 1999), Internat. Assn. Fire Safety Sci. (life mem., exec. com.), Tau Beta Pi, Pi Tau Sigma, Alpha Sigma Nu Democrat. Roman Catholic. Home: 1901 Ascot Dr Moraga CA 94556-1412 Office: U Calif Coll Engring Mech Engring Dept Berkeley CA 94720-1740 Office Phone: 925-376-4288. Business E-Mail: pjpagni@me.berkeley.edu.

PAGON, ROBERTA ANDERSON, pediatrician, educator; b. Boston, Oct. 4, 1945; d. Donald Grigg and Erna Louise (Goettsch) Anderson; m. Garrett Dunn Pagon Jr., July 1, 1967; children: Katharine Blye, Garrett Dunn III, Alyssa Grigg, Alexander Goettsch. BA, Stanford U., 1967; MD, Harvard U., 1972. Diplomate Am. Bd. Pediat., Am. Bd. Med. Genetics. Pediatric intern U. Wash. Affiliated Hosp., Seattle, 1972-73, resident in pediat., 1973-75; fellow in med. genetics U. Wash. Sch. Medicine, Seattle, 1976-79, asst. prof. pediat., 1979-84, assoc. prof., 1984-92, prof., 1992—. Prin. investigator, editor in chief GeneTests (www.genetests.org), Seattle, 1992—; pres. Am. Bd. Med. Genetics, 2002, 03; bd. sci. counselors Nat. Human Genome Rsch. Inst., NIH, 2000—04. Sponsor N.W. region U.S. Pony Club, 1985-94. Mem. Am. Soc. Human Genetics (bd. dirs. 2005—, Excellence award 2006), Am. Coll. Med. Genetics, Western Soc. Pediat. Rsch., Phi Beta Kappa. Avocations: hiking, backpacking, horseback riding. Office: Gene Tests 9725 Third Ave NE Ste 602 Seattle WA 98115 Home Phone: 360-794-5726; Office Phone: 206-221-4674.

PAGONIS, WILLIAM GUS, retired army general; b. Charleroi, Pa., Apr. 30, 1941; s. Constantinos V. and Jennie (Kontos) P.; m. Cheryl Elaine Miller, June 14, 1964; children: Gust, Robert. BS, Pa. State U., 1964, MBA in Bus. Logistics, 1970; D in Pub. Svc. (hon.), Washington Jefferson Coll., 1997. Commd. 2d lt. U.S. Army, 1964, advanced through grades to lt. gen., 1991; comdr. 1097th Transp. Co., Vietnam, 1968; div. transp. officer, then exec. officer 2d bn., 501st inf., 101st Airborne Div., Vietnam, 1970-71; pers. staff officer U.S. Army Mil. Pers. Ctr., Alexandria, Va., 1973-75; staff officer Office Chief of Legis. Liaison, Washington, 1975-76; comdr. 10th transp. bn. 7th Transp. Group, Ft. Eustis, Va., 1977-78; chief of staff 193d Inf. Brigade, Panama, 1980-81, comdr. Logistics Support Command, 1981-82; comdr. Div. Support Command, 4th Inf. Div., Ft. Carson, Colo., 1982-85; dir. transp., energy and troop support Office Dep. Chief of Staff for Logistics, Washington, 1989-90; comdg. gen. 22d Support Command, Dhahran, Saudi Arabia, 1990-91, 1990-92, 21st Support Command Europe, Germany, 1992-93; lt. gen., ret. U.S. Army, 1993; exec. v.p. logistics Sears & Roebuck Co., Hoffman Estates, Ill., 1993—. Author: Moving Mountains (Logistics Leadership and Management of the Gulf War), (one of top 30 best bus. books of 1992, top leadership book 1992 Soundview Exec. Book Summaries, 1992), 1992. Decorated D.S.M., Silver Star, Legion of Merit with oak leaf cluster, Bronze Star with 3 oak leaf clusters, Air medal with 2 oak leaf clusters, Meritorious Svc. medal with 4 oak leaf clusters, King Abdul Aziz 2d Class award Chief of Staff, Saudi Arabian Army, 1991, Kuwait Liberation medal Chief of Staff, Kuwait Army, 1992; recipient Merit and Honor award Govt. of Greece, 1991, Joseph C. Scheleen award Am. Soc. Transp. and Logistics, 1991, Man of Yr. award Modern Materials Handling, 1991, Grad. Man of Yr. award Alpha Chi Rho, 1991, AHEPA Man of Yr., 1992, Disting. Alumni award Pa. State U., 1994; named Hellenic Man of Yr., 1992; Pa. State U. fellow, 1992. Home: 202 Smalstig Rd Evans City PA 16033 Office: C&G Ranch LLC 202 Smalstig Rd Evans City PA 16033 Office Phone: 724-789-7680. Business E-Mail: pagonisg@genco.com.

PAGTER, CARL RICHARD, lawyer; b. Balt., Feb. 13, 1934; s. Charles Ralph and Mina (Amelung) P.; m. Judith Elaine Cox, May 6, 1978; 1 child by previous marriage: Corbin Christopher. AA, Diablo Valley Coll., 1953; BA, San Jose State U., 1955; LLB, U. Calif., Berkeley, 1964. Bar: Calif. 1965, D.C. 1977, U.S. Supreme Ct. 1976. Law clk. Kaiser Industries Corp., Oakland, Calif., 1963-64, counsel, 1964-70, assoc. counsel Washington, 1970-73, counsel Oakland, Calif., 1973-75, dir. govt. affairs Washington, 1975-76; v.p., sec., gen. counsel Kaiser Cement Corp., Oakland, Calif., 1976-88, cons., gen. counsel San Ramon, 1988-98, cons., 1998—. Author: (with A. Dundes) Urban Folklore from the Paperwork Empire, 1975, More Urban Folklore from the Paperwork Empire, 1987, Never Try to Teach a Pig to Sing, 1991, Sometimes the Dragon Wins, 1996, Why Don't Sheep Shrink When It Rains, 2000. Trustee Internat. Bluegrass Music Mus., Owensboro, Ky. With USNR, 1957—61, to comdr. USNR, 1978. Mem. Calif. Bar, Am. Folklore Soc., Calif. Folklore Soc., Calif. Bluegrass Assn. (founder, chmn. bd. emeritus), Mariners Square Athletic Club. Republican. Home and Office: 17 Julianne Ct Walnut Creek CA 94595-2610

PAI, SATISH UPENDRA, publishing executive; b. Udupi, Karnataka, India, Nov. 26, 1941; s. Upendra Anantha and Parvathi Pai; m. Sandhya Satish, July 19, 1970; children: Nandana, Gautham. Dir. Manipal Press Ltd., 1960—; mng. dir. Manipal Media Network Ltd., 1989—. Editor Udayavani Daily, 1970, Tushara Mo., 1973, Roopathra Mo., 1976, Tarango Weekly, 1983. Mem. Graphic Arts Tech. Found., IFRA, Fellow Inst. Printing. Avocations: stamp collecting/philately, photography, travel. Home: 38 Anant Nagar Manipal 576104 India Office: Manipal Media Network Ltd Udayavani Bld, Press Corner Manipal 576104 India Business E-Mail: satishpai@manipalmedia.com.

PAIDOUSSIS, MICHAEL PANDELI, mechanical engineering educator; b. Nicosia, Cyprus, Aug. 20, 1935; emigrated to Can., 1953, naturalized, 1976; s. Pandelis Aristeidis and Parthenope (Leptou) P. B in Engring., McGill U., 1958; PhD in Engring., U. Cambridge, 1963. Overseas fellow Gen. Electric Co., Erith, Kent, England, 1958-60; rsch. officer Atomic Energy of Can., Chalk River, Ont., 1963-67; with McGill U., Montreal, 1967—, prof., dept. mech. engring., 1976—, chmn., 1977-86, Thomas Workman prof., 1986—2000, Thomas Workman emeritus prof., 2000—. Cons. and rschr. in field. Author: 2 books; editor: Jour. Fluids and Structures; contbr. articles and books in field. Pres. Hellenic-Can. Solidarity Com. for Cyprus, 1974-80, Com. Pan-Can. de Solidarite pour Chypre, 1978-83; hon. consul gen. Republic of Cyprus, Montreal, 1983—. Recipient Brit. Assn. medal for high distinction in mech. engring., 1958, George Stephenson prize Inst. Mech. Engrs., 1976, commemorative medal for 125th ann. of Confederation of Can., 1993, medal Can. Congress Applied Mechs., 1995. Fellow Instn. Mech. Engrs., ASME (Fluids Engring. award 1999), Can. Soc. Mech. Engring., Royal Soc. Can., Am. Acad. Mechanics, Can. Acad. Engring., Am. Acaad. Mechanics (pres. 2005); mem. Internat. Assn. Hydraulic Rsch., Internat. Assn. Structural Mechanics in Reactor Tech., Order Engrs. Que. Home: 2930 Edouard Montpetit #PH2 Montreal PQ Canada H3T 1J7 Office: 817 Ouest Rue Sherbrooke Montreal PQ Canada H3A 2K6 Home Phone: 514-735-7233; Office Phone: 514-398-6294. Business E-Mail: mary.fiorilli@mcgill.ca.

PAIER, ADOLF ARTHUR, management consultant; b. Branford, Conn., Oct. 27, 1938; s. Adolf Arthur and Margaret Mary (Almond) P.; m. Geraldine Shnakis, Sept. 17, 1966; children: Nathaniel Jason, Andrew Joseph, Alena Catherine. AA, Quinnipiac Coll., 1958; BS in Econs., U. Pa., 1960. Audit mgr. Touche Ross & Co., Phila., 1960-67; pres., dir. Safeguard Scientifics, Inc., Wayne, Pa., 1967-92; chmn., CEO Healthworks Alliance, Inc., King of Prussia, Pa., 1992—2005; pres., CEO Novus Corp., Radnor, Pa., 1992—. Bd. dirs. Deltapaper, Levittown, Pa., Analytical Graphics, Exton, Pa., Probaris Techs., Inc., Phila. Bd. dirs., treas. Univ. of Arts, Phila. bd. dirs. Lincoln Ctr. Family and Youth, Bridgeport, Pa.; bd. overseers U. Pa. Mus. Archaeology and Anthropology. Mem. Chief Execs. Orgn., Phila. Pres. Orgn., Phila. Country Club (bd. govs., treas.). Office: Novus Corp 5 Radnor Corp Ctr 100 Matsonford Rd Ste 520 Radnor PA 19087-4526

PAIGE, DOROTHY BILLIARD, retired secondary school educator, educational consultant; d. Webb Billiard and Doretha Billiard-Johnson; 1 child, Rochelle Denise Paige-Jones. AA in Polit. Sci., LA Harbor Jr. Coll., Wilmington, Calif., 1978; BA in Polit. Sci., Calif. State U. Dominguez Hills, Carson, 1979, MA in Pub. Adminstrn., 1981. Tchr. Calif. Commn. on Tchg., 1982, cert. Bilingual Edn. Calif. Commn. on Tchg., 2002. History tchr. Compton Unified Sch. Dist., Calif., 1979—2002, resource tchr., program coord., 2002—05; edn. cons. Paige-Schwartz & Assoc., Inc., Carson, Calif., 2005—07. Christian edn. dir., fin. dir. Mt. Pilgrim Missionary Bapt. Ch., Compton, 1987—95. Recipient Woman of Yr. award Compton br., Nat. Assn. U. Women, 2007. Mem.: Compton Edn. Assn. (CTA pres. 1982—, segment dir. mid. sch. 1997—99). Democrat. Baptist. Avocations: reading, surfing the net, travel. Home: 21621 Villa Pacifica Cir Carson CA 90745 Office: Paige-Schwartz & Assoc Inc 21621 Villa Pacifica Cir Carson CA 90745 Office Phone: 310-518-7575. Office Fax: 310-427-0279; Home Fax: 310-427-0279. Personal E-mail: dotpaige47@aol.com.

PAIGE, GLENN DURLAND, political scientist, educator; b. Brockton, Mass., June 28, 1929; s. Lester Norman and Rita Irene (Marshall) P.; m. Betty Gail Grenier, Jan. 2, 1949 (div.); children: Gail, Jan, Donn, Sean, Sharon, Van; m. Glenda Hatsuko Naito, Sept. 1, 1973. Grad., Phillips Exeter Acad., 1947; AB, Princeton U., 1955; MA, Harvard U., 1957; Ph. D., Northwestern U., 1959; PhD (hon.), Soka U., 1992. Asst. prof. pub. adminstrn. Seoul Nat. U., 1959-61; asst. to assoc. prof. politics Princeton U., 1961-67; prof. polit. sci. U. Hawaii, Honolulu, 1967-92, prof. emeritus, 1992—. Author: The Korean Decision, 1968, The Scientific Study of Political Leadership, 1977, To Nonviolent Political Science, 1993, Nonkilling Global Political Science, 2002. Program chmn. Hawaii Gov.'s Conf. on Yr. 2000, 1970; faculty UN Univ. Internat. Leadership Acad., 1997; pres. Non-profit Ctr. for Global Nonviolence, 1994—; convenor First Global Nonkilling Leadership Forum, 2007. With U.S. Army, 1948-52. Decorated Commendation medal; recipient Seikyo Culture prize, 1982, Dr. G. Ramachandran award for internat. understanding, 1986, Anuvrat award for internat. peace, 1987, Jai Tulsi Anuvrat award, 1995, Hawaii Lifetime Peacemaker award Ch. of the Crossroads, Honolulu, 2005; named Woodrow Wilson nat. fellow, 1955-56, Princeton U. Class of 1955 award, 1987, 3rd Gandhi Meml. lectr., New Delhi, 1990. Mem. Internat. Polit. Sci. Assn., Am. Polit. Sci. Assn. (Disting. Career award organized sect. ecol. and transformational politics 2004), Phi Beta Kappa. Home: 3653 Tantalus Dr Honolulu HI 96822-5033 Office Phone: 808-536-7442. E-mail: cgnv@hawaii.rr.com.

PAIGE, HILLIARD WEGNER, corporate financial executive, consultant; b. Hartford, Conn., Oct. 2, 1919; s. Joseph Wegner and Ruth (Hill) P.; m. Dorothea Magner, Dec. 8, 1945; children: Elizabeth, Deborah, Hilliard, Jr. BSME, Worcester Poly. Inst., 1941, D (hon.) of Engring., 1971. Sr. v.p. for aerospace and computer ops. GE, NYC, 1941—71; pres. Gen. Dynamics, St. Louis, 1971—73; chmn., CEO Satellite Bus. Sys., Inc., Washington, 1973—76; vice-chmn. bd. Internat. Energy Assocs., Ltd., Washington, 1976—85; chmn. bd. H.A. Knott, Ltd., Silver Spring, Md., 1984—89. Vice-chmn. The Atlantic Coun. of U.S., 1987—, Gallager Marine Systems, Inc., 1993—. Patentee in field; contbr. articles to profl. jours. Mem. Def. Sci. Bd. U.S. Dept. Def., Washington, 1973-78; trustee Worcester Poly. Inst., Mass., 1974—. Recipient Pub. Service award NASA, 1969, Order of Merit Italy, 1970, Engr. of Year award Greater Phila. Engring Council, 1960 Fellow AIAA (founding dir.), Explorers Club (nat.); mem. NAE. Clubs: Metropolitan, Chevy Chase (Washington); Conquistadores del Cielo. Republican. Congregationalist. Avocations: skiing, tennis, scuba diving, golf. Home and Office: 5834 Williamsburg Landing Dr Williamsburg VA 23185 Office Phone: 757-220-2797. Office Fax: 757-220-2149.

PAIGE, JEFFERY MAYLAND, sociologist, educator; b. Providence, June 15, 1942; s. Charles Warren and Dorothy Frances (Rice) P.; m. Karen Ericksen, Apr. 30, 1966 (div. 1980). AB summa cum laude, Harvard U., 1964; PhD, U. Mich., 1968. Asst. prof. U. Calif., Berkeley, 1968-76; assoc. prof. U. Mich., Ann Arbor, 1976-82, prof., 1982—, dir. ctr. for rsch. on social orgn., 1992-97; vis. scholar MIT, Cambridge, Mass., 1998. Vis. lectr. U. Ctrl. Am., San Salvador, El Salvador, 1990, Fla. Internat. U., Miami, 1992; internat. observer Nicaraguan Nat. Adv. Commn. on Atlantic Coast, Managua, 1986. Author: Agrarian Revolution, 1975 (Sorokin award 1976), Coffee and Power, 1997; co-author: The Politics of Reproductive Ritual, 1981. Fulbright fellow, 1990, Kellog fellow, 1991; rsch. grantee NSF, 1990-92. Mem. Am. Sociol. Assn. (coun. chair polit. econ. of world sys. sect. 1987-89), Latin Am. Studies Assn., Sociol. Rsch. Assn. Democrat. Avocations: hiking, skiing, sailing. Office: U Mich Dept Sociology Ann Arbor MI 48109

PAIGE, KATHLEEN K., naval officer; b. Schenectady, NY, Aug. 31, 1948; m. David Tuma. BS, U. N.H., 1970; MS, Naval Postgrad. Sch., 1976; grad., Def. Sys. Mgmt. Coll.; grad. program for execs., Cornell U. Commd. USN, advanced through grades to rear admiral; acquisition mgr. Navy's Std. Embedded Computer Resource Office; AEGIS C3 warfare officer USN; baseline mgr. combat sys. divsn. AEGIS Shipbuilding Program; chief engr. Naval Surface Warfare Ctr., Port Hueneme; tech. dir. AEGIS Program Office; comdr. Naval Surface Warefare Ctr., Arlington, Va., 1996-98, admiral, 1998—. Decorated Legion of Merit. Office: Naval Sea Systems Command SE#1100 1333 Isaac Hull Ave Washington DC 20376-1100

PAIGE, RODERICK RAYNOR, educational consultant, former secretary of education; b. Monticello, Miss., June 17, 1933; div., one child. BS, Jackson State U., 1955; MS, Ind. U., 1964, PhD, 1969. Head football coach Utica Jr. Coll., 1957—67, Jackson St. U., 1962—69; dean Coll. Edn. Tex. So. U., 1984—94, developer Ctr. Excellence in Urban Edn.; supt. Houston Ind. Sch. Dist., 1994—2000; sec. U.S. Dept. Edn., Washington, 2001—05; co-founder, chmn. Chartwell Edn. Group LLC, NYC, 2005—. Est. Ctr. for Excellence in Urban Edn., Tex. Southern U.; created Peer Exam., Evaluation, Redesign (PEER) program. Co-author: A Declaration of Beliefs and Visions. Mem. NAACP; mem. adv. bd. Tex. Commerce Bank, Am. Leadership Forum. Recipient Harold W. McGraw, Jr. Prize in Edn., 2000; named Supt. of the Yr., Nat. Assn. Black Sch. Educators, 2000, Nat. Supt. Yr., Am. Assn. Sch. Adminstr., 2001. Mem. review coms. Tex. Edn. Agy., State Bd. Edn. Task Force H.S. Edn.; chair, Youth Employment Issues Nat. Com. Employment Policy U.S. Dept. Labor subcom.; mem. Nat. Assn. Advancement Colored People, Edn. Com. States, Coun. Great City Schs.(recipient Richard R. Green award for Outstanding Urban Educator, 1999). Office: Chartwell Education Group LLC Empre State Bldg Ste 7506 New York NY 10118 E-mail: paige@chartwelleducation.com.

PAIGE, SUSAN MARY, adult education educator; b. San Antonio, June 18, 1948; d. Frank Allen Paige and Irene Helen Szalkowski; m. Gary James McPhee, Aug. 26, 1968 (div. Feb. 1, 1972); m. Jimmie Louis Botto, May 13, 1974 (div. May 13, 1978); children: Jennifer Lynn McPhee, Jimmie Louis Botto Jr., Amanda Irene Botto Santell. BS, Buffalo State Coll., NY, 1973; MEd, SUNY, Buffalo, 1976, PhD, 2003. Cert. pub. sch. tchr.-elem. edn. NY State Edn. Dept., 1976, pub. sch. tchr.-children with disabilities NY State Edn. Dept., 2006, pub. sch. tchr.-students with disabilities NY State Edn. Dept., 2006. Head tchr. Buffalo State Child Care Ctr., 1973—75; dir. Dunkirk Cmty. Day Care Ctr., NY, 1976—77; office mgr. Penn Aluminum, Buffalo, 1978—82; traffic supr. Kasson & Keller, Fonda, NY, 1983—88; edn. coord. Fulmont Head Start, Amsterdam, NY, 1988—89; program dir. Children's Svcs. Network, Fonda, 1989—90; asst. prof., coord. early childhood edn. Fulton Montgomery C.C., Johnstown, NY, 1990—94; lectr. Buffalo State Coll., 1999—. Treas., membership chair Fulmont Assn. for the Edn. of Young Children, Fonda, 1992—94; pres. grad. student assn. dept. learning and instrn. SUNY, Buffalo, 1998—99, symposium planning com. grad. student assn., 1998—99. Contbr. chapters to books, articles to profl. jours. Religious edn. tchr. Sacred Heart Ch., Tribes Hill, NY, 1985—88; liturgy com. St. Margarets Ch., Buffalo, 2001—04; edn. adv. com. St. Margaret's Ch., Buffalo, 2004—05; bd. dirs. Literacy Empowerment Action Plan of Western NY, 2007. Grantee, NY State Legislature, 1988—90, Hire Edn. Support Ctr. for Sys. Change, 2003—04. Mem.: Nat. Assn. for the Edn. of Young Children (assoc.), Coun. for Exceptional Children (assoc.; treas. NY state divsn. early childhood coun. 2005—07). Independent. Roman Catholic. Avocations: crocheting, gardening. Office: Buffalo State College 1300 Elmwood Ave Buffalo NY 14222 Office Phone: 716-878-3556.

PAIGE, VIVIAN JO-ANN, accountant; b. Memphis, May 7, 1960; d. Charles Thomas and Mary Elizabeth (Manning) P. BS, Old Dominion U., 1981, MBA, 1994. CPA, Va. With IRS, Norfolk, Va., 1980-85; pres. Individual Returns Svcs. Inc., Norfolk, 1991-95; prin. Vivian J. Paige, CPA, P.C., 1986—; adj. instr. acctg. Old Dominion U., 2000—, mem. adv. coun., dept. acctg., 2000—. Bd. dirs. St. Columba Ecumenical Ministries, Inc., 1989-93, v.p. bd. dirs., 1990-91, pres. bd. dirs., 1992-93, Neighborhood Network steering com.; mem. Real Estate Bd. Equalization, 1999-2005, sec., 1999-2001, pres., 2002-05; co-founder Norfolk United Facing Race, bd. dirs., 2001-04. With USAR, 1979-81. Mem. AICPA, NAFE, AAUW, NAACP, LWV, Urban Leauge, Va. Soc. CPAs. Avocations: music, singing, computers. Business E-Mail: vivian@vjpcpa.com.

PAIGE, WAYNE LEO, visual arts educator, artist; b. Chgo., Mar. 5, 1944; s. Henry and Lucille Mabel Paige; 1 child, Matthew. BFA in Painting, U. Ill., Champaign/Urbana, 1968; MFA in Painting, The George Washington U., Washington, DC, 1971. Lic. tchr. Va. Drafting and art tchr. Eastern HS, Washington, 1971—95; drafting instr. Md. Drafting Inst., Langley Pk., 1979—90; constrn. tech. tchr. Potomac HS, Dumfries, Va., 1995—96; visual arts instr. Notre Dame Acad., Middleburg, Va., 1996—; adj. prof. art Lord Fairfax CC, Warrenton, Va., 2007—. Exhibited in group shows at Corcoran Gallery Art, Washington, DC, 1980, Anderson Art Gallery, Richmond, 1983, Strathmore Art Ctr., Bethesda, 1986, Danville Mus. Art, Va., 1990, Western Mich. U., Kalamazoo, 1990, Md. Coll. Art and Design, Silver Spring, 1998, Katzen Art Ctr., Washington, DC, 2006, 16 one man shows. Recipient Print and Drawing award, Va. Commn. Arts, 1989, Best in Show award, Arts Coun. Fairfax County, 1994. Mem.: Tchr. Inst. Contemporary Art, Mid. St. Gallery (Washington, Va.), Piedmont Environ. Coun., Wash. Tchrs. Union. Home: PO Box 729 Flint Hill VA 22627 Office: Notre Dame Acad 35321 Notre Dame Ln Middleburg VA 20117 Office Phone: 540-687-5581. Personal E-mail: paigeart@waynepaige.com.

PAIK, JI HYE, research scientist; d. B. Kook and S. Ryong Paik. PhD, U. Conn., 2004. Lic. pharmacist Korea FDA, 1997. Rschr. Dana Farber Cancer Inst., Boston, 2004—. Fellow, DRC, 2006—. Mem.: NEBS (assoc.). Achievements include research in cancer. Business E-Mail: jpaik@partners.org.

PAIK, JOHN KEE, structural engineer; b. Seoul; came to U.S., 1955; s. Nam Suk and Kyong Ock (Yun) P.; m. Aine Fenoula Ievers, Feb. 20, 1970; 1 child, Brian Ievers Paik. BSCE, So. Meth. U., 1961; PhD, NYU, 1975. Lic. profl. engr. N.Y., N.J., Conn., Pa., Md., Mass., Vt., Ga., Fla., N.C. Chief engr. T.Y. Lin and Assocs., NYC, 1960-67; chief structural engr. Soros Assocs., NYC, 1967-68; sr. project engr. Stauffer Chem. Co., Dobbs

Ferry, N.Y., 1975-77; prin., founder Paik and Assocs., Westchester County, N.Y., 1977—; chmn., founder The Future Home Tech. Inc., Port Jervis, N.Y., 1986—; chmn., pres. J.K.P. Constrn. Co. Inc., Mohegan Lake, N.Y., 1989—. Adj. assoc. prof. Grad. Sch. Engring. Manhattan Coll., Bronx, 1985; lectr. Grad. Sch. Engring. Polytech. U., Bklyn., 1973-85, Cooper Union, N.Y.C., 1972. Mem. ASCE, NSPE, Am. Inst. Steel Constrn., Prestressed Concrete Inst., N.Y Acad. Scis., Am. Concrete Inst., Post Tensioning Inst., Constrn. Specifications Inst., Am. Arbitration Assn. (dispute arbitrator, constrn.), So. Meth. U. Alumni Club (pres. 1964), Chi Epsilon. Republican. Methodist. Achievements include the design of over 200 million sq. feet of comml., residential, indsl. and instnl. structures including several highrise bldgs. over 40 stories in N.Y.C. and White Plains, N.Y. Personal E-mail: jpaik@tampabay.rr.com.

PAIK, MYUNGHEE CHO, statistician, educator; b. Seoul, Republic of Korea, Nov. 2, 1958; d. Seong-Yun Cho and Yong-Hee You; m. Yi Hyon Paik, Dec. 12, 1981; 1 child, Jane. PhD, U. Pitts., 1987. Prof. Columbia U., NYC, 1988—. Author: (textbook) Statistical Methods for Rates and Proportions (Calderone Prize, 1989). Grantee, NIH. Mem.: Am. Statis. Assn. (regional adv. com. mem.). Office: Columbia U 600 W 168th St New York NY 10032

PAIK, YOUNHEE, artist; b. Korea; BFA, Seoul Nat. U.; MFA, San Francisco Art Inst. Exhibitions include Gallery Hyundai, Seoul, Saint Peter's Church, NYC, Brenda Taylor Gallery, TOTAL Mus., Seoul, Kennedy Arts Ctr., Oakland, Calif., Nat. Mus. Contemporary Art, Seoul, San Jose Mus. of Art, San Jose, Calif., Eloise Pickard Smith Gallery, Santa Cruz, Calif., Art Mus. of South Tex., Venice Biennale, Nat. Mus. Modern Art, Mex., Triton Mus., Santa Clara, Calif., Represented in permanent collections Ho Am Art Mus., Byuck San Corp., Triton Mus., San Jose Mus., Korean Cultural Service Nat. Mus. Contemporary Art, Pacific Bell. Home: 448 W 37 St New York NY 10018

PAIKEDAY, THOMAS M., lexicographer, linguistic consultant; arrived in U.S., 1962, arrived in Can., 1964; m. Mary Kurien Kizhakethottam, Jan. 4, 1967; children: Anthony, Anne-Marie. LPH, Coll. of Jesuits, 1955; BA with 1st class honors, Madras Christian Coll., 1958; MA, U. Madras, 1960; postgrad, Boston Coll., 1962—63, U. Mich., 1963—64. Lectr. English St. Joseph's Coll., Tiruchy, Madras, India, 1958—59, Ramjas Coll., Delhi, India, 1960—61; copy editor Statesman, New Delhi, 1961—62; asst. lexicographer W.J. Gage Ltd., Toronto, Ont., Canada, 1964—66; editor Ont. Min. Edn., Toronto, 1966—67; head lexicography divsn. Holt, Rinehart & Winston, Toronto, 1967—73; chief lexicographer Lexicography, Inc., Brampton, Ont., Canada, 1973—. Cons. Collier-Macmillan Can., Toronto, 1980-81, Can. advisor Collins Publs., Glasgow, Scotland, 1981-82. Chief editor Winston Interm. Dictionary, 1969, Compact Dictionary of Canadian English, 1970, Winston Canadian Dictionary, elem. edit., 1975, New York Times Everyday Dictionary, 1982, The Penguin Canadian Dictionary, 1990, The User's Webster, 2000; author: The Native Speaker is Dead!, 1985; contbr. articles to profl. jours. Mem. Dictionary Soc. N.Am., MLA, Am. Dialect Soc., Am. Name Soc. Roman Catholic. Avocations: computer applications in lexicography, tennis, swimming. Office: Lexicography Inc 83 Sunny Meadow Blvd Brampton ON Canada L6R 1Z3 Office Phone: 905-790-7076. Personal E-mail: thomaspaikeday@yahoo.ca.

PAIKOWSKY, SAMUEL G., civil engineering educator; b. Petah Tikva, Israel, Sept. 17, 1954; came to U.S., 1982; s. Rubin and Zehava (Garber) P.; m. Lynn Gariepy, July 15, 1988; children: Oren, Guy, Dan, Tamar. BSc, Technion, Haifa, Israel, 1979, MSc, 1982; ScD, MIT, 1989. Prof. civil/environ. engring. geotech. engring. rsch. lab. U. Mass., Lowell, 1979—. Registered profl. engr., Israel. Recipient NSF Young Investigator award, 1993—, Hogentogler award ASTM, 1996. Achievements include research in granular material behavior; pile foundation design and construction; probability based Load and Resistance Factor Design (LRFD); established Geosciences and Testing and Rsch, Inc. (GTR) for testing, design, rsch. and analysis in 1995. Office Phone: 978-934-2277.

PAIN, BETSY M., lawyer; b. Albertville, Ala., Aug. 29, 1950; d. Charles Riley and Jean Faye (Rains) Stone; m. William F. Pain, Nov. 18, 1977 (div. July 30, 2003); children: Taylor Holland, Emily Anne Pain. AA, Northeastern Okla. A&M, Miami, 1970; BA, U. Okla., 1974, JD, 1976. Bar: Okla. 1977; U.S. Dist. Ct. (we. dist.) 1979. Staff atty. Okla. Dept. Corrections, Oklahoma City, 1978-79; gen. counsel Okla. Pardon and Parole Bd., Oklahoma City, 1979-84, exec. dir., 1983—88; corp. counsel Roberts, Schornick & Assocs., Inc., Norman, Okla., 1990-2000, Atkins Benham, Inc., 2002; chief legal officer The Benham Cos., LLC, Oklahoma City, 2002—. Editor: (newsletter) RSA Environ. Report, 1991—. With extended family program Juvenile Svcs., Inc. Cleveland County, Okla., 1983-91. Mem. NAFE, Okla. Bar Assn., Assn. Corp. Counsel, Phi Alpha Delta. Democrat. Methodist. Avocations: reading, needlecrafts, church activities. Office: The Benham Cos LLC 9400 N Broadway Oklahoma City OK 73114 Office Phone: 405-478-5353. E-mail: betsy.pain@benham.com.

PAIN, GEORGE H., lawyer; b. Corry, Pa., Nov. 18, 1950; BA, BS cum laude, Bucknell U., 1973; JD cum laude, U. Conn., 1977; LLM, NYU, 1988. Bar: Conn. 1977, U.S. Dist. Ct. Conn. 1981, NY 1986, U.S. Dist. Ct. NY (We dist.) 1986, Ill. 1988. Assoc. Holland & Twachtman, Glastonbury, Conn., 1977—78; sr. counsel Environ. Law Inst., Washington, 1978—80; assoc. counsel Olin Chem. Group, Stamford, Conn., 1980—85; with Jaeckle, Fleischmann & Mugel, 1985—86; of counsel Olin Corp., Clayton, Mo., 1986—88, sr. counsel, 1988—91, chief counsel, 1991—94, dep. gen. counsel, 1995—96, v.p., gen. counsel, sec., 2002—, Primex Technologies, Inc., St. Petersburg, Fla., 1997—2000; v.p., gen. counsel, asst. sec. Gen. Dynamics Ordinance and Tactical Systems Inc., St. Petersburg, Fla., 2001—02. Adj. prof. law Stetson U., 2001—02. Mem. editl. adv. bd.: Environmental Law Reporter, 1982—91. Mem.: ABA, Am. Corp. Counsel Assn., Ill. State Bar Assn. Office: Olin Corp Legal Dept 190 Carondelet Plz Ste 1530 Clayton MO 63105 E-mail: ghpain@olin.com. *

PAINCHAUD, PHILLIP ANDRE, metrologist; b. Somerville, Mass., Apr. 24, 1919; s. Phillip Andre Painchaud and Gertrude Marie Shanley; m. Josephine Daisy Wandschneider, Dec. 18, 1943 (dec. Feb. 1988); children: Phillip A. III, Denise Michele, Valerie Yvonne; m. Arlene Roberts Painchaud, July 12, 1992 (dec. Dec. 1999). Student, MIT and U. Ill., 1943, RI State Coll., 1938-41; BS in Engring., Pacific States U., 1947. Lic. profl. engr., Calif. Gen. supr. metrology Northrop Corp., Anaheim, Calif., 1948-65; dir. corp. stds. E-H Rsch. Labs., Oakland, Calif., 1965-70; sr. scientist Alcon Labs., Ft. Worth, 1970-71; dir. mktg. Metron Corp., Upland, Calif., 1971-72, 78-79; cons. Painchaud Cons., Brea, Calif., 1970—. Vice-chair Calif. Profl. Metrology Com., Sacramento, 1965—74; chair Gov.'s Commn. Metrology, Sacramento, 1967—68; mem. metrology adv. bd. Calif. State Poly. U., San Luis Obispo, 1970—76. Columnist The Std., 1993— Mem. curriculum bd. Calif. State U.-Dominguez Hills, Carson, 1998—. With U.S. Signal Corps, 1942-45. Laureate Woodington award Meas. Sci. Conf. Inc., 1996; disting. vis. scholar Butler County C.C., 1996. Fellow Precision Measurements Assn. (co-founder 1958, exec. dir. 1980-89, life, pres. 1963-64), IEEE (life, sr. mem.); mem. Internat. Soc. Weighing and Measurements (life, sr. mem., gov. precision measurement divsn. 1997-99), Instrument Soc. Am. (life, sr. mem., dir. met. divsn. 1966-70), Am. Soc. for Quality (sr. mem., Max J. Unis award for lifetime achievement in measurement sci., measurement quality divsn. 2006), ENG Club San Francisco. Avocations: computer operations, photography. Home and Office: 1110 W Dorothy Dr Brea CA 92821-2017 Office Phone: 714-529-6604. Office Fax: 714-529-1109. E-mail: painchaud4@cs.com.

PAINE, ALAN, poet; b. Panama City, Fla., Nov. 30, 1956; s. Charles Russell and Edna Pearl (Pierce) Williams. Student, U. Nev., Las Vegas, 1978—80, Taft Coll., Calif., 1975—77. Adj. prof. S. Nev. CC, Las Vegas, 1996—99; pres. Diogenes Prodns., Las Vegas, 2000—. Prodr., dir., actor: (plays) What Happens to a Dream Deferred; author: (screenplays) Clear Skies on Tuesday, Shadow Chasers, The Love Child, What Kind of Fool, (book) Ode to Madonna and Other Poems, 1991, numerous poems; actor: (plays) Raisin in the Sun, Don't Bother Me, I can't Cope, No Place to be Somebody; (films) No Not One. Counselor S. Nev. Suicide Prevention Ctr., Las Vegas, 1992. Recipient Golden Poet award, World Poetry, Inc., 1991, 1992, cert. of spl. recognition, Watermark Press, award of merit, Verses, cert. of honor, Hidden Springs Rev., Critics Choice award, Nat. Libr. Poetry, 1996, Editors Choice award, Poetry website, 2005.

PAINE, JAMES CARRIGER, federal judge; b. Valdosta, Ga., May 20, 1924; s. Leon Alexander and Josie Carriger (Jones) P.; m. Ruth Ellen Bailey, Sept. 8, 1950; children: James Carriger, Jonathan Jones, JoEllen. BS, Columbia U., 1947; LL.B., U. Va., 1950, JD, 1970. Bar: Fla. 1950. Mem. firm Earnest, Lewis, Smith & Jones, West Palm Beach, Fla., 1950-54, Jones Adams Paine & Foster, 1954-60, Jones Paine & Foster, 1960-79; judge U.S. Dist. Ct. (so. dist.) Fla., West Palm Beach, 1979-92, sr. judge, 1992—. Bd. dirs., pres. Children's Home Soc. Fla., 1978-80; mem. bd. Episcopal Diocese S.E. Fla. Served to lt. USNR, 1943-47. Mem. Greater West Palm Beach C. of C. (pres. 1973-74), Palm Beach County Bar Assn. Democrat. Office: US Dist Ct 701 Clematis St West Palm Beach FL 33401-5101

PAINE, ROBERT J., environmental scientist, consultant; s. Norman Emory and Jane T. Paine; m. Beth Stephanie Fuller, Aug. 4, 1979; children: Natalie, Nathan, Emory. BS in Atmospheric Sci., SUNY, Albany, 1973; MS in Meteorology, MIT, Cambridge, Mass., 1975. Cert. qualified environ. profl. Inst. Profls. Environ. Practice. Air quality scientist ENSR Corp., Westford, Mass., 1975—2004, tech. dir., 2004—. Com. mem. Medford Clean Energy Com., 2003—. Mem.: Air and Waste Mgmt. Assn. (chair meteorology com. 2000—03), Am. Meteorol. Soc. (chair com. on meteorol. aspects air pollution 1996—98, cert. consulting meteorologist 1983). Avocations: music, photography, gardening. Office: ENSR Corp 2 Technology Park Dr Westford MA 01886

PAINE, ROBERT TREAT, chemistry educator; b. Colorado Springs, Colo., Dec. 15, 1944; Robert T. and Marietta H. Paine; m. Bonnie Pauly Paine, Aug. 20, 1967; children: Andrew S., Matthew H., Joanna M. BS, U. Calif., Berkeley, 1966; PhD, U. Mich., 1970. Postdoctoral work Northwestern U., Evanston, Ill., 1970-72, Los Alamos (N.Mex.) Nat. Lab., 1972-74, cons., 1974—; asst. prof. U. N.Mex., Albuquerque, 1974-78, assoc. prof., 1978-82, prof., 1982—, Disting. prof., 2005—. Contbr. articles to profl. jours. Trainee NASA, 1966-69. Fellow AAAS; mem. Am. Chem. Soc. Office: U NMex Dept Chemistry Albuquerque NM 87131-0001 Office Phone: 505-277-1661. E-mail: rtpaine@unm.edu.

PAINE, STEVEN L., school system administrator; m. Jackie Paine; 4 children. Grad., Fairmont State Coll.; MS in Ednl. Adminstrn., W.Va. U., PhD in Ednl. Leadership. Tchr. Harrison, Upshur and Morgan Counties, W.Va.; curriculum dir.; asst. prin.; prin.; county supt. Morgan County; dep. state supt. schs. W.Va. Dept. Edn., 2003—05, state supt. schs., 2005—. Recipient Milken Family Found. Nat. Educator Award. Office: W Va Dept Edn 1900 Kanawha Blvd E Charleston WV 25305 E-mail: dvermill@access.k12.wv.us. *

PAINE, WALTER CABOT, journalist, consultant; b. Brookline, Mass., May 9, 1923; s. Richard Cushing and Ellen Eliot Paine; m. Ethel Landon Penzel, Dec. 1948 (div. Aug. 14, 1958); children: Michael, Christopher, Piera; m. Eleanor Cole Meyer, Aug. 27, 1959 (div. June 16, 1970); children: Alita, Benjamin; m. Barbara Ann Moyer, June 10, 1995. Student, St. John's Coll., Annapolis, Md., 1942—43; AB cum laude, Harvard U., 1949; postgrad., Columbia U., 1951. Cert. scuba diver, lic. capt. USCG, 1985. Assoc. editor Balt. Sunpapers, 1951—53; editor-in-chief, pub. Valley News, West Lebanon, NH, 1956—80. Pres. Keene (N.H.) Pub. Co., 1955—80; dir. Chelsea Green Pub., White River Junction, Vt., 1995—; cons. Montshire Mus. Sci., Norwich, Vt., 1990—, founder, chmn., 1974—90. Trustee U. Vt., Burlington, 1963—71. Sgt. USAF, 1943—46. Recipient Granite State award for outstanding pub. svc., N.H. State Univ. Sys., 1991. Avocations: ocean racing, marine research, music, poetry. Home: PO Box 90 213 Palmer Rd Enfield Center NH 03749 Office: Montshire Mus Sci 1 Montshire Rd Norwich VT 05055 Personal E-mail: verve@valley.net.

PAINE, WILLIAM H., lawyer; b. 1961; BA cum laude, Amherst Coll., 1983; JD cum laude, Boston Univ., 1987. Bar: Mass. 1987. Ptnr., co-chmn. Securities Enforcement Litigation group Wilmer Cutler Pickering Hale & Dorr, Boston. Named a Mass. Super Lawyer, Boston Mag., 2004. Office: Wilmer Cutler Pickering Hale & Dorr 60 State St Boston MA 02109 Office Phone: 617-526-6134. Office Fax: 617-526-5000. Business E-Mail: william.paine@wilmerhale.com.

PAINTER, GAYLE STANFORD, research physicist, consultant; b. Columbia, SC, Feb. 27, 1941; s. Garland Lee and Pearl Elizabeth (Marler) P.; m. June Elaine Griffin, June 22, 1962; children: Angela, Jennifer. BS, U. S.C., 1963, PhD, 1967. Postdoctoral researcher Quantum Theory Project U. Fla., Gainesville, 1967-69; rsch. physicist Oak Ridge (Tenn.) Nat. Lab., 1969-74, sr. rsch. physicist, 1975—. Guest scientist H.H. Wills Physics Lab., U. Bristol, U.K., 1974, Inst. for Solid State Physics Kernforschungsanlage, Juelich, Germany, 1975; cons. Consultec, Inc., Knoxville, 1990—. Contbr. 60 articles to profl. jours. Leader youth mission 1st United Meth. Ch., Oak Ridge, 1990. Recipient Tech. Achievement award Martin Marietta Energy Systems, 1987, 89, Publ. award, 1988, 93; Woodrow Wilson fellow, 1963. Fellow Am. Phys. Soc.; mem. Phi Beta Kappa. Democrat. Avocations: woodworking, photography, watercolor, music, home repair. Home: 19 Moore Ln Oak Ridge TN 37830-8309 Office: Oak Ridge Nat Lab PO Box 2008 Oak Ridge TN 37831-2008

PAINTER, JACK TIMBERLAKE, civil engineer; b. Kincaid, W.Va., July 23, 1930; s. Troy Earl and Nannie Bell (Proffit) P. BSCE, W.Va. U., 1950, MSCE, 1955. Instr. civil engring. W.Va. U., 1950-51, 53-55; mem. faculty La. Tech U., Ruston, 1955—; prof. civil engring. La. Tech. U., 1962-92; Alumni Found. prof. La. Tech U., 1977-78; prof. emeritus La. Tech. U., 1992—. Vis. lectr. Manhattan Coll., Coll. Forestry, SUNY, Syracuse, Cornell U., U. Wis., 1954-60 Nat. pres. Circus Fans Assn. Am., 1967; lic. layreader Episcopal Ch. With USNR, 1951-52, comdr. res., 1966-90. Named Man of Year Omicron Delta Kappa, 1972, Jack T. Painter Scholarship in his honor, 1998, The Jack T. Painter Professorship in Engring. in his honor, 2003; Faculty fellow NSF, 1958—59. Fellow ASCE (life, 11 Outstanding Prof. award 1969-90); mem. La. Engring. Soc. (Charles M. Kerr Pub. Rels. award 1990), Am. Soc. Engring. Edn., Tau Beta Pi (Outstanding Prof. award 1963, 68, 74, 78), Chi Epsilon (Nat. Excellent Tchg. award 1985). Address: 101 Biel Lane New Bern NC 28562

PAINTER, JOHN HOYT, engineer; b. Winfield, Kans., Mar. 27, 1934; s. John Paul and Marjorie Marietta (Slack) P.; m. Joy Lou Vaughan, June 7, 1955; children: John Mark, Paul Burton, William Vaughan, Joy Lynn. BS, U. Ill., 1961, MS, 1962; postgrad., Coll. William and Mary, 1967—69; PhD, So. Meth. U., 1972. Apollo comm. engr., tchr. astronauts Manned Spacecraft Ctr. NASA, Houston, 1962—65; sr. engr. Motorola Govt. Electronics divsn., Scottsdale, Ariz., 1965—67; rsch. engr. NASA Langley Rsch. Ctr., Hampton, Va., 1967—74; assoc. prof. elec. engring. Tex. A&M U., College Station, 1974—79, prof. elec. engring., 1979—, prof. computer sci., 1989—, prof. aerospace engring., 1999—. Pres. ALTAIR Corp. cons., College Station, 1980—; tchr. Christian eschatology seminars; adj. instr. Nat. Emergency Response and Rescue Training Ctr., 2003-. Author: The Church Visited, 2002; patentee digital signal processing and fuzzy logic. With USAF, 1953—58. Recipient Recognition cert. NASA, 1975; GE Found. fellow, 1962. Mem.: IEEE (life). Avocation: radio operating. Office: Tex A&M U Dept Aero Engring College Station TX 77843-3141 Business E-Mail: painter@tamu.edu.

PAINTER, MARK PHILIP, judge; b. Cin., Apr. 6, 1947; s. John Philip and Marjorie (West) P.; m. Sue Ann Painter. BA, U. Cin., 1970, JD, 1973. Bar: Ohio 1973, U.S. Dist. Ct. (so. dist.) Ohio 1973, U.S. Supreme Ct. 1980. Assoc. Smith & Schnacke (now part of Thompson Hine), 1973-78; pvt. practice Cin., 1978-82; judge Hamilton County Mcpl. Ct., Cin., 1982-95, Ohio 1st Dist. Ct. Appeals, Cin., 1995—. Adj. prof. law U. Cin., 1990-2006; lectr. in field. Author: Ohio DUI Law, 1988, 16th edit., 2007, The Legal Writer: 40 Rules for the Art of Legal Writing, 2002, 3d edit., 2005, Ohio Appellate Practice, 2003, 4d edit., 2007, William Howard Taft, 2004, Write Well, 2007; mem. editl. bd.: Criminal Law Jour. Ohio, 1989—92; contbr. articles to profl. jours. Mem. bd. commrs. on grievances and discipline Ohio Supreme Ct., 1993—95; mem. Rep. Ctrl. Com., Cin., 1972—82; bd. dirs. Citizens Sch. Com., Cin., 1974—76; trustee Freestore Foodbank, Cin., 1984—90, Friends of William Howard Taft Birthplace, 2001—07, Mary Jo Brueggeman Meml. Found., Cin., 1981—92. Recipient Superior Jud. Svc. award Ohio Supreme Ct., 1982, 84, 85, Superior Writing award Green Bag Legal Jour., 2005, Disting. Alumni award U. Cin. Coll. Arts and Scis., 2007. Mem. ABA, Ohio State Bar Assn., Cin. Bar Assn. (trustee 1988-90), Am. Judges Assn., Am. Judicature Soc., Am. Soc. Writers on Legal Subjects, Potter Stewart Inn of Ct. (master of bench emeritus), Bankers Club. Home: 2449 Fairview Ave Cincinnati OH 45219-1170 Office: Ct of Appeals William Howard Taft Law Ctr 230 E 9th St Cincinnati OH 45202-2174 Office Phone: 513-946-3444. E-mail: JuqPainter@aol.com.

PAINTER, NELL IRVIN, historian, educator, writer; b. Houston, Aug. 2, 1942; BA, U. Calif., Berkeley, 1964; student, U. Bordeaux, France, 1962-63, U. Ghana, 1965-66; MA, UCLA, 1967; PhD, Harvard U., 1974. Teaching fellow Harvard U., Cambridge, Mass., 1969-70, 72-74; asst. prof. history U. Pa., Phila., 1974-77, assoc. prof., 1977-80; prof. history U. N.C., Chapel Hill, 1980-88, Princeton (N.J.) U., 1988-91, acting dir. Afro-Am. Studies Program, 1990-91, Edwards Prof. Am. History, 1991—. Russell Sage vis. prof. history Hunter Coll., CUNY, N.Y.C., 1985-86. Author: Exodusters: Black Migration to Kansas After Reconstruction, 1976, The Narrative of Hosea Hudson: His Life as a Negro Communist in the South, 1979, Standing at Armageddon: The United States 1877-1919, 1987, Sojourner Truth: A Life, A Symbol, 1996, Southern History Across the Color Line, 2002, Creating Black Americans, 2005; editor: Gender and Am. Culture Series; mem. editl. bd. Jour. Women's History, Ency. Americana; contbr. articles to profl. jours. Ford Found. fellow, 1971-72, Am. Coun. Learned Soc. fellow, 1976-77, Charles Warren Ctr. Studies in Am. History fellow, 1976-77, Radcliffe/Bunting Inst. fellow, 1976-77, Nat. Humanities Ctr. fellow, 1978-79, Guggenheim fellow, 1982-83, Ctr. Advanced Study in Behavioral Scis. fellow, 1988-89, Kate B. and Hall J. Peterson fellow Am. Antiquarian Soc., 1991, NEH fellow, 1992-93; recipient Ccoretta Scott King award AAUW, 1969-70, Grad. Soc. medal Radcliffe Coll. Alumnae, 1984, Candace award Nat. Coalition One Hundred Black Women, 1986; named U. Calif. at Berkeley Alumnae of Yr., 1989. Fellow Am. Acad. Arts & Scis.; mem. Am. Coun. Learned Soc., Am. Antiquarian Soc., Am. Hist. Assn. (mem. program com. 1976-78, J. Franklin Jameson fellowship com. 1978-79, Beveridge and Dunning prizes com. 1985-87, mem. coun. 1991-93, Roelker Mentorship award 2001), Am. Studies Assn. (mem. internat. com. 1983-88, mem. nat. coun. 1989-92, mem. adv. coun. 1991-92), Assn. Study Afro-Am. Life and History (mem. program com. 1976, Carter G. Woodson award 2004), Assn. Black Women Historians (mem. rsch. com. 1980—, nat. dir. 1982-84, chair Brown pub. prize com. 1983-86, 88-91), Berkshire Conf. Women Historians (mem. program com. 1976), Inst. So. Studies (mem. exec. com. 1987-88), Orgn. Am. Historians (mem. com. status women 1975-77, mem. program com. 1977-79, 83-85, Frederick Jackson Turner award com. 1983, mem. exec. bd. 1984-87, chair ad hoc com. on minority historians 1985-87, chair Avery O. Craven award 1994-95), Nat. Book Found. (chair non-fiction jury, Nat. Book awards 1994), Social Sci. Rsch. Coun. (mem. com. social sci. pers. 1977-78), So. Hist. Assn. (chair Syndor prize com. 1991-92), So. Regional Coun. (mem. Lillian Smith Book prize com. 1986, mem. exec. com. 1987), Soc. Am. Historians (chair Parkman prize com. 1993—), So. Hist. Assn. (pres. 2006-07), Org. Am. Historians (pres. 2007—). Office: Princeton U History Dept Princeton NJ 08544-0001

PAINTER, RICHARD WILLIAM, lawyer, educator; b. Phila., Oct. 3, 1961; s. William Hall and Marion (Homer) Painter; m. Karen Lindsley; children: Elizabeth Homer, William Hall II, Anne Symmes. BA, Harvard Coll., 1984; JD, Yale U., 1987. Bar: N.Y. 1989, U.S. Dist. Ct. (so. dist.) N.Y., Conn. 1990, U.S. Dist. Ct. Conn., U.S. Supreme Ct. Clk. Judge John T. Noonan, Jr. U.S. Ct. Appeals, San Francisco, 1987-88; assoc. Sullivan & Cromwell, NYC, 1988-91, Finn Dixon & Herling, Stamford, Conn., 1991-93; asst. prof. U. Oreg. Sch Law, Eugene, 1993-97, dir. law and enterpreneurship ctr., 1994-97; prof. law U. Ill., Champaign, 1998—2005, Guy Raymond and Mildred Van Voorhis Jones prof., 2003—05; prof. law U. Minn., Mpls., 2005—; assoc. council to pres. (ethics) The White House, 2005—. Vis. prof. law Boston U., 1997, Cornell U., Ithaca, NY, 1997—98, Warren Knowles; vis. prof. govt. ethics U. Wis, 2001; vis. prof. U. Bielefeld, Germany, 1999, 2000, 01; vis. prof. law U. Mich., Ann Arbor, 2002; vis. scholar Humboldt U., Berlin, 2000, Harvard U. Ctr. European Studies, 2003—04. Co-author: Professional and Personal Responsibilities of the Lawyer, 1997, 2nd edit, 2001, Securities Litigation and Enforcement, 2003; contbr. articles to profl. jours. Mem.: ABA, Am. Law Inst., Cosmos Club (Washington). Republican. Episcopalian. Avocation: classical music. Home Phone: 217-367-3260.

PAINTER, ROBERT LOWELL, surgeon, educator; b. Winchester, Ind., Jan. 13, 1934; s. Lowell Walter and Lillian Genevieve (Pierson) P.; m. Esther Lillian Reece, Sept. 21, 1957 (div. Sept. 1977); children: Elizabeth Haines, Bradley, Robert R., Andrew, Jane Macy-Painter; m. Nancy Sue Macy, Feb. 10, 1980. BA, Earham Coll., Richmond, Ind., 1955; MD, Ind. U., 1959. Intern and resident Hartford (Conn.) Hosp., 1959-65; resident Baylor U. Sch. Medicine, Houston, 1967-68; attending surgeon Day Kimball Hosp., Putnam, Conn., 1962-91; chmn., dir. surgery St. Francis Hosp., Hartford, 1991-98; med. practice, cons., 1999—2001. Cons. Hartford Hosp., 1969-99; assoc. prof. surgery U. Conn., 1991-99, anatomy instr., 2000—. Councilman Ct. Common Coun., Hartford, Conn., 2001—. Capt. USAF, 1965—67. Fellow ACS, Am. Coll. Physician Execs.; mem. New Eng. Surg. Soc., New Eng. Vasc. Soc., Soc. Thoracic Surgery. Republican. Avocations: hiking, gardening, bicycling, birdwatching. Home: 12 Babcock St Hartford CT 06106-1301

PAINTER, THEOPHILUS SHICKEL, JR., internist, allergist; b. Austin, Tex., Apr. 29, 1924; s. Theophilus Shickel and Anna Mary (Thomas) P.; m. Dorothy Bulkley, July 11, 1957; children: Dana Parkey, Amy Hur, Theophilus III. BA, U. Tex., 1944, MD, 1947. Diplomate Am. Bd. Internal Medicine, Am. Bd. Allergy and Immunology. Rotating intern Univ. Hosp., U. Mich., Ann Arbor, 1947-48, resident in internal medicine, 1948-51, fellow, jr. clin. instr., 1956-58; pvt. practice, Austin, Tex., 1958—. Capt. USAF, 1951-53. Fellow ACP, Am. Coll. Allergy and Immunology, Am. Acad. Allergy and Immunology. Avocations: fishing, carving, hunting, painting. Home: 3222 Tarryhollow Dr Austin TX 78703-1639 Office: 800 W 34th St Ste 201 Austin TX 78705-1146 Office Phone: 512-454-5821. Personal E-mail: tspainterjr@cs.com.

PAINTON, RUSSELL ELLIOTT, retired lawyer, mechanical engineer; b. Port Arthur, Tex., Dec. 5, 1940; s. Clifford Elliott and Edith Virginia (McCutcheon) P.; m. Elizabeth Ann Mullins, July 2, 1965 (div. Dec. 1977); 1 child, Todd Elliott; m. Mary Lynn Weber, May 9, 1981. BS in Mech. Engring., U. Tex.-Austin, 1963, JD, 1972. Registered profl. engr., Tex., 1972. Engr. Gulf States Utilities, Beaumont, Tex., 1963-66, Tracor, Inc., Austin, Tex., 1966-70, corp. counsel, 1973-83, v.p., gen. counsel, 1983-98, v.p., gen. counsel, corp. sec., 1991-98; atty. Brown, Maroney, Rose, Baker & Barber, Austin, 1972-73, Childs, Fortenbach, Beck & Guyton, Houston, 1973; corp. sec. Westmark Systems, Inc., Austin, 1990-91; sole practitioner, 1998—2005; ret., 2006. Gen. counsel Paramount Theatre for Performing Arts, 1977-83, 2d vice chmn., 1978-80, 1st vice chmn., 1980-82, chmn. bd., 1982-84, retiring chmn., 1984-85; mem. Centex chpt. ARC; mem. adv. bd. Austin Sci. Acad., 1985-88, 93-95; mem. adv. coun. Austin Transp., 1985-88; bd. dirs. Tex. Industries for the Blind and Handicapped, 1988-95, vice chmn., 1990-91; bd. dirs. Aransas County Ind. Sch. Dist. Found., 2002—, Key Allegro Homeowners Assn., 2002—, pres. 2004-06, dir., 2007. Named Boss of Yr., Austin Legal Secs. Assn., 1981. Mem.: ABA, Am. Electronics Assn. (chmn. Austin coun. 1985—86), Better Bus. Bur. (arbitrator 1983—), Nat. Chamber Litigation Ctr., Tex. Bar Assn. (treas. corp. counsel sect. 1982—83), Houston Yacht Club, Order Blue Gavel, Austin Yacht Club (race comdr. 1968—69, treas. 1970—71, sec. 1972, 1975, vice commodore 1980, commodore 1981, fleet comdr. 1986), Delta Theta Phi. Republican. Episcopalian. Personal E-mail: sailor44@swbell.net.

PAIRO, PRESTON ABERCROMBIE, JR., lawyer; b. June 5, 1927; s. Preston Abercrombie and Blossom Winona (Pritchett) P.; 1 child, Preston Abercrombie III. AA, U. Balt., 1948; JD, 1951. Bar: Md. 1951. Legal investigator Office of City Solicitor, Balt., 1947-50; mem. Md. Ho. Dels., 1950-54; asst. states atty. State of Md., Balt., 1954-58; atty. Liquor Bd. City of Balt., 1958-60; savs. and loan atty., 1960—90. Mem. Md. Criminal Def. Bar (bd. dirs., past pres.), Assn. Trial Lawyers Am., Md. Bar Assn., Howard County Bar Assn. Democrat. Episcopalian. Club: Ellicott City Optimists (pres. 1968). Lodges: Ben Franklin, Masons, Shriners, Jesters. Home: 9032 Overhill Dr Ellicott City MD 21042-5221 Office: Pairo & Pairo 9050 Frederick Dr # A Ellicott City MD 21042-4014 Home Phone: 410-465-2300; Office Phone: 410-461-1800. Personal E-mail: papjr@verizon.net. Business E-Mail: pairo@pairo.com.

PAIROLERO, PETER CHARLES, surgeon, educator; b. Bessemer, Mich., 1938; MD, U. Mich., 1963. Diplomate Am. Bd. Surgeons, Am. Bd. Thoracic Surgeons, Am. Bd. Gen. Vascular Surgeons. Intern St. Mary's Hosp., Duluth, Minn., 1963-64; resident gen. surgery Mayo Grad. Sch. Medicine, Rochester, Minn., 1966-71, fellow cerebral vascular resch., 1968-69, resident thoracic-cardio surgery, 1971-73; fellow cerebral vascular surgery Baylor U., Houston, 1973; chmn. American Board of Thorasic Surgery, 2001—; staff surgeon Mayo Clinic, Rochester, Minn., 1974—, chair vascular surgery, 1987—90, chair gen. thoracic surgery, 1989—93, chair cardiothoracic surgery, 1992—93, chair dept. of surgery, 1993—. Served in US Army, 1964—66. Mem. AMA, Am. Bd. Thorasic Surgery (chmn., 2001-). Office: 200 1st St SW Rochester MN 55905-0001

PAISLEY, BRAD, musician; b. Glen Dale, West Virigina, Oct. 28, 1972; married. Grad., Belmont U., 1995. Musician: (albums) Who Needs Pictures, 1999, Part II, 2001, Mud On The Tires, 2003, Time Well Wasted, 2005 (Album of Yr., Acad. Country Music Awards, Country Music Assn. Awards, 2006), 5th Gear, 2007, (songs) He Didn't Have to Be, 1999 (Song of Yr., Single of Yr. & Video of Yr., Country Music Assn., 2000), I'm Gonna Miss Her, 2001 (Song of Yr., Single of Yr. & Video of Yr., Country Music Assn., 2002, Grammy award for Best Male Country Vocal Performance, 2003), Celebrity, 2003 (Song of Yr., Single of Yr. & Video of Yr., Country Music Assn., 2003), (with Chely Wright) Hard to be a Husband, Hard to be a Wife (Vocal Event of Yr., Country Music Assn., 2001), (with Alison Krauss) Whiskey Lullaby, 2003 (Video of Yr. & Event of Yr., Country Music Assn., 2004, Video of Yr. & Event of Yr., Acad. Country Music, 2005, Collaborative Video of Yr., Country Music TV, 2005), (with Dolly Parton) When I Get Where I'm Going, 2005 (Inspiring Video of Yr., Country Music TV, Video of Yr. & Vocal Event of Yr., Acad. Country Music, Musical Event of Yr., Country Music Assn., 2006). Founder The Brad Paisley Foundation, 2001—. Recipient Male Vocalist of Yr. award, Country Music Assoc., 2000—03, Best New Artist award, Grammy Awards, 2001, Top Male Vocalist award, Acad. Country Music, 2007. Office: William Morris Agency 1600 Division St Ste 300 Nashville TN 37203-2755

PAIVA, CLIFFORD ANTHONY, physicist, consultant; b. Honolulu, Jan. 9, 1947; s. John Albert and Dorothy (Martin) P.; m. Jerrine Dunn, Oct. 15, 1972; children: Antonette, Alexander, Allison, Martin. BS in Geophysics, Christian Heritage Coll., El Cajon, Calif., 1978; MS in Astrogeophysics, Inst. Creation Rsch., El Cajon, Calif., 1988. Physicist Naval Warfare Assessment Ctr. Naval Weapons Sys., Seal Beach, Corona, Calif., 1979-83; physicist USAF Rsch. Lab. Rocket Propulsion Directorate Edwards AFB, Calif., 1986-91; physicist Naval Surface Warfare Ctr. Dahlgren (Va.) Divsn., 1991-2000; founder, pres. Battle Sci. Mgmt., California City, 2001—; engring. physicist, sr. infared scientist SPIRAL Techs., Inc, Lancaster, Calif., 2002—. Mem. East Asia Working Group, Ctr. for Strategic and Internat. Studies, Washington, automatic target recognition working group Def. Advanced Rsch. Agy., Theater Missile Def. Asia Pacific sector, Washington; sr. councilor Atlantic Coun. U.S., Washington, mem. physicist for Global Underwater Search Team, Global Ridge, 2000; cons. in field. Contbr. articles to profl. jours. Tenor Masterworks Chorus, King George, Va., 1996-98, Fredericksburg (Va.) Master Chorale, 1996-98, Antelope Valley Master Chorale, 2000—. With USAF, 1965-69. Mem.: AIAA, Internat. Soc. Optical Engring./Penetrating Radiation Working Group, BSM Assn. (pres., founder), Am. Optical Soc., U.S. Naval Inst. Engrs., Creation Rsch. Soc., Optical Soc. Am., Internat. Soc. Optical Engrs., Am. Geophys. Union, APS, U.S. Naval Intelligence Profl. (life). Republican. Assemblies Of God Ch. Achievements include development of advanced morphological target segmentation and extraction techniques, leading to accurate predictive computer simulations of threat target sets for ballistic missile defense; research in high energy laser interactions with missile exhaust plumes; flash physics for missile defense. Avocations: piano, guitar. Home and Office: Edwards AFB 159 Camp Fire Dr California City CA 93505 Personal E-mail: aanthony@as.net.

PAJAK, DAVID JOSEPH, lawyer, consultant; b. Buffalo, June 19, 1956; s. William H. and Theresa A. (Granato) P.; m. Peggy J. Fisher, Aug. 1, 1981; children: Andrew J., Karl W. BA, State Coll. Buffalo, 1978; JD, U. Buffalo, 1982. Bar: NY 1983, US Dist. Ct. (we. dist.) NY, 1991. Social svcs. counsel Genesee County Dept. Social Svcs., Batavia, NY, 1984-93; pvt. practice Corfu, NY, 1983—93, Amherst, 1993—2006, Alden, NY, 2006—; town justice Town of Pembroke, NY, 1994—2005; with Genesee County Attys. Office, 2001—04. Mem. legis. com. NY Fed. on Child Abuse and Neglect, Albany, 1986—99, bd. dirs., 1987—89; cons. NY Pub. Welfare Assn., Inc., Albany, 1987—92; pres. Social Svcs. Attys. Assn. NY State, 1990—91; instr. Bill Adam's Martial Arts & Fitness Ctr., Buffalo, 1999—2002, Klassic Karate Studios, 1990—98, Filipino Karate Acad., 1989—90. Contbr. articles to profl. jours. Mem.: Genesee County Bar Assn., Erie County Bar Assn., NY State Bar Assn. (chair com. on lawyer referral svcs. 2004—). Republican. Avocations: Karate, martial arts. Home: 17 E Main St Corfu NY 14036-9665 Office: 13179 Broadway Ste 2 Alden NY 14004 Home Phone: 585-599-3890; Office Phone: 716-630-0400. Business E-Mail: dave@pajakpersonalinjury.com.

PAJKA, R. BONNIE, language educator; m. Michael S. Pajka, Sept. 29, 1979; children: Corey N., Adam C., Holly E. BSEd in English, Mansfield State U., Pa., 1978; MSEd in Reading, So. Conn. State U., New Haven, 1983; MS in English, Wilkes U., Wilkes-Barre, Pa., 2003. Cert. reading and English tchr. Pa. English instr. Sayre HS, Pa., 1978—82, West Side Vocat.-Tech. Sch., Pringle, Pa., 1998—99, Lake-Lehman HS, Lehman, Pa., 1999—2000; asst. prof. English Luzerne County CC, Nanticoke, Pa., 2000—. Mem.: ASCD, NEA, Pa. State Edn. Assn., Internat. Reading Assn., Nat. Coun. Tchrs. English. Methodist. Avocations: violin, horseback riding, reading, exercise. Home: 7 Sunset Ave Shavertown PA 18708-1626 Office: Luzerne County CC 1333 S Prospect St Nanticoke PA 18634 Office Phone: 570-740-0545.

PAK, HYUNG WOONG, community advocate; b. Ham-Hoong, Korea, Nov. 6, 1932; came to U.S., 1955, naturalized, 1968; s. Kyung-Koo and Myung-Sook (Lee) P.; m. Diana Lee Stenen Woodruff, 1975; children: Jonathan Tong-Hee, Michelle Hyun-Mi Lee. AB, U. Chgo., 1958. Editor and publisher Chgo. Rev., 1958-63, cons., 1963-65; assoc. editor Ency. Britannica Press, Chgo., 1963-64, sr. editor social scis. and humanities, 1964-66; ednl. dir. Bantam Books, Inc., NYC, 1966-69; gen. mgr. sch. dept. Appleton-Century-Crofts/New Century, NYC, 1970-72; v.p., editorial dir. D. Van Nostrand Co., NYC, 1972-74, pres., 1974-76, Chatham Sq. Press, NYC, 1976-83; pub. Urizen Books, Inc., NYC, 1978-81; exec. v.p. Bus. Software Mag., Palo Alto, Calif., 1983-84; pub., editor Asian High-Tech. Report, 1984-90; exec. dir. The Philip Jaisohn Meml. Found., Inc., Phila., 1990-99; pres. Asian Cmty. Devel. Corp., 2000—. Fellow Hoover Instn., Stanford, Calif., 1984-85. Author: The Pacific Rim, 1990; columnist The Phila. Bus. Rev., 1993-99. Mem. Bd. Sch. Dist. Cheltenham Twp., Pa., 1987-94; mem. Asian task force Phila. Sch. Dist., 1988-95; co-chmn. bus. adv. com. Montgomery County, Pa., 1991-93; del. Citizens' Assembly for a Greater Phila., 1991-95; chmn. Pan Asian Assn. Greater Phila., 1992-96, mem. bd. fellowship commn., 1992-95; bd. dirs. Brandywine Art Ctr., 1995-99, vice chair, 1998-99; Pa. del. The White Ho. Conf. on Aging, 1995; trustee Abington Meml. Hosp. Found., 1995-2000; mem. cmty. adv. com. Keystone Mercy Health Plan, 1998-2002; bd. dirs. Nat. Conf. Cmty. and Justice, 2000-02. Mem. ACLU (life), AHA (mem. comms. com. 1998-2000, mem. Phila. All-Am. city host com. 1998-99), Phila. Mus. Art. Home: 1015 Sharpless Rd Elkins Park PA 19027-3040 Office: PO Box 7167 Elkins Park PA 19027-0167 Office Phone: 267-254-4234. Personal E-mail: hwpak1@gmail.com.

PAK, SE RI, professional golfer; b. Daejeon, Korea, Sept. 28, 1977; Professional golfer LPGA Tour, 1997—. Mem. KLPGA, 1996, 97. Recipient Rolex Rookie of Yr. award, South Korea Order of Merit 1998, Golf Writers Assn. of America Player of the Year, 1998, Vare Trophy 2003. Winner of 24 LPGA events including four Grand Slam titles. Won the LPGA championship 1998, 2002, 2006; won the US Open 1998; won the du Maurier Classic 2001; won the Jamie Farr Owens Corning Classic five times, 1998, 99, 2001, 03, 07; first woman in 58 years to make cut in men's golf tournament, SBS Super Tournament on Korean tour (finished 10th overall); qualified for LPGA Hall of Fame, 2004. Address: LPGA 100 International Golf Dr Daytona Beach FL 32124-1082 Office Phone: 386-274-6200. Office Fax: 386-274-1099. *

PAK, SUCHIN, newscaster; b. Korea, Aug. 15, 1976; Degree in Polit. Sci., U. Calif., Berkeley. Corres. MTV News, NYC, 2001—. Host: (TV series) Trackers, 1999—2000; correspondent Internet Tonight, 1998—2001; film appearances: Deuce Bigalow: European Gigolo, 2005; Deck the Halls, 2006. Office: MTV Networks 1515 Broadway New York NY 10036

PAKALA, JAMES COTTON, library director, minister; b. Pitts., Mar. 6, 1944; s. William Elmer and Edythe Leona (Cotton) Pakala; m. Marie Denise Marchand, June 13, 1975; 1 child, Kent Marchand. BA, Shelton Coll., 1966; MDiv, Faith Theol. Sem., 1970; degree, Bibl. Theol. Sem., 1977; MS, Drexel U., 1979. Ordained minister Presbyn. Ch. Am., 1975. Dir. libr. Bibl. Theol. Sem., Hatfield, Pa., 1974—91, Covenant Theol. Sem., St. Louis, 1991—. Chaplain Pa. Army N.G., Phila., 1975—97. Lt. col. chaplain US Army, 1975—97. Decorated Meritorious Svc. medal U.S. Army, Commendation medal, Meritorious Svc. medal; recipient President's award, Shelton Coll., 1966, William Allen Chamberlin award, Faith Theol. Sem., 1968. Mem.: ATLA, Southeastern Pa. Theol. Libr. Assn. (pres. 1985—87), Mo. Bibliog. Info. User Sys. (exec. com. 2001—05), Am. Theol. Libr. Assn. (bd. dirs. 2004—), Mo. Libr. Assn. (bd. dirs. 1996—98), St. Louis Regional Libr. Network (mem. coun. 2000—03), Beta Phi Mu. Presbyn. Avocations: railroad buff, environmentalism. Home Phone: 636-527-4044; Office Phone: 314-434-4044.

PAKENHAM, ROSALIE MULLER WRIGHT, magazine and newspaper editor; b. Newark, June 20, 1942; d. Charles and Angela (Fortunata) Muller; m. Lynn Wright, Jan. 13, 1962; children: James Anthony Meador, Geoffrey Shepard; m. E. Michael Pakenham, Sept. 29, 2001. BA in English, Temple U., 1965. Mng. editor Suburban Life mag., Orange, NJ, 1960-62; assoc. editor Phila. mag., 1962-64, mng. editor, 1969-73; founding editor Womensports mag., San Mateo, Calif., 1973-75; editor scene sect. San Francisco Examiner, 1975-77; exec. editor New West mag., San Francisco and Beverly Hills, Calif., 1977-81; features and Sunday editor San Francisco Chronicle, 1981-87, asst. mng. editor features, 1987-96; v.p. and editor-in-chief Sunset Mag, Menlo Park, Calif., 1996—2001. Editl. cons., 2002—; tchr. mag. writing U. Calif., Berkeley, 1975—76; participant pub. procs. course Stanford U., 1977—79; chmn. mag. judges at conf. Coun. Advancement and Support of Edn., 1980, judge, 84, Nat. Mag. Awards, 1998, 99, 2005. *During Rosalie Muller Wright Pakenham's five-year editorship of Sunset Magazine (1996-2001), circulation grew from 1.3 to 1.5 million (readership, 5 million): profits from $14 to $25 million, renewal rates to 70%. She won for the magazine a record 12 Maggies, a Folio Gold Award and a Henry Luce Award for editorial excellence. She managed a $5 million budget and was involved in circulation, advertising, and production strategies while managing 65 editors/writers/artists. As executive editor of New West, she assigned and edited the Jim Jones and Peoples Temple story in 1977 and the Firestone 500 expose in 1978, for which New West won a National Magazine Award.* Contbr. numerous mag. articles, critiques, revs., Compton's Ency. Mem.: Internat. Assn. Culinary Profls., Am. Soc. Mag. Editors (nat. mag. awards judge, 1998, 99, 2005), Am. Newspaper Pubs. Assn. (Chronicle minority recruiter 1987—94, pub. task force on minorities in newspaper bus. 1988—89), Am. Assn. Sunday and Feature Editors (treas. 1984, sec. 1985, 1st v.p. 1986, pres. 1987, Hall of Fame 1999), Washington D.C. Women's Forum, Women's Forum West (bd. dirs. 1993—, sec. 1994), Internat. Women's Forum. Office Phone: 717-292-6969. Personal E-mail: RosalieMPakenham@aol.com. *Keep a sharp eye out for talent, recognize it and reward it, and everyone profits.*

PAKTER, JEAN, maternal and child health consultant; b. NYC, Jan. 1, 1911; d. David and Lillian (Kunitz) P.; m. Arnold L. Bachman, Sept. 17, 1939 (dec. Dec. 1992); children: Ellen Bachman Mendelson, Donald M. Bachman. BS, NYU, 1931, MD, 1934; MPH, Columbia U., 1955. Diplomate Am. Bd. Pediat. Intern Mt. Sinai Hosp., NYC, 1934-36, resident in pediat., 1937-39; pvt. practice, NYC, 1939-43; dir. Bur. Dept. Health, Maternity, Newborn and Family Planning, NYC, 1950-82; cons., lectr. maternity, child health Columbia U. Sch. Pub. Health, NYC, 1984—, dep. dir. maternal and child health program, 1984-94, lectr. maternity, child health, 1970—. Contbr. numerous articles to profl. med. jours. Advisor March of Dimes, N.Y.C., 1975—. Recipient Fund for City of N.Y. Pub. Svc. award, 1974, Jacobi medal Mt. Sinai Hosp., 1975, N.Y. State Med. Soc. award, 2006. Fellow APHA (Martha May Eliot award 1990), Am. Acad. Pediatrics, N.Y. Acad. Medicine (trustee 1979-83), N.Y. Obstet. Soc. (assoc.); mem. Pub. Health Assn. N.Y.C. (bd. dirs. 1992-96, The Haven Emerson award 2006), Women's City Club, Alpha Omega Alpha. Avocations: concerts, opera, theater, reading. Home: 1175 Park Ave New York NY 10128-1211

PAKULA, ANITA SUSAN, dermatologist; b. LA, Nov. 20, 1961; BA, Pomona Coll., 1983; BS, Calif. Luth. Coll., 1985; MD, U. Calif., Irvine, 1988. Diplomat Am. Bd. Dermatology, NAt. Bd. Med. Examiners. Intern Evanston (Ill.) Hosp., 1988-89; resident Northwestern U. Med. Sch., Chgo., 1989-92; asst. clin. prof. dermatology UCLA MEd. Ctr., 1993—. Presenter in field. Contbr. articles to profl. jours. Fellow Am. Acad. Dermatology; mem. Soc. Pediatric Dermatology. Office: 267 W Hillcrest Dr Thousand Oaks CA 91360-4923

PAKVASA, SANDIP, physicist; b. Bombay, Dec. 24, 1935; came to U.S. 1961; s. Sirish V. and Sumitra (Surti) P.; m. Heide Miller, Nov. 19, 1978. BSc, M.S. U. Baroda, India, 1954; MSc, M.S. U. Baroda, 1957; PhD, Purdue U., 1966. Rsch. assoc. Syracuse (N.Y.) U., 1965-67; asst. prof. U. Hawaii, Honolulu, 1968-70, assoc. prof., 1970-73, prof. physics, 1974—. Vis. prof. U. Wis., Madison, 1978, 81, Nat. High Energy Physics Lab., Japan, 1983, 89, 2002, U. Melbourne, Australia, 1986, Tata Inst. Fund Rsch., Bombay, 1983, 88; vis. assoc. CERN, Geneva, 1982; McMinn lectr. Vanderbilt U., 1996. Contbr. articles to profl. jours., chpts. to books. Japan Soc. for Promotion of Sci. fellow, 1981, 85. Fellow Am. Phys. Soc. Avocations: music, mysteries. Office: Univ Hawaii 2505 Correa Rd Honolulu HI 96822-2219 Office Phone: 808-956-2970. E-mail: pakvasa@phys.hawaii.edu.

PAL, PRABIR KUMAR (SUNNY PAL), lawyer; b. Chittagong, Bengal, India, Feb. 17, 1936; arrived in Can., 1969; s. Niranjan and Renuka (Mitter) P.; m. Nandinee Majumdar, Dec. 13, 1960; 1 child, Nobina Pal Robinson. BA in Law with honors, Cambridge U., 1958, MA, 1972; diploma in Indsl. Mgmt., Geneva U., 1964. Legal and fin. mgmt. positions Alcan Inc., in Can., Europe and Asia, 1959—99, v.p., chief legal officer, corp. sec., 1988—99; governance counsellor Flavell Kubrick LLP, Ottawa, 1999—2005, Lang Michener LLP, Ottawa, 2005—. Bd. dirs. Ottawa Art Gallery. Fellow Inst. Chartered Secs. and Adminstrs.; mem. Internat. Bar Assn., Rideau Club Ottawa. Avocations: photography, rowing. Office: Lang Michener LLP 50 O Connor St #300 Ottawa ON Canada K1P 6L2 Office Phone: 613-232-7171. Business E-Mail: pkpal@langmichener.ca.

PAL, PRATAPADITYA, curator; b. Bangladesh, Sept. 1, 1935; came to U.S., 1967; s. Gopesh Chandra and Bidyut Kana (Dam) P.; m. Chitralekha Bose, Apr. 20, 1968; children: Shalmali, Lopamudra. MA, U. Calcutta, 1958, DPhil, 1962; PhD (UK Commonwealth Scholar), U. Cambridge, 1965. Rsch. assoc. Am. Acad. Benares, India, 1966—67; keeper Indian collections Mus. Fine Arts, Boston, 1967—69; sr. curator Indian and Southeast Asian art Los Angeles County Mus. Art, 1970—95, acting dir., 1979; vis. curator Indian and S.E. Asian art Art Inst. Chgo., 1995—2003; rsch. fellow Norton Simon Mus., Pasadena, Calif., 1995—2005. Gen. editor Marg Publs., Mumbai, 1993-; adj. prof. fine arts U. So. Calif., 1971-89; vis. prof. U. Calif., Santa Barbara, 1980, Irvine, 1994-95; Sir George Birdwood Meml. lectr., The Royal Asiatic Soc., London, 1973; William Cohn lectr. Oxford U., 1983; Catherine Mead meml. lectr. Pierpont Morgan Libr., NYC, 1986; Ananda K. Coomaraswamy meml. lectr. Prince of Wales Mus., Bombay, 1987; D.J. Sibley prehistoric art lectr. U. Tex., Austin, 1989; Anthony Gardner meml. lectr. Victoria and Albert Mus., London, 1993, keynote spkr. 1st Internat. Conf. on Tibetan Art, 1994; mem. commr.'s art adv. panel IRS, Washington, 1986-96. Author: Vaisnava Iconology in Nepal, 1970, The Arts of Nepal, vol. 1, 1974, vol. 2, 1979, The Sensuous Immortals, 1977, The Ideal Image: Gupta Sculptures and its Influence, 1978, The Classical Tradition in Rajput Painting, 1978, Elephants and Ivories, 1981, A Buddhist Paradise: Murals of Alchi, 1982, Art of Tibet, 1983, Tibetan Painting, 1984, Art of Nepal, 1985, From Merchants to Emperors, 1986, Indian Sculpture, vol. 1, 1986, Icons of Piety, Images of Whimsey, 1987, Indian Sculpture, vol. 2, 1988, Buddhist Book Illuminations, 1988, Romance of the Taj Mahal, 1989, Art of the Himalayas, 1991, Pleasure Gardens of the Mind, 1993; Indian Painting, vol. 1, 1993, The Peaceful Liberators: Jain Art from India, 1994, A Collecting Odyssey, 1997, Divine Images, Human Visions, 1997, Tibet Change and Tradition, 1997, Desire and Devotion, 2001, Himalayas: An Aesthetic Adventure, 2003, Asian Art in the Norton Simon Museum, vols. 1 and 2, 2003, vol. 3, 2004; Painted Poems, 2004, Durga: Avenging Goddess Nurturing Mother, 2005, The Arts of Kashmi, 2007. John D. Rockefeller III Fund fellow, 1964, 69, fellow NEA, 1974; Getty scholar, 1995-96. Fellow Asia Soc. (Bombay, hon.); mem. Asiatic Soc. (Calcutta, B.C. Law gold medal 1993, R.P. Chanda Centenary medal, 2003)

PAL, SUKUMAR, immunologist, researcher; arrived in U.S., 1988; s. Kalipada and Parbati Pal; m. Sima Chaki, June 16, 1987; 1 child, Srijita Chaki. Degree, U. Calcutta, 1979, PhD, 1988. Postdoctoral fellow Johns Hopkins U., Balt., 1988—90; post grad. rschr. U. Calif., Irvine, 1990—91, jr. specialist, 1991—94, asst. specialist, 1994—2000, assoc. specialist, 2000—. Rschr. U. Calif., Irvine, 1990; parent site coun. Turtle Rock Elem. Sch., Irvine, 2002—04. Editor: Kheya Mag., Bengali Assn. So. Calif., 1995—; contbr. articles to profl. jours. Fight for Sight Rsch. fellow, Fight for Sight Inc, 1988—89, Equal Opportunity fellow, U. Calif., Irvine, 2001. Mem.: Am. Soc. for Microbiology (reviewer 2003—, Vector Labs. Young Investigator award. 1995). Achievements include research in Engaged in chalmydial research for last 16 years, developed various animal models to study chlamydial infections in various hosts, developing vaccine to prevent from infection. Office: Univ Calif Irvine Dept Pathology Irvine CA 92697-4800 Home Phone: 949-856-2674; Office Phone: 949-824-7450.

PALACIO, CARLOS, physician, medical educator; s. Eloy Angel and Yolanda Palacio. MD, U. Miami, Coral Gables, Fla., 1993. Cert. internal medicine Am. Bd. Internal Medicine, 1996. Resident U. Fla. Coll. Medicine, Jacksonville, 1993—96, chief resident, 1996—97, asst. prof. medicine, 1997—. Med. student clerkship dir. internal medicine U. Fla. Coll. Medicine, Jacksonville, 1998—. Contbr. articles to profl. jours. Named Resident of Yr., U. Fla. Coll. Medicine, Jacksonville, 1996. Mem.: ACP, AMA (assoc.), Duval County Med. Soc. (assoc.), Clerkship Dirs. Internal Medicine (assoc.). Independent. Office Phone: 904-244-3070.

PALACIOS, RAFAEL, geneticist; b. Mexico City, Sept. 4, 1944; MD, Nat. U. Mex., 1969, PhD in Biochemistry, 1970. Asst. prof. Nat. U. Mex., Cuernavaca, 1969—72, assoc. prof., 1972—78, prof., 1979—96, hon. prof. Ctr. Genomic Scis., 1997—; postdoctoral rschr. molecular biology Stanford U., Calif., 1970—73. Chmn. dept. molecular biology Inst. Biomedical Rsch. Nat. U. Mex., 1976—80, dir. Nitrogen Fixation Rsch. Ctr., 1980—87, 1989—97. Contbr. articles to profl. jours., chapters to books; co-editor: Glutamine, Metabolism, Enzymology and Regulation, 1980, Molecular Plant-Microbe Interactions, 1988, New Horizons in Nitrogen Fixation, 1993, Nitrogen Fixation: Origins, Applications and Rsch. Progress, 2005. Recipient Nat. prize, Scis. and Arts, Pres. of Mex., 1994, Nat. Sci. prize, Pvt. Found. Ricardo J. Zevada, 2001, Internat. prize, Third World Acad. Scis., 2003. Mem.: Mex. Soc. Genomic Scis. (founding mem. 2001), State of Morelos Acad. Scis. (founding mem. 1993), Mex. Acad. Scis. (Nat. prize 1979), Mex. Assn. Microbiol., Mex. Soc. Biochemistry, Latin Am. Acad. Scis., Iberoamerican Molecular Biology Orgn. (founding mem. 1998), Internat. Soc. Molecular Plant-Microbe Interactions (bd. dirs. 1988—92, founding mem. 1989), French Soc. Microbiol., Internat. Soc.

Plant Molecular Biology (bd. dirs. 1984—87), Am. Soc. Biol. Chemists, NAS (fgn. assoc.). Office: Ctr Genomic Scis Nat U Mex Ave Univ s/n Col Chamilpa CP 62210 Cuernavaca Mexico E-mail: palacios@ccg.unam.mx.

PALADE, GEORGE EMIL, research scientist, educator; b. Jassy, Romania, Nov. 19, 1912; arrived in U.S., 1946, naturalized, 1952; s. Emil and Constanta Cantemir Palade; m. Irina Malaxa, June 12, 1941 (dec. 1969); children: Georgia Teodora, Philip Theodor; m. Marilyn G. Farquhar, 1970. Bachelor, Hasdeu Lyceum, Buzau, Romania; MD, U. Bucharest, Romania. Instr., asst. prof., then assoc. prof. anatomy Sch. Medicine, U. Bucharest, 1935—45; vis. investigator, asst. assoc., prof. cell biology Rockefeller U., 1946—73; prof. cell biology Yale U., New Haven, 1973—83, sr. research scientist, 1983—89; prof.-in-residence Med. Sch., U. Calif., San Diego, 1990—2001, dean sci. affairs, 1990—2001, prof. emeritus cellular and molecular med., 2001—. Contbr. articles to sci. jours. Recipient Albert Lasker Basic Rsch. award, 1966, Gairdner Spl. award, 1967, Horwitz prize, 1970, Nobel prize in physiology or medicine, 1974, Nat. Medal Sci., 1986. Fellow: Am. Acad. Arts Scis.; mem.: NAS, Royal Belgian Acad. Medicine, Romanian Acad., Leopoldina Acad. (Halle), Royal Soc. (London), Pontifical Acad. Sci. Achievements include correlated morphological and biochemical studies by electronmicroscopy and cell fractionation of subcellular components; discovery of ribosomes; discovery and elucidation of the secretory, exocytic pathway and studies on membrane biogenesis; discovery of and regulation of proteins and membrane traffic in animal eukaryotic cells.

PALADINO, ALBERT EDWARD, venture capitalist; b. NYC, Aug. 4, 1932; s. Albert E. and Jennie (Fiato) Paladino; m. Dorothy M. Hayes (div. June 1979); children: Thomas A., Robert E., Catherine J., Paul F.; m. Susan Flynn, June 11, 1983. BS in Ceramic Engring., Alfred U., 1954, MS in Ceramic Engring., 1956; ScD in Materials Sci., MIT, 1962. Registered profl. engr., Mass. Staff mem. rsch. divsn. Raytheon Co., Waltham, Mass., 1955-59, mgr. materials and crystal growth lab., 1962-69, mgr. materials and techniques group microwave & power tube divsn., 1969-72, mgr. electronics materials group, 1972-75; program mgr. materials Office of Tech. Assessment U.S. Congress, Washington, 1975-78; asst. dir. tel. ops. tech. ctr. GTE Labs., Waltham, 1978-79; dep. dir. Office Energy Programs U.S. Dept. Commerce, Nat. Inst. Stds. and Tech., Washington, 1979-81; mng. ptnr. Advanced Tech. Ventures, Boston, 1981-98. Bd. dir. TranSwitch Corp.; bd. dirs. Paladino & Co.; chmn. Telaxis Comm. Corp., South Deerfield, Mass., 1988—2003, Electro-Scan Corp., Billerica, Mass., 1990—95, Onex Comm. Corp., 1999—2001, RF Micro Devices, Greensboro, NC, 1992—; telecom. bd. adv. Prism Ventures, 1997—2006, Early Stage Enterprises, 1997—2006; bd. advisers Battelle Ventures, 2004—. Contbr. articles to profl. jours. Pres. West Needham Civic Assn., Mass., 1967—69; mem. Needham Town Meeting, 1973—74, Boston Harbor Angels, 2007—; trustee Alfred U., 1991—. Fellow: Am. Ceramic Soc. (chmn. basic sci. divsn. 1968—69, chmn. New Eng. sect. 1969—70, Disting. New Eng. Ceramic award). Achievements include patents in field. Avocations: painting, music, physical fitness, hiking, reading.

PALADUGU, RAMESH, surgeon; Lic. surgeon Am. Bd. Surgery, 2003, Rvt Am. Registry Diagnostic Med. Sonography, 2004, vascular surgery Am. Bd. Surgery, 2005, endovascular medicine Am. Bd. Vascular Medicine, 2006, Rvpi Am. Registry Diagnostic Med. Sonography, 2006. Surg. resident NY Meth. Hosp., Cornell U., Bklyn., 1998—2002; vascular surgery fellow Baylor Coll. Medicine, The Meth. Hosp., Houston, 2002—04; vascular surgeon Plains Regional Med. Ctr., Clovis, N.Mex., 2002—. Contbr. articles to profl. jours. Recipient Best Resident award, NY Meth. Hosp., 2000, Highest Academic Achievement award in surgery, 2001, Rsch. award in surgery, 2002, S. Timothy String award, So. Assn. Vascular Surgery, 2003. Fellow: ACS; mem.: Am. Coll. Phlebology, Soc. Vascular Ultrasound, Soc. Interventional Radiology, Soc. Vascular Surgery. Office: Plains Regional Medical Ctr 2200 Twenty First St Clovis NM 88101

PALAFOX, BRIAN A., surgeon; s. Anastacio L. and Jesusa A. Palafox. BS, U. Hawaii, Honolulu, 1972; MD, U. Calif., Irvine, 1975. Resident U. Calif., Orange, 1975—76, 1976—81, clin. asst. prof. surgery, 1988—; chmn. dept surgery St. Joseph's Hosp., Orange, 2005—; pres. OCTCS, Orange, 2006—. Chmn. thoracic surgery Children's Hosp., Orange, 2002—06. Mem. found. bd. St. Joseph's Hosp., Orange, 1999—2006. Col. US Army, 1982—2006. Decorated Bronze Star US Army; fellow, U. Calif, Orange, 1981—83. Fellow: ACS. Roman Catholic. Office: Octcs 1310 W Stewart Dr #503 Orange CA 92705 Home Phone: 714-997-2224; Office Phone: 714-997-2224. Personal E-mail: idorca@aol.com.

PALAHNIUK, CHARLES MICHAEL See PALAHNIUK, CHUCK

PALAHNIUK, CHUCK (CHARLES MICHAEL PALAHNIUK), writer, journalist; b. Pasco, Wash., Feb. 21, 1962; s. Fred and Carol Palahniuk. BA, U. Oreg. Sch. Journalism, 1986. Former intern Nat. Pub. Radio; former diesel mechanic Freightliner; journalist Portland, 1986—88. Author: Fight Club, 1996 (Pacific Northwest Booksellers Assn. award, 1997, Oregon Book award for best novel, 1997), Survivor, 1999, Invisible Monsters, 1999, Choke, 2001, Lullaby, 2002 (Pacific Northwest Booksellers Assn. award, 2003), Diary, 2003, Fugitives and Refugees: A Walk in Portland, Oregon, 2003, Stranger Than Fiction: True Stories, 2004, Haunted, 2005, Rant, 2007. Mem.: Cacophony Soc. Office: c/o Random House 20 Vauxhall Bridge Rd London SW1V 2SA England *

PALAMARA, SHERRY A., psychologist; b. Detroit, Sept. 21, 1962; d. Ronald Dominic and Margot Cathrine Palamara. BA in Psychology cum laude, St. Leo Coll., Fla., 1984; MS, Butler U., 1987, Carlos Albizu U., 2000, D in Psychology, 2000. Lic. massage therapist 1991. Behavior specialist Behavior Therapy and Learning Ctr., Long Beach, Calif., 1988—89; program coord. Geriatric Residentail Treatment Sys., Miami, Fla., 1989—95; addictions therapist Families in Transition, Miami, 2002—03, child devel. specialist, 2003—06; pvt. practice clin. and neuro psychology Miami Beach, Fla., 2005—. Counselor Exceptional Children's Found., LA, 1988—89; adj. faculty Miami-Dade Coll., 1999—, Fla. Internat. U., Miami, 2001—; clin. and neuropsychologist Dr.'s and Assocs., Doral, Fla., 2006—. Contbr. articles to profl. jours. Counselor Exceptional Childrens Found., LA, 1988—89. Mem.: APA. Achievements include research in infant massage, trauma, addictions, motivation, employee relations. Avocations: meditation, running, swimming, writing. Office: 407 Lincoln Rd Ste 6K Miami Beach FL 33139 Office Phone: 305-450-1470. Office Fax: 305-271-1633. Personal E-mail: shpalamara@aol.com.

PALANS, LLOYD ALEX, lawyer; b. St. Louis, Aug. 6, 1946; s. Hyman Robert and Mae (Sherman) P.; m. Deborah Regn, Aug. 5, 1972; children: Emily Rebecca, Samantha Jane. BS, Tulane U., 1968; JD, U. Mo., 1972. Bar: Mo. 1972, US Dist. Ct. (ea. and we. dists.) Mo. 1972, US Ct. Appeals (8th cir.) 1972, US Ct. Appeals (5th cir.) 1974, US Supreme Ct. 1975, US Ct. Appeals (9th cir.) 1992. Ptnr. Kramer, Chused, Kramer, Shostak & Kohn, St. Louis, 1972-77, Blumenfeld, Marx & Tureen, P.C., St. Louis, 1978-81, Gallop, Johnson & Neuman, St. Louis, 1981-90, Bryan Cave, LLP, St. Louis, 1990—. Adj. prof. Washington U. Sch. Law, St. Louis, 1989—. Bd. dirs. St. Louis Chpt. ARC, 1987—, St. Louis Chpt. Leukemia Soc., 1988—, Combined Health Appeal Greater St. Louis, 1988—, Combined Health Appeal of Am., 1990. Fellow Am. Coll. Bankruptcy; mem. ABA, Mo. Bar, St. Louis Met. Bar Assn. Office: Bryan Cave LLP 1 Metro Sq 211 N Broadway Saint Louis MO 63102-2733 Office Phone: 314-259-2301.

PALATNICK, FRANK SIDNEY, educational consultant; b. Bklyn., Oct. 13, 1951; s. Abraham (dec. 1998) and Miriam Palatnick. Pres. & founder Inst. for Global Edn. Adminstrn., Scottsdale; dir. Global Edn./Adminstrn. & Higher Edn. (IAED); pres. Global_Ed.Conversations Edn. Cons.; edn./adminstrn. amb. People to People, 2003; prodr. Higher Edn. (TV broadcast/Webcast); keynote spkr. Global Edn. Adminstrn. Conf., Rajahstan, India, 2008, World Edn. Conf., Burj Al Arab, Jumeirah, Dubai, 2007, Global Leadership Conf., 2007, Siberia Acad. for Pub. Adminstrn., Russia, Internat. Edn. Adminstrn. Conf., Washington, 2007, Coll. Bd. of Trustees Conf., Phoenix, 2007, Nat. Inst. on the Assesment of Experiential Learning, Princeton U., 2007; participant Coll. Improvement Conf., U. Ohio, Columbus, 2006, Coll. Exec. Summit, Hampton U., Va., 2006; keynote spkr. Nassau Acad. Law, 2003. Cert. in spl. edn. law Nat. Bus. Inst., 2004, sch. bd. specialist NY State Sch. Bd. Assn., 2005, internat. edn. credentials examiner/evaluator for undergrad. and grad. programs WES, 2007, facilitator sch. leadership stds. ETS. Paralegal Albert Grant Esq., Woodbridge, NJ, 1994—96; chief paralegal Oyster Bay Paralegal Assocs., Muttontown, NY, 1996-99; sr. assoc. Foresight Inst., Palo Alto, Calif., 2000-01; chief paralegal Glen Cove Paralegal Svcs., NY, 2001—02; accreditation examiner Distance Edn. and Tng. Coun., Washington, 2002—. Mem. Presdl. Adv. Com. on Fed. Pay, Washington, 1981-82, Nassau County Task Force Office Mgmt. and Budget, Mineola, NY, 2002; substitute attendance tchr. Wyandanch Sch. Dist., LI, 1997; substitute tchr. BOCES Nassau City, Greenlawn and Plainview, NY, 2000; chief cons. LI Degree Consulting Svc., Uniondale, NY, 2005; spkr., presenter in field. Although qualified in agrl., arts and humanities, bus. and econ. devel., edn., health and medicine, law, diplomacy, science and technology, and in the spirit of globalization, he has embarked on a mission of exchanging ideas on edn. adminstrn. as an amb. through People to People Amb. Programs chaired by Pres. George Bush to countries like China. Attended conf. and gave speech in Sydney with ednl. dels. from around the world, as well as Amman, Jordan, Moscow, Cairo. He is also involved with various other national think tanks i.e. Ctr. for Edn. Policy and Rand. He is co-authoring a book on alternative edn. to be published this year. He was a great lecturer at LI U. C W Post as well as other instns. Through his "Degrees Ahead" he is helping learners with attaining degrees and career devel. as well as giving seminars in portfolio devel. UN advisor, dir. Global Edn. Adminstrn. and Higher Edn. Adminstrn. (IAED), 2006. *Mr. Palatnick traveled to Beijing, China where he gave a lecture, which was filmed by the TV station of No. 8 Middle School, one of Beijing's best schools. A group of high school principals collaborated on establishing a school devoted to the administrative concepts and practices discussed in Mr. Palatnick's lecture. While in Beijing, Mr. Palatnick also attended an invite-only wine reception and dinner in the Great Hall of the People, climbed the Great Wall, visited the Forbidden City, and stood in Tiananmen Square. After attending various seminars, he had an intensive dialogue with the Minister of Education of Jordan, the Deputy Prime Minister of Italy, Princess Aliya of Jordan, and the Ex-Governor of Maryland.* Assoc. editor: Nassau Lawyer, 2001-; asst. editor: The Flying Lady, 2000-02; contbg. editor: Jour. Cardinal Points, 2002. Mem. US Power Squadron, USCG Aux.; active People to People Ambs. Programs; poll taker Nassau County Dem. Com., Mineola. Named Outstanding Intellectual of the 21st Century; life fellow, Internat. Hall of Fame, Lifetime Achievement, Internat. Order of Merit, Order of Internat. Fellowship, v.p. recognition bd. of World Congress of Arts, Scis., and Comm., Internat. Medal of Honor, Laureate of DaVinci Diamond, Life Patronage; nominated Nobel Peace prize, Norway, 2008; nominee NYC Liberty Lifetime Achievement medal, 2005; named to Wall of Tolerance, Civil Rights Mem. Ctr., Ala., 2005; recipient Letter of Appreciation Mayor of Glen Cove, 2001, Letter of Accomplishment Supt. of Schs., Mineola, 2003, Letter of Acknowledgement for expertise in career devel. Cornell U., 2005, Letter of Acknowledgement for expertise in edn. adminstrn. Dir.-Gen. IAED, 2006. Mem. ASCD (cert. assessment edn. adminstrn.), ABA (individual right and responsibilities com., internat. law com., judiciary com.), Am. Assn. for Adult and Continuing Edn., Assn. for Continuing Higher Edn., Edn. Writers Assn., Am. Coun. on Edn. (alumnus course evaluator tng.), NY State Bar Assn., Nat. Career Devel. Assn. (alumnus career devel. facilitator tng.), Nat. Assn. Secondary Sch. Prins., Nat. Assn. for Edn. Young Children, Coun. Adult & Experiential Learning (alumnus), Nat. Inst. Assessment Experiential Learning (alumnus), Am. Soc. Notaries, LI Paralegal Assn., Am. Mgmt. Assn. Suffolk County Bar Assn. (ednl. law com., family law com., real estate com.), Nassau County Bar Assn. (publs. com., ednl. law com., com. on coms., civil rights law com., med. legal com., cmty. and pub. rels. com., county clerks office com.), Foresight Inst. (sr.), Mensa, Amnesty Internat. Avocations: stamp collecting/philately, coin collecting/numismatics. Home: 233-38- 38 Dr Douglaston NY 11363 Office Phone: 516-507-8623. Personal E-mail: fpalatnick@msn.com.

PALAV, ANJALI, neuropsychologist; b. Bklyn., May 7, 1974; d. Aravind Baburao and Helen Lim Palav. AB in Psychology, AM in Psychology, Stanford U., Palo Alto, Calif., 1996; PhD in Clin. Psychology, SUNY, Albany, 2003. Lic. psychologist RI, NY. Psychology intern LI Jewish Med. Ctr., Glen Oaks, NY, 2000—01, pediat. neuropsychology fellow, 2001—02, Meml. Hosp. RI, Brown U. Med. Sch., Pawtucket, 2002—04; clin. neuropsychologist Meml. Hosp. RI, 2004—; clin. asst. prof. dept. psychology and human behavior Brown U. Med. Sch., Providence, 2005—. Co-editor: Practitioner's Guide to Symptom Base Rates in Clinical Neuropsychology, 2003, Practitioner's Guide to Symptom Base Rates in the General Population, 2006. Mem.: Internat. Neuropsychology Soc. Avocations: bicycling, tennis. Office: Meml Hosp RI 555 Prospect St Pawtucket RI 02860

PALAZZI, JOSEPH LAZARRO, manufacturing executive; b. New Haven, July 5, 1947; s. Joseph Anthony and Helen (Volosovich) P.; m. Lorna May Mickiewicz, May 27, 1978. BS in Acctg., Quinnipiac Coll., 1969; MBA, U. New Haven, 1973. CPA Conn.; cert. Turnaround Profl., 2005. Auditor Multer Carlson & Co.; mgr. budgets The Stanley Works, New Britian, Conn., 1972-76; mgr. planning Bangor Punta Corp., Greenwich, Conn., 1976-79; asst. corp. controller Pepperidge Farm, Norwalk, Conn., 1979-81, dir. fin. services, 1981-82, group controller, 1982-83; corp. controller Plessey, Inc., White Plains, NY, 1983-84, v.p. finance, 1984-86, CFO, 1986-89; v.p. fin., CFO BTR Inc., Stanford, Ct., 1990-92; pres. Fasco Industries Inc., Chesterfield, Mo., 1992-98; CEO Fasco Motors Group, Chesterfield, Mo., 1998; mng. dir. Corp. Renewal Services, Inc. Mem. Rep. Town Com., Newtown, Conn., 1981; bd. dirs. Danbury Hosp., 1987-92. Served with US Army, 1969—76. Mem. AICPA, Nat. Assn. Accts., Sigma Six Flying Club. Episcopalian. Avocations: sailing, tennis, golf, flying. Home: Corp Renewal Services Inc Ste 204 W 185 Plains Rd Milford CT 06460 Office Phone: 203-301-9901.

PALAZZO, ROBERT PAUL, lawyer, accountant; s. Joseph Francis and Mickey Palazzo; m. Vivianne Palazzo. BA in Econs., UCLA, 1973; MBA, JD, U. So. Calif., 1976; postgrad., U. Oxford, Eng., 1979. CPA Calif., Nev., Colo.; bar: Calif. 1976, US Dist. Ct. (so. dist.) Calif. 1977, US Tax Ct. 1977, US Ct. Appeals (9th cir.) 1978, US Supreme Ct. 1980. Assoc. Graham & James, LA, 1976-78; ptnr. Rader, Cornwall, Kessler & Palazzo CPAs, LA, 1978-81, Palazzo & Kessler, LA, 1978-81; pvt. practice LA, Darwin, Calif., 1981—. Judge pro tem LA Mcpl. Ct., 1982—2000, L.A. Superior Ct., 2001—; alumni advisor UCLA, 1977—81, adv. and scholarship com., 1978—81; lectr. U. Oxford, 1979, U. So. Calif., LA, 1986, Calif. Poly. Inst., Pomona, 1997; profl. adv. com. West L.A. Coll., 1993—96; session chair Medieval and Renaissance Conf. Ariz. State U., 2000—01, 2003; bd. dirs. Cons. Am. Oil. Co., Fin. Sys. Internat. Inc.; part-time faculty Moorpark Coll., Calif., 2004—; spkr. in field. Author: Inyo County Post Offices and Postmasters 1866-1966, 2007; hist. cons. A&E Civil War Jour., (films) Death Valley Memories, hist. and archival cons. Echoes Through Death Valley, Chasing the Rainbow, hist. cons. (TV series) A&E Biography, Guns of Infamy, archival cons., hist. cons., prodr. Haunted History, Echoes Through Time Death Valley; editor: Gun Report; prodr.: (films) L.A. Bounty, the 20 Mule Team of Death Valley; (TV series) Magnificent Failures, 20th Century Infamous Guns; featured (TV series) Tales of the Gun, 1998—2000, Collector's Cafe; contbr. articles to profl. jours. Treas. Italian Am. Civic Coalition; chmn. dist. bd. dirs. Darwin Cmty. Svcs., 1990—92; mem. ethics bd. Universal Autograph Collectors Club; founder Ohio History Flight Mus.; bd. dirs. Calif. Cancer Found., LA, 1978—85, pres., 1979—80; bd. dirs. Friends William S. Hart Pk. and Mus., 1990—93, v.p. mus. rels. Mem.: NARAS, S.E. Ohio Oil and Gas Assn., Nat. Italian Am. Bar Assn., Century City Bar Assn. (vice-chmn. estate planning, trust and probate com. 1979—80), Italian Am. Lawyers Assn. (bd. govs. 1980—, 1st v.p. 1984—88), LA County Bar Assn. (arbitration com., fee dispute resolution program), Medieval Assn. of the Pacific, Universal Autograph Collectors Club (mem. ethics bd., registered dealer review bd., registered authenticator We. Americana), So. Calif. Autograph Soc. (v.p.), Death Valley History Assn. (life), Western Writers Assn., English Westerners Soc., Am. Numismatic Assn. (dist. rep. Carson City 1981—82, L.A. 1982—83), Medieval Acad. Am. (conf. session chair 2001—02), Mensa, Ariz. Ctr. Medieval Renaissance Studies Conf. (chair 2000—01, 2003), Wig and Pen Club (London), Zeta Phi Eta, Phi Alpha Delta, Pi Gamma Mu, Beta Alpha Psi (pres. 1972), Omicron Delta Epsilon. also: 230 S Main St Darwin CA 93522 Office Phone: 805-777-7223.

PALCHICK, BERNARD S., academic administrator, painter, educator; b. Chgo., Sept. 24, 1945; m. Lisa Palchick; children: Linnea, Benjamin. BA in Painting, Purdue U., 1967; MFA in Sculpture, RISD, 1971. Instr. art Kalamazoo Coll., 1972—74, asst. prof. art, 1974—79, assoc. prof. art, 1979—87, prof. art, 1987—, chair art dept., 1977—85, chair divsn. fine arts, 1982—95, dir. endowed artist-in-residence program, 1984—, assoc. provost, 1987—89, spl. asst. to pres. for comm., 1990, acting chair theatre dept., 1994—95, acting provost, 1996—97, v.p. coll. advancement, 1997—2006, interim pres., 2004—05. Bd. mem. Kalamazoo Inst. of Arts, 1994—99, Plz. Arts Cir., Western Mich. U., 1999—2003, Kalamazoo Cmty. in Schs., 2005—, Greater Kalamazoo Arts Coun., 2005—. Mem.: Mich. Watercolor Soc., Watercolor USA Honor Soc., Coun. for Advancement and Support of Edn. Office: Kalamazoo Coll 1200 Academy St Kalamazoo MI 49006 E-mail: palchick@kzoo.edu.

PALDUS, JOSEF, mathematics professor; b. Bzi, Czech Republic, Nov. 25, 1935; arrived in Can., 1968; s. Josef and Ludmila (Danicek) P.; m. Eva Zdena Bajer, Jan. 26, 1961; 1 dau., Barbara Alice. MSc, Charles U., Prague, 1958, DSc, 1995; PhD, Czechoslovak Acad. Sci., Prague, 1961; Drhc, Comenius U., Bratsilava, Slovakia, 2006. Research scientist Czechoslovak Acad. Scis., Prague, 1961-62, 64-68; postdoctoral fellow NRC, Ottawa, Canada, 1962-64; assoc. prof. applied math. U. Waterloo, Ont., Canada, 1968-75, prof. Ont., 1975-2001, disting. prof. emeritus Ont., 2001—; assoc. dir. Fields Inst., 1992-95. Vis. prof. U. Rheims, 1973, U. Louis Pasteur, Strasbourg, France, 1975-76, 82-83, Cath. U., Nijmegen, Holland, 1981, Technion, Haifa, Israel, 1983, Max Planck Inst. for Astrophysics, Munich, Germany, 1997, 98, 99, 2005; vis. scientist NRC, Ottawa, 1966-68, Free U. Berlin, 1981; adj. prof. chemistry U. Fla., Gainesville, 1984—; fellow Inst. for Advanced Study, Berlin, 1986-87. Mem. editl. bd. Comtex Sci., 1981-83, Advances in Quantum Chemistry, 1986, Jour. Chem. Physics, 1987-89, Can. Jour. Chemistry, 1994-96, Internat. Jour. Quantum Chemistry, 1996; mem. adv. editl. bd. Internat. Jour. Quantum Chemistry, 1977-88, Theoretica Chimica Acta, 1988-94, Jour. Math. Chemistry, 1989; contbr. numerous articles to profl. jours., chpts. to books. Recipient prize Chemistry divsn., Czechoslovak Acad. Scis., 1962, 1967, J. Heyrovsky Gold medal, Czechoslovak Acad. Sci., 1992, Gold medal Faculty of Math and Physics, Comenius U., Slovakia, 1994, Alexander von Humboldt Sr. Scientist award, 1996, Charles U. Gold medal, Prague, Czech Republic, 2005, De Scientia et Humanitate Optime Meritis medal, Czech Republic Acad. of Sci., 2007; Killam Rsch. fellow, 1987—89, Fields Inst. for Rsch. in Math. Scis. fellow, 2002. Fellow Royal Soc. Can.; mem. Internat. Acad. Quantum Molecular Sci., Internat. Soc. Theoretical Chem. Physics (bd. dirs.), European Acad. Scis., Arts and Letters (corr.), Czech Learned Soc. (hon.), Am. Inst. Physics, NY Acad. Scis., Applied Math. Soc. Can. Roman Catholic. Avocations: music, history. Office: U Waterloo Dept Applied Math 200 University Ave W Waterloo ON Canada N2L 3G1 Home Phone: 519-746-4435; Office Phone: 519-888-4567 ext. 36267. Business E-Mail: paldus@scienide.uwaterloo.ca.

PALECEK, MICHAEL R., information technology manager; b. Milw., Feb. 9, 1975; s. Michael H. Palecek and Kimberly S. Karas. Student, U. Phoenix, Brookfield, Wis., 2004—. Cert. profl. Microsoft, 2001. Network adminstr. iNET Computers, Inc., Waukesha, Wis., 2001—05; bus. systems mgr. Quick Cable, Franksville, Wis., 2005—. Author: (web site) Quick Cable Home Page. With US Army, 1993—2000. Decorated Army Commendation medal with 2 oak leaf clusters US Army, Good Conduct medal. Roman Catholic. Avocation: golf. Home: 2167 S 79th St West Allis WI 53219 Office: Quick Cable 3700 Quick Dr Franksville WI 53126 Home Phone: 414-526-1885; Office Phone: 262-824-3100. Personal E-mail: mpalecek@wi.rr.com. Business E-Mail: mpalecek@quickcable.com.

PALEN, J(OSEPH) JOHN, social sciences educator; b. Dubuque, Iowa, Feb. 24, 1939; s. Joseph John Palen and Mary (Rowan) Toner; m. Karen Ann Doody, June 9, 1962; children: Joseph John, Elizabeth Ann, Ellen Marye. BA, U. Notre Dame, 1961; MS, U. Wis., Madison, 1963, PhD, 1967. Demographer UN, Addis Ababa, Ethiopia, 1971—72; assoc. prof. U. Wis., Milw., 1972—77, prof., 1977—80; vis. prof. Nat. U. Singapore, 1983—84; prof. sociology, chmn. dept. Va. Commonwealth U., Richmond, 1980—. Author: Gentrification, Displacement and Revitalization, 1984, Urban World, 7th edit., 2005, City Scenes, 2d edit., 1981, The Suburbs, 1995, Social Problems for the Twenty-First Century, 2001. Leader Boy Scouts Am., Wis., 1973-80; pres. Torch Club, 2006-07. Grantee, Rockefeller Found., 1985, NIH, 1980—82, Ford Found., 1979, NIMH, 1976, NSF, 1985; Sr. Fulbright scholar, Taiwan, 1992, Fulbright Disting. Scholar and Chair in N.Am. Studies, U. Calgary, 1997, Fulbright scholar, Germany, 2002, Disting. scholar, Va. Commonwealth U., 1995. Mem. Fellow Am. Sociol. Assn., So. Sociol. Soc.; mem. Urban Affairs Assn. Avocations: hiking, history, rafting. Home: 500 Gardiner Rd Richmond VA 23229-6919 Office Phone: 804-288-0486. Business E-Mail: jpalen@vcu.edu.

PALEOLOGOS, EVANGELOS, hydrologist, educator; b. Athens, Greece, June 26, 1958; came to U.S., 1983; s. Constantine E. and Kathy A. (Michos) P.; m. Cleo L. Kalemkeris, Apr. 30, 1989; children: Katrina, Demi. BSCE, MSCE, Poly. U., 1986; PhD in Hydrology, U. Ariz., 1994. Sr. staff cons. Intera Inc., Las Vegas, Nev., 1992-95; asst. prof. U. S.C., Columbia, 1995-2001, assoc. prof., 2001—. Organizer internat. confs. Author: Environmental Risk and Liability Management, 2000, Environmental Risk Analysis, 2001; contbr. articles to profl. jours.; mem. editl. bd. Stochastic Environ. Rsch. and Risk Assessment, 1998—, Internat. Jour. Ocean and Oceanography, 2006—; contbr. over 50 articles to profl. jours. Mem. adv. bd. Global Alliance for Disaster Reduction. Mem. Am. Geophys. Union, European Geophys. Soc. Greek Orthodox. Avocations: art collecting, gardening. Office: Dept Geol Scis U So Columbia SC 29208-0001 E-mail: epal@geol.sc.edu.

PALERMO, ANTHONY ROBERT, lawyer; s. Anthony C. and Mary (Palvino) P.; m. Mary Ann Coyne, Jan. 2, 1960; children: Mark Henry, Christopher Coyne, Peter Stuart, Elisabeth Megan McCarthy, Julie Coyne Lawther, Gregg Anthony. BA, U. Mich., 1951; JD, Georgetown U., 1956. Bar: DC 1956, NY 1957, U.S. Supreme Ct. 1961. Trial atty. U.S. Dept. Justice, Washington, 1956-58, asst. U.S. atty. NYC, 1958-60, asst. U.S.

atty. in charge Rochester, NY, 1960-61; ptnr. Brennan, Centner, Palermo & Blauvelt, Rochester, 1962-81, Harter, Secrest & Emery, Rochester, 1981-94, Hodgson, Russ, Andrews, Woods & Goodyear, LLP, Rochester, 1994-97, of counsel, 1998, Woods Oviatt Gilman LLP, Rochester, 1999—. Note editor Georgetown Law Jour., 1956. Bd. dirs. McQuaid Jesuit H.S., Rochester, 1978-84, St. Ann's Home, Rochester, 1974-2001; bd. dirs., sec. St. Ann's Found., Rochester, 1989-2001; trustee, charter chmn. Clients' Security Fund N.Y. (now Lawyer's Fund for Client Protection), 1981-90; chmn. Govs. Jud. Screening Com. 4th Jud. Dept., mem. statewide com., 1987-89; chair magistrate selection com. U.S. Dist. Ct. (we. dist.) N.Y., 1995, 98; mem. N.Y. Chief Judge's Commn. on Jud. Salaries, 1997-2000; mem. N.Y. Office Ct. Adminstrn. Commn. on Fiduciary Appointments, 2000—. With US Army, 1951—54. Fellow Am. Bar Found., N.Y. State Bar Found. (bd. dirs. 1978-91), Am. Coll. Trial Lawyers; mem. ABA (ho. dels. 1980-98, 2004—, state del. 1982-85, bd. govs. 1985-88, 1989-93, sec. 1990-93), N.Y. State Bar Assn. (pres. 1979-80, ho. dels. 1973-75, 77—), Monroe County Bar Assn. (pres. 1973, Rodenbeck award, 1998), Oak Hill Country Club. Roman Catholic. Avocations: golf, travel. Home: 38 Huntington Meadow Rochester NY 14625-1813 Home Phone: 585-381-8847; Office Phone: 585-987-2882. Business E-Mail: apalermo@aol.com.

PALERMO, GREGORY SEBASTIAN, architect; b. Westfield, NY, Oct. 28, 1946; s. Sebastian and Frances Joan (Ciminella) P.;m. Olivia Madison; children: Mark Sebastian, Christopher Anthony. BArch, Carnegie Mellon U., 1969; MArch in Urban Design, Wash. U., 1976. Registered architect, Mo., Calif., N.Y., Iowa. Architect PGAV Inc., St. Louis, 1976-79; sr. v.p. HOK, Inc., St. Louis, 1980-87; sr. assoc. Mackey Assocs., St. Louis, 1987-89; v.p., prin. Stone Marraccini Patterson, St. Louis, 1989-91. Affiliate asst. prof. Washington U. Sch. Arch., 1984-90; vis. assoc. prof. Iowa State U. Dept. Arch., 1992-95, assoc. prof., 1995-2001, prof., 2001—, undergrad. program coord., 1996-98, assoc. chair undergrad. program, 1999—; chair Des Moines Archtl. Adv. Com., 1996-97; mem. Des Moines Gateway Planning Com., 1996. Mem. editl. bd. Iowa Architect mag., 1992—, assoc. ed., 1995—; mem. editl. bd. Jour. Archtl. Edn., 2001-04. Mem. Light Rail Transit Rev. Com., 1985, St. Louis Mayoral Task Force, 1986; exec/coun. Arts in Transit Com., St. Louis, 1987—; chmn. design rev. com.,St. Louis Metrolink Transit System, 1989-91; chair Nat. AIA Edn. Task Force, 1990; mem. Leadership St. Louis, 1990-91, Archtl. Adv. Commn. city of Des Moines, 1992-2000. Fellow AIA (bd. dirs., nat. v.p., pres. St. Louis chpt. 1984, pres. Iowa chpt. 2004); mem. Nat. Archtl. Accreditation Bd (pres. 1993-94). Home: 2048 Pinehurst Dr Ames IA 50010-4561

PALESTRO, CHRISTOPHER J., physician; m. Lynnette V. Stevens, May 24, 1985; children: Christopher J., Sarah Alice, Alexander Steven, Lissette Halle, Vincent Giancarlo. MD, Universidad Autonoma de Guadalajara, Mex., 1975. Diplomate Am. Bd. Nuc. Medicine, 1982. Chief nuc. medicine Norwalk Hosp., Conn., 1982—85; nuc. medicine physician Mt. Sinai Med. Ctr., NYC, 1985—92; chief nuc. medicine LI Jewish Med. Ctr., New Hyde Park, 1992—, North Shore U. Hosp., Manhassett, NY, 2006—; chief nuc. medicine and molecular imaging North Shore LI Jewish Health Sys., 2007—. Prof. nuc. medicine and radiology Albert Einstein Coll. Medicine, Bronx, NY, 1996—; chmn. Am. Bd. Nuc. Medicine, 2006; mem. residency rev. com. for nuc. medicine, 2007—; mem. editl. bd. Quar. Jour. Nuc. Medicine and Molecular Imaging. Assoc. editor: Radiology; contbr. articles to profl. jours. including Jour. Nuc. Medicine, Radiology, Radio-Graphics. Fellow: Am. Coll. Nuc. Physicians; mem.: Internat. Skeletal Soc., Radiol. Soc. N.Am., Soc. Nuc. Medicine. Office: Long Island Jewish Med Ctr 270-05 76th Ave New Hyde Park NY 11040 E-mail: palestro@lij.edu.

PALEVSKY, MAX, industrialist, director; b. Chgo., July 24, 1924; s. Isadore and Sarah (Greenblatt) P.; children: Nicholas, Madeleine, Alexander, Jonathan, Matthew. Ph.B., BS, U. Chgo., 1948; postgrad., U. Calif.-Berkeley, U. Chgo., UCLA, 1951-52. Mathematician Computer div. Bendix Corp., LA, 1952—56; v.p., gen. mgr., dir. Packard Bell Electronics, LA, 1957—61; pres., chmn. bd. Sci. Data Systems; chmn. bd. Xerox Data Systems, Inc., El Segundo, Calif., 1961-72; dir. Xerox Corp., 1969-72, chmn. exec. com. of bd., 1969-72. Bd. dirs. Intel Corp., Santa Clara, Calif., Komag, Inc., Milpitas, Calif. Organized George McGovern's campaign for Pres. of US, 1972; organized and ran Tom Bradley's campaign for Mayor of LA, 1973; mem. Folger com. Folger Shakespeare Libr., Washington, 1977—; mem. Dem. Adv. Com., 1968—; bd. dirs. ACLU, Constl. Rights Found.; trustee The Inst. for Advanced Study, Princeton U., 1988—. With USAAF, 1943-46. Office: 924 Westwood Blvd Ste 700 Los Angeles CA 90024-2928 Personal E-mail: palevsky@mindspring.com.

PALEVSKY, PAUL MARC, nephrologist, educator; b. NYC, Dec. 29, 1957; s. Gerald and Estelle (Moore) P.; m. Sharon Renee Roseman, Sept. 4, 1983; children: Hilary Ilana, Jason Michael. BS, Northestern U., 1979, MD, 1981. Diplomate Am. Bd. Internal Medicine, Am. Bd. Internal Medicine (Nephrology). Intern, resident Internal Medicine Hosp., U. Pa., Phila., 1981-84; fellow nephrology U. Pa., Phila., 1984-88, rsch. assoc., 1988-89; asst. prof. U. Pitts. Med. Sch., 1989-95, assoc. prof., 1995—2001, prof., 2001—. Chief Hemodialysis unit VA Pitts. Health Care Sys., 1989—, chief renal sect., 1993—; med. rev. ESRD Network 4, Pitts., 1989—. Contbr. articles to profl. jours. Fellow ACP, ACCP, Am. Soc. Nephrology; mem. Internat. Soc. Nephrology, Am. Soc. Nephrology, Am. Heart Assn. (Coun. on Kidney in Cardiovasc. Disease), Nat. Kidney Found., Renal Physicians Assn., Alpha Omega Alpha. Home: 109 Bell Farm Ests Sewickley PA 15143-8367 Office: VA Pitts Health Care Sys University Dr Divsn Pittsburgh PA 15240 Home Phone: 412-749-9945; Office Phone: 412-688-6474. E-mail: palevsky@pitt.edu.

PALEY, ALAN H., lawyer; b. Apr. 28, 1950; BA, Case Western Res. U., 1972; JD, NYU, 1975, LLM, 1976. Bar: NY 1976. Fellow securities inst. sch. law NYU, 1975-76; assoc. Debevoise & Plimpton, NYC, 1976—84, ptnr., 1984—, co-chair Securities Practice Group. Mem. Phi Beta Kappa. Office: Debevoise & Plimpton LLP 919 Third Ave New York NY 10022 Office Phone: 212-909-6694. Home Fax: 212-909-6386. E-mail: ahpaley@debevoise.com.

PALEY, GERALD LARRY, lawyer; b. Albany, NY, Sept. 11, 1939; s. Arthur and Mary (Peckner) P.; m. Joyce R., June 25, 1961 (div. June 1985); children: Jonathan, Eric, Suzanne; m. Sheryl Gae, Aug. 14, 1985. BA, Union Coll., 1961; JD with distinction, Cornell U., 1964. Bar: N.Y. 1964. Assoc. Nixon, Hargrave, Devans & Doyle, Rochester, NY, 1964-69; assoc. solicitor Dept. Labor, Washington, 1969-71; ptnr. Nixon, Hargrave, Devans & Doyle, Rochester, 1971-87, Phillips, Lytle, Hitchcock, Blaine & Huber, Rochester, 1987—. Author: Handbook of Federal Labor Relations Laws, 1981, Understand Employee Regulations, 1984. Mem. ABA. Republican. Jewish. Office: Phillips Lytle Hitchcock et al 1400 First Federal Plz Rochester NY 14614-1981 Office Phone: 585-238-2008.

PALEY, MICHAEL A., rabbi; BA in Near Eastern and Judaic Studies, Brandeis U., 1974; grad. work in Jewish and Islamic Philosophy and Sci., Temple U.; grad. work in Medieval Jewish Sci., Hebrew U.; studied at Yeshivat Hamivtar and the Reconstructional Rabbinical Coll. Ordained Yeshivat B'nai Or, Phila., 1981. Jewish chaplin also Rabbi Dartmouth Coll., also dir.; dir. Earl Hall/St. Paul's Chapel, Columbia U., 1987—94; chaplin Columbia U., NYC; former v.p., Rabbi Wexner Heritage Found., mem. permanent faculty; prof. Jewish studies, Dean Bard Coll.; exec dir. Jewish Resources & Synagogue and Cmty. Affairs, Rabbi United Jewish Assn. Fedn. NY, dir., Outreach, scholar in residence, dir., Jewish Resource Ctr. Taught at Akiba Hebrew Acad., Nat. Navuraj Summer Inst., Hillel Eastern Winter Inst. and Temple U.; adj. prof. Columbia Sch. Journalism; founder Edgar M. Bronfman Youth Fellowships, Israel, Conf. Judaism Rural New England, 1983; exec. dir. Jewish Communal Network Commn.; mem. exec. com. United Jewish Communities Rabbinic Cabinet. Mem. editorial bd., Jewish book editor Tikkun. Named one of The Top 50 Rabbis in America, Newsweek Mag., 2007. Mem.: Assn. of Religion and Intellectual Life (former v.p.). Office: United Jewish Assn Fedn NY 130 E 59th St New York NY 10022 Office Phone: 212-980-1000. *

PALEY, VITALY, chef, food service executive; Studied piano, The Juliard Sch.; grand diploma, French Culinary Inst. NY. Chef Union Sq Cafe, Remi, Chanterelle, Moulin de la Gorce. Recipient Best Chef: Northwest/Hawaii, The James Beard Found., 2005. Office: Paley's Place Bistro & Bar 1204 NW 21st Ave Portland OR 97209

PALEY, VIVIAN GUSSIN, writer; b. Chgo., Jan. 25, 1929; d. Harry A. and Yetta M. Gussin; m. Irving O. Paley; children: David, Robert. BA, U. Chgo., 1947, Newcomb Coll., New Orleans, 1951; MA, Hofstra U., NY, 1961; PhD (hon.), Lewis and Clark U., Portland, Oreg., 2007, Erikson Inst., Chgo., 2007. Tchr. Great Neck Pub. Sch., NY, 1963—70, U. Chgo., 1971—95. Author: White Teacher, 1979, Wally's Stories, 1981, Boys and Girls, 1984, Mollie is Three, 1986, Bad Guys Don't Have Birthdays, 1988, The Boy Who Would be a Helicopter, 1990, You Can't Say You Can't Play, 1992, Kwanzaa and Me, 1995, The Girl with the Brown Crayon, 1997, The Kindness of Children, 1999, In Mrs. Tully's Room, 2001, A Child's Work, 2004. Recipient Am. Book award for Lifetime Achievement, Columbus Found., 1998, Outstanding Achievement award, John Dewey Soc., 2000; MacArthur fellow, 1989. Home: 5422 Blackstone Ave Chicago IL 60615

PALFREY, THOMAS ROSSMAN, economics professor, political science professor; b. Lafayette, Ind., Oct. 11, 1953; s. Thomas Rossman and Emily Skillings Palfrey; m. Cheryl Craig, July 9, 1976; 1 child, Rossman Craig. BA in Polit. Sci. magna cum laude, U. Mich., 1975, MA in Polit. Sci., 1976; PhD, Calif. Inst. Tech., 1981. Prof. politics and econs. Princeton U., NJ, 2004—06; prof. econs. and polit. economy Carnegie Mellon U., Pasadena, Pa., 1980—; prof. econs. and polit. sci. Calif. Inst. Tech., Pasadena, 1986—2005, Flintridge Found. prof. econs. and poliitcal sci., 2006—. Author: (book) Bayesian Implementation, 1993, Voting: What is, What Could Be, 2001; editor: Laboratory Research in Political Economy, 1991, Experimental Foundations of Political Science, 1993; contbr. over 100 scholarly articles to profl. jours. Dir. Caltech, MIT Voting Tech. Project, Pasadena, 2000—02. Fellow, Ctr. Advanced Study Behavioral Scis., 1986—87; grant, NSF, 1982—. Fellow: Econometric Soc.; mem.: Pub. Choice Soc., Am. Econ. Assn., Game Theory Soc., Econ. Sci. Assn. (pres., v.p., exec. bd. 1988—99). Avocations: classical guitar, tennis, hiking. Office: Calif Inst Tech Mail Code 228-77 (HSS) Pasadena CA 91125 Office Phone: 626-395-4088.

PALIA, ASPY PHIROZE, marketing educator, researcher, consultant; b. Bombay, Nov. 27, 1944; arrived in US, 1973; s. Phiroze E. and Homai P. (Irani) P. BSME, U. Bangalore, 1966; MBA, U. Hawaii at Manoa, 1976; DBA, Kent State U., 1985. Sales engr. Larsen & Toubro Ltd., 1966—72, export sales engr., 1972—73; tchg. fellow Coll. Bus. Adminstrn. Kent State U., 1977—80, instr. Coll. Bus. Adminstrn., 1982—84; asst. prof. Coll. Bus. Adminstrn. U. Hawaii, Manoa, 1984—89, assoc. prof., 1990—95, prof., 1996—2005, prof. Shidler Coll. Bus., 2006—, pres. faculty coun., 1995—96; senator U. Hawaii Manoa Faculty Congress, 1996—98, 2007—; sr. fellow dept. mktg. Nat. U. Singapore, 1998—99, vis. sr. fellow dept. mktg., 2000—02. Vis. prof. Coll. Mgmt. Nat. Sun Yat-sen U., Kaohsiung, Taiwan, 1992, Chulalongkorn U., Bangkok, 1992, 93, 97, 2003, 2005—06, U. Otago, New Zealand, 1995, Adminstrv. Staff Coll. India, Hyderabad, 1992, Indian Inst. Mgmt., Ahmedabad, 2000, Asian Inst. Tech., Bangkok, 2001; mem. Manoa Ctr. for Teaching Excellence Faculty Adv. Group U. Hawaii, 1991, mem. mktg. plan adv. com., 94, mem. honors and awards com., 1990—91, pres. faculty coun., 1995—96, mem. faculty adv. com. on acad. freedom, 1997; vis. scholar faculty bus. adminstrn. Nat. U. Singapore, 1991, Mktg. Inst. Singapore Exec. Devel. Seminars, 1997, 91, 1994—95, Hong Kong Inst. Mktg. Exec. Devel. Seminar, 1996, Kathmandu Coll. Mgmt. Exec. Devel. Workshop, 2000; sr. fellow dept. mktg. faculty of bus. adminstrn. Nat. U. Singapore, 1998—99, vis. prof., 2000, 01, 02; affiliate faculty Japan Am. Inst. Mgmt. Sci., Honolulu, 1989—; vis. prof. Grad. Sch. Internat. Mgmt., Internat. U. Japan, Uhrasa, Yamato-machi, 1991, U. Internat. Bus. and Econs., Beijing, 1991, U. Kebangsaan Malaysia, Bangi-Selangor, Kuala Lumpur, Malaysia, 1991, 92, Mt. Carmel Inst. Mgmt., Bangalore, India, 1997, Vietnam Nat. U., Hanoi Sch Bus., 2002, Singapore Mgmt. U., 2003, 04; condr., leader exec. devel. workshop on strategic market planning Boston Network, Bangkok, 2003; lectr., cons., presenter in field. Editor: (with Dennis A. Rondinelli) Project Planning and Implementation in Developing Countries, 1976; assoc. editor e-Services Quar., 1999—; contbr. articles to profl. jours. including Indsl. Mktg. Mgmt., Internat. Bus. Jour., Asia-Pacific Jour. Mgmt., Internat. Mktg. Rev., European Jour. Mktg., Fgn. Trade Rev., Internat. Rev. Econs. & Bus., others; chpts. to books; developer various mktg. decision support systems and decision-making tools for use in strategic market planning and in marketing simulations. Program rev. com. Pacific and Asian Mgmt. Inst., Acad. Internat. Bus., Assn. Bus. Simulation and Exptl. Learning, others; bd. examiners Nat. U. Singapore Sch. Postgrad. Mgmt. Studies, 1991; external examiner Bd. Grad. Studies, Nat. U. Singapore, 2001-2002; adv. bd. Soc. Coll. of Bus. Adminstrn. Alumni and Friends Exec. Com., 1991-93, Salvation Army Residential Treatment Facilities for Children and Youth Adv. Coun., 1989-96, vice chair, 1987-89; chair Salvation Army Family Treatment Svcs. Adv. Coun., 1997-98; mem. Salvation Army Honolulu Adv. Bd., 1997-98; treas., bd. dirs. Kings Gate Homeowners Assn., 1994-96; bd. advisors Ctr. for Nat. Competitiveness Inst. Indsl. Policy Studies, Korea, 1998—. Univ. fellow Kent State U., 1983; East-West Ctr. scholar East-West Ctr., 1973-75; Ednl. Improvement Fund grantee, 1989, Instrl. Travel and Devel. Fund grantee Office Faculty Devel. and Acad. Support, 1991, 95, joint rsch. grants U. Kebangsaan Malaysia, Nat. U. Singapore, U. So. Queensland, Australia, U. Otago, New Zealand, Lingnan Coll., Hong Kong; recipient Internat. Agreements Fund award Office Internat. Programs and Svcs., 1990-92, ORA travel award U. Rsch. Coun., 1986, 88-89, 91-92, 94-98. Mem. Am. Mktg. Assn. (academia editor Honolulu chpt. 1986-87), Acad. Internat. Bus. (chair Pacific Basin Region 1995, chair Pacific Basin chpt. 1996-2002, co-chair Asia Pacific Conf. 1997), Pacific Asian Consortium for Internat. Bus. Edn. and Rsch., Assn. for Bus. Simulation and Exptl. Learning, Pan-Pacific Bus. Assn. (charter), Mortar Bd. (Outstanding Educator award 1993, Mentor award 1995), East-West Ctr. Alumni Assn. U.S. (v.p. Hawaii chpt. 1987-89, ad campaign com. 1987-88), Beta Gamma Sigma (faculty advisor, sec.-treas. Alpha of Hawaii chpt. 1990—, Outstanding Svc. award 1992-93, Bd. Govs. Commitment to Excellence award 1997, Prof. of Yr. award 2003), Mu Kappa Tau, Pi Sigma Epsilon. Avocations: music, photography, swimming, reading, hiking. Home: 2724 Kahoaloha Ln # 1605 Honolulu HI 96826-3337 Office: U Hawaii Dept Mktg 2404 Malie Way Honolulu HI 96822-2223 Office Phone: 808-956-8642. Business E-Mail: aspy@hawaii.edu.

PALII, SERGIU PETRU, chemist, researcher; b. Moldova, Aug. 5, 1962; s. Petru Eftimie and Larisa P. (Tomacinschi) Palii; m. Stela Simona Sciuca, Aug. 29, 1987; 1 child, Miorel Lucian. PhD, Ukrainian Acad. Scis., 1991. Head mass spectrometry group, rsch. scientist in lab. of coord. chemistry Inst. of Chemistry, Acad. Scis. of Republic of Moldova, Chisinau, 1991—98; rsch. assoc. dept. chemistry U. Fla., Gainesville, 1999—. Joint faculty dept. chemistry Moldavian State U., Chisinau, 1991—96; mem. organizing com. Conf. on Phys. Methods in Coordination and Supramolecular Chemistry, Chisinau, 1993—99. Actor: (movie) Miorita (Telefilm-Chisinau, Moldova), 1978, In Memoriam: Mihai Eminescu (TV Moldova), 1989; author: (series of essays) Historical Architecture and Monuments of Chisinau City (Essay of Yr., Moldavian Soc. Arch., 1990); contbg. author: Chisinau Encyclopedia; contbr. chpts. to book and articles to profl. jours. Recipient Young Scientists prize, Moldavian Nat. Coun. for Sci. Achievement, 1992, Internat. Sci. Exch. award, Natural Scis. and Engring. Rsch. Coun. Can., 1993, award, French Acad. Scis., 1996, Young Scientists prize, Acad. Scis. Moldova, 1997, Scientia Europaea prize, French Acad. Scis. and Rhone-Poulenc Found., 1999, Recognition cert. and medal, Rsch. and New Techs. Eureka, Belgium, 1999; grantee Vis. fellow, United Kingdom's Royal Soc., 1996; Rsch. grant, Internat. Sci. Found., 1993. Mem.: U. Fla. Alumni Assn., Acad. Scis. Republic of Moldova (Coun. Young Scientists vice chmn. 1992—97), Romanian Inst. Genealogy and Heraldry, Am. Chem. Soc., Internat. Mass Spectrometry Soc., Am. Soc. for Mass Spectrometry, Internat. Union of Pure and Applied Chemistry, Scientia Europaea. Achievements include research in Gas Phase Chemistry of Organometallic, Macrocyclic, Polynuclear and Supramolecular Species; patents in field. Business E-Mail: palii@ufl.edu.

PALIN, SARAH HEATH, governor; b. Sandpoint, Idaho, Feb. 11, 1964; d. Chuck and Sally Heath; m. Todd Palin; children: Bristol, Piper, Track, Willow. BS in Journalism, U. Idaho, 1987. Mem. city council City of Wasila, Alaska, 1992—96, mayor, 1996—2002; chair Alaska Oil and Gas Conservation Commn., 2003—04; mem. Interstate Oil and Gas Compact Commn.; gov. State of Alaska, Juneau, 2006—. Mem. Alaska Resource Devel. Coun. Pres. Alaska Conf. Mayors; mem. steering com. Youth Ct.; bd. mem. Alaska Mcpl. League, Valley Hosp. Assn. Named Miss Wasila, 1984; recipient Person of Yr. award, Am. Pub. Works Assn. (Alaska chpt.), Top 40 Under 40 award, Alaska State Chamber. Mem.: Alaska Miner's Assn., Alaska Outdoor Coun., NRA (life), Rotary (hon.), Sigma Beta Delta. Republican. Achievements include being the youngest person and the first woman to hold the office of governor of Alaska, 2006. Avocations: hunting, fishing, running, history. Office: Office of the Gov State Capitol PO Box 110001 Juneau AK 99811 *

PALINSKY, CONSTANCE GENEVIEVE, hypnotherapist, educator; b. Flint, Mich., May 31, 1927; d. George and Genevieve Treasa Ignace; m. Joseph Palinsky, July 3, 1947; children: Joseph II, Mark Robert. Art student, Flint Inst. Arts, Oriental Artists Sch., others; numerous hypnosis studies including, Ethical Tng. Hypnosis Ctr., NJ and Fla., Mid-West Inst., Hypnodye Found, Ill. and Fla.; tng., Nat. Guild Hypnotists. Cert NLP practitioner, neuro linguistics programmer; registered and cert. hypnotherapist. Owner, operator Palinsky Gallery of Art and Antiques, Flint, 1970-80; art lectr. Genesee County Grade Sch. Sys. Flint Inst. Arts, 1972-74; owner, hypnosis cons. Hypno-Tech. Ctr., Flint, 1975-80; asst. mgr. Wethered-Rice Fine Jewelry, Flint, 1982-83; hypnotherapist, sr. cons. Dailey Life Ctr. Inc., Flint, 1985-99. Mem. Am. Bd. Hypnotherapy, Calif.; numerous radio and TV shows and guest appearances, Flint, 1957—, ABC Nat. Network, 1959, Flint Cable TV, 1972, others. Author: Constructive Personality Development, 1987, Secrets Revealed for Hypnosis Scripting, 1989, Designing Hypnosis Scripts for Relief of Multiple Sclerosis, 1994, Substance Abuse Issues Revealed of Effective Hypnosis Interventions, 1994, Light Touch Therapy for Pain Relief of Chemotherapy Treatment Stress-Headache and Back Pain Relief--A Form of Hypno-Acupressure, 1995, Cues and Clues—Interview Listening Methods for Substance Abuse-Including Questionnaires, 1997; one-woman show Dell's Artcraft Gallery, 1958; group shows at Flint Inst. Arts, U. Mich., Purdue U., Lafayette, Inc., Flint Artist Market, Saginaw, Detroit and Grand Rapids, Mich., Japan, others; contbr. articles to profl. jours.; author scripts and software in hypnosis field. Bd. dirs. The Chapel of The Angles Bldg. Fund for Lapeer County, 1974-75; pub. spkr. various civic orgns. Named Oil Colorist of Yr. Profl. Photographers of Mich., 1959; recipient Pub. Svc. award Genesee County Sheriff's Dept., 1974. Mem. Internat. Soc. Profl. Hypnosis (regional v.p. 1977-79), Internat. Soc. Profl. Hypnotists and Counselors, Internat. Med. and Dental Hypnotherapist Assn., Nat. Guild Hypnotists (rsch. award for hypnosis for relief of multiple sclerosis 1991), Questers Antique Study Group (various offices including pres. 1972-98), Internat. Psychic Arts Rsch. (founder, pres. 1974-75), Flint Artist Market Group (program dir., treas.), Flint Soc. Arts and Crafts (v.p., pres. 1958-59), Quota Club, others. Republican. Roman Catholic. Avocations: writing, painting, sculpting, travel, needlepoint. Office: Dailey Life Ctr Inc 5038 Miller Rd Ste B Flint MI 48507-1071

PALION, PETER THADDEUS, financial planner; b. Warsaw, Jan. 14, 1966; came to U.S., 1982; s. Karol and Zofia (Biernacka) P.; m. Monica Witak, Jan. 18, 1992. Student, CUNY, 1984-85; CFP, Coll. Fin. Planning, Denver, 1993. Fin. cons. Shearson Lehman Bros., NYC, 1987-88; fin. planner IDS Fin. Svcs., Inc., NYC, 1988-94; pres., chmn. bd. dirs. Master Plan Advisory, Inc., NYC, 1994—; registered rep., prin. various ind. broker dealers; registered prin. Comprehensive Asset Mgmt. and Servicing, Mem. NASD/SIPC, 2003—. Stock market cons. Polish Govt., Warsaw, 1990; guest spkr. on East European markets Voice of Am., Washington, 1990-93, on investments N.Y.C. Channel 31 Polish TV, 1991, CNNfn, 1997, 98, Neighborhood News 13; featured spkr. Times/Ledger Newspapers-IAFP Person Finance Day, 1998, 99, 2000; tchr. investment planning courses Hofstra U., 1999-2000. Author article series Kariera, 1990. Avocations: tennis, skiing, reading, motorsports. Office: Master Plan Advisory Inc 60 E 42nd St Fl 46 New York NY 10165-4699

PALISI, ANTHONY THOMAS, psychologist, educator; b. Rahway, NJ, Mar. 8, 1930; s. Anthony Francis and Marianne Catherine (Picone) P.; m. Dyane Cassidy, Apr. 19, 1954; children: Jane, Anthony Francis II, Phyllis, Damian-Marie. BS, Seton Hall U., 1951, MA, 1958; EdD, Temple U., 1973. Cert. secondary tchr., elem. prin., psychologist, rehab. counselor, N.J.; mem. Nat. Register Health Care Profls. in Psychology. Tchr., coach pub. schs., Rahway, 1953-60; sports editor Rahway News-Record, 1950-60; prin. elem. pub. sch. Franklin Twp., NJ, 1960-65; asst. prof. edn. Seton Hall U., 1965-73, assoc. prof., 1974-77, prof., 1977-82, acting grad. dean, 1976-77, dir., 1969-80, indsl. cons. group dynamics, 1967-97; pvt. practice psychology, 1977; dir. cons. divsn. FormTech Graphics, Inc., 1997—. Adj. faculty Brookdale C.C., 2005—, Prevention, Inc. Contbr. articles and short stories to profl. jours. and popular periodicals. Mem. Rahway Bd. Edn. 1961-62; trustee Rahway Libr., 1961-68, pres. 1967-68. Recipient award N.J. Sportswriters' Assn., 1953. Mem. APA, ACA, Am. Mgmt. Assn. (co-author video tng. program), N.J. Psychol. Assn., Assn. for Specialists in Group Work (mem. rsch. com. 1980-82), N.Y. Acad. Scis., Nat. Acad. Counselors and Family Therapists (chmn., exec. dir. 1988-93, co-editor Family Letter 1985-93), Nat. Register of Health Svc. Providers in Psychology, Am. Coll. Counselors., Clin. Hypnosis Soc. NJ. Roman Catholic. E-mail: atu74palisi@verizon.net.

PALIWAL, DINESH C., electronics executive; married; 2 children. BS, St. Johns Coll., Agra, India; MS, MBA, Miami Univ., Ohio. Engring. & mgmt. positions with Ballarpur Industries, Yamunanagar, India, AccuRay Corp., Columbus, Ohio, Combustion Engring., Singapore & Melbourne, Australia; engring. & mgmt. positions through dir. Asia Pacific mktg. & sales ABB Ltd., 1985—94, v.p. industries Beijing, 1994—2001, pres. process industries Zurich, Switzerland, 2001—02, pres. automation tech. worldwide Norwalk, Conn., 2002—04; chmn., CEO ABB No. Am., 2004—06; pres. global markets & tech. ABB Group, Zurich, Switzerland, 2006—07; vice-chmn., pres., CEO Harman Internat. Industries, Washington, 2007—. Econ. adv. to Gov. Guangdong Province, China; bd. dir. Embarq Corp., U.S. India Bus. Council; chmn. Nat. Fgn. Trade Council; mem. U.S. Bus. Roundtable; past dir. U.S. China Bus. Council. Dir. Internat. Swimming Hall of Fame. Office: Harman Internat Industries Ste 1010 1101 Pennsylvania Ave NW Washington DC 20004 *

PALKOVIC, MICHAEL W., broadcast executive; With Times Mirror Cable TV, DIRECTV Group, El Segundo, Calif., 1996—, sr. v.p., CFO US bus., 2001—04, exec. v.p., CFO US bus., 2004—, exec. v.p., CFO, 2005—. Office: DIRECTV Group 2230 E Imperial Hwy El Segundo CA 90245 Office Phone: 310-964-5000. *

PALL, ELLEN JANE, writer; b. NYC, Mar. 28, 1952; d. David B. and Josephine H. (Blatt) P.; m. Richard Holmes Dicker, July 12, 1986; 1 child, Benjamin. BA, U. Calif., Santa Barbara, 1973. Freelance writer for several jours., 1987—. Staff assoc. Bread Loaf Writers Conf., Middlebury, Vt., 1986; instr. UCLA-Ext., 1980-83; adj. asst. prof. Fordham U./Coll. at Lincoln Ctr., N.Y.C., 1990-93. Author (under pen name Fiona Hill): The Trellised Lane, The Wedding Portrait, The Practical Heart, Love in a Major Key, Sweet's Folly, The Autumn Rose, The Love Child, The Stanbroke Girls, 1981, The Country Gentleman, 1987; author: (as Ellen Pall) Back East, 1983, Among the Ginzburgs, 1996, Corpse de Ballet, 2001, Slightly Abridged, 2003; contbr. articles to N.Y.Times Mag., N.Y. Times Arts & Leisure, New Yorker mag., Chgo. Tribune, Washington Post; book reviewer. Shane Stevens fellow, Bread Loaf Writer's Conf., Vt., 1983. Mem. Am. PEN (freedom to write com.). Office: care Mary Evans Inc 242 E 5th St New York NY 10003-8501 Business E-Mail: ellen@ellenpall.com.

PALLADINO-CRAIG, ALLYS, museum director, educator; b. Pontiac, Mich., Mar. 23, 1947; d. Stephan Vincent and Mary (Anderson) Palladino; m. Malcolm Arnold Craig, Aug. 20, 1967; children— Ansel, Reed, Nicholas. BA in English, Fla. State U., 1967; grad., U. Toronto, Ont., Can., 1969; MFA, Fla. State U., 1978, PhD in Humanities, 1996. Editorial asst. project U. Va. Press, Charlottesville, 1970-76; instr. English Inst. Franco Americain, Rennes, France, 1974; adj. instr. Fla. State U., Tallahassee, 1978-79, dir. Four Arts Ctr., 1979-82, dir. U. Mus. of Fine Arts, 1982—, prof. mus. studies. Mem. grad faculty Mus. Studies Cert. Program Fla. State U. Curator, contbg. editor: Nocturnes and Nightmares, Monochrome/Polychrome, Chroma, High Roads & Low Roads-Anthems, Dirges, Myths; contbg. editor: Body Language; guest curator, author: Mark Messersmith: New Mythologies; curator, editor Albert Paley--Sculpture, Drawings, Graphics and Decorative Arts, Trevor Bell: A British Painter in America, and Trial by Fire: Contemporary Glass; curator, author: The Abridged Walmsley--Selections from the Career of William Aubrey Walmsley, co-curator, contbg. author: Terrestrial Forces; author: Jack Nichelson: Micro-Theatres, Alexa Kleinbard: Talking Leaves, Jake Fernandez--Ethereal Journeyman, Jim Roche-Sense of Place; editor: Athanor I-XXVI, 1980—; Represented in permanent collections Fla. Ho. of Reps., Barnett Bank, IBM. Individual artist fellow Fla. Arts Coun., 1979 Mem. Am. Assn. Mus., Fla. Art Mus. Dirs. Assn. (sec. 1989-91), Phi Beta Kappa. Democrat. Avocation: antiques. Home: 1410 Grape St Tallahassee FL 32303-5636 Office: Fla State U Mus of Fine Arts 250 Fine Arts Bldg Tallahassee FL 32306-1140 Home Phone: 850-224-4188. Business E-Mail: apcraig@mailer.fsu.edu.

PALLAM, JOHN JAMES, lawyer; b. Cleve., May 19, 1940; s. James John and Coralia (Gatsos) P.; m. Evanthia Venizelos, Nov. 29, 1969; 1 child, Alethea. BA, Case Western Res. U., 1962; JD, Ohio State U., 1965. Bar: Ohio 1965, U.S. Ct. Claims 1969, U.S. Ct. Mil. Appeals 1969, U.S. Supreme Ct. 1970. Law clk. to presiding justice Cuyahoga County Ct., Cleve., 1965-66; assoc. Burke, Habor & Berick, Cleve., 1970-73; corp. atty. Midland Ross Corp., Cleve., 1973-80, corp. counsel, 1980-87; v.p., gen. counsel Brush Engineered Materials Inc., Cleve., 1987—. Guest lectr. Nat. Foundry Assn., Chgo., 1986—. Contbr. articles on labor and environ. matters to jours. Legal advisor Am. Hellenic and Prog. Assn., Cleve., 1966—. Served to capt. JAGC U.S. Army, 1966-70, Vietnam. Decorated Bronze Star with oak leaf cluster. Mem. Ohio Bar Assn. (committeeman 1984—), Cleve. Bar Assn. (merit svc. award 1972), Hellenic Bar Assn., Hellenic Univ. Club, Rowfant. Greek Orthodox. Avocations: history, antiques, golf, rare books, railroading. Office: 17876 Saint Clair Ave Cleveland OH 44110-2602

PALLASCH, B. MICHAEL, lawyer, director; b. Chgo., Mar. 30, 1933; s. Bernhard Michael and Magdalena Helena (Fixari) P.; m. Josephine Catherine O'Leary, Aug. 15, 1981; children: Bernhard Michael III and Madeleine Josephine (twins). BSS, Georgetown U., 1954; JD, Harvard U., 1957; postgrad., John Marshall Law Sch., 1974. Bar: Ill. 1957, U.S. Dist. Ct. (no. dist.) Ill. 1958, U.S. Tax Ct. 1961, U.S. Ct. Claims 1961, U.S. Ct. Appeals (7th cir.) 1962. Assoc. Winston & Strawn, Chgo., 1958-66, resident mgr. br. office Paris, 1963-65, ptnr. Chgo., 1966-70, sr. capital ptnr., 1971-91; sr. ptnr. B. Michael Pallasch & Assocs., 1991—. Corp. sec. Tanis, Inc., Calumet, Mich., 1972-2000, Greenbank Engring. Corp., Dover, Del., 1976-91, C.B.P. Engring. Corp., Chgo., 1976-91, Arthur Andersen Assocs., Inc., Chgo., 1976-98, Chgo. Cutting Svcs. Corp., 1977-88, L'hotel de France of Ill., Inc., Chgo., 1980-85, Water & Effluent Screening Co., Chgo., 1988-91. Bd. dirs. Martin D'Arcy Mus. Medieval and Renaissance Art, Chgo., 1975—; bd. dirs. Katherine M. Bosch Found., 1978—; asst. sec. Hundred Club of Cook County, Chgo., 1966-73, bd. dirs., sec., 1974—. Served with USAFR, 1957-63. Decorated Knight of Merit with silver star Sacred Mil. Constantinian Order of St. George of Royal House of Bourbon of Two Sicilies, Grand Officer with gold and silver stars Sovereign Mil. Order of Temple of Jerusalem; named Youth Mayor, City of Chgo., 1950; recipient Outstanding Woodland Mgmt. Forestry award, Monroe County (Wis.) Soil and Water Conservation Dist., 1975. Mem. Ill. Bar Assn. (tax lectr. 1961), Advs. Soc., Field Mus. Natural History (life), Max McGraw Wildlife Found., English Speaking Union. Clubs: Travellers (Paris); Saddle and Cycle (Chgo.). Roman Catholic. Home: 737 W Hutchinson St Chicago IL 60613-1519 Office: 35 W Wacker Dr Ste 4700 Chicago IL 60601-1614 *Personal philosophy: We define and measure success in various ways: achievement, position, wealth: and attribute it to the application of various attributes but is there any degree of success that we can achieve that is worthier than the knowledge that we have faithfully served those who depend upon and trust in us?.*

PALLASCH, MAGDALENA HELENA (MRS. BERNHARD MICHAEL PALLASCH), artist; b. Chgo., Sept. 6, 1908; d. Frank and Anna (Meier) Fixari; m. Bernhard Pallasch, Nov. 26, 1931 (dec. Nov. 1977); children: Bernhard Michael, Diana Pallasch Miller Student, Art Inst. Chgo., Chgo. Acad. Fine Arts, 1922-26, Am. Acad. Fine Arts, 1926-30; studied with Joseph Allworthy, 1935-38; student, U. Chgo., 1960; doctorate (hon.), 1985. Contbr. two murals and ten life size figures for Woman's World Fair, Chgo., 1928, Century of Progress Exhbn., Chgo., 1933-34; portrait artist, subjects include Cardinal Cody, Chgo., 1980—, Cardinal Francis George, Chgo., 1998, Carlotta Ames, Boston, Mrs. Timothy Kingston, Arlington Heights, Ill., Dr. Neal Coleman, Hinsdale, Ill., Catherine Eardley Murphy, Lake Forest, Ill., Anita Mangels, Sao Paulo, Brazil, Canon Regis Barwig, Oshkosh, Wis., 2000, Dr. Dale King Phelps, Pittsford, NY, Laurel Cummings, Palm Beach Fla.,2001, Barbara and Robert Pendergast, Lake Forest, Ill., Mara Pallasch, Chgo., 2003, Lois Kay Simanton, Northfield Ill., 2004, Bernhard Anthony Miller, Chgo., 2004; mural St. Mary of the Lake Ch., Chgo., 1987; exhbn. at Montifiori Estate, 1992, 93, 94, Hinsdale Art Ctr., 1995, 96, 97; represented in pvt. and pub. collections Loyola U., Chgo., Barat Coll., Lake Forest, Ill., Internat. Coll. Surgeons, Chgo., Med. Library, Columbus Hosp and others.h Recipient first award for still life Arts Club, NYC, 1960, First award Nat. League Am. Pen Women, 1972, 1st place and best of show State Exhibit, Springfield, Ill., 1973, 1st award Chgo. Woman's Club, 1978, hon. mention for portrait Italian Cultural Ctr., hon. alumna award Loyola U., Chgo., 1983, award of excellence for portrait of author Gail Brook Burket, Wheaton Hist. Mus., 1987, Gold Medal of Honor for disting. lifelong achievements, 1987, award of honor for portrait of sculptor Lisa Gengler, 1989, medallion from Archduke Markus Habsburg of Austria, 2003, first award for still life Vanderpoel Gallery, 2005, Best Classic Art award Vanderpoel Gallery, 2006; named Dame Commandeur with Starbust, 1997, with second Starburst, 2003, Sovereign Mil. Order Temple of Jerusalem, 1995 Mem. Presentation Ball Aux.; mem. President's Club, Loyola U., also mem. women's bd. Nat. League Am. Pen Women (v.p. Chgo. br. 1966-68, art chmn. 1978-80, Margaret Dingle Meml. award 1979), Mcpl. Art League Chgo., Nat. Soc. Arts and Letters (art chmn. chgo. chpt. 1982—, apptd. nat. chmn. 1997—), Friends of Austria, Friends of D'Arcy Gallery of Medieval and Renaissance Art., Ill. Cath. Women Club (gov. 1979-), Cuneo Mus. (Vernon Hills, Ill.). Home and Office: 723 W Junior Ter Chicago IL 60613-1512

PALLIN, SAMUEL LEAR, ophthalmologist, educator, medical director; b. NYC, May 8, 1941; s. Irving and Gertrude (Lear) P.; children: Daniel Jay, Marla Jean, Laura Jane; m. Karen K. King, 2004. BA, Hofstra U., 1963; MD, SUNY, Bklyn., 1968. Diplomate Nat. Bd. Med. Examiners, Am. Bd. Ophthalmology. Intern L.I. Jewish Med. Ctr., 1968-69; resident Bklyn. Eye and Ear Hosp., 1972-75; prin. The Lear Eye Clinic, Ltd., Sun City, Ariz., 1975—, Phoenix, 1998—; asst. prof. dept. ophthalmology Sch. Medicine Midwestern U., 1997—; with White Dog Ranch, LLC, Tonopah, Ariz., 2005—; physician supr., med. dir. Arizona State Prison Complex, Perryville, 2005—. Mem. staff Walter O. Boswell Meml. Hosp., Del E. Webb Meml. Hosp., St. Luke's Med. Ctr., Thunderbird Samaritan Hosp.; presenter in field. Patentee in method of making self-sealing episcleral incision. Trustee Congr. Beth El Endowment Fund, 1987; mem. exec. bd. Ariz. chpt. Israel Bonds, 1988; lt. mounted unit cmty. svcs. posse Maricopa County Sheriff's Office, 1996—. With USAF, 1969-71. Mem. AMA, ACS, Am. Soc. Cataract and Refractive Surgery, Am. Acad. Ophthalmology, Ariz. Med. Assn., Ariz. Easter Seal Soc. (bd. dirs. 1989, life dir.), Maricopa County Med. Assn., Lions; hon. mem. Mex. Ophthalmology Soc. N.E., Mex. Intraocular Implant Soc., Ctrl. Mex. Ophthalmol. Soc.

PALLMEYER, REBECCA RUTH, judge; b. Tokyo, Sept. 13, 1954; arrived in U.S., 1957; d. Paul Henry and Ruth (Schrieber) Pallmeyer; m. Dan P. McAdams, Aug. 20, 1977; 2 children. BA, Valparaiso U., Ind., 1976; JD, U. Ill., Chgo., 1979. Bar: Ill. 1980, U.S. Ct. Appeals (7th cir.) 1980, U.S. Ct. Appeals (11th and 5th cir.) 1982. Judge clk. Minn. Supreme Ct., St. Paul, 1979-80; assoc. Hopkins and Sutter, Chgo., 1980-85; judge, administrv. law Ill. Human Rights Commn., Chgo., 1985-91; magistrate judge U.S. Dist. Ct. (No. Dist.), Chgo., 1991-98, dist. judge, 1998—. Mem. jud. resources com. Jud. Conf. U.S., 1994—2000. Nat. adv. coun. Christ Coll., Valparaiso U., 2001—; bd. dirs. Augustana Ctr., 1990—91; mem. vis. com. U. Chgo. Div. Sch., 2006—. Recipient Profl. Achievement award, Chgo.-Kent Coll. of Law, 2002, Alumni Achievement award, Valparaiso U., 2002, President's Award for Disting. Svc., N.W. Suburban Bar Assn., 2003. Mem.: FBA (bd. mgrs. Chgo. chpt. 1995—2004), Alliance Women Chgo. Bar Assn. (exec. bd. 2007—), Chgo. Bar Assn. (chair devel. law com. 1992—93, bd. mgrs. 2004—06, David C. Hilliard award 1990—91), Fed. Magistrate Judges Assn. (bd. dirs. 1994—97), Womens Bar Assn. Ill. (bd. mgrs. 1995—98), Valparaiso U. Alumni Assn. (bd. dirs. 1992—94). Lutheran. Avocations: choral music, sewing, running. Office: US Dist Ct 219 S Dearborn St Ste 2178 Chicago IL 60604-1877 Office Phone: 312-435-5636.

PALLONE, FRANK, JR., congressman, lawyer; b. Long Branch, NJ, Oct. 30, 1951; m. Sarah Hospodor; 3 children. BA cum laude in Hist. and French, Middlebury Coll., Vt., 1973; MA in Internat. Rels., Tufts U. Sch. Law and Diplomacy, Mass., 1974; JD, Rutgers U. Sch. Law, NJ, 1978. Bar: Fla., NJ, NY, Pa. Coastal law specialist NJ Marine Adv. Svc., 1980—81; asst. prof. sea grant ext. prog. Cook Coll.-Rutgers U., NJ, 1980—81; counsel Monmouth County Protective Svcs. for the Elderly, NJ; instr. Monmouth County Cmty. Coll.; maritime atty. NYC, 1982—84; mem. City Council, Long Branch, NJ, 1982-88, NJ Senate, 1984-88, US Congress from 6th NJ dist., 1988—; mem. energy and commerce com., natural resources com., chmn. health subcommittee. Co-chair Congl. caucus on Armenian issues US Congress, founder Congl. caucus on India and Indian Am., chair Dem. caucus task force on health and medicare. Named Consumer Hero, Consumer Fedn. Am., 1997, Legislator of Yr., NJ Acad. Ophthalmology, 1998, Outstanding Legislator of Yr., VFW, 1999; recipient Cancer Advocacy award, Cancer Inst. NJ, 1998, Internat. Yr. of Ocean award, Clean Ocean Action, 1998. Democrat. Roman Catholic. Address: 504 Broadway Ste 118 Long Branch NJ 07740-5951 Office: US House Reps 237 Cannon House Office Bldg Washington DC 20515-3006 Office Phone: 202-225-4671. Office Fax: 202-225-9665. *

PALLOT, JOSEPH WEDELES, lawyer; b. Coral Gables, Fla., Dec. 23, 1959; s. Richard Allen Pallot and Rosalind Brown (Wedeles) Spak; m. Linda Fried, Oct. 12, 1956; children: Richard Allen, Maxwell Ross. BS, Jacksonville U., 1981; JD cum laude, U. Miami, Coral Gables, Fla., 1986. Bar: Fla. 1986. Comml. lending officer S.E. Bank, N.A., Miami, 1981-83; ptnr. Steel Hector & Davis, Miami, 1986-2000, Devine Goodman Pallot & Wells, P.A., Miami, 2000—. Trustee MOSAIC: Jewish Mus. Fla., Miami Beach, 1993—2002, bd. advisors, 2003—; dir. Fla. Grand Opera, 1996—2003, Beacon Coun., 1997—, exec. com., 2001—04, sec., 2002—04, vice chmn., 2004—06; trustee Temple Judea, 2004—06, v.p., 2006—. Avocations: golf, tennis. Business E-Mail: jpallot@devinegoodman.com.

PALLOTTA, JOHANNA ANTONIA (JOHANNA STEPHEN), endocrinologist, educator; b. Boston, May 7, 1937; d. John and Antonia (Lanni) P.; m. Michael John Stephen, Aug. 13, 1966; children: Jacqueline, Antonia, Michael, Andrew. BS in Chemistry magna cum laude, Boston Coll., 1958; MD, N.Y. Med. Coll., 1962. Diplomate Am. Bds. Internal Medicine, Endocrinology and Metabolism; lic. N.Y., Mass., Calif. Intern St. Elizabeth's Hosp., Boston, 1962-63; resident in medicine N.Y. Med. Coll. Metro. Hosp., NYC, 1963-64; resident in medicine, fellow radioisotope svc. VA Hosp., Bronx, 1964—66; fellow metabolism and endocrinology Yale U. Sch. Medicine, New Haven, 1966-67; instr. medicine Harvard Med. Sch., Boston, 1967-69, Beth Israel Deaconess Hosp. Harvard Med. Sch., 1969-70; asst. prof. medicine Harvard Med. Sch., 1970—2003, assoc. prof. medicine, 2004—. Tutor med. scis. Harvard Med. Sch., 1972-73; dir. endocrinology clinic Beth Israel Deaconess Hosp., Boston, 1967—, dir. radioimmunoassay lab., 1972-83, clin. cons., 1984—, asst. in medicine, 1967-69, assoc. in medicine, 1969-70, asst. physician, 1970-79, assoc. physician, 1979-87, sr. physician, 1987—, dir. clin. rsch. ctr. core radioimmunoassay lab., 1984-93; cons. staff Mount Auburn Hosp., Cambridge, 1974-90; mem. numerous other coms., 1969—. Rschr. in field; contbr. articles to profl. jours. Named Carl Shapiro scholar, BIDMC-Harvard Med. Sch., 2000—; recipient S. Robert Stone Harvard Med. Sch.-BIDMC tchg. award, 1998. Fellow: ACP, Am. Assn. Clin. Endocrinologists; mem.: Am. Fedn. Clin. Rsch., Am. Thyroid Assn., Endocrine Soc., Harvard Aesculapian Club, Alpha Omega Alpha. Roman Catholic. Home: 16 Fresh Pond Ln Cambridge MA 02138-4616 Office: Beth Israel Hosp Harvard Med Sch 330 Brookline Ave Boston MA 02215-5491 Home Phone: 617-868-1494; Office Phone: 617-667-4016. Business E-Mail: jpallott@bidmc.harvard.edu.

PALLOTTI, MARIANNE MARGUERITE, foundation administrator; b. Hartford, Conn., Apr. 23, 1937; d. Rocco D. and Marguerite (Long) P. BA, NYU, 1968, MA, 1972. Asst. to pres. Wilson, Haight & Welch, Hartford, 1964-65; exec. asst. Ford Found., NYC, 1965-77; corp. sec. Hewlett Found., Menlo Park, Calif., 1977-84, v.p., 1985—. Bd. dirs. N.Y. Theatre Ballet, N.Y.C., 1986-98, Austin Montessori Sch., 1993, Djerassi Resident Artists Program, 1998—, Mexican Mus., 1999—; mem. women's adv. com., nat. coun.World Wildlife Fund, 1997—; mem. program com. Ind. Sector, Washington, 1998—. Mem. Women in Founds., No. Calif. Grantmakers. Office: William and Flora Hewlett Foundation 2121 Sand Hill Rd Menlo Park CA 94025-6903

PALLOZOLA, CHRISTINE, not-for-profit executive; b. St. Louis, Mar. 28, 1952; BS, U. Mo., 1974. Purchasing and sales mgmt. computer industry, Mo., 1984-92; exec. dir. Cahokia Mounds Mus. Soc., Collinsville, Ill., 1993—2001, dir. spl. events, mktg. Arts and Edn. Coun., 2001—04; exec. dir. Am. Acad. Comm. Healthcare, St. Louis, 2004—. Sec. Businesspersons Between Jobs, St. Louis, 1998—2004. Mem.: Assn. Fundraising Profls. Home: 150 Burtonwood Ballwin MO 63011

PALM, CHARLES GILMAN, academic administrator; b. Havre, Mont., Apr. 25, 1944; s. Victor F. and Laura (McKinnie) P.; m. Miriam Willits, Sept. 15, 1968. AB, Stanford U., 1966; MA, U. Wyo., 1967; MLS, U. Oreg., 1970. From asst. archivist to dep. dir. Hoover Instn. Stanford (Calif.) U., Palo Alto, Calif., 1971—90; dep. dir. Hoover Instn. Stanford U., 1990—2001, dep. dir. emeritus, 2002—. Adv. bd. Calif. Hist. Records, 2006—. Co-author: Guide to Hoover Institution Archives, 1980, Herbert Hoover, Register of His Papers in the Hoover Institution Archives, 1983. Mem. Calif. Heritage Preservation Commn., Sacramento, 1988-2005, vice chmn., 1993-97, chmn., 1997-2004; mem. Nat. Hist. Records and Publs. Commn., Washington, 1990-96; mem. history and edn. ctr. adv. bd. ARC, 1994-2005; trustee Golden State Mus. Corp., 1997-2004. Fellow: Soc. Am. Archivists; mem.: Soc. Calif. Archivists (pres. 1983—84), Bohemian Club. Republican. Office: Hoover Instn Stanford CA 94305

PALM, GREGORY K., lawyer, investment company executive; b. Binghamton, NY, Sept. 25, 1948; m. Susan Palm; children: Jennifer, Katherine, Eleanor, James. SB, MIT, 1970; MBA, JD, Harvard U., 1974. Bar: N.Y. 1977, DC 1978. Law clk. to Hon. Henry J. Friendly US Ct. Appeals (2nd cir.); law clk. to Justice Lewis F. Powell US Supreme Ct.; assoc. Sullivan & Cromwell, 1976—82, ptnr., 1982—92; gen. counsel, co-head, legal dept. Goldman Sachs LP, NYC, 1992—99; exec. v.p., gen. counsel, co-head of legal dept. Goldman Sachs & Co., NYC, 1992—. Mem. Harvard Law Rev. Mem.: Am. Law Inst., DC Bar. Office: Goldman Sachs and Co Legal Dept 37th Fl 1 New York Plz New York NY 10004 Office Phone: 212-902-1000. Office Fax: 212-902-3876. *

PALM, MARY EGDAHL, mycologist; b. Mpls., Jan. 27, 1954; d. Lauren and Mary E.; children: Natalie Elizabeth, Christopher Steven. BA in Biology, St. Olaf Coll., 1976; MSc in Plant Pathology (mycology), U. Minn., 1979, PhD in Plant Pathology (mycology), 1983. Lab. asst. St. Olaf Coll. Biology Dept., Northfield, Minn., 1974, tchg. asst., 1975-76; rsch. asst. U. Minn. plant pathology dept., Mpls., 1976-83, post doctoral rsch. assoc., 1983-84; mycologist (botanist GS12) USDA/APHIS biol. assessment and support staff, Beltsville, Md., 1984-91; mycologist scientific svcs. USDA/Animal and Plant Health Inspection Svc., Beltsville, 1991—, mycologist, dir. morphology, molecular and biochem. diagnostics lab., 2006—. Instr., coord. seminars and tng. sessions for USDA and ednl. sci. group, 1982—; adj. assoc. prof. plant pathology Pa. State U., State College, 1995. Co-author: Deuteromycetes and Selected Ascomycetes That Occur On or In Wood: An Indexed Bibliography, 1979, An Indexed Bibliography and Guide to Taxonomic Literature, 1988, A Literature Guide for the Identification of Plant Pathogenic Fungi, 1987, Fungi on Rhododendron: A World Reference, 1996, Mycology in Sustainable Development: Expanding concepts, Vanishing Borders, 1997, Cultivation and Diseases of Proteaceae: Leucdendron Leucospermum, and Protea, 2004; contbr. articles to profl. jours. Recipient St. Olaf Coll. Hon. Biology scholarship, 1976, Disting. Alumnus Dept. Plant Pathology U. Minn., 1999; grantee U. Minn. Computer Ctr. 1979, 80, 81, 82, V.P Gores Hammer award, 1998. Fellow Mycological Soc. Am.(sec. 1991-94, Am. Inst. Biol. Scis. rep. 1994—, v.p. 1995-96, pres.-elect 1996-97, pres. 1997-98, other coms.); mem. Am. Phytopathol. Soc. (chairperson mycology com. 1988, 89, vice chairperson 1987, mem. 1985, 86, regulatory plant pathology com. 1993—, organizer, moderator colloquim on systematics of plant pathogenic fungi 1987), L.Am. Mycol. Assn. (U.S. liaison), Internat. Assn. Plant Taxonomy (subcom. C of com. on fungi and lichens 1986, 87, 88). Office: USDA Rm 329 B-011A 10300 Baltimore Ave Beltsville MD 20705-2350 Office Phone: 301-504-5327. Business E-Mail: mary.palm@aphis.usda.gov.

PALMA, JACK D., lawyer; b. NYC, Sept. 15, 1946; BA, Allegheny Coll., 1968; JD with honors, U. Denver, 1974. Bar: Colo. 1975, Wyo. 1976. Ptnr. Holland & Hart, Cheyenne, Wyo., 1984—. Mem. ABA, Colo. Bar Assn., Wyo. State Bar, Order St. Ives. Office: Holland & Hart PO Box 1347 Cheyenne WY 82003-1347 Office Phone: 307-778-4200. E-mail: jpalma@hollandhart.com.

PALMATIER, MALCOLM ARTHUR, editor, consultant; b. Kalamazoo, Nov. 11, 1922; s. Karl Ernest and Cecile Caroline (Chase) Palmatier; m. Mary Elizabeth Summerfield, June 16, 1948 (dec. Oct. 1982); children: Barnabus, Timothy K., Duncan M.; m. Marie-Anne Suzanne van Werveke, Jan. 12, 1985. BS in Math., Western Mich. U., 1945; MA in English, UCLA, 1947; MA in Econs., U. So. Calif., 1971. Instr. English Pomona Coll., Claremont, Calif., 1949-51; editor Naval Ordnance Test Sta., Pasadena, Calif., 1951-54; head editl. unit Rocketdyne, LA, 1954-55; editor RAND Corp., Santa Monica, Calif., 1955-87, cons. editor, 1987—. Instr. English UCLA, 1950; participant Internat. Conf. Corp. Citizenship, Wilton Park, England, 2002. Mng. editor, cons. editor: Studies in Comparative Communism, 1968—80; co-editor: Perspectives in Economics, 1971; contbr. chapters to books, book revs. and articles to profl. jours. Chmn. bd. dirs. New Start, LA, 1982—84. With USNR, 1943—45. Mem.: Jonathan Club. Avocations: music, travel. Home: 516 Avondale Ave Los Angeles CA 90049-4804 Office: 1776 Main St Santa Monica CA 90407-2138 Personal E-mail: Malcolm27@earthlink.net.

PALMEIRO, RAFAEL CORRALES, professional baseball player; b. Havana, Cuba, Sept. 24, 1964; Degree in Comml. Art, Miss. State U. Baseball player Chgo. Cubs, 1986-88, Tex. Rangers, 1988—93, 1999—2003, Balt. Orioles, 1994-98, 2004—. Named Nat. League All-Star Team, 1988, Am. League All-Star Team, 1991, 1998, 1999; recipient Gold Glove award, 1997-1999; led Am. League in runs (124), 1993; hit 500th career home run, May 10, 2003; had his 3,000th career hit, July 15, 2005 Office: c/o Baltimore Orioles Camden Yards 333 W Camden St Baltimore MD 21201

PALMER, ANN THERESE DARIN, lawyer; b. Detroit, Apr. 25, 1951; d. Americo and Theresa (Del Favero) Darin; m. Robert Towne Palmer, Nov. 9, 1974; children: Justin Darin, Christian Darin. BA, U. Notre Dame, 1973, MBA, 1975; JD, Loyola U., Chgo., 1978. Bar: Ill. 1978, U.S. Supreme Ct. 1981. Intern Wall Street Jour., Detroit, 1974; freelancer Time Inc. Fin. Publs., Chgo., 1975—77; extern, Midwest regional solicitor U.S. Dept. Labor, 1976—78; tax atty. Esmark Inc., 1978; counsel Chgo. United, 1978—81; ind. contractor Legal Tax Rsch., 1981—89; fin. and legal news contbr. Chgo. Tribune, 1991—, Bus. Week, 1991—, Automotive News, 1993—97, Crain's Chgo. Bus., 1994—2000; contbg. editor Registered Rep, 2002—. Mem.: Chgo. Club. Home: 1570 Christina Ln Lake Forest IL 60045

PALMER, ANTHONY J., health products executive; BS in Mktg., Monash U., Melbourne, Australia, 1986; MBA, Internat. Mgmt. Inst., Geneva, 1989. Bus. devel. mgr. PA Consulting Group, 1986—91; sr. cons. LEK Partnership, 1991—92; mktg. mgr. Mars Confectionery, Australia, 1992—95, CSR Refined Sugars, Australia, 1995—96; mktg. and gen.

mgmt. positions Minute Maid divsn. Coca-Cola Co., 1996—2000, region dir. Australia; pres. natural, frozen and warehouse club businesses Kellogg Co., mng. dir. UK; sr. v.p., chief mktg. officer Kimberly-Clark Corp., Dallas, 2006—. Office: Kimberly-Clark Corp PO Box 619100 Dallas TX 75261-9100 *

PALMER, ARNOLD DANIEL, professional golfer; b. Youngstown, Pa., Sept. 10, 1929; s. Milfred Jerome and Doris M. Palmer; m. Winnie Walzer, Dec. 20, 1954 (dec. Nov. 1999); children: Peggy Palmer Wears, Amy Palmer Saunders; m. Kathleen Gawthrop, Jan. 26, 2005. Student, Wake Forest Coll., LLD, 1970. Profl. golfer, 1954—; businessman, entrepreneur, 1960—. Nat. spokesman Sears Can., Rolex, Golf Digest, Lexington Furniture, Callaway Golf, Capital Mercury, Encore Bank, Cessna, Ketel One, Administaff, Spectrum Brands, Ez-Go, Jacobsen, Pennington Seed, Luna Vineyards, Golf Channel, Wyndham Hotels. Author: Arnold Palmer's Golf Book, 1961, Portrait of a Professional Golfer, 1964, My Game and Yours, 1965, rev. edit., 1983, Situation Golf, 1970, Go for Broke, 1973, Arnold Palmer's Best 54 Holes of Golf, 1977, Arnold Palmer's Complete Book of Putting, 1986, Play Great Golf, 1987, (with Thomas Hauser) A Personal Journey, 1994, (with James Dodson) Arnold Palmer, A Golfer's Life, 1999, Playing by the Rules, 2002, Arnold Palmer, Memories, Stories, and Memorabilia, 2004. Served USCG, 1951—54. Recipient Bob Jones award U.S. Golf Assn., William D. Richardson award Golf Writers Assn. Am., Herb Graffis award Nat. Golf Found., Presdl. Medal of Freedom, 2004; named Sportsman of Yr. Sports Illustrated mag., 1960, Player of Yr. Profl. Golfers Assn., 1960, 62, AP Athlete of Decade, 1969, others; Profl. Golfers Assn. Tour Money Leader, 1958, 60, 62, 63; named to World Golf Hall of Fame, Profl. Golfers Assn. Hall of Fame. Mem. Latrobe (Pa.) Country Club, Laurel Valley Golf Club, Rolling Rock Club (Ligonier, Pa.), Bay Hill Club, Duquesne Club (Pitts.). Winner of over 90 major golf tournaments since 1955, including Masters Championship, 1958, 60, 62, 64, U.S. Open, 1960, U.S. Amateur, 1954, Brit. Open, 1961, 62. Home and Office: PO Box 52 Youngstown PA 15696-0052 Office Phone: 724-537-7751.

PALMER, BEVERLY BLAZEY, psychologist, educator; b. Cleve., Nov. 22, 1945; d. Lawrence E. and Mildred M. Blazey; m. Richard C. Palmer, June 24, 1967; 1 child, Ryan Richard. PhD in Counseling Psychology, Ohio State U., 1972. Lic. clin. psychologist, Calif. Adminstrv. assoc. Ohio State U., Columbus, 1969—70; rsch. psychologist Health Svcs. Rsch. Ctr. UCLA, 1971—77; commr. pub. health L.A. County, 1978—81; pvt. practice Torrance, Calif., 1985—; prof. psychology Calif. State U., Dominguez Hills, 1973—2006. Author: Interpersonal Skills for Helping Professionals Online Course, 2001, 04, reviewer manuscripts for numerous textbook pubs; contbr. articles to profl. jours. Recipient Proclamation, County of L.A., 1972, 1981, Outstanding Prof. award, Calif. State U., 1995; Fulbright Sr. scholar, Malaysia, 2001, Fulbright scholar, Borneo, 2001, Fulbright Sr. scholar, Malaysia, 2004—05, Fulbright scholar, Barbados, 2005. Mem. APA. Office: Calif State U Dominguez Hills Dept Psychology Carson CA 90747-0001 Office Phone: 310-373-6691. Business E-Mail: bpalmer@csudh.edu.

PALMER, BRIAN EUGENE, retired lawyer; b. Mpls., May 16, 1948; s. Eugene Philip and Virginia Breeze (Rolfshus) P.; m. Julia Washburn Morrison, Dec. 29, 1972; 1 child, Julia Hunter. AB, Brown U., 1970; JD, William Mitchell Coll. of Law, 1974. Bar: Minn. 1974, U.S. Dist. Ct. Minn. 1975, U.S. Dist. Ct. (ea. dist.) Wis. 2001, U.S. Ct. Appeals (8th cir.) 1980, U.S. Ct. Fed. Claims 1984, U.S. Supreme Ct. 1980. Asst. pub. defender Hennepin County Pub. Defender, Mpls., 1974-78; assoc. Dorsey & Whitney LLP, Mpls., 1978-82, ptnr., 1983—2004, of counsel, 2005—06, ret., 2006. Home: 1190 Lyman Ave Wayzata MN 55391-9671 Office Phone: 612-340-2797. E-mail: palmer.brian@dorsey.com.

PALMER, CARSON, professional football player; b. Fresno, Calif., Dec. 27, 1979; s. Bill and Danna Palmer; m. Shaelyn Fernandes, July 5, 2003. BA in Pub. Policy, U. So. Calif., 2002. Quarterback Cin. Bengals, 2003—. Co-founder Carson Palmer Found., 2004—. Named NFL Pro Bowl MVP, 2007; named to Am. Football Conf. Pro Bowl Team, 2005—06; recipient Heisman Meml. Trophy, Heisman Trophy Trust, 2002. Achievements include being the first overall selection in the 2003 NFL Draft. Office: c/o Cincinnati Bengals 1 Paul Brown Stadium Dr Cincinnati OH 45202 *

PALMER, CATHERINE E., lawyer; BA, Boston Coll., 1977; JD, Catholic Univ., 1980. Bar: NY 1981. Asst. US atty., chief of criminal divsn. US Attorney's Office, Ea. Dist. NY, 1985—94, spl. assignment asst. US atty., 1996—98; ptnr. Latham & Watkins, NYC, 1994—96, 1998—, and chair, white collar practice and dep. chair, global litig. dept. Office: Latham & Watkins Ste 1000 885 Third Ave New York NY 10022-4834 Business E-Mail: catherine.palmer@lw.com.

PALMER, CHARLES F., lawyer; b. Rome, Ga., 1957; BS cum laude, Univ. Ga., 1979; JD, Emory Univ., 1986. Bar: Ga. 1986. Assoc. Troutman Sanders LLP, Atlanta, 1986—94, ptnr., telecom. tech., govtl. law, transp., 1995, and practice group leader, govtl. law. Editl. bd. Emory Law Jour., 1985—86. Mem.: State Bar Ga. (chmn., Young Lawyers Sect., legislative affairs com. 1992—93, adv. com. on legislation 1992—93), Gamma Sigma Delta, Phi Kappa Phi. Office: Troutman Sanders LLP Bank of America Plz Ste 5200 600 Peachtree St NE Atlanta GA 30308-2216 Office Phone: 404-885-3402. Office Fax: 404-962-6647. Business E-Mail: charles.palmer@troutmansanders.com.

PALMER, CHARLES FRANCIS, lawyer; b. LA, Oct. 4, 1946; s. John Mason and Selma (Nahama) P.; m. Marylouise Oates, Sept. 22, 1970 (div. 1982); 1 child, Michael. AB, U. Calif., 1969; JD, Yale U., 1973. Bar: Calif. 1973. Assoc. O'Melveny & Myers, LA, 1973-77; exec. dir. Pub. Counsel, LA, 1977-81; ptnr. Johnsen, Manfredi & Thorpe, LA, 1981-88, Perkins Cole, LA, 1988—; judge Clara Shortridge Foltz Criminal Justice Ctr., LA. Pres. Legal Aid Found. L.A., 1993; mem. platform com. Dem. Nat. Conv., N.Y.C., 1992; dep. nat. issues dir. Kennedy for Pres., Washington, 1980. Mem. State Bar Calif. (chair legal svcs. sect. 1982-83), L.A. County Bar Assn. (bd. trustees 1988-90), Beverly Hills Bar Assn., Assn. Bus. Trial Lawyers. Democrat. Office: Clara Shortridge Foltz Criminal Justice Ctr 210 W Temple St Los Angeles CA 90012 Office Phone: 213-974-5785.

PALMER, CHARLIE, chef, restaurant manager; b. NY; m. Lisa Palmer; 4 children. Student, Culinary Inst. Am. Former exec. chef The River Café, NYC; chef, owner Aureole, NYC, 1988—; owner numerous other restaurants including Aureole at Mandalay Bay Resort and Casino, Las Vegas, Nev., Charlie Palmer Steak, Las Vegas, Astra, NYC, Métrazur, NYC, Kitchen 22, NYC, Charlie Palmer Steak, Washington, Dry Creek Kitchen, Sonoma, Hotel Healdsburg, Sonoma, Astra West and The Lounge at Astra, West Hollywood. Author: (books) Charlie Palmer's Casual Cooking, 2001, Great American Food, 2003, Art of Aureole, 2003, Charlie Palmer's Practical Guide to the New American Kitchen, 2006. Recipient Restaurant & Institutions IVY award, 1997, James Beard award for best chef in NY, 1997, James Beard award for Who's Who of Food & Beverage in Am., 1998, Food Arts Silver Spoon award for outstanding service, 2003. Office: Charlie Palmer Group 34 E 61st St Ste 2A New York NY 10021 *

PALMER, CHRISTINE (CLELIA ROSE VENDITTI), vocalist, educator, musician; b. Hartford, Conn., Apr. 2, 1919; d. John Marion and Immacolata (Morcaldo) Venditti; m. Raymond Smith, Oct. 5, 1949 (div. June 1950); m. Arthur James Whitlock, Feb. 25, 1953. Student, Mt. Holyoke Coll., 1937-38, New Eng. Conservatory of Music, 1941-42; pvt. studies, Boston, Hartford, N.Y.C., Florence and Naples, Italy; RN with honors, Hartford Hosp. Sch. Nursing, 1941. Artist-in-residence El Centro Coll., Dallas, 1966-71. Pvt. vocal instr.-coach, specializing in vocal technique for opera, mus. comedy, supper club acts, auditions, Dallas, 1962-94; voice adjudicator San Francisco Opera Co., 1969-72, Tex. Music Tchrs. Assn., 1964-75, others; lectr. in field; appearances with S.M. Chartocks' Gilbert and Sullivan Co. Leading operatic soprano N.Y.C. Opera, Chgo., San Francisco, San Carlo, other cities, 1944-62, N.Y. Town Hall Concert, 1951; soloist with symphony orchs. maj. U.S. Cities, 1948-62; soloist Marble Collegiate Ch., Holy Trinity Ch.; coast-to-coast concert tour, 1948; numerous appearances including St. Louis MUNY Opera, Indpls. Starlight Theatre, Lambertville Music Circus; soloist Holiday on Ice, 1949-50; TV performer, including Home Show on NBC, Telephone Hour on NBC, Holiday Hotel; performer various supper clubs, N.Y.C., Atlanta, Bermuda, Catskills, others, including Number One Fifth Avenue, The Embers, The Carriage Club, Viennese Lantern. Hon. mem. women's bd. Dallas Opera Assn.; mem. adv. bd. Tex. Opera News; mem. Tex. Music Tchrs. Cert. Bd., Collegiate Chorale, Don Craig Singers, The Vikings; mem. women's bd., Dallas Bapt. Univ. Oliver Ditson scholar, 1942; recipient Phi Xi Delta prize in Italian, 1937; named Victor Herbert Girl, ASCAP; Spl. Recognition Gold book of Dallas Soc. Mem. Nat. Assn. Tchrs. of Singing (pres. Dallas chpt. 1972-74), Nat. Fedn. Music Clubs, Tex. Fedn. Music Clubs, Dallas Fedn. Music Clubs (pres. 1972-74), Dallas Symphony League, Dallas Music Tchrs. Assn. (pres. 1971-72, Tchr. of Yr. 1974), Thesaurus Book Club (pres. 1990-91, 97-98), Friday Forum (Dallas, bd. dirs.), Dallas Women's C. of C., Eagle Forum, Pub. Affairs Luncheon Club, Dallas Fedn. Music Club, Pro Am., Wednesday Morning Choral Club, Dallas Knife and Fork Club, Prestoncrest Rep. Club. Presbyterian. Home: 6232 Pemberton Dr Dallas TX 75230-4036

PALMER, CHRISTOPHER E., lawyer; BA cum laude, St. John's U., Minn., 1982; JD magna cum laude, Georgetown Univ., 1986. Bar: Minn. 1986, DC 1988. Ct. law clerk US Dist. Ct., DC; ptnr. Shea & Gardner (merged with Goodwin Procter LLP); ptnr.,chair, bus. law dept. Goodwin Procter LLP, Washington, 2004—. Articles editor Georgetown Law Jour. Office: Goodwin Procter LLP 901 New York Ave NW Washington DC 20001 Office Phone: 202-346-4253. Office Fax: 202-346-4444. Business E-Mail: cpalmer@goodwinprocter.com.

PALMER, CRUISE, newspaper editor; b. Kansas City, Kans., Apr. 9, 1917; s. Thomas Potter and Margaret Scroggs (McFadden) P.; m. Dorraine Humphreys, Sept. 7, 1946; children: Thomas Cruise, Martha D. Sprague. BS in Journalism, Kans. State U., 1938. With Kansas City (Mo.) Star, 1938—, news editor, 1963-64, mng. editor, 1965-66; exec. editor, bd. dirs. Star and Times, 1967—78, cons., 1978—. Bd. dirs. Purtec Systems, Inc. Author: Bosses of the News Room, 1927-2006, 2003. Mem. bd. govs. Am. Royal Live Stock and Horse Show Assn., 1967-91; bd. dirs. ARC, 1978-91, Kansas City Mayor's Corps Progress, 1978-91; found. trustee Kans. State U.; trustee Kansas City Sister Cities Commn., 1978-91. Served to lt. (j.g.) USNR, 1943-46. Recipient Distinguished Service award Kans. State U., 1967; First Place award Pro-Am. Southgate Open Golf Tournament, 1973; Second Place award Pro-Am. Hawaiian Open, 1973, 85; Third Place, 1981; First Place award Jim Colbert Celebrity Tournament, 1981, First Place Team award Kansas City area Am. Cancer Soc. Golf Tournament, 1986. Mem. Am. Soc. Newspaper Editors, Soc. Profl. Journalists, Kansas City Sr. Golf Assn., Kansas City Press Club (pres. 1953-54, 64-65, permanent trustee, pres. scholarship found. 1989), Kansas City Club, Chiefs Red Coat Club, Milburn Golf and Country Club, Beta Theta Pi (Greater Kansas City Beta of Yr. 1980). Episcopalian (former vestryman and lay reader). Home: Lakeview Retirement Village 14100 W 90th Ter Apt 504 Lenexa KS 66215-5430 Office: 1729 Grand Ave Kansas City MO 64108-1413

PALMER, DAVE RICHARD, retired military officer, academic administrator; b. Ada, Okla., May 31, 1934; s. David Furman and Lorena Marie (Clardy) P.; m. LuDelia Clemmer, Apr. 13, 1957; children: Allison, J. Kersten. BS, U.S. Military Acad., 1956; MA in History, Duke U., 1966; postgrad., Army War Coll., 1972-73; PhD (hon.), Duke U., 1990. Commd. U.S. Army, 1956, advanced through grades to lt. gen.; mem. faculty dept. history U.S. Mil. Acad., 1966-69; mem. staff (Pentagon), 1973-76, Joint Chiefs of Staff, 1979-81; comdr. Baumholder Mil. Community, W. Ger., 1981-83; dep. comdt. Command and Gen. Staff Coll., Ft. Leavenworth, Kans., 1983-85; comdg. gen. 1st Armored Div., W.Ger., 1985-86; supt. U.S. Mil. Acad., 1986-91, ret., 1991; pres. Walden U., 1995-99; CEO Walden Corp., 1999-2000. Author: The River and the Rock, 1969, The Way of the Fox, 1975, Summons of the Trumpet, 1978, 1794-America, Its Army, and The Birth of the Nation, 1994, First in War, 2000, Provide for the Common Defense, 2001, Washington and Arnold, 2006. Bd. dirs. Walden U., 1992-2001. Decorated Legion of Merit (3); Bronze Star (2), D.S.M.(2); named Disting. Grad., U.S. Mil. Acad., 2005. Mem. Assn. U.S. Army, Armor Assn., Mil. History, Soc. Cin. Office Phone: 254-933-0554. Personal E-mail: davepalmer@clearwire.net.

PALMER, DAVID GILBERT, lawyer; b. Lakewood, NJ, Jan. 10, 1945; s. Robert Dayton and Lois (Gilbert) P.; m. Susan Edmundson Walsh, Aug. 17, 1968; children: Jonathan, Megan. AB, Johns Hopkins U., 1967; JD, U. Colo., 1970. Bar: Colo. 1970, U.S. Dist. Ct. Colo. 1970, U.S. Ct. Appeals (9th and 10th cirs.) 1970, U.S. Supreme Ct. 1970. Ptnr., mng. ptnr., chmn. litig. dept. Holland & Hart, Denver, 1970-87; ptnr., mng. ptnr. Gibson, Dunn & Crutcher, Denver, 1987-97; mng. ptnr. Zevnik, Horton, Palmer, Denver, 1997-2001; mng. shareholder Greenberg Traurig LLP, Denver, 2001—. Chmn. N.W. region Am. Heart Assn., Dallas, 1986—, bd. dirs., 1986—, sec., 1990—, nat. chmn., 1992-93; pres., bd. dirs. Colo. Heart Assn., Denver, 1974; bd. dirs. C.H. Kempe Nat. Ctr. for Prevention of Child Abuse, Denver, 1984-90, pres., 1989-90; bd. dirs. Goodwill Industries, Denver, 1981-84, Metro Denver Econ. Devel. Corp., 2004—; mem. coun. of advisors U. Colo. Med. Sch., 2004—. Mem. ABA, Colo. Bar Assn., Denver Law Club, Univ. Club of Denver (pres. 2004-05), Mile High Club. Office: Greenberg Traurig Tabor Ctr 1200 17th St Ste 2400 Denver CO 80202 Office Phone: 303-572-6539. Office Fax: 303-572-6540. Business E-Mail: palmerdg@gtlaw.com.

PALMER, DAVID J., library director, municipal official; BA, M, U. Mich. With City of Chula Vista, Calif., 1988—, asst. libr. dir., 1988—93, libr. dir., 1993—, head libr. and recreation dept., 1998—2000, dep. city mgr., 2000—03, asst. city mgr., 2003—. Office: Chula Vista Pub Libr 365 F St Chula Vista CA 91910 Office Phone: 619-691-5069.

PALMER, DAVID KEITH, otolaryngologist; s. Merlin and Elna Palmer; m. Elizabeth Palmer; children: Aimee Palmer Stewart, Erin Palmer Morley, David M., Matt, Whitney. BS magna cum laude, U. Utah, Salt Lake City, 1978; MD, Med. Coll. Pa., Phila., 1986. Diplomate Am. Bd. Otolaryngology; RN Utah, 1978. Intern Penn. State U. Hershey Med., resident; clin. instr. Penn. State U., Hershey, 1991—92; chief otolaryngology St. Mark's Hosp., Salt Lake City, 1995—; adj. clin. prof. U. Utah Sch. Medicine, Salt Lake City, 2001—. Instr. Mormon Tabernacle Choir, Salt Lake City, 2001—. Singer: Mormon Tabernacle Choir (Nat. Medal Arts, 05). Voluntary missionary svc. LDS Ch., Sao Paolo, Brazil, 1972—74, bishop Hershey, Pa., 1989—92. 1st lt. US Army, 1978—83. Scholar, Harvard U., 1982; Delmore scholar, Med. Coll. Pa., 1986. Fellow: Am. Acad. Otolaryngic Allergy (chmn., patient and profl. rels. 2005—, bd. dirs. 1996—), Am. Acad. Otolaryngology Head and Neck Surgery; mem.: AMA (life). Office: ENT Specialists 4000 S 700 E #10 Salt Lake City UT 84107 Home Phone: 801-268-4141; Office Phone: 801-268-4141. Office Fax: 801-261-8609.

PALMER, DAVID SCOTT, political scientist, educator; b. Boston, July 16, 1937; s. Walter S. and Jean (Stuart) P.; m. Sarah Crawford, 1966 (dec. Nov. 1985); children: Walter Scott, Henry Crawford, Asa MacAdam; m. Diane Nagel, 1998. BA in Internat. Rels. cum laude, Dartmouth Coll., 1959; MA in Hispanic Am. Studies, Stanford U., 1962; PhD in Comparative Govt., Cornell U., 1973. Vol. leader Peace Corps, Peru, 1962-64; asst. dean freshmen, asst. to dir. admissions Dartmouth Coll., Hanover, NH, 1964-68; from instr. to asst. prof. dept. govt. Bowdoin Coll., 1972-76; professorial lectr. Sch. Advanced Internat. Studies Johns Hopkins U., Washington, 1977-88; assoc. dean for programs Fgn. Svc. Inst., Dept. State, 1984-88, chair Latin Am. and Caribbean studies, 1976-88; prof. polit. sci. Boston U., 1988—, prof. internat. rels., 1990—, assoc. chair undergrad. studies internat. rels. dept., 1997-99, chair dept. polit. sci., 1998-2001, dir. Latin Am. studies program, 1991—94, 2004—05. Vis. lectr. Princeton U., 1978—79, Georgetown U., 1985; vis. scholar Inter-Am. Dialogue, 2001—02. Author: Peru: The Authoritarian Tradition, 1980, (with Kevin Middlebrook) Military Government and Political Development: Lessons from Peru, 1975 (with Robert Wesson and others) The Latin American Military Institution, 1985; editor, contbr.: Shining Path of Peru, 1992, 2d edit., 1994, U.S. Relations with Latin America during the Clinton Years, 2006; contbr. chpts. to books, articles and revs. to profl. jours. Bd. visitors Tucker Found., Dartmouth Coll., 2005—; mem. Fulbright nat. screening com., 2005—. Recipient Meritorious Honor award U.S. Dept. of State, 1981; Daniel Webster nat. scholar, 1955-59; Edward John Noble Found. leadership grantee 1959-62; Fulbright fellow, 1998. Mem. Latin Am. Studies Assn. (exec. com. 1983-86), New Eng. Coun. Latin Am. Studies (exec. com. 1989-98, 2000—, pres. 1993-94), Phi Beta Delta, Phi Kappa Phi, Sigma Delta Pi. Home: 69 Waverley St Belmont MA 02478-1958 Office: Boston U 152 Bay State Rd Boston MA 02215-1501 Office Phone: 617-353-9388. Business E-Mail: dspalmer@bu.edu.

PALMER, DENISE E., publishing executive; b. Seymour, Ind., Feb. 12, 1957; m. Gregory G. Palmer. BA, U. Dayton, 1977; MS in Mgmt., Northwestern U., 1984. Sr. auditor Coopers & Lybrand, Dayton, Ohio, 1977—80; corp. auditor Tribune, 1980—86, planning analyst, 1983—86, mgr. planning, 1986—88; dir. fin. WGN Radio, Chgo., 1988—93, sta. mgr., 1993; dir. fin. Chgo. Tribune, Chgo., 1994—95, v.p. fin. & adminstrn., 1996—97, v.p. fin. strategy & fin., 1996—98, v.p. devel., strategy, fin., 1998—2000; pres., CEO CLTV, Oakbrook, Ill., 2000—02; pres., pub., CEO Balt. Sun, 2002—06; pres., pub. Tampa Tribune, 2006—. Bd. mem. Greater Baltimore Com., 2003—, Econ. Alliance of Greater Baltimore, 2003—, Md. Bus. Roundtable for Edn., 2003—; bd. visitors U. Md. Baltimore County, 2003—; mem. adv. bd. U. Dayton; mem. Northwestern U. Coun. of 100 Women. Office: Tampa Tribune 200 S Parker St Tampa FL 33606 Mailing: Tampa Tribune PO Box 191 Tampa FL 33601 Office Phone: 813-259-7711. *

PALMER, DENNIS DALE, lawyer; b. Alliance, Nebr., Apr. 30, 1945; s. Vernon D. Palmer and Marie E. (Nelson) Fellers; m. Rebecca Ann Turner, Mar. 23, 1979; children: Lisa Marie, Jonathan Paul. BA, U. Mo., 1967, JD, 1970. Bar: Mo. 1970, U.S. Dist. Ct. (we. dist.) Mo. 1970, U.S. Ct. Appeals (8th and 10th cirs.) 1973, U.S. Supreme Ct. 1980. Staff atty. Legal Aid Soc. Western Mo., Kansas City, 1970-73; assoc. Shughart, Thomson & Kilroy, P.C., Kansas City, 1973-76, ptnr., bd. dirs., 1976—. Contbr. articles on franchise and employment law to legal jours. Bd. dirs., chmn. legal assts. adv. bd. Avila Coll., Kansas City, 1984-87. 2d lt. U.S. Army, 1970. Mem. ABA (litigation com. 1980, forum com. on franchising 1987), Mo. Bar Assn. (antitrust com. 1975—, civil practice com. 1975—), Kansas City Bar Assn. (chmn. franchise law com. 1987—), Univ. Club. Avocations: jogging, golf, tennis, outdoor activities, reading. Home: 13100 Canterbury Rd Leawood KS 66209-1700 Office: Shughart Thomson & Kilroy 12 Wyandotte Plz 120 W 12th St Fl 17 Kansas City MO 64105-1902

PALMER, DERYCK A., lawyer; b. NYC, Nov. 21, 1956; BA, Syracuse U., 1978; JD, U. Mich., 1982. Bar: NY 1984. Ptnr., bus., fin. restructuring dept. Cadwalader, Weickersham & Taft LLP. Adj. prof. law NY Law Sch.; mem. Bureau Nat. Affairs Adv. Bd., Bankruptcy Law Reporter. Co-author: Restructuring: The Search for Value in a Troubled Enterprise, 1993, History of Bankruptcy Law in the Second Circuit, 1995. Bd. dirs. Boys & Girls Harbor, Inc., Insol Internat., Greater NY Couns. Boy Scouts Am., UJA-The Ednl. Alliance, Maplewood Village Alliance, Syracuse U., Cleveland Clinic Found., Coalition Consumer Bankruptcy Debtor Edn. Named one of Am. Top Black Attys., Black Enterprise, 2003. Fellow: Am. Coll. Bankruptcy; mem.: ABA, NY State Bar Assn. Office: Cadwalader Weickersham & Taft LLP One World Financial Ctr New York NY 10281 Office Phone: 212-504-6000. Office Fax: 212-504-6666. Business E-Mail: deryck.palmer@cwt.com.

PALMER, DOUGLAS HAROLD, mayor; b. Trenton, NJ, Oct. 19, 1951; s. George H. and Dorothy (Vaughn) P. BS in Bus. Mgmt., Hampton U., 1973. With C.V. Hill Co., Trenton; civil svc. worker N.J. Dept. Motor Vehicles, Trenton; dir. Community Schs. Trenton; asst. dir. Trenton Bd. Edn., dir. purchasing; small bus. owner Trenton; mayor City of Trenton, 1990—. Bd. dirs. ARC, Urban League Met. Trenton, Forum Project, Rider Coll. Ednl. Opportunity Fund Program, We, Inc., Carver Ctr., NAACP, treas.; freeholder Dem. Party Mercer County, 1981-91; mgr. West End Little League, Trenton, 1965-75, treas., 1975—. Named Outstanding Young Man Am., Del. Valley United Way Bd.; recipient Fai Ho Cha award Omega Psi Phi; recipient City Livability award, US Conf. of Mayors, Twenty Year Alumnus award, Hampton U., Spirit of St. Francis award, St. Francis Hosp., Equal Justice medal, Legal Svcs. NJ, State of Israel Peace medal award, 1993, Tending the Garden State, Cmty. Develop. Leadership award, Worldworks Found. NJ, 1993. Baptist. Office: 319 E State St Trenton NJ 08608-1809 *

PALMER, DOUGLAS S., JR., lawyer; b. Peoria, Ill., Mar. 15, 1945; AB cum laude, Yale U., 1966; JD cum laude, Harvard U., 1969. Bar: Wash. 1969. Mem. Foster Pepper & Shefelman PLLC, Seattle, 1975—2002, Hillis Clark Martin & Peterson, P.S., Seattle, 2002—. Office: Hillis Clark Martin & Peterson PS 500 Galland Bldg 1221 Second Ave Seattle WA 98101-2925 Office Phone: 206-623-1745.

PALMER, EDWARD L., psychologist, educator, writer; b. Hagerstown, Md., Aug. 11, 1938; s. Ralph Leon and Eva Irene (Brandenburg) P.; children: Edward Lee, Jennifer Lynn. BA, Gettysburg Coll., 1960; BD, Luth. Theol. Sem., Gettysburg, 1964; MS, Ohio U., 1967, PhD, 1970. Asst. prof. Western Md. Coll., Westminster, 1968-70, Davidson Coll., NC, 1970-77, assoc. prof. NC, 1977-86, chair, 1985—99, prof. NC, 1986—, Watson prof. NC, 1991—. Guest rschr. Harvard U., Cambridge, Mass., 1977; vis. scholar UCLA, 1984, UNC Chapel Hill, 1991, U. Exeter, 2000, U. Ala., 2005; cons. Council on Children, Media, Merchandising, 1978-79, 1st Union Bank Corp., Charlotte, N.C., 1975-79; NSF proposal reviewer, 1978—. Editl. reviewer Jour. Broadcasting and Electronic Media, 1978—, editl. bd. Media Psychology; editor: Children and the Faces of TV, 1980, Faces of Televisual Media, 2003; author: Children in the Cradle of TV, 1987; contbr. to Wiley Ency. of Psychology, 1984, 2002, Lawrence Erlbaum Assocs., 1991, Sage Pub., 1993-96; author jour. articles and book chpts. Sec. Mecklenburg Child Devel. Assn., Davidson and Cornelius, N.C., 1974-78; bd. mem. pub. radio Sta. WDAV, 1970-90, Telecomms. task force Rutgers U., 1981. Recipient Thomas Jefferson Tchg. award Robert Earl McConnell Found., 1993, Deptl. Psychology in Svc. award, 2007. Mem. APA, Am. Psychol. Soc., Assn. Heads Depts. Psychology (chair 1994-96), Am. Psychol. Assn. (task force on advt. and children 2001-03), Southeastern Psychol. Assn., Southeastern Soc. Social Psychologists, Phi Beta Kappa (pres. Davidson chpt. 1985-86). Avocations: sunrise and sunset walks, poetry, bird watching, music composition and performance. Office: Davidson Coll PO Box 7007 Davidson NC 28035-7007 Office Phone: 704-894-2882. E-mail: edpalmer@davidson.edu.

PALMER, FRANCIS ROGER, III, plastic surgeon; Grad. (hon.), San Diego State U.; MD, U. Calif. Irvine Sch. Medicine. Cert. Am. Bd. Facial Plastic and Reconstructive Surgery, bd. eligible Am. Bd. Cosmetic Surgery. Resident, head and neck surgery U. So. Calif.-LA County Med. Ctr.; fellow Am. Acad. of Facial Plastic and Reconstructive Surgery, Am. Acad. Cosmetic Surgery; dir. facial plastic surgery, head and neck surgery dept. U. So. Calif. Sch. Medicine, 1991—; dir. Beverly Hills Internat. Ctr. for Aesthetic Surgery. Spkr. in field. Guest appearances CNN, ABC, CBS, NBC, FOC, KTLA News, Gabrielle, Hard Copy, GMTV, and Good Day Britain, featured in Cosmopolitan, LA Times, NY Times, Liz Smith's Column and several others. Named one of The World's Best Aesthetic Plastic Surgeons, Tatler Mag. Office: Beverly Hills Internat Ctr for Aesthetic Surgery 8500 Wilshire Blvd Ste 900 Beverly Hills CA 90211 Office Phone: 310-652-9583. Office Fax: 310-652-0009. E-mail: drpalmer1@aol.com.

PALMER, FREDRICK D., lawyer, energy executive; b. Ariz., 1945; BA, JD, U. Ariz. CEO, gen. counsel Western Fuels Assn., Inc., Westminster, Colo., 1986—2000; counsel Shook Hardy & Bacon, Wash., DC, 2001; exec. v.p. legal & external affairs Peabody Energy, Saint Louis, Mo., 2001—05, sr. v.p. govt. rels., 2005—. Chmn. Environ. Info Council; bd. pres. Greening Earth Soc.; chmn. legal com. & climate change task force Nat. Mining Assn. Recipient Erskine Ramsay medal, Soc. for Mining, Metallurgy & Exploration, 2004. Mem.: DC Bar Assn., Calif. Bar Assn. Office: Peabody Energy 701 Market St Saint Louis MO 63101

PALMER, GRANT, medical products executive; b. Parramatta, NSW, Australia, Aug. 11, 1967; s. William Henry and Lorraine May Palmer; life ptnr. Sherilyn N. Lee. BS, U. Sydney, Australia, 1988, B in Engring., 1990. Rsch. asst. U. Sydney, 1990; mgr. clin. systems Telectronics Pacing Systems, Englewood, Colo., 1990—97; sr. CRA Baxter Corp., Oakland, Calif., 1997—98; sr. mgr. Boston Sci., Natick, Mass., 1998—2002; dir. clin. quality and regulatory Alsius Corp., Irvine, Calif., 2002—05; dir. clin. affairs Second Sight Med. Products, Sylmar, Calif., 2005—. Adv. bd. Inst. for Internat. Rsch., 2001—02. Contbr. essays, poetry and articles. Mem.: IEEE, LA Poets and Writers Collective, Regulatory Affairs Profl. Soc., Mensa. Achievements include patents pending for a method of endovascular cooling in humans. Office Phone: 818-833-5092.

PALMER, IRENE SABELBERG, retired dean, retired nursing educator, genealogist; b. Franklin, NJ, May 28, 1923; d. John Joseph and May (Heiser) Sabelberg. BS, N.J. State Tchrs. Coll., 1945; diploma, Jersey City Med. Center Sch. Nursing, 1945; MA, NYU, 1951, PhD, 1963. Edn. dir. Diploma Schs. Nursing NJ and Mass, 1948—52; ednl. dir. Glenn Dale Hosp. and DC Dept. Pub. Health, Md., 1956, dir. nursing svc. and edn., 1956—61; assoc. clin. prof. nursing Georgetown U., Washington, 1960—61; USPHS trainee, 1961—62; assoc. chief nursing svc. for rsch. VA Hosp., San Francisco, 1963—64; rsch. nurse cons. divsn. nursing HEW and USPHS Nursing Rsch. Field Ctr., San Francisco, 1964—66; asst. dean and assoc. prof. nursing U. Colo. Sch. Nursing, Denver, 1966—68; founding dean, prof. nursing Boston U. Sch. Nursing, 1968—74, Hahn Sch. Nursing U. San Diego, 1974—91, prof. emeritus, 1991—; dean emeritus Hahn Sch. Nursing, U. San Diego, 1988—. Lectr. Classical Alliance of Western States, Uskudar, Turkey, 1994, Italy, 95. Editor: Nursing Clinics of North America, 1970; contbr. articles to profl. jours. Served to capt. Nurse Corps US Army, 1953—56. Recipient Excellence in Nursing Scholarship award, Orgn. nurse Execs., 1993; Internat. Nightingale scholar, Nat. Health Svc. fellow. Fellow: Am. Acad. Nursing, Nat. League Nursing (bd. visitors 1977—87); mem.: ANA, German Rsch. Assn. (pres. 1995), Am. Assn. Colls. Nurgins (hon.), Am. Assn. History Nursing, Boston U. Nursing Archives, Sigma Theta Tau (Leadership award Zeta Mu chpt. 1986, Excellence in Nursing award 1991).

PALMER, J. CRISMAN, lawyer; BA, SD State U., 1971; JD, U. SD, 1974. Bar: SD 1974. Ptnr. Gunderson Palmer Goodsell Nelson LLP, Rapid City, SD. Mem. SD Bd. Pardons and Parole, 1991—97, chmn., 1993—97; mem. SD Judicial Qualifications Commn., 2004—08; adj. prof. U. SD. Mem.: Am. Bd. Trial Advocates (sec.-treas. 2005—06, v.p. 2006—07), Fedn. Def. and Corp. Counsel, Def. Rsch. Inst., SD Coun. Sch. Attys., SD Def. Lawyers Assn. (bd. dirs. 1995—98, sec. 1998), SD Trial Lawyers Assn., State Bar SD (commr. 1983—86, mem. disciplinary bd. 1996—2002, pres. 2006—07), ABA, Pennington County Bar Assn. (pres. 1985). Office: Gunderson Palmer Goodsell & Nelson LLP PO Box 8045 Rapid City SD 57709-8045

PALMER, JAMES ALVIN (JIM PALMER), baseball commentator; b. NYC, Oct. 15, 1945; children: Jamie, Kelly. Student, Ariz. State U., Towson State Coll., Md. Pitcher Balt. Orioles, 1966—84; commentator ABC Sports, 1984—; former commentator Home Team Sports, Bethesda, Md.; commentator Balt. Orioles baseball. Performer: TV and print advertisements; author (with Jack Clary): Jim Palmer's Way to Fitness, 1985; author: (with Jim Dale) Together We Were Eleven Foot Nine: The Twenty-Four Year Friendship of Hall of Fame Pitcher Jim Palmer and Orioles Manager Earl Weaver, 1996. Named Am. League Pitcher of Yr., The Sporting News, 1973, 1975, 1976; named to Baseball Hall of Fame, 1990, All Star Game, 1970, 1971, 1972, 1977, 1978; recipient Cy Young Meml. award, Am. League, 1973, 1975, 1976. Office: care Home Team Sports 7700 Wisconsin Ave Bethesda MD 20814-3578 *

PALMER, JAMES DANIEL, information technology educator; b. Washington, Mar. 8, 1930; s. Martin Lyle and Sarah Elizabeth (Hall) P.; m. Margret Kupka, June 21, 1952; children: Stephen Robert, Daniel Lee, John Keith. AA, Fullerton Jr. Coll., 1953; BS (Alumni scholar), U. Calif., Berkeley, 1955, MS, 1957; PhD, U. Okla., 1963; DPS (hon.), Regis Coll., Denver, 1977. Chief engr. Motor vehicle and Illumination Lab. U. Calif., Berkeley, 1955-57; assoc. prof. U. Okla., Norman, 1957-63, prof., 1963-66, asst. to dir. Rsch. Inst., 1960-63, cons. Rsch. Inst., 1966-69, dir. Sch. Elec. Engring., 1963-66, dir. Systems Rsch. Center, 1964-66; dean sci. and engring., prof. elec. engring. Union Coll., Schenectady, 1966-71; pres. Met. State Coll., Denver, 1971-78; rsch. and spl. programs adminstr. Dept. Transp., Washington, 1978-79; v.p., gen. mgr. rsch. and devel. div. Mech. Tech., Inc., Latham, NY, 1979-82; exec. v.p. J.J. Henry Co., Inc., Moorestown, NJ, 1982-85; BDM internat. prof. info. tech. George Mason U., Fairfax, Va., 1985-95, prof. emeritus, 1995—; software cons., 1995—. Bd. dirs. J.J. Henry Co., Inc.; cons. Sym Mgmt. Co., Boston, Higher Edn. Exec. Assocs., Denver, PERI, Princeton; adj. prof. U. Colo. Co-author: (with A.P. Sage) Software Systems Engineering, (with Aseltine, Beam and Sage) Introduction to Computer Systems, Analysis, Design and Application. Bd. dirs., exec. v.p. adv. com. U.S.A. Vols. for Internat. Tech. Assistance, 1967-83, exec. v.p., 1970-71, chmn. exec. com.; trustee, vice chmn. Nat. Commn. on Coop. Edn.; mem. exec. policy bd. Alaska Natural Gas Pipeline, 1978-79; trustee Auraria Higher Edn. Program, Denver; mem. Fulbright fellow Selection Com., Colo.; bd. mgrs., mem. exec. com. Hudson-Mohawk Assn. Colls. and Univs., trustee, chmn. bd., 1970-71; adv. com. USCG Acad., 1972-82, chmn. adv. com., 1979-82; mem. Colo. Gov.'s Sci. and Tech. Adv. Coun.; pres. Denver Cath. Cmty. Svcs. Bd.; mem. Archdiocesan Cath. Charities and Cmty. Svcs.; bd. dirs. U. Okla. Rsch. Inst.; chair bd. dirs. Tri-City Vols. Inc., 2004—; mem. adv. com. Mile-Hi Red Cross; mem. Tri-City Vols., chair. With USMC, 1950-51. Named James D. Palmer scholarship in his honor, George Mason U., 2002; recipient U.S. Coast Guard medal, 1983; Centennial scholar, Case-Western Res., 1981. Fellow IEEE (exec. and adminstrv. coms., v.p. long-range planning and finance, chmn. com. on large scale systems, Joseph E. Wahl Outstanding Career Achievement award 1993, Millennium medal 2000); mem. Systems, Man and Cybernetics Soc. (pres., Outstanding Contbns. award 1981), alumni assns. U. Calif. and U. Okla., Inst. Internat. Edn. (bd. dir. Rocky Mt. sect.), Soc. Naval Architects and Marine Engrs., Am. Soc. Engring. Edn., Am. Mil. Engrs., N.Y. Acad. Sci., Navy League, Sigma Xi, Eta Kappa Nu, Pi Mu Epsilon, Alpha Gamma Sigma. Home: 860 Cashew Way Fremont CA 94536-2646 Office: George Mason U Sch of Info Tech & Engring Fairfax VA 22030 Personal E-mail: jdpalmer@ix.netcom.com.

PALMER, JAMES F., aerospace transportation executive; BS, Southeast Mo. State, 1971. Sr. v.p., CFO McDonnell Douglas Corp., 1995—97; pres., Boeing Shared Services Group The Boeing Co., 1997—2000, sr. v.p.; pres. Boeing Capital Corp., 2000—04; exec. v.p., CFO Visteon Corp., 2004—07; corp. v.p., CFO Northrop Grumman Corp., LA, 2007—. Office: Northrop Grumman Corp 1840 Century Park E Los Angeles CA 90067-2199 Office Phone: 734-710-2020. *

PALMER, JANE G., music educator; d. William Edgar and Mildred Irene (Anthony) Galbraith; m. Merrill Jay Palmer, Dec. 26, 1972; 1 child, Brittany Leigh. BA in Edn., U. North Fla., 1977, MA in Edn., 1981. Music resource tchr. Duval County Pub. Schs., Jacksonville, Fla., 1997—99; choral dir. Fletcher Sr. HS, Neptune Beach, Fla., 1999—. Chmn. performing arts dept. Fletcher HS, 2002—. Choir mem., soloist Palms Presbyn. Ch., Jacksonville, 1976—, mem. pastoral nominating com., 2005—06. Named Tchr. of Yr., San Pablo Elem. Sch., Jacksonville, 1993, Fletcher H.S., 2003; recipient Tchr.'s Choice award, Pine Forest Elem., Jacksonville, 1991. Mem.: Am. Choral Dirs. Assn., Fla. Vocal Assn. (dist. chmn., adjudicator), Music Educators Nat. Conf. Avocations: travel, reading. Office: Fletcher HS 700 Seagate Ave Neptune Beach FL 32266 Office Phone: 904-247-5905 ext 152. Office Fax: 904-247-5920. E-mail: palmerj3@educationcentral.org.

PALMER, JESSICA A., former diversified financial services company executive; 3 children. BA, U. Bristol. V.p. internat. corp. fin. dept. Goldman Sachs & Co., 1976—84; mng. dir. Citigroup, Inc., 1988—2006, v.p., 1984—88, head of risk mgmt. for corp. and investment banking group NYC, 2003—06. Named one of 25 Women to Watch, US Banker mag., 2005; recipient Marjorie Magner Lifetime Achievement award, 2006.

PALMER, JOHN ANTHONY, III, language professor, secondary school educator, music educator; b. Worcester, Mass., May 18, 1955; s. John Jr. and Barbara (Dufresne) P. BA in Spanish, Worcester State Coll., 1977, MEd in Ednl. Adminstrn., 1988. Cert. Spanish, French, German and music tchr., Mass. Tchr., head dept. fgn. langs. Mahar Regional Sch., Orange, Mass., 1979-88; tchr. French, Spanish and German Doherty Meml. HS, Worcester, 1993-99, Burncoat Sr. HS, 1999—. Adj. prof. Spanish, Worcester State Coll., 1988-90, Fla. Atlantic U., 1991-93, Quinsigamond CC, 1997—; instr. voice Worcester Poly. Inst., 1979-81; cantor Ch. of St. Peter, 1977-81, Worcester Eglise Notre Dame des Canadiens, Worcester, 1981-83; adjudicator vocal auditions All-State Music Educators Conf., 1988; dir. Mass. Tchrs. Assn., 2006-; bargaining chair com. colls. of Mass. Tenor soloist Regis Coll., Boston, Worcester Poly. Inst., Worcester Chorus, Salisbury Singers, Simmons Coll., Boston, Ft. Lauderdale Opera Co., Opera Worcester, Smith Coll., North Hampton, Wells Coll., Aurore, N.Y. Mem. ASCD, Am. Coun. Tchrs. Fgn. Langs., Nat. Assn. Secondary Sch. Prins., Mass. Assn. Sch. Supts., Mass. Fgn. Lang. Assn., Mass. Tchrs. Assn. (dir.), Sigma Delta Pi. Democrat. Personal E-mail: jpalmerIII@aol.com.

PALMER, JOHN BERNARD, III, lawyer; b. Ft. Wayne, Ind., May 18, 1952; s. John Bernard and Dorothy Alma (Lauer) P. BA, Mich. State U., 1974; JD, U. Mich., 1977. Bar: Ill. 1977, US Dist. Ct. (no. dist.) Ill. 1977, US Ct. Appeals 2002, US Tax Ct. 1979, US Ct. Claims 2001. Assoc. Mayer Brown & Platt, Chgo., 1977-80, Hopkins & Sutter, Chgo., 1980-83, ptnr., 1983-2001, Foley & Lardner LLP, Chgo., 2001—, chmn. taxation practice group. Adj. prof. Ill. Inst. Tech.- Kent Coll. of Law, Chgo., 1984—. Mem. ABA (tax sect.). Office: Foley & Lardner LLP 321 N Clark St Chicago IL 60610 Office Phone: 312-832-4575. Business E-Mail: jpalmer@foley.com.

PALMER, JOHN DERRY, physiology educator; b. Chgo., May 26, 1932; s. John and Florence (Eley) P.; m. Carla Bianchi, Sept. 15, 1960; 1 child, John Charles. BA, Lake Forest Coll., 1957; MS, Northwestern U., 1959, PhD, 1962. Asst. prof. U. Ill., Chgo., 1961-63; fellow NSF, U. Bristol, Eng., 1963-64; prof., dept. chmn. NYU, 1964-74; prof. U. Mass., Amherst, 1974—, dept. chmn., 1974-80. Edit. bd. Marine Behavior and Physiology, 1998—, Chronobiology Internat., 1986—; author: Textbook of Modern Biology, 1968, The Biological Clock: Two Views, 1970, Biological Clocks in Marine Organisms: The Control of Physiological and Behavioral Tidal Rhythms, 1974, An Introduction to Biological Rhythms, 1976, (with others) Biological Rhythms and Living Clocks, 1977, Human Biological Rhythms, 1983, The Biological Rhythms and Clocks of Intertidal Animals, 1995, The Living Clock, 2000, The Biological Clock, 2003; contbr. articles to profl. jours. With U.S. Army, 1953-55. Fellow AAAS, Explorers Club; mem. Internat. Soc. of Chronobiology, Nat. Assn. of Scholars, Marine Biol. Lab., Phi Beta Kappa, Sigma Xi (pres., v.p., treas. N.Y. chpt., Disting. Rschr. award 1968). Avocation: trout and saltwater fishing. Office: U Mass Dept Biology 611 North Pleasant St Amherst MA 01003 Office Phone: 413-545-4400. Business E-Mail: ftodd@bio.umass.edu.

PALMER, KEKE (LAUREN KEYANA PALMER), actress; b. Harvey, Ill., Aug. 26, 1993; Actor: (films) Barbershop 2: Back in Business, 2004, Akeelah and the Bee, 2006 (Actress in a Motion Picture, NAACP Image Awards, 2007), Madea's Family Reunion, 2006; (TV films) The Wool Cap, 2004, Keke & Jamal, 2005, Knights of the South Bronx, 2005, Jump In!, 2007; guest appearances (TV series) Cold Case, 2004, Strong Medicine, 2004, Second Time Around, 2005, ER, 2005, Law & Order: Special Victims Unit, 2005. Office: c/o Coast To Coast 3350 Barham Blvd Los Angeles CA 90068 *

PALMER, LARRY LEON, foundation administrator, former ambassador; b. Augusta, Ga. BA, Emory U., 1970; MEd in African History, Tex. So. U., 1973; EdD in Higher Edn., Ind. U., Bloomington, 1978. Vol. Peace Corps., Liberua, West Africa, 1971—73; joined Foreign Svc., 1982; vice consul Dominican Republic, 1982—84; personnel officer Montevideo, Uruguay and Asuncion, Paraguay, 1984—86; staff asst. to asst. sec. African Affairs US Dept. State, 1986—87, counselor for adminstrn. Freetown, Sierra Leone, 1987—89, personnel officer Seoul, Republic of Korea, 1991—94, counselor for adminstrn. Dominican Republic, 1994—98, dep. chief of mission to chargé d'affaires Quito, Ecuador, 1999—2002, US amb. to Honduras Tegucigalpa, 2002—05; pres. Inter-Am. Found., Arlington, Va., 2005—. Asst. dir. fin. aid U. Va., Charlottesville, 1973—74; prof. hist. Cuttington Coll., Suakoko, Liberia, 1974—76, Wake Forest U., Winston Salem, NC, 1978—81; Pearson fellow, asst. to pres. U. Tex., El Paso, 1989—91. Office: Inter-Am Found 901 N Stuart St, 10 Fl Arlington VA 22203 Office Phone: 703-306-4301. E-mail: lpalmer@iaf.gov. *

PALMER, LIZA JANE, librarian; b. Pittsfield, Mass., Jan. 5, 1976; d. David Joel and Betty Lillian Shippey; m. Tim Neil Palmer, July 29, 2000; 1 child, Riley Tate. BA, Bard Coll., Annandale, NY, 1999; MA in Comm. Arts, U. Wis., Madison, 2001, MLS, 2003. Reference libr. Cape Fear C.C., Wilmington, NC, 2003—04; pub. svcs. libr. Randall libr. U. NC, Wilmington, 2004—05, creative & fine arts libr. Randall libr., 2006—. Editor: Film Internat., 2004—; contbr. articles to profl. jours. Sec. Cape Fear Crime Festival, Wilmington, 2004—06; chmn. One Book, One Cmty. New Hanover County, Wilmington, 2004—06; bd. dirs. First Book New Hanover County, 2006—. Grantee, NC Humanities Coun., 2005—06. Mem.: ALA (grantee office diversity 2006—07), Assn. Coll. and Rsch. Librs., Soc. Cinema and Media Studies, Beta Phi Mu. Office: UNCW Randall Libr 601 S College Rd Wilmington NC 28403-5616 Office Phone: 910-962-4234. Office Fax: 910-962-3078. Business E-Mail: palmerl@uncw.edu.

PALMER, LYNNE, writer, astrologer; b. El Centro, Calif., Dec. 14, 1932; d. Clarence Lee and Paquita Mae (Hartley) Hafer; m. Bruno Cazzaniga, Mar. 13, 1964 (div. 1965); m. Sidney Latter, Nov. 29, 1997 (dec. Oct. 2004). Student, Ch. of Light, 1957-62, Calif. Sch. Escrows, LA, 1960; theatre mgmt. degree, Mus. Arenas Theatres Assn., NYC, 1963. Asst. teller Western Mortgage, LA, 1957-58; head teller Sutro Mortgage Svc., LA, 1958-61; freelance astrologer NYC, 1961-92, Las Vegas, Nev., 1962—; owner, operator, tchr. astrology sch. NYC, 1970-72; owner Star Bright Pubs., Las Vegas, 1996—. Spkr. in field; interviewed in N.Y. Post and other major newspapers and mags. including Life and Oggi (Italy), Veja (Brazil), Wall St. Jour., People Mag., Globe, Die Welt am Sonntag (West Germany), New Woman Mag., Forbes. Author: Prosperity, Nixon's Horoscope, Astrological Almanac, Astrological Compatibility (Profl. Astrologers award 1976), Horoscope of Billy Rose, ABC Basic Chart Reading, ABC Major Progressions, ABC Chart Erection, Pluto Ephemeris (1900-2000), Daily Positions, Is Your Name Lucky For You?, Do-It-Yourself Publicity Directory, Your Lucky Days and Numbers, Money Magic, Astro-Guide to Nutrition and Vitamins, Gambling to Win, The Astrological Treasure Map, Dear Sun Signs, Are You Compatible With Your Boss, Partner, Coworkers, Employee, Client?, Bet to Win, Special Report: USA Under Attack, Lucky Days and Winning Numbers; columnist: Self, House Beautiful, Gold; record album: Cast and Read Your Horoscope; TV appearances include The Johnny Carson Tonight Show, What's My Line, 60 Minutes, CBS News Night Watch, Cosmos (BBC), Sci. Series (Italian TV), Fantastico (Brazilian TV), Japan TV, News (Nippon), Do We Really Need It? (ASAHI), The World is Calling (Uranai); contbr. articles to mags. and newspapers. Mem. AFTRA, Am. Fedn. Astrologers (cert.). Avocation: travel. Home: 850 E Desert Inn Rd Apt 912 Las Vegas NV 89109 Office: Lynne Palmer 1155 E Twain Ave Ste 108-248 Las Vegas NV 89169 Home Phone: 702-894-9919; Office Phone: 800-615-3352. Business E-Mail: lynnepalmer@lynnepalmer.com.

PALMER, MARC, engineer, lawyer; b. Bklyn., Dec. 12, 1949; s. Victor and Ruth Palmer; m. Beverly Miner, Sept. 24, 1989; 1 child, Wanda. BSEE, Poly. Inst. NY; JD, Bklyn Law Sch., 1989—92. Cert. Pe, NY, 2002; bar: NY 1992, Conn. 1992. Cons. Heimer Engring., Huntington, NY, 1986—97. Fellow: Conn.-Westchester Mycol. Assn. (assoc.; pres. 2005), Nat. Acad. Bldg. Inspection Engrs. (assoc.; exec. 2002). Avocation: Go. Home and Office: Palmer'S Inspections 29 Prospect Park W Brooklyn NY 11215-2307 Home Phone: 718-636-6348; Office Phone: 718-636-6348. Office Fax: 718-636-6348; Home Fax: 718-636-6348. Business E-Mail: morrsarian@msn.com.

PALMER, MARILYN JOAN, English composition educator; b. Mahoning County, Ohio, Mar. 3, 1933; d. Rudolph George and Marian Eleanor Wynn; m. Richard Palmer, Nov. 10, 1956 (dec. 1987); children: Ricky, Larry, Kevin. Phys. therapy cert., UCLA, 1954, BS, 1955; MA in Philosophy, Ohio State U., 1969; PhD, U. Okla., 1996. Phys. therapist Neil Ave. Sch. for Handicapped, Columbus, Ohio, 1968-69; instr. philosophy Ohio State U., Columbus, 1969; instr. English Youngstown (Ohio) State U., 1970-71; writer, editor The Economy Co., ednl. publs., Oklahoma City, 1977-81; grad. asst. in English U. Okla., Norman, 1981-87, lectr. in English, 1988-90, tech. writing instr. ind. studies, 1988-97. Free-lance editing and cons.; cons. for on-line CD-ROM to accompany a textbook, 2002. Author: Technical Writing for Science, Business and Industry, 1988, An Enthymeme as a Platform for Understanding Audience Values, 1997; editor: Kindergarten Keys Teacher's Guidebook, 1982, author parochial supplement, 1982. Fund-raiser Easter Seal Soc., 1965-68; den mother coord. Boy Scouts Am., 1966, 67. Dept. Energy grantee, 1976. Mem. AAUP, Am. Phys. Therapy Assn., Soc. for Women in Philosophy, Alpha Xi Delta (nat. editor Quill 1984-86). Home Phone: 405-360-4795; Office Phone: 405-447-6495. Personal E-mail: doclynn@cox.net.

PALMER, MICHAEL, poet; b. NYC, 1943; Author: (books of poetry) Blake's Newton, 1972, The Circular Gates, 1974, Without Music, 1977, Notes For Echo Lakes, 1981, First Figure, 1984, Sun, 1988, At Passages, 1996, The Lion Bridge: Selected Poems 1972-1995, 1998, The Promises of Glass, 2000, Codes Appearing: Poems 1979-1988, 2001, Company of Moths, 2005. Recipient Wallace Stevens award, Acad. Am. Poets, 2006. Office: c/o Acad Am Poets Ste 604 584 Broadway New York NY 10012-5243

PALMER, PAMELA MURRILL, educator; b. Jacksonville, NC, Apr. 21, 1967; d. Roosevelt Dean Lee and Dorsay Ann Mitchell; m. Alan Wade Palmer, Feb. 19, 2000; 1 child, Joshua Alan. BA, Winston-Salem State U., NC, 1990; MS, NC A&T State U., Greensboro, 1996; cert. in nonprofit mgmt., Duke U. Cmty. and econ. devel. specialist NC A&T State U., 1995—97; prof. High Point U., NC, 1998—. Dir. Nonprofit Leadership Enhancement Program, High Point U., 2005—. Mem., com. leader Love and Faith Christian Fellowship, Greensboro, 2003; sec. United Way of Greater High Point, 2006—; mem. exec. com. Am. Friends Svc. Com.-SERO, Atlanta, 2003; mem. Guilford County Mental Health Bd., Greensboro, 2004. Named Minority Bus. Advocate, High Point C. of C., 2005; recipient Outstanding Faculty award, High Point U. Evening Degree Program, 2004, 2005; grantee Nonprofit Leadership Enhancement Program, Hayden-Harman Found. and High Point U., 2006—. Home: 307 Jackson St Jamestown NC 27282 Office: High Point U 833 Montlieu Ave Campus Box 3471 High Point NC 27262 Home Phone: 336-454-0950; Office Phone: 336-841-4632. Home Fax: 336-454-9009. E-mail: pmurrill@highpoint.edu.

PALMER, PATRICK EDWARD, radio astronomer, educator; b. St. Johns, Mich., Dec. 6, 1940; s. Don Edward and Nina Louise (Kyes) P.; m. Joan Claire Merlin, June 9, 1963; children: Laura Katherine, Aidan Edward, David Elijah. SB, U. Chgo., 1963; MA, Harvard U., 1965, PhD, 1968. Radio astronomer Harvard U., Cambridge, Mass., 1968; asst. prof. astronomy and astrophysics U. Chgo., 1968-70, assoc. prof., 1970-75, prof., 1975—2006, prof. emeritus, 2006—. Vis. assoc. prof. astronomy Calif. Inst. Tech., Pasadena, 1972; vis. radio astronomer Cambridge (Eng.) U., 1973; vis. rsch. astronomer U. Calif., Berkeley, 1977, 86; vis. scientist Nat. Radio Astronomer Obs., 1980-2006. Contbr. articles on radio astron. investigations of comets and interstellar medium to tech. jours. Recipient Bart J. Bok prize for contbns. to galactic astronomy, 1969, Alfred P. Sloan Found. fellow, 1970-72, Helen B. Warner prize, 1975. Fellow AAAS (chmn. sect. D astronomy 1984); mem. AAUP, Am. Astron. Soc. (chmn. nominating com. 1981, mem. publs. bd. 1985-86, mem. Warner Prize selection com. 1977-78), Royal Astron. Soc., Internat. Astron. Union, U. Chgo. Track Club. Home: 5549 S Dorchester Ave Chicago IL 60637-1720 Office: Univ Chgo Astronomy & Astrophysics Ctr 5640 S Ellis Ave Chicago IL 60637-1433 Home Phone: 773-955-2223; Office Phone: 773-702-7972. E-mail: ppalmer@oskar.uchicago.edu.

PALMER, PHILIP EDWARD STEPHEN, radiologist; b. London, Apr. 26, 1921; MBBS, U. London, 1944, DMR, 1946, DMRT, 1947; MD (hon.), U. Tirgu Mures, Romania, 2004. Intern, then resident Westminster Hosp.; cons. radiologist West Cornwall (Eng.) Hosp. Group, 1947-54; sr. govt. radiologist Matabeleland, Rhodesia-Zimbabwe, 1954-64; prof. radiology U. Cape Town, South Africa, 1964-68; prof. U. Pa., 1968-70; prof. diagnostic radiology and vet. radiology U. Calif., Davis, 1970—. Dir. Bd. World Health Imaging; WHO cons. in field. Author: The Imaging of Tropical Diseases, 1980 and 2nd edit.: 2000; contbr. 200plus articles to profl. publs. Recipient German Röentgen award, 1993, 1st Béclère medal Internat. Soc. Radiology, 1996, 1st Antoine Béclère lectr. Internat. Soc. Radiology, 1996, Presdl. award Radiol. Soc. N.Am., 2000. Fellow Calif. Radiol. Assn., Royal Coll. Physicians (Edinburgh), Royal Coll. Radiologists (Eng.), Romanian Soc. Radiol. and Nuclear Med.; mem. Brit. Inst. Radiology, Brit. Med. Assn., Calif. Med. Assn., Internat. Skeletal Soc., Assn. Univ. Radiologists, Radiol. Soc. N.Am. (Spl. Pres.'s award 2000), Kenya Radiol. Soc., South African Coll. Medicine, Egyptian Soc. Radiology and Nuclear Medicine, Yugoslav Assn. for Ultrasound, West African Assn. Radiologists. Address: 821 Miller Dr Davis CA 95616-3622

PALMER, RICHARD N., state supreme court justice; b. Hartford, Conn., May 27, 1950; BA, Trinity Coll., 1972; JD with high honors, U. Conn., 1977. Bar: Conn. 1977, U.S. Dist. Ct. Conn. 1978, D.C. 1980, U.S. Ct. Appeals (2d cir.) 1981. Law clk. to Hon. Jon O. Newman U.S. Ct. Appeals (2d cir.), 1977—78; assoc. Shipman & Goodwin, 1978—80; asst. U.S. atty. Office U.S. Atty. Conn., 1980—83, 1987—90, U.S. atty., 1991, chief state's atty., 1991—93; ptnr. Chatigny and Palmer, 1984—86; assoc. justice Conn. Supreme Ct., Hartford, 1993—. Mem. Phi Beta Kappa. Office: Connecticut Supreme Ct 231 Capitol Ave Hartford CT 06106-1548 Office Phone: 860-757-2115.

PALMER, RICHARD WARE, retired lawyer; b. Boston, Oct. 20, 1919; s. George Ware and Ruth French (Judkins) P.; m. Nancy Fernald Shaw, July 8, 1950; children: Richard Ware Jr., John Wentworth, Anne Fernald. AB, Harvard U., 1942, JD, 1948. Bar: N.Y. 1950, Pa. 1959. Sec., dir. N.Am. Mfg. Co., Natick, Mass., 1946-48; assoc. Burlingham, Veeder, Clark & Hupper, Burlingham, Hupper & Kennedy, NYC, 1949-57; ptnr. Rawle & Henderson, Phila., 1958-79; co-founder, ptnr. Palmer, Biezup & Henderson, Phila., 1979—97, of counsel, 1998—2004; ret., 2004. Sec. Underwater Technics, Inc., Camden, NJ, 1967-85; adv. on admiralty law to U.S. del. Inter-Govtl. Maritime Consultative Orgn., London, 1967, U.S. del. 30th-34th internat. confs.; mem. U.S. Shipping Coord. Com., Washington legal sub com., 1967—; titular mem. Comité Maritime Internat.; v.p., sec., bd. dirs. Phila. Belt Line R.R., Mather (Bermuda) Ltd. Editor: Maritime Law Reporter. Mem., permanent adv. bd. Tulane Admiralty Law Inst., Tulane U. Law Sch., New Orleans, 1975—; trustee Seamen's Ch. Inst., Phila., 1967—2001, pres., 1972—84; mem. exec. com. Harvard Law Sch. Assn., Phila., 1986—2005; bd. dirs. Havrford (Pa.) Civic Assn., 1972—85, pres., 1976—79; consul for Denmark State of Pa., 1980—91, consul emeritus, 1992—. Lt. comdr. USNR, 1942—46. Fellow World Acad. Art and Sci. (treas. 1988-2002); mem. ABA (former chmn. stdg. com. on admiralty and maritime law 1978-79), N.Y.C. Bar Assn., Phila. Bar Assn., Maritime Law Assn. U.S.(chmn. limitation liability com. 1977-83, 2d v.p. 1984-86, 1st v.p. 1986-88, pres. 1988-90, immediate past pres. 1990-92), Assn. Average Adjusters USA and Gt. Britain, Port of Phila. Maritime Soc., Consul Assn. Phila., Colonial Soc. Pa. (treas. 2003-05, bd. govs. 2005—, counselor 2007—), Danish Order of Dannebrog, Merion Cricket Club, Phila. Club, Rittenhouse Club, Geneal. Soc. Pa. (bd. dirs. 1997-2002, v.p. 2003-04, bd. dirs. 2005—, counsel 2007—), Harvard Club NYC and Phila. (exec. com. 1983-86, 94-97). Republican. Episcopalian. Home: 432 Montgomery Ave Haverford PA 19041-1527 Home Fax: 610-649-7824. Personal E-mail: rnspalmer@earthlink.net.

PALMER, ROBERT BAYLIS, librarian; b. Rockville Centre, NY, Apr. 5, 1938; s. John Frederick and Marion (Baylis) P.; divorced; 1 child, Michele Palmer Fracasso. AB, Kenyon Coll., Gambier, Ohio, 1960; MS in L.S, Simmons Coll., Boston, 1965; MA in English, Middlebury Coll., Vt., 1965. Tchr. Brooks Sch., North Andover, Mass., 1960-65, libr., 1961-65; acting libr. Columbia Coll., 1965-66; asst. to dir. libraries Columbia U., 1965-67; dir. Barnard Coll. Libr., 1967-81. Fulbright lectr. Tribhuvan U. Library, Kathmandu, Nepal, 1972-73, Kathmandu, 1980; vol. lectr. USIS, library cons., Asia, 1976; Fulbright lectr. Wuhan, Peoples Republic China, 1984-85; library cons., advisor, Peoples Republic China, 1986-87, Zanzibar, Tanzania, 1988; lectr., cons. Kenya, Ethiopia, Zimbabwe, 1988; English lang. escort officer US Dept. State, 1989—. Mem. ALA. Address: 190 Riverside Dr New York NY 10024-1008 *Keep a discrimintating mind to make the necessary judgements of life's choices and a lightness of humorous spirit.*

PALMER, ROBERT LESLIE, lawyer; b. Porterville, Calif., Apr. 10, 1957; s. Harrison Rowe and Margaret Elizabeth (Witty) P.; m. Huisuk Kim, Feb. 1, 1986; 1 child, Aaron Rowe. BA, Tulane U., 1979; JD, Georgetown U., 1982. Bar: D.C. 1982, U.S. Ct. Mil. Appeals 1985, Tex. 1987, Ala. 1987, U.S. Dist. Ct. (no. dist.) Ala. 1987, U.S. Ct. Appeals (11th cir.) 1987, U.S. Supreme Ct. 2005, U.S. Dist. Ct. (mid. dist.) Ala. 2006; registered lobbyist, Ala. Assoc. Lewis Martin Burnett & Dunkle, P.C., Birmingham, Ala., 1987-89, Lewis and Martin, Birmingham, Ala., 1989-90, Martin, Drummond and Woosley, Birmingham, 1990-91, bd. dirs., 1991-92, Martin, Drummond, Woosley and Palmer, Birmingham, 1992-95; atty. Environ. Litig. Group, P.C., Birmingham, Ala., 1995—. Ala. del. 6th Joint Conf. between Korea and S.E. U.S., Kyongju, Republic of Korea, 1991, 7th Joint Conf., Atlanta, 1992; founder, dir., pres. Ala. Legal Reform Found.; asst. scoutmaster Boy Scouts Am., 2003—; bd. dirs. Jimmie Hale Mission, 2005—. Capt. JAGC, U.S. Army, 1983-87, USAR, 1987-91. Recipient commendation Republic of Korea Ministry of Justice, 1984. Mem. VFW (life mem.), AAJ, Ala. Assn. for Justice (exec.com., sustaining mem.), Tex. Trial Lawyers Assn., Christian Legal Soc. (pres. Birmingham chpt. 2007—), Phi Beta Kappa, Omicron Delta Kappa. Independent. Baptist. Home: 1408 E Whirlaway Helena AL 35080-4102 Office: Environ Litig Group PC 3529 7th Ave S Birmingham AL 35222-3210 Home Phone: 205-663-3137; Office Phone: 205-328-9200. Business E-Mail: bob@elglaw.com.

PALMER, ROBERT TOWNE, lawyer, bank executive; b. Chgo., May 25, 1947; s. Adrian Bernhardt and Gladys (Towne) P.; m. Ann Therese Darin, Nov. 9, 1974; children: Justin Darin, Christian Darin. BA, Colgate U., 1969; JD, U. Notre Dame, 1974. Bar: Ill. 1974, D.C. 1978, U.S. Supreme Ct. 1978. Law clk. to Hon. Walter V. Schaefer Ill. Supreme Ct., 1974-75; assoc. McDermott, Will & Emery, Chgo., 1975-81, ptnr., 1982-86, Chadwell & Keyser, Ltd., Chgo., 1987—88, Connelly, Mustes, Palmer & Schroeder, Chgo., 1988-89; of counsel Garfield & Merel Ltd., Chgo., 1990-2000. Adj. faculty Chgo. Kent Law Sch., 1975—77, Loyola U., 1976—78; adv. com. Fed. Home Loan Mortgage Corp., 1988—89; bd. dirs. Ctrl. Fed. Savs. & Loan Assn. of Chgo., chmn., COO, 2000—; dir. Chgo. Assn. Fin. Insts., 2001—03, sec., 2002—03; mem. Chgo. Crime Commn., 2001—, dir., 2002—. Contbr. articles to legal jours. and textbooks. Mem. ABA, Ill. State Bar Assn. (Lincoln award 1983), Chgo. Bar Assn., Chgo. Club, Dairymen's Country Club, Lambda Alpha. Office: Central Fed Savs 1601 W Belmont Ave Chicago IL 60657-3044 Personal E-mail: rpalmer916@aol.com.

PALMER, ROGER RAYMOND, finance educator; b. NYC, Dec. 31, 1926; s. Archibald and Sophie (Jarnow) P.; m. Martha West Hopkins, June 7, 1986; children by previous marriage: Kathryn Sue, Daniel Stephen, Susan Jo. BS, U. Wis., 1949; MBA, Cornell U., 1951; postgrad., NYU, 1951-54. Auditor, Ernst and Ernst, CPA's, NYC, 1953-54; auditor Gen. Dynamics Corp., 1956-60; mgr. corp. audits Tex. Instruments, 1960-64; auditor 1st Nat. Bank, St. Paul, 1964-68, v.p. planning, 1968-69, v.p., comptr., 1969-75, sr. v.p., contr., 1975-82; chmn. dept. fin. Coll. of St. Thomas (now U. St. Thomas), St. Paul, 1996—; prof. emeritus U. St. Thomas, 2005—. Dir. First Met. Travel, Inc.; guest lectr. U. Minn., 1966; conf. leader, speaker, 1959— Contbr. articles to publs. Bd. dir. Waterford (Conn.) Civic Assn., 1959-60, Friends of St. Paul Pub. Library, 1967, Mpls. Citizens League; chmn. bd. dirs. Film in the Cities, 1983-85; mem. acctg. adv. council U. Minn.; trustee, chmn. fin. com. Hazelton Found. With U.S. Maritime Svc., 1945-47; with U.S. Army, 1954-56. Mem. Inst. Internal Auditors (pres. So. New Eng chpt. 1957-60, edn. chmn. Dallas 1961, Twin City chpt. 1965-66), Nat. Assn. Accts. (dir. Norwich, Conn. chpt. 1958-60), Nat. Assn. Accountants (St. Paul chpt. 1967), Assn. Bank Audit, Control and Operation, Am. Inst. Banking, Fin. Execs. Inst., Planning Forum (pres. Twin Cities chpt. 1984-85), Univ. Club (St. Paul). Clubs: St. Paul Athletic. Home: 415 Oak Ridge Dr San Marcos TX 78666 Business E-Mail: rrpalmer@stthomas.edu.

PALMER, RUSSELL EUGENE, investment company executive, retired dean; b. Jackson, Mich., Aug. 13, 1934; s. Russell E. and Margarite M. (Briles) P.; m. Priscilla G. Palmer; children: Bradley Carl, Stephen Russell, Russell Eugene, III, Karen Jean. BA with honors, Mich. State U., 1956; D in Comml. Sci. (hon.), Drexel U., 1980; MA (hon.), U. Pa., 1984; PhD (hon.), Chulalongkorn U., 1988, Free U. Brussels, 1989, York Coll., 1989. With Touche Ross & Co., NYC, 1956-83, mng. ptnr., CEO, 1972-82, also bd. dirs., exec. coms.; mng. dir., CEO Touche Ross Internat., 1974-83; dean, Reliance prof. mgmt. and pvt. enterprise Wharton Sch. U. Pa., 1983-90, CEO. Bd. trustees Main Line Health, Nat. Constitution Ctr.; bd. dirs. Smithsonian. Mem. Pres.'s Mgmt. Improvement Coun., 1979—80; mem. adv. bd. Salvation Army, past mem. nat. adv. bd.; former mem. adv. coun. Women's Way; bd. dirs. UN Assn. U.S.A.; former mem. adv. panel Comptr. Gen. U.S.; former chmn. bd trustees U. Pa. Health Care Sys.; trustee Acctg. Hall of Fame U. Pa.; bd. dirs. Joint Coun. Econ. Edn., 1978—83, United Fund Greater N.Y., 1980—83; mem. Bus.Com. Arts, 1977—83; bd. dirs. SEI Ctr. for Advanced Studies in Mgmt.; former mem. adv. coun. Sch. Internat. and Pub. Affairs Columbia U., Grad. Sch. Bus. Stanford U.; mem. assocs. coun. Bus. Sch. Oxford U.; mem. U.S. Sec. Labor's Commn. on Workforce Quality and Labor Market Efficiency; pres. Fin. Acctg. Found., 1979—82; pub. mem. Hudson Inst. Recipient Gavin Meml. award Beta Theta Pi, 1956, Disting. Community Svc. award Brandeis U., 1974, Outstanding Alumnus award Mich. State U., 1978, Humanitarian award Fedn. Jewish Philanthropies, 1979, Disting. Aux. Svc. award Salvation Army, 1979, LEAD Bus. award, 1984, Good Scout award Phila. coun. Boy Scouts Am., 1987, Oxford Cup Beta Theta Pi, 2005. Mem. Merion Cricket Club, Conf. Bd. (bd. dirs.), Beta Gamma Sigma (mem. bd. govs.). Presbyterian. Office: The Palmer Group 3600 Market St Ste 530 Philadelphia PA 19104-2649 Office Phone: 215-243-2590. Business E-Mail: rpalmer@palmer-group.com.

PALMER, SAMUEL COPELAND, III, lawyer; b. Phila., June 9, 1934; s. Samuel Copeland Jr. and Vivian Gertrude (Plumb) P.; divorced; children: Samuel C. IV, Sarah Anne, Bryan Douglas. Grad., Harvard Sch., Los Angeles, 1952; student, Yale U., 1953; AB, Stanford U., 1955; JD, Loyola-Marymount U., Marymount, 1958. Bar: Calif. 1959, U.S. Dist. Ct. (cen., ea. and so. dists. Calif.) 1959, U.S. Ct. Appeals (9th cir.) 1970, U.S. Supreme Ct. 1971. Dep. city atty., Los Angeles, 1959-60; assoc. firm Pollock & Deutz, Los Angeles, 1960-63; ptnr. firm Pollock & Palmer, Los Angeles, 1963-70, Palmer & Bartenetti, Los Angeles, 1970-81, Samuel C. Palmer III, P.C., 1981-85; ptnr. Thomas, & Snell, 1985—. Adj. prof. Calif. State U., Fresno, 1993. Trustee Western Ctr. Law and Poverty; bd. dirs. Big Bros./Big Sisters, Fresno, Arte Ams., Lively Arts Found., Nat. Sleep Found., Vols. in Parole; pres., bd. dirs. Poverello House; founder, pres. Fresno Crime Stoppers. Mem. ABA, State Bar Calif. (disciplinary subcom., bar examiners subcom.), Fresno County Bar Assn. (pres., bd. dirs. 1988-93), Pickwick Soc., Am. Bd. Trial Advocates, Chancery Club, Downtown Club, Calif. Club, Fig Garden Tennis Club, Rotary, Delta Upsilon, Phi Delta Phi. Office: Gilmore Wood Vinnard 7108 N Fresno St Ste 410 Fresno CA 93720-2953 Home: 9323 N Saybrook Dr Apt 117 Fresno CA 93720-0830 E-mail: spalmer@thomasnell.com.

PALMER, SHARON-JOY, agricultural research company executive; b. S.I., NY, Oct. 16, 1947; d. James Murdock Palmer and Lillian Elinore (Nelson) Daniels; 1 child, Cameron Nelson Polland. Student, Wayne U., Chgo., 1966-68; student in real estate, Dade Jr. Coll., 1969-73; BS in Edn./Ch. Ministries, Liberty U., 1989, ThM, MAR/Counseling, 1994. Dental asst. Francis J. Byron Jr., DDS, SI, NY, 1966-69; flight attendant Delta Airlines, Miami, 1969-77; realtor D.W. Hyder and Assocs., Albuquerque, 1976-78; sales rep. Postique of Colo., Denver, 1976-78; dir. Combanc Internat., Inc., Albuquerque, 1976-80; mfr.'s rep. Innovative Mktg. Concepts, Albuquerque, 1977-79, owner; developer, owner Angel Skye Investments, Ltd., Angel Fire, N.Mex., 1979—; econ. adv. Am. S.S.T. Corp., Parkersburg, W.Va., 1982-85; founder, pres., CEO Sci. Econ. Environ. Devel. Internat., Inc., Albuquerque, 1981—. Ptnr. Angel Skye Investments, 1980—; bd. dirs. Asia Enterprise Ltd., Tokyo, Condoc-Paraguay Ltd., Asuncion, Victory Internat. Inc., Panama City, Republic of Panama, Sci Econ. Environ. Devel. Kenya Ltd., Nairobi, 1980—, Sci. Econ. Environ. Devel. Internat. Del., Mountains Herbs and Spices, Albuquerque, 1980—; pres. World Solar Seed, 1999-; Native Seed Internat., Native Am. Nations, 2000, Mighty Seed Internat., CEO, 1999, Mighty Seed Corp., 1998-. Inventor agrl. energy efficient units, 1982; inventor, designer above ground and underground "mighty seed" units for food prodn., seed programmable environ. controller and modular housing, disaster hurricane enclosures. Active Embassy Kenya, Washington for Agrl. Devel., Nairobi, Kenya, East Africa, 1982; mem. various childrens' hosps., Miami, 1973, Westside Assn., Coralles, N.Mex., 1980, various children's hosps. Mem. Am. Dental Assts. Assn., Better Bus. Bur., Bd. Realtors, NAFE (nat. dir.), Nat. Platform Assn., Entrepreneur's Assn. Clubs: Angel Fire Country, Rio Rancho (N.Mex.) Country. Republican. Baptist. Home: 3208 Sue Cir Albuquerque NM 87124

PALMER, STACY ELLA, periodical editor; b. Middletown, Conn., Oct. 25, 1960; d. Marvin Jerome Palmer and Eileen Sondra (Cohen) Palmer Burke. B in Liberal Arts and Internat. Rels., Brown U., 1982. Asst. editor Chronicle of Higher Edn., Washington, 1982-86, sr. editor, 1986-88; news editor Chronicle of Philanthropy, Washington, 1988-93, mng. editor, 1993-98, editor, 1998—. Bd. dirs. Brown Alumni Monthly, Providence, 1988-91, vice chmn., 1991-93, mem. 1996—, chmn., 2003. Mem.: Brown U. Alumni Assn. (bd. govs. 1997—2001), Brown Club Washington (bd. dirs. 1993—99, pres. 1994—99). Avocations: swimming, bicycling, travel. Office: Chronicle of Philanthropy 1255 23rd St NW Washington DC 20037-1125 Home: 3131 Connecticut Ave NW Apt 2803 Washington DC 20008

PALMER, STUART HUNTER, sociology educator; b. NYC, Apr. 29, 1924; s. Herman G. and Beatrice (Hunter) P.; m. Anne Barbara Scarborough, June 22, 1946; 1 dau., Catherine. BA, Yale U., 1949, MA, 1951, PhD, 1955; LHD (hon.), Daniel Webster Coll., 1997. Asst. to dean Yale Coll., New Haven, 1949-51; instr. sociology New Haven Coll., 1949-51, 53-55; faculty U. NH, Durham, 1955—, prof., 1964—, chmn. dept. sociology and anthropology, 1964-69, 79-82, dean Coll. Liberal Arts, 1982-95, dir. London program, 1995-96. Disting. vis. prof. SUNY, Albany, 1970-71; vis. behavioral scientist NH Divsn. Mental Health; vis. prof. U. Sussex, Eng., 1976, U. Ga., 1977; cons. U.S. Office Edn., USPHS, U.S. Office Delinquency and Youth Devel., Dept. Justice; mem. adv. com. for sociology Com. on Internat. Exch. of Persons; mem. exec. com. NH Gov.'s Commn. on Crime and Delinquency; co-chmn. Internat. Symposium on Univs. in Twenty-First Century; co-chmn. Internat. Confs. on Stress Rsch., Nat. Commn. Arts and Scis. Author: Understanding Other People, 1955, A Study of Murder, 1960, (with Brian R. Kay) The Challenge of Supervision, 1961, Deviance and Conformity, 1970, (with Arnold S. Linsky) Rebellion and Retreat, 1972, The Violent Society, 1972, The Prevention of Crime, 1973, (with John A. Humphrey) Deviant Behavior, 1980, Role Stress, 1981, Deviant Behavior: Patterns, Sources, and Controls, 1990, The Universities Today, 1998; contbr. articles to profl. jours. Chmn. bd. trustees Daniel Webster Coll., New Eng. Aero. Inst. Served to lt. AC AUS, 1942-45; Served to lt. AC USAF, 1951-53. Decorated Air medal with 3 oak leaf clusters; fellow Henry Page. Mem. Am. Sociol. Assn., Ea. Sociol. Soc., Internat. Sociol. Soc., Internat. Soc. Criminology, Internat. Soc. Forecasters, Am. Assn. Colls., Coun. for Liberal Learning, Am. Assn. Higher Edn., Coun. Colls. Arts and Scis., Nat. Assn. State Univs. and Land-Grant Colls., AAAS, Am. Acad. Polit. and Social Scis., NY Acad. Scis., Am. Assn. Suicidology, Soc. Cross-Cultural Rsch., Am. Soc. Criminology, Assn. Gov. Bds. Univs. and Colls., Phi Beta Kappa (hon.), Sigma Xi, Alpha Kappa Delta. Home: 38A Emerson Rd Durham NH 03824-2110 *Be honest with yourself.*

PALMER, VENRICE ROMITO, lawyer, educator; b. Springfield, Mass., Jan. 11, 1952; s. Venrice Wellesley and Mildred Adlay (Foster) P. Higher diploma, U. Besançon, France, 1973; AB maxima cum laude, King's Coll., Wilkes-Barre, Pa., 1974; JD, Harvard U., 1977. Bar: N.Y. 1978, U.S. Dist. Ct. (so. and ea. dists.) N.Y. 1979, Ill. 1986, Calif. 1997. Spl. asst. atty. gen. Office N.Y. Atty. Gen., NYC, 1977-79; staff atty. SEC, NYC, 1979-82, br. chief, 1982-83, spl. trial counsel, 1983-85, acting asst. regional adminstr., 1984-85; sr. counsel Sears, Roebuck and Co., Hoffman Estates, Ill., 1985-97, Bank of Am., San Francisco, 1997-99; counsel McCutchen, Doyle, Brown & Enersen, LLP, San Francisco, 1999—2002; of counsel Bingham McCutchen LLP, San Francisco, 2002—07; pvt. practice San Francisco, 2007—. Guest lectr. St. John's U. Bus. Sch., N.Y.C., 1984; lectr. Practicing Law Inst., N.Y.C., 1995—, Glasser LegalWorks, Little Falls, N.J., 1997—, Am. Soc. Corp. Secs., 1997-99, Nat. Bus. Inst., Eau Claire, Wis., 2000—. Contbr. articles to various law publs. Recipient cert. of appreciation N.Y. State Bar Assn., 1978, Benaglia award King's Coll., 1974. Mem.: ABA, Calif. State Bar Assn. (mem. fin. instns. com. 2000—03), Alpha Mu Gamma, Delta Epsilon Sigma. Avocations: opera, ballet, reading. Home and Office: 1200 Gough St Apt 7A San Francisco CA 94109-6616 E-mail: steveintel@aol.com.

PALMER, VERNON VALENTINE, law educator; b. New Orleans, Sept. 9, 1940; s. George Joseph and Juliette Marie (Wehrmann) P. BA, Tulane U., 1962, LL.B., 1965; LL.M., Yale U., 1966; PhD, Pembroke Coll., Oxford U., 1985. Bar: La. 1965, U.S. Supreme Ct. 1981. Asst. prof. law Ind. Sch. Law, Indpls., 1966-70; lectr. law U. Botswana, Lesotho & Swaziland, Roma, Lesotho, 1967-69; prof. Tulane Law Sch., New Orleans, 1970—, Clarence Morrow research prof. law, 1980—, Thomas Pickles prof. law, 1989—; external examiner Nat. U. Lesotho, Roma, 1978-81. Dir. Tulane Paris Inst. European Legal Studies, European Legal Studies; reporter for revision of civil code La. Law Inst. 1979; vis. prof. Faculty Law, U. Strasbourg, 1988, The Sorbonne, U. Paris, 1986, 92, U. des Antilles, Martinique, 1998, U. Ramon Llull, Barcelona, 1998, U. Trento, 1999—, U. Laussanne, 2000, U. Geneva, 2000, U. Fribourg, 2005. Author: The Roman-Dutch and Lesotho Law of Delict, 1970, The Legal System of Lesotho, 1971, The Paths to Privity, 1992, The Civil Law of Lease in Louisiana, 1997, Louisiana: Microcosm of a Mixed Jurisdiction, 1999, Mixed Jurisdictions Worldwide: The Third Legal Family, 2001; author: (with Bussani) Pure Economic Loss Europe, 2003, The Louisiana Civilian Experience, 2004, The Boundaries of Strict Liability in European Tort Law, 2004; contbr. numerous articles to profl. jours. Pres. French Quarter Residents Assn., 1973-75, Alliance for Good Govt., 1974-75; del. Nat. Democratic Conv., NYC, 1976; chmn. World Congress on Mixed Jurisdictions, 2002. Decorated chevalier French Legion of Honor and L'ordre des Palmes Académiques. Mem. La. Law Inst., World Soc. Mixed Jurisdiction Jurists (pres.), Titulaire Internat. Acad. Comparative Law (The Hague). Democrat. Roman Catholic. Office: 6329 Freret St New Orleans LA 70118-6231 Home: 1027 Eleonore St New Orleans LA 70115-2401 Office Phone: 504-865-5978. Business E-Mail: vpalmer@tulane.edu.

PALMER, VICKI R., food products executive; b. Memphis; m. John E. Palmer; 1 child, Alexandria. B in Econs. and Bus. Adminstrn., Rhodes Coll., 1975; MBA in Fin., U. Memphis, 1980. Corp. loan officer First Tenn. Bank.; head pension investment FedEx, mgr. corp. fin.; mgr. pension investments Coca-Cola Co., 1983—86; asst. treas. Coca-Cola Enterprises Inc., 1986—93, v.p., 1993—99, treas., 1993—, sr. v.p., spl. asst. to CEO, 1999—2004, bd. dir., 2001—, exec. v.p. fin. & adminstrn., 2004—. Bd. dirs. Spelman Coll., Rhodes Coll., Woodward Acad., First Tenn. Nat. Corp. Named one of 20 Women of Power and Influence in Corp. Am., Black Enterprise Mag., 100 Black Women of Influence, Atlanta Bus. League, 1998; recipient Disting. Alumni award, U. Memphis Alumni Assn. Office: Coca-Cola Enterprises 2500 Windy Ridge Pkwy Atlanta GA 30339 *

PALMER, WILLARD ALDRICH, III, magician, writer, actor; b. Houston, July 25, 1942; s. Willard Aldrich and Ruby Lenoir (Touchstone) P.; m. Carol Ann Houston. BA in Germanics, Rice U., 1964; MA in Letters, Music, Profl. Studies, World U. Advanced Studies of Hawaii, 1995, Phd in Germanics, 2000. Instr. Charlie Cash Music Studios, Houston, 1962-70; performer various venues, Houston, Montreal, Can., 1965—; writer Alfred Music Co., Los Angeles, 1968-86; official magician Todd Mission, Tex., 1984—; owner, operator Bill Palmer Magic Shows, Bellaire, Tex., 1984—. Dir. Tex. Renaissance Festival, Todd Mission, 1978-79; writer, dir. Ren Fair Prodns., Inc., Houston, 1979-81; writer, cons. Exclusive Magical Pubs., Houston, Mexico City, 1986— (mem. editoral bd. 1986). Author: (books) How To Play Folk and Bluegrass Banjo, 1965, A Guide For The Texas Renaissance Festival Performer, 1978, Early History of the Paddle Trick in Print, 1995, How to be a Professional Entertainer, 1996; translator: Magical Adventures and Fairy Tales (Punx) 1987, Punx's Fourth Dimensional Mysteries, 1990, Farewell Performance (Punx), 1990, Paramiracles, 1996, Shenerazade (Borodin), 2001. Dir., pres. Houston Soc. for Psychic Research, 1972—. Mem. Soc. Am. Magicians (pres. Houston chpt. 1985-86), Internat. Brotherhood Magicians (pres. Houston chpt. 1984-85), Tex. Assn. Magicians, Houston Assn. Magicians (pres. 1978-79), Magic Cir. London (MIMC with Gold Star), Phi Mu Alpha (warden 1966-67), Delta Phi Alpha. Lutheran. Avocation: psychic research. Home and Office: Adesso Verlag 7902 Roos Rd Houston TX 77036-6440 E-mail: bill@billpalmer.com.

PALMER, WILLIAM JOSEPH, accountant; b. Lansing, Mich., Sept. 3, 1934; s. Joseph Flammin Lacchia and Henrietta (Yagerman) P.; m. Judith Pollock, Aug. 20, 1960 (div. Nov. 1980); children: William W., Kathryn E., Leslie A., Emily J.; m. Kathleen Francis Booth, June 30, 1990; stepchildren: Blair T. Manwell, Lindsay H. Manwell. BS, U. Calif., Berkeley, 1963. CPA. With Coopers & Lybrand, 1963—80, mng. ptnr. Sacramento, 1976—80; ptnr. Arthur Young & Co., San Francisco, 1980—89, Ernst & Young, San Francisco, 1989—94; prof. U. Calif., Berkeley, 1994—. Bd. dirs. Dutra Group; chair constrn. industry group Coopers & Lybrand, 1973-80, Arthur Young, 1980-89, Ernst & Young, 1989-94; guest lectr. Engrng. Sch. Stanford U., 1976; lectr. Golden Gate Coll., 1975. Author: Businessman's Guide to Constuction, 1981, Construction Management Book, 1984, Construction Accounting and Financial Management, 5th edit., 1994, Construction Litigation-Representing The Contractor, 1992, Construction Insurance, Bonding and Risk Management, 1996. Bd. dirs. Sacramento Met. YMCA, 1976-82, KXPR, Sacramento 1976-85, V.p., 1979-82; bd. dirs. Sacramento Symphony Found., 1977-80; asst. state fin. chmn. Calif. Reagan for Pres., 1980. Lt. USN naval aviator, 1953-59. Mem. AICPA (vice chmn. com. constrn. industry 1975-81), Nat. Assn. Accts. (pres. Oakland/East Bay chpt. 1972, Man of Yr. 1968), Calif. Soc. CPAs, Assn. Gen. Contractors Calif. (bd. dirs. 1971-74), World Trade Club, Del Paso Country Club, Sutter Club, Lambda Chi Alpha. Roman Catholic. Avocations: antique boats, golf, book collecting, pipe collecting. Home: PO Box 60405 Sacramento CA 95860-0405 Office: Ernst & Young 560 Mission St San Francisco CA 94105-2907 Office Phone: 415-894-8850. Personal E-mail: kathpalm@hotmail.com.

PALMIERI, DORA ANN, retired language educator; b. Monmouth, Ill., Dec. 31, 1943; d. Gust John and Ruth Ida Douffas; m. Ronald Ernest Naedele, Feb. 3, 1966 (dec. Sept. 30, 1966); 1 child, Ronnann Naedele-Risha; m. Frank William Palmieri, Jan. 2004. BA in English, Milligan Coll., 1966; MA in English, E. Tenn. State U., 1974. Cert. tchr. Miss., Tenn., N.C., Md., Fla. Editor/asst. editor Courier And Gateway Newspapers, Suitland, Md., 1966—69; English tchr. Long Beach (Miss.) HS, 1969—74, Garinger HS Night Program, Charlotte, NC, 1974—76; curriculum specialist, English instr. Ctrl. Piedmont CC, Charlotte, 1976—81; mgr. tng. and devel. Control Data Corp. and Comml. Credit Corp., Charlotte, Balt., 1980—87; program designer, rschr. Rutledge Coll. Sys., Charlotte, 1987—88; assoc. prof. Daytona Beach (Fla.) CC, 1990—. Lead tchr. adult HS English Daytona Beach CC, 1998—. Co-author: Ecology: The Living World, 1996; author: English All Around Us, vols. 1-4, 1999—2003, Vols. 2, 3, 4. Singles' lay min. South Daytona Christian Ch., 1990—2001. Named Lay Person Of The Yr., Kiwanis Port Orange And South Daytona, 1996. Mem.: Fla. Assn. CCs, Nat. Coun. Tchrs. English. Avocations: photography, theater, writing, crafts, movies. Personal E-mail: hollyhilla@hotmail.com.

PALMIERI, FREDERICK WILLIAM, structural engineer; s. Mario and Maria Palmieri; m. Judy Anna Drystek, Dec. 22, 1973; children: Corey, Caroline. BS, MS, Stanford U., 1961; PhD, Madison U., 2003. Chief structures space sys. divsn. AVCO, Lowell, Mass., 1965—68; head basic loads Lockheed Missiles and Space Sys., Sunnyvale, Calif., 1957—65; dir. Palmieri Co., Phila., 1968—73; sect. head advanced rsch. and devel. Hughes Aircraft Co., Fullerton, Calif., 1973—74; cons. structural dynamics Palmieri Cons. Co., Anaheim Hills, Calif., 1974—92; dir. Marwais Internat., S.A., Luxembourg, 1992—94; pres. Pacific Consol. Co., Inc., Las Vegas, Nev., 1994—. Mem.: ASME, Soc. Exptl. Mech. Democrat. Roman Catholic. Avocation: golf. Office: Pacific Consol Co Inc 4300 Meadows Ln Ste 136 Las Vegas NV 89107 Home: 4302 Callahan Ave Las Vegas NV 89120 Home Phone: 310-640-2515. Office Fax: 702-433-5450. E-mail: fredpalmieri@hotmail.com.

PALMIERI, VICTOR HENRY, lawyer, director, investment advisor; b. Chgo., Feb. 16, 1930; s. Mario and Maria (Losacco) P.; children: Matthew B., John W.; m. Cathryn Connors, July 6, 1990. AB in History, Stanford U., 1951, JD, 1954. Bar: Calif. 1954. Assoc. O'Melveny & Myers, LA, 1955-59; exec. v.p. Janss Investment Corp., LA, 1959-63, pres., 1963-68; chmn. Pa. Co. and its subs. Great S.W. Corp., 1969-77; chmn. bd. Palmieri Co., NYC, 1969—. Chmn. PHL Corp., Inc. (formerly Baldwin-Unitaed Inc.), Phila., 1983—87; trustee, CEO Colo. Ute Electric Assn., Inc., 1990—92; spl. dep. rehabilitator Confedn. Life Ins. Co., 1994—98; dep. rehabilitator, CEO Mut. Benefit Life Ins. Co., 1991—94; pres., CEO MBL Life Assurance Corp., 1994—95; chmn. AlixPalmieri Assocs., 1997—99; bd. dirs. Mullin Cons., Inc., vice chmn., 2002—06; bd. dir. M Fin. Holdings Inc., M Benefit Solutions, M Fin. Investment Advisors, LA Universal Pre-Sch. Ambassador-at-large, coord. refugee affairs US Dept. State, 1979—81; chmn. Am. Learning Corp., 1970—85; dep. exec. dir. Nat. Adv. Commn. on Civil Disorders, 1967—68; mem. Coun. on Fgn. Rels.; trustee Rockefeller Found., 1979—89; pres. bd. dis. Lincoln Ctr. Theater, 1985—89; chmn. Overseas Devel. Coun., 1985—91; bd. trustees The Police Found., 1996—2002. Office: MullinTBG 2029 Century Park E 37th Fl Los Angeles CA 90067 Business E-Mail: victor.palmieri@mullintbg.com.

PALMISANO, SAMUEL J., information technology executive; b. Balt., July 29, 1951; m. Gaier Notman; 4 children. BA in History, Johns Hopkins U., 1973. Joined IBM, Balt., 1973, various sales, mktg. and prod. devel. positions, 1973—89, exec. asst. to IBM CEO John F. Akers, 1989; sr. mng. dir. ops. IBM Japan, 1991; pres., CEO Integrated Systems Solutions Corp., IBM subs., 1993—96; sr. v.p., group exec. IBM Personal Systems Group, 1997, IBM Global Svcs., 1998, IBM Enterprise Systems Group, 1999; pres., COO IBM, White Plains, NY, 2000—02, pres., CEO, 2002—03, chmn., pres., CEO, 2003—. Bd. dirs. IBM, 2000—, ExxonMobil Corp., 2006—. Trustee Johns Hopkins U. Recipient Disting. Alumni award, Johns Hopkins U., 2003. Avocations: golf, history, jogging, skiing. Office: IBM 1133 Westchester Ave White Plains NY 10604 *

PALMORE, JOHN STANLEY, JR., retired lawyer; b. Ancon, C.Z., Aug. 6, 1917; s. John Stanley and Antoinette Louise (Gonzalez) P.; m. Eleanor Anderson, July 31, 1938 (dec. 1980); 1 child, John Worsham (dec.); m. Carol Pate, Jan. 1, 1982. Student, Western Ky. State Coll., 1934-36; LL.B. cum laude, U. Louisville, 1939. Bar: Ky. 1938. Practice law, Henderson, 1939-42, 47-59; judge Ct. Appeals Ky. (name changed to Supreme Ct. Ky. 1975), 1959-82, chief justice, 1966, 73, 77-82; practice law Frankfort, Ky., 1983-84; ptnr. Palmore & Sheffer, Henderson, 1984-86; sr. counsel Jackson & Kelly, Lexington, Ky., 1986-92; ret., 1992. City pros. atty., Henderson, 1949-53, city atty., 1953-55; commonwealth's atty. 5th Circuit Ct. Dist. Ky., 1955-59 Served to lt. USNR, 1942-46, 51-52. Mem. VFW, Ky. Bar Assn., Am. Legion, Ky. Hist. Soc., Frankfort Country Club, Lexington Club, Frankfort Rotary Club (pres. 1993-94), Masons, Shriners, Elks, Phi Alpha Delta. Episcopalian (past vestryman, sr. warden). Home: 2310 Peaks Mill Rd Frankfort KY 40601-9437

PALMORE, RICK (RODERICK A.), lawyer, food products executive; b. Pitts., Feb. 14, 1952; s. Jefferson and Sophie (Spencer) Palmore; m. Lynne Avril Janifer, June 3, 1978; children: Jordan, Adam. BA in Econs., Yale U., 1974; JD, U. Chgo., 1977. Bar: Pa. 1977, Ill. 1982. Assoc. atty. Berkman, Ruslander, Pohl, Lieber & Engel, Pitts., 1977-79; asst. US atty. US Atty.'s Office, Chgo., 1979-82; assoc. atty. Wildman, Harrold, Allen & Dixon, Chgo., 1982-86, ptnr., 1986-93, Sonnenschein, Nath & Rosenthal, Chgo., 1993-96; v.p., dep. gen. counsel Sara Lee Corp., Chgo., 1996-99, sr. v.p., gen. counsel, sec., 1999—2004, exec. v.p., gen. counsel, sec., 2004—. Commr. Oak Park Plan Commn., 1988—, chair, 1994—; lectr. Youth Motivation Prog. Chgo. Coun. Commerce & Industry, 1989—; chair Oak Pk. Pub. Art Adv. Com., 2002—; bd. dirs. Pub. Interest Law Initiative, Legal Assistance Found. Chgo., Chgo. Bd. Options Exch., 2002—, Nuveen Investments, 2003—, United Way Met. Chgo., 2003-07; trustee Chgo. Symphony Orch., 2006—. Named one of Outstanding African-Am. Businessmen, Dollars & Sense mag., Chgo., 1991. Mem. ABA (monirity ptnrs. conf. 1991—), Nat. Bar Assn., Cook County Bar Assn., Chgo. Bar Assn. (bd. dirs. 1992-94, co-chmn. minority clerkshop prog. 1991-92), Chgo. Com. on Minorities in Law Firms (bd. dirs. 1990-92), Chgo. Bar Found. (bd. dirs. 1993-94). Mem. Trinity United Ch. Of Christ. Avocations: running, biking, tennis, reading. Office: Sara Lee Corp 3500 Lacey Rd Downers Grove IL 60515 Office Phone: 630-598-6000.

PALMQUIST, MARK L., energy and food products executive; Grad., Gustavus Adolphus Coll., St. Peter, Minn., 1979; student, U. Minn. Grain buyer Harvest States, Inver Grove Heights, Minn., 1979, v.p., dir. grain mktg. divsn., 1990-93, sr. v.p., 1993; exec. v.p., COO Ag. Bus. CHS Inc. (merger of Cenex and Harvest States), Inver Grove Heights, Minn., 2005—. Bd. dirs. Agriliance LLC, Ventura Foods, LLC, InTrade, Nat. Coop. Refinery Assn., Schnitzer Steel Industries, Inc., Portland, Oreg. Office: CHS Inc PO Box 64089 Saint Paul MN 55164-0089 Office Phone: 651-355-6000. *

PALMS, JOHN MICHAEL, academic administrator, physicist; b. Rijswijk, The Netherlands, June 6, 1935; naturalized, 1956; s. Peter Joannes and Mimi Adele (DeYong) P.; m. Norma Lee Cannon, June 2, 1958; children: John Michael, Danielle Maria, Lee Cannon. BS in Physics, The Citadel, 1958, DSc (hon.), 1980; MS in Physics, Emory U., 1959; PhD, U. N.Mex., 1966. Commd. 2d lt. USAF, 1958, retired capt. Res., 1970; lectr. physics dept. U. N.Mex., 1959-60; instr. physics dept. USAF Acad., 1961-62; staff mem. Western Electric Sandia Lab., 1961-62, U. Calif. Los Alamos Sci. Lab., 1962-66, Oak Ridge Nat. Lab., 1966; asst. prof. Emory U., Atlanta, 1966-69, assoc. prof., 1969-73, chmn., assoc. prof. dept. physics, asso. prof. radiology dept. Med. Sch., 1973-74, prof., chmn. dept. physics, 1969-74, dean Coll. Arts. and Scis., 1974-80, acting chmn. dept. math. and computer sci., 1976-77, v.p. arts and scis., acting chmn. dept. anthropology, 1979-80, acting dean Emory Coll., 1979-80, acting dir. Emory U. Computing Ctr., 1980-82, v.p. acad. affairs, 1982-88, interim dean Grad. Sch., 1985-86, Charles Howard Candler prof. nuclear, radiation and environ. physics, 1988-90; pres., prof. physics Ga. State U., Atlanta, 1989-91, U. S.C., Columbia, 1991—92. Chmn. bd. Assurant Inc., 2003-, Inst. for Def. Analyses; bd. dirs. Fortis, Inc., N.Y.C., Exelon Corp., Chgo., NCAA, Simcom Internat. Holdings, Inc., Atlanta, Computer Task Group, Assurant, 1990-; adv. com. Oak Ridge Nat. Lab., 1985-89; mem. nat. nuclear accredititng bd. Inst. Nuclear Power Ops., 1985-91, mem. nat. adv. coun., 1997-2001; mem. panel for semicondr. detectors NAS/NRC, 1963-74; cons. Acad. Natural Scis., Phila., Hughes, Inc., Santa Barbara, Calif., Tennelec, Inc., Three Mile Island Environ. Study, TRW Space Sys. Divsn., L.A., Ga. Dept. Human Resources, Nat. Cancer Inst.; mem. high tech. task force Atlanta C. of C. Contbr. articles on nuclear, atomic, med. and environ. physics to profl. jours. Mem. adv. bd. The Citadel, Oak Ridge Nat. Lab.; mem. exec. bd. Atlanta Area Coun. Boy Scouts of Am., 1989-90; mem. cmty. rels. bd. U.S. Penitentiary, Atlanta; trustee, chmn. Inst. Def. Analyses, Wesleyan Coll., 1984-89, Pace Acad., 1984-89, St. Joseph's Hosp., Atlanta, 1987-89, Ga. Rsch. Alliance, 1988-89; mem. S.C. Univs. Edn. Found., Devel. Found. and Rsch. Found., S.C. Rsch. Inst. Bds.; bd. dirs. Civic-Atlanta Partnership Bus. and Edn., Inc., 1988-90, United Way; chair Rhodes scholar selection com., 1987, S.C., 1995-99; bd. dirs. Nat. Merit Scholarship Corp. Mem. AAAS, Am. Phys. Soc., Am. Assn. Physics Tchrs., IEEE (Nuclear Sci. Group), Am. Nuclear Soc., Am. Coun. Edn., Coun. Provosts and Acad. V.P.s, Am. Conf. Acad. Deans, Soc. Nuclear Medicine, Health Physics Soc., Greater Columbia C. of C. (bd. dirs.), Rotary, Columbia C. of C., Phi Beta Kappa, Sigma Xi, Phi Kappa Phi, Omicron Delta Kappa, Sigma Pi Sigma. Home and Office: Pres U SCO Osborne Bldg Columbia SC 29208-0001 *

PALMS, ROGER CURTIS, writer, educator, minister; b. Detroit, Sept. 13, 1936; s. Nelson Curtis and Winifred Jessie (Bennett) P.; m. Andrea Sisson, Aug. 22, 1959; children: Grant Curtis, Andrea Jane BA, Wayne State U., 1958; B.D., Eastern Baptist Sem., Phila, 1961, M.Div., 1971, D.D., 1977; MA, Mich. State U., 1971. Ordained to ministry Am. Bapt. Chs., 1961. Pastor Ronceverte Bapt. Ch., W.Va., 1961-64; pastor 1st Bapt. Ch., Highland Park, NJ, 1964-67; chaplain Am. Bapt. Student Found., Mich. State U., East Lansing, 1967-73; assoc. editor Decision mag. Billy Graham Evang. Assn., Mpls., 1973-76, editor, 1976-98. Lectr. in field. Author: Enjoying the Closeness of God, 1989, Let God Help You Choose, 1989, An Unexpected Hope, 1998, Effective Magazine Writing, 2000, Your Best Years, 2003, others; newspaper columnist Trustee No. Bapt. Theol. Sem., 1973— Mem. Evang. Press Assn. (pres. 1991-93). Baptist. Personal E-mail: rcpalms@aol.com. *Investing in people's spiritual lives, giving time and counsel, will bring multiplied results for generations. It is one of the most far-reaching ways I can put faith to work.*

PALOLA, HARRY JOEL, retired international affairs executive, consultant; b. Kaukola, Viipuri, Finland, May 13, 1943; came to U.S., 1961; s. Heikki and Mary Dagmar (Ahokas) P.; m. Rita Hannele Ahokas, Sept. 15, 1968 (div. July 1992); children: Christine, Kathy, Kimberly. AA, LA City Coll., 1966; BS in Mech. Engring., Calif. State U., Long Beach, 1971; MA in Internat. Affairs, Calif. State U., Sacramento, 1995. Registered engr.-in-tng., Calif. Design engr. Northrop Corp., Hawthorne, Calif., 1971-77, Ford Aerospace and Comm. Corp., Newport Beach, Calif., 1977-81, B&M Assocs., San Diego, 1982; mech. engr. Raytheon Corp., Goleta, Calif., 1982-84; electronic packaging engr. LPL Tech. Svc., Seattle, 1984-86; design/test engr. Boeing Co., Seattle and Vandenberg, Calif., 1986-92; CEO Internat. Consultancy Corp., Santa Ynez, Calif., 1993—2003, ret., 2003. Cons. in basic and applied rsch. in human comm., 1993—2003. Author: International Finnish Studies: Language, History and Culture, 1995, The Karjala Question-Thoughts on Religious Directions, 1997. Econ. devel. student intern City of Sacramento, 1992-93. Sgt. USNG, 1966-72. Republican. Lutheran. Avocations: ocean sailing, private flying, Finno-Urgic and Ural-Altaic languages.

PALOW, JAMES ALEXANDER, real estate company executive; b. Miami, Fla., Nov. 25, 1975; s. James Walter Palow, Jr. and Irene Palow. BA in polit. sci., history, U. Fla., Gainesville, 1997. Enlisted USMC, 1990, advanced through grades to sgt., 1996; tchr. history, govt. W.R. Boone HS, Orlando, Fla., 1999—2000; sales mgr., owner Palow Properties Internat., Inc., Orlando, 2002—; dir. Operation Just Gratitude, Inc., Orlando, 2006—. Libertarian. Avocations: travel, bodybuilding. Home Phone: 321-234-2156; Office Phone: 321-234-2156. Office Fax: 407-378-4920; Home Fax: 407-378-4920. Business E-Mail: james@opjg.org.

PALOZZI, DINA, bank executive; b. 1951; BA, U. Toronto; MBA, York U. Dep. registrar of motor vehicles; dep. min. Revenue and Fin. Institutions, Correctional Services; CEO, supt., Fin. Services Fin. Services Commn. Ont.; sr. v.p., CPO BMO Fin. Grp.; exec. v.p., Client Rels. BMO Nesbitt Burns, 2001—. Dir. Providence Healthcare Found., Recycling Coun. Ont. Named one of 25 Women to Watch, US Banker, 2006. Mem.: Inst. Chartered Accountants. Office: BMO Financial Group PO Box 150 Stn 1st Canada Pl Toronto ON Canada M5X 1H3 *

PALSER, BARBARA F., retired botanist; b. Worcester, Mass., June 2, 1916; d. G. Norman and Cora A. (Munson) P. AB, Mt. Holyoke Coll., 1938, A.M., 1940, D.Sc. (hon.), 1978; PhD, U. Chgo., 1942. From instr. to prof. botany U. Chgo., 1942-65; from assoc. prof. to prof. botany Rutgers U., New Brunswick, NJ, 1965-83, dir. grad. program in botany, 1973-80; adj. prof. botany U. Mass., Amherst, 1991—. Erskine fellow U. Canterbury, Christchurch, N.Z. 1969; vis. prof. Duke U., Durham, N.C., fall 1962; vis. research fellow U. Melbourne, Parkville, Victoria, Australia, fall 1984-85 Author lab. manual Principles of Botany, 1973, also numerous research papers in bot. jours.; bot. adviser Ency. Brit., Chgo., 1958-59; editor Bot. Gazette, Chgo., 1960-65 Named Outstanding Tchr., Rutgers Coll., 1977 Mem. Bot. Soc. Am. (sec. 1970-74, v.p. 1975, pres. 1976, Merit award 1985), Torrey Bot. Club (pres. 1968), Internat. Soc. Plant Morphologists, N.J. Acad. Scis. (pres. elect 1987-88, pres. 1988-89, Outstanding Svc. award 1985, 90). Avocations: hiking, stamp collecting/philately, photography. Home: Rockridge Retirement Cmty 37 Coles Meadow Rd #303 Northampton MA 01060

PALSHO, DOROTHEA COCCOLI, information services executive; b. Phila., June 9, 1947; d. John Charles and Dorothy Lucille (Decker) Coccoli; m. Edward Robert Palsho; children: Christopher, Ryan, and Erica (stepchild). BS, Villanova Univ., 1976; MBA, Temple Univ., 1977. V.p. info. svc. Dow Jones and Co., Princeton, NJ, 1977-97, pres. bus. info. svc., 1995-97, v.p. interactive pub. NYC, 1997—2002, v.p. electronic pub., 2000—02, v.p. stragetic mktg., 2002—. Named to Class of Women Achievers, YWCA Acad. of Women Achievers, 1985. Avocation: sports. Office: Dow Jones and Co Inc 200 Liberty St New York NY 10281

PALSSON, BERNHARD O., engineering educator; PhD, U. Wis., 1984. Faculty mem. U. Mich., 1984—95, G.G. Brown assoc. prof., 1989; Olaf Hougen prof. U. Wis.; prof. bioengineering U. Calif., San Diego, adj. prof. medicine. Contbr. articles to profl. jours. Recipient Lindbergh Tissue Engring. award, 2001; grantee Inst. Internat. Edn. Fellowship, 1977, Rotary Fellowship, 1979, NATO Fellowship, 1984, Fulbright Fellow, 1995, Ib Henriksen Fellow, 1996. Mem.: NAE. Office: U Calif 9500 Gilman Dr Mail Code 0412 La Jolla CA 92093-0412 Office Phone: 858-534-5668. E-mail: palsson@ucsd.edu.

PALTER, ROBERT MONROE, humanities educator; b. NYC, June 19, 1924; s. Meyer and Mildred (Gilder) Palter; m. Ruth Rappeport, July 15, 1945 (div. 1953); 1 child, Alixe Daphne Cielo; m. Toni Ann Inman, Apr. 5, 1955 (div. 1977); children: Geoffrey Meyer, Jennifer Thorn Allan, Nicholas Trask, Adam Finch; m. Annette B. Weiner, May 21, 1979 (div. 1982). AB, Columbia U., 1943; PhD, U. Chgo., 1952. From instr. to assoc. prof. phys. scis. and philosophy U. Chgo., 1949-64; prof. philosophy and history U. Tex., Austin, 1964-82; Dana prof. history of sci. Trinity Coll., Hartford, Conn., 1983-91, prof. emeritus, 1991—. Author: (book) Whitehead's Philosophy of Science, 1960, The Duchess of Malfi's Apricots and Other Literary Fruits, 2002; editor: Toward Modern Science, 1961, The Annus Mirabilis of Sir Isaac Newton, 1971. With US Army, 1944—46. Mem.: Phi Beta Kappa. Personal E-mail: rmpalte55@sbcglobal.net.

PALTROW, GWYNETH, actress; b. LA, Sept. 28, 1972; d. Bruce Paltrow and Blythe Danner; m. Chris Martin, Dec. 5, 2003; children: Apple Blythe Alison Martin, Moses Martin. Student, U. Calif. Santa Barbara. Grad. Spence Sch., NYC, 1990. Spokesmodel Estee Lauder. Appeared in films: Shout, 1991, Hook, 1991, Malice, 1993, Flesh and Bone, 1993, Mrs. Parker and the Vicious Circle, 1994, Jefferson in Paris, 1995, Moonlight and Valentino, 1995, Seven, 1995, The Pallbearer, 1996, Emma, 1996, Hard Eight, 1996, Sliding Doors, 1998, Out of the Past, 1998 (voice), Great Expectations, 1998, Hush, 1998, A Perfect Murder, 1998, Shakespeare in Love, 1998 (Academy Award for Best Actress, Golden Globe for Best Actress), The Talented Mr. Ripley, 1999, Duets, 1999, The Intern, 2000, Bounce, 2000, The Anniversary Party, 2001, The Royal Tenenbaums, 2001, Shallow Hal, 2001, Possession, 2002, View From the Top, 2003, Sylvia, 2003, Sky Captain and the World of Tomorrow, 2004, Proof, 2005, Infamous, 2006, Love and Other Disasters, 2006, Running with Scissors, 2006; TV films: Cruel Doubt, 1992, Deadly Relations, 1993; Theatre: Picnic, The Adventures of Huck Finn, Sweet Bye and Bye, The Seagull, Proof. Mem. Screen Actors Guild (Outstanding Performance with others). Office: Creative Artists Agy c/o Rick Kurtzman 9830 Wilshire Blvd Beverly Hills CA 90212-1804 also: Screen Actors Guild 5757 Wilshire Blvd Los Angeles CA 90036-3635 *

PALUDA, ANDREW JOSEPH, lawyer, consultant; b. Ala., Mar. 31; s. Andrew Joseph and Catherine Paluda; m. Stephanie Paluda; children: Drew, Annika, Erik. JD, U. Detroit Sch. of Law, Mich. Bar: Mich. 1989, US Dist. Ct.: ea. dist., Mich. 1989, US Ct. Appeals: Mich. 1998. Shareholder Bigler, Berry, Johnston, et al, Troy, Mich., 1998—2006; founder, pres. Paluda Smolek, P.C., Troy, Mich., 2006—. Guest spkr. Macomb Dental Assn., Clinton Twp., Mich., 2007. Recipient AV rating, LexisNexis/Martindale-Hubbell, 1998—2007. Mem.: Oakland County Bar Assn. (assoc.), Mich. Def. Trial Counsel (assoc.). Achievements include listing in Preeminent Law Firms. Office: Paluda Smolek PC 3150 Livernois Ste 335 Troy MI 48083 Office Phone: 248-740-0203. Office Fax: 248-740-0243. E-mail: apaluda@paludasmolek.com.

PALUMBO, BENJAMIN LEWIS, public relations executive, consultant; b. Boston, Mar. 4, 1937; s. Guido Americo and Stella Marie (Lombardo) P.; m. Magdalene Julia Palinczar, Nov. l8, 1961; children: Matthew, Jason, Guy. BA, Rutgers U., 1959, MA, 1961. Adminstrv. asst. to Gov. Richard J. Hughes, NJ, 1963-65; dir. rsch. NJ Dem. Com., Trenton, 1965-66; asst. to commr. NJ Dept. Transp., Trenton, 1966-70; asst. dean Woodrow Wilson Sch., Princeton U., NJ, 1970—71; adminstrv. asst. to Senator Harrison Williams, US Senate, Washington, 1971-73, staff dir. US Ho. Dem. caucus, 1975-77, Ho. subcom. on govt. activities and transp., 1977-78; nat. campaign dir. Bentsen for Pres., Washington, 1973-75; dir. fed. govt. rels. Phillip Morris, Inc., Washington, 1978-83; chmn., CEO Palumbo & Cerrell, Inc., Washington, 1983—, pres., bd. dirs., 2004—06. Bd. dirs. Copyright Alliance. Bd. dirs., pres. Nyumbani Child of God Hospice and Orphanage; bd. dirs. John Mott Found. Mem.: NJ State Soc., Am. League Lobbyists, Nat. Dem. Club, Rutgers Club Washington, Nat. Press Club. Democrat. Roman Catholic. Office: 1001 G St NE Ste 600E Washington DC 20001 Office Phone: 202-777-0670. Office Fax: 202-879-9340. Business E-Mail: bpalumbo@covad.net.

PALUMBO, JAMES FREDRICK, finance company executive; b. Everett, Mass., Nov. 30, 1950; s. Bruno James and Lillian Elizabeth (Picardi) P.; m. Nancy Laurie Richards, July 24, 1976; children: Elizabeth Richards, Andrew Reid, Alexander Thomas. BA, Lake Forest Coll., Ill., 1973; MBA, Washington U., St. Louis, 1975. Market surveillance analyst Nat. Assn. of Securities Dealers, Washington, 1975-76, asst. treas., 1976-78; regional rep. Student Loan Mktg. Assn., Washington, 1978-79, mgr., 1979-81, dir., 1981-82, asst. v.p., 1982-83, v.p., 1983-87; sr. v.p. Connie Lee Mgmt. Svcs. Corp., Coll. Constrn. Loan Ins. Assn., Washington, 1987-95; with N.Y. Life Ins. Co., NYC, 1995—2000, N.Y. Life Securities Inc., NYC, 1995—2000; prin. Treasury Investment Svcs., Reston, Va., 2000—03; mng. dir. TransCapital Group, Reston, 2000—03, sr. mng. dir., 2003—04; v.p. RyanLabs Fund Mgmt. LLC, 2003—; registered broker Bedminster Fin. Group, 2003—06; prin. TransGlobal Capital LLC, 2004—06, Dynamic Capital Ptnrs. LLC, 2006—. Participant Govt.-Univ.-Industry Rsch. Roundtable, Washington, 1986; chmn. Palumbo Properties L.L.C.; chmn. Capital Holdings Ltd., Great Falls, Va. Actor popular and children's theater, 1973-76. Chmn. sports announcers com. D.C. Spl. Olympics, Washington, 1986, 87, D.C. Regional Counsel, Lake Forest Coll., Washington, 1976-80; mem. Elliott Soc. membership com. Washington U., 1986—, Great Falls (Va.) Hist. Soc., Great Falls Citizens Assn., 1996—; bd. govs. Lake Forest Coll., 1978-82, trustee, 1992-99; trustee Abruzzo and Molise Heritage Soc., 2002-03. Mem.: Washington Soc. Investment Analysts, Nat. Assn. Ins. and Fin. Advisors, Assn. for Investment Mgmt. and Rsch., Great Falls Swim and Tennis Club (bd. dirs. 1988—91), Alpha Psi Omega. Avocations: polo, horseback riding, painting. Office: Dynamic Capital Ptnrs 8120 Woodmont Ave Ste 960 Bethesda MD 20814 Home Phone: 703-759-6467; Office Phone: 301-229-8400. Business E-Mail: jpalumbo@dyncap.com.

PALUMBO, MATTHEW ALOYSIUS, marketing executive; b. Queens, NY, Sept. 17, 1961; s. John Christopher and Seiko (Murakami) P. BS, Cornell U., 1986; MBA in Mktg. Mgmt., St. John's U., 1990. Mortgage clk. Salomon Bros., Inc., NYC, 1986; mut. fund adminstr. Bank of N.Y. Co., Inc., NYC, 1986-88; copywriter Pierce Assocs., NYC, 1988-90; dir. mktg. cons. Palumbo Assocs., SI, 1989-90; adj. prof. St. John's U., SI, 1990; mktg. dir., copy dir. Flaghouse Inc., Mt. Vernon, NY, 1990-93; spl. projects mgr., group product mgr. Global Computer Supplies, Port Washington, NY, 1993-97; dir. product mktg. Cyberian Outpost, Kent, Conn., 1997—2000; pres. Palumbo Consultants, Kent, 2000—. Guest lectr. Am. direct mktg. techniques Sheffield Halleron U. (Eng.), 1993; guest lectr. designed and acquired funding Cornell U., Ithaca, 1992—. NY State Regents scholar, 1979, Annette Brodsky scholar, 1988. Mem. Am. Assn. MBA Execs., Cornell Asian Alumni Assn. (v.p. alumni affairs 1993-95), Cornell ILR Alumni, Direct Mktg. Club N.Y., Cornell Club N.Y., Cornell Club Fairfield County, Cornell U. Quadrangle Club, Beta Gamma Sigma. Avocations: reading, sports, music.

PALUMBO, MICHAEL, investment company executive; b. 1966; Ptnr. Third Millenium Investment Firm, Chgo., 1996—. Named one of Top 100 Fin. Traders in the World, Trader Monthly, 2004, 40 Under Forty, Crain's Bus. Chgo., 2005. *

PALUMBO, ROBERT CRAIG, sports medicine physician, director, not-for-profit developer; BA, Cornell U., Ithaca, NY, 1982; MD, Rutgers U., Piscataway, New Brunswick, NJ, 1986. Lic. physician Nat. Bd. of Med. Examiners, Pa., 1996, diplomate Am. Bd. Orthop. Surgery, 1996. Resident gen. surgery Robert Wood Johnson Med. Sch. (formerly Rutgers Med. Sch.), New Brunswick, NJ, 1988—92, resident orthop. surgery, 1992—93; fellow sports medicine Union Meml. Hosp., Balt., 1993—94; attending physician Orlando Orthopaedic Ctr. Lucerne Med. Plz., Orlando, Fla., 1994—98, Celebration Orthopaedic & Sports Medicine Inst., Fla., 1998—2002; dir. Orthop. Specialists Sports Medicine Inst. Found. Orthop. Assoc. Allentown, Pa., 2002—. Orthop. team leader Walt Disney World Marathon Med. Tent, Orlando, 1997—2002; team physician Browns Gym Metro Gymnastics Jr. Olympic Tng. Ctr., Orlando, 1994—2002, Orlando Cubs AA Farm Team, 1995—96, Chgo. Cub AA Farm Team, 1995—96, Orlando Ballet (formerly the So. Ballet Theater), Orlando, 1996—2002, LGE Sports Medicine Inst., Orlando, 1996—2002, Orlando Columbia Sundogs Soccer Team, Fla., 1997, Orlando Rays Baseball Team (Seattle Mariners & Tampa Bay Devil Rays) AA Farm Club, Orlando, 1997—98, Walt Disney World Wide World of Sports, Orlando, 1997—2002, U.S. Nat. Women's Soccer Team, 1997—, Orlando Nighthawks Soccer Club, Fla., 1998, World Telehealth InPlay Sports Health Mgmt., NFL Players Assn., 1998—, Cirque De Soleil La Nouba, Orlando, 1998—2002, Parkettes Nat. Tng. Ctr., Allentown, 2002—, Muhlenberg Coll. Athletics, Allentown, 2003—; reviewer The Am. Jour. of Sports Medicine, 2002—; med. dir. Orlando Regional Health Sys. Ctr. Performing Arts, Orlando, 1996—2002; cons. in field. Scholar, Cornell U., 1978—82. Mem.: Internat. Assn. Dance Medicine and Sci., Am. Orthop. Foot and Ankle Soc., Arthroscopy Assn. N.Am., Am. Coll. Sports Medicine, Am. Orthop. Soc. Sports Medicine, Am. Acad. Orthop. Surgeons (mem. sports medicine com., mem. sports medicine evaluation com.). Avocations: fishing, exercise, photography. Office: OAA Orthopaedic Specialists 250 Cetronia Road Allentown PA 18104 Office Phone: 610-973-6200.

PALUMBO, RUTH ANN, state legislator; b. Lexington, Ky., July 7, 1949; d. James Keith and Dorothy Calvin (Carrier) Baker; m. John Anthony Palumbo II, June 29, 1974; children: John A. III (dec.), Joseph Edward, James Thomas, Stephen Baker. BA in Secondary Edn., U. Ky., 1972. Sales Chez Lissette Boutique, Leysin, Switzerland, 1966; sales, shoes Purcell's Dept. Store, Lexington, Ky., 1966-70; organist Ctrl. Bapt. Ch., Lexington, Ky., 1968; clk. Good Samaritan Hosp., Lexington, Ky., 1968-73; sec. Dr. Joseph Keith, Lexington, Ky., 1971-73; senate clk. aide Ky. Gen. Assembly, Frankfort, Ky., 1974; pub. rels. Palumbo Properties, Lexington, 1974-92; state rep. Ky. Gen. Assembly, 1991—. Mem. LWV, Lexington, 1990-92, Ky. Women's Polit. Caucus, Louisville, 1991-92, NAt. Order Women Legislators, Washington, 1992; sec. Ctrl. Ky. Caucus, Lexington, 1991-92. Mem. Greater Lexington Dem. Women, fin. v.p., 1982; mem. Nat. Order of Women Legislators, Washington, 1992; legis-.liaison ACS Breast Cancer Detection Task Force, Ky., 1992; adv. coun. Bryan Sta. Youth Svcs. Ctr., Lexington, 1992; ball chmn. Lexington Philharmonic Women's Guild, 1990; govt. affairs Am. Symphony Orch. League Vol. Coun., Washington, 1992; bd. dirs. Philharmonic Women's Guild, pres., 1986-88; bd. dirs. Am. Cancer Soc., pres., 1988-89; bd. dirs. Lexington Phulharmonic Soc. Recipient Dorothy Moomaw Miles Svc. award Sayre Sch., 1986, Govs. Vol. Activist award Gov. Wallace G. Wilkinson, 1989, named Lexington's Outstanding Young Woman Bluegrass Jr. Woman's Club, 1982, Leadership Lexington, C. of C., 1988, Leadership Am. Found. for Women's Resources, Washington, 1989. Fellow U. Ky. Devel. Coun.; mem. Jr. League LExington (sec. 1989-90), Prof. Women's Forum, Gamma Phi Veta (pres. 1980-82). Baptist. Avocations: playing piano, singing, collecting stamps, music boxes, family. Home: 10 Deepwood Dr Lexington KY 40505-2106 Office: House of Reps State Capitol Annex Rm 370B Frankfort KY 40601

PALVINO, JACK ANTHONY, retired broadcasting executive; b. Rochester, NY, May 28, 1934; s. John Charles and Mary Aurelia P.; m. Joyce Ann Vilkaitis, Oct. 8, 1960; children: John Charles, Jill Marie, Jason Allen. BS, St. John Fisher Coll., 1955. Broadcaster, program dir. Sta. WGVA, Geneva, N.Y., 1958-60; radio personality Sta. WBBF, Rochester, N.Y., 1958-78; pres. Sports and Spls. TV, 1970-73; co-owner, exec. v.p. Lincoln Group Ltd., 1978-98; gen. mgr. Stas. WHAM, WVOR, WHTK, WPXY, Rochester, 1978-98; ret., 1998. Chmn. bd. trustees St. John Fisher Coll. Served with U.S. Army, 1957-58. Mem. St. John Fisher Alumni Assn., Nat. Assn. Broadcaster, Rochester Radio Broadcasters Assn. (pres. 1987-97), N.Y. State Broadcasters Assn., Rochester C. of C. Clubs: University, Rochester Press Radio (pres. 1974), Rotary. Roman Catholic. Home: 780 Beach Ave Rochester NY 14612-2028

PAMELA, TAYLOR K., writer, editor; b. Arlington, Va., July 22, 1964; d. Thomas W. and Linda K. Taylor; m. Syed Arif Khalid, Oct. 1, 1988; children: Tasneem Khalid, Saara Khalid, Ameera Khalid, Noora Khalid. BA, Dartmouth Coll., Hanover, NH, 1986; MTS, Harvard U., Cambridge, Mass., 1992. Dir. Islamic Writers Alliance, Phoenix, 2005—; founder Muslims for Prog. Values, LA, 2006—07. Editor Muslim Writers Publs., Phoenix, 2004—; panelist Newsweek-The Washington Post, 2007—. Author poetry. Co-chair Prog. Muslim Union, NYC, 2005—07; founder Muslims for Prog. Values, LA, 2007. Recipient Qalam Poetry award. Mem.: Nat. Writers Union. Democrat. Muslim. Avocations: science fiction, travel, interfaith activities. Home Phone: 513-777-5936. Personal E-mail: momtotsan@yahoo.com.

PAMIES, RUBENS JOHN, dean; s. George and Lillian Pamies. MD, SUNY at Buffalo, Sch. of Medicine, 1982—86. AAMC Health Services Reseaerch Institute ACP, 2004, diplomate Nat. Bd. Examiners, Am. Bd. Internal Medicine. Dir. and founder of minority affairs U. of South Fla. Coll. of Medicine, 1994; vice chancellor for academic affairs U. of Nebr. Med. Ctr., 2004—; program dir. Mt. Sinai Med. Ctr., Cleve., 1994—94; assoc. dean for academic programs and student affairs Case Western Res. U. Sch. of Medicine, Cleve., 1994—2000; chmn. and prof. Meharry Med. Coll., Nashville, 2000—03; prof. of medicine Vanderbilt U. Sch. of Medicine, Nashville, 2001—03; chief of svc. Met. Nashville Gen. Hosp., 2000—03; prof. of internal medicine U. of Nebr. Med. Ctr., 2004—, dean of grad. studies, 2004—. Author: (text book) Multicultural Medicine And Health Disparities. Mem. Va.-Nebr. Alliance, Richmond, Va., 2004, Joslyn Art Mus., Omaha, 2004. Grant, Nat. Heart, Lung, & Blood Inst., 2002, scholarship, Case Western Res. U. SOM, 2000—. Mem.: ACP, AMA, Assn. of Am. Med. Colleges, Internat. Soc. of Hypertension in Blacks, Assn. of Academic Minority Physicians. Achievements include research in early clinical exposure and its effect in performance in the third year clearkship. Office: Univ of Nebr Med Ctr 987810 Nebraska Med Ctr Omaha NE 68198-7810 Home Phone: 402-559-6605; Office Phone: 402-559-5130. Office Fax: 402-559-7845. Personal E-mail: rpamies@unmc.edu.

PAMPLIN, ROBERT BOISSEAU, SR., retired textile manufacturing executive; b. Sutherland, Va., Nov. 25, 1911; s. John R. and Pauline P. (Beville); m. Mary K. Reese, June 15, 1940; 1 child, Robert Boisseau Jr. BBA, Va. Poly. Inst. & State U., 1933; postgrad., Northwestern U., 1933-34; LLD (hon.), U. Portland, Oreg., 1972; LHD (hon.), Warner Pacific Coll., 1976. With Ga.-Pacific Corp., Portland, 1934-76, sec., from 1936, adminstrv. v.p., 1952-55, exec. v.p., 1955-57, pres., 1957-67, chmn. bd., chief exec. officer, from 1967; ret., 1976; with R.B. Pamplin Corp., 1957—, chmn. bd., CEO, to 1996, Mt. Vernon Mills Inc. (subs. R.B. Pamplin Corp.), Greenville, S.C., retired, 1996. Office: R B Pamplin Corp Ste 2400 805 SW Broadway Portland OR 97205-3341

PAMPLIN, ROBERT BOISSEAU, JR., manufacturing company executive, minister, writer; b. Augusta, Ga., Aug. 3, 1941; s. Robert Boisseau and Mary Katherine (Reese) P.; m. Marilyn Joan Hooper; children: Amy Louise, Anne Boisseau. Student, Va. Poly. Inst., 1960-62, BSBA, 1964, BS in Acctg., 1965, BS in Econs., 1966; BS (hon.), Va. Tech., 2001; LHD (hon.), Va. Poly. Inst., 1995, Pacific U., 2001; DHL (hon.), Va. Poly. Inst., 1995; MBA, U. Portland, 1968, LLD (hon.), 1972, MEd, 1975; MA, Western Conservative Bapt. Sem. (name now Western Sem.), 1978, DMin, 1982, D (hon.) of Sacred Letter, 1991, MA, 2000; PhD, Calif. Coast U.; DHL (hon.), Warner Pacific Coll., 1988; LLD (hon.), Western Baptist Coll., 1989, George Fox U., 2005; cert. in wholesale mgmt., Ohio State U., 1970; cert. labor mgmt., U. Portland, 1982; cert. in advanced mgmt., U. Hawaii, 1975; DD (hon.), Judson Baptist Coll., 1984; DBA (hon.), Marquis Giuseppe Scicluna Internat. U. Found., 1986; LittD (hon.), Va. Tech. Inst. and State U., 1987, LHD (hon.), Western Seminary, 1991; DD, Western Evang. Sem., 1994; DBA (hon.), U. S.C., 1996; D Pub. Svc., DHL (hon.), U. Puget Sound, Pacific U., 1999, 2001; BS in Bus. Adminstrn. (hon.), Va. Inst. Tech., 2001. Pres., CEO R.B. pamplin Corp., Portland, Oreg., 1964—. Chmn. bd., CEO Columbia Empire Farms Inc., Lake Oswego, Oreg., 1976—, Pamplin Comms.; chmn. bd., CEO Mt. Vernon Mills Inc.,; pres., CEO Ross Island Sand & Gravel; lectr. bus. adminstrn. Lewis and Clark Coll., 1968-69; adj. asst. prof. bus. adminstrn., U. Portland, 1973-76; pastor Christ Cmty. Ch., Lake Oswego; lectr. in bus. adminstrn. and econs. U. Costa Rica, 1968, Va. Tech. Found., 1986; chmn. bd. dirs. Christian Suppl1y Ctrs. Inc.; prof. with tenure U. Portland, 1999. Author: Everything is Just great, 1985, The Gift, 1986, Another Virginian: A Study of the Life and Beliefs of Robert Boisseau Pamplin, 1986; author: (with others) A Portrait of Colorado, 1976, Three in One, 1974, The Storybook Primer on Managing, 1974, One Who Believed, Vol. I, 1988, vol. II, 1991, Climbing the Centuries, 1993, Heritage the Making of an American Family, 1994, American Heroes, 1995, Prelude to Surrender, 1995, Alaska Gold, 1998, Robert Reese, 1998; editor: Oreg. Mus. Sci. and Industry Press, 1973; trustee Oreg. Mus. Sci. and Industry Press, 1971, 1974—; editor: Portrait of Oregon, 1973; editor: (with others) Oregon Underfoot, 1975. Trustee Lewis and Clark Coll., 1989—, chmn. bd. trustees, 1988-96, life trustee 1996-; hon. life pres. Western Conservative Bapt. Sem.; chmn. regents Western Sem., 1994; mem. nat. adv. coun. on vocat. Edn., 1975—; mem. Western Interstate Com. on Higher Edn., 1981-84; co-chmn. Va. Tech. $50 Million Campaign for Excellence, 1984-87, Va. Tech. Found., 1986—, Va.-Oreg. State Scholarship Commn., 1974—, chmn. 1976-78; mem. Portland dist. adv. coun. SBA, 1973-77; mem. rewards rev. com., City of Portland, 1973-78, chmn., 1973-78; bd. regents U. Portland, 1971-79, chmn. bd., 1975-79, regent emeritus, 1979—; trustee Oreg. Episc. Schs., 1979, Linfield Coll., U. Puget Sound, 1989—; dr. pub. svc., U. Puget Sound, 1999; chmn. bd. trustees Portland Art Mus., 2003-05. Named Outstanding Philanthropist of Yr. award, Nat. Soc. Fund Raising Execs., 1997, Western Conservative Bapt. Sem. Lay Inst. for Leadership, Edn. Devel. and Rsch. named for R.B. Pamplin Jr., 1988, Textile World's Top 10, 1999, Portland First Citizen, Portland Met. Assn. Realtors, 1999, Parents of Yr., Juvenile Diabetes Found., 2001, Entrepreneur of Yr., Oreg. Entrepreneur Forum, 2001, Va. Tech. Coll. Bus. Adminstrn. renamed R.B. Pamplin Coll. Bus. Adminstrn. in his honor, U. Portland Sch. Bus. renamed Dr. Robert B. Pamplin, Jr. in his honor, Civil War Preservationalist of Yr., Civil War Preservation Trust, 2003, Nat. Vol. of Yr., Vols. of Am., 2006; named one of 20 Most Influential Execs. Past 20 Yrs., Bus. Jour.; recipient Disting. Alumnus award, Lewis and Clark Coll., 1974, ROTC Disting. Svc. award, USAF, 1974, bronze medal, Albert Einstein Acad., 1986, Disting. Leadership medal, Freedoms Found., Disting. Bus. Alumnus award, U. Portland, 1990, Nat. Caring award, Caring Inst., 1991, Pride of Portland award, Portland Lions Club, Hero Athlete award, 1994, Herman Lay Entrepreneurship award, 1995, Thomas Jefferson award, Oreg. Hist. Soc., 1998, Aubrey R. Watzek award, Lewis and Clark Coll., 1998, Leadership award, Portland Living Mag., 1998, Unique Contbns. to Comms. award, Portland Advt. Fedn., 2001, Oliver Wendell Holmes, Jr. award for Civil War Preservationalist of Yr., 2001, Govs. Arts award, 2001, Legacy award, Civil War Preservation Trust, 2003, Gov.'s Gold award as Oregonian of Achievement, 2003, Corp. Citizenship award, Woodrow Wilson Internat. Ctr. for Scholars, 2005. Mem. Acad. Mgmt., Delta Epsilon Sigma, Beta Gamma Sigma, Sigma Phi Epsilon, Waverley Country Club (pres. 2003-04), Arlington, Multnomah Athletic Clulb, Capitol Hill Club, Greenville Country Club, Poinsett Club, Eldorado Country Club, Thunderbird Country Club, Rotary. Republican. Episcopalian. Office: RB Pamplin Corp Inc Ste 2400 805 SW Broadway Portland OR 97205-3341

PAMPUSCH, ANITA MARIE, foundation administrator; b. St. Paul, Aug. 28, 1938; d. Robert William and Lucille Elizabeth (Whaley) P. BA, Coll. of St. Catherine, St. Paul, 1962; MA, U. Notre Dame, 1970, PhD, 1972. Tchr. St. Joseph's Acad., St. Paul, 1962-66; instr. philosophy Coll. of St. Catherine, St. Paul, 1970-76, assoc. acad. dean, 1979, acad. dean, 1979-84, pres., 1984-97; Am. Council Edn. fellow Goucher Coll., Balt., 1976-77; pres. Bush Found., St. Paul, 1997—. Bd. dirs. St. Paul Cos.; head Women's Coll. Coalition, 1988-91. Author: (book rev.) Philological Quarterly, 1976; contbr. articles to profl. jours. Mem. adv. com. Instl. Leadership project, Columbia U., 1986—; dist. chmn. Rhodes Scholarship Selection com., Mo., Neb., Minn., Kans., N.D., S.D., 1987—; exec. com. Women's Coll. Coalition, Washington, 1985—. Mem. Coun. for Ind. Colls. (bd. dirs. 1987—, chair 1991—), Am. Philos. Assn., St. Paul C. of C. (bd. dirs. 1986—), St. Paul's Athletic Club, Mpls. Club, Phi Beta Kappa. Roman Catholic. Avocations: swimming, camping, reading, music. Home: 161 Stonebridge Rd Saint Paul MN 55118

PAN, BING, information technology educator, researcher; b. Jining, Shandong, China, Jan. 7, 1974; arrived in US, 1998; s. Yaocai Pan and Shiying Liu; m. Yunfang Jiang, Jan. 15, 1997; 1 child, Alexander. B in Econs., Nanjing U., China, 1995; PhD in Tourism Mgmt., U. Ill., Urbana, 2003. Post-doctoral fellow Cornell U., Ithaca, NY, 2003—05; asst. prof. Coll. Charleston, SC, 2005—. Head rsch. Office Tourism Analysis, Coll. Charleston, 2005—. Grantee, SC Dept. Natural Resources, 2005—06, Inst. Mus. and Libr. Svcs., 2005; Disting. Ill. fellow, U. Ill., 1998—2001. Achievements include research in new conceptual framework and methodology to study online trip planning behavior; design of map-based interface for planning trips to Charleston; map-based handheld device for travel information access. Office: College of Charleston 5 Liberty St Charleston SC 29424 Home Phone: 843-901-9304; Office Phone: 843-953-2025. Office Fax: 843-953-5697; Home Fax: 843-953-5697. Personal E-mail: bp58@cornell.edu. Business E-mail: panb@cofc.edu.

PAN, DEMING, chemistry professor; b. Shanghai, May 9, 1944; arrived in U.S., 1988; d. Han Qing and Jian (Zuo) Pan; 1 child, Xiaosheng Huang. BSChemE, Tian Jing U., China, 1966; MSChemE, Chem. Engring. Inst. East China, 1983; MS in Inorganic Chemistry, Kent State U., Ohio, 1993, PhD in Phys. Chemistry, 1995. Chem. engr. Shanghai Rsch. Inst. Materials, 1983—88; tchg. asst. chemistry Kent State U., 1988—93, vis. asst. prof., 1996—98; prof. chemistry Mid-Plains CC, North Platte, Nebr., 1998—. Contbr. articles to profl. publs. Mem.: Am. Chem. Soc. Office Phone: 308-535-3743. Business E-Mail: pand@mpcc.edu.

PAN, YA-HUI LAURIE, toxicologist, director; m. Larry Swales. BS in Biology & Chemistry, Bethel Coll., N.Newton, Kans., 1983—87; PhD in Toxicology, U. Kans. Med. Ctr., Kans. City, 1987—92. Diplomate of American Board of Toxicology Am. Bd. of Toxicology/North Carolina, 1996. Human safety toxicologist Proctor & Gamble, Co., Hunt Valley, Md., 1992—94; sr. scientist product safety Mary Kay, Inc., Dallas, 1994—95, group leader product safety, 1995—2000, mgr. product safety, 2000—05; dir. regulatory affairs Sally Beauty Holdings, Inc., Denton, Tex., 2006—. Chmn. safety & regulatory toxicology com. Cosmetic, Toiletry & Fragrance Assn., DC, 2002—04. Mem.: Am. Contact Dermatitis Soc. (assoc.), Am. Acad. Dermatology (assoc.), Soc. Toxicology (assoc.).

PAN, YI, computer science educator; b. Wujiang, Jiangsu, China, May 12, 1960; came to U.S., 1987; s. Jun and Xiuzhen (Fei) P.; m. Hong Miao, Aug. 4, 1986; children: Marissa, Anna. BEng, Tsinghua U., Beijing, 1982, MEng, 1984; MSc, U. Pitts., 1988, PhD in Computer Sci., 1991. Rsch. asst. Tsinghua U., 1982-86; tchg. asst. U. Pitts., 1987-89, tchg. fellow, 1989—91; asst. prof. computer sci. U. Dayton, Ohio, 1991-96, assoc. prof. Ohio, 1996-2000; assoc. prof. computer sci. Ga. State U., Atlanta, 2000—, now chair computer sci. Director of Graduate Studies in Computer Science University of Dayton, Dayton, 1998—2000. Contbr. articles to profl. jours. Recipient Rsch. Opportunity award NSF, 1995, Investment Competition Fund award Ohio Bd. Regents, 1996, World Acad. Scis. Achievement award, 2002; Mellon Found. fellow 1990, Summer Rsch. fellow U. Dayton Rsch. Coun., 2000, Air Force Office for Sci. Rsch., JSPS fellow, 1998. Mem.: IEEE (sr.; Secretary of the IEEE Computer Society Dayton Chapter 1996—97, IEEE Computer Society Distinguished Visitor Program Speaker 2000). Home: 615 Summer Breeze Ter Alpharetta GA 30005-6431 Office: Ga State U Computer Sci Dept 34 Peachtree St Ste 1450 Atlanta GA 30303 E-mail: pan@cs.gsu.edu.

PAN, YUE, finance educator; B in Econs., Tsinghua U., 1996; PhD, U. Ga., Athens, 2003. Instr. U. Ga., Athens, 1999—2003; asst. prof. mktg. U. Dayton, Ohio, 2003—. Reviewer profl. jours. Author: Advertising Management, 1999; contbr. articles to profl. jours., chapters to books. Recipient Mary Kay award, Acad. Mktg. Sci., 2002, Grad. Student Outstanding Tchg. award, U. Ga., 2003; grantee, SBA, 2003—07, U. Dayton, 2005—06, 2005—07; scholar, U. Ga., 2002; Cohen scholarship, 2002—03, Comer Rsch. fellowship, 1999—2002. Mem.: Soc. Consumer Psychology, Assn. Consumer Rsch., Am. Mktg. Assn. Office Phone: 937-229-1773.

PANAGIDES, JOHN, pharmacologist; b. NYC, Aug. 15, 1944; s. Chris and Sophie (Marmar) P.; m. Kathleen Ann Heimann, July 9, 1967; children: Christopher, Melissa, Adrienne. BS, CCNY, 1966; MS, U. N.C., 1968; PhD, SUNY, Buffalo, 1972. Rsch. assoc. Rockefeller U., NYC, 1972-73; sr. scientist Lederle Labs., Pearl River, NY, 1973-83; sr. clin. monitor Ayerst Labs., NYC, 1983-87; dir. clin. projects, CNS Organon Pharms. USA Inc., 1987-99, sr. dir. clin. projects, CNS, 1999—. Contbr. articles to profl. jours. NDEA Title IV fellow, Chapel Hill, 1966-68. Mem. AAAS, Am. Soc. Pharmacology and Exptl. Therapeutics, Am. Coll. Neuropsychopharmacology, N.Y. Acad. Scis. Achievements include development of haemophilus influenza vaccine, 23-valent pneumococcal vaccine, fenbufen, lodine, cotazym, cotazym-S, zymase, remeron. Home: 7 Catawba Dr West Nyack NY 10994-2304 Office: Organon Pharms USA Inc 56 Livingston Ave Roseland NJ 07068 E-mail: j.panagides@organonusa.com.

PANAGIOTOPOULOS, ATHANASSIOS ZOIS, chemical engineering educator; b. Thessaloniki, Greece, Mar. 27, 1960; m. Maria Alivisatos, May 30, 1998. PhD, MIT, 1986; grad., Nat. Tech. U. of Athens, 1982. Prof. Princeton U., 2000—. Recipient Presdl. Young Investigator Award, NSF, 1989, Colburn Award, Am. Inst. Chem. Engring., 1995, John M. Prausnitz Award in Applied Chem. Thermodynamics, 1998. Mem.: NAE. Office Phone: 609-258-4591. Office Fax: 609-258-0211. E-mail: azp@princeton.edu.

PANAGOS, STEVEN GREGORY, food products executive; b. Royal Oak, Mich., Nov. 18, 1961; s. George William and Anna (Pappas) P.; m. Joan Kwiatkoski. BS in Acctg., U. Mich., 1983. CPA; cert. insolvency reorganization acct. Sr. acct. KMG Main Hurdman, Stamford, Conn., 1984-86; corp. contr. Van Wagner Comms., Inc., NYC, 1986-88; prin. Zolfo Cooper, LLC, NYC, 1988—; pres., COO Krispy Kreme Doughnuts Inc., 2005—. Mem. adv. bd. CDC Techs., Inc., Newtown, Conn., 1990—, Contract Rec. Co., N.Y.C., 1996—, Eaton Life Ins. Co., N.Y.C., 1995-96. Mem. Patterson Club. Greek Orthodox. Avocations: golf, tennis. Home: 1129 Sasco Hill Rd Fairfield CT 06430-6346 Office: Zolfo Cooper LLC 7th Fl 292 Madison Ave Fl 7 New York NY 10017-6307 also: Krispy Kreme Doughnut Corp PO Box 83 Winston Salem NC 27102

PANARESE, WILLIAM C., civil engineer; b. Framingham, Mass., Mar. 6, 1929; s. Angelo and Stephanie (Di Profio) P. BSCE, Purdue U., 1952. Structural research engr. Assn. Am. Railroads, Chgo., 1952-55; with Portland Cement Assn., Chgo. and Skokie, Ill., 1957-76, 80-94, mgr. concrete tech. sect., 1973-76, assoc. mgr. bldg. constrn. sect., 1980-83, mgr. bldg. tech. dept., 1983-86, mgr. constrn. info. services dept., 1987-94. Author, editor: Concrete Floors on Ground, 1983, Transporting and Handling Concrete, 1987, The Homeowner's Guide to Building with Concrete, Brick and Stone, 1988, Cement Mason's Guide, 1990, Concrete Masonry Handbook for Architects, Engineers, Builders, 1991, Fiber Reinforced Concrete, 1991, High Strength Concrete, 1994, Design and Control of Concrete Mixtures, 2002, Performance of Architectural Concrete Panels in the PCA Outdoor Display, 2004, Environmental Performance of Concrete, 2005, Concrete Floors and Moisture, 2005, Specifier's Guide to Durable Concrete, 2005, Concrete Finisher's Guide, 2006, author, editor: other bldg. guides and handbooks; editor: Concrete Constrn. mag., 1976—80, Concrete Tech. Today newsletter, 1980—94. Served with C.E. U.S. Army, 1955-57. Fellow Am. Concrete Inst. (coms. 302 on constrn. of concrete floors and slabs, 332 on residential concrete work, chmn. 332 1984-88), Chi Epsilon. Roman Catholic. Avocations: music, walking, tennis, skiing, writing. Home and Office: 1625 Glenview Rd Unit 304 Glenview IL 60025-2973 Office Phone: 847-729-5885. Personal E-mail: wmpanarese@aol.com.

PANATIER, CHRISTOPHER J., lawyer; BA, U. Tex., Austin, 1998, JD, 2001. Bar: Tex. 2001. Assoc. asbestos litig. sect. Baron & Budd, P.C., Dallas, 2001—. Contbr. articles to profl. publs. Named a Rising Star, Tex. Super Lawyers mag., 2006. Office: Baron & Budd PC 3102 Oak Lawn Ave Ste 1100 Dallas TX 75219 Office Phone: 214-521-3605. *

PANCHYK, RICHARD ROBERT, writer; b. Elmhurst, NY, Mar. 30, 1970; s. Robert Panchyk and Katherine Arvai; m. Caren Prommersberger, June 11, 1994; children: Matthew, Elizabeth. BA in Anthropology, Adelphi U., Garden City, NY, 1992; MA in Anthropology, U. Mass., Amherst, 1994, postgrad. in anthropology, 1996. Inst. U. Mass., Mass., 1994—95. Author (with Katherine Panchyk): The CADD Department, 1991, CAD Management, 1998; author: (with Matthys Levy) Engineering the City, 2000; author: Archaeology for Kids, 2001; author: (foreword by Senator John McCain) World War II for Kids, 2002 (Notable Book, Children's Lit. Coun., Nat. Tchrs. Social Studies, 2003, 10 Most Popular Student-Selected Books award, Hong Kong, 2006); author: American Folk Art for Kids, 2004; author: (foreword by Buzz Aldrin) Galileo for Kids, 2005; author: (foreword by Senator John Kerry) Our Supreme Court, 2006; author: (foreword by Senator Edward Kennedy) Franklin Delano Roosevelt for Kids, 2007; author: A History of Westbury, Long Island, 2007; editor: Handbook of Amherst, 2008; contbr. (ency.) Americans at War, 2004. Mem.: Author's Guild. Democrat. Episcopalian. Avocations: book collecting, antiques, genealogy. Personal E-mail: panchyk@yahoo.com.

PANDEY, RAMESH CHANDRA, chemist, chemicals executive; b. Naugaon, Uttranchal, India, Nov. 5, 1938; arrived in US, 1967; s. Gauri Dutt and Jivanti Pandey. BSc, U. Allahabad, India, 1958; MSc, U. Gorakhpur, India, 1960; PhD, U. Poona, India, 1965. Jr. rsch. fellow CSIR Nat. Chem. Lab., Poona, 1960-64, rsch. officer, 1965-67, scientist organic divsn., 1970-72; rsch. assoc. dept. chemistry U. Ill., Urbana, 1967-70, vis.

scientist, 1972-77; sr. scientist fermentation program Nat. Cancer Inst. Frederick (Md.) Cancer Rsch. Facility, 1977-82, head chem. sect., 1982-83; sr. scientist Abbott Labs., North Chicago, Ill., 1983-84; pres. Xechem, Inc., Melrose Pk., Ill., 1984-90, pres., CEO, dir. tech. devel. New Brunswick, NJ, 1990—2003; chmn., CEO, pres. Xechem Internat. Inc., 1994—2004, chmn., CEO, 2004—07; chmn., CEO, pres. Xetapharm Inc., 1996—2007; chmn. Pres. G.D. Pandey Ayurved U., 2001—. Cons. Washington U. Sch. Medicine, St. Louis, 1976-85, LyphoMed, Inc., Melrose Park, 1984-85; vis. prof. Waksman Inst. Rutgers U., Piscataway, NJ, 1984-86; mem. life sci. adv. bd. NJTC, 1999—; mem. statewide adv. com. bd. mgrs. NJ Agrl. Exptl. Sta., Rutgers State U. NJ in Biotechnology, 2002—; founder G.D. Padney Ayurved U., New Brunswick, NJ. Mem. editl. bd. Internat. Jour. Antibiotics, 1986—; patentee graft thin layer chromatography; several US and internat. patents for the isolation and purification of antiobiotics and anticancer agents. Mem. Middlesex County (NJ) Work Force Investment Bd., 1999-2005; mem. adv. com. for sci. transfer and sci. tech. program Middlesex County Coll., Edison, NJ, 1999-2001. Fellow Am. Inst. Chemists; mem. Am. Chem. Soc., Am. Soc. Microbiology, Am. Soc. Mass Spectrometry, Am. Assn. Cancer Rsch., Am. Soc. Hosp. Pharmacists, Am. Soc. Pharmacognosy, Soc. Indsl. Microbiology, NY Acad. Scis., Indian Sci. Congress Assn., Am. Acad. Ayurvedic Medicine (founder, exec. trustee), Rotary Club (Paul Harris fellow 1996—, pres. New Brunswick club 1999-2000). Office: Xechem Internat Inc New Brunswick Tech Ctr 100 Jersey Ave Ste B-310 New Brunswick NJ 08901-3200 Home Phone: 732-846-3969; Office Phone: 732-317-8124. Business E-Mail: ramesh@gdpaul.com.

PANDIAN, SHANTHA G., psychiatrist; b. Bklyn., Dec. 19, 1972; d. Dorairaj Sivajothi and Sugirtha Rose Pandian; m. Juan Francisco Rodriguez, Apr. 24, 1998; children: Christopher Rodriguez, Ethan Rodriguez. MBBS, Kasturba Med. Coll., India, 1995. Cert. MD Tenn., Fla., diplomate psychiatry Am. Bd. Psychiatry Neurology. Psychiatry residency E. Tenn. State U., Johnson City, 1997—2001; assoc. chief mental health clin., outpatient psychiatrist James H. Quillen Vets. Admntrn. Med. Ctr., Mt. Home, Tenn., 2001—; asst. prof. psychiatry E. Tenn. State U., 2001—. Chair psychiatry and neurology section Southern Med. Assn., Ala., 2003—. Mem.: Southern Med. Assn. (chair 2003—). Meth. Avocations: reading, exercise, cooking. Office: James H Quillen Vets Adminstrn Med Clinic PO Box 4000 Johnson City TN 37604 Office Phone: 423-926-1171.

PANDINA, GAHAN J., psychologist, researcher; b. Burlington, Vt., Dec. 13, 1968; s. Nancy and Robert Pandina, Valerie Johnson (Stepmother); m. Gillian Roth, Sept. 23, 1995; children: Alexander, Jake. PhD, Binghamton U., NY, 2000. Dir. clin. devel. Janssen, LP, Titusville, NJ, 2001—07; dir., clin. devel. J&J Pharm. R & D, Titusville, 2007—. Bd. dirs. Family Resource Network (Autism Family Svcs.), Trenton, NJ, 2003—07. Mem.: APA. Office: Johnson & Johnson 1125 Trenton Harbourton Road Titusville NJ 08560 Home Phone: 609-918-9554; Office Phone: 609-730-2324. Personal E-mail: gahan@optonline.net. Business E-Mail: gpandina@omjus.jnj.com.

PANDIT, VIKRAM S., investment banker; b. Bombay, 1957; married; 2 children. BS, Columbia U., 1976, MBA, 1980, PhD, 1986. Fin. prof. Columbia U.; mng. dir. Morgan Stanley & Co., 1990—94; head of equity derivatives Morgan Stanley Group Inc., 1994—96; head of instl. equity divsn. Morgan Stanley, 1997—2000, co. pres., COO instl. securities divsn., 2000—03, pres. COO, instl. securities divsn., 2003—05; co-founder Old Lane Capital Mgmt. LLC, 2005—07; CEO, Citi Alternative Investments Citigroup Inc., 2007—. Bd. dirs. NASDAQ, 2000—03, NYC Investment Fund. Office: Citi Alternative Investments 731 Lexington Ave 27th Fl New York NY 10022 *

PANDOLFE, JOHN THOMAS, JR., lawyer; b. Neptune, NJ, Dec. 15, 1941; s. John T. and Jeannette R. (Pullen) P.; m. Linda Lee Fritzsche, July 12, 1969; children: Leslie, Matthew. AB, U. Miami, 1965; MS, Monmouth Coll., 1973; JD, U. Miami, 1975. Bar: Fla. 1976, NJ 1976, U.S. Dist. Ct. NJ 1976. Ptnr. Pandolfe, Shaw & Rubino, Spring Lake, NJ. Mem.: ABA, Monmouth Bar Assn., NJ Bar Assn., Fla. Bar Assn., Spring Lake Golf Club. Office: Pandolfe Shaw and Rubino 215 Morris Ave Spring Lake NJ 07762-1360

PANDOLFI, FRANCES, health facility administrator; b. NYC, Sept. 7, 1944; d. Frank Pandolfi and Rose McGinn; m. Edmund Lewiska Menelik Bobbitt, May 19, 1973. BA, Vassar Coll., 1965; MPA, NYU, 1990. Health planner N.Y.C. Dept. City Planning, 1965-74; planner West Midlands County Coun., Birmingham, Eng., 1974-81, dir. recreation and tourism planning, 1981-85, dir. strategic planning, 1985-86; dep. dir. housing coord. N.Y.C. Mayor's Office, 1987-89; dir. nurses housing N.Y.C. Health & Hosps. Corp., 1989-92, exec. asst. to v.p., 1992-94, asst. v.p., 1994-97; chief of staff N.Y.C. Health and Hosps. Corp., 1998-2001, chief info. officer, 2001—. Dir. Women in Housing and Fin., N.Y.C., 1990-96. Mem.: Am. Soc. Pub. Adminstrn. Office: NYC Health & Hosps Corp 125 Worth St New York NY 10013-4006 Office Phone: 212-788-3437. Business E-Mail: pandolff@nychhc.org.

PANEK, WILLIAM DOMINICK, systems engineer executive; b. Perth Amboy, NJ, Jan. 14, 1970; s. Richard William Panek and Marjaree Marie Mayne; m. Crystal Marie Pellerin, Feb. 11, 1995; children: Paige children: Alexandria. Assoc. degree, Computer Learning Ctr., 1994. MCSE Microsoft, 1997, Microsoft, 2001, cert. trainer Microsoft, 1997, database adminstr. Microsoft, 2000, network assoc. Cisco Corp., 2000. Microsoft cert. instr. The Associates, Shrewsbury, Mass., 1997—98; pres. Stellacon Corp, Farmington, NH, 1998—. Cons. MicroScript, Danvers, Mass., 1994—2000. Firefighter/EMT; spl. advisor to the chmn. Bus. Adv. Coun., Washington, 2002—03. E4 USAF, 1988—92, Spain. Recipient NH Businessman Yr., Bus. Adv. Coun., 2003. Mem.: AOPA (corr.), NRA (assoc.). R-Conservative. Roman Catholic. Avocations: flying, hunting, scuba diving. Home and Office: Stellacon Corp 18 Polliwog Ln Farmington NH 03835

PANELLA, MICHAEL JOSEPH, pathologist, lawyer; b. New Castle, Pa., Aug. 2, 1963; s. Arnold Michael and Joan Frances Panella; 1 child, Parker Nathaniel. BS, U. Mich., Ann Arbor, 1985; MD, Med. Coll. Pa., Phila., 1989; JD, U. Pitts., 2005. Bar: Tenn. 2005; diplomate anatomical and clinical pathology Am. Bd. Pathology. Commd. 2d lt. USAF, 1985, advanced through grades to maj.; staff pathologist Lewis Bale Clinic, Salem, Va., 1999—2000, Med Ctrl. Healthcare Sys., Mansfield, Ohio, 2000—02, Quest Diagnistics, Inc., Pitts., 2002—06; forensic pathology fellow Med. Examiners Office Allegheny County, Pitts., 2006—. Vol. Tenn. Justice Ctr., Nashville, 2006. Decorated Air Force Commendation medal for meritorious svc. Fellow: Coll. Am. Pathologists; mem.: ABA, Tenn. Bar Assn., Order of Coif, Phi Beta Kappa, Alpha Omega Alpha. Home: 222 Sunset Dr New Castle PA 16105

PANERIO, ROBERT MAJOR, SR., music educator, composer; b. Roslyn, Wash., June 28, 1929; s. Major Annible and Margaret Beatrice (Hunter) Panerio; m. Charlotte Ruth Klein, June 10, 1950; children: Deborah Jo, Robert Major Jr. BA in Edn., Ctrl. Wash. U., 1953, BA, 1953, MusM in Edn., 1958; postgrad., Eastman Sch. Music, 1963. Supr. instrumental music Moses Lake (Wash.) Pub. Sch., 1953—62; head arts and humanities Big Bend Coll., Moses Lake, 1962—63; prof. music Ctrl. Wash. U., Ellensburg, 1963—91. Composer: Marauders, Nocturne, Ensenada, Concert March, Passacaglia, Pastorale, Two Contemporary Songs for Children, The Beepers' March, Theme for Band, Concert Suite for Bank, Brassology, Quartal Quartet, Dark Blue, Beguine for Orchestra, Softly. Named Disting. Univ. Prof., Ctrl. Wash. U., 1982; named to Wash. Music Educators Hall of Fame, 1998; recipient Am. Bandmasters Composition award, 1975. Mem.: Am. Soc. Composers, Authors and Publishers, Music Educators Nat. Conf. (adj. clinician). Home: 1309 Radio Rd Ellensburg WA 98926

PANERO, HUGH EDWARD, former broadcast executive; b. NYC, Feb. 26, 1956; s. Julius and Renee (Rubin) P.; m. Mary Beth Durkin, June 21, 1987; 1 child, Sofia. BA in Govt. & Sociology, Clark U., Worcester, Mass., 1978; MBA, Baruch Coll., NYC, 1989. Dep. bur. chief CableVision Mag., NYC, 1980-82; various positions including v.p. mktg. Time Warner Cable of N.Y.C., 1982-93; pres., CEO Request Television, Denver, 1993—98; founder, pres., CEO, dir. XM Satellite Radio Holdings Inc., 1998—2007, also bd. dir., 1998—. Mem.: Cable Television Adminstrv. and Mktg. Soc. Office: XM Satellite Radio Holdings Inc 1500 Eckington Pl NE Washington DC 20002-2194 Office Phone: 202-380-4000. Office Fax: 202-380-4500. *

PANES, JACK SAMUEL, publishing executive; b. NYC, Apr. 6, 1925; s. Max S. and Sophie (Levine) P.; m. Pearl Shaine, Dec. 25, 1949; children—Stephanie Jill, Michael Jonathan. BA, Bklyn. Coll., 1947; MS in Journalism, Northwestern U., 1949. Editor, pub. The Howe Service, Inc., NYC, 1949-54; founder, pub. Publs. for Industry, NYC, 1955—, Panes Publs., Inc., NYC, 1959—; owner Drug Products Display Service Advt. Co., NYC, 1955—, Supplies for Industry Co., NYC, 1956—; pres. Senap Devel. Corp., Great Neck, N.Y., 1972—. Pres. Russell Woods Civic Assn., Great Neck. Served with inf. AUS, 1942-45, ETO. Decorated Silver Star medal, Bronze Star medal. Mem. 94th Infantry Divsn. Assn. (pres.), Deadline Club, Sigma Delta Chi. Home: 21 Russell Woods Rd Great Neck NY 11021-4644 Office: Panes Publications Inc Great Neck NY 11021 Home Phone: 516-487-0991; Office Phone: 516-487-0990.

PANETH, DONALD JOSEPH, editor, writer; b. NYC, Feb. 28, 1927; s. Irving and Maud (Kramer) P.; m. Elma Olans, Apr. 10, 1949 (dec. 1987); children: Thea, Ira. BBA, CCNY, 1948; postgrad., Columbia U., NYC, 1949-50. Reporter NY Times, 1947-49; freelance journalist NYC, 1950-56, 73-75, 77-83, 94—; rewriteman Daily Mirror, NYC, 1956-63; copy editor Morning Telegraph, NYC, 1964-65, L.I. Press, Queens, NY, 1975-77; staff writer Med. Tribune, NYC, 1966-72; editor-in-chief News Dictionary: People, Places, Events, 1977-80; editor, writer Yearbook UN, NYC, 1986-93; documents editor UN Office Conf. Svcs., NYC, 1993-94; recruiting asst., crew leader US Bur. Census, 2000; UN corr. N.Y. Indypendent, 2002—. Adj. lectr. English York Coll., CUNY, 1983-86; cons. study lit. far right extremist groups US, Anti-Defamation League, NY, 1995-96. Author: William Baziotes: A Lit. Portrait, 1961, Current Affairs Atlas, 1979, The Ency. of Am. Journalism, 1983; contbr. articles to Commentary mag., The Nation, Village Voice, Current Biography, Peacework, WorldPaper, others; work included anthologies Commentary on the American Scene, 1953, New York City Folklore, 1956. Mem. Am.-Scandinavian Found., NY Soc. Libr. Avocation: reading. Home and Office: 240 Cabrini Blvd Apt 1E New York NY 10033-1113

PANETTA, JOSEPH DANIEL, biotechnologist, director; b. Syracuse, NY, Mar. 1, 1954; s. Salvatore and Josephine Mary (Sbardella) P.; m. Karin Ann Hoffman, Oct. 21, 1978; children: Lauren Marie, Christopher Daniel. BS, LeMoyne Coll., 1976; MPH, U. Pitts., 1979. Environ. protection specialist EPA, Washington, 1979-82, sr. policy analyst, 1982-84; project leader Schering Corp./NorAm Chem Co., Wilmington, Del., 1984-85; mgr. regulatory affairs agrchems. divsn. Pennwalt Corp., Phila., 1985-88; mgr. corp. regulatory affairs Mycogen Corp., San Diego, 1988-90, dir. corp. regulatory affairs and quality assurance, 1990-92, dir. corp. regulatory, environ. affairs San Diego, 1992-97, v.p. govt. and pub. affair, 1998-99; pres., CEO BIOCOM, San Diego, 1999—. Bd. dirs. Gene Therapy Sys., San Diego (Calif.) Econ. Devel. Corp.; chmn. agr. and environment subcom. Internat. Bioindustry Forum; guest lectr. biotech. U. Calif., San Diego, and Calif. Western Law Sch.; advisor bd. on agr. NAS; mem. San Diego Pub. Utilities Adv. Commn., 2002—; adv. Com. Calif. Food Biotech., 2002-2004, U. Calif. Sch. Pharm. Sci., San Diego, Calif., 2003—; mem. adv. coun. Keck Grad. Inst., 2003—; vice chmn. Coun. State Biotech Assocs., 2002—, chmn. Coun. State Biotechnology Assn., 2004-. Columnist San Diego Daily Transcript, 1999—; contbr. articles to profl. jours. Mem. Rep. State Com. Del., 1987; bd. dirs. San Diego Work Force Partnership; mem. exec. com. Calif. Cmty. Colls. Econ. Devel. Network; mem. adv. bd. UCSD-Connect; bd. dirs. San Diego C. of C.; commissioner San Diego City Pub. Utilities commn., 2002—. Mem. Am. Crop Protection Assn. (chmn. com. biotech.), Nat. Agrl. Chems. Assn. (mem. registrations com. 1986-89), Biotech. Industy Orgn. (mem. food and agr. steering com., chmn. bipesticides com., internat. affairs com.), Calif. Indsl. Biotech. Assn. (mem. agrl. affairs com.), Am. Chem. Soc. (mem. agrl. div.), Am. Seed Trade Assn. (chmn. steering com. biotech.), Gov.'s Biotech. Coun. (Calif.), San Diego C. of C. (mem. pub. policy com.), San Diego Workforce Partnership (mem. youth coun.). Roman Catholic. Avocations: yachting, skiing, classical piano. Home: 5459 Shannon Ridge Ln San Diego CA 92130-4808 Office: BIOCOM San Diego 4501 Executive Dr San Diego CA 92121-3025 Home Phone: 858-481-5336; Office Phone: 858-455-0300. E-mail: jpanetta@biocom.org.

PANETTA, LEON EDWARD, former White House chief of staff, former congressman; b. Monterey, Calif., June 28, 1938; s. Carmelo and Carmelina Panetta; m. Sylvia Marie Varni, July 14, 1962; children: Christopher, Carmelo, James. BA magna cum laude, U. Santa Clara, Calif., 1960, LL.B., JD, 1963. Bar: Calif. bar 1965, U.S. Supreme Ct. 1965, U.S. Dist. Ct. (no. dist.) Calif. 1965, U.S. Ct. Appeals 1965. Legis. asst. to US Sen. Thomas Kuchel, Washington, 1966-69; dir. US Office Civil Rights, HEW, Washington, 1969-70; exec. asst. to mayor NYC, 1970-71; ptnr. Panetta, Thompson & Panetta, Monterey, 1971-76; mem. US Congress from 17th Calif. dist., 1977-93, mem. agr. com., 1976—84, adminstrn. com., 1976—84, com. dep. majority whip budget issues, chmn. budget com., 1989—92, dep. majority whip for budget issues, chmn. select com. hunger, chmn. 95th Congress New Mems. Caucus, vice chmn. Caucus Vietnam Era Vets. in Congress, mem. Pres.'s Com. Fgn. Lang. and Internat. Studies; dir. Office Mgmt. & Budget Exec. Office of the Pres., Washington, 1993-94; chief of staff to Pres. The White House, Washington, 1994-97; founder Panetta Inst., Calif. State U., Monterey bay, Seaside, Calif., 1998—. Mem. Iraq Study Group, 2006. Co-author: Bring Us Together, 1971. Counsel Monterey Regional Park Dists.; counsel NAACP, 1971-76; bd. trustees U. Santa Clara Law Sch.; founder Monterey Coll. Law; mem. Monterey County Dem. Cen. Com., 1972-74; v.p. Carmel Valley Little League, 1974-75; spl. advisor chancellor Calif. State U.; presdl. prof. pub. policy Santa Clara U.; former mem. bd. dirs. NY Stock Exch., chmn. com. rev. bd. dirs., co-chair corp. governance and listing stds. com. bd. dirs.; mem. nat. rev. bd. US Conf. Cath. Bishops; former trustee Nat. Steinback Ctr., Nat. Marine Sanctuary Found., 2005-; former mem. U. Calif. Santa Cruz Found., 2005-; nat. bd. advisors Ctr. Nat. Policy, 2005-; former chmn. Oceans Commn., 2005-; DCO-chair Joint Ocean Commn. Initiative; mem. Iraq Study Group, 2006-; mem. Task Force on Immigration and Am.'s Future, 2005-; bd. dirs. Blue Shield Calif., 2005-, IDT, 2005-, Zenith, 2005-, Connetics, 2005-, Bread for the World, 2005, Close Up, 2005-. Served with AUS, 1964-66. Recipient Army Commendation medal, 1966, Lincoln award NEA, 1970, A. Philip Randolph award, 1971, Disting. Svc. award NAACP, 1972, Bread for World award, 1978, 80, 82, 91, Nat. Hospice Orgn. award, 1984, Golden Plow award Am. Farm Bur. Fedn., 1988, 91, Pres.'s award Am. Coun. on Tchr. of Fgn. Langs., 1991, Coastal and Ocean Mgmt. award Coastal Zone Found., 1991, Food Rsch. and Action Ctr. award, 1991, Disting. Pub. Svc. medal Ctr. Study Presidency, 1995, Peter Burnett award disting pub. svc., 1993, Spl. Achievement award Nat. Italian Am. Found., 1997, John H. Chafer Coastal Stewardship award, 2001, Spl. Achievement award Santa Clara U. Sch. Law, 2002, Julius A. Stratton award coastal leadership, 2003, Coastal Stewarship award Aquarium of the Pacific, 2006, Lifetime Achievement award Nat. Marine Sanctuary Found., 2006, Paul Peck Presdl. award Smithsonian Instn. Nat. Portrait Gallery, 2006; named Lawyer of Yr., Law Sch. U. Santa Clara, 1970. Mem.: Calif. Bar Assn. Roman Catholic. Office: The Panetta Inst Calif State U Monterey Bay 100 Campus Ctr Bldg 86E Seaside CA 93955-8000 Office Phone: 831-582-4200. Business E-Mail: info@panettainstitute.org.

PANETTA, MICHAEL, shadow representative; b. July 14, 1971; m. Cady Panetta; 1 child. BA, Am. U., 1993, MA in Polit. Sci., 1994. Dep. task leader internet devel. Advanced Tech. Sys., 1998—2000; cons. Issue Dynamics Inc., 2000—03; asst. v.p. emerging media and pub. affairs Grassroots Enterprise, Washington, 2003—. DC shadow rep. to US Congress, 2007—. Exec. dir., treas. X-PAC. Office: 1101 17th St NW, Ste 1350 Washington DC 20036 also: John A Wilson Bldg 1350 Pennsylvania Ave, NW Washington DC 20004 Office Phone: 202-727-7891, 202-783-5910. *

PANETTIERE, HAYDEN, actress; b. Palisades, NY, Aug. 21, 1989; d. Skip and Lesley Panettiere. Actor: (TV series) One Life to Live, 1994—97, Guiding Light, 1996—2000, Ally McBeal, 2002, Malcolm in the Middle, 2003—05, Heroes, 2006— (Choice TV Actress: Drama, Teen Choice Awards, 2007); (TV films) How Do You Spell God?, 1996, Too Rich: The Secret Life of Doris Duke, 1999, Chestnut Hill, 2001, Normal, 2003, Tiger Cruise, 2004, Lies My Mother Told Me, 2005; (films) The Object of My Affection, 1998, Message in a Bottle, 1999, Remember the Titans, 2000, The Affair of the Necklace, 2001, Joe Somebody, 2001, Raising Helen, 2004, The Dust Factory, 2004, Racing Stripes, 2005, Ice Princess, 2005, The Architect, 2006, Shanghai Kiss, 2007. *

PANG, DACHLING, neurosurgeon, educator; arrived in US, 1979; m. Lynne Gormley, July 31, 1999; children: Alexis, Colin. BSc, Dalhousie U., Halifax, NS, Can., 1968; MD, U. Toronto, Ont., Can., 1972. Lic. Med. Coun. Can., 1973, diplomate Am. Bd. Neurol. Surgery, 1984, Am. Bd. Pediatric Neurol. Surgery, 1992, specialist cert. in paediatric neurosurgery Royal Coll. Surgeons Eng., 2005. Asst. prof. neurosurgery U. Pitts., 1979—85, assoc. prof., 1985—91, chief pediat. neurosurgery, 1987—93, prof. pediat. neurosurgery, 1991—93, U. Calif., Davis, 1993—, chief pediat. neurosurgery, 1993—99; chief Regional Centre Pediat. Neurosurgery Kaiser Permanente Hosps. No. Calif., Oakland, 1999—. Hon. cons., vis. expert Ministry Health & Nat. U. Singapore, 1998—; hon. cons. Neurosurgical Soc. Hong Kong, 2000—. Author: Disorders of the Pediatric Spine, 1995; editor: Spinal Dystaphism, Neurosurgerial Clinics of North America, 1995; mem. editl. bd. Child's Nervous Sys., Jour. Internat. Soc. Paediatric Neurosurgery, 1996—2003. Mem. adv. bd. Nat. Head Injury Found. Pa., 1986—93. Grantee, Am. Heart Assn. Pa., 1980—82, Nat. Inst. Neurol. and Communicable Disease and STroke, 1986—89. Fellow: ACS, Royal Coll. Surgeons Eng., Royal Coll. Surgeons Can. (specialist cert. neurosurgery 1978); mem.: Am. Soc. Paediatric Neurosurgeons, Congress Neurol. Surgeons, Am. Assn. Neurol. Surgeons, Internat. Soc. Paediatric Neurosurgeons. Avocations: literature, rare book collecting, classical music. Office: Kaiser Permanente Hosp Dept Paediatric Neurosurgery 280 W MacArthur Blvd Oakland CA 94611

PANG, DARREN, hockey analyst, retired professional hockey player; b. Ottawa, Ont., Can., Feb. 17, 1964; m. Lynn Pang; children: Tyler, Samantha. Goaltender Chgo. Blackhawks, 1984—89, ret., 1990, post game show host, 1990—92, pre game show host, 1992—97; guest analyst Norris Divsn. playoffs ESPN, 1988; color analyst, studio analyst, reporter Ctrl. Collegiate Hockey Assn. (CCHA) SportsChannel, Chgo., 1989-94; analyst Internat. Hockey League games Prime Network, 1989-93; NHL game analyst ESPN2, 1993—2005, analyst NHL 2Night; ice level reporter Nagano Olympic Games, CBS, 1998, Salt Lake City Olympic Games, NBC, 2002; color commentator Phoenix Coyotes, 2005—; part-time playoff analyst TSN. Goalie coach Notre Dame U., 1996—99, U. Ill.-Chgo. Flames, Ctrl. Collegiate Hockey Assn., 2002—04. Named to NHL All-Rookie team, 1988. Office: c/o Phoenix Coyotes Hockey Club 5800 W Glenn Dr, Ste 350 Glendale AZ 85301

PANG, SHUO, engineering educator; s. Fengge Pang and Guixiang Zhang; m. Lulu Sun; 1 child, Maggie. BS, Harbin Engring. U., China, 1997; MS, U. Calif., Riverside, 2001—01, PhD, 2004. Sys. engr. China Telecom, Harbin, 1997—99; asst. prof. Embry-Riddle Aero. U., Daytona Beach, Fla., 2005—. Mem.: IEEE, Phi Beta Kappa. Achievements include development of chemical plume mapping algorithms. Office: Embry-Riddle Aero Univ 600 S Clyde Morris Blvd Daytona Beach FL 32114 Home Phone: 386-226-7038; Office Phone: 386-226-7038. Business E-Mail: shuo.pang@erau.edu.

PANG, YUAN-PING, synthetic and computational chemist; b. Shanghai, Sept. 9, 1962; came to U.S., 1987, naturalized, 1999; s. Qi-Yang and Li-Kang (Wang) P.; m. Bee-Darn Chao, July 26, 1996 (div. Oct. 7 2002). BS, Amoy U., Xiamen, China, 1984; PhD, U. Pitts., 1990. Rsch. assoc. Mayo Clinic, Jacksonville, Fla., 1991-92, assoc. cons., 1992-97, chief rational drug design lab., 1996-97, mem. rsch. exec. subcom., 1995-97, sr. assoc. cons. Rochester, Minn., 1997-2001, cons., 2001—; asst. prof. dept. pharmacology Mayo Med. Sch., Rochester, Minn., 1998—2001, assoc. prof., 2001—04, prof., 2004—. Inventor neuroprotectives, drugs for Alzheimer's, drugs for schizophrenia, and antidotes for organophosphate poisonings. Author: (with others) Excitatory Amino Acids, 1991, Trends in QSAR and Molecular Modeling '92, 1993, QSAR and Molecular Modelling: Concepts, Computational Tools and Biological Applications, 1995; contbr. articles to profl. jours. including Nature, Nature Struct. Biol., Procs. NAS USA, Jour. Phys. Chemistry, Jour. Medicinal Chemistry, Jour. Biol. Chemistry, Molecular Pharmacology, Jour. Organic Chemistry, Jour. Am. Chem. Soc., Protein Sci., Protein, others. Grantee NIH, NIMH, NIAID, FNIH, ARO, USAMRAA, Def. Advanced Rsch. Projects Agy. Achievements include inventions of the multiple template approach for developing nonpeptidic mimetics, the cationic dummy atom approach to molecular modeling of metalloproteins and the dimeric analog approach for prototype drug optimization; contbn. to conformational selection mechanism for bindings of biologically active proteins; and leadership in developing automated computer docking program, ligands of cholinesterase and neurotensin receptor, model of ligand binding site of transmembrane receptor for neurotension and in silico screening of chemical databases for drug leads. Office: Mayo Clinic Dept Pharmacology 200 1st St SW Rochester MN 55905-0002 Office Phone: 507-284-7868. Business E-Mail: pang@mayo.edu.

PANICEK, DAVID, radiologist; b. Johnson City, NY, Oct. 7, 1954; MD, Cornell U., 1980. Cert. diagnostic radiology 1984. Intern Lenox Hill Hosp., NYC, 1980—81; resident NY Hosp. Cornell Med. Ctr., NYC, 1981—84; radiologist U. Hosp., Syracuse, NY, 1984—88; asst. prof. radiology SUNY Health Sci. Ctr., Syracuse, 1984—88, Cornell U. Med. Coll., 1988—93; radiologist Meml. Sloan-Kettering, NYC, 1988—; assoc. prof. radiology Cornell U. Med. Coll., 1993—98, prof. radiology, 1999—. Fellow: Am. Coll. Radiology; mem.: Am. Roentgen Ray Soc., Radiological Soc. N.Am., Internat. Skeletal Soc. Office: Meml Sloan-Kettering Cancer Ctr 1275 York Ave New York NY 10021-6007

PANICH, DANUTA BEMBENISTA, lawyer; b. East Chicago, Ind., Apr. 9, 1954; d. Fred and Ann Stephanie (Grabowski) B.; m. Nikola Panich, July 30, 1977; children: Jennifer Anne, Michael Alexei. AB, Ind. U., 1975, JD, 1978. Bar: Ill. 1978, U.S. Dist. Ct. (no. dist.) Ill. 1978, U.S. Dist. Ct. (ctrl. dist.) Ill. 1987, U.S. Ct. Appeals (7th cir.) 1987, U.S. Dist. Ct. (no. dist.) Ind. 2001, U.S. Dist. Ct. (ea. dist.) Mich. 2003, U.S. Ct. Appeals (6th cir.) 2003, U.S. Dist. Ct. (so. dist.) Ill., 2004. Assoc. Mayer Brown & Platt, Chgo., 1978-86, ptnr., 1986—2001, Mayer Brown Rowe & Maw, LLP, Chgo., 2002—. Bd. dirs. Munster (Ind.) Med. Rsch. Found., 1990—, Pub. Interest Law Initiative, 2003—. Mem. ABA, Fed. Bar Assn., Ill. Bar Assn. Republican. Roman Catholic. Office: Mayer Brown Rowe & Maw LLP 71 S Wacker Dr Chicago IL 60606 Office Phone: 312-701-7198. Business E-Mail: dpanich@mayerbrownrowe.com.

PANICHAS, GEORGE ANDREW, language educator, critic, editor; b. Springfield, Mass., May 21, 1930; s. Andrew and Fotini (Dracouli) P. BA, Am. Internat. Coll., Springfield, Mass., 1951, LittD (hon.), 1984; AM, Trinity Coll., Conn., 1952; PhD, Nottingham U., Eng., 1962. Instr., English and comparative lit. U. Md., College Park, 1962-63, asst. prof., 1963-66, assoc. prof., 1966-68, prof., 1968-92. Mem. Richard M. Weaver fellowship awards com., 1984-88, Ingersoll Prizes Jury Panel, 1986; co-chmn. Conf. on Irving Babbitt: Fifty Years Later, 1983. Author: Adventure in Consciousness: The Meaning of D.H. Lawrence's Religious Quest, 1964, Epicurus, 1967, The Reverent Discipline: Essays in Literary Criticism and Culture, 1974, The Burden of Vision: Dostoevsky's Spiritual Art, 1977, The Courage of Judgment: Essays in Criticism, Culture and Society, 1982, The Critic as Conservator: Essays in Literature, Society, and Culture, 1992, The Critical Legacy of Irving Babbitt: An Appreciation, 1999, Growing Wings to Overcome Gravity: Criticism as the Pursuit of Virtue, 1999, Joseph Conrad: His Moral Vision, 2005; editor: (with G.R. Hibbard and A. Rodway) Renaissance and Modern Essays: Presented to Vivian de Sola Pinto in Celebration of His Seventieth Birthday, 1966, Mansions of the Spirit: Essays in Literature and Religion, 1967, Promise of Greatness: The War of 1914-1918, 1968, The Politics of Twentieth-Century Novelists, 1971, The Simone Weil Reader, 1977, Irving Babbitt: Representative Writings, 1981, (with C. G. Ryn) Irving Babbitt in our Time, 1986; Modern Age: The First Twenty-Five Years. A Selection, 1988, In Continuity: The Last Essays of Austin Warren, 1996, The Essential Russell Kirk. Selected Essays, 2007; editl. advisor Modern Age: A Quar. Rev., 1971-77; assoc. editor, 1978-83, editor, 1984—; adv. bd. Continuity: A Jour. of History, 1984-88, Humanitas, 1993—; contbr. articles and revs. to profl. jours. Mem. Acad. Bd. Nat. Humanities Inst., 1985—; trustee Found. for Faith in Search of Understanding, 1987. Grantee Earhart Found., 1982, Henry Regnery award, 2003. Fellow Royal Soc. Arts (U.K.). Eastern Orthodox. Home and Office: PO Box Ab College Park MD 20741-3025 Office Phone: 301-779-6894. *In a profane age of unrest and breakdown, it is not enough for the critic to be purely and simply critical. He must work to conserve what is timeless, time-tested, time-honored. He must fight for causes he believes in, even if they appear to be lost causes. The critic's burden of responsibilty is also his vision of order.*

PANIOTO, RONALD ANGELO, judge; b. Dec. 18, 1935; s. Judith K. Panioto; 1 child, Ronald A. Jr. BBA, U. Cin., 1963; JD, No. Ky. U., Highland Heights, 1967. Bar: Ohio 1967. Constable Ct. Common Pleas, Cin., 1958-63, 1963-67; adminstrv. asst. U.S. Congressman Donald Clancy, Cin. and Washington, 1967-68; asst. pros. atty. Hamilton County Prosecutor's Office, Cin., 1968-75; judge Hamilton County Mcpl. Ct., Cin., 1975-82, Hamilton County Ct. Common Pleas, Cin., 1982-83, adminstrv. judge, 1983—, judge domestic rels. divsn., 1982—. Mem. Ohio State Bar Assn., Order Sons of Italy, Lawyers' Club Cin., Queen City Club, United Italian Soc. Greater Cin. (pres.), DaVinci U. Club, So. OHio Dog and Game Protective Assn., Cin. Athletic Club, Met. Club, Order Sons of Italy (pres.). Republican. Roman Catholic. Avocation: golf. Office: Hamilton County Ct Domestic Rels 800 Broadway Rm 225 Cincinnati OH 45202

PANISH, BRIAN JOSEPH, lawyer; b. Waco, Tex., Apr. 19, 1958; s. Howard Raymond and Mary Patricia (Murphy) P. Student, Calif. State U., 1980; JD cum laude, Southwestern Sch. Law, 1984. Bar: Calif. 1984, U.S. Dist. Ct. (no., ea. and cen. dists.) Tex. 1984. Assoc. Engstrom, Lipscomb & Lack, LA, 1984-86, Greene, Broillet, Taylor & Wheeler and predecessor firm, LA, 1987—93, ptnr., 1993—2005, Panish, Shea & Boyle, LLP, LA, 2005—. Named Trial Lawyer of the Yr., Trial Lawyers for Pub. Justice; named one of 100 Most Influential Lawyers, Nat. Law Jour., 2006; recipient American Jurisprudence Awards in Evidence, Wills and Trusts, Legal Ethics and Sales and Secured Transactions, Fresno State Scholar Athlete Award, 1980, Athletics Directors Award, 1980. Mem. L.A. County Bar Assn., Am. Bar Assn., Assn. Trial Lawyers Am., Calif. Trial Lawyers Assn., L.A. Trial Lawyers Assn., Consumer Attorneys Assn. of Calif. (Bd. Govs.), Internat. Soc. of Barristers, Consumer Attorneys Assn. of L.A., Am. Bd. of Trial Advocates, Western Trial Lawyers Assn., Trial Lawyers for Pub. Justice, Eighth Street Lawyers, Santa Monica Leaders Club. Home: 2527 3rd St Santa Monica CA 90405-3604 Office: Panish, Shea & Boyle, LLP 11111 Santa Monica Blvd Suite 700 Los Angeles CA 90025 Business E-Mail: panish@psandb.com.

PANISH, MORTON B., retired physical chemist; b. NYC, Apr. 8, 1929; s. Isidore and Fanny (Glasser) P.; m. Evelyn Wally Chaim, Aug. 20, 1951; children: Steven, Paul, Deborah. Student, Bklyn. Coll., 1946-48; BS in Chemistry, Denver U., 1950; MS in Chemistry, Mich. State U., 1951, PhD in Phys. Chemistry, 1954. Chemist Oak Ridge (Tenn.) Nat. Lab., 1954-57; mem. tech. staff RAD div. AVCO Corp., Wilmington, Mass., 1957-61, sect. chief, 1961-64; mem. tech. staff Bell Telephone Labs. (now Bell Labs.), Murray Hill, NJ, 1964-69, dept. head, 1969-86, disting. mem. tech. staff, 1986-92; cons., 1992—2003. Mem. com. on microgravity rsch. NRC, 1991-96, mem. com. on future of space sci. rsch. priorities, 1994-95, space studies bd., 1996-98; mem. com. on human rights NAS, 1996-02. Co-author: Heterostructure Lasers, 1978, Gas Source Molecular Beam Epitaxy, 1993; contbr. numerous articles to profl. jours.; patentee in field. Mem. dean's adv. bd. Coll. Natural Sci., Mich. State U., 1990-95. Recipient Electrochem Soc. Electronics Divsn. award, 1972, Solid state medal, 1979, C&C Found. prize, Japan, 1986, Internat. Crystal Growth award Am. Assn. Crystal Growth, 1990, John Bardeen award The Minerals, Metals and Materials Soc., 1994, The Kyoto prize, 2001. Fellow IEEE (Morris N. Liebmann Meml. award 1991), Am. Phys. Soc.; mem. Nat. Acad. Engring., Nat. Acad. Scis. Avocation: photography. Home and Office: 52 Baldwin Rd Freeport ME 04032 Personal E-mail: mort@att.net.

PANITCH, HOWARD BARRY, pediatric pulmonologist; b. Phila., Nov. 7, 1956; s. Jack and Harriet Rhoda (Morrison) P.; m. Mary Lisa Raimondo, Apr. 11, 1987; children: Oren Jacob, Rebecca Alyssa. BA, U. Penn., 1978; MD, U. Pitts., 1982. Intern in pediatrics Children's Hosp. Pitts., 1982-83, resident in pediatrics, 1983-85; fellow in pediatric pulmonary St. Christopher's Hosp. for Children, Phila., 1985-88, attending staff physician, 1988-98; clin. instr. pediatrics Temple U. Sch. of Medicine, Phila., 1985-88, asst. prof. pediatrics, 1988-94, assoc. prof. pediatrics; attending staff physician Children's Hosp. Phila., 1998—; assoc. prof. pediat. MCP-Hahnemann Sch. Medicine, 1997-98, U. Pa. Sch. Medicine, 1998—. Med. dir. Home Mech. Ventilation Program, St. Christopher's Hosp. for Children, Phila., 1989-98; med. dir. pulmonary home mech. ventilation program Children's Hosp. Phila., 1998—; med. dir. Pediat. Ctr. at Plymouth Meeting, 1992-99, Holland Glen, 2000—. Author book chpts.; contbr. rsch. and review articles to profl. jours. Mem. Physicians for Social Responsibility, Pitts., 1984-85. Fellow Am. Coll. Chest Physicians; mem. Am. Thoracic Soc., Pa. Thoracic Soc., Am. Physiol. Soc. Jewish. Avocations: woodworking, photography. Home: 649 Oak Shade Ave Elkins Park PA 19027-1713 Office: Children's Hosp Phila Fl 5 Wood Bldg 34th St and Civic Ctr Blvd Philadelphia PA 19104 E-mail: panitch@email.chop.edu.

PANITCH, RONALD LOUIS, lawyer; b. Newark, Feb. 10, 1941; BSME, NJ Inst. Tech., 1962; JD, Georgetown U., 1965. Patent examiner US Patent and Trademark Off., 1962; mng. ptnr. Panitch, Schwarze, Jacobs & Nadel, P.C., Phila., 1983; now ptnr.-in-charge Phila. Akin Gump Strauss Hauer & Feld LLP. Course chmn. ABA Am. Law Inst., Phila., 1990—. Assoc. editor Georgetown Law Jour. Named one of Best Lawyers in Phila., Phila. Mag., 1994, 1999; recipient Alumni Achievement Honor Roll medal, NJ Inst. of Tech., 2001. Mem. Phila. Bar Assn., Pa. Bar Assn., Phila. Patent Law Assn., Am. Intellectual Property Assn., Am. Law Inst. Office: Akin Gump Strauss Hauer & Feld LLP One Commerce Sq Ste 2200 2005 Market St Philadelphia PA 19103-7013 Office Phone: 215-965-1300. Office Fax: 215-965-1210. Business E-Mail: rpanitch@akigump.com.

PANITZ, DANIEL R., psychologist, consultant; b. Bklyn., May 1, 1945; s. Daniel Panitz and Lilian Victor. BA in Psychology, Rutgers U., 1968; MA in Psychology, New Sch., 1972; PhD Candidate, NYU, 1975; PhD in Pastoral Counselling, Trinity Inst., 2006. Chief psychologist NY State Narcotic Addiction Control Commn., 1970—79; psychologist NY State Alcoholism, 1980—89; dir. Human Svcs., 1990—2004, Eagle Ministeries, 2005; project dir. Hope Internat. Ministeries, 2004—05. Mem. editl. bd.: Am. Jour. Family Therapy, 1990—; composer (album): Songs Carried on Angel's Wings, 2001, River, 2002; author: Other Side of Sun, 2001. Named Humanitarian of Yr., Heno 911, 2002, NY Gov., Pres. Bush; recipient Eleanor Roosevelt award, US Congress, 2002. Mem.: Internat. Soc. Arts Scis. Avocation: writing. Office: 3840 Hillsboro Blvd Deerfield Beach FL 33442

PANITZ, LAWRENCE, physician; b. Apr. 30, 1928; s. Max and Gussie (Gorenstein) Panitz; m. Adrienne Ruth Luke, June 20, 1965; children: Jennifer, Michael. BA, NYU, 1962; MD, Upstate Med. U., Syracuse, 1966. Diplomate Am. Bd. Family Practice. Intern St. Joseph's Hosp., Syracuse, NY, 1966—67; pvt. practice gen. medicine Elmsford, NY, 1967—90, Hawthorne, NY, 1968—. Affiliated with Docs Physicians Beth Israel Med. Ctr., NYC, Shrub Oak, NY, Hartsdale, NY, Larchmont, NY, Yonkers, NY, Thornwood, NY, Crestwood, NY, New City, West Haverstraw, NY; mem. staff New Rochelle Hosp., NY, St. Agnes Hosp., White Plains, NY, Westchester County Med. Ctr., Valhalla, NY, N.Y. Dobbs Ferry Hosp., Beth Israel Hosp. Med. Ctr., NYC, Sound Shore Med. Ctr., Phelps Meml. Hosp., North Tarrytown, NY, dep. dir. dept. family practice; dir. Elmsford Med. Ctr.; police surgeon, Tarrytown, North Tarrytown, Sleepy Hollow, Elmsford, Town of Greenburgh; med. dir. Margaret Chapman Sch. Exceptional Child, Hawthorne; med. dir., prin. rschr. Clin. Tech. Assoc., Elmsford, CNS Bioservices, Pleasantville, NY; physician Westchester County Correctional Health Dept., Valhalla; sch. physician, Elmsford; cons., expert witness Vogel & Rosenberg, NYC, Britcher, Leone & Roth, LLC, Glen Rock, NJ; cons. on malpractice litig. for law firms. With US Army, 1946—48, with US Army, 1982—88, lt. col. Med. Corps USAR. Fellow: AMA, Am. Acad. Family Physicians; mem.: Westchester Acad. Medicine, Westchester County Med. Soc., Med. Soc. NY, Jewish War Vets., Masons, Shriners. Jewish. Home and Office: Riveredge 3 David Ln Yonkers NY 10701-1122 Office: 132 S Central Ave Elmsford NY 10523 Home Phone: 914-968-6033; Office Phone: 914-968-6135. E-mail: lp711md@aol.com.

PANKAU, BARBARA ROPES, lawyer; b. Miami, Apr. 4, 1951; d. Paul Chapman Ropes and Inga Ropes Roberts; m. Stephen Lamarr Pankau, May 1, 1976 (dec. Feb. 2001); children: Jonathan Lamarr, Emmy Ingrid; m. Jonathan L. Alpert, Dec. 4, 2003. Student, Sorbonne, Paris, 1970—71; BA cum laude, Tufts U., 1972; JD cum laude, U. Fla., 1975. Cert.: Fla. Bar (health law), bar: US Dist. Ct. (ctrl. dist.), US Ct. Appeals (11th cir.) 1981, US Ct. Appeals (5th cir.) 1976, US Claims Ct. 1979, US Supreme Ct. 1979. Legal writing instr. U. Fla. Coll. Law, Gainesville, 1975; assoc., litig. practice Trenam, Simmons, Kempker, Scharf, Brakin, Frye & O'Neill, Tampa, Fla., 1975—79; shareholder Carlton, Fields, Warrd, Emmanuel, Smith & Cutler, P.A., Tampa, 1979—89, Stearns Weaver Miller Alhadeff & Shierson, P.A., Tampa, 1989—90; lawyer Law Offices Barbara R. Pankau, P.A., Tampa, 1990—94; ptnr. Honigman, Miller, Schwartz and Cohn, Tampa, 1994—97, Shumaker, Loop & Kendrick, L.L.P., Tampa, 1997—. Lectr. in field of health law. Contbr. articles to profl. jours.; guest editor: health law issue, Fla. Bar Jour., 1998. Past dir. Hospice of Fla. Suncoast; past adv. bd. Burdines; adv. bd. trustees Humana Women's Hosp. Tampa, 1983—93; chmn. Tufts Alumni Admissions Program, Ctrl. Fla., 1986—92; moderator, adv. bd. trustees Humana Hosp., St. Petersburg, Fla., 1990—91, trustee, 1988—91; vice chmn., bd. counselors U. Tampa, 1982—83; adv. bd. Suncoast AIDS Network, 1990—91; adv. com. Tampa Tribune/Health Care Guide, 1989—91. Named an Outstanding Lawyer of Am., 2003; recipient numerous svc. awards, various profl. assns., svc. distinction awards, Tampa C. of C., Jr. League of Tampa, Big Bros./Big Sisters, others. Mem.: ABA (gov. bd. health law forum 1989—92, mem.health law forum, adminstrv. law and regulatory practice, bus. law), Fla. Bar Assn. (chmn. health law com., mem. exec. coun. health law sect. 1988—2003), Athena Soc., Fla. Bar (cert. com. health law sect. 1994—96, mem. health law, adminstrv. law, and bus. law sects.), Suncoast Healthcare Execs., Am. Health Lawyers Assn., Hillsborough County Bar Assn., Fla. Acad. Healthcare Attys. Office: Shumaker Loop & Kendrick LLP Bank of Am Plz Ste 2800 101 E Kennedy Blvd Tampa FL 33602 Office Phone: 813-227-2321. Business E-Mail: bpankau@slk-law.com.

PANKAU, CAROLE, state senator; b. Aug. 13, 1947; m. Anthony John Pankau Jr.; 4 children. BS, U. Ill., 1981. Mem. Ill. House of Rep., 1993—2004, Ill. Senate from 23th dist., 2004—. Mem. DuPage County (Ill.) Bd., 1984-92; committeeman Bloomingdale Twp. Rep. Precinct 70; mem. Keeneyville (Ill.) Sch. Dist. 20; vice chair Bloomingdale Twp. Rep. Orgn. also: One Tiffany Pointe Bloomingdale IL 60108 Office: 105-K State House Springfield IL 62706 E-mail: carole@pankau.org.

PANKEN, PETER MICHAEL, lawyer; b. NYC, Dec. 30, 1936; s. Harold Ira and Sylvia Rita (Haimes) P.; m. Beverly Muriel Goldner, June 19, 1960; children: Aaron, Melinda. BA cum laude, Haverford Coll., 1957; LLB magna cum laude, Harvard U., 1962. Bar: N.Y. 1962, U.S. Dist. Ct. N.Y. 1962, U.S. Ct. Appeals (2d cir.) 1969, (3d cir.) 1988, (10th cir.) 1989, (7th cir.) 2003, U.S. Supreme Ct. 1989. Assoc. Paul Weiss Rifkind Wharton Garrison, NYC, 1962-66, Poletti Freiden Prashker Feldman & Gartner, NYC, 1966-67, Parker Chapin Flattau & Klimpl, NYC, 1967-72, ptnr., 1973-99, chair employment and labor law dept., 1986-99; mem. Epstein Becker & Green PC, NYC, 1999—. Editor: Harvard Law Rev., 1961-62; author: A State-by-State Survey of the Law of Religion in the Workplace, 2001; contbg.: Employment Law Desk Book for Human Resources Professionals; editor-in-chief ALIABA Resource Materials: Employment and Labor Law; mem. bd. editors The Practical Litigator; contbr. articles to profl. jours. Pres., bd. dirs. Fedn. of Handicapped, N.Y.C., 1984-92; bd. dirs. Fedcap Rehab. Svcs., 1993—; pres. metro N.Y. chpt. Soc. for Human Resource Mgmt., 1990-92, gen. counsel, 1993-2003. Mem. ABA (labor and employment sect., com. on NLRB law, contbg. editor The Developing Labor Law), NY State Bar Assn. (labor and employment law sect., continuing legal edn. com.), Am. Law Inst.-ABA (chmn. employment and labor law programs), Am. Law Inst. (com. on restatement of agy. and restatement of employment law), Soc. for Human Resource Mgmt. (com. on employment practices 1990-99). Office: Epstein Becker & Green PC 250 Park Ave Ste 1200 New York NY 10177-1211 Office Phone: 212-351-4840. Business E-Mail: ppanken@ebglaw.com.

PANKEY, GEORGE ATKINSON, internist, educator, researcher; b. Shreveport, La., Aug. 11, 1933; s. George Edward and Annabel (Atkinson) P.; m. Patricia Ann Carreras, Sept. 22, 1972; children: Susan Margaret, Stephen Charles, Laura Atkinson, Edward Atkinson. Student, La. Poly. Inst., 1950-51; BS, Tulane U., 1954, MD, 1957; MS, U. Minn., 1961. Diplomate Am. Bd. Internal Medicine, Am. Bd. Infectious Disease. Intern U. Minn. Hosps., 1957-58, resident in internal medicine, 1958-60, Mpls. VA Hosp., Mpls. Gen. Hosp., 1960-61; asst. vis. physician Charity Hosp. La., New Orleans, 1961-62, vis. physician, 1962-75, sr. vis. physician, 1975-95; ptnr. Ochsner Clinic, New Orleans, 1968—69; head sect. infectious diseases Ochsner Clinic Found., 1972—94, dir. infectious disease training program, 1972—94, dir. infectious disease rsch., 1999—; instr. dept. medicine, div. infectious diseases Tulane U. Sch. Medicine, New Orleans, 1961-63, clin. instr., 1963-65, clin. asst. prof. medicine, 1965-68, clin. assoc. prof., 1968-73, clin. prof., 1973—; clin. prof. dept. medicine La. State U. Sch. Medicine, 1979—; clin. prof. oral diagnosis, medicine and radiology La. State U. Sch. Dentistry, 1983—. Dir., founder Century Nat. Bank, New Orleans; medicine test com. Nat. Bd. Med. Examiners, 1979-83; infectious diseases adv. bd. Hoffman-LaRoche, 1982—; dir. Nat. Found. Infectious Diseases, 2004—; cons. in field. Author: A Manual of Antimicrobial Therapy, 1969; co-author: (with Charles W. Gross and Michael G. Mendelsohn) Contemporary Diagnosis and Management of Sinusitis, 1997, 4th edit., 2004, (with Julia Garcia-Diaz and Layne O. Gentry) Contemporary Diagnosis and Management of Diabetic Foot Infections, 2006; editor: Infectious Diseases Digest, 1983-95, So. Med. Assn. Program for Infectious Diseases Dial-Access, 1983-92, Ochsner Clinic Reports on Serious Hosp. Infections, 1985—, Ochsner Clinic Reports on Geriatric Infectious Diseases, 1990-93, Ochsner Clinic Reports on the Mgmt. of Sepsis, 1991-93, Infectious Disease Clinics of N.Am., 1994, co-editor: (with Geoffrey A. Kalish) Outpatient Antimicrobial Therapy - Recent Advances, 1989; contbg. editor: Antimicrobial Therapy Guide, 18th edit., 2006; mem. editl. bd. Patient Care, 1969-75, Today in Medicine, 1990, Nat. Infectious Disease Info. Network, 1983, Compendium Continuing Edn. in Dentistry, 1984—, Quinolones Bull., 1985-93, Ochsner Jour., 1999—, Infectious Disease News, 2001—; contbr. numerous articles to profl. jours. Dir. Camp Fire Inc.; Pres. New Orleans Young Republican Club, 1969-71; adv. bd. Angie Nall Sch. Hosp., Beaumont, Tex.; trustee Nall Found. for Children, Beaumont. Recipient cert. merit Am. Acad. Gen. Practice, 1969, 70 Master ACP-ASIM (laureate award La. chpt. 1997); fellow Am. Coll. Preventive Medicine, Infectious Disease Soc. Am. (Clinician award 1996), Am. Coll. Chest Physicians, Royal Soc. Medicine; mem. Am. Soc. of Transplantation, Assn. Contamination Control (chpt. pres. 1968-70), Am. Fedn. Med. Rsch., So. Med. Assn. (certificate of award 1970), Am. Soc. Internal Medicine (del. ann. meeting 1971-72), Am. Soc. Microbiology, Am. Thoracic Soc., New Orleans Acad. Internal Medicine (pres. 1977-78, 96-97), AMA, Aerospace Med. Assn., Am. Soc. Tropical Medicine and Hygiene, Am. Venereal Disease Assn., Am. Soc. Parasitologists, Internat. Travel Medicine Soc., La. Soc. Internal Medicine (pres. 1972-73), La. Med. Soc., La. Thoracic Soc. (chmn. program com. 1968, governing council 1976-80), Surg. Infection Soc., Immunocompromised Host Soc., Musser Burch Soc., Orleans Parish Med. Soc., N.Y. Acad. Scis., Pan Am. Med. Assn. (diplomate mem. sect. internal medicine 1971, sect. pres. infectious diseases and virology 1978-85), SAR, Huguenot Soc. Founders Manakin in Colony of Va., Aviation Med. Examiner, Masons (32 deg), Shriners. Home: 5910 Prytania St New Orleans LA 70115-4348 Office: Ochsner Clinic Found 1514 Jefferson Hwy New Orleans LA 70121-2483 Office Phone: 504-842-4006. Personal E-mail: gpankey@ochsner.org.

PANKO, GEORGE, application developer; b. Harwinton, Conn., Nov. 21, 1951; s. John and Marie Rosa Panko; m. Laurel Lyn Childs, Feb. 14, 2004; children: Gabriel Abinadi, Ivan Theodore, Samuel Isaiah, Adam Theodore, Lydia Faith, Eric Christopher Cummings, Tyler Daniel Cummings, Joel Houston Cummings. BS, U. Conn., Storrs, 1973; MS, Rensselaer Poly. Inst., Troy, NY, 1992. Engring. specialist Electric Boat, Groton, Conn., 1996—2004; software engr. Raytheon, Groton, 2006—. Electronics engr. Naval Undersea Warfare Ctr., New London, Conn., 1973—96. Mem.: Mensa (life). Libertarian. Home Phone: 860-447-9990. Personal E-mail: g.panko@usa.net.

PANKO, JESSIE SYMINGTON, education educator; b. Jan. 19, 1935; Student, Hunter Coll., NYC, 1959-62; BA, MS, SUNY, 1969; PhD, Syracuse U., 1974. Tchr. Anderson Elem. Sch., Mariana Islands, Guam, 1964-65; tchr. Herman Ave. Elem. Sch., Auburn, NY, 1969-71; asst. prof. edn. dept. SUNY, Cortland, NY, 1971-76, Utica, Rome, NY, 1974-76; asst. prof. applied scis. dept. Loop Coll., Chgo., 1976-77; assoc. prof. social scis. dept. Truman Coll., Chgo., 1977-81; dir. student teaching St. Xavier Coll., Chgo., 1976—94, dir. undergrad. edn., 1977-79, dir. grad. edn., 1979-81, prof. edn. ctr., 1981-83, dir. grad. prog. in edn., 1983-86, dir. edn. ctr., 1986-89, dean sch. edn., 1989-92. Bd. dirs. Queen of Peace, Acad. of Our Lady; mem. com. grad. programs St. Xavier Coll., 1986-89, tchr. edn. coun., 1976-94, early childhood adv. bd., 1976-92. Moffett SUNY scholar, 1969. Mem. AAUP, ASCD, Am. Assn. Colls. of Tchr. Edn. (instnl. rep. 1987-92), Assn. Ind. Liberal Arts Colls. of Tchr. Edn. (instl. rep. 1986-92), Ill. Assn. of Tchr. Edn. in Pvt. Colls. (instnl. rep. 1985-98), Ill. Assn. Colls. Tchr. Edn. (coll. rep. 1981-98, sec. 1990-92), Assn. Tchr. Educators, Nat. Assn. Educatos Young Children, Ill. Dirs. Student Tchg., Chgo. Consortium Dirs. Student Tchg. (chairperson 1976-79), Ill. Assn. Tchr. Educators, Chgo. Area Dir. Student Tchg. (chmn. 2002-04), Pi Lambda Theta, Kappa Delta Pi. Office: St Xavier U 3700 W 103rd St Chicago IL 60655-3105 Office Phone: 773-298-3215. Business E-Mail: panko@sxu.edu.

PANKOV, GRADIMIR KRUNISLAV, performing company executive; b. Skopje, Macedonia, Yugoslavia, Oct. 25, 1938; s. Krunislav Ivan Pankov and Dragica Isak (Mihajlovska); m. Margret Maria Kaufmann, Dec. 30, 1980. Baccalaureat, Josip Broz Tito Gymnasium, Skopje, 1956; diploma, State Conservatory of Dance & Music, Skopje, 1957. Dancer Nat. Theatre Macedonia, Skopje, 1956-63; guest artist Nat. Theatres, Belgrade, Zagreb, Sarajevo, 1963-67; soloist City Theatres, Nuremberg, Karlsruhe, Wuppertal, Fed. Republic Germany, Theater Am Gärtnerplatz, Munich, 1967-74, Nat. Theatre, Mannheim, Fed. Republic Germany, 1974-76; ballet master City Theatre, Dortmund, 1976-80; artistic dir., tchr. Netherlands Dance Theatre Jr. Co., The Hague, 1980-81; artistic dir. Nat. Ballet of Finland, Helsinki, 1981-84; artistic dir., tchr. Cullberg Ballet, Stockholm, 1984-88; artistic dir. Ballet du Grand Theatre, Geneva, 1988-96, Les Grands Ballets Canadiens de Montreal, 2000—. Dancer (ballets) Mercutio in Romeo and Juliet, 1963, title role in Petrushka, 1965, title role in Pulcinella, 1971, The Faun in Afternoon of a Faun, 1975, choreographer (Operas) Eugene Onegin, 1977, Carmen, 1978, Don Giovanni, 1978. Office: Les Grands Ballets Canadiens de Montreal 4816, rue Rivard Montreal PQ H2J 2N6 Canada *

PANKOVE, JACQUES ISAAC, retired physicist, researcher; b. Chernigov, Russia, Nov. 23, 1922; came to U.S., 1942, naturalized, 1944; s. Evsey Leib and Miriam (Simkine) Pantchechnikoff; m. Ethel Wasserman, Nov. 24, 1950; children: Martin, Simon. BSEE, U. Calif., Berkeley, 1944, MSEE, 1948; PhD in Physics, U. Paris, 1960; DSc (hon.), Nat. Poly. Inst., Grenoble, France, 2000. Mem. tech. staff RCA Labs., Princeton, NJ, 1948-70, physicist, fellow, 1970-85; prof. U. Colo., Boulder, 1985-93, prof. emeritus, 1993—, Hudson Moore Jr. Univ. prof., 1989-93, program mgr. materials and devices Ctr. for Optoelectronic Computing Systems, 1986-89; Disting. Rsch. fellow Nat. Renewal Energy Lab. (formerly Solar Energy Rsch. Inst.), 1985-93; v.p. for rsch. and tech. Astralux, Inc., 1992—2004; ret. Vis. McKay lectr. U. Calif., Berkeley, 1968-69; vis. prof. U. Campinas, Brazil, 1975; Disting. vis. prof. U. Mo., Rolla, 1984; participant NAS sci. exch. program with Romania, 1970, Hungary, 1972,

Yugoslavia, 1976. Mem. hon. editl. bd. Solid State Electronics, 1970-94, Solar Energy Materials, 1984—, Optoelectronics, 1986-95; regional editor Crystal Lattice Defects and Amorphous Materials, 1984-90; author: Optical Processes in Semiconductors, 1971, 75, (ednl. film) Energy Gap and Recombination Radiation, 1962; editor: Electroluminescence, 1977, Display Devices, 1980, Hydrogenated Amorphous Silicon, 1984; co-editor: Hydrogen in Semiconductors, 1991, Wide Bandgap Semiconductors, 1992, III-Nitrides, 1997, Gallium Nitride Vol. I, 1998, Vol. II, 1999; designer: laser sculpture, Bklyn. Mus., 1968; contbr. articles to profl. jours.; patentee in field. Trustee Princeton Art Assn., 1970-82; mem. Experiment-in-Arts-and-Tech., Berkeley, 1968-69. Served with U.S. Army, 1944-46. Recipient RCA achievement awards, 1952, 53, 63, Faculty Rsch. award U. Colo. Coll. Engring. and Applied Sci., 1997, Rank Prize award Optoelectronics, 1998; David Sarnoff scholar, 1956, Disting. Alumnus award U. Calif., Berkeley, 2000. Fellow IEEE (J. J. Ebers award 1975, assoc. editor Jour. Quantum Electronics 1968-77, mem-at-large IEEE awards bd. 1992-95), Am. Phys. Soc.; mem. AAAS, Nat. Acad. Engring. (hon.), Materials Rsch. Soc., Sigma Xi. Home: 809 10th St Boulder CO 80302-7551

PANNALA, SREEKANTH, aerospace engineer; s. Venkat Narayan and Chandrakala Pannala; m. Maria Laura Cavallero, Aug. 29, 2005. B in Aerospace Engring., Indian Inst. Tech., Kharagpur, 1993; MS in Aerospace Engring., Ga. Tech, Atlanta, 1994; PhD in Aerospace Engring., Ga. Inst. Tech., Atlanta, 2000. Summer internship Aero. Devel. Establishment, Bangalore, Karnataka, India, 1991; grad. student asst. Ga. Tech, Atlanta, 1993—99; post-doctoral rsch. fellow Oak Ridge Inst. Sci. and Edn./Oak Ridge Nat. Lab., Tenn., 1999—2001; summer intern Defence R & D Lab., Hyderbad, Andhra Pradesh, India, 1992; rsch. staff mem. Oak Ridge Nat. Lab., Tenn., 2001—. Contbr. articles to profl. jours., chapters to books. Grad. student sen. Ga. Tech, Atlanta, 1995—96; vol. Centennial Olympics, 1996, Paralympics, 1996; founder ASHA and Child Relief and You chpts. Ga. Tech, 1996—96; walk coord. Vibha, Sunnyvale, Calif., 1998—98, project monitoring coord., 2004—, nat. walk advisor, cons., 1999—; philanthrophy chair India Club Ga. Tech, 1997—98. Recipient Person Yr., India Club Ga. Tech, 1998; fellow, ORISE, 1999—2000, 2000—01. Mem.: AIChE, Siam Sac. Achievements include research in open source multiphase flow software; development of realistic simulation models for reacting two-phase flows in order to achieve more efficient and controllable spray combustion; reduced order model for bubbling fluidized beds; a detailed simulation model for simulating spouted bed coaters for nuclear fuel particles. Office: Oak Ridge Nat Lab Bldg 6012 MS-6367 RM-101 Oak Ridge TN 37831 Home Phone: 615-469-5100; Office Phone: 865-574-3129. Office Fax: 865-574-0680. E-mail: pannalas@ornl.gov.

PANNELL, THIERRY EDGARD, engineer, information technology manager; s. Frank James Pannell and Emiliene Eugenie Omont. AAS, Brookdale C.C., 1989; BS, So. Ill. U., 1991; MS, Regis U., 2003. Lic. gen. radio operator, with radar endorsement, FCC, 1991, cert. broadcast engr., Soc. of Broadcast Engrs., 1991, sr. electronics technician, ETA/Iowa State U., 1990, cert. electronics technician, ISCET, 1991. Electronics mechanic U.S. Navy, Colts Neck, NJ, 1983—88; electronics technician U.S. Marine Corps, Cherry Point, NC, 1988—90, U.S. Army Yuma Proving Ground, Yuma, Ariz., 1990—93; grad. tchg., rsch. asst. Ill. State U., Normal, Ill., 1993—94; electromagnetic test technician Delco Electronics, Kokomo, Ind., 1995; electromagnetic interference, electromagnetic compatability technician Ford Motor Co., Dearborn, Mich., 1996—98; sr. electromechnical technician Barry Controls, Brighton, Mass., 1998; assoc. electro-magnetic interference compatibility engr. Sundstrand Aerospace, Rockford, Ill., 1998—2000; hardware engr. Rockwell Automation, Mayfield Heights, Ohio, 2000; info. tech. analyst Caterpillar, Inc., Lafayette, Ind., 2004; train controls sys. engr. GE Rail, Erie, Pa., 2004—06; EMI sys. engr. Ingenium Technologies, Rockford, Ill., 2006—. Cons. 24 Hour Club, Kokomo, Ind., 1999—2003, ClearView Windows, Hastings, Nebr., 2004, Brian's Lawn Svc., Kokomo, Ind., 2006—. Specialist 5th class US Army, 1978—81. Mem.: Internat. Soc. Profl. Electronics Technicians (assoc.). Achievements include development of computer applications. Home: 1701 E Empire St Ste 360 #140 Bloomington IL 61704 Home Phone: 708-450-8237.

PANNER, OWEN M., federal judge; b. 1924; Student, U. Okla., 1941-43, LL.B., 1949. Atty. Panner, Johnson, Marceau, Karnopp, Kennedy & Nash, 1950-80; judge, now sr. judge U.S. Dist. Ct. Oreg., Portland, 1980—, sr. judge, 1992—. Recipient Am. Bd. Trial Advocates Trial Lawyer of Yr., 1973. Mem. Am. Coll. Trial Lawyers, Am. Bd. Trial Advs., Order of Coif. Office: US Courthouse 310 W 6th St Medford OR 97501

PANNETON, JEAN M., vascular surgeon; MD, U. of Montreal, Can., 1987. Lic. surgery Am. Bd. of Surgery, gen. surgery Royal Coll. of Physicians and Surgeons of Can., spl. competence in Vascular Surgery Royal Coll. of Physicians and Surgeons of Can., lic. vascular surgery Am. Bd. of Surgery. Clin. lectr. U. of Glasgow, Scotland, 1994—95; asst. prof. of surgery U. of Man., Winnipeg, Canada, 1995—97, Mayo Clinic Coll. of Medicine, Rochester, Minn., 1997—2002, assoc. prof. of surgery, 2002—04; assoc. prof. of clin. surgery Ea. Va. Med. Sch., Norfolk, Va., 2004—. Dir. of clin. rsch. in vascular surgery Mayo Clinic, Rochester, 2002—04; dir. chief vascular surgery, program dir. Ea. Va. Med. Sch., 2007—. Contbr. articles to profl. jours., chpts. to books. Named Surg. Subspecialty Tchr. of the Yr., Mayo Clinic Grad. Sch. of Medicine, 2000; recipient Prix B.G. Bourgeois Award for Excellence in Surgery, U. of Montreal, 1987, Ctr. Hospitalier de la Baie des Chaleurs Found. scholarship, 1984, Prix Pierre Masson, U. of Montreal, 1983, Excellence in Tchg. Recognition award, Mayo Clinic Coll. of Medicine, 1999—2000, Walter C. MacKenzie, Johnson & Johnson / Ethicon award, Royal Coll. of Physicians and Surgeons of Can., 1994, R.S. McLaughlin Found. fellowship, McLaughlin Found. and U. of Montreal, 1994, Lange Med. Publ. award, U. of Montreal, 1987, Mosby Award for Scholastic Excellence, 1987, Prix E.P. Lachapelle for Scholastic Excellence, 1987, Merck Sharp and Dohme Award for Scholastic Excellence, 1987, Prix T. Parizeau for Excellence in Surgery, 1987. Fellow: ACS, Royal Coll. Surgeons of Can.; mem.: Internat. Soc. for Cardiovasc. Surgery, Internat. Soc. for Endovascular Specialists, Can. Assn. of U. Surgeons, Soc. for Clin. Vascular Surgery, Priestley Soc., Peripheral Vascular Surgery Soc. (mem. program com. 2002—02), Mayo Alumni Assn., Med. Soc. of Va., Chesapeake Med. Soc., Societe Francaise d'Angiologie (cons. of internat. com. 2003—06), Soc. for Vascular Surgery, Christian Med. and Dental Assn., Internat. Union of Angiology (sec. N.Am. chpt. 2002—06), Midwestern Vascular Surg. Soc., Societe de Chirurgie Vasculaire de Langue Francaise, Am. Assn. for Vascular Surgery, Can. Soc. for Vascular Surgery, European Soc. for Vascular Surgery (corr.). Achievements include research in Endovascular repair of aortic aneurysms. Office: Vascular and Transplant Specialists Ste 8620 600 Gresham Dr Norfolk VA 23507 Office Phone: 757-622-2649. Office Fax: 757-961-4992. Business E-Mail: jpanneton@vascularandtransplant.com.

PANNILL, WILLIAM PRESLEY, lawyer; b. Houston, Mar. 5, 1940; s. Fitzhugh H. and Mary Ellen (Goodrum) Pannill; m. Deborah Detering, May 9, 1966 (div. Nov. 1986); children: Shelley, Katherine, Elizabeth. BA, Rice U., 1962; MS, Columbia U., 1963; JD, U. Tex., 1970. Bar: Tex. 1970, U.S. Ct. Appeals (5th cir.) 1973, U.S. Ct. Appeals (DC cir.) 1974, U.S. Dist. Ct. (so. dist.) Tex. 1975, U.S. Supreme Ct. 1975, U.S. Ct. Appeals (10th cir.) 1980, U.S. Dist. Ct. (no. dist.) Tex. 1991. Assoc. Vinson, Elkins, Searls & Connally, 1970-71, Vinson, Elkins, Sears, Connally & Smith, 1972-75; staff asst. to sec. Treasury Dept., Washington, 1971-72; pvt. practice Houston, 1975—76, 1985—88, 2000—; ptnr. Pannill and Hooper, Houston, 1977-80, Pannill and Reynolds, Houston, 1982-85, Pannill, Moser, Mize & Hermann, Houston, 1988-90, Pannill & Moser, L.L.P., Houston, 1990-93, Pannill, Moser & Barnes, L.L.P., Houston, 1993-2000. Assoc. editor Litig. Jour. sect. litig., ABA, 1979—81, exec. editor, 1981—82, editor-in-chief, 1982—84, dir. publs., 1984—86, mem. coun., 1986—89. Contbr. articles to profl. jours. Bd. dirs. Houston Grand Opera, 1989—92, mem. adv. bd., 1995—97, Houston Symphony Soc., 1990—98; pres. ARS Lyrica Houston, 2004—; bd. dirs. Gulf Coast literary jour. U. Houston, 2004—. With USMCR, 1963—64. Mem.: ABA, Houston Bar Assn., Tex. Bar Assn., Rice U. Alumni Assn. (bd. dirs. 1989—92). Episcopalian. Office: 3262 Westheimer PMB 570 Houston TX 77098 Home Phone: 713-622-0846; Office Phone: 713-829-6585. Business E-Mail: william.pannill@williampannill.com.

PANNKE-SMITH, PEGGY, regional vice chairperson; b. Chgo., Oct. 26; d. Victor E. and Leona (O'Leary) Stich; m. Craig D. Smith, July 18, 1998; children from previous marriage: Thomas Scott, David Savonne, Heidi Mireille, Peter. V.p. long term care ins. Sales & Seminars, Des Plaines, 1986-90; pres., founder Nat. Consumer Oriented Agy., Des Plaines, 1990—2007. Cons. on long-term care ins. The Travelers, Tchrs. Inc. & Annuity Assocs., others; spkr. Exec. Enterprises, NYC, 1988—93. Columnist Sr. News, Vital Times, Daily Herald, Sr. Connection, Sr. Marketplace News, Prime Time for Seniors, Pioneer Press, Boulder Daily Camera, Longmont Times-Call, Aurora Sun, Mature Times Lifestyles, 50 Plus Marketplace. Sponsor Ill. Alliance for Aging, Chgo., 1990—, Ill. Assn. Homes for Aging, 1990-91; bd. govs. St. Matthew Luth. Home, Park Ridge, Ill., 1993-95. Recipient Spkrs. awards Health Ins. Assn. Am., Washington, 1990, Ret. Officers Assn., Glenview, Ill., 1991, 93, Nat. Assn. Sr. Living Industries, Denver, 1992, Exec. Enterprises, NYC, 1993, Gov.'s Conf. on Aging, Chgo., 1996, Golden Harvest Long Term Care award Ret. Officers Assn., 2001, Nat. awards UNUM, 2001, AIG 2002, Conseco, 2000, Allianz, 2002, Mut. of Omaha, 2003, Presidents Club, Lincoln Benefit. Mem.: Internat. Soc. for Retirement Planning, Am. Soc. on Aging, Mature Am., Nat. Coun. on Aging (ad hoc com.), Ctr. for Applied Gerontology, Nat. Assn. Long Term Care Profl., Nat. Assn. Sr. Living Industries, Friends of the Colo. Trail, Colo. Mountain Club, Boulder C. of C., Park Ridge C. of C., Kiwanis (bd. dir. Park Ridge 1992—98, pres. 1996—97, Boulder publicity chair 2006—), Am. Mensa (program dir. in Ill. 1983—85, Colo. chpt. 1999—, pres. Boulder chpt. 2003—, regional vice chairperson 2007—, bd. dirs. 2007—). Avocations: showshoeing, travel, sketching wildflowers, hiking, trekking the Colorado Trail. Address: 310 Busse Hwy #305 Park Ridge IL 60068 Office Phone: 800-554-1996. E-mail: rvc7@us.mensa.org, ncoa.pps@sbcglobal.net.

PANSINI, MICHAEL SAMUEL, financial analyst, tax specialist; b. Molfetta, Italy, July 12, 1928; arrived in U.S., 1935; s. Ralph and Isabel (Cirilli) P.; m. Anna D'Angelo, June 5, 1949 (div. 1970); children: Elizabeth, Valerie, Michael; m. Elizabeth Bischoff, Oct. 3, 1970 (div. Feb. 1992); 1 child, Elissa Michelle. BS, NYU, 1950, MBA, 1952, LL.M., 1960; LL.D., Fordham U., 1956. Bar: N.Y. 1956, U.S. Tax Ct. Tax mgr. Pfizer Corp., NYC, 1951-64; asst. treas. Hooker Chem. Corp., NYC, 1964-69; treas., dir. United Indsl. Corp., NYC, 1969-72; sr. v.p., gen. counsel Beker Industries Corp., Greenwich, Conn., 1972-87; pres., dir. Panmer, Inc., 1987—; tax, fin. cons., 1988—; v.p., corp. counsel Champion Energy Corp. and affiliates, 1991-93, Champion Holdings Co. and affiliates, 1993-96. V.p., chmn. various coms. Tax Exec. Inst., N.Y.C., 1963-72; pres., dir. Fed. Tax Forum, Inc., N.Y.C., 1961-72; dir. Intelligent Bus. Communications Corp. Commr., vice chmn. Econ. Devel. Commn., Stamford, Conn., 1994—; mem. Rep. Town Com. 19th Dist., Stamford, 1993—; bd. dirs. Stamford Sr. Ctr., 2000—06, treas., 2007—; bd. dirs., treas. Women's Bus. Devel. Ctr., Inc., 2003—06, chmn. audit com, 2007—; bd. dirs., treas. Food Bank of Lower Fairfield County, 2004—06. Mem.: Sr. Men's Assn. Stamford (bd. dirs., 2d v.p. 2005—06, 1st v.p. 2007—, bd. dirs., 1st. v.p. 2007—), North Stamford Assn. (bd. dirs. 1999—2005, v.p. 2000, pres. 2001). Republican. Home and Office: 76 Lawrence Hill Rd Stamford CT 06903-2120

PANTALEO, JACK, playwright, composer, educator; b. Melrose Park, Ill., Nov. 30, 1954; s. Jack Sam Pantaleo and Sophia Mannozzi Pantaleo Cicero. Psychiat. Tech., C.C., San Francisco, 1981; BA in Humanities, New Coll. Calif., San Francisco, 1986; MA in Writing, U. San Francisco, 1988. Lic. psychiat. technician. Asst. to dean U. San Francisco Sch. Nursing, 1984—88; grammar sch. tchr. St. Michael's Cath. Sch., San Francisco, 1989—91; instr. English Vista C.C., Berkeley, Calif., 1990—93; social worker City and County San Francisco, 1991—. Founder, dir. Evangelicals Concerned, San Francisco, 1978-85; co-founder, co-dir. AIDS InterFaith Network, San Francisco, 1983-88. Author: (novel) Mother Julian and the Gentle Vampire, 2000 (winner cert. of merit Writer's Digest 2001 Nat. Book Awards); Playwright/composer musical The Gospel According to the Angel Julius translated into German and performed in Hamburg, Germany, 1999; (one-act play): Uncle Fred's Ex-Staight Ministry in Wilma Loves Betty, 1999; contbg. author: (collection of meditations) The Road to Emmaus, 1990; author booklet and articles. Caregiver for babies with AIDS, The Bridge, San Francisco, 1989-93. Work included in Silver Quill, The David Ross Meml. Competition, Wichita, 1996. Mem. Social Workers Union, Nat. Writers Union. Democrat. Episcopalian. Avocations: harp, lecturing. Office Phone: 415-401-5004. Personal E-mail: jackp100@onebox.com.

PANTALEO, PETER S., lawyer; BA, U. Wis., 1971; JD with honors, U. ND, 1976. Bar: Pa. 1976, ND 1977, DC 1989. Atty. Verner Liipfert Bernhard McPherson and Hand; ptnr. Piper Rudnick, Washington, 2002—04; ptnr., chair labor and employment law practice group DLA Piper Rudnick Gray Cary LLP, Washington, 2005—. Editor-in-chief ND Law Rev., lectr.; contbr. articles to profl. jours. Mem.: ABA, Inst. of Directors, London. Office: DLA Piper Rudnick Gray Cary LLP 1200 Nineteenth St NW Washington DC 20036-2412 Office Phone: 202-861-3956. Office Fax: 202-223-2085. Business E-Mail: peter.pantaleo@dlapiper.com.

PANTANO, ALESSANDRA, mathematics professor; b. Italy; MS, Univ. Tor Vergata, Rome, 1999; MA, Princeton Univ., 2001, PhD, 2004. H. C. Wang asst. prof. math. Cornell Univ., 2004—. Achievements include being one of 18 top mathematicians and computer scientists (Atlas of Lie Groups Project) from the US to successfully map E8, one of the largest and most complicated structures in mathematics. Office: Dept Math 583 Malott Hall Cornell Univ Ithaca NY 14850 Office Phone: 607-255-9299. Office Fax: 607-255-7149. Business E-Mail: pantano@math.cornell.edu. *

PANTANO, DANIELE, poet, educator; b. Langenthal, Bern, Switzerland, Feb. 10, 1976; U.S. s. Giuseppe Pantano and Katharina Wiest; m. Nicole Renée Boyer, June 23, 1997; children: Fiona, Giacomo. BA in Philosophy, U. South Fla., 2003, MA in Creative Writing, 2005. Instr. U. South Fla., Brandon, 2003—, dir. Writing Ctr., 2007—. Adj. prof. Fla. So. Coll., 2006—. Office: U South Fla 527 Emberwood Dr Brandon FL 33511

PANTEL, GLENN STEVEN, lawyer; b. Plainfield, NJ, Sept. 25, 1953; s. Donald and Sarah Libby (Pearlman) P.; m. Lisa Pamela Krop, June 28, 1981; 1 child, Adam Scott. AB, Johns Hopkins U., 1975; JD, U. Pa., 1978. Bar: N.J. 1978, U.S. Dist. Ct. N.J. 1978, Pa. 1978, Fla. 1980, U.S. Ct. Appeals (3d cir.) 1982. Law clk. to presiding judge U.S. Dist. Ct. (so. dist.), Miami, Fla., 1978-79; from assoc. to ptnr. Shanley & Fisher P.C., Morristown, NJ, 1979-99, also bd. dirs.; ptnr. Drinker Biddle and Reath LLP, Florham Park, NJ, 1999—. Trustee, mem. scholarship com. 200 Club of Somerset County. Mem. ABA, Fla. Bar Assn., N.J. Bar Assn., Morris County Bar Assn., Phi Beta Kappa. Avocations: skiing, sailing. Home: 3 Cross Way Mendham NJ 07945-3120 Office: Drinker Biddle & Reath LLP 500 Campus Dr Florham Park NJ 07932-1047

PANTHAKI, ZUBIN JAL, medical educator, plastic surgeon; b. Bombay, Feb. 26, 1968; arrived in U.S., 2000; s. Jal Minocher Panthaki and Nergish Nanabhoy Sethna. B in Engring., McGill U., Montreal, Quebec, 1991, MD, 1995. Diplomate Am. Bd. Plastic Surgeons, cert. for hand surgery Am. Bd. Plastic Surgeons, lic. N.H., Calif., Fla. Resident in surgery McGill U., Montreal, 1995—2000; microsurgery and hand surgery fellow Buncke Clinic, San Francisco, 2000—01; asst. prof. plastic surgery U. Miami, Fla., 2001—, program dir. plastic surgery, 2005—. Cons. Miami Children's Hosp., Cedar's Hosp., Jackson Meml. Hosp., 2001—, U. Miami Hosps., Miami Vets. Hosp., West Palm Beach Vets. Hosp. Editor: Jour. Craniofacial Surgery, 2004—. Vol. Interplast, 2003—. Capt. mil. engrs., 1987—2000, Can. Fellow: Royal Coll. Surgeons; mem.: Miami Soc. Plastic Surgeons (pres. 2007—), Fellow Am. Coll. Surgeons, Fla. Soc. Plastic Surgeons, Nat. Bd. Med. Examiners, Am. Soc. Plastic Surgeons. Avocation: computers. Office: Univ Miami Jackson Meml 1611 NW 12th Ave ET-3019 Miami FL 33136 Home: 6002 SW 58th St South Miami FL 33143 Office Phone: 305-585-5285. Office Fax: 305-324-7384. Business E-Mail: zpanthaki@med.miami.edu.

PANTOLIANO, JOE, actor; b. Hoboken, NJ, Sept. 12, 1951; s. Dominic and Mary Pantoliano; m. Morga Kester, 1979 (div. 1985); 3 children; m. Nancy Sheppard, Feb. 18, 1994; 1 child. Actor: (stage prodns.) Brothers, 1982, Orphans, 1983, One Flew Over the Cuckoo's Nest, Italian American Reconciliation, The Death Star, Visions of Kerouac, (feature films) The Godfather Part II, 1974, The Idol Maker, 1980, Monsignor, 1982, Risky Business, 1983, Eddie and the Cruisers, 1983, The Mean Season, 1985, Goonies, 1985, Running Scared, 1986, The In Crowd, 1987, The Squeeze, 1987, Scenes from the Goldmine, 1987, Amazon Women on the Moon, 1987, La Bamba, 1987, Empire of the Sun, 1987, Midnight Run, 1988, Downtown, 1990, The Last of the Finest, 1990, Short Time, 1990, Zandalee, 1991, Used People, 1992, Three of Hearts, 1993, The Fugitive, 1993, Baby's Day Out, 1994, Calendar Girl, 1994, Steal Big, Steal Little, 1995, Bad Boys, 1995, Bound, 1996, Top of the World, 1997, Self Storage, 1997, Tinseltown, 1997 (also assoc. prodr.), The Tax Man, 1998, U.S. Marshals, 1998, The Life Before This, 1999, Black and White, 1999, Tinseltown, 1999, The Matrix, 1999, Ready to Rumble, 2000, Memento, 2000, Silver Man, 2000, (voice) Cats & Dogs, 2001, The Adventures of Pluto Nash, 2002, A Piece of My Heart, 2002, Daredevil, 2003, Bad Boys II, 2003, 5-25-77, 2003, Second Best, 2004 (also prodr.), A Piece of My Heart, 2004, (voice) Racing Stripes, 2005, The Check Up, 2005, The Moguls, 2005, (voice) The Easter Egg Adventure, 2005, Larry the Cable Guy: Health Inspector, 2006; (TV movies) More Than Friends, 1978, Alcatraz: The Whole Shocking Story, 1980, Destination: America, 1987, El Diablo, 1990, One Special Victory, 1991, Through the Eyes of a Killer, 1992, (voice) Olive, the Other Reindeer, 1999, (TV mini-series) From Here to Eternity, 1979, Robert Kennedy and His Times, 1985, (TV spl.) Mr. Roberts, 1984 (TV Series) Free Country, 1978, The Fanelli Boys, 1990-91, Sugar Hill, 1999, The Sopranos, 2001-02 (Emmy award best sup. actor drama, 2003), Dr. Vegas, 2004-05; writer, dir. (films) Just Like Mona, 2003; TV appearances include Tales From the Crypt, Amazing Stories, L.A. Law, The Hitchhiker, NYPD Blue, Arlis$, Hill Street Blues, The Hitchhiker, Highlander, The Marshal. Avocations: skiing, jogging, shopping. Office: UTA care Lisa Hellerman 9560 Wilshire Blvd Fl 5 Beverly Hills CA 90212-2401

PANTONE, DAVID, academic administrator; BS in Hospitality Mgmt., Fla. Internat. U.; Assoc. Occupl. Studies degree in Culinary Arts, Culinary Inst. Am. Cert. Exec. Chef, Culinary Educator. Exec. pastry chef Waldorf-Astoria, Pavillion Hotel, Mayfair Hotel, Chef Allen's, Lucky's, Breakers; dean culinary edn. Fla. Culinary Inst., West Palm Beach. Named Educator of Yr., Foodservice Educators Network Internat. Office: Florida Culinary Institute 2410 Metrocentre Blvd West Palm Beach FL 33407 Office Phone: 877-523-7549. Office Fax: 561-688-9882. *

PANTUSO, VINCENT JOSEPH, food service consultant; b. Charleston, W.Va., Aug. 13, 1940; s. Fortunato F. Pantuso and Josephine Malcom (Ginestra) Pantuso Messer; m. Carol Barber, Dec. 10, 1964 (div. 1976); children: Lisa, Barbara, Tina; m. Nancy Josephine Chellman, Sept. 30, 1978 (div. 1995). Student, Drexel U.; BSBA, St. Joseph's U., 1968; postgrad., Rollins Coll., 1984-85. Asst. mgr. Marriott Hotels, Inc., Bethesda, Md., 1962-64; v.p. sales mktg. ARA Services, Inc., Phila., 1964-72; sr. v.p. Interstate United Corp., Chgo., 1972-84; pres. V.J. Pantuso Services, Inc., Orlando, Fla., 1984—, New Vista Services, Inc., 1988-97. Mem. Nat. Assn. Concessionaires (bd. dirs. 1982—, pres. 1989-91, chmn. 1991-94, Master Concessionaire, Chgo. 1985), Nat. Assn. Food Equipment Mfrs. (doctorate 1989). Republican. Episcopalian. Avocation: fishing. Home: Apt 5 120 Monarch Cir Casselberry FL 32730-2718 Office Phone: 407-539-0000.

PANUSKA, JOSEPH ALLAN, retired academic administrator; b. Balt., July 3, 1927; s. Joseph William and Barbara Agnes (Preller) P. BS, Loyola Coll., Balt., 1948; PhD, St. Louis U., 1958; STL, Woodstock Coll., 1961; D of Health (hon.), Trnava U., Slovakia, 1997; LLD (hon.), U. Scranton, 1974; LHD (hon.), Marywood Coll., 1992; LLD (hon.), Alvernia Coll., 2007. Joined S.J., 1948; ordained priest Roman Cath. Ch., 1960. Instr. dept. physiology Emory U. Sch. Medicine, 1962-63; asst. prof. biology Georgetown U., 1963-66, assoc. prof., 1966-72, prof., 1973; provincial, bd. dirs. Jesuit Conf. Md. Province (S.J.), 1973-79; acad. v.p., dean faculties, prof. biology Boston Coll., 1979-82; pres. U. Scranton, Pa., 1982-98, pres. emeritus, 1998—2004; rector Jesuit Ctr., 1988—2003; pres. emeritus, 2004—. Mem. Pa. Commn. Ind. Colls. and Univs., 1982-98, mem. exec. com., treas., 1987-91, vice chmn., 1988-89, chmn., 1990-91; mem. Pres.'s Commn., NCAA, 1989-90; spiritual dir. Scranton Ctrl. City Ministerium, bd. dirs., 2003—. Mem. editl. bd. Crybiology, 1968-88, editor-in-chief, 1971-74; contbr. chpts. to books, articles to sci. rsch. jours. Mem. corp. Am. Found. Biol. Rsch., 1967-85, pres. bd. dirs., 1974-79, v.p., 1979-83; trustee Loyola Coll., 1979-85, St. Joseph's U., 1979-84, U. Scranton, 1970-73, 1982-98, St. Peter's Coll., 1971-72, Woodstock Coll., 1973-76, Fordham U., 1982-88, Cambridge Ctr. for Social Studies, 1973-79 (pres. 1973-79), Corp. Roman Cath. Clergymen, 1973-79 (pres. 1973-79); rector Jesuit Cmty. at Georgetown U., 1970-73; bd. dirs. United Way Pa., 1985-87, Scranton Prep. Sch., 1984-90, Scranton Area Found., 1997-98, John Carroll U., 1992-98, Nat. Inst. Environ. Renewal, 1992-98, Woodstock Theol. Ctr., Washington, 1998-2001, St. Joseph's Prep. Sch., Phila., 1998-2001, Alvernia Coll., 2001-07, Ctrl. Scranton (Pa.) Ministerium, 2004—; chmn. Pa. Commn. for Ind. Colls. and Univs., 1990-91; bd. visitors Panuska Coll. Profl. Studies, U. Scranton, 1998-; pres. emeritus, spiritual dir. and advancement Campus Ministry. NIH postdoctoral fellow, 1962-63; recipient Danforth Found. Harbison prize for disting. tchg., 1969, B'nai B'rith Americanism award, 1997, recipient from 2001, Michelini award Outstanding Svc. to Higher Edn. AICUP (Assoc. Ind. Coll. and U. Pa.), 2001; vis. fellow St. Edmunds Coll., Cambridge U., 1969; college named J.A. Panuska Coll. of Profl. Studies, Univ. at Scranton, Interfaith Person of Yr. Scranton Ctrl. City Ministerium, 2004. Mem. Assn. Jesuit Colls. and Univs. (bd. dirs. 1982-98, treas. 1993-96), Pa. Assn. Colls. and Univs. (exec. com., adv. com. to State Bd. Edn. 1990-91). Home and Office: Jesuit Cmty U Scranton Scranton PA 18510-4623 Office Phone: 570-941-6594. Business E-Mail: panuskaj1@scranton.edu. *In order to be happy in a leadership role and to succeed in it, I have to possess a sense of coherence with my life values. I also need to recognize that my own activity makes a real difference in the empowerment of others so that there is a multiplier effect which extends me beyond my own person and activity.*

PANUTHOS, PETER J., federal judge; b. NY, 1943; BS, Bernard Baruch Sch. Bus., CUNY; diploma, Bryant Coll., Providence, RI, 1966; JD, Suffolk U. Law Sch., Boston, 1969; LLM in Taxation, Boston U. Sch. Law,

1972. Bar: DC, admitted to: Supreme Jud. Ct., Mass., US Supreme Ct. Trial atty., asst. dist. counsel Boston Office of Chief Counsel, IRS, 1970—83; spl. trial judge US Tax Ct., 1983—92, chief spl. trial judge, 1992—. Adj. prof. Bentley Coll., Boston, Cath. U. Am., Columbus Sch. Law, David A. Clarke Sch. Law, U. DC; mem. law rev. Suffolk U. Law Sch. Mem.: ABA, Inns of Ct., Fed. Bar Assn. Office: US Tax Ct 400 2nd St NW Washington DC 20217 Office Phone: 202-521-4707. *

PANWAR, SHIVENDRA SINGH, education educator, researcher; b. Delhi, India, Dec. 15, 1959; came to U.S., 1981; s. Surendra Singh and Lakshmi (Singh) P.; m. Shruti Kumari, Apr. 8, 1988. B Tech., Indian Inst. Tech., Kanpur, India, 1981; MS, U. Mass., 1983, PhD, 1986. Tchr., rsch. asst. U. Mass., Amherst, 1981-85; asst. prof. Poly. U., Bklyn., 1985-90; assoc. prof. Poly U., Bklyn., 1990—2003, prof., 2003—. Vis. scientist IBM Rsch., Yorktown Heights, N.Y., 1987; spl. cons. AT&T Bell Labs., Holmdel, N.J., 1988; dir. N.Y. State Ctr for Adv. Tech. in Telecom., 1996—. Co-author TCP/IP Essentials: A Lab Based Approach, 2004; contbr. articles to profl. jours. Recipient Rsch. Initiation award NSF, Washington, 1989 Fellow IEEE (sr., tech. com. computer comms., Leonard G. Abraham prize 2004); mem. Sigma Xi, Tau Beta Pi. Hindu. Office: Polytechnic Univ Six Metrotech Ctr Brooklyn NY 11201-2907

PANY, KURT JOSEPH, finance educator, consultant; b. St. Louis, Mar. 31, 1946; s. Joseph Francis and Ruth Elizabeth (Westerman) P.; m. Darlene Dee Zabish, June 3, 1971; children: Jeffrey, Michael. BSBA, U. Ariz., 1968; MBA in Mgmt., U. Minn., 1971; PhD in Accountancy, U. Ill., 1977. CPA, Ariz., cert. fraud examiner. Staff auditor Arthur Andersen & Co., Mpls., 1968-69, Touche Ross & Co., Phoenix, 1971-73; teaching asst. U. Minn., Mpls., 1969-71; teaching asst. auditing and acctg. U. Ill., Urbana, 1972-76; asst. prof. acctg. Ariz. State U., Tempe, 1977-81, assoc. prof., 1981-85, Arthur Andersen/Don Dupont prof. acctg., 1985-91. Mem. acctg. and auditing standards com. State of Ariz., Phoenix, 1989—; reviewer Jour. Acctg. and Pub. Policy, 1983—. Contbg. author: CPA Exam. Rev., 1983—; co-author: Principles of Auditing, 1988—, Auditing, 1993—; co-editor Auditing: A Jour. Practice and Theory, 1984-88; mem. editl. bd. Advances in Acctg., 1982—, Jour. Acctg. Edn., 1983—; reviewer Acctg. Rev., 1984—, ad hoc editor, 1989—; contbr. numerous articles to profl. jours. Active various child-related orgns. Peat, Marwick, Mitchell & Co. Found. grantee, 1985. Fellow AICPA (auditing stds. divsn. 1989-90, acctg. lit. selection com. 1989-90, acctg. lit. awards com. 1979-83, mem. auditing stds. bd. 1995—); mem. Am. Acctg. Assn. (tech. program com. 1980-81, chairperson Western region auditing sect. 1981-83, acctg. lit. nominating com. 1982-84, 88-89, acctg. lit. selection com. 1989-90, dir. auditing stds., chmn. auditing stds. com. 1989-90), Ariz. Soc. CPA's (auditing stds. com. 1978-81, ethics com. 1981-84). Avocation: baseball. Address: 7445 S Rita Ln Tempe AZ 85283-4792 Office: Ariz State U Sch Accountancy Tempe AZ 85287 Business E-Mail: kpany@cox.net, kurt.pany@asu.edu.

PANZER, MARK, retail executive; BBA, Northeastern Ill. U.; MBA in Fin., Loyola U. Various positions including asst. store mgr., store mgr., regional sales & mktg. mgr. and regional ops. mgr. Osco Drug, Inc., 1972; dist. mgr. to dir. sales & mktg. to v.p. sales, mktg. & advt. to sr. v.p. mktg. & formats Am. Stores, 1989—98; corp. v.p. mktg., sales and gen. mdse. Albertson's Inc., 1998—2001; exec. v.p. store ops. Rite Aid Corp., 2001—02, sr. exec. v.p. store ops., 2002—05, sr. exec. v.p., chief mktg. officer, 2005. Office: Rite Aid Corp 30 Hunter Lane Camp Hill PA 17011 Office Phone: 717-761-2633. *

PANZER, MARY CAROLINE, historian, museum curator; b. Flint, Mich., May 29, 1955; d. Milton and Caroline Alice (Weis) P. BA, Yale U.; MA, Columbia U., 1980; PhD, Boston U., 1990. Asst. prof. U. Kans., Lawrence, 1989-91; curator photographs Spencer Mus. Art, Lawrence, 1989-91; asst. dir. SMART Mus. Art U. Chgo., 1991; curator photographs Nat. Portrait Gallery Smithsonian Instn., Washington, 1992-2000; ind. historian NYC, 2000—; adj. faculty NYU, 2002—, Hunter Coll., CUNY, 2003. Author: Philadelphia Naturalistic Photography, 1982, Rudolf Eickemeyer, Jr. and the Art of the Camera, 1986, Mathew Brady and the Image of History, 1997, Halsman: A Retrospective, 1998, Brady 55, 2001, Hine 55, 2002 Separate, But Equal, 2002, Nickolas Muray and Miguel Corarrubias, 2004, Things as They Are: Photojournalism in Context Since 1955, 2005 (winner Infinity award, 2006); contbg. editor Am. Photo, 2002. Mem. Am. Studies Assn., Coll. Art Assn., Oracle, Mid-Atlantic Radical Historians Orgn., Orgn. Am. Historians.

PANZER, MILTON, retired orthodontist, volunteer; b. Phila., June 22, 1924; s. Julius Panzer and Tillie (Markowitz) Panzzer; m. Caroline Alice Weis, Sept. 11, 1949; children: Mary, Elizabeth, Kate. BS, Temple U., Phila., 1943, DDS, 1947; MS in Dentistry For Children, U. Mich., Ann Arbor, 1957; MS in Orthodontics, State U. Iowa, Iowa City, 1961. Dental intern US Marine Hosp., Balt., 1947—48; staff dentist US Pub. Health, Richmond, Ind., 1948—49; dir. Mott Children's Health Ctr., Flint, Mich., 1951—60; pvt. practice Flint, 1962—93; ret. Dental cons. Flint Pub. Sch. Sys., 1951—60; lectr. orthodontics and facial growth, dental hygiene program Mott CC, Flint, 1969—89; clin. faculty Loyola U. Sch. Dentistry, Flint, 1988—92; cons. in orthodontics Mott Children's Health Ctr., Flint, 1962—93; bd. mem., fin. com. mem., program com. mem. Motts Children's Health Ctr., Flint, 1993—. Svc. dental vol. Israel Clinic, Jerusalem, 1991—93; com. mem. Flint Art Fair, 1973—; mem. Free Med. Clinic Bd., 1997—; bd. dirs. Temple Beth El, 1965—75, chmn. bd. edn., 1970—76, chmn. adult edn. com., 1977—78; bd. dirs. Flint Inst. Health, 1976—80; mem. bd. friends Sloan Mus., Flint, 1985—, pres. bd friends, 1987—90; program com. mem. Mgmt. Assistance Program, 1998—. Fellow: Am Coll. Dentists; mem.: Mus. Trustes Assn., Mich. Dental Assn. (dental health edn. com. 1964—67, dental care com. 1970—73, ins. com. 1985—88), Mich. Assn. Pub. Health Dentists (pres. 1953—54), Mich. Soc. Orthodontists, Am. Assn. Orthodontists, Great Lakes Soc. Orthodontists, Am. Dental Assn., Mich. Dental Soc., Genesee Dist. Dental Soc. (editor monthly pub. 1962—71, exec. sec., treas. 1962—), Flint Rotary Club. Avocations: tennis, reading, politics.

PAO, BING SHIH, emergency physician; b. Pitts., Oct. 2, 1965; s. Chia-Ven and Mei-Shan Pao; m. Metalane Pao; children: Caroline, Noah. BS in Biology, U NC, Chapel Hill, 1987; MD, Duke U., Durham, NC, 1992. Resident U. Calif., San Diego, 1992—96; attending physician Pinnacell Emergency Cons., Atlanta, 1996—99; ptnr. Calif. Emergency Physicians, San Diego, 1999—. Assoc. clin. prof. U. Calif., San Diego, 1999—; asst. dir. Palonian Emergency Dept., San Diego, 2003—. Recipient Med. Student award, SAEM. Fellow: ACEP. Avocations: martial arts, surfing, soccer, guitar. Office: Calif Emergency Physicians 2100 Powell St Ste 920 Emeryville CA 94608

PAOLETTA, MARK R. A., lawyer; b. 1962; BA, Duquesne U., 1984; JD, Georgetown U., 1987. Bar: DC, US Supreme Ct. Asst. counsel to the Pres. Exec. Office of the Pres., Washington, 1990-93; ptnr. O'Connor & Hannan, Washington, 1993, Keck, Mahin & Cate, Washington, Dickstein Shapiro LLP, Washington, 2007—; counsel oversight and investigations subcommittee, House Com. on Energy & Commerce, 1996—97, chief counsel, 1997—2007. Office: Dickstein Shapiro LLP 1825 Eye St NW Washington DC 20006-5403 Office Phone: 202-420-3447. *

PAOLINI, CLAIRE JACQUELINE, dean, educator; b. Newton, Mass., May 19, 1934; d. Frank and Angelina Landro; m. Gilberto Paolini, June 18, 1960; children: Angela J., John F. BA, Boston U., 1956; MA, Middlebury Coll., Vt., 1958; PhD, Tulane U., 1982. Instr. Spanish U. Mass., Amherst, 1956-60, U. New Orleans, 1970-75; from dir. internat. student affairs to assoc. dean Loyola U., New Orleans, 1975-83, assoc. dean arts and scis., 1983-97; dean coll. arts and scis., prof. spanish Sacred Heart U., Fairfield, Conn., 1997—. Author: The Narrative Art of Domingos Monteiro, 1979, Valle-Inclán's Modernism: Use and Abuse of Religious and Mystical Symbolism, 1986; editor: LA CHISPA '95: Selected Proceedings, 1995, LA CHISPA '97: Selected Proceedings, 1997; co-editor: La CHISPA '99: Selected Proceedings, 1999; assoc. editor: LA CHISPA '93: Selected Proceedings, 1993; mem. editl. bd. LA CHISPA, 1983, 85, 87, 89, NACADA Jour., 1995-97. V.p. Soc. Espanola, New Orleans, 1977-81, bd. mem. 1976-97. Mem. Nat. Assn. Academic Affairs Administrators (Administrator of Yr. award 1996-97), Modern Lang. Assn., Council Colls. Arts Scis., Am. Assn. Tchrs. Spanish and Portuguese, Coll. Consortium Internat. Studies (bd. mem. 1997—), Am. Assn. Higher Edn. Home: 3 Gregory Farm Rd Easton CT 06612-2049 Office: Sacred Heart Univ 5151 Park Ave Fairfield CT 06825-1000 Office Phone: 203-396-8020. Business E-Mail: paolinic@sacredheart.edu.

PAOLINI, GILBERTO, literature educator; b. L'Aquila, Italy; naturalized citizen, 1954; s. John and Assunta Angela P.; m. Claire Jacqueline Landro; children: Angela Janet, John Frank. BA, U. Buffalo, 1957, MA, 1959; postgrad., Middlebury Coll., summer 1960, 61; PhD, U. Minn., 1965. Lectr. Spanish Rosary Hill Coll., Buffalo, 1957-58; instr. Italian and Latin lit. U. Mass., Amherst, 1958-60; instr. Spanish and Italian Syracuse U., 1962-65, asst. prof., 1965-67; assoc. prof. Spanish lit. Tulane U., New Orleans, 1967-76, prof. comparative lit., 1976—, dir. Tulane scholars and honors program, 1981-83, chmn. colloquia dept., 1981-83. Originator Spanish Culture Week, New Orleans, 1977, 79; chmn. adv. com. Jambalaya program Nat. Endowment Humanities, New Orleans, 1975-80; Spanish essay reader Ednl. Testing Svc., Princeton, 1979-85; founder, gen. chmn. La. Conf. on Hispanic Langs. and Lits., 1981, 83, 85, 87, 89, 93, 95, 97, 99. Author: Bartolome Soler: novelista: Procedimientos estilísticos, 1963; An Aspect of Spiritualistic Naturalism in the Novel of B.P. Galdos: Charity, 1969, La Vita Transecolare nel Contado Aquilano, 2003, Complesso Monastico St. Maria Agraiano Sec. X-XXY, 2007; mem. editl. bd.: Forum Italicum, 1967-71, Critica Hispanica, 1979—, Discurso Literario, 1985—, Letras Peninsulares, 1987—, Ojáncano, 1994—; assoc. editor: South Central MLA Bull, 1978-80; editor: La Chispa: Selected Procs., 1981-99, Papers on Romance Literary Relations, 1983; cons. editor South Central Rec., 1988-99; contbr. articles to profl. jours. With AUS, 1952-54, USAF, 1954-57. Recipient Disting. Service award Sociedad Espanola, 1979, Knight Cross of Order of Isabel the Catholic, 1984; subject of Festscrift Studies, Honor of Gilberto Paolini, 1996. Mem. MLA, AAUP, Am. Assn. Tchrs. Spanish and Portuguese (chmn. pub. rels. com. 1981-86, pres. La. chpt. 1979-81, 88-89), Am. Assn. Tchrs. Italian, Am. Assn. Advancement Humanities, Soc. for Lit. and Sci., Asociacion Internacional de Hispanistas, Southeastern Am. Soc. 18th Century Studies (exec. v.p.), Assn. Internat. Galdosistas, Soc. Literatura Española del Siglo XIX, Phi Sigma Iota, Sigma Delta Pi (v.p. for S.W. 1989-92). Office: Tulane Univ 304 Newcomb Hall New Orleans LA 70118 Business E-Mail: gpaolini@tulane.edu.

PAOLINO, RONALD MARIO, clinical psychologist, consultant, psychopharmacologist, pharmacist; b. Providence, Mar. 15, 1938; s. Lawrence and Mary Corinne (Guglielmi) P.; m. Eileen Frances Quimby, June 18, 1960; children: Lisa Katherine, David Lawrence. Student, Providence Coll., 1955—56; BS in Pharmacy, U. R.I., 1959, MS, 1961; PhD in Pharmacology/Toxicology, Purdue U., 1963; postdoctoral studies Exptl. Psychology, Yale U., 1963—65; doctoral studies in clin. psychology, Purdue U., 1972—74; postdoctoral studies in existential analytic psychotherapy, Okla. Inst. Existential Analysis and Psychotherapy, 1974—75; Hostage Negotiation, FBI, 1991, Advanced Hostage Negotiation, 1995; Crisis Negotaition, FBI Acad., 1994; MA (hon.), Brown U., 1977. Lic. psychologist, R.I., pharmacist R.I.; nat. registered health svc. provider in psychology; cert. arbitrator; cert. nat. registered group psycho-therapists; cert. edn. provider N.Y.; diplomate Am. Bd. Forensic Examiners, Am. Bd. Forensic Medicine. Intern dept. psychiatry and behavioral scis. U. Okla. Health Scis. Ctr., 1974—75, NIMH fellow in clin. psychology, 1974-75; David Ross predoctoral fellow dept. pharmacology/toxicology Purdue U., West Lafayette, Ind., 1961—63, assoc. prof. psychopharmacology, 1967—74; NIMH postdoctoral fellow in psychology dept. psychology Yale U., 1963—65; asst. prof. pharmacology U. Conn. Sch. Pharmacy, 1965—67; coord. group psychotherapy tng. program Brown U. Program in Medicine, 1983—85, assoc. prof. psychiatry and human behavior, 1976—90; pvt. practice; chief drug dependency treatment program VA Med. Ctr., Providence, 1975—87, dir. biofeedback clinic, 1977—87, primary hostage negotiator, 1991—. Psychiatric cons. VA Police, alternative Dispute Resolution Mediator, New Eng. Veterans Integrated Svc. Network, 1996—, pain mgmt. bd., 1999—; mem. Pharmacology and Therapeutic Agts. Com., 1979-87, VA Med. Ctr., coord. VA Contracted Half-Way Project for Substance Dependent Vets., 1981-85, chmn. Pain Mgmt. Task Force, 1984-85, mem. Supervisory Level Pharmacy Profl. Standards Bd., 1990—, mem. Mgmt. Suicidal and Violent Patient Task Force, 1990-91, chmn. Com. Prevention & Mgmt. of Disturbed Behaviors, 1991—, chief crisis mgmt. program, 1993-96, advisor FBI Hostage Negotiations, 1991—, Instr. R.I. State Police Acad., 1994, Instr., Drug Recognition Experts Recert PRGM, R.I. Dept Health, 1995, Faculty, Law Enforcement Mgmt. Command Sch. U.R.I., 1991—, Va. Nat. Law Enforcement Tng. Ctr., 1997; chmn. Outpatient Psychiatry Svcs. Reorganization Task Force, 1991, mem. VA DOD Desert Storm Emergency Plan Com., 1991; advisor OSHA Dept. Labor for Violence in the Work Place, 1994-95; mem. E. Prov. Clergy & Mental Health Providers Alliance, 1995—; mem. substance abuse and prevention grant application rev. com. R.I. Adv. Coun. on Substance Abuse, 1982-92, prevention, edn. and tng. com. on substance abuse, 1981—, chmn. 1981-82; adj. assoc. prof. psychology, U. R.I., 1982—, clin. prof. pharmacy U. R.I., 1998—; mem. planning com. State Conf. on Substance Abuse in the Hispanic Community, 1986; mem. alcohol awareness commn. Episc. Diocese of R.I., 1983-85; gubernatorial appointee Gov.'s Permanent Coun. on Drug Abuse Control, 1978-82; mem. rev. com. for funding of state drug abuse programs R.I. Single State Agy. on Drug Abuse, R.I. Dept. Mental Health Retardation and Hosps., 1978-82; cons. Nurses Renewal Com., 1980-81, substance abuse prevention edn. for elem. sch. children R.I. chpt. ARC, 1977, mem. suicide prevention steering com., 1977; mem.Interagy. Drug Abuse Steering Com., Lafayette, Ind. 1969-72; bd. dirs. Providence VA Med. Ctr. Credit Union; mem. bd. cert. for alcoholism counselors R.I. Assn. Alcohol Counselors, 1979-81; mem. Gov.'s Task Force on Substance Abuse at Adult Correctional Instn., 1977-78, Gov.'s Task Force on Mental Health Svcs. at Adult Correctional Instn., 1977-78, chmn. reclassification of inmates com., 1977-78; chmn. com. on edn. and cert. biofeedback practioners Conn. Biofeedback Soc., 1977-78; summer faculty fellow U. Conn., 1967; vis. scientist lectr. Assn. Am. Colls. Pharmacy, 1972-73; cons. to bus., unions, law enforcement. Author: (2 chpts.) Drug Testing: Issues and Options, 1991; contbr. 37 articles to profl. jours. Bd. dirs. R.I. chpt. Samaritans Internat. Suicide Prevention Orgn., 1978-84; v.p. Experience Jesus Inc.; mem. com. adv. bd. Cpina Bifida Assn. R.I., 1980-83; mem. R.I. East Bay Interfaith Mental Health Alliance; congressman appointee (Patrick J. Kennedy); mem. veterans adv. commn., 1995—. Recipient Citation award for svc. and contbns. to formulation of state policy for treatment and prevention of drug abuse Gov. R.I., 1983, Letter of Commendation, Gov.'s R.I. Adv. Coun. on Substance Abuse, 1986, vc. Recognition award DAV, 1990, Spl. Contbn. award Providence VA Med Ctr., 1990, 98, 99, 2000, Outstanding Performance award, 1991, 92, 93, 94, 97, cert. appreciation for continued excellence in patient care, 1999; named to Cranston Hall of Fame, 2001. Fellow Am. Coll. Forensic Examiners; mem. AMA, Am. Psychotherapy Assn., Am. Soc. Pharmacology Exptl. Therapeutics, Internat. Brain Rsch. Orgn., Internat. Narcotic Enforcement Officers Assn., R.I. Group Psychotherapy Soc. (pres. 1991-93, continuing edn. dir. psychologists 1990-95, exec. bd. 1986—, tng. faculty 1985—, co-dir. tng. 1986-87, tng. adv. bd. 1985-86), R.I. Psychol. Assn. (chmn. substance abuse ins. subcom. 1986-87, rep. Gov.'s Coun. on Mental Health State Plan Com. 1982-84), Hostage Negotiators Am. Office: Mental Health and Behavioral Scis Svc VA Med Ctr Providence RI E-mail: ronald.paolinophd@med.va.gov.

PAOLUCCI, ANNE ATTURA, playwright, poet, literature educator, educational consultant; b. Rome; d. Joseph and Lucy (Guidoni) Attura; m. Henry Paolucci(dec.). BA, Barnard Coll; MA, Columbia U., PhD, 1963; D (hon.), Lehman Coll., CUNY, 1995. Mem. faculty English dept. Brearley Sch., NYC, 1957—59; asst. prof. English and comparative lit. CCNY, 1959—69; univ. rsch. prof. St. John's U., Jamaica, NY, 1969—97, acting head dept. English, 1973—74, chmn. dept. English, 1982—91, dir. doctor of arts degree program in English, 1982—97; ednl. cons.; editl. cons. Bagehot Coun. Fulbright lectr. in Am. drama U. Naples, Italy, 1965-67; spl. lectr. U. Urbino, summers 1965-67, U. Bari, 1967, univs. Bari, Bologna, Catania, Messina, Palermo, Milan, Pisa, 1965-67; disting. adj. vis. prof. Queens Coll., CUNY; bd. dir. World Centre for Shakespeare Studies, Globe project, London; spl. guest Yugoslavia Ministry of Culture, 1972; rep. U.S. at Internat. Poetry Festival, Yugoslavia, 1981; founder, exec. dir. Coun. on Nat. Lits., 1974—; mem. exec. com. Conf. Editors Learned Jour.-MLA, 1975—85; del. to Fgn. Lang. Jours., 1977—85; mem. adv. bd. Commn. on Tech. and Cultural Transformation, UNESCO, 1978—80; vis. fellow Humanities Rsch. Centre, Australian Nat. U., 1979; rep. U.S. woman playwright Inter-Am. Women Writers Congress, Ottawa, Ont., Can., 1978; organizer, chmn. profl. symposia, meetings; TV appearances; hostess Mag. in Focus, Channel 31, N.Y.C., 1971-73; mem. N.Am. Adv. Coun. Shakespeare Globe Theatre Ctr., 1981—; mem. Nat. Grad. Fellows Program Fellowship Bd., 1985—87; mem. Nat. Garibaldi Centennial Com., 1981; trustee Edn. Scholarship, Grants Com. of NIAF, 1990-94; guest spkr. with E. Albee Ohio No. State U., 1990; Apptd. by Pres. Reagan to Nat. Coun. on Humanities, 1986-1993; One of the 10 top Women in Bus. in Queens, 2003. Author (with H. Paolucci): Hegel On Tragedy, 1962, new edition, 2001, From Tension to Tonic: The Plays of Edward Albee, 1972, new edit., 2000, Pirandello's Theater: The Recovery of the Modern Stage for Dramatic Art, 1974, 2d edit. 2002; editor: Henry Paolucci: Selected Writings on Literature and the Arts; Sci. and Astronomy; Law, Govt., and Pol. Sci., 1999, Dante's Gallery of Rogues, 2001; author: Do Me a Favor (and other short stories), 2001 (nominated for the Pulitzer Prize), Poems Written for Sbek's Mummies, Marie Menken, and Other Important Persons, Places, and Things, 1977, Eight Short Stories, 1977, Sepia Tones, 1985, 2nd edit., 1986, In Wolf's Clothing, 2004; plays include: Minions of the Race (Medieval and Renaissance Conf. of Western Mich. U. Drama award 1972), video version, 2002, Cipango!, 1985, pub. as book, 1985, 86, videotape excerpts, 1986, revision, 1990; performed NYC and Washington, 1987-88; The Actor in Search of His Mask, 1987, Italian translation and prodn., Genoa, 1987, The Short Season, Naples, 1967, Cubiculo, NY, 1973, German translation, Vienna, 1996, mini-prodn. of Minions of the Race, The Players, 1999, video prodn. 2002, In the Green Room (play), 1999, Three Short Plays, 1995; editor Dino Bigongiari: Backgrounds to the Divine Comedys; editor with introduction: Readings in the Divine Comedy, 2006; poems Riding the Mast Where It Swings, 1980, In the Green Room (orig. play), 1999; Gorbachev in Concert, 1991, Queensboro Bridge (and other Poems), 1995 (Pulitzer prize nominee 1995-96), Terminal Degrees, 1997; contbr. numerous articles, rev. to profl. jour.; editor, author intro. to: Dante's Influence on Am. Writers, 1977; gen. editor tape-cassette series China, 1977, 78; founder Coun. on Nat. Lit.; gen. editor series Rev. Nat. Lit., 1970-2000, CNL/Quar. World Report, 1974-76, semi-ann., 1977-84, ann., 1985-2000; full-length TV tape of play Cipango! and ednl. TV with original music by Henry Paolucci, 1990, grant Queens Pub. TV for 48 Min Videotape of award-winning play, Minions of the Race, 2003, About Thomas More, Thomas Cromwell, and Cardinal Thomas Wolsey, 2003-04; featured in PBS psl. Italian-Americans II: A Beautiful Song, 1998; translations of Selected Poems by Giacomo Leopardi (with Thomas Bergin), 2004 (Italian Ministry Fgn. Affairs prize 2005), The Woman in Dante's "Divine Comedy" and Spenser's "Faerie Quene", 2005. Pres. Reagan appointee Nat. Grad. Fellows Program Fellowship Bd., 1985—86, Nat. Coun. Humanities, 1986—, Ann. award FIERI, 1990; bd. dirs. Am. Soc. Italian Legions of Merit, chmn. cultural com., 1990—; bd. dirs. Italian Heritage and Culture City-wide com., 1986—; pres. Columbus: Countdown 1992 Fedn.; mem. Gov. Cuomo's Heritage Legacy Project for Schs., 1989—; trustee CUNY, 1996—, chairwoman bd. trustees, 1997—99; mem. adv. com. on edn. N.Y. State Senate, 1996—. Decorated cavaliere Italian Republic, commendatore Order of Merit (Italy); named one of 10 Outstanding Italian Ams. in Washington, awarded medal by Amb. Rinaldo Petrignani, 1986; recipient Notable Rating for Mags. in Focus series N.Y. Times, 1972, Woman of Yr. award Dr. Herman Henry Scholarship Found., 1973, Amita award, 1970, award Women's Press Club N.Y., 1974, Gold medal for Quincentenary Can. trustee NIAF, 1990, ann. awards Consortium of Italian-Am. Assns., 1991, Am.-Italian Hist. Assn., 1991, 1st Columbus award Cath. Charities, 1991, Leone di San Marco award Italian Heritage Coun. of Bronx and Westchester Counties, 1992, Children of Columbus award Order of Sons of Italy in Am., 1993, 1st Nat. Elena Cornaro award Order of Sons of Italy, 1993, Golden Lion award, 1997, Can.'s Gold medal Christopher Columbus Can. Commn., 1992, Ann. award Am. Italian Cultural Roundtable, 1997, Am. Italian Tchrs. Lifetime Achievement award, 1997, Italian-Am. Legislator's award, Albany, 1997, N.Y. State Italian-Am. Legis. Lifetime Achievement award, 1997, Columbus Citizens Fedn. Ann. award, 1997, Italian Welfare League award, 1998, Queens Coun. on Arts award, 1998, N.Y. State Conservative Party Bronx com. award, 1998, Woman of Distinction award Kingsborough C.C./CUNY, 1999, Woman of Distinction award N.Y. State Senate, 2000, prize Italian Ministry Fgn. Affairs, 2005; named one of "Ten Top Queens Women in Bus.", 2003; Fulbright scholar U. Rome, 1951-52; Columbia U. Woodbridge hon. fellow, 1961-62; Am. Coun. Learned Socs. grantee Internat. Pirandello Congress, Agrigento, Italy, 1978; Woodbridge fellow Dept. English and Compariitive Literature, Columbia U., 1961. Mem. Internat. Shakespeare Assn., Shakespeare Assn. Am., Renaissance Soc. Am., Internat. Comparative Lit. Assn., Am. Comparative Lit. Assn., MLA, Am. PEN, Hegel Soc. Am., Dante Soc. Am. (v.p. 1976-77), Am. Found. Italian Arts and Letters (founder, pres.), Pirandello Soc. (pres. 1978-85, 1990-2001), Am. Soc. Italian Legions of Merit (bd. dir. 1990-93). Achievements include pioneering work in multi-comparative literary studies. *My own first practical premise has been to organize every task (even routine chores) so that there is always time and energy for whatever important projects come up. There is enough room in the day for doing a number of things—and for creating "space" every so often to do one's own special work (writing fiction or poetry or plays, in my case). Organization is all-important; but perhaps the basic premise in intellectual things is organic growth, letting "in" those things that are meaningful because they already suggest an intrinsic pattern. In my case, I discovered long after the projects and books themselves had taken shape and had been published, that I had been tending for a number of years more and more exclusively toward drama and dramatic criticism and theory. Well, that, obviously, was my own potential "law" organizing from within my various interests. One must continue to allow for new interests to revitalize those already familiar.*

PAONE, PETER, artist; b. Phila., Oct. 2, 1936; s. George and Angelina (Vitrella) P.; m. Alma Alabilikian, 1976. BA, Phila. Mus. Coll. Art, 1958. Head graphics dept. Fleisher Art Meml., 1959—62; instr. Phila. Mus. Coll. Art, 1959—66, Positano Art Sch., Italy, 1961; tchr. Pa. Acad. Fine Arts, 1978—, chmn. graphics dept., 1978; instr. Pratt Inst. One-man shows include Grippi Gallery, 1959—61, Phila. Print Club, 1961—64, Ft. Worth Mus., 1963, Clydie Jessop Gallery, London, 1968, David Gallery, Houston, 1970—72, Kennedy Gallery, NYC, 1970—72, Robinson Gallery, Houston, 1978—79, Hooks Epstein Gallery, 1978, 1980—83, Pa. Acad. Fine Arts,

1983, Phila. Print Club, 1983, Hooks Epstein Gallery, 1985, 1987—88, 1990, Rider Coll., NJ, 1991, Ryder Coll., Pa., 1991, Merlin Verlag, Hamburg, Germany, 1996, Dresden, Germany, 1996, Pascal Robinson Gallery, Houston, 2000, exhibited in group shows at Poets, Phila. Mus. Art, 1960—61, Contemporary Am., 1961, Lehigh U., Pa., 1962, Bklyn. Mus., 1962, Poets, Phila. Mus. Art, 1963, Paris Biennial, 1963, Dallas Mus., 1964, Otis Art Inst., LA, 1964, Syracuse U., NY, 1964, La Escuela Nacional, Mexico City, 1967, Vanderbilt U., 1967, NY World's Fair Exhbn., Pakistan, 1967, 176 Anniv. Nat. Acad. Design, NYC, 2001, Poets, Nat. Acad. of Design Mus., 2003, Jersey City Mus., 2004, James A. Michener Mus., Doylestown, Pa., 2004, Lancaster Mus., 2006, Represented in permanent collections Libr. Congress, Washington, DC, Phila. Mus. Art, NY Mus. Modern Art, Princeton Libr., Phila. Libr., Gen. Mills, Phila. Print Club, Rosenwald Collection, Carl Sandburg Meml. Libr., Syracuse U., Ft. Worth Mus., Victoria and Albert Mus., Brit. Mus., Art Inst. Chgo., Yale U. Recipient award of merit Phila. Print Club, 1983, Painting prize Nat. Acad., 1997; Tiffany Found. grantee, 1962, 64; John Simon Guggenheim fellow, 1965-66; grantee Penn Council for the Arts, 1985, Nat. Portrait Gallery, Washington. Mem. NAD. Home: 1027 W Westview St Philadelphia PA 19119-3718 Personal E-mail: ppaone@aol.com. *Somewhere between the world of realism and surrealism, there is a world that deals with the reality of relationships, favoring the substance of the imagination rather than the substance of everyday vision. Objects that seemingly have no real relationship to each other in their existence are juxtaposed in the life of the artist. They have touched each other and have become part of the vision, and in turn have become his iconography. There is no urgency in this vision. The private reality has always been there and always will be. The viewer is allowed to question his knowledge of it, and in doing so, he often is uneasy and bewildered before the assemblage. This, at first, implies fantasy; this is not true. Instead, this is a reconstruction of reality, not an escape from it.*

PAPA, JOSEPH C., pharmaceutical executive; BS in Pharmacy, U. Conn.; MBA in Mktg. and Fin., Northwestern U. Kellogg Grad. Sch. Mgmt. Pharmacist; with Geneva Pharms., Ciba Geigy Pharms., Novartis Pharms. Corp.; pres. US ops. Searle Pharms.; pres. global country ops. N.Am. Pharmacia Corp.; pres., COO DuPont Pharms., Watson Pharms. Inc., 2001—04; grp. pres. Pharm. Technologies and Svcs. Cardinal Health, 2004—. Office: Cardinal Health 7000 Cardinal Pl Dublin OH 43017

PAPA, MARK GARY, oil and gas industry executive; b. Monroeville, Pa., Sept. 16, 1946; s. Mark W. Papa and Jean Feiler; m. Susan Berryman, Dec. 21, 1970; 1 child, Christine. BS in Petroleum Engring., U. Pitts., 1968; MBA in Econs./Fin., U. Houston, 1980. Registered profl. engr., Tex. Various petroleum engring., supervisory & engring. positions Conoco, Inc., various locations, 1968-81; divsn. prodn. coord. Belco Petroleum, Houston, 1981-82, mgr. ops., 1982-83; v.p. drilling and prodn. Belnorth, Houston, 1983-84, sr. v.p. drilling and prodn., 1984-85; sr. v.p. ops. Enron Oil & Gas, Houston, 1986—94, pres. N.Am. ops., 1994—98, pres., 1996—99, COO, 1997—98, CEO, 1998—99; chmn., CEO EOG Resources, 1999—. Bd. dir. Oil States Internat., Magellan Midstream Partners; chmn. U.S. Oil & Gas Assn. Mem. Soc. Petroleum Engrs., Am. Assn. Petroleum Geologists, Natural Gas Supply Assn., Tex. Ind. Prodrs. Royalty Orgn. Avocation: tennis. Office: EOG Resources 333 Clay St PO Box 4362 Houston TX 77002 *

PAPA, VINCENT T., insurance company executive; b. NYC, Dec. 11, 1946; s. Frank R. and Carmela (Farruggia) P.; m. Karen Ann Conroy, July 4, 1969; children: Kimberly, Jennifer, Kristen. AA, Nassau C.C., 1967; BBA, Hofstra U., 1969. CPA, N.Y. Staff acct. Arthur Andersen & Co., NYC, 1969-72; comptr. Finserv Corp., NYC, 1972-80; sr. v.p. Orion Capital Corp., NYC, 1980-99; chmn. bd. dirs. Wm. H. McGee & Co. Inc., NYC, 1995-99; CEO NYMAGIC Inc., 1999. Mem. AICPAs, Am. Mgmt. Assn. (mem. ins. and risk mgmt. coun.), N.Y. State Soc. CPAs.

PAPACHRISTOU, COSTAS JOHN, physicist, researcher; b. Athens, July 16, 1957; s. John C. and Katherine (Luckmas) Papachristou. BS in Physics, U. Athens, 1981; PhD, Brigham Young U., 1987. Postdoctoral assoc. Brigham Young U., Provo, Utah, 1987—88; faculty Ctr. Naval Edn. for Petty Officers, Athens, 1988—89; faculty dept. physics Naval Acad. Greece, Piraeus, 1989—. Course dir. Athens Inst. Tech., 1989-93, 96—. Contbr. articles to profl. jours. John E. Anderson scholar Brigham Young U., 1981-87. Mem. N.Y. Acad. Scis., Sigma Xi, Phi Kappa Phi. Avocations: music, poetry. Office: Naval Acad Greece Dept Physics 18539 Piraeus Greece Office Phone: 30-210-4581616. Business E-Mail: papachristou@snd.edu.gr.

PAPADAKIS, CONSTANTINE N., academic administrator, civil engineer, educator; b. Athens, Greece, Feb. 2, 1946; came to U.S., 1969; s. Nicholas and Rita (Masciotti) P.; m. Eliana Apostolides, Aug. 28, 1971; 1 child, Maria. Diploma in Civil Engring., Nat. Tech. U. Athens, 1969; MS in Civil Engring., U. Cin., 1970; PhD in Civil Engring., U. Mich., 1973. Registered profl. engr., Ohio, Greece. Engring. specialist, geotechnical group Bechtel, Inc., Gaithersburg, Md., 1974-76, supr. and asst. chief engr. geotechnical group Ann Arbor, Mich., 1976-81; v.p., bd. dirs. water resources div. STS Cons. Ltd., Ann Arbor, 1981-84; v.p. water and environ. resources dept. Tetra Tech-Honeywell, Pasadena, Calif., 1984; head dept. civil engring. Colo. State U., Ft. Collins, 1984-86; dean Coll. Engring. U. Cin., 1986-95, dir. Groundwater Rsch. Ctr., 1986-95; dir. Ctr. Hill Solid and Hazardous Waste Rsch. Ctr. EPA, Cin., 1986-93; pres. Drexel U., Phila., 1995—. Adj. prof. civil engring. U. Mich., 1976-83; cons. Gaines & Stern Co., Cleve., 1983-84, Honeywell Europe, Maintal, Fed. Republic of Germany, 1984-85, Arthur D. Little, Boston, 1984-85, Camargo Assocs., Ltd., Cin., 1986, King Fahd U. Rsch. Inst., Dhahran, Saudi Arabia, 1987, King Abdulaziz City for Sci. and Tech., Riyadh, Saudi Arabia, 1991, Henderson & Bodwell Cons. Engrs. Inc., 1991, Cin. Met. Sewer Dist., 1992, Ohio River Valley Water Sanitation Commn., 1994; acting pres. Ohio Aerospace Inst., 1988-90; interim pres. Inst. Advanced Mfg. Scis. Ohio Edison Tech. Ctr., 1989-90; bd. govs. Edison Materials Tech. Ctr., 1988-95; adv. bd., founding mem. Hamilton County Bus. Incubator, 1988-95; bd. dirs. Nat. Commn. for Coop. Edn., Opera Co. of Phila., Hellenic Coll./Holy Cross Acad., Mace Security Internat., Inc., Met-Pro Corp., Aqua Am., Inc., Amkor Techs., Inc., CDI, Inc., Phila. Stock Exch. Author: Problems on Strength of Materials, 1968, Sewer Systems Design, 1969; editor: Fluid Transients and Acoustics, 1978, Pump-Turbine Schemes, 1979, Small Hydro Power Fluid Machinery, 1982; Megatrends in Hydraulics, 1987; contbr. more than 65 articles to profl. jours. Mem. Greater Cin. C. of C. Blue Chip Campaign for Econ. Devel. Task Force, 1988-93, bd. dirs. Bus. Assistance Ctr., 1989-95; mem. Ohio Coun. on Rsch. and Econ. Devel., 1988, Ohio Sci. and Tech. Commn. Adv. Group, 1989-90, 92-95; coun. mem. St. Nicholas Ch. Parish, Ann Arbor, 1981-84; mem. City of Ft. Collins Drainage Bd., 1984-86; bd. dirs. Dan Beard coun. Boy Scouts Am., 1995, Intelligent Vehicle Hwy. Soc. Ohio, 1994-95; bd. dirs. Liberty Bell Coun. of the Boy Scouts of Am., 1996—. Recipient Horace W. King scholarship civil engring. dept. U. Mich., 1971-73, 6 Bechtel Merit awards, 1974-79, Young Engr. of Yr. award Mich. Soc. Profl. Engrs., Ann Arbor, Mich., 1982, Disting. Engr. award Engrs. and Scientists Cin. Tech. Socs. Coun., 1989, Acad. of Achievement in Edn. award Am. Hellenic Ednl. Progressive Assn., 1995, Hellenic Univ. Club of Phila. Achievement award, 1996, Krikos Disting. Hellene Leader award, 1996, Svc. Learning award, Jr. Achievement Inc., 2001, Congl. medal of Ellis Island, 2001, Heart of Phila. award, Am. Heart Assn., 2001, Silver Beaver award, Boy Scouts Am., 2002, US Dept. Treasury medal of Merit, 2003, Disting. Hellene award, Hellenic Med. Soc. NY, 2003, End. award, Consular Corps Phila., 2003, Dennis Clark Immigrant Achievement award, 2004, Penn Club Ann. award, 2005, Amb. award, YMCA Phila., 2005, Interdependence Day Phila. award, 2006, Gold medal award Pub. Rels. Assn., 2006, Svc. to Humanity award March of Dimes, 2007, Global Citizen award Global Interdependence Ctr., 2007. Fellow ASCE (pres. Ann Arbor br. 1980-81, pres.-elect Mich. sect. 1983-84, hydraulics divsn. publ. com. 1980-83), ASME (chmn. fluid transients com. 1978-80, mem. fluids engring. divsn. awards com. 1981-84), Am. Soc. Engring. Edn.; mem. NSPE (legis. and govt. affairs com. 1994-95, chair profl. engrs. in edn. divsn. 1995), Order of the Engr., Internat. Assn. for Hydraulic Rsch., Ohio Engring. Dean's Coun. (chmn.-elect 1989-91), Rotary, Sigma Xi, Chi Epsilon, Tau Beta Pi. Greek Orthodox. Avocations: photography, classical music, travel, swimming, racquetball. Home: 75 Crestline Rd Wayne PA 19087-2611 Office: Drexel Univ Main Building 3141 Chestnut St Philadelphia PA 19104-2875 Office Phone: 215-895-2100. Business E-Mail: papadakis@drexel.edu.

PAPADAKIS, EMMANUEL PHILIPPOS, physicist, consultant; b. NYC, Dec. 25, 1934; s. Philippos E. and Helen (Eastman) P.; m. Stella Christopher, Sept. 4, 1960; children: Susan H., Philip E., Christopher E., Nicholas E. BS in Physics, MIT, 1956, PhD in Physics, 1962; M.M. in Mgmt, U. Mich., 1979. Mem. tech. staff Bell Telephone Labs., Allentown, Pa., 1962-69; dept. head Panametrics, Inc., Waltham, Mass., 1969-73; prin. staff engr. Ford Motor Co., Detroit, 1973-75, supr., 1975-87; ptnr. E&S Antiques, 1978—; pres. Quality Sys. Concepts Inc., 1991—; assoc. dir. Ctr. for Nondestructive Evaluation, Iowa State U., Ames, 1988-95. Adj. prof. Northeastern U. ext., Waltham, 1970-73, elec. engring. and computer engring. Iowa State U., 1988-95; cons. quality, NDT, TQM, ISO-9000, acoustics and ultrasonic testing sys., 1969-73, 88—. Contbr. numerous articles on electronics, ultrasonics, acoustics, nondestructive testing and quality to profl. jours.; tech. editor Materials Evaluation, 1988—; reviewer various jours. in physics, testing materials and sci. instrumentation; guest editor for Academic Press, 1995-2000; reviewer proposals to various govtl. agencies; patentee in field; author: Financial Justification of Nondestructive Testing- Cost of Quality in Manufacturing, 2007. Fellow: IEEE, Am. Soc. for Nondestructive Testing (Mehl honor lectr. 1979, tutorial award 1993, Mentoring award 2007), Acoustical Soc. Am. (Biennial award 1968); mem.: ASTM, Am. Soc. Quality, Am. Phys. Soc., Sigma Xi. Achievements include developing method and instrument for measuring ultrasonic velocity, method for bonding thin slabs to substrates, instrument for sheet metal texture determination, method using DSSS in ultrasonic flaw detection, method to calculate effect of quality on profitability quantitatively, new economic field of nanoeconomics. Office: QSC Inc 379 Diem Woods Dr New Holland PA 17557-8800 Office Phone: 717-355-2142. Personal E-mail: epp34@comcast.net.

PAPADAKIS, PANAGIOTIS AGAMEMNON, corporate financial executive; b. Athens, Greece, Mar. 29, 1935; s. Agamemnon Ioannou and Anna Karyatis (Kyriakopoulou) P.; m. Alexandra Argyropoulou, July 12, 1959. Student, U. Athens, 1953-57. Registered rep., Del., Athens, Greece, Zurich, Switzerland, Chgo., NY, DC, 50 other countries. Pub., owner newspaper Peristeri, Athens, 1953-64; owner, gen. dir. printing house, advt. office, ins. agy., Athens, 1953-64; leader Nat. Radical Party Youth, Athens, 1958-59; founder, gen. dir. Servis Advt., Athens, 1963-78, Book-Servis, Athens, 1974-78; pres. Investments Promotions and Assocs. of Chgo., Athens, 1979-85; chmn. Internat. Investments World Co. Inc., Athens and Zurich, 1985—, Internat. Bus. Co. Inc., Internat. Comml. Co. Inc., Athens and Zurich, 1985—, Papadakis Internat. Fin. Co. Inc., Guarantor Co. Inc., Athens and Zurich, 1992—, Internat. Banker Fin. Co. Inc., Athens and Zurich, 1992—. Chmn. Internat. Pap Financing and Investment Group, Vaduz Liechtenstein and US, Konekt Financing Investment Group AG; chmn., pres. 30 companies in several countries. Author, editor: Historical Biography of President Karamanlis, 1974-77; author: Why the Revolution of 21 April 1967 Happened, 1968; author numerous articles in Recently Humanity '93, Human Rights. Mem. Democracy Party, Christian Orthodox Ch. Mem. Internat. C. of C., Assn. Bus. Leaders Inc., London Diplomatic Acad., Comml. and Indsl. Chamber Athens, Greece. Mem. New Democracy Party. Christian Orthodox. Office: Internat Invest World Co Inc PO Box 140 88 115 10 Athens Greece also: Bahnhofstrasse 52 8001 Zurich Switzerland also: 24 Pontou St Ilisia 115 28 Athens Greece Office Phone: 30 210 7795444. Business E-Mail: papgroup@otenet.gr. E-mail: papadaki@hol.gr.

PAPADEMOS, LUCAS, bank executive; Gov. Bank of Greece, Athens, 1994—2002; v.p. European Ctrl. Bank, Frankfurt, Germany, 2002—. Mailing: European Central Bank Postfach 16 03 19 D-60066 Frankfurt Germany

PAPADIMITRIOU, DIMITRI BASIL, economist, educator, academic administrator; b. Thessaloniki, Greece, June 9, 1946; s. Basil John and Ellen (Takas) P.; m. Rania Antonopoulos. BA, Columbia U., 1970; PhD, New Sch. for Social Rsch., 1986. V.p., asst. sec. ITT Life Ins. Co. NY, NYC, 1970-73; exec. v.p., sec., treas. William Penn Life Ins. Co. NY, NYC, 1973-78, also dir.; exec. v.p., provost Bard Coll., 1978—, Jerome Levy prof. econs., 1978—; exec. dir. Bard Ctr., 1980—; pres. Levy Econs. Inst., 1988—; disting. scholar Shanghai Acad. Social Scis., 2002. Adj. lectr. econs. New Sch., 1975-76; fellow Ctr. for Advanced Econ. Studies, 1983; Wye fellow Aspen Inst.; bd. dirs. William Penn Life Ins. Co. NY; bd. govs. Levy Econs. Inst., 1986—; mem. subcoun. capital allocation Competitiveness Policy Coun., 1998-2000; mem., vice-chmn. Congl. Commn. to Rev. the Trade Deficit, 2000-02; mem. adv. com. Women's World Banking; radio econs. commentator Sta. WAMC, NPR, PRI, Money Radio, Marketplace. Author: Employment Policy Community Development and the Underclass, 1997, Employment Policy: Theory and Practice, 1998; co-author: Community Development Banking, 1993, A Path to Community Development, 1993, An Alternative in Small Business Finance, 1994, Monetary Policy Uncovered: The Federal Reserve's Experiment with Unobservables, 1994, Targeting Inflation: The Effects of Monetary Policy on the CPI and Its Housing Component, 1996, The Fed Should Lower Interest Rates More, 1998, What to Do With the Surplus, 1998, How Can We Provide for the Baby Boomers in their Old Age?, 1999, Can Social Security Be Saved, 1999, Fiscal Policy for the Coming Recession, 2001, Is Personal Debt Sustainable?, 2002, Understanding Deflation: Treating the Disease not the Symptom, 2003, Is Deficit-Financed Growth Limited? Policies and Prospects in An Election Year, 2004, How Fragile is the US Economy?, 2005, The United States and Her Creditors: Can the Symbiosis Last?, 2005, Are Housing Prices Household Debt and Growth Sustainable?, 2006, Can the Growth in the US Current Account Deficit be Sustained?, 2006, Can Global Imbalances Continue? Policies for the US Economy, 2006, The US Economy, 2007, Cracks in the Foundations of Growth, 207, Perspectives on Aging, 2007; editor, contbr. Profits, Deficits and Instability, 1992, Aspects of Distribution of Wealth and Income, 1994, Stability in the Financial System, 1996, Modernizing Financial Systems, 2000, Employment Policies: Theories and Evidence, 2001, Induced Investment and Business Cycles, 2004, The Distributional Effects of Government Spending and Taxation, 2006, Government Expenditures to the Elderly, 2007; co-editor, contbr.: Poverty and Prosperity in the USA in the Late Twentieth Century, 1993, Financial Conditions and Macroeconomic Performance, 1992; bd. editors Challenge, Rev. of Income and Wealth; book reviewer Econ. Jour., Ea. Econ. Jour. Trustee, treas. Am. Symphony Orch. Mem. Am. Econ. Assn., Royal Econ. Soc., Am. Fin. Assn., Econ. Club NY, The Bretton Woods Com., European Econ. Assn., Eastern Econ. Assn., Econ. Sci. Chamber of Greece, Assn. for Evolutionary Econs. Home and Office: Bard Coll Annandale On Hudson NY 12504-5000 Home Phone: 845-758-8488; Office Phone: 845-758-7426.

PAPADOPOULOS, GREGORY MICHAEL, information technology executive; b. Oakland, Calif., Apr. 30, 1958; s. Michael Nicholas and Imogen (Sherman) P.; m. Elizabeth Ann Woellner, Nov. 26, 1982; children: Michael Gregory, Kathryn Elizabeth. BA in Systems Sci., U. Calif., San Diego, 1979; MS in Elec. Engring. and Computer Sci., MIT, 1983, PhD in Elec. Engring., 1988. Programmer Scripps Inst. Oceanography, La Jolla, Calif., 1977-79; devel. engr. Hewlett-Packard, Inc., San Diego, 1979-81; sr. rsch. scientist Honeywell Inc., Mpls., 1981-84; co-founder, chief systems arch. PictureTel Corp., Danvers, Mass., 1984-86; co-founder, chief tech. officer A.I. Archs., Inc., Cambridge, 1985-88; project mgr. MIT lab. for computer sci., 1988-90, asst. prof. elec. engring. and computer sci., 1990-93, assoc. prof., 1993-95; sr. arch. Thinking Machines Corp., Cambridge, 1993-94; chief scientist server sys. engring. Sun Microsystems Computer Co., Santa Clara, Calif., 1994-95, chief tech. officer, enterprise servers and storage group, 1995-96, v.p. tech. and advanced devel., chief tech. officer, 1996-98, v.p., chief tech. officer, Sun Microsystems Inc., Santa Clara, Calif., 1998-2000, sr. v.p., chief tech. officer, 2000-02, exec. v.p. R & D, chief tech. officer, 2002-, also bd. dirs., 1994-. Dir. Ergo, Inc., 1989-90 (also co-founder); co-founder Exa Corp.; rsch. fellow Charles Stark Draper Labs., Cambridge, 1981-83; vis. prof. elec. engring. and computer sci., MIT, 2002-03; mem. Pres.'s bd. on Sci. and Innovation, U. Calif.; tech. advisor BP, Alien Techs. Contbr. articles to profl. jours. Pres. Meml. chpt. Am. Field Service, Houston, 1975-76; bd. trustees Anita Borg Inst. for Women and Tech. Recipient Spl. distinction award Nat. Forensic League, 1976, Presdl. Young Investigators award, Nat. Sci. Found.; U. Calif. Regents scholar, 1978. Mem. AAAS, Search for Extraterrestrial Intelligence (chmn. bd.), Phi Beta Kappa, Sigma Xi. Republican. Avocations: bicycle touring; soccer, diving. Office: Sun Microsystems 4150 Network Cir Santa Clara CA 95054 Office Phone: 650-960-1300. Office Fax: 408-276-3804. *

PAPADOPOULOS, JOHN K., archaeology educator; arrived in US, 1993; s. Kyriakos J. and Anastasia Papadopoulos; m. Sarah P. Morris, Dec. 1, 1991. BA with honors, U. Sydney, 1980, MA with honors, 1982, PhD, 1987. Dep. dir. Australian Archaeol. Inst., Athens, Greece, 1987—91; lectr. archaeology U. Sydney, 1991—93; assoc. curator JP Getty Mus., LA, 1994—2002; prof. UCLA, 2002—, prof., chair classics, 2005—. Exhbn. organizer antiquity and photography Getty Mus., 2005; exhbn. organizer art of antiquity Benaki Mus., Athens, Greece, 2006—07. Author: Ceramicus Redivivus, 2003, Early Iron Age Cemetery, Art of Antiquity, 2007. Grantee, Instn. for Aegean Prehistory, 1994—, Kress Found., 1994—. Mem.: Archaeol. Inst. Am. Office: Cotsen Inst Archaeology Dept Classics 405 Hilgard Ave Los Angeles CA 90095

PAPAEFTHYMIOU, GEORGIA C., physicist, educator; b. Athens, Greece, Sept. 24, 1946; arrived in US, 1964; d. Christos and Chrysoula Papaefthyiou; children: Hrysoula Davis, Stephanie Davis. BA in Physics, Barnard Coll., NYC, 1968; MA in Physics, Columbia U., NYC, 1974, PhD in Physics, 1976. Physicist F. Bitter Magnet Lab., MIT, Cambridge, Mass., 1976—99; prof. physics Villanova (Pa.) U., 1999—. Peer reviewer, panel reviewer NSF, Washington. Contbr. articles to profl. jours. Grantee, Office Naval Rsch., 1996, NSF, 2000—. Mem.: Materials Rsch. Soc., Am. Phys. Soc. Office: Villanova U Dept Physics 800 E Lancaster Ave Villanova PA 19085 Office Phone: 610-519-4883.

PAPAGAN, HARRY GREGORY, literature and language professor; b. Youngstown, Ohio, Apr. 5, 1948; s. Harry Andrew and Julia Katherine Papagan; m. Sonia Lane Miller Papagan, Aug. 5, 2000; 1 child, Sara Papagan Reville. BA in English, Youngstown State U., Ohio, 1972, MA in English, 1974; post grad., W.Va. U., Morgantown, 1988. Instr. Fort Dix coll. transition Montclair State Coll., Upper Montclair, NJ, 1974—75; instr. then asst. prof. English W. Va. Northern CC, Wheeling, 1976—83, assoc. prof. English, 1983—88, chair humanities dept., 1985—88; assoc. prof. Lord Fairfax CC, Middletown, Va., 1988—2005, dean humanities, social scis., 2000—05; asst. prof. English Macon State Coll., Ga., 2005—. Editl. bd. Inquiry, 2000—05; Title III grant reader US Dept. Edn., Washington, 1998, 90, 98, 2000. Vol. editor local sesquicentennial project, Fort Valley, Ga. Recipient Outstanding Faculty Mem. award, Lord Faifax CC, 1998, NISOD Excellence award, U. Tex., 1999. Mem.: Ga. Coun. Tchrs. English, Nat. Coun. Tchrs. English. Roman Catholic. Avocations: reading, cooking, guitar, songwriting. Office: Macon State Coll 100 Coll Sta Dr Macon GA 31206-5145 Home: 711 Worthington Cir Fort Valley GA 31030 Office Phone: 478-471-2812. Business E-Mail: hpapagan@mail.maconstate.edu.

PAPAI, BEVERLY DAFFERN, retired library director; b. Amarillo, Tex., Aug. 31, 1949; d. Clarence Wilbur and Dora Mae (Henderson) Daffern; m. Joseph Andrew Papai, Apr. 3, 1976. BS in Polit. Sci., West Tex. State U., Canyon, 1972; MSLS, Wayne State U., 1973. Head extension dept. and Oakland County Subregional Libr. The Farmington Cmty. Libr., Farmington Hills, Mich., 1973-79, coord. adult svcs., br. head, 1980-83, asst. dir., 1983-85, dir., 1985—2005; ret., 2005. Cons. U.S. Office of Edn., 1978, Battelle Meml. Inst., Columbus, Ohio, 1980; presenter in field; libr. cons. 2005-. Contbr. articles to profl. jours. Bd. dirs. Mich. Consortium, 1987-91; bd. dirs. Oakland Literacy Coun., 1998—, vice chair, 2000-01, chair, 2001—; trustee Libr. of Mich., 1989-92, vice chair, 1991, 97-98, chair, 1992; del. White House Conf. on Librs. and Info. Svcs., 1991; founder, treas., fiscal agt. METRO NET Libr. Consortium, 1993—; mem. edn. com. Child Abuse and Neglect Coun. of Oakland County, 1998-2000; mem. Commn. on Children, Youth and Families, 1996—, Multiracial Cmty. Coun., 1995—; chair Edn. and Tng. Com., 2000—04. Recipient Athena award Farmington/Farmington Hills C. of C. and Gen. Motors, 1994, Chairperson's Rainbow award, 2001, Spl. Recognition award Oakland County, 2004; Amarillo Pub. Libr. Friends Group fellow, 1972, Wayne State U. Inst. Gerontology fellow, 1972. Mem. ALA (officer), Mich. Libr. Assn. (chair specialized libr. svcs. roundtable 1975, chair conf. program 1982, chair pub. policy com. 1988-89, chair devel. com. 1994-95, chair ann. conf. and program coms. 1995-96, pres. 1996-97, Loleta D. Fyan award 1975, Libr. of Yr. award 2004), LWV of Mich., Farmington Exch. Club, Coun. on Resource Devel. Democrat. Roman Catholic. Home: 6805 Wing Lake Rd Bloomfield Hills MI 48301-2959 Personal E-mail: papaibev@farmlib.org.

PAPALIA, DIANE ELLEN, humanities educator; b. Englewood, NJ, Apr. 26, 1947; d. Edward Peter and Madeline (Borrin) P.; 1 child, Anna Victoria Finlay. AB, Vassar Coll., 1968; MS, W.Va. U., 1970, PhD, 1971. Asst. prof. child and family studies U. Wis., Madison, 1971-75, assoc. prof., 1975-78, prof., 1978-87, coord. child and family studies, 1977-79. Adj. prof. psychology in pediatrics U. Pa. Sch. Medicine, 1987-89. Author (with Sally W. Olds and Ruth D. Feldman): A Child's World: Infancy Through Adolescence, 1975, 10th edit., 2006, Human Development, 1978, 10th edit., 2007; author: (with Harvey Sterns, Cameron J. Camp & Ruth D. Feldman) Adult Development and Aging, 1996, 3rd edit., 2007; author: (with Dana Gross and Ruth D. Feldman) Child Development: A Topical Approach, 2003; co-author: Psychology, 1985, 2d edit., 1988; contbr. articles to profl. jours. NSF fellow, 1971, Am. Coun. on Edn. fellow, 1979-80; U. Wis. grantee. Fellow: Gerontol. Soc.; mem.: APA, Nat. Coun. Family Rels., Soc. Rsch. in Child Devel., Am. Psychol. Soc., Author's Guild, Psi Chi. Home: Apt 6D 253 W 73d St New York NY 10023 Office Phone: 212-724-4244. Personal E-mail: depapalia@aol.com.

PAPALIA, ROCCO DOMINIC, food products executive; b. Walnut Creek, Calif., Sept. 19, 1960; s. Rocco and Carolyn Therese (Corker) P.; children: Dominique Therese, Rocco Anthony. BSChemE, Princeton U., 1982. Engr. Procter & Gamble, Cin., 1982-83, group leader, 1983-87, sect. head, 1987-89; group mgr. Frito-Lay Tech., Dallas, 1989-93; dir. tech. Frito-Lay, Dallas, 1993; head rsch. and devel. tech. PepsiCo, Inc. Indsl. adv. bd. Tex. A&M U. chem. engring. dept., 1992—. Inventor shampoo dispenser. Recipient Textile Vets. Assn. award, 1982. Office: Frito Lay 7701 Legacy Dr Plano TX 75024-4099

PAPANEK, GUSTAV FRITZ, economist, educator; b. Vienna, July 12, 1926; s. Ernst and Helen Papanek; m. Hanna Kaiser, June 13, 1947; children: Thomas H., Joanne R. Papanek Orlando. BA in Agrl. Econs, Cornell U., 1947; MA in Econs, Harvard U., 1949, PhD, 1951. Economist, dep. dir. program planning for Asia, tech. coop. adminstrn. Dept. State, 1951-53; from econ. adv. to dir. adv. group to planning commn. Harvard U., Pakistan, 1954-58, from dep. dir. to dir. devel. adv. svc. Cambridge, Mass., 1958—70, dir. adv. group to planning commn. Indonesia, 1971—73; prof. econs. Boston U., 1974-92, prof. emeritus, 1992—, chmn. dept., 1974-83, interim dir., 1977-80, dir. Ctr. Asian Devel. Studies, 1983-90, dir. Asian program, 1991-92; pres. Boston Inst. Developing Econs., Ltd. (BIDE), 1987—; dir., cons. team devel. studies to planning commn. Govt. of Indonesia, 1987—89; dir. policy adv. team to Federated States of Micronesia, 1995—2002. Cons. Govt. of Indonesia, 1998—2005, Govt. of Liberia, 2006—; co-dir. pro-poor growth study U.S. AID, 2002—03; cons. in field. Author: (book) Pakistan's Development: Social Goals and Private Incentives, 1967, The Indonesian Economy, 1980, Development Strategy, Growth Equity and the Political Process in Southern Asia, 1986; co-author: Decision Making for Economic Development, 1971, The Indian Economy, 1988, others; contbr. articles to profl. jours. With US Army, 1944—46. Grantee, Ford Found., AID, World Bank, UN Devel. Program, UN Univ., HEW, Asian Devel. Bank. Mem.: Pakistan Econ. Assn., Assn. Asian Studies (pres. New Eng. conf. 1975—77), Assn. Comparative Econ. Studies (pres. 1982), Soc. Internat. Devel. (past mem. exec. com.), Am. Agrl. Econs. Assn., Am. Econs. Assn. Home and Office: 2 Mason St Lexington MA 02421-6315 Home Phone: 781-862-4549; Office Phone: 781-862-7776. E-mail: papanek@bide.com.

PAPARELLA, LEON RALPH, psychotherapist, consultant; b. Providence, Dec. 31, 1944; s. Ralph A. and Eleanor Paparella; m. Jacqueline Z. Anderson, Sept. 19, 1987 (div. Aug. 5, 1993). BA, RI Coll., Providence, 1967; MSW, Howard U., Washington, 1969; cert. in group psychotherapy, Washington Sch. Psychiatry, 1972. Lic. psychotherapist Md., Washington, Va. Social worker Cmty. Mental Health Ctr., Washington, 1969—72; psychotherapist Inst. Marriage and Family Rels., Annandale, 1972—74, Va. Cmty. Mental Health Ctr., Fairfax, 1974—78, Treatment Ctr. Washington Sch. Psychiatry, 1977—90; pvt. practice Washington, 1973—. Mem. faculty Washington Sch. Psychiatry, 1974—; cons. Walter Reed Army Hosp., 1984—; support group specialist Parkinson Found. Nat. Capital Area, Washington, 1999—; dean Nat. Group Psychotherapy Inst., 2004—; presenter in field. Named Social Work Mentor of the Yr., Walter Reed Army Hosp., 2002; recipient appreciation, Washingotn Sch. Psychiatry, 1994, Social Work commendation, Walter Reed Army Hosp., 1997. Mem.: NASW, Mid-Atlantic Group Psychotherapy Assn., Nat. Registry Certified Group Psychotherapists, Am. Group Psychotherapy Assn. Avocations: singing, sports. Personal E-mail: leonpaparella@comast.net.

PAPAS, IRENE KALANDROS, English language educator, poet, writer; AA with highest honors, Balt. C.C.; BA magna cum laude, Goucher Coll., 1968; MA in English Lang. and Lit., U. Md., 1974, postgrad., 1980—. Lic. theology profl. Tchr./tutor various schs., Balt., 1965—; tchr. theology U. Md. Free Univ., College Park, 1979—; author/pub. Ledger Publs., Silver Spring, Md., 1982—; TV producer Arts and Humanities Prodns., Silver Spring, 1991—. Lectr. in English, philosophy, Montgomery Coll., Goucher Coll.; instr. English Composition, World Literature, U. Md., College Park, 1968—; adj. faculty various colls.; White House duty, 1997—. Author: Irene's Ledger Songs of Deliverance, 1982, Irene's Ledger Song at Sabbatyon, 1986, Small Meditations, Leaves for Healing, 1996; prodr./dir. tv. progs. Election judge, Montgomery County (Md.) Suprs. Bd. of Elections, 90's; tutor in literacy, 1989, 90. Recipient First Prize Arts and Culture Category Smithsonian Inst., 1991; honored 6th Annual Awards Ceremony Montgomery Community, 1991. Mem. AAUP, Internat. Platform Assn., Nat. Poetry Assn., Phi Beta Kappa. Democrat. Greek Orthodox. Avocations: art/iconography, calligraphy, music, needlepoint. Office: PO Box 10303 Silver Spring MD 20914-0303

PAPATHOMAS, GEORGIA NIKOLAKOPOULOU, technology executive; b. Kato Achaia, Greece, Sept. 11, 1950; d. Andreas and Corina (Fotopoulou) Nikolakopoulos; m. Thomas Vergil Papathomas, Aug. 15, 1976; children: Lia Natassa, Alexander Vergil. BS in Engring. Sci., Columbia U., 1973, MS in Engring. Sci., 1974, PhD in Engring. Sci., 1978; cert. in bus. devel., U. Pa., 1994; cert. in strategic mktg., Harvard U., 1995. Mem. tech. staff Bell Labs., Murray Hill, NJ, 1978-84, supr. Whippany, NJ, 1984-90, program mgr., 1990-93; dir. strategy AT&T, Morristown, NJ, 1993-96, dir. ops. Bedminster, NJ, 1996—2002; v.p. network solutions Lucent Tech., 1998—2002; v.p. info. tech. Pfizer, 2003—. Sloan Found. rsch. fellow, N.Y.C., 1974. Mem. ASCE, Soc. Women Engrs., Sigma Xi. Business E-Mail: georgia.papathomas@pfizer.com.

PAPAZIAN, DENNIS RICHARD, retired historian, educator, commentator; b. Augusta, Ga., Dec. 15, 1931; s. Nahabed Charles and Armanouhe Marie (Pehlevanian) P.; m. Mary Arshagouni. BA, Wayne State U., 1954; MA, U. Mich., 1958; NDG, Moscow State U., 1962; PhD, U. Mich., 1966. Head dept. social and behavioral scis. U. Mich., Dearborn, 1966-69, head div. lit., sci. and the arts, 1969-73, assoc. dean acad. affairs, 1973-74, dir. grad. studies, 1979-85, prof. history, dir. Armenian Rsch. Ctr., 1985—2006, prof., dir. emeritus, 2006—; dir. Armenian Assembly Am., Washington, 1975-79. Fellow Ctr. for Russian and East-European Studies, U. Mich., Ann Arbor, 1982-92; chmn. bd. dirs. Mich. Ethnic Heritage Studies Ctr., U. Mich., 1987-92. Author: St. John's Armenian Church, 1974; editor: The Armenian Church, 1983, Out of Turkey, 1994; editor Jour. of Soc. Armenian Studies, 1994—. Bd. dirs. Armenian Apostolic Soc., Southfield, Mich., 1968-78; chmn. bd. dirs. Alex Manoogian Found., Taylor, Mich., 1969-77; mem. evaluation team Ind. Schs. Assn. Ctrl. States, Chgo., 1985; polit. commentator WXYZ-TV, ABC, Detroit, Southfield, 1984—, WWJ-Radio, Detroit, 1984—; bd. dirs. Southeastern Mich. chpt. ARC, 1988-98, chmn. internat. svcs. com., 1988-98, disaster and mil. family svcs. com., 1988-98; mem. NJ Commn. on Holocaust Edn., 2005—. Scholar/diplomat U.S. Dept. State, Washington, 1976; grantee NEH, Washington, 1977, AID, Washington, 1978. Mem. AAUP (chpt. pres. 1962-65), Nat. Assn. Armenian Studies and Rsch. (bd. dirs. 1961-91), Nat. Ethnic Studies Assn. (bd. dirs. 1976-85), Am. Hist. Assn., Soc. Armenian Studies (pres. exec. com. 1988-91, 97—, sec./treas. exec. com. 1991-97), Am. Assn. Advancement of Slavic Studies, Am. Acad. Polit. Sci., Armenian Students Assn. (Arthur S. Dadian Armenian Heritage award 1993), Knights of Vartan. Armenian Orthodox. Avocations: reading, travel. Home: 9 Blueberry Dr Woodcliff Lake NJ 07677 Office: U Mich 4901 Evergreen Rd Dearborn MI 48128-1491 Office Phone: 313-593-5181. Business E-Mail: papazian@umich.edu.

PAPAZIAN, GEORGE ARA, dentist; b. LA, Jan. 18, 1937; m. Kathleen Annette Weaver, May 12, 1978; children: Charles, Jeffrey M., Steven A. MusB, U. So. Calif., LA, 1959, DDS, 1966. Lic. dentist State Bd. Dental Examiners, 1966. Jr. HS music tchr. LA Unified Sch. Dist., 1959—60; pvt. gen. dentist Long Beach, Calif., 1968—. Contbr. articles to profl. jours. Capt. USAF, 1966—68. Mem.: ADA (licentiate), Harbor Dental Soc. (licentiate; peer rev. chmn. 1988—2007), Calif. Dental Assn. (licentiate). Office: George A Papazian DDS Inc 6226 E Spring St #330 Long Beach CA 90815 Home Phone: 562-598-0361; Office Phone: 562-420-1512. Office Fax: 562-420-8854.

PAPE, GLENN MICHAEL, lawyer, financial planner; b. Aug. 20, 1954; s. Gilbert Thomas and Janine Elizabeth (Beheyt) P.; m. Nancy Ann Vaske, Apr. 7, 1979 (div. 2006); children: Katherine Jo, Courtney Johanna. BA in Classics, U. Chgo., 1978, MBA, 1981; JD, DePaul U., 1979. Cert. fin. planner, Ill., 1979, CPA Ill., 1979, Calif., 2005; CLU Ill., 1979; bar: Ill. 1979; cert. investment mgmt. analyst Investment Mgmt. Cons. Assn., 1998. Cons. tax divsn. No. Trust Co., Chgo., 1980-81, fin. planner, 1981-82; fin. counselor Continental Ill. Nat. Bank, Chgo., 1982—84; tax mgr. Arthur Andersen & Co., Chgo., 1984-88; v.p., ptnr. Fin. Related Svcs., Ayco Co., L.P., Albany, NY, 1988-96; ptnr., nat. svc. leader broad market fin. planning svcs. Ernst & Young, Chgo., 1996—2005, west zone fin. svcs. leader San Francisco, 2003—06; pvt. practice San Mateo, Calif., 2006—. Developer Money in Motion Fin. Edn. System; mem. bd. govs. Cert. Fin. Planning Standards, 2000-05; chair bd. of stds. Cert. Fin. Planning, 2005. Active Five Hosp. Homebound Elderly Program, Chgo., 1981; treas. Chamber Music Coun., Chgo., 1982. Mem. AICPA (accredited pers. fin. specialist), Nat. Spkrs. Assn. (cert.) Home and Office: 207 Mendocino Way Redwood City CA 94065 Home Phone: 408-390-6814; Office Phone: 408-390-6814. Personal E-mail: glenn_pape@hotmail.com.

PAPE, JEAN WILLIAM, physician, researcher; b. Port-au-Prince, Haiti, June 24, 1946; s. William and Marie (Laraque) P.; m. Dominique Pasquis, Dec. 19, 1987. BS, Columbia U., 1971; MD, Cornell U., 1975. Intern North Shore U. Meml. Hosp., NYC, 1975-76, resident, 1976-78; Rockefeller's Found. fellow infectious diseases NY Hosp. Cornell Med. Ctr., NYC, 1978-80; instr. medicine Cornell U. Med. Coll., NYC, 1980-83, asst. prof. medicine, 1983-89, assoc. prof. medicine, 1989—, head infectious diseases unit Port-au-Prince, Haiti, 1983—; assoc. prof. medicine Med. Sch. Haiti, Port-au-Prince, 1983—. Co-founder, dir. Haitian Study Group on Kaposi's Sarcoma and Opportunistic Infections (GHESKIO), 1982-, Port-au-Prince, Haiti; mem. organizing scientific com. III, IV, V, VI Internat. Confs. AIDS, 1985-89; tech. advisor PAHO World Health Orgn., 1987—; cons. Panos Inst., London, 1988—. Reviewer Jour. AIDS, 1988—; contbr. articles to profl. jours. Mem. Nat. Aids Commn., Port-au-Prince, Haiti, 1983—, Nat. Red Cross Blood Bank Commn., Port-au-Prince, 1989—. Mem.: Inst. Medicine. Avocations: arabian horses, german shepherds. Home: PO Box 15267 Port-au-Prince Haiti Office: Cornell ID Unit Inst Nat de Laboratoire et de Recherches 33 Blvd Harry Truman Port-au-Prince Haiti

PAPE, PATRICIA ANN, social worker, consultant; b. Aurora, Ill., Aug. 2, 1940; d. Robert Frank and Helen Louise (Hanks) Grover; children: Scott Allen, Debra Lynn. BA in Sociology, Northwestern U., 1962; MSW, George Williams Coll., 1979. Cert. addictions counselor, Ill.; lic. clin. social worker, sch. social worker, Ill. Pvt. practice family counseling, 1979—; coord. community resources DuPage Probation Dept., Wheaton, Ill., 1977-80; dir. The Abbey Alcoholism Treatment Ctr., Winfield, Ill., 1980-81; prin. Pape & Assocs., Wheaton, 1982—; dir. alcoholism counselor tng. program Coll. of DuPage, Glen Ellyn, Ill., 1982-87. Chgo. affiliate Employee Assistance Program, 1982—; cons. Luth. Soc. Services Ill., 1979-82. Contbr. articles to profl. jours. Mem. alcohol drug task force Ill. Synod Luth. Ch. Am., Chgo., 1985—. Named Woman of Yr., Entrepreneur Women in Mgmt., Oak Brook, Ill, 1986, Social Worker of Yr. Fox Valley Dist., 1998. Mem. Assn. Labor-Mgmt. Adminstrs. Cons. Alcoholism (women's issues com. 1984—), Acad. Cert. Social Workers, Am. Assn. Marriage Family Therapists, Nat. Assn. Soc. Workers, Women in Mgmt. Home: 1330 Shagbark Ln Wheaton IL 60187 Office: Pape & Assocs 618 S West St Wheaton IL 60187-5038

PAPE, STUART M., lawyer; b. Paterson, NJ, Dec. 24, 1948; BA, U. Va., 1970, JD, 1973. Bar: Va. 1973, DC 1980, US Ct. Appeals (6th cir.) 1975, US Supreme Ct. 1976. Law clk. to Hon. Leonard Braman Superior Ct. DC, 1973-74; exec. asst. to commr. FDA, 1979; mng. ptnr., Food & Drug Law, Legis. Affairs practices, mem. exec. com. & mgmt. com. Patton Boggs LLP, Washington. Contbr. articles to profl. jours. Mem. ABA (com. food and drug law, sect. adminstrv. law 1973-2006), Va. State Bar, DC Bar. Office: Patton Boggs LLP 2550 M St NW Washington DC 20037-1350 Office Phone: 202-457-5240. Office Fax: 202-457-6315. Business E-Mail: spape@pattonboggs.com.

PAPE, WILLIAM JAMES, II, newspaper publisher; b. Waterbury, Conn., Aug. 14, 1931; s. William B. and Helen (Cronan) P.; m. Patricia Moran, Oct. 15, 1959; children: William B. II, Andrew J. BS, U.S. Naval Acad., 1953; MBA, Harvard U., 1959; LHD (hon.), Teikyo Post U., 1991. Commd. ensign USN, 1953, advanced through grades to lt., 1955, resigned, 1957; asst. treas. Ea. Color Printing Co., Waterbury, 1959-63, pres., treas. Avon, Conn., 1977-87; v.p., asst. treas. Am.-Republican Inc., Waterbury, 1963-64, asst. publisher, comptroller, v.p., treas., 1964-72, pres., 1972—, treas., 1972-98; pub. Republican-Am., 1972—, editor, 1988—; also bd. dirs.; v.p., asst. treas. & dir. Paper Delivery, Inc., 1972—. Bd. dirs. Platt Bros., Waterbury. Bd. dirs. Conn. Coun. Freedom of Info., 1968-88, Conn. Bus. and Industry Assn., 1980-83, Naugatuck Valley Devel. Corp., Regional Action Coun., Waterbury, 1991; bd. dirs. Conn. Citizens for Jud. Modernization, pres., 1973-75; bd. dirs. Waterbury YMCA, 1970-78, trustee, 1972-2001, chmn. trustees, 1976-85; trustee Northeast Utilities, 1974-2001, Greater Waterbury Health Network Inc., 1993-95; mem. Conn. Pub. Expenditure Coun. Inc., 1974-77, dir. Conn. policy and econ. coun., 1994-2000; trustee Teikyo Post U., 1976-96; grants com. Waterbury Found., 1980-87; pub. affairs com. Waterbury Hosp., 1984-90, past trustee; incorporator Conn. Found. for Open Govt. Inc.; active Conn. Legislature Commn. to Study Modernization and Unification of Cts., 1973-75, Citizens for Better Govt. Through Reorganization, 1977. Mem. Am. Judicature Soc. (assoc. dir. 1975-76), New England Newspaper Assn. (Conn. bd. govs. 1983-87), Conn. Bar Assn. (task force conflict of interest 1979), Conn. Daily Newspaper Assn. (pres. 1970, exec. com. 1971-91), Waterbury C. of C. (exec. com., v.p. 1975, chmn. 1977-79, dir. 1964-2001, vice-chmn. transp. 1981-2001), Navy League U.S. (comms. bd. 1982), Waterbury Club, Madison Beach Club, Highfield, Liverpool Nautical Rsch. Soc., Am. Legion, Vet. Foreign Wars. Republican. Roman Catholic. Avocations: sailing, firearms, walking, carpentry. Home: Old Sherman Hill Rd Woodbury CT 06798 Office: Republic Amer PO Box 2090 389 Meadow St Waterbury CT 06722-2090 E-mail: wjpape@rep-am.com.

PAPELBON, JON (JONATHAN R. PAPELBON), professional baseball player; b. Baton Rouge, Nov. 23, 1980; s. John and Sheila Papelbon; m. Ashley Jeffries. Student, Miss. State U. Draft pick Boston Red Sox, 2003, pitcher, 2005—. Named Sarasota Red Sox Pitcher of Yr., 2004; named to Am. League All-Star Team, 2006—07. Achievements include holding record for most Saves thrown by a rookie pitcher in his first month, 2006. Office: Boston Red Sox 4 Yawkey Way Boston MA 02215-3496 *

PAPELL, HELEN GERTRUDE, poet, retired librarian; b. NYC, Apr. 8, 1924; d. Henry and Anna (Gimpel) Sobel; m. Robert Papell, June 1, 1949; 1 child, David H. BA, U. Mo., 1949; MLS, Pratt Inst., 1969; cert. profl. pub. libr., SUNY, 1973. Libr. trainee Bklyn. Pub. Libr., 1967-69, libr., storyteller, puppeteer, sr. libr., supervising libr., 1969-84; libr., cataloger Jewish Women's Resource Ctr. Nat. Coun. Jewish Women, NYC, 1984-98; ret., 1998. Puppeteer in librs., schls., chs., st. fairs, N.Y.C., Bklyn., 1969-84. Author: (poems) Talking with Eve, Leah, Hagar, Miriam, 1996, Caretaker's Mask, 2003; contbg. editor Jewish Women's Lit. Ann. Grantee Poets and Writers, 1991, 93. Mem. Nat. Coun. Jewish Women, Phi Beta Kappa. Avocations: reading judaica, folklore and mysteries, visiting museums, attending plays. Home: 720 W End Ave New York NY 10025-6299 E-mail: helenpapell@aol.com.

PAPENFUSE, EDWARD CARL, JR., archivist, state official; b. Toledo, Oct. 15, 1943; m. Sallie Fisher; children: Eric, David. BA in Polit. Sci., Am. U., 1965; MA in History, U. Colo., 1967; PhD, Johns Hopkins U., 1973. Assoc. editor Am. Hist. Rev., Washington, 1970-73; asst. archivist Md. Hall of Records, Annapolis, 1973-75, archivist, 1975—, commr. land patents, 1975—. Author: In Pursuit of Profit: The Annapolis Merchants in the Era of the American Revolution, 1975, (with others) Biographical Dictionary of Maryland Legislators, 1635-1789, 1974, (with others) Maryland: A New Guide to the Old Line State, 3d edit., 1999, Doing Good to Posterity, 1995, Maryland State Archives Atlas of Historical Maps of Maryland, 1608-1908, 2003; contbr. articles and revs. to profl. jours. Mem. Johns Hopkins U. Med. Archives. NEH grantee; recipient Disting. Svc. award to State Govt. Nat. Gov.'s Assn., 1985, Marylander of Yr. award Md. Colonial Soc., 1985. Fellow Soc. Am. Archivist, Md. Hist. Soc., Am. Antiquarian Soc. Home: 206 Oakdale Rd Baltimore MD 21210-2520 Office: Md State Archives 350 Rowe Blvd Annapolis MD 21401-1686 Office Phone: 410-260-6401. E-mail: edp@mdsa.net.

PAPER, LEWIS J., lawyer, educator; b. Newark, Oct. 13, 1946; s. Sidney and Dorothy (Nieman) P.; m. Jan Clachko, Sept. 4, 1972; children: Lindsay, Brett. BA, U. Mich., 1968; LLM, Harvard U., 1971; JD, Georgetown U., 1972. Bar: D.C. 1971, Md. 1984. Fellow Inst. Pub. Interest Representation Georgetown U. Law Sch., Washington, 1971-72; staff atty. Citizens Comms. Ctr., 1972—73; legis. counsel to Sen. Gaylord Nelson U.S. Senate, 1973—75; assoc. atty. Lowenstein, Sandler, Brochin, Kohl & Fisher, Newark, 1975—78; asst. gen. counsel FCC, Washington, 1978—79, assoc. gen. counsel, 1979—81; ptnr. Grove Engelberg & Gross, 1981—86, Keck, Mahin & Cate, 1986—95, Dickstein, Shapiro, LLC (formerly Dickstein, Shapiro, Morin & Oshinsky LLP), 1995—. Adj. prof. law Georgetown U. Law Sch., Washington, 1983-86. Author: John F. Kennedy: The Promise and the Performance, 1975, 79, Brandeis: An Intimate Biography, 1983, Empire: William S. Paley and the Making of CBS, 1987, Deadly Risks, 2006; contbr. articles to newspapers, mags., and profl. jours. Office: Disckstein, Shapiro LLC 1825 Eye St NW Washington DC 20006 Office Phone: 202-420-2265. Business E-Mail: paperl@dicksteinshapiro.com.

PAPERNIK, JOEL IRA, lawyer; b. NYC, May 4, 1944; s. Herman and Ida (Titefsky) Papernik; m. Barbara Ann Barker, July 28, 1972; children: Deborah, Ilana. BA, Yale U., New Haven, Conn., 1965; JD cum laude, Columbia U., NYC, 1968. Bar: NY 1969. Assoc. Shea & Gould, NYC, 1968—76, ptnr., 1976—91; ptnr., chmn. corp. and securities dept., mem. mgmt. com. Squadron, Ellenoff, Plesent & Sheinfeld, NYC, 1991—2000; ptnr., mem. opinion and policy com. Mintz, Levin, Cohn, Ferris, Glovsky and Popeo P.C., NYC, 2000—05. Lectr. various panels. With 11th Spl. Forces USAR, 1967—73. Mem.: ABA (sect. corp. law), Negotiated Acquisitions Com., Tri-Bar Opinion Com., Assn. Bar City NY (securities regulation com. 1992—95, chmn., lectr., corp. law com.), NY State Bar Assn. (lectr. various panels, securities law com.), NY Biotech. Assn. (bd. dirs. 2005—), Yale Club. Office: Mintz Levin Cohn Ferris Glovsky and Popeo PC 666 3rd Ave New York NY 10017-4011 Office Phone: 212-692-6774. Business E-Mail: jpapernik@mintz.com.

PAPISOV, MIKHAIL I., chemist; s. Ivan M. Papisov and Valeria I. Naidich; m. Elena A. Tokareva, Aug. 23, 1986; children: Vera M., Eugenia M. MS in Chemistry, Moscow State U., 1982; PhD in Biochemistry and Biology, Inst. Exptl. Cardiology, Moscow, 1988. Rsch. scientist Nat. Cardiology Rsch. Ctr., Moscow, 1988—91; assoc. chemist Mass. Gen. Hosp., Boston. Sci. founder, cons. Mersana Therapeutics, Cambridge, Mass., 2002—. Recipient Outstanding Pharm. Paper, Controlled Release Soc., 1995; grantee Several Rsch. grants, U.S. Govt., The Whitaker Found., Pharm. Industry, 1996—2006. Mem.: Controlled Release Soc., Am. Chem. Soc. Achievements include U.S. and foreign patents in the areas of pharmacology and biomaterials. Home: PO Box 441 Winchester MA 01890 Office: Mass General Hosp 55 Fruit St Boston MA 02114-2696 Home Phone: 617-967-4245; Office Phone: 617-724-9655.

PAPITTO, RALPH RAYMOND, manufacturing executive; b. Providence, Nov. 1, 1926; s. John and Maria (David) P.; m. Norma J. Ewart, June 10, 1943 (div.); children: Andrea (Mrs. Harry Crump), Aurelia (Mrs. William Young), David John; m. Barbara Auger, Apr. 1982. BS in Finance, Bryant Coll., Providence, 1947, DSc Bus. Adminstrn. (hon.), 1987; student, Boston U. Law Sch., 1948-49; DSc Bus. Adminstrn. (hon.), Roger Williams Coll., 1985; LLD (hon.), New Eng. Inst. Tech., 1985, Suffolk U., 1986, New England Inst. Tech. With Arthur Andersen & Co. and Ernst & Ernst, Providence, 1948-51; exec. v.p. fin. Ritz Products, Inc., Providence, 1951-55; founder, pres., chmn., dir. Glass-Tite Industries, Inc., Providence, 1956-63, chmn. bd., 1963—, also bd. dirs.; founder, chief exec. officer, pres., chmn. Nortek Inc., Providence, 1967-90, bd. dirs.; Chair and CEO AFC Cable Systems, Inc., Providence, 1993—. Bd. dirs. Hi-G, Inc. Fin. dir. Town of Johnston, R.I., 1955-59; trustee Roger Williams U., Bristol, R.I., chmn. bd. trustees, 1972-2007; bd. dirs. Meeting St. Sch. Retarded; mem. Gov.'s Blue Ribbon Commn., Roger Williams Hosp.; mem. Aurora Civic Assn. Named Man Yr. in R.I., R.I. C. of C., 1961. Mem. Alpine Country Club (pres. 1966-68, 92—), Jockey Club, Surf Club, LaGorce Country Club (Fla.). Office: AFC Cable Systems Inc 50 Kennedy Plz Providence RI 02903-2393 Office Phone: 401-453-2000. Fax: 401-453-2009.

PAPP, LASZLO GEORGE, retired architect; b. Debrecen, Hungary, Apr. 28, 1929; arrived in USA, 1956; m. Judith Liptak, Apr. 12, 1952 (dec. 2005); children: Andrea, Laszio-Mark(dec.). Archtl. Engr., Poly. U. Budapest, 1955; MArch, Pratt Inst., 1960; D of Liberal Arts, Tech. U. Budapest, 1998. Designer Harrison & Abramovitz, Architects, NYC, 1958—63; ptnr. Whiteside & Papp, Architects, White Plains, NY, 1963—67; pres. Papp Architects, P.C., White Plains, 1967—96, chmn., 1996—2005; exec. dir. Urban Redevel. Commn., Stamford, Conn., 2001—05. Adj. prof. U. Debrecen, Hungary, 1999—2007; chmn. Planning and Zoning Commn., New Canaan, Conn., 2004—. Mem. Pres.'s Adv. Com. on Pvt. Sector Initiatives, 1980-85; mem. adv. com. Westchester C.C., 1971-75, Iona Coll., New Rochelle, N.Y., 1982-87, Norwalk State Tech. Coll., 1983-95; v.p. Clearview Sch., 1985-89, pres., 1990-91, bd. dirs. 2007—; mem. Town Coun. New Canaan, Conn., 1993-99; chmn. Planning and Zoning Commn., New Canaan, 2004—. Fellow AIA (reg. dir. 1983-85); mem. Internat. Union Architects (rep. habitat com. 1986-90), N.Y. State Assn. Architects (v.p. 1977-80, pres. 1981), Am.-Hungarian Engrs. Assn. (bd. dirs. 1978-90), Am. Coun. World Fedn. Hungarians (pres. 1993-97, regional pres. 1996-2000), Hungarian Univ. Assn. (pres. 1958-60), Westchester County C. of C. (bd. dirs. 1968-71, vice chmn. bd. for area devel. 1983-89, chmn. bd. dirs. 1989-90), Am.-Hungarian C. of C. (charter 1989—). Home: 1197 Valley Rd New Canaan CT 06840-2428 Personal E-mail: papparch@aol.com.

PAPPAGALLO, MARCO, neurologist, pain medicine specialist; b. Senigallia, Italy, Sept. 30, 1957; arrived in U.S., 1986; s. Sergio Pappagallo and Fiorella Capomagi. MD, U. Rome, 1982. Diplomate in neuology Am. Bd. Psychiatry and Neurology, in pain mgmt. Am. Bd. Med. Specialties. Clin. instr. Johns Hopkins Hosp., Balt., 1993—95; asst. prof. dept. neurology and neurosurgery Johns Hopkins Sch. Medicine, Balt., 1995; assoc. prof. dept. neurology NYU Sch. Medicine, NYC, 1999—; dir. Pain Treatment Ctr. Hosp. for Joint Diseases, Mt. Sinai-NYU Health, NYC, 1999—; dir. NYU Pain Treatment Ctrs., Hosp. for Joint Diseases, NYC, 1999—2003; dir. divsn. chronic pain Beth Israel Med. Ctr., 2003—06; prof. anesthesiology and neurology dept. pain medicine R&D Mt. Sinai Sch. Medicine, NYC, 2006—. Achievements include invention of therapeutic method with capsaicin; therapeutic method with capsaicin and capsaicin analogues. Office: Mt Sinai Sch Medicine Pain Mgmt Box 1192 5 E 98th St 6th Fl New York NY 10029 Business E-Mail: marco.pappagallo@mssm.edu.

PAPPAJOHN, JOHN G., venture capitalist; b. St. Luke's, Greece, July 31, 1928; s. George and Maria (Zanios) P.; m. Mary; children Ann Vassiliou. BSc, U. Iowa, 1952. Owner Pappajohn Ins. Agy., Mason City, Iowa, 1953-59; pres., founder Guardsman Life Investors, Inc., Des Moines,

1962-69; co-founder, v.p. Guardsman Life Ins. Co., West Des Moines, Iowa, 1962-69; pres. Equity Dynamics Inc., Des Moines, 1969—, Pappajohn Capital Resources, Inc., Des Moines, 1969—. Bd. dirs. United Systems Tech., Dallas, Optimumcare Corp., La Jolla, Calif., Galagen, Inc., BioCryst, Inc., Neose Pharms., Drug Screening Systems. Horatio Alger Assn., Leadership 100. Trustee Anatolia Coll., Thessalonia, Greece, 1988, Pine Manor Coll., Boston, 1990, U. Iowa Found., Iowa City, 1990; mem. adv. bd. Kennedy Ctr. for Performing Arts, Washington, 1986, 90; philanthropic causes with wife: John Pappajohn Bus. Bldg., Univ. Iowa Sch., Pappajohn Pavilion, Univ. Iowa Hosp. and Clinics, John and Mary Pappajohn Clin. Cancer Ctr.; founder, John and Mary Pappajohn Scholarship Fund, 1997; organizer, financer John Pappajohn Entrepreneurial Ctrs. at five different univs. and colls. in the state of Iowa; funder, NIACC Pappajohn Bus. Bldg., Mason City, Iowa, 2001; active mem. Nat. Com. of the Performing Arts; mem. trustee coun., collectors com., Nat. Gallery Art, Washington, DC.; dir. Hirshhorn Mus., Washington, DC; mem. nat. com., Whitney Mus., NYC; hon. trustee, Des Moines Art Ctr., Iowa; bd. visitors Univ. Iowa; mem. Greek Orthodox Archdiocese Exec. Com., 2001-04; coun. mem. Greek Orthodox Archdiocese of Am.; associated with JF Kennedy Ctr. for Performing Arts, Washington, D.C., former mem. advisory bd. Recipient Spl. Achievement award Big Bros., 1972, Big Bro. of Yr. award, 1974, Oscar D. Schmidt Iowa Bus. Leadership award, U. Iowa Coll. Bus., 1993, Horatio Alger award, Horatio Alger Assn., 1995, Brotherhood award, Iowa Region Nat. Conf. of Christian and Jews, 1997, Beta Gamma Sigma Mediallion for Entrepreneur of Yr., 1997, Hellenic Hertiage Achievement award, 1997, Meredith Willson Heritage award, 1998, Ellis Island Medal of Honor, 2000, Greek Orthodox Archon award, 2000, Univ. Iowa Homecoming Honored Guest, 2002; Finkbine award, U. Iowa Bus. Sch., 2004; named Iowa Bus. Leader of Yr., 1993; named to Iowa Hall of Fame, 1996, Central Iowa Bus. Hall of Achievement, 1999; named one of Top 200 Collectors, ARTnews Mag., 2004, 2006. Mem. U. Iowa Alumni Assn. (pres.' club), Des Moines Club, Embassy Club, Univ. Club, Order AHEPA, Masons, Shriners, Phi Gamma Delta. Republican. Greek Orthodox. Avocations: Collector of Modern and Contemporary Art, wines, philanthropy. Office: Pappajohn Capital Resources 2116 Financial Ctr Des Moines IA 50309-3908 Address: John Pappajohn Entrepreneurial Ctr Curris Bus Bldg Stes 5 & 264 U Northern Iowa Cedar Falls IA 50614-0130

PAPPALARDO, A. JOHN, former prosecutor, lawyer; b. Nashua, NH, Dec. 15, 1948; BA in Govt., Bowdoin Coll., 1971; JD, Suffolk Univ., 1974. Asst. dist. atty. Off. of Dist. Atty., Norfolk County, 1975—78; Chief, Public Integrity Unit Off. of Atty. Gen., Commonwealth of Mass., 1981, deputy chief counsel,spl. commn., 1978—81; asst. US atty. Dept. Justice, 1981—86, Chief, Public Corruption Unit, US Attys. Off., 1986—87; dep. atty. gen., chief criminal bur. Office Atty. Gen., Commonwealth of Mass., Boston, 1987—89; 1st asst. US atty, Dist. of Mass. Dept. Justice, 1989—92, U.S. atty. Boston, 1992—93; now co-mng. shareholder Greenberg Traurig LLP, Boston. Roman Catholic. Office: Greenberg Traurig LLP One International Place Boston MA 02110 Office Phone: 617-310-6072. Office Fax: 617-310-6001. Business E-Mail: pappalardoj@gtlaw.com.

PAPPALARDO, ROSA GLORIA, secondary school educator; b. Bklyn., Mar. 10, 1932; d. Angelo Charles and Rose (Paternostro) Borgia; m. Leonard Thomas Pappalardo, Apr. 16, 1955; children: Marianne, Leonard, Charles, Roseanne. BS, NYU, 1952, MA, 1953; postgrad., Seton Hall U., 1980-81, Rutgers U., 1984. Cert. supr. of art K-12, N.J., N.Y. Art edn. tchr. Islip (N.Y.) Bd. Edn., 1953—54, Herricks (N.Y.) Bd. Edn., 1954-57, 61-62; tchr. spl. edn. Passaic Assn. for Mentally Retarded, Passaic, NJ, 1958—60; supr. art/home edn. Randolph (N.J.) Twp. Schs., 1962—95; adj. prof. Jersey City State Coll., 1971—98, N.J. State U., Trenton, 2002—03; prof. Jersey City State U., 2002—. Art cons.; editor GAINS Leadership Curriculum, Jersey City U.; presenter in field. Co-author art and math. curricula for Randolph Twp. Schs. K-12; contbr. chpt. to books Organizer, host children's art exhibits Cmty. Children's Mus., Dover, NJ, 2007. Recipient numerous svc. awards, recognition awards, awards for art edn. and art adminstrn. Fellow: Art Educators N.J. (Disting., pres.); mem.: NABA (pres.), Art Adminstrs. N.J. (pres.), N.J. Art Educators, Arts Coun. of Morris Area (planning com. 2002, Chinese, U.S. and Croatia exhibits in NYC galleries), Kiwanis, Delta Zeta (pres.), Phi Delta Kappa. Republican. Roman Catholic. Avocations: swimming, visual arts. Home: 312 Mountain Way Morris Plains NJ 07950-1910 Office: 73 Evans Ln Lake Placid NY 12946-1605 E-mail: lenpgloria@optonline.net.

PAPPAS, ALCESTE THETIS, consulting company executive, educator; b. Dix Hills, NY, May 5, 1945; d. Costas Ernest and Thetis (Hero) P.; m. Sylvan V. Endich, Sept. 13, 1987. AB, U. Calif.-Berkeley, 1967, PhD, 1978; EdM, Harvard U., 1969. Cert. guidance counselor, Mass., secondary sch. tchr., Mass. Dir. student-young alumni affairs Calif. Alumni Assn., Berkeley, 1969-71; dir. residential programs U. Calif., Berkeley, 1971-73, dir. housing and childcare, 1973-79; sr. cons., mgr. Peat, Marwick, Mitchell & Co., NYC, 1979-80, 80-82, sr. mgr., 1982-84; ptnr. in charge edn., other instns. Peat, Marwick, Main & Co., NYC, 1984-93; pres., CEO Pappas Cons. Group, Inc., Greenwich, Conn., 1993—. Spkr. in field. Author: Reengineering Your Non-Profit Organization: A Guide to Strategic Transformation, 1996; contbr. articles to profl. jours., author monographs. Mem. Merola Opera Bd., San Francisco, 1978-80, Calif. Alumni Council, 1976-79; bd. overseers Regents Coll., 1986-89; bd. dirs., mem. fin. com. Hellenic Coll. and Holy Cross Sch. Theology, Brookline, Mass., 1983-87, Seabury Western Theol. Sem., Evanston, Ill., 1983-89; bd. dirs. N.Y. Chiropractic Coll., 1986-88, Com. on Econ. Devel., 1986-88, Greek Orthodox Archdiocese Council, N.Y.C., 1985-89; bd. dirs., vice chmn. St. Basil Acad., 1983-87; bd. dirs., mem. exec. com. YWCA, N.Y.C., 1985-90, Catalyst, 1988-90; chairperson capital campaign com. U. Calif., Berkeley, exec. v.p. exec. coun. Coll. Letters and Sci.; trustee Clark U., 1993-95, U. Calif. Found., 1993-99; bd. dirs. Nat. Coun. for Rsch. on Women, 1996-98; mem. adv. bd. Grad. Sch. Edn. U. Calif., Berkeley, 2005—. Named mem. Acad. Women Achievers, YWCA, N.Y.C., 1984; recipient award Nat. Mgmt. Assn., 1997. Mem. Mid. States Assn. Schs. and Colls. (bd. dirs., fin. com. 1984-89, planning com. 1988-89), Order of the Ky. Colonels, Mortar Bd., Pi Lambda Theta, Prytanean. Avocations: opera, gourmet cooking, travel, photography. Office: 68 Southfield Ave Stamford CT 06902-7237 Office Phone: 203-357-7058.

PAPPAS, BARBARA ESTELLE, biblical studies educator, author; b. Chgo., July 26, 1941; m. George G. Pappas, Sept. 20, 1964; children: Dheanna Pappas Fikaris, Michele Pappas Glavanovits, Laina Pappas Krabbe. BA in Early Ch. Fathers, DePaul U., Chgo., 2004. Lay asst. Holy Apostles Ch., Westchester, Ill., 1976—. Sec., lectr. Diocese of Chgo. Religious Edn. Commn., 1982—; founder, dir. Holy Apostles Resource Ctr., Westchester, 1984—. Author: Are You Saved?, The Orthodox Christian Process of Salvation, 1984, 5th edit., 2006, The Christian Life in the Early Church and Today, Commentaries on Paul's Epistles to the Corinthians, Vol. I, 1989, Vol. II, 1998, God's Bubbly, Gurgly, Overwhelming, Overflowing Love, 2000, First and Second Corinthians: A Study of Paul's Letters, 2005. Mem. teenage curriculum com. Greek Orthodox Archdiocese. Mem.: ASCD. Greek Orthodox. Home: 379 Arboretum Cir Wheaton IL 60187 E-mail: ayspappas@comcast.net.

PAPPAS, CHARLES ENGELOS, plastic surgeon; b. Phila., May 20, 1946; s. Engelos George and Angelina (Biniaris) Pappas; m. Aprille Pappas; children: Evan, Angela, Chrysten. BA, BS, U. Pa., 1968; MD, Temple U., 1972. Intern, then resident in gen. surgery Johns Hopkins Hosp., Balt., 1972-75; resident in gen. surgery Temple U. Hosp., Phila., 1975-76, resident in plastic surgery, 1976-78, clinical fellow cardiac surgery, 1972-73; clinical fellow transplant Harvard Med. Sch., 1973; chmn. dept. plastic surgery Temple U. Hosp., Phila., 1978-81, clin. assoc. prof. surgery, 1981—; chief dept. plastic surgery Meml. Hosp., Phila., 1986—; clin. assoc. plastic surgery Chestnut Hill Hosp., Phila., 1979—, chief/dir. dept. plastic surgery, 1994—; med. dir. Ft. Washington Surgery Ctr., 1994—. Dir. Inst. for Aesthetic Plastic Surgery, Ft. Washington, Pa., 1985—; chmn. bd. Am. Gaming Industries, 1984—; dir., ptnr. Tristate Quicklube Co., 1982-91, Medars; pres., dir. two carwash cos., Phila., 1989—; med. dir. Fort Washington Surgery Ctr., 1995—, dir., trustee, 1996—; med. dir. Aesthetica, Inc., 1996—; nat. med. dir. Aesthetics Med. Mgmt., Inc., 1996—, med. advisor, 1997—; dir., CEO Spa Aesthetika, 1998—; CEO, dir. Aesthetic Health Care Ctrs., 1999—, SPA Aesthetika, 1999—; founder, CEO Papco Ventures, Inc., 2000—. Contbr. articles to profl. jours. Trustee Germantown Acad., Ft. Washington, 1986—, Commonwealth Nat. Country Club, Horsham, 1988—, Patrons' Charity Found. Fellow ACS, Royal Coll. Surgeons; mem. Am. Soc. Plastic Reconstructive Surgeons (diplomate), Am. Soc. Aesthetic Plastic Surgeons (diplomate), Phila. Soc. Plastic Surgeons (pres. 1990-92). Greek Orthodox. Avocations: golf, tennis, development and investing, skiing. Office: The Aesthetic Health Care Ctr 467 Pennsylvania Ave Ste 202 Fort Washington PA 19034-3420 Personal E-mail: cepmd@att.net.

PAPPAS, CHARLES NICHOLAS, III, dentist, educator; b. Phila., Jan. 14, 1936; s. Charles Nicholas, Jr. and Marie (Pero) Pappas; m. Edith Basedow, Aug. 24, 1974. Student, U. Colo., 1953—55; DDS, Northwestern U., 1959. Assoc. practice dentistry, South Weymouth, Mass., 1962; pvt. practice dentistry Weymouth Heights, Mass., 1962—65; public health dentist Dept. Health and Hosps., Boston, 1965—70; assoc. practice Weymouth, 1965—68, Brookline, Mass., 1969; practicing clin. dentist Harvard U., 1970—71, clin. instr. operative dentistry, 1967—71; clin. rsch. asst. Forsyth Dental Ctr., 1972; asst. prof. restorative dentistry U. Pa., 1972—83; dentist Dept. Pub. Health, City of Phila., 1984—. Clin. instr. Tufts U., 1965. Author: The Life and Times of G.V. Black, 1983, (pamphlet) Self-Control of Tooth Decay, 1967; contbr. articles to profl. publs. Program, fund-raising chmn. Phillips Brooks Club Boston Trinity Ch., 1965—66. Capt. AUS, 1960—62. Recipient Earle Banks Hoyt award for excellence in tchg., 1980. Mem.: AAAS, ADA, Christian Dental Soc., NY Acad. Scis., Pa. Assn. Dental Surgeons, Mass. Dental Soc., Philadelphia County Dental Soc., Harvard Odontological Soc., Yale Libr. Assocs., U.S. Submarine Vets WWII (assoc. Cert. of Appreciation 1982), Goethe Soc. New Eng., English-Speaking Union, 4001 Lit. Union (founder, faculty advisor), New Haven Colony Hist. Soc., Hist. Soc. Pa., Ill. State Hist. Soc., G.V. Black Soc., Northwestern U. of Delaware Valley Club (pres. 1978), Xi Psi Phi, Lambda Chi Alpha. Home: 5723 Charles St Philadelphia PA 19135-3806 Office: City of Phila Dist Health Ctr # 10 Dental Clinic 2230 Cottman Ave Philadelphia PA 19149

PAPPAS, DAVID CHRISTOPHER, lawyer; b. Kenosha, Wis., Mar. 18, 1936; s. theros and Marion Lucille (Piperas) P.; m. Laurie Jean LaCaskey, Nov. 26, 1956 (div. 1969); children: Christopher David, Andrea Lynn; m. Nancy Marie Pratt, June 11, 1983 (div. 1998). BS, U. Wis., 1959, JD, 1961. Bar: Wis. 1961, U.S. Dist. Ct. (ea. and we. dists.) Wis. 1965, U.S. Supreme Ct. 1971; lic. master mariner. Asst. corp. counsel Racine County (Wis.), 1961; atty., advisor U.S. Dept. Labor, Washington, 1961-62; staff atty. U.S. Commn. Civil rights, Washington, 1962-63; asst. city atty. City of Madison (Wis.), 1963-65; atty. pvt. practice, Madison, 1965—. Chmn. Madison Mayor's Citizen Adv. Com., 1964-65; pres. Wis. Cup Assn., Madison, 1965; c0-chmn. 2d Congl. Dist. Humphrey for Pres., Madison, 1972. Recipient commendation for Supreme Ct. work Madison County Coun., 1965, commendation resolution City of Madison, 1965. Mem. Wis. Bar Assn., Dane County Bar Assn., Wis. Acad. Trial Lawyers, Am. Assn. Trial Lawyers, Lawyer-Pilot Bar Assn. (master mariner), Gt. Lakes Hist. Soc., Madison Club, South Shore Yacht Club (Milw.). Home and Office: 1787 Strawberry Rd Deerfield WI 53531-9779 Office Phone: 608-764-8666. E-mail: mooney@midplains.net.

PAPPAS, DAVID WAYNE, guidance counselor, consultant; b. Chgo., May 19, 1958; s. Danny and Roselle Pappas. BS in Adminstrn. Justice, So. Ill. U., 1981, M Bus. Edn., 1988; ednl. specialist degree in curriculum and instrn., No. Ill. U., 1993, MEd in Counseling, 1997, EdD in Curriculum Inst. and Supervision, 2001. Cert. tchr., in bus., technology, and ESL, cert. counsellor in Guidance and ESL assessment, ISBE gen. cert, lic. profl. counselor, Ill.; nat. cert. counselor; cert. in scuba diving. Residence hall coord. So. Ill. U., Carbondale, Ill., 1981—84, grad. asst. Sch. Tech. Careers, 1983; tng. specialist Dawson Tech. Inst., Chgo., 1985-92; coord. coop. edn. Chgo. City-Wide Coll., 1987-89, ast. dir. curriculum and tng., 1989-90, dir. Life Skills Employment Awareness Program, 1990-92; dir. opportunities program Harold Washington Coll., Chgo., 1992-94; tchr. tech. Taft H.S., Chgo., 1994-2001, lead tchr. summer sch., 1999; coord. Chgo. Police and Firefighters Tng. Acad., Chgo. Bd. Edn., 1999—, guidance counselor, 2001—; instr. No. Ill. U., DeKalb, 1997—. Cons. Strategies, Inc., Chgo. Author: The History and Development of Correctional Education in the Correctional Institutions of Southern Illinois, 1988, An Investigation of the Personality Types of Chicago Fire Fighters and High School Students Participating in the Chicago Police and Fire Fighters Training Academy, 2001; contbr. articles to profl. jours. Recipient Outstanding Young Men Am., 1988. Mem. ACA, Am. Sch. Counseling Assn., Ill. Counseling Assn., Phi Delta Kappa, Chi Sigma Iota. Democrat. Roman Catholic. Avocations: international travel, scuba diving, running, swimming, skiing. Home: 700 W Bittersweet Pl Chicago IL 60613-2385 Office: Chgo Bd Edn 6530 West Bryn Mawr Ave Chicago IL 60631 Fax: 773-534-1027. E-mail: dwpappas@ix.netcom.com.

PAPPAS, EDWARD HARVEY, lawyer; b. Midland, Mich., Nov. 24, 1947; s. Charles and Sydell (Sheinberg) P.; m. Laurie Weston, Aug. 6, 1972; children: Gregory Alan, Steven Michael. BBA, U. Mich., 1969, JD, 1973. Bar: Mich. 1973, U.S. Dist. Ct. (ea. dist.) Mich. 1973, U.S. Dist. Ct. (we. dist.) Mich. 1980, U.S. Ct. Appeals (6th cir.) 1983, U.S. Supreme Ct. 1983, U.S. Ct. Appeals (3d cir.) 1994, U.S. Ct. Appeals (1st cir.) 2002. Ptnr. firm Dickinson & Wright, P.L.L.C., Detroit and Bloomfield Hi, Mich., 1973—. Mediator Oakland County Cir. Ct., Pontiac, Mich., 1983—; hearing panelist Mich. Atty. Discipline Bd., Detroit, 1983—, chmn., 1987—; mem. bus. tort subcom. Mich. Supreme Ct. Com. Std. Jury Instrns., 1992-94; bd. commrs. State Bar Mich., 1999-, v.p., 2006-. Trustee Oakland Community Coll., Mich., 1982-90, Oakland-Livingston Legal Aid, 1982-90, v.p., 1982-85, pres., 1985-87; trustee, adv. bd. Mich. Regional Anti-Defamation League of B'nai B'rith, Detroit, 1983-90; planning commr. Village of Franklin, Mich., 1987-91, chmn. 1989-91, councilman, 1991-92, chmn. charter com., 1993-94; chmn. State Bar Mich. Long Range Planning com.; pres.-elect Oakland County Bar Assn., 1996-97, pres., 1997-98, chmn. Jud. Selection Task Force, 1997; bd. dirs. Franklin Found., 1989-92; trustee The Oakland Medication Ctr., 1992-96; treas. State Bar of Mich., 2004-05. Master Oakland County Bar Assn. Inn of Ct.; fellow Mich. State Bar Found., Oakland Bar-Adams Pratt Found., ABA Found., Am. Coll. Civil Trial Mediators; mem. ABA, Fed. Bar Assn., State Bar Mich. (co-chmn. nat. moot ct. competition com. 1974, 76, com. on legal aid, chmn. standing com. on atty. grievances 1989-92, comml. litig. com., civil procedure com. 1992-94, bd. commrs. 1999—, treas. 2004-05, sec. 2005-06, v.p. 2006—), Oakland County Bar Assn. (vice-chmn. CLE com., chmn. CLE com. 1985-86, mediation com. 1989-90, chmn. mediation com. 1990-91, bd. dirs. 1990-98, chmn. select com. Oakland County cir. ct. settlement week 1991, chmn. strategic planning com. 1992-93, editor Laches monthly mag. 1986-88, co-chair task force to improve justice systems in Oakland County 1993—, pres.-elect, bd. dirs. 1996-97, pres. 1997-98), Am. Judicature Soc., Mich. Def. Trial Lawyers, Def. Rsch. and Trial Lawyers Assn. (com. practice and procedure), B'nai B'rith Barristers. Home: 32223 Scenic Ln Franklin MI 48025-1702 Office Phone: 248-433-7228. Business E-Mail: epappas@dickinsonwright.com.

PAPPAS, EFFIE VAMIS, language educator, finance educator, writer, poet, artist; b. Cleve., Dec. 26, 1924; d. James Jacob and Helen Joy (Nicholson) Vamis; m. Leonard G. Pappas, Nov. 3, 1945; children: Karen Pappas Morabito, Leonard J., Ellen Pappas Daniels, David James. BBA, Western Res. U., 1948; MA in Edn., Case Western Res. U., 1964, postgrad., 1964—68; MA in English Lit., Cleve. State U., 1986; postgrad., Ind. U. Pa., 1979—86. Cert. elem. and secondary tchr. Ohio. Tchr. elem. schs., Ohio, 1963-70; office mgr. Cleve. State U., 1970-72, adminstr. pub. rels., 1972-73; med. adminstr. Brecksville VA Hosp., Ohio, 1974-78; lectr. English, econs./bus. mgmt., math., comm., composition Cuyahoga CC, Cleve., 1978-92. Tchg. asst. Case Western Res. U., 1979—80; lectr. bus. comm. Cleve. State U., 1980; participant in sci. and cultural exch. dels. Am. Inst. Chemists, China, 1984, Russia, 89. Feature writer: The Voice, 1970—78, editor, writer: Cleve. State U. newsletter and mag., 1970—73. Cub scout leader Boy Scouts Am., Brecksville, 1960; mem. local coun. PTA, 1965—70; sec. St. Paul's Coun., 1990—91; mem. membership com. St. Paul Ladies Philoptohos, 1990—; active Women's Equity Action League, 1995—2003; mem. Greater Cleve. Learning Project; Sunday sch. tchr., mem. choir Brecksville United Ch. of Christ, 1975—76, mem. bd. missions, 1966—67, mem. membership com., 1993; mem. planning com. edn. Case Western Res. U.; mem. 75th Anniversary steering com. Cleve. Coll. Recipient Editor's Choice award for outstanding achievement in poetry, Nat. Libr. Poetry, 1995, 2000; grantee, Cuyahoga CC, 1982. Mem.: AARP, AAUW (del. meetings, legis. chair 1993—94, co-chair Cleve. br. 1994, 1996—97, legis. chair 1997—98), NAFE, NAE (life named to Nat. Women's Hall Fame), Ohio Edn. Assn. (rep. assembly Columbus 1994, 1999—2001, 2002—03), N.E. Ohio Edn. Assn. (licentiate), Nat. Mus. Women in Arts (hon. roll. mem.). Avocations: travel, art, legal studies, theater, correspondence with national and international friends. Home: 8681 Brecksville Rd Brecksville OH 44141-1912

PAPPAS, ERIC CHARLES, director; b. NYC, Mar. 10, 1950; s. Robert Lester and Betty Pappas; children: Jesse, Angelea. BS in Econ. Theory, Wagner Coll., NYC, 1972; MA in English, Va. Tech., 1987, EdD in English Edn., 1990. Furniture designer, furniture maker, Ithaca, NY, 1973—81; composer, singer Blacksburg, Va., 1979—85; dir., founder Va. Dept. Corrections Sch., Floyd, 1980—82; lit. instr. Va. Tech., Blacksburg, 1985—93; founder, dir. Va. Tech. Engrng. Ctr., Blacksburg, 1993—2003; founder, dir. Inst. Higher Order Thinking James Madison U., Harrisonburg, Va., 2003—. Cons., spkr. in field. Songwriter, singer (record album) All Your Heart, 1983, founder (academic jour.) Cutting Ed, 2001—; contbr. articles to engrng. jours.; editor: Managing Quality and Productivity, 1988; author: A Rural Community Organizer's Manual, 1988. Founding organizer Ithaca (NY) Farmer's Market, 1973—78; cmty. organizer Coalition of Am. Electric Consumers, Va., 1980—82; chair Va. Tech. Commn. on Outreach, Blacksburg, 2001—03. Named Artist of Mo., Swamp Records, 2003; grantee, Honeywell Internat., 1994—2002, State Coun. of Higher Edn., Richmond, Va., 1997. Mem.: AAUP, Am. Soc. Engring. Edn., Phi Kappa Phi (pres. Va. Tech. chpt. 1990—92). Office: James Madison U ISAT 117 MSC 4102 Harrisonburg VA 22807 Office Phone: 540-568-1694. Office Fax: 540-568-2761. E-mail: pappasec@jmu.edu, epappas@cisat.jmu.edu.

PAPPAS, GEORGE DEMETRIOS, anatomist, cell biologist, educator; b. Portland, Maine, Nov. 26, 1926; s. James and Anna (Dracopoulos) Pappatheodoros; m. Bernice Levine, Jan. 14, 1952; children: Zoe Alexandra, Clio Nicollette. BA, Bowdoin Coll., Brunswick, Maine, 1947; MS, Ohio State U., Columbus, 1948, PhD, 1952; DSc (hon.), U. Athens, Greece, 1988. Vis. investigator Rockefeller Inst., NYC, 1952-54; assoc. in anatomy Coll. Physicians and Surgeons, Columbia U., NYC, 1956-57, asst. prof. anatomy, 1957-63, assoc. prof., 1963-66; prof. anatomy Albert Einstein Coll. Medicine, Yeshiva U., NYC, 1967-77, prof. neurosci., 1974-77, vis. prof. neurosci., 1977-97; prof., head dept. anatomy and cell biology U. Ill. Coll. Medicine, Chgo., 1977-96, prof. cell biology and psychiatry, 1996—. Trustee Marine Biol. Lab., Woods Hole, Mass., 1975-81. Author: (with others) The Structure of the Eye, 1961, Growth and Maturation of the Brain, vol. IV, 1964, Nerve as a Tissue, 1966, The Thalmus, 1966, Pathology of the Nervous System, vol. 1, 1968, Structure and Function of Synapses, 1972, Methodological Approaches to the Study of Brain Maturation and Its Abnormalities, 1974, Advances in Neurology, vol.12, 1975, The Nervous System, vol. 1 The Basic Neurosciences, 1975, Cellular and Molecular Basis of Synaptic Transmission, 1988; contbr. over 250 articles to profl. jours.; former mem. editl. bd. Anatomical Record, Biol. Bull., Brain Rsch., Jour. Neurocytology, Microstructure, Neurol. Rsch. Arthritis and Rheumatism Found. fellow, 1954-56; recipient Career Devel. award Columbia U., 1964-66; Rsch. grant NIH. Fellow AAAS, NY Acad. Scis., Inst. Medicine Chgo.; mem. Am. Soc. Cell Biology (pres. 1974-75), Am. Assn. Anatomists (chmn. pub. policy com. 1981-82, Henry Gray award 2003), Assn. Anatomy Chmn. (exec. com. 1978-80, pres. 1981-82), Electron Microscopy Soc. Am. (program chmn. 1984-85), NY Soc. Electron Microscopy (pres. 1967-68), Soc. for Neurosci. (pres. Chgo. chpt. 1985-86), Harvey Soc., Internat. Brain Rsch. Orgn., Cajal Club, Sigma Xi. Achievements include patents for method inducing analgesia by implantation of cells releasing neuroactive substances. Home: Apt 512 S 680 N Lake Shore Dr Chicago IL 60611 Office: U Ill Psychiat Inst MC 912 1601 W Taylor St Chicago IL 60612-4310 Office Phone: 312-413-4562. Business E-Mail: gdpappas@uic.edu.

PAPPAS, GEORGE FRANK, lawyer; b. Washington, Oct. 5, 1950; s. Frank George and Iora Marie (Stauber) P.; m. Susan Elizabeth Bradshaw, Apr. 25, 1980; children: Christine Bradshaw, Alexandra Stauber. BA, U. Md., 1972, JD, 1975. Bar: Md. 1976, D.c. 1991, u.S. Dist. Ct. Md. 1976, U.S. Dist. Ct. (d.C. cir.) 1986, U.S. Dist. Ct. (we. dist.) Tex. 1993, U.S. Ct. Appeals (4th cir.) 1976, U.S. Ct. Appeals (d.c. cir.) 1984, U.S. Ct. Appeals 9fed. cir.) 1991, U.S. Ct. Appeals (2d cir.) 1993, U.S. Ct. Appeals (6th and 7th cirs.) 1994, U.S. Supreme Ct. 1984, U.S. Ct. of Fed. Claims, 1995. Assoc. H. russell Smouse, Balt., 1976-81, Melnicove, Kaufman, Wiener & Smouse, Balt., 1981-83, prin., 1983-88; ptnr. Venable, Baetjer and Howard, Balt., 1986—. Lectr. Wash. Coll. Law, Am. U., Washington, 1980-84; moot ct. bd., 1974-75; Master of the Bench, Inn XIII, Am. Inns of Ct., 1989; mem. U.S. Dist. Ct. of Delaware Judges' Intellectual property Adv. Com., 1998—; mem. Dist. Judge Edn. Adv. Com. for the Fed. Jud. Ctr., 2001—, chmn. Gov. Commn. on Devel. of Advanced Tech. Bus., 2003—. Founding editor-in-chief Internat. Trade law Jour., 1974-75. Mem. bd. vis. U. Md. Sch. of Law, 2000—. 1st lt. USAF, 1972-76. Fellow Am. Coll. Trial Lawyers; mem. ABA, Am. Law Inst. 2002-, Internat. Assn. Def. Counsel, Md. Bar Assn. (chmn. internat. coml. law sect., 1980-81), Am. Intellectual Property Law Assn., US Trademark Assn., Balt. Country Club, Omicron Delta Kappa, Phi Kappa Phi, Phi Beta Kappa, L'Hirondelle Club. Republican. Greek Orthodox. Home: 9 Roland Ct Baltimore MD 21204-3550 Office: Venable Baetjer & Howard 2 Hopkins Plz Ste 2100 Baltimore MD 21201-2982 also: 575 7th St NW Washington DC 20004-1601 E-mail: gfpappas@venable.com.

PAPPAS, JAMES PETE, university administrator; b. Price, Utah, June 30, 1939; s. Pete S. and Dia P. (Metrakis) P.; m. Peggy Ann Kunz, Aug. 30, 1964; children: C. Jennifer, Peter T. AS in Psychology, Coll. Eastern Utah, 1959; BA in Psychology, U. Utah, 1961; MS in Counseling Psychology, Ohio U., 1964; PhD in Clin. Psychology, Purdue U., 1968; cert. in Mgmt., Stanford U., 1979; cert. in adminstrn., Harvard U., 1985. Asst. dir. counseling ctr. U. Utah, Salt Lake City, 1969-72, dir. ctr. for acad. advising, assoc. dean liberal edn., 1975-78, assoc. dean divsn. of continuing edn.,

1978-87; prof. ednl. psychology and liberal studies U. Okla., Norman, 1987—, v.p. for univ. outreach; dean Coll. of Continuing Edn., 1994-00, Coll. of Liberal Studies, 2000—. Author: (book) Windows of Opportunity: Preparing University Based Residential Continuing Education for the Twenty-First Century, 1992, The University's Role in Economic Development: From Research to Outreach, 1997; co-author: (workbook) Promotional Techniques, 1987. Mem. Norman Econ. Devel. Coalition, 1996—; state chmn. Utah Endowment for Humanities, 1985-88; pres. Norman Arts and Humanities Coun., 1994-95. Recipient St. Paul award Greek Orthodox Ch. of N. Am., Denver, 1990, Christopher Outstanding Leadership and Bittner Svc. awards U. Continuing Edn. Assn.; inductee Internat. Adult and Continuing Edn. Hall of Fame, 1997. Mem. Am. Assn. Counseling and Devel. (nat. senator 1975-77), Assn. Acad. Affairs Adminstr. (bd. dirs. 1977-78), Adult Edn. Assn. Utah (bd. dirs. 1979-82), Univ. Continuing Edn. Assn. (pres. 1996-97, Julius M. Nolte award 2006), Nat. Assn. State Univs. and Land Grant Colls. (bd. dirs. 1994-97), Assn. Grad. Liberal Studies Programs (bd. dirs. 2002—). Avocations: reading, community service, writing, sports, travel. Office: Coll Continuing Edn 1700 Asp Ave Rm 111 Norman OK 73072-6407

PAPPAS, JANICE LOUISE, paleontologist, researcher; d. Steve George and Angela Pappas; m. Mark Zerbe Brahce, June 19, 1981. BA in Philosophy, U. Mich., Dearborn, 1979, BS in Environ. Sci., 1979; MA in Biology, Drake U., 1986; PhD, U. Mich., Ann Arbor, 2000. Rsch. asst. Gt. Lakes Rsch. Divsn., Ann Arbor, 1978—81; grad. asst. dept. biology Drake U., Des Moines, 1981—83; rsch. assoc. U. Mich., Ann Arbor, 1988—99, grad. asst., 1997—2000, rsch. assoc. mus. zoology, 2001—06, asst. rsch. scientist mus. paleontology, 2006. Cons. in field. Field worker frog and toad survey Ann Arbor Parks and Recreation Dept., 1995. Mem.: The Avicultural Soc. Achievements include research in using parametric 3D equations in diatom morphological phylogenetic research; using fuzzy set theory to solve problems in biology, ecology, and paleontology. Office: Univ Mich Mus Paleontology Ann Arbor MI 48109-1079

PAPPAS, LEAH AGLAIA, foundation administrator, political organization worker, secondary school educator; b. Ogden, Utah, Mar. 23, 1936; d. George Thomas and Maria (Harames) P. BA, Coll. St. Mary of the Wasatch, 1959. Tchr. Bishop Gorman High Sch., Las Vegas, Nev., 1959-64; with Dist. Atty.'s staff, Las Vegas, 1972-75; tchr. Weber State Coll., Las Vegas, 1985. Civic worker various orgns., including Opera Guild, Heart Fund, City of Hope, March of Dimes, also groups for prevention of blindness, sr. citizens' groups, others, Ogden and Las Vegas, 1955—; cons. numerous polit. campaigns, Ogden, Las Vegas and Boston, L.A., John F. Kennedy campaign, 1959; alt. del. Chgo. Nat. Conv.; vol. Senator Robert Kennedy Campaign, 1968; supr. Senator Edward M. Kennedy Campaign, Boston, 1970, 76, Presdl. Campaign, 1980; campaign worker Gov. Jerry Brown, L.A., 1978, office mgr., Reagan-Bush campaign, 1984, Pres. Bill Clinton, 1996. Greek Orthodox. Home: 1323 Marilyn Dr Ogden UT 84403-0424 E-mail: Leahap@msn.com.

PAPPAS, MARGENE, retired music educator; d. Eugene Wallace and Marietta Joan Kirkwood; m. Peter Michael Pappas, Dec. 30, 1973. BS, U. Ill., Champaign-Urbana, 1969, MS, 1973. Tchr. Oswego Dist. 308, Ill., 1969—2006; band dir. Oswego Cmty. Band, 1994—2006; ret., 2006. Guest conductor Ill. All-State Band, 2001. Contbr. articles to NBA Jour. Named to Hall of Fame, Phi Beta Mu, Ill. Chpt., 2003; recipient Studs Terkel Humanitarian award, Village of Oswego, 2002, Sudler Legion of Honor, John Philip Sousa Found., 2003, John P. Paynter Lifetime Achievement award, Quinlan and Fabish Music Co., 2006. Mem.: Bands of Am. (adv. bd. 2001—), Ill. Music Edn. Assn., Am. Sch. Band Dirs. Assn., Nat. Band Assn. (bd. dirs. 2000—06). Achievements include directing the HS Wind Symphony performance at 2004 IMEA All-State; directing Oswego HS Marching Band in the 2005 Tournament of Roses; Margene Pappas Day named in her honor Village of Oswego, May 28, 2006. Avocations: travel, reading, music, hiking, cross stitch. Home: 2469 Lakeside Dr Aurora IL 60504 Office Phone: 312-501-4610. E-mail: tntohsband@aol.com.

PAPPAS, MARJORIE L., library studies educator; b. Adrian, Mich., Oct. 4, 1938; d. Raymond C. Spielman and Adalene E. Dickey, Alfred Dickey (Stepfather); children: David J, Mark J. BS, U. Toledo, 1961; MEd, Miami U., Oxford, Ohio, 1977, PhD, 1987. Sch. libr. Watts Mid. Sch., Centerville, Ohio, 1970—78; dir. tech. and librs. Troy (Ohio) City Schs., 1978—85; asst. prof. Wright State U., Dayton, Ohio, 1986—95; assoc. prof. U. No. Iowa, Cedar Falls, 1995—98, vis. prof. online, 1998—2001; assoc. prof. Ea. Ky. U., Richmond, 2001—04; adj. prof. Mansfield U., Mansfield, Pa., 2004—05; assoc. prof. sch. libr. and Dept. Info. Tech. Mansfield (Pa.) U., 2005—, chmn. sch. libr. and Dept. Info. Tech., 2005; freelance writer, cons. Danville, Ky., 2005—, Pres., cons. C L Assocs., Inc., Danville, Ky., 1999—2000. Author: (information process model) Pathways to Knowledge, 1997, Searching Electronic Resources, 1998, Pathways to Knowledge and Inquiry Learning, 1998; contbr. articles to profl. jours. Recipient Edgar Dale award, Assn. Ednl. Comm. and Tech., 1995. Mem.: ALA, Ky. Sch. Media Assn., Am. Assn. Sch. Librs. (regional dir. 1993—96), Ohio Ednl. Libr. Media Assn. (life award of merit 2001), Delta Kappa Gamma. Home: 426 Cloverdale Dr Danville KY 40422 Business E-Mail: marjorie.pappas@gmail.com.

PAPPAS, MILTON J., venture capitalist; b. Cleve., Nov. 13, 1928; s. John Milton and Helen Stajos Pappas; m. Christine Kanillos, Nov. 7, 1953; children: Jeannine, William. BBA, Case Western Res. U., 1950; LLB, Cleveland Marshall Law Sch., 1956. Bar: Ohio 1956; cert. Inst. Chartered Analysts. Trust investment officer Cleve. Trust Co., 1954-60; fin. analyst Merrill Turben & Co., Cleve., 1960-62; sr. v.p. First of Mich., Detroit, 1962-66; v.p. Drexel, Harrman Ripley, NYC, 1966-70, Euclid Ptnrs., NYC, 1970—. Bd. dirs. Cubic Wafer, Inc., Austin, Tex. Lt. (j.g.) USCG, 1952-54. Mem. N.Y. Venture Capital Forum. Greek Orthodox. Avocations: opera, ballet, theater, travel, jogging. Office: Euclid Ptnrs Corp 45 Rockefeller Plz Ste 3240 New York NY 10111-0999 Business E-Mail: milton@euclidsr.com.

PAPPAS, PHILIP JAMES, real estate company executive; b. Chgo., Sept. 29, 1954; s. Nicholas James and Ann (Nicholson) P.; m. Ana Lucia Sant'Anna; children: Tiago, Marcelo, Amanda. BA, Shimer Coll., 1975. Mgr. Cook County Hosp., Chgo., 1975-77, purchasing agt., 1977-81; pres. L.G. Properties, Chgo., 1980—, Tiamar Real Estate, 1990—. Docent Chgo. Architecture Found., 1976-78. Pres. Lincoln Park Builders Assn., 1997-99, Lake View Developers, 1988-89; trustee Shimer Coll., 1997-2003. Recipient 1st pl. award for best interior restoration Nat. Trust for Hist. Preservation, 1991. Mem. Nat. Assn. Realtors, Oxford Union Soc. (life), Chgo. Assn. Realtors (Good Neighbor award 1992, 96, 99-2004), Owassippe Staff Assn. Boy Scouts Am. (life). Greek Orthodox. Office: LG Properties 3654 N Lincoln Ave Chicago IL 60613-3536

PAPPAS, SANDRA LEE, state senator; b. Hibbing, Minn., June 15, 1949; m. Neal Gosman, 1976; 3 children. BA, Met. State U., 1986; MPA, Harvard U., 1994. Mem. Minn. Ho. of Reps., St. Paul, 1984-90, Minn. Senate, St. Paul, 1990—. Part-time coll. instr. Mem. Dem. Farmer Labor Party. Home: 182 Prospect Blvd Saint Paul MN 55107-2136 Office: Minn State Senate 120 State Capitol 75 Martin Luther King Jr Blvd Saint Paul MN 55155-1601 Office Phone: 651-296-1802.

PAPPAS-SPEAIRS, NINA, financial planner, educator; d. Steve E. and Martha (Hicks) Kalfas; m. Harry J. Pappas, 1951 (div.); children: John J., Nicholas S., Vivien E. Pappas Unger, Mark A., Carol A. Pappas Siegel; m. Mitchell F. Speairs, 1992 (dec. 2001). BS, U. Cin., 1950; MA, Northwestern U., Evanston, Ill., 1957; PhD, U. Ill., Champaign, 1978. Faculty St. Mary's H.S., Chgo., Sch. Dist. 102, LaGrange, Ill., U. Ill., Chgo., 1969-79, U. Tex., Arlington, 1979-82, Tex. Wesleyan Coll., Ft. Worth, 1982-83; realtor Merrill Lynch Realty, Ft. Worth, 1983-84; fin. planner Cigna Corp., Irving, Tex., 1984-90; pvt. practice fin. planning and investments, Ft. Worth, 1990—. Organizer, condr. 1st U.S. Olympic Acad., Chgo., 1977; collaborator Internat. Olympic Acad., Olympia, Greece, 1977, guest lectr., 77, 78; chief of mission to Greece U.S. Olympic Com., 1977; guest lectr. Nat. Olympic Acad. Republic of China, 1982. Author: History and Development of the International Olympic Academy: 1927-1977, 1978; editor: Perspectives of the Olympic Games, 1979; also articles. Vice chair edn. coun. U.S. Olympic Com., 1977—85; sch. bd. Dist. 107, LaGrange, Ill., 1971—74. Recipient Silver Medal Internat. Olympic Acad., Olympia, Greece, 1981. Mem. Lecture Found., Symphony League, Opera Guild (pres. 1982-83), Round Table, Ft. Worth Woman's Club, Women's Wednesday Club (pres. 2003-04), River Crest Country Club, Ft. Worth Boat Club, Ridglea Rejebian Club, Carousel Club. Republican. Greek Orthodox. Avocations: golf, reading, sailing, dance.

PAPPERT, AMY S., dermatologist, educator; b. Orange, NJ, Nov. 5, 1960; d. Howard Walter and Audrey Smith Pappert; m. Matthew A. Menza, May 27, 1989; children: Daniel Christopher Menza, Andrew Julian Menza. BS in Pharmacy, Rutgers U., Piscataway, NJ, 1983; MD, U. Medicine and Dentistry NJ, New Brunswick, 1989. Diplomate Am. Bd. Dermatology, lic. physician NJ. Clin. asst. prof. U. Medicine and Dentistry NJ/Robert Wood Johnson Med. Sch., New Brunswick, 1995—. Residency program dir. dept. dermatology U. Medicine and Dentistry NJ/Robert Wood Johnson Med. Sch., New Brunswick, 2006—. Advisor Alopecia Areata Support Group, New Brunswick, 2004—. Fellow: Am. Acad. Dermatology; mem.: NJ Dermatol. Soc. (sec. 2005—), Alpha Omega Alpha. Office: U Medicine and Dentistry NJ Robert Wood Johnson Med Sch 1 World's Fair Dr Somerset NJ 08873

PAPPERT, JERRY (GERALD J. PAPPERT), lawyer, former state attorney general; m. Ellen Pappert; 2 children. Grad. with honors, Villanova U., 1985; JD, Notre Dame U., 1988. Atty. Duane, Morris and Heckscher, Phila., 1988—96; first deputy atty. gen. State of Pa., Harrisburg, Pa., 1996—2003, acting atty. gen., 2003—04, atty. gen., 2004—05; ptnr. Ballard, Spahr, Andrews & Ingersoll LLP, Phila., 2005—. Office: Ballard Spahr Andrews & Ingersoll LLP 51st Fl 1735 Market St Philadelphia PA 19103 Office Phone: 215-864-8521. Business E-Mail: pappertg@ballardspahr.com.

PAPPONE, MICHAEL J., lawyer; b. Caledonia, Minn., Sept. 24, 1948; Student, George Washington U.; AB, U. Calif., Berkeley, 1970; JD, Harvard U., 1973. Bar: Mass. 1973, U.S. Dist. Ct. Mass. 1973, U.S. Ct. Appeals (1st cir.) 1980, U.S. Ct. Appeals (11th cir.), U.S. Ct. Appeals (4th cir.) 1986, U.S. Ct. Appeals (3rd cir.) 1987, U.S. Supreme Ct. Mem. Goodwin, Procter & Hoar, Boston; ptnr. Goodwin, Procter LLP, Boston. Mem. editorial adv. bd. Banking Law Rev. and Bankruptcy Law Rev. 1988-1992. Contbr. articles to profl. jours. Named Am's. Leading Bus. Lawyers, by Chambers USA, Best Lawyers Am. Mem. ABA (bus. bankruptcy com. 1980—, comml. fin. svcs. 1983—, chmn. subcom. on creditor's rights 1990-94), Mass. Bar Assn., Boston Bar Assn., Phi Beta Kappa, Am. coll. Comml. Fin. Lawyers; fellow Am. Bar Found., Am. coll. Bankruptcy. Office: Goodwin Procter LLP Exchange Pl State St Boston MA 02109-2803 Office Phone: 617-570-1940. E-mail: mpappone@goodwinprocter.com.

PAPPS, BRUCE WILLIAM, financial analyst, investment company executive; b. Mt. Kisco, NY, Jan. 19, 1962; s. Ernest W. and Annette (Lazration) P. BS in Econs., U. Pa., 1985. CFA Designation, 2000. Pres., CEO Papps Capital Group, Inc., NYC, 1996—. Adj. prof. SUNY, Valhalla, 1996—98. Mentor P.R.I.D.E., Harlem, N.Y., 1996-98. Mem. N.Y. Soc. Securities Analysts (mem. com.), Merrill Lynch Pres.'s Club, Wharton Club. Avocations: sky diving, scuba diving, boating, skiing. Office: Papps Capital Group Inc 67 Wall St Ste 2211 New York NY 10005-3101 Office Phone: 888-727-7769. E-mail: CEO@papps.com.

PAPROCKI, THOMAS JOHN, lawyer, priest; b. Chgo., Aug. 5, 1952; s. John Henry and Veronica Mary (Bonat) P. BA, Loyola U., Chgo., 1974; student Spanish lang. study, Middlebury Coll., 1976, student Italian lang. study, 1987; MDiv, St. Mary of the Lake Sem., 1978; student Spanish lang. study, Instituto Cuannahuac, 1978; Licentiate in Sacred Theology, St. Mary of the Lake Sem., 1979; JD, DePaul U., 1981; JCD, Gregorian U., Rome, 1991; student Polish lang. study, Cath. U. Lublin, Poland, 1989, Jagiellonian U., Cracow, Poland, 2000. Bar: Ill. 1981, U.S. Dist. Ct. (no. dist.) Ill. 1981, U.S. Supreme Ct. 1994. Assoc. pastor St. Michael Ch., Chgo., 1978-83; pres. Chgo. Legal Clinic, 1981-87, 91—; exec. dir. South Chgo. Legal Clinic, 1981-85, bd. dirs., 1987—; adminstr. St. Joseph Ch., Chgo., 1983-86; vice-chancellor Archdiocese of Chgo., 1985-92, chancellor, 1992-2000, titular bishop Vulturara, aux. bishop Chgo., episc. vicar, Vicariate IV, 2003—, archbishop's liaison health and hosp. affairs, 2005—, canonical affairs com., 2003—, chmn. region VII, 2006; adj. faculty Loyola U. Law, 1999—; pastor St. Constance Parish, 2001—03; with canonical affairs com. US Conf. Cath. Bishops, 2003—; v.p. Ill. Cath. Health Care Assn., 2005—. Senator Presbyteral senate Archdiocese of Chgo., 1985-87, mem. Presbyteral coun., 1992-2000, mem. Cardinal's cabinet, 1992-2000, sec. coll. consultors, 1992-2000; chmn. incardination com., 1991-2000, chmn. policy devel. com., 1998-2000, chmn. Fgn. Priests Initiative, 1998-2000; asst. to the Gen. Sec., Vatican Synod of Bishops, Spl. Assembly for Am., Rome, 1997, cardinal's del. to profl. rev. bd., 1991-2003, chmn. profl. conduct adminstrv. com., 1991-2002; bd. dirs. Cath. Conf. Ill., 1985-87. Mem. editl. adv. bd. Chgo. Cath. Newspaper, 1984-85; contbr. articles to profl. jours. Bd. dirs. United Neighborhood Orgn., Chgo., 1982-85, S.E. Community Youth Svc. Bd., Chgo., 1985, Ctr. for Neighborhood Tech., Chgo., 1986-87, Chgo. Area Found. for Legal Svcs., 1994-2002; active Chgo. Cmty. Trust Com. on Children, Youth and Families, 1991-2002, Ill. Family Violence Coordinating Coun., 1994—. Recipient Humanitarian award Polish Am. Congress, 1997, Alumni award for Outstanding Pub. Svc., DePaul Coll. of Law, 2001; named Man of Yr., Nat. Advs., 1999. Fellow Leadership Greater Chgo.; mem. Ill. Bar Assn., Chgo. Bar Assn. (bd. mgrs. 1999-2001, Maurice Weigle award 1985), Advs. Soc. (award of merit 1996), Cath. Lawyers Guild (Cath. Lawyer of Yr. award 2003), Canon Law Soc. Am., Polish Am. Leadership Initiative (bd. dirs. 2001—), Polish Am. Assn. (bd. dirs. 1998—), The Chgo. Jr. Assn. Commerce and Industry (Ten Outstanding Young Citizens award 1986), Union League Club of Chgo., Pi Sigma Alpha, DePaul U. Alumni Assn. Avocations: hockey, running, reading. Office: Aux Bishop of Chgo 1400 S Austin Blvd Cicero IL 60804 Office Phone: 708-329-4040. Business E-Mail: tpaprocki@archchicago.org.

PAPS, BETTY LOU, nursing educator; b. Chrisman, Ill., Nov. 17, 1937; d. Robert Bertram Bonwell and Katherine Carol (Hess) Buchanan; m. Peter George Paps, Apr. 22, 1989 (dec.); children: Jill Stuebe Thompson, Nena Carol Mihailovic. RN, Lakeview Hosp. Sch. Nursing, 1958; BSN, U. Ill., Chgo., 1965; MSN, DePaul U., 1970; PhD, LaSalle U., 1998. Nurse educator Danville Jr. Coll., Ill., 1963-65, Chgo. Pub. Schs., 1966-68, Mt. Sinai Hosp. Sch. Nursing, Chgo., 1970; prof. nursing Kennedy King Coll., Chgo., 1970—96; chief nurse 63d Aeromedical Evacuation Squadron, 1980—92, troop comdr. Persian Gulf War, 1991; evaluator Nat. League Nursing, 1994—98. Col. USAFR, 1974—94. Decorated Commendation award, Air medal, Meritorious Svc. award, Southeast Asia award, Kuwait Liberation medal, Chief Nurse's badge, Chief Flight Nurse award, Nat. Def. medal. Mem.: VFW, Air Force Assn., Res. Officers Assn., Aerospace Med. Assn., Mil. and Hospitallar Order of St. Lazarus of Jerusalem (Dame), Am. Legion. Personal E-mail: bpaps@aol.com.

PAPY, CHARLES C., III, lawyer; b. Miami, Fla., Feb. 16, 1952; s. Charles C. and June (Marlow) Papy; m. Anne Lang, Aug. 6, 1977; children: Jennifer, Ryan, Alyson, Douglas. BBA, U. Miami, 1974, JD, 1977. Bar: Fla., US Dist. Ct. So. Dist. Fla. Atty. Papy Poole & Weissenborn, Miami, 1977-83; ptnr. Papy Weissenborn & Papy, Miami, 1983-92, Eckert, Seamans, Cherin & Mellott, Miami, 1992—98, Duane Morris LLP, Miami, 1999—, mng. ptnr. Miami office. Appointee Jud. Nominating com., Miami, 1986-90, Health Fin. com. Dade County, Miami. Presbyterian. Avocations: fishing, hunting, sports. Office: Duane Morris LLP 200 S Biscayne Blvd Miami FL 33131-2397 Office Phone: 305-960-2222. Office Fax: 305-960-2201. Business E-Mail: ccpapy@duanemorris.com.

PAQUETTE, JACK KENNETH, management consultant, writer, historian; b. Toledo, Ohio, Aug. 14, 1925; s. Hector J. and Nellie (McCormick) P.; m. Jane Russell, Sept. 13, 1947; children: Jan Eriksen, Mark Russell, Mary Beth, John Eric. Student, Baldwin-Wallace Coll., 1943-44, Marquette U., 1944; BA, Ohio State U., 1949, MA, 1951; postgrad., Wayne State U., 1966. Editor monthly pub. Bur. Motor Vehicles, Ohio, 1947-49; asst. city editor, copy editor Ohio State Jour., 1949-51; copywriter Owens-Ill., Inc., Toledo, 1951-53, copy chief mktg. dept., 1953-55, asst. advt. mgr. mktg. dept., 1955-59; advt. mgr. Owens-Ill., Inc. (Libbey div.), 1959-61; mgr. advt. and sales promotion Owens-Ill., Inc. (Libbey products), 1961-64, mgr. customer mktg. services glass container div., 1964-67, dir. corporate orgn. planning, 1967-69, v.p. adminstrv. div., dir. corp. relations, 1969-70, corporate v.p., dir. corp. relations, 1970-80, corp. v.p., asst. to chmn. bd., 1980-84, cons., 1984-86; pres. Paquette Enterprises, 1984—; owner The Trumpeting Angel, antiques, 1985—. Mem. adv. bd. Cresset Chem. Co., 1987—. Author: A History of Owens-Illinois Inc., (1818-1984), 1985, The Glassmakers, 1994, Blowpipes, 2002, A Boy's Journey Through the Great Depression, 2005. Bd. dirs. Toledo YMCA, 1970-74, Vis. Nurse Svc., 1970-73, Children's Svcs., Lucas County, 1973-80, Toledo coun. Boy Scouts Am., trustee, v.p. fin., 1978-84; trustee Owens Tech. Coll. Found, 1978-81; mem. Advt. Club Toledo, 1951-75, trustee, 1960-62; hon. bd. dirs. Greater Toledo area chpt. ARC, 1970—; mem. adv. bd. Mercy Hosp., Toledo, 1981-84, Mary's Adult Day Care Ctr., 1989-93, St. Anthony's Children's Ctr., 1993, Mid-Coast Hosp., Brunswick, Maine, 1998—; mem. pub. rels. com. Cath. U. Am., 1979-82; chmn. U.S. Savs. Bonds, Lucas County, 1977-79; trustee Bowling Green State U. Found., 1976-83, pres., 1980-82; mem. Nat. Commn. on a Free and Responsible Press, 1980-83; v.p. trustee, Toledo Repertoire Theatre, 1984-88; trustee Crosby Gardens, 1983-89, chmn. 1987-88; trustee Toledo Bot. Gardens, 1989-90, chmn. emeritus and hon. lifetime trustee, 1990—; mem. pres.'s coun. Toledo Mus. Art, Bowling Green State U.; trustee Riverside Hosp. Found., 1984-94, chmn. 1986-89; mem. Juvenile Justice Adv. Bd., 1986-87; advisor R.B. Hayes Presdl. Ctr., 1990-92. With USNR, 1943-46, PTO. Recipient Gold Key award Pub. Rel. News, 1970, Silver Anvil award Pub. Rel. Soc., 1971, 72; named to Toledo Clean Hall of Fame, 1983. Mem. Soc. Profl. Journalists (co-founder Columbus and Toledo chpts.), Ohio Mfrs. Assn. (v.p., trustee 1969-84), Keep Am. Beautiful, Inc. (nat. chmn., exec. com., 1978-84, chmn. emeritus, mem. nat. adv. coun. 1984—), Bus. Com. for the Arts (corp. liaison 1980-84), U.S. C. of C. (cons. affairs com. 1980-84), Western Lake Erie Hist. Soc. (life, trustee 1998-2003), USN Armed Guard Assn., Sampson WWII Navy Vets. Assn., OSU Alumni Assn. (life), Maine Maritime Mus., Toy Soldier Collectors of Am. Soc., Toledo Glass Club, Fostoria Glass Club, Toledo Press Club (founding trustee), Toledo Club, Torch Club (trustee), Rotary (Paul Harris fellow), U.S. Navy League, Am. Legion (Toledo post), Pi Sigma Alpha. Home and Office: 2355 Parliament Sq Toledo OH 43617-1256

PAQUETTE, WILLIAM ARTHUR, historian, educator; b. Lawrence, Mass., Aug. 6, 1947; s. Arthur Conrad Paquette and Dorothy Lucille Root; m. Sylvia Lois Kreps, June 14, 1969 (div. 1987). BA, Grove City Coll., Pa., 1969; MA, Duquesne U., Pitts., 1971; PhD, Emory U., Atlanta, 1994. Tchr. Acad. Holy Cross, Kensington, Md., 1972—75, chmn. dept. social sci., 1973—75; from adj. prof. to prof. history Tidewater C.C., Portsmouth, Va., 1975—94, prof., 1994—. Grad. tchg. asst. Duquesne U., Pitts., 1969—71; adj. prof. history Old Dominion U., Norfolk, Va., 1975—78, Spelman Coll., Atlanta, 1983—84, adj. prof., 1989—90; adj. prof. history Ga. Perimeter, Atlanta, 1983—84; adj. prof. edn. Emory U., Atlanta, 1989—90; project historian NEH, 1979—82, 1995—96, 2000—02; reviewer ETS, 1995—2002; chmn. chancellor's prefix review com. Va. CC. Sys., Richmond, 1998—2000; nat. co-editor history Merlot Project, 2000—; mem. adv. bd. history digital project Nat. Humanities Alliance, 2000—, Gale Group Pubs., 2003—, ProQuest Pubs., 2004—, Prentice-Hall, 2004—, Houghton Mifflin, 2005—; cons. in field; grants reviewer Dept. Edn., 2004—; edn. reviewer Nat. Gallery of Art, 2004—. Author: U.S. Colored Troops from Lower Tidewater in the Civil War, 1992, Encyclopedia of African-American Civil Rights, 1992, Ready Reference: Censorship, 1997, Great Events from History, North America Series, 1997, The War of 1812: An Encyclopedia, 1998, Dictionary of World Biography: 20th Century, 1999, Biographical Encyclopedia of Twentieth Century World Leaders, 1999, Encyclopedia of the U.S. Supreme Court, 2000, Encyclopedia of America's Historic Sites, 2000, Putting the World into World History textbooks, Teaching History, 2001, Great Events: 1900-2001, 2002, World Education Encyclopedia, 2002, World Press Encyclopedia, 2003, A Taste of Merlot: The Multimedia Resources for Historians and Others, Perspectives, 2003; co-author: Instructor's Guide to the Teaching of American History, 1979, Readings in Black and White, 1982, Suffolk: A Pictorial History, 1987, Dictionary of World Biography: Renaissance, 1998, Encyclopedia of North America, 1998, Teaching History, A Journal of Methods, 2001; photographer Fashion Doll Wardrobe, 2002, Suffolk: A Celebration of History, 2006, Instructor's Manual, Western Civilization, 2007; contbr. articles to profl. jours. Mem. adv. bd. US Com. World Food Day, 1999—; commr. Mus. Fine Arts, Portsmouth, Va., 1997—2002; mem. adv. bd. Ba. Fest. of the Book, 1998—2004; adv. bd. H-NET, 2005—. Fellow, NEH, 1985; grantee, Tidewater CC, 1992—93, Am. Cities and Pub. Spaces, NEH, 2005—06; Gilder-Lehrman fellow, U. Va., 2005, Landmark grants, NEH, 2007. Mem.: Va. Political Scientists, History of Edn. Soc., Comparative and Internat. Edn. Soc., US Capitol Hist. Soc., Internat. Standing Conf. History Edn., Am. Ednl. Rsch. Assn., Am. Coun. Quebec Studies, Cmty. Coll. Humanities Assn. (v.p. 1991—93, bd. dirs. 1993—97, Disting. Svc. award 1997), Orgn. Am. Historians (com. cmty. coll. 2002—, chmn. 2004—05), Am. Hist. Assn. (Nancy Roelker Mentorship com. 1997—2000, chmn. 1999—2000, joint com. adj. 2000—04), Mayflower Soc. Va. (asst. historian 1992—93, historian 1993—98, dep. gov. 2004—07, gov. 2007—). Avocations: stamp collecting/philately, photography, travel, genealogy. Office: Tidewater CC 7000 Coll Dr Portsmouth VA 23703 Home: 13565 Filly Ct Gainesville VA 20155 Office Phone: 757-822-2386. Business E-Mail: wpaquette@tcc.edu.

PAQUIN, ANNA, actress; b. Winnipeg, MB Canada, July 24, 1982; d. Brian and Mary Paquin. Actor: (films) The Piano, 1993 (Academy Award best supporting actress, 1993), Golden Globe nomination best supporting actress, 1993), Jane Eyre, 1995, Fly Away Home, 1996, Amistad, 1997, A Walk on the Moon, 1988, Hurly-burly, 1998, Begin the Beguine, 1998, Sleepless Beauty, 1998, A Walk on the Moon, 1999, She's All That, 1999, X-Men, 2000, Almost Famous, 2000, Finding Forrester, 2000, Buffalo Soldiers, 2001, Darkness, 2002, 25th Hour, 2002, X2: X-Men United, 2003, Steamboy, 2004, The Squid and the Whale, 2005, X-Men: The Last Stand, 2006; (TV films) Member of the Wedding, 1997, Hercules (voice only), 1988, All the Rage, 1999, (voice) Joan of Arc, 2005,: (plays) After Ashley, 2005. Office: Double Happy Talent c/o Gail Cowan PO Box 9585 Wellington New Zealand also: William Morris Agy One William Morris Pl Beverly Hills CA 90212

PAQUIN, EDWARD H., JR., retired state legislator, not-for-profit developer; b. Bennington, Vt., Feb. 12, 1953; s. Edward H. Sr. and Alice Marie P.; m. Patricia LaRose, July 4, 1981 (div. Dec. 2005); 1 child, Katherine Marie BA, U. Vt., 1975. Various positions including silversmith and factory worker; builder; rep. Vt. Gen. Assembly, Montpelier, 1991—2002; exec. dir. Vt. Protection and Advocacy, Inc., Montpelier, 2002—. Dir. summer camp for low-income rural children CAMP!; bd. dirs. Vt. Ctr. Ind. Living. Recipient Victory award Nat. Rehab. Hosp., 1991. Democrat. Baptist. Home: PO Box 219 Fairfax VT 05454-0219 Office: Vt Protection and Advocacy Inc 141 Main St Ste 7 Montpelier VT 05602

PAQUIN, GERALD CHESTER, retired military officer, retired registrar; b. Mpls., Jan. 8, 1925; s. Chester Amie Paquin and Mildred Estelle McKellip; m. Carol Joan White (dec.); children: Teresa Lynn, Elise Nannette. BS, U. Colo., Boulder, 1958. Lt. col. USAF, 1943—70; registrar Anoka-Ramsey CC, Coon Rapids, Minn., 1972—74. Decorated Disting. Flying Cross, Air medal, Joint Svcs. Commendation medal, 4-Battle Stars. Mem.: DAV, VFW, Disting. Flying Cross Soc., Am. Legion. Roman Catholic. Avocation: genealogy.

PAQUIN, JEFFREY DEAN, lawyer; b. Milw., Dec. 7, 1960; s. James DeWayne and Helen Ann (Walter) P. BA, U. Wis., 1983; JD, U. Ky., 1986. Bar: Ga. 1986, U.S. Dist. Ct. (no. dist.) Ga. 1986, U.S. Ct. Appeals (11th cir.) 1986, U.S. Dist. Ct. (mid. dist.) Ga. 1987, D.C. 1989, U.S. Ct. Appeals (D.C. cir.) 1989, U.S. Supreme Ct. 1990. Assoc. Powell, Goldstein, Frazer & Murphy, Atlanta, 1986—94; chief litigation counsel United Parcel Svc., Atlanta, 1994—98; nat. practice leader ADR and litig. mgmt. Price Waterhouse, Atlanta, 1998; global practice leader Legal Mgmt. Svcs. Ernst & Young, LLP, Atlanta, 1998—2000; practice leader ADR and conflict mgmt. svcs. Kritzer & Levick, Atlanta, 2000—01; ptnr. Paquin Victor LLP, Atlanta, 2001—; exec. dir. Chief Litigation Counsel Assn., 2001—. V.p. Prodn. Values, Inc., Atlanta, 1987-88. Exec. editor U. Ky. Law Rev., 1985-86. Bd. dirs. Children's Motility Disorder Found., 1995-2000, Ctr. Corp. Counsel Innovation, 2000-02. Mem. ABA, FBA, The Ombudsman Assn., Am. Corp. Counsel Assn. (bd. dirs. Ga. 1997-98), D.C. Bar Assn., Ga. Bar Assn., Atlanta Bar Assn. (v.p., dir. alternative dispute resolution sect.), Mortar Board, Phi Delta Phi, Sigma Epsilon Sigma, Psi Chi. Roman Catholic. Home: 3620 Woodshire Chase Marietta GA 30066-8719 Office: Paquin Victor LLP Bldg 9 Ste 250 1640 Powers Ferry Rd Marietta GA 30067 Home Phone: 770-977-3890; Office Phone: 770-321-4367. E-mail: jeff.paquin@adrcms.com.

PAQUIN, THOMAS CHRISTOPHER, lawyer; b. Quincy, Mass., Feb. 12, 1947; s. Henry Frederick and Rita Marie (St. Louis) P.; m. Jean Jacqueline O'Neill, Aug. 5, 1972; children: Martha, Edward. BS in Acctg., Bentley Coll., 1969; JD, U. Notre Dame, 1974. Bar: Mass. 1974, U.S. Dist. Ct. Mass. 1976. Tax atty. Coopers and Lybrand, Boston, 1974-76; assoc. Cargill, Masterman & Cahill, 1976, Wilson, Curran & Malkasian, Wellesley, 1976-77; ptnr. Bianchi and Paquin, Hyannis, 1977-98; shareholder, dir. Quirk and Chamberlain, P.C., Yarmouthport, 1998—2001; of counsel Quirk, Chamberlain & Marsh, P.C., 2002—04; pvt. practice Barnstable, Mass., 2004—; pub. adminstr. Barnstable County, 2006—. Bd. dirs., chmn. nominating com. Elder Svcs. Cape Cod and Islands, Inc., Dennis, Mass., 1986-91; bd. dirs., corporator Vis. Nurse Assn. Cape Cod Found., Inc., Dennis, 1988-97; pres. Life Svcs. Inc., 1991-95; bd. dirs. Woodside Cemetery Corp., 1998—, pres., 1999—. Mem. Bass River Golf Commn., Yarmouth, Mass., 1980-83, chmn., 1982-83; chmn. Yarmouth Golf Course Bldg. Com., 1985-89; mem. hearing com. bd. Bar Overseers of the Supreme Jud. Ct., 1989-95; bd. dirs. Project Coach, Inc., 1990-97, Arts Found. Cape Cod, 2006—; conciliator Barnstable Superior Ct., 1992—, Barstable Dist. Ct., 2000—; trustee, asst. treas. Cape Symphony Orch., 1999-2004, chmn. fin. com., 2003-04; bd. dirs. Arts Found. Cape Cod, 2006—. Fellow Mass. Bar Found.; mem. ABA, Mass. Bar Assn. (del. 1986-87, mem. com. on bicentennial U.S. Constn. 1986-88, fee arbitration bd. 1985-86, chmn. spkrs. and writers subcom. 1986-88), Barnstable County Bar Assn. (chmn. seminar com. 1979-83, mem. exec. com. 1981-84, v.p. 1984-86, pres. 1986-87), Estate Planning Coun. Cape Cod (exec. com. 1985-98, sec. 1991-93, pres.-elect 1993-95, pres. 1995-97), Mass. Conveyancers Assn., Mid-Cape Men's Club (v.p. 1992, pres. 1993), Cummaquid Golf Club (dir. 2003-). Office: PO Box 1145 3010 Main St Barnstable MA 02630-1145 Home Phone: 508-362-4588; Office Phone: 508-375-9004. Personal E-mail: thomaspaquin@verizon.net.

PĀQUIN, TRUDY, gerontological nurse; b. Wantagh, NY, May 23, 1954; d. William Carl and Gertrude Mary (Kryl) Bauer; m. Alfred Joseph Pāquin III, July 30, 1977. AAS, John Tyler C.C., Chester, Va., 1982; BA magna cum laude, So. Conn. State U., New Haven, 1993, MS in Sociology, 2003; gerontol. nurse cert., U. Conn., Storrs, 1994, nurse mgmt. cert., 1995. cert. psychiat. and mental health nurse. Animal trainer, 1972—; pet therapist, 1974—; rschr. Alzheimer's, 1995; nurse therapy dog tng., educator, 1983—; adj. faculty dept. sociology So. Conn. State U., 2001—. Mem. Antarctic Expdn., 1996; qualitative rsch. on psychiat. patient interaction, 2002. Author: Pet Therapy Handbook, 1998, One Man's Journey to America, 1996; composer numerous musical works. Mem. Harness Goat Soc. Avocations: songwriting, fiddling, dog agility and showing dogs, swimming, packing with Llamas, running. Office: Fowler Nursing Ctr 10 Boston Post Rd Guilford CT 06437 Office Phone: 203-453-3725. Personal E-mail: trudy@prodigy.net.

PARA, GERARD ALBERT, lawyer, real estate broker, consultant; b. Oak Park, Ill., June 27, 1953; s. Bruno Joseph and Bernice Agnes Para; m. Gayle Louise Keegan, Sept. 15, 1979; children: Eric, Teresa. BA with honor, De Paul U., 1973, JD, 1976. Bar: Ill. 1977, U.S. Dist. Ct. (no. dist.) Ill. 1977, U.S. Ct. Appeals (7th cir.) 1977, Fed. Trial Bar. 1984; lic. real estate broker, Ill., 1981. Jud. law clk. Ill Appellate Ct. (1st dist.), Chgo., 1977-78; divsnl. counsel Household Internat. Franchisor Divsns., Prospect Heights, Ill., 1978-85; v.p. Bannockburn (Ill.) Pk. Concepts, Inc., 1986-93; dir. real estate ops., asst. gen. counsel Ben Franklin Stores, Carol Stream, Ill., 1994-96; v.p., gen. counsel DiMucci Devel. Corp., Palatine, Ill., 1996-97; gen. counsel Urban Investment Trust Inc., Chgo., 1998-99; prin. Franchise ESQ.sm, Lincolnshire, Ill., 1999—; arbitrator 19th Jud. Cir., Lake County, Ill., 1999—, 18th Jud. Cir., DuPage County, Ill., 2000—, Cir. Ct. of Cook County, Ill., 2000—; candidate 19th Jud. Cir. Judge, Dem. Party, Lake and McHenry Counties, Ill., 2002. Real estate broker, Long Grove, Ill., 1987—; franchise cons. Elliotts' Off Broadway Deli, Oak Brook, Ill., 1993—, Hollywood Tanning Sys., Inc., Sewell, NJ, 2007—; interim exec. dir. YWCA of Rockford, Ill., 2006. Editor: Medical Malpractice, 1975, Trial Technique, 1975. Asst. coach Little League Buffalo Grove Recreation Assn., Ill., 1988—2000; asst. scoutmaster Boy Scouts Am., Long Grove, 1995—2001. Mem. ABA, Internat. Coun. Shopping Ctrs., Internat. Corp. Real Estate Execs. (bd. dirs. Chgo. chpt. 1999-2002), Chgo. Bar Assn., Internat. Franchise Assn., Coun. Franchise Suppliers. Roman Catholic. Avocations: lap swimming, boating, scuba diving, weightlifting. Office: Franchise ESQ sm 125 Shelter Rd #450 Lincolnshire IL 60069 Office Phone: 847-634-2175. Personal E-mail: franchiseesq@aol.com.

PARAD, RICHARD BARRY, pediatrician, researcher; b. Boston, Sept. 29, 1955; s. Sidney and Edna Parad; m. Judy Ann Estroff, Nov. 16, 1951; children: Rebecca Estroff, Matthew Alexander Estroff. BA, Wesleyan U., Middletown, Conn., 1977; MD, U. Calif., La Jolla, 1981; MPH, Harvard U., Boston, Mass., 1997. Diplomate Am. Bd. of Pediat., 1986. Pediat. intern and resident Children's Hosp., Boston, 1981—84, fellow in neonatology, 1984—87, fellow in pediat. pulmonology, 1984—89; neonatologist Harvard Newborn Medicine, Brigham and Women's Hosp., Boston, 1987—2006; assoc. prof. pediat. Harvard Med. Sch., Boston, 2006—07. Co-dir. Mass. Cystic Fibrosis Newborn Screening Program, Boston, 1999—; dir. clin. rsch. dept. newborn medicine Brigham and Women's Hosp., Boston, 2006. Fellow: Am. Acad. of Pediat.; mem.: Soc. for Pediatric Rsch. Achievements include research in Newborn Respiratory Disorders, Cystic Fibrosis, C1 Inhibitor defects and Cystic Fibrosis Newborn Screening. Office: Brigham and Women's Hosp 75 Francis St Boston MA 02115 Office Phone: 617-732-8405.

PARADA, LUIS FERNANDO, science educator; b. Santa Fe de Bogota, Colombia, July 18, 1954; came to the U.S., 1993; s. Alfonso and Clara Parada. BS, U. Wis., 1979; PhD, MIT, 1985. Postdoctoral fellow Pasteur Inst., Paris, 1985-87; group leader Nat. Cancer Inst., Frederick, Md., 1988-91, sect. chief ABL, 1991-94; prof., dir. Ctr. Devel. Biology U. Tex. Southwestern Med. Ctr., Dallas, 1994—, Dana and Richard C. Strauss disting. chmn. in devel. biology, 1994—, dir. Kent Waldrep Ctr. for Basic Rsch. on Nerve Growth, 1997—, Southwestern Bell disting. chair in basic neurosci. rsch., 1998—; prof. Amer. Cancer Soc., 2003. Mem. sci. adv. bd. Rett Syndrome Found., N.Y., 1999—, Christopher Reeve paralysis Found., N.Y.C., 1996—; mem. sci. adv. coun. Damon Runyan-Walter Winchell Cancer Fund., N.Y.C., 1998—, Nat. Neurofibromatosis Found., N.Y.C., 1997—; chmn. bd. sci. counselors Nat. Inst. Neurol. Disorders and Stroke, Bethesda, Md., 1999—; mem. bd. sci. counselors Nat. Cancer Inst., Bethesda, 1995-99; rschr. in field. Patentee in field. Peter A. Steck Memorial ward, Soc. for Neuro-Oncology, 2000 Fellow Am. Acad. Arts & Scis.; mem. AAAS, Soc. for Neuroscience, Amer. Assn. for Cancer Rsch, Soc. for Develp. Biology. Office: U Tex Southwestern Med Ctr 5323 Harry Hines Blvd Dallas TX 75390-9133 *

PARADISE, LOUIS VINCENT, education educator, dean; b. Scranton, Pa., Apr. 19, 1946; s. Louis Benjamin and Lucille P.; children: Christopher, Gabrielle,Victoria. BS, Pa. State U., 1968; MS, Bucknell U., 1974; PhD, U. Va., 1976. Lic. psychologist, profl. counselor; cert. sch. psychologist. Assoc. prof. Cath. U. Am., Washington, 1976-83; prof. edn., chmn. edn. leadership U. New Orleans, 1983-90, dean Coll. Edn., 1990-92, univ. vice chancellor, provost, 1992-94, exec. vice chancellor, provost, 1994—2003, prof. Dept. Ednl. Leadership, Counseling, and Found., 2003—. Author: Ethics in Counseling and Psychotherapy, 1979, Questioning: Skills for the Helping Process, 1979, Counseling in Community College, 1982. 1st lt. U.S. Army, 1968-72. DuPont scholar U. Va., 1974. Mem. APA, ACA (ethics com. 1986-89), Am. Edn. Rsch. Assn., So. Assn. Counselor Edn. (chmn. ethics com. 1988-89), Acad. Counseling Psychology, Chi Sigma Iota (founding chpt. pres. 1985-87). Roman Catholic. Avocations: running, bicycling, music. Office: U New Orleans Dept Ednl Leadership Counseling & Found New Orleans LA 70148-0001 Office Phone: 504-280-6026. Business E-Mail: louis.paradise@uno.edu.

PARAMEKANTHI, SRINIVASAN MANDAYAM, software services executive; b. Mysore City, India, July 1, 1940; arrived in U.S., 1970, naturalized, 1991; s. Appalacharya Paramekanthi and Singamma Budugan; m. Ranganayaki Srirangapatnam, June 18, 1967; children: Srikala, Srilatha, Sriharsha. BS, U. Mysore, 1959, BE in Mech. Engring., 1963; MS in Ops. Rsch., Poly. Inst. NY, 1974, MS in Computer sci., 1983. Costing engr. Heavy Engring. Corp., Ranchi Bihar, India, 1963—70; inventory analyst Ideal Corp., Bklyn., 1970—75; sys. analyst Electronic Calculus, Inc., NYC, 1975—76; cons. in software, project leader Computer Horizons Corp., NYC, 1976—85; pres. Compmusic, Bellerose, NY, 1985—. Tchr. classical Indian Karnatak music theory, acoustics and voice tng. Hindu Temple Soc., NYC; tchr., cons. in-house tng.; presenter seminars on classical Indian music theory. Founding mem. governing coun. Vishwa Hindu Parishad of USA, 1973—, pres. NY State chpt., 1977—86; chmn. Indian/South Asian Comty. Orgn. of Ea. Queens, NYC, 1996—98. Mem.: IEEE, Inst. Engrs. (India), Assn. for Computing Machinery. Democrat. Hindu. Office: Compmusic Inc 8229 251st St Bellerose NY 11426-2527 E-mail: viswamitra@aol.com, ranganayaki@earthlink.net.

PARAMESWARA, VINAY KUMAR, medical educator; b. Bangalore, Karnataka, India, Sept. 2, 1973; s. M. A. and Lalitha Parameswara; m. Aditi Jagdish Sule, Aug. 2, 2002. MBBS, Bangalore Med. Coll., India, 1997; MPH, U. North Tex. Health Sci. Ctr., Fort Worth, 2004, PhD, 2003. Postdoctoral fellow U. Tex. Southwestern Med. Ctr., Dallas, 2003—05, instr., 2005—. Vol. Nat. Pub. Radio, Dallas, 2004. Mem.: Am. Diabetes Assn. (corr.), Am. Physiol. Soc. (assoc.), Karnataka Med. Coun. (life), Rsch. Soc. Study Diabetes India (life), Mensa. Athiest. Achievements include research in diabetes. Avocations: dance, cooking, travel, writing, movies. Home: 1109 Esters Rd Irving TX 75061 Office: U Tex Southwestern Med Ctr 5323 Harry Hines Blvd Dallas TX 75390 Home Phone: 214-441-9802; Office Phone: 214-648-2683. Personal E-mail: vinay.parameswara@gmail.com. Business E-Mail: vinay.parameswara@utsouthwestern.edu.

PARAMESWARAN, RAJU, accountant; b. Aymanam, India, Oct. 5, 1955; s. Raghunatha Iyer and Rajalakshmi Raghunathan; m. Ramaa Ramharith, June 3, 1981; children: Arjun children: Arun. BSc, U. Kerala, India, 1972—75. Chartered acct., Inst. Chartered Accts. India, 1979, CPA Botswana Inst. Accts., 1990. Chmn. Moores Rowland, Gaborone, Botswana, 1981—; dir. Drawtech Pty, Ltd., Lobatse, Botswana, 1995—2005; founder, dir. Flotek, Lobatse, 1999—, Budgetax, Ft. Myers, Fla., 2003—, Capri-Budgetax, Chennai, India, 2003—. Contbr. articles to profl. jours. Chmn. BOCCIM-Lobatse Bus. Coun., Lobatse, 2004—05. Mem.: Rotary Club Lobatse (pres. 1993—94, Paul Harris Fellow 2004). Home Phone: +267 5332262.

PARAN, MARK LLOYD, retired lawyer; b. Cleve., Feb. 1, 1953; s. Edward Walter and Margaret Gertrude (Ebert) P. AB in Sociology cum laude, Harvard U., 1977, JD, 1980. Bar: Ill. 1980, Mass. 1986, Tex. 1993. Assoc. Wilson & McIlvaine, Chgo., 1980-83, Lurie Sklar & Simon, Ltd., Chgo., 1983-85, Sullivan & Worcester, Boston, 1985-92; pvt. practice Boston, 1992, Euless, Tex., 1992—2002. Mem. ABA, State Bar Tex. Avocations: tornado hunting, severe thunderstorms, photography. Home and Office: 1050 W Ash Ln Apt 1015 Euless TX 76039-2171 Office Phone: 817-684-0725. Personal E-mail: f6tornado@tx.rr.com.

PARANJPE, PANKAJ VINAYKUMAR, research scientist; s. Vinaykumar Prabhakar and Vineeta Vinay Paranjpe; m. Prajakta Pankaj Damle. PhD, Rutgers U., Piscataway, NJ, 2004. Rsch. scientist CuraGen Corp., Brandord, Conn., 2004—05; rsch. investigator Bristol-Myers Squibb, New Brunswick, NJ, 2005—. Recipient Gallo Outstanding Cancer Rsch. award, Cancer Inst. NJ, 1999. Achievements include patents pending for improving transcompartmental delivery of medicinal agents. Home Phone: 732-227-5098; Office Phone: 732-227-5098.

PARAVANO, DINO, artist; b. Rome, Nov. 9, 1935; arrived in US, 1992; s. Domenico and Gemma Paravano; m. Maria Grazia Malinverni, Jan. 25, 1964; children: Daniela Maria, Paolo Carlo, Domenico. Co-owner The Sandton Gallery, Johannesburg, 1970—73; owner Kempel's Gallery, Pretoria, South Africa, 1973—75; owner studio Johannesburg, 1956—75, Sandton, 1976—93, Tucson, 1992—. Exhibitions include Pride's Proud Family, Witte Mus., San Antonio (Elliot Lipskin award for representational painting, Soc. Animal Artists, NYC, 1996), Cheetah with Cubs (Soc. Animal Artist's award of excellence, NYC, 1990), North of San Francisco (Master of Wildlife Artist award, Birds in Art, Leigh Yawkey Woodson Art Mus., Wausau, Wis., 1993), exhibited in group shows at Night Games (Second Place award on wild cat art, Frsno, LA, 2001), Big Rock (First Place landscape category award, Artist's Mag. Competition, Cin., 2005). Mem.: Pastel Soc. Am., Soc. Animal Artists. Roman Catholic. Avocation: trap and skeet shooting (won over 30 interclub and nat. trophies). Home: 9030 E Chof Ovi Dr Tucson AZ 85749 Office Phone: 520-749-0197. Home Fax: 520-749-0197. Personal E-mail: dinoparavano@msn.com.

PARAZYNSKI, SCOTT E., astronaut; b. Little Rock, Ark., July 28, 1961; m. Gail Marie Vozzella; 2 children. BS in Biology, Stanford U., 1983, MD with honors, 1989. Intern Brigham and Women's Hosp., 1990; resident in emergency medicine Denver; astronaut NASA, Houston, 1992—, crew rep. for extravehicular activity, Astronaut Office Mission Devel. Br., crew rep. for space shuttle, space station, dep. Astronaut Office ISS Br. Author numerous publs. in the field of space physiology. Team coach for the Philippines Olympic Winter Games, Calgary, Canada, 1988. Recipient Predoctoral Tng. award in cancer biology, NIH, 1983, NASA-Ames Cert. of Recognition, 1990, Space Station Team Excellence award, 1996, NASA Exceptional Svc. medal, 1988, 1999, NASA Space Flight medal, 1994, 1997, 1998, 2001, NASA Disting. Svc. medal, 2002, Ellis Island Family Heritage award in Technology, Statue of Liberty-Ellis Island Found., Inc., 2005. Mem.: Aircraft Owners and Pilots Assn., Exptl. Aircraft Assn., Assn. Space Explorers, Wilderness Med. Soc. (Rsch. award 1991), Am. Soc. Gravitational and Space Biology, Aerospace Med. Assn., Am. Alpine Club. Achievements include logged over 2,000 flight hours in a variety of aircraft; logged over 1.019 hours in space; 20 hours EVA; crew STS-66 (1994), STS-86 Atlantis (1997), STS-95 Discovery (1998) and STS-100 Endeavour (2001); mission specialist reassigned from mission STS-118 to STS-121 to Internat. Space Station, 2006; competed on the US Development Luge Team and was ranked amoung the top 10 competitors in the nation during the 1988 Olympic Trials; served as an Olympic Team Coach for the Phillippines during the 1988 Olympic Winter Games in Calgary, Canada. Avocations: mountain climbing, rock climbing, flying, scuba diving, skiing, woodworking, nature photography. Office: Astronaut Office/CB NASA Johnson Space Ctr Houston TX 77058

PARCELLS, BILL (DUANE CHARLES PARCELLS), sportscaster, retired professional football coach; b. Englewood, NJ, Aug. 22, 1941; s. Charles and Ida (Naclerio) Parcells; m. Judith Parcells, 1962 (div. Jan. 16, 2002); children: Suzy, Jill, Dallas. BA, Wichita State U., 1964. Asst. coach Hastings Coll. (Nebr.), 1964, Wichita State U. (Kans.), 1965, US Mil. Acad., West Point, NY, 1966—69, Fla. State U., Tallahassee, 1970—72, Vanderbilt U., Nashville, 1973—74, Tex. Tech U., Lubbock, 1975—77; head coach USAF Acad., Colorado Springs, Colo., 1978—79; linebackers coach New England Patriots, 1980—81; defensive coord. NY Giants, 1979—80, defensive coord., linebackers coach, 1981—82, head coach, 1983—91, New England Patriots, 1993—97, NY Jets, 1997—2000, chief football ops., 2000—01; head coach Dallas Cowboys, 2003—07; studio analyst NBC Sports, 1991—92, NFL Pregame Show, ESPN, 2002, Monday Night Countdown, ESPN, 2007—; radio co-host ESPN radio, 2007—. Co-author (with Jeff Coplon): Finding a Way to Win: The Principles of Leadership, Teamwork and Motivation, 1995; co-author: (with Will McDonough) The Final Season: My Last Year as Head Coach in the NFL, 2000. Named NFL Coach of Yr., Sporting News, 1986, UPI, 1986, 1994, AP, 1986, 1994, Maxwell Football Club, 1994, Pro Football Weekly, 1994, 1996; named to NFL 1990s All-Decade Team. Achievements include head coach, NFC Champion and Super Bowl Champion New York Giants, 1986, 1990; head coach, AFC Champion New England Patriots, 1996. *

PARCELLS, FREDERICK R., underwriter; b. Chgo., May 14, 1957; s. Charles Hubbard and Winifred Elaine (Summer) P. AA, Barton County C.C., Great Bend, Kans., 1977; BA in Fin., U. Ill., 1980; MBA, Ind. U., 1985. CFP, CPCU; assoc. in risk mgmt., assoc. in reinsurance/Ins. Inst. Am. Actuarial trainee CNA Ins., Chgo., 1980-81; actuarial technician Sentry Ins., Stevens Point, Wis., 1982-83; scouting intern The Buffalo Bills, Orchard Park, Fredonia, N.Y., 1984; underwriting trainee Kemper Group, Chgo., 1986-87, casualty underwriter Chgo. and St. Louis, 1987-88; acct. underwriter Northbrook P&C Ins. (subs. Allstate), Chgo., 1988-91; sr. account underwriter Northbrook Property and Casualty Ins., Chgo./Rolling Meadows, 1991; sr. underwriter Allstate Ins., South Barrington, Ill., 1991-95; product analyst CNA Ins. Cos., Chgo., 1995-97; sr. splty. exec. underwriter Interstate Ins. Group, Chgo., 1997-2000; sr. underwriter Apex Ins. Mgrs., 2001—. Asst. chmn. civic affairs com., Cambridge Forest Assn., Lincolnshire, Ill., 1980-81; treas. Santa Claus Anonymous, Chgo., 1990-91, 91-92, pres., 1992-93; vol. duplex constrn. Habitat for Humanity, Chgo., 1988, 89. Mem. CPCU Soc. (sec. Chgo. chpt. 1994-95, bd. dirs./pub. rels. chmn. 1993-94, mem. nat. underwriting sect. com. 1994-2003, com. chair, 2001-03, treas. Chgo. chpt. 1995-96, v.p. Chgo. chpt. 1996-97, pres. Chgo. chpt. 1997-98, past pres. 1998-2000). Presbyterian. Home: 1957 Barnhill Dr Mundelein IL 60060 Office: Apex Ins Mgrs LLC 200 N Monroe St Ste 1800 Chicago IL 60606 Business E-Mail: fparcells@apexamerican.com.

PARDEE, ARTHUR BECK, biochemist, educator; b. Chgo., July 13, 1921; s. Charles A. and Elizabeth B. (Beck) Pardee; m. Ruth Sager (dec.); m. Ann Goodman; children: Michael, Richard, Thomas. BS, U. Calif., Berkeley, 1942; MS, Calif. Inst. Tech., 1943, PhD, 1947; D (hon.), U. Paris, 1993. Merck postdoctoral fellow U. Wis., 1947—49; mem. faculty U. Calif., Berkeley, 1949—61, assoc. prof., 1957—61; NSF fellow Pasteur Inst., 1957—58; prof. biology, chmn. dept. biochem. scis. Princeton (NJ) U., 1961—67, prof. biochemistry, 1961—75, Donner prof. sci., 1966; prof. Dana Farber Cancer Inst. and biochem. pharmacology dept. Harvard Med. Sch., Boston, 1975—. Co-author: Experiments in Biochemical Research Techniques, 1957; editor: Biochemica et Biophysica Acta, 1962—68; contbr. over 500 articles to publs. Mem. rsch. adv. coun. Am. Cancer Soc., 1967—71; trustee Cold Spring Harbor Lab. Quantitative Biology, 1963—69. Named Princess Takamatu lectr., 1990, hon. faculty mem., Nanjing U., 1999; recipient Young Biochemists travel award, NSF, 1952, Krebs medal, Fedn. European Biochem. Socs., 1973, Rosenstiel award, Brandeis U., 1975, 3M award, Fedn. Am. Socs., Exptl. Biology, 1980, CIIT prize, 1993, Disting. Alumnus award, Calif. Inst. Tech., 1999; fellow, Internat. Inst. for Advanced Studies, 1999. Fellow: AAAS; mem.: NAS (editl. bd. proc. 1971—73, com. on scis. and pub. policy 1973—76), Chem. Industry Inst. Toxicology (Founders award, Boehringer-Mannheim award 1998), Ludwig Inst. Cancer Rsch. (sci. com. 1988—), Japanese Biochem. Soc., Am. Philos. Soc., Am. Soc. Microbiologists, Am. Assn. Cancer Rsch. (pres. 1985—86), Am. Soc. Biol. Chemists (treas. 1964—70, pres. 1980—81), Am. Chem. Soc. (Paul Lewis award 1960). Office: 44 Binney St Boston MA 02115-6013 Office Phone: 617-632-3372. Business E-Mail: arthur_pardee@dfci.harvard.edu.

PARDEE, JEFFREY CLARK, county government official; b. NYC, May 14, 1944; s. Jack Howard II and Florence (Brennan) P.; m. Mary Anna Weil, Dec. 23, 1966; children: Brennan James, Kennedy Clark. BBA, Eastern Mich. U., 1968; MBA in Fin., U. Detroit, 1971; postgrad., Nova U., 1975-81. Cert. pub. fin. officer. Fin. analyst Sterling Axle Plant div. Ford Motor Co., Sterling Heights, Mich., 1968-73; budget dir. Genesee County, Flint, Mich., 1973-76, Oakland County, Pontiac, Mich., 1976-95, dep. dir. mgmt. and budget, 1996-99, dir. mgmt. and budget, 1999—. Treas. Flint-Genesee Corp. for Econ. Growth, 1978-81; pres. Genesee County Econ. Devel. Corp., Flint, 1982-84; bd. dirs. Forward Devel. Corp; chmn. bd. dirs. Communications Services Network, Inc.; adj. prof. pub. budgeting U. Mich., Flint, 1984-85. Editor Statewide News-Mich. Rental Housing Assn. Newsletter, 1985-95. Merit counselor Boy Scouts Am., Grand Blanc, Mich., 1982—, dist. com. chmn. Tall Pines Coun., 1998-2001; councilman

City of Grand Blanc, 1985—; treas. Crime Watch Assn., Grand Blanc, 1985—, Genesee County Met. Alliance, Flint, 1986-91; bd. dirs. Flint-Genesee Revolving Loan Fund, 1980-90; treas. Partnership Saginaw Bay Watershed, 1987-2001, Grand Blanc Vision 2020, 1998—; pres. Mich. Mcpl. Fin. Officers Assn., 1995-96; mem. GFOA Mgmt. Budget Com., 1998—; mem. City Coun., Grand Blanc, Mich., 1985--. Recipient Fin. Officer award CFO Mag., 2000. Mem. Govt. Fin. Officers Assn. U.S. and Can. (review com. 1984—, Disting. Budget Presentation award, Excellence in Fin. Reporting award), Am. Soc. Pub. Adminstrs., G.M.I. Mgmt. and Engring. Inst. (adv. bd. 1984-87). Republican. Mem. Lds Ch. Avocations: racquetball, auto racing. Home: 11390 Grand Oak Dr Grand Blanc MI 48439-1219 Office: Oakland County Dept Mgmt & Budget 1200 N Telegraph Rd Pontiac MI 48341-0407 E-mail: pardeej@co.oakland.mi.us.

PARDEE, OTWAY O'MEARA, computer scientist, educator; b. Seattle, June 26, 1920; s. Otway and Mary Gertrude (O'Meara) Pardee; m. Marilynn Lowrie, Aug. 9, 1946; children: Irene, Loraine, Suzanne. BS in Elec. Engring., U. Wash., 1941; PhD in Elec. Engring., Stanford U., 1948. Instr. math. Syracuse U., NY, 1948-52, asst. to assoc. prof. NY, 1952-69, dir. Computing Ctr. NY, 1962-69, prof. computer sci. NY, 1969-86, prof. emeritus, 1986—. With USNR, 1944—46. Mem.: IEEE, AAUP (pres. Syracuse U. chpt. 1960), Am. Phys. Soc., Math. Assn. Am., Am. Math. Soc., Assn. Computing Machinery (chmn. Syracuse chpt. 1963), Tau Beta Pi, Sigma Xi. Avocations: camping, photography. Home: 843 Maryland Ave Syracuse NY 13210-2502 Office: Syracuse U Ctr for Sci and Tech Ste 2-175 Syracuse NY 13244-0001 Business E-Mail: oopardee@syr.edu.

PARDEE, SCOTT EDWARD, securities dealer; b. New Haven, Oct. 11, 1936; s. William Durley and Catherine (Eames) P.; m. Aida Milagros Fuentes Tavarez, Jan. 29, 1966; 1 child, Alan Alexander. BA, Dartmouth Coll., 1958; PhD, MIT, 1962. Research asst. Fed. Res. Bank, Boston, 1959-62; teaching asst. in econs. MIT, Cambridge, Mass., 1961-62; research economist Fed. Res. Bank N.Y., NYC, 1962-66, mgr. fgn. dept., 1967-70, asst. v.p. fgn. dept., 1970-74, v.p. fgn. dept., 1974-79; tchr. banking and fin. NYU, 1965-67, Am. Inst. Banking, 1969-72; adj. prof. Grad. Sch. Bus. Columbia U., NYC, 1972-75; dep. mgr. fgn. ops. Fed. Res. System Open Market Account, 1975-79, mgr. fgn. ops., 1979-81; exec. v.p., dir. Discount Corp. N.Y., NYC, 1981-86; dir. Am. Internat. Group, 1982-86; vice chmn. Yamaichi Internat. Am. Inc., NYC, 1986-88, chmn., 1988-95, sr. advisor, 1995-97; sr. lect., exec. dir. Fin. Rsch. Ctr., MIT Sloan Scool of Mgmt., 1997-99; adj. prof. Grad. Sch. of Business, U. Chicago, Chicago, Ill., 1997-98; Alan R. Holmes prof. of monetary econs. Middlebury Coll., Vt., 2000—. Bd. dirs. Renaissance Holdings, Ltd. Author: A Study of Inter-City Wage Differentials, 1962. Trustee Woodrow Wilson Fellowship Found., 1994—; mem. Coun. on Fgn. Rels., 1995—. Woodrow Wilson fellow MIT, 1958-59; recipient Dr. Louis M. Spadaro award Fordham U., 1980 Mem. Phi Beta Kappa. Home: 250 South End Ave New York NY 10280-1074 Office: Middlebury Coll Econs Dept Middlebury VT 05753

PARDEN, ROBERT JAMES, engineering educator, management consultant; b. Mason City, Iowa, Apr. 17, 1922; s. James Ambrose and Mary Ellen (Fahey) P.; m. Elizabeth Jane Taylor, June 15, 1955; children: Patricia Gale, James A., John R., Nancy Ann. BS in Mech. Engring, State U. Iowa, 1947, MS, 1951, PhD, 1953. Reg. profl. engr. Iowa, Calif.; lic. gen. contractor Calif. Indsl. engr. LaCrosse Rubber Mills, 1947-50; asso. dir. Iowa Mgmt. Course, 1951-53; asso. prof. indsl. engring. Ill. Inst. Tech., 1953-54; prof. engring. mgmt. Santa Clara U., 1955—, dean Sch. Engring., 1955-82; prin. Saratoga Cons. Group (Calif.), 1982—. Mem. Sec. Navy's Survey Bd. Grad. Edn., 1964 Mem. Saratoga Planning Commn., 1959-61. Served to 1st lt., Q.M.C. AUS, 1943-46. Named to Silicon Valley Engring. Hall of Fame Silicon Valley Engring. Coun., 1993. Mem. ASME (chmn. Santa Clara Valley sect. 1958), Am. Soc. Engring. Edn. (chmn. Pacific N.W. sect. 1960), Am. Inst. Indsl. Engrs. (edn. chmn. 1958-63, dir. ASEE-ECPD affairs 1963-68), Nat. Soc. Profl. Engrs., Engrs. Council Profl. Devel. (dir. 1964-65, 66-69), Soc. Advancement Mgmt., ASEM, Sigma Xi, Tau Beta Pi. Roman Catholic. Home: 19832 Bonnie Ridge Way Saratoga CA 95070-5010 Office: Santa Clara U Sch Engring Santa Clara CA 95053-0001 Office Phone: 408-554-4984. Personal E-mail: bobparden@comcast.net. Business E-Mail: rparden@scu.edu.

PARDES, HERBERT, health facility executive, psychiatrist, educator; b. Bronx, NY, July 7, 1934; s. Louis and Frances (Bergman) P.; m. Juidith Ellen Silber, June 9, 1957; children: Stephen, Lawrence, James. BS, Rutgers U., 1956; MD, SUNY-Downstate Med. Center, Bklyn., 1960; DSc (hon.), SUNY, 1990. Straight med. intern Kings County Hosp., 1960-61, intern & resident in psychiatry Bklyn., 1961-62, 64-66; asst. prof. psychiatry Downstate Med. Ctr., Bklyn., 1968-72, prof., chmn. dept., 1972-75; dir. psychiat. svcs. Kings County Hosp., Bklyn., 1972-75; prof., chmn. dept. psychiatry U. Colo. Med. Sch., 1975-78; dir. psychiat. svcs. Colo. Psychiat. Hosp., Denver, 1975-78; dir. NIMH, Rockville, Md., 1978-84; asst. surgeon gen. USPHS, 1978-84; prof. psychiatry Columbia U., NYC, 1984—, chmn. dept., 1984; dir. Psychiat. Svc. Presbyn. Hosp. (now Columbia Presbyn. Center of NY Presbyn. Hosp.), NYC, 1984-89; dir. NY State Psychiatric Inst., 1984—89; v.p. for health scis., dean faculty medicine Columbia U., NYC, 1989—99; pres., CEO NY-Presbyn. Hosp. and Healthcare Systems, NYC, 2000—. Bd. trustees Healthcare Leadership Coun. Contbr. articles to med. jours. Pres. sci. bd. Alliance for Rsch. on Schizophrenia and Depression. Capt. M.C., AUS, 1972-74. Named Ann. Hon. Lectr. Downstate Med. Ctr. Alumni Assn., 1972; recipient Alumni Achievement medal, 1980, William Menninger award ACP, 1992, Dorothy Dix award Mental Illness Fedn., 1992, Vester Mark award, 1994, Salmon award, 1996. Mem. Assn. Am. Med. Colls. (chair 1995-96), Am. Psychiat. Assn. (v.p. 1986-88, pres. 1989-90, Disting. Svc. award 1993), Inst. Medicine, Am. Psychoanalytic Assn., Coun. of Deans (adminstrv. bd., chair-elect 1993-94, chair 1994-95), Assoc. Med. Schs. NY (pres. 1995-2000), Phi Beta Kappa, Alpha Omega Alpha. Office: NY Presbyn Hosp Pres and CEOs Office 161 Ft Washington Ave New York NY 10032 also: NY Presbyn Hosp 525 E 68th St New York NY 10021 Office Phone: 212-305-8000. Business E-Mail: pardesh@nyp.org.

PARDIECK, ROGER L., lawyer; b. Seymour, Ind., Mar. 1, 1937; s. Martin W. and Lorna (Wente) P.; m. Mary Ann Pardieck; children: Amy, Andrew, Melissa, Duncan. AB, Ind. U., 1959, LLB, 1963; student, Internat. Grad. Sch., Stockholm, 1960. Bar: Ind. 1963, US Dist. Ct. (so. dist.) Ind. 1964, US Ct. Appeals (7th cir.) 1965; diplomate Am. Bd. Trial Advocates. Ptnr. Montgomery, Elsner and Pardieck, Seymour, Ind., 1965-84; prin. Pardieck Law Firm, Seymour, Ind., 1985—. Faculty Nat. Inst. Trial Advocacy, Ind.; lectr. in field. Contbr. articles to profl. jours. Fellow Internat. Acad. Trial Lawyers, Am. Coll. Trial Lawyers, Ind. Trial Lawyers Assn. (bd. dirs. 1969—, pres. 1975), Ind. Coll. Trial Lawyers, Roscoe Pound Found., Ind. Bar Assn.; mem. FBA, ATLA (bd. govs. 1985-88), Ind. State Bar Assn. (bd. govs. 1980-82), Inst. for Injury Reduction (bd. dirs. 1992-95), Nat. Bd. Trial Advocacy, Safety Attys. Fedn. (bd. dirs. 1993-95), Internat. Soc. Primerus Law Firms (bd. dirs. 1995-2004), Am. Bd. Trial Advocates, Trial Lawyers Pub. Justice (Ind. coord. 1991-, bd. dirs. 2005-), Am. Judicature Soc., Inner Cir. Advocates Office: 100 N Chestnut St PO Box 608 Seymour IN 47274-0608 Office Phone: 812-523-8686. Business E-Mail: rlp@pardiecklaw.com.

PARDINGTON, MARY ELIZABETH, elementary school educator; d. John and Elizabeth Curell; m. David Charles Pardington, July 9, 1993; children: Catherine, Sarah, Veronica, Mary Kate. BS in Elem. Edn., Oakland U., Rochester, Mich., 1987, MA in Curriculum, Instrn., and Leadership, 1991. Continuing tchg. cert. Dept. Edn. Mich., 1991. Elem. tchr. Birmingham (Mich.) Pub. Schs., 1987—. Mem. accreditation team Mich. Accreditation Program, 1990—91; co-head tchr. Beverly Elem. Sch., Beverly Hills, Mich., 1995—, svc. squad leader, 1995—. V.p. Concerned Catholics Shelby Twp., Mich., 1993—, catechism tchr., 1995—; soprano soloist Assumption Grotto Choir, Detroit, 1992—, asst. choir dir., 1994—; dir., prodr. Coffee Ho. Fundraiser, Detroit, 1999—2002. Recipient Workplace Excellence award, Birmingham Pub. Schs., 2002, 2003, award, Friends of Different Learners, 2005; Paul Douglas Tchr. scholar, US Congress, 1986—87, Performance grantee, Birmingham Pub. Schs., 1988. Mem.: NSTA. Republican. Roman Catholic. Avocations: music, old movies, logic puzzles. Office: Beverly Elementary School Beverly Hills MI 48025 Home Phone: 586-532-7199.

PARDINI, JAMES CHRISTOPHER, musician, conductor, composer; b. NYC, May 24, 1973; s. James Joseph and Nancy Anne Pardini. MusB in Sacred Music, Rider U., Princeton, NJ, 1996; MusM in Organ Performance and Lit., U. Rochester, NY, 2000. Organist, dir. music First United Meth. Ch., Somerville, NJ, 1992—94, First Bapt. Ch., Moorestown, NJ, 1994—96; organist, dir. music ministries Messiah Luth. Ch., Rochester, NY, 1996—98; sr. organist Crystal Cathedral, Garden Grove, Calif., 1998—2004; organist, dir. music, artistic dir. Music in Gt. Space, Shadyside Presbyn. Ch., Pitts., 2004—. Composer: Toccata on Amazing Grace, 2000, Meditation and Toccata on Hyfrydol, 2007, others, performer various organ recitals. Mem. com. Clarence Mader Scholarship Fund, LA, 2004. Recipient 1st prize, San Marino Organ Competition, Calif., 1998. Mem.: Eastwest Organists, Am. Guild Organists. Office: Shadyside Presbyn Ch 5121 Westminster Pl Pittsburgh PA 15232

PARDO, ROBERT, game designer, video game software company executive; V.p. game design Blizzard Entertainment, Irvine, Calif. Accredited to the following games Voyeur, 1994, Cyberia, 1994, Whiplash, 1995, Descent, 1995, Tempest X3, 1996, Mortal Kombat Trilogy, StarCraft: Brood War, 1998, StarCraft, 1998, Warcraft II: Battle.net Edition, 1999, StarCraft 64, 2000, Diablo II, 2000, Diablo II (Collector's Edition), 2000, Kingdom Under Fire, 2001, Warcraft III: Reign of Chaos, 2002, Warcraft III: The Frozen Throne, 2003, lead designer World of Watercraft, 2004 (WIRED Rave award-Games, 2006). Named one of 100 Most Influential People, Time Mag., 2006. Office: Blizzard Entertainment PO Box 18979 Irvine CA 92623

PARDUE, A. MICHAEL, retired plastic and reconstructive surgeon; b. Nashville, June 23, 1931; s. Andrew Peyton and Ruby (Fly) P. BS, Sewanee U. of the South, 1953; MD, U. Tenn., 1957. Resident in gen. surgery Pittsfield (Mass.) Affiliated Hosps., 1966; resident in plastic surgery N.Y. Hosp./Cornell Med. Ctr., 1968; plastic surgeon A. Michael Pardue, M.D., Thousand Oaks, Calif., 1968-98; ret., 1995. Lt. comdr. USN, 1956-62. Fellow ACS; mem. Am. Soc. Plastic Surgeons, Am. Soc. Aesthetic Plastic Surgery, Calif. Soc. Plastic Surgeons. Episcopalian. Avocations: fly fishing, skiing, golf, horses, African safaris. Home: PO Box 4677 Tubac AZ 85646-4677 Also: 3217 Augusta Dr Bozeman MT 59715-8792

PARDUE, DWIGHT EDWARD, venture capitalist; b. North Wilkesboro, NC, Aug. 3, 1928; s. Gilbert F. and Nina (Glass) P.; m. Annie Eller, Mar. 24, 1951; children: Richard S., Dwight E. Cert., Clevenger Bus. Coll., 1956. Dir. warehousing Lowe's Co., Inc., North Wilkesboro, 1956-57, store mgr. Sparta, NC, 1957-59, Richmond, Va., 1959-70, regional v.p. North Wilkesboro, 1970-75, sr. v.p. store ops., 1975-78, exec. v.p. sales and store ops., 1978-86, sr. exec. v.p., 1986-90; pres., investor D. Pardue & Assocs., Wilkesboro, NC, 1990—. Mem. steering com. Home Ctr. Leadership Coun., Nat. Home Ctr. Home Improvement Congress and Exposition, 1983—86; bd. dirs. Northwestern Nat. Bank, Inc., Wilkesboro, NC, Integrity Fin. Corp., Hickory, NC; chmn. bd. Cmty. Bancshares, Inc., Wilkesboro, 1992—2002. Served with U.S. Army, 1950-52. Mem. Jefferson Landing Golf Club, Masons. Office Phone: 336-667-9411. Personal E-mail: dep0013@aol.com.

PARDUE, MARY-LOU, biology professor; b. Lexington, Ky., Sept. 15, 1933; d. Louis Arthur and Mary Allie (Marshall) P. BS, William and Mary Coll., 1955; MS, U. Tenn., 1959; PhD, Yale U., 1970; DSc (hon.), Bard Coll., 1985, U. Edinburgh, Scotland, 2003. Postdoctoral fellow Inst. Animal Genetics, Edinburgh, Scotland, 1970—72; assoc. prof. biology MIT, Cambridge, 1972—80, prof., 1980—, Boris Magasanik prof. biology, 1995—. Summer course organizer Cold Spring Harbor Lab., NY, 1971—80; mem. rev. com. NIH, 1974—78, 1980—84, nat. adv. gen. med. scis. coun., 1984—86; sci. adv. com. Wistar Inst., Phila., 1976—2004; mem. health and environ. rsch. adv. com. U.S. Dept. Energy, 1987—94; bd. trustees Associated Univs., Inc., 1995—97; mem. Burroughs Wellcome Adv. Com. on Career Awards in Biomed. Scis., 1996—2000, now bd. dirs.; chair Inst. of Medicine Com. on Biol. Basis of Sex and Gender Differences, 1999—2001. Mem. editl. bd.: profl. jours.; contbr. articles to profl. jours. Mem. rev. com. Am. Cancer Soc., 1990-93, Howard Hughes Med. Inst. Adv. Bd., 1993-2000. Recipient Esther Langer award Langer Cancer Rsch. Found., 1977, Lucius Wilbur Cross medal Yale Grad. Sch., 1989; grantee NIH, NSF, Am. Cancer Soc. Fellow AAAS, NAS (chmn. genetics sect. 1991-94, coun. 1995-98), Am. Acad. Arts and Sci. (coun. mem. 1992-96); mem. NRC (bd. on biology 1989-95), Genetics Soc. Am. (pres. 1982-83), Am. Soc. Cell Biology (coun. 1977-80, pres. 1985-86), Phi Beta Kappa, Phi Kappa Phi, Sigma Xi. Office: MIT Dept Biology 68-670 77 Massachusetts Ave Dept 68-670 Cambridge MA 02139-4307 Office Phone: 617-253-6741. Business E-Mail: mlpardue@mit.edu.

PAREDES, JAMES ANTHONY, anthropologist, educator; b. NYC, Sept. 29, 1939; s. Antonio Paredes Piñeiro and Mildred Olene (Brown) P.; m. Anna Hamilton, Nov. 25, 1959 (div. 1984); children: J. Anthony Jr., Anna Teresa P. Lesinski, Sara Caroline P. Campbell; m. Elizabeth Dixon Purdum, Aug. 10, 1985 (div. 1994): 1 stepchild, David Joseph Plante; m. Alleen Dimitroff Deutsch, July 24, 2003. BA, Oglethorpe U., 1961; MA, U. N.Mex., 1964, PhD, 1969. Rsch. coord. Upper Miss. Mental Health Ctr., Bemidji, Minn., 1964-67; asst. prof., acting dir. Am. Ind. Studies Bemidji State Coll., 1967-68; community devel. specialist U. Minn. Agrl. Extension Svc., Bemidji, 1967-68; asst. prof. dept. anthropology Fla. State U., Tallahassee, 1969-74, assoc. prof., 1974-78, prof., 1979-99, emeritus prof., 1999—, chmn. dept., 1974-77, 84-90; chief ethnography and Indian affairs S.E. regional office Nat. Park Service, Atlanta, 1999—2006. Adj. prof. dept. anthropology U. Fla., Gainesville, 1979-2004; cons. Nat. Marine Fisheries Svc., Galveston, Tex., 1987-88, Bur. Indian Affairs, Washington, 1985, 92, Fed. Recognition Panel, Assn. on Am. Indian Affairs, N.Y.C., 1987-88. Author: Indios de los Estados Unidos Anglosajones, 1992; editor: Anishinabe: Six Studies of Modern Chippewa, 1980, Indians of the Southeastern United States in the Late 20th Century, 1992; co-editor: Classics of Practicing Anthropology: 1978-1998, 2000; co-editor: Anthropologists and Indians in the New South, 2001; series editor: Contemporary American Indian Studies; author or co-author numerous articles, chpts. in books, revs. Mem. Sci. and Statis. Com., Gulf of Mex. Fishery Mgmt. Coun., Tampa, Fla., 1978-88. Recipient svc. award Poarch Creek Indians, 1990, Woodrow Wilson Found. fellow U. N.Mex., 1961-62; Nat. Inst. Mental Health predoctoral fellow U. N.Mex., 1968-69; Rockefeller Ctr. for Study of So. Culture and Religion fellow, Fla. State U., 1978. Fellow: Soc. for Applied Anthropology (assoc. editor 1983—88, pres. 1993—95), Am. Anthrop. Assn. (exec. bd. 2004—07); mem.: Fla. Acad. Scis. (sect. chair 1984—85), So. Anthrop. Soc. (pres. 1988—89), Sigma Xi (Fla. State U. chpt. pres. 1977—78). Democrat. Avocation: walking. Home Phone: 404-252-6956; Office Phone: 404-252-6956. Personal E-mail: janthonyparedes@bellsouth.net.

PAREENE, ALEX E., political blog editor; b. July 23, 1985; Attended, NYU. Guest editor Gawker Media, 2004—06; co-editor Wonkette.com, 2006, editor, 2006—. *

PAREKH, DHIRAJLAL GOKALDAS, electrical engineer; b. Mumbai, Maharashtra, India, May 20, 1945; s. Gokaldas Bhagwandas and Lilavatiben Gokaldas Parekh; m. Nirulata Dhirajlal Parekh, July 6, 1973; children: Parag Dhirajlal, Monica Dhirajlal. MSEE, Ga. Inst. Tech., 1970; MBA, Fla. Inst. Tech., 1986. Profl. engr., Ga., 1974. Supervisory mech. engr. Edgewood (Md.) Chem. Biol. Ctr., Edgewood, 1982—. Bd. dirs. Cinemaya Media, NYC, 1999—, Am. Desi Mag., Cockeysville, Md.; founder, chmn. Indian Sch. Performing Arts, Lutherville, Md., 2002—; founder Internat. Sch. Performing Arts, Balt., 2002—; founder, ptnr. A.C. Birox. Internat. Prodr.: (film) Wings Of Hope (Cineview Internat. Film Festival, 2000), Bawandar (San Jose Internat. Film Festival, 2001); author: (book) Reality Check Happiness And Success; exec. prodr.: (tv serial) Dollar Bahu. Author acad. excellence Gujarati Samaj, Balt., 1994—97; founder Internat. Soc. Performing Arts; founding mem. Greater Balt. Temple, Balt., 1989—98; mem. World Gujarati Conf., College Park, Md., 1994, founder, convenor, 2006, convenor Edison, NJ, 2006; founder Olympics Performing Arts For World Peace. Named Internat. Poet, 1995; recipient Civilian Svc. award, Soldier Chem., Biol. Command, 1993, Army Materieal Command, 1995, Pravasi Excellence award, Ind. Orgn., Delhi, 2004, Prodr. award, TV Asia, 2005. Achievements include patents for biological classifier system; office organizer; electro-magnetizing of polymers for decontamination. Home: 9 Westspring Way Lutherville MD 21093 Home Phone: 410-561-1583. Personal E-mail: dparekh001@yahoo.com.

PARELES, JON, music critic; Copy editor Crawdaddy!, NYC, 1977, music editor; asst. music editor Rolling Stone; music writer Village Voice; freelancer NY Times, 1982, chief popular music critic. Author: The Rolling Stone Encyclopedia of Rock and Roll, 1983. Office: NY Times Culture Desk 229 W 43rd St New York NY 10036 Office Phone: 212-556-7304. Office Fax: 212-556-1516.

PARENT, ANNETTE RICHARDS, free lance writer, artist; b. Elizabeth, NJ, May 5, 1924; d. Edward Carrington Mayo and Elizabeth Veech (Coan) Richards; m. Hiram Lincoln Parent, Mar. 23, 1957; children: Laurence Edward, Anne Mayo Parent Fischer Pasqual. BA, Swarthmore Coll., 1946; postgrad., U. Ariz., Western N.Mex. U. Nat. lit. sec. Woman's Internat. League for Peace and Freedom, Phila., 1946-48; free lance writer various, 1948—. Contbr. poems to ann. anthologies Intermountain Friendly Rev., 1990, 91, 92; contbr. non-fiction articles to numerous publs.; painter, photographer, poet, book reviewer, presenter elderhostel commencement addresses, talks about Quakerism to coll. classes and Presbyn. youth groups; slide talks on Russia; editor: The Troglodyte at Carlsbad Caverns Nat. Park, 1966-80. Mem. search com. for Western N.Mex. U. mus. dir., 1987; co-founder Youth Coun. Against Conscription, Phila., 1946-48; organizer Westtown (Pa.) Sch. peace team, 1940-42; mem. Nat. Coun. Fellowship of Reconciliation, N.Y.C., 1941-46; former mem. safety com. Cralsbad Cacerns Nat. Park; charter mem., officer A Christian Ministry in the Nat. Parks, Carlsbad Caverns Nat. Park, N.Mex., 1970-80, centennial com., 1975; founder, leader of Peace Team, Westtown Sch., 1940-42. Winner N.C. Wyeth 1st in Art award Westtown Sch., 1942, Alumni Assn. 1st in Art award 1942; recipient awards in juried and non-juried art shows Carlsbad Area Art Assn., N.Mex., Grant County Art Guild, Black Range Artists Inc., Best of Show award for The Great American Litterbug, Annual N. Mex. State Exhibition, 2005. Mem. AAUW, Nat. League Am. Pen Women (in dual categories of art and letters, v.p., sec., treas., winner non-fiction nat. contest 1955), Soc. Southwestern Authors, Grant County Art Guild, Black Range Artists Inc. (v.p. 1991), Nat. Audubon Soc. (publicity chmn. Southwestern N.Mex. coun. del. 1987-92); mem. many nat. environ., peace, and civil rights organizations. Mem. Religious Soc. of Friends. Avocations: hiking, sewing, piano, swimming, reading, bridge. Home and Office: PO Box 1319 Silver City NM 88062-1319

PARENT, LOUISE MARIE, lawyer, corporate financial executive; b. San Francisco, Aug. 28, 1950; d. Jules D. and Mary Louise (Bartholomew) P.; m. John P. Casaly, Jan. 5, 1980. AB, Smith Coll., 1972; JD, Georgetown U., 1975. Bar: N.Y. 1976, U.S. Dist. Ct. (so. dist.) N.Y. 1976. Assoc. Donovan Leisure, NYC, 1975-77; various positions, then gen. counsel Am. Express Info. Svcs. Corp., NYC, 1977-92; dep. gen. counsel Am. Express Co., NYC, 1992-93, exec. v.p., gen. counsel, 1993—. Bd. dirs. A Better Chance Inc., Cooke Ctr. for Learning and Devel., Nat. Womens Law Ctr; trustee Smith Coll.; mem. adv. bd. Studio in a Sch. Mem. ABA (com. depts. corp. law), NYC Bar Assn., N.Y. State Bar Assn., Coun. on Fgn. Rels. Home: 1170 5th Ave New York NY 10029-6527 Office: Am Express Co Am Express Tower World Fin Ctr New York NY 10285-0001 Office Phone: 212-640-2000. *

PARENT, MARK GORDON, cardiologist; b. Phila., Pa., June 5, 1957; MD, U. So. Fla. Coll. Medicine, 1982. Cert. Internal Medicine, Cardiovascular Disease. Intern, medicine LDS Hosp., Salt Lake City, 1982—83, resident, cardiology, 1983—85; fellow Martinez VA Hosp., 1986; hosp. appointment St. Luke's Regional Med. Ctr., St. Alphonsus Regional Med. Ctr., Boise, Idaho, West Valley Med. Ctr., Weiser Meml. Hosp.; clin. faculty U. Wash., Seattle; founding mem., cardiologist Idaho Cardiology Associates, PA, 1994—. Fellow: Am. Coll. Cardiology. Avocations: boating, fishing, golf, skiing, tennis, financial investing. Office: Idaho Cardiology Assocs PA 6140 Curtisian Ave Ste 200 Boise ID 83704-0107 Office Phone: 208-322-1680. *

PARENT, MARY, film company executive; Past agt. trainee ICM; dir. develop. to v.p. prodn. New Line Cinema, 1994—97; sr. v.p. prodn. Universal Pictures, Universal City, Calif., 1997—2000, exec. v.p. prodn., 2000—01, co-pres. prodn., 2001—03, vice chmn., worldwide prodn., 2003—05, prodr., 2006—. Exec. prodr.: (films) Set It Off, 1996, Trial and Error, 1997, Pleasantville, 1998; prodr.: You, Me and Dupree, 2006; prodn. mgr.: Dangerous Ground, 1997. Named one of 100 Most Powerful Women in Entertainment, Hollywood Reporter, 2004. Office: 100 Universal City Plaza Universal City CA 91608

PARENT, RODOLPHE JEAN, retired Canadian air force officer, pilot; b. Thurso, Que., Can., June 16, 1937; s. Eugène Jean and Eliane Marie (Raby) P.; m. Michelle Marie Masse, Aug. 10, 1963; children: Stéphane, Nathalie, Cynthia Student, Coll. Militaire Royal de St-Jean, 1958-61; B.Sc., Royal Mil. Coll. Can., Kingston, Ont., 1963. Commd. Royal Can. Air Force, 1958; advanced through grades to brig.-gen., 1984; joined 425 Squadron for ops. on CF-101 aircraft Bagotville, Que., 1964-69; worked for Directorate of Recruiting and Selection at Nat. Def. Hdqrs., Ottawa, Ont., Canada, 1969-71; chief of ops. 433 Tactical Fighter Squadron, Bagotville, 1972-75, Can. Forces Base Bagotville, 1975-76; comdg. officer 433 Tactical Fighter Squadron, 1976-80; asst. dir. personnel careers Nat. Def. Hdqrs., Ottawa, 1980-81; base comdr. Can. Forces Base Lahr, Federal Republic Germany, 1981-83; commandant Coll. Militaire Royal de Saint-Jean, Que., 1983-86; dir. gen. personnel careers other ranks Nat. Def. Hdqrs., Ottawa, 1986-89; def. attaché Paris, 1989-92; ret., 1992. Decorated Order of Mil. Merit, Order of St. John of Jerusalem Roman Catholic. Avocations: hockey, tennis, windsurfing. E-mail: rudy.michelle@rogers.com.

PARENTE, ROBERT BRUCE, electrical engineer, consultant; b. Sept. 10, 1936; s. Almerico Elmer and Royda (Boyd) P.; m. Rozalinda Thelma Saturnio, May 28, 1977; children: Jennifer Dee, Jessica Dale, Jacquelyn Dawn. BSEE, MIT, 1959, MS in Engring., 1959, EE, 1961, PhD, 1966.

Registered profl. engr., Calif. Instr. elec. engring. MIT, Cambridge, 1959-65; asst. prof. engring. UCLA, 1965-70; mgr. electric power sys. Sys. Devel. Corp., Santa Monica, Calif., 1970-72, dir. planning, 1973-75, dep. dir. energy devel., 1975-76; sr. cons. Theodore Barry & Assocs., LA, 1976-78; propr. Parente & Assocs., mgmt. cons., LA, 1978—. Expert witness before utility commns.; cons. to U.S. and fgn. electric power cos. Author: Electric Power Pools, 1983; contbr. articles to profl. jours.; patentee in field. Res. lt. sheriff L.A. County Sheriff's Dept., 1970—. Mem. IEEE, Inst. Mgmt. Scis., Ops. Rsch. Soc. Am., Sigma Xi, Tau Beta Pi, Eta Kappa Nu, Hex-Alpha, Theta Chi. Office: 2715 Angelo Dr Los Angeles CA 90077-2142 Office Phone: 310-271-4248.

PARENTE, WILLIAM JOSEPH, political science professor; b. Chgo., July 7, 1937; s. Salvatore S. and Genevieve (Rooney) P.; m. Diane Alpern, Nov. 30, 1963; children: Elizabeth, Margaret, William Joseph, Caroline, Rebecca, Catherine, Abigail, Christopher, Natalya. AB cum laude, Xavier U., Ohio, 1961; PhD (Woodrow Wilson fellow, Woodrow Wilson dissertation fellow), Georgetown U., 1970. Woodrow Wilson intern Wilberforce (Ohio) U., 1965-66; asst. prof., chmn. polit. sci. dept. Antioch Coll., 1966-69, assoc. dean faculty, 1969-70; dean Coll. Arts and Scis., U. Scranton, Pa., 1970-85, assoc. prof. polit. sci., 1970-73, prof., 1973—; Fulbright scholar Chulalongkorn U., Bangkok, Thailand, 1985-86, Inst. for Policy Studies, Washington, 1986-87. Mem. nat. Fulbright screening com. for East Asia, Southeast Asia; mem. adv. com. Inst. Internat. Edn.; cons. on world affairs to Peace Corps. Author articles in field. Fellow Inst. Acad. Deans, 1971, Inst. Ednl. Mgmt., Harvard Bus. Sch., 1972, Fulbright fellow, Korea, 1974, Indonesia, 1978, Germany, 1980, Thailand, 1985-86, fellow NEH Seminar, U. Va., 1976, Harvard U., 1985, Columbia U., 1988, George Mason U., Va., 1990, UCLA, 1991, U. Mich., 1992, William and Mary, 1993, U. Iowa, 1994, U. Accra, Ghana, 1996; scholar-diplomat program State Dept., 1970, 73; vis. scholar in humanities NYU, 1989; named Tchr. of Yr., U. Scranton, 2006. Fellow Union Experimenting Colls. and Univs., Inst. for Policy Studies, Soc. for Religion in Higher Edn.; mem. Am. Polit. Sci. Assn., Assn. Jesuit Colls. and Univs. (chmn. conf. on internat. edn. 1981-85), Alpha Sigma Nu (nat. sec.-treas. 1979-82, nat. pres. 1983-85), Pi Sigma Alpha, Eta Sigma Phi, Alpha Sigma Lambda, Tau Kappa Alpha, Phi Alpha Theta. Roman Catholic. Home: 1608 Summit Pointe Scranton PA 18508-1034 Office: U Scranton Coll Arts & Sciences Scranton PA 18510 Office Phone: 570-941-7644. Business E-Mail: parentew1@scranton.edu.

PARET, PETER, historian; b. Berlin, Apr. 13, 1924; s. Hans and Suzanne Aimée (Cassirer) P.; m. Isabel Harris, Sept. 23, 1961; children: Suzanne Aimée, Paul Louis Michel. BA, U. Calif., Berkeley, 1949; PhD, U. London, 1960, DLitt, 1992; LittD, U. S.C., 1995; HHD, Coll. of Wooster, 1996; PhD (hon.), Humboldt U., 2007. Resident tutor, delegacy of extramural studies Oxford U., 1959-60; research assoc. Center of Internat. Studies, Princeton U., 1960-62, 63; vis. asst. prof. U. Calif., Davis, 1962-63, assoc. prof., 1963-66, prof., 1966-69; prof. history Stanford U., 1969-77, Raymond A. Spruance prof. internat. history, 1977-86; Andrew W. Mellon Prof. in humanities Inst. Advanced Study, Princeton, N.J., 1986-97, Andrew W. Mellon Prof. in humanities emeritus, 1997—. Mem. Inst. for Advanced Study, Princeton, 1966-67; fellow Ctr. for Advanced Study in Behavioral Scis., Stanford, Calif., 1968-69; vis. fellow London Sch. Econs., 1972-73; NEH fellow, 1979-80; sr. fellow Hoover Instn., Stanford U., 1988-93; Lees Knowles lectr. military history Cambridge U., 2008. Author: (with John Shy) Guerrillas in the 1960's, 1962, French Revolutionary Warfare from Indochina to Algeria, 1964, Yorck and the Era of Prussian Reform, 1966, Clausewitz and the State, 1976, rev. edit. 2007; The Berlin Secession, 1980, Art as History, 1988, (with Beth Irwin Lewis and Paul Paret) Persuasive Images, 1992, Understanding War, 1992, Imagined Battles, 1997, German Encounters with Modernism, 1840-1945, 2000, An Artist against the Third Reich: Ernst Barlach, 1933-1938, 2003; editor, translator: (with Michael Howard) On War (C. v. Clausewitz), 1976, (with Daniel Moran) Historical and Political Writings (C. v. Clausewitz), 1992; editor: Frederick the Great, 1968, Frederick the Great: A Historical Profile, 1972, Sisyphus or the Limits of Education, 1973, The Age of German Liberation, 1977, Berliner Secession, 1981, Makers of Modern Strategy, 1986, (with Ekkehard Mai) Sammler, Stifter & Museen, 1993. Served with inf. U.S. Army, 1943-46. Decorated Officer's Cross, Order of Merit, Germany. Fellow AAAS, Leo Baeck Inst., London Sch. Econs. (hon.); mem. Am. Philos. Soc. (Jefferson medal), Hist. Kom zu Berlin, Soc. for Mil. History (Samuel Eliot Morison and Moncado prizes), Clausewitz Gesellschaft (hon.). Office: Sch Hist Studies Inst Advanced Study Princeton NJ 08540 Home Phone: 609-683-5027; Office Phone: 609-734-8344. Business E-Mail: paret@ias.edu.

PARETS, PAUL L., music educator; b. Bangor, Maine, Apr. 29, 1942; s. J. P. and Berneta L. Parets; children: Timothy E. VanderGraaff, Meredith Anne. B of Music Edn., Cen. Mich. U., 1965; postgrad., U. Mich., 1980—83, U. Md., 1980—83. Cert. tchr. Del. Band dir. Sacred Heart H.S., Mt. Pleasant, Mich., 1965—66, Croswell (Mich.)-Lexington H.S., 1966—76; band dir., politics/govt. educator Alexis I. duPont H.S., Greenville, Del., 1976—. Mem. city coun. City of Delaware City, 1998—2006; assoc. mem. Rep. Nat. Com. Named Del. Tchr. of Yr., State of Del., 1987; named to 50 Who Make a Difference, SBO Mag., 2003, 2004; recipient Order of the 1st State, Gov. Michael Castle, 1987. Mem.: Music Educators Nat. Conf. (state pres. 1984—86, Disting. Music Educator award 1988). Anglican. Avocations: astronomy, travel. Home: PO Box 711 Delaware City DE 19706 Office: Alexis I duPont H S 50 Hillside Rd Greenville DE 19807

PARETSKY, SARA N., writer; b. Ames, Iowa, June 8, 1947; d. David Paretsky and Mary E. Edwards; m. S. Courtenay Wright, June 19, 1976; children: Kimball Courtenay, Timothy Charles, Philip William. BA, U. Kans., 1967; MBA, PhD, U. Chgo., 1977. Mgr. Urban Rsch Ctr., Chgo., 1971-74, CNA Ins. Co., Chgo., 1977-85; writer, 1985—. Author: (novels) Indemnity Only, 1982, Deadlock, 1984 (Friends of Am. Writers award 1985), Killing Orders, 1985, Bitter Medicine, 1987, Blood Shot, 1988 (Silver Dagger award Crime Writers Assn., 1988), Burn Marks, 1990, Guardian Angel, 1992, Tunnel Vision, 1994, Ghost Country, 1998, Hard Time: A V.I. Warshawski Novel, 1999, Total Recall, 2001, Blacklist, 2003 (Gold Dagger, Brit. Crime Writers Assn.), Fire Sale, 2005 (Publishers Weekly Bestseller hardcover fiction list, 2005), also numerous articles and short stories. Pres. Sisters in Crime, Chgo., 1986-88; dir. Nat. Abortion Rights Action League Ill., 1987—; mentor Chgo. inner-city schs. Named Woman of Yr. Ms mag., NYC, 1987; recipient Mark Twain award for disting. contbns. to Midwestern lit., 1996, Lifetime Achievement award, Private Eye Writers Am., 2005, Cartier Diamond Dagger for Lifetime Achievement, Brit. Crime Writers Assn., 2005. Mem. Crime Writers Assn. (Silver Dagger award 1988), Mystery Writers Am. (v.p. 1989), Authors Guild, Chgo. Network Achievements include being the founder of two scholarships at U. Kans. Office: c/o Dominick Abel Lit Agy #1B 146 West 82nd St New York NY 10024 Business E-Mail: viwarshawski@mindspring.com.

PARHAM, ELLEN SPEIDEN, nutrition educator; b. Mitchells, Va., July 15, 1938; d. Marion Coote and Rebecca Virginia (McNiel) Speiden; m. Arthur Robert Parham, Jr., Dec. 16, 1961; children: Katharine Alma, Cordelia Alyx. BS in Nutrition, Va. Poly. Inst., 1960; PhD in Nutrition, U. Tenn., 1967; MSEd in Counseling, No. Ill. U., 1994. Registered dietitian; lic. clin. profl. counselor. Asst. prof. to prof. nutrition No. Ill. U., DeKalb, Ill., 1966—2003, coord. programs in dietetics, 1981—86, 1990—2003, coord. grad. faculty sch. family, consumer, nutrition scis., 1985-87, interim chair Sch. Applied Health Professions, 2005—06; state coord. Ill. Homeland Security Ednl. Alliance, 2006—. Cons. on nutrition various hosps., clins. and bus., Ill., 1980-88; founder, dir. Horizons Weight Control Program, DeKalb, 1983-91; founder, leader "Escaping the Tyranny of the Scale" Group, 1994—; co-chair Nutrition Coalition for Ill., 1989-90; ptnr., mgr. Blue Chicory Arts, 1986—; adj. counselor Ctr. for Counsel, Family Svc. Agy. of DeKalb County. Bd. editors Jour. Nutrition Edn., 1985-90, 97—2005, Jour. Am. Dietetic Assn., 1991-97; contbr. articles to profl. jours. Recipient Fisher award, No. Ill. U. Coll. Health and Human Svcs., 2001, Sullivan award, 2002, No. Ill. Amazing Woman award, 2006. Mem. Am. Inst. Nutrition, Soc. Nutrition Edn., Am. Dietetic Assn. (named Ill. Outstanding Dietetics Educator 2001, Excellence in Dietetics Edn. award 2001), Soc. Nutrition Edn. (treas. 1991-94, chair divsn. nutrition and weight realities 1995-96, chair jour. com. 2002—05, Weight Realities Cert. of Achievement 1999), N.Am. Assn. Study Obesity. Democrat. Avocations: painting in watercolor, gardening, reading. Business E-Mail: eparham@niu.edu.

PARHAM, SHEILA D., elementary school educator; BS in Edn., MS in Edn., Duquesne U., Pitts. Cert. tchr. Pa., 2002, Md., 2005. Mem.: Alpha Kappa Alpha (chair social com. 2003—04). Office: Longfields Elem Sch 3300 Newkirk Ave District Heights MD 20747

PARHAM-HOPSON, DEBORAH, health programs administrator; BSN, U. Cin., 1977; MS in Pub. Health, U. NC, 1979, PhD in Pub. Health, 1990. Rear adm. USPHS Commd. Corps.; dep. assoc. adminstr. Health Resources and Svcs. Adminstrn., HIV/AIDS Bur., HHS, 2000—02, acting assoc. adminstr., 2002, assoc. adminstr., 2002—. Office: US Dept Health and Human Svcs Health Resources Svcs Adminstrn 5600 Fishers Ln Rm 7-05 Rockville MD 20857 Office Phone: 301-443-1993. Business E-Mail: dparham@hrsa.gov.

PARHI, KESHAB KUMAR, electrical and computer engineering educator; b. Balasore, Orissa, India, June 15, 1959; came to U.S., 1983; s. Budhiram and Kamalini Parhi; m. Jagruti Mahapatra, Dec. 11, 1988; children: Megha, Rahul B Tech., Indian Inst. Tech., Kharagpur, 1982; MSEE, U. Pa., 1984; PhD, U. Calif., Berkeley, 1988. Tchg. and rsch. asst. U. Pa., Phila., 1983—84; postgrad. rschr. U. Calif., Berkeley, 1984—88; mem. tech. staff T.J. Watson Rsch. Ctrs. IBM, Yorktown Heights, NY, 1986, AT&T Bell Labs., Holmdel, NJ, 1987; asst. prof. U. Minn., Mpls., 1988—92, assoc. prof., 1992—95, prof., 1995—, Edgar F. Johnson prof., 1997—2007, Disting. McKnight U. prof., 2000—. Tech. dir. DSP Sys., Broadcom Corp., Irvine, Calif., 2000-02; vis. rschr. NEC Computer Comm. Lab., Kawasaki, Japan, 1992, 96-97; cons. AT&T Bell Labs., 1987, U.S. West Sci. and Techs., Boulder, Colo., 1989 Editor Jour. VLSI Signal Processing, 1993—; contbr. articles to profl. jours Recipient NSF Young Investigator award, 1992, Eliahu Jury award U. Calif., Berkeley, 1987, Demetri Angelakos award U. Calif., Berkeley, 1987, Frederick Emmons Terman award Am. Soc. Engring. Edn., 2004; IBM grad. fellow, 1987-88, Regents fellow U. Calif., 1986-87 Fellow IEEE (assoc. editor trans. on cirs. and sys. 1990-91, editor-in-chief 2004-05, assoc. editor trans. on signal processing 1993-95, assoc. editor trans. on cirs. and sys. part II 1995-97, 2002-03, trans. on VLSI syss. 1997-98, signal processing letters 1997-99, signal processing mag. 2003-2004, signal processing soc. paper award 1991, Browder J. Thompson Meml. Prize Paper award 1991, W.R.G. Baker prize 2001, Kiyo Tomiyasu Tech. Field award 2003), Cirs. and Sys. Soc. (bd. govs. 2005—, Guillemin-Cauer award 1993, Darlington award 1994, Golden Jubilee medal 1999, Disting. lectr. 1994-99, Design Automation Conf. Best Paper award 1996) Avocations: swimming, gardening, hiking, travel. Office: U Minn Dept Elec/Computer Engring 200 Union St SE Minneapolis MN 55455-0154 Office Phone: 612-624-4116. Business E-Mail: parhi@umn.edu.

PARIENTE, BARBARA J., state supreme court justice; b. NYC, Dec. 24, 1948; m. Frederick A. Hazouri; children: David, Leslie, Josh. Grad. with highest honors, Boston U., 1970; JD with highest honors, George Washington U., 1973. Bar: Fla. 1973; cert. civil trial lawyer Fla. Bar; cert. Nat. Bd. Trial Advocacy. Law clk. to hon. Norman C. Roettger, Jr. US Dist. Ct. (so. dist.) Fla., 1973-75; assoc. Cone Wagner and Nugent, 1975—77, ptnr., 1977—83, Pariente & Silber, P.A., 1983; pvt. practice, 1983—2001; judge US Ct. of Appeals (4th dist.), 1993-97; justice Fla. Supreme Ct., Tallahassee, 1997—, chief justice, 2004—06, liaison, task force on treatment-based drug cts., 1999—2004, chair, steering com. families and children in cts., 2002—04, faculty mem., Justice Tchg. Inst. Participant Twenty-First Century Justice Conf.; mem. Jud. Cir. Grievance Com., 1989-92, chair, 1990-92; appointee gov.'s adv. com. character edn., 1999; second v.p. Conf. of Justices, 2005-06; mem. 15th jud. cir. nominating commn.; mem. nat. judges adv. com. balanced and restorative justice project, Dept. of Justice; bd. dirs. Fla. Bar Found., Legal Aid Soc., Palm Beach County Bar Assn.; conf. organizer in field; spkr. in field. Contbr. articles to profl. jours. in field. Mentor Take Stock in Children, 1992-2003, Communities in Schs.; mentoring program mem. Cities in Schs., 1993; mem. Palm Beach County Commn. on Status of Women; program vol. judge Palm Beach County Youth Ct. Recipient Disting. Svc. to Arts award Palm Beach County Bar Assn., 1987, Civil Litig. Pro Bono award Legal Aid Soc., 1993, Lifetime Achievement award Palm Beach County Jewish Fedn., 1998, Disting. Jud. Svc. award Fla. Coun. Crime and Delinquency, 2000, Breaking the Glass Ceiling award Jewish Mus. Fla., 2002, Good Govt. award Palm Beach County LWV, 2005, Lifetime Achievement award Fla. Assn. Sch. Social Workers, 2005, Disting. Alumni award George Washington U., 2006, Jurist of Yr. award Fla. Chpt. Am. Acad. Matrimonial Lawyers, 2006. Master Am. Inns of Ct. (Palm Beach County chpt.); mem. ABA (mem. coalition for justice com. 2000-03, Law Day Speech award 1998), Nat. Assn. Women Judges, Am. Inns of Ct. (founding mem. Palm Beach County chpt.), Acad. Fla. Trial Lawyers (bd. dirs., chair spkr.'s bur. program 1984-87, outreach com. 1991-92, co-chair workhorse seminar 1991-92), Assn. Trial Lawyers Am. (vice chair profl. rsch. and devel. dept. 1980-82, chair comml. litig. sect. 1984-85, women's trial lawyer caucus 1986-87, mem. ethics com. 1989-90, conv. planning com. 1992-93), Fla. Assn. Women Lawyers (Lifelong Dedication award 2000), Fla. Bar Assn. (civil rules com. 1981-87, commn. legal needs of children 2000-02, Family Law Visionary award 2004, William M. Hoeveler Jud. Professionalism award 2004, Hugh S. Glickstein Child Adv. of Yr. award 2005), Order of Coif. Office: State Supreme Ct of Florida 500 S Duval St Tallahassee FL 32399-1925 Business E-Mail: supremecourt@flcourts.org.

PARIKH, NEEL, library director; b. Pitts., Apr. 20, 1948; d. John White and Virginia Kellogg Kingston; m. Mihir Parikh, Dec. 28, 1968 (div. July 1975). BA in Polit. Sci., U. Calif., Berkeley, 1970, MLS, 1971. Branch mgr. Alameda County Libr., various, Calif., 1977-84; coord. children's svcs. San Francisco Pub. Libr., 1984-90, chief branch librs., 1990-94; libr. dir. Pierce County Libr. Sys., Tacoma, Wash., 1994—. Chair adv. bd. Libr. Coun. Wash., Olympia, 1996—2002, chair Mayor's Adv. Coun. on Child Care, San Francisco, 1985-90; mem. steering com. Calif. Libr. Networking Task Force, San Francisco, 1992-93; instr. U. Calif., Berkeley, 1990; pres. Pierce County AIDS Found., Tacoma, Wash., 1995-2002; bd. dirs. Commns. on Children, Youth and Their Families, Tacoma, 1993-96. Contbr. articles to profl. jours. Bd. dirs. Am. Leadership Forum, Tacoma, 1998—, Lakewood's Promise exec. bd., Tacoma, 1997-2001, 2005—; pres., bd. dirs. YWCA, Pierce County, 2003—, Fund for Women and Girls Adv. Com., 2001-06. Recipient Merit award Calif. Assn. Tchrs. Eng., San Francisco, 1989, Golden Rule award J.C. Penney, San Francisco, 1989. Mem. ALA (John Cotton Dana award 1988, councillor 1999-2002), Calif. Libr. Assn. (pres. 1992), Washington Libr. Assn. (exec. bd. 1995-97), Women Libr. Workers (nat. pres. 1978-79), Urban Librs. Coun., Pub. Library Assn. (bd. dirs. 2007—), City Club Tacoma, Tacoma Rotary. Avocations: reading, rafting, gardening. Office: Pierce County Library System 3005 112th St E Tacoma WA 98446-2200 Home Phone: 253-566-8584; Office Phone: 253-536-6500 ext. 114. Business E-Mail: neelp@pcl.lib.wa.us, nparikh@piercecountylibrary.org.

PARINS, ROBERT JAMES, professional football team executive, judge; b. Green Bay, Wis., Aug. 23, 1918; s. Frank and Nettie (Denissen) P.; m. Elizabeth L. Carroll, Feb. 8, 1941; children: Claire, Andrée, Richard, Teresa, Lu Ann. BA, U. Wis., 1940, LLB, 1942. Bar: Wis. Supreme Ct. 1942. Pvt. practice, Green Bay, Wis., 1942-68; dist. atty. Brown County, Wis., 1949-50, cir. judge Wis., 1968-82, res. judge Wis., 1982—; pres. Green Bay Packers, Inc., 1982-90, chmn. bd., 1990-92; hon. chmn. bd., 1992-94. Mem.: Wis. State Bar Assn. Roman Catholic.

PARIS, DAVID ANDREW, dentist; b. Milw., Jan. 16, 1962; s. John Baptistia and Geraldine Louella (Grosso) P. BA, UCLA, 1985, DDS, 1989. Oral surgery extern VA, Phoenix, 1989; primary practitioner Aids Project L.A. Dental Clinic, 1990-94; assoc. M. Marchese D.D.S., Sun Valley, Calif., 1990-92, D. Pickrell DMD, West Hollywood, Calif., 1992-94, Dental Arts Assocs., Milw., 1994-95, Family Dental Ctr., Milw., 1994-96; pvt. practice Elm Grove, Wis., 1996—. Mem. ADA, Wis. Dental Assn., Calif. Dental Assn., Acad. Gen. Dentistry, Delta Sigma Delta. Avocations: cello, Italian language. Office Phone: 262-784-7770.

PARIS, DAVID C., political science professor; b. Rochester, NY; married; 3 children. BA in Govt., Hamilton Coll., 1971; MA & PhD in Polit. Sci., Syracuse U. Asst. prof. polit. sci. Va. Polytechnic Inst. and State U., 1975—79; asst. prof. govt. Hamilton Coll., Clinton, NY, 1979—, James S. Sherman prof. govt., assoc. dean faculty, chmn. dept. govt., acting dean faculty, 2000—01, v.p. acad. affairs, dean faculty, 2001—06, Leonard C. Ferguson prof. govt., 2006—. Co-author (with James F. Reynolds): The Logic of Policy Inquiry1983, 1983; author: Ideology and Education Reform: Themes and Theories in Public Education, 1995. Fellow: Assn. Am. Colleges & Universities (sr.; work on campaign. Liberal Edn. & America's Promise (LEAP)). Office: Hamilton College 198 College Hill Rd Clinton NY 13323 *

PARIS, DEIDRE EILEEN, artificial intelligence researcher, educator; b. Hammond, Ind., Oct. 7, 1968; d. Elizabeth Paris and Dillard Paris Jr. BSEE, So. U., Baton Rouge, 1992; Masters of Sci., Pub. Policy, Ga. Inst. Tech., 1996; MS in Elec. Engring., Ga. Inst. of Tech., 1994; PhD in Civil & Environ. Engring., Ga. Inst. Tech., 2002. Rschr. Constrn. Rsch. Ctr., Ga. Inst. of Tech., Atlanta; fellow GE Med. Sys., Milw., 1991—93, Army Environ. Policy Inst., Atlanta, 1995—97; rschr. Lawrence Livermore Nat. Lab., Livermore, Calif., 1997; asst. prof. Clark Atlanta U., Atlanta, 2002—04; faculty rschr. Oak Ridge Nat. Lab., Tenn., 2003; rsch. participant (NRC) Nuc. Regulatory Commn., Washington, 2004—05; adminstr. fellow NASA Marshall, Ala., 2004—; prof. coll. engring., architectgure & phys. sci. Tuskagee U. Adminstr. fellow Nasa Marshall Space Flight Ctr., Huntsville, Ala., 2002—04; presenter in field. Author, (exbhn.) 17th Internal Symposium on Polymer Analysis and Characterization; contbr. chapters to books. Resident adv. Atlanta Mut. Housing Assn., Atlanta, 2000—03; grad. senator for civil engring. dept. Ga. Inst. Tech. Student Govt. Assn., 1997—99; coord. ReJOYce In Jesus Ministries, LA, 1995—2001; contractor selection com. mem. Hist. Dist. Devel. Corp., 2003—04. Fellow, NASA, ASEE, 2004, GEM, 2003-2006; scholar Ga. Tech Bd. of Regents, Ga. Bd. of Regents, 1999—2001, GM, 1988—91, Motorola Corp., 1992; Adminstv. fellow, NASA, 2004—06, Presdl. Fellow, Ga. Inst. Tech., 1996—2000. Mem.: ASCE (assoc.), Am. Soc. of Civil Engring. (assoc.). Independent. Avocations: dance, reading, exercise. Home: 3672 Hawthorn Ct Auburn AL 36830 Office: Tuskegee U Coll Engring Architecture & Phys Sci 305 Luther Foster Hall Tuskegee Institute AL 36088 Home Phone: 404-344-4057; Office Phone: 404-429-9469. Office Fax: 256-544-8480; Home Fax: 256-544-8280. Personal E-mail: deidreparis@yahoo.com. E-mail: deidre.e.paris@msfc.nasa.gov.

PARIS, GORDON A., investment banker; b. 1953; MBA, U. Pa., 1977. CPA. Consulting and auditing Deloitte & Touche, Coopers & Lybrand; v.p., head transportation industrials practice GE Capital Corp.; head corp. restructuring group Kidder Peabody, 1989—91; mng. dir. high-yield investment banking group Lehman Brothers, 1991—93, mng. dir. fixed-income investment banking, 1993; mng. dir. leveraged fin. group Credit Suisse First Boston, 1994; mng. dir., group head high yield origination and capital markets TD Securities Inc., 1996—2002; sr. v.p. Toronto-Dominion Bank, 2000—02; interim pres. & CEO Hollinger Internat. Inc. (name changed to Sun-Times Media Group, 2006), NYC, 2003—05, interim chmn., 2004—05, chmn., pres., CEO, 2005—06; mng. dir. Berenson & Co, NYC, 2002—06, advisory dir., 2006—. Dir. Warrantech Corp., 1998—. *

PARIS, NORMA JEAN, psychologist, educator; b. Muskogee, Okla., Jan. 15, 1937; d. Howard Charles and Eleanor Ruth Lewis; m. Barney McKinley Paris, Jr., Feb. 17, 1957; children: Donna Katherine Paris Willis, Cynthia Elizabeth Paris Bickham, Barney McKinley Paris III(dec.). BA summa cum laude, La. State U., 1975, psychologist, 1985, MEd, 1977, PhD, 1997; Edn. Specialist in Counseling, La. Tech. U., 1980. Tchr. Bossier Parish Sch. Bd., Bossier City, La., 1975—84, sch. psychologist, 1984—87, Caddo Parish Sch. Bd., Shreveport, 1987—2001; spl. lectr. Centenary Coll. La., Shreveport, 2001—06. Psychol. advisor Compassionate Friends, Shreveport, 1981—92; cons. Children's Advocacy Ctr. Task Force, Shreveport, 1996—98; spkr. Oxford Round Table, England, 2005, England, 06; presenter in field. Bd. mem. Juvenile Justice Bd. Dirs., Shreveport, 1996—2000; exec. bd. mem. Caddo-Bossier Mental Health Assn. Bd. Dirs., Shreveport, 1996—2000. Mem.: La. Sch. Psychologists Assn. (exec. bd. mem. 2001—, La. Sch. Psychologist of Yr. 2001), Assn. Tchr. Educators, Internat. Reading Assn., Mensa. Republican. Baptist. Avocations: bridge, puzzles, water aerobics, travel. Home: 4406 Curtis Loop Bossier City LA 71112 Personal E-mail: parisn@bellsouth.net.

PARIS, STEVEN MARK, application developer; b. Boston, May 26, 1956; s. Julius Louis and Frances (Keleishik) Paris. BS, Rensselaer Poly. Inst., 1978; MS, Boston U., 1980, postgrad., 1980-84. Sr. software engr. Prime Computer Inc., Framingham, Mass., 1978-82; sr. analyst Computervision Corp., Bedford, Mass., 1982-84; prin. engr. Lotus Devel., Inc., Cambridge, Mass., 1984-88; pres. Tri-Millennium Corp., 1988-91; sr. rschr. Tech. Edn. Rsch. Ctr., Cambridge, 1990-93; prin. engr. Beyond, Inc., Burlington, Mass., 1993, Bus. Matters Inc., Waltham, Mass., 1994—96; v.p. engr. Ambit, Inc., Brighton, Mass., 1996—2002; v.p. product implementation Health Allianze, Inc., Andover, Mass., 2003—. Civil def. capt. City of Somerville, Mass., 1984—2006. Recipient 1st prize, Boston Sci. Fair, 1973, 1974, 3d prize, State of Mass. Sci. Fair, 1973, 2d prize, 1974. Mem.: IEEE, Boston Computer Soc., Assn. Computing Machinery, Planetary Soc. Jewish.

PARIS, ZACHARY T., lawyer; b. Cleve., Aug. 30, 1948; BA summa cum laude (hon.), Yale U., 1970, JD, 1973. Bar: Ohio 1973. Law clk. U.S. Dist. Ct. (no. dist.) Ohio; ptnr. Jones, Day, Reavis & Pogue, Cleve., Jones Day, Cleve. Mem. Phi Beta Kappa. Office: Jones Day N Point 901 Lakeside Ave Cleveland OH 44114 Office Phone: 216-586-7275, 216-579-0212. Business E-Mail: ztparis@jonesday.com.

PARIS-DE MONTE, ILEANA M., assistant principal; d. Alfredo Paris Torres and Margarita Badilla Vega; life ptnr. Roland Wyler; children: Adriana M. De Monte, Leonard Alfredo De Monte. BA in Journalism, Calif. State U., Northridge, 1979, Bilingual Tchg. Credential, 1993, M Ednl. Adminstrn., 2005. Cert. adminstr. Calif. Media release officer Bank of Am., LA, 1980; elem. sch. tchr. Serrania Ave. Elem. Sch., LA Unified

Sch. Dist., Woodland Hills, Calif., 1988—2002; asst. prin. Napa St. Elem. Sch., Northridge, 2002—. Master tchr. Pepperdine Univ., Nat. U., LA, 1992—2002. Elem. tchr. liaison Taft Complex, LA Unified Sch. Dist., Woodland Hills, Calif., 1997—99. Mem.: ASCD. Home Phone: 818-222-8072; Office Phone: 818-885-1441. Office Fax: 818-993-4824. Personal E-mail: idemon1@lausd.k12.ca.us.

PARISH, J. MICHAEL, lawyer, mutual fund executive, writer; b. Decatur, Ill., Nov. 9, 1943; s. John Mitchell and Gladys Margaret (Daulton) P.; m. Susan Lee Sgarlat, July 24, 1976 (div.); m. Ellen R. Harnett, Dec. 3, 1991; children: Margaret Ruth, William Walter. AB cum laude, Princeton U., 1965; LLB, Yale U., 1968. Assoc. LeBoeuf Lamb et al, NYC, 1968-73, ptnr., 1974-89, Winthrop Stimson Putnam & Roberts, NYC, 1989-95, Thelen, Reid & Priest, NYC, 1995—2002, Wolf, Block, Schorr & Solis-Cohen, NYC, 2002—03. Chmn. bd. dirs. Forum Funds, Portland, Maine, Core Trust. Contbr. stories and poetry to mags. Dir. PBS Am. Poetry Project, 1985-90; coord. Yale Law Sch. Clinton Election com.; class sec. Princeton Class of 1965; trustee Hackensack Riverkeeper. Univ. scholar Princeton U., 1965, Nat. scholar Yale U., 1968. Avocation: creative writing. Home: 443 1st St Oradell NJ 07649-1705 Home Phone: 917-328-0402; Office Phone: 201-634-0812. Personal E-mail: mparish@alumni.princeton.edu.

PARISH, JAMES MICHAEL, medical educator; BS in Biology with honors, U. Ill., 1974; MD, U. Ill., Chgo., 1978. Diplomate Am. Bd. Internal Medicine, Am. Bd. Pulmonary Medicine. Resident internal medicine Mayo Clinic, 1978—81, fellow pulmonary medicine, 1981—84; pulmonary and critical care specialist Sharp Meml. Hosp., San Diego, 1984—87; cons., Assoc. Prof. Mayo Clinic Coll. Medicine, Scottsdale, Ariz., 1987—. Fellow: ACP, Am. Acad. Sleep Medicine, Am. Coll. Chest Physicians; mem.: AMA, Am. Thoracic Soc. Achievements include research in sleep disorders. Office: Mayo Clinic 13400 Shea Blvd Scottsdale AZ 85259 Office Phone: 480-301-8000.

PARISH, JAMES ROBERT, writer, cinema historian; b. Cambridge, Mass., Apr. 21, 1944; s. Fred Arthur and Ann Lois (Magilevy) P. BA, U. Pa., 1964, LLB, 1967. Pres. Entertainment Copyright Rsch.Co. Inc., NYC, 1967-68; film reporter, reviewer, interviewer Variety, Motion Picture Daily, 1968-69; entertainment publicist Harold Rand & Co., 1969-70; free-lance writer, publicist, film book cons., film reviewer, novelist, 1970—; acquisition editor Renaissance Books, 1996-99. Author: (with P. Michael) The Emmy Awards: A Pictorial History, 1970, The Fox Girls, 1971, The Great Movie Series, 1971 (with A.H. Marill) The Cinema of Edward G. Robinson, 1972, The Slapstick Queens, 1972, The Paramount Pretties, 1972, (with R. Bowers) The MGM Stock Company, 1973, Actors TV Credits, 1950-72, 73, Good Dames, 1973, (with M.R. Pitts) The Great Spy Pictures, 1973, The RKO Gals, 1973, (with S. Whitney), The George Raft File, 1973, (with M.R. Pitts) Film Directors: A Guide to Their American Pictures, 1974, Hollywood's Great Love Teams, 1974, (with S. Whitney) Vincent Price Unmasked, 1974, The Great Movie Heroes, 1975, (with D. Stanke), The Glamour Girls, 1975, The Debonairs, 1975, (with L. DeCarl) Hollywood Players: The Forties, 1975, (with J. Ano) Liza! (The Liza Minnelli Story), 1975, (with M.R. Pitts) The Great Gangster Pictures, 1975, The Elvis Presley Scrapbook, 1975, (with W. Leonard) Hollywood Players: The Thirties, 1976, (with D. Stanke) The All Americans, 1976, Film Directors: A Guide for Western Europe, 1976, Great Child Stars, 1976, The Jeanette MacDonald Story, 1976, (with D. Stanke) The Leading Ladies, 1977, (with M.R. Pitts) The Great Science Fiction Pictures, 1977, Film Actors Guide: Western Europe, 1977, The Elvis Presley Scrapbook (update), 1977, (with M. Trost) Actors TV Credits: Supplement One, 1977, (with M.R. Pitts) Hollywood on Hollywood, 1978, (with R. Braff et al.) Hollywood Character Actors, 1978, (with G. Mank and D. Stanke) The Hollywood Beauties, 1978, (with W. Leonard) The Funsters, 1979, (with D. Stanke) The Forties Gals, 1980, (with G. Mank) The Hollywood Reliables, 1980, The Great American Movies Book, 1980, (with G. Mank) The Best of MGM, 1981, (with M.R. Pitts) The Great Spy Pictures II, 1986, (with M.R. Pitts) The Great Gangster Pictures II, 1987, (with M.R. Pitts) The Great Western Pictures II, 1988, Black Action Pictures from Hollywood, 1989, (with M.R. Pitts) The Great Science Fiction Pictures II, 1990, (with V. Terrace) Complete Actors TV Credits, 1990, (with M.R. Pitts) Hollywood Songsters, 1990, updated edit., 2002, The Great Cop Pictures, 1990, Prison Pictures from Hollywood, 1991, (with M.R. Pitts) Hollywood's Great Musicals, 1992, (with D. Stanke) Hollywood Baby Boomers, 1992, Prostitution in Hollywood Film, 1992, The Hollywood Death Book, 1992; Let's Talk: America's Favorite Talk Show Hosts, 1993, Gays and Lesbians in Mainstream Cinema, 1993, Hollywood's Celebrity Death Book, updated and expanded, 1994, Ghosts and Angels on the Hollywood Screen, 1995, Today's Black Hollywood, 1995, Pirates and Seafaring Swashbucklers, 1995, The Great Child Stars, 1996, The Unofficial "Murder She Wrote" Casebook, 1997, Rosie: Rosie O'Donnell's Biography, 1997, updated edit., 1998, Whoopi Goldberg: From Poverty to Mega Stardom, 1997, updated edit., 1999, Jason Biggs, 2000, The Hollywood Book of Death, 2001, Gus Van Sant, 2001, Hollywood Bad Boys, 2002, Jet Li, 2002, The Encyclopeida of Ethnic Groups in Hollywood, 2002, Hollywood Divas, 2002, The Hollywood Book of Love, 2003, Whitney Houston, 2003, Steven Spielberg, 2004, The Hollywood Book of Scandals, 2004, Tom Hanks, 2004, Stephen King, 2004, Halle Berry, 2004, Twyla Tharp, 2005, Denzel Washington, 2005, Stan Lee, 2005, Katie Couric, 2005, Katharine Hepburn: The Untold Story, 2005, Jim Henson, 2006, Gloria Estefan, 2006, Fiasco: A History of Hollywood's Iconic Flops, 2006, The Hollywood Book of Breakups, 2006, (with Allan Taylor) Career Opportunities in Writing, 2006, (with Allan Taylor) Career Opportunities in Television and Cable, 2006, It's Good to Be the King: The Serious Funny Life of Mel Brooks, 2007, (with Allan Taylor) Career Opportunities in the Internet, Video Games, and Multimedia, 2007, The Hollywood Book of Extravagance, 2007; assoc. editor: The American Movies Reference Book, 1969, TV Movies, 1969, The Great American Movie Book, 1980. Mem. Phi Beta Kappa. Avocations: docent, reading, writing. Address: 4338 Gentry Ave Unit 1 Studio City CA 91604-1764 Personal E-mail: jrparish@sbcglobal.net. *To succeed in one's ambitions requires an unyielding avoidance of other people's skepticisms.*

PARISH, NORMAN, artist, gallery director; b. New Orleans, Aug. 26, 1937; B in Painting, Sch. of Art Inst. of Chgo., 1960. Draftsman to asst. project leader, to project leader to supr. of computer-aided drafting; founder, dir. Parish Gallery, Washington, 1991—. Contbr. to Wall of Respect, Chgo., 1967. Office: Parish Gallery 1054 31st St Washington DC 20007 Office Phone: 202-944-2310. Business E-Mail: parishgallery@bigplanet.com.

PARISH, RICHARD LEE, engineer, consultant; b. Kansas City, Mo., May 31, 1945; s. Charles Lee and Ruth (Duncan) P.; m. Patricia Ann Erickson, June 2, 1968; children: Christie Lynn White, Kerry Anne Parish-Philp. BS in Agrl. Engring., U. Mo., 1967, MS in Agrl. Engring., 1968, PhD, 1970. Registered profl. engr., Ohio. Asst., then assoc. prof. engring. Univ. Ark., Fayetteville, 1969-74; mgr. mech. research and devel. O.M. Scott & Sons Co., Marysville, Ohio, 1974-83; assoc. prof., then prof. La. State U., Baton Rouge, 1983-97; prof. Hammond Rsch. Sta., 1995—, resident coord. Coastal area rsch. sta., 2005—. Cons. in equipment patents, equipment safety, product liability, personal injury, design and evaluation; expert witness testimony in agrl. and hort. equipment, patents, 1984—. Contbr. over 100 articles to profl. jours.; patentee in field. Bd. dirs. Agrl. Devel. Found. Recipient Quality award, ITT, 1979, Doyle Chambers award for excellence in rsch., La. State U. Agrl. Ctr., 2001; NSF fellow, 1967—69. Mem. Am. Soc. Agrl. Engrs. (chmn. agrl. chem. application com. 1982-83, chmn. power and machinery divsn. program com. 1986-87, chmn. cultural practices equipment com. 1994-95, chmn. fruit and vegetable prodn. engring. com. 1999-2001), Am. Soc. Hort. Sci. Republican. Baptist. Avocations: old tractors, gardening, woodwork, bicycling. Home: 21135 Highway 16 Amite LA 70422-4733 Office: Hammond Rsch Sta 21549 Old Covington Hwy Hammond LA 70403-0533 Office Phone: 985-543-4125. Business E-Mail: dparish@agcenter.lsu.edu.

PARISH, THOMAS SCANLAN, psychology professor; b. Oak Park, Ill., Jan. 24, 1944; s. Robert S. and Florence Catherine (Fleming) P.; children: Robert V., Kimberly E., David G., Thomas P., Kathryn E., Lydia E.; m. Joycelyn G. Parish, Dec. 29, 2000. BA, No. Ill. U., 1968; MA, Ill. State U., 1969; PhD, U. Ill., 1972. Cert. reality therapy Inst. Reality Therapy, LA, 1980. Instr. psychology Parkland Coll., Champaign, Ill., 1971-72; asst. prof. Okla. State U., Stillwater, 1972-76; assoc. prof. Kans. State U., Manhattan, 1976-80, prof., 1980—2005, asst. to dean of edn., 1992-97; assoc. dir. ARIOS-Kan., 1994-96. Rsch. coord. for Midwest Desegration Asst. Ct., 1994-96; regional dir. Excel Comm., 1997-98; assoc. prof. Upper Iowa U., Fayette, 2001-07. Assoc. editor Jour. of Social Studies Rsch., 1994-98; cons. editor Jour. Genetic Psychology, 1984—, Internat. Jour. Reality Therapy, 1992-2003, 2006—, The Genetic, Social and General Psychology Monographs, 1984-2003; contbr. articles to profl. jours. Bd. dirs. Friendship Tutoring Program, Manhattan, 1982-91, Stillwater Awareness Coun., 1973-74; co-founder, bd. dirs. Youth Alternatives, Inc., Champaign, 1971-72; pres. Mid-Western Edn. Rsch. Assn., 1998-99. Fellow Am. Psychol. Soc.; mem. Am. Ednl. Rsch. Assn., APA, Assn. Reality Therapists, Soc. for Rsch. in Child Devel., Phi Delta Kappa, Phi Kappa Phi. Achievements include research in discerning the possible impact of parent loss on children and youth; ways to motivate one's self and others. Avocation: dance. Home Phone: 785-862-1379, 319-230-9970. Personal E-mail: parishthomas@yahoo.com.

PARISH, WILLIAM HENRY, lawyer; b. Oakland, Calif., July 28, 1954; s. Harry and Elaine Katherine (Triplett) P.; m. Kathryn Annette, Aug. 14, 1976; children: Michael Erik, Jennifer Christine, Melissa Ann. AA, Hartnell Coll., 1974; BA, Calif. State U., 1977; JD, U. Pacific, 1980. Bar: Calif. 1980, U.S. Dist. Ct. (ea. dist.) Calif. 1980, U.S. Ct. Appeals (9th cir.) 1980, U.S. Supreme Ct. 1990. Assoc. Cavalero, Bray, Geiger & Rudquist, Stockton, Calif., 1980-82, ptnr., 1982-87, Bray, Geiger, Rudquist, Nuss & Parish, Stockton, 1987; prin. Law Offices of William H. Parish, Stockton, 1987—96, Parish & Nelson, A Profl. Corp., Stockton, 1997—2002, Parish & Small, A Profl. Corp., Stockton, 2003—. Bd. dirs. Cmty. Bus. Bank. Dir. Cmty. Bus. Bank, 2005—. Mem. ABA (litigation sect. 1980—), Am. Bd. Trial Advs., Order of Coif, Am. Heart Assn., San Joaquin County (bd. dirs. 2001—, pres. 2002—). Office: Parish & Small Profl Corp 1919 Grand Canal Blvd Ste A-5 Stockton CA 95207

PARISI, LEAH EVANS, dean, nursing educator, lawyer; d. Leslie Malcom and Elizabeth Stoughton Evans; m. Alfonso Parisi, Oct. 6, 1990; stepchildren: Anne Marie, Joseph, Nancy, Paula; m. Ronald Katz (div.). BSN, Ohio State U., Columbus, 1962; MA in Healthcare Adminstrn., Lindenwood Coll., LA, 1975; EdD in Instl. Mgmt., Pepperdine U., LA, 1982; JD, Loyola Law Sch., LA, 1985. Bar: Calif. 1985; RN Ohio, 1962, N.Y., 1967, Tex., 1967, Ontario, Can., 1989, S.C., 1999, Calif., 1973, CRNA, Am. Assn. Nurse Anesthetists, 1965. Nurse anesthetist cardiac surgery Cleve. Clinic, Cleve., 1960—67, Baylor Coll. Medicine, Houston, 1967—73; dir. nurse anesthesia program Martin Luther King Gen. Hosp., LA, 1973—74, UCLA Sch. Medicine, 1973—85; attorney med. malpractice and staff privileges law Rushfeld Shelley & Drake, 1985—88; prof. sch. nursing Faculty Health Scis. McMaster U., Hamilton, Ontario, Canada, 1989—99; instr. legal asst. and paralegal program Tech. Coll. Lowcountry, Beaufort, SC, 2000—, dean bus. tech., 2000—06. Adj. assoc. prof. dept. anesthesiology UCLA Sch. Medicine, 1974—85; ednl. cons. and sr. on- site visitor Am. Assn. Nurse Anesthetists, Chgo., 1975—85; prof. sch. nursing Faculty Health Scis. McMaster U., Hamilton, Ontario, 1989—99; invited vis. faculty U. Nebr., Lincoln, Henry Ford Hosp. U. Detroit, U. So. Calif., LA; invited participant McMaster U. Faculty Health Scis. Program Academic Leaders, Hamilton, Ontario; dir. Hummingbird Enterprises, Hilton Head, SC. Contbr. to conf. prceedings, chapters to books, scientific papers, articles to profl. jours. Bd. mem St. Josephs Villa, Hamilton, Ontario, 1992—99. Recipient Helen Lamb award Educator of Yr., Am. Assn. Nurse Anesthetists, 1984, Alumni Assn. Ann. award, Ohio State U, Nurse Anesthesia Program, 1985, Faculty Tchg. Excellence award, McMaster U. students, 1999, hon. mention Ann. Grad. Student Supr. award, McMaster U. Mem.: ABA. Achievements include established first graduate level program in nurse anesthesia U.S. Office: Tech Coll Lowcountry 921 Ribaut Rd Beaufort SC 29910 Office Phone: 843-525-8278. Business E-Mail: lparisi@tcl.edu.

PARISI, VALERIE MARIE, former dean, medical educator; b. Bklyn., 1952; m. Gary Strong. BS in Biology, Brown U., 1972, MD, 1975; MPH, U. Calif. Sch. Pub. Health, 1980; MBA, U. NC, 2004. Lic. Calif., 1979, Tex., 1984, NY, 1994, NC, 1998, diplomate Nat. Bd. Med. Examiners, 1976, Am. Bd. Ob-gyn., 1981, Am. Bd. Ob-gyn. Divsn. Maternal-Fetal Medicine, 1987. NIH rsch. fellow, Dept. Chemistry and Physics Brown U., Providence, 1970, Noyes Found. rsch. fellow, Dept. Sociology & Divsn. Reproductive Biology and Medicine, 1971; Noyes Found. rsch. fellow, Dept. Ob-gyn. Women and Infants Hosp. RI, Providence, 1972; intern in categorical gen. surgery Brown U. Affiliated Hospitals, RI Hosp., Providence, 1975—76; resident in ob-gyn. Women and Infants Hosp. of RI, Providence, 1976—79; fellow divsn. maternal-fetal medicine, Dept. Ob-gyn. U. Colo. Health Sci. Ctr., Denver, 1982—83, U. Wis. Ctr. for Health Sciences, Madison, 1983—84; instr. Dept. Human Growth and Reproduction Brown U., 1976—79; lectr., divsn. maternal child health U. Calif. Sch. Pub. Health, Berkeley, 1980—81; clin. instr. Dept. Ob-gyn. and Reproductive Sciences, U. Calif., San Francisco, 1980—81, clin. asst. prof., 1981—82; asst. prof. Dept. Ob-gyn. U. Colo. Health Sci. Ctr., Denver, 1982—83, U. Wis. Health Sci. Ctr., Madison, 1983—84; asst. prof. Dept. Ob-gyn. and Reproductive Sciences U. Texas Med. Sch., Houston, 1984—89, assoc. prof. Dept. Ob-gyn. and Reproductive Sciences, 1989—94, dir. divsn. maternal-fetal medicine, 1984—94, asst. prof. Dept. Pediatrics, 1987—89, assoc. prof. Dept. Pediatrics, 1989—94, co-dir. maternal-fetal medicine fellowship program, 1987—94; vis. prof. divsn. neonatology Dept. Pediatrics U. Cin. Med. Ctr., 1991—92; prof. & chair Dept. Ob-gyn. and Reproductive Medicine U. Med. Ctr. at Stony Brook, NY, 1994—97; Robert A. Ross prof. & chair Dept Ob-gyn. U. NC, Chapel Hill, 1997—2004, residency program dir. Dept. Ob-gyn., 1999—2004, rsch. fellow Cecil G. Sheps Ctr. for Health Sciences Rsch., 2003—; dean medicine U. Tex. Med. Branch, Galveston, 2004—06, chief acad. officer, v.p. acad. program adminstrn. and services, 2004—06, adv., 2006—. Attending staff Providence Neighborhood Health Centers, RI, 1977—79; dir. Ob-gyn. Services Bristol County Cmty. Med. Ctr., RI, 1977—79; dir. gynecological services Brown U. Student Health Services, 1978—79; consulting staff Letterman Army Med. Ctr., Presidio of San Francisco, 1979—82; attending staff Kaiser Found. Hosp., Oakland, Calif., 1980, San Francisco, 1980—82; clin. staff Moffitt Hosp. U. Calif. San Francisco Med. Ctr., 1980—82; med. dir. Ambulatory Care Ctr. Dept. Ob-gyn. U. Colo. Health Sci. Ctr., Denver, 1982—83; attending staff Madison Gen. Hosp., Wis., 1983—84, U. Wis. Clin. Sciences Ctr., Madison, 1983—84; consulting staff St. Mary's Med. Ctr., Madison, Wis., 1983—84; attending staff Hermann Hosp., Houston, 1984—94, dir. Maternal-Fetal Spl. Care Unit, 1985—92, obstetrical dir. labor and delivery, 1987—88, Houston, 1992—94, med. dir. Family Ctr., 1992—94; consulting staff St. Joseph's Hosp., Houston, 1987—94, Meml. Southwest Hosp., Houston, 1990—94; active staff Lyndon Baines Johnson Hosp., Houston, 1990—94; ob-gyn. chief U. Hosp., Stony Brook, NY, 1994—97; consulting staff Southampton Hosp., NY, 1995—97, St. Charles Hosp., Port Jefferson, NY, 1996—97; obstetrician-gynecologist-in-chief NC Women's Hosp., Chapel Hill, 1997—2004; attending staff Dept. Ob-gyn REX Hosp., 2002—04. Bd. dirs. Am. Bd. Family Practice, 1999—2004; fin. and investment com., nominating com. Am. Bd. Med. Specialties, 2004; basic examiner Am. Bd. Obstetrics and Gynecology, 1990—, maternal and fetal medicine examiner, 1992—, divsn. maternal and fetal medicine, 1996—2002, bd. dirs. and divsn. chief maternal and fetal medicine, 1998—2002, exec. com., 1999—2002, fin. com., 2004—; mem. Coun. on Residency Edn. in Ob-gyn., 1995—2000; bd. dirs. Planned Parenthood of Suffolk County, 1994—97; exec. bd. Western Perinatal Collaborative Group, 1986—92, chair membership com., 1986—88, vice pres. & pres.-elect, 1988—90, pres., 1990—92. Fellow: Am. Gynecologic and Obstetrical Soc. (nominating com. 1992, fellowship com. 1992—95), Am. Assn. Advancement Sci.; mem.: Tex. Perinatal Assn., Tex. Med. Found., Tex. Med. Assn., Tex. Assn. Obstetricians and Gynecologists, Soc. for Study of Reproduction, Soc. Obstetric Anesthesia and Perinatology (bd. dirs. 1995—99), Soc. for Maternal Fetal Medicine (bd. dirs. 1989—92, scientific program chair 1993, pres.-elect 1993—94, pres. 1994—95), Soc. Gynecological Investigation, Perinatal Rsch. Soc. (exec. coun. 1993—95), NY Obstetrical Soc., Internat. Soc. for Study of Hypertension in Pregnancy, Houston Gynecological and Obstetrical Soc., Harris County Med. Soc., Assn. Reproductive Health Professionals, Assn. Professors of Gynecology and Obstetrics, Am. Med. Women's Assn., AMA, Am. Coll. Obstetricians and Gynecologists (patient edn. com. 1989—91, scientific program com. 1993, edn. commn. 1995—97), Sigma Xi.

PARIZEK, ELDON JOSEPH, geologist, educator, dean; b. Iowa City, Apr. 30, 1920; s. William Joseph and Libbie S. P.; m. Mildred Marie Burger, Aug. 9, 1944; children: Richard, Marianne, Elizabeth, Amy. BS, U. Iowa, 1942, MS, 1946, PhD, 1949. Instr. U. Iowa, 1947-49; asst. prof. geology U. Ga., 1949-54, assoc. prof., 1954-56, U. Kansas City, 1956-63; prof. U. Mo., Kansas City, 1963—, chmn. dept. geoscis., 1968-78; dean U. Mo. (Coll. Arts and Scis.), 1979-86. Served with USN, 1942-45. Fellow Geol. Soc. Am.; mem. AAUP, Assn. Mo. Geologists, AAAS, Sigma Xi. Roman Catholic. Achievements include research, numerous publs. on mass wasting, slope failure, underground space, geology of West Mo. Home: 6913 W 100th Shawnee Mission KS 66212 Office: 5100 Rockhill Rd Kansas City MO 64110-2481

PARK, CHAN HO, professional baseball player; b. Kongju, South Korea, June 30, 1973; Grad., Hanyang U., South Korea. Player LA Dodgers, 1994—2001, Tex. Rangers, 2002—05, San Diego Padres, 2005—06, NY Mets, 2007—. Player Korean Nat. Team, World Baseball Classic, 2006. Named a mem. of the All-Tourney Team (pitcher), World Baseball Classic, 2006. Achievements include becoming the first South Korean to ever reach 100 Career Wins in the majors; 3 saves (1st in tournament) in the World Baseball Classic 2006, 3 games finished (3rd in tournament, 0.00 (10.0 innings) earned run average (2nd in tournament). Office: NY Mets 123-01 Roosevelt Ave Flushing NY 11368-1699 Office Phone: (619) 795-5000. *

PARK, CHAN HYUNG, cell biologist, physician; b. Seoul, Korea, Aug. 16, 1936; s. Chung Suh and Yoon Sook Yuh; m. Mary Hyungrok Kim, Apr. 16, 1966; 1 child, Christopher Myungwoo. MD, Seoul Nat. U., 1962, MS, 1964; PhD, U. Toronto, 1972. Diplomate in internal medicine and med. oncology Am. Bd. Internal Medicine. Asst. prof. U. Kans. Med. Ctr., 1974—80, assoc. prof., 1980—86, prof., 1986—89; prof., chief divsn. oncology/hematology, dept. internal med. Tex. Tech U. Health Scis. Ctr., 1989—94; dir. Cancer Ctr. Samsung Med. Ctr., Seoul, 1994—2001, head divsn. hematology/oncology dept. medicine, 1994—99; sr. rsch. scientist Ctr. for Improvement of Human Functioning Internat., Inc., Wichita, Kans., 2001—; prof. medicine Sungkyn-Kwan U. Med. Sch., 1997—2001, prof. emeritis, 2007—. Cancer ctr. cons. 2001; adv. com. Samsung Cancer Ctr., 2006—. Transl. novel from German to Korean; mem. editl. bd. Jour. Nutrition, Growth and Cancer, 1986-87; mem. editl. bd. Internat. Jour. Hematology, 1999—; contbr. articles to biomed and sci. jours. Recipient Rsch. Career Devel. award USPHS, NIH, 1979-84. Fellow: ACP; mem.: Am. Soc. Hematology, Internat. Soc. Exptl. Hematology, Am. Soc. Clin. Oncology, Am. Assn. Cancer Rsch. Home: 611 S 291 ST Federal Way WA 98003 Office: The Ctr for the Improvement Human Functioning Internat Inc 3100 N Hillside Wichita KS 67219 Personal E-mail: park.chanh@gmail.com.

PARK, CHONG S., computer company executive; BA in Mgmt., Yonsei U.; MA in Mgmt., Seoul Nat. U.; MBA, U. Chgo.; PhD in Mgmt., Nova Southeastern U. Chmn., pres., CEO Axil Computer, Inc., 1993—95; pres., CEO Hynix Semiconductor Am., Inc., 1996—2000, chmn., 1996—2002; pres., CEO, chmn. Hynix Semiconductor, Inc., 2000—02; pres., CEO Maxtor Corp., Milipitas, Calif., 1995—96, chmn., 1998—2006, CEO, 2004—06. Chmn. MMC Tech. (Maxtor subs.), 1996—2000; bd. dir. Dot Hill Sys. Corp., ChipPAC, Seagate Tech., 2006—. Mailing: Seagate Technology Bd Directors 920 Disc Dr Scotts Valley CA 95066-4544

PARK, CYNTHIA, sociology educator, consultant; b. Schenectady, NY, Feb. 7, 1925; d. Robert Hiram and Miriam Elizabeth Park; m. Robert Wentworth Christy (div.). BA, New Sch. Social Rsch., 1959; MS in Secondary Social Studies, Yeshiva U., 1961; MA in Sociology, Hunter Coll., CUNY, 1969; postgrad., New Sch. U., 1970—75. Permanent lic. secondary social studies N.Y.C. and N.Y. State. Tchr. h.s. sci. and social studies N.Y. Bd. Edn., NYC, 1961, tchr. h.s. social studies Brandeis H.S., 1962—66; tchr. Nassau C.C., LI, NY, 1970; instr. sociology Bloomfield (N.J.) Coll., 1967—70, Quinnipiac Coll., New Haven, 1971—73, U. New Haven, West Haven, Conn., 1973—75; ind. cons. NYC, 1975—. Cons. Paulo Mesdag Gruppe Rec. Yale U. Archives; owner 98 1/2 McDougal St., NYC, 1951; dir. Coop Gallery, NYC, 1960—65, Westerly Gallery, NYC. Prodr.: (mus. recs.) Music of Finland. Local campaign worker Lexington Dem. Club, NYC, 1963—67. Recipient Fulbright grant to Finland, 1959—60, grants in field. Mem.: Soc. Ethnomusicology, Ind. U., Am. Sociol. Assn., Violoncello Soc., Am. Fedn. Musicians. Democrat. Episcopalian. Avocations: art, violincello, singing. Home: 965 Lexington Ave New York NY 10021

PARK, DAVID ALLEN, physicist, researcher; b. NYC, Oct. 13, 1919; s. Edwin Avery and Frances (Paine) P.; m. Clara Justine Claiborne, Aug. 18, 1945; children: Katharine, Rachel, Paul, Jessica. AB, Harvard, 1941; PhD, U. Mich., 1950. Instr. Williams Coll., 1941-44; ops. research on radar countermeasures Harvard U. and Eng., 1944-45; instr. U. Mich., 1950; mem. Inst. Advanced Study, Princeton, 1950-51; mem. faculty Williams Coll., 1952-88, prof. physics, 1960-88, emeritus, 1988—; sr. vis. Cambridge (Eng.) U., 1962-63; vis. lectr. U. Ceylon, 1955-56, 72, Mass. Inst. Tech., 1966; vis. prof. U. N.C., 1964. Author: Quantum Theory, 1964, 3d edit., 1991, Contemporary Physics, 1964, Strong Interactions, 1966, Classical Dynamics and Its Quantum Analogues, 1979, 2d edit., 1990, The Image of Eternity, 1980, (with P.J. Davis) No Way, 1987, The How and the Why, 1988, The Fire Within the Eye, 1997, The Grand Contraption, 2005. Fellow Am. Phys. Soc.; mem. Internat. Soc. for Study Time (pres. 1973-76). Office: Williams Coll Dept Physics Williamstown MA 01267 Business E-Mail: dpark@williams.edu.

PARK, HEE-JUNG (HEE JONG PARK), professional golfer; b. Seoul, Korea, Feb. 27, 1980; Profl. golfer Korean LPGA, 1998—2000, LPGA Tour, 2000—. Winner Australian Jr. Championship, 1996, 97, 98. Achievements include winning several Korean LPGA events including Sports Seoul Ladies Open, 1998, Indonesian Ladies Open, 1999; winner LPGA events including Williams Championship, 2001, Sybase Big Apple Classic, 2002. Avocations: movies, music, video games. Office: LPGA 1000 International Golf Dr Daytona Beach FL 32124-1092

PARK, HYUN, lawyer, utilities executive; BA summa cum laude, Columbia U., NYC; MA, Oxford U.; JD cum laude, Harvard U., 1989. Ptnr. Latham & Watkins, LA, NYC, Hong Kong; sr. v.p., gen. counsel, sec. Sithe Energies Inc., 1998—2005; v.p., gen. counsel Allegheny Energy Inc., Greensburg, Pa., 2005—06; sr. v.p., gen. counsel PG&E Corp., San Francisco, 2006—. Office: PG&E Corp Ste 2400 One Market Spear Tower San Francisco CA 94105-1126 Office Phone: 415-367-7070. Office Fax: 415-267-7268. *

PARK, JOHN THORNTON, retired academic administrator; b. Phillipsburg, NJ, Jan. 3, 1935; s. Dawson J. and Margaret M. (Thornton) P.; m. Dorcas M Marshall; June 1, 1956; children: Janet Ernst, Karen Daily. BA in Physics with distinction, Nebr. Wesleyan U., 1956; PhD, U. Nebr., 1963. NSF postdoctoral fellow Univ. Coll., London, 1963-64; asst. prof. physics U. Mo., Rolla, 1964-68, assoc. prof. physics, 1968-71, prof., 1971-2000, prof. emeritus, 2000—, chmn. dept. physics, 1977-83, vice chancellor acad. affairs, 1983-85, 86-91, interim chancellor, 1985-86, 91-92, chancellor, 1992-2000, chancellor emeritus, 2000—; ret., 2000. Vis. assoc. prof. NYU, 1970-71; pres. Talema Electronics, Inc., St. James, Mo., 1983-99, Tortran Corp., 1990—; prin. investigator NSF Rsch. Grants, 1966-92; bd. dirs. Mo. Tech. Corp., Jefferson City, Mo., 1994—, Mo. Enterprise, 1990—, Phelps County Bank, 1997—, Phelps County Regional Med. Ctr. Contbr. articles to profl. jours. Recipient Most Disting. Scientist award Mo. Acad. Sci., 1994. Fellow Am. Phys. Soc. (mem. divsn. elec. and atomic physics); mem. Am. Assn. Physics Tchrs., Rotary. Methodist. Personal E-mail: parkj@umr.edu.

PARK, JOON BU, biomedical engineer, researcher, educator; b. Pusan, Republic of Korea, June 20, 1944; arrived in U.S., 1964; s. Sung Sub and Jung Ju (Kim) P.; m. Hyonsook Yoo, Apr. 15, 2000; children: Misun, Yoon Ho, Yoon Il, Lajong. Student, Seoul Nat. U., 1962—64; BS, Boston U., 1967; MS, MIT, 1969; PhD, U. Utah, 1972. NIH postdoctoral fellow U. Wash., Seattle, 1972—73; vis. asst. prof. U. Ill., Urbana, 1973—76; asst. prof., assoc. prof. Clemson U., SC, 1976—81; prof. Tulane U., New Orleans, 1981—83; prof. biomed. engrng. U. Iowa, Iowa City, 1983—. Advisor, cons. FDA, Rockville, Md., 1980—. Author: Biomaterials: An Introduction, 1979, 3d edit., 2007, Biomaterials Science and Engineering, 1984, 3d edit., 2007, Biomaterials: Principles and Applications, 2002; contbr. articles to profl. jours. Fellow Am. Inst. Med. and Biol. Engrng.; mem. Soc. for Biomaterials (founding mem.), Biomed. Engrng. Soc., Orthop. Rsch. Soc., NY Acad. Scis. Achievements include patents in field. Home: 1810 Country Club Dr Coralville IA 52241-1183 Office: Univ Iowa Dept Biomed Engrng Iowa City IA 52242 Office Phone: 319-335-5636. Business E-Mail: joon-park@uiowa.edu.

PARK, LEE (LEE PARKLEE), artist; b. Seoul, Republic of Korea; s. Chung-Kun Park and Mil-Hwa Kim; m. Chai Kyung Lim, June 3, 1994. MA, Fla. State U., 1986. Prof. associated academician dept. arts Vinzaglio, Italy, 2002—. Group shows include Shinpara Gallery, LA, Up-Stairs Gallery, LA, Beverly Plz. Hotel, Pacific Mus., Pasadena, Calif., Barnsdall Art Gallery, Hollywood, Calif., Brand XXII The Assn. of Brand Art Ctr., Glendale, Calif., Asia Invitation Art Exhibn., Sejong Cultural Ctr., Seoul, la Peintre Moderne Coreend '93, Paris, Korea-Japan Interchange Exhbn., Tokyo, 1994, Downtown Lives '96 Art Exhbn., LA, City Hall of Paris, 4, Biennale Internat. de Paris, 1994, Musee d'Art Moderne de la Commanderie d'Unet, Paris, 1994, Bridgeport (NY) U., 1995, San Bernardino County Mus., 1995, Kong-Ja Culture Art Exhbn., China, 1995, His Majesty the King's 50th Anniversary Art Exhbn., Thailand, 1996, 1st Venice Ann. Internat. Open Art Exbhn., Venice, 1998, 1st Internat. Biennial Contemporary Art, Perugia, Italy, 1998, Heukyong-gangsung Internat. Art Exhbn., China, 1998, Ting Shao-Kuang Fine Art Ctr., Beverly Hills, Articulture Gallery, Hermosa Beach, Calif., 1998, '99 World Peace Art Exhbn., Sejong Cultural Ctr., Seoul, 1999, The Millennium Art Collection, 2000, Invitational Art Exhbn. Jin-Jiang Gen. Assn. Gallery, Philipines, 2001, Galerie Michelangelo, Las Vegas, 2002, Reasons to Love the Earth, Den Haag, Netherlands, 2002; 2 person shows include Cosmos Gallery, Honolulu, The City of LA Cultural Affairs Dept.; solo exhibits include Modern Art Gallery, LA, Olympic Gallery, LA, Sun Space Gallery, LA, Gallery Nuevo, Pusan, Republic of Korea, Westside Jewish Cmty. Ctr., LA, World Festival of Art Exhbn., Slovenia, Caesars Palace Hotel Michelangelo, Las Vegas, Nev., 49th Toyo Calligraphy Art Assn., Tokyo, Eloge du Petit Fermat Dans L'Art D'Aujourd' Hui, Paris, Singapore, Korea Art Exhbn., Ngee Annual Cultural Ctr., Rubicon Gallery, LA, 2007, LA Mcpl. Art Gallery, Hollywood, 2007; publ. artwork in American References, Art of California mag., Artweek mag., The Biweekly Art Jour., Seoul, Artprint mag., Washington, Art Exposure mag., Calif., Ency. of Living Artists mag., Calif., Art 2000, Seoul, Mag. for World Art & Culture Vergil Quarterly, Seoul, 2004, Art Diary Internat. 1998—, Milan, Italy, Internat. Encyclopaedic Dictionary Modern and Contemporary Art, Ferrara, Italy, 2002-05, Dictionary Internat. Biography Ctr., Cambridge, Eng. (Top 100 artists 2005). Recipient Bronze award Art of Calif., 1993, Gold award Art Addiction, Stockholm, 1997. Avocations: collecting stamps and antiques, music, jogging, playing tennis, reading. Home: 1935 S La Salle Ave Apt 31 Los Angeles CA 90018-1627 E-mail: park@b17.com.

PARK, LEE CRANDALL, psychiatrist; b. Washington, July 15, 1926; s. Lee I. and Alice (Crandall) P.; m. Barbara Ann Merrick, July 1, 1953; children: Thomas Joseph, Jeffrey Rawson; m. Mary Woodfill Banerjee, Apr. 27, 1985; stepchildren: Stephen K., Scott K. Grad., Putney Prep. Sch., Vt.; BS in Zoology, Yale U., 1948; MD, Johns Hopkins U., 1952. Diplomate Nat. Bd. Med. Examiners, Am. Bd. Psychiatry and Neurology. Intern medicine Johns Hopkins Hosp., Osler Clinic, Balt., 1952-53; resident psychiatry USN Hosp., Oakland, Calif., 1953-54, Henry Phipps Psychiat. Clinic, Johns Hopkins Hosp., Balt., 1955-59, asst. psychiatrist, 1955-59, staff psychiatrist, 1959—, staff dept. medicine, 1970—, hon. staff dept. medicine, 1991—, dir. psychiat. outpatient svcs. and community psychiatry program, 1972-74, asst. dir. clin. svcs. dept. psychiatry, 1973-74, mem. departmental coun., 1974-76. Fellow psychiatry Johns Hopkins U., 1955-59, faculty in psychiatry, 1959—, assoc. prof., 1971—, physician charge psychiat. svcs. student health svc., 1961-73; vis. psychiatrist Balt. City Hosp., 1960-61; co-prin., prin. investigator NIMH Psychopharmacology Rsch. Br. Outpatient Study of Drug-Set Interaction, 1960-68, co-dir. (with Eugene Meyer) Time-Limited Psychotherapy Rsch. Grant, 1969-73; pvt. practice psychiatry, 1964—; cons. Met. Balt. Assn. Mental Health, 1961-63, Bur. Disability Ins., Social Security Adminstrn., 1964-81; attending staff Seton Psychiat. Inst., 1966-73, exec. bd., 1970-73; staff Sheppard and Enoch Pratt Hosp., 1974—. Co-author: A Primer on Mental Disorders: A Guide for Educators, Families and Students, 2001; contbr. articles and chpts. to profl. jours. and books. Served to lt. M.C., USNR, 1953-55, div. psychiatrist 1st Marine Div., Korea, staff psychiatrist USN Hosp., Camp Pendelton, Calif., 1954-55; mem. Md. Interdisciplinary Coun. for Children and Adolescents, 1978-98, treas., 1980-87. Fellow: AAAS, Am. Psychiat. Assn. (mem. assembly 1983—93, Psychiat. Rsch. Network 1994—2002, Disting. life fellow); mem.: AAUP, AMA, Johns Hopkins Med. and Surg. Assn., Balt. County Med. Assn., Balt. City Med. Soc., Med. and Chirurg. Faculty Md., Group Therapy Network, N.Y. Acad. Scis., Soc. Psychotherapy Rsch., Md. Psychiat. Soc. (pres. 1978—79), Md. Assn. Pvt. Practicing Psychiatrists, Am. Assn. Pvt. Practicing Psychiatrists, Am. Coll. Neuropsychopharmacology, Am. Soc. Adolescent Psychiatry, Internat. Soc. Study Personality Disorders, Am. Psychosomatic Soc., Md. Found. Psychiatry (bd. dirs. 1995—2003, pres. 2000—03), Nat. Assn. Scholars, St. George's Soc., Avery Assn., Denison Soc., Crandall Assn., Van Kouwenhoven-Conover Assn., Van Voorhees Assn., Parke Soc., Nat. Soc. Sons and Daus. of Pilgrims (gov. State of Md. 2006—), Gen. Soc. War 1812 (pres. State of Md. 2004—06, v.p. gen. 2006—), Nat. Huguenot Soc. (surgeon gen. 2005—), Descendants Mexican War Vets, Sons Union Vets. Civil War, SAR (surgeon State of Md. 2006—), Gen. Soc. Colonial Wars, S.R. (bd. mgrs. State of Md. 2006—), Yale Club NYC, Farmington Country Club, Met. Club (Washington), Johns Hopkins Club, Chevy Chase (Md.) Country Club, Phi Beta Pi. Republican. Episcopalian. Achievements include research in borderline and narcissistic conditions; long-term effects of childhood emotional abuse and neglect; psychotherapy; interrelationships of psychotherapy and pharmacotherapy; genesis and nature of social, personal and emotional intelligence. Home: 308 Tunbridge Rd Baltimore MD 21212-3803 Office: 1205 York Rd Ste 35 Lutherville Timonium MD 21093-6268 Office Phone: 410-321-1276. E-mail: lpark3@jhmi.edu.

PARK, LELAND MADISON, librarian; b. Alexandria, La., Oct. 21, 1941; s. Arthur Harris and Jane Rebecca (Leland) P. Student, McCallie Sch., 1957—59; AB, Davidson Coll., 1963; MLS, Emory U., 1964; postgrad., Simmons Coll., 1968; AdvM in Libr. Sci., Fla. State U., 1973, PhD, 1974. Reference libr. Pub. Libr. of Charlotte and Mecklenburg County, NC, 1964-65; head reference and student pers. Davidson (N.C.) Coll. Libr., 1967-70, asst. dir., 1970-75, dir., 1975—2006. Cons. coll. cons. network So. Assn. Colls and Schs.; vis. lectr. Emory U., summer 1972; temporary instr. Fla. State U., 1973; libr. cons.; conf. spkr.; chmn. state adv. com. Libr. Svcs. and Constrn. Act, 1975-79; mem. N.C. State Libr. Commn., 1983-85, 87-92, chmn., 1989-92; mem. Davidson (N.C.) Town Appearance Commn., 1986-93, design rev. bd. 98—, Hist. Preservation Commn., 1994-96; mem. editl. bd. CHOICE, 2003-06. Editor Southeastern Librarian, 1976-78; acad. sect. editor N.C. Libraries, 1972-77; contbr. articles to profl. jours. Mem. Wake County Citizens for Better Librs., N.C., 1965-67; sec. com. libr. affairs Piedmont U. Ctr., 1969-70, chmn., 1970-72; mem. nat. bd. cons. NEH, 1976-2006; clk. mission com. St. Alban's Episcopal Mission, Davidson, N.C., 1969-72, layreader, 1970-75, treas., 1975-86; bd. dirs. statewide computer libr. resource network NC-LIVE, 1997—2006. Recipient H.W. Wilson Libr. periodical award, 1979, Alumni Achievement award The McCallie Sch., 1989, Order of Long Leaf Pine presented by N.C. Gov. James G. Martin, 1993. Mem. ALA, Southeastern Libr. Assn. (chmn. coll. and univ. sect. 1976-78, exec. bd. 1976-78), N.C. Libr. Assn. (2d v.p. 1975-77, 1st v.p. 1981-83, pres. 1983-85), Metrolina Libr. Assn. (pres. 1969-71), Mecklenburg County Libr. Assn. (treas. 1969-70), Soc. of Cin. (2d v.p. Ga. Soc. 1982-83), SAR, Mil. Order World Wars, Raleigh Jaycees (chmn. libr. com. 1965-67), Res. Officer Assn., SCV, Soc. Colonial Wars, S.C. Huguenot Soc., Rotary, Beta Phi Mu, Sigma Nu, Omicron Delta Kappa. Home: PO Box 777 235 Ney Circle Davidson NC 28036-0777 Home Phone: 704-892-1529. E-mail: lepark@aol.com.

PARK, MARIA, artist, educator; b. Munich, 1972; MFA, San Francisco Art Inst., 2001—03. Asst. prof. Cornell U., Ithaca, NY, 2006—. Exhibitions include Strange Passages, Kemper Mus. Contemporary Art, Stasis, Margaret Thatcher Projects, Discrete Velocity, Toomey Tourell Gallery. Recipient award, Korea Arts Found. Am., 2002; grantee Jack and Gertrude Fine Arts fellowship, San Francisco Found., 2002; MFA grant, Joan Mitchell Found., 2003. Business E-Mail: myp4@cornell.edu.

PARK, MARINA H., lawyer; b. Pasadena, Calif., Nov. 6, 1956; BA with honors, Univ. Calif., Berkeley, 1978; JD, Univ. Mich., 1982. Bar: Calif. 1983. Mng. ptnr. Pillsbury Winthrop LLP, Palo Alto, Calif., 1999—2005; ptnr., Emerging Growth & Tech. practice & mng. ptnr. Pillsbury Winthrop Shaw Pittman, Palo Alto, Calif., 2005—. Office: Pillsbury Winthrop Shaw Pittman 2475 Hanover St Palo Alto CA 94304-1114 Office Phone: 650-233-4770. Office Fax: 650-233-4545. Business E-Mail: marina.park@pillsburylaw.com.

PARK, MARY WOODFILL, information consultant, librarian, writer; b. Nevada, Mo., Nov. 20, 1944; d. John Prossor and Elizabeth (Devine) Woodfill; m. Salil Kumar Banerjee, Dec. 29, 1967 (div. 1983); children: Stephen Kumar, Scott Kumar; m. Lee Crandall Park, Apr. 27, 1985; stepchildren: Thomas Joseph, Jeffrey Rawson. BA, Marywood Coll., 1966; postgrad., Johns Hopkins U., 1983, Goucher Coll., 1986. Asst. to dir. U. Pa. Librs., Phila., 1968-69; investment libr. Del. Funds, Phila., 1969-71; investment officer Investment Counselors Md., Balt., 1980-84, 1st Nat. Bank Md., Balt., 1984-85; founder Info. Consultancy, Balt., 1985—. Lectr. Loyola Coll., Balt., 1991-92, Cath. U., 1993. Author: InfoThink—Practical Strategies for Using Information in Business, 1998; editor, contbr. to profl. publs. Vol. Internat. Visitors' Ctr., Balt., 1979-80, 91; del. White House Conf. on Librs.; v.p. bd. dirs. Friends of Goucher Libr., 1988-90; mem. industry applications com. Info. Tech. Bd., State of Md., 1993-96; mem. info. tech. com. of the Tech. Coun., Greater Balt. Com., 1993-98. Named One of Md.'s Top 100 Women, Warfield's Bus. Publn., 1996. Mem.: DAR, Huguenot Soc. Md. (1st v.p. 2003—05), Nat. Huguenot Soc., Md. Found. for Psychiatry (bd. dirs. 1998—), Assn. Ind. Info. Profls., Info. Futures Inst., Spl. Librs. Assn. (pres. Md. chpt. 1991—92, v.p. network coord. coun. Sailor project 1993—95, govt. rels. chair 1998—2003, pub. rels. chair 2003—), Nat. Soc. Colonial Dames Am., Nat. Soc. Dames Ct. Honor, Nat. Soc. Colonial Dames XVII Century (state rec. sec. 2003—05, 2d v.p. 2005—), Nat. Soc. of the Sons and Daus. of the Pilgrims, Nat. Soc. of U.S. Daus. of 1812 (Md. state rec. sec. 2003—05), Nat. Soc. Daus. Am. Colonists (Md. state regent 2006—), Friends of New Netherlands, Daus. of Colonial Wars, Colonial Dames Am., Nat. Inst. Geneal. Rsch. Alumnae Assn., Soc. Daughters Holland Dames, Descendants of Ancient and Honorable Families of New Netherland (1st directress 2006—), Three Arts Club Homeland, Hamilton St. Club (bd. dirs. 1989—92). Episcopalian. Office: The Information Consultancy 308 Tunbridge Rd Baltimore MD 21212-3803 Business E-Mail: mwpark@informationconsultancy.com.

PARK, MYUNG KUN, medical educator; b. Suhung, Hwanghae, Republic of Korea, Sept. 30, 1934; arrived in U.S., 1962; s. Jung-Jin and Sonnyu (Lee) Park; m. Issun Kim, Jan. 21, 1967; children: Douglas Yongwoon, Christopher Yongchul, Warren Yongsun. Diploma, Seoul Nat. U., Republic of Korea, 1956, MD, 1960. Intern Vassar Brothers Hosp., Poughkeepsie, NY, 1962—63; pediat. resident Georgetown U., Washington, 1963—64; chief resident Univ. Hosp., Morgantown, W.Va., 1964—65; pediat. cardiology fellow U. Washington, Seattle, 1965—68; asst. prof. U. Kans. Coll. Medicine, Kansas City, 1973-76; assoc. prof. U. Tex. Med. Sch., San Antonio, 1976-83, prof., 1983—2003, prof. emeritus, 2003—; prof., chmn. pediat. Arabian Gulf U. Med. Coll., Bahrain, 1995-98. Author: (book) How to Read Pediatric ECG, 1982, 3d rev. edit., 1992, Pediatric Cardiology for Practitioners, 1984, 4th rev. edit., 2002, The Pediatric Cardiology Handbook, 1991, 3d rev. edit., 2002; contbr. articles to profl. jours. Postdoctoral fellow, NIH, 1965—68, Rsch. fellow, 1971—73, Rsch. grantee, Maternal and Child Health Bur., 1991—95. Fellow: Am. Acad. Pediat., Am. Coll. Cardiology; mem.: Am. Assn. Pharmacology Therapy, Soc. Pediatric Rsch. Personal E-mail: drmpark@satx.rr.com.

PARK, MYUNGKARK, publishing company owner, physicist; b. Kangwon Do, Republic of Korea, July 24, 1950; came to U.S., 1977; m. Hyunmi Suh, July 17, 1977; 1 child, Brian. BS, Seoul Nat. U., Repubic of Korea, 1972; MS, Wayne State U., 1979; postgrad., Wash. State U., 1979—83, Kent State U., 1983—85, U. Cin., 1985—87. Teaching asst. Seoul Nat. U., 1974-76; tchr. physics Jeonnong Girl's Mid. Sch., 1976-77; teaching and rsch. asst. Wayne State U., Detroit, 1977-79; tchg. and rsch. asst. Wash. State U., Pullman, 1979-83, Kent (Ohio) State U., 1983-85, U. Cin., 1985-87, Southern Ohio Coll., 1987—88; pres., owner Prompter Publs., Cin., 1988-90, Seoul, 1990—. Author and editor several books and jours.; contbr. over 750 articles to profl. jours. and rsch. notebooks. 1st lt. Republic of Korea Army, 1972-74. Nat. scholar, 1962-68, 70-72, Hamchoon scholar, 1968-70, tchg./rsch. asst. scholar, 1977-87, Am. Vacuum Soc. scholar, 1989, The Knoller Physics-Chemistry scholar 1977-78; faculty fellow Wayne State U., 1977-79. Mem. AAAS, Am. Math. Soc., Korean Phys. Soc., Am. Vacuum Soc., Phi Theta Kappa, Pi Sigma Alpha. Home: PO Box 167 Chongnyangni Tongdaemoon-gu Seoul 130-650 Republic of Korea

PARK, NAEUN, statistician; MS, Columbia U., NYC, 2002. Biostatistician Columbia U., NYC, 2001—. Mem.: Internat. Soc. for Computational Biology, Am. Med. Informatics Assn. Achievements include research in genes predisposing to complex psychiatric diseases, bipolar disorder, psychosis, and schizophrenia. Home Phone: 917-287-4431; Office Phone: 212-305-1710.

PARK, NO-HEE, dean, academic administrator; b. Jan. 30, 1944; m. Yu Bai Yuly, 1969; 1 child, Jennifer. DDS, Seoul Nat. U., 1968, MSD, 1970; PhD, Med. Coll. Ga., 1978; DMD, Harvard U., 1982. Postdoctoral fellow in oral biology and pharmacology Med. Coll. Ga., 1975—78; rsch. assoc., Eye Rsch. Inst. Harvard Med. Sch., Boston, 1978—80, instr., dept. ophthalmology, 1978—82, asst. scientist, Eye Rsch. Inst., 1980—82, assoc. scientist, Eye Rsch. Inst., 1982—83; asst. prof., oral biology and pathophysiology Harvard U. Sch. Dental Medicine, Boston, 1982—83; assoc. prof., oral biology UCLA Sch. Dentistry, LA, 1984—85, prof., 1985—, assoc. dean rsch., 1997—98, dean, 1998—; assoc. dir. UCLA Dental Rsch. Inst., LA, 1986—90, dir., 1995—, UCLA Wound Healing Rsch. Ctr., LA, 1997—. Contbr. articles to profl. jours.; ad-hoc reviewer for various publs., 1990—, editl. bd. Internat. Jour. Oncology, 1996—, Electronic Jour. Biotechnology, 1997—, editor-in-chief Internat. Jour. Oral Biology, assoc. editor Odontology, 2000—. Mem.: Internat. Assoc. for Dental Rsch. (Selection Com. for Distinguished Scientist in Oral Medicine 2001—), Friends of NIDCR (Exec. Com. 2001—), Am. Assn. for Dental Schools Coun. of Deans Exec. Com., Am. Dental Assn., Calif. Dental Assn., Tissue Culture Assn., Am. Assn. for Cancer Rsch., Am. Dental Edn. Assn., Am. Assn. for Dental Schools, Am. Soc. for Microbiology, Am. Assn. for the Advancement of Sci., Internat. Assn. for Dental Rsch., Internat. Coll. Dentistry, Omicron Kappa Upsilon Dental Soc. Achievements include research in the role of telomerase in oral carcinogenesis, gene therapy for oral cancer, molecular mechanism of replicative senescence in normal human oral keratinocytes and viral and chemical oncogenesis; cellular proto-oncogenes and tumor suppressor genes, cell cycle and DNA repair, and antiviral chemotherapy. Office: UCLA 10833 Leconte Ave Rm 53-038 Los Angeles CA 90095

PARK, PENNY SHERAN, retired elementary school educator; b. Tulare, Calif., July 13, 1948; d. Sheridan Lee Roy Harris and Jeanne Avril Lightbody. AA, Coll. of the Sequoias, Visalia, CA, 1968; B in Music Edn., U. of Pacific, 1971; M in Music Edn., U. Calif., Fresno, 1980. Registered music therapist Nat. Assn. Music Therapy, 1971. Music therapist mental health wing Emmanual Hosp., Turlock, Calif., 1971; music therapist Brandel Manor Nursing Home, Turlock, 1971, Kings County Mental Health Day Treatment Ctr., Hanford, Calif., 1971—77; self-employed Hanford, 1977—85; music therapist Lee Richmond Sch. -Spl. Edn., Hanford, 1979—84; resource tchr.- music The Learning Ctr., Hanford, 1984—85; tchr. Hanford Elem. Sch. Dist., 1985—2006; ret., 2006. Cons. music therapist, music educator various, Hanford, 1977—79; program devel. Kings County Supt. Schs.-Spl. Edn., 1979—84; chorale instr. Hanford Elem. Sch. Dist., 1985—90; trainer The Activities In Math & Sci. Found.- Fresno (Calif.) Pacific Coll., 1987—92. Author: Learning Poco a Poco, 1980, Five Merry Santas, 1992; editor: Community Treasures, 2000. Mem.: Hanford Elem. Tchrs. Assn., Calif. Tchrs. Assn., Ea. Star (25 year pin 1997). Avocations: writing, reading, music, scrapbooks, computer games. Home: PO Box 484 Bass Lake CA 93604 Home Phone: 559-641-7296. E-mail: pensterpen@hotmail.com.

PARK, ROGER COOK, law educator; b. Atlanta, Jan. 4, 1942; s. Hugh and Alice (Cook) Park; m. Rosemarie J. Lilliker, June 14, 1967 (div. 1979); 1 child, Matthew; m. Suzanne Nicole Howard, Feb. 18, 1984; stepchildren: Sophie Currier, Nicolas Currier. BA cum laude, Harvard U., 1964, JD magna cum laude, 1969. Bar: Mass. 1969, Minn. 1973. Law clk. to Hon. Bailey Aldrich U.S. Ct. Appeals (1st cir.), Boston, 1969-70; with Zalkind & Silverglate, Boston, 1970-73; prof. Law Sch. U. Minn., Mpls., 1973-95, Fredrikson and Byron prof. law, 1990-95; Disting. James Edgar Hervey prof. law Hastings Coll. Law U. Calif., San Francisco, 1995—. Vis. prof. Law Sch. Stanford U., Palo Alto, Calif., 1977, Sch. Law Boston U., 1981—82, Law Sch. U. Mich., Ann Arbor, 1984; bd. dirs. Ctr. Computer-Aided Legal Instrn., 1982—96; reporter adv. group Civil Justice Reform Act, Dist. Minn.; mem. evidence adv. com. Minn. Supreme Ct., 1988—95. Author: Computer Aided Exercises in Civil Procedure, 1979, 2d edit., 1995, Waltz and Park Casebook on Evidence, 8th edit., 1994; author: (with Leonard and Goldberg) 10th edit., 2005; author: Evidence Law, 1998, 2d edit., 2004; author: (with McFarland) Trial Objections Handbook, 1991, 2d edit., 2001; contbr. articles to profl. jours. Lt. US Army, 1964—66, Vietnam. Mem.: ABA (mem. rules criminal procedure and evidence com. criminal justice sect. 1988—, mem. subcom. fed. rules evidence), Am. Assn. Law Schs. (chairperson evidence sect. 1994), Am. Law Inst. Office: Hastings Coll Law 200 Mcallister St San Francisco CA 94102-4707

PARK, ROY HAMPTON, JR., advertising executive; b. NC, 1938; s. Roy Hampton and Dorothy Goodwin (Dent) P.; m. Elizabeth Tetlow Parham; children: Elizabeth P. Fowler, Roy H. III. BA in Journalism, U. NC, Chapel Hill, 1961; MBA, Cornell U., Ithaca, NY, 1963. Sr. acct. exec., rev. bd. exec., advt. planning dir., J. Walter Thompson Co., NYC and Miami, 1963-70; v.p. mktg. and account mgmt. Kincaid Advt. Agency divsn. First Union Nat. Bank Corp., Charlotte, NC, 1970-71; v.p. Park Outdoor Advt., Ithaca, NY, 1971-75; v.p. advt. and promotion Park Broadcasting Inc., Ithaca, 1976-81; dir., 1993-95; mng. editor Park Comm. Newsletter, Ithaca, 1976-81; mng. dir. Agrl. Rsch. Advt. Agy., Ithaca, 1976-81; v.p., gen. mgr. Park Outdoor Adv., 1981-84; pres., CEO, dir. Park Outdoor Advt. of N.Y. Inc., 1984—; pres. Outdoor Advt. Coun. N.Y. Inc., 1986-91, chmn., dir., 1992-95; dir., sr. v.p. RHP Inc., 1994-96, RHP Properties Inc., 1994-96. Mem. region I planning bd. Inst. Outdoor Advt., 1984—86. Dir. Boyce Thompson Inst. for Plant Rsch. Inc., 1995-2001, dir., vice chmn. 2002-07; trustee, v.p. Park Found. Inc., 1995-2002; pres., chmn. Triad Found., Inc., 2003—; founding mem. alumni exec. com. Cornell U., 1984-88, trustee, 1999-07, trustee emeritus, 2007—; mem. adv. coun. Johnson Grad. Sch. Mgmt., 1996—, named to Johnson Hall Hon., 1999—; bd. vis. U. N.C. Sch. Journalism and Mass Comm., 1994—; chmn. Ithaca Assembly Cotillion, 1979-81; dir. pub. rels. Tompkins County Conf. and Tourist Coun., 1976; exec. com. Tompkins County Rep. Fin. Com., 1983-84; chmn. fin. com. MacNeil for Assembly, 1984-86, co-chmn. 1978-82; bd. dir. Tompkins County Coun. Arts, 1976; chmn. pub. rels. com. United Way Tompkins County, 1973-74, loaned publicity exec., 1977; bd. chmn., publicity dr. Jr. Olympics, 1973-74; dir. pub. rels. United Fund Raleigh, N.C., 1971; fin. com. Spl. Children's Ctr., 1979. Recipient Disting. Alumnus award, U. NC, 2005. Mem. Tompkins County C. of C. (chmn. sign ordinance com., 1975-76, chmn. legis. action com. 1976, acting chmn. nominating com. 1976, pub. rels. coun. 1976, Project of Yr. award 1974, Recognition award 1975), Charlotte C. of C. (pub. rels. com. 1970-71), Boque Banks Beach Preservation Assn., Ithaca Yacht Club, Ithaca Country Club, Boca Bay Pass Club, Gasparilla Inn Beach and Tennis Club. Office: Park Outdoor Advt PO Box 4680 Ithaca NY 14852-4680 Office Phone: 607-257-1477. Business E-Mail: roy.park@parkoutdoor.com.

PARK, THOMAS JOSEPH, biology researcher, educator; b. Balt., June 8, 1958; s. Lee Crandall and Barbara Ann (Merrick) P.; m. Stephanie Suzanne Reynolds, June 22, 1985; 1 child, Nicholas Timothy. BA in Psychology, Johns Hopkins U., 1982; MSc in Exptl. Psychology, U. Md.,

1984, PhD in Exptl. Psychology, 1988. Postdoctoral fellow Inst. Cellular and Molecular Embryology, Paris, 1989; postdoctoral rsch. assoc. dept. zoology U. Tex., 1989—94; asst. prof. dept. biol. scis. U. Ill., Chgo., 1994—2000, assoc. prof. dept. biol. scis., 2000—. Contbr. articles and chpts. to profl. jours. and books. Grantee NIMH, 1986-88, Nat. Ctr. Sci. Rsch., Paris, 1989, NIH, 1989-90, 1997-2003, Nat. Orgn. Hearing Rsch., 1996-97; Alexander von Humboldt Rsch. fellowship, Zool. Inst., U. Munich, 1993-94, Max Planck Inst. Neurobiology, Munich, 2001-02. Mem. AAAS, Soc. Neurosci., Assn. Rsch. in Otolaryngology. Achievements include research in neurobiology of sensory information processing and sensorimotor integration. Office: Univ Ill Chgo Dept Biol Sci Neurobiology Group 840 W Taylor St Chicago IL 60607

PARK, WILLIAM ANTHONY (TONY), lawyer; b. Blackfoot, Idaho, June 4, 1934; s. William Clair and Thelma Edelweiss (Shear) P.; m. Elizabeth Taylor, Aug. 26, 1961 (div.); children: Susan E., W. Adam, Patricia A.; m. Gail Chaloupka, Aug. 6, 1983. AA, Boise Jr. Coll., 1954; BA, U. Idaho, 1958; JD, U. Idaho, 1963. Bar: Idaho 1963. Sole practice, Boise, Idaho, 1963-70, 82-83; atty. gen. State of Idaho, 1971-75; ptnr. Park & Meuleman, Boise, 1975-81, Park & Burkett, Boise, 1983-84, Martin, Chapman, Park & Burkett, Boise, 1984-90, Park, Costello & Burkett, Boise, 1990-93, Park, Redford, Thomas & Burkett, Boise, 1994-97, Park, Thomas, Burkett & Williams, Boise, 1997-99; of counsel Huntley Park (formerly Huntley, Park, Thomas, Burkett, Olsen & Williams), Boise, 1999—. Chmn. Idaho Bicentennial Commn., 1971—77; bd. dirs. ACLU, Idaho, 1996—2000, pres. Idaho, 1997—99; chmn. Idaho State Dem. Party, 1998—99; bd. dirs. Radio Free Europe/Radio Liberty, Inc., 1977—82, Am. Lung Assn., 1978—90, Am. Lung Assn. Washington/Idaho, 1976—96, pres., 1991—95, 2002—04, bd. dirs., 1999—. With US Army, 1956—58. Recipient Disting. Svc. award. Home: 706 Warm Springs Ave Boise ID 83712-6420 Office: PO Box 2188 Boise ID 83701-2188 Office Phone: 208-345-7800. Personal E-mail: gchaloupka@msn.com. Business E-Mail: wap@huntleypark.com.

PARK, WILLIAM H(ERRON), finance company executive; b. Monongahela, Pa., Sept. 19, 1947; s. William M. and Marjorie (Herron) Park; m. Mary Cornell, June 25, 1977; children: William H., Douglas C. BS in Indsl. Engring. with distinction, Cornell U., 1969, MBA, 1970. Engr. True Temper Corp., Geneva, Ohio, 1970-72; with Price Waterhouse & Co., Boston, 1972-82; exec. v.p., CFO United Asset Mgmt. Corp., Boston, 1982—2001; v.p. The UAM Funds, 1982—2001; pres., CEO Prizm Capital Mgmt., 2001—05; CEO Structured Capital Ptnrs., 2005; vice chmn. Comml. Indsl. Fin. Corp., 2006—. Bd. dirs. No. Light Asset Mgmt.; bd. trustees Eaton Vance Group of Mut. Funds, 2003—. Treas., trustee Tower Sch. in Marblehead, 1982—92; trustee Proctor Acad., 1998—2006; bd. dirs. Nat. Com. to Preserve Social Security and Medicare, 1997—2005, chmn., 2000—03; bd. dirs. Chautauqua Found., Inc., 1992—2005. Home: 3 Fort Sewall Ter Marblehead MA 01945-3505 Office: Charlesbank Capital Ptnrs 200 Clarendon St 54th Fl Boston MA 02116 Personal E-mail: parkwilliam@comcast.net. Business E-Mail: wpark@cifc.com.

PARK, WILLIAM WYNNEWOOD, law educator; b. Phila., July 2, 1947; s. Oliver William and Christine (Lindes) Park. BA, Yale U., 1969; JD, Columbia U., 1972; MA, Cambridge U., 1975. Bar: Mass. 1972, DC 1980. Law practice, Paris, 1972-79; prof. law Boston U., 1979—, dir. Ctr. Banking Law Studies, 1990—93. V.p. London Ct. Internat. Arbitration; vis. prof. U. Dijon, France, 1983—84, Inst. U. Hautes Etudes Internat., Geneva, 1983, U. Hong Kong, 1990; arbitrator Claims Resolution Tribunal Dormant Accts., Switzerland, 1998—2002, Internat. Commn. Holocaust Era Ins. Claims, London. Author: International Chamber of Commerce Arbitration, 3d edit., 2000, International Forum Selection, 1995, International Commercial Arbitration, 1997, Arbitration in Banking and Finance, 1998, Income Tax Treaty Arbitration, 2004, Arbitration of International Business Disputes, 2006; gen. editor: Arbitration Internat.; contbr. articles to profl. jours. Trustee Mass. Bible Soc.; sr. warden King's Chapel, Boston. Fellow, Selwyn Coll., Cambridge, Eng., 1975—77. Fellow: Coll. Comml. Arbitrators, Chartered Inst. Arbitrators (U.K.); mem.: ABA (chmn. internat. dispute resolution com.). Home: 36 King St Cohasset MA 02025-1304 Office: Boston Univ Law Sch 765 Commonwealth Ave Boston MA 02215-1401 Office Phone: 617-353-3149.

PARK, WON KUK, foundation administrator; b. Bukchang Dong, Chung-Ku, Korea, Mar. 24, 1929; s. Jun Seop and Kum Sun (Song) P. BA in Economics, Sungkyunkwan U., Seoul, Korea, 1957; MA in Economics, Am. U., 1960; PhD in Economics, Kyunghee U., Seoul, Korea, 1975; PhD (hon.), Caldwell Coll., 1997. Asst. prof. Duksung Women's U., Seoul, Republic of Korea, 1961-63, assoc. prof., 1965-67, v.p., 1965-70, prof., 1967-77, pres., 1970-77, chmn. bd. trustees Duksung Sch. Found., 1979—2001; asst. prof. Kyunghee U., Seoul, Republic of Korea, 1963-65; v.p. Korean Pvt. Ednl. Found., Seoul, Republic of Korea, 1987-90, Korean Assn. for Univ. Found., Seoul, Republic of Korea, 1987-92. Dir. Korean Pvt. Ednl. Found., Seoul, 1978—, Korean Assn. for Univ. Found., 1987—. Chmn. bd. trustees Jungam Found. of Culture in Korea, 2002—. Recipient Choon Kang award, Republic of Korea, 1995. Mem. Korean Sect. World Edn. Fellowship (v.p. 1987—), The Seoul Ctrl. Club of Good Will.

PARK, YONG JIN, lawyer; b. Daejeon, Korea, Oct. 13, 1953; BA Coll. Bus. & Economics, Yonsei U., Korea, 1976; MBA, NYU, 1982; JD, Pa. State U., 1988. Bar: NY 1989, US Dist. Ct. Ea. Dist. NY, US Dist. Ct. No. Dist. NY. Ptnr. Wilson, Elser, Moskowitz, Edelman & Dicker LLP, NYC. Mem.: ABA. Office: Wilson Elser Moskowitz Edelman & Dicker LLP 23rd Fl 150 E 42nd St New York NY 10017-5639 Office Phone: 212-490-3000 ext. 2864. Office Fax: 212-490-3038. Business E-Mail: parky@wemed.com.

PARK, YOUNG H., dean; b. Kyung-Buk, Korea, Aug. 5, 1937; s. Won K. Park and Tae S. Lee; m. Jong-Hwa Park, Oct. 20, 1967; children: Grace, David. BD, Presbyn. Gen. Assembly Theol. Seminary, 1961; BA in English Lit., Kyung Hee U., Seoul, 1963; BD, Covenant Theol. Sem., St. Louis, 1967, M in Theology, 1968; MA in Bibl. Lit., St. Louis U., 1973; PhD in Theology, Calif. Grad. Sch. Theol., 1978. Lic. Midwestern Presbyn., 1970. Minister First Presbyn. Ch., St. Louis, 1970—83; prof. New Testament Chongshin U., Seoul, 1983—86, pres., 1986—92; dean grad. sch. Midwest Theol. U., St. Louis, 1992—93, acad. dean, 2002—; pres. Taeshin Christian U., Taegu, Republic of Korea, 1994—2002. Author: Exegetical Principles of N.T., 1988, A Study of Christological Titles, 1990. Avocations: classical music, reading, walking, travel. Home: 1322 Creve Coeur Mill Saint Louis MO 63146 Office: Midwest Univ 851 Parr Rd Wentzville MO 63385 Personal E-mail: younghpark@sbcglobal.net.

PARKE, DAVID ALAN, lawyer; b. Marlboro, Mass., May 23, 1953; s. Richard Alan Parke and Barbara Ann Morse; m. Patrice Ann Meacham, Aug. 5, 1955; 1 child, Geoffrey David. BA, U. Pa., Phila., 1975; JD, Georgetown U., Washington, 1979. Bar: Mass. 1980. Ptnr. Bulkley, Richardson and Gelinas LLP, Springfield, Mass., 1980—. Bd. dirs. Safety Coun. Western New England, Inc., Springfield, 2004—, Affiliated C. of C. Greater Springfield, Inc., 2006—. Author: Forming a Massachusetts Corporation Under Chapter 156D, 2005; contbg. author: Doing Business in States Other Than State of Incorporation, 2006. Mem. fin. com. Town of Wilbraham, Mass., 2005—. Mem.: Mass. Bar Assn. (mem. bus. law sect. coun. 2004—). Office: Bulkley Richardson and Gelinas LLP 1500 Main St Springfield MA 01115 Office Phone: 413-272-6257.

PARKE, DAVID WILKIN, II, ophthalmologist, educator, health facility administrator; b. Columbus, Ohio, May 19, 1951; s. David William Parke and Eunice Joyce Erikson; m. Julie Diane Thorne, Sept. 15, 1975; children: David W. III, Laura Thorne, Lindsey Diane. AB, Stanford U., 1973; MD, Baylor Coll. Medicine, 1977. Diplomate Am. Bd. Ophthalmology. Resident in internal medicine Baylor Coll. Medicine, Houston, 1977-78, resident in ophthalmology, 1978-81, fellow in med. retina, 1981-82, asst. prof., 1983-90, assoc. prof., 1990-92; fellow diseases and surgery of the retina and vitreous Med. Coll. of Wis., 1982-83; prof., chair dept. ophthalmology U. Okla., Oklahoma City, 1992—; pres., CEO McGee Eye Inst., Oklahoma City, 1992—. Chmn., bd. dirs. Medem, Inc., 2004—; vice chair Ophthalmic Mut. Ins. Co., 2005—. Active Okla. Econ. Devel. Found., 1992, Okla. Health Ctr. Found., 1992—; trustee Presbyn. Health Found., 1995-2006, Casady Sch., 1997-2004, vice chair, 1999-2004; mng. dir. Stephenson Laser Ctr., 1996—; bd. mgrs. Okla. Health Alliance, 1995-97; dir. Oklahoma City C. of C. Fellow: Am. Acad. Ophthalmology (assoc. sec. 1983—92, trustee 2000—, sr. sec. for ophthalmic practice 2002—, pres.-elect 2007, Honor award 1980, Sr. Honor award 1998); mem.: Am. Soc. Ret. Specialists, Retina Soc., Assn. Univ. Profs. Ophthalmology (trustee 1997—2003, pres. 2001—02), Greater Oklahoma City C. of C. (bd. dirs. 1998—99, 2004—), Alpha Omega Alpha. Office: Dean A McGee Eye Institute 608 Stanton L Young Blvd Oklahoma City OK 73104-5065 E-mail: david-parke@ouhsc.edu.

PARKE, M(ARGARET) JEAN, retired business owner, editor; b. Akron, Ohio, Aug. 23, 1920; d. Lawrence William and Rosella (Washburn) Beat; m. Harry Morris Parke, July 25, 1942; children: Richard Blake, Catherine Jean. BA magna cum laude, U. Toledo, 1942, MA, 1959. Adminstrv. asst. Dist. Office Price Adminstrn., Toledo, 1943-45; editing cons. Century Press, Inc., Toledo, 1955-72; cons. women's progs. U. Toledo, 1973-75; reports editor Price-Waterhouse & Co., Cleve., 1976-78; fin. officer, ptnr. Parke Supply Co., Avon Lake, Ohio, 1980-86; co-owner, sec. Woodlark Farms, Inc., Georgetown, Ky., 1978-94. Bd. trustees, past pres. Avon Lake Pub. Libr., 1981-90, Friends of the U. Toledo Libr., past pres. 1971-74; founding trustee Friends of Toledo-Lucas county Pub. Libr., 1970-73; trustee Avon Lake Pub. Libr. Found., Inc., 1991-97; organizer, past pres. Parkview Hosp. Evening Guild, Toledo, 1953; incorporator, sec. Ch. Women United of Toledo area, 1963-66; bd. dirs. LWV, Sylvania, Ohio, Avon Lake; mem. Friends of Avon Lak Libr. Jean Parke Conf. Rm. named in her honor Avon Lake Pub. Libr., 1981. Mem. AAUW (past pres., bd. dirs. Toledo br. 1981-90, Ednl. Found. Prog. honoree 1981), Avon on the Lake Garden Club, U. Toledo Alumni Assn. (trustee, officer Blue T award 1981), Chi Omega Alumnae Toledo (officer), Chi Omega Alumnae Ohio (state bd. dirs. 1983-85, Outstanding Ohio Chi Omega Alumna 1982). Republican. Episcopalian. Avocations: travel, great books, theater, college football, needlecrafts. Home: 32821 Tanglewood Ct Avon Lake OH 44012-1540

PARKE, TERRY RICHARD, state legislator; b. Pittsfield, Ill., Feb. 21, 1944; m. Joanne Toombs; 2 children. BS, 1970. Mem. Ill. Ho. of Reps. from 44th dist., 1985—. Rep. spokesman ins. com., mem. telecom. com.; mem. labor com.; mem. consumer protection, mem. environment and energy com., mem. environ. health com.; co-chmn. Ill. Commn. on Govt. Forecasting and Accountability; mem. Employee Suggestion Award Bd.; past pres. Elgin Area Life Underwriters. Exec. comm. Bus. and Labor Am. Legis. Exch. Coun. Past Pres. and Nat. Coun. of Ins. Legis.; past pres. N.W. Schaumburg Assn. Commerce and Industry; bd. dirs., Boy Scouts Northwest Suburban Coun.; past mem. Girl Scouts Crossroads Coun. Mem. Rotary (past pres. Schaumburg club). Republican. Office: 220 State House Springfield IL 62706-0001 also: 837 W Higgins Rd Schaumburg IL 60195 Home: 6098 Delaney Dr Hoffman Estates IL 60192-4811 Office Phone: 847-882-0270. Personal E-mail: cityparkxx@yahoo.com.

PARKEL, JAMES G., former health association administrator; BS in Elec. Engring., U. Denver; LLD (hon.), Am. Grad. Sch. Internat. Mgmt. Exec. mgmt. IBM Internat. Found., 1961—93; pres.-elect AARP, 2000—02, pres., 2002—04. Chair AARP Andrus Found.; mem. bd. councilors Andrus Gerontology Ctr., U. So. Calif. Mem. Madison Coun. Libr. of Congress; former pres. and CEO Junior Achievement Internat.; former chair Junior Achievement Westchester; former nat. bd. mem. Junior Achievement; bd. dirs. Danbury Hosp., New Fairfield Cmty. Trust, Am. Grad. Sch. Internat. Mgmt. Mem.: Soc. Human Resource Mgmt. (past nat. chair).

PARKER, ALAN JOHN, veterinary neurologist, educator, researcher; b. Portsmouth, Eng., Oct. 28, 1944; arrived in U.S., 1969, naturalized, 2002; s. William Barton and Emily (Begley) P.; m. Heather Margaret Nicholson, Oct. 30, 1971; children: Alyxander John, Robert William. BSc with honors, Bristol U., 1966, BVSc with honors, 1968; MS, U. Ill., 1973, PhD, 1976. Diplomate Am. Coll. Vet. Internal Medicine-Neurology, European Coll. Vet. Neurology. Intern Vet. Coll., U. Calif.-Davis, 1969—70; instr. vet. clin. medicine U. Ill., Urbana, 1970—71, 1972—76, asst. prof., 1976—77, assoc. prof., 1977—82, prof., 1982—2000, prof. emeritus, 2001—. Cons. pharm. cos., seminar presenter; cons. in neurology Berwyn Vet. Hosp., Chgo., 1973—, Lake Shore Animal Hosp., Chgo., 1978-03. Contbr. numerous articles to sci. jours., chpts. to books. Active Boy Scouts Am., Champaign, Ill., 1982—; active Presbyn. Ch., Monticello, Ill., 1979-2006. Recipient Vigil Honor and Founder's award Order of the Arrow, Silver Beaver award Boy Scouts Am.; sci. grantee various orgns., 1972-2000. Mem. AVMA, Am. Animal Hosp. Assn., Brit. Vet. Assn., Ill. State Vet. Assn. Republican. Office: 2845 S Harlem Ave Berwyn IL 60402 Office Phone: 708-749-4200.

PARKER, ALICE, composer; b. Boston, Dec. 16, 1925; d. Gordon and Mary (Stuart) P.; widowed; children: David, Timothy, Katharine, Mary, Elizabeth. BA, Smith Coll., Northampton, Mass., 1947; MS, Juilliard Sch., NYC, 1949; MusD (hon.), Hamilton U., 1979, Macalester Coll., St. Paul, 1989, Bluffton Coll., Ohio, 1991, Westminster Choir Coll., Princeton, NJ, 1996, Shenandoah U., Winchester, Va., 2007. Arranger Robert Shaw Chorale, NYC, 1948-66; artistic dir. Melodious Accord, NYC, 1985—. Tchr., workshop leader Westminster Choir Coll., Princeton, N.J., summers, 1972-98; McDonald chair Emory U., 2003. Composer 4 operas, 41 cantatas, 8 song cycles and numerous anthems and suites. Recipient composer's award ASCAP, 1968—, AGO Disting. Composer of the Yr., 2000, Barlow Endowment, 1992, spl. award Nat. Endowment Arts, 1976, Gottschalk award Pioneer Valley Symphony, 2003, Lifetime Achievement award Choral Arts New Eng., 2004. Fellow Hymn Soc., Hymn Soc. Am. (conf. composer in residence, 2006); mem. Am. Choral Dirs. Assn. (ea. disvn. conf. dedicated in her honor 2006), Am. Condrs. Guild, Chorus Am. (Founders award 1994), Am. Music ctr., Sigma Alpha Iota. Office: Melodious Accord Inc Park West Sta PO Box 20801 New York NY 10025-1523 Personal E-mail: alice@aliceparker.com.

PARKER, BARRINGTON D., JR., federal judge, lawyer; b. Washington, Aug. 21, 1944; BA, Yale U., 1965, JD, 1969. Bar: NY 1971. Law clk. to Hon. Aubrey E. Robinson, US Dist. Ct. for DC, Washington, 1969-70; assoc. Sullivan & Cromwell, NYC, 1970-77; ptnr. Parker Auspitz Neesemann & Delehanty, P.C., NYC, 1977-87, Morrison & Foerster, NYC, 1987-94; judge US Dist. Ct. for so. dist. NY, White Plains, 1994—2001, US Ct. Appeals (2nd cir.), NY, 2001—. Bd. dirs., v.p. NAACP Legal Def. and Educational Fund, Inc., 1980—; com. on grievances, com. on civil discovery US Dist. Ct. (so. dist.) NY, 1983—; com. on pre-trial phase civil cases US Ct. Appeals (2nd cir.) 1983—. Trustee Governance Inst., Greenwich Acad., South Africa Legal Svcs. and Legal Edn. Project, Inc.; successor trustte an mem. Yale Corp. Mem. ABA, Fed. Bar Coun., Assn. Bar City NY (com. on the judiciary 1978-82, exec. com. 1982-86, nominating com. 1987), Coun. on Fgn. Rels. Office: US Courthouse 300 Quarropas St Rm 633 White Plains NY 10601-4150 also: Thurogood Marshall US Courthouse 40 Foley Square New York NY 10007 also: US Courthouse Two Stamford Plz 281 Tresser Blvd Stamford CT 06901 *

PARKER, BOBBY DOUGLAS, radio broadcaster, educator, photographer; b. Anthony, Kans., Feb. 12, 1935; s. Luther Joseph and Inez Beatrice (Lawrence) P.; m. Nelda Arlene Parker, Aug. 23, 1958; children: Steven Douglas, Gregory Allen, Kirby Lynn. Attended Kans. State U., Manhattan, 1953-56; B. Music Edn., Wichita State U., 1960, M. Music Edn., 1964; specialists in edn. cert. U. Colo., 1975; student portraits for small studio Brooks Inst. Photography, Santa Barbara, Calif., 1982; student Nikon Sch. Photography, 1980; grad. with spl. honors Modern Sch. Photography, NYC, 1981, NY Inst. Profl. Photography, 1982. Cert. tchr., Kans.; 3d class radio lic., Kans., Colo. Tchr. elem. and sr. HS vocal music Moscow Pub. Schs., Kans., 1960-64, jr. and sr. high sch. vocal music Sublette Pub. Schs., Kans., 1966-73; salesman, announcer Sta.-KLEY, Wellington, Kans., 1966-73; tchr. vocal music Jefferson County Pub. Sch., Colo., 1973-1993; instr. photography, dark-room techniques, 1981—; owner, photographer Universal Creations, Arvada, Colo., 1979—; tour guide Coors Brewery; dir. ch. choirs, 1958-75, including First United Methodist Ch., Wellington, 1966-73; choir dir. Sumner County Cmty. Chorus, Kans., 1966-73; dir. prize-winning music groups in contests. Mem. Colo. Tchrs. Assn., NEA, Music Educators Nat. Conf., Am. Choral Dirs. Assn., Profl. Photographers Am. (2 Nat. award merits), Wedding Photographers Internat. (Hon. award in photography at convs. 1981, 82), Photographers Soc. Am., Phi Delta Kappa, Phi Mu Alpha. Democrat. Clubs: Masons (Wellington); Shriners (Denver). Home: 9157 W 101st Ave Broomfield CO 80021-3869 Personal E-mail: bobby1406@comcast.net.

PARKER, BONITA M., civil rights organization executive; b. Jan. 23, 1968; married; 2 children. Degree in Fin., DePaul U. Several positions with Urban Fin. Services, Am. Bankers Assn.; intern Northern Trust Co., second v.p.; co-owner Skills For Life Tng. Co.; dir., Investments and Econ. Empowerment Salem Bapt. Ch., Chgo.; COO Rainbow/Push Coalition, Chgo. Fin. specialist USAR. Mem.: Nat. Assn. County Officials. Office: RainbowPush Coaltion 930 E 50th St Chicago IL 60615-2702 Home Phone: 708-331-5473; Office Phone: 773-551-8661. Personal E-mail: bp5225@aol.com.

PARKER, BRENT MERSHON, retired medical educator, internist, cardiologist; b. St. Louis, July 3, 1927; s. William Bahlmann and Florence (Mershon) P.; m. Martha Shelton, Aug. 1, 1953; children: Martha Parker Burgess, Elizabeth, Margaret. MD cum laude, Wash. U., St. Louis, 1952. Diplomate Am. Bd. Internal Medicine. Intern and asst. resident N.Y. Hosp.-Cornell, NYC, 1952-54; asst. resident, fellow Barnes Hosp., Wash. U., St. Louis, 1954-57; cardiology sect. chief VA Hosp., U. Oreg., Portland, 1957-59; asst. prof. to assoc. prof., co-dir. cardiovascular div., chief adult cardiac catherization Wash. U. Sch. Medicine, St. Louis, 1959-73; prof. medicine U. Mo., Columbia, 1973-89, prof. emeritus, 1989-94, chief of staff, assoc. dean, 1976-82, chief of cardiology, 1983-89. Mem. colloquium faculty Merck, Sharp and Dohme, West Point, Pa., 1980-86. Author or co-author 58 papers in referred jours., 6 book chpts., teaching papers, others. Bd. dirs. St. Louis Heart Assn., 1962-73, v.p. 1972-73; bd. dirs. Mo. Heart Assn., 1965-75, pres. 1970-71. Served with USN, 1945-46. Recipient Arthur Strauss award St. Louis Heart Assn., 1973, 3 teaching awards U. Mo. Sch. Medicine, 1974, 75, 86, Preventive Cardiology Acad. award, Nat. Heart Lung and Blood Inst., 1982-87, Alumni Achievement award Washington Univ. Sch. Medicine, 1992; Brent Mershon Parker professorship estab. in honor U. Mo., 1989. Fellow ACP, Am. Coll. Cardiology (Mo., Kans. council rep. 1973-77), Clin. Cardiology Soc. Am. Heart Assn.; mem. Am. Fedn. Clin. Research, Cen. Soc. for Clin. Research, Alpha Omega Alpha, Sigma Xi. Episcopalian. Avocations: choral singing, jogging, camping, back packing.

PARKER, C. ALLEN, lawyer; b. Jacksonville, Fla., Feb. 17, 1955; BA magna cum laude, Duke Univ., 1977; MA, Univ. Chgo., 1980; JD magna cum laude, Columbia Univ., 1983. Bar: NY 1985. Law clk., Hon. Amalya L. Kearse US Ct. of Appeals, 2nd Cir.; assoc. Cravath Swaine & Moore LLP, NYC, 1984—90, ptnr., corp., 1990—. Mem.: NY State Bar Assn. Office: Cravath Swaine & Moore LLP Worldwide Plz 825 Eighth Ave New York NY 10019-7475 Office Phone: 212-474-1765. Office Fax: 212-474-3700. Business E-Mail: aparker@cravath.com.

PARKER, CATHERINE L., theater educator; b. Warren, Mich., Dec. 12, 1973; d. Carl and Elinor Russo; m. Nathan T. Parker; 1 child, Owen Travis. MA, Ea. Mich. U., Ypsilanti, 1996—99. Asst. prof. theatre Rochester Coll., Rochester Hills, Mich., 1997—. Worship team leader Heritage Ch. Christ, Clawson, Mich., 2005—06. Office: Rochester Coll 800 W Avon Rd Rochester Hills MI 48307 Business E-Mail: cparker@rc.edu.

PARKER, CLEA EDWARD, retired university president; b. Talisheek, La., Apr. 2, 1927; s. William A. and Lutritia (Davis) P.; m. Peggy Ann Faciane, June 21, 1953; children: Brian, Stephen, Karen, Robin. BA, Southeastern La. U., 1948; M.Ed., La. State U., 1952, Ed.D., 1965. Coach, tchr. Rugby Acad., New Orleans, 1948-50; tchr., prin., supr. instr., dir. curriculum and instrn. St. Tammany Parish Sch. Bd., 1950-67; prof. edn., head dept. student teaching Nicholls State Coll., Thibodaux, La., 1967-68; acting pres. Southeastern La. U., Hammond, 1968, pres., 1968-80, pres. emeritus, 1980—86. Liaison La. State Dept. Edn., Higher Edn. and Bds. for Edn. in La., 1986; vis. lectr. La. State U. at NC, 1965-69; past pres. St. Tammany Parish Tchrs. Assn., La. Assn. Supervision and Curriculum Devel.; past pres. elementary dept. La. Tchrs. Assn.; chmn. Pres.'s Coun. La. Bd. Edn., 1972-73; v.p. Conf. La. Colls. and Univs., 1973-74, pres., 1974-75; pres. elect Gulf South Conf., 1974-75, pres., 1975-76; mem. Steering Com. on Curriculum Devel. and Revision for Career Edn. for State La., 1973; mem. adv. council for State Plan for Career Edn., 1973 Mem. planning com. Gov.'s Conf. on Aging, 1976; v.p. chpt. 15 La. Good Samaritans, 1987-88; bd. dirs. Assn. for Retarded Citizens, pres.-elect, 1981; mem. Zemurray Park Recreation Commn., Hammond, 1992-95; chmn. bd. dirs. Lallie Kemp Meml. Hosp., 1993-94; bd. dirs. Lallie Kemp Med. Ctr., 1994—, chmn., 1994-95. With USCGR, 1945, 93-94. Named Hon. State Farmer La., 1970, Disting. Alumnus of Yr., Southeastern La. U. Alumni Assn., 1977, 91, 92; inductee La. Spl. Olympics Hall of Fame, 1998. Mem. Am. Assn. State Colls. and Univs. (com. on nat. svc. 1972-73, task force on aging 1975-76, 78-79, nominating com. 1977—, state Rep. for La. 1979—, com. agr. renewable resources and rural devel. 1979-80, Svc. to Edn. award 1980), Hammond C. of C., La. Assn. for Sch. Execs., Ozone Ramblers Camping Club (pres. 1988), KC (lectr. 1982, 85, 90-91, chancellor 1983-84, 87—, dep. grand knight 1995-96), Rotary (bd. dirs. Hammond, internat. svc. dir. 1972), Phi Delta Kappa, Kappa Delta Pi. Home: 10 Golden Dr Hammond LA 70401-1010 Personal E-mail: ceparker10@bellsouth.net.

PARKER, DAVID B., lawyer; b. NYC, Nov. 16, 1947; s. Herman and Beatrice (Dolgins) P.; m. Ronnie Beth Weiss, May 20, 1979. AB cum laude, Brown U., 1969; JD, Yale U., 1973. Bar: NY 1974, US Dist. Ct. (so. and ea. dist.) NY 1975, US Tax Ct. (2d cir.) 1986, US Ct. of Appeals (2nd cir.) 1985, US Tax Ct. 1991, US Claims Ct. & US Ct. of Appeals (fed. cir.). Assoc. Skadden, Arps, Slate, Meagher and Flom, NYC, 1973-81; ptnr. Olshan Grundman and Frome, NYC, 1981-85, Kraver and Parker, NYC, 1985-88, Kleinberg, Kaplan, Wolff & Cohen, P.C., NYC, 1988—. Contbg. author: Business Competitor Intelligence, 1984. Dir. Legal Svs. NYC, 1983—; trustee Horace Mann Sch., 2001—; trustee & officer Pk. Ave. Synagogue, 1991—2003, hon. trustee & v.p., 2003—; mem., bd. dir. NYC Justice Project, 2006—. Mem. Assn. Bar City of NY, Phi Beta Kappa.

Office: Kleinberg Kaplan Wolff & Cohen 551 5th Ave New York NY 10036-7601 Office Phone: 212-986-6000. Office Fax: 212-986-8866.

PARKER, DENNIS GENE, former sheriff, martial arts instructor; b. Kansas City, Kans., Jan. 5, 1956; s. Billy Gene and Lola Ruth (Martens) Parker; m. Brenda Jean Hamre, June 30, 1972 (div. 1989); children: Heatheryn Ruth, Jessica Elise. Student, U. Kans., 1984. Nat. accredited police firearms instr. and expert., police side handle baton instr. Martial arts instr. Northland Tai-Ryuku, Kansas City, Mo., 1974-84; anti-terrorist/hostage rescue specialist ITC CITRO, 1977—80; anti-terrorist team mem. USNSAD, Mid. East, 1980—81; police cpl. Atchison (Kans.) Dept. Police, 1984-90; estate investigator Am. Rsch. Bur., LA, 1990; sheriff Atchison County, Kans., 1990-94; instr. martial arts, including Shito-Ryu Okinawa-TE, Tang Soo Do Mu Duk Kwon, Chinese Wu-Shu Chin Na. Bd. dirs. Atchison County Community Corrections; team mem. Atchison County Multidisciplinary Child Protection Team, 1992—; bd. dirs. N.E. Kans. Drug Task Force, Oskaloosa, 1990-91. Author: Surviving the Badge, 2005. Bd. dirs. N.E. Kans. Community Action Program, Atchison, 1991—, Atchison Area Drug Task Force, 1993—. Recipient Silver Star for Bravery Am. Police Hall of Fame, 1992, Honor award, 1992, John Edgar Hoover Meml. award Nat. Assn. Chiefs of Police and Police Hall of Fame, 1993, State of Kans. medals of valor, 1992, 93, Pres.'s Nat. medal of patriotism, 1993, APD Life Saving award and commendation, 1987, knight chevalier medal Am. Police Hall of Fame, 1992, Medal of Valor Atchison County, 1992, U.S. Cold War Recognition award, 2000. Mem. World Black Belt Bur., Sandan-3d Level Black Shito-Ryu Okinawa Te. Baptist. Home and Office: 5125 NW Parkdale Rd Kansas City MO 64151-3205 Home Phone: 816-728-8087; Office Phone: 816-505-0949. Personal E-mail: dparker20@kc.rr.com.

PARKER, DENNY S., engineering company executive; BA, U. Calif., Berkeley, 1965, MS, 1966, PhD, 1970. Sr. v.p. Brown and Caldwell Inc., Walnut Creek, Calif. Mem.: NAE. Office: Brown & Caldwell PO Box 8045 Walnut Creek CA 94596-1220

PARKER, DIANA LYNNE, restaurant manager, special events director; b. Eureka, Calif., June 21, 1957; d. Carol Dean and Lynne Diane (Havemann) P. BA in English, Humboldt U., Arcata, Calif., 1981, post-grad., 1982—84. Lic. real estate agent, Calif. Retail clk. Safeway, Inc., Eureka, 1977-84; caterer, owner TD Catering, Eureka, 1982-84; asst. buyer Macy's Calif., San Francisco, 1984-85; realtor Mason-McDuffie, Alameda, Calif., 1985-87; host, Rotunda Restaurant Neiman Marcus, San Francisco, 1987-89, asst. mgr. Rotunda Restaurant, 1989—96, dir. spl. events, 1989—96, mgr. dining room Rotunda Restaurant, 1996—2006, gen. mgr. food svc., 2007—. Mem.: Nat. Assn. Catering Execs., San Francisco Visitor and Conv. Bur., Women Chefs and Restaurateurs, Mus. Modern Art, Commonwealth Club Calif. Republican. Avocations: gourmet cooking, art, antiques. Office: Rotunda at Neiman Marcus 150 Stockton St San Francisco CA 94108-5807 Office Phone: 415-362-4777.

PARKER, DOUG (WILLIAM DOUGLAS PARKER, W. DOUGLAS PARKER), air transportation executive; m. Gwen Parker; 3 children. BA in Econ., Albion Coll., 1984; MBA, Vanderbilt U., 1986. Various fin. mgmt. positions Am. Airlines, 1986—91; v.p., fin. planning and analysis, v.p., asst. treas. Northwest Airlines; sr. v.p., CFO Am. West Holdings, 1995—99, exec. v.p., corp. group, 1999—2000, pres., COO, 2000—01, chmn., pres., CEO, 2001—05; interim pres. US Airways Group Inc., Tempe, Ariz., 2005, chmn., CEO, 2005—. Recipient Disting. Alumnus award, Vanderbilt U. Owen Grad. Sch. Mgmt., 2004. Methodist. Office: US Airways 111 W Rio Salado Pkwy Tempe AZ 85281 *

PARKER, EDWIN BURKE, communications executive; b. Berwyn, Alta., Can., Jan. 19, 1932; m. Frances G. Spigai, 1976; children: David Kendall, Karen Liane. BA, U. B.C., Can., 1954; MA, Stanford U., 1958, PhD in Mass Comms., 1960. Staff reporter Vancouver (Can.) Sun., 1954-55; info. officer U. B.C., Vancouver, 1955-57; rsch. asst. Inst. Comms. Rsch. Stanford U., 1957-60, asst. prof., 1962-63, assoc. prof., 1963-71, prof., 1971-79; v.p. Equatorial Comms. Co., 1979-85, chmn. bd. dirs., 1986-87; pres. data networks divsn. CONTEL, 1987-88; pres. Parker Telecomm., Gleneden Beach, Oreg., 1989—. Asst. prof. Communications U. Ill., Urbana, 1960-62. Ctr. for Advanced Studies in Behavioral Sci. fellow, 1969-70; named Leader of Yr., Oreg. Local Econ. Devel., 1995, Man of Yr., Lincoln City, 2005. Avocation: bridge. Office: Parker Telecommunications PO Box 402 Gleneden Beach OR 97388-0402 Office Phone: 541-764-3058. Business E-Mail: edparker@teleport.com.

PARKER, ELIZABETH RINDSKOPF, dean, law educator; b. Detroit, Dec. 2, 1943; d. Arthur C. and Kathryn G. (Rodgers) Roediger; m. Peter E. Rindskopf, May 25, 1968; 1 child; m. Robert Parker. BA in Philosophy cum laude, U. Mich., 1964, JD, 1968. Bar: Ga. 1968, U.S. Dist. Ct. (no. dist.) Ga. 1969, U.S. Ct. Appeals (5th cir.) 1970, U.S. Supreme Ct. 1971, U.S. Ct. Appeals (6th cir.) 1972, U.S. Ct. Appeals (3rd cir.) 1974, U.S. Ct. Appeals (4th cir.) 1977, U.S. Ct. Appeals (9th cir.) 1978, D.C. 1979. Reginald Heber Smith fellow, mng. atty. Emory Legal Svcs., Atlanta, 1968-71; ptnr. Moore, Alexander & Rindskopf, Atlanta, 1971-74; dir. New Haven Legal Assistance Assn., Inc., 1974-76; dep. dir. Lawyers Com. Civil Rights Under Law, Washington, 1978-78; ptnr. Cohen, Vitt & Annand, Alexandria, Va., 1978-79; acting asst. dir. mergers and joint ventures, dep. asst. dir. health care Bur. of Competition, Fed. Trade Commn., 1979-81; of counsel Surrey & Morse, Washington, 1981-84; gen. counsel Nat. Security Agy., Washington, 1984-89; prin. dep. office of the legal adviser US Dept. State, Washington, 1989-90; gen. counsel CIA, Washington, 1990-95; of counsel Bryan Cave, LLP, 1995—99; gen. counsel U. Wis. Sys., 1999—2002; dean, prof. law U. Pacific McGeorge Sch. Law, Sacramento, 2002—. Co-operating atty. NAACP Legal Def. and Edn. Fund, Inc., 1971-74; trustee Monterey Inst. Internat. Studies. Contbr. articles to profl. jours. Mem. ABA (standing com. law and nat. security, counsel sect. internat. law and politics, adv. bd. Ctr. and Eastern European Law Initiative), Coun. Fgn. Rels, NAS (com. on sci. comm. and nat. security, com. on a new govt.-univ. partnership on sci. and security). Office: U of Pacific McGeorge Sch Law 3200 Fifth Ave Sacramento CA 95817 Office Phone: 916-739-7151. E-mail: elizabeth@pacific.edu.

PARKER, ELLIS D., retired military officer; b. Adams, Tenn., Nov. 1, 1932; s. Ellis A. and Lorene (Qualls) P.; m. Judy C. Matthews, Dec. 24, 1952; children: Donald S., Phillip R., David B. BS in Psychology, U. Nebr., 1972; MPA, Shippensburg U., 1979; LLD (hon.), Miles U., 1989. Rated aviator FAA. Commd. 2d lt. U.S. Army, 1957, advanced through ranks to lt. gen., 1992, aviation officer, comdr. 17th aviation brigade Republic of Korea, 1978-80; dir. requirements army staff Pentagon, Washington, 1980-83; asst. divsn. comdr. 101st airborne divsn. U.S. Army, Ft. Campbell, Ky., 1983-84, commdg. gen. Army Aviation Ctr. Sch. Ft. Rucker, Ala., 1984-89; dir. army staff Pentagon, Washington, 1989-92; bd. dirs. Can. Aviation Electronics, 1993—, chmn., CEO Can., 1993—2001, chmn. govt. security com. Bd. dirs. Doss Aviation, Colorado Springs; chmn., bd. dirs. Hammer Constrn. Co., Samson, Ala.; bd. dirs. Aereus Internat., Enterprise, Ala. Contbr. articles to profl. jour. Chmn. Fort Rucker Mus. Found., 1995—; adv. bd. Troy U., Dotham, 1992—; chair retiree coun. for chief of staff U.S. Army, 1993-99; co-chair Dept. of Def. Retiree Coun., 1994-99. Decorated D.S.M. with oak leaf cluster, D.F.C., Legion of Merit, Bronze Star with two oak leaf clusters, Meritorious Svc. medals, 23 Air medals; named to Hall of Honor Bd. by Gov. Ala., 1993—, chmn. Bd. of dirs., Enterprise Cals. C of C. Mem.: Army Assn. Am., Enterprise C. of C. (chmn bd. 1995—), Assn. U.S. Army (mem. exec. com. Ft. Rucker chpt. 1994, named to Army Aviation Hall of Fame 1994), Ret. Officers Assn. (bd. mem.), Army Aviation Assn. Am. (pres., Order of St. Michel, Gold 1992), Enterprise Rotary Club (Paul Harris fellow). Republican. Avocations: flying, hunting, fishing, volunteering in community. Home and Office: 128 Deer Run Strut Enterprise AL 36330-7812

PARKER, ELLIS JACKSON, III, lawyer, broadcaster; b. Haleyville, Ala., Oct. 2, 1931; s. Ellis J. and Elizabeth (Funderburg) P.; m. Nancy Elizabeth Bealer; children: Francis Hill, Ellis Stuart. At, U.S. Mil. Acad., West Point, NY, 1953—57; AB, U. Ala., University, 1958, LLB, 1960, JD, 1961; diploma, Droit Compare, Luxembourg, 1959; cert., Acad. Internat. Law, Hague, Netherlands, 1960. Bar: Ala. 1960, U.S. Tax Ct. 1960, U.S. Supreme Ct. 1966, U.S. Ct. Appeals D.C. 1972, Md. Ct. Appeals 1973, U.S. Ct. Claims 1977. Legis. atty. IRS, Washington, 1961—62; chief of staff to U.S. Congressman Grant Ala., 1963—64; pvt. practice Birmingham, Ala., 1964—84; spl. advisor to Pres. Richard Nixon White House, Washington, 1968—69; v.p., counsel Birmingham Broadcasting Co., 1964—83; ptnr. Taylor, Smith & Parker Law Office, Upper Marlboro, Md., 1970—86; prin., owner Ellis J. Parker, Law Office, Washington, 1986—. V.p., sec. Constrn. Components Corp., Upper Marlboro, Md., 1968-72; pres. Washington-Ala. News Reports, Washington, 1980-01, Parker Real Estate, Birmingham, Bealer-Parker, LLC, Washington; chmn. bd. Blackbelt Broadcasting Co., Selma, Ala., 1986-2000; founding mem. Women's Nat. Bank, Washington; CEO Birmingham Broadcasting Co.; ptnr. Linden Radio Joint Venture, Faunsdale, Ala., 1969-89; pres., bd. dirs. 17th St LLC, N.B. Devel. Co. LLC, Washington, 2006, Hartford E. Bealer Devel. Corp., Washington. Mem. Presdl. Inaugural Com., inaugural protocol officer V.p. Agnew, 1968; mem. steering com. Rep. Party, Balt., 1972; chmn. bd. trustees Prince George's Hist. and Cultural Trust, Upper Marlboro, 1974; chmn. bd. advisors Prince George's Equestrian Ctr., Upper Marlboro, 1980; founder, pres. bd. dirs. Hospice of Prince George's County, Upper Marlboro, 1982; mem. Upper Marlboro Devel. Com. Mem. IEEE, ABA, FCC Bar Assn., Fed. Bar Assn., Inter-Am. Bar Assn., Ala. Bar Assn., Md. Bar Assn., D.C. Bar Assn., Nat. Assn. Broadcasters, Ala. Broadcasters Assn., Balt. Coun. Fgn. Affairs, Assn. Grads. U.S. Mil. Acad., Chevy Chase Club, Md. Club, St. Andrews Soc., Met. Club, Ala. Alumni Assn., Scabbard and Blade (chmn. nat. alumni coun. 1986-2006), Pi Kappa Alpha, Sigma Delta Kappa. Home: Chateau Rambouillet 2165 Ibis Island Palm Beach FL 33480 Personal E-mail: eparker124@aol.com.

PARKER, EUGENE NEWMAN, retired physicist, retired educator; b. Houghton, Mich., June 10, 1927; s. Glenn H. and Helen (MacNair) Parker; m. Niesje Meuter, 1954; children: Joyce, Eric. BS, Mich. State U., East Lansing, 1948, DSc (hon.), 1975; PhD, Calif. Inst. Tech., Pasadena, 1951; DHC in Physics and Math. (hon.), U. Utrecht, The Netherlands, 1986; DHC in Theoretical Physics (hon.), U. Oslo, 1991. Instr. math. and astronomy U. Utah, 1951—53, asst. prof. physics, 1953—55; mem. faculty physics U. Chgo., 1955—95, prof. dept. physics, 1962—95, prof. dept. astronomy and astrophysics, 1967—95, prof. emeritus, 1995—. Author: Interplanetary Dynamical Processes, 1963, Cosmical Magnetic Fields, 1979, Spontaneous Current Sheets in Magnetic Fields, 1994, Conversations on Electric and Magnetic Fields in the Cosmos, 2007. Recipient Space Sci. award, AIAA, 1964, Chapman medal, Royal Astron. Soc., 1979, Gold medal, 1992, Disting. Alumni award, Calif. Inst. Tech., 1980, Karl Schwarzschild award, Astronomische Gesselschaft, 1990, Bruce medal, Astron. Soc. Pacific, 1997, medal, Assn. Internat. Devel. Nice (France) Obs., 1997, Kyoto prize, Inamori Found., 2003, Maxwell prize, plasma physics divsn., Am. Phys. Soc., 2003. Mem.: NAS (H. K. Arctowski award 1969, US Nat. medal of Sci. 1989), Norwegian Acad. Sci. and Letters, Am. Geophys. Union (John Adam Fleming award 1968, William Bowie medal 1990), Am. Astron. Soc. (Henry Norris Russell lectr. 1969, George Ellery Hale award 1978). Achievements include development of theory of the origin of the dipole magnetic field of Earth; prediction and theory of the solar wind and heliosphere; theoretical basis for the X-ray emission from the Sun and stars. Home: 1323 Evergreen Rd Homewood IL 60430-3410 E-mail: parker@oddjob.uchicago.edu.

PARKER, EVA ANNETTE, librarian; b. North Island, Calif., Nov. 27, 1950; d. R.L. and Eva Mae (Helm) Peters; m. Darrell Dwight Parker, Nov. 9, 1970; children: Geoff, Jenny. BS, Okla. Christian Coll., 1974; MEd, Southwestern Okla. State U., 1984. Cert. libr. media specialist. Tchr. Summer Safari program Oklahoma City Zoo, 1973; libr., tchr. Leedey (Okla.) Pub. Sch., 1983-87; prof. Draughon Tng. Inst., Wichita Falls, Tex., 1988-89; tchr. Region IX Edn. Svc. Ctr., Wichita Falls, 1990; libr. media specialist Vernon (Tex.) Mid. Sch., 1990—2003; libr. Burgess Elem. Sch., Wichita Falls, Tex., 2004—; tchr. art and sci. Vernon Kids Kollege, 1999—. Tutor Vernon Intermediate Sch., 1993—; del. alt. to NEA, Leedey, 1987; storm spotter for City of Grandfield, Okla. Contbg. author: What America's Teachers Wish Parents Knew, 1993; contbr. article to profl. jour. Tchr. Bible sch. Ch. of Christ, Iowa Park, Tex., 1987-93, Grandfield, Okla., 1994—; vol. ARC, Wichita Falls, 1987-93; coach bowling Spl. Olympics, 1992-93; coach track and field Spl. Olympics, Vernon, 1993—; bd. mem. Harvest Playhouse; spl. olympics coach. Libr. improvement grantee Okla. State Dept. Edn., Leedey, 1984, Sch.-to-Work grantee, 1996-2001. Mem. Tex. Libr. Assn., Assn. Tex. Profl. Educators, P.E.O. (pres. Okla. orgn.). Avocations: rock collecting, painting, calligraphy, reading, music. Home: 1303 W 1st St Grandfield OK 73546 Office: Kate Burgess Elem Lang and Prep Acad 3106 Maurine St Wichita Falls TX 76306 Home Phone: 580-479-5422; Office Phone: 940-716-2850. Personal E-mail: annettep_1@yahoo.com.

PARKER, EVERETT CARLTON, clergyman; b. Chgo., Jan. 17, 1913; s. Harry Everett and Lillian (Stern) P.; m. Geneva M. Jones, May 5, 1939; children: Ruth A. (Mrs. Peter Weiss), Eunice L. (Mrs. George Kolczun, Jr.), Truman E. AB, U. Chgo., 1935; BD magna cum laude, Chgo. Theol. Sem., 1943, Blatchford fellow, 1944-45, DD, 1964, Catawba Coll., Salisbury, NC, 1958; L.H.D., Fordham U., 1978, Tougaloo Coll., 1987; LLD, Coll. St. Elizabeth, 2000. Pastor Waveland Ave. Congl. Christian Ch., 1943; asst. pub. service and war program mgr. NBC, 1943-45; founder-dir. Protestant Radio Commn., 1945-50; lectr. communication Yale Div. Sch., 1946-58, dir. communications research project, 1950-54; dir. Office Communication United Ch. Christ, 1954-83; sr. research assoc., adj. prof. Fordham U., 1983—; founder citizen movement to protect minority rights in media, 1963—. Chmn. broadcasting and film commn. Nat. Coun. Chs., 1969-72, gen. bd., 1966-72; chmn. Study Commn. on Theology, Edn. and Electronic Media, 1985-87; founder Found. for Minority Interests in Media, 1985—, treas., 1985—, Hispanic Telecommunications Network, 1986-2004; adv. com. on advanced TV svcs., Consumer Adv. Group FCC, 1988-92 Producer-dir.: nat. TV programs including series Off to Adventure, 1956, Tangled World, 1965; originator: series Six American Families, PBS-TV, 1977; Author: Religious Radio, 1948, Film Use in the Church, 1953, The Television-Radio Audience and Religion, 1955, Religious Television, 1961, (with others) Television, Radio, Film for Churchmen, 1969, Fiber Optics to the Home: The Changing Future of Cable, TV and The Telephone, 1989, Social Responsibility of Television in the United States, 1994. Recipient Human Relations award Am. Jewish Com., 1966, Faith and Freedom award Religious Heritage Found., 1966, 77, Alfred I. DuPont-Columbia U. award pub. service in broadcasting, 1969; Roman Cath. Broadcasters Gabriel award pub. service, 1970; Lincoln U. award significant contbn. human relations, 1971; Racial Justice award Com. for Racial Justice, United Ch. Christ, 1973; Ch. Leadership award Coun. for Christian Social Action, 1973; Public Svc. award Black Citizens for a Fair Media, 1979, Pioneer award World Assn. for Christian Comm., 1988, award for Ecumenical Leadership Nat. Coun. Chs., 2000, Ellul award Media Ecology Assn., 2004 Mem.: Yale (N.Y.C.). Home: 11 Midland Ave White Plains NY 10606-2828 Office: Fordham University Dept Communications Bronx NY 10458 Office Phone: 718-817-4859. Personal E-mail: ecparker92@msn.com.

PARKER, GARY DEAN, manufacturing executive; b. Omaha, Mar. 27, 1945; s. Norman and Dolores (Pierce) P.; m. Joanne Baker, Aug. 27, 1966; children: Jason E., Rodney R. BS in BA, Nebr. Wesleyan U., BS in Econs. Dir. sales Lindsay Mfg. Co., Nebr., 1971-73, v.p. sales-mktg. Nebr., 1973-76, sr. v.p. Nebr., 1976-78, exec. v.p. Nebr., 1978-83, pres., 1983—, dir., 1977—. Pres. Irrigation Assocs., Silver Springs, Md., 1981-82, dir., 1978-83; dir. Irrigation Found. & Research, Silver Springs, 1978— Mem. Nebr. Mfg. Assn. (pres. 1982-83), Delta Omicron Epsilon Lodges: Elks. Office: Lindsay Mfg Co PO Box 156 Lindsay NE 68644-0156

PARKER, GERALD M., osteopath, researcher; b. Olean, NY, Nov. 20, 1943; s. Richard and Kathleen (Manwaring) P.; m. Linda Kay Stuart, Dec. 28, 1968; children: Kimberly, Gerald, Cassandra, Kevin. BA, Western Wash. U., 1965; DO, Kirksville Coll. Osteopathy & Surgery, 1969. Intern Art Centre Hosp., Detroit, 1969-70; ptnr. Doctor's Clinic, Amarillo, Tex., 1970. Dir. S.W. Inst. Preventive Medicine, Amarillo, 1978—, Hyperbaric Oxygen Ctr., Amarillo, 1979—; appeared on That's Incredible TV show, 1982. Contbr. articles to profl. jours. Pres. S.W. Amarillo Little Dribblers Assn., 1979—; coach Girls Nat. Champion Basketball Teams, 1981, 83-87, 89. Named Physician of Yr., Nat. Rep. Com. Physician Adv. Bd., 2003. Fellow Am. Acad. Med. Preventics; mem. S.W. Acad. Preventive Medicine (pres. 1980—), Am. Osteo. Assn. Methodist. Avocation: athletics. Office: Doctors Clinic 4714 S Western St Amarillo TX 79109-5950 Office Phone: 806-355-8263.

PARKER, H. LAWRENCE, retired investor, rancher, investment banker; b. Portchester, NY, June 16, 1926; s. Raeburn H. and Alice (Lawrence) P.; m. Eleanor Sage, Mar. 3, 1951 (div. 1967); children: Katherine, Richard, Michael, Douglas (dec.); m. Regine Hawes, Nov. 15, 1994. BA, Yale U., 1949. With Morgan Stanley & Co., NYC, 1950—, ptnr., 1959-75, mng. dir., 1975-83, adv. dir., 1984—; pres. Morgan Stanley Can. Ltd., 1976-79, chmn., 1979-84, ret. Mem. adv. bd. on edn. and tng. Sec. Navy, 1985-87; dir. Jupiter (Fla.) Med. Ctr. Found., vice chmn., 2002—. Trustee Green Mountain Valley Sch., Waitsfield, Vt., 1981-91. Served with USMC, 1944-46. Mem. Investment Bankers Assn. Am. (bd. govs. 1966-70, pres. 1969), Nat. Assn. Securities Dealers (gov. 1981-84), Sublette County Hist. Soc. (trustee 1987-91), Blind Brook Club, Augusta (Ga.) Nat. Golf Club, Jupiter (Fla.) Island Club, Seminole Golf Club, Ekwanok Country Club. Home: One Angas Trail Hobe Sound FL 33455 Home Phone: 772-546-3818; Office Phone: 212-762-8865. E-mail: thepard@aol.com.

PARKER, HAROLD ALLEN, lawyer, real estate company officer; b. Denver, Sept. 14, 1924; s. Hyman and Sophia P.; m. Gertrud Parker; children: David, Rodney, Diana, Jesse, Jonathan. JD, Golden Gate U., 1971. Bar: Calif. 1972.; cert. mediator, Marin County, Calif. Pvt. practice, San Francisco; gen. ptnr. Harold Parker Properties, San Francisco. Legal cons. San Francisco Craft and Folk Art Mus.; past mem. Bay Area Lawyers for the Arts; spkr. in field; prime developer Union St. Comml. Corridor, San Francisco, 1963—; settlement conf. panelist Marin County Superior Cts., Calif. Pub.: Wolfgang Paalen, His Art and His Writings, 1980, Richard Bowman, Forty Years of Abstract Painting, 1986. Chmn. Fine Arts Commn., Tiburon, Calif., 1976-78. Mem. Family Club (San Francisco). Avocations: music, art, tennis. Office: 1844 Union St San Francisco CA 94123-4308 Home Phone: 415-435-2161; Office Phone: 415-563-6900. Personal E-mail: halepo@aol.com.

PARKER, HENRY GRIFFITH, III, insurance executive; b. Plainfield, NJ, Oct. 27, 1926; s. Henry Griffith and Ruth Martin (Van Auken) P.; m. Audrey Lansing Turner, May 11, 1957; children: Henry Griffith, IV, Elizabeth Wright. AB, Princeton U., 1948; postgrad., U. Pa. Sch. Law. With Chubb & Son, Inc., 1949-97, v.p., 1968-70, sr. v.p., dir., 1971-92, mng. dir., 1986-92; cons. to chmn., 1992-97; v.p. Fed. Ins. Co., 1968-73, sr. v.p., 1973-91; v.p. Vigilant Ins. Co., 1966-91, mgr. internat. div., 1967-84; chmn. Parker Assocs., Madison, NJ, 1997—. Adv. bd. Firemark Global Ins. Fund II, L.P., 1997-2005, bd. dirs. Alliance Assurance Co. Am., NYC, Sun Ins. Office Am. Inc., NYC; mem. industry sector adv. com. on svcs. US Dept. Commerce, Washington; bd. dirs. Nat. Fgn. Trade Coun., chmn. declarations com., 1974-81, chmn. ins. com., 1976-81; chmn. internat. policy com. US C. of C., 1970-73; chmn. US del. XII-XIII-XX-XXII-XXII Hemispheric Ins. Conf., Chile, 1969, Paraguay, 1987, Panama, 1985, Buenos Aires, 1989; chmn. Internat. Ins. Adv. Coun., Washington, 1970-73, 85-90, chmn. Internat. Com. Am. Ins. Assn., 1991-93; mem. NJ Commn. on Internat. Trade, 1986—; chmn. bus. adv. com. bus. coun. UN, 1988—; mem. adv. bd. Liaison Office Peoples Ins. Co. China, 1986-94. Appeared on numerous TV and radio programs; contbr. articles to profl. jours. Chmn. bd. Overlook Hosp., Summit, NJ, 1973-80; trustee Drew U., Madison, 1974—. Lt. (j.g.) USNR, 1944-46. Recipient Internat. Ins. award US C. of C., 1981, Disting. Service award Internat. Ins. Council, 1988. Mem. Nat. Assn. Ins. Commrs. (chmn. internat. adv. com.), Am. Ins. Assn. (chmn. internat. com.), Downtown Assn. Club (NYC), Princeton Club (NYC), River Club (NYC), Devon Yacht Club, Morris County (NJ) Golf Club, Hillsboro Club (Fla.), Psi Upsilon. Republican. Episcopalian. Office: Parker Assocs 38 East Ln Madison NJ 07940-2652

PARKER, HENRY HERBIN, humanities educator; s. Ben and Ray Parker; m. Marilyn Irene Crist, July 2, 1987; children: Alicia Erica Maya, Shauna Kay Crist. BA in English, magna cum laude, U. St. Thomas, St. Paul, 1956; MA in English, U. Minn., Mpls., 1958; PhD, U. Ill., Champaign-Urbana, 1977. Cert. hypnotherapist Ameriican Bd. Hypnotherapy, 2006. Prof. U. No. Iowa, Cedar Falls, 1965—90; prin., owner Parker Acad., Waterloo, Iowa, 1970—82, Parker Reading Co., Chgo., 1979—85; prof. modern fgn. language dept. U. No. Iowa, 1985—90; prof. dept. psychology and philosophy U. Tenn., Martin, 1990—95, dir. African Am. studies, 1995—, Cunningham disting. prof., 1998—2007. Nat. dir. curriculum operation push-excel Rev. Jesse Jackson, Chgo., 1979—80; pub. Parker Tribune Newspaper, Waterloo, Iowa, 1974—80; spkr. in field. Prodr.: (TV series) The Hank Parker Show, 1972—77; author (with Marilyn Crist): (book) Teaching Minorities to Play the Corporate Language Game, 1995, Apollo vs. Dionysus: A Philosophy to Increase College Success by 85%, 2001. Mem. com. ethnic, race and gender fairness Tenn. Supreme Ct., Nashville, 1995—98; bd. dirs. Gov. Bredesen's First Families, Nashville, 2004—07. Recipient George Washington Carver award, Simpson Coll., Iowa, 1977, Cert. of Appreciation, Tenn. Supreme Ct., 2000; fellow, Ford Found., 1969, Danforth Assoc., 1975. Mem.: African Am. Leadership Assn. (pres. 1995—2000). Avocations: hypnosis, classical music. Home: 139 Glenwood Dr Martin TN 38237 Office: Univ Tenn Martin 322 Humanities Martin TN 38237 Home Phone: 731-587-9008; Office Phone: 731-881-7545. Office Fax: 731-588-0388. Business E-Mail: hparker@utm.edu.

PARKER, IRA H., Internet company executive, lawyer; b. NYC, 1956; m. Jill Parker; children: David, Gregory. BA, Bklyn. Coll., City U. NY, 1978; JD, Emory U. Sch. Law, Atlanta, 1981. Asst. gen. counsel, litig. and policy FDIC, 1989—92, dep. gen. counsel, Resolution Trust Corp., 1992—93; ptnr. Alston & Bird, Washington, 1993—97; v.p., dep. gen. counsel GTE Corp., 1997—2000; v.p., gen. counsel Genuity Inc., 1997—2000, sr. v.p., gen. counsel, sec., 2000—03, pres., CEO, 2003; v.p., gen. counsel, corp. sec., chief compliance officer Polaroid Corp., 2004—06; exec. v.p., gen. counsel AOL LLC, Dulles, Va., 2006—. Office: AOL LLC 22000 AOL Way Dulles VA 20166 Office Phone: 703-265-1000. Office Fax: 703-433-7263. *

PARKER, JAMES AUBREY, federal judge; b. Houston, Jan. 8, 1937; s. Lewis Almeron and Emily Helen (Stuessy) P.; m. Florence Fisher, Aug. 26, 1960; children: Roger Alan, Pamela Elizabeth. BA, Rice U., 1959; LLB, U. Tex., 1962. Bar: Tex. 1962, N.Mex. 1963. With Modrall, Sperling, Roehl,

Harris & Sisk, Albuquerque, 1962-87; judge U.S. Dist. Ct. N.Mex., Albuquerque, 1987—2000, chief judge, 2000—03. Mem. Standing Commn. on Rules of Practice and Procedures of U.S. Cts., 1993-99, N.Mex. Commn. on Professionalism, 1986-2004; bd. vis. U. N.Mex. Law Sch., 1996-2004; bd. dirs. Fed. Jud. Ctr., 2004—. Articles editor Tex. Law Rev., 1961-62. Mem. Fed. Judges Assn., Am. Judicature Soc., Am. Bd. Trial Advocates, N.Mex. Bar Assn. (Outstanding Judge award 1994), Albuquerque Bar Assn. (Outstanding Judge award 1993, 00, Law Dragon 500 Leading Judges in Am. 2006), Nat. Assn. Criminal Def. Lawyers (Courageous Judiciary award 2001), Order of Coif, Chancellors, Phi Delta Phi. Avocations: ranching, fly fishing, running, skiing. Office: US Dist Ct 421 Gold S W 6th Fl Albuquerque NM 87102-2277 Mailing: PO Box 669 Albuquerque NM 87103 Office Phone: 505-348-2220. Office Fax: 505-348-2225. Business E-Mail: jparker@nmcourt.fed.us.

PARKER, JAMES JOHN, engineer, marketing professional; s. John J. and Marjorie (Grohmann) P.; m. Mary P. Nash, Oct. 21, 1972; children: Elizabeth Ann Parker Fahey, John James, Patricia Mary. BSEE, Marquette U., Milw., 1971; BSBA, Elmhurst Coll., Ill., 1982; MBA, U. Chgo., 1987. Student engr. Motorola Consumer Products, Franklin Park, Ill., 1968—70, engring. assoc., 1972—74; co-op engr. Warwick Electronics, Niles, 1971—72; sr. engr. R&D Quasar Electronics, Inc., Franklin Park, 1974—76; sr. project engr. Motorola Data Products, Carol Stream, 1978—79, Zenith Electronics Co., Glenview, 1979—82, mgr. market rsch., 1982—85, mgr. sect., 1985—86, mgr. program, 1988—95; mgr. displays Zenith Data Sys./Groupe Bull, Buffalo Grove, 1995—96; v.p. mktg. AVC Tech, Niles, 1996—97; mgr. product Visiontek, Gurnee, 1997; dir. product planning Telular, Inc., Vernon Hills, 1997—98; mgr. product mktg. Motorola BCS/SBNS, Schiller Park, 1998—2001; sr. cons. Pro-Team Cons., Palatine, 2001—03; dir. engring. Graphic Solutions Internat., Burr Ridge, Ill., 2003—06. Faculty Wright Jr. Coll., Chgo., 1975-80. Mem. editl. bd. Electronic Products Mag., 1976-77; contbr. to conf. and forums. Adviser Jr. Achievement, Chgo., 1972-78; treas. Immaculate Conception Parish Christian Svc. Commn., 1988-91; vol. Pub. Action to Deliver Shelter, 1987-2000; alderman 5th ward Elmhurst, 1993-2005; vice-chmn. fin. com. City of Elmhurst, 1995-2003, chmn. pub. works and bldg. com., 2003-05, vice-chmn. telecom. and tech. adv. group, 1997. Mem. IEEE Midcon. (vice-chmn. pub. rels. 1979, chmn. spl. exhibits 1981, vice-chmn. spl. exhibits 1983), Hon. Order Ky. Cols., Internat. Microelectronics and Packaging Soc., Tech. Assn. Graphic Arts, Delta Mu Delta (hon.) Roman Catholic. Avocations: ham radio, flying. Home: 421 Berkley Ave Elmhurst IL 60126-3706 Office Phone: 630-742-5756. Personal E-mail: jimparker@ameritech.net.

PARKER, JEFFREY SCOTT, law educator; b. Alexandria, Va., Sept. 6, 1952; s. Clarence Franklin and Mary Florence (Partlow) P. B in Indsl. Engring., Ga. Inst. Tech., 1975; JD, U. Va., 1978. Bar: N.Y. 1979, U.S. Dist. Ct. (ea. and so. dists.) N.Y. 1979, U.S. Ct. Appeals (3d cir.) 1981, U.S. Ct. Appeals (2d cir.) 1984, U.S. Supreme Ct. 1984, U.S. Ct. Appeals (fed. cir.) 1985, U.S. Ct. Appeals (4th cir.) 1992, U.S. Ct. Appeals (D.C. cir.) 1997. Assoc. Sullivan & Cromwell, NYC, 1978-86, Sacks Montgomery, NYC, 1986-87; dep. chief counsel U.S. Sentencing Commn., Washington, 1987-88; of counsel Sacks Montgomery, NYC, 1988-90; assoc. prof. law George Mason U Sch. Law, Arlington, Va., 1990-94; prof. George Mason U. Sch. Law, Arlington, Va., 1994—, assoc. dean acad. affairs, 1994-96. Cons. counsel U.S. Sentencing Commn., Washington, 1988-89. Contbr. articles to law revs.; mem. editorial bd. Va. Law Rev., 1976-78. Mem. ABA, Assn. of Bar of City of N.Y., N.Y. State Bar Assn., Am. Law and Econs. Assn., Am. Econs. Assn., Am. Judicature Soc. Office: George Mason U Sch of Law 3401 Fairfax Dr Arlington VA 22201-4411 E-mail: jparke3@gmu.edu.

PARKER, JOEL LOUISE, nursing administrator; d. Hattie Louise and Joe Nmn Williams. BS in nursing, Tex. Christian U., 1975—77; MS in human resources, Golden Gate U., 1988—90; MS in nursing informatics, U. Md., 1997—99, postgrad., 1997—99. CPA; cert. nursing informatic ANCC, 2001. Dept. head, oper. rm. Naval Hosp., Jacksonville, Fla., 1999—2003; dir., ctrl. credentials quality assurance sys. Resources II Program Office, Falls Church, Va., 2003—. Clin. coord., oper. rm. Nat. Naval Med. Ctr., Bethesda, 1994—97; charge nurse pacu/gen. surgery Naval Hosp., Okinawa, Japan, 1991—94; charge nurse ent Naval Hosp. Camp Lejeune, 1988—91; relief charge nurse sicu Veterans Adminstrn. Hosp., Dallas, 1983—87; oper. rm. staff nurse St. Joseph's Hosp., Fort Worth, 1987—88. Pres. ushers bd. First Bapt. Ch. Of Mandarin, Jacksonville, 2000—02. Comdr. USN, 2003—05. Decorated Navy/Marine Corps Achievement medal, Naval Officers Disting. Svc. award, Navy and Marine Corps Overseas Svc. ribbon, Global War on Terrorism Expeditionary medal, Navy Fleet Marine Force ribbon, Joint Meritorious Unit award, Navy Unit Commendation, Meritorious Unit Commendation, Nat. Def. Svc. medal. Mem.: Nat. Naval Officers Assn. (life; pres. 1995—97, Disting. Svc. award 1996), Sigma Theta Tau. Democrat. Bapt. Home Phone: 202-561-0330. Personal E-mail: texjop@yahoo.com.

PARKER, JOHN CARLYLE, retired librarian and archivist, editor; b. Ogden, Utah, Oct. 14, 1931; s. Levi and Marietta (Parkinson) P.; m. Janet C. Greene, May 31, 1956; children: Denise, Nathan, Bret. BA, Brigham Young U., 1957; MLS, U. Calif., Berkeley, 1958. Cert. jr. coll. life credential, Calif. Spl. svcs. libr. Humboldt State U., 1958-60; cataloger, reference libr. Ch. Coll. Hawaii, 1960-62, acting libr., 1962-63; head Pub. svcs. Calif. State U. Libr., Stanislaus, 1963-68, head pub. svcs., asst. libr. dir., 1968-83, 84-90, acting libr. dir., 1983-84, univ. archivist, 1990-94, libr. and univ. archivist emeritus, 1994—. S ctr. reference svc. for genealogists and geneal. rsch. for genealogists, 1966-98; cons. Bailey's Moving and Storage Co., Allied Van Lines, Bountiful, Utah, 1983-85, Gale Rsch. Co., Detroit, 1986, 92, E & J Gallo Winery, Modesto, Calif., 1990; editor Marietta Pub. Co., 1985—. Author: Library Service for Genealogists, 1981, Going to Salt Lake City to Do Family History Research, 3d rev. and expanded edit., 1996; compiler numerous books, including Directory of Archivist and Librarian Genealogical Instructors, 2d edit., 1990, Rhode Island Biographical and Genealogical Sketch Index, 1991; contbr. articles and book revs. to profl. jours. Founder, vol. libr. Modesto Family History Ctr., 1968-90, Turlock (Calif.) Family History Ctr., 1990-97; chmn. Stanislaus County United Way campaign Calif. State U., Stanislaus Campus, 1980-81; sec. bd. dirs. Turlock Centennial Found., 1971-75; pres. Turlock Cmty. Concert Bd., 1973-75; trustee Turlock Libr., 1969-70; merit badge counselor Yosemite coun. Boy Scouts Am., 1973—. With U.S. Army, 1953-55. Fellow Utah Geneal. Assn., 1984. Mem. ALA (chmn. genealogy com. 1989-92, award reference and adult svcs. divsn., history sect.-Geneal. Pub. Co. award 1994), AAUP, Nat. Geneal. Soc. (award of merit 1984), Calif. Libr. Assn. (pres. Redwood dist. 1959-60, state coll. librs. divsn. 1969, chmn. geneal. librs. round table 1994, 96-97), Calif. State Geneal. Alliance (historian 1991—), Stanislaus County Hist. Soc. (v.p., program chmn. 1972-73), Geneal. Soc. Stanislaus County (founding mem. 1968-70, 1980-84, hon.), Turlock Hist. Soc. Democrat. Mem. LDS Ch. Avocations: birding, travel, singing solos and in choirs. Home: 2115 N Denair Ave Turlock CA 95382-1821

PARKER, JOHN HILL, lawyer; b. High Point, NC, Feb. 1, 1944; s. George Edward and Tullia Virginia (Hill) Parker; m. Lynette Becton Smith, July 7, 1977; children from previous marriage: Alice Lindsey, Elizabeth Shelby(dec.). BA, U. N.C., 1966; JD, U. Tenn., 1969. Bar: N.C. 1969, U.S. Dist. Ct. (ea. dist.) N.C. 1970, U.S. Supreme Ct. 1975. Assoc. Sanford, Cannon, Adams & McCullough, Raleigh, NC, 1969-73; pvt. practice Raleigh, 1974-76; judge N.C. Dist. Ct., Raleigh, 1976-82; ptnr. Cheshire & Parker, Raleigh, 1982—. Instr. judges seminars Inst. Govt., Chapel Hill, NC, 1977—82. Mem. Raleigh Arts Commn., 1981—84, chmn., 1983; parlementarian Wake County Dems., 1971—73. Fellow: Am. Acad. Matrimonial Lawyers (mem. ethics com. 1995—97, pres. N.C. chpt. 1999); mem.: Am. Coll. Family Trial Lawyers (diplomate), Wake County Bar Assn., N.C. Acad. Trial Lawyers, N.C. Bar Assn. (CLE com. family law 1979—, editor newsletter family law sect. 1984—86, chmn. ethics com. 1989—90, gen. curriculum com. 1989—2003, chmn. 1996—97, 1996—98, mem. trial practice curriculum com. 2004—), ABA. Episcopalian. Avocations: travel, backpacking, fishing, reading, music. Home: PO Box 1029 Raleigh NC 27602 Office: Cheshire & Parker PO Box 1029 133 Fayetteville St Mall Raleigh NC 27601-1356 Office Phone: 919-833-3114. Business E-Mail: john.parker@cheshirepark.com.

PARKER, JOHN VICTOR, judge; b. Baton Rouge, Oct. 14, 1928; m. Mary Elizabeth Fridge, Sept. 3, 1949; children: John Michael, Robert Fridge, Linda Anne. BA, La. State U., 1949, JD, 1952. Bar: La. 1952. Atty. Parker & Parker, Baton Rouge, 1954-66; asst. parish atty. City of Baton Rouge, Parish of East Baton Rouge, 1956-66; atty. Sanders, Downing, Kean & Cazedessus, Baton Rouge, 1966-79; chief judge U.S. Dist. Ct., Middle Dist. La., Baton Rouge, 1979—. Vis. lectr. law La. State U. Law Sch. With JAG US Army, 1952—54. Mem.: ABA, Baton Rouge Bar Assn. (past pres.), La. State Bar Assn. (past mem. bd. govs.), Am. Arbitration Assn., Am. Judicature Soc., Baton Rouge Country Club, Kiwanis (past pres.), Masons (32 degree), Order of Coif, Phi Delta Phi. Democrat. Office: Russell B Long Fed Bldg and Courthouse 777 Florida St Ste 355 Baton Rouge LA 70801-1717 Office Phone: 225-389-3568.

PARKER, JOSEPH CORBIN, JR., pathologist, educator, department chairman; b. Richmond, Va., Aug. 1, 1937; s. Joseph Corbin and Alice Cabell (Horsley) P.; m. Patricia Hugh Singleton, June 24, 1961; children: John Randolph, Nancy Jordan. BA, Va. Mil. Inst., 1958; MD, Med. Coll. Va., 1962; MS in Pathology, U. Minn., 1968. Fellow in pathology Mayo Clinic, Rochester, Minn., 1963-68; fellow in neuropathology Duke U., Durham, NC, 1968—69, asst. prof., 1969-70, Harvard U., Boston, 1970-71; assoc. prof. U. Ky., Lexington, 1971-75; prof. U. Miami, Fla., 1975-81; dir. neuroscience lab. U. Tenn., Knoxville, 1981—86, assoc. dean, prof., 1981—83, prof. pathology and med. biology; prof., chmn. dept. pathology U. Mo., Kansas City, 1986—92, U. Louisville Sch. Medicine, 1992—2002, chair, prof., 2002—, dir. pathology residency program, 2007—. Bd. dirs. Truman Med. Ctr., Kansas City, Mo., Hosp. Hill Health Svc., Kansas City; cons. Ky. Stroke Assn., Stroke Coun. Author 4 chpts. in books; contbr. more than 170 articles to profl. jours. Bd. dirs. Multiple Sclerosis Soc., Knoxville, Tenn., 1985, Alzheimers Assn., Kansas City, 1988-91. With Med. Corp, USAR, 1958-67. Recipient 1st Jackson -Hope medal Va. Mil. Inst., 1958; Caldwell award Alzheimers Assn., 1986. Fellow Am. Asns. Neuropathology, Am. Soc. Clin. Pathology, Coll. Am. Pathology, Assn. Clin. Scientists (pres. 2000); mem. So. Med. Assn., Am. Acad. Neurology, Am. Assn. Neurol. Surgeons, Univ. Pathologists (pres. 1993-01). Republican. Unitarian Universalist. Achievements include discovery of autosomal recessive neonatal adrenal leuko-distrophy, and types of cerebral mycoses at autopsy. Home: 4606 Wolf Creek Pky Louisville KY 40241-5502 Office: U Louisville Sch Medicine Dept Pathology Louisville KY 40292-0001 Office Phone: 502-852-6515. Business E-Mail: jcpark01@gwise.louisville.edu.

PARKER, JOSEPH MAYON, retired publishing executive; b. Washington, NC, Oct. 11, 1931; s. James Mayon and Mildred (Poe) Parker; m. Lauretta Owen Dyer, Mar. 23, 1957; children: Katherine Suzanne, Joseph Wilbur. Student, Davidson Coll., 1949-51; BA, U. N.C., 1953, MPA, 1992; postgrad., Carnegie Inst. Tech., 1955-56. From mgr. print divsn. to pres. Parker Bros., Inc., Ahoskie, NC, 1956—77, pres., CEO, 1977—2001; ret., 2001. Editor, columnist: 5 cmty. newspapers; panelist (TV series) NC This Week, 1986—89. Treas. Chowan Graphic Arts Found., Murfreesboro, NC, 1971—90, pres., 1990—92; mem. Ind. Devel. Commn., 1974—86; dir. Gov.'s Hwy. Safety Program, 1993—2001; vice chmn. N.C. Goals and Policy Bd., Raleigh, 1977—84; pres. Com. of 100, Winton, NC, 1984—87; chmn. Northeastern N.C. Tomorrow, Elizabeth City, 1981—84, sec., 1984—90; del. Dem. Nat. Conv., NYC, 1980, platform com., 1988; dist. chmn. N.C. Dem. Ctrl. Com., 1980—82, 2005—; bd. dirs. Wake Dem. Men, 2004—; exec. com. State Dem., 2005—; pres. NC Meth. Bd. Pub., 2004—06; trustee Pitt County Meml. Hosp., 1980—88. With US Army, 1953—54, col. USAR, 1954—88. Mem.: Roanoke Island Hist. Assn. (vice-chmn. 1987—89), Nat. Newspaper Assn. (state chmn. 1976—83), NC Press Assn., East NC Press Assn. (past pres.), Soc. Profl. Journalists, Ea. NC C. of C. (past chmn.), NC Order of Long Leaf Pine, Rotary. Democrat. Methodist. Avocations: golf, reading. Home: 4500 Connell Dr Raleigh NC 27612-5600 E-mail: jpark4173@aol.com.

PARKER, JUSTON SCOTT, travel company executive; s. Gordon J. and Linda J. Parker; m. Lisa Parker, May 19, 1996; children: James Mait, Jamie Brooke Munson, Caitlyn Leigh. Degree in psychology, No. Ariz. U., Flagstaff, 1989; degree in labor rels., U. Wis., Madison, 1999; degree in polit. sci., U. Md., Silver Spring, 1999. Lic. paramedic Colo., 1989; Chrme HSMAI, 2006. Pres., CEO Parker Hospitality Grp., Inc., Colo., 2001—; exec. v.p., supplier svcs. & strategy Gusto, Springfield, Mo., 2006—. Author: (textbook) Revenue Managment. Chmn. Talents Found., Parker, 2001—07. Nominee Pres. award, HEDNA, 2005. Mem.: HSMAI (assoc. Nominee Top 25 Minds in Hospitality Industry award 2006). D-Liberal. Avocations: travel, golf. Office: Parker Hospitality Grp Inc 17063 E Rosebay Cir Parker CO 80134 Office Fax: 720-851-9272. Business E-Mail: juston@parkerhospitality.com.

PARKER, KELLY ANDREW, philosopher, educator; s. Victor Robert Parker Jr. and Margaret Anne Parker; m. Sandra Sue Landstrom, June 2, 1984; children: Elizabeth Drake, William James. PhD, Vanderbilt U., Nashville, 1987—92. Assoc. prof. Grand Valley State U., Allendale, Mich., 1992—. Chair, dept. philosophy Grand Valley State U., Allendale, Mich., 2001—. Mem.: Josiah Royce Soc. (pres. 2007—). Achievements include research in environmental pragmatism. Office: Grand Valley State Univ Department of Philosophy Allendale MI 49401 Office Phone: 616-331-2114.

PARKER, KEVIN JAMES, electrical engineer, educator; BS in Engring. Sci. summa cum laude, SUNY, Buffalo, 1976; MSEE, MIT, 1978, PhD, 1981. Rsch. assoc. lab. for med. ultrasound MIT, Cambridge, 1977-81; asst. prof. dept. elec. engring. U. Rochester, NY, 1981-85, assoc. prof., 1985-91, assoc. prof. dept. radiology, 1989-91, prof., 1992—, chair, 1992-98, dean sch. engring. & applied scis., 1998—, William F. May Prof. Engring., 2005—. Com. mem. Internat. Symposium Ultrasound Imaging, 1989—; dir. Rochester Ctr. Biomedical Ultrasound, 1990—. Mem. editl. bd. Ultras. Med. Biology, 1989—; contbr. articles to profl. jours. Named IBM Supercomputing Contest finalist, 1989; recipient Ultrasound Medicine and Biology prize, World Fed., 1991, Outstanding Innovation award, Eastman Kodak Co., 1991; fellow, NIH, 1979; Lilly Tchg. fellow, 1982. Fellow: IEEE, Am. Inst. Ultrasound Medicine (ethics com. 1987—90, stds. com. 1990—93, bd. govs. 1996—99, Joseph P. Holmes Pioneer award 1999); mem.: Acoustical Soc. Achievements include patents in field of 13 patents, liscened by several companies in field of engring. Office: Univ of Rochester Sch Engring & Applied Scis Lattimore Bldg Rm 309 Rochester NY 14627-0076

PARKER, LEE BRYAN, retired physician; b. Dermott, Ark., May 10, 1929; s. Lee Bryan and Viola Lee Parker; m. Beverly Edith Brosell, Dec. 23, 1951; children: Susan Leigh Brewer, Elizabeth Ann Beecher, Steven Lee, Edith Lynn Hegwood. BS, U. Ark., Fayetteville, 1950; MD, U. Ark., Little Rock, 1954. Lic. physician Ark., 1954. Intern Crawford Long Hosp., Atlanta, 1954—55; pvt. practice Dermott, 1957—59, McGehee, Ark., 1959—67; gen. practice Doctor's Bldg., Fayetteville, Ark., 1967—74; dir. Area Health Edn. Ctr. NW, U. Ark. for Med. Scis., Fayetteville, 1974—96; ret., 1996. Chief med. staff S.t Mary's Hosp., Dermott, 1964—65, McGehee Desha Hosp., Ark., 1965—67, Fayetteville City Hosp., 1975—76, Wash. Regional Med. Ctr., Fayetteville, 1980—81; vis. prof. Kaohsiung Med. U., Taiwan, 1986; bd. dirs. Butterfield Trail Village, Fayetteville, 2001—06, Ark. Regional Med. Program, Little Rock, 1967—70; adv. bd. Area Health Edn. Ctr. NW, Fayetteville, 2004—07; dir. continuing med. edn. U. Ark. Sch. Medicine, Little Rock, 1970—74. Sec. Wash. County Med. Soc., Fayetteville, 1973—74. Capt. USAF, 1955—57. Recipient Disting. Svc. award, McGehee Jaycees, 1963, Distinguised Svc. award, U. Ark. for Med. Scis. Coll. Medicine, 1992, Founders Soc. award, U. Ark. for Med. Scis., 1996, Eagle award, Wash. Regional Med. Found., 1999, Diamond Soc. award, Ark. Cmty. Found., 2004, Doyne Soc. award, U. Ctrl. Ark., 2004, Legacy Soc. award, U. Ark. for Med. Scis., 2005. Mem.: Ark. Acad. Family Physicians (life; bd. dirs. 1962—67, chmn. continuing edn. com. 1971—89, pres. 1982—83, alt. del. 1984—89, Family Dr. of Yr. 1993), Ark. Med. Soc. (life; councilor 4th dist. 1965—67, jour. editor 1993). Independent. Methodist. Avocations: hunting, fishing, golf, gardening. Office: Univ Ark Med Sci 2907 E Joyce Fayetteville AR 72703 Home Phone: 479-756-0115; Office Phone: 479-521-8269.

PARKER, LISA FREDERICK, music educator, Dalcroze specialist; b. NYC, Sept. 17, 1934; d. Karl Telford and Anne (Moore) Frederick; m. Dec. 24, 1966 (div. May, 1979); children: Eden Elizabeth, Wendy Margaret. BA cum laude, Smith Coll., 1956; M of Music in Conducting, New Eng. Conservatory, 1962; Diplôme, Inst. Jacque Dalcroze, Geneva, 1965. Instr. eurythymics, solfége New Eng. Conservatory, Boston, 1959-71; conductor NEC Youth Singers, Boston, 1965-71; dir. Dalcroze Program, Belmont (Mass.) Music Sch, 1970-77; chair Dalcroze dept. Longy Sch. of Music, Cambridge, 1977—. Mem. guest faculty Inst. Jaques Dalcroze, at internat. conf., 1974—; presenter at workshops internationally; tchr., 1999—; founder Boston Ctr. Osteophonie. Author: (children's skit) Curious George Goes to Music School, 1993—; contbr. articles to profl. jours. Recipient George Seamon award Excellence in Tchg., 2003. Mem. Dalcroze Soc. Am. (pres. 1972-75, editor jour. 1975-81), Nat. Music Tchrs. Assn., Dalcroze Soc. Can. Democrat. Episcopalian. Avocations: gardening, french language, travel, reading, chamber music. Office: Longy Sch of Music 1 Follen St Cambridge MA 02138-3599

PARKER, LYNDA CHRISTINE RYLANDER, secondary school educator; b. Bremerton, Wash., Apr. 21, 1949; d. Richard Algot and Marian Ethelyn (Peterson) Rylander; m. Joseph Hiram Parker, Feb. 7, 1981; 1 child, Joseph Hiram IV. BA in English, Sociology, Pacific Luth. U., 1971, MA in Ednl. Administrn., 1981, prin.'s credential, 1982, postgrad. Tchr. lang. arts Cen. Kitsap Schs., Silverdale, Wash., 1971-74; tchr. English gifted Okanagan Schs., Kelowna, B.C., Can., 1974-78; tchr. lang. arts gifted Federal Way (Wash.) Schs., 1978-86; tchr. lang. arts, remedial reading, humanities gifted Bethel Sch. Dist., Spanaway, Wash., 1986—. Counselor Okanagan Sch. Dist., Kelowna, 1974-78; advisor Ski Club, Cheerleaders, Svc. Club, Pep Club, Kitsap Schs., Silverdale, 1971-74, Cheerleaders, Pep Club, Svc. Club, Ski Club, annual, newspaper, class advisor, Okanagan Sch. Dist., Kelowna, 1974-78, newspaper, Cheerleaders, Bethel Schs., Spanaway, 1986—; multi-media, at-risk program, gifted program, video prodns., 1996-; presenter of workshops for parents, tchrs., adminstrs., 1988—. Named Christa McAuliffe Outstanding Tchr. of Yr. State of Wash., 1988, Walmart Tchr. of Yr., 2004; recipient Supts. Superior Svc. award, 2007. Mem. NEA, ASCD, NAFE, Nat. Assn. Secondary Sch. Prins., Wash. Edn. Assn., Wash. Assn. Secondary Sch. Prins., Bethel Educators Assn. Republican. Lutheran. Avocations: piano, skiing, body building. Home: 1721 169th Street Ct S Spanaway WA 98387-9141 Personal E-mail: stefanlay@aol.com. E-mail: lparker@bethdsd.org.

PARKER, LYNDA MICHELE, psychiatrist; b. Sept. 28, 1947; d. Albert Francis and Dorothy Thomasina (Herriott) P. BA, C. W. Post Coll., 1968; MA, NYU, 1970; MD, Cornell U., 1974; postgrad., N.Y. Psychoanalytic Inst., 1977-82. Diplomate Am. Coll. Forensic Examiners. Intern N.Y. Hosp., NYC, 1975; resident in psychiatry Payne Whitney Clinic, NYC, 1975-78; psychiatrist-in-charge day program Cabrini Med. Ctr., NYC, 1978-79, attending psychiatrist, supr. psychiatry residents, 1978-96, supr. long-term psychotherapy, 1980-82; attending psychiatrist N.Y. Hosp., Cornell Med. Ctr., 1979-96; practice medicine specializing in psychiatry NYC, 1979-96; from instr. psychiatry to asst. prof. Cornell U. Med. Coll., 1979-96; instr. psychiatry N.Y. Med. Coll., 1978-96; assoc. prof., regional chair dept. psychiatry Tex. Tech. U. Health Scis. Ctr., Amarillo, 1996-99, No. region dir. correctional mental health scis., 1999—2002, clin. dir. PAMIO, 1999—2002; pvt. practice, 2002—. Assoc. prof. pharmacy practice in psychiatry Tex. Tech U. Sch. Pharmacy, 1996-99; psychiat. cons. Bldg. Service 32BJ Health Fund, 1983-89, Inwood House, N.Y.C., 1983-86, Time-Life Inc., 1986-96, Ind. Med. Examiners, 1986-96, Epilepsy Inst., 1986-87, asst. med. dir., 1987-88, med. dir., 1988; ind. med. examiner Rep. Health Care Rev. Sys. Mem. adv. bd. St. Bartholomew Community Presch., N.Y.C., 1990-96. Martin Luther King Jr. scholar, NYU, 1968—70. Mem.: AAUW, Tex. Med. Assn., Tex. Soc. for Psychiat. Physicians, Am. Womens Med. Assn., Am. Psychiat. Assn. Episcopalian. Office: 1616 S Kentucky Ste C-200 Amarillo TX 79102 Home Phone: 806-356-8824; Office Phone: 806-457-9200. Personal E-mail: LyParker@aol.com.

PARKER, MARIAN F., law librarian, educator; BA, U. NC, Greensboro; MSLS, U. NC, Chapel Hill, 1979; JD, Wake Forest U., 1978. Rsch. libr., instr.and Instructor Duke U., 1979—80; assoc. dir. pub. svcs., asst. prof. SUNY, Buffalo, 1980—83; dir. Law Libr., asst. prof. law U. Tulsa, 1983—86; mgr. legal quality, competitive analysis mgr. Mead Data Ctrl., 1986—90; assoc. law libr. rsch. svcs. Harvard U., 1990—92; dir. Law Libr., prof. law NYU, 1992—94; spl. asst. edn. tech. NC Dept. Human Resources, 1994—96; dir. profl. rels. Lexis-Nexis/Matthew Bender & Co., 1996—99; dir. Profl. Ctr. Libr., prof. law Wake Forest U. Sch. Law, Winston-Salem, NC, 1999—, assoc. dean info. svcs. Office: Wake Forest U Sch Law PO Box 7206, Reynolda Station Winston Salem NC 27109 Office Phone: 336-758-4879. Office Fax: 336-758-4301. E-mail: parkermf@law.wfu.edu. *

PARKER, MARILLA J., school psychologist; b. Durant, Okla., Feb. 2, 1955; d. Charles B. Ladd and C. Joyce (Grimes) Ladd; m. Ricky E. Parker, July 28, 1979; children: Stuart E., Stephanie J. BA, in Edn., Southeastern Okla. State U., 1981, MEd in Counseling, 2000; Cert. in Sch. Psychol. Svcs., East Ctrl. U., Ada, OK, 2003. Lic. Psychologist Okla. State Bd. of Edn., 2003, School Counselor Okla. State Bd. of Edn., 2000, cert. tchr. music Okla. State Bd. of Edn., 1981. Vocal music dir. Atoka Pub. Schs., Atoka, Okla., 1981—84, Caddo Pub. Schs., Caddo, Okla., 1988—91, Rock Creek Pub. Schs., Bokchito, Okla., 1991—98; sch. counselor Caney Pub. Schs., Caney, Okla., 2000—06, Calera Pub. Schs., Okla., 2006—. Co-chair SE All-District Honor Choir, Durant, Okla.; adv. coun. Kiamichi Tech. Ctr., 2000—; state adminstr. Yom Chi Tae Kwon-Do, Okla., 2007—. Mem.: NEA, Okla. Edn. Assn., Okla. Music Educators Assn. (coord. region G 1997—98), Music Educators Nat. Conf., Okla. Sch. Psychologists Assn., Nat. Assn. Sch. Psychologists, Psi Chi. Office: Calera Pub Sch 209 N 3rd Calera OK 74730

PARKER, MARK G., apparel executive; b. Poughkeepsie, NY; BS in Polit. Sci., Pa. State U., 1977. With Nike, Inc., 1979—, designer, devel. mgr. Exeter, NH, 1979—80, mgr. advanced product design, 1980—81, dir. design concepts & engring. Beaverton, Oreg., 1981—82, dir. footwear design, 1982—83, mgr. footware mktg., 1983—85, head, spl. design project teams, 1985—87, divsn. v.p. footware rsch., design and devel.,

1987—88, corp. v.p. rsch. design & devel., 1988—93, v.p. consumer product mktg., 1993—98, v.p., gen. mgr. global footware, 1998—2001, pres. Nike Brand, 2001—06, pres., CEO, 2006—. Avocations: running, rock climbing, mountain biking, sailing, kayaking, drawing, painting, collecting art. Office: Nike Inc One Bowerman Dr Beaverton OR 97005-6453 Office Phone: 503-671-6453. *

PARKER, MARSHA MARIE, dean, actress; b. St. Charles, Mo., Aug. 13, 1949; d. Anthony Gregory and Stella Julia Hollander; m. Ronald E. Parker, Oct. 20, 1979. BA, Lindenwood U., St. Charles, 1971; MFA, Lindenwood U., 1987. Dir. vol. svcs. St. Louis State Sch. and Hosp., 1971—73; dep. juvenile officer 11th Jud. Cir., St. Charles, 1973—76; dir. pers. St. Charles City-County Libr., 1976—87; dir. evening grad. admissions Lindenwood U., St. Charles, 1987—90, dir. alumni svcs., 1990—93, dean fine and performing arts, 1993—. Dir., prodr., actress various plays. Author: (plays) A Christmas Carol - adaptation, 1993. Mem. Higher Edn. Coun.-Theatre, St. Louis, 2004—; adv. bd. The Foundry, St. Charles, 2004—05. Named Outstanding Tchr., Emerson Elec., St. Louis, 1996. Democrat. Roman Catholic. Office: Lindenwood U 209 S Kingshighway Saint Charles MO 63301

PARKER, MARY LOU, lawyer; b. Brockton, Mass., Nov. 16, 1945; BA, Immaculata Coll., Pa., 1967; JD cum laude, Seton Hall U. Sch. of Law, South Orange, NJ, 1975; LLM in Taxation, NYU, 1989. Bar: N.J. 1975, Fla. 1983. Law clk. to Hon. Worrall F. Mountain Supreme Ct. N.J., 1975-76; ptnr. Pitney Hardin LLP, Morristown, NJ, 1982—. Notes editor Seton Hall Law Review, 1974-75; author, Increased Cost of Dying in New Jersey, New Jersey Lawyer, 2002, Estate Administration Checklist, NJSBA Real Property, Probate and Trust Law Section Newsletter, 2003. Named NJ Super Lawyer for trusts and estates, 2005, Best Lawyer in Am. for 2006. Fellow Am. Coll. Trust and Estate Counsel, Am. Bar Found.; mem. ABA, N.J. State Bar Assn. (bd. consultors real property probate and trust law sect. 1986—, chmn., real property, probate and trust law section 1991-92), Fla. Bar Assn., N.J. State Bar Found. (trustee, 1993, sec., 1994, pres. 1995-96), Northwestern N.J. Estate Planning Coun. (pres. 1982-83), Morris County Bar Assn.(named Profl. Lawyer of Yr., 2005) Office: Pitney Hardin LLP PO Box 1945 Park Ave at Morris County Morristown NJ 07962-1945 Office Phone: 973-966-8061. Business E-Mail: mparker@pitneyhardin.com.

PARKER, MARY-LOUISE, actress; b. Ft. Jackson, SC, Aug. 2, 1964; 1 child, William Atticus. Attended, Bard Coll. Actress: (theatre) Hay Fever, 1987, The Miser, 1988, The Art of Success, 1989, The Importance of Being Earnest, 1989, Prelude to a Kiss, Broadway, 1990-91 (Theatre World award, Clarence Derwent Award, Tony nomination, 1990), Babylon Gardens, 1991, How I Learned to Drive, 1997 (Lucille Lortel Award for outstanding actress, OBIE Award, 1997), Proof, Broadway (Tony award for best actress in a play, 2001); (films) Signs of Life, 1989, Longtime Companion, 1990, Grand Canyon, 1991, Fried Green Tomatoes, 1991, Mr. Wonderful, 1993, Naked in New York, 1994, The Client, 1994, Bullets Over Broadway, 1994, Boys on the Side, 1995, A Portrait of a Lady, 1996, Reckless, 1995, Murder in Mind, 1997, The Maker, 1997, Let the Devil Wear Black, 1998, Goodbye, Lover, 1998, Five Senses, 1999, Pipe Dream, 2002, Red Dragan, 2002, The Best Thief in the World, 2004, Saved!, 2004, Romance & Cigarettes, 2005; (TV movies) Too Young the Hero, 1988, A Place for Annie, 1994, Sugartime, 1995, Legalese, 1998, Saint Maybe, 1998, The Simple Life of Noah Dearborn, 1999, Cupid & Cate, 2000, Master Spy: The Robert Hanssen Story, 2002, Miracle Run, 2004, Vinegar Hill, 2005, The Robber Bride, 2007; (TV miniseries) Angels in America, 2003 (Golden Globe for best supporting actress 2004, Emmy award, Outstanding Supporting Actress in a Miniseries or a Movie, 2004); (TV series) Ryan's Hope, 1975, West Wing, 2001-05,(Emmy nomination, 2002), Weeds, 2005- (Best Performance by an Actress in a TV Series-Musical or Comedy, Hollywood Fgn. Press Assn. (Golden Globe award), 2006. Office: William Morris Agy care Scott Henderson 151 S El Camino Dr Beverly Hills CA 90212-2775 *

PARKER, MEL, editor; b. NYC, Feb. 11, 1949; s. David Parker and Mollie (Kantorowicz) Lederman; m. Diane Nancy Goldberg, June 27, 1971; children: Emily, David. AB, Rutgers U., 1971; AM in English, NYU, 1973. Editl. rschr. Esquire Mag., NYC, 1973; grad. asst. NYU Dept. English, 1974-77; adj. lectr. CUNY, 1977-78; editor Leisure Books, NYC, 1978-81; sr. editor Playboy Paperbacks, NYC, 1981-82, Berkley Pub. Group, NYC, 1982-85, exec. editor, 1985-86, editor-in-chief, 1986-87; v.p. editor-in-chief Warner Paperbacks, 1987-90, pub., 1990-96; sr. v.p. Warner Books, NYC, 1996-98, sr. v.p., editor-in-chief Book-of-the-Month Club, 1999-2000; sr. v.p., editl. dir. Bookspan, 2000—03; pres. Mel Parker Books, LLC, 2004—. Co-chair exec. pub. com. United Jewish Appeal Fedn.; mem. faculty Stanford Pub. Course, 1997-98. Mem. Jerusalem Book Fair Com., 1997-99. Mem. Assn. Am. Publs. (chmn. trade exec. com. 1997-99), Book Table, Pub. Lunch Club (sec.-treas. 2000-01, v.p. 2001-02, pres. 2002-03). Office Phone: 718-788-0080. Business E-Mail: mel@melparkerbooks.com.

PARKER, MELISSA BERNICE, advertising executive; d. Marzine Parker, Sr. and Moretha Parker. BS in Agrl. Econs., U. Calif., Davis, 1995; MBA, Calif. State U., Hayward, 2000. Cert. notary pub. Calif., lic. Realtor Calif., property mgmt. Calif. Apt. Assn. Property mgr. M & M Parker & Assocs., Oakland, 1991—; banking officer Citibank F.S.B., San Francisco, 1995—96; sr. claims rep. Farmers Ins. Exch., Pleasanton, Calif., 1996—2000, Richmond, Calif., 1996—2000; applied materials Human Resources Exec. Program, Santa Clara, Calif., 2000; advt. exec. SBC Calif., Oakland, 2001—04, Valley Yellow Pages, Hayward, Calif., 2004—05, Hilltop Learning Corp., 2004—, Jack London Square Realty, Inc., 2005—. Photo journal dvd, Celebrations Article Oakland Tribune Marzine & Moretha Parker Sr. Co-chair Taylor Meml. United Meth. Ch. Ann. Woman's Day; with Marilyn Hickey Ministries; mem. U. Calif.-Davis. Mem.: NAFE, So. Poverty Law Ctr., Pres.'s Cir., Alfred Lepure Soc., Delta Sigma Theta (life). Democrat. United Methodist. Office: 311 Oak St Ste 116 Oakland CA 94607 Home Phone: 510-601-5358, 510-601-5358; Office Phone: 510-459-9062. Personal E-mail: parkermel@aol.com. Business E-Mail: melissa.parker@jacklondonrealty.com.

PARKER, MELISSA EPLEY, psychologist; b. Columbus, Ohio, June 19; BA in Psychology, Wittenberg U., Springfield, Ohio, 2000; MA in sch. psychology, magna cum laude, Ohio State U., Columbus, 2005. Cert. sch. psychologist Ohio. Sch. psychologist Columbus Pub. Schs., 2005—06, Columbus Rsch. Based Edn. for Autistic Children Autism Program, 2006—. Contbr. articles to profl. jours. Recipient McGregor Rsch. Fellow award, Wittenberg U., 1999. Mem.: NASP, Sch. Psychologists Ctrl. Ohio, Ohio Sch. Psychologists Assn. Personal E-mail: melle27osu@yahoo.com. Business E-Mail: mparker684@columbus.k12.oh.us.

PARKER, MICHAEL J., editor, writer, researcher; b. Camden, NJ, Apr. 21, 1959; s. Harry J. and Charlotte D. Parker. BA, Glassboro State Coll., 1981. Mng. editor, regional editor Suburban Newspaper Group, Cherry Hill, NJ, 1980-82; database sketch editor Lehigh Press, Pennsauken, NJ, 1983; copy control editor, assoc. supr. Datapro, Delran, NJ, 1984-95, sr. data quality adminstr., 1996-98; editor Gartner Datapro, Delran, 1998—2005, spl. projects US and abroad, 2002—05, publs. flow coord., 2004—05; editor conf. projects Gartner, 2006. Article writer, columnist Silent Film Monthly, Silent Film Annual-U.S., Canada, Europe, Far East, 1993-00; cons. to film historians- U.S., Europe; contbr. articles to The Grapevine; writer motion picture history various publs., 2007-. Assoc., coord. Homeless Hospitality Network, Merchantville, NJ, 1995-02; rep. Echelon Mall Ministry, Voorhees, NJ, 1975-76; asst. to clergy First Presbyn. Ch., 1992—; editor promotion, Anthony Griggs Found. Advancement of Youth; contbr. Interfaith Homeless Outreach Coun., Angel Tree Program, South Jersey Animal Shelters. Recipient cert. Borough of Haddonfield Commrs., 1981, Commendations Maple Shade Bd. of Edn. Avocations: writing to members of the arts (U.S. and overseas), collecting autographed items, exhibits, stamps, coins. Personal E-mail: mike.parker12@yahoo.com.

PARKER, MICHAEL SETH, technical development manager; b. Norwich, Conn., Jan. 30, 1964; s. Truman Kelly and Loretta (Hebert) P.; m. Cynthia Lynn Beck, May 23, 1998. BS in Mech. Engring., U. Hartford, 1986; MBA in Mgmt., U. N.Mex., 1999. Registered profl. engr., Ariz., N.Mex., Nev.; accredited Leadership in Energy and Environ. Design, 2002. Metal fabricator Crown Mfg. Corp., Waterford, Conn., 1980-86; project engr. Savage Engring., Inc., Bloomfield, Conn., 1986-94, Fletcher Thompson, Inc., Bridgeport, Conn., 1994-95; solutions devel. mgr. Johnson Controls, Inc., Camp Hill, Pa., 1995—. Mem. ASHRAE, Assn. Energy Engrs. (sr.; cert. energy mgr., cert. demand side mgmt. profl., regional v.p. 2000-01, cert. lighting efficiency profl., Internat. Energy Engr. of Yr. 1998, Western Regional Energy Engr. of Yr. 1997), Beta Gamma Sigma. Republican. Avocations: downhill skiing, harley davidsons, travel, guitar. Office Fax: 717-763-9219. Business E-Mail: michael.s.parker@jci.com.

PARKER, NANCY KNOWLES (MRS. CORTLANDT PARKER), publishing executive; b. Buffalo, Aug. 30, 1929; d. Ward Emerson and Barbara Louise (Bull) Knowles; m. Cortlandt Parker, Sept. 8, 1951; children: Elizabeth, Cortlandt, Stephen, Nancy Gray. Student, Chevy Chase Jr. Coll., 1949. Copy girl Washington Evening Star, 1947-49; reporter Newark Evening News, 1949-51; asst. pub. rels. dir. Newark Cmty. Chest, 1951-52; writer Suburban Life mag., Summit, NJ, 1952-55; co-founder, assoc. editor, then editor Observer Tribune, Mendham, NJ, 1955-59; cmty. living editor Recorder Pub. Co., Bernardsville, NJ, 1959-84, v.p., 1960—2002; pub. emerita, 2002—; editor, pub. New Eng., Finger Lakes, L.I. and Va. Wine Gazettes, 1988—. Pres. Greenvale Vineyards, Portsmouth, R.I. Past trustee Somerset Hills Cmty. Chest, North Jersey Tng. Sch., Totowa, Morris-Somerset chpt. UN Assn., Bonnie Brae Ednl. Ctr., Millington, NJ Vis. Homemaker Svc. Somerset County; trustee, bd. dirs. Camp Brett-Endeavor, Clinton, NJ, Morristown (NJ) Meml. Hosp.; mem. Glen Manor House Com., Portsmouth, RI; sec. New Eng. Wine Coun Mem. LWV (chair voters svc. Morris County chpt. 1954-55), Bus. and Profl. Women, Nat. Soc. Arts and Letters, Southeastern New Eng. Grape Growers Assn., Jr. League, Pen and Brush NYC, Friends of Whitehall, Colonial Dames in Am. (bd. dirs. RI chpt.), Newport (RI) Garden Club (past pres.), English Speaking Union (bd. dirs. Newport br. 1990-2000), NJ Hist. Soc. (adv. coun. Newark chpt.) Home: 582 Wapping Rd Portsmouth RI 02871-5306 Office: Greenvale Farm & Vineyard 582 Wapping Rd Portsmouth RI 02871-5306 also: 17 Morristown Rd Bernardsville NJ 07924-2312 Home Phone: 401-847-3268.

PARKER, OLIVIA, photographer; b. Boston, June 10, 1941; d. Harvey Perley and Barbara Ellen (Churchill) Hood; m. John Otis Parker, Apr. 4, 1964; children: John Otis, Helen Elizabeth. BA, Wellesley Coll., 1963. Tchr. photog. workshops, 1975—. Photographer, 1969—; author: (monographs) Signs of Life, 1978, Under the Looking Glass, 1983, Weighing the Planets, 1987; portfolios of black and white photographs Ephemera, 1977, Lost Objects, 1980; one-woman shows include Vision Gallery, Boston, 1976, 1977, 1979, 1982, 1983, 1986, 1987, Friends of Photography, Carmel, Calif., 1979, 1981, Marcuse Pfeifer, N.Y.C., 1980, 1983, George Eastman House, Rochester, N.Y., 1981, Art Inst. Chgo., 1982, Photo Gallery Internat., Tokyo, 1983, 1984, 1987, Fotografie Forum Gallery, Frankfurt, Germany, 1985, Lieberman and Saul, N.Y.C., 1988, Mus. Photgraphic Arts, San Diego, 1988, Photographers' Gallery, London, 1990, Brent Sikkema, N.Y.C., 1990, 1991, Parco, Tokyo, 1991, ICAC/Weston, 1992, Vision, San Francisco, 1993, Robert Klein, Boston, 1993, 1996, 1999, 2005, Wooster Gardens, N.Y.C., 1996, (with Jerry Uelsmann) Isabella Stewart Gardner Mus., Boston, 1997, Huntington (W.Va.) Mus. of Art, 2000, Lancaster (Pa.) Mus. of Art, 2000, Toledo (Ohio) Art Mus., 2002, Visual Arts Ctr. Coll. of Santa Fe, 2003, Edelman Gallery, Chgo., 2004, exhibited in group shows at Mus. Fine Arts, Boston, 1978, 1992, 1993, 1996, 1999, Chgo. Art Inst., 1978, Internat. Ctr. Photography, N.Y.C., 1985, 1987, Fogg Art Mus. Harvard U., 1989, Aldrich Mus. Contemporary Art, 2004, Represented in permanent collections Mus. Modern Art, N.Y.C., Art Inst. Chgo., Boston Mus. Fine Arts, Victoria and Albert Mus., London, TV documentary, Africans in America, 1998. Trustee Art Inst. Boston, 1992—99; bd. dirs. MacDowell Colony, 1988—. Recipient Wellesley College Alumnae Achievement award, 1996; Artists Found. fellow, 1978. Mem.: Soc. for Photog. Edn., Chilton Club. Office: Robert Klein 4th Fl 38 Newbury St Fl 4 Boston MA 02116-3210 E-mail: glasslight@mac.com. *I am interested in the way people think about the unknown. New ideas form, the old are shattered, and sometimes old ideas pop up among the new like graffiti on a wall. All is uncertainty and change, but optimists and bingo players are on the look out for moments of perfect knowledge and perfect cards.*

PARKER, PETER D.M., physicist, educator, researcher; b. NYC, Dec. 14, 1936; s. Allan Ellwood and Alice Francis (Heywood) P.; m. Judith Maxfield Curren, Dec. 27, 1958; children: Stephanie, Gregory, Gretchen. BA, Amherst Coll., 1958; PhD, Calif. Tech., 1963. Physicist Brookhaven Nat. Labs., Upton, NY, 1963-66; prof. Yale U., New Haven, 1966—. Office: Yale U Physics Dept Wright Nuclear Structure 272 Whitney Ave New Haven CT 06520-8124 Office Phone: 203-432-3099. E-mail: peter.parker@yale.edu.

PARKER, R. JOSEPH, lawyer; b. St. Louis, June 29, 1944; s. George Joseph and Ann Rosalie Parker; m. Theresa Gaynor, Aug. 26, 1967; children: Christa Michele, Kevin Blake. AB, Georgetown U., 1966; JD, Boston Coll., 1969. Bar: Ohio 1969. Law clk. to judge U.S. Ct. Appeals (6th Cir.), Akron, Ohio, 1969-70; assoc. Taft, Stettinius & Hollister, Cin., 1970-78, ptnr. Arbitrator Am. Arbitration Assn., Cin., 1980—; faculty Nat. Inst. for Trial Advocacy, 1990—; faculty advanced trial advocacy program IRS, 1993. Editor Law Rev. Ann. Survey Mass. Law, 1967-69; contbg. author: Fed. Civil Procedure Before Trial-6th Circuit. Bd. dirs. West End Health Ctr., Inc., Cin., 1972-76, Legal Aid Soc. Cin., 1982-85; chmn. bd. dirs. Vol. Lawyers for Poor Found., Cin., 1986-88; master Am. Inn of Court, 1984—. Fellow Am. Coll. Trial Lawyers; mem. Ohio State Bar Assn., Cin. Bar Assn., Cin. Country Club, Order of Coif. Democrat. Roman Catholic. Office: 425 Walnut St Ste 1800 Cincinnati OH 45202-3759 E-mail: parker18002000@yahoo.com.

PARKER, RICH, lawyer; b. St. Paul, 1948; AB summa cum laude, U. Calif. Davis, 1970; JD, U. Calif., Los Angeles, 1974. Bar: Calif. 1974, DC 1980. Clerkship with Hon. William Matthew Byrne, Jr. US Dist. Ct., Ctrl. Dist. Calif., 1974—75; former sr. dep. dir. FTC, 1998—99, former dir., Bur. Competition, 1999—2001; ptnr. O'Melveny & Myers LLP, Washington, 2001—, chair antitrust/competition. Comment editor U. Calif. Los Angeles Law Review, 1973—74; contbr. articles to profl. jours. Mem.: DC Bar, ABA (annual mtg. chair 1996—98, spring mtg. chair, antitrust sect. 2002), Phi Kappa Phi, Order of the Coif, Phi Beta Kappa. Office: O'Melveny & Myers LLP 1625 Eye St NW Washington DC 20006 Office Phone: 202-383-5380. Office Fax: 202-383-5414. Business E-Mail: rparker@omm.com.

PARKER, RICHARD DAVIES, law educator; b. Boston, Apr. 3, 1945. BA, Swarthmore Coll., 1967; JD, Harvard U., 1970. Bar: Mass. 1973. Law clk. to Judge J. Skelly Wright, US Ct. Appeals DC Cir., 1970-71; law clk. to Assoc. Justice Potter Stewart, US Supreme Ct., 1971-72; atty. Children's Def. Fund, Cambridge, Mass., 1973-74; asst. prof. law Harvard Law Sch., Cambridge, 1974-79, prof., 1979—98, Paul W. Williams prof. criminal justice, 1998-. Author: The People Rule: A Constitutional Populist Manifesto, 1994. Office: Harvard Law Sch 1563 Massachusetts Ave Cambridge MA 02138 Office Phone: 617-495-7925. Office Fax: 617-496-4913. Business E-Mail: parker@law.harvard.edu.

PARKER, RICHARD WILSON, lawyer, retired rail transportation executive; b. Cleve., June 14, 1943; s. Edgar Gael and Pauline (Wilson) P.; m. Helen Margaret Shober, Jan. 3, 1998; children from previous marriage: Brian Jeffrey, Lauren Michelle, Lisa Christine. BA in Econs. cum laude, U. Redlands, 1965; JD cum laude, Northwestern U., 1968. Bar: Ohio 1968, Va. 1974. Assoc. Arter & Hadden, Cleve., 1968—71; asst. gen. atty. Norfolk & Western Ry. Co., Cleve. and Roanoke, Va., 1971-74, asst. gen. solicitor Roanoke, 1974-78, gen. atty., 1978-84, Norfolk So. Corp., 1985-88, sr. gen. atty., 1988-93, asst. v.p. real estate, 1993-99, v.p. properties, 1999-2000, v.p. real estate, 2000—03. Mem. ABA, Va. State Bar, Norfolk-Portsmouth Bar Assn. Presbyterian. Office: 3 Commercial Pl Norfolk VA 23510-2108

PARKER, ROBERT ALLAN RIDLEY, federal agency administrator, astronaut; b. NYC, Dec. 14, 1936; s. Allan Elwood and Alice (Heywood) P.; m. Joan Audrey Capers, June 14, 1958 (div. 1980); children: Kimberly Ellen, Brian David Capers; m. Judith S. Woodruff, Apr. 2, 1981. AB, Amherst Coll., 1958; PhD, Calif. Inst. Tech., 1962. NSF postdoctoral fellow U. Wis., 1962-63, asst. prof., then assoc. prof. astronomy, 1963-74; astronaut NASA, Johnson Space Ctr., 1967-91; dir. policy plan Office Space Flight, NASA Hdqs., Washington, 1991, dir. space ops. utilization program, 1992-97; dir. NASA Mgmt. Office, JPL, Pasadena, Calif., 1997—. Mem. support crew Apollo XV and XVII, mission scientist Apollo XVII, program scientist Skylab program, mission specialist for Spacelab 1, 1983, ASTRO-1, 1990. Mem. Am. Astron. Soc., Phi Beta Kappa. Office: NMO 180 801 JPL 4800 Oak Grove Dr Pasadena CA 91109-8001 Business E-Mail: rparker@nmo.jpl.nasa.gov.

PARKER, ROBERT CHAUNCEY HUMPHREY, clergyman, publishing executive; b. NYC, Apr. 6, 1941; s. Robert Humphrey and Edith Louise (Corya) P. Student, U. Va., Charlottesville, 1960—61, student, 1962—63; diploma, Inst. Psychorientology, Laredo, Tex., 1973. Ordained to ministry Ch. of Antioch-Malabar Rite, 1975. Law clk. Shearman & Sterling, NYC, 1961-62; owner Parker's Pronto-Pups Inc., NYC, 1962-64; asst. to pres. US Packaging, NYC, 1964-66; asst. nat. sales mgr. Elliott Svc. Co. Inc., Mt. Vernon, NY, 1966-67; pres., cons. Lenfield Assocs. & Cons., NYC and Washington, 1967-71; founder, pres. Occult Comm. Corp., NYC, Washington, and Danbury, Conn., 1971-76, New Awareness Corp., London and Mpls., 1973-81; dir., resident min. The Healing Ctr. at St. Patricia's, Inver Grove Heights, Minn., 1975; lectr., min. Ch. of Antioch-Malabar Rite, 1975—; editor New Awareness News, 1975—2006; founder, pres. Parker/Tofte Comm., Robert Parker Assocs., Minnetonka, Minn., 1977—2005; pres., CEO Am. Energy & Alcohol Corp., Mpls., 1981-84. Cons. Boat Owners Assn. US, Washington, 1967-70, Durance Co., 1994-95; rschr., cons. Am. Marine Corp., Marblehead, Mass.; pres. Field Harmonics Rsch. Group Inc., 1993-97, New Awareness Spkrs. and Pub. Group, Inc., 1997-2005; cons., spkr. in field. Author: Watergate Flight 553, 1974, Reabsorption Energy, 1975, Finding Your Own Four-Leaf Clover, 1993; author Telsa Newsletter, 1979; editor New Awareness Mag., 1973-75, (newsletter) Sunbeams; editor, pub. New Awareness News and Book News, 1977—2006, New Awareness Computer News, 1995—2006, psychic/parapscyhology internat. trade jours., 1971-75; designer, pub.: Henry's Hilarious One Liners, 1991, Henry's Just a Chuckle, 1992, Henry's Just a Laugh, 1992, Henry's Just a Witticism, 1992; contbr. articles to profl. jours.; featured on Dimension WCCO-TV, 1991, 93, Forbes Mag., 1996, Elizabeth Smart Recovery, Sta. WCCO-TV, 2003, Ruth Koscielak Show, Sta. KCCO-AM, 2003, Smart Predictions 100% Correct, 2003; host (cable) Astrology and Mind, Etc., 1994-96; syndicated columnist; ongoing guest WUO-AM, 2006. Bd. dirs. Toutorsky Ednl. Found., Washington, 1988—91. Mem. Nat. Press Club (Washington), Internat. Telsa Soc. Inc., Knickerbocker Greys Vet. Corps (NYC), Browning Sch. Alumni Assn. (NYC), Lenox (Mass.) Sch. Alumni Assn. Avocations: reading, travel.

PARKER, ROBERT M., JR., (BOB PARKER), wine critic, writer; b. Balt., July 23, 1947; m. Patricia Parker; 1 child, Maia. BA in History, U. Md., College Park; JD, U. Md., Balt., 1973. From sr. atty. to asst. gen. counsel Farm Credit Banks of Balt., 1973—84; founder, writer, pub. The Wine Advocate (formerly The Baltimore-Washington Wine Advocate), Parkton, Md., 1978—. Author Bordeaux, 1985 (Glenfiddich Award, 1986, Goldene Feder, 1993, Moët Hennessy Wine and Vine Comm. Award, 1993), 2nd edit., 1991 (Internat. Assn. of Cooking Profls. Award, 1992), 3rd edit., 1998, 4th edit., 2003, Parker's Wine Buyer's Guide, 1987, 2nd edit., 1989, 3rd edit., 1993, 4th edit., 1995, 5th edit., 1999, 6th edit., 2002, The Wines of the Rhone Valley and Provence, 1987 (Tastemaker's Award, 1989, Wine Guild's Wine Book of Yr. Award, 1989), Burgundy, 1990 (Moët Hennessy Wine and Vine Comm. Award, 1993), The Wines of the Rhone Valley, 1997, The World's Greatest Wine Estates: A Modern Perspective, 2005, contbg. editor Food and Wine Mag., contbr. The Field, wine critic L'Express mag., columnist BusinessWeek, 2006—. Named Marylander of Yr., Loyola Coll., 1992, Chevalier, Ordre Nat. du Merite, 1993, Légion d'honneur, 1999, Officer, 2005, Hon. Citizen of Châteauneuf-du-Pape, 1995, Wine and Spirits Profl. of 1997, James Beard Found., 1998, Comdr., Italy's Nat. Order of Merit, 2002. Office: The Wine Advocate PO Box 311 Monkton MD 21111 Office Phone: 410-329-6477. Office Fax: 410-357-4504. E-mail: wineadvocate@erobertparker.com.

PARKER, SARA ANN, librarian, consultant; b. Cassville, Mo., Feb. 19, 1939; d. Howard Franklin and Vera Irene (Thomas) P. BA, Okla. State U., 1961; M.L.S., Emporia State U., Kans., 1968. Adult svcs. librarian Springfield Pub. Libr., Mo., 1972-75, bookmobile dir. Mo., 1975-76; coord. S.W. Mo. Libr. Network, Springfield, 1976-78; libr. developer Colo. State Libr., Denver, 1978-82; state librarian Mont. State Libr., Helena, 1982-88, State Libr. Pa., Harrisburg, 1988-90; Pa. commr. librs., dep. sec. edn. State of Pa., Harrisburg, 1990-95; state libr. State of Mo., Jefferson City, 1995—2005. Cons. and lectr. in field. Author, editor, compiler in field; contbr. articles to profl. jours. Sec. Western Coun. State Librs., Reno, 1984—88; mem. Mont. State Data Adv. Coun., 1983—88, Mont. Telecomm. Coun., 1985—88, WLN Network Coun., 1984—87, Kellogg ICLIS Project Mgmt. Bd., 1986—88; mem. adv. com. Gates Libr. Initiative, 1998—2005; mem. OCLC Strategic Directions and Governance Study Adv. Coun., 2000—01, webjunction adv. coun., 2003—05. Recipient Pres.'s award, Nature Conservancy, 1989, Friends award, Pa. Assn. Ednl. Comms. and Techs., 1989, Friend of Sch. Librs. award, Mo. Sch. Librs. Assn., 2000, Bohley Libr. Cooperation award, 2001; fellow Inst. Ednl. Leadership, 1982. Mem.: ALA, Mountain Plains Libr. Assn. (sec. chmn. 1980, pres. 1987—88, chair MOREnet adv. coun. 2004—05), Mont. Libr. Assn. (bd. dirs. 1982—88), Chief Officers State Libr. Agys. (pres. 1996—98).

PARKER, SARAH ELIZABETH, state supreme court chief justice; b. Charlotte, NC, Aug. 23, 1942; d. Augustus and Zola Elizabeth (Smith) P. AB, U. N.C., 1964, JD, 1969; LHD (hon.), Queens Coll., 1998. Bar: N.C. 1969, U.S. Dist. Ct. (mid., ea. and we. dists.) N.C. Vol. U.S. Peace Corps, Ankara, Turkey, 1964-66; pvt. practice Charlotte, 1969-84; judge N.C. Ct. Appeals, Raleigh, 1985—92; assoc. justice N.C. Supreme Ct., Raleigh, 1993—2005, chief justice, 2006—. Bd. visitors U. N.C., Chapel Hill, 1993—97; pres. Mecklenburg County Dem. Women, Charlotte, 1973; N.C. ct. commr., 1999—; bd. dirs. YWCA, Charlotte, 1982—85. Recipient Disting. Woman of N.C. award, 1997, Woman of Achievement award Nat. Fedn. Women's Clubs, 1997, Humanitarian award N.C. Assn. of Black

County Officials, 2003; Named Judge of Yr., N.C. Women Attorneys Assn., 2002. Mem. ABA, Inst. Jud. Adminstrn., N.C. Bar Assn. (v.p. 1987-88), Mecklenburg County Bar (sec.-treas. 1982-84), Wake County Bar Assn., N.C. Internat. Women's Forum, Women Attys. Assn. (Gwyneth David Pub. Svc. award 1986). Episcopalian. Office: NC Supreme Ct PO Box 1841 Raleigh NC 27602-1841 *

PARKER, SARAH JESSICA, actress; b. Nelsonville, Ohio, Mar. 25, 1965; m. Matthew Broderick May, 1997; 1 child: James. Launched fragrance Lovely perfume, 2005; designer, clothing line Bitten, 2007—. Actress: (theatre) The Innocents, 1976, The Sound of Music, 1977, Annie, 1978, The War Brides, 1981, The Death of a Miner, 1982, To Gillian on Her 37th Birthday, 1983, 84, Terry Neal's Future, 1986, The Heidi Chronicles, 1989, How to Succeed in Business Without Really Trying, 1996, Once Upon a Mattress, 1996, (films) Rich Kids, 1979, Somewhere Tomorrow, 1983, Firstborn, 1984, Footloose, 1984, Girls Just Want to Have Fun, 1985, Flight of the Navigator, 1986, L.A. Story, 1991, Honeymoon in Vegas, 1992, Hocus Pocus, 1993, Striking Distance, 1993, Ed Wood, 1994, Miami Rhapsody, 1995, If Lucy Fell, 1996, Mars Attacks!, 1996, The First Wives Club, 1996, Extreme Measures, 1996, 'Til There Was You, 1997, The Substance of Fire, 1996, (voice) A Life Apart: Hasidism in America, 1997, Isn't She Great, 1999, Dudley Do-Right, 1999, State and Main, 2000, Life Without Dick, 2001, Strangers with Candy, 2005, The Family Stone, 2005, Failure to Launch, 2006; (TV movies) My Body, My Child, 1982, Going for the Gold: The Bill Johnson Story, 1985, A Year in the Life, 1986, The Room Upstairs, 1987, Dadah Is Death, 1988, The Ryan White Story, 1989, Twist of Fate, 1989, In the Best Interest of the Children, 1992, The Sunshine Boys, 1995, Sex and the Matrix, 2000, (TV series) Square Pegs, 1982-83, A Year in the Life, 1987-88, Equal Justice, 1990-91, Sex and the City, 1998-2004 (Best Supporting Actress Golden Globe award 1999, 2000, 01, 02, 04, Emmy nominee for Outstanding Lead Actress 1999-2002, Outstanding Performance by Female Actor in Comedy Series award 2001, Emmy award Outstanding Lead Actress in a Comedy Series, 2004), (TV pilots) The Alan King Show, 1986; guest appearances The Ben Stiller Show, 1992, The Larry Sanders Show, 1992, (video) Sesame Beginnings: Moving Together, 2007; co-exec. prodr. Sex and the City. Nat. amb. US Fund for UNICEF. Recipient, Am. Civil Liberties Union award, 1995. Office: Creative Artists Agy care Jane Berliner 9830 Wilshire Blvd Beverly Hills CA 90212-1804 *

PARKER, SASHA SMILKA, medical educator, nurse, consultant; b. Neustadt, Holstein, Germany, Nov. 3, 1947; arrived in US, 1952; d. Blagoje Blazo and Sofia Soka Dragic; life ptnr. Richard A. Polemeni; 1 child, Peter Joseph. Student, Ind. U., 1978; AS in Nursing, Broward CC, 1982. Lic. massage therapist Fla., cert. electrologist Fla.; RN Fla.; cert. facial specialist Fla. Asst. surg. adminstr. Am. Med. Inst. Surgery, Ft. Lauderdale, Fla., 1988—89; surg. adminstr. Eye Care & Surgery Ctr., Ft. Lauderdale, 1989—91; clin. supr. Spl. Care Home Health, 1991—97; pres., CEO Gem Homecare Svcs., Inc., Ft. Lauderdale, 1997—2005, Eclectic Skin Inst., LLC, Ft. Lauderdale, 1998—2003; pres., CEO, CFO Esthetic Skin Inst., Inc., 2003—. Cons. Innovative Health Svcs., Inc., Ft. Lauderdale, 1997—; faculty spa mgmt. and hospitality program U. Calif., Irvine, Calif. Vol. Women in Distress, Ft. Lauderdale, Adult Congregate Living Assn., Ft. Lauderdale. Named Ultimate Nurse, Ultimate Nurses, Inc., 2004, Businesswoman of Yr., Nat. Rep. Congl. Com., Inc., 2004, 2005, 2006; recipient Spotlight Entrepreneur award, Nursing Spectrum, 2004. Mem.: Am. Massage Therapy Assn., Nat. Bus. Adv. Coun., Fla. Electrology Assn., Fla. Nurses Assn., Assn. Med. Esthetic Nurses (pres., founder 2004). Avocations: dancing, travel, music, cooking. Office: Esthetic Skin Inst Inc 1120 S Fed Hwy Ste 4 Fort Lauderdale FL 33316 Home Phone: 954-779-7248; Office Phone: 954-463-6881. Office Fax: 954-463-4459. Personal E-mail: sashas@bellsouth.net.

PARKER, STUART BLAIN, insurance company executive; BBA in Mgmt., Valdosta State U., Ga.; MA in Polit. Sci., Midwestern U.; MBA, St. Mary's U., San Antonio. CLU; ChFC. CFP practitioner USAA (United Svcs. Automobile Assn.), San Antonio, 1998, v.p. fin. planning svcs., pres. fin. planning svcs., 2004, pres. property & casualty ins. group. Pilot USAF. Mem.: Fin. Planning Assn. Office: USAA 9800 Fredericksburg Rd San Antonio TX 78288 Office Phone: 210-498-8222. *

PARKER, SUSAN BROOKS, government agency administrator; b. Newport, NH, Nov. 7, 1945; d. Ronald Elliott and Elizabeth Louise (Wiggins) P.; m. Allen D. Avery, 1967 (div. 1978); children: Jeffrey Roberts Avery, Mark Brooks Avery. BS in English and French, U. Vt., 1968; MSW/MSP, Boston Coll., 1978. EMT Vt., 1973-76. Resort hotel mgr., retail buyer Avery Vt. Inns, 1967-75; aftercare psychiat. social worker Orange County Mental Health, Bradford, Vt., 1974-76; exec. dir. Grafton County Planning Coun., Lebanon, NH, 1978-80, N.H. Developmental Disabilities Planning Coun., Concord, NH, 1980-87; commr. Dept. of Mental Health, Augusta, Maine, 1987-89; assoc. commr. U.S. Social Security Adminstrn., Balt., 1989-93; sec. gen. Rehab. Internat., NYC, 1993—98; sr. adv., interim dir. disability program Internat. Labor Office, Geneva, 1998—2002; dir. policy and rsch. Office Disability Employment Policy U.S. Dept. Labor, Washington, 2002—. Cons. Nat. Gov.'s Assn., Washington, 1985-86, Office of Health and Devel. Svcs., Washington, 1987; bd. dirs. Nat. Assn. Devel. Disabilities, Washington, 1983-87, Ctrl. NH Mental Health Ctr., Concord, 1985-87, World Com. Disability, Washington, 1997—, Roeher Inst., Toronto, 1997-2000, Orah.com, Geneva, 2002—, NH Devel. Disabilities Coun., 2002—05; hon. coun. Rehab. Internat., mem. World Assembly, NYC, 1998-. Author: poetry; contbr. articles to newspapers and profl. jours. Pres. Parent Tchr. Orgn., Fairlee, Vt., 1972-73; founder and dir. Fairlee Ford Sayre Ski Program, Dartmouth Coll. Skiway, Fairlee, 1972-76, United Way, Concord, 1983-86; bd. dirs. PTO Rundlett Jr. H.S., Concord, 1982-85; pres. U.S. Coun. for Internat. Rehab., Washington, 1993. Named Outstanding Alumnae, Boston Coll., 1991; recipient Children's Disability Pub. Policy award, Assn. Retarded Citizens, 1992, Kathryn C. Arneson award, People to People, 1992, Commr.'s citation, US Social Security Adminstrn., 1992, Commn.'s citation, 1993, Secretary's Exemplary Achievement award, US Dept. Labor, 2003—06. Avocations: skiing, gardening, boating, reading, film and performing arts.

PARKER, THERESA ANN BOGGS, retired special education educator, retired music educator; b. Spencer, W.Va., Jan. 16, 1947; d. Harry Clay and Betty Jean (Richards) Boggs; m. Larry Glen Parker, Apr. 29, 1967; children: Carey Ann, Jill Renee, Timothy Preston, Jeremy David, Leanna Michelle. AA in Secretarial Studies, Glenville State Coll., 1967, BA in Music Edn., 1970; MA in Spl. Edn., Coll. Grad. Studies, 1991; EdS in Ednl. Leadership, W.Va. Grad. Coll., 1996. Cert. tchr. Pvt. practice piano tchr., Spencer, 1967—; sub. tchr. Roane County Schs., Spencer, 1970—71, tchr. spl. edn., 1987—2001, tchr. music K-8, 2001—02, tchr. spl. edn., 2002—06, tchr. music K-8, 2006—, educator team mem.-parent/educator resource ctr., 1989—2002; sub. tchr. Marietta City Schs., Ohio, 1986; adminstr. Sand Hill Day Care Ctr., Reno, Ohio, 1986—87. Spl. edn. rep. W.Va. Dept. Edn., Charleston, 1995-98; dir. Safetytown Roane County, Spencer, 1989-93. Author: (with others) Selected Teaching Models Integrated with West Virginia's Academic Model for Gifted Education, 1991; poet with works appearing in Echoes of Yesteryear, America at the Millennium, 2000, Enlightened Shadows, Miracles of Nature, Best Poems and Poets of 2001, The Road That Never Ends, Internat. Libr. Poetry. Chmn. Cub Scout Pack Boy Scouts Am., Reno, 1983-87, dist. trainer, Parkersburg, W.Va., 1986-87, chmn. Boy Scout Troop, Spencer, 1987-91; Roane County rep. to Clay Ctr. for Arts Charleston, 2005—; organizer First Bapt. Ch. Diabetes Sup. Group, 1995-98. Safetytown grantee W.Va. Dept. Edn., Roane County, 1989, grantee W.Va. Edn. Fund, Roane County, 1992, W.Va. Edn. Fund, Clover Sch., 1992, Diabetes Support Group grantee Benedium Found., Roane and Calhoun/Jackson Counties, 1995, Youth and Edn. grantee Tri-County Partnership, Inc., 1998, W.Va. Humanities Coun., 2000-01, 05, The Edn. Alliance, 2004, 05, Exceptional Tchg. Techniques award RESA V, 2005; named Tchr. of Yr. Spencer Middle Sch., 1999-2000. Mem. MENC, ASCD, W.Va. Profl. Educators, Blue Grass Riding Club, Lions (program chmn., pres. 1997-98, dist. Leo chmn. 1998-00, dist. Flag Day/Peace Poster contest 2000-2001), Roane Arts and Humanities Coun. (charter, pres. 2000—), W.Va. Celtic Soc., Cultural Diversity Soc. Democrat. Baptist. Avocations: reading, sewing, playing piano. Home: 5754 Charleston Rd Walton WV 25286 Office: Roane County Schs 102 Chapman Ave Spencer WV 25276

PARKER, TOM, state supreme court justice, lawyer; b. Montgomery, Ala., Aug. 19, 1951; s. Tom Parker and Gloria Parker Pennington; m. Dottie James. BA, Dartmouth Coll., 1973; JD, Vanderbilt U., 1978; attended, U. Sao Paulo Sch. of Law, Brazil. Prtnr. Parker & Kotouc; asst. atty. gen. State of Ala.; legal adviser, to Chief Justice Ala. Supreme Ct.; dep. administrative dir., gen. counsel Ala. Ct. System, 2001—03; assoc. justice Ala. Supreme Ct., 2004—. Former special projects mgr. Found. for Moral Law. Founding exec. dir. Ala. Family Alliance (now Alabama Policy Institute), Ala. Family Advocates. Grantee Rotary Internat. Fellowship, U. São Paulo Sch of Law, Brazil. Office: Ala Supreme Ct 300 Dexter Ave Montgomery AL 36104-3741 *

PARKER, TONY (WILLIAM ANTHONY PARKER II), professional basketball player; b. Bruges, Belgium, May 17, 1982; s. Tony Parker and Pamela Firestone; m. Eva Longoria, July 7, 2007. Degree in Econ., Nat. Inst. Physical Edn., Paris. Guard San Antonio Spurs, 2001—. Mem. France's Jr. Nat. Team, 1998, 2000. Singer: (albums) Top of the Game, 2007. Named Champion of French Champions, L'Equipe, 2003, NBA Finals MVP, 2007; named to NBA All-Rookie First Team, 2002, NBA We. Conf. All-Star Team, 2006—07. Achievements include mem. NBA Championship Team, 2003, 2005, 2007; has appeared in more playoff games before his 24th birthday than any player in NBA history. Office: San Antonio Spurs One SBC Ctr San Antonio TX 78219 *

PARKER, TOWANA D., entrepreneur, director; d. John Richard Martin and Bernice Eason; m. Towana D. Parker, Sept. 25, 1976; children: Tanaya S., Yoshaundala S., Edmond II M., Gabriel T. Child Evangelism Metro Child Evangelism, 1985. Entrpreneur Special-T Uniform & Embroidery, Detroit, 1995—; pres. Ladies of Destiny and Purpose Internat., 1997—; exec. dir. Destiny and Purpose Cmty. Outreach, 1999—. TV host Public Report Host. Contbr. articles to profl. jours. Master puppeteer Kings Kids Puppet Ministry, Detroit, 1986—2004; mem. Detroit Exch. Club, 2004—. Grantee, Detroit Empowerment Zone Devel. Corp., 2002-2004, City of Detroit Neighborhood Opportunity Fund, 2004-2005. Home Phone: 313-535-8220; Office Phone: 313-533-1931. Office Fax: 313-533-1932; Home Fax: 313-535-8810. Personal E-mail: ladyteedp@aol.com. Business E-Mail: dapco7outreach@aol.com. E-mail: dapcol@sbcglobal.net.

PARKER, TREY, animator; b. Conifer, Colo., Oct. 19, 1969; s. Randy and Sharon Parker. Attended, Colo. Univ. Dir., writer: (films) American History, 1992; prodr., dir., writer, voice of various characters The Spirit of Christmas (also titled Jesus vs. Frosty), 1992; The Spirit of Christmas (also titled Jesus vs. Santa), 1995 (Los Angeles Film Critics Assn. award for Best Animation, 1997); dir., writer, actor Your Studio and You, 1995; prodr., dir., writer, composer, actor Alfred Packer: The Musical (also titled Cannibal! The Musical), 1996; dir.: For Goodness Sake II, 1996; creator, exec. prodr., dir., writer, composer (TV series) South Park, 1997—, voice of Mr. Mackey, Satan, Randy Marsh, Ned Gerbalnski, Mr. Hankey, Officer Barbrady, and others (CableACE award for Animated Programming Special or Series, 1997); prodr., dir., composer, actor: (films) Orgazmo, 1997; composer, actor BASEketball, 1998; prodr., dir., writer, composer (films) South Park: Bigger Longer & Uncut, 1999 (Los Angeles Film Critics Assoc. award for Best Music, 1999, New York Film Critics Circle award for Best Animated Film, 1999, MTV Movie award Best Musical Performance, 1999); exec. prodr.: (films) How's Your News?, 1999; exec. prodr., writer, creator, composer (TV series) That's My Bush, 2001; prodr., dir., writer, composer: (films) Team America: World Police, 2004; exec. prodr., singer: albums Chef Aid: The South Park Album, South Park: Bigger, Longer and Uncut, Mr. Hankey's Christmas Classics, Timmy and the Lords of the Underworld. Office: c/o Comedy Central 1775 Broadway 10th Fl New York NY 10019

PARKER, VIRGINIA MARIE, language educator; b. Boston, Aug. 31, 1950; d. Thomas Gurney Sr. and Marguerite Mary (O'Sullivan) P. BA, Emmanuel Coll., 1972; postgrad. studies in English, Lincoln Coll. U. Oxford, (Eng.) Bread Loaf Sessions, summers 1987-89; MA, Middlebury Coll., 1989. Cert. secondary English tchr., Mass. Vol. Jesuit Vol. Corps N.W., Seattle, 1972-73; tchr. English Blue Hills Regional Tech. Sch., Canton, Mass., 1973—, sch. newspaper advisor, 1973—75. Editl. cons. competency-based vocat. ednl. curriculum Dept. Edn./Occupl. Divsn., Commonwealth of Mass., 1984-88; nat. honor soc. advisor, screening com. mem. William A. Dwyer Chpt., Blue Hills, Canton, 1986-88, 1994-97; mediation trainee, advisor Sch. Mediation Assocs., 1993, 2000-03 Ch. lector, religious educator, youth retreat facilitator various parishes, 1970—; grad. master tchr. program Office of Religious Edn., Archdiocese of Boston, 1977. Recipient Outstanding Educator award, Norfolk County Tchrs. Assn., Blue Hills Regional Sch. Dist., 2007. Mem. NEA, Nat. Coun. Tchrs. English, Mass. Vocat. Assn., Mass. Tchrs. Assn., Blue Hills Ednl. Assn. (sec. 1977-78), Mass. Audubon Soc., Alden Kindred Am., Irish Culture Ctr., Historic Winslow Ho. Soc. Democrat. Roman Catholic. Avocations: travel, theater, beach walking, genealogy, cemetary haunting. Home: 80 Parks St Duxbury MA 02332-4831 Office: Blue Hills Regional Tech Sch 800 Randolph St Canton MA 02021-1358 E-mail: vparker@bluehills.org.

PARKER, WALTER BRUCE, arctic research specialist, consultant; b. Spokane, Wash., Aug. 11, 1926; s. Bruce Velorus and Lucille Kathryn (Chessman) P.; m. Patricia Isabelle Ertman, Jan. 28, 1946; children: Sandra Wassilie, Patrick B., Jeffrey K., Douglas S., Lisa M. BA in History, U. Alaska, Fairbanks, 1964; DSc, U. Alaska, Anchorage, 1998. Air traffic controller FAA, 1946-64, evaluation officer Anchorage, 1964-66, analyst Washington, 1966-68, planner Anchorage, 1968-70; sr. planner Fed. Field Com. for Alaska, Anchorage, 1970-71; rsch. assoc. U. Alaska, Anchorage, 1971-74; commr. Alaska Dept. Hwys., Juneau, 1974-76; chmn. Alaska Fed./State Land Use Planning Commn., 1976-79; disting. practioner in residence U. Alaska, Anchorage, 1979-80; chmn. Alaska Oil Spill Commn., Anchorage, 1989-90; pres., cons. transp. and telecom. sys. Parker Assocs., Inc., Anchorage, 1971—; commr. U.S. Arctic Rsch. Commn., Anchorage, 1995—2001. Sr. fellow Inst. of the North, 2000—; mem. marine bd., com. on advances in pilotage and navigation NRC, 1991-94, North Pacific rsch. bd., 2000-04, Oil Spill Recovery Inst. bd., 1999-; chmn. Alaska Hazardous Substance Spill Coun., 1991-95; chmn. Arctic Coun. Circumpolar Infrastructure Task Force, 2000—. Author: Alaska and The Law of the Sea, 1974, Alaska People's and Alaska Lands, 1977; contbr. reports to profl. publs. Chmn. Alaska Conservation Soc., Anchorage, 1969-71, Alaska Humanties Forum, Anchorage, 1987-93, Anchorage Parks and Recreation Coun., 1971-74; active Alaska Bd. Fish and Game, Juneau, 1971-74; chmn. Prince William Sound Sci. Ctr., 1996-2004, chmn.; assemblyman Anchorage Borough, 1971-74. With USN, 1944-46. Mem. Am. Soc. Pub. Adminstrn. (chmn. Alaska chpt. 1971-73). Democrat. Avocations: skiing, dog mushing and breeding, gardening. Home: 3724 Campbell Airstrip Rd Anchorage AK 99504-4422 Office Phone: 907-343-2444. E-mail: wbparker@gci.net.

PARKER, WILLIAM, education educator; b. Savannah, Ga., May 23, 1965; s. William Robert and Carolyn Parker; m. Maria Susanne Meza-Keuthen, Aug. 4, 1989. PhD, U. Nebr., 1992. Asst. prof. Duke U. Med. Ctr., Durham, NC, 1993—. Co-author: more than 80 sci. articles. Mem. local and state leadership Royal Rangers, Durham, 1981—. Grantee, NIH. Mem.: Fedn. Am. Socs. for Exptl. Biology, Protein Soc., Sigma Xi Sci. Rsch. Soc., AAAS, Am. Soc. Transplant Surgeons, Am. Chem. Soc. Achievements include discovery of new model for host-bacterial interactions in the gut; new model for evaluation of the hygiene hypothesis; evidence for universal protein folding mechanism proposed by Valerie Lim; new member of the family of antibodies that includes isohemagglutinins. Home: 1023 Wells St Durham NC 27707 Office: Duke Univ Med Ctr DUMC Box 2605 Durham NC 27710 Home Phone: 919-419-6226; Office Phone: 919-681-3886. Business E-Mail: bparker@duke.edu.

PARKER-FAIRBANKS, DIXIE, artist; b. Cedar Rapids, Iowa, Aug. 1, 1936; d. James N. and Mary Louise (Mussell) Parker; m. Richard Fairbanks, Aug. 26, 1966 (dec. Mar. 1989) BFA, Drake U., 1958, MFA, 1959. Craft instr. State of Wis., Waukesha, 1960—61; asst. dir. dept. edn. Des Moines Art Ctr., 1961—66; art lectr. Ctrl. Wash. U., Ellensburg, 1967—69; dir. Jr. Art Mus. Des Moines Art Ctr., 1965—66, dir. docent program, 1963—66; dir. Cmty. Art Gallery, Ellensburg, 1968—72. Coord./dir. Richard Fairbanks Project, Ellensburg, 1991-95; guest curator, Richard Fairbanks Retrospective, Nordic Heritage Mus., Ballard, Wash., 1995; guest spkr., Networks in Ceramics, U. Art and Design, Helsinki, Finland, 1966 Author: Essential Passions, Fairbanks-Salmenhaara Letters, 1999, Silent Sunflowers, A Balkan Memoir, 2000, Something Lost, Something Found: Ceramics: Art and Perception, 2000 (Authors Guild award 2003); contbr. articles to profl. jours.; prodr./editor: (biography) Richard Fairbanks, American Potter, 1993; exhibited in one-person shows, 1962-96, two-person shows, 1970-95; ceramic exhbns. include Seattle Free Lances, 2003, N.Y. Authors Guild, 2003; gallery affiliations include Galerie Pelin, Helsinki, City of Sanda, Japan, Galerie Prisma, Vienna, C.G. Rein, Scottsdale, Ariz., Maxwell Galleries, Inc., San Francisco, Des Moines Art Ctr., Percival Galleries, Inc., Des Moines, Greenwood Galleries, Seattle, PANACA, Bellevue, Wash., Louise Matzke Gallery, Seattle, N.W. Craft Ctr., Bellevue, Lynn McAllister Gallery, Seattle, Seattle Art Mus., Richard White Gallery, Seattle, Foster/White Gallery, Seattle, Gallery One, Ellensburg, Allied Arts, Yakima, Wash., Oak Hollow Gallery, Yakima, Larson Gallery, Yakima Established, dir. Richard Fairbanks: Am. Potter Found., 2005—. Address: 19111 SE 47th Pl Issaquah WA 98027-9315

PARKES, WALTER F., film company executive; b. Bakersfield, Calif. m. Laurie MacDonald; 2 children. AB in Anthropology, Yale U.; student, Grad. Sch. Comm., Stanford U. Pres. Amblin Entertainment, 1994; co-head, dir. motion pictures Dreamworks Pictures, 1995—. Prodr., dir.: (films) The California Reich, 1975 (nominated Acad. Award, spl. citation Cannes Film Festival); prodr.: Volunteers, 1985, True Believer, 1987, Awakenings, 1990 (nominated best picture, 1990), Men in Black, 1997, The Peace Maker, 1997, Gladiator, 2000, Artificial Intelligence, 2001; prodr.: (films) The Time Machine, 2002; prodr.: (films) Minority Report, 2002, Men in Black II, 2002, Road to Perdition, 2002, The Tuxedo, 2002, The Ring, 2002, Catch Me If You Can, 2002, The Terminal, 2004, Lemony Snicket's A Series of Unfortunate Events, 2004, The Ring Two, 2005, The Island, 2005, Just Like Heaven, 2005, The Legend of Zorro, 2005; prodr.: (films) The Lookout, 2007; exec. prodr.: (TV series) Birdland, 1994, Men in Black: The Series, 1997; (films) Littler Giants, 1994, Twister, 1996, The Trigger Effect, 1996, Amistad, 1997, Deep Impact, 1998, Small Soldiers, 1998, Mask of Zorro, 1998; writer: WarGames, 1983 (nominated best original screenplay, 1983); prodr., writer: (films) Sneakers, 1992 (nominated Acad. Award, spl. citation Cannes Film Festival). Named one of 50 Most Powerful People in Hollywood, Premiere mag., 2004—05. Office: DreamWorks SKG 1000 Flower St Glendale CA 91201 Office Phone: 818-733-7000. Office Fax: 818-695-7574. *

PARKHURST, BEVERLY SUSLER, lawyer, judge; b. Decatur, Ill. d. Sewell and Marion Susler; m. Todd S. Parkhurst, Aug. 15, 1976. BA with honors, U. Ill., 1966, JD, 1969. Bar: Ill. 1969, U.S. Dist. Ct. (no. dist.) Ill. 1969, U.S. Ct. Appeals (7th cir.) 1975, U.S. Supreme Ct. 1980. Asst. U.S. atty. U.S. Atty.'s Office U.S. Dist. Ct. (no. dist.) Ill., Chgo., 1974-78, exec. asst. U.S. atty., 1978-81; pvt. practice law Offices of Beverly Susler Parkhurst, Chgo., 1982-86; trial judge Cir. Ct. Cook County, 1996-98; of counsel Witwer, Poltrock & Giampietro, Chgo., 1997—2003, Hedlund & Hanley LLC, 2003—04; appt. fed. adminstr. law judge, 2004—. Faculty Nat. Inst. of Trial Advocacy; bd. dirs. Internat. Forum Travel and Tourism Advs., vice chmn. 2d Internat. Conf., Jerusalem, 1986, regional chmn. 3d Internat. Conf., San Francisco, 1987; chmn. inquiry bd. Ill. Atty. Registration and Disciplinary Commn., 1985-87; guest lectr. legal ethics Washington U., St. Louis, 1986; lectr. on travel law, fed. civic procedures and med. malpractice; adj. prof. John Marshall Law Sch., 1999-2002; mediator Jud. Disput Resolution. Contbr. articles to profl. jours.; spkr. in field. Mem. Ill. Toll Hwy. Adv. Com., 1985-90; bd. dirs. Ill. Soc. for Prevention of Blindness, Cook County Ct. Watchers, Chgo. State U. Found., 1997—2003. James scholar U. Ill., 1962-66; recipient Spl. Achievement award U.S. Dept. Justice, 1978, Dir.'s award, 1981, Cert. of Profl. Achievement in Mediation, DePaul U. Dispute Resolution Ctr.; U.S. Utility Patent grantee 1984. Mem. ABA (chmn. subcom. alternatives to discovery litigation sect. 1985-87), Ill. Bar Assn. (com. profl. responsibility), Women's Bar Assn., Fed. Bar Assn., Chgo. Bar Assn. (chmn. judiciary commn. l988-90, bench bar symposium l988-91, exec. com. Alliance for Women), Nat. Inst. Trial Advocacy (faculty N.E. region), Lincoln Inn of Ct. (pres.), Legal Club of Chgo. Avocations: scuba diving, swimming, cooking. Office: Fed Adminstr Law Judge Chicago IL 60603

PARKHURST, CHARLES LLOYD, electronics executive; b. Nashville, Aug. 13, 1943; s. Charles Albert Parkhurst and Dorothy Elizabeth (Ballou) Parkhurst Crutchfield; m. Dolores Ann Oakley, June 6, 1970; children: Charles Thomas, Deborah Lynn, Jere Loy. Student, Hume-Fogg Tech. Coll., 1959—61; AA, Mesa Community Coll., 1973; student, Ariz. State U., 1973—76. Mem. design staff Tex. Instruments, Dallas, 1967; mgr. design Motorola, Inc., Phoenix, 1968—76; pres. LSI Cons., Inc., Tempe, Ariz., 1976—85, LSI Photomasks, Inc., Tempe, 1985—94, Charles Parkhurst Books, Inc., Prescott, Ariz., 1994—; founder IC Photomask, LLC, Chandler, Ariz., 2002—. Founder IC Photomask. Mem. Rep. Congl. Leadership Coun., Washington, 1988; life mem. Rep. Presdl. Task Force, 1990. Served as cpl. USMC, 1961-64. Mem. Ariz. State U. Alumni Assn. (life), Antiquarian Booksellers Assn. Am. Baptist. Achievements include first to design digital watch chip. Avocations: genealogy, coin collecting/numismatics, scuba diving, book collecting. Office: Charles Parkhurst Books Inc PO Box 10850 Prescott AZ 86304-0850

PARKHURST, TODD SHELDON, lawyer; b. Evanston, Ill., Mar. 8, 1941; s. Don A. and Ruth Ellen (Sheldon) P.; m. Karen Judy Huckleberry, Sept. 2, 1968 (dec. Sept. 1969); m. Beverly Ann Susler, Aug. 15, 1976. BS in Gen. Engring., U. Ill., 1963; JD, U. Pa., 1966. Bar: Ill. 1968, U.S. Dist. Ct. (no. dist.) Ill. 1968, U.S. Dist. Ct. (ea. dist.) Wis. 1989, U.S. Ct. Appeals (7th cir.) 1977, U.S. Ct. Appeals Fed. Cir. 1978, U.S. Ct. Mil. Appeals, 1968, U.S. Patent and Trademark Office, 1973, U.S. Supreme Ct. 1973. Assoc. Wolfe, Hubbard, Voit & Osann, 1968-72; assoc. and ptnr. Trexler, Wolters, Bushnell & Fosse, Chgo., 1972-84; ptnr. Jenner & Block, Chgo., 1984-87, Gardner, Carton & Douglas, 1996-98, Hill & Simpson, Chgo., 1998-2000; ptnr., mgr. intellectual property practice Schiff Hardin & Waite, Chgo., 1987-96, Holland & Knight, Chgo., 2000—07, Wildman Harrold Allen & Dixon LLP, 2007—. Adj. prof. John Marshall Law Sch., Chgo., 1980-84, Ill. Inst. Tech.-Chgo. Kent Law Sch., 1989—. Contbr. articles to profl. jours. Mem. Lifeline Pilots, Inc., pres. 1994-96; hearing officer Ill.

Pollution Control Bd., 1972-96. Capt. Corps of Engrs. US Army, 1966—68. Mem. Am. Intellectual Property Law Assn., Licensing Execs. Soc., Chgo. Bar Assn., Patent Law Assn. Chgo., Chgo. Lit. Club (pres. 1989-90), Adventurers Club Chgo. (sec. 1988). Methodist. Avocations: flying, scuba diving, photography, theatrical acting. Office: Wildman Harrold Allen & Dixon LLP 233 W Wacker Dr Ste 3000 Chicago IL 60606 Office Phone: 312-201-2000. Personal E-mail: todd.parkhurst@hklaw.com.

PARKHURST, VIOLET KINNEY, artist; b. Derby Line, Vt., Apr. 26, 1926; d. Edson Frank and Rosa (Beauchiene) Kinney; student Sch. Practical Arts, Boston, 1941-42, Baylor U., Waco, Tex., 1943, Calif. State U., Los Angeles, 1950-51; m. Donald Winters Parkhurst, Apr. 10, 1948. Fgn. corr. 5 Brazilian mags., 1946-53; tech. illustrator, 1954-55; owner five galleries including Ports of Call, San Pedro, Calif.; artist, specializing in seascapes; work included in permanent collection of Stockholm Mus., many pvt. collections including Presidents Richard M. Nixon, Ford, Reagan, Bush, Gov. Wilson, Mayor of Kobe, Japan, Mayor Yorty of L.A., Rory Calhoun, Barbara Rush, Jim Arness, David Rose, President Hu of China, 2005; one-shows shows at prominent galleries; numerous paintings published. Winner 30 blue ribbons for art. Fellow Am. Inst. Fine Arts. Mem. Ch. of Religious Sci. Author: How to Paint Books, 1966; Parkhurst on Seascapes, 1972. Paintings reproduced on covers South West Art, Arizona Living, Hollywood Bowl Easter Sunrise Service program; ltd. edit. prints published, also ltd. edit. plates. The first artist in the world invited to present a painting to Pres. Jiang Zemin, Beisin, China, 2002; the first western artist to have a painting in China Nat. Mus. of Fine Arts and the Hall of the People. Office: Parkhurst Gallery Ports of Call Village San Pedro CA 90731 E-mail: violet@parkhurstartgalleries.com.

PARKIN, FERN AGNES MARVEL, medical/surgical nurse, nursing educator; b. Pocatello, Idaho, Nov. 22, 1931; d. Clarence J. and May Agnes Cuppett; m. Jesse James Marvel, Apr. 16, 1948 (div. Aug. 28, 1973); children: Alexa Ann Adams, Marco Lewis Marvel, Jill Lynn Osburn; m. William Heber Parkin, Jan. 4, 1991. AA, LA Harbor Coll., Wilmington, Calif., 1967; B in Vocat. Edn., Calif. State U., Long Beach, 1978. RN Calif., Idaho, Ariz., Wyoming, Wash., cert. adult cardiopulmonary resuscitation, Calif., coronary care. Staff nurse, clinic nurse Kaiser Found. Hosp., Harbor City, Calif., 1964—65, 1967—69; charge nurse Bishop Randal Hosp., Lander, Wyo., 1970, Needles Hosp., Calif., 1971, Icelandic Rest Home, Blaine, Wash., 1971—, Shuksans Nursing Home, Bellingham, Wash., 1971—72; nursing instr. LA Unified Sch. Dist., 1973—78; charge nurse Pacific Hosp., Long Beach, Calif., 1972—74; acting head nurse L.A. Harbor Gen. Hosp., Torrance, Calif., 1974—76; LVN nurse instr. YWCA Job Corp, LA, 1976—77; intensive care and coronary care nurse Profl. Nurses Bur., Long Beach, Calif., 1971—77; psychiatric facilitation instr. Atascadero State Hosp., Calif., 1979; dir. staff devel. Paso Robles Convalescent, Calif., 1987—88; welfare missionary Church of Jesus Christ of LDS, Ormoc, Cebu, Bohol, Philippines, 1988—90; charge nurse Twin Cities Convalescent Ctr., Templeton, Calif., 1990—92. Painted portraits, Pres. Aquina, Pres. Ronald Regan. Counselor relief soc. Ch. Jesus Christ LDS, Wilmington, 1973, mem. choir Pocatello, Idaho, 1969; pres. PTA, Idaho, 1962—63. Mem.: Alpha Gamma Sigma. Democrat. Mem. Lds Ch. Avocations: painting, writing, reading. Home: 200 N PO Box 220667 Centerfield UT 84622

PARKIN, GERARD FRANCIS RALPH, chemistry educator, researcher; b. Middlesbrough, Cleveland, Eng., Feb. 15, 1959; s. Ralph and Clementine (Gill) P.; m. Rita K. Upmacis. BA with honors, Oxford U., Eng., 1981, MA, 1984, PhD, 1985. NATO/SERC (U.K.) postdoctoral rsch. fellow Calif. Inst. Tech., 1985-88; asst. prof. Columbia U., NYC, 1988-91, assoc. prof., 1991-94; prof., chmn. chemistry dept., 1994—; chmn. dept. chemistry, 1999—2002. Contbr. numerous articles to profl. jours. Recipient Camille and Henry Dreyfus Tchr.-Scholar award, 1991, award in pure chemistry Am. Chem. Soc., 1994, Corday Morgan medal Royal Soc. Chemistry, 1995, Organometallic Chemistry award, 2004; A.P. Sloan rsch. fellow; NSF Presdl. faculty fellow, 1992—. Roman Catholic. Achievements include discovery that bond stretch isomerism in an artifact. Office: Columbia U 116th St And Broadway New York NY 10027

PARKIN, JAMES LAMAR, retired otolaryngologist, educator; b. Salt Lake City, June 2, 1939; s. Elmer Lamar and Mary Ilene (Soffe) Parkin; m. Bonnie Dansie, July 1, 1963; children: Jeffrey, Brett, Matthew, David. BS, U. Utah, 1963, MD, 1966; MS, U. Wash., 1970. Diplomate Am. Bd. Otolaryngology. Resident in otolaryngology U. Wash., Seattle, 1968—72; practice medicine specializing in otolaryngology Salt Lake City, 1972—; chmn. divsn. otolaryngology U. Utah Sch. Medicine, Salt Lake City, 1974—93, prof. surgery, 1981—, acting chmn. dept. surgery, 1984—84, 1993—94, chmn., 1994—96, prof. emeritus, 2004—. Pres. med. bd. Univ. Med. Ctr., Salt Lake City, 1983—85, chmn. exec. com. faculty practice orgn., 1994—96, assoc. v.p. health scis., 1996—97, v.p. sch. medicine alumni, 2003—, v.p. med. alumni, 2003—, chmn. centennial com., 2005—; bd. govs. Utah Med. Ins. Assn., Salt Lake City, 1979—81. Guest editor Ear, Nose and Throat Jour., 1982, assoc. editor Archives of Otolaryngology. Leader Boy Scouts Am.; bishop Ch. of Jesus Christ of Latter-Day Saints, Salt Lake City, 1983—86, stake pres., 1986—96, pres. Eng. London South Mission, 1996—2000. Recipient Honor award, Am. Acad. Otolaryngology, 1980. Fellow: ACS, Am. Neurotology Soc., Am. Soc. Laser Medicine and Surgery, Am. Otol. Soc., Am. Plastic and Reconstructive Surgery, Am. Laryngol, Rhinol. and Otol. Soc.; mem.: Collegium Aesculapium (pres. 2005—), Soc. Otolaryngology-Maxillofacial Surgery (pres. Utah chpt. 1979), Am. Cancer Soc. (pres. Utah chpt. 1984—86), Soc. Univ. Otolaryngologists (pres. 1984—85), Assn. Acad. Depts. Otolaryngology (chmn. nat. faculty survey com. 1980—90, sec.-treas. 1982—84, pres. 1986—88).

PARKIN, STUART STEPHEN PAPWORTH, materials scientist; IBM fellow IBM Almaden Rsch. Ctr., San Jose, Calif., 1983—. Recipient Internat. prize for new materials Am. Phys. Soc., 1994, C.V. Boys prize Inst. Physics, London, 1991, Inaugural Outstanding Young Investigator award Materials Rsch. Soc., 1991, Europhysics prize Hewlett-Packard, 1997, Indsl. Applications of Physics prize Am. Inst. Physics, 1999-2000, Humbboldt award, 2005; named Innovator of Yr., R&D Mag., 2001. Fellow AAAS, IEEE, Am. Phys. Soc., Royal Soc. London, Inst. Physics (London). Office: IBM Almaden Rsch Ctr 650 Harry Rd San Jose CA 95120-6099 Office Phone: 408-927-2390. E-mail: parkin@almaden.ibm.com.

PARKINS, FREDERICK MILTON, dental educator, dean; b. Princeton, NJ, Sept. 8, 1935; s. William Milton and Phyllis Virginia (Plyler) P.; m. Carolyn V. Rude; children: Bradford, Christopher, Eric. Student, Carleton Coll., 1953-56; D.D.S., U. Pa., 1960; MSD. in Pedodontics, U. N.C., Chapel Hill, 1965; PhD in Physiology, 1969. Instr. pedodontics U. N.C., 1965-67; asst. prof. pedodontics U. Pa., 1967-68, dir. Dental Aux. Utilization program, chmn. pedodontics, 1968-69; assoc. prof., head pedodontics U. Iowa, Iowa City, 1969-72, prof., head pedodontics, 1972-75; asst. dean acad. affairs U. Iowa (Coll. Dentistry), 1974-75, asso. dean acad. affairs, 1975-79, dir. continuing edn., 1975-77; prof. pedodontics, dean Sch. Dentistry, U. Louisville, 1979-85, prof. pediatric dentistry, 1985—2003, prof. pediatric dentistry emeritus, 2003—. Mem. Hillenbrand Fellowship adv. com. Am. Fund Dental Health, 1980-85; cons. Div. Dental Health USPHS, 1969-72; dental cons., med. staff Children's Hosp. Phila., 1968-71; med. staff Kosair Children's Hosp. Louisville, 1983—; cons., mem. pedodontic adv. com. Council Dental Edn., 1974-80, chmn. pedodontic adv. com., 1978-80, cons. council on legislation, 1978-79; dental cons. Aux. Utilization VA, 1968-69; cons. Bur. Health Resources Devel., 1974-76, Dept. Army, 1980-, numerous others Assoc. editor Jour. Preventive Dentistry, 1973-79, mem. editl. bd., 1980-83; editl. reviewer Jour. Pediatrics, 1969-, Jour. Dental Edn, 1978-, Jour. AMA, 1979-; assoc. editor Jour. Clin. Preventive Dentistry, 1979-84; mem. editl. bd. Jour. Clin. Laser Medicine and Surgery, 1999-; contbr. chpts. to textbooks, articles to profl. pubis. Bd. govs. Youth Performing Arts Coun., Louisville-Jefferson County Sch. Dist., 1980-89, pres., 1986-88; bd. govs. Regional Cancer Ctr., U. Louisville, 1979-84, Univ. Hosp., 1979-84; mem. human studies com. U. Louisville, 1988-90. Robert Wood Johnson Congl. fellow Inst. of Medicine, 1977-78; USPHS postdoctoral fellow, 1963-67; NIH grantee, 1971-75; Recipient Earle Banks Hoyt Teaching award, 1969 Fellow AAAS, Am. Acad. Pediat. Dentistry (chmn. rsch. com. 1972-73, Ann. Rsch. award 1968, chmn. advanced edn. com. 1974-75, chmn. dental care programs com. 1978-80); mem. ADA, Am. Coll. Dentistry, Am. Soc. Dentistry for Children (exec. bd. Iowa unit 1969-75, award com. 1973-76, edn. com. 1974-77, chmn. rsch. adv. com. 1973-76), Biophys. Soc., Internat. Assn. Dental Rsch., N.Y. Acad. Dentistry, Ky. Dental Assn. (exec. bd. 1979-84), Am. Assn. Dental Schs. (coun. deans 1979-85, chmn. pedodontics sect. 1976, chmn. continuing edn. sect. 1979, legis. com. 1978-83), Louisville Dental Alumni Assn. (bd. govs. 1979-84), Am. Assn. Dental Rsch. (nat. affairs com. 1978-85), Acad. Laser Dentistry (co-chmn. rsch. and edn. 1997, chair 1998-2003, bd. dirs. 1997-2003, cert. com., T.H. Maiman award for excellence in dental laser rsch.), U.S. Power Squadron (bd. govs. 1987-93, sec. 1989, adminstrv. officer 1990, exec. officer 1991, comdr. 1992), Aircraft Owners and Pilots Assn., Omicron Kappa Upsilon (pres. Wa. chpt. 1991-92), Rotary. Unitarian Universalist. Home: 6424 Marina Dr Prospect KY 40059-8846 Office: U Louisville Sch Dentistry Dept Orth and Pediatric Dentistry Rm 240N Louisville KY 40292 Office Phone: 502-228-3389. Business E-Mail: fmpark01@louisville.edu.

PARKINSON, BRADFORD WELLS, astronautical engineer, educator; b. Madison, Wis., Feb. 16, 1935; s. Herbert and Metta Tisdale (Smith) P.; m. Virginia Pinkham Wier, Nov. 26, 1977; children: Leslie, Bradford II, Eric, Ian, Bruce, Jared Bradford. BS, U.S. Naval Acad., 1957; MS, MIT, 1961; PhD, Stanford U., 1966; grad. (disting.), USAF Command and Staff Coll., 1969, Naval War Coll., 1972. Commd. 2d lt. USAF, 1957, advanced through grades to col., 1972; divsn. chief AF Test Pilot Sch., 1966-68; chair dept. astronautics and computer sci. USAF Acad., 1969-71; dir. engring. ABRES, 1972; program mgr. NAVSTAR GPS, 1972-78; ret. USAF, 1978; prof. mech. engring. Colo. State U., Ft. Collins, 1978-79; v.p. advanced engring. Rockwell Internat., Downey, Calif., 1979-80; gen. mgr., v.p. Intermetrics, Inc., Cambridge, Mass., 1980-84; prof. emeritus, assoc. dir. gravity probe-B Stanford (Calif.) U., 1984—; CEO, pres. Trimble Navigation Ltd., 1998-99. Chair adv. coun. JPL NASA; dir. Trimble Navigation Ltd., Sunnyvale, Calif., NTV, Cambridge; past chair bd. dirs. Aerospace Corp., El Segundo, Calif. Decorated Def. Superior Svc. medal, AF Commendation medal with oak leaf cluster, Meritorius Svc. medal, Presdl. Unit citation, Bronze Star, Legion of Merit, Air medal with oak leaf cluster; recipient Pub. Svc. award, Disting. Pub. Svc. award, NASA, 1984, Thurlow award Inst. Navigation, 1986, Burka award, 1987, Kepler award, 1991, Aerospace Contbn. to Soc. award, 1991, Goddard medal, von Karman Lectureship AIAA, 1996, Magellan Premium, Am. Philos. Soc., 1997, Gold medal Space Tech. Hall of Fame of U.S. Space Found., 1998, Williams Space medal Soc. Logistics Engrs., 1996, ASME medal, 2004; named to National Inventors Hall of Fame, 2004. Fellow AIAA, Royal Inst. Navigation (Gold medal 1983), Inst. Navigation, IEEE (Kirchner award 1986, Pioneer award 1994, Sperry award 1999, Simon Remo medal); mem. AAS, NAE (Charles Stark Draper Prize, 2003), Internat. Acad. Astronautics, Sigma Xi, Tau Beta Pi. Avocations: hiking, skiing, sailing. Office: Stanford U 4085 Mail Code Stanford CA 94305 Home: 2360 Camino Edna San Luis Obispo CA 93401

PARKINSON, CLAIRE L., climatologist; b. Bay Shore, NY, Mar. 21, 1948; d. C. V. and Virginia (Hafner) Parkinson. BA, Wellesley Coll., 1970; MA, Ohio State U., 1974, PhD, 1977. Rsch. asst. Inst. Polar Studies, Columbus, Ohio, 1972-74; tchg. asst. Ohio State U., Columbus, 1973-76; rsch. asst. Nat. Ctr. Atmospheric Rsch., Boulder, Colo., 1976-78; rsch. scientist Goddard Space Flight Ctr. NASA, Greenbelt, Md., 1978-87, sr. scientist, 1987—, sr. fellow, 2005—. Sci. colloquium com. mem. Goddard Space Flight Ctr. NASA, 1986—99, project scientist Earth Observing Sys. Aqua Satellite Mission, 1993—, sci. exec. com. Earth Observing Sys., 1996—2000, lead scientist expedition to Resolute Bay and North Pole, 1999; adv. panel climate and global change NOAA, 1990—95; climate rsch. com. NAS, 1994—96; sci. advisor radio series Earth & Sky, 1998—, Soundprint Media Ctr., 1998—; mem. climate variability and change decadal survey panel NAS-NRC, 2005—06. Author: Breakthroughs, 1985, Gospel Cryptograms, 1994, Earth from Above, 1997 (Spl. Act award, 1997); co-author: Antarctic Sea Ice, 1983 (Group award, 1982), Three-Dimensional Climate Modeling, 1986, 2d edit., 2005; lead author Arctic Sea Ice, 1987 (Peer award, 1988); co-editor: Atlas of Satellite Observations Related to Global Change, 1993 (Group award, 1993); lead editor EOS Data Products Handbook, vol. 2, 2000, Earth Science Reference Handbook, 2006, guest lead editor IEEE Transactions on Geoscience and Remote Sensing, 2003, mem. editl. bd. Internat. Glaciological Soc., 1989—92, Earth Obs. Website, 1999—2006 (Webby award, 2003); contbr. articles to profl. jours. Vol. Spl. Olympics, Annapolis, Md., 1989, College Park, Md., 1998—2001; tutor Greenbelt Cares, 1989—94; spkr., sci. fair judge local schs., 1989—. Recipient Gold medal, Md. Sr. Olympics, 2000—03, 2005—06, medal, US Nat. Sr. Olympics, 2001, 2003, Outstanding Leadership medal, 2003, Goldthwait Polar medal, Ohio State U. Byrd Polar Rsch. Ctr., 2004, Excellence in Outreach award, 2006. Fellow: Am. Meteorol. Soc. (com. on polar meterology and oceanography 1984—86, com. on the history atmospheric scis. 1988—90, chair 1990, devel. com. 2005—); mem.: AAAS, Oceanography Soc., Assn. Philosophy Math., Am. Polar Soc., Phi Beta Kappa Fellows, Phi Beta Kappa. Avocation: history of science. Home: 8345 Canning Ter Greenbelt MD 20770-2701 Office: Code 614-1 NASA Goddard Space Flight Ctr Greenbelt MD 20771-0001 Office Phone: 301-614-5715. Business E-Mail: claire.l.parkinson@nasa.gov.

PARKINSON, JAMES THOMAS, III, investment consultant; b. Richmond, Va., July 10, 1940; s. James Thomas and Elizabeth (Hopkins) P.; m. Molly O. Owens, June 16, 1962 (div. June 1998); children: James Thomas, Glenn Walser; m. Caroline Smith Pyle, Oct. 10, 1998. BA, U. Va., 1962; MBA, U. Pa., 1964. Trainee Chem. Bank, NYC, 1964—66; assoc., corp. fin. dept. Blyth & Co., Inc., NYC, 1968—69; v.p., corp. fin. dept. Clark Dodge & Co., Inc., NYC, 1969—72; pvt. practice investment mgmt. NYC, 1972—85, Va., 1987—; v.p. Pleasantville Advisors, Inc., NYC, 1986—87. Instr. corp. fin. Ind. U., 1966-68; bd. dirs. Bowles Fluidics Corp. Sr. warden Ch. of Holy Trinity, NYC, 1978-79; trustee Am. Bible Soc., 1980—, vice chair bd. trustees, 2006-; trustee Funds, Episcopal Diocese of Va., 2000-06, Diocesan Missionary Soc., 2006—, Mus. Bibl. Art, NYC, 2005-06. With AUS, 1966-68. Mem. Univ. Club (N.Y.C.), Va. Country Club. Republican. Episcopalian. Home and Office: PO Box 2247 Middleburg VA 20118-2247

PARKINSON, JUSTIN PAUL, urologist; b. Salt Lake City, Nov. 27, 1973; s. Paul Barry and Kathy Annette Parkinson; m. Chelsy A. Parkinson, June 10, 1993; children: Jordan, Austin, Cooper. BS in Biochemistry, Idaho State U., Pocatello, 1997; MD, U. Utah, Salt Lake City, 2001. Diplomate Urologist. Residency U. Iowa, 2001—06. Mem.: Am. Urological Assn. Republican. Mormon. Avocations: horseback riding, snowboarding. Office: Urology Specialists of Utah 4052 W Pioneer Pkwy Salt Lake City UT 84120 Business E-Mail: parkinsonj@mac.com.

PARKINSON, MARK VINCENT, lieutenant governor, former state legislator; b. Wichita, Kans., June 24, 1957; s. Henry Filson and Barbara Ann (Gilbert) Horton; m. Stacy Abbott Parkinson, Mar. 7, 1983; children: Alex Atticus, Sam Filson, Kit Harlan. BA in Edn., Wichita State U., 1980; JD, Kans. U., 1984. Assoc. Payne and Jones Law Firm, Olathe, Kans., 1984-86; ptnr. Parkinson, Foth & Reynolds, Lenexa, Kans., 1986—96; mem. Kans. Ho. Reps., 1990-92, Kans. State Senate, 1993-97; chmn. Kans. Rep. Party, 1999—2003; lt. gov. State of Kans., Topeka, 2007—. Mem. ABA, Johnson County Bar Found. (pres. 1993—), Kans. Bar Assn. Democrat. Avocations: travel, running, movies. Office: Lieutenant Governor State Capitol 300 SW 10th Ave Ste 2225 Topeka KS 66612 Office Phone: 785-296-2213. Office Fax: 785-296-5669. *

PARKINSON, ROBERT L., JR., medical products executive, health facility administrator; BBA, MBA, Loyola U., Chgo. With Abbott Labs., Abbott Park, Ill., 1976, v.p. European ops., 1990-93, sr. v.p. chem. and agrl. products, 1993-95, pres. internat. divsn., 1995-98, bd. dirs., 1998, pres., COO, 1999-2001; dean Loyola U. Chgo.'s Sch. of Bus. Adminstrn. and Grad. Sch. of Bus., 2002—04; chmn., CEO Baxter Internat., Inc., 2004—. Chmn. Geneva (Switzerland) Proteomics, 2001; bd. trustees Healthcare Leadership Coun. Bd. dirs. Northwestern Mem. Hosp., Northwestern Mem. Found. Office: Baxter Internat Inc One Baxter Pkwy Deerfield IL 60015 Office Phone: 847-948-2000. *

PARKINSON, WILLIAM CHARLES, physics professor, researcher; b. Jarvis, Ont., Can., Feb. 11, 1918; came to U.S., 1925, naturalized, 1941; s. Charles Franklin and Euphemia Alice (Johnston) P.; m. Martha Bennett Capron, Aug. 2, 1944; children: Martha Reed, William Reid. BSE, U. Mich., 1940, MS, 1941, PhD, 1948. Physicist Applied Physics Lab., Johns Hopkins U., 1942-46, OSRD, 1943-44; mem. faculty U. Mich., 1947—, prof. physics, 1958-88, prof. emeritus physics, 1988—, dir. cyclotron lab., 1962-77; mem. subcom. nuclear structure NRC, 1959-68; mem. nuclear physics sub panel mgmt. and costs nuclear program, 1969-70; adv. panel physics NSF, 1966-69. Cons. grad. sci. facilities, 1968, chmn. postdoctoral fellowship evaluation panel, 1969, cons. to govt. and industry, 1955— Quondam mem. Trinity Coll., Cambridge, Eng. Recipient Ordnance Devel. award Navy Dept., 1946; Fulbright research scholar Cavendish Lab., Cambridge U., 1952-53 Fellow Am. Phys. Soc.; mem. N.Y. Acad. Scis., Biophys. Soc., Grad. "M" Club (awarded hon. "M" 1991), Flounders Water Polo, Sigma Xi, Phi Kappa Phi, Kappa Kappa Psi. Achievements include invention of automatic judging and timing for swim meets, fast neutron spectroscopy using cyclotrons; development of high resolution nuclear spectroscopy with cyclotrons. Home: 1600 Sheridan Dr Ann Arbor MI 48104-4052 Office: Univ Mich Dept Physics Ann Arbor MI 48109 Office Phone: 734-764-3458. Business E-Mail: wcpark@umich.edu.

PARKS, A. LAURISTON, lawyer; b. Providence, July 18, 1935; s. Albert Lauriston and Dorothy Isabel (Arnold) Parks; m. Martha Ann Anderson, Jan. 12, 1961; children: Amy Woodward, George Webster, Reed Anderson. BA, Kent State U., 1958; JD, U. Chgo., 1961. Bar: R.I. 1962, U.S. Dist. Ct. R.I. 1963, U.S. Ct. Appeals (1st cir.) 1966, U.S. Supreme Ct. 1980. Assoc. Hanson, Curran, Parks & Whitman, Providence, 1961-65, ptnr., 1966-2000. Town solicitor No. Kingstown, RI, 1978—80, RI, 1997—2006, Jamestown, 1999—2000, 2003—07. Fellow: Am. Coll. Trial Lawyers; mem.: ABA, R.I. Bar Assn., Maritime Law Assn., Wickford Yacht Club, Saunderstown Yacht Club. Republican. Episcopalian. Office: 53 Narragansett Ave Jamestown RI 02835 Home: 14 Church Ln North Kingstown RI 02852-5004 Office Phone: 401-423-8900. E-mail: alp@alparks.net.

PARKS, ARVA MOORE, historian; b. Miami, Fla., Jan. 19, 1939; d. Jack and Anne (Parker) Moore; m. Robert Lyle Parks, Aug. 19, 1959 (div. May 1986); children: Jacqueline Carey, Robert Downing, Gregory Moore; m. Robert Howard McCabe, June 20, 1992. Student, Fla. State U., 1956-58; BA, U. Fla., 1960; MA in History, U. Miami, Coral Gables, 1971; LLD (hon.), Barry U., 1996. Tchr. Rolling Crest Jr. H.S., West Hyattsville, Md., 1960-63, Miami Edison Sr. H.S., Fla., 1963-64; grad. asst. U. Miami, Coral Gables, 1964-65; tchr. Everglades Sch. for Girls, Miami, 1965-66; cons., 1966-70; free-lance rsch. historian Miami, 1970-86; adj. prof. U. Miami, Coral Gables, 1986-87; pres. Arva Parks & Co., Miami, 1986—. Cons. thematic and interpretive rsch. and design Harry S. Truman Little White House, Key West, Fla., 1989-91; pres. Centennial Press, 1991—. Author: Miami the Magic City, 1981, rev. edit., 1991, The Forgotten Frontier, 1977 (rev. edit. 2004), Harry Truman and the Little White House in Key West, 1991, Miami: Then and Now, 1992, The Pathway to Greatness, 2001; co-author: (with Gregory M. Bush) Miami: The American Crossroad, 1996, (with Carolyn Klepser) Miami Then & Now, 2002, George Merrick's Coral Gables, 2006; editor Tequesta Jour. Hist. Soc. Fla., 1986-95; writer: (film) Our Miami: The Magic City, 1994. Bd. advs., Nat. Trust Hist. Preservation, 1984-93, chmn. so. region, 1990-91, Fed. Adv. Coun. Hist. Preservation, 1995-2003; trustee Miami-Dade C.C., 1984-90, U. Miami, 1994—; bd. dirs. Louis Wolfson Media History Ctr., Miami, 1985-90, Orange Bowl Com., 1989—, Bapt. Health Systems of Miami, Inc., 1992—, Dade Found., 1997-2004, Drs. Hosp. Bd., 2004—; cmty. adv. Dade Heritage Trust, Miami, 1988-97, mem. Bi-Racial Tri-Ethnic Adv. Bd., Miami, 1984-99, New World Sch. Arts (exec. com.), Miami, 1986-90, Bok Sanctuary Bd., 2005—, City of Coral Gables Mus. Bd., 2005-; chmn. Vizcaya Trust, 1998-2004, pres. Fla. Forum, 2003-05; chair City of Miami Planning Adv. Bd., 2005—. Recipient Historic Preservation award AIA, 1993, Outstanding Women of History award Cuban Am. Women's Club, 1992, Women Helping Women award Soroptimists, 1992, Am. History award DAR, 1987, Pathfinder's award Women's Com. 100, 1985, Outstanding Citizen award Coral Gables C. of C., 1983, Outstanding Preservationist award Dade Heritage Trust, 1983, Good Faith award Black Archives and Rsch. Found., 1981, Mus. of Sci. award, 1981, Cmty. Headliner award Women in Comm., 1980, Humanitarian award Urban League Guild, 1980, award City of Coral Gables Hist. Preservation Bd., 1978, Women of Impact award Cmty. Coalition for Women's History, 1996, Cmty. Star award Family Counseling Svcs. of Greater Miami, 1996, Edward T. Foote Alumnae of Distinction award U. Miami, 2002, Henriette Harris award Dade Heritage Trust, 2004; named to Alumni Hall of Fame Dade County Pub. Schs., 1985, Fla. Women's Hall of Fame, 1986, one of Women Who Made a Difference YWCA, 1988, City Miami Women's Hall Fame, 1996, Woman of Distinction award Soroptimist Internat. of Ams., Woman of Distinction award Girl Scouts Am., 1996, Alumni Women Distinction U. Fla., 1997, Tebeau prize Fla. Hist. Soc. for Am. Crossroad, 1997, Theodore Gibson Unity award, 1999, Vizcayans Cultural Millennium award, 1999, Miami Herald Spirit of Excellence award, 1999, Joseph R. Narot Cmty. Svc. award, 2003, Olympian award Olympia Theater at Gusman Ctr., 2006, Julia Tuttle award Commn. on the Status of Women, City of Miami, 2006. Mem. Internat. Women's Forum (found. pres., 2001-05, pres. Fla. chpt. 2003-05, bd. dirs. Fla. chpt. 2005-), Jr. League. Democrat. Methodist. Avocation: photography. Home and Office: 1601 S Miami Ave Miami FL 33129-1103 Office Phone: 305-854-8087. Personal E-mail: arvamiami@bellsouth.net.

PARKS, DONALD LEE, mechanical engineer, human factors engineer; b. Delphos, Kans., Feb. 23, 1931; s. George Delbert and Erma Josephine (Boucek) P.; m. Bessie Lou Schur, Dec. 24, 1952; children: Elizabeth Parks Anderson, Patricia Parks-Holbrook, Donna, Charles, Sandra Parks-Bennett. Student, Kans. Wesleyan U., 1948-50; BSME, BSBA, Kans. State U., 1957, MS in Psychology, 1959. Cert. profl. ergonomist. Elem. tchr., 1950-51; with Kans. State U. Placement Svc., 1959-57; human factors engr., sys. engr. Boeing Co., Seattle, 1959-90, sr. specialist engr., 1972-74, sr. engring. supr., 1974-90; pres. D-Square Assocs. Engring. Cons., 1990-95, Venture Worlds, 1995—. Adj. lectr. UCLA Engring. Extension, 1989—; cons., lectr. in field; participant workshops on guidelines in profl. areas, NATO, NSF, Nat. Acad. Sci., NRC. Author Mystery Codes From Ancient Times, 2007; contbr. over 80 articles to profl. publs., 8 book chpts. Mem. Derby (Kans.) Planning Commn., 1961-62, chmn., 1962; del. King

County (Wash.) Rep. Conv., 1972. With AUS, 1952-54. Mem. ASME, APA, Human Factors Soc. (Puget Sound Pres.'s award 1969), Elks. Presbyterian. Home: 6232 127th Ave SE Bellevue WA 98006-3943

PARKS, GARRY LEE, military officer; b. Huntingdon, Pa., Mar. 9, 1947; m. Earlene Knight; children: Garry Lee Jr., Tamara Anne. BS, The Citadel, 1969; MA, Pepperdine U., 1973, Naval War Coll., 1987. Commd. 2nd lt. USMC, 1969, advanced through grades to lt. gen., 2001; platoon comdr., co. exec. officer 1st Reconnaissance Bn. 1st Marine Divsn., Vietnam; co. comdr. 2nd Bn., 3rd Marines; aide-de-camp to comdg. gen. 1st Marine Brig., Kaneohe Bay, Hawaii; co. officer U.S. Naval Acad., 1979-81; comdg. officer recruiting sta. USMC, Raleigh, NC, 1982-85; joint program and budget coordination officer Requirements and Programs divsn. USMC Hdqrs.; exec. officer, then comdg. officer 2nd Bn. 5th Marines, 1st Marine divsn.; officer in charge spl. ops. tng. group USMC, Okinawa, Japan, 1990-91; comdg. officer, camp comdr. Camp Hansen, 1991; dir. presentation team USMC, 1993; chief of staff Marine Forces Pacific, Camp H.M. Smith, 1993-94; comdg. gen. USMC Recuit Depot, Western Recruiting Region, San Diego, 1995-97; dep. dir. politico-mil. affairs global, multilateral issues The Pentagon, Washington, 1997-98; comdg. gen. Marine Corps Recruiting Command, Quantico, Va., 1998-2001; dep. comdt. Manpower and Res. Affairs, 2001—04; pres./CEO SC Credit Union League, Irmo, SC, 2004—. Decorated Dist. Svc. medal, Legion of Merit, Bronze Star, Def. Superior Svc. medal. Office: SC Credit Union League 7440 Broad River Rd Irmo SC 29063 Business E-Mail: gparks@sccul.org.

PARKS, HAROLD RAYMOND, mathematician, educator; b. Wilmington, Del., May 22, 1949; s. Lytle Raymond Jr. and Marjorie Ruth (Chambers) P.; m. Paula Sue Beaulieu, Aug. 21, 1971 (div. 1984); children: Paul Raymond, David Austin; m. Susan Irene Taylor, June 6, 1985; 1 stepchild, Kathryn McLaughlin. AB, Dartmouth Coll., 1971; PhD, Princeton U., 1974. Tamarkin instr. Brown U., Providence, 1974-77; asst. prof. Oreg. State U., Corvallis, 1977-82, assoc. prof., 1982-89, prof. math., 1989—, chmn. dept. math., 2001—04. Vis. assoc. prof. Ind. U., Bloomington, 1982-83. Author: Explicit Determination of Area Minimizing Hypersurfaces, vol. II, 1986; (with Steven G. Krantz) A Primer of Real Analytic Functions, 1992, 2d edit., 2002; (with G. Musser, R. Burton, W. Siebler) Mathematics in Life, Society and the World, 1997, 2d edit., 2000; (with Steven G. Krantz) The Geometry of Domains in Space, 1999; (with Krantz) The Implicit Function Theorem: History, Theory, and Applications, 2002, (with G. Musser, L. Trimpe, V. Maurer, R. Maurer) A Mathematical View of Our World, 2007; contbr. articles to profl. jours. Cubmaster Oregon Trail Coun. Boy Scouts Am., 1990-92. NSF fellow, 1971-74. Mem. Am. Math. Soc., Math. Assn. Am., Soc. Indsl. and Applied Math., Phi Beta Kappa. Republican. Mem. Soc. Of Friends. Home: 33194 Dorset Ln Philomath OR 97370-9555 Office: Oreg State U Dept Math Corvallis OR 97331-4605 Home Phone: 541-929-6822; Office Phone: 541-737-5166. Business E-Mail: parks@math.orst.edu.

PARKS, J. MICHAEL, data processing executive; b. Independence, Mo., Dec. 29, 1950; s. Emory C. and Lorene (Belt) P.; m. Maureen C. Weston; children: Christopher Michael, Daniel John. BS in Edn., U. Kans., 1973. Sales rep. Ingersoll-Rand Corp., Kansas City, Mo., 1973-75; sales rep., then sr. v.p. First Data Resources/Am. Express Info. Svcs. Co., Omaha, San Francisco, Boston, Atlanta, 1976-88; chief exec. officer Call Interactive (joint venture of Am. Express Info. Svcs. Corp. and AT&T), Omaha, 1989—93; pres. First Data Resources, 1993—94; chmn., pres., CEO Alliance Data Systems, Dallas, 1997—2006, chmn., CEO, 2006—. Bd. dirs. Commerce Bank Omaha, Data Transmission Network Inc., Am. Express Info. Svcs. Corp., WATS Mktg. of Am. Inc. Chief YMCA Indian Guide Program, Omaha, 1988-89; Cub Scouts den leader local chpt. Boy Scouts Am., Omaha, 1989—. Methodist. Avocations: golf, tennis, camping. Office: Alliance Data 17655 Waterview Pkwy Dallas TX 75252 *

PARKS, JAMES WILLIAM, II, public facilities executive, lawyer; b. Wabash, Ind., July 30, 1956; s. James William and Joyce Arlene (Lillibridge) P.; m. Neil Ann Armstrong, Aug. 21, 1982; children: Elizabeth Joyce, Helen Frances, James William III. BS, Ball State U., 1978; JD, U. Miami, 1981. Bar: La. 1981, U.S. Dist. Ct. (ea. dist.) La. 1981, U.S. Ct. Appeals (5th and 11th cirs.) 1981. Fla. 1982, U.S. Dist. Ct. (mid. dist. La.) 1982. Atty. Jones, Walker, Waechter, Poitevent, Carrere et al., New Orleans, 1981-83, Foley & Judell, New Orleans, 1983-88, McCollister & McCleary, pc, Baton Rouge, 1988-95; pres., CEO La. Pub. Facilities Authority, Baton Rouge, 1995—. Mem. AICPA, Nat. Assn. Bond Lawyers, La. State Bar Assn., Fla. Bar Assn., Assn. for Gifted and Talented Students, Baton Rouge (treas. 1994-96, pres.-elect 1996-97, pres. 1997-98), Soc. La. CPA (govt. acctg. and auditing com. 1994-95), Nat. Assn. Higher Edn. Facilities Authorities (bd. dirs. 1996-2001, v.p. 1997-99, pres. 1999-2001), Nat. Coun. Health Facilities Fin. Authorities (bd. dirs. 2004—, treas. 2004-06), Coun. of Devel. Fin. Agys. (bd. dirs. 2002—), La. Assistive Tech. Access Network (bd. dirs. 2001—, chmn. 2004—06), La. Pub. Health Inst. (bd. dirs. 2005—). Avocations: travel, computers. Home: 5966 Tennyson Dr Baton Rouge LA 70817-2933 Office: La Pub Facilities Authority 2237 S Acadian Thruway Ste 650 Baton Rouge LA 70808-2380 Office Phone: 225-923-0020. E-mail: jameswparks2@hotmail.com, parks@lpfa.com.

PARKS, JANE DELOACH, retired law librarian, legal assistant; b. Atlanta, June 7, 1927; d. John Keller and Martha Lorena (Lee) deLoach; m. James Bennett Parks, Dec. 28, 1951 (dec. Sept. 1983); children: Carrie Anne Parks-Kirby, Susan Jane, Lora Beth Maury. BA magna cum laude, Vanderbilt U., 1949; postgrad., Emory U., 1950-51; tchr. cert., U. Chattanooga, 1954; postgrad., U. Tenn., Chattanooga, 1971-73. Med. rsch./writing dept. surgery Emory U., Atlanta, 1949-51; sec. to med. dir. Tenn. Tuberculosis Hosp., Chattanooga, 1951-53; tchr. Signal Mountain (Tenn.) Elem. Sch., 1954-55; tchr., dean jr. sch. Cleve. (Tenn.) Day Sch., 1963-70; law firm libr., legal asst. Stophel, Caldwell & Heggie, Chattanooga, 1972-85, Caldwell, Heggie & Helton, Chattanooga, 1985-93, Heiskell, Donelson, Bearman, Adams, Williams & Caldwell, Chattanooga, 1993-94, Baker, Donelson, Bearman & Caldwell, Chattanooga, 1994-99; ret., 1999. Tchr. various seminars on legal rsch. and writing, organizing one-person librs. and ch. librs., Chattanooga Legal Secs. Assn., Chattanooga-Hamilton County Bicentennial Libr. Editor (mag.) The Gadfly, 1947-49; editorial asst.: Studio Collotype, 1988 and to profl. jours., 1949—. Tchr. Chattanooga Area Literacy Movement, 1984-86; exec. coun. Friends of Chattanooga-Hamilton County Bicentennial Libr., 1989-94; del. Gov.'s Conf.-White House Conf. on Librs. and Info. Svcs., Nashville, 1990; libr. vol. Tenn. Aquarium. Environ. Learning Lab. 1993-2004; allocations com. United Way, 1994—, Signal Mountain Cmty. Guild, 1999—, dir. Lit. Dept., 2000—02, pub. chmn., 2002-04, chaplain, 2006-. Mem. Tenn. Paralegal Assn., Chattanooga Area Libr. Assn. (2d v.p. 1989-90, sec. 1992-93), Non-Atty. Profl. Assn. (chmn. 1989-93), Phi Beta Kappa, Mortar Bd. Republican. Methodist. Avocations: reading, needlecrafts, genealogy, ceramics.

PARKS, JEAN ANNE, retired acute care nurse; b. Grand Rapids, Mich., Aug. 3, 1940; d. Edwin Charles and Ruth Katherine (Skellenger) Paepke; m. Charles Wilbur Parks, Nov. 24, 1961; children: Charles Edwin, Catherine Ann, Michael Allan. Diploma in Nursing with highest honors, Blodgett Meml. Hosp., 1961; BS summa cum laude in Health Studies, Western Mich. U., 1987; MA magna cum laude in Health and Humanities, Mich. State U., 1994. RN. Staff nurse Blodgett Meml. Hosp., Grand Rapids, 1961—62; nurse Ctrl. Mich. Cmty. Hosp., Mt. Pleasant, 1962—64; med.-surg. staff Blodgett Meml. Hosp., 1964—70, part-time staff, 1979—2003; part-time Medicaid evaluator for Kent County, Mich. Dept. Pub. Health, Lansing, 1987—88. Mem. Grand Rapids Symphony Chorus, 1987—2003. Baptist. Avocations: travel, music (toured with chorus to several countries).

PARKS, JOE BENJAMIN, entrepreneur, retired state legislator; b. McAlester, Okla., Dec. 17, 1915; s. James Allen and Mary Florence (Youngblood) P.; m. Florence M. Evans, Oct. 25, 1941; children: Anne, Kathryn. BS in Pub. Adminstrn., Okla. State U., 1939. Divsn. dir. U.S. VA, Washington, 1946—56; spl. asst., cons. U.S. GSA, Washington, 1957—58; mgr. dist. EDP divsn. RCA Corp., Washington, 1959—65; mgr. Ea. region Dashew Bus. Machines, Arlington, Va., 1966—68; assoc. adminstr. social and rehab. svc. U.S. Dept. HEW, Washington, 1969—73; dir. mktg. govs. sys. divsn. Booz, Allen & Hamilton, Washington, 1974—75; ptnr. Forbes & Parks, Dover, NH, 1976—2002, PatPar, Inc., 1990—; mem. N.H. State Legislature, Concord, 1984—92, chmn. joint com. on elderly affairs, 1987—92, mem. com. on health, human svcs. and elderly, 1983—90; chmn. subcom. mileage and electronic roll call, 1989—90; vice chmn. legis. adminstrn. com., 1990—91; mem. appropriations com., 1991—92; propr. Portsmouth Athenaeum, Portsmouth, NH, 1992—. Corporator Wentworth Douglas Hosp., Dover, 1980-89; pres. Berr Par, Inc., 1994—. Columnist Nat. Antiques Rev., 1975-77, Boston Globe N.H. Weekly 1987-88, Foster's Daily Democrat (Dover, N.H.), 1988-90; freelance writer, 1990—. Vice-chmn. NH State Rep. Com., 1987-88; chmn. Strafford County, NH, Reps., 1988; Strafford County campaign mgr. George W. Bush for Pres., 1999-2000; bd. dirs. Coastal Maine Bot. Garden, 2001-05, Rockingham Bot. Garden, 2005—, Ageless Dreamer, 2007—. Decorated Bronze Star; recipient Lawmakers award for disting. environ. svc. Sierra Club, 1990, NH State award New England Wildflower Soc., 1998; named Norris Cotton Rep. of Yr., 1993; Paul Harris fellow Rotary Internat. Found., 1998. Mem. Am. Rhododendron Soc. (pres. Mass. chpt. 1995-96, Bronze medal 1992, 2003, Silver medal, 2006). Congregationalist. Avocation: plant breeding. Home and Office: Parkwood Farm 195 Long Hill Rd Dover NH 03820-6108

PARKS, JUDITH TYLER, business executive, consultant; b. Chgo., June 16, 1972; d. Edsel J. and Irma T. Parks. BS, Rensselaer Poly. Inst., Troy, NY, 1995; MS, NC State U., Raleigh, 1997, PhD, 2003. Supply chain mgmt. advisor The Internat. Group, Raleigh, 2004—05; dir. Expense Reduction Analysts, Morrisville, NC, 2006—. Fellow, Office Naval Rsch., 1998—2001. Mem.: Alpha Pi Mu. Achievements include patents pending for cross-selling optimization for the banking industry. Business E-Mail: jparks@era-usa.com.

PARKS, LINDA S., lawyer; b. Oneida, NY, Aug. 19, 1957; BA summa cum laude, Washburn U., 1979, JD cum laude, 1983. Bar: Kans. 1983, Kans. Supreme Ct., US Ct. Appeals (10th Cir.), US Dist. Ct. (Dist. Kans.). Ptnr. Hite Fanning & Honeyman LLP, Wichita, Kans. Bd. mem. YWCA. Fellow: ABA (Kans. Bar Assn. del. 1999—2005); mem.: Kans. Bar Found. (trustee 2000—02), Am. Bar Found., Nat. Assn. Women Bar Assoc. (bd. mem. 2005—), Wichita Women Attys. Assn., Kans. Women Attys. Assn. (pres. 1994—96), Kans. Bar Assn. (mem. bd. gov. 1999—, chair law related edn. com. 2000—02, exec. com. 2000—, v.p. 2005—06, pres.-elect 2006—07, pres. 2007—08), Wichita Bar Assn. Office: Hite Fanning & Honeyman LLP Ste 950 100 N Broadway Wichita KS 67202-2209 Office Phone: 316-265-7741. Office Fax: 316-267-7803. E-mail: parks@hitefanning.com.

PARKS, LLOYD LEE, oil industry executive; b. Kiefer, Okla., Dec. 9, 1929; s. Homer Harrison and Avis Pearl (Motes) P.; m. Mary Ellen Scott, Aug. 20, 1948; children: Connie Jo, Karyn Ann, Rebecca Lee. Student, Okla. State U., 1948-50, Tulsa U., 1950-51, Harvard U. Bus. Sch., 1965. Acct. Deep Rock Oil Corp., 1951-54; chief acct. Blackwell Oil & Gas Co., Tulsa, 1954-60, sec. treas., 1960-62; v.p., controller Amax Oil & Gas Inc., Houston, 1962-67, pres., CEO, 1968—92; v.p. Amax, Inc., 1975-92; pvt. practice oil and gas and real estate imvestment Salado, Tex., 1992—. Served with AUS, 1946-48, 50-51. Mem.: Ind. Petroleum Assn. Am. (dir.), Lions Club, Wildflower Country Club (Temple, Tex.). Republican. Office: PO Box 1021 Salado TX 76571-1021 Personal E-mail: llparks9@aol.com. *Work hard, work smart and believe in yourself. You can and will be successful; if you want to be.*

PARKS, MICHAEL CHRISTOPHER, journalist, educator; b. Detroit, Nov. 17, 1943; s. Robert James and Rosalind (Smith) P.; m. Linda Katherine Durocher, Dec. 26, 1964; children: Danielle Anne, Christopher, Matthew. AB, U. Windsor, Ont., Can., 1965. Reporter Detroit News, 1962-65; corr. Time-Life News Service, NYC, 1965-66; asst. city editor Suffolk Sun, Long Island, NY, 1966-68; polit. reporter, foreign corr. The Balt. Sun, Saigon, Singapore, Moscow, Cairo, Hong Kong, Peking, 1968-80; fgn. corr. L.A. Times, L.A., Peking, Johannesburg, Moscow, Jerusalem, 1980-95, dpty. fgn. editor, 1995-96, mng. editor, 1996-97, editor, 1997-2000, v.p., 1996-97, sr. v.p., 1997-98, exec. v.p., 1998-2000; v.p. Times Mirror Co., 1998-2000; prof. Annenberg Sch. Comm. U. So. Calif., LA, 2000—02, dir. Annenberg Sch. Journalism, 2002—, prof. journalism and internat. rels., 2002—. Disting. fellow Pacific Coun. Internat. Policy, 2000-02, dir. 1998-; dir. L.A. Jewish Jour., 2004-. Recipient Pulitzer prize, 1987. Mem. Am. Soc. Newspaper Editors, AP Mng. Editors, Pacific Coun. Internat., Policy, Radio-TV News Dirs., Soc. Profl. Journalists, Athenaeum (Pasadena, Calif.), Coun. on Fgn. Rels., US Naval Inst., City Club (L.A.), Nat. Press Club. Office: Annenberg Sch U So Calif Los Angeles CA 90089-0281 Office Phone: 213-740-0638. E-mail: mparks@usc.edu.

PARKS, MICHAEL JAMES, editor; b. Spokane, Wash., June 3, 1944; s. Floyd Lewis and Marie (McHugh) Parks; m. Janet K. Holter, Aug. 12, 1967; children: Michael J., Gregory F., Sarah M. BA, Seattle U., 1966. Reporter The Seattle Times, 1966—74, fin. editor, 1974—77; pub., editor Marple's N.W. Letter, Seattle, 1977—. Bd. govs. Seattle U. Alumni Assn.; trustee Seattle Rotary Svc. Found. Fellow, Am. Press Inst., N.Y.C., 1973. Mem.: Rotary. Roman Catholic. Avocations: opera, reading, swimming, walking. Office: Marples NW Letter Ste 200 117 W Mercer St Seattle WA 98119-3960 Personal E-mail: michaeljparks@gmail.com. E-mail: info@marples.com.

PARKS, PATRICIA JEAN, lawyer; b. Portland, Oreg., Apr. 2, 1945; d. Robert and Marion (Crosby) Parks; m. David F. Jurca, Oct. 17, 1971 (div. 1976). BA in History, Stanford U., 1967; JD, U. Pa., Phila., 1970. Bar: N.Y. 1971, Wash. 1974. Assoc. Milbank, Tweed, Hadley & McCoy, NYC, 1970-73, Shidler, McBroom, Gates & Lucas, Seattle, 1974-81, ptnr., 1981-90, Preston, Thorgrimson, Shidler, Gates & Ellis, Seattle, 1990-93; pvt. practice Seattle, 1993-99; spl. counsel Karr Tuttle Campbell, Seattle, 1999—. Active Vashon Allied Arts; former bd. dirs. Seattle chpt. Western Pension and Benefits Conf. Mem.: ABA, Pension Roundtable, Seattle-King County Bar Assn., Wash. Women Tax, Wash. State Bar Assn. (past chair gift and estate tax com.), Wash. Native Plant Soc., Wash. Athletic Club. Avocations: kayaking, hiking, contra dancing, birdwatching. Office: 1201 3rd Ave Ste 2900 Seattle WA 98101-3284 Office Phone: 206-224-8094. Business E-Mail: pparks@karrtuttle.com.

PARKS, ROBERT MYERS, appliance manufacturing company executive; b. Nevada, Mo., July 18, 1927; s. Cecil R. and Marcella (Myers) P.; m. Audrey Lenora Jones, June 18, 1955; children: John Robert, Janet M. Parks Huston. BS, U. Mo., 1949; MBA, Harvard U., 1952. Asst. dept. mgr. Jewett & Sherman Co., Kansas City, Mo., 1949-50; staff cons. Harbridge House, Inc., Boston, 1952; v.p. Electronic Splty. Co., Inc., Los Angeles, 1952-57; founder, chmn. bd. Parks Products, Inc., Hollywood, Calif., 1957—; pres. Generalist Industries, Inc., Hollywood, 1960-73. Chmn. bd. Shaver Corp. Am., LA, 1965—; lectr. mktg. UCLA Extension divsn., 1960-61. Contbr. articles to profl. jours.; patentee in field. Active YMCA; bd. dirs. Hollywood Presbyn. Med. Center Found., Presbyn. Homes Found.; mem. dean's adv. council U. Mo. Bus. Sch., mayor's task force on L.A. River Cahuenga Pass Coalition. With USNR, 1944-45. Named in his honor Grad. Bus. Sch., U. Mo. Mem. Sales and Marketing Execs. Assn., C. of C., Navy League, World Affairs Coun., Calif. Caballeros, Rangers, Vaqueros del Desierto, Los Caballeros, Rancheros Visitadores, E Clampus Vitus, Delta Sigma Pi, Sigma Chi. Clubs: Mason (Shriner), LA Breakfast, Braemar Country, Saddle and Sirloin. Presbyterian. Home: 7421 Woodrow Wilson Dr Los Angeles CA 90046-1322 Office: 3611 Cahuenga Blvd Hollywood CA 90068-1205 Office Phone: 323-876-5454.

PARKYN, JOHN DUWANE, nuclear engineer; b. La Crosse, Wis., Feb. 20, 1944; s. Lionel Eric and Florence Katrina (Klum) P.; m. Betty Christine Tarnutzer, Aug. 13, 1966; children: Christine Peggy, Sarah Katherine, John Martin. Student, Wis. State U., 1962-64, U. N.Mex., 1968-69; BS in Nuclear Engrng. and Physics, U. Wis., 1972. Cert. assessor, Wis.; registered profl. engr., Calif., Wis.; lic. sr. reactor operator; lic. min. United Ch. of Christ. Asst. plant engr. Ohio Med. Products Co., 1966-67; party chief U.S. Geol. Survey, Madison, Wis., 1971-72; asst. ops. gorup Point Beach Nuclear Plant, Two Rivers, Wis., 1972-74; asst. supt. La Crosse Boiling Water Reactor, Genoa, Wis., 1974-82; supt., 1982-95; mem. industry rev. bd. Inst. Nuclear Power Ops.; CEO Great Salt Lake and So. R.R.; pres., CEO Nuclear Three Inc., La Crosse, Wis., 1965—. Past chmn. bd. dirs. BAnks Stoddard, BAnk Ferryville; chmn. bd. dirs. Wis. Masonic Home; chmn. bd., CEO Pvt. Fuel storage LLC; dir. River BAnk; past chmn. bd. Mescalero Fuel Storage LLC; pres. Genoa Fuel Tech Co.; chmn. bd., CEO Great Salt Lake & So. R.R.; mem. atty.'s responsibility investative bd. Wis. Supreme Ct Mem. Two Rivers City Coun., 1974; mem. Vernon County Bd. Suprs., 1976-94, 2002-, past vice chmn. county bd., mem. fin. com., chmn. human svcs. rev. bd., chn. cmty. options program; assessor Bergen Twp. (Wis.), 1977-79; chmn. Vernon County Libr. Com., 1976—; chmn. pers. com. Vernon County Bd. Equalized Values; chmn. Vernon County Com. for Programs of Aging; past pres. Sch. Dist. of La Crosse, pres.; past pres. Riverland coun. Girl Scouts U.S.A.; past mem. exec. bd. Gateway Area coun. Boy Scouts Am., dist. chmn.; advisor, mem. Wis. staff Order of DeMolay; past chmn. Wis. Masonic Home; pres. St. Johns United Ch. Christ; pres. River Rails Inc., Gov. Commn. on Midwest Rail Initiative; vice chmn. Vernon County Jail Study Commn.; bd. dirs. Coffeemill Shi Hul, Wabasha, Minn. Mem. Am. Nuclear Soc. (chmn. Wis. sect., mem. nat. planning com., vice chair decommissiong divsn.), Nat. Assn. R.R. Passengers (nat. bd. dirs.), Wis. Assn. R.R. Passengers (state pres.), Am. Legion, Wis. Legis. Coun., Masons (past worshipful master Frontier Lodge 45), Disabled Am. Veterans Home: Pleasant Vly Stoddard WI 54658 Office: La Crosse Boiling Water Reactor RR 1 Genoa WI 54632-9801

PARKYN, JOHN WILLIAM, editor, writer, columnist; b. London, Dec. 7, 1931; came to U.S., 1967; citizen, 1973; s. James R. and Eva M. (Dix) P.; m. Sybil (Judy) Hetherington; 1 child, Elaine. Student, Dulwich Coll., 1943-48. Staff writer Bus. Mag., London, 1954-56; writer-editor Amalgamated Press, London, 1956-58; features editor Woman's Illustrated mag., London, 1958-60; staff writer Internat. Pub. Corp., London, 1960-61; editor Westward mag. Daily News Ltd., London, 1961-64; assoc. editor Daily Telegraph mag., London, 1964-66; features editor King mag. Europress, Ltd., London, 1966-67; assoc. editor Tropic mag. Miami Herald, 1967-69; editor Tropic mag., 1969-77; editor Calif. Today mag. San Jose Mercury News, Calif., 1977-83; editor Sunshine: The Mag. of South Fla. Sun-Sentinel Co. (subs. Tribune Co.), Ft. Lauderdale, Fla., 1983-96; columnist S. Fla. Sun-Sentinel, 1997—2005; exec. editor, sr. writer Vero Beach Mag., Fla., 1998—; columnist, feature writer City & Shore mag., 2000—05. Cons. Het Parool newspaper, Amsterdam, 1965. Contbr. numerous articles to Am. and European mags. Chmn. Sunday Mag. Editors Conf., Louisville, 1973. With RAF, 1950-52. Recipient Outstanding Use of Editl. Color award Editor & Pub. mag., 1974, 75, 77, Nat. Headliner award, 1976, 79; named Editor Best Weekly Mag. in State Fla. Press Club, 1985-93, 95. Personal E-mail: johnparkyn@aol.com.

PARLAMIS, MICHAEL FRANK, civil engineer, construction executive; b. Bklyn., May 29, 1940; s. Frank Michael and Phyllis (Burnago) P.; m. Marguerite Koskinas, Aug. 21, 1966; children: Franklin, Christine, Alexander. BSCE, MIT, 1962, BS in Indsl. Mgmt., 1962; MSCE, Stanford U., 1963. Registered profl. engr., N.Y. Engr. Port Authority of N.Y. and N.J., 1963-64; asst. to chief engr. George A. Fuller Co., NYC, 1964-67; pres. Frank Parlamis Inc., Bklyn., 1968—, Parlamis Bros. Inc., Bklyn., 1968—, Hermes Constrn. Corp., Bklyn., 1968—; ptnr. City Path LLC, City Jam LLC, 128 MAC LLC, 128 MAPP LLC. Author: CPM/PERT As Basis for Management Information Systems in Building Construction, 1966, Regulation of Building Construction in the City of New York, 1967, Greece and the Panama Canal, 1988. Chmn. expension program Greek Orthodox Cathedral St. John the Theologian, Tenafly, NJ, 1978—; mem. Leadership 100 of Greek Orthodox Ch.; Archon of Ecomenical Patriarcate, Greek Orthodox Ch.; mem. ednl. coun. MIT; trustee Frank Parlamis Sr. Citizens Ctr., Jamaica, NY, Space Camp Turkey, Izmir; founder St. John the Theologian Peace Meml. Gymnasium; exec. dir. St. John the Theologian World Peace Inst.; founding trustee New Hagia Sophia, Hagia Eurine 250 Charitable Trust. Recipient Ellis Island medal of honor, 2002, Gold Key award for best engineered restaurant in USA, Internat. Hotel, Motel an Restaurant Show, 1992. Mem. Am. Hellenic Progressive Assn., Bklyn. Tech. Rsch. Found. (life), Tau Beta Pi, Chi Epsilon. Republican. Avocations: engineering and religious history, peace advocacy, ecumenical religious activities. Home: 128 Downey Dr Tenafly NJ 07670-3006 Office: 328 Atlantic Ave Brooklyn NY 11201-5804 Office Phone: 718-875-6744. Business E-Mail: parlamis@alum.mit.edu.

PARLANGE, JEAN-YVES, environmental engineer, educator; PhD, Brown U., 1962. Asst. prof. Yale U., Dept. Engring. and Applied Sci., 1964—69, assoc. prof., 1969—72; assoc. scientist Conn. Agr. Exp. Station, 1968—71, mathematician, 1971—77; prof. Coll. Forest Resources, U. Wash., 1977—78; prof. applied math. Environ. Scis., Griffith U., 1978—85; prof. biological and environ. engring. Cornell U., 1985—. Vis. prof. U. Grenoble, 1981—82; prof. hydrology Flinders U., 1993—94. Contbr. articles to profl. jours. Recipient Minta Martin Nat. Award, 1962, AGU Horton Award, 1997; Fulbright Grant, 1958. Mem.: NAE, Soil Science Soc. Am., Am. Geophysical Union, Sigma Xi. Office: Cornell U Biological and Environ Engring 228 Riley-Robb Hall Ithaca NY 14853-5701 Office Phone: 607-255-2476. Office Fax: 607-255-4080. Business E-Mail: jp58@cornell.edu.

PARLE, BERTHA IBARRA, writer; b. El Paso, Tex., Nov. 14, 1947; d. Arnulfo and Bertha (Soto) Ibarra; m. Dennis Jerome Parle, Aug. 16, 1969; children: Joseph, Mónica, Angélica Attended, Loretto Acad., 1965; BA in French, Spanish, U. Tex., El Paso, 1968; MA in Spanish, U. Kans., Lawrence, 1970, H.S. tchg. cert., 1971; postgrad. courses in French, U. Houston, 1990—95. Bilingual tchr. Kans. Remedial Edn. Program, Sharon Springs, 1967, 71, 72; Spanish tchr. Ottawa (Kans.) H.S., 1971-74; ESL instr. North Harris Coll., Houston, 1977-83; modern lang. prof. N. Harris Montgomery C.C. Dist., Houston, 1983-97, head lang. inst., 1997—2002. Cultural cons., sponsor Hispanic students North Harris Coll. and Montgomery Coll., 1983-97, organizer Hispanic cultural events, 1983—, sponsor Cath. Newman Club, 1985-95; lectr., slide show The Nahua Mexica Legacy, 1994-96; participant in field seminars; NEH and Fulbright Ecuador field experience. Author numerous poems; Spanish poetry publ. in Tejidos,

Grito al Sol, 1972-94. Hispanic leader St. Leo's Cath. Ch., Houston, 1982-92; del. People to People Am. Program to S. Africa, 2000. Recipient Tchg. Excellence award North Harris Coll., 1997, Excellence award Nat. Inst. for Staff and Orgn. Devel., 1998; Am. Coun. Tchrs. Fgn. Langs. summer scholar U. Montreal, 1999. Mem. AAUW, Am. Coun. Tchrs. Fgn. Langs., Computer Assisted Lang. Instn. Consortium, Am. Assn. C.C. Women, Tex. Fgn. Lang. Assn., Inst. Hispanic Culture., North Harris United Faculty. Avocations: creative writing, study of indigenous language cultures, Hispanic students and Hispanic issues in the community. Office: North Harris Coll 2700 W Thorne Dr Houston TX 77073 Home Phone: 281-586-8821; Office Phone: 281-618-5546. Business E-Mail: bertha.parle@nhmccd.edu.

PARLEE, MARY BROWN, psychology educator; b. Oak Park, Ill., Feb. 11, 1943; d. Grant Sylvester Brown and Esther (Bonter) de Neufville; 1 child, Elizabeth. BA, Harvard U., 1965; PhD, MIT, 1969. Asst. prof. Wellesley Coll., Mass., 1969-72; fellow Bunting Inst. of Radcliffe Coll., Cambridge, Mass., 1972-74; fellow lab. social psychiatry Harvard U., Boston, 1974-75; assoc. prof. Barnard Coll. of Columbia U., NYC, 1975-78; dir. ctr. for study women and soc. CUNY, 1979-84, prof. psychology grad. ctr., 1984-93; vis. prof. MIT, 1993—99, vis. lectr., 2000—. Contbr. articles to profl. jours. Vol. St. Ignatius, NYC, 1987-88. NIH grantee, 1975-78, 79-82; recipient Publ. award Assn. for Women in Psychology, 1978. Fellow APA (pres. divsn. psychology of women 1983-84); mem. Harvard Club NYC, Radcliffe Club NY (bd. dirs. 1989), Radcliffe Club Boston. Episcopalian. Office: MIT 46-2004 Cambridge MA 02139 Business E-Mail: mbparlee@alum.mit.edu.

PARLIER, GREG H., military officer, analyst, engineer, researcher; b. San Luis Obispo, Calif., May 10, 1952; s. Merton B. and Kathleen F. Parlier; m. Judy D. Olson, Aug. 30, 1975; children: Jamie Lynn, Timothy Scott, Steven Hugh. BS, U.S. Mil. Acad., 1974; MS, Naval Postgrad. Sch., 1983; MA, Georgetown U., 1988; postgrad., USMC Command and Staff Coll., 1988—89, U. Va., 1992, U.S. Army War Coll., 1995—96; PhD, Wesleyan U., 2004. Registered profl. engr., Va.; master parachutist, army strategist, battle staff officer, cert. strategy and innovation MIT, 2005, mgmt. and leadership MIT, 2006. Vulcan and redeye platoon leader 3-4 ADAR, 82d Airborne Divsn., Ft. Bragg, NC, 1975—76; exec. officer Battery C, 3-4 ADAR, 82d Airborne Divsn., 1976—77, Battery C, 2-71 ADA, 31st ADA Brigade, Republic of Korea, 1977; battery comdr. Battery D, 3-4 ADAR, 82d Airborne Divsn., 1979—81; asst. prof. dept. engring. U.S. Mil. Acad., West Point, NY, 1983—86; chief officer plans U.S. Army Mil. Pers. Ctr., Alexandria, Va., 1986—88, 3-4 ADAR ops. officer, 1989—90, exec. officer, 1990—91; G-3 air def. element XVIII Airborne Corps, Ft. Bragg, 1991—92; bn. comdr. 5-2 ADAR, 69th ADA Brigade, V Corps, Crailsheim and Bamberg, Germany, 1992—94; chief resource plans and analysis divsn. Office of the Chief of Staff U.S. Army, Washington, 1996—98; dir. program analysis and evaluation U.S. Army Recruiting Command, Ft. Knox, Ky., 1998—2002; dir. for transformation U.S. Army Aviation and Missile Command, Redstone Arsenal, Ala., 2002—03; sr. rsch. scientist U. Ala., Huntsville, 2003—05; def. analyst Inst. for Def. Analysis, 2004—; sr. sys. analyst Sci. Applications Internat. Corp., 2005—; v.p. strategic planning Rsch., Sys., and Analytical Engring., Inc., 2005—. Pres. ops. Rsch. Soc. Ala., 2005. Sr. tactical comdr. McKee Barracks, Crailsheim, 1993; vice chmn. Bamberg (Germany) Scholarship Com., 1993—94; mentor Georgetown U. ROTC, Washington, 1996—98. Col. US Army, 1997. Decorated Bronze Star U.S. Army, Legion of Merit; named Dept. of the Army Rsch. Analyst of the Yr., 1987; recipient German Efficiency Badge (Gold), Bundeswehr (German Army), 1999, 2001, plaque of appreciation, Korean Nat. Assembly, 1978, Can. Parachutist Badge, Can. Forces, 1977, USMC CSC Disting. Grad. and Gen. Clifton B. Cates award, 1989, Jim and Rafer Johnson Outstanding Athlete Award, Kingsburg H.S. Faculty and Coaches, 1970; Nat. Def. Fellow, MIT, 1994—95. Mem.: Mil. Ops. Rsch. Soc. (Grad. Rsch. award 1983), Inst. Ops. Rsch. and Mgmt. Scis., 82nd Airborne Divsn. Assn. (life), Sigma Xi. Avocations: reading, classical music, sports. Home: 255 Avian Ln Madison AL 35758-6863 Personal E-mail: gparlier@knology.net. Business E-Mail: greg.h.parlier@saic.com.

PARMAN, TRACY LE, application developer; d. Noble Robert and Marjorie June Parman. BSBA, Fla. Internat. U., Miami, 1993; MBA, U. S.Ala., Mobile, 1999. Internship Ryder Corp., Miami, 1993—95; computer analyst/programmer Renaissance Cruises, Port Everglades, Fla., 1995—97; contract programmer Long's Human Resources, Mobile, 1997; computer programmer Autry Greer & Sons, Inc., Prichard, Ala., 1997—2003; application analyst Spring Hill Coll., Mobile, 2003—. Mem.: Mobile Bot. Gardens, Mensa (webmaster 2007). Home: 7261 Griffice Rd Mobile AL 36618 Office: Spring Hill Coll 4000 Dauphin St Mobile AL 36608 Business E-Mail: tparman@shc.edu.

PARMELEE, ARTHUR HAWLEY, JR., pediatric medical educator; b. Chgo., Oct. 29, 1917; s. Arthur Hawley and Ruth Frances (Brown) P.; m. Jean Kern Rheinfrank, Nov. 11, 1939; children: Arthur Hawley III, Ann (Mrs. John C. Minahan Jr.), Timothy, Ruth Ellen. BS, U. Chgo., 1940, MD, 1943. Diplomate Am. Bd. Pediatrics (examiner 1966—). Intern U.S. Naval Hosp., Bethesda, Md., 1943-44; extern Yale Inst. Child Devel., 1947, New Haven Hosp., 1947-48, L.A. Children's Hosp., 1948-49; mem. faculty UCLA Med. Sch., 1951—, prof. pediat., 1967-88, prof. emeritus, 1988, dir. divsn. child devel., 1964-88; mem. Brain Rsch. Inst., 1966-88, Mental Retardation Rsch. Ctr., 1970-88. Rsch. prof. pediat. U. Göttingen, Germany, 1967-68; mem. com. child devel. rsch. and pub. policy NRC, 1977-81; cons. Nat. Inst. Child Health and Human Devel., 1963-70, Holy Family Adoption Svc., 1949-80. Author articles, chpts. in books. Trustee Los Angeles Children's Mus., 1979. Served with USN, 1943-47. Recipient C. Anderson Aldrich award in child devel., 1975; Commonwealth fellow Centre de Recherches Biologiques Neonatales, Clinique Obstetricale Baudelocque, Paris, 1959-60; fellow Ctr. Advanced Study in Behavioral Scis., Stanford U., 1984-85; hon. lectr. Soc. for Developmental and Behavioral Pediat., 1996. Mem. AMA, Am. Pediat. Soc., Soc. Pediat. Rsch., Western Soc. Pediat. Rsch., Am. Acad. Pediat. (chmn. com. sect. child devel. 1966), Assn. Ambulatory Pediat. (mem. coun. 1966-69), Soc. Rsch. in Child Devel. (pres. 1983-85, Disting. Sci. Contbns. to Child Devel. award 1993), Assn. Psychophysiol. Study of Sleep, Los Angeles County Med. Soc., Phi Beta Kappa. Home: 764 Iliff St Pacific Palisades CA 90272-3927 Office: Univ Calif Dept Pediatrics Los Angeles CA 90024

PARMENTER, KELLI DENISE, middle school educator, small business owner; b. Dallas, Feb. 10, 1963; d. Ted M. and Grace M. Porter; m. Ernest Eugene Parmenter, Jr., July 26, 1986; children: Joshua Shane, Clint Martin. MusB in Edn., Baylor U., Waco, Tex., 1986; MEd, Tex. A&M, Commerce, 1994. Tchr. elem. music, mid. sch. choir Mesquite Ind. Sch. Dist., Tex., 1986—. Owner Kelli's Angels Animal Sitters, Mesquite, Tex., 2002—. Recipient Featured Tchr. award, Mesquite Daily News, 1993. Mem.: Mesquite Edn. Assn. (com. mem. 2006—), Tex. Music Educators Assn. (assoc.). Baptist. Avocations: reading, gardening, travel, horseback riding. Office Phone: 972-288-6411. Personal E-mail: kellisangels@sbcglobal.net.

PARMESE, GABRIEL J., corporate financial executive; s. James and Martha (Phillips) Parmese; m. Ann C. Mullen, Oct. 20, 2000; children: Norah, Jimmy. BSc in Commerce and Fin., Rider U.; MBA, N.H. Coll., 1987. V.p. fin., corp. contr. Art Tech., Cambridge, Mass., 2001—04; CFO SynQor Inc., Boxboro, Mass., 2004—. Corp. contr. Applix, Westbrough, Mass., 2000—01. Active homeless shelter activities and abuse programs, 1993—2005. Mem.: Fed. Executives Inst. (assoc.). Conservative. Achievements include public reporting, turn around and operational efficiency expert for US based companies. Office: SynQor Inc 155 Swanson Rd Boxboro MA 01719 Home Phone: 508-429-6877; Office Phone: 978-849-0600. Business E-Mail: gabrielparmese@synqor.com.

PARMET, HARRIET ABBEY L., literature educator; b. Phila., July 22, 1928; d. Jacob and Belle Cecil (Popolow) Leibowitz; m. Sidney B. Parmet, June 7, 1950; children: Howard B., Jonathan L. AB, Temple U., 1950, MS, 1960; B in Hebrew Lit., Gratz Coll., 1979; PhD in English, Lehigh U. Cert. secondary edn. tchr., Pa. Tchr. Hebrew Temple U., Phila., 1946-50, Beth Israel, Phila., 1946-51; tchr. English and social studies Gillespie Jr. High Sch., Phila., 1950-55; tchr. Hebrew and Jewish history Temple Beth El, Allentown, Pa., 1964-77; tchr. Hebrew and Israeli lit. Lehigh U., Bethlehem, Pa., 1976—95; prof. emeritus, 1995. Hillel co-advisor, mem. exec. bd. Lehigh U., 1976—. Author: The Terror of Our Days: Four Am. Poets Respond to the Holocaust, 2001; contbr. articles to profl. jours. Vice pres. Temple Beth El Sisterhood, Allentown, 1973-75; mem. exec. bd. Jewish Family Svc., Allentown, 1988—; bd. dirs. Women's Profl. Jewish Fedn., Allentown, 1973-75. Coolodge Colloquim fellow, 1986, Givat Haviva Rsch. fellow, 1987; named Outstanding Alumna Gratz Coll. Centenial Celebration. Mem. Women's Studies Consortium, Lehigh Valley Assn. Ind. Colls., Am. Jewish Congress (pres. Allentown chpt. 1970), Assn. Jewish Studies, Nat. Assn. Hebrew Profs., Temple U. Alumni Assn. (Disting. Alumni award 1995), Gratz Coll. Alumni Assn., Hadassah (life). Home: 1118 N 28th St Allentown PA 18104-2908 Office: Lehigh U Modern Lang Dept Maginnes Hall # 9 Bethlehem PA 18015-3206 Home Phone: 610-433-2484; Office Phone: 610-758-3090. Business E-Mail: hlpo@lehigh.edu.

PARMET, HERBERT SAMUEL, historian, writer; b. NYC, Sept. 28, 1929; s. Isaac and Fanny (Scharf) P.; m. Joan Kronish, Sept. 12, 1948; 1 child, Wendy. BS, SUNY, Oswego, 1951; MA, Queens Coll., 1957; postgrad., Columbia U., 1958-62. Prof. history Grad. Sch. CUNY, 1968-95, disting. prof. history, 1983-95, prof. emeritus, 1995—. Cons. ABC-TV, N.Y.C., 1983, KERA-TV, Dallas, 1986-91, WGBH-TV, Boston, 1988-91, 2007. Author: Aaron Burr: Portrait of an Ambitious Man, 1967, Never Again: President Runs for a Third Term, 1968, Eisenhower and the American Crusades, 1972, The Democrats, 1976, Jack: The Struggles of John F. Kennedy, 1980, JFK: The Presidency of John F. Kennedy, 1983, Richard Nixon and His America, 1990, George Bush: The Life of a Lone Star Yankee, 1997, Presidential Power: From the New Deal to the New Right, 2001, Richard Nixon: An American Enigma, 2007. Cpl. U.S. Army, 1952-54. Grantee, NEH, 1987. Fellow Soc. Am. Historians; mem. Am. Hist. Assn., Orgn. Am. Historians, Authors Guild. Avocation: photography. Home: 36 Marsten Ln Hillsdale NY 12529-5816 E-mail: hparmet@taconic.net.

PARMET, ROBERT DAVID, historian, educator; b. NYC, Dec. 11, 1938; s. Isaac and Fanny (Scharf) Parmet; 1 child, Andrew Charles. BA, CCNY, 1960; MA, Columbia U., 1961, PhD, 1966. Fellow CCNY, 1960-62, lectr., 1962-65; asst. prof. Newark State Coll., Union, NJ, 1965-67, CUNY, Jamaica, NY, 1967-70, assoc. prof., 1971-77, chmn. dept. history, 1972-75, prof., 1978—. Author: Labor and Immigration in Industrial America, 1981, rev. edit., 1986, The Master of Seventh Avenue: David Dubinsky and the American Labor Movement, 2005; co-author: American Nativism 1830-1860, 1971, rev. edit., 1979; contbr. articles to encys., profl. jours. Fellow, Woodrow Wilson Nat. Found., 1960, CUNY, 1994. Mem.: Labor and Working Class History Assn., Immigration History Soc., Am. Jewish Hist. Assn., So. Hist. Assn., N.Y. Labor Hist. Assn. (mem. exec. bd. 1990—), Conn. Hist. Soc., Acad. Polit. Sci., Orgn. Am. Historians, Am. Hist. Assn., Phi Alpha Theta. Democrat. Jewish. Avocations: photography, travel, musical theater, baseball. Home: 1 Highland Pl Great Neck NY 11020 Office: York Coll CUNY 94-20 Guy R Brewer Blvd Jamaica NY 11451 Office Phone: 718-262-2644. Business E-Mail: parmet@york.cuny.edu.

PARMITER, KAREN LYNN, retired education educator; b. McKeesport, Pa., Jan. 8, 1943; d. William and Helen Wolk Barlow; m. Jon Parmiter, Mar. 20, 1965; children: Mechel Ruth Golenberke, Jon Kyle. BS, Edinboro State U., 1964; MA, Allegheny Coll., 1970; PhD, U. Pitts., 1995. Tchr. Linesville HS, Pa., 1964—67, Conneaut Lake HS, 1973—79, 1979—80, pvt. tutoring, 1975—79, Jamestown HS, 1981—98; ret., 2005. Dept. head, class/club advisor Linesville HS, 1964—67, Jamestown HS, 1981—98, curricular cons., designer, 1981—98; faculty liaison Student Academic Ctr. Thiel Coll., 1995—2005; spkr. in field. Author: Fulfilling the Prophecies: The Journey of Education, 1999, Life: The Power of Promise, 2001. Program cons. Penn Lakes Girl Scout Troop 365, Conneaut Lake, 2003; participant Daffodil Drive/Cancer Fundraiser Thiel Coll., 2003—05; vol. tchr. West End. Elem. Sch., Meadville, Pa., 2003; vol. meals to homeless Erie City Mission, Pa., 2003—06; vol. Girl Scout Troops 305 and 250, Meadville, 2006. Recipient Most Memorable Tchr. award, Jamestown HS Graduating Class, 2001; grantee, Nat. Def. Edn., Elmira Coll., 1965. Mem.: AAUP, NEA, Am. Assn. Univ. Profs., Pa. State Edn. Assn., U. Pa. Alumni Assn., Edinboro U. of Pa. Alumni Assn., Red Hat Soc., Allegheny Coll. Alumni Assn., U. Pitts. Alumni Assn., Order Ea. Star, Kappa Delta Pi. Democrat. Greek Orthodox. Avocations: writing, reading, travel. Home: 9361 Free Rd Conneaut Lake PA 16316

PARMLEY, RICHARD TURNER, pediatric hematologist, oncologist; b. Madison, Wis., Sept. 10, 1949; BA, U. Va., 1970; MD, Med. U. S.C., 1973. Diplomate in pediatrics and in pediatric hematology/oncology Am. Bd. Pediatrics; diplomate in hematopathology Am. Bd. Pathology. Intern Med. U. S.C., Charleston, S.C., 1973, resident in pediats., 1974-75; fellow in pediat. hematology-oncology St. Jude Children's Rsch. Hosp., Memphis, 1976-77, U. Ala., Birmingham, 1977; clin. fellow in med. oncology bone marrow transplant svc. Fred Hutchinson Cancer Rsch. Ctr., Seattle, 1986; dir. electron microscopy and histology unit inst. dental rsch. U. Ala., Birmingham, 1978-83, assoc. scientist Comprehensive Cancer Cancert Ctr., 1978-83, asst. prof. pediats. and pathology, 1978-82, assoc. prof. pediats., 1982-83; assoc. prof. pediats. and pathology U. Tex. Health Sci. Ctr., 1983-88, prof. pediats., 1988-94; dir. divsn. pediat. hematology/oncology Carolinas Med. Ctr., Charlotte, NC, 1994—2000; clin. prof. pediat. U. N.C., Chapel Hill, 1994—2000; mem. med. staff Spartanburg (S.C.) Reg. Med. Ctr., 2000—; clin. prof. pediat. Med. Univ. SC, Charleston, 2000—. Mem. Am. Soc. Pediatric Hematology/Oncology, Am. Acad. Pediat., Am. Pediatric Soc., Soc. Pediatric Rsch., Alpha Omega Alpha. Office: Spartanburg Regional Med Ctr Dept Med Edn 101 Eastwood St Spartanburg SC 29303 Home Phone: 803-831-7136; Office Phone: 864-560-6287. Personal E-mail: rparmley@srhs.com.

PARNAFES, ITZIK, Internet company executive; Co-founder, R&D mgr. Class Data Sys. (acquired by Cisco Networks, 1998); co-founder, v.p. products Kagoor Networks; sr. dir. product mgmt. Juniper Networks (formerly Kagoor Networks). Spkr. in field; consul. in field. Office: Juniper Networks 1194 No Mathilda Ave Sunnyvale CA 94089-1206 Office Fax: 408-745-2100.

PARNAS-SIMPSON, MARIANNA, chorus director, singer; arrived in U.S., 1990, naturalized, 1996; d. Abram and Yeva Parnas; m. Robert Louis Simpson, May 29, 1994; 1 child from previous marriage, Faina Goldstein. BA in in Choral Conducting and Music Edn., Coll. Music Leningrad N.A. Rimsky-Korsakov State Conservatory, St. Petersburg, Russia, 1978; MusM in Choral Conducting and Music Edn., Leningrad N.A. Rimsky-Korsakov State Conservatory, St. Petersburg, Russia, 1983. Dir. children's chorus studio Pioneer Ho. State Ednl. Inst., St. Petersburg, Russia, 1980—89; asst. dir. and vocal instr. Houston Children's Chorus, 1994—99; chorus dir. and music appreciation instr. Parker Elem. Sch., 1999—; chorus dir. Revels Houston. Condr. region 23 treble choir Tex. Music Educators Assn., Houston, 2002; clinician in music appreciation Nat. Suzuki Piano Workshop, Texas City, 2005, 06; clinician and adjudicator Children's Music Festival, Houston, 2006. Performer: Tex. Music Educators Assn. Conv., 2003, 2005. Named Tchr. of Yr., Parker Elem. Sch., 2004—05; recipient First pl., Nat. Children's Chorus Competition, Russia, 1988, Nat. Grammy award, Parker Music Acad., Houston, 2002. Mem.: Am. Choral Dir. Assn., Tex. Choral Dir. Assn., Tex. Music Educators Assn. Avocations: Russian folk songs, travel, reading. Office: Parker Elem Sch 10626 Atwell Dr Houston TX 77076 Office Phone: 713-726-3634. Office Fax: 713-726-3660. Business E-Mail: msimpso1@houstonisd.org.

PARNELL, CHARLES L., speechwriter; b. Myrtis, La., Feb. 13, 1938; s. Forrest L. and Dorothy D. (Jones) P. BA, Rice U., 1960; M Bus. and Pub. Adminstrn., Southeastern U., 1977. Commd. ens. USN, 1960, advanced through grades to comdr., 1975, ret., 1987; speechwriter Mead Data Cen., Dayton, Ohio, 1987-89, Nationwide Ins. Co., Columbus, Ohio, 1989-90; exec. speechwriter Miller Brewing Co., Milw., 1990-96; speechwriter, Milw., 1996-98; exec. speechwriter, Dallas, 1998—. Contbr. articles to profl. jours.; frequently quoted in leading speech-related publs.; speeches used as models in 8 college level textbooks in U.S. and Can. Mem. U.S. Naval Inst., Mil. Officers Assn., World Future Soc. Avocations: reading, writing, travel. Home and Office: 1311 Brittany Ln Mansfield TX 76063-4013

PARNELL, FRANCIS WILLIAM, JR., otolaryngologist; b. Woonsocket, RI, May 22, 1940; s. Francis W. and Dorothy V. (Lalor) P.; m. Diana DeAngelis, Feb. 27, 1965; children: Cheryl Lynn, John Francis, Kathleen Diana, Alison Anne, Thomas William. Student, Coll. Holy Cross, 1957-58; AB, Clark U., 1961; MD, Georgetown U., 1965. Diplomate: Nat. Bd. Med. Examiners, Am. Bd. Otolaryngology. Intern Univ. Hosps., Madison, Wis., 1965-66, resident in gen. surgery, 1966-67, otolaryngology, 1967-70; pvt. practice medicine specializing in otolaryngology San Rafael, Calif., 1972-75, Greenbrae, Calif., 1978—2000; chmn., pres., CEO Parnell Pharms., Larkspur, Calif., 1982—. Cons. corp. med. affairs, 1978-82; corp. med. dir. Becton, Dickinson & Co., Rutherford, N.J., 1976-78; clin. instr. U. Calif. at San Francisco, 1972-75, asst. clin. prof., 1975-76; Alt. del., U.S. Del. 27th World Health Assembly WHO, Geneva, 1974. Contbr. articles to profl. jours. Candidate Calif. State Assembly, 1988; bd. dirs. Marin Coalition, 1980-96, 97-01, chmn., 1986-87; trustee Ross (Calif.) Sch. Dist., 1981-89; mem. governing bd. Marin Cmty. Coll. Dist., 1995-03, pres., 1999-00, 02-03; dir. Coll. Marin Found., 2004-, pres., 2006-. Maj. M.C. AUS, 1970-72, lt. col. M.C., USAR, 1985-93. Fellow ACS (gov. 1988-94), Am. Acad. Otolaryngology. Home: PO Box 998 Ross CA 94957-0998 Office: 1100 S Eliseo Dr Greenbrae CA 94904-2017 Office Phone: 415-256-1800.

PARNELL, SEAN, lieutenant governor, former state legislator, lawyer; b. Hanford, Calif., Nov. 19, 1962; m. Sandy Parnell; children: Grace, Rachel. BBA, Pacific Luth. U., 1984; JD, U. Puget Sound, 1987. Comml. atty., 1987—; pvt. bus. owner, 1991—2000; mem. State House of Representatives, 1992—96, Alaska State Senate, 1996—2000, co-chair fin. com., mem. resources com., legis. budget and audit com.; ptnr. Patton Boggs, LLP, Anchorage; lt. gov. State of Alaska, 2007—. Vol. mentor for H.S. youth groups and orgns., 1988-91; mem. Telecom. Info. Coun., Energy Coun., Western Legis. Timber Task Force, Bayshore-Klatt Cmty. Coun., Uniform Code Revision Commn.; dissenting mem. Long Range Fin. Planning Commn. Mem. Nat. Fedn. Ind. Bus. Republican. Avocations: teaching and coaching high school youth, running, reading, softball. Office: 716 W 4th Ave Ste 530 Anchorage AK 99501-2107 also: Lieutenant Governor PO Box 110015 Juneau AK 99811-0015 Office Phone: 907-465-3520. *

PARNELL, THOMAS ALFRED, physicist; b. Lumberton, NC, Nov. 24, 1931; s. Johnathan Alfred and Lula Beale (Lashley) P.; m. Elizabeth G. Brite, June 4, 1955; children: Marc Thomas, Gina Ann. BS in Physics, U. N.C., 1954, MS in Physics, 1962, PhD in Physics, 1965. Rsch. adj., dept. physics U. N.C., Chapel Hill, 1962-65; ops. analyst U.S. Air Force Europe, Wiesbaden, W. Ger., 1965-66; asst. prof. physics Marshall U., Huntington, W.Va., 1966-67; physicist NASA-Marshall Space Flight Center, Huntsville, Ala., 1968—99, chief astrophysics br., 1969-98; prin. rsch. scientist, dir. high energy photonics lab U. Ala., Huntsville, 1999—. Mem. editorial bd. Radiation Measurements; contbr. articles to profl. jours. Served to capt. USNR, 1954-91. Recipient Exceptional Sci. Achievement medal, Outstanding Leadership medal NASA, U.S. Antarctic Svc. medal. Mem. Am. Phys. Soc. Home: 907 Corinth Cir SE Huntsville AL 35801-2064 Office Phone: 256-961-7845. Business E-Mail: tom.parnell@msfc.nasa.gov.

PARNEROS, DEMOS, retail executive; Gen. mgr. Staples, Inc., Framingham, Mass., 1987, various positions in human resources, mktg., merchandising and store ops., v.p. ops., 1996—99, sr. v.p. ops., 1999—2002, pres. US retail, 2002—. Office: Staples Inc 500 Staples Dr Framingham MA 01702 *

PARNES, ALAN P., lawyer; b. NYC, Apr. 7, 1952; BA summa cum laude, Columbia U., 1974; JD, Harvard U., 1977. Bar: NY 1978, US Tax Ct. 1993. Mem. Proskauer, Rose, Goetz & Mendelsohn, NYC; ptnr. Proskauer Rose LLP, NYC. Spkr. in field. Contbr. articles to profl. jours. Office: Proskauer Rose LLP 1585 Broadway Fl 27 New York NY 10036-8299 Office Phone: 212-969-3820. Office Fax: 212-969-2900. Business E-Mail: aparnes@proskauer.com.

PARNES, ANDREW H., financial executive; V.p. fin., treas., CFO Standard Pacific Corp., Costa Mesa, Calif., 1996—. Office: Standard Pacific Corp 15326 Alton Pkwy Irvine CA 92618-2338

PAROBEK, DREW THOMAS, lawyer; b. Lorain, Ohio, Oct. 22, 1957; s. James Stephan and Opal Ann (Kitchens) P.; m. Julie Gail King, Aug. 19, 1983; children: Emily Elizabeth, Andrew Thomas Jr., James Craig. BA summa cum laude, Vanderbilt U., 1980, JD, 1984. Bar: Ohio, U.S. Dist. Ct. (no. and so. dists.) Ohio. Ptnr. Vorys, Sater, Seymour & Pease, Columbus, 1984—; law clk. Ohio Supreme Ct., Columbus, 1985. Examiner State of Ohio Bd. Bar Examiners, Columbus, 1991-94. Contbr. articles to law rev. Trustee Worthington (Ohio) Pub. Libr., 1991-93, Cleve. chpt. Juvenile Diabetes Found.; active Columbus Area Leadership Program, 1991-92; mem. bd. trustees Clev. Bar Assn., Clev. Zoo. Soc. Bay Soccer Club, Contemporary Youth Orches. Mem. ABA, Ohio State Bar Assn., Clev. Bar Assn., Vanderbilt All Stars. Avocations: civil war history, country music, guitar, golf. Office: Vorys Sater Seymour & Pease 2100 One Cleveland Ctr 1375 E 9th St Cleveland OH 44114-1724 Home Phone: 440-892-1751; Office Phone: 216-479-6162. Business E-Mail: dtparobek@vssp.com.

PARODE, ANN, lawyer; b. LA, Mar. 3, 1947; d. Lowell Carr and Sabine Parode. BA, Pomona Coll., 1968; JD, UCLA, 1971. Bar: Calif. 1972, U.S. Dist. Ct. (so. dist.) Calif. 1972, U.S. Ct. Appeals (9th cir.) 1975, U.S. Supreme Ct. 2000. Assoc. Luce, Forward et al, San Diego, 1971-75; gen. counsel, exec. v.p., sec. San Diego Trust & Savs., 1975-94; with First Interstate Bank, 1994—97; campus counsel U. Calif., San Diego, 1997—. Judge pro tem San Diego Mcpl. Ct., 1978—84; campus counsel U. Calif., San Diego, 1997—. Bd. dirs. San Diego Cmty. Found., 1989-97, chmn., 1994-96; bd. dirs. The Burnham Inst., 1995-2001, Girard Found., 1990-. Mem. Calif. Bar Assn. (corp. law com. 1980-83, client trust fund commn. 1986-90, chmn. 1989-90), San Diego County Bar Found. (founder, bd. dirs.

1979-86, 98-2001, pres. 1980-83), San Diego Bar Assns. (bd. dirs. 1977-81, v.p. 1977-78, 80-81, treas. 1979-80), Law Libr. Justice Found. (pres. 1994). Office Phone: 858-822-1236. Business E-Mail: aparode@ucsd.edu.

PARR, CAROLYN MILLER, federal judge; b. Palatka, Fla., Apr. 17, 1937; d. Arthur Charles and Audrey Ellen (Dunklin) Miller; m. Jerry Studstill Parr, Oct. 12, 1959; children: Kimberly Parr Trapasso, Jennifer Parr Turek, Patricia Audrey Smith. BA, Stetson U., 1959; MA, Vanderbilt U., 1960; JD, Georgetown U., 1977; LLD (hon.), Stetson U., 1986. Bar: Md. 1977, U.S. Tax Ct. 1977, D.C. 1979, U.S. Supreme Ct. 1983. Gen. trial atty. IRS, Washington, 1977-81, sr. trial atty. office of chief counsel, 1982; spl. counsel to asst. atty. gen. tax divsn. U.S. Dept. Justice, Washington, 1982-85; judge U.S. Tax Ct., Washington, 1985-2000, sr. judge, 2001—. Nat. Def. fellow Vanderbilt U., 1959-60; fellow Georgetown U., 1975-76; recipient Spl. Achievement award U.S. Treasury, 1979. Mem. ABA, Md. Bar Assn., Nat. Assn. Women Judges, D.C. Bar Assn. Office: US Tax Ct 400 2nd St NW Washington DC 20217-0002

PARR, GRANT VAN SICLEN, surgeon; b. NYC, Dec. 30, 1942; s. Ferdinand Van Siclen and Helene H. P.; m. Helen Mushat Frye, July 1, 1967; children: Kathleen Gage, Helen Johnston. AB with honors, Wesleyan U., 1965; MD, Cornell U., 1969. Diplomate Am. Bd. Thoracic Surgery, Am. Bd. Surgery. Intern, resident U. Hosps. of Cleve., 1969-71; resident in surgery U. Ala. Hosps., Birmingham, 1971-74, chief resident in surgery, 1974-75, resident in cardiovascular and thoracic surgery, 1975-77; practice medicine specializing in thoracic surgery Hershey, Pa., 1978-82; mem. staff Presbyn.-U. Pa. Med. Ctr., Phila., 1982-88, chief div. Thoracic surgery, 1984-88, acting chmn. Dept. Surgery, 1988, chief cardiovascular surgery, 1984-88; asst. prof. cardiothoracic surgery M.S. Hershey Med. Center, Hershey, Pa., 1987-88; chief cardiovascular surgery Morristown (N.J.) Meml. Hosp., 1988-97, co-chmn. dept. cardiovasc. scis., 1997—2004, chmn. dept. cardiovasc. medicine, 2004—06, med. dir. Cardiac Svc. Line, 2004—; asst. prof. Pa. State U., 1978-82; clin. assoc. prof. surgery U. Pa., 1982-89; assoc. prof. clin. surgery Columbia U., 1992—; physician in chief Gagnon Heart Hosp., 2007—. Chief cardiovasc. surgery Overlook Hosp., 1988—, Morristown Meml. Hosp., 1988—98; chmn. cardiovasc. surgery Atlantic Health Sys., 1998—, trustee, 1998—, med. dir. cardiac svcs., 2004—. Contbr. articles to profl. jours. Fellow Am. Coll. Cardiology, ACS, Am. Coll. Chest Physicians, Phila. Coll. Physicians; mem. AMA, Internat. Cardiovascular Soc., Assn. of Acad. Surgeons, Am. Assn. Thoracic Surgery, Phila. County Med. Soc., Soc. Thoracic Surgeons, Soc. Critical Care Medicine Pa., Thoracic Surg. Soc., John W. Kirklin Soc., Pa. Med. Assn., N.J. Soc. Thoracic Surgery, N.Y. Soc. Thoracic Surgery, Morris County Golf Club, NYU Club, Beaverkill Trout Club. Office: 100 Madison Ave Morristown NJ 07960-6136 Office Phone: 973-971-7300. Business E-Mail: gparr@atlantichealth.org.

PARR, ROBERT GHORMLEY, chemistry professor; b. Chgo., Sept. 22, 1921; s. Leland Wilbur and Grace (Ghormley) P.; m. Jane Bolstad, May 28, 1944; children: Steven Robert, Jeanne Karen, Carol Jane. AB magna cum laude with high honors in Chemistry, Brown U., 1942; PhD in Phys. Chemistry, U. Minn., 1947; D (hon.), U. Leuven, 1986, Jagiellonian U., 1996. Asst. prof. chemistry U. Minn., 1947-48; mem. faculty Carnegie Inst. Tech., 1948-62, prof. chemistry, 1957-62, Johns Hopkins U., 1962-74, chmn. dept., 1969-72; William R. Kenan, Jr. prof. theoretical chemistry U. N.C., Chapel Hill, 1974-90, Wassily Hoeffding prof. chem. physics, 1990—. Vis. prof. chemistry, mem. Ctr. Advanced Study, U. Ill., 1962; disting. vis. prof. SUNY, Buffalo, Pa. State U., 1967; vis. prof. Japan Soc. Promotion Sci., 1968, 79, U. Haifa, 1977, Free U., Berlin, 1977, Duke U., 1996-97; Firth prof. U. Sheffield, 1976; Coochbehar prof. Indian Assn. Cultivation of Sci., 1990; Sandoval Vallarta prof. UAM-Iztapalapa, 1992; chmn. com. postdoctoral fellowships in chemistry NAS-NRC, 1961-63; chmn. panel theoretical chemistry Westheimer com. survey chemistry NAS, 1964; mem. coun. Gordon Rsch. Conf., 1974-76; mem. Commn. on Human Resources, NRC, 1979-82; mem. coun. Inst. for Molecular Sci., Okazaki, Japan, 1986-88; bd. trustees Inst. for Fundamental Chemistry, Kyoto, Japan, 1988—. Author: Quantum Theory of Molecular Electronic Structure, 1963, Density-Functional Theory of Atoms and Molecules, 1989, also numerous articles.; Assoc. editor: Jour. Chem. Physics, 1956-58, Chem. Revs, 1961-63, Jour. Phys. Chemistry, 1963-67, 77-79, Am. Chem. Soc. Monographs, 1966-71, Theoretica Chimica Acta, 1966-69, 92-96; Chinese Chem. Letters, 1998—; bd. editors: Jour. Am. Chem. Soc, 1969-77; adv. editorial bd.: Internat. Jour. Quantum Chemistry, 1967—, Chem. Physics Letters, 1967-79. Recipient Outstanding Achievement award U. Minn., 1968, N.C. Disting. Chemist award, 1982; fellow U. Chgo., 1949; research asso., 1957; Fulbright scholar U. Cambridge, Eng., 1953-54; Guggenheim fellow, 1953-54; NSF sr. postdoctoral fellow U. Oxford (Eng.) and Commonwealth Sci. and Indsl. Research Orgn., Melbourne, Australia, 1967-68; Sloan fellow, 1956-60, N.C. award in sci., 1999. Fellow AAAS, Am. Phys. Soc. (chmn. divsn. chem. physics 1963-64); mem. NAS (award in chem. scis., 2004), AAUP, Am. Chem. Soc. (chmn. divsn. phys. chemistry 1978, Irving Langmuir award in chem. physics 1994), Am. Acad. Arts and Sci., Indian Nat. Sci. Acad., Internat. Acad. Quantum Molecular Sci. (pres. 1991-97), Phi Beta Kappa, Sigma Xi, Phi Lambda Upsilon, Pi Mu Epsilon. Home: 701 Kenmore Rd Chapel Hill NC 27514-2019 Office: U NC Dept Chemistry Chapel Hill NC 27599-3290 Office Phone: 919-962-1577.

PARR, ROYSE MILTON, retired lawyer, writer; b. Elk City, Okla., Sept. 11, 1935; s. Clinton Riley and Caroline (Royse) Parr; m. Sheila Ann Harshaw, May 28, 1960; children: Clinton Howard, Reagan Royse. BS, Okla. State U., 1958; JD, U. Tulsa, 1964. Bar: Okla. 1964. Rsch. scout Jersey Prodn. Rsch. Co., Tulsa, 1960-64; atty. Sun Oil Co., 1964-70, White Shield Corp., 1970-71; sec., atty., asst. gen. counsel MAPCO, Inc., Tulsa, 1971-97; gen. counsel, dir. Seminole Pipeline Co., 1989-97. Lectr. in field. Co-author: Glory Days of Summer: The History of Baseball in Oklahoma, 1999, Allie Reynolds: Super Chief, 2002, Native Americans in Sports, 2004. Vice chmn. Tulsa County Election Bd., 1973—97; pres. Ret. Sr. Vol. Program, 1982—83. Served to 1st lt. US Army, 1958—60, capt. USAR, 1960—63. Mem.: ASME, ABA, Soc. Am. Baseball Rsch., Am. Soc. Corp. Secs., Tulsa County Bar Assn., Okla. Bar Assn., Soc. Petroleum Engrs., Oaks Country Club, Phi Delta Phi. Republican. Methodist.

PARR, VIRGINIA HELEN, retired librarian; b. Mansfield, Ohio, May 23, 1937; d. Bernard Franklin and Frances Cole (Downes) P.; m. Marvin E. Lickey, June 14, 1959 (div. 1972); children: Sarah Elizabeth, David Andrew, Rachel Alison; m. Laurence E. Steadman, Nov. 27, 1993 (div. 2007). AB, Oberlin Coll., 1959; AM, U. Mich., 1961; MLS, U. Oreg., 1973. English and social studies tchr. Whittier Jr. High Sch., Livonia, Mich., 1961-64; libr. U. Oreg. Libr., Eugene, 1973-79, head edn. and psychology, 1979-80, acting asst. univ. libr. for pub. svcs., 1980-82; head reference, rsch. and instrn. svcs. U. Cin., 1982-89, reference libr., bibliographer, 1989—2002, ret., 2002—. Chair, mem. budget com. Eugene Sch., 1976-79. Founding editor: Behavioral and Social Scis. Libr., 1978; contbr. articles to profl. jours. Bd. dirs. Eugene Jr. Symphony Assn., 1979-82; mem. adv. bd. various mental health groups, Eugene, 1971-79. Mem. Assn. Coll. and Rsch. Librs. of ALA (various offices edn. and behavioral sci. sect. 1977-86, numerous coms. reference and adult svcs. divsn. 1981-92), Beta Phi Mu, Pi Lambda Theta. Democrat. Avocations: reading, classical music, travel. Home: 5532 S Shore Dr 12F Chicago IL 60637-1990 E-mail: v_parr@sbcglobal.net.

PARRA, RAUL O., urologist, educator; s. Raul F. and Olena Parra; married; 3 children. MD, U. Seville, Spain, 1980. Diplomate Bd. Urology. Chmn. urology St. Louis U., 1989—99, Mayo Clinic, Jacksonville, Fla., 1995—2002; dir. urologic cancer surgery Oreg. Health and Sci. U., Portland, 2002—04; chmn. urology Cooper Health Sys., Robert Wood Johnson Sch. Medicine, Camden, NJ, 2004—. Author med. papers, book chpts., and textbooks. Office: Cooper Urology 3 Cooper Plz Camden NJ 08103 Home Phone: 856-424-0192; Office Phone: 856-963-3577. Business E-Mail: parra-raul@cooperhealth.edu.

PARRA, RO (ROSENDO G. PARRA), former computer company executive; b. Ecuador, Nov. 12, 1959; m. Cheryl L. Parra; 4 children. BA in Mktg., U. Md., 1982. Various sales, mgmt. positions, bus. prod. divsn. Tandy Corp.; various sales, gen. mgmt. positions GRiD Sys. Corp.; v.p. Dell USA, 1993—94; group v.p. sales, mktg. & services Dell Inc., 1994—97, v.p. pub. & Americas internat., 1997—98, sr. v.p. Americas pub. & Americas internat., 1998—2001, sr. v.p., gen. mgr. Americas, 2002—06, sr. v.p., worldwide home & small bus. group, 2006—07. Bd. dirs. Dell Inc., 2004—07. Named one of Most Important Hispanics in Tech., Bus., Hispanic Engineer and Info. Tech. mag., 2005. *

PARRA-ARANGUREN, GONZALO, judge; b. Caracas, Venezuela, Dec. 5, 1928; Degree juridical and political studies, Ctrl. U. Venezuela, 1950; degree, Inter-Am. Law Inst., NYU; LLD, Ludwig-Maximilians U., Munich. Prof. Ctrl. U. Venezuela, Caracas, 1956—96, Andrés Bello Cath. U., Caracas, 1957—96; judge 2d Ct. of 1st Instance Fed. Dist. and State of Miranda, Caracas, 1958-71; 1st assoc. judge Chamber of Cassation Supreme Ct. of Justice, Caracas, 1988-92, alt. judge, 1992—96; judge Internat. Ct. of Justice, The Hague, Netherlands, 1996—. Mem. nat. group for Venezuela Permanent Ct. of Arbitration, The Hague, 1985—; arbitrator, Venezuela and abroad; mem. legal adv. com. Ministry of Fgn. Affairs, 1984-96, Nat. Congress, 1990-96; mem. Acad. Polit. and Social Scis. of Caracas, 1966—, pres., 1993-95; mem. Inst. of Internat. Law, 1979—; Venezuelan rep. several sessions of The Hague Conf. on Pvt. Internat. Law. Author: (books) Die Regel "Locus Regit Actum" und die Fromen der Testamente, 1955, La Nacionalidad Venezolana Originatia, vols. I and II, 1964, La Constitucion de 1830 y los Venzolanos por Naturalizacion, 1969, La Influencia del Matrimonio sobre la Nacionalidad de la Mujer en la Legislacion Venzolana, 1983, Ensayos de Derecho Procesal Civil Internacional, 1986, Estudios de Derecho Mercantil Internacional, 1998, others. Office: Internat Ct of Justice Peace Palace 2517 KJ The Hague Netherlands Business E-Mail: mail@icj-cij.org. *

PARRA-DAVILA, EDUARDO, surgeon, educator; arrived in US, 1992; s. Alfonso Parra and Enma del Socorro Davila; m. Thaisabel Grisolia, May 23, 2003. MD, Universidad de los Andes, Merida, 1988. Gen. surgeon Jackson Meml. Hosp., U. Miami Miller Sch. Medicine, Fla., 1998; colorectal surgeon Colon and Rectal Clinic U. Tex., 1999; minimally invasive surgery fellow Tex. Endosurgery Inst., San Antonio, 2000; clin. asst. prof. surgery U. Miami Miller Sch. Medicine, 2001—03; staff colorectal and gen. surgeon VA Hosp., Miami, 2001—03, chief surgery, 2003; asst. prof. biomedical sci. U. Miami Miller Sch. Medicine, Fla. Atlantic U., Boca Raton, Fla., 2004—; dir. minimally invasive surgery program Boca Raton Cmty. Hosp., Fla., 2004—, co-dir. Abdominal Wall Reconstruction Ctr., 2006—07. Fellow: ACS (licentiate), Am. Soc. Colon and Rectal Surgeons (licentiate). Office: Surgical Assocs Palm Beach County 670 Glades Rd Ste 300 Boca Raton FL 33431 Home Phone: 305-479-3366; Office Phone: 561-395-2626. Personal E-mail: parra11@bellsouth.net.

PARRAGUIRRE, RONALD DAVID, state supreme court justice; b. Reno, July 8, 1959; s. Paul Charles and Iris Mae (Bleick) P.; m. Leslie, 2 children. BBA, San Diego State U., 1982; JD, U. San Diego, 1985. Bar: Pa. 1986, Nev. 1986, D.C. 1987. Legis. asst. U.S. Senator Paul Laxalt, Washington, 1985-86; counsel subcom. on criminal law, judiciary com. U.S. Senate, Washington, 1986-87; lawyer Parraguirre & Parraguirre, Las Vegas, Nev., 1987-91; mcpl. ct. judge Dept. 6 City of Las Vegas, 1991-99; dist. ct. judge Eighth Jud. Dist. Ct., Clark County, Nev., 1999—2004; justice Nev. Supreme Ct., 2004—. Mem. Nev. State-Federal Jud. Council, Nev. Supreme Ct. State Ct. Funding Com.; former mem. Nev. Supreme Ct. Jud. Election Practices Com. Mem. ABA, ATLA, Am. Judges Assn., Nev. Judges Assn., Nev. State Bar Assn. (mem. multi-jurisdictional task force com.), Clark County Bar Assn. (former exec. bd. mem.) Republican. Lutheran. Avocations: skiing, racquetball, hunting, fishing. Office: Nev Supreme Court 201 S Carson St Carson City NV 89701-4702 *

PARRAMORE, BARBARA MITCHELL, education educator; b. Guilford County, NC, Aug. 29, 1932; d. Samuel Spencer and Nellie Gray (Glosson) Mitchell; m. Lyman Griffis Worthington, Dec. 23, 1956 (div. 1961); m. Thomas Custis Parramore, Jan. 22, 1966 (dec. Jan. 2004); children: Lisa Gray, Lynn Stuart. AB, U. N.C., Greensboro, 1954; MEd, N.C. State U., 1959; EdD, Duke U., 1968. Counselor, tchr. Raleigh City Schs., 1954-59, sch. prin., 1959-65; prof. dept. of curriculum and instrn. N.C. State U., 1970-96, prof. emeritus, 1996—. Acad. specialist Office Internat. Edn., U.S. Info. Svcs., sec. sch. initative program, The Philippines, 1987. Author: The People of North Carolina, 1972, 3rd edit. 1983. Japan Inst. Social and Econ. Affairs fellow, 1980; N.C. AAUW award for juvenile lit., 1973, Holladay medal for excellence N.C. State U., 1994. Mem. ASCD, N.C. ASCD (pres. 1994-96), N.C. Coun. for Social Studies (pres. 1985-87), Assn. Tchr. Educators, Delta Kappa Gamma, Kappa Delta Pi. Home: 5012 Tanglewood Dr Raleigh NC 27612-3135

PARRAVANO, AMELIA ELIZABETH (AMY BETH PARRAVANO), recording industry executive; b. Providence, Apr. 5, 1951; d. Olindo Luigi and Violet Carmella (Russo) Izzo; m. Grimaldo Antonio Parravano, July 4, 1979; children: Peter Paul, Paula Elizabeth. AA, Roger Williams Coll., 1972; student, RI Coll., 1972—73, Oral Roberts U., 1986. Owner, operator Aura Arts & Crafts, Cranston, RI, 1985-88; pres. Peridot Caprice Rec. Artist, Cranston, 1990—; president, owner Peridot Records; music pub.; host, prodr. cable TV show Amy Beth Presents!. Freelance artist Artist Letters League, Cranston, 1992—; singer (Amy Beth), songwriter, musician. Active PTA, Cranston, 1991-92; artist mem. RI State Coun. Arts, Providence, 1986-92; active Pawtucket (RI) Arts Coun., 1986-92. Named Ky. Col.; named to Rockabilly Hall Fame. Mem. Am. Soc. Composers, Authors Pubs., Songwriters Guild Am., Gospel Music Assn., County Music Assn., Country Music Showcase Internat., Broadcast Music Inc. (pub.), Retirement Entertainment Orgn., Internat. Fan Club Assn., Greater So. Country Music Assn. (state rep. RI). Avocations: golf, bicycling, entertaining at children's parties, painting, poetry. Home: 17 Woodbine St Cranston RI 02910-1916 Personal E-mail: amybeth_e@yahoo.com.

PARRENT, JONATHAN VINCE, dean; b. Princeton, Ky., July 30, 1973; s. Michael and Vicky Parrent; m. Jennifer Waggener, Sept. 4, 1999; children: Parker, Jacob. BA, Ky. Wesleyan Coll., Owensboro, 1995; MA, Murray State U., Ky., 1998. Registrar Madisonville C.C., Ky., 2002—05, dean student affairs, 2006—. Home: 107 West Legion Dr Princeton KY 42445 Office: Madisonville Cmty Coll 2000 College Dr Madisonville KY 42431 Home Phone: 270-365-7056; Office Phone: 270-821-2250.

PARRETT, JANELLE SWILLEY, secondary school educator; b. Meridian, Miss., Nov. 20, 1922; d. Edgar Rowan and Ada Swilley; m. Leslie Loring Parrett (dec. Nov. 2004); children: Ann Loring, John Edward. BS, La. State U., Baton Rouge, 1945; MA, Ohio State U., Columbus, 1949; elem. conversion, Ind. U., South Bend, 1964. Cert. tchr. La., Ohio. Instr. Ohio State U., 1945—49; tchr. elem. Plymouth Cmty. Schs., Ind., 1960—63, tchr. phys. edn. mid. sch., 1963—72, tchr. phys. edn., coach H.S., 1972—75. Mem.: AAHPERD, Ind. Alliance for Health, Phys. Edn. and Recreation (sec. 1963, v.p. 1964—66, chmn. Girls and Women's Sports divsn. 1969), St. Joseph Valley Golf Assn. (v.p. 1999, pres. 2001). Republican. Presbyterian. Avocations: reading, bridge, swimming, golf. Home: 5710 Hampton Woods Blvd Sebring FL 33872 Personal E-mail: janelleparrett@comcast.net.

PARRETT, SHERMAN O., lawyer; b. Cin., Jan. 8, 1943; s. Earl and Ruby (Angel) P.; m. Rosalind K. Brooks, Sept. 21, 1985; children: Laura, Samantha. BSEE, U. Cin., 1965; JD with honors, George Washington U., 1969. Bar: Calif. 1970, D.C. 1975, Ariz. 1992. Assoc. Flehr, Hohbach et al., San Francisco, 1970-73; ptnr. Cushman, Darby & Cushman, Washington, 1973-86, Irell & Manella, LA, 1986-91, Streich Lang, Phoenix, 1991-94, Snell & Wilmer, Phoenix, 1994-98. Address: 2818 SE 19th Ave Cape Coral FL 33904 Office Phone: 239-945-6209. Personal E-mail: parretts@aol.com.

PARRETT, WILLIAM G., accounting company executive; m. Diane Parrett; six children. BA, St. Francis Coll., NY, 1967. Joined predecessor firm Deloitte & Touche LLP, 1967, named ptnr., 1977, ptnr. Stamford, Conn., group mng. ptnr. NY, regional mng. ptnr. tri-state, mng. ptnr., now sr. mng. ptnr.; co-founding chmn. global fin. services industry practice Deloitte Touche Tohmatsu, regional mng. ptnr. Americas, CEO, 2003—. Mem. bd. Japan Soc., US-Japan Bus. Coun. Bd. trustees Carnegie Hall, United Way of Am.; nat adv. bd. Nat. Underground R.R. Freedom Ctr.; trustee Cath. U. Am.; internat. councillor Ctr. Strategic and Internat. Studies. Mem. Econ. Club NY, Am. Inst. CPAs, Com. to Encourage Corp. Philanthropy, G100 CEO Forum, Transatlantic Bus. Dialogue, US Coun. Internat. Bus.(chmn. 2005-). Office: Deloitte Touche Tohmatsu 1633 Broadway New York NY 10019-6754 *

PARRETTE, JEAN-BRIAC, communications executive; b. 1971; m. Amy Parrette, Oct. 25, 2003. BA in Pub. Policy, Hamilton Coll. Analyst CS First Boston, London, Tokyo; CFO Bravo Cable Network, 2003; v.p., CFO, Bus. Devel. NBC Universal Cable, sr. v.p., New Media, CFO, 2004—. Named one of 40 Executives Under 40, Multichannel News, 2006. Office: NBC Universal Inc 30 Rockefeller Plz New York NY 10112 Office Phone: 212-664-4444. Office Fax: 212-664-4088.

PARRETTE, LESLIE JACKSON, lawyer; b. Mt Pleasant, Mo., Aug. 25, 1961; s. Leslie Jackson and Janet Parrette. AB, Harvard Coll., 1983; JD, Harvard Law Sch., 1986. Assoc. Hale & Dorr, Boston, 1986-89, Watson Ess Marshall & Enggas, Kansas City, Mo., 1989-91, Bryan Cave, Kansas City, Mo., 1991-92; ptnr. Blackwell Sanders Peper Martin, Kansas City, Mo., 1992-2000; gen. coun., sr. v.p., corp. sec. Aquila Inc., Kansas City, Mo., 2000—05. Mem. Sister City Commn. of Kansas City, Mo., 1999—; bd. dirs. Am. Jazz Mus., 2002—03. E-mail: les.parrette@aquila.com.

PARRICK, GERALD HATHAWAY, communications and marketing executive; b. Cushing, Okla., Oct. 27, 1924; s. Gerald H. and Phyllis A. (Sheppard) B.; m. Gail V. Straney, Dec. 5, 1984; children: Gerald Hathaway III, Candace Anne. BJ, U. Mo., 1948. Creative account exec. George Knox & Assoc., Oklahoma City, 1948-51; account exec. Batten, Barton, Durstine & Osborn, San Francisco, 1952-60; account dir. McCann-Erickson, LA, 1960-67, v.p. Portland, Oreg., 1967-72; dir. comm. Pacific Power Co., Portland, 1972-77, spl. asst. to chmn. bd., 1977-79; pres. Entreepublic Comm., West Linn, Oreg., 1979—, Bailey/Parrick, Inc., Portland, 1981-84, Parrick/Milpacher, Inc., Portland, 1984-85, The Laugh Clinic, Inc., Portland, 1984-90, K-KOR, Inc., 1990-93. Author: A 20th Century Miracle, 1981, Touched by a Miracle, 1997. Mem. Oreg. Advt. Rev. Bd., 1974-75. Capt. AUS, 1943-45, 51-52, ETO. Named Oreg. Advt. Man of Yr., Oreg. Advt. Club, 1971. Mem. Am. Advt. Fedn. (chmn. edn. western region 1973-74), Portland Advt. Fedn. (pres. 1974-75), Toastmasters (pres. 1966-67) (Encino, Calif.), Kappa Tau Alpha. Home: 17185 Carlson Ct Lake Oswego OR 97034-5802 Personal E-mail: jergail@aol.com.

PARRIGIN, ELIZABETH ELLINGTON, lawyer; b. Colon, Panama, May 23, 1932; d. Jesse Cox and Elizabeth (Roark) Ellington; m. Perry G. Parrigin, Oct. 8, 1975. BA, Agnes Scott Coll., 1954; JD, U. Va., 1959. Bar: Tex. 1959, Mo. 1980. Atty., San Antonio, 1960-69; law libr. U. Mo., Columbia, 1969-77, rsch. assoc., 1977-82; atty. pvt. practice, Columbia, 1982—. Elder, clk. of session First Presbyn. Ch., Columbia; mem. permanent jud. commn. Presbyn. Ch. U.S., 1977-83, mem. advisory com. on constitution, 1983-90. Mem. ABA, Mo. Bar Assn. (chmn. sub-com. revision of Mo. trust law 1988-92), Columbia Kiwanis Club (pres. 1997-98). Democrat. Presbyterian. Avocations: music, gardening, reading. Home: 400 Conley Ave Columbia MO 65201-4219 Office: 224 N 8th St Columbia MO 65201-4844

PARRILLO, JOSEPH EDISON, JR., allergist, immunologist, cardiologist; b. Paterson, NJ, Jan. 5, 1947; MD, Cornell U., 1972. Diplomate Am. Bd. Allergy and Immunology, Am. Bd. Internal Medicine, Am. Bd. Cardiology. From intern to resident in medicine Mass. Gen. Hosp., Boston, 1972-74, fellow in cardiology, 1978-80; resident in medicine N.Y. Hosp.-Cornell Med. Ctr., NYC, 1977-78; resident in allergy & immunology and infectious disease Clin. Ctr. Nat. Inst. Allergy and Immunology Disease, Bethesda, Md., 1974-77; med. staff Rush-Presbyn.-St. Lukes Med. Ctr., Chgo.; chief divsn. cardiology and critical care medicine Rush Heart Inst.; dir., chief of medicine Cooper Heart Inst.; and prof. medicine UMDNJ-RWJMS at Camden. Mem. Am. Coll. Cardiology, Am. Fedn. Clin. Rsch., Am. Heart Assn., Am. Soc. Clin. Immunology, Am. Coll. Critical Care Medicine, Am. Coll. Chest Physicians, Soc. Critical Care Medicine, Alpha Omega Alpha. Office: Cooper Univ Hosp Dorrance Bldg 3d Fl One Cooper Plaza Camden NJ 08103 also: Ste H 900 Centennial Blvd Voorhees NJ 08043 Business E-Mail: Parrillo-Joseph@cooperhealth.edu. *

PARRIS, MARK ROBERT, former ambassador, policy advisor; b. Mpls. m. Joan Elizabeth Gardner; 2 children. BS magna cum laude, Georgetown U., 1974. With Fgn. Svc., 1972-77, polit. counselor Moscow, 1982-85, dir. Office Soviet Union Affairs, 1985-88; dep. chief mission U.S. Embassy, Tel Aviv, 1989-92; spl. asst. pres., sr. dir. Nat. Security Coun., Washington, 1995-97; amb. to Turkey Ankara, 1997—2000; sr. fgn. policy advisor Baker, Donelson, Bearman and Caldwell, Washington, 2000—. Counselor Turkish Rsch. Program The Washington Inst., 2002—; bd. chmn. Am. Friends of Turkey; bd. mem. Am. Turkish Coun. Mem. policy bd. Una Chapman Cox Found., U.S.-Israel Edn. Found. Phi Beta Kappa. Office: Baker Donelson Bearman and Caldwell 6th Fl 555 Eleventh St Washington DC 20004

PARRIS, MARK S., lawyer, professional athletes consultant; b. Caldwell, Wash., Mar. 22, 1957; s. Wayne Wesley and Helen (Padgett) P. BA, Gonzaga U., 1980; JD, U. Wash., 1983. Bar: Wash. 1983, U.S. Dist. Ct. (we. dist.) Wash. 1983, (ea. dist.) Wash. 1989, U.S. Dist. Ct. (ea. dist.) Wash. 1989, U.S. Ct. Appeals (9th cir.) 1990. Assoc. Syrdal, Danelo, Seattle, 1983-88, Heller, Ehrman, White & McAuliffe, Seattle, 1988-90, ptnr., 1990—. Cons. Athlete Cons. Svcs., Seattle. Pres., Athletes That Care, Seattle; vol. Lake City Legal Clinic, Seattle, Children's Hosp., Seattle. Avocations: cricket, golf, squash, mountain climbing. Office: Heller Ehrman White & McAuliffe 721 5th Ave 6100 Columbia Ctr Seattle WA 98104-7043

PARRISH, CHARLES S., lawyer, oil industry executive; BA in History with honors, U. Va.; JD, U. Houston Law Sch. Pvt. practice, Houston and San Antonio; v.p., asst. gen. counsel, sec. Tesoro Corp., San Antonio,

1994—2005, 2005—06, sr. v.p., gen. counsel, sec., 2006—. Mem.: ABA, State Bar Tex. Office: Tesoro Corp 300 Concord Plz San Antonio TX 78216-6999 Office Phone: 210-828-8484. Office Fax: 210-283-2045. E-mail: cparrish@tsocorp.com. *

PARRISH, D. MICHAEL, manufacturing executive; BSCE, U. Toledo, Ohio, 1975. Engr. Vulcraft divsn. Nucor Corp., St. Joe, Ind., 1975-81, engring. mgr. Vulcraft divsn. Brigham City, Utah, 1981-86, prodn. mgr. Vulcraft divsn. Ft. Payne, Ala., 1986-89, gen. mgr. Vulcraft divsn. Brigham City, 1989-91, gen. mgr. steel divsn. Jewett, Tex., 1991-95, Hickman, Ark., 1995-90, v.p. Charlotte, NC, 1990-98, exec. v.p. steel products, 1998—. Office: Nucor Corp 1915 Rexford Rd Charlotte NC 28211 Office Phone: 704-366-7000. Office Fax: 704-362-4208. *

PARRISH, DAVID WALKER, JR., legal publishing company executive; b. Bristol, Tenn., Feb. 8, 1923; BA, Emory and Henry Coll., 1948, LLD, 1978; BS, US Mcht. Marine Acad., 1950; LLB, U. Va., Charlottesville, 1951. Pres. The Michie Co., Charlottesville, Va., 1969-89, vice chmn., 1989-96; pub. cons., 1996—. Named to Sports Hall of Fame, Emory & Henry Coll. Mem.: Va. Bar Assn. Office: David W Parrish Jr PO Box 7587 Charlottesville VA 22906-7587

PARRISH, EDWARD ALTON, JR., electrical and computer engineering educator, academic administrator; b. Newport News, Va., Jan. 7, 1937; s. Edward Alton and Molly Wren (Vaughn) Parrish; m. Shirley Maxine Johnson, Oct. 26, 1963; children: Troy Alton, Gregory Sinton. BEE, U. Va., 1964, MEE, 1966, DScEE, 1968. Registered Tenn., Va. Group leader Amerad Corp., Charlottesville, Va., 1961—64; asst. prof. elec. engring. U. Va., Charlottesville, 1968—71, assoc. prof. elec. engring., 1971—77, prof. elec. engring., 1977—86, chmn. dept. elec. engring., 1978—86; dean, centennial prof. electrical engring. Vanderbilt U., Nashville, 1987—95; pres., prof. elec. and computer engring. Worcester Poly. U., 1995—2004, pres. emeritus, 2004—. Cons. U.S. Army, Charlottesville, Va., 1971—77, ORS, Inc., Princeton, NJ, 1973—74, Sperry Marine Systems, Charlottesville, 1975—76, Hajime Industries Ltd., Tokyo, 1978—84. Contbr. articles to profl. jours. With USAF, 1954—58. Grantee numerous rsch. grants. Fellow: IEEE (bd. dirs. 1990—91, v.p. ednl. activities 1992—93, engring. accreditation commn. 1989—96, exec. com. 1991—96, officer 1993—96, chmn. elect 1994—95, chmn. 1995—96, past chmn. 1996—97, editor-in-chief IEEE Computer 1995—98), ABET (bd. dirs. 2000—); mem.: IEEE Computer Soc. (sec. 1997, v.p. 1978—81, pres. 1988), Tau Beta Pi, Eta Kappa Nu, Sigma Xi. Baptist. Avocations: music, woodworking. E-mail: eap@wpi.edu.

PARRISH, FRANK JENNINGS, retired food products executive; b. Manassas, Va., Dec. 29, 1923; s. Edgar Goodloe and Alverda (Jennings) Parrish; m. Lorene Lomax, Feb. 11, 1944 (dec. Apr. 1984); children: Edgar Lee, Julia Lorene; m. Mary Jane Biser, Aug. 25, 1984. Student, Va. Poly. Inst., 1942-43; grad., Indsl. Coll. Armed Forces, 1972. Pres. Manassas Frozen Foods, Inc., 1946—2001; pres., mgr. Cert. Food Buyers Svc., Inc., 1953—2001; pres. First Nat. Acceptance Co., 1966—2001; ret., 2001. V.p. Manassas Ice & Fuel Co. Chmn. bd. N. Va. coun. Am. Heart Assn., 1987—88, mem. inaugural com., 1961, vice-chmn. inaugural parade com.; chmn. bd. trustees Meth. Ch., 1958—66; mem. bus. adminstrn. adv. com. No. Va. CC. Maj. USAF, 1943—46, CBI, comdr., dr. 909 TAC Airlift Group USAF, 1969—73, mobilization asst. DCS plans and ops. hdqrs. USAF, 1973—79, ret. brig. gen. USAF, 1983. Decorated Legion of Merit, Air medal. Mem.: Va. Assn. Meat Processors (pres. 1986—90), Hump Pilots Assn., Va. Frozen Foods Assn. (past pres., dir.), Nat. Inst. Locker and Freezer Provisioners Am. (past. pres.), Kiwanis. Methodist. Home: 9107 Park Ave Manassas VA 20110-4350 *Do unto others as you would have them do unto you.*

PARRISH, JENNI, law librarian, educator; b. Houston; BA, Rice U.; MLS, JD, U. Tex., Austin. Assoc. law libr. U. Okla.; dir. Law Libr. U. Pitts., 1980; faculty mem. U. Calif., Hastings Coll. of Law, San Francisco, 1993—, prof. law, dir. Law Libr. Contbr. articles to profl. jours. Office: U Calif Hastings Coll of Law 200 McAllister St San Francisco CA 94102 Office Phone: 415-565-4881. E-mail: parrishj@uchastings.edu. *

PARRISH, JILL NIEDERHAUSER, state supreme court justice; BA, Weber State U., 1982; JD, Yale U., 1985. Bar: Utah 1985, 10th Cir. Ct. Appeals 1987, U.S. Supreme Ct. 2000. Clk. Hon. David K. Winder U.S. Dist. Ct., Utah, 1985; atty. Parr, Wadddoups, Brown, Gee & Loveless, Salt Lake City, 1986—90, shareholder, 1990—95; asst. U.S. atty. Civil Divsn. U.S. Dist. Ct., Utah, 1995—2003; justice Utah Supreme Ct., Salt Lake City, 2003—, mem. tech. com., judicial performance evaluation com., 2003—. Supr. Fin. Litigation Unit U.S. Attys. Office. Mem.: Fed. Bar Assn. (pres.). Office: Utah Supreme Ct PO Box 140210 Salt Lake City UT 84114-0210 *

PARRISH, LORI NANCE, property appraiser; b. Evansville, Ind., July 31, 1948; m. Geoffrey Cohen; children: Gary Brown, Brandi Schmidt. Student, Fin. Inst. Sch., 1968, Fla. Atlantic U., 1969, Clemson U., 1982, Fla. Internat. U., 1988; LHD (hon.), Keiser Coll., 1996; postgrad., U. Ctrl. Fla., 1996—98. Cert. Retail Nurseryman Nova/Davie Cmty. Sch., Fla., 1975, in Credit and Collections Broward CC, Fla., 1980, in Quality Cir. Fla. Atlantic U., 1986, in Target Mgmt. Selection Fla. Internat. U., 1988, County Commrs. Cert. in Fin. Mgmt. Fla. Counties Found., Fla. Assn. Counties, 1997, County Commrs. Cert. in County Govt. Law Fla. Counties Found., Fla. Assn. Counties, 1998, County Commrs. Cert. in Ethics Fla. Counties Found., Fla. Assn. Counties, 1998. Toll operator So. Bell Telephone Co., 1966-68; adminstrv. asst. appraisal and constrn. Loan Dept. Hollywood Fed. Savings & Loan Assn., 1968—72; acct., qualifying agt. Victor Purdo Painting Co., 1972-81; fin. mgr. CRG, Inc., 1982-83; bookkeeper I county and vocat. Sch. Bd. Broward County, South Plantation HS, 1983-84; commr. dist. 5 Broward County, Fla., 1988—2004, vice-chair, 1989—90, 1996—97, chair, 1990—91, 1997—98, 2001—02, property appraiser, 2005—. Citizen's adv. bd. City of Cooper, 1976-77, pers. rev. bd., 1976-77; mem. Property Appraisal Adjustment Bd., 1984-90, 91-94, vice chair, 1987-88, chair 1989-90, 1993-94, 95-96; mem. South Fla. Coordinating Coun., 1985-, Criminal Justice Planning Coun., 1985-90, Nat. Assn. Counties, 1988-2004, Human Svcs. Com., 1988-2004, Broward Econ. Devel. Bd., 1988-89, chair 1991-92; mem. Courthouse Security Com., 1990-93, Pub. Health Trust Com., Environment, Energy Land Use Steering Com., 1991-2004, Health Steering Com. 1989-90, 94-95, Overall Econ. Devel. Planning Com., 1988-90, Met. Planning Orgn., 1988-90, 92-2004, HIV Health Planning Coun., 1992-93, Broward Edn. Planning Initiative Com., Legal, Legis. Subcommittee, 1993, Resource Recovery Bd. 1994-95, 2002-03, vice chair, 1992, chair, 1993, Tourist Devel. Coun. 1997, 2001; mem. select com. water policy, Fla. Assn. Counties', 1995-96, elderly task force mem., 1995; bd. govs. Fort Lauderdale C. of C., 1987-88, 90-91; adv. bd. mem. Water Supply, 1988-94, chair 1991-92; Brady Brigade recruiter, Nat. Orgn. Disability, 1991-93; chair NACO's Subcommittee on Aging, 1993; chair Cooper City Election Reform Com., 1993-94; bd. dirs. Cmty. Health Purchasing Alliance, 1993-96, Fla. Assn. Counties, 1988-2001, South Fla. Regional Transp. Authority, Tri-County Commuter Rail Authority, 1988-2004, vice chair, 1996-97, chair 1997-98; vice chair Broward County Planning Coun., 1991-92, mem. 2002-; spl. projects coord. Davie/Cooper City C. of C.; adminstrv. asst. to bldg. ofcl. City of Cooper City, 1972-81; landscape contractor, owner Earthy Interiors; v.p. Lake Shore Motel and Swap Shop, Inc., 1994-2003, 3290 Sunrise Investments, Inc., 1994-2003, 3291 Sunrise Investments, Inc. (dba Swap Shop), 1994-2003, Fla. Drive-In Theater Mgmt., Inc. 1994-2001, COO Millennium Hollywood's City Pl., 1994-2003; v.p., sec., treas. Swap Shop Mgmt. LLC, 2001-; founder Broward Workshop Criminal Justice Com. Regional Transp. Orgn. Bd. 1996-2003. Adv. bd. Broward County Libr., 1979-85, Mommas and Poppas of Cooper City High, 1982-90, Broward C.C. Women's Programs Adv. Com., 1981-82; sec. Cooper City Elem. Sch. Adv. Com., 1979-80, chair 1980-82, South Ctrl. Area Adv. Com., 1982-83, sec., 1981-82; legis. chair Broward County Libr. Adv. Bd., 1982-84; active Broward County Sch. Bd., 1984-88, vice-chair, 1986-87, chair, 1987-88; bd. dirs. Pembroke Pines Human Resource Ctr. Adv. Com., 1984-88. Recipient Lifetime Membership award Broward County Phys. Edn. Tchrs., 1988, VIP Female award West Broward Dem. Club, 1988, Lifetime Membership award Young Dems., 1988, Outstanding Svc. award Lauderhill Regular Dem. Club, 1988, Disting. Svc. award Plantation Dem. Club, 1988, Disting. and Dedicated Svc. award Broward County Deputies Assn., 1989, 92, Spl. Achievement award Jefferson-Jackson, 1990, Friend of ARC award Assn. Retarded Citizens of Broward, 1990, Tribute to Success award Pembroke Pines Dem. Club, 1991, Leadership and Dedication award Children's Svcs. Bd., 1991, Desert Storm Family Support award 1991, Disting. Svc. award Women in Distress, 1991-92, Appreciation award Mus. Archaeology, 1992, Ann. Appreciation award N.W. Federated Woman's Club, 1992, Mother's Day award Rainbow Crusaders, 1992, Environ. Appreciation award Sunshine Ranches Homeowners Assn., 1992, Woman Leadership award Assn. Retarded Citizens, 1992, Coconut Creek Disting. Svc. award, 1994, Conservation Legislator of Yr. award Broward County Airboat, Halftrack, Conservation Club, 1994, Honoree Sunrise Regular Dem. Club, 1994, Legislator of Yr. award Broward County Fire Fighters and Paramedics, 1994, Woman of Yr. award Plantation Dem. Club, 1995, Humanitarian of Yr. award Soref Jewish Cmty. Ctr., 1995, Pres.'s award Broward County Fair, 1996, award Manatee Survival Found. 1996, Dream Maker award Jr. League Greater Fort Lauderdale, 1996, Jesse Portis Helms award Dolphin Dem. Club, 1996, Par Excellence award Miramar High Cmty. Sch., 1997, Recognition award North Dade C. of C., 1997, Par Excellence award Miramar High Cmty. Sch., 1997, Criminal Justice Image award Cmty. Reconstruction Inst., 1998, Govtl. Dream Builder award Children's Harbor, 1999, Ray Lisanti Meml. award Gays United to Attack Repression and Discrimination, 1999, Gracias award Hispanic Unity, 1999, Polit. Leader of Yr. award The Vanguard Chronicle, 1999, Environ. Merit award EPA, 2000, Third Ann. Student Life Achievement Corp. Ptnr. of Yr. award Nova Southeastern U., 2002, 2002 Arts Collaboration award 13th Ann. ArtServe Encore awards, Karl Clark Cmty. Involvement award, 2002, Commr. Leadership award Fla. Local Environ. Resource Agencies, 2002, Spirit of Excellence award South Broward Chpt. Am. Bus. Women's Assn., 2002, Edee Greene Good Egg award, 2002, Humanitarian award LWV, 2002, Medallion award Unsung Heroine People with AIDS Coalition Broward County, 2002, Dem. Elected Women Honoree N.W. Dem. Club, 2002, Contbn. to Cmty. award, Pine Island Ridge Civic Orgn. award, 2003, Outstanding Svc. award Engring. Profession Broward Chpt. Fla. Engring. Soc., 2003, Women of Valor Broward County award David Posnack Jewish Cmty. Ctr., 2003, Outstanding Svc. award Washington Pk. Neighborhood Preservation and Enhancement Dist., 2003, South Fla. Commuter Svcs. Transp. Leadership award, 2004, David Posnack Hebrew Day Sch. Lifetime Achievement award, 2004, Outstanding Pub. Ofcl. award Fla. Assn. Mus., 2004-05, Pub. Svc. award Davie Merchants and Indsl. Assn., 2005, Cert. Appreciation Coral Springs C. of C., 2005, Cert. Appreciation Poinsettia Heights Civic Assn., 2005; nominee Feminist of Yr. Fedn. Pub. Employees, 1987; finalist Woman of Yr. Govt., 1987; named Woman of Yr. Sunrise Lakes Phase III Women's Club, 1987, Woman of Yr. City of Hope, 1989, Hon. Conch and Citizen of Fabulous Fla. Keys, 1991, Woman of Yr. Metro Broward Fire Fighters, 1992, Dem. of Yr. Jefferson-Jackson, 1992, 2002, Woman of Yr. Women in Distress, 1993, Environ. Legislator of Yr. Environ. Coalition of Broward County, 1993, Polit. Alliance of Yr. Dolphin Dem. Club, 1999, Humanitarian of Yr. E.A.S.E. Found., 2001, Woman of Yr. South Fla. Mus. Natural History and Pyramid Soc., 2002; named to Broward County Women's Hall of Fame, 1997; Paul Harris fellow Rotary Found. Rotary Internat. Davie Rotary Club, 1997. Mem. ALA, Southeastern Libr. Assn., Davie/Cooper City Friends of Libr. (founder), Ft. Lauderdale Friends of Libr., Broward County Friends of Libr., Amalgamated Transit Union (hon. life, Naval Air Sta., Ft. Lauderdale Hist. Assn. (hon.), Broward County Police Benevolent Assn. (hon.). Office: Broward County Property Appraiser 115 S Andrews Ave Ste 111 Fort Lauderdale FL 33301-1801 Home Phone: 954-236-5537; Office Phone: 954-357-6904. Business E-Mail: lori@bcpa.net.

PARRISH, MARK, health products executive; B, U. Calif., Berkeley. Various gen. mgmt. and sales positions Foxmeyer Health Corp., Gen. Med. Coun., Bergen Brunswig Corp., Proctor & Gamble Co.; exec. v.p. sales and mktg. Cardinal Health, Inc., 1997—99, exec. v.p. retail sales and mktg., 1999—2001, pres. medicine shoppe internat., 2001—03, group pres. pharm. supply chain svcs., 2003—, exec. v.p., 2003—. Office: Cardinal Health Inc 7000 Cardinal Pl Dublin OH 43017

PARRISH, MATTHEW DENWOOD, psychiatrist; b. Washington, Apr. 1, 1918; s. Forrest Denwood and Alice Lorena (Flynn) P.; m. Virginia John Bennet, Sept. 24, 1944 (div.); children: Denwood, John, Stephen; m. Marilyn Kay Arney, May 29, 1978; children: Megan, Maxwell. BA, U. Va., 1939; MD, George Washington U., 1950. Diplomate Am. Bd. Psychiatry. Intern Letterman Hosp., San Francisco, 1950-51; resident in psychiatry Walter Reed Hosp., Washingotn, 1951-54; commd. 2d lt. U.S. Army, 1941, advanced through grades to col., 1967, ret., 1971; chief tng. Ill. Dept. Mental Health, Chgo., 1972-74; supt. Singer Mental Health Ctr., Rockford, Ill., 1974-85, med. dir., 1985-93; child and adolescent psychiatrist, 1986-95; ret., 1996. Clin. prof. psychiatry U. Ill., Chgo., 1972-76; clin. asst. prof. psychiatry Coll. Med., Rockford, 1976—. Editor in chief: U.S. Army Vietnam Medical Journal, 1967-68. Decorated Legion of Merit (2). Fellow Am. Psychiat. Assn. (life); mem. Soc. Med. Cons. in Armed Forces, Assn. Mil. Surgeons U.S. Avocations: writing, photography, painting, linguistics, electronics. Office Phone: 815-399-4504.

PARRISH, MAURICE DRUE, museum executive; b. Chgo., Mar. 5, 1950; s. Maurice and Ione Yvonne (Culumns) P.; m. Gail Marie Sims, Sept. 2, 1978; children: Theodore, Andrew, Brandon, Cara. BA in Arch., U. Pa., 1972; MArch, Yale U., 1975. City planner City of Chgo., 1975-81; architect John Hiltscher & Assocs., Chgo., 1981-83, Barnett, Jones & Smith, Chgo., 1983-84; zoning adminstr. City of Chgo., 1984-87, bldg. commr., 1987-89; dep. dir. Detroit Inst. of Arts, 1989-97, interim dir., 1997-99, exec. v.p., 1999—. Bd. dirs. Arts League of Mich., Detroit, 1994-97, Mosaic Youth Theatre Detroit, 2000—, chmn., 2002—; co-chmn. Mayor's Affordable Housing Task Force, Chgo., 1984-89; chmn. Chgo. Elec. Commn., 1988-89; mem. Chgo. Econ. devel. Commn., 1987-89; pres. St. Philip Neri Sch. Bd., Chgo., 1981-85, South Shore Commn., Chgo., 1982-84. King Chavez Parks fellow U. Mich., 1991, H.I. Feldman fellow Yale U., 1972; Franklin W. Gregory scholar Yale U., 1974, Nat. Achievement scholar U. Pa., 1968. Mem. Am. Assn. Mus., Am. Assn. Mus. Adminstrs., Constrn. Specifications Inst., Lambda Alpha. Avocations: sailing, chess, reading, astronomy. Office: Detroit Inst of Arts 5200 Woodward Ave Detroit MI 48202-4094 E-mail: mparrish@dia.org.

PARRISH, OVERTON BURGIN, JR., pharmaceutical corporation executive; b. Cin., May 26, 1933; s. Overton Burgin and Geneva Opal (Shinn) P. BS, Lawrence U., 1955; MBA, U. Chgo., 1959. With Pfizer Inc., 1959-74; salesman Pfizer Labs., Chgo., 1959-62, asst. mktg. product mgr. NYC, 1962-63, product mgr., 1964-66, group product mgr., 1966-67, mktg. mgr., 1967-68, v.p. mktg., 1969-70, v.p., dir. ops., 1970-71; exec. v.p. domestic pharm. div. Pfizer Pharms., 1971-72; exec. v.p., dir. Pfizer Internat. Divsn., 1972-74; pres., chief operating officer G.D. Searle Internat., Skokie, Ill., 1974-75, pres., chief exec. officer, 1975-77; pres. Worldwide Pharm./Consumer Products Group, 1977-86; pres., chief exec. officer Phoenix Health Care, Chgo., 1987—; chmn., CEO, bd. dirs. Wis. Pharmiacal Co., Inc., 1990-96; co-chmn. Inhalon Pharms., 1991-95, also bd. dirs.; chmn. ViatiCare Fin. Svcs. LLC, 1993—, also bd. dirs.; chmn., CEO, bd. dirs. The Female Health Co., 1996—. Bd. dirs., chair Abiant Inc. Author: The Future Pharmaceutical Marketing; International Drug Pricing, 1971. Trustee Mktg. Sci. Inst.; trustee Food and Drug Law Inst., 1979-86, Lawrence U., 1983-87, 98—. Served to 1st lt. USAF, 1955-57. Mem. Beta Gamma Sigma, Phi Kappa Tau. Office: Phoenix Health Care 515 N State St Chicago IL 60610 Home Phone: 312-822-0790; Office Phone: 312-595-9833. Personal E-mail: oparrish@aol.com.

PARRISH, STEVEN C., consumer products company executive; BA in Polit. Sci., U. Mo., 1972, JD, 1975. Joined Philip Morris Cos., 1990, sr. v.p. external affairs, gen. counsel, 1992—94, sr. v.p. worldwide regulatory affairs, 1994—95; sr. v.p. corp. affairs Altria Group, Inc., NYC, 1995—. Vice chmn. bd. dirs. Safe Horizon; bd. dirs. Stamford Symphony Orch. Office: Altria Group Inc 120 Park Ave New York NY 10017-5592 *

PARRISH, THOMAS KIRKPATRICK, III, marketing consultant; b. Richmond, Va., May 18, 1930; s. Thomas Kirkpatrick and Sally Cary (Friend) P.; divorced; children: Linn Cary, Wayne Elizabeth, Susan Scott, Thomas Kirkpatrick IV. AB, Princeton U., 1952. Product mgr. Vick Chem. Co., NYC, 1955-58; v.p. Benton & Bowles Advt. Agy., NYC, 1958-65; pres. Am. Chicle Co. div. Warner-Lambert Co., Morris Plains, NJ, 1965-70, Life Savers Inc. div. Squibb Corp., NYC, 1970-73, Lanvin-Charles of Ritz Inc. subs. Squibb Corp., NYC, 1974-76; dir. parent co. Squibb Corp., 1974-77; group dir. new bus. devel. Gillette Co., Boston, 1977-78; exec. v.p. SSC & B, Inc., NYC, 1978-81; sr. assoc. Am. Cons. Corp., 1982-86; prin. The Parrish Co., NYC, 1986—. Mem. N.Y. State Republican Com., 1962-63; bd. dirs. YMCA Ctr. for Internat. Mgmt. Studies, N.Y.C., 1970-85. Served to lt., jr. grade USN, 1952-55. Home: 231 Elsinore St Apt 7 Concord MA 01742 Home Phone: 978-254-5069.

PARRISH, WILLIAM M., lawyer; b. Springfield, Mass., Feb. 8, 1953; BA with honors, U. Tex., Austin, 1975, JD, 1978. Bar: Tex. 1978, US Dist. Ct. No. & We. Districts Tex. 1978, US Ct. Appeals 5th & 11th Circuits 1978. Named ptnr. Jenkins & Gilchrist, P.C., 1983, now shareholder, litig. practice group Austin, Tex., firm v.p. bd. dirs. Mem. ABA, Tex. State Bar Assn., Dallas Bar Assn., Travis County Bar Assn., Phi Beta Kappa, Omicron Delta Kappa. Office: Jenkens & Gilchrist PC 401 Congress Ave Ste 2500 Austin TX 78701 Office Phone: 512-499-3893. Office Fax: 512-499-3810. Business E-Mail: bparrish@jenkens.com.

PARRISH-ST. JOHN, FLORENCE TUCKER, writer, retired federal agency administrator; b. Greenville, Miss., Nov. 12, 1925; d. Victor Amos and Martha Buchannan (Binkley) Denslow; m. Joseph Nathaniel Tucker Jr., Nov. 9, 1946 (dec. Dec. 1955); children: Joseph Nathaniel Tucker III, Frederick Steven Tucker, James Denslow Tucker; m. Noel Francis Parrish, June 25, 1983 (dec. Apr. 1987); m. Adrian St. John, Jan. 29, 1998. Diploma in piano, Ward-Belmont Coll., Nashville, 1945; studied piano with Michael Field, NYC, 1945—46; B of Music Edn., Delta State U., 1960; MS in Counseling, U. So. Miss., 1971; EdD in Human Resources, George Washington U., 1983. Tchr. music Gulfport Pub. Schs., Miss., 1959—63; recreation therapist VA Hosp., Gulfport, 1964—70; edn. counselor USAF, Miss. and Japan, 1971—74, edn. svcs. officer Kunsan, Republic of Korea, 1974—75; asst. dir. sr. tng. CAP Nat. Hdqrs., 1975—77; EEO officer D.C. Dept. Labor, 1977—80; bur. chief complaints processing and adjudication, EEO U.S. Geol. Survey, Reston, Va., 1980—82; mgr. human resources Dept. Interior, 1982—84; internat. forum coord. Inspire 85 Pres.'s Com. on Employment of Handicapped, 1985; commr., chmn. edn. and cultural affairs com. Alexandria Commn. on Aging, Va., 1985—88, sec., 1987—88; lead scholar pilot project Nat. Coun. Aging. Mem. adv. bd. Inst. Conflict Analysis and resolution George Mason U., 1993—, vice chair adv. bd. Inst. Conflict Analysis and resolution, 1995—97, chmn. adv. bd. Inst. Conflict Analysis and resolution, 1998—2000, adv. bd. mem. emeritus, 2003—. Feature writer on aging issues: Alexandria Gazette-Packet, 1986—92; feature writer Hurricane Katrina and White House Presdl. Families, 2006; contbr. articles to profl. jours. Pianist/organist Sr. Living Cmty., The Fairfax, Ft. Belvoir, Va., 2003—, The Fairfax. Mem.: Nat. Press Club (sr. rep. NPC trip to China and Hong Kong 1998, events com., chmn. oral history com., dir. videos and taped programs, presenter 13 panel programs, Vivian award 1998, 1999, 2000, 2002, 2003), Va. Assn. on Aging, World Affairs Coun., Women in Comm., Nat. Tuskegee Airmen Inc. Orgn., Smithsonian Assocs., Friends of Kennedy Ctr., Ret. Officers Assn., Miss. Soc. Washington, Am. Inst. Wine and Food, NATO Def. Coll. Ancients Assn., USAF Assn. (v.p. for cmty. programs Gen. Charles Gabriel chpt. 1991—98, Pres.'s award 1998, Woman of Distinction award Thomas Anthony chpt.), Washington Opera Guild. Home: 9110 Belvoir Woods Pky Apt 118 Fort Belvoir VA 22060-2717 Home Phone: 703-799-4355; Office Phone: 703-799-3758. Office Fax: 703-799-9530.

PARR-JOHNSTON, ELIZABETH, economist, consultant; b. NYC, Aug. 15, 1939; d. Ferdinand Van Siclen and Helene H. Parr; m. David E. Bond, Dec. 28, 1962 (div. July 1975); children: Peter V.S., Kristina Aline; m. Archibald F. Johnston, Mar. 6, 1982; children: James, Heather, Alexandra, Margaret. BA, Wellesley Coll., 1961; MA, Yale U., 1962, PhD, 1973; postgrad., Harvard U., 1986; DLitt, U. NB, 2004. Various positions Govt. of Can., Ottawa, Ont., Canada, 1973-76, INCO Ltd., Toronto, 1976-79; chief of staff, sr. policy advisor Ministry of Employment and Immigration, Govt. of Can., 1979-80; various positions Shell Can. Ltd., Calgary, Alta., Canada, 1980-90; pres. Parr-Johnston & Assocs., Calgary, 1990-91; pres., vice-chancellor Mt. St. Vincent U., Halifax, Nova Scotia, N.S., Canada, 1991-96, The U. New Brunswick, Fredericton, Canada, 1996—2002; pres. Parr Johnston Econ. and Policy Cons., Chester Basin, N.S., Canada, 2002—. Instr. U. We. Ont., London, 1964—67, U. B.C., Vancouver, 1967—71; vis. scholar Wesleyan U., Middletown, Conn., 1971—72; acad. rsch. assoc. Carleton U., Ottawa, 1972—73; bd. dirs. Nova Scotia Power, Emera Ltd., Bank of Nova Scotia, Social Rsch. and Demonstration Corp., Can. Found. Sustainable Devel. Tech., Can. Millennium Scholarships Found., Coun. Can. Acads.; spkr. and presenter in field. Mem. editl. bd. Can. Econ. Jour., 1980—83; contbr. articles to profl. jours. Planning chmn. John Howard Soc., 1980—84; mem. policy adv. com. C.D. Howe, 1980—85; mem. Ont. Econ. Coun., 1981—84, 2005—06; bd. dirs. Dellcrest Home, 1980—84, Calgary S.W. Fed. Riding Assn., 1985—91, The Learning Ctr., Calgary, 1989—91, Halifax United Way, 1991—92, North/South Inst., 1992—96, Can. Unity Coun., 1993—2005, Vol. Planning N.S., 1992—93, Social Sci. Human Rsch. Coun., 1995—98, FPI Ltd., 1996—2001, Empire Co., 1994—2002, Symphony Nova Scotia, 2003—06, Nat. Theatre Sch. Recipient Canada 125 medal, Queen's Jubilee medal; Hon. Woodrow Wilson fellow, 1962. Mem. Assn. Atlantic Univs. (chair 1994-96), Assn. Univs. and Colls. in Can. (bd. dirs., mem. exec. com. 1994-96), Women in Acad. Adminstrn. (adv. bd. 1991-96), Calgary Coun. Advanced Tech. (exec. 1990-91), Can. Econs. Assn., Inst. Pub. Adminstrn. Can., Sr. Women Acad. Adminstrs. Can., Assn. Commonwealth Univs. (former mem. exec. com.), Phi Beta Kappa. Anglican. Avocations: golf, travel. Home: PO Box 219 Chester Basin NS Canada B0J 1K0 Personal E-mail: epj@chesterbasin.com.

PARROTT, DENNIS BEECHER, retired insurance industry executive; b. St. Louis, June 13, 1929; s. Maurice Ray and Mai Ledgerwood (Beecher) P.; m. Vivian Cleveland Miller, Mar. 24, 1952; children: Constance Beecher, Dennis Beecher, Anne Cleveland. BS in Econs., Fla. State U., Tallahassee, 1954; postgrad., Princeton U., NJ, 1964; MBA, Pepperdine U., Malibu, Calif., 1982. With Prudential Ins. Co. Am., 1954-74, v.p. group mktg. LA, 1971-74; sr. v.p. Frank B. Hall Cons. Co., LA, 1974—83; v.p. Johnson & Higgins, LA, 1983-95; exec. v.p. Arthur J. Gallagher & Co., LA, 1995-98; ret., 1998. Spkr. in field. Chmn. Weekend with the Stars

Telethon, 1976-80; chmn. bd. dirs. United Cerebral Palsy/Spastic Children's Found., LA County, 1979-82, chmn. bd. govs., 1982-83; bd. dirs. Nat. United Cerebral Palsy Assn., 1977-82, pres., 1977-79; bd. dirs. LA Emergency Task Force, 1992; mem. cmty. adv. coun. Birmingham High Sch., Van Nuys, Calif., 1982-85; sect. chmn. United Way, LA, 1983-84; bd. dirs. The Betty Clooney Found. for Brain Injured, 1986-88; mem. com. to fund an endowed chair in cardiology at Cedars-Sinai Med. Ctr., 1986-88; adv. coun. Family Health Program, Inc., 1986-88; bd. deacons Bel Air Presbyn. Ch., 1990-92, chmn., 1991-92, elder, 1993-96; mem. adv. coun. Blue Cross Calif., 1996-98; chmn. Danny Arnold Meml. Golf Classic at Riviera Country Club benefitting John Wayne Cancer Inst., 1997. 1st lt. AUS, 1951-53. Named Tournament Champion, Sunkist Invitational Golf Tournament, 1995. Mem. Am. Soc. CLUs, Internat. Found. Employee Benefits, Mchts. and Mfrs. Assns. 44th Ann. Mgmt. Conf. (chmn. 1986), Employee Benefits Planning Assn. So. Calif., LA Club, Woodland Hills Country Club, Jonathan Club (LA). Republican. Presbyterian. Home: 17023 Encino Hills Dr Encino CA 91436-4009 Personal E-mail: CallParrott@aol.com.

PARRS, MARIANNE M., paper and lumber company executive; b. NYC, 1945; m. Walter Parrs; 3 children. Grad., Brown U. Joined Internat. Paper Co., 1974, sector controller, printing papers Purchase, NY, staff v.p., worldwide responsibility tax planning and compliance, CFO, sr. v.p., 1995—99, exec. v.p. adminstrn., info. tech. and human resources Stamford, Conn., 1999—2005, exec. v.p., CFO, 2005—. Bd. dir. Liaison Tech. (formerly Forest Express), CIT Group, 2003—. Bd. dir. Women's Forum. Office: Internat Paper Co 400 Atlantic St Stamford CT 06921 Office Phone: 203-541-8000. Fax: 914-397-1650. *

PARRY, CLINT, business coaching executive; b. 1970; Owner Action Internat. Bus. Coaching, Tucson. Involved with Northern Pima County Chamber of Commerce. Named one of 40 Under 40, Tucson Bus. Edge, 2006. Mem.: Ariz. Assn. Bus. Brokers, Ariz. Small Bus. Assn., Jr. Achievement of Ariz. (bd. mem.), Tucson Assn. of Executives (pres/). Office: Action International 5670 Wynn Rd Ste A & C Las Vegas NV 89118

PARRY, DALE D., publisher, editor; BS in Journalism cum laude, Ball State U., Muncie, Ind., 1981. Feature writer Richmond (Ind.) Palladium-Item, 1981-84, Cin. Enquirer, 1984-86; editor Today section The Dallas Morning News, 1987-90; assignment editor The Way We Live sect. Detroit Free Press, 1990-92, dep. features editor, 1992-94, features editor, 1993-96, asst. mng. editor, 1997-2000, dep. mng. editor, 2001—06; pub. Signature Media, Detroit, 2007—. Mem. Am. Assn. Sun. and Feature Editors. Office: Signature Media 615 W Lafayette Blvd Detroit MI 48226

PARRY, DAVID C., engineering executive; BSc in Chemistry, U. Manchester, Eng., 1974, MSc in Chemistry, 1975, PhD in Chemistry, 1977. With Ill. Tool Works (ITW), Glenview, Ill., 1994—, gen. mgr. Devon Plexus and ITW Devcon, v.p., gen. mgr. Performance Polymers, 2001—04, pres. Performance Polymers, 2004—06, exec. v.p. polymers and fluids, 2006—. Office: Ill Tool Works 3600 W Lake Ave Glenview IL 60026-1215 Office Phone: 847-657-4575. Office Fax: 847-657-4392.

PARRY, JANET, retired health facility administrator; b. Salt Lake City, Nov. 5, 1943; d. Nathaniel Edmunds Parry and Dortha Nell (Harris) Parry-Miller. BSN, U. Utah, Salt Lake City, 1966. RN Calif. Pres. Med. Mgmt. Cons., Anaheim, Calif., 1970—91; v.p. Parry Devel. Co., Anaheim, 1971—91; property mgr. Parry Profl. Bldg., Anaheim, 1981—95; founding ptnr. Med. Billing Specialist, Anaheim, 1991, PPP Med. Practice Sales, Anaheim, 1995; sales assoc. P & F Investment Property Mgmt., Anaheim, 1994, Boydston Realty, Anaheim, 1994—95; ret., 1995. Pres., chmn. bd. dirs. Anaheim Meml. Hosp. Contbr. articles to profl. publs. V.p. Aspen Hollow Homeowners Assn., 2003—05, pres., 2007—; mem. Caritas Chorale of Sun Valley, 2001—, pres., 2005—06, co-chmn. benefit dinner com., 2003—04, bd. dirs., 2003—07, v.p., 2004—05; asst. dir. Promise Christmas Chorale, 2001—02; mem. St. Luke's Hosp. Aux., Sun Valley, 2000—01; bd. dirs. Anaheim Meml. Hosp. Found., 1987—96, v.p., 1991—96, chmn. bd. dirs., 1994; mem. Anaheim Bd. Realtors, 1987—97; mem., bd. dirs., treas. Tustin Main St. Chorus, 1991—94; mem. med. adv. bd. So. Calif. Coll. Med. and Dental Assts., 1972—85; mem. citizen's adv. com. Anaheim Hills Hosp., 1982—84; mem. Anaheim Sister City Com. to Mito, Japan, 1985; exec. prodr. Miss Anaheim Pageant, 1983—84; mem. Anaheim Halloween Festival Com., 1983; treas. Tu Casa Condo. Assn., Carlsbad, Calif., 1976—77; mem. Mormon Tabernacle Choir, Salt Lake City, 1966—68; bd. dirs. U. Utah Coll. Nursing, 2001—03, Am. Heart Assn., 1993—95. Recipient Annie Accolade award, Women's Divsn. Anaheim C. of C., 1984, Women of Achievement award, YWCA, Orange, Calif., 1985. Home: PO Box 3299 Ketchum ID 83340

PARRY, LANCE AARON, publishing executive; b. Allentown, Pa., Sept. 4, 1947; s. Harwood Clayton Bachman and Iola Mary (Johnson) P.; m. Virginia Eleanor Ford, Apr. 24, 1971; children: Halloran Lee, Christine Ford. BS in English Edn., Kutztown U., 1969; MS in Journalism, W.Va. U., 2003. With Call-Chronicle Newspapers, Allentown, 1970-81, mng. editor, 1979-81; asst. news editor The Phila. Inquirer, 1981-82, systems editor, 1982-84, night news editor, 1984-86, news editor daily edit., 1986-87, news editor Sunday edit., 1987-89, sr. editor/systems and tech., 1989-93, page design dir., 1993-94, features news editor, 1994-96, news editor Sunday edit., 1996-98, features news editor, 1998—2004, news editor, 2005, sr. news editor, 2005—. Recipient 1st Place award for front page design Pa. Newspaper Pubs. Assn./Pa. Soc. Newspaper Editors, 1985, 87, 88, Disting. Alumnus award Kutztown U., 1992; Sigma Delta Chi scholar, 1969. Mem. Soc. Profl. Journalists, Pen and Pencil Club. Democrat. Presbyterian. Home: 16 Salisbury Ln Malvern PA 19355-2836 Office: The Phila Inquirer 400 N Broad St Philadelphia PA 19130-4099

PARRY, MICHAEL, not-for-profit fundraiser, singer, actor; b. Cleve., Sept. 15, 1957; s. George and Eleanor Parry. MusB in Edn., Baldwin-Wallace Coll., Berea, Ohio, 1981. Cert. fundraising exec. 2005. Devel. dir. Svcs. for Ind. Living, Cleve., 1990—95, Hitchcock Ctr. for Women, Cleve., 1995—97; dir. planned giving Salvation Army of NE Ohio, Cleve., 1997—99; sr. mgr., corp. and found. support ARC, Cleve., 1999—. Actor: (solo dramatic presentation) PAUL - Apostle of Christ; singer: (concert soloist) REQUIEM of Giuseppe Verdi, Five Mystical Songs, others. Adv. bd. Found. Ctr., Cleve., 2005—07; v.p., treas. Mary Ministries Found., Westlake, Ohio, 2002—07; sec. Cedarwood Townhouse Assn. #1, Westlake, 2005—07. Named Bd. Mem. of Yr., Mary Ministries Found., 2005; recipient Spirit of Excellence award, ARC Greater Cleve. Chpt., 2006. Mem.: Assn. Fundraising Profls. (v.p. 2005—07, v.p. Greater Cleve. chpt. 2005—, Fundraising Exec. of Yr. 2006). Avocations: art, architecture, antiques. Office: Am Red Cross 3747 Euclid Ave Cleveland OH 44115 Home Phone: 440-871-2476; Office Phone: 216-431-3275. Office Fax: 216-431-3663. Business E-Mail: parrym@redcross-cleveland.org.

PARRY, RICHARD D., lawyer, construction executive; b. LA, July 12, 1952; BA, Calif. State U., 1977; JD, Brigham Young U. J. Rueben Clark Law Sch., 1980. Bar: Utah 1980, Ohio 1983, U.S. Ct. of Appeals, 6th Circuit, U.S. Dist. Ct., Dist. of Utah, U.S. Ct. of Appeals, 10th Circuit. Atty. priv. practice; interim U.S. atty. State of Utah, asst. U.S. atty.; v.p., assoc. gen. counsel Wash. Group Internat., 1993—97, v.p., gen. counsel, 1997—2001, sr. v.p., gen. counsel, 2001—. Assoc. counsel U.S. Senate Select Com. on Iran-Contra, 1987. Mem.: ABA, Ohio State Bar Assn., Utah State Bar Assn. Office: Wash Group Internat PO Box 73 720 Park Blvd Boise ID 83729

PARRY, SCOTT BRINK, psychologist; b. Reading, Pa., Sept. 4, 1932; s. George Raymond and Claire (Blackburne) Parry; m. Joan SantAntonio; 1 child, Christiana Claire. BA, Princeton U., 1954; MS, Boston U., 1960; PhD, NYU, 1969. Account exec. Hill & Knowlton, Inc., NYC, 1960-62; editor Harcourt, Brace, Jovanovich, NYC, 1962-64; ptnr. Parry & Robinson, Inc., NYC, 1964-66; mgr. N.Y.C. office Sterling Inst., 1966-71; v.p., pres., chmn. Tng. House, Inc., NYC, Princeton, 1971—; prof. comms. Mercer County (N.J.) C.C., 2000—05. Educ. cons. UNESCO, Paris, Nigeria, 1963, Ghana, 64; mem. adv. bd. Training Mag. Lakewood Publs., Mpls., 1988—92; adj. prof. NYU, 1968—74; spkr. convs. and meetings in 17 countries on 6 continents; cons. to more than 50 Fortune 500 cos. Author: (book) The Story of Handbells, 1957, A Handbell Handbill, 1963, From Managing to Empowering, 1993, The Managerial Mirror, 2 vols, 1997, Evaluating the Impact of Training, 1997, Training for Results, 2000, 46 training books; contbr. articles to profl jours and newspapers. Lt US Army, 1957—59. Named Hon Chmn, 25th Anniversary Am Guild English Handbell Ringers, 1979; named to Human Resource Develop Hall of Fame, 1999; recipient Best Training Product Award, Human Resource Exec, 1990, 1994. Mem.: ASTD, Instructional Sys Asn, Int Soc Performance Improvement, Int Fedn Training and Develop Orgns. Republican. Presbyterian. Avocations: music (harpsichord, organ, carillon), collecting and restoring antiques, renovating buildings. Office: Training House 96 Bear Brook Rd Princeton NJ 08540-6246 E-mail: jsparry@erols.com.

PARRY, TIMOTHY R., lawyer; b. Syracuse, NY, July 28, 1954; s. Edward Lee and Ruth (Thomas) P.; children: Ryan Edward, Ian Andrew, Erika Isabella. BS, Ariz. State U., 1976; JD, U. Cin., 1980. Bar: Ohio 1980, Fla. 1983, US Dist. Ct. (so. dist.) Ohio 1981, US Dist. Ct. (so. and mis. dists.) Fla. 1983, US Ct. Appeals (11th cir.) 1984. Law clk. to judge John D. Holschuh US Dist. Ct. (so. dist.) Ohio, Columbus, 1980-81; asst. atty. gen. Ohio Atty. Gen.'s Office, Columbus, 1981-83; assoc. Harter, Secrest & Emery, Naples, Fla., 1983-88, ptnr., 1989—96; div. v.p., asst. gen. counsel Health Mgmt. Associates, Naples, Fla., 1996—97, sr. v.p., gen. counsel, sec., 1997—. Past pres., Cath. Social Svcs. Collier County, Naples, Fla. 1988—; dir. Econ. Devel. Coun. Collier County, 2004-; mem. pres.'s adv. coun. Internat. Coll., Naples, Fla., 2005-. Mem. Fla. Bar Assn. (20th jud. cir. bar grievance com. 1989-91), Collier County Bar Assn. (bd. dirs. 1989—). Office: Health Mgmt Associates 5811 Pelican Bay Blvd Naples FL 34108-2710 Home Phone: 239-598-1717; Office Phone: 239-598-3131.

PARRY, WILLIAM DEWITT, lawyer; b. Hartford, Conn., June 4, 1941; s. William Brown and Mary Elizabeth (Caton) p.; m. Andrea Hannah Lewis, June 30, 1973; children: Sara, Jessica. BA, U. Mass., 1963; JD, U. Pa., 1966. Bar: N.J. 1987, Pa. 1967, U.S. Dist. Ct. (ea. dist.) Pa. 1974, U.S. Ct. Appeals (3d cir.) 1980, U.S. Ct. Appeals (9th cir.) 1998, U.S. Supreme Ct. 1980. Assoc. Shapiro, Cook & Bressler, Phila., 1966-67; asst. dir. ABA joint com on continuing legal edn. Am. Law Inst., Phila., 1967-73; assoc. Lowenschuss Assocs., Phila., 1973-85; of counsel Weiss, Golden & Pierson, Phila., 1985-88; pvt. practice Phila., 1988; ptnr. Rubin, Quinn, Moss & Patterson, Phila., 1989-93; pvt. practice Phila., 1993—. Lectr. in field. Author: Understanding and Controlling Stuttering: A Comprehensive New Approach Based on the Valsalva Hypothesis, 1994, 2000; editor U. Pa. Law Rev., 1964-66, The Practical Lawyer, 1967-73. Founder Phila. area chpt. Nat. Stuttering Project, 1985; bd. dirs. Nat. Stuttering Assn., 1996-2002; trustee Unitarian Soc. Germantown, Phila., 1983-86. Mem.: ATLA, ABA, Pa. Trial Lawyers Assn., Phila. Bar Assn., Pa. Bar Assn. Democrat. Avocations: acting, writing. Home: 520 Baird Rd Merion Station PA 19066-1302 Office: 1608 Walnut St Ste 900 Philadelphia PA 19103-5451 Home Phone: 610-664-5139; Office Phone: 215-735-3500. Personal E-mail: wdparry@aol.com.

PARRY-JONES, RICHARD, automotive executive; b. Wales, 1951; Mech. engring. (hon.), Univ. Salford, Manchester, 1973; D (hon.), Loughborough Univ., 1995. Apprentice Ford's European Product Devel. Group, 1969; leading role in devel. of the 1981 European Escort Ford Motor Co., 1981, apptd. mgr. small car programs, 1982, v.p. European vehicle ctr. Dearborn, Mich., 1994—98, group v.p. global product devel. and quality, 1998—2001, group v.p., chief tech. officer, 2001—. Vis. prof. Dept. of Aero. and Automotive Engring. at England's Loughborough U., 2001. Named Exec. Engr.of Ford's Technol. Rsch. in Europe, 1985, Chief Engr. for Vehicle Rngring., 1991, Man of the Yr., Bit. publ. Autocar, 1994, U.S. mag. Automobile, 1997, sr. exec. for Mazda oversight on Nov. 15, 2001; recipient Golden Gear Award, Wash. Motor Press Assn., 2001, Mktg. Statesman of the Yr., Sales and Mktg. Executives of Detroit. Fellow: Inst. of Mech. Engineers, Royal Acad. Engineers. Office: Ford Motor Co One American Rd Dearborn MI 48126-1899 *

PARSA, FEREYDOUN DON, plastic surgeon; b. Tehran, Iran, May 20, 1942; came to U.S., 1970; s. Issa and Zahra (Bismark) P.; m. Touri Akhlaghi, June 17, 1972; children: Natalie, Alan, Sean. MD, Lausanne U., Switzerland, 1969. Diplomate Am. Bd. Plastic Surgery. Chief of plastic surgery, prof. surgery U. Hawaii, Honolulu, 1981—. Contbr. articles to profl. jours. Mem. AMA, Am. Soc. Plastic Surgeons, Hawaii Med. Assn. Avocation: painting. Office: U Hawaii Sch Med Surgery 1329 Lusitana St 807 Honolulu HI 96813-2421 Home Phone: 808-396-0070. Personal E-mail: hawaiiplasticsurgery@yahoo.com.

PARSAPOUR, KOUROSH, medical educator; s. Ali Akbar Parsapour and Manijeh Etebari. BS in Physiology, U. Calif., Davis, 1992; MD, St. Georges U., Grenada, 1998. Lic. in pediatrics Am. Bd. Pediat., 2003, in pediatric critical care medicine Am. Bd. Pediat., 2006. Resident Henry Ford Hosp., Detroit, 1998—2001; fellow Rady Children's Hosp., San Diego, 2002—05; asst. prof. U. Calif., Davis Children's Hosp., Sacramento, 2005—. Co-chair Pediatric Telehealth Colloquium, San Francisco, 2006—. Contbr. chapter to book, articles to profl. jours. Recipient Outstanding Resident award, Henry Ford Hosp., 2001, 10th Ann. People's Choice award, Am. Telemedicine Assn., 2005. Mem.: Am. Telemedicine Assn., Am. Acad. Pediat., Soc. Critical Care Medicine. Office: Univ Calif Davis 2516 Stockton Blvd Sacramento CA 95817 Office Phone: 916-734-3676. Office Fax: 916-456-2235. Personal E-mail: kparsapour@yahoo.com. Business E-Mail: kourosh.parsapour@ucdmc.ucdavis.edu.

PARSHALL, GEORGE WILLIAM, chemist, researcher; b. Hackensack, Minn., Sept. 19, 1929; s. George Clarence and Frances (Virnig) Parshall; m. Naomi B. Simpson, Oct. 9, 1954; children: William, Jonathan, David; m. Anna Mae Buhl, Oct. 28, 2006. BS, U. Minn., 1951; PhD, U. Ill., 1954. Rsch. chemist E.I. duPont de Nemours & Co., Wilmington, Del., 1954—65, rsch. supr., 1965—79, dir. chem. sci., 1979—92, cons., 1992—2004, mem. com. on environ. mgmt. techs., 1994—97; mem. chem. stockpile disposal com. NRC, Washington, 1992—98, mem. non-stockpile com., 1998—99, 2001—06, mem. chem. weapons adv. com., 2004—. Bd. chem. sci. NRC, Washington, 1983—86; Reilly lectr. Notre Dame U., 1980; Ipatieff lectr. Northwestern U., 1994; mem. sci. adv. bd. Phoenix S&T, 2002—. Author: (book) Homogeneous Catalysis, 1980, Homogeneous Catalysis, 2d rev. edit., 1992; editor: Inorganic Syntheses, 1974, Jour. Molecular Catalysis, 1977—80. Recipient Ballar Inorganic Chemistry medal, U. Ill., 1976, Alumni Achievement award, 2005. Mem.: NAS, Am. Acad. Arts Scis., Am. Chem. Soc. (award in inorganic chemistry 1983, award leadership in chem. rsch. mgmt. 1989), Inst. Chemists (Chem. Pioneer award 1992, Gold medal award 1995), Guild Episcopal Scholars (treas. 1994—99). Episcopalian. Home: Apt 714 2401 Pennsylvania Ave Wilmington DE 19806 Personal E-mail: parshallgw@aol.com.

PARSHALL, GERALD, journalist; b. St. Paul, Apr. 24, 1941; s. William Elmer and Evelyn (Steckling) P.; m. Sandra Grant, Dec. 20, 1970. BA, U. Minn., 1963; MA, U. Mich., 1964; grad. fellow, U. Chgo., 1966-67. Reporter York (Pa.) Gazette and Daily, 1968, Balt. Evening Sun, 1968-71; Capitol Hill staff U.S. News & World Report, Washington, 1971-77, sr. editor, 1977-79, asst. mng. editor, 1979-90, sr. writer, 1990-99, contbg. editor, 1999—2004. Mem. Exec. Com. of Periodical Corrs., U.S. Congress, 1974-80, chmn., 1979-80 Served to 1st lt. U.S. Army, 1964-66. Recipient Front Page award Washington-Balt. Newspaper Guild, 1971, Silver Gavel award ABA, 1983 Home: 1004 Congress Ln Mc Lean VA 22101-2116 Personal E-mail: gparshall@verizon.net.

PARSHALL, KAREN VIRGINIA HUNGER, mathematician; b. Virginia Beach, Va., July 7, 1955; d. Maurice Jacques and Jean Kay (Wroton) Hunger; m. Brian J. Parshall, Aug. 6, 1978. BA, U. Va., 1977, MS, 1978; PhD, U. Chgo., 1982. Asst. prof. math. Sweet Briar (Va.) Coll., 1982-87, U. Ill., Urbana, 1987-88; asst. prof. math. and history U. Va., Charlottesville, 1988-93, assoc. prof. math. and history, 1993—99, prof. math. and history, 1999—. Author: (with David Rowe) Emergence of American Mathematics Research Community, 1994; (with others) Experiencing Nature, 1997, James Joseph Sylvester: Life and Work in Letters, 1998, (with others) Mathematics Unbound: The Emergence of an International Mathematical Community, 1800-1945, 2002, James Joseph Sylvester: Jewish Mathematician in a Victorian World, 2006; Years Ago editor Mathematical Intelligencer, N.Y.C., 1990-93; book rev. editor Historia Mathematica, San Diego, 1990-93, mng. editor, 1994-95, editor, 1996-99; contbr. articles to Archive for History Exact Scis., History of Sci., Jour. of the History of Biology, Archives internationales d'histoire des sciences, Annals of Sci., Historia Mathematica, Notices of the Am. Math. Soc., Am. Math. Mo., Revue d'histoire des mathématiques. Scholars award NSF, 1986-87, 90-93, NSF VPW award, 1996-97; John Simon Guggenheim Found. fellow, 1996. Mem. Am. Math. Soc., History Sci. Soc., Académie Internationale d'histoire des sciences (corr.), Internat. Commn. for History Math. (chair), Phi Beta Kappa. Office: U Va Depts Math and History Dept Mathematics P O Box 400137 Charlottesville VA 22904

PARSKY, BARBARA J., utilities executive; BA, Rollins Coll., Winter Park, Fla. Various mgmt. positions in mktg. and strategic comm. GE, mgr. corp. advt.; gen. mgr. Porter Novelli, LA, ptnr.; prin., owner consulting bus.; v.p. corp. comm. Edison Internat., Rosemead, Calif., 2002—07, sr. v.p. corp. comm., 2007—, sr. v.p. corp. comm. So. Calif. Edison subs., 2007—. Office: Edison Internat 2244 Walnut Grove Ave Rosemead CA 91770-3714 *

PARSKY, GERALD LAWRENCE, lawyer; b. West Hartford, Conn., Oct. 18, 1942; s. Isadore and Nettie (Sanders) P.; m. Susan Haas, June 26, 1966; children: Laura, David; m. Robin Cleary, Jan. 27, 1980. AB, Princeton U., 1964; JD, U. Va., 1968. Bar: N.Y. 1969, D.C. 1974, Calif. 1983. Assoc. Mudge Rose Guthrie & Alexander, NYC, 1968-71; spl. asst. to under sec. U.S. Treasury Dept., Washington, 1971-73, exec. asst. to dep. sec. Fed. Energy Office, 1973-74, asst. sec. internat. affairs, 1974-77; sr. ptnr. Gibson, Dunn & Crutcher, LA, 1977-90; of counsel Gibson, Dunn & Cruther, 1990-92; chmn. Aurora Capital Ptnrs., 1990—. Bd. dirs. James A. Baker III Inst. Pub. Policy. Trustee George Bush Presdl. Libr. Found., 1993—, Ronald Reagan Presdl. Found., 1995—; bd. dirs. Music Ctr. Found., 1998—. Recipient Alexander Hamilton award U.S. Treasury, 1976, Woodrow Wilson award, 2000. Mem. ABA, Coun. Fgn. Rels., N.Y. Princeton Club, Calif. Club, Racquet Club N.Y., Rolling Rock Club, Rancho Santa Fe Golf Club. Office: Aurora Capital Group 10877 Wilshire Blvd Ste 2100 Los Angeles CA 90024-4376

PARSLEY, HENRY NUTT, JR., bishop, academic administrator; b. Memphis, Tenn. m. Rebecca Knox Allison; 1 child, Henry Nutt III. B in English magna cum laude, U. of the South, 1970; MDiv, Gen. Theol. Sem., NYC, 1973. Asst. rector Trinity Ch., Myrtle Beach, SC, St. Philip's Ch., Charleston, SC; rector St. Paul's Ch., Summerville, SC, Christ Ch., Charlotte, NC; bishop Episcopal Diocese Ala., 1999—; chancellor U. of the South, Sewanee, Tenn., 2003—. Avocations: reading, fishing. Office: Univ of the South 735 University Ave Sewanee TN 37383

PARSLEY, STEVEN DWAYNE, title company executive; b. Monrovia, Calif., Dec. 31, 1959; BBA magna cum laude, U. Albuquerque, 1985. Lic. agt. to issue title ins. N.Mex. Data processing asst. Orion Corp., Albuquerque, 1978-79; title searcher N.Mex. Title, Albuquerque, 1979; various positions Rio Grande Title Co., Albuquerque, 1979-84, v.p., mgr. title ops., 1984-91, sr. v.p., escrow officer, 1992-94, exec. v.p., 1994-99; pres. Dona Ana Title Co., Las Cruces, N.Mex., 1999—. Bd. dirs. N.Mex Land Title Trust Fund. Mem. state apptd. Title Ins. Task Force State of N.Mex.; mem. Affordable Housing Round Table. Presdl. scholar, U. N.Mex, 1978. Mem.: Las Cruces Homebuilders Assn., N.Mex Land Title Assn. (pres. 1997—98, past v.p.). Avocations: ragtime piano, running. Home: 746 Oro Viejo Las Cruces NM 88011-8071 Office: Dona Ana Title Co 425 S Telshor Blvd Ste B Las Cruces NM 88011-8237 Home Phone: 505-521-4397; Office Phone: 505-521-5800. Personal E-mail: ssppiano@msn.com. Business E-Mail: stparsley@donaanatitle.com.

PARSON, SHAUN D., plastic surgeon; BS, U. Utah; MD, George Washington U. Diplomate Am. Bd. Surgery, Am. Bd. Plastic Surgery. Gen. surgery resident Phoenix Integrated Surg. Residency; plastic & reconstructive surgery trainee Mayo Clinic, Rochester, Minn.; pvt. practice Scottsdale, Ariz.; chief of plastic & reconstructive surgery Scottsdale Healthcare Shea Hosp. Clin. instr. in plastic surgery Mayo Clinic, Rochester, Minn., Phoenix Integrated Surg. Residency; assoc. prof. surgery U. Ariz. Active in Operation Smile. Fellow: Am. Coll. Surgeons. Office: 10210 N 92nd St #200 Scottsdale AZ 85258 Office Phone: 480-282-8386. E-mail: info@drparson.com. *

PARSONAGE, K. SUSAN, artist; b. Mpls., Aug. 8, 1939; d. Karl P. and Amanda J. Hoerschgen; m. William H. Parsonage, May 6, 1961; children: David W., Mark R., Kara L. Martin. BA in Art with highest distinction, Pa. State U., University Park, 1985, MFA, 1988. Instr. visual arts Pa. State U., 1987—98; vis. prof. of art U. Monterrey, Mexico, 1988—89; chmn. images fine art exhibition Ctrl. Pa. Festival of Arts, State College, 1993—98; artist in residence Pa. Coun. on Arts, Harrisburg, 1998—2002. Interim visual arts dir. and cons. Ctrl. Pa. Festival of Arts, 1996—2000; art cons. State College Borough Coun., 2002—04. One-woman shows include Foxdale Gallery, State Coll., Pa., 2005, exhibitions include Gallery 234, York, Pa., 1994—2007, State Mus. Pa., Harrisburg, 1995, 1998, 2004, 2005, Gamble Mill, Bellefonte, Pa., 2004—05, Boston Printmakers Exhbn., 1997 (Hon. mention, 90), Art Alliance Gallery, Lemont, Pa., 2001, 2006. Mem. ad hoc com. State College Borough Coun., 2002—04; developer, coord. Art in Prison, Centre County Prison, Bellefonte, Pa., 1990—92; developer Children's Art Exchange, Partners of Ams. with State College and Bahia, Brazil, 1992; precinct election judge Centre County Election Bd., State College, 1998—2007; charter mem., organizer Printmaker's Studio Workshop, Boalsburg, Pa., 1995—2000. Recipient 1st pl. award, Ellicotville, NY, 1991, Guest Artist award, Beret Internat. Gallery, Chgo., 1992, purchase award, Austin Peay U., 1989, Material prize, HUB Gallery, Pa. State U.; fellow in printmaking, Women's Studio Workshop, Rosendale, NY, 2005. Mem.: Art Alliance Ctrl. Pa. (life; bd. dirs., chmn. com. 1972—2007, developer, coord. workshop series 1989—90, chmn. long range planning com. 1989—95), Friends of Palmer Mus., Phi Kappa Phi. Democrat. Achievements include development of process for collagraph printing. Avocations: travel, reading, crossword puzzles. Home: 798 W Aaron Dr State College PA 16803 Studio: 798 W Aaron Dr State College PA 16803 Office Phone: 814-238-7145. Personal E-mail: whp@psu.edu.

PARSONS, ALEXANDRA CLARE, literature and language educator; b. London, Sept. 3, 1975; arrived in U.S., 1976; d. Andrew and Carol Parsons. BA in English cum laude, Wellesley Coll., 1997; MA, Columbia U., Tchrs. Coll., 2001. Permanent tchg. cert. NY, 2001. TV rsch. analyst Katz Media, Seltel, Inc., NYC, 1997—98; broadcast assoc. CBS News Prodns., NYC, 1998—99; media rels. publicity coord. ABC News, NYC, 1999; asst. kindergarten tchr. Marymount Sch., NYC, 1999—2000; English tchr. The Nightingale-Bamford Sch., NYC, 2001—. Scholar, Japan Fulbright Meml. Fund, 2005. Mem.: Nat. Coun. Tchrs. English, Assn. Tchrs. Ind. Sch., Kappa Delta Pi. Home Phone: 212-639-9446.

PARSONS, ANDREW JOHN, management consultant, corporate administrator; b. Kingston, Surrey, Eng., July 22, 1943; arrived in US, 1968; m. Carol Ann Iannucci; children: Alexandra, Katherine. BA, MA, Oxford U., 1965; MBA, Harvard U., 1970. Acct. exec. LPE/Leo Burnett, London, 1965—68; from strategic planning dir. to v.p. mktg. Prestige Group Ltd. div. Am. Home Products, NYC and London, 1970-76; v.p. mktg. Kurzweil Computer Products div. Xerox Corp., Cambridge, Mass., 1979-80; assoc. McKinsey & Co., Inc., NYC, 1976-82, prin., 1982-88, dir. consumer industries sector, mktg. ctr., sr. ptnr., 1988-2000, dir. emeritus, 2004—; chmn. Kantar Group of WPP, PLC, 2001—03. Underwriting mem Lloyds of London, 1986—; chmn. Gulliver Growth Ptnrs. LLC, 2001—; with McKinsey Adv. Coun., 2001—04; adv. bd. aQuantive, Inc., 2002—05, Quaero, Inc.; pres. Smithfield Estates LLC, 2002—; bd. dirs. A.T. Cross Co., IXI Corp., ENR Svcs., Inc., UST Inc. Contbr. articles to profl jours. Mem. adv. bd. Salvation Army, Greater NY, 1983—, chmn. adv. bd., 1993—97; gov. United Way of Tri-State, 2003—07; bd. dirs. United Way, NYC, 1988—; trustee Sarah Lawrence Coll., Bronxville, NY, 1993—2001. Scholar Baker, Harvard Bus Sch, 1970. Mem.: Shelter Harbor Golf Club, Weekapaug Golf Club, Watch Hill Yacht Club, Siwanoy Country Club. Home: 56 Hereford Rd Bronxville NY 10708-5408 also: 2 Arraquat Rd Westerly RI 02891 E-mail: andrew_parsons@mckinsey.com.

PARSONS, BOB (ROBERT R. PARSONS), entrepreneur, domain register and web host company executive; b. Balt., Md., 1950; BS in Acctg., U. Balt., 1975. CPA. Founder Parsons Technology (sold to Intuit, Inc.), 1984—96; founder, CEO The Go Daddy Group, Inc., Scottsdale, Ariz., 1997—. Rifleman USMC, 1969, Vietnam War. Decorated Combat Action Ribbon, Vietnamese Cross of Gallantry, Purple Heart Medal; recipient Ed Denison Bus. Leader of the Yr., Ariz. Governor's 2005 Innovation Celebration, 2005. Office: The Go Daddy Group Inc 14455 N Hayden Rd Ste 219 Scottsdale AZ 85260-6947 Office Phone: 480-505-8800. Office Fax: 480-505-8844. *

PARSONS, CHARLES ALLAN, JR., lawyer; b. Mpls., July 16, 1943; s. Charles Allan and Grace Adelaide (Covert) P.; m. JoAnne Ruth Russell, Oct. 16, 1965; children: Charles, Daniel, Nancy. BS, U. Minn., 1965, JD cum laude, 1972. Bar: Minn. 1972, U.S. Dist. Ct. Minn. 1972, U.S. Supreme Ct. 1995. Ptnr. Moss & Barnett, P.A., 1972—. Bd. dirs. Legal Advice Clinics Ltd., Mpls., 1975-93, Legal Aid Soc. Mpls., 1999-2004, first v.p., 2000-02, pres., 2002-04; bd. dirs. Mid-Minn. Legal Assistance, 2001-04; chair steering com. S.E. Asian Legal Assistance Project, Mpls., 1988-93. Capt. USMCR, 1968—69, Vietnam. Named Vol. Atty. of Yr., Legal Advice Clinics, Ltd., Mpls., 1990, Top 100 Super Lawyers in Minn., 2004, 05, 06, 07. Mem. ABA, Am. Coll. Real Estate Lawyers, Am. Coll. Mortgage Attys., Minn. State Bar Assn. (co-chair legis. com. real property sect. 1986-06, coun. mem. 1986-06, chair real property sect. 1993-94), Hennepin County Bar Assn. (chair real property sect. 1988-89, Van Valkenburg award for pub. svc. 2002). Roman Catholic. Avocations: reading, walking, biking, hiking. Office: Moss & Barnett PA 4800 Wells Fargo Ctr 90 S 7th Minneapolis MN 55402-4129 Office Phone: 612-877-5276. Business E-Mail: parsonsc@moss-barnett.com.

PARSONS, DANIEL LANKESTER, pharmaceutics educator; b. Biscoe, NC, Sept. 10, 1953; s. Solomon Lankester and Doris Eva (Bost) P. BS in Pharmacy, U. Ga., Athens, 1975, PhD, 1979. Asst. prof. pharmaceutics U. Ariz., Tucson, 1979-82; asst. prof. Auburn U., Ala., 1982-86, assoc. prof. Ala., 1986-91, chmn. divsn. Ala., 1990—, prof. Ala., 1991—. Cons. Wyeth-Ayerst, Phila., 1989—93, Technomics, Ardsley, NY, 1990—93, Murty Pharm., Lexington, Ky., 1996—99; presenter in field. Author (with G.V. Betageri and S.A. Jenkins): Liposome Drug Delivery Systems, 1993. Named Disting. Alumni, Sandhills Coll., 1990, Tchr. of Yr., Pharmacy Student Coun., 1987, Grad. Faculty Mem. of Yr., Grad. Student Orgn., 1994. Mem. Am. Pharm. Assn., Am. Assn. Pharm. Scientists, Phi Kappa Phi, Kappa Psi (advisor 1990-95, nat. grad. devel. com. 1993-95, nat. scholarship com. 1995-99, nat. grand coun. dep. com. 1997-05, Svc. award 1990, 95, Advisor award 1992, Prof. of Yr., 2000, Outstanding Faculty award, 2007). Achievements include research in plasma protein binding of drugs, effects of perfluorochemical blood substitutes on such binding, and development of orally disintegrating tablets. Office: Auburn U Harrison Sch Pharmacy Auburn AL 36849 Business E-Mail: parsodl@auburn.edu.

PARSONS, DONALD FRANCIS, judge; b. Phila., June 28, 1948; BSEE cum laude, Lehigh U., 1970, MA, 1972; JD, Georgetown U., 1977. Bar: Del. 1977. Law clk. to Hon. James L. Latchum U.S. Dist. Ct. Del., 1977-79; ptnr. Morris, Nichols, Arsht & Tunnell, Wilmington, Del., 1979—2003; vice chancellor Del. Ct. of Chancery, Wilmington, 2003—. Case and note editor Georgetown Law Jour., 1976-77. Mem. ABA, Am. Intellectual Property Law Assn., Intellectual Property Owners Assn., Am. Coll. Del. Bar Assn. (pres. 1999-2000), Am. Coll. Bus. Ct. Judges (dir. 2006—). Office: NCC Courthouse 500 N King St Wilmington DE 19801-3734 Office Phone: 302-255-0509. Business E-Mail: donald.parsons@state.de.us.

PARSONS, DONALD JAMES, retired bishop; b. Phila., Mar. 28, 1922; s. Earl and Helen (Drabble) P.; m. Mary Russell, Sept. 17, 1955; children—Mary, Rebecca, Bradford. BA, Temple U., 1943; MDiv, Phila. Div. Sch., 1946, ThD, 1951, DD (hon.), 1964; postgrad., U. Nottingham, Eng., 1968; DCL, Nashotah House, wIS., 1973. Ordained priest Episcopal Ch., 1946, consecrated bishop, 1973; curate Immanual Ch., Wilmington, Del., 1946-49; rector St. Peter's Ch., Smyrna, Del., 1949-50; prof. N.T. Nashotah House, 1950-73, pres., dean, 1963-73, Ramsey prof. ascetical theology, 2000—; bishop Diocese of Quincy, Ill., 1973-88. Author: A Life-time Road to God, 1966, In Time with Jesus, 1973, Holy Eucharist: Rite Two, 1976. Episcopalian. Home: 6901 N Galena Rd Apt 111 Peoria IL 61614-3158

PARSONS, DONALD OSCAR, economics professor; b. Pitts., Oct. 22, 1944; s. Leonard J. and Marion (Williams) P.; m. A. Cristina Cunha; children: Donald Williams, Christopher Milne, Madalena Cunha. AB, Duke U., 1966; PhD, U. Chgo., 1970. Asst. prof. econs. Ohio State U., Columbus, 1970-73, assoc. prof., 1973-77, prof., 1977-95, prof. emeritus, 1995—; prof. George Washington U., 1998—, dir. program labor studies, 1998—, chmn. dept., 2003—. Fulbright disting. prof. econs., Siena, Italy, 1991; vis. prof. Copenhagen Bus. Sch., 1997. Author: Poverty and the Minimum Wage, 1980; bd. editors Jour. Econs. and Bus., 1973-91; contbr. articles to Jour. Polit. Economy, Am. Econ. Rev. Rsch. fellow Nat. Bur. Econ. Rsch., 1975-76; grantee NIH. Mem. Am. Econ. Assn., Soc. Labor Economists, So. Econ. Assn. Achievements include rsch. in modelling and estimation of relationship between job turnover and training in the employment contract, measurement of impact of social insurance programs, on labor force participation and income security. Office: George Washington U Econs Dept 1922 F St NW Ste 208 Washington DC 20052-0001 Home Phone: 202-338-5599. Business E-Mail: dopars@gwu.edu.

PARSONS, DONNA LYNN, artist; b. Richmond, Va., July 16; d. Emmett Loraine and Dorothy Louise Parsons; life ptnr. William Kennedy Matthews. BA with high honors, Eckerd Coll., St. Petersburg, Fla., 1997. Owner, mng. dir. Sunny Monday Flowers, Seattle, 1983—86; owner, buyer Balinese art Zephyr, Roadtown, British Virgin Islands, 1988—92; owner, artistic dir. Maiden Studio, Maidens, Va., 2001—. Tchr. art Ettrick Elem. Sch., Va., 2007. Reproductive rights activist Feminist Womens Health Ctr.-Nat. Abortion Rights Action League, Tallahassee, 1980—81, San Diego, 1982—83; environ. activist Seattle Non-Violent Action Group, 1983—86. Recipient Irving G. Foster award for academic excellence, Eckerd Coll., 1997. Mem.: Soc. Am. Mosaic Artists. Avocations: travel, sailing, hiking, sewing, yoga. Office: Maiden Studio PO Box 712 Goochland VA 23063 Office Phone: 804-556-3799. Office Fax: 707-516-3799. E-mail: donna@maidenstudio.com.

PARSONS, EDMUND MORRIS, investment company executive; b. Houston, Oct. 19, 1936; s. Alfred Morris and Virgina (Hanna) P. AB, Harvard U., 1958; MBA, U. Pa., 1961; MS, MIT, 1970. Pres. Fredonia Enterprises, Inc., Houston, Tex., 1990—; fgn. service officer U.S. Dept. State, Washington, 1965-90; 1st sec. Am. Embassy, Mexico City, 1973-76; economist Fed. Res. Bank N.Y., NYC, 1976-77; chief food aid div. U.S. Dept. State, Washington, 1977-80, dir. office devel., 1981-82, dir. office econ. policy, 1983-84; dep. chief mission U.S. Mission to FAO, Rome, 1985-86; dir. Office Ecology and Natural Resources U.S. Dept. State, Washington, 1986-88; dir. Office of Internat. Narcotics Control Programs, 1988-89; min.-counselor for econ. affairs Am. Embassy, Mexico City, 1989-90; pres. Fredonia Enterprises, Inc., Houston, 1990—. Dep. U.S. rep. UN FAO, Rome, 1985-86; alt. U.S. rep. to environ. program U.S. Del. Nairobi, Kenya, 1987. Capt. USAF, 1962—72. Mem. Am. Fgn. Svc. Assn., Houston World Affairs Coun. Republican. Methodist. Avocation: genealogy. Home: 11823 Poplar Creek Dr Houston TX 77077-6118

PARSONS, EDWIN SPENCER, clergyman, educator; b. Brockton, Mass., Feb. 16, 1919; s. Edwin Webber and Ethel Faunce (Marsh) P.; m. Eleanor Millard, Nov. 3, 1944; children: William Spencer, Ellen, James Millard, Bradford Delano. AB, Denison U., Granville, Ohio, 1941, DD, 1967; BD, Andover Newton Theol. Sch., 1945; DD, Kalamazoo Coll., Mich, 1966; LHD, Chgo. Coll. Osteo. Medicine, 1978. Ordained to ministry Am. Baptist Ch., 1944; asst. minister First Bapt. Ch., Newton Centre, Mass., 1945-47; exec. dir. Bapt. Student Found., Inc., Cambridge, Mass., 1947-59; pastor Hyde Park Union Ch., Chgo., 1959-65; assoc. prof. ethics U. Chgo. Div. Sch., 1965-78, prof., 1978-81; dir. ministerial field edn., 1977-79; asst. to dean, 1981-88; dean Rockefeller Meml. Chapel, 1965-79; v.p., dir. New Eng. office Health Resources Ltd., Kansas City, Mo., 1979-89; ret. Cons. dept. ch. and soc. Am. Bapt. Chs. of Mass., 1979-86, also editor Mass. Bapt. News, 1983-85; chmn. strategy and action com., bd. dirs. Mass. Coun. Chs., 1983-85; adj. prof. Andover Newton Theol. Sch., 1981-85 Author: The Christian Yes or No, 1964; contbr. chapters to books. Pres. Coun. Hyde Park-Kenwood Chs. and Synagogues, 1963; chmn. Abortion Rights Assn. Ill., 1974-79; founder, chmn. Ill. Religious Coalition for Abortion Rights, 1975, Ill. Clergy Consultation Svcs. on Problem Pregnancies, Chgo. Clergy Consultation Svcs., 1969-73; bd. dirs., chmn. clergy adv. com. Planned Parenthood Assn., Chgo., 1977-79; bd. dirs. Hyde Park YMCA, Facing History and Ourselves Nat. Found., 1983-87; bd. govs. Internat. House, Chgo., 1969-79; trustee Packard Manse (Mass.), Bapt. Theol. Union, U. Chgo., 1960-70, 81-96, hon. trustee, 1996—; pres., bd. mgrs. Ministers and Missionaries Benefit Bd., 1975-81; mem. policy coun. Religious Coalition for Abortion Rights of Mass., 1980-86; sec., treas. Bolton Inst. for Sustainable Future, 1983-87; mem. gen. bd., mem. exec. com., mem. commn. on Christian unity Am. Bapt. Chs., 1963-72, 74-81; bd. dirs. Planned Parenthood League of Mass., 1984-92. Democrat. Baptist. Home: 65 Briarwood Cir Apt 410 Worcester MA 01606-1254 Office Phone: 508-856-0577.

PARSONS, ERIC E., insurance company executive; Degree, Lewis & Clark Coll., Northwestern U. V.p. Standard Ins. Co., pres. mortgage and real estate subs.; sr. v.p., CFO, then COO StanCorp Fin. Group/Standard Ins. Co., Portland, Oreg.; pres., CEO StanCorp Fin. Group, Portland, Oreg., 2003—04, chmn., pres., CEO, 2004—. Vice-chmn. Oreg. Health & Sci. Univ. Found.; chmn. OSHU Cancer Inst. Council; trustee Oreg. Zoo Found.; bd. dirs. Oreg. Bus. Council, Portland Opera, Portland Art Mus. Fellow: Life Mgmt. Inst. Office: StanCorp Fin Group Inc 1100 SW 6th Ave Portland OR 97204 *

PARSONS, ESTELLE, actress, director, theater producer; b. Lynn, Mass., Nov. 20, 1927; d. Eben and Elinor (Mattson) P.; m. Richard Gehman, Dec. 19, 1953 (div. Aug. 1958); children: Martha and Abbie (twins); m. Peter L. Zimroth, Jan. 2, 1983; 1 child, Abraham. BA in Polit. Sci., Conn. Coll. Women, 1949; student, Boston U. Law Sch., 1949-50; DFA (hon.), Conn. Coll., 2005. Stage appearances include Happy Hunting, 1957, Whoop Up, 1958, Beg, Borrow or Steal, 1960, Threepenny Opera, 1960, Mrs. Dally Has a Lover, 1962, Ready When You Are C.B, 1964, Malcolm, 1965, Seven Descents of Myrtle, 1968, And Miss Reardon Drinks a Little, 1971, Mert and Phil, 1974, The Norman Conquests, 1975-76, Ladies of the Alamo, 1977, Miss Margarida's Way, 1977-78, The Pirates of Penzance, 1981, The Shadow Box, 1994; adapted, dir., performer Orgasmo Adulto Escapes from the Zoo, 1983, The Unguided Missile, Baba Goya, 1989, Shimada, 1992, Grace & Glorie, 1996, The Last of the Thorntons, 2000-01, Morning's At Seven, 2002, The Bay at Nice, 2004, Harold & Maude, 2005; film appearances include Bonnie and Clyde, 1966 (Acad. award), Rachel, Rachel, 1967, I Never Sang for My Father, 1969, Dick Tracy, 1990, Boys On The Side, 1995, Looking for Richard, 1996, That Darn Cat, 1997; TV appearances include Roseanne, 1990—, NBC Today, 1951-56; artistic dir. NY Shakespeare Festival Players, 1986, Actors' Studio, 1997-2003; dir. (Broadway play) Salome, the Reading, 2003. Recipient Theatre World award, 1962-63, Obie award, 1964, Motion Picture Acad. Arts and Scis. award, 1967, Medal of Honor, Conn. Coll., 1969; named to Theatre Hall of Fame, 2004. Home: 924 West End Ave Apt T5 New York NY 10025-3543
It's in attempting all, that one succeeds.

PARSONS, GARY M., broadcast executive; m. Kathy. B in Engring., Clemson U.; MBA, U. So. Carolina, 1978. With Bellsouth; prin. Telecom USA, 1984—90; with MCI Comm. Corp., 1990—96, CEO, MCImetro Inc., exec. v.p. telecommunications; joined Motient Corp., 1996, CEO, pres., chmn., 1998—2002; chmn., CEO Am. Mobile Satellite Ventures LP; CEO XM Satellite Radio, chmn., 1997—. Bd. dirs. Sorrento Networks Corp. Office: XM Satellite Radio 1500 Eckington Pl NE Washington DC 20002 Office Phone: 202-380-4000. Office Fax: 202-380-4500.

PARSONS, IRENE ADELAIDE, management consultant; b. North Wilkesboro, NC; d. Everett T. and Martha (Minton) P. BS in Bus. Edn. and Adminstrn., U. N.C., 1941, LLD (hon.), 1967; MS in Pub. Adminstrn., George Washington U., 1965. Tchr. Roanoake Rapids (N.C.) High Sch., 1941-42; rep. U.S. Civil Svc. Commn., 1942-43; with VA, 1946-74, asst. adminstr. vets. affairs, dir. personnel, dir. equal employment opportunity, 1965-74; mgmt. cons., 1974—. Exec. com. Pres.'s Study Group Careers for Women. Served to lt. USCGR, 1943-46. Recipient Fed. Woman's Outstanding Achievement award, 1966, Silver Helmet award Amvets, 1971, Career Svc. award Nat. Civil Svc. League, 1972, Disting. Alumni Achievement award George Washington U., 1973; named to Brevard Coll. Hall of Fame, 1984 Mem. Assn. Fed. Woman's Award Recipients (chmn. 1972-76) Address: PO Box 2046 North Wilkesboro NC 28659-2046

PARSONS, JEFFREY ROBINSON, anthropologist, educator; b. Washington, Oct. 9, 1939; s. Merton Stanley and Elisabeth (Oldenburg) P.; m. Mary Thomson Hrones, Apr. 27, 1968; 1 child, Apphia Hrones. BS, Pa. State U., 1961; PhD, U. Mich., 1966. Asst. prof. anthropology U. Mich., Ann Arbor, 1966-71, assoc. prof., 1971-76, prof., 1976—2006, dir. mus. anthropology, 1983-86, emeritus prof., 2006—. Vis. prof. Universidad Nacional Autonoma de Mexico, 1987; vis. prof. Universidad Buenos Aires, 1994, Univ. Nac de Catamarca, Argentina, 1996, Univ. Nac de Tucuman, Argentina, 1996, Univ. Mayor de San Andres, Bolivia, 1999. Author: Prehistoric Settlement Patterns in the Texcoco Region, Mexico, 1971; (with William T. Sanders and Robert Santley) The Basin of Mexico: The Cultural Ecology of a Civilization, 1979; (with E. Brumfiel) Prehispanic Settlement Patterns in the Southern Valley of Mexico, 1982; (with M. Parsons) Chinampa Agriculture and Aztec Urbanization in the Valley of Mexico, 1985; (with Mary H. Parsons) Maguey Utilization in Highland Central Mexico, 1990; The Production and Consumption of Salt During Postclassic Times in the Valley of Mexico, 1994; (with E. Brumfiel and M. Hodge) The Developmental Implications of Earlier Dates for Early Aztec in the Basin of Mexico, 1996; (with C. Hastings and R. Matos) Rebuilding the State in Highland Peru, 1997; A Regional Perspective on Inca Impact in the Sierra Central, Peru, 1998; (with C. Hastings and R. Matos) Prehispanic Settlement Patterns in the Upper Mantaro-Tarma Drainage, Peru, 2000; The Last Saltmakers of Nexquipayac, Mexico, 2001; (with Luis Morett) Recursos aquaticos en la subsistancia Azteca; 2004, The Last Pescadores of Chimalhuacan, Mexico, 2006. Rsch. grantee NSF, 1967, 70, 72-73, 75-76, 81, Nat. Geog. Soc., 1984, 86, 88, 2003. Mem. Am. Anthrop. Assn. (Alfred V. Kidder award 1998), Soc. Am. Archaeology, AAAS, Inst. Andean Rsch., Inst. Andean Studies, Sociedad Mexicana de Antropologia, Sociedad Argentina de Antropologia. Office: Museum of Anthropology U Mich Ann Arbor MI 48109 Business E-Mail: jpar@umich.edu.

PARSONS, LEONARD JON, marketing educator, consultant; b. Pitts., Sept. 1, 1942; s. Leonard J. and Marion Jane (Williams) P.; m. Julia Grieve, Jan. 23, 1965; children: Lorelei, Leonard Jon Jr. BSChemE, MIT, 1964; MS in Indsl. Adminstrn., Purdue U., 1965, PhD in Indsl. Adminstrn., 1968. Asst. prof. Ind. U., Bloomington, 1968-70; assoc. prof. Claremont (Calif.) Grad. Sch., 1970-77; prof. marketing Ga. Inst. Tech., 1977—. Vis. scholar MIT, Cambridge, fall 1973; Fulbright-Hays sr. scholar Cath. U. Leuven, Belgium, spring 1977; vis. prof. INSEAD, France, fall 1984, Norwegian Sch. Mktg., Oslo, fall 1989, UCLA, spring 1990, Advt. Edn. Found., Anheuser Busch, St. Louis, summer 1993, CREER/FUCAM, Belgium, Fall 1995; mem. rsch. and test devel. com. Grad. Mgmt. Admissions Coun., 1988-90. Author: Using Microcomputers in Marketing, 1986; co-author: Marketing Management, 7th edit., 2000, Market Response Models, 2d edit., 2001, others; edtl. bd. Jour. Mktg. Rsch., 1970-80, 83-85, Jour. Bus. Rsch., 1973-79, Jour. Mktg., 1978-80; assoc. editor: Decision Scis., 1976-79; mktg. dept. editor: Mgmt. Sci., 1980-82; contbr. numerous chpts. to books, articles to profl. jours. Recipient first prize rsch. design contest Am. Mktg. Assn., 1971-72. Mem. Am. Mktg. Assn. (mem. adv. bd. mktg. rsch. spl. interest group 1998), Am. Statis. Assn. (chmn. stats. in mktg. sect. 1995), European Mktg. Acad. (mem. exec. com. 1981-84), Theta Delta Chi, Beta Gamma Sigma, Phi Kappa Phi. Office: Ga Inst Tech Coll Mgmt Atlanta GA 30308-0520 Office Phone: 404-894-4381. Business E-Mail: len.parsons@mgt.gatech.edu.

PARSONS, RICHARD DEAN, communications executive; b. NYC, Apr. 4, 1948; s. Lorenzo Locklair and Isabelle (Judd) Parsons; m. Laura Ann Bush, Aug. 30, 1968; children: Gregory, Leslie, Rebecca. Student, U. Hawaii, 1968; JD, U. Ala. Law Sch., 1971; LLD (hon.), Adelphi U., 1990, Medgar Evers Coll., NYC, 1991; LHD (hon.), U. Hawaii, 2003. Bar: NY 1972. Asst. counsel to gov. State of NY, Albany, 1971-73, 1st asst. counsel to gov., 1973-74; dep. counsel to v.p. Office of V.P., Washington, 1975; gen. counsel, assoc. dir. domestic coun. White House, Washington, 1975-77; ptnr. Patterson, Belknap, Webb & Tyler, NYC, 1979—88; pres., COO Dime Savs. Bank NY, NYC, 1988-90, chmn., CEO, 1990-94; dir. Time Warner, NYC, 1991—; pres. Time Warner Inc., NYC, 1995—99; co-COO AOL Time Warner, Inc., NYC, 1999—2002; CEO Time Warner Inc., NYC, 2002—, chmn., 2003—. Bd. dirs. Citigroup, Estee Lauder, Fed. Nat. Mortgage Assn., Philip Morris Co.; trustee, Rockefeller Bros. Fund. Mem. Presdl. Drug Task Force; mayor-elect transition coun., head, 1993; chmn. Wildcat Svc. Orgn., NYC Econ. Devel. Corp.; bd. dir. NY Zool. Soc., Am. TV & Comm. Inc., Colonial Williamsburg Found., Com. to Encourage Corp. Philanthropy, Mus. Modern Art; trustee Howard U., Met. Mus. Art. Named one of Most Influential Black Americans, Ebony mag., 2006; recipient Disting. Alumnus award, U. Hawaii, 2003. Apollo Theatre Found. (chmn.). Office: Time Warner Inc 75 Rockefeller Plz New York NY 10019-6990 *

PARSONS, RICHARD HUGO, lawyer; b. Okla., June 9, 1936; s. Alfred Richard and Veronica Cecilia (Hugo) Parsons; m. Catherine Ann Logan; children: Karen Ann (Parsons) Voss, Anne Logan (Parsons) Muren, Alfred Richard Parsons II. BA, Bradley U., Peoria, Ill., 1958; JD, Wash. & Lee, Lexington, Va., 1961; Cert., Harvard Law Sch. Bar: Ill., DC. Asst. sec. Chgo. Title and Trust, 1961—68; pvt. practice Peoria, Ill., 1968—95; fed. pub. defender Ctrl. Dist. of Ill., Peoria, 1995—. Commr./trial judge Ill. Ct. of Claims, Springfield, Ill., 1975—95; pres. Ill. Assn. of Criminal Def. Lawyers, 1994, Clarence Darrow Inn of the Am. Inns of Ct., Peoria, Ill.; chmn. ABA Criminal Justice Sect. Amicus Curiae Com., 2000—03; dir. Peoria County Bar Assn., Peoria, Ill. Author: Possible Issues for Review in Criminal Appeals, 2d edit., Warrants and Motions to Suppress: Inst. CLE Fed. Criminal Practice; editor: (newsletter) The Back Bencher. Founder, pres., grand marshall City of Peoria St. Patrick's Day Parade, Peoria, Ill., 1981; screening com. mem. Ill. Capital Litigation Trial Bar, 2004—06; del. Dem. Nat. Conv., 1972; pres. Ancient Order of Hibernians, Peoria, Ill., 1981; precinct committeeman Dem. Precinct Committeeman, Peoria, Ill.; lector Sacred Heart Ch., Peoria. Mem.: Ill. Assn. Criminal Def. Lawyers (pres. 1994—95, Lawyer of the Yr. 2000), Nat. Assn. Criminal Def. Lawyers (life), KC (3d degree knight), Union League Club Chgo., Mt. Hawley Country Club, Sigma Phi Epsilon. Democrat. Avocations: tennis, golf, literature, crossword puzzles. Office: Federal Public Defender 401 Main Street - Suite 1500 Peoria IL 61602 E-mail: richard_parsons@fd.org.

PARSONS, RICHARD WALTER, construction executive; b. Washington, Sept. 24, 1943; s. William Walter and Lois Shattuck Parsons; children from previous marriage: Jemma Maguire, Brewster William. BBA, Bucknell U., Lewisburg, Pa., 1966; MA in Planning, U. So. Calif., LA, 1973, MPA, 1973. Environ. planning coord. City of Redondo Beach, Calif., 1972—74, planning assoc., 1974—75, asst. planning dir., 1975—76, harbor dir., 1976—82; gen. mgr. Ventura Port Dist., Calif., 1982—96; owner RWP Dredging Mgmt., Ojai, Calif., 1996—. Comdr. USCG, 1967—87. Home and Office: 2271 Los Encinas Rd Ojai CA 93023

PARSONS, STUART W., librarian; m. Kathy Parsons; children: David, Geoffrey, Suzy, Timmy. Student, Bridgewater State Coll., Mass. Naturalist Green Briar Nature Ctr., Sandwich, Mass.; children's libr. Sandwich Pub. Libr. Mem. exec. bd. Sandwich Cmty. Partnership Coun. Recipient NY Times Libr. award, 2006. Mem.: Wildlands Trust Southeastern Mass. Office: Sandwich Pub Libr 142 Main St Sandwich MA 02563 Office Phone: 508-888-0625. Office Fax: 508-833-1076.

PARSONS, TERENCE DWIGHT, linguist, educator; b. 1939; BS in Physics, Univ. Rochester; PhD, Stanford Univ., 1966. Faculty Univ. Pitts., Univ. Calif., Berkeley, Univ. Ill-Chgo. Cir., Univ. Mass., Amherst; prof. philosophy, dean of humanities Univ. Calif., Irvine; disting. prof. philosophy, linguistics UCLA. Fellow: Am. Acad. Arts & Scis. Office: Dept Philosophy UCLA Los Angeles CA 90095-1451 Office Phone: 310-825-4641. Business E-Mail: tparsons@ucla.edu. *

PARSONS, VINSON ADAIR, retired computer company executive; b. Frankfort, Ky., Oct. 22, 1932; s. Richard Adair and Nina (Mefford) P.; m. Elizabeth Ann Peltier, June 2, 1956. AS, Mitchell Coll., 1959; BS, U. Conn., 1960; Advanced Mgmt. Program cert., Harvard U., 1985. Auditor, Price Waterhouse & Co. (C.P.A.s), Hartford, Conn., 1960-65; controller Pervel Industries Inc., Plainfield, Conn., 1965-70; v.p., controller Akzo Am. Inc., Asheville, NC, 1970-71, 73-83, v.p., chief fin. officer, 1983-86, System Software Assocs. Inc., Chgo., 1986-89, also bd. dirs.; ret., 1990. Bd. dirs. Am. Tape Co., BRIntec Co., Control Tech. Corp. Elected commr. Town of Weaverville Bd. Commrs., 1994-2000. With USN, 1953-57. Mem. Am. Mgmt. Assn., Fin. Execs. Inst., Inst. Mgmt. Accts. (pres. local chpt. 1969-70) Clubs: Asheville Country; University (N.Y.C.); Reems Creek Golf. Personal E-mail: ssn571@charter.net.

PARSONS, WILLIAM JONATHAN, cardiologist; b. Apr. 3, 1955; married; 3 children. BA, Dartmouth Coll., 1977, MD, 1980. Diplomate Am. Bd. Internal Medicine, Am. Bd. Cardiovascular Diseases, Am. Bd. Nuclear Cardiology, Nat. Bd. Echocardiography. Resident in internal medicine Strong Meml. Hosp. U. Rochester (N.Y.), 1983-85; cardiology fellow Duke U. Med. Ctr., Durham, 1985-88, asst. prof., 1988-91; asst. prof. medicine Southwestern Med. Ctr. U. Tex., Dallas, 1991-93; attending cardiologist Baylor U. Med. Ctr., Dallas, 1993—2001, Rex Hosp., Raleigh, NC, 2001—. Contbr. articles to profl. jours. Gen. med. officer USPHS-IHS, 1981-83. Fellow Am. Coll. Physicians, Am. Coll. Cardiology, Am. Soc. Echocardiography. Office: Carolina Cardiology Cons 3324 Six Forks Rd Raleigh NC 27609 Home Phone: 919-845-6743; Office Phone: 919-781-7772. Personal E-mail: wjpdnp@aol.com.

PART, HOWARD MITCHELL, dean; b. NYC, Apr. 26, 1949; m. Kristine Kunesh-Part. BS, Ohio U.; MD, Ohio State U., 1982. Cert. Am. Bd. Internal Medicine. Intern Ohio State U. Hospitals, Columbus, 1982—83, resident in internal medicine, 1983—85; voluntary faculty mem. Wright State U. Sch. Medicine, Dayton, Ohio, 1986—88, mem. faculty, 1988—, chief of gen. medicine consult svc., dir. internal medicine residency program Dayton VA Med. Ctr., assoc. dean faculty and clin. affairs, 1995—98, acting dean, 1998—99, dean, 1999—. Recipient Dean's Award for Excellence in Med. Edn., Wright State U. Sch. Medicine, 1992, Disting. Teaching award, 1996, Master Teacher of Medicine award, Am. Coll. of Physicians, 2000. Fellow: Am. Coll. Physicians (Gov.'s Award - Ohio Chpt.); mem.: Am. Bd. of Internal Medicine. Office: 115 Med Scis Bldg Wright State U 3640 Colonel Glenn Hwy Dayton OH 45435-0001 Office Phone: 937-775-3010. Office Fax: 937-775-2211.

PARTAIN, CLARENCE LEON, radiologist, nuclear medicine physician, educator, health facility administrator; b. Memphis, July 12, 1940; s. Archie Leon and Vergie (Young) P.; m. Judith Stafford, Jan., 1964; children: David Blane, Teri Ellyn, Amy Leigh. BSNE, U. Tenn., 1963; MSNE, Purdue U., 1965, PhD in Nuc. Engring., 1967; MD, Washington U., St. Louis, 1975. Diplomate Am. Bd. Nuc. Medicine, Am. Bd. Radiology; registered profl. engr., Mo. Asst. prof. nuc. engring. U. Mo.-Columbia, 1968-71, assoc. prof., 1971-75; resident NC Meml. Hosp., Chapel Hill, 1975-79; assoc. prof. radiology U. NC-Chapel Hill, 1978-79; assoc. prof. Vanderbilt U., Nashville, 1980-85, prof. radiology and biomed. engring., 1985—, vice chmn. radiology, 1989-92, dir. nuc. medicine, 1981-85, dir. magnetic resonance imaging, 1983-92, chmn. radiology, radiologist in chief, 1992-2000, dir. Ctr. for Imaging Rsch., 2000—; cons. NIH, Bethesda, Md., 1980—; Carol D. and Henry P. Pendegrass prof. radiology and radiol. scis. Vanderbilt U., 1997—. Author: Nuclear Magnetic Resonance (NMR) Imaging, 1983, NMR Imaging: Clinical Utility and Correlation, 1984, Thyroid and Parathyroid Imaging, 1986, Magnetic Resonance Imaging, 2d edit., 1988, Correlative Image: Nuclear Medicine, Magnetic Resonance, Computer Tomography, Ultrasound, 1988; editl. bd. Acad. Radiology, Magnetic Resonance Imaging, Jour. Magnetic Resonance Imaging, Jour. Nuclear Medicine; editor-in-chief Jour. of Magnetic Resonance Imaging. Scientific adv. coun. Whitaker Found. AEC Spl. fellow, 1964-66; grantee Nat. Inst. Neurosci., Communicative Diseases and Stroke, 1977-78 Fellow Am. Coll. Nuc. Physicians, Am. Coll. Radiology, Soc. Magnetic Resonance Imaging (bd. dirs.), Internat. Soc. of Magnetic Resonance in Medicine, Accreditation Coun. for Grad. Med. Edn., Residency Rev. Com. Nuc. Medicine; mem. AMA, IEEE, Radiol. Soc. N.Am. (chair rsch. devel. com., trustees, R&E Found.), Assn. Univ. Radiologists (exec. com.), Radiology Rsch. Alliance (pres.), Soc. Nuc. Medicine (trustee, Benedict Casson lectr. 1981), Am. Roentgen Ray Soc. (exec. coun.), Soc. Magnetic Resonance in Medicine (trustee), Internat. Soc. Magnetic Resonance in Medicine (governance coun., bd. dirs.), Soc. Chmn. Acad. Radiology Depts. (bd. dirs.), Am. Bd. Radiology (examiner in nuc. medicine, Disting. Svc. award), Sigma Phi Epsilon. Baptist. Home: 5485 Pinewood Rd Franklin TN 37064-9235 Office: Vanderbilt U Med Ctr Dept Radiology RM RR-1223 MCN Nashville TN 37232-0001

PARTAN, DANIEL GORDON, lawyer, educator; s. Toivo Antero and Lempi Sivia (Adamson) P.; m. Doris Liepmann, June 8, 1957; children: Andrew Stewart, Matthew Alexander, Sarah Ruth, Iliana Maria, Juan Carlos. AB, Cornell U., 1955; LLB, Harvard U., 1958, LLM, 1961. Bar: Mass. 1959. Rsch. assoc. Harvard Law Sch., 1961, Rule of Law Ctr., Duke U. Law Sch., 1962-65; assoc. prof. U. N.D., 1964-65; assoc. prof. law Boston U., 1965-68, prof., 1968—, prof. London Inst., 2003, 2006. NAFTA dispute settlement roster and binat. dispute panel U.S.-Can. Free Trade Agreement; dispute settlement panel roster World Trade Orgn.; sr. specialist roster U.S. Fulbright Commn.; cons. Dept. State, UN Devel. Program, Am. Acad. Arts and Sci.; pres., chmn. Bd. dirs. UN Assn. Greater Boston, 1969-71, 76-77; chmn. Brookline Selectmen's Com. on Harvard Energy Plant, 1976—; vis. scholar Harvard Law Sch., 1977-78; vis. fellow Cambridge (Eng.) U., 1972; vis. prof. Peking U., Beijing, 2000, 05; Fulbright prof. Tsinghua U. Law Sch., Beijing, 2003-04; vis. prof. Xiamen U., China, 2006, 07. Author: Population in the United Nations System, 1973, Documentary Study of the Politicization of UNESCO, 2 vols., 1975, The International Law Process, 1992, Documents Supplement to the International Law Process, 1999; co-author: Legal Problems of International Administration, 1968, The United States and the International Labor Organization, 1980; co-editor: Corporate Disclosure of Environmental Risks: U.S. and European Law, 1990; contbr. chpts. to books, articles to profl. jours. Past elected mem. town meeting, Brookline, Mass.; appointed chair Brookline Selectmen's Harvard Energy Plant Com. Mem. ABA (amicus brief com. sect. internat. law and practice), Bretton Woods Com., Commn. to Study the Orgn. Peace, Am. Law Inst., Acad. Coun. UN System, Am. Soc. Internat. Law, Internat. Law Assn., European Communities Studies Assn., UN Assn., Coalition for a Strong UN, Trade Law Consultative Group, Boston Area Tchrs. Internat. Law (convenor). Office: 765 Commonwealth Ave Boston MA 02215-1401 Business E-Mail: partan@bu.edu.

PARTANEN, CARL RICHARD, biology professor; b. Portland, Oreg., Nov. 23, 1921; s. Emil and Ellen (Engstrom) P.; m. Jane Nelson, June 24, 1961; children: Karen, Kirsten, Richard (dec.) Student, Multnomah Jr. Coll., 1946-48; BA, Lewis and Clark Coll., 1950; MA, Harvard, 1951, PhD, 1954. Am. Cancer Soc. postdoctoral research fellow Columbia, 1954-55, Harvard, 1955-57; research asso. Childrens Cancer Research Found., Boston, 1957-61; asso. prof. biology U. Pitts., 1961-64, prof. biology, 1964-86, chmn. biology, 1964-70, prof. emeritus, 1987—; Research fellow U. Edinburgh, Scotland, 1971-72, U. Nottingham, Eng., 1978-79. Contbr. articles to profl. jours. Served with AUS, 1942-45, ETO. Recipient Distinguished Achievement award Lewis and Clark Coll., 1968 Mem. AAAS, Bot. Soc. Am., Soc. for Devel. Biology, Soc. for In Vitro Biology. Home: 112 Farragut St Pittsburgh PA 15206-1746 Office: U Pitts Dept Biol Scis Pittsburgh PA 15260 Personal E-mail: cpartanen@comcast.net.

PARTH, FRANK R., consulting company executive, educator; b. Eichendorf, Germany, Aug. 26, 1949; came to US, 1952. s. Frank and Erna (Framelsberger) P.; m. Jane Hoppe, Dec. 27, 1974 (div. Jan. 1985); children: Katherine, Frank. BS in Physics, Creighton U., 1972; MS in Physics, U. Wyo., 1978; MS in Sys. Mgmt., U. So. Calif., LA, 1986; MBA, Peter Drucker Inst., 2000. Design engr. Tex. Instruments, Dallas, 1978-81; asst. tech. dir. Martin-Marietta Space Sys., Long Beach, Calif., 1981-92; pres. InterVolve Mgmt. Sys., Mission Viejo, Calif., 1993-95; dir. sys. engring. Experian, Orange, Calif., 1995-97; mgr. Deloitte & Touche, Santa Ana, Calif., 1997-98; practice mgr. Keane, Inc., Long Beach, 1998-99; v.p. devel. Overstock Market (e-commerce), 2000—01; pres. Project Auditors, LLC, 2001—. Faculty U. So. Calif. Inst. Safety and Sys. Mgmt., LA, 1993-97, U. Calif. Irvine, 1996—, Claremont Grad. U., 2000—; vis. prof. Am. U. Sharjah, United Arab Emirates; spkr. in field. Author: Introduction to IT Project Management, 2006; contbr. articles to profl. jours. Bd. dirs. Orange County Search and Rescue, Calif., 1989-2002, OC Project Mgmt. Inst., 1996-2004 v.p. membership, 2003, v.p. profl. devel., 2004; constitutional rev. officer Mensa, 1993—. Mem. Internat. Coun. Sys. Engring., Mensa Internat. (pres. Orange County chpt. 1993), Project Mgmt. Inst. (Spkr.'s award 1998). Avocations: sailing, skiing, wine. Home: 21901 Palanca Mission Viejo CA 92692-1012 Office: PO Box 80688 Rancho Santa Margarita CA 92688-0688 Home Phone: 949-452-0579; Office Phone: 800-545-1340. Business E-Mail: Fparth@projectauditors.com.

PARTHASARATHY, VINOD, manufacturing engineer, consultant; b. Bombay, Aug. 17, 1979; arrived in U.S., 2001; s. Gopalan and Vedha Parthasarathy. B in Engring. (hon.), U. E. London, 2000; MBA, Harvard U., 2005. Project engr. Ford Motor Co., London, 1999, Dormer Tools, Sheffield, England, 1999—2001; product engr. Freudenberg-Nok, Laconia, NH, 2001—04, sys. mgr., 2005—. Mng. ptnr. Digitized Artisan, Perth, Australia, 2005—. Contbr. articles to profl. jours. Vol. Red Cross, London, 1997—2000, Rep. Party, Concord, 2004—. Recipient Six Sigma Black Belt award, Freudenberg-Nok, 2005. Mem.: IEEE (chartered). Republican. Hinduism. Achievements include patents for drill detection transducer. Avocations: skydiving, writing, travel, surfing. Office: Freudenberg-Nok 51 Growth Rd Laconia NH 03246 Office Phone: 603-527-6431. E-mail: iamvinny@hotmail.com.

PARTHEMORE, JACQUELINE GAIL, internist, educator, hospital administrator; b. Harrisburg, Pa., Dec. 21, 1940; d. Philip Mark and Emily (Buvit) Parthemore; m. Alan Morton Blank, Jan. 7, 1967; children: Stephen Eliot, Laura Elise. BA, Wellesley Coll., 1962; MD, Cornell U., 1966. Diplomate Am. Bd. Internal Medicine. Resident in internal medicine N.Y. Hosp./Cornell U., 1966-69; fellow in endocrinology Scripps Clinic and Rsch. Found., La Jolla, Calif., 1969-72; rsch. ednl. assoc. VA Hosp., San Diego, 1974-78; staff physician VA San Diego Health Care Sys., 1978-79, asst. chief, med. svc., 1979-83, acting chief, med. svc., 1980-81, chief of staff, 1984—; asst. prof. medicine U. Calif. Sch. Medicine, San Diego, 1974-80, assoc. prof. medicine, 1980-85, prof. medicine, assoc. dean, 1985—. Mem. nat. rsch. resources coun. NIH, Bethesda, Md., 1990—94; mem. VHA Performance Measures Work Group, 2006—, Blue Ribbon Panel Acad. Affiliations, 2007—. Contbr. chapters to books, articles to profl. jours. Mem. adv. bd. San Diego Opera, 1993—2007; mem. Roundtable and Channel 10 Focus Group, San Diego Millennium Project, 1999; v.p. bd. dirs. San Diego Vets. Med. Rsch. Found., 1989—. Recipient Bullock's 1st Annual Portfolio award, 1985, San Diego Pres.'s Coun. Woman of Yr. award, 1985, YWCA Tribute to Women in Industry award, 1987, San Diego Women Who Mean Bus. award, 1999, Excellence in Leadership award Am. Hosp. Assn., 2002, Local Legend award AMWA/Nat. Libr. Medicine, 2005. Fellow ACP (gov. 2005-, mem. edn. com. 2006-), Am. Assn. Clin. Endocrinologists; mem. Endocrine Soc., Nat. Assn. VA Chiefs Staff/Physician Execs. (pres. 1989-91), Assn. Am. Med. Colls. (mem. steering group chief med. officers, 2005—), Wellesley Coll. Alumnae Assn. (1st v.p. 1992-95), San Diego Wellesley Club (pres. 1997-99), San Diego Herb Soc. (co-pres. 2003-04), Nat. Assn. VA Rsch. and Edn. (found. bd., 2003—). Avocations: gardening, reading, sailing, cooking, travel. Office: VA San Diego Healthcare Sys 3350 La Jolla Village Dr San Diego CA 92161-0002 Home Phone: 858-756-2917; Office Phone: 858-552-7419. Business E-Mail: jparthemore@ucsd.edu.

PARTIE, DAVID JOHN, language educator; b. Detroit, Apr. 14, 1944; s. William Richey and Arlene Esther Partie; m. Janice Sue Stanage, June 14, 1975; 1 child, Elizabeth Catherine. BA, U. of Redlands, 1966; postgrad., U. Heidelberg, Germany, 1967—68; MA, UCLA, 1971; MDiv, Talbot Theol. Sem., 1978; MA, U. of So. Calif., 1982, PhD, 1988. C.C. Instr. Credential in German Calif. Cmty. Colleges, 1974, Cert. of Completion, World Travel Counselor Tng. Program Automobile Club of So. Calif., 1981, Apollo Travel Services Tng. Cert. United Airlines, 1982, Qualification Cert. as an ESL Tchr. for Speakers of Japanese Japanese Cross Cultural Ctr./ LA, Calif., 1984, sys. direct access tng. program cert. Ea. Airlines, 88. Tchg. asst. in German UCLA, 1968—70; instr. in German, French, Spanish and English LA Bapt. Coll., Newhall, Calif., 1969—73; instr. in German Santa Monica City Coll., 1974—77; instr. in German and French Biola Coll., La Mirada, Calif., 1974—78; instr. in French and Spanish Baymonte H.S., Santa Cruz, Calif., 1978—79; tchg. asst. in freshman writing U. of So. Calif., 1979—82; tour counselor/world travel agt. Automobile Club of So. Calif., LA, 1979—82; account exec. Agnew Tech-Tran, Woodland Hills, Calif., 1982—84; instr. in ESL and German Berlitz Sch. of Langs., Pasadena, 1984—85; prof. English and modern langs. Liberty U., Lynchburg, Va., 1985—. Chmn. dept. of modern langs. Liberty U., 1985—93, co-chair Writer's Conf., 1999, mem., adv. bd. for the ctr. for global ministries, 2001—, moderator of the faculty senate, 2002—03, chair, faculty senate exec. com., poetry editor Lamplight, 2003—, mem. pres.' com. on faculty devel. and welfare, 2004—, mem. modern langs. com. dept. English, 2004—; adj. prof. English Ctrl. Va. CC, Lynchburg, 1997—; presenter in field. Author: The Poet's Domain; actor: (films) The Gathering, 1998, Pilgrim's Progress, 2006, The Great Sacrifice of Jefferson Davis, 2007; (plays) U. Redlands, 1963—66, Cmty. Theater, Coll. Theater (outstanding contbn. to theater at Sweet Briar Coll., 1999, 2000), Morgan Theatre, 1967, Biola Coll., 1976, U. So. Calif., 1980, Lynchburg Fine Arts Ctr., 1990—2004, Sweet Briar Coll., 1999—2000; guest poet: TV series All the Arts, 1996, Joe Campbell Show, 1991, Riverviews, 2006, Focus on the Phrase, 2006, radio guest author: Literary Pages of the Air, 1986; contbr. poems to mags. and jours. (Hon. Mention, Poet's Choice Award, vol. 13 of The Poet's Domain, 1997), acad. papers presented at numerous conf. Roving reader Lynchburg Pub. Schools, 1995—96; tchr. of creative writing Lynchburg Parks and Recreation Dept., 1995—95; forensics judge Va. Orgn. of German Students, Lynchburg, 1997—97; crisis counselor Centinella Valley Hotline, 1977—78, Suicide Prevention Ctr., LA, 1985, Life Aid, 1988—89; mem. com. readers judging poems Maier Mus. of Art, 2005; mem. Lynchburg Rep. City Com., Lynchburg, 1988—2000; del. to state polit. conventions Rep. Party, Richmond, Va., 1988—96; legis. liaison to Va. state del. Joyce Crouch Va. Soc. for Human Life, Lynchburg, 1991—92; mem., mission selection com. Heritage Bapt. Ch., Lynchburg, 1991—98, 2002—04; student poetry contest judge Poetry Soc. of Va., Williamsburg, 1996—96. Recipient William Ward Bass award, Talbot Theol. Seminary, 1978, First Pl. In The Serious Poem Category, Lynchburg Poetry Festival, 1987, 1991, 1994, 2000, Karma Deane Ogden Prize for Poetry, Poetry Soc. of Va., 1991, Brodie Herndon Meml. Prize for Poetry, 1997, Carleton Drewry Meml. Prize for Poetry, 2000; Walter Loewy fellow for Grad. Study Abroad, U. of Heidelberg, 1967-68, Chancellor's Tchg. fellow, UCLA, 1966—70. Mem.: Poetry Soc. of Va. (assoc.; regional v.p. 2002—06), Assn. for the Interdisciplinary Study of the Arts (assoc.), F. Scott Fitzgerald Soc. (assoc.), MLA (assoc.), Alpha Mu Gamma (life). Avocations: travel, athletics, church work, drama, book collecting. Office: Liberty U 1971 University Blvd Lynchburg VA 24502-2269 Office Phone: 434-582-2439. Business E-Mail: djpartie@liberty.edu.

PARTLETT, DAVID F., dean, law educator; b. 1947; LLB, Sydney U., 1970; LLM, Mich. U., 1972-74; SJD, U. Va., 1980. Bar: New South Wales 1971, Australian Cap. Terr. 1978. Vis. asst. prof. U. Ala., 1972-73; legis. officer Australia Atty. Gen.'s Office, 1974—75; dir, rsch. Australian Law Reform Commn., 1975—78; lectr. Australian Nat. U., 1978-80, sr. lectr., 1980-87, assoc. dean, 1982—85; vis. prof. Vanderbilt U., Nashville, 1987-88, prof. law, 1988-2000, acting dean, 1996-97; v.p., dean, prof. Sch. Law Washington & Lee U., Lexington, Va., 2000—06; dean Emory U. Sch. Law, Atlanta, 2006—. Sparkman Dist. vis. prof. Ala. U., 1986-87. Office: Emory University School of Law G546 Gambrell Hall 1301 Clifton Rd Atlanta GA 30322 Business E-Mail: david.partlett@law.emory.edu. *

PARTNOY, RONALD ALLEN, lawyer; b. Norwalk, Conn., Dec. 23, 1933; s. Maurice and Ethel Marguerite (Roselle) P.; m. Diane Catherine Keenan, Sept. 18, 1965. BA, Yale U., 1956; LL.B., Harvard U., 1961; LL.M., Boston U., 1965. Bar: Mass. 1962, Conn. 1966. Atty. Liberty Mut. Ins. Co., Boston, 1961-65; assoc. counsel Remington Arms Co., Bridgeport, Conn., 1965-70, gen. counsel, 1970-88, sec., 1983-93; sr. counsel E.I. du Pont de Nemours & Co., Wilmington, Del., 1985-95. Served to capt. USNR, 1956-85. Mem.: ABA, Naval Res. Assn. (nat. exec. com. 1981—85, 1997—99, nat. v.p. 1997—99, nat. exec. com. 2001—03, nat. v.p. 2001—03, 3d dist. pres.), U.S. Navy League (pres. Bridgeport coun. 1975—77, Conn. pres. 1977—80, v.p. Empire region 1980—85, nat. dir.), Am. Judicature Soc., Sporting Arms and Ammunition Mfrs. Inst. (chmn. legis. and legal affairs com. 1971—86), Assn. of Yale Alumni (del. 1997—2000), Yale Club of N.Y.C., Harvard Club of Phila., Harvard Club of Boston, Chancery Club. Home: 24 Cove View Rd New London CT 06320-3006

PARTON, DOLLY REBECCA, singer, composer, actress; b. Sevier County, Tenn., Jan. 19, 1946; d. Robert Lee and Avie Lee (Owens) P.; m. Carl Dean, May 30, 1966. Country music singer, rec. artist, composer, actress, radio and TV personality. Entrepreneur, owner entertainment park Dollywood, established 1985. Radio appearances include Grand Ole Opry, WSM Radio, Nashville, Cass Walker program, Knoxville; TV appearances include Porter Wagoner Show, from 1967, Cass Walker program, Bill Anderson Show, Wilburn Bros. Show, Barbara Mandrell Show; rec. artist, Mercury, Monument, RCA, CBS record cos.; albums include Here You Come Again (Grammy award 1978), Real Love, 1985, Just the Way I Am, 1986, Portrait, 1986, Think About Love, 1986, Trio (with Emmylou Harris, Linda Ronstadt) (Grammy award 1988), 1987, Heartbreaker, Great Balls of Fire, Rainbow, 1988, White Limozeen, 1989, Home for Christmas, 1990, Eagle When She Flies, 1991, Slow Dancing with the Moon, 1993 (Grammy nomination, Best Country Vocal Collaboration for Romeo (with Tanya Tucker, Billy Ray Cyrus, Kathy Mattea, Pam Tillis, & Mary-Chapin Carpenter), (with Tammy Wynette and Loretta Lynn) Honky Tonk Angels, 1994, The Essential Dolly Parton, 1995, Just the Way I Am, 1996, Super Hits, 1996, (with others) I Will Always Love You & Other Greatest Hits, 1996, Hungry Again, 1998, Trio II, 1998, Grass is Blue, 1999 (Grammy award for best bluegrass album), Best of the Best-Porter & Doll, 1999, Halos and Horns, 2002, For God and Country, 2003, Makin' Believe, 2003; appears on song "Creepin' In" with Norah Jones, 2004; composer numerous songs including Nine to Five (Grammy award 1981, Acad. award nominee and Golden Globe award nominee 1981); Film appearances include Nine to Five, 1980, The Best Little Whorehouse in Texas, 1982, Rhinestone, 1984, Steel Magnolias, 1989, Straight Talk, 1991; (TV films) A Smoky Mountain Christmas, 1986, Wild Texas Wind, 1991, Unlikely Angel, 1996, Blue Valley Songbird, 1999; (TV series) Heavens to Betsy, 1994, Mindin My Own Business, 1996; Author: Dolly, 1994. Recipient (with Porter Wagoner) Vocal Group of Yr. award, 1968, Vocal Duo of Yr. award All Country Music Assn., 1970, 71, Nashville Metronome award, 1979, Am. Music award for best duo performance (with Kenny Rogers), 1984, Grammy awards for best female country vocalist, 1978, 81, for best country song, 1981, for best country vocal performance with group, 1987, People's Choice award, 1980, 88, Nat. Medal of Arts Nat. Endowment for the Arts, 2005, Kennedy Ctr. Honor, John F. Kennedy Center for Performing Arts, 2006; co-recipient (with Emmylou Harris and Linda Ronstadt) Acad. Country Music award for album of the yr., 1987, (with Brad Paisley) Most Inspiring Video of Yr. for When I Get Where I'm Going, CMT Awards (Country Music TV), 2006, Video of Yr. and Vocal Event of Yr., Acad. Country Music award, 2006; named Female Vocalist of Yr., 1975, 76, Country Star of Yr., Sullivan Prodns., 1977, Entertainer of Yr., Country Music Assn., 1978, Female Vocalist of Yr., Acad. Country Music, 1980; Dolly Parton Day proclaimed, Sevier County, Tenn., designated Oct. 7, 1967, Los Angeles, Sept. 20, 1979; named to Small Town of Am. Hall of Fame, 1988, East Tenn. Hall of Fame, 1988. Address: RCA 6 W 57th St New York NY 10019-3901 Office: Dollywood Co 1020 Dollywood Ln Pigeon Forge TN 37863-4101

PARTOYAN, GARO ARAKEL, lawyer; b. Toledo, Dec. 6, 1936; s. Garo and Vartoohi Partoyan; children: Garo Linck, Elizabeth Margaret, Martin Joseph. BS in Chem. Engring., Northwestern U., 1959; JD, U. Mich., 1962; LLM, NYU, 1964. Bar: N.Y. 1963, U.S. Dist. Cts. (so. dist.) N.Y. 1964, U.S. Ct. Claims 1966, U.S. Ct. Appeals (2nd cir.) 1966, U.S. Dist. Ct. (ea. dist.) N.Y. 1968. Ptnr. Curtis, Morris & Safford, NYC, 1962-76; gen. counsel mktg. and tech. Mars, Inc., McLean, Va., 1976-98; pres. Mgmt. of Intellectual Property, Inc., Sarasota, Fla., 1998—. Mem. Dobbs Ferry (N.Y.) Bd. Edn., 1972-76, pres., 1975-76; chmn. Fairfax Citizens Group, Fairfax County, Va., 1988-90. Mem. ABA, Licensing Execs. Soc., Am. Intellectual Property Law Assn., N.Y. Intellectual Property Law Assn., Internat. Trademark Assn. (pres. 1990-91, bd. dirs. 1983—), Intellectual Property Owners (bd. dirs. 1992-99), Armenian Bar Assn. Avocations: sailing, curling. Office: 464 MacEwen Dr Osprey FL 34229 Home Phone: 941-918-0720; Office Phone: 941-918-0595. Fax: 941-918-0678. Personal E-mail: partoyanga@aol.com.

PARTRIDGE, BRUCE JAMES, lawyer, educator, writer; b. Syracuse, NY, June 4, 1926; arrived in Can., 1969; s. Bert James and Lida Marion (Rice) P.; m. Mary Janice Smith, June 13, 1948 (dec. 1986); children: Heather Leigh, Eric James, Brian Lloyd, Bonnie Joyce; m. May S. Archer, May 28, 1988; stepchildren: Sheila Archer, Laurel Archer. AB cum laude, Oberlin Coll., Ohio, 1946; LLB, Blackstone Coll., Chgo., 1950, JD, 1952; LLB, U. B.C., 1974. Bar: B.C. 1976, N.W.T. 1980. Rsch. physicist Am. Gas Assn., Cleve., 1946-48; bus. mgr. Cazenovia (N.Y.) Coll., 1948—51; bus. mgr., purchasing agt., asst. treas. Rochester Inst. Tech., NY, 1953—58; bus. adminstr. Baldwin-Wallace Coll., Berea, Ohio, 1951-53; v.p. bus. and mgmt. U. Del., Newark, 1958-63; v.p. adminstrn. Johns Hopkins U., Balt., 1963-69; pres. U. Victoria, B.C., Can., 1969-72; assoc. Clark, Wilson & Co., Vancouver, B.C., Can., 1975-78; successively solicitor, mng. solicitor, gen. solicitor, v.p. law and gen. counsel, sec. Cominco Ltd., Vancouver, 1978-88; exec. dir. Baker & McKenzie, Hong Kong, 1988-90; v.p. Pacific Creations, Inc., 1990-92; faculty Camosun Coll., 1992-99. Author: Management in Canada: The Competitive Challenges, 2000; co-author: College and University Business Administration, 1968; chmn. editl. com. Purchasing for Higher Education, 1962; contbr. numerous articles to profl. jours. Chmn. commn. on adminstrv. affairs Am. Coun. on Edn., Washington, 1966-69; mem. Pres.'s Com. on Employment of Handicapped, Washington, 1967-69; mem. adv. coun. Ctr. for Resource Studies, Queen's U., 1983-88; bd. dirs. L'Arche in the Americas, 1984-88; mem. adv. coun.

Westwater Rsch. Ctr., U. B.C., 1982-88. Mem. Assn. Can. Gen. Counsel, Def. Rsch. Inst. (product liability com.), Am. Inst. Parliamentarians, Nat. Assn. Parliamentarians. Fair Vote Can. Party. Unitarian Universalist. Business E-Mail: brucepart@telus.net.

PARTRIDGE, GAROLD CLYDE, marketing executive; b. Coryden, Iowa, Nov. 20, 1929; s. David Claude Partfidge and Hazel Irene Partridge; m. Kay Kathleen Krieigsman; children: Carla Joan, Caren Jean. PhD, U. Md., Balt., 1960; LLB, Blackstone Coll., Chgo., 1968. Commd. 2nd lt. US Army, 1951, advanced through the grades to maj., 1971; with Colorado City Rairty, Colorado Springs, 1971—76; mktg. dir. Cantury of Rocky Mountains, Denver, 1974—90; mktg. cons. JD Mktg., Colorado Springs, 1990—2001; owner, pres. Maxcare, Colorado Springs, 1990—. Author: (training tapes) Affirmation of Profession, 1995, 31 Keys, 1997, My Success Plan, 1997. Home: 111 Dartmouth St Colorado Springs CO 80911

PARTRIDGE, LOREN WAYNE, art historian, educator; b. Raton, N.Mex., Apr. 11, 1936; s. Don F. and Ruth (Isaacson) P.; widowed; children: Wendy, Amy; married. BA in English Lit., Yale U., 1958; cert. in L.Am. lit., U. Buenos Aires, 1959; diploma in Russian, U.S. Army Lang. Sch., Monterey, Calif., 1961; MA in Fine Arts, Harvard U., 1965, PhD in Fine Arts, 1969. Tchg. fellow Harvard U., Cambridge, Mass., 1964-66; lectr. U. Calif., Berkeley, 1968, acting asst. prof., 1969-70, asst. prof., 1970-76, assoc. prof., 1976-80, prof., 1980—, chmn. Dept. Art History, 1978—87, 1990—93, 1999, chmn. Dept. Art Practice, 2002—03, 2004—. Resident in art history Am. Acad. in Rome, 1985; reviewer Art Bull, 1972, 78, 80, 83, Renaissance Quar., 1984, 87, 90, 99, Design Book Rev., 1987, Master Drawings, 1987, Am. Hist. Rev., 1993, Apollo, 1996. Author: John Galen Howard and the Berkeley Campus: Beaux-Arts Architecture in the Athens of the West, 1978, Caprarola, Palazzo Farnese, 1988, (with Randolph Starn) A Renaissance Likeness: Art and Culture in Raphael's Julius II, 1980, (with Randolph Starn) Arts of Power: Three Halls of State in Italy 1300-1600, 1992, The Art of Renaissance Rome, 1400-1600, 1996, Michelangelo: The Sistine Chapel Ceiling, Rome, 1996, Michelangelo Last Judgement: A Glorious Restoration, 1997; contbr. author: Ency. of Italian Renaissance, 1981, Internat. Dictionary Art and Artists, 1990, Dictionary of Art, 1996; contbr. articles to profl. jours. With U.S. Army, 1960-63. Scholar Yale U., 1955-58, Harvard U., 1964-66; Fulbright fellow, 1958-59, 75, Am. Acad. in Rome fellow, 1966-68, Kress fellow Inst. for Advanced Studies, 1974-75, U. Calif., 1972, 77, 82, 85, 93-94, 99-2000, 2003-04, Guggenheim fellow, 1981-92; grantee Kress Found., 1968-69, 71-72, Getty. sr. rsch. grantee, 1988-89. Office: U Calif Dept Art History 6020 416 Doe Libr Berkeley CA 94720-6020 Office Phone: 510-643-6301. Business E-Mail: lpart@berkeley.edu.

PARTRIDGE, MARK VAN BUREN, lawyer, educator, mediator, writer; b. Rochester, Minn., Oct. 16, 1954; s. John V.B. and Constance (Brainerd) P.; m. Mary Roberta Moffitt, Apr. 30, 1983; children: Caitlin, Lindsay, Christopher. BA, U. Nebr., 1978; JD, Harvard U., 1981. Bar: Ill. 1981, U.S. Dist. Ct. (no. dist.) Ill. 1981, U.S. Dist. Ct. (ea. dist.) Mich. 1983, U.S. Ct. Appeals (1st. cir) 2003, U.S. Ct. Appeals (4th cir.) 1986, U.S. Ct. Appeals (7th cir.), 1992, U.S. Ct. Appeals (5th cir.) 1993, U.S. Ct. Appeals (3rd cir.) 1998. Assoc. Pattishall, McAuliffe, Newbury, Hilliard & Geraldson, LLP, Chgo., 1981-88, ptnr., 1988—, exec. com., 2003—. Adj. prof. John Marshall Law Sch., Chgo., 1987—; arbitrator Cook County Mandatory Arbitration Program, 1989-2003; v.p. Harvard Legal Aid Bur., 1980-81; mediator no. dist. Ill. Voluntary Mediation Program, 1997—; panelist World Intellectual Property Orgn., Domain Name Dispute Resolution Svc., 1999—; neutral Nat. Arbitration Forum, Intellectual Property Mediation and Arbitration Panel, 2004—; mediator Internat. Trademark Assn. Panel of Neutrals, 2005—; bd. adv. N.W. Law Sch., Jour. Tech. and Intellectual Property. Author, Guilding Rights Trademarks, Copyright and the Internet, iUniverse, 2003, Contbr. articles to profl. jours.; mem. editl. bd. The Trademark Reporter, 1994-97; adv. bd. IP Litigator, 1995—. Vol. Chgo. Vol. Legal Svcs., 1983—. Fellow Am. Intellectual Property Law Assn. (com. chmn. 1989-91, 96-98, bd. dirs. 1998-2001); mem. ABA (com. chmn. 1989-91, 94-99, rep. 2006—), Internat. Trademark Assn. (com. vice chmn. 1996), World Intellectual Property Orgn. (experts panel internet domain name process 1998-99), Intellectual Property Law Assn. Chgo. (com. chmn. 1993-96), Brand Names Ednl. Found. (moot ct. regional chmn. 1994-96, nat. vice-chmn. 1997-98, nat. chmn. 1998-99), Nat. Spkrs. Assn. (Ill. chpt. pres.-elect 2006), Legal Club (v.p. 1998, pres. 1999), Lawyers Club Chgo. (pres. 2000, bd. dirs. 2000-01), Execs. Club, Union League Club, Harvard Club Chgo., Bagatelle Club. Avocations: writing, music, genealogy, travel, internet. Office: Pattishall McAuliffe Newbury Hilliard & Geraldson LLP 311 S Wacker Dr Ste 5000 Chicago IL 60606-6631 Office Phone: 312-554-8000. Business E-Mail: mpartridge@pattishall.com.

PARTRIDGE, WILLIAM FRANKLIN, JR., lawyer; b. Newberry, SC, July 16, 1945; s. William F. and Clara (Eskridge) P.; m. Ilene S. Stewart, Aug. 16, 1969; children: Allison, William F. BA in History, The Citadel, 1967; JD, U. S.C., 1970. Bar: S.C. 1970, U.S. Ct. Claims 1971, U.S. Ct. Mil. Appeals 1971, U.S. Tax Ct. 1971, U.S. Supreme Ct. 1973, U.S. Dist. Ct. S.C. 1980. Instr. internat. law Chapman Coll., 1973-74; pub. issue com. S.C. Bar, 1982-83. Lt. Col. USAFR. Mem. Newberry Bar Assn. (pres. 1982-83), Palmetto Club, County of Newberry Club, Cotillion Club, Assn. Citadel Mens Club, Masons, Phi Delta Phi. Democrat. Methodist. Home: 2029 Harrington St Newberry SC 29108-3055 Office: 1201 Boyce St Newberry SC 29108-2705 Office Phone: 803-276-5968.

PARVEEN, NIKHAT, microbiologist, educator; d. Misbah ul-Haq Abbasi and Qudsia Begam. PhD, U. Hawaii, Manoa, 1995; student, U. Delhi. Scientist Indian Agrl. Rsch. Inst., New Delhi, 1991; postdoctoral fellow U. Mass. Med. Sch., Worcester, 1996—2000, rsch. asst. prof., 2000—05; asst. prof. U. Medicine and Dentistry of NJ. NJ Med. Sch., Newark, 2005—. Grantee, Am. Heart Assn., 2002—04, NIH, 2003—06, Nat. Rsch. Fund for Tick Borne Diseases, 2006—07, U. Medicine and Dentistry NJ Found., 2006—07; rsch. fellow, Nitrogen Fixation in Tropical Agrl. Legumes, 1991—95. Mem.: AAAS, Am. Soc. Microbiology. Office: U Medicine and Dentistry NJ/ NJ Med Sch 225 Warren St ICPH Bldg Newark NJ 07103 Home Phone: 973-325-8041; Office Phone: 973-972-4483 ext 25218.

PARVIS, PETER P., lawyer; b. NYC, Aug. 10, 1945; BA with honors, U. Md., 1968, JD with honors, 1977. Bar: Md. 1977. Ptnr., health care, pharm. Venable LLP (formerly Venable, Baetjer and Howard), Balt. Mem. ABA, Md. State Bar Assn., Bar Assn. Balt. City, Am.Health Lawyers Assn., Order of Coif. Office: Venable LLP Ste 2100 1800 Mercantile Bank & Trust Bldg 2 Hopkins Plz Baltimore MD 21201-2982 Office Phone: 410-244-7644. Office Fax: 410-244-7742. Business E-Mail: ppparvis@venable.com.

PASACHOFF, JAY MYRON, astronomer, educator; b. NYC, July 1, 1943; s. Samuel S. and Anne (Traub) P.; m. Naomi Schwartz, Mar. 31, 1974; children: Eloise Hilary, Deborah Donna. AB, Harvard U., 1963, AM (NSF fellow), 1965, PhD (NSF fellow, N.Y. State Regents fellow for advanced grad. study), 1969. Rsch. physicist Air Force Cambridge Rsch. Labs., Bedford, Mass., 1968-69; Menzel rsch. fellow Harvard Coll. Obs., Cambridge, Mass., 1969-70; rsch. fellow Hale Obs., Carnegie Instn., Washington, and Calif. Inst. Tech., Pasadena, 1970-72; from asst. prof., dir. Hopkins Obs. to prof. Williams Coll., Williamstown, Mass., 1972—84, Field Meml. prof. of astronomy, 1984—, chmn. astronomy dept., 1972—77, 1991—92, 1997—2001, 2004—. Adj. asst. prof. astronomy U. Mass., Amherst, 1975-77, adj. assoc. prof., 1977-83, adj. prof., 1986-90; vis. colleague and vis. assoc. prof. astronomy Inst. for Astronomy, U. Hawaii, 1980-81; vis. scientist Inst. d'Astrophysique, Paris, 1988; mem. Inst. Advanced Study, Princeton, 1989-90, Harvard-Smithsonian Ctr. for Astrophysics, 1993-94, 2001-02; total and other solar eclipse expdn. leader numerous locations, Pluto, Charon and Triton occultation expeditions, 1997—, transit of Venus expedition, 2004, transit of Mercury expedition, 2006; guest investigator NASA, 1975-79, 1999-2000, 2004—; lectr. in field. Author: Contemporary Astronomy, 1977, 4th edit., 1989, Astronomy Now, 1978, Astronomy: From Earth to the Universe, 1979, 6th edit., 2002, A Brief View of Astronomy, 1986, First Guide to Astronomy, 1988, 2006, First Guide to the Solar System, 1990, 2006, Journey Through the Universe, 1992; co-author: (with Marc L. Kutner, Naomi Pasachoff) Student Study Guide to Contemporary Astronomy, 1977, (with Kutner, Pasachoff and N.P. Kutner) Student Study Guide to Astronomy Now, 1978; (with M.L. Kutner) University Astronomy, 1978, Invitation to Physics, 1981; (with N. Pasachoff, T. Cooney) Physical Science, 1983, 2d edit., 1990, Earth Science, 1983, 2d edit., 1990; (with D.H. Menzel) A Field Guide to the Stars and Planets, 4th edit., 2000, 2006; (with R. Wolfson) Physics, 1987, 3rd edit., 1999 (Extended with Modern Physics, 1989, 3rd edit. 1999), (with N. Pasachoff, R.W. Clark, M.H. Westermann) Physical Science Today, 1987; (with N. Pasachoff and others) Discover Science, 7 vols., 1989; (with Michael Covington) Cambridge Eclipse Photography Guide, 1993; (with Len Holder and James DeFranza) Calculus, 1994, Single Variable Calculus, 1994, Multivariable Calculus, 1995; (with Edward Cheng, Patrick Osmer and Hyron Spinrad) The Farthest Things in the Universe, 1994; editor (with J. Percy) The Teaching of Astronomy, 1990, (with Leon Golub) The Solar Corona, 1997, rev. edit., 1998, (with Roberta J. M. Olson) Fire in the Sky: Comets and Meteors, the Decisive Centuries, 1998, rev. edit., 1999, Science Explorer: Astronomy, 1998, rev. edit., 2004, Sound and Light, 1999, (with J. Percy) Teaching and Learning Astronomy: Effective Strategies for Educators Worldwide, 2005; (with Alex Filippenko) The Cosmos: Astronomy at the New Millennium, 2000, 3d edit., 2007, The Complete Idiot's Guide to the Sun, 2003; assoc. editor: Jour. Irreproducible Results, 1972-94, Annals of Improbable Rsch., 1994—; abstractor from Am. jours. for Solar Physics, 1968-78; cons. editor McGraw-Hill Ency. Sci. and Tech., 1983—; co-editor-in-chief (with S.P. Parker), McGraw-Hill Ency. of Astronomy, 1993; cons. Random House Dictionary, 1983-86, Nat. Geographic Atlas, 5th edit., 1981, 6th edit., 1990; phys. sci. com. World Book Ency., 1989-95, cons., 1996—; contbr. articles to profl. jours. Recipient bronze medal Nikon Photo Contest Internat., 1971, photograph aboard NASA Voyagers, 1977, Dudley award Dudley Obs., 1985; grantee NSF, 1973-75, 79-83, 88—2002, Nat. Geog. Soc., 1973-86, 91—2001, 2004—06, Rsch. Corp., 1973-78, 82-88, 2001, Getty Found., 1994-95, NASA, 1999-2000, 2004—. Fellow AAAS (chair sect. D 1987-88, 97-98), Royal Astron. Soc., Am. Phys. Soc. (mem.-at-large thrs. forum edn. 1995-98), Internat. Planetarium Soc.; mem. AAUP (chpt. pres. 1977-80), Internat. Astron. Union (U.S. nat. rep. Commn. tchg. astronomy 1976-2000, chair eclipse working group 1991—, rep. com. tchg. sci. internat. coun. sci. unions 1991-93, v.p. com. on edn. and devel. 2000-2003, pres. 2003—06, US nat. liaison commn. on edn. and devel., 2000—), Am. Astron. Soc. (astronomy edn. adv. bd. 1990-97, astronomy news com. 1991-96, rep. to AAAS 2004—, Edn. prize 2003), Astron. Soc. Pacific, Union Radio Sci., Am. Assn. Physics Tchrs. (astronomy com. 1983-87), Sigma Xi (chpt. pres. 1973-74, 95—, nat. lectr. 1993-97), Phi Beta Kappa. Home: 111 Park Street Williamstown MA 01267-2116 Office: Williams Coll Hopkins Obs 33 Lab Campus Dr Williamstown MA 01267-2565 E-mail: jay.m.pasachoff@williams.edu.

PASAHOW, LYNN HAROLD, lawyer; s. Samuel and Cecelia (Newman) P.; m. Leslie Aileen Cobb, June 11, 1969; 1 child, Michael Alexander. AB, Stanford U., 1969; JD, U. Calif., Berkeley, 1972. Bar: Calif. 1972, U.S. Ct. Appeals (9th cir.) 1972, U.S. Dist. Ct. (no. dist.) Calif. 1973, U.S. Dist. Ct. (ctrl. dist.) Calif. 1974, U.S. Supreme Ct. 1976, U.S. Dist. Ct. (ea. dist.) Calif. 1977, U.S. Ct. Appeals (fed. cir.) 1990. Law clk. judge US Dist. Ct. (no. dist.) Calif., San Francisco, 1972—73; with McCutchen, Doyle, Brown & Enersen, 1973—2001; ptnr. Fenwick & West LLP, Mountain View, Calif., 2001—. Bd. dirs. Alzheimer's Assn., Greater San Francisco Bay area. Co-author: Civil Discovery and Mandatory Disclosure: A Guide to Effective Practice, 1994, Berkeley Center for Law & Technology Patent Case Management Judicial Guide, 2007; author: Pretrial and Settlement Conferences in Federal Court, 1983; contbr. articles to profl. jours. Bd. dirs. Bay Area Biosci. Ctr. Mem. ABA, Calif. Bar Assn. Democrat. Office: Fenwick & West LLP Silicon Valley Ctr 801 California St Mountain View CA 94041 Office Phone: 650-335-7225. Business E-Mail: lpasahow@fenwick.com. *Notable cases include: Amazon.com v. BarnesandNoble.com, duPont vs. Cetus, PCR patent litigation, Elan Pharmaceutical transgenic mouse litigation, Iomega Zip Disk litigation, nicotine patch patent litigation, University of California & Vysis v. Oncor FISH litigation.*

PASCAL, AMY BETH, film company executive; b. LA, Mar. 1958; d. Tony and Barbara Pascal; m. Bernard Weinraub, Aug. 9, 1997; 1 adopted child, Anthony. BA in Internat. Rels., UCLA. With Kestral Films; v.p. prodn. 20th Century Fox, 1986—87, Columbia Pictures, 1987—89, exec. v.p. prodn., 1987—94; pres. prodn. Turner Pictures, 1994—96; pres. Columbia Pictures, Culver City, Calif., 1996-99, chmn., 1999—2002; vice chmn. Sony Pictures Entertainment, Culver City, Calif., 2002—06, co-chmn., 2006—; chmn. Sony Pictures Entertainment Motion Picture Group, Culver City, Calif., 2003—. Bd. trustees Rand Corp. Bd. trustees AFI; mem. UCLA Sch. Theater, Film & Television. Named one of 100 Most Powerful Women in Entertainment, Hollywood Reporter, 2004—06, 100 Most Powerful Women, Forbes mag., 2005—06, 50 Most Powerful People in Hollywood, Premiere mag., 2004—06, 50 Most Powerful Women in Bus., Fortune mag., 2006. Office: Sony Pictures Entertainment 10202 Washington Blvd Culver City CA 90232 *

PASCAL, C(ECIL) BENNETT, classics educator; b. Chgo., May 4, 1926; s. Jack and Goldie (Zeff) P.; m. Ilene Joy Shulman, Feb. 1, 1959; 1 child, Keith Irwin. BA, UCLA, 1949, MA, 1950, Harvard U., 1953, PhD, 1956. Instr. U. Ill., Champaign, 1955-56, Cornell U., Ithaca, NY, 1957-60; asst. prof., then assoc. prof. U. Oreg., Eugene, 1960-75, prof. classics, 1975-96, prof. emeritus, 1996—, head dept., various years - 1965-85. Author: Cults of Cisalpine Gaul, 1964; contbr. articles to profl. jours. Active Eugene Bicycle Com., 1971-83. Wwith USN, 1944-46. Traveling fellow, Italy, Harvard U., 1956-57, Fulbright-Hays fellow, Rome, 1967-68. Mem. Am. Philol. Assn., Classical Assn. Pacific N.W. (pres. 1965-66), AAUP, Archeol. Inst. of Am. (past pres., sec. Eugene Soc.) Democrat. Jewish. Avocations: skiing, fly fishing, novel writing. Home: 330 Fulvue Dr Eugene OR 97405-2788 Office: U Oreg Dept Classics Eugene OR 97403 Business E-Mail: cbpasc@uoregon.edu.

PASCAL, ROGER, lawyer; b. Chgo., Mar. 16, 1941; s. Samuel A. and Harriet E. (Hartman) P.; m. Martha Hecht, June 16, 1963; children: Deborah, Diane, David AB with distinction, U. Mich, 1962; JD cum laude, Harvard U., 1965. Bar: Ill. 1965, US Dist. Ct. (no. dist. Ill.) 1965, US Ct. Appeals (7th cir.) 1969, US Supreme Ct. 1976, Wis. 1985, US Ct. Appeals (2nd, 6th, 9th and 10th cirs.) 1986. Lic. pilot, FAA, 1977, instrument rating, 1979. Assoc. Schiff Hardin, LLP, Chgo., 1965-71, ptnr., 1972—. Adj. prof. law Northwestern U. Law Sch., 1994—; bd. dirs. Evanston Cmty. Defender; instr. Nat. Inst. for Trial Advocacy, 1989-. Bd. dirs., mem. exec. com. Chgo. Law Enforcement Study Grp., 1975-80, pres., 1978-80; pres. Harvard Law Soc. Ill., 1976-78; bd. dirs. ACLU of Ill., 1984—, gen. counsel, 1986—. Recipient Roger Baldwin Lifetime Achievement award, 2003. Fellow Am. Bar Found.; mem. ABA (antitrust, intellectual property, and litig. sects.), Pub. Interest Law Initiative (bd. dirs. 1989—, v.p. 1995-97, pres. 1997-98), Fund for Justice (v.p., bd. dirs. 1986-97), Chgo. Coun. Lawyers (bd. dirs. 1970-74, 80-84, 2004—), Chgo. Legal Assistance Found. (bd. dirs. 1985-88), Chgo. Bar Found.(recipient Edward Lewis II Pro Bono Svc. award, 2003), Univ. Club, Met. Club, Phi Beta Kappa. Avocation: flying. Office: Schiff Hardin LLP 6600 Sears Tower Chicago IL 60606-6473 Office Fax: 312-258-5600. E-mail: rpascal@schiffhardin.com.

PASCAL, TRACEY MICHELE, software engineer, director; d. Harold Saunders and Dinah Lee Pascal. BBA, Tex. Tech U., Lubbock, 1986. Lic. nursing home adminstr. Tex., 1986. Adminstr. ARA Living Ctrs., Weatherford, Tex., 1986—87, Beverly Enterprises, Van, Tex., 1987—88; CFO Carter Nursing Homes, Inc, Corsicana, Tex., 1988—90; sr. software engr./tech. lead Sprint, Irving, Tex., 1990—. Employee trainer and mentor Sprint, Irving, Tex., 2002—06. Author: (manual) Sprint Operatons for Offshore Employees, (training manual) How to Complete and Fix Production Codes, (flash cards) Sprint History Past and Present; contbr. articles to profl. jours. Mem.: Project Mgmt. Inst., Am. Acad. Med. Adminstrs., Nat. Soc. DAR, Golden Key, Pi Beta Phi. Office: Sprint/Nextel 1300 East Rochelle Blvd Irving TX 75062 Home Phone: 817-354-3061; Office Phone: 972-536-6628. Personal E-mail: valinese@aol.com.

PASCALE, DANIEL RICHARD, lawyer; b. Racine, Wis., Mar. 22, 1940; s. Domenic and Fannie Colette (Julian) P.; m. Mary Sara McDonald, June 28, 1986; 1 child, Alexander. AB cum laude, Harvard U., 1962; JD, U. Chgo., 1965. Bar: Ill. 1966, U.S. Ct. Appeals (7th cir.) 1967, U.S. Dist. Ct. (no. dist.) Ill. 1969, U.S. Supreme Ct. 1972. Asst. corp. counsel City of Chgo., 1966-72, chief appellate atty., 1972-79, 1st dep. corp. counsel, 1979-84; assoc. Rudnick & Wolfe, Chgo., 1984-87, ptnr., 1987-90; judge Circuit Ct. of Cook County, Ill., 1990-94, 96-98; adminstrv. dir. Adminstrv. Office of Ill. Cts., Chgo., 1995-96; sr. corp. atty. Dean Foods Co., 1999—2002; instr. Northeastern Ill. U., 2004—. Counsel to the chmn. com. on fin. Chgo. City Coun., 2005—. Bd. dirs. DeKoven Found., Racine, 1986—, The Church Home/Montgomery Pl., 1998-2007; adv. bd. Art Resources in Teaching, Chgo., 1987-94; v.p. Episcopal Homes Mgmt., Inc., Milw., 1988-94. Mem. Ill. Bar Assn., English-Speaking Union. Independent. Episcopalian.

PASCALE, MARK, curator, educator; b. New Haven, Conn., Mar. 10, 1954; s. Joseph Dante and Leola Sonn Pascale; m. Susan Lynn Mathews, Aug. 11, 1979; 1 child, Arthur. BA, So. Conn. State U., New Haven, 1976; MFA, Ohio State U., Columbus, 1978. Asst. prof. U. Mo., St. Louis, 1979—81; rsch. asst. Art Inst. Chgo., 1989—90, asst. curator, 1990—99, assoc. curator, 1999—. Vis. artist Sch. Art Inst., Chgo., 1981—92, adj. assoc. prof., 1992—2000, adj. prof., 2000—. Panelist visual arts grants Chgo. Dept. Cultural Affairs, 1995—99. Mem.: Print Coun. Am. (trustee 1996—). Office: Art Inst Chgo 111 S Michigan Ave Chicago IL 60603

PASCARELLA, HENRY WILLIAM, lawyer; b. New Haven, Aug. 15, 1933; s. John Manlio and Mary (Iannotti) P.; m. Tessa Peruzzi, Jan. 28, 1967; children: Averardo, Leonora, Cassandra. BS in Econs., U. Pa., 1955; LLB, Yale U., 1958. Bar: Conn. 1958, U.S. Supreme Ct. 1963. Ptnr. Badger, Fisher, Cohen & Barnett and predecessors, Greenwich, Conn., 1959-73; sr. counsel to Taylor Cooper & Alcorn, Greenwich, Conn., 1978—2005. Pres., dir. The Timber Trails Corp. Sherman, Conn.; dir. Nine West Group, Inc., 1995-99. Author column, theater critic Greenwich Times, 1964-67. Dir. Planned Parenthood League of Conn., Greenwich coun. Boy Scouts Am., 1990-96. Served to lt. (j.g.) USCG, 1959. Me.m ABA, Greenwich Bar Assn. (pres. 1967), Conn. Bar Assn., Yale Club (N.Y.C.), Belle Haven Club (Greenwich). Home: 675 Steamboat Rd Greenwich CT 06830-7140 E-mail: henry@pascarellalaw.com.

PASCARELLA, PERRY JAMES, editor, writer; b. Bradford, Pa., Apr. 11, 1934; s. James and Lucille Margaret (Monti) P.; m. Carol Ruth Taylor, May 4, 1957; children: Cynthia, Elizabeth. AB, Kenyon Coll., 1956; Coll. William and Mary, William and Mary Coll., 1957; postgrad., George Washington U., 1958. Credit reporter Dun & Bradstreet, Cleve., 1956, 60; from asst. editor to mng. editor Steel mag., Cleve., 1961-69; mng. editor Industry Week mag., Cleve., 1970-71, exec. editor, 1971-86, editor-in-chief, 1986-89; v.p. editorial Penton Pub. Inc., 1989-96. Lectr. in field. Author: Technology-Fire in a Dark World, 1979, Humanagement in the Future Corporation, 1981, The New Achievers, 1984, The Purpose-Driven Organization, 1989, The Ten Commandments of the Workplace, 1996, Leveraging People and Profit, 1998, Christ-Centered Leadership, 1999; co-author: Optimistic Outlooks, 1982, Creating a Global Agenda, 1984, Leadership in a New Era, 1994, The New Bottom Line, 1996. Lt. comdr. USNR, 1957-60. Recipient Disting. Service award Kenyon Coll., 1975, 81, Am. Bus. Press Crain award, 1992; Carnegie scholar, 1952-56 Mem. World Future Soc., U. Akron Inst. for Future Studies (bd. advisors). Presbyterian (elder). Home: 694 Coronado Cir Avon Lake OH 44012

PASCH, ALAN, philosopher, educator; b. Cleve., Dec. 1, 1925; s. P. Jerome and Esther (Broverman) P.; m. Eleanor Kudlich Berna, Dec. 27, 1950; 1 child, Rachel. BA, U. Mich., 1949; MA, New Sch. Social Research, 1952; PhD, Princeton U., 1955; Bamford fellow, 1955-56. Instr. philosophy Ohio State U., 1956-59, asst. prof., 1959-60; assoc. prof. philosophy U. Md., College Park, 1960-67, prof., 1967-97, prof. emeritus, 1997—. Author: Experience and the Analytic, 1958; also articles, revs. Served with AUS, 1944-46, PTO. Mem. Am. Philos. Assn. (exec. dir. 1969-72, sec.-treas. Eastern div. 1965-68), Metaphys. Soc. Am., Washington Philosophy Club (pres. 1978-79), Washington Rare Book Group. Office: Dept Philosophy Univ Md College Park MD 20742 Business E-Mail: pasch@umd.edu.

PASCHALL, LEE MCQUERTER, retired communications executive; b. Sterling, Colo., Jan. 21, 1922; s. Lee McQuerter and Agnes (Woldridge) P.; m. Bonnie Jean Edwards, Oct. 24, 1942; children: Patricia Ann Grillos, Stephen Lee, David Edward. BA, U. Ala., 1957; MA, George Washington U., 1964. Served with U.S. Army, 1940-46; communications engr. Colo. Air N.G., Denver, 1946-51; commd. maj. U.S. Air Force, 1951, advanced through grades to lt. gen., 1974, ret., 1978; ind. cons. Springfield, Va., 1978-81; pres., chief exec. officer Am. Satellite Co., Rockville, Md., 1981-84, chmn., 1984-85. Dir. Gen. Data Comm. Industries. Contbr. numerous articles to profl. publs. Mem. com. rev. nat. communications system initiatives NRC, 1982-88. Decorated Legion of Merit with oak leaf cluster; decorated disting. service medals; recipient Eascon IEEE, 1979 Mem. Armed Forces Comms.-Electronics Assn. (chpt. pres., nat. bd. dirs. Disting. Svc.), Air Force Assn., Phi Beta Kappa. Mem. Christian Ch. (Disciples Of Christ). Home and Office: 1513 Hampton Hills Cir Mc Lean VA 22101-6018 Personal E-mail: lmpaschall@prodigy.net.

PASCHEN, STEPHEN H., archivist, historian; b. Pekin, Ill., Nov. 17, 1949; s. Richard Gordon and Marguerite Hinds Paschen; m. Mary Lynn LaMarco, Sept. 10, 1977; children: Kristin Anne, Richard Stephen. BS in Landscape Architecture, Iowa State U., Ames, 1972; MA in History, U. Akron, Ohio, 1987; M in Libr. and Info. Sci., Kent State U., Ohio, 2002. Cert. archivist Acad. Cert. Archivists, 2000, landscape arch. State Bd. Landscape Architecture, 1979. Landscape arch. City of Akron Dept. Planning, 1975—83; pvt. practice landscape arch. Akron, 1983—85; curator Summit County Hist. Soc., Akron, 1985—90, exec. dir., 1990—97; sr. archives assoc. U. Akron Archives, 1997—2002, subject libr., 2002—06; u. archivist, asst. prof. Kent State U., Librs. and Media Svcs., Ohio, 2006—. Part-time faculty history dept. U. Akron, 1998—2006; part-time faculty Kent State U. Sch. Libr. and Info. Sci., 2004; faculty Oral History Inst., Columbus, Ohio, 2001—06; project historian Cmty. History Tchr. Workshops, Ohio Literacy Resource Ctr., Kent, 1999—2001. Author: Shootin' the Chutes: Amusement Parks Remembered, 1988, Speaking of Summit: An Oral History Handbook, 1989, Molding a Legacy: A Centennial History of the Akron Porcelain & Plastics Company, 1990, Order in the

Court: The History of the Courts and the Practice of Law in Akron, Ohio, 1997, Quarrytown: The History of Amherst, Ohio 1811-1900, 2003, Traces of Akron: Old and New, 2004, The 1890s in America: Documenting the Maturation of a Nation, 2006, The Ballyhoo Years: The United States in the 1920s As Observed Through Contemporary Documents, 2007; mem. edit. bd.: NE Ohio Jour. History, 2001—. Curator, bd. mem., co-founder The Dr. Shirla R. McClain Gallery of Akron's History and Culture, 1995—2006; local history tour presenter Leadership Akron, 2004—06; advisor Cmty. Adv. Coun., Akron, 2005—06. Recipient George Popp Hall of Fame Svc. award, Greater Akron Baseball Hall of Fame, 1990, Cert. of Commendation, Am. Assn. for State and Local History, 1993, Sch. Improvement award, Akron Pub. Schs., 1995, J. Crawford Meml. award, Kent State U. Sch. Libr. and Info. Sci., 2002. Mem.: Oral History in Ohio Assn. (pres. 1995—96), Ohio Assn. Hist. Socs. and Museums (treas. 2005—06, pres. 1998—99, Outstanding Achievement award local history publ. 1993, Outstanding Achievement award edn. program 1987, Outstanding Achievement award local history publ. 1989, Outstanding Achievement award regional history publ. 1990, Outstanding Achievement award newsletter design 1993), Soc. Ohio Archivists (treas. 2006), Women's History Project Akron (bd. mem. 1990—94). Achievements include design of Discovery Trunks Museums. Avocations: vintage baseball, reading, drawing and design, sports. Office: Kent State University PO Box 5190 1 Eastway Dr Kent OH 44242-0001 Office Phone: 330-672-1639. Office Fax: 330-672-9318. Business E-Mail: spaschen@kent.edu.

PASCHETTO, JOHN J., lawyer; b. Long Branch, NJ, Sept. 18, 1959; s. Edward and Elizabeth McCue Paschetto; m. Katherine Anne Dobrosky, Feb. 20, 1982. BA, Rutgers U., 1981; MA, U. Del., 1988; JD, Harvard U., 1998. Bar: Del. 1998, U.S. Dist. Ct. Del. 1999. Ptnr. Young Conaway Stargatt & Taylor, LLP, Wilmington, Del., 1998—. Contbr. chapters to books. Mem.: ABA, Del. State Bar Assn., Harvard Law Sch. Assn. Del. (treas. 1998—). Office: Young Conaway Stargatt & Taylor LLP 1000 West St Wilmington DE 19801 Office Phone: 302-571-6608. Business E-Mail: jpaschetto@ycst.com.

PASCHKE, DONALD VERNON, music educator; b. Menominee, Mich., Oct. 22, 1929; s. Leo Carl Ferdinand and Augusta O. (Fritz) P.; m. Helen Inez Burton, Feb. 17, 1951; children: David Vernon, Celeste Eileen. MusB in Voice, U. Ill., 1957, BS in Choral Music Edn., 1957, MusM in Voice, 1958; D Mus. Arts, U. Colo., 1972. Instr. music Berea (Ky.) Coll., 1958-62; asst. prof. music Eastern N.Mex. U., Portales, 1962-71, assoc. prof., 1971-76, prof., 1976-94; prof. emeritus, 1994. Translator, editor: A Complete Treatise on the Art of Singing, Part Two (Manuel Garcia II), 1975; Part One, 1984. Songleader Portales Christian Breakfast, 1976—, pres., 1975-76, 90-91, v.p. 1974-75, 89-90; chancel choir dir. 1st Presbyn. Ch., Clovis, N.Mex., 1976-95. With U.S. Army, 1951-53. Mem. Nat. Assn. Tchrs. Singing (lt. gov. N.Mex. 1968-72, v.p. Gt. Plains chpt. 1972-74, chpt. pres. 1974-78), Am. Legion, Pi Kappa Lambda, Phi Kappa Phi. Republican. Presbyterian. Avocations: photography, do-it-yourself projects. Home: 228 Kansas Dr Portales NM 88130-7121

PASCIUTO, JOSEPH DORIA, priest; b. Bklyn., June 27, 1945; s. Carmine Michael Pasciuto, Rose Marie (Doria) Pasciuto. BA, St. John's U., 1968, MBA, 1981; MDiv, Immaculate Conception Sem., Huntington, NY, 1991; MA in Theology, Immaculate Conception Sem., 1999; theol. studies, Pontifical N.Am. Coll., Vatican City, 2003. Ordination Roman Cath. Diocese Bklyn., 1991. CFO Local 371 AFSCME, NYC, 1981—84; mgr. pers./labor rels Child Welfare Adminstrn., NYC, 1984—87; vicar Our Lady Help of Christians, Bklyn., 1991—99, Our Lady of Hope, Queens, NY, 1999—2000, St. Brendan, Bklyn., 2000—03; adminstr. Holy Cross Roman Cath. Ch., Bklyn., 2003—. Chaplain Boy Scouts Am., Bklyn., 2000—, Internat. Firefighters Assn., NYC, 2001. Mem.: KC (chaplain 1995—, 4th degree L.I. Assembly 2001), Montauk Club. Democrat. Avocations: music, reading, cooking. Home: 451 Abingdon Ave Staten Island NY 10308

PASCO, HANSELL MERRILL, retired lawyer; b. Thomasville, Ga., Oct. 7, 1915; s. John and Katherine (Merrill) P.; m. Williamine Carrington Lancaster, June 28, 1941; children: Hansell Merrill, Dabney, Robert, Elizabeth, Carrington. BA, Va. Mil. Inst., 1937; LL.B., U. Va., 1940. Bar: Va. bar 1939. Ptnr. Hunton & Williams, Richmond, Va., 1948-81, sr. counsel, 1981—2005, mng. partner, 1968-76; ret., 2005. Chmn. State Counsel Higher Edn. for Va., 1978-80; trustee Protestant Episcopal Sem., Alexandria, Va., 1980-85. Served with U.S. Army as staff officer, first asst. and then sec. war dept.gen. staff, sec., 1940-45.

PASCOE, B. LYNN, international organization official, former ambassador; b. Mo., July 7, 1943; m. Diane Pascoe; 2 children. BA, U. Kans.; MA, Columbia U. Spl. asst. to dep. sec. state US Dept. State, dep. exec. sec., Am. dep. chief of mission Beijing China, prin. dep. asst. sec. East Asian and Pacific Bur.; dir. Am. Inst. Taiwan, Taipei, 1993—96; US spl. negotiator for Nagorno-Karabakh & regional conflicts, US co-chair for Orgn. for Security & Cooperation in Europe's Minsk Grp. US Dept. State, 1997—98, US amb. to Malaysia Kuala Lampur, 1999—2001, dep. asst. sec. Bur. European and Eurasian Affairs Washington, 2001—04, US amb. to Indonesia Jakarta, 2004—07; under-sec. gen. for polit. affairs UN, NYC, 2007—. Fluent in Mandarin Chinese. Office: UN Dept Political Affairs Room S-3755A New York NY 10017 *

PASCOE, PATRICIA HILL, former state legislator; b. Sparta, Wis., June 1, 1935; d. Fred Kirk and Edith (Kilpatrick) Hill; m. D. Monte Pascoe, Aug. 3, 1957; children: Sarah, Edward, William. BA, U. Colo., 1957; MA, U. Denver, 1968, PhD, 1982. Tchr. Sequoia Union H.S. Dist., Redwood City, Calif. and Hayward (Calif.) Union H.S. Dist., 1957-60; instr. Met. State Coll., Denver, 1969-75, Denver U., 1975-77, 81, rsch. asst. bur. ednl. rsch., 1981-82; tchr. Kent Denver Country Day Sch., Englewood, Colo., 1982-84; freelance writer Denver, 1985—; mem. Colo. Senate, Dist. 32, Denver, 1989—93, Colo. Senate, Dist. 34, Denver, 1995—2003; chair minority caucus Colo. Senate, Denver, 1996-2000, chair policy and planning com., 2001, chair edn. com., 2002. Commr. Edn. Commn. of the States, Denver, 1975-82, 01-05. Contbr. articles to numerous publs. and jours. Bd. dirs. Samaritan House, 1990-94, Cystic Fibrosis Found., 1989-93, 2007—, chmn. legis. com.; pres. East HS Parent Tchr. and Student Assn., Denver, 1984-85; mem. Moore Budget Adv. Com., Denver, 1966-72; legis. chmn. alumni bd. U. Colo., Boulder, 1987-89; del. Dem. Nat. Conv., San Francisco, 1984, NYC, 1992; mem. Denver Woman's Press Club, 1996—, pres., 2005-06, Colo. Arts Coalition, 1988-97, Conflict Ctr. Bd., 2003-05; bd. dirs. Opera Colo., 1996-02; mem. bd. ACLU Colo., chair legis. com. Mem. Soc. Profl. Journalists, Common Cause (bd. dirs. Denver chpt. 1986-88), Lions Club (dir. 2003-05), Phi Beta Kappa. Democrat. Presbyterian.

PASCOTTO, ALVARO, lawyer; b. Rome, Mar. 8, 1949; came to U.S., 1984; s. Antonio and Anna Ludovica (Habig) P.; m. Linda Haldan, July 20, 1985. JD, U. Rome, 1973. Bar: Italy 1976, Calif. 1987, U.S. Dist. Ct. (cen. dist.) Calif. 1987, U.S. Ct. Appeals (9th cir.) 1987. Ptnr. Studio Legale Pascotto, Rome, 1976-86, Pascotto, Gallavotti & Gardner, LA and Rome, 1986-90, Pascotto & Gallavotti, LA, 1990—; of counsel Irell & Manella LLP, LA, 1994—2003, Morrison & Foerster, LLP, LA, 2003. Ofcl. counsel Consulate Gen. Italy, L.A., 1987—. Mem. ABA, Calif. Bar Assn., Italian-Am. Bar Assn., Am. Mgmt. Assn., Consiglio dell'Ordine Degli Avvocati e Procuratori di Roma. Clubs: Circolo del Golf (Rome); Malibu (Calif.) Racquet Club, Regency Club (L.A.), L.A. Country Club, Calif. Club. Home: 6116 Merritt Dr Malibu CA 90265-3847 Office: 555 W 5th St Ste 3500 Los Angeles CA 90013 Office Phone: 213-892-5635. Office Fax: 213-892-5637. Business E-Mail: apascotto@mofo.com.

PASCRELL, WILLIAM J., JR., congressman; b. Paterson, NJ, Jan. 25, 1937; s. William J. Sr. and Roffie (Loffredo) Pascrell; m. Elsie Marie Botto; children: William III, David, Glenn. BA in Journalism, Fordham U., NY, 1959, MA in Philos., 1961; postgraduate student, Fairleigh Dickinson U. Tchr. Jr. HS, Clifton, NJ, 1962, Paramus HS, NJ, 1962-74; adj. prof. Fairleigh Dickinson U., Madison, NJ, 1964—69; ophthalmic technician Seymour Pollack Opticians, 1968—74; adult sch. tchr. Dwight Morrow HS, Englewood, NJ, 1969-70; dir. Dept. Pub. Works, Paterson, NJ, 1974-77, Dept. Policy, Planning and Devel., Paterson, NJ, 1979—87; mem. Paterson Planning Bd., NJ, 1975—77; pres. Bd. Edn., Paterson, NJ, 1979—82; mem. NJ Gen. Assembly, 1987—90; mayor Paterson, NJ, 1990—96; mem. US Congress from 8th NJ dist., 1997—. Co-chair Congl. Brain Injury Task Force US Congress, mem. ways and means com. Bd. dirs. Passaic County Cmty. Coll., 1973-79, Boys Club, 1975-; campaign coord. Robert A. Roe for Gov., NJ, 1977; regional coord. James Florio for Gov., Hudson County, NJ, 1981; active County Chairmen for Sen. Frank Lautenberg, NJ, 1982; chmn. Passaic County Democrats, NJ, 1982-1990. Enlisted US Army, 1961—62, sgt. USAR, 1962—67. Named Man of Yr., Mother Cabrini Soc., 1979, Fedn. Italian Socs., 1981, Unico Passaic County, 1982, Am. Legion John Raad Post, 1983, Passaic County Young Democrats, 1983; recipient Congl. Recognition award, Internat. Assn. Fire Fighters, 2001. Mem.: Pat Mone Assn., Charles Alfano Assn., Riverside Vets., KC, Fordham U. Alumni Assn., Am. Cancer Soc., Italian-Am. Fedn., Paterson Taxpayers Assn., Elks. Democrat. Roman Catholic. Office: US House Reps 2464 Rayburn House Office Bldg Washington DC 20515-3008 Office Phone: 202-225-5751. Office Fax: 202-225-5782. *

PASCU, DAN, astronomer; b. Arad, Romania, July 20, 1938; came to U.S., 1941; s. Danila and Maria (Pojar) P.; m. Julia Fay Stephens, Aug. 28, 1965; children: David, Mark, Adam. BS in Astronomy, Case Western Res. U., 1961, MS in Astronomy, 1964; PhD in Astronomy, U. Va., Charlottesville, 1972. Astronomer U.S. Naval Obs., Washington, 1963—. Specialist in planetary satellite studies and solar sys. astrometry. Contbr. rsch. and rev. articles to profl. jours. Recipient NASA Group Achievement award, 1981, 86, Inaugural Newcomb award U.S. Naval Obs., 1983. Mem. Internat. Astron. Union, Am. Astron. Soc., Sigma Xi. Baptist. Achievements include developing techniques for astrometric observation of the planetary satellites; produced largest astrometric archive and observational database for the planetary satellites; co-discoverer 14th moon of Saturn, Calypso, and 10th moon of Saturn, Janus, 1980. Home Phone: 301-530-5258; Office Phone: 202-762-1490. Business E-Mail: pascu.dan@usno.navy.mil.

PASCUAL, CARLOS E., think-tank executive, former ambassador; b. Cuba; BA in Internat. Rels., Stanford U., 1980; MA in Pub. Policy, Harvard U., 1982. With USAID, South Africa, Mozambique, Washington, project devel. officer Sudan, 1983—92, dir., Office of Program Analysis and Coordinatoin for New Ind. States Task Force, 1994—94, dep. asst. adminstr. for Europe and New Ind. States, 1994—95; dir. for Russian, Ukrainian and Eurasian Affairs Nat. Security Coun., 1995—98, spl. asst. to Pres., sr. dir. for Russia, 1998—2000; US amb. to Ukraine US Dept. State, Kiev, 2000—03, coordinator for U.S. assistance to Europe and Eurasia, 2003—04, dir. Office of Reconstruction and Stabilization, 2004—06; v.p., dir. fgn. policy studies The Brookings Instn., Washington, 2006—. Office: The Brookings Instn 1775 Massachusetts Ave NW Washington DC 20036

PASEK, MARK EDWARD, manufacturing executive; b. Chgo., Jan. 23, 1951; s. Edward Joseph and Mary Elizabeth Pasek; m. Elizabeth M. Pasek, Oct. 6, 1974; children: Edward, Mark J., Samantha. Student, Chgo. City Coll., 1969, student, 1970, Advanced Coll. Traffic, Chgo., 1971, student, 1972. Distbn. ctr. mgr. Martin-Brower, various locations, 1971—78; warehouse mgr. B.A. Railton, Northlake, Ill., 1979—80, Jovan, Bensenville, Ill., 1980—90; pvt. cons. Hickory Hills, Ill., 1990—93; warehouse mgr. Gurensey-Bel, Chgo., 1994—2000; plant dir. Tampico Beverages, Chgo., 2000—. Author: (software) Formula Warehouse, 1998. With USAR, 1970—76. Mem.: Coun. Supply Chain Mgmt. Profls., Intertel, Mensa. Achievements include patents for lift alone; builder several SCCA sports racecars with two invitations to the National Championships in 1999 and 2002; current member of a Grand Am Cup Team (Fall Line Motorsports); designer and builder of a three wheel concept car. Avocations: SCCA sportscar racing, ATV riding, jet ski, inventing.

PASETTI, LOUIS OSCAR, retired dentist; b. Tampa, Fla., Dec. 27, 1916; s. Joseph G. and Carmen (Gonzalez) P.; m. Mary Mendez, Jan. 11, 1942; children: Louis M., Arleen Pasetti Mariotti. BS, U. Fla., 1937; DDS, Emory U., 1941; postgrad., U. Pa., 1978. Capt. U.S. Army, 1942—46; pvt. practice Tampa, Fla., 1947—2002; ret., 2002. Past. pres. Tampa Civitan Club, 1953; past lt. gov. Civitan Clubs of Tampa, 1962; past dep. gov. Civitan Internat., Fla., 1964; fin. officer Am. Legion Post 248. Named Fla. Dentist of the Yr., Fla. Acad. Gen. Dentistry, 1983; recipient meritorious Svc. award Fla. Acad. Gen. Dentistry, 1989, Disting. Svc. award, 1985. Fellow Acad. Gen. Dentistry (Lifetime Achievement award 2004), Am. Coll. Dentists, Internat. Coll. Dentists, Acad. Dentistry Internat.; mem. ADA, Fla. Dental Assn., Fla. Acad. Gen. Dentistry (pres. 1981, Lifetime Achievement award 1996, mem. emeritus 2002), Tampa Bay Acad. Gen. Dentistry (pres. 1977-78), Elks, Round Table of Civic Clubs of Tampa (sec. 1953), Palma Ceia Golf and Country Club. Democrat. Roman Catholic. Avocations: photography, orchid culture. Home: 10023 Hampton Pl Tampa FL 33618-4227

PASHGIAN, MARGARET HELEN, artist; b. Pasadena, Calif., Nov. 7, 1934; d. Aram John and Margaret (Howell) P. BA, Pomona Coll., 1956; student, Columbia U., 1957; MA in Fine Arts, Boston Univ., 1958. Art instr. Harvard-Newton Program Occidental Coll., 1977-78; artist in residence Calif. Inst. Tech., 1970-71. Grants panelist Calif. Arts Coun., Sacramento, 1993. One-woman shows include Rex Evans Gallery, LA, 1965, 67, Occidental Coll., 1967, Kornblee Gallery, NYC, 1969-72, U. Calif., Irvine, 1975, U. Calif. Santa Barbara, 1976, Stella Polaries Gallery, LA, 1981-82, Kaufman Galleries, Houston, 1982, Modernism Gallery, San Francisco, 1983, Works Gallery, Long Beach, Costa Mesa, Calif., 1986-92, Malka Gallery, LA, 1997; exhibited in group shows at Pasadena Art Mus., 1965, Carson Pirie Scott, Chgo., 1965, Calif. Palace of Legion of Honor, San Francisco, 1967, Esther Bear Gallery, Santa Barbara, 1967, 69, Lytton Ctr. of the Visual Arts, LA, 1968, Salt Lake Art Inst., Salt Lake City, 1968, Mus. Contemporary Crafts, 1969, Second Flint (Mich.) Invitational, 1969, Milw. Art Ctr., 1969, U.S.I.S. Mus., NYC, Mus. Contemporary Art, Chgo., 1970, Studio Merconi, Milan, 1970, Calif. Inst. Tech., Baxter Art Galley, 1971, 1980, Calif. Innovations, Palm Springs Dessert Mus., 1981, Calif. Internat. Arts Found. Mus. Modern Art, Paris, 1982, LA Artists in Seoul, Donsangbang Gallery, 1982, An Artistic Conversation, 1931-82, Poland, USA, Ulster Mus., Belfast, Ireland, 1983, Madison Art Ctr., Wis., 1994, Calif. State U., Fullerton, 1995, Oakland Mus., Calif., 1995, Molly Barnes Gallery, LA, Calif., 2000, Pasadena Mus. Calif. Art, 2002, Patricia Faure Gallery, LA, 2006, Norton Simon Mus., Pasadena, Calif., 2006; represented in pub. collections at River Forest State Bank, Ill., Atlantic Richfield Co., Dallas, Frederic Weisman Collection, L., Security Pacific Bank, LA, Singapore, Andrew Dickson White Mus. Art, Cornell U., Ithaca, NY, LA County Mus. Art, Santa Barbara Art Mus., Laguna Beach Mus. Art, Portland Art Mus., Oreg., Palm Springs Art Mus., Calif. Trustee, Pomona Coll, Claremont, Calif., 1987—; parade judge Tournament of Roses Centennial Parade, Pasadena, 1987; bd. dirs. LA Master Chorale, 1992—, Ojai Music Festival, 2004— NEA grantee, 1986. Home: 731 S Grand Ave Pasadena CA 91105-2424

PASHMAN, SUSAN ELLEN, writer; b. NYC, Dec. 17, 1942; d. Jonas Charles and Pearl (Steinberg) Greenfield; m. Louis Jonathan Pashman, Sept. 17, 1964 (div. Feb. 1978); children: Joshua, Benjamin. BA, NYU, 1963; MPhil, Columbia U., 1966; JD, Bklyn. Law Sch., 1982; cert. in landscape design, Harvard U. Bar: NY 1983. Tch. fgn. langs. N.Y.C. Pub. Schs., 1963-65; instr. philosophy Adelphi U., Garden City, NY, 1965-77; dir. humanities project N.Y. Coun. Humanities, NYC, 1977-79; dean coll. rels. Douglass Coll., New Brunswick, NJ, 1978-79; assoc. atty. Proskauer, Rose, Goetz & Mendelsohn, NYC, 1982-84, Moses & Singer, NYC, 1984-86, Cravath, Swaine & Moore, NYC, 1986-91; freelance writer Sag Harbor, NY, 1991—. Program dir. Pub. Access Continuing Edn., Sag Harbor, 1991—; lectr. in philosophy and ethics Jewish Ctr. of Hamptons, L.I. U. Ctr. for Creative Retirement. Author: The Speed of Light, 1997. Jewish. Avocations: gardening, cooking, tennis. Home: PO Box 2530 Sag Harbor NY 11963-0116

PASHOLK, PAUL DOUGLAS, retail executive, government official; b. Columbus, Ohio, Mar. 24, 1968; s. Jerome Joseph and Norma Anne (Weigand) Pasholk; m. Rebecca Jean Eaton, June 10, 1995; children: Rachel Marie, Victoria Elizabeth, Teresa Anne, Julia Louise. BA in History, Ohio State U., 1990, BA in Polit. Sci., 1990. Dept. supr. Kohl's Dept. Stores, Columbus, 1991-96; market news reporter U.S. Dept. of Agriculture, Fruit and Vegetable Division, Phoenix, 1996—. Author: The Columbus Public Schools and 75 Years of School Board Elections, 1992; co-author (with Rebecca Pasholk): U.S. Senate Elections: The Numbers, and the Story Behind Them; author: King of the Hill - U.S. Presidential Elections, 1992. Vol., rschr. Bill Moss for Columbus Sch. Bd., 1985, 1989, 1991, 1997, Bill Buckel for Columbus Sch. Bd., 1987, treas., 1989, 1991, 1993; presdl. elector cand. Eugene McCarthy for Pres., Columbus, 1988; vol. Bruce Babbitt for Pres., Cedar Rapids, Iowa, 1988, Jesse Jackson for Pres., Columbus, 1988, Richard Letts for Judge, Columbus, 1989, Jerry Brown for Pres., Columbus, 1992; local organizer Hands Across Am., Columbus, 1986; vol. recruiter AFL-CIO Support Group Frontlash, Columbus, 1988—90; mem. Indsl. Workers of the World, San Francisco/Ypsilanti, 1991—; organizer, chmn. West H.S. Class Reunion, Columbus, 1991; Ohio state campaign chmn. Ray Rollinson for Pres., Columbus, 1992; non-voting del. numerous Nat. Market News Assn. Confs.; mem. Friends of Freedom and Justice, Columbus, 1998—; contact Ariz. state John B. Anderson for Pres., 2000; mem. We The People, 2000—; contbr. Kirtland Reorganized LDS Ch. Temple Restoration, Kirtland, Ohio, 1996. Libertarian. Avocations: collecting buffalos, political election statistics, public speaking, editorial letters, religious collectibles. Office: 230 N First Ave Ste 404 Phoenix AZ 85003 Personal E-mail: voteforwalker@yahoo.com.

PASI, GEETA, diplomat; BA, Duke U., Durham, NC; M in French Studies, NYU. Instl. fin. market rschr., NYC; with US Fgn. Svc. US Dept. State, 1988—, assignments in Cameroon, Romania, Ghana and India, mem. Sec. of State's advance team Washington, desk officer for Afghanistan, 2001—03, dep. prin. officer Am. Consulate Gen. Frankfurt, Germany, US charge d'affaires, a.i. to Bangladesh. Office: US Embassy 3120 Dhaka Pl Washington DC 20521-3120

PASIC, HAJRUDIN, mathematician, educator; b. Sarajevo, Bosnia-Herzegovina, Mar. 13, 1945; s. Suljo and Zada Pasic; m. Nadja Osmic, Feb. 21, 1948; children: Faruk, Mirza. BS, U. Sarajevo, 1968; MS, U. Belgrade, 1976; PhD, Stanford U., Calif., 1979. From asst. prof. ro prof. U. Sarajevo, Bosnia-Herzegovina, 1980—94; prof. Ohio U., Athens, 1994—. Fellow, Fulbright Com., 1976—77. Mem.: ASME. Liberal. Muslim. Achievements include patents for electrostatic precipitators. Avocation: trumpet. Home: 47 Charles St Athens OH 45701 Office: Ohio U 261 Stocker Athens OH 45701 Home Phone: 740-592-6344; Office Phone: 740-593-9471. Office Fax: 740-593-0476. Business E-Mail: pasic@ohio.edu.

PASICH, KIRK ALAN, lawyer; b. La Jolla, Calif., May 26, 1955; s. Chris Nick and Iva Mae (Tormey) P.; m. Pamela Mary Woods, July 30, 1983; children: Christopher Thomas, Kelly Elizabeth, Connor Woods. BA in Polit. Sci., UCLA, 1977; JD, Loyola Law Sch., LA, 1980. Bar: Calif. 1980, U.S. Dist. Ct. (no., so., ea. and cen. dists.) Calif. 1981, Mich. (ea. dist.) 1997, Tex. (ea. dist.) 2001, U.S. Ct. Appeals (9th cir.) 1981, U.S. Ct. Appeals (1st cir.) 1992. Assoc. Paul, Hastings, Janofsky & Walker, LA, 1980-88, ptnr., 1988-89, Troop Steuber Pasich Reddick & Tobey, LLP, 1989-2000, Howrey Simon Arnold & White LLP, 2001—03, Pasich & Kornfeld LLP, 2003—05, Dickstein Shapiro LLP, 2005—. Author: Casualty and Liability Insurance, 1990, 2000, 03; co-author: Officers and Directors: Liabilities and Protections, 1996, 2000, 03, The Year 2000 and Beyond: Liability and Insurance for Computer Code Problems, 2000; contbg. editor: West's California Litigation Forms: Civil Procedure Before Trial, 2000; co-author, co-editor: ABA Manual for Complex Insurance Coverage Litigation, 1999, 2000, 04; entertainment law columnist, ins. law columnist L.A. and San Francisco Daily Jour., 1989—; contbr. articles to profl. jours. Active bd. dirs. Nat. Acad. Jazz, L.A., 1988-89, chmn. bd. dirs. Woody Herman Found., L.A., 1989-92, Constnl. Rights Found., 2000; active L.A. City Atty's. Task Force for Econ. Recovery, 1992-93. Named to Calif's. Legal Dream Team as 1 of state's top 25 litigators, Calif. Law Bus., 1992; named one of the nation's top 45 lawyers under age 45, Am. Lawyer, 1995, market leader for policyholder representation in California, Chambers Am. Leading Bus. Lawyers, 2003-07; named one of 500 Leading Lawyers in Am., Lawdragon, 2005, 06. Mem. ABA (mem. Task Force on Complex Insurance Coverage Litigation), Risk & Insurance Mgmt. Soc., Def. Rsch. Inst. Democrat. Avocations: reading, music, basketball. Office: Dickstein Shapiro LLP 2049 Century Park East Ste 700 Los Angeles CA 90067 Home Phone: 310-475-5374; Office Phone: 310-772-8305. Business E-Mail: pasichk@dicksteinshapiro.com.

PASIERB, STEPHEN JOHN, advertising executive, marketing professional; b. Ramsey, NJ, Oct. 9, 1962; s. Stephen Anthony and Leila Joy (Gommoll) P.; m. Wendy Ann Wiethorn, June 11, 1988. BS in Criminology, Ind. U., Ind., Pa., 1984, MEd (with honors), 1986. On-air personality Sta. WCLG, Morgantown, W.Va., 1981-83, Sta. WWVU, 1981-83, Sta. WGLU, Johnstown, Pa., 1983-85; ops. dir. Sta. WIUP, Ind., Pa., 1984-86; account exec. Sta. WLTJ, Pitts., 1986; dir. media svcs. GNVC Comm., Pitts., 1986-87; acct. mgr., new bus. Freed & Assocs., Balt., 1987-91; mgr. media comm. Md. Gov.'s office, Towson, 1991-93; from sr. v.p., dep. dir. to pres., chief exec. Partnership for a Drug-Free Am., NYC, 1993—. Adv. bd. mem. Sta. WMAR-TV, Balt., 1994-96. Mktg. vol. Balt. Coalition Against Drugs, 1993-95; media vol. D.C. Cmty./Coalition Against Drugs. Recipient Markee awards Nat. Assn. Addictions Comm., Seattle, 1992, award of excellence Internat. Assn. Bus. Communicators, Balt., 1993, Discovery Health Channel Med. Honors, 2004; named to Advt. Hall of Fame, Am. Advt. Fedn., 2003. Mem. Advt. Assn. Balt. (sec. 1987—), Balt. Area Soaring Soc. (bd. dirs. 1991—, pres. 1992, newsletter editor 1993-97). Avocations: sailplanes, soaring, wine collecting, racquetball. Office: Partnership For A Drug-Free Am 405 Lexington Ave Rm 1601 New York NY 10174 Office Phone: 212-922-1560. Office Fax: 212-922-1570.

PASIK-DUNCAN, BOZENNA JANINA, mathematics professor, researcher; b. Radom, Warsaw, Poland, June 30, 1947; d. Janina and Antoni Pasik; m. Tyrone Edward Duncan, May 21, 1983; 1 child, Dominique Duncan. MS, Warsaw U., 1970, PhD, 1978, D, 1986. Asst. prof. Warsaw Sch. Econ., 1970—84; instr. U. Kans., Lawrence, 1984—87, asst. prof., 1987—89, assoc. prof., 1989—93, prof. math., 1993—. Lectr. Warsaw Tech. U., 1973—75. Contbr. scientific papers to profl. jours. Membeer of the bd. of governors IEEE Control Systems Soc., Piscataway, NJ, 1996—2002. Recipient Excellence in Rsch. and Tchg., Ministry of Higher Edn. and Sci., 1975; fellow, IREX, 1982—83; Rsch. grant, NSF, 1987—. Mem.: AAUW, IEEE (v.p. 1999, bd. govs. 1996, medal 2000, Dist. Mem. award 2000, fellow 2001), Internat. Stats. Inst., Soc. Indsl. and Applied Math., Bernoulli Soc., Am. Math. Soc., Polish Math. Soc., Assn. Women in

Math. (L. Hay award 2004), Math. Assn. Am. Achievements include research in stochastic adaptive control of continous time systems. Avocations: travel, music, poetry. Home: 1208 Schwarz Rd Lawrence KS 66049 Office: Univ Kans Dept Math Lawrence KS 66045 Home Phone: 785-841-2086; Office Phone: 785-864-5162. Office Fax: 785-864-5255. Business E-Mail: bozenna@math.ku.edu.

PASINETTI, NINA DENTON, dance educator, choreographer; b. Charleston, W.Va., July 27, 1943; d. Oliver Berman and Lelia Bernice Denton; m. Thomas Patrick Pasinetti, Mar. 10, 2000; stepchildren: Thomas Jr., Terri Brannan. BS, U. Charleston, W.Va.; MA, Ohio U., Athens. Grad. asst. math. tchr. Ohio U., 1965—66; math. tchr. Glouster HS, Ohio, 1968; math. and theater tchr. George Washington HS, Charleston, 1968—99, choreographer, dir. musicals, 1968—; choreographer Charleston Light Opera Guild, 1971—, artistic dir., 1983—; choreographer Kanawha Players, Charleston, 1968, 1969, 1974, W.Va. State Coll. Fine Arts, Institute, 1969, 1970; theater adjudicator W.Va. State Thespian Festival, 2000—. Tchr., dir. dance studio YWCA, Charleston, 1970—82; choreographer, dir. Jenny Wiley Profl. Music Theatre, Prestonburg, Ky., 1983—85; dir., founder George Washington Dance Co., Appalachian Youth Jazz Ballet Co., 1968—93; owner, tchr. Ballet and Mus. Theatre Dance Arts Inc., Charleston, 1983—93; dir. Charleston Theatre Festival, 2000—03. Choreographer W.Va. dance festivals, dinner theaters, sr. programs. Pres. Dance W.Va., 1981—85; program chmn. Clay Ctr. Arts, Charleston, 2004—; v.p., dance chair Festivall Charleston, 2004—. Named Outstanding Individual Artist, Mayor's Arts Awards, 1996, East Bank HS Alumnus of Yr., Charleston, 1999; recipient recognition at Gov.'s Arts Awards, Gov. of W.Va., 2006. Avocations: movies, pets, antiques, travel, theater. Home: 1603 Clark Rd Charleston WV 25314 Personal E-mail: pasinettindrudi@aol.com.

PASINETTI, PIER MARIA, author; b. Venice, Italy, June 24, 1913; came to U.S., 1946, naturalized, 1952; s. Carlo and Maria (Ciardi) P. Dottore in Lettere, U. Padua, Italy, 1935; PhD in Comparative Lit., Yale U., 1949. Fellow La. State U., 1935-36, U. Calif. at Berkeley, 1936-37; lectr. U. Stockholm, 1942-46; prof. Italian and comparative lit. UCLA, 1949—. Author: L'ira di Dio, 1942, Venetian Red, 1960, The Smile on the Face of the Lion, 1965, From the Academy Bridge, 1970, Suddenly Tomorrow, 1971, Dall' Estrema America, 1975, Il Centro, 1979, Dorsoduro, 1983, Life for Art's Sake: Studies in the Literary Myth of the Romantic Artist, 1985, Melodramma, 1993, Piccole Veneziane Complicate, 1996, Astolfo, 1999; also articles, revs., film scripts. Recipient Fiction award Nat. Inst. Arts and Letters, 1965, Prix Écureuil Li. Etrangère, 1996. Mem. Authors Guild. Clubs: Elizabethan Yale. Office: 1259 Dorsoduro Venice Italy 30123

PASK, SCOTT, set designer; Grad., Yale Sch. Drama. Broadway: Cabaret, 1998, Urinetown (Lucille Lortel nom.), 2001, Amour, 2002, Take Me Out, 2003, Little Shop of Horrors (Touring Broadway award, best prodn. design, 2005), La Cage aux Folles, 2004, Pillowman, (Tony award, best scenic design, 2005), Sweet Charity, 2005, The Wedding Singer, 2006, Fame Becomes Me, 2006, The Lieutenant of Inishmore, 2006, The Coast of Utopia, 2006 (Outer Critics Cir. award outstanding set design, 2007, Drama Desk award outstanding set design of a play, 2007, Tony award best scenic design of play, 2007); in London: On an Average Day, Tales from Hollywood, Albert Herring, Pillowman; also appeared at Almeida Theatre, Royal Nat. Theatre, Donmar Warehouse, Opera North, Atlantic Theater Co., The Pub. Theatre, Roundabout Theatre, Yale Rep., South Coast Rep., Ctr. Stage, Williamstown, NY Theatre Workshop, Classic Stage Co., Playwrights Horizons, Chgo. Opera Theater, Bklyn. Acad. Music. Recipient Lucille Lortel award, 1999, Henry Hewes award, Am. Theater Wing, 1999, Bessie award, 2001. Office: 4 Times Sq #15 New York NY 10036-6518 *

PASKACH, DAVID M., lawyer, food products executive; BS in Acctg., Iowa State U., 1980; JD, U. Ill., 1983. Bar: Iowa 1983, Ill. 1983, Minn. 1989. Atty., Iowa; corp. atty. Schwan Food, Marshall, Minn., 1989—93, sr. atty., 1993—97, gen. counsel, 1997, v.p. adminstrn., exec. v.p., gen. counsel, sec., 1997—2004; pres. Schwan's Venture Group, Marshall, 2005—. Lt. col. USAFR, ret. Office: Schwan Food 115 W College Dr Marshall MN 56258

PASKIN, MICHAEL A., lawyer; b. Phila., Jan. 23, 1970; BA cum laude, Univ. Pa., 1992; JD, Fordham Univ., 1995. Bar: NY 1996. Law clk., Hon. Paul J. Kelly, Jr. US Ct. of Appeals, 10th Cir.; assoc. Cravath Swaine & Moore LLP, NYC, 1996—2003, ptnr., litig., 2003—. Assoc. editor Fordham Law Rev. Office: Carvath Swaine & Moore LLP Worldwide Plz 825 Eighth Ave New York NY 10019-7475 Office Phone: 212-474-1760. Office Fax: 212-474-3700. Business E-Mail: mpaskin@cravath.com.

PASKY, GARY JEROME, consumer products company executive; b. Burbank, Calif., Feb. 26, 1964; s. Norman Jeroma Pasky and Norma Lee Phillips; m. Angela Marie Nilsby, Apr. 29, 1995; children: Bryce, Miranda, Aubrey. BS in Computer Sci., U. Calif., Santa Barbara, 1986. Developer Computer Sci. Corp., Pt. Mugu, Calif., 1986—88; product mgr. Softool Corp., Santa Barbara, 1988—92; devel. mgr. QAD, Inc., Calif., 1992—95; product svcs. mgr. PICS, Inc., Calif., 1995—. Author: (software) Auto Pac, 2006. Mem.: Tau Beta Pi, Mensa. Avocations: Karate, volleyball. Home: 523 Laruelwood Dr Paso Robles CA 93446

PASNICU, CORNEL, mathematician, educator; b. Bucharest, Romania, Sept. 6, 1953; arrived in U.S., 1992; s. Tanasa Pasnicu, Xenia Adina Pasnicu; m. Adina Melania Truta; 1 child, Nastasia Laura. BA, U. Bucharest, 1976, MS, 1977, PhD, 1987. Rsch. fellow INCREST (IMAR), Bucharest, Romania, 1980—91; vis. scholar U. Copenhagen, 1991—91; vis. assoc. prof. U. Toronto, Ont., Canada, 1992—92; assoc. prof. U. P.R., San Juan, 1992—97, full prof., 1997—. Mem. operator algebras/operator theory panel NSF, Arlington, Va., 2002. Contbr. articles to profl. jours. Recipient S. Stoilov prize, Romanian Acad., 1988; grantee, NSF, 1994—96, 1996—2000, 2001—, Army Rsch. Office, 2000—. Mem.: Am. Math. Soc. Avocations: reading, music, sports.

PASQUIER, JOËL, music educator; b. Montmorency, France, Sept. 25, 1943; arrived in Can., 1967; s. Jean and Raymonde (Gourdin) P.; m. Anne Vachon, Nov. 28, 1970; 1 child, Ariane. Grad. in piano and chamber music, Conservatoire Nat. Superieur de Musique, Paris, 1962. Prof. Conservatoire de Musique de St. Germain-en-Laye, France, 1964-65; grad. asst. Sch. Music, Ind. U., Bloomington, 1965-67; tchr. piano U. Laval, Quebec, Canada, 1967—2003, dir., 1988-91. Recording artist ATMA Records. Appeared as solo pianist concert halls, radio, TV, with chamber and symphony orchs. in France, U.S., Can., The Netherlands. Fulbright scholar Ind. U., 1965. Mem. Que. Yacht Club. Personal E-mail: orion_556@hotmail.com.

PASS, CHARLOTTE LOUISE, literature educator, consultant; b. Oneonta, Ala., Sept. 2, 1966; d. James Arnold and Betty Jo Pass. Cert. English Edn. Ala., 1998, ESL Ala., 2005. Acad. tutor, supr. U. Ala. Athletic Dept., Tuscaloosa, 1986—93; English/journalism tchr. Tuscaloosa Acad., 1989—91; grad. tchg. asst. U. Ala., Tuscaloosa, 1988—91, grad. instr., 2002—; English/music appreciation tchr. Hillcrest HS, Tuscaloosa, 1998—2001; home sch. tchr. Victory Christian Sch., Tuscaloosa, 2002—04. Literacy cons. Eastwood Mid. Sch., Ala., 2003—; presenter and cons. in field. Mem.: Am. Assn. Applied Linguistics (assoc.), Am. Ednl. Rsch. Assn. (assoc.), Mid-South Ednl. Ednl. Rsch. Assn. (assoc.), Tchrs. of English to Speakers of Other Languages (assoc.), Internat. Reading Assn. (assoc.), Nat. Reading Conf. (assoc.), Nat. Coun. Tchrs. of English (assoc.), Assn. Tchr. Educators (assoc.), ASCD (assoc.), Ala. Reading Assn. (assoc.), Ala. Coun. Tchrs. of English (assoc.), ASPCA, Amnesty Internat., Peta, Nat. Humane Soc., Phi Delta Kappa (assoc.), Phi Kappa Phi (life). Independent. Episcopalian. Avocations: reading, piano, singing. Home: 1022 Fairfax Dr Tuscaloosa AL 35406 Office: Univ Ala PO Box 870232 204 Graves Hall Tuscaloosa AL 35487 Home Phone: 205-758-7567; Office Phone: 205-758-7567.

PASSAIC, JOSEPH G., lawyer; b. Newark, Aug. 23, 1953; BA, Pa. State Univ., 1975; JD, Widener Univ., 1979. Bar: Pa. 1979, DC 1985. Atty. Office of Gen. Counsel, FDIC, Washington, 1979—82, sr. atty., 1982—83; ptnr., Securities, Tech. Law, Banking practices, mem. mgmt. com. Patton Boggs LLP, Washington. Adj. prof. Georgetown Univ. Sch. Bus.; mem. editl. bd. Banking Law Report. Co-author: Banking Law in the U.S. Office: Patton Boggs LLP 2550 M St NW Washington DC 20037-1350 Office Phone: 202-457-6104. Office Fax: 202-457-6315. Business E-Mail: jpassaic@pattonboggs.com.

PASSANO, E. MAGRUDER, JR., management consultant; b. Balt., Oct. 2, 1942; s. Edward M. and Mildred P. (Nelson) P.; m. Helen C. Marikle, Sept. 4, 1971; children: Catherine, Tammy, Sarah. BS, Johns Hopkins U., 1967, MA, 1969. With Waverly Inc., Balt., 1965-98, salesman, 1970-73, v.p., 1973-75, v.p. adminstrn., sec., 1975-90, vice chmn., sec., 1990-98; pres., CEO One Waverly LLC, Balt., 1998—. Chmn. Passano Found., Balt., 1982—; pres. Am. Lung Assn., Md., 1982-84; mem. exec. com. Vol. Coun. Equal Opportunity, Balt., 1978-2002, chmn., 1995-2002; bd. dirs. Combined Health Appeal Am., 1994-97; pres. (CHA) Combined Health Agys., Md., 1985-87, chmn. exec. com., 1987-95; pres. 12:30 Club Balt., 1981-83; mem. exec. com. Balt. City Life Mus., 1982-93, v.p. 1987-93; trustee emeritus, 1993-98; mem. adv. coun. Johns Hopkins U. Sch. Profl. Studies in Bus. and Edn., 1984—, exec. chair alumni chpt., 1986-89, chair edn. cmty. devel. iniative, 1995—2006; mem. Md. Gov.'s Commn. on High Blood Pressure and Related Cardiovascular Risk Factors, 1986-2002; bd. govs. Md. New Directions, Inc., 1987-94; bd. dirs., mem. exec. com. YMCA Ctrl. Md., 1988-96; treas., bd. dirs., chmn. edn. com. Pride of Balt., 1990—; bd. dirs. Ind. Coll. Fund Md., 1994—; mem. bd. visitors Towson State U., 1994—2006, chmn. 1997-2001, Sch. Medicine U. Md., 1995—; mem. planning com., bd. vis. Md. Bus. Responsive Govt., 1994-2002. With USN, 1963-65. Recipient Prince Hall Bicentennial award Masons, 1975; citations Mayor of Balt., 1976, City of Balt., 1977, Vol. of Yr. award for outstanding svc. to CICHA, 1984-85, Presdl. award for outstanding svc. to Am. Lung Assn. Md., 1985, Outstanding Vol., 1988, Disting. Svc. award Soc. Profl. Journalists, 1987, Outstanding Svc. award Am. Heart Assn., 1988, Outstanding Vol. Svc. award Balt. Assn. Retarded Citizens, 1990, Vol. of Yr./Outstanding Leadership and Dedication award Combined Health Agys., 1991-92, Outstanding Family of the Century, Am. Lung Assn. Md., 2003, Outstanding Bd. Mem., Ind. Coll. Fund Md., 2004. Mem. Purchasing Mgmt. Assn. Md. (chmn. com. 1968-70), Balt. Jaycees (v.p. 1974-76, internat. senator 1975), Greater Balt. Minority Purchasing Coun. (Svc. award 1978), Soc. Colonial Wars (chpt. gov. 1989-91), Johns Hopkins U. Alumni Assn. (pres. Balt. 1984-86, Univ. Heritage award 1987). Democrat. Episcopalian. Home: 3925 Linkwood Rd Baltimore MD 21210-3001 Office: One Waverly LLC 1122 Kenilworth Dr Ste 115 Towson MD 21204-2142 E-mail: macpassano@verizon.net.

PASSANTINO, BENJAMIN ARTHUR, marketing executive; b. Bklyn., Feb. 26, 1956; s. Anthony Frank and Ann Marie (Ruggerio) Passantino. Mgr. pub. rels. AT&T, NYC, mgr. mktg. comm. and new techs.; pres. B. Arthur Comm., Morristown, NJ, 1984-89; sr. v.p. bus. devel. IMEDIA Creative Corp. Mktg., Morristown, 1989-94, also dir.; mng. ptnr., CEO, Tribeca Global, Inc., Hackettstown, NJ; dir. media and comm. onProject-.com, Morristown, NJ, 2000—01; pres. Avid Records, Inc., NYC, 2002—; COO Avid Listener, Inc., NYC, 2002—. Bd. dir. Dieknowlogist, Inc., N.Y.C., One World Botanicals, Inc., Red Bank, N.J., Lasercomb Am., Inc., N.Y.C., The Perfect Supply Co., Inc., N.Y.C., Imedia, Morristown, Medicines Global. Co-author: One with the Flame, NFL Quarterbacks; contbr. articles to mags. Bd. dir. Am. Cancer Soc., Morristown, Jr. Achievement, Basking Ridge, NJ; mem. Washington Twp. (Morris County) Planning Bd., chairperson econ. devel. com.; trustee Drakestown United Meth. Ch. Mem. IEEE, Internat. Assn. Bus. Communicators, Am. Mktg. Assn., Bus. Profls. of Advt. Assn., Conf. Bd. Office: 375 Mt Prospect Ave Ste 7BE Newark NJ 07104 Office Phone: 201-456-6500. E-mail: bap@avidrecords.com.

PASSARO, PAUL CHARLES, strategic planning consultant; b. Ridgewood, NJ, June 6, 1967; s. Richard Paul and Barbara (Brown) Passaro; m. Kristi-Anne Tolo, June 25, 1994; children: Peter James, Anne Marie, Charles Andrew. BA in History cum laude, Williams Coll., Williamstown, Mass., 1989; MBA, U. N.C., 1993. Mcpl. bond trader and salesman Roosevelt & Cross, Inc., NYC, 1989—91; v.p. The Fraser Co., Hilton Head, SC, 1992—94; CFO Pine Needles and Mid Pines Resorts, Southern Pines, NC, 1994—2003; COO EastWest Ptnrs. Club Mgmt., Chapel Hill, NC, 2003—06; pres. Pansado Cons., 2004—. Bd. dirs. small bus. adv. bd. NC Citizens for Bus. and Industry, Raleigh, 1999—2002; v.p. The Toppers, NYC, 1991; founder Habitat for Humanity Charity Golf Classic, Chapel Hill, 1992—2004; mem. fin. com. Trinity Sch., Durham and Chapel Hill, 1999—2002; bd. dirs. Leadership NC, 1999—2005; mem. audit com. NC Rep. Party, Raleigh, 1999—2003, chmn., 2001—03; alt. del. 2004 Rep. Nat. Conv.; elder Christ Cmty. Ch., Chapel Hill, 2006—. Mem.: Christmas Fore Moore (treas. 1997—2003, Charity Golf Tourney), Theodore Roosevelt Assn. Republican. Avocations: bible study, golf, reading history, bird hunting. Home Phone: 919-932-6404. Personal E-mail: pcpassaro@yahoo.com.

PASSEY, GEORGE EDWARD, psychologist, educator; b. Stratford, Conn., Sept. 28, 1920; s. Henry Richard and Elizabeth (Angus) P.; m. Algie Aldridge Ashe, Nov. 18, 1950; children— Richard Ashe, Elizabeth Aldridge, Mary Louise. BS, Springfield Coll., 1942; MA, Clark U., 1947; PhD, Tulane U., 1950. Asst. prof. U. Ala., Tuscaloosa, 1952-55, assoc. prof., 1955-56, 57-59, prof., 1959-63, prof. psychology, chmn. div. social and behavioral scis. Birmingham, 1967-73, prof. engring., 1969-84, Disting. Service prof. psychology, 1984-85, Disting Service prof. emeritus, 1985—; dean U. Ala. (Sch. Social and Behavioral Scis.), 1973-84. Research scientist Lockheed Ga. Co., Marietta, Ga., 1956-57, 63-65, cons., 1965-67; prof. Ga. Inst. Tech., 1965-67 Served with USNR, 1942-46, PTO; with USAF, 1951-52. Fellow Am. Psychol. Assn.; mem. So. Soc. for Philosophy and Psychology, Southeastern Psychol. Assn., Ala. Psychol. Assn., Pine Harbor Golf and Racquet Club, Sigma Xi. Home: 7141 Skyline Dr Pell City AL 35128-6936 E-mail: gpassey@centurytel.net. *Whatever success I have enjoyed ought to be attributed to the attempt I have made to carry out the admonitions of my parents to make choices only after having appraised the alternatives in terms of their consequences, to weigh ethical considerations above all others, never to demand of others what one is unwilling to give of himself, and to work untiringly for those causes to which one is committed.*

PASSLEY, JOSEF ANTONIO, psychologist, educator, writer; b. Kingston, Jamaica, Oct. 22, 1974; s. Harold Arnold and Yvonne Claire Passley; m. Staci Latreese Manago, July 29, 2005. AS, Lancaster Bible Coll., 1995, BS, 1996; MA, Towson U., Md., 1999; PhD, Walden U., 2004. Licensed Clinical Professional Counselor Md., 2004. Mental health worker Sheppard and Enoch Pratt Hosp., Towson, 1996—99, spl. edn. tchr., 1999—2000; child adolescent therapist Johns Hopkins Bayview Med. Ctr., Balt., 2000—05, sr. child/adolescent therapist Baltimore, Md., 2005—; psychotherapist Cedar Ridge Counseling Ctr., Eldersburg, Md., 2005—. Radio guest WOLB Radio, Lanham, Md., 2004—; cons. Johns Hopkins Hosp., Balt., 2005—; adj. prof. Lancaster Bible Coll., Pa., 2004—, U. Balt., 2005—; assoc. prof. Ctrl. Mich. U., 2006—; faculty assoc. Johns Hopkins U., 2006—, 2006—. Co-author: (tng. manual) Keeping Families Strong: A Clinic Based Intervention, Single Parenting in the 21st Century and Beyond; author (book), 2006. Recipient Psi Chi Nat. Honor Soc., Walden U., 2000, Outstanding Clinician award, Johns Hopkins Bayview Med. Ctr., 2003, Employee Excellence award, 2003. Mem.: Media Psychology (assoc.), Soc. Child and Adolescent Psychology (assoc.), Am. Assn. Christian Counselors (assoc.), APA (assoc.). Avocations: reading, travel. Office: Johns Hopkins Bayview Med Ctr 4940 Eastern Ave Baltimore MD 21224 Office Phone: 443-621-7260. Business E-Mail: jpassle1@jhmi.edu.

PASSLOF, PAT, artist, educator; b. Brunswick, Ga. m. Milton Resnick. Student, Queens Coll., Flushing, 1946—48, Black Mountain Coll., NC, 1948, Willem de Kooning, 1948—50; BFA, Cranbrook Coll., Bloomfield Hills, Mich., 1951. Prof. art Coll. of Staten Island, CUNY, 1972—. One-woman shows include Elizabeth Harris Gallery, 1993, 1996, 1998, 2000, 2002, 2005; contbr.: di Suvero Peace Tower, Whitney Biennial, 2006. Fellow John Simon Guggenheim Meml. Found., 1999-2000; recipient award of Merit for painting, Am. Acad. of Arts and Letters, 2000, Purchase award Hassam, Speicher, Betts and Symons Fund of the Am. Acad., 2000, award for achievement in the arts Coun. on Arts and Humanities for S.I., 2001. Mem.: Nat. Acad. (Edwin P. Palmer award 2006). Address: c/o Elizabeth Harris Gallery 529 W 20th St 6E New York NY 10011

PASSMAN, MARC A., vascular surgeon; b. Hartford, Conn., Dec. 25, 1965; m. Cora Passman; children: Corinne, Isabelle. MD, U. Vt., 1991. Cert. Am. Bd. Surgery, 1998. Intern Oreg. Health Scis. U., 1991—92, resident, 1992—97; vascular fellow U.N.C. Chapel Hill, 1997—99; attending physician VA Hosp., 1999—; asst. prof. surgery Vanderbilt U. Med Ctr., Nashville, 1999—. Recipient Chief Resident Teaching award, Oreg. Health Scis. Ctr., 1997; scholar James Bowdoin scholar, Bowdoin Coll., Brunswick, ME, 1984—87. Fellow: Am. Coll. Surgeons. Office: Vanderbilt U Med Ctr 1161 22d Ave S D-5237 MCN Nashville TN 37232 Office Phone: 615-322-2343. Office Fax: 615-343-4251. Business E-Mail: marc.passman@vanderbilt.edu.

PASSON, RICHARD HENRY, retired academic administrator, language educator; b. Hazleton, Pa., Aug. 18, 1939; s. Henry Richard and Grace Miriam (Bernstein) P.; m. Margaret Rose Ferdinand, Aug. 14, 1965; children— Michael, Rebecca, Christopher. BA (Bishop Hafey scholar), King's Coll., Pa., 1961; MA, U. Notre Dame, 1963, PhD (NDEA fellow), 1965. From instr. to prof. English U. Scranton, 1964-73, chmn. English dept., 1970-73, fgn. student adviser, 1965-67; dean Coll. Arts and Scis., Creighton U., Omaha, 1973-77; acad. v.p. St. Joseph's U., Phila., 1977-84; provost U. Scranton, Pa., 1984-2000, prof. English Pa., 2000—02, Pa., 2004—; interim acad. v.p. St. Joseph's U., Phila., 2002—04. Contbr. articles profl. jours. Recipient grant Nat. Assn. Fgn. Students, 1966 Mem. MLA, Am. Assn. Higher Edn., Am. Assn. Acad. Deans, Nat. Coun. Tchrs. English. Democrat. Roman Catholic. Office: U Scranton 402 Brennan Hall Scranton PA 18510 Home Phone: 570-586-1880; Office Phone: 570-941-4327. Business E-Mail: passonr1@scranton.edu.

PASSTY, JEANETTE NYDA, literature and language professor, writer; b. LA, Jan. 19, 1947; d. Walter Isaac and Mollie Sarah Nyda; m. Gregory Bohdan Passty, June 18, 1976; 1 child, Benjamin. AA, L.A. Valley Coll., 1966; BA, UCLA, 1968; MA, U. So. Calif., 1974, PhD, 1982. Cert. c.c. instr., Calif. Tchg. asst., lectr., assoc. dir. freshman English program U. So. Calif., 1971—78; lectr. English dept. U. Tex., Austin, 1983—85; vis. asst. prof., adj. assoc. prof. Tex. Luth. U., Seguin, 1983, 1985—87; from instr. to asst. prof. St. Philip's Coll., San Antonio, Calif., 1988—92, assoc. prof., 1992—. Lectr. UCLA, U. Tex., Austin, Western Mich. U., U. Louisville, Salisbury State U., Morehead State U., Tex. Tech. U., U. Wales, Bangor; humanities book reviewer CHOICE (ALA Jour.), 1985—86; manuscript reviewer Fairleigh Dickinson U. Press, 1991—; editl. cons. CONNECTIONS: Online Distance Learning Faculty Forum, 2002—. Author: Eros and Androgyny: The Legacy of Rose Macaulay, 1988, The Lion Tells Her Story: A Biography of the Honorable N.P. Brooks Hinton, 1998, Bringing Denis Home: The Hero from Hope, Kansas, 2001; annotator: Alice Crawford's Paradise Pursued, 1995; contbr. articles to encyclopedia and profl. jours.; guest Sta. KSPL Radio in Touch With, 1989; appearance Sta. KENS-TV, 1992; Channel 12 Morehead, KY, 1998; CNN, 1995, Roadside (entr'acte with G.S. Bailey), 2000. Mem. Nat. Abortion Rights Action League, Tex. Abortion Rights Action League, Greenpeace, Environ. Def. Fund, The Nature Conservancy, NOW, Sierra Club, Handgun Control Inc., Orgn. Internat. Conf. on the Holocaust, San Antonio, 2000. Recipient Elizabeth K. Pleasants Tchg. award, U. So. Calif., 1974, letters of appreciation, Lord Bonham-Carter, 1987, HRH Princess Margaret, 1989—90, Oustanding Acad. Book award, ALA, 1989, Women Honoring Women award, Am. Assn. Women in C.C.s, 1997, Katherine Anne Porter Lit. prize, 1999, NISOD Internat. Conf. on Tchg. and Leadership Excellence Award, 2003, St. Philip's Coll. Tchg. Excellence award, 2003—04; Vierling Kersey scholar, L.A. Valley Coll., 1964—66, NEH grantee, Tex. Luth. U., 1986. Mem. AAUW, MLA, Nat. Coun. Tchrs. English, South Ctrl. Soc. 18th Century Studies, Victorians Inst., Virginia Woolf Soc. Avocations: Tae Kwon Do, travel. Office: St Phillips College Bookstore Tbc 951 County Road 769 Devine TX 78016-4422 Home Phone: 512-396-5968; Office Phone: 210-531-3373. Business E-Mail: jpassty@accd.edu.

PASSUT, CHRISTINE DIANA, special education educator; b. Fairfax, Va., Dec. 9, 1974; d. Robert Charles and Barbara Ann Passut. BA in Psychology, Roanoke Coll., Salem, Va., 1997; M in Spl. Edn., Marymount U., Arlington, Va., 2002. Lic. tchr. learning disabled/emotionally disabled Va. Dept. Edn., 2002. Lead tchr. for four and five yr. olds Child Time Child Care Ctr., Faifax, 1997—98; pub. health tng. asst. Fairfax County Pub. Schs. - Langley HS, McLean, Va., 1998—99, instrnl. asst. for students with autism, 1999—2000, tchr. for students with autism; tchr. for students with autism and mild mental retardation Fairfax County Pub. Schs. - Annandale HS, Va., 2003—. Support tchr. Tech. Outreach Program, Annandale H.S., 2004, co-sponsor B-Buddies club, 2005—; co-sponsor interlinks club Langley H.S. Mem.: Sierra Club, World Wildlife Fedn., Fairfax Edn. Assn., Endometriosis Assn., Gardening Club Am. (life), Cooking Club Am. (life). Lutheran. Avocations: reading, gardening, cooking, playing with my dogs. Office: Annandale HS 4700 Medford Dr Annandale VA 22003 Home Phone: 703-978-0156; Office Phone: 703-642-4945. Business E-Mail: cpassut@fcps.edu.

PASSWATER, BARBARA GAYHART, real estate broker; b. Phila., July 10, 1945; d. Clarence Leonard and Margaret Jamison; m. Richard Albert Passwater, June 2, 1964; children: Richard Alan, Michael Eric. AA, Goldey-Beacom Coll., 1963; BA, Salisbury State U., 1981. Notary pub., Md. Sec. DuPont, Wilmington, Del., 1963-65, Nuclear-Chgo., Silver Spring, Md., 1965-67; office mgr. Montgomery County Sch. System, Wheaton, Md., 1977-79; adminstrv. asst. Solgar Nutritional Rsch. Ctr., Berlin, Md., 1979-94, asst. to v.p. R&D, 1995—2001; assoc. broker Prudential-Groff Realty, Berlin, Md., 1983-87, ReMax, Inc., Berlin, Md., 1987-88; broker, mgr., developers rep. River Run Sales Ctr., Berlin, Md., 1988-96; broker Solgar Realty LLC, Berlin, Md., 1997—98, CAMBR Realty LLC, Berlin, 1998—. Treas. Ocean Pines (Md.) Vol. Fire Dept. Aux., 1981—84, emergency med. tech., 1983—95, life mem., 1996—; sec. Ocean Pines Fire Dept., 1990—95; mem. Citizens Rev. Bd., Snow Hill, Md., 1984—; state bd. del. Child Protection Sys.; bd. dirs. Worcester Gold, 2002—; mem. Worcester County Panel on Child Abuse and Neglect, 2002—; Worcester County organizer Rainbows, 2003—; mem. com. Worcester County YMCA, 2005; Sunday sch. tchr. Cmty. Ch. of Ocean Pines, 1999—2005, co-chair nuture and edn. com., 2001—05. Recipient Woman of the Yr., Worcester County Commn. for Women, 2006. Mem.

Coastal Assn. Realtors of Md., Inc., Beta Sigma Phi, Phi Kappa Phi. Avocations: photography, golf. Office: CAMBR Realty LLC 11017 Manklin Meadows Ln Berlin MD 21811-9340 Office Phone: 410-208-9006. Business E-Mail: cambr@dmv.com.

PASSWATER, RICHARD ALBERT, biochemist, author; b. Wilmington, Del., Oct. 13, 1937; s. Stanley Leroy and Mabel Rosetta (King) P.; m. Barbara Sarah Gayhart, June 2, 1964; children: Richard Alan, Michael Eric. BS, U. Del., 1959; PhD, Bernadean U., 1976. Cert. firefighter. Supr. instrumental analysis lab. Allied Chem. Corp., Marcus Hook, Pa., 1959-64; tech. svcs. rep. F&M Sci. Corp., Avondale, Pa., 1965; dir. applications lab. Am. Instrument Co., Silver Spring, Md., 1965-77; dir. Am. Gen. Enterprises, Minn.; former daily broadcaster Sta. WMCA, NYC, 1980-88, Sta. WRNG, Atlanta, 1982-85; rsch. dir. Solgar Nutritional Rsch. Ctr., Berlin, Md., 1978—. Corp. v.p. Solgar Co., Inc.; mem. health, edn., rsch. coun. adv. bd. ICCC, NGO, UN, 2003—; chmn. Worcester County Emergency Planning Com., 1995-96; bd. dirs. Worcester Meml. Hosp., Atlantic Gen. Hosp., River Run Assn.; pres. 1989-92, Subaqueous Exploration and Archeology Ltd.; apptd. Md. State One Md. Com. and the Eastern Shore Econ. Task Force, Md. Gov. Glendenning, 1999, 2000. Author: Guide to Fluorescence Literature, vol. 1, 1967, vol. 2, 1970, vol. 3, 1974, Supernutrition, 1975, Supernutrition for Health Hearts, 1977, Super Calorie, Carbohydrate Counter, 1978, Cancer and Its Nutritional Therapies, 1978, 83, 93, The Easy No-Flab Diet, 1979, Selenium as Food and Medicine, 1980, The Slendernow Diet, 1982, (with Dr. E. Cranton), Trace Elements, Hair Analysis and Nutrition, 1983, The New Supernutrition, 1991, The Longevity Factor, 1993, Cancer Prevention and Nutritional Therapy, 1993, (with Ben Friedrich and Hans Kugler) Heart Health, 1994, Pycnogenol: The Super Protector Nutrient, 1994, Lipoic Acid: The Metabolic Antioxidant, 1995, numerous others; contbg. author: Fire Protection Guide to Hazardous Materials, 1991; editor Fluorescence News, 1966-77, Jour. Applied Health Scis., 1982-83; mem. editl. bd. Nutritional Perspectives, 1978-96, The Body Forum, 1979-80, Jour. Holistic Medicine, 1981-88, VIM Newsletter, 1979—99; contbg. Firehouse Mag., 1988-94, Jour. Applied Nutritrion; contbr. over 400 health articles to mags.; co-editor booklet series Your Good Health; sci. adv. and columnist Whole Foods mag.; patentee in field. Bd. dirs. Sci. Documentation Ctr., Dunfermline, Eng.; Am. Found. Firefighter Health and Safety; chief Ocean Pines Vol. Fire Dept., 1984-93; active Emergency Med. Tech.; adviser Nat. Inst. Nutrition Edn.; past adv. bd. Stephen Decatur High Sch., Worcester County Dept. Edn. Cubmaster, 1975-79. Named Citizen of Yr. Ocean Pines, Md., 1987; recipient 5th Ann. Achievement award, 1989, VFW Cert. of Commendation, 1988, Industry award Nat. Inst. Nutritional Edn., 1991, Pres.'s award Nat. Nutritional Foods Assn., 1999, James Lind Scientific Achievement award, 2004, James Peter Zarger Free Press award, 2004; named to Delmarva Fireman's Hall of Fame, 1993. Fellow Internat. Acad. Preventive Medicine, Am. Inst. Chemists; mem. ASTM, AAAS, Am. Chem. Soc., Gerontology Soc., Am. Geriatric Soc., Am. Aging Assn., Internat. Found. Preventive Medicine (v.p.), Internat. Union Pure and Applied Chemistry, Royal Soc. Chemistry (London), Internat. Acad. Holistic Health and Medicine, Capital Chem. Soc., Nutrition Today Soc., Am. Acad. Applid Health Sci. (pres., bd. dirs.), Internat. Found. Preventive Medicine (v.p., dir.), Inst. Nutritional Rsch., N.Y. Acad. Scis., Nat. Fire Protection Assn. (cert. firefighter level III, com. on properties of hazardous chemicals), Pi Kappa Alpha. Office: 11017 Manklin Meadows Ln Berlin MD 21811-9340

PASSY, CHARLES, writer; b. NYC, Jan. 9, 1964; s. Victor and Beverly (Green) P.; m. Leslie M. Olsen, Dec. 15, 1989; two children: Jacob E., Emma F. BA, Columbia U., 1985. Assoc. Jay K. Hoffman and Assocs., NYC, 1983-87; sr. editor, mng. editor Ovation Mag., NYC, 1988-89; editor Classical Mag., NYC, 1989-91; editor-in-chief Musical Am. Pub., NYC, 1991-92; staff writer The Palm Beach Post, West Palm Beach, Fla., 1992—. Announcer, prodr. WNYC FM, N.Y., 1984-85; entertainment stringer N.Y. Newsday, 1987-92. Author (with others): New Voices: Selected University and College Prize Winning Poems, 1989, The New Grove Dictionary of Jazz, 1988, The New Grove Dictionary of American Music, 1986, The New Grove Dictionary of Music and Musicians, 2d edit., 2001; editor: The Letters of Virgil Thomson, 1988; contbr. numerous articles to publs. in field, columns in newspapers, articles to various newspapers and mags. Recipient Poetry award Acad. Am. Poets Columbia U., 1985, Criticism awards Soc. Profl. Journalists, 1995, 97, 99, 2001, 03, 05, Fla. Press Club, 1993, 2004, Fla. Soc. Newspaper Editors, 1993, 2001, Cox Newspapers, 2001, Am. Assn. Sunday and Feature Editors, 2002, 05, award Mo. Lifestyle Journalism, 2005; fellow Knight Ctr. for Specialized Journalism, 1993. Home: 180 Bent Tree Dr Palm Beach Gardens FL 33418-3597 Office: Palm Beach Newspapers Inc 2751 S Dixie Hwy West Palm Beach FL 33405-1298 Office Phone: 561-820-4589. Personal E-mail: chazpbg@aol.com. Business E-Mail: charles_passy@pbpost.com.

PASTAN, LINDA OLENIK, poet; b. NYC, May 27, 1932; d. Jacob L. and Bess (Schwartz) Olenik; m. Ira Pastan, 1953; children: Stephen, Peter, Rachel. BA, Radcliffe Coll., 1954; MLS, Simmons Coll., 1955; MA, Brandeis U., 1957. Author: (poetry) A Perfect Circle of Sun, 1971, On the Way to the Zoo, 1975, Aspects of Eve, 1975, The Five Stages of Grief, 1978 (Alice Fay di Castagnola award Poetry Soc. Am. 1978), Setting the Table, 1980, Waiting for My Life, 1981, PM/AM: New and Selected Poems, 1982 (Am. Book award nomination 1982), A Fraction of Darkness: Poems, 1985, The Imperfect Paradise, 1988, Heroes in Disguise, 1991, An Early Afterlife, 1995, Carnival Evening: New and Selected Poems, 1968-98 (nat. Book award nomination 1998), The Last Uncle, 2002, Queen of a Rainy Country, 2006. Recipient Dylan Thomas Poetry award Mademoiselle, 1958, Virginia Faulkner award Prarie Schooner, 1992, Charity Randall citation Internat. Poetry Forum, 1996, Ruth Lilly Poetry prize, 2003; NEA fellow; grantee Md. Arts Coun.; poet laureate of Md., 1991-95. Jewish. Office: 11710 Beall Mountain Rd Potomac MD 20854-1105 Personal E-mail: lpastan@att.net.

PASTER, BENJAMIN G., lawyer; b. St. Louis, July 8, 1948; Student, London Sch. Econs., Eng.; BS magna cum laude in Econs., U. Pa., 1970; LLM, U. Cambridge, 1972; postgraduate student, Academie De Droit Internat. de la Haye, The Hague, The Netherlands; JD, Yale U., 1974. Bar: NY 1975, US Tax Ct. 1975, RI 1976. With Adler Pollock & Sheehan Inc., Providence; ptnr. Paster & Harpootian, Ltd., 1974. Asst. instr. law Yale U., 1973-74; adj. prof. Bryant Coll., 1980-81; vis. mem. faculty U. Cambridge, 1984. Contbr. articles to profl. jours. Recipient Gregson-Benn award, Dorothy Lohmann Cmty. Svcs. award; Trinity Hall scholar, Thouron Scholar, Curatorium Scholar. Fellow Am. Coll Trust and Estate Counsel; mem. ABA (real property, probate and trust com., taxation sect.) RI Bar Assn., Am. Soc. Fin. Svc. Profl., Beta Gamma Sigma, Omicron Delta Epsilon. Office: Paster & Harpootian Ltd 121 S Main St Providence RI 02903-7104 Office Phone: 401-455-9800. Office Fax: 401-455-9801. E-mail: ben@ph-estplan.com. *

PASTER, HOWARD G., public relations and public affairs company executive; b. NYC, Dec. 23, 1944; BA with honors, Alfred U., 1966; MS in Journalism, Columbia U., 1967. Legis. dir. UAW, 1977-80; exec. v.p. Timmons & Co., 1980-92; asst. to pres. and dir. Office Legis. Affairs White House, Washington, 1993; chmn., CEO Hill and Knowlton, Inc., NYC, 1994—2002; exec. v.p. WPP Group, NYC, 2002—. Office: WPP Group 125 Park Ave 4th Fl New York NY 10017-5529

PASTERNAC, ANDRÉ, cardiologist, educator; b. Toulouse, France, July 22, 1937; came to Can., 1971, naturalized, 1978. s. Jacques and Règine P. BA, Lycée Henri IV, Paris, 1956; BA in Polit. Sci., Toulouse U., 1963, MD Med. Sch., 1968; grad. in Mgmt. Program, Columbia U., 2000. Cert. Ins. and Disability Assessment U. Montreal, 2002. Intern Toulouse Univ. Hosp., 1962-63, resident, 1963-64, Edouard-Herriot Hosp., Lyon, France, 1965-66; Fulbright scholar in cardiology Harvard U., 1968-71; research fellow Peter Bent Brigham Hosp., Boston, 1968-69; Milton fellow Children's Hosp., Boston, 1969-71; fellow in cardiology Toronto (Ont., Can.) U., 1971-72; staff cardiologist Montreal (Que., Can.) Heart Inst., 1972—; asst. prof. medicine U. Montreal, 1972-78, clin. assoc. prof., 1978—, clin. prof. medicine, 1994—. Vis. lectr. U. Liège (Belgium), 1977, U. Madrid, 1977, U. Warsaw, 1979, 83; cons. Harley St. Clinic, Cromwell Hosp., Wellington Hosp., London; vis. assoc. prof. McGill U., Montreal, 1975-76; medico-legal and ins. expert U. Montreal, 2002. Contbr. articles to profl. jours. Bd. dirs. Heart-Brain Rsch. Found. Inc., NYC, Cardiostat Inc., Montreal, Cardiostat USA Inc., West Palm Beach, Fla. Am. Field Svc. grantee, Oreg., 1954-55. Mem. French Cardiac Soc., European Soc. Cardiology, Canadian Cardiovasc. Soc., Am. Coll. Cardiology, Am. Heart Assn., Internat. Soc. Heart Rsch., Am. Fedn. Clin. Rsch., NY Acad. Scis. Research in stress-related myocardial ischemia and dysfunction, mitral valve prolapse, cardiovascular drugs, cardiomyopathies, catecholamines, neuroendocrine control of the heart, stress and the heart, prevention of cardiovascular disease. Home: Port Royal 1455 Sherbrooke St W # 703 Montreal PQ Canada H3G 1L2 Office: Montreal Heart Inst 5000 Belanger E Montreal PQ Canada H1T 1C8 Home Phone: 514-989-4534; Office Phone: 514-376-3330. E-mail: andre.pasternac@sympatico.ca.

PASTERNACK, ROBERT FRANCIS, chemistry professor; b. NYC, Sept. 20, 1936; 2 children. BA, Cornell U., 1957, PhD in Chemistry, 1962. Research assoc. in chemistry U. Ill., Champaign, 1962-63; from asst. to prof. chemistry Ithaca Coll., NY, 1963-66, Charles A. Dana Endowed prof. chemistry NY, 1976-82; Edmund Allen prof. chemistry Swarthmore Coll., Pa., 1984—. Invited speaker seminars, colls., univs., nat., internat. meetings, confs. including Bioinorganic Chem., Italy, Portugal, Gordon Rsch. Confs., Spanish Royal Soc. Chem., many others; lectr. series Nankai U., China, U. Messina, Italy; mem. adv. com. Rsch. Corp.; mem. sci. & art com. Franklin Inst.; co-organizer, chmn. workshop on rsch. at undergrad. instn. NSF, mem. undergrad. curriculm chem.; vis. prof., vis. rschr. U Messina, U. Paris, Nakai, Rome, King's Coll., London, Fritz Haber Inst., Berlin, Doshisha U., Kyoto; co-developer A Unified Lab. Program; initiator, chmn. C.P. Snow Lectr. Series. Author, co-author more than 100 sci. publs. Mem. com. on sci. and the arts Franklin Inst., 1992-98. Grantee NSF, 1965-66, 69-72, 77-78, 83-84, 86-94, 95-03, Petroleum Rsch. Fund, 1967-74, 86-88, NIH, 1971-82, 85-89, 2001-05, Monsanto Corp., 1986-92, Rsch. Corp., 1974-75, 78-79, 84-85, Danforth Assocs., 1978-84, Camille and Henry Dreyfus Found., 1981, 95, NATO, 1979, 88-89, 95-96; recipient Camille and Henry Dreyfus Tchg./Scholar award, 1987-89, NSF Manpower Improvement award, King's Coll., U. London, 1977-78, Commemorative medal for sci. contbns. U. Catania, 1994, Excellence in Tchg. award, Am. Chem. Soc., Phila. Section, 2005, Conspicuous Sci. Achievement Through Rsch. award, Am. Chem. Soc., 2005; NSF sci. faculty fellow U. Rome, 1968-70. Mem. AAAS, Am. Inst. Chemists (Hon. Scroll award 1998), Am. Chem. Soc. (award for rsch. at an undergrad. instn. 2001, Excellence award 2005, award conspicuous sci. achievement through rsch. 2005), NY Acad. Sci., Sigma Xi. Office: Swarthmore Coll Dept Chemistry Swarthmore PA 19081 Office Phone: 610-328-8559. Business E-Mail: rpaster1@swarthmore.edu.

PASTERNACK, ROBERT HARRY, former federal agency administrator; b. Bklyn., Nov. 30, 1949; s. William and Lillian Ruth (Levine) P.; m. Jeanelle Livingston, Apr. 10, 1980; children: Shayla, Rachel. BA, U. South Fla., 1970; MA, N.Mex. Highlands U., 1972; PhD, U. N.Mex., 1980. Dir. Eddy County Drug Abuse Program, Carlsbad, N.Mex., 1972-73; adminstrv. intern U.S. Office Edn., Washington, 1975-76; exec. dir. Villa Santa maria, Cedar Crest, N.Mex., 1976-78; clin. dir. Ranchos Treatment Ctr., Taos, N.Mex., 1978-79; sch. psychologist N.Mex. Boys Sch., Springer, 1980—, supt., 1991; pres. Ensenar Health svcs., Inc., Taos, 1980—; CEO Casa de Corazon, Taos, N.Mex., 1994-98; state dir. spl. edn. N.Mex. State Dept. Edn., Santa Fe, 1998—2001; asst. sec. spl. edn. & rehab. services US Dept. Edn., Washington, 2001—03; v.p. edn. services Maximus Inc., 2004—. Instr. N.Mex. Highlands U., Las Vegas, 1980—, U. N.Mex., Albuquerque, 1980—; cons. N.Mex. Youth Authority, Santa Fe, 1988—, N.Mex. Devel. Disabilities Bur., Santa Fe, 1986—, various sch. dists.; state dir. spl. edn., N.Mex., 1998—. Author: Growing Up: The First Five Years, 1986; contbr. articles to profl. publs. Pres., bd. dirs. Children's Lobby, N.Mex., 1978, N.Mex. Spl. Olympics, 1986-88, Child-Rite, Inc., Taos, 1990; mem. Gov.'s Mental Health Task Force, Albuquerque, 1988—. Mem.: N.Mex. Coun. on Crime and Delinquency, Nat. Alliance Mentally Ill, Correctional Edn. Assn., Nat. Assn. Sch. Psychologists. Avocations: tennis, racquetball, skiing, cooking.

PASTERNACK, STEFAN ALAN, psychiatrist, psychoanalyst; b. Jersey City, Nov. 5, 1939; BA, Cornell U., 1961; MD, Georgetown U., 1965. Diplomate in psychiatry Am. Bd. Neurology and Psychiatry; lic. physician, D.C., Md. Resident in psychiatry U. Cin. Gen. Hosp., 1966-69; psychiat. cons. North Cmty. Mental Health Ctr., Washington, 1971-97; asst. prof. psychiatry Georgetown U. Sch. Medicine, Washington, 1971-79, assoc. clin. prof. psychiatry, 1979-86, clin. prof. psychiatry, 1986—, co-dir. advanced studies prog. in psychiatry/psychoanalysis, 1995—. Pvt. practice psychiatry and psychoanalysis, Washington, 1978—; attending. Fla. Psychoanalytic Inst., 2006. Editor: Violence and Victims, 1975; contbr. articles to profl. jours. Bd. dirs. Nat. Capital Med. Found., Washington, 1973-76, Forum for Psychoanalytic Study of Film, Washington, 1989—. Lt. comdr. USN, 1969-71. Mem.: Fla. Psychiat. Assn., Washington Psychiat. Soc. (mem. coun. 1987—99), Am. Psychoanalytic Assn., Am. Psychiat. Assn. (disting. life fellow), Cosmos Club. Avocations: motorboating and yachting, piano, writing. Home: 6924 Balboa Island Ct Delray Beach FL 33446-5641 Office: 4800 N Federal Hwy Ste E-102 Boca Raton FL 33431 Office Phone: 561-706-9584. Personal E-mail: sp39@aol.com.

PASTERNAK, JILL MARGOT, radio producer, host, musician, educator; b. Newark, Mar. 9, 1934; d. Albert Aaron and Dorothy Vera Bengelsdorf; children from previous marriage: Amy Lydia Pasternak Hendry, William. BS in Harp, Juilliard Sch. Music, NYC, 1955; MA in Pub. Media, Montclair State U., NJ, 1981. Radio broadcasting lic. FCC. Freelance musician, prin. harp Little Orch. Soc. NY, NYC, 1954—56; prin. harp Radio City Music Hall, NYC, 1955—56, 1960—63, 1977—79; prin. harp, soloist Halifax Symphony Orch., NS, Canada, 1956—57, Orlando Symphony Orch., Fla., 1960—63; prin. harp Kennett Symphony Orch., Kennett Square, Pa., 1991—2001; exec. prodr., classical host WMHT-FM, Schenectady, NY, 1984—87; exec. prodr. WFLN-FM, Phila., 1987—97, WRTI-FM, Phila., 1997—. Asst. to pres. Nonesuch Records, NYC, 1977—79; mgr. tng. & devel. Exxon, East Millstone, NJ, 1979—84; coord. MD/PhD program Thomas Jefferson U., Phila., 1987—96; lectr. Arcadia U., Phila., 2003—05, Jewish Cmty. Ctrs., Phila., 2003—; bd. dirs. Strings for Schs., Phila., 1999—2002. Freelance music, prin. harp: albums Broadway shows recs., editl. asst.: Hi-Fi/Stereo Rev. Mag., 1960—62, lit. editl. asst.: New World Records, 1975—77, prodr., host: Crossover, 1998—, Riccardo Muti, 2005, Thomas Hampson American Songbook, 2006 (Excellence in Broadcasting award Pa. Assn. Broadcasters, 2005, 2006). Mem. World Wildlife Fund, 2006, Physicians Ethical Medicine, 2006. Recipient Sarah award, Assn. Women in Comm., 1999, Svc. award, Darlington Arts Ctr., 2004, Crossover award, Pa. Assn. Broadcasters, 2005; Fublright scholar, Ecole Normale de Musique, 1956—57. Mem.: Musicians Union, Mu Phi Epsilon. Avocations: travel, dance. Office: WRTI FM Temple Pub Radio 1509 Cecil B Moore Ave Philadelphia PA 19121 Office Phone: 215-204-8405.

PASTIN, MARK JOSEPH, health science association administrator, educator; b. Ellwood City, Pa., July 6, 1949; s. Joseph and Patricia Jean (Camenite) Pastin; m. Joanne Marie Reagle, May 30, 1970 (div. Mar. 1982); m. Carrie Patricia Class, Dec. 22, 1984 (div. June 1990); m. Christina M. Brecto, June 15, 1991. BA summa cum laude, U. Pitts., 1970; MA, Harvard U., 1972, PhD, 1973. Asst. prof. Ind. U., Bloomington, 1973-78, assoc. prof., 1978-80; founder, bd. Compliance Resource Group, Inc., 1983—; chmn., CEO, pres. Coun. Ethical Orgns., Alexandria, Va., 1986—; prof. mgmt., dir. Ariz. State U., Tempe, 1988-92, prof. emeritus, 1996—; chair Health Ethics Trust, 1995—. Dir. Learned Nicholson, Ltd., 1990-91; bd. Japan Am. Soc. Phoenix, Found. for Ethical Orgns.; cons. GTE, Interim Healthcare, 1997-2000, U.S. Dept. Edn., 2002, Tex. Instruments, MicroAge Computers, Med-Tronic, Blood Sys., Inc., Opus Corp., GTE, NyNex, Am. Express Bank, Kaiko Bussan Co., Japan, Arex Co., Japan, Century Audit Co., U.S. Dept. Edn., Japan, Scottsdale Meml. Hosp., Cosanti Found., Lincoln Electric Co., Tenet Healthcare, The Williams Co.; vis. faculty Harvard U., 1980; presenter Australian Inst. Mgmt., Nippon Tel. & Tel., Hong Kong Commn. Against Corruption, 1984, Young Pres.'s Orgn. Internat. U., 1990, Nat. Assn. Indsl. & Office Parks, 1990, ABA, 1991, Govt. of Brazil, 1991. Author: Hard Problems of Management, 1986 (Book of Yr. Armed Forces Mil. Comtrs. 1986, Japanese edit. 1994), Power by Association, 1991, The Hotline Handbook, 1996, Planning Forum, 1992; editor: Public-Private Sector Ethics, 1979; mem. editl. bd. Report on Medicare Compliance; pub. Pastin Report on Best Compliance Practices, 1998—, Guerin Lect. on Philanthropy, 1996. Founding bd. mem. Tempe Leadership, 1985-89; bd. mem. Ctr. for Behavioral Health, Phoenix, 1986-89, Tempe YMCA, 1986—, Valley Leadership Alumni Assn., 1989-92; mem. Clean Air Com., Phoenix, 1987-90. Nat. Sci. Found. fellow, Cambridge, Mass., 1971-73; Nat. Endowment for the Humanities fellow, 1975; Exxon Edn. Found. grant, 1982-83. Mem.: Am. Assn. Physician Specialists (exec. com.), Found. Ethical Orgns. (chmn. 1988, pres.), Am. Soc. Assn. Execs. (presenter 1987—97), Mt. Vernon Country Club, Harvard Club D.C., Phi Beta Kappa, Golden Key. Avocations: golf, running. Office: 214 S Payne St Alexandria VA 22314-3530 Home: 7205 Regent Dr Alexandria VA 22307-2044 Office Phone: 703-683-7916. Personal E-mail: councile@aol.com.

PASTIZZO, FRANK ANTHONY, writer, educator; b. Gouverneur, NY, Nov. 26, 1957; s. Anthony Pastizzo and Faith Gwendolyn Johnson Day, Peter Patrick Day (Stepfather) and Carol C. Pastizzo (Stepmother); m. Susan Gayle Bertram, Jan. 21, 1996; children: Jesse Loring Billow, Natasha Anne Hill, Danielle Marie Anthony, Laura Lee. BS in Edn., U. Maine, Presque Isle, 1986. Tchr. English and drama Dept. Def. Dependent Schs., Cambridge and Suffolk, England, 1986—90; program mgr. United Helpers Care, Inc., Ogdensburg, Morristown, Lisbon, NY, 1990—95; dir. comm. United Helpers, Ogdensburg, 1996—2001, Rural No. NY Behavioral Inst., Saranac Lake, 2001—03; pres. Warm Up The Workplace, Inc., Saranac Lake, NY. Musical comedian Frank Pastizzo Presentations, Waddington, NY, 1990—2001. Author: (plays) A Class Act, FIGMO; actor: (plays) The Strolling Players, A Thousand Clowns, The Arkansaw Bear; dir.: Once Upon A Playground. State assembly candidate and nominee 112th Assembly Dist., Canton, 1998; dir., bd. pres. St. Lawrence Child Care Coun., Ogdensburg, 1996—2001; dir. St. Lawrence Leadership Inst., Canton, NY, 1996—2000. Sgt. USAF, 1976—81. Home Phone: 518-891-9276; Office Phone: 518-891-9276. Business E-Mail: frankpastizzo@warmuptheworkplace.com.

PASTOOR, ROBERTUS ANTONIUS, academic administrator; b. Maastricht, The Netherlands, Jan. 6, 1953; arrived in U.S., 1961; s. Johannes Pastoor and Maria Van der Pas; m. Ann Marie Lynch, June 8, 1985; children: Thomas Lynch-Pastoor, Tully Lynch-Pastoor, Marijka Lynch-Pastoor. BS in History and Edn., Mount St. Mary's Coll., Emmitsburg, Md., 1976; MEd in Counseling, McDaniel Coll., Westminster, Md., 1979; EdD in Ednl. Leadership, U. Mont., Missoula, 2003. Asst. dean of students Mount St. Mary's Coll., Emmitsburg, Md., 1979—81, assoc. dean of students, 1981—83, dean of students, 1983—87, v.p. student affairs, 1987—95; v.p. student life Carroll Coll., Helena, Mont., 1985—2002; v.p. student affairs U. San Diego, 2002—05; pres. St. John's Cath. Prep, Frederick, Md., 2005—. Chair, bd. dirs. St. Johns Lit Inst. at Prospect Hall, Frederick, Md., 1989—95; pres., bd. dirs. ASACCU, 1998—2003. Vol. Project Concern, Inc., Vienna, Va., 1968—71. Mem.: Assn. Student Affairs at Cath. Colls., ACPA, NASPA. Democrat. Roman Catholic. Avocations: tennis, music, reading. Office: St Johns Cath Prep 889 Butterfly Ln Frederick MD 21703 Home: 7022 Summerfield Dr Frederick MD 21702 Home Phone: 301-620-0403; Office Phone: 301-662-4210.

PASTOR, EDWARD, congressman; b. Claypool, Ariz., June 28, 1943; m. Verma Mendez; children: Yvonne, Laura. BA in chemistry, Ariz. State U., 1966, JD, 1974. Former chem. teacher N. High Sch.; former dep. dir. Guadalupe Org., Inc.; mem. Maricopa County Bd. Suprs., Phoenix, 1976-91, U.S. Congress from 4th Ariz. dist. (formerly 2nd), Washington, 1991—; mem. appropriations com., steering & policy com. Mem. Arts Caucus, Biotechnology Caucus, Border Caucus, Congressional Caucus on Women's Issues, Congressional Children's Caucus. Democrat. Office: US Ho Reps 2465 Rayburn Ho Office Bldg Washington DC 20515-0304 *

PASTOR, STEPHEN DANIEL, chemistry professor, researcher, consultant; b. New Brunswick, NJ, Feb. 15, 1947; s. Stephen and Irene (Bors) P.; m. Joan Ordemann, Apr. 3, 1971 (div. 1979); 1 child, Melanie; m. Joanne Behrens, July 13, 1985 (div. 1990). BA in Chemistry, Rutgers U., 1969, MS in Chemistry, 1978, PhD in Chemistry, 1983. Chemist Nat. Starch and Chem. Corp., Bridgewater, NJ, 1972—79; rsch. group leader CIBA-Geigy Corp., Ardsley, NY, 1979—84, rsch. mgr., 1985—87; group leader Ctrl. Rsch. Labs. CIBA-Geigy Ag, Basel, Switzerland, 1987—89, rsch. fellow Ardsley, 1989—90, rsch. mgr., 1990—97, sr. rsch. fellow, 1997—2003; cons. Mayhill, N.Mex., 2003—. Asst. adj. prof. Pace U., Pleasantville, NY, 1984—, assoc. adj. prof., 1989-93, adj. prof., 1994—. Contbr. articles to profl. jours. 1st lt. US Army, 1969—71, Vietnam. Sr. Rsch. Fellow, Ciba Specialty Chemicals Corp., 1998—2003. Mem.: Am. Chem. Soc. (Westchester sect. Disting. Scientist award 1977). Achievements include research on organophosphorous and organosulfur chemistry, conformational analysis, germanium chemistry, organometallic chemistry, asymmetric synthesis, homogeneous catalysis, hypercoordinated compounds, spectroscopy, astronomy. Home: PO Box 195 Mayhill NM 88339-0195 E-mail: astro3d@pvtnetworks.net.

PASTOREK, PAUL G., school system administrator, lawyer; b. Anchorage, Alaska, June 27, 1954; m. Kathy Pastorek; children: Ryan, Jeffery, Kaitlin. BA, Loyola U., 1976, JD, 1979. Bar: La. 1979. Former ptnr. Adams and Reese, New Orleans; gen. counsel NASA, Washington, 2002—04; ptnr., spl. bus. svcs. Adams & Reese, LLP, New Orleans, 2004—07; supt. of edn. State of La., Baton Rouge, 2007—. Served La. State Bd. Elem. and Secondary Edn., 1996—2004, pres., 2000—04; mem. various state bds. and commns. Chair, coun. exec. com. New Orleans Regional C. of C. area. Mem.: La. State Bar Assn. Office: La Dept Edn Office of Supt PO Box 94064 Baton Rouge LA 70804-9064 Office Phone: 877-453-2721. Office Fax: 225-342-0193. E-mail: paulpastorek@la.gov. *

PASTORES, GREGORY MCCARTHY, pediatrician, medical geneticist, researcher; b. Bklyn., Sept. 4, 1959; s. Jovito Camara and Annie Harrington (McCarthy) P. BS in Biology, U. St. Thomas, 1979, MD, 1983. Diplomate Am. Bd. Pediat., Am. Bd. Med. Genetics in Clin. Genetics and Clin. Molecular Genetics. Resident in pediat. Mt. Sinai Med. Ctr., NYC, 1986-89; fellow med. genetics Mayo Clinic Found., Rochester, Minn., 1989-91; fellow med. and molecular genetics Mt. Sinai Sch. Medicine, NYC, 1991-92, instr. pediatrics, genetics, 1992-93, asst. prof. human genetics and pediatrics, 1993-97; asst. prof. neurology and pediatrics NYU Sch. Medicine, NYC, 1997—2004, assoc. prof. neurology and pediatrics, 2004—. Roman Catholic. Home: 215 W 90th St Apt 6G New York NY 10024-1224 Office: NYU at Rivergate 493 E 34th St 2d Fl New York NY 10016 Office Phone: 212-263-8344. Business E-Mail: gregory.pastores@med.nyu.edu.

PASTORES, STEPHEN M., internist; b. NYC, Sept. 5, 1958; s. Jovito Camara and Annie McCarthy Pastores; m. Maria Teresa Desancho; children: Steven Michael, Monica Cristina. MD, Lyceum Northwestern Coll. Medicine, Philippines, 1982. Diplomate Am. Bd. Internal Medicine, Am. Bd. Pulmonary Disease, Am. Bd. Critical Care Medicine. Resident Met. Hosp. Ctr., 1989; attending critical care physician Montefiore Med. Ctr., Bronx, NY, 1993—96; dir. emergency svcs. Dept. VA Med. Ctr., Bronx, 1996—99, asst. dir. surg. ICU, 1996—99; attending critical care physician Meml. Sloan-Kettering Cancer Ctr., NYC, 1999—, dir. critical care rsch. and critical care fellowship program; assoc. prof. medicine and anesthesiology Weill Med. Coll. Cornell U., NYC, 2001—. Editor: (book) ICU Bedside Technology, 2000; contbr. articles to profl. jours. Fellow: ACP (2000-Present), Am. Coll. of Critical Care Medicine, Am. Coll. Chest Physicians (1997-Present). Office: Meml Sloan-Kettering Cancer Ctr 1275 York Ave M-210C New York NY 10021 Business E-Mail: pastores@mskcc.org.

PASTORIZA, JULIO, lawyer; b. Havana, Cuba, Sept. 22, 1948; came to U.S., 1960; s. Julio S. and Emilia P.; m. Gloria M. Alvarez-Pedroso, Jan. 5, 1974; 1 child, Gloria Cristina. AA, Miami Dade CC, 1967; BA, U. Fla., 1969; JD, U. Miami, 1973. Bar: Fla. 1973, US Tax Ct. 1974, US Supreme Ct. 1977. Assoc. Miguel A. Suarez P.A., Miami, Fla., 1973-77; ptnr. Sulli, Pastoriza & Hill, Miami, 1977-82; shareholder Julio Pastoriza, P.A., Coral Gables, Fla., 1982-85; ptnr. LaCapra & Wiser, Miami, 1985-87; pvt. practice Coral Gables, 1987—. Agent Attys. Title Ins. Fund, Miami, 1979—; instr. Biscayne Coll., Miami, 1972-76. Spkr. pre-marital conf. St. Theresa Cath. Ch., Coral Gables, 1981-88, mem. adv. bd. St. Theresa Cath. Sch., 1987-89; mem. adv. bd. Our Lady of Lourdes Acad., Miami, 1991-95; counselor St. Robert Bellarmine Cath. Ch., 2000-01. Avocations: fishing, photography. Home: 2601 San Domingo St Coral Gables FL 33134-5534 Office: 7101 SW 99 Ave Ste 109B Miami FL 33173-4661 Office Phone: 305-273-7890. Office Fax: 305-273-4511. Personal E-mail: pastorizajulio@hotmail.com.

PASTRANA, RONALD RAY, theology studies educator, science educator, department chairman, psychotherapist, retired school system administrator; b. NYC, Sept. 5, 1939; s. Anthony and Mildred Pastrana; m. Josephine Pastrana; children: Christine, Therese. BA in History/Sci. Edn., Queens Coll., 1963; advanced sci. cert., Pace U., NYC, 1964-68; MS in Counseling Edn., St. John's U., 1967; diploma, US Acad. of Health Sci., 1975, US Army Command and Gen. Staff Coll., 1979; D Ministry, Sch. Bible Theology Sem., 1996, ThD, 2000. Ordained min. Pentecostal Assemblies of God of Am.; diplomate Am. Bd. of Psychotherapy; cert. life support sys. in internat. space NOAA, NASA. Tchr. sci. Marie Curie Jr. HS, Bayside, NY, 1963-68; guidance counselor Half Hollow Hills HS, Dix Hills, NY, 1969-71, Walt Whitman HS, Huntington Station, NY, 1968-69, coord. occupl. svcs., 1971-74; guidance coord. Dutchess County Bd. Coop. Ednl. Svcs. Tech. Edn. Ctr., Poughkeepsie, NY, 1974-86; asst. prin., supr. sci. and math. Career and Tech. Inst. and Tech. Shop Programs, Poughkeepsie, 1986-96; asst. dir. Reach Out Sch. of Ministry, Hyde Park, NY, 1996—; prof. Bibl. theology Sch. Bible Theology Sem., San Jacinto, Calif., 1999—. Ednl. cons. NY State Edn. Dept., Albany, 1975-83, Armed Forces Vocat. Testing Group, Dept. of Def., Washington, 1975-77; cert. educator Lunar Edn. Project, NASA, 1986-87, Asteroids, Lunar Rocks, Meteorites Edn. Projects, 1999—; earth and space sci. cons., 1998; pub. Reach Out Ministries; rschr. NASA Astronauts and Space Program. Author: Career Guidance in the Classroom, 1974, A Curriculum Guide to the Study of the Seven Dispensations and Eight Covenants, 1996, Dispensational Theology, 1997, Pentecostal Doctrine and Theology, 1998, Student Guide to the Seven Dispensations and Eignt Covenants, 1999, The Greek Fathers of the Early Christian Church, 2000, The Latin Fathers of the Early Christian Church, 2000, The Reformers of the Christian Church, 2001, Reach Out Ministries. Lt. col. USAR, ret. 1992. NSF Sci. Geology, Biochemistry, Biology, Genetics, Cell Physiology, Physics, Astronomy and Advanced Biol. Lab. Techniques Study grantee, 1964-68, grantee NASA and Nat. Ocean. and Atmos. Adminstrn., 1999; recipient Recognition award oustanding cultural and hist. achievement Town of Hyde Pk., 1987, Recognition award oustanding performance guidance and counseling Dutchess County Counseling Assn., 1990, Dutchess Counselor of Yr. award Dutchess County Counseling Assn., 1995, Commemorative Recognition award NASA Space Project and Jason Space Project Wappingers Ctrl. Sch. Dist., 2001, NASA medallion NASA Hdqrs., Washington, 2005; decorated Joint Svc. Commendation medal, Army achievement medal, Selective Svc. Meritorious medal, Army Res. Components Achievement medal, Nat. Def. Svc. medal, NY State medal Meritorious Svc., Meritorious Svc. award for civilian svc. USN, 2000. Mem. Am. Counselors Assn., Am. Mental Health Counselors Assn., Nat. Career Devel. Assn., Am. Assn. Christian Counselors, Am. Psychotherapy Assn., Planetary Soc., Nat. Space Soc., NY Acad. Scis., NY State Assn. Counseling and Devel., Sch. Adminstrs. Assn. NY State, Dutchess County Counseling Assn. (exec. bd. 1989-96), Sci. Tchrs. Assn. NY State, Phi Delta Kappa, Nat. Tech. Honor Soc. (founder career and tech. ctr. chpt.). Avocations: rock and mineral collecting, exercise, canoeing, hiking. Home: 24 Meadow Dr Red Hook NY 12571-1200

PASTUCH, BORIS MAX See MAX, BUDDY

PASUKINIS, CHERYL RENEE, elementary school educator; b. Danville, Pa., Feb. 10, 1960; d. William Wayde and Janet Marie (Thomas) Beishline; m. William Albert Pasukinis, Dec. 14, 1985; children: William Beishline, Joseph Albert, Benjamin Thomas, Stanislaus Edward. BS in Elem. Edn., Bloomsburg U., Pa., 1983, MEd, 1985. Cert. reading specialist Bloomsburg U., profl. tchg. cert. Bloomsburg U., cert. tutor Laubach Literacy Action. Title I reading specialist So. Columbia Sch. Dist., Catawissa, Pa., 1983—84; remedial reading specialist, math instr., gifted instr. Cen. Susquehanna Intermediate Unit, Montandon, Pa., 1985; title I reading, remedial reading specialist Milton Area Sch. Dist., Pa., 1985—2003, lang. arts instr. 6th grade mid. sch., 2003—04; title I reading, Reading is Fundamental coord. Berwick Area Sch. Dist., Pa., 2004—. Fed. programs monitor Pa. Dept. Edn.'s Divsn. of Fed. Programs, Harrisburg, 1988—94; cooperating tchr. for grad. assts. and student tchrs. Milton Area Sch. Dist.; tchr. edn. course rev. com. Pa. Power and Light, Berwick; mem. instrnl. support team Milton Area Sch. Dist., 1996—2004, tchr. trainer, 1996—2004, peer coaching mentor model; mem. reading conf. planning com. Bloomsburg U.; mem. parent and child planning conf. com. Bloomsburg U. and Cen. Susquehanna Intermediat Unit #16, Bloomsburg; intergenerational program coord. Milton Elem. Sch., 1999—2004; ARC cmty. project coord. Milton Area Sch. Dist., 2003—04; mem. planning com., early childhood com., kindergarten transition conf. planning com., early childhood conf. planning com., presch. rep. Columbia County Early Childhood Conf., 2006—. Mem. elem. by-laws com. Benton Elem. Parent Tchr. Assn.; asst. coach Am. Youth Soccer Orgn., Benton; actor Bloomsburg U. Cmty. Theater Group, soloist; mem. Columbia County Covered Bridge Soc.; mem. com. Cmtys. that Career; stake seminar supr. Ch. of Jesus Christ of Latter-Day Saints, Ch. Ednl. Sys., Williamsport, Pa., 2005—; stake primary 1st counselor Ch. of Jesus Christ of Latter-Day Saints, Williamsport, 1998—2005, primary 1st counselor Berwick Ward, music chairperson, dir. Berwick Ward choir. Recipient music scholarship, Bloomsburg U., Preschooler R.E.A.D.Y. Kits grant, Berwick Health and Wellness Found., Vocal Music award, Benton Area Sch. Dist. Chorus, Gift of Time Tribute award, Am. Family Inst., 1996, 1997. Mem.: Internat. Reading Assn., Pa. State Edn. Assn. (assoc.), Berwick Area Edn. Assn. (assoc.), Pa. Assn. of Fed. Programs Coords. (life), Women's Relief Soc. (life). Home: 439 State Rte 239 Benton PA 17814 Office: Berwick Area Sch Dist 500 Line St Berwick PA 18603 Home Phone: 570-925-6952; Office Phone: 570-759-6400 3558. Office Fax: 570-759-6439. Business E-Mail: cpasukinis@berwicksd.org.

PASUPATHY, KALYAN SUNDER, education educator, consultant; s. N. K. and Lalithambal Pasupathy. BS in Engring. with honors, Bharathiar U., Coimbatore, India, 1999; MS, Va. Poly. Inst. & State U., Blacksburg, 2002; PhD, Va. Poly. Inst. & State U., Falls Church, 2006. Design engr. Roots Multiclean Ltd., Coimbatore, Tamil Nadu, India, 1998—99; grad. rsch., tchg. asst. Va. Poly. Inst. & State U., Falls Church, 1999—2003; mgr., sr. analyst ARC, Washington, 2003—06; asst. prof. U. Mo., Columbia, 2006—. Logistics engr. intern Menlo Logistics, Redwood City, Calif., 2000; simulation engr. intern Wash. Post, Springfield, Va., 2001; adj. rsch. faculty Va. Poly. Inst. & State U., Falls Church, 2002; steering com. Inter-professional Curriculum on Quality & Safety, Columbia, 2006—07. Grantee, ARC, 2006—07, Mo. Cancer Registry, 2007, Dept. Health and Sr. Svcs., 2007; scholar, Va. Poly. Inst. & State U., 1999—2003, ARC, 2002. Mem.: Sys. Dynamics Soc., Inst. Ops. Rsch. Mgmt. Sci. Achievements include design of conceptualization of service evaluation; development of mathematical models for service evaluation. Office Phone: 573-882-7683.

PASUPULETI, VENUMADHAV, information technology executive; s. Srinivas Rao and Rama Kumari P.; m. Marilyn L. Miller, May 7, 1992; 1 child, Teja. Grad., Bur. of Data Processing Sys., Hyderabad, 1985; student, Wright State U., 1988-92. Info. tech. cons., 1984-93; mgr. Info. Horizons, Parsippany, NJ, 1993-95; exec. v.p. Globe Tech. Exch., Dayton, Ohio, 1995; COB/CEO Megasoft, Dayton, 1995—. Pres. Indian Student Assn. Wright State U., Dayton, 1989-92; vol. India Literacy Project, Dayton, 1990-95, Ohio India Project, Dayton, 1990-95, Project Outreach, Dayton, 1999—, Day of Caring, Dayton, 1990-95. Mem. IEEE, South Ctrl. Ohio Minority Bus. Coun. (coun. mem. 2000—), Assn. for Computing Machinery, Math. Assn. of Am. Office: Megasoft PO Box 340591 Beavercreek OH 45434-0591 Home Phone: 801-305-8735. Business E-Mail: ceo@megasoft.us.

PASURKA, CARL A., JR., economist; b. Elgin, Ill., Sept. 15, 1953; s. Carl A. Pasurka, Sr., Lorraine Pasurka. AA, Harper Jr. Coll., Palatine, Ill., 1973; BS, No. Ill. U., 1975; MS, PhD, U. Ill., 1981. Vis. asst. prof. dept. econs. So. Ill. U., Carbondale, 1981—85, vis. asst. prof. dept. fin., 1983; asst. prof. dept. econs. Loyola U., Chgo., 1985—92; economist U.S. EPA, Washington, 1992—. V.p. Chgo. Energy Economists, 1988—89, pres., 1989—90, bd. advisors, 1990—91; adj. prof. Sch. Pub. Policy George Mason U., 2005—07. Assoc. editor: Jour. Environ. Econs. and Mgmt., 1994—96; contbr. chapters to books, articles to profl. jours. Grantee, U.S. EPA, 1991—92. Mem.: Internat. Input-Output Assn., Productivity Analysis Rsch. Network, Assn. Environ. and Resource Economists, Am. Econs. Assn. Home: 320 23rd St S Apt 623 Arlington VA 22202-3806 Office: EPA 1301 Constitution Ave NW Washington DC Office Phone: 202-566-2275. Business E-Mail: PASURKA.CARL@EPA.GOV.

PASVOLSKY, RICHARD LLOYD, retired parks, recreation, and environment educator; b. Englewood, NJ, Feb. 16, 1924; s. Valentine and Ellen Isabel (Stoughton) P.; m. Jo Anne Evans, June 16, 1968. BEd, Panzer Coll., 1950; MA in Edn., NYU, 1955; D in Recreation, Ind. U., 1973. Asst. supt. recreation City of Rutland, Vt., 1951-53; supt. recreation City of Montpelier, Vt., 1953-55; dir. parks and recreation Twp. of Parsippany-Troy Hills, NJ, 1955-62; asst. prof. outdoor and environ. edn. NJ State Sch. Conservation, Branchville, NJ, 1962-71; assoc. prof. edn. Ramapo Coll. NJ, Mahwah, NJ, 1972-84, coach archery, 1973-84; adj. prof. Kean Univ., Union, NJ, 1985—2003; ret., 2003. Instr. archery, dir. dance and recreation World Archery Ctr., Pomfret, Conn., 1964-92; dir. NJ State Coll. divsn. Nat. Archery Assn., 1978-84. Advisor to choreographer, cons. prodn. office closing ceremonies Statue of Liberty Centennial Celebration, 1986; rec. artist: Square Dances, 1961, 91, mag. articles, 1954-66; columnist Lines About Squares, 1983—. Instr. dance camp staff Lloyd Shaw Found., 1981—, bd. dirs., 1982-88; bd. trustees Sussex County Sr. Legal Resources Ctr., 1992-94. With U.S. Army, 1943-46, ETO. Recipient Alumni award Panzer Coll. NJ, 1979, Spl. Alumni award, 1987; named to Ramapo Coll. Athletic Hall of Fame, 1993, Lakewood (NJ) HS Hall of Fame, 1998. Mem. AAHPERD (Recreator of Yr. Ea. Dist. 1977), NJ Alliance Health, Phys. Edn., Recreation and Dance, Callers Coun. NJ, Callerlab, North NJ Sq. Dance Callers Assn. (pres., 1960-1963), Phi Delta Kappa. Avocations: calling square dances, ballroom dancing, skiing, golf, tennis. Home: 31 Newton Ave Branchville NJ 07826-4203

PATAKI, ANDREW, bishop; b. Palmerton, Pa., Aug. 30, 1927; Student, St. Vincent Coll., St. Procopious Coll., Lisle, Ill., Sts. Cyril and Methodius, Byzantine Cath. Sem., Grigorian U., Rome. Ordained priest Roman Cath. Ch., 1952. Apptd. aux. bishop of Passaic, N.J. Byzantine Cath. Diocese, 1983; bishop of Parma (Ohio) Diocese of Passaic, NJ, 1984—96, bishop NJ, 1996—. Home: 445 Lackawanna Ave West Paterson NJ 07424-2969

PATAKI, GEORGE ELMER, lawyer, former governor; b. Peekskill, NY, June 24, 1945; s. Louis P. Pataki and Margaret (Lagana) P.; m. Elizabeth (Libby) Rowland, 1973; children: Emily, Teddy, Allison, George Owen. BA, Yale U., 1967; JD, Columbia U. Sch. Law, 1970. Mayor City of Peekskill, NY, 1981—84; mem. NY State Assembly, 1985-92, NY State Senate from dist. 37, 1993—95; assoc. Dewey, Ballantine, Bushby, Palmer & Wood LLP, 1970-74; ptnr. Plunckett & Jaffe, P.C., NYC, White Plains, Albany and Peekskill, 1974-89; co-proprietor Pataki Farm, Peekskill, NY; gov. State of NY, Albany, NY, 1995—2007; counsel Chadbourne & Parke LLP, NYC, 2007—. Co-author (with Daniel Paisner): Pataki: An Autobiography, 1998. Advanceman Friends of Rockefeller Team, 1970; upstate campaign coord. Com. to Elect Gov. Wilson, 1974; mem. Peekskill Rep. City Com., 1974—, chmn. 1977-83; mem. N.Y. State Rep. Com., 1980-85. Republican. Office: Chadbourne & Parke LLP 30 Rockefeller Plz New York NY 10112 E-mail: gpataki@chadbourne.com. *

PATAKY, PAUL ERIC, ophthalmologist; b. Phila., May 19, 1945; s. Andrew and Helen (Koffler) P.; m. Aimee Janet Margoles, June 13, 1971; Meryl Corinne, Lisa Ann. BS, Trinity Coll., 1966; MD, Pa. State U., 1971. Diplomate Am. Bd. Ophthalmology. Resident ophthalmology Mass. Eye and Ear Infirmary, Boston, 1972-76; asst. in ophthalmology Harvard Med. Sch., Boston, 1976-79; ophthalmologist Dedham (Mass.) Med. Assocs., 1976-79, Paul E. Pataky M.D. P.A., Boynton Beach, Fla., 1979—. Chmn. dept. surgery Bethesda Meml. Hosp., Boynton Beach, 1988-89; pres. med. staff, 1990-91, chmn. credentials chmn., 1992-93, chmn. surg. care com., 1993-97. Named One of Am.'s Top Ophthalmologists 2004-07, Consumer Rsch. Coun. Am., 2004. Fellow: Am. Acad. Ophthalmology; mem.: AMA, Pan-Am. Assn. Ophthalmology. Avocations: travel, fine art. Office: 2623 S Seacrest Blvd Ste 102 Boynton Beach FL 33435-7531 Home Phone: 561-381-4486; Office Phone: 561-734-5056.

PATCH, LISA E., health services director, nurse; b. Macomb, Ill., Jan. 19, 1967; d. Lyle Marlin Swearingen and Mildred Fern Swearingen-Engel; m. Allan Trent Patch, May 25, 1986; children: Breckon Nicole, Brighton Ellen, Brooklyn Leigh. AA in Nursing, N.Mex., 1997; BS, Western Ill. U., 1989. Intern Dona Ana Pub. Health, Las Cruces, N.Mex., 1990—91; pediatric registered nurse Mem. Med. Ctr., Las Cruces, 1997—2000; dir. health svcs. Alamogordo Pub. Schs., Alamogordo, N.Mex., 1999—; registered nurse Dr. Paul's Family Practice, 2000. Adv. bd. N.Mex. State U., Alamogordo, N.Mex., 2002—, preceptor, 2005. Mem. Otero Path, Alamogordo, N.Mex., 2000—03, Otero County Health Coalition, Alamogordo, 2000—, Leadership Alamogordo, 2004; youth leader Wesley United Meth. Ch., Alamogordo, 2004—. Mem.: N.Mex. Sch. Nurse Assn. (exec. bd. mem. 2000—), Am. Sch. Health Assn., Nat. Assn. Sch. Nursing, Sigma Theta Tau. Avocation: travel. Office: Alamogordo Pub Schs 1211 Hawaii Ave Alamogordo NM 88310

PATCHEN, KELLY A., elementary school educator; b. Cleve., Dec. 20, 1970; d. Dennis Malcher and Beverly Fick; m. Michael C. Patchen, Nov. 22, 1997; children: Blake, Ryan. BA, Alverna Coll., Reading, Pa., 1992; MEd, Seattle U., 1998. Cert. curriculum and instrn. specialist Wash., reading specialist Wash., early childhood specialist N.C. Tchr. Balt. City Pub. Schs., 1992—93; tchr. and wedding coord. Villa Acad., Seattle, 1993—2002; tchr. Cabarrus County Sch., Concord, NC, 2004—05; 0lead tchr. Carolina Internat. Sch., Harrisburg, NC, 2005—06, asst. prin. elem. edn., 2006—. Vol. Literacy Coun.; active ch. youth group. Named Tchr. of Yr., Balt. City Pub. Schs., 1992—93, Student Tchr. of Yr., Alverna Coll., 1992. Mem.: ASCD, Nat. Assn. Edn. of Young Children, Internat. Reading Assn. Avocations: scrapbooks, crafts, sports. Office: Carolina Internat Sch 8810 Hickory Ridge Rd Harrisburg NC 28075

PATCHETT, ARTHUR ALLAN, medicinal chemist, pharmaceutical executive; b. Middletown, NY, May 28, 1929; s. Arthur Allan and Anna Gertrude (Vossler) P.; m. Lois Rhoda Mc Neil, Aug. 18, 1962; Thomas John, Steven Edward. BA, Princeton U., 1951; PhD, Harvard U., 1955; DSc (hon.), Bloomfield Coll., 2001. Rsch. assoc. NIH, Bethesda, Md., 1955-57; rsch. chemist Merck Rsch. Labs., Rahway, NJ, 1957-62, dir. synthetic chem. rsch., 1962-69, sr. dir. synthetic chem. rsch., 1969-71, sr. dir. new lead discovery, 1971-76, exec. dir. new lead discovery, 1976-88, v.p. exploratory chemistry, 1988-95, v.p. medicinal chemistry, 1995-2000, cons., 2000—. Contbr. over 170 papers to profl. jours., sci. confs. Named to N.J. Inventors Hall of Fame, N.J. Inst. Tech., 1990; recipient Discoverers award, Pharm. Mfrs. Assn., 1992, Smissman Bristol-Myers Squibb award, 2001, NAS award for Chemistry in Svc. to Soc., 2007. Fellow AAAS; mem. Am. Chem. Soc. (chmn. div. medicinal chemistry 1971, E.B. Hershberg Important Discoveries in Medicinally Active Substances award 1993, Alfred Burger award in medicinal chemistry 2002). Achievements include 180 U.S. patents (co-holder); co-inventor antihypertensive drug Vasotec; key contbr. to discovery of cholesterol lowering drug Mevacor.

PATCHIN, REBECCA J., anesthesiologist, educator, administrator; b. Detroit, Dec. 8, 1949; d. Robert Ira and Doris J. (Hubert) P.; m. Carl W. Anderson, 1988. ASN, Pacific Union Coll., 1969; BSN, Walla Walla Coll., 1971; MD, Loma Linda U., 1989. Diplomate in anesthesiology and pain mgmt. Am. Bd. Anesthesiology. Resident in internalmedicine Loma Linda U. Med. Ctr., Calif., 1989-90, resident in anesthesiology Calif., 1990-93, fellow in pain mgmt. dept. anesthesiology Calif., 1993-94, asst. prof. anesthesiology, 1994—; assoc. med. dir. Ctr. for Pain Mgmt., Loma Linda, 1995—. Presenter in field. Contbr. abstracts to profl. jours. Mem. AMA (mem. credentials com. 1986—, mem. awards com. bd. trustees 1988-89, del. ho. of dels. 1990—, mem. reference com. 1994—, chair coun. on med. edn. 2002-03, trustee 2003-, Internat. Anesthesiology Rsch. Soc., Internat. Assn. for Study of Pain, Am. Soc. Anesthesiology, Am. Pain Soc., Am. Soc. Regional Anesthesia, Am. Acad. Pain Medicine, Calif. Soc. Anesthesiology (del. resident component 1991-93, mem. com. on young physicians 1994—96, chair com. on young physicians 1996—), Calif. Med. Assn. (mem. reference com. 1988, trustee 1991-93, mem. com. on health professions and licensure 1992—, chair com. on health professions and licensure 1993-96, mem. coun. on legislation 1995-96, chair coun. on legislation 2000—), So. Calif. Cancer Pain Initiative, Riverside County Med. Assn. (sec.-treas 2002, pres. 2004), San Bernardino County Med. Soc. Home Phone: 951-780-8121; Office Phone: 951-413-0200.

PATE, LISA M., transportation services executive, lawyer; b. 1969; m. Hank Pate; children: Riley, Bealie, Casey. BS, Northwestern U.; JD, Cornell U. Bar: Tenn. 1996. Assoc. Witt, Gaither & Whitaker, PC, Chattanooga, 1996—2002, named shareholder, 2002; now gen. counsel US Xpress Enterprises, Inc., Chattanooga. Office: US Xpress Enterprises Inc 4080 Jenkins Rd Chattanooga TN 37421 Office Phone: 423-510-3000. Office Fax: 423-510-3318. *

PATE, MICHAEL LYNN, lawyer; b. Ft. Worth, July 9, 1951; s. J.B. and Mary Anna (Hable) P.; m. Barbara Ann Linch, May 28, 1977. AA, Schreiner Coll., 1971; BS, Tex. Wesleyan Coll., 1973; JD, U. Tex., 1975. Bar: Tex. 1976, DC 1983, US Tax Ct. 1986, US Supreme Ct. 1987. Adminstrv. asst. to Senator Sherman, counsel natural resources com. Tex. Senate, 1976-77; adminstrv. asst. to Lt. Gov. Bill Hobby, Austin, Tex., 1977-79; legis. asst. Senator Bentsen, Washington, 1979-81, legis. dir., 1981-86; ptnr., head Washington office Bracewell & Giuliani LLP, Washington, 1986—. Trustee Schreiner U. Mem. ABA, Tex. Bar Assn., DC Bar Assn. Democrat. Methodist. Avocations: basketball, tennis, golf. Office: Bracewell & Giuliani LLP 2000 K St NW Ste 500 Washington DC 20006-1872 Office Phone: 202-828-5841. Business E-Mail: michael.pate@bgllp.com.

PATE, PAUL DANNY, mayor; b. Ottumwa, Iowa, May 1, 1958; s. Paul Devern and Velma Marie (McConnell) P.; m. Jane Ann Wacker, July 15, 1978; children: Jennifer Ann, Paul Daniel III, Amber Lynn. AA in Bus., Kirkwood Coll., 1978; cert. fin. mgmt. program, U. Pa., 1990. Exec. dir. Jr. Achievement, Cedar Rapids, Iowa, 1978-82; pres. PM Systems Corp., Cedar Rapids, 1982—; senator Iowa State Senate, Des Moines, 1989-93; Sec. of State State of Iowa, 1994-98; mayor City of Cedar Rapids, 2002—. Chmn. Iowa Young Reps., Des Moines, 1989-93, Recipient Guardian Small Bus. award Nat. Fedn. Independent Bus., 1990; named Young Entrepreneur of Yr. U.S. Small Bus. Adminstrn., Iowa, 1988, Alumnus of Yr. Kirkwood Coll., Cedar Rapids, 1990. Republican. Methodist. Avocation: water-skiing. Home: 6801 Bowman Ln NE Cedar Rapids IA 52402-1575 Office: Pm Pate Asphalt 3285 3rd Ave Marion IA 52302-3928

PATE, ROBERT HEWITT, JR., counselor educator; b. Abingdon, Va., Apr. 5, 1938; s. Robert Hewitt and Esther Frances (Kirk) P.; m. Ellen O'Neal Pope, Dec. 11, 1960; children: Robert Hewitt III, Mary Ellen Pate Barton. AB, Davidson Coll., 1960; MEd, U. Va., 1965; PhD, U. N.C., 1968. Lic. prof. counselor, Va. Marketer Sinclair Refining Co., Abingdon, Va., 1960-61, 63-64; counselor St. Andrews Presbyn. Coll., Laurinburg, NC, 1965-66; prof. edn., William Clay Parrish Jr. prof. edn. U. Va., Charlottesville, 1968—, interim dean, 1994-95, assoc. dean, 1995—. Mem. adj. faculty Fed. Exec. Inst., Charlottesville, 1978—. Author: Being A Counselor, 1983. 1st lt. U.S. Army 1961-63. Mem. ACA, Va. Counselors Assn. (pres. 1983-84), Nat. Bd. Cert. Counselors (chair 1996-97), Raven Soc. Avocation: reading. Home: 552 Dryden Pl Charlottesville VA 22903-4666 Office: Curry Sch Dean's Office 405 Emmet St S PO Box 400260 Charlottesville VA 22904-4260

PATE, R(OBERT) HEWITT (III), lawyer, former federal agency administrator; b. Ft. Sill, Okla., June 14, 1962; s. Robert and Ellen Pate; m. Lindsey Haines, Aug. 2, 1986; children: Elizabeth, Ellen. BA, U. NC, 1984; JD, U. Va., 1987. Bar: Va. 1989, DC 2000, bar: Brussels 2006. Law clk. for Hon. J. Harvie Wilkinson, US Ct. Appeals (4th cir.), Charlottesville, Va., 1987—88; law clk. for Justice Lewis F. Powell, Jr., US Supreme Ct., Washington, 1988—89, law clk. for Justice Anthony M. Kennedy, 1989—90; assoc. Hunton & Williams, Richmond, Va., 1990—95, ptnr., 1995—2000, 2005—; dep. asst. atty. gen., antitrust divsn. U.S. Dept.

Justice, Washington, 2001—03, asst. atty. gen., 2003—05. Mem. Commn. on Future of Higher Edn. in Va., Richmond, 1994—95, Governor's Commn. on Self-Determination and Federalism, Richmond, 1994—96; Ewald disting. vis. prof. U. Va. Sch. Law, Charlottesville, Va., 1999; chmn. competition com. working party 3 Orgn. for Econ. Cooperation and Devel., Paris, 2003—05; chair internat. working group U.S. Atty. General's Task Force on Intellectual Property, Washington, 2004—04. Contbr. numerous articles to legal jours. Gen. counsel Children's Mus. Richmond, 1996—2000; bd. gov. St. Catherine's Sch., 2006—; bd. dir. John Marshall Found., 2007—. Recipient Alumni Award for Academic Excellence, U. Va. Sch. Law, 1987, Roger and Madeline Traynor prize, 1987. Mem.: ABA, Fourth Circuit Jud. Conf., The Federalist Soc., Raven Soc., Omicron Delta Kappa. Republican. Episcopalian. Office: Hunton & Williams LLP 1900 K St NW Washington DC 20006 Home Phone: 804-285-0650; Office Phone: 202-955-1921. Business E-Mail: hpate@hunton.com.

PATE, STEPHEN PATRICK, lawyer; b. Beaumont, Tex., May 6, 1958; s. Gordon Ralph and Shirley Jean (Riley) P.; m. Jean Janssen; 1 child, Teddy. BA, Vanderbilt U., 1980, JD, 1983. Bar: Tex. 1984, U.S. Dist. Ct. (ea. dist.) Tex. 1984, U.S. Dist. Ct. (so. dist.) Tex. 1985. Law clk. to judge Joe J. Fisher U.S. Dist. Ct. Tex., Beaumont, 1983-84; ptnr. Fulbright & Jaworski, Houston. Contbr. articles to profl. jours. Fellow Houston Bar Found., Tex. Bar Found.; mem. Fedn. Defense and Corp. Counsel (v.p., chair, property ins. sect., 2003-05, John Applemon award, 2004), Tex. Bar Assn., Tex. Young Lawyers Assn. (bd. dirs. 1992-94), Houston Young Lawyers Assn. (bd. dirs. 1990-92, sec. 1992-93, chmn. professionalism com., mem. sunset rev. com. 1990), Am. Bd. Trial Advocates, Sons of the Republic Tex., SAR (pres. Paul Carrington chpt. 2001-02), Soc. Colonial Wars, Manitoba Master Angler, Billfish Found. (Top Angler 1993), Knight of Momus, The Briar Club, Phi Beta Kappa. Republican. Roman Catholic. Avocations: hunting, fishing. Home: 2740 Arbuckle St Houston TX 77005-3932 Office: Fulbright & Jaworski 1301 Mckinney St Houston TX 77010-3031 E-mail: spate@fulbright.com.

PATE, WILLIAM PATRICK, city manager; b. Duplin County, NC, July 30, 1962; s. William Atlas and Bonny Lou (O'Leary) P.; m. Sandra Martin, Aug. 17, 1985; children: William Glenn, Andrew Patrick. BA in Polit. Sci. and Religion, U. N.C., 1984, MPA, 1986. Budget and evaluation analyst intern City of Winston-Salem, NC, 1985-86, budget and evaluation analyst NC, 1986-87, lead budget and evaluation analyst NC, 1987; budget and rsch. mgr. City of Greensboro, NC, 1987-90, budget and evaluation dir. NC, 1990-99; asst. city mgr. City of High Point, NC, 1999—. Inst. of Govt. intern N.C. Office Coastal Mgmt., Raleigh, N.C., 1984; rsch. asst. U. N.C., Chapel Hill, 1984-85. Mem. Chmns. Soc. United Way of High Point, 1998—; mem. Leadership Greensboro, 1993-99, Leadership High Point, 2000—; elder, clk. session Faith Presbyn. Ch., Greensboro; mem. Salem Presbyn. World Ministries Cluster, 1997-99; chair staff parish rels. team Covenant Ch., 2005—. Recipient Disting. Svc. award Alpha Phi Omega, 1984. Mem. Internat. City Mgrs. Assn., Am. Soc. Pub. Adminstrn. (pres. Piedmont Triad chpt. 1994), Gov. Fin. Officers Assn. U.S. and Can. (exec. bd. 1998-2004, nat. com. on govtl. budgeting and mgmt. 1993-98, nat. com. on debt and fiscal policy 1998-2001, pres. 2002-03, Disting. Budget Presentation award reviewer, Disting. Budget Presentation award 1992-98), N.C. Local Govt. Budget Assn. (bd. dirs. 1990-92, 95, 1st v.p. 1992-93, pres. 1993-94), N.C. City/County Mgrs. Assn., U. N.C. MPA Alumni Assn. (program chmn. 1992, pres-elect 1993, pres. 1994, Scholarship award 1985), U. N.C. Gen. Alumni Assn. (bd. dirs. 1994-95), Kiwanis Club (v.p. 2006—). Methodist. Home: 4509 Calabria Ct High Point NC 27265-9595 Office: City of High Point PO Box 230 High Point NC 27261-0230 E-mail: pat.pate@highpointnc.gov.

PATÉ-CORNELL, MARIE-ELISABETH LUCIENNE, finance, engineering educator; b. Dakar, Senegal, Aug. 17, 1948; arrived in U.S., 1971; d. Edouard Pierre Lucien and Madeleine (Tournissa) Paté; m. C. Allin Cornell, Jan. 3, 1981; children: Phillip Cornell, Ariane Cornell. Eng. Degree, Inst. Polytechnique de Grenoble, France, 1971; MS in Ops. Rsch., Stanford U., 1972, PhD in Engring.-Econ. Systems, 1978. Asst. prof. in civil engring. MIT, 1978-81; asst. prof. indsl. engring. Stanford (Calif.) U., 1981-84, assoc. prof. indsl. engring., 1984-91, prof. indsl. engring., 1991—, chmn. dept. indsl. engring., 1997-99, chmn. dept. mgmt. sci. and engring., 2000—. Cons. SRI Internat., 1993, Electric Power Rsch. Inst., 1995, Atty. Gen. of N.Mex., 1995, Swiss Re, 2002, Boeing, 2003—; mem. adv. coun. NASA, 1995—98; mem. Marine Bd. NRC, 1995—97; mem. Army Sci. Bd., 1995—97, Air Force Sci. Bd., 1998—2002, Calif. Coun. on Sci. and Tech., 2000—, Pres.'s Adv. Bd. on Fgn. Intelligence, 2001—; chmn. bd. advisors Naval-Postgrad. Sch., 2004—06. Contbr. numerous articles to profl. jours. Numerous rsch. grants. Fellow: Inst. for Mgmt. Scis.; mem.: Nat. Acad. Engring. (councilor 2001—), Ops. Rsch. Soc. Am., Soc. for Risk Analysis (councilor 1985—86, pres. 1995). Avocations: tennis, swimming, chess, music. Home: 110 Coquito Way Menlo Park CA 94028-7404 Office: Stanford U Dept Mgmt Sci and Engring Stanford CA 94305 E-mail: mep@leland.stanford.edu.

PATEK, SHEILA N., biologist, educator; MA/AB with honors in Biology, Harvard U., Cambridge, Mass., 1994; PhD in Biology, Duke U., Durham, NC, 2001. Postdoctoral fellow Miller Inst. Basic Rsch. in Sci. U. Calif., Berkeley, 2001—04, asst. prof. dept. integrative biology, 2004—. Contbr. articles to sci. jours. Named one of Brilliant 10, Popular Sci. mag., 2004. Office: Dept Integrative Biology U Calif Berkeley 3060 Valley Life Scis Bldg Number 3140 Berkeley CA 94720-3140 Office Phone: 510-643-9159. Office Fax: 510-643-6264. E-mail: patek@berkeley.edu. *

PATEL, AJAY, dean; m. Aparna Patel; 2 children. BS, St. Joseph's Coll., India; MBA, U. Balt.; PhD, U. Ga. Faculty appointments U. Mo., Bentley Coll.; faculty mem. Babcock Grad. Sch. Mgmt., Wake Forest U., 1993, Babcock rsch. prof. fin., 2001—, interim dean, 2003—04, dean, 2004—. Office: Babcock Grad Sch Mgmt Wake Forest Univ PO Box 7659 Winston Salem NC 27109-7659 Home Phone: 336-760-2862; Office Phone: 336-758-5419. E-mail: ajay.patel@mba.wfu.edu.

PATEL, CHANDRA KUMAR NARANBHAI, communications executive, educator, entrepreneur, researcher; b. Baramati, India, July 2, 1938; came to U.S., 1958, naturalized, 1970; s. Naranbhai Chaturbhai and Maniben P.; m. Shela Dixit, Aug. 20, 1961; children: Neela, Meena. BS in Engring., Poona U., 1958; MS, Stanford U., 1959, PhD, 1961. Mem. tech. staff Bell Telephone Labs., Murray Hill, NJ, 1961-93, head infrared physics and electronics rsch. dept., 1967-70, dir. electronics rsch. dept., 1970-76, dir. phys. rsch. lab., 1976-81, exec. dir. rsch. physics and acad. affairs div., 1981-87, exec. dir. rsch., materials sci., engring. and acad. affairs div., 1987-93; trustee Aerospace Corp., LA, 1979-88; vice chancellor rsch. UCLA, 1993-2000, prof. dept. physics and astronomy, dept. chemistry, 2000—, prof. dept. elec. engring., 2000—; chmn., CEO Pranalytica, Inc, Santa Monica, Calif., 2001—. Mem. governing bd. NRC, 1990-91; bd. dirs. Newport Corp.; chmn. bd. Calif. Accuwave Corp., 1994-98; founder, chmn. bd. Pranalytica, Inc., Santa Monica, Calif.; co-founder Photuris, Inc. Contbr. articles to tech. jours. Chmn. Calif. Biomed. Found., 1994-2000; mem. exec. bd. Calif. Healthcare Inst., 1995-2000; mem. LA Regional Tech. Alliance, 1997-2003. Recipient Ballantine medal Franklin Inst., 1968, Nat. Sci. medal 1996, Coblentz award Am. Chem. Soc., 1974, Honor award Assn. Indians in Am., 1975, Founders prize Tex. Instruments Found., 1978, award N.Y. sect. Soc. Applied Spectroscopy, 1982, Schawlow medal Laser Inst. Am., 1984, Thomas Alva Edison Sci. award N.J. Gov., 1987, William T. Ennor Manufacturing Technology award ASME, 1995, Nat. Medal of Sci., Pres. of US, 1996, prize Internat. Photoacoustic and Photothermal Assn. prize, 2007. Fellow AAAS, IEEE (Lamme medal 1976, medal of honor 1989, Millennium medal 2000), Am. Acad. Arts and Scis., Am. Phys. Soc. (coun. 1987-91, exec. com. 1987-90, George E. Pake prize 1988, pres. 1995), Optical Soc. Am. (Adolph Lomb medal 1966, Townes medal 1982, Ives medal 1989, Lifetime Achievement award Def. and Security Symposium 2006), Indian Nat. Sci. Acad. (fng.); mem. NAS (coun. 1988-91, exec. com. 1989-91), NAE (Zworykin award 1976), Def. and Security Symposium (Lifetime Achievement award 2006), Gynecol. Laser Surgery Soc. (hon.), Am. Soc. for Laser Medicine and Surgery (hon.), Third World Acad. Scis. (assoc.), Calif. Biomed. Found. (pres. 1994-00), Calif. Healthcare Inst. (exec. com. 1995-00), Fedn. Am. Scientists (bd. dirs. 2002-),Sigma Xi (pres. 1994-96). Achievements include invention of many lasers including the Carbon Dioxide laser. Office: Pranalytica Inc 1101 Colorado Ave Santa Monica CA 90401 Business E-Mail: patel@pranalytica.com.

PATEL, CHINTAN, adult education educator; PhD, UMBC, Balt., 2004. Lectr. UMBC, Balt, 2001—04, rsch. asst. prof., 2004—. Mem.: IEEE. Achievements include patents for system and method for testing integrated circuits by transient signal analysis. Office: UMBC 1000 Hilltop Circle Baltimore MD 21250 Office Phone: 410-455-3963.

PATEL, HOMI BURJOR, apparel executive; b. Bombay, June 28, 1949; s. Burjor Ratan and Roshen Burjor (Marfatia) P.; married; children: Neville H., Cyrus H., Natasha E. BS in Stats., U. Bombay, 1973; MBA in Fin. and Mktg., Columbia U., 1975. Exec. asst. to pres. Corbin Ltd., NYC, 1976, dir. mktg., 1978; with subs. Hartmarx Corp., Chgo., 1979—; v.p., gen. mgr. Fashionaire Apparel Inc., Chgo., 1979-81; exec. v.p. Austin Reed of Regent St., Chgo., 1981-82, M. Wile and Co., Buffalo, 1982-84; pres., chief exec. officer M. Wile & Co., Johnny Carson Apparel, Intercontinental Apparel, Buffalo, 1984—; group exec. v.p. Hartmarx Mens Apparel Group Corp., Buffalo, 1987-91, chmn., ceo Chgo., 1991-92; pres., COO Hartmarx Corp., Chgo., 1992—, bd. dirs., 1994—2001, CEO, 2002—. Mem. Clothing Mfrs. Assn. Am. (bd. dirs. 1984—, chief labor negotiator for U.S. tailored clothing industry), Univ. Club N.Y., Chgo. Club. Office: Hartmarx Corp 101 N Wacker Dr Fl 23 Chicago IL 60606-1718

PATEL, KIRAN, manufacturing executive; BEE; MBA, U. Tenn. CPA. With Cummins Inc., 1974—2000; CFO iMotors, 2000; exec. v.p. Solectron Corp., Milpitas, Calif., 2001—, CFO, 2001—. CFO iMotors, 2000. Mem.: Fin. Exec. Inst., Tenn. Soc. CPAs, Am. Inst. CPAs. Office: Solectron Corp 777 Gibraltar Dr Milpitas CA 95035

PATEL, MANU V., physics educator; b. Jhalod, India, Jan. 4, 1934; arrived in US, 1965; s. Valabhai L. and Revaben V. Patel; m. Shashikala Patel, Sept. 27, 1940; children: Sonna M., Rupa M. BS in Physics, Gujarat U., India, 1955, EdB, 1958; MEd, Maharaja Sayajira U., Gujarat, 1960; MS in Physics, U. Conn., Storrs, 1970, PhD in Atomic Physics, 1975. Cert. tchr. Va. Tchr., asst. prin. various schs., Gujarat, 1955—64; tchr. sci. and math. Ballston Spa Ctrl. Schs., NY, 1965—66; asst. prof. Coll. Edn., Gujarat, 1967—68; grad. asst. U. Conn., Storrs, 1968—75; physics tchr. Alexandria City Schs., Va., 1976—. Test ctr. supr. Ednl. Testing Svc., Coll. Bd., Princeton, NJ, 1982—, mem. advanced placement test devel. com., 1988—92, SAT subject test, 1985—88. Author: AP Exam Tests and Solution Manual, 1994; author: (in Gujarati) Temple of Inspiration for Poor Students, 2006. Organizer Sonna-Rupa Charity Trust, Jhalod, India, 1999—. Recipient honors, Alexandria Sch. Bd., City Coun., Va. State Ho. and Senate, Minority Tchg. award, RCA, 1987, Tchg. award, NSF, 1987, Excellence in Tchg. award, Alexandria C. of C., 1998; Fulbright scholar, 1965. Mem.: NEA, Va. Edn. Assn. Avocations: travel, gardening. Home: 6153-A Edsall Rd Alexandria VA 22304 Office: TC Williams HS Alexandria VA 22302 Office Phone: 703-824-6800. Business E-Mail: mpatel@acps.k12.va.us.

PATEL, MARILYN HALL, judge; b. Amsterdam, NY, Sept. 2, 1938; d. Lloyd Manning and Nina J. (Thorpe) Hall; m. Magan C. Patel, Sept. 2, 1966; children: Brian, Gian. BA, Wheaton Coll., 1959; JD, Fordham U., 1963. Bar: N.Y. 1963, Calif. 1970. Mng. atty. Benson & Morris, Esq., NYC, 1962-64; sole practice NYC, 1964-67; atty. U.S. Immigration and Naturalization Svc., San Francisco, 1967-71; sole practive San Francisco, 1971-76; judge Alameda County Mcpl. Ct., Oakland, Calif., 1976-80, U.S. Dist. Ct. (no. dist.) Calif., San Francisco, 1980—; now chief judge U.S. Dist. Ct. for No. Dist. Calif., San Francisco, 1998—. Adj. prof. law Hastings Coll. of Law, San Francisco, 1974-76 Author: Immigration and Nationality Law, 1974; also numerous articles Mem. bd. visitors Fordham U. Sch. Law. Mem. ABA (litigation sect., jud. adminstrn. sect.), ACLU (former bd. dirs.), NOW (former bd. dirs.), Am. law Inst., Am. Judicature Soc. (bd. dirs.), Calif Conf. Judges, Nat. Assn. Women Judges (founding mem.), Internat. Inst. (bd. dirs.), Advs. for Women (co-founder), Assn. Bus. Trial Lawyers (bd. dirs.). Democrat. Avocations: piano, travel. Office: US Dist Ct PO Box 36060 450 Golden Gate Ave Ste 36052 San Francisco CA 94102-3482

PATEL, MULCHAND SHAMBHUBHAI, biochemist, researcher; b. Sipor, India, Sept. 9, 1939; came to U.S., 1965; s. Shambhubhai J. and Puriben (Patel) P.; m. Kankuben M. Patel; children: Sumitra, Yashomati, Mayank. BS, Gujarat U., 1961; MS, U. Baroda, 1964; PhD, U. Ill., 1968. Asst. prof. pediat. rsch. Sch. Medicine Temple U., Phila., 1970-72, rsch. asst. prof. medicine, 1972-75, rsch. asst. prof. biochemistry, 1970-75, rsch. assoc. prof. biochem. medicine, 1975-78; assoc. prof. biochemistry Sch. Medicine Case Western Res. U., Cleve., 1978-86, prof., 1986-93; prof., chmn. biochemistry SUNY, Buffalo, 1993-98, assoc. dean biomed. rsch. edn., 1999—, prof., 1999—2004, disting. prof., 2004—. Mem. NIH biochem. study sect. 2, 1984-88; mem. editl. bd. Jour. Biol. Chem., 1991-97, 99-2004, 06-. Contbr. articles to profl. jours. Recipient gold medal in biochemistry U. Baroda, 1973, Fulbright Rsch. Scholar award to India, 1987; prin. investigator, rsch. grantee NIH. Mem. Am. Soc. for Biochemistry and Molecular Biology, Am. Soc. Nutritional Scis. Office: SUNY-Dept Biochemistry Sch Medicine 140 Farber Hall 3435 Main St Buffalo NY 14214-3001 Office Phone: 716-829-3074. Business E-Mail: mspatel@buffalo.edu.

PATEL, NARESH PRATAP, medical educator, physician, consultant; b. Oct. 26, 1969; married. BA in Biology and Govt., Cornell U., 1991; MD, Baylor Coll. Medicne, 1995. Diplomate Am. Bd. Neurol. Surgery, lic. medicine and surgery N.Y., physician and surgeon Calif.; cert. BCLS, ACLS, advanced pneumatic instrumentation, microvascular surgery, med. lic. Ariz., lic. Drug Enforcement Agy. Intern in surgery Mt. Sinai Hosp., NYC, 1995—96, resident in neurosurgery, 1996—2001; intra-residency complex spine fellowship UCLA Med. Ctr./Cedars Sinai Med. Ctr., LA, 2000—01; clin. instr. Mayo Med. Sch., 2001—02, asst. prof. neurosurgery, 2003—, clin. cons., 2002—. Sr. assoc. cons. Mayo Clinic, 2001—; mem. CME com. Mayo Clinic Scottsdale, 2002—; presenter in field. Contbr. articles to profl. jours., chapters to books. Recipient Pi Kappa Phi Scholar award. Mem.: AMA (Physician Recognition award), World Spine Soc., N.Am. Spine Soc. (CME com. 2002—), Am. Assn. Neurol. Surgeons, Congress Neurol. Surgeons, Ariz. Med. Assn. Office: Mayo Clinic-Scottsdale 5777 E Mayo Blvd Phoenix AZ 85054 Business E-Mail: patel.naresh@mayo.edu.

PATEL, NIMA P., surgeon; d. Praful R. and Nayna P. Patel. MD, SUNY, Stony Brook, 2003. Resident surgery NJ med. sch. U. Medicine and Dentistry NJ, Newark, 2003—. Personal E-mail: illin79@aol.com.

PATEL, NIRAJ B., information technology executive; BBA in Computer Sci., Fin., Temple Univ. Network analyst to chief tech. officer Capmark Financial Group (formerly GMAC Holding Group), 1992—96, exec. v.p., chief info. officer, 1996—2006; mng. dir. Musser Group LLC fin. cons., Wayne, Pa., 2006—. Bd. dir. MISMO. Named Top Fin. IT Exec., CIO Forum, 2001—02, 2004; named one of Top 25 People to Watch in Real Estate, Realcomm, 2004, 2005, Top 25 Chief Tech. Officers, InfoWorld mag., 2006. Office: Musser Group LLC 435 Devon Pk Dr Bldg 500 Wayne PA 19087 Office Phone: 610-975-4912. *

PATEL, SNEHAL RAMAN, oral surgeon; s. Raman Kashibhai and Bhanu Raman Patel; m. Nisha Raman Patel, June 17, 2006. BS, Boston U., 1996; DDS, Columbia U., NYC, 2001, MD, 2004. Cert. Oral and Maxillofacial Surgery Columbia Presbyn. Med. Ctr., NY, 2007. Pvt. practice oral and maxillofacial surgery, Rockville, Md., 2007—. Vol. surgeon Healing the Children, Nieva, Colombia, 2006, Guaranda, Bolivar, Ecuador, 2007—. Mem.: AMA, ADA, Med. State Soc. NY, Am. Assn. Cosmetic Surgery, Acad. Osseointegration, Am. Cleft-Palate Assn., Am. Assn. Oral and Maxillofacial Surgery. Home Phone: 212-305-4552.

PATEL, TILLIAN K., critical care nurse; b. Columbus, Ohio, June 1967; d. William Theodore and Catherine Rose (Burke) Smith; m. Omar Hussain Patel, July 16, 1994; children: Aisha K., Ali Hussain, Yasmeen Zara. BS in Nursing, Bowling Green State U., Ohio, 1990. Emergency room nurse Riverside Mercy Hosp., Waterville, Ohio, 1990—99; critical care nurse Meriks County Hosp., Rapid City, Mich., 1999—2004, head nurse, 2004—. Named Nurse of Yr., Riverside Mercy Hosp., 1995, 1997. Mem.: Delta Delta Delta (life). Independent. Avocations: reading, travel, dollhouses, piano.

PATEL, UPTAL DINESH, nephrologist, researcher; BA, U. Calif. San Diego, 1993; MD, U. Calif. San Francisco, 1997. Diplomate Am. Bd. Internal Medicine, 2001, Diplomate, Subspecialty in Nephrology Am. Bd. Internal Medicine, 2005, Diplomate Am. Bd. Pediat., 2001, Diplomate, Subspecialty in Pediat. Nephrology Am. Bd. Pediat., 2005. Robert Wood Johnson clin. scholar U. Mich., Ann Arbor, 2003—05; asst. prof. medicine and pediat. Duke U., Sch. Medicine, Durham, NC, 2005—. Mem. editl. bd.: Jour. Am. Soc. Nephrology, 2007—. Rsch. Career Devel. award, NIH, 2006—. Office Phone: 919-668-8008.

PATEL, VIMLA L., research scientist; b. Nadi, Fiji Islands; d. Harvovind Mavji and Kantaben Lodhia; m. Yogesh C Patel (dec.); children: Sunil, Camille. BSc, Otago U., New Zealand, 1976; MA, McGill U., Montreal, 1980, MA, 1990, PhD, 1982; DSc (hon.), U. Victoria, B.C., Can., 1990. Prof. psychology and medicine McGill U., Montreal, 1991—2000, asst. prof. medicine and psychology, assoc. prof. medicine and psychology, 1997—2000; prof. psychiatry and biomed. informatics Columbia U., NYC, 2000—07, adj. prof. psychology and edn., 2000—; prof., chair dept. biomed. informatics Ariz. State U., Phoenix, 2007—, dir. med. edn. rsch. Coll. Medicine, 2007—; prof. basic med. scis. U. Ariz. Coll. Medicine, Phoenix, 2007—. Dir. med. edn. McGill U., Montreal, 1993—2000, dir. cognitive sci. ctr., 1993—97; dir., lab. of decision making and cognition Columbia U., 2000—07; vis. scholar Stanford U., Palo Alto, Calif., 1999—2000; vis. prof. Universty of Tex., Houston, 1998—99. Contbr. articles to profl. jours. Recipient Woman of Sci. award, Rsch. Coun., Sweden, 1994. Fellow: N.Y. Acad. Sci.; mem.: Acad. of Humanities and Social Sci. of Can., Royal Soc. Can., Am. Med. Informatics Assn. (assoc.), Cogniitve Sci. Soc. (assoc.), Psychonomics Socoety (assoc.), Am. Ednl. Rsch. Assn. (corr.), Am. Coll. Med. Informatics. Office: Ariz State U 699 S Mill Ave Ste 553 Tempe AZ 85281 Office Phone: 480-965-1496. Business E-Mail: vimla@asu.edu.

PATEL, VIRENDRA CHATURBHAI, mechanical engineer, educator; b. Mombasa, Kenya, Nov. 9, 1938; arrived in US, 1969, naturalized, 1975; s. Chaturbhai S. and Kantaben N. (Rai) Patel; m. Manjula Patel, May 29, 1966; children: Sanjay, Bindiya. BSc with honors, Imperial Coll., London, 1962; PhD, Cambridge U., Eng., 1965; Dr. honoris causa, Tech. U. Civil Engring., Bucharest, Romania, 1994. Sr. asst. in rsch. Cambridge U., 1965-69; vis. prof. Indian Inst. Tech., Kharagpur, 1966; cons. Lockheed Ga. Co., Marietta, 1969-70; from mem. faculty to disting. prof. U. Iowa, Iowa City, 1971—90, disting. prof., 1990—, Edwin B. Green chair in hydraulics, 2000—; rsch. engr. Iowa Inst. Hydraulic Rsch., 1971—, dir., 1994—2004, hon. prof. Dharamsinh Desai Inst. Tech., 2002—, dir. Ctr. Computer Aided Design, 2003—05. Mem. Iowa Gov. Sci. Adv. Coun., 1977—83; mem. resistance com. Internat. Towing Tank Conf., 1978—87; vis. prof. U. Karlsruhe, Germany, 1980—81, Ecole Nationale Superieure de Mechanique, Nantes, France, 1984, Nantes, 96; jubilee prof. Chalmers Inst. Tech., Goteborg, Sweden, 1988; dir. Ctr. for Computer Aided Design, 2003—; cons. in field. Author: (book) Three Dimensional Turbulent Boundary Layers, 1972; contbr. articles to profl. jours.; assoc. editor: AIAA Jour., 1987—90. V.p. internat. com. Anooram Mission, Mogri, India. Recipient Sr. Scientist award, Alexander von Humboldt Found., 1980, 1993. Fellow: ASME (Fluids Engring. award 1997), AIAA (assoc.); mem.: Soc. Naval Archtl. Marine Engrs., Am. Soc. Engring. Edn., Pi Tau Sigma, Sigma Xi. Home: 60 Kennedy Pkwy Iowa City IA 52246-2780 Office: IIHR Hyrdoscience and Engring U Iowa 302 Hydraulics Laboratory Iowa City IA 52242-1585 Home Phone: 319-351-5426. Business E-Mail: v-c-patel@uiowa.edu.

PATENAUDE, PAMELA HUGHES, federal agency administrator; BA, St. Anselm Coll., 1983; MA, So. NH U. Liaison, spl. asst. to dep. asst. sec. for multifamily housing The White House, Washington, exec. asst. to dep. undersec. field coord.; v.p. Manor Homes Builders, Inc., Bedford, NH, 1988—96; mktg. and training dir. NH Small Bus. Ctr.; state dir. and dep. chief of staff Office of U.S. Senator Bob Smith; asst. dep. sec. field policy & mgmt. US Dept. Housing & Urban Devel., Washington, asst. sec. for community planning & devel., 2005—. Former chmn. Bedford Housing Adv. Com.; held leadership positions in various profl. and civic organizations. Office: 451 Seventh St SW Rm 7100 Mall Code D Washington DC 20410 Office Phone: 202-708-2690. Office Fax: 202-708-3336.

PATERAKIS, ANGELA GREGORY, art educator, consultant, writer; b. Oak Park, Ill., June 1, 1932; d. Kostas and Sophia (Spiliotou) Gregory; m. George A. Paterakis, July 31, 1958. B.A.E., Sch. of Art Inst. Chgo., 1954; M.A., U. Ill., 1955; art therapy cert., 1985. Tchr. jr. high sch., Oak Park, Ill., 1955-60; prof. emerita art edn. and art therapy Sch. of Art Inst. Chgo., 1961—; mem. arts advocacy groups, Ill. Author numerous articles, pamphlets on art edn.; pres. Ill. Alliance for Arts Edn.; bd. dirs. Hellenic Mus. and Cultrual Ctr., Chgo., 1990—. mem. Ill. Arts Adv. Com., 1989-91. Recipient Svc. Recognition award Ill. Alliance for Arts Edn., 1985; U. Ill. fellow, 1954-55. Mem. NEA (life), Nat. Art Edn. Assn., Ill. Art Edn. Assn. (named Outstanding Art Educator 1981, Disting. mem., 2000). Office: Sch of the Art Inst Chgo 37 South Wabash Ave Chicago IL 60603-3103

PATERIK, FRANCES SUE, secondary school educator, actress; b. Bloomington, Ill., Feb. 10, 1953; d. Francis LaVerne and Magaline Wilken. Student, Am. Cons. Music, Chgo., 1976—78, N.W. Ind. Opera Co., 1980, Hinsdale Opera Co., Ill., 1981; BA, MA, Western Ill. U., 1984. Tchg. asst. Western Ill. U., Macomb, 1982—84; music tchr. Cardinal Cmty. Schs., Eldon, Iowa, 1985—89, Johnston (Iowa) Cmty. Schs., 1990—94; music/performing arts tchr. Colfax (Iowa)-Mingo Cmty. Sch., 1995—2002, Merrill Middle Sch., Des Moines, 2002—. Dir. handbell choir 1st Christian Ch., Des Moines, 1996—2000; soprano soloist Des Moines Concert Singers, 1989—, Des Moines Choral Soc., 2002—; alto sect. leader St. John's Luth. Ch., 2004—, bell choir dir., 2006—. Actress: (various comedic roles) Ingersoll Dinner Theatre; Playhouse; Drama Workshop; Stage West; actress (various comedic roles) Ankeny Cmty. Theatre, St. John's Luth. Ch., Shoestring Prodns., Indianola, Iowa, music dir. Children's Theatre, 2007. Mem.: Des Moines Choral Soc., Iowa Choral Dirs. Assn., Am. Choral Dirs. Assn., Music Educators Nat. Conf., Nat. Wildlife Fedn., Sierra Club. Democrat. Avocations: gardening, dance. Office: Des Moines Pub Schs Des Moines IA 50312 Business E-Mail: f.paterik@mchsi.com.

PATERNO, JOE (JOSEPH VINCENT PATERNO), college football coach; b. Bklyn., Dec. 21, 1926; s. Angelo Lafayette and Florence (de LaSalle) P.; m. Suzanne Pohland, May 12, 1962; children: Diana Lynne, Mary Kathryn, David, Joseph Vincent, George Scott. BA, Brown U., Providence, 1950, LLD, 1975. Asst. football coach Pa. State U., 1950-66, head coach, 1966—. Author (with Bernard Asbell): The Paterno Principle, 1989; Paterno: By the Book, 1989. Served with AUS, 1945-46. Recipient Coach of Yr.award Am. Football Coaches Assn, 1968, 78, 82, 86, 2005, Paul "Bear" Bryant award, Nat. Sportscasters & Sportswriters Assn., 1978, 82, 86, Amos Alonzo Stagg award, 2002, Gold Medal, Nat. Football Fedn. awards, 2006; Named Coach of Yr. Walter Camp Football Found., 1972, 2005, Coach of Yr. Washington Touchdown Club, 1973, 86; named Sports Illustrated's 1986 Sportsman of the Yr.; inducted into Coll. Football Hall of Fame, 2006 Mem. Am. Football Coaches Assn. (dir., Coach of Yr. awards 1968, 78, 82, 86). won Nat. Championship, 1982, 1986; Ranked 4th in All-Time Divsn. I-A Coaching Victories, 1st among active coaches. Office: Pa State U Lasch Football Bldg University Park PA 16802-7101 *

PATERSON, BASIL ALEXANDER, lawyer; b. NYC, Apr. 27, 1926; s. Leonard J. and Evangeline (Rondon) P.; m. Portia Hairston, 1953; children: Daniel, David. BS, St. John's Coll., 1948; JD, St. John's U., 1951. Bar: N.Y. 1952. Ptnr. Paterson, Michael, Dinkins and Jones, NYC, 1956—77, Meyer, Suozzi, English & Klein, P.C., Garden City, NY, 1983—; mem. N.Y. State Senate, 1965-70; dep. mayor for labor rels. City of N.Y., 1978; sec. of state State of N.Y., 1979-82. Pres. Inst. Mediation and Conflict Resolution, 1971-77; chmn. 2d Jud. Screening Com., 1985-95; assoc. chmn. N.Y. State Sentencing Guidelines Com.; commr. Port Authority N.Y. and N.J., 1989-95; mem. commn. to promote confidence in judicial elections, 2003-. Bd. dirs. St. Benedict's Day Nursery, 1999—; vice chmn. Dem. Nat. Com., 1972-78, mem., 1972-78; chmn. KeySpan Found., 2003—. Recipient Eagleton Inst. Politics award, Disting. Svc. award Guardians Assn. N.Y. Police Dept., City Club N.Y. award, Black Expo award, Excellence medal St. John's U., Kibbe award CUNY. Roman Catholic. Office: Meyer Suozzi English Klein Pc PO Box 9194 Garden City NY 11530-9194

PATERSON, DAVID ALEXANDER, lieutenant governor, former state legislator; b. Bklyn., May 20, 1954; s. Basil and Portia (Hairston) P.; m. Michelle Paige; 1 child, Alexander Basil; 1 stepchild, Ashley Dennis. BA, Columbia U., NYC, 1977; JD, Hofstra U., 1983. Mediator Inst. Mediation and Conflict Resolution, NYC, 1975; legal asst. Mcpl. Credit Union, NYC, 1976-78; asst. grants officer Bronx CC, NY, 1981; dir. Housing Preservation Dept. Fair Housing Office, 1982; asst. criminal law Queens Dist. Atty.'s Office, NY, 1983-85; mem. NY State Senate, 1985—2006, dep. minority leader, 1985—2002, minority leader, 2002—06; lt. gov. State of NY, Albany, 2007—. Bd. dirs. Mil-Gar Home Care Service, NY; mem. adv. coun. Lower Manhattan Devel. Corp. Contbr. articles to profl. jours. Fundraising chmn. George McGoverns Presdl. Campaign, N.Y., 1972, Herman Badillo's Mayoral Campaign, N.Y., 1973, Black Citizens for Fair Media, N.Y., 1976, Manhattan Borough Pres. David Dinkins, N.Y., 1985; mem. Martin Luther King Dem. Club, N.Y., 1977—, Jewish Guild for the Blind, N.Y., 1986; mem. bd. trustees Am. Found. for Blind; bd. dirs. Achilles Track Club; mem. fed. steering com. African Burial Ground. Recipient Cmty. Svc. award N.H. Hairston Clan, 1984, Achievement award Courtsman A.A., Inc., 1986, Spl. award Profl. Archaeologists N.Y.C., 1993, Migel award Am. Found. for Blind, 1996; named Senator of Yr., N.Y. State NOW, 1989. Mem. NAACP (bd. dirs. Mid-Manhattan br. 1981—), N.Y. State Bar Assn. on Minorities, Macon B, Allen Black Bar Assn., Met. Com. of 100 (legal advisor 1979—). Democrat. Avocations: basketball, theater, baseball, history. Office: Office Lt Gov Exec Chamber State Capitol Rm 326 Albany NY 12224 E-mail: paterson@senate.state.ny.us. *

PATERSON, DAVID J., paper company executive; b. Washington, Aug. 15, 1954; BS, Cornell U., 1976; MBA, U. Mich., 1978. Mktg. analyst Continental Forest Industries, 1978—79, supr. fibre supply, 1979—80, shift foreman, 1980—82, mgr. quality control, 1982—83; sales mgr. containerboard S.W. Forest Industries, 1983—87; export sales mgr. containerboard Ga.-Pacific Corp., Atlanta, 1987—88, dir. export pulp sales, 1988—92, dir. pulp sales & mktg., 1992—94, v.p. sales & mktg. pulp & bleached bd., 1994—95, v.p. market pulp and recycling ops., 1995—96, v.p. market pulp, 1996—2000, v.p. electronic commerce, 2000, sr. v.p. comm. papers, 2000—01, pres. paper, 2001, pres. paper & bleached bd., 2001, exec. v.p. pulp & paperboard, 2001—03, exec. v.p., pres. bldg. products, 2003—06; pres., CEO Bowater Inc., Greenville, SC, 2006, chmn., pres., CEO, 2007—. Bd. mem. Rsch. Atlanta, Inc.; mem. ISAC12 U.S. Dept. Commerce. Mem.: Japan-Am. Soc. Ga. Office: Bowater Inc 55 E Camperdown Way Greenville SC 29601 *

PATERSON, EVA, legal association director, educator; b. 1949; BA, Northwestern U.; JD, Boalt Hall Sch. Law, U. Calif., Berkeley. Bar: 1975. Assoc. Legal Aid Soc. Alameda County; staff mem. Lawyers' Com. Civil Rights, 1977—90, exec. dir., 1990—2003; exec. dir., founder Equal Justice Soc., 2003—. Adj. prof. U. San Francisco Sch. Law, Hastings Sch. Law. Co-founder A Safe Place, Oakland, Calif., Calif. Coalition Civil Rights, chair; v.p. ACLU Nat. Bd.; chair Equal Rights Advocates. Named one of Top 25 Lawyers, San Francisco Chronicle, 2002; recipient Fay Stender award, Calif. Women Lawyers, Woman Yr. award, Black Leadership Forum, Earl Warren Civil Liberties award, ACLU No. Calif., Alumni award Merit, Northwestern U. Mem.: San Francisco Bar Assn. (chair). Achievements include first African Am. pres. student govt. at Northwestern U. Office: Equal Justice Soc 220 Sansome St 14th Fl San Francisco CA 94104 Office Phone: 415-288-8700.

PATERSON, KATHERINE WOMELDORF, writer; b. Huaiyin, China, Oct. 31, 1932; came to U.S., 1940; d. George Raymond and Mary Elizabeth (Goetchius) Womeldorf; m. John Barstow Paterson, July 14, 1962; children: Elizabeth Polin, John Barstow, David Lord, Mary Katherine Nah-he-sah-pe-che-a. AB, King Coll., Bristol, Tenn., 1954; post grad., Kobe Sch. Japanese Lang., 1957-60; MA, Presbyn. Sch. Christian Edn., 1957; MRE, Union Theol. Sem., 1962; LittD. (hon.), King Coll., Bristol, Tenn., 1978; LHD (hon.), Otterbein Coll., 1979; LittD (hon.), St. Mary's of the Woods, 1981; LittD, Washington and Lee U., 1982; LittD (hon.), U. Md., 1982, Shenandoah Coll., 1982; LHD, Washington and Lee U, 1982; LHD (hon.), Norwich U., 1990, Mount St. Vincent U., Halifax, NS, Can., 1994; LittD, Hope Coll., 1997; DLitt (hon.), Prebyn. Coll., 2002. Tchr. Lovettsville Elem. Sch., Va., 1954-55; missionary Presbyn. Ch., Japan, 1957-61; master sacred studies and English Pennington Sch. for Boys, NJ, 1963-65. Author: The Sign of the Chrysanthemum, 1973, Of Nightingales That Weep, 1974, The Master Puppeteer, 1976, Bridge to Terabithia, 1977, The Great Gilly Hopkins, 1978, Angels and Other Strangers, 1979, Jacob Have I Loved, 1980, Rebels of the Heavenly Kingdom, 1983, Come Sing, Jimmy Jo, 1985, (with John Paterson) Consider the Lilies, 1986, Park's Quest, 1988, The Tale of the Mandarin Ducks, 1990, The Smallest Cow in the World, 1991, Lyddie, 1991, The King's Equal, 1992, Who Am I?, 1992, Flip-Flop Girl, 1994, A Midnight Clear: Stories for the Christmas Season, 1995, A Sense of Wonder, 1995, The Angel and the Donkey, 1996, Jip: His Story, 1996, Marvin's Best Christmas Present Ever, 1997, (with John Paterson) Images of God, 1998, Parzival, 1998, Celia and the Sweet, Sweet Water, 1998, Preacher's Boy, 1999, The Wide-Awake Princess, 2000, The Field of the Dogs, 2001, Marvin One Too Many, 2001, The Invisible Child, 2002, The Same Stuff as Stars, 2002, (with John Paterson) Blueberries for the Queen, 2004, Bread & Roses, Too, 2006; translator: The Crane Wife, 1981, The Tongue-Cut Sparrow, 1987. V.p. Nat. Children's Book and Literacy Alliance. US nominee for Hans Christian Andersen award, 1979, 89, 97, 98; recipient Nat. Book award, 1977, 79, Newbery medal, 1978, 91, Newbery honor, 1979, New Eng. Book award New Eng. Booksellers Assn., 1982, Union medal Union Theol. Sem., 1992, Scott O'Dell award for hist. fiction, 1997, May Hill Arbuthnot Lectr. award, 1997, Lion award NY Pub. Libr., 1998, Literary Light award Boston Pub. Libr., 2000, Living Legend award Libr. of Congress, 2000, Jefferson cup Va. Libr. Assn., 2000, Vt. Gov.'s award for excellence in arts, 2001, Astrid Lindgren Meml. award Swedish Govt., 2006, Christopher award, 2007, NHK Newstadt award, 2007. Mem. Authors Guild, Children's Book Guild Washington. Democrat. Office: Clarion Books 215 Park Ave S New York NY 10003-1603

PATERSON, PAUL CHARLES, retired private investigator, security consultant; b. Bethlehem, Pa., Dec. 31, 1927; s. Thomas and Ida (Weiss) P.; m. Estelle Marie Nabors; children: Linda Ann, Thomas Scott, Terry Maurice Leard. Grad., Inst. Applied Sci., Chgo., 1950. Jr. credit analyst Bethlehem Steel Corp., Pa., 1947-50; inspector claim spec., claim dir., field supr. Equifax Svcs., Inc., Allentown, Pa., 1953-61, field claim supr. St. Louis, 1961-63, regional claims mgr. Phila., 1963-71, spl. claim sales, sales exec.-claims Atlanta, 1971-89; pvt. investigator, pres. Paterson Investigations, Inc., Douglasville, Ga., 1989-2001. Editor CFE newsletter The Ga. Examiner, 1994-95. With U.S. Army, 1950-53. Mem. VFW, Am. Legion, Life, Accident and Health Claims Assn. Phila. (life, pres. 1969-70), Mktg. Ins. Claims Assn. (life, v.p. 1985—, pres. 1989-90), So. Loss Assn., Nat. WWII Meml. Assn. (charter), Atlanta Claims Assn., Ga. Assn. Profl. Pvt. Investigators (chair ethics com. 1999, treas. 2000), Assn. Cert. Fraud Examiners (cert., past pres. Ga. chpt. 1990, 93, bd. dirs. 1991-92, faculty 1995-96, bd. regents 1996, Disting. Achievement award 1994, 95, Regent Emeritus, life mem.), Criminal Investigation Divsn. Agts. Assn. Inc., Ga. Sheriffs' Assn., Ga. Claims Assn., Ga. Fire Investigators Assn., Ret. Mil. Police Assn. (assoc.), Am. Legion, Chapel Hills Golf Club. Republican. Avocations: golf, music, swimming, physical conditioning. Home: 5235 Stilesboro Rd NW 215 Kennesaw GA 30152-3968 E-mail: paulpaterson@earthlink.net.

PATERSON, RICHARD DENIS, corporate financial executive; b. Ottawa, Ont., Can., Oct. 13, 1942; m. Antoinette Paterson; children: Christopher, Russell, Kathlyn, Victoria, Connor. B in Commerce, Concordia U., Montreal, Que., Can., 1964. Auditor Coopers & Lybrand, Montreal, 1964-67; acct. Genstar Corp., Montreal, 1967-69; dir. fin. and adminstrn. Indussa Corp. (subs. Genstar Corp.), NYC, 1969-73; v.p., comptroller Genstar Corp., Montreal and San Francisco, 1973-83, sr. v.p., CFO San Francisco, 1983-87; exec. v.p. Genstar Investment Corp., San Francisco, 1987-95; mng. dir. Genstar Capital LP, San Francisco, 1996—. Bd. dirs. Installs Inc., Am. Pacific Enterprises, Inc., Altra Indsl. Motion, Inc., Propex Fabrics, Inc., Woods Equipment Co., North Am. Constrn. Group., Inc. Mem. Order Chartered Accts. Que. Office: Genstar Capital LP Four Embarcadero Ctr Ste 1900 San Francisco CA 94111-4191 E-mail: rpaterson@gencap.com.

PATERSON, ROBERT E., retail executive; b. Kearny, NJ, 1926; s. Robert McKinley and Ethel Paterson; m. Eileen Josephine Connolly; children: Carol Joan, Robert, Richard, Donald, Jeffrey. MBA, Columbia U., 1971. Sr. v.p. fin., treas. The Sperry & Hutchinson Co., Inc., NYC, 1952-87, also bd. dirs. Bd. dirs. Govt. Obligations Fund, 1986—87. Mem. Borough Coun., 1991—98, 2002—04, coun. pres., 1995—98, 2002. With US Army, 1944—45, PTO.

PATHAK, ANANT MADHAV, retired anesthesiologist; arrived in US, 1956; s. Madhav B. and Annapurna M. Pathak; m. Meera Anant Paranjape, Feb. 12, 1978; children: Arjun A., Anuja A. MBBS, Nagpur Med. Coll., Nagpur, India, 1955. Lic. Ariz., 1972. Instr. anesthesiology We. Res. Med. Sch., Cleve., 1959—62; intern Deaconess Hosp., Cleve., 1956—57; resident in anesthesiology U. Hosps. Cleve., 1957—59; resident in gen. surgery Lakewood Hosp., Ohio, 1959—61; fellowship in anesthesiology U. Hosps. Cleve., 1961—62, instr. anesthesiology, 1962—64; pvt. practice Lakewood, Ohio, 1964—72; mem. staff various hosps., Tucson, 1972—97, ret., 1997. Mem.: Homeowners Assn. (sec. 2002—07). Conservative.

PATHAK, SANJEEV, psychiatrist, researcher; b. Shimla, Himachal Pradesh, India; MD, All India Inst. Med. Sci., 1993. Diplomate Am. Bd. of Psychiatry and Neurology. Resident in psychiatry U. Cin., 1996—99, fellowship in child and adolescent psychiatry, 1999—2001; asst. prof. psychiatry and neurology Cin. Children's Hosp., U. Cin. Coll. Medicine, Cin., 2001—. Contbr. articles to profl. jours. Achievements include research in pediatric mood disorders. Office: Cin Children's Hosp 3333 Burnet Ave D-3014 Cincinnati OH 45229 Office Phone: 513-636-4788. E-mail: sanjeev-pathak@cchmc.org.

PATIENCE, GREGORY SCOTT, chemical engineer, educator; b. Victoria, BC, Can., Aug. 19, 1961; s. Danny Alexander Patience and Margaret Puczko; m. Nadine Aboussouan; children: Paul Alexander, Christian Alexander, Nicolas Alexander, Brendan Alexander. BSc, U.Calgary, Alta., Canada, 1983; MSc, U. Calgary, Alta., Canada, 1987; PhD, Ecole Polytechnique de Montreal, Que., Can., 1990. Rsch. engr. DuPont Chems., Wilmington, Del., 1990—94; sr. engr. Lycra/Terathane DuPont, Gijon, Asturias, Spain, 1996—2000, rsch. assoc. apparel and textile scis. Meyrin, Geneva, Switzerland, 2000—04; prof. Agregé Ecole Polytech., Montreal, 2004—. Scholar, NSERC, Can. Govt., 1987—90, Alta./Can. Energy Resources Rsch. Fund, Govt. of Alta., 1983, Home Oil Co. Ltd., 1986, Ecole Polytechnique de Montreal, 1987—90, Bourse d'Etude Superieures Fonds, Govt. Que., 1987—90. Achievements include patents for new reactor type based on membrane technology and fluidization technology - Membrane Reactor; catalyst process; research in gas-solid hydrodynamic model; laminar entry length model for non-Newtonian fluids; laminar start-up time for fluids in pipes; design of fundamental principle related to scaling up a chemical process - scale-up factors; development of kinetic model to describe partial oxidation catalysis. Office Phone: 154 340 4711 x 3439.

PATIENT, WILLIAM F., chemicals executive; V.p. sales and mktg. Borg-Warner Chemicals, v.p. mfg.; pres. Borg-Warner Chemicals Europe; sr. v.p. BF Goodrich Company, pres. Geon Vinyl divsn.; CEO Geon (now PolyOne Corp.), 1993—99; chmn. PolyOne, Corp., 2003—06, lead dir., 2006—. Bd. dir. Navistar Internat. Corp. Bd. dir. Wash. U.; chmn. of bd. Cleve. State U. Found. Office: 33587 Walker RD Avon Lake OH 44012-1145

PATINKIN, MANDY, actor, singer; b. Chgo., Nov. 30, 1952; s. Lester and Doris (Sinton) P.; m. Kathryn Grody, June 15, 1980; children: Isaac, Gideon. Student, U. Kans., 1970-72, Juilliard Sch. Drama, 1972-74, NC Sch. of Arts. Actor N.Y. Shakespeare Festival, 1975-81; plays include Hotspur in Henry IV, Part 1, Hudson Guild, N.Y.C., Rebel Women, Hamlet, Leave it to Beaver is Dead, Savages; (Broadway) Evita (Tony award 1980), Shadow Box, Sunday in the Park with George, 1984, The Knife, 1987, The Winter's Tale, 1989, Mandy Patinkin in Concert: Dress Casual, 1989, The Secret Garden, 1991, Man of La Mancha, 1996, Forbidden Broadway, 1999, The Wild Party, 2000; (films) The Big Fix, 1978, Last Embrace, 1979, French Postcards, 1980, Night of the Juggler, 1980, Ragtime, 1981, Yentl, 1983, Daniel, 1983, Maxie, 1985, The Princess Bride, 1987, The House on Carroll Street, 1988, Alien Nation, 1988, Dick Tracy, 1990, The Doctor, 1991, True Colors, 1991, The Music of Chance, 1993, Life with Mikey, 1993, Squanto: A Warrior's Tale, 1994, Men with Guns, 1997, Lulu on the Bridge, 1998, The Adventures of Elmo in Grouchland, 1999, Piñero, 2001, Choking Man, 2006, (voice) Everyone's Hero, 2006; (TV appearances): That Thing on ABC, That Second Thing on ABC, Taxi, Midnight Special, (TV series) Chicago Hope, 1994-95, 1999-2000 (Emmy award, 1995), Dead Like Me, 2003-04, Criminal Minds, 2005-; TV movies include Charleston, 1979, Sunday in the Park with George, 1986, Broken Glass, 1996, The Hunchback, 1997, Strange Justice, 1999, NTSB: The Crash of Flight 323, 2004; albums: Mandy Patinkin, 1984, Sunday in the Park with George, 1986, Dress Casual, 1990, Oscar and Steve, 1995, Experiment, 1994, Mamaloshen, 1998, Kidults, 2001. Recipient Music Achievement award Drama League, 1989. Mem. AFTRA, Screen Actors Guild, Actors Equity Assn. Office: United Talent Agy care Adam Isaacs 9560 Wilshire Blvd Ste 500 Beverly Hills CA 90212-2427 also: care Dodger Touring Ltd 501 Broadway Ste 2015 New York NY 10036

PATINKIN, TERRY ALLAN, physician; b. Oak Park, Ill., Feb. 1, 1950; s. Lester D. and Marcella Jaqueline (Steynburg) P.; m. Sandra Lee Friedman, Apr. 21, 1985; children: Jonathan, Zachary. BS, U. Ill., 1971; MD, U. Calif., San Francisco, 1975; MPH in Health Care Mgmt., Harvard U., 1996. Diplomate Am. Bd. Emergency Medicine, Am. Bd. Family Medicine; cert. physician exec. Intern, resident in family practice U. Calif. San Francisco/Natividad Med. Ctr., Salinas, Calif., 1975-78, assoc. dir. family medicine residency program, 1978-90; dir. emergency dept. Natividad Med. Ctr., Salinas, 1985-91, dir. continuing med. edn., 1978-91, dir. undergrad. edn., 1978-90, emergency physician, 1979-91, Sturdy Meml. Hosp., Attleboro, Mass., 1991-94; dir., chmn. emergency dept. Roger Williams Hosp., Providence, 1994-99, Landmark Med. Ctr., Woonsocket, RI, 2000—02; med. dir. urgent care East Boston Neighborhood Health Ctr., 2002—. Asst. clin. prof. U. Calif., San Francisco, 1981-88, assoc. clin. prof., 1988-91; clin. asst. prof. Stanford U., 1990-93; asst. clin. prof. Brown U., Providence, 1995—, Boston U., 1999—. Fellow Am. Coll. Emergency Physicians; mem. Am. Coll. Physician Execs., Mass. Coll. Emergency Physicians, Mass. Med. Soc., U. Ill. Alumni Assn. (life), U. Calif. San Francisco Alumni Faculty Assn. Office: 10 Gove St East Boston MA 02128 Home Phone: 617-332-3752; Office Phone: 617-568-4639. Business E-Mail: patinkit@ebnhc.org.

PATINO, DOUGLAS XAVIER, government agency administrator, academic administrator; b. Calexico, Calif., Apr. 11, 1939; s. Jose Luis and Maria Teresa (Seymour) P.; m. Barbel Wilma Hoyer, Aug. 13, 1970; 1 child, Viktor Xavier. AA, Imperial Valley Coll., 1960; BA, Calif. State U., San Diego, 1962, MA, 1966; PhD, U.S. Internat. U., 1972. Deputy dir. Sacramento Concilio, Inc., Calif., 1968-69; v.p. student affairs U. So. Colo., Pueblo, 1973-75; dep. dir. for planning and rev. svc. br. to dir. Calif. Employment Devel. Dept., dir.; sec. Calif. Health & Welfare Agy., 1975-83; dir. Ariz. Dept. of Econ. Security, Phoenix, 1983-87; pres., chief exec. officer Marin Community Found., Larkspur, Calif., 1987-91; pres. New Partnership Found. and Patino Group, San Rafael, Calif., 1991; vice chancellor Calif. State U. Sys., Long Beach, 1993—2002; prof. social welfare Calif. State U., LA, 1998—2004. Commr. W.T. Grand Found., 1986—88, Enterprize for the Ams., Washington, 1994—; trustee C.S. Mott Found., Flint, Mich., 1995—, Calif. Wellness Found., Woodland Hills, 1997—; chmn., treas. Hispanics in Philanthropy, 1993—2002. Mem. Sec. of U.S. Dept. of Labor Task Force, Ariz., 1985-86, Staff Adv. Com. of the Human Resource Com., Nat. Gov. Assn., Washington, 1983-86; bd. dirs. Calif. Leadershp, Santa Cruz, Calif., 1985-95, No. Calif. Grantmakers, 1990-91, Ariz. Assn. Bus., 1984; chair U.S. Savs. Bond Dr. for State of Calif., 1982; trustee Nat. Hispanic U., Oakland, Calif., 1987-90, Hispanic Community Fund, San Francisco, 1989-95, bd. dirs. Calif. Sch. Profl. Psychology, 1989-94, Coun. on Found., Washington, 1990-96, Found. Ctr., N.Y., 1993; pres. Calif. State U. Found. Recipient Monty Disting. Alumni award San Diego State U., 1997, Simon Bolivar award Hispanic Cmty. Found. and Bay Area United Way, 1996, Azteca award Human Devel. Corp., 1991, Leadership award Nat. Concilors Am. and United Way of Bay Area, 1990, Disting. Performance award Nat. Alliance of Bus., Washington, 1985, Superior Svc. Mgmt. award Am. Soc. Pub. Adminstrn., 1985, Humanitarian award Los Padrinos, Inc., 1981, Small and Minority Bus. award for the State of Calif. 1982, Disting. Alumni award Calif. Jr. CC Assn., Sacramento, 1982, Silver Spur award Nat. Fedn. Charros in Guadalajaro, Jalisco, Mex., 1974, Calif. Cmty. Svc. award Former Gov. Ronald Reagan, Sacramento, 1973; named to 100 Most Influential Hispanics, Hispanic Bus., 1995, 97; named one of 100 Most Influential Latinos, Latino Leaders Mag., 2005-06. Mem. Am. Pub. Welfare Assn. (bd. dirs., Leadership award 1987), Assn. Black Found. Execs. (dir. 2003-07), Rotary, 1987-93. Office: The Patino Group Sacramento CA 95822

PATINO-BRANDFON, SYLVIA, retired psychologist; d. Alfonso and Zenobia Moeller Patino; children: Andrea, Thea. AB in English, U. N.Mex., 1956; MS in English, Wis. U., 1958; student, Tavistock Inst., London, 1970—71; MA in Child Study, Tufts U., 1975; PhD in Psychology, Boston Coll., 1980; student in Psychopharmacology, Internat. Coll. Prescribing Psychologist, 1995—97. Lic. psychologist Mass., 1981. Intern psychotherapy Judge Baker Guidance Ctr., Boston, 1972—74; intern McLean Hosp., Belmont, Mass., 1979—80, post doctoral fellow, 1980—81; pvt. practice Quincy and Taunton, Mass., 1982—99; ret., 1999. Spkr. in field. Author: (newsletter) ADHD and Other Behavior Problems, 1994—98. Mem. com. superior cts. Ariz. Supreme Ct., 2004—, mem. jud. performance rev. commn., 2004—, bd. overseeing reporters, 2004; mem. Ariz. Commn. Jud. Conduct, 2007—. Fellow: APA (life).

PATKI, KIRAN C., pharmacologist, researcher; s. Chandrakant S. and Prabhavati C. Patki; m. Leena K. Patki, Nov. 20, 2003. MBBS, Grant Med. Coll., Bombay, India, 1994; MD, Seth GS Med. Coll., Bombay, 1997. Resident med. officer Seth GS Med. Coll., Bombay, 1994—97; sr. clinician Pfizer Internat. Clin. Rsch. Group, 1997—2001; fellow clin. investigations Harvard-MIT, Boston, 2001—03; fellow clin. pharmacology Tufts U. Sch. of Medicine, 2001—. Recipient Troika award best rsch. paper presentation, Indian Pharm. Soc. (Gujrat chpt.), 1996; scholar, Govt. of Maharashtra, India, 1988—94. Mem.: Am. Coll. Clin. Pharmacology, Am. Soc. Clin. Pharmacology and Therapeutics. Achievements include research in clin. pharmacology; identification of potential effects of polymorphisms; other factors in explaining the variability associated with CYP3A metabolism. Personal E-mail: kirancp@yahoo.com.

PATMOS, MARCIA, apparel designer; Grad. in Apparel Design, Rhode Island Sch. of Design. Designer, NYC, 1991—; co-owner, designer (with Tina Lutz) Lutz & Patmos, NYC, 2000—. Work featured in Vogue, Elle, Cosmopolitan, Town & Country, WWD, Glamour, NY Mag., NY Times, Marie Claire; work shown in Cooper Hewitt Museum, Pasadena Museum of Calif. Arts, Royal Museum of Scotland, San Francisco Modern Museum of Art. Office: Lutz & Patmos Ste 406 425 W 13th St New York NY 10014

PATNAIK, PRADEEP KUMAR, science educator; arrived in US, 1980; s. Prafulla K. Patnaik; m. Maria De Lourdes Villar, May 19, 1986. BSc with honors, Bombay U., 1974; MA, SUNY, Buffalo, 1983; PhD, Ind. U., Bloomington, 1989. Rsch. asst. Roswell Pk. Mem. Hosp., Buffalo, 1981—83, Ind. U., Bloomington, 1983—89; rsch. assoc. Rockefeller U., NYC, 1990—95; scientist Nat. Inst. Med. Rsch., London, 1996—99; assoc. prof. William Paterson U., Wayne, NJ, 1999—. Adj. faculty Rockefeller U., NYC, 2000—. Contbr. scientific papers. Mem. selection com. Prafulla Mukerji Found., NY, 2005—. Recipient Ctr. for Rsch. award, William Paterson U., 2001, 2002; grantee, NIH, 2002—05; scholar, Indian's People's Theatre Assn. Independent. Avocations: travel, hiking, photography. Office: William Paterson Univ Dept Biology 300 Pompton Rd Wayne NJ 07470

PATNAUDE, WILLIAM EUGENE, architect; b. Sanger, Calif., Sept. 24, 1937; s. Eugene Joseph Patnaude and Vera Mae (Giles) Patnaude Fagan; m. Mary Esther Simerly, Aug. 22, 1971 (div. 1987); children: Nathaniel, Matthew BArch, U. Calif., Berkeley, 1961; postgrad., Calif. State U., Fresno, 1968-72. Registered arch., Calif., Wash., Idaho, Nev., Colo., Utah, Ariz., Mont., Ind., Nebr., Ohio, N.Y., N.J. Draftsman, arch. Robert Stevens Assoc., Santa Cruz, Calif., 1963-66; arch. Llewelyn Davies, Weeks & Ptnrs., London, 1966, Allen Y. Lew, Fresno, Calif., 1967-69, assoc., 1969-74; v.p., arch. Lew & Patnaude, Inc., Fresno, Calif., 1978-84, pres., 1985—. Instr. Calif. State U., Fresno, 1968-81 Constrn. arbitrator Am. Arbitration Assn., 1976-96; chair ctrl. area plan citizen's adv. com. City of Fresno, 1991-93, chair gen. plan update com., 1994-97; bd. dirs. Fresno Arts Ctr., 1971-74, Fresno County Alliance for the Arts, 1986-88, 91-94. With USNR, 1961-63. Recipient Merit award Calif. Hist. Preservation Conf., Orange County, 1983, Excellence award Woodwork Inst. Calif., 1982, Recognition cert. City Fresno, 2004, Calif. State Assembly commendation City Fresno, 2004. Fellow AIA (nat. dir. 1983-85, pres. Calif. Coun. 1982, San Joaquin chpt. 1978, Awards of Excellence, 1972-95); mem. Constrn. Specifications Inst. (pres. Fresno chpt. 1977). Democrat. Avocations: photography, fine wines. Home: 4190 N Van Ness Blvd Fresno CA 93704-4213 Office: Lew & Patnaude Inc 1050 S St Fresno CA 93721-1497 Business E-Mail: billp@csufresno.edu.

PATON WALSH, JILL, writer; b. London, Apr. 29, 1937; d. John Llewelyn and Patricia (Dubern) Buss; m. Antony Edmund Paton Walsh, Aug. 5, 1961; Children: Edmund, Margaret, Clare. Author: Hengest's Tale, 1966, The Dolphin Crossing, 1967, Fireweed, 1969, (World Book Festival award 1970), Wordhoard, 1969, Goldengrove 1972, Farewell Great King, 1972, Toolmaker, 1973, The Dawnstone, 1973, The Emporer's Winding Sheet, 1974 (Whitbread prize 1974), The Huffler, 1975, The Island Sunrise: Preshistoric Culture in the British Isles, 1975, Unleaving, 1976 (Boston Globe, Horn Book award 1976), Children of the Fox: Crossing to Salamis, 1977, The Walls of Athens, 1978, Persian Gold, 1978, A Chance Child, 1978, The Green Book, 1981, Babylon, 1982, Parcell of Patterns, 1983 (Universe prize 1984), Lost and Found, 1984, Gaffer Samson's Luck, 1984 (Smarties Grand prix 1984), Lapsing, 1985, A School for Lovers, 1989, Birdy and the Ghosties, 1990, "Grace", 1991, Matthew and the Sea Singers, 1992, When Grandma Came, 1992, The Wydham Case, 1993, Knowledge of Angels, 1994, A Piece of Justice, 1995, Connie Came to Play, 1995, Thomas and the Tinners, 1995, The Serpentine Cave, 1997, When I Was Little Like You, 1997, (with Dorothy L. Sayers) Thrones, Dominations, 1998, A Desert in Bohemia, 2000, (with Dorothy L. Sayers) A Presumption of Death, 2002, Debts of Dinosaur, 2006, The Bad Quarto, 2007. Fellow Royal Soc. of Lit. (CBE award 1996). Address: care David Higham Assocs 5-8 Lower John St Golden Sq London W1R 3PE England

PATRICK, ALAN K., artist; b. Richmond, Ind., June 16, 1942; s. Paul and Edythe (Kackley) P.; m. Dianne Childers, Apr. 5, 1966 (div. June 1977); m. Cynthia Hope Gill, Oct. 12, 1985. Owner Bethel Pottery, Albany, Ind., 1966—. Represented in permanent collections Ball State U., Minnetrista Cultural Ctr., Richmond Art Mus., others. Recipient Best of Show award Minn. Cultural Ctr., 1972, Hoosier Salon, 1991, Richmond Art Mus., 1996. Mem. Ind. Artists Club (Best of Show 2000). Home: 5809 E Pottery Rd Albany IN 47320-9714 Office Phone: 765-282-7848. Personal E-mail: apatrick@prodigy.net.

PATRICK, BRENDA JEAN, educational consultant; b. Dallas, Aug. 24, 1955; d. Gene Everett and Peggy Rose Patrick; 1 child, Michael Everett. BS in Elem. Edn., Tex. A&M U., Commerce, 1981, MS, 1984, postgrad., 1989—. Cert. Tex. Edn. Agy. Tchr. Garland Ind. Sch. Dist., 1982-87, acad. coach, 1983-86; with Austin Acad. for Excellence, 1987-88; program coord., master cons. Region 10 Edn. Svc. Ctr., 1988—. Coord. Tchr. Expectation Student Achievement; trainer Devel. Capable People; trainer of trainers Profl. Devel. and Appraisal Sys.; developer, presenter workshops and seminars in field. Author: Better Teaching, Texas Secretary. Past bd. dirs. Dallas Arboretum's Fan Club; mem. adv. bd. Tex. Edn. Support Staff Assn.; contbg. sponsor Friends of Tex. Pub. Schs., mem. adv. bd. Recipient Tex. History Tchr. award Daus. of Republic of Tex., Am. History Tchr. award DAR; named Vol. with a Heart, YWCA, Adminstr. of Yr., Tex. Ednl. Support Staff Assn., 2007. Mem. Tex. PTA (hon. life). Office Phone: 214-693-2411. Personal E-mail: bjp@brendajeanpatrick.com.

PATRICK, CHARLES WILLIAM, JR., lawyer; b. Monroe, NC, Oct. 9, 1954; s. Charles William and Louise (Nisbet) P.; m. Celeste Hunt, June 5, 1976; children: Laura Elizabeth, Charles William III. BA magna cum laude, Furman U., 1976; JD, U. SC, 1979. Bar: S.C. 1979, U.S. Dist. Ct. S.C. 1981, U.S. Ct. Appeals (11th cir.) 1981, U.S. Ct. Appeals (10th cir.) 1983, U.S. Ct. Appeals (4th cir.) 1986. Law clk. to presiding judge 9th Cir. Ct. State of S.C., Charleston, 1979—80; assoc. Ness, Motley, Loadholt, Richardson and Poole and predecessor firm Blatt and Fales, Charleston, 1980—2002, 1980—84, ptnr., 1984—2002, Richardson, Patrick, Westbrook & Brickman, LLC, Charleston, 2002—. Exec. editor S.C. Law Review, 1978; contbr. articles to profl. jours. Mem. ABA, Assn. Trial Lawyers Am., S.C. Assn. Trial Lawyers, Trial Lawyers for Pub. Justice, Phi Beta Kappa. Democrat. Presbyterian. Avocations: boating, skiing, jogging. Home: 38 Church St Charleston SC 29401-2742 Office: Richardson Patrick Westbrook & Brickman LLC PO Box 879 174 East Bay St Charleston SC 29402-0879 Home Phone: 843-853-8601; Office Phone: 843-727-6500. Business E-Mail: cpatrick@rpwb.com.

PATRICK, CONNIE L., federal official; m. John Patrick; 4 children. BA in Criminal Justice, U. Ctrl. Fla.; Grad., FBI Nat. Acad., Fla. Criminal Justice Exec. Inst., Fed. Exec. Inst. Dep. Sheriff's Office Brevard County, 1976—81; various positions including spl. agent, spl. agent supr., asst. spl. agent in charge of Tampa reg. ops. bur., dir. Fla. Criminal Justice Inst. Fla. Dept. Law Enforcement, 1981—95, dir. divsn. human resources & training, 1995—96; dir. gen. training Fed. Law Enforcement Training Ctr., 1996—98, assoc. dir. planning & resources, 1998—2001, assoc. dir. planning & workforce devel., 2001—02, dir., 2002—. Recipient Presdl. Meritorious Rank award, 2001. Office: Fed Law Enforcement Training Ctr 1131 Chapel Crossing Rd Brunswick GA 31524

PATRICK, CRAIG, former professional hockey team executive; b. Detroit, May 20, 1946; s. Lynn P.; m. Sue Patrick; children— Erin, Taylor, Ryan, CJ. MBA, U. Denver. Hockey player Calif. Golden Seals, 1971-74, St. Louis Blues, 1974-75, Kansas City Scouts, 1975-76, World Hockey Assn., Minn., 1976-77, Washington Capitals, 1977-79; v.p., gen. mgr. NY Rangers, NYC, 1981-86; dir. athletics and recreation Univ. Denver, 1987-89; gen. mgr., exec. v.p. Pitts. Penguins, 1989—2006. Named Exec. of Yr., The Sporting News, 1998, 1999; named to US Hockey Hall of Fame, 1996; recipient Lester Patrick Trophy, 2000. Achievements include being capt., US Nat. Team, World Championships, Moscow, 1979; asst. mgr. and asst. coach US Olympic Hockey Team, 1980.

PATRICK, DAN, sportscaster; b. May 15, 1957; married; 2 children. BA in Broadcasting, U. Dayton, 1979. Morning sports and news reporter WTUE Radio, Dayton, Ohio, 1979-81; weekend sports anchor, reporter WDTN-TV, Dayton, Ohio, 1981-83, CNN, 1983-89; sports dir. WKLS, Atlanta, 1987-91; reporter weekday sports Laser 103, Milw., 1989-91, WLVQ-AM, Columbus, 1989-91; anchor, reporter SportsCenter ESPN, Bristol, Conn., 1989—2007; reporter weekday sports KSEG, Sacramento, 1991. Guest host ABC Good Morning Am., 1996. Recipient Sports Emmy award for studio host, 1998. *

PATRICK, DANE HERMAN, lawyer; b. San Antonio, Oct. 18, 1960; s. Kae Thomas and Joyce Lynn (von Scheele) P.; m. Kelly Marie Carlson, May 17, 1986. BA in Econs. with honors, U. Tex., 1983; JD, So. Meth. U., 1987. Cert.: Tex. Bd. of Legal Specialization (personal injury trial law). Assoc. Law Office of Earl Luna, Dallas, 1987-88, Veitch & Davis, San Antonio, 1988-91; pvt. practice, San Antonio, 1991—. Mem.: San Antonio United Shareholder Assn. (chmn. 1988—92), San Antonio Trial Lawyers Assn. Democrat. Methodist. Avocations: weightlifting, hunting, fishing. Office: Colonnade I 9901 IH 10 West Ste 800 San Antonio TX 78230 Office Phone: 210-226-7782. Personal E-mail: dane@danepatrick.com.

PATRICK, DANICA SUE, race car driver; b. Beloit, Wis., Mar. 25, 1982; d. T.J. and Bev Patrick; m. Paul Hospenthal, Nov. 19, 2005. With Team Rahal Letterman, 2002—; debut Formula Vauxhall Winter Series, England, 1998, Toronto, Canada, 2002; made her IndyCar Series debut Toyota Indy 300, 2005; signed with Andretti Green Racing, 2006. Co-author (with Laura Morton): Danica: Crossing the Line, 2006. Recipient numerous World Karting Assn. titles including National Points titles in WKA Manufacturs Cup, 1994, 96, five Great Lakes Sprint Series titles and Midwest Spring Series titles, 1996, Grand National championship and Summer National Championship, 1997; Gorsline Scholarship award, 2001 Won 39 of 49 feature karting races, 1996; finished 9th in Formula Vauxhall Championship, Eng., 1991, 2d in Formula Ford Festival (highest finish for an American), 2000, 4th in first appearance in the Indianapolis 500, 2005; became the first female to post a top three result in Atlantic Series, Monterrey, Mex., 2003; first female driver to win pole position in Toyota Atlantic, Portland, 2004.

PATRICK, DEVAL LAURDINE, governor, lawyer; b. Chgo., July 31, 1956; s. Laurdine Kenneth and Emily Mae (Wintersmith) Patrick; m. Diane Louise Bemus, May 5, 1984; children: Sarah Baker, Katherine Wintersmith. AB cum laude, Harvard Coll., 1978, JD, 1982; JD (hon.), Dist. Columbia Law Sch., 1994, Morris Brown Coll., 1996, Curry Coll., 1997, Clark U., 1999, New Eng. Sch. Law, 1999, Suffolk U., 2000, Northeastern U., 2002. Bar: Calif. 1983, DC 1985, Mass. 1987, US Dist. Ct. Mass. 1987, US Dist. Ct. (ctrl. dist.) Calif. 1983, US Ct. Appeals (1st and 5th cirs.) 1984, US Ct. Appeals (9th and 11th cirs.) 1984, US Supreme Ct. 1988. Law clk. to Hon. Stephen Reinhardt US Ct. Appeals (9th cir.), LA, 1982-83; asst. counsel NAACP Legal Def. Fund, NYC, 1983-86; assoc. Hill & Barlow, Boston, 1986—90; ptnr. Hill & Barlow LLP, Boston, 1990—94; asst. atty. gen. civil rights divsn. US Dept. Justice, Washington, 1994-97; ptnr. Day, Berry & Howard LLP, Boston, 1997-99; v.p., gen. counsel Texaco Inc., White Plains, NY, 1999-2001; exec. v.p., gen. counsel, mem. exec. com. The Coca-Cola Co., Atlanta, 2001—04, corp. sec., 2002—04; gov. Commonwealth of Mass., Boston, 2007—. Herman Phleger disting. vis. prof. Stanford Law Sch., 1997; lectr. Boston Coll. Sch. Law, 1997, Harvard Law Sch., 1998; mem. various corp. bd. dirs.; bd. overseers Harvard U., 1998-2003; dir. UAL Corp., 1997-2001, Reebok Internat. Ltd., 2001-05, Coca-Cola Enterprises Inc., 2001-04, ACC Capital Holdings (Ameriquest), 2004-06 Dir., mem. exec. com., chmn. New Eng. steering com. NAACP Legal Def. and Edn. Fund., Inc., 1991-94, vice chmn. Mass. Jud. Nominating Coun., 1991-93; trustee, mem. exec. com. Milton Acad., 1985-97; overseer WGBH, 1993-94; trustee Nathan Cummings Found., 1998-2000, Ford Found., 2000-05 Recipient George Leisure award Harvard Law Sch., 1981; Rockefeller Traveling fellow, 1978. Mem. ABA (numerous bds. and coms.), Mass. Bar Assn., Mass. Black Lawyers Assn., Boston Bar Assn. (coun. mem. 1993), Harvard Alumni Assn. (dir. 1993-96). Democrat. Avocations: squash, cooking, gardening. Office: Office Gov 56 Roland St Ste 100D Boston MA 02129 *

PATRICK, DONALD LEE, sociologist, educator; b. Eugene, Oreg., Sept. 23, 1944; s. Lawrence Leonard and Marie Esther (Bell) P.; m. Shirley Anne Alexander Beresford, May 31, 1980; children: Alistair Lawrence Beresford, Mira Yvonne Bell. AB with distinction, Northwestern U., 1966; MSPH, Columbia U., 1968, PhD, 1972. Rsch. assoc. U. Calif., San Diego, 1970-72; lectr. Yale U., New Haven, 1972-76; sr. lectr. U. London, 1976-82; assoc. prof. U. N.C., Chapel Hill, 1982-87; prof. and dir. social and behavioral scis. program U. Wash., Seattle, 1987—. Adj. prof. sociology, U. Wash., 1988—, dept. rehab. medicine, 1987—. Author: Health Status and Health Policy, 1993; editor: Sociology as Applied to Medicine, 1976, Disablement in Community, 1989. Mem. APHA (mem. coun. 1993-96), Spina Bifida Assn. Am. (chair profl. adv. bd. 1990-93, Pres.' award 1995), Internat. Soc. for Quality of Life Rsch. (pres. 1994-96, Pres. award 2001), Inst. Medicine. Democrat. Unitarian Universalist. Avocations: gardening, music, travel. Home: 5427 43rd Ave W Seattle WA 98199-1061 Office: Univ Wash PO Box 358852 Seattle WA 98103 Office Phone: 206-685-7252. E-mail: donald@u.washington.edu.

PATRICK, H. HUNTER, retired judge, lawyer; b. Gasville, Ark., Aug. 19, 1939; s. H. Hunter Sr. and Nelle Frances (Robinson) P.; m. Charlotte Anne Wilson, July 9, 1966; children: Michael Hunter, Colleen Annette. BA, U. Wyo., 1961, JD, 1966. Bar: Wyo. 1966, U.S. Dist. Ct. Wyo. 1966, Colo. 1967, U.S. Supreme Ct. 1975. Mcpl. judge City of Powell, 1967-68; sole practice law Powell, 1966-88; atty. City of Powell, 1969-88; justice of the peace County of Park, Wyo., 1971-88; bus. law instr. Northwest C.C., Powell, 1968-98; dist. judge State of Wyo. 5th Jud. Dist., 1988—2006; drug ct. judge Park County, Wyo., 2001—06; ret, 2006; sole practice law Powell, 2006—. Mem. Wyo. Dist. Judges Conf., sec.-treas., 1993-94, vice chair, 1994-95, chair, 1995-96. Editor: Bench Book for Judges of Courts of Limited Jurisdiction in the State of Wyoming, 1980-90. Dir. cts. Wyo. Girls State, Powell, 1982—85, 1989—99, 2005—; mem. Wyo. Commn. Jud. Conduct and Ethics, 1997—2003; judge, chair mgmt. com. Park County Drug Ct., 2001—06; elder, deacon, moderator of deacons Powell Presbyn. Ch., 1997; bd. dirs. Heart Mountain Vol. Med. Clinic, 2007. Recipient Wyo. Crime Victim Compensation Commn. Judicial award, 1995, Wyo. Criminal Justice Assn. Svc. award, 2005. Fellow Am. Bar Found. (life), Wyo. Jud. Adv. Coun.; mem. ABA (Wyo. state del. to ho. of dels. 1994-2001, Wyo. del. jud. adminstrn. divsn., exec. com. nat. conf. trial ct. judges representing Wyo., Colo., Kans., Nebr., N.Mex. 1996-2000, bd. govs. 2001-04, Pub. Svc. award for ct.-sponsored Law Day programs 1990, 92, standing com. judges adv. com. on ethics in profession 2004-07), Wyo. Bar Assn. (Cmty. Svc. award 1999, Ann. Pub. Svc. award 1999), Colo. Bar Assn., Park County Bar Assn. (sec. 1969-70, pres. 1970-71), Wyo. Assn. Cts. Ltd. Jurisdiction (pres. 1973-80), Wyo. Dist. Judges Conf. (chair 1996), Am. Judicature Soc. (mem. jud. adv. coun.). Avocations: photography, travel, fishing, reading, writing. Home: PO Box 941 Powell WY 82435-0941 Personal E-mail: hpatrick2778@msn.com.

PATRICK, HUGH TALBOT, economist, educator; b. Goldsboro, NC, Feb. 22, 1930; s. Talbot and Paula (Miller) P.; children: Stephen, Matthew, Catherine. BA, Yale U., 1951; MA in Far Eastern Studies, U. Mich., 1955, MA in Econs., 1957, PhD in Econs., 1960; MA (hon.), Yale U., 1968; PhD (hon.), Lingnan U., 2000. Econ. analyst U. S. Govt., 1951-52; lectr. econs. U. Mich., 1958-60; asst. prof. econs. Yale U., New Haven, 1960-64, assoc. prof., 1964-68, prof. Far Eastern econs., 1968-84; dir. Yale U. Econ. Growth Ctr., 1976-79, 80-83; R.D. Calkins prof. internat. bus. Columbia U., NYC, 1984—2001, prof. emeritus, 2001—. Vis. prof. U. Bombay, 1961-62; mem. Japan-U.S. Econ. Rels. Group, 1978-81, U.S. Com. for Pacific Econ. Coop.; dir. Ctr. on Japanese Econ. and Bus., Columbia U., 1986—. Editor: Japanese Industrialization and Its Social Consequences, 1976, Japanese High Technology Industries-Lessons and Limitations of Industrial Policy, 1986; contbr. chpt. and co-editor (with Henry Rosovsky): Asia's New Giant-How the Japanese Economy Works, 1976, (with Masahiko Aoki): The Japanese Main Bank System: Its Relevance for Developing and Transforming Economies, 1994, (with Takatoshi Ito and David Weinstein) Reviving Japan's Economy: Problems and Prescriptions, 2005; co-editor (with Larry Meissner): Pacific Basin Industries in Distress: Structural Adjustment and Trade Policy in Nine Industrialized Economies, 1991 (Masayoshi Ohira Meml. prize 1992), (with Yung Chul Park) The Financial Development of Japan, Korea and Taiwan: Growth, Repression and Liberalization, 1994, (with Takeo Hoshi) Crisis and Change in the Japanese Financial System, 2000. Ford Found. fellow 1957-58; grantee Am. Coun. Learned Socs., 1962; Guggenheim fellow, 1964-65; Fulbright rsch. prof., 1964-65; Fulbright-Hays NDEA fellow, 1968-69; Assn. Asian Studies Disting. lectr., 1977. Mem. Japan Soc. (dir. 1973-79, 81-2000), Social Sci. Rsch. Coun. (dir., chmn. 1985-88), Pacific Trade and Devel. Confs. (chmn.). Democrat. Office: Columbia U 320 Uris Hall 3022 Broadway New York NY 10027-6945 Office Phone: 212-854-3497. Business E-Mail: htp1@columbia.edu.

PATRICK, JAMES DUVALL, JR., lawyer; b. Griffin, Ga., Dec. 28, 1947; s. James Duvall and Marion Wilson P. BS in Indsl. Mgmt., Ga. Inst. Tech., 1970; JD, U. Ga., 1973. Bar: Ga. 1973, U.S. Dist. Ct. (mid. dist.) Ga. 1973, U.S. Dist. Ct. (so. dist.) Ga. 1983, U.S. Ct. Appeals (5th cir.) 1974, U.S. Ct. Appeals (11th cir.) 1981, U.S. Tax Ct. 1985, U.S. Supreme Ct., 1977. Assoc. Cartledge, Cartledge & Posey, Columbus, Ga., 1973-74; ptnr. Falkenstrom, Hawkins & Patrick, Columbus, 1975, Falkenstrom & Patrick, Columbus, 1975-77; sole practice Columbus, 1977—. Instr. bus. law Chattahoochee Valley C.C., Phenix City, Ala., 1975-77; instr. paralegal course Columbus Coll., 1979, 84; del. U.S./China Joint Session on Trade, Investment, and Econ. Law, Beijing, 1987, Moscow Conf. on Law and Bilateral Econ. Rels., Moscow, 1990; U.S. del. U.S./Cuba Law Initiative, Havana, 2000. Mem. Hist. Columbus Found., Mayor's Com. for the Handicapped, 1987-88; local organizer, worker Joe Frank Harris for Gov. Campaign, Columbus, 1982; bd. dirs. Columbus Symphony Orch., 1988-94. Fellow Am. Bar Found.; mem. ATLA, ABA (fellow found.), Am. Judicature Soc., State Bar Ga., Fed. Bar Assn., Ga. Trial Lawyers Assn., Columbus Lawyers Club, Columbus Kappa Alpha Alumni Assn. (sec.), Civitan (bd. dirs. 1975-77), Country Club of Columbus, Georgian Club (Atlanta), Buckhead Club, Chattahoochee River Club, Phi Delta Phi, Kappa Alpha. Methodist. Office: PO Box 2745 Columbus GA 31902-2745

PATRICK, JOHN JOSEPH, social sciences educator; b. East Chicago, Ind., Apr. 14, 1935; s. John W. and Elizabeth (Lazar) P.; m. Patricia Grant, Aug. 17, 1963; children: Rebecca, Barbara AB, Dartmouth Coll., 1957; Ed.D., Ind. U., 1969. Social studies tchr. Roosevelt High Sch., East Chicago, 1957-62; social studies tchr. Lab. High Sch., U. Chgo., 1962-65; research assoc. Sch. Edn., Ind. U., Bloomington, 1965-69, asst. prof., 1969-74, assoc. prof., 1974-77, prof. edn., 1977—2004, prof. emeritus edn., 2004—, dir. social studies devel. ctr., 1986—2004, dir. ERIC clearinghouse for social studies, social sci. edn., 1986—2003. Bd. dirs. Biol. Scis. Curriculum Study, 1980-83; ednl. cons. Author: Progress of the Afro-American, 1968, The Young Voter, 1974; (with L. Ehman, Howard Mehlinger) Toward Effective Instruction in Secondary Social Studies, 1974, Lessons on the Northwest Ordinance, 1987; (with R. Remy) Civics for Americans, 1980, rev. edit. 1986; (with Mehlinger) American Political Behavior, 1972, rev. edit. 1980, (with C. Keller) Lessons on the Federalist Papers, 1987; America Past and Present, 1983; (with Carol Berkin) History of the American Nation, 1984, rev. edit., 1987; Lessons on the Constitution, 1985, James Madison and the Federalist Papers, 1990, How to Teach the Bill of Rights, 1991, Ideas of the Founders on Constitutional Government: Resources for Teachers of History and Government, 1991, Young Oxford Companion to the Supreme Court of the United States, 1994, Founding the Republic: A Documentary History, 1995, (with Gerald Long) Constitutional Debates on Freedom of Religion: A Documentary History, 1999, (with Richard M. Pious and Donald A. Ritchie) The Oxford Essential Guide to the U.S. Government, 2000, The Bill of Rights: A History in Documents, 2002, Understanding Democracy, 2006, (with Kermit L. Hall) The Pursuit of Justice: Supreme Court Decisions That Shaped America, 2006. Bd. dirs. Law in Am. Soc. Found., 1984-88, Social Sci. Edn. consortium, 1984—; mem. Gov.'s Task Force on Citizenship Edn., Ind., 1982-87; active Ind. Commn. on Bicentennial of U.S. Constn., 1986-92; bd. dirs. Coun. for the Advancement of Citizenship, Nat. History Edn. Network, 1994-96; mem. Natr. Coun. for History Standards, 1991-94. Recipient John W. Ryan award for disting. svc. in internat. programs and studies, Ind. U., 2002, Civic Edn. award, Ind. State Bar Assn., 2005. Mem. ASCD, Nat. Coun. Social Studies, Social Sci. Edn. Consortium (v.p. 1985-87), Coun. for Basic Edn., Am. Polit. Sci. Assn., Am. Hist. Assn., Orgn. Am. Historians, Ind. State Bar Assn. (recipient Civic Edn. award 2005), Phi Delta Kappa. Home: 1209 E University St Bloomington IN 47401-5045 Office: Ind U 2805 E 10th St Bloomington IN 47408-2601 Business E-Mail: patrick@indiana.edu.

PATRICK, NICHOLAS J.M., astronaut; b. North Yorkshire, Eng., 1964; naturalized, U.S., 1994; s. Stewart Patrick, Gillian Patrick; married. BA in Engring., U. Cambridge, Eng., 1986; MA in Engring., U. Cambridge, 1990; SMME, MIT, 1990, PhDME, 1996. Registered profl. engr. (mech.). Astronaut, mission specialist candidate NASA, Johnson Space Ctr., Houston, 1998—; mem. Cambridge U. Air Squadron RAF; civil engr. (summers) NY, Conn.; engr. divsn. aircraft engines GE, Boston; tchg. and rsch. asst. Human-Machine Sys. Lab. dept. mech. engring. MIT, Cambridge, Mass.; statistician, programmer med. and robotic products co., Mass.; sys. and human factors engr. Boeing Comml. Airplane Group, Seattle. Flight instr. Hanscom Field's E. Coast Aero Club, Boeing Field's Galvin Flying Svc., Seattle; bd. stockholders Harvard Cooperative Soc.; crew mem. STS-116 Mission (Discovery), 2006. Recipient Project award, GE Aircraft Engines Devel. Program, 1988; scholar, U. Cambridge, 1983. Mem.: Nat. Space Soc., Aircraft Owners and Pilots Assn. Achievements include patents for telerobotics, display design and integrated aircraft alerting systems; logged over 1600 hours as a pilot, 750 hours as a flight instructor in over 20 types of airplanes and helicopters. Avocations: flying, reading, automotive work, hiking, skiing, building and fixing things, Tae Kwon Do. Office: Astronaut Office/CB NASA Johnson Space Str Houston TX 77058 *

PATRICK, PAULINE MARGARET, secondary school educator; b. Mpls., Oct. 18, 1949; d. Melvin H. and Margaret P. (Calvelage) Boone; m. Mark H. Patrick, Dec. 18, 1971; children: Lance, Megan. BS, U. Mankato, 1971; MEd, St. Mary's Coll., Winona, Minn., 1993; MA (hon.), Minnetonka U., 1990. Cert. tchr., Minn. Tchr. Edina (Minn.) Sch., 1972-79, Minnetonka (Minn.) Schs., 1986—. Adj. prof. U. St. Thomas, St. Paul, 1989—, mem. T.E.A.C.H., 1991—. Recipient Apple award Ashland Oil Co., 1989. Mem. ASCd, Nat. Coun. Tchrs. English, Nat. Coun. Tchrs. Social Studies. Office Phone: 952-401-5000. E-mail: pelly.patrick@minnetonka.k12.mn.us.

PATRICK, RICHARD M., professional hockey team executive; b. Victoria, BC, Can., Oct. 20, 1946; married; 3 children. Student, Dartmouth Coll., Am. U. Washington. Exec. v.p. Washington Capitals Hockey Team, Landover, Md.; now pres, gov. Washington Capitals, 1992—. Office: Washington Capitals MCI Center 601 F St NW Washington DC 20004-1605

PATRICK, ROBERT, playwright; b. Kilgore, Tex., Sept. 27, 1937; s. Robert and Beulah (Goodson) O'Connor. Author numerous plays produced off-off Broadway, off-Broadway, Broadway, also abroad including Robert Patrick's Cheep Theatricks (23 plays), 1972, Simultaneous Transmissions, 1973, Play-By-Play, 1975, The Golden Circle, 1975, Kennedy's Children, 1975, Let Me Tell It To You, Dr. Paroo, 1976, One Man, One Woman (6 plays), 1978, T-Shirts, 1979, Mutual Benefit Life, 1980, Mercy Drop and Other Plays (5 plays), 1980, My Cup Ranneth Over, 1984, Big Sweet, 1985, Untold Decades (7 plays), 1988, Drowned Out, 1990, Connie, 1991, Michaelangelo's Models, 1994, Bread Alone, 1994, The Trial of Socrates,

1994, Evan on Earth, 1995, Hollywood at Sunset, 2004, Pouf Positive (CD), 1996; author: (novels) Temple Slave, 1986, Echo, 1990, (book on CD) Film Moi, 2003, (films) Resident Alien, 1990, The O Boys Documentary, 1999; teleplays include: High Tide, 1994, Robin's Hoods, 1995, Ghost Story, 1997, (essay) Film Moi, 1999, Caffe Cino Picture Pages, 2006; contbr. poems, articles, stories to profl. jours. Rockefeller grantee, 1974, N.Y. State CAPS grantee, 1975; recipient Show Bus. Best Playwright award 1968-69, Glasgow Citizens' Theatre Best World Playwright award, 1974, Omni-Act One award, 1975, Robbie award, 1976, Founders award Internat. Thespians Soc., 1980, Blue is for Boys weekends in Manhattan, 1983, 86, Lifetime Achievement award for Gay Playwriting Robert Chesley Found., 1996. Home and Office: 1837 N Alexandria Ave Apt 211 Los Angeles CA 90027-4068 Personal E-mail: rbrtptrck@aol.com. *No object or action has any meaning except that given to it by a writer. Writers create the consciousness of humanity, which in turn creates our world. Writers write the world.*

PATRICK, ROBERT HERBERT, JR., economist, educator; BA magna cum laude, Blackburn Coll., 1978; PhD in Econs., U. N.Mex., 1985. Mgr. Burroughs Corp., Fairbanks, Alaska, 1978-80; rsch. assoc. Purdue U., West Lafayette, Ind., 1985-87; asst. prof. Colo. Sch. Mines, Golden, 1987-91, assoc. prof., 1991-93; project mgr. Electric Power Rsch. Inst., Palo Alto, Calif., 1992-94. Vis. scholar Stanford U., Calif., 1992-94, assoc. prof. Rutgers U., 1994—; reviewer US EPA, US Dept. Energy, Calif. Energy Commn., NSF, ISF, NY Mec. Exch.; coun. of acad. policy advisors NJ Legis. Contbr. articles to profl. jours. and chpts. to books.; mem. editorial bd. Jour. Regulatory Econs., Jour. Environ. Econs. and Mgmt. Grantee Elec. Power Rsch. Inst., 1994-98, NSF, 1994-96, Gas Rsch. Inst., 1990-92, EPA, 1989-92, USDA, 1985-87. Mem. Am. Econ. Assn., Assn. Environ. and Resource Econs., Econometric Soc., Internat. Assn. for Energy Econs. (v.p. Rocky Mountain chpt. 1992, bd. dirs. 1990-91), Mineral Econs. and Mgmt. Soc. (bd. dirs. 1992), N.J. Coun. Acad. Policy Advisors. Office: Grad Sch of Mgmt Rutgers U Newark NJ 07102 Home: 70 Wendover Ct Bedminster NJ 07921 Office Phone: 973-353-5247. Business E-Mail: rpatrick@rutgers.edu.

PATRICK, RUTH (MRS. RUTH HODGE VAN DUSEN), botany educator, curator; b. Topeka; d. Frank and Myrtle (Jetmore) Patrick; m. Charles (IV) Hodge, July 10, 1931; 1 child, Charles (V). BS, Coker Coll., 1929; MS, U. Va., 1931, PhD, 1934; LLD (hon.), Coker Coll., 1971; LHD (hon.), Chestnut Hill Coll, 1974; DSc (hon.), Beaver Coll., 1970, PMC Colls., 1971, Phila. Coll. Pharmacy and Sci., 1973, Wilkes Coll., 1974, Cedar Crest Coll., 1974, U. New Haven, 1975, Hood Coll., 1975, Med. Coll. Pa., 1975, Drexel U., 1975, Swarthmore Coll., 1975, Bucknell U., 1976, Rensselaer Poly. Inst., 1976, St. Lawrence U., 1978, U. Mass., 1980, Princeton U., 1980, Lehigh U., 1983, U. Pa., 1984, Temple U., 1985, Emory U., 1986, Wake Forest U., 1986, U. S.C., 1989, Clemson, 1989, Glassboro State Coll., 1992. Assoc. curator microscopy dept. Acad. Natural Scis., Phila., 1939-47; curator Leidy Micros. Soc., 1937-47, curator limnology dept., 1947—, chmn. limnology dept., 1947-73; occupant Francis Boyer Research Chair Acad. Natural Scis., Phila., 1973—, chmn. bd. trustees, 1973-76, hon. chmn. bd. trustees, 1976—; lectr. U. Pa., 1950-70, adj. prof., 1970—; guest Fellow of Saybrook Yale, 1975. Participant Am. Philos Soc. limnology expdn. to Mexico, 1947; leader Catherwood Found. expdn. to Peru and Brazil, 1955; del. gen. assembly Internat. Union Biol. Scis., Bergen, Norway, 1947; bd. dirs. E.I. Du Pont, Pa. Power and Light Co.; chmn. algae com. Smithsonian Oceanographic Sorting Ctr., 1963—68; mem. panel on water blooms Pres. Sci. Adv. Com., 1966; mem. panel on water resources and water pollution Gov.'s Sci. Adv. Com., 1966; mem. nat. tech. adv. com. on water quality requirements for fish and other aquatic life and wildlife Dept. Interior, 1967—68; mem. citizen's adv. coun. Pa. Dept. Environ. Resources, 1971—73; mem. hazardous materials adv. com. EPA, 1971—74, exec. adv. com., 1974—79; chmn. com.'s panel on ecology, 1974—76; mem. Pa. Gov.'s Sci. Adv. Coun., 1972; mem. exec. adv. com. nat. power survey FPC, 1972—75; mem. coun. Smithsonian Instn., 1973—; mem. Phila. Adv. Coun., 1973—76; mem. energy R&D adv. coun. Pres.s Emergy Policy Office, 1973—74; mem. adv. coun. Renewable Nat. Resources Found., 1973—76, Elecric Power Rsch. Found., 1973—77; mem. adv. com. for rsch. NSF, 1973—74; mem. gen. adv. com. ERDA, 1975—77; mem. adv. bd. Sec. Energy, 1975—89; mem. com. on human resources NRC, 1975—76; trustee Biological Abstracts, 1974—76; mem. adv. coun. dept. biology Princeton U., 1975—80; mem. com. on sci. and arts Franklin Inst., 1978—; mem. univ. coun. com. Yale Sch. Forestry and Environ. Studies, 1978—80; mem. sci. adv. coun. World Wildlife Fund-US, 1978—80; trustee Aquarium Soc., Phila., 1951—58, Henry Found.; bd. dirs. Wissahickon Valley Watershed Assn.; bd. govs. Nature Conservancy; bd. mgrs. Wistar Inst. Anatomy and Biology. Author: (series of volumes) Rivers of the United States Vol. 1, 1994, Rivers of the United States Vol. 2, 1997, Chemical and Physical Characteristics Vol. 3, 1995, Rivers of Atlantic and Eastern Gulf Drainage Vol. 4, The Mississipi River and Major Tributaries; co-author (with C.W. Reimer): Diatoms of the United States Vol. 1, 1966, Vol. II, Part 1, 1975; co-author: (with others) (books) Ground Water Contamination in the United States, 1983, 2nd edit.; co-author: (with others) (book) Surface Water Quality: Have the Laws Been Successful?, 1992; mem. editorial bd.with C. W. Reimer: sci. jours. Science, 1974—76, mem. editorial bd.: sci. jours. American Naturalist; contbr. articles over 150 to profl. jours. Recipient Disting. Dau. of Pa. award, 1952, Richard Hopper Day Meml. medal, Acad. Nat. Scis., 1969, Gimbel Phila. award, 1969, Gold medal, YWCA, 1970, Lewis L. Dollinger Pure Environment award, Franklin inst., 1970, Pa. award for excellence in sci. and tech., 1970, Eminent Ecologist award, Ecol Soc. Am., 1972, Phila. award, 1973, Gold medal, Pa. State Fish and Game Protective Assn., 1974, Internat. John and Alice Tyler Ecology award, 1975, Gold meda;, Phila. Soc. for Promoting Agr., 1975, Pub. Svc. award, U.S. Dept. Interior, 1975, Iben award, Am. Water Resources Assn., 1976, Outstanding Alumna award, Coker Coll., 1977, Francis K. Hutchinson medal, Garden Club of Am., 1977, Golden medal, Royal Zool. Soc., Antwerp, 1978, Green World award, N.Y. Bot. Garden, 1979, Hugo Black award, U. Ala., 1979, Sci award, Gov. Pa., 1988, Founders award, Soc. Environ. Toxicology and Chemistry, 1982, Environ. Regeneration award, Rene DuBois Ctr., 1985, Disting. Citizen award, Pa., 1989, Excellence award, N. Am. Benthological Soc., 1993, Benjamin Frankln medal, Am. Philosophical Soc., 1993, U.S. medal of svc., Pres. Bill Clinton, 1996, Nat. medal for sci., 1997, Nat. Wetlands award, 2000, Sci. Edn. Ctr. named in her honor, U. S.C., 1989. Fellow: AAAS (com. environ. alternatives 1973—74); mem.: Internat. Phycol. Soc., Am. Inst. Biol. Scis., Ecol. Soc. Am., Am. Soc. Naturalists (pres. 1975—76), Am. Soc. Limnology and Oceanography (Lifetime Achievement award 1996), Am. Soc. Plant Taxonomy, Internat. Soc. Plant Taxonomists, Internat. Limnological Soc., Phycol Soc. Am. (pres 1954), Bot. Soc. Am. (mem. Darbarker prize com. 1956, Merit award 1971), Am. Acad. Arts and Scis., Assn. Metro. Sewage Agys. (Environ. award 1995), Am. Philos. Soc. (Benjamin Franklin Outstanding Sci. Achievement award 1993), Nat. Acad. Engring. (com.environ. engr. study explicit criteria for power plant siting 1973), Nat. Acad. Scis. (chmn. panel com. on pollution 1966, mem.environ. measures panel com. remote sensing earth resources survey 1973—74, mem. nominating com. 1973—75, mem. com. sci. and public policy 1973—77), Water Pollution Control Fedn. (hon.), Soc. Study Evolution, Sigma Xi. Presbyterian. Office: Acad Natural Scis 19th at Benjamin Franklin Pkwy Philadelphia PA 19103 Office Phone: 215-299-1098. Business E-Mail: Patrick@acnatsci.org.

PATRICK, STEPHEN C., consumer products company executive; Mgr. Price Waterhouse; mgmt. positions through v.p., corp. contr. and v.p. fin. Colgate - L.Am. Colgate-Palmolive Co., NYC, 1982—96, CFO, 1996—. V.p. Fin. Acctg. Found.; bd. dirs. Arrow Electronics, 2003—. Office: Colgate-Palmolive Co 300 Park Ave New York NY 10022-7499 Office Fax: 212-310-3284. *

PATRICK, SUSAN D., educational association administrator, former federal agency administrator; B in English, Colo. Coll.; M in Comm. Mgmt., U. So. Calif. Dir. distance learning campus Old Dominion U.; coord. Digital State Survey 2002 State of Ariz.; dep. dir. Office Edn. Tech. US Dept. Edn., Washington, dir. Office Edn. Tech., 2004—05; pres., CEO North American Coun. for Online Learning (NACOL), Vienna, Va., 2005—. Office: NACOL 1934 Old Gallows Rd, Ste 350 Vienna VA 22182-4040 Office Phone: 703-752-6216. Office Fax: 703-752-6201. E-mail: spatrick@nacol.org. *

PATRICK, VICTOR PHILLIP, lawyer, construction executive; b. Lake Forest, Ill., Jan. 7, 1958; s. Rodger Ralph Patrick and Phyllis Elaine Bachler; m. Elizabeth Fletcher, Aug. 9, 1985; children: Kathryn Elaine, Stephen James, Diane Elizabeth, Marie Christine, Thomas Grant, John Wallace, Daniel Victor, Emily Frances. AB in Politics magna cum laude, Princeton U., 1982; JD cum laude, Harvard U., 1985. Bar: DC 1986, NY 1986, U.S. Ct. Appeals (10th cir.) 1986. Law clk. U.S. Ct. Appeals 10th Cir., Denver, 1985-86; assoc. Cleary, Gottlieb, Steen & Hamilton, Washington, 1986-88, 92-94, Brussels, 1988—91; from asst. gen. counsel to v.p., sec. and dep. gen. counsel Honeywell Internat. Inc. (formerly AlliedSignal Inc.), Morristown, NJ, 1994—97, 1999—2002, Torrance, Calif., 1997—99; sr. v.p., gen. counsel, sec. Walter Industries, Inc., Tampa, Fla., 2002—06, vice chmn., gen. counsel, sec., 2006—. Pres. Tampa Fla. Stake; mem. bd. BS Gulf Ridge Coun. Mem. ABA. Republican. Lds Ch. Business E-Mail: vpatrick@walterind.com.

PATRICOF, ALAN JOEL, investment company executive; b. NYC, Oct. 22, 1934; s. Martin and Dorine (Glass) Patricof; m. Susan Patricof; children: Jonathan, James, Mark. BS in Fin., Ohio State U., 1955; MBA, Columbia U., 1957. Various positions Naess & Thomas, NYC, 1957-58, Lambert & Co., NYC, 1958-60; asst. v.p. to v.p. Ctrl. Nat. Corp., NYC, 1960-68; asst. to chmn. N.W. Industries, NYC, 1968-70; co-founder, chmn. Apax Ptnrs., Inc. (formerly Alan Patricof Assocs.), NYC, 1969—2001; dir. Boston Properties, Inc., 1997—; founder, mng. dir. Greycroft Ptnrs., L.P., 2006—. Bd. dirs. Harman Internat. Industries, Inc., Datascope, Inc., Quantronics Corp., Cellular Comm., Inc.; founder, former chmn. bd. NY mag.; chmn. pvt. equity grp. Global Corp. Governance Forum; bd. mem. NY Small Bus. Venture Fund; mem. NY adminstrv. com. Fleet Nat. Bank. Trustee NY Sci. and Tech. Found.; bd. trustees Columbia U. Grad. Sch. Bus. Served in US Army, 1958, served in US Army, 1961—62. Mem. NY Acad. Scis. (former mem. bd. govs., former treas.). Clubs: Friars. Office: Apax Ptnrs LP 153 E 53rd St 53rd Fl New York NY 10022 *

PATRIE, CHERYL CHRISTINE, elementary school educator; b. Dobbs Ferry, NY, June 8, 1947; d. Edward F. and Antoinette C. (Patrie) P. BA in Edn., U. Fla., 1969; MS in Edn., U. Miami, 1979. Cert. assoc. master tchr., Fla. Tchr. Marion County Sch. Bd., Ocala, Fla., 1970, Dade County Sch. Bd., Miami, 1973—. Mem. faculty coun. Lorah Park Elem. Sch., Miami, 1979-89, 1991—95, career lab. cons., 1983-85, human growth and devel. cons., 1983—87, phys. fitness co-chmn., 1984-90, chair dept., 1993—, coord. quality instrn. incentives program, 1984-89, faculty adv. com., 1990-; mem. Dade County Elem. Sch. Day Task Force, 1987-88. Mem. United Tchrs. Dade (bldg. union steward 1979-89, mem. crisis in inner city task force 1984-85, mem. sch. adv. com., 1987—, Disting. Svc. award 1984). Office: Lorah Park Elem 5160 NW 31st Ave Miami FL 33142-3439 Home: 555 NE 15th St #28-I Miami FL 33132 Office Phone: 305-633-1424.

PATRIKIS, ERNEST T., lawyer; b. Lynn, Mass., Dec. 1, 1943; s. Theodore A. and Ethel (Stasinopolous) Patrikis; m. Emily Herrick Trueblood, Mar. 18, 1972. BA in Econs. with honors, U. Mass., Amherst, 1965; JD, Cornell U., Ithica, 1968. Bar: N.Y. 1969. Exec. v.p., gen. counsel Fed. Res. Bank N.Y., NYC, 1968—95, 1st v.p., 1995—98; spl. adv. to chmn. Am. Internat. Group Inc., NYC, 1998—2000, sr. v.p., gen. coun., 1998—2006; ptnr. Pillsbury Winthrop Shaw Pittman LLP, NYC, 2006—, head fin. svc. & regulatory practice, 2006—. Dep. gen. counsel Fed. Open Market Com., 1988—95, alternative mem., 1995—98; bd. dirs. Atlantic Legal Found. Contbr. articles to legal jours. Mem.: ABA (subcom. gen. banking matters 1986), Internat. Inst. Conflict Prevention & Resolution (mem. banking and fin. svc. com.), Internat. Law Assn. (monetary law com. 1990—), Fed. Bar Assn. (banking law exec. com. 2006—), Internat. Swaps and Derivatives Assn. (dir. 1999—2006), Coun. Fgn. Rels., N.Y. State Bar Assn. (banking law com. 1986—, chmn. com. internat. banking, securities and fin. transaction 1987—91, vice chmn. internat. practice sect. 1991—2003, derivatives and structured products com. 2006—), Assn. Bar City N.Y. (banking law com. 1982—84, 1990—, ins. com. 2000—03, corp. law com. 2003, European law com. 2004—06, futures regulations com. 1986-89 2007—, Joint Yr. 2000 Coun.). Office: Pillsbury Winthrop Shaw Pittman LLP 1540 Broadway New York NY 10036 Home Phone: 212-677-5178; Office Phone: 212-858-1317. Personal E-mail: erniepatrikis@yahoo.com. Business E-Mail: ernest.patrikis@pillsburylaw.com.

PATRINOS, ARISTIDES, environmental scientist, federal agency administrator; b. July 18, 1947; Diploma in Mech. Engring. & Electrical Engring., Nat. Tech. U., Athens, 1970, PhD (hon.), 2001; PhD in Mech. Engring. and Astronautical Scis., Northwestern U., 1975. Asst. prof. mechanical & aerospace sciences U. Rochester, 1975—76; rsch. scientist Engring. Tech. Div., Oak Ridge Nat. Lab., 1976—80, Dept. Applied Scis., Brookhaven Nat. Lab., 1980—88; staff mem. EPA, Nat. Acid Deposition Assessment Program, Washington, 1984—86; dir. Environ. Sciences Divsn. Office of Biological & Environ. Rsch., US Dept. Energy, 1991—93; acting assoc. dir. Biological & Environ. Rsch. Office of Biological & Environ. Rsch., US Dept. Energy, 1993—95; assoc. dir. Office of Biological & Environ. Rsch., US Dept. Energy, 1995—. Ex-offico mem. Nat. Cancer Adv. Bd., NIH. Contbr. articles to profl. jours. Recipient Sec.'s Gold Award, US Dept. Energy, 2001, 2003. Fellow: Am. Meteorological Soc.; mem.: AAAS, ASME, Nat. Tech. Soc. Greece, Am. Geophysical Union. Office: Office Biological and Environ Rsch US Dept Energy 19901 Germantown Rd Germantown MD 20874-1207 also: SC-23 / Germantown Bldg 1000 Independence Ave SW Washington DC 20585-1290 Office Phone: 301-903-3251. Office Fax: 301-903-5051. E-mail: ari.patrinos@science.doe.gov.

PATRON, JUNE EILEEN, retired government agency administrator; b. NYC, May 15; d. Irving B. and Mollie Patron. BA in Govt. with honors, Clark U., Worcester, Mass., 1965; MA, Am. U., 1967. With U.S. Dept. Labor, 1966-95, dir. Black Lung benefits program, 1976-79, asst. adminstr. pension and welfare benefit programs, 1979-84, assoc. dir. pension and welfare benefit programs, 1984-88, dir. program svcs., 1988-95; ret., 1995. Mem. Sr. Exec. Svc.; ind. contracotr, mgmt. cons., 1997—2003. Vol. Neighbor Network, 2003—; vol. alumni and parent admissions program Clark U., 1998—. Recipient various awards, Dept. Labor. Mem.: Sr. Execs. Assn., Nat. Assn. Ret. Fed. Employees. Home: 3001 Veazey Ter NW Washington DC 20008-5405 E-mail: jpdcny@aol.com.

PATRON, SUSAN HALL, librarian, writer; b. San Gabriel, Calif., Mar. 18, 1948; d. George Thomas and Rubye Denver Hall; m. René Albert Patron, July 27, 1969. BA, Pitzer Coll., 1969; MLS, Immaculate Heart Coll., 1972. Children's libr. LA Pub. Libr., 1972-79, sr. children's libr., 1980—, juvenile materials collections devel. Reviewer Sch. Libr. Jour., 1980-90, Pubs. Weekly, 1986-91, The Five Owls, 1987-95. Author: (with Christopher Weiman) Marbled Papers, 1979, Burgoo Stew, 1991, Five Bad Boys, Billy Que, and the Dustdobbin, 1992, Maybe Yes, Maybe No, Maybe Maybe, 1993 (ALA Notable Book 1994), Bobbin Dustdobbin, 1993, Dark Cloud Strong Breeze, 1994, The Higher Power of Lucky, 2006 (winner Newbery medal 2007.) Mem. ALA (Caldecott award com. 1988, Laura Ingalls Wilder award com. 2001), PEN (mem. West Lit. awards jury 1997, 2006), Calif. Libr. Assn. (Patricia Beatty award com. 1987-89, 91-92), Internat. Bd. on Books for Young Children, Soc. Children's Book Writers and Illustrators, So. Calif. Coun. on Lit. for Children and Young People (awards com. 1985), Authors Guild, Friends of Children and Lit. (mem. award com. 1984). Office: LA Pub Libr Childrens Svcs 630 W 5th St Los Angeles CA 90071-2002 *

PATRUSKY, BEN, writer; b. Bklyn., Nov. 30, 1935; s. Herman and Sylvia Patrusky; m. Judith M. Mortlock, Dec. 27, 1988. BEE, CCNY, 1958; grad. in Sci. Writing, Columbia U., 1962. News editor Electronic Design Mag., NYC, 1958—60; sci. editor, rsch. writer Am. Heart Assn., NYC, 1962—75; ind. sci. writer NYC, 1975—. Exec. dir. Coun. Advancement Sci. Writing, 1988—. Author: (books) The Laser: Light That Never Was Before, 1966, Living With Your Heart, 1972. Mem. bd. dirs. Sci. Svc., Washington, 1989—2007. Named to CCNY Alumni Comm. Group Hall of Fame, 2007; recipient Sci. Writers award, Am. Chem. Soc., 1985, Am. Physics Soc., 1985. Mem.: Nat. Assn. Sci. Writers, Sigma Xi (hon. life). Avocations: jazz, piano, travel.

PATSICOSTAS, SUSAN JOANNA, mental health services professional, psychotherapist; d. Gordon Howard and Melba Christine Williams; m. Nicholas Patsicostas, May 31, 1970 (div.); children: Thanos Nicholas, William Nicholas, Anthony Nicholas. AA, Ctrl. Fla. C.C., 1989; BA, Stetson U., 1991; MS in Mental Health Counseling, Nova Southeastern U., 1997. Lic. profl. counselor La., mental health counselor Fla., cert. parent trainer Boys and Girls Town, 2001, anger mgmt. and domestic violence counselor 2003. Psychotherapist Lake County Boys Ranch, Ocala, Fla., 1996—2000; clin. dir. Right Choice, LLC, Opelousas, La., 2001—02; owner, dir. New Way Mental Health Resources, LLC, Ville Platte, 2002—. Ct. apptd. adv. for foster children Guardian Ad Litem Program, Ocala, 1993—98. Recipient Above and Beyond award, Guardian Ad Litem Program, 1996. Mem.: Am. Counseling Assn., Assn. Play Therapy (licentiate), Psi Beta, Phi Theta Kappa. Office: New Way Mental Health Resources LLC 1769 West Main St Ville Platte LA 70586 Home Phone: 337-945-5031; Office Phone: 337-363-3703. Office Fax: 337-363-4008. E-mail: susantexas10@aol.com.

PATT, HERBERT JACOB, lawyer; b. Chgo., Feb. 12, 1935; s. Abraham and Esther Blanch (Kuchinsky) P.; m. Yvonne Phyllis Shavell, Oct. 9, 1958 (dec. Mar. 1986); children: Aldon Wayne, Bradley Earl, Colette Emile; m. Lynn Cheryl Feingold, December 26, 1993. BA, Northwestern U., 1956, JD, 1958; Diploma, Indsl. Coll., Johannesburg, South Africa. Bar: Ill. 1959, U.S. Dist. Ct. (no. dist.) Ill. 1959, U.S. Supreme Ct. 1977, Calif. 1986, U.S. Dist. Ct. (ctrl. and so. dists.) Calif. 1987, U.S. Ct. Appeals (9th cir.) 1987, U.S. Ct. Appeals (4th cir.) 2002. Assoc. Andres & Andres, Santa Ana, Calif. Pres. Jewish Nat. Fund Orange Co., Santa Ana, 1994-95, chmn., 1996-98, nat. bd. dirs., N.Y., 1994-98; pres. Temple Judea, Laguna Hills, Calif., 1992-93. Office: Andres & Andres 2041 N Main St Santa Ana CA 92706 Home Phone: 949-643-1441; Office Phone: 714-558-7775. Business E-Mail: hjpatt@andrewslaw.com. E-mail: pattlaw@aol.com.

PATTEE, STEVEN D., lawyer; b. Harlan, Iowa, Jan. 8, 1971; s. Donald E. and Carol A. Pattee; m. Nicole Boutell, Aug. 5, 1995; children: Megan, Kathleen. BS, U. Iowa, Iowa City, 1993, JD, 1996. Assoc. Cousineau, McGuire & Anderson, Chartered, St. Louis Pk., Minn., 1996—97, Waldeck & Lind, PA, Mpls., 1997—2005; CEO Pattee & Assocs., LLC, Lakeville, Minn., 2005—. Dir. Minn. Def. Lawyers Assn., Minneapolis, Minn., 2000—04; chair Minn. Def. Lawyers Association-No-Fault Com., Minneapolis, Minn., 2004—06. Contbr. articles to profl. jours. Commr. Planning Commn., Lakeville, 2003. Named Rising Star, Minnesota Law & Politics. Mem.: Minn. Def. Lawyers Assn. (dir. 2000—04, chmn. 2004—06), Dakota County Bar Assn., Def. Rsch. Inst., Wis. State Bar Assn., Minn. State Bar Assn. Office: Pattee & Associates LLC 17595 Kenwood Trl Ste 150 Lakeville MN 55044 Home Phone: 952-997-2560; Office Phone: 952-898-5552. Office Fax: 952-898-2775. Business E-Mail: steve@patteelaw.com.

PATTEN, BERNARD MICHAEL, neurologist, writer, educator; b. NYC, Mar. 23, 1941; s. Bernard M. and Olga (Vaccaro) P.; m. Ethel Doudine, June 18, 1964; children: Allegra, Craig. AB summa cum laude, Columbia Coll., 1962; MD, Columbia U., 1966. Med. intern N.Y. Hosp. Cornell Med. Ctr., NYC, 1966-67; resident neurologist Columbia Presbyn. Med. Ctr., NYC, 1967-69, chief resident neurologist, 1969-70; assoc. prof. neurology Baylor Coll. Medicine, Houston, 1973-95; ret., 1995. Asst. chief med. neurology NIH, Bethesda, Md., 1970-73; mem. med. bd. Nat. Myasthenia Gravis Found., 1973—, Nat. AmyoTrophic Lateral Sclerosis Found., 1982—, Nat. Myositis Assn., 1995—; invited faculty Rice U., 1999—; faculty Women's INst. Houston. Author: One or Two Things I Remember About Her, 1999, Tristan and Iseult: Modern Version, 2000, Investment Pearls for Modern Times Expressed in Meter and in Rhymes, 2000, The Great Cotzias, 2001, Ascent to Heaven, 2001, Quia Imperfectum, 2001, Truth, Knowledge or Bull: How to Tell the Difference, 2004, The Blood of a Million Christs, 2004, Cruising Around the World on the Queen Elizabeth 2, 2006; contbr. articles to profl. jours. With USPHS, 1970-73. Rsch. grantee NIH, pvt. founds., nat. health orgns. Fellow ACP, Royal Coll. Physicians, Tex. Neurol. Soc. Achievements include discoverer (with others) L-Dopa for Parkinson's disease; pioneered use of immune suppression for myasthenia gravis, diagnosis and treatment of medical and neurologcal complications of breast implants. Home: 1019 Baronridge Dr Seabrook TX 77586-4001 Home Phone: 281-474-7670; Office Phone: 713-252-1306. Personal E-mail: dadpatten@aol.com.

PATTEN, BETSEY LELAND, state legislator; b. Newton, Mass., Apr. 26, 1945; m. Richard C. Patten (dec.); 1 child. Student, Kings Coll. With publ. dept. Raytheon Co., 1978—84; rec. sec. Planning and Zoning Bds. of Moultonborough, 1985—91; state rep. N.H. Ho. Reps., former chmn. mcpl. and county govt. com. Former chmn. Joint Legis. Com. on Administrv. Rules; chmn. Assessing Standards Bd., Carroll County Rep. Com., 1996—. Home: 46 Patten Hill Rd Moultonborough NH 03254 Office Phone: 603-271-3317. E-mail: blpatten@worldpath.net.

PATTEN, CHARLES ANTHONY, management consultant, retired manufacturing company executive, writer, publisher; b. Allentown, Pa., May 12, 1920; s. Charles Henerie and Mae (Doyle) P.; m. Kathleen Marie Breene, Jan. 6, 1951 (dec. 1999); children: Charles Anthony Jr., Amy Elizabeth Goddard, Nancy Kathleen Hansen. BSM.E., Lehigh U., 1942. With Joy Mfg. Co., 1947-63, works mgr., 1956-63; v.p. mfg. White Motor Corp., 1963-68, Colt Industries, 1968-69; With Dravo Corp., Pitts., 1942-47, 69-85, gen. mgr. engring. works div., 1970-71, corp. v.p., gen. mgr. engring. works div., 1971-75, corp. group v.p., chief exec. officer Dravo Mfg. Group, 1975-81, corp. sr. v.p., mem. corp. policy com., chief exec. officer Dravo Mfg. Group, 1981-83, corp. sr. v.p., asst. to pres. and chief exec. officer, mem. exec. com., 1984-85; pres. C.A. Patten Enterprises, 1985—. Bd. dirs., v.p. Dravo (Can.) Ltd., 1975-85; dir., pres.

Dravo-Okura Co. Ltd., 1974-79; dir. Dravo Mfg. (Can.) Ltd., 1975-83, Tru Weld Grating Inc., 1983-85; v.p. Dravo Internat., Inc., 1974-85; adv. com. Nat. Mgmt. Assn., 1973-85; chief devel. officer Western Pa. Model RR. Mus., 2001-, corp. mem., Am. Mgmt. Assn., 1954-85 Seminar spkr. in field, contbr. publs. Trustee Ohio Valley Gen. Hosp., McKees Rocks, Pa., 1975-82, Marietta (Ohio) Coll., 1979-89, emeritus trustee, 1989—; bd. dirs. Vocat. Rehab. Ctr. of Allegheny County, 1972-79, Jr. Achievement of S.W. Pa., 1975-80, Sherwood Oaks Residents Assn., 2003—. Recipient Silver Knight of Mgmt. award Nat. Mgmt. Assn., 1976. Mem. ASME, Neville Island Mfrs. Assn. (pres. 1975-85), Am. Arbitration Assn. (panel of arbitrators, 1989-95), Shipyard Steering Com. of Am. Waterways Operators, Inland Waterways Am. Bur. of Ships. Republican. Roman Catholic. Home and Office: 204 Norman Dr Cranberry Township PA 16066-4233 Office Phone: 724-776-8204. *The successful manager is a time-oriented goal setter. Without waiting for others to ask, envisions things that should happen and thinks through possible paths to reach the goals. When the goals are reached, is quick to laud and praise people for their accomplishments.*

PATTEN, DUNCAN THEUNISSEN, ecologist educator; b. Detroit, Oct. 13, 1934; s. Marc T. and Doris (Miller) P.; m. Eva Chittenden, July 27, 1957; children: Michael, Marc, Robin, Scott. BA, Amherst Coll., 1956; MS, U. Mass., Amherst, 1959; PhD, Duke U., 1962. Asst. prof. ecology Va. Poly. Inst., Blacksburg, 1962-65, Ariz. State U., Tempe, 1965-67, assoc. prof., 1967-73, prof., 1973-95, prof. emeritus, 1995—, dir. ctr. environ. studies, 1980-95. Rsch. prof. Mont. State U., 1995—. Contbr. articles to profl. jours. Fellow AAAS, Ariz.-Nev. Acad. Sci.; mem. Ecol. Soc. Am. (bus. mgr. 1979-95), Brit. Ecol. Soc., Soc. Range Mgmt., Am. Inst. Biol. Scis., Soc. Wetland Scientists (pres. 1996-97), Am. Water Resource Assn., Am. Geophys. Union, Sigma Xi Office: Mont State U Land Resources and Environ Scis Box 173120 Bozeman MT 59717-3120 Personal E-mail: dtpatten@starband.net.

PATTEN, LANNY RAY, gas industry executive; b. St. Joseph, Mo., July 31, 1934; s. E.L. and Sarah Catherine (Langner) P.; m. Ann Rogers Hall, Oct. 26, 1957; children: David, John, Jeffrey, Mark. BS in Engring., Iowa State U., 1956; AMP, Harvard U., 1976. Net sr. v.p. gases and equipment Air Products and Chems., Inc., Allentown, Pa., 1960—90; pres., COO Airgas Inc., Radnor, Pa., 1990-91; founder, pres. CylServ, Inc., West Conshohocken, Pa., 1992—. Chmn. Lehigh U. Parents Assn., Bethlehem, Pa., 1977—90. Officer USAF, 1957—60. Recipient PACE award for Engring. Achievement Iowa State U., 1990, Friend of Lehigh award, 1991. Mem.: SAR (chpt. pres. 2006—07), Allentown C. of C. (exec. bd. dirs. 1978—82), Internat. Oxygen Mfg. Assn., Compressed Gas Assn. (exec. bd. dirs. 1977—91), Pa. Soc. SAR (v.p. 2005—), Pa. Soc. SR (bd. dirs.), Union League of Phila., Phila. Country Club, Kappa Sigma (Alumni Hall of Fame). Republican. Episcopalian. Avocations: baseball, golf, reading. Home: 1306 Club House Rd Gladwyne PA 19035-1006

PATTEN, ROBERT LOWRY, language educator; b. Oklahoma City, Apr. 26, 1939; s. Charles H. and Helen (Lowry) P.; m. Faith L. Harris, June 12, 1960 (div. 1974); children: Jocelyn S., Christina S. BA, Swarthmore Coll., 1960; MA, Princeton U., 1963, PhD, 1965. Lectr. Bryn Mawr (Pa.) Coll., 1964-66, asst. prof. English, 1966-69; asst. prof. Rice U., Houston, 1969-71, assoc. prof., 1971-76, prof. English, 1976-96, chair, dept. of English, 1991-92, master Grad. House, 1992-95, Lynette S. Autrey prof. humanities, 1996—. Pres. PEN S.W., Houston, 1989—92. Author: Charles Dickens and His Publishers, 1978, George Cruikshank's Life, Times and Art, vol. 1, 1992, vol. 2, 1996 (best biography of the decade Guardian); editor: (book by Charles Dickens) Pickwick Papers, 1972, George Cruikshank: A Revaluation, 1974, 2d edit., 1992, (with John O. Jordan) Literature in the Marketplace, 1995, (with John Bourn) Palgrave Advances in Charles Dickens Studies, 2005; editor SEL: Studies in English Lit., 1978-84, 90—. Bd. dirs. Cultural Arts Coun., Houston, 1979-80, Tex. Com. for the Humanities, 1979-80; pres., bd. dirs. Houston Ctr. for the Humanities, 1976-84; v.p. Houston Philanthropical Soc., 2007—. NEH fellow, 1968-69, 77-78, 87-88; Guggenheim fellow, 1980-81; Nat. Humanities Ctr. fellow, 1987-88; Nat. Gallery of Art Assoc., 1988-89. Mem. AAUP, MLA, PEN Am. Ctr., Dickens Fellowship, Dickens Soc., Soc. for the History of Authorship, Reading and Pub. (bd. dirs. 1992-2003, treas. 1997-2003, v.p. 2003-05, pres. 2005—), Coun. Editors of Learned Jours., Phi Beta Kappa (pres. Beta chpt. Tex. 1991-94, 97-2002, 07—, bd. dirs. Houston chpt. 1997-2000, adv. dir. 2000-03, senator 2002-03, Couper scholar, 2004-06). Episcopalian. Avocations: travel, classical music. Office: Rice U Dept English MS 30 PO Box 1892 Houston TX 77251-1892 Home Phone: 713-524-1485; Office Phone: 713-348-4697. Business E-mail: patten@rice.edu.

PATTEN, RONALD JAMES, university dean; b. Iron Mountain, Mich., July 17, 1935; s. Rudolph Joseph and Cecelia (Fuse) Pataconi; m. Shirley Ann Bierman, Sept. 5, 1959; children: Christine Marie, Cheryl Ann, Charlene Denise. BA, Mich. State U., East Lansing, 1957, MA, 1959; PhD, U. Ala., Tuscaloosa, 1963. Acct. Price Waterhouse & Co., Detroit, 1958; instr. No. Ill. U., 1959-60; asst. prof. U. Colo., 1963-65; assoc. prof. Va. Poly. Inst. and State U., 1965-67, prof., 1967-73, head dept. accounting, 1966-73; dir. research Financial Accounting Standards Bd., Conn., 1973-74; dean Sch. Bus. Adminstrn., U. Conn., Storrs, 1974-88; chief of party-Eastern Caribbean Arthur D. Little Internat., 1988-89; dean Coll. Commerce and Kellstadt Grad. Sch. Bus. De Paul U., Chgo., 1989-99; dean Ritsumeikan Asia Pacific U. Grad. Sch. Mgmt., Beppu, Japan, 2003—06. Individual investors adv. com. NY Stock Exch., 1993—98; cons. in field. Contbr. chapters to books, articles to profl. jours. Bd. dirs. US com. UNICEF, Chgo., 1996—99. Recipient Nat. Quartermaster award Nat. Quartermaster, Assn., 1956; Earhart Found. fellow, 1962-63. Mem. AICPA, Am. Acctg. Assn., Inst. Mgmt. Accts., Acad. Internat. Bus. (Internat. Dean of Yr. award 1987), Internat. Assn. for Acctg. Edn. and Rsch., Ill. Coun. Econ. Edn. (Chgo., trustee 1989-2006, chmn. bd. trustees 1997-2000), Pacioli Soc., Internat. Trade and Fin. Assn., dir. 1998-2000, Heidelberg Club Internat., Scabbard and Blade, Golden Key, Beta Gamma Sigma (mem. bd. govs. 1975-90, nat. sec.-treas. 1980-82, nat. v.p. 1982-84, nat. pres. 1984-86), Beta Alpha Psi (bd. dirs. 1992-94), Delta Sigma Pi, World Assn. for Case Method Rsch. and Application, Adv Bd., 1998-, Phi Kappa Phi, Delta Mu Delta. Avocations: hiking, softball, golf, travel, singing. Home: PO Box 190 Newfield ME 04056 Business E-Mail: rpatten@depaul.edu.

PATTEN, THOMAS HENRY, JR., retired finance educator, personnel director; b. Cambridge, Mass., Mar. 24, 1929; s. Thomas Henry and Lydia Mildred (Lindgren) Patten; m. Rosalie Medina, May 23, 2002. AB, Brown U., 1953; MS, Cornell U., 1955, PhD, 1959. Dir. program planning Ford Motor Co., Dearborn, Mich., 1957-65; prof. mgmt. and sociology U. Detroit, 1965-67; prof. orgnl. behavior and personnel mgmt. Sch. Labor and Indsl. Relations, Mich. State U., E. Lansing, 1967-84; prof. mgmt. and human resources Calif. State Poly. U., Pomona, 1984—2003, prof. emeritus, 2003—07; ret., 2007. Cons. in field. Author: The Foreman: The Forgotten Man of Management, 1968, Manpower Planning and the Development of Human Resources, 1971, OD-Emerging Dimensions and Concepts, 1973, A Bibliography of Compensation Planning and Administration, 1960-1974, 2d rev. edit., 1981, 3d rev. edit., 1987, Pay: Employee Compensation and Incentive Plans, 1977, Classics of Personnel Management, 1979, Organizational Development Through Teambuilding, 1981, A Manager's Guide to Performance Appraisal, 1982, Fair Pay: The Managerial Challenge of Comparable Job Worth and Job Evaluation, 1988, Exercises for Developing Human Resources Management Skills, 1996. With USMC, 1946—51. Mem. ASTD (chmn. orgn. devel. div. 1972), Indsl. Rels. Rsch. Assn. (chpt. pres. 1970-71), Am. Sociol. Assn., Internat. Pers. Mgmt. Assn., Internat. Indsl. Rels. Assn., Inst. Applied Behavioral Sci., Am. Compensation Assn. Home: 407 Mossy Ct Lincoln CA 95648-8158 *Human values come first.*

PATTEN, VALERIE LYNN, lawyer; b. LA, Apr. 8, 1950; d. Russell Carl and Donna D. Patten; 1 child, Elizabeth Nicole Wood. AB, Stanford U., 1972; MFA, San Jose State U., 1981; JD, Georgetown U., 1992. Bar: Calif. 1992. Legal intern Washington Area Lawyers for the Arts, 1990—90; law clk. Garfinkle & Assocs., Washington, 1990—92; staff atty. Legal Advocates for Children and Youth, San Jose, Calif., 1992—93; assoc. atty. Law Offices of Robert L. Hoover, San Jose, 1994—96; pvt. practice Law Offices of Valerie L. Patten, Palo Alto, Calif., 1996—. Freelance writer Bay Area (Calif.) Art Publ., 1980—84; writer arts & entertainment Palo Alto (Calif.) Weekly, 1982—84; instr. art dept. U. Mont., Missoula, 1984—84; lectr. continuing edn. art dept. legal issues for artists San Jose State U., Calif., 1993; referral atty., lectr. Calif. Lawyers for the Arts, San Francisco, 1993—; asst. prof. art dept. San Francisco State U., 1994—95; atty. mem. Graphic Artists Guild, 1997—; presenter, continuing edn. seminar on custody and visitation in Calif. Nat. Bus. Inst., Eau Claire, Wis., 2003, Eau Claire, 06. One-woman shows include DeSaisset Mus., Pro Arts Gallery, Oakland, Henry Art Gallery, Seattle, exhibited in group shows at Am. Acad. and Inst Arts and Letters, N.Y. (selected for Hassam and Speicher fund Purchase Exhbn., 1983). Pro tem judge Superior Ct. Santa Clara County, San Jose, 1999—, property divsn. mediator, 1998—2001; pro bono panel mem. Santa Clara County Bar Assn. Law Found., San Jose, 1993—; vol. tchr. Prisoners' Info. Svcs., Palo Alto, 1977—84; vol. atty. Pro Bono Project, San Jose, 2002—; bd. mem., sec. Young Audiences San Jose, 1998—2001; bd. mem. DanceVisions, Palo Alto, 1993—. Recipient Am. Jurisprudence award, Lawyers Coop. Pub., 1991; Charles Warren Kendrick Meml. scholar, Stanford U., 1968—72. Mem.: San Mateo County Bar Assn. (family law sect. 2003—), Calif. State Bar Assn., ABA (family law sect. 1992—), Santa Clara County Bar Assn. (family law sect. com. 1995—), State Bar Calif. Episcopalian. Avocations: painting, art history, hiking. Home: 1528 Rosita Rd Pacifica CA 94044 Office: Law Offices Valerie L Patten Ste 7 744 San Antonio Rd Palo Alto CA 94303 Office Phone: 650-855-9570. E-mail: valpatten@prodigy.net.

PATTENAUDE, RICHARD LOUIS, academic administrator, educator; b. Seattle, Feb. 22, 1946; s. Joseph Arthur and Alice June (Vrooman) P.; m. Michele Arlen Stevenson, May 31, 1975; children: Lauren, Lisa, Dylan, Joshua. BA with honors in Econs., San Jose State U., 1968; PhD in Polit. Sci., U. Colo., 1974. Asst. to assoc. prof. Drake U., Des Moines, 1974-80, assoc. dean liberal arts, 1976-80; asst. v.p. acad. affairs SUNY-Binghamton, 1980-82, assoc. v.p., 1982-86; v.p. acad. affairs; prof. polit. sci. Ctrl. Conn. State U., New Britain, 1986-91; pres., prof. polit. sci. U. So. Maine, Portland, 1991—2007; chancellor U. Maine Sys., 2007—. Cons. in field; panelist, presenter various nat. higher edn. meetings. Contbr. numerous articles to profl. jours., chpts. to books in field. Commr. Occupational and Licensing Commn., Iowa, 1978-80; mem. Gov.'s Com. Efficiency, 1979; mem. adv. coun. planning dept. City of Binghamton, 1984-1986; bd. dirs. Broome County United Way, 1985, Greater Hartford Red Cross, 1991-93, Mercy Hosp., Portland, 1992-94, Portland Symphony Orch., Maine Devel. Found., 1991-97, Maine Sci. & Tech. Found., 1992-98, Portland Mus. Art, 1993-99, Pmt. Symphony 1998-, Lee Altomalls, 2000—, Maine Med. Ctr., 2002-05, Maine Health, 2005—, Inst. Civic Leadership, 1992-94, Greater Portland United Way, 1998-2002. With U.S. Army, 1969-71, Vietnam. Fanny W. Ames scholar, 1965; Title II fellow, 1970. Mem. Assn. Instl. Rsch. and Planning Officers (v.p. 1983-84, pres. 1984-85), Am. Assn. State Colls. and Univs. (state rep. 1995—, bd. dirs. 1999—2003), Greater Portland C. of C. Office: U Maine System 16 Central St Bangor ME 04401 Business E-Mail: pattenaude@maine.edu.

PATTERSON, AMANDA MARGARET, music educator; b. Luxemburg, Wis., May 15, 1931; d. Alois Milton Arendt and Martha Anastacia Dorner-Arendt; m. Neil A. Patterson (dec.); children: Debra Lee, Patrick Neil, Dean Michael, Jane Marie Mlenar. Student, Milw. State Tchrs. Coll., 1949—53. Tchr. music Walworth County, Elkhorn, Wis., 1953—56; tchr. Milw. Music City, 1956—57; tchr. instrumental music City of Milw., 1956—68; tchr. music Greendale, 1968—2006. Musician Anita McKnights All Women Orch., Milw., 1970—81, West Allis Adult Band, Wis., 1972—80. Pres. Wis. State Podiatry Aux. Soc., Milw., 1972—73, Greendale PTA, Wis., 1968—69, active, 1968—85; chmn. Ballet Co. Friends, Milw., 1973—76; pres. Greendale VFW Aux., Wis., 1980—82, 4th Dist. VFW Aux., Milw., 1992—93; bd. dirs. Milw. Ballet Co., 1973. Mem.: VFW (pres. auxiliary Greendale chp. 2004—), Am. Legion. Roman Catholic. Home: 5342 Lakeview Dr Greendale WI 53129-1928 Personal E-mail: amandamp515@aol.com.

PATTERSON, ANNE WOODS, ambassador, former federal agency administrator; b. Ft. Smith, Ark., 1949; m. David R. Patterson; children: Edward, Andrew. BA in Econs., Wellesley Coll., Mass.; grad. student, U. NC. With US Fgn. Svc., 1973—, econ. officer Ecuador, 1974-77, desk officer Nicaragua, analyst for C.Am., trade specialist Canada, econ. counselor Riyadh, Saudi Arabia, 1984-88, polit. counselor US Mission to UN Geneva, dir. Office Andean Affairs, 1991-93, dep. asst. sec. C.Am. and the Caribbean, 1993-95, prin. dep. asst. sec. for inter-Am. affairs, 1995—97, US amb. to El Salvador San Salvador, 1997—2000, US amb. to Colombia Bogota, 2000—03; dep. insp. gen. US Dept. State, Washington, 2003—04, asst. sec. Bur. Internat. Narcotics and Law Enforcement Affairs, 2005—07, US amb. to Pakistan Islamabad, 2007—; dep. permanent US rep. UN, NYC, 2004—05, acting permanent US rep., 2005. Recipient Superior Honor award, US Dept. State, 1981, 88 Meritorious Honor award, 1977, 83, Presdl. award, 1993; Order of the Congress, Congress of Colombia, Order of Boyaca, Govt. Colombia, Order of Jose Matias Delgado, Govt. El Salvador. Office: DOS Amb 8100 Islamabad Pl Washington DC 20521-8100 *

PATTERSON, CARLY, Olympic gymnast; b. Baton Rouge, Feb. 4, 1988; d. Ricky and Natalie. Mem. TOPS Nat. Team, 1996, 1997, U.S. Nat. Gymnastics Team, 2000—; gymnast Team USA, Athens Olympic Games, 2004. Achievements include member of US World Championships Gold medal team, 2003; winning silver medal, all-around, World Championships, 2003; won Visa Am. Cup Championship by winning all four events, 2004; winning gold medal, all-around, Athens Olympic games, 2004; member of US Women's Silver medal Gymnastics team, Athens Olympic games, 2004. Office: c/o USOC One Olympic Plz Colorado Springs CO 80909

PATTERSON, CHARLES DAROLD, librarian, educator; b. Wahpeton, ND, Aug. 8, 1928; s. Charles Irwin and Inez Fern (Slagg) P. BSc, Bemidji State U., 1950; MA, U. Minn., 1956; MusM, W.Va. U., 1964; advanced cert., U. Pitts., 1968, PhD, 1971. Tchr. music Fargo (N.D.) Pub. Schs., 1950; jr. reference libr. U. Minn. Librs., 1954-55; head libr. Bemidji (Minn.) State U., 1955-58; dir. librs., asst. prof. Glenville (W.Va.) State Coll., 1958-62; asst. prof. W.Va. U., 1962-66; instr. Grad. Sch. Libr. and Info. Scis. U. Pitts., 1966-71, asst. prof., 1971-72; assoc. prof. Sch. Libr. and Info. Sci. La. State U., Baton Rouge, 1972-78, prof., 1978-93, prof. emeritus, 1993—. Del. La. Gov.'s Conf. on Libr. and Info. Svcs., 1978. Author: Analysis of Library of Congress Music Subject Headings, 1971, JEL Cumulative Index, 1979, supplement, 1982, (with D.G. Davis) ARBA Guide to Library Science Literature, 1987, Letters from the Far East, 2003; editor W.Va. Libraries, 1963-66; mem. editl. bd. Jour. Edn. for Librarianship, 1975-79, editor, 1980-84; editor Jour. Edn. for Libr. and Info. Sci., 1984-88; asst. editor Reference Svcs. Rev., 1986-93; contbr. articles to profl. jours. Served with U.S. Army, 1950-52. Recipient La. State U. Faculty Excellence award, 1984 Mem. ALA (chmn. scholarship jury 1972-73, award 1989, Disting. Mem. medal 2005), W.Va. Libr. Assn. (chmn. coll. and univ. libr. sect. 1960-61, exec. bd. 1960-61, 64-66), Assn. Coll. and Rsch. Librs. (pres. Tri-state chpt. 1972), Assn. Am. Libr. Schs. (exec. bd. 1980-88), La. Libr. Assn., Southeastern Libr. Assn., AAUP (pres. chpt. 1985-86), Am. Guild Organists (dean chpt. 1985-86), Pitts. Bibliophiles, Univ. Chamber Music Soc. (pres., dir. 1979-80), La. Sinfonietta (exec. bd. 1994—), Beta Phi Mu (dir.-at-large 1982-85). Methodist. Home: 1480 Kenmore Ave Baton Rouge LA 70808-1130 also: Birchmont Beach Bemidji MN 56601 Office: La State U Sch Libr And Info Sci Baton Rouge LA 70803-0001 *When one is confident in his own mind that he has, with given abilities, done his very best, then perhaps he has paid for his niche in eternity.*

PATTERSON, CHRISTOPHER NIDA, lawyer; b. Washington Courthouse, Ohio, Apr. 17, 1960; s. Donis Dean and JoAnne (Nida) O.; m. Vicky Patterson; children: Travis, Kirsten. BA, Clemson U., 1982; JD, Nova U., 1985. Bar: Fla. 1985, U.S. Dist. Ct. (mid. dist.) Fla. 1985, U.S. Ct. Mil. Rev. 1986, U.S. Ct. Appeals Armed Forces 1987, U.S. Dist. Ct. (ea. dist.) Va. 1987, U.S. Supreme Ct. 1989, U.S. Ct. Appeals (11th cir.) 1992, U.S. Dist. Ct. (no. dist.) Fla. 1992, U.S. Dist. Ct. (so. dist.) Tex. 1995; cert. criminal trial specialist Fla. Bar., 1995, cert. criminal trial advocate Nat. Bd. Trial Advocacy, 1995.; cert. dependency mediator, family law mediator, county ct. mediator, arbitrator. Pros. Fla. State Attys. Office, Orlando, Fla., 1985; spl. asst. U.S. Atty. U.S. Dist. Ct. (ea. dist.) Va., 1987-90; pvt. practice, 1991—. Adj. prof. law Gulf Coast CC, 1994—95; mem. Fla. Supreme Ct. Mediators Qualifications Bd.; family law mediator Fla. Supreme Ct., dependency law mediator, county ct. mediator, mem. mediators qualifications bd.; mediator County Ct.; on-air legal analyst Nex Media-WYOO-FM. Author: Queen's Pawn, 1996, Treasure Trove, 1997, Krysha, 2006; contbr. Nat. DAR Mag., Fla. Defender mag. Chancellor St. Thomas Episcopal Ch.; bd. dirs. Bay County Teen Ct., Inc., Gulf Coast, Girs Inc. Svc. Orgn., Widowed Persons Svc., The Unlimited Path, Inc. With judge advocate gen. corps U.S. Army, 1986—91. Recipient U.S. Army Chief of Staff award for legal excellence, 1989, Guardian ad litem commendation, Fla. Supreme Ct., 1999. Mem. ABA, FBA, SAR, NACDL (life), Am. Coll. Barristers, Fla. Assn. Criminal Def. Lawyers, Acad. Fla. Trial Lawyers, Assn. Fed. Def. Attys., Fla. Acad. Profl. Mediators, Fla. Bar Spkrs. Bur. (criminal law sect., del. 11th cir. jud. conf. 1999, Pro Bono Svc. award, nominee Jefferson award for pub. svc. 1999), Bay County Bar Assn., The Ret. Officers' Assn., Christian Legal Soc., Am. Legion, Fellowship of Christian Athletes, Nat. Triathlon Fedn., Soc. Colonial Wars, Mil. Order Fgn. Wars, Rotary Internat. (past pres., Paul Harris fellow). Episcopalian. Avocations: athletics, travel, writing. Office: 335 Magnolia Ave Panama City FL 32401 Office Phone: 850-872-0226. Business E-Mail: pattersonlaw@knology.net.

PATTERSON, DAVID ANDREW, computer scientist, educator, consultant; b. Evergreen Park, Ill., Nov. 16, 1947; s. David Dwight and Lucie Jeanette (Ekstrom) P.; m. Linda Ann Crandall, Sept. 4, 1967; children: David Adam, Michael Andrew. BS in Math., UCLA, 1969, MS in Computer Sci., 1970, PhD, 1976. Mem. tech. staff Hughes Aircraft Co., LA, 1972-76, Thinking Machines Corp., Cambridge, Mass., 1979; prof. computer sci. divsn. U. Calif., Berkeley, 1977—, chmn., 1990-93, E.H. and M.E. Pardee chair computer sci., 1992—. Cons. Sun Microsystems, Inc., Mountain View, Calif., 1984—. Author: A Taste of Smalltalk, 1986, Computing Unbound, 1989, Computer Architecture: A Quantative Approach, 2d edit., 1996, 4th edit., 2007, Computer Organization & Design: The Hardware/Software Interface, 2d edit., 1998, 3rd edit., 2005. Recipient Disting. Tchg. award U. Calif., Berkeley, 1982, Diane S. McEntyre award, 1998, Outstanding Alumnus award UCLA Computer Sci. Dept.; named to Silicon Valley Engring. Hall of Fame, 2006. Fellow IEEE (undergrad. tchg. award 1996, tech. achievement award 1995, co-recipient Reynold B. Johnson Info. Storage award, John Von Neumann medal 2000, James H. Mulligan Edn. medal, 2000), Assn. Computer Machinery (Karl V. Karlstrom Outstanding Educator award, 1991, co-recipient, Sigmod Test of Time award 1998), Computer Soc., Am. Acad. Arts & Sciences; mem. NAE, AAAS, Computing Rsch. Assn. (bd. dirs. Washington 1991-2003, chair 1993-97, spl. interest group on computer architecture), Assn. Computer Machinery (bd. dirs. 1987-90, chair 1993-95, pres. 2004-2006), NAS (computer sci. and telecomm. bd.). Avocations: biking, soccer, weightlifting, body surfing. Office: Univ Calif Computer Sci Computer Sci Divsn 1776 465 Soda Hall Berkeley CA 94720-1776 Office Phone: 510-642-6587. Office Fax: 510-643-7352. Business E-Mail: patterson@cs.berkeley.edu.

PATTERSON, DEB, women's college basketball coach; Grad., Rockford Coll., 1979. Coach Hononegah HS, Ill., 1982—86; asst. coach No. Ill. U., 1986—87, asst. coach, recruiting coord., 1987—91, Vanderbilt U., 1992-96; asst. coach So. Ill. U., 1991-92; head coach Kans. State U., 1996—. Asst. coach World U. Games, 1997, World Championships, 1998, Jr. World Championship Qualifying Team, 2000; asst. coach Women's Sr. Nat. Team USA Invitational Tournament of Champions, 1997. Named Coach of Yr. Ill. HS Assn., 1985, Conf. Coach of Yr., 1985, 86, Women's Coll. Basketball Coach of Yr. Kans. Basketball Coaches Assn., 1997, 2002, ESPN The Mag. Coach of Yr., 2002, Big 12 Coach of Yr., 2002, Women's Basketball Coaches Assn. Dist. V Coach of Yr., 2002, Dallas Morning News, Austin-Am. Statesman and San Antonio Express News Big 12 Coach of Yr., 2002. Achievements include leading Kansas State to Women's National Invitational Tournament Championship as head coach, 2006. Office: Kansas State U Womens Basketball 1800 College Ave Manhattan KS 66502-3308 Office Phone: 785-532-6970. E-mail: dlpip@k-state.edu. *

PATTERSON, DENNIS JOSEPH, retired management consultant; b. Honolulu, Apr. 13, 1948; s. Joseph John and Dorothy Elizabeth (Snajkowski) P.; divorced; children: Valerie Jean, Christina Elizabeth. BA, Elmhurst Coll., Ill., 1970; MA, George Washington U., 1973. Asst. dir. Vancouver (B.C.) Gen. Hosp., 1973-76, dir., 1975-76; v.p. Shaugnessy Hosp., Vancouver, 1976-79; pres. Westcare, Vancouver, 1979-84; mgr. Ernst & Whinney, Chgo., 1984-86, sr. mgr., 1986-88, ptnr., 1988-93; pres. FHP Internat. Cons. Group, Inc., Fountain Valley, Calif., 1993-95; ptnr. KPMG Peat Marwick, 1996-97; sr. cons. Hay Group, 1997-98; chmn., CEO IMC Rsch. Inst. (now Healthcare Net); ptnr. Wellspring Ptnrs.; ret., 2007. Author: Indexing Managed Care, 1997; contbr. articles to profl. jours. Fin. mgr. Electoral Action Movement, Vancouver, 1978; trustee George Washington U., 1992-96, Calif. Sch. Profl. Psychology, 1993-96, Alliant U., 1999-2003, Elmhurst Coll., 2006—. Mem. Royal Vancouver Yacht Club, Union League Chgo., Chgo. Yacht Club, Phi Gamma Mu. Republican. Anglican. Avocations: sailboat racing, golf. Home Phone: 310-386-0995. Personal E-mail: djpdennis@yahoo.com.

PATTERSON, DENNIS M., bank executive; Grad., Ga. Inst. Tech., Atlanta, 1971. Corp. exec. v.p. corp. sales adminstrn., mem. mgmt. com. SunTrust Banks, Inc. Mem. adv. bd. Ga. Inst. Tech. Coll. Mgmt. Named to Acad. Disting. Alumni, Ga. Inst. Tech. Coll. Mgmt., 2006. Office: SunTrust Banks Inc PO Box 4418 Atlanta GA 30302-4418 Office Phone: 404-588-7711. Office Fax: 404-827-6173. *

PATTERSON, DONALD EUGENE, research scientist; b. El Paso, Tex., Feb. 7, 1958; s. Donald M. Patterson and Beverly Lee (Viles) McElroy; m. Mary Jane Ingram, May 6, 1989. BS, U. Tex., 1982, MS, 1984; MA, Rice U., 1987, PhD, 1989. Rsch. scientist Rice U., Houston, 1989-91; sr. rsch. scientist Houston Advanced Rsch. Ctr., The Woodlands, Tex., 1989-93, TSA, Inc., The Woodlands, 1991-95; sr. scientist SI Diamond Tech. Inc., Houston, 1991-95, dir. R & D, 1995-96; edn. supr. ITT Tech. Inst.,

Houston, 1996-97; prin. scientist Sys. & Processes Engring. Corp., Austin, Tex., 1997-98; founder, sr. v.p. product devel. Extreme Devices, Inc., Austin, 1998—2003; sr. scientist Nanohmics, Inc., Austin, 2004—. Contbr. articles to profl. jours. Recipient Harry B. Weiser award, Rice U., 1988; Grad. fellow, 1984, VFW Voice Democracy scholar, 1974, Davis and Bertha Green scholar, 1982, Grad. scholar, U. Tex. El Paso, 1983. Mem.: SID, AAAS, Am. Chem. Soc., Sigma Xi, Phi Kappa Phi. Achievements include patents in field. Home: 4728 Interlachen Ln Austin TX 78747 Office: Nanohmics Inc 6201 E Olfort St 400 Austin TX 78741 Home Phone: 512-292-8769; Office Phone: 512-389-9990. Business E-Mail: dpatterson@nanohmics.com.

PATTERSON, DONALD ROSS, lawyer, educator; b. Sept. 9, 1939; s. Sam Ashley and Marguerite (Robinson) P.; m. Peggy Ann Schulte, May 1, 1965; children: D. Ross, Jerome Ashley, Gretchen Anne. BS, Tex. Tech U., 1961; JD, U. Tex., 1964; LLM, So. Meth. U., 1972. Bar: Tex. 1964, U.S. Ct. Claims 1970, U.S. Ct. Customs and Patent Appeals 1970, U.S. Ct. Mil. Appeals 1970, U.S. Supreme Ct. 1970, U.S. Dist. Ct. (ea. dist.) Tex. 1982, U.S. Ct. Appeals (5th cir.) 1991, U.S. Ct. Appeals (D.C. cir.) 1994; bd. cert. in immigration and naturalization law, Tex. Commd. lt. (j.g.) USN, 1964, advanced through grades to lt. comdr., 1969; asst. officer in charge Naval Petroleum Res., Bakersfield, Calif., 1970-72; staff judge adv. Kenitra, Morocco, 1972-76; officer in charge Naval Legal Svcs. Office, Whidbey Island, Wash., 1976-79; head mil. Justice divsn., Subic Bay, The Philippines, 1979-81; ret. USN, 1982; pvt. practice Tyler, Tex., 1982—. Former instr. U. Md., Chapman Coll., U. LaVerne, Tyler Jr. Coll., Jarvis Christian Coll., U. Tex., Tyler. Mem. East Tex. Estate Planning Coun. Mem. Coll. of State Bar of Tex., Tex. Bar Assn., Smith County Bar Assn., Am. Immigration Lawyers Assn., Masons, Rotary (past pres.), Shriners, Toastmasters (past pres.), Phi Delta Phi. Republican. Baptist. Home: 703 Wellington St Tyler TX 75703-4666 Office: 777 S Broadway Ave Ste 106 Tyler TX 75701-1648 Office Phone: 903-592-8186. Personal E-mail: oneworldtogether@sbcglobal.net.

PATTERSON, DONNA E., lawyer; b. Greensboro, NC, Mar. 4, 1949; BA cum laude, Yale U., 1971, JD, 1981. Bar: DC 1981. Dep. asst. atty. gen. US Dept. of Justice, 1997—2000; ptnr. Arnold & Porter, Wash, 2000—. Contbr. articles to profl. jours. Office: Arnold & Porter 555 12th St NW Washington DC 20004-1206 Office Phone: 202-942-5000. Office Fax: 202-942-5999. Business E-Mail: donna.patterson@aporter.com.

PATTERSON, DOUGLAS MACLENNAN, finance educator; b. Jan. 16, 1945; s. Thomas and Ruth (MacLennan) P.; m. Sara Louise Lucas; children: Cara Beth, John Douglas BSEE, U. Wis., 1968, MBA, 1972, PhD, 1978. Elec. engr. Westinghouse Electric, Balt., 1968—71; asst. prof. U. Mich., Ann Arbor, 1976—80, Va. Tech., Blacksburg, 1980—86, assoc. prof., 1986—98, prof., 1998—. Vis. prof. U. Calif., Santa Barbara, 1989; vis. scholar U. Tex., Austin, 1994; dir. PhD program fin. Va. Tech., 1991—95; invited spl. spkr. Statis. Inference and Non-Linear Dynamics in Time Series conf., Bressanone, Italy, 2005; presenter, spkr. in field. Co-author: A Nonlinear Times Series Workshop: A Tool Kit for Detecting and Identifying Nonlinear Serial Dependence; contbr. articles to profl. jours Mem. ad hoc com. Detroit Area Hosp. Assn., 1978-79 Recipient Tchg. Excellence award Va. Tech., 1983; U. Mich. fellow, 1979; USN grantee, 1984, 85, 90 Mem. Am. Fin. Assn., Am. Econ. Assn., Fin. Mgmt. Assn., Beta Gamma Sigma Methodist. Home: 702 Crestwood Dr Blacksburg VA 24060-6006 Office: Va Poly Inst Dept Finance 0221 Blacksburg VA 24061 Business E-Mail: docfin@vt.edu.

PATTERSON, EDWARD PALMER, retired physicist; b. Kansas City, Kans., Sept. 5, 1921; s. Sidney Edward and Dura (Palmer) P.; m. Eula Mae Bennett, Oct. 15, 1945; children: Nona Marie, Wilma Jean Patterson Graham. BS in Metall. Engring., U. Mo., Rolla, 1944, MS in Metall. Engring., 1947, prof. degree of engring., 1957. Registered profl. engr., Kans. Instr. Nat. Sch. Aeronautics, Kansas City, Mo., 1947-50; metall. engr. Boeing Airplane Co., Wichita, Kans., 1950-51; sr. rsch. engr. GM Corp., Kansas City, Kans., 1951-52; sr. staff engr. White Motors Co., Cleve., 1952-54; sr. engr. Westinghouse Elec. Co., Kansas City, Mo., 1954-59; sr. staff rschr. Cessna Aircraft Corp., Wichita, 1959-60; project engr., project leader Bendix Corp./Allied Signal Corp., Kansas City, Mo., 1960-87; ret., 1987. Vol. Hospice Mesquite Med. Ctr., 1997-98, Nat. Hospice Orgn., Dallas, 1998. With USAF, 1944-46. Mem. AIME, Am. Soc. Materials Internat., Am. Rocket Soc., Am. Phys. Soc., Masons (master, York Rite Cross of Hon. & Red Cross of Constantine, High Priest), Knights of Kadosh (comdr. 1968). Republican. Mem. Lds Ch. Achievements include discovery of the unitron, basic command unit for life and non-life; established new values for the Planck time, mass, and length; calculated the speed of gravity.

PATTERSON, EDWIN, minister; b. Andalusia, Ala., Sept. 6, 1921; s. Walter Levi and Kate Edline (Aughtman) P.; m. Margaret Alice Hall, May 14, 1966. Degree, Brennan Bus. Sch., 1940; postgrad., Samford U., 1950-57. Ordained to ministry So. Bapt. Conv., 1947. Pastor various chs., Ala., 1947—; including Hopewell Bapt. Ch., 1949-67, Harmony Bapt. Ch., Andalusia, 1967-80, Searight Bapt. Ch., Dozier, Ala., 1980—; acct. C.G. Tomberlin, M.D., Andalusia, 1985—. Mem. bd. regents Liberty U., Lynchburg, Va. Home: 407 Lakeview Dr Andalusia AL 36420-3542 Office: PO Box 486 Andalusia AL 36420-1209 *In Him, we live and move and have our being. Therefore, my heart's desire is to honor Christ in all things, for He is the way, the truth, and the life.*

PATTERSON, ELAINE WILCOX, art educator; b. Newburgh, NY, Nov. 16, 1948; d. William Thomas and Julia B. Wilcox; m. Russell Saunders Patterson, Dec. 23, 1974; children: John Russell, Heath Tyler. BA English Art, Delta State Univ., 1970. Nat. bd. cert. tchr. 2004. Mutal funds liaison Merrill Lynch, Memphis, 1969—71; flight attentant Delta Airlines, Memphis, 1971—74; adminstr. asst. Pikeville Coll./Tchr. Corps, Pikeville, Ky., 1974—79; art tchr. East Jr. HS, Gaffney, SC, 1981—86, W.C. Friday Jr. HS, Dallas, NC, 1986—93; missionary Honduras Bapt. Med. Dental Mission, Tegucigalpa, Honduras, 1992—99; tchr. Forestview HS, Gastonia, NC, 1999—. Presenter NC Art Educators Assn., 2002—. Various local and state level exhbns., 1999—. Sun. sch. tchr. East Bapt. Ch., Gastonia, NC, 1999—, choir mem., 1999—, banner ministry dir., 1999—. Named Outstanding Young Woman of the Yr., Tchr. of Yr., W.C. Friday Jr. HS, 1992. So. Bapt. Office: Forestview HS 5545 Union Rd Gastonia NC 28056

PATTERSON, ELIZABETH C., choir director; b. Lakeland, Fla., Mar. 1, 1938; d. Jewell King Patterson and Loreta Marie Woodruff; m. Richard Pugsley; children: Richard Pugsley, Wendy Saran. B, 1960; MusM, Milliken U., 1962; postgrad., Cambridge U., Eng. Dir. Gloriae Dei Cantores, Orleans, Mass., 1988—. CEO Paraclete Press, Brewster, Mass., 1983—90, cons., 1990—. Co-author: (book) The Sound Eternal, 1987. Prioress Cmty. of Jesus Inc., 1990—. Mem.: NARAS, Am. Choral Dirs. Assn. Avocations: needlepoint, knitting, painting, sewing. Office: Gloriae Dei Cantores PO Box 2831 11 Bayview Dr Orleans MA 02653

PATTERSON, ELIZABETH JOHNSTON, retired congresswoman; b. Columbia, SC, Nov. 18, 1939; d. Olin DeWitt and Gladys (Atkinson) Johnston; m. Dwight Fleming Patterson, Jr., Apr. 15, 1967; children: Dwight Fleming, Olin DeWitt, Catherine Leigh. BA, Columbia Coll., 1961; postgrad. in polit. sci., U. S.C., 1961, 62, 64; LLD (hon.), Columbia Coll., 1987; D Pub. Svc. (hon.), Converse Coll., 1989, M in Liberal Arts, 1999; LLD (hon.), Wofford Coll., 1999. Pub. affairs officer Peace Corps, Washington, 1962-64, VISTA, OEO, Washington, 1965-66; D Pub. Svc. Head Start and VISTA, OEO, Columbia, 1966-67; tri-county dir. Head Start, Piedmont Community Actions, Spartanburg, SC, 1967-68; mem. Spartanburg County Coun., 1975-76, S.C. State Senate, 1979-86, 100th-102nd Congresses from 4th S.C. dist., 1987-93; dir. continuing edn., converse II program Converse Coll., 1993—2003; ret. Adj. prof. Spartanburg Meth. Coll., 1993—2001. Trustee Wofford Coll., 1978—90, Columbia Coll., 1991—2003, Spartanburg Meth. Coll., 2004—; pres. Spartanburg Dem. Women, 1968; v.p. Spartanburg County Dem. party, 1968—70, sec., 1970—75, pres., 2004—; bd. dirs. S.C. Ind. Colls. and Univs., 1995—99, Charles Lea Ctr., 1978, Spartanburg Coun. on Aging; chmn., bd. dirs. Bethlehem Cmty. Ctr., 1998—. Mem.: Bus. and Profl. Women's Club, Alpha Kappa Gamma. Democrat. Methodist. E-mail: lizjpatterson@charter.net.

PATTERSON, EUGENE CORBETT, retired editor, publishing executive; b. Valdosta, Ga., Oct. 15, 1923; s. William C. and Annabel (Corbett) P.; m. Mary Sue Carter, Aug. 19, 1950; 1 child, Mary Patterson Fausch. Student, North Ga. Coll., Dahlonega, 1940-42; AB in Journalism, U. Ga., 1943; LL.D., Tusculum Coll., 1965, Harvard U., 1969, Duke U., 1978, Stetson U., 1984, Ind. U., 1990; Litt.D., Emory U., 1966, Oglethorpe Coll., 1966, Tuskegee U., 1966, Roanoke Coll., 1968, Mercer U., 1968, Eckerd Coll., 1977, U. South Fla., 1986, Dillard U., 1992, Colby Coll., 1994, North Ga. Coll. & State U., 1999. Reporter Temple (Tex.) Daily Telegram and Macon (Ga.) Telegraph, 1947-48; mgr. for S.C. United Press, 1948-49, N.Y. night bur. mgr. NYC, 1949-53, mgr. London bur., also chief corr. U.K., 1953-56; v.p., exec. editor Atlanta Journal-Constitution, 1956-60; editor Atlanta Constitution, 1960-68; mng. editor Washington Post, 1968-71; prof. polit. sci. Duke U., 1971-72; editor, pres. St. Petersburg (Fla.) Times, 1972-84, chmn., chief exec. officer, 1978-88, editor emeritus, 1988—; editor, pres. Congl. Quar., Washington, 1972-86, chmn., chief exec. officer, 1978-88. Chmn. bd., chief exec. officer Fla. Trend mag., 1980-88, Ga. Trend mag., 1984-88, Ariz. Trend mag., 1986-88, Governing mag., 1987-88, Modern Graphic Arts, Inc., 1978-88, Poynter Inst. Media Studies, 1978-88, Poynter Fund, 1978-88. Author: The Changing South of Gene Patterson, 2002. Vice chmn. U.S. Civil Rights Commn., 1964-68; mem. Pulitzer Prize Bd., 1973-84; trustee ASNE Found., 1981-84, U. Ga. Found., 1982-88, North Ga. Coll. Found., 1991-93, Am. Press Inst., Reston, Va., 1983-88, Duke U., 1988-94, Fla. Bar Found., 1992-93, LeRoy Collins Ctr. for Pub. Policy, 1990-93. Decorated Silver Star, Bronze Star with oak leaf cluster in 10th Armored Divsn., Gen. Patton's 3rd Army; recipient Pulitzer prize for editl. writing Columbia U., 1967, William Allen White Nat. Citation award U. Kans., 1980, Elijah Parish Lovejoy award Colby Coll., 1994; inducted into Fla. Newspaper Hall of Fame Fla. Press Assn., 1997. Fellow Soc. Profl. Journalists; mem. Am. Soc. Newspaper Editors (pres. 1977-78), St. Petersburg Yacht Club. Home: Snell Isle 1967 Brightwaters Blvd NE Saint Petersburg FL 33704-3007 E-mail: Ecp1015@aol.com.

PATTERSON, GARY, college football coach; b. Larned, Kans., Feb. 13, 1960; m. Kelsey Patterson; children: Josh, Cade, Blake. BS in Phys. Edn., Kans. State, 1983; MEd, Tenn. Tech., 1984. Grad. asst. Kans. State, 1982; linebackers coach Tenn. Tech., 1983—84, Univ. Calif.-Davis, 1986, Pitts. State, Kans., 1988; defensive coord. Cal Lutheran, 1987, Sonoma State, Calif., 1989—91; secondary coach Utah State, 1992—94, Navy, 1995; defensive coord., safeties coach New Mexico, 1996—97, TCU, 1998—2000, head football coach, 2000—. Office: TCU Athletics PO Box 297600 Fort Worth TX 76129

PATTERSON, JAMES BRENDAN, JR., writer, former advertising executive; b. Newburgh, NY, Mar. 22, 1947; s. Charles H. and Isabelle (Morris) P. BA, Manhattan Coll., 1969; MA, Vanderbilt U., 1970. With J. Walter Thompson Co., NYC, 1971—96; chmn. J. Walter Thompson U.S., 1990—96. Author: (children's books) santaKid, 2004, Maximum Ride: The Angel Experiment, 2005, Maximum Ride: School's Out-Forever, 2006, Maximum Ride: Saving the World and other Extreme Sports, 2007, (novels) The Thomas Berryman Number, 1976 (Edgar Allen Poe award Mystery Writers Am.), Season of the Machete, 1977, The Jericho Commandment, 1979, Virgin, 1980, Black Market, 1986, The Midnight Club, 1988, Along Came a Spider, 1992, Kiss the Girls, 1995, Hide and Seek, 1996, Jack and Jill, 1996, Miracle on the 17th green, 1996, See How They Run, 1997, Cat and Mouse, 1997, When the Wind Blows, 1998, Pop! Goes the Weasel, 1999, Black Friday, 2000, Cradle and All, 2000, Roses are Red, 2000, 1st to Die, 2001, Suzanne's Diary for Nicholas, 2001, Violets are Blue, 2001, 2nd Chance, 2002, The Beach House, 2002, Four Blind Mice, 2002, The Jester, 2003, The Lake House, 2003, The Big Bad Wolf, 2003, 3rd Degree, 2004, Sam's Letters To Jennifer, 2004 (Publishers Weekly Bestseller), London Bridges, 2004, Honeymoon, 2005 (NY Times Bestseller); co-author (with Maxine Paetro) 4th of July, 2005 (Publishers Weekly Bestseller); author Lifeguard, 2005, Mary, Mary, 2005, The 5th Horsemen, 2006, Beach Road, 2006, Judge & Jury, 2006, Cross, 2006, Step on a Crack, 2007; co-author (with Maxine Paetro) The 6th Target, 2007. Recipient 6 Clio awards, 1983; recipient Effie awards, 1983. Mem. Phi Beta Kappa. Mailing: c/o Author Mail Hachette Book Group USA 237 Park Ave New York NY 10017 *

PATTERSON, JAMES RANDOLPH, physician; b. Lancaster, Pa., Jan. 30, 1942; m. Linda Lewis Patterson, Nov. 22, 1969. AB, U. Pa., 1964; MD, Columbia U., 1968. Diplomate Nat. Bd. Med. Examiners, Am. Bd. Internal Medicine, Subsplty. of Pulmonary Disease. Pulmonary and critical care specialist The Oreg. Clinic, Portland, 1975—; clin. prof. medicine Oreg. Health Scis. U., Portland, 1978—. Mem. Am. Bd. Internal Medicine, Phila., 1995—, sec.-treas., 2002--; trustee Collins Med. Trust, Portland, Oreg., 1992—, chair subsplty. bd. pulmonary disease, 1998-2002. Contbr. numerous articles to profl. jours. Recipient Class of 1964 award U. Pa., Van Loan award Am. Lung Assn. Oreg., 1990, Meritorious Achievement award Oreg. Health Scis. U., 1991; named Class Pres. Coll. Physicians and Surgeons of Columbia U., 1968, Tchr. of Yr. Providence Med. Ctr., Portland, Oreg., 1976, Internist of Yr., 1983, Best Doctors in Am., 1992—, Consumers Guide to Top Doctors, 2002-. Mem. AMA, Am. Thoracic Soc., Am. Coll. Chest Physicians, Oreg. Lung Assn., North Pacific Soc. of Internal Medicine, Pacific Interurban Clin. Club, Multnomah County Med. Soc., Oreg. Med. Assn., Oreg. Soc. Critical Care Medicine. Office: The Oregon Clinic 1111 NE 99th St Ste 200N Portland OR 97220 Office Phone: 503-963-3030. Business E-Mail: jpatterson@orclinic.com.

PATTERSON, JAN EVANS, epidemiologist, educator; b. Ft. Worth, May 13, 1956; d. C. Wayne and Zona (Horn) Evans; m. Thomas F. Patterson, June 22, 1985. BA, Hardin-Simmons U., 1978; MD, U. Tex., 1982. Diplomate Am. Bd. Internal Medicine, Am. Bd. Infectious Diseases. Asst. prof. medicine and lab. medicine Yale U. Sch. Medicine, New Haven, 1988-92; assoc. prof. medicine and pathology Health Sci. Ctr. U. Tex., San Antonio, 1993—99, prof. medicine and pathology, assoc. chair medicine, 1999—2005, prof. medicine and pathology, vice chair medicine, 2005—06, prof. medicine and pathology, interim chair medicine, 2006—; chief med. svc. Audie Murphy Vets. Hosp., 2004—06. Hosp. epidemiologist Univ. Health Sys., San Antonio, 1993-2005, Audie Murphy Meml. Vets. Hosp., San Antonio, 1993-95, S. Tex. Vets. Healthcare System, San Antonio and Kerrville, 1995-2005. Contbr. articles to profl. jours. Fellow ACP, Infectious Disease Soc. Am.; mem. Soc. Hosp. Epidemiologists, Am. Soc. Tropical Medicine and Hygiene, Exec. Leadership in Academic Medicine, Alpha Omega Alpha Office: Health Sci Ctr U Tex Divsn Infectious Diseases 7703 Floyd Curl Dr San Antonio TX 78284-6200 Office Phone: 210-567-4810. Business E-Mail: pattersonj@uthscsa.edu.

PATTERSON, JIM, economist, writer; b. Ft. Belvoir, Va., Jan. 1, 1955; s. James G. and Helen L. Patterson; m. Sheryl Rene Alexander (div.); children: James H., Alexandra Baker. BS in Econs., Auburn U., 1977, MS in Econs., 1980. Economist Dept. Agrl. Econs., Auburn, Ala., 1978—80; sys. analyst Ind. Employment Security Divsn., Indpls., 1981—84; economist /statistician U.S. Dept. of Commerce, 1984—87; sr. economist USDA, 1987—92, diplomat/fgn. svc. officer, 1992—98; freelance writer, 1999—. Prof. econs. Grad. Sch., USDA, 1989—91; adj. prof. econs. No. Va. C.C., Woodbridge, 1987; instr., cons. mktg. Fairfax County Adult Edn. Dept., Va., 1985—87. Author: (newspaper column) Washington Scene, 1995; contbr. articles to mags. Mem. Fed. GLOBE; mem. nat. adv. com. Lillian Gish Theater, Bowling Green State U.; coord. USDA AIDS Walk, Wash., 1994. Named one of Outstanding Young Men of Am., 1989; recipient Spl. Svc. award, US Dept. Commerce, 1986, Productivity award, 1987, Performance award, 1989, Presdl. Point of Light award, USDA, 1992, certs. from, EEO award. Mem.: GLAAD, Nat. Book Critics Cir., Nat. Lesbian & Gay Journalist Assn., Integrity, William J. Clinton Found., Gerald R. Ford Found., Am. Foreign Svc. Assn., Nat. Gay & Lesbian Task Force, Rock & Roll Hall Fame & Mus., Alpha Zeta (sec., treas., VP 1988—92). Episcopalian. Achievements include being profiled in New York Times, Wall Street Journal, The Washington Times, American Writer and The Foreign Service Journal. Avocations: travel, writing, reading.

PATTERSON, JOHN DE LA ROCHE, JR., lawyer; b. Schenectady, NY, July 8, 1941; s. John de la Roche Sr. and Jane C. (Clay) P.; m. Michele F. Demarest, Nov. 28, 1987; children: Daniel C., Sara R., Amy C. BA, Johns Hopkins U., 1963; LLB, Harvard U., 1966. Bar: Mass. 1968. Vol. Peace Corps, Chad, 1966-67; assoc. Foley Hoag LLP, Boston, 1967-73, ptnr., 1974—, mem. exec. com., 1989-97. Chmn. Kodaly Ctr. Am. Inc., Newton, Mass., 1977-87. Mem. ABA, Boston Bar Assn. Democrat. Avocations: sailing, tennis, travel, reading. Office: Foley Hoag LLP 155 Seaport Blvd Boston MA 02210- Office Phone: 617-832-1144. Business E-Mail: jpatterson@FoleyHoag.com.

PATTERSON, JOHN MALCOLM, judge; b. Goldville, Ala., Sept. 27, 1921; s. Albert Love and Agnes Louise (Benson) P.; m. Florentine M. Sawyers, Oct. 17, 1975; children— Albert L., Barbara Louise. JD, U. Ala., 1949. Bar: Ala. bar 1949. Practiced in, Phenix City, 1949-51, 53-55; atty. gen., securities commr. State of Ala., 1955-59; gov. Ala., 1959-63; practice law Montgomery, Ala., 1963-84; judge Ala. Ct. Criminal Appeals, 1984-97, part-time judge, 1997—. Chief judge Ct. of the Judiciary, 1989-97; cattle farmer. Bd. editors: Ala. Law Review, 1948-49. Chmn. bd. Lyman WArd Mil. Acad. Served to maj., F.A. AUS, 1940-45; maj. 1951-53. Nominated one of 10 outstanding young men of U.S., 1956, one of four outstanding young men of Ala. Jr. C. of C. Mem. ABA, Ala. Bar Assn., VFW, Am. Legion. Farrar Order of Jurisprudence, Ala. Acad. Honor, Alpha Tau Omega, Phi Alpha Delta, Sigma Delta Kappa, Phi Eta Sigma, Omicron Delta Kappa. Office: PO Box 301555 Montgomery AL 36130-1555

PATTERSON, KATHERYN CLEWS, lawyer; b. Glen Cove, NY, Jan. 29, 1954; AB with distinction, in comm. & polit. sci., Stanford U., 1974; JD cum laude, Harvard Law Sch., 1977. Bar: N.Y. 1978. Assoc. Coudert Bros., NYC, 1977—85, ptnr., 1986—96; bd. mem. NYC Campaign Fin. Bd., NYC, 1996—. Co-editor, contbg. author: A Practical Guide to Letters of Credit, 1990. Trustee Juilliard Sch., Trinity Sch.; vol. Am. Mus. of Natural Hist. Mem. ABA, Phi Beta Kappa, NYC Charter Revision Commn., 2003. Office: NYC Campaign Fin Bd 40 Rector St 7th Fl New York NY 10006 Office Phone: 212-306-7100. Office Fax: 212-306-7143.

PATTERSON, KENNETH, nurse; b. Milledgeville, Ga., Dec. 14, 1968; s. William Thomas and Dotsie Mae Patterson; m. Daphne Marie Wise; children: Alexander, Kendra, DeAmber, Lucas, Ryan. Diploma in practical nursing, Macon Tech. Inst., 2003; BA in criminal justice, Mercer U., 2005. Lic. LPN. LPN, charge nurse Ctrl. State Hosp., Milledgeville, Ga., 1993—96, Macon Manor Nursing Rehab, Macon, Ga., 1996—99; resident care coord. Bel Arbor Nursing Ctr., Macon, Ga., 2000—02; intake coord. Regency Hosp. Co., Macon, 2004—05; dir. admissions Macon Manor Nursing Rehab, Macon, Ga., 2005—. Cons. Tri State Health Corp., Macon, Ga., 2005—. Bd. mem. Family Counseling Ctr., Macon, Ga., 2005—; vol. Vista Care Hospice, Macon, Ga., 2005—; co-coord. Mentor Leadership Program, Ballard Mid. Macon, Ga., 2001—02. Mem.: NAACP Mercer Chapter. Republican. Bapt. Avocation: youth mentoring. Home: 2858 Hwy 49 W Haddock GA 31033 Office: Macon Manor Nursing and Rehab 4373 Houston Ave Macon GA 31206 Office Phone: 478-784-1500. Office Fax: 478-784-1528. E-mail: pdaphne2@aol.com.

PATTERSON, M. BRETT, musician; b. Vancouver, BC, Canada, July 4, 1985; s. Myron B. and Robin L. Patterson. MusB, Pacific Luth. U., Tacoma, 2007. Resident asst., head resident asst. Pacific Luth. U., Tacoma, 2004—07. Organist recitalist, various cities, 2003—; choir coun. mem. Choir of the West Pacific Luth. U., Tacoma, 2004—05, u. chorale sect. leader, 2006—07; choir sect. leader St. Mary's Episcopal Ch., Lakewood, Wash., 2006—07. Singer: (PBS TV spl.) A Cathedral Christmas, (choir CD) Let the Bright Seraphim, A Radiant Light; singer: (featured soloist) (TV broadcast) Music and the Spoken Word. Vol. benefit organ recital Bountiful Food Bank, Utah, 2005; vol. Primary Children's Med. Ctr., Salt Lake City, 2002—03; weather broadcaster KCNS TV-Pacific Luth. U., Tacoma. Recipient President's Student Svc. award, Pres. of the US, 2001; scholar Roy A. Johnson scholar, Tucson AGO Chpt., 2005, David P. Dahl Organ scholar, Pacific Luth. U. Music Dept., 2005—07. Mem.: Nat. Assn. Pastoral Musicians, Am. Guild Organists. Avocations: travel, reading. Home: 2036 Kensington Ave Salt Lake City UT 84108 Home Phone: 253-820-4264. Personal E-mail: diapason16@rbmp.aros.net.

PATTERSON, NEAL L., information systems company executive; BS in Fin., Okla. State U., MBA. Sys. cons., mgr. Arthur Andersen & Co., Kansas City, Mo.; co-founder, CEO, chmn. bd. dirs. Cerner Corp., Kansas City, Mo., 1979—. Trustee Midwest Rsch. Inst.; mem. steering com. Coun. Growing Cos. Named Entrepreneur of Yr., Ernst & Young, 1991. Mem. Health Execs. Network. Office: Cerner Corp 2800 Rockcreek Pkwy Ste 601 Kansas City MO 64117-2521

PATTERSON, NICHOLAS NOEL, language educator, journalism educator; s. Howard Russell Patterson and Marjorie Magdalene Striegel; m. Barbara Lynn Renz, Aug. 14, 1971; children: Trent Alexis, Elizabeth Ann Downend. BA in Spanish, Grinnell Coll., Iowa, 1962; MEd, U. Pa., Phila., 1967; MA in Spanish, U. Kans., Lawrence, 1972. Lic. Tchr. Iowa, 1973. Peace corps vol. English instr. U. Andes, Bogota, Colombia, 1963—65; Spanish tchr. Sch. Dist. Lower Merion Twp., Rosemont, Pa., 1967—68; tchr. intern Sch. Dist. Phila., 1967—68, Spanish and bilingual-bicultural tchr., 1968—69, Spanish tchr., 1972—73; asst. instr. Spanish U. Kans., Lawrence, 1969—72; lectr. Spanish for med. personnel and Chicano lit. Marycrest Coll., Davenport, 1978—92; Spanish and English tchr. Davenport Cmty. Schs., Iowa, 1973—; lectr. comml. Spanish John Deere Internat., Moline, Ill., 1980; tchr. creative writing and Spanish Miss. Bend Area Edn. Agy., Bettendorf, Iowa, 1993—; cons. for Spanish textbook McDougall Littell, 1999; Spanish textbook reader McDougal Littell, 2005; Spanish and edn. instr. St. Ambrose U., Davenport, 2002—05; all cultural achievement journalism program tchr. U. Iowa, Davenport, Iowa, 2002—; lang. arts and social studies tchr. Sch. Dist. Cedar Rapids. Spkr. on multilingual pub. and judge Journalism Edn. Assn., Nat. Scholastic Press Assn. Conv., Chgo., Atlanta, San Diego, 2004—05; environ. devel., rsch. and vol. tchr. at one-room elem. schoolhouse in a tropical rain forest Assn. Ambiental VIDA, Playa Hermosa, Costa Rica, 2004; coord. for student travel to Spain and Morocco Davenport Ctrl. HS, 2004; blackhawk journalism exch. program in Brazil, Argentina, and Uruguay Davenport Cmty. Sch. Dist., Brazil, 2006; mentor youth inst. World Food Prize, Des Moines, 2006. Fellow King Juan Fellowship, Fundacion Ortega y Gassett, Spain, 1994; Grant, US Office Edn., 1968, Advanced Rsch. Grant, Mellon

Found., 1980, Fellowship for fgn. lang. tchrs. in the HS, Rockefeller Found., 1986, Fellowship, Iowa Carver Trust, 1991. Mem.: NEA, Iowa State Edn. Assn., Am. Assn. Tchrs. Spanish and Portuguese, Am. Coun. on Tchg. Fgn. Langs. Office: Davenport Ctr HS 1120 Main St Davenport IA 52803 Office Phone: 563-323-9900. Office Fax: 563-324-9129. Business E-Mail: pattersonn@davenportschools.org.

PATTERSON, OSCAR, III, academic administrator; b. July 25, 1945; s. Oscar Jr. and Frances (Killian) P.; m. Kathy E. Gibson, June 6, 1966 (div. Apr. 1979); 1 child, Elizabeth Anne Patterson Cassel; m. Julie Ann Holmes, Dec. 28, 1990. BA, Pfeiffer U., Misenheimer, NC, 1967; MFA, U. Ga., Athens, 1973; PhD, U. Tenn., 1982. Asst. prof. architecture and fine arts Auburn (Ala.) U., 1972-75; chairperson BFA in Theatre program Western Carolina U., Cullowhee, NC, 1975-79; dir. telecom. U. NC, Pembroke, NC, 1984—98; chair comm. and visual arts U. North Fla., Jacksonville, Fla., 1998—2006, prof. comm., 2006—. Juvenile probation officer Cleveland Ct. Sys., Shelby, NC, 1967-68; gen. mgr., news dir. WNCP-TV, NC, 1984-98. Contbr. articles to profl. jours.; host pub. tv program, 1989-98. Served US Army, 1968-75, Vietnam. Mem. AEJMC, Soc. Profl. Journalists, Phi Kappa Phi. Republican. Avocations: historical reenactment, beach exploration. Home: 248 Patrick Mill Cir Ponte Vedra Beach FL 32082-4013 Personal E-mail: opatters@comcast.net. Business E-Mail: opatters@unf.edu.

PATTERSON, PEYTON R., bank executive; b. Weisbaden, Germany; m. Thomas Patterson; 1 child. Degree in Polit. Sci., European Inst. Study, 1977; AB in Polit. Sci., Kenyon Coll., 1978; MBA in Mktg., George Washington U., 1983. From asst. v.p. group product mgr. retail deposit products to v.p. Corestates Fin. Corp., Phila., 1983—85, v.p., 1985—89; from v.p. group product mgr. to sr. v.p. Chemical Banking Corp., NYC, 1989—90, sr. v.p., 1990—95; sr. v.p., dir. nat. fin. svcs. group Chase Manhattan Bank, NYC, 1995—96; exec. v.p., gen. mgr. consumer fin. svcs. Dime Bank Corp., NYC, 1996—2001; chmn., pres., CEO New Haven Savings Bank (now NewAlliance Bancshares, Inc.), 2002—. Co-chmn. Greater N.Y. March of Dimes; mem. Regional Leadership Coun., Arts Coun. Greater New Haven; bd. dirs. United Way. Named One of 25 Most Powerful Women in Banking, US Banker mag., 2003, 2004, 2005; named one of 25 Women to Watch, 2006; Rockefeller fellow, 2000—01, Henry Crown fellow, Aspen Inst. Office: NewAlliance Bancshares 195 Church St New Haven CT 06510 *

PATTERSON, P(ICKENS) ANDREW, lawyer; b. Cotton Plant, Ark., Aug. 1, 1944; s. Pickens Andrew and Willie Mae (Miller) P.; m. Gloria Neltine Peebles, Nov. 25, 1967; children— Pickens Andrew, Staci Elizabeth. B.A., Fisk U., 1965; J.D., Harvard U., 1968. Bar: Ga. 1969, N.C. 1978, U.S. Dist. Ct. (no. dist.) Ga. 1969, U.S. Dist. Ct. (mid. dist.) N.C. 1978, U.S. Ct. Appeals (11th cir.) 1983. Vice pres. Urban East Housing Consl. Atlanta, 1968-69; mng. atty. Atlanta Legal Aid, 1968-70; sr. ptnr. Patterson, Parks, Jackson & Howell, Atlanta, 1970-77; atty. adviser HUD, Greensboro, N.C., 1977-81; exec. v.p. Arrington, Patterson & Thomas, P.C., Atlanta, 1982—; ptnr. Thomas, Kennedy, Sampson & Patterson, 1985—. Pres. Atlanta Legal Aid Soc., 1976, Central Carolina Legal Services, Greensboro, 1980; chair State Bd. Bar Examiners. Co-author pamphlet. Mem. Atlanta Charter Study Commn., 1972; bd. dirs. Louisville Presbyn. Theol. Sem., 1983—86, Heritage Fund, Atlanta Med. Assn., 2006; trustee Fisk U., Nashville. Recipient Key to City Atlanta, 1972, plaque awards Atlanta Legal Aid Soc., 1977, Central Carolina Legal Services, 1981, Cert. of Spl. Achievement, Office of Gen. Counsel, HUD, 1980. Mem. Nat. Bar Assn., State Bar Ga., N.C. Bar Assn., Atlanta Bar Assn., Gate City Bar Assn., Alpha Phi Alpha, Sigma Pi Phi. Democrat. Methodist. Home: 3905 Somerled Trl Atlanta GA 30349-2035 Office: 3355 Main St College Park GA 30331 Home Phone: 404-763-1521; Office Phone: 404-688-4503. Business E-Mail: pa.patterson@tksp.com.

PATTERSON, RICHARD NORTH, writer, lawyer; b. Berkeley, Calif., Feb. 22, 1947; s. Richard Wallace and Marjorie Frances (North) P.; children: Shannon Heath, Brooke North, Katherine Amber, Adam Chandler, Chase Kenyon. BA History, Ohio Wesleyan U., 1968; JD, Case Western Reserve, 1971. Bar: Ohio, 1971, D.C., 1973, Ala., 1975, Calif., 1984. Asst. atty. gen. State of Ohio, 1971-73; with divsn. enforcement SEC, Washington, 1973-75, San Francisco, Calif., 1878-81; assoc. atty. Berkowitz, Lefkovits & Patrick, Birmingham, Ala., 1975-77, ptnr., 1978; assoc. McCutchen, Doyle, Brown & Enerson, San Francisco, Calif., 1985-87, ptnr., 1987-93, of counsel, 1993-94. Author: The Lasko Tangent, 1979, The Outside Man, 1981, Escape the Night, 1983, Private Screening, 1985, Degree of Guilt, 1993, Eyes of a Child, 1995, The Final Judgement, 1995, Silent Witness, 1997, No Safe Place, 1998, Dark Lady, 1999, Protect and Defend, 2000, Balance of Power, 2003, Conviction, 2005, Exile, 2007, The Race, 2007. Chmn. Common Cause; bd. mem. Brady Campaign Nat. Partnership for Women and Families, Ohio Wesleyan U. Named Man of Yr., WWRAP, 2001; recipient Edgar Allan Poe award for best 1st novel, Mystery Writers Am., 1979, Grand Prix de Literateur Policiere, 1995, Pres.'s award for Disting. Alumni, Case Western Res. U., 1997, Maggie award, Planned Parenthood, 2001.

PATTERSON, ROBERT ARTHUR, physician, health care consultant, retired health care company executive, retired air force officer; b. Palestine, Ill., Sept. 3, 1915; s. Robert Bruce and Nera (McColpin) P.; m. Judith Scheirer, May 15, 1961; children: Mary Kay, Elaine Alice Mills, Robert Arthur II, Victoria Patterson Goodrum. Student, U. Ill., 1933-35; MD, U. Louisville, 1939. Diplomate: aerospace medicine Am. Bd. Preventive Medicine. Intern Detroit Receiving Hosp., 1939-40; joined Mich. N.G., 1940; commd. USAAF, 1946; advanced through grades to lt. gen. USAF, 1972; rated chief flight surgeon and command pilot; assigned U.S. and ETO, 1940-45; assigned U.S., Spain, Japan, Philippines, 1945-63; dep. dir. plans and hospitalization Office Surgeon Gen., USAF, Washington, 1963-65, dir. plans and hospitalization, 1965-68; surgeon Hdqrs. USAFE, Lindsey Air Sta., Germany, 1968-71, Hdqrs. SAC, Offutt AFB, 1971-72; surgeon gen. USAF, 1972-75, ret., 1975; health care cons. Arlington, Va., 1975; sr. v.p. sci. affairs Baxter Travenol Labs., Inc., Deerfield, Ill., 1976-86, health care cons., 1987—. Decorated D.S.M. with oak leaf cluster, Legion of Merit with two oak leaf clusters, Air Force Commendation medal; recipient citation of honor Air Force Assn., citation of distinction Fed. Hosp. Execs., citation of distinction Am. Hosp. Assn. Fellow Am. Coll. Preventive Medicine, Aerospace Medicine Assn., Am. Coll. Physician Execs. (founder); mem. Assn. Mil. Surgeons (pres. 1972), AMA, Am. Acad. Med. Dirs., Ret. Officers Assn., Soc. Mil. Cons. to Armed Forces, Soc. Armed Forces Med. Labs. Scis., NIH Alumni, U. Ill. Alumni Assn., Aircraft Owners and Pilots Assn., Order Daedalians, Assn. for Advancement of Med. Instrumentation, Exptl. Aircraft Assn., Deutsch Kurzhaar Verband, N.A. Versatile Hunting Dog Assn., Uniformed Services U. Health Scis. Alumni Assn., Air Safety Found., Mid-America (Chgo.), Cen. Fla. Conservation and Hunt (Lake Wales, Fla.), Yacht and Country (bd. govs., 1993-95, pres., 1996-97, Stuart, Fla.), Sunshine Gun, Yacht (Stuart), Willoughby Golf Club (Stuart). Home and Office: Yacht & Country Club 3474 SE Fairway E Stuart FL 34997-6160

PATTERSON, ROBERT EDWARD, lawyer; b. LA, Sept. 14, 1942; s. Ellis Elwood and Helen (Hjelte) Patterson; m. Christina Balboni Patterson, Oct. 2, 1971; 1 child, Victor Ellis. BA, UCLA, 1964; JD, Stanford U., 1972, grad. bus. exec. program, 1986. Bar: Calif. 1972. Sr. counsel Squire Sanders & Dempsey LLP, Palo Alto, Calif., 1972—. Bd. dirs. Peninsula Equity Ptnrs., Ctr. Pvt. Equity; bd. dirs. Amos Tuck Sch. Dartmouth Coll.; bd. dirs. Sumida Corp., Synzyme Techs., LLC, Calif. State Pks. Found., Acuity Ventures, EARN Corp., Inst. Tech. Innovation-Energy, Scotland, Calif. Airlines, Greater China Project Stanford Project Regions Innovation and Entrepreneurship. Bd. dirs. John Ernest Found. Lt. comdr. USN, 1964—69. Vis. scholar, Amos Tuck Sch. Dartmouth Coll., 1998. Mem.: Bohemian Club, Menlo Circus Club, Palo Alto Club, Band of Angels. Democrat. Office: Squire Sanders & Dempsey LLP 600 Hansen Way Ste 100 Palo Alto CA 94304-1043 Office Phone: 650-856-6500. Business E-Mail: rpatterson@ssd.com.

PATTERSON, ROBERT PORTER, JR., federal judge; b. NYC, July 11, 1923; s. Robert Porter and Margaret (Winchester) P.; m. Bevin C. Daly, Sept. 15, 1956; children: Anne, Robert, Margaret, Paul, Katherine. AB, Harvard U., 1947; LLB, Columbia U., 1950. Bar: N.Y. 1951, D.C. 1966. Law clk. Donovan, Leisure, Newton & Lumbard, NYC, 1950-51; asst. counsel N.Y. State Crime Commn. Waterfront Investigation, 1952-53; asst. U.S. atty. Chief of Narcotics Prosecutions and Investigations, 1953-56; asst. counsel Senate Banking and Currency Com., 1954; assoc. Patterson, Belknap, Webb & Tyler, NYC, 1956-60, ptnr., 1960-88; judge U.S. Dist. Ct. (So. Dist.), NY, 1988—98, sr. judge NY, 1998—. Counsel to minority select com. pursuant to house resolution no. 1, Washington, 1967; mem. Senator's Jud. Screening Panel, 1974-88, Gov.'s Jud. Screening Panel, 1975-82, Gov.'s Sentencing Com., 1978-79. Contbr. articles to profl. jours. Chmn. Wm. T. Grant Found., 1974-94, Prisoners' Legal Services N.Y., 1976-88; dir. Legal Aid Soc., 1961-88, pres., 1967-71; chmn. Nat. Citizens for Eisenhower, 1959-60, Scranton for Pres., N.Y. State, 1964; bd. mgrs. Havens Relief Fund Soc., 1994—, Millbrook Sch., 1966-78, Vera Inst. Justice, 1981-99, New Sch. for Social Rsch., 1986-94, George C. Marshall Found., 1987-93; mem. exec. com. Lawyers Com. for Civil Rights Under Law, 1968-88; mem. Goldman Panel for Attica Disturbance, 1972, Temporary Commn. on State Ct. System, 1971-73, Rockefeller U. Council, 1986-88, exec. com. N.Y. Vietnam Vets. Meml. Commn., 1982-85, Mayor's Police Adv. Com., 1985-87. Served to capt. USAAF, 1942-46. Decorated D.F.C. with cluster, Air medal with clusters. Mem. ABA (ho. of dels. 1976-80), N.Y. State Bar Assn. (pres. 1978-79), Assn. Bar City N.Y. (v.p. 1974-75), N.Y. County Lawyers Assn., Am. Law Inst., Am. Judicature Soc. (bd. dirs. 1979). Republican. Episcopalian. Home: Fair Oaks Farm 1657 Route 9D Cold Spring NY 10516-3543 Office: US Dist Ct So Dist NY US Court House 500 Pearl St New York NY 10007-1316

PATTERSON, RONALD R(OY), management consultant; b. Baton Rouge, Mar. 4, 1942; BS, U. Houston, 1965; MS, Trinity U., San Antonio, 1973. Asst. adminstr. U. Tex. Med. Br., Galveston, 1972-75; asst. v.p. Hosp. Affiliates Internat., Nashville, 1975-81; chief oper. officer Affiliated Hosp. Systems, Houston, 1981-82; sr. v.p. Republic Health Corp., Dallas, 1982-88; pres. Miller Patterson Inc., Plano, Tex., 1988-89; ind. healthcare mgmt. cons. Plano, 1989-90; sr. v.p. Harris Meth. Health System, Ft. Worth, 1990-91; exec. v.p., COO Champion Healthcare Corp., Houston, 1991-96; exec. v.p., pres. healthcare ops. Paracelsus Healthcare Corp., Houston, 1996-99; pres. R. Patterson Assocs., 1999—. Bd. dirs. Tarrant County Hosp. Dist., 2002—05, sec., 2002—05; bd. chair Metrowest Health Plan, 2002—04, Tex. Health Facilities Devel. Corp., 2002—05. Fellow Am. Coll. Healthcare Execs. (life), Tex. Hosp. Assn. (vice-chmn. multi-hosp. constituency 1987), Fedn. Am. Health Sys. (bd. govs. 1996-99, bd. dirs., sec. 1997-99). Office: R Patterson Assocs PO Box 489 Jacksboro TX 76458 Office Phone: 817-692-5132.

PATTERSON, SALLY JANE, communications executive, consultant; b. Ontario, Calif., May 28, 1948; d. James Lowell and Barbara Verle (Griffin) Swain; 1 child, Robert Elias Sandoval. BA, Calif. State U., Fullerton, 1970, MA, 1974. Adminstrv. asst. Congressman Jerry Patterson, U.S. House of Reps., Washington, 1978-81; v.p. Pub. Response Assocs., Washington, 1981-87, Hamilton & Staff, Washington, 1987-90; v.p. pub. affairs Planned Parenthood Fedn. of Am., NYC, 1990-93; internat. cons. Mgmt. Sys. Internat., Washington, 1993—; v.p. Wagner & Assocs. Pub. Affairs Cons., Inc., NYC, Washington, 1994-99; pres. Radiant Comms. Inc., 2000—. Cons. Nat. Dem. Inst., Washington, 1994—. Author: Supporting Democracy in The Newly Independent States of The Former Soviet Union, 1994, Women in Government Relations: 20 Years of Vision, Leadership, Education and Networking, 1995, Pursuing a Paradox: Public Attitudes vs. Public Action on Campaign Finance Reform, How does Congress Approach Population and Family Planning Issues?, 1999, Generating Buzz Strategic Communication for Nonprofit Boards, 2006. Bd. dirs Round House Theatre, 2004—, Sewall Belmont House and Mus. Recipient Gold Key award PR Soc. Am., 1992; named one of 74 Women Shaping Am. Politics, Campaigns and Elections, 1993. Mem. NARAL, Women in Govt. Rels., Inc. (disting. mem., chair leader found. 1985-87, v.p. 1987-88, pres. 1988-89), Coun. Excellence in Govt. (prin.), NARAL Found. (bd. 1993-2005, chair 2001-2004, found. bd. 2001—). Democrat. Episcopalian. Office: Radiant Comm Inc 1250 Connecticut Ave NW Ste 200 20036

PATTERSON, SAMUEL C., retired political science professor; b. Omaha, Nov. 29, 1931; s. Robert Foster and Garnet Marie (Jorgensen) P.; m. Suzanne Louise Dean, June 21, 1956; children— Polly Ann, Dean Foster, Grier Edmund. BA, U. S.D., 1953; MS, U. Wis., 1956, PhD, 1959. Asst. prof. polit. sci. Okla. State U., Stillwater, 1959-61; asst. prof. U. Iowa, Iowa City, 1961-64, assoc. prof., 1964-67, prof., 1967-85, Roy J. Carver prof., 1985-86; prof. Ohio State U., Columbus, 1986-98, prof. emeritus, 1998—; ret., 1998. Vis. prof. U. Wis., 1962, U. Okla., 1968-78, U. Essex, Colchester, Eng., 1969-70, U. S.D., 2001. Author: (with others) Representatives and Represented, 1975, A More Perfect Union, 4th edit., 1989; co-author: The Legislative Process in the United States, 4th edit., 1986, Comparing Legislatures, 1979; editor: American Legislative Behavior, 1968; co-editor: Comparative Legislative Behavior: Frontiers of Research, 1972, Handbook of Legislative Research, 1985, Political Leadership in Democratic Societies, 1991, Parliaments in the Modern World, 1994, Great Theatre: The American Congress in the 1990s, 1998, Senates: Bicameralism in the Contemporary World, 1999; editor Am. Jour. Polit. Sci., 1970-73; co-editor Legis. Studies Quar., 1981-85; mng. editor Am. Polit. Sci. Rev., 1985-91. Served with U.S. Army, 1953-55 Recipient Disting. Scholar award Ohio State U., 1990; fellow Social Sci. Rsch. Coun., 1961, 67, Guggenheim, 1984-85; vis. fellow Brookings Instn., 1984-85, Ctr. Advanced Study in Behavioral Scis., 1993-94; Fulbright Bologna chair, 1995. Mem. Am. Polit. Sci. Assn. (Frank J. Goodnow award, 2000), Midwest Polit. Sci. Assn. (pres. 1980-81), Phi Beta Kappa, Phi Kappa Phi, Pi Sigma Alpha. Personal E-mail: patpat851@earthlink.net.

PATTERSON, SCOTT DAVID, lawyer; b. Phila., Feb. 15, 1954; s. Walter Blake Jr. and Rosemary Jeanne (Sheehy) P.; m. Susan Patricia Brestrup, June 27, 1981; children: Julia Connell, Amanda Macaulay. AB magna cum laude, Princeton U., 1974; JD cum laude, Harvard U., 1977. Bar: Pa. 1977, US Ct. Appeals (3d cir.) 1977, US Dist. Ct. (ea. dist.) Pa. 1977, US Dist. Ct. (mid. dist.) Pa. 1988, US Ct. Appeals (4th cir.) 1989. Assoc. Saul, Ewing, Remick & Saul, Phila., 1977-85, ptnr., 1985, Saul, Ewing, Wayne, Pa. Panelist. Pa. Bar Inst. tech. Mem. Healthcare Information Mgmt. Sys. Soc. Mem. ABA, Pa. Bar Assn., Assn. of U Tech. Mgrs. Avocations: computers, photography, hiking, piano, genealogy. Office: Saul Ewing 1200 Liberty Ridge Dr Ste 200 Wayne PA 19087 Office Phone: 610-251-5089. Office Fax: 610-408-4407.

PATTERSON, STEVE, former professional sports team executive; b. Beaver Dam, Wis., Sept. 21, 1957; BBA with honors, U. Tex., 1980, JD, 1984. Bar: Tex. 1984. Gen. mgr., profl. basketball team counsel Houston Rockets, NBA, 1984-89, profl. basketball mktg. exec. group ticket sales, mgr., bus. ops. exec., gen. mgr., 1989-94; pres. profl. hockey team Houston Aeros, 1994-97; pres. Arena Oper. Co., Houston, 1995-99; exec. v.p. Houston NFL Holdings, 1997—2003; pres. Portland Trail Blazers, NBA, Oreg., 2003—07, gen. mgr., 2006—07.

PATTERSON, W. MORGAN, college president; b. New Orleans, Oct. 1, 1925; s. E. Palmer and Jess Margaret (Wood) P.; m. Ernestine North, June 10, 1948; children— W. Morgan, II, Jay North BA, Stetson U., 1950, D.D. (hon.), 1979; M.Div., New Orleans Baptist Theol. Sem., 1953, Th.D., 1956; postdoctoral, Oxford U., 1965-66, 72-73. Prof. ch. history New Orleans Bapt. Theol. Sem., 1956-59; prof. ch. history, David T. Porter prof. ch. history, dir. grad. studies So. Baptist Theol. Sem., Louisville, 1959-76; dean acad. affairs Golden Gate Bapt. Theol. Sem., Mill Valley, Calif., 1976-84; pres. Georgetown Coll., Ky., 1984-91; asst. to pres. Coll. of Ozarks, Mo., 1994—. Vis. prof. Midwestern Bapt. Theol. Sem., Kansas City, Mo., La. Coll., Pineville, 1991—92, Golden Gate Bapt. Theol. Sem., Mill Valley, Calif., 1992—94, 1997, 2003—05, Okla. Bapt. U., 1997, Fla. Bapt. Theol. Coll., 1998—99, New Orleans Bapt. Sem., 1995—96, 1999—2000; vis. scholar Campbellsville U., Ky., 2000—03, 2006, 07; chmn. hist. commn. So. Bapt. Conv., Nashville, 1969—72; honored guest 2d Vatican Coun., Rome, 1965. Author: Baptist Successionism: A Critical View, 1969; co-editor: Professor in the Pulpit, 1963; contbr., editor: Ency. Southern Baptists; book rev. editor Review and Expositor, 1965-70 Served as flight officer USAF, 1943-46 Recipient Disting. Alumnus award Stetson U., 1992, Disting. Svc. award for outstanding contbn. to Bapt. history Hist. Commn., So. Bapt. Conv., 1993; Am. Assn. Theol. Schs. fellow, 1965-66. Mem. Am. Soc. Ch. History, So. Bapt. Hist. Soc. (pres. 1979-80), William H. Whitsitt Bapt. Heritage Soc., Commn. on Bapt. Heritage of Bapt. World Alliance. Avocations: travel, stamp collecting/philately, collecting books. Home: 7 Pierce Dr Novato CA 94947-4450

PATTERSON, WAYNE K., historian, educator; b. Phila., Dec. 20, 1946; s. George M. and Marjorie K. Patterson; m. Marlene B. Patterson, Aug. 13, 1977. BA in History, Swarthmore Coll., 1968; MA in Internat. Rels., U. Pa., 1969, MA in History, 1974, PhD, 1977. From asst. prof. to assoc. prof. history St. Norbert Coll., DePere, Wis., 1977—95, prof. history, 1995—. Vis. prof. history Harvard U., Cambridge, Mass., 2001. Author: The Korean Frontier in America, 1994, The Ilse, 2000, The Koreans in Hawaii, 2003. Mem.: Am. Hist. Assn., Assn. for Asian Studies (com. on Korean studies 1999—2002). Office: St Norbert Coll 100 Grant St De Pere WI 54115 Office Phone: 920-403-3096.

PATTERSON, WILLIAM BROWN, dean, history professor; b. Charlotte, NC, Apr. 8, 1930; s. William Brown and Eleanor Selden (Miller) P.; m. Evelyn Byrd Hawkins, Nov. 27, 1959; children: William Brown Patterson, Evelyn Byrd Donatelli, Lucy Patterson Murray, Emily Patterson Higgs. BA, U. South, 1952; MA, Harvard U., 1954, PhD, 1966, cert. ednl. mgmt., 1982; BA, Oxford U., Eng., 1955, MA, 1959; MDiv., Episc. Div. Sch., Cambridge, Mass., 1958. Ordained to ministry Episcopal Ch. as deacon, 1958, as priest, 1959. Asst. prof. history Davidson (N.C.) Coll., 1963-66, assoc. prof., 1966-76, prof. history, 1976-80, U. of South, Sewanee, Tenn., 1980—2005, dean Coll. Arts and Scis., 1980-91; Francis S. Houghteling prof. hist., 2001. Author: (with others) Discord, Dialogue, and Concord, 1977, This Sacred History: Anglican Reflections for John Booty, 1990, King James VI and I and the Reunion of Christendom, 1997; mem. bd. editors St. Luke's Jour. Theology, Sewanee, 1982-90; contbr. numerous articles to profl. jours. Trustee U. South, 1968-71; mem. internat. adv. com. U. Buckingham, Eng., 1977-93; pres. So. Coll. and Univ. Union; organizer Associated Colls. of South, 1988-89. Danforth Found. grad. fellow, 1952, Mellon Appalachian fellow U. Va., 1992-93, rsch. fellow NEH, 1967, Folger Shakespeare Libr., Washington, 1975, Inst. for Rsch. in Humanities, U. Wis., Madison, 1976, Newberry Libr., Chgo., 1979; Rhodes scholar, 1953. Mem. Am. Hist. Assn., Am. Soc. Ch. History (Albert C. Outler prize for best book in ecumenical ch. history 1999), N.Am. Conf. on Brit. Studies, Eccles. History Soc. Eng., Royal Hist. Soc. Eng., So. Hist. Assn., Soc. for Values in Higher Edn., Episcopal Div. Sch. Alumni/ae Assn. (mem. exec. com. 1984-87), Phi Beta Kappa, Beta Theta Pi. Avocations: gardening, tennis. Home: 195 N Carolina Ave Sewanee TN 37375-2040 Office: U of South Dept History 735 University Ave Sewanee TN 37383-0001 Business E-Mail: bpatters@sewanee.edu.

PATTERSON, WILLIAM S., lawyer; b. Kings Mountain, NC, July 16, 1947; BA, Wake Forest U., 1969; JD with honors, U. N.C., 1973. Bar: N.C. 1973. Staff atty. interpretive divsn. Office Chief Counsel U.S. Dept. Treasury, 1973-75, staff atty. tax ct. litigation divsn., 1975-77; mng. ptnr. Raleigh office Hunton & Williams LLP, NC. Office: Hunton & Williams 1 Hanover Sq Ste 1400 421 Fayetteville St Raleigh NC 27601 Office Phone: 919-899-3022. Office Fax: 919-833-3233. Business E-Mail: bpatterson@hunton.com.

PATTILLO, MANNING MASON CALVERT, academic administrator; b. Charlottesville, Va., Oct. 11, 1919; s. Manning Mason and Margaret (Camblos) P.; m. Martha A. Crawford, June 8, 1946 (dec.); children: Manning Mason III (dec.), Martha Crawford, John Landrum. Student, Johns Hopkins U., 1937-38; BA with highest honors, U. of South, 1941, DCL, 1993; student, U. Calif., Berkeley, 1941—42; AM, U. Chgo., 1947, PhD, 1949; LLD, LeMoyne Coll., 1967, St. John's U., 1968, Oglethorpe U., 1994; LHD, U. Detroit, 1968, Coll. New Rochelle, 1967, Park Coll., 1973; LittD, St. Norbert Coll., 1967. From instr. to assoc. prof. higher edn. U. Chgo., 1949-56; assoc. dir. Lilly Endowment, Inc., Indpls., 1956-60, exec. dir. for edn., 1961-62; dir. Danforth commn. on ch. colls. and univs., 1962-66; assoc. dir. The Danforth Found., 1964-66, v.p., 1966-67; pres. The Found. Center, NYC, 1967-71; adj. prof. NYU, 1968-71; dir. spl. projects U. Rochester, 1972-75; pres. Oglethorpe U., Atlanta, 1975-88, hon. chancellor, 1988—. Cons. in field; tech. asst., then assoc. sec. commn. on colls. and univs. North Ctrl. Assn. Colls. and Secondary Schs., 1948-56; cons. USAF Acad., 1952, Phillips Exeter Acad., 1974; chmn. IBM Incentive awards com., 1970-75; adv. com. Brookings Instn., 1970-71; vis. prof. Inst. Higher Edn., U. Ga., 1988-90; bd. dirs. Fidelity Nat. Bank. Author: (with D.M. Mackenzie) Church Sponsored Higher Education in the United States, 1966, (with D.M. Mackenzie) Eight Hundred Colleges Face the Future, 1965, Private Higher Education in the United States, 1990, The Episcopal Church: Diagnosis and Reform, 1989; contbr. articles to profl. jours. Mem. pres.'s adv. coun. Wellesley Coll., 1969-72; trustee Seabury Press, Japan Internat. Christian U., 1970-72, Le Moyne Coll., 1970-83, Sacred Heart U., 1968-75, U. of South, 1984-88, St. Martin's Episc. Sch.; bd. dirs., interim pres., chmn. Atlanta Coll. Art, 1984-95, Howard Sch.; trustee Greater Rochester Cmty. Found., 1973-75, pres., 1975; trustee, chmn. Nat. Coun. on Philanthropy, 1968-80; trustee, chmn. bd. trustees Park Coll., 1967-74; bd. visitors Evangeline Booth Coll., 1997—; provost St. Mary's Coll. of Md., 1975; bd. visitors Kanuga Confs., Inc.; pres., life trustee Ga. Found. for Ind. Colls., 1977—; chmn. Univ. Center in Ga., 1978-79; pres. Assn. Pvt. Colls. and Univs. of Ga., 1980-81; trustee, chmn. Ga. Spl. Olympics; trustee, mem. exec. com. Nat. Assn. Ind. Colls. and Univs., Ind. Coll. Funds of Am., 1982-86; co-dir. Coll. Ctrs. Network, So. Assn. Colls. and Schs., 1988-96; mem. De Kalb County Cmty. Rels. Commn.; chmn. De Kalb Cmty. Coun. on the Aging; mem. commn. on colls. and steering com. on revision accrediting procedures So. Assn. Colls. and Schs.; vice-chmn bd. and life trustee, Woodruff Arts Ctr.; mem. adv. coun. ARC. With AUS, 1942-46. Mem.: English Speaking Union (dir., pres. br., nat. bd. dirs.), Guild of Scholars, Nat. Assn. Ind. Schs. (bd. dirs.), Nat. Assn. Scholars, Country Day Sch. Headmasters Assn. US (hon.), DeKalb C. of C. (dir., chmn.), Atlanta Hist. Ctr., St. Andrew's Soc., High Mus. Art, Am. Anglican Coun. (chmn. Atlanta chpt.), Phi Beta Kappa Assn. of Atlanta (pres., chmn., fellow nat. soc.), Kappa Sigma, Omicron Delta Kappa. Episcopalian (vestryman, sr. warden, mem. cathedral chpt., diocesan council, standing com.). Clubs: Century (NYC); Capital City. Lodge: Rotary.

PATTIPATI, SREENIVASULU NAIDU, science educator; b. Tirupati, Andhra Pradesh, India, May 21, 1975; s. Krishnaiah Naidu and Chandramma Pattipati; m. Pushpa Pattipati, Apr. 25, 2002; 1 child, Saaketh. PhD, Panjab U., Chandigarh, 2004. Sr. rsch. fellow Panjab U., Chandigarh, India, 2000—02, asst. prof., 2003—. Achievements include research in antipsychotic-induced movement disorders, and cognitive dysfunction: development and validation of Animal models, dopamine-glutamate modulation, excitatory mechanisms and oxidative stress. Office: Univ Inst of Pharm Sci Panjab Univ Chandigarh 160014 India E-mail: psnadiu2004@yahoo.com.

PATTIS, S. WILLIAM, publishing executive; b. Chgo., July 3, 1925; s. William Robert and Rose (Quint) P.; m. Bette Z. Levin, July 16, 1950; children: Mark Robert, Robin Quint Himovitz. BS, U. Ill., 1949; postgrad., Northwestern U., 1949-50. Exec. v.p., pub. United Bus. Publs., 1949-59; chmn., CEO 3M/Pattis, 1959-88; pres. NTC Pub. Group, Lincolnwood, Ill., 1961-96, Next Chapter Holdings, L.P., Highland Park, Ill., 1996—; dir. P-B Comm., Winnetka, Ill., 1978-98; vice-chmn. Profl. Media Group, Norwalk, Conn., 1999—. Bd. dirs. 1st Colonial/Highwood; mem. book and libr. com. USIA, Washington, 1986—89, chmn., 1989—93; mem. exec. com. Pub. Hall of Fame, 1987—2000; chmn. U.S.-USSR Bilateral Media Confs., Washington and Moscow, 1990—91. Author: Opportunities in Advertising Careers, 1984, 1988, 1995, Opportunities in Magazine Publishing Careers, 1992, 2001, VGM Career Planing, 1988, Careers in Advertising, 1996, 2d edit, 2002, 3d edit., 2003, 4th edit., 2004; co-author: Opportunities in Publishing Careers, 1995, 2001. Mem. Pres.'s Coun. Youth Opportunity, 1968-70; bd. dirs. Photography Youth Found., 1968-70, Expt. in Internat. Living, 1970, Inst. Human Creativity, 1983—, Fund for Am.'s Libraries, 1996-99; vice chmn. bd. dirs. Annenberg Ctr. for Health Scis., 1991—, vice chmn., 1996-99; trustee Eisenhower Med. Ctr., Rancho Mirage, Calif., 1989—, exec. com. mem., 1996—, chmn. investment com., 2000-03; trustee Am. Coun. Tchrs. Russian, 1992-96; bd. dirs. Nat. Security Edn. Act, Washington, 1993-94, Knapp Sch. Entrepreneurship, Ill. Inst. Tech., 2005-; bd. dirs. resource bd. Coll Comm. U. Ill., 2006-; lord of manor, Kirkbride, Eng., 1989—. Recipient Human Rels. award Am. Jewish Com., 1971, Paul Simon award Ctrl. States Conf. on Tchg. Fgn. Langs., 1992. Mem. Standard Club (Chgo.), Club Internat. (Chgo.), Northmoor Country Club (Highland Park, Ill.), Tamarisk Country Club (Rancho Mirage). Office: Next Chpt Holdings Port Clinton Sq 600 Central Ave Highland Park IL 60035-3211 Home (Winter): 70843 Tamarisk La Rancho Mirage CA 92270 Office Phone: 847-432-8700. Business E-Mail: bpattis@nextchapterholdings.com.

PATTON, ALTON DEWITT, electrical engineering consultant; b. Corpus Christi, Tex., Feb. 1, 1935; s. Alton G. and Civilia Louise (Taylor) P.; m. Nancy Jo Elder, Mar. 1, 1959; children: Elizabeth, Carolyn. BEE, U. Tex., 1957; MEE, U. Pitts., 1961; PhD in Elec. Engring., Tex. A&M U., 1972. Registered profl. engr., Tex.; diplomate Am. Bd. Forensic Engring. and Tech. Engr. Westinghouse Electric Corp., Pitts., 1957-65; prof. elec. engring. dept. Tex. A&M U., College Station, 1965-79, 82-2000, head elec. engring. dept., 1992-96, Brockett prof., 1986, Dresser prof., 1987, dir. Electric Power Inst., 1976-79, 85-92, prof. emeritus, 2005—; rsch. fellow Tex. Engring. Expt. Sta., College Station, 1985, dir. Ctr. for Space Power, 1987-92; pres. Associated Power Analysts Inc., College Station, 1973—. Mem. panel for assessment of NIST Elec. and Electronics Engring. Lab., 1995-2000, NRS. Contbr. articles to elec. engring. jours. Fellow IEEE (life, tech. com., Prize Paper award 1975, 94, Richard Harold Kaufmann award 2000); mem. NSPE. Republican. Presbyterian. Avocations: fishing, hunting, photography, stamp and coin collecting. Home: 8411 Spring Crk College Station TX 77845-4608 Office: Associated Power Analysts Inc 303 Anderson St College Station TX 77840-3114 Home Phone: 979-693-1918; Office Phone: 979-696-0010. Business E-Mail: adpatton@tca.net. E-mail: adewittpatton@msn.com.

PATTON, ANTWAN ANDRE (BIG BOI), vocalist; b. Savannah, Ga., Feb. 1, 1975; children: Jordan Alexus, Bamboo. Performer Outkast, 1992—. Singer: (albums) Southernplayalisticadillacmuzik, 1994, ATLiens, 1996, Aquemini, 1998, Stankonia, 2000 (Grammy awards: Best Rap Album, 2001, Best Rap Performance By A Duo Or Group for song "Ms Jackson", 2001), Big Boi and Dre Present...Outkast, 2001 (Grammy award: (with Killer Mike) Best Rap Performance By A Duo Or Group for song "The Whole World", 2002), Speakerboxxx/The Love Below, 2003 (Grammy awards: Album Of The Yr., 2003, Best Urban/Alternative Performance for song "Hey Ya!", 2003, Best Rap Album, 2003, Am. Music Awards Favorite Album-Rap/Hip-Hop, 2004), Idlewild, 2006; actor: (films) ATL, 2006, Idlewild, 2006. Recipient Best New Rap Group of Yr., Source award, 1995, Favorite Band, Duo or Group-Pop or Rock, Am. Music Awards, 2004, Favorite Band, Duo or Group-Rap/Hip-Hop, 2004, Duo/Group Artist of Yr., Billboard Music Awards, 2004, Billboard 200 Duo/Group Album Artist of Yr., 2004, Hot 100 Duo/Group of Yr., 2004, R&B/Hip-Hop Duo/Group of Yr., 2004, Digital Track of Yr., 2004. Address: Arista Records Inc 8750 Wilshire Blvd Beverly Hills CA 90211-2713

PATTON, BRUCE M., law educator, management consultant; b. Terre Haute, Ind., Oct. 14, 1956; s. William Eugene and Carol Ann P.; m. Diana McLain Smith, Oct. 21, 1994. AB, Harvard U., 1977, JD, 1984. Bar: Mass. Co-founder, assoc. dir. Harvard Negotiation Project, Cambridge, Mass., 1979-84, dep. dir., 1984—; co-founder, assoc. dir. Program on Negotiation at Harvard Law Sch., Cambridge, Mass., 1983—2002; co-founder, ptnr. Vantage Partners, LLC, Cambridge, 1997—. Co-founder, prin. Conflict Mgmt. Inc., Cambridge, 1984—; co-founder, dir. Conflict Mgmt. Group, Cambridge, 1984-2000; Thaddeus R. Beal lectr. Harvard Law Sch., Cambridge, 1985-99. Co-author: The Mainstream of Alegbra and Trigonometry, 2d edit., 1980, Getting To Yes, 2d edit., 1991, Difficult Conversations, 1999; contbr. articles to profl. jours. Fellow: Coll. of Trial Mediators (hon.). Avocations: squash, hiking, tennis. Office: Harvard Negotiation Project Pound Hall 524 Harvard Law Sch Cambridge MA 02138 also: Vantage Ptnrs Brighton Landing W Ste 350 10 Guest St Boston MA 02135 Home Phone: 781-642-1211; Office Phone: 617-354-6090. E-mail: bpatton@post.harvard.edu.

PATTON, CARL VERNON, academic administrator, educator; b. Coral Gables, Fla., Oct. 22, 1944; s. Carl V. and Helen Eleanor (Benkert) Patton; m. Gretchen West, July 29, 1967. BS in Cmty. Planning, U. Cin., 1967; MS in Urban Planning, U. Ill.-Urbana, 1969, MS in Pub. Adminstrn., 1970; MS in Pub. Policy, U. Calif.-Berkeley, 1975, PhD in Pub. Policy, 1976. From instr. to prof. U. Ill., 1968—83, dir. Bur. of Urban and Regional Planning Rsch., 1977—79, prof., chmn. dept., 1979—83; prof., dean Sch. Architecture and Urban Planning U. Wis., Milw., 1983—89; v.p. acad. affairs, prof. polit. sci., geography and urban planning U. Toledo, 1989—92; pres. Ga. State U., Atlanta, 1992—. Author: Academia in Transition, 1979; co-author: The Metropolitan Midwest, 1985; co-author: (with David Sawicki) Basic Methods of Policy Analysis and Planning, 1986, rev. 2d edit., 1993 Chinese translations, 2001, 2002; co-author: (with Kathleen Reed) Guide to Graduate Education in Urban and Regional Planning, 1986, 1988; editor: Spontaneous Shelter: International Perspectives and Prospects, 1988; co-editor (with G. William Page): Quick Answers to Quantitative Problems: A Pocket Primer, 1991; assoc. editor: Jour. of Planning Edn. and Rsch., 1983—87, editl. bd.: Habitat International, 1993—99, Intertrade and Investment (formerly Atlanta Internat. Mag.), 1993—2000; contbr. articles to profl. jours. Chmn. Cmty. Devel. Commn., Urbana, 1978—82; mem. Civic Design Ctr., Milw., 1983—87, City of Milw. Art Commn., 1988—89, Toledo Vision, 1989—92, City of Toledo Bd. Cmty. Rels., 1990—92, Ga. Rsch. Alliance, Atlanta Convention and Vis. Bur., 1995—2005, Woodruff Art Ctr., 1996—2006, Fox Theatre, Ga. Coun. on Econ. Edn., Atlanta Neighborhood Devel. Partnership; chair Centennial Olympic Park Area Inc., 1998—2000, Ctrl. Atlanta Progress, 2000—03, Grady (Hosp.) Healthcare, Inc., 1998—2000, Atlanta Reg. Coun. for Higher Edn., 1998—; fellow U. Ill. Ctr. for Advanced Studies, 1973—74; bd. dirs., chair The Atlanta Downtown Partnership, 1997—2000. Fellow, NIMH, 1973—75. Fellow: Am. Inst. Cert. Planners; mem.: Met. Atlanta C. of C., Assn. Collegiate Schs. of Planning (v.p. 1985—87, pres. 1989—91), Am. Planning Assn. Avocations: racquetball, gardening, travel. Home: 250 Park Ave West NW # 908 Atlanta GA 30313 Office: Ga State U PO Box 3999 Atlanta GA 30302-3999 Office Phone: 404-651-2560. Business E-Mail: cpatton@gsu.edu.

PATTON, CHARLES HENRY, lawyer, educator; b. Asheville, NC, Jan. 13, 1953; s. Charles Robert and Sarah (Gulledge) Patton. BA, Memphis State U., 1975, JD, 1979. Bar: Tenn. Assoc. Holt, Bachelor, Spicer & Ryan, Memphis, 1979-80; fin. exec. Felsenthal Planning Service Co., Memphis, 1980-81; sole practice Memphis, 1981—; prof. Memphis State U., 1982—. Mem. Planned Giving Coun., Memphis; planned giving dir. Christ United Meth. Ch., Memphis, 1986. Mem.: Estate Planning Coun. Memphis, Memphis Bar Assn., S.E. Regional Bus. Law Profs. Assn. Republican. Avocations: auto restoration, model building. Office: 5100 Poplar Ave Ste 2701 Memphis TN 38137-4000 Office Phone: 901-685-8475. E-mail: services@clarktower.com, cpatton@interactiveoffices.com.

PATTON, DIANA LEE WILKOC, artist, educator, illustrator; b. New Rochelle, NY, June 28, 1940; d. August E. and Meta Diane (Neuburg) Wilkoc; m. Gardner C. Patton, Aug. 10, 1963; children: Michael, Talryn, Shawn. AB cum laude, Brown U., 1962; postgrad., Pan-Am. Art Inst., 1962-63. Svc. mgr. Lord and Taylor, NYC, 1962-63; tchr. adult edn., Mountain Lakes, NJ, 1972-74, Somerville, NJ, 1978-82, Jointure for Cmty. Adult Edn., 1982—. Artist in watercolors, pen and ink and acrylics; writer, illustrator of children's books; card designer; instr. in field; developer art appreciation courses for children and adults; toymaker, 1973-76. Exhibited N.E. US, Perth, Australia, 1977, spl. bicentennial exhibit, Trenton, NJ, 1976, Rutgers U., 1980, Brookdale Coll., 1982, Camden County Coll., 9186, Moris County Coll., 1988, Bergen Mus. Arts and Scis., 1987-88, 90-91, Princeton Med. Ctr., 1993-94, 96, Madison Gallery--Morristown Hosp., 2001, 03, 05, Salmagundi Club, NYC, 2002, Gallery Capital Health Mercer, 2005; one-woman show SAA Pluckemin Galleries, 1998; represented in pvt. and pub. collections in US, Australia, NZ, Germany, Luxembourg, Japan, Eng.; designer ofcl. poster NJ Festival Ballooning, 1990, Arc Challenge Races, 1993-94, Capital Health Sys. Hosp., Trenton, NJ 2004, 07. Recipient Bronze medal in watercolor Nat. Mystic (Conn.) Outdoor Art Festival, 1977, Mayor's purchase prize Franklin Twp., 1976, Tri-State Watercolor award Somerset County Coll., 1978, Best in Show award Raritan Valley Art Assn., 1978, 94, award Garden State Watercolor Soc., 1979, 84-85, 1st, 2d and Best in Show award Somerset and Westfield Art Assns. shows, 1st place for profl. watercolor Plainfield Tri-State Arts Festival, 1983, 85, 87, 96, 2001, N.E. Art Festival, Caldwell Coll., 1990, 95, Tewksbury award, 1990, 2d place in watercolor Internat. Miniature Art Show, Washington, 1983, Best in Show and Grumbacher award Caldwell State show, 1984, 1st place Carrier Clinic Tri-State, 1984, Grumbacher Bronze award, 1984, Grumbacher silver award, 1985, 88, 94, watercolor award Artists League Ctrl. NJ Show, Cornelious Lowe Mus., 1986, Winsor-Newton award Am. Artists Proleague, 1987, Robert Simmons award, 1989, Basking Ridge Environ. Ctr. award, 1994, Best in Show award NJ State Juried, Piscataway, 1988, 2d place NJ Miniature Art Soc., 1989, 1st Pro award Raritan Valley, 1992-93, 1st mixed media award Basking Ridge Environ. Ctr., 1994, award Essex Watercolor Club, 1999, Grumbacher Gold award Essex Watercolor Club, 2000, 1st Pro award Bridgewater Arts, 2001, 03; artist-in-residence grantee Middlesex Librs., 1983-92, watercolor demonstrator, 1983—; TV appearances State of Arts-NJ, 1986, Midday (spl. art shows), 1986, TKR, 1995; finalist ABC's children's picture book internat. competition, 2007; Elisha Benjamin scholar Brown U., 1960. Mem. Garden State Watercolor Soc. (writer, editor 1994—), Miniature Art Soc., Washington, NJ Watercolor Soc., AAUW (life, various offices 1963-73), Art Assn. Raritan Valley (pres. 1980-82, writer, editor newsletter 1993—), Art Assn. Somerset, Art Assn. North Haven (Maine), Essex Watercolor Club, Am. Artists Profl. League Nat., Soc. Children's Book Writers and Illustrators, Bee Sharps Square Dance Club. Presbyterian. Home: 497 Stony Brook Dr Bridgewater NJ 08807-1945 Personal E-mail: diana@dianapatton.com.

PATTON, GREGORY KENNETH, management educator; b. Sheridan, Wyo., Dec. 20, 1960; s. Philip Kenneth and Martha Jane Patton; children: Christopher Kenneth, Gentina Leigh. BA, Northwestern Coll., Orange City, Iowa, 1984; MBA, U. S.D., Vermillion, 1993; PhD, U. Iowa, Iowa City, 2002. Rsch. asst. bus. rsch. bur. U. S.D., Vermillion, 1992—93; instr. econs. Buena Vista Coll., Storm Lake, Iowa, 1993—95; grad. tchg./rsch. asst. U. Iowa, Iowa City, 1995—2000; asst. prof. mgmt. U. N.D., Grand Forks, 2000—. Retail store mgmt. Duckwall-ALCO Stores, Inc., Abilene, Kans., 1984—92; adj. instr. Northwestern Coll., Orange City, Iowa, 1993—95, Western Iowa Tech. CC, Sioux City, Iowa, 1994—95. Contbr. articles to profl. jours. Second v.p. Kiwanis, Alliance, Nebr., 1989—92; com. mem. parish health ministries Bethel Luth. Ch., Grand Forks, ND, 2004. Named Vol. of Yr., YMCA of Alliance, Nebr., 1992, Outstanding Student Orgn. Advisor, 2006, Nat. award excellence in advising, Mortar Bd., 2006; recipient Superior Instrn. and Noteworthy Devotion to the Advancement of Students, Quo Vadis Chpt. of Mortar Bd., 2003; Rsch. grantee, Small Bus. Devel. Ctr. ND, 2003—04. Mem.: APA, Soc. Indsl. and Orgnl. Psychology, Acad. Mgmt. (assoc. Scholarly Achievement award (Human Resources divsn.) 2002), Golden Key, Beta Gamma Sigma. Avocations: running, architecture. Office: Univ ND Box 8377 Grand Forks ND 58202 Office Phone: 701-777-3632. Business E-Mail: gregory_patton@und.nodak.edu.

PATTON, JACK THOMAS, family practice physician; b. Rogers, Ark., Feb. 18, 1941; s. Jack Marcus and Jewell Selah (Pense) P.; m. Lynette Anne Carr, Sept. 2, 1960; children: Robert, John, Mark, Christopher. BA in History, Calif. State U., Long Beach, 1963; MA in History, Calif. State U., Fresno, 1993; MD in Medicine, U. So. Calif., 1967; MA in Bibl. Studies, Mennonite Brethren Bib. Sem., Fresno, Calif., 1980. Cert. Bd. Med. Examiners, Calif., Hawaii. Intern Tripler Army Med. Ctr., Honolulu, 1967-68; resident in gen. practice Walson Army Hosp., Ft. Dix, NJ, 1968-70; med. supt. Nazarene Hosp., Papua New Guinea, 1973-80; chmn. family practice dept. Sharp Rees-Stealy, San Diego, 1981-86; chmn. occupational medicine Kaiser Permanent, Fresno, 1986-87; assoc. med. dir. Sharp Rees-Stealy, San Diego, 1987-92; med. dir. Summer Inst. Linguistics, Papua New Guinea, 1993-94; with family practice dept. Sharp Rees-Stealy Med. Group, San Diego, 1994-97, Northwest Med. Group, Fresno, Calif., 1997—; chmn. dept. family practice St. Agnes Med. Ctr., 2002—05. Family practice residency liaison Tripler Army Med. Ctr., Honolulu, 1972-73; chief medicine, dep. commr. Schofield Army Med. Clinics, Wahiawa, Hawaii, 1970-72; lectr. Calif. State U., Fresno, 1978-79, Pt. Loma Nazarene Coll., 1982-85, San Jose Christian Coll., 1997-2003; v.p. Patton Industries, Inc., 2005—. Mem. med. sch. support Salerni Collegium, U. So. Calif. Sch. Medicine, 1967-85; lectr. Ch.-Mission Inst., Mennonite Brethren Bib. Sem., 1984-92; sec. S.E. Asian task force Mennonite Brethren Ch. Fresno, 1990-93. Maj. U.S. Army, 1966-73. Mackenzie scholar U. So. Calif. Sch. Medicine, 1966-67; decorated Meritorious Svc. medal. Fellow Am. Acad. Family Physicians; mem. Am. Bd. Family Practice (diplomate), Calif. Acad. Family Physicians, Royal Soc. Medicine (assoc., London). Avocations: history, travel, hiking. Home: 1566 S Adler Ave Fresno CA 93727-5101 Office: 4770 W Herndon Ave Fresno CA 93722-8401 Office Phone: 559-271-6308.

PATTON, JAMES RICHARD, JR., lawyer; b. Durham, NC, Oct. 27, 1928; s. James Ralph and Bertha (Moye) P.; m. Mary Margot Maughan, Dec. 29, 1950; children: James Macon, Lindsay Fairfield. AB cum laude, U. N.C., 1948; postgrad., Yale U., 1948; JD, Harvard U., 1951. Bar: D.C. bar 1951, U.S. Supreme Ct. 1963. Attache of Embassy; spl. asst. to Am. ambassador to, Indochina, 1952-54; with Office Nat. Estimates, Washington, 1954-55; atty. Covington & Burling, Washington, 1956-61; founding ptnr., chmn. exec. com. Patton Boggs, LLP, Washington, 1962—. Lectr. internat. law Cornell Law Sch., 1963-64, U.S. Army Command and Gen. Staff Coll., 1967-68; Mem. Nat. Security Forum, U.S. Air War Coll., 1965, Nat. Strategy Seminar, U.S. Army War Coll., 1967-70, Global Strategy Discussions, U.S. Naval War Coll., 1968, Def. Orientation Conf., 1972; mem. Com. of 100 on Fed. City, Washington; mem. adv. council on nat. security and internat. affairs Nat. Republican Com., 1977-81; bd. dirs. Security Nat. Bank (Wash.), Signet, N.A., Madeira Sch., Greenway, Va., 1975-81, Lawyers Com. for Civil Rights Under Law, Washington, Legal Aid Soc. Washington; mem. Industry Policy Adv. Com. for Trade Policy Matters, 1984-87; mem. nat. adv. bd. Ackland Art Mus. U. N.C., 1987—; chmn. exec. com. Anderson Ranch Arts Ctr., 2002-05. Adv. coun. mem. Johns Hopkins U. Sch. Advanced Internat. Studies, 1989-92; nat. bd. dirs. Aspen Mus., 1987-90; nat. coun. mem. Whitney Mus., 1992—; bd. dirs., exec. com. Nat. Mus. Natural History, Smithsonian, 1992—; bd. dirs. Smithsonian Nat. Bd., 1999-2002; trustee Aspen Music Festival and Sch., 1993-2003; chmn. Ariz. astronomy Bd. U. Ariz., 2003—, mdm. dean's bd. Coll. Sci., 2004—; chmn. Patton Boggs Found., 2000—. Fellow U.N.C. Wilson Library, 1996—. Mem. ABA (past com. chmn.), Inter-Am. Bar Assn. (past del.), Internat. Law Assn. (past com. chmn.), Am. Soc. Internat. Law (treas., exec. coun.), Washington Inst. Fgn. Affairs, Nat. Gallery (collectors com. 1988-91), Gerrard Soc., Met. Club (Washington), Phi Beta Kappa, Alpha Epsilon Delta.

PATTON, JODY, management company executive; With Pacific Northwest Ballet; pres., CEO Vulcan, Inc., Seattle; pres. Vulcan Prodns. Vice-chair First & Goal, Inc.; exec. dir. Experience Music Project, Seattle; co-founder Sci. Fiction Mus. and Hall of Fame, Seattle, Allen Inst. for Brain Sci., Wash.; bd. dir. Charter Comm. Exec. prodr.: The Blues. Exec. dir. Paul G. Allen Family Found.; bd. dir. U. Wash. Found., Internat. Glass Mus., Oreg. Shakespeare Festival, Theatre Comm. Group. Office: Vulcan Inc 505 Fifth Ave S Ste 900 Seattle WA 98104 Office Phone: 206-342-2000. Office Fax: 206-342-3000. *

PATTON, JOSEPH DONALD, JR., management consultant; b. Washington, Pa., Jan. 4, 1938; s. Joseph Donald and Priscilla Ann (Johnson) P.; m. Susan Oertel, June 3, 1967; children: Jennifer Ann, Joseph Donald III (dec.). BS in Phys. Scis. and Math. Edn., Pa. State U., 1959; MBA in Mktg., U. Rochester, NYC, 1970. Registered profl. quality engr., Calif.; cert. profl. logistician; cert. quality engr.; cert. reliabilty engr. Tchr. Aschaffenburg (W.Germany) Am. Sch., 1963-64; with Xerox Corp., Rochester, 1964-75, mgr. field engring., 1975-93; CEO Patton Cons., Inc., Rochester, NY, 1993—, Hilton Head, SC, 1993—. Chmn., Mgmt. Metrics Svcs., Inc., 1996-2001; mem. adj. faculty Rochester Inst. Tech., SUNY, Geneseo. Author 8 textbooks; contbr. over 200 articles to profl. jours. Capt. U.S. Army, 1959-63. Recipient Leadership and Svc. award Pa. State U. Coll. Edn., 1999, Lifetime Achievement award, Service Industry Assn., 2007. Fellow Am. Soc. Quality Control (reliability and maintainablity tech. award 1982), Soc. Logistics Engrs. (Sole Armitage medal 1980, 82, 97); mem. Instrument Soc. Am. (sr.), Assn. Field Svc. Mgrs. (publs. award 1981, Pres.'s Club 2005), Nat. Assn. Svc. Mgrs. (life cert. svc. exec.). Republican. Presbyterian (elder). Office: Patton Consultants Inc 36 Blue Heron Pt Hilton Head Island SC 29926-1209 Office Phone: 843-384-6232. Personal E-mail: JDPatton@aol.com.

PATTON, JUNE ODESSA, writer, consultant, educator, researcher; d. Joe Edward Patton and Nancy Odessa Britt. BA, Roosevelt U., Chgo., MS in Tchg.; PhD, postgrad., U. Chgo. Tchg. asst. U. Ill., Chgo.; rsch. assoc. U. Chgo.; vis. prof. Governors State U., University Park, Ill.; instr. Roosevelt U., Chgo.; instr. Lab. H.S. U. Chgo., testing asst., rsch. assoc.; program officer Nat. Endowment for Humanities, Washington; prof. Governors State U., University Park, Ill. Midwestern regional dir. Assn. Black Women Historians, Washington, acting-nat. membership chairperson; program chair 75th ann. meeting Assn. for Study of African Am. Life and History, Washington; treas. and nat. membership chair Assn. of Black Women Historians, Washington; adv. reviewer Jour. African Am. History, Washington, mem. editl. bd.; exec. coun. Assn. for Study of African Am. Life and History, Washington; treas. Women's Edn. Network, Chgo.; cons. in field. Contbr. biographical American National Biography, biographical Encyclopedia of African-American Educators, biographical Black Women in the United States: An Historical Encyclopedia, educational Harcourt Brace Jovanovich Resource Guide for Multicultural Classroom; author: (book review) History of Education Quarterly; contbr. book The Closing Door: Conservative Policy and Black Opportunity; author: (documentary essay) The Journal of Negro History; contbr. articles to profl. jours. Charles Hubbard Judd centennial planning com. U. Chgo., 1975—78; rschr. and del. US-Africa Partnership for Bldg. Stronger Communities, Albany, NY, 1999—2003; com. mem., Katherine Dunham golden anniversary tribute festival Inst. for Intercultural Comm., Chgo.; bd. dirs. Catalyst for Youth, Chgo., 1973—78; cons. and spkr. Chgo. Humanities Festival, 1999—2002, DuSable Mus., Chgo., 1987—2002, Harold Wash. Libr. Reading Group, Chgo., 1999—2002; cons. and judge Chgo. Metro History Fair, Chicago, Ill., 1982—91; cons. and spkr. Ill. Humanities Coun., Chgo., 1984—91; bd. dirs. African Am. Geneal. Soc. of Chgo., 1979—89; bd. dirs., George E. Kent Meml. and Scholarship Fund U. Chgo., 1982—87; com. mem. Women's Com. for 1992 Chgo. World's Fair, 1990—91; planning com., Ill. and Chgo. Salute to Katherine Dunhamgo State of Ill. and City of Chgo., 1982—83; planning com. City of Chgo.'s women's history week City of Chgo., 1982—83; advisor Chgo. Film Symposium, 1975—78. Recipient Achievement award, NAACP, 1980, Chairman's Cert. of Appreciation, Nat. Endowment for Humanities, 1993, Faculty Excellence award, Govs. State U., 1997 and 2000, Students Cert. of Appreciation, 1997 and 1998; scholarship, State of Ill., 1965-1967, Roosevelt U. Grad. Grant-in-Aid, Roosevelt U., 1967-1968, PhD assistantship, U. Ill., 1968-69; 1969-70 (unable to accept), Ednl. fellowship, U. Chgo., 1970-71, Contingency grant, 1972, Ford Found. fellowship, The Ford Found., 1972, Nat. Dissertation Yr. Fellow, Ford Found., 1974-75; 1975-1976, Carter G. Woodson Disting. Scholar-In-Residence, Assn. for Study of African Am. Life and History, 1991—94, Adminstrv. fellowship, State of Ill., 1991-1992 (unable to accept), Profl. Devel. grant, Govs. State U. Alumni Assn., 2001. Mem.: So. Hist. Assn. (life), Orgn. of Am. Historians (life), Assn. of Black Women Historians (life; treas. and nat. membership chair 1993—95), Assn. for Study of African Am. Life and History (life; exec. coun. 1993—2000, 2005—). Avocations: tennis, white water rafting, bicycling, travel, golf. Office: Govs State Univ 1 University Pky University Park IL 60466-3165 Office Phone: 708-534-4574. Business E-Mail: j-patton@govst.edu.

PATTON, KASSIE (KATHLEEN MORONEY PATTON), former principal, director; BA, Northeastern Ill. U., 1983; MA in English, Saint Xavier U., 1992; PhD in Ednl. Adminstrn., Govs. State U., 1996. English instr. St. Joseph HS, Chgo., 1986—91, Crete-Monee HS, 1991, dean students, asst. prin.; adminstr. Bremen HS, Midlothian, 2000—01; dean academic affairs, asst. prin. Hales Franciscan HS, Chica, 2001—03, interim prin., 2002; dir., prin. Univ. Lab HS, Urbana, Ill., 2003—07. Named Adminstr. of Yr., Ill. Journalism Edn. Assn., 2006. Mem.: U. Ill. Edn. Adminstrn. Alumni Assn. Office Phone: 217-333-2870. E-mail: kapatton@uni.uiuc.edu. *

PATTON, LAURIE LOUISE, religious studies educator, writer; b. Boston, Mass., Nov. 14, 1961; d. Anthony Seavey and Christine Card Patton. BA, Harvard U, Cambridge, Mass, 1983; MA, U of Chgo., Chgo., Ill, 1985, PhD, 1991. Asst. prof. Bard Coll., Annandale, 1991—96, Emory U., Atlanta, 1996—98, assoc. prof., 1998—2003, full prof., 2003, chair dept. religion, 1999—, Winship Disting. Rsch. prof., 2003—. Fellowship selection com. Am Coun. of Learned Societies, New York, NY, 2000—02; academic adv. bd. Carlos Mus., Atlanta, 2000—; mem. exec. bd. Am. Soc. Study of Religion, 2001—; academic task force Am. Acad. Religion, Atlanta, 2003—. Editor: Authority, Anxiety Canon; Myth & Method; Jewels of Authority; Notes from a Mandala; author: Myth as argument (DeGruyter Press), 1996, Bringing the Gods to Mind, 2003, Fires Goal: Poems from a Hindu Year; translator: The Bhagavad Gita, 2004. Exec. bd. Atlanta Interfaith Alliance, Atlanta, 2001—04; edn. com. Ahavath Achim Synagogue, Atlanta, 2002—. Grantee rsch., Am. Inst. of Indian Studies/Pure, India, 1992, Nat. Endowment for the Humanities/Pure, India, 1995, Fulbright, Jerusalem, 1999, Fulbright, India, 2004. Fellow: Am. Coun. Learned Socs., Gustafson Seminar (dir. 1999—2002); mem.: South Asia/Am. Acad. Religion (secretary 1998—2001), Humanities Coun. (chair 2000—03). Democrat. Judaism. Avocations: embroidery, photography. Office: Emory Univ Dept of Religion 537 Kilgo Circle Atlanta GA 30322-0001

PATTON, LYNN RADONIC, pharmacist, educator; d. Peter R. and Ines M. Radonic; m. Kurt A. Patton, 1975. BS in Pharmacy, St. John's U., Jamaica, NY, 1975, MS in Instl. Pharmacy Practice, 1978. Registered pharmacist NY, 1976, cert. in nutrition support pharmacy Bd. Pharm. Specialties, 1992. Asst. prof. coll. pharmacy St. John's U., 1980—85; mgr. nutrition support New Eng. region Caremark, Albany, NY, 1986—93; assoc. prof., dir., postgraduate profl. edn. Albany Coll. Pharmacy, NY, 1993—98; prof., vice chmn. coll. pharmacy Midwestern U., Downers Grove, Ill., 1998—2005, prof. coll. pharmacy Glendale, Ariz., 2005—, assoc. dean coll. pharmacy, 2005—. Contbr. articles to profl. jours. Mem.: NY State Bd. Pharmacy (chmn. 1995—96), Am. Soc. Health-Sys. Pharmacists (dir. profl. affairs Ill. coun. 2001—05), Am. Soc. Parenteral and Enteral Nutrition (pres. upstate NY chpt. 1994—95), Ariz. Pharmacy Alliance, Am. Assn. Colls. Pharmacy. Office: Midwestern Univ Coll Pharmacy 19555 N 59th Ave Glendale AZ 85308 Home Phone: 623-572-8487; Office Phone: 623-572-3506. Office Fax: 623-572-3510. Business E-Mail: lpatto@midwestern.edu.

PATTON, RICHARD WESTON, retired mortgage company executive; b. Evanston, Ill., Sept. 26, 1931; s. Robert Ferry and Sue Buckley P.; m. Lynda A. Kruse, Feb. 2, 1971; 1 child, Robert Weston BA, Amherst Coll., 1954. Sales engr. Thermo Fax Sales Corp., Chgo., 1958-60; account exec. Nat. Mortgage Investors, Inc., Chgo., 1960-61, sales mgr. Pasadena, Calif., 1962-66, asst. v.p., 1966-67, v.p., 1967-69, exec. v.p., 1969-73, pres., chief exec. officer, dir., 1973-84, vice-chmn. bd., 1984-90; pres. Richard W. Patton Enterprises, Pasadena, 1990—2004; ret., 2005. Pres., chmn. exec. com., dir. Ocean Park Restaurant Corp., Santa Monica, Calif., 1977-88; dir. Cenfed Bank, Cenfed Fin. Corp. Bd. dirs. Pasadena Boys' Club, 1963-66, Opera Assocs., 1984-90; mem. steering com. Amherst Coll. Capital Fund Drive, 1963-66; mem. citizens adv. com. L.A. County Sheriffs Dept. 1st lt. USMCR, 1955-58. Mem. Amherst Coll. Alumni Assn. (bd. dirs. 1963—2001, pres. 1977-79, 86-89), Kroenstadt Ski Club (past pres.). Office: Rich W Patton Enterprises 3644 San Pasqual St Pasadena CA 91107-5419

PATTON, SHARON F., museum director; BA, Roosevelt U., 1966; MA, U. Ill., 1969; PhD in Art History, Northwestern U., 1980. Mem. faculty U. Houston, 1976—79, U. Md., 1979—85; dir. art galleries Montclair State Coll., NJ, 1986—87; chief curator Studio Mus., NYC, 1988—91; assoc. prof. art history U. Mich., Ann Arbor, 1991—98, dir. Ctr. for Arfoamerican and African Studies, 1996—98; dir. Allen Meml. Art Mus. Oberlin Coll., 1998—2003; mem. adv. bd. Nat. Mus. African Art, Washington, 2000—, dir., 2003—. Author: Memory and the Metaphor, the Art of Romare Bearden, 1991, African-American Art, 1998 (Choice Outstanding Book of Yr. award); contbr. articles to publs. in field. Mem. Rapid Transit Pub. Art Commn., Cleve., ArtTable, Cleve.; mem. visual arts jury Cleve. Arts Prize, 2000—02; mem. African Am. adv. coun. and Acquisition adv. com. Cleve. Art Mus. Mem.: ArtTable, Assn. Art Mus. Dirs., Am. Assn. Museums. Office: Nat Mus African Art Smithsonian Instn MRC 708 PO Box 37012 Washington DC 20013-7012

PATTON, STUART, biochemist, educator; b. Ebenezer, NY, Nov. 2, 1920; s. George and Ina (Neher) P.; m. Colleen Cecelia Lavelle, May 17, 1945; children: John, Richard, Gail, Thomas, Mary Catherine, Patricia, Joseph. BS, Pa. State U., 1943; MS, Ohio State U., 1947, PhD, 1948. Chemist Borden Co., 1943-44; rsch. fellow Ohio State U., Columbus, 1946-48; faculty Pa. State U., University Park, 1949-80, prof., 1959-80, Evan Pugh rsch. prof. agr., 1966-80; adj. prof. neurosci. Sch. Medicine U. Calif., San Diego, 1981—99; ret., 1999. Vis. scientist Scripps Instn. Oceanography; cons. in field. Author: (with Robert Jenness) Principles of Dairy Chemistry, 1959; (with Robert G. Jensen) Biomedical Aspects of Lactation, 1975; Milk: Its Remarkable Contribution to Human Health and Well-Being, 2004. Lt. (j.g.) USNR, 1944-46. Recipient Borden award chemistry milk Am. Chem. Soc., 1957, Agrl. and Food Chemistry award, 1975, Alexander von Humboldt sr. scientist award, 1981, Macy-Gyorgy award Internat. Soc. for Rsch. on Human Milk and Lactation, 1997, Distinguished Alumnus award, Pa. State U., 2002, Distinguished Svc. award Am. Dairy Sci. Assn., 1999, fellow Pa. State Alumni Assn., 2001. Fellow Am. Dairy Sci. Assn.; mem. Am. Chem. Soc., Am. Soc. Biochemistry and Molecular Biology, Am. Soc. Cell Biology. Home and Office: 6208 Avenida Cresta La Jolla CA 92037-6510 E-mail: spatton@ucsd.edu.

PATTON, SUSAN OERTEL, clinical social worker, educator; b. Syracuse, NY, May 18, 1946; d. Robert William and Jane (VanWormer) Oertel; m. Joseph D. Patton, Jr., June 3, 1967; children: Jennifer, Joseph D. III. BA, SUNY, Geneseo, 1984; MSW, SUNY, Buffalo, 1987. Cert. social worker, NY; lic. ind. social worker, S.C.; qualified clin. social worker; diplomate in clin. social work. Counselor Profl. Counseling Svc., Gowanda, NY, 1987-88, Mental Health Mgmt., Rochester, NY, 1988-93, The Health Assn., Rochester, 1988-89, sr. counselor, 1989-90, asst. dir. mktg. and tng., 1990-92; pvt. practice Rochester, 1988-93; employee assistance program dir. Recovery Ctr. EAP, Hilton Head, SC, 1993-95; pres., dir. Employee Assistance Program, Inc., Hilton Head Island, SC, 1995-2001. Instr. Medaille Coll., Buffalo, 1990-93. Co-author: Treating Perpetrators of Sexual Abuse, 1990. Mem.: NASW, Acad. Cert. Social Workers.

PATTON, THOMAS EARL, lawyer; b. Nov. 25, 1940; s. Thomas E. and Alice F. (Rodarmel) P.; m. Patricia Mann, Aug. 12, 1965 (dec.); m. Barbara Wood, Sept. 21, 1974 (div. 2005); 1 child, David Earl; m. Yogi Yogan, 2006. AB, Cath. U. Am., 1962, JD summa cum laude, 1965. Bar: NY 1966, DC 1966, Va. 1982. Assoc. Sullivan & Cromwell, NYC, 1965-69; mem. Williams Connolly & Califano, Washington, 1970-75; asst. gen. counsel US Dept. Energy, Washington, 1977-78; ptnr. Schnader, Harrison, Segal & Lewis, Washington, 1979-94. Disting. lectr. Cath. U. Am., 1970-90, 95—, bd. regents; nat. arbitrator Am. Arbitration Assn.; bd. dirs. Elcotel, Inc., IXI, Inc., Vanguard Found. Author: Securities Litigation, 1989, Federal Procedure Casebook, 1990; contbr. articles to profl. jours.; editor in chief Cath. U. Am. Law Rev. Mem. Washington World Affairs Coun., 1980—. Mem. ABA, DC Bar (founder and chair litigation sect.), Cosmos Club. Roman Catholic. Office: Tighe Patton Armstrong Teasdale 1747 Pennsylvania Ave NW Washington DC 20006-4688 Office Phone: 202-454-2840. Business E-Mail: tpatton@tighepatton.com.

PATTON, THOMAS JAMES, marketing executive, sales executive; b. Cleve., Nov. 2, 1948; s. Michael Anthony and Delores (Bammerlin) Patton; m. Thomasina Bernadette Cavallaro, Aug. 9, 1969; children: Thomasina, Thera V. A in Transp., Cleve. State U., 1971, BA in Mktg., 1973; BA, SUNY, Empire State, 1994. CLU; ChFC; registered health underwriter; registered employee benefit cons. Ins. salesman Manulife, Cleve., 1972-75, Mass. Mut., Cleve., 1976-80, Patton Ins. Assn., Inc., Avon Lake, Ohio, 1976—; ins. cons. Diversified Benefit Plans, Inc., Avon Lake, 1978-93, dir. sales and mktg., 1993—; pres. commerce Benefits Group, Inc. and Ins. Mktg. Group, Inc., 1995; prin. Cmty. Health Ptnrs., Ltd., Ill., 1994. Pres. Commerce Benefits Group, Inc.; cons. Regional Sch. Consortium, Lorain County, Ohio, 1986—, County of Lorain, 1984—, City of Lorain, 1986—, County of Lorain, 1984—, City of Lorain, 1984—; prin. Comty. Health Ptnrs. Ltd.; bd. Italian Cultural Found.; founder 1-888 Ohiocomp w/c MCO-Ohio, 1997; co-founder VocRehabOne, Ltd., w/c Vocat. Rehab. Co.; founder MedAudits Inc., Cardinal Utilization Mgmt., Cardinal Preferred Cave, Imaging Workflows Sys. Pres. Lake Erie Rate Coun., Cleve., 1970-71; mem. Lorain County Dem. Ctrl. Com., Avon Lake, Ohio, 1986—; mem. com. Cleve. Leukemia Soc., 1985; bd. dirs. Villa Serena Sr. Housing, St. Francis Soc., Italian Cultural Found.; bd. trustees Found. Am. Coll., Bryn Mawr, Pa., 2002—. Mem. Nat. Assn. Life Underwriters, Profl. Ins. Agts. Assn., Cert. Profl. Ins. Agts. Soc., Soc. Benefit Plan Adminstrn., Lorain County Life Underwriters, Irish Heritage, Order Italian Sons and Daus., Profl. Assn. Dive Instrs./Nat. Assn. Underwater Instrs. (SCUBA diving instr.). Roman Catholic. Avocations: fishing, skin and scuba diving, photography. Office: Commerce Group PO Box 900 Elyria OH 44036-0900 Office Phone: 440-930-7500 203. Business E-Mail: tompatton@thecommercegroup.com.

PATTON-NEWELL, JANET LAVELLE, minister; b. Sharon, Pa., Jan. 15, 1965; d. Henry Elbert and Flora Lee Newby; m. Derrick Lamount Newell, June 17, 2000; children: Flora Evette Harris, Kellen Dauntae Newby, Kent Michael Patton, Kaston Moneke Patton, Grace Newell. Diploma in Bible studies, Full Bible Inst. Farrell, Pa., 2002; HHD, diploma in biblical studies, NCI Bible Coll. and Sch. Prophets, 2005; cert., Cambria County Prison Tng. Acad., Pa. Lic. ordained World Missions Ministerial Assn., minister Ranha Outreach Internat. Orders clk. Mercer County Domestic Rels., (Child Support Bur.), Mercer, Pa., 1996—98; youth and young adult activities coord. Americorp Vista, (Mercer County Housing Authority), Sharon, Pa., 1998—99; evangelist New and Living Way Apostolic Ch. of Jesus Christ, Farrell, Pa., 1998—2000; overseer Paramount Ctr. for Learning, Farrell, Pa.; pastor Rivers Living Water Outreach Ministry, Farrell, Pa., 2000—01, Wind in the Word Worship Ctr., Farrell, Pa., 2001—. Correction officer Mercer County Prison. Author: (self help) You are a Woman of Excellence, 2001, You are a Man of Excellence, 2001, Our Weapons are not Carnal, 2001; The Three Dimensions of the Prophetic, 2005. Mem. E.R.A.S.E. Anti Drug Coalition, Farrell, 1999, Wheels To Work, (Prince of Peace), Farrell, Pa., 1999; dir. New and Living Way Edn. Dept., Farrell, 1998—2000, Wind in the Word Outreach Ministry Edn. Dept., Farrell, 2001—05; mem. Walking in Black History, Erie, Pa., 1999. E-5 US Army, 1987—2001, Fort Bragg, N. Carolina and Ansbach, Germany. Recipient Appreciation cert., Anointed Call to Singleness, 1999, Wind in the Word Worship Ctr., 2002, 2003, 2004, Congratulations cert., New and Living Way Apostolic Ch. Jesus Christ, 2000. Mem.: Women In Truth Fellowship, Women Speakers, Prophetic Women, Women N Power. Democrat. Apostolic. Avocations: computers, writing. Office: Wind in Word Worship Ctr 712 Martin Luther King Blvd Farrell PA 16121 Office Phone: 724-734-1904. Business E-Mail: dr.janetl.newell@windintheword.com.

PATTY, CLAIBOURNE WATKINS, JR., lawyer; b. Cleve., Feb. 19, 1934; s. Claibourne Watkins and Eleanor (Todd) P.; m. Barbara Benton, May 4, 1968; children— Claibourne Watkins III, William Jordan. BA, U. of South, 1955; JD, U. Ark., 1961. Bar: Ark. 1961. Law clk. U.S. dist. judge, Ft. Smith, 1961-63; pvt. practice Little Rock, 1963-68; asst. ins. commr. State of Ark., 1968-69; trust officer Union Nat. Bank of Little Rock, 1969-77; asst. dean U. Ark. Sch. Law, Little Rock; also exec. dir. Ark. Inst. for Continuing Legal Edn., 1977-86; law clk. 2d Div. Chancery Ct., Pulaski County, 1986-89; of counsel Gruber Law Firm, North Little Rock, 1989-2001; prin. Patty Law Firm, North Little Rock, 2001—. Lectr. law Ark. Sch. Law, 1965; bd. dirs., chmn. Pulaski County Legal Aid Bur., 1966—69; mem. com. on civil practice Ark. Supreme Ct., 1998—2004. Bd. dirs., pres. Family Svc. Agy. of Ctrl. Ark., 1976—81, 1986—93, 1999—2004, Good Shepherd Ecumenical Retirement Ctr., 1975—2002; mem. Ark. adv. com. U.S. Commn. on Civil Rights, 1985—89; bd. dirs. Am. Diabetes Assn., Ark. Affil., 1996—2005, Ark. Gerontol. Soc., 1996—. With AUS, 1955—57. Mem.: Phi Alpha Delta, Beta Theta Pi. Office: Patty Law Firm 315 N Broadway St North Little Rock AR 72114-5379 Home Phone: 501-663-0604; Office Phone: 501-375-5061. Personal E-mail: clairgpm@swbell.net.

PATTYN, SUE, publishing executive; b. Sept. 1, 1958; Pub. The Nat. Infectious Disease Directory, 1994—2006. Mem.: Guides for Living LLC. Home: 1658 Saint St SE Palm Bay FL 32909 Office: PO Box 101203 Palm Bay FL 32910 Home Phone: 321-243-5437.

PATURIS, E(MMANUEL) MICHAEL, lawyer; b. Akron, Ohio; s. Michael George and Sophia (Manos) P.; m. Mary Ann Toompas, Febr. 28, 1965. BS, U. N.C., 1954, JD with honors, 1959. Bar: NC 1959, DC 1969, Va. 1973; CPA. Acct., Charlotte and Wilmington, N.C., 1960-63; assoc. Poyner, Geraghty, Hartsfield & Townsend, Raleigh, N.C., 1963-64; atty. advisor Chief Counsel's Office, Washington, 1964-66, sr. trial atty. Richmond, Va., 1966-69; ptnr. Reasoner, Davis & Vinson, Washington, 1969-78; sole practitioner Alexandria, 1978—. Acctg. lectr. U. N.C., Chapel Hill, 1959-60; acctg., econs. lectr. N.C. State U., Raleigh, 1963-64; business law lectr. George Mason U., Fairfax County, Va., 1978-79. Mem. bd. editors U. N.C. Law Rev. With U.S. Army, 1954-56. Recipient U. N.C. Law Sch. Block award, 1959. Mem.: Washington Golf and Country Club, Beta Gamma Sigma, Phi Beta Kappa. Home: 6326 Stoneham Ln Mc Lean VA 22101-2345 Office: Law Offices of E Michael Paturis 431 N Lee St Alexandria VA 22314-2301 Office Phone: 703-836-2501.

PATZ, EDWARD FRANK, retired lawyer; b. Balt., Aug. 25, 1932; s. Maurice A. and Violet (Furman) P.; m. Betty Seldner Levi, Nov. 18, 1956; children— Evelyn Anne, Edward Frank, Thomas L. BS, U. Md., 1954, LLB, 1959. Bar: Md. 1959, U.S. Dist. Ct. Md. 1959, U.S. Ct. Appeals (4th cir.) 1959, U.S. Supreme Ct. 1980. Ptnr. Weinberg and Green and predecessor firms (now merged into Saul Ewing), Balt., 1959—97; ret., 1997. Bd. dirs. Jewish Family and Children's Service, 1965-71; regional bd. dirs. NCCJ; pres. Suburban Club Balt. County, 1977-79; bd. trustees, exec. com. Flagler Ecumenical Social Svcs. Ctr., Inc., 1999-2002. Mem.: Gov.'s Club. Home: 19032 Stone Brook Chapel Hill NC 27517 Personal E-mail: espesq@earthlink.net.

PAUKEN, THOMAS WEIR, venture capital executive, mediator; b. Victoria, Tex., Jan. 11, 1944; s. Thomas N. and Patricia (Weir) P.; m. Ida Ayala; children: Thomas II, Michelle, Angela, Elizabeth, Daniel, Victoria, Monica. AB in Polit. Sci., Georgetown U., 1965, postgrad., 1966-67; JD, So. Meth. U., 1973. Bar: Tex., 1975. White House staff asst., dep. dir. White Ho. fellows, Washington, 1970-71; pvt. practice atty. Dallas, 1974-80; dir. ACTION, Washington, 1981-85; pres. Sta. KRZI-Radio, Waco, Tex., 1985-86; v.p., corp. counsel Garvon, Inc., Dallas, 1986-91; pres. TWP, Inc., Dallas, 1991—. Bd. dirs. TOR Minerals, Inc. Author: The Thirty Years War - The Politics of the 60s Generation, 1994. Mem. Reagan transition team Counsel's Office, Washington, 1980-81; Tex. Rep. State chmn., 1994-97; chmn. Gov.'s Tex. Task Force on Appraisal Reform, 2006-07. With US Army, 1967—70. Recipient Drug Edn. Leadership award PRIDE, 1985, Dir.'s award U.S. Office of Personnel Mgmt., 1985; Weaver fellow 1965. Mem. State Bar Tex., VFW (life). Roman Catholic. Avocation: reading. Office Phone: 214-378-9340. Business E-Mail: twpauken@sbcglobal.net.

PAUL, ANDREW MITCHELL, investment advisor; b. NYC, Feb. 10, 1956; s. John William and Bobba Lorraine (Ice) P.; m. Margaret Rae Batchelor, Sept. 19, 1987. BA, Cornell U., 1978; MBA, Harvard U., 1983. Mktg. rep. IBM Corp., NYC, 1978-81; assoc. Hambrecht & Quist Venture Capital Co., San Francisco, 1983-84; gen. ptnr. Welsh, Carson, Anderson & Stowe, NYC, 1984—2000; chmn. Enhancee Capital Ptnrs.; mng. gen. ptnr. Enhanced Equity Fund. Mem. Nat. Venture Capital Assn., NY Venture Capital Assn., Bronxville Field Club, Siwanoy Country Club, Roaring Fork Club, Aspen., Blind Brook Country Club, Commanderie de Bordeaux, Chevaliers du Tastevin. Avocations: golf, skiing, biking, travel. Home: 283 Pondfield Rd Bronxville NY 10708-4936 Office: Enhanced Capital Partners 350 Park Ave 24th Fl New York NY 10022

PAUL, ANDREW ROBERT, defense and government consultant; b. NYC, Aug. 14, 1938; s. Andrew B. and Maria (Filotas) P.; m. Britt-Marie Hagelbrant, Feb. 6, 1988. AB in French, Dartmouth Coll., 1960; MS in Fgn. Svc., Georgetown U., 1967. Dir. govt. rels. Motorola, Inc., Washington, 1968-75, Paramount Communications, Washington, 1975-90; sr. v.p. Satellite Broadcasting and Communications Assn., Alexandria, Va., 1990—2001; def. and legis. cons. Mem. GATT adv. com. on Intellectual Property, Washington, 1988-94; mem. adv. com. MS in Fgn. Svc. program Georgetown U., Washington, 1981-2004. Presdl. campaign advance man Rep. Nat. Com., 1964; pres. chpt. XI Spl. Forces Assn., Washington, 1981-82; chmn. Alternative House Crisis Intervention Ctr., Vienna, Va., 1983-84. Capt. U.S. Army, 1960-65. Roman Catholic. Home: 1450 Emerson Ave Mc Lean VA 22101-2024

PAUL, ANNEGRET, mathematics professor; PhD, Univ. Md., College Park, 1996. Adj. asst. prof. Univ. Calif., Berkeley, 1996—99; now assoc. prof. math. We. Mich. Univ., Kalamazoo. Mem.: Assn. Women in Math., Am. Math. Soc., Pi Mu Epsilon. Achievements include being one of 18 top mathematicians and computer scientists (Atlas of Lie Groups Project) from the US to successfully map E8, one of the largest and most complicated structures in mathematics. Office: Dept Math 6619 Everett Tower Western Mich Univ Kalamazoo MI 49008-5248 Business E-Mail: annegret.paul@wmich.edu, paul@wmich.edu. *

PAUL, ARA GARO, university dean; b. New Castle, Pa., Mar. 1, 1929; s. John Hagop and Mary (Injejikian) P.; m. Shirley Elaine Waterman, Dec. 21, 1962; children: John Bartlett, Richard Goyan. BS in Pharmacy, Idaho State U., 1950; MS, U. Conn., 1953, PhD in Pharmacognosy, 1956. Cons. plant physiology Argonne Nat. Lab., Ill., 1955; asst. prof. pharmacognosy Butler U., Indpls., 1956-57; faculty U. Mich., Ann Arbor, 1957—, prof. pharmacognosy, 1969—; dean U. Mich. Coll. Pharmacy, 1975-96, dean emeritus, Hans W. Vahlteich prof. pharmacognosy, 2001—04, prof. emeritus, 2005—. Vis. prof. microbiology Tokyo U., 1965-66; mem. vis. chemistry faculty U. Calif., Berkeley, 1972-73; del. U.S. Pharmacopeial Conv., 1980, 90; scholar-in-residence Am. Assn. Colls. Pharmacy, 1996; bd. grants Am. Found. Pharm. Edn., 1997—, chmn., 1999, 2007, co-chmn. endowment com., 2002—, bd. dirs., 2003—; mem. organizing com. Millennial World Congress Pharm. Scis., 1996-2000; mem. FIP Found., 2000—05, chmn. bd. trustees, 2001—05. Contbr. articles to profl. jours. Recipient Outstanding Tchr. award Coll. Pharmacy, U. Mich., 1969, Outstanding Alumnus award Idaho State U., 1976, Profl. Achievement award Coll. Pharmacy, Idaho State U., 1990; G. Pfeiffer Meml. fellow Am. Found. Pharm. Edn., 1965-66, Disting. Svc. Profile award Am. Found Pharm. Edn., 1992; fellow Eli Lily Found., 1951-53, Am. Found. Pharm. Edn., 1954-56, NIH, 1972-73. Fellow AAAS; mem. Am. Pharm. Assn., Am. Soc. Pharmacognosy, Acad. Pharm. Scis., Am. Assn. Colls Pharmacy, Am. Assn. Pharm. Scientists, Phi Lambda Upsilon, Sigma Xi, Phi Delta Chi, Phi Sigma Kappa, Rho Chi. Home: 1415 Brooklyn Ave Ann Arbor MI 48104-4496 Office: U Mich Coll Pharmacy Ann Arbor MI 48109-1065 Office Phone: 734-763-4267. Business E-Mail: arapaul@umich.edu.

PAUL, ARTHUR, artist, illustrator, graphics designer, design consultant; b. Chgo., Jan. 18, 1925; m. Beatrice Miller, Dec. 24, 1949 (div. 1973); children: William Warren, Fredric; m. Suzanne Seed, Mar. 8, 1975; 1 stepdaughter, Nina. Student, Inst. Design, 1947-51. Vice-pres., art dir. HMH Pub. Co., Playboy, Chgo., 1953-82; also sr. art dir., corp. art dir. Playboy mag.; pres. Art Paul Design; freelance artist Chgo., 1984—. Lectr. in field. Freelance illustrator, designer, 1951-53; designer 1st issue: Playboy mag, 1953, Playboy Rabbit symbol, 1953; one-man shows include Etc. Gallery, 1949, 500D Gallery, 1965, U. Ill., 1965, Visual Identity Chgo., 1991, Chgo. Cultural Ctr., 1997-98; organizer, exhibitor: travelling exhbn. Beyond Illustration-The Art of Playboy; museums, Europe, Asia, U.S., 1971-73, Can., 1976-77; author: Vision-Art Paul, 1983, Art of Playboy, 1986, Sex Appeal, 2000; designer PBS-TV title Sence of Humor for humorous feature film presentations on American Playhouse; prodn. design cons. (PBS-TV movie) Who Am I This Time?; featured in Contemporary Master Works, 1991, Print mag., 2000, Graphis mag., 2004, Picturing Text, 2004. Trustee Chgo. Mus. Contemporary Art, 1970-86; apptd. trustee by Gov. of Ill. to Ill. Summer Sch. of Arts, 1987—. With USAAF, 1943-46. Recipient numerous art awards, including Outstanding Achievement in Trademark Design for Playboy Mag. award Soc. Typographic Arts, 1970, Gold medal for exhbn. Beyond Illustration City of Milan, 1971, Polycube award Art Dirs. Club Phila., 1975, Art Direction Mag. award, 1975, Top Midwest Mktg. award Playboy TV Subscription Ad, 1979, 82, Gold medal for Chgo. Film Festival poster Art Dirs. Club N.Y., 1980, Profl. Achievement award IIT Inst. Design Alumni Assn., 1983, Herb Lubecin Lifetime Achievement award Soc. Publ. Designers, 2006; Art Inst. scholar, 1943; named to Art Dirs. Hall of Fame, 1986. Mem. Alliance Graphique Internat. *Design is more than a sense of order for me. It is beauty and common sense. To draw, to paint and to look at art is in the fabric of my life. I enjoy working with ideas and seeing them develop into a reality, after which I am fortunate enough to learn whether they have performed as intended.*

PAUL, BESSIE MARGRETTE, retired weather forecaster; b. Absher, Mont., June 24, 1926; d. Fredrick Ernest Bergman and Margrette Marie Daly; m. Theodore Eugene Paul, Dec. 1, 1949 (dec. 1964); 1 child, Barbara Marie. AS, Eastern Montana Coll., 1988; BSBA in bus. adminstrn., Eastern Mont. Coll., 1992. Weather observer, map plotter US Weather Bur., Billings, Mont., 1944—53, map plotter San Francisco, 1955—56; forecaster Nat. Oceanic and Atmospheric Adminstrn., 1956—81; ret., 1981. Mem.: AAUW, Order of Eastern Star, Nat. Assn. Active and Ret. Fed. Employee. Avocations: cooking, baking, gardening, exercise, reading. Home: 2425 Ave B Billings MT 59102

PAUL, BIPUL C., research scientist; s. Dasarathi and Sephali Paul; m. Manjulika Saha, Jan. 19, 2001. MTech, U. Calcutta, India, 1993—95; PhD, Indian Inst. Sci., Bangalore, 1996—99. Design engr. Alliance Semiconductor, Bangalore, 1999; rsch. assoc. Purdue U., W.Lafayette, Ind., 2000—05; rsch. scientist Toshiba Am. Rsch. Inc., San Jose, Calif., 2005—; vis. scientist Stanford U., Calif., 2005—. Editor: IET Digital Technologies on Computers, 2007—, Jour. Low Power Electronics, 2007—. Sr. Rsch. fellow, Coun. Sci. & Indsl. Rsch., Govt. India, 1995. Mem.: IEEE (sr.; Best Paper award 2006), Giga Scale Silicon Rsch., Assn. Computing Machinary. Achievements include invention of device design for ultra-low power subthreshold circuit operation; design of robust circuit design techniques in the nanoscale regime; research in state-of-the-art memory design; patents pending for high performance circuit design; modeling of nanoscale device such as carbon nanotubes and nanowires for high performance circuit applications. Personal E-mail: bipul_paul@hotmail.com.

PAUL, CAROL ANN, retired academic administrator, biology educator; b. Brockton, Mass., Dec. 17, 1936; d. Joseph W. and Mary M. (DeMeulenaer) Bjork; m. Robert D. Paul, Dec. 21, 1957; children: Christine, Dana, Stephanie, Robert. BS, U. Mass., 1958; MAT, R.I. Coll., 1968, Brown U., 1970; EdD, Boston U., 1978. Tchr. biology Attleboro (Mass.) High Sch., 1965-68; asst. dean., mem. faculty biology North Shore Community Coll., Beverly, Mass., 1969-78; master planner N.J. Dept. for Higher Edn., Trenton, 1978-80; assoc. v.p. Fairleigh Dickinson U., Rutherford, N.J., 1980-86; v.p. acad. affairs Suffolk Community Coll., Selden, N.Y., 1986-94, prof. biology, 1994-98; ret., 1998. Faculty devel. cons. various colls., 1979-98, title III evaluator, 1985-98. Author: (lab. manual and workbook) Minicourses and Labs for Biological Science, 1972 (rev. edit., 1975); (with others) Strategies and Attitudes, 1986; book reviewer, 1973-77, 94-98. V.p. LWV, Beverly, 1970—74, Cranford, NJ, 1982—83; alumni rep. Brown U., 1972—92; mem. Cape Cod Area LWV, 2001—03; mem. bd. dirs. YMCA of Cape Cod, 2004—07, bd. dirs., clk. of bd., 1998—2003. Commonwealth Mass. scholar, 1954-58; recipient Acad. Yr. award NSF, 1968-69, Proclamation for Leadership award Suffolk County Exec., 1989. Mem.: AAUW, AAWCC, AAHE, Nat. Coun. for Staff (nat. exec. bd. 1979—80), Profls. and Orgn. Developers (planning com. 1977—79), Brown Alumni Club of Cape Cod (sec. 2001—04, bd. dirs. 2001—07), Pi Lambda Theta, Phi Theta Kappa. Roman Catholic. Avocation: swimming. Home: 640 Washington ST East Walpole MA 02032 Personal E-mail: artrdpaul@verizon.net.

PAUL, CHRIS, professional basketball player; b. Winston-Salem, NC, May 6, 1985; Attended, Wake Forrest Univ., NC, 2002—05. Guard New Orleans Hornets, 2005—. Recipient ACC Rookie Yr., 2003—04, ACC Player Yr. award, 2004—05, Best Breakthrough, Espy award, 2006. Achievements include Rookie Yr. honors with nearly unanimous vote for top ten league ratings in assists, steals, top rookie ratings in points, steals, assists, 2005-2006. Office: New Orleans/Oklahoma City Hornets Ste 1850 Olahoma Tower 210 Park Ave Oklahoma City OK 73102

PAUL, DEBAJYOTI, geologist, educator; s. Anil Kumar and Kananbala Paul; m. Rumjhum Arora, Dec. 16, 2005. PhD in Geology, Cornell U., 2002. Postdoctoral fellow Max-Planck-Institut fur Chemie, Mainz, Germany, 2002—04; asst. prof. U. Tex., San Antonio, 2004—. Reviewer: Jour. Geochemistry, Geophysics, Geosystems, Jour. Geophysical Rsch., NSF. Recipient Gold medal for securing 1st position in MSc in Geology, Andhra U., India, 1994, Faculty Rsch. award, U. Tex. at San Antonio, 2005; Long fellow, Cornell U., 1998—99, Grad. Rsch. Assistantship, NSF, 2001—02, Alexander von Humboldt Rsch. fellow, Alexander von Humboldt Found., Germany, 2004. Mem.: Alexander von Humboldt Assn. Am., Geol. Soc. Am., Am. Geophys. Union, Geochemical Soc. Home Phone: 12107241204. Office Fax: 210-458-4469. Business E-Mail: debajyoti.paul@utsa.edu.

PAUL, EVE W., retired lawyer; b. NYC, June 16, 1930; d. Leo I. and Tamara (Sogolow) Weinschenker; m. Robert David Paul, Apr. 9, 1952; children: Jeremy Ralph, Sarah Elizabeth. BA, Cornell U., 1950; JD, Columbia U., 1952. Bar: N.Y. 1952, Conn. 1960, U.S. Ct. Appeals (2nd cir.) 1975, U.S. Supreme Ct. 1977. Assoc. Botein, Hays, Sklar & Herzberg, NYC, 1952-54; pvt. practice Stamford, Conn., 1960-70; staff atty. Legal Aid Soc., NYC, 1970-71; assoc. Greenbaum, Wolff & Ernst, NYC, 1972-78; v.p. legal affairs Planned Parenthood Fedn. Am., NYC, 1979—91, v.p., gen. counsel, 1991—2003; ret., 2003. Bd. dirs. Ctr. Advancement of Women, Inc. Contbr. articles to profl. jours Trustee Cornell U., Ithaca, N.Y., 1979-84; mem. Stamford (Conn.) Planning Bd., 1967-70; bd. dirs. Stamford LWV, 1960-62. Harlan Fiske Stone scholar Columbia Law Sch., 1952. Mem.: ABA, Fairfield County Bar Assn., Assn. Bar of City of N.Y., Conn. Bar Assn., Phi Kappa Phi, Phi Beta Kappa. Personal E-mail: evewpaul@aol.com. *The ability to plan the number and timing of my children has made it possible for me to enjoy career, marriage and family.*

PAUL, GARY WAYNE, music educator; b. Tulsa, July 15, 1954; s. Bill and Ellen Ada Paul; m. Bonnie Jean McIntosh, May 22, 1981; children: Jeanette Ellen, Marisa Nicole. BA in Edn., East Ctrl. U., 1977. Dir. bands Joliet H.S., Mont., 1987—88, Yale H.S., Okla., 1988—91, Hominy H.S., 1991—93, Wetumka H.S., 1993—96, Pocola H.S., 1996—99, Chelsea H.S., 1999—2003, Inola H.S., 2003—. Chair Mid-East Honor Band, Glenpool, Okla., 2000; adjudicator Northeastern A&M Coll. Contest, Miami, 1992; mem. staff ARk. Tech. U. Band Camp, Russellville, 1996—99. Mem. Tulsa Cmty. Band, 2001—. Mem.: Music Edn. Nat. Conf., Okla. Music Educators Assn., Okla. Bandmasters Assn. Democrat. Avocations: tennis, golf, camping. Home: 107 E 9th Pl S Claremore OK 74017 Office; Inola High Sch Inola OK 74036 Office Phone: 918-543-3122. Personal E-mail: bdpaul@olp.net. E-mail: gpaul3@cox.net.

PAUL, GEORGE, television director; b. 1929; Studied Acctg., Northwestern U. Stage mgr. WBKB-TV, Chgo., 1954—57, local staff dir., 1957—69, KNBC-TV, LA, 1969; with Am. Broadcasting Co., 1989—. Dir.: (TV series) Polka Go-Round, 1959—61, The Nancy Wilson Show, El Teatro Campesino, The Tomorrow Show with Tom Snyder, 1976, The Today Show, 1982, 20/20, 1989—, Primetime, Good Morning Am., This Week With David Brinkley, 20/20 Downtown; (documentaries) The Slow Guillotine. Mem.: Directors Guild of Am. (Nat. Bd. mem., Midwest Exec. Sec., 2006 Lifetime Achievement award in News Direction). Office: c/o ABC-News 7 W 66th St New York NY 10023 *

PAUL, GERALD D., electronics executive; D in Physics, Tech. U. Munich. Asst. to mgr. capacitor plant Draloric Electronic GmbH, Selb, Germany, 1978; from prodn. mgr. to mng. dir. Vishay Intertechnology, Malvern, Pa., 1987-94, pres. electronic components Europe, 1994-96, COO, 1996—2006, pres., 1998—, CEO, 2004—. Office: Vishay Intertechnology 63 Lancaster Ave Malvern PA 19355 *

PAUL, GORDON LEE, behavioral scientist, psychologist; b. Marshalltown, Iowa, Sept. 2, 1935; s. Leon Dale and Ione Hickman (Perry) P.; m. Joan Marie Wyatt, Dec. 24, 1954; children: Dennis Leon, Dana Lee, Joni Lynn. Student, Marshalltown Community Coll., 1953-54, San Diego City Coll., 1955-57; BA, U. Iowa, 1960; MA, U. Ill., 1962, PhD, 1964. Social sci. analyst VA Hosp., Danville, Ill., 1962; counseling psychologist U. Ill., Urbana, 1963; clin. psychologist VA Hosp., Palo Alto, Calif., 1964-65; pvt. practice clin. psychology, 1964-65; asst. prof. psychology U. Ill., Champaign-Urbana, 1965-67, assoc. prof., 1967-70, prof., 1970-80; Cullen disting. prof. psychology U. Houston, 1980—; pvt. practice psychology Champaign, 1965-80, Houston, 1980—. Psychotherapy rsch. cons., Palo Alto, 1964-65; cons. Ill. Dept. Mental Health, 1965-73, 78-82, NIMH, 1968-78; adviser Ont. (Can.) Mental Health Found., 1968-69, NSF, 1968-69, Can. Coun., 1969-75, VA, 1972, 80—, APA, 1970—, UCLA/VA Med. Ctr./Camarillo Schizophrenia Rsch. Ctr., 1978-93, Alliance for Mentally Ill, 1980—. Author: Insight vs. Desensitization in Psychotherapy, An Experiment in Anxiety Reduction, 1966, Anxiety and Clinical Problems, 1973, Psychosocial Treatment of Chronic Mental Patients, 1977, Assessment in Residential Treatment Settings, Part 1, 1986, Observational Assessment Instrumentation for Service and Research, Part 2, 1987, Part 3, 1988; mem. editl. bd. Behavior Therapy, 1969-75, Behavior Therapy and Exptl. Psychiatry, 1969—, Schizophrenia Bull., 1971-99, Jour. Abnormal Psychology, 1972-76, Jour. Behavioral Residential Treatment, 1983—96, Jour. Psychopathology and Behavioral Assessment, 1985—; cons. editor Jour. Applied Behavior Analysis, 1966-77, 81—, Psychol. Bull., 1967—, Jour. Abnormal Psychology, 1970-72, 76—, Psychosomatic Medicine, 1971-77, Psychophysiology, 1971—77, Archives Gen. Psychiatry, 1973-74, Behavior Therapy, 1976-87, Profl. Psychologist, 1977-87, Psychiat. Svcs. (formerly Hosp. Cmty. Psychiatry), 1980—, Biobehavioral Revs., 1980-84, Jour. Cmty. Psychology, 1983, Am. Psychologist, 1983—, Brit. Jour. Clin. Psychology, 1985-87, Jour. Nervous and Mental Disease, 1992, Current Directions in Psychol. Sci., 1992—; contbr. articles to profl. jours. Served with USN, 1954-58. Recipient Creative Talent award Am. Inst. Rsch., 1964, Teaching award U. Ill., 1968, 75; rsch. award Mental Health Assn., 1985; listed one of 327 Best Mental Health Experts in Nation, Good Housekeeping, 1994; NIMH fellow, 1963-64. Fellow APA (corr. com. 1965-70, pres. sect. III div. 12 1972-73, exec. coun. div. 12 1974-77, Disting. Scientist award sect. III, div. 12 1977, Disting. Sci. Contbns. to Clin. Psychology award Soc. Clin. Psychology divsn. 12 1999), Am. Psychol. Soc., Assn. Clin. Psychosocial Rsch., Am. Assn. Applied and Preventive Psychology; mem. Midwestern Psychol. Assn., Tex. Psychol. Assn., Houston Psychol. Assn., Assn. for Advancement Psychology, Phi Beta Kappa, Chi Gamma Iota. Achievements include being subject of NIMH sci. report monograph, 1981: Treating and Assessing the Chronically Mentally Ill: The Pioneering Research of Gordon L. Paul. Office: U Houston Dept Psychology 126 Heyne Bldg Houston TX 77204-5022 Home: 3402 Parkside Dr Pearland TX 77584 Home Phone: 281-692-9543; Office Phone: 713-743-8564. Business E-Mail: gpaul@uh.edu.

PAUL, HERBERT MORTON, lawyer, accountant, educator; b. NYC; s. Julius and Gussie Paul; m. Judith Paul; children: Leslie Beth, Andrea Lynn. BBA, Baruch Coll.; MBA, LLM, NYU; JD, Harvard U. Ptnr. Touche Ross & Co. (predecessor Deloitte Touche), NYC, assoc. nat. dir. tax, dir. fin counseling; mng. ptnr. Herbert Paul, P.C., NYC, 1983—. Prof. taxation, trustee NYU. Author: Ordinary and Necessary Expenses; editor: Taxation of Banks; adv. tax editor The Practical Acct.; mem. adv. bd. Financial and Estate Planning, Tax Shelter Insider, Financial Planning Strategist, Tax Shelter Litigation Report; bd. dirs. Partnership Strategist, The Business Strategist; cons. Profl. Practice Mgmt. Mag.; mem. panel The Hot Line; advisor The Partnership Letter, The Wealth Formula; cons. The Insider's Report for Physicians; mem. tax bd. Business Profit Digest; cons. editor physician's Tax Advisor; bd. fin. cons. Tax Strategies for Physicians; tax and bus. advisor Prentice Hall; contbg. editor. Jour. of Accountancy; mem. editl. bd. Family Bus. Advisor. Life trustee NYU, mem. bd. overseers Grad. Sch. Bus.; mem. com. on trusts and estates Rockefeller U.; trustee Alvin Alley Am. Dance Theatre, Assoc. Y's of N.Y.; mem. accts. divsn. Fedn. Philanthropies; mem. adv. bd. Family Bus. Advisor. Mem. ABA, Inst. Fed. Taxation (adv. com. chmn.), Internat. Inst. on Tax and Bus. Planning (adv. bd.), Assn. Bar City N.Y., NYU Tax Soc. (pres.), Bur. Nat. Affairs-Tax Mgmt. (adv. com. on exec. compensation), Am. Inst. CPAs (com. on corp. taxation), Tax Study Group, N.Y. County Lawyers Assn., N.Y. State Soc. CPAs Dir. (chmn. tax div. com. on fed. taxation, gen. tax com., furtherance com., com. on rels. with IRS, bd. dirs.), Nat. Assn. Accts., Assn. of Bar of City of N.Y., Accts. Club of Am., Pension Club, Nat. Assn. Estate Planners (bd. dirs.), N.Y. Estate Planning Coun. (bd. dirs.), N.Y. C. of C. (tax com.), Grad. Sch. Bus. of NYU Alumni Assn. (pres.), NYU Alumni Assn. (pres.), Wall St. Club, City Athletic Club (N.Y.C.), Inwood Country Club. Office: Herbert Paul PC 450 7th Ave Ste 3000 New York NY 10123 Office Phone: 212-752-3700.

PAUL, JAMES CAVERLY NEWLIN, law educator, retired dean; b. Chestnut Hill, Pa., Apr. 30, 1926; s. William Allen Butler and Adelaide Sims (Newlin) P.; m. Margaret Morris Clausen, June 25, 1948; children: Nicholas Newlin, Martha Morris, Adelaide Sims. BA, Princeton U., 1948; JD, U. Pa., 1951. Bar: Pa. 1952. Legal sec. to Chief Justice US, 1951-53; asst. prof. U. NC, 1953-55; asst. dir. Inst. Govt., U. NC, 1953-55; prof. law, dir. Inst. Legal Research, U. Pa., 1955—67; prof. law, dean and founder of faculty of law Haile Selassie U., Ethiopia, 1962—67, v.p. acad. affairs, 1967-69; exec. v.p. Ednl. and World Affairs, NYC, 1969-70; dean Sch. Law, Rutgers U., Newark, 1970-74, prof. law, 1970-96, Newhouse scholar in law, 1984-88, William J. Brennan prof., 1988-96; exec. sec., trustee Internat. Ctr. for Law in Devel., NYC, 1974—. Founding mem., sec.-treas. Internat. Third World Legal Studies Assn., NYC, 1980—96; adj. prof. Columbia U., 1973—95; cons. US Peace Corps, 1961—62, Constl. Commn. Transitional Govt. of Ethiopia, 1992—95, UN Devel. Programme, 1994—96, 2005; commr. Internat. Eritrean-Ethioplan Claims Commn., The Hague, 2001—; chmn. Fund for Assistance to Legal Edn. in Ethiopia and Eritrea, 2006—. Author: Rift in the Democracy, 1951, The School Segregation Decision, 1954, 9with others) Federal Censorship, 1961, Ethiopian Constitutional Development, 1969, Lawyers in the Third World, 1981, The International Context of Rural Poverty in the Third World, 1986, Incorporating Human Rights Into the World Summit for Social Development, 1995; editor-in-chief U. Pa. Law Rev., 1950-51. Candidate for US Congress from 9th Dist. Pa., 1958; del. Dem. Nat. Conv., 1960. Served with USNR (Amphibious forces), 1943-46, PTO. Recipient Spl. medal for distinguished service to the devel. of law and univ. edn. in Ethiopia, Emperor Haile Sellassie 1st, 1969; Eisenhower Exch. fellow, Africa, 1960. Mem. ABA, NJ Bar Assn., Pa. Bar Assn., Am. Soc. Internat. Law, Internat. Third World Legal Studies Assn. (sec.-treas. 1980-96), Orgn. Am. Historians, Am. Law and History Assn., Order of Coif, Princeton Club (NYC). Home: 1352 Chancellor Pt Trappe MD 21673-1540 Personal E-mail: jpaul@goeaston.net. *My life in law and teaching about law gives satisfaction because it enables me to direct my energies towards thinking about social justice, individual dignity, and the possibilities of attaining more of the conditions enabling these ideals. But that satisfaction is tempered by constant realization of my own frailities and the failure everywhere of people, particularly those most fortunately endowed, to be guided by principled thinking.*

PAUL, JAMES WILLIAM, lawyer; b. Davenport, Iowa, May 3, 1945; s. Walter Henry and Margaret Helene (Hillers) P.; m. Sandra Kay Schmid, June 15, 1968; children: James William, Joseph Hillers. BA, Valparaiso U., 1967; JD, U. Chgo., 1970. Bar: N.Y. 1971, U.S. Ct. Appeals (2d cir.) 1971, U.S. Dist. Ct. (so. and ea. dists.) N.Y. 1972, U.S. Supreme Ct. 1977, U.S. Ct. Appeals (6th cir.) 1981, Ind. 1982, U.S. Dist. Ct. (no. dist.) Ind. 1982, U.S. Claims Ct. 1989, U.S. Dist. Ct. (ea. dist.) Mich. 1989, U.S. Ct. Appeals (fed. cir.) 1991. Assoc. Rogers & Wells, NYC, 1970-78, ptnr., 1978—; ptnr., gen. counsel Clifford Chance US LLP, NYC, 2000—. Officer Musica Sacra, Inc., 1972—81. Bd. dirs. Turtle Bay Music Sch., Am. Luth. Publicity Bur., Wartburg Found., chmn. bd., 2004—06. Recipient Disting. Alumnus award, Valparaiso U., 1994. Mem. ABA (antitrust sect. ins. com.), Assn. Bar City N.Y. (com. legal and jud. ethics, com. on civil ct., com. profl. discipline), Fed. Bar Coun. Democrat. Home: 360 E 72nd St Apt A-710 New York NY 10021-4755 also: 5 Curtis Dr Sherman CT 06784-1220 Office: Clifford Chance US LLP 31 W 52nd St New York NY 10019-6131 Home Phone: 212-472-1459; Office Phone: 212-878-8227. Business E-Mail: james.paul@cliffordchance.com.

PAUL, JERALD S., former federal agency administrator, state legislator; b. Lancaster, Ohio, Feb. 26, 1966; m. Kristina L. Paul; children: Jared, Lauren. BS, Maine Maritime Acad.; MS, U. Fla.; JD, Stetson U. Nuclear engr. E.I. Hatch Nuclear Plant; ptnr. McKinley, Ittersagen, Gunderson and Berntsson, PA; mem. Fla. Ho. of Reps.; prin. dep. adminstr. Nat. Nuclear Security Adminstrn., US Dept. Energy, Washington, 2004—06; Disting. Fellow on Energy Policy, Howard H. Baker Ctr. on Pub. Policy U. Tenn., Knoxville, 2007—. Office: Howard H Baker Ctr on Pub Policy Rm 217 James D Hoskins Libr Knoxville TN 37996 *

PAUL, JOHN CHARLES, lawyer; b. Norwalk, Conn., Mar. 3, 1954; s. John Andrew and Alberta (Miserendino) P. AB, Brown U., 1976; JD, Case Western Res. U., 1979. Bar: Ohio 1979, DC 1981, US.Patent and Trademark Office 1981, US Ct. Appeals (DC Cir.) 1981, US Ct. Appeals (Fed. Cir.) 1982, US Dist. Ct. DC 1982, US Supreme Ct. 1983. Patent examiner U.S. Patent and Trademark Office, Arlington, Va., 1980-81; assoc. Bacon & Thomas, Arlington, 1981-84, Finnegan, Henderson, Farabow, Garrett & Dunner LLP, Washington, 1984-91, ptnr., 1991--, leader, Intellectual Property Mgmt. Sect. Adj. faculty Cath. U. Law Sch., 1999—2003. Mem. ABA (young lawyers div. vice chmn. patent, trademark, copyright law com. 1989-90), Fed. Bar Assn. (young lawyers div., bd. dirs. 1982-85), DC Bar Assn. (young lawyers sect., exec. coun. 1987-90), Licensing Execs. Soc. (trustee 2005—). Office: Finnegan Henderson Farabow Garrett & Dunner LLP 901 New York Ave NW Washington DC 20001-3315 Office Phone: 202-408-4109. Office Fax: 202-408-4400. Business E-Mail: john.paul@finnegan.com.

PAUL, KENNETH, newspaper editor; b. NYC, June 7, 1948; s. Samuel D. and Rose (Markoff) P.; m. Sevara Jeleva, Dec. 5, 1993; 1 child, Kathryn Hannah. BA in English, Dartmouth Coll., Hanover, NH, 1969; spl. diploma in social studies, Oxford U., Eng., 1973. Tchr. Concord HS, NH, 1969-71; dep. European editor LA Times/Washington Post News Svc., London, 1972-73; reporter, news editor Riverside Press Enterprise, Calif., 1973-76; specialists editor, copy editor, asst. nat. and day nat. editor Newsday, NY, 1976—87; mng. editor NY Observer, NYC, 1987-91; editor The Litchfield County Times, New Milford, Conn., 1993—2002, Housatonic Pubs., New Milford, 2001—02; editor-in-chief Manhattan Media, NYC, 2002—04; day editor The NY Sun, NYC, 2004—05; staff editor New York Times, 2005—. Business E-Mail: kenpaul@nytimes.com.

PAUL, LAURENCE M., editor; BA, Drake U., Des Moines, IA. Asst. mng. editor Des Moines Register; with NY Times, 1989—98; dep. editor NY Times News Svc., 1998—99, exec. editor, 1999—, NY Times Syndication Sales Corp., 2000—. Office: NY Times News Svc 9th Fl 229 W 43rd St New York NY 10036 also: NY Times Syndication Sales Corp 14th Fl 122 E 42nd St New York NY 10168 Office Phone: 212-556-4149. Office Fax: 212-556-3535, 212-499-3382. E-mail: lmpaul@nytimes.com.

PAUL, LES, entertainer; b. Waukesha, Wis., June 9, 1915; s. George and Evelyn (Stutz) Polfuss; m. Mary Ford; children: Lester, Gene, Colleen, Robert, Mary. Student pub. schs., Waukesha. Appeared on numerous radio programs throughout Midwest, in 1920's and 1930's, formed Les Paul Trio, 1936—37, and appeared with Fred Waring, N.Y.C., appeared on first television broadcast with an orch. from NBC, N.Y.C., 1939; mus. dir: WJJD and WIND, 1941; appeared with Mary Ford on own television show, Mahwah, N.J., 1953—57, host Edison 100th Anniversary of invention of phonograph at Edison Home, West Orange, N.J, 1977, numerous TV, club appearances especially Fat Tuesday's, N.Y.C, recs. include Lover and Brazil, 1948, Nola, 1949, Goofus, 1950, Tennessee Waltz, 1950, Little Rock Getaway, 1950, Mockin' Bird Hill, 1951, Just One More Chance, 1951, Walkin' and Whistlin' Blues, 1951, How High The Moon, 1951 (Hall of Fame award 1979), Smoke Rings, 1952, The World's Waiting For The Sunrise, 1952, Tiger Rag, 1953, Meet Mr. Callaghan, 1953, Jazz Me Blues, 1952, Vaya Con Dios, 1954, Chester and Lester, 1976 (Grammy award), Guitar Monsters, 1977 (Grammy nominee), The Legend and the Legacy, 1991, The Best of the Capitol Masters with Mary Ford, 1992, The Guitar Artistry of Les Paul, Greatest Hits!, 1994. Served with Armed Forces Radio Service, World War II. Named to Grammy Hall of Fame Les Paul and Mary Ford, 1977, Rock 'N' Roll Hall of Fame, 1988, Wis. Performing Artists Hall of Fame, 1990, Nat. Inventors Hall of Fame, 2005; recipient Grammy Achievement award for contbns. to rec., musical instruments industry. Mem.: SAG, ASCAP, AFTRA, Am. Fedn. Musicians, Audio Engring. Soc. Achievements include consultant, Gibson Guitar Corp., Nashville; invention of multi-track tape recorder; first 8-track tape recorder; sound-on-sound recording; design of Les Paul electric solid body guitars. Address: Columbia Records Sony Music Entertainment 550 Madison Ave Fl 24 New York NY 10022-3211 *To be successful requires hard work, determination, a positive attitude, believing in one's self, a God given talent and luck.*

PAUL, NORMAN LEO, psychiatrist, educator; b. Buffalo, July 5, 1926; s. Samuel Joseph and Tannie (Goncharsky) P.; m. Betty Ann Byfield, June 6, 1951 (dec. May 1994); children: Marilyn, David Alexander; m. Janet Athos, Aug. 16, 2002. MD, U. Buffalo, 1948. Fellow pharmacology U. Cin. Coll. Medicine, Ohio, 1949-50; resident psychiatry Mass. Mental Health Ctr., Boston, 1952-55; fellow child psychiatry James Jackson Putnam Children's Ctr., Boston, 1957-59, Mass. Gen. Hosp., Boston, 1958-59; chief psychiatrist Day Hosp. Mass. Mental Health Ctr., Boston, 1960-64; dir. conjoint family therapy Boston State Hosp., 1964-65, cons. in family psychiatry, 1965-70; assoc. clin. prof. dept. neurology Boston U. Sch. Medicine, 1977—. Cons. Mental Health Ctr., Alaska Native Hosp., Anchorage, 1967-68; cons. family psychiatry Boston VA Hosp., 1967-71, Mass. Soc. for the Prevention of Cruelty to Children, Boston, 1993—; vis. family therapist St. George's Med. Sch., London, 1996-97; lectr. in psychiatry Harvard Med. Sch., Boston, 1976-2003; faculty assoc. Mgmt. Analysis Corp., Cambridge, Mass., 1979-82; presenter Internat. Conf. on Telemedicine and Telecare, London, 1996 Family therapist: (tv documentary) PBS-Trouble in the Family, 1965 (George Foster Peabody award 1965); co-author A Marital Puzzle, 1977, 86, German edit., 1987, French edit., 1995, Chinese edit., 1997, contbr. articles to profl. jours. Sponsor Mass. Orgn. to Repeal Abortion Laws, Boston, 1965-70; chair Audio Unit of Child Devel. and Mass Media, White House Conf. on Children and Youth, Washington, 1970; bd. trustees Cambridge (Mass.) Coll., 1977-89; bd. dirs. Let's Face It, 1990—, Ctr. for Family Connections, 1998—2002. Capt. USAF, 1950-52. Recipient Edward A. Strecker, M.D. award for young psychiatrist of yr., 1966, Cert. of Merit, Mass. Coun. on Family Life, Boston, 1967, Cert. of Commendation, Mass. Assn. for Mental Health, Boston, 1967, Disting. Achievement award Soc. for Family Therapy and Rsch., Boston, 1973, Lifetime Achievement award Mass. Assn. for Marriage and Family Therapy, 1998, Disting. Svc. award Physician Health Svcs., 1998. Fellow Royal Soc. Medicine, Am. Psychiat. Assn. (life); mem. Am. Assn. Marriage and Family Therapy (bd. dirs. 1983-86), Am. Family Therapy Assn. (v.p. 1982-83, Disting. Contbn. award 1984), Assn. for Rsch. in Nervous and Mental Disorders, Group for the Advancement Psychiatry (chair com. on the family 1982-84). Avocations: study of codes, travel. Office Phone: 978-369-3754. Personal E-mail: nlpaul@aol.com.

PAUL, OGLESBY, cardiologist, educator; b. Villanova, Pa., May 3, 1916; s. Oglesby and Laura Little (Wilson) P.; m. Marquerite Black, May 29, 1943 (dec. Jan. 1979); children: Rodman, Marquerite; m. Jean Lithgow, Jan. 17, 1981. AB, Harvard Coll., 1938; MD, Harvard Med. Sch., 1942. Intern Mass. Gen. Hosp., Boston, 1942-43, resident, 1946-48; prof. medicine Northwestern U., Evanston, Ill., 1963-77; sr. physician emeritus Brigham & Womens Hosp., Boston, 1977—; prof. medicine emeritus Harvard Med. Sch., Boston, 1977—. V.p. health scis. Northwestern U., Evanston, 1974-75; dir. admissions Harvard Med. Sch., Boston, 1977-82. Author: Take Heart, 1986, The Caring Physician, 1991. Pres. Am. Heart Assn., Dallas, 1960-61. Lt. USNR. Home: 10 Longwood Dr Apt 322 Westwood MA 02090-1142 Office: Harvard Med Sch Countway Libr 10 Shattuck St Boston MA 02115-6011 Personal E-mail: oleypaul@aol.com.

PAUL, OUIDA FAY, music educator; b. Deatsville, Ala., Jan. 18, 1911; d. Elza Bland and Martha Eleanor (Hinton) P. AB in Math. and English, Huntingdon Coll., 1930, BS in Music Edn., 1933; MA in Music and Music Edn., Columbia U., 1943, EdD in Music and Music Edn., 1957; postgrad., U. Ill., 1968; studied oil painting, Gloria Foss Sch. of Art, 1978—83. Tchr. math., English and music pub. schs., Ala., 1930—42; tchr. math. Sacred

Heart Convent Sch., NYC, 1942-43; tchr. h.s. choral music Kingsport, Tenn., 1943-45; instr., asst. prof. music edn. Greensboro (N.C.) Coll., 1945-49; asst. prof. U. Fla., Gainesville, 1949-61, U. Hawaii, Honolulu, 1961-68; tchr. musicology and voice Leeward C.C., Pearl City, Hawaii, 1968-77; pvt. tchr. voice, Honolulu, 1977-95, Gainesville, 1996—. Choir dir. 1st Presbyn. Ch., Gainesville, 1950-61, Protestant Chapel, USN, Honolulu, 1962-68, Cmty. Ch., Honolulu, 1969-78, Wesley United Meth. Ch., Honolulu, 1978-94; contralto soloist various chs., 1950-94; adjudicator solo and choral auditions and festivals, 1945-94; tchr. adults with singing problems, 1950-. One-woman art shows include Honolulu Cmty. Theatre, 1980, 84, First United Meth. Ch., 1980; group shows with Honolulu Artists, others; permanent collections René Malmezac, Tahiti; contbr. articles to profl. jours. Cons. to com. on edn. Hawaii Gov.'s Commn. on Status of Women, 1965; English lang. tutor Hawaii Literacy, Inc., Honolulu, 1978-95. Recipient Alumni Achievement award, Huntingdon Coll. Alumnae Assn., 1998. Mem. Music Educators Nat. Conf. (1st v.p. Hawaii 1969-70), Am. Choral Dirs. Assn. (Hawaii chmn. 1963-66), Nat. Assn. Tchrs. Singing, Altrusa (pres. Gainesville 1960-61, past pres. Honolulu), Delta Kappa Gamma (pres. Hawaii Theta chpt. 1963-64, past state music chmn., named one of Makers of Destiny Hawaiian Style 2002.). Methodist. Avocation: painting. Home: 8015 NW 28th Pl Apt B210 Gainesville FL 32606-8607

PAUL, RICHARD WRIGHT, lawyer; b. Washington, May 23, 1953; s. Robert Henry Jr. and Betty (Carey) P.; m. Paula Ann Coolsaet, July 25, 1981; children: Richard Haven, Timothy Carey, Brian Davis. AB magna cum laude, Dartmouth Coll., 1975; JD, Boston Coll., 1978. Bar: Mich. 1978, U.S. Dist. Ct. (ea. dist.) Mich. 1978, U.S. Ct. Appeals (6th cir.) 1982, U.S. Supreme Ct. 1989, U.S. Dist. Ct. (we. dist.) Mich. 1991. Assoc. Dickinson, Wright, Moon, Van Dusen & Freeman, Detroit, 1978-85, ptnr., 1985—. Case evaluator Wayne County Cir. Ct., Oakland County Cir. Ct.; mediator Mich. State Ct. Adminstrv. Office. Co-author, Barbarians At The Gate: Daubert Two Years Later, 1995; contbr. articles to profl. publs. Trustee Bloomfield Village Assn., Birmingham, Mich., 2001-04, sec., 2003-04, bd. dirs; mem. Little League, Birmingham, 2000-07, treas. 2005-07; treas. Seaholm Baseball Boosters, 2005—, v.p., 2006, pres., 2007—. Mem. ABA, State Bar of Mich. (treas. litig. sect. 1998-99, sec. litig. sect. 1999-2000, chmn. elect litig. sect. 2000-01, chairperson litigation sect. 2001-02, mem. representative assembly 2004—), Def. Rsch. Inst., Detroit Met. Bar Assn., Mich. Def. Trial Counsel, Dartmouth Lawyers Assn., Oakland County Bar Assn., Assn. Def. Trial Counsel, Alumni Coun. Dartmouth Coll., Dartmouth Detroit Club (pres. 1980—). Avocations: tennis, bicycling. Office Phone: 248-433-7200. Business E-Mail: rpaul@dickinsonwright.com.

PAUL, ROBERT ARTHUR, steel company executive; b. NYC, Oct. 28, 1937; s. Isadore and Ruth (Goldstein) P.; m. Donna Rae Berkman, July 29, 1962; children: Laurence Edward, Stephen Eric, Karen Rachel. AB, Cornell U., 1959; JD, Harvard U., 1962, MBA, 1964. With Ampco-Pitts. Corp. (formerly Screw & Bolt Corp. Am.), 1964—, v.p., 1969-71, treas., 1973-79, exec. v.p., 1972-79, pres., COO, 1979-94, pres., CEO, 1994—2004, dir., 1969—, chmn., CEO, 2004—. Pres., bd. dirs. Louis Berkman Co.; bd. dirs. ECHO Real Estate Svs.; gen. ptnr. Romar Trading Co.; instr. Grad. Sch. Indsl. Adminstrn. Carnegie Mellon U., 1966-69; trustee emeritus Cornell U.; bd. dirs. Pitts. br. Fed. Res. Bank Cleve. Trustee H.L. and Louis Berkman Found., U. Pitts. Med. Ctr. Sys., Jewish Healthcare Found., U. Pitts.; trustee, pres. Fair Oaks Found. Mem. ABA, Mass. Bar Assn., Harvard Club (NY), Pitts. Athletic Club, Duquesne Club, Laurel Valley Golf Club, Fox Chapel Golf Club. Republican. Jewish. Office: Ampco-Pitts Corp 600 Grant St Pittsburgh PA 15219-2702 Office Phone: 412-456-4400. Personal E-mail: rpaul@ampcopgh.com.

PAUL, ROBERT CAREY, lawyer; b. Washington, May 7, 1950; s. Robert Henry and Betty Jane (Carey) Paul. AB, Dartmouth Coll., 1972; JD, Georgetown U., 1978. Assoc. Milbank, Tweed, Hadley & McCloy, NYC, 1978—85; ptnr. Dechert Price & Rhoads, NYC, 1986—89, Kelley Drye & Warren, Brussels, 1989—93; counsel Rockefeller & Co., Inc., NYC, 1995—2003; cons. NYC, 2003—05; corp. coun. Rockefeller Group Internat., Inc., 2005—; v.p. Rockefeller Group Tech. Solutions, Inc., 2005—, corp. coun., 2005—, chief adminstrv. officer, 2007—. Editor-in-chief Real Property Probate and Trust Jour., 2001—06. Mem.: ABA (real property, probate and trust law sect. coun. 2006—), Am. Coll. Real Estate Lawyers. Home: 310 E 46th St Apt 19E New York NY 10017-3029 Office: 1221 Ave of the Americas New York NY 10020 Office Phone: 212-282-2650. Business E-Mail: rpaul@rockgrp.com.

PAUL, ROLAND ARTHUR, lawyer; b. Memphis, Jan. 19, 1937; s. Rol and Hattye (Mincer) P.; m. Barbara Schlesinger, June 10, 1962; children: Deborah Lynn, Arthur Eliot. BA summa cum laude, Yale U., 1958; LL.B. magna cum laude, Harvard U., 1961. Bar: N.Y. 1962, Mich. 1978, Conn. 1989. Law clk. to judge U.S. Ct. Appeals, 1961-62; fgn. affairs officer, spl. asst. to gen. counsel Dept. Def., 1962-64; assoc. firm Cravath, Swaine & Moore, NYC, 1964-69; counsel fgn. relations subcom. security commitments U.S. Senate, 1969-71; assoc. firm Simpson Thacher Bartlett, NYC, 1971-73; v.p., gen. counsel Howmet Corp., Greenwich, Conn., 1976-2000, Howmet Internat. Inc., 1997-2000; v.p., gen. counsel, dir. Pechiney Corp., Greenwich, Conn., 1984-95; counsel Day, Berry & Howard, Stamford, Conn., 2000—03, Ivey, Barnum & O'Mara, Greenwich, 2003—. Author: American Military Commitments Abroad. Mem. ABA, Coun. Fgn. Rels. Home: 8 Ellery Ln Westport CT 06880-5202 Office: 170 Mason St Greenwich CT 06832 Office Phone: 203-862-7740.

PAUL, RONALD ERNEST, congressman; b. Pitts., Aug. 20, 1935; m. Carol Paul; 5 children. BA, Gettysburg Coll., Pa., 1957; MD, Duke U. Med. Ctr., Durham, NC, 1961. Intern, resident Henry Ford Hosp., Detroit, 1961, 1962; ob-gyn. tng. U. Pitts., 1965—68; physician pvt. practice Brazoria County, Tex., 1968; mem. US Congress from 14th Tex. dist., 1976—77, 1979—85, 1997—, mem. internat. rels. com., mem. joint econ. com., mem. fin. svcs. com., vice chmn. oversight and investigations subcommittee. Author: Challenge to Liberty, The Case for Gold, A Republic: If You Can Keep It. Flight surgeon USAF, 1963—65, flight surgeon US Air N.G., 1965—68. Recipient Taxpayer's Best Friend award Nat. Taxpayers Union, Mises Inst. Groseclose Prize and Leadership award, Leadership award Coalition for Peace Through Strength, Disting. Svc. award Am. Constl. Action, Torch Freedom award Young Conservatives Tex., Guardian Freedom award Young Am. Freedom. Republican. Office Phone: 202-225-2831. *

PAUL, RONALD NEALE, management consultant; b. Chgo., July 22, 1934; s. David Edward and Frances (Kusel) P.; m. Nona Maria Moore, Dec. 27, 1964 (div. Oct. 1981); children: Lisa, Karen, Brenda; m. Georgeann Elizabeth Lapkoff, Apr. 10, 1982. BS in Indsl. Engring., Northwestern U., 1957, MBA, 1958. Asst. to pres. Victor Comptometer Co., Chgo., 1958-64; cons. Corplan, Chgo., 1964-66; pres. Technomic Inc., Chgo., 1966—. Mng. ptnr. L/P Ptnrs., Chgo., 1978-84; bd. dirs. Summit Restaurants, Salt Lake City, 1990-96. Co-author: The 101 Best Performing Companies in America, 1986, Winning the Chain Restaurant Game, 1994. Mem. Am. Mktg. Assn., Am. Mgmt. Assn., Planners Forum, Pres.'s Assn., Product Devel. Mgmt. Assn., Beta Gamma Sigma. Avocations: reading, racquetball. Office: Technomic Inc 300 S Riverside Plz Ste 1200 Chicago IL 60606-6613 Office Phone: 312-876-0004. Business E-Mail: rpaul@technomic.com.

PAUL, STEPHEN HOWARD, lawyer; b. Indpls., June 28, 1947; s. Alfred and Sophia (Nahmias) P.; m. Deborah Lynn Dorman, Jan. 22, 1969; children: Gabriel, Jonathan. AB, Ind. U., 1969, JD, 1972. Bar: Ind. 1972, US Dist. Ct. (so. dist.) Ind. 1972. Assoc. Baker & Daniels, Indpls., 1972-78, ptnr., 1979—, chmn. mgmt. com., 2004. Mem. bd. visitors Ind. U. Sch. Law, Bloomington. Editor in chief Ind. U. Law Jour., 1971. Pres. Belle Meade Neighborhood Assn., Indpls., 1974-78; v.p., counsel Brentwood Neighborhood Assn., Carmel, Ind., 1985-88, pres., 1988-91. Mem. ABA (state and local tax com. 1985—, sports and entertainment law com.), Am. Property Tax Counsel (founding mem.), Counsellors to Real Estate, Ind. State Bar Assn., Order of Coif. Office: Baker & Daniels 300 N Meridian St Ste 2700 Indianapolis IN 46204-1782 Office Phone: 317-237-0300. Business E-Mail: stephen.paul@bakerd.com.

PAUL, STEVEN M., pharmaceutical executive; BA magna cum laude in Biology and Psychology, Tulane U., New Orleans, 1972, MS in Anatomy and Neuroanatomy, 1975, MD, 1975. Intern neurology Charity Hosp., New Orleans; resident psychiatry, instr. dept. psychiatry U. Chgo. Pritzker Sch. Medicine; prof. psychiatry Tulane U. Sch. Medicine; chief clin. neuroscience br., chief preclinical studies sect. NIH NIMH, Bethesda, sci. dir. intramural rsch. program; v.p. ctrl. nervous sys. discovery and decision phase med. rsch. Lilly Rsch. Labs. Eli Lilly and Co., Indpls., 1993—96, v.p. therapeutic area discovery rsch. and clin. investigation Lilly Rsch. Labs., 1996—98, group v.p. therapeutic area discovery rsch. and clin. investigation Lilly Rsch. Labs., 1998, exec. v.p. sci. and tech., pres. Lilly Rsch. Labs., 2003—, mem. corp. policy and strategy, ops. coms., mem. sr. mgmt. coun. Chmn. exec. bd. Pharm. Rsch. and Mfrs. Am. Sci. and Regulatory Com.; bd. mem. Biotechnology Industry Orgn. Contbr. articles to profl. jours., chapters to books. Bd. dirs. Lilly Found., Found. of NIH, Butler U., Indpls., Indpls. Zoological Soc. Named Chief Sci. Officer of Yr., 2005; recipient A.E. Bennett award, Soc. Biol. Psychiatry, Foundations' Fund prize for Rsch., Am. Psychiat. Assn., Disting. Svc. medal, US. Mem.: NAS Inst. Medicine, Tulane Scholars and Fellows, Alpha Omega Alpha Med. Soc., Phi Beta Kappa, Sigma Xi, Alpha Epsilon Delta, Phi Eta Sigma. Office: Eli Lilly and Co Lilly Corp Ctr Indianapolis IN 46285 Office Phone: 317-276-2000. *

PAUL, T. V., social sciences educator; b. Kottayam, India, Nov. 10, 1956; m. Rachel Paul, Dec. 30, 1984; children: Kavya, Leah. PhD, UCLA, 1991. Asst. prof. McGill U., Montreal, Que., Canada, 1991—95, assoc. prof., 1995—2000, prof., 2000—02, James McGill prof. internat. rels., 2003—. Vis. scholar Harvard U., Cambridge, Mass., 1997—98; vis. prof. Naval Postgrad. Sch., Monterey, Calif., 2002—03; sr. vis. assoc. Ctr. for Nonproliferation Studies, MIIS, Monterey, 2002—03; dir. Rsch. Group in Internat. Security, Montreal, 2000—02. Author: Assymetric Conflicts: War Initiation by Weaker Powers, 1994, Power versus Prudence: Why Nations Forgo Nuclear Weapons, 2000 (Outstanding Academic Title, Choice Mag., 2001), India in the World Order: Searching for Major Power Status, 2003; editor: The Absolute Weapon Revisited: Nuclear Arms and the Emerging International Order, 1998, International Order and the Future of World Politics, 1999, The Nation-State in Question, 2003, Balance of Power: Theory and Practice in the 21st Century, 2004, The India-Pakistan Conflict: An Enduring Rivalry, 2005. Named a Popular Prof., MacLean's Mag. Guide to Can. Univs., 2005; recipient Peace Scholar award, US Inst. for Peace, 1989; grantee, Rockefeller Found., 1993—96, SSHRC, 1994—2004, Que. Provincial Granting Agy., 1997—. Mem.: Am. Polit. Sci. Assn., Brit. Internat. Studies Assn., Internat. Studies Assn. Office: McGill U 855 Sherbrooke St W Montreal PQ Canada H3A 2T7

PAUL, THOMAS FRANK, lawyer; b. Aberdeen, Wash., Sept. 23, 1925; s. Thomas and Loretta (Ounstead) P.; m. Dolores Marion Zaugg, Apr. 1, 1950; children: Pamela, Peggy, Thomas Frank. BS in Psychology, Wash. State U., Pullman, 1951; JD, U. Wash., Seattle, 1957. Bar: Wash. 1958, US Dist. Ct. (no. and so. dist.) Wash. 1958, US Ct. Appeals (9th cir.) 1958, US Supreme Ct. 1970, Oreg. 2004, Alaska 2004. Ptnr., shareholder, pres. LeGros, Buchanan & Paul, Seattle, 1958—. Lectr. on admiralty and maritime law; mem. mediation and arbitration panel U.S. Dist. Ct. Seattle. Mem. bd. adv. U. San Francisco Law Jour., 1996—2002. Named one of Best Lawyers in Am., Woodward White, Inc., 2005—07. Mem.: ATLA, ABA (chmn. com. on admiralty and maritime litig. 1982—86), Fed. Bar Assn., Asia Pacific Lawyers Assn., Am. Arbitration Assn., Transp. Lawyers Assn., Wash. Def. Trial Lawyers, Def. Rsch. Inst., Wash. State Trial Lawyers Assn., Maritime Law Assn. U.S.A., Million Dollar Advocates Forum, Propeller Club. Republican. Home: 1323 Willard Ave W Seattle WA 98119-3460 Office: LeGros Buchanan & Paul 701 5th Ave Ste 2500 Seattle WA 98104-7051 Office Phone: 206-623-4990. Business E-Mail: tpaul@legros.com.

PAUL, WILLIAM, physicist, researcher; b. Deskford, Scotland, Mar. 31, 1926; came to U.S., 1952; s. William and Jean (Watson) P.; m. Barbara Anderson Forbes, Mar. 28, 1952; children: David, Fiona. MA, Aberdeen U., Scotland, 1946; PhD, Aberdeen U., 1951; A.M. (hon.), Harvard U., 1960; D Honoris Causa, Paris, 1994. Asst. lectr., then lectr. Aberdeen U., 1946-52; mem. faculty Harvard U., 1953—, Gordon McKay prof. applied physics, 1963-91, Mallinckrodt prof. applied physics, 1991—2000, prof. physics, 1980-2000, Mallinckrodt rsch. prof. applied physics, 2000—04, rsch. prof. physics, 2000—04, Mallinckrodt prof. applied physics emeritus, prof. physics emeritus, 2004—. Professeur associé U. Paris, 1966-67; cons. solid state physics, 1954—; Ripon prof., Calcutta, 1984 Author: Handbook on Semiconductors: Band Theory and Transport Properties, 1982; coeditor: Solids Under Pressure, 1963, Amorphous and Liquid Semiconductors, 1980, Physics of Semiconductor Materials and Applications, 1986, High Pressure in Semiconductor Physics, Vols. 1 and 2, 1998. Carnegie fellow, 1952-53; Guggenheim fellow, 1959-60; Humboldt awardee, 1990; fellow Clare Hall Cambridge U., 1974-75. Fellow Am. Phys. Soc., Brit. Inst. Physics, N.Y. Acad. Scis., Royal Soc. Edinburgh Home: 57 Dartmouth Ct Bedford MA 01730 Office: Harvard U Pierce Hall Cambridge MA 02138 Home Phone: 781-275-6787. Business E-Mail: paul@seas.harvard.edu.

PAUL, WILLIAM DEWITT, JR., retired art educator, photographer, videographer, museum director; b. Wadley, Ga., Sept. 26, 1934; s. William DeWitt and Sonoma Elizabeth (Tinley) Paul; m. Dorothy Hefling Paul, Sept. 2, 1962; children: Sarah Elizabeth, Barbara Susan, Dorothy Ann. Student, Emory U., Atlanta, summer 1952, U. Rome, summer 1953, Ga. State Univ., Atlanta, 1953—; BFA, Atlanta Coll. Art, 1955; AB, U. Ga., Athens, 1958, MFA, 1959. Instr. art and art history Park Coll., Parkville, Mo., 1960-61; dir. exhbns., instr. art history Kansas City Art Inst., 1959-64, curator study collections, asst. prof. art, 1964-65; coordinator basic courses dept. art, asst. prof. art U. Ga., Athens, 1965-67; curator Ga. Mus. Art, assoc. prof. art, 1967-69, dir., asso. prof., 1969-80, prof., 1997—2002, gen. Sandy Beaver tchr. prof., 2000—02, prof. emeritus, 2002—. Lectr. Boston, LA, New Orleans, San Antonio, Memphis, Birmingham; chmn. visual arts rev. panel Ga. Council for Arts and Humanities, 1976-77; v.p. Arts Festival Atlanta, 1982, 84, 85, trustee, 1982-93; guest artist Arts Festival Atlanta, 1987; mem. parents council Randolph-Macon Woman's Coll., Lynchburg, Va., 1986-87. Exhibited in one man shows at Ga. Mus. Art, 1959, Atlanta Art Assn., 1959, Unitarian Gallery, Kansas City, 1960, Palmer Gallery, Kansas City, 1965, Heath Gallery, Atlanta, 1976, Hunter Mus. Art, Chattanooga, 1976, Forum Gallery, NYC, 1977, Madison, Ga., Morgan Cultural Ctr., 1980, Columbus, Ga., Mus. Arts and Scis., 1980, Macon, Ga., Mus. Arts and Sci., 1980, Banks Haley Gallery, Albany, Ga., 1980, Augusta Richmond County, Ga., Mus., 1980, Heath Gallery 1982, Moon Gallery, Berry Coll., Rome, Ga., 1983, Bathhouse Gallery, Atlanta, 1987, MIA Gallery, Seattle, 1988, Valencia CC, Orlando, Fla., 1991, Gasperi Gallery, New Orleans, 1993, Contemporary Arts Ctr., New Orleans, 1994, Lyndon House Art Ctr., Athens, Ga., 2005, Averitt Art Ctr., Statesboro, Ga., 2006; numerous site-specific installations, 1986-97; exhibited group shows, New Arts Gallery, Atlanta, 1961, Kansas City Art Inst., 1960-64, Park Coll., 1960, Mulvane Art Ctr., Topeka, 1965, Palazzo Venezia, Rome, 1984, Elaine Benson Gallery, Bridgehampton, LI, NY, 1986, Dulin Gallery Art, Knoxville, Tenn., 1986, 1987 Atlanta Biennale, Nexus Contemporary Art Ctr., Atlanta, Valencia CC, Orlando, 1988, Greg Kucera Gallery, Seattle, 1992, King Plow Arts Ctr., Atlanta, 1994, Leslie-Lohman Found., NYC, 1995, Mus. Fine Arts, Tallahassee, 1996, Art Ctr., Miami Beach, Fla., 1997, Lebanon Valley Coll., Annville, Pa., 1998, others; represented in permanent collections Gen. Mills, Inc., Mpls., Hallmark Cards, Kansas City, Little Rock Arts Ctr., Ga. Mus. Art, U. Ga., The Kinsey Inst., Ind. U., Calif. State U., Tom of Finland Found. Ford Found. faculty enrichment grantee, 1978; recipient numerous awards for paintings. Mem. Am. Fedn. Arts (trustee 1969-81), Coll. Art Assn., Am. Assn. Museums (coun. 1981), Lovis Corinth Meml. Found., Ga. Alliance Arts Edn. (dir. 1975-77), Phi Kappa Phi. Home: 150 Bar H Ct Athens GA 30605-4702 Office: 4900 Barnett Shoals Rd Athens GA 30605 Office Phone: 706-613-2312. Business E-Mail: bpaul@uga.edu.

PAUL, WILLIAM ERWIN, immunologist; b. Bklyn., June 12, 1936; s. Jack and Sylvia (Gleicher) Paul; m. Marilyn Heller, Dec. 25, 1958; children: Jonathan M. Carmel, Matthew E. BA summa cum laude, Bklyn. Coll., 1956; MD cum laude, SUNY, Bklyn., 1960, DSc (hon.), 1991; PhD (hon.), Hebrew U., Jerusalem, 2003, Med. U. Cluj-Naporca, Romania, 2003, Nat. U. Athens, Greece, 2007; Laurea hon. causa, U. Rome, 2005. Intern, asst. resident Mass. Meml. Hosp., Boston Med. Ctr., 1960—62; clin. assoc. Nat. Cancer Inst., NIH, Bethesda, Md., 1962—64; post doctoral fellow, instr. NYU Sch. Medicine, NYC, 1964—68; prin. investigator lab. immunology Nat. Inst. Allergy and Infectious Diseases, NIH, Bethesda, Md., 1968—70, chief lab. immunology, 1970—; dir. office of AIDS rsch. NIH, Bethesda, Md., assoc. dir. AIDS rsch., 1994—97. Awards jury mem. Albert Lasker Med. Rsch. Awards Program, 1993—; chmn. selection com. Irene Diamond Fund Professorship in Immunology; Sackler sr. prof. Tel Aviv U., Israel; chair sci. adv. bd. Lupus Rsch. Inst.; mem. Novartis Sci. Bd., 2001—05; adj. prof. U. Pa., 2002—; governing dir. Am. Found. for AIDS Rsch., 2002—05, mem. program adv. bd., 2006—; vis. com. chair for assessment of basic biomed. rsch. in Israel; with Israel Acad. of Sci. and Humanities, 2007; mem. sci. adv. bd. Trudeau Inst. Adv. editor Jour. Exptl. Medicine, 1974—2006; editor: Ann. Rev. Immunology, Volumes 1-25, 1983—, Fundamental Immunology, 1st - 6th edits., 1984—, Immunity, 2003—06; assoc. editor Cell, 1985—96, transmitting editor Internat. Immunology, 1989—96, corr. editor Procs. Royal Soc. Series B, 1989—93, mem. editl. bd. Molecular Biology of Cell, 1990—93; contbg. editor: Procs. NAS U.S.A., 1992—94; mem. editl. bd. Procs. NAS U.S.A., 2004—; contbr. numerous articles to sci. journals. With USPHS, 1962—64, with USPHS, 1975—96. Recipient Founders' prize, Tex. Instruments Found., 1979, Alumni medal, SUNY Downstate Med. Ctr., 1981, DSM, USPHS, 1985, Life Sci. Award, 3M, 1988, Tovi Comet - Wallerstein prize, CAIR Inst., Bar Ilan U., 1992, 6th ann. Excellence Award in Immunologic Rsch., Duke U., 1993, Alumni Honors, Bklyn. Coll., 1994, Abbott Labs. Award in Clin. and Diagnostic Immunology, Am. Acad. Microbiology, 1998, Lifetime Achievement award, Am. Assn. Immunologists, 2002, Sci. Achievement in award, The Irvington Inst., 2002, Rsch. in Action award, Treatment Action Group, 2003, Scientific Leadership award, Lupus Found., 2005, Hon. Lifetime Achievement award, Internat. Cytokine Soc., 2007. Fellow: Am. Acad. Arts and Sci.; mem.: NAS, Am Assn. Immunologists (pres. 1986—87, Lifetime Achievement award 2002), Assn. Am. Physicians, Scandinavian Soc. Immunology (hon.), Am. Soc. Clin. Investigation (pres. 1980—81), Inst. Medicine NAS. Achievements include discovery of interleukin-4 and demonstration of its central role in allergic inflammatory responses; determination of mechanisms of Th2 differentiation. Office: NIH Bldg 10 Rm 11n311 Bethesda MD 20892-1982 Office Phone: 301-496-5046. Business E-Mail: wpaul@niaid.nih.gov.

PAUL, WILLIAM GEORGE, lawyer; b. Pauls Valley, Okla., Nov. 25, 1930; s. Homer and Helen (Lafferty) P.; m. Barbara Elaine Brite, Sept. 27, 1963; children: George Lynn, Alison Elise, Laura Elaine, William Stephen. BA, U. Okla., 1952, LL.B., 1956. Bar: Okla. bar 1956. Pvt. practice law, Norman, 1956; ptnr. Oklahoma City, 1957-84; with Crowe & Dunlevy, 1962-84, 96—; sr. v.p., gen. counsel Phillips Petroleum Co., Bartlesville, Okla., 1984-95; ptnr. Crowe & Dunlevy, Oklahoma City, 1996—. Assoc. prof. law Oklahoma City U., 1964-68; adv. bd. Martindale Hubbell, 1990—. Author: (with Earl Sneed) Vernon's Oklahoma Practice, 1965. Bd. dirs. Nat. Ctr. for State Cts., 1993-99, Am. Bar Endowment, 1986—, Bank 2, 2005-; trustee Nat. Constitution Ctr., 2000—. 1st lt. USMCR, 1952-54. Named Outstanding Young Man Oklahoma City, 1965, Outstanding Young Oklahoman, 1966, Okla. Hall of Fame, 2003. Fellow Am. Bar Found. (chmn. 1991), Am. Coll. Trial Lawyers; mem. ABA (bd. govs. 1995—, pres. 1999), Okla. Bar Assn. (pres. 1976), Oklahoma County Bar Assn. (past pres.), Okla Lottery Commn., Nat. Conf. Bar Pres. (pres. 1986), U. Okla. Alumni Assn. (pres. 1973), Order of Coif, Phi Beta Kappa, Phi Delta Phi, Delta Sigma Rho. Democrat. Presbyterian. Home: 13017 Burnt Oak Rd Oklahoma City OK 73120-8919 Office: Crowe & Dunlevy 20 N Broadway Ave Ste 1800 Oklahoma City OK 73102-8273 Office Phone: 405-239-6676.

PAUL, WILLIAM MCCANN, lawyer; b. Cambridge, Mass., Feb. 9, 1951; s. Kenneth William and Mary Jean (Lamson) P.; m. Janet Anne Forest, Feb. 25, 1984; children: Emily L'Engle, Andrew Angwin, Elizabeth Seton. Student, U. Freiburg, Fed. Republic of Germany, 1971-72; BA, Johns Hopkins U., 1973; JD, U. Mich., 1977. Bar: D.C. 1978, U.S. Dist. Ct. D.C. 1978, U.S. Ct. Claims 1984, U.S. Ct. Appeals (4th cir.) 1980, U.S. Ct. Appeals (fed. cir.) 1983, U.S. Tax Ct. 1990. Law clk. to judge U.S. Ct. Appeals (5th cir.), Austin, Tex., 1977-78; assoc. Covington & Burling, Washington, 1978-87, ptnr., 1987-88, 89—; dep. tax legis. counsel U.S. Treasury Dept., 1988-89. Mem. ABA (asst. sec. tax sect. 1995-97, sec. 1997-99, coun. mem. 1999-2002, vice chair govt. rels. 2005-07), D.C. Bar Assn., Am. Law Inst., Am. Coll. Tax Counsel, Order of Coif. Presbyterian. Home: 5604 Chevy Chase Pkwy NW Washington DC 20015-2520 Office: Covington & Burling PO Box 7566 1201 Pennsylvania Ave NW Washington DC 20004-2401 E-mail: wpaul@cov.com.

PAULEY, BRUCE FREDERICK, retired history professor; b. Lincoln, Nebr., Nov. 4, 1937; s. Carroll Righter and Blanche Marie (Hulsebus) P.; m. Marianne Barbara Utz, Dec. 21, 1963; children: Mark Allan, Glenn Hamilton. BA, Grinnell Coll., 1959; MA, U. Nebr., 1961; PhD, U. Rochester, 1966. Instr. history Coll. of Wooster, Ohio, 1964-65, U. Nebr., Lincoln, 1965-66; asst. prof. history U. Wyo., Laramie, 1966-71; from assoc. prof. to prof. history U. Ctrl. Fla., Orlando, 1971—2006, chmn. faculty senate, 1978-79, prof. emeritus, 2006. Vis. prof. history U. Nebr., Lincoln, 2002, 06; cons., expert witness war crimes divsn. Can. Justice Dept., 1998-99. Author: The Habsburg Legacy, 1867-1939, 1972, Hahnenschwanz und Hakenkreuz: Steirischer Heimatschutz und österreichischer Nationalsozialismus, 1918-1934, 1972, Hitler and the Forgotten Nazis: A History of Austrian National Socialism, 1981, Der Weg in den Nationalsozialismus: Ursprünge und Entwicklung in Österreich, 1988, From Prejudice to Persecution: A History of Austrian Anti-Semitism, 1992 (Charles Smith prize So. Hist. Assn. best book European history, 1992, best book Austrian studies Austrian Cultural Inst., 1993), Eine Geschichte des österreichischen Antisemitismus: Von der Ausgrenzung zur Auslöschung, 1993, Hitler, Stalin and Mussolini: Totalitarianism in the Twentieth Century, 1997, 2d edit., 2003. Chmn. parents' adv. com. Oviedo (Fla.) High Sch., 1981-82. Named Disting. Alumnus, U. Nebr., Lincoln, 1996; Fulbright fellow, 1963-64, rsch. fellow NEH, 1972, 87, Lifetime Achievement award, U. Nebr., Lincoln, 2005. Mem.: Soc. Austrian and Habsburg Historians, German Studies Assn. (exec. com. 1986—89). Avocations: traveling to historical sites, photography, golf. Business E-Mail: bpauley@pegasus.cc.ucf.edu.

PAULEY, JAMES LEROY, JR., retired lawyer; b. Mason City, Iowa, Dec. 6, 1916; s. James Leroy and Clara May (Lampson) Pauley; m. Viola Jennie Lemker; children: James Donald (Don), Richard (Dick) Joseph. BA, U. Iowa, 1938, JD, 1940. Bar: (Iowa) 1940. Sole practitioner law, Scranton, Iowa, 1940—42; spl. agt. Fed. Bur. Investigation, Washington, 1942—43, NYC, 1943—45, Louisville, 1945; practitioner law Pauley, Horak & Mumma, Jefferson and Scranton, Iowa, 1946—82; ret., 1982. Dir., v.p. Security Nat. Bank, Jefferson, Scranton, Iowa, 1955—95. Contr. articles to periodicals including: U.S. Specialist, Iowa Postal History Soc. Bull. Mayor City of Jefferson, Iowa, 1967—71; pres., dir. Jefferson Cmty. Sch. Dist., Iowa, 1959—67; mem. Jefferson Plan Commn., 1971—75, chmn. Mem.: Am. Diabetes Assn., Internat. Carnival Glass Assn., Inc., Univ. Iowa Alumni Assn., Iowa State Hist. Soc., Iowa Postal History Soc., Am. Philatelic Soc., U.S. Stamp Soc., Trans-Miss. Philatelic Soc., ABA, Iowa State Bar Assn., 16th Judicial Dist. Bar Assn. (pres. 1940—70), Greene County Bar Assn. (pres. 1940—), Lions Club (pres., zone chmn. 1947—). Republican. Congregational. Avocations: genealogy, antique collector, stamp collecting/philately. Home: 300 Edgewood Ave Jefferson IA 50129

PAULEY, JANE, newscaster, journalist; b. Indpls., Oct. 31, 1950; m. Gary Trudeau; 3 children. BA in Polit. Sci, Ind. U., 1971; D of Journalism (hon.), DePauw U., 1978. Reporter Sta. WISH-TV, Indpls., 1972—75; co-anchor WMAQ-TV News, Chgo., 1975—76, The Today Show, NBC, NYC, 1976—90; from co-anchor to corr. NBC News, NYC, 1976—; prin. writer, reporter NBC Nightly News, 1980—82, substitute anchor, 1990—2003; co-anchor Early Today, NBC, 1982—83; prin. corr. Real Life With Jane Pauley, NBC, 1991; co-anchor Dateline NBC, NYC, 1992—99, prin. anchor, 1999—2003; anchor Time & Again MSNBC, 1999—2003; host The Jane Pauley Show, 2004—05. Author: Skywriting: A Life Out of the Blue, 2004 (Publishers Weekly Bestseller). Mem. adv. bd. Childrens Health Fund, Internat. Coun. Freedom From Hunger; bd. dirs. Pub. Edn. Needs Civic Involvement in Learning. Named Broadcaster of Yr., Internat. Radio and TV Soc., 1986, Best in Bus., Washington Journalism Rev., 1990; named to Broadcasting and Cable Hall of Fame; recipient Emmy award, Edward R. Murrow award, Gabriel award, Nancy Susan Reynolds award, Maggie award, Humanitas award, Commendation award, Am. Women in Radio and TV, Gracie Allen award, Clarion award, Assn. for Women in Comm., Wilbur award, Religious Pub. Rels. Coun., Salute to Excellence award, Nat. Assn. Black Journalists, Leonard Zeidenberg First Amendment award, Radio TV News Dirs. Found., Paul White award, NTNDA. Fellow: Soc. for Profl. Journalists (hon. chair Jane Pauley task force on mass comm. edn.).

PAULEY, SHIRLEY STEWART, religious organization executive; b. Boston, Sept. 13, 1938; d. Charles Norris and Nellie Consuelo (Yorke) Stewart; m. Edward Haven Pauley, May 29, 1964; children: David Stewart, Deborah Jeanne. BA, Gordon Coll., 1960; postgrad., Ariz. State U., 1961, Boston U., 1963. Sec./receptionist Atwell Co., Boston, summer 1956; sec., typist Kelley Girl, Boston, 1956-60; asst. office mgr. Radiator Chem. Corp., Scottsdale, Ariz., 1960-62; sec., clerical worker GM, Westwood, Mass., 1962-64; v.p. Truth Alive Ministries, Dallas, 1995—. Spkr. At Large, Boston, 1956-60; Sunday sch. tchr. Blaney Meml. Bapt. Ch., Boston, 1956-60; choir dir. Sherwood Bapt. Ch., Phoenix, 1961-62, co-youth dir., 1961; co-youth dir. Blaney Meml. Ch., Boston, 1964-66; messenger Bapt. Gen. Conv. Tex., Ft. Worth, 1996; leader bible study Prestonwood Bapt. Ch., Dallas, 2006—; v.p. Truth Alive Ministries, 1996—. Republican. Avocations: photography, reading, music. Office: Truth Alive Ministries PO Box 794945 Dallas TX 75379-4945 Personal E-mail: sspauley@prodigy.net.

PAULIKAS, GEORGE ALGIS, retired physicist; b. Pagegiai, Lithuania, May 14, 1936; came to U.S., 1949, naturalized, 1955; s. George and Olga (Pacas) P.; m. Joan Marie Gross, Sept. 7, 1957; 1 child, Nancy Marie. BS in Engring. Physics, U. Ill., Chgo. and Urbana, 1957, MS (univ. fellow 1957-58), 1958; PhD in Physics (NSF fellow 1958-61), U. Calif., Berkeley, 1961. With Aerospace Corp., El Segundo, Calif., 1961-98; ret., head space particles and fields dept., 1968, dir. space scis. lab., 1968-81, v.p. labs., 1981-85, sr. v.p. devel., 1985-89, sr. v.p. programs, 1989-94, exec. v.p., 1992-98. Mem. various ad hoc coms. NAS, 1970—, ann., 1984—2007; mem. adv. coun. geophysics U. Calif., 1973—75, exec. com. space scis. lab., 1978—81; mem. sci. adv. bd. USAF, 1975—82, 1991—95; mem. def. space tech. com. NRC, 1987—92; mem. NAS/NRC Space Studies Bd., 1999—2006, vice chair, 2003—06; cons. in field. Author papers in field; asso. editor: Jour. Geophys. Research, 1972-75. Trustee Calif. Sci. Ctr., 1994-2000, Boy Scouts Am., L.A., 1996-2000. Recipient Aerospace Corp. Trustees Disting. Achievement award, 1980, Meritorious Civilian Svc. award USAF, 1982, 95, U. Ill. Alumni Disting. Engring. award, 1992, Nat. Reconnaissance Office Gold Medal, 1998; named U. Ill. (Navy Pier) Hall of Fame, 1996. Fellow AIAA (chmn. tech. com. space sci. and astronomy 1976-77), Am. Phys. Soc.; mem. Am. Geophys. Union, Sigma Xi. Home: 1537 Addison Rd Palos Verdes Estates CA 90274 Office Phone: 310-336-7076. E-mail: george.a.paulikas@aero.org.

PAULISON, R(OBERT) DAVID, federal agency administrator; b. Miami, 1947; m. Kathy Paulison. BA, Fla. Atlantic U.; postgrad., Harvard U. Rescue firefighter, lt., battalion comdr., dist. chief ops., divsn. chief, asst. chief, deputy dir. adminstrn. Miami-Dade Fire Rescue Dept., chief, 1992—2001; adminstr. US Fire Adminstrn. US Dept. Homeland Security, Emmitsburg, Md., 2001—, dir. preparedness divsn. Emergency Preparedness & Response Directorate (FEMA) Washington, 2003—05, acting under sec. of emergency preparedness & response, 2005—06, acting under sec. for Fed. Emergency Mgmt. (FEMA dir.), 2005—06; under sec. for Fed. Emergency Mgmt. (FEMA dir.) US Dept Homeland Security, Washington, 2006—. Pres. Internat. Assn. Fire Chiefs, 1996—97. Named Fire Chief of the Year, State of Fla., 1993; named to The Miami-Dade Community Coll. Hall of Fame; recipient Motorola Mason Lankford Fire Svc. Leadership award, Congl. Fire Svc. Inst., 2004, Leroy Collins Disting. Alumni award. Office: FEMA US Dept Homeland Security Fed Ctr Plz 500 C St SW Rm 828 Washington DC 20472

PAULISSEN, JAMES PETER, retired pediatrician, county official; b. Chgo., Aug. 14, 1928; s. Joseph Edward and Louise Catherine (Muno) P.; m. Lorraine Antoinette Polly, Sept. 11, 1954; children: Linda, Steven, Mark, Daniel. Student, Loyola U., 1946-49, MD cum laude, 1953; MPH, Johns Hopkins U., 1966. Diplomate Am. Bd. Pediat. Intern Milw. County Hosp., 1953-54; resident Milw. Children's Hosp., 1957-58; practice medicine specializing in pediats. Wauwatosa Children's Clinic, Wis., 1959-65; pediat. fellow Johns Hopkins U., 1965—66; chief Bur. Maternal and Child Health Ill. Dept. Pub. Health, Springfield, 1966-70, chief Divsn. Family Health, 1970-76; exec. dir. DuPage County Health Dept., Wheaton, Ill., 1976-93. Bd. dirs., mem. exec. com. Suburban Cook-DuPage Health Sys. Agy., Oak Park, Ill., 1976-82; bd. dirs., past pres. Comprehensive Health Coun. Met. Chgo., 1977-87; dir. Sr. Home Sharing, Inc., Wheaton, 1981-83; mem. Ill. Commn. on Children, 1971-85, vice chmn., 1983-85; chmn. Ill. Perinatal Adv. Com., 1981-84, mem., 1981-92; mem. Ill. Sch. Health Adv. Com., 1982-93, Gov.'s Adv. Coun. on Devel. Disabilities, 1973-76, Ill. Med. Determinations Bd., 1985-93; vice chmn. Ill. Pub. Health Advisors, 1988-91; mem. adv. bd. divsn. Svcs. Crippled Children U. Ill., 1986-94; trustee DuPage County Med. Found., 1976-82, 86-92, 1999-2006, treas. 2002-06; bd. dirs. DuPage Cmty. Clinic, 1993—, Cmty. Nursing Svc. of DuPage, 1993-99, vice chair, 1997-99; mem. cmty. health com. Ctrl. DuPage Health Sys., 1993-98; del. White House Conf. for Children, 1970. Capt. USAF, 1954-56. Recipient Dir.'s award for Sustained Excellence Ill. Dept. Pub. Health, 1988, Ill. Pediatrician of Yr. award, 1992, Humanitarian award DuPage County Health Planning Coun., 1994. Fellow Am. Acad. Pediats. (exec. com. Ill. chpt. 1978-81, sec. 1988-92), APHA, Am. Coll. Preventive Medicine; mem. Ill. Pub. Health Assn. (pres. 1977-78, Disting. Svc. award 1983), Ill. Assn. Maternal and Child Health (pres. 1975-76). Avocation: model building. Home: 28w660 Hawthorne Ln West Chicago IL 60185-2472

PAULL, MATTHEW H., food service executive; BA, U. Ill., M in Acctg. Ptnr. Ernst & Young; with McDonald's Corp., 1993—, v.p. corp. tax, sr. v.p., fin. Oak Brook, Ill., 1999—2001, exec. v.p., CFO, 2001—04, sr. exec. v.p., CFO, 2004—. Adv. dir. bd. dirs. McDonalds Corp., 1999—2000, mem. chmns. coun., mem. Japan Bd., 2002—03; mem. adv. coun. Fed. Res. Bank, Chgo.; bd. dirs. Best Buy Co., Inc. Active Kohl Children's Mus., Chgo. Symphony Orch.; trustee Ravinia Festival Assn.; bd. mem. Loyola Ronald McDonald House. Office: McDonalds Corp McDonalds Plaza Oak Brook IL 60523 *

PAULL, RICHARD ALLEN, geologist, educator; b. Madison, Wis., May 20, 1930; s. Ethra Harold and Martha (Schaller) P.; m. Rachel Kay Krebs, Mar. 6, 1954; children: Kay Marie, Lynn Ellen, Judith Ann. BS, U. Wis., 1952, MS, 1953, PhD, 1957. Party chief Pan Am. Petroleum Co., 1955-57; research group leader Jersey Prodn. Research Co., 1957-62; mem. faculty U. Wis.-Milw., 1962-97, chmn. dept. geol. scis., 1962-66, prof., 1966-97, prof. emeritus, 1997—. Cons. in field, 1966— Author books, papers in field. Co-exec. sec. NAGT/USGS/AASG-Coop. Summer Field Tng. Program, 1994-99. Served with USAF, 1953-55. Recipient Amoco Disting. Tchg. award, 1975 Fellow Geol. Soc. Am. (chmn. ann. meeting 1970, tech. program com. 1970, 77, membership com. 1977-80, chmn. 1980); mem. Am. Assn. Petroleum Geologists (chmn. sci. fair award com. 1980, membership com. 1981-87, vis. petroleum geologists com. 1982-87, pub. affairs com. 1982-85), Soc. Econ. Paleontologists and Mineralogists, Nat. Assn. Geology Tchrs. (v.p. 1976-77, pres. 1977-78), Am. Geol. Inst. (governing bd. 1977-79, sec. and exec. com. 1986-88. Home: 1657 W Canal Ct Littleton CO 80120-4515 Personal E-mail: rocdox@comcast.net.

PAULOS, JOHN ALLEN, mathematics educator, writer; b. Denver, July 4, 1945; s. Peter George and Helen (Sanavas) P.; m. Sheila Schwartz, Aug. 12, 1972; two children. PhD in Math., U. Wis., 1974. Prof. math. Temple U., Phila., 1973—. Spkr. in field; adj. prof. journalism Columbia U. Author: Mathematics & Honor, 1980, I Think Therefore I Laugh, 1985, Innumeracy, 1989, Beyond Numeracy, 1991, A Mathematician Reads the Newspaper, 1995 (100 Best Nonfiction Books of Century Random House Modern Libr.), Once Upon a Number, 1998 (Best Book of 1998, L.A. Times), A Mathematician Plays the Stock Market, 2004; columnist ABCNews.com, the Guardian; mem. editl. bd. Philadelphia Daily News; contbr. book reviews, columns in newspapers, sci. papers. Notable TV appearances include: The NewsHour with Jim Lehrer, 20/20, Larry King Live, Late Night with David Letterman. Recipient Pub. Understanding Sci. and Tech. award, AAAS, 2003. Fellow Com. Sci. Investigation of Claims of the Paranormal; mem. Math. Assn. Am., Assn. for Symbolic Logic, Authors' Guild. Office: Temple Univ Dept Math Philadelphia PA 19122 Business E-Mail: paulos@math.temple.edu.

PAULOSE, RACHEL K., prosecutor; b. 1973; Grad., U. Minn., 1994; JD, Yale Law Sch., 1997. Law clk. to Hon. James B. Loken US Ct. Appeals (8th Cir.), 1997—98; trial atty. Civil Rights Divsn. US Dept. Justice, Washington, 1998—99, asst. US atty. Dist. Minn. Mpls., 1999—2002; atty. Williams & Connolly LLP, Washington; atty Dorsey & Whitney LLP, Mpls.; sr. counsel to atty. gen. US Dept. Justice, Washington, 2006, interim US atty. Dist. Minn. Mpls., 2006, US atty., 2006—. Mem.: Nat. Asian-Am. Bar Assn. (bd. mem.), Fed. Bar Assn. (bd. mem.). Office: US Attys Ofce 600 US Courthouse 300 S Fourth St Minneapolis MN 55415 *

PAULRAJ, AROGYASWAMI JOSEPH, engineering educator, consultant; b. Coimbatore, Tamilnadu, India, Apr. 14, 1944; came to U.S., 1992; s. Sinappan Arogyaswami and Rose (Gounder) P.; m. Nirmala Paulraj, Feb. 5, 1973; children: Mallika, Nirupa. BTech, Naval Engring. Coll., 1966; PhD, Indian Inst. Tech., 1973. Divsn. head NPOL, Cochin, 1977-83; vis. scientist Stanford U., Calif., 1984-85; dir. CAIR, Bangalore, India, 1986-88; chief scientist Bharat Electronics, Bangalore, India, 1988-91; vis. scientist Stanford U., Calif., 1984-85, prof. elec. engring. Calif., 1992—. Bd. dirs. numerous cos. in India and U.S. Editor 14 books; contbr. more than 150 articles to profl. jours. Patentee in field. With Indian Navy, 1961-76. Recipient medal Vaswik Found., 1986, Disting. Svc. medals Govt. India, 1973, 84. Fellow IEEE, Inst. Engrs. (India), Inst. Telecom. Engrs. (India), Indian Nat. Acad. Engring.; mem. NAE. Home: 59 Peter Coutts Cir Stanford CA 94305-2507

PAULSEN, BRIAN OLIVER, art educator, artist; b. Seattle, Mar. 29, 1941; s. Edward and Sylvia Paulsen; m. Dianne C. Coulter, Sept. 1963; children: Geoffrey E., Erica L. Knudsvig. BA, U. Wash., 1963; MFA, Wash. State U., 1966. Asst. prof. Chico (Calif.) State Coll., 1966—71; sessional instr. U. Calgary, Canada, 1971—73; prof. U. ND, Grand Forks, 1973—, Chester Fritz disting. prof., 1990. Vis. artist 12 venues; juror nat. art exhbns. 86 one-man shows, more than 1000 group exhbns., more than 200 invitational exhibits. Artist fellowship award, Nat. Endowment Arts, Washington, 1981—82. Mem.: Nat. Acad. Design. Avocations: photography, biking. Business E-Mail: brian_paulsen@und.nodak.edu.

PAULSEN, FRANK ROBERT, college dean emeritus; b. Logan, Utah, July 5, 1922; s. Frank and Ella (Ownby) P.; m. Marye Lucile Harris, July 31, 1942; 1 son, Robert Keith; m. Lydia Ransier Lowry, Nov. 1, 1969. BS, Utah State U., 1947; MS, U. Utah, 1948, Ed.D., 1956; Kellogg Found. postdoctoral fellow, U. Oreg., 1958; Carnegie Found. postdoctoral fellow, U. Mich., 1959-60. High sch. prin., Mt. Emmons, Utah, 1948-51; supt. schs. Cokeville, Wyo., 1951-55; from asst. prof. to assoc. prof. edn. U. Utah, 1955-61; prof. edn., dean Sch. Edn. U. Conn., 1961-64; dean Coll. Edn. U. Ariz., Tucson, 1964-84, dean emeritus, prof. emeritus higher edn., 1984—. Scholar-in-residence Fed. Exec. Inst., Charlottesville, Va., 1970; Disting. prof. edn. U. Bridgeport, summer 1972. Author: The Administration of Public Education in Utah, 1958, Contemporary Issues in American Education, 1966, American Education: Challenges and Images, 1967, Changing Dimensions in International Education, 1968, Higher Education: Dimensions and Directions, 1969, also numerous articles. Trustee Joint Council Econ. Edn., 1962-70; v.p., dir. Southwestern Coop. Ednl. Lab., 1965-67; bd. dirs. Nat. League for Nursing, 1967-69, mem. com. on perspectives, 1966-72; dir., chmn. exec. com. ERIC Clearinghouse on Tchr. Edn., 1968-70; bd. dirs. Tucson Mental Health Center, 1968-70. Served with AUS, 1942-46, PTO. Mem. Aerospace Med. Assn., Am. Assn. Sch. Adminstrs., Am. Acad. Polit. and Social Sci., Utah Acad. Letters, Arts and Scis., Ariz. Acad., Am. Assn. Colls. Tchrs. Edn. (Conn. liaison officer 1962-64, mem. studies com. 1962-68, dir.), Ariz. Assn. Colls. Tchr. Edn. (pres. 1972-80), AAAS, Am. Ednl. Research Assn., Kappa Delta Pi, Pi Sigma Alpha, Pi Gamma Mu., Phi Delta Kappa. Lodges: Rotary.

PAULSEN, RUTH ANN, French and Spanish language educator; b. Cosby, Mo., Dec. 9, 1940; d. Ernest Raymond and Ollie Hasque (Clouse) Thornton; m. Reuben Ray Paulsen, June 15, 1962 (div. 1982); children: Terrill Kent, Jeffrey Alan. AA, St. Joseph's Jr. Coll., Mo., 1960; BS in Edn., N.W. Mo. State U., 1962; MA, Baker U., 1985; postgrad., U. de Dijon, France, 1982, U. de l'Ouest, 1988-92. Cert. tchr. French and Spanish 7-12. Tchr. French, Spanish Highland Park High Sch., Topeka, 1962-68, Cen. N. Jr. High Sch., Kansas City, Mo., 1968-70; adult edn. instr. French Johnson County Community Coll., Overland Park, Kans., 1971-73; tchr. French, Spanish Cen. S. Jr. High Sch., Kansas City, 1974-77; tchr. French Ctr. Sr. HS, Kansas City, 1977—95, chair fgn. lang. dept., 1980—86, 1993—95; tchr. French and Spanish Blue Valley North HS, Overland Park, Kans., 1996—2002. Lectr. French, U. Mo., Kansas City, 1987-95; life mem. Mo. PTA. Author, photographer: (slide and video units with script) France at a Glance, 1989; co-editor: (book) Introduction to Language, 1976. Cub scout den mother Boy Scouts Am., 1969-74; sec. Brookridge Homes Assn., 1980-84. Grantee NDEA, 1964, 65, Rockefeller Found., Angers, France, 1988; Alliance Française scholar, Paris, 1983. Mem. NEA (life), NOW, Am. Coun. Teaching Fgn. Langs., Am. Assn. Tchrs. French, Alliance Française (bd. dirs. 1991-93, scholar Paris 1983), Fgn. Lang. Assn. Mo., Kans. Fgn. Lang. Assn. (sec. 1989—), Mo. Edn. Assn., Cen. Edn. Assn. (pres. 1988-89, chief negotiator 1989-90), Planned Parenthood, Phi Theta Kappa, Alpha Delta Kappa. Democrat. Baptist. Avocations: photography, travel. Home: 10932 Rosehill Rd Overland Park KS 66210-1178 Personal E-mail: rpaulsen@aol.com.

PAULSEN, SERENUS GLEN, retired architect, educator; b. Spooner, Wis., July 27, 1917; s. Serenus Justin and Edna Anne (Dalton) P.; m. Virginia C. Habel, Jan. 26, 1944; children: Thomas J., Nancy Lee (Mrs. John Marshall). Student, U. Ill., 1938-42; B.Arch. cum laude, U. Pa., 1947; Diploma in Architecture and City Planning, Royal Acad. Art, Stockholm, 1948. With Carroll, Grisdale & Van Alan (Architects), Phila., 1946-47, Eero Saarinen & Assos., Bloomfield Hills, Mich., 1949-51, 53-57; chief designer Reisner & Urbahn (Architects), NYC, 1951-52; archtl. coordinator Knoll Assos., NYC, 1952-53; prin. Glen Paulsen Assos., Birmingham, Mich., 1958-69; prin., v.p. Tarapata-MacMahon-Paulsen Assos., Inc. (Architects), Bloomfield Hills, 1969-77; pres. Cranbrook Acad. Art, head dept. architecture, 1966-70; prof., chmn. Masters Program in Architecture U. Mich., 1976-78, Emil Lorch prof. architecture, 1982-85, prof. emeritus, 1985—. Mem. Nat. Com. on Urban Planning and Design, 1971-72; archtl. commn. U. Wash., Seattle, 1968-76 (Recipient 3d prize Bi-Nat. Competition for Design Rainbow Center Plaza, Niagara Falls, N.Y. 1972). Gov. emeritus Cranbrook Acad. Art. Served with C.E. USAAF, 1942-46. Fellow AIA (honor awards Detroit chpt. for Shapero Hall of Pharmacy 1965, Our Shepherd Lutheran Ch. 1966, Ford Life Sci. Bldg. 1967, Birney Elementary Sch., Detroit 1971, Fed. Bldg., Ann Arbor, Mich. 1978, gold medal for 1980 Detroit chpt.); mem. Mich. Soc. Architects, (Robert F. Hastings award 1985).

PAULSEN, VIVIAN, editor; b. Salt Lake City, May 10, 1942; d. Paul Herman and Martha Oline (Blattmann) P. BA, Brigham Young U., 1964, postgrad., 1965, U. Grenoble, France, 1966. Cert. tchr., Utah. Tchr. French Granite Sch. Dist., Salt Lake City, 1966-67; assoc. editor New Era mag., Salt Lake City, 1970-82; mng. editor Friend mag., Salt Lake City, 1982—. Am. Field Service scholar, 1959; grad. fellow Brigham Young U., 1964-66 Republican. Mem. Ch. of Jesus Christ of Latter-day Saints Office: The Friend 50 E North Temple # F23 Salt Lake City UT 84150-0002

PAULSON, BELDEN HENRY, political scientist, educator; s. Henry Thomas and Evelina (Belden) P.; m. Louise D. Hill, Jan. 9, 1954; children: Eric, Steven AB, Oberlin Coll., 1950; MA, U. Chgo., 1955, PhD, 1962. With Italian svc. mission, Naples, 1950—53; organizer Homeless European Land Program, Sardinia, 1957—59; with UN High Comm. Refugees, Rome, 1960—61; mem. faculty U. Wis., Milw., 1962—; prof. polit. sci. U. Wis. ext., 1969—; founder and chmn. Ctr. Urban Cmty. Devel., 1967—90; co-founder and pres. High Wind Assn. for Modeling Cmty. for Sustainable Living, 1980—; pres. Plymouth Inst., 1995—98. Hon. rsch. prof. Internat. Tech. and Economy Inst, Inst. for Sci. of Scis., Shanghai, China, 1990—; mem. edn. task force Pres.'s Coun. on Sustainable Devel., 1995-98; co-founder Global Learning Ctr., 1998-2004 Author: The Searchers, 1966; also articles Served with USNR, 1945-46 Findhorn Found. fellow; grantee Social Sci. Rsch. Coun., 1967-68; recipient Lifetime Disting. Achievement award Oberlin Coll., 2004 Mem.: World Future Soc. Home: W7122 County Rd U Plymouth WI 53073-4538 Office: U Wis Dept Urban Cmty Devel 161 W Wisconsin Ave Fl 6 Milwaukee WI 53203-2602 E-mail: paulson@dotnet.com.

PAULSON, BERNARD ARTHUR, oil industry executive, consultant; b. Lakeview, Mich., July 12, 1928; s. Arthur Bernard and Genevieve Talbard (Bushley) P.; m. Joan Lee Curtiss, Dec. 4, 1954; children: James, Joseph (dec.), Ann, Thomas (dec.), Bernadette, Patricia, Steven. BS in Chem. Engring., Mich. State U.-East Lansing, 1949. Registered profl. engr., Tex. Process engr. Mid-West Refineries Inc., Alma, Mich., 1949-57; plant mgr. Kerr-McGee Corp., Cleve. and Wynnewood, Okla., 1957-66; v.p. Coastal States Petrochemical, Corpus Christi, Tex., 1966-71, Koch Industries Inc., St. Paul and Wichita, 1971-88, cons. Corpus Christi, Tex., 1988-94; pres. Koch Refining Co., Wichita, 1981-88; chmn. The Automation Group Inc.; chmn., CEO The Inspection Group Inc. CEO Tor Minerals Internat., 1997, also bd. dirs; dir. Orion Refining Corp., 1999—. Chmn., pres. Cleve. Area Hosp. Corp., 1962; bd. govs. Water Devel. Bd. Tex. Region 10 Water JCom.; pres. Corpus Christi Bd. Trade; commr. Port of Corpus Christi Authority, vice chmn., 1997; bd. dirs. Ada Wilson Hosp. Found., Driscoll Hosp. Found., Coastal Bend Cmty. Found., Del Mar Coll. Found., Tex. A&M U. Corpus Christi Found., Art Mus. South Tex. 1st lt. USAF, 1955—57. Recipient Claud R. Erickson Disting. Alumnus award Mich. State U., 1994. Mem.: AIChE (fuels and petrochem. award 1989), Bd. Trade, Refining Am. Petroleum Inst., Nat. Petroleum Refiners Assn., Corpus Christi Town Club, Elks. Home and Office: Tor Minerals 3 Ocean Park Dr Corpus Christi TX 78404-1600

PAULSON, DONALD ROBERT, chemistry professor; b. Oak Park, Ill., Sept. 6, 1943; s. Robert Smith and Florence Teresa (Beese) P.; m. Elizabeth Anne Goodwin, Aug. 20, 1966; children: Matthew, Andrew. BA, Monmouth Coll., 1965; PhD, Ind. U., 1968. Asst. prof. chemistry Calif. State U., Los Angeles, 1970-74, assoc. prof., 1974-78, prof., 1979—, chmn. dept., 1982-90. Vis. prof. U. B.C., Vancouver, Can., 1977-78, U. Sussex, Brighton, Eng., 1984-85. Author: Alicyclic Chemistry, 1976; contbr. articles to profl. jours. Named Outstanding Prof., Calif. State U., Los Angeles, 1978, 84, 96. Mem. Am. Chem. Soc., Chem. Soc. (London), InterAm. Photochem. Soc., Nat. Assn. Sci. Tchrs., Sigma Xi. Democrat. Episcopalian. Avocations: photography, hiking, soccer. Office: Calif State U Dept Chemistry 5151 State University Dr Los Angeles CA 90032-4226 Home: PO Box 1168 Ouray CO 81427 Home Phone: 970-325-0931; Office Phone: 323-343-2300. Business E-Mail: dpaulso@calstatela.edu.

PAULSON, ERIC J., literacy education educator; s. Steven King and Sally Anne Paulson; m. Christina Toscidis, Aug. 21, 1993; children: Marina Grammatiki, Alexandros Steffen. BA with honors, Eckerd Coll., St. Petersburg, Fla., 1991; MS, Fla. State U., Tallahassee, 1993; PhD, U. Ariz., Tucson, 2000. English as fgn. lang. program developer, instr. Rotary Internat. English Lang. Program, Izamal, Mexico, 1991; English as fgn. lang. instr. ELS Internat. Kangnam, Seoul, 1993—94, academic dir., 1994—96; instr. reading Pima CC, Tucson, 1997—2000; assoc. prof. literacy edn. Coll. Edn., Criminal Justice and Human Svcs. U. Cin., 2001—. Author: Entrance, A Communicative Text for Learners of English, 1995, Insight from the Eyes: The Science of Effective Reading Instruction, 2003; editor: College Reading Research and Practice, 2003, Scientific Realism in Studies of Reading, 2007. V.p. Literacy Vols. Pima County, 1998—99, mem. adv. bd., 1999—2000. Recipient Profl., Scholarly Activity award, Ctr. Access and Transition U. Cin., 2006. Mem.: Ctr. Expansion Lang. and Thinking, Nat. Coun. Tchrs. English, Internat. Reading Assn. (mem. coll. literacy and learning spl. interest group 2000—02, chmn. coll. literacy and learning spl. interest group 2003—04). Office: U Cin Divsn Tchr Edn PO Box 210022 Cincinnati OH 45221-0022 Office Phone: 513-556-2943.

PAULSON, GWEN O. GAMPEL, government relations consultant, life and leadership coach; b. Detroit, Mar. 16, 1945; d. Maurice V. and Lilyan

Victor; div.; children: Jill Susan, Mindy Beth; m. Jerome A. Paulson, July 2, 1989. BA, Mich. State U., 1966; MA, Wayne State U., 1974; postgrad., U. Mich., 1981; cert. in Leadership Coaching, Georgetown U., 2005. Lectr. Oakland U., Mich., 1979—80, U. Mich., Ann Arbor, 1981; legis. asst. U.S. Rep. Pete Stark, Washington, 1982—85; mem. profl. staff, ways and means health subcom. U.S. Ho. of Reps., Washington, 1985—89; v.p. for health Capitol Assocs., Washington, 1989—90; pres. Congl. Cons., Washington, 1990—2005, Coaching and Cons. LLC, 2005—. Author: Women and the Structure of Society, 1984. Edward S. Beck fellow U. Mich., Ann Arbor, 1978-79; Rackham Dissertation grant U. Mich., Ann Arbor, 1980. Mem. Coun. for Excellence Govt., Bus. and Profl. Women, Fedn. Am. (co-chair 1999-2001), Internat. Coaching Fedn., Phi Alpha Theta, Tau Sigma Avocations: collecting contemporary glass, travel, history, politics, reading. Office: Coaching and Consulting LLC 1113 N Howard St Alexandria VA 22304-1627 Office Phone: 703-461-7683. Personal E-mail: gwencc@comcast.net.

PAULSON, HANK (HENRY MERRITT PAULSON JR.), secretary of the treasury, former diversified financial services company executive; b. Palm Beach, Fla., Mar. 28, 1946; s. Henry Merritt and Marianna (Gallaeur) Paulson; m. Wendy Judge, Sept. 6, 1969; children: Henry Merritt III, Amanda Clark. BA in English, Dartmouth Coll., 1968; MBA, Harvard U., 1970. Staff asst. to the asst. sec. def. (comptroller) US Dept. Def., Washington, 1970-72; staff asst. to Pres. Domestic Policy Coun. The White House, Washington, 1972-73; assoc. Goldman Sachs & Co., Chgo., 1974-77, v.p., 1977-82, ptnr., 1982—88, ptnr. in charge investment banking services Midwest region, 1983—88, mng. ptnr., 1988—90, co-head investment banking divsn. NYC, 1990—94, pres., COO, 1994—98, co-CEO, 1998—99; chmn., CEO The Goldman Sachs Group, Inc., NYC, 1999—2006; sec. US Dept. Treasury, Washington, 2006—. Mem. exec. com. NYC Investment Fund. Named Outstanding Coll. Lineman, Divsn. I, New Eng. Football Coaches, 1967; named to 1st team All-Ivy, All New Eng., All-East; NCAA Scholar Athlete, 1967. Republican. Mem. Christian Science Ch. Avocations: skiing, fishing, canoeing, tennis. Office: US Dept Treasury 1500 Pennsylvania Ave NW Rm 3330 Washington DC 20220 Office Phone: 202-622-2000. Office Fax: 202-622-6415. *

PAULSON, JAMES MARVIN, retired engineering educator; b. Wausau, Wis., Jan. 1, 1923; s. Gustav Victor and Susanna (Dracy) P.; m. Marjorie Beulah Burton, May 11, 1946; children— Vicki Rae, Michael James. BS in Civil Engring, The Citadel, 1947; MS in Civil Engring, Ill. Inst. Tech., 1949; PhD, U. Mich., 1958. Registered profl. engr., Mich. Draftsman Wausau Iron Works, 1946; engr. Charles Whitney Cons. Engr., Milw., 1948-49; faculty Wayne State U., Detroit, 1949—, prof., 1961-85, chmn. dept. civil engring., 1967-72, assoc. dean Coll. Engring., 1973-83, prof. emeritus, 1985—; ret., 1985. V.p. Civil Engrs., Inc., 1954—; cons. in field. Served with AUS, 1943; Served with USMCR, 1943-46. Mem. ASCE (life), Mich. Soc. Profl. Engrs. (life), Am. Soc. for Engring. Edn., Sigma Xi, Tau Beta Pi, Chi Epsilon. Presbyterian. Home: PO Box 23 Greenbush MI 48738-0023

PAULSON, JANE, lawyer; JD, U. Va., Charlottesville, 1990. Ptnr. Paulson Coletti Trial Atts. PC, Portland, 1995—. Office: Paulson Coletti Trial Attys PC 1000 SW Broadway #1660 Portland OR 97205 Office Phone: 503-226-6361.

PAULSON, JEROME AVROM, pediatrician; b. Balt., July 31, 1949; s. Robert R. and Edna (Brenner) P.; m. Susan Miller, 1973 (div. 1986); m. Gwen Victor Gampel, July 2, 1989. BS in Biochemistry, U. Md., 1971; MD, Duke U., 1974. Diplomate Am. Bd. Pediatrics, Nat. Bd. Med. Examiners. Resident in pediatrics Johns Hopkins Hosp., Balt., 1974-76, Sinai Hosp., Balt., 1976-77, fellow in ambulatory pediatrics, 1977-78; asst. prof. pediatrics Case Western Res. U., Cleve., 1978-86; dir. sci. rsch. and pub. policy devel. Joseph P. Kennedy Jr. Found., Washington, 1986-87; dir. pediatrics Regional Inst. for Children and Adolescents, Rockville, Md., 1987-89; clin. assoc. prof. pediatrics Georgetown U., Washington, 1987—; exec. dir. Research!America, Alexandria, Va., 1989-90; assoc. prof. medicine (formerly healthcare scis.) George Washington U., Washington, 1990—2002, assoc. prof. pediats., 1991—, fellow Ctr. Health Policy Rsch., 1991—98, assoc. prof. prevention and cmty. health, 1997—, assoc. rsch. prof. environ. and occupl. health, 2003—; co-dir. Mid-Atlantic Ctr. for Children's Health and the Environment George Washington U. Med. Ctr., 2000—. Mem. conf. on methodology and std. definitions for childhood injury rsch. Nat. Inst. Children & Human Devel., 1989; health adv. com. Congressman James Moran, 8th Congl. Dist., Va., 1992—94; mem. benefits working group Nat. Drinking Water Adv. Coun. EPA, 1989—99; adv. Health Pages, 1994—97; spl. asst. to dir. Nat. Ctr. for Environ. Health, Ctrs. for Disease Control, Washington, 1999—2001; Soros advocacy fellow Children's Environ. Health Network, 2000—02; bd. dirs. Crative Glass Ctr. Am. Author: Pediatrics: Review for New National Boards, 2000; editor Pediat. Clinics N.Am., 2001, 07; contbr. articles to profl. jours., chpts. to books. Profl. adv. bd. Nat. Safety Town Ctr., Cleve., 1981-85; bd. dirs., pres. James Renwick Alliance, Washington, 1986-93, 95-98; bd. dirs. Jewish Social Svcs. Agy Greater Washington, 2002—, chmn. No. Va. com., 2002— Recipient Cert. for Ednl. and Pub. Policy Activity, Ohio State Senate/Ho. of Reps., 1985; Robert Wood Johnson Health Policy fellow, 1985-86, Soros Advocacy fellowship 2000-02. Fellow Am. Acad. Pediat. (mem. com. environ. health 2007—); mem. Ambulatory Pediatric Assn. Jewish. Avocation: collecting contemporary american crafts. Office: CP & A Foggy Bottom 2141 K St NW # 401 Washington DC 20037-1866 Home Phone: 703-461-7683; Office Phone: 202-833-4543. Business E-Mail: jpaulson@cnmc.org.

PAULSON, KENNETH ALAN, editor-in-chief; b. Chgo., Dec. 3, 1953; s. Knut Norman and Helen Elizabeth (Beardsley) P.; m. Peggy Jean Foot, June 12, 1976; children: Carrie Ann, David. BA in Journalism, U. Mo., 1975; JD, U. Ill., 1978. Bar: Ill., 1978, Fla. 1979. Reporter, bur. chief Fort Myers News-Press, Fla., 1978—80; metro editor to mng. editor Courier-News, Bridgewater, NJ, 1980—84; founding staff member USA Today, McLean, Va., 1982; editor Green Bay Press-Gazette, Wis., 1985—86; spl. asst./chief of staff to chmn. Gannett Co., 1986—88; exec. editor Florida Today, Brevard County, 1988—92; exec. editor, v.p. news Gannett Suburban Newspapers, White Plains, NY, 1992—96; exec. dir. 1st Amendment Ctr. Vanderbilt U., Nashville, 1997—2004; sr. v.p., exec. dir. Freedom Forum, Arlington, Va., 1997—2004; sr. v.p., editor USA Today, McLean, Va., 2004—; editor USAToday.com. Adj. prof. Vanderbilt U. Law Sch.; host TV show Speaking Freely; trustee Freedom Forum Bd; juror, Pulitzer Prize awards, 2007. Office: USA Today 7950 Jones Branch Dr Mc Lean VA 22108 *

PAULSON, LORETTA NANCY, psychoanalyst; b. LA, Nov. 5, 1943; d. Frank Morris and Rose (Kaufman) Fargo; m. Maurice Krasnow; 1 child, Kira. BA, U. So. Calif., 1966; MS in Social Work, Columbia U., NYC, 1969; cert. psychoanalyst, C.G. Jung Inst., NYC. LCSW; lic. clin. social worker, N.Y., Conn., N.J. Pvt. practice psychoanalysis, NYC, 1976—. Past vice chmn. CGJ Inst. Tng. Bd. Mem. NASW (diplomate in clin. social work), Internat. Assn. for Analytical Psychology (past del., bd. dirs.), N.Y. Assn. for Analytic Psychology (past pres., past chair program com.), Conn. Soc. Clin. Social Work (com. on psychoanalysis), C.G. Jung Inst. Address: 334 W 86th St Apt 1A New York NY 10024-3130 Home Phone: 212-595-5445; Office Phone: 212-595-4111. E-mail: lnp222@aol.com.

PAULSON, PAUL JOSEPH, advertising executive; b. White Plains, NY, Sept. 25, 1932; s. Paul and Ann (Loughlin) P.; m. Kathryn P. Keeler, June 30, 1962; children: Thomas, Mark, Kathryn, John, Clifford. BSBA, Ohio State U., 1954; MBA, U. Pa., 1959. With Compton Advt. Inc., NYC, 1959-78, mgmt. supr., 1965-78, sr. v.p., 1968-78, also dir.; pres., dir. Doyle Dane Bernbach Inc., NYC, 1978-83; pres., chief exec. officer Isidore & Paulson, Inc., NYC, 1983-93; chmn., pres., CEO Paulson & Co. Mktg. Svcs., Greenwich, 1993—. Chmn. Mktg. Exec. Networking Group, 2000—03; mem. Ohio State U. Alumni Adv. Coun., 1982—; pres. coun. mem. Ohio State U., 1993—. Author: Fundamentals of Consumer Goods Marketing, 1966. Founder, chmn. Christmas for Underprivileged Children, N.Y.C., 1963—. Served to lt. (j.g.) USNR, 1955-58, MTO, ETO. Recipient Commendation letter, MTO, 1957. Mem. Wharton Grad. Bus. Sch. Alumni Assn. (pres. N.Y.C. club 1963-65, dir. 1972—), Ohio State U. Alumni Assn., Wharton Grad. Bus. Sch., Milbrook Owners Assn. (pres.). Clubs: N.Y. (dir.), Milbrook, Sigma Chi. Roman Catholic. Home: 45 W Brother Dr Greenwich CT 06830-6726 Office Phone: 203-629-3347. Personal E-mail: pjpmrktg@verizon.net, pjpmrktg@ortonline.net. E-mail: pjpmrktg@aol.com.

PAULSON, RAYMOND ARNOLD, science engineering executive; b. Eagle Rock, Calif., Dec. 29, 1921; s. Arnold Edwin and Clara (Martin) P.; m. Beverly Doris, Sept. 21, 1941; children: Larry, Jerry, Celeste. JD, Calif. Coll. Law, 1966; postgrad., Citrus Coll., Nat. U., U. S.C. Law instr. U.S. Armed Forces Inst.; dir., mgr. nat. maj. mfr., prodr. first tactical army missile The Corporal, 1959; sales mgr., asst. dir. So. Calif. Credit. Bur.; engr., designer radiation and chem. evaluation test labs. USAF; dir., mgr. electro-mech. bus.; founder Calif. Coll. Law; pres. chmn. bd. Paulson Internat. Corp., 1971-90, ret., hon. chmn., 1990—; pres. World Trust Agy. (div. Paulson Devel. Corp.); founder Paulson Products Co.; sole proprietor Paulson Co.; established pvt. trust Paulson Trust; established Guatemala Pvt. Sector Country Trust Fund. Devel., instr. exec. leadership tng. program dept. adult edn. Baldwin Pk. Schs.; founder Paulson Zero Emission Energy Rsch. and Devel. Found. Talent locator, stage mgr. "I Love Lucy Show"; designer, assoc. dir. World Internat. Air and Space Show, 1995, Sky Harbor and McCarron Airports, Hdqs. World Air and Space Tours; assoc. designer thermal battery and developer 1st semi-perpetual electric vehicle; pioneered color telecasting; 1st color stage mgr. with Carlton Winkler-Ed Wynn on Union Pacific show Sta. CBS-TV; joint originator USMC Christmas program for underprivileged kids Toys for Tots; surveyor, designer congress-approved U.S. Canal, Brownsville, Tex., Nat. City, San Diego; designer Direct Fly by Wire Flight Control Sys.; mfr. 1st all composite single engine bullet proof two place jet spacecraft in world Mach 3 Plus; designer, developer VAC-PAC All Purpose Shipping Container for ship, rail and truck; designer, prodr. semi-perpetual self-contained charging sys. for electric vehicle battery sources, containers and vehicles too way sea level water way; designed concept for congress-approved Gulfo-Pacific Canal, Mex.; designer-mfr. pacemaker cs. for MedTronics Leadership tng. dir. Boy Scouts Am., Monte Vista dist.; founding mem. Air-Space Mus. Smithsonian Instn., 1994. B-29 radar navaigator pilot USAAF, 1944—45, WWII, Hiroshima Atomic Bombing and Nagaski. Decorated Air Medal and Battle Stars with presdl. citation; recipient Merit award, div. rsch. and sci. guidance LA County Supt. Schs. Mem. TV Acad. Arts and Sci. (co-originator, life assoc.). Achievements include designing and developing the first hybrid-electric jet with semi-perpetual electric charging syste(specs.); operates with 80-9o percent less jet fuel. Office: Paulson Co Internat World Trust Agy PO Box 4369 Covina CA 91723-4369 Office Fax: 626-332-4346.

PAULSON, ROBERT LAWRENCE, aerospace engineer, consultant; b. Jan. 7, 1937; BSEE, Mich. Tech. U., Houghton, 1958; MSEE, Air Force Inst. Tech., Wright Patterson AFB, Ohio, 1964. Commd. 2d lt. USAF, 1959, advanced through grades to col., ret., 1989; pres., CEO Geodynamics Corp., Torrance, Calif., 1989—95; mission 2 dir. TRW, Redondo Beach, Calif., 1995—2001. Recipient Space Pioneer award, Nat. Reconnaissance Orgn., Chantilly, Va., 2002. Mem.: AIAA, AF Assn. Address: 2133 W 235th Pl Torrance CA 90501-6045

PAULSON, RONALD HOWARD, language educator, humanities educator; b. Bottineau, ND, May 27, 1930; s. Howard Clarence and Ethel (Tvete) P.; m. Barbara Lee Appleton, May 25, 1957 (div. 1982); children: Andrew Meredith, Melissa Katherine. BA, Yale U., 1952, PhD, 1958. Instr. U. Ill., 1958-59, from asst. to assoc. prof., 1959-63; prof. English Rice U., Houston, 1963-67, Johns Hopkins U., Balt., 1967-75, chmn. dept., 1968-75, Andrew W. Mellon prof. humanities, 1973-75, Mayer prof. humanities, 1984—2005, chmn. dept., 1985-91; prof. English Yale U., New Haven, 1975-84, Thomas E. Donnelly prof., 1980-84, Ward Phillips lectr., 1978, Alexander lectr., 1979, Brown and Haley lectr., 1979, Hodges lectr., 1980. Author: Theme and Structure in Swift's Tale of a Tub, 1960, Fielding, 1962, Hogarth's Graphic Works, 1965, rev. edits., 1970, 89, Fictions of Satire, 1967, Satire and the Novel, 1967, (with Thomas F. Lockwood) Fielding: The Critical Heritage, 1969, Satire: Modern Essays in Criticism, 1971, Hogarth: His Life, Art and Times, 1971, Rowlandson: A New Interpretation, 1972, Emblem and Expression: Meaning in Eighteenth Century English Art, 1975, The Art of Hogarth, 1975, Popular and Polite Art in the Age of Hogarth and Fielding, 1979, Literary Landscape: Turner and Constable, 1982, Book and Painting: Shakespeare, Milton and the Bible, 1983, Representations of Revolution, 1983, Breaking and Remaking, 1989, Figure and Abstraction in Contemporary Painting, 1990, Hogarth Vol. 1: The Making of the Modern Moral Subject, 1991, Hogarth Vol. 2: High Art and Low, 1991, Hogarth Vol. 3: Art and Politics, 1993, The Beautiful, Novel, and Strange: Aesthetics and Heterodoxy, 1996, Don Quixote in England: The Aesthetics of Laughter, 1998; editor: The Analysis of Beauty, 1997, The Life of Henry Fielding: A Critical Biography, 2000, Hogarth's Harlot: Sacred Parody in Enlightenment England, 2003, Sin and Evil: Moral Values in Literature, 2007; mem. editl. bd.: English Lit. History, 1967-2005, sr. editor, 1985-2002. 1st lt. AUS, 1952-54. Sterling fellow 1957-85, Guggenheim fellow 1965-66, 1986-87, NEH fellow 1977-78. Fellow Am. Acad. Arts and Scis.; mem. Am. Soc. for 18th Century Studies (pres. 1986-87). Home: 2722 Saint Paul St Baltimore MD 21218-4332 Office: Johns Hopkins U Dept English Baltimore MD 21218

PAULSTON, CHRISTINA BRATT, linguistics educator; b. Stockholm, Dec. 30, 1932; arrived in US, 1951; d. Lennart and Elsa Bratt; m. Rolland G. Paulston, July 26, 1963 (dec. Jan. 2006); children: Christopher-Rolland, Ian Rollandsson. BA, Carleton Coll., 1953; MA in English and Comparative Lit., U. Minn., 1955; Ed.D., Columbia U., 1966. Cert. tchr., Minn. Tchr. Clara City and Pine Island High Schs., Minn., 1955-60, Am. Sch. of Tangier, Morocco, 1960-62, Katrineholm Allmanna Larovерk, Katrineholm, Sweden, 1962-63, East Asian Library, Columbia U., NYC, 1963-64; asst. instr. Tchrs. Coll., Columbia U., 1964-66; instr. U. Punjab, Chandigarh, India, summer 1966, Pontificia Universidad Catolica Del Peru, Lima, 1966-67; cons. Instituto Linguistico de Verano, Lima, 1967-68; asst. prof. linguistics U. Pitts., 1969-75, prof., 1975-99, prof. emerita, tchg. pro bono, 1999—, asst. dir. English Lang. Inst., 1969-70, dir. English Lang. Inst., 1970-97, acting dir. Lang. Acquistion Inst., fall 1971, acting chmn. dept. gen. linguistics, 1974-75, chmn., 1975-89. Apptd. internat. advisor in sociolinguistics to Summer Inst. of Linguistics, 1997. Author numerous books and articles on linguistics. Recipient research award Am. Ednl. Research Assn., 1980; Fulbright-Hays grantee, Uruguay, 1985. Mem. Assn. Tchrs. English to Speakers of Other Langs. (2d v.p., conv., chmn. 1972, exec. com. 1972-75, rsch. com. 1973-75, 78-80, chmn. 1973-75, 1st v.p. 1975, pres. 1976), Linguistics Soc. Am. (com. linguistics and pub. interest 1973-77), Internat. Assn. Tchrs. of English as a Fgn. Lang., Am. Coun. on Tchg. of Fgn. Langs., MLA (exec. com. lang. and soc. 1975-76), Ctr. Applied Linguistics (trustee 1976-81, exec. com. 1980, publs. com. 1981, rsch. com. 1981). Democrat. Episcopalian. Office: U Pitts Linguistics Pittsburgh PA 15260 Office Phone: 412-624-5900.

PAULU, FRANCES BROWN, retired international center administrator; b. Hastings, Minn., June 22, 1920; d. Thomas Andrew and Florence Ida (Tuttle) Brown; m. Burton Paulu, June 29, 1942; children: Sarah Leith Paulu Boittin, Nancy Jean Paulu Hyde, Thomas Scott. BA magna cum laude, U. Minn., Mpls., 1940. Case worker Family Welfare Assn., Mpls., 1943—45; interviewer County Health and Welfare Coun., Mpls., 1963; sch. social worker Project Head Start, Mpls., 1966; program dir. Minn. Internat. Ctr., Mpls., 1970—72, exec. dir., 1972—89; mem. tourism adv. com. City of Mpls., 1976—83; mem. adv. coun. Minn. World Trade Ctr., 1984—86. Pres. UN Rally, 1970—72; chmn. Mpls. Charter Commn., 1972—74; dir. Minn. World Trade Week, 1977—81; del. Nat. Coun. World Affairs, Taipei-Manila, 1988; coord. Voices from Around the World, 1996—2000; bd. dirs. Urban Coalition of Mpls., 1967—70; sec. Becketwood Coop., 2001—04; mgmt. team Minn. Awareness Project, 1982—89; participant Intercultural Comm. Project Japan, 1974; dir. Elder Learning Inst., 1995—2000. Fellow, U. Min. Sch. Social Work, 1942—44; DeWitt Jennings Payne scholar, 1939—40. Mem.: LWV (pres. Mpls. chpt. 1967—69), Nat. Coun. Internat. Visitors (mem. exec. com. 1975—81, sec. 1976—77, v.p. 1977—78, leader fact-finding team N. Africa, Mid. East, India 1978, conf. chair 1989), Alliance Française (bd. dirs. 1991—94), People to People Internat. (Disting. Membership award 1987), UN Assn. Minn. (mem. adv. coun. 1979—92, sec. 1994—96, mem. adv. coun. 1996—2004), U. Minn. Women's Club (pres. 1992—94), Phi Beta Kappa, Lambda Alpha Psi, Alpha Omicron Pi. Home: 4300 W River Pkwy Apt 444 Minneapolis MN 55406-3681 Personal E-mail: paula86@msn.com. Business E-Mail: paulu005@umn.edu.

PAULUS, MICHAEL JOHN, government official, economist, bank executive; b. Port Washington, Wis., Feb. 18, 1957; s. John Peter and Elizabeth Jane (Streff) P.; m. Christine H. Kwon, Apr. 29, 2000; children: Alexandra, Veronica. BA, U. Wis. Milw., 1980; cert., U. Freiburg, 1979—80; M Internat Affairs, Columbia U., 1982. Economist Fed. Res. Bank, NYC, 1982—85, sr. fgn. exch. trader, 1985—87, dep. chief fgn. exch. trader, spl. asst., 1987—88, mgr., chief fgn. exch. trader, 1988—90; v.p. capital markets group 1st Nat. Bank Chgo., 1990—92; v.p. treasury dept. Dresdner Bank, NYC, 1992—94; v.p., mgr. instnl. mktg. desk Bank of Am., NYC, 1994—97, v.p., mgr. sales and mktg., 1997—98, prin., mgr. mktg. and bus. devel. U.S. Fgn. Exch., 1998—2000; dep. asst. sec. for fed. fin. U.S. Dept. Treasury, Washington, 2000—01; mng. dir. head of U.K. investor sales fixed income, currencies and commodities Citi, London, 2001—05, mng. dir., head pub. sector group Asia, Hong Kong, 2005—. Vice chmn. Ams. com. Hong Kong Gen. C. of C., 2007—. Fgn. Student scholar U. Freiburg, 1979; Sch. of Internat. Affairs fellow Columbia U., 1980-81, Internat. fellow Columbia U., 1981; recipient U.S. Dept. Treasury exceptional Svc. award, 2001. Mem. Hong Kong Gen. C. of C. (vice chmn. Am.'s com. 2007—), Phi Beta Kappa, Phi Kappa Phi. Roman Catholic. Avocations: sports, history. Address: Apt 23-A The Summit 41-C Stubbs Rd Wanchai Hong Kong Fax: 852-2868-8911. E-mail: michael.paulus@citigroup.com.

PAULY, JOHN EDWARD, retired anatomist; b. Elgin, Ill., Sept. 17, 1927; s. Edward John and Gladys (Myhre) P.; m. Margaret Mary Oberle, Sept. 3, 1949; children: Stephen John (dec.), Susan Elizabeth, Kathleen Anne, Mark Edward; m. Dola S. Thompson, Jan. 7, 2006. BS, Northwestern U., 1950; MS, Loyola U., Chgo., 1952, PhD, 1955. Grad. asst. gross anatomy Stritch Sch. Medicine, Loyola U., 1953-54; rsch. asst. anatomy Chgo. Med. Sch., 1952-54, rsch. instr., 1954-55, instr. in gross anatomy, 1955-57, assoc. in gross anatomy, 1957-59, asst. prof. anatomy, 1959-63, asst. to pres., 1960-62; assoc. prof. anatomy Tulane U. Sch. Medicine, 1963-67; prof., head dept. anatomy U. Ark. for Med. Scis., Little Rock, 1967-83, prof., head dept. physiology and biophysics, 1978-80, vice chancellor for acad. affairs and sponsored rsch., 1983-92, assoc. dean Grad. Sch., 1983-92, prof. anatomy, 1992-95, prof. emeritus, 1995—. Flight instr. Ctrl. Flying Svc., Little Rock, 1997—2002; tech. adviser Ency. Brit. Films, 1956; mem. safety and occupl. health study sect. Nat. Inst. Occupl. Safety and Health, Ctr. for Disease Control, 1975—79; vis. prof. faculty medicine Kuwait U., 1993, 94; vis. prof. anatomy U. Nev., 1996; chief of staff Ark. wing Civil Air Patrol, 2002—05. Author: (with Hans Elias) Human Microanatomy, 1960, 3d edit. 1966, (with Elias and E. Robert Burns) Histology and Human Microanatomy, 1978; editor: (with Lawrence E. Scheving and Franz Halberg) Chronobiology, 1974, (with Heinz von Mayersbach and Lawrence E. Scheving) Biological Rhythms in Structure and Function, 1981, The American Association of Anatomists, 1888-1987. Essays on the History of Anatomy in America and a Report on the Membership-Past and Present, 1987, (with Lawrence E. Scheving) Advances in Chronobiology, 1987, (with Dora K. Hayes and Russel J. Reiter) Chronobiology: Its Role in Clinical Medicine, General Biology and Agriculture, 1990; editor Am. Jour. Anatomy, 1980-92; co-mng. editor Advances in Anatomy, Embryology and Cell Biology, 1980-95; mem. adv. editl. bd. Internat. Jour. Chronobiology, 1973-83; contbr. articles to profl. jours. Chief of staff, mission pilot, instr. pilot and check pilot Ark. Wing Civil Air Patrol, 2002—05. With USNR, 1945—47. Recipient merit certificates AMA, 1953, 59; Bronze award Ill. Med. Soc., 1959; Lederle Med. Faculty award, 1966 Fellow AAAS, Am. Assn. Anatomists (sec.-treas. 1972-80, pres. 1982-83, Centennial award 1987, Henry Gray award 1995); mem. So. Soc. Anatomists (pres. 1971-72), Assn. Anatomy Chmn. (sec.-treas. 1969-71), Am. Physiol. Soc., Internat. Soc. Chronobiology, Pan-Am. Assn. Anatomy, Internat. Soc. Electrophysiol. Kinesiology, Internat. Soc. Steriology, Consejo Nacional de Profesores de Ciencias Morfologicas (hon.), Quiet Birdmen, Sigma Xi, Sigma Alpha Epsilon. Roman Catholic. Office Phone: 501-376-1729. Personal E-mail: flydoc1@comcast.net.

PAUP, MARTIN ARNOLD, securities investor, real estate investor; b. Seattle, Aug. 30, 1930; s. Clarence Jacob and Emaline Ethel (Lodestein) P.; m. Mary Jean Iske, Apr. 4, 1959; children: Barbara Ann Paup Soriano, Jennifer Marie, Elizabeth Paup-Byrnes. BS, U. Wash., 1952. Indsl. engr. Boeing Airplane Co., Seattle, 1954—60; owner Coopers Unfinished Furniture, Seattle, 1960—63; claims rep. Unigard Ins., Seattle, 1963—66; asst. benefits mgr. Equitable Life Assurance, Seattle, 1966—85; owner Paup Ventures, Seattle, 1974—, Paup Investment Co., Seattle, 1963—, Ella Paup Properties, Seattle, 1963—. Bd. dirs. Denny Regrade Property Owners' Assn., Seattle, Denny Regrade Bus. Assn., Seattle, First Ave. Assn., Seattle. Grantee, Seattle Dept. Cmty. Devel., 1980. Mem. Greenwood C. of C., Seattle Opera Guild. Democrat. Roman Catholic. Avocations: opera, travel, literature, history.

PAUSA, CLEMENTS EDWARD, electronics company executive; b. South Gate, Calif., Oct. 18, 1930; s. Oscar Clements and Kathleen Patricia (O'Toole) P.; m. Janice Mary Hanson, Jan. 22, 1955; children: Geoffrey Clements, Ronald Edward. Student, UCLA, 1948-50; BS, U. Calif., Berkeley, 1953, MS, 1954, cert. in bus., 1960. Product mgr. Fairchild Semiconductor Corp., 1959-62, mgr. plant, 1962-64; gen. mgr. Fairchild Hong Kong Ltd., 1964-67, dir. plant group, 1967-68; dir. internat. mfg. Nat. Semiconductor Corp., Santa Clara, Calif., 1968-70, gen. mgr. Far East ops., 1970-73, v.p. internat. mfg., 1973-86, corp. v.p. internat. mfg., 1986-90, corp. v.p. internat. mfg. emeritus, 1991—. Dir. Price Waterhouse Coopers STS; v.p. ops. Power Integrations, Inc., 1997-99; bd. dirs. 8 subs. cos., 2 J.V. cos. Mem. internat. adv. bd. U. Santa Clara, 1984—. Capt. USNR, 1952-81. Mem. Naval Res. Assn., Res. Officer's Assn., Sons in Retirement, Calif. Alumni Assn., Delta Chi Alumni Assn. (v.p., pres. 1978-86). Republican. Roman Catholic. Office: Ste 1600 10 Almaden Blvd San Jose CA 95113 Office Phone: 408-817-5738. E-mail: clements.e.pausa@us.pwc.com.

PAUSTIAN, PAUL ROBERT, librarian; b. Kansas City, Mo., July 29, 1949; s. Paul Louis and Marguerite (Semstead) P.; m. Elisabeth Wilma Kalbach, June 12, 1971; children: Nathan Adam, Megan Elisabeth, Lauren Ingrid. BA, U. Mo., 1971; MA, U. Kans., 1975; postgrad., U. Toronto, 1977-78; MA, U. Mo., 1979. Libr. asst. U. Mo. Librs., Kansas City, Mo., 1972-73, 75-76, Columbia, Mo., 1978-79; asst. instr. U. Kans., Lawrence, 1973-75, grad. rsch. asst., 1976-77; asst. dir. Kansas City Pub. Libr., Kans., 1979; collections libr. U. Mo., Kansas City, 1979-82, asst. dir. librs., 1982-84; dir. libr. Wilkes Coll., Wilkes-Barre, Pa., 1984-88, U. SD, Vermillion, 1988-91, Lebanon Valley Coll., Annville, Pa., 1991—2006; project mgr. OCLC Preservation Svc. Ctr., Bethlehem, Pa., 2007—. Contbr. articles to profl. jours. Mem. Twp. Planning Commn., North Lebanon (Pa.) Twp., 1992-94. Mem. ALA, Assn. Coll. and Rsch. Librs. (bd. dirs. Delaware Valley chpt. 1986-88, 93-99, chair bylaws com., 1996-2001, others), PALINET (fin. com. 1999-2001, chair spl. com. on bylaws 2001-04, trustee 2001-04, exec. com. 2002-04), Beta Phi Mu. Home: 821 Calico Ct Lebanon PA 17046-8254 Office: OCLC Preservation Svc Ctr 9 S Commerce Way Bethlehem PA 18017 Office Phone: 610-758-8700. Business E-Mail: paustiar@oclc.org.

PAUWELS, COLLEEN KRISTL, library director, educator; AB, Barat Coll., 1968; MLS, Ind. U., 1975, JD, 1986. Pub. svcs. libr. Ind. U. Sch. Law, Bloomington, 1975—78, acting dir. Law Libr., 1978—80, interim dir., 1980—83, dir., 1983—, assoc. prof. Office: Ind U Sch Law Indiana U Sch Law Bloomington IN 47405-7001 Office Phone: 812-855-9666. E-mail: pauwels@indiana.edu. *

PAUWELS, JUDITH, physician, medical educator; d. Maurice and Martha Pauwels; m. Tom Truesdell, Oct. 12, 1996. MD, U. Wis., Madison, WI, 1983. Diplomate Am. Bd. Family Medicine, 2006. Program dir. Tacoma Family Medicine Residency Program, 1995—2001, U. Wash. Family Medicine Residency Program, Seattle, 2002—. Cons. Residency Assistance Program of the AAFP, Kansas City, Mo., 2001. Recipient Family Physician Educator Yr., Wis. Acad. Family Physicians, 1990. Mem.: Soc. Tchrs. Family Medicine (licentiate). Avocations: flyfishing, hiking, skiing. Office: Univ Wash 4245 Roosevelt Way NE Seattle WA 98122 Office Phone: 206-598-2883.

PAVALON, EUGENE IRVING, lawyer; b. Chgo., Jan. 5, 1933; m. Lois M. Frenzel, Jan. 15, 1961; children: Betsy, Bruce, Lynn. BSL, Northwestern U., 1954, JD, 1956. Bar: Ill. 1956. Sr. ptnr. Pavalon, Gifford & Laatsch, Chgo., 1970—. Adj. prof. Northwestern U. Sch. Law; mem. com. on discovery rules Ill. Supreme Ct., 1981—; lectr., mem. faculty various law schs. Author: Human Rights and Health Care Law, 1980, Your Medical Rights, 1990; contbr. articles to profl. jours., chpts. in books. Mem. bd. overseers Inst. Civil Justice, Rand Corp., 1993-99; mem. vis. com. Northwestern U. Law Sch., 1990-96. Capt. USAF, 1956-59. Fellow Am. Coll. Trial Lawyers, Internat. Soc. Barristers, Internat. Acad. Trial Lawyers, Am. Bd. Trial Advs., Inner Cir. Advs., Roscoe Pound Found. (life mem., pres. 1988-90); mem. ABA, Chgo. Bar Assn. (bd. mgrs. 1978-79), Ill. Bar Assn., Ill. State Bar Assn., Ill. Trial Lawyers Assn. (pres. 1980-81, Lifetime Achievement award 1996), Trial Lawyers for Pub. Justice (founding mem., v.p. 1991-92, pres.-elect 1992-93, pres. 1993-94, Champion of Justice award 2000), ATLA (parliamentarian 1983-84, sec. 1984-85, v.p. 1985-86, pres.-elect 1986-87, pres. 1987, pres., bd. trustees 2003-05, Champion of Justice award 2003), Am. Bd. Profl. Liability Attys. (diplomate), Laureate, Ill. Acad. Lawyers, Chgo. Athletic Assn., Std. Club. Home: 1540 N Lake Shore Dr Chicago IL 60610-6684 Office: Pavalon Gifford et al 2 N La Salle St Chicago IL 60602-3702 Home Phone: 312-280-2331; Office Phone: 312-419-7400. Business E-Mail: pavalon@pglmlaw.com.

PAVARINI, PETER ALFRED, lawyer; b. NYC, Feb. 21, 1952; s. Alfred S. and Anne M. (Pertusi) Pavarini; m. Colleen A. Wulf, Apr. 12, 1980. BA summa cum laude, SUNY-Albany, 1973; JD, Boston Coll., 1977. Bar: Mass. 1977, D.C. 1979, Ohio 1981. Aide N.Y. State Office of Gen. Svcs., Albany, 1973—74; rsch. asst. Boston Coll., 1975—76; intern Office of Mass. Atty. Gen., Boston, 1976—77; atty. HHS, Washington, 1977—81; assoc. Murphey Young & Smith, Columbus, 1981—85, ptnr., 1986—88, Squire, Sanders & Dempsey, Columbus, 1988—90. Lectr. Capital U. Law Sch., 1993—95, Fisher Sch. Bus., 2004—; chmn. adv. bd. Ohio Health Law Insider; editor-in-chief Health Law Jour. of Ohio, 1989—95. Editor: U.S. Health Care Law and Rules. Trustee Friends of the Homeless, 1991—94, Goodwill Columbus, 2003—. Recipient Congressman's medal of Merit, 1970, Gen. Counsel's award, HEW, 1979. Fellow: Am. Acad. Hosp. Attys.; mem.: ABA (Health Law sect.), Ohio Bar Assn. (chmn. 1991—93), Am. Health Lawyers Assn. (bd. dirs.). Avocations: music, skiing, bicycling, songwriting. Home Phone: 740-548-5508; Office Phone: 614-462-5016. Business E-Mail: peter.pavarini@szd.com.

PAVAROTTI, LUCIANO, lyric tenor; b. Modena, Italy, Oct. 12, 1935; s. Fernando and Adele (Venturi) Pavarotti; m. Adua Veroni, Sept. 30, 1961 (separated 1996); children: Lorenza, Cristina, Giuliana; m. Nicoletta Mantovani, Dec. 13, 2003; 1 child, Alice. Diploma magistrale, Istituto Magistrale Carlo Sigonio, 1955; studied with Arrigo Pola, studied with Ettore Campogalliani, degree. Formerly tchr. elem. schs.; salesman ins. Singer: (Operas) (debut) as Rodolfo in La Bohème, 1961, (roles) Edgardo in debut Lucia di Lammermoor, 1963, the Duke in debut Rigoletto, 1961, Rodolfo in La Bohème, 1963, Tonio in debut The Daughter of the Regiment, 1966, (appeared) Lucia di Lammermoor, 1965, (Am. debut) Miami, Fla., 1965; performer (numerous): European performances including Italy, Vienna Staatsoper, Paris; performer: with San Francisco Opera, 1967; singer: (Operas) (debut) Met. Opera, 1968; appeared (Operas) The Daughter of the Regiment, Met. Opera, 1971, Elisir d'Amore, 1973, La Bohème, Chgo. Opera, 1973, La Favorita, San Francisco Opera, 1973, Il Trovatore, 1975, Bellini I Puritani, Met. Opera, 1976, Ponchielli La Gioconda, San Francisco Opera, 1979, Aida, 1981, Mozart, Idomeneo, Met. Opera, 1982, Verdi, Ernani, Met. Opera, 1983, Tosca, Met. Opera, 1995, numerous internat. performances La Scala, Milan, Hamburg, Teatro Colon, Buenos Aires, Australian Opera, Sydney, concert series of Am. and internat. cities Carnegie Hall, 1973, Buenos Aires, Moscow, Beijing, Hong Kong, Tokyo, including arena concerts Madison Square Garden, 1984, and major cities in America, Europe, South America, performance in Central Park, NY, 1993, appeared (films) Yes, Giorgio, 1983, established Opera Co. Philadelphia/Luciano Pavarotti Vocal Competition, 1980, rec. artist (albums) Winner Concorso Internationale, Reggio Emilia, 1961, O Solo Mio, 1979, Mamma, 1984, Passione, 1985, Tutto Pavarotti, 1989, The Essential Pavarotti, 1990, Carreras, Domingo, Pavarotti in Concert, 1990, Amore, 1992, Ti Amo Puccini's Greatest Love Songs, 1993, Pavarotti and Friends, 1993, Pavarotti Plus-Deluxe Edit., 1995, The Three Tenors in Concert, 1994, Pavarotti and Friends 2, 1995, Pavarotti Plus, 1997, Pavarotti Greatest Hits: The Ultimate Collection, 1998, The Three Tenors in Paris, 1998, Arias & Duets Freni Pavarotti, 1998, Donizetti Arias, 1998, Notte d' Amore, 1998, Verdi Arias-La donna é mobile, 1999, I tre tenor L'album di Natule, 2000, The Three Tenors Arias, 2000, Quarant' anni pe la Lirica, 2001, Live Recital, 2001, Nessumdorma Arias & Duets, 2001, Amore: The Essential Romantic Collection, 2001, The Pavarotti Edit., 2001, Luciano Pavarotti-The Singers, 2002, The Best of the Three Tenors, 2002, Ti Adoro, 2003, The Millenium Collection: The Three Tenors, 2005, appeared (PBS TV spl. TV series) (with Placido Domingo & Jose Carreras) The Three Tenors, 1994; performer: Three Tenors Tour, Worldwide Farewell Celebration Tour, 2004—. Established teaching facility for young singing students, Mondena, Italy; created annual charity concert, Pavarotti & Friends, 1993—; UN Messenger for Peace. Named Artist of Yr. Gramophone, 1992; named to Italian Am. Hall of Fame in Music, Nat. Italian Am. Found., 2004; recipient Grammy award, Best Classical Vocal Soloist Performance for Luciano Pavarotti-Hits From Lincoln Ctr., 1978, Grammy award, Best Classical Vocal Soloist Performance for O Solo Mio-Favorite Neapolitan Songs, 1979, Grammy award, Best Classical Vocal Soloist Performance, Live From Lincoln Ctr.-Sutherland/Horne/Pavarotti, 1981, Grammy award, Best Classical Vocal Soloist Performance for Luciano Pavarotti In Concert, 1988, Grammy award, Best Classical Vocal Performance for Carreras, Domingo, Pavarotti in Concert, 1990, Commendatore Cross and Grand Offical Cross for services to the Italian Republic, Nansen award, UN High Commissioner for Refugees, 2001, World Social award, Pres. Gorbachev, Vienna, 2001, John F. Kennedy Ctr. Honor award, 2001, Eisenhower Medallion, People to People Internat., 2004, Freedom of the City of London, Corp. of London, 2005, Red Cross award for Services to Humanity, 2005. Achievements include performance at opening ceremonies of Winter Olympics, Torino, 2006. Office: care Herbert Breslin 119 W 57th St New York NY 10019-2303

PAVELICH, DANIEL L., retired account and tax management consulting executive; CEO BDO Seidman LLP, Chgo.; ret., 1999. Office: BDO Seidman LLP Two Prudential Plaza 130 E Randolph St Fl 2800 Chicago IL 60601-6300

PAVELICH, JUDITH, retired secondary school educator; b. Bklyn., July 10, 1924; d. Abraham and Anna (Chaikin) Goldstein; m. Martin Pavelich, Dec. 5, 1948; children: Alyce, Susan, Sharon. BA, Moravian Coll., 1954; MA, Lehigh U., 1961; postgrad., Pa. State U., Mainland Inst., Marywood Coll. Tchr. spl. edn., Bethlehem, Pa., 1961—62; counselor Northampton Area Jr. H.S., Pa., 1962—. Coord., sec. Big Bros. and Sisters Northampton Area; mem. cataract support group, treas. Israel Cancer Rsch. Fund; bd. dirs. Lehigh Social Svc. Exch.; vol. Lehigh Valley Ecumenical Soup Kitchen; vol. coord. Reibman for Congress Campaign, Reibman for Judge Campaign; campaign coord. Alan Black for Judge; aide leisure group B'rith Sholom Synagogue; mem. friendship cir. Jewish Cmty. Ctr. With WAVES USNR, 1943—48. Mem.: NEA, Am. Sch. Assn., Pa. Sch. Counselors Assn. (unit rep.), Lehigh Valley Guidance Assn. (sec.), Pa. Educators Assn., Northampton Area Educators Assn., Pa. Pers. and Guidance Assn., Am. Pers. and Guidance Assn. Home: 2235 W Highland St Allentown PA 18104-3631

PAVELKA, ELAINE BLANCHE, mathematics professor; b. Chgo. d. Frank Joseph and Mildred Bohumila (Seidl) P. BA, MS, Northwestern U.; PhD, U. Ill. With Northwestern U. Aerial Measurements lab., Evanston, Ill.; tchr. Leyden Cmty. H.S., Franklin Park, Ill.; prof. math. Morton Coll., Cicero, Ill. Invited prof. Internat. Congress on Math. Edn., Karlsruhe, Germany, 1976. RecipientSci. Talent award Westinghouse Electric Co. Mem. Am. Edn. Rsch. Assn., Am. Math. Assn. 2-Yr. Colls., Am. Math. Soc., Assn. Women in Math., Can. Soc. History and Philosophy of Math., Ill. Coun. Tchrs. Math., Ill. Math. Assn. C.C., Math. Assn. Am. Math. Action Group, Ga. Ctr. Study and Tchg. and Learning Math., Nat. Coun. Tchrs. Math., Sch. Sci. and Math. Assn., Northwestern U. Alumni Assn., U. Ill. Alumni Assn., Am. Mensa Ltd., Intertel, Sigma Delta Epsilon, Pi Mu Epsilon. Home: PO Box 7312 Westchester IL 60154-7312

PAVER, ROBERT L., lawyer; b. St. Petersburg, Fla., May 1956; BA, U. Fla., Gainesville, 1978; JD, Stetson U. Coll. Law, Gulfport, Fla., 1981. Bar: Fla. 1981, US Fed. Ct. 1982, US Supreme Ct. 1985. Adj. law prof. Stetson U., 1985—; atty. Holland & Knight, St. Petersburg, Fla., 1994—97; gen. counsel, corp. sec. Jabil Circuit Inc., St. Petersburg, Fla., 1997—. Pres. Pinellas County Criminal Def. Lawyers, 1987—88. Recipient Victor D. Wehle Trial Practice award. Office: Jabil Circuit Inc 10560 Dr Martin Luther King Jr St N Saint Petersburg FL 33716 Office Phone: 727-577-9749. Office Fax: 727-579-8529. *

PAVIA, GEORGE M., lawyer; b. Genoa, Italy, Feb. 14, 1928; s. Enrico L. and Nelly (Welisch) P.; m. Ellen Salomon, June 15, 1952; children: Andrew, Alison; m. 2d, Antonia Pearse, Dec. 2, 1976; children: Julian, Philippa. BA, Columbia U., 1948, LL.B., 1951; postgrad. U. Genoa, 1954-55. Bar: NY 1951, US Supreme Ct. 1956, US Dist. Ct. (so. and ea. dists.) NY 1956. Assoc., Fink & Pavia, NYC, 1955-65; sr. ptnr. Pavia & Harcourt, NYC, 1965—. Served to capt. JAGC, US Army, 1951-54. Mem. ABA, Internat. Law Soc., Consular Law Soc. Home: 18 E 73rd St New York NY 10021-4130 Office: 600 Madison Ave New York NY 10022-1615

PAVIET-HARTMANN, PATRICIA, chemist, researcher; b. Cormeilles, France, June 8, 1964; came to U.S., 1997; d. Roland Jean and Josette Juliette (Camus) Paviet; m. Thomas Hartmann, Apr. 27, 1996; children: Josephine Caroline, Katarina Virginia. BS, U. Nice, France, 1986, MS, 1988; PhD Chemistry, U. Paris XI, 1992. Rsch. scientist Commissariat a l'Energie Atomique, Cadarache, France, 1990—92; postdoctoral fellow Lawrence Livermore Nat. Lab., Calif., 1992—93; mem. staff Forschungszentrum, Karlsruhe, Germany, 1993—97; project leader in actinide chemistry Los Alamos Nat. Lab., 1997—2003; sr. scientist adv. MOX Project, Areva NP, Inc., Aiken, SC; with Savannah River Site, Aiken, 2003—06; rsch. assoc. prof. Idaho State U., Idaho Falls, 2007—. Contbr. articles to profl. jours.; patentee in field. Mem. Am. Chem. Soc., Am. Nuclear Soc. Roman Catholic. Avocations: painting, piano, languages (french, english, german, italian, spanish). Home: 2350 S Rimrock Dr Idaho Falls ID 83401 Office: Idaho State U 1776 Sci Ctr Dr Idaho Falls ID 83402 Office Phone: 208-282-7874. Business E-Mail: pph@isu.edu.

PAVIN, COREY ALLEN, professional golfer; b. Oxnard, Calif., Nov. 16, 1959; Mem. US Team Ryder Cup, 1991, 1993, 1996, Presidents Cup, 1994, 1996. Achievements include winning PGA Tour events including the Houston Coca-Cola Classic, 1984, Colonial Nat. Invitation Tournament, 1985, Hawaiian Open, 1986, 87, Greater Milw. Open, 1986, Bob Hope Chrysler Classic, 1987, 91, Tex. Open, 1988; winner, PGA Tour events including the Bell South Atlanta Golf Classic, 1991, Honda Classic, 1992, LA Open, 1994, Nissan Open, 1995, US Open, 1995, Mastercard Colonial, 1996, US Bank Championship, 2006; set a PGA Tour nine-hole record score of 26 at the US Bank Championship, 2006; finished number 1 on the PGA Tour money list, 1991. Address: c/o PGA TOUR 112 PGA TOUR Blvd Ponte Vedra Beach FL 32082

PAVLAKOS, ELLEN TSATIRI, sculptor; b. Athens, May 25, 1936; d. Andrew and Katherine (Fliskanopoulou) Tsatiri; m. Andrew George Pavlakos, Nov. 2, 1952; children: James, John Andrew. Student, Arsakeion, Athens, 1952, Norton Sch. Art, West Palm Beach, Fla., 1975-79, Nat. Acad. Design, NYC, 1980-81. Solo shows include Brevard Art Mus., 1981, Hess Galleries, Allentown, Pa., 1983, Cultural Ctr. Athens, 1990, 5th Ave. Art Gallery, Melbourne, Fla., 1994, 98; group shows include Le Salon des Nations, Paris, 1984, Nat. Exhbn. of Contemporary Realism in Art, Springfield, Mass., 1984, Springville Mus. Art, Utah, 1985, Capitol Gallery, Fla. Dept. Cultural Affairs, Tallahassee, 1988, Outstanding Am. Women Artists Invitational, Sarasota, 1993, Chamber of fine Arts and Min. of Edn. and Civilization Symposium, Nicosia, Cyprus, 1994, Mus. of Art and Sci., Melbourne, 1996, Appleton Mus. Art, Ocala, Fla., 1997, Sculpture '97, Thessaloniki, Greece, 1997, Dunedin (Fla.) Fine Arts Ctr., 1998, Orlando City Hall Gallery, 1998, 621 Gallary, Tallahassee, Fla., 1999, Lee County Alliance of the Arts, Fort Myers, Fla., 1999, La. State U., Shreveport, 2000, Mt. Dora (Fla.) Art Ctr., 2000, U. Fla. Arts Ctr., Gainesville, 2001, DeLand (Fla.) Mus. Art, 2001, Oceola Art Ctr., Kissimmee, 2002, Visual Arts Ctr. of NW Fla., Panama City, Fla., 2002, Brevard Mus. of Arts and Sci., Melbourne, Fla., 2002, Gadsen Arts Ctr., Lake Wales, Fla., 2004, Atlantic Ctr. for the Arts at Harris, 2004, Seminol Com. Coll., Sanford, Fla., 2004, Lake Wales Art Ctr., Fla., 2004, South Fla. Coll. Mus. Art, Avon Park, 2005, Albany Mus., Ga., 2006, Turner Ctr. Arts, Valdosta, Ga., 2006; bronze sculpture commd. The Harry T. Moore Monument, Titusville Social Svcs. Ctr., 1985, wall relief Knowledge, Brevard Libr., 1993, bronze sculpture Mother Earth, Penakotheke, Athens, 1990, painting Interlude, Penakotheke, Hydrostone sculpture The Flame Keeper, Kennedy Space Ctr., Fla., 1992, Stephen Girard relief Girard Coll., Phila., 1999, Welcoming Christ, bronze sculputre, Holy Name of Jesus CH., Fla., 2004. Recipient best of Show award Brevard Art Mus., 1980; grantee Brevard County Art in Pub. Places, 1990, 93. Mem. Acad. Artists Assn., Medalic Sculpture Assn., Chamber of Visual Arts in Greece, Ten Women in Art. Greek Orthodox. Avocations: art collecting, gardening. Studio: 331 Coral Way W Indialantic FL 32903-4401 Office Phone: 321-773-5046. Personal E-mail: pavlakosstudio@cfl.rr.com.

PAVLATH, ATTILA ENDRE, chemist, researcher; b. Budapest, Hungary, Mar. 11, 1930; came to U.S., 1958; s. Eugene Rudolph and Yolanda Elizabeth (Hortobagyi) P.; m. Katalin Wappel, July 27, 1951; children: George, Grace. Diploma in chem. engring., Tech. U., Budapest, 1952; D in Chemistry, Hungarian Acad. of Sci., Budapest, 1955. Asst. prof. Tech. U., Budapest, 1952-56; group leader Cen. Chem. Rsch. Inst., Budapest, 1954-56; rsch. fellow McGill U., Montreal, Can., 1957-58; sr. group leader Stauffer Chem. Co., Richmond, Calif., 1958-67; project leader Western regional rsch. ctr. USDA, Albany, Calif., 1967-78, rsch. leader Western regional rsch. ctr., 1979—. Author three books; contbr. articles to profl. jours; patentee in field. Fellow Am. Inst. Chemists (councilor 1985-95, dir. 1993-95); mem. Am. Chem. Soc. (councilor 1973-90, dir. 1991-99, pres.-elect 2000, pres. 2001, immediate past pres. 2002), Royal Chem. Soc. Great Britain, Internat. Union of Pure and Applied Chemistry, German Chem. Soc., Hungarian Chem. Soc. Avocations: flying, bridge, tennis, ping pong/table tennis, computers. Office: USDA Western Regional Rsch Ctr 800 Buchanan St Berkeley CA 94710-1105 Office Phone: 510-559-5620. Business E-Mail: apavlath@pw.usda.gov.

PAVLATOS, ARTHUR L., retired social studies educator; b. Lancaster, Pa., Apr. 21, 1942; s. August Constantine and Chrysanthy Grace Pavlatos; m. Mary Jane Pavlatos, Mar. 5, 1967; children: Constantina, Georgina. BS, Millersville U., Pa., 1970, MEd, 1979. Airman USAF, 1962—66; adminstrv. asst. Redevel. Authority, Lancaster, 1967—70; secondary social studies tchr. Lampeter-Strasburg Sch. Dist., Pa., 1970—97. Dept. chmn. Lampeter-Strasburg HS, 1989—95. Editor: The Quiet in the Land, 2003. Pres. Lancaster/Lebanon Coun. for Social Studies, 1985—87; bd. dirs. Friends of Gauser Libr., Millersville, 1999—2001. Mem.: VFW (life), Pa. State Edn. Assn. (life), Am. Legion (licentiate). Greek Orthodox. Avocation: collecting art and books. Home: 1984 Wilderness Rd Lancaster PA 17603

PAVLEY, FRAN J., state representative; b. LA, Nov. 11, 1948; m. Andy Pavley; children: Jennifer, David. BA, Calif. State U., Fresno, 1970; MA, Calif. State U., 1985. Cert. tchr. Calif. Tchr., 28 yrs.; mem. Calif. Assembly, 2000—. Founder Agoura Hills Disaster Response Team, 1987; mem. adv. com. Santa Monica Mountains Conservancy, 1990—; mem. Coastal Commn., State of Calif., 1995—2000; mem. coun., mayor Agoura Hills, Calif., 1982—97. Democrat. Office: PO Box 942849 Rm 3120 Sacramento CA 95814 Address: 6355 Topanga Canyon Blvd Ste 205 Woodland Hills CA 91367-2108 Office Phone: 916-319-2041.

PAVLICK, JOHN J., JR., lawyer; b. Wurzburg, Germany, Mar. 30, 1948; BS, US Military Acad., 1970; JD, Univ. Pa., 1978. Bar: Pa. 1978, US Supreme Ct. 1982, US Ct. Fed. Claims 1989, DC 1991. Ptnr., govt. contracts, regulatory law and compliance Venable LLP, Washington. Contbr. articles profl. journals. To lt. col. US Army, 1970—90, ret. Mem.: ABA, Nat. Contract Mgmt. Assn., Fed. Bar Assn., Phi Kappa Phi. Office: Venable LLP 575 Seventh St NW Washington DC 20004 Office Phone: 202-344-4894. Office Fax: 202-344-8300. Business E-Mail: jpavlick@venable.com.

PAVLIK, WILLIAM BRUCE, psychologist, educator; b. Cleve., Feb. 29, 1932; s. William Frank and Mary (Maco) P.; m. Mary Katherine Findley, May 22, 1979; children by previous marriage: William James, Heather Ann, Russell Matthew, James Clark; 1 child, Amelia Katherine. BS, Western Res. U., 1953; MA, Ohio State U., 1955, PhD, 1956. Asst. prof. psychology Western Mich. U., 1956-60; asst. prof., then asso. prof. Rutgers U., 1960-68; prof. psychology Va. Poly. Inst. and State U., 1968-77, chmn. dept., 1968-72; prof. psychology U. Ga., Athens, 1977-94; ret., head dept., 1977-84. Author articles in field. Mem. Eastern Psychol. Assn., Southeastern Psychol. Assn. (pres. 1985-86), Psychonomic Soc. Home: 2509 Heidi Loop Flagstaff AZ 86004-1843

PAVLISH, CATHERINE ANN, language educator, writer; d. Theodore Joseph and Dorothy Mae Pavlish; m. Gregory A. Carpenter, July 22, 1991; children: Skylar Pavlish Carpenter, Aurora Pavlish Carpenter. BA, Calif. State U., Long Beach, 1985, MA, 1989; PhD, U. North Dakota, Grand Forks, 1998. Cert. secondary tchg. Calif. State U. Long Beach, 1986. Academic advisor, supr. Calif. State U., Long Beach, 1987—92; instr. English Palomar C.C., Vista, Calif., 1999—2001, Mira Costa C.C., Oceanside, Calif., 2000—01, Oreg. Coast C.C., Newport, 2004—. Editor, advisor Waves Literary Program, Newport, 2004—; mem. bd. Writers on the Edge, Newport, 2005—, Internat. Baccalaureate Program, Newport, 2006—. Author: (screenplays) Enough, 2004, Out of the Darkness: An Anthology of Women's Poetry Against Women, 2004, (poetry) A Certain Uncertainty, 2006. Activist anti-poverty programs; advocate human and civil rights, women's rights, consumer rights/protection. Mem.: Am. Fedn. Tchrs., Am. Assn. U. Women, Modern Lang. Assn. Office: Oreg Coast CC 332 SW Coast Hwy Newport OR 97365 Office Phone: 541-574-7129. Business E-Mail: cpavlish@occc.cc.or.us.

PAVONY, WILLIAM H., financial consultant, management consultant; s. Harry and Mollie (Leibel) Pavony; m. Geraldine Rice; 1 child, Sheryl. BBA cum laude, Hofstra U., 1960. CPA, NY. Mgr. Arthur Andersen & Co. Inc., NYC, 1960-73; group sr. v.p. Purolator Svcs. Inc., New Hyde Park, NY, 1973-75; v.p., contr. Purolator Inc., Piscataway, NJ, 1975-78; sr. v.p. Zale Corp., Dallas, 1978-85; sr. v.p. fin., chief fin. officer Alexander's Inc., NYC, 1985-88, exec. v.p., chief fin officer, 1988-89; exec. v.p. adminstrn. The Kobacker Co., Columbus, Ohio, 1989-93; also bd. dirs.; exec. v.p. Arthur Rutenberg Homes, Clearwater, Fla., 1993-94; CFO Color Tile, Inc., Ft. Worth, 1994-95; pres. Pavony Assocs., Corona Del Mar, Calif., 1995-99, Newport Coast, Calif., 1999, 2001—; exec. bus. cons. The Netplex Group, Newport Coast, Calif., 1999-2001; pres. Pavony Assocs., Newport Coast, 2001—. Treas., bd. dirs. Tex. Vis. Nurses Assn., Dallas, 1984-85. Mem AICPA, Fin. Execs. Internat. (past bd. dirs. North Tex. chpt., sec. Columbus chpts.), N.Y. Soc. CPAs, Inst. Mgmt. Accts., Turnaround Mgmt. Assn. Home: 5 Adriana Newport Coast CA 92657-1224 Home Phone: 949-376-1613; Office Phone: 949-497-8026. Personal E-mail: Bpavony@aol.com.

PAVSEK, DANIEL ALLAN, banker, educator; b. Cleve., Jan. 18, 1945; s. Daniel L. and Helen A. (Femec) P. AB, Maryknoll Coll., Glen Ellyn, Ill., 1966; MA, Maryknoll Sch. Theology, Ossining, NY, 1971, Cleve. State U., 1972; PhD, Case Western Res. U., 1981; MS, George Washington U., 2000. Pres. Coun. Richmond Heights, Ohio, 1972-75; lectr. econs. Cleve. State U., 1972-75; asst. prof. Baldwin-Wallace Coll., Berea, Ohio, 1975-81; v.p., economist Ameritrust Co., Cleve., 1981-91; dean, prof. econs. Harry F. Byrd Jr. Sch. Bus. Shenandoah U., Winchester, Va., 1992-99, Durell prof. money and banking H.F. Byrd Jr. Sch. Bus., 1999—. Adj. prof. bus.

adminstrn. Baldwin-Wallace Coll., Berea, Ohio, 1981-91 Mem. Am. Econ. Assn., Nat. Assn. Bus. Econs. Democrat. Home: 21343 Sawyer Sq Ashburn VA 20147-4728 Office Phone: 540-665-4526. E-mail: dpavsek@su.edu.

PAWEL, NANCY EMMA RAY, oil industry executive, educator, artist; b. Boston, Feb. 14, 1928; d. Carlon Weston and Anna Urban Ray; m. Thomas Ernst Pawel, Sept. 1, 1951 (dec.); children: Margaret Pawel Moore, Elizabeth Thompson, Charlotte Ray Pawel Jonas. BA, Wellesley Coll., Mass., 1949; MA, U. Incarnate Word, San Antonio, Tex., 1989. Lab. asst. Med. Sch. Tufts Coll., Boston, 1949—51; biochemist Sch. Aviation Medicine, Tex., 1952—55; instr. U. The Incarnate Word, 1968—99; pres. Concord Oil Co., San Antonio, 2004—. Adj. faculty S.W. Sch. Art and Craft, San Antonio, 2000—; mem. art adv. com. U. Tex., San Antonio, 1990—95; bd. dirs. San Antonio (Tex.) Art League Mus. Prin. works include Wall Natatorium, U. Incarnate Word, Sleeping Beauty's Castle Garden for Blind, San Antonio (Tex.) Botanic Garden, Towers of San Antonio (Tex.) Children's Mus., Ctrl. Gateway, St. Mary's Hall, San Antonio, exhibitions include Taipei, Taiwan, 1998. Named Outstanding Woman in Art, San Antonio (Tex.) Express News, 1970, Artist of Yr., San Antonio (Tex.) Art League, 1977; recipient Lynn Ford Craftsman award, San Antonio (Tex.) Conservation Soc., 2002. Home: 123 Geneseo Rd San Antonio TX 78209 Office: Concord Oil Co Houston St 1500 Frost Bank Tower San Antonio TX 78205 E-mail: Nerpawel@aol.com.

PAWL, RONALD PHILLIP, neurosurgery educator; b. Chgo., July 26, 1935; s. Phillip Joseph and Ruby Helen (Graham) P.; m. Mary M. Rohner, July 11, 1959; children: Mary, Linda, Diane, Julie, Matthew, Michael. BS in Biology, Loyola U., Chgo., 1957, MD, 1961. Diplomate Am. Bd. Neurol. Surgery, Am. Bd. Pain Med. Intern Resurrection Hosp., 1961-62; resident in gen. surgery and orthopedics Hines VA Hosp., 1962-63; resident in neurology and neurosurgery U. Ill., Chgo., 1963-66, asst. prof. neurosurgery, 1968-73; asst. chief neurosurgery Tripler Army Med. Ctr., Honolulu, 1966-68; assoc. prof. neurosurgery U. Ill., Chgo., 1973—; dir. pain treatment ctr. Lake Forest (Ill.) Hosp., 1978—. Pres. Am. Bd. Pain Medicine, 1995, residency rev. com. chmn., 1997-2002, appeals com. 2001-. Author: Chronic Pain Primer, 1979; editor Seminars in Neurology, 1989; editor Clin. Jour. Pain, 1988—, Surg. Neurology, 1994—, Clin. Rev. of Pain, 1997-2002, Currant Rev. of Pain, 1995-2001; contbr. articles to profl. jours. Capt. US Army, 1966—68. Named Physician of Yr., Ill. Masonic Med. Ctr., Chgo., 1973. Mem. Ctrl. Neurosurg. Soc. (pres. 1979), Midwest Pain Soc. (pres. 1986), Am. Acad. Pain Medicine (treas. 1990), Ill. Neurosurg. Soc. (pres. 1982), Chgo. Neirological Soc. (pres. 1980). Roman Catholic. Avocations: anthropology, archaeology. Office: 900 N Westmoreland Rd Lake Forest IL 60045-1674 Home Phone: 847-234-6564; Office Phone: 847-535-6132. E-mail: ron@pawl.com.

PAWLACZYK, GEORGE, reporter; Reporter Belleville (Ill.) News-Dem. Co-recipient Best Cmty. Svc. award, So. Ill. Editl. Assn. Better Newspaper Contest, 2003, Nat. Headliner Grand award for Print, 2007, Robert F. Kennedy Journalism award for Domestic Print, 2007; recipient Best Cmty. Svc. award, So. Ill. Editl. Assn. Better Newspaper Contest, 2002. Office: Belleville News-Democrat 120 S Illinois St Belleville IL 62220-2130 Office Phone: 618-239-2625. E-mail: gpawlaczyk@bnd.com.

PAWLENTY, TIMOTHY JAMES, governor; b. South St. Paul, Minn., Nov. 27, 1960; m. Mary Elizabeth Anderson, 1987; children: Anna, Mara BA, U. Minn., 1983; JD, U. Minn.Law Sch., 1986. Chmn. Eagan Planning Commn., 1988-89; mem. Minn. Ho. of Reps. from Dist. 38, St. Paul, 1993—2002, majority leader, 1999—2002; gov. State of Minn., St. Paul, 2003—. Active Eagan city coun., 1990-92. Fannie Gilbertson Coll. scholar. Republican. Lutheran. Office: Office of the Gov 130 State Capitol 75 Rev Dr Martin Luther King Jr Blvd Saint Paul MN 55155 Office Phone: 651-296-3391. Office Fax: 651-296-2089. E-mail: tim.pawlenty@state.mn.us. *

PAWLEY, RAY L., retired zoological park administrator, curator; b. Midland, Mich., Nov. 7, 1935; s. Lynn Richard and Alice Marie (Skelton) P.; m. Ethel Marie Condon, Feb. 19, 1955 (div. 1974); children: Ray Allyn, Shanna Sue, Cynthia Ann, Dawn Marie, Brandon Earl, Dareen Joy; m. Hedda P. Saltz, Mar. 16, 1997. Student, Mich. State U., 1954—57. Asst. curator, lectr. Black Hills Reptile Gardens, Rapid City, SD, 1952—53; owner, adminstr. Reptile Exhibit, St. Ignace, Mich., 1957—59; animal coord. Don Meier Prodns. Marlin Perkin's Wild Kingdom, Chgo., 1961—62; zoologist Lincoln Park Zool. Gardens, Chgo., 1961—64; curator Brookfield Zoo, Ill., 1964—97; ret., 1997. Formerly assoc. dept. zoology Field Mus. Natural History, Chgo.; internat. zoo and conservation cons., Russia, Latvia, Mex., Kenya, China, Ecuador, Galapagos Islands; past instr. herpetology Field Mus., Coll. of DuPage, Triton Coll.; assoc. zoologist Moscow Zool. Pk., Russia; info. resource for fed. and state wildlife agys.; lectr., cons. in field. Contbr. over 100 articles to profl. jours. and popular mags.; co-creator money bench Chgo. Children's Mus. Past v.p. Ill. Endangered Species Protection Bd., Springfield; liaison Endangered Species Tech. Adv. Com., Springfield. Mem. Am. Zoo Assn. (3 Outstanding Svc. awards), Chgo. Acad. Scis. (life), Chgo. Herpetological Soc. (life), Nat. Herpetological Alliance (past pres.), Mensa. Achievements include development of several new live animal exibit concepts; research in fossil urolite identification; rattlesnake hibernation physiology; discovery and documentation of parthenogenisis in snakes; discovery and documentation of Goliath frog calls; designed and built air-powered water craft prototype for island biological surveys in lakes Huron and Michigan. Avocations: hiking, archaeology, art, paleontology. Home and Office: PO Box 12 Hondo NM 88336 Business E-Mail: raypawley@pvtnetworks.net.

PAWLICZKO, GEORGE IHOR, academic administrator; b. Rochester, NY, Oct. 26, 1950; s. Roman and Irene Olha (Zubryckyj) P.; m. Ann Maria Lencyk, June 10, 1978. BA, St. John Fisher Coll., 1972; MA, Fordham U., 1974, MBA, 1986, PhD, 1989. Admissions counselor Fordham U., Bronx, N.Y., 1977-78, asst. dean Grad. Sch. of Bus. NYC, 1978-81; asst. to pres., dir. mgmt. info. systems Marymount Coll., Tarrytown, N.Y., 1981-82; exec. dir. N.Y. Inst. Credit, NYC, 1982-94, The Global Inst. Fin. and Banking (formerly Am. Inst. Banking Greater N.Y.), NYC, 1994—. Trustee St. Andrew's Ch., Hamptonburgh, N.Y., 1986-2002; bd. trustees St. Basil Coll., Stamford, Conn., 2006-. Mem. Shevchenko Scientific Soc., Beta Gamma Sigma, Phi Alpha Theta. Office: The Global Inst Fin and Banking 80 Maiden Ln New York NY 10038-4811 Office Phone: 212-480-3200.

PAWLITSCHEK, DONALD PAUL, management consultant; b. Heron Lake, Minn., Aug. 5, 1941; s. Paul P. and Marion (Erickson) Pawlitschek; m. Korrine Kunerth, Oct. 9, 1965; children: Andrew, Jennifer, Heidi, Sarah, Benjamin. Student, Southwest Tech. Inst., 1960, Mankato State Coll., 1965—66. Farmer, Heron Lake, 1967—73; pres. Dundee Steel, Inc., 1973—75, Alpha Prime, Inc., Heron Lake, 1975—80, Prime Ventures, Inc., Lake Crystal, Minn., 1980—. Bd. dirs. Am. Search and Referral Co. With US Army, 1960. Mem.: Am. Entrepreneurs Assn., Nat. Assn. Fin. Cons., Elks, Am. Legion. Conservative. Roman Catholic. Achievements include patents for livestock flooring. Home and Office: Prime Ventures Inc 1801 499th Ave Lake Crystal MN 56055-9700

PAWSON, ANTHONY J., molecular biologist; b. Maidstone, Eng., Oct. 18, 1952; BA in Biochemistry, Cambridge U., 1973; PhD in Molecular Biology, London U., 1976. Postdoctoral rsch. fellow U. Calif., Berkeley, 1976—80; asst. prof. Dept. Microbiology U. Brit. Columbia, Vancouver, Canada, 1981—85; sr. scientist Nat. Cancer Inst. Can., 1985—88, Terry Fox Cancer Rsch. scientist, 1988—99; assoc. prof. Dept. Med. Genetics U. Toronto, Canada, 1985—88, prof., dept. medical genetics and microbiology, 1989—, sr. fellow Massey Coll., 2003—; sr. investigator, Samuel Lunenefeld Rsch. Inst. Mount Sinai Hosp., Toronto, 1985—, Apotex chair in molecular oncology, 1991, head rsch. molecular biology and cancer, Samuel Lunenfeld Rsch. Inst., 1994—, dir. rsch. Samuel Lunenfeld Rsch. Inst., 2002—06. Mem. sci. adv. bd. Inst. Molecular and Cell Biology, Singapore, 1998—2004, Jane Coffin Childs Meml. Fund for Med. Rsch., 1997—2004, MGH Cancer Ctr., 1999—, Argonex Discovery Inc., 1999—; mem. sci. planning com. Nat. Human Genome Rsch. Inst., 1997—98; mem. sci. review bd. Howard Hughes Med. Inst., 1997—2000; mem. med. adv. bd. Gairdner Found., 1998—; mem. adv. bd. Ariad Pharm. Inc., 1992—97; lectr. in field; spkr. in field. Mem. editl. bd.: Trends in Genetics, Oncogene, Molecular and Cellular Biology, Cell Growth and Differentiation, Chemistry and Biology, Current Opinion in Cell Biology, Developmental Cell, Molecular Biology of the Cell, European Jour. Biochemistry; editor: Jour. Cellular Physiology, Progress in Biophysics and Molecular Biology. Decorated Officer of the Order of Can.; recipient Internat. award, Gairdner Found., 1994, Robert L. Noble prize, Nat. Cancer. Inst. Can., 1995, George Drummond Meml. award, U. Alberta, 1995, John Colter award, U. Calgary, 1996, Boehringer Mannheim prize, Can. Soc. Biochemistry and Molecular and Cellular Biology, 1997, Disting. Sci. award, Med. Rsch. Coun., 1998, Dr. H.P. Heineken prize for biochemistry and biophysics, Royal Netherlands Acad. Arts and Scis., 1998, Henry Friesen award, Can. Soc. Clin. Investigation, 1998, Pezcoller Internat. award for Cancer Rsch., Am. Assn. for Cancer Rsch./Pezcoller Found., 1998, J. Allyn Taylor Internat. prize in medicine, U. Western Ont., 2000, Killam prize for health scis., 2000, Michael Smith prize in Health Rsch., 2002, Prix Galien Can., 2002, Ernst W. Bertner Meml. award, MD Anderson Cancer Ctr., 2004, Louisa Gross Horwitz prize, 2004, Disting. Investigator award, Can. Inst. Health Rsch., 2004, Poulsson medal, Norwegian Soc. Pharmacology and Toxicology, 2004, Louisa Gross Horwitz prize, Columbia U., 2004, Spl. award Nature Biotech. Winter Symposium, U. Miami, 2005, Wolf prize in medicine, Jerusalem, 2005, Daniel Nathans Meml. award, Van Andel Rsch. Inst., 2005; Internat. Rsch. scholar, Howard Hughes Med. Inst., 1991—2001. Fellow: Am. Acad. Microbiology, Royal Soc. Can. (Flavelle medal 1998), Royal Soc. London (Royal medal 2005); mem.: NAS (assoc.), EMBO (assoc.; mem. editl. bd.), Japanese Biochem. Soc. (hon.), Am. Acad. Arts and Scis. (hon.; fgn.). Office: Mt Sinai Hosp 600 University Ave Rm 1084 Toronto ON Canada M5G 1X5 Mailing: Samuel Lunenfeld Rsch Inst Mt Sinai Hosp 600 Univ Ave Rm 1084 Toronto ON M5G 1X5 Canada Office Phone: 416-586-4800 ext. 8262. Office Fax: 416-586-8869. E-mail: pawson@mshri.on.ca.

PAXON, L. WILLIAM, former congressman; b. Buffalo, Apr. 29, 1954; s. Leon W. and Mary P. (Sellers) P.; m. Susan Molinari, July 3, 1994; children: Susan Ruby, Katherine Mary. BA, Canisius Coll., 1977. Mem. Erie County Legis., N.Y., 1978-82, N.Y. State Assembly, 1983-89, 101st-105th Congresses from 31st (now 27th) N.Y. dist., 1989-98; chair Nat. Rep. Congrl. Com.; mem. com. on commerce; sr. advisor Akin, Gump, Strauss, Hauer & Feld, Washington, 1999—. Roman Catholic. Office: Akin Gump Strauss Hauer & Feld Ste 400 1333 New Hampshire Ave NW Washington DC 20036-1564

PAXSON, JOHN, professional sports team executive, retired professional basketball player; b. Dayton, Ohio, Sept. 29, 1960; s. Jim Paxson; m. Carolyn Paxson; children: Ryan, Drew. Grad., U. Notre Dame, 1983. Player San Antonio Spurs, 1983—85, Chgo. Bulls, 1985—94, radio and TV color analyst, asst. coach, 1995—96, exec. v.p. basketball ops., 2003—. Achievements include winning NBA Championships as a member of the Bulls, 1991, 92, 93. Office: Chgo Bulls United Ctr 1901 W Madison St Chicago IL 60612-2459 *

PAXSON, SAM M., judge; s. Audion H. and Dorothy M. Paxson; m. Gloria de la Ganza Paxson; children: Peyton, Kurt, Christian, Tita, Marie. BBA, Tex. We. U., El Paso, 1955; JD, U. Tex., Austin, 1957. Atty. Paxson & Santiesteban, El Paso, 1959—73; judge 210th Dist. Ct., El Paso, 1973—2003; sr. dist. judge El Paso County Ct. Ho., 2003. Presiding judge 6th Adminstrv. Jud. Dist. Tex., 1986—90. 1st lt. US Army, 1957—59, Tex. Democrat. Office: El Paso County Courtho Ste 1005 El Paso TX 79901

PAXTON, BILL, actor, film director; b. Ft. Worth, May 17, 1955; s. John Lane and Mary Lou (Gray) P.; m. Louise Newbury, 1987, children: James, Lydia Student, NYU; studies with Stella Adler, Vincent Chase. Actor: (films) Crazy Mama, 1975, Stripes, 1981, Taking Tiger MOuntain, 1983, The Lords of Discipline, 1983, Night Warning, 1983, Streets of Fire, 1983, Mortuary, 1983, Impulse, 1983, Terminator, 1984, Weird Science, 1985, Commando, 1985, Aliens, 1985 (Saturn award Acad. of Sci. Fiction, Fantasy, and Horror Films 1986), Near Dark, 1986, Pass the Ammo, 1987, Slipstream, 1989, Next of Kin, 1989, Back to Back, 1990, Brain Dead, 1990, The Last of the Finest, 1990, Navy Seals, 1990, Predator 2, 1990, The Dark Backward, 1991, One False Move, 1992, The Vagrant, 1992, Trespass, 1992, Future Shock, 1993, Indian Summer, 1993, Boxing Helena, 1993, Tombstone, 1993, True Lies, 1994, Apollo 13, 1995, Twister, 1995, Evening Star, 1996, The Last Supper, 1996, Titanic, 1997, A Simple Plan, 1998, Mighty Joe Young, 1998, U-571, 2000, Vertical Limit, 2000, Spy Kids 2: Island of Lost Dreams, 2002, Resistance, 2003, Spy Kids 3-D: Game Over, 2003, Ghosts of the Abyss, 2003, Club Dread, 2004, Thunderbirds, 2004, Haven, 2004; actor, dir. (films) Frailty, 2001, dir. only, The Greatest Game Ever Played, 2005; actor, prodr. (films) Traveler, 1997; actor, dir., prodr., writer, (theatrical short) Fish Heads, 1982 (Spl. Award Melbourne Film Festival 1982); actor (TV movies) Deadly Lessons, 1983, An Early Frost, 1985, Frank and Jesse, 1994, A Bright Shining Lie, 1998; actor (TV mini-series) The Atlanta Child Murders, 1985, Fresno, 1986; actor (TV series) The Six O'Clock Follies, 1980, Big Love, 2006-; (TV appearances) The Hitch-Hiker, 1986, Miami Vice, 1986, Tales From the Crypt, 1993, Frasier (voice only), 2003; (theatrical short) Fish Heads, 1982 (Spl. Award Melbourne Film Festival 1982); prodr., co-author (theatrical short) Scoop, 1983. Mem. Screen Actors Guild. Office: c/o Endeavor Agency 9601 Wilshire Blvd, 3rd Fl Beverly Hills CA 90212

PAXTON, GARY L., auto rental company executive; Positions with Dollar Rent a Car, 1968—72, v.p. ops., 1972—74, v.p. properties, 1974—82, v.p. properties & facilities, 1982—86, sr. v.p. ops. & properties, 1986—90, pres., 1990—2002; pres., COO corp. ops. Dollar Thrifty Automotive Group, Inc., Tulsa, Okla., 2002—03, pres., CEO, 2003—. Office: Dollar Thrifty Automotive Group 5330 E 31st St Tulsa OK 74135 Office Phone: 918-665-3930. *

PAXTON, GLENN GILBERT, composer; b. Chgo., Dec. 7, 1931; s. Glenn G. and Florence A. (Nosek) P.; m. Leslie H. Davis, Dec. 8, 1962; children: Alexandra, Eben. BA, Princeton U., 1953. Freelance composer Broadway, opera, TV and film, 1959—. Composer: (theater prodns.) First Impressions, 1959, The Adventures of Friar Tuck, 1983 (Pulitzer prize nomination 1984), W.R. and Daisy, 2003, (opera) Monticello, 2000, (film) When the Legends Die, 1972, (concert pieces) Four Character Pieces for Piano, 1962, Sara's Diary, 9/11, 2003, The Evening Sing, 1981, (TV movies) Charlie and the Great Balloon Chase, 1981, Vital Signs, 1986, Dark Night of the Scarecrow, 1981, Isobel's Choice, 1981, The Two Worlds of Jenny Logan, 1979, The Clone Master, 1978, (TV shows) Amazing Stories, 1986, Willa Cather's America, 1976, Andy Rooney Takes Off, 1983, An American Christmas: Words and Music, 1971, The Hill Country: Lyndon Johnson's Texas, 1967, The Stately Ghosts of England, 1968, Barry Goldwater's Arizona, 1968, New World Visions, 1984, The American Image, 1969, others; (TV Special) Which Mother Is Mine, (1980 Emmy nominee) (multi-media) Walking Home, 1991; (CD) Prairie Indigo, 1995, Hymns From the Little Stone Church, 2006. Served to lt. (j.g.) USCG, 1953-56. Mem. ASCAP, Am. Fedn. Musicians. Home and Office: 230A Saddle Ln Ojai CA 93023-4204 Home Phone: 805-640-9449; Office Phone: 805-640-9449. Personal E-mail: gpaxton@alumni.princeton.edu.

PAXTON, J. WILLENE, retired academic administrator; b. Birmingham, Ala. d. Will and Elizabeth (Davis) P. AB, Birmingham So. Coll., Ala., 1950; MA, Mich. State U., East Lansing, 1951; EdD, Ind. U., Bloomington, 1971; postgrad., U. Tex., Austin, 1965. Dormitory dir. Tex. Tech U., Lubbock, 1951-53; dir. univ. ctr. and housing SUNY, Fredonia, 1953-56, assoc. dean of students, 1956-57; asst. dean of women U. N.Mex., Albuquerque, 1957-63; dean of women East Tenn. State U., Johnson City, 1963-68, 70-78, dir. Counseling Ctr., 1978-93, initiated Paxton lectureship for learning and leadership, 2007. Tng. dir. CONTACT Teleministries, Tenn., 1984-92, chmn. bd. dirs., 1986, 95. Chmn. social concerns Munsey United Meth. Ch., 1989-92, sec. adminstrv. bd., 1980-84, vice chair, 1993, chair, 1994, coun. on ministries, 1980-94, chair stewardship campaign, 1995, chair promotion and publicity subcom. bldg. campaign, 1996-2001, chair scholarship com., 1997-2004, lay leader, 2001-04, sec. staff parish rels. com., 2001-2004, nominations com., 2001-04, sec. ch. coun., 2003-06, mem. SEND team, Circle tchr., 2000-06; visitor for Mended Hearts, 2000—; recording sec. United Meth. Women, 2005—, corr. sec., 2004; mem. Philip D. Cooper Meml. Rsch. Trust Fund Inc., 2006—. U.S. Ednl. Profl. Devel. Act grantee, 1968-69; chosen One of Ten in Tenn. as Cmty. Quarterback Nat. Football League Tenn. Titans, 2004. Mem.: Watauga Pers. and Guild Assn. (pres.-elect 1967—68, chair ETEA guidance divsn. 1968), Tenn. Assn. Women Deans Counselors (pres. 1966—68), Tenn. Coll. Pers. Assn. (legis. chair 1974), Am. Coll. Pers. Assn. (media com., newsletter editor com. XVI 1977—79), East Tenn. State U. Retirees Assn. (bd. dirs. 1993—2000, program com. 1994—95, pres. 1995—96, chair com. to compile Tales of the Univ. 1999—2005, sec. 2000, bd. dirs. 2003—06), Asbury Retirement Ctrs. Tenn. and Va. (bd. dirs., policy com. 1991—96, nomination com. 1994—96, chair 1995—96, fin. com. 1996), Gen. Federated Women's Club Monday Club (co-chair edn. dept. 2005—06, chair internat. affairs dept. 2007—), Gen. Federated Woman's Club Monday Club Aux. (corr. sec. 1979—80, pres. 1980—81, 1988—89, v.p. 1993—99, pres. 1995—96, 1999—2000), Univ. Women's Club (pres. 1994—96), Delta Kappa Gamma Soc. Internat. (chpt. pres. 1972—74, state rec. sec. 1975—77, state v.p. 1977—79, chair state nominating com. 1979—81, internat. rsch. com. 1982—84, chair state ad hoc com. to study feasibility exec. sec. 1987—89, internat. exec. bd., state pres. 1989—91, internat. chair rules com. 1992, internat. constn. com. 1992—94, state pers. com. 1995—97, chair 1997—99, archives com. 1999—2001, pers. com. 2001—03, awards com. 2003—05, area dir. 2005—07, State Achievement award 1987). Avocations: reading, bridge, travel, needlecrafts. Personal E-mail: willenepj@charter.net.

PAXTON, JAY L., lawyer; b. Ft. Worth, Dec. 24, 1947; s. Carl C. Paxton and Mildred F. (Fawver) Shepherd; m. Carolyn P. Paxton, June 21, 1969; 1 child, Laura. BA, U. Calif., Berkeley, 1970, JD, 1973. Bar: Calif. 1973. Spl. asst. to chancellor U. Calif., 1973-74; ptnr., mng. ptnr. Bianchi, Paxton, Engel, Keegin & Sherwood, San Rafael, Calif., 1974—90; mem., mng. dir. Ellman, Burke, Hoffman & Johnson, San Francisco, 1990—. Bd. dirs., v.p. Internat. House, U. Calif., Berkeley, 1974—, mem. exec. com. Fisher Ctr. for Real Estate and Urban Econs., 2004—; trustee U. Calif. Berkeley Found., 1997—, Marin Cmty. Found., 2005—; mem., chair exec. com. San Francisco Dist. Coun., Urban Land Inst., 1976-; bd. dirs. Bay Area Coun., 1996—. Mem. ABA, Calif. Bar Assn., Urban Land Inst., Lambda Alpha. Office: Ellman Burke Hoffman Johnson 601 California St Ste 1900 San Francisco CA 94108-2824 Business E-Mail: jpaxton@ellman-burke.com.

PAXTON, ROBERT OWEN, historian, educator; b. Lexington, Va., June 15, 1932; s. Matthew W. and Nell B. (Owen) P.; m. Sarah Plimpton, Dec. 9, 1983 BA, Washington and Lee U., 1954, LittD (hon.), 1974; BA, Oxford U., Eng., 1956, MA, 1961; PhD, Harvard U., 1963; DHL (hon.), SUNY, Stony Brook, 1994; DL (hon.), U. Caen, France, 1994; DL (hon.), U. Lyon, France, 2003. Instr. history U. Calif., Berkeley, 1961-63, asst. prof., 1963-67; asso. prof. SUNY, Stony Brook, 1967-69; prof. history Columbia U., 1969—, chmn. dept., 1980-82, dir. Inst. on West Europe, 1991-95. Author: Parades and Politics at Vichy, 1966, Vichy France: Old Guard and New Order, 1940-44, 1972, 2d edit., 2001, Europe in the Twentieth Century, 1975, 4th edit., 2001, French Peasant Fascism, 1997, Anatomy of Fascism, 2004; co-author: Vichy France and the Jews, 1981, 2d edit., 1995; co-editor: De Gaulle and the U.S., 1995. Served with USNR, 1956-58. Decorated comdr. Ordre National des Arts et des Lettres (France), officer Ordre Nat. du Mérite (France); recipient Scholarly Distinction award Am. Hist. Soc., 1998; Rhodes scholar, 1954-56; Am. Coun. Learned Socs. fellow, 1974-75; Rockefeller Found. fellow, 1978-79; German Marshall Fund fellow, 1986. Fellow Am. Acad. Arts and Letters; mem. Am. Philos. Soc., Linnaean Soc. NY (pres. 1978-80), Century Assn. Home: 460 Riverside Dr Apt 72 New York NY 10027-6801 Office: Columbia U Dept History New York NY 10027 Business E-Mail: rop1@columbia.edu.

PAYACK, PAUL J.J., marketing professional, writer; b. Morristown, NJ, Jan. 3, 1950; BA in Comparative Lit., Harvard U., 1974, cert. advanced study in fine arts, 1983. Asst to pres., asst. dir. admissions Newbury Coll., Boston, 1975-78; tech. writer Digital Equipment Corp., Maynard, Mass., 1978-79, Wang Labs., Lowell, Mass., 1980-82; mktg. mgr., sales promotion Apollo Computer Inc. (now Hewlett-Packard Workstations), Chelmsford, Mass., 1982-87; corp. dir., mktg. Unisys Corp., Blue Bell, Pa., 1987-90; v.p., global comm. A.C. Nielsen, Unit of Dun & Bradstreet, Northbrook, Ill., 1990-93; dir., worldwide network mktg. Network Systems Corp., Mpls., 1994—95; v.p. corp. mktg. Intersolv, Rockville, Md., 1995-96; sr. v.p. strategic mktg. Intelliguard Software, Dublin, Calif., 1997; v.p. worldwide mktg. Legato Sys., Mountainview, Calif., 1998-99; pres., wordman yourDictionary.com, Paoli, Pa., 2000—; sr. v.p. Alacritus Software, 2002—05; pres. Global Lang. Monitor, San Diego, 2003—. Cons., lectr. San Diego U., Babson Coll., GM/Hughes, Fed. Res. Bank of NY, Shandwick, Bunting's Window TV show, Bus. Week's Digital Economy, CIO conf.; adj. prof. Babson Coll., Harvard U., Mass State Coll., U. Tex. Author: A Ripple in Entropy, 1973, The Star-Tales Cycle (Solstice 1-3), 1979, Children of the Mind, 1984; (short stories) Mythomania, 1978, Shortest Tomas, 1980, A Plague of Darkness, or the Unseen and the Unseeable, 2003; Anatomical Plates, 1989, The Wind Turbine Studies, 2000, The Pacific Plates, 1999, The Paris Plates, 1999, The End of Empire, 1999, The Perspective Series, 1986, The Land of Orth, 1977, Unexpected Twist Series, 1976, The Book of Hours, 1986, The Idea Mine, A Brief Note on Metafiction, 2000; (play) Worlds to Shatter, Shattered Worlds, 2003, Conversations with the Wordman, and Other Words on Words, 2004, One Million Words and Counting, 2007; contr. articles to profl. jours. Office: #103 11184 Vista Sorrento Pkwy San Diego CA 92130 Office Phone: 925-367-7557. E-mail: pjjp@post.harvard.edu.

PAYARD, FRANCOIS, food service executive; b. Nice, France; With Au Nid de Friandises, Riviera, France; pastry chef La Tour d'Argent, Paris, 1988; pastry chef under Alain Senderens Lucas Carton, 1989; pastry chef Le Bernardin, NYC, 1990; pastry chef with chef Daniel Boulud Restaurant Daniel, 1993; pastry chef, owner Payard, NYC, 1997—. Named Pastry Chef of Yr., James Beard Assn., 1995, Bon Appétit Food & Entertainment Awards, 1998, Isignia of Chevalier de l'ordre de mérite agricole, French Govt., 2004; named one of 85 Best Pastry Chefs in World, Relais Desserts, 2006. Office: Payard 1032 Lexington Ave New York NY 10021 Office Phone: 212-717-5252. E-mail: francois@payard.com.

PAYN, CLYDE FRANCIS, technology company executive; b. Auckland, New Zealand, Jan. 17, 1952; came to U.S., 1973; s. Phillip Francis and Ngaire Eunice P.; m. Betsy Ann Dannels, June 17, 1978; children: Tamara, Brittany, Erik. Cert., Auckland Inst. Tech., 1971; MBA, Vanderbilt U., 1980. Tech. mgr. Carborundum (N.Z.) Ltd., Auckland, 1968-73; mem. product application tech. staff Carborundum Co., Niagara Falls, NY, 1973-78; mgr. product mktg. Universal Abrasives, Phila., 1978-80; bus. mgr., catalyst advocate Johnson Matthey, Inc., Phila., 1980-84; pres. Catalyst Cons., Inc., Phila., 1984—2004; CEO Catalyst Group, Phila., 1988—. Pres. Hideaway Hill Civic Assn., Maple Glen, Pa., 1988, 89. Mem. AIChE, Am. Chem. Soc., Catalysis Soc., Comml. Devel. Assn., Chem. Mktg. Rsch. Assn., Polymer Mfg. Engrs. Assn. Achievements include development of new process technology, catalyst and product development for petroleum, petrochemical, chemical, polymer, pharmaceutical, fine chemical and environ. industries. Office: The Catalyst Group Inc PO Box 637 Spring House PA 19477-0637 Office Phone: 215-628-4447. Office Fax: 215-628-2267. Business E-Mail: cfp@catalystgrp.om.

PAYNE, ALEXANDER, film director, writer; b. Omaha, Nebr., Feb. 10, 1961; m. Sandra Oh, Jan. 1, 2003. BA in history and Spanish lit., Stanford U., 1984; MFA in filmmaking, UCLA, 1990; LHD (hon.), U. Nebr., 2004. Prodr., writer, dir.: (films) The Passion of Martin, 1991; dir., writer Citizen Ruth, 1996; dir., writer (screenplay) Election, 1999; About Schmidt, 2002 (Golden Globe award for best screenplay (with Jim Taylor), 2003); Sideways, 2004 (Golden Globe award for best adapted screenplay, 2005, Writers Guild award for best adapted screenplay, 2005, Academy award for best adapted screenplay, 2005); writer Jurassic Park III, 2001; exec. prodr.: (films) The Assassination of Richard Nixon, 2004.

PAYNE, ANITA HART, reproductive endocrinologist, researcher; b. Karlsruhe, Baden, Germany, Nov. 24, 1926; came to U.S., 1938; d. Frederick Michael and Erna Rose (Hirsch) Hart; widowed; children: Gregory Steven, Teresa Payne-Lyons. BA, U. Calif., Berkeley, 1949, PhD, 1952. From rsch. assoc. to prof. U. Mich., Ann Arbor, 1961-96, prof. emeritus, 1996—; assoc. dir. U. Mich. Ctr. for Study Reproduction, Ann Arbor, 1989-94; sr. rsch. scientist Stanford U. Med. Ctr., Calif., 1995—2007. Vis. scholar Stanford U., 1987-88; mem. reproductive biology study sect. NIH, Bethesda, Md., 1978-79, biochem. endocrinology study sect., 1979-83, population rsch. com. Nat. Inst. Child Health and Human Devel., 1989-93. Assoc. editor Steroids, 1987-93; contbr. book chpts., articles to profl. jours. Recipient award for cancer rsch., Calif. Inst. for Cancer Rsch., 1953, Acad. Women's Caucus award, U. Mich., 1986, Mentor award, Women in Endocrinology, 1999. Mem. Endocrine Soc. (chmn. awards com. 1983-84, mem. nominating com. 1985-87, coun. 1988-91), Am. Soc. Andrology (exec. coun. 1980-83), Soc. for Study of Reproduction (bd. dirs. 1982-85, sec. 1986-89, pres. 1990-91, Carl G. Hartman award 1998, Disting. Svc. award 2004).

PAYNE, BARBARA ANN, artist, educator; b. Marionville, Mo., Jan. 14, 1938; d. Lewis Michel and Velma Etta Rapp; m. Kenneth L. Payne, Nov. 25, 1956 (dec.); children: Kevin James, Kendra Lynne, Keli Song. AA, Fort Scott Cmty. Jr. Coll., Kans., 1965—67; BS in Edn., Kans. State Coll., Pittsburg, 1967—69. Tchr. Dept. Def. Schs., Yokosuka, Japan, 1969—72, Seoul, Republic of Korea, 1972—74, Spangdahlem, Germany, 1974—75, Bitburg, Germany, 1975—76, West Berlin, 1976—83, Doddea, ret., 1984; artist. art instr. Bonn, Königswinter, Germany, 1983—88; artist Würzburg, Germany, 1988—2001, Brussels, Erps Kwerps, 2001—02. Contbr. articles to profl. jours.; one-woman shows include Galerie Fasanenstrasse 71, Berlin, 1983, Am. Embassy Club, Bonn, Germany, 1986, Mobau Wittemann, Aegidienberg, Germany, 1986, Spar-und Darlenhskasse, Aegidienberg, 1987, Stadtbücherei (City Libr.), Bonn-Dottendorf, Germany, 1988, Mehrzweckhalle, Unterpleichfeld, Germany, 1989, 1990, 1991, 1992, 1993, 1994, 1995, 1996, 2001, Kultur Stüble, Höchberg, Germany, 1991, 1992, Hotel Rebstock, Würzburg, Germany, 1993, Firme Volk, Am Markt, 1994, Farewell to Europe exhbn. Erps Kwerps, Brussels, 2002, exhibited in group shows at Berlin Am. Art Guild, West Berlin, Germany and Berlin Am. Cmtys. inside West Berlin, 1977—83, Bildungscentrum des Deutschen Beamtenbundes, Königswinter, Germany, 1986, Akademie Führungskraefte Deutsche Post, Bad Honnef, Germany, 1987, Alte Kirche, Waldbüttelbrunn, Germany, 1990, 1993. Mem. Berlin Am. Art Guild, 1977—83, pres., 1981—82. Mem.: Nat. Mus. Women in the Arts. Avocations: piano, antiques, poetry, art.

PAYNE, BILLY (WILLIAM PORTER PAYNE), real estate lawyer, sports association executive; b. Athens, Ga. m. Martha Payne. BA in polit. sci., U. Ga.; JD, U. Ga. Joseph Henry Lumpkin Sch. of Law; D (hon.), U. SC, Emory U., Mercer U., Oglethorpe U., Presbyn. Coll., U. Ga. Comml. real estate atty. in pvt. practice; dir. Healtheon/WebMD, Premiere Technols.; vice chmn. NationsBank, Bank of Am.; head Atlanta Com. for the Olympic Games 1996, 1992; ptnr. Gleacher Ptnrs.; chmn. Augusta Nat. Golf Club and The Masters, 2006—. Founding mem. Ga. State Games; adv. bd. Nat. Distbg. Co.; chmn. Centennial Investment Properties; bd. dirs. Crown Crafts, Atlanta C. of C., Commerce Club, Convex Grp., Atlanta Falcons, ILD Telecom., Lincoln Financial Grp. (was Jefferson-Pilot Corpn.), Cousins Properties, Anheuser-Busch, 1997—; head The Masters media com., 2000—06; pres., CEO Ga. Amateur Athletic Found. Trustee U. Ga. Found.; mem. State of Ga. Internat. Edn. Task Force; bd. deacons, ruling elder St. Luke's Presbyn. Ch. Recipient Nat. Sports Marketeer of Yr., Washington, DC Touchdown Club, 1990, Presdl. citation, Morehouse Coll., 1996, Theodore Roosevelt award, NCAA, 1997, Olympic Order in Gold, Internat. Olympic Com., Disting. Svc. award, Martin Luther King, Jr. Ctr. for Non-violent Social Change, Cmty. Svc. Governor's award for Unique and Outstanding Vol. Svc. Mem.: ABA. Achievements include induction to Ga. Sports Hall of Fame, 1996. Office: US Olympic Com 1750 E Boulder St Colorado Springs CO 80909-5724 *

PAYNE, BRETT H., lawyer; b. Jan. 18, 1969; BA, U. Tex., Austin, 1991; JD, Tex. Tech U., 1994. Bar: Tex. 1994, US Dist. Ct. (ea. dist. Tex.). Ptnr. Walters, Balido & Crain, Dallas. Named a Rising Star, Tex. Super Lawyers mag., 2006. Mem.: East Tex. Claims Assn., Dallas Bar Assn. Office: Walters Balido & Crain 900 Jackson St Founders Sq Ste 600 Dallas TX 75270 Office Phone: 214-347-8370. E-mail: brett.payne@wbclawfirm.com. *

PAYNE, DANIEL HAROLD (HAROLD PAYNE), real estate developer, small business owner; b. Caddo Mills, Tex., Feb. 12, 1921; s. Flavy Malone and Sally Ella Payne; m. Wanda Louise Lyday, Aug. 3, 1941; 1 child, Kyle Steven. At, Tex. A&M, Commerce, 1940—41; grad., Tex. Real Estate Sch., Dallas, 1971. Sales J.C. Penney, Greenville, Tex., 1940—41, A&P Grocery, Greenville, 1940—41; office and credit mgr. Firestone Tire Co., Ft. Worth, 1941—42; office mgr. Guy F. Atkinson Co., Denison, 1942—43; co-owner Payne Bros. Super Markets, 1945—55; owner Payne's Famous Furniture Village, Caddo Mills, Tex., 1955—90, Payne Magnavox Ctr., Garland, Tex., 1960—61, Harold Payne Land Sales & Devel., Caddo Mills, Tex., 1970—. Adv. bd. Tex. Retail Grocery Assn., Dallas, 1951—55; bd. mem. State Nat. Bank, Caddo Mills, 1972—99; adv. mem. Tex. Retail Furniture Assn., Dallas, 1967—88. Contbr. articles to trade periodicals. Pres. Lions Club Internat., Caddo Mills, Tex., 1955—56; treas. Hunt County Fair Bd., Greenville, 1966—, publicity chmn., 1966—87; public spkr. civic, military and ch. groups in Tex. and Okla., 1963—83; elder Faith Bible Ch., Caddo Mills, Tex.; bd. mem. and publicity chmn. Sky Ranch Christian Youth Camp, Van, 1962—63; founding mem. 390th Bomb Group Meml. Mus., Tucson. 2d lt. USAF, 1942—45. Recipient Advt. award, Tex. Furniture Assn., 1969, Nat. Sales award, Nat. Furniture Assn., 1976, numerous manufacturers' sales awards. Mem.: Hunt County Freedom Forum (chmn. 1957—63, chmn. of bd. 1959—81), Masons (32 degree 1973). Republican. Avocations: youth work, civic activities, church, scouting, athletics.

PAYNE, DAVID EMER, university administrator; b. Salt Lake City, Mar. 29, 1944; s. John W. and Sara (Harris) P.; m. Grettle Haglund, Mar. 16, 1973; children: Sara, John, Samuel, Daniel, James, David. BS, Brigham Young U., Provo, Utah, 1968; MS, U. N.C., 1970, PhD, 1972. Asst. prof. U. Iowa, Iowa City, 1972-76; assoc. prof. U. N.D., Grand Forks, 1976-80, prof., 1980-81; fellow Am. Coun. Edn., New Orleans, 1981-82; dean social sci. S.E. Mo. State U., Cape Girardeau, 1982-88; v.p. acad. affairs Sangamon State U., Springfield, Ill., 1988-89, Emporia (Kans.) State U., 1989-96, Sam Houston State U., Huntsville, Tex., 1997—. Vis. prof. U. Iceland, Reykjavik, 1974-75. Contbr. articles to profl. jours. Dist. commr. Boy Scouts Am. Am. Coun. Edn. fellow, 1981-82, Bush Found. sr. fellow, 1982. Mem. Lds Ch. Office: Sam Houston State U Huntsville TX 77340 Home: 4 Rushing Oak Ct Huntsville TX 77320 Office Phone: 936-294-1001. Business E-Mail: payne@shsu.edu.

PAYNE, DAVID L., bank executive; b. 1956; Chmn., pres., CEO Westamerica Bancorporation; gen. mgr. Gibson Publishing Co., Gibson Radio and Publishing Co., Vallejo, Calif. Office: Westamerica Bancorp 1108 5th Ave San Rafael CA 94901-2916 *

PAYNE, DEBORAH ANNE, retired medical company officer; b. Norristown, Pa., Sept. 22, 1952; d. Kenneth Nathan Moser and Joan (Reese) Dewhurst; m. Randall Barry Payne, Mar. 8, 1975 (div.). AA, Northeastern Christian Jr. Coll., 1972; B in Music Edn., Va. Commonwealth U., 1979. Driver, social asst. Children's Aid Soc., Norristown, Pa., 1972—73; mgr. Boddie-Noell Enterprises, Richmond, Va., 1974—79; retail food saleswoman Hardee's Food Systems, Inc., Phila., 1979—81; supr., with tech. tng. and testing depts. Cardiac Datacorp., Phila., 1981—95; tng. supr. Raytel Cardiac Svcs., Forest Hills, NY, 1995—98, supr. tech. support Haddonfield, NJ, 1998—2000; ret., 2000. Mem. NAFE, Delta Omicron (pres. Alpha Xi chpt. 1978-79, pres. Epsilon province 1980-85, chmn. Eastern Pa. alumni 1986-88, Star award 1979), Am. Soc. Profl. and Exec. Women. Democrat. Avocations: music, sports. Home: Park Ter Apts 8040 Rowland Ave Apt A14 Philadelphia PA 19136 Personal E-mail: d.a.payne@att.net.

PAYNE, DONALD MILFORD, congressman; b. Newark, July 16, 1934; 3 children. BA in Social Studies, Seton Hall U., NJ, 1957; grad. student, Springfield Coll., Mass.; D (hon.), Chgo. State U., Drew U., Essex County Coll., William Paterson U. Educator Newark Pub. Schs.; exec. Prudential Ins. Co.; v.p. Urban Data Systems, Inc.; mem. Essex County Bd. Chosen Freeholders, 1972—78, Newark Mcpl. Coun., 1982—88, US Congress from 10th NJ dist., 1989—. Mem. edn. and labor com. US Congress, mem. fgn. affairs com., chmn. subcommittee on Africa and Global Health, mem Dem. whip orgn. Nat. pres. YMCA, 1970—73, chmn. world refugee and rehab. com., 1973—81; bd. dirs. Nat. Endowment Democracy, TransAfrica, Discovery Channel Global Edn. Fund, Congl. Award Found., Boys and Girls Club Newark, Newark Day Ctr., Fighting Back Initiative, Newark YMCA. Named one of Most Influential Black Ams., Ebony mag., 2006, 2007 People to Watch, Sunday Star Ledger; recipient Leadership award, Hudson County Urban League, NJ, 2003; Visionaries for Africa award, Africa Soc., 2004, Humanitarian Svc. award, Isaac Hayes Found., 2004, Bishop John T. Walker Disting. Humanitarian Svc. award, Africare, 2004. Mem.: NAACP (life). Democrat. Baptist. Office: US House Reps 2209 Rayburn House Office Bldg Washington DC 20515-0001 Office Phone: 202-225-3436. Office Fax: 202-225-4160. *

PAYNE, ELTON CURTIS, JR., adult education educator; b. Beaumont, Tex., Mar. 12, 1969; s. Elton Curtis and Annie Pearl Payne; m. Nitashia Renita Tennarse, Apr. 3, 2001; children: Elton Curtis, Aubren Nichille. BA, Prairie View A&M, Tex., 1992. Occupl. tng. dir. SE Tex. Regional Planning Commn., Port Arthur, Tex., 1992—97; program dir. Lamar U., Beaumont, Tex., 1997—. Pres. Bay Area Cmty. Devel. Corp., Baytown, Tex., 2004—. Mem.: Tex. Assn. Cmty. Svc. and Continuing Edn. (Excellence award 2003), Assn. Continuing Higher Edn. (minority affairs com., Minority Affairs award 2004), Meridian Estates Homeowners Assn. (pres.), Omega Psi Phi (intake com. mem. 1994—95). Progressive. Home and Office: Po Box 10008 Beaumont TX 77710 Home Phone: 409-880-7983; Office Phone: 409-880-1983. Personal E-mail: payneec@hal.lamar.edu.

PAYNE, EUGENE C., III, lawyer; b. San Francisco, May 15, 1947; AB, Georgetown U., 1969; JD, Harvard U., 1973. Bar: Calif. 1973. Office of gen. counsel Bank of Am.; mem. Tobin & Tobin, San Francisco, atty. Past pres. (bd.) St. Thomas More Soc., San Francisco. Mem. Bar Assn. San Francisco (co-chair banking, bus. and corp. law sect. 1981-82), San Francisco Bank Attys. Assn. (chair) 1989, mem. ABA (bus. law sect.). Office: Tobin & Tobin 500 Sansome St San Francisco CA 94111 Office Phone: 415-772-9613. Office Fax: 415-433-3883. Business E-Mail: ecpayneiii@tobinlaw.com.

PAYNE, FRED J., epidemiologist, educator; b. Grand Forks, ND, Oct. 14, 1922; s. Fred J. and Olive (Johnson) P.; m. Dorothy J. Peck, Dec. 20, 1948; children: Chris Ann Payne Graebner, Roy S. William F., Thomas A. BS, U. Pitts., 1948, MD, 1949; MPH, U. Calif., Berkeley, 1958. Diplomate Am. Bd. Preventive Medicine. Intern St. Joseph's Hosp., Pitts., 1949-50; resident Charity hosp., New Orleans, 1952-53; med. epidemiologist Ctr. Disease Control, Atlanta, 1953-60; prof. tropical medicine Med. Ctr. La. State U., New Orleans, 1961—66, dir. Internat. Ctr. for Med. Rsch. and Tng. Costa Rica, 1963—66; exec. sec. 3d Nat. Conf. on Pub. Health Tng., Washington, 1966-67; epidemiologist Nat. Nutrition Survey, Bethesda, Md., 1967-68; chief pub. health professions br. NIH, Bethesda, 1971-74; med. officer, sr. rsch. epidemiologist Nat. Inst. Allergy and Infectious Diseases, 1974-78; asst. health dir. Fairfax County (Va.) Health Dept., 1978-94; dir. HIV/AIDS case mgmt. program, 1988-94; cons. epidemiologist, 1994—; med. advisor Ams. for Sound AIDS Policy, 1996—, Childrens AIDS Fund, 1997—. Clin. prof. La. State U., 1966-76; cons. NIH, 1979-81; leader WHO diarrheal disease adv. team, 1960. Contbr. articles to profl. jours. Served with AUS, 1942-46, 49-52. Decorated Combat Medic Badge. Fellow Am. Coll. Preventive Medicine, Am. Coll. Epidemiology; mem. AAAS, AMA, Am. Soc. Microbiology, Internat. Epidemiology Assn., Soc. Epidemiol. Rsch., USPHS Commd. Officers Assn., Sigma Xi. Office: PO Box 16433 Washington DC 20041 Office Phone: 703-433-1640. Personal E-mail: fdpayne6@email.msn.com. Business E-Mail: jjiyd@ibm.net.

PAYNE, GARELD GENE, vocal music educator, medical transcriptionist; b. Colony, Okla., Aug. 27, 1931; s. Eugene A. and Agnes D. (Chastain) P.; children: Gareld, S. Raymond, Lynn Dita, Jana Lee. MusB, Oklahoma City U., 1965; MusM in Edn., North Tex. State U. (name change to U. North Tex.), 1969; ednl. specialist, Pitts. State U., 1989; EdD, Okla. State U., 2007. Ind. organist, pianist numerous nightclubs, nationwide, 1956-64; instr. vocal, instrumental music Muenster Ind. Sch. Dist., Tex., 1965-69; tchr. vocal music Dallas Ind. Sch. Dist., 1966-74, Carrizo Springs Ind. Sch. Dist., Tex., 1976-79, Coffeyville Unified Sch. Dist., Kans., 1979-91; tchr. elem. vocal music Oklahoma City Pub. Schs., 1996—. Rec. artist (album) Evening With Gareld, 1984; composer publ. anthems. With USAF, 1950—53. Scholar Oklahoma City U., 1949. Mem. Am. Fedn. Musicians, NEA, Am. Orff-Schulwerk Assn., Am. Recorder Soc., Am. Theater Organ Soc., Am. Guild Organist Orgns. of Am. Kodaly Educators, Phi Mu Alpha Sinfonia Frat., Phi Delta Kappa. Republican. Methodist. Avocations: astrology, oil and water color painting, cooking, reading, computers. Home: 3643 NW 15th St Oklahoma City OK 73107-4423 Personal E-mail: pgareld_osu@brightok.net.

PAYNE, GEORGE FREDERICK, academic administrator; b. Summerville, SC, Jan. 29, 1941; s. Fred N. and Lota (Griffith) Payne; m. Kay Martin, June 23, 1963; children: John F., Mark C., Janet E. Student, Ga. Inst. Tech., 1959-60, U.S. Naval Acad., 1960-62; BS, U. S.C., 1963, MA, 1966; MRE, Luth. Theol. Sem., 1968; postgrad., U. Ga., 1969-71; LLD (hon.), Lincoln Meml. U., 1988. Cert. fund raising exec. 2000. From instr. to asst. prof. Ga. So. Coll., Statesboro, 1966-78; dir. admission Brewton-Parker Coll., Mt. Vernon, Ga., 1978-80; v.p. devel. North Greenville Coll., Tigerville, SC, 1980-86; pres. Limestone Coll., Gaffney, SC, 1986-91, dir. various grants, 1976-91; spl. agt., registered rep. Prudential Fin. Svcs., 1991-92; dir. ITT Tech. Inst., Greenville, SC, 1992-95; exec. dir. Inst. Adv. Greenville Tech. Coll., 1996—2006; mng. dir. Greenville Tech. Found., 2007—; exec. dir. GTF McAlister LLC, 2003—, GTF Student Housing LLC, 2004—, Greenville County Coun., Dist. 28. Author: An Introduction to the Principles of Geography: Facts, Skills, Concepts, and Models, 1973; contbr. articles to profl. jours. Active Leadership Greer, SC, 1980—81, regent, 1982—84; active AACTion Consortium, 1980—82, Leadership Greenville, 1982—83; bd. dirs. Greenville County unit Am. Cancer Soc., 1985—86; advisor Cherokee County Arts Coun., 1986—91; trustee Rolling Green Village Continuing Care Ret. Cmty., 1996—2006, sec., 1998, 2003; trustee Baptist Found. S.C., 2001—05, 2007—. Oakwood Sch., Va., 2002—; bd. dirs. Greenville Redevel. Authority, 2005—06, chair adminstrn. com., 2006. With USN, 1960—62. Recipient Disting. Svc. award, Brewton-Parker Coll., 1980, North Greenville Coll., 1986. Mem.: Coun. Advancement Support Edn. (Circle of Excellence award for ednl. fundraising 2001, 2004), Assn. Fund-Raising Profls. (cert. fund-raising exec.), Greater Greer C. of C. (bd. dirs. 1981—84), Rotary. Baptist. Avocation: reading. Office: Greenville Tech Coll McAlister Ste B-12 225 S Pleasantburg Dr Greenville SC 29607 Office Phone: 864-884-8899. Business E-Mail: Fred.Payne@GvlTec.edu. E-mail: fpayne@greenvillecounty.org.

PAYNE, GLORIA MARQUETTE, business educator; b. Elkins, W.Va., Dec. 21, 1923; d. Anthony and Roselyn Marquette; m. Carl Wesley Payne, Mar. 6, 1950; 1 child, Mary Debra Payne Moore. BA, Davis and Elkins Coll., MHL (hon.); MA, W.Va. U.; PhD, U. Pitts., 1975; postgrad., NYU Fashion Inst. Tech. Cert. designed appearance cons. Sec. Equitable Ins. Co., Elkins, 1943-44; tchr., dept. head Spencer (W.Va.) H.S., 1944-45; prof. bus. Davis & Elkins Coll., Elkins, 1945-93; image cons. Elkins, 1988-93; bus. cons., 1970-93; mgr. Elkins Wallpaper Shop, 1945-65; owner Merle Norman Cosmetic Studio, Elkins, 1950-56. Dir. tchr. workshops W.Va. U., Marshall U., State Dept. Edn., Charleston, W.Va., summers; dir. machine shorthand workshops for tchrs. throughout the U.S.; dir. designer appearance World Modeling Assn., N.Y.C., 1989—; instr. modeling Davis & Elkins Coll., 1980-93. Author: A Methods Class is Interesting and Challenging, 1970, The Oak or the Pumpkin; mem. editl. bd. Nat. Assn. of Business Teachers Edn. Pub., 1993, 94; contbr. articles to profl. jours. Chair Bi-Centennial, City of Elkins; dir. Elkins Fair, City of Elkins; pres. St. Brendans Parish; judge Mountain State Forest Festival Parades, 1988-2004; rep. Region I at Dallas Nat. Conv., 1994 (one of five nat. finalists); div. chair bus., econs., and tourism. Recipient Outstanding Prof. award Sears-Roebuck Co., Lois Latham award for Excellence in Tchg., Cmty. Svc. award Elkins C. of C., 1992, Outstanding Educator award BPW, 1997, W.Va. Bus. Edn. Assn., W.Va. Vocat. Assn., 1994, 97, Region I award for Outstanding Vocat.Educator, Outstanding Collegiate Tchr. Bus. award, 1997, award of merit Assn. Career and Tech. Edn., 2003-04, Outstanding Prof. of Region award, 2003, 04, 05, Humanitarian award Odd Fellows Lodge, 2004, Disting. Svc. award Internat. Order Odd Fellows, 2004, 05, 06, 07, Outstanding Citizen citation Gov. of W.Va., 2006; 1st recipient James S. McDonnell Found. Fully Endowed Acad. Chair in Bus. and Econs.; named Educator of Yr., W.Va. Women's Club, Outstanding Educator AAUW, Randolph County C. of C. Citizen of Yr., 1998, Disting. Citizen, Gov. W.Va., W.Va. Women in Bus. Champion, Small Bus. Assn., 2005, Outstanding Prof., W.Va. State Legis., Charleston, Va., 2005, Bus. Champion, Small Bus. Assn., 2007. Mem. Am. Bus. Writers Assn., W.Va. Edn. Assn. (past pres., Outstanding Prof., Outstanding Svc. award, Outstanding Bus. Educator award, Outstanding Prof. of Region 2003, 04, 05, 06, 07), Tri-State Bus. Edn. Assn. (historian, outstanding svc. award, Tchr.-Educator of the South award 1991), World Modeling Assn. (v.p. 1988-95, Modeling award 1989), Designed Appearance U.S. (dir. 1990-98), W.Va. Bus. Edn. Assn. (award 1977, 85, 94, 97), Bus. and Profl. Women's Orgn., W.Va. C. of C., The Fashion Club (advisor), Beta Sigma Phi (advisor), Beta Alpha Beta (advisor), Pi Beta Phi, Phi Beta Lambda (advisor), Sigma Beta Delta (advisor). Democrat. Roman Catholic. Avocations: flower arranging, modeling. Home: 301 Davis St Elkins WV 26241-4030 Office: Davis & Elkins Coll 100 Sycamore St Elkins WV 26241-3996 Office Phone: 304-637-1247.

PAYNE, HARRY MORSE, JR., architect; b. Norwood, Mass., Nov. 3, 1922; s. Harry Morse and Edna May (Beardsley) P.; m. Helen Marion Beasley, Aug. 29, 1946; children: Harry Morse, Thomas Beasley, Amelia Morse. Student, Boston Archtl. Center, 1946—49, MIT, 1949—50. Draftsman William G. Upham, Norwood, 1946-47; designer William Riseman Assos., Boston, 1947-49, Harry J. Korslund, Norwood, 1949-51, William Hoskins Brown, Boston, 1951-52; designer, prin. dir. The Architects Collaborative, Cambridge, Mass., 1952-86, pres., 1975-77, emeritus, 1986—, Boston Archtl. Center, 1963-65, 71-73; asst. prof. Harvard U. Grad. Sch. Design, 1954-63. Prin. works include U.S. Embassy, Athens, Greece, U. Baghdad, Iraq, Temple Israel, Boston, Quincy Sch., Boston, Nauset Regional H.S., Cape Cod, Mass.; author: The Survey System of the Old Colony, 1985, Name Change--Paine to Payne, 1992, Cape Cod Land Strategy, 1994, New England 17th Century Land Strategy, 1997, America's Stonehenge As Architecture, 1998, Payne Paine Family—England and Cape Cod, 1999, The Ordering of Towns: Massachusetts Bay Colony 17th Century Land Strategy, 2002. Served with USN, 1943-46. Recipient Cascieri Lectureship in Humanities medal, Boston Archtl. Ctr., 2002. Fellow AIA; mem. Soc. Archtl. Historians, N.E. Antiquities Rsch. Assn., Boston Soc. Architects, Mass. State Assn. Architects, New Eng. Hist. and Geneal. Soc., The Colonial Soc. Mass., Mass. Soc. Genealogists (pres. 1986-88), Lincoln Hist. Soc. (pres. 1990-92). Home: 303 Winthrop Terr Bedford MA 01730

PAYNE, JOHN ROSS, archivist, educator, library and information scientist, educator; b. Clarksville, Tex., Dec. 4, 1941; BA, Tex. Christian U., 1963; MLS, North Tex. State U., 1967. Successively acting dir., asst. to dir., assoc. libr. for acquisitions, assoc. libr. for ops., rsch. assoc. Harry Ransom Humanities Rsch. Ctr. U. Tex., Austin, 1969—85, prof. Grad. Sch. Libr. and Info. Sci., 1988—89, 1991—92, tchr. course in rare books and lit. manuscripts; dir. Payne Assocs., 1979—. Rare books and hist. archives appraiser. Author: A Bibliography of W. H. Hudson, 1977, Modern British Fiction: An Exhibit, 1972; co-author: (with Elizabeth Johnson) Katherine Mansfield: An Exhibit, 1973, (with Adrian Goldstone) A Bibliographical Catalogue of John Steinbeck, 1975; contbr. articles to profl. jours. Lilly fellow Ind. U., 1967-68. Mem. Manuscripts Soc., Tex. Libr. Assn., Tex. State Hist. Assn., Book Club of Tex., Tex. and Southwestern Collectors' Assn. Address: 2309 Camino Alto Austin TX 78746-2404 Home Phone: 512-328-4534; Office Phone: 512-328-4535. Business E-Mail: payne@payne-associates.com.

PAYNE, JOHNNY F., minister; s. Floyd and Audrey L. (Gregory) Payne. AA in Indsl. Security/Criminal Justice, CC Air Force, 1989; BA in Bible and Theology, Appalachian Bible Coll., Bradley, W.Va., 1997; postgrad.,

Liberty Bapt. Theol. Sem., Lynchburg, Va., 2006—. Ordained to ministry Stanford Rd. Bapt. Ch., 1997. Dept. leader Riverdale Bapt. Ch., Malboro, Md., 1989—91; youth pastor Faith Bapt. Ch., Enterprise, W.Va., 1991—93; asst. pastor Stanaford Rd. Bapt. Ch., Beckley, W.Va., 1993—97; evangelist, preacher Appalachian Bible Coll., Bradley, 1993—97, Can You Reach My Friend Ministries, 1997—2001; pastor Lac Du Flambeau Bible Bapt. Ch., Wis., 2000—01; asst. pastor Berean Bapt. Ch., Fairmont, W.Va., 2001—02; guest preacher W.Va., Ky., Va., 2002—03; tchr., guest preacher Integrity Christian Sch., Kingwood, W.Va., 2003—04; preacher W.Va., Ky., 2004—. Guest preacher, Wis., Ill., Minn., 2001. Mem. Civil Air Patrol; Sunday sch. asst. tchr., deacon Norris City Bapt. Ch., Ill., 1980—82; chapel guide, Bible study tchr. Lackland AFB, Tex., 1982—83; asst. tchr. Calvary Bapt. Ch., Anchorage, 1983—85; Sunday sch. tchr. Emmanuel Bapt. Ch., Netherlands, 1985—87; deacon Emmanuel Baptist Ch., Netherlands; evangelist Ind. Bapt. Ch., Clinton, Md., 1985—89; Bible study tchr. Andrew AFB, Md., 1985—89. With USAF, 1983—89. Decorated Joint Svc. Commendation medal, Commendation medal USAF, Two Good Conduct medals; named Hosp. Svc. Coordinator of the Yr., W.Va. Disabled Am. Vets.; recipient various letter and certs. of appreciation, Disabled Am. Vets., Am. Vet., Dept. Vet. Affairs Med. Ctr., others. Republican. Office: 916 W Pike St Apt 708 Clarksburg WV 26301

PAYNE, LADELL, retired academic administrator; b. Birmingham, Ala., Dec. 6, 1933; s. Clyde Ladell and Martha Gerusia (McBrayer) P.; m. Mary Jean Taylor, Aug. 23, 1954; children: Lisa, Jennifer BA with honors, Samford U., 1955; MA in English, La. State U., 1956; PhD in English, Stanford U., 1966; LittD, Samford U., 1996; DHL, Randolph-Macon Coll., 1998. From instr. to prof. English, chmn. dept. lit. and presdl. asst. Claremont McKenna Coll., Calif., 1960-79; pres. Randolph-Macon Coll., Ashland, Va., 1979-97, prof. emeritus, 1997—, pres. emeritus, 1998—. Fulbright lectr. U. Vienna, Austria, 1971-72; nat. cons. Ctr. for Study So. Culture, U. Miss., Oxford, 1980—; adminstrv. assoc. Am. Coun. on Edn., Washington, 1979, mem. nat. panel, commn. on women in higher edn., 1981-97; founding mem. pres.'s commn. Nat. Collegiate Athletic Assn., 1984-97. Author: Thomas Wolfe, 1969, Black Novelists and the Southern Literary Tradition, 1981; contbr. articles on William Faulkner, Robert Penn Warren, Thomas Wolfe, and Ellen Glasgow to profl. jours. Mem. Va. bd. dirs. NCCJ, 1980-92, chmn. Va. region, Richmond, 1982-85; trustee, mem. exec. com. The Collegiate Schs., Richmond, 1986-89; bd. dirs. Music in the Mountains, Nevada City, Calif., 2000-02, Congregational Homes: Mt. San Antonio Gardens, Pomona, Calif., 2007—. NEH fellow, 1973. Mem. Nat. Assn. Ind. Colls. and Univs. (bd. dirs. 1990-93), Coun. on Postsecondary Accreditation (bd. dirs. 1991-93), Pi Kappa Phi, Phi Beta Kappa. Methodist. Avocation: classical music.

PAYNE, LELAND HOWARD, lawyer; b. NYC, Dec. 4, 1933; s. Edward DeMille and Candace Leland (Howard) P.; m. Bendel Tracy, July 18, 1959; children: Candace Tracy Payne Conte, David Whitney Payne. BA in Am. History, Yale U., 1956; LLB, Cornell U., 1959. CLU 1982; bar: N.Y. 1959, Fla. 1961, U.S. Dist. Ct. (no. dist.) N.Y. 1959, U.S. Ct. Appeals (2d cir.) 1961, U.S. Ct. Appeals (5th cir.) 1969, U.S. Dist. Ct. (mid. dist.) Fla. 1988, U.S. Tax Ct. 1979. Atty. Breed, Abbott & Morgan, NYC, 1959-61; atty. Icard, Merrill, Cullis & Timm, Sarasota, Fla., 1961-64, Nelson, Stinnett, Surfus, Sarasota, Fla., 1964-75, Isphording, Korp & Payne, Sarasota, Fla., 1975-93, Kirk Pinkerton, Sarasota, Fla., 1993—2005, Payne Law Group PA, Sarasota, Fla., 2005—. Bd. dirs. ARC, Sarasota, 1989, Boys & Girls Club Found., Sarasota, 1990. Named one of Best Lawyers in Am., Fla. Super Lawyers. Fellow Am. Coll. Trust & Estate Counsel; mem. Am. Soc. Fin. Svc. Profls., Fla. Bar Assn. (chair ins. com., real property probate trust law sect.). Republican. Avocations: sailing, skiing, travel. Office Phone: 941-487-2807. Personal E-mail: lhpayne@yahoo.com. Business E-Mail: hpayne@lawnav.com.

PAYNE, LUCY ANN SALSBURY, law librarian, educator, lawyer; b. Utica, NY, July 5, 1952; d. James Henry and Dorothy Eileen (Seavy) Salsbury; m. Albert E. Payne, June 2, 1973 (div. 1983); 1 child, Joni Eileen. MusB, Andrews U., 1974; MA, Loma Linda U., Calif., 1979; JD, U. Notre Dame, Ind., 1988; MLS, U. Mich., 1990. Bar: Ind. 1988, Mich. 1988, U.S. Dist. Ct. (no. and so. dists.) Ind. 1988, U.S. Ct. Appeals (7th cir.) 1992, N.Mex., 2003. Rsch. specialist Kresge Libr. Law Sch. U. Notre Dame, 1988—90, asst. libr., 1990—91, assoc. libr., 1991—96, libr., 1996—2002; asst. pub. defender N.Mex. Met. Ct. Divsn., 2004—. Vis. prof. Notre Dame London Law Programme, 2001. Contbr. articles to profl. jours. Recipient Rev. Paul J. Foik award, 2001, Commitment award Notre Dame Black Student Law Assn., 2002. Adventist. Home: 4420 Barrett NW Albuquerque NM 87114 Office: 200 Third St NW Ste 740 Albuquerque NM 87102

PAYNE, MARGARET ANNE, lawyer; b. Aug. 10, 1947; d. John Hilliard and Margaret Mary (Naughton) P. Student, Trinity Coll., Washington, 1965-66; BA magna cum laude, U. Cin., 1969; JD, Harvard U., 1972; LLM in Taxation, NYU, 1976. Bar: N.Y. 1975, U.S. Dist. Ct. (so. dist.) N.Y. 1975, Calif. 1979, U.S. Dist. Ct. (so. dist.) Calif. 1979. Assoc. Mudge, Rose, Guthrie, and Alexander, NYC, 1972-75, Davis, Polk and Wardwell, NYC, 1976-78, Seltzer, Caplan, Wilkins and McMahon, San Diego, 1978-79, Higgs, Fletcher and Mack, San Diego, 1980-82, ptnr., 1983-90, of counsel, 1991—. Adj. prof. grad. tax program U. San Diego Sch. Law, 1979-89, Calif. Western Sch. Law, San Diego, 1980-82; judge pro tem Mcpl. Ct., San Diego Jud. Dist., 1983, 92. Bd. dirs. Artist Chamber Ensemble, Inc., 1983-86, Libr. Assn. La Jolla, Calif., 1983-86, San Diego County Crimestoppers, Inc., 1993-95, San Diego Crime Commn., 1994-95, St. Augustine's H.S., 1994-95, San Diego Hist. Soc., 1993-95. Mem. ABA, Calif. State Bar Assn., San Diego County Bar Assn., Mortar Bd., Guidon Soc., Charter 100, Phi Beta Kappa. Office: Higgs Fletcher & Mack 401 W A St Ste 2600 San Diego CA 92101-7913 Office Phone: 619-595-4292. Business E-Mail: maggie@hggslaw.com.

PAYNE, MARY LIBBY, retired judge; b. Gulfport, Miss., Mar. 27, 1932; d. Reece O. and Emily Augusta (Cook) Bickerstaff; m. Bobby R. Payne; children: Reece Allen, Glenn Russell. Student, Miss. U. for Women, 1950-52; BA in Polit. Sci. with distinction, U. Miss., 1954, LLB, 1955. Bar: Miss. 1955. Ptnr. Bickerstaff & Bickerstaff, Gulfport, 1955-56; sec. Guaranty Title Co., Jackson, Miss., 1957; assoc. Henley, Jones, & Henley, Jackson, Miss., 1958-61; freelance rschr. Pearl, Miss., 1961-63; solo practitioner Brandon, Miss., 1963-68; exec. dir. Miss. Judiciary Commn., Jackson, 1968-70; chief drafting & rsch. Miss. Ho. Reps., Jackson, 1970-72; asst. atty. gen. State Atty. Gen. Office, Jackson, 1972-75; founding dean, assoc. prof. Sch. Law Miss. Coll., Jackson, 1975-78, prof., 1978-94, scholar in residence, prof. emerita, 2003—; judge Miss. Ct. Appeals, Jackson, 1995—2001; ret., 2001. Mem. bd. disting. alumnae Miss. U. Women, 1988—2000. Contbr. articles to profl. jours. Founder, bd. dirs. Christian Conciliation Svc., Jackson, 1983-93; bd. dirs. Exchange Club's Child Abuse Prevention Ctr. of Jackson, 1999-2001; counsel Christian Action Com. Rankin Bapt. Assn., Pearl, 1968-92; advisor Covenant Ministerial Fellowship, 1995-2002. Named Miss. Coll. Lawyer of Yr., Miss. Coll. Sch. Law Alumni Assn., 1998, Outstanding Woman Lawyer, Miss. Women Lawyers Assn., 1999, Susie Blue Buchanan award, Women in Profession Com. of Miss. Bar, 2000; recipient Book of Golden Deeds award, Pearl Exch. Club, 1989, Excellence medallion, Miss. U. Women, 1990, Woman of Yr. award, Miss. Assn. Women Higher Edn., 1989, Power of One award, Miss. Govs. Conf., 1996, Disting. Jurist award, Miss. State U., 2004, Lifetime Achievement award, Miss. Bar, 2005. Fellow Am. Bar Found.; mem. Miss. Bar Found., Christian Legal Soc. (nat. bd. dirs. 1992-2001, Skeeter Ellis Svc. to Law Students award 1999, Lifetime Achievement award 2002). Baptist. Avocations: public speaking, travel, needlepoint, sewing, reading.

PAYNE, MEREDITH JORSTAD, physician; b. St. Louis, Feb. 7, 1927; d. Louis Helmar and Cleone Gladys (Branian) Jorstad; m. Spencer Payne, 1948 (div. 1959); m. James McGarity, 1965 (div. 1977); children: Maureen Meredith, James Louis. AB, Washington U., St. Louis, 1947, MD, 1950; MBA, Lindenwood U., 1999. Diplomate Am. Bd. Surgery, Am. Bd. Plastic Surgery. Intern gen. surgery St. Louis City Hosp., 1950-51, asst. resident surgery, 1951-54; chief surg. resident Roswell Park Meml. Hosp., Buffalo, 1954-55; chief plastic surgery resident Allentown (Pa.) Gen. Hosp., 1955-57; clin. instr. surgery Washington U. Med. Sch., 1957-70; vis. surgeon Homer G. Phillips Hosp., St. Louis, 1957-70; staff St. Luke's, St. Louis and Bethesda, 1957—, St. Mary's, 1988—; chief plastic surgery Vets. Hosp., 1986-98; assoc. prof. plastic surgery (clin.) St. Louis U. Sch. Medicine, St. Louis, 1986—. Med. dir. Unity Clft Palate Clinic; asst. dir. Bethesda Delworth Nursing Home, 1997—2001; attending physician Concentra Med. Ctrs., 1994—. Contbr. articles to profl. jours. Fellow ACS; mem. AMA, Am. Soc. Plastic and Reconstructive Surgery, Mo. Med. Assn. (del., councillor 1988—), St. Louis Met. Med. Soc. (councillor 1983-86, sec. 1998-99, v.p. 1999-00), Am. Cleft Palate Assn., Roswell Park Surgery Assn., So. Med. Assn., Washington U. Med. Alumni Assn., Am. Geriatrics Soc., Midwestern Assn. Plastic Surgeons, Pan Am. Med. Assn., City Hosp. Alumni Assn., Soc. Head and Neck Surgeons, St. Louis Area Soc. Plastic Surgeons (pres. 1990-93), City Hosp. Alumni Assn. (v.p. 1995-97, pres. 1997-99, sec. 2005), Mo. Assn. Plastic Surgery (treas. 1995—, v.p. 1997, pres. 1998), St. Louis Surg. Soc. (v.p. 1998), AMWA (treas. St. Louis chpt. 1995), Order Eastern Star, Zonta (St. Louis pres. 1968-69), College Club (bd. dirs. St. Louis 1983-85). Avocations: skiing, tennis, sewing, knitting, gardening. Home: 7314 Westmoreland Dr Saint Louis MO 63130-4240

PAYNE, MICHAEL DAVID, English language educator; b. Dallas, Jan. 17, 1941; s. Fred G. Payne and Jocie Marie (Kirkham) Lundberg; children: Jeffrey, Jennifer, Albert, Edward. Student, U. Calif.-Berkeley, 1958-59, 61; BA, So. Oreg. Coll., 1962; PhD, U. Oreg., 1969. Tchr. English, Medford (Oreg.) Sr. High Sch., 1962-63; instr. English, U. Oreg., Eugene, 1963-69; asst. prof. to prof. English, Bucknell U., Lewisburg, Pa., 1969—, chmn. dept. history, 1980-82, chmn. dept. English, 1982-88, 92-94, chair faculty, 2000—04, Presdl. prof., 1982-86, John P. Crozer prof. English lit., 1986—2006; dir. Bucknell Univ. Press, 1972-76; assoc. editor Bucknell Rev., 1970-85, editor, 1985-88. Author: Irony in Shakespeare's Roman Plays, 1974, Reading Theory, 1993, Reading Knowledge, 1997; editor: Contemporary Essays on Style, 1969, Shakespeare: Contemporary Critical Approaches, 1979, Text, Interpretation, Theory, 1985, Self, Sign and Symbol, 1986, Perspective, 1986, Criticism, History and Intertextuality, 1987, New Interpretations of American Literature, 1987, The Senses of Stanley Cavell, 1988, Dictionary of Cultural and Critical Theory, 1996, Renaissance Literature: An Anthology, 2003, Life.after.theory, 2003, The Greenblatt Reader, 2005; gen. editor Bucknell Lectures in Lit. Theory, 1990-95. Recipient Lindback award for disting. teaching, 1976, Disting. Svc. award CEA, 1988, Profl. Achievement award, 1993; Folger Shakespeare Libr. fellow, 1973, NEH fellow, 1974, Bucknell Alumni fellow, 1978-79. Mem.: MLA, Children's Lit. Assn., Coll. English Assn., Inst. Romance Studies (U. London), Johnson Soc. London, Phi Beta Kappa (hon.). Home: 24 S Water St Lewisburg PA 17837-1562 Office Phone: 570-577-3020. E-mail: payne@bucknell.edu.

PAYNE, ROGER LEE, geographer; b. Winston-Salem, NC, Oct. 26, 1946; s. Irvin Lee and Gladys Odel (Binkley) P.; m. Sara Lucinda Parker, Aug. 16, 1970 (div. Feb. 1992); 1 child, Jennifer Nicole; m. Anne F. Remen, June 11, 1995. BA, East Carolina U., 1969, MA, 1972. Geographer, chief geog. names U.S. Geol. Survey, Reston, Va., 1974—2006; instr. geography and history Pan Am. Inst./U.S. Geog. Survey, 1989—; exec. sec. U.S. Bd. Names, U.S. Geol. Survey, Washington, 1990—2006, emeritus, 2006—. Instr. East Caroline U., Greenville, N.C., 1969-71, George Washington U., Washington, 1977-90, George Mason U., Fairfax, Va., 1979-83, 1998—2003, Benjamin Franklin U., Washington, 1985-87, Old Dominion U., 2005—; del. UN, N.Y.C., 1987—2006, instr., 1995—; mem. scientist exch. Geol. Survey, Beijing, 1989; instr. Nat. Black Colls., Howard U., 1985; book reviewer AAAS, 1975—; mem. Antarctica Sci. Field Program, 1999-2000; cons. in field. Author: Urban Development in South Africa, 1972, Place Names of Outer Banks, 1985, Manuals on Auto Names, 1987, 89, 97; coord., editor: (book series) National Gazetter U.S., 1982—; contbr. articles to profl. jours. Chmn. E. Carolina Blood Dr., Greenville, 1969. Lt. USAF, 1970-72. Recipient Guy Buzzard award Gamma Theta Upsilon, 1970; Superior Svc. award Geol. Survey, 1988, Outstanding Achievement award, 1985, 86, 88, 97, 2004. Fellow Explorers Club; mem. Assn. Am. Geographers (various coms. 1969-95, pres. mid-Atlantic divsn. 1981-82, treas., sec.), Am. Name Soc. (pres. 1989), Am. Nat. Std. Inst. (rep. 1986-2001), Cosmos Club (cons. 1986—, manuscript reviewer 1975—). Achievements include Mount Payne, Antarctica, named in his honor. Avocation: hiking. Home: 1462 Gleasons Landing Dr Saint Helena Island SC 29920 Office: US Geol Survey 523 National Ctr 12201 Sunrise Valley Dr Reston VA 20192-0523 Business E-Mail: rpayne@usgs.gov.

PAYNE, ROGER SEARLE, zoologist, researcher, science administrator, conservationist; b. NYC, Jan. 29, 1935; m. Katy Boynton, 1960 (div. 1985); children: John, Holly, Laura Sam; m. Lisa Harrow, Aug. 18, 1991. AB in Animal Behavior, Harvard U., 1957; PhD, Cornell U., 1961. Rsch. zoologist Inst. for Rsch. in Animal Behavior N.Y. Zool. Inst., NYC, 1968-71; asst. prof. biology Rockefeller U., NYC, 1968-71; founder, pres. Ocean Alliance, Lincoln, Mass., 1971—. Author: Among Whales, 1995; host (TV documentary) In the Company of Whales, 1992 (series) Ocean Planet, 1994-95; co-writer, co-dir. (film) Whales, 1995. Co-recipient Albert Schweitzer medal Animal Welfare Inst., 1980; recipient Joseph Wood Krutch medal Humane Soc. U.S., 1989, Lyndhurst prize Lyndhurst Found., 1984; genius grantee John D. and Catherine T. MacArthur Found., 1984, Global 500 award UN, 1988; knighted, Netherlands, 1977. Home: 2141 Biscuit Hl South Woodstock VT 05071-9530 Office: Ocean Alliance 191 Weston Rd Lincoln MA 01773-4516 E-mail: rpayne@oceanalliance.org.

PAYNE, ROY STEVEN, lawyer; b. New Orleans, Aug. 30, 1952; s. Fred J. and Dorothy Julia (Peck) P.; m. Laureen Fuller, Sept. 8, 1973; children: Julie Elizabeth, Kelly Kathryn, Alex Steven, Michael Lawrence. BA with distinction, U. Va., 1974; JD, La. State U., 1977; LLM, Harvard U., 1980. Bar: La. 1977, US Dist. Ct. (we. dist.) La. 1980, US Ct. Appeals (5th cir.) 1980, US Supreme Ct. 1983. Law clk. to judge U.S. Dist. Ct., Shreveport, La., 1977-79; assoc. Blanchard, Walker, O'Quin & Roberts, Shreveport, 1980-83, ptnr., 1984-87; U.S. Magistrate judge We. Dist. La., Shreveport, 1987—2005; pvt. practice Shreveport, 2005—. Instr. New Eng. Sch. Law, Boston, 1979-80. Contbr. articles to profl. jours. Chmn. Northwest La. Legal Svcs. Assn., Shreveport, 1984-85; pres. Shreveport Bar Found., 2003-06. Mem. 5th Cir. Bar Assn., 5th Cir. Jud. Coun. (magistrate judges com. 1992-2000), La. State Bar Assn. (editl. bd. Forum jour., 1983-87, legal aid com.), Fed. Magistrate Judges Assn. (circuit dir. 2003-05), Shreveport Bar Assn., La. Assn. Def. Counsel (bd. dirs. 1987), Harry V. Booth Am. Inn of Ct. (pres. elect 1994-95, pres. 1996-98), Order of Coif, Rotary, Phi Kappa Phi, Phi Delta Phi. Republican. Methodist. Home: 12494 Harts Island Rd Shreveport LA 71115-8505 Office: 2800 Youree Dr Ste 120 Shreveport LA 71104 Home Phone: 318-798-0814; Office Phone: 318-865-8680. Office Fax: 318-865-8565.

PAYNE, SIDNEY STEWART, retired archbishop; b. Fogo, Nfld., Can., June 6, 1932; m. Selma Carlson, 1962; children: Carla Ann, Christopher Stewart, Robert Clement, Angela Marie Louise. BA, Meml. U., St. John's, Nfld., 1958; lic. of theology, Queen's Coll., St. John's, 1958; BDiv, Gen. Synod, 1968; DDiv (hon.), King's Coll., Halifax, NS, Can., 1981. Ordained priest Anglican Ch., 1958, bishop, 1978, archbishop, 1990. Deacon Mission of Happy Valley, Goose Bay, Labrador, Nfld., Canada, 1957-65; rector Parish of Bay Roberts, Nfld., Canada, 1965-70, Parish of St. Anthony, 1970-78; bishop Diocese of Western Nfld., 1978-90, archbishop of Western Nfld. and Met. Eccles. Province of Can., 1990-97; ret., 1997. Pres. Diocesan Synod, chmn. exec. com., mem. ex-officio diocesan coms.; pres. Provincial Synod, Provincial Coun.; chair Provincial House of Bishops; mem. long range planning com., ministry com., mem. nat. exec. coun. Partners in World Mission, Stewardship and Fin. Devel. Com.; mem. Anglican/Roman Cath. Bishops' Dialogue, Can.; active Provincial and Nat. House of Bishops. Mem. Internat. Grenfell Assn. (past bd. dirs.). Anglican. Avocations: reading, walking, gardening, cross country skiing. Home: PO Box 2255 R R 1 Stn Main Corner Brook NL Canada A2H 2N2 E-mail: sspayne@nf.sympatico.ca.

PAYNE, STANLEY E., mathematics professor; b. Chgo., Sept. 26, 1939; s. Don Ivan Payne and Agnes Eileen Craven - Payne; life ptnr. Angelika Adamic; m. Shirley Ann Ellison, Aug. 22, 1961 (div. Sept. 26, 1983); children: Tanya Marie Ker, Rahn Kenneth, Brian Curtis, Brett Ivan. MS in Math., Fla. State U., Tallahassee, 1963, PhD in Math., 1966. Prof. math. Miami U., Oxford, Ohio, 1966—84, U. Colo., Health Sci. Ctr., Denver, 1984—. Contbr. articles to profl. jours. Mem.: Inst. Combinatorics and Its Applications, Am. Math. Soc. (life). Achievements include discovery of new examples of ovals and generalised quadrangles. Office: U Colo at Denver CB 170 POBox 173364 Denver CO 80217-3364 Home Phone: 303-693-8259; Office Phone: 303-556-8443. Office Fax: 303-556-8550. Business E-Mail: stanpayne@mac.com.

PAYNE, TIMOTHY D., information technology executive; b. Oct. 25, 1958; BS, Univ. Calif., Santa Barbara, 1981. Pres., CEO Openware Technologies Inc., 1994—97; pres., COO Modis Inc., 1997—2000; pres., CEO MPS (Modis Profl. Services) Group Inc., Jacksonville, Fla., 2001—. Bd. dir. ITFlorida.com Inc. Office: MPS Group Inc 1 Independent Dr Jacksonville FL 32202 *

PAYNE, TYSON ELLIOTT, JR., retired insurance executive; b. Dallas, May 25, 1927; s. Tyson Elliott and Winnie Claris (Denman) P.; m. Billie Jane Spears, Aug. 28, 1948; children: David Tyson, Sally Jane. B.J., U. Tex., 1949. CLU, ChFC. Sports editor Lufkin (Tex.) News, 1949-51, Tyler (Tex.) Courier Times, 1951-53; with Am. Nat. Ins. Co., Galveston, Tex., 1953-88, v.p. health ins. ops. St. Louis, 1965-1970, v.p. mktg. Galveston, 1970-86; pvt. practice ins. agt. Austin, Tex., 1987-88; exec. v. p., dir. Sch. of Ins. & Fin. Svcs. at U. Houston, 1988-92; ret., 1992. Elder Presbyn. Ch. With USNR, 1945-46. Home: 8110 Cardin Dr Austin TX 78759-8704 Personal E-mail: tpaynejr1927@sbcglobal.net.

PAYNE, URSULA OCTAVIA, choreographer, educator; b. Charlotte, NC, Aug. 11, 1969; d. James Oliver and Octavia Clark Payne. BA in Dance, Slippery Rock U., Pa., 1992; MFA in Dance, Ohio State U., 1995. Cert. movement analyst Laban Bartenieff Inst. Movement Studies, N.Y., 1996. Tchr. Slippery Rock (Pa.) U., 1995—. Cons., panelist Dance Advance, Phila., 2003—; faculty Am. Dance Festival, Durham, NC, 2002—. Named one of Top 25 to Watch, Dance Mag.; recipient President's Internat. Initiative award, Slippery Rock (Pa.) U., 2001, Young Alumni award, 2005; fellow, Pa. Coun. of the Arts, 2004, 2006. Mem.: Delta Sigma Theta. Democrat. Avocations: travel, theater. Home: 1707 Highland Ave New Castle PA 16105 Office: Slippery Rock University of Pennsylvania Morrow Field House Slippery Rock PA 16057 Home Phone: 724-652-7260; Office Phone: 724-738-4509. Office Fax: 724-738-4524. Business E-Mail: ursula.payne@sru.edu.

PAYNE, WILLIAM ALBERT, JR., agronomist, educator; b. Indpls., Dec. 17, 1958; s. William and Aline Payne; married, June 30, 1984; children: Will, Matt, Ken. BA in Chemistry, Wabash Coll., 1981; MS in Soil Sci., Tex. A&M U., 1986, PhD in Soil Sci., 1990. Vol. Peace Corps, Mauritania, 1981-84; rsch. asst. Tex. A&M U., College Sta., 1984-90, postdoctoral rschr., 1990-91, assoc. prof. crop physiology Bushland, 2000—05, prof. crop physiology, 2005—; prin. scientist ICRISAT, Niger, 1991-97; asst. prof. agronomy Oreg. State U., Pendleton, 1997-2000. Assoc. editor: Agronomy Jour., 1998-; contbr. articles to profl. jours. Fellow AAAS, Am. Soc. Agronomy (chair internat. divsn. 1997-98); mem. Soil Sci. Soc. Am., Crop Sci. Soc. Am., Sigma Xi. Democrat. Achievements include work on crop water use and water-use efficiency. Office: Tex A&M U Sys Tex Agrl Exptl Sta 2301 Experiment Sta Rd Bushland TX 79012 Office Phone: 806-354-5801. Business E-Mail: w-payne@tamu.edu.

PAYNE, WILLIAM BRUCE, lawyer, director; b. Tulsa, Apr. 18, 1943; s. Marvin Ream and Audrey Arlene (Jones) P.; m. Suzanne Cooper, June 4, 1966; children: Allison, Stephanie. BS, U. Okla., 1965, JD, 1968. Bar: Minn. 1968, U.S. Dist. Ct. Minn. 1968, U.S. Ct. Appeals (8th cir.) 1968. Ptnr. Dorsey & Whitney LLP, Mpls., 1968—, head M&A group, 1992—. 1st lt. USAR, 1968—74. Mem. ABA, Minn. Bar Assn. Office: Dorsey & Whitney LLP 50 S 6th St Minneapolis MN 55402-1498 Office Phone: 612-340-2722. Office Fax: 612-340-2868. Business E-Mail: payne.bill@dorsey.com.

PAYRI, JOEL, pharmaceutical marketing executive; b. Sidi-Bel-Abbes, Algeria, Nov. 29, 1961; s. Rene and Marie P. DVM, Nat. Vet. Sch., Toulouse, France, 1985, diploma of anatomo-pathology, 1988; diploma of med. stats., U. Paris VI, 1989; MBA, INSEAD, Fontainebleau, France, 1991. Pvt. vet. practice, St. Gaudens, France, 1985-86; study dir. Searle Rsch. and Devel., Sophia Antipolis, France, 1986-87; head exptl. cardiology Rhone Poulenc Sante, Vitry sur Seine, France, 1988-90; mktg. mgr. Pharmuka-Rhone Poulenc, Paris, 1991-92; worldwide product mgr. Taxotere Rhone Poulenc Rorer, Paris, 1992-96; internat. mktg. dir. GlaxoSmithkline, London, 1996—2001; v.p. internat. Biogen Idec, Paris, 2001—06, Johnson & Johnson, 2006—. Surg. asst. Nat. Vet. Sch., Toulouse, 1984-85; pres. new mgmt. team Rhone Poulenc Sante, Paris, 1989-91; interviewer INSEAD MBA cands. Biogen Idec, Paris, 1995-2006. Author: Telemetry and Gastric pH Measurements, 1985 (gold medal 1985); contbr. to websites and pubs. for Internat. Herpes Alliance. Capt. French Army, 1987-90, Paris. Grantee Ministry Agr., 1985. Mem. Am. Social Health Assn., Infectious Disease Soc. Am. Home: La petite Ourse Anse de Maldorme Bouches du Rhone 13007 Marseilles France Office: Johnson and Johnson 1 rue Camille Desmoulins 92787 Paris France Fax: 33-147-217535. Business E-Mail: jpayri@jnjfr.jnj.com.

PAYSON, MARTIN F., lawyer; b. Bklyn., Dec. 25, 1940; m. Rhoda Shapiro, Oct. 8, 1961; children: Jacqueline, Marla. BBA, CCNY, 1961; JD, Bklyn. Law Sch., 1966. Bar: N.Y. 1967, Pa. 1989, U.S. Ct. Appeals (1st cir.) 1971, U.S. Ct. Appeals (2d and 3d cirs.) 1968, U.S. Ct. Appeals (4th cir.) 1969, U.S. Supreme Ct. 1970. Gen. ptnr. Jackson Lewis L.L.P. (formerly Jackson, Lewis, Schnitzler & Krupman), White Plains, NY, 1967—. Lectr. in field. Contbr. articles to various pubs. With U.S. Army, 1961-62. Mem. N.Y. State Bar Assn. (labor and employee rels. sects.), Soc. for Human Resource Mgmt. Avocations: photography, bicycling, model railroading, gardening. Office: Jackson Lewis LLP One N Broadway White Plains NY 10601 Home Phone: 914-319-5914; Office Phone: 914-328-0404. Business E-Mail: paysonm@jacksonlewis.com.

PAYTON, GARY DWAYNE, professional basketball player; b. Oakland, Calif., July 23, 1968; m. Monique Payton; children: Raquel, Gary Dwayne, Julian. Grad., Oreg. State U., 1990. Drafted NBA, 1990; guard Seattle Supersonics, 1990—2003, Milwaukee Bucks, 2003, L.A. Lakers, 2003—04, Boston Celtics, 2004—05, Miami Heat, 2005—. Author: (novels) Confidence Counts, 1999. Founder Gary Payton Foundation,

1996—. Named NBA All-Star, 1994—98, 2000—01, NBA Defensive Player of the Year, 1996; named to All-Am. 1st team, The Sporting News, 1990, NBA All-Def. 1st team, 1994—2001, All-NBA 1st team, 1998, 2000, All-NBA 2nd team, 1995—97, 1999; recipient Gold Medal, Atlanta Olympic Games, 1996, Sydney Olympic Games, 2000. Office: Miami Heat Am Airlines Arena 601 Biscyane Blvd Miami FL 33132

PAYTON, PAUL MAX, application developer; b. San Francisco, Aug. 31, 1961; s. Gertrude Lychenheim; m. Patricia Egan, Dec. 27, 2003. AS summa cum laude, Coll. San Mateo, Calif., 1980; BS magna cum laude, San Francisco State U., 1982. Cassoc. engr. Lockheed Martin, Palo Alto, Calif., 1982—84, sci. programmer, 1984—85, sr. sci. programmer, 1985—86, sci. programmer analyst, 1986—90, sci. programming specialist, 1990—96, staff engr., 1996—99, cons. software engr., 1999—2002, prin. software engr., 2002—. Lectr. in field. Contbr. articles to profl. jours.; Represented in permanent collections PARC, Amnesty Internat., NYC, Space Imaging Inc., Thornton, Colo., numerous pvt. collections, Calif.; contbr. poetry to profl. jours. Mem.: Mensa (life), San Francisco State U. Alumni Assn., Alpha Gamma Sigma (life). Achievements include patents in field. Avocations: creative writing, poetry, mathematical research, algorithmic art. Home: PO Box 194391 San Francisco CA 94119-4391 Office: Lockheed Martin Missiles and Space 1111 Lockheed Martin Way Bldg 153 Sunnyvale CA 94089 Office Phone: 408-756-2792. Business E-Mail: paul.payton@lmco.com.

PAYTON, ROBERT See PROUD, ROBERT

PAYTON, SALLYANNE, law educator; b. 1943; BA, Stanford U., 1964, LLB, 1968. Bar: Calif. 1969, DC 1969. Staff asst. to Pres. of U.S. White House Domestic Coun., Washington, 1971-73; chief counsel urban mass transp. adminstrn. U.S. Dept. Transp., Washington, 1973-76; assoc. prof. U. Mich. Law Sch., Ann Arbor, 1976-85, prof., 1985—; William W. Cook Prof. Law. Trustee Stanford U., 1972-82; mem. Adminstrn. Conf. U.S., 1980—; bd. dirs. Roosevelt Ctr. Am. Policy Studies, 1982—. Fellow: Nat. Acad. of Pub. Adminstrn. Office: U Mich Law Sch 336 Hutchins Hall 625 S State St Ann Arbor MI 48109-1215 Office Phone: 734-763-0220. Office Fax: 734-763-9375. E-mail: spayton@umich.edu.

PAYTON, SEAN (PATRICK SEAN PAYTON), professional football coach; b. San Mateo, Calif., Dec. 29, 1963; m. Beth Payton; children: Meghan, Connor Thomas. BS in Comm., U. Ea. Ill., 1987. Quarterback Arena Football League Chgo. Bruisers, 1987, Chgo. Bears, 1987; grad. asst. San Diego State U., 1988—89, running backs coach, 1992—93; offensive coach Ind. State U., 1990—91; quarterbacks coach, co-offensive coord. Miami U., Ohio, 1994—95; quarterbacks coach U. Ill., 1996, Phila. Eagles, 1997—98, NY Giants, 1999—2000, offensive coord., 2000—03; quarterbacks coach Dallas Cowboys, 2003, asst. head coach, offensive coord., 2004—05; head coach New Orleans Saints, 2006—. Named NFL Coach Yr., AP, 2006; named to U. Ea. Ill. Hall of Fame, 2000. Office: New Orleans Saints 5800 Airline Dr Metairie LA 70003 *

PAYTON, SUE C., civilian military employee; b. 1950; BS in Edn., Ea. Ill. U., 1972; MS in System Acquisition Mgmt. & Systems Tech., U. So. Calif., 1985; grad. exec. program, Goizueta Bus. Sch. Emory U., 1998. Sr. site systems integration mgr. Martin Marietta, Reston, Va., 1989—94; mgr. advanced tech., Office of V.P. Bus. Devel. Lockheed Martin Corp., Reston, Va., 1994—98; dir. Nat. Ctr. Applied Tech., Springfield, Va., 1999—2001; v.p. applied tech. ImageLinks, Inc., Springfield, Va., 2000—01; acting dir. def. rsch. & engring. US Dept. Def., Washington, dep. under sec. for advanced systems & concepts, 2001—06, asst. sec. for acquisition, Dept. Air Force, 2006—. Mem.: Nat. Correlation Working Group, Open Geospatial Consortium, Ea. Ill. Alumni Assn., Def. Sci & Tech. Adv. Group. Office: USAF 1060 Air Force Pentagon Rm 4E964 SAF/AQ Washington DC 20330-1060 Office Phone: 703-697-6446. Office Fax: 703-693-6400. E-mail: sue.payton@osd.mil. *

PAYTON, THOMAS WILLIAM, finance company executive; b. Toronto, Ont., Can., Sept. 7, 1946; With Can. Imperial Bank of Commerce, Toronto; dir. Bramalea Ltd., Toronto, 1981-82, v.p., 1982-88, sr. v.p., 1988-90, sr. v.p., treas., 1991-93; dir. Cadillac Fairview, Inc., 1994-95; pres. Sunnybrook Properties Inc., 1997-2000, DelLyn Advisors Inc., 1993—; v.p. Hawthorne Realty Advisors Inc., 2003—. Personal E-mail: dellynadvinc@aol.com.

PAYTON-WRIGHT, PAMELA, actress; b. Pitts., Nov. 1, 1941; d. Gordon Edgar and Eleanor Ruth (McKinley) Payton Wright; m. David Arthur Butler, May 8, 1978 (div. 1989); 1 child, Oliver Dickon Hedley. Grad., St. Mary's Jr. Coll., 1961; BA, Birmingham So. Coll., 1963; postgrad., Royal Acad. Dramatic Arts, London, 1963-65. Actress (Broadway plays) The Show-Off, 1968, Exit the King, 1968, The Cherry Orchard, 1968, Jimmy Shine, 1969, The Crucible, 1972, Mourning Becomes Electra, 1972, All Over Town, 1975, The Glass Menagerie, 1976, Romeo and Juliet, 1977, A Streetcar Named Desire, 1988, Night of the Iguana, 1988, M. Butterfly, 1988—90, Something Unspoken, 1995, Long Day's Journey Into Night, 2003, (off-Broadway) The Effect of Gamma Rays on Man-In-The Wood Marigolds, 1970—71, Jesse and the Bandit Queen, 1975, The Seagull, 1980, Don Juan, 1982, Hamlet, 1982, Mrs. Warren's Profession, 1992, The Replacement, 1995, Richard III, 'Til the Rapture Comes, 1998, What You Get and What You Expect, 2000, Fifth of July, 2003, Duet, 2004, The Day Emily Married, 2004, Indian Blood, 2006, (plays) Skin of Our Teeth, 1972, Aimee, 1973, Othello, Troilus and Cressida, As You Like It, 1976, Lunch Girls, 1977, Summerfolk, 1978, The Greeks, 1982, The Misanthrope, 1982, Tobacco Road, 1984, Passion, 1984—85, Cat on a Hot Tin Roof, 1985, Little Eyolf, 1985, On the Verge, 1986, Our Town, 1987, The Road to Mecca, 1990, Picnic, 1991, The Way of the World, 1991, Quartermaine's Terms, 1993, Misalliance, 1993, Six Degrees of Separation, 1993, Ghosts, 1994, Sea Gull, 1994, The Rivals, 1996, Touch of the Poet, 1996, Glass Menagerie, 1997, Voir Dire, 1997, She Stoops to Conquer, 1997, Blithe Spirits, 1998, Transit of Venus, 1998, Sweet Bird of Youth, 1999, A Fair Country, 2000, Philadelphia Story, 2001, Seascape, 2002, Outward Bound, 2002, Hay Fever, 2005, Equus, 2005, The Learned Ladies of Park Avenue, (films) At the Dark End of the Street, 1980, Going in Style, 1981, Starlight, 1985, My Little Girl, 1985, Ironweed, 1987, The Freshman, 1989, In Dreams, 1999, Saving Face, 2004. Nominee Emmy, 1972, Lucille Lortel, 2003; recipient Fulbright award, 1963, Spl. medal, Edmund Gray prize for high comedy, Herbert Beerbohm Tree citation, Royal Acad. Dramatic Art, 1963—65, Obie award, 1970, 1975, 1976, Clarence Derwent award, Variety Critics' Poll citation, 1970, Drama Desk award, 1972, Best Actress citation, Dallas Theater Critics' Forum, 1994, Balt., 1997, Dean Goodman award, 1999, Joseph Jefferson award, 1996; Fox Grant fellow, 1999. Mem.: Screen Actors Guild, AFTRA, Actors Equity Assn. Episcopalian. Office: Bauman & Assocs 250 W 57th St New York NY 10019-3741

PAZ, GEORGE, health products executive; b. St. Louis, Aug. 27, 1955; s. Geronimo and Collen May (Hart) P.; m. Georgene Marie Wade, July 27, 1974; children: Stacy, Kelly, Rebecca. BSBA, U. Mo., St. Louis, 1982. CPA, Mo. Jr. acct. Gen. Am., St. Louis, 1980-82, sr. acct., 1982-83, acctg. adminstr., 1983-85, tax planning analyst, 1985-87, dir. tax planning, 1987; ptnr. Coopers & Lybrand, 1988—93, 1996—98; exec. v.p., CFO Life Ptnrs. Group, 1993—95; sr. v.p., CFO Express Scripts Inc., St. Louis, 1998—2003, pres., 2003—, bd. dirs., 2004—, CEO, 2005—, chmn., 2006—. Bd. dirs. Gen. Am. Employees Fed. Credit Union, 1985. Fellow Life Office Mgmt. Assn.; mem. AICPA, Mo. Soc. CPA, Pharm. Care Mgmt. Assn. Lutheran. Avocations: golf, running, softball. Office: Express Scripts Inc 13900 Riverport Dr Maryland Heights MO 63043 Office Phone: 314-770-1666. Office Fax: 314-702-7037. *

PAZ, HAROLD LOUIS, hospital administrator, internist, educator; b. NYC, Jan. 3, 1955; BA in Biology and Psychology, U. Rochester, 1977, MD, 1982; MS in Life Sci. Engring., Tufts U., 1979. Diplomate subspecialty in pulmonary medicine Am. Bd. Internal Medicine. Intern in internal medicine Northwestern U. Med. Ctr., Chgo., 1982—83, resident in internal medicine, 1983—85, chief med. resident, 1985—86; instr. clin. medicine Northwestern U., Chgo., 1985—86; fellow in pulmonary and critical care Johns Hopkins U., Balt., 1986—88, fellow in environ. health scis., 1986—88; asst. prof. medicine Hahnemann U., Phila., 1988—92, asst. prof. anesthesia, 1989—92, assoc. dean grad. med. edn., 1992—94, assoc. prof. medicine, 1992—94, dir. med. ICU, 1988—94, assoc. hosp. med. dir., 1992—94, dir. Ctr. for Clin. Outcomes, 1992—94; med. dir., assoc. dean for clin. affairs U. Medicine and Dentistry N.J. Robert Wood Johnson Med. Sch., New Brunswick, 1994—95, assoc. prof. medicine, 1994—2003, dean, 1995—2006; CEO U. Medicine and Dentistry N.J. Robert Wood Johnson U. Med. Group, New Brunswick, 1995—2006; prof. medicine U. Medicine and Dentistry N.J. Robert Wood Johnson Med. Sch., New Brunswick, 2003—06; CEO Penn State Milton S. Hershey Medical Ctr. and Penn State Coll. of Medicine, 2006—. Editor: Jour. Undergrad. Rsch., 1976, Med. Staff News newsletter, 1992—94; cons.: Annals Internal Medicine, Clin. Immunology and Immunopathology, Chest, Intensive Care Medicine, Physician Execs., N.Y. State Med. Jour., mem. editl. bd.: Jour. Disease Mgmt. and Clin. Outcomes, 1996—, Chest, 1998—2003. Named to Gold Humanism Honor Soc., 2005; recipient Disting. Svc. award, Motolinsky Rsch. Found., 1998, Cmty. Leaders of Distinction award, County C. of C., 1999, Sir William Oster Humanitarian award, 2005; Eudowood fellow, Johns Hopkins U., 1987—88, U. Rochester scholar, 1979. Fellow: ACP, Am. Coll. Chest Physicians; mem.: AMA, Laennec Soc. (pres. 1994—95), Philip Drinker Soc. for Critical Care (pres. 1992—94), Am. Thoracic Soc. Office: Penn State Hershey Med Ctr 500 University Dr Hershey PA 17033 Office Phone: 717-531-8323.

PAZNOKAS, LYNDA SYLVIA, elementary school educator; b. Portland, Oreg., Feb. 19, 1950; d. Marley Elmo and Undine Sylvia (Crockard) Sims. BA, Wash. State U., Pullman, 1972; MS, Portland State U., Oreg., 1975; EdD, Oreg. State U., Corvallis, 1984. Cert. tchr. Oreg. Tchr. 5th grade, outdoor sch. specialist Clover Park Sch. Dist. 400, Tacoma, 1971-72; tchr. 6th grade, outdoor sch. specialist Hillsboro Elem. Dist. 7, Oreg., 1972-78, Bend-La Pine Sch. Dist., Oreg., 1978-82, elem. curriculum specialist Oreg., 1983-85, tchr. 4th grade gifted and talented Oreg., 1985-90; grad. teaching asst. Oreg. State U., Corvallis, 1982-84; asst. prof., assoc. prof. No. Ariz. U., 1990-99, chair instnl. leadership, 1997-98; Boeing disting. prof. sci. edn. Wash. State U., Pullman, 1999—, assoc. dean sch. and cmty. collaboration, 2006—. Ednl. cons., tchr. workshops, 1973—; presenter workshop Soviet-Am. Joint Conf., Moscow State U., 1991, Meeting of Children's Culture Promoters, Guadalajara, Mex., 1994, internat. conf. Sci., Tech. and Math. Edn. for Human Devel., UNESCO, Panaji, India, 2001, Nishinomiya Joint Rsch. Conf., Japan, 2001, internat. workshop Promoting Sci. and Tech. Literacy Through Sci. Toys & Out-of-Sch. Sci. Activities, Pattaya, Thailand, 2005, Scientifically Literate Students as World Citizens, Singapore, 2006, World Environ. Edn. Congress, Durban, South Africa, 2007, others; faculty Ariz. Journey Schs. for Math. and Sci. Tchg. Improvement; coord. Odyssey of the Mind, Bend, 1985-89, tchr. mentor program for 1st yr. tchrs., Beaverton, Oreg., 1982-83; reviewer Sci. Books and Films AAAS, 1992-2006; presenter Social Edn. Assn. of Australia, 1997, Nat. State Tchrs. of Yr., Guam, 2005; steering com. Wash. LASER (Leadership and Assistance for Sci. Edn. Reform), 2002—, mem. sci. drafting team sci. curriculum instrnl. frameworks; mem. Nat. Ecol. Obs. Network Design Consortium. Author: Pathways of America: Lewis and Clark, 1993, Pathways of America: The Oregon Trail, 1993, Pathways of America: The California Gold Rush Trail, 1994, Pathways of America: The Santa Fe Trail, 1995, Fifty States, 1997, U.S. Presidents, 1997, U.S. Map Skills, 1997, Human body, 1998, National Parks and Other Park Service Sites, 1999, Our National Parks, 1999, Pathways of America: The California Mission Trail, 2000, Circling the World: Festivals and Celebrations, 2000, Endangered Species, 2001; mem. adv. bd. (jour.) Sci. and Children; contbr. articles to profl. jours.; reviewer Turkish Jour. Sci. Edn. Vol., leader, bd. dirs. Girl Scouts US, 1957—; elder First Presbyn. Ch., Bend, 1980—; vol. hist. interpretation High Desert Mus., Bend, 1987-91; docent Mus. No. Ariz.; pres. bd. dirs. The Arboretum at Flagstaff; former sec. and v.p. bd. dirs. Palouse Discovery Sci. Ctr. (pres. bd. dirs.); past pres. Arboretum bd.; mem. Ptnrs. Achieving Leadership in Sci., Wash., DC, Leadership and Assistance for Sci. Edn. Reform, Wash., DC. Recipient Excellence in Teaching award Bend Found., 1985-86, 86-87; named Tchr. Yr. Oreg. Dept. Edn., 1982, Higher Edn. Tchr. Yr., Wash. Sci. Tchrs. Assn. (WSTA), 2003; Celebration Teaching grantee Geraldine Rockefeller Dodge Found., 1989, 90, 91, 92, 93, 94, 95, EPA grantee, 1997-99, 2006-, Eisenhower Math and Sci. Edn. Act grantee, 1997, 99, Grand Canyon Assn. grantee, 1996, 97, 98; commd. Ky. Col., 1993. Mem. NEA, Internat. Coun. Assns. Sci. Edn. (chair pre-secondary and informal sci. edn. of the exec. com. 2004—, editor Stepping Into Sci. Internat. Quar. jour. 2004—, jour/advisor), Nat. Coun. Tchrs. Math., NSTA (past mem. nat. supervision com., internat. com., mem. sci. and children bd.), Nat. State Tchrs. of Yr. (nat. pres. 1988-90), Nat. Assn. Rsch. in Sci. Tchg., Oreg. Coun. Tchrs. Math. (bd. dirs. 1981-82), Oreg. Coun. Tchrs. English (bd. dirs. 1981-82), Ariz. Reading Assn. (bd. dirs.), Nat. Coun. for Social Studies, Coun. for Elem. Sci. Internat. (bd. dirs. 1995-98, 99—2003, chair informal edn. com.), Internat. Reading Assn., Oreg.-Calif. Trails Assn., Nat. Sci. Edn. Leadership Assn., Assn. for Sci. Tchr. Edn., Sch. Sci. and Math. Assn. (publs. com.), Nat. Assn. for Rsch. in Sci. Tchg., Assn. for Sci. Edn., Wash. Sci. Tchrs. Assn. (higher edn. rep. bd. dirs. 2004—, co-chair WSTA-Wash. Orgn. for Reading Devel. Joint Conf., 2006), N.W. Oreg.-Calif. Trails Assn., Lewis and Clark Trail Heritage Found., PEO (past corr. sec.), Delta Kappa Gamma (1st v.p.), Phi Delta Kappa (found. rep. 1991-92, v.p. programs 1992-93, historian 1993-94, v.p. membership 1994-95), Golden Key Hon., Pi Lambda Theta, Phi Kappa Phi, Kappa Delta Pi (chpt. counselor, mem. spkrs. bur., nat. Web com., sci. specialist), others. Avocations: cross country skiing, photography, hiking, researching immigrant trails, gardening. Home: 101 Enman-Kincaid Rd Pullman WA 99163

PAZOUR, DON, publishing executive; Pres. Miller Freeman, Inc., San Francisco. CEO Access Intelligence, LLC. Office: c/o Miller Freeman Inc 600 Harrison St San Francisco CA 94107-1387

PEA, ROY, education educator; BA in Philosophy and Psychology, Mich. State U., 1974; DPhil Oxon. in Developmental Psychology, Oxford U., Eng., 1978. NIMH postdoctoral fellow psycholinguistics Rockefeller U., 1978—79; asst. prof. psychology Clark U., 1979—81; assoc. dir. Ctr. for Children and Tech., Bank St. Coll. Edn., 1984—86, sr. rsch. scientist, 1981—86, Inst. for Rsch. on Learning, 1988—91; John Evans prof. edn. an dlearning scis. Northwestern U., 1991—96, dean Sch. Edn. and Social Policy, 1992—96; dir. Ctr. for Tech. in Learning SRI Internat., 1996—2001; prof. edn. and learning scis. Stanford (Calif.) U., 2001—. Co-founder Teachscape, 1999, bd. dirs.; established, dir. Stanford Ctr. for Innovations in Learning. Office: Stanford U Sch Edn 485 Lasuen Mall Stanford CA 94305-3096

PEABODY, ARLENE L. HOWLAND BAYAR, retired enterostomal therapy nurse; b. Deposit, NY, June 26, 1931; d. Burt and Olive (Oralls) Howland; m. Atilla C. Bayar, Dec. 8, 1956 (div.); m. Norman R. Peabody, Feb. 1, 1975 (dec.); children: Tildy Anne Bayar Sparrow, Carol A. Digilio; m. Robert A. Ehlers, Feb. 15, 2003. Diploma, Ridley's Sec. Sch., Binghamton, NY, 1949, Binghamton Sch. Practical Nursing, 1970, Harrisburg Hosp. Sch. Enterostomal Therapy, Pa., 1971; AAS, Empire State Coll., Saratoga Springs, NY, 1985; BS in Edn., SUNY, Oneonta, 1990. RN, N.Y.; cert. therapeutic touch practitioner, natural force healing practitioner, enterostomal nurse. Sec. pres.'s office Cornell U., Ithaca, NY, 1949—55; exec. sec. Rudolph Lang, Office Execs. Assn. N.Y. and Prestige Expositions Inc., NYC, 1955—69; enterostomal therapy nurse M.I. Bassett Hosp., Cooperstown, NY, 1972—89; pvt. practice enterostomal therapy nurse Oneonta, NY, 1989—2002. Spkr. in field. Vol. Am. Cancer Soc., 1972-2002, Catskill Area Hospice, 1990-02, Glimmerglass Opera, 1975-2002; bd. dirs. Del. Heritage Inc., 1996-2002; trustee Unitarian Universalist Soc.; active Storytelling Ctr. of Oneonta, Oneonta Concert Assn., Oneonta Contradance. Mem. AARP (bd. dirs. 1986-2002), N.Y. State Hist. Assn., Delaware County Hist. Soc., Wound Ostomy and Continence Nurses Soc., United Ostomy Assn. (N.Y. state field svcs. rep.), Order Ea. Star. Avocations: heirloom quilting, traditional folk music, coutourier clothing, costuming, dance. Home: 13511 Pebblebrook Dr Houston TX 77079-6023

PEACE, H. W., II, small business owner, retired oil industry executive; b. Clinton, Okla., May 21, 1935; s. Herman Wilbern and Bernice (Mitchell) P.; m. Norma June Williams; children: Hugh William, Susannah Lee. BS in Geology, U. Okla., 1959, MS in Geology, 1964; postgrad., U. S.W. La., 1968. Jr. geologist Union Oil Co. Calif., Houston, 1964-65, area geologist Lafayette, La., 1965-70, geologist dist. exploration Oklahoma City, 1970-77, mgr. Rocky Mountain exploration Casper, Wyo., 1977-80; mgr. divsn. exploration Cotton Petroleum Corp., Tulsa, 1980-83; v.p. exploration Hadson Petroleum Corp., Oklahoma City, 1983-85, exec. v.p., COO, 1985-88, also bd. dirs.; exec. v.p., COO Mosswood Oil and Gas Co., Oklahoma City, 1985-88, Anadarko Supply Co., Oklahoma City, 1986-88, also bd. dirs.; mng. ptnr. EXAD, Oklahoma City, 1988-91, owner, 2006—; pres., CEO, dir. Panhandle Royalty Co., Oklahoma City, 1991—2006; pres., CEO Wood Oil Co. subs. Panhandle Royalty Co., 2001—06. Mgmt. com. PLC Energy Data, LLC, 1994—2001; bd. dirs. OIL Law Recs. Corp., chmn. bd. dirs., 2006—. Dir. sch. geology adv. com. U. Okla., Norman, 1984—, vice chmn. 1988-89, chmn. 1989-90, 2006-, exec. com. 1990—. Lt. USN 1959-63, capt. USNR, 1963-82, ret. list 1995. Mem. Am. Assn. Petroleum Geology (rep. del. or alt. 1984—), Soc. Exploration Geophysicists, Soc. Econ. Paleontologists and Mineralogists, Petroleum Assn. Wyo. (v.p. 1979-80), Tulsa Geol. Soc., Oklahoma City Geol. Soc. (chmn. profl. affairs 1976-77, rep. to mid. continent sec. 2007—), Naval Res. Assn., Cherokee Hills Homeowners Assn. (pres. 1971-73), Fieldstone Homeowners Assn. (pres. 1983), Navy League, Okla. Corp. Commn. (royalty adv. com. 1998—), Okla. Nat. Royalty Owners (bd. dirs. 2006—, pres, 2007—), Rotary. Republican. Avocations: golf, swimming, hiking. Office: EXAD Bradley Sq Ste 22 2932 NW 122d St Oklahoma City OK 73120 Office Phone: 405-286-5538.

PEACH, PAUL E., physician, health facility administrator; b. Owensboro, Ky., June 2, 1943; s. Elbert B. and Ermal M. (Bennett) P. Student, So. Meth. U., 1961-63; BS, Ind. U., 1965, JD, 1969; student, U. New Orleans, 1977-79; MD, La. State U., 1983. Bar: Ind., 1970; diplomate Am. Bd. Phys. Medicine and Rehab. Atty. pvt. practice, Indpls., 1970-72; staff atty La. Dept. Health & Human Svcs., New Orleans, 1972-77; resident La. State U. Charity Hosp., New Orleans, 1983-84, Wadsworth VA Hosp., Cedars-Sinai Hosp., LA, 1984-86; med. dir. Roosvelt Warm Springs (Ga.) Inst. for Rehab., 1986-97, Palmyra Post-Polio Clinic, Albany, Ga., 1997—; med. dir. rehab. medicine Palmyra HCA Hosp., 2003—; med. dir. Palmyra Rehab. Ctr., 2002—. Pvt. practice atty., New Orleans, 1972-77; clin. assoc. prof. Ctr. for Rehab. Medicine Emory U., Atlanta, 1987—. Author: (with others) Late Effects of Poliomyelitis, 1991, Effect of Compliance in Treatment Outcomes in Patients with Post-Polio Syndrome, 1991. Fellow Am. Acad. Phys. Medicine and Rehab.; mem. Med. Assn. Ga., Tri-County Med. Assn. Ga. (pres. 1990-91, 93-96), Ga. Soc. Phys. Medicine and Rehab. (pres. 1989-90, 95-96), Am. Acad. Electrodiagnostic Medicine (assoc.), Am. Hosp. Assn. (governing bd. 1988-91, del. rehab. sect. 1990), So. Soc. Physical Medicine & Rehab. (pres. 2001—). Avocations: photography, music. Home: 1230 Rawson Dr Albany GA 31701-1852 Office: 810 13th Ave Ste 105 Albany GA 31701-1333 Office Phone: 229-446-8960.

PEACH, ROBERT WESTLY, retired small business owner, engineer; b. Balt., May 5, 1921; s. Eggelston Westly Peach and Ola English; m. Margaret Jean McClure, July 11, 1953 (dec.); children: John, Helen. AB, Ctrl. High, Phila., 1937; BSE, Univ. Mich., Ann Arbor, 1944, MSE, 1949. Registered profl. engr., Conn., 1958, Md., 1963. Engr. Toledo Shipbuilding, 1942; jr. engr. Bethlem Steel, Quincy, Mass., 1944—46; engr. Rocket Motors, Inc., Dover, NJ, 1950—52; engr. supr. Electric Boat Co., 1952—62; engring. mgr. Md. Drydock, Balt., 1962—67; engring. supr. Westinghouse Electric, Annapolis, 1967—73; owner R.W. Peach Engring. Assoc., Arnold, Md., 1973—90. Contbr. scientific papers. Mem. investment com. Ann Arundel Cmty. Coll., Arnold, 2005; founder, chmn., advisor, Chesapeake Sailing Yacht Symposium. Sgt. US Army, 1946—47, Korea. Recipient Bill Zimme, Univ. Mich., 2002. Mem.: Marine Tech. Soc., Am. Soc. Naval Engr., Soc. Naval Arch. and Marine Engrs. Achievements include invention of 1974, 76. Avocations: sailing, swimming.

PEACOCK, A(LVIN) WARD, textile company executive; b. Durham, NC, June 17, 1929; s. Erle Ewart and Vera Louise (Ward) P.; m. Barbara Sheppard White, July 2, 1955; children: Alvin Ward, Stephen White, Nancy Lay. BS in Commerce, U. N.C., 1950; MBA, Harvard U., 1952. Asst. to v.p. Erwin Mills, Inc., Durham, 1953-55, sec., 1957-62, sec.-treas., 1962-64; v.p. Dixie Yarns, Inc., Chattanooga, 1964-76, sr. v.p., 1976-81, Springs Industries, Fort Mill, SC, 1981-86, exec. v.p., 1986-92. Bd. dirs. Palmetto Seed Capital Corp.; regional dir. First Wachovia Corp., Charlotte, N.C., 1988-92. Trustee Holston Conf. Colls., Tenn., 1968-79, Sci. Mus. Charlotte, 1990-94; bd. dirs. Chattanooga Meml. Hosp., 1979-81, Charlotte Symphony, 1990-94, Greater Carolinas chpt. ARC, 1988-94; dir. Allied Arts Fund, 1978-81, Metrolina Food Bank, 1994-2003; mem. Chattanooga Wastewater Regulation Bd., 1978-81. 1st lt. USAF, 1955-57. Mem. Tenn. Mfrs. Assn. (chmn. bd. dirs. 1980-81), Chattanooga Mfrs. Assn. (pres. 1968-69), Am. Textile Mfrs. Inst., Univ. Club, River Hills Club, Phi Beta Kappa, Alpha Kappa Psi, Sigma Nu. Republican. Methodist. Home: 6618 Seton House Ln Charlotte NC 28277-4520

PEACOCK, ERLE EWART, JR., surgeon, lawyer, educator; b. Durham, NC, Sept. 10, 1926; s. Erle Ewart and Vera Louise (Ward) P.; m. Mary Louise Lowrey, Apr. 17, 1954; children: James Lowrey, Susan Louise, Virginia Gayle. Cert. in Medicine, U. N.C., 1947, BS, 1990, JD, 1999; MD, Harvard U., 1949. Bar: N.C. 1993. Intern, asst. resident surgery Roosevelt Hosp., NYC, 1949-51; from asst. resident gen. surgery U. N.C. Hosps., Chapel Hill, 1953-54, chief resident gen. surgery, 1954-55; resident in plastic surgery Barnes Hosp., St. Louis, 1955-56; mem. faculty dept. surgery U. N.C., Chapel Hill, 1956-69, prof. surgery, head divsn. plastic surgery, 1965-69; prof., chmn. dept. surgery U. Ariz., Tucson, 1969-77; prof. surgery Tulane U., New Orleans, 1977-82; pvt. practice surgery Chapel Hill, 1982-93; vis. prof. surgery U. Va., Charlottesville, 1988-97; clin. prof. surgery U. N.C., Chapel Hill, 1996—. Chief hand surgery Valley Forge Army Hosp., Phoenixville, Pa., 1951-53. Author: Wound Repair, 1977, 3d edit., 1982; assoc. editor: Am. Jour. Surgery, 1967—, Surgery Yearbook, 1970-89, Plastic and Reconstructive Surgery, 1972-78; asst. editor: Jour. Surg. Rsch., 1970-76. Served with U.S. Navy, 1945-46; served to capt. M.C. U.S. Army, 1951-53. Recipient Yandell medal Louisville Surg. Soc., 1972, McGraw medal Detroit Surg. Soc., 1973, Disting. Svc. award U. N.C., 1979, Jacob Markowitz award Acad. Surg. Rsch., 1993, Lifetime Achievement award Wound Healing Soc., 1994. Mem. AAAS, ACS, ABA, Womack Sur. Soc. (pres. 1979-80), Soc. U. Surgeons (treas.

1965-68), Plastic Surgery Rsch. Coun. (pres. 1966), Am. Surg. Assn., Am. Bd. Plastic Surgery (pres. 1976), Am. Bd. Gen. Surgery, Am. Assn. Plastic Surgeons (Clinician of Yr. 1985), Am. Soc. Surgery Hand, Internat. Soc. Surgeons, So. Surg. Assn., Am. Coll. Legal Medicine, Rotary, Alpha Omega Alpha. Republican. Methodist. Home and Office: 645 Rock Creek Rd Chapel Hill NC 27514-6714 Home Phone: 919-967-0347. E-mail: eepeacockmd@aol.com.

PEACOCK, LAMAR BATTS, retired physician; b. Albany, Ga., Sept. 21, 1920; s. Herbert A. and Helen Marian (LeVan) P.; m. Jane Bonner, June 7, 1947; children: Helen Lee Wade, Linda Jane Gossage, Lamar Bonner BA, Emory U., 1941; MD, Med. Coll. Ga., 1946. Diplomate: Am. Bd. Internal Medicine. Intern U. Hosp., Augusta, 1946—47, resident, 1947—48, 1948—50; fellow internal medicine U. Va. Hosp., Charlottesville, 1948—49; practice medicine specializing in internal medicine and allergy Atlanta, 1950—91. Mem. staff St. Joseph's Hosp., Crawford Long Hosp., Piedmont Hosp., Grady Meml. Hosp., Hughes Spalding Pavilion, Northside Hosp., All Atlanta, Cobb Gen. Hosp., Austell, Ga., Douglasville (Ga.) Hosp.; instr. internal medicine Ga. Bapt. Hosp., Atlanta, 1950-58, chief medicine, 1958-72; mem. faculty Emory U. Sch. Medicine, Atlanta, 1950—, asst. clin. prof. medicine, 1962—; instr. internal medicine Sch. Dentistry, 1958— Chief med. br., health svcs. Atlanta Met. Area Civil Def., 1960-63; mem. Ga. Pub. Health Assn., 1967-69, Ga. Bd. Health, 1966-72, Ga. Vocat. Rehab. Coun., 1973—; pres. trustees Med. Coll. Ga. Found., 1963 Recipient Physicians Physician award, MCG, 1984. Fellow ACP, Am. Coll. Allergy, Asthma and Immunology (nat. pres. 1972-73), Am. Acad. Allergy, Asthma and Immunology; mem. AMA, Am. Heart Assn., Ga. Heart Assn., Am. Soc. Internal Medicine, Ga. Soc. Internal Medicine, 5th Dist. Med. Soc., Ga. Thoracic Soc., Med. Assn. Atlanta (prs. 1965), Med. Assn. Ga. (1st v.p. 1966-67), Southeastern Allergy Assn. (pres. 1963-64), So. Med. Assn., Cherokee Town and Country Club Episcopalian. Home: 3120 Verdun Dr NW Atlanta GA 30305-1940 Personal E-mail: strutjbp@webtv.net.

PEACOCK, MARCUS C., federal agency administrator; b. 1960; BS, U. So. Calif.; MS, Harvard U. Registered profl. engr., DC. Line supr., indsl. engr. R.R. Donnelly & Sons, LA, 1982—84; various positions including dep. chief nat. resources br. U.S. Office Mgmt. and Budget, Office Adminstrn. and Regulatory Affairs, 1986—90; divsn. mgr. environ. policy analysis and forecasting Jellinek, Schwartz & Connolly, Inc., 1990—95; subcom. staff mem. of water resources and environ. subcom.of ho. com. on transp. and infrastructure U.S. Ho. of Reps., 1995—98, staff dir. oversight and emergency response subcom. of com. on transp. and infrastructure, 1999—2001; assoc. dir. nat. resource programs, Office Mgmt. & Budget Exec. Office of the Pres., 2001—05; dep. adminstr. EPA, 2005—. Mem.: AAAS, Inst. Indsl. Engrs. (sr.). Office: EPA Ariel Rios Fed Bldg 1200 Pennsylvania Ave NW Rm 3000 Washington DC 20460 Office Phone: 202-564-4711. Office Fax: 202-501-1450.

PEACOCK, MARILYN CLAIRE, retired primary school educator; b. Harvey, Ill., Aug. 2, 1952; d. Carmen Anthony and Helen Elaine (Welch) R. AA with high honors, Thornton C.C., 1972; BS in Edn. with high honors, Ill. State U., 1974; MEd, Nat.-Louis U., 1990. Cert. K-9, Ill. Tchr. kindergarten Primary Acad. Ctr., Markham, Ill., 1976-91, tchr. K-3, 1991—2007; ret., 2007. Ill. State scholar, 1969. Mem. Ill. Edn. Assn. (assn. rep. 1976-88), Kappa Delta Pi, Phi Theta Kappa. Republican. Avocations: music, travel. Home: 2447 Clyde St Homewood IL 60430-3103 Office: Acad Ctr 3055 W 163rd St Markham IL 60426-5626 Personal E-mail: mcrpeacock@hotmail.com.

PEACOCK, MARY WILLA, magazine editor, consultant; b. Evanston, Ill., Oct. 23, 1942; d. William Gilbert and Mary Willa (Young) P. BA, Vassar Coll., 1964. Assoc. lit. editor Harper's Bazaar mag., NYC, 1964-69; staff editor Innovation mag., NYC, 1969-70; editor in chief, co-founder Rags mag., NYC, San Francisco, 1970-71; co-founder, features editor Ms. mag., NYC, 1971-77; pub., pres. Rags mag., NYC, 1977-80; sr. editor Village Voice, NYC, 1980-85, style editor, 1985-89; editor-in-chief Model mag., NYC, 1989—, editorial cons., 1991—; fashion dir. Lear's Mag., NYC, 1992-93; dep. editor In Style Mag., 1993-94, Mirabella mag., 1994-95; pvt. practice, 1995—2002; internat. editor InStyle, 2002—06. Cons. in field. Contbr. articles to popular mags.

PEACOCK, MOLLY, poet, educator; b. June 30, 1947; d. Edward Frank and Pauline Ruth (Wright) P. BA magna cum laude, Harpur Coll., Binghamton, NY, 1969; MA with hons., Johns Hopkins U., 1977. Adminstr., lectr. in english SUNY, Binghamton, 1970-76; instr. english Friends Sem., NYC, 1981-92; poet-in-residence Bucknell U., 1993-94, Cathedral St. John the Divine, 2000—04; mem. grad. faculty Spalding U., 2001—. Author: And Live Apart, 1980, Raw Heaven, 1984, Take Heart, 1989, Original Love, 1995, Paradise, Piece by Piece, 1998, How To Read A Poem and Start A Poetry Circle, 1999, The Private I: Privacy in A Public World, 2001, Cornucopia: New and Selected Poems, 2002, The Shimmering Verge: A One-Woman Show in Poems, 2003; contbg. writer House and Garden mag., 1996-2001; contbr. poems to The New Yorker, The New Republic, The Nation, articles to O, the Oprah Mag., Elle, N.Y. Mag. Named Tennessee Williams Playwright in Residence, Sewanee U., 2006, Elliston poet U. Cin., 2006; Danforth Found. fellow, 1970, Yaddo fellow, 1980, 82, 89, Ingram Merrill Found. fellow 1981, 86, Lila Wallace/Woodrow Wilson fellow 1994, 95, 96, 2001; grantee Creative Artists Pub. Svc. Program, 1977, N.Y. Found. for Arts, 1985, NEA, 1991; Regents scholar U. Calif., Riverside, 1998. Mem. PEN, Poetry Soc. Am. (governing bd. 1988—, pres. emeritus). Home: 109 Front St E #1041 Toronto ON M5A 4P7 Canada Office Phone: 212-677-3535. Personal E-mail: molly@mollypeacock.org.

PEACOCK, PENNE KORTH, ambassador; b. Hattiesburg, Miss., Nov. 3, 1942; m. Fritz-Alan Korth, Dec. 15, 1965 (div. 1997); children: Fritz-Alan Jr., Maria Korth Chieffalo, James Frederick; m. Andrew Peacock, Sept. 21, 2002. Student, U. Tex., 1960—64. Sr. Washington assoc., client liaison and rep. trust and estate div. Sotheby's, 1986-89; amb. to Mauritius, Port Louis, 1989-92; pres. Firestone and Korth Ltd., Washington, 1993-97; commr. US Adv. Commn. Pub. Diplomacy, 1997—. Bd. dir. Chevy Chase Bank, 1993—; rep. Sotheby's Internat., 1997—; adv. com. Sydney (Australia) Cancer Ctr., 2003—. Sr. advisor Ptnrs. in Performance Internat., 2005—; co-chmn. Am. Bicentennial Presdl. Inauguration, Washington, 1988—99; mem. adv. bd. Washington Ballet, 2002—; mem. adv. com. Sydney Cancer Ctr.; bd. dirs. Hillwood Mus. and Gardens; counselor Meridian Internat. Ctr.; bd. dirs. Coun. of Am. Ambs., 1994—. Mem.: Assn. for Diplomatic Studies and Tng. (bd. dir. 1996—2002). Office: 11 Gladswood Gardens Double Bay 2028 NSW Australia

PEACOCK, S. WAYNE, insurance company executive; BA in Econs., U. New Orleans, 1981. Cert. comml. investment mgr. With Merrill Lynch, Coldwell Banker, USAA (United Svcs. Automobile Assn.), San Antonio, 1992—, v.p. portfolio mgmt., sr. v.p. corp. real estate, 2001, exec. v.p. enterprise bus. ops. Bd. mem. CoreNet Global. Mem. editl. adv. bd.: Jour. Facilities Mgmt. Office: USAA 9800 Fredericksburg Rd San Antonio TX 78288 Office Phone: 210-498-5384. E-mail: wayne.peacock@usaa.com. *

PEACOCK, SCOTT, chef; Founding chef Horseradish Grill, Atlanta; exec. chef Watershed Restaurant, Decatur, Ga. Featured in Newsweek, NY Times, Wine Spectator, Bon Appetit, Food & Wine Mag., USA Today, Atlanta Mag., Gourmet Mag., Cooking Light, Southern Living; author: The Gift of Southern Cooking: Recipes and Revelations from two Southern Chefs. Named Best Chef: Southeast, James Beard Found., 2007. Office: Watershed Restaurant 406 West Ponce De Leon Ave Decatur GA 30030 Office Phone: 404-378-4900. *

PEAKE, RYAN, musician; b. Can., Mar. 1, 1973; m. Treanna Peake; children: Dax, Adair. Lead guitarist Nickelback, 1995—; signed to Roadrunner Records, NYC. Musician: (albums) Curb, 1996, The State, 2000, Silver Side Up, 2001 (Juno award for Best Album, 2002), The Long Road, 2003, All the Right Reasons, 2005 (Juno award for Best Rock Album, 2006, Favorite Rock Album, Am. Music Awards, 2006, Billboard Rock Album of Yr., 2006), (songs) How Your Remind Me (Juno award for Best Single, 2002, Billboard Top 100 Single & Track, Top Hot 40 Track, Top Hot 100 Airplay Track, 2002). Named Top Hot 100 Singles Artist, Billboard, 2002, Favorite Group, People's Choice Awards, 2007; recipient Best New Group award, Juno Awards, 2001, Best Group award, 2002, 2006, Songwriters of Yr. award, 2003, Group of Yr., Billboard Music Awards, 2006, Hot 100 Group of Yr., 2006, World's Best Rock Group, World Music Awards, 2007, Best-Selling Canadian Artist, 2007. Office: c/o Bryan Coleman Union Entertainment Group 1323 Newbury Rd Ste 104 Thousand Oaks CA 91320 also: c/o Ron Burman Roadrunner Records 902 Broadway New York NY 10010 *

PEALE, RUTH STAFFORD (MRS. NORMAN VINCENT PEALE), not-for-profit executive; b. Fonda, Iowa, Sept. 10, 1906; d. Frank Burton and Anna Loretta (Crosby) Stafford; m. Norman Vincent Peale, June 20, 1930; children: Margaret Ann (Mrs. Paul F. Everett), John Stafford, Elizabeth Ruth (Mrs. John M. Allen). AB, Syracuse U., 1928, LLD, 1953; LittD, Hope Coll., 1962; LHD (hon.), Judson Coll., 1988. Tchr. math. Cen. High Sch., Syracuse, NY, 1928—30; nat. pres. women's bd. domestic missions Ref. Ch. Am., 1936-46; sec. Protestant Film Commn., 1946-51; chmn. Am. Mother's Com., 1948-49; pres., editor-in-chief, gen. sec., CEO, chmn. bd. trustees, chmn. emeritus Guideposts Peale Ctr. Christian Living, 1940—; nat. pres. bd. domestic missions Ref. Ch. in Am., 1955-56; mem. bd. N. Am. Missions, 1963-69, pres., 1967-69; mem. gen. program coun. Ref. Ch. in Am., 1968—; mem. com. of 24 for merger Ref. Ch. in Am. and Presbyn. Ch. U.S., 1966-69; v.p. Protestant Council NYC, NYC, 1964-66; co-founder, pub. Guideposts, NYC, 1945—, pres., 1985-92, chmn. bd., 1999—2003, chmn. emeritus, 2003—; pres. Fleming H. Revell, Tarrytown, NY, 1985-92. Appeared on: (nat. TV program) What's Your Trouble, 1952—68; author: I Married a Minister, 1942, The Adventure of Being a Wife, 1971, Secrets of Staying in Love, 1984, A Lifetime of Positive Thinking, 2001; founder, pub. (with Dr. Peale) Guidepost mag., 1945—, co-subject with husband (film) One Man's Way, 1963. Named N.Y. State Mother of Yr., 1963, Disting. Woman of Yr., Nat. Art Assn., Religious Heritage Am. Ch. Woman of Yr., 1969, Woman of Yr., AAUW, 2000; recipient Cum Laude award Syracuse U. Alumni Assn. N.Y., 1965, Honor Iowans award Buena Vista Coll., 1966, Am. Mother's com. award for religion, 1970, Disting. Svc. award Coun. Chs., N.Y.C., 1973, Disting. Citizen award Champlain Coll., 1976, Disting. Svc. to Cmty. and Nation award Gen. Fedn. Women's Clubs, 1977, Horatio Alger award, 1977, Religious Heritage award, 1979, joint medallion with husband Soc. for Family of Man, 1981, Soc. Family of Man award, 1981, Alderson-Broaddus award, 1982, Marriage Achievement award Bride's mag., 1984, Gold Angel award Religion in Media, 1987, Adela Rogers St. John Roundtable award, 1987, Disting. Achievement award Am. Aging, 1987, Paul Harris award N.Y. Rotary, 1989, Leader's award Arthritis Found. Dutchess County, 1992, Dave Thomas Well Done! award, 1994, Norman Vincent Peale award for positive thinking, 1994, Master of Influence award, 1995, The Leadership award Worldwide Leadership Coun., 1998, Cert. for Disting. Svc., N.Y. State Fedn. Women's Clubs, 1999, Light award CANDL Found., 2000, Woman of Distinction awd RCA Women, 2001. Mem. Blanton-Peale Inst. (bd. exec. com.), Am. Bible Soc. (trustee 1948-93, hon. trustee 1993—, bd. dirs.), Nat. Bible Assn. (bd. dirs.), United Bible Soc., Interch. Ctr. (bd. dirs. 1957-92, chmn. 1982-90), Nat. Coun. Chs. (v.p. 1952-54, gen. bd.; treas. gen. dept. United Ch. Women, vice chmn. broadcasting and film commn. 1951-55, program chmn. gen. assembly 1966), N.Y. Fedn. Women's Clubs (chmn. religion 1951-53, 57-58), Home Missions Coun. N.A. (nat. pres. 1942-44, nat. chmn. migrant com. 1948-51), Internat. Platform Orgn. (bd. govs. 1994-2000), Cmty. Action Network (adv. bd. 1998—), Wainwright House (hon. trustee, advisor 2001), PEO, Sorosis (pres. 1953-56, hon. pres.), Alpha Phi (Frances W. Willard award 1976). Republican. Office: Guideposts 66 E Main St Pawling NY 12564-1409 Office Phone: 845-855-5000. Business E-Mail: rpeale@guideposts.org.

PEALE, STANTON JERROLD, physics educator; b. Indpls., Jan. 23, 1937; s. Robert Frederick and Edith May (Murphy) P.; m. Priscilla Laing Cobb; June 25, 1960; children: Robert Edwin, Douglas Andrew. BSE, Purdue U., 1959; MS in Engring. Physics, Cornell U., 1962, PhD in Engring. Physics, 1965. Research asst. Cornell U., Ithaca, N.Y., 1962-64, research assoc., 1964-65; asst. research geophysicist, asst. prof. astronomy UCLA, 1965-68; asst. prof. physics U. Calif., Santa Barbara, 1968-70, assoc. prof., 1970-76, prof., 1976-94, prof. emeritus, rsch. prof., 1994—. Mem. com. lunar and planetary exploration NAS-NRC, Washington, 1980-84, lunar and planetary geosci. rev. panel, 1979-80, 86-89, 94-96, Planetary Sys. Sci. Working Group, 1988-93, Lunar and Planetary Sci. Coun., 1984-87, mem. com. astronomy and astrophysics, 1997—; lunar sci. adv. group NASA-JPL, Pasadena, Calif., 1970-72; mem. Keck time allocation com. NASA, 1996-98. Assoc. editor: Jour. Geophys. Research, 1987; contbr. articles to profl. jours. Recipient Exceptional Scientific Achievement medal NASA, 1980, James Craig Watson award Nat. Acad. Scis., 1982; vis. fellowships U. Colo., Boulder, 1972-73, 1979-80. Fellow AAAS (Newcomb Cleveland prize 1979), Am. Geophys. Union; mem. Am. Astron. Soc. (divsns. planet sci. and dynamic astronomy, Dirk Brouwer award 1992, chair dynamical astronomy 1999-2000), Internat. Astron. Union. Avocation: gardening. Office: U Calif Santa Barbara Dept Physics Santa Barbara CA 93106

PEAPPLES, GEORGE ALAN, retired automotive executive; b. Benton Harbor, Mich., Nov. 6, 1940; s. Arthur L. and Kathleen C. (Peters) Peapples; m. Rebecca Dean Sowers, June 27, 1962; children: Lucia Christine, Sarah Bouton. BA in Econs., U. Mich., 1962, MBA in Fin., 1963. Fin. analyst GM Corp., Detroit, 1964-68, fin. analyst treas. office NYC, 1968—72, dir. capital analysis and investment, 1972—73, asst. divsn. comptr. Delco Moraine divsn. Dayton, Ohio, 1973-75, asst. treas. bank rels. Detroit, 1975-77, asst. comptr., 1980-82; v.p., fin. mgr. GM Can. Ltd., Oshawa, Ont., 1982-84; group dir. strategic bus. planning Chevrolet-Pontiac-Can. group GM Corp., Warren, Mich., 1984-86; v.p. GM Corp., pres., gen. mgr. GM Can. Ltd., Oshawa, 1986-94; v.p. pub. policy GM Corp., Washington, 1994-99; ret., 2000; asst. sec. of Navy US Dept. Def., 1977-80. Bd. dirs. The Ark. Recipient Disting. Pub. Svc. award, Washington, 1980. Personal E-mail: gapeapples@aol.com.

PEAR, CHARLES E., JR., lawyer; b. Macon, Ga., June 18, 1950; s. Charles Edward and Barbara Jane P.; children: Jennifer Sue, Charles Edward III, Stephanie Sue. BA, U. Hawaii, 1972; JD, U. Calif., Berkeley, 1975. Bar: Hawaii 1976, Fla. 1977, Colo. 1994, U.S. Ct. of Appeals (9th cir.). Assoc. Rush, Moore, Craven, Sutton, Morry & Beh, Honolulu, 1976-77, of counsel, 1987-90; assoc., ptnr. Carlsmith & Dwyer, Honolulu, 1977-82; ptnr. Burke, Sakai, McPheeters, Bordner & Gilardy, Honolulu, 1983-87; vis. prof. law and computers U. British Columbia, 1990-93; of counsel Holland & Hart, Denver, 1993-96; counsel, ptnr. McCorriston, Miller, Mukai, MacKinnon, Honolulu, 1996—. Mem. Hawaii Real Estate Commn. com. on condominium and resort real estate legis., 1978-79; spl. counsel to consumer protection com. Hawaii State Ho. of Reps., 1981-82; chair real property and fin. svcs. sect. Hawaii State Bar Assn., ABA; lectr. in field. Editor-in-Chief Hawaii Conveyance Manual II, 1987; editor Hawaii Commercial Real Estate Manual, 1988; bd. editors Hawaii Inst. of Continuing Legal Edn.; co-author: Nat. Assn. of Real Estate Licensing Law Officials and Nat. Timesharing Coun. Model Timesharing Act, 1981-82; contbr. chpts. to books. Named one of Ams. Leading Bus. Lawyers, Chambers USA, 2004—07, Best Lawyers in Am., 2005—07. Mem. ABA.

PEARCE, ALAN S., lawyer; BS, Lehigh U., 1963; LLB, NYU, 1966. Bar: NY 1966. Ptnr. Bryan Cave LLP, NYC, mem. operating group, 2002—05. With IRS, US Treasury Dept., 1966—67. Mem.: ABA (com. on Partnerships & Unincorporated Bus. Orgns. 1977—), NY State Bar Assn., Assn. of the Bar of the City of New York. Office: Bryan Cave LLP 1290 Ave of the Americas New York NY 10104 Office Phone: 212-541-2111. Office Fax: 212-541-1411. E-mail: aspearce@bryancave.com.

PEARCE, CAROLE ANN, poet; d. Franklin Richard Markham and Mary Priscilla Jensen; m. Ronald Kent Chirrick, July 12, 1958 (div. 1964); children: Kenneth Scott Chirrick, Ronda Lee Buhler; m. Edwin Garth Pearce, Nov. 26, 1966; 1 child, Edwin Ryan. Degree in bus., Salt Lake Trade Tech. Coll., 1965; AS, Salt Lake C.C., 1998. Lic. real estate assoc. Utah. Real estate assoc. Utah Dept. Bus. Regulation, Salt Lake City, 1976—80. Writer, editor fed. women's coord. U.S. Geol. Survey, Salt Lake City, 1989—94, equal employment opportunities officer, 1993. Contbr. poetry to Great Poems of the Western World, 1990, The Fountain of Peace, 2000, Nature's Gentle Kiss, 2003. Mem.: Dixie Newcomers of St. George (corr.), Acad. Am. Poets, Internat. Soc. Poetry (corr. Poet of Merit 2000, 2002, 2003, 2004). Avocations: swimming, dance, reading. Home and Office: 1831 Lazy River Dr Saint George UT 84790-4420 E-mail: lazypearce@aol.com.

PEARCE, DONALD JOSLIN, retired librarian; b. Southampton, Eng., May 31, 1924; came to US, 1949, naturalized, 1952; s. Alfred Ernest and Constance May (Jeffrey) P.; m. June Inez Bond, Dec. 7, 1946; children: Kristin, Kim. Student, Sch. Oriental and African Studies, U. London, 1942-43; AB, George Washington U., 1953; MS in L.S, Cath. U. Am., 1954. Part-time libr. asst. U.S. Dept. Agr., 1949-54; student asst. George Washington U. Libr., 1950-53; circulation libr. Denison U., 1954-56; staff Ohio State U. Libr., 1956-59, asst. acquisition libr., 1958-59; head libr., asst. prof. U. ND, 1959-69, chief bibliographer, 1969-73, asst. dir. libraries, 1973-75, asst. prof. Oriental philosophy, 1969-75; libr. dir., asst. prof. philosophy U. Minn., Duluth, 1975-88, ret., 1988. Chmn. staff orgn. round table Ohio Libr. Assn., 1958-59 Served with Brit. Army, 1943-47. Mem. ALA, ND Libr. Assn. (pres. 1965-67), Minn. Libr. Assn. (sec. 1978-80, v.p. 1985, pres. 1986), Assn. Coll. Reference Librarians, Mountain Plains Libr. Assn. (v.p. 1968-69), Buddhist Assn., Phi Beta Kappa, Beta Phi Mu. Home: 70 E St Marie St Apt 127 Duluth MN 55803 Personal E-mail: dpearce2310@inbox.com.

PEARCE, DRUE, federal official, former state legislator; b. Fairfield, Ill., Apr. 2, 1951; d. H. Phil and Julia Detroy (Bannister) P.; m. Michael F.G. Williams; 1 child, Tate Hanna Pearce-Williams. BA in Biol. Scis., Ind. U., 1973; MPA, Harvard U., 1984; cert. exec. program Darden Sch. Bus., U. Va., 1989. Sch. tchr., Clark County, Ind., 1973-74; curator of edn. Louisville Zoo, 1974—76; dir. Summerscene, Louisville, 1976—77; asst. v.p., br. mgr. Alaska Nat. Bank of the North, 1977-82; legis. aide to Rep. John Ringstad Alaska Ho. of Reps., Juneau, 1983, mem., 1984-88, minority whip, 1987—88; mem. Alaska Senate, 1989—2001, chmn. com. oil and gas, mem. exec. com. energy coun., 1989-90, chmn. com. labor and commerce, mem. exec. coms. western state conf., coun. state govts., energy coun., 1991-92, co-chmn. senate fin., chmn. energy coun., vice chmn. com. energy, nat. coun. state govts., 1993-94, mem. select com. legis. ethics and legis. coun., pres. senate, mem. exec. com. energy coun., vice chmn. senate coms. resources and rules, 1995-96, co-chmn. com. senate fin., mem. exec. com. energy coun., vice chmn. com. senate judiciary, 1997—98; sr. adv. to sec. for Alaska affairs US Dept. Interior, 2001—; fed. coord. for Alaskan Natural Gas Transp. Projects Fed. Energy Regulatory Commn., 2006—. Senate pres., 1995-96, 1999-2000, senate rules chmn., 2001; ptnr. Cloverland N., Anchorage, 1993—; resources cons. Arctic Slope Regional Corp., Anchorage, 1987-91, 95-96; sr. adv. Sec. Interior for Alaska Affairs, 2001-. Former bd. dirs. Alaska Women's Aid in Crisis, Anchorage Econ. Devel. Coun., Alaska Aerospace Devel. Corp., Alaska Spl. Olympics, Gov.'s Bd. Mem. DAR, Commonwealth North, Resource Devel. Coun., Alaska Miners Assn., Alaska Fedn. Rep. Women, Aircraft Owners & Pilots Assn., U.S. Trotting Assn. Republican. Office: Office of the Secretary Dept of the Interior 1849 C St NW MS 6020 Washington DC 20240

PEARCE, ELIZABETH NIEWOEHNER, endocrinologist, researcher; arrived in U.S., 1968; d. Dennis Erwin and Catherine Beattie Niewoehner; m. Richard A. Pearce, May 24, 1997; children: Alexander, Ian. BA, Harvard U., Cambridge, Mass., 1990; student, Bryn Mawr Coll., 1991—92; MD, Harvard U., 1997; MSc in Epidemiology, Boston U., Mass., 2004. Diplomate internal medicine, endocrinology, diabetes and metabolism. Intern internal medicine Beth Israel Deaconess Med. Ctr., Boston, 1997—98, resident internal medicine, 1998—2000; from fellow in endocrinology to asst. prof. medicine Med. Ctr. Boston (Mass.) U., 2000—04, asst. prof. medicine Med. Ctr., 2004—. Contbr. chapters to books, articles to profl. jours. Recipient K-23 Mentored Career award, NIH, 2003; grantee Pfizer Scholars in Endocrine, 2002. Mem.: Mass. Med. Soc., Am. Thyroid Assn., Endocrine Soc. Avocation: singing. Office: Boston Med Ctr Evans 201 88 E Newton St Boston MA 02118 Office Phone: 617-414-1348. Business E-Mail: elizabeth.pearce@bmc.org.

PEARCE, HARRY JONATHAN, lawyer, manufacturing executive; b. Bismarck, ND, Aug. 20, 1942; s. William R. and Jean Katherine (Murray) P.; m. Katherine B. Bruk, June 19, 1967; children: Shannon Pearce Baker, Susan J., Harry M. BS, USAF Acad., Colorado Springs, Colo., 1964; JD, Northwestern U., 1967; Degree in Engring. (hon.), Rose-Hulman Inst. Tech., 1997; LLD (hon.), Northwestern U., 1998. Bar: N.D. 1967, Mich. 1986. Mcpl. judge City of Bismarck, 1970-76, U.S. magistrate, 1970-76, police commr., 1976-80; sr. ptnr. Pearce & Durick, Bismarck, 1970-85; assoc. gen. counsel GM, Detroit, 1985-87, v.p., gen. counsel, 1987-92, exec. v.p., gen. counsel, 1992-94, exec. v.p., 1994-95, vice chmn., 1996—2001; chmn. Hughes Electronics, El Segundo, Calif., 2001—03; non exec. chmn. Nortel Networks Corp., Brampton, Ont., 2005—. Bd. dirs. GM Corp., Hughes Electronics Corp., GM Acceptance Corp., Delphi Automotive Sys. Corp., Alliance of Automobile Mfrs. of Am., Marriott Internat. Inc., Nortel Networks Corp., Econ. Strategy Inst., Theodore Roosevelt Medora Found., MDU Resources Group, Inc., Nat. Def. U. Found., Detroit Investment Fund. Mem. law bd. Sch. Law, Northwestern U.; mem. bd. visitors U.S. Air Force Acad.; chmn. Product Liability Adv. Coun. Found.; founding mem. minority counsel demonstration program Commn. on Opportunities for Minorities in the Profession, ABA; chmn. The Sabre Soc., USAF Acad.; trustee Howard U., U.S. Coun. for Internat. Bus., New Detroit, Inc.; mem. The Mentor's Group Forum for U.S.-European Union Legal-Econ. Affairs, The Conf. Bd., Network of Employers for Traffic Safety's Leadership Coun., Pres.'s Coun. on Sustainable Devel., World Bus. Coun. for Sustainable Devel., World Economic Forum Coun. Innovative Leaders in Globalization. Capt. USAF, 1964-70. Named Michiganian of Yr., The Detroit News, 1997; Hardy scholar Northwestern U., Chgo., 1964-67, recipient Alumni Merit award, 1991. Fellow Am. Coll. Trial Lawyers, Internat. Soc. Barristers; mem. Am. Law Inst. Avocations: amateur radio, woodworking, sailing. Office: Bowman and Brooke LLP 50 W Big Beaver Rd Ste 600 Troy MI 48084

PEARCE, JODY ANN, mathematics educator; b. Wynne, Ark., Nov. 26, 1955; d. Nathan Edward and Mary Mae Williams; m. Billy Burdette Pearce, May 7, 1976; children: Stevey Kathleen, Eric Jason, Kelly Nicole. BS in Elem. Edn., Tex. A&M U., Texarkana, 1984; MEd, Harding U., Searcy, Ark., 2005. 4th grade tchr. De Queen Pub. Schs., Ark., 1985—99; elem. math. specialist De Queen-Mena Ednl. Coop., Gillham, Ark., 1999—. Team capt. Race for Cure, Texarkana, 2002—05; com. chair Relay for Life, De Queen, 2006—07. Mem.: ACTM, NCSM, NCTM. Meth. Avocations: singing, travel.

PEARCE, JOHN Y., lawyer; b. New Orleans, Mar. 26, 1948; s. John Young, II and Marina (Harris) Pearce; m. Marjorie Pamela Doyle, May 22, 1971 (div.); children: Andrea Elizabeth, Roger Wellington; m. Julia Evans Reed, May 10, 2003. BA, La. State U., 1973, JD, 1976. Bar: La. 1977, US Dist. Ct. (ea., mid. and we. dists.) La., US Ct. Claims, US Ct. Appeals (5th and 11th cirs.), US Supreme Ct. 2003. Assoc. Doyle, Smith & Doyle, New Orleans, 1977-79, ptnr., 1979-80, mng. ptnr., 1980-84; ptnr. Montgomery, Barnett, New Orleans, 1984—2003, mng. ptnr., 2003—. Pres. New Orleans Legal Assistance Corp., 1999—2002, S.E. La. Legal Svcs. Corp., 2002—04. Bd. dir. Children's Hosp., New Orleans, 1993—, chmn., 2006—. Sgt. US Army, 1969—71. Mem.: ABA (ho. of dels. 1998—2003), New Orleans Bar Assn. (pres. 1997—98, exec. com.), La. Bar Assn. (chmn. mineral law sect. 1994—95). Republican. Presbyterian. Office: Montgomery Barnett 3300 Energy Ctr New Orleans LA 70163 Office Phone: 504-585-3200. Business E-Mail: jpearce@monbar.com.

PEARCE, PAUL FRANCIS, retired electronics executive, aerospace engineer; b. Boston, Sept. 17, 1928; s. George Hamilton and Marie Louise (Duval) P.; m. Gilda Troisi, Apr. 11, 1953; children: Janet, Theresa, Diane. BSEE (Edwards scholar), MIT, 1950; MS, Mass. Inst. Tech., LA, 1952; postgrad. (Hughes fellow), U. Calif., Los Angeles, 1957-58, U. So., Calif., 1958-59, Inst. Mgmt. Northwestern U., 1966. Project engr. Trans-Sonics, Inc., Burlington, Mass., 1952-55; sect. head application engring., strategic systems Hughes Aircraft Co., Culver City, Calif., 1955-59; with Lockheed Electronics Co., Plainfield, NJ, 1959-67, gen. mgr. div. mil. systems, 1964-65, v.p., gen. mgr., 1965-67; v.p., div. mgr. Tele-Dynamics div. AMBAC Industries, Inc., Ft. Washington, Pa, 1967-74; group v.p. comml. and aerospace electronics group AMBAC Industries, Inc., Carle Place, NY, 1973-80; pres. James G. Biddle Co., Blue Bell, Pa., 1980-93, ret. Bd. dirs. AVO Internat. Ltd., 1987-91. Mem. Armed Forces Communications and Electronics Assn. (pres. 1969-71), Inst. Nav., Delaware Valley Mfrs. Assn. (sr. vice chmn. 1987-89, chmn. 1990-92—), Greater Phila. C. of C., Ft. Washington Indsl. Park Mgmt. Assn. (gov. 1973-74), Sigma Xi. Clubs: Mfrs'. Golf and Country (Oreland, Pa.) (handicap chmn. 1987-90), St. David's Golf Club (Wayne, Pa.). E-mail: pfpearce@att.net.

PEARCE, RICHARD LEE, lawyer; b. Racine, Wis., Apr. 11, 1959; s. John Wallace and Betty Jane Pearce; m. Cynthia Davis, June 11, 1983; 1 child, Melissa Lauren. BS in Chemistry, U. S.C., 1981, JD, 1984. Bar: S.C. 1984, U.S. Dist. Ct. S.C. 1985, U.S. Ct. Appeals (4th cir.) 1985. Law clk. to resident cir. judge Edward B. Cottingham, 1984-85; assoc. Fox, Zier, Burkhalter & Verenes, Aiken, S.C., 1985-86; ptnr. Toole & Toole, Aiken, 1986-96; asst. pub. svcs. dir., legis. liaison S.C. Bar, 1996-98; city solicitor, staff atty. City of Aiken, 1998—. Instr. Am. Banking Inst., Nat. Advocacy Ctr., Nat. Dist. Attys. Assn.; guest lectr., adj. instr. U. SC, Aiken, pro bono divsn. law sch. non lawyers, IMLA program; legal advisor Bd. Zoning Appeals, Design Rev. Bd., Neighborhoods Com., Tourism Bd., Arts Commn., City Dept. Dirs., Bldg. Code Bd. Appeals, Pks. Commn.; coord. Aiken Youth Ct.; organizer Aiken Livability Ct.; bd. dirs. Leadership Aiken County Class of 2003, 03-06, Hitchcock Health Svcs., 2004-05; adv. bd. Soc. Prevention of Cruelty to Aminals, 2000-01; mem. spl. commn. on domestic violence, SC Atty. Gen.; mem. US Dept. Justice Operation Cease Fire. Contbr. columns in newspapers The Aiken Standard, South Carolina Bar News, The State, Le Rotarien, articles to profl. pubs., newspapers, magazines. Emcee Sch. Bd. Acad. Tournament, Aiken, 1986; bd. dirs. Tri-Devel. Ctr., Aiken, 1985—86; spl. events com. Downtown Aiken Devel. Corp.; fundraising com. Am. Cancer Soc., 1985—2000, Am Heart Assn., 2000—01; legal advisor Children's Place, Inc.; judge mock trial h.s. competition, 1991—96; trustee Aiken, Barnwell, Bamberg and Edgefield Libr. Sys.; organizer, coord. Llandrindod Wales exch. program Aiken H.S.; active Ptnrs. in Friendship, Sister Cities, Orvieto, Italy and Schoalhaven, Australia, Mex./SC Govt. Study Exch. Seminars, Internat. Youth Exch., Groundhog Day Job Shadowing, Tech-Prep Career Advisor. Mem.: SC Mcpl. Attys. Assn. (v.p. 2007), SC Solicitors Assn., Nat. Coll. Dist. Attys., Nat. Dist. Attys. Assn., Internat. Mcpl. Lawyers Assn., Aiken C. of C. (legal liaison 1986), Aiken County Bar Assn. (pres. 1990—92), SC Bar Assn. (ho. of dels. 1989—95, pro bono program 1989—97, resolution of fee disputes bd., lawyers' fund for client protection, task force on justice for all, ethics adv. com., unauthorized practice law com., co-editor Legis. Update, editor Ethics Adv. Opinion summaries, coord. annual jud. evaluation, sec. chmn. govt. law sect. 2007—), Leadership Aiken County (disting. grad. 2003, bd. dirs. 2003—06), Hitchcock Woods Axe Club, Rotary Internat. (pres.-elect 1994—95, bd. dirs. 1994—96, pres. 1995—96, team leader group study exch. with France 2006, group study exch. coord., various offices exchange programs, active numerous projects, chmn. internat. group study exch. hosting teams, Paul Harris fellow, Sustaining Paul Harris fellow), Omicron Delta Kappa. Presbyterian (vice-chair bd. deacons 1999-2000, chair 2001-02). Avocations: antique phonographs/records, grilling and barbecuing, outdoor activities, historical research, bicycling. Office: City of Aiken PO Box 1177 Aiken SC 29802-1177 Home Phone: 803-642-0636; Office Phone: 803-642-7658. Business E-Mail: rpearce@aiken.net.

PEARCE, RONALD, retired cosmetic company executive; b. Apr. 29, 1920; s. Fernley Charles and Medora Kate (Lissenden) P.; m. Olive Stacey, Apr. 4, 1942; children: David Fernley, Jane Ryding Robertson. Cambridge matriculation, Lindisfarne Coll., Ruabon, North Wales, UK, 1937. Chief cashier Westminster Bank, Croydon, Eng., 1947-48; comml. officer Brit. Consulate, Dallas, 1949-52; v.p. World Gift Co., Dallas, 1953-63, Nelson Electronics, Dallas, 1963-68; stockbroker Walston & Co., Dallas, 1968-73; dir. purchasing Mary Kay Cosmetics, Inc., Dallas, 1973-85; pres. Global Water Techs., Inc., 1992-95; chmn. bd. Alpha Aqua, 1996—, Concha Holdings LTD, 2002—. Chmn. bd. Dallas Lighthouse for the Blind, 1987. Flight lt. RAF, 1940-46. Republican. Episcopalian. Home: 5455 La Sierra Dr Apt 1014 Dallas TX 75231 Office Phone: 214-363-9064.

PEARCE, STEVE (STEVAN E. PEARCE), congressman; b. Lamesa, Tex., Aug. 24, 1947; m. Cynthia Pearce. BBA in Econs., N.Mex. State U., Las Cruces, 1970; MBA, Ea. N.Mex. U., Portales, 1991. Owner-operator crop dusting flying svc., Blytheville, Ark., 1975—78; chief pilot, check pilot Marshall Aviation, 1978—81; chief pilot RUNCO, Inc.; co-owner, operator Lea Fishing Tools, Inc., 1989—2002; mem. N.Mex. State Ho. Reps., 1997—2000, chmn. Rep. Caucus; mem. US Congress from 2nd N.Mex. dist., 2003—. Mem. fin. svcs. com. US Congress, dep. ranking mem. subcommittee on housing and cmty. opportunity, mem. natural resources com., ranking mem. subcommittee on energy and mineral resources, asst. Rep. whip. Pilot USAF, 1970—76, Philippines. Decorated DFC, Air medal; co-recipient VIVA award, Assn. Commerce and Industry, 2001; named Outstanding Legislator, N.Mex. Tech. Showcase. Republican. Baptist. Office: US House Reps 1607 Longworth House Office Bldg Washington DC 20515-3102 Office Phone: 202-225-2365. *

PEARCE-MOSES, RICHARD, librarian; B in Journalism, with honors, U. Tex., Austin, 1976; MA, U. Tex., 1987; MLIS, U. Ill., Urbana-Champaign, 2001. Asst. to curator U. Tex. at Austin Harry Ransom Humanities Rsch. Ctr., 1981—84; hist. photography project coord. Tex. Hist. Found., 1984—87, asst. editor Heritage mag., 1984—87; records cons. Tex. State Libr. & Archives, 1987—88; photographs curator Dept. Archives & Manuscripts, Ariz. State U. Librs., 1988—92, assoc. archivist, 1992—94; documentary collections archivist & automation coord. Heard Mus., Phoenix, 1993—99; coord. cultural inventory project Ariz. State Libr., Archives & Pub. Records, 1999—2001, dir. digital govt. info., 2001—. Adv. com. Electronic Records Archives, Nat. Archives & Records Adminstrn.; mem. InterPARES 2 Glossary Cross-Domain Team, 2003—; researcher U. Ill. & Online Computer Libr. Ctr. ECHO DEPository rsch. project, 2004—. Recipient Leadership award, U. Ill. Urbana-Champaign Libr. Sch. Alumni Assn., 2006, Frederick G. Kilgour award, Online Computer Libr. Ctr./Libr. & Info. Tech. Assn., 2007; fellow Archival Rsch. fellow, Nat. Hist. Pubs. & Records Adminstrn., 2002—03. Mem.: Soc. Am. Archivists (mem. coun. 1999—2002, v.p./pres. elect 2004—05, pres. 2005—06), Acad. Certified Archivists (fellow 2005), Beta Phi Mu. Office Phone: 602-542-4035. E-mail: rpm@lib.az.us.

PEARL, JUDEA, computer scientist, educator; b. Tel-Aviv, Sept. 4, 1936; U.S. citizen; m. Ruth Pearl; 3 children. BSc, Israel Inst. Tech., 1960; MSc, Newark Coll. Engring., 1961; PhD in Elec. Engring., Poly. Inst. Bklyn., 1965. Rsch. engr. Dental Sch., NYU, 1960-61; mem. tech. staff RCA Rsch. Labs., 1961-65; dir. advanced memory devices Electronic Memories, Inc., Calif., 1966-69; prof. Sch. of Engring./Dept. Computer Scis. UCLA, 1969—; co-founder, pres. Daniel Pearl Found., 2002—. Instr. Newark Coll. Engring., 1961; cons. Rand Corp., 1972, Integrated Sci. Corp., 1975, Hughes Aircraft, 1989. Author: Heuristics, 1984, Probabilistic Reasoning in Intelligent Systems, 1988, Casuality: Models, Reasoning, Inference, 2000. Recipient: Outstanding Achievement award RCA Labs., 1965, Rsch. Excellence award, IJCAI, 1999; co-recipient: Purpose prize, Civic Ventures, 2006. Fellow IEEE, ACM, Am. Assn. Artificial Intelligence (Classical Paper award 2000, Lakatos award 2001), Acad. Engring. (Allen Newell award, 2003), Nat. Acad. Engring; corr. mem. Spanish Acad. Engring. Office: UCLA Dept Computer Sci 4532 Boelter Hl Los Angeles CA 90095-0001

PEARL, LAURENCE DICKSON, retired federal government executive; b. Phila., Mar. 2, 1934; s. Simon and Dorothy (Lichtig) P.; m. Ruth Switzer, Dec. 22, 1959 (div. Apr. 1972); children: Natasha, Lisa Talbott, Thomas Simon; m. Anne Womeldorf, Dec. 20, 1972. AB, Antioch Coll., 1955; postgrad., Harvard U., 1955-56; LLB, Yale U., 1959. Bar: D.C. 1959, U.S. Supreme Ct. 1983. Assoc. Trammell, Rand & Nathan, Washington, 1960-61; rsch. assoc. George Washington U., Washington, 1961; atty., advisor HUD, Washington, 1961-67, exec. asst. to gen. counsel, 1967-69, spl. asst. to asst. sec. for equal opportunity, 1969-72, dir. program standards and data analysis, 1972-74, dir. program compliance, 1974-86, dir. program standards and evaluation, 1986-98; ret., 1998. Pres. Capitol Hill Restoration Soc., Washington, 1990-92. Ford Found. fellow, 1955-56. Mem. Am. Bar Assn., Sr. Execs. Assn. (pres. HUD chpt. 1990-91). Avocations: music, gardening, cross country skiing.

PEARL, MARY CORLISS, wildlife conservationist; b. NYC, July 5, 1950; d. George Carleton and Margaret Lyon (Scheuer) Pearl; m. Don Jay Melnick, Oct. 3, 1981; children: Meredith, Seth. BA, Yale U., 1972, MPhil, 1976, PhD, 1982; DSc (hon.), Marist Coll., 2006. Dir. corp. devel. World Wildlife Fund, NYC, 1983-85, head NY office, 1984-85; adminstr. conservation progs. Wildlife Conservation Soc., NYC, 1985-87, asst. dir., 1988—; exec. dir., pres. Wildlife Trust (formerly Wildlife Preservation Trust Internat.); vis. scholar dept. biol. sci. Stanford U., 1987-88; assoc. dir. Ctr. Environ. Rsch. and Conservation Columbia U. Co-founder Consortium for Conservation Medicine, 1997; adj. rschr. Columbia U., NYC. Editl. adv. Wildlife Conservation mag., 1988; editor: Conservation for the 21st Century, 1989, Conservation Medicine: Ecosystem Health in Practice, 2002; co-editor: Conservation for the 21st Century; columnist Discover Magazine, 2006—; contbr. articles to profl. jour. Founding mem. Cons. in Higher Edn. Group of the Rainforest Alliance, NYC, 1988; trustee Gomez Found., NYC, 1985—; founder Calvin Hill Daycare Ctr., New Haven, 1970. Recipient David Lapham award, Yale U., 1971. Mem.: AAAS, Internat. Ecol. Rsch. (Brazil), Ecohealth Soc., Soc. for Conservation Biology (bd. gov. 1990—93), Internat. Union for Conservation of Nature (primate specialist group species survival commn.), Internat. Women's Forum, Cosmos Club (Belizean Grove). Avocations: squash, birdwatching, reading, history. Office: Wildlife Trust 460 West 34th St 17th Floor New York NY 10001 Office Phone: 212-380-4460. Personal E-mail: marypearl@aol.com. E-mail: pearl@wildlifetrust.org.

PEARL, NANCY LINN, librarian; b. Detroit, Jan. 12, 1945; d. Sidney and Anne Linn; m. Joseph Harold Pearl; children: Eily Raman, Katie. Grad., U. Mich., 1965, MLS, 1967. Head collection devel. Tulsa City County Libr., Okla.; exec. dir. Washington Ctr. Book Seattle Pub. Lib., 1993—2004. Author: Now Read This: A Guide to Mainstream Fiction, 1978-1998, 1999, Now Read This II: A Guide to Mainstream Fiction, 1990-2001, 2002, Book Lust: Recommended Reading for Every Mood, Moment and Reason, 2003, More Book Lust: Recommended Reading for Every Mood, Moment and Reason, 2005. Named Fiction Reviewer of Yr., Libr. Jour. Magazine, 1998; recipient Open Book award, Pacific Northwest Writer's Conf., 1997, Allie Beth Martin award, Pub. Libr. Assn., 2001, Humanities Washington award, 2003, Ontario Library Assn. Media and Communications award, 2004, Louis Shores Greenwood Publishing award for Reviews, ALA, 2004, Women's Nat. Book Assn. award, 2004—05, Louis Shores Greenwood Publishing award for Reviews, ALA, 2004—05. Achievements include the shushing librarian action figure based on her likeness. Office: Sasquatch Books 119 S Main Suite 400 Seattle WA 98104

PEARL, SHARRONA HYLA, science educator; b. Toronto, Ont., Can., May 3, 1977; d. Susan and Ernest Pearl; m. Ben Knepler, Aug. 12, 2007. PhD, Harvard U., Cambridge, Mass., 2005. Tchg. fellow, resident tutor Harvard U., Cambridge, Mass., 2001—05, lectr., 2005—. Contbr. chapters to books. Organizer Nat. Weekend of Prayer and Solidarity for the Suffering in Darfur, Mass., 2005—07; co-founder Out of the Cold, Holy Blossom, Toronto, 1998—99; hotline counselor Boston Area Rape Crisis Ctr., Cambridge, 2006—07. Recipient Marshall award, Grad. Sch. Arts and Sci., Harvard U., 2006; fellow, Social Sci. and Humanities Rsch. Coun. Can., 2000—04; Krupp Found. fellow, Ctr. for European Studies, Harvard U., 2002—03. Fellow: Kirkland Ho. Sr. Common Rm. (assoc.); mem.: NACBS (assoc.), History Sci. Soc. (assoc.), Jewish. Home Phone: 617-395-8439.

PEARLMAN, JERRY KENT, electronics company executive; b. Des Moines, Mar. 27, 1939; s. Leo R. Pearlman; married; children: Gregory, Neal. BA cum laude, Princeton U., 1960; MBA, Harvard U., 1962. With Ford Motor Co., 1962-70; v.p. fin. dir. Behring Corp., 1970-71; from contr. to chmn. Zenith Electronics Corp., Glenview, Ill., 1971-95. Bd. dirs. Smurfit-Stone Container Corp, Ryerson Inc., Nanophase Techs., Evanston Northwestern Healthcare. Bd. dirs. Northwestern U. Office: 21 Linden Ave Wilmette IL 60091-2837 E-mail: jpearl@northwestern.edu.

PEARLMAN, MARK, medical educator, researcher; s. Joseph and Rebecca Pearlman; m. Susan Pearlman; children: Aaron, Allison, Zachary, Hannah. BS, U. Mich., Ann Arbor, 1979; MD, Mich. State U., East Lansing, 1984. Diplomate Am. Bd. Ob-Gyn., 2000. Assoc. chief clin. affairs U. Mich. Hosps., Ann Arbor, svc. chief dept. ob-gyn., 2002; prof. surgery U. Mich. Med. Sch., Ann Arbor, S. Jan Behrman prof. in reproductive medicine, 2001—. Assoc. chief clin. affairs U. of Mich. Health Sys., Ann Arbor, 2002—. Author: (textbook) Obstetric and Gynecologic Emergencies (n). Fellow: Am. Coll. Ob-Gyn. (chair patient safety com. 1999—2004); mem.: Alpha Omega Alpha. Achievements include invention of anthropomorphic pregnant crash dummy. Office: Univ Mich Health Sys 1500 E Medical Center Drive Ann Arbor MI 48109-0276 Home Phone: 734-709-0057; Office Phone: 734-764-8429.

PEARLMAN, PETER STEVEN, lawyer; b. Orange, NJ, June 11, 1946; s. Jack Kitchener and Tiela Josephine (Fine) P.; m. Joan Perlmutter, June 19, 1969; children: Heather, Christopher, Megan. BA, U. Ill., 1967; JD, Seton Hall U., 1970. Bar: N.J. 1970, U.S. Dist. Ct. N.J. 1970, U.S. Dist. Ct. (so. dist.) N.Y. 2003, U.S. Dist. Ct. S.D., 2003, U.S. Dist. Ct. N.Y., 2003, U.S. Tax Ct. 1973, U.S. Supreme Ct. 1974, U.S. Ct. Appeals (2d cir.) 1981, U.S. Ct. Appeals (3d cir.) 1983, U.S. Ct. Appeals (7th cir.) 1985, U.S. Ct. Appeals (D.C. cir.) 1998, U.S. Ct. Appeals (4th cir.) 1999, U.S. Ct. Claims 2000; cert. civil trial atty., 1982. Assoc. Cohn & Lifland, Esquires, Saddle Brook, N.J., 1970-72; ptnr. Cohn, Lifland, Pearlman, Herrmann & Knopf, Saddle Brook, 1972—. Lectr. Nat. Inst. Trial Advocacy, Hempstead, N.Y., 1988—; active trial advocacy program Widener Law Sch.; adj. faculty mem. trial advocacy program Hofstra Law Sch.; master C. Willard Heckel Inn of Ct.; guest lectr. appellate advocacy Roger Williams Law Sch., 1995—; mem. panel arbitrators Am. Arbitration Assn.; lectr. for Inst. Continuing Legal Edn. for State of N.J. Mem. ABA, NJ Bar Assn., Fed. Bar Assn. of N.J. (trustee). Home: 9 Harvey Dr Short Hills NJ 07078-1122 Office: Cohn Lifland Pearlman Herrmann & Knopf 1 Park 80 Plz W Ste 4 Saddle Brook NJ 07663-5808 Home Phone: 973-564-7637; Office Phone: 201-845-9600. Business E-Mail: psp@njlawfirm.com.

PEARLMAN, RONALD ALAN, lawyer, educator; b. Hamilton, Ohio, July 10, 1940; AB with honors, Northwestern U., 1962, JD cum laude, 1965; LL.M. in Taxation, Georgetown U., 1967. Bar: D.C. 1991, U.S. Tax Ct. 1969, U.S. Supreme Ct. 1968. Atty. office chief counsel IRS, Washington, 1965—69; assoc. Thompson & Mitchell, St. Louis, 1969—70, ptnr., 1970—83; dep. asst. sec. for tax policy Dept. Treasury, Washington, 1983—84, asst. sec. tax policy, 1984—85; ptnr. Bryan, Cave, McPheeters & McRoberts (now Bryan Cave), St. Louis, 1986—88; chief of staff joint com. on taxation U.S. Congress, Washington, 1988—90; ptnr. Covington & Burling, Washington, 1991—2000; prof. Georgetown U. Law Ctr., Washington, 1999—. Ind. trustee Eaton Vance Mut. Funds, 2003—; vis. prof. Georgetown U. Law Ctr., Washington, 1998, Harvard U. Law Sch., Cambridge, Mass., 2002; adj. prof. Sch. Law Wash. U., St. Louis, 1972—83; vis. instr. Sch. Law U. Va., Charlottesville, 1995—98; mem. BNA Tax Mgmt. Adv. Bd., 1986—88, 1993—; participant ednl. seminars. Mem. bd. editors Northwestern U. Law Rev.; contbr. articles to various publs. Trustee Am. Tax Policy Inst., 1998—2006, pres., 2003—04. Fellow Am. Coll. Tax Counsel; mem. ABA (vice chair govt. rels. 1997-99, chair govt. rels. com. 1996-97, mem. coun., tax sect. 1986-88), Am. Law Inst. (tax adv. group, cons. pass-through entities project and tax integration project), Order of Coif. Office: Georgetown U Law Ctr 600 New Jersey Ave NW Washington DC 20001-2022 Home Phone: 202-342-2335; Office Phone: 202-662-9882. Business E-Mail: pearlman@law.georgetown.edu.

PEARLMAN, SAMUEL SEGEL, lawyer, educator; b. Pitts., May 28, 1942; s. Merle Maurice and Bernice Florence (Segel) P.; m. Cathy Schwartz, Aug. 16, 1964; children: Linda P. Kraner, Caren E. AB, U. Pa., 1963, LLB magna cum laude, 1966. Bar: Pa. 1966, Ohio 1967, U.S. Ct. Appeals (3d cir.) 1967. Law clk. U.S. Dist. Ct. for Ea. Dist. Pa., Phila., 1966-67; assoc. Burke, Haber & Berick, Cleve., 1967-72, prin., 1973-86, Berick, Pearlman & Mills, Cleve., 1986-99; ptnr. Squire, Sanders & Dempsey L.L.P., Cleve., 2000—. Lectr. law Case Western Res. U. Sch. Law, 1978-82; mem. registration com. Ohio Div. Securities, 1979-89; adv. dir. Midland Title Security, Inc.; trustee Realty ReFund Trust, N.Y. Stock Exch., 1990-98. Author: Cases, Forms and Materials for Modern Real Estate Transactions, 1978, 82. Mem. ABA, Ohio Bar Assn., Greater Cleve. Bar Assn. (chmn. securities law sect. 1985-86), Order of Coif. Republican. Jewish. Office: Squire Sanders & Dempsey 4900 Key Tower 127 Public Sq Ste 4900 Cleveland OH 44114-1304 Office Phone: 216-479-8500, 216-479-8025. Business E-Mail: spearlman@ssd.com.

PEARLMAN, STEVEN JAY, otolaryngologist, surgeon, educator; b. NYC, 1956; BA (magna cum laude with high honors) in Biology, Brandeis U., 1978; MD, Mt. Sinai Sch. Medicine, 1982. Cert. Am. Bd. Otolaryngology-Head and Neck Surgery, 1987, Am. Bd. Facial Plastic and Reconstructive Surgery. Resident gen. surgery Mt. Sinai Med. Ctr., NYC, 1982-83, resident otolaryngology-head and neck surgery, 1983-87; fellow facial plastic surgery St. Luke's Roosevelt Hosp., NYC, 1987-88, otolaryngologist, assoc. dir., head and neck surgery, now dir., facial plastic surg. divsn.; attending surgeon Lenox Hill Hosp., NY, Manhattan Eye Ear and Throat Hosp., NY; private practice NYC. Asst. prof. clin. otolaryngology, Columbia U. Hosp. Ctr. of Physicians and Surgeons, clin. assoc. prof.; tchr. facial plastic surgery to residents, Columbia U. Med. Sch. and NY Eye and Ear Infirmary. Contbr. to numerous medical and sci. publs., to chpts. in books.; appeared on nat. and local television talk and news programs (including CNN, WABC, Eyewitness News, Good Day NY, The Food Network, Fox-Channel 5, Montel Williams Show, E! and performed "live" face lift on CNBC's "The Real Story".), frequently quoted in Allure, Elle, Harper's Bazaar, Marie-Claire, W, Fitness Plus, Cosmopolitan, In Style, More, YM, NY Mag., Redbook, NY Times, Daily News, Chicago Tribune and Newsday. Pro bono surgeon Face to Face; pro bono facial reconstructive surgeon Nat. Domestic Violence Project. Named an Top 12 Plastic Surgeons in NYC, NY Mag., 2002. Mem. AMA, Am. Acad. Otolaryngology-Head and Neck Surgeons, Am. Acad. Facial Plastic and Reconstructive Surgery (past eastern region v.p. and nat. com. chmn., pres. 2004-05), NY State Med. Soc., NY Facial Plastic Surgery Soc. (founder, 1993 and past pres.). Office: 521 Park Ave New York NY 10021-8140 Office Phone: 212-262-4444, 212-223-8300. Office Fax: 212-644-8655, 212-523-6364. *

PEARLSTEIN, PHILIP, artist; b. Pitts., May 24, 1924; s. David and Libbie (Kalser) Pearlstein; m. Dorothy Cantor, Aug. 20, 1950; children: William, Julia, Ellen. BFA, Carnegie Inst. Tech., 1949; MA, NYU, 1955. Instr. Pratt Inst., 1959-63; vis. critic Yale U., 1962-63; from asst. prof. to prof. art dept. Bklyn. Coll., 1963-88, disting. prof. emeritus; pres. Am. Acad. Arts Letters, 2003—06. Exhibited in group shows at Carnegie Internat., 1955, 1964, 1967, Whitney Mus. Am. Art, 1955—56, 1958, 1962, 1965, 1967, 1970, 1972—74, 1979, 1991, U. Mich. Mus., 1965, U. Ill., 1965, 1967—68, Providence Art Club, 1965, Corcoran Gallery, 1967, Vassar Coll., 1968, Milw. Art, 1969, Pa. Acad. Fine Arts, 1971—72, Indpls. Mus. Art, 1972, Galerie Lowenadler, Stockholm, Sweden, 1973, Nat. Acad. Arts, Letter, NYC, 1973 (award, 1973), Yale U., 1973—74, Hofstra U., 1973, Helsinki Mus. Art, Finland, 1974, Art Inst. Chgo., 1974, Cleve. Mus. Art, 1974, US Dept. Interior, 1976, Wildenstein Gallery, NYC, 1976, Tokashima Art Mus., Japan, 1992, exhibitions include retrospective U. Tex., Austin, 1974, Finch Coll., 1974, Cranbrook Acad. Art, Mich., 1974, Miami Art, 1975, Kalamazoo Inst. Arts, Tampa Bay Art, Tampa, Fla., 1975, Grand Rapids Art Mus., Mich., 1975, Notre Dame U., 1975, exhibitions include Bicentennial, Am., 1976, exhibitions include retrospective Chryler Mus., 1980, Philbrook Art, 1980, San Antonio Mus., 1981, Akron Art Mus., 1981, Honolulu Acad. Art, 1994, exhibitions include Fahnemann Galerie, Berlin, 2003, Michael Hass, Zurich, 2004, Haas and Fuchs, Berlin, 2004, Robert Miller Gallery, NY, 2004, Betty Cunningham Gallery, 2005, Represented in permanent collections Columbus Mus., Ga., Phila. Mus. Art, San Antonio Mus. Assn., Pa. State U., Whitney Mus., Mus. Modern Art, NY, Met. Mus. Art, Bklyn Mus., Carnegie Mus., Syracuse U., James A. Michener Found., Hirshhorn Mus., Corcoran Gallery, Art Inst. Chgo., Milw. Art Ctr., Ludwig Collection, Aachen, Germany, Sydney and Frances Lewis Found., Richmond, Va., Cleve. Mus. Art, Milw. Mus. Grantee, NAD, 1983; Fulbright fellow, Italy, 1958—59, Guggenheim fellow, 1971—72, Nat. Endowment Arts grantee, 1968. Mem.: Am. Acad. Arts, Letters. (pres. 2003—06, grantee 1992).

PEARLSTEIN, SEYMOUR, artist; b. Bklyn., Oct. 14, 1923; s. Morris Lazarus and Anna (Bassiur) P.; m. Toby Tessie Rubinstein, Mar. 21, 1943; children: Judith Helene, Lawrence Jonathan. Cert., Pratt Inst., Bklyn., 1950, Art Students League N.Y., 1954; student of Jack Potter. Owner, illustrator, designer Sy Pearlstein Advt. Art Studio, NYC, 1946-71; artist-painter rep. by Far Gallery, NYC, 1969-81; prof. N.Y.C. Tech. Coll., CUNY, Bklyn., 1971-94, prof. emeritus, 1994—, chmn. art and advt. design dept., 1985-88. One-man shows Silvermine Guild of Artists, New Canaan, Conn., 1973, Far Gallery, 1973, 75, 78, Klitgord Ctr., N.Y.C., C.C., 1974, De Mers Gallery, Hilton Head, S.C., 1975, Adelphi U., Garden City, N.Y., 1979, Grace Gallery, N.Y.C. Tech. Coll., 1992; group shows A.M. Sachs Gallery, N.Y.C., 1971, Springfield (Mo.) Art Mus., 1971, Am. Acad. Arts and Letters, N.Y.C., 1975, 76, 77, NAD, N.Y.C., 1986, 87, 89, 91, 92, Butler Inst. Art, Ohio, 1975, Ball State U., Queens Mus., N.Y.C., 1978, 81, Dept. State Art in Embassies Program, N.Y. Hist. Soc., 1981, Colo. Heritage Mus., Denver, 1981, 82, 86, Am. Watercolor Soc., N.Y.C., Ingber Gallery, N.Y.C., 1985, Audubon Artists, N.Y.C., 1990, 92, 97, Allied Artists Am., N.Y.C., 1991, 95, 2002, Nat. Arts Club, N.Y.C., 1989, Grace Gallery, N.Y.C. Tech. Coll., CUNY, 1998, 99, 2000, others; represented in permanent collections Mus. N.Mex., Santa Fe, Mint Mus. Art, Charlotte, N.C., NAD, N.Y.C., Fine Arts Gallery, San Diego, Adelphi U., Queens Mus., N.Y.C., Munson-Williams-Proctor Inst., Utica, N.Y., N.Y.C. Tech. Coll., Bklyn. Served with AUS, 1942-46. Recipient Gold medal Nat. Acad. Design, 1969, Hassam Fund Purchase award Am. Acad. Arts and Letters, 1969, 77, Gold medal of honor Nat. Arts Club, 1970, Ranger Fund Purchase award NAD, 1971, 82, Gold medal Soc. Illustrators, 1972, Nat. Inst.-Am. Acad. Arts and Letters grant, 1975 Mem. NAD (sec. coun.) 1980-84, W.H. Leavin prize 1985), Am. Watercolor Soc. (bd. dirs. 1979-80, Watercolor U.S.A. award 1971), Art Students League of N.Y. (life), Allied Artists Am. (bd. dirs. 1976-79, E. Lowe award 1969, gold medal 1980, George Tweed Meml. award 1989, 92), Audubon Artists (bd. dirs. 1986-89, 91-93, Grumbacher award 1971, Fabri medal 1980), Alliance Figurative Artists (c0chmn. 1976-77), Profl. Staff Congress. Home: 52 Dartmouth St Forest Hills NY 11375-5142 Office: NYC Tech Coll AD Dept CUNY 300 Jay St Brooklyn NY 11201-1909

PEARLSTINE, NORMAN, communications consultant, former editor; b. Phila., Oct. 4, 1942; s. Raymond and Gladys (Cohen) Pearlstine. BA, Haverford Coll., 1964; LLB, U. Pa., 1967. Staff reporter Wall Street Jour., Dallas, 1968—73, Detroit, 1968—73, LA, 1968—73, Tokyo bur. chief, 1973—76; mng. editor Asian Wall Street Jour., Hong Kong, 1976—78; exec. editor Forbes Mag., LA, 1978—80; nat. news editor Wall Street Jour., NYC, 1980—82; editor, pub. Wall Street Jour./Europe, Brussels, 1982—83; mng. editor, v.p. Wall Street Jour., NYC, 1983—91, exec. editor, 1991—92; pres., CEO Friday Holdings, L.P., NYC, 1993—94; editor-in-chief Time Inc., NYC, 1995—2005; sr. adv. Time Warner Inc., NYC, 2006; sr. adv. to telecom & media team The Carlyle Group, NYC, 2006—. Author: Off the Record: The Press, the Government, and the War Over Anonymous Sources, 2007. Pres. Atsuko Chiba Found.; bd. councilors USC Annenberg Sch. Comm.; pres. adv. bd. Neiman Found. at Harvard U.; mem. adv. bd. CUNY Grad. Sch. Journalism, Arthur F. Burns Fellowship Program; bd. dir. The Carnegie Corp., The Arthur F. Burns Fellowship Program, Com. to Protect Journalists, 2004—, Internat. Ctr. for Journalists, The Berlin Sch. of Creative Leadership Steinbeis U.; trustee NY Hist. Soc., 1985—2005, chmn., 1989—93; pres. Am. Acad. in Berlin, 2006—. Named to, Mag. Editors Hall of Fame, 2005; recipient Editor of Yr. award, Nat. Press Found., 1989, Lifetime Achievement award, ASME, 2005, Loeb Lifetime Achievement award for disting. bus. and fin. journalism, 2000. Mem.: ABA, Am. Acad. Arts and Scis., Japan Soc., Coun. Fgn. Rels., D.C. Bar Assn., Tribeca Film Inst. (bd. dirs.). Office: The Carlyle Group 520 Madison Ave 42nd Fl New York NY 10022

PEARMAN, RAVEN-SYMONÉ CHRISTINA See SYMONE, RAVEN

PEARSALL, GEORGE WILBUR, materials scientist, mechanical engineer, consultant, educator; b. Brentwood, NY, July 13, 1933; s. Milo Dickerson and Margaret Elizabeth (White) P.; m. Patricia Louise Stevens, Oct. 11, 1962. B. Metall. Engring., Rensselaer Poly. Inst., 1955; Sc.D. (Am. Soc. Metals fellow), MIT, 1961. Registered profl. engr., NC. Rsch. engr. Dow Chem. Co., Midland, Mich., 1955-57; rsch. asst. MIT, 1959-60, asst. prof. metallurgy, 1960-64; assoc. prof. mech. engring. Duke U., 1964-66, prof., 1966-81, prof. mech. engring. and materials sci., 1981—2001, prof. pub. policy studies, 1982—2001, acting dean Sch. Engring., 1969-71, dean, 1971-74, 82-83, prof. emeritus, 2001—. Trustee Triangle Univ. Ctr. for Advanced Studies, 1976-92, chmn. exec. com., 1983-88; dir. Duke-IBM Product Safety Inst., 1979-90. Author: (with W.G. Moffatt and J. Wulff) The Structure and Properties of Materials, 1964; mem. editl. bd. Jour. Products Liability, 1977-92, Jour. Products and Toxics Liability, 1993-96, Proceedings of the IEEE, 1994-96; contbr. articles to profl. jour. Served with AUS, 1957. Mem. ASME (Triodyne Safety Award 2001), Am. Soc. Metals (life), Phi Lambda Upsilon, Tau Beta Pi, Pi Tau Sigma. Home: 2941 Welcome Dr Durham NC 27705-5555 Office Phone: 919-660-5344. Personal E-mail: page1212@msn.com. Business E-Mail: pearsall@duke.edu.

PEARSALL, GLENN LINCOLN, brokerage house executive; b. Huntington, NY, June 19, 1949; s. Alan W. and Jean (Doubrava) Pearsall; m. Carol Ann Ciesla, June 19, 1971; children: Adam, Heather. BA in English, SUNY, Oswego, 1971; cert. in investment mgmt. analyst, U. Pa., 1994. V.p. Pearsall Realty Inc., Wevertown, NY, 1975-85; investment exec. E. F. Hutton, Glens Falls, NY, 1985-87; fin. cons. Shearson, Lehman, Hutton, Glens Falls, Saratoga, NY, 1987-90; fin. advisor UBS (formerly PaineWebber), Glens Falls, 1990—, br. mgr., 1990—2002, divsional v.p., 1994—. Daily stock market reporter Stas. WLPW-FM, WIRD-AM, Lake Placid, 1985—90, Sta. WKBE-FM, Glens Falls, 1992—95, Sta. WWSC-AM, 1995, Sta. WCKM-FM, 1995—2002; fin. commentator TV 8 Monday Night News, Glens Falls, 1988—2002; mem. 1991 stock pickers coun. Capital Dist. Bus. Rev., Albany, NY, 1991; spkr. in field. Fin. columnist: several weekly newspapers, 1988—2002. Bd. dirs. Adirondack coun. Girl Scouts U.S., fund-raising chmn., 1990; bd. dirs., v.p. Lake George Opera Festival; bd. dirs. Adirondack Ensemble, 1997—, v.p., 1999, chair fin. com., 1998—, pres., 2000—01; co-founder, pres. Glenn and Carol Pearsall Adirondack Found.; trustee Town of Johnsburg Libr. Found., 2001—, pres., 2003—06; trustee Adirondack Cmty. Trust, 2006—; commencement spkr. Paul Smith's Coll., 2006; mem. Assemblyman Glenn Harris legis. adv. coun. Assembly Dist. 109 N.Y. State, 1985—90; pres. bd. dirs. North Creek (N.Y.) C. of C., 1978—86; trustee Adirondack Mus. Blue Moutain Lake, 2001—, chmn. personnel com., 2005—; trustee, pres. Johnsburg Pub. Libr. Endowment, 2002—; trustee Adirondack Cmty. Trust, 2006—; mem. Cornell Coop. Ext. Adv. Coun., 1982—91; bd. dirs. Warren County Coop. Ext., pres., 1985, 1986, Adirondack Civil War Round Table, 1997—99. With US Coast Guard, 1971—75. Republican. Avocations: white water canoeing, skiing, fishing, reading. Office: UBS One Broad St Pla Glens Falls NY 12801 Office Phone: 800-526-3763. Business E-Mail: glenn.pearsall@ubs.com.

PEARSALL, JOHN WESLEY, lawyer; b. Richmond, Va., Aug. 21, 1914; BS, Randolph-Macon Coll., 1935; LLB, U. Richmond, 1941. Bar: Va. 1940. Assoc. McGuire, Riely & Eggleston, Richmond, 1941-50; ptnr. McGuire, Eggleston, Bocock & Woods, Richmond, 1950-53; gen. counsel Va.-Carolina Chem. Corp., Richmond, 1953-56; pvt. practice Richmond, 1956-60; ptnr. McCaul, Grigsby & Pearsall, Richmond, 1960-86, Pearsall & Pearsall, 1986—; gen. counsel, dir. Estes Express Lines, 1972—. Chpt. chmn. ARC, Chesterfield County, Va., 1944-49, campaign chmn., 1949, campaign chmn. Richmond, Henrico, and Chesterfield, Va., 1950, nat. vice chmn. fund dr., 1956, nat. gov., 1953-55; mem. budget com. Richmond Area Cmty. Chest, 1946-47, mem. exec. com., 1947-55, trustee, 1946-50, campaign chmn., 1951, pres., 1955, United Giver's Fund, 1970; v.p. Children's Aid Soc., Richmond, 1950-55, trustee, 1948-55; active Boy Scouts Am., 1953-56; mem. exec. com. Randolph-Macon Coll., 1958-76, chmn. long range plan com., 1960-76, trustee, 1955-76, mem. alumni bd., 1994-99, trustee emeritus, 2006; mem. Chesterfield County Welfare Bd., 1951-55; trustee Sheltering Arms Hosp., Richmond, 1949-80; dir. Jr. Achievement, 1975-81; vestryman St. Stephens Ch., 1967-70, ch. bearer, 1986-87; mem. exec. com. Hist. Richmond Found. (1965-70), Falls of James adv. bd., 1979—, Chesterfield Hist. Soc., 1985-95. Served to lt. j.g. USNR, 1944-46. Mem. ABA, Va. Bar Assn., Richmond Bar Assn., Chesterfield County Bar Assn. (pres. 1963-64), Am. Judicature Soc., Va. State Bar Council (chmn. judicial ethics com. 1970-71), Am. Archaeol. Soc. (local chpt., pres. 1976), Phi Beta Kappa (pres. Richmond area chpt. 1976-77), Jr. C. of C. (Disting. Svc. award 1948, state pres. 1948-49), Omicron Delta Kappa, Lambda Chi Alpha. Office: Ellen Glasgow House 1 W Main St Richmond VA 23220-5623 Home: 1550 Westbrook Ct Apt 6205 Richmond VA 23227-3356 Home Phone: 804-200-1189; Office Phone: 804-644-5491. Personal E-mail: jwpearsall@comcast.net.

PEARSALL, OTIS PRATT, retired lawyer; b. Bklyn., Apr. 25, 1932; s. Willard Hall and Marilla Houghton (Pratt) P.; m. Nancy Jeanne Boden, July 7, 1956; 1 child, Melissa Mather BA, Yale U., 1953, LL.B., 1956. Assoc. Hughes, Hubbard, Blair & Reed, NYC, 1956-59, 60-63; asst. U.S. atty. US Atty.'s Office So. Dist. NY, 1959-60; ptnr. Hughes Hubbard & Reed, NYC, 1964-91, Arnold & Porter, NYC, 1991—2002; ret., 2002. Mem. Art Commn. of the City of N.Y., 2001—; dir. Bridgehampton (N.Y.) Assocs., Inc., 1973—, pres., 2004—. Bd. dirs. Mcpl. Art Soc. NY, NYC, 1967-74, v.p., 1973-74; trustee Soc. for Preservation of L.I. Antiquities, Setauket, NY, 1969-77, Bklyn. Mus., 1986-92, 93—, mem. adv. bd., 1992-93; bd. dirs. LI Hist. Soc., Bklyn., 1971-82; mem. historic city com., NYC, 1987-88; trustee The Green-Wood Cemetery, Bklyn., 1992—; dir. NY Preservation Archive Project, 2003-. Recipient Green Star award Environ. Action Coalition, Inc., 1989, Landmark Lion award NY Hist. Dists. Coun., 1993, Lucy G. Moses Preservation Leadership award, NY Landmarks Conservancy, 2000, Forsythia award Bklyn. Botanic Garden, 2007. Fellow Am. Coll. Trial Lawyers; mem. Bklyn. Heights Assn. (gov., adv. com. 1960-), mem. ABA, Bridgehampton Club (pres. 1989-91), India House Club, Calif. Club, Univ. Club, Phi Beta Kappa. Republican. Congregationalist. Avocation: historic building restoration. Home: 157 Willow St Brooklyn NY 11201-2201

PEARSALL, SAMUEL HAFF, III, ecologist, geographer, foundation administrator; b. Nashville, Sept. 2, 1949; s. Sam H. Jr. and Margaret Isabelle (Ikard) P.; m. Patricia Davenport, July 1973 (div. 1978); 1 child, Rachel Claire; m. Linda Louise Parrish, Sept. 4, 1982; 1 child, Paul Samuel. BS, U. Tenn., 1942; M of Prof. Studies, Cornell U., 1982; PhD, U. Hawaii, 1993. Exec. dir. Coastal Resources Ctr., Bar Harbor, Maine, 1975-77; program dir. Natural Areas and Natural Heritage Survey Tenn. Dept. Conservation, Nashville, 1978-81, dir. Ecol. Svcs. divsn., 1982-85; dir. Pacific Sci. The Nature Conservancy, Honolulu, 1989-91, dir. sci. and stewardship Durham, NC, 1992-99, dir. sci. and Roanoke River Project, 2000—07, dir. sci. and climate change adaptation, 2007—. Adj. faculty U. NC, 1993—, Nicholas Sch. Environment Duke U., 1999—, founder Pacific Sci. program Nature Conservancy, 1989, founding mem. conservation com., 1994-96, Ecoregions working group, 1996-97; mem. So. Blue Ridge Ecoregional Planning Team, 1996-97; leader Mid-Atlantic Coastal Plain Ecoregional Planning Team, 1997—; founding mem. Ga.-Pacific/Nature Conservancy Roanoke Ecosys. Partnership, 1995-97; sci. and tech. adv. com. Albermarle-Pamlico Nat. Estuari Program, 2004-05; adv. com. coastal elevations and sea level rise US EPA, 2007-; mem. Nat. Park Svc. Cape Hatteras Regulatory Negotiation Com., 2007-. Author: Terrestrial Coastal Environments and Tourism in Western Samoa, 1993, Managing for Future Change on the Albemarle Sound, 2005, Adapting Coastal Lowlands to Rising Seas, 2005; (with others) Wildlife Conservation Evaluation Methods in U.S., 1985; contbr. articles to profl. jours. Bd. dirs. Tenn. Environ. Coun., Nashville, 1980-85, Natural Areas Assn., Rockford, Ill., 1984-87, Bend, Oreg., 97-2000, treas., 1999-2000; counselor Conservation Trust for N.C., 1993-98; founder Tenn. Protection Planning Com.; student fellow East-West Ctr., 1985-90. Recipient Hodgson award Assn. Am. Geographers, 1988, Wiens award U. Hawaii, 1993, Conservation by Design award Nature Conservancy, 2003. Achievements include research in nature conservation, adaptive ecosystem management and landscape ecology in Western Samoa and North Carolina, coastal climate change and sea level rise in North Carolina; co-author FERC Lic. Settlement among Dominion Generation, Inc. and stakeholders at Lake Gaston and Roanoke Rapids dams. Home: 1307 Chaney Rd Raleigh NC 27606-2736 Office: Nature Conservancy Ste 209/One University Pl 4705 University Dr Durham NC 27707 Home Phone: 919-859-6297; Office Phone: 919-403-8558 x 1022. Business E-Mail: sampearsall@tnc.org.

PEARSON, ANDREW R., lawyer; married; 2 children. BA in Govt., St. John's U., Collegeville, Minn., 1992; JD cum laude, William Mitchell Coll. Law, St. Paul, 1998. Bar: Minn. 1998. Assoc. counsel Bradshaw & Bryant, P.L.L.C., St. Cloud, Minn. Vol. Peace Corps. Named a Rising Star, Minn. Super Lawyers mag., 2006. Mem.: Benton/Stearns County Bar Assn., Assn. Trial Lawyers of Am., Minn. Trial Lawyers Assn., Minn. Criminal Def. Lawyers (Spl. Achievement award 2005), Nat. Assn. Criminal Def. Lawyers, Minn. State Bar Assn. Office: Bradshaw & Bryant PLLC 1505 Division St Waite Park MN 56387 Office Phone: 320-251-6889. *

PEARSON, APRIL VIRGINIA, lawyer; b. Martinsville, Ind., Aug. 11, 1960; d. Clare Grill and Sheila Rosemary (Finch) Rayner; m. Randall Keith Pearson, Dec. 10, 1988; children: Randall Kyle, Austin Finch, Autumn Virginia. BA, Calif. State U., Long Beach, 1982; JD, Pepperdine U., 1987; cert. indsl. fire brigade, Tex. A&M U. Bar: Calif. 1987, Idaho 1993, D.C. 1989. Assoc. counsel Union Oil Co. Calif., LA, 1988—2001; owner Avrilex, Chino Hills, Calif., 2001—. V.p. Pa's Bier, Long Beach, Calif., 1988—98, Ammonia Safety Tng. Inst., 1995—98, gen. counsel, 1997—; mem. Pub. Works Commn. City of Chino Hills, 1999—. Mem.: Calif. State Bar (mem. agribusiness com. 2006—), Chem. Industry Coun. Calif. (chair regulatory affairs com. 1995), Am. Corp. Counsel Assn., Women Lawyers Long Beach (v.p. 1990—93). Avocations: running, Tae Kwon Do. Office: Avrilex 13462 Montserrat Ct Chino Hills CA 91709-1327 Office Phone: 909-517-3838. Business E-Mail: april@avrilex.com.

PEARSON, CHARLES THOMAS, JR., lawyer, director; b. Fayetteville, Ark., Oct. 14, 1929; s. Charles Thomas and Doris (Pinkerton) P.; m. Wyma Lee Hampton, Sept. 9, 1988; children: Linda Sue, John Paddock. BS, U. Ark., 1953, JD, 1954; postgrad., U.S. Naval Postgrad. Sch., 1959; A.M., Boston U., 1963. Bar: Ark. bar 1954. Practice in, Fayetteville, 1963—. Dir. officer N.W. Comms., Inc., Dixieland Devel., Inc., Jonlin Investments, Inc., World Wide Travel Svc., Inc., Oklania Farms, Inc., N.W. Arl. Land & Devel., Inc., Garden Plaza Inns, Inc. Word Data, Inc., M.P.C. Farms, Inc., Fayetteville Enterprises, Inc., NWA Devel.Co., Delta Comm., Inc.; past. dir., organizer N.W. Nat. Bank. Adviser Explorer Scouts, 1968—; past pres. Washington County Draft Bd.; past pres. bd. Salvation Army. Served to comdr. Judge Adv. Gen. Corps USNR, 1955-63. Mem. ABA, Ark. Bar Assn., Washington County Bar Assn., Judge Advs. Assn., N.W. Ark. Ret. Officers Assn. (past pres.), Methodist Men (past pres), U. Ark. Alumni Assn. (past dir.), Sigma Chi (past pres. N.W. Ark. alumni, past chmn. house corp.), Alpha Kappa Psi, Phi Eta Sigma, Delta Theta Phi. Clubs: Mason (32 deg., K.T., Shriner), Moose, Elk, Lion, Metropolitan. Republican. Methodist. Office: 9 N College Ave Fayetteville AR 72701-5301 Office Phone: 479-521-4300. Personal E-mail: tpesq1101@aol.com. Business E-Mail: tpesq@cox.net.

PEARSON, CLARENCE EDWARD, management consultant, educator; b. Chgo., Apr. 22, 1925; s. Edward and Irene (Silander) P.; m. June Waldhe, Apr. 21, 1951 (dec. 1967); 1 child, Scott (dec.); m. Laurie Norris, Apr. 25, 1995. BS, No. Ill. U., 1950; MPH, U. N.C., 1952. Instr. Mt. Prospect (Ill.) Pub. Schs., 1950-51; dir. health edn. DuPage County Health Dept., Wheaton, Ill., 1952-55; chief health edn. St. Louis Health Dept., 1955-57; dir. health and hosps. Health and Welfare Council, St. Louis, 1957-61; dir. health and safety Met. Life Ins. Co., NYC, 1961-87. Prof. edn. Columbia Tchrs. Coll., 1975—; pres. Universal Health Concepts, N.Y.C., 1984-87; Coun. Internat. Health, Washington, 1981-84; chmn. Profl. Exam. Svc., N.Y.C., 1996-99; v.p. Peter Drucker Found. for Nonprofit Mgmt., 1994-96; adv. bd. C. Everett Koop Inst.; bd. overseers Dartmouth Med. Sch., 1992-96, 99—; adj. prof. cmty. health Rober Wood Johnson Med. Sch., 1996-2003; pres., CEO Nat. Ctr. for Health Edn., 1997-2001; sr. adv. Who office, U.N Co-author: Managing Health Promotion, 1982; co-editor: (with C. Everett Koop) Critical Issues in Global Health, 2000; exec. editor: Global Health Mgmt. and Leadership; contbr. chpts. to books Co-chmn. Scandinavian-Ams. for Rockefeller presdl. campaign, N.Y., 1968; co-dir. Salzburg Seminar Spl. Session: Critical Issues in Global Health. Served as staff sgt. U.S. Army, 1943-46. Recipient Disting. Career award APHA, Washington, 1981, Gold Medal for Achievement, Columbia U., N.Y.C., 1984, Internat. Health award Asia Pacific Consortium, Honolulu, 1984, Porter Prize, Pitts. Health Ctr., 1986, Disting. Alumni award Sch. Pub. Health, U. N.C., 2001. Fellow APHA (governing coun. 1970-78, pres. conf. emeritus members 2002—, Internat. Health Lifetime Achievement award), AARP (bd. dirs. 2002—), Advt. Coun. (adv. bd.), The Univ. Club (N.Y.C.), Advertising Council Adv. Bd Home: 530 E 23rd St New York NY 10010-5022 Home Phone: 212-254-3309; Office Phone: 212-254-3309. Personal E-mail: nyvikings@aol.com. Business E-Mail: cpearson@aarp.org.

PEARSON, DANIEL R., federal official; m. Cindy Pearson; 2 children. BS in Agrl. Econs., MS in Agrl. Econs., U. Minn. Farmer, Ogilvie, Minn., 1979—80; agrl. legis. asst. to Senator Rudy Boschwitz US Senate, 1981—87; policy analyst Pub. Affairs Dept., 1987—98; asst. v.p., pub. affairs Cargill, Inc., 1998—2003; commr. US Internat. Trade Comm., Washington, 2003—, chmn., 2006—. Republican. Office: US Internat Trade Comm 500 E St SW Washington DC 20436 Office Phone: 202-205-2000. *

PEARSON, DAVID PETRI, chemist; b. Oct. 24, 1926; s. Brewer Petri and Laura Alvine (Johnson) P.; m. Patricia Margaret Cowan, June 4, 1949; children: Kathryn A., James P., Rebecca L., Kristine R., Judith G. BA in Chemistry, Reed Coll., 1949; MS in Phys. Chemistry, Oreg. State U., 1953; PhD in Phys. Chemistry, U. So. Calif., 1960. Rsch. chemist Phillips Petroleum Co. (AEC), Idaho Falls, Idaho, 1957-62, Bartlesville, Okla., 1962-69; lectr. in chemistry Portland State U., 1969-71; asst. prof. chemistry So. Oreg. State Coll., Ashland, 1971-72; rsch. assoc. Oreg. Grad. Ctr., Beaverton, 1972-74; sr. chemist Portland Gen. Electric Co., 1975-87, ret., 1987. Patentee in field. Cpl. USAAF, 1946-47. Mem. Am. Chem. Soc. (treas. Portland sect. 1979-82, chmn. 1983). Clubs: Am. Alpine, Idaho Alpine (sec. Idaho Falls 1961, pres. 1962), Sigma Xi. Republican. Presbyterian. Home: 6324 SW Radcliffe St Portland OR 97219-5749 Personal E-mail: pdpearson49@comcast.net.

PEARSON, GERALD LEON, food products executive; b. Mpls., June 24, 1925; s. Perry and Lillian (Peterson) P.; m. Beverly Mary Schultz, Nov. 10, 1946; children: Steven, Perry, Liecia. Treas. Trimont Packing Co., 1946-52; v.p. Spencer Foods, Iowa, 1952-68, pres., chief exec. officer Iowa, 1969-80, chmn. bd., chief exec. officer Iowa, 1972-80; chmn. Beef Specialists of Iowa Inc., 1983-94. Bd. dirs. Graffaloy, Inc.; chmn., CEO World Champions of Golf Inc.; owner Brooks Golf Club, Okoboji, Iowa. Pres. Pearson Art Found.; bd. dirs. Bethany Coll., Lindsborg; commr. Nat. Mus. Am. Art-Smithsonian Instn., 1995-99; founder Internat. Ctr. for Jazz Found. With USN, 1943-46. Mem. Swedish Royal Roundtable, Swedish Council Am. (bd. dirs.). Office: Brooks Golf Club PO Box 948 Okoboji IA 51355-0948 Home: 5209 Lake Shore Dr Okoboji IA 51355-2597 Home Phone: 712-382-5571; Office Phone: 712-332-7873. E-mail: bud.pearson@worldnet.att.net, bpearson@iowaone.net.

PEARSON, HENRY CLYDE, retired judge; b. Ocoonita Lee County, Va., Mar. 12, 1925; s. Henry James and Nancy Elizabeth (Seals) P.; m. Jean Calton, July 26, 1956; children: Elizabeth, Frances, Timothy Clyde. Student, Union Coll., 1947-49; LLB, U. Richmond, 1952. Bar: Va. 1952, U.S. Ct. Appeals (4th cir.) 1957, U.S. Supreme Ct. 1958. Sole practice, Jonesville, Va., 1952-56; asst. U.S. atty. Western Dist. Va., Roanoke, 1956-61; ptnr. Hopkins, Pearson & Engleby, Roanoke, 1961—70; so. states presdl. campaign mgr. Nelson A. Rockefeller, 1964; judge U.S. Bankruptcy Ct. Western Dist. Va., Roanoke, 1970-98; ret., 1998. Adv. com. fed. rules bankruptcy procedure; mem. Va. Ho. of Reps., 1954-56, Va. Senate, 1968-70; Republican nominee Gov. of Va., 1961. Editl. bd. Am. Survey Bankruptcy Law, 1979. With USN, 1943—46, PTO. Mem. Va. State Bar, ABA, Va. Trial Lawyers Assn., Assn. Trial Lawyers Am., Am. Judicature Soc., Am. Judges Assn., Fed. Bar Assn., Delta Theta Phi, Tribune Jefferson Senate, Am. Legion, VFW, Masons, Shriners. Methodist.

PEARSON, JENNIE SUE, retired government administrator; b. Washington, Jan. 26, 1928; d. Orville Louis and Jennie (Rogers) Ganbin; m. Eugene Ryder Pearson, Feb. 3, 1945 (div. 1955); 1 child, Ronald Eugene. AA, Frederick CC, Md., 1987. Title examiner Md. Motor Vehicle Adminstrn., Glen Burnie, 1970-74, title advisor, 1975-80, title supr., 1980-84, asst. br. mgr., 1984-91; ret., 1991. Pres. Rebekah Assembly Md., 1968-69, Internat. Assn. Rebekah Assemblies, Winston-Salem, N.C., 1973-74; v.p. Citizens Nursing Home Aux. Vols., 1997-98, pres., 1999—; vice chmn. bd. dirs. Md. Odd Fellows Home, 1991-92; mem. Srs. and Law Enforcement Together Coun.-Frederick City Police Dept.; mem. adv. bd. Inst. Learning in Retirement Frederick Cmty. Coll., bd. dirs.; trustee Schuyler Colfax Mus., Winston Salem, N.C.; bd. dirs. Frederick C.C. Found., Inc., Md. Sr. Citizens Hall Fame, 2003; mem. vol. Frederick Ret. Srs. Vol. Program, 2003; mem. Tng. for Future Disasters, Ret. Srs. Vol. Program. Recipient Outstanding Alumni award for significant contbns. Coll. Mission and Alumni Assn., 1991, 98, Meritorious Jewel Rebekah Assembly of Md. Outstanding Svc. in Fraternal Order and Cmty., Vol. of Month, Frederick Sr. Mag.; inductee Md. Sr. Citizens Hall of Fame, Inc. Mem. AARP (pres. Frederick chpt. 1997-99, Andrus award pin for vol. cmty. svc. 2003), Frederick CC Alumni Assn. (pres. 1991-98, bd. dirs., 2006), Montgomery County Agrl. Ctr., Inc. (life), Frederick County Commn. for Women, Rebekah Lodge (past noble grand mem. 1997-98, Meritorious Jewel award 2000), Frederick Woman's Civic Club, Inc. (mem. com. 1992-2003, 1st v.p. 2006—), Md. Sr. Citizens Hall of Fame, Inc. (bd. dirs. 2003), 1902 Club, Ret. Srs. Vol. Program. Republican. Methodist. Avocations: volunteer work, travel, ice skating, walking.

PEARSON, JIM BERRY, JR., human resources specialist; b. Wichita Falls, Tex., Sept. 25, 1948; s. Jim Berry and June Louise (Young) P.; m. Cynthia Ann Medlin, Nov. 9, 1985 (div. Jan. 1999). Cert. mediator. Community organizer VISTA, Pitts., 1969-71; youth dir. East Liberty YMCA, Pitts., 1971-72; aide, therapist technician Austin (Tex.) State Sch., 1972-80; labor organizer Comm. Workers Am., Austin, 1980-90; employee resource officer Austin State Hosp., 1990-96; human resource dir. Capital Area State-Operated Cmty. MHMR Svcs., Austin, 1996-97; human resources dir. Bluebonnet Trails Cmty. Mental Health/Mental Retardation Ctr, Round Rock, Tex., 1997-2001; employee rels. specialist Tex. Dept. Mental Health and Mental Retardation, Austin, 2001—03, Tex. Health and Human Svcs. Commn., Austin, 2003—05; dir. tng. and competency devel. Austin State Hosp., 2005—. Exec. bd. rep. Communications Workers

Am./Tex. State Employees Union, Austin, 1987-90; trustee Austin Cen. Labor Coun. AFL-CIO, Austin, 1983-84. Vol. AFL-CIO Polit. Action Com., 1980—; del. founding conv. Labor Party, 1996. Recipient Vols. in Politics award Nat. ALF-CIO, Washington, 1984, Peacemaker award Travis County Dispute Resolution Ctr., 1993. Mem. Comm. Workers Am./Tex. State Employees Union Local 6186 (founding mem.). Avocation: pre-colombian archaeology. Home: 1118 Mclain St Taylor TX 76574-2343 Office: Austin State Hosp 4110 Guadalupe St Austin TX 78751 Office Phone: 512-419-2305. Personal E-mail: dzul@texas.net. Business E-Mail: jimb.pearson@dshs.state.tx.us.

PEARSON, JOHN YEARDLEY, JR., lawyer; b. Norfolk, Va., July 23, 1942; BA, Washington & Lee U., 1964; JD, U. Va., 1971. Bar: Va. 1971. Atty. Willcox & Savage P.C., Norfolk. Mem editl. bd.: Va. Law Rev., 1969—71. Fellow Am. Coll. Trial Lawyers; mem. ABA (litig. sect.), Internat. Assn. Def. Counsel, Order of Coif. Office: Willcox & Savage PC 1800 Bank of America Ctr Norfolk VA 23510-2197 Office Phone: 757-628-5503. Business E-Mail: jpearson@wilsav.com.

PEARSON, LYNDA ANN, music educator; b. Washington, June 1, 1950; d. Frederick Joseph and Nancy Lee Pearson. AA in Music Edn., Luther Rice Coll., Alexandria, Va., 1971, BA in Music Edn., 1973; M in Music Edn., Cath. U. of Am., Washington, 1977. Substitute tchr. Alexandria City Pub. Schs., 1973—77, vocal music tchr., 1977—. Adjudicator Bland Music Competition, Alexandria, 1985. Recipient Good Apple award, Children Together, Alexandria, 2004. Mem.: NEA, Alexandria Edn. Assn., Va. Edn. Assn., Music Educators Nat. Conf., Va. Music Educators Assn. (Dist. 10 rep. 2006—). Baptist. Avocations: counted cross stitch, rubber stamping, collecting bells and Longaberger baskets. Home: 1018 Beverley Dr Alexandria VA 22302-2420 Office: Lyles-Crouch Traditional Acad 530 S Saint Asaph St Alexandria VA 22314 Office Phone: 703-706-4430. Office Fax: 703-684-0252. Personal E-mail: misslap@aol.com. Business E-Mail: lpearson@acps.k12.va.us.

PEARSON, MARGIT LINNEA, management consultant; b. Weymouth, Mass., Nov. 6, 1950; d. Eric Gustav and Evelyn (Forest) P. BA, Simmons Coll., 1972; MBA, Harvard U., 1975. With McKinsey & Co., Inc., NYC, 1975-83; pres. Berkey, Inc., Conn., 1987-89, APC Corp., NJ, 1990-91, Sunset Mgmt., NY, 1993-97; prin. CFN, NY, 1998—; CEO Neoptis, Inc., NY, 2000, HipnTasty, Inc., NY, 2001—; CIO Sidney Frank Family Office, 2004—, FDIC, LLC, 2005—. Bd. dirs. Desert Chorale, N. Mex., 1994—, Tchrs. Network, NY, 1996—, iKindi, NY, 2002—. Avocations: art, skiing, travel. Home: 1590 Canyon Rd Santa Fe NM 87501 Office: 689 Fifth Ave 14th Fl New York NY 10021 Personal E-mail: margitp@att.net.

PEARSON, MICHAEL P., lawyer; b. Houston, June 9, 1953; BA, U. Tex., 1975, JD, 1978. Bar: Tex. 1978, U.S. Ct. Appeals (5th cir.) 1981. Assoc. Jackson & Walker LLP, Houston, 1978—84; ptnr. Jackson Walker LLP, Houston, 1984—. Assoc. editor: Tex. Law Rev., 1977-78; contbr. articles to profl. jours. Mem. ABA, Internat. Bar Assn., State Bar Tex., Houston Bar Assn. (chair elect oil, gas and energy resources law sect.), Phi Beta Kappa, Phi Kappa Phi. Office: Jackson Walker LLP 1401 McKinney St #1900 Houston TX 77010-1900 Office Phone: 713-752-4311. E-mail: mpearson@jw.com.

PEARSON, NATHAN WILLIAMS, communications, investment executive; b. Sewickley, Pa., Aug. 1, 1951; s. Nathan Williams Sr. and Kathleen Patricia (McMurtry) P.; m. Jane Ruth Wallace, Oct. 12, 1985; children: Nathan McMurtry, Howe Quinn, Henry Wallace. BA and MA in Music, Conn. Wesleyan U., 1974; MBA, Columbia U., NYC, 1982. Pvt. practice cons., NYC and Washington, 1974-82; with McKinsey & Co., NYC and LA, 1982-88; exec. v.p., chief fin. officer, mng. prin., sec., treas. Broadcasting Ptnrs., Inc., NYC, 1988-95; chmn. Broadcasting Ptnrs., LLC, Rye, NY, 1995—; pres., CEO and chmn. RadioWave.com Inc., Chgo., 1999—2001; mng. dir. Manursing Group, Rye, NY, 2002—. Vice chmn. No. Light Comms., Reykjavik, 1995-2003; mng. dir. Commonwealth Holdings, Inc., NYC, 1996-99; operating affiliate McCown DeLeeuw & Co., NYC, 1997-99; ptnr. Windale Group, 2004-, 1105 Media Inc., 2006—; bd. dirs. Archway Broadcasting Group, Las Vegas TV Ptnrs., LLC, Tranzact, Inc., Ft. Lee, NJ, 2007—. Author: Goin' to Kansas City, 1987; producer LP records, TV and radio programs; contbr. articles to profl. jours. Sec., bd. dirs. CityLore, Inc., NYC, 1986—, pres., 1990-92; pres. Young Audiences/NYC, 1995-96; bd. dirs. Young Audiences, 1986—, Young Audiences, Inc., 1995—, Rye Nature Ctr., 2004—, The Osborn, 2005—. Mem. Soc. for Ethnomusicology, Am. Folklore Soc., Wadawanuck Club, Nat. Assn. Broadcasting, Manursing Island Club, Hillsboro Club, Rolling Rock Club, Beta Gamma Sigma. Avocations: boardsailing, river running, hiking. Home: 3 Holly Ln Rye NY 10580-3953 Office: Broadcasting Ptnrs Rye NY 10580 Office Phone: 914-643-3278. Personal E-mail: bill_pearson@prodigy.net. Business E-Mail: bpearson@manursingllc.com.

PEARSON, NELS KENNETH, retired manufacturing executive; b. Algonquin, Illinois, May 2, 1918; s. Nels Pehr and Anna (Frye) P.; m. Louise Mary Houston (Lenox), June 28, 1941 (dec. Dec. 1996); children: Lorine Marie Pearson Walters, Karla Jean; m. Ethel Jane Pearson, July 26, 1997. High Sch. grad. Assembly line foreman Oak Mfg. Co., Crystal Lake, Ill., 1935—43; served in U.S. Army, 1943—46; apprentice tool and die maker Oak Mfg. Co., Crystal Lake, Ill., 1946—50; co-founder, pres. Wauconda Tool and Engring. Co., Algonquin, Ill., 1950—86; co-founder, treas. Kenmode Tool and Engring. Co., Inc., Algonquin, 1960—72; founder, owner Kar-Lor Enterprises, Crystal Lake, 1986—. Avocation: restoring, showing and travelling in antique automobiles 1911 thru 1927. Home: 125 Dole Ave Crystal Lake IL 60014-5837 Office: 910 Pyott Rd Crystal Lake IL 60014

PEARSON, P. DAVID, dean; BA, U. Calif., Berkeley, 1963; PhD, U. Minn., 1969. Dean Coll. Edn. U. Ill., Urbana-Champaign, co-dir. Ctr. for Study of Reading; John. A. Hannah Disting. prof. edn. Mich. State U., co-dir. Ctr. for Study of Reading; dean Grad. Sch. Edn. U. Calif., Berkeley, 2001—. Recipient Oscar Causey Award, Nat. Reading Conf., 1989, William S. Gray Citation of Merit, 1990. Mem.: Nat. Acad. Edn., Phi Beta Kappa. Office: Grad Sch Edn 1501 Tolman Hall #1670 Berkeley CA 94720-1670 Office Phone: 510-643-6644. Office Fax: 510-643-8904. E-mail: ppearson@berkeley.edu.

PEARSON, PAUL DAVID, lawyer, arbitrator, mediator; b. Boston, Jan. 22, 1940; s. Bernard J. and Ruth (Bayla) Horblit; children: David Todd, Lisa Kari, Grant M. BA, Bucknell U., 1961; LLB, U. Pa., 1964. Bar: Mass. 1966, N.Y. 1987. Staff atty., tech. assoc. lab. cmty. psychiatry dept. Med. Sch. Harvard U., Boston, 1966—68; assoc. Snyder Tepper & Berlin, Boston, 1969—71, ptnr., 1971—77; ptnr., chmn. family law dept. Hill & Barlow, 1977—87; ptnr. chmn. family law dept. Hodgson, Russ, LLP, Buffalo, 1987—96; of counsel Sullivan Oliverio & Gioia, Buffalo, 1996—2006; with Law Offices Kevin A. Ricotta, 2006—. Lectr. Mass. CLE, New Eng. Law Inst., 1975-1987, dept. psychiatry SUNY Sch. Medicine, Buffalo, 1989—; instr. law and mental health Boston Psychoanalytic Soc. and Inst., 1975-87; lectr. law, mental health, alternative dispute resolution Contbr. articles to profl. jour. and interdisciplinary publs Founding mem. Alliance for Dispute Resolution, 1996, Buffalo Collaborative Law Coun., 2002; bd. dir. Jewish Cmty. Ctr. Greater Buffalo, 1991-96, Am. Jewish Com. Buffalo, pres., 1995-97, nat. bd. govs., 1997—; bd. dir. Arts Coun. Buffalo and Erie County, 1992-99; legal coord. Parent Edn. and Custody Effectiveness program N.Y. 8th jud. dist.; pres., trustee, legal counsel Wayland (Mass.) Townhouse; trustee Family Counseling Svc. (region West); mem., chmn., clk. Wayland Zoning Bd. Appeals, 1970-80; v.p., counsel Arts Wayland Found., 1982-87; vis. fellow Woodrow Wilson Found., 1985-87, Mass. Gov. Spl. Commn. on Divorce, 1985-87. Capt. Mil. Police Corps USAR. Fellow Am. Acad. Matrimonial Lawyers (cert., pres., bd. mgr. Mass); mem. ABA (chair ADR family com.), Mass. Bar Assn. (chmn. family law sect.), Assn. Conflict Resolution (advanced practitioner), N.Y. State Coun. on Divorce Mediation, Assn. Family and Conciliation Ct., Boston Bar Assn. (family law com., legis. chmn.), N.Y. Bar Assn. (family law sect., ADR com.), Erie County Bar Assn. (chair ADR com. 1992-96, family law com., judiciary com.) Office: 1100 Main Place Tower 350 Main St Buffalo NY 14202-3711 Office Phone: 716-854-6424. Office Fax: 716-854-6425.

PEARSON, PAUL HOLDING, insurance company executive; b. Worcester, Mass., Feb. 14, 1940; s. Malcolm D. and Myra L. (Holding) P.; m. Judith N. Howe, July 13, 1958 (div. June 1974); children: Scott D., Todd E.; m. Anne Beck, July 26, 1974. BA in Bus. and Econs., U. Maine, 1961. C.L.U., 1971. Jr. life underwriter State Mut. Am., Worcester, 1961-63, life underwriter, 1963-67, sr. life underwriter, 1967-69; dir. life underwriting Security Mut. Life Ins. Co., Binghamton, NY, 1969, 2d v.p. underwriting, 1970, v.p., 1971-75, sr. v.p. ins. services div., 1975-79, exec. v.p., 1979-81, pres., 1981-96, chief exec. officer, 1987-97; chmn. Security Mutual Life Ins. Co. of N.Y., Binghamton, 1996-97. Chmn., CEO, bd. dirs. SML Properties corp., Binghamton, Security Equity Life Ins. Co., Binghamton, 1987-93; vice chmn. Generalife, 1997-99. Trustee, treas. Lourdes Meml. Hosp., Binghamton, 1978-92; mem. SUNY Found., Binghamton, 1982-89; trustee, chmn. fin. com. Elmira Coll., 1983-87; bd. dirs. Broome C.C. Found., 1982-91, pres. 1985-86; pres. New Industries for Broome, Binghamton, 1985-95, N.Y. State Bus. Devel. Coun., 1987-96; bd. dirs. Valley Devel. Found., 1987-91, Bus. Coun. N.Y., 1988-97, Am. Coun. Life Ins., 1990-96; bd. dirs., treas. Fiddlesticks C.C., 2002-05. Mem. Assn. for Advanced Life Underwriting, Nat. Assn. Life Underwriters, Broome County C. of C. (bd. dirs. 1980-88, chmn. 1986), Binghamton C/C Live Wire Club, Fiddlesticks Country Club (bd. dirs., treas. 2002-05). Office Phone: 239-768-0162. Personal E-mail: phapearson@aol.com.

PEARSON, REBECCA E., lawyer; b. Balt., Jan. 14, 1964; AB, Duke Univ., 1985; JD, Univ. NC, Chapel Hill, 1989; LLM in Govt. Procurement with highest honors, George Washington Univ., 1996. Bar: Fla. 1989, DC 2000. Assoc. Venable LLP, Washington, ptnr., govt. contract litig., 2004—. Articles editor NC Jour. Internat. Law and Comml. Regulation, 1988—89, student editor-in-chief ABA Public Contract Law Jour., 1995—96; contbr. articles to profl. journals. With USAF, 1989—99. Mem.: ABA. Office: Venable LLP 575 Seventh St NW Washington DC 20004 Office Phone: 202-344-8183. Office Fax: 202-344-8300. Business E-Mail: repearson@venable.com.

PEARSON, RICHARD JOSEPH, archaeologist, educator; b. Kitchener, Ont., Can., May 2, 1938; s. John Cecil and Henrietta Anne (Wallwin) P.; m. Kazue Miyazaki, Dec. 12, 1964; 1 child, Sarina Riye. BA in Anthropology with honours, U. Toronto, 1960; PhD, Yale U., 1966. Asst. prof., then assoc. prof. archaeology U. Hawaii, 1966-71; mem. faculty U. B.C., Vancouver, 1971-2000. Sr. rsch. advisor Sainsbury Inst. Japanese Arts and Cultures, 2007. Author: The Archaeology of the Ryukyu Islands, 1969, Higashi Ajia no Kodai Shakai to Kokogaku, 1984, Windows on the Japanese Past, Studies in Archaeology and Prehistory, 1986, Ancient Japan, 1992; contbr. articles to profl. jours. Guggenheim fellow.

PEARSON, ROBERT LAWRENCE, executive recruiter; b. Chgo., Apr. 19, 1939; s. Jonas Peter and Caroline Margaret (Reilly) P.; m. Norma Eloise Dale, April 27, 1963; children: Jill C., Keith D. BSEE, Mich. State U., 1961; MS magna cum laude, MIT, 1963. Cons. McKinsey and Co., Inc., Chgo., 1964-68; v.p. Raymond James and Assoc., St. Petersburg, Fla., 1968-70; pres. Pearson Wade and Co., Inc., Ft. Lauderdale, Fla., 1970-71, Pearson, Inc., Racine, Wis., 1971-81; exec. dir. Russell Reynolds Assoc., Inc., Dallas, 1981-83; mng. dir. Lamalie Assoc., Inc., Dallas, 1984-89, chmn., 1989-94; pres. Lamalie Amrop Internat., Dallas, 1994-98, chmn., CEO, 1994—99; CEO Pearson Ptnrs. Internat., Inc., 1999—; mem., bd. dirs. Tatum CFO Inc., 1999—2003; mem. bd. dirs. Pentagon Techs. Inc., 2000—, Baird Capital Ptnrs. Inc., 2000—. Mem. fund raising com. Dallas Mus. of Art, 1983-85; mem. Dallas Mus. Natural History, 1985—, bd. dirs., 1988-90; mem. YMCA, Dallas; patron Ronald McDonald House of Dallas; speech writer Gov.'s Campaign, Chgo., 1968. Contbr. articles to profl. jours. Mem. MIT Enterprise Forum, Dallas C. of C., Phi Delta Theta (pres. 1959-61), Tower Club (Dallas), MIT (Dallas, pres. 1993-96), Gilda's Club North Tex. (founding sponsor), Dallas Nat. Golf Club, Broadmoor Golf Club. Episcopalian. Avocations: squash, jogging, deep sea fishing, hunting, marathon running. Office: Pearson Ptnrs Internat Inc Ste 1200 8080 N Central Expy Dallas TX 75206 Home: Apt 9D 3510 Turtle Creek Blvd Dallas TX 75219 Office Phone: 214-292-4130. Business E-Mail: rpear@pearsonpartners.intl.com.

PEARSON, ROGER, organization executive; b. London, Aug. 21, 1927; s. Edwin and Beatrice May (Woodbine) P.; m. Marion Primrose Simms, June 3, 1959; children: Edwin, Sigrid, Emma, Rupert BS with honors, U. London, 1951, MS, 1954, PhD, 1969. Chmn. Pakistan Tea Assn., 1963-64; mng. dir. Octavius Steel & Co. of Pakistan Ltd., Chittagong, East Pakistan, 1959-65; chmn. Plummer Bros., Ltd., Chittagong, East Pakistan, 1959-65, Chittagong Warehouses, Ltd., Chittagong, East Pakistan, 1960-65; chmn. dept. sociology and anthropology Queens Coll., Charlotte, NC, 1970-71; chmn. dept. anthropology U. So. Miss., Hattiesburg, 1971-74; dean acad. affairs, dir. research Mont. Coll. Mineral Sci. Tech., Butte, 1974-75; exec. dir. Council for Econ. and Social Studies, Washington, 1975—. Author: Eastern Interlude, 1954, Introduction to Anthropology, 1978, Anthropological Glossary, 1985, Race, Intelligence and Bias in Academe, 1991, Shockley on Eugenics and Race, 1992, Heredity and Humanity, 1996, Cultural Anthropology, 2002; editor: Ecology and Evolution, 1982, (jour.) Social Polit. and Econ. Studies, 1976—. Trustee, Benjamin Franklin U., Washington, 1984-87. Served to lt. Brit. Indian Army, 1945-48. Office: Coun Econ and Social Studies 1133 13th St NW Washington DC 20005-4203

PEARSON, ROGER LEE, library director; b. Galesburg, Ill., Dec. 7, 1940; s. Clifford Emmanuel and Lillian Louise (Fisher) P. BA, Knox Coll., 1963; MA in Sociology, U. Nebr.-Omaha, 1968; MA in Library Sci., Rosary Coll., 1974. Vol. U.S. Peace Corps, Brazil, 1964-66; extension service supr. Brown County Libr., Green Bay, Wis., 1974-75; system adminstr. Nicolet Libr. System, Green Bay, 1976-77; exec. dir. South Central Libr. System, Madison, Wis., 1977-81; dir. Corpus Christi Pub. Librs., Tex., 1981-84, Naperville (Ill.) Pub. Librs., 1984-95, Sonoma County Libr., Santa Rosa, Calif., 1996-2001; interim dir. Spokane (Wash.) Pub. Libr., 2001; interim libr. dir. Coll. of Marin, Kentfield, Calif., 2002; interim dist. libr. Dixon (Calif.) Pub. Libr., 2002—03; interim dir. Kans. City (Mo.) Pub. Libr., 2004—05, Sonoma County Libr., Santa Rosa, 2005, Berkeley Pub. Libr., Calif., 2006. Lectr. Grad. Sch. Libr. and Info. Sci., Dominican U., River Forest, Ill., 1991-95. Mem. ALA, Train Riders Assn. Calif., Calif. Libr. Assn., Wine Libr. Assocs. Sonoma County. Avocations: power walking, travel research, train travel. Home: 1451 Country Manor Dr Santa Rosa CA 95401

PEARSON, RONALD DALE, retail food stores corporation executive; b. Des Moines, 1940; married. BS in Bus. Adminstrn., Drake U., 1962. With Hy-Vee Food Stores, Inc. (name changed to Hy-Vee, Inc. in 1996), Chariton, Iowa, 1962—; pres. Hy-Vee, Inc., Chariton, Iowa, 1983—, chmn., pres., & CEO, 1989—2001, chmn., CEO, COO West Des Moines, Iowa, 2001—. Dir. Beverage Mfrs., Inc., Civic Ctr. Cts., Inc.; chmn. Food Marketing Inst. Found., Washington. Bd. dir. Keep Iowa Beautiful Inc., Greater Des Moines Partnership. Office: Hy-Vee Inc 5820 Westown Pkwy West Des Moines IA 50266-8223

PEARSON, RONALD K., mathematical data analyst; s. Robert S. and Beatrice I. Pearson; m. Pamela L. Pearson, Mar. 22, 1997. PhD, MIT, Cambridge, 1973—81. Sr. scientist ProSanos Corp., Harrisburg, Pa., 2004—; adj. rsch. asst. prof. Jefferson Med. Coll., Phila. Author: (books) Mining Imperfect Data, Discrete-Time Dynamic Models; co-author: (book) Identification and Control Using Volterra Models. Mem.: IEEE, Soc. Indsl. & Applied Math., Math. Assn. Am., Classification Soc. N.Am. Avocation: poetry. Office: ProSanos Corp 225 Market St Harrisburg PA 17101 Business E-Mail: ronald.pearson@prosanos.com.

PEARSON, ROY LAING, business administration educator; b. Victoria, Hong Kong, Oct. 18, 1939; s. Roy Ross and Martha Ann L.; m. Louise Elliott Johns, June 11, 1960; 1 child, Cynthia Laing. BS in Commerce, U. Va., 1961, PhD in Econs., 1968. Asst. prof. U. Ark. Sch. Bus. Adminstrn., Fayetteville, 1964-68; assoc. prof. Centenary Coll. La., Shreveport, 1968-71; assoc. prof. bus. adminstrn. Coll. William and Mary, Williamsburg, Va., 1971-76, prof. bus. adminstrn., 1976-87, dir. Bur. Bus. Rsch., 1985-98, Chancellor prof. bus. adminstrn., 1987—2005, prof. emeritus, 2005. V.p. Wessex Group, Inc., Williamsburg, Va., 1979—; sec.-treas. McKinley Land Co., Inc., Williamsburg, 1969-2001. Editor, author: (newsletter) Virginia Business Report, Virginia Outlook, 1984-99. Bd. dirs. Williamsburg Community Hosp., 1985-90; gov.'s adv. bd. economists Commonwealth of Va., Richmond, 1984-98, 2002-; mem. trust fund adv. com. Va. Employment Comm., 1984—. NSF fellow, 1963. Mem. Va. Assn. Economists (pres. 1990-91, bd. dirs. 1985-91, disting. fellow 1998), Assn. for Univ. Bus. and Econ. Rsch. (bd. dirs. 1991-92, v.p. 1992-94, pres. 1994-95, hon. mem. 1999—), Nat. Assn. Bus. Economists, Internat. Inst. Forecasters (bd. dirs. 2001-2004), Nat. Bus. and Economics Soc. (v.p. 2004-), Richmond Assn. Bus. Economists. Avocations: scuba diving, underwater photography, science fiction. Home and Office: 4400 Chickasaw Ct Williamsburg VA 23188-8020 Business E-Mail: roy.pearson@mason.wm.edu.

PEARSON, SCOTT ROBERTS, retired economics professor; b. Madison, Wis., Mar. 13, 1938; s. Carlyle Roberts and Edith Hope (Smith) P.; m. Sandra Carol Anderson, Sept. 12, 1962; children: Sarah Roberts, Elizabeth Hovden. BS, U. Wis., Madison, 1961; MA, Johns Hopkins U., 1965; PhD, Harvard U., 1969. Asst. prof. Stanford U., Calif., 1968-74, assoc. prof., 1974-80; assoc. dir. Food Rsch. Inst., 1977-84, dir., 1992-96, prof. food econs., 1980—2002; ret., 2002. Cons. AID, World Bank, Washington, 1965—; staff economist Commn. Internat. Trade, Washington, 1970-71. Author: Petroleum and the Nigerian Economy, 1970; (with others) Commodity Exports and African Economic Development, 1974, (with others) Rice in West Africa, Policy and Economics, 1981, (with others) Food Policy Analysis, 1983, (with others) The Cassava Economy of Java, 1984, (with others) Portuguese Agriculture in Transition, 1987, (with Eric Monke) The Policy Analysis Matrix, 1989, (with others) Rice Policy in Indonesia, 1991, (with others) Structural Change and Small-Farm Agriculture in Northwest Portugal, 1993, (with others) Agricultural Policy in Kenya, 1995, (with others) Small Farm Agriculture in Southern Europe, 1998, (with others) Applications of the Policy Analysis Matrix in Indonesian Agriculture, 2004. Mem. Am. Agrl. Econs. Assn., Am. Econ. Asn. Home: 691 Mirada Ave Stanford CA 94305-8477 E-mail: pearson@stanford.edu.

PEARSON, SELA, poet, speaker; b. Bklyn., Aug. 10, 1952; d. Thomas Turner and Thelma (Brown) Razor; children: Nassar (dec.), Anwar, Jonathan BS, St. Joseph's Coll., Bklyn., 1988; MBA in Healthcare Mgmt., U. Phoenix, 2006. LPN. Psychiat., pediat. nurse Syosset Hosp., NY, 1974—78; sales agent Combined Life Ins. Co. N.Y., Albany, 1978—80; med., surg. nurse Bapt. Med. Ctr., Bklyn., 1980—86; nurse counselor Riker's Island Prison Hosp., Queens, NY, 1986—88; clinic nurse St. Christopher Ottilie, Queens, 1988—90; mgr. intensive case AIDS Ctr. Queens County, 1990—92; quality assurance, utilization rev. nurse Vanderbilt U. Med. Ctr., Nashville, 1992—94; program dir. Boys and Girls Club, Franklin, Tenn., 1994—95; spkr., writer, nurse Akanke Creations, Brentwood, Tenn., 1996—; ind. health contractor Clayton County Crisis Unit, 1997—98; nurse Phoenix Program FHC of Nashville, 1998—99; nurse Murci Homes, 1999—. Cons. Murphy Alternative Ctr., Nashville, 1996, Serendipity House, Nashville, 1996, Family and Ednl. Adv. Assocs., Inc., Nashville, 1996, Growing In Grace Leadership Sch., Nashville, 1996; storyteller, presenter poetry recitals; ind. contractor Crisis Group Home, Riverdale, Ga.; faculty mem. Antara Ctr., 2004. Author: New York Poetry Foundation Anthology, 1986, Beyond the Stars, 1995 (Editors Choice 1995), Sela's Sounds of Silence, 1995, A Soulful Journey, 2000; performer (video) A Soulful Journey, 1995, The Magic of Peace, 1996, Our Voices, 1996; author numerous poems; contbr. articles to profl. jours., mags Vol. Williamson County Libr., Franklin, 1995—, Boys and Girls Club, Franklin, 1996—, TPAC; bd. dirs. Nashville Peace Action, 1996—; mem. New Gospel Singers Choir, 1995—; storytelling del. to South Africa People to People Amb. Programs, invited Women in Sec. rep., Egypt, 2000—; mem. Coun. for the Written Word. Recipient Vol. Svc. award Berksheire Nursing Ctr., West Babylon, N.Y., 1977, Mayor's award for svc. in cmty. in arts, 2001; inclusion of poem Faith to Wm. Kings Regl. Art Ctr., 1999, Cmty. Svc. award Edith Taylor Langster, Ho. of Reps., 54th Dist., 2003. Mem. Nat. Spkrs. Assn., Brentwood Early Risers Toastmasters (v.p. membership 1996—, various awards), Tenn. Writers Alliance, Harpeth Storytelling Group, Nat. Storytelling Assn., Internat. Soc. Poets (Poets Choice award 1995, Internat. Poet of Merit award 1995), Tenn. Writers Group Franklin, Tenn. Assn. Perpetuation Preservation Storytelling, Ga. Writers Group, Creative Artists Tenn., Tenn. Spkrs. Assn., Women Vision Enhancing Network (cert., dir. pub. rels.), Cherokee Wolf Clan (tribal coun.). Avocations: piano playing, travel, reading. Address: PO Box 111341 Nashville TN 37222-1341 Office Phone: 615-365-3187. Personal E-mail: selaperson@bellsouth.net. Business E-Mail: sela@akankecreations.com.

PEARSON, THOMAS SPENCER, academic administrator; b. Rockville Center, NY, Sept. 19, 1949; s. Donn Spencer and June Leonora Pearson; m. Susan Louise Frankus, July 24, 1971; children: Timothy Spencer, Mark Thomas. BA in History (magna cum laude), Santa Clara U., 1971; MA in Russian History, U. N.C., Chapel Hill, 1973, PhD in Russian History, 1977. Asst. prof. history Auburn (Ala.) U., 1977—78, Monmouth Coll., West Long Branch, NJ, 1978—81, asst. prof., chair of history, 1981—85, assoc. prof., chair of history, 1985—92, acting provost, assoc. prof. history, 1992—94, provost, v.p. acad. affairs, prof. history, 1994—. Co-chair Two River Film Festival Bd. Dirs., West Long Branch, NJ, 2003—. Author: (book) Russian Officialdom in Crisis: Autocracy and Local Self-Government, 1861-1900, 1989, 2004. Sec. bd. trustees Rumson (N.J.) County Day Sch., 1990—92, v.p. bd. trustees, 1992—95; vice chair bd. trustees ECI Sch. for Children, Eatontown, NJ, 2001—07. Grantee Fellowship to Russia, Internat. Rsch. and Exch. Bd., 1975—76. Mem.: Am. Assn. for Advancement of Slavic Studies. Roman Catholic. Avocations: film collector, tropical fish collector. Home: 184 Chatham Ave Oakhurst NJ 07755 Office: Monmouth Univ Provost's Office 400 Cedar Ave West Long Branch NJ 07764 Office Phone: 732-571-3405. E-mail: pearson@monmouth.edu.

PEARSON, WALTER DONALD, editor, columnist; b. Pittsfield, Mass., Feb. 5, 1916; s. Edgar C. and Edna (Scott) P.; divorced; children: Florence, Donald, Sharon; m. Elsa Swanson (dec.); 1 child, Richard Scott. Student, Dartmouth Coll., 1941-43. Advt. salesman, 1935-41; securities broker Charles A. Day Co., Boston, 1947-55; founder, owner, mgr. First New Eng.

Securities Co., Inc., Southbridge, Mass., 1955-71; now owner, editor Pearson Investment Letter, Dover, Fla.; ptnr. Pearson Capital Inc.; fin. columnist World Intelligence Rev., CDL Report, Nationalist Times; free-lance columnist various publications; fin. advisor, investment mgr. Author: Investing for the Millions, 1990, Bridge Made Easy, 1995 With inf. U.S. Army, 1943-45, ETO. Decorated Bronze star, Croix de Guerre (France), Combat Infantry badge. Home: 1628 White Arrow Dr Dover FL 33527-5741 Office Phone: 813-659-2560. Personal E-mail: PearsonCap@aol.com.

PEARSON, W(ILLIAM) ROBERT, former federal agency administrator, former ambassador; b. Bells, Tenn., June 28, 1943; s. Marion Robert and Louise (Wilson) P.; m. Margaret Coplin, June 20, 1975; 1 child, Matthew. BA, Vanderbilt U., 1965; LLB, U.Va., 1968. Vice consul U.S. Consulate Gen., Auckland, New Zealand, 1976-78; staff asst./Conf. Asia Bur. US Dept. State, Washington, 1978-79, Chinese lang. tng. officer Washington and Taiwan, 1979-81; polit. officer US Embassy, Beijing, 1981-83; dep. dir. Ops. Ctr. US Dept. State, Washington, 1983-85; dep. exec. sec. NSC, Washington, 1985-87; dept. asst. sec. gen. NATO, Brussels, 1987-90; dep. exec. sec. US Dept. State, Washington, 1990-91, exec. sec., 1991—93; dep. permanent rep. to US mission NATO, 1993—97; dep. chief mission US Embassy, France, 1997—2000; US amb. to Turkey US Dept. State, Ankara, 2000—03, dir. gen. US Fgn. Svc. Washington, 2003—06, dir. human resources, 2003—06. Mem. Internat. Inst. of Strategic Studies.

PEART, SANDRA JOAN, dean; b. Stratford, Canada, Apr. 4, 1959; d. Donald MacLean and Beverley Joan Peart; m. Craig Warren Heinicke, June 4, 1988; children: Nathan Casey Heinicke-Peart, Matthew Warren Heinicke-Peart. BA, U. Toronto, Ont., Can., 1982, PhD, 1989. Asst. prof. Coll. William and Mary, Williamsburg, Va., 1989—91; prof. econs. Baldwin-Wallace Coll., Berea, Ohio, 1991—2007; dean Jepson sch. leadership studies U. Richmond, Va., 2007—. Vis. scholar Ctr. Study of Pub. Choice George Mason U., Fairfax, Va., 2004—05, dir. Summer Inst. Ctr. Study of Pub. Choice, 2004—. Co-author (with David Levy): The Vanity of the Philosopher: From Equality to Hierarchy in Post-Classical Economics, 2005; contbr. articles to profl. jours. Fellow, Am. Coun. Edn., 2005—06. Mem.: History Econs. Soc. (exec. com. 2000—05, pres. 2007—, Best Dissertation award 1990). Achievements include research in the transition from egalitarian thinking to notions of race and hierarchy in economics; the role of sympathy in economics and social science; the role of the expert in social science. Office: Jepson Sch Leadership Studies Univ Richmond Richmond VA 23173 Office Phone: 804-289-8008. Personal E-mail: sandrajpeart@gmail.com. Business E-Mail: speart@richmond.edu.

PEASE, DAVID GORDON, artist, educator; b. Bloomington, Ill., June 2, 1932; s. Gordon A. and June (Stephens) P.; m. Julie Jensen, Mar. 29, 1956; children: Lisa Kay, Kerry Susan. BS, U. Wis., 1954, MS, 1955, M.F.A., 1958. Instr. audio visual ctr. Mich. State U., 1958-60; mem. faculty Tyler Sch. Art, Temple U., Phila., 1960-83, prof., 1970-83, chmn. painting dept., 1968-77, dean, 1977-83; prof. of painting Yale U. Sch. Art, New Haven, 1983-2000, Street prof., dean emeritus, 2000—, dean, 1983-96, dir. grad. studies/painting, 1997-2000. Vis. faculty mem. Yale U. Summer Sch. Music and Art, 1970-72, Ohio State U., spring 2001. One-man shows include Baylor U., 1972, U. Wis., 1972, Pa. Acad. Fine Arts, 1977, Terry Dintenfass Inc., N.Y.C., 1969, 71, 76, Phila. Art Alliance, 1961, 70, Vassar Coll., 1999, Ohio State U., 2001; group exhbns. include Carnegie Internat., Pitts., 1961, Corcoran Biennial, Washington, 1961, 63, Whitney Annual, N.Y.C., 1963; represented in permanent collections Whitney Mus. Am. Art, Phila. Mus. Art, Pa. Acad. Fine Arts, Des Moines Art Center, Pa. State U., U. Wis., Temple U., Hallmark Cards Inc., Columbia Pictures, Yale U. Art Gallery, others. Trustee Louis Comfort Tiffany Found., 1988-97, 98—; bd. trustees Lyme Acad. Coll. Fine Arts, 1999-2007. With U.S. Army, 1955-57. Recipient William A. Clark award Corcoran Biennial, 1963, Lindbeck Found. Disting. Teaching award, 1968, Disting. Alumni award U. Wis., 1991; Guggenheim Found. fellow, 1965-66; Tiffany Found. grantee, 1975-76 Mem. Assn. Ind. Colls. Art and Design (trustee 1992-96). Home: 95 Thankful Stow Rd Guilford CT 06437-2529 Personal E-mail: david.pease@yale.edu.

PEASE, EDWARD A., former congressman; b. Terre Haute, Ind., May 22, 1951; BA with distinction, Ind. U., 1973, JD cum laude, 1977; postgrad. in English, Ind. State U. Past city atty. City of Brazil, Ind.; past gen. counsel Ind. State U., v.p. univ. advancement, 1993; past ptnr. Thomas Thomas & Pease; senator Ind. Gen. Assembly, 1980-92, past chmn. senate jud. com., past chmn. Ind. commn. trial cts., past chmn. Ind. code revision commn.; mem. U.S. Congress from 7th Ind. dist., 1997—2001, mem. jud. com., mem. transp. and infrastructure com.; sr. v.p. Rolls-Royce N.Am. Past mem. adv. coun. on nat. coun. Boy Scouts Am., chmn. com. Nat. Order of Arrow; bd. trustees Nature Conservancy. Recipient numerous awards Boy Scouts Am. Mem. Nat. Interfraternity Conf. (past nat. pres.), Pi Kappa Alpha (nat. dir. alumni affairs, chpt. advisor, nat. pres., pres. ednl. found.). Republican.

PEASE, JOHN ALAN, sociology educator; b. Grand Rapids, Mich., Mar. 8, 1936; s. Homer R. and P. Leola (Dulyea) P.; m. Barbara Ann Limpus, Feb. 22, 1958 (dec. 1980); children: Leah Kay, Jay Robert. BS in Sociology, Western Mich. U., 1960; MA in Sociology, Mich. State U., 1963, PhD in Sociology, 1968. Rsch. assoc. Mich. State Univ., 1961—64, asst. instructor, 1964—67, instructor, 1968; asst. prof. U. Md., College Park, 1967-71, assoc. prof. sociology, 1971—. Asst. instructor Western Mich. U., 1960; part-time lectr. Hood Coll., 1975, 1978-80, 83-84; temporary, part-time instructor Md. Coll. of Art and design, 1977; reader/cons. Allyn and Bacon, William C. Brown Pub., Gordon and Breach Pub., Harper and Row, Harper Collins, F.E. Peacock Pub., Macmillan Co., McGraw-Hill Book Co., Oxford U. Press, D. Van Nostrand Co., Wadsworth Pub. Co., West Pub. Co., Pine Forge Press and several others; program cons./referee Acad. Ednl. Devel., Am. Sociol. Assn., NSF, Social Scis. and Humanities Rsch. Coun. of Can., others.; facilitator, The Maryland Experience, 2005; spkr. in field. Contbr. numerous articles to profl. jours.; co-author: Sociology and Social Life, 1973, 2d edit. 1979; co-author monograph: Attrition of Graduate Students at the PhD Level in the Traditional Arts and Sciences, 1964; editor, The Sociologist, 1971-73; assoc. editor, Social Problems, 1974-78; referee, reviewer The Sociol. Quar., 1970, Am. Jour. Sociology, 1971-72, Social Problems, 1974-78, Am. Sociologist, 1977, Housing Educator's Jour., 1977, The Sociologist, 1977, Sociol. Focus, 1978, Teaching Sociology, 1983, Am. Sociol. Rev., 1991. Recipient numerous campus teaching awards various orgns.; assoc. Danforth Found., 1980-86. Mem. D.C. Sociol. Soc. (treas., 1969-71, Sec., 1971-73, pres. 1974-75, historian/archivist, 2000-2002), Armed Forces Soc., Alpha Kappa Delta, Phi Kappa Phi. Office: Univ of Maryland Dept Sociology 2112 Art-Sociology Bldg College Park MD 20742-1315 Office Phone: 301-405-6436. E-mail: pease@umd.edu.

PEASE, NEAL, history professor; m. Ewa Barczyk; children: Andrew, Krystyna, Alexander. PhD in History, Yale U., 1982. Assoc. prof. history U. Wis., Milw., 1983—.

PEASE, WILLIAM STOESS, physiatrist, educator; b. Cin., Jan. 7, 1955; s. Burton Reiman and Elizabeth Stoess Pease; m. Margaret E. Ginn, Dec. 29, 1979; children: James Burton, Katherine Elizabeth. MD, U. Cin., 1977—81. Lic. dr. Am. Bd. Phys. Medicine & Rehab., 1985, Am. Bd. Electrodiagnostic Medicine, 1989. Faculty Ohio State U. Coll. Medicine, Columbus, 1984—94, prof., dept. chair, 1994—. Bd. dir. Am. Bd. Electrodiagnostic Medicine, Rochester, Minn., 2003—. Assoc. editor: medical textbook Physical Medicine and Rehabilitation: Principles and practice; assoc. editor Am. Jour. Phys. Medicine & Rehab., Phila., 2005—; contbr. chapters to books. Bd. mem. St. Joseph Montessori Sch., Columbus, 1999—2001. Recipient Faculty Tchg. award, Ohio State U. Coll. Medicine, 2005, Disting. Clinician award, Am. Acad. Phys. Medicine & Rehab., 2006. Fellow: Am. Assn. Neuromuscular & Electrodiagnostic Medicine, Assn. Academic Physiatrists, Am. Acad. Phys. Medicine & Rehab.; mem.: AMA (alt. del., ho. delegates 2004—), Tau Beta Pi (life), Beta Theta Pi (pres. 1976—76). Meth. Office: Ohio State Univ Med Ctr 480 Medical Center Dr Columbus OH 43210 Office Phone: 614-293-3433.

PEASE-PRETTY ON TOP, JANINE B., community college administrator; b. Nespelam, Wash., Sept. 17, 1949; d. Benjamin and Margery Louise (Jordan) Pease; m. Sam Vernon Windy Boy, July 30, 1975 (div. Jan. 1983); children: Rosella L. Windy Boy, Sam Vernon Windy Boy; m. John Joseph Pretty On Top, Sept. 15, 1991. BA in Sociology, Anthropology, Ctrl. Wash. U., 1970; MEd, Mont. State U., 1987, EdD, 1994; HHD (hon.), Hood Coll., 1990; LLD (hon.), Gonzaga U., 1991; DHL (hon.), Teikyo/Marycrest U., 1992; EdD (hon.), Whitman Coll., 1993; HHD (hon.), Rocky Mountain Coll., 1998. Dep. dir. Wash. State Youth Commn., Olympia, 1971; tutor student svcs. Big Bend C.C., Moses Lake, Wash., 1971-72, upward bound dir., 1972-75; women's counselor Navajo C.C., Many Farms, Ariz., 1972; dir. adult & continuing edn. Crow Ctrl. Edn. Commn., Crow Agy., Mont., 1975-79; ednl. cons. Box Elder, Mont., 1979-81; dir. Indian career svc. Ea. Mont. Coll., Billings, 1981-82; pres. Little Big Horn Coll., Crow Agency, 1982—; with Rocky Mountain Coll., Billings, Mont. Exec. com. Am. Indian Higher Ednl. Consortium, Washington, 1983—; bd. dirs. Am. Indian Coll. Fund, N.Y.C., 1988—; sec. Indian Nations at Risk U.S. Dept. Edn., Washington, 1990-91, collaborator task force, 1990-91; 2d vice chmn. Nat. Adv. Coun. Indian Edn., Washington, 1994—. Chmn. Bighorn County Dem. Ctrl. Com., Hardin, Mont., 1983-88; mem. coun. First Crow Indian Bapt. Ch., 1989—; bd. dirs. Ctr. for Rocky Mountain West, 1998—; chmn. Mont. State Reappt. an Distructing Commn., 1999—. MacArthur fellow John D. & Catharine MacArthur Found., 1994. Mem. Nat. Indian Edn. Assn. (Indian educator of yr. 1990), Mont. Assn. Chs. (bd. dirs. 1997—), Crow Tribe Nighthawk Dance Soc.

PEASLEE, ROBERT LEON, metallurgical engineer, consultant; b. Milw., Jan. 4, 1917; m. Betty Kirby Peaslee, Jan. 4, 1941 (dec.); children: Bonnie Jean, Robert Leon Peaslee II. ChE, U. Cin., 1940. V.p. Wall Colmonoy Corporaation, Madison Heights, Mich., 1952—2003; cons. to wall colmonoy corp. Wall Colmonoy Corp., Madison Heights, Mich., 2003—. Dir. Wall Colmonoy Corp., Mont., 1952—95; v.p., dir. Wall Colmonoy Can. Ltd., Montreal, Canada, Wall Gases Inc, Morrisville, Pa., Wall Colmonoy Ltd. (GB), Pontardawe, Swansea. Fellow: Am. Welding Soc. (life); mem.: ASME (life), Am. Chem. Soc. (life), ASM Internat. (life). R-Consevative. Baptist. Achievements include patents for 2, 588.566 Electrolytic Process for Stripping Copper (AC); 3, 275, 240 Spray Apparatus (US); 3, 809, 553 Metal Foil-Making Process (US); 3, 809, 556 Metal-Foil Making Process; 1, 448, 008 Process for Making Sintered Metal Foils (GB); 506, 364 Spray Aparatus (JP); 2, 833, 030 Brazing Method (Lithium Atmosphere) (US); 2, 833, 030 Method of Joining Metal Parts with Flexible Composit Joining Material (US); 3, 188, 203 Brazing Alloy (US); 3, 275, 240 Spray Apparatus (US); 2, 588, 566 Electrolytic Process for Stripping Copper (US); 2, 800, 711 Brazing Method (Lithium Atmosphere) (US); Method of Joining Metal Parts eith Flexable Joining Material (US); 3.188.203 Brazing Alloy (Ni-Cr-P) (US). Home: 217 Linden Royal Oak MI 48073 Office: Wall Colmonoy Corp 30261 Stephenson Hwy Madison Heights MI 48071 Home Phone: 248-585-0226.

PEAT, RANDALL DEAN, military analyst, retired military officer; b. Chgo., July 6, 1935; s. Thomas R. and Lulu M. (Ray) P.; m. Joyce Enid Hunter, Sept. 15, 1956; children: Brian James, Sondra Lee Peat Gadell BS in Journalism, Medill Sch. Journalism Northwestern U., Evanston, Ill., 1956, MS in Journalism Mgmt., 1957. Commd. officer U.S. Air Force, 1957, advanced through ranks to maj. gen.; pilot, instr. Strategic Air Command, Westover AFB and Clinton-Sherman, Okla., 1958-66; asst. air attache Am. Embassy, Djakarta, Indonesia, 1967; pilot Pacific Command Airborne Command Post, Hickam AFB, Hawaii, 1968-70; staff officer 7th Air Force, Saigon, Vietnam, 1971, Hdqrs. U.S. Air Force, Pentagon, DC, 1972-75, SHAPE, Belgium, 1976-79, Hdqrs. U.S. Air Force, Pentagon, DC, 1980-81; dep. dir. plans Office Joint Chief of Staff, Pentagon, DC, 1982-84; asst. chief of staff ops. Supreme Hdqrs. Allied Powers Europe, Belgium, 1984-87; chief of staff Strategic Air Command, Offutt AFB, Nebr., 1987-89; v.p. R&D Assocs., Europe, 1989—2002. Bd. dirs. Santa Fe Farmer's Market. Decorated Air medal, Bronze Star, Meritorious Service medal, Def. Superior Service medal, Def. Disting. Service medal; Republic of Vietnam Cross of Gallantry with Palm, Republic of Vietnam Campaign medal Mem. Daedalians (vice flight capt. 1976), Air Force Assn., Arroyo Hondo Neighborhood Assn. (pres.), Pi Alpha Mu Avocations: cooking, hiking, painting, british mystery writers. Home: 28 Likely Rd Santa Fe NM 87508

PEAVY, JAKE (JACOB EDWARD PEAVY), professional baseball player; b. Mobile, Ala., May 31, 1981; m. Katie Peavy; children: Jacob Edward II, Wyatt. Draft pick San Diego Padres, 1999, pitcher, 2002—. Named to Nat. League All-Star Team, Maj. League Baseball, 2005, 2007. Achievements include leading the Nat. League in earned run average (2.27), 2004, strikeouts (216), 2005. Mailing: San Diego Padres PO Box 122000 San Diego CA 92112-2000 *

PEAY, J.H. BINFORD, III, academic administrator, career military officer; b. Richmond, Va., May 10, 1940; m. Pamela Jane Pritchett; children: James, Ryan. BS, Va. Mil. Inst., 1962; MA, George Washington U., 1975; grad., U.S. Army Command and Gen. Staff Coll., U.S. Army War Coll. Commd. 2d lt. US Army, 1962, advanced through grades to gen., 1993, commd. gen., 101st Airborne Divsn., 1989—91, vice chief staff Washington, 1993; comdr. in chief US Ctrl. Command, MacDill AFB, Fla., 1994-97; ret., 1997; chmn. bd. Allied Def. Group, 2001—; supt. Va. Mil. Inst., 2003—. Served in Viet Nam, 1967-68, 71-72, Desert Storm, 1991. Decorated Def. D.S.M., Silver Star, Legion of Merit with oak leaf cluster, Army D.S.M. with three oak leaf clusters, Def. D.S.S.M., Purple Heart, Bronze Star medal with three oak leaf clusters. Home: 412 VMI Parade Lexington VA 24450-2115 Office: Va Military Inst Supt Office 201 Smith Hall Lexington VA 24450 Office Phone: 540-464-7311.

PECA, MICHAEL, professional hockey player; b. Toronto, Ont., Can., Mar. 26, 1974; m. Kristin Peca; children: Trevor, Emily. Center Vancouver Canucks, 1993—95, Buffalo Sabres, 1995—2000, NY Islanders, 2001—05, Edmonton Oilers, 2005—06, Toronto Maple Leafs, 2006—07, Columbus Blue Jackets, 2007—. Mem. Team Can., Olympic Games, Salt Lake City, 2002. Recipient Frank J. Selke Trophy, 1997, 2002. Achievements include being a member of gold medal Team Canada, World Junior Championships, 1994; being a member of gold medal Canadian Hockey team, Salt Lake City Olympic Games, 2002. Office: Columbus Blue Jackets Nationwide Arena 200 W Nationwide Blvd Columbus OH 43215 *

PECANO, DONALD CARL, automotive manufacturing executive; b. LA, Dec. 2, 1948; s. Domenick Lawrence and Carlotta Noble (Martello) P.; m. Sandra Ann Tuminello, Apr. 26, 1969; children: Julia Ann, Melissa Ann, Donald Carl. BS in Acctg, Pa. State U., 1970; MBA in Mktg., Youngstown State U., 1981. CPA, Pa.; cert. mgmt. acct., cert. fin. mgr. Contr. Atlas Guard Svc. subs. SERVISCO, East Orange, NJ, 1974-76; asst. to pres. SERVISCO, Hillside, NJ, 1976-77; v.p. fin. Columbus Svcs., Inc. subs. SERVISCO, New Castle, Pa., 1977-82; dir. fin. East Mfg. Corp. and subs. cos., 1982-88, v.p. fin. and adminstrn., 1988-99, also mem. exec. com., exec. v.p., CFO, 1999—; v.p. fin. Intermodal Techs. Inc., 1991—. Bd. dirs. Intermodal Techs. Inc. Weatherhead fellow Case Western Res. U., 1995. Republican. Roman Catholic. Office: 1871 State Route 44 Randolph OH 44265 *Placing the best interests of the company ahead of your own is ultimately in your own best interest.*

PECHA, BRIAN S., physician; b. Salt Lake City, Feb. 18, 1961; s. Robert L. and Laura Boone Pecha; m. Kari S. Pecha, Dec. 29, 1985; children: Elizabeth Ann Anderson, Robert Hayden, Mary Katherine Meyer, Mary Bridget Finn, Nancy Marie Byrne, Margaret Louise Conroy. BS, U. San Francisco, 1983; MD, Stanford U., Calif., 1988; diploma with distinction, Naval War Coll., 2005. Diplomate Am. Bd. Internal Medicine, 2001. Internist, hospitalist Sonoma Devel. Ctr., Eldridge, Calif., 1996—. Clin. asst. prof. medicine U. Calif., Davis Med. Ctr., Sacramento; chief residents, internal medicine Naval Hosp. San Diego, 1990—91; dir. med. svcs. Naval Hosp. Naples Italy, 1992—94; bn. surgeon USN, 2004—06. Officer KC, Sonoma, Calif., 2000. Decorated Navy Commendation medal with 2 gold stars USN. Fellow: ACP; mem.: Assn. Mil. Surgeons the US. Roman Catholic. Avocation: woodworking. Home Phone: 707-287-0181; Office Phone: 707-938-6000.

PECHURA, CONSTANCE MARY, foundation administrator; BS, Va. Commonwealth U., 1980; PhD, Uniformed Svcs. U. Health Scis, 1987. Lab. asst. dept. pharmacology Med. Coll. Va., Richmond, 1977-79, rsch. asst. dept. surgery, divsn. neurosurgery, 1979-81; staff fellow NIH-NINDS, 1987-88; sr. program officer Inst. Medicine, Washington, 1989-98, dir. divsn. neurosci. & behavioral health, 1994-98; sr. program officer Robert Wood Johnson Found., Princeton, NJ, 1998—. Contbr. chpts. to books and articles to profl. jours. Bd. dirs., trainer, counselor Richmond Hotline, 1975-78; dir., counselor Rape Crisis Outreach, Richmond, 1976-78; mem., chair bd. dirs. Student Pugwash, Washington, 1995-2000. Office: Robert Wood Johnson Found PO Box 2316 Rte 1 and College Rd E Princeton NJ 08543-2316

PECINA, JULIE H., education educator; b. Edinburg, Tex., Feb. 17, 1972; d. Francisco and Ofelia C. Pecina; m. Pablo Martinez, Aug. 7, 1999; children: Mara Lisa Martinez, Miran Aurelio Martinez. M Ednl. Diagnostician, U. Tex.-Pan Am., Edinburg, 1997. Cert. elem. spl. edn. tchr. Tex., 1994. Dir. field experience office U. Tex.-Pan Am., 2003—05, program coord., advisor, 2004—. Vol. Spl. Olympics, Weslaco, Tex., 1997—2007. Recipient Outstanding Svc. award, Tex. Spl. Olympics, 2006. Mem.: Coun. Exceptional Children (student club advisor U. Tex.-Pan Am. 1998—). Home: 2212 River Dr Edinburg TX 78539 Office: UT-Pan Am 1201 W University Dr Edinburg TX 78539 Home Phone: 956-386-1012; Office Phone: 956-292-7352. Office Fax: 956-381-2395; Home Fax: 956-381-2395. Personal E-mail: j_pecina@yahoo.com. Business E-Mail: pecinaj@panam.edu.

PECK, ABRAHAM, editor, writer, educator, media consultant; b. NYC, Jan. 18, 1945; s. Jacob and Lottie (Bell) Peckolick; m. Suzanne Wexler, Mar. 19, 1977; children: Douglas Benjamin, Robert Wexler. BA, NYU, 1965; postgrad., CUNY, 1965-67; cert. in advanced exec. program, Northwestern U., 1997. Engaged in cmty. organizing and tutoring, 1962-64; with NYC Welfare Dept., 1965—67; free-lance writer, 1967—; writer, organizer Chgo. Action Youth Internat. Party, 1968; editor Chgo. Seed, 1968-70; treas. Seed Pub., Inc., 1968-70; mem. coordinating com. Underground Press Syndicate, 1969; assoc. editor Rolling Stone mag., San Francisco, 1975-76, contbg. editor, 1976-2001; feature writer Chgo. Daily News, 1977-78; with features dept. Chgo. Sun-Times, 1978-81; from asst. prof. to prof. Northwestern U., Evanston, Ill., 1981—2001, Sills prof. journalism, 2001—06, Helen Gurley Brown prof. journalism, 2006—, chair mag. dept., 1981—2006, dir. mag. programs Media Mgmt. Ctr., 2002—, chair journalism and cross-media storytelling, 2006—. Editor, co-founder Sidetracks, alt. newspaper supplement, Chgo. Daily News, 1977—78; critic at large Sta. WBBM, 1979—82; mem. exec. com. mag. divsn. Assn. Edn. Journalism and Mass Communication, 1987—89, 1992—96, 2003—04, pres., 1994—95; mem. adv. bd. Academe mag., AAUP, 1990—2000, Heartland Jour., 1990—2002, Technos, 1992—; editl. co-auditor Advanstar Comm., 1999—; mem. adv. bd. Chgo. chpt. Asian Am. Journalists Assn., 2002—; chair ethics subcom. Am. Bus. Media, 2002; cons., lectr. in field. Editor: Dancing Madness, 1976; author: Uncovering the Sixties: The Life and Times of the Underground Press, 1985, 1991; contbg. editor: Satisfaction Mag., 2005—06, consulting editor, contbr.: The Sixties, 1977; contbr. chapters to books. With US Army, 1967. Named to Chgo. Journalism Hall of Fame, 2006; recipient Mag. Divsn. Educator of Yr., Assn. Edn. Journalism and Mass Comm., 2003—04. Office: Northwestern U Medill Sch Journalism 1845 Sheridan Rd Evanston IL 60208-0815 Office Phone: 847-491-2068. Business E-Mail: a.peck@northwestern.edu.

PECK, ANDREW JAY, federal judge; b. 1953; AB, Cornell U., 1974; JD, Duke U., 1977. Bar: N.Y. 1978, U.S. Dist. Ct. (so. dist.) N.Y., U.S. Ct. Appeals (2d thru 11th cirs.), U.S. Supreme Ct. Law clk. to Hon. Paul Roney, U.S. Ct. Appeals for 5th Circuit, St. Petersburg, Fla., 1977-78; from assoc. to counsel Paul, Weiss, Rifkind, Wharton & Garrison, NYC, 1978-95; magistrate judge US Dist. Ct. (So. Dist.) NY, NYC, 1995—, chief magistrate judge, 2004—05. Adj. prof. Cardozo Law Sch., 2003—. Editor Duke Law Jour., 1976-77. Mem. ABA, N.Y. State Bar Found., Fed. Magistrate Judges Assn., Mystery Writers Am. Inc. (bd. dirs.), Order of Coif. Office: Daniel P Moynihan US Courthouse Rm 1370 500 Pearl St New York NY 10007-1312 Office Phone: 212-805-0036. Office Fax: 212-805-7933.

PECK, ART, retail executive; Grad., Occidental Coll., LA; MBA, Harvard Bus. Sch. Fin. and mktg. position Avery Denison, Pasadena, Calif.; sr. v.p. Boston Consulting Group, 1982—2005, dir., 1988—2005; exec. v.p. strategy and ops. Gap, Inc., San Francisco, 2005—. Office: Gap Inc 2 Folsom St San Francisco CA 94105 Office Phone: 650-952-4400. *

PECK, ARTHUR JOHN, JR., retired manufacturing executive, lawyer; b. Trenton, NJ, Mar. 2, 1940; s. Arthur John and Mary Ellen (Kelly) P.; m. Susan Williams Lodge, July 18, 1970; children: David A., Margaret E. BA in Hist., Yale U., 1962; LLB, Washington & Lee U., 1968. Admissions officer Lawrenceville Sch., NJ, 1962-65; atty. Shearman & Sterling, NYC, 1968-72; asst., assoc. counsel Corning (N.Y.), Inc., 1972-81, asst. sec., 1981—88, sec., v.p., 1988—2000, sr. v.p., 2000-01; ret., 2001. Sec. Teddington Co., Ltd., 1989-2001, Corning Inc. Found. 1981-01, Corning Europe, Inc., 1989-97, Corning Inc., 1988-2001, Corning Internat. Corp., 1991-2001; dir., Corning Inc. Fgn. Sales Corp., 1992-01, Corning Enterprises, Inc., 1974-97; asst. sec. Market St. Restoration Corp., 1974-01, Corning Mus. of Glass, 1981-98, sec., 1998-2001; trustee Rockwell Mus., sec., 1983-01, v.p., 2001—, pres. 2007-; trustee, sec. Corning Classic Charities, Inc., 1977-; bd. dirs. Guthrie Healthcare Sys., vice chmn., 2005-; bd. dirs. Guthrie Health; trustee Elmira-Corning Cmty. Found., 2005-, pres. 2007—. E-mail: jpeck@stny.rr.com.

PECK, BERNARD SIDNEY, lawyer; b. Bridgeport, Conn., July 26, 1915; s. James and Sadie Peck; m. Marjorie Eloise Dean, Apr. 10, 1943; children: Daniel Dean, Constance Lynn. BA, Yale U., 1936, LLB, 1939. Bar: Conn. 1939, Fla. 1979, N.Y. 1982. Pvt. practice, Bridgeport, 1939-84; ptnr. Goldstein and Peck, 1946-84, Peck & Peck, Naples, Fla., 1983-87, 97—, Porter, Wright, Morris & Arthur, Naples, 1987-90, Peck, Peck & Volpe, Naples, 1990-92, Peck, Volpe & Sullivan, Naples, 1992-94, Peck & Faga, Naples, 1994-97; judge Mcpl. Ct., Westport, Conn., 1951-55; ptnr. Peck & Peck, 1997—. Moderator town meeting, Westport, 1950—51; pres.

Westport YMCA, 1957, trustee, 1964—84; pres. endowment bd. YMCA, Naples, 1987—88; mem. Westport Rep. Town Com., 1951—79. Capt. US Army, 1942—46. Fellow: Internat. Acad. Trial Lawyers, Am. Coll. Trial Lawyers; mem.: ABA, Collier County Bar Assn., Royal Poinciana Golf Club (bd. dirs. 1983—90, pres. 1987—89), Park Meadows Country Club (Park City, Utah), Yale Club SW Fla. (trustee 1985—), Phi Beta Kappa. Office: Peck & Peck 5801 Pelican Bay Blvd Ste 103 Naples FL 34108-2709 Home: Apt 702 4151 Gulf Shore Blvd N Naples FL 34103-2296 Office Phone: 239-566-3600.

PECK, CHARLES EDWARD, retired construction and mortgage executive; b. Newark, Dec. 1, 1925; s. Hubert Raymond and Helen (White) P.; m. Delphine Murphy, Oct. 15, 1949; children: Margaret Peck Iovino, Charles Edward, Katherine Peck Koustmer, Perry Anne Peck Flanagan. Grad., Phillips Acad., 1943; student, MIT, 1944; BS, U. Pa., 1949; PhD in Pub. Svc. (hon.), Univ. Md. Univ. Coll., 1995. With Owens-Corning Fiberglas Corp., 1949-81, from sales mgr. home bldg. products to exec. v.p. Toledo, 1975-81; co-chmn. The Ryland Group, Columbia, Md., 1981-82, chmn., CEO, 1982-91; dir. The Delaware Group of Funds, 1991-2000; sec. Enterprise Homes, Inc., 1992-2000, New Homes by Enterprise, Inc., 2000-01; ret., 2001. Statutory vis. com. U.S. Nat. Bur. Standards, 1972-77; adv. com. Fed. Nat. Mortgage Assn., 1977-78, 85-86; vis. com. MIT-Harvard Joint Ctr. for Urban Studies; chmn. Prodrs. Adv. Forum, 1977-81; mem. nat. adv. bd. Way Sta., 2004—. Vis. com. Harvard U. Grad. Sch. Design, 1981-86; chmn. Howard County United Way Campaign, Md., 1987; chmn. Cmty. Partnerships, 1991-94; bd. dirs. Nat. Inst. for Urban Wildlife, 1986-90, United Way Ctrl. Md., 1987-91, Howard County Gen. Hosp., 1988-94, NAHB Rsch. Found., 1989-92, Alliance to End Childhood Lead Poisoning, 1990-93, Meml. Hosp. Found., 2004—; adv. bd. U. Md. Engring. Sch., 1990-2003, Continuing Edn. Johns Hopkins U., 1988-91; policy adv. bd. Harvard Joint Ctr. Housing Studies, 1984-94; chancellor's adv. com. U. Md. Sys., 1988-2001, chmn., 1988-99; chmn. U. Md. Found., 1990-94, bd. dirs., 1990—; bd. visitors U. Md. Ctr. Environ. Sci., 2001—; exec. fellow Kennedy Sch., Harvard U., 1990-92; chmn. Affordable Housing Initiative, Columbia, Md., 1990-92; bd. overseers U. Md., College Park, 1994-97; bd. visitors Sch. Law U. Md., Balt., 1996-2004; vis. com. U. Md. Univ. Coll., 1997—; bd. dirs. Ctr. for Grant Devel., 1994-98, Victory '94 com. Md. State Rep. party, chmn. election inquiry funding com., 1994-95; chmn. Children of Separation and Divorce Ctr., 1995-2000; pres. adv. coun. Washington Coll., Chestertown, Md., 1997-2005, chmn., 2000-05; mem. Commn. on Future, Howard C.C. bd. visitors, 1999-2002; mem. Howard County Delta Project; pres. Peck Family Found., 1992—; co-chmn. Smart Growth Forum, 2001; bd. dirs. Columbia Festival of Arts, Md., 1988-91, 2002-03; active Marylanders for Coll. Opportunity, 2005-06; co-chair psychiat. adv. bd. Johns Hopkins Med. Inst., 2005-07. Mem. U.S. C. of C. (bd. dirs. 1975-81), Ohio C. of C. (bd. dirs. 1975-81), Depression and Related Affective Disorders Assn. (pres. 1986-89, bd. dirs. 1986-2000, pres. 1993-94), Ctr. Club, Phi Gamma Delta. Home and Office: 6855 Pea Neck Rd Saint Michaels MD 21663-2725 Office Phone: 410-745-3205. Personal E-mail: tpeck123@toad.net.

PECK, DOUGLAS CATON, dean, educator; b. Sturgis, Mich., Feb. 12, 1945; s. Herman Darwin and Volga Marceille Peck; m. Anna Kay Abraham, Aug. 23, 1969. BSChemE, Tri-State U., Angola, Ind., 1967; BA, U. Akron, 1972, MA, 1979, MS in Edn., 1997, PhD, 1993; grad., Ohio Statewide Leadership Acad. Cert. computing profl. Inst. for Certification of Computing Profls., 1990. R & d mgmt. trainee The Goodyear Tire & Rubber Co., Akron, Ohio, 1967—68, staff compunder, tire devel. divsn., 1968—70, tech. services engr., plant 2 tire prodn., 1970—72, programmer/analyst, product performance and field engring., 1972—74, engring. analyst, task force on radial passenger tire uniformity, 1974—80, systems analyst, tire devel. info. systems, 1980—82, systems analyst, tech. computer ops., 1982—91, sr. program designer, computer tng., computer applications analyst, exec. compensation and succession planning, 1996—97; vis. asst. prof. of sociology U. Akron, 1998—2000, adj. asst. prof. of sociology, 2000—01; dir. - evening, weekend and summer programs Ashland U., Ashland, Ohio, 2001—03; dean - gen. studies and pub. svc. technologies Stark State Coll. Tech., Canton, Ohio, 1993—. Cons. on statis. analysis, data utilization, and orgnl. analysis. Exhibition, Oculis Sinistris; author: (book review) The Journal of Higher Education (Shaping the College Curriculum: Academic Plans in Action), musician university band and summer concert band; drawings, Old and Young / Noble and Commonplace - Portraits in Color Pencil, sculptures in steel and plaster, Sharp and Pointy / Soft and Rounded, metalworking, Metamorphosis: Ancient, Early Scientific and Advanced Scientific Views of Matter; contbr. articles and papers to jours., confs. Team mem. Summit Edn. Initiative, Akron, Ohio, 2000; mem. - career tech. adv. com.: career paths for the tchg. profession Perry H.S., Massillon, Ohio; judge Canton Artists' League, Canton, Ohio; pres. Hampton Ridge Homeowners' Assn., Akron, Ohio; adv. bd. Akron Chpt. of the Arthritis Found., Akron, Ohio, 1994—98, Dept. Chem. and Bioprocess Engring., Tri-State U., Angola, Ind.; trustee Tau Kappa Epsilon, Beta-Rho Chpt., Akron, Ohio, The Arthritis Found. of NE Ohio, Cleveland, Ohio, 1989—95; grant reader - fund for the improvement of postsec. edn. US Dept. of Edn.; grant reviewer (small bus. innovation program) NSF; peer reviewer Social Sci. Computer Rev. - NC State U., NC; merit reviewer (course, curriculum, and lab. improvement program) The NSF, Washington; co-chair, social sci. transfer and articulation guide project Ohio Bd. of Regents, Columbus, Ohio, 2004—05; steering com. mem. Stark County Coll. Tech Prep Consortium, Canton, Ohio; mem. - tchr. acad. adv. com. Wash. H.S., Massillon, Ohio; facilitator ARC - Akron Chpt., Akron, Ohio; area dir. coord. for united way campaign The Goodyear Tire & Rubber Co.; vol. Home at Last Animal Rescue, Akron, Ohio, 1998—2004. Recipient Cert. of Faculty Appreciation, Interfraternity Coun./Panhellenic Coun., The U. of Akron; scholar Trustees' scholar, Bd. of Trustees, Tri-State U., 1967. Mem.: Am. Tech. Edn. Assn., Am. Conf. of Academic Deans (assoc.), Kappa Delta Pi, Phi Alpha Theta, Alpha Kappa Delta, Omicron Delta Kappa, Golden Key (hon.). Avocations: playing saxophone and flute, reading. Home: 370 Goodhue Dr Akron OH 44313 Office: Stark State College of Tech 6200 Frank Ave NW Canton OH 44720-7299 Home Phone: 330-864-6084; Office Phone: 330-966-5457. Office Fax: 330-494-0571. Personal E-mail: dpeck1@neo.rr.com. Business E-Mail: dpeck@starkstate.edu.

PECK, DOUGLAS EDWARD, lawyer; b. Bloomington, Ill., Apr. 15, 1961; s. Richard Ray and Sarah Josephine (Wilhoit) P.; m. Martha Elaine Jones. BA, U. N.C., 1983, JD, 1986. Bar: NC 1986, Tenn. 1987, US Dist. Ct. (ea. dist.) Tenn. 1987, US Ct. Appeals (6th cir.) 1991, US Tax Ct. 1990. Shareholder Shumacker Witt Gaither & Whitaker, P.C., Chattanooga, 1986—2006. Editor N.C. Law Rev., 1985-86.

PECK, EDWARD LIONEL, retired foreign service officer, corporate executive; b. LA, Mar. 6, 1929; s. Alexander George and Rae (Lee) P.; m. Heather Dianne Hicks-Beach, Jan. 20, 1957 (div. July 1971); m. Ann Day Slevin, May 5, 1974; children: Heather Anne, Brian Michael, Thomas William, Julia Katherine BS, UCLA, 1956; MBA, George Washington U., 1973. Joined Fgn. Service Dept. State, Washington, 1957, intelligence specialist, 1968-71, spl. asst., 1971-74; econ. counselor U.S. Embassy, Cairo, 1974-77; chief of mission U.S. Interests Sect., Baghdad, Iraq, 1977-80; dir. Office of Egyptian affairs Washington, 1980-82; ambassador U.S. Embassy, Nouakchott, Mauritania, 1983—85; dep. dir. cabinet task force combating terrorism White Ho., 1985-86; dir. Office of Career Transition, 1986-88; ret., 1989; pres. Fgn. Svcs. Internat., 1989—; exec. sec. Am. Acad. Diplomacy, 1989-92. Trainer, lectr., cons. on fgn. affairs, internat. bus., 1990—; dir. polit. tradecraft program Nat. Fgn. Affairs Tng. Ctr., Arlington, Va., 1991-96; sr. assoc. Global Bus. Access Ltd., Washington, 1991—; Woodrow Wilson vis. fellow, 1993—. Bd. dirs. Ams. for Middle East Understanding, 1999—; chmn. Coun. for the Nat. Interest Found., 2001-03. Served to capt. U.S. Army, 1946-49, 50-52 Recipient Meritorious Honor award Dept. State, 1967, 73, 77, 79, Superior Honor award Dept. State, 1974, 88, Wilbur J. Carr award, 1989; Rivkin award Am. Fgn. Svc. Assn., 1973 Home and Office: 106 Grafton St Bethesda MD 20815-3426 Home Phone: 301-654-8472; Office Phone: 301-652-8318. Personal E-mail: peckfsi@erols.com.

PECK, ERNEST JAMES, JR., academic administrator; b. Port Arthur, Tex., July 26, 1941; s. Ernest James and Karlton Maudean (Luttrell) P.; children: David Karl, John Walter, Michael R. Peck. BA in Biology with honors, Rice U., 1963, PhD in Biochemistry, 1966. Rsch. assoc. Purdue U., West Lafayette, Ind., 1966-68, asst. prof., 1968-73, Baylor Coll. Medicine, Houston, 1973-74, assoc. prof., 1974-80, prof., 1980-82; prof., chmn. biochemistry Sch. Med. Sci., U. Ark., Little Rock, 1982-89; dean sci. and math. U. Nev., Las Vegas, 1989-95; vice chancellor acad. affairs U. Nebr., Omaha, 1995-98; exec. dir. Coun. Colls. of Arts and Scis., rsch. prof. Ariz. State U., Tempe, 1998—. Adj. prof. U. Ark., Pine Bluff, 1986-88; program dir. NSF, Washington, 1988-89; mem. editl. bd. Jour. Neurosci. Rsch., N.Y.C., 1982-92. Co-author: Female Sex Steroids, 1979, Brain Peptides, 1979. Recipient Rsch. Career award NIH, Nat. Inst. of Child Health and Human Devel., 1975-80; NIH fellow, 1964-66. Fellow AAAS; mem. Am. Chem. Soc., Am. Soc. Biochemistry and Molecular Biology, Endocrine Soc., Sigma Xi. Avocations: fishing, hunting.

PECK, FRED NEIL, economist, educator; b. Bklyn., Oct. 17, 1945; s. Abraham Lincoln and Beatrice (Pikholtz) P.; m. Jean Claire Ginsberg, Aug. 14, 1971; children: Ron Evan, Jordan Shefer, Ethan David. BA, Binghamton U., NY, 1966; MA, SUNY, Albany, 1969; PhM, NYU, 1984; PhD, Pacific Western U., 1984; MS in Edn., Coll. New Rochelle, NY, 1993. Lectr. SUNY, Albany, 1969-70; rsch. asst. NY State Legislature, Albany, 1970; sales and rsch. staff Pan Am. Trade Devel. Corp., NYC, 1971; v.p., economist The First Boston Corp., NYC, 1971-88; mng. dir. Sharpe's Capital Mkt. Assocs. Inc., NYC, 1988-89; pres., chief economist Hillcrest Econs. Group, NYC, 1989-93; dir. edn. The Ednl. Advantage, Inc., New City, NY, 1990-95; dir. Robert F. Kennedy Acad., NYC Dept. Edn., 1998—. Adj. prof. Hofstra U., Hempstead, NY, 1975, Mercy Coll., 2004-07, Touro Coll., 2004-; lectr. NYU, 1982; faculty New Sch. Social Rsch., NYC, 1974-94; coord. ednl. tech. NYC Bd. Edn., 1990-98. Author, editor: Handbook of Securities of U.S. Government, 1972-86. Mem. ASCD, Am. Econ. Assn., Ea. Econ. Assn., Econometric Soc., Nat. Assn. Bus. Economists, Am. Statis. Assn., Coun. Exceptional Children, Doctorate Assn. of NY Educators, Beta Gamma Sigma (hon. soc.), Phi Delta Kappa. Lodges: Knights Pythias, Knights Khorassan. Democrat. Jewish. Office: Robert F Kennedy Sch 110 East 88th St New York NY 10128 Office Phone: 212-348-6140. Personal E-mail: docfnp@bigfoot.com. *March in one place long enough and eventually you will wind up leading the parade of progress...No one grows old. When you tire of learning, of experiencing new things you are old.*

PECK, GARNET EDWARD, pharmacist, educator; b. Windsor, Ont., Can., Feb. 4, 1930; s. William Crozier and Dorothy (Marentette) P.; m. Mary Ellen Hoffman, Aug. 24, 1957; children: Monique Elizabeth, Denise Anne, Philip Warren, John Edward. BS in Pharmacy with Distinction, Ohio No. U., 1957; MS in Indsl. Pharmacy, Purdue U., 1959, PhD, 1962. Sr. scientist Mead Johnson Research Center, 1962-65, group leader, 1965-67; assoc. prof. indsl. and phys. pharmacy Purdue U., West Lafayette, 1967—73, prof., 1973—2003, dir. indsl. pharmacy lab., 1975—, assoc. dept. head, 1989-96, prof. emeritus, 2003—. Cons. in field. Contbr. articles to profl. jours. Mem. West Lafayette Mayor's Advisory Com. on Community Devel., 1973-; mem. West Lafayette Citizen's Safety Com., 1974-81; mem. West Lafayette Park Bd., 1981-, pres., 1983-96. Served with U.S. Army, 1951-53. Recipient Lederle Faculty award Purdue U., 1976 Fellow APHA, AAAS, Am. Inst. Chem., Am. Assn. Pharm. Scientists; mem. Am. Chem. Soc., Acad. Rsch. and Sci. (Sidney Riegelman award 1994), Am. Assn. Colls. Pharmacy, Cath. Acad. Sci. (founding mem.), KC, Knight of Holy Sepulchre, Sigma Xi, Rho Chi, Phi Lambda Upsilon, Phi Kappa Phi, Phi Sigma Lambda, Phi Lambda Sigma. Roman Catholic. Office: Purdue U Sch Pharmacy & Pharm Scis Dept Industrial & Physical Pharm West Lafayette IN 47907 Office Phone: 765-494-1400. Business E-Mail: gepeck@pharmacy.purdue.edu.

PECK, H. DANIEL, literature educator; b. Milw., July 15, 1940; s. Henry Edward and Carmen (Barbulesco) P.; m. Patricia B. Wallace, Apr. 3, 1982; 1 child, Jennifer Peck; stepchildren: Christopher Wallace, Matthew Wallace. BA, Ohio Wesleyan U., 1962; MA, U. Iowa, 1971, PhD, 1974. Asst. prof. to assoc. prof. U. Calif., Santa Barbara, 1972—80; assoc. prof. Vassar Coll., Poughkeepsie, NY, 1980—83, prof. lit., 1983—. Dir. Am. culture program Vassar Coll., Poughkeepsie, 1989—92, John Guy Vassar chair, 1999—, founding dir. environ. studies program, 2000—03; dir. NEH Summer Insts. for Coll. and Univ. Faculty, 1993, 97. Author: Thoreau's Morning Work, 1990, A World by Itself: The Pastoral Moment in Cooper's Fiction, 1977; editor: The Green American Tradition, 1989, New Essays on the Last of the Mohicans, 1992, World's Classics edit. Fenimore Cooper's Deerslayer, 1993, A Year in Thoreau's Journal: 1851, 1993, Thoreau's A Week on the Concord and Merrimack Rivers, 1998, Mark Twain's The Adventures of Tom Sawyer, 2003; contbr. Columbia Lit. History of the U.S., 1988, Health Anthology of Am. Lit., 1996—; mem. editl. bd. Hudson River Valley Rev., 2006— Fellow Am. Coun. Learned Socs., 1977-78, NEH, 1984, 94, Georgia O'Keeffe Mus. Rsch. Ctr., 2002; grantee Mellon Found., 2006— Mem. MLA (chmn. divsn. 19th Century Am. Lit. 1986), Am. Studies Assn., New Eng. Am. Studies Assn. (coun. 1991-93), Assoc. for Study Lit. of Environ. (editl. bd., 1995—), John Burroughs Assoc. (bd. dir. 1994-2001) Office: Vassar Coll Box 226 Poughkeepsie NY 12604-0226 Home: 19 Watson Rd Poughkeepsie NY 12603 Office Phone: 845-437-5662. E-mail: peckd@vassar.edu.

PECK, KENNETH E., lawyer; b. Carson City, Nev., June 20, 1950; s. Donald Leon and Thelma Louise (Robinson) P.; m. Katherine Louise Weeks, Oct. 20, 1973 (div. 1991); children: Jason Z., Jennifer D., Joy H., Jessica K. BA in Polit. Sci. cum laude, U. Colo., 1971; MA in Pub. Adminstrn., U. Va., 1975; JD, Georgetown U., 1979. Bar: Colo. 1979, U.S. Dist. Ct. Colo. 1979, U.S. Ct. Appeals (10th cir.) 1980, U.S. Supreme Ct. 1983. Rsch. analyst Va. Hwy. Rsch. Coun., Charlottesville, 1972-73; budget and mgmt. analyst Prince Georges County Schs., Upper Marlboro, Md., 1974-76; chief legis. asst. U.S. Rep. Paul Trible, Washington, 1977-79; atty. Holland & Hart, Denver, 1979-83, Hopper & Kanouff, Denver, 1983-85, Phelps, Singer & Dunn, Denver, 1985-90, Law Firm of Kenneth E. Peck, Denver, 1990-98, Bushell & Peck, L.L.C., Denver, 1999—. Mem. nat., regional and state adv. councils SBA, 1981-86; mem. bd. appeals U.S. Dept. Edn., Washington, 1982-84; profl. lobbyist Colo. Legis., Denver, 1983-84; nat. commr. of econ. policy 1986 White House Conf. on Small Bus. Asst. campaign mgr. Jim Tate for Congress, Fairfax, Va., 1976; bd. dirs. Jefferson County Srs.' Resource Ctr., Wheatridge, Colo., 1982-88; pres. Arvada Rep. Club, Colo., 1982; mem. bd. mgrs. Northwest YMCA, Arvada, 1982-88; active Foothills Cmty. Ch. William McIntyre fellow U. Va., 1971-72; law fellow Georgetown U. Law Ctr., 1976-77. Mem. ABA (litigation sect., various coms.), Colo. Bar Assn. (various coms.), Colo. Assn. Comml. Industry (chmn. small bus. legis. com. 1983-85), Denver Bar Assn. (various coms.). Republican. Avocations: golf, hiking, coaching youth sports. Home: 10935 W 68th Ave Arvada CO 80004-2744

PECK, LEONARD WARREN, JR., lawyer; b. El Paso, Tex., June 3, 1948; s. Leonard Warren and Perry Elizabeth (Lewis) Peck; m. Johanna Lee Blaschke, July 23, 1976; 1 child, Margaret Elizabeth. AB, Harvard U., 1970; JD, U. Tex., 1973; PhD, Sam Houston State U., 2004. Bar: Tex. 1973, US Dist. Ct. (so. dist.) Tex. 1980, US Dist. Ct. (ea. dist.) Tex. 1980, US Dist. Ct. (we. dist.) Tex. 1980, US Dist. Ct. (no. dist.) Tex. 1984, US Ct. Appeals (11th cir.) 1981, US Supreme Ct. 1980. Analyst Tex. Gov.'s Office, Austin, 1974—75; cons. Atty. Gen. Tex. Office, Austin, 1976—80, asst. atty. gen., 1981; dir. R & D Tex. Dept. Corrections, Huntsville, Tex., 1981—82, legal counsel, 1982—2002; asst. prof. Tex. A&M U., Texarkana, Tex., 2006—. Trustee Tri-County MHMR Svcs., 1985—2005; pres. Ind. Communities Inc., 2004—. Home: PO Box 6106 Texarkana TX 75505-6106 Home Phone: 903-223-3011. Business E-Mail: leonard.peck@tamut.edu.

PECK, LOUIS MOSES, editor; b. NYC, Apr. 16, 1951; s. Seymour and Susan (Lustig) P.; m. Nancy Jean Schwerzler, Sept. 5, 1987. BA in Am. History, Brown U., 1973. Govt. and politics reporter Frankfort (Ind.) Times, 1974-76, Poughkeepsie (N.Y.) Jour., 1976-78; regional corr. Gannett News Svc., Washington, 1978-82, congl. and polit. corr., 1983-87; editor Campaigns and Elections, Washington, 1988-89; freelance writer editor Washington, 1989-91; editor Congress Daily, Washington, 1991—2007, editor-in-chief, 2007—, Nat. Jour.'s Tech. Daily, 2000—. Vis. instr. Medill Sch. Journalism, Northwestern U., Washington, 1988, 90. Editorial cons.: Reform and Reality: The Financing of State and Local Campaigns, 1990, Financing Politics: Money, Elections and Political Reform, 1991. Mem. Washington Ind. Writers. Office: Nat Jour 600 New Hampshire Ave NW Washington DC 20037 Business E-Mail: lpeck@nationaljournal.com.

PECK, MARYLY VANLEER, retired academic administrator, chemical engineer; b. Washington, June 29, 1930; d. Blake Ragsdale and Ella Lillian (Wall) VanLeer; m. Jordan B. Peck, Jr., June 15, 1951; children: Jordan B. III, Blake VanLeer, James Tarleton VanLeer, Virginia Ellaine.; m. 2d, Walter G. Ebert, Sept. 3, 1983 (dec. June 1990); m. 3d Edwin L. Carey, Apr. 13, 1991. Student, Ga. Inst. Tech., 1948, 55-58, Duke U., 1947-48; B.Ch.E., Vanderbilt U., 1951; MSE., U. Fla., 1955, PhD, 1963. Chem. engr. Naval Research Lab., Washington, 1951-52; chem. engr. Med. Field Research Lab., Camp LeJeune, NC, 1952; asso. research and instr. U. Fla., Gainesville, 1953-55; chem. engr., research asso. Ga. Tech. Expt. Sta., Atlanta, 1956-58; lectr. Ga. State Coll., Atlanta, 1957-58; lectr. math. East Carolina Extension, Camp Lejeune, 1959; sr. research engr. Rocketdyne div. N.Am. Aviation Co., 1961-63; self-employed as lectr., 1963; assoc. prof. Campbell Coll., Buie's Creek, NC, 1963-66, prof., 1966; acad. dir. St. John's Episcopal Sch., Upper Tumon, Guam, 1966-68; chmn., prof. phys. scis. U. Guam, Agana, 1968-73, dean Coll. Bus. and Applied Tech., 1973-74, dean Community Career Coll., 1974-77; pres. Cochise Coll., Douglas, Ariz., 1977-78; systems planning analyst Urban Pathfinders, Inc., Balt., 1978-79; dean undergrad. studies U. Md. Univ. Coll., College Park, 1979-82; pres. Polk Community Coll., Winter Haven, Fla., 1982-97, pres. emeritus, 1997—; headmaster All Saints' Acad., 1997-99. Cons. in field. Founder, pres. Guam Acad. Found., 1972-77; bd. dirs. Cochise Coll. Found., 1977-78; charter bd. dirs. Turnaround Inc., 1987-91, chmn. 1990-93; bd. dirs. United Way Ctrl. Fla., 1986-95, vice-chmn., 1992, chair elect, 1993, chmn. 1994; founding mem. Prince George's Ednl. TV Cable Coalition; mem. Prince George's Cable TV Ednl. Adv. Group, 1980-82, Polk County Coun. Econ. Edn., 1982; sec. Polk C.C. Found., 1982-97; mem. Polk County Coord. Coun. Vocat. Edn., 1982-91, PRIDE Adv. Coun.; vice-chmn. Fla. Job Tng. Coord. Coun., 1983-87, Fla. Edn. Fund Bd., 1988-93; active Girls Inc. Bd., 1992—, pres., 2000-2001, hon. mem., 2005; trustee All Sts.'s Acad. 1994-2002; trustee Vanguard Sch., 2001—06, mem. Fdn. Bd., 2001—06; bd. dirs. Theater Winter Haven, 2000—, chair, 2002-03. Named Disting. Alumnus U. Fla., 1992, Woman of Distinction Girls Scouts U.S.A., 1994, Woman of Distinction, 1997; fellow NSF, 1961-63; recipient She Knows Where She's Going award Girls Inc. of Winter Haven, 1995, Cmty. Svc. award Jr. League Winter Haven, 2002, Disting. Citizen award Lake Region dist. Gulf Ridge coun. Boy Scouts Am., 2005, NDAR Cmty. Svc. award, 2005; named to Fla. Women's Hall of Fame, 2007. Fellow Soc. Women Engrs. (nat. v.p. 1962-63); mem. AAUW, AIChE, DAR (Cmty. Svc. award 2005), Am. Chem. Soc., NSPE, Am. Assn. for Higher Edn., Am. Assn. Cmty. and Jr. Colls., Am. Assn. Univ. Adminstrs., Rotary of Winter Haven (hon., sec. 1999-2000, pres.-elect 2003-04, centennial pres. 2004-05), Rotary of Palm Beach Gardens, Sigma Xi, Tau Beta Pi, Chi Omicron Gamma, Phi Kappa Phi, Delta Kappa Gamma. Episcopalian. Home: 5390 Woodland Lakes Dr 206 Palm Beach Gardens FL 33418-3959 E-mail: marylypeck@bellsouth.net.

PECK, MERTON JOSEPH, economist, educator; b. Cleve., Dec. 17, 1925; s. Kenneth Richard and Charlotte (Hart) P.; m. Mary McClure Bosworth, June 13, 1949 (dec. Aug. 2004); children: Richard, Katherine, Sarah, David. AB, Oberlin Coll., 1949; AM, Harvard U., 1951, PhD, 1954; AM (hon.), Yale U., 1963. Teaching fellow, instr. econs. Harvard U., Boston, 1951-55, asst., then assoc. prof. bus. adminstrn., 1956-61; asst. prof. econs. U. Mich., Ann Arbor, 1955-56; dir. systems analysis Office Sec. Def., Washington, 1961-63; prof. econs. Yale U., New Haven, 1963—81, chmn. dept., 1968—74, 1977—84, acting dean sch. of orgn. and mgmt., 1986—88, Thomas DeWitt Cuyler prof., 1981—, prof. emeritus, 2002. Mem. Council Econ. Advisers, Exec. Office of Pres., 1968-69; cons. in field, 1954— Author: (with others) The Economics of Competition in the Transportation Industries, 1959, Competition in the Aluminum Industry, 1945-58, 1961, (with F. Scherer) The Weapons Aquisition Process, An Economic Analysis, 1962, (with others) Technological Change, Economic Growth and Public Policy, 1967, Federal Regulation of Television, 1973; editor The World Aluminum Industry in a Changing Energy Era, 1988; co-editor: What Is To Be Done? Proposals for the Soviet Transition to the Market, 1991, Competitiveness, The Impact of Public Policy, 1992; contbr. (with others) articles to profl. jours. With AUS, 1944-46. Mem. AAUP, Am. Econ. Assn., Lawn Club, Yale Club. Home: 5000 SW 25th Blvd # 3109 Gainesville FL 32608

PECK, MIRA P., lawyer; b. Minsk, USSR, Mar. 31, 1946; d. Wolf and Zofia (Wlaznik) Paszko; m. David O. Peck, May 15, 1971; children: Lena Ruth, Benjamin Jay. BEChemE, RMIT Univ., Australia, 1972; MS in Indsl. Adminstrn., Union Coll., 1976; JD, Rutgers U., 1984. Bar: N.J. 1984, U.S. Dist. Ct. N.J. 1984. Tchr. sci. Victoria Edn. Dept., 1971-72; process engr. GAF Corp., Rensselaer, NY, 1974-77; design engr. BASF Corp., Parsippany, NJ, 1977-80, product mgr., 1980-86, mgr. corp. strategic planning, 1986-92, v.p. tech. purchasing Mount Olive, NJ, 1993-2000; pvt. law practice Denville, NJ, 1984—. Mem., counsel Protect Wildlife Water and Woods, Denville, 1987—; mem. Mus. Modern Art, N.Y.C. Mem. ABA, NOW, N.J. Bar Assn., Am Inst. Chem. Engrs., Am. Humanist Assn., Amnesty Internat., Simon Wiesenthal Ctr., So. Poverty Law Ctr. Democrat. Avocations: art, writing, music, hiking, bicycling.

PECK, PAUL LACHLAN, minister; b. Glens Falls, NY, Sept. 11, 1928; s. Paul Lee and Caroline Jeannette (Stanton) Peck; children: Paul Barrett, Kathryn Elizabeth, Gretchen, Kole W. BS, U. Conn., 1952; ThD, Bernadean U., 1976; MEd, Westfield State Coll., 1983. Ordained to ministry Truth Ctr., 1972. With Proctor and Gamble Co., Watertown, NY, 1956-60; dir. deferred giving programs Syracuse (N.Y.) U., 1960-68, v.p., 1968-70, Fairleigh-Dickinson U., NJ, 1970-71, Manhattan Coll., Bronx, NY, 1971-75; founder, pastor Arete' Truth Ctr., San Diego, 1975—. Author: Footsteps Along the Path, 1978, Inherit the Kingdom, 1978, Milestones of the Way, 1978, Freeway to Health, 1980, Freeway to Work and Wealth, 1981, Freeway to Human Love, 1982, Freeway to Personal Growth, 1982, Your Dreams Count, 1990, Heroic Love Poems, 1990, Worth The Room: An Autobiography of Survival and Service, 2005 Bd. dirs. Girl Scouts U.S.A., Syracuse, 1967-70; trustee, bd. dirs. Erickson Ednl. Found., 1970-75; vol. chaplain Auburn (N.Y.) State Prison, 1967-68; mem. chaplains' coun.

Syracuse U., 1960-70; co-founder suicide and drug abuse prevention program Syracuse U., 1968-71, Fairleigh-Dickinson U., 1970-71, Manhattan Coll., 1971-75. Staff sgt. USNG, 1947-50. Mem. Internat. New Thought Alliance, SAR, Rotary, Knights of Malta (svc. award 1973), Masons, Shriners, Spiritual Frontiers Fellowship. Avocations: golf, book collecting.

PECK, RALPH BRAZELTON, civil engineering educator, consultant; b. Winnipeg, Man., Can., June 23, 1912; (parents Am. citizens); s. Orwin K. and Ethel Indie (Huyck) Peck; m. Marjorie Elizabeth Truby, June 14, 1937; children: Nancy Jeanne Peck Young, James Leroy. D in Civil Engring., Rensselaer Poly. Inst., 1937; postgrad., Harvard U., 1938; D Eng. (hon.), Rensselaer Poly. Inst., 1974; DSc (hon.), Laval U., 1987. Registered Ill., structural engr., Ill., civil engr., Calif. Structural detailer Am. Bridge Co., Ambridge, Pa., 1937; asst. subway engr. City of Chgo., 1939—43; chief engr. testing Holabird & Root, Scioto Ordnance Plant, Marion, Ohio, 1943; research asst. prof. soil mechanics U. Ill., Champaign-Urbana, 1943—48, research prof. found. engring., 1948—57, prof. found. engring., 1957—74, prof. emeritus, 1974—. Cons. in field. Author (with K. Terzaghi and G. Mesri): Soil Mechanics in Engineering Practice, 1948, 3rd edit., 1996; author: (with T.H. Thornburn and W.E. Hanson) Foundation Engineering, 1953, 2d edit., 1973, Judgment in Geotechnical Engineering: The Professional Legacy of Ralph B. Peck, 1984; contbr. articles to profl. jours. Named to Hall of Fame, Rensselaer Poly. Inst., 1998; recipient Disting. Civilian Svc. award, Dept. of Army, 1973, Moles Non-mem. award, 1973, Nat. Medal Sci., Pres. Gerald Ford, 1974, Golden Beaver award, 1983, Disting. Svc. award, Deep Founds Inst., 1984, Merit award, Am. Cons. Engrs. Coun., 1988, John F. Parmer award, Structural Engrs. Assn. Ill., 2004. Fellow: Geol. Soc. Am. (sr.); mem.: NSPE (award 1972), ASCE (hon.; nat. dir. 1962—65, Norman medal 1944, Wellington prize 1965, Terzaghi award 1969, Washington award 1976, Pres.'s award 1986, John Fritz medal 1987, Rickey medal 1988, Geo-Inst. award 2000, Outstanding Projects and Leaders award 2001), NAE, Can. Geotech. Soc. (Spl. award 2002), Internat. Soc. Soil Mechanics and Geotech. Engring. (pres. 1969—73), Am. Acad. Arts and Scis., Mexican Soc. Soil Mechanics (hon.), Japanese Soc. Soil Mechanics (hon.), Southeast Asian Soc. Soil Mechanics (hon.), Tau Beta Pi, Sigma Xi, Phi Kappa Phi, Chi Epsilon. Home: 1101 Warm Sands Dr SE Albuquerque NM 87123-4328

PECK, ROBERT A., publishing executive, state legislator; b. Riverton, Wyo., Oct. 7, 1924; s. LeRoy E. and Elvira Eugenia (Sostrom) P.; m. Cordelia S. Peck, Oct. 5, 1949 (dec. Feb. 1996); children: Christopher, George, Steven. BA, U. Wyo., 1949. Pub. The Riverton Ranger, 1949—; mem. Wyo. Senate, Dist. 26, Cheyenne, 1991—. Pres. Central Wyo. Coll. Bd., Riverton, 1966-81; sec. CWC Found., Riverton, 1968—. Staff sgt. U.S. Army, 1943-46, ETO. Mem. Soc. Profl. Journalists, Masons, Phi Beta Kappa. Republican. Methodist. Office: The Riverton Ranger 421 E Main PO Box 993 Riverton WY 82501-0993 Home Phone: 307-856-2751; Office Phone: 307-856-2244. E-mail: bpeck@wyoming.com, ranger@wyoming.com.

PECK, ROBERT MCCRACKEN, naturalist, historian, writer; b. Phila., Dec. 15, 1952; s. Frederick William Gunster and Matilda (McCracken) P. BA in Art History, Princeton U., 1974; MA, U. Del., 1976. Dir. Pocono Lake (Pa.) Preserve Nature Ctr., 1971, 72; asst. to dir. Natural History Mus. Acad. Natural Scis., Phila., 1976-77, spl. asst. to pres., 1977-82, acting v.p. Nat. History Mus., 1982-83, fellow, 1983—, curator Art and Artifacts, 2000—, editor sci. publs., 2001—03, sr. fellow, libr., 2003—; tech. dir. Bartram Heritage Study U.S. Dept. Interior and Bartram Trail Conf., Atlanta and Montgomery, Ala., 1977-78. Cons. BBC, Eng., 1987-92; bd. dirs. Phila. Conservationists, Natural Lands Trust, Phila., Libr. Co. of Phila., Phila. City Inst.; mng. editor Frontiers, 1979-82, editor Proceedings of The Acad. of Natural Scis., 2001-04; lectr. in field. Author: A Celebration of Birds: The Life and Art of Louis Agassiz Fuertes, 1982, Headhunters and Hummingbirds: An Expedition Into Ecuador, 1987, Wild Birds of America: The Art of Basil Ede, 1991, Land of the Eagle: A Natural History of North America, 1991, German edit., 1992; author: (with others) John James Audubon in the West: The Last Expedition, 2000, William Bartram's Travels, 1980, John Cassin's Illustrations of the Birds of California, Texas, Oregon, British and Russian America, 1991; author: (forward) The Birds of America by John James Audubon, 1985; editor: Bartram Heritage Report, 1978; author (with others), editor: Philadelphia Wildfowl Exposition Catalog, 1979; contbr. chpts. to books, articles to mags. and newspapers including The New York Times. Recipient Richard Hopper Day Meml. award Acad. Natural Scis. of Phila., 1991, Wyck-Strickland award for contbns. to cultural life of Phila., 2003; Eleanor Garvey fellow in printing and graphic arts Houghton Libr., Harvard U., 1995; Yale Ctr. for Brit. Art fellow, 1997. Fellow Royal Geog. Soc., Explorers Club (various coms. 1983—, Explorers award 1988); mem. Soc. History of Natural History, Sigma Xi. Achievements include discovery of new species of frog, Eleutherodactylus pecki; research in orthoptera indigenous to the Caribbean; status of invasive African Desert Locust in the West Indies; the Orinoco River and its tributaries, botanical, entomological, ichthyological, herpetological and malacological specimens for the Smithsonian Institution and the Academy of Natural Sciences; participation in expeditions which discovered several new species of fish in Guyana Shield, Venezuela; discovery of several new species of amphibians and insects; current projects include biological and cultural research in Mongolia, the natural history illustrations of Edward Lear; research in 19th century exploration. Office: Acad Natural Scis 1900 Benjamin Franklin Pkwy Philadelphia PA 19103-1195 Office Phone: 215-299-1138. Business E-Mail: peck@acnatsci.org.

PECK, ROBERT STEPHEN, lawyer, educator; b. Bklyn., Dec. 11, 1953; s. Irwin and Edith Rose (Welt) P.; m. Terre Garcia; 1 child, Zachary Madison. BA in Polit. Sci., George Washington U., 1975; JD, Cleve.-Marshall Law Sch., 1978; postgrad., NYU, 1978; LLM, Yale U., 1990. Bar: N.Y. 1979, U.S. Dist. Ct. (so. and ea. dists.) N.Y. 1979, D.C. 1989, U.S. Ct. Appeals (9th and 11th cirs.) 2004, U.S. Ct. Appeals (2d cir.) 2006, U.S. Supreme Ct. 2002. Congl. aide U.S. Ho. of Reps., Washington, 1972-74; divsn. dir. Automated Correspondence, Washington, 1974-75; law clk. to presiding justice Cleve. Mcpl. Ct., 1976; editor Matthew Bender & Co., NYC, 1977-78; legal dir. Pub. Edn. Assn., NYC, 1978-82; staff dir. ABA, Chgo., 1982-87, Washington, 1987-89; jud. fellow U.S. Supreme Ct., 1990-91; legis. counsel ACLU, 1991-95; adj. prof. Am. U., Washington, 1991—, George Washington U., Washington, 2000—; dir. legal affairs Assn. Trial Lawyers Am., 1995-98, sr. dir. legal affairs, 1998—2003; pres. Ctr. for Constl. Litigation, 2001—. Legal advisor Freedom to Read Found., Chgo., 1986-2002, exec. com. bd. trustees, 1987-90, 93-97, pres., 1988-90, v.p., trustee, 1993-97; bd. dirs. Nat. Constl. Ctr., 1990-93; bd. overseers RAND Inst. Civil Justice, 2001—; mem. lawyers com. Nat. Ctr. for State Cts., 2002—, bd. dirs., 2005—; lectr. on constl. law, legal ethics. Author: We the People, 1987, The Bill of Rights and the Politics of Interpretation, 1991, Libraries, the First Amendment and Cyberspace, 1999; co-author: Speaking and Writing Truth, 1985; editor: Understanding the Law, 1983, Blessings of Liberty, 1986, To Govern A Changing Society, 1990; contbr. articles to profl. jours. Mem. N.Y. State Edn. Adv. Bd., Albany, N.Y., 1979-81; bd. dirs. Nat. Com. on Pub. Edn. and Religious Liberty, 1995-97, Ams. for Religious Liberty, 1995-2000, Citizens for Constitution, 1997—; nat. chair Lawyers for Libr., 1996-2002; chair legal adv. com. Nat. Ctr. for Sci. Edn., 1996-2000; mem. first amendment adv. coun. Media Inst., 1996—. NEH grantee 1983, 85. Mem.: ABA (chmn. pub. election law com. 1983—85, 1987—90, vice chmn. access to justice com. 1997—98, program chmn. consumer and personal rights litigation com. 1997—2000, chmn. 1998—99, chmn. first amendment com. 1999—2005, chmn. appellate adv. com. 2001—02, chmn. com. Am. Law Inst. and Uniform Laws 2002—03, spl. advisor Commn. on 21st Century Judiciary 2002—03, governing coun. tort, trial and ins. law sect. 2003—06, chmn. 20/20 vision task force 2004—06, mem. Commn. Am. Jury 2005—06, chmn. task force disaster relief 2005—07), Am. Law Inst., US Supreme Ct. Fellows Alumni Assn. (pres. 2004—06). Democrat. Jewish. Avocations: tennis, music, travel. Office: Ctr for Constl Litigation 1050 31st St NW Washington DC 20007-4499 Home Phone: 703-690-6006; Office Phone: 202-944-2874. Business E-Mail: robert.peck@cclfirm.com.

PECK, SHELDON, orthodontist, educator, dental anthropologist, historian; b. NYC, Sept. 12, 1941; s. Max A. and Sylvia Peck; m. Leena Kataja, Apr. 20, 1986; children: Mark Alvar, Anya Elizabeth. BS, U. NC, Chapel Hill, 1963, DDS, 1966; MSc in Dentistry, Boston U., 1968. Pvt. practice orthodontics Doctors Peck, Peck and Savusalo, Boston, Newton, 1968—; asst. prof. Boston U., 1971—75, adj. prof., 1976—80; asst. prof. Harvard U., Boston, 1992—99, assoc. prof., 1999—2006, clin. prof. devel. biology, 2007—. Exec. sec. The Angle Soc., 1995—. Author: Rembrandt Drawings: Twenty-Five Years in the Peck Collection, 2003; co-author: Fresh Woods and Pastures New: Seventeenth-Century Dutch Landscape Drawings from the Peck Collection, 1999; editor: The World of Edward Hartley Anglè, MD, DDS, His Letters, Accounts and Patents, 2007; assoc. editor: The Angle Orthodontist, 1997—. Adv. bd. mem. Met. Mus. Art, NYC, Mus. Fine Arts, Boston, Ackland Art Mus., Chapel Hill, NC, Harvard U. Art Museums, Cambridge, Mass. Mem.: St. Botolph Club (gov. 2005), Omicron Kappa Upsilon, Phi Beta Kappa, Alpha Chi Sigma, Phi Eta Sigma. Achievements include discovery of genetic linkage in dental anomaly patterns; research in radiographic and graphic-stroke analysis of old artworks; orofacial morphogenetic fields; dental anthropology. Office: 1400 Centre St Newton Centre MA 02459 Office Phone: 617-969-1416.

PECK, SUZANNE J., transit authority administrator; b. St. Paul, Jan. 20, 1943; d. John Christopher and Margaret (Theisen) Janes; m. Paul Leonard Peck, 1965. BA, Notre Dame Coll., Balt., 1964; MBA, U.Pa., Phila., 1966. Dir. Honeywell Info. Systems, Washington and Boston, 1971-84; v.p. Bankers Trust Co., NYC, 1984-85; sr. v.p. Student Loan Mktg. Assn., Washington, 1985; chief tech. officer District of Columbia, 1998—2007; asst. gen. mgr., info. tech. Washington Met. Area. Transit Authority (Metro), Washington, 2007—. Named one of 25 Chief Tech. Officers, InfoWorld mag., 2006. Office: Metro 600 Fifth St NW Washington DC 20001

PECK, WILLIAM ARNO, internist, educator, dean, academic administrator; b. New Britain, Conn., Sept. 28, 1933; m. Patricia Hearn, July 10, 1982; children by previous marriage: Catherine, Edward Pershall, David Nathaniel; stepchildren: Andrea, Elizabeth, Katherine. AB, Harvard U., 1955; MD, U. Rochester, NYC, 1960; DSc (hon.), U. Rochester, 2000. Intern, then resident in internal medicine Barnes Hosp., St. Louis, 1960-62; fellow in metabolism Washington U. Sch. Medicine, St. Louis, 1963; mem. faculty U. Rochester Med. Sch., 1965-76, prof. medicine and biochemistry, 1973-76, head divsn. endocrinology and metabolism, 1969-76; John E. and Adaline Simon prof. medicine, co-chmn. dept. medicine Washington U. Sch. Medicine, St. Louis, 1976-89; physician in chief Jewish Hosp., St. Louis, 1976-89; prof. medicine and exec. vice chancellor med. affairs, dean sch. medicine, pres. univ. med. ctr. Washington U., St. Louis, 1989—2003, Wolff disting. prof., dean emeritus and dir. ctr. for health policy, 2003—. Chmn. endocrinology and metabolism adv. com. FDA, 1976-78; chmn. gen. medicine study sect. NIH, 1979-81; chmn. Gordon Conf. Chemistry, Physiology and Structure of Bones and Teeth, 1977, Consensus Devel. Conf. on Osteoporosis, NIH, 1984; co-chmn. Workshop on Future Directions in Osteoporosis, 1987; chmn. Spl. Topic Conf. on Osteoporosis, U.S. FDA, 1987; bd. dirs. Allied Healthcare Products, Rsch! Am., St. Louis Regional Chamber and Growth Assn., TIAA-CREF Trust Co., Centene Health Policy Adv. Coun. Editor Bone and Mineral Rsch. Anns., 1982-88. Pres. Nat. Osteoporosis Found., 1985-90. Served as med. officer USPHS, 1963-65. Paul Harris fellow Rotary Found., 2001; recipient Lederle Med. Faculty award, 1967, Career Program award NIH, 1970-75, Commr.'s Spl. citation FDA, 1988, Humanitarian award Arthritis Found. Ea. Mo., 1995, Crohn's and Colitis Fedn. Am., 1999, Founders award Nat. Osteoporosis Found., 1996, Huntington Disease Soc. Am. award, 2002, Juvenile Diabetes Rsch. Found. Lifetime Achievement award, 2003, Internat. Brotherhood award Bikur Cholim Hosp., Jerusalem, 2003, Nat. Children's Cancer Soc. Legacy award, Disting. Svc. award Washington U. Sch. Medicine, Lifetime Achievement award health care. Fellow AAAS, ACP; mem. Internat. Bone & Mineral Soc., Royal Soc. Medicine, Am. Assn. Clin. Endocrinologists, Am. Geriatrics Soc., Am. Soc. Biochemistry & Molecular Biophysics, Am. Soc. Bone and Mineral Rsch. (councilor 1978-81, pres.-elect 1982-83, pres. 1983-84), Am. Soc. Clin. Investigation, Am. Soc. Internal Medicine, Assn. Am. Med. Colls. (coun. deans adminstrv. bd. 1992—, chmn. 1996-97, chair elect 1997-98, chair 1998—, immediate past chair 1999), Assn. Am. Physicians, Endocrine Soc., Orthopaedic Rsch. Soc., Soc. Med. Adminstrs., St. Louis Metro. Med. Soc., St. Louis Soc. Internal Medicine (pres. 1986), Inst. Medicine Nat. Acad. Sci., Washington U. Health Adminstrn. Program Alumni Assn. (hon.), Research! Am. (vice chair 1999—), Pi Theta Epsilon (hon.), Sigma Xi, Alpha Omega Alpha (bd. dirs 1992-95). Home: 32 Huntleigh Downs Saint Louis MO 63131 Office: Washington U Sch Medicine #1 Brookings Dr Box 1133 Saint Louis MO 63130

PECK, WILLIAM HENRY, curator, archaeologist, educator, art historian, writer; b. Savannah, Ga., Oct. 2, 1932; s. William Henry Peck and Mildred (Bass) Peck Tuten; m. Ann Amelia Keller, Feb. 2, 1957 (dec. 1965); children: Alice Ann, Sarah Louise; m. Elsie Holmes, July 8, 1967; 1 child, William Henry IV. Student, Ohio State U., 1950-53; BFA, Wayne State U., 1960, MA, 1961. Jr. curator Detroit Inst. Arts, 1960-62, asst. curator, 1962-64, assoc. curator, 1964-68, curator ancient art, 1968—2004, acting chief curator, 1984-88, sr. curator, 1988—2004; lectr. art history Coll. Creative Studies, 2004—. Lectr. art history Cranbrook Acad. Art, Bloomfield Hills, Mich., 1963-65; vis. lectr. U. Mich., Ann Arbor, 1970, U. Mich., Dearborn, 2005—; adj. prof. art history Wayne State U., Detroit, 1966—; excavations in Egypt, Mendes, 1964-66, Precinct of Mut, Karnak, 1978—; adj. faculty art history Coll. Creative Studies, Detroit, 2004—, U. Mich., Dearborn, 2005—; sessional instr. U. Windsor, Ont., 2006. Author: Drawings from Ancient Egypt, 1978, The Detroit Institute of Arts: A Brief History, 1991, Splendors of Ancient Egypt, 1978; co-author: Ancient Egypt: Discovering its Splendors, 1978, Mummies, Diseases and Ancient Cultures, 1980, Arts and Humanities Through the Ages: Ancient Greece and Rome, 2005; contbr. articles to profl. publs. With U.S. Army, 1953-55. Recipient award in the arts Wayne State U., 1985; Ford Motor Co. travel grantee, 1962; Am. Rsch. Ctr. Egypt fellow, 1971; Smithsonian Instn. travel grantee, 1975. Mem. Archaeol. Inst. Am., Am. Rsch. Ctr. Egypt, Internat. Assn. Egyptologists, Soc. Study Egyptian Antiquities, Assn. Study Travel in Egypt and the Near East, Am. Assn. Mus., Oriental Inst.-U. Chgo. Democrat. Episcopalian. Avocations: oragami, early music performance, collecting T.E. Lawrence material. Office: 1901 Orleans Detroit MI 48207-2718 Personal E-mail: whpeck@yahoo.com.

PECKENPAUGH, ROBERT EARL, investment advisor; b. Potomac, Ill., July 17, 1926; s. Hilery and Zella (Stodgel) P.; m. Margaret J. Dixon, Sept. 21, 1945; children: Nancy Lynn, Carol Sue, David Robert, Daniel Mark, Jeanne Beth, Douglas John. Student, Ind. U., 1946—47; BS, Northwestern U., 1949, MBA with distinction, 1952. Chartered fin. analyst. With First Nat. Bank Chgo., 1949—52; pres. Security Suprs., Inc., Chgo., 1952—73; v.p. Chgo. Title & Trust Co., 1973—77; pres. Hotchkiss & Peckenpaugh, Inc., Chgo., 1977—84; v.p. Morgan Stanley Asset Mgmt. Inc., Chgo., 1984—86, Morgan Stanley & Co., Inc., Chgo., 1986—91; pres. Peckenpaugh Asset Mgmt. Inc., Chgo., 1991—2006; sr. v.p. Whitnell & Co., Oak Brook, 2006—. Chmn., Evang. Covenant Ch. of Hinsdale, Ill., 1981-84. Served with USN, 1944-46. Mem. CFA Soc. Chgo. (pres. 1963-64), Mid-Day Club, Hinsdale Golf Club. Home: 429 S County Line Rd Hinsdale IL 60521-4724 Office: Whitnell & Co 701 Harger Rd Oak Brook IL 60523

PECKER, DAVID J., magazine publishing company executive; b. NYC, Sept. 24, 1951; m. Karen Balan, Oct. 31, 1987. BBA, postgrad., Pace U. CPA, N.Y. Sr. auditor Price Waterhouse & Co.; mgr. fin. reporting Diamandis Communications, Inc., NYC, 1979, dir. fin. reporting, dir. acctg., asst. contr., 1983; COO, CFO, exec. v.p. pub. Hachette Mags., Inc., NYC, 1990-91, pres., COO, 1991-92, pres. and CEO, 1992-99; chmn., CEO Am. Media Inc., 1999—, pres., CEO, COO Lake Worth, Fla., 1999—. Mem. Fashion Group's Internat. Adv. Bd., The N.Y. City Partnership Com.; mem. bd. dirs. The Madison Square Boys & Girls Club. Bd. dirs. Pace U., N.Y.C., Drug Enforcement Agents Found., 1995—. Mem. Am. Mgmt. Assn.

PECKERMAN, BRUCE MARTIN, lawyer; b. Milw., Sept. 28, 1949; s. Joseph and Doris (Kassel) P.; m. Jeanette Chrustowski. BA, U. Wis., 1971; JD, Washington U., St. Louis, 1973. Bar: Wis. 1974, U.S. Dist. Ct. (we. dist.) Wis. 1974, U.S. Ct. Appeals (7th cir.) 1977. Sole practice, Milw., 1985—2002; ptnr. Peckerman & Klein, Milw., 2002—. Recipient young leadership award Milw. Jewish Fedn. Mem. ABA, Wis. Bar Assn. (past chmn. family law sect.), Milw. Bar Assn. (bench/bar com. 1987-88), Am. Acad. Matrimonial Lawyers (past pres.). Office: 920 E Mason St Milwaukee WI 53202-4015 Home Phone: 414-351-3866; Office Phone: 414-271-9300. Business E-Mail: bmp@peckermanlaw.com.

PECKHAM, DONALD, computer company executive; b. Aberdeen, SD, Feb. 8, 1932; s. Donald Seth and Crystal (Maytum) P.; m. Jeanette G. Mackenzie, June 20, 1967 (div. Jan. 1995); children: Dean, Deanna Jean. BSEE, U. Wash., 1957; MSEE, Calif. Inst. Tech., 1958. Engr. Hughes Aircraft Co., Culver City, Calif., 1957-60; sr. engr. Nortronics divsn. Northrop Corp., Hawthorne, Calif., 1960-61, rsch. scientist Nortronics divsn., 1965-67, tech. dir. Aircraft divsn., 1985-92; v.p. Digitek Corp., Inglewood, Calif., 1961-63, v.p., gen. mgr. LA, 1963-65; mem. staff Decade Computer Corp., Huntington Beach, 1967-71; mgr. software Pertec Computer Corp., Santa Ana, Calif., 1971-81; mgr. software tools CXC Corp., Irvine, Calif., 1981-85; instr. U. So. Calif., 1960-61; pres. Modern Computer, Carlsbad, Calif., 1992-2001, Modern.net, Oceanside, Calif., 2001—. With USN, 1950-54. Mem. IEEE, Assn. Computing Machinery, Tau Beta Pi. Home and Office: Unit 85 3890 Vista Campana S Oceanside CA 92057-8160 E-mail: donaldpeckham@cox.net.

PECKHAM, ELLEN, artist, poet; b. Rochester, NY, Sept. 28, 1938; d. Walter Fredrick and Florence Albertina (Schmanke) Stoepel; m. Anson Wheeler Peckham, Sept. 10, 1976 Exhibitions include Atelier A/E Enterprises, NYC, 1994—, Instituto Cultural Peruano Norteamericano, Peru, 1997—, Art Internat., NYC, 1998, Boston Printmakers, 1999—, Katonah Mus., NY, 1999—, Collage/Assemblage Soc., NYC, 2000—02, Brand Libr. and Art Ctr., Glendale, Calif., 2001—, Springfield Art Mus., Mo., 2001, Stocker Ctr., Elyria, Ohio, 2001, U. Richmond, Va., 2002, NW Arts Coun./Ill. Arts Coun., Woodstock, 2002, Sothebys, NY, 2002, Pacific States Biennial, Hilo, Hawaii, 2002, No. Ariz. U., Flagstaff, 2002, Multisensory Hera Gallery, Warwick, RI, 2003, Warwick, 2004, Solarplate Traveling Exhibits, NY, Mass., Va., Maine, Conn., 2003, 2004, 2005, Zimmerli Mus., Rutgers U., NJ, 2004, Robert Blackburn Printmaking Workshop, NY, 2004, Taller Boricua, 2005, NY Soc. Etchers, 2005, Gualala Arts Ctr., Calif., 2006, Bright Hills Art Ctr., NY, 2006;, author numerous poems. Avocations: gardening, theater.

PECKHAM, EUGENE ELIOT, judge, lawyer; b. Stamford, Conn., Aug. 11, 1940; s. Joseph E. and Margaret (Nabors) P.; m. Judith Alice Chamberlain, Dec. 19, 1964; children: Margaret, Joseph, Elizabeth. BA with honors, Wesleyan U., Middletown, Conn., 1962; JD, Harvard U., 1965. Bar: N.Y. 1965, Fla. 1981, U.S. Tax Ct. 1974, U.S. Ct. Appeals (2d cir.) 1975, U.S. Dist. Ct. (no. dist.) N.Y. 1965. Assoc. Hinman, Howard & Kattell, Binghamton, N.Y., 1965-72, ptnr., 1972-2000; surrogate judge Broome County, N.Y., 2001—; acting justice N.Y. Supreme Ct. (6th jud. dist.), 2003—. Instr. Broome C.C., Binghamton, 1968-69, Am. Coll. Life Underwriters, Bryn Mawr, Pa., 1969-70, Am. Coll. Property and Casualty Underwriters, Bryn Mawr, 1970-71; adj. lectr. SUNY, Binghamton, 1972-77, adj. asst. prof., 1977-81, adj. assoc. prof., 1981-87, adj. prof. acctg., 1987—2003; vis. lectr. Cornell U., Ithaca, N.Y., 1978, adj. prof., 1984. Author: Warren's Heaton Surrogate's Courts, Federal and New York Estate Taxes, vol., revised, 1988, 89, Bender's Federal Tax Service " Income Taxation of Estates & Trusts", 1989; mem. bd. editors Warren's Heaton on Surrogate Courts, 2001-; contbr. articles to profl. jours. Peace Corps vol. tchr. Santa Maria U., Arequipa, Peru, 1966-67, treas. Joint Legis. Adv. Com. on Estates, Powers and Trusts Law and The Surrogates Ct. Procedure Act, 1990—; pres. Binghamton Girls Club, N.Y., 1974-76, bd. dirs., 1970-77; chmn. bd. Binghamton Boys and Girls Club, 1977, trustee, 1987-2000, chmn. bd. trustees, 1996-2000; bd. dirs. A. Lindsay and Olive B. O'Connor Found., 1982—, Dr. G. Clifford and Florence B. Decker Found., 1984-2001; bd. dirs. Comty. Found. South Ctrl. N.Y., 1996-2002; mem. trust fund. com. Broome County United Way, N.Y., 1979-94; pres. SUNY Found., Binghamton, 1977-79, bd. dirs., 1975-82; bd. dirs. Estate Planning Coun. So. Tier, 1983-87, treas., 1983, sec., 1984, v.p., 1985, pres., 1986; bd. dirs. Samaritan Counselling Ctr. So. Tier, Inc., 1982-87, v.p., 1986, pres., 1987; co-chmn. sta. WSKG-TV auction, 1983; treas. Roberson Ctr. Arts & Scis., 1980, bd. dirs., 1977-80, 87-95; bd. dirs. Twin Tier Home Health, Inc., 1990-97, v.p., 1991-93, pres., 1993-95; chmn. Broome County Cmty. Ambassador Project, 1970-71; mem. Broome Bd. Ethics, 1985-89, chair, 1999-2000; mem. Broome County Arena Bd., 1987-89; deacon 1st Presbyn. Ch., Binghamton, 1971-74, moderator, 1974, elder, 1975-78, 87-90, trustee, 1980-83, 92-95; exec. com. Broome County Rep. Com., 1980-83, 96-2000, co-chmn. fin. com., 1982-83, vice chmn., 1996-2000; pres. Broome County Young Rep. Club, 1969-70. Recipient SUNY-Binghamton Alumni Recognition award, 1984. Fellow Am. Coll. Trust and Estate Coun.; mem. N.Y. State Bar Assn. (exec. com. trusts and estates sect. 1980-84, 86-92, treas. 1986, sec. 1987, chmn. elect 1988, chmn. 1989, tax sect. 1972-2000, chmn. spl. commn. on alt. sources funding legal svcs. 1976-78, action unit 6 1984-86, ethics com. 1979-82, bd. editors N.Y. State Bar Jour. 1998—, v.p. 1999-2002, ho. dels. 1990-94, 95-2002), Fedn. Bar Assns. 6th Jud. Dist. (pres. 1984-85), Broome County Bar Assn. (chmn. prepaid legal ins. com. 1976-80, ethics com. 1981-87, chmn. jud. rating com. 1988-90). Home: 1 Stonecrest Ct Binghamton NY 13903 Office: Broome County Surrogate Ct PO Box 1766 Binghamton NY 13902-1766 Office Phone: 607-778-2118.

PECKHAM, JOHN MUNROE, III, investment executive, author, lecturer; b. Abington, Mass., July 25, 1933; s. John Munroe and Mildred P.; m. Ann M. Murphy, Apr. 30, 1995; children: Lisa, Holly, John M. IV. AB, Tufts U., 1955; postgrad., Columbia U., 1962—. Pres. Peckham Boston Adv. Co., 1964—; pres., chmn. Boston Hall Corp., Boston, 1987—; pres. Boston Hall Pub. Co., 1988—; founder, exec. dir. Real Estate Cyberspace Soc., 1996—. Founder Realtors Concerned for Realtors, Chgo., 1986—; mem. bd. advisors Kids Stop, Boston, 1988-89; bd. dirs. Am. Fedn. for Children and Youth, L.A., 1988-89. Lt. comdr. USN, 1956-62. Mem. Nat. Assn. Realtors (v.p.), Realtors Nat. Mktg. Inst. (v.p. 1988), Internat. Fedn. Realtors, Inst. Real Estate Mgmt., Ten Club (pres. Boston chpt. 1974-79), Friends of Bill W. Republican. Baptist. Avocations: bicycling, swimming, cribbage, speaking, reading. Office: Real Estate Cyberspace Soc 4 Longfellow Pl Ste 2003 Boston MA 02114-2817

PECKHAM, THOMAS ELWOOD, lawyer; b. Arlington, Mass., Apr. 25, 1947; s. Alford S. and Janet (Gates) P.; m. Ellen A. Petersen, July 16, 1994; children: Samuel, Anne, Tavish, Duncan. BA, Brown U., 1969; JD, Boston U., 1972, LLM, 1976. Bar: Mass. 1972, U.S. Ct. Claims, U.S. Tax Ct. 1979, U.S. Supreme Ct. 1979, U.S. Dist. Ct. Mass., U.S. Ct. Appeals (1st cir.) 1982. Assoc. Goodwin, Procter & Hoar, Boston, 1976-83; ptnr. Segal, Moran, Feinberg, Peckham & Lobel, Boston, 1983-85; mng. ptnr. Peckham, Lobel, Casey, Prince & Tye LLP, Boston, 1985-99; ptnr. Bingham McCutchen LLP, Boston, 1999—, chmn. estate planning practice group. Adj. prof. grad. tax program Boston U., 2007. Contbr. articles to profl. publ. including Fun & Games with Split Interest Gifts, ALI-ABA Jour., others; lectr. in field. Pres. Friends of the Marblehead (Mass.) Pub. Schs. Inc., 1994-97, mem. adv. bd., 1997—. Fellow Am. Coll. Trust and Estate Counsel; mem. ABA, Mass Bar Assn., Boston Bar Assn., Boston Estate Planning Coun., Boston Probate and Trust Forum. Office: Bingham McCutchen LLP 150 Federal St Boston MA 02110 Home Phone: 617-306-9644; Office Phone: 617-951-8954. Office Fax: 617-345-5094. Business E-Mail: tom.peckham@bingham.com.

PECKOL, JAMES KENNETH, consulting engineer; b. Cleve., Oct. 24, 1944; s. William John and Elinor Elizabeth (Bustard) P.; children: Erin, Robyn. BS Engring., Case Inst. Tech., 1966; MSEE, U. Wash., 1975, PhDEE, 1985. Cons. GE, Raytheon, Ling Temco Vought, RCA, Boeing Co., 1966-72; sr. staff engr. indsl. products bus. unit John Fluke Mfg. Co., Seattle, 1972-83, sr. staff engr. automated systems bus. unit, 1983-86, sr. staff engr. MR&D Bus. unit, 1986-93; founder Oxford Cons., Edmonds, Wash., 1987—. Affiliate asst. prof. dept. elec. engring., affiliate asst. prof. dept. computers and software sys. U. Wash., Seattle, 1984-87, 95—, prof. dept. elec. engring., 1997—; sr. lectr., assoc. prof. dept. elec. engring. U. Aberdeen, Scotland, 1987; lectr. dept. math. and sci. Shoreline C.C., Seattle, 1989—; lectr. dept. computer sci. Edmonds (Wash.) C.C., 1992—; assoc. prof. dept. engring./computer sci. U. Nantes, Frances, 1993, 96; mem. computer sci. and elec. engring. curriculum adv. bd. Wash. State U., 1990—; lectr. various confs. and univs. Contbr. articles to profl. jours.; patentee in field. Mem. IEEE, Am. Assn. Artificial Intelligence, Assn. Computing Machinery, Tau Beta Pi. Home and Office: Oxford Cons Ltd 859 14th St SW Edmonds WA 98020-6611

PECKOLICK, ALAN, painter, graphics designer, photographer; b. NYC, Oct. 3, 1940; s. Charles and Belle (Binenbaum) P.; m. Jessica Margot Weber, June 3, 1984. AAS, Pratt Inst., Bklyn., 1968. Art dir. McCann-Erickson, 1964-68; graphic designer Herb Lubalin, 1968-72; v.p., creative dir. Lubalin, Smith, Carnase, Inc., NYC, 1972-74, LCS & P Design Group, Inc., NYC, 1974-76; pres. Lubalin Peckolick Assoc., NYC, 1976-81, Pushpin, Lubalin, Peckolick, NYC, 1981-86, Peckolick and Ptnrs., NYC, 1986-89; design dir. Addison Design Cons., NYC, 1989-91; chmn. Peckolick Inc., NYC, 1991—; painter, 2000—. Bd. adv. Designworld mag., Victoria, Australia, 1983—, Herb Lubalin Study Ctr., NYC; lectr. Pratt Inst., Parsons Sch. Design, Sch. Visual Arts, others. Co-author, designer Herb Lubalin Graphic Designer, 1986; exhibitions include Sony Gallery, Tokyo, 1989, one-man shows include Gallery 468, N.Y.C., 2000, Agora Gallery, 2002, Lucky St. Gallery, Key West, Fla., 2001, 2003, 2004, Salamagundi Club Invitational, 2002, Gallery 468, N.Y.C., 2002, Agora Gallery, 2003, Photo Dist. Gallery, 2004, Fales Libr. at NYU, 2005, Cosa Gallery, London, 2004, Atlantic Gallery, N.Y.C., 2006, Hermes Gallery, 2006. Bd. dirs. Glaucoma Found., 1993, Whale Conservation Inst., 1994. Recipient awards AIGA, Art Directors Club awards. Mem. N.Y. Art Dirs. Club (6 gold medals, over 50 awards), N.Y. Type Dirs. Club (bd. dirs.), Alliance Graphique Internationale, Art Dirs.Club Bergen (Norway) (hon.). Avocations: collecting art and prints, cooking, travel, photography, antique Corvetts. Home: 30 E 10th St New York NY 10003-6202 Personal E-mail: alanart@verizon.net.

PECORA, ANDREW LOUIS, hematologist, oncologist; b. Newark, 1957; B magna cum laude, Seton Hall U.; MD, U. Medicine and Dentistry NJ, 1983. Diplomate Am. Bd. Internal Medicine, Am. Bd. Hematology, Am. Bd. Med. Oncology. Intern NY Hosp.-Cornell Med. Ctr., NYC, 1983—84, resident in internal medicine, 1984—86; fellow in hematology and oncology Meml. Sloan Kettering Cancer Ctr., NYC; asst. dir. adult stem cell/bone marrow transplantation program Hackensack U. Med. Ctr., NJ, 1990—93, chief, program dir., 1993—, dir. stem cell collection and storage svc., 1993—, chmn., 1999—, chmn., dir. Cancer Ctr., 2001—. Clin. asst. hematology/oncology Hackensack U. Med. Ctr.; prof. medicine U. Medicine and Dentistry NJ Med. Sch. Named one of Top Drs. in NY Metro Area, Castle Connolly, Top Drs., NJ Monthly Mag., 2003, Top Drs. in Am., 2005, Top Drs. in Am. for cancer, 2006. Office: The Cancer Ctr Hackensack U Med Ctr 20 Prospect Ave Ste 400 Hackensack NJ 07601-1962

PECORA, DAVID VICTOR, retired surgeon; b. Yonkers, NY, Oct. 2, 1916; s. Michael and Tulia (Muzi) Pecora; m. Dorothy Edith Beavers, July 22, 1944; children: Ann Charlene Diamond, Michele. BA, Columbia U., 1937; MD, Yale U., 1941. Diplomate Am. Bd. Gen. Surgery, Am. Bd. Thoracic Surgery. Intern Lakeside Hosp., Western Res. U., Cleve., 1941-42; grad. fellow in surgery NY Med. Coll., NYC, 1946-47; asst. resident in surgery Sch. Medicine, Yale U., New Haven, 1947-49, resident surgeon in thoracic surgery Uncas-on-Thames, Conn., 1949-51; chief thoracic surgery, sect. chief second surg. svc. VA Hosp., Providence, 1951-54, McGuire VA Hosp., Richmond, Va., 1967-72; prin. thoracic surgeon Ray Brook State Tb Hosp., NY, 1954-65; chief surgery Sunmount VA Hosp., Tupper Lake, NY, 1964-65, VA Hosp., Altoona, Pa., 1965—67; chief surg. svc. VA Ctr., Wilmington, Del., 1972-82; pvt. practice in thoracic, vascular and gen. surgery Newark, Del.; mem. staff Med. Ctr. Del., Wilmington, Cmty. Hosp., Chester, Pa., Crozer-Chester Hosp., Pa., Union Hosp., Elkton, Pa., Riverside Hosp., Wilmington; ret., 1995. Instr. in surgery Boston U., 1953-54; clin. assoc. prof. in surgery SUNY, Syracuse, NY, 1961-70; asst. prof. surgery Med. Coll. Va., Richmond, 1967-70, assoc. prof. surgery, 1970-72; prof. surgery Thomas Jefferson U., Phila., 1972—; adj. prof. surgery Hahnemann U., Phila., 1988—; supv. tng. surg. residents numerous hosps. Mem. editl. bd. Del. Med. Jour.; author: Memoir: Between the Raindrops, 1998; contbr. over 130 articles to sci. jours. Capt. med. corps U.S. Army, 1942-46. Fellow ACS (instr. advanved trauma life support); mem. AMA, IEEE, Am. Assn. for Thoracic Surgery, Am. Coll. Chest Physicians, Am. Thoracic Soc., Am. Soc. Microbiology, Am. Med. Writers Assn., Am. Lung Assn. (ea. sect.), Royal Soc. Medicine, Pa. Assn. Thoracic Surgery, Del. Valley Vascular Soc., Md. State Med. Assn., Del. State Med. Assn., Del. Acad. Medicine, Va. Thoracic Soc., New Castle County Med. Assn., Phila. Acad. Surgery, Phila. Coll. Physicians, So. Thoracic Surg. Assn., Soc. Thoracic Surgeons (founder), Soc. Laparoendoscopic Surgeons, Soc. Neurovascular Surgery, Upstate NY Soc. Thoracic Surgery (past pres.), Saranac Lake Med. Soc. (past pres.). Home Phone: 703-462-9733.

PECTOR, MICHELLE D., lawyer; b. San Antonio; BA cum laude, U. Tex., Austin, 1997; JD cum laude, U. Houston Law Ctr., 2000. Bar: Tex. 2000, US Dist. Ct. (all dists. Tex.), US Supreme Ct., US Ct. Appeals Fifth Cir. Assoc. Baker Hostetler, Houston. Named a Rising Star, Tex. Super Lawyers mag., 2006. Mem.: Tex. Bar Assn., Assn. Women Attys., Houston Young Lawyers Assn., ABA. Office: Baker Hostetler 1000 Louisiana Ste 2000 Houston TX 77002 Office Phone: 713-646-1326. E-mail: mpector@bakerlaw.com. *

PEDDICORD, ROLAND DALE, lawyer; b. Van Meter, Iowa, Mar. 29, 1936; s. Clifford Elwood and Juanitas Irene (Brittain) P.; m. Teri Linn O'Dell; children: Erin Sue, Robert Sean. BSBA with honors, Drake U., 1961, JD with honors, 1962. Bar: Iowa 1962; cert. civil trial specialist Nat. Bd. Trial Advs.; cert. mediator Am. Acad. ADR Attys., 2000. Asst. atty. gen. State of Iowa, 1962-63; assoc. Steward, Crouch & Hopkins, Des Moines, 1962-65; ptnr. Peddicord, Wharton, Spencer, Hook, Barron & Wegman LLP, Des Moines, 1965—. Lectr. in law Drake U., 1962-68; lectr. law Coll. Osteo. Medicine, Des Moines, 1965-72. Editor and chief Drake Law Rev., 1961-62 Past mem. nat. bd. dirs., nat. coun. YMCA of U.S.A., past vice chmn. nat. bd.; bd. dirs., past chmn. Greater Des Moines YMCA, 1968-89. With USMC, 1954-57. Mem. ABA, ATLA, Iowa Bar Assn., Polk County Bar Assn., Iowa Trial Lawyers Assn., Iowa Acad. Trial Lawyers, Am. Bd. Trial Advs. (mem. nat. bd., past pres. Iowa chpt.), Am. Acad. ADR Attys. (past pres.). Republican. Methodist. Office: 405 6th Ave Ste 700 Des Moines IA 50309-2415 also: Peddicord Wharton Spencer Hook Barron & Wegman LLP 405 6th Ave Ste 700 Des Moines IA 50309 Office Phone: 515-243-2100. Business E-Mail: dale.peddicord@peddicord-law.com.

PEDDIE, RICHARD, professional sports team executive; b. Windsor, Ont., Can. m. Colleen McAnoy, 2005. Grad., U. Windsor, Ont., 1970, D (hon.), 2001. With Colgate-Palmolive, 1970—73, Gen. Foods, 1973—83, pres. Hostess Foods, 1983—85; pres., CEO Pillsbury Can., 1985—89, Stadium Corp. Ont. (Skydome), 1989; with The Palestra Grp., Toronto, 1993—96; pres., COO NetStar Comm. (formerly Labatt Comm.); pres. Toronto Raptors, 1996—98; pres., CEO, alternate NHL gov. Maple Leaf Sports & Entertainment Ltd. (owns NHL Toronto Maple Leafs, NBA Toronto Raptors and Maj. League Soccer Toronto FC), Toronto, 1998—, bd. dirs., 2003—. Recipient North Am. Facility Mgr. of Yr., 1992, Donald B. McCaskill award for Mktg. Excellence in Can. Office: Maple Leaf Sports & Entertainment Ltd 40 Bay St Ste 400 Toronto ON M5J 2X2 Canada *

PEDEN, KEITH J., human resources specialist; b. Mich., May 1950; BA, Western Mich. U.; MA, Ea. Mich. U. Human resources staff Honeywell, Prime Computer; dir. worldwide compensation, benefits and human resources info. systems Lotus Devel. Corp.; v.p., head human resources Alexander & Alexander Consulting, Boston; dir. benefits, compensation, human resources mgmt. systems Raytheon Co., Lexington, Mass., 1993—97, v.p., dep. dir. human resources initiatives, 1997—2001, sr. v.p. human resources, 2001—. *

PEDERSEN, ARLENE, web design company executive; b. 1974; Creative dir., owner Pedersen Design Grp. Involved with Tanque Verde Sch. Dist.; mem. Leukemia and Lymphoma Soc. Team in Tng.; mentor Nike Women's Marathon. Named one of 40 Under 40, Tucson Bus. Edge, 2006. Office: Pedersen Design Group 1160 N Craycroft Rd Tucson AZ 85712 Office Phone: 520-270-7863. Office Fax: 520-270-7957.

PEDERSEN, DARHL MAX, psychology professor; b. Orem, Utah, Oct. 12, 1935; s. Max Barlow and Edith (Aiken) P.; 1 child, Clark. BS, Brigham Young U., 1957, MS, 1958; PhD, U. Ill., 1962. From asst. prof. psychology to prof. Brigham Young U., Provo, Utah, 1962—71, prof., 1971—, chmn. Dept. Psychology, 1967—77. Postdoctoral assoc. Ames Research Ctr., NASA, Moffett Field, Calif., 1969-70. Author: Psychological Tests and Measurements, 1965, Essentials for Understanding Statistics, 1978, Environmental Psychology, 1978, Learning Statistics, 1988; contbr. over 100 papers to profl. jours. V.p. Provo Coun. Boy Scouts Am., 1978-81, coun. commr., 1981-86. NSF fellow, 1962; recipient Creative Talent award Am. Inst. Rsch., 1962. Mem. Soc. for Sci. Study of Religion, Sigma Xi (ann. lecture 1973), Phi Kappa Phi, Psi Chi. Republican. Mem. Lds Ch. Avocation: outdoor activities. Home: 1815 N 1550 E Provo UT 84604-5709 Office: Brigham Young U 1090 SWKT Provo UT 84602 Home Phone: 801-377-8965; Office Phone: 801-422-6364. Business E-Mail: darhl_pedersen@byu.edu.

PEDERSEN, DARLENE DELCOURT, publishing executive, writer, psychotherapist; b. Westbrook, ME; 1 child, Jorgen David. BSN, U. Conn., 1967; postgrad., U. B.C., 1974-75; MSN, U. Penn., 1996—97. RN bd. cert. clinical specialist, advanced practice registered nurse, bd. cert. in adult psychiatric and mental health nursing, Am. Nurses Credentialing Ctr. Various nursing positions, psychiat. cmty. health, 1967-79; assoc. editor JB Lippincott Co., Phila., 1979-84; sr. acquisition editor WB Saunders Co., Phila., 1984-88, v.p., editor in chief, 1988-91, sr. v.p., editorial dir. books divsn., liaison to London office, 1991-95; domestic and internat. pub. cons. Phila., 1995—; psychotherapist pvt. practice, 1997—. Team leader Northwestern Human Svcs. Delaware County, 1998—99; dir. PsychOptions, 2000—; v.p. content ops. MedCases, Phila., 2000—03; exec. editor Thomson Physicians World, 2003—04; dir. content devel. FA Davis Co., Phila., 2004—. Author: Canadian Nurse, 1976, PsychNotes, 2005, 2nd Ed., 2007; contbg. editor: (book) Basic Nursing Skills, 1977; acquisition editor: book Saunders Manual of Medical Practice, Comprehensive Cytopathology; contbr. chapters to books. Recipient Book of the Year award (for PsychNotes), Am. Jour. Nursing, 2005. Mem.: ANA, Internat. Soc. Traumatic Stress Studies, U.S. Dressage Fedn., Inc., Am. Orthopsychiat. Assn., Internat. Platform Assn., Assn. Profl. Comm. Cons., Manuscript Soc., Forum Exec. Women, Internat. Soc. Psychiat. Mental Health Nurses, Med. Mktg. Assn., Assn. Am. Pubs., Med. Mktg. Assn., Am. Med. Writers Assn., Am. Med. Pubs. Assn., Am. Psychiat. Nurses Assn., Am. Group Psychotherapy Assn., Emily's List, U. Club Penn., Sigma Theta Tau (Xi chpt.). Avocations: autograph and art collection, travel, music, reading, movies. Office: FA Davis Co 1915 Arch St Philadelphia PA 19103 Office Phone: 215-568-2074. Business E-Mail: ddp@fadavis.com.

PEDERSEN, JAMES F., lawyer; b. Wayne, Nebr., Jan. 26, 1949; BA Journalism with distinction, U. Nebr., 1971; JD, Harvard U., 1975. Bar: Minn. 1975, Registered Fgn. Lawyer, Eng. & Wales. Mem. Oppenheimer Wolff & Donnelly, Mpls.; grp. head Dorsey & Whitney LLP, 1996—2000, ptnr. Mem. editorial bd.: Harvard Internat. Law Jour., 1974-75. Mem. ABA (mem. corp., banking and bus. law sect., chair pub. com. sect. internat. law and practice 1987-89), Minn. State Bar Assn., Phi Beta Kappa, dir. Minn. Internat. Ctr. 1996-2002, mem. Minn. State Bar Assn. Internat. Bus. Law Sect. and Corp. Counsel Sect., Swedish Am. C. of C. of Minn., Internat. Bar Assn. Office: Dorsey & Whitney LLP 50 S 6th St Ste 1500 Minneapolis MN 55402-1498 Office Phone: 612-340-2600. Office Fax: 612-340-2868. Business E-Mail: pedersen.james@dorsey.com.

PEDERSEN, JAMIE D., lawyer; b. Puyallup, Wash., Sept. 9, 1968; s. Douglas Kirk and Audrey Mary (Draheim) P. BA summa cum laude, Yale U., 1990, JD, 1994. Bar: Wash. 1994. Law clk. Hon. Stephen F. Williams US Ct. Appeals, DC Cir.; ptnr. Preston Gates & Ellis LLP, Seattle; co-chair nat. bd. dirs Lambda Legal Defense & Edn. Fund, Inc. Outside gen. counsel McKinstry Co., Pacific Med. Ctr., Parametrix, Inc. Pres. Yale Russian Chorus, New Haven, 1992-94. Recipient Charles G. Albom prize Yale Law Sch., 1994; Nat. Merit scholar, 1986. Mem. Phi Beta Kappa. Democrat. Lutheran. Avocations: swimming, flute. Office: Preston Gates & Ellis LLP Ste 2900 925 Fourth Ave Seattle WA 98104-1158 Office Phone: 206-370-7987. Office Fax: 206-370-6152. E-mail: jamiep@prestongates.com.

PEDERSEN, KAREN SUE, electrical engineer; b. Indianola, Iowa, Apr. 27, 1942; d. Donald Cecil and Dorothy Darlene (Frazier) Kading; m. Wendell Dean Pedersen, May 6, 1961; children: Debra Ann Pedersen Schwickerath, Michael Dean. AA in Math., Grand View Coll., Des Moines, 1975; BSEE, Iowa State U., 2007; MBA in Econ., Bentley Coll., Waltham, Mass., 1989. Registered profl. engr., Iowa, Mass., Ill. Engr. Iowa Power & Light Co., Des Moines, 1978—80, rate engr., 1980—84; sr. rsch. engr. Boston Edison Co., Boston, 1984—87, sr. engr., 1987—94, prin. rsch. analyst, 1994—98; sr. engr. MidAmerican Energy Co., Davenport, Iowa, 1998—2006; prin. Pedersen Power Solutions, Davenport, 2006—. Ops. chmn. Old South Ch., Boston, 1989-98. Recipient Disting. Svc. award, Iowa Engring. Soc., 2004. Mem. IEEE (chmn. Iowa ctrl. sect. 1983-84, sec. Iowa-Ill. sect. 2003), NSPE (v.p. 1999-2000, v.p. North Ctrl. region 2001-03, Outstanding Svc. award), Mass. Soc. Profl. Engrs. (pres. 1992-93), Eta Kappa Nu. Independent. Congregationalist. Avocations: golf, gardening. Office Phone: 563-340-2139. Personal E-mail: kspedersen@mchsi.com.

PEDERSEN, KNUD GEORGE, retired economics professor, academic administrator; b. Three Creeks, Alta., Can., June 13, 1931; s. Hjalmar Neilsen and Anna (Jensen) P.; m. Joan Elaine Vanderwarker, Aug. 15, 1953 (dec. 1988); children: Greg, Lisa; m. Penny Ann Jones, Dec. 31, 1988. Diploma in Edn., Provincial Normal U., 1952; BA, U. B.C., 1959; MA, U. Wash., 1964; PhD, U. Chgo., 1969; LLD (hon.), McMaster U., 1996; DLitt (hon.), Emily Carr Inst. of Art and Design, 2003; LLD (hon.), Simon Fraser U., 2003, U. No. B.C., 2005. Asst. prof. econs. of edn. U. Toronto; asst. prof. econs. of edn., assoc. dir. U. Chgo., 1970-72; dean, assoc. prof., then prof. U. Victoria, B.C., 1972-75, acad. v.p., prof., 1975-79; pres., vice-chancellor, prof. Simon Fraser U., Vancouver, B.C., 1979-83, U. B.C., Vancouver, 1983-85; pres., vice-chancellor U. Western Ont., London, Can., 1985-94, prof. econs. of edn., 1985-96; interim pres. U. No. B.C., 1995; founding pres., vice-chancellor Royal Roads U., 1995-96; chancellor U. No. B.C., 1998—2004; vice chmn. bd. govs. Emily Carr Inst. Art and Design, 2004—05, chmn. bd. govs., 2005—. Bd. dirs. Assn. Univs. and Colls., Canada, 1979—84, chmn., Canada, 1989—91; bd. dirs. Vancouver Bd. Trade, 1983—85; pres. Can. Club Vancouver, 1983—84; mem. coun. trustees Inst. for Rsch. on Pub. Policy, Ottawa, Ont., Canada, 1983—89; chmn. Coun. Ont. Univs., 1989—91. Author: The Itinerant Schoolmaster, 1972; contbr. chpts. to books, numerous articles to profl. jours. Chmn. B.C. (Can.) Region Can. Cystic Fibrosis Found.; mem. Min. Advanced Edn. Adv. Com. Decorated officer Order of Can., Order of Ont., Order of B.C.; recipient 125th Anniversary of Confedn. of Can. medal, Queen's Jubilee medal; fellow Ford Found., 1965-68, Can. Coll. Tchrs., 1977, Royal Soc. for Encouragement of Arts, 1984; also 11 major scholarships. Mem. Semiahmoo Golf and Country Club, Loomis Trail Golf and Country Club. Avocations: golf, fishing, gardening, cooking, art. Personal E-mail: pgpedersen@telus.net.

PEDERSEN, PAUL BODHOLDT, psychologist, educator; b. Ringsted, Iowa, May 19, 1936; BA in History and Philosophy, U. Minn., 1958, MA in Am. Studies, 1959; ThM, Luth. Sch. Theology, Chgo., 1962; MA in Ednl. Psychology, U. Minn., 1966; PhD in Asian Studies, Claremont Grad. U., Calif., 1968. Asst. prof. dept. psychoednl. studies, psychologist U. Minn., Mpls., 1971-75; sr. fellow Culture Learning Inst. East-West Ctr., Honolulu, 1975-76, sr. fellow coord., 1975-76; assoc. prof. dept. psychoednl. studies, psychologist U. Minn., 1975-79, higher edn. coord., 1976-77; sr. fellow Culture Learning Inst. East-West Ctr., 1979-81; prof., chmn. dept. counselor edn. Syracuse (N.Y.) U., 1982-90, prof. edn. dept. counseling and human svcs., 1989—95, adj. prof. dept. internat. rels., 1993—95, prof. emeritus, 2000—; prof. counseling edn. U. Ala., Birmingham, 1996-2001. Vis. lectr. Nommensen U., Medan, Sumatra, Indonesia, 1962—65, U. Malaya, 1969—71; vis. prof. dept. psychology U. Hawaii, 1978—81, 2000—; spkr. in field. Author numerous books, chpts. in books, articles to profl. jours.; mem. editl. bd. Am. Jour. Multicultural Counseling and Devel.; editl. advisor Jour. Profl. Psychology, Jour. Simulation and Games, Internat. Jour. Intercultural Rels. Sr. Fulbright fellow Nat. Taiwan U., Taipei, 1999-2000. Mem. APA, Am. Assn. Counseling and Devel. Internat. (mem. rels. com., editl. bd. Jour. Counseling and Devel., editor Internationally Speaking newsletter, mentor media com.), Internat. Assn. for Cross Cultural Psychology, Internat. Coun. Psychologists, Soc. Intercultural Tng. and Rsch. (exec. com., program chairperson 1977, chairperson Pacific Com. 1977, pres. 1978-80, editl. bd. Jour. Intercultural Rels.). Home: 1330 Ala Moana Blvd Apt 1306 Honolulu HI 96814-4221 Home Phone: 808-721-1568; Office Phone: 808-589-2662.

PEDERSEN, PAUL MARK, sportswriter, educator, columnist; b. Stratton, Nebr., Sept. 21, 1970; s. Harold Clifford and Cassandra Sue Pedersen; m. Jennifer Lynn Estes, May 31, 1991; children: Hallie Susannah, Zack Paul, Brock Victor, Carlie Elizabeth. AA in Bibl. Studies, Hobe Sound Bible Coll., Hobe Sound, Fla, 1990; BSBA, Palm Beach Atlantic U., West Palm Beach, Fla., 1992; MA in History, U. Ctrl. Fla., Orlando, 1993; MA in Bus. Comm. and Pub. Rels., Emerson Coll., Boston, 1997; PhD in Sport Mgmt., Fla. St. U., Tallahassee, 2000. Lic. FCC Broadcasting Fed. Comm. Commn./Washington, 1993. Sportswriter, agate clk. Palm Beach Post, West Palm Beach, Fla., 1996—98, sports corr., 1998—2002; comm. instr. Palm Beach Atlantic U., 1997—98, asst. prof. sport mgmt., 2003—05; grad. tchg., rsch. asst. Fla. State U., Tallahassee, 1988—2000, sport mgmt. instr., 2001—01; asst. prof. sport mgmt. Bowling Green State U., Ohio, 2001—03; assoc. prof. sport com. Ind. U., Bloomington, 2005—. Book rev. editor Academic Athletic Jour., 2001—03; sports bus. columnist Treasure Coast Bus. Jour., Stuart, 2003—05; mem. editl. bd. Internat. Jour. Sport Mgmt., 2004—, Internat. Jour. Sport Mgmt. and Mktg., 2005—; pres., founder Premier Sports Cons., LLC, 2004—. Author: Build It and They Will Come: Arrival of the Tampa Bay Devil Rays, 1997, Bobby Bowden: Win by Win, 2003, Stragegic Sport Communication, 2007; editor: Human Kinetics, 2007, Internat. Jour. Sport Comm., 2007; contbr. articles to profl. jour. Recipient Outstanding BS Grad., Palm Beach Atlantic U., 1992. Mem.: North Am. Soc. for Sport Mgmt., Phi Kappa Phi, Phi Alpha Theta. Office: Ind U 1025 E 7th St HPER 170 Bloomington IN 47405 Office Phone: 812-855-4066.

PEDERSEN, PEER, lawyer; BS, U. Ill., 1947, JD, 1948. Bar: Ill. 1949. Assoc. Arrington & Healy; founding ptnr. Pedersen & Houpt, 1957—. Bd. dirs. Delray Farms, Inc., Fla. Office Property Co., Inc., Home Access Health Corp., Martin Brower Co., River East Devel., Spraying Systems Co., Tempel Steel Co., Tennis Corp. Am. Pres. Robert R. McCormick Boys and Girls Club; bd. dirs. Boys and Girls Club Chgo., Children's Meml. Hosp., Children's Meml. Found., Rehabilitation Inst. Chgo., Lyric Opera Chgo., U. Ill. Law Sch. Served USN, WWII. Mem.: ABA, Ill. State Bar Assn., Chgo. Bar Assn., Law Club. Office: Pedersen & Houpt 161 N Clark Ste 3100 Chicago IL 60601-3242

PEDERSEN, RICHARD FOOTE, diplomat, academic administrator; b. Miami, Ariz., Feb. 21, 1925; s. Ralph Martin and Gertrude May (Foote) P.; m. Nelda Newell Napier, May 9, 1953; children: Paige Elizabeth, Jonathan Foote, Kendra Gayle. BA summa cum laude, Coll. of Pacific, 1946; MA, Stanford U., 1947; PhD, Harvard U., 1950; LLD (hon.), George Williams Coll., 1964, U. of Pacific, 1966; DHL (hon.), Am. U., Cairo, 1997. Teaching fellow, tutor Harvard U., Cambridge, Mass., 1949-50; with UN econ. and social affairs Dept. State, Washington, 1950-53; adviser econ. and social affairs U.S. Mission to UN, NYC, 1953—55, adviser polit. and security affairs, 1956-59, sr. advisor polit. and security affairs, 1959-64, minister, counselor, 1964-66, ambassador, sr. adviser to U.S. rep., 1966-67; ambassador, dep. U.S. rep. UN Security Coun., NYC, 1967—69; counselor Dept. State, 1969-73; ambassador to Hungary, 1973-75; sr. v.p. internat. U.S. Trust Co., 1975-78; pres. Am. U., Cairo, 1978-90; dir. internat. programs Calif. Poly Pomona U., 1990-95. Mem. adv. bd. Nat. Coun. U.S.-Arab Rels., 1985—; trustee Consortium for Internat. Devel., 1990—95; mem. adv. bd. Ctr. Near Eastern Studies UCLA, 1996—99; adv. bd. Sch. Internat. Studies, U. Pacific, 1997—. Mem. Nat. Coun. YMCAs, 1961-73; bd. dirs. Ctr. for Civic Edn., 1995—, Physicians for Peace, 1988-90; mem. Fulbright bd., Egypt, 1980-82, adv. bd. Fulbright Cultural Enrichment Program, So. Calif., 1991—2001. With US Army, 1943—45, ETO. Recipient Sumner Peace prize Harvard U., 1950, Outstanding Alumnus award U. Pacific, 1962, Order of Sacred Treasure, Gold and Silver Star, Govt. of Japan, 1987; named One of 10 Outstanding Young

Men, U.S. Jr. C. of C., 1956; awarded Order of Scis. and Arts, first class Govt. of Egypt, 1990. Mem. Coun. Fgn. Rels., Am. Soc. Internat. Law, L.A. World Affairs Coun., Am. Fgn. Svc. Assn., Mid. East Inst., Oriental Inst., UN Assn. Am., Internat. Assn. Univ. Pres., Pacific Coun. Internat. Policy, Asia Soc. Clubs: Harvard (N.Y.); Cosmos (Washington). Democrat. Congregationalist. Avocations: swimming, tennis, egyptology, local history. Home: 2503 N Mountain Ave Claremont CA 91711-1545 Personal E-mail: rfpdrsn@earthlink.net.

PEDERSEN, WESLEY NIELS M., public relations and public affairs counselor; b. South Sioux City, Nebr., July 10, 1922; s. Peder Westergaard and Marie Gertrude (Sorensen) P.; m. Angeline Kathryn Vavra, Oct. 17, 1948; 1 son, Eric Wesley. Student, Tri-State Coll., Sioux City, Iowa, 1940-41; BA summa cum laude, Upper Iowa U., Fayette; postgrad. in Russian, George Washington U., 1958—59. Editor, writer Sioux City Jour., 1941-50; corr. N.Y. Times, Life, Time, Fortune, 1948-50; editor Dept. State, 1950—52, fgn. svc. officer Hong Kong, 1960-63; fgn. affairs columnist, roving corr., counselor summit meetings and fgn. ministers confs. USIA, 1952—60, chief, worldwide spl. publs. and graphics programs, 1963-69; chief Office Spl. Projects, Washington, 1969-78, Office Spl. Projects, Internat. Comm. Agy., 1978-79; v.p. Fraser Assocs., pub. rels., Washington, 1979-80; dir. comm. and pub. rels. Pub. Affairs Coun., Washington, 1980—2006; prin. Wes Pedersen Comms., 2006—. Lectr. creative comm. Upper Iowa U., 1975; chmn., Europe, Ambassadorial Internat. Affairs Seminar, Fgn. Svc. Inst., 1975; lectr. internat. pub. rels. Pub. Rels. Inst., Am. U., 1976; lectr. bus. and mgmt. divsn. NYU, 1976-78; cons. pub. rels., editl. and design; del. founding sessions 1st Amendment Congress, Phila. and Williamsburg, Va., 1980, exec. com., 1980. Columnist: (as Paul L. Ford) The World Today, 1952-60; (as Benjamin E. West) Behind the Curtain, 1952-60; White House Report, 1966-69 (as Wesley Pedersen), Washington Report-Pub. Rels. Jour., 1980-85; author: Mr. President: Lyndon B. Johnson, 1964, Legacy of a President, 1964, Journey to the Pacific, 1965, Mr. President: Richard M. Nixon, 1969, American Heroes of Asian Wars, 1969; co-author: Effective Government Public Affairs, 1981; editor: The Imam's Story, 1961, Escape at Midnight and Other Stories (Pearl S. Buck), 1962, Exodus From China (Harry Redl), 1962, Macao, 1962, The Dividing Line (Arturo Gonzalez), 1962, China's Men of Letters (K.E. Priestley), 1963, Children of China (Pearl S. Buck and Margaret Wylie), 1963, Destination the Moon (William Howard), 1964, Man on the Moon, 1964, Nine From Little Rock, 1964, To the Moon and Beyond, 1965, Bounty From the Land, 1965, Workers Paradise Lost (Eugene Lyons), 1967, The Americans and the Arts (Howard Taubman), 1969, The Dance in America (Agnes de Mille), 1969, Getting the Most From Grassroots Public Affairs Programs, 1980, Computer Applications in Public Affairs, 1984, Cost-Effective Management for Today's Public Affairs, 1984, Making Community Relations Pay Off: Tools and Strategies, 1988, Winning at the Grassroots: How to Succeed in the Legislative Arena by Mobilizing Employees and Other Allies, 1989, Leveraging State Government Relations, 1990, Managing the Business-Employee PAC, 1992, Adding Value to the Public Affairs Function, 1994, Winning at the Grassroots (with Tony Kramer), 2000, Managing the Corporate Political Action Committee, 2001; Pub. Affairs Rev. Mag., 1980-86, 2000, 01, 02, 03, 04, 05, Impact newsletter on nat. and internat. pub. affairs, 1980—2006; contbr. to The Commissar, 1972, Informing the People: A Public Affairs Handbook, 1981, The Practice of Public Relations, 1984, 2d edit., 2003, Legislative Careers: Why and How We Should Study Them, 1999, Encyclopedia of Public Relations, 2004, Corporate Public Affairs: Interacting with Interest Groups, Media, and Government, 2006; mem. editl. bd. Pub. Rels. Quar., 1975—, Washington editor, Pub. Rels. Quar., 1998—, Fgn. Svc. Jour., 1975-81; mem. editl. adv. bd. Pub. Rels. News, 1991-98, contbg. editor Pub. Affairs News Mag., London, 2004—; author scripts Uncle Walter's Doghouse radio show, 1938; contbr. articles to profl. jours. Founding chmn. bd. dirs. Nat. Inst. for Govt. Pub. Info. Rsch., Am. U., 1977-80. Served with Air Corps, US Army, 1943-46. Recipient 3 awards A.P. Mng. Editors Assn., Iowa, 1948-49, Meritorious Svc. award USIA, 1963, Superior Svc. award USIA, 1964, Presdl. commendation, 1964, 70, 1st prize Fed. Editors Assn., 1970, 74-75, Agy. Dir.'s citation USIA, 1965, 74, 78, Soc. Tech. Comm., 1974-76, Gold award Internat. Newsletter Conf., 1982, Silver award, 1985, Eddi award for design excellence Editor's Workshop, 1983, Gold Circle award Am. Soc. Assn. Execs., 1983-89, 97-2000, Ten Cool award Am. Soc. Assn. Execs., 2001, Editors' Forum award, 1988-90, 94-96, Assn. Trends award, 1989-2005, Lifetime Great Assn. Communicator award, Assn. Trends, 1999, Best of Century Comm. award, Assn. Trends, 2001, spl. citation Assn. Trends, 2001, 07, Silver award 2004, 05, Gold award, 2004, Excellence award, 2006, Grand prize Internat. Ann. Report Conf., 1989, Gold award 1997, Comm. Concepts awards, 1989-2006, Grand Comm. Concepts awards, 1992, 95, 2000, 02, 04, 05, 06, MerComm awards, 1990-2000, Nat. Media Conf. award, 1989, 90, Internat. Acad. Comm. Arts and Scis. award, 1994-98, 2000, Grand prize, 1995, awards Printing and Graphic Assn., 1987, 91, 96-97, 2000, Excell award Soc. of Nat. Assn. Publishers, 2000, Judges' award 2000; named Most Outstanding Info. Officer in Exec. Br. Govt. Info. Orgn., 1975, Ky. Col. and Adm. Nebr. Navy, 1984; inducted into PRSA Hall of Fame Nat. Capital Divsn., 2005. Mem. DAV, Am. Fgn. Svc. Assn., Am. Legion, Internat. Assn. Bus. Communicators (Communicator of Yr. Washington chpt. 1978, various awards 1973, 76-78, 84, 90, 94-2004, Winners' Circle awards dist. III 1996-2003), Nat. Assn. Govt. Communicators (pres. 1978-79, Communicator of Yr. 1977, Disting. Svc. award 1978), Pub. Rels. Soc. Am. (mem. Counselor's Acad. 1980—, chmn. 1st Amendment task force 1980-81, co-recipient Thoth award 1980-81, 94, twin Thoth awards 1995-97, 2003, Thoth awards 1998-2003, Bronze Anvil award 2000, named to Hall of Fame 2005), Am. Soc. Profl. Communicators (Colonial award 2002, Masters award 2004), World Affairs Coun., Soc. Profl. Journalists, The Acad. Polit. Sci., Fgn. Svc. Club, Nat. Press Club, Overseas Press Club. Episcopalian. Office: Wes Pedersen Comms and Pub Rels 4701 Willard Ave Ste 1007 Chevy Chase MD 20815-4622 Office Phone: 301-718-9191. Personal E-mail: wesped@comcast.net. Business E-Mail: editorwes@hotmail.com. *Keenness of mind and an abundance of luck, it is said, are the key ingredients of personal success. The truth be told, however, I've performed only one act of brilliance in my lifetime: the selection of my parents. But I've had an enormous amount of good fortune, a fact manifestly clear to anyone who has ever met my wife, my son and my granddaughters. They, thank goodness, chose me.*

PEDERSEN, WILLIAM FRANCIS, lawyer; b. NYC, Apr. 4, 1943; s. William F. and Priscilla S. (Auchincloss) P.; m. Ellen L. Frost, Feb. 2, 1974; children: Mark Francis, Claire Ellen. BA, Harvard U., 1965, LLB, 1968. Bar: Mass. 1969, D.C. 1978. Assoc. Ropes & Gray, Boston, 1969-72; staff atty. EPA, Washington, 1972-75, dep. gen. counsel, then assoc. gen. counsel, 1976-85; staff counsel Senate Com. on Govt. Ops., Washington, 1975-76; lectr. Harvard Law Sch., 1985-86; of counsel Perkins Coie, Washington, 1987—89, ptnr., 1989-94, Shaw, Pittman, Potts & Trowbridge, Washington, 1994-2001; pvt. practice Washington, 2001—. Vis. prof. Law Sch., U. Mich., 1997-98. Contbr. articles to profl. jours. Mem. ABA (standing com. on environ. law 1987-89). Republican. Episcopalian. Office: William F Pedersen PLLC Ste 1350 1615 L St NW Washington DC 20036 Office Phone: 202-296-8884. Business E-Mail: bill.pedersen@billpedersen.com.

PEDERSON, GORDON ROY, state legislator, retired military officer; b. Gayville, SD, Aug. 8, 1927; s. Roy E. and Gladys F. (Masker) P.; m. Betty L. Ballard, Mar. 8, 1955; children: James D., Carol A. Pederson Niemann, Nancy G. Pederson Holub, Gary W. Student, Yankton Coll., 1948-50, Fla. State U., 1963; advanced course, Infantry Sch., 1958-59. Drafted U.S. Army, 1945-47, commd. 2nd lt., 1952, advanced through grades to lt. col., 1967, served CONUS World War II, platoon leader 17th infantry regiment, 7th infantry divsn. Korea, 1953-54, served Korean War, 1950-54, rifle co. commdr. 10th mountain divsn. Germany, 1955-58, instr., dir. instrn. U.S. Army Jungle Warfare Tng. Ctr. Ft. Sherman, Canal Zone, 1961-63, comdr. post, 1963-64, 1st brig., 1st infantry divsn. Vietnam, 1965—66, dir. tng. hdqs. G3, Ft. Leonard Wood, 1966—68; advisor Ministry of Nat. Def., Rep. China on Taiwan, 1969-70; retired U.S. Army, 1970; operator Elkton Ho. Post, 1971—78; rep. S.D. Ho. Reps., Pierre, 1977-99, 2001—; operator Dairy Queen, Wall, SD, 1990-95. Chmn. transp. com. S.D. Ho. Reps., 1979-93, vice chair state affairs com., 1994-98, vice chair commerce com., 1998, chmn. budget audit com., 2001-2002, chmn. transp. com., 2002—; exec. bd. Legis. Rsch. Coun., 2002—. Del. S.D. Rep. Conv., 1974-78, 80, 82, 84, 87-98, 2002-04, vice chair, 2004-06; del. Nat. Rep. Conv., 1976, 80, 84, 88, 92, 96, 2000, 04; bd. dirs. Legis. Rsch. Coun., 1988, 90, 92, 96, 98, 2001-02, 05-06. Decorated Bronze Star, Medal of Merit, U.S. Presdl. Unit Citation, Rep. Korea Presdl. Unit Citation, Rep. Vietnam Presdl. Unit Citation, Combat Infantry Badge with Star, Legion of Merit, Air Medal with 2 Oak Leaf Clusters, Army Accomodation medal with 2 oak leaf clusters, Cross of Gallantry with Palm, Republic Vietnam. Mem. VFW, DAV, Am. Legion, Retired Officers Assn., Wall C. of C., Internat. Lions Club, Sons of Norway. Lutheran. Home: PO Box 312 116 W 7th St Wall SD 57790 Office: SD Ho of Reps State Capitol Bldg Pierre SD 57501 Office Phone: 605-279-2610. Fax: 605-279-2609. Business E-Mail: bpers@gwtc.net, rep.gordonpederson@state.ussd.

PEDERSON, JOHN MARTIN, education educator; b. Lanigan, Saskatchewan, Can., Nov. 23, 1969; s. Lee Denise Pederson and Marjorie Christine Benson Pederson. BA, Concordia Coll., 1992; MA, U. N.D., 1994; PhD, U. Nebr., 1998. Asst. prof. Mayville State U., ND, 1998—2004, assoc. prof., 2004—. V.p., coun. coll. facilities ND U. Sys., 2003—04, faculty rep. to Acad. Affairs Coun., 2003—04, pres. coun. coll. faculties, 2004—05, faculty advisor, state bd. of higher edn., 2005—07. Coun. pres. Mayville Luth. Ch., ND, 2005—06; v.p. Mayville Luth. Ch. Found., 2007—; synod coun. mem. Ea. ND Synod of the Evang. Luth. Ch. in Am., Fargo, 2005—. Mem.: Sons of Norway (v.p. 2005). Lutheran. Home: 114 6th Ave SE Mayville ND 58257 Office: Mayville State Univ 330 Third St NE Mayville ND 58257

PEDERSON, SALLY J., former lieutenant governor; b. Muscatine, Iowa, Jan. 13, 1951; d. Gerald and Wineva Pederson; m. James A. Autry, Feb. 6, 1982; children: Rick, Jim Jr., Ronald. Grad., Iowa State U., 1973. With Meredith Corp., 1973-84; sr. food editor Better Homes & Gardens mag.; lt. gov. State of Iowa, Des Moines, 1999—2007. Pres. Polk County Health Svcs.; bast bd. trustees Nat. Alliance for Autism Rsch.; pres. bd. trustees Autism Soc. Iowa; founding pres. The Homestead Living and Learning Ctr. for Adults with Autism; past cmty. bd. svcs. includes Des Moines Cmty. Playhouse, Very Spl. Arts Iowa, YWCA Aliber Child Care Ctr., YMCA Ctr. Br.; parent rep. Heartland AEA Autism Steering Com.; mem. Iowa State Spl. Edn. Adv. Bd; bd. dirs. Blank Children's Hosp., Mid-Iowa Health Found.; gov.'s appointee State Spl. Edn. Adv. Panel. Democrat. *

PEDERSON, WILLIAM CHRISTOPHER, plastic surgeon; b. Texas City, Tex., July 15, 1952; s. Alton Curtis and Lucy Vernor (Windham) P.; m. Cynthia Lea Anderson, June 17, 1978; children: Liv, Anton, Candice. BA, U. Tex., 1974, MD, 1978. Hand fellow U. Louisville, 1984; rsch. fellow Duke U. Med. Ctr., Durham, N.C., 1985; microsurgery rsch. fellow St. Vincent's Hosp., Melbourne, 1986; asst. prof. plastic surgery Duke U. Med. Ctr., Durham, 1087-89; chief of plastic surgery U. Tex. Health Sci. Ctr., San Antonio, 1989—. Contbr. articles to profl. jours. Bd. dirs. C.E. Homeowner's Assn., San Antonio, 1990—. Fellow ACS (assoc.); mem. Am. Soc. Plastic and Reconstructive Surgery, Am. Assn. Hand Surgery, Am. Soc. Reconstructive Microsurgery.

PEDESCLEAUX-MUCKLE, GAIL, retired business analyst, writer, artist, consultant; b. Cleve., June 20, 1949; d. Alfonso Pedescleaux and Belle Pinkard Pedescleaux; m. Kirk Muckle, Oct. 24, 1997; 1 stepchild, Christopher Corey Muckle. BA in English Lit., Ctrl. Mich. U., 1971. Acct. asst. Travelers Ins. Co., Southfield, Mich., 1972—79, underwriter Garden City, NY, 1979—81, Commerce and Industry, NYC, 1981—83; sr. underwriter Firemans' Fund, NYC, 1983—85; bus. analyst Am. Internat. Group, NYC, 1985—94, sr. quality assurance analyst Livingston, NJ, 1994—2000, sr. bus. analyst Parsippany, NJ, 2000—04; ret., 2004. Cons. in field; patient rep. JFK Family Practice, 2005—; coord. creative arts programs, 2006. Author: (anthology) America at the Millennium, 2000 (Editor's Choice, 2000), Poetry's Elite: The Best Poets of 2000, 2001 (Editor's Choice, 2001), Throwing Stardust, 2003 (Editor's Choice, 2003), Celebrating Poetry, 2003, Theatre of the Mind, 2003, The Best Poems and Poets of 2003, 2003, Colours of the Heart, 2004, Twilight Musings, 2005 (Editors Choice award, 2005). Mem. DAV: Comdr.'s Club, 1993—, Nat. Multiple Sclerosis Soc., 1994—, Nat. Trust, 1993—, Am. Mus. Natural History, 1996, Nat. Civil Rights Mus., 2002, So. Poverty Law Ctr., 2002, Susan G. Komen Breast Cancer Found., 2003; patient rep. JFK Family Medicine, 2005—. Mem.: Acad. Am. Poets, N.Y.C. Ballet Guild, Nat. Mus. Women in the Arts, Met. Mus. Art. Avocations: jazzercise, photography, theater, writing children's stories and poetry, gardening. Home: 54 Rainford Rd Edison NJ 08820-2903 Personal E-mail: pedymuck@msn.com.

PEDIGO, PAUL F., lawyer; b. Chattanooga, Tenn., Oct. 22, 1954; BA in English, Vanderbilt Univ., 1976, BS in Chem. Engring., 1980; JD, Loyola Univ., 1985. Bar: Ill. 1986, NC 1988, registered: US Patent and Trademark Off. 1984. Ptnr., leader, Chem. and Pharm.Patent Solicitation Group Alston & Bird LLP, Charlotte, NC. Mem.: Am. Intellectual Property Law Assn., Carolinas Patent, Trademark and Copyright Law Assn. Office: Alston & Bird LLP Ste 4000 Bank of Am Plz 101 S Tryon St Charlotte NC 28280-4000 Office Phone: 704-444-1021. Office Fax: 704-444-1111. Business E-Mail: ppedigo@alston.com.

PEDINI, EGLE DAMIJONAITIS, radiologist; b. Kaunas, Lithuania, July 22, 1943; d. Vytautas and Elena Damijonaitis; m. Kenneth Pedini, June 4, 1966; children: David Durand, Julian Adam. BA cum laude, Boston U., 1967, MD, 1967. Diplomate Am. Bd. Radiology. Intern St. Elizabeth's Hosp., Brighton, Mass., 1967—68; resident in radiology Boston City Hosp., 1968—71; radiologist St. John's Hosp., Lowell, Mass., 1972, Chelmsford X-Ray, Mass., 1979—80, Amesbury Hosp./Amesbury Health Ctr., Mass., 1973—98, New Eng. Meml. Hosp./Boston Regional Med. Ctr., Stoneham, Mass., 1973—98, Anna Jacques Hosp., Newburyport, Mass., 1973—98. Ptnr. NE Radiology Assocs., Brockton, Mass., 1980-98; chief radiology Anna Jacques Hosp., Newburyport, Mass., 1984, Amesbury Hosp., 1988-90. Founder, bd. dirs. Andover Sch. Montessori, Mass., 1974-79; parent ann. fundraising com. Phillips Exeter (N.H.), 1985, 86, 87. Mem. Am. Coll. Radiology, Mass. Radiol. Soc., New Eng. Roentgen Ray Soc., Stonehorse Yacht Club, Chatham Women's Club, Garden Club Harwich, Naples Garden Club, Allen Harbor Yacht Club.

PEDINI, KENNETH, radiologist; b. Hartford, Conn., Mar. 19, 1940; s. Daniel Victor and Elizabeth Catherine Pedini; m. Egle Damijonaitis; children: David D., Julian A. AB in Philosophy, Trinity Coll., 1962; MD, Boston U., 1966. Diplomate Nat. Bd. Med. Examiners, Am. Bd. Radiology. Resident in radiology Boston City Hosp., 1967—70, chief resident in radiology, 1969—70, jr. staff radiologist, 1970—71, U. Hosp., Boston, 1970—71; ptnr. Shawsheen Radiology, Andover, Mass., 1971—98; sr. radiologist Lawrence Gen. Hosp., Mass., 1971—, dir. radiology, 1976—87; sr. radiologist Melrose-Wakefield Hosp., Mass., 1971—99, chief radiologist, 1993—97, emeritus staff, 1999; pres. L & M Radiology Inc, Andover, Mass., 1994—98. Bd. trustees Lawrence Gen. Hosp., 1984-89, fin. com., 1986-03. Mem. Townwide Water Quality Mgmt. Task Force, 2001—, Class XI, Greater Naples Leadership, Inc., 2006; trustee Lawrence Gen. Hosp. Health Enterprises, Inc., 1990—93; mem. fin. com. Lawrence Gen. Regional Health Sys., 1996—2003; mem. alumni adv. com. Trinity Coll., 1995; co-founder Andover Sch. Montessori, 1975—. Fellow Am. Coll. Radiology (councilor 1979-81); mem. New Eng. Roentgen Ray Soc., Mass. Radiol. Soc. (pres. 1985-86, pres.-elect 1984-85, v.p. 1983-84, exec. com. 1977-87), Mass. Med. Soc., Stonehorse Yacht Club, Algonquin Club, Allen Harbor Yacht Club (Harwichport, Mass.). Personal E-mail: wychview@comcast.net.

PEDLEY, JOHN GRIFFITHS, archaeologist, educator; b. Burnley, Eng., July 19, 1931; arrived in U.S., 1959, naturalized, 2002; s. George and Anne (Whitaker) Pedley; m. Mary Grace Sponberg, Aug. 30, 1969. BA, Cambridge U., Eng., 1953, MA, 1959; postgrad. (Norton fellow), Am. Sch. Classical Studies, Greece, 1963-64; PhD, Harvard U., 1965. Loeb rsch. fellow in classical archaeology Harvard U., Cambridge, Mass., 1969-70; asst. prof. classical archaeology and Greek U. Mich., Ann Arbor, 1965-68, assoc. prof., 1968-74, acting chmn. dept. classical studies, 1971-72, 75-76; dir. Kelsey Mus. Archaeology, 1973-86, prof., 1974—2002, prof. emeritus, 2002—. Guest scholar J. Paul Getty Mus.; mem. staff excavations, Sardis, Turkey, 1962—64, Pylos, Greece, 1964; co-dir. excavations, Apollonia, Libya, 1966—68; field dir. Corpus Ancient Mosaics, Tunisia, 1972—73; co-prin. investigator excavations, Carthage, North Africa, 1975—79; dir. excavations, Paestum, Italy, 1982—85, Paestum, 1993, Paestum, 95; vis. scholar UCLA, 1989; resident in archaeology Am. Acad., Rome, 1990. Author: (book) Sardis in the Age of Croesus, 1968, Sardis in the Age of Croesus, reprint, 1999, Ancient Literary Sources on Sardis, 1972, Greek Sculpture of the Archaic Period: The Island Workshops, 1976, Paestum: Greeks and Romans in Southern Italy, 1990, Greek Art and Archaeology, 1992, Greek Art and Archaeology, 3d edit., 2002, Greek Art and Archaeology, 4th edit., 2007, Sanctuaries and the Sacred in the Ancient Greek World, 2005; co-author: Apollonia, the Port of Cyrene, 1977, The Sanctuary of Santa Venera at Paestum, Vol. 1, 1993, Corpus des Mosaiques de Tunisie, Vol. III, 1996; editor: New Light on Ancient Carthage, 1980; co-editor: Studies Presented to GMA Hanfmann, 1971. Fellow Am. Coun. Learned Socs., 1972—73, NEH, 1986; grantee, Am. Philol. Soc., 1979, Nat. Endowment Arts Mus., 1974, 1977, 1979, 1980, NEH, 1967, 1975, 1983, 1984. Home: 1720 Morton Ave Ann Arbor MI 48104-4522 Office: Dept Classical Studies Univ Mich Ann Arbor MI 48109 E-mail: jpedley@umich.edu.

PEDLEY, TIMOTHY ASBURY, IV, neurologist, educator, researcher; b. Phoenix, Aug. 31, 1943; s. Timothy Asbury Pedley III and Mary Adele (Newcomer) Melis; m. Barbara S. Koppel, Mar. 17, 1984. BA, Pomona Coll., 1965; MD, Yale U., 1969. Cert. neurology, electroencephalography, clin. neurophysiology; diplomate Am. Bd. Psychiatry and Neurology. Intern Stanford U. Hosp., 1969-70, resident in neurology, 1970—73, postdoctoral fellow, 1973-75; asst. prof. neurology Stanford U., 1975-79; from assoc. prof. neurology to prof., vice chmn. Columbia U., 1979-98, Henry and Lucy Moses prof., chmn. neurology, 1998—; neurologist-in-chief Columbia U. Med. Ctr., NYC, 1998—. Dir. comprehensive epilepsy ctr. Columbia U. Med. Ctr., 1983-97. profl. adv. bd. Epilepsy Found Am., 1984-98, chmn. profl. adv. bd., 1985-87, pres. bd. dirs., 1991-93, chmn. 1993-95. mem. rev. com. NIH Nat. Inst. Neurol. and Chronic Diseases and Strokes, 1985-89, chmn., 1988-89; various adv. coms. NIH/NINDS, 1990-98; vis. fellow in exptl. neurology Inst. Psychiatry, London, 1978-79; mem. merit rev. bd. neurobiology rsch., VA, 1992-96, chmn., 1995-96; vis. prof. various univs., U.S. and abroad. Editor-in-chief: Epilepsia, 1993—2001; contbr. articles to profl. jours. Fellow AAAS, N.Y. Acad. Medicine; Recipient various honors and awards. Fellow Am. Acad. Neurology (bd. trustees 2001—, sec., 2003-07), Am. Electroencephalographic Soc. (pres. 1989-90, bd. dirs. 1981-85), Royal Soc. Medicine; mem. Am. Neurol. Assn. (coun. 1992-94, treas. 1995-98, first v.p. 2003-04, pres. 2007-), Am. Epilepsy Soc. (treas. 1980-83, pres. 1991-92), Soc. Neurosci., Internat. League Against Epilepsy (exec. com. 1994-02), Vidonian Club, Yale Club, N.Y. Med. Surg. Soc., Shenorock Shore Club, Alpha Omega Alpha. Office: The Neurological Inst 710 W 168th St New York NY 10032-2603 Office Phone: 212-305-6489. Office Fax: 212-305-6978. Business E-Mail: tap2@columbia.edu.

PEDOWITZ, MARK, broadcast executive; b. Bklyn., 1953; m. Carolyn Martin. BA in history, Rockford Coll.; JD, John Marshall Law Sch. Atty. MCA Inc., 1979—80; v.p. bus. affairs Reeves Entertainment Group/Alan Landsburg Prodns., 1980—85; v.p. bus. affairs, gen. counsel Landsburg Co., 1985—87; sr. v.p. bus. affairs & adminstrn. MGM/UA TV Prodn. Group, 1987—91; sr. v.p. bus. affairs & contracts ABC Entertainment; sr. v.p. bus. affairs ABC Entertainment TV Group Walt Disney Co., exec. v.p. bus. affairs & adminstrn., ABC Entertainment TV Group, 1998—, pres. Touchstone TV Burbank, Calif., 2004—. Mem.: Hollywood Radio and TV Soc. (past mem. exec. bd.), Acad. TV Arts and Scis. (found bd. dirs., past mem. exec. bd.). Office: Touchstone TV 500 S Buena Vista St Burbank CA 91521

PEDOWITZ, ROBERT ALAN, orthopaedic surgeon, researcher; b. NYC, Aug. 1, 1959; s. Irving and Beverly Pedowitz; m. Loraine Pedowitz, Sept. 28, 1986; children: Rachel, Jason. BS in Psychobiology, UCLA, 1981; MD, U. Calif., San Diego, 1985; PhD, U. Gothenburg, Sweden, 1991. Diplomate Am. Bd. Orthopaedic Surgery. Resident, orthopaedic surgery U. Calif., San Diego, 1985—92; fellow, sports medicine Duke U., Durham, NC; faculty, dept. orthopaedics U. Calif., San Diego, 1992—, chief, sports medicine, 1998—2006, residency dir., dept. orthop., 2001; co-dir. San Diego Arthroscopy and Sports Medicine Fellowship, San Diego, 2001—06; chmn., dept. orthop. surgery Univ. S. Fla. Coll. Medicine, Tampa, 2007—. Cons. Orthop. Mfg. Cos., 1995—2003; internat. adv. bd. Doha Orthop. and Sports Medicine Hosp., Qatar. Author; contbr. articles to profl. jours. Named a San Diego Top Doctor, 2005, 2006; Various rsch. grants and awards, 1987—. Fellow: Am. Acad. Orthopaedic Surgeons; mem.: Orthopaedic Rsch. Soc., Arthroscopy Assn. N.Am., Am. Orthopaedic Soc. Sports Medicine, Am. Orthopaedic Assn. Avocations: golf, travel, skiing. Office: Orthop & Sports Medicine 4202 E Fowler Ave Tampa FL 33620 Office Phone: 813-974-2011. *

PEDROTTI, LENO STEPHANO, physics professor; b. Zeigler, Ill., May 21, 1927; s. Celeste Louis and Dolores (Galeaz) P.; m. Wilma Jean Sullivan, June 23, 1951; children: Daro Stephano, Michael Louis, Sandra Maria, Laura Jean, Catherine Ann, Leno Matthew, Mary Ann, John Owen. BS in Edn, Ill. State U., 1949; MS in Physics, U. Ill., 1951; PhD, U. Cin., 1961. Teaching asst. U. Ill., Urbana, 1949-51; prof. physics, chmn. dept. Air Force Inst. Tech., Wright-Patterson AFB, Ohio, 1951-82, prof. emeritus, 1982—; cons., editor Ctr. Occupational Rsch. & Devel., Waco, Tex., 1975-82, sr. v.p., 1982—. Presenter in field, 1982—; author, editor, lectr. laser and electro-optics Engring. Tech., Inc., Waco, 1978—; mem. indsl. adv. com. laser electro-optics program Cin. Tech. Coll., 1981-82; tech. cons. Univ. Eye Surgeons, Inc., Ohio State U., 1979-82; mem. exec. com. joint svcs. optical program Optical Scis. Ctr., U. Ariz., 1975-82. Author: Principles of Technology, 1986, Introduction to Optics, 1987, rev. edit., 2007, Applied Mathematics, 1988, Optics and Vision, 1998; contbg. author Technical Prep Associate Degree: A Win/Win Experience, 1991, The Science Technology, Society Movement, 1993; contbr. articles to profl. jours. Fellow Faculty fellow, NSF, 1959. Fellow Optical Soc. Am.; mem. Am. Nuclear Soc., Am. Phys. Soc. (vice chmn. then chmn. Ohio sect. 1974-76), Laser Inst. Am. (bd. dirs. 1974-84), Am. Assn. Physics Tchrs., Am. Soc. Engring. Edn., Am. Vocat. Assn. (Outstanding Mem. award 1988 vocat. instrnl. materials affiliate Ednl. Exhibitor Assn.-SHIP citation for outstanding commitment to vocat.-tech. edn. 1994), Nat. Coun. Tchrs. Math., Sigma Xi, Tau Beta Pi (Outstanding Tchr. award 1961, 62, 63, 68),

Sigma Pi Sigma. Home: 11006 Trailwood Dr Waco TX 76712-3131 Office: CORD 601 Lake Air Dr Waco TX 76710-5841 Office Phone: 254-741-8392. Business E-Mail: pedrotti@cord.org.

PEDROW, BRENDA M., retired language educator; b. NYC, Aug. 31, 1942; d. Howard and Stella Stevenson; m. Donald P Pedrow, Aug. 25, 1962; 1 child, Brian D; 1 child, Bradley D. BA in history, Millersville U., 1980. Tutor Millersville U., Millersville, Pa., 1978—80; tchr. Adult Sch. for Cuban Refugees, Lebanon, Pa., 1980, Linden Hall Sch. for Girls, Lititz, Pa., 1981—82; tutor Conestoga Valley Sch. Dist., Lancaster, Pa., 1984—87; tchr. Lancaster Sch., 1985; ESL tchr. Am. Home Life Internat., Lancaster, Pa., 1989; tchr. Manheim Twp. Sch. Dist., Lancaster, 1986—2000; ret. Bd. mem. Lancaster Lit. Coun., 1980—86. Rschr. Interfaith Rels. Lancaster County Human Rels. Commn., 1972; org. fundraiser Lancaster Cmy. Action Program, 1976; founder First Internat. Club, Manheim Twp. H.S. Recipient Cert. Appreciation, Adult Edn. Cuban Refugees, 1980, Exceptional Svc. award, Boy Scouts Am., 1971, Cmty. Svc. award, Cmty. Action Program, 1980. Mem.: Pa. Assn. Sch. Retirees, Nat. Edn. Assn. Avocations: exercise, travel, reading. Home: 6121 Geneva Dr East Petersburg PA 17520

PEDUZZI, CLAUDIA CLAIRE, elementary school educator; b. Westerly, RI, Apr. 10, 1952; d. Everett Orlando and Claire Eve Peduzzi. BA, U. RI, 1974; MEd, RI Coll., 1991, MEd, 1993. Reading specialist, cons. East Providence (RI) Sch. Dist., 1990—93, Chariho Sch. Dist., Wood River Junction, RI, 1993—. Mem.: RI Reading Assn., Internat. Reading Assn. Avocations: reading, gardening, walking, cooking, sewing. Business E-Mail: Claudia.Peduzzi@chariho.k12.ri.us.

PEEBLES, ALLENE KAY, manufactured housing company executive; b. Waukegan, Ill., Feb. 9, 1938; d. Allan Laverne and Kathryn Bernice (McGill) Sedlmayr; m. William Ross Peebles, July 9, 1960; children: Ross William, Robb Allan, Raymond John, Renda Kay (Mrs. Christopher Sivak). BS with high honors, U. Wis., 1960, MS, 1967; grad., Realtors Inst., 1968. Cert. home economist. Tchr. Horicon (Wis.) High Sch., 1960-61, Oconomowoc (Wis.) High Sch., 1961-67; freelance writer, 1967-70; v.p. Luxury Homes, Inc., Watertown, Wis., 1970-93, Land Devel. Plus Devel. Inc., Watertown, 1970—; co-developer Hidden Meadows Condominium Community, Watertown, 1976-96; gen. ptnr. W and A Elderly Housing Ltd. Partnership, Watertown, 1988—; pres. Housing Am., Inc., Watertown, 1991—2003. Gen. ptnr. Sunrise Housing Ltd., 1990—; builder new and rehab low-income housing, 1983-2003 Active Wis. Gov.'s Conf. on Family, 1980, long range planning team, 1996—2003; dist. membership chmn. Boy Scouts Am., 1984—90; chmn. Ams. Abroad Am. Field Svc., Oconomowoc, 1982—87; del. Wis. Rep. Conv., 1997—; chmn. adminstrv. bd. United Meth. Ch., Oconomowoc, 1974—77, 1996—99, lay leader, 2000—03, pres. United Meth. Women, 2002—06, chmn. family ministry Wis. Conf., del. Wis. conf., 2000—03. Recipient Dist. award of Merit Potawatomi Area coun. Boy Scouts Am., 1986; named Woman of Yr., United Meth. Women, 2003. Mem.: AAUW (pres. Oconomowoc br. 1981—83, pres. Oconomowoc 1983—85, officer's bd. 1984—93, fin. advisor 1995—2002), NAFE, Wis. Assn. Family and Consumer Scis. (state bd. 1999—, state housing chmn. 2000—02), Met. Builders Assn. Greater Milw., Internat. Fedn. Home Economists (USA internat. del. 1997—), Wis. Manufactured Housing Assn. (bd. dirs. 1979—90, chmn. bd. 1985—88, Mem. of Yr. award 1986), Wis. Builders Assn., Waukesha Bd. Realtors, Wis. Assn. Realtors, Am. Assn. Family and Consumer Scis., Nat. Assn. Realtors, Wis. Home Economists in Bus. (state chmn. 1987—88, internat. rep. 1998—2000, Home Economist in Bus. of Yr. 1987), Internat. Profl. and Bus. Women, Nat. Assn. Home Builders, Nat. Home Economists in Bus. (internat. com. 1985—87, regional U.S. advisor 1990—92), Wis. Home Econs. Assn. (parliamentarian 1988—90), Am. Home Econs. Assn., Phi Lambda Theta, Kappa Omicron Nu, Phi Upsilon Omicron, Phi Kappa Phi. Republican. Avocation: writing. Home: 37788 Mapleton Rd Oconomowoc WI 53066

PEEBLES, CHRISTOPHER SPALDING, anthropologist, educator, dean, academic administrator; b. Clearwater, Fla., May 26, 1939; s. Frederick Thomas and Corinne deGarmendia (Stephens) P.; m. Laura Ann Wisen, Oct. 6, 1993. AB, U. Chgo., 1963; PhD, U. Calif., Santa Barbara, 1974. Asst. prof. U. Windsor, Ont., Canada, 1970-74; asst. curator U. Mich., Ann Arbor, 1974-81; prof. prehistory U. Amsterdam, Netherlands, 1981-82; prof. Ind. U., Bloomington, 1983—, dean acad. computing, assoc. v.p., 1992—. Author: Excavations at Moundville, 1974, Representations in Archaeology, 1992. With USAF, 1956-60. Mem. Cosmos Club. Avocation: flying. Office: Ind U Glenn A Black Lab 423 N Fess Bloomington IN 47408-3800 Home Phone: 812-334-7823; Office Phone: 812-855-9544. Business E-Mail: peebles@indiana.edu.

PEEBLES, E(MORY) B(USH), III, lawyer; b. Hattiesburg, Miss., May 3, 1943; s. E.B. Jr. and Lee (Baldwin) P.; m. Celeste H. Hodges; children: E.B. IV, Catharine Celeste, Thomas Hill. BA, Vanderbilt U., 1965; JD, U. Ala., 1967. Bar: Ala. 1967, U.S. Dist. Ct. (so. dist.) Ala., U.S. Ct. Appeals (5th and 11th cirs.), U.S. Supreme Ct. Assoc. Armbrecht, Jackson, DeMouy, Mobile, Ala., 1967-72, ptnr., 1972—. Bd. dirs. South Ala. area bd. Regions Bank. Mem. Ala. Securities Commn., 1989-93; chmn. sports com. Mobile Area C. of C., 1988-90; bd. dirs. Am.'s Jr. Miss Orgn., Mobile, 1983-90; active Mobile area coun. Boy Scouts Am., 1979—; mem. Sr. Bowl Com., Mobile, 1978—; chmn. trustees Nat. Maritime Mus. of the Gulf of Mexico; trustee United Way, Mobile, 2003— bd. dirs. Mobile Area Conv. and Visitors Bur., 2003—. Mem. ABA (chmn. fin. svcs. com., tort and ins. practice sect. 1989-90, comml. fin. svcs. com. bus. law sect. 1984—), Ala. Bar Assn., Maritime Law Assn. U.S., Southea. Admiralty Law Inst., Internat. Bar Assn., Am. Soc. Internat. Law, Inter-Am. Bar Assn., Ala. Law Inst. (mem. governing coun. 1975—, corp. law com., letters of credit com.), Mobile Touchdown Club (pres. 1987-88), Mobile Area C. of C. (bd. dirs. 2000—). Office: 1300 Riverview Plz Mobile AL 36602

PEEBLES, PEYTON ZIMMERMANN, JR., electrical engineer, educator; b. Columbus, Ga., Sept. 10, 1934; s. Peyton Zimmermann Peebles Sr. and Maida Erlene Dials; m. Barbara Ann Suydam, Sept. 6, 1969; children: Peyton Zimmermann III, Edward Arlen. BSEE, Evansville Coll., 1957; MSEE, Drexel Inst., 1963; PhD, U. Pa., 1967. Design engr. RCA, Moorestown, NJ, 1958-64, systems engr., 1966-69; prof. U. Tenn., Knoxville, 1969-75, 76-81; vis. prof. U. Hawaii, Honolulu, 1975-76; prof. U. Fla., Gainesville, 1981-84, 90-96, assoc. chmn., 1984-90, prof. emeritus, 1996—. Cons. in field. Author: Communication System Principles, 1976, Probability, Random Variables and Random Signal Principles, 1980, 4th edit., 2001, Digital Communication Systems, 1987; prin. author: Principles of Electrical Engineering, 1991, Radar Principles, 1998; contbr. articles to profl. jours.; patentee in field. Capt. USAFR, 1957-61. David Sarnoff fellow, 1964-66. Fellow IEEE (life); mem. Sigma Xi, Eta Kappa Nu, Tau Beta Pi, Sigma Pi Sigma, Phi Beta Chi. Methodist. Avocations: fishing, painting, woodworking. Business E-Mail: ppeeb@ece.ufl.edu.

PEEK, JEFFREY M., finance company executive; BA in Internat. Affairs, Princeton U., 1969; MBA, Harvard Bus. Sch., 1972. With Merrill Lynch, 1983—2002; exec. v.p. Merrill Lynch & Co., Inc., 1997—2001; pres. Merrill Lynch Investment Managers, 1997—2001; vice chmn. Credit Suisse First Boston LLC, 2002—03; pres., COO CIT Group Inc., Livingston, NJ, 2003—04, pres., CEO, 2004—05, chmn., CEO, 2005—. Treas. NYC Ballet; chmn. advisory coun. Bendheim Ctr. for Fin.; bd. dirs. CIT Group, Travelers Property Casual Corp., Freddie Mac, 2005—, NJ Performing Arts Ctr.; bd. trustees Teachers Coll, Columbia U. Office: CIT Group 1 CIT Dr Livingston NJ 07039 *

PEEL, HARRIS, retired small business owner; b. Decatur, Ill., Nov. 14, 1923; s. Wilbur David Peel and Ruth Harris; m. Margaret Backus, Oct. 11, 1946 (dec. Nov. 1990); children: Susan Harris, Jane Peel Fuller, David Harris. BS, Columbia U., 1950; MS, George Washington U., 1967. Editor War Dept., Frankfurt, Germany, 1946; writer Holiday Mag., Europe, 1947-48; fgn. svc. officer U.S. Dept. State and USIA, various locations, 1950-74; owner Peel Gallery Fine Art, Danby, Vt., 1976—2005. Author: (book) History of 254th Infantry Regiment, 1945. Advisor on psychol. warfare U.S. Army and USN, Ft. Bragg, N.C., 1971-74. Cpl. U.S. Army, 1943-45. Decorated Bronze star with oak leaf cluster U.S. Army, 1945, Disting. Civilian Svc. medal U.S. Army; 4-yr. scholar Chgo. Tribune, 1941. Mem. Vt. Assn. Galleries (pres. 1978-98), Overseas Press Club. Avocation: astronomy. Home: 1 Peel Rd Danby VT 05739 Office: Peel Gallery Peel Rd Danby VT 05739 E-mail: hpeel@vermontel.net.

PEEL, MARK, chef, restaurant owner; b. Calif. m. Daphne Brogdon; children: Vanessa, Benjamin, Oliver, Vivien Tiana. Student, Calif. Poly. U., Pomona; studied Agrl. Econ., U. Calif. Davis. Former apprentice Ma Maison, LA; former mem. staff La Tour d'Argents, Moulin de Mougins; former sous chef Michael's, Santa Monica, Calif., 1979; former mem. staff Chez Panisse, Berkeley, Calif.; head chef Spago, Hollywood, Calif., 1982—85; chef Maxwell's Plum, NYC, 1985—89; co-owner, chef Campanile, LA, 1989—, La Brea Bakery, LA, 1989—. Author (with Nancy Silverton): Mark Peel and Nancy Silverton at Home, Two Chefs Cook for Family and Friends, The Food of Campanile. Nominee Best Am. Chef, Calif., James Beard Found., 1990, 1995, 1996, 2001, 2002, 2004; named Restaurateur of Yr., So. Calif. Restaurant Writers, 1995, Chef of Yr., Calif. Restaurant Assn., 2005; named one of Best New Chefs, Food & Wine Mag., 1990. Office: Campanile 624 S La Brea Ave Los Angeles CA 90036 *

PEELER, FORREST EDWARDS, retired physician; b. NC, Nov. 25, 1922; s. Summey Alfred Andrew Peeler and Mattie Dixon Stamey; m. Kathryn Mozelle Peeler, Apr. 2, 1944; children: Carol Peeler de Perczel, Michael Forrest. BA, Lenoir Rhyne Coll., Hickory, NC, 1949; MD, Med. Coll. Va., Richmond, 1950. Intern Charlotte Meml. Hosp., NC, 1950—51; pvt. practice Lenoir, NC, 1951—52, Maiden, NC, 1952—2005; ret., 2005. Lt. (j.g.) USN, 1943—46. Fellow: Am. Acad. Family Practice; mem.: AMA, NC Med. Soc., Catauspa County Med. Soc. (past pres. 1950—59). Home: 1975 E Maiden Rd Maiden NC 28650

PEELER, STUART THORNE, gas industry executive, consultant; b. Los Angeles, Oct. 28, 1929; s. Joseph David and Elizabeth Fiske (Boggess) P.; m. Sylvia Frances Townley, Nov. 5, 1985. BA, Stanford U., 1950, JD, 1953. Bar: Calif. 1953. Ptnr. Musick, Peeler & Garrett, LA, 1958-73; with Santa Fe Internat. Corp., Orange, Calif., 1973-81, v.p., sec., assoc. gen. counsel, 1973-74, sr. v.p., gen. counsel, dir., 1975-81; vice-chmn. bd., chmn. exec. com. Supron Energy Corp., 1978-82; chmn. bd., CEO Statex Petroleum, Inc., 1982-89; chmn., pres., CEO Putumayo Prodn. Co., Tucson, 1989—. Bd. dirs. Chieftain Internat. Inc. Trustee J. Paul Getty Trust, 1963-99; mem. U.S. Tuna Team, 1957-67, capt., 1966. Served with U.S. Army, 1953-55. Decorated Army Commendation medal. Mem. AIME, State Bar Calif., Am. Judicature Soc., Theta Chi, Phi Delta Phi, Skyline Country Club. Republican. Congregationalist. Office: PO Box 35852 Tucson AZ 85740-5852 Office Phone: 520-575-0709. Office Fax: 520-544-0632.

PEELER, WILLIAM JAMES, lawyer; b. Highland Park, Mich., Nov. 27, 1927; s. Herb and Beulah (Wells) P.; m. Nancy Jean Bradley, Dec. 26, 1949; children: Nannette Peeler Bradley, Jeana Peeler Hosch, Jacqueline Peeler Safstrom. LLB, Cumberland U., 1952. Bar: Tenn. 1952. Ptnr. Porch, Peeler, Williams & Thomason, Waverly, Tenn., 1952—. Mem. Tenn. Ho. of Reps., 1959-63; majority leader Tenn. Senate, 1967-75; trustee emeritus Cumberland U., Lebanon, Tenn., 1985—. Fellow Am. Coll. Trial Lawyers, Tenn. Bar Found.; mem. Am. Judicature Soc., ABA, Tenn. Bar Assn., Humphreys County Bar Assn., Masons (32 deg.), Shriners, Elks, Cumberland Club, City Club. Democrat. Mem. Ch. of Christ. Home: 2351 Ogden Rd Waverly TN 37185 Office: Porch Peeler Williams & Thomason 102 S Court Sq Waverly TN 37185-2198

PEEPLES, MARY ANNE BAUMANN, science educator; b. Binghamton, NY, July 2, 1941; d. Emmanuel Patrick and Ella Lucille (Woods) Baumann; m. Horace Timothy Peeples, Aug. 21, 1993; children: Charles David Steinkuehler, Ayne Elizabeth Steinkuehler Ray. BS in Edn., Ctrl. Mo. State U., Warrensburg, 1962, MS in Edn., 1969. Cert. Tchr. Mo. Bd. Edn., Kans. Bd. Edn., N.C. Bd. Edn. Sci. tchr., N. Kansas City, Mo., 1962—64, Immaculata HS, Leavenworth, Kans., 1964—72, Easton, Kans., 1972—73, Topeka Pub. Schs., 1973—79, Cumberland County Schs., Fayetteville, NC, 1979—2003; ret., 2003; adj. chemistry tchr. Fayetteville Tech. CC, 1983—. Med. transcriber, radiology Highsmith-Rainey Meml. Hosp., Fayetteville, 1983—97; med. transcriber, orthopedics Cape Fear Orthopaedics, Fayetteville, 1998—2001. With USAR, 1974—80. Recipient NSF award, Tex. A&M, Emporia (Kans.) Coll., 1965, 1972, Citizen Soldier award, 89th ARCOM, USAR, Wichita, Kans., 1977; grantee Merit fellowship-chemistry, Shell Oil Co., Stanford U., 1966. Mem.: DAR (state corr. sec. 2005—06, chpt. regent, state chmn., state officer), Fayetteville Rep. Women, Woman's Club of Fayetteville (v.p. 2005—). Republican. Roman Catholic.

PEEPLES, WILLIAM DEWEY, JR., mathematics professor; b. Bessemer, Ala., Apr. 19, 1928; s. William Dewey and Thelma Jeannette (Chastain) P.; m. Katie Ray Blackerby, Aug. 30, 1956; children: Mary Jeannette, William Dewey III, Gerald Lewis, Stephen Ray. BS, Samford U., 1947; MS, U. Wis., 1949; PhD, U. Ga., 1951. Rsch. mathematician Ballistics Rsch. Lab., Aberdeen, Md., summer 1951; mem. faculty Samford U., Birmingham, Ala., 1951-56, prof. math., 1959-95, head dept., 1967-95; prof. emeritus, 1995; mem. faculty Auburn U., 1956-59. Cons. Hayes Internat. Corp. Co-author: Modern Mathematics for Business Students, 1969, Finite Mathematics, 1974, Modern Mathematics with Applications to Business and the Social Sciences, 4th edit, 1986, Finite Mathematics with Applications to Business and the Social Sciences, 1981, 2d edit., 1987; Contbr. articles to profl. publs. Served to 1st lt. AUS, 1954-56. Mem. Am. Math. Soc., Math. Assn. Am., Nat. Council Tchrs. Math., Ala. Coll. Tchrs. Math. (pres. 1969), Sigma Xi, Pi Mu Epsilon, Phi Kappa Phi (pres. 1977), Lambda Chi Alpha. Baptist (deacon, chmn. 1986). Club: Mason (Shriner). Home: 419 Poinciana Dr Birmingham AL 35209-4129 E-mail: wdpeeples@peoplepc.com.

PEER, LARRY HOWARD, literature educator; b. Ogden, Utah, Jan. 2, 1942; s. Howard Harvey and Edna Celina (Baron) P.; m. Janet Priday; 9 children. BA, Brigham Young U., 1963, MA, 1965; PhD, U. Md., 1969. From asst. to assoc. prof. U. Ga., Athens, 1968-75; assoc. prof. Brigham Young U., Provo, Utah, 1975-78, prof., 1978—. Acting head dept. comparative lit. U. Ga., Athens, 1973-74, Brigham Young U., Provo, 1978-81; pres. Western Regional Honors Coun., 1978-79; exec. dir. Am. Conf. on Romanticism, 1992—. Author: Beyond Haworth, 1984, The Reasonable Romantic, 1986, The Romantic Manifesto, 1988. Mem. MLA, Am. Comparative Lit. Assn. (exec. officer 1988-94), Am. Soc. for Aesthetics, Rocky Mountain Soc. for Aesthetics (pres. 1986-87), Internat. Byron Soc., Internat. Brontë Soc. Mem. Lds Ch. Avocation: travel. Office: Brigham Young U Comparative Lit Dept Provo UT 84602

PEERCY, PAUL STUART, engineering educator; s. Robert L. and Ernest (Bell) P.; m. Catherine B. Christen, July 17, 1965; children: Michael, Mark. BS in physics, Berea Coll., 1961; MS in physics, U. Wis., Madison, 1963, PhD in physics, 1966. Postdoctoral fellow Bell Labs., Murray Hill, NJ, 1966-68; mem. tech. staff Sandia Nat. Labs., Albuquerque, 1968-76, divsn. supr., 1976-82, mgr. ion-solid rsch. dept., 1982-86, mgr. compound semicondr. and device rsch. dept., 1986-91, dir. microelectronics and photonics, 1991-95; pres. SEMI/SEMATECH, 1995—99; dean Coll. Engring. U. Wis., Madison, 1999—, prof. dept. materials sci. and engring., 1999—. Mem. solid state sciences com. NRC, Washington, 1989-91; mem. external adv. bd. U. Ill. elec. engring. dept.; mem. microelectronics sci. bd. Jet Propulsion Lab., Calif. Inst. Tech., Pasadena, Calif., 1992—; mem. indsl. adv. coun. U. Ariz. Coll. Engring., Tucson, 1992—; mem. external rev. bd. Carnegie Mellon Rsch. Inst., Pitts., 1992-97; mem. Roadmap Coordinating Group for the Nat. Tech. Roadmap for Semiconductors Semiconductor Industry Assn., 1994; mem. policy bd. NSF Engring. Rsch. Ctr. in Semiconductor Environment and Safety, 1997-99, Nat. Nanofabrication Users Network, 1998-; chair U. Wis. Tech. Enterprise Coop., 1999-; mem Wis. Tech. and Entrepreneurship Coun., 2000-; bd. dirs. Meriter Hosp. and Health Services, Madison, Wis., 2000-, Mason-Wells, Milw., 2003-. Editor 3 books; prin. editor: Jour. Materials Rsch., 1986-91; contbr. more than 175 articles to profl. jours. Recipient Sandia Award for Excellence, Woody award for Exceptional Svc., Materials Rsch. Soc. Fellow IEEE, AAAS (councilor, 1998-, Am. Phys. Soc. (chair divsn. material physics 1994, councilor 1998—, mem. exec. com. 1999—2000); mem. NAE, The Minerals, Metall., and Materials Soc. (chair electronics materials com. 1991-92), Materials Rsch. Soc. (v.p. 1987, councilor and mem. exec. com., 2001-; Woody Award for Exceptional Svc.), Phi Kappa Phi, Sigma Pi, Tau Peta Pi (disting. mem.); Nat. Acad. Engineers. Achievements include 2 patents in field. Office: U Wis 2610 Engring Hall 1415 Engineering Dr Madison WI 53706-1691 Home Phone: 608-833-0370; Office Phone: 608-262-3482.

PEERMAN, DEAN GORDON, magazine editor; b. Mattoon, Ill., Apr. 25, 1931; s. Staley Jacob and Irene (Monen) P. BS with highest distinction, Northwestern U., 1953; postgrad., Cornell U., 1953-54; B.D., Yale, 1959; D.D., Kalamazoo Coll., 1967. With Christian Century Found., 1959—; copy editor Christian Century mag., 1959-61, assoc. editor, 1961-64, mng. editor, 1964-81, exec. editor, 1981-85, sr. editor, 1985-98, contbg. editor, 1998—. Author: (with M.E. Marty) Pen-ultimates, 1963, (with Marty, L.M. Delloff, J.M. Wall) A Century of The Century, 1987; editor: Frontline Theology, 1967; co-editor: (with Marty) New Theology 1-10, 1964-73, A Handbook of Christian Theologians, 1965, enlarged edit., 1984, (with Alan Geyer) Theological Crossings, 1971; contbg. author: Chile: Under Military Rule, 1974; editor, contbr. Faithful Witness, 2002. Active Chgo. cmty. theater groups. Recipient award for distinction in lay ministry within the church Yale Div. Sch., 1995. Mem. ACLU, Fellowship of Reconciliation, Amnesty Internat., Chgo. Religious Leadership Network on Latin Am., Phi Beta Kappa. Democrat. Baptist. Office: Christian Century Mag 104 S Michigan Ave Ste 700 Chicago IL 60603-5901 Office Phone: 312-263-7510 ext. 236. E-mail: dpeerman@christiancentury.org.

PEERY, SHELLEY, psychologist; d. Catherine and Donald Peery (Stepfather), Stephen Paul Grosse. Degree, U. Calif., Santa Cruz, 1993; PhD, CUNY, NYC, 2004. Lic. psychologist NY State Bd. Edn., 2005. Staff psychologist Rusk med. ctr. NYU, 2003—. Mem.: APA, Nat. Acad. Neuropsychology, Internat. Neuropsychol. Soc., NY Neuropsychology Group (sec. 2006—), Hispanic Neuropsychological Soc., NY State Psychol. Assn. (sec. neuropsychology divsn. 2006). Office: Rusk NYU Medical Center 400 East 34th St New York NY 10016 Home Phone: 917-446-9849; Office Phone: 212-263-6156.

PEET, AMANDA, actress; b. NYC, Jan. 11, 1972; d. Charles and Penny Peet; m. David Benioff, Sept. 30, 2006; 1 child, Frances Pen. BA in History, Columbia U., 1994. Actor: (films) Animal Room, 1995, Winterlude, 1996, She's the One, 1996, Virginity, 1996, Grind, 1997, Touch Me, 1997, One Fine Day, 1996, Sax and Violins, 1997, 1999, 1998, Southie, 1998, Playing by Heart, 1998, Origin of the Species, 1998, Simply Irresistible, 1999, Jump, 1999, Two Ninas, 1999, Body Shots, 1999, Isn't She Great?, 2000, The Whole Nine Yards, 2000, Takedown, 2000, Whipped, 2000, Saving Silverman, 2001, High Crimes, 2002, Changing Lanes, 2002, Igby Goes Down, 2002, Whatever We Do, 2003, Identity, 2003, Something's Gotta Give, 2003, The Whole Ten Yards, 2004, Melinda and Melinda, 2004, A Lot Like Love, 2005, Syriana, 2005, Griffin and Phoenix, 2006, The Martian Child, 2005, The Ex, 2007; (TV films) Ellen Foster, 1997, Date Squad, 2001; (TV series) Central Park West, 1995—96, Jack & Jill, 1999—2001, Partners, 1999, Studio 60 on the Sunset Strip, 2006—07, (TV appearances) Law & Order, 1995, The Single Guy, 1996, Spin City, 1997, Seinfeld, 1997; (plays) Whale Music, Winter Lies, 27 Sketches: Fear and Misery in the Third Reich, The Country Club, This Is How It Goes, 2005, Escape: 6 Ways to Get Away, 2005, Barefoot in the Park, 2006. Office: The Gersh Agy Ste 201 232 N Canon Dr Beverly Hills CA 90210

PEET, CHARLES D, JR., lawyer; b. NYC, Sept. 3, 1935; s. Charles D and Margaret Louise (Sherman) P.; children: Alisa, Amanda. BA, Yale U., 1957; JD, Harvard U., 1960. Bar: N.Y. 1962. Assoc. Milbank, Tweed, Hadley & McCloy, NYC, 1960-68, ptnr., 1969-98; of counsel Freshfields Bruckhaus Deringer LLP (and predecessor firm), NYC, 1998—. Mem. Assn. Bar N.Y.C. Office: Freshfields Bruckhaus Deringer LLP 520 Madison Ave Fl 34 New York NY 10022-4213 Office Phone: 212-277-4000. E-mail: charles.peet@freshfields.com.

PEET, PHYLLIS IRENE, women's studies educator; b. Winnipeg, Man., Can., Mar. 3, 1943; came to the U.S., 1948; d. Harold Parsons and Gladys Mae (Riley) Harrison; m. Thomas Peter Richman, June 14, 1963 (div. 1969); m. Charles Francis Peet, Sept. 9, 1972. BA in Art, Calif. State U., Northridge, 1972; MA in Art History, U. Calif., LA, 1976, PhD in Art History, 1987. Sec. L.A. County Supr. Kenneth Hahn, 1960-68; assoc. in art history L.A. County Mus. Art, 1974-75; asst. dir., curator Grunwald Ctr. for the Graphic Arts, U. Calif., LA, 1975-78; Am. art scholar High Mus. Art, Atlanta, 1984-90; instr. women's studies Monterey (Calif.) Peninsula Coll., 1986—; dir., instr. women's programs/women's studies Re-entry and Multicultural Resource Ctr. Monterey Peninsula Coll., Calif., 1989—. Dirs.' adv. com. Art Mus. Santa Cruz County, 1981-84, 89-96; vis. lectr. Calif. State U., Fresno, 1984; program coord. conf. Inst. for Hist. Study, San Francisco, 1987; lectr. bd. studies in art U. Calif. Santa Cruz, 1991-95; coord. Monterey County Women's Multicultural Conf., 1993-2007. Author, co-curator, editor, compiler: (book and exhbn.) The American Personality: The Artist Illustrator of Life in the United States, 1860-1930, 1976; author, curator: (book and exhbn.) American Women of the Etching Revival, 1988; co-author: American Paintings in the High Museum of Art, 1994; contbr. articles to profl. jours. including Am. Nat. Biography, Fitzroy Dict. of Women Artists, 1997, Dict. Literary Biography, 1998. Vol., activist Dem. Party, L.A., 1960-66, Peace and Freedom Party, L.A., 1967-71; vol. Dem. Party Candidates, Santa Cruz, Calif., 1979-96, Santa Cruz Action Network, 1980-85; mem. nominating com. Girl Scouts of Am., Monterey Bay, 1991-93. Rockefeller Found. fellow UCLA, 1978-80, Dickson grantee U. Calif. LA, 1981-82; recipient Women Helping Women award Soroptimists, Monterey and Carmel, Calif., 1991, 95, Allen Griffin for Excellence in Edn. award Cmty. Found. Monterey County, 1993, Quality of Life award Econ. Devel. Corp., Monterey, 1994, Excellence in Edn. award Monterey Peninsula Coll. Found., 2004-06; named Tchr. of Yr., Tchrs. of Tomorrow, 2004. Mem.: NAACP, ACLU, AAUW, NOW, Nat. Mus. Women in the Arts (founding mem.), Coll. Art Assn., UN Assn., Western Assn. Women Historians, Inst. for Hist. Study, Nat. Women's Studies Assn., Planned Parenthood, Monterey Bay Women's Caucus for Art (founder, bd. dirs. 1988—93), Women's Internat. League for Peace and Freedom. Avocations:

print collecting, photography. Office: Womens Programs Monterey Peninsula Coll 980 Fremont St Monterey CA 93940-4704 Personal E-mail: ppeetcat@comcast.net. Business E-Mail: ppeet@mpc.edu.

PEETZ, KAREN B., bank executive; b. Sept. 15, 1955; married; 2 children. BS, Penn State. U.; MS, Johns Hopkins U. Various client services, sales, credit and risk mgmt. positions JP Morgan Chase (formerly Chase Manhattan Bank and Chemical Bank); sales mgr. global trust services then head global client mgmt. Chase Manhattan Bank, NYC, sr. v.p., bus. mgr. global trust services London; sr. v.p., divsn. head domestic corp. trust bus. Bank of NY, 1998, head global payments services group, haed corp. trust, 2003, sr. exec. v.p., 2006—. Mem. Women's Leadership Initiative Penn State U.; bd. trustees Brooklyn Acad. Music; steering com. Women United in Philanthropy United Way NYC. Named one of 25 Women to Watch, US Banker, 2006. Mem.: Women's Bond Club. Office: Bank of NY One Wall St 10th Fl New York NY 10286 *

PEFANIS, HARRY N., oil industry executive; b. Buffalo, 1957; Grad., U. Okla., 1979. Exec. v.p. Plains All American Pipeline LP, Houston, 1998, pres., COO, 1999—. Office: Plains All American Pipline LP 333 Clay St Ste 1600 Houston TX 77002 *

PEFLEY, NORMAN GORDON, bank executive; b. Eugene, Oreg., Dec. 15, 1955; s. Gordon Vergne Pefley and Jean Pefley (Lee) Hawley; m. Emma Ginete Lacuesta, July 5, 1986. BA, U. Calif., Davis, 1977; MA, Johns Hopkins U., 1979; MBA, U. Chgo., 1981; MA, Golden Gate U., 2001. CFA, CPHQ. Rsch. analyst Chgo. Bd. Options Exch., 1981-83; sr. fin. analyst Bank of Am., San Francisco, 1983-89, v.p., 1989-99. Referee Jour. Futures Markets, N.Y.C., 1984-87. Mem.: ASTD, Nat. Assn. Healthcare Quality, The Security Analysts of San Francisco, Internat. Soc. Performance Improvement, CFA Inst., Toastmasters Internat., Omicron Delta Epsilon, Delta Phi Alpha, Phi Beta Kappa. Avocation: languages.

PEGALIS, STEVEN E., lawyer; b. NYC, Apr. 12, 1942; BA, Queens Coll. of City of NY, 1962; LLB, NY Law Sch., 1965, JD, 1979. Bar: NY 1966, Pa. 1992, US Ct. Appeals (2nd cir.) 1969, US Dist. Ct. (ea. dist. NY) 1969. Founding ptnr. Pegalis & Erickson, LLC, Lake Success, NY, 1972—. Adj. prof. med. malpractice NY Law Sch. Author: American Law of Medical Malpractice (2nd edit.); bd. editors: Cancer Litigation published by NY Law Jour. Pub. Co. Bd. dirs. NY Law Sch. Named one of Top 10 Trial Lawyers in Am., Nat. Law Jour., 2005. Fellow: Roscoe Pound Found.; mem.: ABA, Am. Soc. Law and Medicine, Am. Coll. Medicine (assoc. in law), Assn. Trial Lawyers Am., NY State Trial Lawyers Assn., Nassau County Bar Assn., Queens County Bar Assn., Assn. Bar City of NY. Office: Pegalis & Erickson 1 Hollow Ln Ste 107 New Hyde Park NY 11042 Office Phone: 516-684-2900. Office Fax: 516-684-2939. *

PEGELS, C. CARL, management consultant, educator; b. Barendrecht, Holland, The Netherlands, Feb. 26, 1933; came to U.S., 1962, naturalized, 1968; s. Bertus and Adriana Maria (Denotter) P.; children: Janice Joy, Kevin Carl. BS in Mech. Engring., Detroit Inst. Tech., 1961; MS, Purdue U., 1963, PhD in Mgmt., 1966. Prodn. engr. Ford Motor, Windsor, Can., 1955-62; instr. Purdue U., W. Lafayette, Ind., 1962-66; prof. SUNY, Buffalo, 1966—. V.p. Ctr. Mgmt. Sys., Buffalo, 1978—91. Author: Basic for Business, 1973, Health Care & Elderly, 1980, Japan vs The West, 1984, Q.C. in Health Care, 1985, Decision Support Systems for Production and Operations Management, 1986, Management and Industry in China, 1987, Strategic Management for Hospitals and Health Care Corporations, 1987, Health Care and the Older Citizen, 1988, Decision Support Systems for Management Science/Operations Research, 1989, Strategic Information Systems, 1993, Total Quality management, 1995, Strategies and Tools for the Learning Company, 1998, Proven Solutions for Reducing Health Care Costs, 2003; Proven Solutions for Improving Supply Chain Management, 2005. Krannert fellow, 1966; Krannert scholar Purdue U., 1963. Mem. Acad. of Mgmt., Prodn. and Ops. Mgmt. Soc., Am. Inst. Decision Scis. Avocation: running. Home: 150 Arielle Ct Apt D Buffalo NY 14221-1969 Office: Sch of Mgmt SUNY at Buffalo Buffalo NY 14260-0001 Personal E-mail: cpegels@yahoo.com. Business E-Mail: cpegels@buffalo.edu.

PEGG, RICHARD ANDERSON, curator; b. Bronxville, NY, Dec. 11, 1960; s. Robert Richard and Judith Benson Pegg; m. Ellen Rose Healy, May 18, 1990; 1 child, Lily Rose. BA, George Wash. U., Washington, 1983, MA, 1990, Columbia U., NY, 1995, MPhil, 1999, PhD, 2001. Rsch. asst, gallery lectr. The Met. Mus. Art, NY, 1989—2004; curator asian art MacLean Collection, Libertyville, Ill., 2004—. Author: Kaikodo Journal; author: (editor) Passion for Form: Selections of Southeast Asian Art from the MacLean Collection, A Walk through the Ages: Archaic Chinese Art from the Collection of Sondra Landy Gross (First prize Am. Assn. Mus. Publications Design, 2004); editor (contbr.): Crosscurrents: Masterpieces of East Asian Art from New York Private Collections; contbr. articles to profl. jours. Mem.: Am. Assn. Museums, Coll. Art Assn., Assn. Asian Studies. Avocation: martial arts. Home: 190 Leonard Wood South Highland Park IL 60035 Office: MacLean Collection 15330 West Old Sch Rd Libertyville IL 60048 Home Phone: 847-681-0459; Office Phone: 847-816-0901. Office Fax: 847-816-0948. Personal E-mail: richardapegg@aol.com.

PEGIS, ANTON GEORGE, retired language educator; b. Milw., Feb. 21, 1920; s. George Anton and Eugenia (Stathas) Pegis; m. Harriet Louise Stevens, June 1, 1949; children: Stefani Elizabeth, Penelope Eugenia. AB, We. State Coll. Colo., 1949; MA, Denver U., 1951, PhD, 1956. Jr. engr. North Shore Gas Co., Waukegan, Ill., 1946—47; instr. Ft. Lewis Coll., 1952—53; process control technician Gates Rubber Co., Denver, 1953—54; prof. English Colo. Sch. Mines, Golden, 1954—82, asst. to pres., 1964—68, v.p. devel., 1968—73, v.p. external affairs, 1973—74, prof. emeritus, 1982—. Cons. Office Mineral Reports U.S. Bur. Mines, Washington, Civil Svc. Commn., San Francisco, 1974—94, Regional Tng. Ctr. Office Pers. Mgmt., Denver, 1983. Author: Social Theory in the Novels of Ford Madox Ford, 1956, An Intensive Course in English for Foreign Engineering Students, 1957, Humanism and the Practical Order, 1964, Excellence and the Odyssean Philosophy, 1965, Platonism in the Renaissance Lyric, 1965, Education for Leadership, 1966, Totality in Engineering Education, 1968, Course Recommendations for the Resource Engineer, 1968, Encroachment of Competing Land Uses on Mineral Development, 1976. Chmn. United Way Fund; sec. Colo. Sch. Mines Found.; pres. Roland Valley Civic Assn., 1974—75. With US Army, 1940—46, maj. AUS Ret. Named Disting. Sgt., 121st Field Arty. Rgt., 1988, Outstanding Prof., Tau Beta Pi, 1963, Hon. Col., 115th Engring. Rgt., 1988; recipient Outstanding Prof. award, Colo. Sch. Mines, 1976, Amoco Found. awards. Mem.: MLA, Am. Soc. Engring. Edn. (chmn. Rocky Mountain sect.), Am. Alumni Coun. (chmn. dist. VII 1971—72), Golden C. of C. (pres. 1968), Blue Key, Alpha Psi Omega, Theta Chi. Home: 415 Scenic Ct Golden CO 80401-2533

PEGO, MARGARET M., utilities executive; BA in Bus. Adminstrn., William Paterson Coll., Wayne, NJ; MBA in Mgmt. and Labor Rels., Seton Hall U., South Orange, NJ; grad. Human Resources Exec. Program, U. Mich., Ann Arbor. Cert. sr. human resources profl. Various mgmt. positions in human resources PSEG, 1974; v.p. human resources PSEG Svcs. Corp., sr. v.p. human resources, chief human resources officer, 2006—. Mem. EEI Chief Human Resources Execs. Policy Com., NY/NJ Industry Liaison Group; mem. human resources policy com. Am. Gas Assn.; mem. Coun. Human Resources Execs. Conf. Bd. Adv. Coun. Human Resources Mgmt.; bd. trustees Am. Conf. Diversity, Boys and Girls Club Concert for Kids Com. Mem.: Soc. Human Resources Mgmt. Office: PSEG Svcs Corp PO Box 570 Newark NJ 07101 Office Phone: 973-430-7000. *

PEGRAM, JOHN BRAXTON, lawyer; b. Yeadon, Pa., June 29, 1938; s. William Bement and Marjorie (Rainey) P.; m. Patricia Jane Narbeth; Aug. 21, 1965; children: Catherine, Stephen. AB in Physics, Columbia U., 1960; LLB, NYU, 1965. Bar: N.Y. 1965, U.S. Dist. Ct. (ea. and so. dists.) N.Y. 1967, U.S. Supreme Ct. 1971. Engr. Fairchild Camera and Instrument Corp., Clifton, NJ, 1960-66; assoc. Davis Hoxie Faithfull and Hapgood, LLP, NYC, 1966-71; ptnr. Davis Hoxie Faithfull and Hapgood, NYC, 1972-95; prin. Fish & Richardson P.C., NYC, 1995—2002, sr. counsel, 2003—. Mem. intellectual property litig. adv. com. U.S. Dist. Ct. for the Dist. Del., 1994-96; mem. neutral evaluation and mediation panels U.S. Dist. Ct. for the Eastern Dist. of N.Y., 1994-97; mem. mediation panel U.S. Dist. Ct. for the So. Dist. N.Y., 1994-97. Editor The Trademark Reporter jour., 1984-86, mem. editl. adv. bd., 1986—; contbr. articles to profl. jours. Fellow Am. Bar Found. (life), Am. Intellectual Property Law Assn. (chmn. fed. practice and procedure com. 1974-76, chmn. unauthorized practice com. 1977-79, chmn. trade secrets com. 1992-94, mem. Japan practice com. 1992—, mem. editl. bd. Quar. Jour., 1994-95, chmn. fed. litig. com. 1995-97, chmn. internat. com. 1998-00, bd. dirs. 2000-03, mem. amicus com. 2003—06, mem. spl. com. legis. strategies 2003-05, mem. profl. responsibility com. 2005—); mem. IEEE, ABA (chmn. antitrust law sect. com. on patents, trademarks and know how 1986-89, mem. legal econs. sect., bus. law sect., chmn. intellectual property law divsn. IV 1995-96), Am. Phys. Soc. (life), Fed. Bar Coun., Fed. Cir. Bar Assn., N.Y. State Bar Assn., Assn. Bar City of N.Y., NY Intellectual Property Law Assn. (sec. 1981-84, dir. 1984-86, pres. 1989-90), US Bar-European Patent Office Liaison Coun. (del. 2003-), Japan Patent Office Liaison Coun. (del. 1990—), Internat. Intellectual Property Soc., Internat. Patent and Trademark Assn. (U.S. group AIPPI), Internat. Trademark Assn. (bd. dirs. 1985-87, fin. com. 1987-95, pub. com. 1997-98). Office: Fish & Richardson PC Citigroup Ctr 153 E 53rd St 52d Fl New York NY 10022-4611 Office Phone: 212-765-5070.

PEHLKE, RICHARD W., real estate company executive; BA, Valparaiso U.; MBA, DePaul U. Dir. invester relations, fin. planning and fin. reporting Beatrice Co.; dir. investor relations Household Internat.; v.p., treas. and v.p. investor relations Ameritech Corp., 1986—99; exec. v.p. and CFO ONE, Inc., 2000; founder, pres. pvt. consulting firm, 2001—03; exec. v.p., CFO, bd. dirs. Hudson Highland Group, 2003—07; exec. v.p., CFO Grubb & Ellis Co., 2007—. Bd. dirs. Edward Health Services Corp., Naperville, Ideal Industries, Sycamore, Ill., Valparasio U. Named an Outstanding Alumni, DePaul U., 1999. Office: Grubb & Ellis Co 500 W Monroe St Ste 2880 Chicago IL 60661 *

PEHRSON, GORDON OSCAR, JR., lawyer, venture capitalist; b. San Antonio, Feb. 18, 1943; s. Gordon Oscar and Frances (Burns) Pehrson; m. Janice Sue Hagedorn, May 17, 1969; children: Christopher Wells, Ashley Stewart; m. Sharon Ann McNellage, Jan. 1, 1983; m. Maria Terresa Sitvin Basso del Pont, Mar. 25, 1997. AB, Coll. William and Mary, 1964; JD cum laude, U. Mich., 1967; postgrad., U. London, 1967-68. Bar: Ill. 1968, DC 1969, US Ct. Claims 1968, US Ct. Mil. Appeals 1968, US Ct. Appeals (DC cir.) 1976, US Supreme Ct. 1976, US Ct. Appeals (3d and 5th cirs.) 1979, US Ct. Appeals (fed. cir.) 1982, US Tax Ct. 1990. Assoc. Sutherland, Asbill & Brennan, Washington, 1970-75, ptnr., 1975—97; sr. tax and corp. ptnr. Hopkins & Sutter, Washington, 1997—2000; founder, mng. ptnr. Potomac Capital LLP, Washington, 2000—. Adj. prof. law Georgetown U., Washington, 1977—81; vis. prof. law Coll. Ins., NYC, 1997—98; founder, bd. advisors The Inst. Tax Rev., 1986—. Contbr. articles on tax law to profl. jours.; editor The Ins. Tax Rev., 1986-94. Trustee U.S. Supreme Ct. Hist. Soc., 1993—, Food for Christmas Found., 1992-94; bd. advisors Hartford Inst. Ins. Taxation, 1993—, U.S. Humane Soc., 1994-96, Coll. William and Mary Sch. Bus., 1995-99. Fellow in internat. law U. Mich., 1967 Master: ABA (co-chair investment, fin. and taxation, com. sect. torts and ins. practice 1994—96, chair tax procedure com.,sect. adminstrv. law and regulatory practice 1994—); mem.: FBA, Am. Law Inst., DC Bar Assn., Fed. Cir. Bar Assn. (chair tax appeals com. 1994—96), Knickerbocker Club (NYC), Econ. Club Washington, Met. Club (Washington), Nat. Press Club (Washington), Order of Coif. Episcopalian. Home: Apt 1176 198 Halpine Rd Rockville MD 20852 Address: Ave Libertador 2602 6A Buenos Aires Argentina Office Phone: 301-984-4202. E-mail: gopehrson@netzero.com.

PEI, I.M. (IEOH MING PEI), architect; b. Canton, China, Apr. 26, 1917; arrived in US, 1935, naturalized, 1954; s. Tsu Yee Pei and Lien Kwun Chwong; m. Eileen Loo, June 20, 1942; children: Ting Chung, Chien Chung, Li Chung, Liane. BArch, MIT, Cambridge, 1940; MArch, Harvard U., 1946; DFA (hon.), U. Pa., 1970, Rensselaer Poly. Inst., 1978, Carnegie Mellon U., 1980, U. Mass., 1980, Brown U., 1980, NYU, 1980, Dartmouth Coll., 1991, Northeastern U., Harvard U., U. Rochester; LLD (hon.), Chinese U., Hong Kong, 1970, Pace U.; LHD (hon.), Columbia U., NYC, 1980, U. Colo., 1982, U. Rochester, 1982, U. Hong Kong, 1990, Am. U., Paris, 1990. Arch., NYC, 1939—42; with Nat. Def. Rsch. Com., 1943—45; asst. prof. Harvard Grad. Sch. Design, 1945—48; dir. archtl. divsn. Webb & Knapp, Inc., 1948—55; founding ptnr. Pei Cobb Freed & Ptnrs. (formerly I.M. Pei & Ptnrs., I.M. Pei & Assocs.), NYC, 1955—90; ind. arch. NYC, 1990—. Prin. works include Mile High Ctr., Denver, Nat. Ctr. Atmospheric Rsch., Boulder, Colo., Dallas City Hall, John Fitzgerald Kennedy Libr., Boston, Can. Imperial Bank Commerce Complex, Toronto, Overseas Chinese Banking Corp. Ctr., Singapore, Dreyfus Chemistry Bldg., MIT, East-West Ctr. U. Hawaii, Honolulu, Mellon Art Ctr. and Choate Rosemary Hall Sci. Ctr., Wallingford, Conn., Univ. Plz., NYU, Johnson Mus. Art Cornell U., Ithaca, NY, Washington Sq. East, Phila., Everson Mus. Art, Syracuse, NY, Nat. Gallery Art, East Bldg., Washington, Wilmington Tower, Raffles City, Singapore, West Wing Mus. Fine Arts, Boston, expansion and modernization of Louvre Mus., Paris, Morton H. Meyerson Symphony Ctr., Dallas, MIT Arts and Media Ctr., Jacob K. Javits Conv. Ctr., NYC, Fragrant Hill Hotel, Beijing, Tex. Commerce Tower, Houston, Bank of China, Hong Kong, Creative Artists Agy., Beverly Hills, Calif., Guggenheim Pavilion, Mount Sinai Med. Ctr., NYC, Rock n' Roll Hall of Fame and Mus., Cleve., Mus. Modern Art, Athens, Greece, Miho Mus. of Art, Shiga, Japan, Bilbao Estuary Project, Spain, Four Seasons Hotel, NYC, planning projects include, SW Washington Redevelopment Plan, Govt. Ctr. Redevelopment Plan, Boston, Oklahoma City Downtown Redevelopment Plan, Bedford Stuyvesant Super Block, Bklyn., master plan Columbia U. Mem. Nat. Coun. Humanities, 1966—70, Nat. Coun. on Arts, 1981—84. Recipient Thomas Jefferson Meml. medal for Architecture, 1976, gold medal for architecture, AAAL, 1979, Nat. Arts Club Gold medal of honor, 1981, Mayor's award of Honor for Art and Culture, NYC, 1981, La Grande Medaille D'or L'Académie d'Architecture, 1981, Pritzker Architecture prize, 1983, Medal of Liberty, 1986, Medal of French Legion of Honor, 1988, Nat. Medal of Art, 1988, Praemium Imperiale, Japan Art Assn., 1989, UCLA Gold medal, 1990, Colbert Found. first award for excellence, 1991, Excellence 2000 award, 1991, Freedom medal, 1993, Thomas Jefferson medal for Disting. Achievement in the Arts, Humanities or Social Scis., Am. Philos. Soc., 2001, Legion of Honor, France, 2006, Oreint und Okzident Preis, Erwin Wickert Found., 2006; fellow MIT traveling, 1940, Wheelwright, Harvard U., 1951. Fellow: AIA (Medal of Honor NY chpt. 1963, Gold Medal 1979), ASID (hon.); mem.: NAD, Urban Design Coun., Royal Inst. Brit. Archs., Am. Acad. and Inst. Arts and Letters (chancellor 1978—80), Am. Acad. Arts and Scis., Nat. Inst. Arts and Letters (Arnold Brunner award 1961). *

PEIPERL, ADAM, sculptor, photographer; b. Sosnowiec, Poland, June 4, 1935; arrived in US, 1953, naturalized, 1958; s. Jacob and Fanny (Alster) P.; m. Martha Rose Dorf, June 15, 1958; children: Maury, Laurence, Linda. Grad., Cours Complementaire Gen, Paris, 1952; BS in Chemistry, George Washington U., 1957; postgrad., Pa. State U., 1959. Cons. in Russian sci. lit. Libr. Congress, Washington, 1959-61, 66-67; chemist Nat. Bur. Standards, Washington, 1961-63; sci. translator Am. Inst. Physics, NYC, 1973-94, Plenum Pub., 1993-98. One-man shows include Balt. Mus. Art, 1969, Pa. Acad. Fine Arts, 1969, Marlborough Gerson Gallery, NYC, 1969, Smithsonian Mus. History and Tech., 1972, Phila. Art Alliance, 1978; group shows include Washington Gallery Modern Art, 1968, Corcoran Gallery Art, 1968, Kent State U., McKay Art Inst., San Antonio, 1969, NASA Manned Spacecraft, Houston, 1970-71, Nat. Mus. Am. Art, 1972-82, Meml. Art Gallery, U. Rochester, 1978, Art of the Sixties, Fred Jones Jr. Mus. of Art, U. Okla., 2002, Radicals and Conservatives: Abstraction 1945 to the Present, Pa. Acad. Fine Arts, 2004, Refract, Reflect, Project: Light Works from the Collection, Hirshhorn Mus. and Sculpture Garden, 2007; represented in permanent collections Kreeger Mus., Pa. Acad. Fine Arts, Mus. Boijmans-Van Beuningen, Fred Jones Jr. Mus. Art, U. Okla., Hirshhorn Mus. and Sculpture Garden; with choreographer Denise Vale collaboration involving projections of sculpture video, U. Okla., 2003. Home: 1135 Loxford Ter Silver Spring MD 20901-1130 E-mail: digitall@comcast.net.

PEIRCE, BONNIE, librarian; MS Internat. Mgmt., Thunderbird, 1993; MLIS, Simmons Coll., 2003. Former bookstore mgr.; head of children's svcs. Dover Town Libr., Mass. Co-founder & chief tech. officer TheBestKidsBooksite.com; continuing edn. instr. Simmons Grad. Sch. Libr. & Info. Sci., Boston. Co-author (blogs) Library Goddesses. Named one of the Movers & Shakers, Libr. Jour., 2007. Mem.: Mass. Libr. Assn. Office: Dover Town Libr 56 Dedham St PO Box 669 Dover MA 02030 Office Phone: 508-785-8117. Personal E-mail: bonnie@thebestkidsbooksite.com. Business E-Mail: bpeirce@minlib.net.

PEIRCE, CAROLE, elementary school educator; b. Oshkosh, Wis., June 11, 1943; d. Charles J. and Bernadette (Graf) P.; m. Jack McDowell, Nov. 18, 1982. BS, U. Wis., Oshkosh, 1965; MA, U. Wis., Madison, 1966. Instr. U. Wis. Ctr. System, Marinette & Fond Du Lac, 1966-70, Concordia Coll., Milw., 1970-71; tchr. of French Behavioral Rsch. Labs., Palo Alto, Calif., 1971-73; elem. tchr. Nido De Aguilas Internat. Sch., Santiago, Chile; elem. bilingual tchr. Alum Rock Sch. Dist., San Jose, Calif., 1978-87; elem. tchr. Huntsville (Ark.) Sch. Dist., 1987-95; French, Spanish, and ESL tchr. Huntsville (Ark.) H.S., 1995-2000. Presenter Bay Area Sch. Dists. Calif., 1984-87, Springdale Tchrs. Co-op, Little Rock, Arkadelphia, Ark., Dallas, Albuquerque, St. Paul, Dominican Republic; tchr., cons. Nat. Geog. Soc., 1990-96. Author Social Studies Review Article 1985. Grantee Environ. Edn. State of Calif., 1986, NSTA to Internat. Geographical Congress, Washington, 1992, NASA Ednl. Workshop for Elem. Sci. Tchrs., 1993; Christa McAuliffe fellow, 1993-94; recipient Nat. Disting. Teaching award Nat. Achievement Coun. Geographic Edn., 1993. Mem. NEA, Nat. Coun. for Social Studies, Nat. Coun. for Geog. Edn., Ark. Geog. Alliance (newsletter editor, Geography Tchr. of Yr., 1993-94), Ozark Soc. Avocations: global studies, geography, outdooring, travel. Home: 2046 Madison 8325 Hindsville AR 72738-9727

PEIRCE, DWIGHT A(LEXANDER), JR., music educator; s. Dwight Alexander and Helen Frances (Shockley) Peirce. BMus, Cin. Coll. Conservatory, 1969, MusM, 1972. Asst. prof. Howard Payne U., Brownwood, Tex., 1977—81; lectr. in accompaniment Lamar U., Beaumont, Tex., 1982—. Lectr. in field; pianist Beaumont Symphony Orch., Tex., 1982—90; organist Wesley United Meth. Ch., Beaumont, 1983—, Temple Emanuel, 2001—. Rehearsal pianist, organist Beaumont Interfaith Choir, 1988—2003; rehearsal pianist Beaumont Civic Opera, 1984—2000. Recipient Svc. award, Delta Omicron, Lamar U., 1989, Orpheus award, Phi Mu Alpha Sinfonia, Lamar U., 1996, Arts award for outstanding achievement, S.E. Tex. Arts Coun., 1998. Mem.: Tex. Music Educators Assn., Am. Guild Organists (dean Beaumont chpt. 1999—). Methodist. Avocations: opera, photography, films, collecting records, reading. Office: Lamar U PO Box 10044 Beaumont TX 77710 Office Phone: 409-880-8076.

PEIRCE, FREDERICK FAIRBANKS, lawyer; b. Torrington, Conn., Jan. 28, 1953; s. Everett L. and Frederica (Fairbanks) P.; m. Sandra Marie MacMillan, Dec. 16, 1989. BS with high honors, Colo. State U., 1975; JD, U. Colo., 1979. Bar: Colo. 1979, U.S. Dist. Ct. Colo. 1979. Assoc. Bratton & Zimmerman, Gunnison, Colo., 1979-80; staff atty. Holland & Hart, Aspen, Colo., 1980-82; assoc. Austin, McGrath & Jordan, Aspen, 1982-84, Austin & Jordan, Aspen, 1984-87; ptnr. Austin, Jordan, Young & Peirce, Aspen, 1987-89, Austin & Peirce, Aspen, 1989-92, Austin, Peirce & Smith, P.C., Aspen, 1992—. Bd. dirs. Aspen Nordic Coun. Inc., 1985-88, Aspen Velo Club Inc., 1986-88, Aspen Cycling Club, Inc., 1988-93, Aspen Ctr. for Environ. Studies, 1991-97, v.p., 1992-94, pres., 1994-97; bd. dirs. Pitkin County Pks. Assn., Inc., 1990-98, v.p., 1991-92, pres., 1992-95; bd. dirs. Aspen Valley Land Trust, 1990-98, v.p., 1991-92, pres., 1992-95; bd. edn. Aspen Sch. Dist., 1997-2005, v.p., 2003-04, pres., 2004-05; open space and trails adv. bd. City of Aspen, 2002—, pres., 2002—; Kids First adv. bd. City of Aspen, 1997-2004, pres., 1998-2004. NSF grantee, 1975. Mem. Colo. Bar Assn. (bd. govs. 1989-93, exec. coun. 1993-95, v.p. 1995-96, ethics com., 1995-97), Pitkin County Bar Assn. (v.p. 1985-86, pres. 1986-88, bd. govs. rep. 1989-93), Phi Kappa Phi. Avocations: skiing, hiking, fly fishing, bicycling, golf. Office: Austin Peirce & Smith PC Ste 205 600 E Hopkins Ave Aspen CO 81611-2933 Home Phone: 970-925-1242; Office Phone: 970-925-2600. Business E-Mail: fpeirce@aps-pc.com.

PEIRCE, KAREN PATRICIA, education educator; b. Providence, July 12, 1971; d. Raymond Fales and Patricia Kay Peirce. ABH, Rollins Coll., Winter Park, Fla., 1993; MA, Carnegie Mellon U., Pitts., 1997; PhD, U. Ariz., Tucson, 2006. Peer writing cons. Rollins Coll. Writing Ctr., Winter Park, Fla., 1990—93; Fulbright English tchg. asst. Korean Am. Edn. Commn., Ulsan, 1993—94; pub. rels. asst. Embassy of the Republic of Korea, Washington, 1995—96; rsch. asst. Carnegie Mellon U., Pitts., 1996—97; English instr. The Sawyer Sch., Warwick, RI, 1997—98; upper divsn. English tchr. Berkeley Prep. Sch., Tampa, Fla., 1998—2001; grad. assoc. tchg. U. Ariz., Tucson, 2001—06; asst. prof. English U.S. Mil. Acad., West Point, NY, 2006—. Mem.: MLA, Coun. Writing Program Adminstrs., Coll. English Assn., Rhetoric Soc. Am., Internat. Writing Ctr. Assn., Conf. on Coll. Composition and Comm., Nat. Coun. Tchrs. English. Home: 281 Hudson St Ste 2 Cornwall On Hudson NY 12520-1039

PEIRCE, NEAL R., journalist; b. Phila., Jan. 5, 1932; s. J. Trevor and Miriam deS. (Litchfield) P.; m. Barbara von dem Bach-Zelewski, Apr. 18, 1959; children: Celia, Andrea, Trevor. BA, Princeton U., 1954; postgrad., Harvard U., 1957-58. Polit. editor Congl. Quar., 1960-69; co-founder, contbg. editor Nat. Jour., Washington, 1969-97. Cons. and commentator elections CBS News, 1962, 67-76, NBC News, 1964-66; lectr. in field; syndicated newspaper columnist Washington Post Writers Group; chmn. The Citistates Group; mem. faculty Salzburg (Austria) Seminar, 1980, 84, 97; 1st Weinberg prof. Princeton U.'s Woodrow Wilson Sch. Pub. and Internat. Affairs, 1992. Author: The People's President, 1968, 2d edit., 1981, The Megastates of America, 1972, The Pacific States of America, 1972, The Mountain States of America, 1972, The Great Plains States America, 1973, The Deep South States of America, 1974, The Border South States, 1975, The New England States, 1976, The Mid-Atlantic States of America, 1977, The Great Lakes States of America, 1980, The Book of America: Inside Fifty States Today, 1983, Citistates: How Urban America Can Prosper in A Competitive World, 1993, Breakthroughs: Recreating The American City, 1993; Corrective Capitalism, 1987; editor Peirce Report series on 24 regions' Citistate futures starting with Phoenix Republic and Gazette, 1987, including New England Futures Project, 2005-06. Founder, chmn. S.W. Neighborhood Assembly, Washington, 1963-65; mem. exec. com. Nat. Civic League, 1990-95; trustee German Marshall Fund U.S., 1987-97. With CIC, U.S. Army, 1954-57. Fellow

Woodrow Wilson Internat. Center Scholars, 1971-74 Fellow Nat. Acad. Pub. Adminstrn.; mem. Newfound Lake Region Assn. (v.p. 1989-92), Phi Beta Kappa. Episcopalian. Home and Office: 610 G St SW Washington DC 20024-2440 Business E-Mail: npeirce@citistates.com.

PEIRIS, SUHITHI MAHESICA, chemist, researcher; b. Colombo, Sri Lanka, Nov. 23, 1965; d. Suran A. and Marguerite M. Peiris; m. Brett M. Goodman, Apr. 28, 2001. BS with honors, U. Mich., 1991; PhD in Inorganic Chemistry, U. Chgo., 1996. Postdoctoral fellow U. Chgo., 1996-97; staff scientist Nova Rsch. Inc., Alexandria, Va., 1997-98; rsch. chemist Naval Rsch. Lab., Washington, 1998-2000, Naval Surface Warfare Ctr., Indian Head, Md., 2000—06, Def. Threat Reduction Agy., Ft. Belvoir, Va., 2007—. Contbr. articles to profl. jours. Sci. fair judge, Washington, 1999, Indian Head, 2000. Recipient Outstanding Young Scientist award, Gordon Rsch. Conf., 2000. Mem. Am. Chem. Soc. Avocations: swimming, reading.

PEIRSOL, AARON, Olympic swimmer; b. Irvine, Calif., July 23, 1983; s. Tim Hartig and Wela Peirsol. Grad., U. Tex., 2006. Mem. US Olympic Swim Team Sydney Olympic Games, 2000, Athens Olympic Games, 2004. Named NCAA Swimmer of Yr., 2003. Silver medal, 200m backstroke, Sydney Olympic games, 2000, Gold medal, 200m backstroke, World Championships, 2001, Gold Medal, 100m, 200m backstroke, 400m relay, Pan American games, 2002, Gold Medal, 100m backstroke, 200m backstroke, 4x100m medley relay, Athens Olympic Games, 2004, Gold medal, 100m, 200m, and 4x100m medley relay, Pan Pacific Championships, 2006, Gold medal, 100m and 200m backstroke, USA Swimming National Championships, 2006, Gold medal, 100m and 200m backstroke, Texas A&M Grand Prix, 2006, Gold medal, 100m backstroke, World Championships, 2007, Holds world record in the 100m backstroke and 200m backstroke (long and short course meters), mem. Gold Medal US 400m medley relay team, World Championships, 2003, Gold Medal, 200m backstroke, World Championships, 2003, Youngest American (age 15) to break two minutes in 200m backstroke. Office: c/o USA Swimming One Olympic Plz Colorado Springs CO 80909 *

PEITHMAN, ROSCOE EDWARD, physicist, educator; b. Hoyleton, Ill., Feb. 26, 1913; s. Edward Henry Peithman and Sarah Jane Smith; m. Laura Jane Davenport, Apr. 3, 1936 (dec. Oct. 13, 1987); children: Ann Davenport, Stephen Edward. BS, So. Ill. U., 1935; MS, U. of Ill., 1939; EdD, Oreg. State U., 1955. Tchr. various HS, Ill., 1935—42; prof. of physics Humboldt State U., Arcata, Calif., 1946—77, chmn. divsn. of phys. scis., 1960—69, dean Sch. Scis., 1969—70, emeritus prof. of physics, 1977—. Academic senator Calif. State U. Sys., Calif., 1963—66. Lt. comdr. USNR, 1942—73. Fellow: Am. Men and Women of Sci. (life); mem.: Am. Assn. of Physics Tchrs. Avocation: amateur radio. Home: 2704 Sunny Grove Ave Mckinleyville CA 95519-7912 Personal E-mail: w6bme@suddenlink.net.

PEIXOTO NETO, JOSE ULYSSES, internist, researcher; b. Crato, Ceará, Brazil, Aug. 29, 1930; s. Adérito de Aquino Silva and Adelite Alencar Peixoto; m. Maria Isolda Teles Cartaxo, May 23, 1958; children: Jose Ulysses Peixoto Filho, Eunice Ulysséia Peixoto Maia, Jorge André Cartaxo Peixoto. 1st degree, State Coll. Goias, Brazil, 1942, postgrad., 1942-49; 2d degree, St. John Coll., Fortaleza, Brazil, 1949; postgrad., Fed. U., Recife, Brazil, 1955; Laurel, Cearense Med. Ctr., 1994. Med. resident St. Michael Hosp., Rio de Janeiro, 1956; intern St. Anthony Hosp., Iguatú, Ceará, 1957; founder Social Providence, Crato, Ceará, 1958-64; attendent St. Frances Hosp., Crato, 1958-69; founder St. Michael Hosp., Crato, 1967-93, pres., dir., 1983-93, internist, researcher, 1993—; founder Faculty of Law, Crato, 1977-78. Lectr. faculty of medicine The Fed. U. of Ceará, 1976—. Recipient Good Svc. award Lyons Club, 1992, Laurel Cearense Med. Ctr., 1994, Cert. Merit Health Care Profls. Juazeiro North Profl. Health Assn., 1998, Gold Medal of Profl. Merit, Ceara Estate Regional Coun. Medicine, 1999, Plaque of profl. merit Cariri sect. Coun. of Ceara, 2002, Diploma of Ethical Profl. Merit Fed. Medicine Coun., 2006, Jubilee of Gold, Diploma of Fifty Yrs. as Med. Doctor, Medice Meml. Pernam Buco, 2006. Fellow Brazilian Med. Assn. (specialist); mem. AAAS, ACP, Brazilian Soc. Clin. Medicine (specialist), NY Acad. Sci. Roman Catholic. Avocations: reading, walking, movies, farming.

PEKARSKY, MELVIN HIRSCH, artist; b. Chgo., Sept. 18, 1934; s. Abe and Inda (Levin) P. Student, Sch. of Art Inst., Chgo., 1951-52; BA, Northwestern U., 1955, MA, 1956. Faculty Northwestern U., 1955-56; faculty Kendall Coll., 1960-67, chmn. art dept., 1965-67; asst. dean Sch. Visual Arts, NYC, 1967-68, assoc. dean, 1968-69; grad. faculty NYU, 1970-71; assoc. prof. art SUNY, Stony Brook, 1975-84, prof. art, 1984—, chmn. dept., 1977-78, 84-89, dir. MFA and studio programs, 1990—2003. Chmn. SUNY, 2005—07. One-man shows include Gimpel and Weitzenhoffer, N.Y.C., 1974, Lehigh U., 1975, Ball State U. Gallery, Muncie, Ind., 1975, G.W. Einstein Co., Inc., N.Y.C., 1975, 77, 78, 80, 81, 82, 84, 86, 88, 91, 95, 97, Hull Gallery, Washington, 1978, Centro Colombo-Americano, Bogotá, Colombia, 1980, 112 Greene St. Gallery, N.Y.C., 1980, 82, Marianne Deson Gallery, Chgo., 1987, Butler Inst. Am. Art, Youngstown, Ohio, 1990, The Mus. at Stony Brook, 1993, Nev. Mus. Art, Reno, 2001, Nielsen Gallery, Boston, 2002-03, Van Deb Editions, 2007; group shows include Chgo. Art Inst., 1966, Whitney Mus., N.Y.C., 1971, Bklyn. Mus., 1974, Cleve. Mus., 1978, Cooper-Hewitt Mus., 1971, Mus. Modern Art Corp., Lending and Adv. Svc. Exhbns., Kuznetsky-Most Galleries, Moscow, 1989, NAD, N.Y.C., 1990, Fogg Mus. Art/Harvard U., 2000, 06, Am. Acad. Arts and Letters, N.Y.C., 2001, Nielsen Gallery, Boston, 2001, 02, 03, 04, 05, 07, public murals commns., Houston and Crosby Sts., N.Y.C., 1972, Lafayette and Bleecker Sts., N.Y.C., 1969; represented in permanent collections, Cleve. Mus., Fogg Mus. Art, Harvard U., Indpls. Mus., Nev. Museum of Art, Roswell Mus. Art, N.Mex., Westinghouse Corp., Corcoran Gallery Art, Yale U., Notre Dame U., AT&T, Chase Manhattan Bank, Fidelity Corp., Zimmerli Mus., Rutgers Univ., other pub. and corp. collections, also pvt. collections Founding mem., v.p., bd. dirs. City Walls, 1969-77. Served with Combat Engrs. AUS, 1957-59. Recipient grants in public art through City Walls Kaplan Fund, 1969, City Walls Bernhard Found., 1971, City Walls N.Y. State Council on Arts, 1970, City Walls Nat. Endowment for the Arts, 1971 Mem. Coll. Art Assn., Pub. Art Fund. Home: PO Box 1575 Stony Brook NY 11790-0875 Office: SUNY Art Dept Stony Brook NY 11794-5400 Home Phone: 631-476-1890; Office Phone: 631-689-9586. Personal E-mail: pekarsky@aol.com. Business E-Mail: mpekarsky@ms.cc.sunysb.edu.

PEKER, ELYA ABEL, artist; b. Moscow, June 15, 1937; came to U.S. 1972; s. Aba Z. and Frieda I. (Warshavsky) P.; m. Katrina Friedman, May 19, 1977; 1 child, Benjamin E. Diploma of Artist for Theater Decoration, Art Inst., Moscow, 1956. Comml. artist, NYC, 1972-88. One-man shows include Nakhamkin Fine Art Gallery, N.Y.C., 1980-85; exhibited in group shows in Basel, Switzerland, Hong Kong, others; represented in permanent collections of Kennedy-Onassis family, Emil Wolf, Frank L'Angella, Campbell family, Benjamin family, others; contemporary flower and still-life poster series published 1991, reproductions published worldwide. Mem. Am. Biog. Inst. (dep. gov., order internat. ambs., Gold Record Achievement 1995, 20th Century Achievement award 1995, Internat. Cultural Diploma Honor 1996), Internat. Platform Assn., Licensing Industry Merchandiser's Assn. Home: 1610 E 19th St # 297-196 Brooklyn NY 11229

PELACCIO, ZAKARY, chef; Grad., U. VT, French Culinary Inst. Cook Seri Melayu, Kuala Lumpur, Malaysia, Westin Hotel, Chiang Mai, Thailand, The French Laundry, Daniel, Chickenbone Café, Brooklyn; owner, mgr. wiredkitchen.com; mgr., purchasing agt. Myriad Restaurant Grp.; script writer, field prodr. Dining Around, Food Network; exec. chef 5 Ninth, NYC, Fatty Crab, NYC. Adv. bd. Heritage Foods USA. Named one of NYC's Rising Stars, StarChefs.com, 2006. Mem.: Slow Food. Office: 5 Ninth 5 9th Ave New York NY 10014 Office Phone: 212-929-9460.

PELAVIN, SOL HERBERT, research company executive; b. Detroit, Dec. 16, 1941; s. Norman J. and Alice A. Pelavin; m. Diane Christine Blakemore, Aug. 14, 1966; 2 children. BA in Math., U. Chgo., 1965, MAT in Math., 1969; MS in Stats., Stanford U., 1974, PhD candidate in mathematical models of edn. research, 1975. Tchr. pub. schs., 1965-70. teaching rsch. asst. Stanford (Calif.) U., 1972-74; cons. Rand Corp., Santa Monica, Calif., 1975; policy analyst SRI Internat., Menlo Park, Calif., 1975-78; exec. officer NTS Research Corp., Durham, N.C., 1978-82; pres. Pelavin Assocs., Inc., Washington, 1982-94; exec. v.p., COO Am. Inst. Rsch., 1994-2001, pres., CEO, 2001-; dir. Data Analysis and Tech. Support Ctr., Washington, 1989-93, Policy Analysis Support Ctr., Washington, 1993—; expert witness to U.S. Congress, 1977, 79, Cabinet briefing, 1983; cons. Frank, Bernstein, Conway and Goldman, Balt., 1980-81; dir. Ednl. Analysis Ctr., Washington, 1982-85. Author: (with P. Barker) A Study of the Generalizability of the Results of Standardized Achievement Tests, 1976, (with J.L. David) Research on the Effectiveness of Compensatory Education Programs: A Reanalysis of Data, 1977, (with others) Federal Expenditures for the Education of Children and Youth With Special Needs, 1981, (with D.C. Pelavin) An Evaluation of the Fund for the Improvement of Postsecondary Education, 1981, 83, (with others) Evaluation of the Commodity Supplemental Food Program, 1982, An Evaluation of the Bilingual Education Evaluation, Dissemination and Assessment Centers, 1984, A Study of a Year-Round School Program, 1978, Teacher Preparation: A Review of State Certification Requirements, 1984, Analysis of the National Availability of Mathematics and Science Teachers, 1983, Minority Participation in Higher Education, 1988, Changing the Odds, 1990, others; contbr. articles to profl. jours. NSF fellow U. Chgo., 1968-69; Cuneo fellow Stanford U., 1973. Mem. Am. Ednl. Research Assn., Am. Psychol. Assn. Democrat. Jewish. Office: American Inst Rsch 1000 Thomas Jefferson Washington DC 20007-3500 Home Phone: 301-299-6681; Office Phone: 202-342-5000. Business E-Mail: spelavin@air.org.

PELEG, AVNER, physicist, mathematician; BS cum laude, Israel Inst. Tech., Haifa, 1990; MS, Hebrew U., Jerusalem, 1997, PhD, 2001. Rsch. assoc. Los Alamos Nat. Lab., N.Mex., 2001—04, U. Ariz., Tucson, 2004—. Contbr. articles to profl. jours. Recipient Racah award, Hebrew U., Jerusalem, 2001, Travel award, Soc. Indsl. and Applied Math., 2006. Achievements include research in nonlinear optics; optical communications; statistical physics; plasma physics. Office Fax: 520-621-1510.

PELFREY, D. PATTON, lawyer; b. Ky., 1941; BA, Calif. State U., LA, 1963; JD, U. Louisville, 1968. Bar: Ky. 1968. Trial atty. region 9 NLRB, Cin., 1968-72; mem. Frost Brown Todd LLC, Louisville, 1972—. Prof. labor law sch. law U. Louisville. Fellow Coll. Labor and Emloyment Lawyers; mem. ABA (sect. labor and employment law), Ky. Bar Assn. (labor sect.), Louisville Bar Assn. (mem. labor com. 1983—), Delta Theta Phi. Office: Frost Brown Todd LLC 400 W Market St Ste 3200 Louisville KY 40202-3363 Office Phone: 502-589-5400. E-mail: ppelfrey@fbtlaw.com.

PELHAM, ANN, publishing executive, department chairman; BA, Duke Univ., 1974. Reporter The News & Observer, Raleigh, NC, Congl. Quarterly, Washington, Governing Mag.; reporter through exec. editor Legal Times, Washington, 1988—96, assoc. pub., 1996—98, publisher, 1998—; v.p. Duke U. Alumni Assn., 2004—; chmn. Duke Student Pub. Co., 2003—. Editor: The Chronicle (Duke Univ. newspaper). Office: Legal Times Ste 800 1730 M St NW Washington DC 20036 Office Phone: 202-457-0686. Office Fax: 202-457-0718.

PELHAM, JUDITH, health system administrator; b. Bristol, Conn., July 23, 1945; d. Marvin Curtis and Muriel (Chodos) Pelham; m. Jon N. Coffee, Dec. 30, 1992; children: Rachel Welch, Molly, Edward. BA, Smith Coll., 1967; MPA, Harvard U., 1975. Various govt. postions, 1968-72; prin. analyst Urban Systems, Cambridge, Mass., 1972-73; dir. devel. and planning Roxbury Dental and Med. Group, Boston, 1975-76; asst. to dir. for gen. medicine and ambulatory care Peter B. Brigham Hosp., Boston, 1976-77, asst. dir. ambulatory care, 1977-79; asst. v.p. Brigham and Women's Hosp., Boston, 1980-81; dir. planning and mktg. Seton Med. Ctr., Austin, Tex., 1980-82, pres., 1982-92, CEO, 1987-92; pres., CEO Daughters of Charity Health Svcs., Austin, 1987-92, Mercy Health Svcs., Farmington Hills, Mich., 1993—2000, Trinity Health (merger of Mercy Health Svcs. and Holy Cross Health Sys.), Novi, Mich., 2000—04, pres. emeritus, 2005—. Bd. dirs. Amgen, 1995—, Cath. CEO Healthcare Connection, 1998—2004; cons. Robert W. Johnson Found., 1979—80; mem. mgmt. bd. Inst. for Diversity in Health Mgmt., 1994—97; chair Coalition for Non-Profit Healthcare, 1997—2000, exec. com., 1997—2002; mem. Healthcare Rsch. and Devel. Inst., 1998—2005, bd., 2003—05; mem. adv. com. RAND Health Compare Strategic Policy, 2005—; mem. strategic adv. bd. Shattuck Hammond, 2005—; mem. strategic adv. com. for comprehensive assessment of reform efforts RAND Corp., 2006—. Contbr. articles to profl. jours. Trustee A. Shivers Radiation Therapy Ctr., Austin, 1982—92, Marywood Maternity and Adoption Agy., 1982—86; bd. dirs. Quality of Life Found., Austin, 1985, Austin Rape Crisis Ctr., adv. bd. mem., 1986—88; bd. dirs., trustee League House, 1992—93, Seton Fund, 1982—93, Greater Detroit Area Health Coun.; mem. Gov.'s Job Tng. Coordinating Coun., 1983—85; mem. adv. coun. U. Tex. Social Work Found., 1983—85; charter mem. Leadership Tex., Austin, 1983—93. Named one of Detroit's 100 Most Influential Women, Crain's Detroit Bus., 1997, 2002; recipient Leadership award, YWCA Austin, 1986, CEO IT Achievement award, Modern Healthcare, Healthcare Info. Mgmt. Sys. Soc., 2004. Fellow: Am. Hosp. Assn., Am. Coll. Healthcare Execs. (bd. dirs. 1987—95); mem.: Cath. Health Assn. (sec., treas. 1982—95, com. on govt. rels. 1984—91, chair fin. com. 1992—95, bd. dirs. 1987—95), Tex. Conf. Health Facilities (bd. dirs. 1985—89, pres. 1988), Austin Area Rsch. Orgn., Tex. Hosp. Assn. (various couns. 1982—87). Home (Winter): 9939 E Celtic Dr Scottsdale AZ 85260

PELIKAN, DONNA MAE, retired secondary school educator; m. Richard R. Pelikan, Jr.; children: Brian, Mark, Tim. BS in Edn., Webster U., St. Louis, 1987; MAT in Comm. (emphasis on reading), Webster U., 1990. Cert. elem. tchr., Mo; cert. 6-8 social studies, K-12 reading specialist, 1997; chancellor's certificat in conflict mediation for youth svc. providers, U. Mo. Elem. tchr. Immaculate Heart of Mary, St. Louis, 1966-68, St. Mary Magdalen, St. Louis, 1968-69, Carman Trls. Sch. Pkwy. Dist., Manchester, Mo., 1989—99; tchr. asst. Ladue Sch. Dist., Mo., 1988—89; tchr. Alternative Discipline Ctr., St. Louis, 1999—2006; ret., 2006. Adj. prof. St. Louis CC, Meramec, Mo., 2006—; founder Pelikan Instrnl. Enterprises, 2007—. Scholar Webster U., 1987. Mem. ASCD, Internat. Reading Assn.

PELKEY, LAWRENCE MICHAEL, school psychologist; b. Oswego, NY, Sept. 24, 1964; s. Richard David and Elizabeth Anne Pelkey. BA, SUNY, Oswego, 2001, MS, 2004. Nat. cert. sch. psychologist. Asst. coord. disability svcs. office SUNY, Oswego, 2001—03; sch. psychologist Syracuse (N.Y.) City Sch. Dist., 2003—04, Canastota (N.Y.) Cen. Sch. Dist., 2003—04, Cayuga-Onondaga Bd. Coop. Edn. Svcs., Auburn, NY, 2004—. Team coord. sch.-based intervention Cayuga-Onondaga Bd. Coop. Edn. Svcs., Auburn, 2004—; sch. bd. intervention team coord. Syracuse City Sch. Dist., 2003—04. Vol. pet visitor VA Hosp., Syracuse, 2002—; Babe Ruth coaching asst. North Syracuse Youth Baseball; umpire Cen. Sq. Youth Softball. Recipient William G. McGarvey award for Outstanding Sr. in Psychology, Oswego State U., 2000, presdl. scholarship, SUNY Oswego, 2002, Donald Snygg Grad. award, 2003. Mem.: N.Y. Assn. Sch. Psychologists, Nat. Assn. Sch. Psychologists, Psi Chi, Phi Kappa Phi. Avocations: sewing, camping, motorcycling, hiking. Office: Cayuga Onondaga Bd Coop Edn Svcs 5980 South St Rd Auburn NY 13021 E-mail: limpelkey@hotmail.com.

PELL, ARTHUR ROBERT, human resources specialist, consultant, writer; b. NYC, Jan. 22, 1920; s. Harry and Rae (Meyers) P.; m. Erica Frost, May 19, 1946; children— Douglas, Hilary. AB, NYU, 1939, MA, 1944; PhD, Calif. Coast U., 1977; diploma, Cornell U., 1943. Personnel dir. Eagle-Electric Mfg. Co., Long Island City, NY, 1946-50, North Atlantic Constructors, NYC, 1950-53; v.p. Harper Assos., Inc., NYC, 1953-75; cons. Human Resources Mgmt., Hempstead, NY, 1975—2004; writer, editor Hartsdale, NY, 2004—. Adj. assoc. prof. mgmt. NYU Sch. Continuing Edn., 1962-84, St. John's U. Coll. Bus. Adminstrn., 1971-76; lectr. Baruch Sch. Bus. and Pub. Adminstrn. Coll. City N.Y., 1948-67. Author: (with W.B. Patterson) Fire Officer's Guide to Leadership, rev. edit., 1963, Placing Salesmen, 1963, Placing Executives, 1964, Police Leadership, 1967, How to Get the Job You Want After 40, 1967, Recruiting and Selecting Personnel, 1969, (with M. Harper) Starting and Managing an Employment Agency, 1970, Recruiting, Training and Motivating Volunteer Workers, 1972, Be a Better Employment Interviewer, 1972, rev. edits., 1978, 86, 94, The College Graduate Guide to Job Finding, 1973; (with Wilma Rogalin) Women's Guide to Executive Positions, 1975; (with Albert Furbay) College Student's Guide to Career Planning, 1975; (with Dale Carnegie Assocs.) Managing Through People, 1975, rev. edits., 1978, 1987, Choosing a College Major: Business, 1978, Enrich Your Life: The Dale Carnegie Way, 1979, The Part Time Job Book, 1984, Making the Most of Medicare, 1987, rev. edit., 1990; (with George Sadek) Resumes for Engineers, 1982, Resumes for Computer Professionals, 1984, How to Sell Yourself on an Interview, 1982, The Job Finder's Kit, 1989, Getting the Most from Your People, 1990, Diagnosing Your Doctor, 1991, The Supervisor's Infobank, 1994, The Complete Idiot's Guide to Managing People, 1995, 3d edit., 2003, The Pocket Idiot's Guide to One Minute Management, 1999, The Complete Idiot's Guide to Team Building, 1999, The Complete Idiot's Guide to Recruiting The Right Stuff, 2000, The Complete's Idiot Guide to Human Resources Management, 2001, (with Franklin C. Ashby) Embracing Excellence, 2001; editl. cons. for revision Dale Carnegie's How to Win Friends and Influence People, 1981; author syndicated feature The Human Side; editor: Dale Carnegie's: Public Speaking for Success, 2004, Napoleon Hill's: Think and Grow Rich, 2005; contbr. articles to profl. jours. With AUS, 1942-46. Home and Office: 400 High Point Dr Apt 101 Hartsdale NY 10530-1125 Office Phone: 914-949-1382. Personal E-mail: arpell22@optonline.net.

PELL, CLAIBORNE, former senator; b. NYC, Nov. 22, 1918; s. Herbert Claiborne and Matilda (Bigelow) P.; m. Nuala O'Donnell, Dec. 1944; children: Herbert Claiborne III, Christopher T. Hartford, Nuala Dallas Yates, Julia L.W. Student, St. George's Sch., Newport, RI; AB cum laude, Princeton U., 1940; AM, Columbia U., 1946; 51 hon. degrees. Enlisted USCGR, 1941; served as seaman, ensign North Atlantic sea duty, Africa, Italy; hospitalized to, 1944; instr. Navy Sch. Mil. Govt., Princeton, 1944-45; capt. USCGR; ret.; on loan to State Dept. at San Francisco Conf., 1945, State Dept., 1945-46, US embassy, Czech Republic, 1946-47; established consulate gen. Bratislava, Czechoslovakia, 1947-48; vice consul Genoa, Italy, 1949; assigned State Dept., 1950-52; v.p., dir. Internat. Rescue Com.; senator from RI, 1961-96; US del. to UN, 97—. Ranking minority mem. Fgn. Rels. Com., Labor and Human Resources Subcom. on Edn., Arts, and Humanities; mem. Rules and Adminstrn. Com., Joint Com. on Libr. and Congl. Intern Program, Senate Dem. Policy Com.; US del. Internat. Maritime Consultative Orgn., London, 1959, 25th Gen. Assembly, 1970; disting. vis. prof. Salve Regina U., Newport, RI, 1997. Author: Megalopolis Unbound, 1966, (with Harold L. Goodwin) Challenge of the Seven Seas, 1966, Power and Policy, 1972. Hon. bd. dirs. World Affairs Council RI; trustee St. George's Sch.; trustee emeritus Brown U.; Cons. Democratic Nat. Com., 1953-60; exec. asst. to chmn. RI State Dem. Com., 1952-54; chmn. RI Dem. Fund drive, 1952, Dem. nat. registration, chmn., 1956, co-chmn., 1962; chief delegation tally clk. Dem. Nat. Conv., 1956, 60, 64, 68. Decorated knight Crown of Italy, Grand Cross Order of Merit Italy, Red Cross of Merit Portugal, Legion of Honor France, comdr. Order of Phoenix Greece, Grand Cross Order of Merit Liechtenstein, Grand Cross Order of Christ Portugal, Order of Henry the Navigator, Portugal, Grand Cross Order of N. Star Sweden, Grand Cross of Merit Knights of Malta, Grand Officer of Merit Luxembourg, Grand Comdr. Lebanon; recipient Caritas Elizabeth medal Cardinal Franz Koenig, Grand decoration of honor in silver with sash Austria, Gold medal of St. Barnabas (Cyprus), recipient Pres.'s Fellow award RI Sch. Design, medal Nat. Order of Cedar, Hugo Grotius Commemorative medal The Netherlands, recipient Harold W. McGraw, Jr. Prize in Education, McGraw-Hill, 1988; named to Centennial Honor Roll, Am. Assn. Museums, 2006. Mem. Soc. Cin. Clubs: Hope (Providence); Knickerbocker (NYC), Racquet and Tennis (NYC), Brook (NYC); Metropolitan (Washington); Travellers (Paris); Reading Room (Newport); White's (London). Democrat. Episcopalian. *I have a seven word definition of my job and of my life: "Translate ideas into events, and help people.".* *

PELL, JONATHAN LAURENCE, performing company executive; b. Memphis, Oct. 20, 1949; s. Burton Marshall and Eleanor (Leopold) P. BA, U. So. Calif., 1971. Interior designer Gene Morse Assocs., Wichita, Kans., 1971-77; mgr. Internat. Artists Mgmt., NYC, 1977-79, Robert Lombardo Assocs., NYC, 1979-80; TV producer Sta. WNET, NYC, 1980-83; dir. publicity John Curry Skating Co., NYC, 1983; prodr. Jerome Kern Centennary Gala Town Hall, NYC, 1984; dir. artistic administration The Dallas Opera, 1984—. Vocal competition judge Met. Opera Nat. Coun. Auditions, Pavarotti Competition, Bidu Sayao Internat. Competition, Brazil, Ottavio Ziino Internat. Competition, Rome, Patronesses of the Opera Competition, Miami, Fla., George London Awards, Ctr. for Contemporary Opera, Jensen Found. Competition, Dallas Opera Guild, Denver Lyric Opera Guild, Ft. Worth Opera, Marguerite McCammon Competition, San Antonio Opera Guild, Richard Tucker Award, others; tchr. master classes for young singers Opera Am., Nat. Opera Assn., Can. Opera Co., S.W. Chpt. NATS, Performing Arts Assistance Corp., U. North Tex., Internat. Sch. Performing Arts, Amarillo Opera, So. Meth. U.; host Dallas Opera Radio Hour, WRR, 1994—97, Inside the Dallas Opera, WRR, 2004—; advisor singer svcs. com. Opera Am.; lectr. on opera Crystal Cruises. Bd. dirs., chmn. nat. auditions com., mem. award selection com. Richard Tucker Music Found.; mem. adv. bd. Awards Recognizing Individual Artistry; advisor to singer svcs. com. Opera Am. Office: Dallas Opera Campbell Ctr I LBI-11 8350 N Central Expy Ste 210 Dallas TX 75206-1601 Home Phone: 214-821-6339; Office Phone: 214-443-1043.

PELL, SIDNEY, epidemiologist; b. NYC, Dec. 13, 1922; m. Lola May, July 2, 1950. MBA, CCNY, 1952; PhD, U. Pitts., 1956. Biostatistician E.I. Du Pont de Nemours and Co., Wilmington, Del., 1955-76, mgr. epidemiology sect., 1976-82, sr. cons., 1982-85; epidemiology cons. Wilmington, 1985—. Epidemiology cons. Del. Divsn. Pub. Health, Dover, 1986-95. Contbr. articles to New Eng. Jour. Medicine, Jour. Occupational Medicine, Jour. AMA. With U.S. Army, 1943-45, ETO. Recipient Merit in Authorship Hon. Mention, Inds. Med. Assn., 1959. Fellow Am. Coll. Epidemiology, Am. Heart Assn., Am. Pub. Health Assn., Delta Omega. Home: 1416 Emory Rd Wilmington DE 19803-5120 E-mail: pell104@aol.com.

PELLA, MILTON ORVILLE, science educator; b. Wilmot, Wis., Feb. 13, 1914; s. Charles August and Ida Marie (Pagel) P.; m. Germaine Marie Reich, Dec. 9, 1944. B.E., Milw. State Tchrs. Coll., 1936; MS, U. Wis., 1940, PhD, 1948. Tchr. sci. and math. Wyler Mil. Acad., 1937-38; tchr.

elementary sch. Delavan Pub. Schs., 1938-39; tchr. sci. U. Wis. High Sch., 1939-42; prof. sci. edn. U. Wis., Madison, 1946-80, prof. emeritus, 1980—; With Fgn. Ednl. Service, 1959—81. Author: Physical Science for Progress, 3d edit, 1970, Science Horizons— The Biological World, (with Branley and Urban), 1965-70. Served with AUS, 1942-46. Fellow AAAS; mem. Ctrl. Assn. Sci. and Math. (pres. 1955), Nat. Assn. for Rsch. in Sci. Tchg. (pres. 1966), Nat. Sci. Tchrs. Assn. (dir. 1950, 60), Masons. Home: 6175 Mineral Point Rd Rm 328 Madison WI 53705

PELLEGRINI, JOHN B., lawyer; b. Leominster, Mass., Jan. 1, 1942; AB cum laude, Boston Coll., 1963; LLB, Columbia U., 1966; LLM in Internat. Law, NYU, 1973. Bar: NY 1970, US Ct. Internat. Trade 1971. Atty. US Customs Svc., 1970-73, J.C. Penny Co. Inc.; ptnr. Kaplan & Pellegrini, NYC, Baskin & Steingut, NYC; joined Ross & Hardies, NYC, 1985; now co-mng. ptnr. NYC office McGuireWoods LLP. Mem. ABA (internat. trade com., internat. law sect. 1976—), Customs and Internat. Trade Bar Assn. (adminstrv. practice com. 1981-84, bd. dirs. 1984-88). Office: McGuire-Woods LLP 7th Fl 1345 Ave of the Americas New York NY 10105-0106 Office Phone: 212-548-7020. Office Fax: 212-715-2301. Business E-Mail: jpellegrini@mcguirewoods.com.

PELLEGRINO, EDMUND DANIEL, internist, educator, retired academic administrator; b. Newark, June 22, 1920; s. Michael J. and Marie (Catone) Pellegrino; m. Clementine Coakley, Nov. 17, 1944; children: Thomas, Virginia, Michael, Andrea, Alice, Leah. BS, St. John's U., 1941, DSc (hon.), 1971; MD, NYU, 1944; 39 hon. degrees. Diplomate Am. Bd. Internal Medicine. Intern Bellevue Hosp., NYC, 1944—45, asst. resident medicine, 1948—49; resident medicine Goldwater Meml. Hosp., NYC, 1945—46; fellow medicine NYU, 1949—50; supervising Tb physician Homer Folks Hosp., Oneonta, NY, 1950—53; dir. internal medicine Hunterdon Med. Center, Flemington, NJ, 1953—59, med. dir., 1955—59; prof., chmn. dept. medicine U. Ky. Med. Center, 1959—66; prof. medicine SUNY, Stony Brook, 1966—72, v.p. for health scis., dir. Health Scis. Center, 1968—73, dean Sch. Medicine, 1968—72; v.p. health affairs U. Tenn. System; chancellor U. Tenn. Med. Units, Memphis, 1973—75; prof. med. Yale U., New Haven, 1975—78; pres. Yale-New Haven Med. Center, 1975—78, Cath. U. Am., Washington, 1978—82, prof. philosophy and biology, 1978—82; John Carroll prof. medicine and med. ethics Georgetown U., Washington, 1982—; dir. Kennedy Inst. Ethics, Washington, 1983—88; dir. Ctr. for Advanced Study Ethics Georgetown U., Washington, 1988—94, dir. Ctr. for Clin. Bioethics, 1991—, acting chief Divsn. Gen. Internal Medicine, 1993—94, chief Gen. Internal Medicine, 1995. Founding editor: Jour. Medicine and Philosophy, 1983—. Chmn. Pres.'s Coun. on Bioethics, Washington, 2005—. With USAF, 1946—48. Master: ACP; fellow: N.Y. Acad. Medicine; mem.: Inst. Medicine NAS, AMA, Am. Clin. and Climatol. Assn., Assn. Am. Physicians (chmn. pres. coun. 2005—). Office: Georgetown U Ctr for Clin Bioethics Washington DC 20007

PELLEGRINO, PETER, retired surgeon; b. Camden, NY, July 7, 1934; s. Peter and Alice (Alchin) Pellegrino; m. Barbara Ann Haldon, June 18, 1960; children: Peter Scott, Kathleen Ann, Lisa Marie. AB in Psychology, Franklin & Marshall Coll., Lancaster, Pa., 1960; MD, Hahnemann Med. Coll., Phila., 1960. Diplomate Am. Bd. Surgery. Intern Hahnemann Hosp., Phila., 1960—61, surg. resident, 1961—62, 1965—67, 1968, attending surgeon, 1969—2006; chief dept. surgery Kessler Hosp., Hammonton, NJ, 1969—2006. Assoc. prof. surgery Hahnemann Hosp., Phila., 2003—06. Capt. US Army, 1962—65. Fellow: ACS; mem.: N.J. Med. Soc., Hahnemann Alumni Assn. (1st v.p. 1984). Republican. Office Phone: 856-767-8980.

PELLEGROM, DANIEL EARL, health and development executive; b. Three Rivers, Mich., May 29, 1944; s. Francis Robert and Regina Elizabeth (Valentine) P.; m. Sally Margaret Stukenbroeker, Nov. 30, 1968; children: Daniel, Jr., Benjamin, Sara. BA, Western Mich. U., 1966; MDiv, Union Theol. Seminary, 1969. Ordained to ministry, Presbyn. Ch., 1970. Dir. coll. programs Planned Parenthood Fedn., NYC, 1969-71; exec. dir. Memphis Planned Parenthood, 1971-75, Md. Planned Parenthood, Balt., 1975-85; pres. Pathfinder Internat., Watertown, Mass., 1985—. Mem. Gov.'s conf. on children and youth State of Md., Balt., 1978-80; assoc. Sch. Hygiene and Pub. Health Johns Hopkins U., Balt., 1984-85; pres. bd. mgrs. Brush Found., Cleve.; bd. dirs. InterAction, WAshington, World Neighbors, Oklahoma City, Planned Parenthood League of Mass., Boston. Recipient Leadership award Greater Balt. Com., 1983-84, UN Population award Pathfinder Internat., 1996, Internat. award Nat. Family Planning and Reproductive Health Assn., 1997, Friendship award Pathfinder Internat. Govt. Vietnam, 2005. Mem. APHA. Democrat. Avocations: baseball, travel, hiking. Home: 48 Bound Brook Rd Newton MA 02461-2036 Office: Pathfinder Internat 9 Galen St Ste 217 Watertown MA 02472-4523 E-mail: dpellegrom@pathfind.org.

PELLETIER, ARTHUR JOSEPH, state legislator, educator; b. Dec. 13, 1946; s. Joseph Telesphor and Elsie Jane (Dillon) Pelletier; m. Marsha Lynn Mingle, May 19, 1973; 1 child, John. Diploma, N.H. Vocat. Tech. Inst., 1966; BA, Kans. State U., 1970, MS, 1972. Asst. to dir. Kans. State U. Divsn. Contbg. Edn., Manhattan, 1971-74; tchr. drafting Portsmouth (N.H.) HS, 1974-86; tchr. computer programming McIntosh Coll., Dover, NH, 1982-84; assoc. prof. N.H. Vocat.-Tech. Coll., Stratham, 1986-87; kitchen designer Area Kitchen Ctr., Portsmouth, 1987; mem. N.H. Ho. of Reps., 1993—2004; asst. to archivist Berwick Acad., South Berwick, Maine, 2005—. Mem. legis. sci., tech. and energy com. N.H. Ho. of Reps., 1993—96, 2003—04, mem. legis. edn. com., 1997—2000; co-founder N.H. Coalition Edn.; mem. Dover Ready to Learn Task Force, 1995—2001; mem. evaluation and rev. com. Dover Schs., mem. curriculum com., 1997—2001; bd. advs. Hub Family Support Ctr., 1996—97. Mem. Partnership Healthier Cmty., 1995—97, Ams. Non-Smoker's Rights, 1996—; chmn. Friends Dover Libr., 2004—. Avocations: radio-controlled model aircraft, tennis, photography. Home: 94 Back River Rd Dover NH 03820-4411

PELLETIER, JOHN B., JR., mathematics professor, consultant; s. John B. and Doris B. Pelletier; m. Judi B. Pelletier, June 12, 1971; children: Jennifer Ann, Sara D. BS, Castleton State U., Vt., 1973, M in Art Edn., 1978. Middle sch. math. tchr. Rockingham Sch. Dist., Bellows Falls, Vt., 1973—2003, math coord. grades 5-8, 2003—04; math. tchr. Leland & Grey Union High Sch., Townshend, Vt., 2004—05, Sch. Adminstrn. Unit, 29 Keene H.S., 2005—. Network math leader Vt. Dept. Edn., Montpelier, 2001—04, per-diem cons., 2003—04. Recipient Sportsmanship award, Vt. Soccer Ofcls. Orgn., 1999. Mem.: KC (grand knight 753 2001—04, 4th degree color guard 2000—). Roman Catholic. Avocations: fly fishing, fishing, bus driving, coaching. Home: 3 Overpass Rd Chester VT 05143 Office: Keene HS Arch St Keene NH Office Phone: 603-352-0640 X3301.

PELLETIER, LOUIS CONRAD, surgeon, educator, health facility administrator; b. Montreal, Que., Can., Mar. 15, 1940; s. Conrad L. and Lucienne (Rochette) P.; m. Louise Montpetit, June 26, 1965; children: Conrad R., Marie-Helene. BA, Brébeuf Coll., Montreal, 1959; MD, U. Montreal, 1964, MBA, 1996. Resident in cardiovascular and thoracic surgery U. Montreal, 1964-70, chmn. dept. surgery, 1986-94; rsch. asst. Mayo Clin. Found., Rochester, Minn., 1970-72; mem. dept. surgery Maisonneuve-Rosemont Hosp., Montreal, 1972-76, Sacré-Coeur Hosp., Montreal, 1972-80, Montreal Heart Inst., 1979—2000, head dept. surgery, 1979-87; dir. rsch. Ctr. Sacre-Coeur Hosp., 1998—2002; pres. Cardianove, Inc., 1998—; dir. med. affairs Sacrè-Coeur hosp., 2000—02; cons. in health adminstrn. and mgmt. of emergency wards, 2002—. Contbr. articles to profl. jours. Mem. adminstrv. bd. College Stanislas, Montreal, 1979-86, Que. Heart Found., 1980-84, regional healthcare bd., 1991-92, Hotel-Dieu Hosp., 1993-95. Recipient Young Investigator's award Am. Coll. Cardiology, 1972; Med. Rsch. Coun. Can. scholar U. Montreal, 1973-78. Fellow Royal Coll. Physicians and Surgeons Can.; mem. ACS, Association des Medecins de Langue Francaise du Canada, Can. Med. Assn., Royal Coll. Can., Assn. Cardiovascular and Thoracic Surgery Que., Can. Cardiovascular Soc., Montreal Cardiac Soc., Clin. Rsch. Club Que., Soc. Thoracic Surgeons, Can. Assn. Clin. Surgeons, Sociedad de Cardiocirujanos, Coun. on Cardiovasular Surgery, Am. Heart Assn., Internat. Soc. for Heart Transplantation, Can. Soc. Cardiovascular and Thoracic Surgeons, Am. Assn. Thoracic Surgery, Am. Surgical Assn. Roman Catholic. Avocations: skiing, bicycling.

PELLETIER, MARSHA LYNN, secondary school educator, poet; b. Mt. Pleasant, Mich., July 29, 1950; d. Eugene Russell and Mary Ellen (Edde) Mingle; m. Arthur Joseph Pelletier, May 19, 1973; 1 child, John Frederick. BS in Home Econs. and Edn., Kans. State U., 1971, MS in Edn. Guidance and Counseling, 1972. Lic. real estate broker N.H. Conf. coord., guidance counselor Kans. State U., Manhattan, 1971-73; tchr. home econs. Franklin (Mass.) HS, 1974, Exeter (N.H.) HS, 1974-75, Barrington (N.H.) Mid. Sch., 1975-81, Pentucket Regional Jr. HS, West Newbury, Mass., 1981-82; realtor assoc. Century 21 Ocean and Norword Realty, Portsmouth, NH, 1983-86; tchr. interior design, cons. U. N.H., Durham, 1986-87; tchr. family and consumer sci. Dover (N.H.) Mid. Sch., 1983—2001; tchr. Dover HS, 2001—; mem. legis. adminstrn. com. N.H. Ho. of Reps., Concord, 1992—94, 1996—2002; ind. real estate broker Dover, 1986-2000. Bd. dirs. N.H. State Profl. Bd. Stds., 1999—2004; assessor Nat. Bd. Profl. Tchg. Stds., 2001; tchr. assessor Nat. Tchrs. Bd. Cert., 2002—. Author: Portsmouth Unabridge: New Poems for an Old City, 2002, Arriving at the Crossroads, 2003, Exeter, New Hampshire: Where the River Meets the Tide, 2005; costume dir. & designer: Guys and Dolls, 2004; actor: (plays) Factory on Fire, 2006; contbr. poems to books. Bd. dirs. Dover Adult Learning Ctr., 1995—98; mem. Health Task Force, Dover, Concord, 1993—94, Cornerstone Dancers, Dover Friends of Pub. Libr., 1996—, bd. supt. adv. com., 2001—06, poetry judge, 2003—, bd. principal's adv. com., 2004—; mem. faculty coun. Dover H.S., 2004—; trustee St. John's Meth. Ch., 1995—97. Named to Nat. Honor Roll for Outstanding Am. Tchrs., 2006; recipient Best Poets award, Internat. Soc. Poetry, 2000, 2001, 2002, 2004. Mem.: NEA (local pres., negotiator, v.p., membership chair, mem. leadership exec. com., bldg. rep. 1979—, N.H. del. to nat. conv.), Poetry Soc. NH, Seacoast Writers Assn., Nat. Coalition Consumer Econ., Alpha Delta Kappa (v.p., historian, altruistic chmn. 1984—89). Democrat. Avocations: gardening, aerobics, poetry, sewing, cooking. Home: 94 Back River Rd Dover NH 03820-4411

PELLETIER, SHO-MEI, musician, educator; b. Tucson, July 25, 1952; d. Harold W. and Mary Pelletier; m. Dwight E. Shambley, Aug. 12, 1979; children: Aaron Joshua Pelletier-Shambley, Alexis Jessica Pelletier-Shambley. Student, No. Ariz. U., 1965—66, Ariz. State U., 1965—66; MusB in Violin, Ind. U., 1974; student with, Josef Gingold, 1970—75, Ivan Galamian, 1969—75, Sally Thomas, 1969, Sydney Harth, 1967, Angel Reyes, 1968, Dr. Frank Spinosa, 1965—70, Dr. Harold W. Pelletier, 1966. Asst. prin. violinist Dallas Symphony Orch., assoc. prin. violinist, 1975—, solo violinist, 1993, 1995; assoc. prin. violinist Santa Fe Opera, Santa Fe, 1973—98; prin. violinist Dallas Chamber Orch., 1975—92, Dallas Bach Soc., 1975—95. Mem. youth edn. svc. quintet Dallas Symphony Orch., 1978—, charter tchr. Young Strings Minority Scholarship program, 1988; part-time tchr. Booker T. Washington Arts Magnet HS, Dallas, 1982—85. Musician (solo violinist): Sun Valley Music Festival, 1966—67, Interlochen, 1968, Meadowmount, 1969, Walden Ensemble, 1975—, New Arensky Piano Trio, 1975—, Anton A Piano Trio, 1975—, Kodaly Duo, 1975—, Voices Change Ensemble, 1975—, Haydn's Double Concerto for Violin & Harpischord, 1993, The Arensky Violin Concerto in Am. with Dallas Symphony Orchestra as Violin Concerto Soloist, 1995; author: (book) The Simple Dictionary for Classical Musicians, 2000. Charter mem. Nat. Mus. Women Art, Washington; mem. Klanwatch So. Poverty Law Ctr. Named concertmaster, Ariz. All-State Orch., 1968, 1969, Outstanding Young Women of Am., 1982; recipient awards, Plano Art Soc., 1980—, Richardson Art Soc., 1980—. Mem.: Nat. Geog. Soc. Avocations: painting, drawing, photography. Home: 9648 Whitehurst Dr Dallas TX 75243 Office: Dallas Symphony Orch 2301 Flora St Dallas TX 75201-2497 Office Phone: 214-871-4000. Personal E-mail: dwightshambley@sbcglobal.net.

PELLETT, JON MICHAEL, lawyer; b. Orlando, Fla., Nov. 16, 1961; s. Milton Francis and Jean Ellen (Avery) P.; m. Karen Walker, July 21, 1984 (div. Sept. 1990). BS in Biology, U. Ctrl. Fla., Orlando, 1984, BS in Stats., 1985; JD, Fla. State U., 1993. Bar: Fla. 1995. Legal trainee Dept. Bus. and Profl. Regulation, Tallahassee, 1993-95; staff atty. Agy. for Health Care Adminstrn., Tallahassee, 1995-96; assoc. Freeman, Hunter & Malloy, Tampa, Fla., 1996-2000, Barr, Murman, Tonelli et al, Tampa, 2000—. Vol. guardian ad litem Guardian ad Litem Program, Tallahassee, 1991-95; mem. Coun. for Licensure Enforcement and Regulation, 2003—; bd. dirs. Suncoast Healthcare Execs., Tampa, Fla., 2003-06. Bd. dirs. Friends of Arboretum, Orlando, 1998—2003, Sun Coast Healthcare Execs., Tampa, Fla., 2004—06, treas., 2004—06. Mem. ABA, ATLA, Hillsborough County Bar Assn. Avocations: racquetball, beach volleyball. Office: Barr Murman Tonelli Et Al 201 E Kennedy Blvd Ste 1750 Tampa FL 33602-5829 Office Phone: 813-223-3951.

PELLI, CESAR, architect; b. Tucuman, Argentina, Oct. 12, 1926; arrived in US, 1952, naturalized, 1964; s. Victor V. and Teresa S. Pelli; children: Denis G., Rafael A. BArch cum laude, U. Tucuman, 1949; MS in Architecture, U. Ill., 1954. Assoc. Eero Saarinen & Assocs., 1954-64, Daniel, Mann, Johnson & Mendenhall, 1964-68, Gruen Assocs. Inc., LA, 1968-77, Pelli Clarke Pelli Arch., New Haven, 1977—; dean Yale U. Sch. Architecture, New Haven, 1977-84. Works include Pacific Design Ctr. and Expansion, LA (Honor award So. Calif. chpt. AIA 1976), US Embassy, Tokyo, Mus. Modern Art Expansion, NYC, World Fin. Ctr. and Winter Garden, NYC (Bard award 1992), Cleve. Clinic (Honor award AIA 1986), Herring Hall, Rice U., Houston (Honor award AIA 1986), Carnegie Hall Tower, NYC (Honor award AIA 1994, Design award AIA/Conn. 1991), Boyer Ctr. Molecular Medicine Yale U. (Design award AIA/Conn. 1991), Bank of Am. Corp. Ctr., Charlotte, NTT Corp. Hdqrs., Tokyo (Design award AIA/Conn. 1997), Terminal B/C Reagan Washington Nat. Airport (Design award AIA/Conn. 1998, NE Design award 1999, Design for Transp. award 2000), Aronoff Ctr. for the Arts, Cin. (USITT Honor award 1996, Design award AIA/CIN 1996, Design award AIA/Conn. 1997), Petronas Towers, Kuala Lumpur, Malaysia (Design award AIA/Conn. 1999, NE Design award 2000, Honor award AIA 2000), Frances Lehman Loeb Art Ctr. Vassar Coll., Poughkeepsie, NY (Design award AIA/Conn. 1996), Internat. Fin. Ctr., Hong Kong, Nat. Mus. of Art, Osaka, Japan (Design award AIA/Conn. 2005), Overture Ctr., Madison, Cira Ctr., (AIA award 2006), The Solaire (AIA/Conn. award 2005), Carnival Ctr. Performing Arts, Fla., Mpls. Ctrl. Libr. Bank of Okla. Ctr., Tulsa, Conn. Sci. Ctr., Hartford, Torre de Cristal, Madrid, Torre Libertad, Mexico City, South Sta. Air Rights Devel., Boston, Torre Iberdrola, Bilbao, Paradise St. Devel. & One Park West, Liverpool, Eng., Gran Torre Costanera, Santiago, Brazil, Project CityCtr. Hotel and Casino, Las Vegas, Torre Puerto Triana, Seville, Spain, Winnipeg Airport Terminal, Nat. Children's Mus., Wash., DC; editor Yale Seminars on Architecture, 1981-82; author Observations for Young Architects, 1999 Fellow AIA (Firm award 1989, named to top ten list of living Am. archs. 1991, Gold medal 1995, Aga Khan award, 2004); mem. NAD (Arnold M. Brunner Meml. prize 1978), Am. Acad. Arts and Letters (academician), Internat. Acad. Architecture (academician). Office: Pelli Clarke Pelli Archs 1056 Chapel St New Haven CT 06510-2402 Office Phone: 203-777-2515. Office Fax: 203-787-2856. *

PELLITTERI, JOHN STEVEN, psychologist, psychotherapist, educator; b. Bklyn., Feb. 19, 1964; s. Horace Mario and Lorraine (LoNano) Pellitteri; m. Leda Sabio, June 21; children: Alexander Rafael, Maya Paloma. BS in Music Edn., NYU, 1985, MA in Music Therapy, 1988; MEd in Psychol. Counseling, Columbia U., 1993; PhD in Counseling Psychology, NYU, 1999. Lic. psychologist N.Y., 2000, cert. sch. counselor N.Y., 1998, lic. music educator N.Y., 1985, cert. music therapist Am. Music Therapy Assn., 1988, martial arts instr. 1985-96. Music tchr. Leif Ericson Day Sch., Bklyn., 1986—87; crisis counselor Postgrad. Ctr. for Mental Health, NYC, 1986—89; music therapist Northside Ctr. for Child Devel., NYC, 1987—91; sch. counselor Archdiocese Drug Prevention Program, Bronx, NY, 1991—93; clin. supr. and music therapist Heartsong Music Therapy Program, Bronxville, NY, 1993—2000; pvt. psychotherapy practice Bklyn., 2000—. Program dir. Queens Coll. City U. N.Y., Flushing, NY, 2000—, asst. prof. Queens Coll., 1998—2005, assoc. prof., 2006—; cons. Bay Ridge Prep. Sch., Bklyn., 2000—02; mem. adv. bd. N.Y.C. Bd. Edn., 2001—03; bd. dir. Heartsong Music/Art Therapy Program, 2000—05. Lead editor Emotionally Intelligent School Counseling, 2006; contbr. articles to profl. jours. Recipient Student Rschr. award, NYU, 1994; scholar, 1983—85. Mem.: Am. Psychol. Assn., World Martial Arts Assn. Avocations: martial arts, music, marathon running. Office: Queens College City Univ NY 65 30 Kissena Blvd Flushing NY 11367 Office Phone: 718-997-5246. Business E-Mail: John.Pellitteri@qc.cuny.edu.

PELOFSKY, JOEL, lawyer; b. June 23, 1937; s. Louis J. and Naomi (Hecht) Pelofsky; m. Brenda L. Greenblatt, June 19, 1960; children: Mark, Lisa, Carl. AB, Harvard U., 1959; LLB, Harvard Law Sch., 1962. Bar: Mo. 62, U.S. Dist. Ct. (we. dist.) Mo. 62, U.S. Ct. Appeals (8th cir.) 68, U.S. Ct. Appeals (10th cir.) 70. Law clk. to judge U.S. Dist. Ct. (we. dist.) Mo., 1962—63; mem. Miniace & Pelofsky, Kansas City, Mo., 1965—80; asst. pros. atty. Jackson County, Mo., 1967—71; mem. Kansas City (Mo.) City Coun., 1971—79; judge U.S. Bankruptcy Ct. Western Dist. Mo., Kansas City, 1980—85; ptnr. Shughart, Thomson & Kilroy P.C., Kansas City, 1986—95; U.S. Trustee Ark., Mo., Nebr., 1995—2003; of counsel Spencer, Fane, Britt and Browne, LLP, Kansas City, Mo., 2003—. Intermittent lectr. in law U. Mo. Bd. dirs., mem. exec. com. Truman Med. Ctr., Kansas City, Mo., pres. bd., 1988—90, chmn. bd., 1990—92; pres., trustee JVS, 2000—04; mem. Kansas City (Mo.) Sch. Bd., 2002—. Lt. US Army, 1963—65. Mem.: ABA, Am. Coll. Bankruptcy, Kansas City Met. Bar Assn., Mo. Bar. Office: 1000 Walnut Ste 1400 Kansas City MO 64106-2140 Office Phone: 816-292-8189. E-mail: jpelofsky@spencerfane.com.

PELOSI, MARCO ANTONIO, obstetrician and gynecologist, plastic surgeon; b. Lima, Peru, Oct. 5, 1942; came to the U.S., 1968; m. Luisa Garcia-Pacheco, 1962; children: Marco, Carla, Monica. BS, U. Peruana Mayor de San Marcos, Lima, 1962; MD, U. Peruana Cayetano Heredia, Lima, 1968. Cert. Am. Bd. Ob-Gyn. Intern Navy Med. Ctr., Lima, 1967-68; intern dept. ob-gyn. U. Medicine and Dentistry of N.J., Martland Hosp., Newark, 1968-69; resident dept. ob-gyn. CMDNJ-NJMC/Martland Hosp., Newark, 1969-72, fellow oncology dept. ob-gyn., 1972-74; pvt. practice, 1975—. Instr. dept. ob-gyn. UMDNJ-N.J. Med. Sch., Newark, 1972-75, clin. asst. prof., 1975-80, 80—; clin. asst. prof. dept. ob-gyn. Hahnemann Med. Coll. Phila., Pa., 1980—; attending physician dept. ob-gyn. UMDNJ-N.J. Med. Sch., Newark, 1972—, Bayonne (N.J.) Hosp., 1974—, St. Joseph Hosp., Paterson, N.J., 1974—, St. Elizabeth Hosp., Elizabeth, N.J., 1979-87, Meadowlands Hosp., Secaucus, N.J., 1979—, Greenville Hosp., Jersey City, N.J., 1980—; dir. dept. ob-gyn. Bayonne (N.J.) Hosp., 1987—; presenter; pres. Bayonne Hosp. Med. Staff, 1996—. Contbr. chpts. to books and articles, abstracts to profl. jours. Recipient 1st prize The Female Patient's 1st Annual Photo Contest, The Female Patient Mag., 1988, Physician's Recognition award AMA, 1979, 81, 84, 87, 90, 93, 96, 99, Sci. Exhibit Recognition award, Sci. Exhibit Achievement award 83rd Annual Sci. Assembly, So. Med. Assn., Washington, 1989, Physician's Recognition award Med. Soc. N.J., 1999. Fellow: ACOG (Philip F. Williams award 1972, Cont. Edn. award 1972, 1979, 1982, 1984, 1987, 1990, 1993, 1996, 1999, 2nd prize winner film festival 1999), ACS, Am. Inst. Ultrasound in Medicine, N.J. Ob-Gyn. Soc., Am. Fertility Soc., Internat. Coll. Surgeons; mem.: Internat. Soc. Cosmetogynecology (pres., founder), Med. History Soc. N.J., Royal Soc. Medicine, Am. Assn. Gynecol. Laparoscopists (1st place surg. videos 1996, winner Golden Laparoscope award 1996, Golden Laparoscope award 2001, 3rd place best surg. video 1997, first place/Golden Laparoscope award best surg. video 1998, award best surg. video 2001, 2002), Internat.Soc. Physician Historians, Am. Assn. History Medicine, Med. Collectors Assn., Gynecol. Urology Soc., Pan Am. Cancer Cytology Soc., Am. Soc. Cytology, Passaic County Med. Soc., N.J. Med. Soc., N.J. Med. Soc., Soc. Laparoendoscopic Surgeons, Soc. Minimally Invasive Surgery, Am. Soc. Profs. Ob-Gyn., One Kilo Club Soc. (pres., founder). Office: Pelosi Womens Med Ctr 350 Kennedy Blvd Bayonne NJ 07002-1313 Office Phone: 201-858-1800. E-mail: mpelosi@aol.com.

PELOSI, NANCY PATRICIA, congresswoman; b. Balt., Mar. 26, 1940; d. Thomas J. D'Alesandro Jr. and Annunciata M. Lombardi; m. Paul Pelosi, 1963; children: Nancy Corinne, Christine, Jacqueline, Paul, Alexandra. AB in Polit. Sci., Trinity Coll., 1962. Chair No. Calif. Dem. Party, 1977—81; chmn. Calif. State Dem. Com., 1981—83; committeewoman Dem. Nat. Com., 1976, 1980, 1984; fin. chmn. Dem. Senatorial Campaign Com., 1987; mem. US Congress from 5th Calif. dist., 1987-93, US Congress from 8th Calif. dist., 1987—, minority whip, 2002, minority leader, 2002—07, spkr. of the House, 2007—, mem. appropriations com., intelligence com.; vice chmn. Dem. Nat. Conv., 1996, co-chmn., 2004. Pub. Svc. award, Fedn. of Am. Societies for Experimental Biology, 1997, Congl. Svc. award, InterAction (Am. Coun. for Voluntary Internat. Action), 1999, Alan Cranston Peace award, Global Security Inst., 2003, Cesar E. Chavez Legacy award, Cesar E. Chavez Found., 2003, Nat. Legis. award, League of United Latin Am. Citizensm 2004, Golden Plate award from Acad. Achievement, 2006; named One of 100 Most Powerful Women in World, Forbes Mag., 2005, Barbara Walters-Most Fascinating Person of 2006, The World's Most Influential People, TIME mag., 2007 Democrat. Achievements include being the first woman in US history to be elected Speaker of the House, 2006. Office: US Ho Reps 2371 Rayburn Ho Office Bldg Washington DC 20515-0508 *

PELOSO, JOHN FRANCIS XAVIER, lawyer; b. NYC, Oct. 7, 1934; s. Rocco C. and Victoria P.; m. Elizabeth Byrne Peloso, Oct. 7, 1961; children: Alycia, John, Matthew. BA, Fordham U., 1956, LLB, 1960. Bar: NY 1960, US Dist. Ct. (so. dist.) NY 1962, US Ct. Appeals (2nd cir.) 1967, US Supreme Ct. 1968. Law clk. to judge U.S. Dist. Ct. (so. dist.) N.Y., 1960-61; asst. U.S. Atty. U.S. Atty.'s Office, NYC, 1961-65; assoc. Carter Ledyard & Milburn, NYC, 1965-70; chief trial counsel NYRO-SEC, NYC, 1970-75; ptnr. to chmn. Sage Gray Todd & Sims, NYC, 1975-87; ptnr. to mng. ptnr. Morgan, Lewis & Bockius, LLP, NYC, 1987-95, 95-99, sr. counsel, 2000—. Adj. prof. law Fordham Law Sch., 2000—; spkr. in field. Contbr. articles to profl. jours. Capt., inf. USAR, 1956—61. Mem. ABA (sect. corp., banking and bus. law, com. fed. regulation securities 1975—, com. bus. and corp. litig., chair subcom. securities litig. 1993-99, litig. co-chmn. com. securities 1983-87, com. on liaison with jud. 1987-88, coun. 1989-91, co-chmn. com. trial evidence 1994-95, co-chmn. task force on the ind. lawyer 1995-99), Assn. Bar of City of NY (arbitration com. 1970-73, fed. legis. com. 1975-78, fed. cts. com. 1982-86), Nat. Assn. Securities Dealers (nat. panel arbitrators 1975—, nat. arbitration com. 1982-85, fixed income com. 2005—), CPR Inst. for Dispute Resolution (Disting. Neutral). Office: Morgan Lewis & Bockius LLP 101 Park Ave Fl 44 New York NY 10178-0060 Home Phone: 203-454-4630; Office Phone: 212-309-6240. Business E-Mail: jpeloso@morganlewis.com.

PELPHREY, JOHN, men's college basketball coach; b. July 18, 1968; m. Tracy Lyon; children: Jaxson Hamilton, Ann-Marie Grace Donovan. Grad., U. Ky., Lexington, 1992. Profl. basketball player France and Spain, 1992—93; asst. coach Okla. State U., Stillwater, 1993—94, Marshall U., Huntington, W.Va., 1994—96, U. Fla., Gainesville, 1996—2002; head coach U. South Ala., Mobile, 2002—07, U. Ark., Fayetteville, 2007—. Named Sun Belt Conf. Coach of Yr., 2006; named to Ky. Hall of Fame, 2005. Office: U Ark Mens Basketball Broyles Athletic Ctr PO Box 7777 Fayetteville AR 72702 *

PELSTER, WILLIAM CHARLES, lawyer; b. St. Louis, May 11, 1942; s. William R. and Marie C. (Graefe) P.; m. Terry C. Cuthbertson, Aug. 9, 1969. BA, Oberlin Coll., 1964; JD, U. Mich., 1967. Bar: Mo. 1967, N.Y. 1968, U.S. Dist. Ct. (so. dist.) N.Y. 1968, U.S. Ct. Appeals (2d cir.) 1968, U.S. Supreme Ct. 1972. Law clk. to judge Lenord P. Moore U.S. Ct. Appeals (2d cir.), NYC, 1967-68; assoc. Donovan, Leisure, Newton & Irvine, NYC, 1968-75; ptnr. Skadden, Arps, Slate, Meagher & Flom, LLP, NYC, 1976—. Trustee Cancer Care Inc., N.Y.C., 1975—. Mem. ABA, Assn. of Bar of City of N.Y. Office: Skadden Arps Slate Meagher & Flom LLP 4 Times Sq Fl 24 New York NY 10036-6595 E-mail: wpelster@skadden.com.

PELTIER, RONALD JAMES, real estate corporation officer; b. St. Paul, Mar. 18, 1949; s. George Anthony and Shirley (Peterson) P.; m. Arlyce Corrine Brink, Feb. 15, 1970; children: Jean Paul, Janeé. BA with honors, U. Minn., 1971; MBA, St. Thomas U., 1974. Tchr. Annoka Hennepin Schs., Blaine, Minn., 1974-77; salesman Edina Realty, Mpls., 1977-78, br. mgr., 1979-80, regional mgr. St. Paul, 1980-83; gen. mgr. Edina Realty & Fin., Inc., First Realty Iowa, Mpls., St. Paul, 1983—91, v.p. & gen. mgr., 1991—92; pres., CEO Edina Realty, Mpls., St. Paul, 1992—, HomeServices of America, Inc., Edina, Minn., 1999—; founder and dir. Realty Alliance. Pres. Peltier Devel. Corp., Dellwood, Minn., 1985, White Bear (Minn.) Lake Hotel, 1987; owner Peltier Homes Contracting, 1982, ptnr. J.R. Farms, Inc., 1988, Advanced Soil Tech., 1991, Thermo Remediation of Contaminated Soil, 1991; chmn. bd. RELO. Coach Community Receation Programs, White Bear; bd. dirs. U. Minn., 1984-86, St. Andrews Lutheran Ch., Mahtomedi, Minn., 1986-87, Fairview Found., Augsburg Coll. Named Master Entrepreneur of Yr., Ernst & Young, 2002; named one of Real Estate's 25 Most Influential Thought Leaders, Realtor Mag., 2001, 2006, 5 Most Admired Individuals in Real Estate, REALTrends, 2002. Mem. Nat. Assn. Realtors, Minn. Assn. Realtors, St. Paul Bd. Realtors, Mpls. Bd. Realtors, Anoka County Bd. Realtors, Rotary Club, M Club of Univ. Minn. Avocations: golf, tennis, hockey, investing. Office: HomeServices of America 333 S 7th St 27th Floor Minneapolis MN 55402 also: Edina Realty Corp 6800 France Ave S Minneapolis MN 55435 E-mail: ronpeltier@edinarealty.com. *

PELTO, GRETEL H., nutritional anthropologist, educator; b. Mpls., May 6, 1940; d. Isaac L. and Deana (Harris) Hoffman; m. Pertti J. Pelto, July 27, 1968 (div. Dec. 1995); children: Jonathan, Dunja, Ari; m. Jean-Pierre Habicht, June 13, 1997. Student, Bennington Coll., Vt., 1957—60; BA, U. Minn., Mpls., 1963, MA, 1967, PhD, 1970; DSc (hon.), U. Helsinki, Finland, 1996. Clin. assoc. U. Conn. Sch. Medicine, Farmington, 1970-74; asst. prof. anthropology U. Conn., Storrs, 1974-77, prof. nutritional scis., 1977-92, prof. emerita, 1992—; scientist, child health divsn. WHO, Geneva, 1992-98; prof. nutritional scis. Cornell U., Ithaca, NY, 1998—2006, vis. prof., 2006. Mem. adv. bd. divsn. diarrheal disease control WHO, 1987-92; mem. adv. bd. subcom. on maternal and infant nutrition NAS, Washington, 1980-83; cons. UN U., Washington and Tokyo, 1985, Population Coun., NYC, 1980-82; vis. prof. Cornell U., Ithaca, NY, 2006-. Co-author: Anthropological Research, 1978, Community Assessment of Natural Food rces of Vitamin A; co-editor: Nutritional Anthropology, 2000; symposium editor: Jour. Nutrition, 2006; mem. editl. bd. Ecology of Food and Nutrition, Maternal and Child Nutrition, Human Orgn. Bd. dirs. Parent-Child Rsch. Ctr. for Eastern Conn., 1974-79; mem. task force Hartford Area Health Edn. Ctr., Conn., 1980-82; mem. adv. com. Travelers Ctr. on Aging, Hartford, 1988-89. Fulbright grantee, 1984; hon. rsch. fellow U. Birmingham, Eng., 1994-97; U.S. AID rsch. grantee, Mex., 1982-87. Fellow Soc. for Applied Anthropology (Malinowski award 2007), Am. Soc. for Nutrition (mem. long range planning com. 2001-05, coun. mem. 2004-05, councilor 2004—06, symposium editor 2006), Soc. for Internat. Nutritional Rsch. (bd. dirs. 1989-92); mem. Coun. on Nutritional Anthropology (pres. 1982-84, v.p. 1998-2000), Soc. for Med. Anthropology (bd. dirs. 1980-82). Avocations: photography, cooking. Home: 129 Eastlake Rd Ithaca NY 14850-9700 Office: Cornell U Div Nutritional Sci MVR 3M1 Ithaca NY 14853 Home Phone: 607-272-3262; Office Phone: 607-255-6277. Business E-Mail: gp32@cornell.edu.

PELTON, ALAN ROY, engineer, researcher, engineering educator; b. Seattle, Oct. 26, 1953; s. Claude LaVerne and Rose Marie Pelton; m. Sandra Jean Wells, July 15, 1978; children: Shannon Leigh Pelton-Topham, Sean Michael. PhD, U. Calif., Berkeley, 1982. Rsch. scientist Stanford U., Calif., 1982—83, Ames Lab., Iowa State U., 1983—86; faculty U. Notre Dame, Ind., 1986—89; tech. mgr. Raychem Corp., Menlo Park, Calif., 1989—92; dir. rsch. Nitinol Devices & Components, Fremont, Calif., 1992—; instr. U. Calif., Berkeley, 2004—. Co-founder, officer Shape Memory and Superelastic Technologies, Fremont. Editor: (book) Images of Materials; editor: (author) Proceedings of Shape Memory and Superelastic Technologies. Pres. Fremont Youth Soccer League, 1989—2003. Democrat. Roman Catholic. Achievements include patents for shape memory alloy treatment; intravascular device with improved radiopacity; radiopacity intraluminal medical device. Avocations: hiking, kayaking, camping. Office: Ndc 47533 Westinghouse Dr Fremont CA 94539 Office Phone: 510-413-1677. E-mail: apelton@ndcus.jnj.com.

PELTON, ERIK MICHAEL, lawyer; b. Boston, Nov. 12, 1972; s. Stephen Ira and Irene (Fromberg) Pelton; m. Rebecca D. Tax, Oct. 11, 2003; 1 child, Elijah I. BA, Boston U., 1994; JD, Cath. U. Am., 1997. Bar: NJ 1999. Trademark examiner US Patent and Trademark Office, Arlington, Va., 1997—99; pvt. practice Arlington, 1999—. Bd. dirs. Clarendon Alliance, Arlington, 2004—05. Named one of Top 20 Trademark Filers, Nameprotect's Trademark Insider, 2004; recipient, 2005, 2006. Office: PO Box 100637 Arlington VA 22210 Office Phone: 703-525-8009. Business E-Mail: emp@tm4smallbiz.com.

PELTON, JAMES RODGER, library director; b. St. Louis, Mar. 21, 1945; s. Norman C. and Leona V. (Schulte) Pelton; m. Sandra Lee Birdsell, Jan. 29, 1969; children: Joni Lee, Vicki Sue. BA, U. Mo., 1967, MLS, 1969. Br. libr. Scenic Regional Libr., Union, Mo., 1968—71; adminstr. Daniel Boone Regional Libr. - Columbia Ctr., Mo., 1971—78; cons. La. State Libr., Baton Rouge, 1978—80; dir. Shreve Meml. Libr., Shreveport, La., 1980—. Mem.: ALA, La. Libr. Assn. Office: Shreve Meml Libr PO Box 21523 424 Texas St Shreveport LA 71101 Office Phone: 318-226-5897. Office Fax: 318-226-4780. E-mail: jpelton@shreve-lib.org.

PELTON, JEFFREY J., surgeon; b. Milw., Feb. 21, 1957; s. Jerry E. and Jennie J. Pelton; m. Elissa E. Emmons, June 28, 1980; children: Douglas T., Gregory J., Christine E., Katharine A. MD, Uniformed Services U. Health Scis., Bethesda, Md., 1984. Diplomate Am. Bd. Surgery, 1990, Nat. Bd. Med. Examiners, 1984. Commd. 2d lt. USAF, 1980, advanced through grades to col., ret., 2004; resident in gen. surgery Wilford Hall USAF Med. Ctr., San Antonio, 1980—84, chief surg. oncology, 1991—99; fellow surg. oncology Fox Chase Cancer Ctr., Phila., 1989—91; chief surg. oncology David Grant USAF Med. Ctr., Fairfield, Calif., 1999—2004, Kaiser Permanente Mid-Atlantic Group, Washington, 2005—; med. dir. Mercy Cancer Ctr., Sacramento, 2004—05. Author: (med. textbook) ECG Essentials; contbr. articles to med. jours. Col. USAF, 1980—2004, San Antonio, TX and Fairfield, CA. Recipient Physician's Recognition award with commendation, AMA, 1994—2003. Fellow: ACS, Soc. Surg. Oncology. Office: Washington Hosp Ctr 106 Irving St NW Ste 108 Washington DC 20010 Home Phone: 301-913-2845; Office Phone: 202-877-9835.

PELTON, M. LEE, academic administrator; B magna cum laude, Wichita U., 1974; D, Harvard U., 1984. Tchg. fellow, English instr. Harvard U., 1980—86; sr. tutor Winthrop Ho., 1986; dean of student to dean of coll. Colgate U., 1986—91; dean of coll., adj. prof. Dartmouth Coll., 1991—98; pres. Willamette U., 1998—. Mem. bd. Oregon Ind. Coll. Fund, 1998—, Oregon Ind. Coll. Assn., 1998—; bd. overseers Harvard U., 2000; mem. Commn. on Minorities in Higher Edn., 2000—02. Mem.: Governor's Commn. on Financing Higher Edn. (Ore.), President's Coun. of Nat. Collegiate Athletic Assn. (Div. III), Nat. Assn. of Ind. Colleges and Universities (com. on policy analysis and pub. rels. 2000—03), Am. Coun. on Edn., Am. Assn. of Higher Edn. Office: Willamette U Office of Pres 900 State St Salem OR 97301 Office Phone: 503-370-6300, 503-370-6209. E-mail: president@willamette.edu.

PELTON, MARGARET MARIE MILLER, retired art educator, academic administrator, artist; b. Charlotte, NC, Nov. 5, 1934; d. William Andrew Miller and Helen Cook Miller Margolin; m. Donald Wesley Pelton Jr.; children: Donald W. III, Charles F. BS, U. Miami, 1956; MS, Fla. State U., 1957; EdD in Coll. Adminstrn., Southeastern Nova U., 1979. Art tchr. Miami Dade Pub. Sch., Fla., 1957—70; art instr. Kendall Campus, Miami-Dade Coll., Fla., 1970—79, dept. chair, 1971—79, assoc. dean humanities, Rank prof., 1979—86; founder, vice provost New world Sch. Arts, 1987—96; ret., 1996. Bd. mem. Fla. Very Spl. ART, 1986—96; founder Louis Wolfsou II Fla. Moving Image Archive, Miami, 1986—96, pres., 1986—, v.p., 1996—. Exhibitions include Miami Water Color Soc., Spring Exhbn., 1999, 2001, 2002, 2003 (Outstanding award), Miami Water Color Soc., Fall Exhbn., 2001 (Peoples Choice award), Macon County Fair, Franklin, NC, 2000, Watercolor Soc. NC, Western Regional Show, Asheville, 2001, Watercolor Soc. NC, New Bern, 2003, Macon County Fair, Franklin, NC, 2001, Bet Breira Gallery, 2002 (First award), Fla. Profl. Art Guild, 2003 (Second award), Bascon Louise Gallery, Highlands, NC, 2003, Art League Highlands, 2003, one-woman shows include Kendall Campus Gallery, Miami-Dade Cmty. Coll., 2002, Richmond Cottage Deering Estate, Miami, 2006, two-person exhibition, Highlands, NC, 2006, 55 other exhbns. Mem. Dade Commn. Status of Women, Fla., 1983—86; bd. mem. Dade Heritage Trust, Fla., 1995—2001. Recipient Fla. Art Educator of Yr. award, Fla. Art Edn. Assn., 1989. Mem.: DAR (regent Coral Gables chpt. 2006—), Miami Watercolor Soc. (trustee), Macon County Art Assn., NC Watercolor Soc., Fla. Watercolor Soc., United Daus. Confederacy. Republican. Presbyterian. Home (Winter): 11725 SW 82nd Rd Miami FL 33156-5104

PELTON, RUSSELL MEREDITH, lawyer; b. Chgo., May 14, 1938; BA, DePauw U., 1960; JD, U. Chgo., 1963. Bar: Ill. 1963, U.S. Supreme Ct. 1979. Assoc. Peterson, Ross, Schloerb & Seidel, Chgo., 1966—72, ptnr., 1972-90, Oppenheimer, Wolff & Donnelly, Chgo., 1990-2000, Chgo. mng. ptnr., 1992-95, 98-2000; ptnr. Ross & Hardies, Chgo., 2000—03, McGuire-Woods LLP, Chgo., 2003—. Co-founder, gen. counsel Chgo. Opportunities Industrialization Ctr., 1969—83; gen. counsel Delta Dental Plan Ill., 1979—96, Am. Assn. Neurol. Surgeons, 1983—; bd. dirs. First United Life Ins. Co., 1979—82. Pres. Wilmette Jaycees, 1970; chmn. Wilmette Sch. Bd. Caucus, 1970-71; Wilmette Dist. 39 Bd. Edn., 1972-80; bd. dirs. Wilmette United Way, 1980-86, campaign chmn., 1983-85, pres., 1985-86; Wilmette Zoning Bd. Appeals, 1989-2000, chmn., 1990-2000. Served to capt. USAF, 1963-66. Mem.: ABA, Am. Soc. Med. Assn. Counsel, Am. Health Lawyer Assn., Soc. Trial Lawyers, Chgo. Bar Assn., Ill. Bar Assn., Ill. State Dental Soc. (hon.), Plaza Club (chair 2003—06). Office: McGuireWoods LLP 77 W Wacker Dr Ste 4100 Chicago IL 60601-1815 Home Phone: 847-251-8480; Office Phone: 312-750-8652. Business E-Mail: rpelton@mcguirewoods.com.

PELTON, VIRGINIA LUE, small business owner; b. Utica, Kans., Apr. 15, 1928; d. Forrest Selby and Nellie (Simmons) Meier; m. Theodore Trower King Jr., Oct. 27, 1956 (div.); m. Harold Marcel Pelton, July 11, 1970; children: Mary Virginia Joyner, Diana Jean. Student, Kans. State U., 1946-47, Ft. Hays U., 1947-48, Washington U., St. Louis, 1950-51. Instr. Patricia Stevens Modeling Sch., Kansas City, Mo., 1948-50; model various cos., Calif. and NY, 1951-53; fashion cons. Giorgio, Beverly Hills, Calif., 1967-68, Charles Gallay, Beverly Hills, 1975-77, Dorso's, Beverly Hills, 1977-79; buyer, mgr. giftware Slavick's, Laguna Hills, Calif., 1980-83; owner P.J. Secretarial Svcs., Laguna Hills, 1980—; v.p. H.P. Fin. Inc., Laguna Hills, 1983—. Editor Profl. Network newsletter, 1980—. Sec. Leukemia Soc. Am., Santa Ana, 1985—; mem. Laguna Beach Art Mus., 1986—. Mem. Profl. Network Assn. (sec. 1986-96), Market Plus The Consumer Network, Saddleback C. of C., Laguna Hills Club, Kappa Delta. Republican. Methodist. Avocations: gourmet cooking, sewing. Home: 24942 Georgia Sue Laguna Beach CA 92653-4323

PELTZ, CISSIE JEAN, art gallery director, cartoonist; d. Morton Dunbar Liebshutz and Myrtle Jewel Friedman; m. Richard Walter Peltz, Jan. 1, 1953 (dec. Feb. 21, 1975); 1 child, David Lee. BA, U. Chgo., 1947. Freelance cartoonist Milw. Jour., 1975—77, Chgo. Tribune, 1948—68, Today's Health, Chgo., 1959—71, Cosmopolitan mag., NYC, 1950—85, Look Mag., NYC, 1950—85, N.Y. Times, NYC, 1950—85, Saturday Rev., NYC, 1950—85, Chgo. Mag., 1950—85, Great Books Found., Chgo., 1950—85; owner, dir. Peltz Gallery, Milw., 1989—. Illustrator: book Everyday Speech, 1949, Laugh Your Way to Work, 1977, illustrator: booklets, advt. filmstrips. Named Communicator of Yr., Univ. Chgo., 1963. Mem.: Milw. Art Mus. Contemporary Art Soc., Mil. Art Mus. Print Forum (v.p., pres. 1987—89, bd. dirs. 1989—2002), Milw. Art Dealers Assn. Democrat. Avocations: collecting art, theater, movies. Office: Peltz Gallery 1119 E Knapp St Milwaukee WI 53202 Office Phone: 414-223-4278. E-mail: peltzgallery@sbcglobal.net.

PELTZ, NELSON A., investment company executive; b. NYC, June 24, 1942; s. Maurice Herbert and Claire (Wechsler) P.; m. Claudia H. Peltz, 1980, 8 children; two children by previous marriage. Student, U. Pa., 1962. With A. Peltz & Sons, Inc., NYC, 1963-70; pres., CEO APS Food Systems, Inc., NYC, 1970-72, Flagstaff Corp., NYC, 1972-78, Coffee-Mat Corp. (merged with Flagstaff Corp.), Kenilworth, NJ, 1975-76; chmn. bd., CEO Triangle Industries, Inc., NYC, 1983—88, Avery Inc., 1989—93, Triarc Companies, Inc., 1993—; CEO, founding ptnr. Trian Fund Mgmt., L.P., 2005—. Chmn. bd. NPM Group, Inc.; bd. dirs., Encore Capital Group, Inc., 2003-, H. J. Heinz Co., 2006-; gen. ptnr. Brook Fund. Trustee U.S. Olympic Ski Team, 1975—. Named one of Forbes Richest Americans, 2006. Mem. Young Pres.'s Orgn., Madison Sq. Garden Club, Old Oaks Country Club, City Athletic Club. Office: Triarc Group 280 Park Ave New York NY 10017 *

PELTZER, DOUGLAS LEA, manufacturing executive; b. Clinton, Iowa, July 2, 1938; s. Albert and Mary Ardelle (Messer) P.; m. Nancy Jane Strickler, Dec. 22, 1959; children: Katharine, Eric, Kimberly. BA, Knox Coll., 1960; MS, N.Mex. State U., 1964; MBA, U. Phoenix, 1990. Rsch. engr. Advanced Computer Lab., GE, Sunnyvale, Calif., 1964—67; engr. large scale integrated circuit R&D Lab., Fairchild Camera & Instrument, Palo Alto, Calif., 1967—70, bipolar memory divsn. Mountain View, Calif., 1970—83, dir. tech., 1977—83; v.p. tech. ops. Trilogy Sys. Corp., Cupertino, Calif., 1983—85; pres. Tactical Fabs, Inc., Cupertino, 1985—89; v.p. process devel. Chips and Techs. Inc., Cupertino, 1988—92; pres., CEO Camlan, Inc., San Jose, Calif., 1992—94; staff Chip Express, Santa Clara, Calif., 1994—98; prin. Corp. Tech. Devel., Santa Clara, 1994—2004, Ft. Lauderdale, Fla., 2001—. NSF fellow, 1962-63; recipient Sherman Fairchild award for tech. excellence, 1980, Semiconductor Equipment and Materials Inst. award, 1988; Inventor of Yr. award Peninsula Patent Law Assn., 1982. Mem. IEEE, Sigma Pi Sigma. Achievements include patents in field. Home: 340 San Marco Dr Fort Lauderdale FL 33301

PELTZMAN, SAM, economics professor; b. Bklyn., Jan. 24, 1940; s. Benjamin Raphael and Ceil (Heller) P.; m. Nancy Virginia Bradney, Sept. 7, 1952; children: Shira Malka, Talya Rose. BBA, CCNY, 1960; PhD, U. Chgo., 1965. Prof. econs. UCLA, 1964-73; sr. staff economist Coun. Econ. Advisers, Washington, 1970-71; prof. econs. grad. sch. bus. U. Chgo., 1973-87, Sears, Roebuck prof., 1987-2001, dir. George J. Stigler Ctr. Study of Economy and the State, 1992—2005, Ralph and Dorothy Keller disting. svc. prof., 2001—05, Ralph and Dorothy Keller prof. emeritus, 2005—. Vis. fellow Inst. for Advanced Study Hebrew U., Jerusalem, 1978; dir. CMP Industries LLC, 1995—; mem. coun. acad. advisers Am. Enterprise Inst., 1995—. Author: Political Participation and Government Regulation, 1998; co-author: Public Policy Toward Mergers, 1967; editor Jour. Law and Econs.; contbr. articles to profl. jours. Mem. Am. Econ. Assn., Mt. Pelerin Soc. Jewish. Office: U Chgo Grad Sch Bus 5807 S Woodlawn Ave Chicago IL 60637-1620 Home Phone: 773-752-4246; Office Phone: 773-702-7457. Business E-Mail: samp@uchicago.edu.

PELUSO, JOHN, lawyer, insurance company executive; b. 1947; BA in English, St. John's U.; MBA in Mktg., Bernard Baruch Coll. (CUNY); JD, St. John's U. Law Sch. Bar: N.Y., 1987. Mgr. advt. & sales promotion Guardian Life Ins. Co. of Am., 1974—83, legal asst., 1983—87, asst. counsel, 1987—89, counsel, 1989—96, second v.p., ins. ops. counsel, 1994—96, v.p. & assoc. gen. counsel, 1996—97, v.p. & gen. counsel, 1997—. Mem. ABA. Office: Guardian Life Ins Co of Am 7 Hanover Sq New York NY 10004-2616 *

PELUSO, MICHELLE, Internet company executive, travel company executive; b. Middletown, NY; B. in Finance and Multinational Mgmt., U. of Pa. Wharton Sch. Bus.; M. in Economics, Phil. and Politics, Pembroke Coll., Oxford U. Mgmt. cons., case leader Boston Consulting Group, NYC, 1995—98; White House Fellow, sr. advisor to sec. of labor, 1998—99; founder, CEO Site59.com (acquired by Travelocity), NYC, 1999—2002; sr. v.p. product strategy and distribution Travelocity, 2002, COO, 2003, pres., CEO, 2003—. Founder A New Generation for Peace. Named Technol. Person of the Year, Travel Agent mag., 2001; named one of 50 Women to Watch, Wall Street Jour., 2004; named to Fast 50, Fast Co. mag., 2004; recipient Thoroun scholarship, Ernst and Young Entrepreneur of the Year award, 2002, Spl. Achievement Award in Bus., Nat. Italian Am. Found., 2005. Office: Travelocity 3150 Sabre Dr Southlake TX 76092 *

PELYPENKO, ELIZABETH, lawyer; b. Chgo., Dec. 17, 1961; d. Mykola and Lydia Pelypenko; m. Arthur Italo, May 31, 1997; 1 child, Valentino Italo. BA Polit. Sci., Northwestern U., Evanston, Ill., 1984; JD, U.Ga., Athens, Ga., 1988. Atty. Pelypenko Law Firm, P.C., Atlanta, 1992—. Lectr. in field. Editor: Calendar Call mag., Verdict mag.; contbr. articles to profl. jours. Named a Ga. Super Lawyer, Atlanta Mag., 2005; named Pre-eminent Lawyer, Martindale-Hubbell Registry, 2005—06. Fellow: Litig. Counsel Am., Melvin Belli Soc., Knights of the Bar; mem.: ABA, ATLA, MENSA, So. Trial Lawyers Assn., Roscoe Pound Inst., State Bar of Ga., Ga. Trial Lawyers Assn. (chair CLE com. 2004—), Million Dollar Advs. Forum, Ga. Assn. Women Lawyers, Athletic Club NE Fencing, Lawyers Club of Atlanta. Independent. Avocation: fencing. Office: Pelypenko Law Firm PC 100 Galleria Pkwy Ste 1320 Atlanta GA 30339 Office Phone: 770-937-0800. Business E-Mail: ep@pelypenkolawfirm.com.

PELZ, ROBERT LEON, lawyer; b. NYC, Nov. 18, 1918; s. Leon S. and Fanny M. (Berk) P.; m. Mary Jane Gips, Feb. 11, 1949; children: Kathryn Louise, Robert Leon Jr. AB, Columbia U., 1939, JD, 1942. Bar: N.Y. 1942. Since practiced in, NYC; ptnr. Hess Segall Guterman Pelz Steiner & Barovick, 1953-86, Loeb and Loeb, NYC, 1986-2000. Life trustee, former v.p. Fedn. Jewish Philanthropies; bd. dirs., former chmn. bd. dirs. Fedn. Jewish Philanthropies Svc. Corp.; past trustee Coll. Pharm. Scis. Columbia U.; former chmn. bd. trustees Am. Jewish Com. Capt. AUS, WWII. Office: Loeb and Loeb 345 Park Ave Fl 18 New York NY 10154-1895

PELZER, CHARLES FRANCIS, human molecular geneticist, biologist, educator, research scientist; b. Detroit, June 5, 1935; s. Francis Joseph and Edna Dorothy (Ladach) P.; m. Veronica Ann Killeen, July 7, 1972; 1 child, Mary Elizabeth. BS in Biology, U. Detroit Mercy, 1957; PhD in Human Genetics, U. Mich., 1965. Postdoctoral fellow Wabash Coll., Crawfordsville, Ind., 1965-66; instr. U. Detroit, 1966-68; asst. prof. biology dept. Saginaw Valley State U., University Center, Mich., 1969-74, assoc. prof., 1974-79, prof., 1979—, chmn. biology dept., 2002—. Rsch. assoc. Mich. State Univ., 1976-79; rsch. fellow Henry Ford Hosp., Detroit, 1982-83, 88-92; v.p. Saginaw Valley Retinitis Pigmentosa Found., Mich., 1979-81; vis. scientist Am. Inst. Biol. Scis., Washington, 1975-78; grant reviewer U.S. Dept. Edn., Washington, 1984-87, 91. Contbr. articles to profl. jours. Recipient Alumni award Saginaw Valley State U. Alumni Assn., 1971, Outstanding Svc. award Mich. Assn. Biology Tchrs., 1995; grantee Kellogg Found., 1961, NIH, 1961-64, Kettering Found., 1965-66, Mich. State U., 1977, Saginaw Valley State U. Found., 1979-82, 83-85, 86-89, Fund for Ford Hosp., 1983, Dow Chem. Co., 1988, 89, Dow Corning Co., 1988, 89, Mich. Rsch. Excellence Fund, 1993, rsch. grantee Monsanto Co., 1987. Mem. Am. Soc. Human Genetics, Genetics Soc. Am., Nat. Assn. Biology Tchrs. (dir. for Mich. Outstanding Biology Tchr.'s award), Internat. Electrophoresis Soc., Coun. for Undergrad. Rsch., N.Y. Acad. Scis., also others. Home: 43 Sawmill Creek Trail Saginaw MI 48603 Office: Saginaw Valley State U Dept Biology 7400 Bay Rd University Center MI 48710-0001 Home Phone: 989-792-0324; Office Phone: 989-964-4358. Business E-Mail: cfp@svsu.edu.

PEMBERTON, ALAN A., lawyer; b. Nov. 4, 1952; BA with honors, U. Chgo., 1974; MA in English Lit., U. Mich., 1977, JD cum laude, 1981. Ptnr. Covington & Burling, Washington, coord. Govt. Contracts Practice Group, vice chmn. pub. svc. com. Adj. prof. law Georgetown U. Law Ctr., Washington. Co-author: Obtaining Adequate Compensation for Delay, 1999, 2d edit., 2006. Bd. dirs. Indigent Civil Litig. Fund, Inc., Covington & Burling Public Sch. Project. Mem.: US Dist. Ct. DC (pro se litig. com.). Achievements include run the Boston marathon ten times. Office: Covington & Burling 1201 Pennsylvania Ave NW Washington DC 20004-2401 Office Phone: 202-662-5642. Office Fax: 202-662-6291. Business E-Mail: apemberton@cov.com.

PEMBERTON, BARBARA BUTLER, religious studies educator; d. William Bradley Butler and Elizabeth Ann McGee; m. James Beck Pemberton, Jr., Dec. 7, 1974; children: William Patrick, John David, Michael Beck. BA, U. Miss., Oxford, 1973; MA, Southwestern Bapt. Theol. Sem., Ft. Worth, 1996; PhD, Baylor U., Waco, Tex., 2000. Asst. prof. Christian missions Ouachita Bapt. U., Arkadelphia, Ark., 2001—. Sponsor Chi Rho Phi, Arkadelphia, 2002—, Pruet Sisterhood, Arkadelphia, 2006—; fellow Inst. Ch. and Theology, New Orleans Bapt. Theol. Sem., New Orleans; presenter, spkr. in field. Named Most Inspirational Prof., Ouachita Bapt. U., 2001—02. Fellow: Inst. Ch. and Theology; mem.: Soc. Bibl. Lit., Am. Acad. Religion, Evang. Theol. Soc. Office: Ouachita Bapt U 410 Ouachita street Arkadelphia AR 71998 Home Phone: 870-246-2444; Office Phone: 870-245-5541. Business E-Mail: pembertonb@obu.edu.

PEMBERTON, BRADLEY POWELL, lawyer; b. Ft. Scott, Kans., June 15, 1952; s. Howard Duane and Juanita Lucille (Powell) P.; m. Kathleen Frances Querrey, May 22, 1976 (div. Feb. 1984); m. Lori Scott, June 18, 1994. BSBA, U. Mo., Columbia, 1974; JD, U. Mo., Kansas City, 1977. Bar: Mo. 1977, U.S. Dist. Ct. (we. dist.) Mo. 1981, U.S. Tax Ct. 1981; CPA, Mo. Tax acct. Alexander Grant & Co., Kansas City, Mo., 1977-79; shareholder Polsinelli Shalton Flanigan Suelthaus, Kansas City, 1979—; also bd. dirs. Kansas City. Active Vol. Atty. Project, Kansas City, 1984—; bd. dirs. Synergy House Inc., Kansas City, 1985-88, Youth Vol. Corps of Am., 1991—, March of Dimes, 1995—. Mem. ABA, Internat. Entrepreneurs Coun. (bd. dirs.), Mo. Bar Assn., Kansas City Bar Assn., AICPAs, Mo. Soc. CPAs, Kansas City C. of C. Avocations: tennis, golf, private aviation. Home: 5806 W 131st St Shawnee Mission KS 66209-3639 Office: Polsinelli Shalton Flanigan Suelthaus 700 W 47th St Ste 1000 Kansas City MO 64112-1805 Office Phone: 816-753-1000. Business E-Mail: bpemberton@polsinelli.com.

PEMBERTON, S. MACPHERSON, govt. ofcl., educator; b. St. Kitts, W.I.; s. Abraham Ebenezer and Rachel Adelaide (Benjamin) P.; came to U.S., 1961, naturalized, 1978; Fulbright scholar in Ednl. Adminstrn., U. Utah, 1961-62; M.A. in History (Can. Govt. scholar), U. Alta., Edmonton, 1966; Ph.D. in History and Philosophy of Edn. (Univ. scholar 1967-68), U. Calif., Berkeley, 1969; m. Janette Emelda Matthew. Sch. prin., St. Kitts, 1958-61; researcher Carnegie Commn. Higher Edn., Berkeley, 1967-68, Office Instl. Research, U. Calif., Berkeley, 1968-69; research asso. NEA, Washington, 1969-70; research dir., asst. prof. higher edn. U. Pitts., 1970-71; sr. researcher, project officer Nat. Inst. Edn., HEW, Washington, 1973-76; liaison rep. for program evaluation Bur. Postsecondary Edn., Office of Edn., Washington, 1976-77; spl. asst. to asst. sec. for edn. HEW, Washington, 1977-78; v.p. Edn. Forum, U.S. Dept. Edn., 1981-82, now writer/editor office of gen. counsel assigned White House Task Force on Internat. Cultural Programs, 1978; Nat. Inst. Edn. rep. 1st Internat. Conf. Gen. Cultural Theory Edn., Wis., 1973; dep. commr. higher edn. rep. Fed. Adv. Council State Stats., 1977; asst. sec. edn. rep. Nat. Council Ednl. Research, 1978; v.p. internat. coordination, UN liaison Oppenheimer Remediation Svcs. Corp.; vis. scholar Harvard U., 1969. Recipient 1st class cert. Erdiston Tchrs. Coll., Barbados, W.I., 1958; Summer award Lincoln U., 1962; Carnegie Commn. Higher Edn. grantee, 1967; Sec. of Edn. award, 1982; Presdl. Achievement award; Hall of Fame award for contbns. to edn., Commemorative medal of honor for outstanding achievements and dedication to personal and profl. goals. Mem. Internat. Platform Assn., Am. Hist. Assn., Phi Beta Kappa. Seventh-Day Adventist. Author: Disestablishment and Educational Equity in Ireland, 1869-1879, 1979; The Federal Government and Equality of Educational Opportunity, 1981; contbr. articles to profl. jours. Home: 7620 Old Georgetown Rd Bethesda MD 20814-6150

PEÑA, AMADO MAURILIO, JR., artist, curator, lecturer; b. Laredo, Tex., Oct. 1, 1943; s. Amado Maurilio and Maria Baldomera (Arambula) P.; children: Marcos, Jose Luis, Amado Maurilio III. BA, Tex. A&I U., 1965, MA in Art, 1971. Tchr. Laredo Ind. Sch. Dist., 1965-70, Tex. A&I U., Kingsville, 1970-72, Crystal City Ind. Sch. Dist., Tex., 1972-74, Austin Ind. Sch. Dist., Tex., 1974-80; resident artist El Taller, Inc., Austin, 1985—. One man shows include Squash Blossom, Denver, 1985, Lincoln Sq. Gallery, Arlington, Tex., 1985, Galeria Capistrano, San Juan Capistrano, Calif., 1985, Andrews Gallery, Albuquerque, N.Mex., 1985, Joy Tash Gallery, Scottsdale, Ariz., 1985, Byrne-Getz Gallery, Aspen, Colo., 1985, Parke Gallery, Vail, Colo., 1985, Am. West Gallery, Chgo., 1985, Adagio Gallery, Palm Springs, Calif., 1985, Houshang's Gallery, Dallas, 1985, Mus. Native Am. Art, Spokane, Wash., 1985, El Taller, Taos, N.Mex., 1985, Austin, 1985, Kauffman Gallery, Houston, 1985, now Peña Studio Gallery, Santa Fe, N.Mex.; represented in permanent collection: Palacio del Gobernador, Baja California, Mex., Hist. Creative Arts Ctr., Lufkin, Tex., Mus. Nuevo Santander, Laredo, Smithsonian Inst., Washington, Whitney Mus., San Antonio, Tex., also corp., univs., and pvt. collections. Commd. by civic and arts orgns. for fund-raising events and spl. presentations. Avocations: purchasing quarter horses; horseback riding. Office: Peña Studio Gallery 235 Don Gaspar Santa Fe NM 87501 Office Phone: 505-820-2286. Business E-Mail: penastudios@earthlink.net.

PENA, ANTONIO FRANCISCO (TONY PENA), professional athletics coach; b. Monte Cristy, Dominican Republic, June 4, 1957; m. Amaris Pena; children: Tony, Jennifer Amaris. Profl. baseball player Pitts. Pirates, Nat. League, 1980-86, St. Louis Cardinals, 1986-89, Boston Red Sox, 1989—93, Cleveland Indians, 1994—97; mgr. Astros AAA farm club, New Orleans, 1997—2001, Kansas City Royals, 2002—05; first base coach NY Yankees, 2005—. AL Mgr. of the Year, 2003. Player Major League All-Star Game, 1982, 84; winner Gold Glove. Office: New York Yankees 161st St and River Ave Bronx NY 10451

PEÑA, JUAN JOSÉ, retired interpreter; b. Hagerman, N.Mex., Dec. 13, 1945; s. Rosa Peña; m. Petra Cervantes, Dec. 22, 1974 (div. 1982); children: Federico Ezequiel, Margarita María Blea. BA, N.Mex. Highlands U., 1968, MA, 1972, postgrad. With Albert Garcia Gen. Contr., Las Vegas, N.Mex., 1955-67; tchg. asst. N.Mex. Highlands U., Las Vegas, Nev., 1971-72, prof. Spanish, Chicano studies, 1972-78; teaching asst. U. N.Mex., Albuquerque, 1978-79; attendant N.Mex. State Mental Hosp., Las Vegas, Nev., 1982-83; staff and supervisory interpreter US Dist. Ct. N.Mex., Albquerque, N.Mex., 1983—2005; ret., 2005. Head Raza Unida del to PLO in Lebanon, 1981; head negotiator with Iranians for release of 2 Chicanos and 1 Indian; supr ct. interpreters and reporters sect. US Dist. Ct. N.Mex.; co-chmn. Cuatro-Centennial Com., Inc.; mem. exec. com. N.Mex. Human Rights Coalition. Author: (poetry) Angustias y Remembranzas; contbr. articles to profl. jour.; playwright: Canto a La Raza, 1978. Pres. Dads Against Discrimination, Albuquerque, 1993—; chmn. bd. trustees No. N.Mex. Legal Svc., Las Vegas, 1972-81; exec. com. Ind. Socialist Parties of Latin Am.; exec. commn. N.Mex. Human Rights Coalition; vice chmn. Barelas Cmty. Devel. Corp.; Barelas rep. Hist. Neighborhoods Alliance; cmty. coun. on equity Albuquerque Pub. Sch.; active N.Mex. Cmty. Loan Fund; bd. dir. Albuquerque Downtown Action Team, N.Mex. Land Grant Forum; textbook rev. commn. N.Mex. Dept. Edn., bilingual edn. adv. com.; commr. N.Mex. Textbook Selection Commn., 2001—; nat. sec. Am. GI Forum of US, 2000-01, 03-04, state comdr., 2006-07; v.p. Cmty. Enrichment Svc. Orgn., Inc.; bd. trustees, Nat. Hispanic Cultural Ctr. N.Mex., 2003—; vice-chmn., Hispano Round Table N.Mex., 1999-2003, chmn. 2003-04, 2007, co-exec. vice-pres., 2007; v.p. Cmty. Enrichment Svcs. Orgn., Inc.; bd. dir., bd. trustees Nat. Hispanic Cultural Ctr. N.Mex., v.p. 2005-06, U. N.Mex. Coll. Edu. Advancement Coun.; adv. com. U. N.Mex Coll. Edn.; chmn. N.Mex. Voter Registration Project; bd. dir. Albuquerque Downtown Action Team. Decorated Bronze Star; recipient Human Rights award City of Albuquerque Human Rights Bd., N.Mex. State Coun. Profile of Courage award Vietnam Vets. Am., 1995, N.Mex. Nat. Guard Cinco de Mayo award, 1995, Hispanics for U N.Mex. Achievement award, 1999, Human Rights award Albuquerque Human Rights Bd., 2000. Mem. N.Mex. Translator and Interpreters Assn. (pres. 1984-86), Nat. Assn. Judiciary Interpreters (sec. 1986-88), Nat. Partido Raza Unida (pres. 1976-81), N.Mex. Partido Raza Unida (pres. 1972-75, 77-78), Vietnam Vets. Am. (vice chmn. chpt. 1993—), Vietnam Vets. N.Mex., U. N.Mex. Sch. Ed. Adv. comm. mem., Nat. Assn. Chicano Studies (founding mem.), N.Mex. Chicano Studies Assn. (pres. 1972-78), Barelas Neighborhood Assn. (pres.), Hist. Neighborhoods Assn., Barelas Cmty. Devel. Corp. (rep., chmn. bd. 2006-07), Phi Sigma Iota. Democrat. Roman Catholic. Avocations: weightlifting, swimming, ice skating, hiking, camping. Home: 1115 9th St SW Albuquerque NM 87102-4027 Office: US Dist Ct Dist NMex 333 Lomas Blvd NW Albuquerque NM 87102-2272 Office Phone: 505-220-9139. Personal E-mail: jpena71@comcast.net, jjp3000@aol.com.

PEÑA, MICHAEL ANTHONY, actor; b. Chgo., Jan. 13, 1976; Actor: (films) Running Free, 1994, My Fellow Americans, 1996, Boogie Boy, 1998, La Cucaracha, 1998, Bellyfruit, 1999, Gone in Sixty Seconds, 2000, United States of Leland, 2003, Love Object, 2003, The Calcium Kid, 2004, Crash, 2004 (ALMA award for Outstanding Actor in a motion picture, 2006), Million Dollar Baby, 2004, Little Athens, 2005, Sueño, 2005, Fifty Pills, 2006, Babel, 2006, World Trade Center, 2006, Shooter, 2007, (TV films) Semper Fi, 2001, Untitled David Diamond/David Weissman Project, 2005, Walkout, 2006, (TV appearances) The Sentinel, 1998, Moesha, 1998, Profiler, 1999, Felicity, 1999-2000, The District, 2000, Roswell, 2001, Men, Women and Dogs, 2001, American Family 2002, Andy Richter Controls the Universe, 2002, Twilight Zone, 2003, ER, 2003, NYPD Blue, 1997, 2004, CSI, 2005, The Shield, 2005. Mailing: c/o Innovative Artists Talent & Lit Agy 1505 Tenth St Santa Monica CA 90401 *

PENA, RAYMUNDO JOSEPH, bishop; b. Corpus Christi, Tex., Feb. 19, 1934; s. Cosme A. and Elisa (Ramon) P. DD, Assumption Sem., San Antonio, 1957. Ordained priest Roman Cat. Ch., 1957. Asst. pastor St. Peter's Ch., Laredo, Tex., 1957—60, St. Joseph's-Our Lady of Fatima, Alamo, Tex., 1960—63, Sacred Heart, Mathis, Tex., 1963—67, Christ the King and Our Lady of Pillar Parishes, Corpus Christi, 1967—69; pastor Our Lady of Guadalupe Parish, Corpus Christi, 1969—76; v.p. Corpus Christi Diocesan Senate of Priests, 1970—76; aux. bishop San Antonio, 1976—80; bishop El Paso, 1980—95, Brownsville, Tex., 1995—. Mem. secretariat Prep. Synod of Bishops for Am., 1996—97; Synodal Father Synod of Bishops for Am., 1995. Mem.: U.S. Conf. Cath. Bishops (chmn. bishops' com. for Hispanic affairs 1987—90, bishops' com. for ch. in L.Am. 1994—97, 2000). Roman Catholic. Home: 741 Bowie Alamo TX 78516 Office: PO Box 2279 Brownsville TX 78522-2279 Office Phone: 956-542-2501. Business E-Mail: rjpena@cdob.org.

PENA, RICHARD, lawyer; b. San Antonio, Feb. 13, 1948; s. Merced and Rebecca (Trejo) P.; m. Carolyn Sarah Malley, May 25, 1979; 1 stepchild, Jason Charles Schubert. BA, U. Tex., 1970, JD, 1976. Bar: Tex. 1976, Colo. 1986. Pvt. practice, Austin, Tex., 1976—. Instr. bus. law St. Edwards U., Austin, 1983, Austin C.C., 1981-82; broker Tex. Real Estate Commn., 1980—; sports editor Austin Light, 1982. Bd. dirs. Ctr. for Battered Women, Austin, 1979-82, Austin Assn. Retarded Citizens, 1980-82; chmn. Austin Travis County Mental Health/Mental Retardation Pub. Responsibility Com., 1979-84; chmn. pvt. facilities monitoring com. Austin Assn. Retarded Citizens, 1981; bd. dirs. Boys Club of Austin, 1987-88; chair Homeless Task Force Austin, 1999—. Named one of Outstanding Young Men of Am., 1982. Fellow Tex. Bar Found. (sustaining life; trustee 1994, sec., treas. 1994, vice-chmn. 1995, chmn. 1996); mem. ABA (ho. dels., nominating com. 1998—, immigration bono com. 2000—, chair 2004-07, vice chair credentials com. 2001, state del. 2002-07), Am. Bar Found. (bd. dirs. 2000, fellows officer 2003-04, chair 2004-05, vice pres. 2006), Nat. Conf. Bar Pres. (exec. com. 2001-03), State Bar Tex. (bd. dirs. Dist. 9 1991-94, exec. com. 1992—, chmn. minority representation com. 1991-92, chair James Watson Inn 1997-98, pres. 1998-99, chmn. profl. devel. com. 1991-92, policy manual com. 1993, fed. jud. appts. com. 1984-86, opportunities for minorities in the profession com. 1990-91, mem. advt. rev. com., pres.-elect 1997, pres. 1998-99), Travis County Bar Assn. (trustee lawyer referral svc. 1984-85, bd. dirs. 1986-88, sec. 1988, pres. 1990-91, chmn. jud. screening com. 1987, chmn. 1988-89, ins. com. 1988, 89, chmn. law day banquet com. 1988-89, lawyer referrel svc. com. 1983-84, trustee 1984-86, membership com. 1989), Capitol Area Mex. Am. Lawyers (pres. 1985, Outstanding Hispanic Lawyer Austin 1989), Legal Aid Soc. Ctrl. Tex. (bd. dirs. 1984), Austin Young Lawyers Assn., Tex. Trial Lawyers Assn., Austin C. of C. (Leadership Austin 1985-86). Democrat. Office: 2028 E Ben White #220 Austin TX 78741 Office Phone: 512-327-6884. Business E-Mail: richard@rpenalaw.com.

PENBERTHY, STANLEY JOSIAH, JR., publisher; b. Des Moines, Sept. 3, 1921; s. Stanley Josiah and Beatrice Ann (Voith) P.; m. Dorothea Oehmke, July 7, 1945; 1 child, Robert Bruce. Student, Drake U., 1940—43. Engaged in broadcasting WJR, Detroit, 1941—56; freelance radio, TV, motion picture, actor, narrator, 1956—95. V.p. Fed. I-D Equipment Corp., Dearborn, Mich., 1951-62; pres. Publishers, Inc., Detroit, 1976-99. Author, prodr., narrator nat. radio series These Were Our Presidents, 1975; contbr. Mich. Sesquintennial hist. articles; author: Living Under Cover, Episodes of Life and other Relatives, Cottage Industry, The Photographs of William A. Roeser: A Talent Unfulfilled, From the Golden Tower of the Fisher Building. Past mem. bd. dirs. Sleeping Bear Dunes Citizens Coun., Traverse City, Mich., 1968-72, Cass Park Area Devel. Corp., City of Detroit, 1989; pres. Heritage Village Condominium Assn.; trustee Detroit Masonic Temple Assn.; mem. Founders Soc. Detroit Inst. Arts. Mem. AFTRA (past dir.), Adcraft Club Detroit, Detroit Execs. Assn. (dir.), Am. Film Inst., Detroit Prodrs. Assn., Broadcast Pioneers, Screen Actors Guild, Masons (33rd degree), Alpha Tau Omega (past alumni pres.). Home: 35560 Heritage Ln Farmington MI 48335-3136

PENCALL, CONSTANCE MCCONNELL, retired secondary school educator; b. New Brunswick, NJ, July 21, 1929; d. John Ernest and Frieda Ash McConnell; m. Edwin Michael Pencall; children: Steven, Brian. BA in English, Hope Coll., Holland, Mich., 1951; MA in English, U. So. Calif., LA, 1963. English tchr. Antelope Valley H.S., Lancaster, Calif., 1956—59, Arroyo H.S., El Monte, Calif., 1961—88, dept. chmn., 1984—88; ret., 1988. Master tchr. Arroyo H.S., El Monte, 1980—88, mentor tchr., 1984—85. Mem.: Mark Twain Dem. Club (vol. 2006). Avocations: travel, theater. Home: 13636 Mulberry Dr Whittier CA 90605

PENCE, HOBERT LEE, physician; b. Campton, Ky., July 14, 1941; s. Bruce Elmer and Elva (Banks) P.; m. Marsha Lee Sweet, June 29, 1962; children: Robert, Ryan, Stefanie. BS, Ohio State U., Columbus, 1963, MD, 1968. Residency Walter Reed Gen. Hosp., Washington, 1969-71, fellowship in allergy and clin. immunology, 1971-73; pvt. practice pvt. practice, Louisville, 1975—. Asst. clin. prof. medicine U. Louisville, 1976-81, assoc. clin. prof. medicine, 1981—; assoc. clin. prof. Pediat. U. Louisville, 1995—. Contbr. articles to profl. jours. V.p. Jefferson County Med. Soc., Louisville, 1984-86; pres. Greater Louisville Allergy Soc., 1990-92. Major U.S. Army, 1969-75. Fellow ACP, Am. Acad. Allergy Asthma and Immunology, Am. Coll. Allergy and Immunology; mem. Southeastern Allergy Assn. (1st v.p., pres. elect, pres. 1996). Avocations: golf, tennis, reading. Office: Kentuckiana Allergy 9113 Leesgate Rd Louisville KY 40222-5003 Office Phone: 502-426-1621.

PENCE, IRA WILSON, JR., engineering executive, researcher; b. Pontiac, Mich., June 18, 1939; s. Ira Wilson and Fern Elizabeth (Fraser) P.; m. JoAnna Springer, Sept. 5, 1959; children: Ira W. III, Teresa Ann, Deidre Lynn. BS, U. Mich., 1962, MSEE, 1964, PhD, 1970. Rsch. engr. Willow Run Labs., Ypsilanti, Mich., 1960-67, Dow Lab., Ann Arbor, Mich., 1967-70, GE, Schenectady, NY, 1970-80, engring. mgr. Charlottesville, Va., 1980-83; v.p. engring. Unimation, Inc., Danbury, Conn., 1983-87; dir. MHRC Ga. Inst. Tech., Atlanta, 1987-97, dir., pres. Intelligent Integrated Info. Sys., 1999—. Cons. Superior Motor, Hartford, 1987—89; bd. dirs. Wesley Found.; mem. adv. coun. Westinghouse, Pitts., 1983—87; treas. Wesley Comm. Ctrs., Inc., 1999—2007; exec. pres. Intelligent Integrated Info. Sys., 1999—; dir. 21iii.com, 2000—. Editor: Progress in Material Handling and Logistics, 1988; Material Handling for 90's, 1990. Trustee United Meth. Ch., 1988—, Camp Wesley, Inc. 1998— (treas. 2003-). Recipient New Product of Yr. award Innovation Today, 1985. Mem. IEEE (sr., sect. chmn. 1978), ASME (Materials Handling Engring. divsn. chair 1994). Republican. Methodist. Avocations: cabinet making, golf. Office Phone: 770-435-3183. Office Fax: 770-435-0493. Business E-Mail: ipence@isye.gatech.edu.

PENCE, JEAN VIRGINIA (JEAN PENCE), retired real estate broker; d. William Roscoe and Sophie Cottrell; m. Robert Albert Pence, June 14, 1947; children: Marjorie Pence Tuinstra, Robert J. Grad., Realtors Inst., Ill. Assn. Realtors. Cert. in real estate Central YMCA Coll., 1976. Sales assoc. William Knight Co., Realtors, LaGrange, Ill., 1962—70, sales mgr., 1970—76; pres. Pence & Co., Realtors, LaGrange, 1976—86; freelance writer Sun City Center, Fla., 1999—. Chmn. LaGrange Go-Getters Com. Channel 11 WTTG, Chgo., 1973—74. Author: (genealogy) The Cottrell Adventure With the Wright Connection, (novel) The Apprentice Angel, short stories. Sec. bd. deacons St. Andrew Presbyn. Ch., Sun City Center, 2003—05. Mem.: DAR (vice regent Clearwater chpt. 1984—86), Women's Coun. Realtors (pres. West suburban chpt. 1979—81), DuPage Bd. Realtors, LaGrange Bd. Realtors (sec.-treas. 1973—75, dir. multiple listing service 1978, chmn. profl. standards com. 1985—86), Nat. Assn. Realtors, Coterie (pres. 1982—83), LaGrange Park Woman's (sec. 1967—68), Pierre Chastain Family Assn. (press chmn. 1998—2001).

PENCE, LINDA LEE, lawyer; b. Indpls., Dec. 24, 1949; d. Woodrow Wilson and Patsy Mae (Kelley) P. BA in Polit. Sci., Ind. U., 1971, JD, 1974. Bar: Ind. 1974, DC 1982, US Dist. Ct. (no., so. dist. Ind.), US Ct. Appeals (4th, 7th, 9th, 10th, Fed. cir.), US Supreme Ct. Trial atty., chief U.S. Dept. Justice, Washington, 1974-83; assoc. Akin, Gump, Strauss, Hauer & Feld, Washington, 1983-84; ptnr. Spriggs, Bode & Hollingsworth, Washington, 1985-86, Johnson Smith Pence Densborn Wright & Heath, Washington, 1994; dir., ptnr., bus. litig., white collar criminal def. practices Sommer Barnard, Indianapolis. Bd. dir. Indianapolis Symphony Orch.; mem. & past pres. bd. vis. Ind. Univ. Sch. Law; founding mem. & past pres. Ind. Fed. Cmty. Defenders; mem. adv. council Ind. Zoological Soc. Recipient Atty. award Assn. Fed. Investigators, 1982, Atty. Gen. Spl. Commendation award, 1981. Mem. ABA (co-chmn. complex crimes com. 1987-90), Nat. Assn. Criminal Def. Lawyers, D.C. Bar Assn., Ind. State Bar Assn. (chmn. Fed. Judiciary com. 1988-91), Indianapolis Bar Assn. Office: Sommer Barnard Ste 3500 1 Indiana Sq Indianapolis IN 46204 Office Phone: 317-713-3500. Office Fax: 317-713-3699. Business E-Mail: lpence@sommerbarnard.com.

PENCE, MICHAEL RICHARD, congressman; b. Columbus, Ind., June 7, 1959; m. Karen; 3 children. Grad., Hanover Coll., 1981; JD, Ind. U. Sch. Law, 1986. Atty., 1986—91; pres. Ind. Policy Rev. Found., 1991; mem. US Congress from 2nd Ind. dist., 2001—, mem. judiciary com., internat. relations com., agr. com., chmn. Ho. Rep. Study Com., 2004—. Host (radio shows) The Mike Pence Show, 1992—99. Republican. Office: US Ho Reps 426 Cannon Ho Office Bldg Washington DC 20515-1406 Office Phone: 202-225-3021. Office Fax: 202-225-3382. *

PENCE, ROBERT DUDLEY, biomedical researcher, consultant, hospital administrator; b. Hillsboro, Ohio, June 16, 1928; s. Glenn Roush and Mildred (Wright) P. BA cum laude, Miami U., Oxford, Ohio, 1950; postgrad., U. Montpellier, France, 1950-51. Mktg. rep. Tex. Petroleum Co., West Africa, 1956-58; mgr. lab. and office svcs. Sloan-Kettering Inst. for Cancer Rsch., NYC, 1958-68; bus. mgr., cancer rsch. inst. New Eng. Deaconess Hosp., Boston, 1968-72, adminstr. Shields Warren Radiation Lab., 1970-78, asst. dir., 1972-86, adminstrv. dir., cancer rsch. inst., 1974-88, adminstrv. dir. Shields Warren Radiation Lab., 1978-88, dir. div. of rsch., 1986-88, cons., 1988—. Field liaison fellow ACS, Chgo., 1981-88. Pres. Am. Cancer Soc., Brookline, Mass. Served to lt. (j.g.) USN, 1951-55. Fulbright scholar, Montpellier, 1950. Mem. Assn. Community Cancer Ctrs. (del.), Internat. Union Against Cancer (U.S. standing com.), Assn. Am. Cancer Insts., Soc. Rsch. Adminstrs. (charter), Nat. Coun. Univ. Rsch. Adminstrs., Nat. Tumor Registrars Assn. (advisor 1980—), Tumor Registrars Assn. New Eng. (bd. dirs. 1975—), Phi Beta Kappa. Home: 30 Driftwood Cir Norwood MA 02062-5505

PENCE, STEPHEN BEVILLE, lieutenant governor; b. Dec. 22, 1953; m. Ruth Ann Cox; 5 children. BS, Ea. Ky. U., 1976, MBA, 1978; JD, U. Ky., 1981; PhD (hon.), Eastern Ky. U., 2004. Asst. atty. gen. State of Ky., 1981—82; assoc. Taustine and Post, 1987—88, Borowitz and Goldsmith, 1988—90; ptnr. Sheffer and Hoffman, 1995—96, Pedley, Zielke, Gordinier and Pence, Louisville, 1996—2001; U.S. Atty. We. Dist. Ky U.S. Dept. Justice, 2001—03; lt. gov Commonwealth of Ky., 2003—. JAG Corps US Army, 1982—87. Recipient Ky Bar Assn.'s Outstanding Lawyer award, 1995. Republican. Office: Office Lt Governor 700 Capitol Ave Ste 142 Frankfort KY 40601 Office Phone: 502-564-2611. Office Fax: 502-564-2849.

PENCOLA, ANNAMARIA REGINA, elementary school educator; d. Patrick Andrew and Regina Burnette Pencola. BS, Longwood Coll., Farmville, Va., 1977—81, MS, 1988. Sch. leadership team Smithfield Mid. Sch., 2004—05; treas. Isle of Wight Edn. Assn., Va., 2003—. Music director (original musical) A Crack in the Sidewalk; editor: (newsletter) The Real Smithfield Jaycees Newsletter (Best in State- 1st Pl., 1990). Choir dir. Good Shepherd Cath. Ch., Smithfield, 2005—06. Mem.: Women of the Moose, Chi Sigma Iota. Episcopalian/Roman Catholic. Avocations: gardening, animals, music. Home Phone: 757-357-6991; Office Phone: 757-357-3021. Home Fax: none.

PENDAS, DEVIN OWEN, history professor; b. Colorado Springs, Colo., Oct. 24, 1966; m. Christine McAllister, Sept. 2, 1996; children: Olivia Fiona, Owen James. BA, Carleton Coll., Northfield, Minn., 1989; MA, U. Chgo., PhD, 2000. Collegiate asst. prof. U. Chgo., 2000—03; asst. prof. history Boston Coll., Chestnut Hill, Mass., 2003—06, assoc. prof. history, 2006—. Author: (book) The Frankfurt Auschwitz Trial, 1963-1965. Recipient doctoral rsch. grant, German Acad. Exch. Svc., 1996—97, dissertation grant, MacArthur Found., 1998—99. Office: Boston Coll Dept History 140 Commonwealth Ave Chestnut Hill MA 02467 Home Phone: 508-545-0510; Office Phone: 617-552-6881.

PENDER, MARTHA HELEN, retired dramatic soprano; b. Abilene, Tex., Nov. 8, 1927; d. Herman Arthur and Mary (Paxton) Pender. MusB, North Tex. State U., 1949; MusM, U. Tex., 1970; pvt. studies, Rome, 1950—67. Voice tchr. Ind. U., 1967—68, Tex. Tech U., Lubbock, 1968—73; pvt. practice in studio, 1973—95. Organizer reopening Paramount Theater, Abilene, 1981, organizer concert series, 1981—83. Opera debut with world famous tenor Beniamino Gigli: Cavaleria Rusticana, 1953, soprano: numerous concert recs. and roles in Norma, AIDA, Nabucco, Tosca, 1953—67, Lady MacBeth, 1964, Requiem, Tex. Tech. U., 1970—73. Organizer reopening Paramount Theater, Abilene, Tex., 1981, organizer concert series, 1981—83. Recipient Patron of Arts award, Abilene Cultural Affairs Coun., 1989, Disting. Svc. award, Harmony Club, 2002. Mem.: Nat. Assn. Tchrs. Singing (life), Abilene Opera Assn. (founder, first pres.), Alpha Psi Omega (life), Sigma Alpha Iota (life). Republican. Baptist. Home: 1209 Musken Rd Apt H Abilene TX 79601

PENDERGRAFT, DAVID, management consultant; s. Ray Daniel and Sue Pendergraft; m. Wendy Alexander, Nov. 16, 1991; 1 child, Kelsey. BS in Math., USAF Acad., Colorado Springs, Colorado, 1987; MS in Mgmt. Sci., U. Dayton, Ohio, 1992. Commd. 2d lt. USAF, 1987, advanced through grades to capt., 1999; mgr. Accenture, Reston, Va., 1999—2002, sr. mgr., 2002—; advanced through grades to maj. USAFR, 2001. Decorated

Meritorious Svc. medal USAF, Nat. Def. Svc. medal, Air Force Commendation medal, Air Force Achievement medal. Achievements include patents for security checkpoint simulation, mobile security unit; patents pending for effective security scheduler. Office: Accenture 11951 Freedom Dr Reston VA 20190 Personal E-mail: david.r.pendergraft@accenture.com.

PENDERGRAFT, JANICE GAYLE, volunteer; b. San Antonio, Mar. 9, 1950; d. Janice Gayle and John Joseph Pendergraft (Stepfather); m. Pete E. Kraus, Nov. 3, 1973 (dec. Aug. 3, 1987); 1 child, Heather Kraus; m. John Joseph Pendergraft, June 18, 1988. Cert. dental asst., L.A. Coll. Med. and Dental Assts., San Bernardino, Calif., 1969. Cert. dental asst. Vol. M.A.D.D., San Bernardino, 1995—, Ronald McDonald House, Loma Linda, Calif., 1998—. Author poetry. Active Yucaipa Edn. Bd., Calif., 1980—98. Recipient several poetry awards, 1998—2002. Office: Ronald Mcdonald House Barton Rd Loma Linda CA 92353

PENDERGRASS, HENRY PANCOAST, radiologist, nuclear medicine physician; b. Bryn Mawr, Pa., Jan. 29, 1925; s. Eugene Percival and Rebecca (Barker) P.; m. Carol Lowe Dodson, Aug. 27, 1960 (dec. Aug. 1993); children: Sharon (dec. Aug. 1993), Lisa (dec. Aug. 1993), Deborah, Margaret; m. Carol Minster Roberts, Oct. 2, 1994. Student, U.S. Naval Acad., 1944-46; AB, Princeton U., 1948; MD, U. Pa., 1952; MPH, Harvard U., 1969. Diplomate Am. Bd. Radiology, Am. Bd. Nuc. Medicine. Intern Pa. Hosp., 1952—53; resident Hosp. U. Pa., 1953—56; mem. staff and faculty U. Pa. Med. Sch. and Univ. Hosp., Phila., 1956—58, U. Pa. Med. Sch. & U. Hosp., 1960—61; clin. asst. in neuroradiology Inst. Neurology Queen Sq., London, 1959-60; mem. staff and faculty Harvard U. Med. Sch. and Mass. Gen. Hosp., Boston, 1958-59, 61-76; prof. radiology Vanderbilt U. Sch. Medicine, Nashville, 1976-95, prof. emeritus, 1995—, vice chmn., 1976-89; adj. prof. radiology U. Pa. Sch. Medicine, Phila., 1996—. Mem. editorial bd. Am. Family Physician, 1980-94, Jour. Digital Imaging, 1987-96; contbr. chpts. to books, articles to med. jours. Mem. cancer control rev. com. Nat. Cancer Inst., 1975-79; Bd. dirs. state and local div. Am. Cancer Soc., 1976-85; mem. Project Hope Med. Mission, Peru, 1962; trustee Harpeth Hall Sch., Nashville, 1983-88. With U.S. Army, USN, 1943-46. Am. Cancer Soc. grantee, 1956-57; Nat. Cancer Inst. grantee, 1957-58; Nat. Inst. Neurol. Disease and Blindness grantee, 1959-60; Nat. Inst. Gen. Med. Scis. grantee, 1968-69. Fellow: AMA (sect. coun. on radiology 1979—99, chair 1997-99, sect. on med. schs. 1979—99, sec. 1986—97, mem. ho. of dels. 1986—99, specialty and svc. sect. 1986—99, grad. med. edn. adv. com. 1994—97, chair 1996, Gold medal 1994), Tenn. Radiol. Soc. (exec. com. 1984—88, pres.-elect then pres. 1985—86, Disting. Svc. award 1993), Soc. Magnetic Resonance in Medicine, Soc. Thoracic Imaging, Mid. Tenn. Radiol. Soc. (pres. 1984—85), Tenn. Med. Assn., Am. Soc. Emergency Radiology, Radiol. Soc. N.Am. (bd. dir. 1972—77, chmn. 1975—76, pres.-elect then pres. 1977—78, appointee to AMA ho. dels. 1986—97, sec.-treas. Edn. Found. 1988—90, trustee 1984—90, Gold medal 1984), Nashville Acad. Medicine (chmn. com. on ethics 1981—82), Mass. Med. Soc. (counselor 1968—76), Mass. Radiol. Soc. (v.p. 1967—68, 1975—76, sec.-treas. 1985—94), Assn. U. Radiologists, Ea. Radiol. Soc. (sci. program chmn. 1964, pres. 1968—72, trustee 1968—72), Coun. on Med. Specialty Socs., Brit. Inst. Radiology, Am. Roentgen Ray Soc., Am. Coll. Radiology (coun. steering com. 1968—73, bd. chancellors 1977—81, appointee to AMA ho. of dels. 1977—99, coun., Gold medal 2002); mem.: Cap & Gown Club (Princeton, NJ), Merion Golf Club, Belle Meade Country Club, Merion Cricket Club, Amateur Ski Club NY, Delta Psi, Sigma Xi. Home: 1400 Waverly Rd Villa 25 Gladwyne PA 19035-1273

PENDLETON, AUSTIN, actor, theater director; b. Warren, Ohio, Mar. 27, 1940; m. Katina Commings; 1 child, Audrey Christine. BA, Yale U., 1961. Apprentice Williamstown Theatre Festival, Mass., 1957—58; actor & dir. Steppenwolf Co., 1970; artistic dir. Circle Repertory Co., NYC, 1995—. Actor: (plays) Oh Dad, Poor Dad, Momma's Hung You in the Closet and I'm Feeling So Sad, 1962, Fiddler on the Roof, 1964, Hail Scrawdyke, 1966 (Clarnece Derwent award), The Little Foxes, 1967, The Last Sweet Days of Isaac, 1970 (Obie award, Drama Critic's Poll award), An American Millionaire, 1974, The Sorrows of Frederick, 1976, The Three Sisters, 1977, Julius Caesar, 1978, Waiting for Godot, 1979, Doubles, 1985, Booth, Uncle Bob, Orson's Shadow, 2001, 2005; dir.: Shelter, 1973, Little Egolf, 1974, Benita Cereno, 1976, The Runner Stumbles, 1976, After the Fall, 1980; (TV films) Say Goodnight Gracie, 1979; actor: Alice in Wonderland, 1983, Lethal Innocence, 1991, Four Eyes and Six-Guns, 1992, Don't Drink the Water, 1994, Long Island Fever, 1995; (films) Skidoo, 1968, Catch-22, 1970, What's Up, Doc?, 1972, Every Little Crook and Nanny, 1972, The Thief Who Came to Dinner, 1973, The Muppet Movie, 1979, Starting Over, 1979, Simon, 1980, First Family, 1980, Off Beat, 1986, Short Circuit, 1986, Mr. & Mrs. Bridge, 1990, The Ballad of the Sad Cafe, 1991, True Identity, 1991, My Cousin Vinny, 1992, My Boyfriend's Back, 1993, Mr. Nanny, 1993, Guarding Tess, 1994, Two Much, 1995, Sgt. Bilko, 1996, The Proprietor, 1996, The Associate, 1996, The Mirror Has Two Faces, 1996, Amistad, 1997, Brokendown Love Story, 1999, Joe the King, 1999, Fast Food, Fast Women, 2000, A Beautiful Mind, 2001, (voice) Finding Nemo, 2003, Uptown Girls, 2003, Christmas with the Kranks, 2004, Dirty Work, 2005.

PENDLETON, ELISHA DONSHELL, molecular biologist, researcher; d. Riley and Lenora Pendleton. BS in Chemistry, So. U., Baton Rouge, 1998; MS, U. Iowa, Iowa City, 2003. Rsch. tech. U. Chgo., 2003—. Coord. Rock Ages Baptist Ch., Maywood, Ill., 2003. Fellow, GAANN, 1998. Office: U Chgo 5841 S Maryland Ave Chicago IL 60637 Home Phone: 630-338-9218. E-mail: ependlet@uchicago.edu.

PENDLETON, FLORENCE HOWARD, former shadow senator; b. Columbus, Ga., Jan. 1928; d. John Milton and Elease Brooks Howard; m. Oscar Henry Pendleton, 1943; children: Oscar Henry Jr., Howard Thompson. BS, Howard U., 1949, MS, 1957. Tchr. Columbus Pub. Sch., Ga., 1951—55; instr. Morgan State Coll., Balt., 1957—58; tchr. DC Pub. Sch., Washington, 1958—70, asst. prin., 1970—80, prin., 1980—93; ret., 1993; chmn. Ward Five Dem. Com., Washington, 1979—82; mem. DC Dem. State Party, Washington, 1979—90; DC shadow senator to U.S. Congress, 1995—2006. Alt. delegate Dem. Nat. Convention, NYC, 1980; commr. Ward Five C07 Advisory Neighborhood Com. Clerk Berean Baptist Ch., 1965—94, clerk emeritus, 1994—. Named Disting. Citizen, Washington, 1980, Outstanding Cmty. Leader Ward Five, Berean Baptist Ch., 1981. Mem.: South St. And Affiliate Streets Block Club (pres. 1975—), Bloomingdale's Civic Assn. (edn. chmn. 1978—80), Ctr. City Cmty. Corp. (mem. chmn. exec. com. 1976—79). Democrat. Home Phone: 202-232-2010; Office Phone: 202-727-8099. Office Fax: 202-483-6301. *

PENDLETON, MARY CATHERINE, retired foreign service officer; b. Louisville, June 15, 1940; d. Joseph S. and Katherine R. (Toebbe) Pendleton. BA, Spalding Coll., 1962; MA, Ind. U., 1969; cert., Nat. Def. U., 1990; D (hon.), U. N. Testemitanu, Moldova, 1994. Cert. secondary tchr. Ky. Tchr. Presentation Acad., Louisville, 1962-66; vol. Peace Corps, Tunis, Tunisia, 1966-68; employment counselor Ky. Dept. for Human Resources, Louisville, 1969-75; gen. svcs. Am. Embassy, Khartoum, Sudan, 1975-77, counsular officer Manila, 1978-79, adminstrv. officer Bangui, Central African Republic, 1979-82, Lusaka, Zambia, 1982-84; post mgmt. officer Dept. of State Bur. European and Can. Affairs, Washington, 1984-87; adminstrv. counselor Am. Embassy, Bucharest, Romania, 1987-89; dir. adminstrv. tng. divsn. Fgn. Svc. Inst., Arlington, Va., 1990-92; ambassador Am. Embassy, Chisinau, Moldova, 1992-95, adminstrv. counselor Brussels, 1995-98; consul gen. U.S. Consulate Gen., Montreal, 1998-2001; mgmt. counselor Am. Embassy, Cairo, 2001—04; diplomat in residence U. Memphis, 2004—05; ret., 2005. Bd. dirs. Cairo Am. Coll., 2001—04; vol. instr. Presdl. Classroom, 2006—; bd. dirs. Am. Sch. Bucharest, 1987—89. Named to, Hon. Order Ky. Cols., 1988. Democrat. Roman Catholic. Avocation: outdoor activities. Home: 1946 N Cleveland St Arlington VA 22201 Personal E-mail: pendletonmc@gmail.com.

PENDLETON, MILES STEVENS, JR., diplomat; b. Montclair, NJ, Mar. 22, 1939; s. Miles Stevens and Lucille (Bond) P.; m. Elisabeth Morgan, Aug. 13, 1967; children: Constance Morrow, Nathaniel Palmer. BA magna cum laude, Yale U., 1961; MPA, Harvard U., 1967; diploma, Nat. War Coll., 1980. Tchr. Ghana Secondary Sch., Koforidua, 1962-63, Adisadel Coll., Cape Coast, Ghana, 1963-64; vice consul Am. Embassy, Tel Aviv, 1968-70, polit. and econ. officer Bujumbura, Burundi, 1970-72; watch officer Ops. Ctr. Dept. State, Washington, 1972-73, staff officer Secretariat Staff, 1973-74, spl. asst. to Dep. Sec. of State Office Dep. Sec., 1974-76, dep. dir. Office of No. European Affairs, 1980-82, dir. Office of Israel and Arab-Israel Affairs, 1982-83, exec. asst. to under sec. of state for polit. affairs, 1983-85, dir. Office of Ecology and Terrestrial Conservation, 1995-97; polit. officer U.S. Mission to NATO, Brussels, 1976-79; min.-counselor for polit. affairs Am. Embassy, London, 1985-89, min., counselor for polit. affairs Paris, 1989-93; prof. strategy Indsl. Coll. Armed Forces Nat. Def. U., Washington, 1993-95. Mem. Am. Fgn. Svc. Assn., North Haven (Maine) Yacht Club, Met. Club (Washington), Phi Beta Kappa. Avocations: sailing, reading. Home: 3410 Lowell St NW Washington DC 20016-5023 Office Phone: 202-363-2601. E-mail: milespendelton@hotmail.com.

PENDLETON, ROBERT GRUBB, pharmacologist; b. Kansas City, Mo., Apr. 24, 1939; AA, Kansas City Jr. Coll., 1959; AB in Chemistry, U. Mo., 1961; PhD in Pharmacology, U. Kans., 1966. Sr. scientist SmithKline and French, Phila., 1966-67, assoc. sr. investigator, 1967-69, sr. investigator, 1969-74, asst. dir., 1974-79, assoc. dir., 1977-80, dir. pharmacology, 1980-81, Rorer Ctrl. Rsch., King of Prussia, 1986-90, Sepracor, Marlborough, Mass., 1991—96; dir. gastroenterology Merck, West Point, 1981-86; lectr. pharmacology Thomas Jefferson U., 1997—2006; assoc. prof. Temple U., Phila., 1993—. Lab. sci. cons. Office Surgeon Gen., U.S. Army, Washington, 1989—96, Ft. Detrick, Md., 1996—99. Col. US Army. Decorated Legion of Merit. Mem.: Soc. Armed Forces Med. Lab. Scientist, Am. Chem. Soc., Am. Soc. Pharmacology and Exptl. Therapeutics. Achievements include patents for dopamine receptor agonists; discovery of new drugs to activate dopamine reactors in CNS and kidney, PNMT inhibitors; new drugs to inhibit epinephrine biosynthesis in adrenal gland and CNS; new drugs to block histamine receptors insurmountably including Pepcid; tricyclic antidepressants DMI act in CNS to decrease gastric acid secretion; roles of DMI in gut; research in pharmacology of chiral molecules including Xopenex and in transgenic Drosophila models of Parkinson's disease and neurodevelopment. Avocation: ballroom dancing. Home and Office: 1312 Sumneytown Pike Lower Gwynedd PA 19002-1303 Office Phone: 215-654-5022. Personal E-mail: robertpendleton@comcast.net.

PENDLEY, DONALD LEE, association executive; b. Jersey City, Nov. 5, 1950; s. Donald L. and Loretta M. (Purcell) P.; m. Donna Lynn Meade, Oct. 14, 1984; 1 child, Katelyn. BA, Montclair State Coll., 1972; MA, Syracuse U., 1974. Reporter/rewriter The Herald-News, Passaic, N.J., 1969-72; reporter The Dispatch, Union City, N.J., 1973; writer Keep America Beautiful, Inc., NYC, 1974-75, comm. dir., 1976-78, v.p. comm. program devel., 1979-84; sr. v.p. comm. Greater Newark C. of C., 1985-86; dir. pub. rels. Internat. Coun. Shopping Ctrs., NYC, 1987-92; exec. dir. N.J. Hospice and Palliative Care Orgn., Scotch Plains, N.J., 1993-97, pres., 1997—. Creator, dir. theatre composer series William Carlos Williams Ctr., 1987-91; creator, dir. SRO Cabaret Series, 1991-99. Pres. State Repertory Opera, South Orange, N.J., 1981-85, 92-99, Ars Musica Chorale, Englewood, N.J., 1979-81; mem. steering com. Coun. of States, 1999—2003, chmn. 2000—03; bd. dirs. Nat. Hospice Orgn., 2000—03; pres. Cmty. Health Charities of NJ, 2003—06. Recipient Award of Excellence Am. C. of C. Execs. 1986, Gold Key awards, Pub. Rels. News, 1982, 86. Mem. PRSA (accredited, sec.-treas. assn. sec. 1989-90, vice-chmn. assn. sect. 1990-91, chmn. 1991-92), Am. Soc. Assn. Execs. (cert., Gold Circle award 1988, comm. sect. coun. 1994-96, dean Sch. Pub. Rels. 1998-2000), Am. Mensa, Ltd. (nat. devel. officer 1985-89, 96-2003, regional tng. officer 1989-93), Intertel. Avocations: music, photography. Home: 32 Hamilton Rd Glen Ridge NJ 07028-1109 Business E-Mail: don@njhospice.org.

PENDLEY, STEPHEN, social studies educator, department chairman; Degree with honors in history, SUNY, New Paltz, 2003. Dept. chair social studies NY Mil. Acad., Cornwall on Hudson, 2003—07. Home and Office: 78 Academy Ave Cornwall On Hudson NY 12520 Home Phone: 845-534-3710; Office Phone: 845-534-3710. Business E-Mail: spendley@nyma.org.

PENDLEY, WILLIAM TYLER, military officer, educator; b. Paris, Ky., June 21, 1936; s. Louis Tyler and Virginia Lorene (Poplin) P.; m. Anne Carroll Cooke, Dec. 13, 1958; children: Stephen Tyler, Robert Randolph, Lisa Carroll, Leslie Brooks. BS in Engring., U.S. Naval Acad., 1958; MA, Am. U., Washington, 1965. Commd. ensign USN, 1958, advanced through grades to rear adm., 1983; comdg. officer Patrol Squadron 45, Jacksonville, Fla., 1975-76; ops. officer Patrol Wing 11, U.S. Atlantic Fleet, Jacksonville, 1976-78, comdr., 1979-81; exec. sec. for joint chief of staff matters Chief Naval Ops., Washington, 1978-79, planner for joint chief of staff matters, 1981-82, dir. plans policy and strategy divsn., 1985-86; exec. asst. to comdr. in chief U.S. Pacific Fleet, Pearl Harbor, Hawaii, 1982-83; comdr. patrol wings U.S. Atlantic Fleet, Brunswick, Maine, 1983-85; commdr. Naval Forces Korea, Seoul, 1986-89; sr. mem. UN Mil. Armistice Commn., 1986-89; dir. strategic plans and policy USCINCPAC, Camp H. M. Smith, Hawaii, 1989-91; dep. asst. sec. def. for East Asia and Pacific affairs Dept. Def., Washington, 1992-93; prof. internat. rels. Air War Coll., Maxwell AFB, Ala., 1993-98. Lectr. and cons., 1998—; fellow Georgetown U. Leadership Seminar, Washington, 1985. Co-author: Nuclear Coexistence, 1994; contbr. articles to profl. jours. Decorated Def. D.S.M. with oak leaf cluster, Legion of Merit with 4 gold stars; named hon. Ky. Col., 1975; recipient Def. medal for disting. pub. svc., 1993. Mem. Phi Kappa Phi, Pi Gamma Mu. Methodist. Avocations: golf, travel. Home: 10 Walden Ln Bluffton SC 29909 Office Phone: 843-589-9080. E-mail: pendleyw@yahoo.com.

PENDRY, PATTIE LOUISE, writer; b. Raleigh, NC, Sept. 11, 1946; d. William Henry and Tempie Lee Walker; m. Michael Leigh Pendry, Nov. 12, 1978; children: Keith, Patrick, Elizabeth. Author: You Are Never Alone, 1997, A View from Afar, 1997, Lord Teach Me How to Pray, 1999, Poems of Blessing and Encouragement, 2003. Republican. Avocations: camping, fishing, mountain climbing. Home: 3653 Wickersham Way Raleigh NC 27604-4064 Office: Internat For Jesus Ministries PO Box 13007 Raleigh NC 27605-3007 Office Phone: 919-755-1547.

PENFIELD, PAUL LIVINGSTONE, JR., electrical engineering educator; b. Detroit, May 28, 1933; s. Paul Livingstone and Charlotte Wentworth (Gilman) P.; m. Martha Elise Dieterle, Aug. 24, 1956 (dec. Apr. 1988); children: David Wesley, Patricia Jane, Michael Baldwin; m. Barbara Jean Buehrig Lory, July 22, 1989. BA, Amherst Coll., 1955; ScD, MIT, 1960. Asst. prof. elec. engring. MIT, Cambridge, 1960-64, assoc. prof., 1964-69, prof., 1969—2005, head dept. elec. engring. and computer sci., 1989-99. Author: Frequency-Power Formulas, 1960, MARTHA User's Manual, 1971; co-author: Varactor Applications, 1962, Electrodynamics of Moving Media, 1967, Tellegen's Theorem and Electrical Networks, 1970. Sr. postdoctoral fellow NSF, 1966-67. Fellow IEEE (chmn. Boston sect. 1971-72, Darlington award 1985, Centennial medal 1984, Golden Jubilee award 1999); mem. Nat. Acad. Engring., Am. Phys. Soc., Assn. for Computing Machinery, Audio Engring. Soc., Sigma Xi. Avocation: field identification of ferns and fern hybrids. Office: MIT Dept EECS Cambridge MA 02139

PENG, JUNHUA, molecular biologist, botanist; b. Sichuan, China, Sept. 4, 1962; BS in Agronomy, Sichuan Agrl. U., China, 1983, MS in Plant Genetics & Breeding, 1986; PhD in Molecular Biology/Plant Genomics (scholar 1996-2000), U. Haifa, Israel, 2001. Asst. scientist Crop Inst. Sichuan Acad. Agrl. Scis., Chengdu, China, 1986—92, rsch. assoc. prof., 1992—94; assoc. prof. dept. agronomy Guangdong Ocean U., China, 1994—96; sr. rsch. assoc. dept. soil and crop scis. Colo. State U., Ft. Collins, Colo., 2000—05, asst. prof., 2005—. Co-author: Crop Breeding, 1996, Crop Breeding Research, 1994; reviewer numerous jour. manuscripts; contbr. over 80 articles to profl. jours. Grantee, Fgn. Ministry Israel, 1997; scholar, Israel-China Friendship Soc., 1998, China Friendship Soc., 1999; vis. scholar, Govt. of Japan, 1989; EMBO Short Term fellow, Germany, 1998. Mem.: AAAS, Genetics Soc. Am., China Crop Sci. Soc., Internat. Genetics Soc., China Genetics Soc., Soc. Advancement Breeding Rsch. Asia and Oceania, Israelis Soc. Plant Sci. and Plant Molecular Biology. Achievements include research in plant genomics; molecular marker techniques; genomic mapping; bioinformatics; QTL analysis; quantitative genetics and biostatistics; plant breeding. Office: Colo State U Dept Soil and Crop Scis Fort Collins CO 80523-1170 Business E-Mail: jpeng@lamar.colostate.edu.

PENG, LIANG-CHUAN, mechanical engineer; b. Taiwan, Feb. 6, 1936; came to U.S., 1965, naturalized, 1973; s. Mu-Sui and Wang-Su (Yang) P.; m. Wen-Fong Kao, Nov. 18, 1962; children: Tsen-Loong, Tsen-Hsin, Lina, Linda. Diploma, Taipei Inst. Tech., 1960; MS, Kans. State U., 1967. Registered profl. engr., Tex., Calif. Project engr. Taiwan Power Co., 1965—66; asst. engr. Carlson & Sweatt, NYC, 1966—67, Pioneer Engrs., Chgo., 1967—68; mech. engr. Bechtel, San Francisco, 1969—71; sr. specialist Nuc. Svcs. Co., San Jose, Calif., 1971—75; sr. engr. Brown & Root, Houston, 1975; stress engr. Foster Wheeler, Houston, 1976; staff engr. AAA Technologists, Houston, 1977; prin. engr. M.W. Kellogg, Houston, 1978—82; pres., owner Peng Engring., Houston, 1982—. Instr. U. Houston; condr. piping tech. seminars. Developer: (computer programs) SIMFLEX. Chmn. South Bay Area Formosan Assn., 1974, No. Calif. Formosan Fedn., 1975. Mem. ASME, NSPE. Buddhist. Home: 3010 Manila Ln Houston TX 77043-1312 Business E-Mail: lcpeng@pipestress.com.

PENG, STANFORD LEE-YU, physician; s. Syd and Felicia Peng; m. Andrea Jeanne Gerth, Sept. 8, 2001; children: Avery, Charlotte. PhD, Yale U., New Haven, Conn., 1991—96, MD, 1991—97. Cert. in internal medicine ACP, 2000, in rheumatology ACP, 2002, diplomate Am. Bd. Internal Medicine, Am. Bd. Rheumatology. Intern Hosp. U. Pa., Phila., 1997—98, resident in internal medicine, 1998—99; rsch. assoc. immunology and infectious diseases Harvard U. Sch. Pub. Health, Boston, 2002; clin. rsch. fellow in rheumatology Brigham and Women's Hosp., Boston, 1999—2002; asst. prof. Wash. U. Sch. Medicine, St. Louis, 2002—05; clin. asst. prof. U Calif., San Francisco, 2005—. Group leader Roche, Palo Alto, 2005, dir. arthritis rsch., 2005—07, sr. dir. translational med. leader, rheumatology, 2007—. Named Keck Disting. Young Scholar, 2005; recipient Arthritis Investigator, Arthritis Found., 2003. Mem.: Am. Assn. Immunologists, Am. Coll. Rheumatology. Office: 3431 Hillview Ave M/S R7-101 Palo Alto CA 94304 Office Phone: 650-855-5649. Business E-Mail: stanford.peng@roche.com.

PENG, SYD S., mining engineer, educator; arrived in US, 1965; Diploma in Mining Engring., Taiwan; M, SD Sch. Mines; PhD in Mining Engring., Stanford U., Calif., 1970. Mining engr. Twin Cities Rsch. Ctr. US Bur. Mines, 1970—74; asst. prof. mining engring. W.Va. U., Morgantown, 1974—78, chmn. dept. mining engring., 1978—2006, dir. Longwall Mining and Ground Control Rsch. Ctr., 1985—, Charles T. Holland disting. prof., 1987—, Charles E. Lawall chair mining engring. Morgantown, 2006—. Contbr. articles to sci. jours.; author: Coal Mine Ground Control, 1978, Longwall Mining, 1984, Surface Subsidence Engring., 1992. Recipient Instn. Overseas Medal award, Instn. Mining Engrs., UK, 1992, Howard N. Eavenson award, Soc. Mining, Metallurgy and Exploration, 1999, Donald S. Kingery Meml. award, Pitts. Coal Mining Inst. Am., 2001, Erskine Ramsey Medal award, AIME, 2002, Medal for Excellence, Inst. Materials, Minerals and Mining, UK, 2004, R & D 100 award, R & D Mag., 2004, 2005, 2006. Mem.: NAE. Achievements include patents in field. Office: Dept Mining Engring PO Box 6070 365 Mineral Resources Bldg Morgantown WV 26506-6070 Office Phone: 304-293-7680 ext. 3301. E-mail: sspeng@mail.wvu.edu. *

PENG, WEIMIN, biochemist, molecular biologist; s. Shansi and Chunzhao (Ren) Peng; m. Lijie Di, Mar. 17, 2003; 1 child, Andy Henry. PhD, Tsinghua U., Beijing, 2001. Rsch. assoc. Duke U., Durham, NC, 2001—04; rschr. U. Calif., LA, 2004—. Contbr. articles to profl. jours. Agrl. technique support Ji'an Agrl. Bur., 1993—95. Recipient Young Investigator Travel award, ISTH, 2003; scholar, Dupont, 2000; Guanghua scholar, Tsinghua U., Beijing, 1999, Travel fellow, Am. Soc. for Biochemistry and Molecular Biology, 2007. Mem.: Am. Soc. for Biochemistry and Molecular Biology, Sigma Xi. Achievements include research in regulators of histone acetylation; interactions of blood coagulation factor V and other molecules in prothrombinase complex; thermochemical & biochemical characteristics of microalgae. Office: Univ Calif Le Conte Ave Los Angeles CA 90095 Home Phone: 310-439-1003. Business E-Mail: wpeng@mednet.ucla.edu.

PENG, ZHONG-REN, education educator; PhD, Portland State U., 1994. Assoc. prof. U. Wis., Milw., 2001—05, prof., 2005—. Dir. Ctr. for Advanced Spatial Info. Rsch. U. Wis., Milw., 2003—. Author: Internet GIS: Distributed Geographic Information Services for the Internet and Wireless Networks, 2003; contbr. articles to profl. jours. Recipient Excellence in Rsch. award, U. Wis. Found., 2002. Mem.: Soc. Chinese Am. Professors and Scientists (v.p., bd. dirs. 2006), Transp. Rsch. Bd., Am. Planning Assn., Urban and Regional Info. Systems Assn. (bd. dirs. 2005—), Inst. Transp. Engs. (life). Office: U Wis SARUP PO Box 413 Milwaukee WI 53201-0413 Office Phone: 1-414-229-5887.

PENG CHEN, HSIU-HUI, music educator; b. Kaosiung, Taiwan, Jan. 12, 1957; arrived in U.S., 1993; d. San-Jen Chen and Jin-Ju Shi; m. Chin-Yuan Perng, Sept. 13, 1981; children: Wei Perng, Powell Perng. BA, Nat. Cheng-Chi U., Taiwan, 1979. Pvt. piano tchr., Taipei, Taiwan, 1975—83; choir dir., piano accompanist Acctg. Dept. Cheng-Chi U., Taipei, 1976—78; piano tchr. Palo Alto, Calif., 1984—89; pvt. piano tchr. Ann Arbor (Mich.) Piano Tchr. Guild, 1994—. Mem.: Am. Coll. Musicians, Mich. Music Tchrs. Assn., Nat. Guild Piano Tchrs., Music Tchrs. Nat. Assn. (chmn. Students Achievement Test Day N.E. Ctr. Sr. Finals 2003—). Home: 2515 Whitetail Run Ct Ann Arbor MI 48105

PENGRA, R. RENE, lawyer; b. 1967; BA, U. Wyo., 1988; JD, NYU, 1993. Bar: Ill. 1995, N.Y. 2000. Law clk. to Hon. David B. Sentelle U.S. Ct. Appeals, D.C. Cir., 1993; with Sidley Austin Brown & Wood, Chgo., 1993—, ptnr., 2002—. Office: Sidley Austin Brown and Wood Bank One Plz 10 S Dearborn St Chicago IL 60603

PENHOET, EDWARD, foundation administrator, former biochemicals company executive, former dean; b. Oakland, Calif., Dec. 11, 1940; AB in Biology, Stanford U., 1963; PhD in Biochem., U. Wash., 1968. Prof. biochem. U. Calif., Berkeley, 1971—81; co-founder, CEO Chiron Corp.,

1981—98; dean Sch. Pub. Health U. Calif., Berkeley, 1998—2002, dean emeritus, 2002—; sr. dir., Sci. & Higher Education Gordon and Betty Moore Found., 2002—04, pres., 2004—. Bd. dirs., sr. adv. to CEO Chiron Corp. Recipient Outstanding Philanthropist award, Assn. of Fundraising Professionals, No. Calif. Entrepreneur of the Yr. award, Ernst & Young and Inc. Mag. Mem.: Am. Soc. of Biological Chemists, Nat. Acad. of Sci., Inst. Medicine. Office: Gordon and Betty Moore Found Presidio of San Francisco PO Box 29910 San Francisco CA 94129 also: Chiron Corp 4560 Horton St Emeryville CA 94608-2900

PENHOLLOW, TINA MARIE, health science researcher, educator; b. Dunkirk, NY, Sept. 24, 1980; d. Duane Wesley and Christine Ann Penhollow. BS, SUNY Coll. Fredonia, 2001; MS, U. West Fla., Pensacola, 2003; PhD, U. Ark., Fayetteville, 2006. Cert. Health Edn. Specialist Nat. Commn. Health Edn. Credentialing, Inc. Tutor SUNY Coll. at Fredonia, 1999—2001; substitute tchr. Santa Rosa County Sch. Dist., Pensacola, Fla., 2001—02; grad. tchg. and rsch. asst. U. West Fla., 2001—03; health educator women infants and children program Escambia County Health Dept., 2002—03; doctoral acad. fellow and sr. grad. asst. U. Ark., Fayetteville, 2003—06; asst. prof. health promotion Fla. Atlantic U., Davie, 2006—. Presenter in field. Contbr. scientific papers, articles to nat. and internat. periodicals, in profl. jours. Recipient Outstanding Doctoral Student in Health Sci. award, U. Ark., 2005; grantee, U. West Fla., 2001, 2002, 2003; scholar, Western Divsn. Credit Union NY, 1997—98; Pace Grad. scholar, U. West Fla., 2001—03, Doctoral fellow, U. Ark., 2003—06. Mem.: AAHPERD, Soc. Sci. Study of Sexuality, Am. Assn. Health Edn. (Horizon Award 2007). Achievements include youngest PhD graduate from the University of Arkansas's program in Health Science. Office: Florida Atlantic Univ ES Building #286 2912 College Ave Davie FL 33314 Office Phone: 954-236-1260. Business E-Mail: tpenholl@fau.edu.

PENICK, ANGELA LUCAS, elementary school educator; b. Roanoke Rapids, NC, Sept. 7, 1950; d. George Alexander and Carrie Louise (Hinson) Lucas; m. Charles Inglesby Penick, Jr. (div.); 1 child, Carrie Hayes. AA, Marjorie Hebster Jr. Coll., Washington, 1970; BA in Edn., U. N.C., Chapel Hill, 1972. Cert. tchr. phys. edn., health, presch. handicap. Accounts payable clk. Boddie-Noell Ent., Rocky Mount, NC, 1973—75; tchr. Rocky Mount City Schs., 1975—80; admissions counselor N.C. Wesleyan Coll., 1980—81; dropout counselor Nash C.C., 1981—85; social worker Britthaven Nursing Home, Nags Head, 1988—89; early childhood interventionist Halifax County Mental Health Ctr., Poanoke Rapids, 1989—99, Edgecombe-Nash Mental Health Ctr., Rocky Mount, 1989—99; tchr. Nash-Rocky Mount Schs., 1999—. Chmn. Good Shepherd Day Sch., Rocky Mount, 2000—02; mem. Tar River Orch. & Chorus, Rocky Mount, 2004—05; vol. Episc. Ch. Women, Am. Cancer Soc., March of Dimes; leader Bible Study Fellowship, Rocky Mount, 2004—05; mem. vestry Ch. of the Good Shepherd, Rocky Mount, 1999—2002, mem. search com., 2003—04, mem. youth coun.; bd. dirs., sec. My Sister's House, Rocky Mount, SC, 1995—98. Mem.: Women's Tennis League, U.S. Tennis Assn., Benvenue Country Club. Republican. Episcopalian. Avocations: tennis, gardening, drawing, weight training, jogging. Office: Nash-Rocky Mount Schools 930 Eastern Ave Nashville NC 27856 Office Phone: 252-937-5622. E-mail: anjo950@aol.com.

PENICK, ANN CLARISSE, minister, counselor; b. Woodstock, Ill., Feb. 17, 1951; d. Preston Edwin and Marjorie Jane Yeoman; m. John William Schoenberger (div.); m. James Lal Penick, Jr., Aug. 9, 1986; stepchildren: Michael Andrew, Katherine Leona. BA in History, No. Ill. U., DeKalb, 1977; MA in History, Loyola U., Chgo., 1987; MA in Counseling, U. Ala., Birmingham, 1995. Cert. minister Diocese Birmingham, Ala., 1993; lic. counselor S.C., 1997, cert. Nat. Bd. Certified Counselors, 1999, lic. mental health counselor Mass., 2006. Substitute tchr. Regina Dominican HS, Wilmette, Ill., 1987—88; adj. faculty Birmingham So. Coll., 1988—91; tchr. theology John Carroll Cath. HS, Birmingham, 1993—94; chaplain intern Bon Secours St. Francis Hosp., Charleston, 1996—97; minister Cath. Campus Diocese Charleston, Coll. of Charleston, SC, 1997—2000; pastoral assoc. St. Ann U. Parish, Archdiocese Boston, 2000—02, assoc. cath. chaplain Tufts U., 2002—. Adj. faculty Nat. U., Chgo., 1988; coord. sexual abuse awareness Archdiocese Boston, 2002—, facilitator marriage preparation, 2002—. Contbr. articles to profl. jours. Aid worker Polish Refugee Camp, Vienna, 1982; spokesperson Nat. Night Out, Charleston, 1996; vol. Dem. Nat. Com., Boston, 2004; vol. pastoral counselor Hospice Charleston, 1995—98. Named Advisor of Yr., Emerson Coll., 2001. Mem.: Assn. for Spiritual, Ethical and Religious Values in Counseling, Mass. Mental Health Counselors Assn., Cath. Campus Ministry Assn., Am. Counseling Assn. (bd. dir. 2001—04, Svc. award 2004). Democrat. Roman Cath. Avocations: dance, guitar, singing. Home: 5 Walden Mews Cambridge MA 02140 Office: Tufts Cath Chaplaincy Goddard Chapel 3 on the Green Medford MA 02155 Personal E-mail: annpenick@hotmail.com.

PENICK, ELIZABETH C., psychologist; b. New Orleans, July 17, 1934; d. Rawley M. Penick and Marie G. Sells. BA, Newcomb Coll., 1957; MS, Tulane U., 1960; PhD, Washington U., St. Louis, 1975. Diplomate clin. psychology Am. Bd. Profl. Psychology. Prof. dept. psychiatry Kans. U. Med. Ctr., Kansas City, 1980—, dir. divsn. psychology. Rsch. grantee Nat. Assn. Alcohol Abuse and Alcoholism, Washington, 1980-97. Mem. APA, Kans. Psychol. Assn. (dir.). Home: 12231 Charlotte Kansas City MO 64146 Office: Kans U Med Ctr Dept Psychiatry 3901 Rainbow Blvd Kansas City KS 66160 E-mail: epenick@kumc.edu.

PENICK, JOHN E., education educator; b. Langley, Va., Jan. 2, 1944; s. Edgar Cohen and Bessie (Beene) P.; m. Nell Inman, July 23, 1966; children: Lucas T., Megan J. Penick. BS, U. Miami, 1966, MA, 1969; PhD, Fla. State U., 1973. Sci. dept. head Miami (Fla.) Jackson High Sch., 1967-70; instr. Miami-Dade Community Coll., 1968, Fla. State U., Tallahassee, Fla., 1970-73; dir. tchr. edn. Loyola U., Chgo., 1973-75; prof. U. Iowa, Iowa City, 1975-97, head Sci. Edn. Ctr., 1982, 89-93; prof., head dept. math., sci. and tech. edn. N.C. State U., Raleigh, 1998—. Editor: (monograph series) Focus on Excellence, 1983—89; author: Biology: A Community Context, 2003; contbr. numerous articles to profl. jours. Named Disting. Alumnus Fla. State U., 1987; recipient Burlington No. award for outstanding career achievement U. Iowa, 1992; Fulbright fellow USIA, Portugal, 1985. Fellow Iowa Acad. Sci.; mem. NSTA (bd. dir. 1986-88, pres. 2003, Ohaus awards), Nat. Assn. for Rsch. in Sci. Tchg. (assoc. editor 1979-84), Coun. Sci. Soc. Prs. (sec. 1991-92, treas. 2003-04), Nat. Assn. Biology Tchrs. (pres. 1989, hon. mem. award, 2004), Assn. Sci. Tchr. Educators (pres. 2002, Outstanding Paper 1978, Outstanding Sci. Educator 1987, Outstanding Mentor 1997), Sigma Xi, Esilon Pi Tau (Dist. Svc. Citation, 2003). Office: NC State U 326 Poe Hl Raleigh NC 27695-7801

PENIKETT, TONY, mediator, negotiator, writer; b. Nov. 14, 1945; s. Erik John Keith and Sarah Ann (Colwell) P.; m. Lula Mary Johns, 1974 (div. 1997); children— John Tahmoh, Sarah Lahlil, Stephanie Yahsan Exec. asst. to nat. leader New Dem. Party, Ottawa, Ont., Canada, 1975-76, nat. pres., 1981-85, fed. councillor, 1973—, leader Whitehorse, Y.T., Canada, 1980—, campaign mgr. N.W.T., Canada, 1972; alderman City of Whitehorse, Y.T., Canada, 1977-79; elected mem. Yukon Legis. Assembly, 1978-95, opposition leader Y.T., Canada, 1982-85, 92-95, elected premier Yukon Terr., 1985-92; sr. policy advisor Govt. of Sask., 1995-97; dep. min. negotiations Ministry of Fin. and Corp. Rels., Govt. of B.C., Victoria, 1997-2000; dep. min. labor Ministry of Fin., Govt. of B.C., Victoria, 2000—01; propr. Tony Penikett Negotiations Inc., Vancouver, B.C., Canada, 2001—. Author (film): The Mad Trapper, 1972, La Patrouille Perdue, 1974, (books) Breaking Trail, 2004, Reconciliation: First Nations Treaty Making in British Columbia, 2006. Office: Tony Penikett Negotiations Inc 550 Beatty St Unit 7-8 Vancouver BC Canada V6B 2L3 Office Phone: 604-724-6720. E-mail: tony_penikett@telus.net.

PENINGER, MICHAEL J., insurance company executive; Actuary Northwestern Nat. Life, 1977—85; corp. actuary Assurant Employee Benefits, 1985—91, sr. v.p., CFO, 1991—93, sr. v.p. fin., 1993—98, exec. v.p., 1998—99, pres., CEO, 1999—; exec. v.p. Assurant Inc., NYC, 1999—, interim CFO, 2007—. Fellow: Soc. Actuaries; mem.: Am. Acad. Actuaries. Office: Assurant Inc 1 Chase Manhattan Plz New York NY 10005 *

PENISTEN, GARY DEAN, entrepreneur; b. Lincoln, Nebr., May 14, 1931; s. Martin C. and Jayne (O'Dell) P.; m. Nancy Margaret Golding, June 3, 1951; children: Kris D., Janet L., Carol E., Noel M. BS in Bus. Adminstrn., U. Nebr., Omaha, 1953; LLD (hon.), Concordia Coll., 1993. With Gen. Electric Co., 1953-74, mgr. group fin. ops. power generation group NYC, 1973-74; asst. sec. navy fin. mgmt., 1974-77; sr. v.p. fin., chief fin. officer, dir. Sterling Drug Inc., NYC, 1977-89; sr. v.p. fin., health group Eastman Kodak Co., NYC, 1989-90. Chmn. bd. dirs. Acme United Corp., 1996—2006, chmn. emeritus, 2007—. Mem. corp. adv. bd. U. Nebr. Coll. Bus., Omaha. Recipient Disting. Public Service award Navy Dept., 1977; Alumni Achievement citation U. Nebr., Omaha, 1975. Mem. Fin. Execs. Inst., Navy League of U.S., Army and Navy Club (Washington), Rotary, Union League (N.Y.), Ft. Lauderdale (Fla.) Country Club, White Eagle Golf Club (Naperville). Republican. Unitarian Universalist. Home and Office: 1409 Aberdeen Ct Naperville IL 60564-9787 Home Phone: 630-978-7092; Office Phone: 630-978-7093. Personal E-mail: asnfm@aol.com.

PENLAND, JOHN THOMAS, retired import/export and development company executive; b. Guntersville, Ala., Mar. 31, 1930; s. James B. and Kathleen (Bolding) P.; m. Carolyn Joyce White, May 30, 1961; children: Jeffrey K., Mark A., Michael J. BA, George Washington U., 1957. Vice pres., dir. Rouse, Brewer, Becker & Bryant, Inc., Washington, 1957-63; staff mem. SEC, Washington, 1963-67; pres., dir. INA Trading Corp., Phila., 1968-69; v.p. INA Security Corp., Phila., 1967-69; from v.p. to pres. Shareholders Mgmt. Co., LA, 1969—75, v.p., dir. several mut. funds managed by, 1970-75; v.p. Shareholders Capital Corp., LA, 1972-73; pres., chmn., CEO, HMO Internat. and its subs., LA, 1975; founder, pres., chmn. Pendlar Corp., Atlanta, 1977-97; chmn., pres. Bella Vista Developers, Inc., Albuquerque, 1977-98; chmn., CEO, CompuComp Corp., Atlanta, 1977-81; chmn., pres. Fran Stef Corp., NYC, 1982-89; pres., chmn. Engineered Products Corp., Dandridge, Tenn., 1983-90; founder, chmn., CEO Am. Accessories Inc., Covington, Ga., 1983-98; founder, pres., chmn. United Am. Products Corp., Dandridge, 1983-89; founder, chmn., pres. Chamisa Properties, Inc., Albuqueque, 1988-94; founder, chmn. Glorieux Ltd., Atlanta, 1988-96; founder, pres. Ga. Ptnrs. Ltd., Covington, 1988—94; founder, chmn. Premier Trading Internat., Inc., Atlanta, 1989—98; founder, pres. Chamisa Enterprises, Inc., Covington, 1990—2001; founder, mng. ptnr. Ft. Hill Ptnrs., Knoxville, Tenn., 1990-93; chmn. Einson Freeman & Detroy Corp., Fair Lawn, NJ, 1978-83; founder, dir., pres. West Point Contract Packaging, Inc., Martinsville, Va., 1991-98; founder, mng. ptnr. Harbor View, Ltd., Fernandina Beach, Fla., 1992-94; founder, chmn. West Point Tech. Assembly, Inc., Winston-Salem, NC, 1993—2002; dir., pres. BKP Industries, Inc., Monroe, Ga., 1995-97. With US Army, 1948—55. Republican. Episcopalian. Home: PO Box 549 Social Circle GA 30025-0549 Office Phone: 770-634-6817. Personal E-mail: cjpenland@bellsouth.net.

PENLEY, JULIE ANNE, psychologist, educator; d. John and Marcheta Isabelle Dietien; m. Howard Lawson Penley. PhD, U. Tex., 2001. Tchg. asst. U. Tex., El Paso, 1995—96, rsch. asst., 1996—2001; instr. Dona Ana CC, Sunland Park, N.Mex., 1999; part-time instr. El Paso CC, 2000—02, asst. prof., 2002—07, assoc. prof., 2007—; evaluation coord. U. Tex., El Paso, 2001—02. Mem.: APA, Am. Assn. Women in Cmty. Colls. Lutheran. Office: El Paso Community Coll PO Box 20500 El Paso TX 79998-0500 Office Phone: 915-831-3210. Business E-Mail: jpenley@epcc.edu.

PENLEY, LARRY EDWARD, academic administrator, finance educator; b. Bristol, Va., Feb. 9, 1949; s. William Edward and June (Caudill) P.; m. Yolanda Elva Sanchez, Nov. 25, 1977; children: Jonathan Andrew, Josephine Anna. BA, Wake Forest U., 1971, MA, 1972; PhD, U. Ga., 1976. Vis. prof. ITESM, Monterey, Mexico, 1977, Universidad de Carobobo, Valencia, Venezuela, 1978; assoc. dean U. Tex., San Antonio, 1980-85; prof., chmn. dept. Ariz. State U., Tempe, 1985—90, dean Coll. Bus., 1990—2003; pres. Colo. State U., 2003—; chancellor Colo. State U. Sys., 2003—. Contbr. articles to profl. jours. Mem. NCAA Task Force on Future of Athletics, Nat. Western Stock Show and Rodeo, Citizen of West Com.; mem. adv. counsel Group Ecole Superieure De Commerce de Toulouse, 1997; chmn. Assn. Advance Collegiate Sch. of Bus., 2000—01; bd. mem. dir. Greater Phoenix Econ. Coun., 1993—2003. Recipient Frank C. Carr Founders award, INROADS, 1997, Disting. Svc. award, Greater Phoenix Econ. Coun., 2002. Mem.: Assn. Advance Collegiate Schs. of Bus. (chmn. 2001—02), Rocky Mountain Bd., Inst. Internat. Edn., Mountain States Employers Coun. Bd., Greater Denver Metro Chamber Bd., Acad. Mgmt. (chmn. divsn. program 1986), Mountain West Conf. Bd., Colo. Inst. of Tech. Bd., Colo. Concern. Roman Catholic. Home: 3001 Hearthstone Dr Fort Collins CO 80528-9171 Office: Colo State U Office of the Pres Fort Collins CO 80523-0100 Office Phone: 970-491-6211. E-mail: presofc@lamar.colostate.edu. *

PENLEY, VIRGINIA LONG, social worker; b. Statesville, NC, July 3, 1955; d. Robert Long and Mary Joyce Broussard; m. Jeffrey Michael Penley. AA, Mitchell C.C., 1975; BA in Social Work, Greensboro Coll., 1977. LCSW; cert. Dir. Vol. Svcs. Social worker Moses H. Cone Hosp., Greensboro, 1987—94; dir. vol. svcs. and patient rels. Women's Hosp. Greensboro, NC, 1994—. Mem.: NASW (Piedmont rep. 1991—92), N.C. Soc. Dirs. Vol. Svcs. (chair publicity 2000—, corr. sec., edn. co-chair 1997—99), N.C. Zoologica. Presbyterian. Avocations: travel, antiques, reading. Office: Women's Hosp Greensboro 801 Green Valley Rd Greensboro NC 27408 Home Phone: 336-855-0353; Office Phone: 336-832-6586. Business E-Mail: ginger.penley@mosescone.com.

PENLIDIS, ALEXANDER, chemical engineering professor; b. Kozani, Greece, Feb. 12, 1957; Diploma in engring., U. Thessaloniki, 1980; PhD in Chem. Engring., McMaster U., 1986. Rsch. assoc. Polymer Prodn. Techs., McMaster Inst., Canada, 1985-86; from asst. prof. to assoc. prof. chem. engring. U. Waterloo, Ont., Canada, 1986-90, assoc. prof. Ont., 1990—95, prof. Ont., 1995—, assoc. dir. Inst. Polymer Rsch. Ont., 1990-95, dir., 1995—, assoc. dean rsch. & grad. studies, faculty engring. Ont., 1998—2004. Can. rsch. chair in poly. engring., 2002—; cons. in field. Founding co-editor Polymer Reaction Engring. Jour., 1990-2003. Fellow Chem. Inst. Can., Can. Acad. Engring.; mem. Can. Soc. Chem. Engring. Office: Univ Waterloo Inst Polymer Rsch Chem Engring Dept Waterloo ON Canada N2L 3G1 Office Phone: 519-888-4567 x36634. Business E-Mail: penlidis@uwaterloo.ca.

PENMAN, ROBBIE MAE, volunteer, political organization worker; b. Memphis, Feb. 25, 1903; d. Robert Rudolph and Emma Jimmie Franklin; m. Edward Thaddeus Penman Sr., June 28, 1922 (dec.); children: Vincent Robert, Edward Thaddeus Jr., Wallace Abraham, Horace Eugene. Student in English and Journalism, Alleghany Coll., Meadville, Pa.; student in Bus. Adminstrn., John Hay Bus. Coll., Cleve.; student in Social Svcs., Case Western Res. U., Cleve.; student in Housing and Cmty. Devel., Cleve. State U. Social svc. outreach worker; dir. day care ctr. Fellowship Bapt. Ch., Cleve. Author: Call Me Russell, 1995. Pres. George Washington Carver Elem. PTA, Cleve., John Borroughs Elem. PTA, Ctrl. Jr. H.S. PTA, East Tech. H.S. PTA; mem. Econ. Opportunity Anti-Poverty Bd., 1962—67; v.p. Model Cities Program, 1972—77, supr. dist. connectors; organizer Cmty. Responsive Dial A Bus; mem. bd. RTA; Am. rep. World Conf. Women, Copenhagen, 1980; asst. to Rev. Donald Jacobs Cleve. Black Ch. Ptnrs. in Ecumenism; mem. Cleve. Econ. Opportunity Anti-Poverty Bd., 1962—71; bd. mem. United St. Club, 1953, Cuyahoga County Welfare Bd., 1961, Vocational Guidance Rehabilitation Ctr., 1971, Regional Transit Authority, 1976, Sr. Project Cath. Commn., 1977, Hope House, St. Citizen Drop-In Ctr., United Labor Agency, 1980, Stop and Start Multi Purpose Homeless Ctr., 1981. Named Outstanding Grandparent of Yr., Ch. LDS, 2005; named to Wall of Tolerance, Montgomery, Ala., 2005; recipient Outstanding Svc. honors, Rep. Louis Stokes. Democrat. Ch. Lds. Achievements include first congressional sr. intern. Avocations: reading, exercise. Home: 6003 Thackeray Ave Cleveland OH 44103

PENN, BUDDIE J. (B.J. PENN), civilian military employee; b. Peru, Ind. BS, Purdue U.; MS, George Washington U. Cert. Aerospace Safety U. So. Calif., Nat. Security for Sr. Officials Harvard U. Former naval aviator; EA-6B pilot, 1972; held various leadership assignments including exec. officer/commdg. officer VAQ 33; battalion officer U.S. Naval Acad.; air officer USS Am.; spl. asst. to Cheif of Naval Ops.; commdg. officer NAS N. Island, Calif.; dep. dir. Navy Office Tech. Transfer and Security Assistance; dir. internat. bus. Loral Fed. Sys., 1995—98; with Naval Electronics and Surveillance Sys. Dept. Navy, US Dept. Def., 1998, dir. indsl. base assessments, 2001—05, asst. sec. for installations & environ., 2005—. Office: US Dept Def 1000 Navy Pentagon Rm 4E739 Washington DC 20350-1000 Office Phone: 703-693-4530. Office Fax: 703-693-1165.

PENN, DARREN W., lawyer; BA, U. Ga., 1990, JD, 1994. Bar: Ga. 1994. Trial atty. State Farm Mutual Auto. Insurance Co.; founding ptnr. Penn & Pate, LLP; merged with Scherffius, Ballard Still & Ayres LLP, 2000; founding ptnr. Harris Penn & Lowry, LLP, Atlanta, 2005—. Instr. law courses. Contbr. articles to numerous profl. jours. Named Rising Star, Ga. SuperLawyer Mag., 2005. Office: Harris Penn and Lowry Ste 1105 817 W Peachtree St Atlanta GA 30308 Office Phone: 404-961-7650.

PENN, J. B., economist, former federal agency administrator; b. Lynn, Ark., Dec. 18, 1944; s. Jacob Bernard and Virginia Lucille (Martin) P.; m. Martha Ann Brannon (div.); children: Penny Alane, Kristin J. Rens. BS, Ark. State U., 1965; MS, La. State U., Baton Rouge, 1967; PhD, Purdue U., 1973. Rsch. economist Econ. Rsch Svc., USDA, Baton Rouge, W. Lafayette, Ind., 1967-75, leader policy group Washington, 1975-76, dep. adminstr. for econs., 1979-81; mem. sr. staff, Coun. Econ. Advisers Exec. Office of the Pres., Washington, 1977-78; pres. Econ. Perspectives, Inc., Washington, 1981-88; sr. v.p. Sparks Commodities, Inc., Washington, 1988—2001; under sec. for farm & foreign agr. services USDA, Washington, 2001—06; chief economist Deere & Co., Moline, Ill., 2006—. Co-author: (textbook) Agriculture and Food Policy, 3d edit., 1995. Mem. adv. bd. Ctr. for Nat. Policy, Washington, 1990; bd. dirs. Found. for Devel. of Polish Agr., Warsaw, 1990, Farm Found., 1995. Mem. Am. Agrl. Econs. Assn., Am. Econs. Assn. Office: Deere & Co 1 John Deere Rd Moline IL 61265-8098

PENN, LEE, information scientist, consultant, journalist; b. Midland, Tex., Jan. 19, 1953; s. Rhesa and Dorothy Penn. BA, Harvard U., 1976; MBA, MPH, U. Calif., Berkeley, 1986. Freelance journalist Oregon mag. and others, Portland, 1975-79, San Francisco, 1998—; rsch. asst. Kaiser Permanente Ctr. for Health Rsch., Portland, 1979-83; sys. planner Alta Bates Corp., Berkeley, 1985—86; sr. fin. analyst St. Mary's Hosp., San Francisco, 1987; mgr. assoc., cons. JDA/SAIC, San Francisco, 1992-96; prin. Penn Cons., San Francisco, 1988—. Adj. faculty, lectr. Golden Gate U., San Francisco, 1990-98 Author: False Dawn: The United Religions Initiative, Globalism, and the Quest for a One-world Religion, 2005; contbr. articles to profl. jours. and mags. including Jour. Ambulatory Care Mgmt., chpts. to books Vestryman, chmn. fin. com., mem. search coms. Episcopal Parish St. John the Evangelist, San Francisco, 1989-94 Edgar F. Kaiser Sr. fellow U. Calif., 1983-84, Regents fellow, 1984-85 Mem. IEEE Computer Soc., Soc. Profls. in Healthcare, Am. Coll. Health Care Execs., Phi Beta Kappa. Office: PO Box 20050 Stanford CA 94309-0050 Office Phone: 650-566-1547. Personal E-mail: leepenn@aol.com.

PENN, SEAN, actor; b. Burbank, Calif., Aug. 17, 1960; s. Leo and Eileen (Ryan) P.; m. Madonna Louise Ciccone, Aug. 16, 1985 (div. Jan. 10, 1989); m. Robin Wright Penn, April 27, 1996; 2 children: Dylan Frances, Hopper Jack. Actor: (plays) Heartland, 1981, Slab Boys, 1983, Hurlyburly, 1988; (films) Taps, 1981, Fast Times at Ridgemont High, 1982, Summerspell, 1983, Bad Boys, 1983, Crackers, 1984, Racing with the Moon, 1984, The Falcon and the Snowman, 1985, At Close Range, 1986, Shanghai Surprise, 1986, Color Blue, 1988, Colors, 1988, Judgment in Berlin, 1988, Casualties of War, 1989, We're No Angels, 1989, State of Grace, 1990, Carlito's Way, 1993, Dead Man Walking, 1995 (Golden Globe award nominee for best actor, 1995, Best Actor award Berlin Film Festival, 1996, Acad. award nominee for best actor, 1996), The Game, 1997, U Turn, 1997, Hugo Pool, 1997, The Thin Red Line, 1998, Hurly Burly, 1998, As I Lay Dying, 1998, Up at the Villa, 2000, Before Night Falls, 2000, The Weight of Water, 2000, I Am Sam, 2001, It's All About Love, 2003, Mystic River, 2003, (Golden Globe for best dramatic actor, 2004, Acad. Award for best actor, 2004, Golden Satellite award, 2004, London Critics Circle Film awards, 2004, Screen Actors Guild Award nomination for best actor, 2004), 21 Grams, 2003, The Assassination of Richard Nixon, 2004, The Interpreter, 2005, All the King's Men, 2006; actor, prodr.: Loved, 1997; actor, exec. prodr.: She's So Lovely, 1997; dir., writer: The Indian Runner, 1991; dir., prodr., writer: The Crossing Guard, 1995; dir., prodr.: The Pledge, 2001; actor (TV movies) Hellinger's Law, 1981, The Killing of Randy Webster, 1981. Recipient John Steinbeck award, San Francisco Chronicle, 2004. Office: Ste 2500 2049 Century Park E Los Angeles CA 90067-3127

PENN, STANLEY WILLIAM, journalist; b. NYC, Jan. 12, 1928; s. Murray and Lillian (Richman) P.; m. Esther Aronson, July 12, 1952; children— Michael, Laurel. Student, Bklyn. Coll., 1945-47; B. Journalism, U. Mo., 1949. With Wall St. Jour., 1952-90; investigative reporter N.Y. bur., 1957-90. (Co-recipient Pulitzer prize for nat. reporting 1967). Home: 380 Riverside Dr New York NY 10025-1858 Personal E-mail: estan380@hotmail.com.

PENNAMPED, BRUCE MICHAEL, lawyer; b. Kearney, Nebr., July 16, 1948; s. Matthew Paul and Betty Fern (Harper) P.; m. Victoria A. Crull, May 13, 1972 (div. Dec. 1980); 1 child, Katheryn A.; m. Melissa J. Barth, July 22, 1985. BS in Mgmt., Ind. U., 1970, JD, 1972. Bar: Ind. 1972, U.S. Dist. Ct. (no. and so. dists.) Ind. 1972, U.S. Ct. Appeals (7th cir.) 1978; cert. family law specialist. Assoc. Rocap Rocap Reese & Young, Indpls., 1972-76; pvt. practice Indpls., 1976-78, 88-91; ptnr. Forbes & Pennamped, Indpls., 1978-88, Lowe Gray Steele & Hoffman, Indpls., 1991-96, Lowe Gray Steele & Darko, Indpls., 1996—2001, Pennamped & Assocs., Indpls., 2001—. Chair and panelist Ind. Continuing Legal Edn. Forum; mem. Ind. Child Custody and Support Adv. Commn. Contbr. articles to profl. jours. Majority atty. Ind. Ho. of Reps., Indpls. Cpl. USMCR, 1967-69. Fellow Am. Acad. Matrimonial Lawyers, Ind. Family Law Specialist Bd. (co-chair). Home: 9662 Decatur Dr Indianapolis IN 46256-9654 Office: Pennamped & Associates 3925 River crossing Pky Ste 280 Indianapolis IN 46240 Home Phone: 317-845-4130; Office Phone: 317-815-9736. Business E-Mail: bruce@pennamped-associates.com.

PENNELL, DANIEL MARK, researcher; b. Valparaiso, Ind., July 14, 1971; s. Lawrence Foster Pennell and Nancy Lea Rogan. BA, Ind. U., Bloomington, Ind., 1989—93, MA, 1997—99, MLS, 1999—2001. Bibliographer for Russian, east European, and Germanic studies U. of Pitts., Pitts., 2001—; asst. slavic bibliographer Ind. U., Bloomington, Ind., 1996—2001; program mgr. for edn. US Peace Corps., Saratov, Russia, 1995—96. Asst. dir. Inst. for the Study of Russian Edn., Bloomington, Ind., 1996—98; reviews editor Balkan Academic News, 2002—04, East European Politics and Societies, 2004—. Fgn. Lang. Area Studies fellowship, Ind. U., 1997-2000. Mem.: Southeastern European Studies Assn., Soc. for Romanian Studies, Am. Libr. Assoication, Am. Assn. for the Advancement of Slavic Studies, Phi Beta Kappa. Achievements include development of Slavic, East European, and Germanic Studies Research Collections; research in Modern Russian and Eastern European History. Office: University of Pittsburgh 3960 Forbes Avenue G-20X Hillman Library Pittsburgh PA 15260 Home: 1517 S Negley Ave Pittsburgh PA 15217 Office Phone: 412-606-3795. Personal E-mail: pennell@pitt.edu.

PENNELL, DANNY JOE, social worker; b. Aug. 31, 1945; s. Donald Louis and Lela Geneva (Murray) P.; m. Janis Evelyn Reynolds, Dec. 26, 1984; children: Joel, Jason, Jaime, Chad, Colter. BA, U. Ill., 1970, MSW, 1972. Social worker Dept. Child and Family Svcs., Danville, Ill., 1971-72, social worker supr. Rockford, Ill., 1972-74; instr. Rockford Coll., 1977-78; pres., CEO Goldie B. Floberg Ctr., Rockton, Ill., 1974—. Exec. dir. Found. Ft. Lewis Coll., Durango, Colo., 1986-87; bd. dirs. Winnebago County Child Protection Assn., Rockford, 1974-76; bd. dirs., mem. legis. affairs com., chmn. mental health devel. disabilities com., spl. edn. com. Child Care Assn. Ill., Springfield, Ill., 1980—; mem. child welfare adv. com. Ill. Dept. Children and Family Services; mem. devel. disabilities adv. com. Dept. Mental Health, mem. children's svcs. subcom.; cons. in field. Bd. dirs., v.p. H.O.P.E. Found., 2001—. Grantee Ill. Dept. Children and Family Svcs., 1970-72. Mem. Nat. Soc. Fund Raising Execs. (bd. dirs., sec. 1984-85, v.p. 1986-87), Nat. Soc. Fund Raising Dirs. (pres. bd. dirs. 1988, v.p. 1987, v.p. 1986, bd. mem. various coms. 1984, 85), Am. Assn. Mental Deficiency, Nat. Assn. Retarded Citizens, Coordinating Council for Handicapped Children, Nat. Assn. Devel. Disabilities Mgrs., Roscoe C. of C. (bd. dirs. 2000—). Home: 12080 N Ledges Dr Roscoe IL 61073-9600 Office: Goldie B Floberg Ctr PO Box 346 Rockton IL 61072-0346 Personal E-mail: dpenn58@aol.com.

PENNELL, WILLIAM BROOKE, lawyer; b. Mineral Ridge, Ohio, Oct. 28, 1935; s. George Albert and Katherine Nancy (McMeen) P. AB, Harvard U., 1957; LLB cum laude, U. Pa., 1961; m. Peggy Polsky, June 17, 1958; children: Katherine, Thomas Brooke. Bar: NY 1963, US Dist. Ct. (so. dist.) NY 1964, US Dist. Ct. (ea. dist.) NY 1964, US Ct. Appeals (2d cir.) 1966, US Ct. Claims 1966, US Tax Ct. 1967, US Supreme Ct. 1967. Clk. US Dist. Ct., (so. dist.) NY, NYC, 1961-62; assoc. Shearman & Sterling, NYC, 1962-71, ptnr., 1971-91. Recent case editor U. Pa. Law Rev., 1960-61. Bd. govs. Bklyn. Heights Assn., 1964-74, pres., 1969-71; chmn. bd. Willoughby House Settlement, 1972-95. Served with US Army, 1957. Fellow Salzburg Seminar Am. Studies, 1965. Mem. Rembrandt Club. Home and Office: PO Box 249 Canaan NY 12029-0249

PENNER, DUSTIN, professional hockey player; b. Winkler, Man., Can., Sept. 28, 1982; Attended, U. Maine, 2002—04. Left wing Cin. Mighty Ducks, 2004—05, Portland Pirates, 2005—06, Anaheim Ducks, 2005—07, Edmonton Oilers, 2007—. Named to All-Tournament Team, NCAA, 2004. Achievements include being a member of Stanley Cup Champion Anaheim Ducks, 2007. Office: Edmonton Oilers Hockey Club 11230 - 110 St Edmonton AB T5G 3H7 Canada *

PENNER, KEITH, former Canadian government official; b. Sask., Can., May 1, 1933; BA, U. Alberta, Can., 1955; MDiv, Toronto U., 1959; MEd, U. Ottawa, Can., 1971. Secondary sch. tchr., Dryden, Ont., Canada, 1961-68; mem. parliament Cochrane-Superior, Ont., 1968-88; mem. Can. Transp. Agy., Ottawa, 1988—2003; pres. dispute resolution Keith Penner & Assocs., Ottawa, 2003—. Past parliamentary sec. to Min. of State Sci. and Tech., past parliamentary sec. to Min. of Indian Affairs and No. Devel., past chmn. Standing Com. on Indian Affairs and No. Devel.; vis. fellow Sch. of Polit. Sci., Queen's U., 1987-88; chmn. Chartered Inst. Logistics and Transport, N.Am., 2004. Fellow: Chartered Inst. Logistics and Transport (chmn. 2004—); mem.: Lic. Appeal Tribunal Ont. Office: Ottawa ON Canada Home Phone: 613-828-6070; Office Phone: 613-828-3067. Personal E-mail: keith.penner@rogers.com. E-mail: keith.penner@disputeres.ca.

PENNER, STANFORD SOL, engineering educator; b. Unna, Germany, July 5, 1921; arrived in US, 1936, naturalized, 1943; s. Heinrich and Regina (Saal) P.; m. Beverly Preston, Dec. 28, 1942; children: Merilynn Jean, Robert Clark. BS, Union Coll., 1942; MS, U. Wis., 1943, PhD, 1946; Dr. rer. nat. (hon.), Technische Hochschule Aachen, Germany, 1981. Rsch. assoc. Allegany Ballistics Lab., Cumberland, Md., 1944-45; rsch. scientist Standard Oil Devel. Co., Esso Labs., Linden, NJ, 1946; sr. rsch. engr. Jet Propulsion Lab., Pasadena, Calif., 1947-50; mem. faculty Calif. Inst. Tech., 1950-63, prof. divsn. engring., jet propulsion, 1957-63; dir. rsch. and engring. divsn. Inst. Def. Analyses, Washington, 1962-64; prof. engring. physics, chmn. dept. aerospace and mech. engring. U. Calif., San Diego, 1964-68, vice chancellor for acad. affairs, 1968-69, dir. Inst. for Pure and Applied Phys. Scis., 1968-71, dir. Energy Ctr., 1973-91, disting. prof. engring. physics emeritus, 1991—. Bd. dirs. Optodyne Corp.; US mem. adv. group aero. rsch. and devel. NATO, 1952-68, chmn. combustion and propulsion panel, 1958-60; mem. adv. com. engring. scis. USAF-Office Sci. Rsch., 1961-65; mem. subcom. on combustion NACA, 1954-58; mem. rsch. adv. com. on air-breathing engines NASA, 1962-64; mem. coms. on gas dynamics and edn. Internat. Acad. Astronautics, 1969-80; nat. lectr. Sigma Xi, 1977-79; chmn. fossil energy rsch. working group Dept. Energy, 1978-82, chmn. advanced fuel cell commercialization working group, 1993-95; mem. assembly engring. NAE, 1978-82; chmn. NAS-NRC U.S. Nat. Com. IIASA, 1978-82; mem. commn. engring. tech. sys. NRC, 1982-84; spl. guest Internat. Coal Sci. Confs., 1983, 85, 87, 89, 91; mentor Def. Sci. Studies Group, 1985-93; chmn. studies mcpl. waste incineration NSF, 1988-89, Calif. Coun. Sci. Tech., 1992; pub. info. adv. com. Nat. Acad. Engring., 1994-98, Ind. Commn. on Environ. Edn., 1995-97, Environ. Literacy Coun., 1998-2005; sci. adv. bd., San Diego County, 1997—, chair, 2004-07. Author: Chemical Reactions in Flow Systems, 1955, Chemistry Problems in Jet Propulsion, 1957, Quantitative Molecular Spectroscopy and Gas Emissivities, 1959, Chemical Rocket Propulsion and Combustion Research, 1962, Thermodynamics, 1968, Radiation and Reentry, 1968; sr. author: Energy, Vol. I (Demands, Resources, Impact, Technology and Policy), 1974, 81, Energy, Vol. II (Non-nuclear Energy Technologies), 1975, 77, 84, Energy, Vol. III (Nuclear Energy and Energy Policies), 1976; editor: Chemistry of Propellants, 1960, Advanced Propulsion Techniques, 1961, Detonations and Two-Phase Flow, 1962, Combustion and Propulsion, 1963, Advances in Tactical Rocket Propulsion, 1968, In Situ Shale Oil Recovery, 1975, New Sources of Oil and Gas, 1982, Coal Combustion and Applications, 1984, Advanced Fuel Cells, 1986, Coal Gasification: Direct Applications and Syntheses of Chemicals and Fuels, 1987, CO2 Emissions and Climate Change, 1991, Commercialization of Fuel Cells, 1995, Advanced Nuclear Techs., 1998; assoc. editor Jour. Chem. Physics, 1953-56; founding editor Jour. Quantitative Spectroscopy and Radiative Transfer, 1960-92, Jour. Def. Rsch., 1963-67, Energy (The Internat. Jour.), 1975-98; sect. editor Energy and Power Systems, Ency. Phys. Sci. and Tech., 1998-2002. Recipient spl. award People-to-People Program, pub. svc. award U. Calif., San Diego, N. Manson medal Internat. Colloquia on Gasdynamics of Explosions and Reactive Systems, 1979, internat. Columbus award Internat. Inst. Comm., Genoa, Italy, 1981, disting. assoc. award US Dept. Energy, 1990, Edward Teller award for def. of freedom, 1997, Rockwell medal, 2003, Nat. Acad. Engring. Founders award, 2007. Fellow Am. Phys. Soc., Optical Soc. Am., AAAS, NY Acad. Scis., AIAA (dir. 1964-66, past chmn. com., G. Edward Pendray award 1975, Thermophysics award 1983, Energy Systems award 1983), Am. Acad. Arts and Scis.; mem. Nat. Acad. Engring., Internat. Acad. Astronautics, World Level Hall of Fame for Engring., Sci. and Tech., Am. Chem. Soc., Sigma Xi. Home: 5912 Avenida Chamnez La Jolla CA 92037-7402 Office: U Calif San Diego 9500 Gilman Dr La Jolla CA 92093-0411 Office Phone: 858-534-4281. Business E-Mail: spenner@ucsd.edu.

PENNER, SUSANNE MARY, communications executive; arrived in US, 1974; d. Franklyn Thomas and Paulette Penner; m. Gene Aaron Milleson, Oct. 17, 2003. BS, Calif. Poly. State U., San Luis Obispo, 1998. With Weber Group, Palo Alto, Calif., 1998—99; rschr. Egon Zehnder Internat., Palo Alto, 1999—2000; mktg. mgr. Silicon Graphics, Mountain View, Calif., Trolltech, Palo Alto, Calif.; sr. mgr. Oracle, Redwood Shores, Calif. Author (contributor): (book) After the Morning Calm, 2002. Vol. Big Bros. Big Sisters, San Francisco, 1998—2003. Democrat-Npl. Avocations: travel, writing, reading. Office: Oracle 500 Oracle Pkwy Redwood City CA 94065

PENNEY, ALEXANDRA, magazine editor-in-chief, writer; b. May 23, 1939; married; 1 child. Grad., Smith Coll.; MA, Hunter Coll., 1977. Editor health and beauty Glamour mag.; editor at large Bantam Doubleday; editor-in-chief Self mag., 1989. Author: How to Make Love to a Man, 1981, Great Sex, 1985, How to Keep Your Man Monogamous, 1989; co-author (with Howard Kaminsky): Magic Words: A Collection of Workplace Wisdom for Spectacular Results on the Job, 2004, Magic Words at Work, 2004; contbr. (articles) to N.Y. Times Mag., Vogue, others.

PENNEY, CHARLES RAND, lawyer, civic worker; b. Buffalo, July 26, 1923; s. Charles Patterson and Gretchen (Rand) P. BA, Yale U., 1945; JD, U. Va., 1951; DFA (hon.), SUNY, 1995, Niagara U., 2007. Bar: Md. 1952, NY 1958, U.S. Supreme Ct. 1958. Law sec. to US Dist. Ct. Judge W.C. Coleman, Balt., 1951-52; dir. devel. office Children's Hosp., Buffalo, 1952-54; sales mgr. Amherst Mfg. Corp., Williamsville, NY, 1954—56, Delevan Electronics Corp., East Aurora, NY; mem. firm Penney & Penney, Buffalo, 1958-61; pvt. practice Niagara County, NY, 1961—. Exhbns. include Mus. Modern Art, NYC, 1962, Whitney Mus. Am. Art, NYC, 1963, 79, 80, Burchfield-Penney Art Ctr., 1973, 92-2003, Meml. Art Gallery, Rochester, 1976, 78, 83, 88, U. Iowa, 1978, Columbus Gallery Fine Arts, Ohio, 1976, 78. Hon. life trustee Burchfield-Penney Art Ctr.; adv. bd. Found. Study of Arts and Crafts Movement at Roycroft; hon. bd. dirs. Buffalo-Lille/France Assn., Inc. 2d lt. U.S. Army, 1943-46. Recipient Pres.'s Disting. Svc. award Buffalo State Coll., 1991, Disting. Svc. to Culture award Coll. Arts and Scis., SUNY, Potsdam, 1983; named Disting. fellow Cultural Studies of the Burchfield-Penney Art Ctr., 1994, Outstanding Individual Philanthropist, Nat. Soc. Fund Raising Execs. Western NY, 1996, Individual Patron of the Arts award Buffalo and Erie County Arts Coun. and Buffalo C. of C., 1997, Citation for Outstanding Achievements and Svc. to Lockport Cmty., NY State Assembly, 1997; awarded Key to City of Lockport, 1997; named to Lockport Hist. Walk of Fame, 1999. Fellow The Explorers Club; mem. AARP, YWCA Niagra (life), Albright-Knox Art Gallery Buffalo (life), Buffalo Mus. Sci. (Life), Buffalo and Erie County Hist. Soc. (life, Red Jacket award 2000), Niagara County Hist. Soc. (life), Old Ft. Niagara (life), Buffalo Soc. Artists (hon. trustee), Hist. Lockport (life), Landmark Soc. Western NY (life), Am. Ceramic Cir., Hist. Lewiston (life), Friends of U. Rochester Librs. (life) Meml. Art Gallery U. Rochester (hon. bd. mgrs., hon. life), Winslow Homer Soc. of Dirs. Cir. (hon. life), Smithsonian Instn. (benefactors cir.), Rochester Hist. Soc. (life), Am. Hist. Print Collectors Soc. (life), Burchfield Homestead Soc. (hon. life), Charles E. Burchfield Nature and Art Ctr., Archives Am. Art, Mark Twain Soc. (hon.), U. Rochester's Pres.'s Soc. (hon. life), U. Iowa's Pres.'s Club (hon. life), Va. Law Found., Nat. Geog. Soc. (life), World's Fair Collectors Soc., Hist. Soc. of Tonawandas (life), Pres.'s Cir. Buffalo State Coll. (hon. life), Buffalo State Alumni Assn. (life), Yale Sailing Assocs., Yale Glee Club Assocs., Peanut Pals, Grolier Club, Pan Am. Expo Collectors Soc., Buffalo Indsl. Heritage Com., Roycrofters-at-Large Assn. (life), Arctic Cir. Club, Order of the Alaska Walrus, Automobile Club (Lockport), Niagara County Antiques Club (hon.), Rochester Art Club (hon. life), Fine Arts Mus. San Francisco (patron), De Young & Legion of Honor Museums (patron), U. Cir., SUNY Buffalo, Chi Psi, Phi Alpha Delta. Office: 538 Bewley Building Lockport NY 14094-2944 Home Phone: 716-733-2524; Office Phone: 716-433-2524. Personal E-mail: charliepenney@aol.com. *I have tried to strive for excellence in whatever I undertake, be it small or large. What success I may have achieved has required initiative, imagination, and dedication to the task at hand. Satisfaction comes from the hard work that leads to an objective. In all that I do I adhere to the Golden Rule and to fairness, honesty, and understanding in human relationships. I try to maintain a sense of humor at all times. And I enjoy living in a small community because it is from such areas that the strength of America comes.*

PENNEY, SHERRY HOOD, academic administrator, consultant; b. Marlette, Mich., Sept. 4, 1937; d. Terrance and B. Jean (Stoutenburg) Hood; m. Carl Murray Penney, July 8, 1961 (div. 1978); children: Michael Murray, Jeffrey Hood; m. James Duane Livingston, Mar. 30, 1985. BA, Albion Coll., 1959; MA, U. Mich., 1961; PhD, SUNY, Albany, 1972; LLD (hon.), Albion Coll., 1989; degree (hon.), Quincy Coll., 1999. Vis. asst. prof. Union Coll., Schenectady, NY, 1972-73; assoc. higher edn. NY State Edn. Dept., Albany, 1973-76; assoc. provost Yale U., New Haven, 1976-82; vice chancellor acad. programs, policy and planning SUNY System, Albany, 1982-88; acting pres. SUNY, Plattsburgh, 1986-87; chancellor U. Mass., Boston, 1988-95; pres. U. Mass. Sys., Boston, 1995; chancellor U. Mass. Boston, 1996-2000, endowed prof., 2001—. Chmn., bd. dirs. Nat. Higher Edn. Mgmt. Sys., Boulder, Colo., 1985-87; mem. commn. on higher edn. New Eng. Assn. Schs. and Colls., Boston, 1979-82, Mid. States Assn. Schs. and Colls., Phila., 1986-88; mem. commn. on women Am. Coun. Edn., Washington, 1979-81, commn. on govt. rels., 1990-94; bd. dirs. NSTAR, South Shore Hosp. Author: Patrician in Politics, 1974; co-author (with James D. Livingston) A Very Dangerous Woman: Martha Wright and Women's Rights, 2004; editor: Women and Management in Higher Education, 1975; contbr. articles to profl. jours. Nat. adv. com. Nat. Initiative for Women in Higher Edn., 2001—05; active Internat. Trade Task Force, 1994—96; exec. com. Challenge to Leadership, 1988, chair, 1995—98; trustee Berkeley Div. Sch., Yale U., 1978—82, John F. Kennedy Libr. Found., 1988—2001; chair Met. Affairs Coalition, 1999—2001; bd. trustees New Eng. Aquarium, 1990—2004; chair The Ednl. Resource Inst., 1996—; bd. visitors WEIU, 2002—06; bd. dirs. HERS, 1992—, Mary Baker Eddy Libr., Boston, 2001—06, Albany Symphony Orch., 1982—88, U. Mass. Found., 1988—2000, Mcpl. Rsch. Bur., Boston, 1990—2001, New Eng. Coun., 1990—2000, Greater Boston C. of C., 1989—2002, Met. Affairs Coalition, Greater Boston One to One Leadership Coun., 1990—2000, NASULGC Commn. Urban Affairs, 1990—2000, The Environ. Bus. Coun., 1991—97, South Shore Hosp., Mass., 2006—. Recipient Disting. Alumna award Albion Coll., 1978, Disting. Citizen award for racial harmony Black/White Boston, 1994, Am. Coun. on Edn./Nat. Identification Program award, Mass., Leadership award, 1995, New Eng. Women's Leadership award, 1996, Pinnacle award for Lifetime Achievement Greater Boston C. of C., 1998, Abigail Adams award, Mass. Women's Polit. Caucus, 2003. Mem. Orgn. Am. Historians, Comml. Club (Boston). Unitarian Universalist. Office: U Mass Boston 100 Morrissey Blvd Boston MA 02125-3300 Office Phone: 617-287-3890.

PENNIMAN, NICHOLAS GRIFFITH, IV, retired newspaper publisher; b. Balt., Mar. 7, 1938; s. Nicholas Griffith Penniman III and Esther Cox Lony (Wight) Keeney; m. Linda Jane Simmons, Feb. 4, 1967; children: Rebecca Helmle, Nicholas G. V. AB, Princeton U., 1960; MA, Washington U., 1999. Asst. bus. mgr. Ill. State Jour. Register, Springfield, 1964-69, bus. mgr., 1969-75; asst. gen. mgr. St. Louis Post-Dispatch, 1975-84, gen. mgr., 1984-86, pub., 1986-99; sr. v.p. newspapers ops. Pulitzer Pub. Co., 1986-99; pres., CEO Pulitzer Comm. Newspapers Inc., 1997-99; chmn. bd. Penniman & Browne, Inc., Balt., 2001—. Chmn. Downtown St. Louis, Inc., 1988-90, Mo. Health and Ednl. Facilities Adminstrn., 1982-85, Ill. State Fair Bd., Springfield, 1973-75, Forest Pk. Forever, 1991-93, Pks. and Open Space Task Force St. Louis 2004, 1996-00, St. Louis Sports Com., 1992-93, Gateway Pks. and Trls. 2004, 1999-04; pres. Caring Found. Children, 1988-91; trustee St. Louis Country Day Sch., 1983-86, Nat. Recreation Found., 2003—, Merc. Libr. St. Louis, 1997-00; bd. dirs. Mo. Coalition for Environment, 1997-2000, Randall Rsch. Ctr., Pineland, Fla., 2001—, Friends of Rookery Bay, 2004—; chmn. bd. Am. Rivers, 2004-06, Conservancy of SW Fla., 2007—; mem. Collier County Environ. Adv. Coun., Fla., 2005—. With US Army, 1962—67. Mem.: Rolling Rock Club, Elkridge Club, Noonday Club (pres. 1994), Grey Oaks Country Club. Home: 611 Portside Dr Naples FL 34103-4118 E-mail: ngpiv@aol.com.

PENNIMAN, RICHARD WAYNE See LITTLE RICHARD

PENNINGER, FRIEDA ELAINE, retired literature educator; b. Marion, NC, Apr. 11, 1927; d. Fred Hoyle and Lena Frances (Young) Penninger. AB, U. N.C., Greensboro, 1948; MA, Duke U., 1950, PhD, 1961. Copywriter Sta. WSJS, Winston-Salem, NC, 1948-49; asst. prof. English Flora Macdonald Coll., Red Springs, NC, 1950-51; tchr. English Barnwell, SC, 1951-52, Brunswick, Ga., 1952-53; instr. English U. Tenn., Knoxville, 1953-56; instr., asst. prof. Woman's Coll., U. N.C., Greensboro, 1956-58, 60-63; asst. prof., assoc. prof. U. Richmond (Va.), 1963-71; chair. dept. English Westhampton Coll., Richmond, 1971-78; prof. English U. Richmond, 1971-91, Bostwick prof. English, 1987-91, ret., 1991. Author: William Caxton, 1979, Chaucer's "Troilus and Criseyde" and "The Knight's Tale": Fictions Used, 1993, (novel) Look at Them, 1990; compiler, editor: English Drama to 1660, 1976; editor: Festschrift for Prof. Marguerite Roberts, 1976. Fellow Southeastern Inst. of Mediaeval and Renaissance Studies, 1965, 67, 69. Mem.: Friends of The Libr. U. NC Greensboro (bd. dirs. 2005—). Democrat. Presbyterian. Home: 2701 Camden Rd Greensboro NC 27403-1438

PENNINGTON, AUBREY EL, director; s. Elhanan and Rosie Mae Pennington; m. Kathy Lee Alstott, Dec. 28, 1985; children: Zachary El, Tyler Ray. BS, Campbellsville U., 1993; MA, Western Ky. U., 1999; Rank I, Union Coll., 2002. Cert. provisional secondary tchr. Ky. Dept. Edn., 1994, curriculum cons. Ky. Dept. Edn., 2005. History/social studies tchr. Casey Co. Pub. Schs., Liberty, Ky., 1993—99; region six social studies cons. Ky. Dept. Edn., Corbin, 2000—03; curriculum specialist Pulaski Co. Pub. Schs., Somerset, Ky., 2003—. Program cons. Am. Legacies Fed. History Grant, Frankfort, Ky., 2003—; mid. sch. social studies textbook editor McGraw-Hill Publishers, Inc., Englewood, NJ, 2005; vol. hist. interpreter Stones River Nat. Battlefield Pk., Murfreesboro, Tenn., 2006—; vol. oral historian U. Tex. Tech: Vietnam Oral History Project, Austin, 2005—. Mem.: Ky. Assn. Sch. Adminstrs. (assoc.), Assn. Supr. for Curriculum Devel. (assoc.), Ky. Assn. Tchrs. of History (assoc.), Ky. Coun. for Social Studies (assoc.), Nat. History in Edn. Assn. (assoc.), Am. Hist. Assn. (assoc.), Ky. Hist. Soc. (assoc.). Avocations: local historical research, photography, hiking. Office: Pulaski County Public Schools 500 University Dr Somerset KY 42502 Home Phone: 606-787-0221; Office Phone: 606-679-1123. Personal E-mail: history2234@yahoo.com.

PENNINGTON, BEVERLY MELCHER, financial services company executive; b. Vermillion, SD, Feb. 8, 1931; d. Cecil Lloyd and Phyllis Cecelia (Walz) M.; m. Glen D., Sept. 1, 1965 (dec. Aug. 1986); 1 child, Terri Lynn. BS, U. S.D., Vermillion, 1952. Enrolled agt. cert. IRS 1989. Sec. budget dept. Bur. of Indian Affairs, Aberdeen, S.D., 1952-53, pvt. sec., 1953-54, U.S. P.H.S. Indian Health, Aberdeen, 1954-55; adminstr. asst. U.S. Pub. Health Svc., Anchorage, 1955-58, U.S. Pub. Health, Dental Pub. Health, Washington, 1958-61; grant adminstr. Dental Pub. Health, Washington, 1961-65; co-owner Pen Mel Marina, Platte, S.D, 1965-74, Pennington Tax Service, Platte, 1974-86, owner, 1986-93; pres., CEO, White Tiger Fin. Svc., Inc., Platte, 1994—. Contbr. articles to profl. jours. Mem. Platte Women's Club, sec., 1965-68, pres., 1968-70, 89-91; mem. Libr. Bd., Sec., 1982-85, treas., 1995—. Fellow Am. Soc. Tax Profls. (sec. 1989-91, 2d v.p. 1995, 1st v.p. 1996, pres. 1997); mem. NAFE, Platte C. of C. (v.p. 1989, pres. 1990), Lyric Theatre Mus. Soc. (pres. 1988-92, v.p. 2005—), U.S. C. of C., Washington Dakota Cen. Com. Republican. Presbyterian. Avocations: collecting jewelry, reading, dress designing, gourmet cooking. Office: White Tiger Fin Svc Inc 420 Main St Platte SD 57369 Office Phone: 605-337-2603. Business E-Mail: whitetigerfinancial@inbox.com.

PENNINGTON, CHAD (JAMES CHADWICK PENNINGTON), professional football player; b. Knoxville, Tenn., June 26, 1976; s. Elwood and Denise Pennington; m. Robin Hampton; children: Cole, Luke. BA in Broadcast Jour., Marshall U., 2000. Quarterback N.Y. Jets, 2000—. Co-founder Share Your Soles Charity, 2003—. Named NFL Comeback Player of Yr., AP, 2006. Achievements include being a Rhodes Scholar finalist, graduating with 3.75 GPA; holds Marshall U. school records for touchdown passes & passing yards; set NY Jets team record for passer rating (104.2), 2002. Office: NY Jets 1000 Fulton Ave Hempstead NY 11550 *

PENNINGTON, JODIE A., education outreach educator; b. Danville, Ky., Oct. 27, 1949; s. Emmett Clair and Edna Davis Pennington; m. Melinda Snider Pennington, June 10, 1972; children: Sara E., Ellen M. Pennington Steinmiller. BS, Western Ky. U., Bowling Green, 1971; MS, U. Ill., Urbana-Champaign, 1974, PhD, 1976. Asst. prof. animal sci. U. Wisconsin-River Falls, 1976—81, Purdue U., West Lafayette, Ind., 1981—85; asst. to assoc. prof. agr. Western Ky. U., Bowling Green, 1986—92; prof./dairy specialist Univ Ark. Coop Ext. Svc., Little Rock, 1993—. Contbr. more than 400 articles to profl. jours. Active United Meth. Ch., Conway, Ark., 1993—. Rsch. grantee, 1976—86. Mem.: Nat. Mastitis Coun., Dairy Shrine (state coord. 2000—06), Am. Dairy Sci. Assn. (3 com. chairmanships, bd. dirs. So. region), Am. Dairy Sci. Assn. Found. (charter mem.), Holstein Assn. Am., Ark. Assn. Registered Profl. Animal Scientists (pres. 1998—99), Ark. Assn. Coop. Ext. Specialists (pres., bd. mem. 1998—2002), Omicron Delta Kappa (life), Epsilon Sigma Phi (life), Gamma Sigma Delta (life), Sigma Xi (life), Phi Eta Sigma (life; advisor 1981—86), Alpha Gamma Rho (life; chpt. advisor 1976—81, Cert. of Merit 1981). Methodist. Avocations: gardening, landscaping, cattle and goat shows. Office: Univ Arkansas Coop Ext Svc 2301 S Univ Ave PO Box 391 Little Rock AR 72203 Home Phone: 501-336-8986; Office Phone: 501-671-2190. Office Fax: 501-671-2185. Business E-Mail: jpennington@uaex.edu.

PENNINGTON, KAREN HARDER, lawyer; b. Amarillo, Tex., June 7, 1956; d. Alvin L. and Rosemary Herskowitz Harder; BS in Biology, W. Tex. State U., 1977; JD, U. Tex., 1986. Bar: Calif. 1986, Tex. 1998, US Patent and Trademark Office 1993, Hopi Tribal Ct. 1993. Assoc. atty. Thelen, Marrin, Johnson & Bridges, LA, 1986—89, Quinn, Emanuel & Urquhart, LA, 1989—91, Crosby, Heafey, Roach & May, LA, 1991—92; atty. Law Office of Karen H. Pennington, Long Beach, Calif., 1993—97, Cath. Charities Immigration Counseling Svcs., Dallas, 1998—2000; immigration atty. Law Office of Karen H. Pennington, Dallas, 2000—.

Recipient cover story, Sept. 9 issue, Tex. Lawyer mag., 2002. Mem.: Dallas Bar Assn., LA County Bar Assn., Tex. Bar Assn., Calif. Bar Assn., Am. Immigration Lawyers Assn., North Tex. Coalition Just Peace, United For Peace and Justice, Dallas Peace Ctr. Roman Catholic. Achievements include representation of post-Sept. 11 immigration/national security detainees both before the courts and in FBI interrogations. Office: Law Office of Karen H Pennington Ste 410 701 Commerce St Dallas TX 75202 Office Phone: 214-741-7711. Office Fax: 214-741-7733. Business E-Mail: penningtonlaw@yahoo.com.

PENNINGTON, RICHARD J., police chief; m. Renee Pennington; 1 child. BA, American U.; MA, U. Dist. Columbia. Asst. police chief Met. Police Dept., Washington, 1993—94; chief of police New Orleans Police Dept., 1994—2002, Atlanta Police Dept., 2002—. Named an Most Influential Black Americans, Ebony mag., 2006. Mem.: Nat. Orgn. of Black Law Enforcement Execs. (NOBLE) (v.p., pres., immediate past pres. 2006). Office: Atlanta Police Dept 675 Ponce De Leon Ave Atlanta GA 30308

PENNINGTON, WILLIAM MARK, sportswriter; b. Hartford, Conn., Dec. 12, 1956; s. Albert William and Lillian Anne (Lewis) P.; m. Joyce Hand, July 14, 1990; children: Anne D'Amour, Elise Holly, John Taylor. BS, Boston U., 1978. Reporter The Bristol Press, Bristol, Conn., 1976-77, The Associated Press, Boston, 1977, The Providence Jour.-Bull., Providence, 1977-79, The Stamford Advocate, Stamford, Conn., 1979-84, The Record, Hackensack, NJ, 1984-89, syndicated columnist, sr. writer, 1989-97; reporter The New York Times, 1997—. Author: The Winning Spirit, 1991, The Heisman, 2004; contbg. author: (book) Best Sports Stories, 1983, 85, 87, 94. Recipient Best Story award Associated Press Sports Editors, 1985, 89, 91, 93, 96, Best Columnist award, 1983, 89, 95, 96, 2004; Best Story award, 1999. Mem. Baseball Writers Assn. of Am., Boston U. Football Alumni Assn., New England Hist. Genealogical Soc. Roman Catholic. Office: The NY Times 229 W 43rd St New York NY 10036-3959 Office Phone: 212-556-7371.

PENNISI, LIZ, women's health nurse; b. Bklyn., Nov. 20, 1953; d. Alexander and Marjorie (Soviero) Perillo; children: Stephen, Scott, Greg. Diploma, Beth Israel Sch. Nursing, NYC, 1974. RN, N.Y.; cert. ambulatory women's health nurse. Staff nurse Montefiore Hosp., Bronx, NY, 1974-75; mem. staff Beth Israel Med. Ctr., NYC, 1975-77; office nurse Martin Kurman, M.D., NYC, 1977-80, Adam Romoff, M.D. and Suzanne Yale, M.D., P.C, 1984—. Mem. AWHONN. Avocations: tennis, horseback riding, reading. Office: Drs Romoff and Yale 768 Park Ave New York NY 10021-4153 E-mail: lizpennisi@hotmail.com.

PENNISTEN, JOHN WILLIAM, computer scientist, actuary, linguist; b. Buffalo, Jan. 25, 1939; s. George William and Lucy Josephine (Gates) P. AB in Math. and Chemistry with honors, Hamilton Coll., 1960; postgrad., Harvard U., 1960-61, U.S. Army Lang. Sch., 1962-63; MS in Computer Sci. with honors, NY Inst. Tech., 1987. Cert. Application Developer IBM, 2006, assoc. developer Oracle Corp., 2006; in Taxation NYU, 1982, in Asian Langs. NYU, 1992, in Profl. Banking Am. Inst. Banking, Am. Bankers Assn., 1988. Actuarial asst. New Eng. Mut. Life Ins. Co., Boston, 1965-66; asst. actuary Mass. Gen. Life Ins. Co., Boston, 1966-68; actuarial assoc. John Hancock Mut. Life Ins. Co., Boston, 1968-71; asst. actuary George B. Buck Cons. Actuaries, Inc., NYC, 1971-75, Martin E. Segal Co., NYC, 1975-80; actuary Laiken Siegel Co., NYC, 1980; cons. Bklyn., 1981—; timesharing and database analyst banklink corp. cash mgmt. div. Chem. Bank NYC, 1983-85; programmer analyst Empire Blue Cross and Blue Shield, NYC, 1986-88, Mt. Sinai Med. Ctr., NYC, 1988-89, French Am. Banking Corp. (subs. Banque National de Paris), NYC, 1989; sr. programmer analyst Dean Witter Reynolds, Inc., NYC, 1989-92; computer specialist for software NYC Dept. Fin., 1992—97, computer specialist, 2003—; sr. cons. Pinkerton Computer Cons., Inc., NYC, 1997-99; tech. officer J.P. Morgan Chase Co., NYC, 1999—2003. Enrolled actuary U.S. Fed. Pension Legis. Bklyn., 1976—. Contbr. articles to profl. jours. With US Army, 1961-64. Fellow: Soc. Actuaries; mem.: IEEE Computer Soc., MLA, AAAS, Harvard Grad. Soc., Am. Friends of Covent Garden, Bklyn. Heights Assn., Nat. Ry. Hist. Soc., Am. Chem. Soc., Math. Assn. Am., Nat. Model R.R. Assn. (life), Ry. and Locomotive Hist. Soc. (life), Am. Math. Soc., Assn. Computational Linguistics, Linguistic Soc. Am., Am. Assn. Artificial Intelligence, Assn. Computing Machinery, Met. Opera Guild, Nat. Rep. Club Capitol Hill, Am. Legion, Phi Beta Kappa. Republican. Presbyterian. Office: NYC Dept Fin 345 Adams St 12th Fl Brooklyn NY 11201 Business E-Mail: pennistenj@finance.nyc.gov.

PENNOYER, PETER MORGAN, architect; b. NYC, Feb. 19, 1957; s. Robert Morgan and Victoria (Parsons) P.; m. Katherine Lee Ridder, Sept. 24, 1988; children: Jane Delano, Anthony Ridder. BA, Columbia U., NYC, 1979, MArch, 1983. Registered arch., NY. Designer Robert A.M. Stern Archs., NYC, 1979-83; pres. Peter Pennoyer Archs. P.C., NYC, 1990—. Contbg. author: Inside Architecture, 1997; prin. works include Mark Hotel, NYC, Waldorf Astoria, Mandarin Oriental, Hong Kong. Bd. dirs. Mcpl. Art Soc., NYC, 1994, Sir John Soane's Mus. Found., 1999, Morgan Libr.; pres. poetry project St. Marks Ch., NYC, 1994-97. Recipient award Friends of Upper East Side Hist. Dists., 1992, NYC Landmarks award, 1994. Mem. AIA. Office: Peter Pennoyer Archs 432 Park Ave S 11th Fl New York NY 10016 Office Phone: 212-779-9765. E-mail: peter@ppapc.com.

PENNOYER, ROBERT M., lawyer; b. NYC, Apr. 9, 1925; BA, Harvard U., 1946; LL.B., Columbia U., 1950. Bar: N.Y. 1951, U.S. Supreme Ct. 1971. Asst. US atty. criminal divsn. (so. dist.) NY US Dept. Justice, 1953-55; asst. to gen. counsel US Dept. Def., Washington, 1955-57, spl. asst. to asst. sec. for internat. security affairs, 1957-58; ptnr. Patterson, Belknap, Webb & Tyler, NYC, 1962-95, of counsel, 1995—. Trustee Carnegie Instn., Washington, 1968-79, John Merck Fund, 1982—, Mrs. Giles Whiting Found., 1970—2000, Met. Mus. Art, 1966—, Pierpont Morgan Libr., 1969—, Columbia U., 1982-88, Boyce Thompson Inst. for Plant Rsch., Cornell U., 1974-97, Inst. Democracy Studies, 1999-2002. Lt. (j.g.) USNR, PTO, 1944-46. Recipient Lifetime Achievement award, Am. Lawyer mag., 2006. Mem. ABA, N.Y. State Bar Assn., Assn. Bar City N.Y., Century Assn. Office: Patterson Belknap Webb & Tyler Rm 2200 1133 Ave of the Americas New York NY 10036-6731 Office Phone: 212-336-2700. Business E-Mail: rmpennoyer@pbwt.com.

PENNY, BRAD (BRADLEY WAYNE PENNY), professional baseball player; b. Blackwell, Okla., May 24, 1978; Draft pick Ariz. Diamondbacks, 1996; pitcher Fla. Marlins, 2000—04, LA Dodgers, 2004—. Named to Nat. League All-Star Team, Maj. League Baseball, 2006—07. Achievements include leading the Nat. League in wins (16), 2006; pitched two career complete game shutouts, 2001, 02. Avocations: fishing, hunting. Office: LA Dodgers 1000 Elysian Park Ave Los Angeles CA 90012-1199 *

PENNY, NICHOLAS BEAVER, museum curator; b. London, Dec. 21, 1949; s. Joseph Noel and Anges Celia (Roberts) P.; m. Anne Philomel Udy (div.); children: Caroline Emil, Elizabeth Joan. MA, St. Catharines Coll., Cambridge, Mass., 1971, Courtauld Inst., London, 1973, PhD, 1975. Leverhulme fellow Cambridge U., 1973-75; lectr. history of art dept. U. Manchester, 1975-82; sr. rsch. fellow King's Coll., Cambridge, 1982-84; keeper dept. Western art Ashmolean Mus., Oxford, Eng., 1984-89; Clore curator Renaissance painting Nat. Gallery, London, 1990—2007; sr. curator sculpture Nat. Gallery of Art, Washington, 2002—. Slade prof. U. Oxford, 1980-81. Author: Church Monuments in Romantic England, 1977; co-author: Taste and The Antique, 1981, Raphael, 1983; editor exh. catalog and book, Reynolds, 1984. Fellow Am. Acad. Arts & Scis. Mailing: Sr Curator Sculpture Nat Gallery of Art 2000B S Club Dr Landover MD 20785 *

PENNY, ROGER PRATT, retired management consultant; b. Buffalo, July 13, 1936; s. George Albert and Louise (Mings) P.; m. Judith Stevens, Aug. 25, 1957; children: David, Sarah, Julia. BA in Adminstrv. Engring., Union Coll., 1958; grad., Wharton Bus. Sch., 1993. From supt. to pres. Bethlehem Steel Corp., Lackawanna, NY, 1958—91, pres., 1991—99, vice chmn., 1999—2000, ret., 2000. Mem. United Way, Buffalo, 1960-82; chmn. campaign United Way Porter County, Valparaiso, Ind., 1986; mem. Orchard Park Town Bd., 1970-82; mem. adv. bd. Purdue U., West Lafayette, Ind., 1985-86, Bus. Sch., Valparaiso U., 1986; bd. dirs. Minsi Trails coun. Boy Scouts Am., Lehigh Valley, Pa., 1988—, pres., 1996; trustee St. Luke's Hosp., 1998-2001. Mem. Am. Iron and Steel Inst., Assn. Iron and Steel Engrs., Valparaiso C. of C. (dir. 1985-86), Orchard Park C. of C., Buffalo C. of C., Sand Creek Club (pres. 1983-86), Buffalo Soccer Club (pres., sec. 1960-75), Saucon Valley Country Club, Wynstone Golf Club. Republican. Episcopalian. Office Phone: 847-756-4211.

PENNY, SIMON, art educator; Prof. art and robotics Carnegie Mellon U., Pitts., 1993—99; European prof. interactive environments Merz Akademie, U. Portsmouth, Stuttgart/Portsmouth, England, 2000—01; prof. arts and engring. U. Calif., Irvine, 2001—. Internat. bd. ISEA, Rotterdam, 1990—98; new media inst., rsch. adv. bd. Banff Ctr., Alberta, Canada, 2003—. Prodr.(curator, editior, director): Machine Culture, Siggraph93. Recipient Cyberstar, GMD and WDR, Germany, 1998, Australian Ctr. for Moving Image, 2000—03; fellow, Zentrum fur Kunst und Medientechnologie, 1997; grantee, Langlois Found. for Sci. and Art. Achievements include invention of traces 3D machine vision system. Office: Arts Computation Engring Univ Calif Irvine CA Home Phone: 949-725-9890. Business E-Mail: penny@uci.edu.

PENROD, MARIAN PENUEL, wellness consultant, retired school librarian; b. Statesville, Tenn., May 11, 1930; d. Hayden L. Penuel and Zoie L. Cunningham; m. William T. Penrod, Jr., June 8, 1954 (div. Oct. 1979); children: Cheryl Anne Penrod Puryear, Paula Wynn, Laura Lynn Penrod Moseng. BS, Middle Tenn. State Coll., 1952; M of Religious Edn., So. Bapt. Theol. Sem., Louisville, 1955; EdM, U. Miami, 1958. Cert. specialist in pastoral care Pastoral Counseling Ctrs. Tenn., Inc., 2002. Tchr. Parma Elem., Mich., 1953—54, Golden Pond Elem., Ky., 1955—57, West Jackson Bapt., Tenn., 1965—66; tchr., libr. Madison County, Jackson, 1967—69; tchr. Dyer County, Dyersburg, Tenn., 1969—70; sch. libr. Murfreesboro City Schs., Tenn., 1972—98; wellness cons. Nikken, Inc., 1998—. Baptist. Avocations: reading, writing, travel, continued education. Office Phone: 615-893-7398.

PENROD, STEVEN DAVID, law educator; b. Ft. Wayne, Ind., Apr. 15, 1947; s. Kenneth David Penrod and Loretta Elaine (Green) Slater; m. Marcia Gilley, June 11, 1969 (div. 1979); m. Joan Dobrof, June 14, 1980; 1 child, Rachel Dobrof. BA, Yale Coll., 1969; JD, Harvard U., 1974, PhD, 1979. Asst. prof. psychology U. Wis., Madison, 1979-85, assoc. prof. psychology, 1985-88, prof. psychology, 1988-89; prof. law U. Minn. Law Sch., Mpls., 1989—95; dir. of law & psych. prog., prof of psych. & prof of Law U. Nebraska, 1995—2001; disting. prof. of psych. John Jay Coll. of Criminal Justice, NYC, 2001—. Vis. prof. law U. Wis., Madison, 1983, Ind. U., Bloomington, 1985; rsch. cons. Calif. Jud. Coun., San Francisco, 1988-90, Nat. Ctr. State Cts., Williamsburg, Va., 1988-; adj. prof. of psych. U. Minn. 1990-1995. Author: Inside the Jury, 1983, Social Psychology, 1986, The Question of Pornography, 1987, Psychology, 1988. Lt. USN, 1971—73. Mem. Am. Psychol. Assn. (disting. early career award 1986), Am. Psychol. Soc., Am. Sociol. Assn., Am. Psychology-Law Soc. (sec.-treas. 1988-90). Office: John Jay Coll of Criminal Justice 445 W 59th St New York NY 10019 Office Phone: 212-237-8877. E-mail: spenrod@jjay.cuny.edu.

PENROSE, CYNTHIA C., retired health care consultant; b. Manila, Philippines, Nov. 24, 1939; d. Douglas Lee Lipscomb Cordiner and Jane (Sturgeon) Edises; m. Douglas Francis Penrose, July 11, 1959 (div. 1981); children: Vicki, Lee Douglas; m. Alan Harrison Magazine, Aug. 30, 1984. BA, U. Calif., Berkeley, 1963; MBA, U. Santa Clara, 1977. LCSW. V.p., dir. employment Resource Ctr. for Women, Palo Alto, Calif., 1973-78; bus. planner Raychem Corp., Menlo Park, Calif., 1979; adminstrv. mgr. Electric Power Rsch. Inst., Palo Alto, 1979-83; sr. ptnr. MB Assocs., Washington, 1983-88; dir. ops. Utility Data Inst., Washington, 1984-85, Randmark, Inc., 1986-87; coord. market devel. for Mid-Atlantic states Kaiser Found. Health Plan, Washington, 1987-88, asst. to assoc. regional mgr., 1988-94; market planner MetraHealth, Vienna, Va., 1995; exec. staff asst. United Health-Care, Vienna, 1995, dir. strategic planning, splty. cos., 1996-97; dir. spl. projects MetraComp subs. United HealthCare, Vienna, 1995, v.p. regulatory affairs and compliance, 1997-99; ptnr. Penrose Mag. LLC, 2000—01; ret., 2001. Bd. dirs., treas. Unique Enterprises, Washington, 1985-87; sec. Wesley Property Mgmt. Co., 1987-89; bd. dirs. Wesley Housing Devel. Corp., 1988-89. Chair vol. com. Habitat for Humanity, No. Va., 2002—03, bd. dirs., 2003—06, chair Restore adv. com., 2003—05, v.p., exec. com., 2005—06; mem. Affirmative Action Adv. Com., Palo Alto, 1975—76; bd. dirs., sec. Am. Hospice Found., 1995—97, treas., 1998—2000; bd. dirs. Nat. Inst. for Med. Options, 1999—2001; bd. dirs., v.p. LWV, Berkeley and Palo Alto, 1966—73; chmn. program adv. com. Resource Ctr. for Women, Palo Alto, 1980—83; bd. dirs. HFHNV, 2003—06. Mem. Peninsula Profl. Women's Network (v.p. 1981-82), U. Calif. Alumni Assn., AAUW (Bicentennial br. sec. 1986-88), Capitol Area Soc. Healthcare Planning and Mktg., Nat. Capital Healthcare Execs., LWV. Democrat. Episcopalian. Avocations: swimming, nutrition and health, reading. Home and Office: 28 Fillingame Way PO Box 740 Rehoboth Beach DE 19971 Personal E-mail: ccpenrose@comcast.net.

PENSABENE, JUDITH K., lawyer; b. 1945; BA, U. Mo., Kansas City; postgrad., U. Houston, 1971; JD, U. Tulsa, 1975. Bar: Okla. 1975, D.C. 1978. Assoc. Holliman Langholz Runnels & Dowart, Tulsa, 1974—78; cons. environ. issues, 1980—89; sr. minority counsel Com. Energy & Natural Resources, U.S. Senate, 1990—95; v.p. & counsel Constellation Energy Group, Washington, 1995—2002; dep. chief counsel Com. Energy & Natural Resources, U.S. Senate, 2002—03, chief counsel, 2003—. Articles editor: U. Tulsa Law Jour. Mem.: Phi Delta Phi, Order of Curule (chair). Office: Committee on Energy and Natural Resources Room 364 Senate Dirksen Office Building Washington DC 20510-6150 Office Phone: 202-224-4971.

PENSE, ALAN WIGGINS, metallurgical engineer, academic administrator; b. Sharon, Conn., Feb. 3, 1934; s. Arthur Wilton and May Beatrice (Wiggins) P.; m. Muriel Drews Taylor, June 28, 1958; children: Daniel Alan, Steven Taylor, Christine Muriel. B.Metall. Engring., Cornell U., 1957; MS, Lehigh U., 1959, PhD, 1962. Research asst. Lehigh U., Bethlehem, Pa., 1957-59, instr., 1960-62, asst. prof., 1962-65, asso. prof., 1965-71, prof., 1971-96, chmn. dept. metallurgy and materials engring., 1977-83, assoc. dean Coll. Engring. and Applied Scis., 1984-88, dean, 1988-90, v.p., provost, 1990-96, prof. emeritus, 1996—. Assoc. dir. Ctr. Advanced Tech. for Large Structural Systems NSF, 1986-89; cons. adv. com. on reactor safeguards NRC, 1965-86; rsch. engr., 1997—; cons. Lehigh U., 1997—. Author: (with D. Henkel) Structure and Properties of Engineering Materials, 5th edit, 2001; also articles. Recipient Robinson award Lehigh U., 1965, Stabler award, 1972, Hillman award 1997, Materials Sci. and Engring. Disting. Alumni award, 2002; Danforth fellow, 1974-86. Fellow Am. Soc. Metals, Am. Welding Soc. (William Spraragan award 1963, Adams Membership award 1966, Jennings award 1970, Adams lectr. 1980, William Hobart medal 1982, Plummer lectr. 1995); mem. ASTM, Am. Soc. Engring. Edn. (Western Elec. award 1986), Internat. Inst. Welding, Nat. Acad. Engring. Republican. Evang. Congregationalist (bd. trustees Evang. Sch. Theology). Home: 2586 Lynhurst Dr Bethlehem PA 18017-3940 Office: The ATLSS Rsch Ctr 117 Atlss Dr Bethlehem PA 18015-4728 Office Phone: 610-758-6104. Business E-Mail: awp0@lehigh.edu. *Achievement of significant goals in our life must be balanced by the quality of that life itself, for what we are is as important as what we do.*

PENSHORN, JOHN S., health facility administrator; Stock analyst Piper Jaffray; dir. Capital Markets Comm. and Strategy UnitedHealth Grp., Minnetonka, Minn., 1998—, sr. v.p. Office: UnitedHealth Grp 9900 Bren Rd E Minnetonka MN 55343

PENSKA, KEITH HENRY, psychiatrist; b. Riviera Beach, Fla., Sept. 18, 1979; s. Ken Kern and Beth Jill Penska; m. Mary Christine Prahme, June 4, 2006. BS in Psychology, U. Fla., Gainesville, 2002; MD, U. Health Scis., Bethesda, 2006. Psychiatric intern Walter Reed Med. Ctr., Washington, 2006—. Capt. US Army, 2006—. Mem.: Mensa, Phi Beta Kappa. Avocations: reading, movies, bicycling. Home: 14317 Vivaldi Ct Burtonsville MD 20866

PENSKAR, MARK HOWARD, lawyer; b. Detroit, Mar. 4, 1953; s. Sol Leonard and Frances (Rosenthal) P.; m. Carol Ann Stewart, Aug. 7, 1977; children: David, Rebecca. BA, U. Mich., 1974, M in Pub. Policy, 1975, JD cum laude, 1977. Bar: Calif. 1977, U.S. Dist. Ct. (no. dist.) Calif. 1977, U.S. Dist. Ct. (ea. and ctrl. dists.) Calif. 1983, U.S. Dist. Ct. (so. dist.) Calif. 1988, U.S. Ct. Appeals (9th cir.) 1987, U.S. Tax Ct. 1993. Assoc. Pillsbury, Madison and Sutro, San Francisco, 1977-84, ptnr., 1985-96; sr. bus. litig. atty. Pacific Gas and Electric Co., San Francisco, 1996—, dir. and counsel, 2006—. Mediator Superior Ct. early settlement program, San Francisco; mediator and early neutral evaluator U.S. Dist. Ct. Alternative Dispute Resolution Program; bd. dirs. Legal Aid Soc. of San Francisco Employment Law Ctr. Mem. ABA, San Francisco Bar Assn., Commonwealth Club, Phi Gamma Delta (past pres. Bay Area grad. chpt.). Avocations: camping, golf, wine collecting, fishing. Home: 29 E Altarinda Dr Orinda CA 94563-2415 Office: Pacific Gas & Electric Co Law Dept B30A PO Box 7442 San Francisco CA 94120-7442 E-mail: MHP5@pge.com.

PENSLER, JAY MICHAEL, plastic surgeon, educator; b. Detroit, Apr. 29, 1954; s. Paul and Joyce (Keywell) P.; m. Laurie Ellen Olson, May 1985; children: Arielle, Alexander. BS Microbiology, U. Mich., 1976; MD, U. Chgo., 1980. Diplomate Am. Bd. Plastic Surgeons, Nat. Bd. Med. Examiners; lic. N.Y., Calif., Mass., Ill. Resident gen. surgery NYU Med. Ctr., 1980-83; resident plastic surgery U. Tex. Med. Br., Galveston, 1983-86; fellow craniofacial surgery Harvard U., Boston, 1986-87; plastic surgeon Northwestern Meml. Hosp., Chgo., 1987—; and assoc. prof. clin. plastic surgery Northwestern Univ. Med. Sch., Chgo. Assoc. prof. surgery Northwestern U., Chgo., 1987-93; plastic surgeon Children's Meml. Hosp., Chgo., 1987—; surf. staff Columbus-Cabrini Med. Ctr., Chgo., 1990—, Evanston (Ill.)-Glenbrook Hosps., 1992—. Featured on NBC, CBS, ABC, Fox-TV; contbr. more than 100 articles to profl. jours. Named one of Chgo.'s Top Doctors, Chgo. mag., 2003. Fellow Am. Coll. Surgeons (Met. Chgo. chpt.), Internat. Coll. Surgeons (Plastic Surgery); mem. AMA, Am. Acad. Pediatrics, Am. Assn. Pediatric Plastic Surgeons, Am. Burn Assn., Am. Cleft Palate-Craniofacial Assn., Am. Fedn. Clin. Rsch., Am. Soc. Bone and Mineral Rsch., Am. Soc. Maxillofacial Surgeons, Am. Soc. Plastic and Reconstructive Surgeons, Bioelec. Repair and Growth Soc., Blocker-Lewis Plastic Surgery Soc., Midwestern Assn. Plastic Surgeons, Chgo. Med. Soc., Chgo. Soc. Plastic Surgery. Office: 680 N Lake Shore Dr Ste 1125 Chicago IL 60611-8701 *

PENTCHEVA, BISSERA V., art history educator; b. Sofia, Bulgaria, Nov. 11, 1972; d. Vladimir J. Pentchev and Olga Z. Zaharieva; m. Atkinson Stephen A., May 23, 1998; 1 child, Olivia M. Atkinson. BA, Dartmouth Coll., Hanover, NH, 1991—95; MA, Harvard U., Cambridge, Mass., 1995—98, PhD, 1998—2001. Postdoctoral fellow Columbia U., NYC, 2001—03; asst. prof. art history Stanford U., Stanford, 2003—. Author: (book) Icons & Power: The Mother of God in Byzantium, 2006. Fellow, Onassis Found., 2002; jr. fellow, Dumbarton Oaks, 2000—01, rsch. fellow, Alexander von Humboldt Found., 2006—. Mem.: Internat.Ctr. for Medieval Art, Coll. Art Assn., Medieval Acad. Am. Office: Stanford Univ Cummings Art Bldg Stanford CA 94305

PENTIUK, RANDALL ALAN, lawyer; b. Garden City, Mich., Mar. 15, 1955; s. Eugene Otto and Marjorie Bernice (Baynes) P.; children: Amanda Rene, Kristen Lynne, Stephanie Joyce; m. Cynthia Marie West, July 29, 1999; 1 child, Katheryn Alexandra. BSBA, Wayne State U., 1976; JD magna cum laude, Detroit Coll. Law, 1981. Bar: Mich. 1981, U.S. Dist. Ct. (ea. dist.) Mich. 1981, U.S. Ct. Appeals (6th cir.) 1984, U.S. Supreme Ct. 1984, D.C. 1985. Rsch. atty. Mich. Ct. Appeals, Detroit, 1981; ptnr. Logan, Huchla, Wycoff & Pentiuk and predecessor Logan, Huchla & Wycoff, P.C., Riverview, Mich., 1981-84, ptnr., 1984-89, Pentiuk, Miller & Waterman, P.C., 1989-93, Pentiuk, Couvreur & Kobiljak, 1993—; atty. City of Riverview, Mich.; corp. counsel City of Melvindale, Mich. Contbr. to profl. jours. Mem. Trenton Planning Commn., Mich., 1982-92, chmn. 1985-87. Down River Rep. Club, Trenton, 1983-85; exec. com. 16th Dist. Rep. Party Mich., 1989-91; pres. Rutherford Inst. Mich., 1987-89; bd. dirs. Detroit City Rescue Mission, chmn., 1992—; bd. dirs. Promise Village, chmn., 1996-97. Mich. Consol. Gas scholar Detroit Coll. Law, 1978, Burton scholar, 1979, Alumni scholar, 1980. Mem. ABA, State Bar Mich., Comml. Law League Am., Fed. Bar Assn., Nat. Inst. Mcpl. Legal Officers (com. federalism, sect. zoning and planning law), Nat. Assn. Housing Coops (bd. dirs.), Midwest Assn. Housing Coops. (bd. dirs.), Mich. Assn. Mcpl. Attys., Christian Legal Soc. Baptist. Home: 20460 Coachwood Cir Riverview MI 48192-7910 Office: 2915 Biddle Ste 200 Wyandotte MI 48192 Home Phone: 734-552-3600; Office Phone: 734-281-7100. Business E-Mail: rpentiuk@pck-law.com. E-mail: kuitnep@aol.com.

PENWELL, REBECCA ANN, science educator; b. Dayton, Ohio; d. Harold Russell Penwell, Jr. and Karen Ann Penwell. BS, Allegheny Coll., 1996; MS, Fla. Internat. U., 1999; MEd, U. Fla., 2001, PhD, 2003. Asst. prof. Brenau U., Gainesville, Ga., 2003—. Content specialist Ga. Profl. Stds. Commn., Atlanta, 2003—04. Contbr. articles to profl. jours. Mem.: NSTA, Am. Ednl. Rsch. Assn., Ga. Acad. Sci. Avocations: scuba diving, snorkeling, reading. Office Phone: 770-534-6218. Business E-Mail: rpenwell@brenau.edu.

PENZER, MICHÈLE OLIVIER, lawyer; b. Nov. 22, 1968; AB, Harvard U., 1990; JD, Yale U., 1993. Bar: NY 1994. Ptnr. Latham & Watkins LLP, NYC, 2001—, mem. exec. com., 2004—. Named one of 40 Under 40, Crain's NY Bus., 2007. Mem.: ABA, State Bar NY, NY State Bar Assn. Office: Latham & Watkins LLP 885 Third Ave, Ste 1000 New York NY 10022-4802 Office Phone: 212-906-1200. Office Fax: 212-751-4864. *

PENZIAS, ARNO ALLAN, astrophysicist, information scientist, researcher; b. Munich, Apr. 26, 1933; arrived in U.S., 1940, naturalized, 1946; s. Karl and Justine (Eisenreich) Penzias; m. Sherry Chamove Levit, Aug. 2, 1996; children: David Simon, Mindy Gail, Laurie Shifra. BS in Physics, CCNY, 1954; MA in Physics, Columbia U., 1958, PhD in Physics, 1962; DHC (hon.), Observatoire de Paris, 1976; ScD (hon.), Rutgers U., 1979, Wilkes Coll., 1979, CCNY, 1979, Yeshiva U., 1979, Bar Ilan U.,

1983, Monmouth Coll., 1984, Technion-Israel Inst. Tech., 1986, U. Pitts., 1986, Ball State U., 1986, Kean Coll., 1986, U. Pa., 1992, Ohio State U., 1988, Iona Coll., 1988, Drew U., 1989, Lafayette Coll., 1990, Columbia U., 1990, George Washington U., 1992, Rensselaer Univ., 1992, U. Pa., 1992, Bloomfield Coll., 1994, Rankin Tech. U., 1997, Hebrew Union Coll., 1997, Oxford U., 2002. Mem. tech. staff Bell Labs., Holmdel, NJ, 1961—72, head radiophysics rsch. dept., 1972—76, dir. radio research lab., 1976—79, exec. dir. rsch., communications scis. div., 1979—81, v.p. rsch., 1981—85; v.p., chief scientist Lucent Technologies, 1995—98, sr. tech. adv., 1998—2000; venture ptnr. New Enterprise Assocs., 1997—. Sr. advisor New Enterprise Assocs., 1997—98; adj. prof. earth and scis. SUNY, Stony Brook, 1974—84, Univ. Disting. lectr., 1990; lectr. dept. astrophys. Scis. Princeton U., 1967—72, vis. prof., 1972—85; rsch. assoc. Harvard Coll. Obs., 1968—80; Edison lectr. U.S. Naval Rsch. Lab., 1979; Kompfner lectr. Stanford U., 1979; Gamow lectr. U. Colo., 1980; Jansky lectr. Nat. Radio Astronomy Obs.1983, 1983; Michelson Meml. lectr., 85; Grace Adams Tanner lectr., 87; Klopsteg lectr. Northwestern U., 1987; grad. faculties alumni Columbia U., 1987—89; Regents' lectr. U. Calif., Berkeley, 1990; Lee Kuan Yew Disting. vis. Nat. U. Singapore, 1991; mem. astronomy adv. panel NSF, 1978—79, mem. indsl. panel on sci. and tech., 1982—92, disting. lectr., 1987; affiliate Max-Planck Inst. for Radio-astronomy, 1978—85; chmn. Fachbeirat, 1981—83; rschr. in astrophysics, info. tech., its applications and impacts; bd. dirs. Konarka Techs., Glacier Bay, Inc., Bloom Energy Corp. Patentee auction-based selection of telecom. carriers, participant tracking in conference call, computer-based transportation system, fraud prevention in calling cards, identifying telephone extensions in residence environment, double-encrypted identity verification sys.; author: Ideas and Information Managing in a High-Tech World, 1989, Harmony-Business, Technology and Life After Paperwork, 1995; editl. bd. Ann. Rev. Astronomy and Astrophysics, 1974—78, AT&T Bell Labs. Tech. Jour., 1978—84, chmn., 1981—84, assoc. editor Astrophys. Jour., 1978—82, contbr. over 100 articles to tech. jours. Bd. overseers U. Pa. Sch. Engring. and Applied Sci., 1983—86; mem. vis. com. Calif. Inst. Tech., 1977—77; mem. Com. Concerned Scientists, 1975—, vice chmn., 1976; mem. adv. bd. Union of Couns. for Soviet Jews, 1983—95; bd. dirs. Coun. on Competitiveness, 1989—92; bd. trustees Trenton (N.J.) State Coll., 1977—79. With US Army, 1954—56. Named to N.J. Lit. Hall of Fame, 1991; recipient Herschel medal, Royal Astron. Soc., 1977, Nobel prize in Physics, 1978, Townsend Harris medal, CCNY, 1979, Newman award, 1983, Joseph Handleman prize in the scis., 1983, Grad. Faculties Alumni award, Columbia U., 1984, Achievement in Sci. award, Big Bros. Inc., N.Y.C., 1985, Priestly award, Dickinson Coll., 1989, Pender award, U. Pa., 1992, N.J. Sci. and Tech. medal, 1996, Internat. Eng. Cons. Fell. award, 1997, Indsl. Rsch. Inst. medal, 1998. Mem.: AAAS, NAS (Henry Draper medal 1977), IEEE (hon.), NAE, World Acad. Arts and Sci., Internat. Astron. Union, Am. Phys. Soc. (Pake prize 1990), Am. Astron. Soc. Office: New Enterprises Assocs 2490 Sand Hill Rd Menlo Park CA 94025-6940

PENZIEN, JOSEPH, structural engineering educator; b. Philip, SD, Nov. 27, 1924; s. John Chris and Ella (Stebbins) Penzien; m. Jeanne Ellen Hunson, Apr. 29, 1950 (dec. 1985); children: Robert Joseph, Karen Estelle, Donna Marie, Charlene May. Student, Coll. Idaho, 1942—43; BS, U. Wash., Seattle, 1945; ScD, MIT, Cambridge, Mass., 1950. Staff Sandia Corp., 1950—51; sr. structures engr. Consol. Vultee Aircraft Corp., Fort Worth, 1951—53; asst. prof. U. Calif. at Berkeley, 1953—57, assoc. prof., 1957—62, prof. structural engring., 1962—88, prof. emeritus, 1988—; dir. Earthquake Engring. Rsch. Ctr., 1968—73, 1977—80. Cons. engring. firms; chief tech. adv. Internat. Inst. of Seismology and Earthquake Engring., Tokyo, Japan, 1964-65; chmn. bd. Ea. Internat. Engrs., Inc., 1980-90, Internat. Civil Engring. Cons., Inc., 1990—. NATO Sr. Sci. fellow, 1969. Fellow Am. Acad. Mechanics; hon. mem. ASCE (Walter Huber Rsch. award, Alfred M. Freudenthal medal, Nathan M. Newmark medal, Ernest E. Howard award), Earthquake Engring. Rsch. Inst. (hon., Hausner medal), IAEE (hon.), EERI (Alfred E. Alquist award, Dist. Lectr. 2000); mem. Am. Concrete Inst., Structural Engrs. Assn. Calif., Seismol. Soc. Am., Nat. Acad. Engring. Home: 800 Solana Dr Lafayette CA 94549-5004 Office: Int Civil Engr Cons Inc 1995 University Ave Berkeley CA 94704 Office Phone: 510-841-7328. Business E-Mail: penzien@icec.com. E-mail: josephpenzien@yahoo.com.

PEOPLES, JOHN ARTHUR, JR., former university president, consultant; b. Starkville, Miss., Aug. 26, 1926; s. John Arthur and Maggie Rose (Peoples) P.; m. Mary E. Galloway, July 13, 1951; children: Kathleen, Mark Adam. BS, Jackson State U., 1950; MA, U. Chgo., 1951, PhD, 1961. Tchr. math. Froebel Sch., Gary, Ind., 1951-58; asst. prin. Lincoln Sch., Gary, 1958-62; prin. Banneker Sch., Gary, 1962-64; asst. to pres. Jackson (Miss.) State U., 1964-66, v.p., 1966-67, pres., 1967-84; Trustees disting. prof. Univs. Ctr. of Jackson, 1984-85; asst. to pres. SUNY, Binghamton, 1965-66; cons. in higher edn., 1985—. Lectr. summers numerous univs. and colls. Contbr. articles to profl. jours. Active Boy Scouts Am.; bd. govs. So. Regional Edn. Bd.; bd. visitors Air U.; adv. com. U.S. Army Command and Gen. Staff Coll.; mem. Commn. Excellence Am. Assn. State Colls. and Univs.; bd. commrs. Jackson Airport Authority. Served with USMCR, 1944-47. Recipient Disting. Am. award Nat. Football Found., Presdl. citation, Lifetime Achievement award Nat. Black Coll. Alumni Found., 1993—; named to Southwestern Athletic Hall of Fame. Mem. Am. Council Edn. (chmn. dir. 1975), Am. Assn. Higher Edn. (dir. 1971-74), NEA, Miss. Tchrs. Assn., Jackson C. of C. (econ. council), Alpha Kappa Mu, Phi Kappa Phi, Phi Delta Kappa, Omega Psi Phi (Man of Year, Sigma Omega chpt. 1966), Sigma Pi Phi. Lodges: Masons (33 deg.).

PEOPLES, JOHNNY RAY, music educator; b. West Plains, Mo., Sept. 24, 1964; s. James and Brenda Peoples; life ptnr. Steve Downey; children: Adam Miles, Nathaniel Ronald, Logan Scott, Abbey Christine. B in Music Edn., Ark. State U., 1987, M in Music Edn., 1988. Music educator Mt. View Birch Tree Schs., Mo., 1989—90; choral dir. Westminster Presbyn. Ch., Des Moines, 1991—93, Valley H.S., West Des Moines, 1992—93, Marked Tree Schs., Ark., 1994—95; music educator Nettleton Schs., Jonesboro, Ark., 1995—99, Plainview Rover Schs., 1999—2000; choral dir. Forrest City HS, 2000—01, East Jr. HS, West Memphis, Ark., 2001—. Organist Cornerstone United Meth. Ch., Jonesboro, Ark., 1995—2001; music dir. First United Meth. Ch., West Memphis, 2001—03; asst. condr. Memphis Vocal Arts Ensemble, 2004—; tenor soloist St. John's United Meth. Ch., Memphis, 2004—. Recipient Outstanding Young Men in Am. award, 1999, Nat. Multicultural Honors Choir, Am. Choral Dirs. Assn., 2001, State, Reg. Finalist, Nat. Assn. Tchrs. of Singing, 1988. Mem.: Ark. Choral Dirs. Assn., Am. Choral Dir. Assn. D-Liberal. Methodist. Home: 87 N Highland Memphis TN 38111 Office: East Jr H S 1151 Goodwin Ave West Memphis AR 72301-2714 Personal E-mail: choirman41@hotmail.com.

PEPE, FRANK A., cell and developmental biology educator; b. Schenectady, May 22, 1931; s. Rocco and Margherita (Ruggiero) P. BS, Union Coll., 1953; PhD, Yale U., 1957. Instr. anatomy U. Pa., Phila., 1957-60, assoc. in anatomy, 1960-63, asst. prof., 1963-65, assoc. prof., 1965-70, prof., 1970-92, chmn. dept. anatomy, 1977-90, prof. cell. and devel. biology, 1992-96, emeritus prof., 1996—. Editor: Motility in Cell Function, 1979. Recipient Rsch. Career Devel. award USPHS, 1968-73, Raymond C. Truex Disting. Lecture award Hahneman U., 1988. Fellow AAAS; mem. Am. Assn. Anatomists, Am. Chem. Soc., Biophys. Soc., Microscopy Soc. Am., Sigma Xi. Home: 4614 Pine St Philadelphia PA 19143-1808 E-mail: fpepe@mail.med.upenn.edu.

PEPER, CHARLOTTE ANN, educational consultant; b. Tucson, Oct. 30, 1949; d. Horace Eric and Marion Monier Bounds; children: Sonya, Jesse, Julie, John, Tina. AA, Pima C.C., Tucson, 1986; BA in Therapeutic Recreation, Prescott Coll., Ariz., 1994, MA in Counseling and Psychology, 2005. Therapeutic recreation provider City of Tucson, 1991—92; tchr. recreation therapy Ariz. Sch. for Deaf, 1992—95; cons. therapeutic recreation Westcenter Rehab. Ctr., 1999—2000; activity dir. Carondelet Holy Family Ctr., 1995—2000; dir. cmty. life Fountains at La Challa, 2000—02; tchr. music San Xavier Mission, 2002—04; exec. dir., cons. The Healing Bow, 1994—. Therapist homeless teens Teens is Transition, 2006—; psychiatric assessor Carondelet Hosp., 2007—, Tuscon Heart Hosp., 2007—. Recipient Canondelet Mission award, Canondelet Health Network, Tucson, 1998. Mem.: Ariz. Assn. Activity Profls. (co-chair 2002), Am. Counseling Assn. Democrat. Roman Catholic. Personal E-mail: healingbow2@yahoo.com.

PEPER, CHRISTIAN BAIRD, lawyer; b. St. Louis, Dec. 5, 1910; s. Clarence F. and Christine (Baird) Peper; m. Ethel C. Kingsland, June 5, 1935 (dec. Sept. 1995); children: Catherine K. Peper Larson(dec.), Anne Peper Perkins, Christian B.; m. Barbara C. Pleiter, Jan. 25, 1996. AB cum laude, Harvard U., 1932; LLB, Washington U., 1935; LLM, Yale U., 1937. Bar: Mo. 1934. Pvt. practice, St. Louis; of counsel Blackwell Sanders LLP, St. Louis. Instr. Washington U. Law Sch., St. Louis, 1943—61; ptnr. A. G. Edwards & Sons, 1945—67; pres. St. Charles Gas Corp., 1953—72; bd. dirs. El Dorado Paper Bag Mfg. Co., Inc. Editor: (book) An Historian's Conscience: The Correspondence of Arnold J. Toynbee and Columba Cary-Elwes, 1986. Mem. vis. com. Harvard Div. Sch., 1964—70. Sterling fellow, Yale U., 1936. Mem.: ABA, East India Club (London), St. Louis Bar Assn., Mo. Bar Assn., Harvard Club, Noonday Club, Order of Coif, Phi Delta Phi. Roman Catholic. Home: 1454 S Mason Rd Saint Louis MO 63131-1211 Office: Blackwell Sanders LLP 720 Olive St Saint Louis MO 63101-2338 Office Phone: 314-345-6000. Business E-Mail: cpeper@blackwellsanders.com.

PEPICELLO, WILLIAM J., academic administrator; b. Erie, Pa., 1949; B in Classics, Gannon U.; M in Linguistics, PhD in Linguistics, Brown U. Faculty position U. Del., U. Pacific, Temple U., chair, classics dept.; regional dean Southern Calif., Nat. U.; dean, coll. gen. and profl. studies U. Phoenix, 1995—2000, v.p., academic affairs, 1995, dean, sch. adv. studies, 2002—03, vice provost, academic affairs, 2003—06, provost, 2006, acting pres., 2006, pres., 2006—, U. Sarasota, 2000—02. Commr. Ariz. Comm. Postsecondary Edn. Office: University of Phoenix 4615 E Elwood St Phoenix AZ 85040 *

PÉPIN, JACQUES G., chef; b. Bourg-en-Bresse, France, Dec. 1935; arrived in U.S., 1959; m. Gloria Pépin. MA in 18th Century French Lit., Columbia U., 1972. Personal chef to three French heads of state, including Charles de Gaulle, 1956—58; employee Le Pavillon restaurant, NYC; dir. of rsch. and new devel. Howard Johnson Co.; dean French Culinary Inst., NYC. Adj. faculty mem. Boston U.; Founder Am. Inst. of Wine and Food; mem. Nat. Assn. of Cooking Profls.; bd. trustees James Beard Found. Former columnist New York Times, columnist Food & Wine mag., Host with daughter (PBS TV series) Jacques Pépin's Kitchen: Cooking with Claudine, 1998, Jacques Pépin's Kitchen: Encore with Claudine, 1998, Host with Julia Child, Julia and Jacques Cooking at Home (James Beard Found. award for Best Nat. Cooking Show, 2001; Daytime Emmy award, 2001); author: (cookbooks) La Technique, 1976, La Methode, 1979, Jacques Pépin Celebrates (James Beard award, 2002), 2001, Jacques Pépin's Complete Techniques, 2001, The Apprentice: My Life in the Kitchen, 2003, Jacques Pépin's Fast Food My Way, 2004. Recipient Chevalier de L'Ordre du Mérite Agricole, France, 1992, Chevalier de L'Ordre des Arts et des Lettres, 1997, Disting. Alumni, Columbia Univ. Sch. of General Studies, Lifetime Achievement award, The James Beard Found., 2005. Avocation: painting.

PEPINE, CARL JOHN, physician, educator; b. Pitts., June 8, 1941; s. Charles John and Elizabeth (Hovan) P.; m. Lynn Dives, Aug. 3, 1963; children: Mary Lynn, Anne, Elizabeth. BS, U. Pitts., 1962; MD, N.J. Coll. Medicine, 1966. Intern Allegheny Gen. Hosp., U. Pitts., 1966-67; resident in internal medicine Jefferson Med. Coll. Hosp., Phila., 1967-68, naval med. ctr., 1968-69, fellow in physiology and cardiovasc. disease, 1969-71; asst. prof. medicine Jefferson Med. Coll., Phila., 1972-74, U. Fla., Gainesville, 1974-75, assoc. prof., 1975-79, prof., 1979—, co-dir. divsn. cardiovasc. medicine, 1982-88; chief cardiology VA Regional Med. Ctr., Gainesville, 1979-94, chief divsn. cardiovasc. medicine, 1998—. Dir. cardiology catheterization lab. Shands Hosp., U. Fla., Gainesvile, 1974-86. Mem. editl. bds. Am. Heart Jour., 1997—, Am. Jour. Cardiology, 1981-94, 97—, Am. Jour. Geriat. Cardiology, 1992—, Geriat. Cardiology, 1996—, Clin. Cardiology, 1995—, Circulation, 1980-83, 93—, Cardiac Chronicle, 1989—, Heart Disease: A Jour. of Cardiovasc. Medicine, 1999—, Hypertension, 1999—, Jour. Am. Coll. Cardiology, 1981-85, 91-95, 98—, Jour. Preventive Cardiovasc. Medicine, 1997—, Preventive Cardiology, 1998-2000; chief med. editor Cardiology Today, 1997—; contbr. articles to profl. jours.; developer catheters to measure blood flow and heart circulation. Comdr. USN, 1968-74. Recipient Racuity Rsch. prize in clin. sci., U. Fla., 1989-90, Piioneer Investigator award Internat. Soc. Holter Monitoring, 1990, Rsch. Achievement awards U. Fla., 1990-93, Paul Dudley whhite award Assn. Mil. Surgeons, 1991; grantee Dept. of Def., 1971-74, VA, 1975-90, NHLBI, 1985—. Fellow Am. Coll. Cardiology (master; trustee 1986-88, 90-95, 2001—, v.p. 2001—, chmn. cardiac catheterization com. 1990-96, chmn. Fla. chpt. found. 1992—, chmn. bd. govs. 1986-87, chmn. ann. sci. sessions 1990), Am. Heart Assn. (coun. on clin. cardiology and on circulation, bronze award 1983), Am. Fedn. Clin. Rsch., Soc. Cardiac Angiography, Am. Soc. Clin. Investigation; mem. Assn. Univ. Cardiologists, Am. Clin. and Climatol. Assn. (Theodore E. Woodward award 1998), Assn. of Profs. of Cardiology, European Soc. Cardiology, Pi Kappa Alpha, Alpha Omega Alpha. Office: U Fla 1600 SW Archer Rd PO Box 100277 Gainesville FL 32610-0277 Office Phone: 352-846-0620. Business E-Mail: pepincj@medicine.ufl.edu. *

PEPINE, MARY, dermatologist; b. Jersey City, Apr. 27, 1966; d. Carl and Lynn Pepine; m. Daniel Oli Haight, June 3, 1995; 1 child, Emily Lynn Haight. BS magna cum laude, Duke U., Durham, NC, 1988; MD, U. Fla., 1992. Cert. Nat. Bd. Med. Examiners, 1993, diplomate Am. Bd. Dermatology, 1996, lic. Fla., 1995. Internal medicine internship U. Ala., Birmingham, 1992—93; dermatology resident U. South Fla., Tampa, 1993—96; dermatologist Office of John Millns, Tampa, 1996—98, Watson Clinic, LLP, Lakeland, Fla., 1998—2000, Assocs. in Dermatology, Kissimmee, Fla., 2000—02; pres., owner, dermatologist Adult and Pediat. Dermatology Ctrl. Fla., Lakeland, 2002—. Melanoma/skin cancer screener H. Lee Moffitt Cancer Ctr. and Rsch. Inst., Tampa, 1994, Tampa, 95, Tampa, 96, U. South Fla. Med. Clinics, Tampa, 1994, Tampa, 95, Tampa, 96, Incarnation Cath. Ch., Tampa, 1996, Lakeland Regional Med. Ctr., 1999, Combined Care for Cancer and Rsch., Lakeland, 2003—06; with Town and Country Hosp., Tampa, 1997—98, Lakeland Regional Med. Ctr., 1998—2000, 2002—04, Fla. Hosp., 2000—02; clin. asst. faculty U. South Fla., 1996—98; presenter in field. Contbr. articles to profl. jours. Fellow: Am. Acad. Dermatology; mem.: Fla. West Coast Dermatology Soc., Fla. Soc. Dermatologic Surgeons, Fla. Soc. Dermatology, Polk County Med. Assn. Office: Adult and Pediatric Dermatology of Ctrl Fla 727 S Fla Ave Lakeland FL 33801 Office Phone: 863-687-2055.

PEPONIS, HAROLD ARTHUR, insurance agent, portfolio manager; b. Chgo., Dec. 12, 1928; s. Arthur Harold and Ethel (Karambis) P.; m. Toula H. (Preketes), Mar. 1, 1952 (dec. Dec. 1984); one child, Arthur Harold II; m. Aphrodite E. (Stavros), May 26, 1990. BS, Loyola U., Chgo., 1950, postgrad., 1991. Treas. Plaza Cleaners and Dyers, Inc., Chgo., 1950—58; owner Exch. Cleaners, Chgo., 1958—63, Park West Plaza Cleaners, Chgo., 1963—69; ins. agt. Aetna Life and Casualty, Lisle, Ill., 1969—2006; ind. broker Registered Rep., Chgo., 1995—; ptnr. lecture series, pub. co. Images of Orthodoxy; instr. religion Plato Acad., Chgo., 1998—99. Pres. Tesera Assoc., Evanston, Ill., 1973-2004; dir. Faith Net, Inc., 2003-. Mem. editl. bd. Christianity and Arts mag., 1996-98; columnist Coyote Chronicle Newsletter, 2003-. Pres. parish coun. United Greek Orthodox Ch. of Chgo., 1963—64, Annunciation Cathedral, 1991—92, 1994; archon Order of St. Andrew, Greek Orthodox Ch., state comdr., 1994—2001, regional comdr., 2001—; mem. Greek Orthodox Metropolis Coun., 1998—; sec. Metroplis Coun. Greek Orthodox Metroplis of Chgo., 2004—07; mem. Ecumenical Millennium Com., 2006—; mem. local planning com. Nat. Workshop on Christian Unity, 2006—. Recipient Medal of St. Paul, Greek Orthodox Archdiocese, 1999. Mem. Pan Arcadian Fedn. Am. (nat. pres. Chgo. 1963-64), Du Page Life Underwriters Assn., 2626 North Lakeview Condominium Assn. (bd. dirs. 2004-05, sec. bd. dirs. 2005-06, v.p. bd. dirs., 2006-, lectr. Chgo. neighborhood tours 2005—). Home: 2626 N Lakeview Apt 2503 Chicago IL 60614-1821 Office: 2626 No Lakeview Ste 806 Chicago IL 60614 Office Phone: 630-291-6865. Business E-Mail: hapeponis26@aol.com.

PEPONIS, JOHN, architect, educator; b. Athens, Greece, June 21, 1955; s. Anastassios Peponis and Mavra Kanaris; m. Evlabia Periklaki, Oct. 15, 1957; children: Elpida, Mavra Maria. BS in Architecture, U. Coll., London, 1976, MS in Architecture, 1977, PhD in Architecture, 1983. Assoc. prof. Ga. Inst. Tech., Atlanta, 1989—2003, prof., 2003—. Author: (book) Chorographies - Descriptions of Space (in Greek); editor: Contemporary Industrial Buildings in Greece, Proceedings, 3rd International Conference on Space Syntax; contbr. articles to profl. jours., chapters to books; mem. editl. bd. Jour. Arch., Environ. and Planning (B): Planning and Design. With Greek Mil., 1984—85. Grantee, Minsitry Energy, Industry and Rsch., Greece, 1986—88, NSF, 2000—01, GSA, 2002—04, Steelcase Corp., 2004—05. Office: Georgia Inst Tech 247 Fourth St Atlanta GA 30332-0155 Home Phone: +302108640199; Office Phone: + 1 404 894 7667. Business E-Mail: john.peponis@coa.gatech.edu.

PEPPAS, NICHOLAS ATHANASSIOU, chemical and biomedical engineering educator, consultant; b. Athens, Greece, Aug. 25, 1948; s. Athanassios Nikolaou Peppas and Alice Petrou Rousopoulou; m. Lisa Brannon, Aug. 10, 1988; children: Katherine, Alexander. Diploma in Engring., Nat. Tech. U., Athens, 1971; ScD, MIT, 1973; D honoris causa, U. Parma, Italy, 1999, U. Ghent, Belgium, 1999, U. Athens, 2000. Asst. prof. chem. engring. Purdue U., West Lafayette, Ind., 1976-78, assoc. prof., 1978-81, prof., 1981—2002, Showalter Disting. prof. of chem. and biomed. engring., 1993—2002; prof. chem. engring. U. Tex., Austin, 2003—, prof. biomed. engring., 2003, prof. pharmaceutics, 2003—, Fletcher S. Pratt disting. prof., 2003—. Vis. prof. U. Geneva, 1982-83, Calif. Inst. Tech., Pasadena, 1983, U. Paris, 1986, Hoshi U., Japan, 1994, Hebrew U., Jerusalem, 1994, U. Naples, 1995, Free U. Berlin, 2001, Complutense U. Madrid, 2001; adj. prof. U. Parma, Italy, 1987; cons. in field; mem. adv. bd. several cos. Author: Biomaterials, 1982, Hydrogels in Medicine and Pharmacy, 1987, One Hundred Years of Chemical Engineering, 1989, Pulsatile Drug Delivery, 1993, Biopolymers, 1993, Superabsorbent Polymers, 1994, Biomaterials for Drug and Cell Delivery, 1994, Polymer/Inorganic Interfaces, 1995, Physicochemical and Cellular Foundations of Biomaterials, 2004; contbr. over 900 articles and over 300 abstracts to jours. Active Austin Symphony Orch., Transfiguration Orthodox Ch. Austin. Recipient APV medal, Herbert McCoy award Purdue U., 2000. Fellow: AIChE (chmn. materials divsn. 1988—90, dir. bioengring. divsn. 1994—97, bd. dirs. 1999—2002, Inst. lectr. 2007, Materials Engring. Sci. award 1984, Bioengring. award 1994, Best Paper award 1994, William Walker award 2006, Jay Bailey award 2006), Am. Phys. Soc., Italian Soc. Medicine and Scis., Soc. Biomaterials (pres.-elect 2002, pres. 2003—04, Founders award 2005), Am. Phys. Soc., Am. Inst. Med. Biol. Engrs., Am. Assn. Pharm. Scientists (Rsch. Achievements Pharm. Tech. award 1999, Dale Wurster award 2002); mem.: Tex. Acad. Scis., NAE, French Acad. Pharmacy, Biomed. Engring. Soc. (Best Rsch. award 2002), Polymer Pioneer, Am. Soc. Engring. Edn. (AT&T award 1982, Curtis McGraw award 1988, G. Westinghouse award 1992, GE Sr. Rsch. award 2002, Dow Chem. Engring. award 2006), Soc. Biomaterials (Clemson award 1992), Controlled Release Soc. (pres. 1987—88, Founders award 1991, Eurand award 2002), NY Acad. Sci., Am. Chem. Soc. (Newsmaker of Yr. award 2002), Sigma Xi. Avocations: linguistics, opera, rare maps, classical record collecting, wine collecting. Office: U Tex Dept Chem Engring Austin TX 78712 Office Phone: 512-471-6644. Business E-Mail: peppas@che.utexas.edu.

PEPPE, RON, lawyer; b. Frederick, Md. m. Elizabeth Peppe; children: Matthew, Laura. B in Internat. Studies, M in Internat. Studies, John Hopkins U.; JD, U. Md., 1987. With Kutak Rock, Omaha, Prudential Ins.Co., Frederick, Md.; v.p. law and tech. Assn. of Corp. Counsel, 2004—06; with Canam Steel Corp., Point of Rocks, Md., 1996—2004, gen. counsel, corp. sec., chief compliance officer, 2006—. Office: Canam Steel Corp 4010 Clay St Point Of Rocks MD 21777 *

PEPPER, ALLAN MICHAEL, lawyer; b. Bklyn, July 5, 1943; s. Julius and Jeanette (Lasovsky) P.; m. Barbara Benjamin, Aug. 30, 1964; children— Leslie Anne, Joshua Benjamin, Adam Richard, Robert Benjamin BA summa cum laude, Brandeis U., 1964; LL.B. magna cum laude, Harvard U., 1967. Bar: N.Y. 1968, U.S. Dist. Ct. (so. and ea. dists.) N.Y. 1968, U.S. Ct. Appeals (2d cir.) 1968, U.S. Supreme Ct. 1988. Law clk. U.S. Ct. Appeals for 2d Circuit, NYC, 1967-68; assoc. Kaye, Scholer, Fierman, Hays & Handler LLP, NYC, 1968-74; ptnr. Kaye, Scholer LLP, NYC, 1975—2006, spl. counsel, 2007—. Lectr. in field. Exec. com., assoc. nat. chmn. Brandeis U. Alumni Fund, 1979-82, nat. chmn., 1982-85, chmn. 25th reunion gift com., 1989, devel. com., trustee, 1982-85, pres., councillor, 1980—, 35th reunion gift com., 1999; trustee Brandeis U., 1985-95, sec., 1992-93, budget and fin. com., 1988-95, chmn. com. strategic plan, 1990-91, acad. affairs com., 1985-92, student life and phys. facilities com., 1985-89, vice-chmn. ad hoc by-laws com., 1988-89, long range planning com., 1989-91, chmn. audit com., 1991-95, exec. com., 1990-91; bd. dir. Styles Brook Homeowners Assn., 1990—, exec. com., 1994—, 2d v.p., 2002—; mem. nominating com. Edgemont Sch. Bd., 1992-93; trustee Edgemont Sch. Found., 1994-2002, 2003-06; 30th reunion gift com. Harvard Law Sch., 1996-97, class agt., 1998-2001, 40th reunion gift com., 2006-; mem. bd. edn. Edgemont Union Free Dist., Scarsdale, NY, 2006—. Recipient Henry Jones-Golda Meier Bnai Brith Youth Services award, 1986, LI Press Valedictory medal, 1960; Felix Frankfurter scholar Harvard U. Law Sch., 1964-65; Louis D. Brandeis hon. scholar Brandeis U., 1964 Mem. ABA, Assn. Bar City N.Y. (law firm mgmt. com. 1987-91, litig. com. 1998-2001), N.Y. State Bar Assn. (comml. and fed. litig. sect., com. on discovery 1993-97, 2004—), Brandeis U. Alumni Assn. (exec. com. 1982-87, alumni giving strategic planning com., 1992, Alumni Svc. award 1988), Phi Beta Kappa (LI Alumni award 1960), B'nai B'rith (pres. Henry Jones Lodge 1982-84, Westchester-Putnam coun. 1982-85, bd. gov. dist. 1, 1985-86). Democrat. Jewish. Office: Kaye Scholer 425 Park Ave New York NY 10022-3506 Home Phone: 914-472-4351; Office Phone: 212-836-8665. E-mail: apepper@kayescholer.com.

PEPPER, BARRY, actor; b. Campbell River, BC, Can., Apr. 4, 1970; m. Cindy Pepper, Nov. 1997; 1 child, Annaliese. Actor: (films) Urban Safari, 1996, Firestorm, 1998, Saving Private Ryan, 1998, Enemy of the State, 1998, The Green Mile, 1999, Battlefield Earth: A Saga of the Year 3000, 2000, We All Fall Down, 2000, Knockaround Guys, 2001, We Were Soldiers, 2002, 25th Hour, 2002, Mr. Ripley's Return, 2004, Ripley Under

Ground, 2005, The Three Burials of Melquidades Estrada, 2005, Flags of Our Fathers, 2006; (TV films) A Killer Among Friends, 1992, Johnny's Girl, 1995, Titanic, 1996, 61*, 2001, others; actor, exec. prodr.: (films) The Snow Walker, 2003; actor, co-exec. prodr: (TV films) 3: The Dale Earnhardt Story, 2004. Office: c/o 9100 Wilshire Blvd W Tower 6th Fl Beverly Hills CA 90212 *

PEPPER, DAVID M., scientist, educator, writer, inventor, consultant; b. LA, Mar. 9, 1949; s. Harold and Edith Pepper; m. Denise Danyelle Pepper, Mar. 19, 1992. BS in Physics summa cum laude, UCLA, 1971; MS in Applied Physics, Calif. Inst. Tech., 1974, PhD in Applied Physics, 1980. Mem. tech. staff Hughes Rsch. Labs., Malibu, Calif., 1973—87, sr. staff physicist, 1987—91, head nonlinear and electro-optic devices sect., 1989—91, sr. scientist, 1991—94; sr. rsch. scientist HRL Labs. (formerly Hughes Rsch. Labs.), Malibu, 1994—2004; owner, tech. cons., scientist Malibu Scientific, 2004—. Adj. prof. math. and physics Pepperdine U., Malibu, 1981—; adv. panel NSF, Washington, 1997; panel advanced signal processing U. Va., 1999; mem. Def. Sci. Rsch. Coun., US Govt., Washington, 1999; presenter in field Author: Scientific American, 1986, 1990; co-author: Optical Phase Conjugation, 1983, Laser Handbook, Vol. 4, 1985, Optical Phase Conjugation, 1995, Spatial Light Modulator Technology, 1995, CRC Handbook of Laser Science and Technology, 1995; contbr. articles to profl. jours. Mem. Sons and Daughters of 1939 Club, 2d Generation of Martyrs Meml., Mus. Holocaust Recipient Rudolf Kingslake award Soc. Photo-Optical Instrumentation Engrs., 1982, Publ. of Yr. award Hughes Rsch. Lab., 1986, Inventor of Yr. award, 1997-2006; NSF trainee Calif. Inst. Tech., 1971; Howard Hughes fellow Hughes Aircraft Co., 1973-80 Fellow Optical Soc. Am. (conf. chair 1996-2001, adv. bd. topical conf. on nonlinear optics, Hawaii 1996, 98, 2000, invited tutorial meeting laser ultrasound 2001, Top 10 cited Paper award); mem. AAAS, IEEE (guest editor, assoc. editor, program com. US CLEO laser conf. 1997-2001, 2005, instr. laser tech. 1994-2000, invited tutorial laser tech. 2001, European CLEO laser conf. program com. 2003), SPIE (guest editor, conf. co-chmn. 1998-2000), NY Acad. Scis., Am. Phys. Soc., Laser Inst. Am., Internat. Coun. Sci. Unions (com. sci. and tech. in developing countries), Sigma Xi (v.p. 1986-87, chpt. pres. 1987-88, 90-92), Sigma Pi Sigma Jewish. Achievements include 50 patents in field; 15 patents pending in field. Avocations: classical music, travel, sports, astronomy. Office: Malibu Scientific P O Box 126 Malibu CA 90265-0126 Personal E-mail: dmpepper@charter.net. *Personal philosophy: We all have a profound, meaningful purpose and mission in life—the challenge is to identify, appreciate, realize and embrace our dreams and goals.*

PEPPER, J. DAVID, II, (DAVE PEPPER), construction executive; Pres., COO Pepper Constrn. Group, LLC, Chgo., chmn., CEO. Vol. officer Builders Assn., 2007—. Mem. exec. bd. NW Suburban Coun. Boy Scouts Am.; mem. rsch./edn. com. Associated Gen. Contractors Found.; treas. Builders Assn. Found.; pres. bd. dirs. United Cerebral Palsy Chgo., 2002—03; bd. dirs., mem. exec. com. Jr. Achievement Chgo.; mem. adv. bd. dirs. Good Shepherd Hosp. Office: Pepper Constrn Group LLC 643 N Orleans Ave Chicago IL 60610-3690 Office Phone: 312-266-4700. *

PEPPER, JEFFREY MACKENZIE, publishing executive; b. Dallas, June 11, 1957; s. Doris Jane (Mackenzie) P.; m. Christy Dale Pepper, Nov. 5, 2004; children: Katherine McRaven, Anne Mackenzie. BA, Coll. Wooster, 1979. Sales rep. Acad. Press, NYC, 1979-82; program editor Addison-Wesley Pub. Co., Reading, Mass., 1982-83, acquisitions editor, 1983-86; sr. editor Osborne McGraw-Hill, Berkeley, Calif., 1986-90, editor-in-chief, 1990-95; v.p., editl. dir. Acad. Press Profl., Chestnut Hill, Mass., 1995-97; v.p., editor-in-chief computer books Prentice Hall PTR, Upper Saddle River, NJ, 1997-98, v.p., pub., 1999—2005; exec. editor O'Reilly Media, Inc., 2005—. Contbr. articles to profl. jours. Avocations: storytelling, computers, gardening. Home: 5331 Burriss Ct Southport NC 28461

PEPPER, JOHN ENNIS, JR., former consumer products company, historical museum executive; b. Pottsville, Pa., Aug. 2, 1938; s. John Ennis Sr. and Irma Elizabeth (O'Connor) P.; m. Frances Graham Garber, Sept. 9, 1967; children: John, David, Douglas, Susan BA, Yale U., 1960; PhD (hon.), Mt. St. Joseph Coll., St. Petersburg U., Russia, Xavier U. Staff asst. Procter & Gamble Co., Cin., 1963-64, asst. brand mgr., 1964-66, brand mgr., 1966-68, copy supr., 1968-69, brand promotion mgr., 1969-72, advt. mgr. bar soap and household cleaning products divsn., 1972-74, gen. mgr. Italy subs., 1974-77, divsn. mgr. internat., 1977-78, v.p. packaged soap and detergent divsn., 1978-80, group v.p. bar soap and household cleaning products divsn., 1980-81, group v.p. Europe, 1981-84, exec. v.p. U.S. bus., 1984-86, pres. U.S. Bus., 1986-90, pres. internat. bus., 1990-95, chmn., CEO, 1995-99, chmn., 1999—2002, mem. exec. com. of bd., 2000—03; v.p. fin. & adminstrn. Yale U., New Haven, 2004—05. Bd. dirs. Xerox Corp., 1990-2005, Motorola, Inc., 1994-2005, Boston Scientific Corp., 1999-2001, The Walt Disney Co., 2006-, non-exec chmn. 2007-. Chmn. U.S. Advisory Com. for Trade Policy and Negotiations; group chmn. Cin. United Appeal Campaign, 1980; bd. trustees Xavier U., 1985-89, mem. exec. com., 1989; trustee Cin. Coun. World Affairs, Cin. Art Mus., Ctr. Strategic & Internat. Studies, Christ Ch. Endowment Fund; fellow Yale Corp.; gen. chmn. United Way Campaign, 1994; mem. Gov.'s Edn. and Bus. Advisory Group, State of Ohio; mem. adv. coun. Yale Sch. Mgmt.; mem. schs. com. Cin. Bus. Com.; co-chmn., mem. exec. com. Cin. Youth Collaborative; mem. Total Quality Leadership steering com.; mem., bd. dirs. United Negro Coll. Fund; former v.p. Am. C. of C., Brussels, Belgium (1981-84); former mem. Cin. Symphony Bd. (1979-81), Cin. Art Mus; bd. mem. Population Services Internat.; honorary co-chair, Nat. Underground Railroad Freedom Ctr, CEO 2006-. Served to lt. USN, 1960—63. Mem. Am. Soc. Corp. Execs., Grocery Mfrs. Am., Nat. Alliance Businessmen (chmn. communication com.), Partnership for a Drug-Free Am., Soap and Detergent Assn. (bd. dirs.), The Bus. Coun., Bus. Roundtable, Yale Club, Queen City Club, Commonwealth Club, Comml. Club (former pres.). Office: Nat Underground Railroad Freedom Ctr 50 E Freedom Way Cincinnati OH 45202 *

PEPPER, JOLINE ROMANO, psychologist, educator; b. Malden, Mass., Nov. 4, 1971; d. Leo Richard and Geraldine Kathleen Romano; m. Eric Edward Pepper; children: Erica Jade, Alexa Jo. BA, Merrimack Coll., 1993; MEd, U. Mass., 1995. Sch. psychologist North Reading Pub. Schs., Mass., 1996—; lisason between dept. pub. health and dept. revenue Mass. Adj. faculty mem. Western New Eng. Coll., Mass., 1999—. Vol. food pantry outreach and citizenship com. Recipient Allen J. Ash award, Nat. Honor Soc. in Psychology. Mem.: Nat. Assn. Sch. Psychologists, Mass. Assn. Sch. Psychologists, Psi Chi. Democrat. Avocations: reading, skiing, rollerblading, travel. Personal E-mail: jolinepepper@msn.com.

PEPPER, JONATHON L., media executive; b. Dearborn, Mich., Aug. 23, 1955; s. Joseph Daniel and Norma (McIntyre) P.; m. Diane Sharon Garelis, May 12, 1984; children: Jonathon Jay, Lauren Claire, Scott Joseph. BA, Mich. State U., 1977. Copywriter Detroit Free Press, 1977-84, reporter, 1984-87; nat. corr. Detroit News, 1987-91, bus. columnist, 1991-2000; host talk show Sta. WXYT, 1995-96; assoc. bus. editor Detroit News, 1997-2000; pres. Small Times Media LLC, Ann Arbor, Mich., 2000—. Mem. Writers Guild Am., The Fairlane Club (vice chmn.). E-mail: jonpepper@ardesta.com.

PEPPER, LATONGIA KENYETTA, physicist, curator; b. Talladega, Ala., Feb. 15, 1977; d. Elvis Gene Groce and Shirley Carter Croce; m. Marcus Cleveland Pepper, Apr. 19; children: Christopher, Caitlyn, Camille. BS in Physics, SC State U., Orangeburg, 1999; MA in Info. Tech. Mgmt., Webster U., Greenville, SC, 2002. Physics instr. ITT Tech. Inst., Greenville, 1999—2004; phys. sci. curator Roper Mountain Sci. Ctr., Greenville, 2004—. Sci. PLUS instr. Furman U., 2006—. Named Instr. of Yr., ITT Tech. Inst., 2001. Avocations: reading, public speaking, travel. Home: 1 Bates Lake Ct Fountain Inn SC 29664 Office: Roper Mountain Sci Ctr 402 Roper Mountain Rd Greenville SC 29615

PEPPER, MAURY, computer consultant; Masters in Computer Sci. Co-founder DRA Libr. Sys., 1975; works with Mass. Gen. Hosp. Utility Multi Programming Sys. (MUMPS), 1970—, mem. develop. com., 1991—; co-founder WorldVistA, 2002, chmn., dir.; computer cons. M-Tech. Co-recipient Rave award-medicine, WIRED Mag., 2007. Achievements include being part of team responsible for a medical-records program called, VistA at US Department Veterans Affairs.

PEPPER, PAMELA POE, psychologist; b. Erwin, NC, Feb. 21, 1953; d. Thomas Wesley Poe, Jr. and Norma Jean (Ferrell) Poe; m. Eugene Vance Pepper, Jr., May 15, 1976; children: Katherine McIver, Anna Faison. BA in Psychology & English, Salem Coll., 1975; MA in Counseling, U. NC, 1980; PhD in Sch. Psychology, U. NC-Chapell Hill, 1992. Lic. psychologist NC, health svcs. provider, psychologist NC, registered electroencephalography tech. Duke U., cert. provider psychol. svcs. traumatic brain injured students NC Dept. Public Instruction. Postdoctoral fellow in neuropsychology Wake Forest U., Bowman Gray Sch. Med., Winston-Salem, NC, 1993—95; rsch. technologist electroencephalography Epilepsy Rsch. Ctr., Va. Med. Ctr., Durham, NC, 1975—76; clin. assoc. biological psychiatry, program dir. electrophysiological tech. Duke U., Durham, 1978—81; mgr. staff edn. & devel. Durham Regional Med. Ctr., 1981—82; postdoctoral fellow in neurology, divsn. neuropsychology Wake Forest U. Bapt. Med. Ctr., Bowman Gray Sch. Medicine, 1993—95; adj. asst. prof. grad. studies edn. Salem Coll., Winston-Salem, 1994; clin. neuropsychologist Salem Psychiatric Assocs., P.A., Winston-Salem, 1995—97; clin. neuropsychologist, found. ptnr. TriCare, P.A., Winston-Salem, 1997—2003; clin. neuropsychologist Pepper Neuropsychol. Consulting., PLLC, Winston-Salem, 2004—. Spkr. in field. Bd. advisors quality assurance Qual Choice Behavioral Health, Winston-Salem, 1996—2001; mem. Jr. League Durham, 1975; pres. Durham/Chapel Hill Salem Coll. Alumnae Assn., 1975—76; bd. dirs. So. Soc. Electroencephalographic Technologists, Atlanta, 1980—81, Mental Health Assn. Forsyth County, Winston-Salem, 2000—02. Recipient Order of Scorpion, Salem Coll., 1973—75. Mem.: APA Clin. Neuropsychology Divsn., APA, Internat. Neuropsychol. Soc., Brain Injury Assn. NC (spkrs. bureau 1998—). Democrat. Presbyterian. Avocations: reading, writing, gardening, rock collecting, birdwatching. Office Phone: 336-409-4705. Business E-Mail: drpampepper@aol.com.

PEPPERMAN, RICHARD C., II, lawyer; b. Camden, NJ, 1964; AB, Dartmouth Coll., 1987; JD, U. Pa. Law Sch., 1990. Bar: NY 1993. Clerk US Ct. of Appeals, Third Cir., 1990—91, US Supreme Ct., 1992—93; ptnr. Sullivan & Cromwell LLP, NYC, 1999—. Named Leading Antitrust Lawyer, NY Super Lawyers, 2006; named one of Litigation's Rising Stars, The Am. Lawyer, 2007; named to Lawdragon 500: New Stars, New Worlds, 2006. Mem.: Am. Law Inst. Office: Sullivan & Cromwell LLP 125 Broad St New York NY 10004-2498 Office Phone: 212-558-4000. Office Fax: 212-558-3588. Business E-Mail: peppermanr@sullcrom.com.

PEPPERS, JERRY P., lawyer; b. Cleve., Mar. 8, 1946; s. Jerry P. and Katherine M. Peppers; m. Sue E. Schafer, June 14, 1969; children: Amy E., Erica K., Christina A., Michele S. BBA, Ohio U., 1968; JD, Duke U., 1971. Bar: N.Y. 1972, U.S. Dist. Ct. (so. dist.) N.Y. 1972, U.S. Ct. Appeals (2nd cir.) 1972. Assoc. Pillsbury Winthrop Shaw Pittman LLP, NYC, 1971-81, ptnr., 1982—; co-chair Mergers and Acquisitions Group, 2006—. Editor (booklet): Outline of Mergers and Acquisitions in the United States, 15th edit., 2003. Trustee emeritus, mem.alternative investment com. Ohio Univ. Found., Athens, 1991—; trustee Scarsdale Youth Soccer Club, Inc.; bd. dirs. Atheneum Venture Fund, Athens, 1996—; com. mem. Fields for Kids. Mem.: ABA, Soc. Automotive Engrs., Assn. Bar City NY, Internat. Bar Assn., India House, Fox Meadow Tennis Club (Scarsdale, NY). Avocation: coaching soccer. Office: Pillsbury Winthrop Shaw Pittman LLP 1540 Broadway New York NY 10036-4039 Office Phone: 212-858-1205. Business E-Mail: jerry.peppers@pillsburylaw.com.

PEPPERS, JULIUS, professional football player; b. Wilson, NC, Jan. 18, 1980; BA in Afro-Am. Studies, U.N.C., Chapel Hill, 2002. Defensive end Carolina Panthers, 2002—. Named to Freshman All-Am. Team, Sporting News, 1999, NFC Pro Bowl Team, 2005, NFL, 2007, NFL All Pro Team, 2006; recipient NFL Def. Rookie Yr., 2002—03, Lombardi award for Nations Top Lineman, NCAA, 2001. Office: Carolina Panthers 800 So Mint St Charlotte NC 28202 *

PEPPET, RUSSELL FREDERICK, accountant; b. Chgo., Oct. 3, 1939; s. George Russell and Elizabeth (Foster) P.; m. Rosemary Meyer, June 18, 1960 (dec. 2000); children: Cynthia, Jeffrey, Scott; m. Sandra S. Wharton, Feb. 2, 2002. BS in Math, Mich. State U., 1960; MBA, Northwestern U., 1963. C.P.A., Ill., Minn. Cons. Peat, Marwick, Mitchell & Co., Chgo., 1961-68, head mgmt. cons. dept. Mpls., 1968-72, partner, 1969-88; sr. cons. partner for Continental Europe, Paris, 1972-78, partner-in-charge mgmt. cons. dept., N.Y. office, 1978-81, vice chmn. mgmt. cons., 1981-86; mng. ptnr. San Jose Bus. Unit, 1986-88; v.p. internat. devel. Towers Perrin, NYC, 1989-90; vice-chmn. Quirk Carson Peppet Inc., NYC, 1990-98; prin. Churchill Capital Inc., NYC, 1999—2001; ptnr. Park Ave. Equity Ptnrs., 2005—; dir. Armstrong World Industries. With U.S. Army, 1962-64. Mem. AICPA, Country Club of Darien (Conn.). Home: 5 Topping Ln Norwalk CT 06854-3418 Office: 399 Park Ave New York NY Office Phone: 212-758-4446.

PEPYNE, EDWARD WALTER, lawyer, psychologist, educator; b. Springfield, Mass., Dec. 27, 1925; s. Walter Henry and Frances A. (Carroll) P.; m. Carol Jean Dutcher, Aug. 2, 1958; children— Deborah, Edward, Jr., Susan, Byron, Shari, Randy, David, Allison, Jennifer, Jaymie Page. BA, Am. Internat. Coll., 1948; MS, U. Mass., 1951, Ed.D., 1968; postgrad., NYU, 1952-55; prof. diploma, U. Conn., 1964; JD, Western New Eng. Coll., 1978. Bar: Mass. 1978, U.S. Supreme Ct. 1981, Vt. 2004. Prin., tchr. Gilbertville Grammar Sch., Hardwick, Mass., 1948-49; sch. counselor West Springfield High Sch., Mass., 1949-53; instr. NYU, 1953-54; supt. schs. New Shoreham, RI, 1954-56; asst. prof. edn. Mich. State U., 1956-58; sch. psychologist, guidance dir. Pub. Sch. System, East Long, Mass., 1958-62; lectr. Westfield State Coll., 1961-65; dir. pupil services Chicopee Pub. Sch., 1965-68; assoc. prof. counselor edn. U. Hartford, West Hartford, Mass., 1968-71, prof., 1971-85, dir. Inst. Coll. Counselors Minority and Low Income Students, 1971-72, dir. Div. Human Services, 1972-77; cons. Aetna Life & Casualty Co., Hartford, 1962-75; hearing officer Conn. State Bd. Edn., 1980-99; exec. dir. Sinapi Assocs., 1959-78; pvt. practice, Derby, Vt., 1978—. Co-author: Better Driving, 1958; assoc. editor: Highway Safety and Driver Education, 1954; chmn. editorial com.: Man and the Motor Car, 5th edit., 1954; contbr. numerous articles to profl. jours. Chief welfare svcs. Civil Def., Levittown, NY, 1953-54; chmn. Ashfield Planning Bd., Mass., 1979-83; moderator Town Ashfield, 1980-81, town counsel, Charlemont, Mass., 1983-84; mem. jud. nominating coun. Western Regional Com., 1993-99; mem. Mohawk Regional Sch. Com., 1999-2000; program chmn. Osher Lifelong Learning Inst., 2006-. Mem. ABA, APA, Mass. Bar Assn., Vt. Bar Assn., Mass. Acad. Trial Attys., Am. Pers. and Guidance Assn., New Eng. Pers. and Guidance Assn. (bd. dirs.), New Eng. Ednl. Rsch. Orgn. (pres. 1971), Am. Assn. Sch. Adminstrs., Am. Ednl. Rsch. Assn., Mt. Tom Amateur Radio Assn., Franklin County Amateur Radio Club, Elks, Kiwanis (pres. 1988-89, lt. gov. div. 12, 1991-92), Masons (master 1994-96, sec. 2007—), Shriners, Phi Delta Kappa. Home: 1585 Pine Hill Rd Newport VT 05855-9830

PERA, RENEE REIJO, biology professor; BS, U. Wis., 1983; PhD, Cornell U., 1993; postdoc., Whitehead Inst. Biomed. Rsch. MIT, 1997. Damon-Runyan fellow Whitehead Inst. Biomed. Rsch. MIT, 1993—97, instr. biology, 1995; asst. prof. in residence U. Calif., San Francisco, 1997—2003, assoc. prof. in residence, 2003—, co-dir. program in human stem cell biology, 2004—, assoc. dir. ctr. reproductive scis., 2004—. Spkr. in field. Contbr. articles to profl. jours. Office: USCF 513 Parnassus Ave Rm HSE 1636 Box 0556 San Francisco CA 94143-0556 Office Phone: 415-476-3178. Office Fax: 415-476-3121.

PERADOTTO, JOHN JOSEPH, retired classics educator, editor; b. Ottawa, Ill., May 11, 1933; s. John Joseph and Mary Louise (Giacometti) P.; m. Noreen Doran, Aug. 29, 1959 (div. 1982); m. Marlene Rosen, Aug. 29, 1992; children: Erin, Monica, Noreen, Nicole. BA, St. Louis U., 1957, MA, 1958; PhD, Northwestern U., 1963. Instr. classics and English Western Wash. U., Bellingham, 1960-61; instr. Georgetown U., 1961-63, asst. prof. classics, 1963-66, SUNY, Buffalo, 1966-69, asso. prof., 1969-73; prof., chmn. classics U. Tex., Austin, 1973-74; prof. classics SUNY-Buffalo, 1974-2000, Andrew V.V. Raymond prof. classics, 1984-99, Disting. tchg. prof., 1990-2000, Disting. tchg. prof. emeritus, 2000—, chmn. dept., 1974-77, dean div. undergrad. edn., 1978-82. Benedict Disting. vis. prof. Carleton Coll., 2003; Martin lectr. Oberlin Coll., 1987; dir. summer seminar for coll. tchrs. NEH, 1976, for secondary sch. tchrs., 1984; vis. scholar winter quarters U. Calif., San Diego, 2000—. Author: Classical Mythology: An Annotated Bibliographical Survey, 1973, Man in the Middle Voice: Name and Narration in the Odyssey, 1990, also articles and revs.; founding assoc. editor: Arethusa, editor-in-chief:, 1974—95, mem. bd. editors: SUNY Press, 1978—81; editor: SUNY Press Classical Series, 1981—2000, Classical Literature and Contemporary Literary Analysis, 1977, Women in the Ancient World, 1978, 1983, Studies in Latin Literature, 1984, Under the Text; co-editor: Population Policy in Plato and Aristotle, 1975, The New Archilochus, 1976, Augustan Poetry Books, 1980, Indo-European Roots of Classical Culture, 1980, Vergil: 2000 Years, 1981, Texts and Contexts: American Classical Studies in Honor of J.P. Vernant, 1982, Semiotics and Classical Studies, 1983, Audience-oriented Criticism and the Classics, 1986, Herodotus and the Invention of History, 1987, Gonimos: Neoplatonic and Byzantine Studies Presented to L.G. Westerlink at 75, 1988, The Challenge of Black Athena, 1989, Pastoral Revisions, 1990, Reconsidering Ovid's Fasti, 1992, Bakhtin and Classical Studies, 1993, Rethinking the Classical Canon, 1994, Horace: 2000 Years, 1995, The New Simonides, 1996, The Iliad and its Contexts, 1997. Fellow Center for Hellenic Studies, 1972-73; recipient Chancellor's award for teaching excellence State U. N.Y., 1975, Disting. Retiring Editor award Coun. of Editors of Learned Jours., 1995. Mem. Am. Philol. Assn. (dir. 1974-77, pres. 1990), Classical Assn. Atlantic States (exec. com. 1976-78). Office: Dept Classics State U Ny Buffalo NY 14261-0011 Home Phone: 716-688-1086; Office Phone: 716-645-2154 ext. 115. Business E-Mail: peradott@buffalo.edu.

PERALTA, EVERETT FIGUEROA, education educator, department chairman; came to U.S., 1958; s. Everado Grijalva and Dora (Figueroa) P. BS in Soc. Sci., SUNY, Albany, 1985; MA in Edn. Administrn. and Supervision, U. Phoenix, 2000; EdD, Ariz. State U. Coll. Edn., Tempe, 2005. Cert. global edn. program U. London, Eng., 2003, in elem. edn. K-8, in secondary edn. 7-12, in endorsement social studies, supt., supr., prin., subsitute tchr., in std. adult edn., ESL tchr. Resident asst. Ariz. State U., Tempe, 1979—81; coord. leadership devel. program, summer conf. mgr., resident hall dir. U. Bridgeport, Conn., 1981—85; exec. dir. Grad. Student Assn. Ariz. State U., Tempe, 1985-87; vice-chmn. Ariz. State Bd. Econ. Planning and Devel., Phoenix, 1987-88; v.p., provost, registrar Ariz. Investment Insurance Sch., 1987—89; sr. mgmt. cons. Crystal Resources, Tempe, 1988—94; substitute tchr. Wilcox, Cochise, Pearce Sch. Dists., 1989—94; exec. dir. Coun. Family Concerns Resources, 1993—95; with Papago Elem. Sch., 1995—97; tchr., prin. Maricopa County Regional Schs., 1997—2001; prof. edn. Am. Indian Coll., Phoenix, 2001—, chmn. dept. edn., 2005—; prof. edn., soc. sci. Western Internat. U., Ottawa U., Phoenix, 2005—. Bd. dirs. FBI Citizens Acad.; bd. dirs. law related edn. We the People Program Ariz. Bar Assn.; exec. dir. Coun. Family Concerns and Resources, 1993—95; prof. Cochise C.C., 1990—94, We. Internat. U., 2005—; presenter in field; cons. in field. Author: College Study Skills, 1992, Organizational Development and Leadership Skills, 1985. Delegate Ariz. Boys State Am. Legion, 1971; bd. dirs. Rural Schs. Project, Willcox, 1972-73, ASU Bd. Equal Opportunity, ASU Task Force Student Recruitment Retention, ASU Student Affairs Bd., ASU Graduate Student Rsch. Grants Bd., ASU res. hall. govt., 1985, Cochise County Literacy Coun., Bisbee, Ariz., 1991-1994; election bd. clk. City of Willcox, 1992; mem. Tempe City Transp. Commn., 1989; precinct committeeman, dep. registrar Maricopa County, 1983-; Wilcox City Election Bd., 1994, state bd. Family Soc. Svcs., 1994, state bd. dir. Prevent Child Abuse, 1995; founder Bilingual Middle 5-8 Sch. Program 1997; Congressional adv. com. Soc. Security Nat. Health Plan, 1998, faculty senate academic affairs com., Am. Indian Coll. 2001. Mem. UN Assn. (state treas., bd. dirs. Conn. chpt. 1984-85), Ctr. for Study of Presidency, K.C. (3d degree knight), Am. Assn. Univ. Prof., Nat. Edn. Assn., Nat. Coun. Soc. Studies, Am. Ednl. Rsch. Assn., Assn. Study of Higher Edn., Omicron Delta Kappa, Phi Delta Kappa, Theta Kappa Epsilon. Conservative. Avocations: reading, writing, politics, public speaking, carpentry. Home: 10020 North 15th Avenue Phoenix AZ 85021 Office Phone: 602-944-3335 ext. 237. Business E-Mail: eperalta@aicag.edu.

PERALTA, LUIS FRANCISCO, language educator; BA in Modern Langs., U. Autonoma Santo Domingo, 1992; MEd, Am. Intercontintal U., 2004. Spanish coord. Cultural Inst. Dominico Americano, Santo Domingo, 1996—99; lectr. Spanish Millikin U., Decatur, Ill., 1999—. Contbr. articles to profl. jours. Named Most Appreciated Profs., Ill. Edn. Assn. Students Program, Millikin U., 2005. Mem.: Am. Coun. Tchrs. Fgn. Langs.

PERALTA-VIDEA, JOSE R., environmental scientist, researcher; b. Pueblo Nuevo, Nicaragua; MS, Tropical Agrl. Rsch. & Higher Edn. Ctr., Costa Rica, 1978; PhD, Postgraduate Coll., Mex., 1986, U. of Tex. at El Paso, 2002. Cert. Agronomist Nat. Sch. of Agrl., Managua, Nicaragua, 1975. Rschr. coffee program Ministry of Agr., Managua, Nicaragua, 1974—76; leader cocoa program Ctrl. Bank of Nicaragua, Managua, 1978—79; sub-leader agrl. rsch. Agrl. Devel. Ministry, Managua, Nicaragua, 1979—82; prof., rschr. grad. coll., plant breeding dept. "Hermanos Escobar" Agricultrural Sch., Ciudad Juarez, Mexico; HS prin. Monterey Inst. of Tech., Ciudad Juarez, Mexico, 1992—95; assoc. prof. Monterrey Inst. of Tech., Ciudad Juarez, Mexico, 1995—99; rsch. asst. U. of Tex. at El Paso, 1999—2001, rsch. specialist, 2001—. Recipient Best H.S. full prof., Monterrey Inst. of Tech., 1993, 1997, Outstanding Doctoral Student award, U. of Tex. at El Paso, 2002; grantee, U.S. Dept. of Energy, 2003—05, SW Ctr. For Environ. Rsch. and Policy, 2005—06, Stanford Synchrotron Radiation Lab. (Ssrl), 2005—. Mem.: Soc. for Advancement of Chicanos and Native Ams. in Sci. (assoc.), Am. Chem. Soc. (assoc.). Achievements include patents for Production of gold and silver nanoparticles by living plants; research in uptake and translocation of inorganic elements within the transport system of vascular plants exposed to excess heavy metals; use of growth factors and chelating agents to enhance the metal translocation from the roots to the leaves and the effects produced on the whole-plant element accumulation. Office: Univ of Texas at El Paso 500 West Univ Ave El Paso TX 79968 Home Phone: 915-842-9178; Office Phone: 915-747-8998. Business E-Mail: jperalta@utep.edu.

PERCUS, JEROME KENNETH, physicist, researcher; b. NYC, June 21, 1926; s. Philip M. and Gertrude B. (Schweiger) P.; m. Ora Engelberg, May 20, 1965; children: Orin, Allon. BSE.E., Columbia U., 1947, MA, 1948, PhD, 1954. Instr. elec. engring. Columbia U., NYC, 1952-54; asst. prof. Stevens Inst. Tech., Hoboken, NJ, 1955-58; assoc. prof. NYU, NYC, 1958-65, prof. physics, 1965—. Dir. Nat. Biomed. Research Found. Author: (book) Many-Body Problem, 1963, Kinetic Theory and Statistical Mechanics, 1969, Combinatorial Methods, 1971, Combinatorial Methods in Developmental Biology, 1977, Mathematical Methods in Developmental Biology, 1978, Mathematical Methods in Enzymology, 1984, Lectures on the Mathematics of Immunology, 1986, Mathematics of Genome Analysis, 2001; editor: (Jours.) Pattern Recognition, Jour. Statis. Physics, Jour. Statis. Mechanics, Open Math. Jour. With USN, 1944-46. Recipient Pregel Chemistry Physics award N.Y. Acad. Scis., 1975, Joel Henry Hildebrand award in the Theoretical and Exptl. Chemistry of Liquids, Am. Chem. Soc., 1993, Pattern Rec. Soc. award, 1992. Fellow AAAS, Am. Phys. Soc.; mem. Am. Math. Soc., Sigma Xi. Office: NYU 251 Mercer St New York NY 10012-1110 Business E-Mail: percus@cims.nyu.edu.

PERCY, HELEN SYLVIA, physician; b. Atlanta, May 7, 1923; d. George L. and Sophia (Toulchin) P.; 1 child, Valentina Stewart-Annor. BS, U. San Francisco, 1951; MD, Med. Coll. Pa., 1958. Intern Harbor Gen. Hosp., Torrance, Calif., 1958-59, resident, 1959; physician Maui Med. Group, Lahaina, Hawaii, 1968—; asst. prof. medicine U. Hawaii, Honolulu, 1978—2000. Adv. bd. Maui Community Health Ctr., 1986-89; v.p. Maui AIDS Found., 1986-89. Mem. AMA, Maui County Med. Soc. (councilor 1988—), Hawaii Med. Assn. (Maui councilor). Democrat. Buddhist. Avocation: dance. Office: Maui Med Group 130 Prison St Lahaina HI 96761-1247 Office Phone: 808-661-0051.

PERCY, LEE EDWARD, motion picture film editor; b. Kalamazoo, Feb. 10, 1953; s. Richard Noyes and Helen Louise (Sheffield) P. Student, Goodman Sch., Chgo., 1971, Juilliard Sch., NYC, 1972; AB, U. Calif., Santa Cruz, 1977. Radio news reporter McGovern Campaign, Chgo., 1972; cons. Kjos Pub. Co., Chgo., 1973-74; dir. VisArt, Ltd., San Francisco, 1977; ind. film editor LA, 1978—. Editor: (films) Re-Animator, 1984, Kiss of the Spiderwoman, 1985 (Acad. award Best Actor), Slam Dance, 1987, Checking Out, 1988, Blue Steel, 1989, Reversal of Fortune, 1990 (Acad. award Best Actor), Year of the Gun, 1991, Single White Female, 1992, Against the Wall, 1993 (Eddie award, 1995, nominated for Cable ACE award), Corrina, Corrina, 1994, Kiss of Death, 1995, Before and After, 1996, Desperate Measures, 1997, "54", 1998, Boys Don't Cry, 1999 (Acad. award Best Actress), The Center of the World, 2001, Lift, 2001, The Believer, 2001 (winner Sundance Film Festival), Our Lady of the Assassins (La Virgen de los Sicarrios), 2001, Murder by Numbers, 2002, Maria Full of Grace, 2003 (Sundance Film Festival Audience award, Best Actress at Venice Film Festival), A Home at the End of the World, 2004, A Love Song for Bobby Long, 2004, The Ice Harvest, 2005, Mrs. Harris, 2006 (nominee ACE Eddy award), Wind Chill, 2006, Noise, 2007, Bernard and Doris, 2007, A Dog Year, 2007, Sleep Dealer, 2007, Taking Chance, 2007. Mem. Am. Cinema Editors, Acad. of Motion Picture Arts and Scis., Motion Picture Editor's Guild.

PERDEW, JOHN PAUL, physics professor; b. Cumberland, Md., Aug. 30, 1943; BS, Gettysburg Coll., 1965; PhD, Cornell U., 1971. Postdoctoral fellow U. Toronto, 1971-74, Rutgers U., New Brunswick, NJ, 1974-77; prof. physics Tulane U., New Orleans, 1977—, chair physics dept., 1991—94, 2001—03. Vis. scientist Nordita, Copenhagen, Argonne Nat. Lab., ETH Zurich, ITP Santa Barbara, Naval Rsch. Lab., Washington, Rice U.; invited lectr. numerous internat. confs. Contbr. more than 200 sci. articles to profl. jours. NSF Rsch. grantee, 1978—, Petroleum Rsch. Fund grantee 1998-2000; recipient Tulane LAS award for excellence in rsch., 1990. Fellow Am. Phys. Soc.; mem. Am. Chem. Soc., Am. Assn. Physics Tchrs., Internat. Acad. Quantum Molecular Sci., Phi Beta Kappa. Office: Tulane U Dept Physics New Orleans LA 70118 Business E-Mail: perdew@tulane.edu.

PERDIGÓ, LUISA MARINA, foreign language and literature educator; b. Havana, Cuba, Dec. 25, 1947; came to U.S. 1962; d. Mario and Hortensia Dolores (Alvarez) P. AB, CUNY, 1971, MA, 1974, PhD, 1981; MA, Columbia U., 1987. LPN, 2005; cert. translator English/Spanish Am. Translators Assn., ins. and coding specialist. Asst. prof. Spanish, asst. dean St. Thomas Aquinas Coll., Sparkill, NY, 1982-87; asst. prof. Spanish and French CUNY, La Guardia, 1987-88, asst. prof. Spanish, City Coll., 1988-89; asst. prof. Spanish St. Peter's Coll., Jersey City, 1989-91; asst. prof. Spanish and French Clarion U., Pa., 1992-94, Rockland Coll. SUNY, 1995-96, Mercy Coll., 1998—2007, assoc. prof. Spanish and French, dir. fgn. languages program, 2007—. Author: La Estética de Octavio Paz, 1975, The Origins of Vicente Huidobro's Creacionismo (1911-1916) and its Evolution (1917-47), 1994, The Lyrics of the Troubadour Perdigon, 2002, (poetry) Desde el Hudson/From the Hudson, 1993, Huellas/Footprints, 1997, 2d edit., 2006, America at the Millenium, 2000, The Best Poems and Poets of 2002, Theatre of the Mind, 2003, The M Poems, 2006, Songs of Honour, 2007; contbr. poetry to anthologies, articles to profl. jours. Participant seminar in poetry, NEH, U. Kans., 1991; Rsch. fellow Orgn. Am. States, Chile, 1981; grantee CUNY, 1975; scholar Columbia U., 1982-84. Mem.: MLA, Acad. Am. Poets, Clarion Hist. Soc., Circulo de Cultura Panamericano, Pi Delta Phi, Sigma Delta Pi.

PERDIKIS, GALEN, plastic surgeon; MB BCh, U. Witwatersrand, South Africa, 1988. Asst. prof. dept. plastic surgery Mayo Clinic, Jacksonville, Fla., 2001—. Contbr. articles to profl. jours. Recipient Trubshaw prize, Coll. of Medicine, South Africa, 1993, Golden Apple, Student Body, Creighton U., 1999; Herbert Davis scholarship, Creighton U., 1999. Fellow: ACS; mem.: Southeastern Soc. of Plastic and Reconstructive Surgeons, Greater Jacksonville Soc. of Plastic Surgeons, Am. Soc. of Plastic Surgery, Alpha Omega Alpha. Office: Mayo Clinic 4500 San Pablo Rd Jacksonville FL 32224 Office Phone: 904-953-2073.

PERDUE, BEVERLY EAVES, lieutenant governor, geriatric consultant; b. Grundy, Va., Jan. 14, 1948; d. Alfred P. and Irene E. (Morefield) (dec.) Moore; m. Robert W. Eaves, Jr.; children: Garrett, Emmett. BA, U. Ky., 1969; MEd, U. Fla., 1974, PhD, 1976. Pvt. lectr., writer, cons., 1980-86; pres. The Perdue Co., New Bern, N.C., 1985—; rep. N.C. State Gen. Assembly, Raleigh, 1986-90; senator N.C. Gen. Assembly, Raleigh, 1990-2001; lt. gov. State of N.C., 2001—. Bd. dirs. Nations Bank, New Bern. Bd. dirs. N.C. United Way, Greensboro, 1990-92; exec. mem. N.C. Dem. Party, Raleigh, 1989—; mem. N.C. travel bd. Nat. Conf. State Legislators. Named Outstanding Legislator, N.C. Aging Network, 1989, 92, 100 to Watch, Dem. Leadership Coun. 2003; Toll fellow Nat. Conf. State Legislators, Lexington, Ky., 1992. Mem. Nat. Coun. on Aging, Bus. and Profl. Women, Rotary. Democrat. Episcopalian. Office: Office of Lt Governor 310 N Blount Blvd 20301 Raleigh NC 27699-0401 Office Fax: 919-733-7350, 919-733-6595. E-mail: bperdue@ncmail.net.

PERDUE, DAVID A., JR., retail executive; b. Macon, Ga., Dec. 10, 1949; s. David A. Sr. and Gervaise (Wynn) P.; m. Bonnie Dunn Perdue, Aug. 26, 1972; children: David A. III, Blake R. BS, Ga. Inst. Tech., 1972, M in Ops. Rsch., 1975. Registered securities principal; cert. fin. planner; cert. mgmt. cons. Staff cons. Kurt Salmon Assocs., NYC, 1972-75, ptnr., 1976—83; v.p. Profl. Planning Assocs., Atlanta, 1983-86, Paul R. Ray and Co., Atlanta, 1986-87; pres. Westar Holding Co., Atlanta, 1987—92; sr. v.p. ops. Sara Lee Corp., Hong Kong, China, 1992—94; sr. v.p. Haggar Inc., 1994—98; sr. v.p. Global Supply Chain Reebok Intern. Ltd., 1998—99, exec. v.p. Global Oper. Units, Reebok Brand, 1999—2001, exec. v.p Global Supply Chain, 2001—02, pres., CEO Reebok Brand, 2001—02; chmn., CEO Pillowtex Corp., 2002—03, Dollar General Corp., 2003—. Mem. investor liaison com. Mortgage Banking Assn., Atlanta, 1989—; bd. dirs. Carl R. Young Sr. Trust, Johnson City, Tenn., Alliant Energy Corp., Ga. Tech. Adv. Bd. Mem. Ga. Coun. on Youth, Atlanta, 1972, Atlanta Care Adv. Bd., 1983-85, Atlanta Athletic Club House Com., 1988—. Mem. Mortgage Banking Assn., Inst. Cert. Fin. Planners, Inst. Mgmt. Cons., Atlanta Athletic Club. Republican. Baptist. Avocations: tennis, golf, sailing, reading. Office: Dollar General Corp 100 Mission Ridge Goodlettsville TN 37072 *

PERDUE, GEORGE (SONNY PERDUE), governor, former state legislator; b. Perry, Ga., Dec. 20, 1946; s. Ervin and Ophie Perdue; m. Mary (Ruff); children: Leigh, Lara, Jim, Dan. PhD in Vet. Medicine, U. Ga. Mem. Ga. Senate (dist. 18), Atlanta, 1990—2002; pres. pro tem; mem. appropriations, ethics, rules, reapportionment coms.; also fin. and pub. utilities, health and human svcs. coms.; former chmn. higher edn., def. conversion com.; co-chair joint commn. legis. info. mgmt.; gov. State of Ga., Atlanta, 2003—. Capt. USAF, 1971-74, Vietnam. Democrat. Baptist. Office: Office of the Gov 203 State Capitol Atlanta GA 30334 Office Phone: 404-656-1776. *

PERDUE, JAMES A. (JIM PERDUE), food products executive; b. 1949; BS, Wake Forest U., 1973; MA in Marine Biology, Southeastern Mass. U., 1976; PhD in Fisheries, U. Wash., 1983. With U. Md., Cambridge, 1976-78; chmn. bd. Perdue Transp., Inc., Salisbury, Md., 1983—, Perdue Farms Inc., 1983—, CEO, 1991—. Dir. Nat. Chicken Coun. Office: Perdue Farms Inc 31149 Old Ocean City Rd Salisbury MD 21804 Office Phone: 410-543-3743. Office Fax: 410-543-3874. E-mail: jim.perdue@perdue.com.

PERDUE, JOHN D., state official; b. Manila, W.Va. s. Glenn and Mary Perdue. BS in Agriculture, W.Va. U., 1972. State treas. State W.Va., 1997—. Mem.: Nat. Assn. State Treas. (pres. 2004—05), W.Va. Forestry Assn., Alpha Gamma Rho, Alpha Tau Alpha. Office: WVa State Treasurers Office 1900 Kanawha Blvd Capital Complex Bldg 1 Rm E-145 Charleston WV 25305 Office Phone: 304-558-5000. Business E-Mail: john.perdue@wvsto.com.

PERDUE, PETER C., history professor; PhD, Harvard Univ., 1981. T.T. and Wei Fong Chao prof.Asian civilizations, prof. history MIT. Author: Exhausting the Earth, 1987, China Marches West, 2005. Fellow: Am. Acad. Arts & Scis. Office: MIT Bldg E51-291 77 Massachusetts Ave Cambridge MA 02139 Office Phone: 617-253-3064. Business E-Mail: pcperdue@mit.edu. *

PEREIRA, JOHN WILLIAM MILLER, theater educator; s. John Pereira and Madeline Miller. BA, Queens Coll., Flushing, NY, 1975; MA, CUNY, NYC, 1979, MPhil, 1982, PhD, 1986. Adj. assoc. prof. dept. drama, theatre and dance Queens Coll., Flushing, 1978—; asst. prof./adj. assoc. prof. dept. theatre and dance Nassau C.C., Garden City, NY, 1989—. Coord. PhD Alumni Assn. CUNY, NYC, 1980—; cons. CUNY-TV, NYC, 1985—, McGraw-Hill Pub. Co., NYC, 1993—2003, Nat. Com. on Am. Fgn. Policy, NYC, 1993—2002, Am. Theatre Wing, NYC, 2004—05; contbg. writer Theater Week Mag., NYC, 1986—88; manuscript reviewer St. Martin's Press, NYC, 1999; external examiner PhD dissertation James Cook U., Townsville, Australia, 2001. Author: Opening Nights: 25 Years of the Manhattan Theatre Club; dir.: (plays) Twelfth Night, 1987, A Midsummer Night's Dream, 1989, What the Butler Saw, 1990, It's Only a Play, 1999, Death Knocks, 2006, The Typists, 2006, The Harry and Sam Dialogues, 2006, Self Help, 2007, Three Viewings, The Long Weekend, Art, Office Hours, Say Goodnight, Gracie, Luv, Album, Sylvia; actor: The Imaginary Invalid, 1991, The Palace of the Dead, 1995, Dr. Faustus, 1996; co-editor: (jour.) Nonprofit and Voluntary Sector Quarterly; contbr. articles to profl. jours. Mem.: PhD Alumni Assn. CUNY (bd. dirs.). Office: Nassau Community College One Education Dr Garden City NY 11530-6793 Home Phone: 718-423-6225; Office Phone: 516-572-8069. Business E-Mail: pereirj@ncc.edu.

PEREIRA, JULIO CESAR, middle school educator; b. Vila Nova Sintra, Cape Verde, Cape Verde, Oct. 12, 1937; came to U.S., 1983; s. Julio Feijoo Pereira and Beatriz Feijoo Pereira. Student, Mil. Sch., Coimbra, Portugal, 1958-61; MAEE, U. Lisbon, Portugal, 1976; cert. in teaching, Afonso Domingues, Lisbon, 1979, Ea. Nazarene Coll., Quincy, Mass., 1988. Registered profl. engr., Portugal. Vocat. sch. tchr. Portuguese Sch., Lisbon, 1969-83, dir. instrn., 1980-81; social studies tchr. Madison Park H.S., Boston, 1984-85; math. tchr. Dearborn Mid. Sch., Boston, 1985—. Inventor slide model for algebraic addition. Lt. Portuguese Army, 1961-65. Recipient Tchr. Appreciation award Algebra Project Boston, 1992, Multicultural Recognition award Mass. Dept. Edn., 1992, Ofcl. citation Mass. Senate, 1993, Presdl. award for Excellence in Math. Teaching, Pres. of U.S., 1994. Mem. Coun. Presdl. Awardees in Math. Avocations: reading, research, computer programming, gardening, travel. Office: Dearborn Mid Sch 35 Greenville St Boston MA 02119-2315 Mailing: PO Box 2450 Mashpee MA 02649-8450

PEREIRA, P.J., media consultant; b. Brazil, 1974; Joined DM9, 1996—99, Midialog, 1999—2005; founder AgenciaClick, 1999; exec. creative dir. AKQA, San Francisco, 2005—. Jury pres. Cyber Lion's jury for the Cannes Internat. Advt. Festival, 2005—. Named one of 40 Under 40, Advt. Age, 2007. Achievements include winning 13 Cyber Lions and a Cyber Lion Grand Prix at Cannes, along with eight One Show Pencils. Office: AKQA Hdqs 118 King St 6th Fl San Francisco CA 94107 Office Phone: 415-645-9400. *

PEREL, DAVID, editor; Sports editor Washington Post; editor-in-chief Nat. Enquirer, 1986—2005, 2006—; pres. AMI Books, 2005—; editor-in-chief Looking Good Now mag., 2005; exec. v.p. & editl. dir. Globe, 2005, Nat. Examiner, 2005, Sun, 2005, Weekly World News, 2005. Co-author: Freak! Inside the Twisted World of Michael Jackson, 2003, Bat Boy Lives! The Weekly World News Guide to Politics, Culture, Celebrities, Alien Abductions, and the Mutant Freaks That Shape Our World, 2005. Office: National Enquirer 1000 American Media Way Boca Raton FL 33464-1000

PEREL, JAMES MAURICE, pharmacology and psychiatry educator, researcher; b. Buenos Aires, Mar. 30, 1933; came to U.S., 1947, naturalized, 1954; s. Aria and Bella (Silverberg) P.; m. July 18, 1959 (div. 1971); 1 child, Allan B.; m. Audrey Feldman, Apr. 9, 1972; children: Alissa A., Stephen M. BS, CUNY, 1956; MS, NYU, 1961, PhD, 1964. Nuclear chemist NY Naval Shipyard Lab., Bklyn., 1956—58; assoc. rsch. scientist Goldwater Meml. Hosp. NYU, 1964—67; asst. prof. medicine and chemistry Emory U., Atlanta, 1967-70; asst. prof. psychiatry, pharmacology Columbia U. Coll. Physicians and Surgeons, NYC, 1970-76; assoc. rsch. scientist NY State Psychiat. Inst., NYC, 1970—76, assoc. prof. clin. pharmacology, chief psychiat. rsch., 1976-80; chief clin. pharmacology VA Med. Ctr. Highland Drive, Pitts., 1979-83; prof. psychiatry U. Pitts. Sch. Medicine, 1980—2001, acting chmn. dept. pharmacology, 1985-88, prof. pharmacology, 1980—, prof. emeritus psychiatry, 2001—; dir. clin. pharmacology Western Psychiat. Inst. and Clinic, Pitts., 1980—; prof. grad. neurosci., 1988—; postdoctoral fellow in clin. pharmacology NIH, 1964-67, NYU. Adj. faculty in chemistry CUNY, 1963-67; cons., mem. grant-awarding study sects. NIH, NIMH. Mem. editorial bd. Psychopharmacology, Neuropsychobiology, Therapeutic Drug Monitoring, Focus on Schizophrenia and Bipolar Disorders, Applied PHarmacokinetics and Pharmacodynamics, 4th edit.; contbr. over 400 articles to sci. jours., chpts. to books. Named Psychopharmacologist of Yr., U. Toronto, 1993; named to Honor Roll, Century of Therapeutics and Sci. 1900-2000, Am. Soc. Clin. Pharmacology and Therapeutics; recipient Founders Day award, NYU, 1974, Julius Koch Meml. award, Rho Chi, 1983; predoctoral fellow, NSF, 1958—60, numerous rsch. grants, including NIH, NIMH, Founds. Fund for Rsch. in Psychiatry, pharm. cos., pvt. founds. Fellow: Am. Inst. Chemists; mem. Am. Chem. Soc., World Fed. Neurology (founder, mem. neurotoxicology group), Internat. Assn. Therapeutic Drug Monitoring and Clin. Toxicology (com. chair), Am. Soc. Pharmacology and Exptl. Therapeutics, Am. Soc. Clin. Pharmacology and Therapeutics (sect. chair), Sigma Xi Jewish. Achievements include discovery of several widely-used pharmacotherapeutic agents. Office: U Pitts Sch Medicine 3811 Ohara St Pittsburgh PA 15213-2593 Office Phone: 412-246-6600. Business E-Mail: pereljm@upmc.edu, pereljm@pitt.edu.

PERELLA, JOSEPH ROBERT, investment banker; b. Newark, Sept. 20, 1941; s. Dominic A. and Agnes P.; m. Amy Gralnick, Jan. 20, 1974 BS, Lehigh U., 1964; MBA, Harvard U., 1972. C.P.A., N.Y. Pub. acct. Haskins & Sells, NYC, 1964-70; cons. Internat. Bank for Reconstruction & Devel., Washington, 1971; assoc. The First Boston Corp., NYC, 1972-74, asst. v.p., 1974-75, v.p., 1975-78, mng. dir., 1978-88; chmn. Wasserstein, Perella & Co., NYC, 1988—2001; head, investment banking div. Morgan Stanley & Co., Inc., NYC, 1997—2000, chmn., instl. securities, 2000—05; co-founder Perella Weinberg Partners, NYC, 2006—. Trustee Lehigh U. Office: Perella Weinberg Partners 767 Fifth Ave New York NY 10153 Office Phone: 212-287-3200. Office Fax: 212-287-3201.

PERELMAN, JEFFREY E., real estate company executive; BA with hon., Univ. Ill.; JD, Ill. Inst. Tech. Chgo. Kent Coll. Law. Former owner, mgr. Commodities Brokerage Firm; with Sterling Real Estate Ptnrs., Chgo., 1996—, now prin. Named one of TOP 200 Art Collectors ARTnews Mag., 2006. Avocation: collecting art. Office: Sterling Real Estate Ptnrs Ste 600 1033 Skokie Blvd Northbrook IL 60062

PERELMAN, RONALD OWEN, consumer products company executive; b. Greensboro, NC, Jan. 1, 1943; s. Raymond and Ruth (Caplan) P.; m. Faith Golding, 1965 (div. 1983), 4 children; m. Claudia Cohen, Jan. 11, 1985 (div. 1994), 1 child, Sammantha; m. Patricia Duff, Dec. 20, 1995 (div. Sept. 10, 1998), 1 child, Caleigh Sophia; m. Ellen Barkin, June 28, 2000 (separated. Jan. 19, 2006) BA, U. Pa., 1964; MBA, Wharton Sch. Fin., 1966. With Belmont Industries Inc., 1966-78; chmn., chief exec. officer, dir. MacAndrews & Forbes Holdings Inc., Wilmington, Del., 1983—; chmn., chief exec. officer MacAndrews & Forbes Group Inc. (subs.), NYC, 1978—; chmn., chief exec. officer, dir. Revlon Group Inc. (subs. MacAndrews & Forbes Group Inc.), NYC, 1985—, Revlon Inc. (subs.), NYC, 1985—; also chmn. Nat. Health Labs. Inc., La Jolla, Calif., 1985—, Andrews Group Inc., La Jolla, 1985—; pres. bd. of trustees Solomon R. Guggenheim Mus., La Jolla, 1995—. Named one of Top 200 Collectors, ARTnews Mag., 2004, Forbes Richest Americans, 1999—, World's Richest People, Forbes Mag., 1999—. Jewish. Avocation: Collecting Contemporary Art. also: Solomark Guggenheim Mus 1071 5th Ave New York NY 10128-0173 Office: Revlon Consumer Products Corp 466 Lexington Ave Fl 13 New York NY 10017-3227 *

PERENCHIO, ANDREW JERROLD, film and television executive; b. Fresno, Calif., Dec. 20, 1930; s. Andrew Joseph and Dorothea (Harvey) P.; m. Robin Green, July 16, 1954 (div.); children: Candace L., Catherine M., John Gardner; m. Jacquelyn Claire, Nov. 14, 1969 (div.); m. Margaret McHugh, 1987. BS, UCLA, 1954. V.p. Music Corp. Am., 1958-62, Gen. Artists Corp., 1962-64; pres., owner theatrical agy. Chartwell Artists, Ltd., LA, from 1964; chmn. bd. Tandem Prodns., Inc. and TAT Communications Co., LA, 1973-83; pres., CEO Embassy Pictures, LA, 1983—85; pres. Chartwell Partnerships Group, LA; chmn., CEO Univision Communications, 1992—2007. Promoter Muhammad Ali-Joe Frazier heavyweight fight, 1971, Bobby Riggs-Billie Jean King tennis match, 1973. Served to 1st lt. USAF, 1954-57. Named one of Richest Americans, Forbes Mag., 1999—, World's Richest People, 2001—. Mem.: Bel-Air Country Club (LA); Westchester Country Club, NY; Friars Club, NYC. *

PEREPEZKO, JOHN H., engineering educator; BS, Polytechnic Inst. of NY, 1967, MS in Metallurgical Engring., 1968; PhD in Metallurgical and Materials Sci., Carnegie-Mellon U., 1973. Prof. materials sci. and engring. physics U. Wis., Madison, 1975—. Contbr. articles to profl. jours. Recipient Bruce Chalmers Award, 1997. Fellow: ASM-Internat.; mem.: AIME, NAE, Electrochemical Soc., Sigma Xi, Alpha Sigma Mu. Office: U Wis Dept Materials Sci & Engring 1509 University Ave Madison WI 53706 Office Phone: 608-263-1678. Office Fax: 608-262-8353. E-mail: perepezk@engr.wisc.edu.

PERERA, LAWRENCE THACHER, lawyer; b. Boston, June 23, 1935; s. Guido R. and Faith (Phillips) P.; m. Elizabeth A. Wentworth, July 5, 1961; children: Alice V. Perera Lucey, Caroline F. Perera Barry, Lucy E.Perera Adams, Lawrence Thacher, Jr. BA, Harvard U., 1957, LL.B., 1961. Bar: Mass. 1961, U.S. Supreme Ct. 1973. Clk. Judge R. Ammi Cutter, Mass. Supreme Jud. Ct., Boston, 1961-62; assoc. Palmer & Dodge, Boston, 1962-69, ptnr., 1969-74; judge Middlesex County Probate Ct., East Cambridge, Mass., 1974-79; ptnr. Hemenway & Barnes, Boston, 1979—. Mem. nat. coun. Hon. Nat. Jud. Coll., Reno, prof., pres. Mass. CLE, Inc., 1988-90; trustee Mass. Investors Trust., 1981—; trustee, vice chmn. Boston Found., 1981-1996. Chmn. Boston Fin. Commn., 1969-71; overseer Boston Lyric Opera; chmn. bd. overseers Boston Opera Assn.; chmn. Back Bay Archtl. Commn., 1966-72; trustee emeritus Sta. WGBH Ednl. Found., Boston Athenaeum, Wang Ctr. Performing Arts, Social Law Libr. Fellow Am. Acad. Matrimonial Lawyers, Am. Coll. Trust and Estate Counsel; mem. ABA, Am. Bar Found., Am. Law Inst., Mass. Bar Assn., Mass. Bar Found., Boston Bar Assn., Boston Bar Found. Home: 18 Marlborough St Boston MA 02116-2101 Office: 60 State St Boston MA 02109-1800

PERERA, UNIL A.G., physics educator, researcher; b. Colombo, Sri Lanka, Nov. 12, 1956; came to U.S., 1982; s. Weymen and Daya (Daluwatta) P.; m. Shrima Y. Samaranayake, July 1, 1983; children: Nuwan, Nirosha. BS in Physics, U. Colombo, 1981; MS, U. Pitts., 1983, PhD, 1987. Asst. lectr. U. Colombo, 1981-82; tchg. asst. U. Pitts., 1982-83, rsch. asst., 1983-87, rsch. assoc., 1987-88, rsch. asst. prof., 1988-92; asst. prof. physics Ga. State U., Atlanta, 1992-95, assoc. prof., 1995-2001, prof., 2001—, grad. dir. physics, 1995—, dir. IRML, 1995—. Lectr. Nat. Rsch. Coun., Ottawa, Ont., Can., 1990, Indiana U. Pa., 1991, Calif. Inst. Tech., 1995, AAAS, Colombo, 1995, Emory U., Atlanta, 1995, U. Colombo, 1997, U. Peradeniya, Sri Lanka, 1997, Tech. U., Vienna, Austria, 1997, U. Linz, Austria, 1997, U. Ill., Chgo., 1998, U. Turkey, Istanbul, 1998, UCLA, 1998, CRL, Tokyo, 1998, Nat. U. Singapore, 1999, Inst. Fund Studies, Sri Lanka, 1999, Inst. for Physics of Microstructure, Nizhny Novogorod, Russia, 2000. Editor: Handbook of Thin Film Devices; contbr. more than 100 articles to profl. jours.; patentee in field. Mentor McNair Program, Atlanta, 1994-97. Grantee NASA, 1997—, NSF, 1990—, Ga. State U., 1992—, others. Fellow Am. Phys. Soc.; mem. IEEE (sr.), Soc. Photo Instrumentation Engrs. Buddhist. Office: Ga State U Dept Physics 29 Peachtree Center Ave NE Atlanta GA 30303-2515 Home Phone: 770-948-1505. Business E-Mail: uperera@gsu.edu.

PERES, FRANK J., healthcare administrator; b. Havanna, Cuba, Oct. 4, 1943; arrived in U.S., 1962; s. Julian N. and Silvia N. (Hernandez) P.; m. Carmen Rosario Perez, Apr. 10, 1966; children: Shelley, Vanessa, Karen. BS, Columbia Union Coll., 1970; M in Health Care Administrn., George Washington U., 1974. Exec. v.p. Christ Hosp., Jersey City, 1974-79; exec. dir. Bella Vista Hosp., Mayaquez, PR, 1979-85, Caribe Hosp. Affiliates,

Bayamon, PR, 1985-88; pres. Atlantic Adventist Healthcare, Stoneham, Mass., 1988-94, Cmty. Hosps. of Ea. Middlesex, Stoneham, 1992-94, New England Meml. Hosp., Stoneham, 1988-94; pres., CEO Kettering (Ohio) Med. Ctr., 1994—. Pres. State Health Facilities Com., Mayaquez, 1985-90; bd. dirs. New Am. Hosp. Assn. Co-author: The Conference Board, 1995; contbr. articles to profl. jours. Trustee Hospice of Dayton, Ohio, 1995-96, Dayton Ballet, 1995-96; bd. dirs. Ohio Quality Cardiac Care Found., Columbus, 1996. Recipient Presdl. Citation for Sustained Bus. Leadership Atlantic Union Coll., 1993; named one of Top 10 Latino Leaders LatinoLeaders mag., 2004 Fellow Am. Coll. of Healthcare Execs., Am. Hosp. Assn., Kettering Coll. of Med. Arts (bd. dirs. 1994-96), Greater Dayton Area Hosp. Assn. (bd. dirs. 1994-96), Dayton Area C. of C. (trustee 1996), PPS State Hosp. Assn. (bd. dirs., v.p., chmn. 1985-88) Office: Kettering Med Ctr 3535 Southern Blvd Kettering OH 45429-1221

PERES, JUDITH MAY, journalist; b. Chgo., June 30, 1946; d. Leonard H. and Eleanor (Seltzer) Zurakov; m. Michael Peres, June 27, 1972 (div. 2004); children: Dana, Avital. BA, U. Ill., 1967; M Studies in Law, Yale U., 1997. Acct. exec. Daniel J. Edelman Inc., Chgo., 1967-68; copy editor Jerusalem (Israel) Post, 1968-71, news editor, 1971-75, chief night editor, 1975-80, editor, style book, 1978-80; copy editor Chgo. Tribune, 1980-82, rewriter, 1982-84, assoc. fgn. editor, 1984-90, nat. editor, 1990-95, nat./fgn. editor, 1995-96, specialist writer, 1997—; Yale Law fellow, 1996-97. Recipient Media award, U. Mich., 2000, Soc. Women's Health Rsch., 2004. Office: Chicago Tribune 435 N Michigan Ave Chicago IL 60611-4066 Office Phone: 312-222-4330. Business E-Mail: jperes@tribune.com.

PERET, KAREN KRZYMINSKI, health facility administrator; b. Springfield, Mass., Mar. 8, 1950; d. Edward S. and Doris L. (Beaudry) Krzyminski; m. Robert J. Peret, June 19, 1971 (div. Sept. 2003); children: Heather, James, Kaitlin, Matthew. BSN, St. Anselm's, 1972; MS in Nursing Adminstrn., Boston U., 1980; EdD in Orgnl. Devel., U. Mass., 1993. RN, Mass. Staff nurse Boston VA's Hosp., 1972—73; staff nurse pediat. Harrington Meml. Hosp., Southbridge, Mass., 1973—74, instr. edn., 1974—75, relief day asst. dir. nursing, 1975; coord. continuing edn. Ctrl. Maine Med. Ctr., Lewiston, 1975—76; asst. dir. nursing Monson Devel. Ctr., Palmer, Mass., 1977—83, DON, 1983—94; exec. nursing cons. Liberty Healthcare, Waltham, Mass., 1994—98, v.p. ops. Phila., 1998—; ind. mgmt. cons., 1993—. Instr. Quinsigamond Cmty. Coll., Worcester, Mass., 1972-73. Contbr. articles to profl. jours. Mem. ANA, Mass. Nurses' Assn., Am. Assn. on Mental Retardation, Sigma Theta Tau. Home: 79 Sturbridge Rd Holland MA 01521-3123 Office: 401 E City Ave Ste 820 Bala Cynwyd PA 19004-1130 Home Phone: 413-245-9452; Office Phone: 800-331-7122. Personal E-mail: karenperet@aol.com.

PERETSMAN, NANCY B., investment banker; b. Worcester, Mass., Mar. 27, 1954; d. George Peretsman and Norma (Burofsky) O'Haire; m. Robert Scully, Sept. 17, 1988. AB with hons., Princeton U., 1976; MPPM, Yale, 1979. V.p. Blyth, Eastman, Dillon & Co., NYC, 1979—83; dir., head of media group Salomon Bros., NYC, 1983—95; exec. v.p., mng. dir. Allen & Co., NYC, 1995—. Bd. mem. Charter Comm., Inc. Charter trustee Princeton U., 1976. Named one of 50 Women to Watch, Wall St. Jour., 2005, 50 Most Powerful Women in Bus., Fortune mag., 2006. Office: Allen & Co Inc 711 5th Ave New York NY 10022 *

PERETTI, PETER ORAL, psychology professor, researcher; s. Peter Charles and Estelle Agnes (Janas) Peretti; children: Robert Peter, Kathryn June. BA, Lake Forest Coll., 1962; MA in Sociology, Roosevelt U., 1964, MA in Psychology, 1967; PhD in Psychology, Walden U., 1974. Prof. Purdue North Ctrl. U., Westville, Ind., 1964—66, Ill. Benedictine Coll., Lisle, 1966—69, North Park Coll., Chgo., 1969—72, City Coll. Chgo., 1972—. Author: 8 books, numerous poems, jour. articles. Recipient Regional and All City Science Fair Judge awards, 1974—, Golden Apple award for Tchg., 2002. Mem.: Assn. Advancement of Ethical Hypnosis, Assn. Supervision and Curriculum Devel., Assn. Rsch. Animal Behavior, Criterion Bar Assn., Quill and Scroll, Hugo's Companions, Mystery Writers Am., Chgo. Acad. Scis. (life), Field Mus. (life), The Hounds, Internat. Soc. Poets (Disting. Mem. award, Found. Laureate award 2005), Western Writers Am., Caxton Club, Phi Theta Kappa (hon.). Avocations: book clubs, bicycling, jogging.

PERETZ, MARTIN, publishing executive, educator; b. NYC, July 30, 1939; s. Julius and Ellen (Weberman) P.; m. Anne Labouisse, June 16, 1967; children— David, Anne Elise, Jesse, Evgenia. BA, Brandeis U., 1959; MA, Harvard U., 1965, PhD, 1966; DHL (hon.), Bard Coll., 1982; DLL (hon.), Coe Coll., 1983; PhD (hon.), Hebrew U., Jerusalem, 1987; DLL (hon.), Long Island Univ, 1988, Brandeis Univ, 1989, Hebrew Coll, 1990, Chgo. Theol. Sem., 1994. Instr. Harvard, 1965-68, asst. prof., 1968-72, lectr. social studies, 1972—; master Cabot House, 1972-75; chmn. editorial bd. New Republic mag., 1974-75; editor-in-chief New Republic, 1975—, chmn., 1998—. Bd chm Digital Learning Group; dir. Dreyfus Money Market Instruments, Dreyfus A Bonds, Dreyfus Instl. Money Market Fund, Dreyfus Balanced Fund, Dreyfus Global bond Fund, Dreyfus Growth and Income Fund, Dreyfus Internat. Funds, Dreyfus Variable Investment Fund and Premier Equity Funds. Bd. govs. Hebrew U. Jerusalem; hon. chmn. Jerusalem Found.; dir. Leukosite; trustee Ctr. for Blood Rsch., Harvard Med. Sch.; co-chmn. THEStreet, Inc. Woodrow Wilson fellow, 1959-61; recipient medal excellence in journalism U. Mo. Sch. Journalism, 1982 Democrat. Jewish. Office: New Republic Ste 700 1331 H St NW Washington DC 20005

PEREYRA-SUAREZ, CHARLES ALBERT, lawyer; b. Paysandu, Uruguay, Sept. 7, 1947; arrived in U.S., 1954, naturalized, 1962; s. Hector and Esther (Enriquez-Sarano) Pereyra-Suarez; m. Susan H. Cross, Dec. 30, 1983. BA in History magna cum laude, Pacific Union Coll., 1970; postgrad., UCLA, 1970-71; JD, U. Calif., Berkeley, 1975. Bar: Calif. 1975, DC 1980. Staff atty. Western Ctr. Law and Poverty, Inc., LA, 1976; trial atty. civil rights divsn. U.S. Dept. Justice, Washington, 1976—79, asst. U.S. atty., criminal divsn. LA, 1979—82; sr. litig. assoc. Gibson, Dunn & Crutcher, LA, 1982—84; pvt. practice LA, 1984—86, 1998—; ptnr. McKenna & Cuneo, LA, 1986—95, Davis Wright Tremaine, LA, 1995—98. Democrat. Avocations: tennis, jogging, travel. Office Phone: 213-623-5923. Business E-Mail: cpereyra@cpslawfirm.com.

PEREZ, ANNIE RIVERA, elementary school educator; d. Francisco Bontugan and Isabel Rivera Perez. BA in elem. edn., U. of Guam, 1975; MEd, U. Portland, 1994. Cert. Profl. II Elem.K-5, P.E. K-6 Guam Pub. Sch. Sys., 2005. Elem. tchr. Guam Pub. Sch. Sys., Hagatna, Guana Island, 1975—2000; elem. tchr. 5th grade San Vicente Cath. Sch., Barrigada, 2001—. Coord. elem. divsn. adminstrv. team San Vicente Cath. Sch., Barrigada, 2001—. Commr. Chamorro Land Trust, Hagatna, Guam, Guam, 2004—06. Mem.: Internat. Reading Assn. (assoc.). Roman Catholic. Office: San Vicente Cath School 196 Bejong Guam Barrigada 96913 Guana Island Home Phone: 671-734-0737; Office Phone: 671-735-4240. Personal E-mail: arp@guam.net.

PEREZ, ANTONIO M., imaging company executive; b. Spain; BSEE, Madrid U. Corp. v.p., mem. exec. coun., pres. consumer bus. Hewlett-Packard Co., pres., CEO inkjet imaging bus., 1995—99; pres., CEO Gemplus Internat., 2000—01; pres., COO Eastman Kodak Co., Rochester, NY, 2003—05, CEO, 2005—, chmn., 2006—. Bd. dirs. Eastman Kodak Co.; dir. Schering-Plough Corp.; vice chair, chmn. Diversity Best Practices, 2007. Trustee George Eastman House. Mem.: Bus. Roundtable, Bus. Coun. *

PEREZ, BEATRIZ R., marketing executive; BA in Mktg., U. Md. Account supr. DMB&B/Sosa, Bromley, Aguilar, Noble & Associates, 1994—96; assoc. brand mgr. Classic Coke, 1996—2005; v.p. sports & entertainment mktg. N. Am. divsn., The Coca-Cola Co., Atlanta, 2005—07, v.p., integrated mktg., 2007—. Bd. dirs. HSBC N. Am. Holdings Inc., 2007—. Mem. Girls Outdoor Adventure for Leadership, The Victory Junction Gang, Grammy Found. Named one of Forty Under 40, Sports Bus. Jour., 2001—03; named to Elite Women, Hispanic Bus., 2005. Office: The Coca-Cola Co PO Box 1734 Atlanta GA 30301 *

PEREZ, DAVID, utilities executive; b. Mexico, 1970; arrived in US, 1976; Grad., U. Ill., Chgo. Tech. investigations mgr. Commonwealth Edison Co., Chgo., maintenance mgr., regional dir. distbn. ops., 2005—. Named one of 40 Under 40, Crain's Chgo. Bus., 2006. Office: ComEd PO Box 805379 Chicago IL 60680-5379 also: Exelon Corp PO Box 805398 Chicago IL 60680 Office Phone: 800-334-7661.

PEREZ, GLAD M., marketing professional; d. Luis and Delia Perez. BBA in Gen. Bus., Pace U., NYC, 1985; attended MBA mini-program, Am. Mgmt Assn., 1987; grad. Advanced Exec. Program, Northwestern U. J.L Kellogg Grad. Sch. Mgmt., 1998, grad. International Mktg. Program, 2000. Brand mgr. McGraw-Hill, NYC, 1977—85; dir. mktg. comm. AT&T, Basking Ridge, NJ, 1985—2004; v.p. mktg. and e-commerce Affinity Fed. Credit Union, Basking Ridge, 2005—. Bd. mem. Affinity Investment Svcs., Basking Ridge. Recipient Golf EFFIE award, Am. Mktg. Assn., 1992, Internat. award, Advertising and Mktg. Effectiveness, 1995, 2 Clio awards, Clio, 1996, NJ Gold medal, Art Dirs. Club NJ, 1996, Best Theme award, 1997, Gold Echo award, Direct Mktg. Assn., 1999, ADDY award, Am. Advt. Fedn., 1999, Multicultural Excellence award, Assn. Nat. Advertisers, 1999, 2001, Telly award, 2004; scholar, Regents, 1976. Mem.: NAFE, Credit Union Executives Soc., Advt. Women NY, The Advt. Club, Mktg. Execs. Networking Group, Nat. Assn. for Multi-ethnicity in Comm., Direct Mktg. Assn., Am. Mgmt. Assn., Am. Mktg. Assn., Ctr. for Creative Leadership (life). Home: 132 Constitution Way Basking Ridge NJ 07920 Office: Affinity Federal Credit Union 73 Mountain View Blvd Basking Ridge NJ 07920 Home Phone: 908-658-4266; Office Phone: 908-860-7306. Personal E-mail: gmperez@gmp-associates.com. Business E-Mail: gladp@affinityfcu.com.

PEREZ, JORGE M., real estate developer; b. Argentina; arrived in U.S., 1968; M in urban planning, Univ. Mich. Chmn., CEO Related Group of Fla., Miami, 1979—. Bd. dir. Regions Fin. Corp. Past. mem. Dem. Nat. Com.; trustee Univ. Miami; vice chmn. Miami Dade Cultural Affairs Council; dir. Miami Film Festival, Miami Downtown Develop. Authority. Named one of 25 Most Influential Hispanics, Time Mag., 2005, Forbes' Richest Americans, 2006. Democrat. Avocations: art collecting, especially Latin Am. contemporary art, tennis. Office: Related Group of Florida 2828 Coral Way Miami FL 33145

PEREZ, JOSEPHINE, psychiatrist, educator; b. Tijuana, Mex., Feb. 10, 1941; came to the U.S., 1960, U.S. citizenship, 1968. BS in Biology, U. Santiago de Compostela, Spain, 1971, MD, 1975. Nuc. medicine technician, EEG technician, supr. Electrographic Labs., Encino, Calif., 1963—69; clerkships in internal medicine, gen. surgery, otorhinolaryngology, dermatology and venereology Gen. Hosp. of Galicia, Spain, 1972-75; resident in gen. psychiatry U. Miami, Jackson Meml. Hosp. and VA Hosp., Miami, Fla., 1976-78; practice medicine specializing in psychiatry, marital and family therapy, individual psychotherapy Miami, 1979—. Emergency room physician Miami Dade Hosp., 1975; attending psychiatrist Jackson Meml. Hosp., 1979—, asst. dir. adolescent psychiat. unit, 1979-83; mem. clin. faculty U. Miami Sch. Medicine, 1979—, clin. instr. psychiatry, 1979—. Mem. AMA (Physicians' Recognition award 1980, 83, 86, 89, 98, 2000, 01, 05), Am. Assn. for Marital and Family Therapy (cert. clin. mem., treas. 1982-84, pres.-elect 1985-87, pres. 1987-89), Am. Psychiat. Assn., Am. Med. Women's Assn., Assn. Women Psychiatrists, Fla. Psychiat. Soc., South Dade Women Physicians Assn. Office: 420 S Dixie Hwy Ste 4A Coral Gables FL 33146-2228 Office Phone: 305-666-7766.

PEREZ, LOUIS ANTHONY, radiologist; b. NYC, June 11, 1939; s. Salvatore Lawrence and Valvadina Rose (Ruscillo) P.; divorced, 1988; children: Lisa, Gregg, Nicole; m. Patricia Ann McVey, May 19, 1990; 1 child, Kelsey. BEE, Manhattan Coll., 1962; MD, SUNY, Bklyn., 1966. Diplomate Am. Bd. Radiology (oral examiner), Am. Bd. Nuclear Medicine. Chief nuc. medicine Misericordia Hosp., Bronx, 1973-75, Norwalk Hosp., Conn., 1975-82; cons. Manhattan Coll., Radiology Inst., Riverdale, N.Y., 1974-81; dir. radiology Lawrence Hosp., Bronxville, NY, 1982—2004; asst. clin. prof. radiology Columbia U. Coll. Physicians and Surgeons, NYC, 1995—2006; with NE Radiology, Brewster, 2006—. Contbr. articles to profl. jours., chpts. to books. Lt. comdr. USN, 1963-77. Grantee, Am. Cancer Soc., 1968-70, USPHS, 1974-75. Fellow Am. Coll. Radiology; mem. Soc. Nuc. Medicine (trustee 1985-89, 92—, chmn. sci. subcom. 1988—, chpt. pres. 1982), NY State Med. Soc. Republican. Roman Catholic. Office: NE Radiology 3839 Danbury Rd Brewster NY 10509-5412

PEREZ, MARITZA E., elementary school educator; b. Bklyn., Nov. 18, 1977; d. Perez A. Jose and Carmen A. Perez (Stepmother), Irma Diaz; m. Steven Brown. Bachelor's, Clayton State U., Morrow, Ga., 2000; Master's, Ctrl. Mich. U., Atlanta, 2003; cert. ednl. specialist, postgrad., Argosy U., Atlanta, 2006—. Tchr. Kendrick Mid. Sch., Jonesboro, Ga., 2000—. Coach swimming Kendrick Mid. Sch., Jonesboro, Ga., 2000—, grade level chair, 2002—06, 1:1 wireless tchr., 2005—; profl. devel. facilitator Clayton County Pub. Schs., Jonesboro, 2002—, Ga. Performance Stds. trainer, 2004—. Named Tchr. of Month, Kendrick Mid. Sch., 2000, 2001, 2003, 2004, 2005, 2006; Hope grantee, State of Ga., 1995. Avocations: swimming, reading. Home: 222 Brannan's Walk Mcdonough GA 30253 Office: Kendrick Middle School 7971 Kendrick Rd Jonesboro GA 30238 Home Phone: 678-984-1198; Office Phone: 770-472-8400. Business E-Mail: mperez@clayton.k12.ga.us.

PEREZ, MIGUEL A., industrial engineer, researcher; m. Myra Blanco, Dec. 28, 1996. BS in Indsl. Engring., U. PR, Mayaguez, PR, 1996; MS in Indsl. Engring., Va. Tech, Blacksburg, 1999, PhD in Indsl. Engring., 2005. Cert. profl. ergonomist, Bd. Certification Profl. Ergonomics, 2006. Sr. rsch. assoc. Va. Tech Transp. Inst., Blacksburg, 2002—. Adj. faculty grad. dept. indsl. and sys. engring. Va. Tech., 2006—. Fellow, Ford Found., 1999—2002. Mem.: Am. Soc. Biomechanics, Human Factors and Ergonomics Soc., Tau Beta Pi. Office: Virginia Tech Transp Inst 3500 Transp Rsch Plz Blacksburg VA 24061 Home Phone: 540-731-1899; Office Phone: 540-231-1537. Office Fax: 540-231-1555.

PEREZ, PAUL IGNATIUS, prosecutor, lawyer; b. Cuba, 1955; Bachelor, Jacksonville U.; Master, U. Fla.; grad. in Law, George Washington U. Assoc. Smith & Hulsey, P.A., Jacksonville, 1985—88; ptnr. Mahoney, Adams, & Criser P.A., Jacksonville, 1988—89, 1992—94, Booth, Arnold & Perez P.A., Jacksonville, Fla., 1994—2002; US atty. (mid. dist.) Fla. US Dept. Justice, Jacksonville, Fla., 1988—92, 2002—07. *

PEREZ, PETER MICHAEL, food products executive; b. Aurora, Ill., Sept. 24, 1953; s. Peter Joseph and Marie Frances (Rogacs) P.; m. Cynthia Lou Perez, May 3, 1976; children: Peter Charles, Lisa Marie. BSBA, Ea. Ill. U., Charleston, 1976; MBA, Northwestern U., 1986. Mgr. plant Emerson Electric Co., Denver, 1985-86, Kraft, North Bergen, NJ, 1986-88, Allentown, Pa., 1988-91; regional mgr., dir. human resources Kraft/Phillip Morris, Deerfield, Ill., 1991-95; sr. v.p. human resources Pepsi-Cola Gen. Bottlers, Rolling Meadows, Ill., 1995—2000, W.W. Granger, 2001—03, ConAgra Foods, Inc., Omaha, 2003—; chief human resources officer Alliant Foodservice, 2001. Mem. Biltmore Country Club. Republican. Roman Catholic. Avocations: sports, guitar. Office: ConAgra Foods Inc 1 ConAgra Dr Omaha NE 68102-5001 Office Phone: 402-595-4000. Office Fax: 402-595-4709. *

PEREZ, VICTOR MANUEL, physician, plastic surgeon; b. Cosamaloapan, Veracruz, Mex., Aug. 18, 1967; s. Tomas and Manuela Perez; m. Diana Marie Bobovnyik, July 14, 2000; 1 child, Victor Manuel Jr. BS, U. Autonomous Nuevo Leon, Guadalupe, N.L. Mex., 1990. Cert. Am. Bd. Plastic Surgery, 2003. Gen. practitioner Ministry of Health, Benito Juarez, Nuevo Leon, Mexico, 1990—91, Mexican Inst. Social Security, Pal, Coahuila, 1991—92; resident Cook County Hosp., Chgo., 1994—95; resident in gen. surgery Western Res. Care Sys., Youngstown, Ohio, 1995—98; burn surgery fellow Shriners Burn Hosp., Galveston, Tex., 1998—99; resident in plastic surgery Loma Linda U. Med. Ctr., Calif., 1999—2002; chief, plastic surgery sect. VA Hosp., Kansas City, Mo., 2002—; asst. prof. plastic surgery U. Kans. Med. Ctr., Kansas City, 2002—. Presenter in field. Contbr. articles to profl jours. and book chpts. in field. Grant, Plastic Surgery Ednl. Found., 2001. Fellow: ACS; mem.: Kans. City Plastic Surgery Soc., Am. Burn Assn., Am. Soc. Plastic Surgeons. Roman Catholic. Achievements include invention of new techniques in abdominoplasty-umbilical inset. Avocation: dog shows. Office: Univ Kansas Medical Ctr 3901 Rainbow Blvd Kansas City KS 66160 Office Fax: 913-588-2061. Business E-Mail: vperez@kumc.edu.

PEREZ, WILLIAM D. (BILL PEREZ), candy company executive, former sports apparel company executive; b. Akron, Ohio, 1947; m. Catherine A. Perez; 2 children. BA in Govt., Cornell U., 1969; BIM, American Grad. Sch. of Internat. Mgmt., 1970. Joined Johnson Wax SC Johnson & Son, Inc., 1970, gen. mgr. Spanish Johnson, v.p., regional dir. Americas, v.p. home care bus., exec. v.p. N. American consumer products, pres., COO worldwide consumer products Racine, Wis., 1993-97, pres., CEO, 1997—2004, Nike, Inc., Beaverton, Oreg., 2004—06, William Wrigley Jr. Co., Chgo., 2006—. Bd. dirs. May Dept. Stores Co., 1998—2004, Kellogg Co., 1999—, Hallmark Cards, Inc., Grocery Mfr. Am. Mem. Cornell U. Council; advisory bd. Racine Youth Leadership Acad.; bd. dirs. Sustainable Racine. Recipient Out & Equal Champion for Workplace Equality award, Out & Equal Workplace Advocates, 2002. Mem.: Grocery Manufacturers of Am. (bd. dirs.). Achievements include 11 marathons. Avocation: running. Office: William Wrigley Jr Co 410 N Michigan Ave Chicago IL 60611 *

PEREZ, ZIOMARA DARLENE, pre-school educator; d. Maria Estela Perez Carrillo. BA in Early Childhood Edn., Nat. Louis U., Chgo., 1997; M in Child Devel., Erikson Inst., Chgo., 2007. Tchr. Jahn Sch., Chgo., 1997—2006, Nettelhorst Sch., Chgo., 2006—. Recipient Tchg. award, Golden Apple Found., 2006. Office: Nettelhorst Sch 3252 N Broadway Chicago IL 60657 Office Phone: 773-534-5810.

PEREZ-CRUET, JORGE, geriatric psychiatrist, researcher; b. Santurce, PR, Oct. 15, 1931; s. Jose Maria Perez-Vicente and Emilia Cruet-Burgos; m. Anyes Heimendinger, Oct. 4, 1958; children: Antonio, Mick, Graciela, Isabelle. BS magna cum laude, U. PR, 1953, MD, 1957; diploma in psychiatry, McGill U., Montreal, Que., Can., 1976. Diplomate Am. Bd. Geriat. Psychiatry, Am. Bd. Psychiatry and Neurology, Nat. Bd. Med. Examiners, lic. Can. Coun. Med. Examiners, Med. Coun. Can., cert. in quality assurance, profl. in healthcare quality Health Quality Cert. Bd., eligible Am. Bd. Psychiatry and Neurology, in geriatric psychiatry Am. Bd. Psychiatry and Neurology, 1991, re-cert. Am. Bd. Psychiatry and Neurology, 2001, in addiction psychiatry Am. Bd. Psychiatry and Neurology, 2006. Rotating intern Michael Reese Hosp., Chgo., 1957-58; fellow in psychiatry Johns Hopkins U. Med. Sch., 1958-60, instr., then asst. prof. psychiatry, 1962-73; psychiatrist neurophysiology and psychosomatic lab. Walter Reed Army Inst. Rsch., Washington, 1960—62, cons., 1963-65; rsch. assoc. lab. chem. pharmacology Nat. Heart Inst., NIH, Bethesda, Md., 1969-71; med. dir. USPHS adult psychiatry sect. lab. clin. sci. NIMH, Bethesda, 1971-73; psychiatry resident diploma course in psychiatry McGill U. Sch. Medicine, Montreal Gen. Hosp., 1973-76, Montreal Children's Hosp., 1975; prof. psychiatry, chief psychopharmacology lab. U. Mo.-Mo. Inst. Psychiatry, St. Louis, 1976—78; chief psychiatry svc. San Juan VA Hosp., PR, 1978—92, pharmacy and therapeutic com., 1978—2004; prof. psychiatry U. PR Med. Sch., 1978-92, U. Okla. Health Sci. Ctr., 1992—2004, Okla. City VA Med. Ctr., 1992—2004; pvt. practice. Spl. cons. NASA, Moffettfield, Calif., 1965-69; cons. divsn. narcotic addition and drug abuse NIDA, 1972-73; drug adv. com. FDA/NIDA, 1976-80, pharmacy and therapeutic com., 1992—; local organizer Internat. Coll. Neuropsychiatry, San Juan, PR, 1986, CINP, 1986; spl. advisor mental health PR Senate, PR sec. health, 1989; prin. investigator NASA biosatellite project JH Sch. Med., 1963-65.; staff sr. psychiatrist and supt. psychiatry ward, VA Med. Ctr., Oklahoma City, 1992-1995, sr. staff psychiatrist and physician substance abuse clinic, 1995-2004, med. dir. opioid treatment program, 2001-2004. Editor: Catholic Physicians Guild Archiocese of Okla., 1997-98. Mem. Rep. Nat. Com., 1995; mem. Eisenhower Commn., 2001. Capt. M.C. USAR, 1960-62; sr. surgeon USPHS, 1969-71, med. dir., 1971-73. Recipient Coronas award, 1957, Ruiz-Arnau award, 1957, Diaz-Garcia award 1957, Geigy award, 1975, 76, AMA Recognition award 1971, 76, 81, Horner's award 1975, 76, Pavlovian award, 1978, Recognition cert. VA Svc. awards and commendations, 1980-98, Senate of PR, 1986, Cert. of Merit Gov. of PR, 1986, Cert. Recognition, Sec. Health, San Juan, Puerto Rico, Appreciation plaque Fifth World Congress of IRMA, Manila, Philippines, Eisenhower Commn., 1995; nominee Eisenhower Commn. award, 1995, 2001. Fellow Interam. Coll. Physicians and Surgeons, Royal Coll. Physicians and Surgeons Can. (sr., cert.), Am. Psychiat Assn. (Disting., life); mem. AAAS, Am. Coll. Med. Quality (bd. dirs. 2004), Am. Physiol. Soc., Am. Coll. Psychiatrists, Pavlovian Soc., Am. Fedn. Clin. Rsch., Am. Fedn. Med. Rsch., Am. Assn. Geriat. Psychiatry, Am. Geriat. Soc., Am. Coll. Preventive Medicine, Am. Soc. Clin. Pharmacology and Therapeutics, Am. Soc. Pharmacology and Exptl. Therapeutics, Am. Soc. Addiction Medicine (cert.), Am. Acad. Addiction Psychiatry (dir. Area VIII, 2002-), Soc. Neurosci., Nat. Assn. Healthcare Quality (mem. editl. bd. Jour. Health Quality, 2005), Internat. Soc. Rsch. Aggression, Okla. Psychiat. Assn., Am. Soc. Clin. Psychopharmacology, Menninger Found., Charles F. Menninger Soc., Okla. Assn. Health Care Quality, Alumni, UPR Sch. Med., Johns Hopkins Med. Surg. Inst., NY Acad. Scis., NIH Alumni (life), McGill, Okla. Hist. Soc.(life). Republican. Roman Catholic. Avocations: painting, writing. Home: 3304 Rosewood Ln Oklahoma City OK 73120-5604 Home Phone: 405-751-0243; Office Phone: 405-834-3001. Personal E-mail: jperezcrue@aol.com.

PEREZ-CRUET, MICK JORGE (MIGUELANGELO JORGE PEREZ-CRUET), neurosurgeon, educator; b. Washington, May 3, 1961; s. Jorge Fortunato and Anyes Lilly Perez-Cruet; m. Donna Jeanne Roggenbuck, July 9, 1994; children: Kristin Magdalene, Joshua Michael, Rachel Elizabeth, David Gabriel. BA, Grinell Coll., 1983; MSc in Chemistry, U. South Fla., 1986; MD, Tufts U., 1991. Commd. 2d lt. USAF, 1987, advanced through grades to maj., 1997, ret., 2001; intern surg. svc. Baylor Coll. Medicine, Houston, 1991-92, resident in neurosurgery, 1992-97; attending neurosurgery, v. chmn. Wilford Hall Med. Ctr., San Antonio, 1997—2001; spinal fellow Rush U./CINN, Chgo., 2001—02; asst. prof., dir. minimally invasive spine surgery Rush U., Chgo., 2002—03; assoc. dir. Inst. Spine Care/CINN; dir., spinal surgery Mich. Head and Spine Inst., 2003—; assoc. prof. Oakland Univ.; dir. minimally invasive spine surgery Providence Med. Ctr., 2003—, dir. spine fellowship program, 2004—; pres., CEO, MI4Spine, LLC. Prin. investigator clin. trials; presenter in field; appointee Coun. State Neurosurg. Socs., 1997, chmn. young physicians com., chmn. workforce com., corr. sec., publs. com.; mem. sci. adv. bd. Neospine; founding surgeon US Spine CNS Publs. Com., 2002—; dir. socioecon. peer rev. articles AANS Bull. Editor: (textbooks) Outpatient Spinal Surgery, An Anatomical Approach to Minimally Invasive Spine Surgery, (DVD) AANS Minimally Invasive Spine Techniques; asst. editor: AANS Bull. Com.; contbr. chapters to books, articles to profl. jours. Chmn. class reunion Tufts Sch. Medicine, 1995-96; dir. class fund Grinnell Coll., 1999—. Air Force Health Professions scholar, 1987—91. Mem. AMA, ACS, AAAS, Congress Neurol. Surgeons, Am. Assn. Neurol. Surgeons (dir. spine courses, editor-in-chief AANS Bull. Socioecon. Jour. 2005—), Mich. Med. Soc., Mich. Assn. Neurol. Surgeons (treas., pres. 2006—), Sigma Xi (grantee 1985). Achievements include invention of spine instrumentation. Avocations: hunting, fishing, scuba diving, archery, poetry. Office: Mich Head and Spine Inst 22250 Providence Dr Ste 300 Southfield MI 48075 Office Phone: 248-440-2162. Personal E-mail: perezcruet@yahoo.com.

PEREZ DE ALONSO, MARCELA, human resources specialist, information technology executive; b. Chile; Grad., Cath. U., Chile. Various sr. level positions in human resources and ops. Citigroup, global consumer head human resources, 1996—99; divsn. head Citigroup North L.Am. Consumer Bank, 1999—2004; exec. v.p. human resources and workforce devel. Hewlett-Packard Co., Palo Alto, Calif., 2004—. Mem. adv. bd. Marshall Bus. Sch. U. So. Calif.; spkr. in field; bd. dirs. Catalyst, NYC, Hewlett-Packard Co. Fin. Svcs. Mem. adv. bd. U. So. Calif. Marshall Bus. Sch.; bd. mem. Next Door Solutions to Domestic Violence. Named Corp. Exec. of Yr., Hispanic-Net, 2005; named one of 50 Most Important Hispanics in Tech. and Bus., Hispanic Engr. & Info. Tech. mag. Office: Hewlett Packard Co 3000 Hanover St Palo Alto CA 94304 *

PEREZ DE LA MESA, MANUEL JOSE, swimming pool company executive; b. Havana, Cuba, Mar. 20, 1957; came to the U.S., 1961; s. Manuel Adolfo Oscar and Olga Marta (Cuervo) Perez de la Mesa; m. Ana Lidia Vidal, June 19, 1982; children: Rosario, Manuel, Cristina. BBA in Fin., Fla. Internat. U., 1977; MBA in Controllership, St. John's U., 1980. Fin. analyst Latin Am. Sea-Land Svc., Inc., Ft. Lauderdale, Fla., 1977-79, sr. fin. analyst Edison, N.J., 1979-80, regional contr. Latin Am. Ft. Lauderdale, 1980-82; ops. auditor IBM, San Jose, Calif., 1982-85, advisory pricing staff Bethesda, Md., 1985-87; asst. corp. contr. Del Monte Fresh Produce Inc., Coral Gables, Fla., 1987-88, v.p. fin. and ops. Latin Am. San Jose, Costa Rica, 1988-90, v.p. ops. S.Am. Santiago, Chile, 1990-91, v.p. planning and devel. Coral Gables, 1991-94; v.p. fin. and ops. Gemaire Distbrs. Inc., Deerfield Beach, Fla., 1994-96; v.p. ops. Watsco, Inc., Miami, Fla., 1996—99; pres. and COO SCP Pool Corp., Covington, La., 1999—2001, pres., CEO, 2001—. Chmn. Agribusiness, Caribbean/Latin Am. Action, Washington, 1991-93; dir., investment banking consulting Latin Fin. Inc., N.Y.C., Miami, Mexico City, 1993—. Mem. Inst. Mgmt. Acctg. Avocations: sports, investment analysis, family. Office: SCP Pool Corp 109 Northpark Blvd Covington LA 70433-5005 *

PÉREZ-DÍAZ, VÍCTOR MIGUEL, sociology educator; b. Madrid, Dec. 8, 1938; s. Miguel Pérez-Poyo and Victoria Díaz-Alonso; m. Marina González Olivares, Apr. 2, 1938. PhD in Sociology, Harvard U., 1976, Complutense U., Madrid, 1978, PhD in Law, 1978. Fellow Inst. Advanced Study, Princeton U., 1976-77; rsch. dir. INI Found., Madrid, 1977-80, FIES Found., Madrid, 1980-86; founding dir. Ctr. Social Sci. Juan March Inst., Madrid, 1987-92; dir. rsch. ctr. Analistas Socio-Políticos, 1993; prof. sociology Complutense U., Madrid, 1978—. Vis. prof. MIT, Cambridge, 1988-89, U. Calif., LaJolla, 1987-93, Harvard U., Cambridge, 1992-93, Inst. for Advanced Study, Princeton, 1975-76, Inst. nat. des Scis. & Politiques, Paris, 1994-95; mem. adv. com. PRISA, Madrid, 1991, Spanish Min. Health, 1996, New Sch. for Social Rsch., N.Y., 1999, Hans Spier vis. prof., 1999; mem. adv. com., prof. King Juan Carlos Ctr., NYU, 2000; mem. adv. bd. REPSOL, Madrid, 1993. Author: State, Bureaucracy and Civil Society, 1978, Castilian Peasants, 1992, The Return of Civil Society, 1993, Spanish Democracy, 1996, Public Sphere and Civil Society, 1997, Spain at the Crossroads, 1999, La lezione spagnola, 2003. Mem. Commn. on Unemployment Spanish Govt., Madrid, 1987-88, Study Group on Social Policy: European Communities Brussels, 1991-93; com. mem. Social Sci. Rsch. Coun., N.Y., 1983-89; mem. Nat. Com. Rules Ethical Behavior, 1997-2000, Prize Libre Empresa, 2002, Fund Rafael del Pino. Mem. Acadmia Europaea, Am. Acad. Arts and Scis. (fgn. hon. mem.). Home: Comandante Fortea 3 28008 Madrid Spain Office: Analistas Socio-Políticos Gabinete de Estudios c/Quintana, 24-5 dcha 28008 Madrid Spain Home Phone: 34-91-5413959; Office Phone: 34 91 5414746. Personal E-mail: asp@ctv.es.

PEREZ-FIRMAT, GUSTAVO FRANCISCO, writer, language educator; b. Havana, Cuba, Mar. 7, 1950; came to U.S., 1960; s. Gustavo Perez and Luz Maria Firmat; m. Rosa Perelmuter, Aug. 12, 1973 (div. 1990); children: David, Miriam; m. Mary Anne Adamson, Feb. 9, 1991. AB, MA, U. Miami, 1973; PhD, U. Mich., 1979. Instructor, dept. Romance studies Duke U., Durham, NC, 1978—79, asst. prof., 1979—83, assoc. prof., 1983—88, prof., 1988—99, 1988-89; David Feinson prof. in Humanities Columbia Univ., NYC, 1999—. Author: Idle Fictions, 1982, Literature and Liminality, 1986, Carolina Cuban, 1986, The Cuban Condition, 1989, Equivocaciones, 1989, Life on the Hyphen, 1994, Next Year in Cuba, 1995, Bilingual Blues, 1995, My Own Private Cuba, 1999, Anything but Love, 2000, Vidas en vilo, 2000, Cincuenta lecciones de exilio y desexilio, 2000, Tongue Ties, 2003, Scar Tissue, 2005; editor: Do the Americas Have a Common LIterature?, 1991. Fellow Am. Coun. Learned Socs., 1981, Guggenheim Found., 1986; sr. fellow NEH, 1985. Fellow: Am. Acad. Arts & Sci.; mem. MLA, Am. Assn. Tchrs. Spanish and Portuguese, Am. Studies Assn., Phi Beta Kappa. Office: Dept Spanish & Portuguese Columbia Univ New York NY 10027 Business E-Mail: gpf@columbia.edu.

PÉREZ-RIVERA, FRANCISCO (FRANK RIVERA), writer; b. Vertientes, Cuba, Oct. 3, 1938; came to U.S., 1968, naturalized, 1974; s. Francisco Daniel Pérez and María Eloísa Rivera. BA, Camagüey Coll., Cuba, 1955; MA in Romance Langs., U. Munich, 1967. Newsman, script writer Bavarian Radio, Munich, 1964-68; newsman AP, NYC, 1968-92, arts and entertainment editor, 1992—2006, ret., 2006; dir. Spanish programs for lang. labs., 1987. Author: (poetry) Constructions, 1979; (novel) Bells Over the Prairies, 1986, 2d edit., 2004; (short stories) Cuban Short Stories, 1992; (short stories) Varadero and Other Cuban Short Stories, 1998; co-author: Introduction to Spanish Literature, 1976, 2d edit, 1982; short stories in the anthologies New Cuban Storytellers (in Spanish), 1961, Cuba: Nouvelles et contes d'aujourd'hui, 1985, Narrative and Liberty: Cuban Tales of the Dispersion, 1996, Prosa moderna del mundo hispánico, 1997; author, narrator audio books The Golden Age of Spanish Literature, 2002. Grantee German Academic Exchange Svc., Munich, 1961-67; fellow Cintas Found., N.Y., 1980; 1st prize short story Círculo de Escritores y Poetas Latinoamericanos, N.Y., 1997, Internat. Short Story award Círculo de Cultura Panamericano, N.J., 1997. Home: 212 E 77th St Apt 1G New York NY 10021-2111 Personal E-mail: fprivera@yahoo.com.

PERFETTI, ROBERT NICKOLAS, educational consultant; b. Staples, Minn., Jan. 8, 1937; s. Nickolas Albert and Lila Bertha (Beurge) P. BS, St. Cloud State U., Minn., 1960; postgrad., Bemidji State U., Minn., 1961-62, Calif. State U., LA, 1964-68, Pepperdine U., Malibu, Calif., 1967-68; MA, La Verne U., 1970; postgrad., U. So. Calif., 1972-73, Point Loma U., Pasadena, Calif., 1974-75; EdD, Pacific States U., L.A., 1975. Cert. admistr., counselor, secondary, community coll., jr. high sch., adult, and elem. edn. Calif. Prin. Richmond Pub. Schs., Minn., 1960-62; elem. tchr. Sebeka Sch. Dist., Minn., 1962-63; team leader lang. arts, social sci. and summer sch. Rowland Unified Sch. Dist., Rowland Heights, Calif., 1965-76, coord. math. lab., 1976-79, secondary counselor, 1979-81, coord. work experience edn., career edn. and career ctr., 1981-95, home ind. study coord., ednl. cons., 1992-95; mental health counselor St. Gabriel's Hosp., Little Falls, Minn., 1999. Coord. Gender Equity, 1980-95, Job Tng. Partnership Act, 1980-95; advisor Nat. Vocat. Tech. Honor Soc., 1991-95; alumni dir. Sacred Heart Sch., Staples. Editor: (profl. newspaper) Reaction. Officer parish coun. Our Lady of the Assumption Ch., Claremont, Calif., chmn. edn. com.; chmn. PTA, Rowland Heights; rep. fed. project, Rowland Heights; scoutmaster, chmn. troop com. Boy Scouts Am. Recipient Svc. Commendation Rowland Unified Sch. Dist., 1978; named. L.A. County Tchr. of Yr. Calif. State Dept. Edn., 1975, Outstanding Secondary Educator of Am., 1974, Giano Tchr. of Yr. Giano Intermediate Sch., 1973, Tchr. of Yr. Rowland Unified Sch. Dist., 1974. Mem. NEA (life), Calif. Tchrs. Assn., Assn. Rowland Educators (v.p.), Calif. Assn. Work Experience Educators (Alpha chpt. v.p.), Alpha Phi Omega (pres.), Pi Delta Epsilon (pres.), KC (3d degree). Roman Catholic. Avocations: water sports, travel, research, writing. Home: 200 4th St SE Little Falls MN 56345-3116 E-mail: perfetti7@msn.com.

PERGER, DONNA SPAGNOLI, retired secondary school mathematics educator; b. Portsmouth, Va., Apr. 24, 1951; d. Delmo John and Lurline M. (Smith) Spagnoli; m. Steve John Perger Jr., June 9, 1980; 1 stepchild, Stephanie Lee. BS in Secondary Edn., Old Dominion U., 1973. Tchr. math. Manor H.S., Portsmouth, Va., 1973—74, Bettie Williams Sch., Virginia Beach, Va., 1974—78, Virginia Beach Jr. H.S., 1978—80, Queens Lake Sch., York County, Va., 1980—2003, chair dept. math. Lead tchr. VQUEST. Art work published in Stampers Sampler, Somerset Studio and Gallery mags. Elder Olive Br. Christian Ch. Named Mid. Sch. Tchr. of Yr. Daily Press Newspaper, Newport News, 1993. Avocations: paper embossing (repousse), needlecrafts, sewing, gardening. Personal E-mail: cardorft@cox.net.

PERHACH, JAMES LAWRENCE, pharmaceutical executive; s. James Lawrence and Elizabeth Louise (Hoffman) P.; m. Judith Irene Selter, Apr. 15, 1967; children: Laura Anne, Amy Elizabeth. BS, U. Dayton, 1966; MS, U. Pitts., 1969, PhD, 1971. Sr. scientist dept. pharmacology Mead Johnson Rsch. Ctr., divsn. Bristol Myers, 1971—74, sr. investigator dept. biol. rsch., 1974—76, sr. rsch. assoc. dept. biol. rsch., 1976—77, sr. rsch. assoc. dept. pathology and toxicology, 1977—78, prin. rsch. assoc. dept. pathology and toxicology, 1978—80; from dir. pharmacology to dir. biol. rsch. to dir. clin. investigation Wallace Labs. Divsn. Carter-Wallace, Inc., Cranbury, NJ, 1980—87, v.p. clin. pharmacology and pharmacokinetics, 1987—2001; sr. dir. clin. pharmacology Purdue Pharma, L.P., 2001—04; sr. dir. CNS Therapeutic Area Forest Rsch. Inst, 2004—05, exec. dir. clin. devel., 2005—. Adj. asst. prof. dept. pharmacy practice and adminstrn. Ernest Mario Coll. Pharmacy Rutgers U., 1993—; adv. bd. clin. rsch. ctr. U. Medicine and Dentistry NJ Robert Wood Johnson Med. Sch., 1995-2003; drug utilization rev. coun. State of NJ, 1983-2003, med. pharmacologist, 1983, sec., 1984, chmn., 1985-87. Fellow: Am. Coll. Clin. Pharmacology; mem.: Am. Soc. Pharmacology and Exptl. Therapeutics, Am. Coll. Clin. Pharmacology, Drug Info. Assn., Am. Soc. Clin. Pharmacology and Therapeutics. Achievements include research in drug discovery, elucidation of mechanism of action and safety evaluation of new therapeutic agents. Office: Forest Rsch Inst Harbor Side Fin Ctr Plaza V Jersey City NJ 07311 Home Phone: 609-716-9228; Office Phone: 201-427-8465. Business E-Mail: james.perhach@frx.com.

PERHACS, MARYLOUISE HELEN, musician, educator; b. Teaneck, NJ, June 15, 1944; d. John Andrew and Helen Audrey (Hosage) P.; m. Robert Theodore Sirinek, Jan. 27, 1968 (div. Jan. 1975). Student, Ithaca Coll., NY, 1962-64; BS, Juilliard Sch., 1967, MS, 1968; postgrad., Hunter Coll., 1976, St. Peter's Coll., Jersey City, NJ, 1977. Cert. music tchr., N.Y., N.J. Instr. Carnegie Hall, NYC, 1966-69; program developer, coord., instr. urban edn. program Newburgh (N.Y.) Pub. Sch. System, 1968-69; adj. prof. dept. edn. St. Peter's Coll., Jersey City, 1976-92; tchr. brass instruments Indian Hills High Sch., Oakland, NJ, 1976; tchr. Jersey City Pub. Schs., 1976-77, N.Y.C. Pub. Sch., Bronx, 1980-84; pvt. tchr. Cliffside Park, NJ, 1976—; vocal music tchr. East Rutherford, NJ, 1990; tchr. music Bergen County Spl. Svcs. Sch. Dist., 1990-91; tchr. gen. music Little Ferry (N.J.) Pub. Schs., 1991-92; tchr. mid. sch. instrumental Paramus (N.J.) Pub. Schs., 1993-94; tchr. vocal music West New York (N.J.) Pub Schs., 1995—. Tchr. music summer enrichment program, West New York, NJ, 1999-2000, tchr. summer instrumental music program Park Ridge (NJ) HS, 1995-96, Waldwick Concert Band, 2003-04; singer, trumpeter Norwegian Caribbean Lines, 1981-82, Jimmy Dorsey Band, Paris and London, 1974; lectr. in field. Singer with Original PDQ Bach Okay Chorale, 1966, Live from Carnegie Hall Recordings, 1970, St. Louis Mcpl. Opera, 1970, Ed Sullivan Show, 1970; singer, dancer, actress (Broadway shows) Promises, Promises, 1969-71, Sugar, 1971-72, Lysistrata, 1972; trumpeter (Broadway shows) Jesus Christ Superstar, 1973, Debbie!, 1976, Sarava!, 1979, Fiddler on the Roof, Lincoln Ctr., 1981, Sophisticated Ladies, 1982; writer, host series on women in music Columbia Cable/United Artists, 1984; recordings: Carnegie Hall Live, Avery Fisher Hall, Lincoln Ctr. Cons. to cadette troop Girl Scouts U.S., Jersey City, 1967-68, Bergen County N.J. Coun., 1995—. Mem. NEA, AFTRA, Actors Equity Assn., Am. Fedn. Musicians (mem. theatre com. local 802 N.Y.C. 1972—, chmn. 1973), Music Educators Nat. Conf., N.J. Music Educators Assn., N.J. Sch. Music Assn., N.J. Edn. Assn., Internat. Women's Brass Conf. (charter mem.), Internat. Trumpet Guild, Mu Phi Epsilon. Democrat. Episcopalian. Avocations: cats, cake decorating, food sculpting, horticulture, sewing. Home and Office: 23 Crescent Ave Cliffside Park NJ 07010-3003

PERHAM, ROY GATES, III, industrial psychologist; b. Hackensack, NJ, Apr. 22, 1958; s. Roy Gates Jr. and Titania Joan (Robbitts) P. BA with honors, Bates Coll., 1980; MS, Stevens Inst. Tech., 1982, PhD, 1989. Intern Sen. Edmund S. Muskie, Washington, 1978; psychometrician Lab. Psychol. Studies Stevens Inst. Tech., Hoboken, NJ, 1981-83, instr., 1985, adj. asst. prof., 1990—95, Fairleigh Dickinson U., Rutherford, NJ, 1986; sr. assoc. AAI Orgnl. Performance Cons., Florham Park, NJ, 1990-94; assessment projects mgr. Tech. Employee Selection and Tng. Inc., Hasbrouck Heights, NJ, 1995—. WordStar coord. NY Computer Soc., NYC, 1985-88; adj. asst. prof. psychology John Jay Coll. Criminal Justice, NYC, 2006-. Chmn. Juvenile Conf. Com., Hasbrouck Heights and Wood-Ridge, NJ, 1985-95; mem. NJ State Juvenile Delinquency Commn., Trenton, NJ, 1988-91; county exec.'s rep. Bergen County Youth Svcs. Commn., 1990-2002, chair, 1994-96; chair Bergen County Task Force on Youth Violence, 1993-95; asst. Bergen County Exec. for Juvenile Justice, NJ, 1999—2002; mem. NJ Gov's. Juvenile Justice and Delinquency Prevention Com., 2001—. Named Citizen of Yr., Lions Club of Hasbrouck Heights, NJ, 1988. Mem. APA, Am. Psychol. Soc., Met. NY Assn. for Applied Psychology, NJ Property Owners Assn., Soc. for Indsl./Orgnl. Psychology, Inc., Phi Beta Kappa, Psi Chi. Home: 269 Raymond St Hasbrouck Heights NJ 07604-1723 Office: Technical Employee Selection & Tng Inc The Profl Bldg 248 Blvd Hasbrouck Heights NJ 07604 Office Phone: 201-288-0730. Personal E-mail: rgperham@cs.com.

PERIASWAMY, PADMINI, materials scientist, researcher; d. Periaswamy Nanjappa and Amirthavalli Periaswamy. BS in Applied Scis., PSG Coll. Tech., Coimbatore, 1988, MS in Materials Sci., 1990; PhD, Indian Inst. Sci., Bangalore, India, 1996. Postdoctoral rschr. Technische Universitaet, Dresden, Germany, 1997—98; asst. rsch. engr. U. Calif., Santa Barbara, 1998—2000; postdoctoral rschr. U. Ala., Tuscaloosa, 2000—01, asst. rsch. engr., 2001—02, assoc. rsch. engr., 2002—. Contbr. articles to profl. jours. Grantee, Dept. of Energy Exptl. Program to Stimulate Competitive Rsch., 2003—06, Office of Naval Rsch., 2003—06; Humboldt Rsch. fellow, Humboldt Found., Germany, 1997—98. Mem.: IEEE, Materials Rsch. Soc., Am. Phys. Soc. Achievements include patents in field. Avocations: travel, music, tennis, reading. Office: U Alabama 317 Houser Hall Tuscaloosa AL 35487 Home Phone: 205-752-2153; Office Phone: 205-348-1685. Office Fax: 205-348-1685; Home Fax: 205-348-1685. Business E-Mail: padmini@bama.ua.edu.

PERIBERE, JEROME A., agricultural products executive; M in Bus. Econs. and Fin., Inst. D'Etudes Politiques, Paris. With Dow Chem. Co., 1977—, regional mktg. mgr. Ea. Europe, 1982—85, regional mgr. Mid. East and Africa, 1985—88, dir. European agr. bus., 1988—89, comml. dir. agr. bus. Europe, 1989—93, global comml. dir. Indpls., 1993—97, corp. strategy leader Dow AgroSciences, 1997—98, global leader Weed Mgmt. Global Bus. Unit European Trade area, 1998—2002, global leader agr. chems., 2002—04, pres., CEO Dow AgroSciences, 2004—, mem. Office of the Chief Exec., 2006—. Mem. bd. BioCrossroads. Named a Power Player in Life Sci. and Tech., Indpls. Bus. Jour., 2005. Office: Dow AgroSciences LLC 9330 Zionsville Rd Indianapolis IN 46268

PERICAK-VANCE, MARGARET A., medical geneticist, educator, health facility administrator; b. Buffalo, June 28, 1951; m. Jeff Pericak-Vance; 1 child. PhD in Med. Genetics, Ind. U., 1978. Dir. Ctr. Human Genetics Duke U. Med. Ctr., Durham, NC, 1996—2006, James B. Duke prof. medicine, chief, med. genetics sect.; prof. Dept. Medicine, dir. Inst. Human Genomics U. Miami, 2007—. Co-recipient McKnight Memory & Brain Disorders award, 2001; named to Century Club: 100 People to Watch as We Move to the Next Millennium, Newsweek Mag., 1997; recipient Louis D. scientific prize, Inst. France Acad. Sci., 2001. Mem.: Inst. Medicine, Am. Coll. Med. Genetics (founding fellow). Office: U Miami Dept Medicine PO Box 016760 Miami FL 33101-6760 E-mail: m.pericakvance@miami.edu. *

PERICH, TERRY MILLER, retired secondary school educator; b. Greensburg, Pa., Sept. 22, 1948; s. Miller and Eleanor Ann (Schmuck) P.; m. Kathleen Ann Ferrari, July 26, 1975. BA in Elem. Edn., Edinboro U., 1970; elem. cert., Pa. State U., 1973; Masters equivalency degree, U. Pitts., 1994; postgrad., Carlow Coll., 1994. Trained student assistance profl., Pa.; cert. tchr. elem. edn. Tchr. sci. and math. Penn Trafford Schs., Harrison City, Pa., 1970—2003; v.p. Jeannette Area Hist. Soc., 2003—06. Mentor, tchr. Tchr. Enhancement Inst. St. Vincent Coll., Latrobe, Pa.; selected tchr. Watershed Restoration St. Vincent Coll., Latrobe. Author: Image of America, 2005; co-author: Postcard History, 2005, Postcard History Series. County committeeman Dem. Party, Penn Twp., Pa., 1994—; lion tamer Bushy Run Lions Club, Claridge, Pa., 1993—, 3rd v.p., 1995, 2d v.p., 1996, 1st v.p., 1997—. Recipient Commendation, Pres.-elect Clinton, Student Assistance Program award for working with students at risk St. Vincent Coll. Prevention Projects, 1991. Mem. NEA, ASCD, PACE, Nat. Sci. Tchrs. Assn., Pa. Tchrs. Edn. Assn., Pa. Sci. Tchrs. Assn., Westmoreland County Assn. Student Assistance Profls. (bd. dirs. 1992-94, mem. Westmoreland county student assistance team 1995-96, 96-97), Penn Trafford Edn. Assn. (exec. bd. dirs. 1990-91). Roman Catholic. Avocations: travel, education. Home: 13 Rizzi Dr Irwin PA 15642-8902 Office Phone: 724-205-1983. E-mail: middie22@aol.com.

PERICH, THOMAS J., lawyer; b. Galveston, Tex., 1945; BS, Georgetown U., 1967; MA with honors, in Economics, U. Tex., 1971, JD with honors, 1975. Bar: Tex. 1976, admitted to practice: US Ct. Appeals (5th Cir.), bar: US Ct. Appeals (11th Cir.). Ptnr. Dept. Bus. Transactions Andrews & Kurth LLP, Houston, mem. policy com. Mem. Tex. Law Rev., 1974—75. Mem.: Tex. Assn. Bank Counsel, Houston Comml. Lawyer Forum, Houston Bar Assn., State Bar Tex., ABA, Order of Coif. Office: Andrews & Kurth LLP 600 Travis St Ste 4200 Houston TX 77002-3090 Home Phone: 713-818-3650; Office Phone: 713-220-4268. Office Fax: 713-238-7175. Personal E-mail: tperich@akllp.com. Business E-Mail: tperich@andrewskurth.com.

PERIK, MICHAEL J., educational organization executive; b. Aug. 1957; m. Elizabeth Beretta Perik. Grad., U. Toronto, Harvard U. Chief of staff Govt. Can., Ont.; with Ontario Hydro Corp., Canada; chmn., CEO The Learning Co. (formerly SoftKey Software), 1994—99; founder, bd. dirs. Achievement Technologies, 2000—06, CEO, 2002—06; chmn. assessment mgmt. divsn. Houghton Mifflin Co., 2006—07; CEO The Princeton Review, Inc., NYC, 2007—. Bd. dirs. John F. Kennedy Presdl. Libr.; bd. trustees, treas. RI Hosp., 2005. Democrat. Office: The Princeton Review 2315 Broadway New York NY 10024 Office Phone: 212-874-8282. Office Fax: 212-874-0775.

PERILLO, SALVATORE J., lawyer; b. Apr. 25, 1945; m. Elizabeth E. Perillo. BS, SUNY, Albany; JD, Woodrow Wilson Coll. Law. Gen. counsel Mohawk Industries Inc., Calhoun, Ga. Mem.: Am. Corp. Counsel Assn. Office: Mohawk Industries Inc 160 S Industrial Blvd PO Box 12069 Calhoun GA 30701 Office Phone: 706-624-2660. Office Fax: 706-624-3825. *

PERIN, NOEL I., neurosurgeon; arrived in US, 1984; s. Rajes Perinpanayagam; m. Frances J. Baker, Nov. 30, 1985; children: Christopher D., Michelle N. MD, U. Colombo, Sri Lanka, 1973. Cert. neurosurgery Am. Assn. Neurol. Surgeons, 1994. Neurosurgeon, gen. surgeon Middlesex Hosp., London, 1986—90; spine fellowship NYU Med. Ctr., 1991; dir. trauma U. Cin., 1991—94; dir. spinal neurosurgery Mt. Sinai Med. Ctr., NYC, 1994—2001; dir. spine and minimally invasive spinal surgery St. Luke's- Roosevelt Hosp. Ctr., NYC, 2001—. Clin. assoc. prof. Roosevelt Hosp. Ctr., NYC. Co-author: Thoracoscopic Spinal Surgery, 1999. Fellow: ACS (assoc.), Royal Coll. Surgeons Edinburgh. Achievements include research in pharmacological treatment in spinal cord injury. Avocations: golf, tennis, travel. Office: Roosevelt Hosp Ctr Ste 5G 80 1000 10th Ave New York NY 10019 Home Phone: 914-381-3017; Office Phone: 212-523-6720. Office Fax: 212-523-6115. E-mail: nperin@slrhc.org, nperin@chpnet.org.

PERINGIAN, LYNDA ANN, dietician, writer; d. Mike and Clara A. Peringian. BS in Dietetics, U. Detroit, 1974; MS in Foods and Nutrition, Wayne State U., Detroit, 1976. Registered dietitian, cert. personnel cons. Clin. dietitian North Oakland Gen. Hosp.; chief dietitian Drs. Hosp., Detroit; dir. Healthcare divsn. Roth Young, Detroit, 1977—88; pres. Peringian & Assoc., Dryden, Mich., 1988—. Author: Healthcare Textbook, 1989, THE MIRACLE ROSES - A True Story, 2005. Vol. Birmingham (Mich.) Cmty. House. Avocations: sports, piano, cooking, reading, gardening.

PERINO, DANA MARIE, White House press secretary; b. Evanston, Wyo., May 9, 1972; m. Peter McMahon. BA in Mass Comm., U. So. Colo., 1994; postgrad., U. Ill. Staff asst. for Rep. Scott McInnis US Congress, Washington, press sec. to Rep. Dan Schaefer; spokesperson US Dept. Justice; dir. comm. White House Coun. on Environ. Quality; spl. asst. to pres., dep. press sec. The White House, dep. asst. to Pres., dep. press sec., 2006—07, acting press sec., 2007, asst. to Pres., press sec., 2007—. Office: The White House 1600 Pennsylvania Ave NW Washington DC 20500 *

PERKEL, ROBERT SIMON, photojournalist, educator; b. Jersey City, Apr. 23, 1925; s. Louis Leo and Flora Sonia (Levin) Perkel. BS, NYU, 1948; MS, Barry U., 1964; postgrad., Columbia U. Owner, operator Gulfstream Color Labs., Miami Beach, Fla., 1955-61; graphics instr. Dade County Pub. Schs., 1962-66; freelance photojournalist, 1967—. Rep. News Events Photo Svc., Ft. Lauderdale, Fla.; instr. photography Broward CC,

1982—92; rep. Patch Comm., Titusville, Fla., 1985—88; pub. Biograph/Comm., North Miami Beach, Fla., 1987—90. Contbr. photos stories and photographs to numerous mags. and indsl. trade publs.; exhibitions include Met. Mus. and Art Ctr., Coral Gables, Fla., Mus. Fine Arts, Boston. Former publicity dir. Coun. Internat. Visitors Greater Miami. With US Army, 1943—46, ETO. Recipient Cmty. Spirit award, Zonta Club Greater Miami, 1980, Found. medal, Nat. Press Photographers Found., 2000. Mem.: VFW (life), DAV (life; trustee Jack Schwartz chpt., past comdr. Miami Beach-Surfside chpt., nat. citation for disting. svc. 1969, nat. svc. plaque 2000), Covenant Soc., Guardian Soc., Nielsen Media Rsch., Nat. Press Photographers Assn. (life), Barry U. Alumni Assn., Steamship Hist. Soc. Am. Found. (life; S.E. Fla. chpt.), NYU Alumni Fedn. (Leadership award for 1982-1983 fund campaign), World Ocean and Cruise Liner Soc., Silver Leader, Commander's Club, Am. Legion, Order of the Flame, Alpha Mu Gamma. Home: 3619 NE 207th St Apt 2107 Aventura FL 33180-3805

PERKIEL, MITCHEL H., lawyer; b. NYC, Oct. 26, 1949; s. Frank and Ella Perkiel; m. Lois E. Perkiel, June 24, 1984; children: Joshua L., Alexa Kim, Griffin. BA, SUNY, Stony Brook, 1971; JD, New York Law Sch., 1974. Bar: N.Y. 1975, U.S. Dist. Ct. (so. and ea. dists.) N.Y. 1975, U.S. Ct. Appeals (2d cir.) 1975, Conn. 1988, Utah 1999. Law clk. to presiding justice N.Y. County Civil Ct., 1975; assoc. Levin & Weintraub & Crames, NYC, 1975-80, ptnr., 1980-90, Kaye, Scholer, Fierman, Hayes & Handler, NYC, 1990—2001, Jenkens & Gilchrist, Parker Chapin, NYC, 2001—05, Troutman Sanders LLP, NYC, 2005—. Notes and comments editor New York Law Rev., 1973-74. With USAR, 1969-73. Mem. ABA, Assn. of Bar of City of N.Y., Am. Bankruptcy Inst., Turnaround Mgmt. Assn. (dir.). Office Phone: 212-704-6016. Business E-Mail: mitchel.perkiel@troutmansanders.com.

PERKINS, BRADFORD, historian, educator; b. Rochester, NY, Mar. 6, 1925; s. Dexter and Wilma (Lord) P.; m. Nancy Nash Tucker, June 18, 1949 (dec.); children: Dexter III, Matthew Edward, Martha Nash. James Bradford (dec.). AB, Harvard U., 1946, PhD, 1952. From instr. to asso. prof. history U. Calif. at, Los Angeles, 1952-62; prof. history U. Mich., 1962-97, chmn. dept.; 1971-72, 80-81, prof. emeritus, 1997—. Commonwealth Fund lectr. Univ. Coll., London, Eng., 1964; vis. prof. history Brandeis U., 1970, Ecole des Hautes Etudes en Sciences Sociales, Paris, 1983; Albert Shaw lectr. Johns Hopkins U., 1979; mem. council Inst. Early Am. History and Culture, 1968-71; program dir. Nat. Endowment for Humanities Fellowships in Residence for Coll. Tchrs., 1974-75 Author: The First Rapprochement: England and the United States, 1795-1805, 1955, Youthful America, 1960, Prologue to War: England and the United States, 1805-1812, 1961, Causes of the War of 1812, 1962, Castlereagh and Adams: England and the United States, 1812-1823, 1964, The Great Rapprochement: England and the United States, 1895-1914, 1968, The Creation of a Republican Empire, 1993. Served with AUS, 1943-45, ETO. Decorated Bronze Star.; Recipient Bancroft prize, 1965, Disting. Faculty award U. Mich., 1986; Warren fellow, 1969-70; Faculty Rsch. fellow Social Sci. Rsch. Council, 1957-60; Guggenheim fellow, 1962-63 Mem. Am. Hist. Assn., Soc. Am. Historians, Orgn. Am. Historians (coun. 1969-72), Soc. Historians Am. Fgn. Rels. (coun. 1967-72, pres. 1974, Graebner award 1992), Mass. Hist. Soc., Am. Antiquarian Soc. Home: 1200 Earhart Rd #410 Ann Arbor MI 48105 Home Phone: 734-327-0080. Business E-Mail: bperkins@umich.edu.

PERKINS, CHARLES, III, newspaper and website editor; b. Brockton, Mass., July 25, 1952; s. Charles II and Barbara Perkins; m. Linda C. Burroughs, Jan. 4, 1985. BA, Dartmouth Coll., 1975. Editor Journal-Opinion, Bradford, Vt., 1977-78; reporter, editor The Union Leader and N.H. Sunday News, Manchester, 1978-81; Sunday editor N.H. Sunday News, Manchester, 1981-84; mng. editor The Union Leader and N.H. Sunday News, Manchester, 1984-92, exec. editor, 1992—; v.p. editl. N.H. Union Leader and UnionLeader.com, Manchester, 2000—. Recipient Andrzeja Drawicza award, Pres. Poland, 2005. Office: PO Box 9555 Manchester NH 03108-9555

PERKINS, CHERYL A., paper company executive; b. Aug. 1960; m. Mark D. Perkins; 2 children. BS in Chemistry, Ga. Inst. Tech., 1983, M in Polymers, Chemical Engring. Dept., 1989. With Smith-Kline Laboratories, Atlanta; researcher Kimberly-Clark Corp., Roswell, Ga., 1984—87, with nonwovens tech. and product develop. grp., 1987—94, rsch. mgr., absorbent tech. Neenah, Wis., 1994—96, dir., absorbent tech., 1996, dir., feminine care R&D, 1996, v.p., global feminine care R&D, 1999—2000, v.p., sr. tech. officer, 2000—01, chief technical officer, 2001—02, sr. v.p., chief innovation officer Tex., 2002—. Mem. adv. com. Inst. Paper Chemistry Rsch., Atlanta; mem. external adv. bd. for textile and fiber engring. Ga. Inst. Tech.; spkr. in field. Bd. dir. Fox Cities Children's Mus., Appleton, Wis. Named Outstanding Young Engring. Alumni, Ga. Inst. Tech., 2000; named one of 25 Masters of Innovation, BusinessWeek. Achievements include patents in field.

PERKINS, DAVID L., music educator; adopted s. Dallas and Sagemary Perkins; m. Beth Ellen Kutzner, Nov. 19, 1994; children: Michael, Ellen, Spencer. BS in Music Edn., West Chester U., West Chester, Pennsylvania, 1980—84. Instructional II Commonwealth of Pa, 1989, Instructional I Commonwealth of Pa, 1984. Jr. h.s. choral dir. Lehighton Area Sch. Dist., Lehighton, Pa., 1985—93, h.s. choral dir., 1993—. Dir. of ch. music First Presbyn. Ch. of Panther Valley, Summit Hill, Pa., 1989—. Scenic and lighting designer (off-broadway production (set/lights) Holy Heists; actor: (college musical production) Oklahoma. Elected to music/worship com. Lehigh Presbytery, Allentown, Pa., 1993—96; elected as ch. elder First Presbyn. Ch. of Panther Valley, Summit Hill, Pa., 1986—89, pres. of ch. corp., 1988—89. Recipient Kappa Delta Pi, Kappa Delta Pi, 1984, Tchr. of the Yr., Lehighton Area Chamber of Commerce, 1991, Outstanding Music Student, UNICO, 1980, Ministerial Award, Panther Valley Ministerium, 1980; scholar The Swope Found. Scholarship, Swope Found. West Chester U., 1983, Off-Campus Student Assn. Scholarship, Off-Campus Student Assn. West Chester U., 1983, Summer Sch. of the Arts, Lehigh CC, 1977 & 1978, Leadership Camp at Keystone CC, Panther Valley Rotary, 1978, Fred Waring Music Workshop, Panther Valley Chamber of Commerce, 1979. Mem.: Pa, State Educators Assn. (assoc.), Music Educators Nat. Conf. (assoc.), Pa, Music Educators Assn. (assoc.), Kappa Delta Pi (assoc.), Phi Mu Alpha Sinfonia (assoc.; choral dir. 1983—84). R-Consevative. Presbyterian. Achievements include 1991 Educator of the Year; Winner of Talent Search at Easton State Theatre. Avocations: travel, magic, lighting and sets, horse back riding. Office: Lehighton Area High School 1 Indian Lane Lehighton PA 18235 Personal E-mail: musiktime@hotmail.com.

PERKINS, DWIGHT HEALD, economics professor; b. Chgo., Oct. 20, 1934; s. Lawrence Bradford and Margery (Blair) P.; m. Julie Rate, June 15, 1957; children: Lucy Fitch, Dwight Edward, Caleb Blair. BA, Cornell U., 1956; AM, Harvard U., 1961, PhD, 1964. From instr. to assoc. prof. Harvard U., Cambridge, Mass., 1963-69, prof. econs., 1969-81, assoc. dir. East Asian Rsch. Ctr., 1973-77, chmn. dept. econs., 1977-80, H.H. Burbank prof. polit. economy, 1981—2006, dir. Asia Ctr., 2002—05; dir. Harvard Inst. Internat. Devel., Cambridge, 1980-95; H.H. Burbank Rsch. prof. of polit. economy Harvard U., 2006—. Trustee China Med. Bd., 1995—2004, chair, 2000—04; cons. permanent subcom. on investigations US Senate, 1974—80; H.M. Jackson vis. prof. Chinese studies U. Wash., 1985, Phi Beta Kappa lectr., 1992—93, Faculty Salzburg seminar, 1996; lectr. Fulbright tchg. policy program, Vietnam, 1997—2007; mem. Internat. Adv. Group to Prime Min. of Papua, New Guinea, 1991—92, 2000—02; cons. Korea Devel. Inst., 1972—80, 2006—, Govt. Malaysia, 1968—69, 2005. Author (with M. Halperin): Communist China and Arms Control, 1965, Agricultural Development in China, 1368-1968, 1969, Market Control and Planning in Communist China, 1966, China: Asia's Next Economic Giant?, 1986; author: (with E.S. Mason and others) The Economic Modernization of Korea, 1980; author: (with S. Yusuf) Rural Development in China, 1984; author: (with S. Radelet and others) Economics of Development, 1983, 6th edit., 2006; editor: China's Modern Economy in Historical Perspective, 1975; editor: (with M. Roemer) Reforming Economic Systems in Developing Countries, 1991; editor: (with J. Stern and others) Industrialization and the State: The Korean Heavy and Chemical Industry Drive, 1995; editor: (with others) Assisting Development in a Changing World, 1997, Industrialization and the State: The Changing Role of the Taiwan Government in the Economy, 1945-1998, 2001, Innovative East Asia: The Future of Growth, 2003; editor: (with S. Yusuf and others) Under New Ownership: Privatizing China's State-Owned Enterprises, 2006. Vis. com. Far Ea. studies U. Chgo., 1973-77; bd. govs. East-West Ctr., Honolulu, 1979-82; co-moderator Aspen Inst. Seminar on Korea, Colo., 1980-83. Lt. (j.g.) USNR, 1956-58. Fgn. Area Tng. fellow, Ford Found., NY, 1958—62, NSF Sci. Faculty fellow, Tokyo, 1968—69. Mem. Am. Philos. Soc., Assn. Asian Studies, Assn. Comparative Econ. Systems (pres. 1999-2000), Am. Econ. Assn., Phi Beta Kappa. Home: 64 Pinehurst Rd Belmont MA 02478-1504 Office: Harvard Univ Dept Econs Cambridge MA 02138-5781 Business E-Mail: dwight_perkins@harvard.edu.

PERKINS, EDDIE, boxer; b. Clarksdale, Miss., Mar. 3, 1937; Profl. boxing circuit, 1956—75. Named to Profl. Boxing Hall of Fame, 2006. Achievements include holding Jr. World Welterweight Title, 1961, 1963-1965; holding No. Am. Weleter Weight Title, 1973-1974; 22 career knock-outs. *

PERKINS, EDWARD A., JR., secondary school educator; s. Edward A. and Shirley S. Perkins; 1 child, Krista. BS, Wayland Bapt. U., Plainview, Tex., 1981; MBA, East Tex. A&M, 1983; MS, Tex. Tech. U., 2004. Tchr. Ecotr County Ind. Sch. Dist., Odessa, Tex., 1996—2000, Lubbock Ind. Sch. Dist., Tex., 2000—05, 2006—, Frisco Ind. Sch. Dist., Tex., 2005—06. Meteorol. observer US Army, 1974—77. Named Tchr. of Yr., Staked Plains Coun. for the Social Studies, Lubbock, 2005. Mem.: ACLU, ASCD, Nat. Coun. for the Social Studies, Amnesty Internat., Sierra Club. Avocations: hiking, camping.

PERKINS, EDWARD S., ophthalmologist; b. London; arrived in US, 1979; s. Edward Walter and Gertrude Perkins; m. Eileen Anne Rammell; children: Stephen, Richard, Juliet, Helena. PhD, Inst. Ophthalmology, London, 1957, MD, 1959. Reader in ophthalmology U. London, 1954—63, prof. exptl. ophthalmology, 1963—79; prof. U. Iowa, Iowa City, 1979—86, prof. emeritus, 1986—. Founder Internat. Soc. Eye Rsch., 1963; Middlemore lectr. Author: An Atlas of Diseases of the Eye, 1957, Uveitis and Toxoplasmosis, 1961; editor: Disease of the Uveal Tract, 1966; contbr. articles to profl. jours. Capt. Royal Army Med. Corp, 1942—46. Recipient Treacher Collins prize, Ophthal. Soc. U.K., 1968, Nettleship prize. Fellow: Royal Coll. Surgeons; mem.: Royal Coll. Physicians. Avocation: music. Home: 889 Park Pl Iowa City IA 52246

PERKINS, FRANK OVERTON, academic administrator, marine biologist; b. Fork Union, Va., Feb. 14, 1938; s. Frank Otie and Mary Ella Perkins; m. Beverly Anne Weeks. BA, U. Va., 1960; MS, Fla. State U., Tallahassee, 1962, PhD, 1966. Marine scientist Va. Inst. Marine Sci., Coll. William and Mary, Gloucester Point, 1966-69, sr. marine scientist, 1969-77, asst. dir., 1977-81, dir., dean Sch. Marine Sci., 1981-91, prof. marine sci., 1991-97; asst. v.p. rsch. and grad. edn. U. Hawaii, Honolulu, 1997—. Baptist. Home: 7519 Olowalu Pl Honolulu HI 96825-2950 Office: U Hawaii 223 Crawford Hall Honolulu HI 96822 Office Phone: 808-956-6635. E-mail: fperkins@hawaii.edu.

PERKINS, GEORGE, writer, educator; b. Lowell, Mass., Aug. 16, 1930; s. George Burton Perkins and Gladys Beatrice Jones; m. Barbara Miller Perkins, May 9, 1964; children: Laura, Suzanne, Alison. AB, Tufts U., Medford, Mass., 1953; MA, Duke U., Durham, NC, 1954; PhD, Cornell U., Ithaca, NY, 1960. Instr. Wash. U., St. Louis, 1957—60; asst. prof. Baldwin-Wallace Coll., Berea, Ohio, 1960—63, Fairleigh Dickinson U., Rutherford, NJ, 1963—66; lectr. U. Edinburgh, Scotland, 1966—67; prof. Ea. Mich. U., Ypsilanti, 1967—2001. Lectr. Peking U., 2006, Zhengzhou U., 2006, Chinese U. Hong Kong, 2006. Author, editor: The American Tradition in Literature, The Reader's Encyclopedia of American Literature, Stones Stand, Waters Flow: A New England Story, others. Fellow Inst. for Advanced Studies in the Humanities, U. Edinburgh, 1981; Sr. Fulbright scholar Australia Coun. for Internat. Exch. of Scholars, 1989. Avocations: travel, tennis, literature, basketball. Home: 1316 King George Blvd Ann Arbor MI 48108-3212 Personal E-mail: george.perkins@emich.edu.

PERKINS, HOMER GUY, manufacturing executive; b. New Haven, Oct. 23, 1916; s. Frank W. and Emily (Oesting) P.; m. Dorothy C. Stock, Jan. 24, 1942; children: Maribeth Perkins Grant, Homer Guy Jr., Hazel Mary Perkins Adolphson, Dorothy Catherine, Caroline Anne, Faith Elizabeth Perkins Crotteau, Ruth Emily Perkins Sico. BA in Internat. Rels., Yale U., 1938; LLD (hon.), Westfield U., Mass., 1977. With Enesco Group, Inc. (formerly Stanhome, Inc.), Westfield, 1939—, v.p., 1965-66, exec. v.p., 1966-70, pres., CEO, 1970-78, chmn., 1978-81. Treas. Stanley Park of Westfield, 1949-2005; pres. Citizens Scholarship Found., Easthampton, Mass., 1966-67, Easthampton Cmty. Chest, 1960-61; chmn. fin. com., bd. dirs. Western Mass. coun. Girl Scouts U.S., 1966-69; devel. com. Clarke Sch. Deaf, Northampton, 1965-68; fin. com. Town of Easthampton, 1962-70, chmn. fin. com., 1967-68; dir. Frank Stanley Beveridge Found., Westfield, 1956-95, pres., 1966-87; trustee Cooley Dickinson Hosp., Northampton, 1963-70, 84-92, chmn. bd. trustees, 1989-91; pres. bd. trustees Northampton Sch. for Girls, 1964-73; bd. dirs. Porter Phelps Huntington Found., Hadley, Mass., 1960-92, Guild of Holy Child, Westfield, 1969-76; bd. overseers Williston Acad., Easthampton, 1961-64, Old Sturbridge Village, Mass., 1970-76; v.p. bd. trustees Williston-Northampton Sch., 1970-75, pres., 1975-78; dir. Lathrop Communities, 2000-07, chair fin. com., 2001, pres. bd. dirs., 2005. With USAAF, 1942-46. Mem. Direct Selling Assn. (chmn. 1975, bd. dirs., mem. Hall of Fame), Paperweight Collectors Assn. (pres. 1991-95), Lions (past pres. Easthampton club). Home: 112 Bassett Brook Dr Easthampton MA 01027-1096

PERKINS, JACK EDWIN, lawyer; b. Portola, Calif., May 25, 1943; s. Charles James and Vira Almena (Wing) P.; m. Barbara Kay Nielson, Jan. 18, 1969; children: Jill Christy, Kelli Anne. BA, San Jose State Coll., 1966; JD, Hastings Coll. Law, 1972. Bar: Calif. 1972, D.C. 1989. From asst. U.S. atty. to dir. ops. bd. immigration appeals Exec. Office Immigration Rev. Dept. Justice, 1972—2004, dir. ops. bd. immigration appeals Exec. Office Immigration Rev., 2004—. Served to capt. USMC, 1966-69, Vietnam. Recipient John Marshall award Dept. Justice, 1986. Office: Exec Office Immigration Rev 5107 Leesburg Pike Ste 2519 Falls Church VA 22041-2400

PERKINS, JOHN ALLEN, lawyer; b. New Bedford, Mass., Sept. 13, 1919; s. Ralph Chamberlain and Louise Bartlett (Allen) P.; m. Lydia Bullard Cobb, Sept. 9, 1944; children: John A., Susan W., Robert C., William B. AB, Harvard U., 1940, LL.B., 1943. Bar: Mass. Of counsel Edwards Angell Palmer & Dodge LLP, Boston; clk. Social Law Library, 1961-83; grad. researcher Univ. Coll., Oxford U., 1978. Bd. dirs. Greater Boston Legal Services, Inc., 1972-91. Author: The Prudent Peace— Law as Foreign Policy, 1981, The Heart of the Art: Reflections on the Human Side of Estate Planning, 2006; contbr. articles to profl. jours. Mem. Dedham (Mass.) Sch. Com., 1959-65, chmn., 1963-65, town counsel, Dedham, 1971-72. Mem. Am. Law Inst., Am. Coll. Trust and Estate Counsel, Mass. Bar Assn. (dir. 1973-75), Internat. Acad. Estate and Trust Law (exec. coun. 1990-94), Boston Bar Assn. (council 1972-75, v.p. 1981-82, pres. 1982-84). Home: 100 Newbury Court Ste 610 Concord MA 01742-5835 Office: Edwards Angell Palmer & Dodge LLP 111 Huntington Ave at Prudential Ctr Boston MA 02199-7613

PERKINS, JON DOUGLAS, accountant, educator; b. Portsmouth, Va., Mar. 31, 1969; s. Robert Caldwell and Kay Steinhauser Perkins; m. Michelle Christine Hamilton, Jan. 2, 1993; 1 child, Jon Douglas Jr. BS in Acctg., U. Mo., Columbia, 1991, BS in Bus. Adminstrn., 1991, JD, 1995; PhD in Acctg., U. Ill., Champaign, 2003. CPA Mo. State Bd. of Accountancy, 1993, cert. Inst. Cert. Mgmt. Accts., 2005; bar: Mo. 1995. Vis. lectr. U. Ill., Champaign, 2002—03; asst. prof. Fla. State U., Tallahassee, 2003—07; vis. asst. prof. U. Ill., Urbana-Champaign, 2007—. Contbr. articles to profl. jorus.; mem. editol bd.: Issues in Accounting Education. Fellow, U. Ill., 1996—2002; Victor L. Bernard Meml. scholar, 2000—04, Lillian and Morrie Moss fellow, 2000—02, Richard D. and Anne Marie Irwin fellow, U. Ill. Coll. Bus., 2000—01. Mem.: AICPA, Inst. Mgmt. Accts., Mo. Bar Assn., Am. Acctg. Assn., Internat. Taekwondo Alliance, Alpha Kappa Psi (pres. 1990—91). Avocation: taekwondo. Personal E-mail: jondperkins@gmail.com.

PERKINS, LAWRENCE BRADFORD, JR., architect; b. Chgo., Jan. 13, 1943; s. Lawrence Bradford and Margery Isabella (Blair) P.; m. Phyllis Barbara Friedman, Sept. 11, 1966; children: Rachael Naomi, Judith Eve, Rebecca Abigail. BA, Cornell U., 1967; MBA, Stanford U., 1969; BArch, CCNY, 1976. Registered architect, N.Y., Conn., Md., Ohio, Ill., Conn., Pa., Mass., Ill., N.J., Ga., Fla., Mo., Ariz., Tex. Pres. Perkins Eastman Archs., NYC, 1983—, Omnidata Svcs., NYC, 1971-73; mng. ptnr. Llewelyn-Davies Assocs., NYC, 1973-77, Perkins & Will, NYC, 1977-81; ptnr. Attia & Perkins, NYC, 1981-83. Author: Design of K-12 Schools; contbr. chpts. to books and articles to profl.jours. Bd. dirs. Castle Gallery Coll. New Rochelle, N.Y., 1985—, Settlement Housing Fund, N.Y.C., 1991—, Helen Keller Internat., N.Y.C., 1993—, various other Scarsdale village bds. and coms.; chmn. bd. Hudson Planning Group. Fellow AIA (mem. various coms.), Am. Inst. Cert. Planners, Cornell U. Coun., Epsilon Assn. (pres. 1993-96). Home: 4 Rectory Ln Scarsdale NY 10583-4314 Office: Perkins Eastman Archs 115 5th Ave New York NY 10003-1004

PERKINS, LEEMAN LLOYD, musicologist, educator; b. Salina, Utah, Mar. 27, 1932; s. Milton Lloyd and Ida Margaret (Johnson) P.; m. Marianne Suzanne Contesse, Nov. 14, 1956; children: Eric Raymond, Bruce Philippe, Marc Christian (dec.), Patrick Thierry. BFA, U. Utah, 1954; PhD, Yale U., 1965. Instr. Boston U., 1964, Yale U., 1964-67, asst. prof., 1967-71, dir. undergraduate studies in music history, 1969-70; assoc. prof. music history, coord. for musicology U. Tex., Austin, 1971-75, grad. adv. for musicology, 1976; prof. music Columbia U., NYC, 1976—2003, prof. emeritus, 2003—, chmn. dept music, 1985-90. Instr. advanced seminar in Medieval History, Smith Coll., 1968; vis. assoc. prof. music Columbia U., 1975; vis. prof. Boston U., 1978; dir. NEH Summer Seminar, 1977. Editor: Johannes Lheritier Opera Omnia, 1969, (with Howard Garey) The Mellon Chansonnier, 1979, Music in the Age of the Renaissance, 1999; gen. editor: Masters and Monuments of Renaissance Music, 1978—. Chmn. grad. musicology com., Columbia U., 1980-84, 1993-96, 97-2001. Sgt., 7th Army Symphony, U.S. Army, 1957-59. Recipient James Morris Whiton Fund award Yale U., 1965, The Otto Kinkeldey award Am. Musicological Soc., 1980, la Médaille de la Ville de Tours, 1997; Trumbull Coll. fellow Yale U., 1966-71, Lewis-Farmington fellow Yale U., 1962-63, Morse fellow Yale U., 1967-68, Am. Coun. Learned Soc. fellow, 1973-74, NEH fellow, 1979, 1984-85, French Archival Scis. fellow Newberry Libr. Center for Renaissance Studies, 1991; Martha Baird Rockefeller grantee, 1963-64, Paul Mellon Found. grantee, 1972, Am. Coun. Learned Soc., 1972, 82, U. Tex. grantee, 1975, Mem. Am. Musicological Soc. (chmn. program com. 1979, bd. dirs. 1980-81, adv. bd., 1985-86, chmn. ad hoc sub com., 1985-86, exec. com. delegate, 1989-92, mem. fellowship com. 1995-98), Internat. Musicological Soc., The Renaissance Soc. of Am., Phi Beta Kappa, Phi Kappa Phi. Mem. Lds Ch. Business E-Mail: LLP1@columbia.edu.

PERKINS, LUCIAN, photographer; Grad., U. Tex. Intern The Washington Post, 1979, now staff photographer. Founder InterFoto (U.S./Russian photography orgn.). Author: (photography book) Runway Madness, 1998. Named Newspaper Photographer of Yr., Pictures of Yr. competition, 1993; recipient Pulitzer prize for explanatory journalism, 1995, Pulitzer prize for feature photography, 2000, Photo of Yr. award, World Press, 1996.

PERKINS, NANCY JANE, industrial designer; b. Phila., Nov. 5, 1949; d. Gordon Osborne and Martha Elizabeth (Keichline) P. Student, Ohio U., 1967—68; BFA, U. Ill., 1972. Indsl. designer Peterson Bednar Assocs., Evanston, Ill., 1972-74, Deschamps Mills Assos., Bartlett, Ill., 1974-75; dir. graphic design Cameo Container Corp., Chgo., 1975-76; indsl. design cons. Sears Roebuck & Co., Chgo., 1977-88; cons. indsl. design, 1988—; program mgr. indsl. design Jarden Consumer Solutions, Boca Raton, Fla., 2007—. Lectr. CUNY, 1995; founder Perkins Design Ltd., Anna Wagner Keichline Gallery, Bellefonte, Pa.; adj. prof. grad. design seminar U. Ill. Chgo., 1982, 88, 91, 93, adj. instr. undergrad. design, 1984, 88, 91, 93; adj. instr. Ill. Inst. Tech., 1987, 91; vis. assoc. prof. Carnegie-Mellon U., 1991; juror annual design rev. Indsl. Design mag., 1986; tech. rev. com. Ben Franklin Partnerships, 1991—; spkr. in field. Contbg. author: Design and Feminism, 1999; featured in Bard Grad. Ctrs.' Exhibit, NYC, 2000; contbr. articles to profl. jours. Co-leader Cadette troop DuPage County coun. Girl Scouts US, 1978-79. Recipient Outstanding Alumni award U. Ill. Alumni Jour., 1981, Goldsmith award, 1992; profiled in Indsl. Design mag., 1986, Feminine Ingenuity (by Anne L. Macdonald), 1992, Dun & Bradstreet Reports, 1993; profiled The Phila. Inquirer Mag., 1994; featured in Chgo. Athenaeum "33 plus 20", 1993, Pratt Manhattan Gallery, NYC, 1994. Fellow Indsl. Designers Soc. Am. (treas. Chgo. chpt. 1977-79, vice chmn. 1979-80, chmn. 1981, dist. membership com. 1982, ann. conf. com. 1983, publs. com. 1985-86, dir.-at-large 1987-88, v.p. Midwest dist. 1989-90, nat. sec.-treas. 1991-92, del. Internat. Coun. of the Socs. Indsl. Design 1989, co-founder women's sect. 1992, pres. design found. 2007, bd. dirs. design found.). Achievements include patents in field. Office Phone: 888-223-5211. Personal E-mail: perkinsnancy1@bellsouth.net.

PERKINS, NANCY LEEDS, lawyer; b. Washington, June 19, 1956; d. Roswell Burchard and Joan (Titcomb) P. AB, Harvard U., 1979, M in Pub. Policy, 1987, JD, 1987. Bar: Pa. 1988, D.C. 1989, U.S. Dist. Ct. D.C. 1990. Jud. clk. U.S. Dist. Ct. (ea. dist.) N.Y., Bklyn., 1987—88; counsel Arnold & Porter, Washington, 1988—. Contbr. articles to profl. jours. Recipient Pro Bono svc. award Internat. Human Rights Law Group, 1990. Democrat. Avocation: tennis. Office: Arnold & Porter 555 12th St NW Washington DC 20004-1206 Office Phone: 202-942-5065. Business E-Mail: nancy_perkins@aporter.com.

PERKINS, RAYMOND LAMONT, retired government official; b. New Rochelle, NY, Apr. 8, 1924; s. Raymond Lamont and Dorothy Marie (Porter) P.; m. Margaret Johnson, Aug. 25, 1946; children: Deborah, Doriane, Amy. AB, U. Denver, 1946, LLB, 1948. Bar: Colo. Pvt. practice, Springfield, Colo., 1949-54; fgn. svc. officer Dept. State, various locations, 1954-86; ret., 1986. Lmem. Fgn. Svc. Grievance Bd., Washington, 1990-2000. Contbr. articles to profl. jours. County atty. Baca County, Colo., 1949-54, dep. dist. atty., 1949-52. Capt. USAR. Mem. Kiwanis. Methodist. E-mail: rperkpeg@aol.com.

PERKINS, RITA WADE, historian, educator; b. Burlington, NJ, Aug. 11, 1948; d. Leo Thomas and Anna Dement Wade; m. James Perkins, Dec. 5, 1981; children: David Wesley, Jeffrey Wade, Elise Marie. BA, Rutgers U., Camden, NJ, 1970; MA, Rutgers U., 1979, Villanova U., Pa., 1972. Assoc. prof. Camden County Coll., Blackwood, NJ, 1972—. Lectr./presenter in field, 2003—. Photographer (photography exhibitions with lectures) Bridge of Tears (NJ. Coun. for Humanities Grants, 2003). Fellow, NEH, 1979. Mem.: Am. Conf. of Irish Studies. Achievements include research in Irish Famine Memorials. Office: Camden County College College Dr Box 200 Blackwood NJ 08012 Home Phone: 856-547-6562; Office Phone: 856-227-7200. E-mail: rperkins@camdencc.edu.

PERKINS, ROBERT EDWARD, retired secondary school educator; b. Hartford, Conn., Mar. 22, 1939; s. Alfred Warren and Montez Ordell (Rideout) P.; m. Jane Richmond Dickey; children: Ann, Margaret. BA, Harvard Coll., 1961; MA, U. Maine, 1964. M of French Deerfield (Mass.) Acad., 1968—90; tchr. French Flint Hill Sch., Oakton, Va., 1990—2004; ret., 2004. Organist, choir dir. South Congl. Ch., Amherst, Mass., 1966—80, 1st Ch. Deerfield, Mass., 1980—90; organist Little Falls Presbyn. Ch., Arlington, Va., 1991—2005; ret., 2005. Pres. PTO Old Deerfield (Mass.) Grammar Sch., 1972; treas., bd. dirs. Pioneer Valley Symphony, Greenfield, Mass., 1975—85; pres. Ballet Arts Regional Rep. Ensemble, Greenfield, 1978—82. Lt. comdr. USNR, 1961—63. Mem.: Am. Guild Organists (treas. Nova 1998—2001). Democrat. Home: 404 Lennox Rd W Palm Harbor FL 34683 Personal E-mail: vaorganguy@aol.com.

PERKINS, ROGER ALLAN, lawyer; b. Port Chester, NY, Mar. 4, 1943; s. Francis Newton and Winifred Marcella (Smith) P.; m. Katherine Louise Howard, Nov. 10, 1984; children: Marshall, Morgan, Matthew, Justin, Ashley. BA, Pa. State U., 1965; postgrad., U. Ill., 1965-66; JD with honors, George Washington U., 1969. Bar: Md. 1969, Mass. 1975. Trial atty. Nationwide Ins. Co., Annapolis, Md., 1969-72; assoc. Arnold, Beauchemin & Huber, PA, Balt., 1973; from assoc. to ptnr. Goodman & Bloom, PA, Annapolis, 1973-76; ptnr. Luff and Perkins, Annapolis, 1976-78; pvt. practice Anapolis, 1978—. Temp. adminstrv. hearing officer Anne Arundel County, 1984—; asst. city atty., Annapolis, 1980-82; atty. Bd. Appeals of City of Annapolis, 1986-2003, 2005—; mem. Appellate Jud. Nominating Commn., 1995—. Editl. adv. bd. Daily Record, 1996-97. Mem. Gov.'s Task Force on Family Law, 1991-94; adv. coun. on family legal need of low income persons MLSC, 1991; coach youth sports. Fellow Am. Acad. Matrimonial Lawyers, Am. Bar Found., Md. Bar Found. (bd. dirs. 1992-95); mem. ABA (ho. dels. 1991-93, 94-96, standing com. on solo and small firm practitioners 1993-97, chair 1996-97), Md. State Bar Assn. (pres. 1992-93, treas. 1988-91, bd. govs. 1985-87, chair membership com. 2002-04, chair spl. com. on lawyer profl. responsibility 1994-95, family and juvenile law sect. coun. 1983-89, chair 1987-88), Anne Arundel County Bar Assn. (pres. 1984-85). Home: 503 Bay Hills Dr Arnold MD 21012-2001 Office: The Courtyards 133 Defense Hwy Ste 202 Annapolis MD 21401-8907 Office Phone: 410-266-3558. E-mail: roger@perkinslaw.com.

PERKINS, ROSWELL BURCHARD, lawyer; b. Boston, May 21, 1926; AB cum laude, Harvard U., 1945, LLB cum laude, 1949; LLD, Bates Coll., 1988. Bar: Mass. 1949, N.Y. 1949. Assoc. Debevoise, Plimpton & McLean, NYC, 1949-53; ptnr. Debevoise & Plimpton and predecessor firm, NYC, 1957-96; of counsel, head rep. office Debevoise & Plimpton LLC, Moscow, 1997-01. Asst. sec. U.S. Dept. HEW, 1954-56; counsel to Gov. Nelson A. Rockefeller State of N.Y., 1959; asst. counsel spl. subcom. Senate Commerce Com. to investigate organized crime in interstate commerce, 1950; chmn. N.Y.C. Mayor's Task Force on Transp. Reorgn., 1966; mem. Pres.'s Adv. Panel on Pers. Interchange, 1968, chmn. adv. com. Medicare Adminstrn. Contracting, Subcontracting HEW, 1973-74; dir. Fiduciary Trust Co., N.Y., 1963-2000; trustee Bowery Savs. Bank, 1975-82; mem. legal com. to bd. dirs. N.Y. Stock Exch., 1995-2000. Editor Harvard Law Rev., 1948-49. Mem. N.Y. Lawyers Com. Civil Rights, 1970-73; mem. nat. exec. com., 1973-1980, co-chmn. 1973-75; mem. adv. coun. Woodrow Wilson Sch. Pub. and Internat. Affairs, Princeton U., 1967-69; bd. dirs. The Commonwealth Fund, 1974-97, Sch. Am. Ballet, 1974-85, chmn. bd. 1976-80; dir., sec. N.Y. Urban Coalition, 1967-74; trustee Pomfret Sch., 1961-76; The Brearley Sch., 1969-75; dir. Salzburg Seminar Am. Studies, 1970-80; mem. overseers vis. com. Kennedy Sch. Govt., Harvard U., 1971-77, Harvard and Radcliffe Colls., 1958-64, 1971-77, Davis Ctr. for Russian and Eurasian Studies, 2000-05 Recipient Spl. Merit citation Am. Judicature Soc., 1989, Harvard Law Sch. Assn. award, 1994, 50 Yr. award Fellows of ABA, 2002. Mem. ABA (commn. on law and economy, 1975-79, mem. ho. of dels. 1980-93), N.Y. State Bar Assn., Assn. of the Bar of the City of N.Y. (chmn. spl. com. on fed. conflict of interest laws 1958-60). Harvard Alumni Assn. (pres. 1970-71), Am. Law Inst. (mem. coun. 1969, pres. 1980-93, chmn. coun. 1993—), Am. Arbitration Assn. (bd. dirs. 1966-71), Russian Inst. Dirs. (mem. expert coun. 2002-06), Ind. Dirs. Assn. (mem. adv. com. Russia 2002-06). Home: 1120 5th Ave New York NY 10128-0144 Office: Debevoise & Plimpton 919 3rd Ave 46th Fl New York NY 10022-3916 Home Phone: 212-722-3673; Office Phone: 212-909-6421. Business E-Mail: rbperkins@debevoise.com.

PERKINS, SAMUEL SWENSON, education educator; b. Cornelia, Ga., Aug. 28, 1960; s. George Swenson and Mary Anne Perkins. AA in Bus. Adminstrn., Gainesville Jr. Coll., Ga., 1979; BA in Acctg., North Ga. Coll., Dahlonega, 1981; MEd, Mercer U., Atlanta, 1994; PhD in Higher Edn., Ga. State U., Atlanta, 1997. Instr. Mercer U., 1994—97; lectr. U. Miami, Coral Gables, Fla., 1997—99; asst. prof. edn. Barry U., Miami Shores, Fla., 2000—. Cons. in field. Recipient Apple award of appreciation, Barry U. commuter students, 2004, VIP award, Mass. Indemnity and Life Ins. Co. Mem.: TESOL (sec. internat. convention 2004—06), Fla. Assn. Tchr. Educators (sec. 2004—06), Sunshine State TESOL (sec. 2006—07), Assn. Tchr. Educators (mem. Leadership Acad. 2006—). Avocations: exercise, reading, travel, bicycling, tennis.

PERKINS, SAMUEL THOMAS, lawyer; b. Ft. Leavenworth, Kans., Sept. 26, 1946; s. David Mural and Helene Mathilde (Berg) P.; m. Ruth Ann Nelson, July 29, 1967 (div. 1975); m. M. Carolyn Cox, Sept. 23, 1978; children: William Frank Cox Perkins, Leni Camille Mermod Perkins. AB summa cum laude, Brown U., 1967; JD, Yale U., 1974. Bar: DC 1975, US Dist. Ct. DC 1975, US Ct. Appeals (fed. cir.) 1993. Ptnr. Steptoe & Johnson, Wash., DC, 1974—, of counsel. With US Army, 1968—70. Woodrow Wilson Found. scholar, 1967-68. Republican. Avocations: travel, historical studies, coaching youth sports teams. Office: Steptoe & Johnson 1330 Connecticut Ave NW Washington DC 20036-1704 Office Phone: 202-429-6299. Office Fax: 202-429-3902. Business E-Mail: sperkins@steptoe.com.

PERKINS, STEPHEN W., plastic surgeon; b. Dec. 15, 1951; BA, DePauw U., Greencastle, Ind., 1974; MD, Ind. U., 1977. Cert. Am. Bd. Facial Plastic and Reconstructive Surgery, Am. Bd. Otolaryngology-Head and Neck Surgery. Gen. surgery internship St. Vincent Hosp. Indpls., 1977—78, resident otolaryngical head & neck surgery, 1978—79; resident facial plastic & reconstructive surgery Ind. U. Hosps., 1979—82; fellowship Am. Acad. Facial Plastic and Reconstructive Surgery, Birmingham, Ala., 1982—83; pvt. practice, 1983—90; chief med. officer, surgeon Meridian Plastic Surgery Ctr., 1990—2002; surgeon Perkins Van Natta Ctr. for Cosmetic Surgery and Med. Skin Care, Indpls., 2002—. Clin. assoc. prof. Ind. U. Med. Ctr.; sr. advisor Am. Bd. Facial Plastic and Reconstructive Surgery; presenter in field. Contbr. articles to profl. jours. Fellow: ACS, Am. Acad. Otolaryngology; mem.: Ind. State Med. Assn., Indpls. Med. Soc., Am. Acad. Facial Plastic and Reconstructive Surgery (pres. 1998, fellowship dir.), Internat. Burgundy Wine Assn. Avocations: travel, skiing, running, scuba diving, golf. Office: 170 W 106th St Indianapolis IN 46290 Office Phone: 317-575-0330, 800-345-1962. Office Fax: 317-571-8667. *

PERKINS, THOMAS P., JR., lawyer; b. 1953; BA, Harvard U.; JD, Loyola Univ., New Orleans. Bar: La., Tex. 1979. Former staff atty. Dallas Regional Office FTC; former special asst. atty. gen. Tex. Atty. Gen.'s Office; atty. Dallas City Atty. Office, 1999—, 1st asst. city atty. Litig. Div., formerly, interim city atty., 2005—, city atty. Adj. professor law So. Methodist Univ. Dedman Sch. Law, LSU Law Sch. Bd. mem. Tex. Appleseed. Mem.: Tex. State Bar Assn. (dir. Antitrust & Bus. Litig. Sect., formerly). Office: Dallas City Atty Office 1500 Marilla St Suite 7-BN Dallas TX 75201-6622

PERKINS, TOM (THOMAS JAMES PERKINS), venture capital company executive; b. Oak Park, Ill., Jan. 7, 1932; s. Harry H. and Elizabeth Perkins; m. Gerd Thune-Ellefsen, Dec. 9, 1961 (dec.); children: Tor Kristian, Elizabeth Siri; m. Danielle Steel, 1998 (div. 1999). BSEE, MIT, 1953; MBA, Harvard U., 1957. Founder Univ. Lab. (merged with Spectra Physics in 1960's); gen. mgr. computer div. Hewlett Packard Co., Cupertino, Calif., 1965-70, dir. corp. devel., 1970-72; co-founder, gen. partner Kleiner & Perkins, San Francisco, 1972-80; sr. ptnr. Kleiner Perkins Caufield & Byers, San Francisco, 1980—; chmn. bd. Tandem Computers, Inc., Cupertino, Calif., 1974—97. Founder, chmn. Genentech; bd. dirs. Spectra Physics., Symantec, Corning Glass Works, Collagen Corp., LSI Logic Corp., Hybritech Inc., Econics Corp., Vitalink Communications Corp., News Corp., Iolon, Philips Electronics NV, Compaq Computer, Hewlett Packard Co., 2002-04, 2005-06; chmn. Acuson, Tandem Computers. Author: Classic Supercharged Sports Cars, 1984, Sex and the Single Zillionaire, 2006. Trustee San Francisco Ballet, 1980—. Mem. Nat. Venture Capital Assn. (chmn. 1981-82, pres. 1980-81) Clubs: N.Y. Yacht, Links, Am. Bugatti (pres. 1983—). Office: Kleiner Perkins Caufield & Byers 2750 Sand Hill Rd Menlo Park CA 94025

PERKINS, WILLIAM CLINTON, manufacturing executive; b. Decatur, Ill., Mar. 7, 1920; s. Glen Rupert and Frances Lola (Clinton) P.; m. Eunice Cagle, Sept. 7, 1939 (div. 1954); stepchildren: William Rea Cagle, Howard Christy Cagle; 1 child, Clinton Colcord; m. Lillian Wuollet, Sept. 7, 1955 (div. 1965); m. Shirley Thomas, Oct. 24, 1969. BS Mil. Sci. and Meteorology, U. Md., College Park, 1954; MS in Bus. and Pub. Adminstrn., Sussex Coll., Eng., 1975. Commd. USAF, 1943—73, advanced through grades to col.; with Ship Sys. divsn. Litton Ind., Culver City, Calif., 1973—75; dir. material Hughes Aircraft Co., Tehran, Iran, 1974—78; mgr. internat. s/c Northrop Corp., Dhahran, Saudi Arabia, 1979—81; dir. materiel CRS, Riyadh, Saudi Arabia, 1981—83; head major subcontracts Lear Ziegler Corp., Santa Monica, Calif., 1984—88; pres., chmn. bd., CEO Snowtech, Inc., LA, 1984—. Bd. dirs. Ice Village Ctrs., Inc., LA, Forefront Industries, Maywood, Calif. Bd. dirs. World Children's Transplant Fund, LA, 1987-95; mem. Mayor's Space Adv. Com., LA, 1970-74; mem. Aerospace Hist. Com. Aerospace Hist. Soc., LA, 1988-, Mus. of Flying, 1998—. Mem. AIAA (sec. chmn. 1970), Ret. Officers Assn. (pres. 1992-95), Military Officers Assn. of Am. (chpt. pres. 2003-2005), Soc. for Non-destructive Testing (program chmn. 1973), Aerospace Hist. Soc., Am. Soc. Quality Control, Am. Meterol. Soc., Sigma Alpha Epsilon (alumni chpt. pres. 1974-76). Avocations: golf, scuba diving, sailing, flying, gardening. Home: 8027 Hollywood Blvd Los Angeles CA 90046-2510 Office Phone: 323-876-1412. Personal E-mail: snowtech@pacbell.net.

PERKINS, WILLIAM H., JR., retired finance company executive; b. Rushville, Ill., Aug. 4, 1921; s. William H. and Sarah Elizabeth (Logsdon) P.; m. Eileen Nelson, Jan. 14, 1949; 1 child, Gary Douglas. Student, Ill. Coll., Jacksonville. Pres. Howlett-Perkins Assos., Chgo. Mem. Ill. AEC, 1963-84, sec., 1970-84; apptd. by Pres. to adv. bd. Nat. Armed Forces Mus., Smithsonian Instn., 1964-82; army aide to Anthony Eden and Lord Halifax of Great Britain, UN Conf., 1945. Sgt.-at-arms Democratic Nat. Conv., 1952, 56, del.-at-large, 1964, 68, 72; spl. asst. to chmn. Dem. Nat. Com., 1960; mem. Presdl. Inaugural Com., 1961, 65, 69, 73, ins. policy agent, 1961. With US Army, 1944-46 Mem. Ill. Ins. Fedn. (pres. 1965-84), Ill. C. of C. (chmn. legis. com. 1971), Chgo. Assn. Commerce and Industry (legis. com., Raoul Wallenberg Humanitarian award 1993), Sangamo Club, Masons, Shriners. Methodist. Home: 726 Community Dr La Grange Park IL 60526-1555

PERKINS-BANAS, MELISSA VERONICA, neuropsychologist; d. Roy Dennis and Marian Dana Perkins; m. Joseph Paul Banas, July 3, 1999. BA, U. RI, 1992; MA, U. Hartford, 1995, MS, 1996; PsyD, Yeshiva U., 2004. Cert. Psychologist 1999. Sch. psychologist Norwich Pub. Schools, Norwich, Conn., 1999—2003; neuropsychologist Wheeler Clinic, Conn., 2003—. Post- doctoral neuropsychology fellowship Fielding Inst., NYC, 2004—. Sponsored athlete Adidas Woodbridge Racing Team, Woodbridge, Conn., 2000—02. Recipient Conn. Distance Runner of the Yr., Hi Tek Racing Team, 2001; Cecilia Rothenberg scholarship, Yeshiva U., 2002—03. Mem.: Assn. Advancement of Applied Sport Psychology, Conn. Assn. Sch. Psychologists, NASP, Am. Psychology Assn. (Divsn. 60, clin. neuropsychology), Psi Chi Nat. Honor Soc. Psychology. Roman Catholic. Office: Wheeler Clinic 91 Northwest Dr Plainville CT 06062 Home: 22 Hill St Southington CT 06489 Home Phone: 860-889-8211.

PERKINSON, ROBERT RONALD, psychologist, consultant; b. Richmond, Va., Aug. 8, 1945; s. Gordon Archibald and Sarah (Haskins) P.; m. Elizabeth Godfrey Fly, July 27, 1968 (div. 1984); children: Robert Reps, Nyshie Page, Shane William; m. Angela Kaufman, Sept. 20, 1991. BS, Colo. State U., 1968; MS, Ea. Wash. State U., 1970; PhD, Utah State U., 1974. Lic. psychologist, S.D.; cert. chem. dependency counselor level III, S.D.; nat. cert. gambling counselor; nat. cert. alcohol and drug counselor; lic. marriage and family counselor, S.D. Juvenile ct. psychologist, Cedar City, Utah, 1971-72; psychologist in pvt. practice Jackson, Wyo., 1974-83; dir. psychol. svcs. Western Wyo. Mental Health Assn., Jackson, 1977-78, psychologist, 1983—; psychologist, clin. dir. Keystone Treatment Ctr., 1988—. Cons. in field; chief psychologist Grand Teton Nat. Pk., Teton County Sheriff's Office and Police Dept. Copyrights: The Yellowstone Park Game, The Good Health Game, The Grizzly Control Team, Communication from God, Chemical Dependency Counseling, The Mystics, God Talks CD, Peace Will Come CD, The Treatment of Pathological Gambling: A Step By Step Approach. Author: Chemical Dependency Counseling: A Practical Guide, 1997, The Chemical Dependency Treatment Planner, 1998, God Talks to You, 2000, The Addiction Treatment Planner, 2001, 2006, Chemical Dependency Counseling: A Practical Guide, 2d edit., 2002, The Alcoholism and Drug Abuse Patient Workbook, 2003, The Gambling Addiction Patient Workbook, 2003, Treating Alcoholism: Helping Your Clients Find the Road to Recovery, 2004; contbr. articles to profl. jours. Mem. APA, S.D. Psychol. Assn., S.D. Chem. Dependency Assn., Biofeedback Soc. Am. (bd. dirs. Wyo. br.), Wyo. Bd. Psychologist Examiners (pres. 1997, bd. dirs. S.D. coun. problem gambling), Nat. Registere of Health Svc. Providers in Psychology. Address: PO Box 159 Canton SD 57013-0159 Personal E-mail: perk@iw.net.

PERKNER, STANISLAV, academic administrator, educator; b. Kladno, Czech Republic, Oct. 12, 1946; arrived in US, 1992; s. Alois Perkner and Karolina Poslednikova-Perknerova; m. Jitka Pulkrabkova, Oct. 1, 1966 (div.); m. Christine D. Willbanks, Feb. 6, 2006; children: Eva Mazankova, Stanislav, Radim. MA in Social Scis. and Journalism, Charles U., Prague, 1970, PhD in History of Czechoslovakia, 1971; PhD in Gen. History, Comenius U., Bratislava, 1982. From asst. to assoc. prof. Sch. Journalism Charles U., Prague, 1971—90, head of radio and TV dept., dean Sch. Journalism, 1974—90; dir., assoc. prof. Internat. Inst. for the Tng. of Journalists, Prague, 1990—91; dir. libr. and learning ctr., prof. Humphreys Coll., Stockton, Calif., 2001—. Rsch. dir. Internat. Assn. for Mass Comm. Rsch. - Czechoslovak Nat. Com., Prague, 1983—90; vis. lectr. Indian Inst. for Mass Comm. Rsch., New Delhi, 1982; vis. rschr. Ind. U., Bloomington, 1986, vis. prof.; mass media rsch. cons. Fed. Ministry of Fgn. Affairs, Prague, 1983—86; vis. prof. Calif. State U., Univ. of the Pacific, Am. Univ., U. Pitts., Brigham Young U., U. Okla., Wichita State U., San Joaquin Delta Coll.; mem. editl. bd., chmn. The Journalist, Prague, Czech Republic, 1980—91, The Isues of Journalism, Prague, Czech Republic, 1980—91, The Journalist's Quar., Prague, Czech Republic, 1980—91. Co-author: (textbook) Theory and Practice of Radio Journalism (Czechoslovak Radio Ann. award, 1987), (non-fiction) The Language of Drama, Vols. I and II (Guild of Czech Dramatists Ann. award, 1989), A Passion for Radio, (specialized ency.) An Encyclopedia of Journalism. Mem., chair acad. coun. Humphreys Coll., Stockton, 1998—2006; mem. lit., arts, and media Nat. Com. for the State Awards, Prague, 1988—90. Office Phone: 209-235-2933. Business E-Mail: sperkner@humphreys.edu.

PERKO, FRANCIS MICHAEL, church administrator, researcher; b. Chgo., Nov. 6, 1946; s. Frank and Mary (Potochnik) P. BA, MA, Boston Coll., Chestnut Hill, Mass., 1970; MDiv, Loyola U., Chgo., 1975; MA, Stanford U., Calif., 1976, PhD, 1981. Prof. Loyola U., Chgo., 1981—2005; Canon to the Ordinary Episcopal Diocese of the Rio Grande, Albuquerque, 2006—. Adj. asst. prof., Xavier U., Cin. Author: American and Catholic: A Popular History, 1989, To Enlighten the Rising Generation, 1988, A Time to Favor Zion, 1987. Scholar Stanford U., U. London, Ecumenical Inst., Jerusalem; fellow U. Chgo. Mem. AERA, Internat. Soc. Edn. Biography (past pres.), Midwest Hist. Edn. Soc. (past pres.), Altantic Theol. Conf. Episcopalian. Home Phone: 505-286-7877.

PERKO, KENNETH ALBERT, JR., lawyer, art dealer; b. Iron Mountain, Mich., Feb. 9, 1943; s. Kenneth Albert and Alice Ellen (Hamad) P.; m. Susan Jane Roodenburg, Oct. 5, 1968; children: Kathryn Ann, Kenneth Albert. AB in Math. with honors magna cum laude, Princeton U., 1964; JD, Harvard U., 1967. Bar: Ohio, N.Y.; cert. real estate broker, N.Y. Assoc. Milbank, Tweed, Hadley & McCloy, NYC, 1967-79; asst. sec. The Rockefeller Group, NYC, 1979—96, 1998—2002; counsel Radio City Music Hall, NYC, 1985-96, Tishman Speyer Properties, 1996-97; pres. Petrarch LLC, 2002—. Lectr. Cambridge U., 1979, U. Paris, 1979; reviewer Math. Revs., 1980—. Contbr. articles to profl. jours. Trustee Princeton Libr., NYC, 1968—, Rockette Alumnae Found., 1992-2006. Grantee NSF, Blacksburg, Va., 1982. Democrat. Roman Catholic. Home: 325 Old Army Rd Scarsdale NY 10583-2643

PERKOVIC, ROBERT BRANKO, retired international management consultant; b. Belgrade, Yugoslavia, Aug. 27, 1925; came to U.S., 1958, naturalized, 1961; s. Slavoljub and Ruza (Pantelic) P.; m. Jacquelyn Lee Lipscomb, Dec. 14, 1957; children: Bonnie Kathryn, Jennifer Lee. MS in Econs, U. Belgrade, 1954; B.F.T., Am. Grad. Sch. Internat. Mgmt., 1960; grad. Stanford exec. program, Stanford U., 1970. Auditor Gen. Foods Corp., White Plains, NY, 1960-62, controller Mexico City, 1962-64; dir. planning Monsanto Co., Barcelona, 1964-67, dir. fin. Europe, Brussels, 1967-70, dir. fin. planning-internat. St. Louis, 1970-71, asst. treas., 1971-72, Brussels, 1972-74; corp. treas. Fiat-Allis Inc. & BV, Deerfield, Ill., 1974-78; v.p., treas. TRW Inc., Cleve., 1978-88; pres. RBP Internat. Cons., Cleve., 1988—. Former dir. U.S. Bus. Coun. for Southeastern Europe, Inc. Active Cleve. Commn. on Fgn. Relations. Inc. Served with Yugoslavian Army, 1944-47. Mem. Fin. Execs. Inst., Cleve. Treas. Club (past bd. dirs., pres.), Latin Am. Bus. Assn. (co-founder), Mayfield Village (Ohio) Racquet Club. Office: RBP Internat Cons 26 Pepper Creek Dr Cleveland OH 44124-5248

PERKOWSKI, JAN LOUIS, language, literature and folklore educator; b. Perth Amboy, NJ, Dec. 29, 1936; m. Liliana Asenova Daskalova, May 24, 1989. AB magna cum laude, Harvard U., 1959, AM, 1960, PhD, 1965. Asst. prof. U. Calif., Santa Barbara, 1964-65; assoc. prof. U. Tex., Austin, 1965-74; prof. U. Va., Charlottesville, 1974—. Author: A Kashubian Idiolect in U.S., 1969, Vampires, Dwarves & Witches Among the Ontario Kashubs, 1972, Vampires of the Slavs, 1976, Gusle & Ganga Among the Hercegovinians of Toronto, 1978, The Darkling-A Treatise on Slavic Vampirism, 1989, Vampire Lore, 2006; contbr. over 65 articles to profl. jours. Grantee, fellow Ford Found., Harvard U., Kościuszko Found., U. Tex., Am. Philos. Soc., Nat. Mus. Man, U. Va., NEH, Kennan Inst., I.R.E.X., Fulbright, others. Mem. Am. Assn. for the Advancement of Slavic Studies, Am. Assn. Tchrs. of Slavic and East European Langs., Am. Assn. S.E. European Studies, Bulgarian Studies Assn. Office: U Va Dept Slavic Langs & Lits PO Box 400783 Charlottesville VA 22904 Office Phone: 434-924-3548.

PERL, HAROLD, neonatologist, pediatrician; b. July 24, 1950; m. Esther Jayde Strauss, June 18, 1972; children: Ari, Sharona, Gil, Doniel. BA, Yeshiva Coll., 1972; MD, Albert Einstein Coll Medicine, 1975. Diplomate Am. Bd. Pediatrics, cert. in neonatal and perinatal medicine. Intern, resident Montefiore Hosp. and Med. Ctr., NYC, 1975-78; dir. neonatology Hackensack (NJ) U. Med. Ctr., 1991—2005; co-dir. SIDS Ctr. NJ; pres. Gateway-N.W. Consortium NJ, 2005—. Mem. biomed. ethics com. Hackensack U. Med. Ctr., 1985—. Mem. health profls. adv. com. March of Dimes, No. N.J., 1982-97. Home Phone: 201-837-9182; Office Phone: 201-996-5362. E-mail: hperl@humed.com.

PERL, MARTIN LEWIS, physicist, educator, chemical engineer; b. NYC, June 24, 1927; children: Jed, Anne, Matthew, Joseph. B in Chem. Engring., Poly. Inst. Bklyn., 1948; PhD, Columbia U., 1955; ScD (hon.), U. Chgo., 1990. Chem. engr. Gen. Electric Co., 1948—50; asst. prof. physics U. Mich., 1955—58, assoc. prof., 1958—63; prof. Stanford U., 1963—. Author: High Energy Hadron Physics, 1975, Reflections on Experimental Science, 1996; contbr. articles on high energy physics and on relation of sci. to soc. to profl. jours. With U.S. Mcht. Marine, 1944—45, with US Army, 1946—47. Recipient Wolf prize in physics, Wolf Found., Israel, 1982, Nobel prize in physics, 1995. Fellow: Am. Phys. Soc.; mem.: NAS, Am. Acad. Arts and Scis. Home: 3737 El Centro Ave Palo Alto CA 94306-2642 Office Phone: 650-926-2652. Business E-Mail: martin@slac.stanford.edu.

PERL, PETER, editor; b. 1951; With Washington Post, 1981—; staff writer Washington Post Mag., 1996—2004; dir. training & career devel. Washington Post, 2004—06, asst. mng. editor, 2006—. Mem. exec. coun. Washington-Baltimore Newspaper Guild, 2001—; prof. journalism Georgetown U., Washington, Poynter Inst., St. Petersburg, Fla. Recipient over 35 journalism awards. Office: Washington Post 1150 15th St NW Washington DC 20007-0070 Office Phone: 202-334-6000.

PERLBERG, JULES MARTIN, lawyer; b. Chgo., Jan. 28, 1931; s. Maurice and Louise Mae (Schonberger) P.; m. Dora Ann Morris, Dec. 22, 1968; children: Julia, Michael. BBA with high distinction, U. Mich., 1952, JD with high distinction, 1957. Bar: Ill. 1958, D.C. 1964; C.P.A., Ill. Acct. Arthur Andersen & Co., Chgo., 1954-55; faculty U. Mich. Law Sch., Ann Arbor, 1957-58; assoc. Sidley & Austin and predecessor firm, Chgo., 1958-65, ptnr., 1966-98, sr. counsel, 1998—. Mem. Glencoe (Ill.) Bd. Edn., 1980-87, pres., 1985-86; bd. dirs. Juvenile Diabetes Found., Chgo., 1981-2001, v.p. 1983-85, treas., 1988-90, 96-98; exec. bd. Am. Jewish Com., Chgo., 1978-88, v.p., 1981-83; trustee New Trier Twp. Schs., 1987-91, pres., 1989-91; class co-chairperson parents com. Duke U.,

1992-94. 1st lt. U.S. Army, 1952-54. Recipient Gold medal Ill. Soc. C.P.A.s, 1955 Mem. ABA, Chgo. Bar Assn., Lawyers Club, Mid-Day Club (Chgo.), Std. Club, Legal Club, Longboat Key Club. Home (Summer): 568 Westley Rd Glencoe IL 60022-1071 Home (Winter): 1281 Gulf of Mexico Dr Longboat Key FL 34228 Personal E-mail: djperlberg@com.net.

PERLE, EUGENE GABRIEL, lawyer; b. NYC, Dec. 21, 1922; s. Philip and Simme (Meschenberg) P.; m. Ellen Carlotta Kraus, Nov. 26, 1953 (dec. 1964); 1 child, Elizabeth Anne Perle; m. Ruth Friedberg Lerner, May 23, 1972 (div. 1977); m. Patricia Fitzpatrick Sinnott, Jan. 24, 1981. BA, Queens Coll., 1943; JD, Yale U., 1949. Bar: NY 1950, Conn. 1995. Assoc. Cravath, Swaine & Moore, NYC, 1949-53; asst. counsel NY State Moreland Commn. Investigation Harness Racing, NYC, 1953-54; assoc. Gordon, Brady, Caffrey & Keller, NYC, 1954-56; assoc. gen. atty. Time Inc., NYC, 1956-66, pub. counsel, 1966-73, v.p. law, 1973-80, corp. v.p. law, 1980-85; counsel Proskauer & Rose, NYC, 1985-92, Chapman & Fennell, 1992-94; mem. Ohlandt, Greeley, Ruggiero & Perle, Stamford, Conn., 1995-97, sr. counsel, 1998—. Co-author: Perle & Williams Publishing Law, 1988-2006; mem. editl. bd. Yale Law Jour., 1948-49; mem. adv. bd. Bur. Nat. Affairs Patent, Trademark and Copyright Jour., 1972-86; contbr. to Bull. Copyright Soc. USA. Trustee Baron deHirsch Fund, 1959-87, hon. trustee, 1988—; commr. Nat. Commn. New Technol. Uses Copyrighted Works, 1975-78; bd. dirs. NY Sch. Circus Arts, Inc., 1979-87, Am. Arbitration Assn., 1979-84; justice of peace City of Norwalk, Conn., 1960-63. Lt. USNR, 1943-46. Mem. ABA (chmn. copyright divsn. 1970-71, 86-87, chmn. com. copyright new tech. 1971-73, chmn. com. econs. profession 1976, coun. patent, trademark copyright sect. 1979-83, governing bd. forum com. comms. law 1979-85, chmn. related fields future devels. divsn. forum com. entertainment sports industries 1979), Copyright Soc. USA (trustee 1962-64, 69-70, 71-74, pres. 1976-78, hon. trustee 1978—), US Trademark Assn. (bd. dirs. 1969-72, 74-77, v.p. 1972-73), Assn. Bar City NY, Sunningdale Country Club, Century Assn., Banyan Golf Club of Palm Beach. Democrat. Office: Ohlandt Greeley Ruggiero & Perle One Landmark Sq Stamford CT 06901 Office Phone: 203-327-4500. E-mail: egperle@ix.netcom.com, egperle@ogrp.com.

PERLE, GEORGE, composer; b. Bayonne, NJ, May 6, 1915; s. Joseph and Mary (Sanders) Perlman; m. Laura Slobe, 1940; m. Barbara Philips, Aug. 11, 1958 (dec.); children: Kathy, Annette; 1 stepchild, Max Massey; m. Shirley Gabis Rhoads, June 6, 1982; stepchildren: Paul Rhoads, Daisy Rhoads. MusB, DePaul U., 1938; MusM, Am. Conservatory of Music, 1942; PhD, NYU, 1956. Faculty U. Louisville, 1949-57, U. Calif., Davis, 1957-61, Juilliard Sch. Music, 1963, Yale U., 1965-66, U. So. Calif., summer 1965, Tanglewood, summers 1967, 80, 87; from asst. prof. to prof. CUNY, 1961-85, prof. emeritus, 1985—; composer-in-residence San Francisco Symphony, 1989-91. Vis. Birge-Cary prof. music SUNY, Buffalo, 1971-72; vis. prof. U. Pa., 1976, 80, Columbia U., 1979, 83; vis. Ernest Bloch prof. music U. Calif., Berkeley, 1989; vis. disting. prof. music NYU, N.Y.C., 1994. Author: Serial Composition and Atonality 1962, 6th edit., 1991, Twelve-Tone Tonality, 1977, 2d edit., 1996, The Operas of Alban Berg, vol. 1, 1980, vol. 2, 1985, The Listening Composer, 1990, The Right Notes, 1995, Style and Idea in the Lyric Suite of Alban Berg, 1995, 2d edit., 2001; contbr. articles in Am., fgn. mus. jours.; composer: Pantomime, Interlude and Fugue, 1937, Little Suite for Piano, 1939, Two Rilke Songs, 1941, Sonata for Solo Viola, 1942, Three Sonatas for Clarinet, 1943, Piano Piece, 1945, Hebrew Melodies for Cello, 1945, Lyric Piece for Cello and Piano, 1946, Six Preludes for Piano, 1946, Sonata for Solo Cello, 1947, Solemn Procession for Band, 1947, Sonata for Piano, 1950, Three Inventions for Piano, 1957, Quintet for Strings, 1958, Wind Quintet I, 1959, Sonata I for Solo Violin, 1959, Wind Quintet II, 1960, Fifth String Quartet, 1960-67, Three Movements for Orchestra, 1960, Monody I for flute, 1960, Music for The Birds of Aristophanes, 1961, Monody II for double bass 1962, Serenade I for Viola and Chamber Ensemble, 1962, Three Inventions for Bassoon, 1962, Sonata II for Solo Violin, 1963, Short Sonata for Piano, 1964, Solo Partita for Violin and Viola, 1965, Six Bagatelles for Orch., 1965, Concerto for Cello and Orch., 1966, Wind Quintet III, 1967, Serenade II for Chamber Ensemble, 1968, Toccata for Piano, 1969, Suite in C for Piano, 1970, Fantasy-Variations for Piano, 1971, Sonata Quasi una Fantasia for Clarinet and Piano, 1972, Seventh String Quartet, 1973, Songs of Praise and Lamentation for chorus and orch. 1974, Six Etudes for Piano, 1976, 13 Dickinson Songs, 1978, Concertino for Piano, Winds, and Timpani, 1979, A Short Symphony, 1980; Ballade for Piano, 1981, Sonata a quattro, 1982, Serenade III for Piano and Chamber Ensemble, 1983, Six New Etudes for Piano, 1984, Wind Quintet IV, 1984, Sonata for Cello and Piano, 1985, Sonatina for Piano, 1986, Sonata a cinque, 1986, Dance Fantasy for Orch., 1986, Lyric Intermezzo for fifteen players, 1987, Lyric Intermezzo for piano, 1987, New Fanfares for brass ensemble, 1987, Sinfonietta, 1987, Windows of Order for string quartet, 1988, Sextet for winds and piano, 1988, Concerto for Piano and Orch., 1990, Sinfonietta II, 1990, Concerto No. 2 for Piano and Orch., 1992, Adagio for Orch., 1992, Transcendental Modulations (commd. for 150 anniversary N.Y. Philharmonic), 1993, Phantasyplay for Piano, 1994, Duos for French horn and string quartet, 1995, Six Celebratory Inventions for Piano, 1995, Critical Moments for Six Players, 1996, Chansons Cachées for Piano, 1997, Musical Offerings for Piano (left hand alone), 1998, Brief Encounters for string quartet, 1998, Nine Bagatelles for Piano, 1999, Critical Moments (2) for Six Players, 2001, Triptych for Solo Violin and Piano, 2003, Bassoon Music for Solo Bassoon, 2004, Lyric Suite, Universal, 2005, The Operas of Alban Berg, 2005 (Otto Kinkeldey award); writer, editor: Preface of Berg's Lyric Suite, 2005. Served with AUS, 1943-46, ETO, PTO. Recipient award Nat. Inst. Arts and Letters, 1977, Pulitzer prize, 1986; Guggenheim fellow, 1966-67, 74-75, MacArthur fellow, 1986; grantee Am. Council Learned Socs., 1968-69, NEA, 1978-79, 85. Fellow Am. Acad. Arts and Scis.; mem. Am. Musicol. Soc., ASCAP (Deems Taylor award 1973, 78, 81), Am. Acad. Arts and Letters. Home Phone: 212-663-6556. Personal E-mail: gxperle@aol.com.

PERLE, RICHARD NORMAN, former federal agency administrator; b. NYC, Sept. 16, 1941; s. Jack Harold and Martha Gloria Perle; m. Leslie Joan Barr, July 31, 1977; 1 child, Jonathan. BA, U. So. Calif., 1964; postgrad. in econs., U. London, 1962-63; MA, Princeton U., 1967. Prof. staff mem. subcom. nat. security Senate Com. on Govt. Ops., Washington, 1970-72; profl. staff mem. to Senator Henry M. Jackson committee on armed services U.S. Senate, Washington, 1969-80; asst. sec. internat. security policy US Dept. Def., Washington, 1981-87; resident fellow Am. Enterprise Inst. for Pub. Policy Rsch., Washington, 1987—. Mem. Def. Policy Bd., 1987—2004, chmn., 2001—03; co-founder Project for the New Am. Century. Prodr.: (TV miniseries) The Gulf Crisis: The Road to War, 1992; author: (non-fiction) Hard Line, 1992; author: (with David Frum) An End to Evil: How to Win the War on Terror, 2004; editor: Reshaping Western Security, 1991. Office: Am Enterprise Inst Pub Policy Rsch 1150 17th St NW Washington DC 20036-4603 E-mail: rperle@aei.org.

PERLEGOS, GEORGE, electronics executive; b. Greece; BS Electrical Engring., 1972. With American Microsystems; design engr. Intel, 1974—81; co-founder, v.p., tech. Seeq Technology, 1981—84; founder, pres., CEO, chmn. Atmel Corp., San Jose, 1984—2006, bd. dirs., 1984—. Achievements include inventing EEPROM technology, the basic technology for flash memory. Office: Atmel Inc 2325 Orchard Pkwy San Jose CA 95131-1034

PERLER, BRUCE ALAN, vascular surgeon; b. New Bedford, Mass., Mar. 12, 1950; s. J. Leonard and Muriel Marcia (Katzman) P.; children: Mason, Rachel. AB in Zoology summa cum laude, Duke U., Durham, NC, 1972, MD, 1976; MBA, Johns Hopkins U., Balt., 2004. Diplomate Am. Bd. Gen. Surgery, cert. spl. qualificatons in gen. vascular surgery; lic. physician, Mass., Md. Surg. intern Mass. Gen. Hosp., Boston, 1976-77, surg. resident, 1977-81, clin. and rsch. fellow in vascular surgery, 1981-82; clin. fellow surgery Harvard Med. Sch., 1977-82; asst. prof. surgery Johns Hopkins U. Sch. Medicine, Balt., 1982-88, assoc. prof., 1988—97, prof., 1997—; asst. surgery Mass. Gen. Hosp., Boston, 1981-82; dir. noninvasive lab., mem. med. bd., vice-chmn. med. staff com. Johns Hopkins Hosp., Balt., 1982—, chief divsn. vascular surgery, 2002—, attending vascular surgeon, 1982—, med. dir. intermediate care unit, 1989-91, mem. med. bd., 1995—99; Julius H. Jacobson II prof. Johns Hopkins U. Sch. Medicine, Balt., 2002—. Cons. vascular surgery Johns Hopkins Bayview Med. Ctr., Balt., 1982—, circulatory system devices panel Ctr. Devices and Radiologic Health, FDA, Washington, 1989—, Rsch. Adv. Group, VA, Washington, 1993—; mem. diagnostic and therapeutic tech. assessment panel AMA, 1991; lectr. throughout U.S. and Can. Mem. editl. bd. Jour. Vascular Surgery, asst. editor, assoc. editor, 2006—; editl. bd. Jour. Vascular Endovascular Surgery, Annals of Vascular Surgery; contbr. articles to profl. jours., chpts. to books. Rsch. grantee NIH, 1986-87, 92-94. Mem. ACS, Am. Surg. Assn., Soc. Vascular Surgery (bd. dirs.), So. Assn. Vascular Surgery (program com. 1992-95, exec. coun. 2004—), Ea. Vascular Soc. (membership com. 1991-94, sec. 2001-, pres. 2004-), Soc. Univ. Surgeons, Assn. Acad. Surgery, Chesapeake Vascular Soc. (pres. 1992-93), Balt. Acad. Surgery, Duke Med. Alumni Assn., Phi Beta Kappa. Office: Johns Hopkins Hosp - Harvey 611 Dept Surgery 600 N Wolfe St Dept Surgery Baltimore MD 21287-8611

PERLESS, ELLEN, advertising executive; b. NYC, Sept. 9, 1941; d. Joseph B. and Bertha (Messinger) Kaplan; m. Robert L. Perless, July 2, 1965. Student, Smith Coll., 1958-59; BA, Bard Coll., 1962. Copywriter Doyle, Dane Bernbach, NYC, 1964-70, Young & Rubicam, NYC, 1970-74, creative supr., 1974-76, v.p., creative supr., 1977, v.p., assoc, creative dir., 1978, sr. v.p., assoc. creative dir., 1979-84; v.p., assoc. creative dir. Leber Katz Ptnrs., 1984-85, sr. v.p., creative dir., 1986-87; sr. v.p., sr. creative dir. Foote Cone & Belding, NYC, 1987-93, sr. v.p., group creative dir., 1994—2002; sr. v.p., sr. creative dir. Euro RSCG Life Becker, NYC, 2003—04; creative cons. pvt. practice Greenwich, Conn., 2004—. Author: numerous poems. Recipient Clio awards, Andy awards, awards Art Dirs. Club N.Y., N.Y. Festivals, One Club. Home: 37 Langhorne Ln Greenwich CT 06831-2611 E-mail: ellen@perless.com.

PERLGUT, MARK RALPH, public relations executive; b. New Brunswick, NJ, Oct. 4, 1942; s. Louis Eliot and Mildred Ruth (Shapiro) P.; m. Phyllis Norma Hershon, May 21, 1946; children: Lauren, Andrew. AB in History, Rutgers U., 1964; MS in Journalism, Columbia U., 1965. Investigative reporter Atlantic City (N.J.) Press, 1965-67; nat. and local reporter N.Y. Times, 1967-72; assoc. editor McGraw-Hill Inc., 1973-77; dir. new ventures Instnl. Investor, Inc., 1977-78; editl. mgr., personal speechwriter Donald T. Regan Merrill Lynch & Co., Inc., 1978-80; sr. policy writer N.Y. Stock Exch., Inc., 1980-82; v.p., dir. policy comms. Chem. Bank, 1982-84, v.p., dep. head of corp. comms. divsn., 1984-85; pres. Mark Perlgut Pub. Rels., 1985-87; v.p., editorial dir., account group supr. Fin. Rels. Bd., Inc., 1987-90; pres. Perlgut Pub. Rels., Inc., 1990-96, Investor Rels. Co. N.Y., 1992-96; sr. v.p., mng. dir. investor rels. divsn. Lobsenz Stevens, Inc., NYC, 1996-99; exec. prin., mng. dir., investor rels. Publicis Dialog, NYC, 1999—2001; mng. dir. Stern & Co. Comm., NYC, 2001—02; pres. Perlgut Group Comms., NYC, 2002—. Author: Electricity Across the Border: The U.S.-Canadian Experience, 1978. Chmn. Fair Harbor (N.Y.) Community Assn., 1980-82. Recipient 1st pl. award Fin. World Ann. Report Competition, 1st pl. award ARC awards Ann. Report Competition, 1989. Mem. Nat. Investor Rels. Inst. Office: 230 W 41st St New York NY 10036 Business E-Mail: mark@perlgutgroup.com.

PERLICK, RICHARD ALLAN, steel company executive; b. Chgo., June 23, 1947; s. Allan Arthur and Lorraine Perlick; m. Sharon Behrendt, Mar. 29, 1969; children: Jill Sharon, Timothy Richard, David Matthew. BS in Metall. Engring., Mich. Tech. U., 1969. Corrosion engr. CarTech Specialty Steel Corp., Reading, Pa., 1969-71, nondestructive test engr. Union, NJ, 1971-75; quality control sr. engr. heavy products AlTech Specialty Steel Corp., Watervliet, NY, 1975-78, gen. supt. bar finish Dunkirk, NY, 1978-79, sr. supr. metallurgist rod mill, 1979-86, mgr. product metallurgy, 1986-87, wire mill supt., 1987-89, sr. product metallurgist, 1989-90; gen. mgr. wire plant Techalloy Co. (now Ctrl. Wire Group), Union, Ill., 1990—94, 1994—96, v.p. metallurgy, process and quality depts., 1997—. Pub. spkr. and trainer on metallurgy of stainless steels; expert in field. Contbr. articles on stainless steel wire products to profl. jours. Cubmaster, scoutmaster Boy Scouts Am., Fredonia, N.Y., 1982-90; mem. ch. choir St. Paul Luth., Dunkirk, 1980-82. Recipient Pres.'s Scoutmaster's award Boy Scouts Am., 1988. Mem. AIChE, ASTM, Nat. Assn. Corrosion Engrs., Indsl. Forming and Fasterner Inst., Am. Soc. Materials, Wire Assn. Internat. (bd. dir. WAI Midwest), Am. Soc. Surface Finishing, Soc. Automotive Engrs., Kiwanis. Conservative. Avocations: vegetable gardening, woodworking, fishing, golf, camping. Home: 1758 Woodhaven Dr Crystal Lake IL 60014-1940 Office: Ctrl Wire PO Box 423 Olson And Jefferson St Union IL 60180 Office Phone: 815-923-2131 x143. Business E-Mail: rperlick@centralwire.com.

PERLIN, ARTHUR SAUL, chemistry professor; b. Sydney, NS, Can., July 7, 1923; s. Benjamin and Eva (Gaum) P.; m. Ruth Laurel Freedman, Nov. 18, 1950; children: Anna, Louise, Deborah, Myra, David BSc, McGill U., Can., 1944, MSc, 1946, PhD, 1949. Rsch. officer Nat. Rsch. Council Can., Ottawa, Ont., Can., 1948-67; E.B. Eddy prof. chemistry McGill U., Montreal, Que., Can., 1967-91, prof. chemistry emeritus, 1991—; rsch. scientist Pulp and Paper Rsch. Inst. Can., Montreal, Que., 1967—. Contbr. articles to profl. jours., chpts. to books; patentee in field Fellow Royal Soc. Can., Chem. Inst. Can.; mem. Am. Chem. Soc. (C.S. Hudson award 1979) Office: McGill U Dept Chemistry Montreal PQ Canada H3A 2K6 Office Phone: 514-398-6188.

PERLIN, GARY LAURENCE, diversified financial services company executive; b. Chgo., May 8, 1951; s. Maurice and Berna (Bardige) P.; m. Amy R., July 4, 1976; children: Jonah, Jacob. BS in Fgn. Svc., Georgetown U., 1972; MS, London Sch. Econs., 1974; MPA, Princeton U., NJ, 1975. Staff aide to US Senator Adlai Stevenson III, Washington, 1972-73; economist The World Bank, Washington, 1975-78, dir. fin. sector devel. dept., 1993—96, v.p., treas., 1996—99, sr. v.p., CFO, 1999—2003; trader J. Aron & Co., NYC, 1978-80; cons., v.p. Hadley Lockwood, NYC, 1980-82; v.p. risk mgmt. Fed. Nat. Mortgage Assn. (Fannie Mae), Washington, 1982-85, sr. v.p. fin., treas., 1985—93; sr. v.p., CFO, prin. acctg. officer Capital One Fin. Corp., McLean, Va., 2003—. Mem. Commodity Futures Trading Commn., Fin. Products Adv. Com., Washington, 1986-91; dir. Future Industry Assn., 1991—; treas. The European Inst., 1991—. Office: Capital One Fin Corp 1680 Capital One Dr Mc Lean VA 22102 *

PERLIN, JONATHAN BRIAN, health services company executive, former federal agency administrator; b. 1961; s. Seymour Perlin; m. Donna Perlin; 1 child, Benjamin. MS in Health Adminstrn., Va. Commonwealth U., Ph.D in Pharmacology & Toxicology. Med. dir. quality improvement Med. Coll. Va. Hosps. Va. Commonwealth U., assoc. dir. internal medicine residency tng. prog.; chief quality and performance officer US Dept. Veterans Affairs, Washington, 1999—2002, dep. under sec. health, 2002—04, acting chief rsch. & devel. officer, 2003—04, acting under sec. for health (Veterans Health Adminstrn.), 2004—05, under sec. for health, 2005—06; sr. v.p. quality, chief med. officer HCA Inc., Nashville, 2006—. Contbr. articles to profl. jours. Fellow: ACP. Office: HCA Inc One Park Plz Nashville TN 37203

PERLIN, SEYMOUR, psychiatrist, educator; b. Passaic, NJ, Sept. 27, 1925; s. Samuel and Fanny (Horowitz) P.; m. Ruth Joan Rudolph, Aug. 21, 1958; children: Jonathan Brian, Steven Michael, Jeremy Francis. Student, Johns Hopkins U., 1943-44; BA summa cum laude, Princeton U., 1946; MD, Columbia U., 1950; grad., Washington Psychoanalytic Inst. Diplomate Am. Bd. Psychiatry and Neurology. Intern Univ. Hosp., Ann Arbor, Mich., 1951-52; resident N.Y. State Psychiat. Inst., 1950-51, 53-54, Manhattan State Hosp., 1952; practice medicine specializing in psychiatry and psychoanalysis Bethesda, Md., 1954-59, Stanford, Calif., 1959-60, NYC, 1960-63, Balt., 1964-72, Bethesda, 1974—; chief div. psychiatry Montefiore Hosp., 1960-63; dir. clin. care and tng. Henry Phipps Psychiat. Clinic, Johns Hopkins Hosp., 1964-72; sr. research scholar Ctr. for Bioethics, Kennedy Inst., Georgetown U., Washington, 1974-78; clin. prof. psychiatry UCLA Sch. Medicine, 1973-74, George Washington U. Sch. Medicine, 1974-76, prof. to prof. emeritus, 1977-97, 97—, also dir. residency tng., 1977-93; lectr. psychiatry Columbia U., 1963-64; assoc. prof. psychiatry Johns Hopkins Sch. Medicine, 1964-65, prof., 1966-72, dep. chmn. dept. psychiatry and behavioral scis., 1969-72; program dir. Fellowship Program in Suicidology, 1967-72; adv. council Univ. health services Princeton, 1970-82. Vis. fellow Princeton U., 1973, Oxford U., 1974; Joseph P. Kennedy fellow medicine, law and ethics, 1974-75; chief sect. psychiatry Lab. Clin. Sci., NIMH, 1955-59, mem. clin. program-project com., 1967-70; fellow Ctr. Advanced Study in Behavioral Scis., 1959-60; chmn. mental health study sect. B, div. research grants NIH, 1964-66; cons. Community Mental Health Services, Md. Dept. Mental Hygiene, 1964-72; chmn. bd. dirs. Youth Suicide Nat. Ctr., 1985-87. Cons. editor: Jour. Suicide and Life Threatening Behavior, 1970-89; editorial bd.: Johns Hopkins Med. Jour, 1970-72; editor: Handbook for the Study of Suicide; co-editor: Ethical Issues in Death and Dying; contbr. numerous articles to med. jours. Served with USNR, 1944-46, with USPHS, 1954-58. Recipient Meirhoff award in pathology, 1950, Bicentennial Silver medal for achievement in psychiatry, 1967, both Coll. Phys. and Surg. Columbia. Fellow Am. Psychiat. Assn. (named Disting. Life fellow 2003); mem. Am. Coll. Psychiatry, Washington Psychoanalytic Soc., Med. Soc. D.C., Washington Psychiat. Soc., Am. Assn. Suicidology (pres. 1969-70, Dublin award 1978, ann. lectureship in suicidology in his name George Washington U. 1995), Phi Beta Kappa. Home and Office: 5125 Westbard Ave Bethesda MD 20816-1413 Office Phone: 301-229-5330.

PERLINGIERI, ILYA SANDRA, art historian, writer; b. NYC; d. Nathaniel Gordon and Naomi Miller Coval-Apel; children: Blake Andrew, Chemynne Alida. BA, U. Mo., 1966; MA, San Diego State U., 1984; PhD, Columbia Pacific U., 1999. Dir. Ilya Sandra Perlingieri Sewing and Design Sch., San Diego and Miami, Fla., 1973-92; asst. prof., chmn. dept. fashion design Marist Coll., Poughkeepsie, N.Y., 1984-85; mem. faculty Fashion Inst. Design, San Diego, 1986-87, LA, 1999—2000. Adj. prof. San Diego State U., 1989—92; dir. Textile Arts and Conservation Ctr., San Diego, 1979—83; guest lectr. Met. Mus. Art, NYC, Nat. Gallery, London, Art Inst. Chgo., Los Angeles County Mus. Art, Nat. Gallery, Washington, NYU, Yale U., others; environ. writer; guest Sta. PBS-TV, Sta. NPR, Sta. NBC-TV, BBC, London. Author: Sofonisba Anguissola: The First Great Woman Artist of the Renaissance, 1992, French. edit., 1992, The Uterine Crisis, 2003; contbg. editor: Threads mag.; contbr. articles to profl. jours.; environ. columnist:. Dir. edn. Nomad Mus. Tribal Art, Portland, 1999—2001. Recipient award, Prague Quadriennale, 1979, Gildred Found., 1980, Sameul H. Kress Found., 1989, 1999; grantee, Thanks be to Grandmother Winifred Found., 2001; French Fgn. Ministry Lecture grantee, 1995. Mem.: Am. Bot. Coun., Early Modern Women (charter), Met. Mus. Art Huntington Libr. and Art Collections, Royal Hort. Soc. (London), Costume Soc. Am. (charter), Renaissance Soc. Am. Avocations: playing classical piano, lyric soprano, organic gardening.

PERLIS, DONALD M., artist; b. NYC, July 29, 1941; s. Herman and Sylvia M. (Marks) P.; m. Theresa Brown, June 9, 1968. Student, Art Students League, 1961, Sch. Visual Arts, NYC, 1965, Skowhegan Sch., 1965. One-man show Sindin Gallery, N.Y.C., 1994, 95, Walter Wickiser Gallery, N.Y.C., 1996-97, Claudia Carr Gallery, N.Y.C., 1999; exhibited in group shows Whitney Mus., N.Y.C., Graham Gallery, 1971, 75, Sindin Galleries, 1993, 95, Charas-Elbohio, 1993; exhbns. include Nat. Mus. Poland, Gdansk, 2007, NAD, 2007; represented by Denise Bibro Gallery, N.Y.C.; documentary film on artist produced by Time Capsule Films, 1993; author: (monograph) Allegories of Love, 1995. Mem. NAD. Home: 110 Duane St #5R New York NY 10007

PERLIS, MICHAEL FREDRICK, lawyer; b. NYC, June 3, 1947; s. Leo and Betty F. (Gantz) P.; children: Amy Hannah, David Matthew, William Garrison, Grace Joanne; m. Colleen M. DeLee, Sept. 8, 2003; children: William G., Grace J. BS in Fgn. Svc., Georgetown U., 1968, JD, 1971. Bar: DC 1971, NY 1993, US Dist. Ct. DC 1971, U.S. Ct. Appeals 1971, DC Ct. Appeals 1971, Calif. 1980, US Dist. Ct. (no. dist.) Calif. 1980, US Dist. Ct. (cen. dist.) Calif. 1985, US Ct. Appeals (9th cir.) 1980, US Supreme Ct., 1980, NY 1993. Law clerk DC Ct. Appeals, Washington, 1971-72; asst. corp. counsel DC, Washington, 1972-74; counsel US SEC, div. enforcement, Washington, 1974-75, br. chief, 1975-77, asst. dir., 1977-80; ptnr. Pettit & Martin, San Francisco, 1980-89, ptnr., fedl. securities law litig., Stroock & Stroock & Lavan, LA, 1989—, mem. operating exec. com.; adj. prof. Cath. U. Am., 1979-80. Mem. ABA (co-chmn. subcom. securities and commodities litigation 1982-83), DC Bar Assn., Calif. State Bar Assn. Office: Stroock & Stroock & Lavan 2029 Century Park E Ste 1800 Los Angeles CA 90067-3086 Office Phone: 310-556-5821. Business E-Mail: mperlis@stroock.com.

PERLIS, SHARON A., lawyer; b. New Orleans; d. Rogers I. and Dorothy Perlis. BA in French, Principia Coll., 1967; JD, Tulane U., 1970. Officer, dir. Perlis, Inc., New Orleans, 1973—2003; pres. SILREP Internat. Co., Metairie, 1984—; officer, dir. Internat. Adv. Svcs., Inc., New Orleans, 1985-89; prin. Perlis & Assocs., Metairie, 1985—2005; pres. Sharon A. Perlis P.C., 1981—2005. Legal counsel La. Ins. Rating Commn., 1980-84; adminstrv. law judge State of La., 1980-84, mem. Econ. Devel. Adv. Coun., 1982-84; exec. com. small bus. coun. Bd. of Trade, 1987-89, chmn. small bus. coun., 1988, exec. com. East Jefferson coun., 1989-96; dir. World Trade Ctr., 1985-2005, vice chmn. internat. bus. com.; dir. New Orleans br. Fed. Res. Bank of Atlanta, 1982-88, chmn., 1984, 86, 88; dir. Metairie Bank & Trust, 1997-2005; bd. of commr. Port of New Orleans, 1992-96, vice chmn., 1995, chmn. bd., 1996; del. U.S. Def. Dept.'s Joint Civilian Orientation Conf., 1997; adj. prof. A.B. Freeman Sch. Bus., Tulane U.; mem. Coun. for a Better La.; mediator U.S. Postal Svc., Econ. Devel. Commn.; mem. La. Econ. Devel. Commn., Inst. Women in Govt., Nicholls State U.; mem. internat. adv. bd. A.J. Butts Sch. Bus., Loyola U. Mem. human rels. commn. City of New Orleans, 1992-93, Commn. To Reorganize City Govt., Leadership La., 2001; mem. exec. bd. La. Coun. Econ. Edn., 1986-89, Pvt. Enterprise Edn. Found., 1986-89; state del. White House Conf. on Small Bus., La. rep. internat. trade issues, 1986; dir. Metro YMCA, 1990-97; exec. com. agy. rels. United Way, 1987-90; mem. exec. com. Jr. Achievement Project Bus., 1987; vice chmn. La. Dist. Export Coun.; bd. dirs. Bur. Govtl. Rsch.; bd. dirs. La. Internat. Trade Commn.; mem. adv. bd. Internat. Program for Non-profit Leadership; mem. Econ. Devel. Commn., State of La.; mem. New Orleans Leadership Inst.; vice chmn. bus.-higher edn. coun. U New Orleans; trustee New Orleans Pub. TV Found.; mem. New Orleans Pub. R.R. Commn.; mem. Jefferson Econ Devel. Commn.; commr. New Orleans Pub. Belt RR. Recipient Achiever's award Woman Bus. owners Assn., 1994, Jefferson Econ. Devel. Commn. award, 1994, Advocacy of Yr. award Small Bus. Adminstrn., 1988, 89, Iberville award New Orleans Pub. Group, 1996, Women of the Yr. award New Orleans Pub. Group, 2000, Patty Strong award Jefferson-25, 2000; named Young Leadership Coun. Role Model, 2001. Fellow Loyla Inst. of

Politics, U. New Orleans Govt. Leadership Inst.; mem. ABA, Bankers Assn., Am. Arbitration Assn. (arbitrator/mediator), Jefferson Bar Assn., Orleans Bar Assn., Federal Bar Assn., Adv. Coun. Federalist Soc., La. Estate Planning Coun., La. Bar Assn., Gov.'s Commn. on Internat. Trade Devel., New Orleans Regional C. of C. (bd. dirs. 1990-2001), New Orleans Regional Leadership Inst., New Orleans Area Polit. Action Coun. (pres.), Leadership La., Greater New Orleans Found., New Orleans Estate Planning Coun. Avocations: reading, sailing, tennis. Office: Perlis & Assocs 6069 Magazine St New Orleans LA 70118-6006

PERLMAN, BARRY STEVEN, sociologist, educator; b. Bklyn., Aug. 25, 1944; s. Aubrey and Grace Perlman; m. Joan Paul Perlman, Apr. 29, 1984; children: Adam, Ryan. AA, Queensborough C.C., 1964; BA, Queens Coll., CUNY, 1966; postgrad., Adelphi U., 1966—68, Temple U., 1968—71. Lectr. Chestnut Hill Coll., Phila., 1968—69, LaSalle U., Phila., 1968—70; instr. Temple U., Phila., 1968—71; assoc. prof. C.C. Phila., Phila., 1971—, chmn. Dept. Social Scis., 1983—89. Chmn. coms. C.C. Phila., 1973—; reviewer articles various publs.; presenter and session chair profl. meetings and confs. Contbr. articles to profl. jours. Founding mem. Am. Cancer Rsch. Ctr., 1978; key communicator Bensalem Twp. Schs., Pa., 1976—79. Recipient Outstanding Contbn. award, Human Svcs. Careers Student Assn., 1990; fellow, NIMH. Mem.: Human Svcs. Career Assn., Am. Sociol. Assn., Am. Fedn. Tchrs., Nat. Social Sci. Assn. Jewish. Office: Community College Phila 1700 Spring Garden St Philadelphia PA 19130 Office Phone: 215-751-8560.

PERLMAN, BARRY STUART, electrical engineer, researcher, director; b. Bklyn., Dec. 5, 1939; s. Harold Wallace and Jane (Cohen) P.; m. Carolyn Amelia Francis; 1 child, David Matthew. BEE, CCNY, 1961; MSEE, Poly. U. N.Y., 1964; PhD in Electrophysics, Poly. Inst. N.Y., 1973. Mem. tech. staff, comms. lab. RCA Corp., NYC, 1961-68; mem. tech. staff RCA Labs., Princeton, NJ, 1968-81, mgr. microwave rsch. lab., 1981-86, head design automation rsch., 1986-88; chief microwave photonic devices br. Electronics and Power Source Directorate, Army Rsch. Lab., Ft. Monmouth, NJ, 1988-95; dir. electronics divsn. Phys. Scis. Directorate, Army Rsch. Lab., Ft. Monmouth, 1995-96; chief RF and electronics divsn. Sensor and Electron Devices Directorate, Army Rsch. Lab., Ft. Monmouth and Adelphi, Md., 1996-97; R&D Engring. Ctr. staff Comm.-Electronics Command, Ft. Monmouth, 1997-98, chief applied comm., 1998-99; assoc. dir. for tech., prin. scientist Intel and Info Directorate, 1999—2002; assoc. dir. DARPA liaison office Comm. Electronics Rsch., Devel. and Engring. Ctr. Hdqrs. Rsch., Devel. and Engring. Command. Pres., mem. bd. dirs. INTEREX, Los Altos, Calif., 1981—83; rep. adv. group on electron devices, chmn. subpanel on RF Components Office of Undersec. of Def.; chmn. Computational Electronics and Nanoelectronics tech. area High Performance Computing Modernization Program, 1995—2005, program mgr. modeling and simulation Electronic Battlefield Environ. Portfolio, 2000—05, agt. Intelligent RF Front End Program and Tech. Efficient Agile Microsys. Program, 2002—07, chmn. Def. Advanced Rsch. Projects Agy. working group, program mgr., agt. Nanomechanical Array Signal Processors, MTO, sys. study team, modeling/simulation team for FCS comm. Def. Advanced Rsch. Projects Agy.; Def. Advanced Rsch. Projects Agy. agt. analog Spectral Processors, 2006—; Def. Advanced Rsch. Projects Agy. agt. Trusted Electronics, 2006—; NASA/JPL adv. com. for SATCOM sys. on a chip U. Mich.; tech. adv. bds. UCLA; ind. adv. bd. Computer Applications to Electromagnetics Edn. NSF and U. Utah, 1990—94; mem. ind. adv. bd. Computer Applications to Electromagnetics Edn. MIMICAD Ctr., U. Colo., 1989—95; adv. bd. Elec. Engring./WAMI U. So. Fla.; ind. adv. bd. Wireless Comm. NJ Inst. Tech.; Ctr. prof. microwave/lightwave engring. Drexel U., Phila., 1992—2002; ind. adv. bd. U. Hawaii, Manoa, 2003—; advisor to NSF Connection One Inc. Ariz. State U., 2004—; advisor NJ Nanotech. Consortium; mem. R&D Coun. NJ; mem. TAB Informal Antennas and Arrays Using Novel Electronic Materials Ohio State U., 2005—; mem. indsl. adv. bd. Multischale Physics IMPACT Ctr U. Ill. Urbana-Champagne; advisor mobile radio program group Va. Tech., 2006—; advisor Ga. Electronic Design Ctr. Ga. Inst. Tech., 2006—. Editor: Advances in Microwaves, 1974; mem. editl. bd. Wiley Jour. MW.MMW CAD, 1992—; contbr. articles to profl. jours.; patentee in field. Bd. dirs. YMCA, Princeton, 1975-78; pres. Home Owners Assn., E. Windsor, N.J., 1976-78; instr. Am. Heart Assn., N.J., 1978-82; chief rescue squad, E. Windsor, 1978-82. Fellow: IEEE (life; admission and advancement com. 1987—, tech. program chair Sarnoff Symposium 1999—2002); mem.: Comm., Antennas & Propagation, Automated RF Techniques Group (treas. 1984—88, v.p. 1990—91), Cirs. and Sys., Ultrasonics, Ferroelectrics and Frequency Control, Microwave Theory and Tech. Soc. of IEEE (IMS tech. program com. 1980—, editl. bd. chmn. CAD com. MTT-1 1985—92, MTT adcom. 1990—94, chmn. Instersoc. Liaison 1995—97, MTT adcom. 2002—, chmn. meetings and symposia com. 2002—04, chmn. membership svcs. com., repcom tech. adv. bd. 2005—). Avocations: woodworking, photography, pistol/rifle target competition, gardening, gourmet cooking. Office: Army Comm-Electronics Ctr RDEC Hdqrs AMSRD CER TSP Bldg 2700 Fort Monmouth NJ 07703-5000 Office Phone: 732-427-4883. Personal E-mail: bperlman@comcast.net. Business E-Mail: barry.perlman@us.army.mil.

PERLMAN, BETH S., information technology executive; b. NY; BS in Mgmt. Info. Sys., Fin., Syracuse Univ. With JP Morgan, 1982—90; group mgr., fin., acctg. sys. Kidder Peabody & Co., 1990—93; project mgr., equity derivatives tech. Lehman Brothers, 1993—95; dir. to v.p. Enron Wholesale Trading Tech., 1995—2002; chief info. officer Constellation Energy, Balt., 2002—, and sr. v.p., 2004—. Bd. dir. Am. Technion Soc. Bd. dir. Women's Ctr., Md. Devel. Ctr. Named Oracle Applications Implementer of Yr., 2005; named one of Top 25 Chief Tech. Officers, InfoWorld mag., 2006. Office: Constellation Energy 750 E Pratt St Baltimore MD 21202 Office Phone: 410-783-2800. *

PERLMAN, BURTON, judge; b. Dec. 17, 1924; s. Phillip and Minnie Perlman; m. Alice Weihl, May 20, 1956; children: Elizabeth, Sarah, Nancy, Daniel. BE, Yale U., 1945, ME, 1947; LLB, U. Mich., 1952. Bar: Ohio 1959, N.Y. 1953, Conn. 1952, U.S. Dist. Ct. (so. and ea. dists.) N.Y. 1954, U.S. Dist. Ct. (so. dist.) Ohio 1959, U.S. Ct. Appeals (2d cir.) 1953, U.S. Ct. Appeals (6th cir.) 1959. Assoc. Armand Lackenbach, NYC, 1952—58; pvt. practice Cin., 1958—61; assoc. Paxton and Seasongood, Cin., 1961—67; ptnr. Schmidt, Effton, Josselson and Weber, Cin., 1968—71; U.S. magistrate U.S. Dist. Ct. (so. dist.) Ohio, 1971—76, U.S. bankruptcy judge, 1976—. Chief bankruptcy judge so. dist. Ohio, 1986—93; adj. prof. U. Cin. Law Sch., 1976—. With US Army, 1944—46. Mem.: ABA, Cin. Bar Assn., Am. Judicature Soc., Fed. Bar Assn. Office: US Bankruptcy Ct Atrium 2 8th Fl 221 E 4th St Cincinnati OH 45202-4124

PERLMAN, DAVID, journalist; b. Balt., Dec. 30, 1918; s. Jess and Sara Perlman; m. Anne Salz, Oct. 15, 1941 (dec. 2002); children: Katherine, Eric, Thomas. AB, Columbia U., 1939; MS, Columbia U. Sch. Journalism, 1940. Reporter Bismarck Capital, ND, 1940, San Francisco Chronicle, 1940—41, reporter, sci. editor, 1952-77, city editor, 1977-79, assoc. editor, sci. editor, 1979—; reporter New York Herald Tribune, Paris, NYC, 1945-49; European corr. Colliers mag. and New York Post, 1949-51. Regents prof. human biology U. Calif., San Francisco, 1974; vis. lectr. China Assn. Sci. and Tech., Beijing, Chengdu, Shanghai; sci. writer-in-residence U. Wis., 1989. Contbr. articles to maj. mags. Founding dir. Squaw Valley (Calif.) Cmty. Writers; bd. dirs. Alan Guttmacher Inst., 1990—99; trustee Scientists Inst. Pub. Info., 1986—94; chmn. pub. svc. award com. Nat. Sci. Bd., 1998—2001. With inf. USAAF, 1941—45. Recipient Atomic Indsl. Forum award, 1975, Sci. Writing award, AAAS, Exploratorium award, 1977, Ralph Coates Roe medal, ASME, 1978, Margaret Sanger Cmty. Svc. award, 1981, Fellows' medal, Calif. Acad. Scis., 1984, Career Achievement award, Soc. Profl. Journalists, 1989, Glenn T. Seaborg award, Internat. Platform Assn., 1993, Sustained Achievement award for sci. journalism, Am. Geophys. Union, 1997, medal, U. Calif., San Francisco, 2000, Journalism award, Columbia U., 2000, award for disting. med. reporting, San Francisco Med. Soc., 2000, Grady-Stack award for sci. journalism, Am. Chem. Soc., 2001, John Wesley Powell award, U.S. Geol. Survey, 2004, Hearst Eagle award, 2004; Poynter Inst. fellow, Yale U., 1984, Carnegie Corp. fellow, Stanford U., 1987. Fellow: Calif. Acad. Scis.; mem.: AAAS (mem. com. Pub. Understanding Sci. 1985—90, adv. bd. Science-81-86 mag.), Astron. Soc. Pacific (bd. dirs. 1976—78), Nat. Assn. Sci. Writers (pres. 1970—71, Disting. Sci. Journalism award 1994), Coun. Advancement Sci. Writing (pres. 1976—80), Sigma Xi. Office: San Francisco Chronicle 901 Mission St San Francisco CA 94103-2905 Business E-Mail: dperlman@sfchronicle.com.

PERLMAN, DOUG, sports association executive; m. Lisa Perlman; 1 child, Taylor; 1 child, Carson. BA, Duke Univ., 1990; JD, Univ. Va., 1993. Assoc. atty. Proskauer Rose, 1993—95; assoc. couns. NHL, 1995, sr. councilor legal and bus. affairs, group enterprises, v.p. bus. affairs, spl. asst. to COO, now sr. v.p. television and media ventures. Office: NHL 4th Fl 1251 Ave Americas New York NY 10020

PERLMAN, HARVEY STUART, academic administrator; b. Lincoln, Nebr., Jan. 17, 1942; s. Floyd Ted and Rosalyn (Lashinsky) P.; m. Susan G. Unthank, Aug. 27, 1966; children: Anne, Amy. BA, U. Nebr., 1963, JD, 1966. Bar: Nebr. 1966, Va. 1980. Teaching fellow U. Chgo. Law Sch., 1966-67; mem. faculty U. Nebr. Sch. Law, 1967-74, prof., 1972-74; prof. law U. Va., Charlottesville, 1974-83; dean law sch. U. Nebr., Lincoln, 1983—98, interim sr. vice chancellor, 1995—96, interim chancellor, 2000—01, chancellor, 2001—; exec. dir. Nebr. Commn. on Law Enforcement. Author: (with Edmund Kitch) Legal Regulation of the Competitive Process, 1972, 79, 86; asso. editor: Jour. Law and Human Behavior, 1974-86. Named Ida Beam Distinguished Vis. Prof. Law, U. Iowa, 1981-86. Mem. Am. Bar Assn., Nebr. Bar Assn., Law-Psychology Assn., Am. Law Inst. Office: U Nebr Office of the Chancellor 201 ADM UNL Lincoln NE 68588 E-mail: hperlman1@unl.edu. *

PERLMAN, ITZHAK, violinist; b. Tel Aviv, Aug. 31, 1945; arrived in U.S., 1958; s. Chaim and Shoshana P.; m. Toby Lynn Friedlander, 1967; children: Noah, Navah, Miriam, Leora, Ariella. Student, Tel Aviv Acad. Music; studied with Ivan Galamian & Dorothy DeLay, Juilliard Sch.; student, Meadowmount Sch. Music.; degree in music (hon.), Tufts U., 1986; degree (hon.), Harvard U., Yale U., Brandeis U., Roosevelt U., Yeshiva U., Hebrew U. Appeared with numerous orchs. including NY Philharm., Cleve. Orch., Phila. Orch., Nat. Symphony Orch., Berlin Philharm., English Chamber Orch., London Symphony, London Philharm., Royal Philharm., BBC Orch., Vienna Philharm., Israel Philharm.; founder Perlman Music Program, NY, 1998—; prin. guest condr. Detroit Symphony, 2001—; participant numerous music festivals including Ravinia Festival, Tanglewood Music Festival, Aspen Music Festival, Israel Festival, Wolf Trap Summer Festival; recital tours US, Can., S.Am., Europe, Israel, Australia, Far East; recorded for Angel, London, RCA Victor, DG, Telarc, Teldec, Sony. Albums include Vivaldi: The Four Seasons, 1977 (Grammy award best classical performance 1977), Beethoven: Sonatas For Violin And Piano, 1978 (Gramy award best chamber music performance 1978), Brahms: Concerto For Violin In D, 1978 (Grammy award best classical album 1978), The Spanish Album, 1980 (Grammy award best classical performance 1980), Brahms: Violin And Cello Concerto In A Minor, 1980 (Grammy award best classical performance 1980), Berg: Violin Concerto/Stravinsky: Violin Concerto In D, 1980 (Grammy award best classical performance 1980), Music For Two Violins, 1980 (Grammy award best chamber music performance 1980), Isaac Stern: 60th Anniversary Celebration, 1981 (Grammy award best engineered recording 1981, Grammy award best classical performance 1981), Tchaikovsky: Piano Trio In A Minor, 1981 (Grammy award best chamber music performance 1981), Elgar: Violin Concerto In B Minor, 1982 (Emmy award best classical performance 1982), Chausson: Violin Concerto, 1984, An Isaac Stern Vivaldi Gala, 1985, Beethoven: The Complete Piano Trios, 1987 (Grammy award best chamber music performance 1987), Bach: Double Concerto, 1987, Mozart Violin Concertos Nos.1 & 2, 1987 (Grammy award best classical performance 1987), Paganini & Giuliani: Duos for Violin and Guitar, 1987, The Italian Album, 1989, Brahms: The 3 Violin Sonatas, 1990 (Grammy award best small ensemble performance 1990), Dvorák In Prague: A Celebration, 1994, Bach: Violin Concertos, 1995, The American Album: Works Of Bernstein, Barber, Foss, 1995 (Grammy award best instrumental soloist performance with orch. 1995), Cinema Serenade, 1997, John Williams Greatest Hits 1969-1999 Cinema Serenade 2, 1999, Classic Yo-Yo, 2001, Classic Perlman: Rhapsody, 2002; appeared in PBS documentary Fiddling for the Future, 1998 (Emmy award outstanding cultural music-dance program 1999); TV specials Perlman in Russia, 1992 (Emmy award outstanding classical program 1992), Itzhak Perlman: In the Fiddler's House, 1996 (Emmy award outstanding cultural music-dance program 1996). Founder Perlman Music Program, 1995. Recipient Leventritt prize, 1964, Medal of Liberty, 1986, Nat. Medal of Arts, 2000, Kennedy Ctr. Honor, 2003, Golden Plate award, Acad. Achievement, 2005; named Musician of Yr., Musical Am., 1981; inductee Am. Classical Music Hall of Fame, 2001. *

PERLMAN, JERALD LEE, lawyer; b. Baton Rouge, Feb. 25, 1947; s. Ralph Robert and Carol Mayer (Herzberg) P.; m. Francine Evonne McKelvey, May 8, 1984; children: Louise, Lee, Kevin. BA, Washington & Lee U., 1969; JD, La. State U., 1972. Bar: La. 1972, Tex. 1994, U.S. Dist. Ct. (we. dist.) La. 1972, U.S. Dist. Ct. (ea. and we. dists.) Ark. 1991, U.S. Ct. Appeals (5th cir.) 1977, U.S. Supreme Ct. 1990. Assoc. Blanchard, Walker, O'Quin & Roberts, Shreveport, La., 1972-76, ptnr., 1976-83, Walker, Tooke, Perlman & Lyons, Shreveport, 1983-94; regional office chief litigation divsn. La. Dept. Justice, Shreveport, 1994—. Assoc. editor La. State U. Law Rev., 1971-72. Bd. dirs. Broadmoor Southside YMCA, Shreveport, 1984-88, vice chmn., 1986, chmn., 1987; bd. dirs. Shreveport Met. YMCA, 1987, N.W. La. chpt. ACLU, 1987-93, N.W. La. Ctr. for Families, 2005—. Capt. USAR, 1972 Named to La. State U. Law Ctr. Hall of Fame. Mem. La. Bar Assn. (com. on uniform court rules 1998-2002), Shreveport Bar Assn., La. Assn. Def. Counsel (bd. dirs. 1979-81), Order of Coif, Phi Beta Kappa, Omicron Delta Kappa. Jewish. Avocations: tennis, reading. Office: La Dept Justice Litigation Divsn 330 Marshall St Ste 777 Shreveport LA 71101-3016 Office Phone: 318-676-5711. E-mail: perlmanj@ag.state.la.us.

PERLMAN, JON ARTHUR, plastic surgeon; b. NYC, Dec. 17, 1948; Bachelor, Lafayette Coll.; MD, Cornell U., 1973. Diplomate Am. Bd. Plastic Surgery, cert. Am. Bd. Surgery. Intern Mass. Gen. Hosp., Boston, 1973—74, resident in surgery, 1974—78; resident in plastic surgery UCLA Med. Ctr., 1978—80; pvt. practice plastic surgery Beverly Hills, Calif., 1980—. Attending plastic surgery Cedars-Sinai Med. Ctr., LA; chief divsn. plastic surgery Brotman Med. Ctr., 1985—; asst. clin. prof. plastic surgery UCLA Med. Ctr.; featured plastic surgeon ABC's Extreme Makeover. Fellow: Am. Coll. Surgeons; mem.: L.A. Soc. Plastic Surgeons, Calif. Soc. Plastic Surgeons, Am. Soc. Plastic Surgeons, Am. Soc. Aesthetic Plastic Surgeons. Office: 414 N Camden Dr 8th Fl Beverly Hills CA 90210 Office Phone: 310-854-0031. Office Fax: 310-275-5079. E-mail: jonap@ucla.edu. *

PERLMAN, LAWRENCE, retired information technology executive; BA, Carleton Coll., 1960; JD, Harvard U., 1963. Bar: Minn. 1963. Law clk. for fed. judge, 1963; assoc., ptnr. Fredrikson & Byron, Mpls., 1964-75; gen. counsel, exec. v.p. U.S. pacing ops. Medtronic, Inc., Mpls., 1975-78; sr. ptnr. Oppenheimer, Wolff & Donnelly, Mpls., 1978-80; exec. Control Data Corp. (now Ceridian Corp.), 1980—2000, CEO, 1990—92, chmn., CEO, 1992—2000; ret., 2000. Dir., chmn. Seagate Tech., 1989-2000; bd. dirs. Carlson Cos., Inc., The Valspar Corp.; chmn. Arbitron Inc.; trustee Carleton Coll. Bd. dirs. Walker Art Ctr.; regent Univ. of Minn., 1993-95; chmn. 21st Century Workforce Commn., 1999-2000. Address: 818 W 46th St 201 Minneapolis MN 55419

PERLMAN, MATTHEW SAUL, lawyer; b. Washington, Aug. 30, 1936; s. Jacob and Helen (Aronson) P.; m. Julia Gertrude Hawks, June 22, 1966; children: Penelope Leah, Deborah Jane Osofsky, Sarah Louise, Jacob Henry AB, Brown U., 1957; LLB, Harvard U., 1960. Bar: DC 1960, Md. 1960, US Supreme Ct. 1965. Atty. Air Force Gen. Counsel's Office, Washington, 1960-65; mem. Armed Services Bd. of Contract Appeals, Washington, 1965-67; gen. counsel Pres.' Commn. on Postal Orgn., Washington, 1967; asst. gen. counsel Dept. Transp., Washington, 1967-69; ptnr. Arent, Fox PLLC, Washington, 1969—2001, arbitrator, 2002—. Mem. Pres. Reagan's Transition Team for GSA, Washington, 1980-81; mem. adv. bd. Fed. Contracts Report, Washington, 1970-97; overseas corr. Internat. Constn. Law Rev., London, 1983—. Contbr. articles to profl. jours. Pres. Civic Assn. River Falls, Potomac, Md., 1975-77; mem. Montgomery County Md. Citizens Adv. Commn. for Rock Run AWT Plant, 1979-85. Served to capt. USAF, 1960-63 Mem. ABA (pub. contracts sect.), Fed. Bar Assn., Cosmos Club. Republican. Jewish. Home: 10517 Stable Ln Potomac MD 20854-3867 Office: Arent Fox PLLC 1050 Connecticut Ave NW Ste 500 Washington DC 20036-5303 Home Phone: 301-299-5618; Office Phone: 202-857-6279. Personal E-mail: mspjgp@gmail.com. Business E-Mail: perlmanm@arentfox.com.

PERLMUTH, WILLIAM ALAN, lawyer; b. NYC, Nov. 21, 1929; s. Charles and Roe (Schneider) P.; m. Loretta Kaufman, Mar. 14, 1951; children: Carolyn, Diane. AB, Wilkes Coll., 1951; LLB, Columbia U., 1953. Bar: N.Y. 1954. Assoc. Cravath, Swaine & Moore, NYC, 1955-61; ptnr. Stroock & Stroock & Lavan, NYC, 1962—97, of counsel, 1998—. Editor Columbia U. Law Rev., 1952-53. Trustee Aeroflex Found., NYC, 1965—, Harkness Found. for Dance, NYC, 1976—, Wilkes U., Wilkes-Barre, Pa., 1980—, Hosp. for Joint Diseases Orthopaedic Inst., NYC, 1980—, Weininger Found., 1985—, NYU Hosps. Ctr., 1994—, NYC Ctr., 1995—, Sch. Am. Ballet, 1997—, Bklyn. Acad. Music, 2004—; chmn. bd. trustees Hosp. Joint Diseases Orthop. Inst., 1994—2005. Mem. N.Y. State Bar Assn., Assn. of Bar of City of N.Y. Jewish. Home: 880 5th Ave New York NY 10021-4951 Office: Stroock & Stroock & Lavan 180 Maiden Ln Fl 34 New York NY 10038-4982 Office Phone: 212-806-5001. Business E-Mail: bperlmuth@stroock.com.

PERLMUTTER, ALVIN HOWARD, television and film producer; b. Poughkeepsie, NY, Mar. 24, 1928; s. Fred and Jennie (Albert) P.; children: James F., Stephen H., Tom W. Student, Colgate U., 1945-47; BA, Syracuse U., 1949. Dir. pub. affairs Sta. WNBC, also Sta. WNBC-TV, NYC, 1957-59; program mgr. Sta. WNBC-TV, 1959-61; exec. producer Nat. Ednl. TV, 1961—; v.p. news documentaries NBC, from 1975; pres. Alvin H. Perlmutter Inc., NYC; instr. TV news and pub. affairs NYU, 1957, Fairleigh Dickinson U., 1962; pres., CEO, Sunrise Media LLC, NYC, 1997—. Cons. John and Mary Markle Found., Pub. Agenda Found.; chmn. Dore Schary Awards for film and TV, Anti-Defamation League. Producer: series Assignment America; Great American Dream Machine, Consumer Reports Presents, Money Matters, Cover Story, Black Journal; various spl. programs including: Native Land, The Primal Mind, Adam Smith's Money World series, Family Computing series, Priceless Treasures of Dresden, The Perpetual People Puzzle; exec. producer: Report From Philadelphia, The Secret Government, The Power of Myth, Muslims (PBS spl. documentary). Chair Dore Schary awards, Anti-Defamation League; bd. dirs. N.Y. Open Ctr., Citizens for Ind. Pub. Broadcasting, Rockland Ctr. for the Arts. 1st lt. AUS, 1950-53; mem. adv. bd. CUNY TV. Recipient various citations and awards including 6 Emmy awards, Peabody award, Robert Kennedy award. Mem. Acad. TV Arts and Scis. (gov. N.Y. chpt., nat. trustee, chmn. awards com. 1968), Assn. Pub. TV Producers (chmn. 1969) Clubs: Overseas Press (N.Y.C.), University, Coffee House, The Econ. Club of N.Y.C., N.Y. Athletic Club. Home: 200 Central Park S New York NY 10019 Office: 155 W 46th St New York NY 10036

PERLMUTTER, BARBARA S., retired public relations executive; b. Hartford, Conn., Oct. 7, 1941; d. Leon and Ethel (Zinman) Sondik; m. Louis Perlmutter, Dec. 11, 1966; children: Kermit, Eric. BA, Smith Coll., 1963; MA in History, Columbia U., 1965; MBA, NYU, 1979. Analyst Celanese Internat. Co., NYC, 1965-69; sr. econ. analyst Nat. Econ. Rsch. Assoc., White Plains, N.Y., 1979-85; dir. pub. affairs Marsh & McLennan Companies, Inc., NYC, 1985-88, v.p. pub. affairs, 1988-99, sr. v.p. pub. affairs, 1999—2006; ret., 2007. Avocations: aerobics, reading, tennis.

PERLMUTTER, DAVID H., physician, educator; b. Bklyn., May 11, 1952; s. Herman Arthur and Ruth (Jacobs) P.; m. Barbara Ann Cohlan, Feb. 7, 1981; children: Andrew, Lisa. BA, U. Rochester, 1974; MD, St. Louis U., 1978. Intern then resident in pediatrics U. Pa. Sch. Medicine, Phila., 1978-81; fellow in pediatric gastroenterology Harvard U. Sch. Medicine, Boston, 1981-84, instr. pediatrics, 1983-85, asst. prof. pediatrics, 1985-86; Donald Strominger prof. of pediatrics Washington U. Sch. Medicine, St. Louis, 1986-89, prof. cell biology, physiology, 1989—. Editor: Pediatric Rsch., 1990—; editl. bd. Gastroenterology, 1990—; dir. divsn. gastrology and nutrition and pediatrics; contbr. articles to profl. jours. Recipient Established Investigator award Am. Heart Assn., 1987, Rsch. Scholar award Am. Gastroent. Assn., 1985, RJR Nabisco Co., 1986. Mem. Soc. Pediatric Rsch. (coun. rep. 1990—), Am. Soc. Cell Biology, Am. Soc. Clin. Investigation.

PERLMUTTER, DIANE F., marketing executive; b. NYC, Aug. 31, 1945; d. Bert H. and Frances (Smith) P. Student, NYU Grad. Sch. of Bus., 1969—70; BA in English, Miami U., Oxford, Ohio, 1967. Writer sales promotion Equitable Life Assurance, NYC, 1967-68; bus. adminstr. de Garmo, Inc., NYC, 1968-69, asst. account exec., 1969-70, account exec., 1970-74, v.p., account supr., 1974-76; mgr. corp. advt. Avon Products, Inc., NYC, 1976-79, dir. comm. Latin Am., Spain, Can., 1979-80, dir. brochures, 1980-81, dir. category merchandising, 1981-82, group dir. motivational comm., 1982-83, group dir. sales promotion, 1983-84, v.p. sales promotion, 1984, v.p. internat. bus. devel., 1984-85, area v.p. Latin Am., 1985, v.p. advt. and campaign mktg., 1985-87, v.p. U.S. operational planning, 1987; cons. NYC, 1987-88; sr. v.p. Burson-Marsteller, NYC, 1988-90, exec. v.p., mng. dir. consumer products, 1991-93, bd. dirs., 1992—98, co-chief oper. officer, 1993-94, chief oper. officer, 1994-96, chmn. mktg. practice/U.S., 1996-98; vice chmn., CEO Cohn & Wolfe, NYC, 1998—2000; CEO Gilda's Club Worldwide, 2001—05, bd. dirs., 2002—; prin. Oxford Hall Assocs., 2005—. Chair ann. meeting Direct Selling Assn., Washington, 1982; v.p. Nat. Home Fashions League, NYC, 1975—76; adj. instr. SUNY/ Fashion Inst. Tech., 1992—; vice chmn. Columbia-Greene Hosp. Found., 2000—; vice chmn., bd. dirs. Olana Partnership, 2000—03; bd. dirs. Double L.P. Industries, Inc. Bd. dirs. Hudson Opera House, 2002—. Named to YWCA Acad. Women Achievers, 1996. Mem.: Women in Comm., Advt. Women of N.Y., Pub. Rels. Soc. Am., Women's Econ. Round Table (bd. dirs. 1998—2000), Miami U. Alumni Assn. (pres., chair 1986), The Women's Forum (bd. dirs. 1998—2000, pres. 2002—04), YMCA of Greater N.Y. (bd. dirs. 1996—2003), Publicity Club N.Y. (bd. dirs. 1994—96). Home Phone: 864-895-5854. Personal E-mail: dianefperlmutter@yahoo.com.

PERLMUTTER, ED (EDWIN GEORGE PERLMUTTER), congressman, former state legislator; b. Denver, May 1, 1953; m. Deana M.

Perlmutter; children: Alexis, Abbey, Zoey. BA, U. Colo., 1975, JD, 1978. Atty. Berenbaum, Weinshienk & Eason, P.C., 1978—; mem. Colo. Senate, Dist. 20, Denver, 1995—2003, pres. pro tempore, 2001—03; mem. pub., policy and planning com., joint legal svcs. com.; mem. US Congress from 7th Colo. dist., 2007—, mem. fin. svcs. com., homeland security com. Trustee First Jud. and Jud. Performance Commn., 1989-91, chair, 1991-93. Mem. Maple Grove Elem. Sch. PTA. Mem. ABA, Am. Bankruptcy Inst., Colo. Bar Assn. (bd. govs.), Colo. Trial Lawyers Assn., Associated Gen. Contractors Colo., Colo. Oil and Gas Assn., Denver Bar Assn., Applewood Bus. Assn., Golden C. of C., N.W. Met. C. of C., West C. of C., U. Colo. Alumni Assn. (former dir.). Democrat. Office: 415 Cannon House Office Bldg Washington DC 20515 also: 12600 W Colfax Ave Ste 8400 Lakewood CO 80215 *

PERLMUTTER, ISAAC, entertainment company executive; b. 1946; m. Laura Perlmutter. Ind. fin. investor; with Marvel Entertainment, Inc., NYC, 1990—, chmn., 1993—95, vice chmn., 2001—, CEO, 2005—. Bd. dirs. Marvel Entertainment, Inc., 1993—, Ranger Industries, Inc. Established (with Laura Perlmutter) the Laura and Isaac Perlmutter Professorship and Chair in Cell Biology (now Pathology) Skirball Inst. Biomolecular Medicine. Office: Marvel Entertainment Inc 417 5th Ave New York NY 10016 *

PERLMUTTER, LOUIS, investment banker, lawyer; b. Cambridge, Mass., Oct. 3, 1934; s. Kermit H and Rachel P (Ehrlich) Perlmutter; m. Barbara Patricia Sondik, Dec. 11, 1966; children: Kermit, Eric. BA, Brandeis U., Waltham, Mass., 1956, LHD (hon.), 1995; JD, U. Mich., 1959. Bar: Mass 1959, NY 1961. Law practice, NYC, 1960-65; asst. to pres. New Eng. Industries, NYC, 1965-67; pres. Octagon Assocs., NYC, 1967-75; sr. v.p. White Weld, NYC, 1975-78; mgn. dir. Merrill Lynch, White, Weld, NYC, 1978; exec. mng. dir. Lazard Freres & Co. LLC, NYC, 1978-99, ltd. mng. dir., 2000—05; sr. adv. Corp. Ptnrs., 2005—. Contbr. articles to profl jours. Bd. dirs. Charles H. Revson Found.; chmn. Transatlantic Inst.; bd. dirs., treas. World Fedn. UNA; chmn. bd. trustees Brandeis U., Waltham, Mass., 1988—95, Am. Jewish Congress, NYC, 1988—94; bd. dirs., chmn. exec. com. UN Assn. USA, 1993—96; com. visitors U. Mich. Law Sch.; bd. fellows Harvard Med. Sch.; adv. bd. Fgn. Affairs, Medis Techs.; mem. coun. fgn. rels., adminstrv. coun. Blaustein Inst. Advancement Human Rights; bd. dirs. Harvard Med. Internat. Recipient Human Rels. award, Am. Jewish Con., 1995, Pub. Svc. award, Phoenix H.S., 1999, tribute dinner, Israel Policy Forum, 2001, honoree, World Fedn. UN Assn., 2003. Home: 39 E 79th St New York NY 10021-0216 Office: Lazard 30 Rockefeller Plz New York NY 10112-5900 Business E-Mail: louis.perlmutter@lazardai.com.

PERLMUTTER, ROGER, medical products executive; Chmn. dept. immunology U. Wash., 1989—97, prof. depts. immunology, biochemistry and medicine, 1991—97; investigator Howard Hughes Med. Inst., 1991—97; various positions including exec. v.p. Worldwide Basic Rsch. and Preclinical Devel. Merck Rsch. Labs., 1997—2000; exec. v.p. R & D Amgen, Inc., 2001—. Bd. dirs. Stem Cells, Inc. Office: Amgen Inc One Amgen Center Dr Thousand Oaks CA 91320-1799 Office Phone: 805-447-1000. Office Fax: 805-447-1010. *

PERLMUTTER, SAUL, astrophysicist, educator; AB in Physics (magna cum laude), Harvard U., 1981; PhD in Physics, U. Calif. Berkeley, 1986. Postdoctoral rschr. Space Sci. Lab., Lawrence Berkeley Nat. Lab., 1987—88; sr. staff scientist, astrophysicist Lawrence Berkeley Nat. Lab.; prof., physics dept. U. Calif. Berkeley, 2004—. Leader Internat. Supernova Cosmology Project, 1998—. Contbr. articles to profl. jours., to Sky and Telescope mag.; guest appearances Pub. Broadcasting Sys., BBC documentaries on astronomy and cosmology. Co-recipient Shaw prize in Astronomy, Shaw Found., Hong Kong, 2006, Gruber Cosmology prize, 2007; named Scientist of Yr., Calif., 2003; recipient Henri Chretien award, Am. Astronomical Soc., 1996, Breakthrough of Yr. award, Science Mag., 1998, E.O. Lawrence award in Physics, Dept. Energy, 2002, John Scott award, 2005, Padua prize, 2005, Feltrinelli Internat. prize, Phys. and Math. Scis., Lincei Acad., Rome, 2006. Fellow: Am. Acad. Arts & Scis. Achievements include discovery of the universe's accelerating expansion using supernovae as "standard candles" to measure the cosmic expansion rate. Office: Lawrence Berkeley Lab 50-232 Univ Calif 392 LeConte Berkeley CA 94720 Office Phone: 510-486-5203, 510-642-3596. Office Fax: 510-486-5401. Business E-Mail: saul@lbl.gov. *

PERLOFF, JEAN MARCOSSON, property manager, retired lawyer; b. Lakewood, Ohio, June 25, 1942; d. John Solomon and Marcella Catherine (Borngen) Marcosson; m. Lawrence Storch, Stpe. 8, 1991. BA magna cum laude, Lake Erie Coll., 1965; MA in Italian, UCLA, 1967; JD magna cum laude, Ventura Coll. Law, 1976. Bar: Calif. 1976, U.S. Dist. Ct. (cen. dist.) Calif. 1978. Assoc. in Italian U. Calif.-Santa Barbara, 1967-70; law clk., paralegal Ventura County Pub. Defender's Office, Ventura, Calif., 1975; pvt. practice Ventura, 1976-79; co-prin. Clabaugh & Perloff, A Profl. Corp., Ventura, 1979-82; sr. jud. atty. to presiding justice 6th divsn. 2d Dist. Ct. Appeals, LA, 1982-97; ret., 1997; comml. property mgr. Santa Barbara, Calif., 1997—. Instr. Ventura Coll. Law, 1976-79. Pres., bd. dirs. Santa Barbara Zool. Gardens, 1987-88; bd. dirs. Montecito Found., 1999—; trustee Lake Erie Coll., 1993—; mem. 19th Agrl. Dist. Bd., 2001—. Named Woman of Yr., 18th Senatorial dist. and 35th Assembly dist. Calif. Legislature, 1993; recipient Disting. Alumnae award Lake Erie Coll., 1996; sesquicentennial fellow Lake Erie Coll., 2001. Mem. Calif. Bar Assn. (appellate ct. com. 1993-95), Fiesta City Club, Kappa Alpha Sigma. Democrat. Avocations: reading, music, hiking, horses. Home: 1384 Plaza Pacifica Santa Barbara CA 93108-2877

PERLOFF, MARJORIE GABRIELLE, literature educator; b. Vienna, Sept. 28, 1931; arrived in U.S., 1998; d. Maximilian and Ilse (Schueller) Mintz; m. Joseph K. Perloff, July 31, 1953; children: Nancy Lynn, Carey Elizabeth. AB, Barnard Coll., 1953; MA, Cath. U., 1956, PhD, 1965. Asst. prof. English and comparative lit. Cath. U., Washington, 1966-68, assoc. prof., 1969-71, U. Md., 1971-73, prof., 1973-76; Florence R. Scott prof. English U. So. Calif., LA, 1976—; prof. English and comparative lit. Stanford (Calif.) U., 1986—, Sadie Dernham prof. humanities, 1990—, prof. emerita, 2000. Vis. prof. U. Utah, 2002; scholar-in-residence U. So. Calif., 2004—; guest prof. Beijing Lang. and Culture U., 2004. Author: Rhyme and Meaning in the Poetry of Yeats, 1970, The Poetic Art of Robert Lowell, 1973, Frank O'Hara, Poet Among Painters, 1977, 2nd edit., 1998, The Poetics of Indeterminacy: Rimbaud to Cage, 1981, 2d edit., 1999, The Dance of the Intellect: Studies in the Poetry of the Pound Tradition, 1985, 2d edit., 1996, The Futurist Moment: Avant-Garde, Avant-Guerre and the Language of Rupture, 1986, 2d edit., 2003, Poetic License: Essays in Modern and Postmodern Lyric, 1990, Radical Artifice: Writing Poetry in the Age of Media, 1991, Wittgenstein's Ladder: Poetic Language and the Strangeness of the Ordinary, 1996, Frank O'Hara, 2d edit., 1998, Poetry On and Off the Page: Essays for Emergent Occasions, 1998, Twenty-first Century Modernism, 2001, The Vienna Paradox, 2004, Differentials, 2004; editor: Postmodern Genres, 1990; co-editor: John Cage: Composed in America, 1994; contbg. editor: Columbia Literary History of the U.S., 1987; contbr. preface to Contemporary Poets, 1980, A John Cage Reader, 1983. Guggenheim fellow, 1981-82, NEA fellow, 1985; Phi Beta Kappa scholar, 1994-95. Fellow Am. Acad. Arts and Scis.; mem. MLA (exec. coun. 1977-81, Am. lit. sect. 1993—, 1st v.p. 2005, pres. 2006), Comparative Lit. Assn. (pres. 1993-94, mem. adv. bd. Libr. of Am.), Lit. Studies Acad. Home: 1467 Amalfi Dr Pacific Palisades CA 90272-2752 Personal E-mail: mperloff@earthlink.net.

PERLOFF, ROBERT, psychologist, educator; b. Phila., Feb. 3, 1921; s. Myer and Elizabeth (Sherman) P.; m. Evelyn Potechin, Sept. 22, 1946; children: Richard Mark, Linda Sue, Judith Kay. AB, Temple U., 1949; MA, Ohio State U., 1949, PhD, 1951; DSc (hon.), Oreg. Grad. Sch. Profl. Psychology, 1984; DLitt (hon.), Calif. Sch. Profl. Psychology, 1985. Diplomate Am. Bd. Profl. Psychology. Instr. edn. Antioch Coll., 1950—51; with pers. rsch. br. Dept. Army, 1951—55, chief statis. rsch. and cons. unit., 1953—55; dir. R & D Sci. Rsch. Assocs., Inc., Chgo., 1955—59; vis. lectr. Chgo. Tchrs. Coll., 1955—56; mem. faculty Purdue U., 1958—59, prof. psychology, 1964—69; 1961field assessment officer univ. Peace Corps Chile III project, 1962; Disting. Svc. prof. bus. adminstrn. and psychology U. Pitts. Joseph M. Katz Grad. Sch. Bus., 1969—90, Disting. Svc. prof. emeritus, 1991—; dir. rsch. programs U. Pitts. Grad. Sch. Bus., 1969—77; dir. Consumer Panel, 1980—83. Bd. dirs. Book Ctr.; adv. com. assessment exptl. manpower R & D labs. NAS, 1972-74; mem. rsch. rev. com. NIMH, 1976-80, Stress and Families rsch. project, 1976-79; cons. in field. Contbr. articles to profl. jours.; editor Indsl. Psychologist, 1963-65, Evaluator Intervention: Pros and Cons; book rev. editor Personnel Psychology, 1952-55; co-editor: Values, Ethics and Standards Sourcebook, 1979, Improving Evaluations; bd. consulting editors Jour. Applied Psychology; bd. advs. Archives History Am. Psychology, Psychol. Svc. Pitts., Recorded Psychol. Jours.; guest editor Am. Psychologist, 1972, Edn. and Urban Soc., 1977, Profl. Psychology, 1977; adv. editor Contemporary Psychology, 1994—. Bd. dirs., v.p. Sr. Citizens Svc. Corp., Calif. Sch. Profl. Psychology; bd. dirs. Greater Pitts. chpt. ACLU, sec., 1997-98; chmn. nat. adv. com. Inst. Govt. and Pub. Affairs, U. Ill., 1986-89, sec. nat. adv. com., 1997—; mem. adv. com. Cornell Inst. for Rsch. on Children, 2002—. Decorated Bronze Star; named in his honor, Robert Perloff Grad. Rsch. Assistantship in Inst. Govt. and Pub. Affairs, U. Ill., 1990, in his honor, Robert Perloff Career Achievement award, Knowledge Utilization Soc., 1991; recipient Legacy award, Greater Pitts. Psychol. Assn., 2001, Hist. Preservation award, City of Pitts., 2002. Fellow: APA (mem.-at-large exec. com. divsn. consumer psychology 1964—67, coun. reps. 1965—68, pres. divsn. 1967—68, chmn. sci. affairs com., divsn. consumer psychology 1968—69, edn. and tng. bd. 1969—72, mem.-at-large exec. com. divsn. consumer psychology 1970—71, coun. reps. 1972—74, dir. 1974—82, chmn. fin. com., treas. 1975—84, chmn. investment com. 1977—82, pres. 1985, adv. bd., bd. sci. affairs 1994—96, task force intelligence and Intelligence Tests, author column Std. Deviations in jour., pres. address selected as one of 50 over 50 yrs.), AAAS, Ea. Psychol. Assn. (dir. 1977—80, pres. 1980—81); mem.: Coun. of Sci. Soc. (found. alumnus, pres. 1998—), Knowledge Utilization Soc. (pres. 1993—95), Soc. Psychologists in Mgmt. (pres. 1993—94, Disting. Contbn. to Psychology Mgmt. award 1989), Am. Evaluation Assn. (pres. 1977—78), Am. Psychol. Found. (v.p. 1988—89, pres. 1990—92, trustee 1995—98, Lifetime Achievement in Psychology Gold Medal award 2000), Assn. for Consumer Rsch. (chmn. 1970—71), Pa. Psychol. Assn. (Disting. Svc. award 1985), Internat. Assn. Applied Psychology, Am. Psychol. Soc., Phi Beta Kappa, Psi Chi, Beta Gamma Sigma, Sigma Xi (pres. U. Pitts. chpt. 1989—91). Home: 815 Saint James St Pittsburgh PA 15232-2112 Office Phone: 412-648-1554. Personal E-mail: rperloff@katz.pitt.edu. *Experiment. Innovate responsibly. Take risks judiciously. Do not shrink from new ventures for fear of failure. No one is immune from adversity. The hallmark of a successful achieving person is his or her ability to snap back after misfortune, and to benefit from and not be immobilized by failure.*

PERLROTH, MARK GUIDO, medical educator; b. Turin, Italy, Nov. 17, 1937; arrived in US, 1941; s. Solomon and Dora Perlroth; m. Karen A. deVries; children: Victor, Nina, Nicole. AB, U. Rochester, NY, 1956; MD, Harvard U., Boston, 1960. Diplomate Am. Bd. Internal Medicine, 1968, Am. Bd. Cardiovasc. Disease, 1974. Prof. medicine Stanford U., Palo Alto, Calif., 1965—. Author: 50 Diseases, 1981. Lt. comdr. USPHS, 1963—65. Fellow: ACP, Am. Heart Assn. Avocations: reading, skiing, swimming. Office: Stanford U CVRB 263 300 Pasteur Dr Palo Alto CA 94305 Office Phone: 650-723-2984. Business E-Mail: mgp@stanford.edu.

PERLSTEIN, WILLIAM JAMES, lawyer; b. NYC, Feb. 7, 1950; s. Justin Sol and Jane (Goldberg) P.; m. Teresa Catherine Lotito, Dec. 20, 1970; children: David, Jonathan. Student, London Sch. Econs., 1969-70; BA summa cum laude, Union Coll., 1971; JD, Yale U., 1974. Bar: Conn. 1974, D.C. 1976, U.S. Dist. Ct. D.C. 1977, U.S. Ct. Appeals (D.C. cir.) 1978, U.S. Supreme Ct. 1993, N.Y. 2000. Law clk. to judge Marvin Frankel U.S. Dist. Ct., NYC, 1974-75; assoc. Wilmer, Cutler & Pickering, Washington, 1975-82, ptnr., 1982—2004, mem. mgmt. com., 1995—2004, chmn., 1998—2004; co-mng. ptnr. & co-chmn. mgmt. com. Wilmer Cutler Pickering Hale & Dorr, Washington, 2004—. Mng. editor Yale Law Jour., 1973-74; contbg. author The Workout Game, 1987. Dir. Neighborhood Legal Svcs. program. Mem.: Am. Bar Found., Am. Coll. Bankruptcy (gen. counsel), Am. Law Inst., Am. Bankruptcy Inst. (chmn. legis. com. 1986—89, bd. dirs. 1989—93, 1997—2002), ABA (bus. bankruptcy com 1983—, v.chmn. executory contracts subcom. of bus. bankruptcy com. 1988—90, bankruptcy cts. subcom. 1990—97, chmn. legislation subcom. 1997—), Phi Beta Kappa. Jewish. Office: Wilmer Cutler Pickering Hale & Dorr 2445 M St NW Washington DC 20037 Office Phone: 202-663-6274. Office Fax: 202-663-6363. Business E-Mail: william.perlstein@wilmerhale.com.

PERNICIARO, CHARLES VINCENT, dermatologist, educator, entrepreneur; b. New Orleans, June 15, 1957; s. Ernest Gabriel and Phereby Sheppard Perniciaro; children: Jamie Lynn, Kelly Gabrielle. BS, U. La., Lafayette, 1979; MD, La. State U., New Orleans, 1983. Diplomate Am. Bd. Dermatology, Am. Bd. Dermatology and Pathology. Staff physician Ochsner Clin. of Baton Rouge, La., 1987-90; sr. assoc. cons. and staff dermatologist Mayo Clinic, Jacksonville, Fla., 1990-93, cons., staff dermatologist and dermatopathologist, 1993-99; pvt. practice dermatology Brunswick, Ga., 1999—, Neptune Beach, Fla., 1999—2006, Ponte Vedra Beach, Fla., 2006—. Pres., CEO Holiday Lighting Concepts, Inc., 1996-2000; lectr., presenter in field; adj. clin. assoc. prof. pathology U. Fla. Shands Jacksonville Med. Ctr., 1999-2001; dir. dermatopathology Bernhardt Labs., Jacksonville, Fla., 2001—. Contbr. articles to profl. jours. Founder, bd. dirs. S.W. La. Skin Cancer Found., 1987. Recipient Outstanding Paper award Noah Worcester Dermatol. Soc., 1993, First Place Poster award 17th Internat. Colloquium Dermatopathology, 1996; named one of Best Doctors, 2000-06, How to Find the Best Fla. Doctors, 2000, Am. Top Physicians, 2003-05. Fellow: Am. Soc. Dermatopathology (chmn. membership com., bd. dirs. 2000—01), Am. Acad. Dermatology (com. on preventive dermatology 1988—90, task force on dermatologic oncology 1990—93, environ. coun. 1994—96, adv. coun. 1995—2001, adv. bd. 2006—); mem.: So. Med. Assn. (vice chair sect. dermatology 1995—96, chair-elect 2001—06, chair 2006—, Resident-in-Tng. award 1994), Fla. Soc. Dermatology (bd. dirs. 1998—2006, chmn. membership com. 1999—2002, v.p. 2002—03, pres. 2003—04), Jacksonville Dermatology Soc. (sec.-treas. 1995, pres. 1996, webmaster 2003—04), Lions (charter, bd. dirs. Ponte Vedra Beach 1997—98). Avocations: tennis, computers. Home: 514 Midway St Neptune Beach FL 32266 Office: Brunswick Dermatology Clinic 3008 E Park Ave Brunswick GA 31520-4241

PERNICK, MARTIN STEVEN, history professor; b. NYC, June 2, 1948; s. Louis W. and Florence P. (Goldberg) P. m. Marie R. Deveney, July 8, 1983; 1 child, Benjamin William. BA, Brandeis U., 1968; MA, Columbia U., 1969, PhD, 1979. Lectr. Coll. Medicine Pa. State U., Hershey, 1972-79; from asst. prof. to prof. U. Mich., Ann Arbor, 1979—. Vis. lectr. Harvard U., Cambridge, Mass., 1975-76; creator, dir. Hist. Health Film Collection, Ann Arbor, 1986—. Author: A Calculus of Suffering, 1985, The Black Stork, 1996; contbr. chpt. to Death: Beyond Whole-Brain Criteria, 1988. Nat. Libr. Medicine fellow, 1984-85, NEH fellow, 1985-88. Mem. Am. Assn. History Medicine (exec. coun. 1992-95). Office: U Mich Dept History Ann Arbor MI 48109-1003

PERONTO, JANICE LYNN, principal; d. Richard A. and Bonnie J. Sinkenbring; m. Karl Eric Peronto, June 10, 1995; children: Kolton Richard, Kolby Eric, Konnor Walter. BA in Edn., Purdue U., West Lafayette, Ind., 1991; MEd (hon.), Tarleton State U., Ctrl. Texas, Tex., 2001. Tchr. Cedar Valley Elem., Killeen, Tex., 1992—2002; campus instrnl. specialist Clifton Pk. Elem., 2002—05; asst. prin. Cedar Valley Elem., 2005—. Adv. panel Tex. SBEC, Austin, 1999—; goal III action rsch. coord. Killeen Ind. Sch. Dist., 2002—, mentor coord., 2002—; adv. panel Cedar Valley Elem., 1993—. Mem. Killeen Svc. League, 2003—04. Recipient Excellence Tchg., Killeen Daily Herald, 1997—98, Tchr. of Yr., Walmart Found., 1997—98, Tchr. of Quarter, Exch. Club Killeen, 2001—02. Mem.: Tex. Edn. Assn., Tex. Elem. Prin. Assn. (assoc.), Delta Kappa Gamma (assoc.). Office: Cedar Valley Elementary 4801 Chantz Drive Killeen TX 76542 Home Phone: 254-634-6418; Office Phone: 254-501-1480. Office Fax: 254-680-6600. E-mail: janice.peronto@killeenisd.org.

PEROT, ROSS (H. ROSS PEROT, HENRY ROSS PEROT), real estate company, investment company, data processing executive; b. Texarkana, Tex., June 27, 1930; s. Gabriel Ross and Lulu May Perot; m. Margot Birmingham, 1956; children: Ross Jr., Nancy, Suzanne, Carolyn, Katherine. Ed., US Naval Acad., 1949—53. Data processing salesman IBM Corp., 1957-62; founder Electronic Data Systems Corp., Dallas, 1962-84, sold to GM, 1984, chmn., CEO, also dir., to 1986; founder The Perot Group, Dallas, 1986—, Perot Systems Corp., Washington, 1988—, bd. mem. Dallas, 1988—94, Plano, 1997—, chmn. Dallas, 1988—92, Plano, 2000—04, chmn. emeritus, 2004—. Ind. candidate US Presdl. Election, 1992, Reform Party candidate, 96. Author (books) United We Stand: How We Can Take Back Our Country, 1992, Not for Sale at Any Price: How We Can Save America for Our Children, 1993, Intensive Care: We Must Save Medicare and Medicaid Now, 1995, Preparing Our Country for the 21st Century, 1995, Ross Perot: My Life & the Principles for Success, 1996; co-author (with Pat Choate) Save Your Job, Save Our Country: Why NAFTA Must Be Stopped-Now!, 1993, (with Senator Paul Simon) The Dollar Crisis: A Blueprint to Help Rebuild the American Dream, 1996. Served with USN, 1953-57. Recipient Winston Churchill Award, 1986, Internat. Disting. Entrepreneur Award, U. Man., 1988, Raoul Wallenberg Award, Jefferson Award, Patrick Henry Award, Nat, Bus. Hall of Fame Award, Sarnoff Award, Eisenhower Award, Smithsonian Computerworld Award, Horatio Alger Award.; named one of Forbes' Richest Americans, 1999—, World's Richest People, Forbes mag., 1999—. Office: Perot Systems Corp 2300 W Plano Pkwy Plano TX 75075 also: Perot Family Trust PO Box 269014 Plano TX 75026-9014 *

PEROT, ROSS, JR., (HENRY ROSS PEROT JR.), real estate developer, professional sports team executive; b. Arlington, Tex. m. Sarah Fullinwider, 1984. BBA, Vanderbilt U., 1981. With Petrus Oil Co., Okla., 1981-83; mng. ptnr. The Perot Group, 1983—; owner Hillwood Devel., Dallas, 1988—; majority owner Dallas Mavericks basketball, 1996—2000; pres., CEO Perot Systems, Dallas, 2000—04, chmn., 2004—. Exec. com. Prince of Wales Bus. Leaders' Forum, Winston Churchill Found. Pilot, USAFR, 1983-1991. Achievements include completing first flight around the world in a helicopter. Office: Perot Systems 2300 W Plano Pkwy Plano TX 75075 *

PEROTTI, ROSE NORMA, lawyer; b. St. Louis, Aug. 10, 1930; d. Joseph and Dorothy Mary (Roleski) Perotti. BA, Fontbonne Coll., St. Louis, 1952; JD, St. Louis U., 1957. Bar: Mo. 1958. Trademark atty. Sutherland, Polster & Taylor, St. Louis, 1958-63, Sutherland Law Office, 1964-70, Monsanto Co., St. Louis, 1971-85, sr. trademark atty., 1985-91, assoc. trademark counsel, 1991-94, trademark counsel, 1994-96, Polster, Lieder, Woodruff & Lucchesi, 1996—. Honored with dedication of faculty office in her honor, St. Louis U. Sch. Law, 1980. Mem. ABA, Mo. Bar, Bar Assn. Met. St. Louis, Am. Judicature Soc., Friends St. Louis Art Mus., Mo. Bot. Garden. Office: Polster Lieder Woodruff & Lucchesi 12412 Powerscourt Dr Ste 200 Saint Louis MO 63131-3615 Office Phone: 314-238-2400. Business E-Mail: rperotti@patpro.com.

PEROULIS, DIMITRIOS, engineering educator, consultant; s. Emilios and Katerina Peroulis. BSc in Elec. Engring. and Computer Sci., Nat. Tech. U. Athens, Greece, 1993—98; MS in Elec. Engring., U. Mich., Ann Arbor, 1998—99, PhD, 2000—03. Asst. prof., elec. and computer engring. Purdue U., West Lafayette, Ind., 2003—. Contbr. articles to profl. jours. Mem.: IEEE. Achievements include patents pending for reconfigurable slot antennas for VHF/UHF applications. Avocations: travel, chess, ballroom dancing. Office: Purdue Univ 465 Northwestern Ave EE Bldg West Lafayette IN 47906 Home Phone: 765-743-6993; Office Phone: 765-494-3491. Office Fax: 765-494-3371. E-mail: dperouli@purdue.edu.

PERRAM FRANK, HEATHER, editor-in-chief; Grad., Tulane U., New Orleans. With CBS, E! Entertainment, Oprah Winfrey's Harpo Prodns., Warner Bros.; exec. dir. creative programming AOL; editor-in-chief Women's Lifestyle & Parenting Group Interactive Media, NYC; site dir. MORE.com Meredith Corp., 2005, editor-in-chief LHJ.com; v.p. programming Revolution Health, 2007—. Bd. dirs. Patricia M. Sitar Ctr. for the Arts. Office: LHJ Meredith Corp 375 Lexington Ave New York NY 10017 *

PERREAULT, WILLIAM DANIEL, JR., business administration educator; b. NYC, Apr. 7, 1948; s. William Daniel Sr. and Barbara Louise (Peckham) P.; m. Pamela Pittard, May 27, 1972; children: Suzanne Elizabeth, William Daniel III. BS, U. N.C., 1970, PhD, 1973. Asst. prof. U. Ga., Athens, 1973-76, U. N.C., Chapel Hill, 1976-79, assoc. prof., 1979-81, prof., 1981-83, Hanes prof., 1983-88. Vis. prof. Stanford (Calif.) U., 1986-87, assoc. dean, 1988-92. Kenan prof., 1988—; vis. prof. Cambridge (Eng.) U., 1997. Co-author: Essentials Marketing, 2003, The Marketing Game, 2001, Basic Marketing, 2007; editor: Jour. Mktg. Rsch., 1982-85; contbr. articles to profl. jours. Chmn. adv. com. Bur. Census, Washington, 1982—86. Mem. Am. Mktg. Assn. (v.p. 1986, 95, bd. dirs. 1986-89, 94-95, Odell award 1985, Disting. Educator award 1997, Churchill award 1997), Acad. Mktg. Sci. (Outstanding Edn. award 1995), Decision Scis. Inst. (coun. 1977), Assn. Dir. Consumer Rsch. Conf. (chmn. 1976—), Mktg. Sci. Inst. (trustee 1989-94), Phi Beta Kappa. Republican. Presbyterian. Office: U NC CB 3490 Mccoll Bldg Chapel Hill NC 27599-3490 Business E-Mail: bill_perreault@unc.edu.

PERRET, GERARD ANTHONY, JR., orthodontist; b. New Orleans, Feb. 13, 1959; s. Gerard A. and Marie M. (Gamino) P.; m. Catherine J. McMahon, 1996; 1 child, Caroline Marie. BS in Chemistry, U. N.C., 1981; DDS, La. State U., 1986, cert. orthodontics, 1989. Diplomate Am. Bd. Orthodontists. Clin. asst. prof. La. State U. Sch. Dentistry, New Orleans, 1986-87; pvt. practice dentistry Lakeside Dental Group, Metairie, La., 1986-87; pvt. practice orthodontics Jacksonville, Fla., 1989-91, Tampa, Fla., 1991—; founder, pres. Orthogap, Inc., Tampa, 1993—, Rodent Realty, Inc., 2001—. Patentee in field. Active mem. New Tampa Cmty. Coun.; chmn. New Tampa Rotary Found., Inc., 2003—04. Mem. ADA, Am. Assn. Orthodontists, Fla. Assn. Orthodontists, Hillsborough County Dental Soc., Hillsborough County Dental Rsch. Clinic, So. Assn. Orthodontists, Rotary (pres. New Tampa chpt. 1997-98), Omicron Kappa Upsilon. Avocations:

sailing, fishing, music, golf. Home: 16014 Penwood Dr Tampa FL 33647-1137 Office: 15283 Amberly Dr Tampa FL 33647 Home Phone: 813-972-7483; Office Phone: 813-977-2828.

PERRILLES, ANGELA TERESE, physical therapist; b. Peoria, Ill., Apr. 27, 1969; d. William Ernest and Marilyn June Perrilles. BS in Fitness Leadership/Cardiac Rehab., No. Ill. U., DeKalb, 1992; MS in Athletic Tng./Exercise Physiology, Ill. State U., Normal, 1998; AAS, Ill. Ctrl. Coll., East Peoria, 2000. Aide phys. therapy St. Francis Med. Ctr., Peoria, 1988—89; front desk clerk/med. records Health Ctr. No. Ill. U., DeKalb, 1990—95; aide phys. therapy No. Rehab., DeKalb, 1993—95; fitness dir., personal trainer Landmark Health Club, Peoria, 1995—2002; athletic trainer Mustangs Jr. Hockey League, Peoria, 1999—2002; phys. therapist asst. Profl. Therapy Svcs., Peoria, 2000—02; phys. therapist asst./athletic trainer Orthop. Inst./Great Plains, Peoria, 2002—. Coord. cardiac rehab., therapist Jasper County Hosp., Rensselaer, Ind., 1996—97. Contbr.: newsletter Orthop. Inst. Ill., 2004—. Vol. spl. events Peoria Park Dist., 1997—; mem. Peoria Jaycees, 1998—; runner St. Jude Children's Hosp., Peoria, 1999—; chair, organizer Red Kettle campaign Salvation Army, Peoria, 2004—; vol. MS Soc., Arthritis Found., ARC, Peoria Humane Soc., Race for the Cure, Race for Life, Arthritis Walk, Diabetes Walk. Recipient Cmty. Svc. award, Peoria Park Dist., 2002. Mem.: Nat. Athletic Trainers Assn. Avocations: running, hot air ballooning, cross stitch, outdoor activities. Home: 617 Rohmann Ct Peoria IL 61604 Office: Orthopedic Inst Ill-Great Plains Rehab 303 N Kumpf Blvd Peoria IL 61605 E-mail: atpatc@insightbb.com.

PERRIN, EDWARD BURTON, biomedical researcher, public health educator; b. Greensboro, Vt., Sept. 19, 1931; s. J. Newton and Dorothy E. (Willey) P.; m. Carol Anne Hendricks, Aug. 18, 1956; children: Jenifer, Scott. BA, Middlebury Coll., 1953; student in Stats., Edinburgh U., Scotland, 1953—54; MA in Math. Stats., Columbia U., 1956; PhD, Stanford U., 1961. Asst. prof. dept. biostats. U. Pitts., 1959-62; asst. prof. dept. preventive medicine U. Wash., Seattle, 1962-65, assoc. prof., 1965-69, prof., 1969-70, prof., chmn. dept. biostats., 1970-72, prof. dept. health svcs., adj. prof. dept. biostats., 1975-98, chmn. dept., 1983-94, prof. emeritus, 1999—; hon. prof. West China U. of Med. Scis., Szechwan, China, 1988-98; overseas fellow Churchill Coll., Cambridge U., 1991-92; sr. scientist Seattle Vets. Affairs Med. Ctr., 1994—2001. Biometrician VA Co-op Study on Treatment of Esophageal Varices, 1961—73; sr. cons. biostatistics Wash., Alaska regional med. programs, 1967—72; mem. epidemiology & disease control study sect. NIH, 1969—73; clin. prof. dept. cmty. medicine and internat. health Sch. Medicine, Georgetown U., Washington, 1972—75; dep. dir. Nat. Ctr. Health Stats. HEW, 1972—73, dir., 1973—75; rsch. scientist Health Care Study Ctr. Battelle Human Affairs Rsch. Ctr., Seattle, 1975—76, dir., 1976—78, Health & Population Study Ctr. Battelle Human Affairs Rsch. Ctr., 1978—83; chmn. health svcs. rsch. study sect. HEW, 1976—79; chmn. health svcs. R & D field program rev. panel VA, 1988—91; chmn. health svcs. info steering com. State of Wash., 1993—94; mem. nat. adv. coun. Agy. for Health Care Policy & Rsch. Dept. HHS U.S. Govt., 1994—97; mem. com. on nat. stats. NRC, NAS, 1994—2000; chmn. sci. adv. com. Med. Outcomes Trust, 1994—99; mem. report rev. com. NAS, 2005—. Contbr. articles on biostats., health svcs. and population studies to profl. publs.; mem. editl. bd.: Jour. Family Practice, 1978-90, Pub. Health Nursing, 1992-98. Mem. tech. bd. Milbank Meml. Fund, 1974-76, Health Svcs. and Outcomes Rsch. Methodology, 1999-04. Recipient Outstanding Svc. citation HEW, 1975; Fulbright scholar 1953-54. Fellow AAAS, APHA (Spiegelman Health Stats. award 1970, program devel. bd. 1971, chmn. stats. sect. 1978-80, governing coun. 1983-85, stats. sect. recognition award 1989), Am. Statis. Assn. (mem. adv. com. to divsn. statis. policy 1975-77); mem. Assn. Health Svcs. Rsch. (pres. 1994-95, bd. dirs. 1991-2000), Inst. Medicine of NAS (chmn. membership com. 1984-86, mem. bd. on health care svcs. 1987-96, forum health stats. 1994-95, chmn. com. on clin. evaluation 1990-93), Biometrics Soc. (pres. Western N.Am. Region 1971), Wash. State Acad. Scis. (bd. dirs. 2007—), Sigma Xi, Phi Beta Kappa. Home: 4900 NE 39th St Seattle WA 98105-5209 Office: U Wash Dept Health Svcs PO Box 358852 Seattle WA 98195-8852 Office Phone: 206-524-9410. E-mail: perrin@u.washington.edu.

PERRIN, MICHAEL WARREN, lawyer; b. Cameron, Tex., Nov. 10, 1946; s. Frank W. and Mary Ann (Green) P.; m. Melinda Elizabeth Hill, Aug. 9, 1969; children: Elizabeth, Carter, Hunter. BS, U. Tex., Austin, 1969, JD, 1971. Bar: Tex. 1972, U.S. Dist. Ct. (no., ea., we. and so. dists.) Tex., U.S. Ct. Appeals (5th and 11th cirs.), U.S. Supreme Ct. Assoc. Vinson & Elkins, Houston, 1972-73; assoc. Fisher, Roch & Gallagher, Houston, 1973-76; ptnr. Fisher, Gallagher, Perrin & Lewis, Houston, 1976-91; sole practice Houston, 1991-96; ptnr. King & Spalding, Houston, 1996—. Fellow Am. Coll. Trial Lawyers, Internat. Acad. Trial Lawyers, Internat. Soc. Barristers; mem. Am. Bd. Trial Advocates, Am. Bar Found., Houston Young Lawyers Assn. (sec. 1974-75), Tex. Young Lawyers Assn. (dir. 1976-78, chmn. bd. 1978-79), Houston Trial Lawyers Assn. (pres. 1987-88), Tex. Trial Lawyers Assn. (pres. 1989-90), Tex. Bar Found. (Houston chpt.), U. Tex. Devel. bd. Methodist.

PERRIN, ROBERT, writer, consultant; b. Ann Arbor, Mich., Aug. 21, 1925; m. Barbara J. Groom, June 25, 1949; children: Stephen, Jennifer Perrin Hummel. BS, U. Minn., 1945. Reporter United Press Assn., Detroit, 1948-49, Detroit Free Press, 1949-55; adminstrv. asst. U.S. Senate, Washington, 1955-66; asst. dir. U.S. Office Econ. Opportunity, Washington, 1966-68, dep. dir., 1968-70; v.p. Mich. State U., East Lansing, 1970-79; vice-chancellor SUNY System, Albany, 1979-85; exec. v.p. Tchrs. Ins. and Annuity Assn.-Coll. Retirement Equities Fund, NYC, 1987-92; cons. Dept. State, 1993-94. Author: Piggy's Luck and More Tales of Evildoing, 1998, Keeping in Practice, 2001; contbr. articles to mags., newspapers. Mem. U.S.-Mex. Commn. on Border Devel., Washington, 1967-68. Lt. USNR, 1943-46, PTO. Fellow Reid Found., 1954; Pulitzer prize nominee Detroit Free Press, 1956. Home: 2435 Emerald Lake Dr East Lansing MI 48823-7256

PERRINE, RICHARD LEROY, environmental engineer, educator; b. Mountain View, Calif., May 15, 1924; s. George Alexander and Marie (Axelson) P.; m. Barbara Jean Gale, Apr. 12, 1945; children: Cynthia Gale, Jeffrey Richard. AB, San Jose State Coll., 1949; MS, Stanford U., 1950, PhD in Chemistry, 1953. Cert. environ. profl., 1987. Research chemist Calif. Research Corp., La Habra, 1953-59; assoc. prof. UCLA, 1959-63, prof. engring. and applied sci., 1963-92, prof. emeritus, 1992—, chmn. environ. sci. and engring., 1971-82; prin. Aspen Environ. Group, 1990-93. V.p. Sage Resources, 1988-91; cons. environ. sci. and engring., energy resources, flow in porous media; mem. Los Angeles County Energy Commn., 1973-81; mem. adv. council South Coast Air Quality Mgmt. Dist., 1977-82; mem. air conservation com. Los Angeles County Lung Assn., 1970-84; mem. adv. com. energy div. Oak Ridge Nat. Lab., 1987-90; mem. policy bd. William D. Ruckelshaus Inst. Environ. and Natural Resources U. Wyo., 1994-2004. Editor in chief The Environ. Profl., 1985-90. Served with AUS, 1943-46. Recipient Outstanding Engr. Merit award in environ. engring. Inst. Advancement Engring., 1975; ACT-SO award in field of chemistry West Coast region NAACP, 1984. Fellow AAAS; mem. Am. Chem. Soc., Soc. Petroleum Engrs., Am. Inst. Chem. Engrs., Can. Inst. Mining and Metallurgy, N.Am. Assn. Environ. Edn., Nat. Assn. Environ. Profls. (cert.), Air and Waste Mgmt. Assn., Assn. Environ. Engring. and Sci. Profs., Sierra Club, Wilderness Soc., Audubon Soc., Sigma Xi, Tau Beta Pi, Phi Lambda Upsilon. Home: 22611 Kittridge St West Hills CA 91307-3609 Office: Univ Calif Engring Bldg I Rm 3066D Los Angeles CA 90095-0001 E-mail: rperrine@ucla.edu.

PERRINEAU, HAROLD, actor; b. Bklyn., Aug. 7, 1963; s. Harold Williams; m. Brittany Perrineau; 1 child, Aurora. Studied, Shenandoah Conservatory. Actor: (films) Shakedown, 1988, King of NY, 1990, Smoke, 1995, Flirt, 1995, Blood and Wine, 1996, The Edge, 1997, Come To, 1998, Lulu On The Bridge, 1998, The Tempest, 1998, A Day in Black and White, 1998, The Best Man, 1999, Woman on Top, 2000, Overnight Sensation, 2000, Someone Like You, 2001, Prison Song, 2001, On Line, 2002, The Matrix Reloaded, 2003; (TV series) Fame, 1982, Oz, 1997, Lost, 2004 (Outstanding Performance by an Ensemble in a Drama Series, Screen Actors Guild award, 2006).

PERRON, EDWARD ADRIAN, lawyer; b. Washington, Jan. 19, 1954; s. Edward Joseph and Irene (Lum) P.; m. Julie Cornman, June 29, 1980; children: Kelly Elizabeth, Christopher Edward. BA in Economics and East Asian Studies, Harvard U., 1975, JD, 1979. Bar: Calif. 1979, US Dist. Ct. (ctrl. dist.) Calif. 1979, US Ct. Appeals (9th cir.) 1980, DC 1995, NY 1996. Assoc. Lillick & McHose, Los Angeles, 1979-85, ptnr., 1985-90; ptnr., mem. exec. com., chair office mgmt. com. Pillsbury Madison & Sutro, Los Angeles, 1991—2001, vice chmn., ptnr. compensation com., 1996, chmn., ptnr. compensation com., 1997—98; (Pillsbury Madison & Sutro merged with Winthrop, Stimson, Putnam, 2001); ptnr., mem. mng. bd. & ptnr. compensation com. Pillsbury Winthrop LLP, Los Angeles, 2001—06; (Pillsbury Winthrop LLP merged with Shaw Pittman LLP, 2005); ptnr., corp. & securities dept., mem. mng. bd. & ptnr. compensation com. Pillsbury Winthrop Shaw Pittman LLP, Los Angeles, 2005—06. Co-chmn. ptnr. compensation com. Pillsbury Winthrop LLP, 2004, chmn. ptnr. compensation com., 07. Mem. exec. adv. bd. Japan Am. Cmty. & Cultural Ctr., LA, 1990—, Asian Pacific-Am. Legal Ctr., LA, 1995—. Mem. Japan Am. Soc. So. Calif. (gen. counsel, dir. 1985-2006, chmn. 2007—), Japan Bus. Assn. So. Calif., ABA, Calif. Bar Assn., Los Angeles County Bar Assn. Office: Pillsbury Winthrop Shaw Pittman LLP 725 S Figueroa St Los Angeles CA 90017-5524 Office Phone: 213-488-7352. Office Fax: 213-629-1033. Business E-Mail: edward.perron@pillsburylaw.com.

PERRONE, NICHOLAS, engineering company executive; b. NYC, Apr. 30, 1930; B. Aero. Engring., Poly. Inst. Bklyn., 1951, MS, 1953, PhD, 1958. Research asst., then assoc. applied mechanics Bklyn. Poly. Inst., 1951-58; asst. prof., then assoc. prof. Pratt Inst., 1958-62; sr. scientist Structural Mechanics br. Office Naval Research, Washington, 1962-67, acting head dept., 1967-68, dir. program, 1968-69, 71-82; pres. CASA Gifts Inc., 1983-85; dep. to pres. Advanced Tech. and Research Inc., 1986-87; pres. Perrone Forensic Cons. Inc., 1987—. Lectr. civil engring. Cath U. Am., 1962-64, adj. prof., 1965-91; spl. research fellow NIH, Georgetown U., 1969-70; participant numerous workshops, confs., symposia; lectr. in field. Contbg. author: Biodynamics, 1980; editor or co-editor numerous monographs; editorial adv. bd.: Advances in Engring. Software, Computers and Structures, Engineering Fracture, Pressure Vessels and Piping; contbr. numerous articles to profl. jours. Fellow AAAS, ASME, Am. Acad. Mechanics; mem. ASCE, AIAA, N.Y. Acad. Sci., Am. Soc. Engring. Edn., Soc. Automotive Engrs., Soc. Mfg. Engrs. Address: 8 Cherry Ln Newtown Square PA 19073-3949 Home Phone: 610-325-7324; Office Phone: 610-325-4447. E-mail: nicholasperrone@comcast.net.

PERROT, PAUL NORMAN, museum director; b. Paris, July 28, 1926; came to US, 1946, naturalized, 1954; s. Paul and K. Norman (Derr) P.; m. Joanne Stovall, Oct. 23, 1954; children— Paul Latham, Chantal Marie Claire, Jeannine, Robert. Student, Ecole du Louvre, 1945-46, N.Y. U. Inst. Fine Arts, 1946-52. Asst. The Cloisters, Met. Mus. Art, 1948-52; asst. to dir. Corning (NY) Mus. Glass, 1952-54, asst. dir. mus., 1954-60, dir., 1960-72; editor Jour. Glass Studies, 1959-72; asst. sec. for mus. programs Smithsonian Instn., Washington, 1972-84; dir. Va. Mus. Fine Arts, 1984-91, Santa Barbara Mus. Art, 1991-94, mus. cons., 1995—. Lectr. glass history, aesthetics, museology; past v.p. Internat. Coun. Mus. Found.; past pres. N.E. Conf. Mus.; past pres. Internat. Centre for Study of Preservation and Restoration of Cultural Property, Rome, mem. coun., 1974-88. Author: Three Great Centuries of Venetian Glass, 1958, also numerous articles on various hist. and archael. subjects. Former trustee Winterthur Mus.; former trustee, treas. Mus. Computer Network; former mem. Internat. Cons. Com. for the Preservation of Moenjodaro; former chmn. adv. com. World Monuments Fund; former chmn. vis. com. Getty Conservation Inst. Mem. Am. Assn. Mus. (past v.p., coun. 1967-78, named to Centennial Honor Roll, 2006), NY State Assn. Mus. (past pres.), Internat. Assn. History Glass (past v.p.) Corning Friends of Library (past pres.), So. Tier Library System (past pres.). E-mail: paulnperrot@comcast.net. *

PERROTTA, ANTONIO, trust company executive; arrived in U.S., 1993; BS in Engring., Mil. Inst. Engring., Rio de Janeiro, 1981; BS in Econs., Rio de Janeiro State U., 1982; MS in Computer Sci., Mil. Inst. Engring., Rio de Janeiro, 1985. Sr. tech. mgr. Bamerindus Bank, Rio de Janeiro, Rio de Janeiro, 1981—93; sr. mgr. Price Waterhouse, NYC, 1993—95; v.p. J.P.Morgan, NYC, 1995—2003; chief tech. officer Bessemer Trust, Woodbridge, NJ, 2003—.

PERRUCCI, ROBERT, sociologist, educator; b. NYC, Nov. 11, 1931; s. Dominic and Inez (Mucci) P.; m. Carolyn Land Cummings, Aug. 4, 1965; children: Mark Robert, Celeste Ann, Christopher Robert, Alissa Cummings, Martin Cummings. BS, SUNY, Cortland, 1958; MS, Purdue U., West Lafayette, Ind., 1959, PhD, 1962. Asst. prof. sociology Purdue U., West Lafayette, Ind., 1962-65, assoc. prof., 1965-67, prof., 1967—, head dept., 1978-87. Vis. Simon prof. U. Manchester (Eng.), 1968-69; Bd. dirs. Ind. Center on Law and Poverty, 1973-76 Author: Sociology, 1983, Circle of Madness, 1974, Divided Loyalties, 1980, The Triple Revolution, 1971, Profession Without Community, 1968, The Engineers and the Social System, 1968, Mental Patients and Social Networks, 1982, Plant Closings: International Context and Local Consequences, 1988, Networks of Power, 1989, Japanese Auto Transplants in the Heartland: Corporatism and Community, 1994, The New Class Society, 1999, Science Under Siege?, 2000, The New Class Society: Goodbye American Dream, 2003, The Transformation of Work in the New Economy,2007; editor: The American Sociologist, 1982—84, Social Problems, 1993-96, Contemporary Sociology, 2000-2005; contbr. articles to profl. jours. Served with USMC, 1951-53. Recipient grants, NSF, 1966—68, 1976—78, NIMH, 1969—72, Sloan Found., 2002—05; fellow, Social Sci. Rsch. Coun., 1962. Mem. Am. Sociol. Assn., Soc. Study Social Problems (dir. 1980-83, v.p. 1996-97, pres. 1999-2000), N. Central Sociol. Assn. (pres. 1973-74) Home: 305 Leslie Ave West Lafayette IN 47906-2411 Office: Dept Sociology Purdue U West Lafayette IN 47907

PERRY, ANNE MARIE LITCHFIELD, secondary school educator; b. LaJunta, Colo., June 20, 1943; d. Robert Silas and Anne (Kennedy) Hovey, Robert Latta Litchfield (Stepfather); m. Franklin Haile Perry, Dec. 21, 1968; children: Kristina Marie, Tad Kennedy. BE, Drake U., 1966; MA, U. Tex., 1969; PhD, Tex. A&M U., 1977. Grade sch. tchr., San Antonio, 1966—67, Austin, 1967—68; rsch. assoc. R&D Ctr., U. Tex., Austin, 1968; grad. asst., instr. Tex. A&M U., 1969—70; kindergarten tchr., 1970—72; instr. U. St. Thomas, 1973—74; spl. edn. tchr., supr. Cypress, Cypress-Fairbanks Ind. Sch. Dist., Houston, 1974—77, supr. gifted/.talented, bilingual, English lang. devel. programs, 1977—80; mem. adj. grad. faculty U. Houston, 1979—80; lower sch. dir. curriculum and ednl. resources Kinkaid Sch., Houston, 1980—85, dir. young writers workshops, 1985—; tchr., chair lang. arts dept. Klein Intermediate Sch. Dist., Tex., 1986—2001. Vis. asst. prof. Tex. A&M U., 1988—89; cons. in field. Author (photographer): Riders Ready, 1985; author: Teacher Guide and Student Packet for Frindle, 2002, Just Like Always, 2005; editor: Travels in Mexico and California, 1988, Bluebonnet Books-Activities for 1996, Lonestar Books-Activities for 1993-1994 and 1994-1995. Named Tchr. of Yr., Hancock Elem. Sch., 1975. Mem.: NEA, Harley Owners Group-Branzos de Dios, Soc. of Children's Book Writers and Illustrators, Tex. State Tchrs. Assn., Run for the Wall. Methodist. Home: 10965 Clyde Acord Rd Franklin TX 77856-5821 Home Phone: 979-828-4374. Personal E-mail: aperry@flash.net.

PERRY, BARRY W., manufacturing executive; b. South Dartmouth, Mass., May 1946; s. Antone and Adelaide Perry; m. Janice G. Perry; 3 children. BS in plastics engring., U. Mass., 1968. With GE; group v.p., gen. mgr. latex specialty polymers divsn. Rhone-Poulenc, 1991—93; group v.p., gen. mgr. pigments and additives group Engelhard Corp., 1993—97, pres., 1997—2001, CEO, 1997—, chmn., 2001—. Bd. dirs. Arrow Electronics Inc., Cookson Group PLC, 2002—. Mem. corp. coun. Conservation Fund. Avocations: antique weapons, bicycling, walking. Office: 101 Wood Ave Iselin NJ 08830

PERRY, BROOKE ELIZABETH, public relations executive; d. Jack Lee and Patricia Suzy Perry. BJ, Marshall U., Huntington, NY, 1999. Publicist Lane Bryant, NYC, 2000—01; media rels. mgr. Charming Shoppers, NYC, 2001—. Mentor Big Bros. Big Sisters, NYC, 2005—. Recipient Gold award, Event Mktg., 2006. Mem.: Internat. Assn. Bus. Comm., Pub. Rels. Soc. Am., Am. Mensa. Office: Charming Shoppes 463 7th Ave 14th Fl New York NY 10018

PERRY, CHARLES OWEN, sculptor; b. Helena, Mont., Oct. 18, 1929; s. Owen Hindmarch and Margaret Carroll (Bache) P.; m. Sheila Alicia Henry, June 22, 1962; children— Paul, Carlo, Daniela, Patrick, Marco. Student, Columbia U., 1953; M.Arch., Yale U., 1958. Architect Skidmore Owings & Merrill, San Francisco, 1958-64, Prix de Rome Architecture, 1964-66. Sculptor-in-residence Dartmouth Coll., 1973. One-man shows include Hansen Gallery, San Francisco, 1964, Waddell Gallery, N.Y.C., 1967, 70, Dartmouth Coll., 1973, Arts Club, Chgo., 1973, Auguste st-Gaudens Mus., N.H.; exhibited in group shows at Whitney Mus., 1964, 66, Spoleto Festival, 1967, Venice Biennale, 1970, Quadrienalle di Arte de Roma, 1977, Katonah Gallery, N.Y.; represented in permanent collections at Mus. Modern Art, N.Y.C., Art Inst. Chgo., San Francisco Mus. Art, U. Ind. Mus. Art, Dartmouth Coll., U. Mich., Nat. Air and Space Mus., IBM, Charlotte, N.C., Hyatt Regency, San Francisco, Fed. Res. Bank, Mpls., Barnett Plaza, Tampa, Lincoln Ctr., Dallas, Shell Oil Bldg., Melbourne, Australia, GE Hdqrs., Fairfield, Conn., Bushnell Park, Hartford, Conn., Crystal City, Arlington, Va., Zeimu U., Tokyo, Kokubu Civic Ctr., Japan; patentee in furniture design field. Served with U.S. Army, 1951-53. Decorated Bronze star, Am. Iron & Steel Inst Citation for Excellende in Fine Art, 1969, 1971, Prix de Rome in Arch., 1964, Best of Show Nat. Acad. Design award sculpture, 1987, Product Design award, Inst. Bus. Designers, 1992, Internat Design Expo., Canada, 1990, 1998. Fellow Am. Acad. Rome, Nat. Acad. Design; mem. Century Assn. (N.Y.C.), Internat. Sculpture Ctr. Roman Catholic. Studio: 3 Raymond St Norwalk CT 06854-3107 Office Phone: 203-820-1011. Personal E-mail: coperry@aol.com. Business E-Mail: charles@charlesperry.com.

PERRY, CHRIS NICHOLAS, retired advertising executive; b. Pitts., Dec. 25, 1945; s. Nicholas and Georgia (Demas) P.; Kathleen Clarke, June 19, 1971; children: Damien, Adam, Dana. BA, U. Pitts., 1968. With Youngstown (Ohio) Steel, 1968-70; creative supr. Ketchum Communications, Pitts., 1970-74; pres., creative dir. Hedding, Perry, Davis Inc., Charlotte, N.C., 1974-76; v.p., creative dir. Fahlgren & Swink Advt., Marion, Ohio, 1976-79, Meldrum and Fewsmith Communications, Inc., Cleve., 1979-82, sr. v.p. creative services, 1982-85, exec. v.p. creative services, 1985-86, pres., chief operating officer, 1986-87, chmn., chief exec. officer, creative dir., 1987-98, also bd. dirs. Mem. bd. disting. judges and advisors The N.Y. Festivals, 1988—. Recipient numerous awards for creative excellence. Mem. Am. Assn. Advt. Agys. (sec.-treas. cen. region 1990-91, chmn. 1992-93), Cleve. Advt. Club, Cleve. Soc. Communicating Arts (pres. 1985-87, Disting. Communicator award 1991), The Hermit Club, Columbia Hills Country Club, The Union Club, Firestone Country Club.

PERRY, DALE LYNN, chemist; b. Greenville, Tex., May 12, 1947; s. Francis Leon and Violet (Inabinette) P. BS, Midwestern U., 1969; MS, Lamar U., Beaumont, Tex., 1972; PhD, U. Houston, 1974. NSF fellow dept. chemistry Rice U., Houston, 1976-77; Miller Research fellow dept. chemistry U. Calif.-Berkeley, 1977-79; prin. investigator solid state chemistry and spectroscopy Lawrence Berkeley Lab. U. Calif., 1979—, sr. scientist, 1987—. Lectr. Ana G. Mendez Ednl. Found., 1988; rsch. mem. G.T. Seaborg Inst. for Transactinium Sci. Author, editor: Instrumental Surface Analysis of Geologic Materials, 1990, Applications of Analytical Techniques to the Characterization of Materials, 1992, Applications of Synchrotron Radiation Techniques to Materials Science, 1993, II, 1995, III, 1996, IV, 1998, V, 2001, VI, 2002, Handbook of Inorganic Compounds, 1995, Materials Synthesis and Characterization, 1997; contbr. articles to profl. jours. Named Outstanding Mentor for Undergrad. Rsch., US Dept. Energy, 2002. Fellow AAAS, Royal Soc. Chemistry (London); mem. Am. Chem. Soc. (chmn. materials chemistry and engring. subdivsn., indsl. and engring. chemistry divsn., 1992-96), Soc. Applied Spectroscopy, Coblentz Soc., Materials Rsch. Soc. (corp. participation com. 1991-96), Sigma Xi (nat. rsch. award 1974). Office: U Calif Lawrence Berkeley Nat Lab Mail Stop 70A 1150 Berkeley CA 94720-0001

PERRY, DAVID ANTHONY, ecologist; b. Kansas City, Kans., Sept. 19, 1938; s. Everett Cecil Perry and Maxine Leona (Sharkey) Cartwright; m. Peggy Louise Cayton, Nov. 21, 1962 (dec. Nov. 1981); children: Kyna, David Jr., Maia; m. Carol Ivy Rosenblum, Aug. 7, 1982; 1 child, Michael. BS in Forestry, U. Fla., 1961, MS in Forest Econs., 1966; MS in Physics, Mont. State U., 1971, PhD in Ecology, 1974. Range ecologist Mont. Dept. Natural Resources, Helena, 1974-75; rsch. forester U.S. Forest Svc., Bozeman, Mont., 1975-77; asst. prof. Oreg. State U., Corvallis, 1977-81, assoc. prof., 1981-86, prof. dept. forest sci., 1986-97, prof. emeritus, 1997—. Mem. adv. bd. Pub. Forestry Found., Eugene, Oreg., 1993-97, Ecoforestry Inst., Victoria, B.C., Can., 1993—; mem. sci. adv. bd. Oreg. Biodiversity Project, 1994-97; bd. dirs. Nat. Ctr. Conservation Sci. and Policy; mem. commn. sci. sustainable forestry, 2002—. Editor: Nitrogen Fixing Plants in Management, 1979, Maintaining Long-Term Productivity, 1989; author: Forest Ecosystems, 1994; co-author: Forest Ecosystems, 2d edit., 2007; mem. editl. bd. Conservation Biology, Corvallis, 1994-97; contbr. over 75 articles to profl. jours. Mem. adv. bd. Sitka Ctr. for Art and Ecology, Niskowin, Oreg., 1988-97; bd. dirs. Ka Makani o Kohala, Kapa'au, Hawaii, 1999—. With USMC, 1956-57. Grantee NSF, U.S. Forestry Svc., U.S. Dept. Energy, Bur. of Land Mgmt., Nat. Biol. Survey. Mem. Ecol. Assn. Am., Soc. for Conservation Biology, Sigma Xi. Democrat. Avocations: spiritual exploration, shamanism. Office: Oreg State U Dept Forest Svc Corvallis OR 97331

PERRY, DOUGLAS, opera singer; B.M., Wittenberg U.; MA, Ball State U. Made debut as Don Basilio in Marriage of Figaro, with N.Y.C. Opera; appeared as King Kaspar in: Amahl and the Night Visitors; appeared as Timothy in: Help! Help! The Globolinks; appeared as Guillot in: Manon; Dancing Master and Brighella in: Ariadne auf Naxos; Met. Opera debut as scientist/first mate in: The Voyage (Philip Glass); European debut with Netherlands Opera as Mahatma Gandhi in Satyagraha (Philip Glass); appeared as analyst in A Quiet Place (Bernstein), La Scala and Vienna Stadtsoper, as Sailor 1, Scientist 3, Traveler 2 world premier Corvo Bronco, Teatro Camô, Lisbon, Portugal, Teatro Real, Madrid; featured soloist on tours and recs. with Gregg Smith Singers and Camerata Singers; performed with Sante Fe Opera, also performed with Ft. Worth Opera, Chatauqua Opera, N.Y.C. Opera, Opera Co. of Boston, Houston Grand Opera, Balt.

Opera., Miami Opera, Chgo. Lyric Opera, Seattle Opera, San Francisco Opera, Opera Co. Phila.; recs. include Satyagraha, Songs from Liquid Days, A Quiet Place, Mother of Us All. Address: 170 W End Ave New York NY 10023-5401 Office: Pinnacle Arts Mgmt 889 9th Ave Ste 1 New York NY 10019-0999

PERRY, E. LYNN, lawyer; d. Eldon G. Perry and Doris E. Noonan BA, U. Ariz., 1970; JD, Loyola U., 1976. Bar: Ill. 1977, US Dist. Ct. (no. dist.) Ill. 1977, NY 1980, US Dist. Ct. (so. and ea. dists.) NY, Calif. 1980, US Dist. Ct. (no., ea. and cen. dists.) Calif., US Ct. Appeals (9th cir.), US Supreme Ct. Flight attendant Pan American World Airways, NYC and L.A., 1971-75; asst. state's atty. Cook County State's Atty., Chgo., 1977-79; assoc. Kass, Goodkind, Wechsler & Labaton, NYC, 1980-81; assoc. counsel MasterCard Internat., Inc., NYC, 1981-84; assoc. Townsend and Townsend and Crew, San Francisco, 1984-89, ptnr., 1989—2002, Thelen Reid & Priest, 2002—06, Perry IP Group, Greenbrae, Calif., 2006—. Adj. prof. U. Calif. Hastings Coll. Law, 2005—; spkr. in field. Scholar U. Ariz., Tucson, 1970, Loyola U., L.A., 1976. Mem. ABA (Governing Com. Forum Franchising 1991-93), Internat. Trademark Assn. (editl. bd. Trademark Reporter 1985—, profl. writing competition judge 1988-2005, panel of neutrals 2003—), Calif. State Bar (trademarks chair 1990-91, Exec. Com. Intellectual Property Sect. 1991-94), San Francisco Intellectual Property Law Assn. (program chair 1987-88). Avocations: tennis, yoga, skiing. Office: Perry IP Group Ste 3900 4 Embarcadero Ctr San Francisco CA 94111

PERRY, GEORGE, neuroscientist, educator; s. George Richard and Mary Arlene (George) P.; m. Paloma Aguilar, May 21, 1983; children: Anne, Elizabeth. AA in Liberal Arts, Allan Hancock Coll., Santa Maria, Calif., 1973; BA in Zoology with honors, U. Calif., Santa Barbara, 1974; PhD in Marine Biology, U. Calif., San Diego, 1979. Postdoctoral fellow Baylor Coll. Medicine, Houston, 1979-82; from asst. prof. to prof. pathology Case Western Res. U., Cleve., 1982-94, prof., 1994—2005, interim chair dept., 2001—05; affiliated prof. chemistry and biochemistry U. Alaska, Fairbanks, 2001—; dean Coll. of Scis. U. Tex., San Antonio, 2006—. Tchg. asst. U. Calif., San Diego, 1977, Stanford U., 1978—79; memory task force on Alzheimer's disease Ohio Gov., 1987, 90; mem. sci. adv. bd. Familial Alzheimer's Disease Rsch. Found., 1988—; mem., chair neurology scis. study sect. NIH, Bethesda, Md., 1989—95; cons. Nymox, Inc., Panacea Pharms., Inc., Prion Devel. Labs., Voyager, Takada Pharms., Alzheimer Rsch. Disease and Regeneration Forum; mem. Faculty of 1000 Biology, Neurobiology Sect., 2004—; spkr. in field; mem. numerous rev. bds. nationally/internationally. Author: The Neuronal Cytoskeleton, 1992, numerous publs. in field; co-author: Frontiers in Biosciences, 2002, Neurosignals, 2002, Brain Pathology, 2004, Microscopy Rsch. and Technique, 2005, Internat. Jour. Exptl. Pathology, 2005; assoc. editor: Am. Jour. Pathology, 1994-2000, Jour. Biomedicine and Biotechnology, 2004—; sr. assoc. editor: Microscopy Rsch. and Technique, 2002—; mem. editl. bd. Am. Jour. Pathology, 1992—, Alzheimer Disease and Associated Disorders, 1994—, Alzheimer's Disease Rev., 1995-98, Jour. Alzheimer's Disease, 1997—, Jour. Exptl. Neurol., 1997-99, Molecular Chem. Neuropathology, 1997-99, Jour. Neural Transmission, 1998-2003, Investigational Drugs Jour., 1998—, Brain Pathology, 1999—, Jour. Molecular Neurosci., 1999-2001, Antioxidant and Redox Signaling, 2000—, Research Signpost, 2000, Lab. Investigation, 2000—06, Brain Rsch., 2002—, Current Medicinal Chemistry, 2002—, Neurobiology of Lipids, 2003—, Jour. Biomed. Biotech., 2002—, Pathology, 2003—, Pharm. Devel. Regime, 2003—, Med. Chemistry Rev.-Online, 2003-05, Current Alzheimer Rsch., 2003—, NeuroSignals, 2003—, Disease Markers, 2003—, Neurobiology Disease, 2004—, Lett Drug Design Discovery, 2004—; reviewer: Expert Review of Neurotherapeutics, 2004—, Mini-Reviews in Medicinal Chemistry, 2005—, Future Neurology, 2005—, Jour. Biological Chemistry, 2006—, Developmental Microbiology and Molecular Biology, 2006—, CNS Agents in Medicinal Chemistry, 2006—, Jour. Clin. Pathology, 2007—, Molecular Neurodegeneration, 2007—, Open Medicinal Chemistry Jour., 2007—, Acta Neuropathol., Alan Liss Publ. Co., Am. Jour. Pathol., Ann Neurol, others; contbr. articles to Exptl. Cell Rsch., Jour Cell Biology, Devel. Biology, Brain Rsch., Am. Jour. Pathology, Jour. Neurosci., European Jour. Cell Biology, Nature, Annals Neurology, Lancet, Acta Neuropathology, Jour. Neurochemistry, Neurosci. Letters, Neuroreport, Med. Hypotheses, Nature Medicine, Neurodegeneration, Sci., others. Pres. Serra Club, 1995-97. Tng. corps. USAR, 1972—74, U. Calif. Santa Barbara. Recipient Bausch and Lomb medal, 1971, Rsch. Career Devel. award, NIH, 1988—93, Career Devel. award, 1988, Temple award, Alzheimer's Assn., 1999, Disting. Am. Portuguese Ancestry award, Portuguese-Am. Hist. Found., Inc., 2001, Mensch award, Alzheimer Rsch. Forum, 2003, Cmty. Svc. award, Cleve. Area Chpt. Alzheimer's Assn., 2004; fellow, Kennecott Copper, 1974—75, Muscular Dystrophy Assn., 1980—82, Philip Morris, USA, 2003—06; grantee, NIH, 1985—, Am. Health Assistance Found., 1988—90, 1997—99, Alzheimer's Assn., 1989—90, 1998—2002, 2004—, United Mitochondrial Disease Fund, 2000—02. Fellow AAAS; mem. AAUP (exec. com. 1996—2006, membership chair 1996-98, v.p. 1998-99, pres. 1999—2006), Am. Soc. Cell Biology, Electron Microscopy Soc. N.E. Ohio (treas. 1986-88, trustee 1988-90, pres. 1990-91), Soc. Neurosci., Am. Assn. Neuropathologists (awards com. 1992-93, 95-2002, chmn. 2001-02, internat. congress neuropathology concilator 1995-2000, sec.-treas. 2003-), Am. Soc. Investigative Pathology (program com. 1998-2001), Am. Soc. Neurochemistry, U.S. and Can. Acad. of Pathology, Hispanic Med. Assn. (com. on status of Portuguese in medicine and sci.), Soc. for Neurosci., Sigma Xi (pres. chpt. 2004-06). Democrat. Roman Catholic. Avocation: genealogy. Office: U Tex San Antonio Coll Scis One UTSA Circle San Antonio TX 78249-0661 Office Phone: 210-458-4450. Business E-Mail: george.perry@utsa.edu.

PERRY, GEORGE LEWIS, research economist, consultant; b. NYC, Jan. 23, 1934; s. Lewis G. and Helen L.P.; m. Jean Marion West, 1956; children: Elizabeth, Lewis G., George A.; m. 2d, Dina Needleman, 1987. BS, MIT, 1954, PhD, 1961. Editor Brookings Papers on Econ. Activity, 1970—; columnist L.A. Times, 1981-93. Bd. dirs. State Farm Mut. Automobile Ins. Co., Bloomington, Ill., Dreyfus Mut. Funds, N.Y.C.; co-dir. Brookings Panel Econ. Activity. Author: Unemployment, Money Wage Rates and Inflation, 1966, Curing Chronic Inflation, 1978, Economic Events, Ideas and Policies, 2000; contbr. articles to profl. jours. With USAF, 1955—57. Mem. Am. Econs. Assn. Office: Brookings Instn 1775 Massachusetts Ave NW Washington DC 20036-2103 E-mail: gperry@brookings.edu.

PERRY, GEORGE WILLIAMSON, lawyer; b. Cleve., Dec. 4, 1926; s. George William and Melda Patricia (Arther-Holt) P. BA in Econs., Yale U., 1949; JD, U. Va., 1953. Bar: Ohio 1953, DC 1958, US Supreme Ct. 1958, US Ct. Appeals (DC cir.) 1959. Atty. US Dept. Justice, Washington, 1954—56; assoc. Roberts and McInnis, Washington, 1957-59; atty. assoc. counsel Com. on Interstate Fgn. Commerce, US Ho. Reps., Washington, 1960—65; atty., advisor ICC, Washington, 1965-68; assoc. dir. devel. Yale U., New Haven, 1968-70; trust officer The No. Trust Co., Chgo., 1970-71; dir. tax rsch. Pan Am. World Airways, NYC, 1973-75; hearing officer Indsl. Commn. Ohio, Cleve., 1978-81; sole practice Cleve., 1981—. With US Army, 1945-46. Mem. Soc. Cin. in State of Conn., Ancient and Hon. Artillery Co. (mem. Boston-hereditary), Phi Delta Phi, Chi Delta Theta. Home: 1801 E 12th St #1522 Cleveland OH 44114-3541 Personal E-mail: gperryxyz@yahoo.com.

PERRY, GEORGE WILSON, oil and gas company executive; b. Pampa, Tex., July 18, 1929; s. Frank M. and Ruth (Ingersoll) P.; m. Patricia Carberry Bowen, 1950; children: Sally Jett Perry Pemrick, Susan Jeanne Perry Bynder-Schrier, Virginia Anne Perry Haynie, Tobe Jackson Perry. BS in Petroleum Engring., U. Tulsa, 1952. Registered profl. engr., Tex. Engr. Stanolind Oil & Gas Co., Oklahoma City, 1952—53, Parker Drilling Co., Tulsa, 1953—54, Holm Drilling Co., Tulsa, 1954—55; drilling engr. Mobil Oil, Victoria, Tex., 1955—61, engr. Lake Charles, La., 1955—61, Paris, 1961—68; ops. mgr. Anaco, Venezuela, 1968—72, NYC, 1972—73, Tehran, Iran, 1973—74, Stavanger, Norway, 1974—78, New Orleans, 1978—79; exec. v.p. Loffland Bros. Co., Tulsa, 1979—89; pres., CEO Gas Well Properties, Inc., Dallas, 1989—. Mem. Delta Tau Delta. Avocation: astronomy. Office: Gas Well Properties Inc PO Box 795302 5995 Summerside Dr Dallas TX 75379

PERRY, GLENN, orthopedic surgeon; Undergraduate degree, Dickinson Coll., 1973; MD, Temple U. Sch. Medicine. Diplomate Am. Bd. Orthop. Surgery. Intern Abington Meml. Hosp.; resident, orthop. Temple. U. Hosp.; group practice Perry & Barron Orthop., NC, 1987—. Head team physician Charlotte Hornets, 1987—2002; team physician U.S.A. Men's World Championship Basketball Team, 1998, U.S.A. Basketball Pre-Olympic Tournament, Am. Team, 1999, U.S.A. Men's Sr. Nat. Basketball Team, Olympic Games, Sydney, 2000, Charlotte Bobcats and Sting, 2004—; team physician, Women's Nat. Basketball League Charlotte Checkers, Charlotte Knights, Davidson Coll. Named one of Golf Digest 2006 Top Golf Doctors in Am. Mem.: NC Med. Soc., Arthroscopy Assn. N.Am., Am. Orthop. Soc. for Sports Medicine, Nat. Basketball Assn. Team Physician Soc. (pres. 1995—2000). Achievements include performing the first Autologous Carticel Transplantation in the Charlotte area; developing and training the first sports medicine fellow in Charlotte. Office: Perry & Barron Orthop 2826 Randolph Rd Charlotte NC 28211 Office Phone: 704-358-0308. *

PERRY, HAROLD OTTO, dermatologist; b. Rochester, Minn., Nov. 18, 1921; s. Oliver and Hedwig Clara (Tornow) P.; m. Loraine Thelma Moehnke, Aug. 27, 1944; children— Preston, Oliver, Ann, John. AA, Rochester Jr. Coll., 1942; BS, U. Minn., 1944, MB, 1946, MD, 1947; MS, Mayo Grad. Sch. Medicine, 1953. Diplomate Am. Bd. Dermatology with spl. competence in dermatopathology. Intern Naval Hosp., Oakland, Calif., 1946-47; resident in dermatology Mayo Grad. Sch. Medicine, 1949-52; practice medicine specializing in dermatology Rochester, 1953-86; mem. staff Mayo Clinic, 1953-86, mem. emeritus staff, 1987—; instr., asst. prof., assoc. prof. Mayo Med. Sch., 1953-86, prof., 1978-83, Robert H. Kieckhefer prof. dermatology, 1978-83, head dept. dermatology, 1975-83, emeritus prof. dermatology, 1987—. Civilian cons. dermatology to surgeon gen. USAF, 1973-84. Contbr. articles to med. jours. and, chpts. to books. With USNR, 1943-45, 46-49. Inducted into Rochester (Minn.) C.C. Alumni Hall of Fame, 1993; recipient Disting. Alumnus award Mayo Found., 1995. Mem. AMA, Am. Acad. Dermatology (pres. 1981, Sulzberger internat. lectr. 1986, Gold Medal for visionary leadership 1998), Am. Dermatol. Assn. (bd. dirs. 1985-89, pres. 1989-90), Am. Bd. Dermatology (bd. dirs. 1979-90, v.p. 1989, pres. 1990), Noah Worcester Dermatol. Soc. (pres. 1969), Minn. Dermatol. Soc. (pres. 1967), Chgo. Dermatol. Soc., Internat. Soc. Tropical Dermatology, Minn. Med. Assn.; hon. mem. French Dermatol. Soc., Spanish Acad. Dermatology, Brazilian Dermatol. Soc., Ga. Dermatol. Soc., Iowa Dermatol. Soc., Korean Dermatol. Soc., Bolivar Soc. Dermatology, Jacksonville Dermatol. Soc., N.Am. Clin. Dermatol. Soc., Pacific Dermatol. Assn. Office: Mayo Clinic Emeritus Staff Ctr 10th Fl Plummer Bldg Ctr Rochester MN 55905-0001 Office Phone: 507-284-2691.

PERRY, HELEN, medical/surgical nurse, secondary school educator; b. Birmingham, Ala., Mar. 4, 1927; d. Van Mary Ellenol (Thornton) Curry; m. Charlie Pitts, May 1960 (div.); 1 child, Charlenia Pitts; m. George Perry (dec. 1989); children: Hattie Mae(dec.), George Jr., Bishop, Jose Sr. Student, LaSalle Extension U., Chgo., 1968, Georgetown U., 1979; Doctorate/Mayanuis Mosaic Soc., Duke Univ., San Antonio, 1979; student in Nursing, Syracuse U. Cert. paramedic, of completion Ptnrs. in Health Sheperd Ctr. Am. South Side, 2006; LPN. Tchr. Wenona HS City Bd. Edn., Birmingham, 1977—2005, supply tchr., 2005—. Notary pub., Ala., 1975—; home health nurse U. Ala. Birmingham Hosp., 1988—; math. and reading tutor Princeton Elem. Sch., 2004. Composer: (songs) Twas the Hour of Midnight, 1950. Trustee Nat. Crime Watch, 1989; mem. adv. bd. Am. Security Coun., Va., Washington, 1969—91; mem. Coalition for Desert Storm; others; vol. ARC, Birmingham, 1970—; mem. crime watch Am. Police, Washington, 1989; mem. Hall of Fame Pres. Task Force, Washington, 1983—91, Image Devel. Adv. Bd.; nominee Nat. Rep. Com., Washington, 1991, 1992; selected VIP guest del. Rep. Nat. Conv., Houston, 1992; life mem. Rep. Presdl. Task Force, Washington, 1992; mem. Jefferson Com., 2001; mem. adv. bd. Nat. Congl. Com., Washington; mem. fin. com. fundraiser Middleton for Congress Campaign, 1994, Dist. # 59 Bd. Reps.; mem. exec. com. Jefferson County Rep., chairperson legis. dist. 52; chair Harriet Tubman Rep. Com.; del. Commonwealth of Ky. So. Rep. Leadership Conf., 2000; min. Greater Emmanuel Temple Holiness Ch., Birmingham, 1957—, ordained elder, vice champion mother bd.; mem. Nat. Law Enforcement Assn., 1989. Nominee Presdl. Election Registry, Rep. Presdl. Task Force, 1992; named Good Samaritan, Law Envforcement Officers; recipient award, Ala. Sheriff Assn., 1989, Navy League, 1989—91, cert. of appreciation, Pres. Congl. Task Force, 1990, Rep. Nat. Com., 1994, Diamond award, U.S.A. Serve Am., 1992, Rep. Presdl. award, Legion of Merit, 1994, Royal Proclamation, Royal Highness Kevin, Prince Regent of Hutt River Province, 1994, Royal Ceremonial jewel, Svc. award, Ala. Bd. Nursing, Outstanding Sr. Citizen's cert. of recognition. Mem.: Ala. Nurses Assn., Nat. Assn. Unknown Players, Nat. Rep. Women Assn., LaSalle Ext. U. Alumni (life). Avocations: singing, writing, reading, gardening. Home: 2021 10th Ave S Apt 513 Birmingham AL 35205-2716

PERRY, I. CHET, petroleum company executive; b. Phila., Jan. 18, 1943; s. Irving Chester Sr. and Erma Jackson (McNeil) P.; m. Eve Evenson Perry; 1 child, London Schade. BA in Psychology, Bus., Lake Forest Coll., 1965. Lic. real estate broker, Ill. Sr. mgmt. trainee British Overseas Airways Corp., London, 1968—69; owner Itec Internat. Ltd., Barrington, Ill., 1970—, Itec Refining & Mktg. Co., Ltd., Barrington, 1970—, CEO, mng. dir., 1986—. Lt. U.S. Army, 1965-68, Vietnam. Decorated Bronze Star, Purple Heart. Mem. Am. Petroleum Inst., European Petrochem. Assn., Internat. Ethanol Trade Assn. Brazil, Ethanol Assn. London, Barrington Bd. Realtors (bd. dirs. 1974-78), Forest Grove Club, Barrington Tennis Club. Republican. Mem. Soc. Of Friends. Avocations: tennis, photography. Home: 3 Porter School Rd Barrington IL 60010 Home Phone: 847-381-2636; Office Phone: 847-304-4700. Business E-Mail: chetperry@itecref.com.

PERRY, J. WARREN, health facility administrator, educator; b. Richmond, Ind., Oct. 25, 1921; s. Charles Thomas and Zona M. (Ohler) Perry. BA, DePauw U., 1944; postgrad., Harvard U., 1948—49; MA, Northwestern U., 1952, PhD, 1955; DSc (hon.), 1959, D'Youville Coll., 1990, Med. Coll. Ohio, 1996, DePauw U., 1998. Instr. St. John's Mil. Acad., Delafield, Wis., 1944—47; counselor, asst. prof. psychology U. Ill.-Chgo., 1953—56; dir. prosthetic-orthotic edn., asst. prof. orthopaedic surgery Northwestern U. Med. Sch., 1957—61; lectr. psychology U. Chgo., 1957—61; asst. chief div. tng. Vocat. Rehab. Adminstrn., HEW, 1961—64, dep. asst. commr. research and tng., 1964—66; prof. health scis. adminstrn. SUNY-Buffalo, 1966—95, founding dean Sch. Health Related Professions, 1966—77, dean and prof. emeritus, 1985—. Mary E. Switzer Meml. lectr., Dallas, 1977, Lexington, 91; mem. Task Force for Legislation for Allied Health Professions, 1966—67; com. edn. allied health professions and svcs., coun. med. edn. AMA, 1968—73; nat. adv. com. Am. Dietetic Assn., 1970—75, chmn., 1972—75; nat. rev. com., regional med. programs HEW, 1969—72; mem.steering com. on manpower policy for primary care bd. health promotion and disease prevention Inst. of Medicine-NAS, 1981—83, sr. advisor com. to study role allied health, com. to study med. manpower in VA, 1988—91; spl. med. adv. com. VA, 1974—77; mem. task force on manpower for prevention Fogarty Internat. Inst., NIH, 1975—76; mem. acad. planning com. Mass. Gen. Hosp. Founding editor Jour. Allied Health, 1972—78, editor emeritus, 1985—; contbr. articles to profl. jours. Mem. Legacy Soc.; charter mem. Cmty. Found. for Greater Buffalo, 1998—; patron of the arts Coun. of Buffalo and Erie County, 2000; bd. dirs., dir. com. opera edn. Lyric Opera Guild, Chgo., 1957—61; chmn. acad. divsn. dr., coun. trustees Buffalo Philharm. Orch., 1987—93; bd. dirs. Goodwill Industries, Buffalo, 1969—76; trustee Cmty. Music Sch. Buffalo, 1977—80; adv. bd., v.p. Sisters of Charity Hosp., Buffalo, 1969—87, pres., 1986—88; bd. visitors U. Pitts., 1977—80; coun. trustees D'youville Coll., Buffalo, 1978—88, trustee emeritus, 1989—95; bd. dirs. Am. Lung Assn. Western N.Y., 1975—92, pres., 1983; bd. dirs. ARC, Buffalo, Artpark State Performing Arts Ctr., Lewiston, NY, 1986—96, Am. Lung Assn. N.Y.State, 1981—85, exec. com., 1989—92; chmn. N.Y. State Coalition Smoking or Health, Albany, NY, 1987—91; trustee Theodore Roosevelt Inaugural Site Found., 1987, pres., 1991—94; bd. advisors Buffalo Coun. on World Affairs, 1987—88; trustee Buffalo Opera Co., 1989—94, chmn. opera adv. coun., 1995—97. Named Outstanding Individual Philanthropist, Nat. Soc. Fundraising Execs. Western N.Y., 1992, Ky. Col., 1969, Nebr. Admn., 1964, Man of the Yr., Opera Found. Buffalo, Inc., 2000, J. Warren Perry Disting. Author award in his honor, Jour. Allied Health, Perry Scholarship in his honor, U. Buffalo Found., J. Warren Perry Outstanding Vol. Leadership award in his honor, Western N.Y. chpt. ALA, J. Warren Perry Meml. lectr. in his honor, SUNY, Buffalo, Buffalo Philharmonic Chorus, 2003; recipient Sustained Superior Svc. award, HEW, 1965, Disting. Svc. award, Am. Orthotics-Prosthetics Assn., 1966, Buffalo Opera Co., 1995, Chancellor's award for adminstrv. svc., SUNY, 1977, 1st Allied Health Leadership award, 1988, Disting. Author award, Jour. Allied Health, 1978, Cert. of Merit, AMA, 1979, Pres. Cir. Pin, Buffalo State Coll., 1993, 50th Anniversary Alumni citation, De Pauw U., 1994, Outstanding Svc. award, Theodore Roosevelt Inaugural Site Found., 1994, Theodore Roosevelt Exemplary Citizenship award, 1997, Brotherhood/Sisterhood award in health, NCCJ Western N.Y., 1995, Christmas Seal Hall of Fame award, ALA N.Y. State, 1995, Disting. Citizenship award, Mayor of Buffalo, 1995, Patron of the Arts award, Arts Coun. of Buffalo and Erie County, 2000, Alumni Achievement award, SUNY-Buffalo, 2000, Wisdom award of honor, 1999, Humanitarian award, Coordinated Care Assn. Buffalo, 2002, Clara Barton award, ARC (Greater Buffalo chpt.), 2004; fellow Wisdom Hall of Fame fellow, Wisdom Soc., 1999; Perry Lecture Hall, D'Youville Coll. named in his honor, 2004. Fellow: Assn. Schs. of Allied Health Professions (pres. 1969—70, Cert. of Merit 1977, Pres.'s award 1978, Honors of Soc. award 1984); mem.: Nat. Rehab. Assn., Am. Pers. and Guidance Assn., Am. Dietetics Assn. (hon.), APA, Phi Beta Kappa, Delta Tau Delta, Phi Delta Kappa (pres. 1955). Home: 705 Renaissance Dr Apt 208 Williamsville NY 14221

PERRY, JACQUELIN, orthopedist, surgeon; b. Denver, May 31, 1918; d. John F. and Tirzah (Kuruptkat) P. BE, U. Calif., LA, 1940; MD, U. Calif., San Francisco, 1950; DSc (hon.), U. So. Calif., 1996. Intern Children's Hosp., San Francisco, 1950-57; resident in orthop. surgery U. Calif., San Francisco, 1951-55; orthop. surgeon Rancho Los Amigos Hosp., Downey, Calif., 1955—, chief stroke svc., 1972-75; chief pathokinesiology Rancho Los Amigos Med. Ctr., 1961—; mem. faculty U. Calif. Med. Sch., San Francisco, 1966—, clin. prof., 1973—; mem. faculty U. So. Calif. Med. Sch., 1969—, prof. orthop. surgery, 1972—, dir. polio and gait clinic, 1972—. Disting. lectr. for hosp. for spl. surgery and Cornell U. Med. Coll., NYC, 1977-78; Packard Meml. lectr. U. Colo. Med. Sch., 1970; Osgood lectr. Harvard Med. Sch., 1978; Summer lectr., Portland, 1977; Shands lectr.; cons. USAF; guest spkr. symposia; cons. Biomechanics Lab. Centinela Hosp., 1979—. Served as phys. therapist U.S. Army, 1941-46. Recipient Disting. Svc. award Assn. Rehab. Facilities, 1981, Pres.'s award, 1984, Isabelle and Lenard Goldensen award for tech. United Cerebral Palsy Assn., 1981, Jow Dowling award, 1985, Profl. Achievement award UCLA, 1988, Milton Cohen award Nat. Assn. Rehab., 1993, Tribute Pres. award Ruth Jackson Orthop. Soc., 2004; named Woman of Yr. for Medicine in So. Calif. LA Times, 1959, Alumnus of Yr. U. Calif. Med. Sch., 1980, Physician of Yr. Calif. Employment Devel. Dept., 1994; Jacquelin Perry Neuro Trauma Inst. Rancho Clin. Bldg. named in her honor, 1996. Mem. AMA, Am. Acad. Orthop. Surgeons (Kappa Delta award for rsch. 1977, orthop. rsch. svc., 1976), Am. Orthop. Assn. (Shands lectr. 1988), Western Orthop. Assn., Calif. Med. Soc., LA County Med. Soc., Am. Phys. Therapy Assn. (hon. Golden Pen award 1965), Am. Acad. Orthotists and Prosthetists (hon.), Scoliosis Rsch. Soc., LeRoy Abbott Soc., Am. Acad. Cerebral Palsy, Gait & Clin. Movement Analysis Soc. (mem. emeritus, Lifetime Achievement award 2000), Orthop. Rsch. Soc. (Shands award 1998, 99). Home: 12319 Brock Ave Downey CA 90242-3503 Office: Rancho Los Amigos Med Ctr 7601 Imperial Hwy Downey CA 90242-3456 Office Phone: 562-401-7177. E-mail: pklab@larei.org.

PERRY, JAMES ALFRED, environmental scientist, consultant, science educator, academic administrator; b. Dallas, Sept. 27, 1945; BA in Fisheries, Colo. State U., 1968; MA, Western State Coll., 1973; PhD, Idaho State U., 1981. Sr. water quality specialist Idaho Div. Environ., Pocatello, 1974-82; area mgr. Centrac Assocs., Salt Lake City, 1982; H.T. Morse disting. prof. water quality U. Minn., 1982—, head dept. fisheries, wildlife, conservation biol., 2000—06, dir. natural resources policy and mgmt., 1985—2002, spl. asst. to dean grad. sch., 1996-2000, interim assoc. v.p., dean internat. programs, 2006. Vis. scholar Oxford U., Green Coll., England, 1990—91; dep. dir. AID-funded Environ. Tng. Project for Ctrl. and Ea. Europe, 1992—96; assoc. Internat. Inst. Sustainable Devel., 2007—; cons. in field. Author: Water Quality Management of a Natural Resource, 1996, Ecosystem Management for Central and Eastern Europe, 2001; editor: Jour. Natural Resources and Life Scis. Edn., 1996—2004; mem. editl. bd. Mitigation and Adaptation Strategies for Global Change, 1998—2005. Charter mem. Leadership Devel. Acad., Lakewood, Minn., 1988; bd. dirs. Minn. Ctr. for Environ. Advocacy, 1995-2006, vice chmn., 2005. Fellow Pres.'s Academic Leadership Initiative, 2003-05; recipient Richard C. Newman Art of Tchg. award, 1998, Morse-Alumni award, 1999, Outstanding Svc. award U. Minn., 2001, Ctr. Integrative Study Writing award interdisciplinary tchg. of writing, 2003, Juror Brock Internat. Edn. prize, 2006; ACOP/ESCOP nat. leadership fellow, 1995-96, CIC acad. leadership fellow, 2000-01, Gordon L. Starr Leadership award, 2003-05. Fellow: Am. Inst. Fish Resource Biology; mem.: Acad. Disting. Tchrs., Nat. Assn. Univ. Fish and Wildlife Programs (sec./treas. 2001—), Soc. for Conservation Biology, Wildlife Soc., Am. Fisheries Soc., N.Am. Benthol. Soc. (exec. bd. Albuquerque 1990—91), Internat. Soc. Theoretical and Applied Limnology, Internat. Water Resources Assn., Am. Water Resources Assn., Minn. Acad. Scis. (bd. dirs. 1987—90), Gamma Sigma Delta (merit award 2001), Xi Sigma Pi, Sigma Xi. Office: Univ Minn Dept Fisheries Wildlife and Conservation Biology 320 Hodson Hall 1980 Folwell Ave Saint Paul MN 55108-1037 Office Phone: 612-625-4717. Business E-Mail: jperry@umn.edu.

PERRY, JAMES BENN, former casino and hotel executive; b. New Castle, Pa., Jan. 15, 1950; s. Samuel Wesley Jr. and Grace Elizabeth (Brumbaugh) P.; m. Cathy Ann Jackson, Dec. 27, 1982; children: James Benn Jr., Lauren Elizabeth, Julie Ann. BA in History, Ohio Wesleyan U., 1972; postgrad., Ariz. State U., 1975-76; student, Tulane U., 1968-70. CPA, N.J. Internal auditor Ramada Inns, Phoenix, 1976-78, regional controller, 1978-79, v.p., contr., 1985-87; asst. controller Tropicana Hotel & Casino, Las Vegas, Nev., 1979-80, controller Atlantic City, 1980-82, v.p. fin., 1982-85, sr. v.p., casino ops., 1987-89; exec. v.p./asst., gen. mgr. ops. TropWorld Casino and Entertainment Resort, Atlantic City, 1989-92, pres., gen. mgr., 1992—96; pres. Hospitality Group, Keating Bldg. Group,

1996—97, Argosy Gaming Co., Alton, Ill., 1997—2002, CEO, 1997—2003, Trump Entertainment Resorts, Inc., Atlantic City, 2005—07. Mem. AICPA, N.J. Soc. CPAs (chmn. gaming conf. com. 1985-86). Avocation: golf. *

PERRY, JAMES E., marketing executive, consultant; b. Franklin, NJ, Dec. 18, 1957; s. Evan and Emeline (Norman) Hendershot. Student, Kansas Wesleyan U., 1975—79; BA in Pastoral Studies, Southwestern Coll., 2003. Exec. dir. Hospice Green Country, Tulsa, 1989-92; dir. devel. Stop AIDS, Chgo., 1993-94; pres. Genesis Assocs., Chgo., 1994-96; dir. devel. Voices for Ill. Children, Chgo., 1996—2004; dir. philanthropy Nature Conservancy, 2005; ind. cons., 2006—. Pres. Tulsa Oklahomans for Human Rights, 1987-88; chair Tulsa Human Rights Commn., 1990-93; trustee, pres. Eagle Condor Inst., 2000-02. Mem. Assn. of Fundraising Profls., Am. Mktg. Assn., am. Psychotherapy Assn. (co-chair Human Rights Campaign Ann. Dinner, 2005). Democrat. Episcopal. E-mail: jasperry@charter.net.

PERRY, JAMES FREDERIC, philosophy educator, writer; b. Washington, Jan. 21, 1936; s. Albert Walter and Helene Anna Maria (Neumeyer) P.; m. Sandra Jean Huizing, Feb. 18, 1957 (div. May 1972); children: Sandra Elaine, James Frederic Jr., Bartholomew; m. Roberta Schofield, June 6, 1984. Student, Princeton U., 1953-56, Marietta Coll., Ohio, 1958-60; BA with honors in Philosophy, Ind. U., 1962, PhD in Philosophy of Edn., 1972. NDEA fellow in philosophy U. N.C., 1962—65; instr. N.C. State U., Raleigh, 1965-66; Univ. fellow Ind. U., 1971, adj. lectr. Bloomington, 1972-75; prof. philosophy Hillsborough C.C., Tampa, Fla., 1975-97, 2005—, honors prof. philosophy, 1997—2005. Adj. prof. U. South Fla., 2000—, adj. honors prof., 2006—. Author: Random, Routine, Reflective, 1989; contbr. articles to profl. jours. Precinct committeeman Dem. Party, Tampa, Fla., 1988—2004. Mem. AAUP (pres. Fla. conf. 1986-89, chair com. "A" on acad. freedom 1989-2002), C.C. Humanities Assn. (so. divsn. exec. bd. 1981-89), Am. Philos. Assn., Fla. Philos. Assn. (pres. 2004-05), Internat. Soc. Philos. Enquiry, Internat. Congress for Critical Thinking and Moral Critiques (founding mem. S.E. coun. 1991), World Congress Philosophy (Boston 1998, Istanbul 2003), Princeton Alumni Assn. of Fla. Suncoast (sec. 1983-86, pres. 1986-95), Mensa, Authors Guild, Textbook and Acad. Authors Assn. Avocations: travel, genealogy. Office: Hillsborough C C PO Box 10561 Tampa FL 33679-0561 Office Phone: 813-253-7357. Business E-Mail: jperry@hccfl.edu.

PERRY, JEAN LOUISE, academic administrator; b. Richland, Wash., May 13, 1950; d. Russell S. and Sue W. Perry. BS, Miami U., Oxford, Ohio, 1972; MS, U. Ill., Urbana, 1973, PhD, 1976. Cons. ednl. placement office U. Ill., 1973-75; adminstrv. intern Coll. Applied Life Studies, 1975-76, asst. dean, 1976-77, assoc. dean, 1978-81, asst. prof. dept. phys. edn., 1976-81; assoc. prof. phys. edn. San Francisco State U., 1981-84, prof., 1984-90, chair, 1981-90; dean Coll. Human and Cmty. Scis. U. Nev., Reno, 1990—2006, spl. asst. to pres. for athletics, academics and compliance, 2006—. Named to Excellent Tchr. List, U. Ill., 1973—79. Mem.: AAHPERD (fellow rsch. consortium, pres. 1988—89), Nat. Assn. Girls and Women in Sports (guide coord., pres.), Nat. Assn. Phys. Edn. in Higher Edn., Am. Ednl. Rsch. Assn., Am. Assn. Higher Edn., Phi Delta Kappa, Delta Psi Kappa. Home: 3713 Ranchview Ct Reno NV 89509-7437 Office: U Nev Legacy Hal/ 232 Reno NV 89557-0001 Office Phone: 775-784-3505.

PERRY, JON ROBERT, lawyer; b. Kane, Pa., May 14, 1965; s. James Felix and Judith Rose (Zelina) P.; m. Joni Lee Detrick, Aug. 10, 1991; children: Alex Joseph, Trevor James. BA summa cum laude, Pa. State U., 1987; JD magna cum laude, Duquesne U., 1991. Bar: Pa. 1991, U.S. Dist. Ct. (we. dist.) Pa. 1991, U.S. Ct. Apppeals (3d, 6th, 7th and fed. cirs.). Assoc. Reed Smith Shaw & McClay, Pitts., 1990-94; ptnr. Betts & Perry, Pitts., 1994-97, Rosen Louik & Perry, Pitts., 1998—. Bd. dirs. Flying Pig Theatre, Pitts., J's Place, Inc., Kane, RBCI, Inc., Cranberry, Pa., CDS, Inc., Pitts., adj. prof., U. Pitts. Sch. Law. Exec. editor Duquesne Law Rev., 1991. Vol. mentor/spkr. elem. and high schs., Pitts., 1992—; founder Pennies From Heaven Children's Charity. Named Pa. Super Lawyer. Mem. ATLA, Pa. Trial Lawyers Assn., Pa. Bar Assn., Allegheny County Bar Assn., Allegheny County Acad. Trial Lawyers, Million Dollar Advs., Phi Beta Kappa. Office: Rosen Perry & Louik 437 Grant St Ste 200 Frick Bldg Pittsburgh PA 15219-6002

PERRY, JUNE CARTER, ambassador; b. Texarkana, Ark., Nov. 13, 1943; d. Bishop W. and Louise (Pendleton) Carter; m. Frederick Majette Perry; children: Chad Douglass, André Frederick. BA cum laude, Loyola U./Mundelein Coll., Chgo., 1965; MA, U. Chgo., 1967. Nat. teaching fellow NC A&T State U., Greensboro, 1967-68; grad./undergrad. lectr. U. Md., College Park, 1969-70; dir. pub. affairs WGMS/RKO Radio, Washington, 1974-77; spl. asst. to dir. pub. affairs Cmty. Svcs. Adminstrn., Washington, 1977-79; dir. pub. affairs ACTION/Peace Corps, Washington, 1979-83; gen. svcs. officer US Embassy, Lusaka, Zambia, 1984-86, polit./labor officer Harare, Zimbabwe, 1986-87; country office for Botswana Bur. African Affairs, Dept. State, Washington, 1987-89; spl. asst. to dep. sec. US Dept. State, Washington, 1989, sr. advisor to asst. sec., 1997—98, amb. to Kingdom of Lesotho, 2004—, dep. amb. to Ctrl. African Rep., 1996—97, dep. amb. to Madagascar, 1998—2000; chief internal polit. affairs and narcotics coord. Embassy Paris, 1990—93; diplomat-in-residence Howard U., 2001—02; dir. Office Social and Humanitarian Affairs Internat. Orgn. Bur., 2002—04; dep. dir. Office of Policy and Plans, Polit. Mil. Affairs Bur. Adv. coun. The Women's Inst., Bethesda, Md., 1983—. Producer, host: Soul of the Classics, WGMS Radio, 1974-77, Heritage Series, RKO Radio, 1974-77, DC Schs. Radio Project, 1973. Bd. dirs. Sign of the Times Art Gallery and Workshop, 1975-77, others in past. Recipient Spl. Achievement award, ACTION, 1981, Mundelein Disting. Alumnae, Mundelein Coll., 1981, Superior Achiever award, RKO Radio, 1977, Superior Honor, Sr. Performance awards State Dept., 1997, 98 2003, 04, 05, 06; Diplomat-in-Residence of Yr. award, US Dept. State, 2002; Woodrow Wilson fellow, 1965, UN Human Rights awardee, 1977, others. Mem. Am. Fgn. Svc. Assn., Cosmos Club, Assn. Black Am. Ambs., Delta Sigma Theta, Nat. Coun. Negro Women. Avocations: African art collecting, African-Am. and French history, classical music. Office: US Embassy 2160 Freetown Pl Dulles VA 20189 Business E-Mail: perryjc2@state.gov.

PERRY, KENNETH WILBUR, finance educator; b. Lawrenceburg, Ky., May 21, 1919; s. Ollie Townsend and Minnie (Monroe) P.; m. Shirley Jane Kimball, Sept. 5, 1942; 1 dau., Constance June (Mrs. Linden Warfel). BS, Eastern Ky. U., 1942; MS, Ohio U., 1949; PhD, U. Ill., 1953; LL.D., Eastern Ky. U., 1983. C.P.A., Ill. Instr. Berea Coll., 1949-50, U. Ky., summer 1950; teaching asst. U. Ill. at Champaign, 1950-53, asst. prof. accounting, 1953-55, asso. prof., 1955-58, prof., 1958—, Alexander Grant prof., 1975—. Vis. prof. Northeastern U., summer 1966, Parsons Coll., 1966-67, Fla. A. and M. U., fall 1971; Carman G. Blough prof. U. Va., fall 1975; dir. Illini Pub. Co. Author: Accounting: An Introduction, 1971, Passing the C.P.A. Examination, 1964, (with N. Bedford and A. Wyatt) Advanced Accounting, 1960; contbg. author: Complete Guide to a Profitable Accounting Practice, 1965, C.P.A. Review Manual, 1971; Editor: The Ill. C.P.A, 1968-70; contbg. editor: Accountants' Cost Handbook, 1960. Served to maj. AUS, 1942-46; col. Res. ret. Named outstanding alumnus Eastern Ky. U., 1969 Mem. Am. Accounting Assn. (v.p. 1963, Outstanding Educator award 1974), Am. Inst. C.P.A.'s, Am. Statis. Assn., Nat. Assn. Accountants (dir. 1969-71), Ill. Soc. C.P.A.s (chair in accountancy), Beta Alpha Psi, Beta Gamma Sigma (Distinguished scholar 1977-78), Omicron Delta Kappa. Methodist. Home: 2314 Fields South Dr Champaign IL 61822-9302 Office: Commerce W U Ill Champaign IL 61822

PERRY, LEE ROWAN, retired lawyer; b. Chgo., Sept. 23, 1933; s. Watson Bishop and Helen (Rowan) P.; m. Barbara Ashcraft Mitchell, July 2, 1955; children: Christopher, Constance, Geoffrey. BA, U. Ariz., 1955, LLB, 1961. Bar: Ariz. 1961. Since practiced in, Phoenix; clk. Udall & Udall, Tucson, 1960-61; mem. firm Carson, Messinger, Elliott, Laughlin & Ragan, 1961-99. Mem. law rev. staff, U. Ariz., 1959-61. Mem. bd. edn. Paradise Valley Elem. and H.S. Dists., Phoenix, 1964-68, pres., 1968; mem. bd. edn. Osborn Elem. Sch. Dist., Phoenix, 2002; bd. dirs. Osborn Sch. Dist. Found., 2003—; treas. troop Boy Scouts Am., 1970-72; mem. Ariz. adv. bd. Girl Scouts U.S.A., 1972-74, mem. nominating bd., 1978-79; bd. dirs. Florence Crittenton Services Ariz., 1967-72, pres., 1970-72; bd. dirs. U. Ariz. Alumni, Phoenix, 1968-72, pres., 1969-70; bd. dirs. Family Service Phoenix, 1974-75; bd. dirs. Travelers Aid Assn. Am., 1985-89; bd. dirs. Vol. Bur. Maricopa County, 1975-81, 83-86, pres., 1984-85; bd. dirs. Ariz. div. Am. Cancer Soc., 1978-80, Florence Crittenton div. Child Welfare League Am., 1976-81; bd. dirs. Crisis Nursery for Prevention of Child Abuse, 1978-81, pres., 1978-80; Ariz. dir. Devereux Found., 1996-2000, vice chmn. 1996-98. 1st lt. USAF, 1955-58. Mem. State Bar Ariz. (conv. chmn. 1972), Rotary (dir. 1971-77, 95-96, pres. 1975-76, West Leadership award 1989), Ariz. Club (bd. dirs. 1994-2002, pres.-elect 1997-98, pres. 1998-99), Phoenix Country Club, Phi Delta Phi, Phi Delta Theta (pres. 1954). Republican. Episcopalian. Home: 106 N Country Club Dr Phoenix AZ 85014-5443

PERRY, LEWIS CHARLES, emergency medicine physician, osteopath; b. La Plata, Mo., Apr. 22, 1931; s. Lewis C. and Emily B. Perry; m. M. Sheryl Gupton, Oct. 30, 1953; children: David, Susan, Stephen, John. BS, U. Mo., 1958; postgrad., Louisville Presbyn. Sem., 1958-60; DO, Kirksville Coll. Osteo. Medicine, 1967. Intern Midcities Meml. Hosp., Arlington, Tex.; parish min. Presbyn. Bd. Nat. Missions, Canada, Ky., 1960-62; intern Mid Cities Meml. Hosp., Arlington; pvt. practice, Ingleside, Tex., 1968-72, Tucson, 1972-81; emergency physician Tucson Gen. Hosp., 1981-88, pres. med. staff, 1978-79, clin. instr., 1981-88; emergency physician Meml. Med. Ctr. East Tex., Lufkin, 1988—. Clin. instr. Osteo. Coll. Pacific, Pomona, Calif., 1985-88. Pres. Helping Hands, Ingleside, 1969-72; bd. dirs., pres. Salvation Army, Tucson, 1978-81; commr. Cub Scouts Am., Tucson, 1975-76; bd. dirs. Unity of Tucson, Inc., 1986-88; pres. bd. dirs. Unity of Nacogdoches, 1993-94; Eagle Scout Boy Scouts Am. 1st lt. USAF, 1952-56. Named Physician of Yr., Tucson Gen. Hosp., 1978; recipient God and Country award Boy Scouts of Am., 1960. Mem. Am. Legion, Rotary (recipient God and Country award), Masons, Scottish Rite, Shrine. Avocations: cooking, gardening. Home: 64251 Whispering Tree Ln Tucson AZ 85739

PERRY, LOUIS BARNES, retired insurance company executive; b. LA, Mar. 4, 1918; s. Louis Henry and Julia (Stoddard) P.; m. Genevieve Patterson, Feb. 8, 1942; children: Robert Barnes, Barbara Ann, Donna Lou. BA, UCLA, 1938, MA, 1940, PhD, 1950; fellow in econs., Yale U., 1941; LL.D., Pacific U., 1964; L.H.D., Whitman Coll., 1967, Linfield Coll., 1981; D.C.S., Willamette U., 1977. Teaching asst. UCLA, 1940-41, research teaching asst., 1946-47; faculty Pomona Coll., 1947-59, asst. to pres., 1955-57, prof. econs., 1957-59; pres. Whitman Coll., Walla Walla, Wash., 1959-67; v.p., treas. Standard Ins. Co., Portland, Oreg., 1967-68, exec. v.p., 1968-71, pres., 1972-83, chmn., 1983-85, also bd. dirs. Investment counselor, broker Wagenseller & Durst, L.A., 1951-59; rsch. coord. So. Calif. Rsch. Coun., 1952-54; cons. Carnegie Survey Bus. Edn., 1957-58. Author: (with others) Our Needy Aged, 1954, A History of the Los Angeles Labor Movement, 1963; Contbr. (with others) articles to profl. jours. Mem. Oreg. Bd. Higher Edn., 1975-87, pres., 1975-80. Served to maj. AUS, World War II; lt. col. Res. Mem. Am. Coll. Life Underwriters (trustee 1972-81), Rotary, Phi Beta Kappa, Beta Gamma Sigma, Phi Delta Kappa, Pi Gamma Mu, Alpha Gamma Omega, Artus. Methodist. Home: 1585 Gray Lynn Dr Walla Walla WA 99362-9282 *In looking back over the years, an unspoken and oftentime subliminal guiding principle has been to reach beyond one's realistic grasp. This concept coupled with an interest in treating others as one would like to be treated has made it possible to react to new challenges. Successfully meeting the latter has provided a varied career in a number of different fields of activity.*

PERRY, MALCOLM BLYTHE, biologist, researcher; b. Birkenhead, Cheshire, Eng., Apr. 26, 1930; s. Cyril A. and Hilda P. (Blythe) Perry; m. Eileen M. Perry, Aug. 10, 1956 (dec. Nov. 1981); children: Sara Jane, Judith Anne; m. Philomena C. Kingsley, July 25, 2001. B.Sc., U. Bristol, Eng., 1953; PhD, U. Bristol, 1956, D.Sc., 1969. Banting rsch. fellow Queen's U., Kingston, Ont., Canada, 1955, asst. prof., 1956-60, R.S. McLaughlin research prof., 1960-62; sr. resch. officer Nat. Rsch. Coun., Ottawa, 1962—81, prin. rsch. officer, 1981—. Scientist U. Cambridge, Eng., 1969, U. Paris, 1979; prof. U. Ottawa, 1982 Contbr. articles to profl. jours. Fellow Royal Soc. Can., Royal Inst. Chemistry; mem. Can. Soc. Microbiology (award 1991), Am. Soc. Microbiology, Internat. Endotoxin Soc. (award 2002). Home: 769 Hemlock Rd Ottawa ON Canada K1K 0K6 Office: NRC 100 Sussex Dr Ottawa ON Canada K1A 0R6 Office Phone: 613-990-0837. Business E-Mail: malcolm.perry@nrc.ca.

PERRY, MARGARET, librarian, writer; b. Cin., Nov. 15, 1933; d. Rufus Patterson and Elizabeth Munford (Anthony) P. AB, Western Mich. U., 1954; Cert. d'etudes Francaises, U. Paris, 1956; MSLS, Cath. U. Am., 1959. Young adult and reference libr. N.Y. Pub. Libr., NYC, 1954-55, 57-58; libr. U.S. Army, France and Germany, 1959-63, 64-67; chief circulation U.S. Mil. Libr., West Point, NY, 1967-70; head edn. libr. U. Rochester, NY, 1970-75, asst. prof. NY, 1973-75, assoc. prof. NY, 1975-82, asst. dir. librs. for reader svcs. NY, 1975-82, acting dir. librs. NY, 1976-77, 80; univ. libr. Valparaiso U., Ind., 1982-93; ret., 1993. Mem. Task Force on Coop. Edn., Rochester, 1972; freelance writer Mich. Land Use Inst., 1995-01. Author: A Bio-bibliography of Countee P. Cullen, 1903-1946, 1971, Silence to the Drums: A Survey of the Literature of the Harlem Renaissance, 1976, The Harlem Renaissance, 1982, The Short Fiction of Rudolph Fisher, 1987, short stories; contbr. articles to profl. jours. and children's mags. Bd. dirs. Urban League, 1978-80 Recipient 1st prize short story contest Armed Forces Writers League, 1966; 2d prize Frances Steloff Fiction prze, 1968, 1st prize short story Arts Alive, 1990, 2d prize short story Willow Rev., 1990; seminar scholar Schloss Leopoldskron, Salzburg, Austria, 1956, 3d prize short story West Shore C.C., Scottville, Mich., 1995. Mem. ALA. Democrat. Roman Catholic. Avocations: violin and viola, collecting book marks, gardening, reading, travel. Home: 8 Muriel St Ithaca NY 14850 Office Phone: 607-257-3997. Personal E-mail: mperry515@yahoo.com.

PERRY, MARK BRADLEY, lawyer, minister; b. Ft. Worth, Mar. 14, 1966; s. James Paul and Dorothy Nelle Perry; m. Cassie Lue Bond, Jan. 2, 2003; children: Michael Dean Marquez, Christian Lee Marquez, Madison Lue Marquez, Alexandria Rebecca Marquez, Ashley Danielle. BBA, Baylor U., Waco, Tex., 1988; JD, U. Wis., Madison, 1992; MDiv, Yale U., New Haven, 1995. Founding atty. Trustlaw Assocs., Farmington, N.Mex., 1996—; founding pastor United Ch. Farmington, 1998—; founding chaplain, bereavement counselor NW N.Mex. Hospice, Farmington, 1998—; pres., CEO BP Realty, LLC, Farmington, 2002—. Pres. Otero County Bar Assn., Alamogordo, N.Mex., 1997, San Juan County Bar Assn., Farmington, 2000. Maj. N.Mex. Air Nat. Guard, 2006—. Mem.: Masons, Sigma Chi. Presbyterian. Avocations: German shepherds, firearms. Office: Trustlaw Associates 412 W Arrington Ave Farmington NM 87401 Home Phone: 505-801-5697; Office Phone: 505-599-8172. Business E-Mail: trustlawassociates@yahoo.com.

PERRY, MATTHEW, actor; b. Williamstown, Mass., Aug. 19, 1969; s. John Bennett Perry and Suzanne Morrison. Actor: (films) A Night in the Life of Jimmy Reardon, 1988, She's Out of Control, 1989, Getting In, 1994, Fools Rush In, 1997, Edwards and Hunt: The First American Road Trip, 1997, Almost Heroes, 1998, Three to Tango, 1999, The Whole Nine Yards, 2000, Disney's THe Kid, 2000, Serving Sarah, 2002, The Whole Ten Yards, 2004; actor, exec. prodr. (films) Numb, 2007; actor (TV series) Second Chance, 1987, Sydney, 1990, Home Free, 1993, Friends, 1994-2004, Studio 60 on the Sunset Strip, 2006-07; writer (films) Imagining Emily, 1999; actor (TV movies) Dance 'Til Dawn, 1988, Call Me Anna, 1990, Deadly Relations, 1993, L.A.X. 2194, 1994 Parallel Lives, 1994, The Ron Clark Story, 2006; (TV appearances) 240-Robert, 1979, Charles in Charge, 1985, Silver Spoons, 1986, The Tracey Ullman Show, 1987, Mr. Belvedere, 1988, Highway to Heaven, 1988, Empty Nest, 1988, Just the 10 of Us, 1988, Growing Pains, 1989, Who's the Boss?, 1990, Beverly Hills, 90210, 1990, Dream On, 1992, The John Larroquette Show, 1993, Caroline in the City, 1995, Ally McBeal, 2002, The West Wing, 2003, Scrubs, 2004; theater debut Sexual Perversity in London, 2003. *

PERRY, MICHAEL CLINTON, internist, educator, academic administrator; b. Wyandotte, Mich., Jan. 27, 1945; s. Clarence Clinton and Hilda Grace (Wigginton) P.; m. Nancy Ann Kaluzny, June 22, 1968; children: Rebecca Carolyn, Katherine Grace. BA, Wayne State U., 1966, MD, 1970; MS in Medicine, U. Minn., 1975. Diplomate Am. Bd. Internal Medicine, Am. Bd. Hematology, Am. Bd. Oncology. Intern in internal medicine Mayo Grad. Sch. Medicine, Rochester, Minn., 1970-71, resident, 1971-72, fellow, 1972-75; instr. Mayo Med. Sch., Rochester, 1974-75; asst. prof. U. Mo., Columbia, 1975-80, assoc. prof., 1980-85, prof., 1985—, chmn. dept. medicine, 1983-91, sr. assoc. dean, 1991-94, Nellie A Smith chair oncology, dir. div. hematology/oncology, 1994—. Prin. investigator Cancer and Leukemia Group B, Nat. Cancer Inst., Chgo., 1982—, exec. com., 1982-84, 1987-90. Author, co-author 30 book chpts.; editor: Toxicity of Chemotherapy, 1984, The Chemotherapy Source Book, 1992, 96, 2001, Comprehensive Textbook of Thoracic Oncology, 1996; contbr. articles to profl. jours. Recipient Faculty Alumni award U. Mo., Columbia, 1985, Disting. Alumnus award Wayne State U., 1995, Disting. Oncologist of Yr. award So. Assn. Oncology, 2000. Fellow ACP; mem. Am. Soc. Hematology, Am. Soc. Clin. Oncology, Cen. Soc. Clin. Research, Am. Soc. Internal Medicine (Young Internist of Yr. 1981), Sigma Xi, Alpha Omega Alpha. Home: 1112 Pheasant Run Columbia MO 65201-6254 Office: U Mo-Columbia 516 Ellis Fischel Cancer Ctr 115 Business Loop 70 W Columbia MO 65203-3244 E-mail: perrym@health.missouri.edu.

PERRY, MICHAEL W., bank executive; BBA with honors, Calif. State U., Sacramento. CPA. With Commerce Security Bank, 1987—92, sr. exec. v.p. Mortgage Banking Divsn.; joined IndyMac Bancorp, Pasadena, Calif., 1993, COO, 1993—97, pres., 1997—99, bd. dirs., 1997—, CEO, 1997—, vice chmn. bd., 2000—03, chmn. bd., 2003—. Bd. trustees, mem. acad. affairs com. Mayfield Jr. Sch.; bd. dirs. YMCA of Pasadena. Named LA Bus. Jour. Hall of Fame; recipient Fin. Industry Leader of Yr. award, LA Bus. Jour., 2002, Entrepreneur of Yr., fin. services, LA Ernst & Young, 2002. Mem.: Young Presidents' Org. (San Gabriel chpt.), Calif. Soc. CPAs, Am. Inst. CPAs. Office: IndyMac Bancorp 888 E Walnut St Pasadena CA 91101 E-mail: michael.perry@indymac.com. *

PERRY, NANCY BLAND, accountant; b. Houston, Miss., Aug. 17, 1955; d. Charles Edward Bland, Minnie Lou Bland; 1 child, Cheryl Elizabeth Crisco; m. Paul D Perry. BS in Edn. with distinction, Miss. Coll., 1975, cert. acctg., 1988. CPA Miss. CPA, acct. various CPA firms, Jackson, Miss., 1983—89; pvt. practice CPA Clinton, Miss., 1989—91; sr. acct. Chem. First Inc., Jackson, 1991—2003; asst. v.p. acctg. Denmiss Corp., 2003—. Bd. dirs., various offices Girl Scouts U.S. Mid. Miss., Jackson, 1992—; team mem. Leadership Clinton, 1997—98; bd. dirs., various positions Clinton Pub. Sch. Dist. PTA, 1988—96; bd. dirs., sec. treas. ChemFirst Found., Inc., Jackson, 1996—2002; trustee Clinton Pub. Sch. Dist., 1998—; bd. dirs. Clinton Jr. Miss, 1997—2004; trustee Frances Rushton Meml. Scholarship Trust, 1998—, chair, 2001—. Nominee GIVE, Gov. of Miss., 1995; named Parent of the Yr., Clinton Pub. Sch. Dist., 1995; recipient Metro Jackson's Finest award, Cystic Fibrosis Foundation, 1999, Thanks Badge, Girl Scouts U.S. Mid. Miss., 1995. Mem.: AICPA, Miss. Soc. CPAs, Am. Soc. Women Accts. (bd. dirs., various positions 1996—2001), Jr. Aux. Clinton (bd. dirs., treas. 1996—2000, trustee Francecs Rushton Meml. Scholarship Trust 1999—, chair 2001—), Clinton C. of C. Ch. Of Christ. Business E-Mail: nperry@denkmann-ms.com.

PERRY, NORAH D., language educator; b. Nurnburg, Germany, Mar. 13, 1973; d. Rosemary and Don Perry. BA, U. Cin., 1995; MA in Tchg., U. Louisville, 1998. Cert. Rank 1 Ind. Wesleyan U., 2006. Lead tchr. fgn. langs. South Oldham HS, Crestwood, Ky., 2002—; reading com. mem. Ednl. Profl. Stds. Bd., Frankfort, Ky., 2002—. Bd. examiner Nat. Coun. for the Accreditation Tchr. Edn., 2004—. Mem.: Phi Kappa Phi (life). Office: South Oldham HS 5900 Hwy 329 ByPass Crestwood KY 40014 Home Phone: 502-241-3817; Office Phone: 502-241-6681. Office Fax: 502-241-0955. Personal E-mail: professafly@insightbb.com. Business E-Mail: norah.perry@oldham.kyschools.us.

PERRY, PHILIP J., lawyer, former federal agency administrator; b. San Diego, 1964; m. Elizabeth Cheney Perry, 1993; children: Katherine, Elizabeth, Grace, Philip, Richard. BA, Colo. Coll., 1986; JD, Cornell U., 1990. Ptnr. Latham & Watkins LLP, 1993—97; counsel US Senate Spl. Investigation of Campaign Fin. Abuses, 1997—98; policy adv. Bush-Cheney presidential transition team, 2000; acting assoc. atty. gen. US Dept. Justice, 2001—02, prin. dep. assoc. atty. gen., 2001—02; gen. counsel. Office Mgmt. & Budget Exec. Office of the Pres., 2002—03; ptnr. Latham & Watkins LLP, Washington, 2003—05, 2007—; gen. counsel US Dept. Homeland Security, Washington, 2005—07. Office: Latham & Watkins LLP 555 Eleventh St NW Ste 1000 Washington DC 20004 Business E-Mail: phil.perry@lw.com.

PERRY, RALPH BARTON, III, lawyer; b. NYC, Mar. 17, 1936; s. Ralph Barton Jr. and Harriet Armington (Seelye) P.; m. Mary Elizabeth Colburn, Sept. 2, 1961; children: Katherine Suzanne, Daniel Berenson. AB, Harvard U., 1958; LLB, Stanford U., 1963. Bar: Calif. 1964. Assoc. and mem. Keatinge & Sterling, L.A., 1963—68; mem. firm Graven Perry Block Brody & Qualls, L.A., 1968—2006, Perry & Grossman, L.A., 2006—. Bd. dirs. Planning and Conservation League, 1968-2005, PLC Found., 2005—, Coalition for Clean Air, 1970—, pres. 1972-80, 85-88. Served with U.S. Army, 1956-58. Mem. ABA (ho. of dels. 1975-95), State Bar Calif., L.A. County Bar Assn., Lawyers Club L.A. County (gov. 1968-82), Nat. and Internat. Wildlife Fedns., Sierra Club, L.A. Athletic Club. Home: 296 Redwood Dr Pasadena CA 91105-1339 Office: Graven Perry 523 W 6th St Ste 723 Los Angeles CA 90014-1223 Office Phone: 213-680-9770. Personal E-mail: rbp3@earthlink.net.

PERRY, RICHARD C., financier; b. 1955; m. Lisa Perry. BA, Wharton Sch. U. Pa., 1977; MBA, NYU. Equity trader Goldman, Sachs & Co., 1977—88; founder, chmn., CEO Perry Capital LLC, 1988—. Adj. prof. Stern Sch. Bus. NYU; chmn. bd. FTD Corp.; dir. Radio & Records, Inc., Capital Bus. Credit LLC, Endurance Specialty Holdings, Sears Holding Corp., MedGroup Inversiones SL. Bd. trustees Facing History and Ourselves, Allen-Stevenson Sch., Milton Academy, Harlem Children's Zone; mem. Wharton Undergrad Exec. Bd. Office: Perry Capital 767 5th Ave New York NY 10153 Office Phone: 212-583-4000. *

PERRY, RICK, governor; b. Paint Creek, Tex., Mar. 4, 1950; m. Anita Thigpen; children: Griffin, Sydney. B.Animal Sci., A&M U., 1972. Farmer/rancher; mem. Tex. Ho. of Reps., 1985-90, mem. appropriations and calendars com.; commr. of agr. State of Tex., 1991-98, lt. gov. Austin, 1999-2000, gov., 2000—. Active Boy Scouts Am. Capt. USAF, 1972-77 Named One of the Most Effective Legislators, Dallas Morning News, 1989. Mem. Am. Legion. Republican. Methodist. Office: Office of Governor 1100 San Jacinto PO Box 12428 Austin TX 78711 Office Fax: 512-463-5571. *

PERRY, ROBERT MICHAEL, lawyer, consultant, rancher; s. John Robert and Katherine Marie (McManus) Perry. BA in History, St. Mary's U., San Antonio, 1959, JD, 1959; LLM, Georgetown U., Washington, 1964; diploma, US Army Arty. and Missile Sch., Ft. Sill, Okla., 1959, JAG Sch. U. Va., Charlottesville, 1962, US Army Command and Gen. Staff Course, 1978. Bar: Tex. 1961, US Supreme Ct., US Ct. Appeals (2d cir.), US Ct. Appeals (3d cir.), US Ct. Appeals (4th cir.), US Ct. Appeals (5th cir.), US Ct. Appeals (7th cir.), US Ct. Appeals (9th cir.), US Ct. Appeals (10th cir.), US Ct. Appeals (DC cir.), US Ct. Mil. Appeals, US Ct. Claims, US Tax Ct. Served to col. US Army, 1959—94, legal officer 1st armored divsn. Ft. Hood, Tex., 1959—61; staff officer JAG Dept. of Army, Washington, 1961—64; trial atty. Land and Natural Resources Divsn. Dept. of Justice, 1964—69; trial counsel Exxon Co. USA, Houston, 1969—80; gen. counsel and adminstr. enforcement US EPA, Washington, 1981—83; legal cons. San Antonio, Washington and Garrison, NY, 1983—. Mobilization designee US Army, Washington, 1964—94; chmn. Oil and Gas Industry Litigation Com. Trans Alaskan Pipeline, Alaska Native Claims and Offshore Oil and Gas Leasing Litigation, Houston, Washington and Anchorage, 1971—80; co-chmn environ. orgn. study com. US Army, Washington, 1984—94. Co-author: Fed. Condemnation Handbook 3 vols., 1964—69; editor-in-chief: US Dept. Justice Land and Natural Resources Divsn. Jour., 1967—68, The Forum (Fed. Bar Assn. DC), 1967—68; contbr. articles to govt. jours. Pres. and CEO Perry-Gething Found., San Antonio and Garrison, NY, 1975—; event pres. San Antonio Fiesta Commn., 1978—; pres. and CEO Frontier Times Mus., Bandera, 2001—07. Decorated Legion of Merit, Commendation medal with oak leaf cluster US Army, Meritorious Svc. medal; recipient Spl. Achievement award, Adminstr. US EPA, 1982. Mem.: Tex. and Southwestern Cattle Raisers Assn., Tex. Bar Assn. Avocation: raising rare Jacob sheep and hybrid cattle. Home: Perrymount Ranch PO Box 531 Bandera TX 78003 Office: Perry-Gething Found PO Box 830233 San Antonio TX 78283-0233 Office Phone: 210-227-9498.

PERRY, STEPHEN A., museum administrator, former federal agency administrator; b. Ohio, 1945; m. Sondra Perry; 5 children. B in Acctg., U. Akron; M in Mgmt., Stanford U.; attended, U. Mich. Exec. Develop. program. Various acctg. positions including dir. acctg., dir. purchasing, sr. v.p. Timken Co., Canton, 1964, v.p. human resources, purchasing and communications, 1993—97, sr. v.p., 1997—2001; dir. Dept. Adminstrv. Services State of Ohio, 1991—93; adminstr. US Gen. Services Adminstrn., Washington, 2001—05; pres., exec. dir. Pro Football Hall of Fame, Canton, Ohio, 2006—. Chmn. Human Resources Coun. of the Mfrs. Alliance for Productivity and Innovation; served on Human Resources Policy Com. Steering Group, Nat. Assn. of Mfrs.; bd. dir. Labor Policy Assn. Chmn. Canton Scholar Fund, Stark County Dist. Libr. Bd., United Way Campaign Ctrl. Stark County, 1996, Jr. Achievement, 1999, Leadership Stark County Selection Com.; mem. Ohio Bd. Regents, 1993—2002; bd. trustees Canton Urban League, 1968—83, Profl. Football Hall of Fame, 1993—2001; gen. chmn. Profl. Football Hall of Fame Festival, 1999; bd. trustees Timken Mercy Med. Ctr., 1984—91; mem. Walsh U. Adv. Bd., 1987—91; served on the Mgmt. Improvement Commn. appointed by Ohio Gov. Bob Taft. Named Man of Yr., Canton Christian Hall of Fame, 2000; recipient Disting. Svc. award, Jaycees, 1977, Pres. Social Responsibility award, Kent State U., 1995, Disting. Alumni award, Kent State U., Stark Campus Alumni Coun., 1996, Dr. Frank L. Simonetti Disting. Bus. Alumnus award, U. Akron, Coll. Bus. Alumni Assn., 1999, Disting. Alumni award, Trimken High Sch. Alumni Assn., 1999, U. Akron, 2001. Office: Pro Football Hall of Fame 2121 George Halas Dr NW Canton OH 44708

PERRY, STEVEN WAYNE, statistician; b. Edenton, NC, Feb. 9, 1971; s. Allen Ray and Josephine Spruill Perry; children: Dominique Lavon, Jullian Nolan. BA in Sociology, Norfolk State U., Va., 1996; MA in Sociology, Ohio State U., Columbus, 1998. Survey statistician US Dept. Commerce, Census Bur., Washington, 1998—2004; statistician US Dept. Justice, Bur. Justice Stats., Washington, 2004—. Author: (book) Census of Tribal Justice Agencies, 2002, (booklet) American Indians and Crime, A BJS Statistical Profile, 2002. Mem. New Creation AME Ch., Ft. Washington, Md., 2006. With US Army, 1990—92. Decorated Army Achievement medal US Army, Nat. Def. Svc. medal; recipient ROTC Cadet Outstanding Acad. Achievement award, Gen. Soc. War 1812, 1994, Spl. Achievement award, US Census Bur., 1999—2002, Spl. Activity award, Bur. Justice Stats., 2004—06; fellow, Va. Poly. and State U., 1994, Coll. William and Mary, 1995. Mem.: Am. Legion (assoc.). Achievements include development of tribal criminal history record improvement program. Avocations: coin collecting/numismatics, kite collecting. Office: US Dept Justice 810 Seventh St NW Washington DC 20531 Home Phone: 240-394-0037; Office Phone: 202-307-0777.

PERRY, TIMOTHY SEWELL, lawyer; b. Hamlet, NC, Feb. 28, 1947; s. Edwin Fleetwood and June Faye (Sewell) P.; children: Courtney, Kate, Bart, Carrie, Jeff, Kevin. BA, Princeton U., 1969; JD, Yale U., 1972. Bar: Ga. 1972. Assoc. Alston & Bird and predecessor firms, Atlanta, 1972—, ptnr., 1977—; of coun. Miller & Martin, Atlanta. Leader Metro Atlanta Chamber's Internat. Partners Coun.; vice chmn. Metro Atlanta Chamber's Global Commerce Coun.; hon. consul Brazil in Atlanta. Sec., Urban Study Inst., Atlanta, 1979—; pres. Andover Reg. Attn./Atlanta, 1987-89. Mem. Atlanta Bar Assn., Ga. Bar Assn. (corp. law sect.), Phillips Acad. Alumni Assn. Presbyterian. Avocation: spanish. Office: Miller & Martin PLLC 1170 Peachtree St NE Atlanta GA 30309-7706 Office Phone: 404-962-6493. Office Fax: 404-962-6393. Business E-Mail: tperry@millermartin.com.

PERRY, TROY D., minister, religious organization administrator; divorced; 2 children; m. Phillip Ray De Blieck, July 16, 2003. Student, Midwest Bible Sch., 1959; D in Ministry (hon.), Samaritan Coll., LA, 1982; D in Human Svcs., Sierra U., Santa Monica, Calif., 1985; DDiv (hon.), Episcopal Div. Sch., Cambridge, Mass., 2003. Former pastor Ch. of God of Prophecy, Santa Ana, Calif.; founder, moderator Universal Fellowship Met. Cmty. Chs., LA, 1968; ret., 2005. Rep. Met. Community Chs. and gay and lesbian rights movement numerous TV shows including 60 Minutes, Phil Donahue, The Mike Douglas Show; author: The Lord is My Shepherd and Knows I'm Gay, Don't Be Afraid Anymore, 1991, (video) God, Gays and The Gospel: This is Our Story; contbg. editor Is Gay Good? Mem. LA County Commn. Human Rels.; del. 1st White House Conf. on AIDS, 1993; del. 1st White House Conf. on Hate Crimes, 1997; trustee Chgo. Theol. Sem., 2002-06. Recipient Humanitarian award Gay Press Assn., Equality award Human Rights Campaign, 1996. Mem. Universal Fellowship Ch. Office: Universal Fellowship MCC PO Box 1374 Abilene TX 79604 Personal E-mail: revtroyperry@aol.com.

PERRY, TYLER, playwright, actor, theater director, theater producer; b. New Orleans, Sept. 13, 1969; Author: (plays) I Know I've Been Changed, I Can Do Bad All By Myself, 2000, Why Did I Get Married, Meet the Browns, 2004; author & actor (plays) Diary of a Mad Black Woman, 2001, author, actor & dir. Madea's Family Reunion, 2002, Madea's Class Reunion-The Class That Had No Class, 2003, Madea Goes to Jail, 2005, co-author (with Bishop T. D. Jakes), director, producer Woman, Thou Art Loosed, 1999, Behind Closed Doors, 2001; dir., writer, prodr.: (films) Daddy's Little Girls, 2007; author: (books) Don't Make a Black Woman Take Off Her Earrings: Madea's Uninhibited Commentaries on Love and Life, 2006 (Quills award humor The Quills Literacy Found., 2006). Named one of Most Influential Black Americans, Ebony mag., 2006. *

PERRY, WILLIAM BRIAN, colorectal surgeon; b. Natchitoches, La., Dec. 18, 1963; s. William Nathaniel and Joyce Hargis Perry; m. Holly Christine Hundemer, June 27, 1987; children: Katherine Mitchell, Patrick William, Austin Joseph. BS, La. State U., 1986; MD, Duke U., 1990. Lic. colon and rectal surgery Am. Bd. of Colon and Rectal Surgery, gen. surgery Am Bd. of Surgery, Tex. State Bd. of Med. Examiners. Chief of colorectal surgery Wilford Hall Med. Ctr., Lackland AFB, Tex., 1997—2006, gen. surgery residency program dir., 2002—06. Cons. to USAF surgeon gen. for colorectal surgery USAF Med. Corps, Bolling AFB, DC, 1997—2004; chief med. ops., chief of staff 4407th Med. Group, Prince Sultan Air Base, Saudi Arabia, 1998; chief trauma surgeon 332d Expeditionary Med. Group, Balad Air Base/LSA Anaconda, Iraq, 2005, 07. Contbr. articles to med. jours. and texts. Lt. col. USAF, 1990—2006. Decorated Commendation Medal USAF. Fellow: ACS, Am. Soc. of Colon and Rectal Surgeons; mem.: VFW, Soc. of Air Force Clin. Surgeons (pres. 2004—06), Delta Tau Delta (treas. 1983—84). Office: 859 Msgs/Mcsg 2200 Bergquist Dr Lackland Afb TX 78236-5300 Home Phone: 210-509-4088; Office Phone: 210-292-5906. E-mail: william.perry.1@us.af.mil.

PERRY, WILLIAM JAMES, engineering educator, former secretary of defense; b. Vandergrift, Pa., Oct. 11, 1927; s. Edward Martin and Mabelle Estelle (Dunlap) Perry; m. Leonilla Green, Dec. 29, 1947; children: David, William, Rebecca, Robin, Mark. BS in Math., Stanford U., 1949, MS, 1950; PhD, Pa. State U., 1957. Instr. math. Pa. State U., 1951—54; sr. mathematician HRB-Singer Co., State College, Pa., 1952—54; dir. electronic def. labs. GTE Sylvania Co., Mountain View, Calif., 1954—64; founder, pres. ESL, Inc., Sunnyvale, Calif., 1964—77; tech. cons. US Dept. Def., Washington, 1967—77, under sec. for rsch. & engring., 1977—81; mng. dir. Hambrecht & Quist, San Francisco, 1981—85; chmn. Tech. Strategies & Alliances, Menlo Park, Calif., 1985—93; prof., co-dir. Ctr. for Internat. Security and Arms Control Stanford U., Calif., 1989—93, prof. mgmt. sci. & engring., 1997—, sr. fellow, Hoover Inst., 1997—, Michael and Barbara Berberian prof., co-dir. Preventive Def. Project, 1997—; dep. sec. US Dept. Def., Washington, 1993—94, sec., 1994—97. Chmn. Global Tech. Ptnrs. LLC; mem. Iraq Study Group, 2006. Served in US Army, 1946—47. Recipient Def. Disting. Svc. medal, U.S. Govt., 1980, 1981, Achievement medal, Am. Electronics Assn., 1980, Forrestal medal, 1994, Henry Stimson medal, 1994, Arthur Bueche medal, NAE, 1996, Eisenhower award, 1996, Presdl. Medal Freedom, 1997, Outstanding Civilian Svc. medals, U.S. Army, 1997, USN, 1997, USAF, 1997, USCG, 1997, NASA, 1981, Def. Intelligence Agy., 1997; sr. fellow, Freeman Spogli Inst. Internat. Studies, Stanford U., 1997—. Office: Stanford Univ CISAC Encina Hall Rm C229 Stanford CA 94305-6165 Office Phone: 650-725-6501. Office Fax: 650-725-0920.

PERRY-BÖTTINGER, LYNNE VALENCIA, interventional cardiologist; b. Washington, June 1, 1961; d. Levi V. and Eula F. Perry; m. Erwin Paul Böttinger, Nov. 26, 1994; 2 children. AB cum laude, Harvard-Radcliffe U., 1982; MD cum laude, Yale U., 1986. Resident in internal medicine Yale-New Haven Hosp., 1986-89, chief med. resident, 1989-90; fellow in cardiology Johns Hopkins Hosp., Balt., 1990-94; instr. medicine Georgetown Univ. Hosp., Washington, 1996-97; asst. prof. medicine Albert Einstein Coll. Medicine, Bronx, 1997-2000; interventional cardiologist N.Y. Hosp. Queens, Flushing, NY, 2000—, Columbia-Presbyn. Hosp., 2002—; clin. asst. prof. medicine Cornell U. Weill Med. Coll.; asst. dir. cardiac cath lab., interventional cardiologist N.Y. Hosp., Queens; asst. prof. clin. medicine Columbia U. Fellow: Am. Coll. Cardiology. Democrat. Roman Catholic. Office: 140A Lockwood Ave New Rochelle NY 10801-Office Phone: 914-576-7577. Personal E-mail: dr.perry-bottinger@savehearts.com.

PERRYMAN, JONATHAN RICHARD, orthopedist, surgeon; b. London, Apr. 8, 1968; m. Brett Whitney Scoll, Aug. 3, 1996. BS, Dartmouth Coll.; MD, Georgetown U. Resident orthop. surgery Duke U.; rsch. asst. Dept. Orthops. Hosp. for Spl. Surgery, NYC; orthopedist New England Orthop. Specialists, Peabody, Mass.; staff mem. North Shore Med. Ctr., Beverly Hosp. Former team physician NY Jets, NY Rangers, Hofstra U. Athletic Teams. Office: New England Orthop Specialists 4 Centennial Dr Ste 201 Peabody MA 01960 Office Phone: 978-531-0800. Office Fax: 978-531-2929. *

PERSAD, ANAND BHOPRAJ, entomologist; s. Doon and Sumatee Persad. BS, U. West Indies, 1992, PhD, 2001. Asst. lectr. U. WI, St. Augustine, Trinidad and Tobago, 2000—01; rsch. entomologist U. Fla., Gainesville, 2001—04. Regional tech. advisor Davey Inst., Kent, Ohio, 2004—. Contbr. rsch. articles in field. Mem.: Entomol. Soc. of Am. Achievements include discovery of initiation and propagation of parasitoid colonies. Home Phone: 330-673-9511; Office Phone: 330-673-9511.

PERSAD, CHADEE, information technology manager; b. Rio Claro, Trinidad and Tobago; s. Chandrika and Indardaye Persad; m. Tara Gopaul, Aug. 4, 1974; children: Govind, Geeta. BSME, U. West Indies, 1974; MSME, City U., London; PhD, U. Tex. at Austin, 1983. Rsch. assoc. Ctr. Materials Sci., U. Tex., 1984—90; rsch. scientist U. Tex., Austin, Tex., 1990—2000; sr. rsch. scientist U. Tex. Inst for Advanced Technology, Austin, Tex., 2001—; faculty, dept. mech. engring. U. West Indies. Vis. faculty U. Netherlands, Antilles, Currcao, 1983—84. Author: (technical publications) Performance of Advanced Materials (US State Dept. for contributions to the ISTC, 1996). Grantee Multidisciplinary - Friction and Wear Scis., Office of Naval Rsch., 2004-2007. Mem.: ASME. Achievements include research in high performance materials for sliding electrical contacts. Avocation: travel. Home Phone: 512-251-2850; Office Phone: 512-232-4492.

PERSANS, PETER DAVID, physics educator, researcher; b. NYC, Mar. 25, 1953; BS in Physics, Poly. Inst. N.Y., 1975; SM in Physics, U. Chgo., 1977, PhD in Physics, 1982. Rsch. scientist Exxon Corp. Rsch., NJ, 1981; asst. prof. physics Rensselaer Poly. Inst., Troy, NY, 1986-89, assoc. prof., 1989—98, prof., 1998—, assoc. dept. head, 2007—. Contbr. more than 150 articles to sci. and tech. jours. Mem. Materials Rsch. Soc., Am. Phys. Soc. Home: Rensselaer Poly Inst Physics Dept Troy NY 12180 Office Phone: 518-276-2934. E-mail: persap@rpi.edu.

PERSAUD, TAREK O., ophthalmologist; b. Belleville, Ontario, Canada, Sept. 13, 1975; m. Smitha R. Rao, May 4, 2002; 1 child, Shaun Rao. MD, U. Ala., Birmingham, 2002. Ophthalmology resident George Wash. U., DC, 2003—06; vitreoretinal surgery fellow Retina Consultants Ala., U. Ala. Sch. Medicine, 2006—. Office: Retina Consultants Ala 700 18th St S Birmingham AL 35233 Office Fax: 205-918-0902.

PERSAUD, TRIVEDI VIDHYA NANDAN, anatomy educator, researcher, consultant; b. Port Mourant, Berbice, Guyana, Feb. 19, 1940; arrived in Canada, 1972; s. Ram Nandan and Deen (Raggy) P.; m. Gisela Gerda Zehden, Jan. 29, 1966; children: Indrani Uta and Sunita Heidi (twins), Rainer Narendra. MD, Rostock U., Germany, 1965, DSc, 1974; PhD in Anatomy, U. West Indies, Kingston, Jamaica, 1970. Intern, Berlin, Germany, 1965-66; govtl. med. officer Guyana, 1966-67; lectr., sr. lectr. anatomy dept. U. West Indies, 1967-72; assoc. prof. anatomy dept. U. Man., Winnipeg, 1972-75, prof., 1975—, prof. ob-gyn., reproductive scis., 1979-99, prof. emeritus, 1999—, prof. pediatrics and child health, 1989—, prof., chmn./head dept. human anatomy & cell sci., 1977-93, dir. Teratology Rsch. Lab., 1972-97. Cons. in teratology, Children's Centre, Winnipeg, 1973—; mem. sci. staff Health Scis. Centre, Winnipeg, 1973—. Author, editor 22 med. textbooks, including: Early History of Human Anatomy: From Antiquity to the Beginning of the Modern Era, 1984, (with others) Basic Concepts in Teratology, 1985, Environmental Causes of Human Birth Defects, 1991, History of Human Anatomy: The Post-Vesalian Era, 1997, (with K.L. Moore) The Developing Human, 8th edit., 2007, Before We Are Born, 7th edit., 2007; rev. Medical Embryology, 6th edit., 2003; contbr. numerous chpts. to books, over 200 articles to profl. jours. Recipient Carveth Jr. Scientist award Can. Assn. Pathologists, 1974, Albert Einstein Centennial medal German Acad. Scis., 1975, Dr. & Mrs. H.H. Saunderson award U. Manitoba, 1985, 12th Raymond Truex Disting. Lectureship award Hahnemann U., 1990, Queen Elizabeth II Golden Jubilee medal Govt. Can., 2003. Fellow Royal Coll. Pathologists of London; mem. Can. Assn. Anatomists (pres. 1981-83, J.C.B. Grant award 1991), Am. Assn. Anatomists, Teratology Soc., European Teratology Soc. Office: U Man Dept Anatomy & Cell Sci 730 William Ave Winnipeg MB Canada R3E OW3 Office Phone: 204-789-3333. Business E-Mail: persaud@cc.umanitoba.ca.

PERSAVICH, WARREN DALE, diversified manufacturing company executive; b. Cleve., Dec. 15, 1952; s. Nick and Sophie (Makris) P.; m. Anita Geraldine Zeleznik, Oct. 12, 1974; children: Nicholas, Katherine. BBA, Kent State U., 1975. CPA, Ohio. Staff acct. Price Water House, Cleve., 1975-76; asst. contr. Banner Industries Inc., Cleve., 1976-79, contr., 1979-86, treas., 1986-88, v.p., treas., 1988-90; sr. v.p., chief fin. officer Banner Aerospace Inc., 1990-98, sr. v.p., chief oper. officer, 1998-99; pres. Banner Aerospace Distbn. Group, 2000—. Pres. aerospace divsn. The Fairchild Corp., McLean, Va. Mem. AICPA, Ohio Soc. CPAs. Republican. Office: The Fairchild Corp Ste 1400 1750 Tysons Blvd Mc Lean VA 22102

PERSCHBACHER, REX ROBERT, dean, law educator; b. Chgo., Aug. 31, 1946; s. Robert Ray and Nancy Ellen (Beach) P.; children: Julie Ann, Nancy Beatrice. AB in Philosophy, Stanford U., 1968; JD, U. Calif., Berkeley, 1972. Bar: Calif. 1972, U.S. Dist. Ct. (no. dist.) Calif. 1973, U.S. Dist. Ct. (so. dist.) Calif. 1979, U.S. Ct. Appeals (9th cir.) 1980, U.S. Dist. ct. (ea. dist.) Calif. 1985. Law clk. to judge U.S. Dist. Ct. (no. dist.) Calif., San Francisco, 1973-74; asst. prof. law U. Tex., Austin, 1974-75; assoc. Heller, Ehrman, White & McAuliffe, San Francisco, 1975-78; asst. prof. law U. San Diego, 1978-79, assoc. prof. law, 1980-81; mem. faculty Inst. on Internat. and Comparative Law, London, 1984—88; acting prof. law U. Calif., Davis, 1981-85, prof., 1988—, assoc. dean, 1993-98, dean Law Sch., 1998—. Dir. clin. edn. Univ. Calif., Davis, 1981-93, acad. senate, law sch. rep., 1989-91; vis. prof. law Univ. Santa Clara (Calif.), summer 1986. Co-author: California Civil Procedure and Practice, 1996, The United States Legal system-An Introduction, 2002, 2d edit., 2007, California Legal Ethics, 7th edit., 2007, Problems in Legal Ethics, 9th edit., 2007, Cases and Materials on Civil Procedure, 5th edit., 2005; contbr. articles to legal jours. Bd. dirs. Legal Svcs. of No. Calif., 1990-96. Recipient Disting. Teaching Award, 1992. Mem. ABA (Section of Legal Edn. and Admissions to Bar, Accreditation Com., 2000-), Calif. Bar Assn., Am. Assn. Law Schs., Inn of Ct. Democrat. Avocation: travel. Office: UC Davis Sch Law Dean Office 400 Mrak Hall Dr Davis CA 95616 Office Phone: 530-752-0243. E-mail: rrperschbacher@ucdavis.edu.

PERSCHETZ, MARTIN L., lawyer; b. Bklyn., Sept. 15, 1952; s. Louis and Edith (Sandhaus) Perschetz; m. Babs D. Hanfling, Mar. 23, 1980; children: Monica, Keith, Evan. BA, U. Md., 1974; JD, SUNY, Buffalo, 1977. Bar: NY 1978, US Dist. Ct. (So. Dist.) NY 1978, US Dist. Ct. (Ea. Dist.) NY 1979, US Ct. Appeals (2nd Cir.) 1984, US Dist. Ct. (No. Dist.) NY 1989, US Dist. Ct. Colo. 1998, US Dist. Ct. (Ea. Dist.) Mich. 2003, US Ct. Appeals (6th Cir.) 2003. Assoc. Obermaier, Morvillo & Abramowitz, NYC, 1977—80; asst. U.S. atty. So. Dist. N.Y., NYC, 1980—86, chief major crimes unit, 1985—86; chief counsel N.Y.C. Spl. Commn. to Investigate City Contracts, NYC, 1986; dep. commr. N.Y.C. Dept. Investigation, NYC, 1986; spl. counsel Schulte, Roth & Zabel, NYC, 1986—87; ptnr. Schulte, Roth & Zabel, LLP, NYC, 1988—. Contbr. articles to profl. jour.; spkr. in field. Recipient Joseph Halpern award, Buffalo Law Rev., 1977. Mem.: NY Coun. Def. Lawyers, NYC Bar Assn., ABA. Office: Schulte Roth & Zabel LLP 919 Third Ave New York NY 10022-4774 Office Phone: 212-756-2247. E-mail: martin.perschetz@srz.com.

PERSELL, CAROLINE HODGES, sociologist, educator, author, researcher, consultant; b. Ft. Wayne, Ind., Jan. 16, 1941; d. Albert Randolph and Katherine (Rogers) Hodges; m. Charles Bowen Persell III, June 17, 1967; children: Patricia Emily, Stephen David. BA, Swarthmore Coll., 1962; MA, Columbia U., 1967, PhD, 1971. Sr. assoc., then nat. coord. Nat. Scholarship Svc. and Fund for Negro Students, NYC, 1962-66; project dir. Bur. Applied Social Rsch., NYC, 1968-71; asst. prof. NYU, 1971-76, assoc. prof., 1976-86, prof., 1986—, dir. grad. studies dept. sociology, 1984-87, chair dept. sociology, 1987-93, Robin Williams Disting. lectr., 1993-94. Author: Education and Inequality, 1977, Understanding Society, 1984, 3d edit., 1990; author: (with Cookson) Preparing for Power, 1985, Making Sense of Society, 1992; author: (with Maisel) How Sampling Works, 1996; assoc. editor: Tchg. Sociology, 1983—85, Sociology of Edn., 1991—95, Gender & Society, 1992—95; contbr. articles to profl. jours. Carnegie scholar Advancement of Tchg., 2000-01; grantee Fund for Improvement of Postsecondary Edn., 1989-92, NSF Equipment Fund, 1993-96; recipient Faculty Devel. award NSF, 1978-79, Women Educators' Rsch. award, 1978. Mem.: Sociologists for Women in Soc., Ea. Sociol. Soc. (pres. 1995—96), Am. Sociol. Assn. (chair sect. 1983—84, chmn. publs. com. 1987—89, chair sect. 1988—89, v.p. 2004—05). Avocations: violin, gardening, opera, sports, photography. Office: NYU Dept Sociology 295 LafayetteSt New York NY 10012 Home Phone: 914-922-1602; Office Phone: 212-998-8350. Business E-Mail: chp1@nyu.edu.

PERSELLIN, ROBERT HAROLD, physician; b. Fargo, ND, July 3, 1930; s. James Harry and Bessie (Hoffman) P.; m. Bonnie Feibleman, June 27, 1957 (dec. 1983); children: Kathleen, Jamie; m. Diane Cummings, June 14, 1986 BS, Northwestern U., 1952, MD, 1956, MS, 1959. Diplomate: Am. Bd. Internal Medicine, Am. Bd. Rheumatology. Intern Charity Hosp., New Orleans, 1956-57; resident in internal medicine Northwestern U. Med. Center, 1957-60; fellow in rheumatology Southwestern Med. Sch., 1962-64; asst. prof. medicine U. Oreg. Med. Sch., 1964-68; prof. medicine, head div. rheumatology U. Tex. Health Sci. Ctr., San Antonio, 1968—81, prof. family practice, 1993—2003. Cons. rheumatology VA Hosps., U.S. Army, Internat. Med. Corps, Kosovo and Republic of Moldova; vis. prof. rheumatology Kingstown Med. Coll.; vis. scholar Corpus Christi Coll., Cambridge U., 1979-80; vis. scientist Strangeways Rsch. Lab., Cambridge. Contbr chpts. to books, articles to profl. jours. Bd. dirs. San Antonio Chamber Music Soc., 1970-75, 80-96, pres., 1983-85; bd. dirs. Friends of Strings, 1972-75, San Antonio Bot. Soc., 1985-87; Dem. precinct committeeman Washington County, Oreg., 1966-68. Served to capt. M.C. U.S. Army, 1960-62. Fellow ACP, Am. Coll. Rheumatology (exec. com. mem.); mem. Arthritis Found. (chmn. med. and sci. com. South Ctrl. Tex. chpt.), Heberden Soc., Am. Fedn. Clin. Rsch., So. Soc. Clin. Investigation, Tex. Rheumatism Assn. (pres.), Nat. Soc. Clin. Rheumatology, Mex. Rheumatology Soc. (hon.). Office: 635 E Olmos Dr San Antonio TX 78212-2504

PERSHAD, ASHISH, cardiologist; b. Hyderabad, India, Jan. 7, 1971; s. Kailash and Sheela Pershad; m. Nisha Waghray, Oct. 11, 1970; 1 child, Yash. MD, U. Bombay, 1994. Interventional cardiologist Heart and Vascular Ctr. Ariz., Phoenix, 2001—. Cons. WL Gore Inc, Flagstaff, Ariz., 2002—05, Care Hospitals, Hyderabad, Ap, India, 2003—. Med. adv. bd.

Boston Sci. Inc, Natick, Mass., 2003—05. McLennon Acad. scholar, U. Bombay, 1994—95. Mem.: Soc. Coronary Angiography and Interventions, Am. Coll. Physicians, Am. Coll. Cardiology, Maricopa Med. Soc. (licentiate), Ariz. Med. Assn. (licentiate). Office: Heart and Vascular Ctr Ariz 1331 N7th St Ste #375 Phoenix AZ 85006 Office Phone: 602-307-0070. Office Fax: 602-307-0080. Business E-Mail: apershad1@cox.net.

PERSHAN, RICHARD HENRY, lawyer; b. NYC, Jan. 4, 1930; s. Benjamin and Sadie (Aronowsky) P.; m. Kathryn Schaefler, June 11, 1952; children: Lee S., Richard H. Jr., Pamela P. Hochman, Julia B. BA, Yale U., 1951, LLB, 1956. Bar: NY 1956, US Supreme Ct.1969. Assoc. Davis, Polk & Wardwell, NYC, 1956-60; ptnr. Finch & Schaefler, NYC, 1960-85, LeBoeuf, Lamb, Greene & MacRae, NYC, 1986-94, of counsel, 1995—. Counsel Mcpl. Art Soc., NYC, 1965-70, Fine Arts Fedn., NYC, 1975-80. Served to 1st lt. USAF, 1951-53. Fellow Am. Coll. Trust and Estate Counsel (author, editor, articles and studies 1960—); mem. Assn. of Bar of City of NY, Yale Club (NYC). Democrat. Avocation: fitness. Home: 1435 Lexington Ave New York NY 10128-1630 Office: LeBoeuf Lamb Greene & MacRae 125 W 55th St New York NY 10019-5389 Office Phone: 212-424-8523. Personal E-mail: rpershan@yahoo.com. Business E-Mail: rpershan@llgm.com.

PERSHING, ROBERT GEORGE, retired telecommunications industry executive; b. Battle Creek, Mich., Aug. 10, 1941; s. James Arthur and Beulah Francis P.; m. Diana Kay Prill, Sept. 16, 1961 (div. Jan. 1989); children: Carolyn, Robert; m. Charlene Jean Reed Wallis, Mar. 18, 1989 (div. Dec. 1995); m. Luz F. Villalon Dreisbach, July 23, 2006. BSEE, Tri-State Coll., 1961. Comm. engr. Am. Elec. Power, Ind., NY, and Ohio, 1961-69; design supr. Wescom, Inc., Ill., 1969-74; dir. engring. Tellabs, Inc., Lisle, Ill., 1974-78; pres., CEO Teltrend, Inc., St. Charles, Ill., 1979-89, chmn. bd., 1979-88; CEO DKP Prodns., Inc., St. Charles, Ill., 1986-89; exec. cons. Teltrend, St. Charles, Ill., 1979-93; asst. treas. Magnekopy, inc., Villa Park, Ill. Bd. dirs. TI Investors, Inc.; advisor entrepreneurial studies U. Ill.; engring. cons. Recipient Chgo. Area Small Bus. award, 1986., INC 500 awards, 1987, 88. Mem. IEEE. Office: PO Box 3377 Show Low AZ 85902 Home Phone: 928-537-8952; Office Phone: 928-537-8952. E-mail: rpershing@frontiernet.net.

PERSICHILLI KEOGH, KAREN MARY, political organization worker; b. 1966; d. Joseph and Barbara Persichilli; m. Michael P. Keogh, Mar. 13, 1999; 1 adopted child, Jessica. Grad., State U. Stony Brook; M in Social Work, Columbia U., 1989. With Dist. Coun. 37, NYC, 1989—93; chief of staff to Councilman Albanese NYC, 1993—2002; dir. NY ops., sr. advisor for Sen. Hilary Rodham Clinton, 2002—; campaign dir. for Sen. Hilary Rodham Clinton's re-election campaign, 2006. Adj. prof. social work Columbia U. Office: State Dir for Senator Hilary Rodham Clinton 780 Third Ave Ste 2601 New York NY 10017

PERSICO, JOSEPH EDWARD, historian, biographer; b. Gloversville, NY, July 19, 1930; s. Thomas Louis and Blanche (Perrone) P.; m. Sylvia La Vista, May 23, 1959; children: Vanya, Andrea. BA, SUNY-Albany, 1952, PhD (hon.), 1996; postgrad., Columbia U., 1955. Writer on staff of gov. N.Y. State, Albany, 1955-59; commd. fgn. service officer USIA, 1959, served in Buenos Aires, Rio de Janeiro, 1959-62; speechwriter Commr. N.Y. State Health Dept., Albany, 1963-66; chief speechwriter for gov. N.Y. State, Albany, 1966-74; speechwriter for Vice Pres. Nelson Rockefeller The White House, Washington, 1975-77. Commr. Am. Battle Monuments Commn. Author: My Enemy My Brother: Men and Days of Gettysburg, 1977, (novel) The Spiderweb, 1979, Piercing the Reich: The Penetration of Nazi Germany by American Secret Agents During World War II, 1979, The Imperial Rockefeller: A Biography of Nelson A. Rockefeller, 1982, Edward R. Murrow: An American Original, 1988, Casey: William J. Casey, From the OSS to the CIA, 1990, Nuremberg: Infamy on Trial, 1994, Roosevelt's Secret War: FDR and World War II Espionage, 2001, Eleventh Month, Eleventh Day, Eleventh Hour: Armistice Day, 1918, 2004; co-author: Colin Powell: My American Journey, 1995. Served to lt. (j.g.) USN, 1952-55. Recipient Disting. Alumnus award SUNY-Albany, 1982 Mem.: Coun. Fgn. Rels., Authors Guild, Inc. Office Phone: 518-452-5429.

PERSING, JOHN ARTHUR, surgeon; b. Burlington, Vt., Apr. 16, 1948; s. Raymond Maurice and Natalie (Vespucci) P.; m. Susan Powers Light, June 22, 1971; children: Sarah Merriman, John Scott. BA cum laude, U. Vt., 1970, MD, 1974; MA (hon.), Yale U., 1992. Diplomate Am. Bd. Plastic and Reconstructive Surgery, Am. Bd. Neurol. Surgeons. Resident gen. surgery Hosp. of U. Ariz., Tuscon, 1974-76; resident neurol. surgery Hosp. of U. Va., Charlottesville, 1976-82, resident plastic surgery, 1982-84, dir. cranial base surgery, 1988-92, vice chmn. dept. of plastic surgery, 1988-92, chief divsn. of craniofacial surgery, 1988-92; asst. prof. plastic and neurosurgery U. Va., Charlottesville, 1984-87, assoc. prof. of plastic and neurosurgery, 1987-89, prof. plastic and neurosurgery, 1989-92; prof. plastic surgery and neurosurgery Yale U. Sch. of Medicine, New Haven, Conn., 1992—, chief sect. of plastic surgery, 1992—; fellow Trumbull Coll. Yale U., New Haven, 1994—. Editor: Clinics in Plastic Surgery, July, 1995; co-editor Jour. of Craniofacial Surgery, 1992—, Scientific Foundations and Surgical Treatment for Craniosynostosis, 1989, Neurosurgery Clinics of North America, July, 1991; assoc. editor Plastic and Reconstructive Surgery, 1997-2005. Recipient Donald D. Matson award Am. Assn. of Neurol. Surgeons, 1981. Mem. Am. Assn. Pediatric Plastic Surgeons (pres. 1995-97), Am. Assn. Plastic Surgeons (membership com. 1994-95), Am. Soc. Plastic and Reconstructive Surgeons (coms.), Am. Cleft Palate-Craniofacial Assn. (coms.), Am. Soc. Maxillofacial Surgeons (coms., v.p. 2000-01,pres. 2002-03, Bernd Speissl award 1991, Maxillofacial Surgeons Found. Rsch. award 1992), Plastic Surgery Edn. Found. (sec. 2005-), Assn. Acad. Chmn. of Plastic Surgery (plastic surgery residency tng. evaluation com. 1993, chair issues com. 1994, v.p. 2002-03, pres. 2004-05), Northeastern Soc. Plastic Surgeons (program com. 1995), Plastic Surgery Rsch. Coun. (program com. 1991-94), Am. Bd. Plastic Surgery (chmn. 2005). Office: Yale Plastic Surgery 330 Cedar St # 2 New Haven CT 06510-8041 Office Phone: 203-785-2570. Business E-Mail: john.persing@yale.edu.

PERSINGER, DEL LOUIS, pharmaceutical company executive; b. Whiting, Iowa, Aug. 2, 1949; s. Ardell L. and Doris L. Persinger; m. Mary L. Tabor, Sept. 16, 1984; children: Christopher, Benjamin Hammerschlag, Sarah Hammerschlag. BSChemE with distinction, Iowa State U., 1971, MS in Journalism and Mass. Comm., 1975; MBA in Fin., Am. U., 1990. Refinery process engr. Exxon Co., Baton Rouge, 1971-73; environtl. and pub. affairs mgr. Am. Petroleum Inst., Washington, 1975-89, sr. assoc. refining, 1989-92, dep. dir. mfg., distbn. and mktg., 1992-94, dir. mgmt. and budget, 1994-96; v.p. fin. ops. Pharm. Rsch. and Mfrs. of Am., Washington, 1996—2006, sr. v.p., CFO, 2006—; pres., CEO PhRMA Found., Washington, 1999—. Trustee, past pres. Bethesda Jewish Congregation, 1992—2000. Mem. Fin. Execs. Inst., Am. Soc. of Assn. Execs., Am. Found. for Pharm. Edn. (bd. dirs. 1999—), Phi Kappa Phi, Tau Beta Pi, Omega Chi Epsilon. Office: Pharm Rsch and Mfrs of Am Ste 300 950 F St NW Washington DC 20004

PERSKY, MARLA SUSAN, lawyer; b. Pitts., Feb. 15, 1956; d. Bernard and Elaine (Matus) P.; m. Craig Heberton IV, May 20, 1984. BS, Northwestern U., 1977; JD, Washington U., St. Louis, 1982. Bar: Ill. 1982. Asst. dir. med. records Chgo. Lake Shore Hosp., 1978; sales/mktg. rep. Colgate-Palmolive Co., Chgo., 1978-79; mem. Lurie Sklar & Simon, Chgo., 1982-86; corp. counsel Baxter Healthcare Corp., Deerfield, Ill., 1986-91; lead litigation counsel Baxter Internat. Inc., 1991-94; assoc. gen. counsel Baxter Healthcare Corp., Deerfield, 1994—98, dep. gen. counsel, 1998—2004, gen. counsel, corp. sec., 2004—. Dir. Cytyc Corp. Sr. editor Urban Law Ann., 1981-82; contbr. articles to profl. jours. Mem. Chgo. Bar Assn., Ill. Bar Assn. (writing contest award 1983), ABA (vice chmn. medicine and law com. 1984-86), Am. Soc. Law and Medicine, Am. Acad. Hosp. Attys. Democrat. Office: Baxter Internat Inc One Baxter Pkwy Deerfield IL 60015-5281

PERSLIDEN, JAN R. G., physicist; b. Norrkoping, Sweden, July 13, 1950; s. Rune E.B. and Ruth E.M. (Roxne) P.; m. Lena K. Åman, Aug. 1, 1976; children: Sara, Hanna, Mikael, Persliden. PhD, Linkoping U., 1986. Rsch. asst. dept. radiation physics U. Linkoping, 1976-82; med. physicist Univ. Hosp., Linköping, Sweden, 1982-88, prin. med. physicist, 1988-99, assoc. prof., 1993, prof., 2002—. Cons. med. physicist Norrkoping Hosp., Motala Hosp., Sweden, 1994-99; head med. physics dept. U. Hosp., Orebro, Sweden, 1999-. Contbr. articles to profl. jours. Mem. Swedish Soc. of Radiation Physics (bd. dirs. 1994-2001, pres. 1999-2001), Swedish Electrotech. Commn. Baptist. Avocations: church activities, cross country skiing. Office: Dept Radiation Physics Univ Hosp 701 85 Örebro Sweden Office Phone: +46 19 602 1000. Personal E-mail: Jan.Persliden@orebroll.se.

PERSOFF, MYRON MAYER, plastic surgeon; b. West Palm Beach, Fla., Apr. 26, 1941; BS, U. Fla., Gainesville, 1963; MD, U. Miami, Fla., 1967. Cert. Am. Bd. Plastic Surgery, 1977. Rotating-2 intern Phila. Naval Hosp., 1967—68; resident gen. surgery U. South Fla. Sch. Medicine, Tampa, 1971—73, St. Joseph Hosp., Houston, 1973—74, resident plastic surgery, 1974—76; fellow Cronin-Brauer Clin. Assn., Houston, 1974—76; staff mem. North Broward Hosp., 1976—90, West Boca Med. Ctr., 1985—94, Northridge Med. Ctr., Ft. Lauderdale, Fla., 1993—95, Mercy Hosp., Coconut Grove, Fla., 1994—, Coral Gables Hosp., Fla., 1998—2001; active staff mem. Boca Raton Cmty. Hosp., Fla., 1976—93; clin. asst. U. Miami Sch. Medicine, 1977—2001. Contbr. articles to med. jours.; featured: magazines Plastic Surgery Products. Orthopedic surgeon USN, 1968—69, Navy Hosp., Pensacola, Fla., sea duty USN, 1968, USS Speigel Grove, attended Flight Surgeons Sch. USN, 1969, Pensacola, Fla., served in USN, 1969—71, US Naval Air Sta., Cubi Point, Philippines. Fellow: Am. Coll. Surgeons; mem.: AMA, Broward County Soc. Plastic Surgeons, Lipolysis Soc. N.Am., Miami Soc. Plastic Surgeons, Dade County Med. Assn., Palm Beach County Med. Soc., Fla. Med. Assn., Palm Beach County Soc. Plastic and Reconstructive Surgeons, Fla. Soc. Plastic and Reconsructive Surgeons, Southeastern Soc. Plastic and Reconstructive Surgeons, Am. Soc. Plastic and Reconstructive Surgeons, Am. Soc. Aesthetic Plastic Surgery. Office: Coconut Grove Plastic Surgery Mercy Output Ctr 3659 S Miami Ave Ste 4006 Miami FL 33133 Office Phone: 305-858-5255. Office Fax: 305-858-5235.

PERSOFF, NEHEMIAH, actor, artist; b. Jerusalem, Aug. 2, 1919; came to U.S., 1929; s. Samuel and Puah (Holman) P.; m. Thia Persov; children: Jeffrey Jonathan, Dan Deckel, Perry Erez, Dahlia. Student, Hebrew Tech. Inst., NYC, 1934-37. Ind. stage, screen and TV actor, 1945—. Actor: (Broadway prodns.) Sundown Beach, Galileo, Richard the 3d, King Lear, Peer Gynt, Peter Pan, Reclining Figure, Flahooly, Montserrat, Tiger at the Gate, Only in America, (local, regional prodns.) Fiddler on the Roof, Man of La Mancha, Oliver, I'm Not Rappaport, 1988, Death of a Salesman (Stratford, Ont.), Two, Drinking America, Rosebloom, Dybbuk (Best Actor L.A. Critics 1975), Glass Menagerie (Israeli prodn.), Volpone, Of Mice and Men, (films) In Search of the Real Jesus, The Harder They Fall, The Wrong Man, This Angry Age, Men in War, Some Like It Hot, Al Capone, Green Mansions, The Commancheros, The Greatest Story Ever Told, Voyage of the Damned, Yentl, The Hook, The Last Temptation of Christ, Twins, numerous TV shows including For Whom the Bell Tolls (Sylvania award for best supporting actor 1958), The Big Knife, Alfred Hitchcock Presents, Rawhide, Twilight Zone, The Untouchables, The Wild, Wild West, I Spy, Gunsmoke, Police Story, Columbo, Barney Miller, Six Million Dollar Man, Delta House, Littlest Hobo, Magnum P.I., Hotel, Adderly; (TV miniseries) The French Atlantic; (one-man show) Aleichem Sholem-Sholem-Alecheim, 1971 (L.A. Critics award, San Francisco Critics Circle award 1979); paintings exhibited at George Krevsky Fine Arts, San Francisco, Seago Gallery, Cambria, Calif. With US Army, 1942—45. Jewish.

PERSON, CURTIS S., JR., judge, former state legislator, lawyer; b. Nov. 27, 1934; married; 6 children. BS, Memphis State U., 1956; LLB, U. Miss., 1959. Chief legal officer Juvenile Ct. Memphis and Shelby County; former mem. Tenn. Ho. Reps.; mem. Tenn. Senate, 1969—2007, Senate Rep. whip, 1973-76, minority caucus chmn., 1976-82; judge Juvenile Ct. Memphis and Shelby County, Tenn., 2006—. Chmn. Senate Judiciary com. 95th-104th Gen. Assemblies. Pres. Memphis-Shelby County Mental Health Assn., 1969-73, Handicapped Inc., 1972-74; chmn. Memphis Commn. Drug Abuse, 1970-71; charter pres. Memphis State Tiger Rebounders; past trustee Memphis State U.; exec. committeeman St. Jude's Memphis Open Golf Classic; co-chmn. Shelby County Legis. Del., 1973-74, vice chmn., 1970, 75, 76, 85-88; chmn. Shelby Rep. Del., 1977, 83-84; mem. adv. bd. Jr. League Memphis, 1995-98; vice chmn. Select Com. Children and Youth, 1997-2002, ex officio Senate Mem., Juvenile Justice Reform Commn., 1998. Named Memphis and Tenn. Outstanding Young Man of Yr., Jaycees, 1969, Outstanding Legis. of Yr., Govt. Leader Against Drunk Driving, Tenn. MADD, 1988, Legis. of Yr., Tenn. Alcohol and Drug Assn., 1988, Legislator of Yr. Tenn. Juvenile Svcs. Yr., 2001; recipient Liberty Bell Freedom award Memphis/Shelby County Bar Assn., 1969, Tenn. Adv. of Yr. Handicapped Children, 1978, Outstanding Svc. Children award Tenn Coun. Juvenile Ct. Judges, 1981, Pres.' Svc. award Tenn. Juvenile Ct. Svcs. Assn., 1981, Americanism award Memphis Civitan Club, 1986, Disting. Svc. award County Ofcls. Assn. Tenn., 1989, Cmty. Svc. award Tenn. Med. Assn., 1989, Eagle award Eagle Forum, 1994, Bill Bates Legis. award United Tenn. League, 1994, Champion for Children award Tenn. Assn. Child Care, 1995, Outstanding Legis. award County Ofcls. Assn. Tenn., 1996, Tenn. Juvenile Svcs. Assn. Pres. Svc. award, 1997, Tenn. Trial Lawyers Assn. Legis. of Yr. award, 1997, Shelby County Rep. Party Chmn. of Yr. award, 1999, Am. Lung Assn. Tenn. Legis. of Yr. award, 1999, Tenn. Task Force Against Domestic Violence Outstanding Legis. of Yr. award, 1999, Tenn. Dispensing Opticians Assn. Legis. of Yr. award, 2000, award Tenn. Juvenile Ct. Svcs. Assn., 2001, Spl. Honor Elvis Presley Meml. Martial Arts Hall of Fame, 2002, Lifetime Achievement award Defenders of Freedom, 2002, Animal Advocacy award Metro Animal Svcs., 2002, Legislator of Yr. award Tenn. Trial Lawyers Assn., 2003; named Legislator of Yr. Tenn. Devel. Dists., 2003, Hon. Fellow and Legislator of Yr., Opticians Assn. Am., 2003, Legislative Leadership award, Tenn. Cable Telecommunications Assn., 2003-2004, Friend of the Family award Tenn. Home Edn. Assn., 2004, Humane Legislator award Humane Soc. U.S., 2004, Thomas B. Murphy Longevity of Svc. award Southern Legislative Conf., 2004, Legislator of Yr., Animal Control Assn. of Tenn., 2004, award of appreciation Tenn. Silica Justice Coalition, 2006; named Champion Tenn. Disability Coalition, 2003-04, Outstanding Legislator, Co. Ofcls. Assn. Tenn., 2004. Office: 616 Adams Ave Memphis TN 38105 Home Phone: 901-767-8659; Office Phone: 901-405-8574. Business E-Mail: person-c@shelbyjuvenilecourt.com.

PERSON, EVERT BERTIL, retired newspaper and radio executive; b. Berkeley, Calif., Apr. 6, 1914; s. Emil P. and Elida (Swanson) P.; m. Ruth Finley, Jan. 26, 1944 (dec. May 1985); m. 2d, Norma Joan Betz, Mar. 12, 1986. Student, U. Calif., Berkeley, 1937; LHD, Calif. State Univ., 1983, LHD, 1993, Sonoma State U., 1993. Co-publisher, sec.-treas. Press Democrat Pub. Co., Santa Rosa, Calif., 1945-72, editor, 1972-73, pres., pub., editor-in-chief, 1973-85; sec.-treas. Finley Broadcasting Co., Santa Rosa, 1945-72, pres., 1972-89, Kawana Pubs., 1975-85; pub. Healdsburg Tribune, 1975-85; prin. Evert B. Person Investments, Santa Rosa, 1985—. Pres. Person Properties Co., Santa Rosa, 1945-70; v.p. Finley Ranch & Land Co., Santa Rosa, 1947-72, pres., 1972-79; pres. Baker Pub. Co., Oreg., 1957-67, Sebastopol (Calif.) Times, 1978-81, Russian River News, Guerneville, Calif., 1978-81; pres. publ. Kawana Pubs., 1978-85; mem. nominating com. AP, 1982-84, mem. auditing com., 1984-85 Bd. dirs Empire Coll., Santa Rosa, 1972-98, Sonoma County Taxpayers Assn., 1966-69, San Francisco Spring Opera Assn., 1974-79; bd. dirs. San Francisco Opera, 1986-95, v.p., 1988-95; pres. Calif. Newspaperboy Found., 1957-58; chmn. Santa Rosa Civic Arts Commn., 1961-62; pres. Santa Rosa Sonoma County Symphony Assn., 1966-68, Luther Burbank Meml. Found., 1979, Santa Rosa Symphony Found., 1967-77; adv. bd. Santa Rosa Salvation Army, 1959-67; commodore 12th Coast Guard Dist. Aux., 1969-70; trustee Desert Mus., Palm Springs, 1987-92, v.p. Nat. Bd. Canine Companions, Inc., 1989-92. Decorated Knight of the Holy Sepulchre. Mem. Calif. Newspaper Pubs. Assn. (pres. 1981-82), Internat. Newspaper Fin. Execs. (pres. 1961-62), Bohemian Club, Sonoma County Press Club, Santa Rosa Golf and Country club, The Springs Club, Santa Rosa Rotary (past pres.), Masons (33 degree, Legion of Merit), Shriners. Roman Catholic. Home: 775 White Oak Dr Santa Rosa CA 95409-6155 Office: The Oaks 1400 N Dutton Ave Ste 12 Santa Rosa CA 95401-4644

PERSON, TAMMY, psychologist; b. Fort Ord, Calif., Nov. 1, 1971; d. Merl and Autrice Taylor; m. Audie Person, Apr. 2, 1994; children: Autumn, Audie Person, Jr. BA in Psychology, NC State U., Raleigh, 1993; MS in Counseling Psychology, U. Ctrl. Tex., Killeen, 1996; EdS in Curriculum and Instrn., Mid. Tenn. State U., Murfreesboro, 2006. Cert. sch. psychologist NASP, 2006. Cmty. svcs. coord. Smyrna Police Dept., Tenn., 2002—05; sch. psychology specialist Killeen Ind. Sch. Dist., Tex., 2006—. Mem.: Phi Kappa Phi. Personal E-mail: tam122@hotmail.com.

PERSONS, JOHN WADE, lawyer; b. Fitchburg, Mass., Dec. 6, 1953; s. Roger W. and Vivian A. (Boudreau) P.; m. Marjorie L. Smith, July 18, 1980; children: Katherine A., Elizabeth W. BA in History magna cum laude, U. Conn., 1975, MA, 1977; JD, Albany Law Sch., 1980. Bar: N.Y. 1981, U.S. Dist. Ct. (no. dist.) N.Y. 1981, U.S. Dist. Ct. (ea. dist.) N.Y. 1985. From law clk. to assoc. Cade & Saunders, Albany, NY, 1978—84; legal rschr., writing instr. Albany Law Sch., 1979—80; assoc. Glynn and Mercep, Stony Brook, NY, 1984—86; ptnr. Glynn, Mercep and Persons, Stony Brook, NY, 1987—91; assoc. Faruolo, Caputi, Weintraub & Neary, Huntington, NY, 1991—96; from assoc. to ptnr. Grey & Grey, LLP, Farmingdale, NY, 1996—2003; assoc. Montfort, Healy, McGuire and Salley, Garden City, NY, 2004—. Law guardian Albany County Family Ct., 1984. Mem. N.Y. State Bar Assn. (ins. sect., negligence and compensation law sect.), Suffolk County Bar Assn. (ins., negligence and compensation), Killington Sch. for Instrs; Clubs: Stony Brook Yacht. Democrat. Home: 53 Cedar St Stony Brook NY 11790-1732 Office: Montfort Healy McGuire & Salley PO Box 7677 1140 Franklin Ave Garden City NY 11530-7677 Office Phone: 516-747-4082. Business E-Mail: john_persons@mhmslaw.com.

PERSONS, (W.) RAY (W. RAY PERSONS), lawyer, legal association administrator; b. Talbottan, Ga., July 22, 1953; s. William and Frances (Crowell) P.; m. Wendy-Joy Mottley, Sept. 24, 1977; children: Conrad Ashley, April Maureen. BS cum laude, Armstrong State Coll., 1975; JD, Ohio State U., 1978. Bar: Ga. 1979, US Dist. Ct. (so. dist.) Ga. 1980, US Dist. Ct. (no. dist.) Ga. 1986, US Ct. Appeals (11th cir.) 1986. Assoc. Troutman, Sanders, Lockerman & Ashmore, Atlanta, 1978-79; atty. NLRB, Atlanta, 1980-82; legis. counsel U.S Ho. Reps., Washington, 1983-86; atty. Mack & Bernstein, Atlanta, 1986-87; ptnr. Arrington & Hollowell LLP, Atlanta, 1987-95, Swift, Currie, McGhee & Hiers LLP, Atlanta, 1995-99, Hunton & Williams LLP, Atlanta, 1999—2001, King & Spalding LLP, Atlanta, 2001—. Adj. prof. litigation Ga. State U., Atlanta, 1989—; spl. asst. atty. gen. State of Ga., Atlanta, 1988—. Master Am. Inns of Ct. (Lamar chpt.); fellow Am. Coll. Trial Lawyers; mem. ABA, Internat. Soc. Barristers, Am. Bd. Trial Advocates, State Bar Ga., Atlanta Bar Assn. (bd. dirs., 1996-97, 2000-, sec., 2003-04, treas., 2004-05, 2nd v.p., 2005-06, pres.-elect, 2006-07, pres., 2007-) Lawyers Club of Atlanta. Roman Catholic. Office: King & Soalding LLP 1180 Peachtree St NE Atlanta GA 30309 Office Phone: 404-572-2494. Business E-Mail: rpersons@kslaw.com. *

PERSSON, ERLAND KARL, electrical engineer, executive; b. Soderala, Sweden, Oct. 9, 1923; arrived in U.S., 1949, naturalized, 1953; m. Elaine Darm; children: Ann Monn, Eric. BSEE, U. Minn., 1955. Registered profl. engr., Minn. Prin. engr. Gen. Mills, Mpls., 1956-61; v.p. engring. Electro-Craft Corp., Hopkins, Minn., 1961-72, v.p. R & D, 1972-83, sr. v.p., chief tech. officer, 1983-86; pres. Erland Persson Co., Mpls., 1987—. Contbr. articles to profl., chapters to books. Mem. mech. engring. adv. com. U. Minn.; bd. dirs. Minn. High Tech. Coun., 1984—86, mem., 1987. Fellow: IEEE (life; mem. indsl. drives com.), Audio Engring. Soc. (life; founder midwest chpt. 1974); mem.: Eta Kappa Nu. Achievements include patents in field. Office: 216 Janalyn Cir Minneapolis MN 55416-3321 Home Phone: 763-377-2531.

PERTH, ROD, network entertainment executive; b. LA; s. Milford Robert Martinson and Phyllis (Hove) Perth; m. Jill Sunderland, Apr. 27, 1974; children: Chelseah, Lauren, Eric. BS in Mgmt., San Jose State U., 1966. V.p., gen. mgr. spot sales CBS TV, NYC, 1974—86; v.p., station mgr. WBBM-TV, Chgo., 1986—89; sr. v.p. late night non-network programming CBS-TV, LA, 1989—94; pres. entertainment USA Network, LA, 1994—95; pres. HRTS, LA, 1995—99, Jim Henson T.V.; programming dir. USA Network. Account exec. KNXT, LA, 1968—71; ea. mgr. spot sales CBS, NYC, 1971—74, dir. midwest spot sales, Chgo., 1974—76; dir. sales KMOX-TV, St. Louis, 1976—79; bd. dirs. HRTS. Contbr. L.E.A.R.N. program, LA, 1995, Alliance for Children, LA, 1996; bd. mem. State St. Coun., Chgo., 1988. Lt. j.g. USN, 1968—74. Named Man of Yr., Alliance for Children, L.A., 1996. Mem.: Hollywood (Calif.) Radio and TV Soc. (pres. 1995—). Avocations: skiing, motorcycling, photography. Office: Jim Henson Television 1416 N Labrea Ave Hollywood CA 90068

PERTHOU, ALISON CHANDLER, interior designer; b. Bremerton, Wash., July 22, 1945; d. Benson and Elizabeth (Holdsworth) Chandler; m. A. V. Perthou, III, Sept. 9, 1967 (div. Dec. 1977); children: Peter T. R., Stewart A. C. BFA, Cornish Coll. Arts, 1972. Pres. Alison Perthou Interior Design, Seattle, 1972—, Optima Design, Inc., Seattle, 1986-89; treas. Framejoist Corp., Bellevue, Wash., 1973-90; pres. Classics: Interior Design and Constrn., Inc., 1988—, Gemini Holdings LLC, 2004—. Cons. bldg. and interiors com. Children's Hosp., Seattle, 1976—; guest lectr. U. Wash., Seattle, 1980—81. Mem. procurement com. Patrons N.W. Cultural and Charitable Orgn., 1985—, mem. antiques com., 1991—; trustee Cornish Coll. Arts, Seattle, 1973—80, sec. exec. com., 1975—77. Mem.: Am. Soc. Interior Design, Sunset Club, Seattle Tennis Club (mem. house and grounds com. 1974—75). Office: 563 Lake Washington Blvd E Seattle WA 98112-4226 Office Phone: 206-322-7909. Office Fax: 206-322-2335.

PERTZOFF, MARGARET HENDERSON, history professor; b. July 4, 1926; AB, Elmira Coll., NY, 1946; MA, U. Va., Charlottesville, 1958, PhD, 1960. Prof. history Randolph-Macon Woman's Coll., Lynchburg, Va., 1967—98; ret. Mem.: Am. Assn. Slavic Studies, Am. Hist. Assn. Home: 250 Pantops Mountain Rd Charlottesville VA 22911-8686

PERUMAL, OMATHANU PILLAI, research scientist, medical researcher, educator; b. Madurai, Tamil Nadu, India, June 29, 1974; s. Perumal and Velammal. BPharm, Tamil Nadu Dr. M.G. R. Med. U., Chennai, India, 1995; MPharm, Birla Inst. Tech., India, 1997; PhD, Nat. Inst. Pharm. Edn. and Rsch. (NIPER), Chandigarh, India, 2002. Jr. rsch. fellow Birla Inst. Tech., Ranchi, Jharkhand, India, 1995—97; lectr. Ultra

Coll. Pharmacy, Madurai, Tamil Nadu, India, 1997—98; sr. rsch. fellow Nat. Inst. Pharm. Edn. and Rsch. (NIPER), Chandigarh, Punjab, India, 1998—2002; rsch. scientist Ranbaxy Rsch. Laboratories, Grugaon, Haryana, India, 2002—03; post doctoral scientist Coll. pharmacy, U. Ky., Lexington, Ky., 2003—04; rsch. assoc. Wayne State U., Detroit, 2004—05; asst. prof. Coll. Pharmacy, SD State U., Brookings, SC, 2005—. Reviewer Internat. Jour. TB and Lung Diseases, AAPS Pharm. Sci., Current Drug Delivery, Biorganic and Medicinal Chemistry, Biomacromolecules, Jour. Investigative Dermatology, Transactions of the Royal Soc. Tropical Medicine and Hygiene, others; presenter in field. Editl. asst. (magazine) Current Rsch. in Pharm. Scis.; contbr. articles to profl. jours. Sec. Jr. Jaycess Wing of Madurai Jr. Chamber, Madurai, Tamil Nadu, India, 1993—94, chmn., 1994—95. Jr. rsch. fellow, U. Grants Commn., India, sr. rsch. fellow, Dept. Sci. and Tech., India, post-doctoral scholar, NIH. Mem.: Am. Assn. Colls. Pharmacy, Indian Pharm. Assn. (assoc.), Am. Assn. Pharm. Scientists (assoc. Travel award 2004), Rho Chi, Sigma Xi. Achievements include development of new modified radioimmuno assay for analysis of insulin; new gel system for the transdermal delivery of insulin; identifying new crystal forms of drugs like azithromycin, rifampicin and mefenamic acid using various techniques; research in insulin delivery through skin using electrical current (iontophoresis) and chemical enhancers. Findings demonstrated that large peptides can be delivered through skin; new ways to improve the drug delivery across skin using various chemical and physical strategies; salt forms, solubility enhancement, stabilization and formulations for new chemical entities in new drug discovery and development; novel nanopolymers for intracellular drug delivery; dendrimer based intracellular drug delivery; intracellular drug delivery sys. for cancer, cardiovascular drugs and neurological diseases using nanovehicles. Avocations: table tennis, reading, cricket. Office: SD State U Coll Pharmacy Box 2202C Brookings SD 57007 Home Phone: 605-697-7455; Office Phone: 605-688-4745. Personal E-mail: omathanu@yahoo.com.

PERUZZO, ALBERT LOUIS, actuary, accountant; b. Chgo., Dec. 27, 1951; s. Anthony L. and Annette Peruzzo. BS Math., No. Ill. U., 1973, BS Accountancy, 1974, MBA, 1975. CPA Ill.; CLU 2003; chartered fin. cons. 2005. Auditor Deloittes CPA, Chgo., 1976—79; valuation analyst IV CNA Ins., Chgo., 1979—89, mgr. valuation compliance, 1989—92, valuation analyst, 1992—97, asst. actuary, 1998—2000, actuarial dir., 2000—02, actuarial cons. dir., 2002—04, Valley Forge Life Ins., 2004—05; actuarial cons. Jacobsen Solutions, 2005—. Treas., bd. dirs. Dignity/Chgo., 1982-84, Integrity/Chgo., 1988-93; dep. vol. Voter's Registrar Bd. Elections, Chgo., 1984-86; bd. dirs. Colonial Condo, 1990-99 Fellow Conf. Cons. Actuaries, Soc. Actuaries (edn. and exam. com. 1998-99), Life Mgmt. Inst. (with distinction); mem. AICPA (exam hon. mention 1975), Am. Acad. Actuaries (participant valuation task force 1998-99), Ill. CPA Soc. (Silver medal 1975), Beta Gamma Sigma (life charter Chgo. chpt.), Mensa (life), ACLU Democrat. Roman Catholic.

PERVAIZ, MOHAMMAD HASSAN, cardiologist; b. Lahore, Punjab, Pakistan, May 2, 1978; arrived in U.S., 2003; s. Pervaiz Akhtar Butt and Riffat Pervaiz; m. Maimoona Qamar. Degree, Govt. Coll., Lahore, Pakistan, 1997; MD, King Edward Med. Coll., Pakistan, 2002. Cert. Ednl. Commn. Fgn. Med. Grad., 2003. Clin. instr. Coll. Human Medicine Mich. State U., East Lansing, 2004—, resident internal medicine dept. medicine, 2004—, cardiology fellow, 2007—. Contbr. articles to med. jours. Grantee, Boston Sci., 2006. Mem.: AMA (assoc.), ACP (assoc.). Avocation: Aikido. Home: 2728 Trappers Cove Tr Apt 1A Lansing MI 48910 Office: Mich State U Dept Medicine B301 Clinical Ctr East Lansing MI 48823 Home Phone: 517-803-9528; Office Phone: 517-353-5100. Business E-Mail: pervaiz@msu.edu.

PERZ, SALLY, former state legislator, former academic administrator; m. Joseph Perz; children: Allison, Julie, Melanie, Andrea, Brian. BA, Siena Heights. Ohio State rep. Dist. 52, 1993; mgmt. cons. Perz, Inc., 1996—; exec. dir. govt. rels. U. Toledo. Active Boy Scouts Am. Recipient Carlson Counyt Mktg. award, 1984-93, Women of Achievement award, 1993. Mem. Toledo Club, Toledo C. of C., Toledo Rotary, Toledo Sisters Cities (exec. bd.). Home: 3245 River Rd Toledo OH 43614-4218

PERZEK, PHILIP JOHN, lawyer; b. Chgo., Sept. 25, 1960; s. Thomas John and Dorothy (Malis) P.; m. Gayle Karon Scott, Aug. 17, 1985; 1 child, Rachel Karon. BS, No. Ill. U., 1982; JD, Northwestern U., 1986. Bar: Ill. 1986, U.S. Dist. Ct. (no. dist.) Ill. 1986. Law clk. to Hon. Nicholas J. Bua U.S. Dist. Ct. (no. dist.) Ill., Chgo., 1986-88; ptnr. Latham & Watkins LLP, Chgo., 1988—. Mem. Ill. State Bar Assn., Nat. Comml. Fin. Assn. Home: 207 W 8th St Hinsdale IL 60521-4448 Office: Latham & Watkins 5800 Sears Tower Chicago IL 60606 Office Phone: 312-876-7699. Business E-Mail: Philip.Perzek@lw.com.

PERZEL, JOHN MICHAEL (JAY PERZEL), state legislator; b. Phila., Jan. 7, 1950; s. Michael Joseph and Susan Mary (Delatour) P.; m. Sheryl Stokes; children: Andrew, David, John Jr., Samuel. AA, Enterprise State Jr. Coll., 1972; student, Temple U., 1973; BS, Troy State U., 1975; postgrad., Auburn U. Ward chmn. Rep. Com., 1975—, ward leader, 1979—; mem. Pa. Ho. of Reps. from Dist. 172, Harrisburg, 1978—, spkr. of the House, 2003—07, mem. appropriations com., chmn. Rep. policy com. Active Consumer Action of the N.E. Mem. Sandybord Civic Assn., KC, Optimists, Moose. Republican. Address: Pa Ho of Reps 110 Main Capitol Bldg House Box 202020 Harrisburg PA 17120-2020

PESAVENTO, GARY D., psychologist; b. Pitts., Apr. 15, 1946; s. Esward J. and Johanna M. Pesavento; m. Kaye Kos Pesavento, Aug. 14, 1971; children: Joshua D., Zachary J. BA, Duquesne U., Pitts., 1968; MS in Edn., Ft. Hays State U., Kans., 1969; PhD, US Internat. U., San Diego, 1972. Clin. psychologist pvt. practice, Bonita, Calif., 1983—, Calif. State Dept. Corrections, San Diego, 1992—. Mem. Am. Legion, 2006—. With USAF, 1969—73. Mem.: APA, Calif. Marriage and Family Therapists Assn. Avocations: reading, travel, photography. Office: 180 Otay Lakes Rd Bonita CA 91902

PESCATORE-SHIREY, HOPE JEAN, middle school reading educator; b. Hollywood, Fla., Sept. 12, 1966; d. Earle Milton Sr. and Faith Lucille Pescatore. BS, Nova U., 1987, MS, 1990. Cert. tchr., Fla. Tchr. 1st, 2d and 3d grades Sunland Park Elem. Sch., Ft. Lauderdale, Fla., 1987—92; tchr. reading Omni Mid. Sch., Boca Raton, Fla., 1992—99; tchr. reading I, II, III Lake Worth H.S., Fla., 1999—2001; reading coach Okeeheelee Cmty. Mid. Sch., Greenacres, Fla., 2001—. Facilitator Regional League Mid. Sch. Conf., 2003, 04, Fla. Online Reading Devel., 2002—; prof. Fla. OnLine Reading Devel., 2002—; spkr. in field; trainer in field. Acad. scholar Nova U., Success grantee Citibank, 1995; named Greenacres Tchr. of Yr. Wal-Mart, 2005 Mem. Internat. Reading Assn. (session trainer 1995). E-mail: shirey@palmbeach.k12.fl.us.

PESCH, ELLEN P., lawyer; BA, Barat Coll., 1986; JD, John Marshall Law Sch., 1989; LLM, DePaul U., 1991. Bar: Ill. 1989, U.S. Dist. Ct. (no. dist.) Ill. With Sidley Austin Brown & Wood, Chgo., 1989—, ptnr., 2001—. Mem.: ABA, Internat. Swaps and Derivatives Assn., Stable Value Investment Assn.

PESCI, JOE, actor; b. Newark, Feb. 9, 1943; m. Claudia Haro, 1988 (div. 1992); m. Garrett Warren; 1 child, Tiffany. Film appearances include Death Collector, 1976, Raging Bull, 1980 (Best Supporting Actor award Nat. Bd. Review, 1980), I'm Dancing as Fast as I Can, 1982, Easy Money, 1983, Dear Mr. Wonderful, 1983, Eureka, 1983, Once Upon a Time in America, 1984, Tutti Dentro, 1984, Man On Fire, 1987, Moonwalker, 1988, Backtrack, 1988, Lethal Weapon II, 1989, Goodfellas (Acad. award Best Supporting Actor, 1991, D.W. Griffith Award, 1990, Best Supporting Actor award Nat. Bd. Review, 1990), Home Alone, 1990, The Super, 1991, JFK, 1991, Lethal Weapon III, 1992, Home Alone II, 1992, The Public Eye, 1992, My Cousin Vinny, 1992, A Bronx Tale, 1993, With Honors, 1994, Jimmy Hollywood, 1994, Casino, 1995, Gone Fishin, 1997, 8 Heads in a Duffel Bag, 1997, Lethal Weapon 4, 1998, The Good Shepherd, 2006; appeared in TV series Half Nelson, 1985. *

PESERIK, JAMES E., electrical engineer, consultant, safety engineer, computer engineer; b. Beloit, Wis., Sept. 30, 1945; s. Edward J. and G. Lucille Peserik; m. Elaine L. Peserik, May 6, 1972. BSEE, U. Wis., 1968; MS, St. Joseph's U., 1990. Registered profl. engr., registered profl. land surveyor; cert. fire and explosion investigator, cert. fire investigation instr.; diplomate Am. Coll. Forensic Examiners. Development and instrumentation engr. Square D Co., Milw., 1968-71; product engr. I-T-E Imperial Corp., Ardmore, Pa., 1971-72; project engr. Harris-Intertype Corp., Easton, Pa., 1972-74; elec. engr. Day & Zimmerman, Inc., Phila., 1974-76; sr. elec. engr. S.T. Hudson Engrs., Inc., Phila., 1980-81; pvt. practice James E. Peserik Assoc., Coopersburg, Pa., 1976—. Mem. adv. coun. Swenson Skills Ctr., Phila., 1990—95; lectr. in field. Contbr. articles to profl. jours. Treas. Salford-Fraconia Joint Parks Commn., Montgomery County, Pa., 1980-83. Fellow: Am. Coll. Forensic Examiners; mem. IEEE (sec. indsl. applications group Phila. chpt. 1980, chmn. 1981, chmn. Lehigh Valley computer sect. 1999—), NSPE, Pa. Soc. Profl. Engrs., Del. Assn. Profl. Engrs. (external affairs com. 1995—), Nat. Fire Protection Assn., Internat. Assn. Arson Investigators, Nat. Assn. Fire Investigators. Office: PO Box 181 Coopersburg PA 18036-0181 Office Phone: 215-234-8901. E-mail: jepeserik@enter.net.

PESHKIN, MURRAY, physicist; b. Bklyn., May 17, 1925; s. Jacob and Bella Ruth (Zuckerman) P.; m. Frances Julie Ehrlich, June 12, 1955; children— Michael, Sharon, Joel. BA, Cornell U., 1947, PhD, 1951. Instr., then asst. prof. physics Northwestern U., 1951-59; physicist, then sr. scientist Argonne (Ill.) Nat. Lab., 1959—, assoc. dir. physics div., 1972-83. Fellow Weizmann Inst. Sci., Rehovoth, Israel, 1959-60, 68-69. Served with AUS, 1944-46. Home: 838 Parkside Ave Elmhurst IL 60126-4813 Office: Argonne Natl Lab Argonne IL 60439 Business E-Mail: peshkin@anl.gov.

PESHKIN, SAMUEL DAVID, retired lawyer; b. Des Moines, Oct. 6, 1925; s. Louis and Mary (Grund) P.; m. Shirley R. Isenberg, Aug. 17, 1947; children: Lawrence Allen, Linda Ann. BA, State U. Iowa, 1948, JD, 1951. Bar: Iowa 1951. Ptnr. Bridges & Peshkin, Des Moines, 1953-66, Peshkin & Robinson, Des Moines, 1966-82. Mem. Iowa Bd. Law Examiners, 1970—. Bd. dir. State U. Iowa Found., 1957—, Old Gold Devel. Fund, 1956—, Sch. Religion U. Iowa, 1966—. Fellow Am. Bar Found., Internat. Soc. Barristers; mem. ABA (chmn. standing com. membership 1959—, ho. of dels. 1968—, bd. govs. 1973—), Iowa Bar Assn. (bd. govs. 1958—, pres. jr. bar sect. 1958-59, award of merit 1974), Inter-Am. Bar Assn., Internat. Bar Assn., Am. Judicature Soc., State U. Iowa Alumni Assn. (dir., pres. 1957) Office Phone: 480-607-3136.

PESIN, ELLA MICHELE, journalist, public relations executive; b. North Bergen, NJ, Aug. 29, 1956; d. Edward and Helene Sylvia (Rattner) P. BA, Sarah Lawrence Coll., 1978. Press rep. CBS-TV News and Entertainment, NYC, 1978-80; publicist Newsweek Mag., NYC, 1980-81; freelance journalist NYC, 1982-85; publicist Universal Studios MCA Inc., LA, 1982-83; with publicity and mktg. NBC-TV News, NYC, 1985-86; media exec. Burson Marsteller Pub. Rels., NYC, 1986-87; prin. Pesin Pub. Rels., 1987—. Contbg. editor Cable Age mag., TV Radio Age mag., Advt. Forum, Facts Figures & Film, Advt. Compliance Svc.; syndicated newspaper columnist. Active Israel Bonds/United Jewish Appeal, N.Y.C., Rudolph Giuliani for N.Y.C. Mayor campaign. Mem. Pub. Rels. Soc. Am., Women in Comm., Publicity Club N.Y., Healthcare Pub. Rels. and Mktg. Soc. Avocations: photography, sculpture, modern dance, tennis, skiing.

PESKOV, VLADIMIR DMITRIEVICH, physicist, consultant, physics professor; b. Karaganda, Russia, Jan. 30, 1947; s. Dmitri S. and Olga D. (Petrova) Peskov; m. Tatiana R. Zabotina, May 3, 1973; children: Dmitri, Tatiana. MS in Physics, Phys. and Tech. Inst., Moscow, 1971; PhD in Physics, USSR Acad. Sci., Moscow, 1976, DSc, 1981. Rschr. Inst. Phys. Problems, Moscow, 1971-76, sr. rschr., 1976-97, leading scientist, 1981-97, prof., 1998—2005; chief scientist Inst. Applied Mechanics, Russian Acad. Sci., 1997—2000; assoc. scientist European Ctr. Nuc. Rsch., Geneva, 1986-92; application physicist II Fermi Nat. Accelerator Lab., Batavia, Ill., 1992-95; invited prof. Coimbra U., Portugal, 1995-98; NRC sr. rsch. assoc. Marshall Space Ctr., Huntsville, Ala., 1995-98; guest prof. Royal Inst. Tech., 1998—2004; prof. Leonardo da Vinci U., Paris, 2004—06; chief scientist Inst. Chem. Physics, Russian Acad. Sci., 2005—; assoc. scientist CERN, Geneva, 2006—; prof. Ecole des Mines Superieures, St. Etienne, France, 2006—. Mem. adv. bd. numerous internat. confs.; mem. org. com. Internat. Conf. Imaging, Stockholm, 2000, Stockholm, 03; mem. neutron time flight experiment European Orgn. Nuc. Rsch. Contbr. articles to profl. jours.; inventor (exhibitions) INNOVACT, Reims, France, 2004, Internat. Exhbn. Inventions, Geneva, 2007. Participant Internat. Meeting Chem. Disarmament, Rome, 1989, Forum di Amore, Italy, 1991, Internat. Meeting Our Nature, 1991. Recipient prize of World Fedn. Scientists, World Lab./Italian Physics Soc., 1993—2002, P.L. Vapitzc medal, Moscow, 1997, Bronze medal, Polexy Exhbn. for Invention. Mem.: Italian Phys. Soc., Am. Phys. Soc. Achievements include discovery of plasma instability, connected to accumulation of excited atoms and molecules, a flux-induced breakdown, cathode excitation effect; invention of device for magnetic field measurement of landing spacecraft, position sensitive gas scintillating detector; detectors and methods for radiation measurement and med. imaging (some demonstrated at INNOVACT and Polexpo); patents in field. Office: CERN PH Div 23 Geneva Switzerland Office Phone: 41227674643. Business E-Mail: vladimir.peskov@cern.ch.

PESKOWITZ, ED, professional sports team owner, communications executive; married; 2 children. Grad., SUNY; M in Internat. Rels., Grad. Sch. Pub. and Internat. Affairs, Pitts. Writer numerous publs. including NY Post and Stars and Stripes; co-founder United Comm. Grp., Rockville, Md., 1977—; prin. Atlanta Spirit, LLC (parent co. of NBA Atlanta Hawks and NHL Atlanta Thrashers). Served in 25th Inf. Divsn. US Army, Vietnam. Office: United Comm Grp Ste 1100 11300 Rockville Pike Rockville MD 20852-3030 *

PESMEN, SANDRA (MRS. HAROLD WILLIAM PESMEN), editor, educator; b. Chgo., Mar. 26, 1931; d. Benjamin S. and Emma (Lipschultz) Zuckerman; m. Harold W. Pesmen, Aug. 16, 1952; children: Bethann, Curtis. BS, U. Ill., 1952. Reporter Radio and Community News Service, Chgo., 1952-53; wire editor Champaign-Urbana (Ill.) Courier, 1953; reporter, feature writer Lerner Chgo. N. Side Newspapers, 1953-55; stringer corr. Wayne (Mich.) Eagle, 1958-61; reporter, feature writer Chgo. Daily News, 1968-78; features editor Crain's Chgo. Business mag., 1978-89; corp. features editor Crain Communications, Inc., 1989-95; tchr. feature writing Northwestern U. Evening Sch., 1972-81. Author: Writing for the Media, 1983, Dr. Job's Complete Career Guide, 1995; editor: Career News Service; author syndicated column Dr. Job, 1985—. Recipient Golden Key award Ill. Mental Health Dept., 1966, 71, award Inst. Psychoanalysis, 1971, Penny Mo. award, 1978, Stick o'Type award Chgo. Newspaper Guild, 1978, award AP, 1975, Peter Lisagor award Soc. Profl. Journalists, 1991; inductee Chgo. Journalism Hall of Fame, 1997. Home: 2811 Fern Ave Northbrook IL 60062-5809

PESNER, CAROLE MANISHIN, art gallery owner; b. Boston, Aug. 5, 1937; m. Robert Pesner (dec. 1983); children: Ben, Jonah; m. Martin Cherkasky, 1995 (dec. 1997). BA, Smith Coll., 1959. Asst. dir. Kraushaar Galleries, Inc., NYC, 1959-86, dir., 1986-90, pres., 1991—. Author, editor publs., catalogues in field. Mem. Art Dealers Assn. Am., Internat. Fine Print Dealers Assn. Office: Kraushaar Galleries Inc 74 E 79th Ste 9B New York NY 10021 Office Phone: 212-288-2558. Business E-Mail: info@kraushaargalleries.com, gallery@kraushaargalleries.com.

PESOLA, GENE RAYMOND, physician; b. Hancock, Mich., Oct. 21, 1952; s. Raymond Lloyd and Helen Eleanor Pesola; m. Helen Rostata, Jan. 5, 1991; children: Gene Richard, Glen Raymond, Gary Roger. BS in Biology magna cum laude, Mich. Technol. U., Houghton, 1974; MD, Wayne State U., 1979; MPH in Biostats. magna cum laude, Columbia U., 1998, MPhil in Epidemiology, 2006. Diplomate Am. Bd. Internal Medicine, also sub-bds. pulmonary medicine and critical care medicine; cert. BCLS, ACLS, ATLS, PALS. Intern Harlem Hosp., NYC, 1979-80; resident U. Tenn. Affiliated Hosps., Memphis, 1980-82; fellow in pulmonary medicine Mt. Sinai Hosp. and Affiliates, NYC, 1982-84; fellow in critical care medicine Meml. Sloan-Kettering Cancer Ctr., NYC, 1984-85, rsch. fellow, 1985-87; asst. prof. medicine and anesthesia Albert Einstein U., Bronx, NY, 1988-89; attending physician Mt. Vernon Emergency Room, NY, 1989-90; rschr. cell/molecular pharmacology and exptl. therapeutics Med. U. SC, Charleston, 1991-94; attending physician critical care and emergency medicine N.Y. Cmty. Hosp., Bklyn., 1989—; attending physician dept. emergency medicine St. Vincent's Hosp., NYC, 1994—2000; asst. prof. emergency medicine NY Med. Coll., 1995-2000, assoc. prof. emergency medicine, 2000; assoc. attending physician Divsn. Pulmonary and Critical Care Medicine, Harlem Hosp./Columbia U., NYC, 2001—; assoc. clin. prof. medicine Columbia U., NYC, 2001—; co-prin. investigator ACRN, NYC, 2001—04. Mem. editl. bd. Academic Emergency Medicine, 2002—, assoc. editor, 2006—, Internet Jour. Asthma, Allergy and Immunology, 2002—; contbr. chapters to books, articles to profl. jours.; reviewer numerous jours. including CHEST, Catheterization and Cardiovasc. Interventions, Annals of Emergency Medicine, The Lancet, Academic Emergency Medicine. Grantee Am. Fedn. Clin. Rsch., 1992; Pharm. Mfr. Found. fellow, 1992-94; named one of Am.'s Top Physicians Consumer's Rsch. Coun., 2004-06; named Tchr. of Yr. Dept. Medicine Harlem Hosp., 2006.

PESOLA, WILLIAM ERNEST, restaurant management executive; b. Marquette, Mich., Mar. 2, 1945; s. Ernest Ensio and Janice Mary (LeDuc) P.; m. Kathleen Mary Deschaine, July 9, 1966; children: Christie Lynn, Laurie Anne. BS, No. Mich. U., 1968, MS, 1971. Route driver Coca Cola Co., Marquette, 1963-68; tchr. Gwinn (Mich.) Schs., 1968-78, pub. Sch. News, 1969; pres. Pesola Mgmt., Marquette, 1974—, Humboldt Ridge, Marquette, 1977—; treas. Elite Bar, Inc., Marquette, 1978—; v.p., dir. Marquette Cablevison, 1981-85; pres. Upper Peninsula Big Boy, Marquette, 1990—. Cons. cable TV, 1985—, Bresnan Comm., 1984—. Pres. Gwinn Edn. Assn., 1975-77; regional pres. Upper Peninsula Edn. Assn., 1977-78; mem. Marquette City Commn., 1977-81. Mem. NEA, Marquette Econ. Club, Mich. Edn. Assn., Marquette C. of C. (Exemplary Citizen award 1990), Rotary. Roman Catholic. Home: 1026 N Front St Marquette MI 49855-3514 Office Phone: 906-228-7200. Personal E-mail: bepesola@chartermi.net.

PESSIN, JEFFREY E., physiology educator; b. NYC, Jan. 2, 1953; s. Al Pessin; m. Rene Debra Bronner, June 23, 1975; children: Jacob, Lauren, Melanie. BA in Chemistry, MA in Chemistry, CUNY, 1975; PhD in Biochemistry, U. Ill., 1980; postgrad., U. Mass., 1980. Grad. rsch. asst. U. Ill., Urbana, 1975-80; asst. prof. physiology U. Iowa, Iowa City, 1983-88, assoc. prof., 1988-91, prof., 1991—, assoc. dir. Diabetes and Endocrinology Rsch. Ctr., 1991—. Contbr. articles to Molecular and Cellular Biology, Endocrinology. Basil O'Connor rsch. scholar March of Dimes Birth Defects Found., 1987-90; grantee NIH, 1988-93. Mem. AAAS, NIH (mem. metabolism study sect. 1989-93), Am. Chem. Soc., Am. Diabetes Assn. (R & D award 1985-87, rsch. award 1995), Sigma Xi. Office: U Iowa Dept Physiology and Biophysics Bowman Sci Bldg 5-530 Iowa City IA 52242 Home: 51 Woodchuck Hollow Ct Port Jefferson NY 11777-2093

PESSL, MARISHA, writer, artist; b. Asheville, NC; married. BA, Columbia Univ., NYC. Author: (novels) Special Topics in Calamity Physics, 2006 (recipient John Sargent Sr. First Book Award, 2006). Achievements include being New York Times Best-Selling Author, several weeks. Office: The Penguin Group 80 Strand London WC2R ORL England *

PESTA, BEN W., II, lawyer, writer; b. Hagerstown, Md., Oct. 15, 1948; s. Ben W. and Ethel Irene (Kirkpatrick) P.; m. Monique Raphel High, Dec. 7, 1987; 1 stepchild, Nathalie Carroll. AB, UCLA, 1969; JD, U. Calif., Berkeley (Boalt Hall), 1972. Bar: US Supreme Ct., US Ct. Appeals, 9th Appellate Cir., US Dist. Cts. Central and Eastern Dist. Calif., Eastern Dist. Wis., Dist. Ariz., all Calif. Cts. Assoc. editor Esquire Mag., 1972—74; instr. grad. profl. writing program U. So. Calif., 1980—82; assoc. pub. Weider Health & Fitness, Woodland Hills, Calif., 1984—90; pvt. practice law LA, 1990—. Freelance writer. Contbr. articles and reviews to Esquire, Playboy, Rolling Stone, Crawdaddy, Sport, TV Guide, Cosmopolitan, Self, LA Style mags., etc., LA Times, LA Daily News, LA Weekly, and profl. jours. Capt. USAF, 1973, 438th MAW. Mem.: ACLU, Authors Guild, Calif. Pub. Defenders Assn., Calif. Atty. for Criminal Justice, Nat. Assn. Criminal Def. Lawyers, Fed. Bar Assn., LA County Bar Assn., State Bar Calif. Office: 1901 Ave of the Stars Ste 390 Los Angeles CA 90067 Office Phone: 310-201-0666. Business E-Mail: pestalaw@aol.com.

PESTANA, CARLOS, surgeon, retired dean, educator; b. Tacoronte, Tenerife, Canary Islands, Spain, June 10, 1936; came to U.S., 1968, naturalized, 1973; s. Francisco and and Blanca (Suarez) P.; m. Myrna Lorena Serrato, Aug. 25, 1966; children— Becky Elizabeth, George Byron. BS, Nat. U. Mex., 1952, MD, 1959; PhD in Surgery, U. Minn., 1965. Intern St. Mary of Nazareth Hosp., Chgo., 1959-60; resident Mayo Clinic, Rochester, Minn., 1961-65; surgeon Hosp. 20 de Noviembre Mexico City; asst. prof. surgery Nat. U. Mex., 1966-67, U. Tex. Med. Sch. at San Antonio, 1968-70, asso. prof., 1970-74, prof., 1974—, asso. dean for acad. devel., 1971-73, asso. dean for student affairs, 1973-86, assoc. dean acad. affairs, 1986-97, clin. prof. surgery, 1998-2000, prof. emeritus, 2000—. Recipient Edward John Noble Found. award, 1965, Piper Prof. award Minnie Stevens Piper Founds., 1972, Nat. Golden Apple award Am. Med. Student Assn., 1999. Mem. Alpha Omega Alpha (Robert J. Glaser Disting. Tchr. award 1997). Home: 10123 N Manton Ln San Antonio TX 78213-1932 Office: 7703 Floyd Curl Dr San Antonio TX 78284-6200

PESTELLO, FRED P., academic administrator; BA in Sociology, John Carroll U.; MA in Sociology, PhD in Sociology, U. Akron. Joined U. Dayton, Ohio, 1984, prof. sociology, assoc. dean, 1997—2001, sr. v.p. for ednl. affairs and provost, 2001—. Office: Office of the Provost Univ Dayton 300 College Park St Marys Hall 212 Dayton OH 45469-1634 *

PESTILLO, PETER JOHN, auto parts company executive, lawyer; b. Bristol, Conn., Mar. 22, 1938; s. Peter and Ruth (Hayes) P.; m. BettyAnn Barraclough, Aug. 29, 1959; children: Kathleen, Karen, Kerry. BSS, Fairfield U., Conn., 1960; LLB, Georgetown U., 1963. Bar: D.C. 1964. Mgr. union relations planning Gen. Electric Co., NYC, 1968-74; v.p. employee relations B.F. Goodrich Co., Akron, Ohio, 1974-80; v.p. labor relations Ford Motor Co., Dearborn, Mich., 1980-85, v.p. employee relations, 1985-86, v.p. employee and external affairs, 1986—90, v.p. corp.

rels. and diversified businesses, 1990—93, exec. v.p. corp. rels., 1993, vice chmn., chief of staff; chmn. Visteon Corp., Dearborn, 2000—, CEO, 2000—04. Mem. adv. bd. United Found., Detroit. Mem. Am. Arbitration Assn. (dir.), U.S. C. of C. (labor relation com.), D.C. Bar, Bus. Roundtable, Labor Policy Assn., Nat. Assn. Mfgs., UBA. Office: Visteon Corp 17000 Rotunda Corp Dearborn MI 48120

PESTOVA, EKATERINA, scientist; b. Moscow, Sept. 27, 1966; life ptnr. Peter Ferro; 1 child, Anna. BS in Biology, Moscow U., 1988, MS in Microbiology, 1991; PhD, U. Ill., Chgo., 1997. Sr. application scientist Motorola, Northbrook, Ill., 1999—2001; adj. asst. prof. dept. pathology Northwestern U. Med. Sch., Chgo., 2000—04; sr. scientist Abbott Molecular, Inc. divsn. Abbott Labs., Des Plaines, Ill., 2001—. Mem.: Am. Soc. Microbiology (Sustaining Mem. Student Travel grantee 1998), Am. Soc. Human Genetics, Delta Mu Delta, Phi Kappa Phi. Achievements include patents for single nucleotide polymorphism biochip analysis; research in competence for genetic transformation in streptococcus pneumoniae, elements of the quorum-sensing pathway; discovery of energetic metabolism of gram-positive methylotrophic bacteria utilizing methanol, novel methanol dehydrogenase. Office: Abbott Molecular Inc 1300 E Touhy Ave 1D Des Plaines IL 60018 Personal E-mail: epestova@gmail.com.

PESZKE, MICHAEL ALFRED, psychiatrist, writer; b. Deblin, Poland, Dec. 19, 1932; arrived in U.S., 1956; s. Alfred Bartlomiej and Eugenia Halina (Grebocka) Peszke; m. Alice Margaret Sherman, Sept. 20, 1958; children: Michele Halina Olender, Michael Alexander. BA, Trinity Coll., Dublin, Ireland, 1956; MB, BCh, BAO, Dublin U., 1956. Cert. Bd. cert. psychiatrist. Staff psychiatrist Yale Student Health Svc., New Haven, 1961-64; asst. prof. sch. medicine U. Chgo., 1964-68; cons. psychiatrist Wesleyan U., Middletown, Conn., 1968-70; asst. prof. Sch. Medicine U. Conn., Farmington, 1970-73, assoc. prof., 1973-80, prof. psychiatry, 1980-90; clin. prof. U. Md. Sch. Medicine, Balt., 1991-99; chief Psychiatry Svc. Perry Point (Md.) VA Med. Ctr., 1990-98, co-coord. R&D, 1998-99. Dir. psychiat. clin. svcs. John Dempsey Hosp. U. Conn. Health Ctr., Farmington, 1983—87; chief VA Med. Ctr., Newington, Conn., 1987—90; ind. rschr., 1999—; chmn. adv. com. to the endowed chair of Polish and Polish Am. studies Ctrl. Conn. State U., 2001—06; advisor Am. Polish Adv. Coun. Author: Involuntary Treatment of the Mentally Ill: The Problem of Autonomy, 1975, Battle for Warsaw, 1939-44, 1995, Poland's Navy: 1918-1945, 1999; co-author (edited by L.A. Pervin, L.R. Reik, W. Dalrymple): The College Drop-out and the Utilization of Talent, 1966; co-author: (edited by J. Zusman, E. Bertsch) The Future of Psychiatric State Hospitals, 1975; co-author: The Polish Underground Army, The Western Allies and the Failure of Strategic Unity in World War II, 2005; contbr.; book reviewer U. Chgo. Law Rev., 1968, Conn. Law Rev., 1976, Am. Jour. Psychiatry, 1976—99. Advisor Am. Polish Adv. Coun., 2003—. Fellow: APA (life; disting.); mem.: Polish Inst. Arts and Scis. Am., Inc., Am. Coll. Psychiatrists, Royal United Svc. Inst. (London), Soc. for Mil. History.

PETACH, ANN MARIE, diversified financial services company executive; B, Muhlenburg Coll.; MBA, Carnegie-Mellon Univ. Fin. mgmt. positions Ford Motor Co., 1984—2007; asst. treas. Autolatina; treas. AutoEuropa; dir. global banking Ford Motor Co.; asst. treas. Ford Credit, Ford Motor Co., v.p., treas., 2004—07; mng. dir., head bus. fin. BlackRock Inc., NYC, 2007—. Office: BlackRock Inc 40 E 52d St New York NY 10022 *

PETAK, WILLIAM JOHN, systems management educator; b. Johnstown, Pa., June 23, 1932; s. Val Andrew and Lola Agatha (Boroski) P.; m. Ramona Janet Cayuela, Dec. 28, 1957; children: Elizabeth Ann Petak-Aaron, William Matthew, Michael David. BS in Mech. Engring., U. Pitts., 1956; MBA, U. So. Calif., 1963, DPA, 1969. Engr. Northrop Corp., Hawthorne, Calif., 1956-59; test engr. Wyle Labs., El Segundo, Calif., 1959-63; we. regional mgr. Instrument div. Budd Co., Phoenixville, Pa., 1963-69; v.p., dir. J.H. Wiggins Co., Redondo Beach, Calif., 1969-81; prof. systems mgmt. U. So. Calif., LA, 1982-98, exec. dir. Inst. Safety and Sys. Mgmt., 1987-98, prof. policy, planning and devel., 1998—2005, emeritus prof., 2006. Chmn. earthquake mitigation com. Nat. Com. on Property Ins., Boston, 1990-92; mem. com. on natural disasters NRC, Washington, 1985-91, mem. U.S. nat. com. for the decade for natural disaster reduction, 1989-92. Co-author: Natural Hazard Risk Assessment and Public Policy, 1982, Politics and Economics of Earthquake Hazard Reduction, 1986, Disabled Persons and Earthquake Hazards, 1988; editor spl. issue Pub. Adminstrn. Rev., 1985. Commr. County of Los Angeles, 1994—; mem. policy bd. So. Calif. Earthquake Prep. Project, L.A., 1986-92; trustee Marymount Coll., Palos Verdes, Calif., 1974—. Sgt. U.S. Army, 1950-52. Mem. Soc. for Risk Analysis, Earthquake Engring. Rsch. Inst., Am. Soc. for Pub. Adminstrn., Sigma Xi. Republican. Roman Catholic. Avocations: skiing, fishing, hiking. Office: U So Calif MC 0626 Sch Policy Planning & Devel Los Angeles CA 90089-0001 Business E-Mail: petak@usc.edu.

PETCHESKY, ROSALIND POLLACK, social and political scientist, educator; b. Bay City, Tex., Aug. 16, 1942; BA, Smith Coll., 1964; MA, Columbia U., 1966, PhD, 1974. Prof., polit. sci. and women's studies, Hunter Coll. CUNY, 1987—, head, women's studies program, Hunter Coll., 1987—91. Bd. dirs. Women's Environ. and Develop. Orgn., 2000—. Author: The Individual's Rights and the International Organization, 1966, Abortion and Women's Choice: The State, Sexuality and Reproductive Freedom, 1984 (Joan Kelly Meml. prize Am. Hist. Assn., 1984), Abortion and Women's Choice: The State, Sexuality and Reproductive Freedom, 2d edit., 1990; co-editor: Negotiating Reproductive Rights: Women's Perspectives Across Countries and Cultures, 1998; serves governing bd. Jour. Reproductive Matters. Founder, first internat. coord. Internat. Reproductive Rights Rsch. Action Group. Fellow, MacArthur Found., 1995. Office: CUNY Hunter Coll Dept Polit Sci Hunter West 1726 695 Park Ave New York NY 10021-5024 Office Phone: 212-772-5500, 212-772-5682. E-mail: rpetches@igc.org.

PETE, ERIC E., writer, claims representative; b. Seattle, Oct. 1, 1968; s. Earl Joseph Pete and Edna Mae Bushnell; m. Marsha Bluin; 1 child, Chelsea. BS, McNeese State U., 1993. Assoc. in mgmt., assoc. in claims, sr. claims law assoc. Claim rep. State Farm Cos., 1994—; owner E-fect Pub., Houston, 2000—. Author: (novels) Real for Me, 2000, Someone's In the Kitchen, 2002, Gets No Love, 2004, Don't Get It Twisted, 2005, Lady Sings the Cruels, 2006, Blow Your Mind, 2007. With US Army, 1987—89. Mem.: Toastmasters Internat., Delta Sigma Pi. Avocations: reading, travel, dance, weightlifting, art. Office: PO Box 670562 Houston TX 77267-0562 Home: 3139 Crossout Cr Spring TX 77373 Business E-Mail: heyeric@att.net.

PETER, BERNARD GEORGE, lawyer; b. Balt., July 28, 1949; S. Bernard George and Ella (Galvin) P.; m. Ellen Cherobina Carosselli; children: Kyle, Jared. AB, Coll. Holy Cross; JD, U. Md. Bar: Md. 1969, Ill. 1974. Lawyer, asst. sec. C.F. Industries, Inc., Long Grove, Ill., 1974-78; assoc. gen. counsel Joslyn Corp., Chgo., 1978-80; asst. gen. counsel Marshall Field & Co., Chgo., 1980-84; atty./cons. William M. Mercer Inc., Chgo., 1984-89; atty./sr. cons. Alexander & Alexander Cons. Group, Chgo., 1989-94; atty., sr. cons. Watson Wyatt and Co., Chgo., 1994—. Bd. dirs. John T. Galvin, Inc., Balt., treas., 2000. Contbr. articles to profl. jours. Usher St. Mary's Ch., Lake Forest, 1983—; recruiter high sch. athletes. Mem. Ill. State Bar Assn. (com. mem. sect. coun. corp. law), Chgo. Bar Assn. (vice-chmn. corp. law depts. 1988-90), John Purdue Club. Avocations: swimming, tennis. Home: 622 Timber Ln Lake Forest IL 60045 Office: Watson Wyatt Co 191 N Wacker Dr Ste 2100 Chicago IL 60606-1615

PETER, PHILLIPS SMITH, lawyer; b. Washington, Jan. 24, 1932; s. Edward Compston and Anita Phillips (Smith) P.; m. Jania Jayne Hutchins, Apr. 8, 1961; children: Phillips Smith Peter Jr., Jania Jayne Hutchins Stone. BA, U. Va., 1954, JD, 1959. Bar: Calif. 1959. Assoc. McCutchen, Doyle, Brown, Enerson, San Francisco, 1959-63; with GE (and subs.), various locations, 1963-94, v.p. corp. bus. devel., 1973-76, v.p. Washington, 1976-79, v.p. corp. govtl. rels., 1980-94; counsel, head govt. rels. dept. Reed Smith Shaw & McClay, Washington, 1994—. Chmn. bd. govs. Bryce Harlow Found., 1990-92, bd. dirs. Mem. editl. bd. Va. Law Rev., 1957-59. Trustee Howard U., 1981—89; bd. dirs., exec. com. Nat. Bank of Washington, 1981—86; v.p. Fed. City Coun., Washington, 1979—85; bd. dirs. Carlton, 1987—90, 1995—98, pres., 1995—96; bd. dirs. Tudor Place Found., 1999—, v.p., 2001—02, pres., 2002—03. Mem. Calif. Bar Assn., Order of Coif, Wee Burn Club, Ea. Yacht Club, Farmington Country Club, Landmark Club, Congl. Country Club, Georgetown Club, Chevy Chase Club, Carlton Club (bd. dirs. 1990-98), Coral Beach and Tennis Club, Johns Island Club, The Windsor Club, Omicron Delta Kappa. Episcopalian. Home: 10805 Tara Rd Potomac MD 20854-1341 Address: Johns Island 1000 Beach Rd 690 Ocean Rd & 10656 Eton Way Windsor Vero Beach FL 32963-3429 Business E-Mail: ppeter@reedsmith.com.

PETERLE, TONY JOHN, zoologist, educator; b. Cleve., July 7, 1925; s. Anton and Anna (Katic) P.; m. Thelma Josephine Coleman, July 30, 1949; children: Ann Faulkner, Tony Scott. BS, Utah State U., 1949; MS, U. Mich., 1950, PhD (univ. scholar), 1954; Fulbright scholar, U. Aberdeen, Scotland, 1954-55; postgrad., Oak Ridge Inst. Nuclear Studies, 1961. With Niederhauser Lumber Co., 1947—49, Macfarland Tree Svc., 1949—51; rsch. biologist Mich. Dept. Conservation, 1951—54; asst. dir. Rose Lake Expt. Sta., 1955—59; leader Ohio Coop. Wildlife Rsch. unit U.S. Fish and Wildlife Svc., Dept. Interior, 1959—63; asso. prof., then prof. zoology Ohio State U., Columbus, 1959—89, prof. emeritus, 1989, chmn. faculty population and environ. biology, 1968—69, chmn. dept. zoology, 1969—81, dir. program in environ. biology, 1970—71; liaison officer Internat. Union Game Biologists, 1965—93; chmn. internat. affairs com., mem. com., ecotoxicology co-organizer XIII Internat. Congress Game Biology, 1979—80; propr. The Iron Works, 1989—. Pvt. cons., 1989—; mem. com. rev. EPA pesticide decision making Nat. Acad. Scis.-NRC; mem. vis. scientists program Am. Inst. Biol. Scis.-ERDA, 1971-77; mem. com. pesticides Nat. Acad. Scis., com. on emerging trends in agr. and effects on fish and wildlife; mem. ecology com. of sci. adv. council EPA, 1979-87; mem. research units coordinating com. Ohio Coop. Wildlife and Fisheries, 1963-89; vis. scientist EPA, Corvallis, 1987. Author: Wildlife Toxicology, 1991; editor: Jour. of Wildlife Mgmt., 1969-70, 84-85, 2020 Vision Meeting the Fish and Wildlife Conservation Challenges of the 21st Century, 1992. Served with AUS, 1943-46. Named Internat. Scientists of Yr., 2002. Fellow AAAS, Am. Inst. Biol. Scis., Ohio Acad. Sci.; mem. Wildlife Disease Assn., Wildlife Soc. (regional rep. 1962-67, v.p. 1968, pres. 1972, Leopold award 1990, hon. mem. 1990, Profl. award of merit North Ctrl. sect. 1993), Nat. Audubon Soc. (bd. dirs. 1985-87), Ecol. Soc., INTECOL-NSF panel U.S.-Japan Program, Xi Sigma Pi, Phi Kappa Phi. Home: 4072 Klondike Rd Delaware OH 43015-9513 Office: Ohio State U Dept Evolution Ecology Organismal Bi 318 W 12th Ave Columbus OH 43210

PETERMAN, DONNA COLE, communications executive; b. St. Louis, Nov. 9, 1947; d. William H. Cole and Helen A. Morris; m. John A. Peterman, Feb. 7, 1970. BA in Journalism, U. Mo., 1969; MBA, U. Chgo., 1984. Mgr. employee comm. Sears Merchandise Group, Chgo., 1975-80; affairs and mktg. comm. Seraco Real Estate, Chgo., 1980-82; dir. corp. comm. Sears, Roebuck and Co., Chgo., 1982-85; sr. v.p., dir. corp. comm. Dean Witter Fin. Svcs. Group, NYC, 1985-88; sr. v.p., mng. dir. Hill and Knowlton, Inc., Chgo., 1988-94, exec. v.p. NYC, 1994-96; sr. v.p., dir. corp. comm. Paine Webber Group, Inc., NYC, 1996-2000; mng. dir., regional head comms. and mktg. The Americas, UBS Americas Inc., 2000—03; chief comm. officer PNC Fin. Svcs. Group Inc., 2003—. Media chair DeKalb County Comm., Ga., 1975; media dir., Mo. Atty. Gen., 1971, Rep. Govs. Conf., 1974; copywriter Govt. of Mo., 1971. Chmn. bd. trustees Found. for Investor Edn. Mem. Pub. Rels. Soc. Am., Arthur Page Soc., Pub. Rels. Seminar, Edgewood Country Club, Palmetto Pines Country Club, The Wise Men. Republican. Roman Catholic. Avocations: tennis, golf, sailing, skiing, bridge. Office: The PNC Fin Svcs Group Inc 1 PNC Plaza 249 5th Ave Pittsburgh PA 15222-2707

PETERMANN, HANS JÜRGEN, research scientist; b. Vienna, Feb. 2, 1942; MA in German, Calif. State U., 1971; PhD in Physics, 2d Phys. Inst., Vienna, Austria, 1976; PhD in Botany (hon.), Bot. Inst., Berlin, Germany, 1980. Prof. phys. scis. Coll. of Desert, Palm Desert, Calif.; rsch. scientist Palm Springs, Calif., 1991—. Chmn., sr. v.p. Galaxy Energy Sys., Inc. Author: The Esoteric Sciences Vol. 1, 2d edit., 2001, Curiosities of Plant Kingdom Vol. 1, 2d edit., 2003, The Esoteric Sciences Vol. 2, 2003, Gravitation, Matter and Space Travel, 3d edit., 2006. With US Army, 1963—66. Achievements include development of magnetic generator; advanced gravity converter; patents in field. Avocations: hiking, tennis, scuba diving, mountain climbing, swimming. Office: PO Box 4513 Palm Springs CA 92263-4513 Office Phone: 760-778-4254.

PETERS, ALAN, anatomy educator; b. Nottingham, Eng., Dec. 6, 1929; came to U.S., 1966; s. Robert and Mabel (Woplington) P.; m. Verona Muriel Shipman, Sept. 30, 1955; children: Ann Verona, Sally Elizabeth, Susan Clare. BSc, Bristol U., Eng., 1951, PhD, 1954. Lectr. anatomy Edinburgh (Scotland) U., 1958-66; vis. lectr. Harvard, 1963-64; prof., chmn. dept. anatomy and neurobiology Boston U., 1966-98, Waterhouse prof., 1998—. Anatomy com. Nat. Bd. Med. Examiners, 1971-75; mem. neurology B Study sect. NIH, 1975-79, chmn., 1978-79; affiliate scientist Yerkes Regional Primate Rsch. Ctr., 1984—. Author (with S.L. Palay and H. deF Webster): The Fine Structure of the Nervous System, 1970, The Fine Structure of the Nervous System, 3rd edit., 1991; author: Myelination, 1970; mem. editl. bd.: Anat. Record, 1972—81, Jour. Comparative Neurology, 1981—97, Neurocytology, 1972—89, 1993—2006, Cerebral Cortex, 1990—2005, Studies of Brain Function, Anat. and Embryology, 1989—92; editor (with E.G. Jones): (book series) Cerebral Cortex, 1984—2000; exec. prodr.(with B. Payne): Cat Visual Cortex, 2001; contbr. articles to profl. jours. Served to 2d lt. Royal Army Med. Corps, 1955-57. Recipient Henry Gray award, 1998, Sanford L. Palay award Jour. Comparative Neurology, 2004; grantee NIH, 1986. Mem. Anat. Soc. Gt. Britain and Ireland (Symington prize anatomy 1962, overseas mem. coun. 1969), Assn. Anatomy Chmn. (pres. 1976-77), Am. Anat. Assn. (exec. com. 1986-90, pres. 1992-93, Henry Gray award 1998), Am. Soc. Cell Biology, Soc. Neurosci., Internat. Primatological Soc., Cajal Club (Harman lectr. 1990, Cortical Discoverer award 1991). Home: 1010 Waltham St # 589 Lexington MA 02421 Office: Boston U Sch Medicine Dept Anatomy and Neurobiology 80 E Concord St Roxbury MA 02118-2307 Home Phone: 781-862-1492; Office Phone: 617-638-4235. Business E-Mail: valan@bu.edu.

PETERS, BARBARA WATERMAN, artist, educator; b. Topeka, Nov. 3, 1944; d. L.E. Clifton Bailey and Gertrude Minnie McFarland; m. John Herman Waterman, Dec. 21, 1965 (div. Dec. 1985); m. Larry Dean Peters, May 30, 1986. BFA, Washburn U., 1973; MFA, Kans. State U., 1998. Adj. instr. Washburn U., Topeka, 1985—88, adj. asst. prof., 1989—96, 1999—2001; grad. tchg. asst. Kans. State U., Manhattan, 1997—98, temporary asst. prof., 2004—, asst. prof. painting, 2004—05. Mus. specialist ednl. svcs. Mulvane Art Mus., Topeka, 1987; faculty advisor Washburn Art Students Assn., Topeka, 1994-96; guest curator Water Marks exhbn. Mulvane Art Mus., Topeka, 1995-96; exhbn. juror in field; spkr., reviewer in field. One-woman shows include Bedyk Gallery, Kansas City, Mo., 1983, 88, Collective Art Gallery, Topeka, 1988-90, 96-97, 1999-2000, 2002-2004, 2006, 07, Yost Gallery-Highland (Kans.) C.C., 1989, 95, Art Craft Gallery, Denver, 1994-95, 97, Fourth St. Gallery, Kansas City, 1997, Michael Cross Gallery, Kansas City, 1999-2000, Wichita Ctr. Arts, 2001, Kanas Artist Gallery, Mulvane Art Mus., 2002-07; group shows include Holman Art Gallery-Trenton State Coll., 1979, N.Mex. Art League, Albuquerque, 1980, Nat. Soc. Painters, N.Y., 1980 (Michael Engle Meml. award), Ball State U. Art Gallery, Muncie, Ind., 1981, Portsmouth (Va.) Cmty. Ctr., 1982, Nelson-Atkins Mus., Kansas City, 1982, Owensboro (Ky.) Mus. Fine Art, 1982 (award), Joslyn Art Mus., Omaha, 1988, others, Women's Conf., Beijing, 1995, Jan Weiner Gallery, Kansas City, 1995, The Columbian Art Gallery, Wamego, Kans., 1997, 2002, Topeka and Shawnee County Pub. Libr., 1997, 2002, 05, Strecker Gallery, Manhattan, Kans., 1999-2000, Cedar Rapids (Iowa) Mus. Art, 1997, Wichita Ctr. for the Arts, 2000, 02, Birger Sandzen Gallery, Lindsborg, Kans., 2001, 2006, U. Kans. Art and Design Gallery, 2002, Strecker-Nelson Gallery, Manhattan, Kans., 2002, 05, 06, 07, Mulvane Art Mus., Topeka, 2003, 07, Emporia Art Ctr., Kans., 2003, Gallery of Framewoods, Topeka, 2004, 05, 07, Beauchamp Gallery, 2003-07, Kemper Gallery, Kans. State U., 2005, Ctrl. Mo. State U., 2006, Nat. League Am. PEN Women, 2006, Foundry Art Centre, St. Charles, Mo., 2006 (award), Kans./Mo. Artists, Carter Art Ctr., Kansas City, Mo., 2006, Internat. Miniature Print Exhbn., Norwalk, Conn., 2007, Kans. Masters Invitational Exhbn., Manhattan, 2007; visual artist Andrew J. and Georgia Neese Gray Theatre, Washburn U., 1999—; contbr. articles to profl. jours. Vol. art gallery Topeka and Shawnee County Pub. Libr., 1986—; panelist Kans. Arts Commn., Kans. Presswomen, 1990—, N.E. Kans. Music Tchrs. Assn./Topeka Music Tchrs. Assn., 2004; mem. ad hoc com. Kans. Arts Commn., 2002—04, mem. fellowship selection panel, 2004, mem. arts in edn. grants selection panel, 2006; mem. ad hoc com. Topeka Cmty. Found., 2002—03; bd. dirs. Arts Coun. Topeka, 2002—. Recipient Outstanding Achievement award, Am. Inst. Banking, Topeka, 1977, assistantship in lithography, Kans. Arts Commn., 1981, Woman of Distinction in the Arts award, Kaw Valley Girl Scouts, Topeka, 1996, Artist's Residency award, The Raymer Soc., 2001—04, Cert. of Recognition Outstanding Contributions, State Kans., 2003. Mem.: Kemper Mus. Contemporary Art, Am. Arts Action Fund, Nat. League Am. PEN Women, Birger Sandzén Meml. Gallery, Am. Craft Coun., Manhattan Arts Ctr., Assn. Cmty. Arts Agys. of Kans. (bd. dir. 2004—06, sec.-treas. 2006—), Lawrence Art Ctr., The Collective (charter, treas. 1987—89, v.p. 1990—94, 1999—2000, newsletter editor 2000—, pres. 2001—06), Mulvane Art Mus., St. Louis Artists Guild, Kansas City Artists Coalition, Chgo. Artists' Coalition, Nat. Mus. Women in the Arts, Raymer Soc. (bd. dir.), Kans. Authors' Club (conv. workshop presenter 2004, selection com. J. Donald Coffin award 2004—05, v.p. dist. 1 2005—, pres. dist. 1 2006), Kans. Citizens for Arts, Libr. Friends of Art Topeka and Shawnee County Pub. Libr., Friends of Art Bd. Beach Mus. Art (collections com. 1997—), Catharine Lorillard Wolfe Art Club (assoc.). Avocations: reading, writing, travel. Home: 2223 SW Knollwood Dr Topeka KS 66611-1623 E-mail: barbara.r.peters@att.net.

PETERS, BERNADETTE (BERNADETTE LAZZARA), actress; b. Queens, NY, Feb. 28, 1948; d. Peter and Marguerite (Maltese) Lazzara; m. Michael Wittenberg, July 20, 1996 (dec. Sept. 26, 2005). Student, Quintano Sch. for Young Profls., NYC. Ind. actress, entertainer, 1957—. Appeared on TV series All's Fair, 1976-77; frequent guest appearances on TV; (films) The Longest Yard, 1974, Silent Movie, 1976, Vigilant Force, 1976, W.C. Fields and Me, 1976, Silent Movie, 1976, The Jerk, 1979, Heartbeeps, 1981, Tulips, 1981, Pennies from Heaven, 1981 (Golden Globe award best actress), Annie, 1982, Slaves of New York, 1989, Pink Cadillac, 1989, Impromptu, 1991, Alice, 1990, Anastasia (voice), 1997, Cinderella, 1997, Snow Days, 1999, Prince Charming, 2001, Bobbie's Girl, 2002, A Few Good Years, 2002, It Runs in the Family, 2003; (TV movies) Cinderella, ABC-TV, 1997, Holiday in Your Heart, 1997; (stage appearances) This is Google, 1957, The Most Happy Fella, 1959, Gypsy, 1961, Curly McDimple, 1967, Johnny No-Trump, 1967, George M!, 1968 (Theatre World award, 1968), Dames at Sea, 1968 (Drama Desk award, 1968), La Strada, 1969, On the Town, 1971, Tartuffe, 1972, Mack and Mabel, 1974, Sally and Marsha, 1982, Sunday in the Park with George, 1983-85 (Tony nom., 1983), Song and Dance, 1985-86 (Drama League award best actress, 1985, Tony award best actress, 1986, Drama Desk award best actress, 1986), Into the Woods, 1987, The Goodbye Girl, 1992-93, Annie Get Your Gun 1998-1999 (Tony award best actress, 1999, Outer Critics Circle award best actress, 1999, Drama Desk award best actress, 1999), Gypsy, 2003; TV mini-series The Odyssey, 1997; rec. artist: (MCA Records) Bernadette Peters, 1980, Now Playing, 1981; CD's include I'll Be Your Baby Tonight, Angel Records, 1996 (Grammy nomination), Sondheim Etc: Bernadette Peters Live at Carnegie Hall, Angel Records, 1997 (Grammy nom.), solo concert Radio City Music Hall, 2002. Founder Ann. Broadway Barks fundraiser. Recipient Hasty Pudding Theatrical award, 1987 Woman of Yr. award, Sara Siddons Actress of Yr. award, 1993-94, Actors Fund medal for artistic achievement, 1999, NYC Parks Citizen award, 2006; named Woman of Yr., Police Athletic League, 1999; named to Theatre Hall of Fame. Office: William Morris Agency c/o Jeff Hunter 1325 Ave of the Americas 15th Fl New York NY 10019

PETERS, CAROL ANN DUDYCHA, counselor; b. Ripon, Wis., Dec. 23, 1938; d. George John and Martha (Malek) Dudycha; m. Milton Eugene Peters, Aug. 27, 1960 AB, Wittenberg U., 1960, MEd, 1963; leadership devel. cert., Ctr. for Creative Leadership, Greensboro, NC, 1986; postgrad., U. Toledo, 1973—97, U. Findlay, 1997—99. Lic. profl. counselor, Ohio; nat. cert. counselor, nat. cert. career counselor Nat. Bd. Cert. Counselors, Inc.; cert. basic critical incident stress mgmt. Internat. Critical Incident Stress Found., 1999. Tchr. Springfield City Schs., Ohio, 1960—62, Mad River-Green Local Schs., Springfield, 1962—63; counselor Napoleon Area Schs., Ohio, 1963—70, Findlay City Sch., Ohio, 1970—2000; field counselor Career Relocation Corp. Am., Armonk, 1992—95, 1998—99; sr. lectr. U. Findlay, 1999—2002. Cons., prin. Peters and Peters, Findlay, 1979—; leader Creative Edn. Found., Buffalo, 1980-91, colleague, Hadley, Mass., 1985—; founder ednl. corp. Career Info. Bur. Hancock County, 1974 Pres. Big Bros./Big Sisters Hancock County, 1982-83; bd. dirs. Citizens Opposing Drug Abuse, Findlay, 1982-2005; advisor, leader Hancock Addictions Prevention for Youth, 1985-91; edn. com. Hancock County Cmty. Devel. Found., 1990-93, Findlay/Hancock County Am. 2000 New Sch. Design Team, 1991-92; mem. Hancock County Crisis Response Team, 1991-97, 99—; assets/needs assessment com. United Way, 1997-98; mem. Findlay Juvenile Diversion Task Force, 1997-98; mem. City of Findlay Mayor's Cmty. Issues Visioning Com., 2004-05, Findlay Hancock County Prosperity Summit, 2007. Named One of Outstanding Young Women Am., 1967, Outstanding Woman in Edn., Bus. and Profl. Women, 1983; recipient Outstanding Citizenship award The Lincoln Ctr., Findlay, 1989, Meritorious Svc. award Big Bros./Big Sisters Hancock County, 1988 Mem. ACA, AAUW, NEA (life), Nat. Career Devel. Assn., Ohio Ret. Tchrs. Assn. (life), Ohio Counseling Assn., Findlay-Hancock County C. of C. (sec. edn. com. 1984-90), Ohio Career Devel. Assn., Black Studies and Libr. Assn. (trustee 2005—, sec. bd. trustees 2006—). Lutheran. Avocations: flower arranging, cooking.

PETERS, CHARLES H.R., lawyer; BS magna cum laude, Miami U., 1982; JD cum laude, Northwestern U., 1986. Bar: Ill. 1986, US Dist. Ct. (no. dist. Ill.) 1986, US Ct. Appeals (7th cir.) 1992, US Supreme Ct. 2001. Ptnr. Schiff Hardin, LLP, Chgo. Mem.: ABA, Chgo. Coun. Lawyers. Office: Schiff Hardin LLP 6600 Sears Tower Chicago IL 60606-6473 Office Phone: 312-258-5683. Office Fax: 312-258-5600. E-mail: cpeters@schiffhardin.com. *

PETERS, CHARLES WILLIAM, nuclear energy industry executive; b. Pierceton, Ind., Dec. 9, 1927; s. Charles Frederick and Zelda May (Line) Peters; m. Katharine Louise Schuman, May 29, 1953; 1 child, Susan Kay; m. Patricia Ann Miles, Jan. 2, 1981; stepchildren: Bruce Miles Merkle, Leslie Ann Merkle Sanaie, Philip Frank Merkle, William Macneil Merkle. AB, Ind. U., 1950; postgrad., U. Md., 1952—58. Supervisory rsch. physicist Naval Rsch. Lab., Washington, 1950—71; physicist EPA, Washington, 1971—76; mgr. advanced sys. EATON-Consol. Controls Corp., Springfield, Va., 1976—89; v.p. Nuc. Diagnostic Sys., Inc., Springfield, Va., 1989—92; cons. Am. Tech. Inst., Memphis, 1993—. With US Army, 1945—47. Mem.: AAAS, IEEE, Am. Phys. Soc. Home and Office: 5235 N Whispering Hills Ln Tucson AZ 85704-2510

PETERS, CHRISTOPHER ALLEN, systems analyst, consultant; b. Syracuse, NY, Apr. 26, 1967; s. William F. and Mary Jo (N.) P. BA, Syracuse U., 1989, MLS, 1994. Info. analyst Syracuse U., 1990-96, asst. dir. devel. for sys. mgmt., 1996-99; sr. sys. analyst The Salvation Army, Syracuse (N.Y.) Area Svcs., 1999—. Mem. Assn. Profl. Rschrs. for Advancement.

PETERS, CONNIE JANE, librarian, media specialist; b. Decatur, Ill., Oct. 21, 1949; d. Sylvester Thomas and Kathryn Harriet (Wittig) Peters. BA in History, Millikin U., 1971; MA in History, Sangamon State U., 1972; MS in Libr. Sci., Ea. Ill. U., 1973, Edn. Specialist degree in Inst. Media, 1985; Basic Cert. in Electronics, Richland C.C., 1992. Cert. elem.and secondary tchr. Ill. Grad. asst. Ea. Ill. U., Charleston, Ill., 1972—73; instr. media ctr. libr. Decatur Pub. Schs., 1974—76; libr. St. Teresa HS, Decatur, 1976—77; media specialist Thomas Jefferson Mid. Sch., Decatur, 1978, Cerro Gordo Unit Schs., Ill., 1980—81, St. Teresa HS, Decatur, 1982—92; instrnl. media specialist Stephen Decatur HS, Decatur, 1995—2000; tchr. social studies MacArthur HS, Decatur, 2000—01, Mound Mid. Sch., Decatur, 2001—04; libr. Eisenhower HS, Decatur, 2004—. Mem. NEA, Ill. Edn. Assn., Decatur Edn. Assn., (bd. dirs., secondary dir., ins. com., sick leave bank com.), Ill. Assn. for Ednl. Comms. and Tech., Ill. Sch. Libr. and Media Assn., Ill. Computing Educators, Ill. State Hist. Soc., Foursquare Gospel. Pentecostal. Avocations: photography, stamp collecting/philately, coin collecting/numismatics, web page design. Office Phone: 217-424-3104. Personal E-mail: conniepeters@juno.com. Business E-Mail: cpeters@dps61.org.

PETERS, DAVID ALLEN, mechanical engineering educator, consultant; b. East St. Louis, Ill., Jan. 31, 1947; s. Bernell Louis and Marian Louise (Blum) P.; children: Michael H., Laura A., Nathan C. BS in Applied Mechanics, Washington U., St. Louis, 1969, MS in Applied Mechanics, 1970; PhD in Aeros. and Astronautics, Stanford U., 1974. Assoc. engr. McDonnell Astronautics, 1969-70; rsch. scientist Army Aeronautics Lab., 1970-74; asst. prof. Washington U., 1975-77, assoc. prof., 1977-80, prof. mech. engring., 1980-85, chmn. dept., 1982-85; prof. aerospace engring. Ga. Inst Tech., Atlanta, 1985-91; dir. NASA Space Grant Consortium Ga. Inst. Tech., Atlanta, 1989-91; dir. Ctr. for Computational Mechanics Washington U., 1992—, prof. dept. mech. engring. St. Louis, 1991—, chmn. dept. mech. engring., 1997—2007, McDonnell Douglas prof. engring., 1999. Contbr. 150 articles to profl. jours. Recipient sci. contbn. award NASA, 1975, 76, Disting. Faculty award Washington U., 2006. Fellow AIAA, ASME, Am. Acad. Mechanics, Am. Helicopter Soc. (jour. editor 1987-90); mem. Am. Soc. for Engring. Edn., Internat. Assn. for Computational Mechanics (charter), Pi Tau Sigma (gold medal 1978). Baptist. Home: 7629 Balson Ave Saint Louis MO 63130-2150 Office: Wash U Dept Mech Engr Campus Box 1185 Saint Louis MO 63130 Office Phone: 314-935-4337. Business E-Mail: dap@me.wustl.edu.

PETERS, DENNIS GAIL, chemist; b. LA, Apr. 17, 1937; s. Samuel and Phyllis Dorothy (Pope) P. BS cum laude, Calif. Inst. Tech., 1958; PhD, Harvard U., 1962. Mem. faculty Ind. U., 1962—, prof. chemistry, 1974—, Herman T. Briscoe prof., 1975—. Co-author textbooks, contbr. articles profl. jours. Woodrow Wilson fellow, 1958-59; NIH predoctoral fellow, 1959-62; vis. fellow Japan Soc. for Promotion Sci., 1980; recipient Ulysses G. Weatherly award disting. teaching Ind. U., 1969, Disting. Teaching award Coll. Arts and Scis. Grad. Alumni Assn. Ind. U., 1984, Nat. Catalyst award for Disting. Teaching Chem. Mfrs. Assn., 1988, Henry B. Linford award The Electrochem. Soc., 2002; grantee NSF. Fellow Ind. Acad. Sci., Am. Inst. Chemists; mem. ACS (grantee, Div. of Analytical Chemistry award for excellence in teaching 1990, James Flack Norris award 2001). Home: 1401 S Nancy St Bloomington IN 47401-6051 Office: Dept Chemistry Ind U Bloomington IN 47405 Home Phone: 812-334-2487; Office Phone: 812-855-9671. Business E-Mail: peters@indiana.edu.

PETERS, DOUGLAS ALAN, risk management and compliance consultant; b. Portsmouth, Va., Oct. 4, 1968; s. Terrance Gene and Pamela (Haffner) P. BA in Philosophy, Va. Poly. Inst. and State U., 1992; BSN summa cum laude, James Madison U., 1995; JD, U. Md., Balt., 2003. RN DC, Tenn., Md.; cert. case mgr., legal nurse cons. Photojournalist CVNI/The Greene County Record, Stanardsville, Va., 1992; nursing asst. Rockingham Meml. Hosp., Harrisonburg, Va., 1993-95; clin. nurse Bapt. Hosp., Pensacola, Fla., 1995-96; nurse mgr. quality assurance Escambia County Jail Infirmary, Pensacola, 1996-97; case mgr./U.R. Total Health Care, Balt., 1997-98; case mgr. Blue Cross/Blue Shield of Md., Balt., 1998-2000, appeals analyst, 2000—01, sr. appeals analyst, 2001—04; jud. law clk. 23d Jud. Cir., W.Va., 2004—05; legal cons. CareFirst Blue Cross Blue Shield, 2005; nurse, case mgr. George Washington U. Hosp., 2006—07. Vol. hospice unit Rockingham Meml. Hosp., 1994-95, Alley Cat Allies, Montgomery County Med. Rescue Corps. Mem.: ABA (health law sect.), Am. Soc. Healthcare Risk Mgmt., Am. Assn. Legal Nurse Cons., Phi Alpha Delta, Sigma Theta Tau, Alpha Chi Sigma. Avocations: Civil War history, darts, photography. Personal E-mail: dapeters2006@yahoo.com.

PETERS, DOUGLAS SCOTT, health care executive; b. Columbus, Ohio, Nov. 2, 1943; s. Edward Alvin and Jane (Appleman) P.; m. Karen Ann Jones, June 19, 1965; children: Brian Edward, Laura Kathleen. BS, Ohio State U., 1965; MHA with distinction, U. Mich., 1967. Assoc. dir. U. Mich. Hosp., Ann Arbor, 1969-74; dir. U. Nebr. Hosps. and Clinics, Omaha, 1974-77; exec. dir. Henry Ford Hosp., Detroit, 1977-83, pres. ceo., 1983-87; exec. v.p. Henry Ford Healthcare Corp., Detroit, 1983-87; pres. ceo. Main Line Health, 1991—. Cons. PanAm. Health Orgn., Washington, 1971-73; asst. prof. dept. med. and edn. adminstrn. U. Nebr., 1974-77. Bd. dirs. New Detroit, Inc., 1985—; co-chmn. Multiple Sclerosis Testimonial Dinner, Detroit, 1985; big bro. Big Bros./Big Sisters, Omaha, 1975. Served to lt. USNR, 1967-69. Fellow Am. Coll. Healthcare Execs. (regent 1984); mem. Young Pres. Orgn., Mich Hosp. Assn. (bd. dirs.), Frontiers in Health Services Mgmt. (mem. editorial bd. 1983), mem. The Pennsylvania Soc, Amer. Hosp. Assoc. Regency Policy Bd, Foster G. McGaw Prize Review Panel, AHA, 1989-; Katahdin Medical and Philosophical Soc., 1992-; Amer. Healthcare Sys. Risk Purchasing Grp, 1993-; Amer. Healthcare Sys. Insur. Assoc., 1993-; bd of dirs: Healthshare Inc., 1988-; Amer. Healthcare Sys., 1991-; The Philadelphia Contributionship, 1992-; Amer. Red Cross, 1992-; First Fidelity Bank, 1994-; Radnor Education Found., 1994-; Amer. Heart Assoc., 1995. Republican. Office: Main Line Health 130 S Bryn Mawr Ave Bryn Mawr PA 19010-3121

PETERS, EDWARD MURRAY, history professor; b. New Haven; BA, Yale U., 1963, MA, 1965, PhD, 1967. Instr. English and history Quinnipiac Coll., Hamden, Conn., 1964-67; asst. prof. history U. Calif., San Diego, 1967-68, U. Pa., Phila., 1968-70, assoc. prof., 1970-81, Henry Charles Lea prof. history, 1981—, curator Henry Charles Lea Library, 1968—; vis. prof. Cath. U. Leuven, Belgium, 1992, 2004. Vis. prof. history Yale U., 1998, 2001-02. Author: The Shadow King, 1970; author: (with A.C. Kors) Witchcraft in Europe, 1100-1750, 1972, 2d edit., 2000; author: (with Jeanne Krochalis) The World of Piers Plowman, 1975, 2d edit., 2006; author: Europe: The World of the Middle Ages, 1977, The Magician, The Witch and The Law, 1978, Europe and the Middle Ages, 1983, 4th edit., 2003, Torture, 1985, expanded edit., 1996, Inquisition, 1988, Limits of Thought and Power in Medieval Europe, 2001, (TV series) The World of the Middle Ages, 1974, The World Around the Revolution, 1977; editor, transl. (series) The Middle Ages, 1970—95; editor: Heresy and Authority in Medieval Europe, 1980; author: also articles, revs. and introductions. Served with AUS, 1956-59. Woodrow Wilson fellow, 1963-64, dissertation fellow, 1966-67, hon. Sterling fellow, 1966-67, ACLS fellow, 1981-82, Guggenheim fellow, 1988-89. Fellow Medieval Acad. Am., Royal Hist. Soc.; mem. Am. Hist. Assn., Medieval Acad. Am., Am. Soc. Legal History, Maiestas, Iuris Canonici Medii Aevi Consociatio, Soc. Jean Bodin, Dante Soc. Am., Renaissance Soc. Am. Office: U Pa Dept History Philadelphia PA 19104-6228 E-mail: empeters@sas.upenn.edu.

PETERS, ELLEN ASH, retired judge; b. Berlin, Mar. 21, 1930; arrived in U.S., 1939, naturalized, 1947; d. Ernest Edward and Hildegard (Simon) Ash; m. Phillip I. Blumberg; children: David Bryan, James Douglas, Julie Haden Dreisch. BA with honors, Swarthmore Coll., 1951, LLD (hon.), 1983; LLB cum laude, Yale U., 1954, MA (hon.), 1964, LLD (hon.), 1985, U. Hartford, 1983, Georgetown U., 1984, Conn. Coll., 1985, N.Y. Law Sch., 1985; HLD (hon.), St. Joseph Coll., 1986; LLD (hon.), Colgate U., 1986, Trinity Coll., 1987, Bates Coll., 1987, Wesleyan U., 1987, DePaul U., 1988; HLD (hon.), Albertus Magnus Coll., 1990; LLD (hon.), U. Conn., 1992, U. Rochester, 1994, Detroit Mercy Coll. Law, 2001. Bar: Conn. 1957, US Dist. Ct. Conn. 1965. Law clk. to judge U.S. Circuit Ct., 1954-55; assoc. in law U. Calif., Berkeley, 1955-56; prof. law Yale U., New Haven, 1956-78, adj. prof., 1978-84; assoc. justice Conn. Supreme Ct., Hartford, 1978-84, chief justice, 1984-96; ret., 1996. Judge trial referee Appellate Ct., Hartford, Conn., 2000—. Author: Commercial Transactions: Cases, Texts, and Problems, 1971, Negotiable Instruments Primer, 1974; contbr. articles to profl. jours. Bd. dirs. Nat. Ctr. State Cts., 1992—96, chmn., 1994; bd. mgrs. Swarthmore Coll., 1970—81; trustee Yale-New Haven Hosp., 1981—86, Yale Corp., 1986—92; mem. conf. Chief Justices, 1984—, pres., 1994; hon. chmn. U.S. Constl. Bicentennial Com., 1986—91; mem. Conn. Permanent Commn. on Status of Women, 1973—74, Conn. Bd. Pardons, 1978—80, Conn. Law Revision Commn., 1978—84; bd. dirs. Hartford Found., 1997—2002. Named Laura A. Johnson Woman of the Yr., Hartford Coll., 1996; recipient Ella Grasso award, 1982, Jud. award, Conn. Trial Lawyers Assn., 1982, citation of merit, Yale Law Sch., 1983, Pioneer Woman award, Hartford Coll. Women, 1988, Disting. Svc. award, U. Conn. Law Sch. Alumni Assn., 1993, Raymond E. Baldwin Pub. Svc. award, Quinnipiac Coll. Law Sch., 1995, Disting. Svc. award, Conn. Law Tribune, 1996, Nat. Ctr. State Cts., 1996. Mem.: ABA, Am. Philos. Coun., Am. Acad. Arts and Scis., Am. Law Inst. (coun.), Conn. Bar Assn. (Jud. award 1992, Spl. award 1996). Office: Appellate Ct 75 Elm St Hartford CT 06106-4431 Home Phone: 860-232-2719. Office Fax: 860-713-2216.

PETERS, FREDERICK WHITTEN, lawyer; b. Omaha, Aug. 20, 1946; s. Jordan Holt and Elizabeth (O'Bryant) P.; children: Mary Irvin, Elizabeth Holt, Margaret Etheridge, Finian O'Bryant, Fiona Whitten. BA magna cum laude, Harvard U., 1968; MS with distinction, London Sch. Econs., 1973; JD magna cum laude, Harvard U., 1976. Bar: D.C. 1978, U.S. Dist. Ct. D.C. 1978, U.S. Dist. Ct. Md., 1994, U.S. Ct. Appeals (3d and D.C. cirs.) 1979, U.S. Ct. Claims 1981, U.S. Ct. Appeals (11th cir.) 1986, U.S. Ct. Mil. Appeals 1993. Law clk. to Hon. J. Skelly Wright U.S. Ct. Appeals (D.C. cir.), Washington, 1976-77; law clk. to justice William J. Brennan U.S. Supreme Ct., Washington, 1977-78; assoc. Williams & Connolly, Washington, 1978-84, ptnr., 1984-95, 2001—; prin. dep. gen. counsel Dept. of Defense, 1995-97, undersec., acting sec. USAF, 1997-99, sec. USAF, 1999-2001; ptnr. Williams & Connolly LLP, Washington, 2001—. Legal ethics com. DC Bar, 1988-94, chmn. rules rev. com., 1991-96; rules com. US Ct. Mil. Appeals, 1993-95. Pres. Harvard Law Rev., 1975-76. Bd. dirs. Cleveland Park Hist. Soc., Washington, 1986-91, 2001-02, Washington Area Lawyers for the Arts, 1987-93, Air Force Enlisted Found., 2001-06, Air Force Aid Soc., 2002—; adv. com. on streamlining procurement laws DOD, 1991-93, vice chmn. adv. com. on future of US aerospace industry, 2001-2002. Lt. USNR, 1969-72. Fellow Am. Bar Found.; mem. ABA. Democrat. Episcopalian. Avocations: sailing, computer science, golf. Office: Williams & Connolly 725 12th St NW Washington DC 20005 Home: 2220 Windsor Rd Alexandria VA 22307-1020 Office Phone: 202-434-5440. Business E-Mail: wpeters@wc.com.

PETERS, GEOFFREY WRIGHT, lawyer, fundraising executive; b. Wilmington, Del., Oct. 30, 1945; s. William Ernest and Ann Miller Peters; m. Cecelia Felicia Dziekonski, Aug. 26, 1967; children: Gregory Kent, Jessica Mohr. AB, Northwestern U., 1967; MA, JD, U. Denver, 1972. Bar: Colo. 1972, Nebr. 1972, Va. 1978, Minn. 1980, U.S. Supreme Ct. 1980. Sole practice, Denver, 1972; prof. law Creighton U., Omaha, 1972-78; dep. dir. Nat. Ctr. State Cts., Williamsburg, Va., 1978-80; pres., dean law William Mitchell Coll. Law, St. Paul, 1980-83; exec. v.p., gen. counsel Minn. Protective Life Ins. Co., Eden Prairie, 1983—86; v.p. ops. Garvey Industries, Wichita, 1986—90; pres. Corp. Investment Internat. (Garvey subs.), Phoenix, 1988-89, Firm One, Inc., Phoenix, 1988-89; chmn. Mid-Am. World Trade Ctr., Wichita, Kans., 1986—91; pres. Pres.'s Coll., 1989—91, Vigurie Co., Falls Ch., Va., 1990—91; exec. v.p. Amortibanc (Garvey subs.), 1989—91; pvt. practice Vienna, Va., 1991—; pres., mng. dir. Creative Dir. Mktg. Internat., Crofton, Md., 1995—2001; pres. Creative Direct Response, 2001—. Cons. Nat. Wiretap Commn., Washington, 1973—74; adj. prof. law William & Mary-Marshall Wythe Sch. Law, Williamsburg, 1978—80; gen. counsel Am. Charities Reasonable Fundraising Regulation, Vienna, 1995—; chmn., dir. Coun. Govt. Reform, Arlington, Va., 1992—2002; spkr. in field. With U.S. Army, 1969—71, West Point, NY. Decorated Army Commendation medal U.S. Army; named one of 50 Most Influential Persons in Nonprofit Sector, The Nonprofit Times, 2005, 2006; recipient Pub. Svc. award, DMA Nonprofit Fedn.; grantee prin. investigator more than 20 various grant funded projects, 1972-1980. Fellow: Am. Bar Found.; mem.: Minn. Bar Assn. (bd. govs. 1980—83). Achievements include first to create an international direct response fundraising agency operating in 15 countries. Avocations: flight instructing, commercial piloting, scuba diving, travel. Office: Am Charities for Reasonable Fundraising Regulation 9112 Tetterton Ave Vienna VA 22182 also: 16900 Science Dr Ste 210 Bowie MD 20715 Office Phone: 703-938-1809. Office Fax: 703-938-2207. Personal E-mail: gpeters@gpeters.net. E-mail: gpeters@cd-nfl.com.

PETERS, GORDON BENES, retired musician; b. Oak Park, Ill., Jan. 4, 1931; s. Arthur George and Julia Anne (Benes) P.; children: Rénee Kemper, Erica Kemper. Student, Northwestern U., 1949-50; studied with Pierre Monteux, 1952—63; MusB, Eastman Sch. Music, 1956, MusM, 1962. Founder, dir. Marimba Masters, 1954—59; percussionist Rochester (NY) Philharm. Orch., 1954—59; prin. percussionist, asst. timpanist Grant Park Symphony Orch., Chgo., 1954—58; mem. faculty Rochester Bd. Edn., 1956-57, Geneseo State Tchrs. Coll., 1957-58; acting prin. percussionist Rochester Philharm., NY, 1958-59; prin. percussionist and assoc. prin. timpanist Chgo. Symphony Orch., 1959—2001; condr., adminstr. Civic Orch. Chgo., 1966-87; condr. Elmhurst Symphony Orch., 1968-73. Instr. percussion instruments Northwestern U., 1963-68, lectr., 1991; guest condr. Bangor Symphony, Maine, 1993; lectr. Winthrop U., SC, 2006. Author, pub. Treatise on Percussion, 1962, rev., 1975 as The Drummer: Man, 1975, rev., 2003 (CD); arranger-pub. Marimba Ensemble arrangements; composer-pub.: Swords of Moda-Ling; editor: percussion column Instrumentalist mag, 1963-69; contbr. articles to profl. jours. Bd. dirs. Pierre Monteux Sch., Hancock, Maine, 1965-95. With U.S. Mil. Acad. Band, 1950-53. Recipient Pierre Monteux Disciple Conducting award, 1962, Prin. Timpani chair named GBP, Chgo. Youth Symphony Orch., 2000. Mem. Percussive Arts Soc. (pres. 1964-67, bd. dirs. Hall of Fame 2004), Am. Symphony Orch. League, Condrs. Guild (treas., exec. com. 1979-82, 86-90), Japan Xylophone Assn., Phi Mu Alpha Sinfonia (life). Home (Winter): 824 Hinman Ave Evanston IL 60202-5906 Home (Summer): PO Box 403 Hancock ME 04640-0403

PETERS, HOWARD NEVIN, foreign language educator; b. Hazleton, Pa., June 29, 1938; s. Howard Eugene and Verna P.; m. Judith Anne Griessel, Aug. 24, 1963; children: Elisabeth Anne, Nevin Edward. BA, Gettysburg Coll., 1960; PhD, U. Colo., 1965. Asst. prof. fgn. langs. Valparaiso (Ind.) U., 1965-69, assoc. prof., 1969-75, dir. grad. divsn., 1967-70, acting dean Coll. Arts and Scis., 1970-71, assoc. dean Coll. Arts and Scis., 1971-74, dean Coll. Arts and Scis., 1974-81, prof. fgn. langs., 1975—, prof. fgn. langs. and lits., chair dept. fgn. langs. and lits., 1994—95, prof. emeritus fgn. langs. and lits., 1995—. Author (poetry) Espejo De Son, 1997. NDEA fellow, 1960-63 Mem. Midwest MLA, Phi Beta Kappa, Sigma Delta Pi, Phi Sigma Iota. Lutheran. Home: 860 N Cr 500 E Valparaiso IN 46383 Office: Meier Hall Rm 113 Valparaiso U Valparaiso IN 46383 Business E-Mail: Howard.Peters@valpo.edu.

PETERS, JOHN DOUGLAS, lawyer, artist; b. Dover, NH, Jan. 23, 1948; s. John Philip Peters, Helen Irene Hurst; m. Christine K. Consales, June 23, 1973. BA, U. NH, 1971; JD, U. Toledo, 1975. Commd. col., Ky., 2006; exec. dir. Profl. Stds. Review Orgn. 4th Ohio Area Profl. Stds. Review Coun., Toledo, 1974—75; shareholder Charfoos & Christensen, P.C., Detroit, 1975—. Legal dir. Mich. Med. Schs. Coun. of Deans, Ann Arbor, 1978—80; lectr. law U. Toledo, 1978—88; assoc. prof. Sch. Medicine Wayne State U., Detroit, 1978—; cons. Georgetown U. Inst. for Health Policy, Washington, 1989, Office of Tech. Assessment, Washington, 1992—96, Robert Wood Johnson Found., Washington, 1994—98. Author: The Law of Medical Practice in Michigan, 1981, Anesthesiology and the Law, 1983, Obstetrics/Gynecology and the Law, 1984, The Law of Medical Practice in Pennsylvania and New Jersey, 1984, Detroit: Freight Cars Before Automobiles, 2005, Social Security Disability Claims, 2006; editor: Legal and Ethical Aspects of Treating Terminally Ill Patients, 1982; contbr. articles to profl. jours. Bd. dirs. Am. Lung Assn., Detroit, 1978—83, Vis. Nurse Assn., Detroit, 1987—96, Preservation Wayne, 1992—. Avocations: Persian textiles, folk art, collecting and studying antiquities. Office: Charfoos and Christensen PC 5510 Woodward Ave Detroit MI 48202 Business E-Mail: jdpeters@czlaw.com.

PETERS, JUANITA TEAL, music educator; b. Dallas, Aug. 4, 1929; d. William Mosely and Vashti Elizabeth Teal; m. Dale Hugh Peters, June 4, 1960; children: Derek, Todd. MB, North Tex. State Coll., 1951; postgrad., U. Minn., 1952—53, Royal Acad. Music, London, 1956—57. Instr. Southeastern Okla. State U., Durant, 1967—79; lectr. U. North Tex., Denton, 1974—. Soloist: Dallas Symphony, Corpus Christi Symphony, Abilene Symphony, Wichita Falls Symphony, Ft. Worth Opera. Recipient G.B. Dealey award, Dallas Symphony, 1954, Wallace award, Wichita Falls Symphony, 1954, 1959. Home: 2818 Glenwood Denton TX 76209 Office: Univ North Tex Denton TX 76203 E-mail: jpeters@music.unt.edu.

PETERS, JULIE ANNE, writer; b. Jamestown, NY, Jan. 16, 1952; BA, Colo. Women's Coll. Rsch. asst., computer programmer Tracom Corp., Denver, 1975—84; computer sys. designer Electronic Data Sys., 1985—88; ednl. asst. Jefferson County Sch. Dist., Lakewood, Colo., 1990—94; writer, 1994—. Author: The Stinky Sneakers Contest, 1992, Risky Friends, 1993, B.J.'s Billion-Dollar Bet, 1994, How Do You Spell G-E-E-K?, 1996, Revenge of the Snob Squad, 1998, Romance of the Snob Squad, 1999, Love Me, Love My Broccoli, 1999, Define Normal, 2000, A Snitch in the Snob Squad, 2001, Keeping You a Secret, 2002, Luna: A Novel, 2004 (Nat. Book Award finalist, 2004), Far from Xanadu, 2005, Between Mom and Jo, 2006, Grl 2 Grl, 2007. Recipient Top Hand Award, Colo. Authors' League. Address: 14 Twilight Dr Lakewood CO 80215 E-mail: juliepeters@juno.com.

PETERS, LEE IRA, JR., public defender; b. Jamestown, NY, Dec. 17, 1946; s. Lee Ira and Carrie Irene (Roberson) P.; m. Mabel Luisa Thompson, June 21, 1969; children: Tammy M., Lee III, Ryan J. BA in Criminology, Fla. State U., 1971; JD, U. Fla., 1984. Bar: Fla. 1984, U.S. Dist Ct. (mid. dist.) Fla. 1989. Sr. intern Pub. Defender State of Fla., Gainesville, Fla., 1983; spl. asst. U.S. Atty No. Dist. Fla., Tallahassee, 1987-89; asst. states atty. 3d cir. State's Atty. Office, Live Oak, Fla., 1984-89; asst. pub. defender, felony divsn. chief 3rd cir. Pub. Defender's Office, Live Oak, 1989—. Spl. agt. crim. investigation Bur. ATF- U.S. Treas., Anniston, Ala., Boise, Idaho, 1971-77, resident agt.-in-charge Portland, Oreg, 1977-81; assoc. counsel (pro bono) Nat. Assn. Fed. Agts., 1993—. With USN, 1965-67, Vietnam, maj. U.S. Army Res., 1981-2006 Recipient Disting Svc. award Fla. Coun. Crime & Delinquency, Chpt. XV, 1989; Meritorious Svc. Sec. Army U.S., 1997. Mem. ACLU, Fla. Assn. Criminal Def. Lawyers, Fla. Bar Assn. (3d cir. grievance com. 1993-96), Acad. Fla. Trial Lawyers, 3d Cir. Bar Assn., Mil. Officers Assn. Am. (life), Am. Legion (life mem. Post 107, Live Oak), McAlpin Cmty. Club (pres. 1990-96), Rotary, Elks, Phi Alpha Delta. Avocation: cattle and arabian horse raising. Office: Third Cir Pub Defender 106 Ohio Ave S Live Oak FL 32064-3212 Home Phone: 386-935-6846; Office Phone: 386-362-7235. E-mail: pd3liveoak@hotmail.com.

PETERS, LEO FRANCIS, environmental engineer; b. Melrose, Mass., Aug. 14, 1937; s. Joseph Leander and Mary Gertrude (Phalen) Peters; m. Joan Catherine Anderson, May 20, 1961; children: Elizabeth M., Susan J., Carolyn A., Jennifer L. BSCE, Northeastern U., Boston, 1960, MSCE, 1966; postgrad., Harvard U., 1989. Registered profl. engr., Mass., N.H., diplomate, Am. Acad. Environ. Engrs. Jr. engr. N.Y. Dept. Transp., Albany, 1960-61; chief engr. John M. Cashman, Weymouth, Mass., 1961-62; project engr. Metcalf & Eddy, Inc., Boston, 1962-65, Weston & Sampson, Boston, 1965-67, assoc., 1967-70, ptnr., 1970-76; exec. v.p. Weston & Sampson Engrs., Inc., Boston, 1976-82, pres., CEO Wakefield and Peabody, Mass., 1982-99, chmn., 1999—2002, chmn. emeritus, 2002—. Treas. Engring. Ctr., 1991—93; mem. corp. Northeastern U., Boston, 1992—, dir. nat. coun., 1993—; treas. Engring Ctr. Edn. Trust, 1992—94, chmn., 1994—95. Clk., mem. Melrose (Mass.) Planning Bd., 1969—91; mem. Conservation Commn., 2003—06, Designer Selection Bd. Commonwealth of Mass., 2004—, vice chair, 2006—07, chair, 2007—; bd. dir. Environ. Bus. Coun. New Eng., 1997—2002. Named Outstanding Civil Engr., Northeastern U. Civil Engring. Alumni, Young Engr. of the Yr., Mass. Soc. Profl. Engrs., Disting. Engring. Alumnus, Northeastern U., 2005; recipient Environ. Merit award, Environ. Bus. Coun. New Eng., Leadership award, Engring. Ctr., 2001. Fellow: Am. Coun. Engring. Cos. (v.p. 1995—96, sr. v.p. 1996—97, pres. 1999—2000); mem.: ASCE (life), Boston Soc. Civil Engrs. (hon. life), New Eng. Water Works Assn. (hon. life) (pres. 1989—90), Am. Coun. Engring. Couns. New Eng. (pres. 1990—91), Water Environ. Fedn., Am. Pub. Works Assn., Am. Water Works Assn. Roman Catholic. Home: 187 E Emerson St Melrose MA 02176-3534 Office: Weston & Sampson Engrs Inc 5 Centennial Dr Peabody MA 01960-7985 E-mail: leopeters@comcast.net.

PETERS, LEON, JR., retired engineering educator; b. Columbus, Ohio, May 28, 1923; s. Leon P. and Ethel (Howland) Pierce; m. Mabel Marie Johnson, June 6, 1953; children: Amy T. Peters Thomas, Melinda A. Peters Todaro, Maria C. Cohee, Patricia D., Lee A., Roberta J. Peters Cameruca, Karen E. Peters Ellingson. BSE.E., Ohio State U., 1950, MS, 1954, PhD, 1959. Asst. prof. elec. engring. Ohio State U., Columbus, 1959-63, assoc.

prof., 1963-67, prof., 1967-93, prof. emeritus, 1993—, assoc. dept. chmn. for rsch. Columbus, 1990-92, dir. electro sci. lab., 1983-94. Contbr. articles to profl. jours. Served to 2d lt. U.S. Army, 1942-46, ETO. Fellow: IEEE. Home: 2087 Ellington Rd Columbus OH 43221-4138 Office: Ohio State U Electrosci Lab 1320 Kinnear Rd Columbus OH 43321-1156 Business E-Mail: peters.6@osu.edu.

PETERS, LEONARD K., environmental scientist; BS, MS, PhD, U. Pitts. Joined U. Ky., 1974, asst. prof. chem. engrng. to v.p. rsch. and grad. studies; rschr. Alcoa Rsch. Labs., Cleve. State U.; with Va. Tech., 1993—2003, mgr. rsch. and grad edn. programs, sr. exec. rsch. divsn.; dir. Pacific NW Nat. Lab. operated by Battelle U.S. Dept. Energy, 2003—; sr. v.p. Battelle, 2003—. Mem. adv. bd. Wash. State U. Coll. Engrng. and Architecture; bd. dirs. Heritage Coll., VITEX Sys., Inc., Wash. Tech. Alliance, Wash. Roundtable, Wash. State U. Rsch. Found., Tri Cities Devel. Coun.; chmn. bd., pres. Va. Tech. Intellecutal Properties, Inc.; chmn. rsch. com. Va. Rsch. and Tech. Adv. Commn. Adv. bd. Jr. Achievement Greater Tri-Cities; bd. dirs. United Way Benton and Franklin Counties; Tri-Cities Indsl. Devel. Coun. Recipient Recognition award for contributions to Sci. and Tech., Nat. Sci. Found., 1990. Mem.: AIChE, Oreg. Coun. Knowledge and Econ. Devel., Am. Soc. Engrng. Edn., Am. Assn. Aerosol Rsch., Air and Waste Mgmt. Assn., Sigma XI. Office: Pacific NW Nat Lab PO Box 999 Richland WA 99352

PETERS, LEROY RICHARD, materials management consulting company executive; b. Milw., June 26, 1943; s. LeRoy Edwin and Eleanor Hedwig (Bensing) Peters; m. Barbara Jean Hackney, Nov. 18, 1964 (div. July 1970); 1 child, Neal; m. Nancy Elizabeth Till, July 17, 1971; children: Richard, Brenda, Eric, Linda. BS, U. Wis., 1966; Grad., U.S. Army/Command and, Gen. Staff Coll., Ft. Leavenworth, Kans., 1977. Cert. fellow in prodn. and inventory mgmt. Inventory supr. Bucyrus Erie, Erie, Pa. and Pocatello, Idaho, ach3-76; inventory mgr. Am. Microsystems, Pocatello, 1976-78; prodn. mgr. Worthington Compressor, Buffalo, 1978-80; mfg. mgr. St. Regis WPM Div., Denver, 1980-82; materials mgr. Robinson Brick Co., Denver, 1982-86; prodn. mgr. Merritt Equipment Co., Denver, 1986-89; instructional designer Martin Marietta, Denver, 1989-90; sr. cons. J.D. Edwards, Denver, 1990-93; sr. cons. mgr. AMX Internat., 1993-97; v.p. The Thompson Group, 1997-98; CEO, Enterprise Resource Mgmt., Inc., 1998—. Editorial com.: Aerospace and Defense Dictionary, 1990; contbr. articles to profl. jours. Scoutmaster Boy Scouts Am., Denver, 1989, cubmaster, 1988, outdoor chmn., Denver, 1990; dist. capt. Adams County Colo. Reps., Denver, 1986. Col. U.S. Army, 1966-94, Vietnam, Desert Storm. Decorated Legion of Merit, Bronze Star, Meritorious Svc. medal, Army Commendation medal. Fellow Am. Prodn. and Inventory Control Soc. (bd. dirs. region VI 1990—, pres. Colo. chpt. 1989-90); mem. Am. Def. Preparedness Assn., Moose. Lutheran. Avocations: fishing, reading, music, photography, geology.

PETERS, MARGARET ANNETTE, English language educator; BA in English, Tex. A&M U., College Station, 1988; MA in English, Claremont Grad. Sch., Calif., 1993. Asst. prof. English, Santa Fe C.C., 1996—, chair dept. English and speech, 2004—. Adviser Phi Theta Kappa, Santa Fe, 2001—03. Achievements include Gov. of New Mexico declared December 12, 2001, Margaret A. Peters Day throughout the state of New Mexico to commend her work as a teacher. Avocations: book arts, crafts, painting and drawing, journaling. Office: Santa Fe CC 6401 Richards Ave Santa Fe NM 87508 Home Phone: 505-992-2636; Office Phone: 505-428-1372. Personal E-mail: margpeters@gmail.com. Business E-Mail: mpeters@sfccnm.edu.

PETERS, MARGARET MYRL, retired music educator; d. Wilmer Jasper and Mary Esteleen (Bradford) Peters; m. Robert Lee Sayre, May 31, 1941; children: Patricia Ann, Michael Lee, Kathryn Eileen. MusB, Ill. Wesleyan U., Bloomington, 1941. Cert. min. music, diaconal min. Meth. Ch. Min. music 1st Meth. Ch., Peoria, Ill., 1954—; pvt. tchr. piano Peoria, 1954—99; tchr. organ Bradley U., Peoria, 1970—84; ret., 1999. Musician University Ave. Meth. Ch. Mem.: Peoria Area Music Tchrs. Assn., Ill. Music Tchrs. Assn., Music Tchrs. Nat. Assn., Am. Guild Organists (dean), Current Events (pres.), Fellowship Meth. Musicians (jurisdictional rep.). Home: 202 W Ridgemont Rd Peoria IL 61614

PETERS, MARY ELIZABETH, secretary of transportation; b. Phoenix, Dec. 4, 1948; d. Rose Peters; m. Terry Peters; children: Tammy, Terry, Tina. BA in Mgmt., U. Phoenix; attended, John F. Kennedy Sch. Govt. Program for State & Local Govt. Executives, Harvard U., 2000. Various positions Ariz. Dept. Transp., 1985—98, dir., 1998—2001; adminstr. Fed. Highway Adminstrn., US Dept. Transp., Washington, 2001—05; nat. dir. for transp. policy, cons. HDR, Inc., Phoenix, 2005—06; sec. US Dept. Transp., Washington, 2006—. Vice chairwoman Nat. Surface Transp. Policy & Revenue Study Commn., 2006. Past bd. dirs. Project Challenge, Nat. Guard; past chair adv. bd. Hwy. Expansion Loan Program; mem. Gt. Ariz. Develop. Authority; past mem. Growing Smarter Commn. Named Women of Yr., Women's Transp. Seminar, 2004; named one of Most Influential Person in Ariz. Transp., Ariz. Bus. Jour.; recipient George S. Bartlett award, 2005. Mem.: We. Assn. State Hwy. Transp. Officials, Am. Assn. State Hwy. Officials (past chair standing com. on planning, assest mgmt. task force, reauthorization steering com. 2001). Office: US Dept Transp 400 7th St SW Rm 10200 Washington DC 20590 *

PETERS, MARYBETH, copyrights register; b. Pawtucket, RI, June 12, 1939; Student, U. R.I., 1957-58; BSc in Edn., R.I. Coll., 1961; JD (hons.), George Washington U., 1971. Bar: D.C. 1973. Tchr., Cranston, R.I., 1961-65; examiner Music Section, Cranston, R.I., 1966-69, sr. examiner, 1969-75; from sr. attorney to register Copyright Office, Washington, 1975-94, register of copyrights, 1994—. Cons. copyright law World Intellectual Property Orgn., Geneva, 1989—90; lectr. Communications Law Inst. Catholic U. Am. Columbus Sch. Law; adj. prof. U. Miami Sch. Law, Georgetown U. Law Ctr. Mem. ABA, Copyright Soc. U.S.A., Computer Law Assn. (bd. dirs.), D.C. Computer Law Forum. Office: Copyright Office Library of Congress 101 Independence Ave SE Rm 403 Washington DC 20540-0002 *

PETERS, MERCEDES, psychotherapist; b. NYC; BS, L.I. U., 1945; MS, U. Conn., 1953; tng. in psychotherapy, Am. Inst. Psychotherapy, 1960-70; PhD in Psychoanalysis, Union Inst., 1989. Cert. in psychoanalysis. Sr. psychotherapist Cmty. Guidance Svc., 1960-75; staff affiliate Postgrad. Ctr. for Mental Health, 1974-76; pvt. practice psychoanalysis and psychotherapy, Bklyn., 1961—; tchr., supr. psychoanalytic psychotherapy at various psychotherapeutic tng. ctrs., 1975—; cons. to advanced tng. program Jewish Bd. Family and Children's Svcs., 2000—. Contbr. articles to profl. jours. Past bd. dirs. Brookwood Child Care Assn. Fellow: Am. Orthopsychiat. Assn.; mem.: NASW, LWV, NAACP, Postgrad. Psychoanalytic Soc., Nat. Assn. Advancement Psychoanalysis (past bd. dirs., chair UN com.), Wednesday Club. Office: 142 Joralemon St Brooklyn NY 11201-4709 Office Phone: 718-875-9874.

PETERS, MILTON EUGENE, retired educational psychologist; b. Anderson, Ind., July 22, 1938; s. Olen A. and Dorothy LaVerne (Lambert) P.; m. Carol Ann Dudycha, Aug. 27, 1960. BA, Wittenburg U., 1960; M in Div., Hamma Sch. Theology, 1963; MA, Bowling Green State U., 1965; PhD, U. Toledo, 1975. Lic. psychologist, Ohio. Pastor Luth. Ch. Am., 1966-69; instr. psychology Defiance (Ohio) Coll., 1969-70, Bluffton (Ohio) Coll., 1970-72; tchr., rsch. asst. U. Toledo, 1973-75, prof., 1975-76; dir. instl. rsch., asst. prof. psychology U. Findlay, Ohio, 1976-85, assoc. prof. psychology, 1985-89, prof., 1989—. Cons., lectr. in field; ednl. rschr. Contbr. articles to profl. and religious jours. Mem. APA, Am. Assn. Univ. Prof. (pres. U. Findlay), Midwestern Psychol. Assn., Creative Edn. Found. (colleague), Findlay Beacon Club, Fostoria Power Squadron. Home: 1130 Country Club Dr Findlay OH 45840-6342 Home Phone: 419-424-0224; Office Phone: 419-434-4523. Business E-Mail: peters@findlay.edu.

PETERS, RALPH EDGAR, architectural firm, engineering executive; b. Harrisburg, Pa., Feb. 20, 1923; s. George Edward and Rebecca Flavia (Michener) P.; m. Roberta Jane Shaffer, June 12, 1948; children: Sheila Jane, Gail Marie, Ralph Jr., Bret Edward. Student, U. Pa., 1942; BA in Bus. Adminstrn., Pa. State U., 1948. From payroll supt. to asst. budget supr. Pa. State U., 1948-52; chief acct., pers. officer Haller, Raymond & Brown, State College, Pa., 1952-54; from contr. to CEO and chmn. bd. Benatec Assocs., Inc. (formerly Berger Assocs., Inc.), Camp Hill, Pa., 1954—. Chmn. bd. advisors Pa. State U., Harrisburg, 1979—; chmn. bd. dirs. Holy Spirit Hosp., Camp Hill, 1982—; past pres. Tri-County United Way, Harrisburg, 1978—; chmn. Pvt. Industry Coun., Harrisburg, 1982-87. With U.S. Army, 1943-45, ETO, 1952-53, Korea. Recipient Comty. Svc. award Salvation Army, 1980, Disting. Pennsylvanian award Greater Phila. C. of C., 1981, Catalyst award Capital Region Econ. Devel., 1992, James Skelly award for exceptional svcs. to the hwy. program Associated Constructors of Pa., 1993, Alexis de Tocqueville Humanitarian award United Way, 1999; named Transp. Adv. of Yr., Pa. Hwy. Info. Assn., 1994; finalist Ctrl. Pa. Entrepreneur of Yr., 1996; Paul Harris fellow Rotary Internat., 1997. Mem. Pa. C. of C. (bd. dirs., transp. com. chmn. 1972-90), Harrisburg Area C. of C. (pres., chmn. 1979-83), Ams. for Competitive Enterprise Sys. (pres. 1981-83), Cumberland County Transp. Authority, Susquehanna Valley Regional Airport Authority, Lions, Masons, Pa. Jaycees (pres. 1955-56, nat. v.p. 1956-57), Delta Sigma Pi. Lutheran. Office: Benatec Assocs Inc 200 Airport Rd New Cumberland PA 17070-2467 Home Phone: 717-737-4178; Office Phone: 717-901-7055. Business E-Mail: rpeters@benatec.com.

PETERS, RAYMOND EUGENE, historian, writer; b. New Haven, Conn., Aug. 24, 1933; s. Raymond and Doris Winthrop (Smith) P.; m. Millie Mather, July 14, 1978 (div. Nov. 1983); life ptnr. Mamie L. Romero, 1986—. Student, San Diego City Coll., 1956-61; cert., Lumbleau Real Estate Sch., 1973, Southwestern Coll., Chula Vista, Calif., 1980. Cert. quality assurance engr., Southwestern Coll., 1980. Founder, pub. Silhouette Pub. Co., San Diego, 1960-75; co-founder, news dir. Sta. XEGM, San Diego, 1964-68; news dir. Sta. XERB, Tijuana, Mex., 1973-74; founder, chief exec. officer New World Airways, Inc., San Diego, 1968-77; co-founder, exec. vice chmn. bd. San Cal Rail, Inc.-San Diego Trolley, San Diego, 1974-77; founder, pres., CEO Ansonia Sta., micro systems, San Diego, 1986—. Cons. on multimedia and electronic commerce sys., 1995—; co-founder, dir. S.E. Cmty. Theatre, San Diego, 1960-68; commr. New World Aviation Acad., Otay Mesa, Calif., 1971-77; co-founder New World Internat. Trade and Commerce Commn., Inc., 1991-94, New World Airways Inc, 1968-77 Author: Profiles in Black American History, 1971, Black Americans in Aviation, 1975, Eagles Don't Cry, 1988, Forgotten Renaissance, African American History, 2005, Diss-Function, The Self Genocide of Negro's in America, 2005; founder, pub., editor Oceanside Lighthouse, 1958-60, San Diego Herald Dispatch, 1959-60 Co-founder, bd. dirs. San Diego County Econ. Opportunity Commn., 1964-67; co-founder Edn. Cultural Complex, San Diego, 1966-75; co-founder, exec. dir. S.E. Anti-Poverty Planning Coun., Inc., 1964-67; mem. U.S. Rep. Senatorial Inner Circle Com., Washington, 1990—; mayoral candidate, city of San Diego, 1986; mem. bus. adv. bd. Value Add Reseller, 1995; ambassador Sycuan Casino and Singing Hills Golf Resort, 2000-05 With US Army, 1950—53, Korea. Decorated (2) Bronze Svc. stars, UN medal, US Presl. Unit Citation 630th Ordinance and Ammo Co., Korea, 1951-52; recipient Pres. of Korea award medal. Mem. Am. Soc. Quality Control, Nat. City C. of C., Afro-Am. Micro Sys. Soc. (exec. dir. 1987—), Negro Airmen Internat. (Calif. pres. 1970-75, nat. v.p. 1975-77), Tuskegee Airmen (charter, bd. dirs. Benjamin O. Davis San Diego chpt. 1995—), Internat. Platform Assn., U.S. C. of C., Greater San Diego Minority C. of C. (bd. dirs. 1974—, past chmn. bd.), Masons (most worshipful grand master, supreme coun.), Shriners (Al Kadosh Disting. Cmty. Svc. award 1975), North Highlands VFW. Republican. Methodist. Achievements include being first African American to co-found a jet powered transcontinental airline that set a national safety record. Avocations: creative writing, golf, world history, public speaking. Home: Meadowbrook Estates # 245 8301 Mission Gorge Rd Santee CA 92071-3500 Personal E-mail: ray_peters@sbcglobal.net.

PETERS, ROBERT K., dean, newscaster, newswriter, journalist; b. Tyler, Tex., June 2, 1941; s. Robert K. and Ruth Bailey Peters; m. Judy D. Loden, Feb. 23, 1980; children: Jonathan W., Anne E. AA, Tyler Jr. Coll., 1961—; BA, Tex. Christian U., 1962; M in History, Stephen F. Austin State Coll., 1964; PhD, U. Tex., 1977. Staff writer, weather, and sci. Tyler Courier Times Telegraph, 1962—; newsreader weather KTBB Radio Sta., Tyler, 1962—; dean univ. studoes Tyler Jr. Coll., 1966—; observer, sta. keeper Nat. Weather Svc., Tyler, 1992—. Dir. bd. dirs. Horizon, Tyler, 1977—; trustee Tyler Mus. Art, 1999—. Author: Texas from Annexation to Succession: 1846-1861, 1977, Practicing Texas Politics, Instructor Resource Manual, 1994, 1995, 1997, 1998, 2000, 2001, 2003. Mem. Tex. Coun. Workforce and Econ. Competitiveness, Austin, 1999—2003, N.E. Tex. State Sub-Comms. Revision, Austin, 1973—74, Tex. Commn. Blind Bd., Austin, 1985—91, 1999—2004, Tex. Coun. Disabilities, Austin, 1990—91, City of Tyler Rev. Bd., 1990—94, Tex. Planning Coun. Disabilities, Austin, 1991—93. Recipient Piper Prof. award, Piper Found., San Antonio, 1993, Nat. Weather Svc. Cooperating Observer award, Nat. Weather Svc., Shreveport, La., 2002. Mem.: Tex. State Hist. Soc., So. Hist. Soc., Orgn. Am. History, Am. Hist. Soc. Republican. Episcopalian. Avocations: reading, cooking. Home: 3813 Brookwood Tyler TX 75701 Office: Tyler Jr Coll 1400 E 5th St Tyler TX 75711 Fax: 903-510-2708. E-mail: rpet@tjc.edu.

PETERS, ROBERT TIMOTHY, judge; b. Memphis, Dec. 28, 1946; s. Rhulin Earl and Bertie Nichols (Moore) P.; m. Ruth Audrey Allen, Dec. 11, 1973; children: Lindsay Elizabeth, Christopher Andrew. AA, St. Petersburg Jr. Coll., 1969; BA, U. Fla., 1971, JD, 1973. Bar: Fla. 1973, U.S. Dist. Ct. (mid. dist.) Fla. 1977, U.S. Ct. Appeals (5th cir.) 1981; cert. real estate lawyer. Ptnr. Goza, Hall & Peters P.A., Clearwater, Fla., 1973-84; sole practice Clearwater, 1984-95; apptd. cir. judge Fla., 1995—. Gov. Fla.'s appointee Condominium Study Commsn., Clearwater, 1990-91. Columnist Clearwater Sun newspaper, 1985—. 1st Lt. U.S. Army, 1966-68, Vietnam. Decorated Silver Star, Purple Heart, Bronze Star with oak leaf cluster. Avocations: reading, exercise. Office: Criminal Justice Ctr 14250 49th St N Clearwater FL 33762 Address: PO Box 6316 Clearwater FL 33758-6316 Office Phone: 727-464-6222.

PETERS, ROBERT WAYNE, small business owner; b. LaPorte, Ind., Jan. 2, 1950; s. Harry Carl and Dorothy May (Fischer) P.; m. Frances Kay Cooley, Aug. 21, 1971; children: Carolyn Marie, Angela Lynn. BA, Purdue U., 1972. CLU. Mgr. pension adminstrn. Gen. Life Ins. Corp., Milw., 1973-75; dir. qualified plan devel. Cen. Life Assurance Co., Des Moines, 1976-84; v.p. individual ops. First Farwest Ins. Co., Portland, Oreg., 1984-90; pres. CAF Enterprises, Inc., Portland, 1990—. Lectr. in field. Contbr. articles to profl. jours. Mem. N.W. Vintage Thunderbird (v.p. 1988, pres. 1989-90, exec. bd. 1991, sec. 1992-93, 97-2002, treas. 1995-96, sec.-treas. 2000), N.W. Car Collectors Assn. (treas. 2002-07). Avocations: reading, vintage thunderbirds. Office: CAF Enterprises Inc PO Box 1529 Tualatin OR 97062-1529 Personal E-mail: bob@tbirdsanctuary.com.

PETERS, ROBERT WOOLSEY, retired architect; b. Mpls., Mar. 24, 1935; s. John Eugene and Adelaide Elizabeth (Woolsey) P. BArch., U. Minn., 1958; MArch., Yale U., 1964. Registered architect, N.Mex. Participating assoc. Skidmore Owings & Merrill, Chgo., 1961-74; dir. design Schaefer & Assocs., Wichita, Kans., 1975-76; ptnr. Addy & Peters, Albuquerque, 1979-82; owner, sole proprietor Robert W. Peters AIA Architect, 1982—2004, ret., 2004. Exhibited work Centre Georges Pompidou, Paris, 1980, U. Art Mus., Albuquerque, 1982, 92, Albuquerque Mus., 1988; contbr. articles to Century Mag., Progressive Architecture, House & Garden, House Beautiful, also others. Recipient honor awards N.Mex. Soc. Architects, 1980-83, 86, 87, 92, HUD, 1980; 5th Nat. Passive Solar Conf., Amherst, Mass., 1981. Fellow AIA; mem. Contemporary Art Soc. N.Mex. (bd. dirs., pres.), N.Mex. Arch. Found. (pres. 2004-), Yale N.Mex. Democrat. Roman Catholic.

PETERS, ROBERTA, soprano; b. NYC, May 4, 1930; d. Sol and Ruth (Hirsch) Peters; m. Bertram Fields, Apr. 10, 1955; children: Paul, Bruce. Litt.D., Elmira Coll., 1967; Mus. D., Ithaca Coll., 1968, Colby Coll., 1980; L.H.D., Westminster Coll., 1974, Lehigh U., 1977; D.F.A., St. John's U., 1982; LittD, Coll. New Rochelle, 1989; MusD, U. R.I., 1992, Fla. Atlantic U., 1997. Author: Debut at the Met; singer: (Operas) Met. Opera debut as Zerlina in Don Giovanni, 1950, recorded numerous operas, (appeared motion pictures including) Tonight We Sing, 1996, frequent appearances radio and TV, (stage appearances include) The King and I, 1973, Bittersweet, Merry Widow, The Sound of Music, Royal Opera House, Vienna State Opera, Munich Opera, West Berlin Opera, Salzburg Festival, The White House, debuts at festivals in Vienna and Munich, premiered Ani M'amin, Carnegie Hall, 1973, concert tours in U.S., Soviet Union, Scandinavian countries, Israel, China, Japan, Taiwan, South Korea, (debut) Kirov Opera, sang at Bolshoi Opera (1st Am. recipient Bolshoi medal). Trustee, bd. dirs. Carnegie Hall; trustee Ithaca Coll.; dir. Met. Opera Guild; chmn. Nat. Inst. Music Theater, 1991—; apptd. by Pres. Bush to Nat. Coun. Arts, 1991; overseer Colby Coll., Bklyn. Coll. Performing Arts Ctr.; past chair Nat. Cystic Fibrosis Found.; active Israel Bonds, AIDS rsch. Named Woman of Yr., Fedn. Women's Clubs, 1964; recipient honored spl. ceremony on 35th anniversary with Met. Opera Co., 1985, Nat. Medal of Arts, Pres. Clinton, 1998. Avocation: tennis. Office: ICM Artists Ltd 40 W 57th St Fl 16 New York NY 10019-4098 *I believe that life is a series of just one darn thing after another. If we can learn that, we can expect, meet, and solve our problems.*

PETERS, SAMMY, artist; Vis. prof. U. Ark. Little Rock, 1988, 1990, Memphis Coll. Art, 1989, 1991, Stephen F Austin, Nacogdoches, Tex., 1994. One-man shows include Shidoni Gallery, Santa Fe, 1986, 1987, 1989, 1991, The Heights Gallery, Little Rock, 1986, 1988, 1994, 1998, The Wright Gallery, Dallas, 1987, The New Gallery, Houston, 1989, 1995, 2002, The Lowe Gallery, Atlanta, 1991, 1994, Santa Monica, 1992, Allen Lapides Gallery, Santa Fe, 1992, 1994—96, Cindric Meyer Gallery, Boca Raton, 1997, Stephen F. Austin U., 1994, Cindric Meyer Gallery, 1998, LewAllen Contemporary, Santa Fe, 1999, 2001, 2003, 2005, 2007, Perry Nicole Gallery, Memphis, 2002, Bentley Gallery, Scottsdale, 2005, catalog, Portals and Intentions, LewAllen Contemporary, 2001, exhibited in group shows at 24th Delta Ann., Ark. Arts Ctr., Little Rock, 1985, 8th Ann. Hot Springs Fine Art Ctr. Ann., 1985, Foster Goldstrom Gallery, Dallas, 1986, Southern Contemporary Art Invitational, Jacksonville, Ala., 1986, Ark. Artists Registry, Little Rock, 1987, Mona Berman Fine Arts, New Haven, Conn., 1987, Contemporary Art Fair, LA, 1987, 1989—90, AES Gallery, Chgo., 1988, Alice Bingham Gallery, Memphis, 1989, Tibor de Nagy Gallery, NYC, 1993, Paintings from America's Heart, Berlin, Bremen, Germany, 1994—95, Anita Shapolsky Gallery, NYC, 1995, 1997, 1999, Ann. US Print & Drawing Exhbn., 1998, LewAllen Contemporary, Santa Fe, 1998—2000, Perry Nicole Gallery, Memphis, 2001, Stephen F. Austin U., 2005, Bentley Projects, Phoenix, 2005. Recipient Juror's Spl. Mention award, 6th Dixie Ann., 1965, Juror's Top award, 10th Ann. Mid-South Exhbn., 1965, Juror's award, 10th Delta Ann., 1967; M-AAA/NEA fellowship, 1992, MacDowell fellowship, 2000, Vt. Studio Ctr. fellowship, 2001. *

PETERS, SARAH WHITAKER, art historian, writer; b. Kenosha, Wis., Aug. 17, 1924; d. Robert Burbank and Margaret Jebb (Allen) Whitaker; m. Arthur King Peters, Oct. 21, 1943; children: Robert Bruce, Margaret Allen, Michael Whitaker. BA, Sarah Lawrence Coll., Bronxville, NY, 1954; MA, Columbia U., NYC, 1966; student, L'Ecole du Louvre, Paris, 1967-68; diplome, Ecole des Trois Gourmandes, Paris, 1968; PhD, CUNY, 1987. Freelance critic Art in Am., NYC. Lectr.-in-residence Garrison Forest Sch., Owings Mills, Md.; adj. asst. prof. art history C.W. Post, U. L.I.; lectr. Bronxville (N.Y.) Adult Sch., Internat. Mus. Photography, 1979, Tufts U., 1979, Madison (Wis.) Art Ctr., 1984, Meml. Art Gallery, Rochester, N.Y., 1988, 91, Caramoor Mus., Katonah, N.Y., 1988, Yale U. Art Gallery, New Haven, 1989, The Cosmopolitan Club, N.Y.C., 1977, 91, Sarah Lawrence Coll., Bronxville, 1992, The Phillips Collection, Washington, 1993, 2006, Mpls. Inst. Arts, 1993, Whitney Mus. Am. Art, Champion, 1994, U. Wis., Parkside, 1994, Nat. Mus. Wildlife Art, Jackson Hole, Wyo., 1995, The Georgia O'Keeffe Mus., Santa Fe, 1997, 2006, Bronxville Pub. Libr., 1998, Weatherspoon Art Mus., Greensboro, NC, 2003, Amon Carter Mus, Ft. Worth, 2003, Vassar Coll., 2003, Pa. Acad. Fine Arts, Phila., 2004. Author: Becoming O'Keeffe: The Early Years, 1991, 2d edit., 2001, Pattern of the Past: A Kenosha Memoir, 2001; contbr. essays to Portraits of American Women, 1991, The Dictionary of Art, 1996, Frames of Reference; Works from the Whitney Museum of American Art, 1999, American Art Review, 2003, Georgia O'Keeffe: Color and Conservation, 2006, N.Mex. Hist. Rev., 2006, Seeing America: Painting and Sculpture, 2006; TV appearances include: BBC, London, The Late Show, 1993, A&E Network Biography series on Georgia O'Keeffe, 2004; radio interview: Art Today, Australia Broadcasting Corp., 1999; contbr. articles to profl. jours. Mem. Coll. Art Assn., Bronxville Field Club, The Cosmopolitan Club. Avocations: horseback riding, rock climbing, tennis, cooking. Home: 14 Village Ln Bronxville NY 10708-4806

PETERS, STEPHEN C., lawyer; b. Kansas City, Mo., Apr. 8, 1957; BA cum laude, Kans. State U., 1979; JD, Duke U., 1983. Bar: Colo. 1983, US Dist. Ct. (dist. Colo.), US Ct. Appeals. Asst. US atty. Dist. Colo., 1987—94; instr. Nat. Inst. Trial Advocacy, 1990—2001; atty. Lindquist & Vennum, PLLP, Denver. Mem. criminal justice act panel US Dist. Ct. (dist. Colo.). Named a Colo. Super Lawyer, 2006; recipient Dir.'s award, US Dept. Justice, 1994. Mem.: N.W. Colo. Bar Assn., Colo. Trial Lawyers Assn., Colo. Bar Assn., ABA (criminal justice sect.), Phi Beta Kappa. Office: Lindquist & Vennum PLLP Ste 1800 S 600 17th St Denver CO 80202-5441 Office Phone: 303-454-0519. Office Fax: 303-573-1956. E-mail: speters@lindquist.com. *

PETERS, SUSAN P., human resources specialist; married; 1 child. BA, St. Mary's Coll., Univ. Notre Dame, 1975; M Edn., Univ. Va., 1978. Mgmt. positions Gen. Electric, 1979—82; mgr. union rels., profl. rels. mgr. Trane Co., 1982—84; mgr. non-exempt rels. GE Plastics, Pittsfield, Mass., 1984—86, HR mgr. worldwide mktg., prod. mgmt., 1986—89, HR mgr. Europe Bergen op Zoom, Netherlands, 1989—90; mgr. HR staffing & develop. Gen Electric, Fairfield, Conn., 1990—91; mgr. human resources GE Plastics, Pittsfield, Mass., 1991—93; sr. human resources mgr. GE Appliances, Louisville, 1993—2000; exec. v.p. human resources NBC, 2000—01; v.p. exec. develop. Gen. Electric, Fairfield, Conn., 2001—. Office: General Electric 3135 Easton Turnpike Fairfield CT 06828 *

PETERS, THOMAS, foundation administrator; BA, San Francisco State U., 1966; PhD, U. Minn., 1973. Various positions including assoc. dir. of health Dept. of Public Health, San Francisco, 1974—90; dir. Health and Human Services, Marin County, 1991—98; pres., CEO Marin Community

Found., 1998—. Mem. Cmty. Leadership Team Council on Foundations; bd. mem. Cmty. Foundations of Am., League of Calif. Cmty. Foundations; fellow NIH, 1968—71. Office: Marin Cmty Found 5 Hamilton Landing Novato CA 94949

PETERS, THOMAS ANDREW, library and information scientist, writer; m. Vicki Peters. BA with honors in English and Philosophy, Grinnell Coll., Iowa, 1980; MA in Libr. and Info. Sci., U. Iowa, Iowa City, 1987; MA in English, U. Mo., Kans. City, 1992. Humanities reference libr., coord. bibliog. instrn. Miller Nichols Libr. U. Mo., Kans. City, 1987—91; collection devel. coord. Meml. Libr. Mankato State U. (now Minn. State U. at Mankato), 1991—94; assoc. dir. collections and tech. svcs. univ. librs. No. Ill. U., 1994—98; dean univ. librs. Western Ill. U., 1998—99; dir. Ctr. Libr. Initiatives, Com. Instl. Cooperation, 2000—03; CEO TAP Info. Svcs., Blue Springs, Mo., 2003—. Author: The Online Catalog: A Critical Examination of Public Use, 1991, Computerized Monitoring and Online Privacy, 1999, Library Programs Online: Possibilities and Practicalities, 2006; contbr. chapters to books, articles to profl. publs. Named one of the Movers & Shakers, Libr. Jour., 2005. Mem.: ALA, Phi Beta Kappa. Office: TAP Info Svcs 1000 SW 23rd St Blue Springs MO 64015-4754 Office Phone: 816-228-6406. E-mail: tpeters@tapinformation.com.

PETERS, THOMAS M., lawyer; b. Saginaw, Mich., Apr. 10, 1943; s. Donald James and Jean Eleanor (Kelly) P.; m. Jane Caryl Fetters, Jan. 6, 1968; children: Jenifer Caryl, Thomas Jr. Grad., Syracuse East European Language Sch., NY, 1966; BA, Mich. State U., 1969; JD, Wayne State U., 1973. Assoc. Vandeveer, Garzia, Tonkin, Kerr, Heaphy, Moore, & Sills, Detroit, 1973-80, prin., ptnr., 1980—. Mem. local and state bar coms. U.S. Dist. Ct. and U.S. Ct. Appeals. Served to staff sgt. USAF, 1965-69. Mem. ABA, Def. Research Inst., Mich. Def. Trial Counsel, Assn. Def. Trial Counsel (bd. dirs. 1978—, pres. 1985-86, award for valuable service 1986), Mediation Tribunal Assn., Am. Arbitration Assn. Clubs: Port Huron (Mich.) Golf, Otsego Ski (Gaylord, Mich.), Beachwood Swim and tennis (Troy, Mich.), Tournament Players (Jacksonville, Fla.). Lodges: Elks. Home: 4906 Rivers Edge Dr Troy MI 48098-4137 Office: Vandeveer Garzia, PC Ste 100 1450 W Long Lake Rd Troy MI 48098-6330 Office Phone: 248-312-2900. E-mail: tpeters@VGpcLAW.com.

PETERSEN, ANNE C. (CHERYL PETERSEN), foundation administrator, educator; b. Little Falls, Minn., Sept. 11, 1944; d. Franklin Hanks and Rhoda Pauline (Sandwick) Studley; m. Douglas Lee Petersen, Dec. 27, 1967; children: Christine Anne, Benjamin Bradfield. BA, U. Chgo., 1966, MS, 1972, PhD, 1973. Asst. prof., rsch. assoc. Dept. Psychiatry U. Chgo., 1972-80, assoc. prof., rsch. assoc., 1980-82; prof. human devel., head Dept. Individual and Family Studies Pa. State U., University Park, 1982-87, dean Coll. Health and Human Devel., 1987-92, prof. health and human devel., 1987-92; dean grad. sch., v.p. for rsch. throughout state U. Minn., Mpls., 1992-94, prof. adolescent devel. and pediatrics, 1992-96; dep. dir., COO NSF, Arlington, Va., 1994-96; sr. v.p. programs W.K. Kellogg Found., 1996—2005; dep. dir. Ctr. Advanced Study Behavioral Scis. Stanford U., 2006—, prof. Dept. Psychology, 2006—. Vis. prof., fellow Coll. Edn., R&D Psychology, Roosevelt U., Chgo., 1973-74; cons. Ctr. for Health Adminstrn. Studies U. Chgo., 1976-78, Ctr. for New Schs., Chgo., 1974-78, Robert Wood Johnson Found., Mathtech, Inc., 1987-89; coord. clin. rsch. tng. program Michael Reese Hosp. and Med. Ctr., Chgo., 1976-80, dir. Lab. for Study of Adolescence, 1975-82; faculty Ill. Sch. for Profl. Psychology, 1978-79; statis. cons. Coll. Nursing U. Ill. Med. Ctr., 1975-83; assoc. dir. health program MacArthur Found., 1980-82, also cons. health program, 1982-88; chair sr. adv. bd. NIMH, 1987-88; nat. adv. mental health coun. NIH, 1997-2003; trustee Nat. Inst. Statis. Scis., 1998-2004. Author: Sex Related Differences in Cognition Functioning: Developmental Issues, 1979, Promoting Adolescent Health: A Diolog on Research and Practice, 1982, Firls at Puberty: Biological and psychosocial Perspectives, 1983, Brain Maturation and Cognitive Development: Comparative and Cross Cultural Perspectives, 1991, Narrowing the Margins: Adolescent Unemployment and the lack of a social role, 1991, Grofit: A Fortran Program for the Estimation of Parameters of a Human Growth Curve, 1972, Girls at Puberty: Biological and Psychosocial Perspectives, 1983, Adolescence and Youth: Psychological Development in a Changing World, 1984, Youth Unemployment and Society, 1994, Transitions Through Adolescence: Interpersonal Domains and Context, 1996; reviewer Jour. Youth and Adolescence, 1975-80, Devel. Psychology, 1979—, Sci., 1979—, Jour. Edn. Psychology, 1979—, Child Devel., 1980—, Jour. Edn. Measurement, 1980, Ednl. Rschr., 1980, Am. Ednl. Rsch. Jour., 1981—, Jour. Mental Imagery, 1982-92, Sex Roles, 1984—; cons. editor Psychology of Women Quar., 1978-82, assoc. editor, 1983-86; adv. editor Contemporary Psychology, 1985-86; mem. editl. bd. various profl. jours.; contbr. chpts. to books and articles to profl. jours. Bd. overseers Lewis Coll., Ill. Inst. Tech., 1980-82; mem. adv. bd. longitudinal data archive project Murray Ctr., Radcliffe Coll., 1985-91, mem. sci. adv. bd., 1983-91 Fellow: APA (chmn. task force on reproductive freedom 1979—81, program chmn. 1981—82, chmn. task force on long range planning 1986—89, pres. divsn. 7 1992—93), AAAS; mem.: NAS (nat. forum on future children and their families 1987—91, chmn. panel on child abuse and neglect 1991—93, mem. forum on adolescence Inst. of Medicine 1997—2000, chair bd. on behavioral, cognitive and sensory scis. 1997—, mem. nat. academics com. sci., engring., and policy 2003—), Global Phys. Therapy Alliance (pres. 2005—), Soc. for Rsch. on Adolescence (pres. 1990—92, past pres. 1992—94, chmn. nominations com. 1992—94, mem. fin. com. 2004—), Acad. Europaea, Psychometric Soc., Behavior Genetics Assn., Assn. Women in Sci. (bd. dirs. 1996—2000), Am. Ednl. Rsch. Assn. (various offices), Internat. Soc. for the Study of Behavioral Devel. (coun. mem. 1995—, pres.-elect 2002—06, pres. 2006—), Inst. for Medicine. Home: 3715 Blackberry Ln Kalamazoo MI 49008-3333 Office Phone: 650-321-2052. E-mail: globalphilliance@yahoo.com.

PETERSEN, ARNE JOAQUIN, chemist, consultant; b. LA, Jan. 27, 1932; s. Hans Maria Theodore and Astrid Marie (Pedersen) Petersen; m. Sandra Joyce Sharp, Aug. 12, 1961; children: Christina Lynn, Kurt Arne. AA, Compton Coll., 1957; BS, Calif. State U., Long Beach, 1959; BA, U. Calif., Irvine, 1975. Lic. comml. pilot. Chemist, scientist Beckman Instruments, Inc., Fullerton, Calif., 1959—62, engr., scientist, 1962—65, project, sr. project engr., 1965—74; project/program mgr. clin. divsn. Beckman Clin. Ops., Fullerton/Brea, 1974—80; ops. mgr. Graphic Controls Corp., Irvine, 1980—82; engr./mgr. R&D Carle Instruments Chromatography, Anaheim, Calif., 1982—84; mgr. ops. Magnaflux/X-Ray Devel., LA, 1984—85; dir. R&D, new products Am. Chem. Sys., Irvine, 1985—86; rsch. assoc. U. Calif., Irvine, 1987—89; ind. cons., contractor, sales real estate investment, 1989—. Career guidance counselor U. Calif., Irvine, 1976; co-founder Cak, Inc., 2001. Contbr. articles and sci. papers in field to profl. jours. Exec. svc. A.I.D. Internat. Exec. Svc. Corps, Egypt, 1993—94; vol. F.I.S.H., Costa Mesa, Newport Beach, Calif.; basketball coach Boys-Girls Club, Newport Beach, 1975—78; baseball coach Newport Beach Parks, 1975—78; adv. com. Newport/Costa Mesa Sch. Bd., 1974—75. Mem.: AAAS, AMA, Am. Chem. Soc., Biomed. Engring. Soc., U. Calif. Univ. Club (bd. dirs.), Chi Gamma Iota (pres. Compton Coll. chpt. 1956), Kappa Sigma (founder Calif. State U. Long Beach chpt.). Achievements include publications; patents in field. Avocations: flying, photography, travel, bridge, surfing. Personal E-mail: ajpetersen@earthlink.net.

PETERSEN, BARRY REX, news correspondent; b. Norfolk, Va., Jan. 14, 1949; s. Kermit and Mavis Lucille (Sutton) P.; m. Sandra H. Petersen, June 7, 1971 (div. Dec. 1984); children: Emily Jensine, Juliette Rose; m. Jan Chorlton, Feb. 14, 1985. BS in Journalism, Northwestern U., 1970, MS in Journalism, 1972. Sports columnist Sidney (Mont.) Herald, 1964-66; city hall reporter Arlington Heights (Ill.) Day, 1968-69; columnist, copy editor Chgo. Today, 1970-71; pub. Daily Northwestern, Evanston, Ill., 1970-71; reporter Milw. (Wis.) Jour., 1971-72; investigative reporter Sta. WITI-TV, Milw., 1972-74; reporter, anchor Sta. WCCO-TV, Mpls., 1974-78; corr. CBS News, LA, 1978-81, San Francisco, 1981-85, Tokyo, 1986-88, Moscow, 1988-90, London, 1991-95, Tokyo, 1995—. Pres. AFRTA, Milw., 1973-74; Josephine B. and Newton N. Minow vis. prof. in communications Northwestern U., Evanston, Ill., 1991. Recipient Investigative Reporting award Wis. Press Assn., 1973, Nat. Emmy award, 1994, 97, World gold medal radio breaking news N.Y. Festivals, 1999, Edward R. Murrow award, 2004. Mem. Fgn. Corrs. Club Japan, Fgn. Club of China. Lutheran. Avocations: sailing, travel, international real estate. also: CBS News 5-3-6 Akasaka Minato-ku Tokyo 107 Japan Office Phone: 212-975-3019. Business E-Mail: bp3@cbsnews.com.

PETERSEN, BENTON LAURITZ, paralegal; b. Salt Lake City, Jan. 1, 1942; s. Lauritz George and Arleane (Curtis) P.; m. Sharon Donnette Higgins, Sept. 20, 1974 (div. Aug. 9, 1989); children: Grant Lauritz, Tashya Eileen, Nicholas Robert, Katrina Arleane. AA, Weber State Coll., 1966, BA, BA, Weber State Coll., 1968; M of Liberal Studies, U. Okla., 1980; diploma, Nat. Radio Inst. Paralegal Sch., 1991; JD, Monticello U., 1999. Registered paralegal. Announcer/news dir. KWHO Radio, Salt Lake City, 1968-70, KDXU Radio, St. George, Utah, 1970-73, KSOP Radio, Salt Lake City, 1973-76; case worker/counselor Salvation Army, Midland, Tex., 1976-84; announcer/news dir. KBRS Radio, Springdale, Ark., 1984-86; case worker/counselor Office of Human Concern, Rogers, Ark., 1986-88; announcer KAZM Radio, Sedona, Ariz., 1988-91; paralegal Benton L. Petersen, Manti, Utah, 1991—. Cons. Sanpete County Srs., Manti, 1992—. Award judge Manti City Beautification, 1992-96; treas. Manti Destiny Com., 1993-98; tourism com. Sanpete County Econ. Devel., Ephraim, Utah, 1993-96. Served with U.S. Army N.G., 1959-66. Mem.: Nat. Assn. Attys. in Fact (past pres.), Am. Assn. Individual Investors. Mem. Lds Ch. Avocation: reading. Home: 120 N 470 E Manti UT 84642 Office Phone: 435-835-8689. Personal E-mail: bpfreedom@hotmail.com.

PETERSEN, CAROLYN ASHCRAFT, retired psychologist; b. Waxhaw, NC; d. J. Carl and Carolyn (Ray) Wolfe; m. Thomas L. Ashcraft (div. 1973); children: Anne C., Thomas Wolfe; m. Marvin E. Petersen, Nov. 14, 1982. BS, U. N.C.; MA, Vanderbilt U., PhD, 1963. Lic. psychologist, Pa., Fla. Psychologist Peabody Child Study Ctr., Nashville, 1963-64; rschr. U.S. Dept. Edn.-Peabody, Nashville, 1964-65; assoc. prof. Tenn. State U., Nashville, 1965-66; asst. prof. U. Tenn., Nashville, 1966-69, LaSalle Coll., Phila., 1970-72; adj. instr. U. Pa., Phila., 1970-73; clin. psychologist Overbrook Sch. for Blind, Phila., 1974-76, Fla. Sch. for Deaf and Blind, St. Augustine, 1976-78; asst. prof. psychology U. Tampa, Fla., 1979-82; assoc., adj. prof. S.D. State U., Brookings, 1983-89; ret., 1995. Cons. Tenn. Dept. Edn., Cookeville, 1966-69, Charter Hosp., Tampa, 1979-82; organizer symposia for profl. meetings. Contbr. to profl. publs. Bd. dirs. Brookings Hosp. Aux., 1985-88; v.p. S.D. Art Mus. Guild, 1988-89. Fellow Am. Psychol. Soc., Pa. Psychol. Assn.; mem. APA, Southeastern Psychol. Assn., Nat. Register Psychologists. Republican. Avocations: bridge, travel, art. Home: 103 Silverbell Ct Sun City Center FL 33573-6215 Personal E-mail: drcarolpetersen@yahoo.com.

PETERSEN, CHRIS, college football coach; b. 1964; m. Barbara Petersen; children: Jack, Sam. BA in Psychology, U. Calif. Davis, 1988, M in Edn. & Psychology. Freshman football coach U. Calif. Davis, 1987—88, receivers coach, 1989—91; quarterbacks coach U. Pitts., 1992, Portland St. U., 1993—94; offensive coord. U. Oreg., 1995—2000, Boise State U., 2000—05, head football coach, 2006—. Recipient Paul "Bear" Bryant award, Nat. Sportscasters & Sportswriters Assn., 2006. Achievements include coaching Boise St. to a perfect 12-0 record, 2006. Office: Boise State U Dept Athletics Boise ID 83725 *

PETERSEN, DAVID L., lawyer; AA, Concordia Jr. Coll., Milw., 1963; BA, Concordia Sr. Coll., Ft. Wayne, Ind., 1965; JD, Valparaiso U., Ind., 1968. Bar: Wis. 1968, U.S. Dist. Ct. (ea. dist.) Wis. 1969, U.S. Ct. Appeals (7th cir.) 1972, U.S. Supreme Ct. 1988, Fla. 1989. Ptnr. Quarles & Brady, Milw. and Naples, Fla., 1968—. Author: Wisconsin Condominium Law, 1988, 98, 2003, 06; editor Valparaiso U. Law Rev., 1967-68; contbr. articles to profl. jours. Mem. Greater Milw. Com. Cmty. Devel., 1983; bd. dirs. Goals for Greater Milw. 2000, 1982, Broward Com. of 100; mem. nat. adv. bd. Nat. Ctr. for Missing and Exploited Children, Washington, Adam Walsh Children's Fund, Palm Beach, Fla.; dir. Boys and Girls Club Collier County. Lt. col., instr. pilot USAF/Wis. Air N.G., 1970-90. Mem. ABA, Wis. Bar Assn., Milw. Bar Assn., Fla Bar Assn., Broward County Bar Assn., Palm Beach County Bar Assn., Collier County Bar Assn., Am. Coll. Real Estate Lawyers, Milw. Yacht Club, Palm Beach Yacht Club. Office: Quarles & Brady LLP 1395 Panther Ln Naples FL 34109 also: Quarles & Brady LLP 411 E Wisconsin Ave Ste 2550 Milwaukee WI 53202-4409 Office Phone: 239-434-4959.

PETERSEN, DONALD SONDERGAARD, lawyer; b. Pontiac, Ill., May 14, 1929; s. Clarence Marius and Esther (Sondergaard) P.; m. Alice Thorup, June 5, 1954; children: Stephen, Susan Petersen Schuh, Sally Petersen Riordan. Student, Grand View Coll., 1946—48; BA, Augustana Coll., Rock Island, Ill., 1951; JD, Northwestern U., 1956. Bar: Ill. 1957. Assoc. Norman & Billick and predecessors, Chgo., 1956-64, ptnr., 1965-78; counsel Sidley & Austin, Chgo., 1978-80, ptnr., 1980-93, ret., 1993. Pres. Chgo. Exhibitors Corp., Chgo., 1972-85. Bd. dirs. Mount Olive Cemetery Co. Inc., Chgo., 1972-90; bd. dirs. Augustana Hosp., 1983-87, The Danish Home, 1976—; bd. dirs. Luth. Gen. Hosp., Park Ridge, Ill., 1968-2005, chmn., 1979-81, 89-91; bd. dirs. Luth. Gen. Health System and predecessors, Park Ridge, 1980-95, chmn., 1980-81, 83-85; bd. dirs., chmn. Parkside Health Mgmt. Corp., Parkside Home Health Svcs., 1985-88. With U.S. Army, 1951-53. Mem. Chgo. Bar Assn., Ill. State Bar Assn. Clubs: Union League (Chgo.). Home: 241 N Aldine Ave Park Ridge IL 60068-3009 Office: 9th Fl One S Dearborn St Chicago IL 60603 Office Phone: 312-853-7232.

PETERSEN, DOROTHY VIRGINIA, investment company executive; b. Milw., Sept. 22, 1929; d. Carl Arndt and Loretta Louise Laura (Bremer) Scherer; m. Glenn Charles Petersen, Aug. 27, 1949; children: Vicki Lynn Taylor, Larry Dean, Rick Randall. BS magna cum laude, U. Wis.-Parkside, 1975. Repair dept. clk. Eastman Kodak Co., Milw., 1946—47; sec. First Wis. Trust Co., Milw., 1947—49; head sec. art edn. dept. U. Wis., Madison, 1949—50; sec. and asst. Red Star Yeast Co., Milw., 1950—51; exec. sec. Boy Scouts Am., Milw., 1963—65, Applied Power, Pewaukee, Wis., 1965—67; sec., treas. Westshore Muffler Shops, Milw., 1983—2002; asst. sec., treas. Fastrack, Inc., Mequon, Wis., 2002—. Paintings (Honorable Mention, Wis. Art Show, Twin Lakes, 1976). Head fund drive Town of Greenfield ARC, 1956, helper fund drive, 1955, helper fund, 1957—59; leader Girl Scouts Am., Wauwatosa, Wis., 1960—61; cub pack sec. Boy Scouts Am., Wauwatosa, 1962—63; children's class tchr. Baha'i World Faith, Greenfield, Milw., Burlington, 1959—72, spkr. Milw., Burlington, 1970—99; mem. Baha'i Faith. Mem.: Order Ea. Star (Wauwatosa chpt. 219). Avocations: day trading, genealogy, reading, photography, miniature poodles. Personal E-mail: dvpetersen29@hotmail.com.

PETERSEN, FREDERICK J., lawyer; b. 1975; Grad., Gonzaga U.; degree in law, U. Ariz. Atty. Mesch, Clark & Rothschild, 1999—. Bd. mem. Greater Tucson Leadership; mem. Vol. Lawyers Prog., Southern Ariz. Legal Aid; former pres. Handidogs Inc. Mem. Lawyers for Literacy. Named one of 40 Under 40, Tucson Bus. Edge, 2006. Mem.: Pima County Bar Assn. Young Lawyers Divsn. Office: Mesch, Clark & Rothschild 259 N Meyer Ave Tucson AZ 85701 Office Phone: 520-624-8886. Office Fax: 520-798-1037.

PETERSEN, JAMES L., lawyer; b. Bloomington, Ill., Feb. 3, 1947; s. Eugene and Cathryn Theresa (Hemmele) P.; m. Helen Louise Moser, Nov. 20, 1971; children: Christine Louise, Margaret Theresa. BA, Ill. State U., 1970; MA, U. Ill., Springfield, 1973; JD magna cum laude, Ind. U., 1976. Bar; Ind. 1976, Fla. 1980, U.S. Dist. Cts. (no. and so. Ind.), U.S. Ct. Appeals (7th cir.), U.S. Supreme Ct. Admissions officer U. Ill., Springfield, 1970-71, asst. to v.p., 1971-72, registrar, 1972-73; assoc. Ice Miller, Indpls., 1976-83, ptnr., 1983—. Pres. United Cerebral Palsy of Ctrl. Ind., 1981-83, pres. Found., 1988-90, Stanley K. Lacy Leadership Series participant. Mem. ABA, Fla. Bar Assn., Ind. Bar Assn., Am. Coll. Trial Lawyers, Intl. Franchise Assn. (bd. mem. Symposium Organizing Cmte., 2003-04), Defense Trial Coun. Ind. (past co-chair, Prods. Liability Cmte; elected 1997 Diplomat), The Business Council, Inc., Ill. State U. Alumni Assn. (pres. 1990-92), Ind. U. Law Alumni Assn. (bd. dirs. 1992—, pres. 1998-99), Ind. U. Bd. Visitors 1998-99, Order of Coif. Home: 11827 Sea Star Dr Indianapolis IN 46256-9400 Office: Ice Miller LLP PO Box 82001 One American Sq Indianapolis IN 46282 Office Phone: 317-236-2308.

PETERSEN, JEAN SNYDER, educational association administrator; b. NYC, Oct. 16, 1931; d. Peter Eugene and Helyn Brownell (Parker) Snyder; m. Elton Reed Petersen, Sept. 16, 1954; children— Bruce Brownell, Craig Reed. Student, N.Y. U., 1949-51; degree fgn. banking, Am. Inst. Banking, 1952. Fgn. credit investigator Chase Nat. Bank Hdqrs., NYC, 1952-56; nat. exec. dir. Assn. Children and Adults with Learning Disabilities (name changed to Learning Disabilities Assn. of Am.), Pitts., 1972—. Mem. exec. com., treas. Jr. League, Pitts.; bd. dirs. Found. for Children with Learning Disabilities, N.Y.C., Children's Hosp., Pitts., Music for Mt. Lebanon, Vocat. Rehab. Ctr., Pitts.; bd. dirs., v.p., mem. exec. com. Assn. Retarded Citizens Pa.; ptnr. UN Internat. Yr. of Disabled; ruling elder Presbyn. Ch.Assn. Retarded Citizens Pa.; mem. exec. com. Pat Buckley Moss Nat. Children's Charity Found; chmn. bd. dirs. Masonic Learning Ctrs. for Children. Recipient Sustainers award Jr. League, 1977, Recognition award, 1975, Pres.'s award, 1978. Mem. AAUW, Meeting Planners Internat. (treas.), Am. Soc. Assn. Execs. Republican. Presbyterian. Office: 4156 Library Rd Pittsburgh PA 15234-1349

PETERSEN, JOHN D., academic administrator; m. Carol Petersen; 2 children. BS in Chemistry, UCLA, 1970; PhD in Inorganic Chemistry, U. Calif., Santa Barbara, 1975. Asst. prof. chemistry Kans. State U., 1975—80; head dept. chemistry, assoc. dean rsch. Coll. Scis. Clemson U., 1980—93; prof. chemistry, dean Coll. Sci. Wayne State U., 1994—2000; provost, exec. v.p. univ. affairs U. Conn., Storrs, 2000—04; pres., CEO U. Tenn. Sys., Knoxville, Tenn., 2004—. Mem.: Nat. Assn. State Univ. and Land Grant Coll. (exec. com. for chief academic officers), Coun. Chem. Rsch., Am. Chem. Soc. Office: U Tenn Office of Pres 800 Andy Holt Tower Knoxville TN 37996-0180 Office Phone: 865-974-2241. Office Fax: 865-974-3753. *

PETERSEN, JONATHAN CHRISTIAN, elementary school educator, music educator; s. Gary W. and Joanne Petersen; m. Katie Lewis Petersen, July 10, 2004. MusB, Lawrence U., Appleton, Wisc., 2003. Cert. tchr. DPI, Wis., 2004. Tchr. music Kettle Moraine Mid. Sch., Dousman, Wis., 2003—. Musician bass sect. Oshkosh Symphony Orch., Wis., 2003—. Recipient Instrumental Music Excellence cert., Milw. Civic Music Assn., 2005. Mem.: Wis. ASTA (assoc.). Office: Kettle Moraine Middle School 301 Ottawa Ave Dousman WI 53118 Home Phone: 920-205-1437; Office Phone: 262-965-6500 2209.

PETERSEN, MARTIN EUGENE, curator; b. Grafton, Iowa, Apr. 21, 1931; s. Martin S. and Martha Dorothea (Paulsen) P. AA, Mason City Jr. Coll., Iowa; BA, State U. Iowa, 1951, MA, 1957; postgrad., The Hague (Netherlands), 1964. Curator San Diego Mus. Art, 1957-96; advisor Olaf Wieghorst Mus., El Cajon, Calif., 1996—. Extension instr. U. Calif., 1958, lectr., 1960 Author art catalogues, books, articles in field. Served with AUS, 1952-54. Mem. So. Calif. Art Historians. Achievements include specialist in early southern California art. Home: 2003 Bayview Heights Dr Spc 138 San Diego CA 92105-5537

PETERSEN, ROLAND, artist, printmaker; b. Endelave, Horsens, Denmark, 1926; came to US, 1928; m. Caryl Ritter, Mar. 4, 2003; children from previous marriage: Dana Mark, Maura Brooke, Julien Conrad, Karena Caia. BA, U. Calif., Berkeley, 1949, MA, 1950; postgrad., Han Hofmann's Sch. Fine Arts, 1950-51, S.W. Hayter's Atelier 17, Paris, 1950, 63, 70, Islington Studio, London, 1976, The Print Workshop, 1980. Tchr. State Coll. Wash., Pullman, 1952-56; faculty U. Calif., Davis, 1956-91, prof. art, 1991; ret., 1991. Exhibited one-man shows: Oakland At Mus., 1954, Calif. Palace Legion of Honor, San Francisco, 1961, Gump's Gallery, San Francisco, 1962, Staempfli Gallery, N.Y.C., 1963, 65, 67, Adele Bednarz Gallery, Los Angeles, 1966, 69, 70, 72, 73, 75, 76, Crocker Art Gallery, Sacramento, 1965, de Young Mus., San Francisco, 1968, La Jolla Mus., 1971, Phoenix Mus., 1972, Santa Barbara Mus., 1973, USIS sponsored touring one-man exhbn., Turkey, U. Reading, Eng., 1977, 80, U. Calif., Davis, 1978, 92, Brubaker Gallery, Sarasota, Fla., 1979, Rorick Gallery, San Francisco, 1981, 82, 83, 84, 85, Himovitz-Salomon Gallery, Sacramento, 1987-88, 91, Vanderwoude Tananbaum Gallery, N.Y.C., 1987-89, Harcourts Gallery, San Francisco, 1989, 91, 93, U. Calif., Davis, 1992, Maxwell Galleries, San Francisco, 1995, Endelave (Denmark) Mus., 1996, John Natsoulas Gallery, Davis, Calif., 1998, Hackett-Freedman Gallery, San Francisco, 2002, 2004; group shows include Calif. Palace Legion of Honor, San Francisco Art Inst., 1962, Mus. Art, Carnegie Inst., Pitts., 1964, Obelisk Gallery, Washington, John Herron Art Inst., Indpls., 1964, Pa. Acad. Fine Arts, Phila., Crocker Art Gallery, Sacramento, 1965, 81, Art Inst. Chgo., 1965, Va. Mus. Fine Arts, Richmond, 1966, U. Ariz. Art Gallery, Tucson, 1967, Am. Cultural Center, Paris, 1971, Nat. Gallery, Washington, 1972, Otis Art Inst. Gallery, Los Angeles, 1974, Auerbach Fine Art Gallery, London, 1977, U. Wis., Madison, 1977, Bklyn. Mus., 1978, U. Ill., 1978, U. Nev., Las Vegas, 1980, Brubaker Gallery, Sarasota, Fla., 1983, U.S.A. World Print Council, San Francisco, Nat. Mus., Singapore, Nat. Gallery, Bangkok, Thailand, Amerika Haus, Berlin, Malmo Konsthall, Sweden, Museo Carrillo Gil, Mexico City, all 1984-86, Crocker Art Mus., 1991, Fresno Met. Mus., 1992, Hall of Pictures, Uman, Russia, 1992, Calif. State U., L.A., 1992, San Bernardino, 1993 Pence Gallery, Davis, Calif., 1993, Artists Contemporary Gallery, Sacramento, 1994, Andre Milan Gallery, Sao Paulo, Brazil, 1995; represented in permanent collections: de Young Mus., San Francisco, San Francisco Mus. Modern Art, Va. Mus. Fine Arts, Richmond, Mus. Modern Art, N.Y.C., Phila. Mus. Art, Whitney Mus. Am. Art, Phoenix Mus., Santa Barbara Mus., Musée Municipal, Brest, France, Smithsonian Instn. Nat. Collection Fine Arts & Archives of Am. Art, Hirschorn Coll., Washington, San Jose Mus. Art, Calif., others. With USN, 1944-46, PTO. Guggenheim fellow, 1963, U. Calif. creative arts fellow, 1967, 70, 77; Fulbright grant, 1970. Mem. AAUP, San Francisco Art Assn., Calif. Soc. Printmakers. Home: 1148 Crespi Dr Pacifica CA 94044-3539 Office: Hackett Freedman Gallery 250 Sutter St Fl 4 San Francisco CA 94108 Office Phone: 415-362-7152.

PETERSEN, ULRICH, geology educator; b. Negritos, Peru, Dec. 1, 1927; s. Georg and Harriet (Bluhme) P.; m. Edith Martensen, Apr. 27, 1952 (dec. Aug. 1978); children: Erich, Armin (dec.), Heidi.; m. Eileen Bourque, June 19, 1982. Mining Engr., Escuela Nacional de Ingenieros, Lima, Peru, 1954; MA, Harvard U., 1955, PhD, 1963. Geologist Instituto Geológico del Peru and Instituto Nacional de Investigación y Fomento Mineros, 1946-51; geologist Cerro de Pasco Corp., Peru, 1951-54, asst. chief geologist, 1956-57, chief geologist, 1958-63; lectr. Harvard, 1963-66; assoc. prof. Harvard U., 1966-69, prof. mining geology, 1969-81, Harry C. Dudley prof. econ. geology, 1981-95; cons. geologist, 1963—; prof. emeritus, 1996—. Named Knight Comdr. Merit Order Disting. Svcs., Peru, 1968;

recipient A. von Humboldt rsch. award, 1992-93, 2003-04; Merit award Colegio de Ingenioros del Peru, 2000, Torch Habich award U. Nacional de Ingenieria del Peru, 2005; named Engr. of Yr., Soc. de Ingenieros del Peru, 1996. Mem. Soc. Econ. Geologists (pres. 1988-89), Geol. Soc. Am., Soc. Geologica del Peru (hon.) Home: 414 Marsh St Belmont MA 02478-1109 Office: 20 Oxford St Cambridge MA 02138-2902 E-mail: ulrichp@aol.com.

PETERSEN-FREY, ROLAND, manufacturing executive; b. Hamburg, Germany, Aug. 17, 1937; arrived in U.S., 1958; s. Georg and Erna (Coltzau) Petersen-Frey; m. Pamela Susan Mobley, Feb. 2, 1993; children: Martin, Anya, Daniel. BA in Fin., CUNY, 1967, MA in Fin., 1970. Asst. v.p. Mfrs. Hanover, NYC, 1961-70; v.p. gen. mgr. Rusch Inc., NYC, 1970-75; CEO, chmn. bd. dirs. Inmed Corp., Atlanta, 1975-89; chmn. bd. dirs. Burrellco, Inc., Atlanta, 1989-90; pres., chmn., CEO A4, Inc., Atlanta, 1997—; pres., CEO The Ga. Contractor LLC. Bd. dirs. Albert Int; chmn. bd. dirs. A4, Inc; mng. ptnr. Bunter Holdings Ltd, Atlanta, chmn. bd. dirs.; bd. dirs. Albert Holdings USA, Inc., Canton, Ga., v.p.; chmn. TGC Pub., LLC. With US Army, 1959—61. Fellow: Inst Dirs. Republican. Avocations: tennis, hiking, swimming. Office Phone: 770-521-8877. Business E-Mail: r.frey@a4inc.com.

PETERSON, ANDREA, elementary school educator; b. BC, Canada; d. Victor and Darlene Rahn; m. Joel Peterson. BA in Music Edn., U. Wash., 1996. Cert. in early and mid. childhood music Nat. Bd. Tchg. Standards, 2002. Music tchr. to elem. music specialist Monte Cristo Elem. Sch., Granite Falls, Wash., 1997—. Named Wash. Tchr. of Yr., Coun. Chief State Sch. Officers, 2007, Nat. Tchr. of Yr., 2007. Avocations: saxophone, singing (mezzo soprano). Office: Monte Cristo Elem Sch 1201 100th St NE Granite Falls WA 98252 Business E-Mail: apeterso@gfalls.wednet.edu.

PETERSON, ANN SULLIVAN, physician, consultant; b. Rhinebeck, NY, Oct. 11, 1928; AB, Cornell U., 1950, MD, 1954; MS, MIT, 1980. Diplomate Am. Bd. Internal Medicine. Intern Cornell Med. Divsn.-Bellevue Hosp., NYC, 1954—55, resident, 1955—57; fellow in medicine and physiology Meml.-Sloan Kettering Cancer Ctr., Cornell Med. Coll., NYC, 1957—60; instr. medicine Georgetown U. Sch. Medicine, Washington, 1962—65, asst. prof., 1965—69, asst. dir. clin. rsch. unit, 1962—69; assoc. prof. medicine U. Ill., Chgo., 1969—72, asst. dean, 1969—71, assoc. dean, 1971—72; assoc. prof. medicine, assoc. dean Coll. Physicians and Surgeons, Columbia U., NYC, 1972—80, Cornell U. Med. Coll., NYC, 1980—83; assoc. dir. divsn. med. edn. AMA, Chgo., 1983—86, dir. div. grad. med. edn., 1986—89, v.p. mgmt. cons. corp., 1989—93; ind. cons. Chgo., 1993—2005. Contbr. articles to med. jours. Mem. bd. regents Uniformed Svcs. U. of Health Scis., 1984—90. John and Mary R. Markle scholar, 1965—70, Alfred P. Sloan fellow, MIT, 1979—80. Fellow: ACP; mem.: Mortar Bd., Alpha Omega Alpha, Alpha Epsilon Delta.

PETERSON, ANNE ELIZABETH WALLACE, music educator, composer; b. Aurora, Ill., June 17, 1949; d. Vernon Ammon and Marjorie Lois (Loudon) Wallace; m. Thomas Leonard Peterson (dec. 1990); m. Tim Allen Gasser, Feb. 27, 1993. Attended, Macphail Sch. Music, 1964—67, San Francisco Conservatory Music, 1974—77, U. Edinburgh, 1979, Baroque Performance Inst., 1992; studied with Martha Ivory, 1970, studied with Charlene Brendler, 1978; BA in English and Music, U. Minn., 1971; MA in Music, Lone Mountain Coll., 1978; studied harpsichord, with Laurette Goldberg, 1974—78; studied harpsichord with Peter Williams. Cert. in Tech. Writing De Anza Coll., Cupertino, Calif., 1981. Music tchr. Pillsbury-Waite Cultural Arts Ctr., Mpls., 1971—72, Music Sch., Sunnyvale, Calif., 1991—; tech. writer, editor, rschr. SRI Internat., Menlo Park, Calif., 1973—90. Music tchr. Cmty. Sch. Music and Arts, Mountain View, Calif., 1973—78, Mountain View, 1979—2001; harpsichord performer No. Calif. Renaissance Faire, 1979—85, Minn. Renaissance Festival, 1982; mem. Soc. Tech. Communication, 1979—90, conv. spkr., 1983; keyboard gen. music instr. Boys' and Girls' Club, Redwood City, Calif., 1990—92; pvt. piano and harpsichord tchr., Redwood City, 1980—; musician, Palo Alto, San Francisco, Calif.; conf. workshop presenter in field. Author: (book) Harpsichord Tuning: An Easy Start, 1978, (book, CD) Follow the Rainbow, 2003; composer: (children's book and CD) 4 Cats, 2006, 3 Cats and a Dog, 2007; musician (harpsichordist): (albums) Then, 1997, Harpsichord at Hampstead, 1999, Starspirations, 2000; musician: Good Company (with Tudor Rose Ensemble), 1997; musician: (harpsichordist) Come and Adore! (Christmas-variety) Starspirations, 1999; musician: (harpsichordist, ensemblist, vocalist) Elizabeth Gambarini, 2000, Cougar Love, 2005. Mem.: Music Tchrs. Assn. (Appreciation award 2000), Music Tchrs. Assn. Calif. (program chair 2000—01), Toastmasters Internat. (Achievement award 1989), Phi Beta (pres. Pi Lambda chpt. 1993—95, program chair 1974—85, 2002—03, Grad. Grant-In Aid award, Marie Logan award 1979, Nat. Historian award 2004). Office Phone: 650-365-5375. Personal E-mail: awpgmusic@yahoo.com.

PETERSON, ARTHUR LAVERNE, foundation administrator; b. Glyndon, Minn., June 27, 1926; s. John M. and Hilda C. (Moline) P.; m. Connie Lucille Harr, June 14, 1952 (dec. July 26, 2002); children: Jon Martin, Rebecca Ruth, Donna Harr, Ingrid Bliss; m. Mary Kinum, Sept. 12, 2003. AB, Yale U., 1947; MSPA, U. So. Calif., 1949; postgrad., U. Chgo., 1949-50; PhD, U. Minn., 1962; LLD, Lebanon Valley Coll., 1988. Mem. Wis. State Legislature, 1951-55; from instr. to asst. prof. polit. sci. U. Wis., Eau Claire, 1954-60; assoc. prof. to prof. polit. sci. Ohio Wesleyan U., Delaware, 1961-65, 70-80; pres. Am. Grad. Sch. Internat. Mgmt., Phoenix, 1966-70; dean spl. programs Eckerd Coll., St. Petersburg, Fla., 1980-84, dir. Acad. Sr. Profls., 1987-94; pres. Lebanon Valley Coll., Annville, Pa., 1984-87; pres., CEO Ctr. for the Study of the Presidency, 1997-99; Scott prof. leadership Rocky Mountain Coll., Billings, Mont., 1999—2002; mem. Mont. Ho. Reps., 2001—; pres. Thomas Wathen Found. Acad., Riverside, Calif., 2002—. Bd. dirs. Arnold Industries; asst. to chmn. Rep. Nat. Com., Washington, 1960-61; founding dir. Ctr. Internat. Bus., L.A., 1969-70; cons. Novin Inst. Polit. Affairs, Tehran, Iran, 1973; exec. dir. Fla. Assn. Colls. and Univs., 1988—. Author: McCarthyism: Ideology and Foundations, 1962; co-author: Electing the President, 1968; contbr. articles to profl. jours. Chmn. Ohio Civil Rights Commn., 1963-65; dep. chmn. Republican Nat. Com., 1965-66; mem. Ohio Ethics Commn., 1976-80. Capt. USMC, 1951-52, Korea Citizenship Clearing House Nat. Faculty fellow, 1960; recipient citation for excellence Sigma Phi Epsilon, 1977, Marshall award Ohio Wesleyan Students, 1979. Mem. Am. Polit. Sci. Assn., Am. Judicature Soc. (dir. 1975—), Soc. Polit. Enquiries (pres. 1985—), Acad. Polit. Sci., Rotary, Masons, Pi Sigma Alpha (dir. 1972—), Phi Mu Alpha Sinfonia, Omicron Delta Kappa Republican. Mem. United Ch. of Christ. Avocations: sailing, flying, music. Home: 26555 Chambers Ave Sun City CA 92586-2132 Office: Wathen Found 4130 Minner Ave Riverside CA 92509 E-mail: apeter333@aol.com. *Give the most you can give, of what you are and what you believe, both talent and treasure - where you are - now!.*

PETERSON, BART, mayor; b. June 15, 1958; m. Amy Minick; 1 child, Meg. Grad., Purdue U., 1980; JD, U. Mich., 1983. Atty. Ice Miller Donadio & Ryan, Indpls.; from exec. asst. for environ. affairs to chief of staff Ind. Gov. Evan Bayh, 1989-95; pres. and co-founder Precedent Cos., 1995; mayor City Indpls., 2000—. Bd. mem. Ind. Nature Conservancy, Regenstrief Found. Office: 2501 City-County Bldg 200 E Washington St Indianapolis IN 46204-3307 Office Phone: 317-327-4622, 317-327-3601. Office Fax: 317-327-3980. E-mail: mayor@indygov.org. *

PETERSON, BETTY W., language educator, writer; b. Phil, Ky., Nov. 15, 1944; d. James Delno Withers and Mae Berniece Withers (Luttrell) Emerson, Glen Emerson (Stepfather); m. Danny F. Peterson, Aug. 11, 1962; children: Angela Yvette Jones, Alisa Yvonne Noritis, Brenton Franklin, Danny Keith. BA English high distinction, U. Ky., Lexington, 1982, MA English, 1986. Instrnl. specialist Somerset C.C., Ky., 1986—89, asst. prof. English, 1989—91, assoc. prof. English with tenure, 1991—2000; prof. English Somerset Cmty. and Tech. Coll., 2000—, tchg. cons., 2006—. Co-editor Ky. writing Somerset C.C., 1989—94, tchg. cons., 2006—. Contbr. articles short stories and poems to profl. jours.;, author plays. Tchr. Gov.'s Scholars Program No. Ky. U., 1996. Named to Who's Who Among Am. Tchrs., 2002, 2005, 2006; recipient Oswald Rsch. and Creativity Award, U. Ky., 1981, Dantzler-Dantzler Acad. Achievement award, 1982, Tchg. Assistantship, U. Ky., 1984—86, Commd. Ky. Col., Hon. Order Ky. Cols., 1996, NISOD Tchg. Excellence Award, Somerset C.C., 2001; scholar, U. Ky. Alumni Assn., 1976—77; Va. Ctr. for Creative Arts Fellow, Ky. Found. for Women, 1993, Al Smith fellow, Ky. Arts Coun., 2007. Mem.: Dramatists Guild Am., Inc. (assoc.), U. Ky. Alumni Assn., Jesse Stuart Found. Independent. Roman Catholic. Avocations: writing, reading, aerobics, theater, guitar.

PETERSON, BRUCE D., lawyer, energy executive; b. Chgo., Nov. 1956; BA, North Park Coll., 1978; JD, U. Notre Dame Law Sch., 1982. Fgn. svc. officer US State Dept., Washington, 1982; ptnr. Hunton & Williams, Washington, 1989—2002; sr. v.p., gen. counsel DTE Energy Co., Detroit, 2002—05. Mem. legal com. Am. Gas Assn., Edison Electric Inst. Bd. dirs. Detroit Symphony Orch.; trustee Cranbrook Ednl. Cmty.; bd. govs. Cranbrook Inst. Sci. *

PETERSON, CARL ERIC, metal products executive, banker; b. Wareham, Mass., Apr. 8, 1944; m. Frances Harkness, Sept. 7, 1966; children: Robin, Alec Harkness. BA, Brown U., 1966; MA, U. Pa., 1971. With R.I. Hosp. Trust Nat. Bank, Providence, 1971-82; with Engelhard Corp., Iselin, NJ, 1982-85, Dryvit System, Inc., West Warwick, RI, 1986, Gerald Metals, Inc., Stamford, Conn., 1987—2002. Mem. corp. Woods Hole Oceanographic Instn., 1981—92, 2004—, trustee, 2005—; pres. Woods Hole Oceanographic Inst. Assocs., 2005—. With USN, 1967—70. Mem.: NY Yacht Club.

PETERSON, CHARLES HAYES, lawyer; b. St. Louis, May 8, 1938; s. Edmund Herbert and Dorothy Marie (Brennan) P.; m. Auli Irene Ahonen, Nov. 28, 1981; children: Mika, Charles, Michael, Katja. BS, U.S. Naval Acad., 1960; MBA, Stanford U., 1971, JD, 1974. Commd. midshipman USN, 1956, advanced through grades to capt., resigned, 1969; with USNR, 1969-89, ret., 1998; counsel Gen. Electric, San Jose, Calif., 1973-79; divsn. counsel Syracuse, NY, 1980-83; v.p. COGEMA, Inc., Washington, 1983-87; pres. NUEXCO Trading Co., Washington, 1987-95; of counsel Morgan, Lewis & Bockius, LLP, 1995—2001; ptnr. Pillsbury Winthrop Shaw Pittman, Washington, 2001—. Recipient Meritorious Service medal State of Calif., 1986. Mem. Calif. Bar Assn., Washington DC Bar Assn. Lutheran. Office: Pillsbury Winthrop Shaw Pittman 2300 N'St NW Washington DC 20037 Office Phone: 202-663-8083. Office Fax: 202-663-8007.

PETERSON, CHARLES MARQUIS, medical educator; b. NYC, Mar. 8, 1943; s. Charles William and Elisabeth (Marquis) P.; m. Karen Pielop, Dec. 26, 1996; children: Caroline, Elisabeth, Christopher. BA in cum laude, Carleton Coll., 1965; MD, Columbia Coll., 1969; MBA, U. Calif., Irvine, 2000. Intern Harlem Hosp., NYC, 1969-70, resident, 1970-73, chief resident, 1972-73; guest investigator, asst. physician Rockefeller U., NYC, 1971-73, assoc. physician, 1973-78, asst. prof., 1973-78, assoc. prof., 1978-84; clin. prof. medicine U. So. Calif., LA, 1985-98; program dir. blood diseases program Nat. Heart, Lung and Blood Inst., NIH, Bethesda, Md., 1998—. Vis. clin. fellow Columbia Coll. Physicians and Surgeons, 1970-73; asst. vis. physician Harlem Hosp., 1973-84; cons. pediatrics Cornell U. Med. Ctr., 1975-84; assoc. attending medicine Beth Israel Med. Ctr., 1976-84; lectr. Mt. Sinai Sch. Medicine, 1977—; adj. assoc. prof. dept. medicine Cornell U. Med. Ctr., 980-84; assoc. attending physician dept. medicine N.Y. Hosp., 1980-84; attending physician in medicine Cottage Hosp., Santa Barbara, Calif., 1984-98; dir. rsch., med. dir. Sansum Med. Rsch. Found., 1984-96, sr. scientist, 1997-98; dir. diabetes Endocrine Clinic, Santa Barbara County, 1989-98; CEO, Sansum Med. Rsch. Found., 1995-96; program dir. Blood Diseases Program Nat. Heart Lung Blood Inst., NIH, 1998-2000, acting dir. and dir. divsn. blood diseases and resorces, 2000—. Author: Self Monitoring of Blood Glucose: A Physician's Guide, 1981, Take Charge of Your Diabetes, 1982, Diabetes Management in the 80's, 1982; co-author: The Diabetes Self-Care Method, 1990, A Touch of Diabetes, 1991, Vivere con il Diabete, 1992, and many others; mem. editorial bd. Diabetes Care, 1980-84, Diabetes in the News, 1985—, Diabetes News Bureau, 1985—, Diabetes Profl., editor-in-chief, 1988-91, Diabetic Nephropathy/Jour. of Diabetic Complications, 1982-91; contbr. numerous articles to Prensa Medica, Jour. Lab. and Clin. Medicine, New England Jour. Medicine, Annals of Internal Medicine, Archives of Neurology, Blood, Jour. Nat. Med. Assn., Am. Jour. Obstetrics and Gynecology, many others. Mem. med. adv. bd. Cooley's Anemia Vols., 1975-84; bd. mem. Diabetes Control Found., 1980-88; dir. Diabetes Self Care Program, 1978-84, med. dir., 1981-84; bd. mem. Leake and Watts, 1978-84, Gifts for Life, 1986-89; bd. dirs. Sports Tng. Inst., 1984-86, others. Fellow ACP; mem. AAAS, Am. Chem. Soc., Am. Diabetes Assn., Am. Fedn. Clin. Rsch., Am. Med. Writers Assn., Am. Soc. Clin. Investigation, Am. Soc. Hematology, Am. Soc. Pharmacology and Experimental Therapeutics, Coun. Biology Editors, Diabetes and Pregnancy Study Group West (founder), N.Y. Acad. Scis., Rsch. Soc. Alcoholism, Soc. Experimental Medicine and Biology, Am. Med. Writers Assn., Am. Diabetes Assn. (founding bd. mem. Santa Barbara chpt. 1988-98, pres. 1991-92), Sigma Xi. Office: 6701 Rockledge Dr # 7950 Bethesda MD 20817-1813

PETERSON, CLARK C., announcer, writer, poet, speaker; b. Pine City, Minn., Dec. 27, 1947; s. Carl A. and Bernice C. Peterson. AA, U. Minn., 1967, B Econs., 1969; PhD in Bibl. Studies, Grace Bible Coll., Morrisville, NC, 2004. Announcer Sta. KOLM/KWWK Radio, Rochester, Minn., 1974-84; pub. affairs specialist US Army, Fort Sill, 1985—86, Oklahoma City, 1986—97; corr. Pro Wrestling Illustrated Mag., 1992-97, Wrestling Tribune, 1993—2004; announcer, writer Power Zone Wresting Fedn., Oklahoma City, 1992-97, New Mid-South Wrestling Fedn., Oklahoma City, 1998—2002, New Mid-South Wrestling Alliance, 2002—06, All-Am. Championship Wrestling, 2007—; host weekly pro wrestling radio talk show "The Three Count" aired throughout one-half of continental U.S., 2001. Parade announcer Mora's (Minn.) Centennial, 1982; announcer Richards-Gebaur AFB Open House, Kansas City, Mo., 1973, Nat. Drum and Bugle Corps Contest, Stillwater, Minn., early 1980's; announcer, entertainment Rochester's (Minn.) 125th Anniversary, 1983; announcer, writer, entertainment, flags & decorations Korn & Klover Karnival, Hinckley, Minn., 1973-87, 90-91, 2005-06; judge Miss Teen Minn. Pageant, St. Paul, 1984, Miss Minn. & Miss Teen. Minn. Internat. Pageants, St. Cloud, 2007. Author: The Great Hinckley Fire, 1978, Blasted Unto a Pile of Rubble, 1995, Blasted Onto a Pile of Rubble, Surviving the Oklahoma City bombing and its controversies, 2006, The Devouring Rages of Fire, the two most terrifying forest fires in North American History, 2006, Outdoor Christmas Lighting Spectaculars, 2007; co-author: In Their Name, 1995, We Will Never Forget, 1996, Forever Changed, 1998, Outdoor Christmas Lighting Spectaculars, 2007, Hinckley's Classic Celebrations, 2007; contbg. author: Wrestling Title Histories, 2000. Mem., survivor Apr. 19, 1995 Oklahoma City Bombing, Family and Survivors United, 1995—; bd. dirs. Grace Bible Coll., Morrisville, NC, 2002—; Served with USAF, 1970-74. Recipient Best Coverage of a Local Story in the U.S., AP, 1978, Civil Svc. Achievement medal U.S. Army, 1997, 14 New Idea/Suggestion awards (one of the highest numbers in U.S. Civil Svc.), 1997; co-recipient Best Advt. and Pub. Affairs Office U.S. Army Recruiting Command, 1989; named #2 Broadcast Journalist of Yr.-Civilian U.S. Army Training and Doctrine Command, 1985, among 25 winners Turner Broadcasting's Nationwide Wrestling Announcing Contest, 1992; inducted into Profl. Wrestling's Wall of Fame, 1998; scholarship Grace Bible Coll., 2003. Avocations: outdoor Christmas lighting displays, state, territorial, and city flag collections, coin collecting/numismatics.

PETERSON, COLLIN C., congressman; b. Fargo, ND, June 29, 1944; children: Sean, Jason, Elliott. BA in Bus. Adminstrn. and Acctg., Moorhead State U., 1966. CPA Minn. Senator State of Minn., 1976-86; mem. US Congress from 7th Minn. dist., 1991—; mem. agrl. com., subcoms. gen. farm commodities, specialty crops and natural resources, livestock, environ. credit and rural devel.; mem. permanent select Com. Intelligence, 2001—; mem. govt. ops. com., chmn. subcom. employment housing and aviation; mem. resource conservation com., rsch. and forestry subcom., livestock, dairy and poultry subcom., govt. reform and oversight com.; nat. econ. growth com., nat. resources and regulatory affairs com.-ranking minority mem., vet. affairs com. With U.S. Army N.G., 1963-69. Mem. Am. Legion, Ducks Unltd., Elks, Sportsmen's Club, Rural Caucus, Mainstream Forum, Cormorant Lakes Sportsmen Club, Congl. Sportsmen's Caucus, Mainstream Forum, Congl. Rural Caucus. Democrat. Office: US Ho Reps 2159 Rayburn Ho Office Bldg Washington DC 20515-2307 also: Lake Ave Plaza Bldg Ste 107 714 Lake Ave Detroit Lakes MN 56501 *

PETERSON, COURTLAND HARRY, law educator; b. Denver, June 28, 1930; s. Harry James and Courtney (Caple) P.; m. Susan Schwab, Gisvold, Jan. 28, 1966; children: Brooke, Linda, Patrick. BA, U. Colo., 1951, LLB, 1953; MCL, U. Chgo., 1959; JD, U. Freiburg, Germany, 1964. Bar: Colo. 1953. Mem. faculty U. Colo. Law Sch., 1959—, prof., 1963—, dean, 1974-79, Nicholas Rosenbaum prof., 1991-94, Nicholas Doman prof. emeritus, 1995—. Vis. prof. UCLA Law Sch., 1965, Max Planck Inst., Hamburg, Germany, 1969-70, U. Tex. Law Sch., Austin, 1973-74, Summer Program, Tulane U., Rodos, Greece, 1993, Summer Program, La. State U., Aix-en-Provence, France, 1996; bd. dirs. Continuing Legal Edn. in Colo., 1974-77. Author: Die Anerkennung Auslaendischer Urteile, 1964; Translator: (Bauer) An Introduction to German Law, 1965. Served to 1st lt. USAF, 1954-56. Fgn. Law fellow U. Chgo., 1957-59; Ford Found. Law Faculty fellow, 1964; Alexander von Humboldt Stiftung fellow, 1969-70. Mem. ABA, Colo. Bar Assn. (bd. govs. 1974-79), Boulder County Bar Assn., Am. Soc. Comparative Law (dir., bd. editors, treas. 1978-89, hon. pres. 1996-98), Internat. Acad. Comparative Law, Am. Law Inst., Boulder County Bar Found. (trustee 1995-2000), U. Colo. Ret. Faculty Assn. (pres. 1998-2000). Home: 4135 Caddo Pky Boulder CO 80303 Office: U Colo Law Sch Boulder CO 80309-0001 Personal E-mail: courtpeterson@comcast.net.

PETERSON, DAVID C., lawyer; b. 1970; BS in Materials Sci. and Engring., U. Minn. Inst. Tech., 1993; JD, U. Minn., 2000. Bar: Minn. 2000. With intellectual property dept. Toro Co.; engr. Hutchinson Tech., Inc.; lawyer Schwegman, Lundberg, Woessner & Kluth, P.A., Mpls. Named a Rising Star, Minn. Super Lawyers mag., 2006. Mem.: Minn. Intellectual Property Law Assn. (chair by-laws com.), Am. Intellectual Property Law Assn. Office: Schwegman Lundberg Woessner & Kluth PA 1600 TCF Tower 121 S 8th St Minneapolis MN 55402 Office Phone: 612-373-6944. E-mail: dpeterson@slwk.com. *

PETERSON, DAVID FREDERICK, retired government agency administrator; b. Washington, Apr. 4, 1937; s. Victor Henry and Alice Augusta (Vogle) P.; m. Laurie A. Cadigan, June 11, 1988. AB, Harvard U., 1959; LL.B., Cornell U., 1962. Bar: D.C. 1963. With Metromedia Inc., NYC and Los Angeles, 1963—70; exec. dir. consumer info. ctr. GSA, Washington, 1970—76, dir. consumer affairs, 1976—82, assoc. archivist for mgmt. Nat. Archives and Records Service, 1982—83; asst. archivist for Fed. Records Ctrs. Nat. Archives and Records Adminstrn., Washington, 1983—96; asst. archivist Presdl. Librs., 1996—2001; ret., 2001. Served with U.S. Army, 1963 Home: 2730 NE Sewalls Landing Way Jensen Beach FL 34957

PETERSON, DAVID MAURICE, retired physiologist; b. Woodward, Okla., July 3, 1940; s. Maurice Llewellyn and Katharine Anne (Jones) P.; m. Margaret Ingegerd Sundberg, June 18, 1965; children: Mark David, Elise Marie. BS, U. Calif., Davis, 1962; MS, U. Ill., 1964; PhD, Harvard U., 1968. Rsch. biologist Allied Chem. Corp., Morristown, NJ, 1970-71; plant physiologist U.S. Dept. Agr.-Agrl. Rsch. Svc., Madison, Wis., 1971—2004; from asst. prof. to prof. U. Wis., Madison, 1971—2004; ret., 2004. Capt. U.S. Army, 1968-70. Capt. US Army, 1968—70. Fellow AAAS; mem. Am. Soc. Plant Biologists (editorial bd. 1984-86), Am. Assn. Cereal Chemists (assoc. editor 1988-91), Crop Sci. Soc. Am. (assoc. editor 1975-78).

PETERSON, DAVID ROBERT, lawyer, former Canadian government official; b. Toronto, Can., Dec. 28, 1943; s. Clarence and Laura Marie (Scott) P.; m. Shelley Peterson, Jan. 16, 1974; children: Benjamin David, Chloe Matthews, Adam Drake Scott BA, U. Western Ont., 1964; LLB, U. Toronto, 1967; LLD (hon.), U. Ottawa, Am. U. of Caribbean, U. Tel Aviv, U. Toronto. Bar: Ont. 1969, Queens counsel 1981. Chmn., pres. C.M. Peterson Co. Ltd., 1969-75, Cambridge Acceptance Corp., 1969-75; M.P. Ont. Parliament, Canada, 1975—; leader Ont. Liberal Party, 1982; premier Province of Ont., 1985-90; chmn. Cassels Brock & Blackwell LLP, Toronto, 1991—; chancellor U. Toronto. Bd. dirs. Rogers Comms., Inc., Industrielle-Alliance Life Assurance Co., BNP Paribas (Can.), others; founding chmn. Chpts. Inc., Cassels-Pouiliot Noriega. Leader of the ofcl. opposition party, Liberal Party, Ont., 1982-85; dir. Legal Svcs., Yorkville; mem. Kidney Found. Can., Ont., Cystic Fibrosis Found. Fellow McLaughlin Coll., 1985; appointed Knight of Order of Legion of Honor, Govt. France, 1994; recipient Ordre de la Pléiade, Internat. Assembly French-Speaking Parliamentarians, 1995. Mem. Law Soc. U.C., Young Pres. Orgn., London C. of C., London Hunt Country Club, London Racquets Club, Can. Club, Toronto Raptors Basketball Club Inc. (founding chmn.). Mem. United Ch. Of Christ. Avocations: theater, riding, jogging, skiing, tennis. Office: Cassels Brock Blackwell LLP 40 King St W Ste 2100 Toronto ON Canada M5H 3C2 E-mail: dpeterson@casselsbrock.com.

PETERSON, DAWN MICHELLE, entrepreneur, writer; b. Rochester, Minn., Oct. 28, 1962; d. Kenneth Eugene and Lois Ann Silker; m. Bud Lamont Peterson, Feb. 14, 1981; children: Jacquline Ann Peterson, Holly Marie Schill, Cassie Jan Wilson. Student, Internet Svcs. Corp. Continuing Bus. Edn., 1985—2005, Legacy Bus. Group Bus. Edn., 2005—. Mgr. of fine dining restaurant and pvt. club Hilton Hotels, Ogden, Utah, 1983—85; pres. B & D Enterprise, Layton, Utah, 1985—; dir. of internat. divsn. Wilson Enterprises, Inc., Ogden, 1991—98; pres. Amma's Daycare, Layton, 2002—, D. S. Peterson Lit. Co., Layton, 2004—. Directorship, Brazilian divsn. Wilson Enterprises, Inc., Ogden, Utah, 1993—95, directorship, Turkish divsn., 1994—96, directorship, Ctrl. Am. divsn., 1994—96, directorship, Polish divsn., 1993—96, directorship, UK divsn., 1993—98, directorship, German divsn., 1993—98, directorship, Mex. divsn., 1993—98, directorship, Australian divsn., 1994—98; US overseer Wilson Enterprises, Inc. and World Wide Dvsn., 1993—98, seminar spkr., 1993—; sr. bus. cons. Victory Devel., Guadalajara, Mexico, 1998—; com. mem. for internet services corp. India launch team Internet Services Corp./Wilson Enterprises, Inc., 1998; organizer and key note spkr. Germany's Women in Bus. Conf., 1996. Author: (novels) Code Breakers; author: (also actor and dir.) (plays) The Tale of the Pigs with the Folders on Their Heads, Barn Yard Animals (Sch. Creativity award, 1970), Laverne and Shirley go into Business; author/speaker (audio presentation) Empowering Women Business Owners, It's an Amazing Trip. Mem. Women In Bus.,

Ogden, Utah, 1983—85, Ogden C. of C., 1983—85, Rep. Nat. Com., 1987—2005; del. Utah Rep. Party, 1986. Recipient All Around Title, Buckaroo Rodeo, 1974, 1976, Appaloosa Horsemen's Assn., 1980, Endurance Champion, Utah Endurace Racing Assn., 1980, Lake Powell Fesitval of Lights Parade, Lake Powell Festival Com., 2002, 5th in Top 25 Producers, Quixtar Corp., 2002. Mem.: Ind. Bus. Owners Assn. (assoc.). R-Consevative. Christian. Avocations: travel, writing, reading. Office Phone: 801-510-9336. Personal E-mail: bpeterson5673@msn.com.

PETERSON, DELAINE CHARLES, lawyer, bank executive; b. Villisca, Iowa, July 28, 1936; s. Reuben Merrill and Margaret Helena (Sederquist) P.; m. Marcia Joan Hitchcock, Aug. 18, 1962; children: Robert, Paul, Janet BBA, U. Iowa, 1963, JD, 1966. Bar: Iowa 1966. Asst. trust officer Security Nat. Bank, Sioux City, Iowa, 1966—73, mgr. trust dept., 1974—82, sr. v.p., 1983—92, sr. v.p., chief trust officer, 1992—2001; assoc. atty. Corbett Anderson Law Firm, Sioux City, 2001—. Bd. dirs. Siouxland Easter Seals, Sioux City, 1983-91, St. Luke's Health Sys., Inc., 1987-2000, chmn. 1989-91; bd. dirs. St. Luke's Regional Med. Ctr., chmn. 1988-89; bd. dirs. St. Luke's Coll. Nursing and Health Scis., 1991-2000, chmn., 1991-93; trustee Prairie Gold coun. Boy Scouts Am., 1987—, pres., 1989-92; mem. Iowa Coll. Found., 1975-85; com. mem. Morningside Coll. Found., 1989-95 Mem.: ABA, Iowa Bar Assn., Woodbury Bar Assn., Iowa Trust Assn. (pres. 1978), Rotary (pres. 1984), Masons (past master 1988). Republican. Methodist. Office: Corbett Anderson Law Firm 423 Sixth St Ste 400 Sioux City IA 51101

PETERSON, DONALD KENT, former telecommunications industry executive; b. Worcester, Mass., Aug. 13, 1949; s. John Ludwig and Ruth Ingeborg (Anderson) P.; m. Maureen Mack, Aug. 27, 1976; children: Janine Marie, Daniel Thomas. BS in Mech. Engring., Worcester Poly. Inst., 1971; MBA, Dartmouth Coll., 1973. CLU; chartered fin. analyst. Investment analyst State Mut. Life Assurance Co. Am., Worcester, 1973-76; cash and credit mgr. No. Telecom, Nashville, 1976-78, asst. treas., 1978-80, Mississauga, Ont., 1980-81, controller, 1981-83, v.p. fin. Nashville, 1983-85, v.p. ops., 1985-86, sr. v.p. fin., CFO Mississanga, Ont., 1986—87, pres. Nortel Communications Sys. Inc., 1994—95; CFO Communication Svc. Group AT&T, 1995—96; exec. v.p., CFO Lucent Technologies, 1996—2000, CEO enterprise networks group, 2000; pres. & CEO Avaya Inc., Basking Ridge, NJ, 2000—02, chmn. & CEO, 2002—06, chmn., 2006. Bd. dir. Reynolds & Reynolds & Co., 1998—2005. Mem. Coun. on Fgn. Relations, World Economic Forum; trustee Teachers Ins. & Annuity Assn. Am., Com. for Economic Development; chmn. bd. trustees Worcester Polytech. Inst.; bd. overseers Amos Tuck Sch. Bus. Adminstrn. Dartmouth Coll. Recipient Washburn Achievement award, Worcester Poly. Inst., 1986. Mem.: Fin. Execs. Forum of Conf. Bd., Fin. Execs. Inst. Lutheran. Avocation: woodworking. *

PETERSON, DONALD ROBERT, editor, vintage automobile consultant; b. Sandstone, Minn., Apr. 1, 1929; s. Martin Theodore and Margaret Mildred (Dezell) P.; m. Lois Taylor, Dec. 31, 1951 (div. 1975); children: Wyatt A., Winston B., Whitney C. (dec.), Westley D., Webster E.; m. Edie Tannenbaum, Aug. 31, 1975; 1 child, Ryan Kerry. Student, U. Minn., Mpls., 1947—50; BS, Gustavus Adolphus Coll., St. Peter, Minn., 1952. Asst. underwriter Prudential Ins. Co. Am., Mpls., 1953—64; chief health underwriter North Ctrl. Life, St. Paul, 1964—66; pres. 1st State Bank Murdock, Minn., 1967—73, EDON, Inc., Roswell, Ga., 1974—; editor Car Collector mag., Roswell, 1977—91, editor emeritus, 1992—; v.p., dir. Classic Pub. Inc., Atlanta, 1979—97. Contbr. chpt. to book. Councilman, City of Murdock, 1968-72, mayor, 1972-74; del. State Republican Conv., 1970-72; treas. Swift County Rep. Com., 1970-73. Served with U.S. Navy, 1946-47. Recipient citation for disting. service Classic Car Club Am., 1965, Hemmings Motor News Hobby Hero Award, 2002. Mem. Internat. Soc. Philos. Enquiry, Swift County Bankers Assn. (pres. 1970-73), Soc. Automotive Historians, Am. Legion, Mensa (pres. Ga. chpt. 1976-78), Classic Car Club Am. (chpt. pres. 1959, 60, 63, nat. bd. dirs. 1978-81, 97-2005), Rolls-Royce Owners Club, Antique Automobile Club, Vet. Motor Car Club Am., Packard Club, Cadillac-La Salle Club, Lincoln and Continental Owner's Club, Horseless Carriage Club Am. Republican. Avocations: automobile collecting, travel. Home: 1400 Lake Ridge Ct Roswell GA 30076-2869 Home Phone: 770-993-5622; Office Phone: 770-993-5622.

PETERSON, DONALD ROBERT, psychologist, educator, academic administrator; b. Pillager, Minn., Sept. 10, 1923; s. Frank Gordon and Ruth (Friedland) P.; m. Jean Hole, Feb. 10, 1952 (div.); children: Wendy, Jeffrey, Roger, Lisa; m. Jane Snyder Salmon, Dec. 21, 1974. BA, U. Minn., 1948, MA, 1950, PhD, 1952. Mem. faculty U. Ill., Urbana, 1952-75, prof. clin. psychology, 1963-75, head div. clin. psychology, 1963-70, dir. Psychol. Clinic, 1961-70, dir. D. Psychology program, 1970-75; dean Grad. Sch. Applied and Profl. Psychology Rutgers U., New Brunswick, 1975-89. Pres. Nat. Coun. Schs. of Profl. Psychology, 1981-83. Author: The Clinical Study of Social Behavior, 1968, reissued with new intro., 2004, Educating Professional Psychologists, 1997, Twelve Years of Correspondence with Paul Meehl, 2005; co-author: Close Relationships, 1983, reissued with new intro., 2002; also articles; editor Jour. Abnormal Psychology, 1970-72. With AUS, 1943-46. Mem. N.J. Psychol. Assn., Am. Psychol. Assn. (awards for disting. contbns. to practice of psychology 1983, disting. contbns. to edn. and tng. 1989) Office: Rutgers U Grad Sch Applied & Profl Psychology Piscataway NJ 08854-8085 Office Phone: 732-445-2000. Business E-Mail: drpeters@rci.rutgers.edu.

PETERSON, DONN NEAL, forensic engineer, engineering company executive; b. Northwood, ND, Jan. 1, 1942; s. Emil H. and Dorothy (Neal) Peterson; m. Lorna Jean Kappedal, July 8, 1962 (div. July 1966); m. Donna Sue Butts Daiker, Aug. 26, 1967; children: Barbara Daiker, Elizabeth Plamondon, Phoebe, Phaedra Howard, Rosalind Ward. BSME, U. N.D., 1963; MSME, U. Minn., 1972. Registered profl. engr., cert. forensic engr., Internat. Inst. Forensic Engring. Scis. Advanced engring. courses student GE, Evendale, Ohio, 1963-66; systems engr. GE Aircraft Engine Group, Evendale, Ohio, 1963-70; prin. Donn N. Peterson & Assocs., Mpls., 1971-74; pres. Donn N. Peterson & Assocs., Inc., Mpls., 1974-85, Peterson Engring., Inc., Mpls., 1985—. Instr. GE Edn. Program, 1968—69; presenter State Bd. Registration, Mpls., 1980; seminar leader Minn. Fedn. Engring. Socs., Mpls., 1990—91; spkr., expert witness in field. Del. Minn. 6th Dist. Rep. Convs., Brooklyn Park, 1982. Fellow: Nat. Acad. Forensic Engrs. (v.p. 1996, sr. v.p. 1997—98), Am. Acad. Forensic Scis. (sect. chmn. 1989—90, Founders award 1991); mem.: NSPE, ASME (state chmn. 1979—80, Young Engr. of the Yr. 1976), Internat. Inst. Forensic Engring. Scis., Internat. Inst. Forensic Engring. Sci. (pres. 2004—), Profl. Engrs. Pvt. Practice (state pres. 1987—88, Svc. award 1988), Soc. Automotive Engrs., Brooklyn Park C. of C. (city hwy. 610 corridor com. 1992—94), Rotary (Brooklyn Park chpt. sec. 1990—93, v.p. 1993—94, pres.-elect 1994—95, pres. 1995—96, Svc. award 1992, 2005). Lutheran. Achievements include development of mathematical models to simulate jet engine transient performance and wave dynamics in gas flow; computer simulations for vehicle and occupant dynamics during collisions. Office: PO Box 664 Brainerd MN 56401-0664 Office Phone: 218-765-3556. Personal E-mail: donnnpeterson@aol.com.

PETERSON, DONNA RAE, health facility administrator, gerontologist, director; b. Wichita, Kans., Aug. 29, 1948; d. Raymond Houston and Edna Brooks (Waddell) Hobbs; m. William E. Peterson, Nov. 7, 1993; 1 child, Shauna Layne Heath. Student, Wichita State U., 1968—70; BS in Mgmt., N.W. Christian Coll., 1996, MA in Interdisciplinary Studies Gerontology, 2000. Adminstrv. asst. postgrad. edn. Med. Sch. U. Kans., Wichita, 1974—80; activity coord. continuing med. edn. Wesley Med. Ctr., Wichita, 1980—84; mgr. support svcs. 9th dist. Farm Credit Svcs., Wichita, 1984—88; mgr. sales and mktg. Amb. Travel, Eugene, Oreg., 1988—93; dir. mktg. Peterson Design Devel., Eugene, 1993—95; pres. Davinci Designs, Eugene, 1996—2000; owner 2d Half Dynamics, 2000—; dir. Alzheimer's program Sunwest Mgmt., Inc., 2002—04; adult/elder specialist, life coach United Behavioral Health, 2004—06; adminstr. Bayberry Commons Assisted Living and Memory Care, Springfield, Oreg., 2006—. Cons. Jr. League Wichita, 1983, Plancon, Inc., Martinsville, NJ, 1987-88, Changing Creatively, 1997; continuing edn. instr. Lane C.C., 2000—; mem. adv. bd. Lane C.C. Ctr. for Leisure and Learning, 2000—. Mem. Wichita Conv. and Visitors Bur., 1987; mem. events com. Wichita Festivals, Inc., 1987; mem. Eugene Conv. and Visitors Bur., 1988—; mem. Eugene Airport Commn., 1991—, chmn., 1992-93; bd. dirs. Campus Life, chmn., 1993-94; mem. steering com. Eugene Celebration, 1991-94, Oreg. Women Bus. Owners Conf., 1997; bd. pres. Of Coun. for Bus. Edn., 1999-2000. Mem. AAUW, Am. Mktg. Assn. (pres. S.W. chpt. 1991—, pres. 1992-94, bd. dirs.), Soc. Travel Agt. in Govt., Adminstrv. Mgmt. Soc., Forum for Exec. Bus. Women, Gt. Plains Bus. Adminstrn. Group, Assn. Travel Exec., Eugene C. of C. (bus. devel. com. 1990-91), The Gerontol. Soc. Am. (student campus rep. 1999), Alzheimers Assn. (Oreg. chpt., edn. com., 2002—), Eugene High Ground Assn. (chmn.), Delta Gamma Alumni Assn. Republican. Avocations: decorating, writing, skiing, water-skiing, camping. Home: 1460 Olive St Apt 32 Eugene OR 97401-3991 Personal E-mail: gerovision@comcast.net, donna@bayberrycommons.com.

PETERSON, DOROTHY HAWKINS, artist, educator; b. Albuquerque, Mar. 14, 1932; d. Ernest Lee and Ethel Dawn (Allen) Hawkins; m. John W. Peterson, July 9, 1954; children: John Richard, Dorothy Anne. BS in Edn., U. N.Mex., Albuquerque, 1953; MA, U. Tex., 1979. Freelance artist, 1960—; educator, instr. Carlsbad (N.Mex.) Ind. Elem. Sch. Dist., 1953-54; instr. Charleston (S.C.) County Schs., 1955-56; instr. in painting Midland (Tex.) Coll., 1971-76, Roswell (N.Mex.) Mus. Sch., 1981-83, 91—; instr. in art history Ea. N.Mex. U., Roswell, 1989—2000; instr. painting N.Mex. Mil. Inst., Roswell, 1992—94. Bd. dirs. N.Mex. Arts Commn., Santa Fe; cons. Casa de Amigos Craft Guild, Midland, Tex., 1971-73. One woman shows include Art Inst., Permian Basin, Odessa, Tex., 1994. Tutor Roswell Literacy Coun., 1988-89; bd. dirs. N.Mex. Arts & Crafts Fair, Albuquerque, 1983-85. Named Best of Show, Mus. of the S.W., 1967, 69; recipient Top award, 1973, 75, Juror award N.Mex. Arts & Crafts Fair, 1986, 1st pl. award Profl. Watercolor N.Mex. State Fair, 1988, Talens-d' Arches award Tex. Watercolor Soc., 1998, Bd. Dirs. award San Diego Watercolor Soc., 1998, N.Mex. Watercolor Soc., 1998, others. Mem. Nat. Watercolor Soc. (San Diego Watercolor Soc. award 1988), N.Mex. Watercolor Soc. (2d pl. award 1981, 1st pl. award state fair 1988, Grumbacher award 1993, Wingspread award 1994, 1st pl. award 1995, 1st, 3rd and Graham award 1997, Best of Show 2001, Best of Show 2004, Masterworks award N.Mex. Tricentennial 2005, 3d pl. award 2006, 1st pl. Masterworks, 2006). Office: Dorothy Peterson Studio PO Box 915 Roswell NM 88202-0915 Personal E-mail: dhpeterson@dfn.com.

PETERSON, DOUGLAS PETE (PETE PETERSON), former ambassador, retired congressman; b. Omaha, June 26, 1935; m. Carlotta Ann Neal (dec.); children: Michael, Paula, Douglas (dec.); m. Vi Peterson. Grad., Nat. War Coll., 1975; BA, U. Tampa, 1976; postgrad., U. Ctrl. Mich., 1977. Commd. USAF, 1954, advanced through grades to col., ret., 1980; exec. CRT Computers, 1984-90; mem. faculty Fla. State U., 1985-90; mem. US Congress from 2d Fla. Dist., 1991-96; mem. appropriation com.-energy and water, agrl.; US amb. to Vietnam US Dept. State, Hanoi, 1997—2001; pres. Peterson Internat., Inc., 2001—. Founder, CEO The Alliance for Safe Children. Prisoner of war, Vietnam. Mem.: VFW, Am. Acad. Diplomacy, Coun. Am. Ambs., Am. Legion. Roman Catholic. Office: 27 Bowen St Camberwell VIC 3124 Australia Office Phone: 66-2-655-4811. E-mail: petevi@bigpond.net.au.

PETERSON, EDWARD ADRIAN, lawyer; b. St. Louis, May 19, 1941; s. Adrian J. and Virginia (Hamlin) P.; m. Catherine Frances Younghouse, Dec. 17, 1960; children: Kristin, Kendra. BSBA, Washington U., St. Louis, 1963; LLB, So. Methodist U., 1966. Bar: Tex. 1966, U.S. Dist. Ct. (no. and so. dists.) Tex. Instr. bus. law and acctg. Midwestern U., Wichita Falls, Tex., 1966-67; assoc. Schenk & Wesbrooks, Wichita Falls, 1966-67, Newman & Pickering, Dallas, 1967-72; ptnr. Moore & Peterson, Dallas, 1972-89, Winstead Sechrest & Minick P.C., Dallas, 1989—. Spkr. in field. Contbr. articles to legal jours. Bd. dirs. Leukemia Soc., 1970-71, North Tex. Commn., 1992-96, South Dallas/Fair Park Trust Fund, 1992, Tex. Ch. Extension Fund, Tex. Dist., Tex. Dist. Luth. Ch. Mo. Synod., 2002-07, Luth. HS, Dallas, 2007—. Fellow Am. Coll. Mortgage Attys., Tex. Bar Found. (life), Dallas Bar Found., Coll. State Bar Tex.; mem. ABA, Am. Coll. Real Estate Lawyers (title ins. com., common interest com.), State Bar Tex., Tex. Coll. Real Estate Attys., Dallas Bar Assn., Phi Alpha Delta, Sigma Alpha Epsilon. Lutheran. Home: Ste 617 2808 McKinney Ave Dallas TX 75204-2562 also: 131 Hilton Head Island Dr Mabank TX 75147-9325 Office: Winstead PC 5400 Renaissance Tower 1201 Elm St Dallas TX 75270-2199 Office Phone: 214-745-5642. Business E-Mail: epeterson@winstead.com.

PETERSON, EDWIN J., retired judge, mediator, educator; b. Gilmanton, Wis., Mar. 30, 1930; s. Edwin A. and Leora Grace (Kitelinger) P.; m. Anna Chadwick, Feb. 7, 1971; children: Patricia, Andrew, Sherry. BS, U. Oreg., 1951, LLB, 1957. Bar: Oreg. 1957. Assoc. firm Tooze, Kerr, Peterson, Marshall & Shenker, Portland, Oreg., 1957-61, mem. firm, 1961-79; assoc. justice Supreme Ct. Oreg., Salem, 1979-83, 91-93, chief justice, 1983—91; ret., 1993; disting. jurist-in-residence, adj. instr. Willamette Coll. of Law, Salem, 1994—. Chmn. Supreme Ct. Task Force on Racial Issues, 1992-94, Oreg. Law Enforcement Contacts Policy and Data Review Com., 2005-; standing com. on fed. rules of practice and procedure, 1987-93; bd. dirs. Conf. Chief Justices, 1985-87, 88-91; founder Understanding Racism Found., 1998; mem. Oreg. Joint Bench-Bar Commn. on Professionalism, 1996-, chair, 1996-97. Chmn. Portland Citizens Sch. Com., 1968-70; vice-chmn. Young Rep. Fedn. Oreg., 1951; bd. visitors U. Oreg. Law Sch., 1978-83, 87-93, chmn. bd. visitors, 1981-83; pres., bd. dirs. Understanding Racism Found., 1999-2002, bd. dirs., 2002—. 1st lt. USAF, 1952-54. Mem. Oreg. State Bar (bd. examiners 1963-66, gov. 1973-76, vice chmn. profl. liability fund 1977-78), Multnomah County Bar Assn. (pres. 1972-73), Phi Alpha Delta, Lambda Chi Alpha. Episcopalian. Home: 3365 Sunridge Dr S Salem OR 97302-5950 Office: Willamette Univ Coll Law 245 Winter St SE Salem OR 97301-3916 Office Phone: 503-375-5399. Business E-Mail: epeterso@willamette.edu.

PETERSON, ELIZABETH HOLLY, art association administrator; b. Nyack, NY, Dec. 30, 1967; d. John Lawrence and Holly Winifred Peterson; life ptnr. Jean Dolan, Sept. 18, 2004. BA in Studio Art, Wells Coll., Aurora, NY, 1989; MS in Theory, Criticism and History of Art, Design and Architecture, Pratt Inst., Bklyn., 1997; postgrad., NYU, 2003. Exhbn. coord., asst. to the dep. dir. The Mus. of Modern Art, NYC, 1997—2004; dir. The Print Rsch. Found., Stamford, Conn., 2005—. Exhbn. coord. Masterworks from the Mus. Modern Art, Strangely Familiar: Approaches to Scale in the Collection of The Museum of Modern Art, Masterworks from MoMA, 1900-1955, project coord. CAFE/ETC. Recipient award, Art Students League, 1986, Nat. Acad. Design, 1996, Distinction in the Spl. Field of Studio Art award, Wells Coll., 1989, Cert. of Excellence award for Outstanding Merit, Pratt Inst., 1997. Mem.: Coll. Art Assn., Am. Assn. of Mus. Avocations: singing, painting, travel, yoga. Office: The Print Research Foundation 258 Atlantic St Stamford CT 06901 Home Phone: 203-772-0245. E-mail: epeterson@printresearch.org.

PETERSON, ERIC F., headmaster; m. Krista Peterson; children: Sam, Jake, Will. BA, Dartmouth Coll.; JD, Northwestern U. Sch. of Law. Asst. dir. admissions Middlesex Sch., Deerfield Acad.; dir. admissions Sewickley Acad.; former asst. headmaster & English teacher & dir. upper sch. Forsyth Country Day Sch., Lewisville, NC; headmaster St. George's Sch., Middletown, RI, 2004—. Mailing: St George's School PO 1910 Newport RI 02840 *

PETERSON, ERIK CHARLES, prosecutor; BA, Drake U., 1992; JD, Marquette U. Law Sch., 1995. Asst. dist. atty. Richland County, 1995—98; dist. atty. Iowa County, 1999—2006; US atty. (we. dist.) Wis. US Dept. Justice, Madison, 2006—. Office: US Atty PO Box 1585 Madison WI 53701 *

PETERSON, EVONNE STEWART, elementary school educator; d. Richard Allen and Theresa Johnson Stewart; m. Kelvin Osborne Peterson (div.); 1 child, Chelsey Denise. BA in Art Edn., N.C. Ctrl. U., 1979; MA in Art Edn., Winthrop U., 1998; MEd in Reading, Lang., and Literacy, U. N.C., 2001; postgrad., Western Carolina U., 2006—. Cert. K-12 Reading Education Charlotte-Mecklenburg Schools, Charlotte, NC, 2001, K-12 Art Education Charlotte-Mecklenburg Schools, Charlotte, NC, 1991. Adminstrv. svcs. clk. Bachelor Enlisted Quarters, Rota, Spain, 1985—88; tour cons. Am. Airlines, Cary, NC, 1989—90; tchr. afterschool enrichment program Bruns Ave. Elem., Charlotte, 1991—92; tchr. art Lincoln Heights Elem., 1992—2004, tchr. Title I literacy, 2004—, Title I summer sch. site coord., lead tchr., 2005—. Sch. leadership team chair Lincoln Heights Elem., Charlotte, 2002—, tchr. adv. coun. rep., 2001—, mentor, 2000—, literacy/writing com., 2002—, key communicator, 2002—04, diversity facilitator, 2002—04; selected participant Tchg. Fellows Inst., White Oaks, Charlotte, 2005; presenter in field. Recipient Tchr. of Month award, Coca-Cola, 2003; grantee, World Affairs Coun., 1998, IMPACTII, 2000, Charlotte-Mecklenburg Schs., 2001. Mem.: N.C. Educators Assn. (corr.), Internat. Reading Assn. (corr.), Kappa Delta Pi, Phi Kappa Phi. Baptist. Avocations: aerobics/strength training, travel, reading, arts and crafts. Office: Lincoln Heights Elem Sch 1900 Newcastle St Charlotte NC 28216 Home Phone: 704-372-9178.

PETERSON, FRANKLIN DELANO, lawyer; b. Braham, Minn., Nov. 11, 1932; s. John Erick and Myrtle M. (Anderson) P.; m. Beverly Ann Crabb, Aug. 2, 1958; children: Heidi, Durward, Heather. Student, Augsburg Coll., Mpls., 1950—51; BA, St. Cloud State Coll., Minn., 1955; LLB, William Mitchell Coll. Law, St. Paul, 1961. Bar: Minn. 1961. Field claims adjuster Farmers Mut. Ins. Co., St. Paul, 1955-57; asst. dist. claims mgr. Minn. Farmers Ins. Group, Mpls., 1957-62; sole practice Kenyon, Minn., 1963—. Atty. City of Kenyon, 1964—82; v.p. Kenyon Devel. Corp., bd. dirs.; sec. Tri-Valley Constrn. Co., Kenyon, bd. dirs. Chmn. Goldwater for Pres. campaign, Village of Kenyon Reps., 1964, Goodhue County LeVander for Gov., 1966, Goodhue County Reps, 1969-70; sec. Goodhue Selective Service Bd., 1968—; pres. Mineral Springs Chem. Dependency Ctr., 1974-85; mem. Kenyon Pub. Sch. Bd. Edn., 1976-82, treas. 1980-82, Kenyon Booster Club (charter), v.p. 1983; mgr. mgr. Kenyon Legion Baseball, 1979—; bd. dirs. Kenyon Roseview Apts., 1967—, pres. 1985—; potentate Osman Shrine, St. Paul, Minn., 2007. Served with USAF, 1950-52. Mem. ABA, Minn. Bar Assn. (jud. dist. del., pres. 1st dist. 1979-80), Goodhue County Bar Assn., Minn. Assn. Plaintiffs Attys., Nat. Assn. Claimants Counsel, Sons of Norway (pres. Kenyon lodge 1969), Kenyon Comml. Club, Kenyon Country Club (pres. Osman Shrine Clowns 1993), Masons, Shriners, (potentate Osman Shrine, 2007), Lions (pres. Kenyon chpt.), Royal Order Jesters, Ct. of St. Paul and Shriner Clowns. Lutheran. Office: 634 2nd St Kenyon MN 55946-1334 Office Phone: 507-789-6141.

PETERSON, FRED MCCRAE, retired librarian; b. Mpls., Dec. 29, 1936; BA, U. Minn., 1958, MS, 1960; PhD in L.S., Ind. U., 1974. Asst. to dir. Iowa State U. Library, 1961-64, head catalog dept., 1964-67, asst. dir. library, 1967-69, assoc. dir. library, 1969-70; with Catholic U. Am., Washington, 1970-82, asst. prof., assoc. chairperson, 1973-77, acting dir. libraries, 1977-78, dir., 1978-82; univ. librarian Ill. State U., Normal, 1982-96, univ. libr. emeritus, 1996—. Mem. ALA, Ill. Libr. Assn. (past pes., Libr. of Yr. award 1994). Home: 32792 Via Malaga San Juan Capistrano CA 92675-4455 E-mail: fmpeterson@cox.net.

PETERSON, G. P. (BUD PETERSON), academic administrator; b. Prairie Village, Kans. BS in Mech. Engring. and Math., Kans. State U., 1975, MS in Engring., 1980; PhD, Tex. A&M U., 1985. Engring. prof. Tex. A&M U., College Station, 1981—2000; provost Rensselaer Poly. Inst., Troy, NY, 2000—06; chancellor U. Colo., Boulder, 2006—. Editor: Jour. Exptl. Thermal and Fluid Scis.; assoc. editor: ASME Jour. Heat Transfer, AIAA Jour. Thermophysics and Heat Transfer, Internat. Jour. Heat and Fluid Flow, Microscale Thermophysical Engring.; contbr. articles to profl. jours. Recipient Best Paper award, AIAA, 1990, award for outstanding mgmt., NSF, 1994, Ralph James and the O. L. (Andy) Lewis awards, ASME, Dow Outstanding Young Faculty award, ASEE, Pi Tau Sigma Gustus L. Larson Meml. award, ASME, Thermophysics award, AIAA, Meml. award, ASME, Sustained Svc. award, AIAA; fellow, Tex. Engring. Expt. Sta., 1986, 1988; sr. fellow, 1989. Fellow: Am. Inst. of Aeronautics and Astronautics, Am. Soc. of Mech. Engrs.; mem.: Phi Kappa Phi, Sigma Xi, Tau Beta Pi, Pi Tau Sigma. Office: U Colo Office of Chancellor 17 UCB, Regent 301 Boulder CO 80309 Office Phone: 303-492-8908. E-mail: chanchat@spot.colorado.edu. *

PETERSON, GALE EUGENE, historian; b. Sioux Rapids, Iowa, May 23, 1944; s. George Edmund and Vergene Elizabeth (Wilson) P. BS, Iowa State U., 1965; MA, U. Md., 1968, PhD, 1973. Instr. dept. history U. Md., College Park, 1971-72, Cath. U. Am., Washington, 1972-73; prin. investigator Gregory Directory project Orgn. Am. Historians, Bloomington, Ind., 1973-75; instr. dept. history Purdue U., West Lafayette, Ind., 1975-76; dir. U.S. Newspaper Project, Orgn. Am. Historians, Bloomington, Ind., 1976-78; exec. dir. Cin. Hist. Soc., 1978-96, exec. dir. emeritus, 1996—; exec. dir. Ohio Humanities Coun., 1998—. Author: (with John T. Schlebecker) Living Historical Farms Handbook, 1970, Harry S Truman and the Independent Regulatory Commissions 1945-52, 1985. Mem. Cin. Bicentennial Commn., 1983-88. Mem. Orgn. Am. Historians (treas. 1993-2003), Am. Assn. State and Local History, Am. Hist. Assn., Am. Assn. Mus., Assn. Midwest Museums (v.p.-at-large 1993-95, exec. v.p. 1995-96, pres. 1996-98), Nat. Coun. on Pub. History (bd. dirs. 1992-95). Office: Ohio Humanities Coun Ste 1620 471 E Broad St Columbus OH 43215-3857 Office Phone: 614-461-7802. Personal E-mail: galep@one.net.

PETERSON, GARY ANDREW, agronomics researcher; b. Holdrege, Nebr., Apr. 30, 1940; s. Walter Andrew and Evelyn Christine (Johnson) P.; m. Jacquelyn Charlene Flick, June 18, 1965; children: Kerstin, Ingrid. BS, U. Nebr., 1963, MS, 1965; PhD, Iowa State U., 1967. Research assoc. agronomy Iowa State U., Ames, 1964-67; prof. U. Nebr., Lincoln, 1967-84; prof. soil and crop scis. Colo. State U., Ft. Collins, 1984—, head dept. soil and crop scis., 2003—. Assoc. editor AGronomy Jour., 1979-81, tech. editor, 1981-83, editor, 1984-89, editor-in-chief, 1991-96; contbr. articles to profl. jours. Fellow Am. Soc. Agronomy (Ciba-Geigy Agr. Achievement award 1974, Agronomic Achievement award-Soils 1990), Soil Sci. Soc. Am. (prs.-elect 2007, Applied Rsch. award 1987); mem. Soil Conservation Soc. Am. Republican. Avocations: reading, hiking, skiing. Office: Colo State U Dept Soil Crop Scis Fort Collins CO 80523-0001 Home Phone: 970-224-5752; Office Phone: 970-491-6501. Business E-Mail: gary.peterson@colostate.edu.

PETERSON, GEORGE EMANUEL, JR., retired lawyer; b. Mt. Vernon, NY, Mar. 8, 1931; s. George E. and Lydia Evelyn (Peterson) P.; m. Barbara Ritter, Aug. 30, 1957; children— Lisa Manvel, George Emanuel III. BA, Yale, 1953; LL.B., U. Va., 1958. Bar: N.Y. State 1959, Conn. 1974. Assoc. firm Reid & Priest, NYC, 1958-68, ptnr., 1968-70; v.p., gen. counsel Insilco Corp., Meriden, Conn., 1970-72, v.p. fin., 1972-76, v.p., sec., 1976-79, v.p., gen. counsel, 1976-89; pvt. practice North Haven, Conn., 1989-90. Served to lt. USNR, 1953-55. Mem. ABA, N.Y. State Bar Assn., Conn. Bar Assn. Home: 225 Blue Trl Hamden CT 06518-1601

PETERSON, GEORGE FOLKE, retired insurance company executive, writer; b. Racine, Wis., June 4, 1926; s. George Edwin Peterson and Anna Zetterquist; m. Evelyn Marie Malcolm, Dec. 29, 1959. Student, Carthage Coll., 1945—48; BA, Ariz. State U., 1949. Mng. ptnr., co-pub. Opportunities Pub. Co., Racine, 1949—50; dir. mkt. rsch., dir. circulation Watson Publs., Chgo., 1955—58; circulation dir., rsch. mgr. Am. Aviation Pub. Co., Washington, 1958—62; editor, pub. Astrosci. News, Washington, 1962—64; mgmt. cons. Alexander Proudfoot Co., Chgo., 1964—66; field exec. Blue Cross of Fla., Inc., St. Petersburg, 1968—84; freelance writer Holiday, Fla., 1984—. Co-founder, CEO Inst. Cons. Engrs., Chgo., 1956—58; CFO Corp. Treas. Anchor Det. Co., Bristol, Va., 1962—64. Editor, pub.: Sci. Newsletter, 1964; author: Accounts Receivable Management, 1984; author: (as Lane Stevenson) (novel) To Las Vegas With Love, 2002, Searching for Krisztina, 2004. Bd. dirs. Health Sys. Agy., Fla., 1980—83; former mem. Fla. Health Sys. Agy. With Med. Corp US Army, 1950—52. Recipient Pub.'s Achievement award, Am. Aviation Pub. Co., 1960, Cert. of Recognition, Sec. of Def. William Cohen, 2000, Sec. of Def. Donald Rumsfeld, 2005. Mem.: NY Acad. Scis. Avocations: astronomy, cosmology, particle physics, string theory physics. Home and Office: 3538 Burntwood Ct Holiday FL 34691 Personal E-mail: pgeorge347@yahoo.com.

PETERSON, GERALD ALVIN, physics professor; b. Chesterton, Ind., Apr. 12, 1931; s. Gustaf Albert and Esther Josephine (Carlson) P.; m. Doris Lee DeJonge, Dec. 22, 1953; children— Curtis Mark, Thomas Andrew, Anna Beth. BS, Purdue U., 1953, MS, 1955; PhD, Stanford U., 1962. Lectr. Yale U., New Haven, 1962-64; asst. prof., 1964—68; research scientist Inst. voor Kernphysisch Onderzoek, Amsterdam, 1967-68; assoc. prof. physics U. Mass., Amherst, 1968-73, prof., 1973-2000, prof. emeritus, 2000—. Vis. prof. U. Mainz, Fed. Republic Germany, 1975, Japan Soc. Promotion Sci., 1972, 89; U.S.-Israel Binat. Sci. Found. vis. prof. Tel Aviv U., 1983; cons. in field. Contbr. articles to profl. jours. Served with U.S. Army, 1955-57. NATO fellow, 1969, U.K. sr. rsch. fellow, 1970. Fellow Am. Phys. Soc. (chmn. New Eng. sect. 1996); mem. Sigma Xi. Congregationalist. Achievements include research in electron scattering; nuclear structure; energy and environmental problems. Home: 10 Old Briggs Rd Leverett MA 01054-9759 Office: U Mass Nuclear Physics Grad Rsch Ctr Amherst MA 01003 Office Phone: 413-545-2008. E-mail: peterson@physics.umass.edu.

PETERSON, GERALD JOSEPH, aerospace executive, consultant; b. Decatur, Ill., Oct. 27, 1947; s. Raymond Gerald (dec.) and Mary Louise (Johnson) P.; m. Layla Ambrosia Fikes, June 9, 2006. AA, Lincolnland C.C., Springfield, Ill., 1969; student, Schiller Coll., Heidelberg, Germany, 1973, Sangamon State U., Springfield, 1974, U. Minn., 1975. Cert. aircraft pilot, engring. tech. Author LOGIC IV commodities futures trading program, 1996; patentee in field. Served with USAF, 1965, French Foreign Legion, 1979. Mem.: Internat. Platform Assn., U.S. Naval Inst. (life). Avocation: Shaolin Kung Fu. Office: Peterson Aerospace Corp PO Box 1294 Mountain View HI 96771-1294 Personal E-mail: TheGeraldPeterson@hotmail.com.

PETERSON, H. DALE, lawyer; b. Amherst, Wis., Jan. 4, 1951; s. Harold C. and Eva I. (Hansen) P.; m. Julie A. Goplin, Jan. 1, 1995; children: Matt, David, Alex, Ellen. BS with honors, U. Wis., Stevens Point, 1973; JD cum laude, U. Wis., 1978. Bar: U.S. Dist. Ct. (we. dist.) Wis., U.S. Ct. Appeals (7th cir.) Wis. Rsch. analyst U.S. Dept. Justice, Washington, 1973-75; ptnr. Stroud, Willink & Howard, LLC, Madison, Wis., 1978—. Dir. Wis. Farm Bur. Svc. Bd., Inc., Madison, 1994—. Co-author: Contract Law in Wisconsin, 1995. Mem. Dane County Bar Assn. (dir./treas. 1987-91, pres. 2004-05). Office: Stroud Willink & Howard LLC PO Box 2236 Madison WI 53701-2236 Office Phone: 608-257-2281. E-mail: hdpeterson@stroudlaw.com.

PETERSON, HOWARD COOPER, lawyer, accountant; b. Decatur, Ill., Dec. 12, 1939; s. Howard and Lorraine (Cooper) P. BEE, Ill., 1963; MEE, San Diego Sate Coll., 1967; MBA, Columbia U., 1969; JD, Calif. Western Sch. Law, 1983; LLM in Taxation, NYU, 1985. Bar: Calif.; solicitor Eng. and Wales; CFP; CPA, Tex.; cert. neuro-linguistic profl.; registered profl. engr., Calif.; lic. real estate broker Calif., Nev. Elec. engr. Convair divsn. Gen. Dynamics Corp., San Diego, 1963-67, sr. electronics engr., 1967-68; v.p., dirl Equity Programs Corp., San Diego, 1973-83; gen. ptnr. Costumes Characters & Classics Co., San Diego, 1979-86; pres., dir. Coastal Properties Trust, San Diego, 1979-89, Juno Securities, Inc., 1983-96, Juno Real Estate Inc., 1974—, Juno Fin. Svcs., Inc., 1999—, Scripps Mortgage Corp., 1987-90, Juno Transport Inc., 1988-89. CFO, dir. Imperial Screens of San Diego, 1977-96, Heritage Transp. Mgmt. Inc., 1989-91, A.S.A.P. Ins. Svcs. Inc., 1983-85. Mem.: ABA, Am. Assn. Atty.-CPAs, Assn. Enrolled Agts., Internat. Assn. Fin. Planning, Interam. Bar Assn. Office Phone: 619-276-9800.

PETERSON, JAMES KENNETH, manufacturing executive; b. Sioux City, Iowa, Oct. 17, 1934; s. David Winfield and Beulah Lillian (Johnson) P.; m. Nanette Kay Olin, Feb. 2, 1957; children: Kimberly, Kristin, David. BA in Econs, Mich. State U., 1956. R & D engr. Reynolds Metals Co., Richmond, Va., 1957-59, sales rep., 1959-61, dist. sales mgr., 1961-65, regional sales mgr., 1965-67, asst. to exec. v.p., 1968, mktg. dir., 1969-71; dir. nat. account sales The Continental Group, Stamford, Conn., 1971, gen. mgr. sales, 1972-73, div. gen. mgr., 1974-78, v.p., corp. officer, 1974-80, v.p., gen. mgr. global bus. devel., 1979; pres., COO, Ludlow Corp., Needham, Mass., 1980-82, also bd. dirs.; pres., CEO, dir. Graphic Packaging Corp., Paoli, Pa., 1982-89; pres., CEO, Peterson Group, Easton, Md., 1989—. Bd. dirs. Jenard Co., Graphic Packaging Corp., South Chester Tube Co. Served to 1st lt. U.S. Army, 1957. Mem. Merion Golf Club, Merion Cricket Club, Talbot Country Club. Home: 27779 Waverly Rd Easton MD 21601-8121

PETERSON, JAMES ROBERT, engineering psychologist; b. St. Paul, Apr. 16, 1932; s. Palmer Elliot and Helen Evelyn (Carlson) P.; m. Marianna J. Stockvig, June 26, 1954; 1 child, Anne Christine. BA in Psychology cum laude, U. Minn., 1954, MA in Exptl. Psychology, 1958; PhD in Engring. Psychology, U. Mich., 1965. Devel. engr. Honeywell Inc., 1961-65, sr. devel. engr., 1965-67, staff engr., 1967-90, sr. project staff engr., 1990-93, retired, 1993. Honeywell sponsor rep. Shuttle Student Involvement Program, 1982, 84. Contbr. articles to profl. jours. With USMC, 1954-57, USMCR, 1957-62. Mem. Human Factors and Ergonomics Soc. (life), Air and Space Mus. (charter), Smithsonian Inst., Masons, Am. Legion, Delta Upsilon (life). Achievements include invention of Apollo translation hand controller; participation in development work in all U.S. Manned Space Programs (Mercury, Gemini, Apollo, Lunar Excursion Module, Manned Orbiting Laboratory, Space Shuttle and Space Sta.) as member/manager of associated human factors groups. Home: 3303 San Gabriel St Clearwater FL 33759-3341 Personal E-mail: bpeteputt@aol.com.

PETERSON, JAMES SCOTT (JIM PETERSON), Canadian government official; b. Ottawa, Can., 1941; married Heather Peterson. BA, LLB, U. We. Ont.; Diploma, L'Acad. de Droit Internat., The Hague and La Sorbonne; DCL, McGill U.; LLM, Columbia U. Mem. faculty of law U. Toronto, 1974-79; elected mem. of parliament Willowdale, 1980—; chair Cambridge Acceptance Corp. Ltd., 1984-87; chair standing com. on fin. Minister of State, Minister of Justice, 1993-97; sec. of state Internat. Fin. Instns., Ottawa, 1997—2002; min. internat. trade Govt. of Canada, Ottawa, 2003—. Legal counsel and cons. UN. Office: Office of the Min for Internat Trade 515S Ho of Commons Rm 359 West Block K1A 0A6 Ottawa ON Canada Office Phone: 613-992-7332. Business E-Mail: james.peterson@international.gc.ca.

PETERSON, JAN ERIC, lawyer; b. Seattle, Apr. 28, 1944; s. Theodore Dare and Dorothy Elizabeth (Spofford) P.; children: Nels Andrew, Anne Elizabeth; m. Marguerite Victoria Caggiano, Mar. 31, 1984. AB in History, Stanford U., 1966; JD, U. Wash., 1969. Bar: Wash. 1969, U.S. Dist. Ct. (we. and ea. dists.) Wash. 1970, U.S. Ct. Appeals (9th cir.) 1970. Gen. counsel ACLU, Seattle, 1969-71; assoc. Daniel F. Sullivan, Seattle, 1972-73; sr. ptnr. Peterson Young Putra (formerly Peterson, Young, Putra, Fletcher, Knopp & Wampold), Seattle, 1973—. Mem. Wash. State Salary Commn., 2002—04. Drafter (state statute) Tap Water Regulation Act, 1983. Fellow Am. Coll. Trial Lawyers; mem. ABA (editor assoc. 1976-78), Damages Attys. Round Table (founding, pres. 1997-98), ATLA (del. 1985-86), Wash. State Trial Lawyers Assn. (bd. 1973-85, pres. 1982-83, Trial Lawyer of Yr. 1999), Wash. State Bar Assn. (jud. selection 1985-87, bd. govs. 1992-95, pres. 2000-01), Wash. State Bar Found. (bd. dirs. 2001-06), Am. Bd. Trial Adv. (diplomate, pres. Wash. chpt. 1990), ACLU. Democrat. Avocations: piano, baseball, basketball, golf. Office: Peterson Young Putra 1501 4th Ave Ste 2800 Seattle WA 98101-1609 E-mail: janeric@pypfirm.com.

PETERSON, JOHN E., congressman; b. Titusville, Pa., Dec. 25, 1938; s. Axel Benjamin and Mary Elizabeth (Baker) Peterson; m. Saundra June Watson, 1968; children: Richard D., Florence Waychoff. Grad. from rural leadership prog., Pa. State U. Owner retail food market, Pleasantville, Pa., 1958-84; mem. City Coun., Pleasantville, Pa., 1969—77, Pa. State Ho. Reps., 1977-84, Pa. State Senate, 1984-96, US Congress from 5th Pa. dist., 1997—, mem. appropriations com., co-chair Congl. Rural Caucus. Mem. Pub. Health and Welfare Com., now chmn.;active PENNVEST Bd., Pa. Hardwoods Devel. Coun.; sec. Ctr. Rural Pa. Mem. regional adv. coum. Pitts. Cancer Inst.; bd. advs. Foxview Manor, Inc.; mem. adv. bd. U. Pitts., Titusville and Bradford campuses; mem. adv. coun. Ind. U. of Pa. Culinary Sch.; active Pa. Trauma Ctr. Found., Venango County Indsl. Bd. Served in US Army, 1957—63. Recipient John Heinz Meml. award; Presdl. Distinction medal U. Pitts. at Bradford, Recognition award Pa. Acad. Family Physicians, Appreciation award, Better Life award Pa. Health Care Assn., Guardian of Small Bus. award Nat. Fedn. Ind. Bus., Spl. Achievement award Pa. Bar Assn., Elected Officials award Pa. Home Health Assn., 1994, Congl. Partnership award Nat. Assn. Devel. Orgns.; named Senator of Yr. Jewish Coalition, Legislator of Yr., Pa. Assn. County Human Svc. Adminstrs., 1993, Pa. Home Health Care Assn., 1993, Nat. Rural Health Assn., 2002, Policymaker of Yr. Assn. Career and Tech. Edn. Mem. Titusville Area C. of C., Pleasantville PTA, Lions. Republican. Methodist. Office: US House Reps 123 Cannon House Office Bldg Washington DC 20515-0001 Office Phone: 202-225-5121. Office Fax: 202-225-5796. *

PETERSON, KENT WRIGHT, physician; b. Portsmouth, Va., Apr. 16, 1943; s. Gerald Milton and Julia Elizabeth (Hoover) P.; children: Liesl Lynn, Owen Sonne. BA, U. N.C., Chapel Hill, 1964; MD, U. Pa., 1968. Diplomate Am. Bd. Preventive Medicine, Am. Bd. Occupl. Medicine. Intern U. Wis., 1968-69, resident, 1970-71; Robert Wood Johnson clin. scholar George Washington U., 1975-77; family physician E. Madison Clinic, Madison, Wis., 1969; chief med. officer policy devel. U.S. Cost of Living Council, Washington, 1973-74; assoc. dir. Assn. Univ. Programs in Health Adminstrn., Washington, 1974-77; exec. v.p. Am. Coll. Preventive Medicine, Washington, 1977-81; corp. mgr. preventive and environ. medicine IBM Corp., White Plains, NY, 1981-84; corp. med. dir. Am. Standard, NYC, 1984-86; pres. Occupational Health Strategies, Charlottesville, Va., 1984—. Clin. asst. prof. Georgetown U. Sch. Medicine, 1979-85; clin. assoc. prof. NYU dept. environ. medicine, 1985-2004; rep. to Coun. Med. Specialty Socs., 1980-86; mem. Accreditation Coun. for Continuing Med. Edn., 1981-86; vice chmn. Med. Rev. Officer Cert. Coun., 1992—; v.p. Am. Bd. Ind. Med. Examiners, 1995-98; sr. v.p. Inst. for Health and Productivity Mgmt., 1997-02. Author of 8 books including Handbook of Occupational Health Informatics, 11th edit., 2000, SPM Handbook of Health Assessment Tools, 4th edit., 1999; contbr. numerous articles to profl. jours. and chpts. in books. Pres. Children of the Americas Found., 1979-84; treas. Alliance for Transforming the Lives of Children, 2000—; bd. dirs., Conserve Va., 1996-2000. Served to maj. M.C. U.S. Army, 1971-73. Fellow Am. Coll. Preventive Medicine, Am. Coll. Occupl. and Environ. medicine (pres. 1996-97); mem. APHA, Metadocs (gen. sec. 1984—), Ramazzini Soc., Soc. Prospective Medicine (officer), World Future Soc., Coun. for Liveable World, Va. Occupl. Medicine Assn. (pres. 1988-90). Home: 1314 Dunlora Dr Charlottesville VA 22901 Office: Occupational Health Strategies Inc 901 Preston Ave Ste 400 Charlottesville VA 22903-4491 Personal E-mail: kent@healthyself.org.

PETERSON, KURT C., lawyer; b. Salem, NJ, Mar. 31, 1953; BA in economics & polit. sci., Stanford U., 1975; JD, U. Calif. Hastings Coll. Law, 1978. Bar: Calif. 1978, US Dist. Ct. Dist. Calif., US Dist Ct. Ctrl. Dist. Calif. Law clk. to Hon. Robert Kane Calif. Ct. Appeal 1st Dist., 1978; with Crosby Heafey Roach & May (combined with Reed Smith in 2003), 1978—2003, opened L.A. office & served as first mng. ptnr., 1990, opened Century City office, 1997, mng. ptnr., 2000—03; ptnr., mem. exec. com. Reed Smith LLP, 2003—. Contbr. ABA Profl. Liability Litig. Newsletter. Bd. trustees Ctr. for Law in the Pub. Interest; bd. dirs. Music Ctr. of LA County. Named Alumnus of Yr., Hastings Alumni Assn. LA Chpt., 2001; named one of the top 25 lawyers under 45 in Calif., Calif. Law Bus., 1993. Mem.: ABA (vice chair litig. sect. legal malpractice subcom. 1989—92), Assn. Bus. Trial Lawyers, L.A. Bar Assn. Office: Reed Smith LLP 1901 Ave of the Stars, Ste 700 Los Angeles CA 90067-6078 Office Phone: 310-734-5201. Office Fax: 310-734-5299. Business E-Mail: kpeterson@reedsmith.com.

PETERSON, LANCE ROBERT, physician; b. Mpls., Sept. 2, 1947; s. Alvin Robert and Norma Lorraine (Soderlin) P.; m. LoAnn Charlotte Liukonen, Aug. 24, 1968; children: Anja Kristine, Kari Elizabeth. BS, U. Minn., 1970, MD, 1972. Diplomate Am. Bd. Internal Medicine, Am. Bd. Infectious Diseases, Am. Bd. Med. Microbiology. Intern U. Minn., 1972—73, resident, 1973—75; med. dir. home care VA Med. Ctr., Mpls., 1975—77, staff infectious diseases, 1977—92; dir. clin. microbiology Northwestern Meml. Hosp., Chgo., 1992—2002; dir. microbiology and infectious diseases rsch. Evanston Northwestern Healthcare, 2002—. Prof. medicine U. Minn., Mpls., 1990—92, prof. lab. medicine, 1990—92; prof. pathology and medicine Northwestern U., Chgo., 1992—; healthcare epidemiologist Evanston Northwestern Healthcare, 2005—; chief microbiology VA Med. Ctr., Mpls., 1979—92, assoc. chief molecular biology, 1987—89; staff infectious diseases Northwestern Meml. Hosp., Chgo., 1992—2002, dir. prevention epicenter, 1999—2002. Co-editor: Diagnostic Microbiology, 9th edit.; editor: The Biologic and Clinical Basis of Infectious Diseases, 5th edit.; contbr. chpts. to books and articles to profl. jours. Pres. Greater Mpls. Day Care Assn., 1985-86; bd. dir. Cmty. Child Care Ctr., Mpls., 1986-89, VA Employees Child Care Ctr., Mpls., 1987-92, chair fundraising com., 1987-92. Grantee, VA Dept., 1978—88, Bayer, Inc., 1985—2006, R.W. Johnson Rsch. Instn., 1990—2004, Ctrs. Disease Control, 1999—2004, Wyeth, Inc., 2003—, Wash. Sq. Health Found., 2003—04, 2006—, Gene Ohm Scis., 2006—, Cepheid, Inc., 2006—, Nanosphere, Inc., 2006—, others. Fellow: Ctrl. Soc. Clin. Rsch. (chair. infectious diseases sect. 1995—97), Am. Soc. Clin. Pathologists, Infectious Diseases Soc. Am. (regional bd. 1991—92, sec.-treas. Chgo. area 2003—), Am. Acad. Microbiology; mem.: Brit. Soc. Antimicrobial Chemotherapy, Am. Soc. Microbiology (BD Rsch. Clin. Microbiology award 2005). Avocations: travel, jogging, dining, gardening. Office: Evanston Northwestern Healthcare 2650 Ridge Ave Evanston IL 60201 Home Phone: 847-835-2971; Office Phone: 847-570-1637. Business E-Mail: lpeterson@enh.org.

PETERSON, LESLIE RAYMOND, barrister; b. Viking, Alta., Can., Oct. 6, 1923; s. Herman S. and Margaret (Karen) P.; m. Agnes Rose Hine, June 24, 1950; children: Raymond Erik, Karen Isabelle. Student, Camrose Luth. Coll., Alta., McGill. U., Can., London U.; LLB, U. B.C., Can., 1949; LLD (hon.), U. B.C., 1993; LLD, Simon Fraser U., Can., 1965; EdD, Notre Dame U., Nelson, Can., 1966; diploma tech. (hon.), B.C. Inst. Tech., 1994. Bar: B.C. 1949; called to Queens Counsel, 1960. Pvt. practice barrister, Vancouver, B.C., 1949-52; with Peterson & Anderson, 1952, Boughton & Co., 1953—55; mem. B.C. Legislature for Vancouver Centre, 1956—63, Vancouver-Little Mountain, 1966; min. of edn., 1956-68; min. of labour, 1960-71; atty. gen., 1968-72; bd. govs. U. B.C., Vancouver, 1979-83, chancellor, 1987-93. Bd. dirs. Can. Found. Econ. Edn., Inst. Corp. Dirs. Can., West Vancouver Found., Inst. for Pacific Ocean Sci. and Tech.; trustee Peter Wall Inst. for Advanced Studies; chmn. U. B.C. Found., 1990—96. Bd. dirs. Portland unit Shriners Hosp. for Children, 1994-96; past bd. dirs. Western Soc. of Rehab., YMCA, Victoria B.C.; past pres. Twenty Club; hon. mem. Vancouver Jr. C. of C.; former v.p. Normanna Old People's Home; founding mem. Convocation, Simon Fraser U. and U. Victoria; hon. dep. French Nat. Assembly, Paris; hon. commr. labor State of Okla.; gov. Downtown Vancouver Assn. With Can. Army, 1942-46, ETO. Recipient Disting. Alumnus award Camrose Luth. Coll., 1980. Fellow: Royal Soc. Arts; mem.: Internat. Assn. Govt. Labour Ofcls. (chmn. standing com., Can. mins. of edn. 1965—66), Law Soc. B.C., Vancouver Bar Assn., Wesbrook Soc. of U. B.C. (chmn. 1987), Union Club (Victoria), Terminal City Club (pres. 1991—92), Scandinavian Bus. Men's Club (past pres.), Order of Can., Venerable Order of Saint John (comdr.), Order of B.C., Freemason (potentate Gizeh Temple Shrine 1988), Order of St. Lazarus (knight comdr.). Avocations: skiing, golf, fishing, tennis. Home: 814 Highland West Vancouver BC Canada V7S 2G5 Office: Boughton Peterson Law Corp 595 Burrard St Ste 1000 PO Box 49290 Vancouver BC Canada V7X 1S8 Home Phone: 604-922-0667; Office Phone: 604-647-4156. Personal E-mail: lpeterson@bpya.com. Business E-Mail: lpeterson@boughton.ca.

PETERSON, LINDA ELLEN, lawyer; b. Kearny, NJ, Feb. 8, 1960; d. Walter Raymond and JoAnn Evelyn Peterson; m. Domenic James Valentine, Oct. 2, 1988 (div. Apr. 1991); m. Nicholas Joseph Mango, Aug. 17, 1996; 1 child, Jessica Lynn Mango. BA with honors, Rutgers U., 1983; JD, Pace U., 1987. Bar: N.J. 1987. Law clk. to Hon. Bruce A. Gaeta, Hackensack, NJ, 1987-88; asst. county counsel Bergen County Counsel, Hackensack, 1988-91; asst. dep. pub. defenders Passaic County Pub. Defenders, Paterson, NJ, 1991-93, Bergen County Pub. Defenders, Hackensack, 1993—. Ranking scholar Pace U., 1986. Mem. Nat. Assn. Criminal Def. Lawyers, N.J. State Bar. Avocations: dance, yoga, antiques, gardening, moutain biking. Office: Office Pub Defender 60 State St Hackensack NJ 07601-5469 Office Phone: 201-996-8030.

PETERSON, LINDA H., English language educator; b. Saginaw, Mich., Oct. 11, 1948; BA in Lit. summa cum laude, Wheaton Coll., 1969; MA in English, U. R.I., 1973; PhD in English, Brown U., 1978; DHL, Quinnipiac U., 2004. From lectr. to assoc. prof. Yale U., New Haven, 1977-92, prof., 1992—, dir. undergrad. studies English, 1990-94, chair, 1994-2000, acting chair, 2003, Niel Gray Jr. prof. of English, 2002—, dir. grad. studies, 2005—. Dir. Bass writing program Yale Coll., 1979-89, 90-2004; mem. various departmental and univ. coms. Yale U., 1977—; presenter in field. Author: Victorian Autobiography: The Tradition of Self-Interpretation, 1986, Traditions of Victorian Women's Autobiography: The Poetics and Politics of Life Writing, 1999; co-author: Writing Prose, 1989, A Struggle for Fame: Victorian Women Artists and Authors, 1994; editor: The Life of Charlotte Bronte, 2006, The Autobiography of Harriet Martineau, 2007; co-editor: Wuthering Heights: A Case Study in Contemporary Criticism, 1992, 2d edit., 2003, The Norton Reader, 11th edit., 2004, Instructor's Guide to the Norton Reader, 2004; mem. editl. bd. Writing Program Adminstrn., 1983-85, Coll. Composition and Comm., 1986-88, Auto/Biography Studies, 1990—, Victorian Poetry, 2002—, Nineteenth-Century Gender Studies, 2005—, Victorian Rev., 2006—; contbr. articles to profl. jours. Resident fellow Branford Coll., 1979-87, Mellon fellow Whitney Humanities Ctr., 1984-85, fellow NEH, 1989-90, fellow Harry Ransom Humanities Rsch. Ctr., U. Tex., 1997; life fellow Clare Hall, Cambridge, Eng., 1998—. Mem. MLA (del. assembly 1984-86, mem. program com. 1986-89, mem. non-fiction divsn. com. 1988-92, mem. nominating com. 1993-94, mem. teaching of writing divsn. 1993-98, mem. Victorian lit. divsn. 2004-), Nat. Writing Program Adminstrs. (mem. cons.-evaluator program 1982-95, mem. exec. bd. 1982-84, 89-90, v.p. 1985-86, pres. 1987-88), Nat. Coun. Tchrs. English (mem. CCCC nominating com. 1985, mem. coll. sect. com. 1987-90). Home: 53 Edgehill Rd New Haven CT 06511-1343 Office: Yale U Dept English PO Box 208302 New Haven CT 06520-8302 Office Phone: 203-432-2226. Business E-Mail: linda.peterson@yale.edu.

PETERSON, LINDA LOU, special education educator; b. Bakersfield, Calif., Oct. 17, 1939; d. Wiley Karl and Chrystine Walker Peterson. AA, El Camino Coll., Gardena, Calif., 1959; BS, U. So. Calif., LA, 1961; postgrad., San Jose State U., 1988—96. Chpt. I tchr. Mt. Pleasant Unified Sch. Dist., Calif., 1986—88; resource specialist in spl. edn. Hayward Unified Sch. Dist., Calif., 1988—. Advisor, dir. Russian Hill Neighbors Bd., San Francisco, 1993—, hospitality and raffle chmn. Named Merit Tchr., San Marino Unified Sch. Dist., 1967. Mem.: NEA (del. to conf. 2004), Hayward Edn. Assn., Vintner's Club. Avocations: reading, exercise, fine dining, travel, jazz. Home: 1001 Pine St #1407 San Francisco CA 94109 Home Phone: 415-776-4892. Personal E-mail: l_peterson888@hotmail.com.

PETERSON, LINDA S., lawyer; b. Grand Forks, ND, Mar. 15, 1952; BA summa cum laude, U. N.D., 1973; JD, Yale U., 1977. Bar: N.D. 1977, D.C. 1978, U.S. Dist. Ct. D.C. 1979, U.S. Ct. Appeals (D.C. cir.) 1979, U.S. Ct. Appeals (3d cir.) 1982, Calif. 1986, U.S. Ct. Appeals (fed. cir.) 1986. Law clk. Ct. of Appeals for D.C., Washington, 1977-78; ptnr. Sidley & Austin, LA, 1978—. Dep. counsel Webster Commn., 1992; mem. bd. trustees Southwestern U. Sch. Law, 1995. Recipient Dean Phillips Memorial Award, Vietnam Veterans of America. Mem. State Bar Calif. (rules of ct. com. 1988-91), L.A. County Bar Assn. (conf. dels. 1987-90, trustee 1998-99), Women Lawyers Assn. L.A. (bd. dirs. 1989-99, pres. 1998-99), Phi Beta Kappa. Office: Sidley Austin Brown & Wood LLP 555 W 5th St Ste 4000 Los Angeles CA 90013-3000

PETERSON, LLOYD, JR., academic administrator, consultant; b. San Antonio, July 20, 1958; s. Lloyd Peterson, Sr. and Dorothy Garrett Phifer; m. Debra Gay Culbertson; 1 child, Jaela Culbertson Grayson. AB in Medieval Lit., Colo. State U., Fort Collins, 1976—80, MS in Applied Human Scis., 1980—82. Sr. admissions officer Yale U., New Haven, 1987—96; dir., admissions Vassar Coll., Poughkeepsie, NY, 1996—2000; v.p., edn. Coll. Coach, LLC, Boston, 2000—. Co-chmn. Black Admissions Officers, Ivy League and Sister Schs., Cambridge, Mass.; chair, minority rels. com. Colo. Coun. HS & Coll. Rels., Colorado Springs. Author: (book) College Admissions. Edn. cons. Horizons Initiative, Boston; pres. El Paso County Black Caucus, Colorado Springs, Colo.; chair, edn. com. Urban League, Pikes Peak Region, Colorado Springs, Colo. Recipient Best Writers Award, Mt. Holyoke Coll., Blue Key Award, City of Colo. Springs; scholar, Sachs Found. Mem.: New Eng. Assn.Coll. Admissions Counseling, Nat. Assn. Coll. Admissions Counselors. Liberal. Avocations: cooking, writing, classical music, jazz. Office: Coll Coach LLC 233 Needham St Newton MA 02464 Office Phone: 617-527-4441. Office Fax: 617-527-8882. E-mail: volvolp@rcn.com.

PETERSON, M. JEANNE, historian, educator; b. Minn., Nov. 26, 1937; d. Clifford Woodrow and Mildred Amelia (Kukas) P.; divorced. BA, U. Calif., 1966, PhD, 1972. Lectr., asst., assoc. prof. Ind. U., Bloomington, 1971-87, prof. history, 1987—, chairperson dept. history, 1987—93, exec. assoc. dean Coll. Arts and Scis., 1993—99, acting chair gender studies dept., 1999—2000, prof. emerita history, found. prof. emerita gender studies, 2001—. Cons. Jour. Women's History, Bull. Hist. Medicine, U. Mich. Press, Butler U., Indpls., Harvard U. Press, Princeton U. Press, Columbia U. Press, Ind. U. Press, SUNY Press, Food and Foodways, Med. History, ACLS, Am. Hist. Rev., Victorian Studies, NEH, NIH, Can. Coun., Adam Matthew Ltd., Johns Hopkins U. Press, U. Va. Press, U. Toronto Press, Ligature, Inc., Am. Philos. Soc., Wellcome Trust (U.K.); external review com. U. Nebr., Lincoln, 1992, U. Iowa, Iowa City, 1995; MA review com. U. N.C., Greensboro, 1993. Author: The Medical Profession in Mid-Victorian London, 1978, Family, Love, and Work in the Lives of Victorian Gentlewomen, 1989; assoc. editor: Oxford Dictionary of National Biography; co-editor: Lizzie Borden: A Case Book of Family and Crime in the 1890s, 1980; contbr. articles to profl. jours. NEH fellow, 1978-79, Guggenheim Found. fellow, 1984-85, Inst. for Advanced Study fellow Ind. U., 1984-85. Mem. Am. Hist. Assn., Soc. for the Social History Medicine, N.Am. Conf. Brit. Studies, Am. Assn. History Medicine, N.Am. Victorian Studies Assn. Home: 1311 S Rechter Ct Bloomington IN 47401-6173 Office: Ind U Dept Gender Studies 742 Ballantine Rd Bloomington IN 47401-5022 Home Phone: 812-332-0458; Office Phone: 812-855-0101. Business E-Mail: petersom@indiana.edu.

PETERSON, MARJORIE, former mayor; b. Chisholm, Minn., Aug. 16, 1924; d. Martin and Catherine Mihelich Champa; m. Andrew Levchak, July 6, 1946 (dec. Mar. 2, 1975); children: Carol, Andrea, Richard, Lisbeth; m. Walter C. Peterson, Sept. 25, 1976. Bookkeeper Ford Sales & Svc., Chisholm, Minn.; dental asst. Office of Dr. J.E. Hoffman, Chisholm, 1960—65; podiatrist asst. Office of Dr. Larson, Hibbing, Minn., 1967; divsn. sec. Fin. Programs, Hibbing, 1967—74; mem. city coun. City of Chisholm, 1977—85, 1989—95, ofcl., 1989—95, mayor, 1996—98. Mem. Pub. Utilities Bd., Chisholm. Contbr. poetry to anthologies. Pres. Range Assn. Sch. and City, Chisholm; bd. dirs. Chisholm-Hibbing Airport Authority, Hibbing, Minn., 1991—2007, chmn., 1991—2001; v.p. bd. dirs. Mus. Mining, 2002—07; mem. Friends of Libr.; bd. dirs. League Minn. Cities, St. Paul, 1984. Recipient C.C. Ludwig award, League Minn. Cities, 1984, Silver award, World of Poetry, 1990, Golden Poet award, 1998, Famous Poet, Famous Poet Soc., 2000. Mem.: Moose. Democrat. Roman Catholic. Achievements include being first woman elected to City Council in Chisholm, and first woman elected as mayor. Avocations: reading, volunteer work, travel, cards. Home: 405 7th St NW Chisholm MN 55719

PETERSON, MARY ELIZABETH DREISBACH, mechanical engineer; b. New Haven, Nov. 27, 1966; d. Raymond Allen and Dorothy Louise (Seal) Dreisbach; m. Brian Peter Peterson, 2005. AS in Plastics Engring., Quinebaug Valley Cmty. Tech.; BSME and Materials Sci., U. Conn., 1989; MS in Materials Engring., Rensselaer Poly. Inst. Lic. profl. engr., Conn. Mfg. engr. United Technologies Corp., Pratt & Whitney, East Hartford, Conn., 1988—93; sr. mfg. engr. Haydon Switch and Instrument Inc., Waterbury, Conn., 1993—97, sr. project engr., 1997—98, mgr. mfg. engring., 1998—2003; mgr. engring. MTU Aero Engines N.Am., Newington, Conn., 2003—05, mgr. estimating and contracts, 2005—. Bd. dirs. Airpax Fed. Credit Union, Cheshire, Conn., 1996-98, supervisory com., 1993-96, chmn., 1996-98, pres., 1998-2001; advisor Holy Trinity Greek Orthodox Church Junior GOYA. Mem. Am. Soc. Materials, Materials Rsch. Soc., Soc. Mfg. Engrs. (cert. mfg. engr.). Office: MTU AENA 275 Richard St Newington CT 06111 Home: 49 Harrison Ln Bethlehem CT 06751 Home Phone: 203-266-5491; Office Phone: 860-667-6623. Personal E-mail: medreisbach@charter.net.

PETERSON, MERRILL DANIEL, historian, educator; b. Manhattan, Kans., Mar. 31, 1921; s. William Oscar and Alice Dwinell (Merrill) P.; m. Jean Hymphrey, May 24, 1944 (dec. Nov. 1995); children: Jeffrey Ward, Kent Merrill. Student, Kans. State U., 1939-41; AB, U. Kans., 1943; PhD in History of Am. Civilization, Harvard U., 1950. Teaching fellow Harvard U., Cambridge, Mass., 1948-49; instr., then asst. prof. history Brandeis U., Waltham, Mass., 1949-55; asst. prof., bicentennial preceptor Princeton U., N.J., 1955-58; mem. faculty Brandeis U., Waltham, Mass., 1958-62, dean students, 1960-62; Thomas Jefferson Found. prof. U. Va., Charlottesville, 1962-87, prof. emeritus, 1987—, chmn. dept. history, 1966-72, dean faculty Arts and Scis., 1981-85; Mary Ball Washington prof. Am. History University Coll., Dublin, Ireland, 1988-89; vol. Peace Corps, Armenia, 1997. Scholar in residence Bellagio Study Ctr., 1974; faculty Salzburg Seminar in Am. Studies, 1975; Lamar lectr. Mercer U., 1975; Fleming lectr. La. State U., 1980; lectr. at 20 European univs., 40 Am. colls. and univs. Author: The Jefferson Image in the American Mind, 1960 (Bancroft prize, Gold medal Thomas Jefferson Meml. Found.), Major Crises in American History, 2 vols., 1962, Democracy, Liberty and Property: The State Constitutional Convention Debates of the 1820s, 1966, Thomas Jefferson and the New Nation: A Biography, 1970, James Madison: A Biography in His Own Words, 1974, Adams and Jefferson: A Revolutionary Dialogue, 1976, Olive Branch and Sword: The Compromise of 1833, 1982, The Great Triumvirate: Webster, Clay and Calhoun, 1987; editor: Thomas Jefferson: A Historical Profile, 1996, The Portable Thomas Jefferson, 1975, Thomas Jefferson Writings, 1984, Thomas Jefferson: A Reference Biography, 1986, The Virginia Statute for Religious Freedom: Its Evolution and Consequences in American History, 1988, Visitors to Monticello, 1989, Lincoln in American Memory, 1994 (History finalist, Pulitzer prize, PBK Book award U. Va.), Coming of Age with the New Republic, 1938-1950, 1999, The John Brown Legend Revisited, 1859-2000, 2002, Starving Armenians: America and the Armenian Genocide. 1915-1930 and After, 2004, The President and His Biographer: Woodrow Wilson and Ray Stannard Baker, 2007. Bd. dirs. Thomas Jefferson Found.; chmn. Thomas Jefferson Commemoration Commn., 1993-94. Guggenheim fellow, 1962-63, Ctr. for Advanced Study in Behavioral Scis. fellow, 1968-69, NEH and Nat. Humanities Ctr. fellow, 1980-81; recipient 20th Anniversary award Va. Found. for Humanities, 1994, Nat. First Freedom award First Freedom Coun., 1997, Career Achievement award, 2005, Libr. Va. Fellow Am. Acad. Arts and Scis.; mem. Am. Hist. Assn., Am. Antiquarian Soc., Mass. Hist. Soc., Phi Beta Kappa. Home and Office: 250 Pantops Mountain Rd Apt 6 Charlottesville VA 22911-8600

PETERSON, MILLIE M., state senator; b. Merced, Calif., June 11, 1944; BS, U. Utah, 1979, MSW, 1984. Mem. Utah Senate Dist. 12, Salt Lake City, 1991—2002. Susa Young Gates Award, 1998. Mem. NASW. Democrat. Address: 7131 W 3800 S West Valley City UT 84128-3416 Office Phone: 801-566-4423. Personal E-mail: mpeter7131@aol.com.

PETERSON, NAD A., retired lawyer; b. Mt. Pleasant, Utah, 1926; m. Martha Peterson, 1948 (dec. 2004). AB, George Washington U., 1950, JD, 1953. Bar: D.C. 1953, Calif. 1960, U.S. Supreme Ct. 1958. Law practice, Washington, 1953-60; sec., asst. gen. counsel Dart Industries, LA, 1960-67; chief counsel Fluor Corp., 1967-73, gen. counsel, 1973-79, v.p. law, 1979-82, sr. v.p. law, 1983-84, sr. v.p., sec. Irvine, Calif., 1984-93; sr. v.p., gen. counsel San Diego Gas & Electric Co., 1993-95. With USNR, PTO, 1944-46. Mem. ABA, Calif. Bar Assn., Phi Delta Phi. Home: PO Box 9101 Rancho Santa Fe CA 92067-4101 E-mail: sanpete1@aol.com.

PETERSON, NANCY, special education educator; AS, Webster State Coll., 1963; BS in Elem. Edn. magna cum laude, Brigham Young U., 1964, MS in Ednl. Psychology, 1966, PhD in Ednl. Psychology, 1969. Instr. in tchr. edn. Brigham Young U., Provo, Utah, 1966-69; asst. prof. edn. dept. spl. edn. U. Kans., Lawrence, 1969-74, dir. spl. edn. classes for handicapped children Clin. Tng. Ctr., 1969-89, project dir. head start tng., 1973-74, coord. edn. univ. affiliated facility Clin. Tng. Ctr., 1969-74, coord. pers. tng. programs in mental retardation, 1973-76, assoc. prof. edn., 1974-88, project dir. pers. tng. programs, 1986-93, prof. edn. dept. spl. edn., 1988—, dept. chair, 1994—. Rsch. sci. Bur. Child Rsch., U. Kans., 1969—; prin. investigator for Kans. U. Kans. Early Childhood Rsch. Inst., 1977-82; Matthew Guglielmo Endowed Chair, Charter Sch. Edn., Calif. State U., LA, 1998-2000; Mary Ann Alia lectureship Charter Sch. Edn. Calif. State U. LA, 1999; prof. spl. edn. U. Kans., 2000—. Recipient J.E. Wallace Wallin award Internat. Coun. Exceptional Children, 1993. Office: U Kans Dept Spl Edn 521 Pearson Hall Lawrence KS 66045-3101

PETERSON, NEAL N., lawyer; b. 1968; BA summa cum laude, St. Olaf Coll., 1990; JD, Cornell Univ., 1993. Bar: Conn. 1993, Minn. 1996. Assoc., health law dept. Murtha, Cullina, Richter and Pinney, 1993—96; assoc. Dorsey & Whitney LLP, Mpls., 1996—2000, ptnr., health care practice group, 2001—, head, health care practice group. Writer, lectr. in field. Named a Rising Star, Minn. Law & Politics Mag. Mem.: Minn. State Bar Assn. (governing coun., health sect.), Am. Health Lawyers Assn. Office: Dorsey & Whitney LLP Ste 1500 50 S Sixth St Minneapolis MN 55402-1498 Office Phone: 612-343-7943. Office Fax: 612-340-2868. Business E-Mail: peterson.neal@dorsey.com.

PETERSON, OSLER LEOPOLD, lawyer; b. Mpls., Oct. 19, 1946; s. Osler Luther and Delores (Kealy) P.; m. Sandra Ann Freeto, Jan. 2, 1971 (div. Dec. 1983); m. Deborah Jean Bero, July 30, 1989; one child: Kristen Ruth. BA, Brown U., 1969; JD cum laude, Suffolk U., 1976. Bar: Mass. 1976, US Dist. Ct. Mass. 1976. Pvt. practice, Newton, Mass., 1976—, Medfield, Mass., 1976—2000. Bd. dirs. Riverside Cmty. Care (formerly Neww Ctr., Inc.), 1976-96, clk., 1978-84, pres., 1984-89, Lasell Coll. (formerly Lasell Jr. Coll.), 1983-97, 98—, clk., 1984-91, Lasell Village, Inc., 1990—, chmn., 1992-2000, Beth Israel Deaconess Hosp.-Needham, 2001-2005; mem. Medfield Zoning Bd. Appeals, 1993-2000; selectman Town of Medfield, 2000—, chair, 2002-03, 05-06; mem. Medfield Found., Inc., 2002—. Mem. ABA, AAJ, Mass. Bar Assn., Real Estate Bar Assn. Mass. Home: 10 Copperwood Rd Medfield MA 02052-1034 Office: 580 Washington St Newton MA 02458-1416 also: 66 North St PO Box 358 Medfield MA 02052-0358 Office Phone: 617-969-1500, 508-359-9190. Business E-Mail: osler.peterson@verizon.net.

PETERSON, PAMELA CARMELLE, language educator; b. Bakersfield, Calif., Sept. 24, 1954; d. Bob Eugene and Carmelita Denyse (Coodey) York; m. Robert Leroy Peterson, Feb. 9, 1979; children: Aimee, Sara, Matthew, Hannah. AA, Bakersfield Coll., 1992; BA in History, Calif. State U., Bakersfield, 1994. Exec. adminstr. Kern Bldg. Materials, Bakersfield, 1973—95; prin. Rosewall Christian Acad., Bakersfield, 1994—; prin., tchr. Dynasty Christian Schs., Bakersfield, 1995—97; instr. ESL Calif. State U., Bakersfield, 1997—2006; instr. English Santa Barbara Bus. Coll., Calif., 1998—. Pres. bd. Dynasty Christian Schs., 1995; exec. sec. bd. dirs. Kern Bldg. Materials, 1983-95; adj. prof. English Bakersfield Coll., 2006-. Mem. Assn. Christian Schs., Inc., Assn. Christian Sch. Adminstrs., Cherokee Nation, Phi Alpha Theta (sec. 1994-95, v.p. 1995-96), Cherokee Cmty. Ctrl. Calif. (meeting facilitator 2007-). Avocations: history, reading, needlecrafts, gardening, baking. Home: 6309 Juniper Rd Lake Isabella CA 93240-2529 Office: Rosewail Christian Acad 7850 White Ln # E149 Bakersfield CA 93309-7689 Home Phone: 760-549-0098; Office Phone: 661-549-0098. E-mail: rcateach@aol.com.

PETERSON, PAUL AMES, lawyer, educator; b. LA, Feb. 17, 1928; s. Ames and Norma (Brown) P.; m. Cynthia Peterson, June 21, 1953 (div.); children: Daniel C., Andrew G., Matthew A., James F.; m. Barbara J. Henderson, Sept. 12, 1976. BS in Econs., U. Calif., Berkeley, 1953, JD, 1956. Bar: Calif. 1956, US Ct. Appeals (9th cir.) 1956, US Supreme Ct. 1964. Of counsel Peterson & Price, San Diego, 1958—. Assoc. prof. Calif. Western Coll. Law, San Diego, 1960—63, U. San Diego Law Sch., 1958—60, U. Calif., San Diego, 1984—87, chmn. bd. overseers, 1994—, chmn., 2000—02; bd. trustees U. Calif. Found., San Diego; bd. dirs. Children's Advocacy Inst., San Diego Regional Airport Authority, 2002—06. Contbr. articles to profl jours. Bd. dirs. San Diego Conv. Ctr. Corp., 1985—90, San Diego Stadium Authority, 1964—72, San Diego County Water Authority, 1984—90, San Diego Regional Govt. Efficiency Commn., 2001—02. Fellow Am. Judicature Soc.; mem. State Bar of Calif., Phi Beta Kappa, Order of Coif. Democrat. Home: 7020 Neptune Pl La Jolla CA 92037-5328 Office: Peterson & Price 7979 Ivanhoe Ave Ste 520 La Jolla CA 92037-4513 Office Phone: 858-551-2338. Business E-Mail: ppeterson@price-entities.com.

PETERSON, PENELOPE LORAINE, dean, education educator; b. Moline, Ill., Nov. 25, 1949; d. Leroy P.; m. W. Patrick Dickson; children: Andrew, Joshua, Elissa. BS, Iowa State U., 1971; MS, PhD, Stanford U., 1976. Asst. prof. dept. ednl. psychology U. Wis., Madison, 1976-80, assoc. prof., 1980-81, prof. ednl. psychology, 1982-85, Sears-Bascom Prof., 1985-87; prof. ednl. psychology & tchr. edn. Mich. State U., East Lansing, 1987—97, co-dir. Inst. Rsch. on Teaching, 1987—97, co- dir. Elem. Subjects Ctr., 1987-92, co-dir. Ednl. Policy Practice Study, 1992—97; dean Northwestern U. Sch. Edn. & Social Policy, Evanston, Ill., 1997—, Eleanor R. Baldwin prof. edn., 1997—. Author chpts. to books; editor: Rev. Ednl. Rsch, 1984-90; contbr. articles to profl. jours. Recipient Palmer O. Johnson award Am. Edn. Rsch. Assn., 1980, Raymond B. Cattell Early Career award Am. Ednl. Rsch. Assn., 1986, Disting. Rsch. award Assn. Tchr. Edn., 1992. Fellow Am. Psychol. Soc. Office: Northwestern U Sch Edn & Social Policy Annenberg Hall Rm 252 2120 Campus Dr Evanston IL 60208 E-mail: p-peterson@northwestern.edu.

PETERSON, PER A., health products executive; V.p. drug discovery R.W. Johnson Pharm. Rsch. Inst. Johnson & Johnson, 1994—98, grp. v.p. Pharm. Rsch. Inst., 1998, pres. Pharm. Rsch. Inst., 1998—2000, chmn. rsch. and devel. Pharms. Grp., 2000—, mem. exec. com., 2001—. Office: Johnson & Johnson 1 Johnson & Johnson Plz New Brunswick NJ 08933

PETERSON, PETER GEORGE, investment company executive; b. Kearney, Nebr., June 5, 1926; s. George and Venetia P.; m. Sally H., May 1953 (div. 1979); children: John, Jim, David, Holly, Michael; m. Joan Ganz Cooney, Apr. 26, 1980. BS, Northwestern U., 1947; MBA, U.Chgo., 1951; PhD (hon.), Colgate U., George Washington U., Northwestern U., Georgetown U., U. Rochester, New School U., Southampton Coll. at L.I. Exec. v.p. Market Facts, Chgo., 1948-52; v.p. McCann Erickson, Chgo., 1952-58; pres. Bell and Howell, Chgo., 1961—63, exec. v.p., 1961—63, chmn., CEO, 1963-71; asst. to Pres. for internat. econ. affairs The White House, Washington, 1961-63; sec. US Dept. Commerce, Washington, 1972-73; CEO, chmn. bd. Lehman Bros. and Lehman Bros., Kuhn, Loeb, Inc., NYC, 1973-84; sr. chmn., co-founder The Blackstone Group, 1985—. Chmn. Fed. Res. Bank NY, 1999-2003; founding pres. The Concord Coalition co-chmn, The Conf. Bd. Comm. on Publ. Trust and Pvt. Enterprise. Author: Facing Up: How to Rescue the Economy from Crushing Debt and Restore the American Dream, 1993, Will America Grow Up Before it Grows Old: How the Coming Social Security Crisis Threatens You, Your Family, and Your Country, 1996, Gray Dawn: How the Coming Age Wave Will Transform America--and the World, 1999, Running on Empty: How the Democratic and Republican Parties Are Bankrupting Our Future and What Americans Can Do About It, 2004; editor: Readings in Market Organization and Price Policies; co-author: On Borrowed Time: How The Growth In Entitlement Spending Threatens America's Future, 1989. Founding mem. Bi-Partisan Budget Appeal; pres. The Concord Coalition; trustee Commn. for Econ. Devel., Mus. Modern Art, NYC; bd. dir. Pub. Agenda. Recipient Outstanding Service award Phoenix House, NYC, 1976, Stephen Wise award Am. Jewish Congress, 1981, U. Chgo. Alumni medal, 1983, Man of Vision award, 1994, Nebraskalander award, 1994, Harvard Bus. Sch. Leadership award, 2004, Coro N.Y. Leadership award, 2004; named to Pres. Clinton's Bi-Partisan Comm. on Entitlement Reform, 1994. Mem. Coun. on Fgn. Rels. (chmn. bd. 1985—), Inst. Internat. Econ. (chmn. bd 1980), Nat. Bur. Econ. Rsch. (trustee), Japan Soc., Blind Brook Club (Purchase, NY), Deepdale Club (Manhasset, NY), Maidstone Club (East-hampton, NY), Chgo. Club, River Club, Links, Augusta Nat. Club, Friar's Head Golf Club (Riverhead, NY), Burning Tree (Washington), Quail Valley Golf Club, Atlantic Club, Windsor Club; fellow Am. Acad. Arts & Sciences Republican. Office: The Blackstone Group 345 Park Ave Ste 3101 New York NY 10154-0004 Home Phone: 212-752-9383; Office Phone: 212-583-5817. *

PETERSON, RALPH RANDALL, engineering executive; b. Hayti, Mo., Oct. 12, 1944; s. James Tony and Helen Irene (Webb) P.; m. Betty Shoemaker, Nov. 7, 1964; children: Jamie Marie Jones, Jeffrey Scott. BSCE, Oreg. State U., 1969; MS in Environ. Engring., Stanford U., 1970; AMP in Bus., Harvard U., 1991. Registered profl. engr., Oreg., Wash., Colo. Engring. aide Johnson, Underkofler & Briggs, Boise, Idaho, 1962—63; surveyor Smith, Keyes, & Blakely, Caldwell, Idaho, 1963—64; with Chronic & Assocs., Boise, Idaho, 1964—65; various project devel. and dept. mng. roles CH2M Hill Cos., Corvallis, Oreg., 1965-78, v.p. indsl. process divsn., 1978-87, sr. v.p., tech. dir. Denver, 1987-90, CEO, 1990—, chmn., 2000—. Bd. dirs. Std. Ins. Co., Portland, Oreg.; bd. advisors Constrn. Industry Pres. Forum, Washington, 1994—; co-chair Nat. Congress Advancement of Minorities in Environ. Professions, Atlanta, 1993-94; industry co-chair tech. for sustainable future White House Office Sci. and Tech. Policy, 1995-96. Bd. dirs. Stapleton Devel. Corp., Denver, 1994—, World Trade Ctr., Denver, 1990—; corp. patron Smithsonian Instn. Corp. Patron. Recipient Colo. Gov.'s award for internat. trade devel., 1995. Mem. ASCE, Am. Water Works Assn., Water Environment Fedn., Colo. Environ. Bus. Assn. (co-chair 1993—), Oreg. State U. Alumni Assn. (bd. dirs. 1992—). Avocations: skiing, camping, fishing, performing arts. Office: CH2M Hill 9191 S Jamaica St Englewood CO 80112 *

PETERSON, RANDALL THEODORE, law librarian, educator; b. Sioux City, Iowa, Aug. 27, 1944; s. Theodore Melvin and Ileann Grace (Wendrich) Peterson; m. Judith Ashcroft, Aug. 24, 1967; children: Kristin, Randall, Heidi, Travis, Robert, Quinn. Student, Dixie Coll., 1962—63; BS, Brigham Young U., Provo, Utah, 1968, MLS, 1974; JD, U. Utah, 1972. Asst. law libr. Brigham Young U., Provo, Utah, 1972—74, assoc. law libr., 1974—77; asst. prof. law and dir. libr. svcs. John Marshall Law Sch., Chgo., 1977—86, assoc. prof. law and dir. libr. svcs., 1986—90, assoc. prof. law, 1990—. Mem.: ABA. Mem. Lds Ch. Office: John Marshall Law Sch 315 S Plymouth Ct Chicago IL 60604-3968 Home Phone: 630-505-0874; Office Phone: 312-978-2372. Business E-Mail: 7rtp@jmls.edu.

PETERSON, RICHARD J., surgeon; b. Mpls. s. James R. Peterson and Betty C. Windham; m. Julie Hasper Peterson, Oct. 1, 1983; children: Lindsay, Bret, Kelise. BA, St. Olaf Coll., Northfield, Minn., 1975; MD, Mayo Med. Sch., Rochester, Minn., 1979. Resident Duke U. Med. Sch., Durham, NC, 1979—88; tchg. scholar Duke U. Med. Ctr., Durham, 1988—89; advanced fellow Mayo Clinic, Rochester, 1989—90; faculty U. Fla., Jacksonville, 1990—92; surgeon SW Cardiology Assocs., Albuquerque, 1992—2000; pvt. practice Bradenton, Fla., 2000—. Fellow: ACS; mem.: Soc. Thoracic Surgeons. Avocations: sailing, travel, scuba diving. Office: Manatee Cardiac Surgery 623 39th St W Ste 2 Bradenton FL 34205

PETERSON, RICHARD WILLIAM, retired judge, lawyer; b. Council Bluffs, Iowa, Sept. 29, 1925; s. Henry K. and Laura May (Robinson) Peterson; m. Patricia Mae Fox, Aug. 14, 1949; children: Katherine Ilene Peterson Sherbondy, Jon Eric, Timothy Richard. BA, U. Iowa, 1949, JD with distinction, 1951; postgrad., U. Nebr.-Omaha, 1972-80, 86. Bar: Iowa 1951, U.S. Dist. Ct. (so. dist.) Iowa 1951, U.S. Supreme Ct. 1991, U.S. Ct. Appeals (8th cir.) 1997. Pvt. practice law, Council Bluffs, 1951—; U.S. commr. U.S. Dist. Ct. (so. dist.) Iowa, 1958-70, U.S. magistrate judge, 1970—99; ret., 2005. Nat. faculty Fed. Jud. Ctr., Washington, 1972—82; emeritus trustee Children's Sq., U.S.A., 1969—; verifying ofcl. Internat. Prisoner Transfer Treaties, Mexico City, 1977, La Paz, Bolivia, 1980—81, Lima, Peru, 1981. Author: The Court Moves West: A Study of the United States Court Decision of Appeals from the United States Circuit and District Court of Iowa, 1846-1882, 1988, West of the Nishnabotna: The Experience of Forty Years of a Part-Time Judicial Officer as United States Commissioner, Magistrate and Magistrate Judge, 1958-1998, 1998; author: (with George Mills) No One is Above the Law: The Story of Southern Iowa's Federal Court, 1994; contbr. articles to legal publs. Bd. dirs. Pottawattamie County chpt. ARC, Iowa, state fund chmn. Iowa, 1957—58; dist. chmn. Trailblazer dist. Boy Scouts Am., 1952—55; state chmn. Radio Free Europe, 1960—61; mem. exec. coun. Mid-Am. Ct., 1976—; pres. St. John Found., 1986; Sunday sch. tchr. St. John Luth. Ch., Council Bluffs, 1952—72, coun. mem., 1955—75. With US Army, 1943—46. Decorated Purple Heart, Bronze Star; named Outstanding Young Man, Council Bluffs C. of C., 1959; recipient Jason award, Children's Sq., 2005. Fellow: Am. Bar Found. (life); mem.: ABA, Hist. Soc. U.S. Cts. 8th Jud. Cir. (pres. 1989—99, ct. historian U.S. Dist. Ct. S.D. and Iowa 2000—), Iowa Conf. Bar Assn. (pres. 1985—87), Fed. Magistrate Judges Assn. (pres. 1978—79), Inter-Am. Bar Assn., Fed. Bar Assn., Pottawattamie County Bar Assn. (pres. 1979—80), Iowa Bar Assn. (chmn. com. fed. practice 1978—80, probate and trust coun. and sect. 1997—), Am. Judicature Soc., Supreme Ct. Hist. Soc., Masons, Kiwanis (pres. Coun. Bluffs), Omicron Delta Kappa, Delta Sigma Rho, Phi Delta Phi. Republican. Lutheran. Home: 1007 Arbor Ridge Cir Council Bluffs IA 51503-5000 Office: PO Box 248 25 Main Pl Ste 200 Council Bluffs IA 51503-0790

PETERSON, ROBERT AUSTIN, retired manufacturing executive; b. Sioux City, Iowa, July 5, 1925; s. Austen W. and Theresa Peterson; m. Carol May Hudy, May 17, 1952; children: Roberta, Richard., Bruce. BS, U. Minn., 1946, BBA, 1947. Credit mgr. New Holland Machine div. Sperry Rand Corp., Mpls., 1952-61; from credit mgr. to treas. Toro Co., Mpls., 1961-70, v.p., treas. internat. fin., 1970-83; v.p. fin., pres. Toro Credit Co., 1983-93. Chmn. Prior Lake Spring Lake Watershed Dist., 1970-80; chmn., bd. dirs. Prior Lake Bd. Edn., 1965-71; chmn. Scott County Republican Party, 1969-70; bd. dirs. Scott Carver Mental Health Center, 1969-73, Minn. Watershed Assn., 1972-76. Served to ensign USNR, 1943-46. Mem.: Prior Lake Yacht Club (bd. dirs.).

PETERSON, ROBERT SCOTT, electrical engineer; b. McKeesport, Pa., Mar. 24, 1930; s. William James and Emma Elizabeth (Scott) P.; m. Betty Louise Oleska, Aug. 11, 1962 (dec. 1995). BSEE, Pa. State U., 1952; MSEE, U. Pitts., 1961. Lic. profl. engr., Pa. Sr. application, design engr. Westinghouse Elec., Pitts., 1952-63, devel. engr. Buffalo, 1963-85, Pitts., 1985-89, AEG Automation Corp., Pitts., 1989-94; cons. engr. CDI-Ctrl. Corp., Pitts., 1994—. Holder 30 U.S. patents. Coach Midget Footbal

League, McKeesport, 1953-55. With U.S. Army, 1955-57. Mem. IEEE, NY Acad. Scis., Assn. Iron Steel Engrs. Achievements include patents in field. Avocations: gardening, woodworking, painting, dance, sports. Home and Office: 719 Heathergate Dr Pittsburgh PA 15238-1000 Office Phone: 412-767-4690.

PETERSON, ROBIN TUCKER, marketing educator; b. Casper, Wyo., July 31, 1937; s. Walfred Arthur and Mary Lurene Peterson; m. Marjorie K. Greenwald, June 25, 1963; children: Timothy, Kimberly. BS, U. Wyo., 1959, MS in Bus., 1961; PhD, U. Wash., 1967. Mem. faculty Idaho State U., Pocatello, 1963-73; prof. mktg., head mktg. dept. St. Cloud (Minn.) State U., 1973-76; prof. mktg. N.Mex. State U., Las Cruces, 1976—2007, head dept. mktg., 1976—, endowed disting. prof., 2007—. Fulbright lectr., Yugoslavia, 1973; vis. scholar Ea. Mont. State Coll., 1985; Sunwest Fin. Svcs. Disting. Centennial prof. N.Mex. State U., 1991, 92; Norwest Disting. prof. N.Mex. State U., 1999, Wells Fargo Disting. prof., 2002; vis. lectr. Nirma Inst. Ahmedabad, India, 1999, Chiang Moi U., Thailand, 2000; Fulbright lectr. Kathmandu U., Nepal, 2001. Author: Marketing-A Contemporary Introduction, 1976, Forecasting, 1976, edit., 1983, Personal Selling, 1977, Marketing in Action, 1977, Lernbook Marketing, 1984, Marketing: Concepts and Decision Making, 1987, Principles of Marketing, 1989, Argentina, 1990, Managing the Distributor Sales Network, 1990, Business Forecasting, 1992, Getting New Products to Market Rapidly, 1994; exec. editor Bus. Forecaster, 1993-94; editor Jour. Bus. and Entrepreneurship, 1994-98; contbr. articles to profl. publs. Served with USAR, 1962-63. Fellow Assn. Small Bus. Entrepreneurship; mem. Am. Mktg. Assn., Sales and Mktg. Execs. Internat., Acad. Mktg. Sci. (pres. 1977-78, 80-82), Am. Arbitration Assn. (Outstanding Educators Am. award), S.W. Small Bus. Assn. (pres. 1983-84, Outstanding Mktg. Educators award, Outstanding Educator, Assn. of Small Bus., 2002), S.W. Mktg. Assn., Western Mktg. Educators, Las Cruces C. of C., Las Cruces Sales and Mktg. Club, Beta Gamma Sigma, Phi Kappa Psi, Alpha Kappa Psi, Alpha Mu Alpha. Republican. Presbyterian. Home: 4350 Diamondback Dr Las Cruces NM 88011-7539 Office: NMex State U PO Box 5280 Las Cruces NM 88003-5280 Office Phone: 505-646-5748. Business E-Mail: ropeters@nmsu.edu.

PETERSON, ROBYN GAYLE, museum director; b. San Francisco, Jan. 17, 1958; BA, UCLA, 1979; MA, U. Wis., 1982, PhD, 1987. Goldsmith, 1974-80; collections acquisition asst. social studies bibliographer Meml. Libr./U. Wis., 1984-86; curator of collections The Rockwell Mus., Corning, N.Y., 1988-99; sr. dir. exhbns. and programs Turtle Bay Exploration Park, Redding, Calif., 1999—2006; exec. dir. Yellowstone Art Mus., Billings, Mont., 2006—. Author: American Frontier Photography, 1993, Edward Borein, 1997, Warp and Weft: Cross-cultural Exchange in Navajo Weavings, 1997, Transforming Trash: Bay Area Fiber Art, 2000, Second Nature: the Art of Michael Haykin, 2006; contbg. author: Allgemeines Künstlerlexikon, 1998—; editor/contbr.: Collector's Choice Review: Masterpieces of Glassmaking; Frederick Carder and the Steuben Glass Works, 1993, Brilliance in Glass: The Lost Wax Glass Sculpture of Frederick Carder, 1993, Journey to Justice: The Wintu People and the Salmon, 2002, The Other Side of the Looking Glass: The Glass Body and Its Metaphors, 2003, Bug-Eyed: Art, Culture, Insects, 2004; mng. editor: Frederick Carder and Steuben Glass: American Classics (Thomas P. Dimitroff), 1998; contbr. articles to profl. jours.; peer reviewer IMLS. Mem. Coll. Art Assn., Am. Assn. Mus. (peer reviewer accreditation). Office: Yellowstone Art Mus 401 N 27th St Billings MT 59101 Office Phone: 406-256-6804. E-mail: director@artmuseum.org.

PETERSON, ROGER, community bank executive, retired international investment banker, manufacturing executive, air force officer; b. Chgo., June 7, 1929; s. Milton Albert and LaVergne P.; m. Sally Ann Alder, Apr. 25, 1952; children: Bruce Roger, Dale Alder, Drew Alan. BS in Acctg., UCLA, 1955; MS in Mgmt., U. Colo., 1964; grad., Air Command and Staff Coll. Air U., Ala., 1965; grad. Exec. Program for Internat. and Nat. Security, J.F. Kennedy Sch. Govt., Harvard U., Cambridge, Mass., 1983. Joined USAF, 1955, advanced through grades to maj. gen., 1981, pilot, 1956-61, mgr. tactical missile site constrn., 1961; air officer comdg. 11th Cadet Squadron, Air Force Cadet Wing USAF Acad., 1961-64; asst. sec. Joint Chiefs of Staff and NSC matters for Hdqrs. Pentagon, 1965-68; transport pilot USAF, Vietnam, 1968, asst. chmn. US-Japan Joint Com., Adminstrn. of Status of Forces Agreement, 1968-73, chief program cost, dir. budget, 1973-76, chief plans, comptroller of Air Force, 1976-78, dir. mgmt. analysis, 1978-79, dir. programs, asst. chief of staff for research and devel., 1979-81; asst. dir. plans, policies and programs Def. Logistics Agy., Alexandria, Va., 1981-82, dep. dir., 1982-83; asst. dep. chief staff for logistics and engring. Hdqrs. USAF, Washington, 1983-84; pres., chief exec. officer advanced tech. factory, 1984-85; strategic planner United Techs. Corp., 1985-88; v.p., chief oper. officer Sikorsky Support Svcs. Inc., 1988-90; exec. asst. to mng. ptnr. O'Connor & Assocs., 1990-92; mng. dir. global ops. and svcs. Swiss Bank Corp., Zurich, 1992-96, chief of staff Chgo., 1996-99, br. mgr. Chgo. N.Am. and S.Am., 1996-99; mng. dir. UBS A.G. (formerly Swiss Bank Corp.), NY, 1996-99, UBS AG, NYC, 1999—2001; mng. dir. mktg. and strategic planning SunSouth Bank, Dothan, Ala., 2002—. Decorated D.S.M., Legion of Merit, Air medal with oak leaf cluster, Joint Service Commendation medal, Air Force Commendation medal with two oak leaf clusters. Mem. Air Force Assn., Beta Gamma Sigma, Sigma Iota Epsilon. Presbyterian. Achievements include designing and negotiating consolidation of US Air Force bases in Tokyo, 1970-73; negotiating mil. and civil aviation agreement for return of Okinawa to Japan; created global bus. mgmt. system for Swiss Bank Corp. Home: 1602 Deerpath Rd Dothan AL 36303-2173 Office: SunSouth Bank 108 Jamestown Blvd Dothan AL 36302 Office Phone: 334-677-4411. Personal E-mail: sbcrogerp@aol.com. *Always with honor.*

PETERSON, RONALD R., health service administrator; b. New Brunswick, NJ, 1948; m. Elizabeth Rooney; children: Joey, Susie. MA in Hosp. Adminstrn., Johns Hopkins U., Balt., 1970. Adminstrv. resident Johns Hopkins U., Balt., 1973, adminstr. Henry Phipps Psychiatric Clinic, 1974, adminstr. cost improvement program, 1975, adminstr. Children's Ctr., 1978, adminstr. Balt. City Hosps., 1982, exec. v.p., COO Johns Hopkins Health Sys., 1995—, acting pres. Hopkins Hosp. and Health Sys., 1996, pres., John Hopkins Health Sys., 1997—. Mem. bus. adv. coun., Balt.; vol. ARC, United Way, Am. Heart Assn. Mem. Md. Hosp. Assn. (mem. exec. com.), Md. C. of C. Office: Johns Hopkins Hosp 600 N Wolfe St Baltimore MD 21287-0005 also: Johns Hopkins U 720 Rutland Ave Baltimore MD 21205-2109 Office Phone: 410-955-5000.

PETERSON, RONALD ROGER, lawyer; b. Chgo., July 27, 1948; married; children: Elizabeth G., Ronald W. AB, Ripon, 1970; JD, U. Chgo., 1973. Bar: Ill. 1974, US Dist. Ct. (no. dist.) Ill. 1974, US Ct. Appeals (7th cir.) 1974, US Dist. Ct. (ea. dist.) Wis. 1975, US Dist. Ct. (no. dist.) Ind. 1978, US Dist. Ct. (ctrl. dist.) Ill. 1980, US Ct. Appeals (8th cir.) 1984, US Ct. Appeals (6th cir.) 1990, US Ct. Appeals (9th cir.) 1996, US Dist. Ct. (we. dist.) Mich. 1999, US Ct. Appeals (3d cir.) 2001, US Dist. Ct. (ea. dist.) Mich. 2004. Commd. 2d lt. US Army, 1968, advanced through grades to 1st lt., 1973, with mil. intelligence, 1968-78; ptnr. Jenner & Block, Chgo., 1974—. Editor: Consumer Bankruptcy in Illinois; contbr., articles to profl. jours. Trustee Ripon Coll.; mem. exec. bd. Northeast Ill. Coun. Boy Scouts of Am. Named to, Best Lawyers in Am., Chambers USA: Ill. Super Lawyer. Mem.: ABA, Fed. Bar Assn., Am. Coll. Bankruptcy Lawyers, Am. Bankruptcy Inst., Comml. Law League, Internat. Soc. Insolvency Practitioners, Chgo. Bar Assn., US Supreme Ct. Hist. Soc. Avocation: skiing. Office: Jenner & Block 330 North Wabash Fl 4000 Chicago IL 60611-7603 Office Phone: 312-923-2981. Business E-Mail: rpeterson@jenner.com.

PETERSON, ROSETTA HICKS, retired music educator; b. Memphis, Dec. 23, 1932; d. Homer Jackson Hicks and Loretta Jones Hicks Kateo. BA, Spelman Coll., Atlanta, 1954; M in Music Edn., Memphis State U., 1975. Cert. tchr. Ga., Tenn. Music tchr. T.H. Slater Elem. Sch., Atlanta, 1954—60, Porter Jr. HS, Memphis, 1961—71, Vance Jr. HS, Memphis, 1971—94; elem. tchr. Douglas Elem. Sch., Memphis, 1960—61; ret., 1994. Organist Rush Meml. Ch., Atlanta, 1957—60; organist, dir. Mt. Pisgah Christian Meth. Episcopal Ch., Memphis, 1966—88, St. John Bapt. Ch., Memphis, 1988—. Singer: (opera chorus) Aida, Memphis Opera, 1969, Porgy and Bess, Lyric Theatre, 1972. Vol. VA Hosp., Memphis, 1964—88, Friends of the Orpheum, Memphis, 1978—82. Named Outstanding Secondary Tchr. Am., Washington, 1974. Mem.: Music Educators Nat. Conf., Zoo Soc., Zeta Phi Beta (life; state dir. 1969—71), Phi Delta Kappa (life; pres. Beta Eta chpt.).

PETERSON, RUSSELL WILBUR, environmental services administrator, retired governor; b. Portage, Wis., Oct. 3, 1916; s. John Anton and Emma (Anthony) P.; m. E. Lillian Turner, June 30, 1937 (dec. Apr. 28, 1994); children: Russell Glen, Peter Jon, Kristin, Elin; m. June B. Jenkins, Oct. 21, 1995. BS, U. Wis., 1938, PhD, 1942, LLD (hon.), 1984; DSc (hon.), Williams Coll., 1975, Butler U., Springfield Coll., Stevens Inst. Tech., 1979, Gettysburg Coll., 1980, Alma Coll., 1981, Ohio State U., SUNY-Syracuse, Northland Coll., Fairleigh Dickinson U., 1981; LLD (hon.), Monmouth Coll., 1982, Salisbury State U., 1988; LHD, Meadville-Lombard Theol. Sch., 1992; DHL, Colby-Sawyer Coll., 2000; DSc (hon.), U. Del., 2006. With E. I. DuPont de Nemours & Co., Inc., 1942-69, rsch. dir. textile fibers dept., 1954-55, 56-59, merchandising mgr. textile fibers, 1955-56, dir. new products divsn. textile fibers, 1959-62, dir. R & D divsn. devel. dept., 1963-69; chmn. exec. com. Textile Research Inst., Princeton, NJ, 1959-61, chmn. bd. dirs., 1961-63, fellow, 1969; gov. State of Del., 1969—73; chmn. exec. com. Nat. Commn. Critical Choices for Am., 1973; chmn. U.S. Council on Environ. Quality, 1973-76; pres. Nat. Audubon Soc., 1979-85; mem. Nat. Commn. Critical Choices for Am., 1973-74; dir. Office Tech. Assessment, U.S. Congress, 1978-79. Pres. New Directions, 1976-77; regional v.p. Nat. Mcpl. League, 1968-78; chmn. Edn. Commn. States, 1970; chmn. com. nuclear energy and space tech. So. Govs. Conf., 1970-71; chmn. Nat. Adv. Commn. on Criminal Justice Standards and Goals, 1971-73; chmn. com. law enforcement, justice and pub. safety Nat. Govs. Conf., 1970-73; v.p. Council State Govts., 1970-71; chmn. adv. bd. Solar Energy Research Inst., 1979-83; vis prof. Dartmouth Coll., 1985, Carleton Coll., 1986, U. Wis., Madison, 1987; chmn. Centennial Internat. Symposium, Nat. Geog. Soc., 1986-88. Author: Oral History, Russell W. Peterson, 1995, Rebel with a Conscience, 1999, Delaware Heritage Series, 1999, Patriots, Stand Up!, 2004, (CD) We Can Save the Earth, 2000; contbr. articles to profl. jours. Chmn. Del. River Basin Commn., 1971-72; founding chmn. Bio-Energy Coun., 1976-78; bd. dirs. World Wildlife Fund, 1976-82, Population Action Internat., 1973-97, Alliance to Save Energy, 1979-93, Global Tomorrow Coalition, 1981-91, chmn., 1981-87; regional councillor Internat. Union Conservation Nature and Natural Resources, 1981-88, v.p., 1984-88; mem. Pres.'s Commn. on Accident at Three Mile Island, 1979; pres. Nat. Audubon Soc., 1979-85, Internat. Coun. Bird Preservation, 1982-90; chmn. Ctr. on Consequences of Nuclear War, 1983-87; vice-chmn. Better World Soc., 1985-90, pres., 1985-87; vis. com. John F. Kennedy Sch. Govt., 1979-85; Goodwill amb. UN Environ. Program, 1984-2002, world environ. prize com., 1989-2002; mem. Gov. Cuomo's Environ. Adv. Bd., 1985-94; adv. bd. Pace U. Sch. Law, 1988-98, Earth Island Inst., 1988-2002; chmn. bd. Earth Lobby, 1992-96; co-chmn. gov.'s task force on rejuvenating Wilmington waterfront, 1992-95; exe. com. Del. Riverfront Devel. Corp., 1995-2006, mem. 2006—; founder Stand Up For What's Right & Just, 2001, hon. chmn. 2002—. Decorated Order of Golden Ark (The Netherlands); Disting. fellow U. Del., 2000; recipient Ann. award NCCJ, 1966, Gold medal World Wildlife Fund, 1971, Ann. award Comml. Devel. Assn., 1971, Gold Plate award Nat. Acad. Achievement, 1971, Audubon award Nat. Audubon Soc., 1977, Frances K. Hutchinson medal Garden Club Am., 1980, Spl. Recognition award Population Reference Bur., 1983, Robert Marshall award Wilderness Soc., 1984, Nat. Conservation medal DAR, 1989, Human and Civil Rights award Del. Human Rights Commn., 1989, Spl. Recognition award Del. State Human Rels. Commn., 1989, Environ. Law Inst. award, 1990, Dr. Martin Luther King, Jr. Citation, Mt. Joy Meth. Ch., 1991, Ann. award Am. Civil Liberties Found. Del., 1992, Lawrence Solid Waste award Assn. N.Am., 1993, Kiwanis Cmty. Svc. award, 1993, Lifetime Achievement award Global Tomorrow Coalition, 1994, Lifetime Achievement award League of Conservation Voters, 1995, Del. Nature Soc., 1997, Liberty Bell award Del. State Bar Assn., 1998, Green Century award Resource Renewal Inst., 1999, Spl. Recognition award Med. Soc. Del., 2000, Samuel Baxter Meml. award Water Resources Assn., 2002, Presdl. medal Del. State U., 2003, Holmes Weatherly award Unitarian-Universalist Assn., 2004; Paul Harris fellow Rotary Internat., 2002; named Conservationist of Yr., Nat. Wildlife Fedn., 1972, Swedish-Am. of Yr., Vasa Order of Am. In Sweden, 1982, Lifetime Achievement award Creative Grandparenting, 1999, NAACP, 1999; named to Wis. Conservation Hall of Fame, 2007; Del. refuge named in his honor Russell W. Peterson Wildlife Refuge, 2000; bronze statue in his honor on Wilmington Waterfront, 2002; papers on file Libr. of Congress, 2006. Fellow Am. Inst. Chemists (hon.), AAAS (past bd. dirs.); mem. Am. Ornithologists Union, Linnaean Soc., Fedn. Am. Scientists, Am. Chem. Soc. (Parsons award 1974), Del. Acad. Sci., U.S. Assn. for Club of Rome, Cosmos Club (Cert. of Appreciation 2001), Phi Beta Kappa, Sigma Xi (Proctor prize 1978), Phi Lambda Upsilon, Phi Kappa Phi. Unitarian Universalist. Address: 11 E Mozart Dr Wilmington DE 19807-1942

PETERSON, RUTH D., sociologist; BA, Cleve. State U., 1969, MA, 1973; PhD, U. Wis., Madison, 1993. Asst. prof. U. Iowa, 1982—85, Ohio State U., 1985—89, assoc. prof., 1989—96, prof., 1996—, dir. Criminal Justice Rsch. Ctr., 1999—. Mem. editl. bd. Race and Society, 1998—2002. Co-editor: Crime and Inequality, 1995; editor (assoc.): Criminology, 1997—2000; contbr. articles to prof. jour. Fellow: Am. Soc. Criminology (v.p. 1999—2000, Herbert Bloch award 1995); mem.: Am. Sociol. Assn. Office: Ohio State U Sociology Dept 300 Bricker Hall 190 N Oval Mall Columbus OH 43210 Office Phone: 614-247-6379. Business E-Mail: peterson.5@osu.edu. *

PETERSON, STEPHEN JOSEPH, internist; b. Bellerose, NY, Mar. 17, 1953; s. Robert Francis and Veronica Mae (Burns) P. BS in Biology, Fairfield U., Conn., 1975; MD, Cebu Drs. Coll. Medicine, Cebu City, The Philippines, 1982. Diplomate Am. Bd. Internal Medicine, 1985. Intern internal medicine Met. Hosp. Ctr. N.Y. Med. Coll., 1982—83, resident to chief resident internal medicine Valhalla, NY, 1983—86, dir. medicine clerkship, 1994—2003; assoc. program dir. Met. Hosp. Ctr., NYC, 1986—88; dep. dir. dept. medicine Lincoln Med. & Mental Health Ctr., Bronx, 1988—93; attending physician Westchester Sq. Hosp Med. Ctr., Bronx, 1993—94; dir. internal medicine residency tng. program Westchester Med. Ctr., Valhalla, 1994—, chief gen. internal medicine, 1994—. Bd. dirs. St. Agnes Hosp., White Plains, NY, 1995—2003; asst. prof. medicine NY Med. Coll., 1986—96, assoc. prof. clin. medicine, 1996—99, adj. prof. pharmacology, 2001—06; mem. med. edn. coms. N.Y. Med. Coll., Westchester Med. Ctr.; prof. clin. medicine NY Med. Coll., 1999—2006, vice chmn. dept. medicine, 2002—06, exec. vice chair, 2006—, prof. medicine and pharmacology, 2006—, prof. clin. public health, 2006—. Contbr. articles to profl. jours. Recipient Advisor award Med. Explorers Boy Scouts Am., 1986, 88. Mem. AMA, ACP (gov. Hudson Valley region 2004-), Clerkship Dirs. Internal Medicine, Assn. Program Dirs. Internal Medicine, Assoc. Chiefs Gen. Internal Medicine, Soc. Gen. Internal Medicine, Assn. Profs. Medicine. Rep. Roman Cath. Avocations: singing, exercise. Office: NY Med Coll Munger Pavillion # 256 Valhalla NY 10595 Home Phone: 914-455-2214; Office Phone: 914-493-8370. Business E-Mail: stephen_peterson@nymc.edu.

PETERSON, TERRY NORRIS, lawyer; b. Wichita, Kans. BA, U. Tex., Austin, 1994; JD, South Tex. Coll. Law, 1998. Bar: Tex. 1998. Assoc. Johnson, Spalding, Doyle, West & Trent, L.L.P., Houston. Named a Rising Star, Tex. Super Lawyers mag., 2005; recipient, 2006. Mem.: Greater Houston Soc. Health Risk Mgmt., Garland Walker Inns of Ct., ABA, Houston Bar Assn. Office: Johnson Spalding Doyle West & Trent LLP 919 Milam St Ste 1700 Houston TX 77002 Office Phone: 713-222-2323. Business E-Mail: tpeterson@js-llp.com.

PETERSON, THOMAS W., engineering educator; b. Tucson, June 15, 1950; BS in Chem. Engring., Tufts U., 1972; MS in Chem. Engring., U. Ariz., 1973; PhD, Calif. Inst. Technology, Pasadena, 1977. From asst. prof. to prof., dean chem. engring. dept. U. Ariz., Tucson, 1977—, head dept. chem. and environ. engring., 1990—98, dean Coll. Engring. and Mines. Office: U Ariz Coll Engring Engring Rm 200 PO Box 210020 Tucson AZ 85721

PETERSON, VICTOR LOWELL, aerospace engineer, consultant; b. Saskatoon, Sask., Can., June 11, 1934; came to U.S., 1937; s. Edwin Galladet and Ruth Mildred (McKeeby) P.; m. Jacqueline Dianne Hubbard, Dec. 21, 1955; children: Linda Kay, Janet Gale, Victor Craig. BS in Aero. Engring., Oreg. State U., 1956; MS in Aerospace Engring., Stanford U., 1964; MS in Mgmt., MIT, 1973. Rsch. scientist NASA-Ames Rsch. Ctr., Moffett Field, Calif., 1956-68, asst. chief hypersonic aerodyns., 1968-71, chief aerodyns. br., 1971-74, chief thermo and gas dynamics div., 1974-84, dir. aerophysics, 1984-90, dep. dir., 1990-94; pvt. mgmt. cons., 1994—. Mem. nat. adv. bd. U. Tenn. Space Inst., Tullahoma, 1984-94. Contbr. numerous articles to profl. jours. Treas. Woodland Acres Homeowners Assn., Los Altos, Calif., 1978—. Capt. USAF, 1957-60. Recipient medal for outstanding leadership NASA, 1982; Alfred P. Sloan fellow MIT, 1972-73. Fellow AIAA. Republican. Methodist. Achievements include development of numerical aerodynamic simulation system for aerospace, of method for reconstructing planetary atmosphere structure from accelerations of body entering atmosphere, of theory for motions of tumbling bodies entering planetary atmospheres. Home: 484 Aspen Way Los Altos CA 94024-7100 Personal E-mail: vicpeterson@comcast.net. *Achievements in life are maximized by creating visions of success and focussing relentlessly on successful accomplishment of intermediate objectives.*

PETERSON, WALTER FRITIOF, retired academic administrator; b. Idaho Falls, Idaho, July 15, 1920; s. Walter Fritiof and Florence (Danielson) P.; m. Barbara Mae Kempe, Jan. 13, 1946; children: Walter Fritiof III, Daniel John. BA, State U. Iowa, 1942, MA, 1948, PhD, 1951; HHD (hon.), Loras Coll., 1983; LHD (hon.), Clarke Coll., 1991; DHum (hon.), U. Dubuque, 1997. Asst. prof. history, chmn. dept. history Milw. Downer Coll., 1952-57, assoc. prof. history, chmn. social sci. div., 1957-64; assoc. prof. history Lawrence U., Appleton, Wis., 1964-67, prof. history, Alice G. Chapman libr., 1967-70; pres. U. Dubuque, 1970-90, chancellor, 1990—2000, chancellor emeritus, 2000. Regional tng. officer Peace Corps, 1965-68; cons. history Allis-Chalmers Mfg. Co., 1959-75, Secura Ins. Group, 1968-92, Wm. C. Brown Pub. Co., 1981-92, bd. dirs. Editor: Transactions of Wis. Acad. Scis., Arts and Letters, 1965-72, The Allis-Chalmers Corporation: An Industrial History, 1977, A History of Wm. C. Brown Cos., 1994, A History of Hawkeye Bancorporation, 1996. Advisor Templeton Prize for Progress in Religion, 1986-91; bd. dirs. Finley Hosp., pres., 1983-84; chmn. Finley Health Found., 1986-95, Finley Health Found. Hall of Fame, 2000; bd. dirs. Dubuque Symphony Orch., Dubuque Art Assn., Jr. Achievement, Nat. River Hall of Fame, 1984; chmn. Iowa Assn. Coll. and Univ. Pres., 1975-76; chmn. Iowa Coll. Found., 1982-83; chair Grand Opera House Found., 1998—. With USAAF, 1942-45, PTO. Recipient Dubuque 1st Citizen award, 1990, Disting. Civic Svc. award, 1991, Benjamin Franklin award Nat. Soc. Fundraising Execs., 1994, Paul Harris fellowship, Duduque Rotary Club, 1993; named to Dubuque Bus. Hall of Fame, 1990 Mem. Iowa Assn. Ind. Colls. and Univs. (chmn. 1988-89), Dubuque County Hist. Soc. (bd. dirs.), Dubuque Shooting Soc., Dubuque Golf and Country Club, Phi Alpha Theta, Kappa Delta Pi, Phi Delta Kappa, Dubuque Shooting Soc Office Phone: 563-556-4365.

PETERSON, WILLIAM T., oceanographer; b. Vancouver, Wash. PhD, Oreg. State U., Corvallis, 1979. Asst. prof. SUNY, Stony Brook, 1980—87; sr. rsch. officer U. Cape Town, South Africa, 1987—; oceanographer NOAA, Newport, Oreg., 1989—. Contbr. articles to profl. jours. Mem.: WAC, AGU, ASLO. Office: NOAA Fisheries/Hatfield Marine Sci Ctr 2030 S Marine Science Dr Newport OR 97365 Office Phone: 541-867-0201. Business E-Mail: bill.peterson@noaa.gov.

PETERSON GERSTNER, JANET, English professor; b. Normal, Ill., Nov. 5, 1963; d. Carroll Valleen and Lillian Maxine Peterson; m. Clinton J. Gerstner, Aug. 1, 1992; children: Isabelle Olivia Gerstner, Alec James Gerstner. BA in English, Colo. State U., Denver, 1991; MA in English, Ariz. State U., Tempe, 1994, PhD in English, 2000. Prof. of English San Juan Coll., Farmington, N.Mex., 2001—, English program coord., 2007—. Recipient Tchg. Excellence award, Nat. Inst. for Staff and Orgnl. Devel., 2003; fellow, Preparing Future Faculty, Fall 1997-Spring 1999. Mem.: MLA, Nat. Coun. of Tchrs. of English, Two-Year Coll. Assn., League for Innovation in the C.C. Office: San Juan Coll 4601 College Blvd Farmington NM 87402 Home Phone: 505-327-3075; Office Phone: 505-566-3140.

PETH, HOWARD ALLEN, law educator; b. Calif., Apr. 20, 1955; s. Howard Allen and Diane Marie (Munyan) P.; m. Gloria Gene Stockton, Aug. 9, 1992; children: Andrew Howard, Rachel Gloria. BA, U. Calif., San Diego, 1980; MD, U. Santiago, 1984; JD, U. Mo., 1991. Bar: Calif. 1993, U.S. Ct. Appeals (9th cir.) 1993, U.S. Ct. Claims, U.S. Ct. Appeals (fed. cir.) 1993, U.S. Dist. Ct. (so. dist.) Calif. 1993, U.S. Supreme Ct. 1997; diplomate Am. Bd. Internal Medicine, Be. Cert. Emergency Medicine; lic. physician, Calif., Mo., Wis.d. Asst. prof. U. Mo. Sch. Medicine, Columbia, 1997—2005; ptnr. Lake Emergency Specialists, Osage Beach, Mo., 2005—. Fellow Am. Coll. Legal Medicine; mem. AMA, ABA (health law sect.), ACP, Am. Coll. Emergency Physicians. Republican. Episcopalian. Office: Lake Regional Hosp Dept Emergency Medicine 54 Hospital Dr Osage Beach MO 65065 Home: PO Box 357 Osage Beach MO 65065-0357 Office Phone: 573-434-2791. Personal E-mail: hpethmdjd@aol.com.

PETHICK, CHRISTOPHER JOHN, physicist; b. Horsham, Sussex, Eng., Feb. 22, 1942; s. Richard Hope and Norah Betty (Hill) P. BA, Magdalen Coll., Oxford U., Eng., 1962, DPhil, 1965. Fellow Magdalen Coll., Oxford U., 1965-70; research assoc. U. Ill., Urbana, 1966-68, research asst. prof., 1968-69, assoc. prof. physics, 1970-73, prof. physics, 1973-95, Nordita, Copenhagen, 1975—. A.P. Sloan research fellow, 1970-72. Fellow Am. Phys. Soc.; mem. European Phys. Soc. Office: Nordita Blegdamsvej 17 DK-2100 Copenhagen Denmark Office Phone: 45 35 32 52 26.

PETIET, CAROLE ANNE, psychologist; b. Newport News, Va., Mar. 1, 1952; d. Gaston Kaleski and Ann (Snyder) Pettit Johnson; m. Lawrence Phillip Bischoff III, Dec. 29, 1973 (div. 1979); m. Robert Jomax Brooks, May 4, 1984 (div. 1989); 1 child, Nicole; stepchildren: Gregory, Randall. BS in Nursing, Baylor U., 1975; MA, Calif. Sch. Profl. Psychology, Berkeley, 1980, PhD, 1982. RN Calif.; lic. psychologist Calif., Colo. Charge nurse Elizabeth Knutsson Hosp., Estes Park, Colo., 1975-76; nurse coordinator, staff nurse Alta Bates Hosp., Berkeley, Calif., 1976-83; pvt.

practice psychotherapy, cons., sports psychology Berkeley, Calif., 1982—; tng./clin. cons., rsch. cons. Phoenix Recovery Ctrs., Alameda, Calif., 1980-88; staff psychologist Kaiser Permanente Med. Ctr., Vallejo, Calif., 1982-84. Sports psychology cons. Women's Ski Programs, Aspen, Colo., and B.C., Can., 1986-93; coord. women's studies splty., mem. faculty Rosebridge Grad. Sch., Walnut Creek, Calif., 1986-94; supr., mem. adj. faculty CSPP, Berkeley/Alameda, 1986-89; intern Eden Youth and Family Svcs., Hayward, Calif., 1978-79, No. Calif. State Correctional Med. Facility, Vacaville, 1979-80, Kaiser Vallejo, 1980-81, Kaiser San Francisco, 1981-82; rschr. in field. Contbr. articles, presentations to profl. publs. Scholar Baylor Hosp. Women's Aux., 1974, Soroptimists, 1981; recipient Am. Coll. Scholarship, 1979. Mem. APA, Assn. Women in Psychology, World Fedn. Mental Health, NOW, Amnesty Internat. Democrat. Achievements include research on neuropsychological effects of altitude on women climbers. Office: 2340 Ward St Ste 105 Berkeley CA 94705-1146 Office Phone: 510-843-6760.

PETILLO, JOHN J., former academic administrator, priest; b. Montclair, NJ, Mar. 19, 1947; s. Gennaro and Geraldine (Illaria) Petillo; m. Sabina M. Porcaro; 1 child. Earned undergraduate degree, Seton Hall U., 1969, MA in Counseling, 1971; profl. diploma in counselor edn., Fordham U., 1973, PhD in Counseling and Personnel Services, 1976; M.Div. in Pastoral Theology, Darlington Sch. Theology, 1975; M.P.A., Rutgers U., 1977. Ordained priest Roman Catholic Ch., 1973; left priesthood in 1990. Asst. dir. office research and planning Archdiocese Newark, Roman Cath. Ch., 1975-77, chancellor for adminstrn., 1978-83; dep. dir. Cath. Community Services, NJ, 1976-78; asst. to pres. Seton Hall U., South Orange, NJ, 1978, chancellor, chief exec. officer, 1983-90, also mem. bd. trustees and bd. regents, 1983—; chancellor, chief exec. officer Immaculate Conception Sem., 1983; CEO for several insurance companies Tribus Companies, Care Advantage, Inc., Blue Cross and Blue Shield, NJ (also pres.), 1990—2001; pres., CEO Newark Alliance, 2001—04; chmn. bd. trustee U. Medicine and Dentistry NJ, 2003—, interim pres., 2004, pres., 2004—06. Mem. Archdiocesan Bd. Adminstrn. Mem. long range-strategic planning com. United Way Am.; bd. dirs. Blue Cross NJ, Nat. Soc. Prevention Blindness, Nat. Commn. on Coop. Edn., Found. Ednl. Alternatives, Ind. Coll. Fund NJ, NJ State Police Meml. Library and Mus. Assn., labor-higher edn. council Am. Council on Edn. and AFL-CIO, Commn. for Pub. Responsibility for Ednl. Success, Washington Ctr. NJ Scholarship Program, Statue of Liberty Centennial Commn. State NJ, NJ Performing Arts Ctr., St. Joseph's Health System, Wachovia Regional Found., Lincoln Educational Svcs.; chmn. bd. Essex County Coll. Found. Mem. Assn. Ind. Colls. and Univs. NJ (bd. dirs.) Office: The Univ Med Dentistry 65 Bergen St Newark NJ 07103 Office Phone: 973-972-4400. Business E-Mail: petillo@umdnj.edu.

PETILLON, LEE RITCHEY, lawyer; b. Gary, Ind., May 6, 1929; s. Charles Ernest and Blanche Lurene (Mackay) Petillon; m. Mary Anne Keeton, Feb. 20, 1960; children: Andrew G., Joseph R. BBA, U. Minn., 1952; LLB, U. Calif., Berkeley, 1959. Bar: Calif. 1960, U.S. Dist. Ct. (so. dist.) Calif. 1960. V.p. Creative Investment Capital, Inc., LA, 1969—70; corp. counsel Harvest Industries, LA, Calif., 1970—71; v.p., gen. counsel, dir. Tech. Svcs. Corp., Santa Monica, Calif., 1971—78; ptnr. Petillon & Davidoff, LA, 1978—92, Gipson Hoffman & Pancione, 1992—93; pvt. practice Torrance, Calif., 1993—94; ptnr. Petillon & Hansen, Torrance, 1994—2003, Petillon & Hiraide LLP, Torrance, 2004—06, Petillon, Hiraide Loomis & Katz, LLP, Torrance, 2006—. Co-author: R&D Partnerships, 2d edit., 1985, Representing Start-Up Companies, 1992, 14th edit., 2006; contbr. chapters to books. Chmn. Neighborhood Justice Ctr. Com., 1983-85, Middle Income Co., 1983085; active Calif. Senate Commn. on Corp. Governance, State Bar Calif. Task Force on Alternative Dispute Resolution, 1984-85; chmn. South Bay Sci. Found., Inc.; vice-chmn. Calif. Capital Access Forum, Inc.; dir., legal counsel ACE-Net.org, Inc. Recipient Cert. of Appreciation L.A. City Demonstration Agy., 1975, United Indian Devel. Assn., 1981, City of L.A. for Outstanding Vol. Svcs., 1984, Outstanding Vol. award Torrance C. of C., 2000, Small Bus. Adv. of Yr. award Torrance C. of C., 2001, Marvin Greene award Los Angeles County Bar Assn., 2005; named Small Bus. Adv. of Yr. Calif. C. of C., 2001. Mem.: ABA (venture capital and pvt. equity com.), Los Angeles County Bar Assn. (trustee 1984—85, alt. dispute resolution sect. 1992—94, bus. and corp. law sect. 2000—, chmn. law tech. sect., Griffin Bell Vol. Svc. award 1993), Los Angeles County Bar Found. (bd. dirs.), Calif. State Bar Assn. (pres., Pro Bono Svcs. award 1983). Avocations: backpacking, reading, music, painting. Home: 1636 Via Machado Palos Verdes Estates CA 90274-1930 Office: Petillon Hiraide Loomis & Katz LLP 21515 Hawthorne Blvd Ste 1260 Torrance CA 90503-6503 Home Phone: 310-378-1852; Office Phone: 310-543-0500. Business E-Mail: lpetillon@corplawp-h.com.

PETINGA, CHARLES MICHAEL, transportation executive; b. Atlantic City, July 9, 1946; s. Thomas Joseph and Rose Marie (Merindino) P.; m. Velna Mae McVicker, June 7, 1969; children: Scott, Jeffery. BS in Geology, Geography, U. Wis., Superior, 1969. Ops. supr. Schneider Transport, Inc., Green Bay, Wis., 1973-74, prodn. mgr., 1974-76, safety dir., 1976-79; dir. safety Schneider Nat., Inc., Green Bay, Wis., 1979-82, dir. risk mgmt., 1982-87; gen. mgr. Petinga Candy Co., Atlantic City, 1987-89; sr. v.p., midwest practice leader Transp. Industry, Appleton, Wis., 1989-2000; exec. v.p. Smith Transport Inc., Roaring Spring, Pa., 2003—; prin. Transp. Assocs., Appleton, Wis., 2005—06; exec. dir. transp. HNI Risk Svcs., New Berlin, Wis., 2006—. Cons. local charitable groups, Green Bay, 1985-88; preactice leader freight/logistics Global Transp. Industry; adviser, cons. Small Bus. Execs., Green Bay, 1989; mem. worker compensation task force Wis. Motor Carriers, Madison, 1991; nat.-internat. spkr. at univs., bus. schs., vocat. schs. and high schs.; speaker to motor carrier assns., bd. directors, and industry mgmt. groups, nat. and state assns. Co. liaison Green Bay United Way, 1985, 86. With US Army, 1971—73. Mem. Wis. Coun. Safety Suprs., Nat. Safety Mgmt. Soc., Wis. Motor Carriers Assn., Risk and Ins. Mgmt. Soc., Nat. Safety Coun., Am. Trucking Assn. Avocations: martial arts, physical fitness, weightlifting. Home: 842 Whisper Falls Ln Menasha WI 54952 Office: HNI Risk Svcs 4650 W Spencer St Ste 13 Appleton WI 54914-8230 Office Phone: 920-540-0647. Personal E-mail: cpetinga@new.rr.com. Business E-Mail: cpetinga@hni.com.

PETIT, EMMANUEL J., architecture educator; MArch, Swiss Fed. Inst. Tech., Zürich, 1998; PhD, Princeton U., NJ, 2006. Lectr., critic Yale U., New Haven, 2001—05, asst. prof., 2005—.

PETIT, WILLIAM ARTHUR, JR., endocrinologist; b. Southington, Conn., Sept. 24, 1956; m. Jennifer Hawke-Petit (dec. July 2007); children: Hayley(dec.), Michaela(dec.). AB cum laude, Dartmouth Coll., 1978; MD cum laude, U. Pitts., 1982. Diplomate Am. Bd. Internal Medicine, Am. Bd. Endocrinology, Diabetes and Metabolism. Postdoctoral fellow Sch. Medicine Yale U., New Haven, 1985-87, assoc. rsch. scientist, 1987-89, asst. clin. prof., 1989—; chief sect. endocrinology, dir. Joslin Diabetes Ctr. New Britain (Conn.) Gen. Hosp., 1997—; asst. prof. clin. medicine Sch. Medicine U. Conn., 1997—2002, assoc. prof. clin. medicine Sch. Medicine, 2002—. Spkr. in field. Contbr. articles to sci. jours.; co-author (with C. Adamec): Encyclopedia of Diabetes, 2002, Encyclopedia of Endocrine Diseases and Disorders, 2005. Chmn. com. on advt. Am. Diabetes Assn., 1996-2002, pres. Conn. affiliate, 1991-93, bd. dirs., 1987-97. Named to Hall of Merit, Am. Diabetes Assn., Hartford, Conn., 1994. Fellow ACP, Am. Assn. Clin. Endocrinologists; mem. AMA, Endocrine Soc., Hartford County Med. Soc. (Cmty. Svc. award 1994), Conn. Endocrine Soc. (pres. 1999-2001). Republican. Roman Catholic. Avocations: golf, horticulture. Office: 100 Grand St New Britain CT 06050 also: Po Box 886 Plainville CT 06062-0886 Office Phone: 860-747-4377. *

PETITAN, DEBRA ANN BURKE, elementary school educator, counselor, design engineer, writer; b. Chgo., Mar. 12, 1932; d. James Marcellus and Susan Florence (Hines) Burke; m. Kenneth Charles Petitan, Aug. 9, 1952; 1 child, Susan Florence. AA, Wilson Jr. Coll., Chgo., 1951, N.Y. Inst. Photography, 1952; BS in Primary Edn., Chgo. State U., 1956, MS in Indsl. Edn., 1967; DSc in Applied Sci. and Tech., London Inst. Tech., 1971; postgrad., U. Wis., Bradley U., U. Calif., U. Ill.; grad., Inst. Children's Lit., West Redding, Conn., 1991; cert. in Childrens' Portraiture, North Light Art Sch., 1997. Tchr. Chgo. Bd. Edn., 1958-71, guidance counselor, 1976-84, now tchr., cons.; nat. dir. edn. Nation of Islam, 1971-75; design engr. Fed. Sign and Signal Corp., Chgo., 1975-76; CEO, owner Petitan's Creative Projects, Inc. Nat. adv. bd. Nat. Right to Work Orgn., 1976-85; cons. ednl. devel., 1978; computer libr. cons.; owner, CEO, Fayzah's Fin. Svcs., Instrn. Svcs. in Trading and Investing, Fayzah's Creative Projects, Inc.; ednl. cons. tech. analysis and chart reading stock market; participant summer writing festival U. Iowa, 1991. Photographer VISTA News, 1969-70; writer children's lit.; author curriculum introducing computer-aided design techniques in the pub. schs., 1965. Cmty. svc. rec. sec. 9600 Block Club; navigator, pub. rels. officer IL wing Squadron 8, capt. Civil Air Patrol, 1953—56; chmn. Career Women for Johnson/Humphrey, Chgo., 1965; dir. Christian edn. Trinity United Ch. Christ, Chgo., 1978—81, family counselor, 1978—81; organizer, leader family counseling ministry, lic. lay Eucharistic min. Episcopal Ch. St. Edmund, Chgo. Episc. Diocese, 1989. Named Woman of Yr. Iota Phi Lambda, 1978; recipient 250 Hr. medal Ground Observer Corps, 1952, 25 Yr. Service medal Chgo. Bd. Edn., 1987. Mem. Off-Campus Writer's Workshop (editor newsletter), Soc. of Children's Book Writers, Am. Contract Bridge League, Am. Bridge Assn. (sr. life master; rec. sec.), Children's Reading Roundtable, Green River Writers, Epsilon Pi Tau. Achievements include introduction of Computer Aided Design curriculum to field of education. Office: Fayzah's Analytical Guidance Svc Chicago IL 60628 E-mail: drdap1@ameritech.net.

PETITO, MARGARET L., foundation president; b. Dallas, Sept. 28, 1950; d. Jacob Charles and Eileen (Shank) Loehr; m. John Haven Petito, 1978 (div. 1984); children: John Christian Robert, David Nelson. BA, So. Meth. U., 1972; MA, Georgetown U., 2006. Mem. Action/Vista Program U.S. Govt., Middlesex, NY, 1972—74; dir., curator Oliver House Mus., Penn Yan, NY, 1975—77; staff asst. Williams & Jensen, P.C., Washington, 1986—89; dir. fed. rels. Chambers Devel. Co., Inc., 1989—92; dir. fed. affairs DSSI-U.S. Biotech., Washington, 1992—94; cons., dir. pub. affairs Embassy Ecuador, Govt. Ecuador, Washington, 1994—96; prin. Petito & Assocs., Washington, 1994—. Dir. external events Internat. Cancer Alliance, Bethesda, Md., 1996—97, Sch. of Bus., Georgetown U., Washington, 1998—99; pres., exec. dir. Friends of Rule of Law in Ecuador, Inc., 2001—. Spl. legis. advisor Drugwatch Internat., Chgo., 1993—; bd. dirs. Nyumbani Orphanage for Kenyan Children with AIDS, Washington, 1989—99; dir. Marshall Ho. Mus., Lambertville, NJ, 1980—82; founder, co-chair Forum for Environ., Washington, 1989—91; pres. Cultural Partnership of the Ams., Washington, 1999—. Mem.: Tex. State Soc. Roman Catholic. Avocations: squash, needlepoint, fishing. Home and Office: Friends of Rule of Law in Ecuador Inc 6008 34th Pl NW Washington DC 20015-1607 Office Phone: 202-537-1327. Business E-Mail: mlp3@starpower.net.

PETIT-PHARE, VANESSA, secondary school educator; d. Emmanuel and Yolene J. Petit-Phare. BS in Environ. Studies, St. John's U., Jamaica, NY, 2000; M, CUNY. Cert. biology and gen. sci. NY, 2000. Sci. tchr., grade leader Gerald R. Dever Mid. Sch. 180Q, Rockaway Park, NY, 2000—04; lead sci. educator Russell Sage JHS 190Q, Forest Hills, NY, 2004—; lead sci. educator Sci. Exit Project Initiative Urban Advantage Mid. Sch., NYC, 2004—. Sci. profl. devel. workshop facilitator NY Hall Sci. and Am. Mus. Natural History, Queens, NY, 2005—; presenter Math and Sci. Edn. Sharing Our Success Conf. NYU, NYC, 2007; lead educator rep. for urban advantage program Channel Thirteen's Ann. Celebration of Learning Conf., NYC, 2007—. Recipient Emerging and Established Leaders awards, St. John's U., 1997—99, Excellence in Sci. Edn. award, Siemen's Found., Hall Sci., 2006, Demonstration/Model Classroom award, Urban Advantage, NY Dept. Edn., 2007—; Tchg. Opportunity Program scholar, CUNY/NY Dept. Edn., 2001, Tchg. Renewal for Urban Sci. Tchg. scholar, Am. Mus. Natural History, 2005—. Mem.: Nat. Sci. Tchrs. Assn. (lead educator rep. for urban advantage program ann. conf. 2007—). Home Phone: 917-749-4227; Office Phone: 718-830-4970. Business E-Mail: ourschoolteacher@aol.com.

PETITTO, LAURA-ANN, cognitive neuroscience educator; b. NYC; m. Kevin Dunbar; children: Eva-Molly Dunbar, Annafaye Dunbar, Maaraluisa Dunbar. PhD, EdD, Harvard U., 1984; MA (hon.), Dartmouth Coll., 2004. Rsch. project coord. and primary tchr. project nim chimpsky Columbia U., NYC, 1973—76; staff lectr. N.Y. Soc. for the Deaf, NYC, 1978—79; asst. prof. dept. psychology McGill U., Montreal, 1983—89, assoc. prof., dept psychology, 1989—99, prof. dept psychology, 1999—2001; prof. Dartmouth Coll., Hanover, NH, 2001—, chmn., dir. cognitive neuroscience NIRS Brain Imaging lab. for lang. and child devel., 2001—. Rschr. in neurolinguistics lab. for am. sign lang. The Salk Inst. for Biol. Studies, San Diego, 1980—85; rsch. scientist, McDonnell-pew ctr. for cognitive neuroscience Montreal Neurol. Inst., 1983—2001, rsch. scientist, 1983—2001; prof. of psychology and dir. of cognitive neuroscience lab. for lang., sign, & cognition McGill U., Montreal, Quebec, Canada, 1983—2001. Contbr. articles to profl. jours., chapters to books. Recipient Career Develop. award, Natural Sciences and Engring. Rsch. Coun. of Can., 1985—95, Young Psychologist award, APA, 1988, Outstanding Tchg. & Sci. Achievements award, Golden Key Nat. Hon. Soc., 1997, Pub. Achievement award, Boys Town Med. Ctr. /U. of Nebr., 1997, Justine and Yves Sergent Fund Internat. prize cognitive neurosci., 2004; fellow, The John D. and Catherine T. MacArthur Found, 1983—84, The John Simon Guggenheim Meml. Found., 1998; grantee, Social Sciences and Humanities Rsch. Coun. of Can., 1997—2000, 2000—03, The Spencer Found., 2000—03, Montreal Neurol. Inst., Brain Imaging Ctr., 2000—. Mem.: AAAS (mem.-at-large), Soc. Lang. Devel., Internat. Mind, Brain, Edn. Soc., Soc. Rsch. in Child Devel., Soc. Neuroscience, Can. Deafness Rsch. & Tng. Inst. Coop. Coun. (assoc.; exec. adv. com. mem. 1983—2003), Phi Beta Kappa (hon.). Office: Dartmouth Coll Dept Edn 110 Raven House Hanover NH 03755 E-mail: laura-ann.petitto@dartmouth.edu.

PETKANICS, DONNA M., lawyer; BA, Northwestern U., 1980; JD, U. Calif., Boalt Hall Law Sch., 1985. Staff economist President Carter Administrn., Washington; with Wilson Sonsini Goodrich & Rosati, Palo Alto, Calif., 1985—, assoc. mng. ptnr., 1996—97, co-chmn., nominating com., 1997, 1998, mng. dir. - ops., ptnr., mem. exec. mgmt. com. & policy com. Office: Wilson Sonsini Goodrich & Rosati 650 Page Mill Rd Palo Alto CA 94304-1050 Office Phone: 650-493-9300. Office Fax: 650-493-6811. Business E-Mail: dpetkanics@wsgr.com.

PETKOVIC, LUCIA M., research scientist; PhD, U. Nebr., Lincoln, 1999. Assoc. prof. Universidad Nacional San Juan, Argentina, 1999—2003; staff scientist Idaho Nat. Lab., Idaho Falls, 2003—. Mem.: AIChE, Am. Chem. Soc. Achievements include research in Heterogeneous Catalysis.

PETKOVSKA, IVA, medical researcher; d. Blagoja Petkovski and Liljana Petkovska; m. Aleksandar Markovski; 1 child, Kristijan Dzekov. MD. Postdoctoral rsch. fellow Mass. Gen. Hosp., Boston, 2001—03; postdoctoral rsch. fellow dept. radiol. scis. UCLA, 2003—06, staff rsch. assoc. Thoracic Imaging Rsch. Group, 2006—. Recipient Magna Cum Laude, European Congress Radiology, 2005. Mem.: Macedonian Soc. Radiology, Acad. Molecular Imaging, Radiol. Soc. N.Am. Achievements include research in lung cancer. Personal E-mail: drluna93@hotmail.com.

PETKUS, ALAN FRANCIS, microbiologist; b. Chgo., Feb. 4, 1956; s. Frank Anthony and Valeria (Shimkus) P.; m. Karan Elaine Blakeley, Apr. 21, 1990; children: Sabrina Marie, Alexandra Louise, Emerson Alan. BS, Ill. Benedictine Coll., Lisle, 1979; PhD, Chgo. Med. Sch., North Chicago, 1986. Technologist Palos Community Hosp., Palos Heights, Ill., 1973-79, med. technologist, 1979-86; microbiologist South Bend (Ind.) Med. Found., 1986-91; dir. microbiology and immunology Metro Health Hosp., Grand Rapids, Mich., 1991—. Mem. AAAS, Am. Soc. Clin. Pathologists, Am. Soc. Microbiology, N.Y. Acad. Sci., Ill. Soc. Microbiology, South Ctrl. Assn. Microbiology (Mich. state dir. 2000). Roman Catholic. Avocations: designing computer programs, fishing, skiing. Office: Metro Health Hosp 1919 Boston St SE Grand Rapids MI 49506-4199

PETNO, DOUGLAS B., investment company executive; b. Feb. 7, 1965; Mng. dir., group head energy JPMorgan Chase & Co., NYC, 2005—. Recipient Top Dealmaker, Dealmaker mag., 2006. Office: JPMorgan Chase & Co 1 Chase Manhattan Plaza Fifth Fl New York NY 10081 Office Phone: 212-622-6774. E-mail: douglas.b.petno@jpmorgan.com. *

PETO, SIR RICHARD, medical researcher; b. May 14, 1943; s. Leonard Huntley and Carrie Clarinda Peto; m. Sallie Messum, 1970 (dissolved); 2 children; m. Gale Mead (dec. 2001); 2 children. MA in Natural Sci., Trinity Coll.; MSc in Statistics, Imperial Coll., London. Rsch. officer Med. Rsch. Coun., 1967—69, U. Oxford, 1969—72, lectr., 1972—75, reader in cancer studies, 1975—92, founder, co-dir. Clin. Trial Svc. Unit, 1975—, prof. med. statistics and epidemiology, 1992—. Co-recipient King Faisal International prize (medicine), King Faisal Found., 2005; recipient Charles S. Mott prize, GM Cancer Rsch. Found., 2002; knighted for services to epidemiology and cancer prevention, 1999. Fellow: Royal Soc. (Royal medal 2002), Acad. Med. Sciences; mem.: Inst. Medicine (fgn. assoc.). Achievements include research in the causes of cancer in general, the effects of smoking, the establishment of large-scale randomized trials of the treatment of heart disease, stroke, cancer, and a variety of other diseases; introduced combined "meta-analyses" of results from related trials that achieve uniquely reliable assessment of treatment effects. Office: Clin Trial Svc Unit Richard Doll Bldg Old Road Campus Oxford OX3 7LF England Office Phone: 44-1865-743801. Office Fax: 44-1865-743985. Business E-Mail: secretary@ctsu.ox.ac.uk.

PETOSA, JASON JOSEPH, publisher; b. Des Moines, Apr. 26, 1939; s. Joseph John and Mildred Margaret (Cardamon) P.; m. Theodora Anne Doleski, Aug. 12, 1972; 1 son, Justin James. Student, Marquette U., 1957-59, St. Paul Sem., 1959-63, 65-67, Colegio Paolino Internationale, Rome, 1963-65. Asso. editor Cath. Home Mag., Canfield, Ohio, 1965-67, editor, 1968; dir. Alba House Communications, Canfield, 1968-71; with Office of Radio and TV, Diocese of Youngstown, Ohio, 1969-71; dir. pub. relations, instr. Alice Lloyd Coll., Pippa Passes, Ky., 1971-76; writer, cons. Bethesda, Ohio, 1976-79; pres., pub. Nat. Cath. Reporter, Kansas City, Mo., 1979-85; v.p., gen. mgr. Towsend-Kraft Pub. Co., Liberty, Mo., 1985-86; pres., pub. Steadfast Pub. Co., Kansas City, 1986—. Bd. dirs. David (Ky.) Sch., 1973-79; mem. Mayor's UN Day Com., Kansas City. Mem. Kansas City Direct Mktg. Assn., UN Assn. (bd. dirs. Met. Kansas City chpt., pres. 2000). Roman Catholic. Office: 19 W Linwood Blvd PO Box 410265 Kansas City MO 64141-0265 Office Phone: 816-561-4561.

PETRAEUS, DAVID HOWELL, career military officer; b. Cornwall, NY, Nov. 7, 1952; s. Sixtus and Miriam Sweet (Howell) P.; m. Hollister Knowlton, July 6, 1974; children: Anne, Stephen. BS, U.S. Mil. Acad., 1974; grad., U.S. Army Command and Gen. Staff Coll., Ft. Leavenworth, Kans., 1983; M in Pub. and Internat. Affairs, Princeton U., 1985, PhD, 1987. Commd. 2d lt. US Army, 1974, advanced through grades to gen., 2007; platoon leader, adjutant 1-509th Inf. (Airborne), Vicenza, Italy, 1975—79; co. comdr., ops. officer, aide-de-camp 24th Inf. Divsn., Ft. Stewart, Ga., 1979—87; asst. prof. internat. relations US Mil. Acad., West Point, NY, 1985-87; mil. asst. to supreme allied comdr. Europe NATO, Brussels, 1987-88; bn. and brigade ops. officer 3rd infantry divsn. US Army, 1988-89, asst. divsn. comdr. for ops., 82nd Airborne divsn., chief of staff, XVIII Airborne Corps. Ft. Bragg, NC, asst. chief of staff for military ops. Joint HQ Ctr., Allied Command Europe, 2001—02, comdr., 101st Airborne Divsn. Ft. Campbell, Ky., 2002—04, comdr. Multinational Security Transition Commd. Iraq Baghdad, Iraq, 2004—05, comdr. Combined Arms Ctr. Ft. Leavenworth, Kans., 2005—07; comdr. Multi-Nat. Force-Iraq, Baghdad, Iraq, 2007—. Mem. NATO Tng. Mission, Iraq. Author: The American Military and the Lessons of Vietnam, 1987; contbr. to: Strategy, Democracy, and Vietnam, 1987; co-editor: NATO At Forty, 1989; contbr. articles to profl. jours. Decorated DSM U.S. Army, Def. Disting. Svc. medal, Bronze Star with v, Meritorious Svc. medal NATO; named one of The World's Most Influential People, TIME mag., 2007; recipient Golden award of the Iraqi Order of the Date Palm, 2005. Mem. Council on Fgn. Relations, Assn. U.S. Army, Phi Kappa Phi. Clubs: Army-Navy (Arlington, Va.). Presbyterian. Avocations: distance running, writing. Office: Multi-Nat Force-Iraq 7115 S Boundary Blvd MacDill AFB Tampa FL 33621 *

PETRAITIS, KAREL COLETTE, lawyer; b. Chgo., Apr. 4, 1945; d. Ferdinand John and Dolores (Karroll) P.; BA, U. Md., 1967, postgrad., 1967-68; JD, George Washington U., 1971. Bar: Md. 1972, U.S. Supreme Ct. 1977. Law clk. Prince George's County Office of Law, Md., 1971-72, atty., 1972-80; real estate agt. Harloff & Perkins, Riverdale, Md., 1978-82; pvt. practice law, College Park, Md., 1980—; past pres., v.p., treas, bd. dirs. Coll. Park Bd. Trade. Youth coord. Agnew for Gov., 1966, Mathias for Senate, 1968, Beall for Senate, 1970; nat. committeewoman Md. Young Reps., 1971-79, dir., 1979-81, legal counsel, 1972-79; mem. bd. trustees Elizabeth Seton H.S., 1991-95. Recipient cert. appreciation Prince George County Circuit Ct., 1979; cert. public service Prince George County, 1980; pres. Friends of Md. Summer Inst. for Creative and Performing Arts, 1983-86, 1997-98, trustee, 1986-2001. Mem. AAUW, Md. Bar Assn., Prince George County Bar Assn., George Washington Law Alumni Assn. (bd. dirs. 1979-94, sec. 1982-84, pres. Md. chpt. 1985-87), U. Md. Alumni Assn. (pres. young alumni 1978-80, pres. Prince George's 1986-88, 2007—, bd.dirs. 1988-96, treas, 2004-07, mem. arts and humanities bd. 1999-2004, legis. com. advocacy 2003—), Balt County Young Rep. Assn., Gridiron Club (membership com.), Terrapin Club (bd. dirs., 2005-), Fastbreakers, Rebounders, Balt. County Rep. Women's Club, Gamma Phi Beta Alumnae (treas. DC 2006—). Roman Catholic. Home: 7307 Radcliffe Dr College Park MD 20740-3023 Office: 7100 Baltimore Ave Ste 205 College Park MD 20740 Office Phone: 301-277-1443. Personal E-mail: karelcp@aol.com.

PETRAKIS, HARRY MARK, author; b. St. Louis, June 5, 1923; s. Mark E. and Stella (Christoulakis) P.; m. Diane Perparos, Sept. 30, 1945; children: Mark, John, Dean. Student, U. Ill., Champaign, 1940—41, LHD (hon.), 1971, Gov.'s State U., Chgo., 1980, Hellenic Coll., Brookline, Mass., 1984, Roosevelt U., Chgo., 1987, Am. Coll. Greece, Athens, 2004, Ind. U., Bloomington, 2006. Freelance writer, tchr., lectr.; tchr. workshop classes in novel, short story; McGuffey vis. lectr. Ohio U., Athens, 1971; writer-in-residence Chgo. Pub. Library, 1976-77, Chgo. Bd. Edn., 1978-79; Kazantzakis Prof. San Francisco State U., 1992. Author: Lion at My Heart, 1959, The Odyssey of Kostas Volakis, 1963, Pericles on 31st Street, 1965 (nominated for Nat. Book award), The Founder's Touch: The Life of Paul Galvin of Motorola, 1965, A Dream of Kings, 1966 (Nat. Book award nomination), The Waves of Night, 1969, Stelmark: A Family Recollection,

1970, In the Land of Morning, 1973, The Hour of the Bell, 1976, A Petrakis Reader, 28 Stories, 1978, Nick the Greek, 1979, Days of Vengeance, 1983, Reflections on a Writer's Life and Work, 1983, Collected Stories, 1986, Ghost of the Sun, 1990, Tales of the Heart, 1999, Twilight of the Ice, 2003, The Orchards of Ithaca, 2004, Legends of Glory and Other Stories, 2007; writer (films) A Dream of Kings, 1969, Picture Windows, 1995; contbr. short stories to mags. including, Atlantic Monthly, Sat. Eve. Post, Harper's Bazaar, Country Beautiful. (Story included in Prize Stories, also O. Henry Award 1966). Recipient awards Friends of Am. Writers, Friends of Lit., Soc. Midland Authors, Carl Sandburg award, Ellis Island medal of honor, 1995, O'Henry award; named Kazantzakis chair in Modern Greek Studies San Francisco State U., 1992. Mem. Authors Guild, PEN, Writers Guild Am.-West. Address: Dune Acres 80 East Rd Chesterton IN 46304-1035 Personal E-mail: hmp801@comcast.net. *"...The older I become, the more clearly I see that there is a stunning purity in the writing of a book that I cannot achieve in my own life with its frailty and desperation. The work takes over with a life of its own. In those moments, I wouldn't trade writing with all its loneliness and sometimes with its pain, for any other profession in the world.*

PETRAKIS, MYRON TITOS, retired mechanical engineer; b. Chgo., Apr. 6, 1922; s. Titos Myron and Elpis Lagovardos Petrakis; m. Catherine Theresa Rinaldi, Sept. 20, 1952; children: Stephen Paul, Barbara Jean, Mary Ann. BSME, Ill. Inst. Tech., Chgo., 1951. Tool and dye maker Republic Flow Meters Co., Chgo., 1941—44; project engr. Gen. Am. Plastics, East Chicago, Ind., 1951—53; mgr. plastic molding Fed. Tool Corp., Lincolnwood, Ill., 1953—67; sales engr. Application Engring. Corp., Elk Grove, Ill., 1967—69; pres. B/P Plastic Equipment Co., Rosemont, Ill., 1969—91. Civil def. dir. Village of Norridge, Ill., 1964—66; commn. sec. Bd. of Fire and Police Commn., Norridge, 1959—; publicist Norridge H.S. Problems Com., 1957—59; historian Village of Norridge, 1996—. With USN, 1944—46. Recipient Sheriff's Sr. Medal of Honor, Cook County Sheriff, Chgo., 2003. Mem.: Soc. Plastic Engrs. (dir., chair edn. 1970—73), K.C. (4th deg.). Achievements include design of accessories for plastic injection molding. Avocations: photography, woodworking, stained glass, fishing. Home: 4437 N Ottawa Ave Norridge IL 60706 Office: Norridge Board of Fire and Police Commrs 4000 N Olcott Ave Norridge IL 60706

PETRAKIS, NICHOLAS LOUIS, epidemiologist, medical researcher, educator; b. San Francisco, Feb. 6, 1922; s. Louis Nicholas and Stamatina (Boosalis) P.; m. Patricia Elizabeth Kelly, June 24, 1947; children: Steven John, Susan Lynn, Sandra Kay. BA, Augustana Coll., 1943; BS in Medicine, U. S.D., 1944; MD, Washington U., St. Louis, 1946. Intern Mpls. Gen. Hosp., 1946-47; physician, researcher U.S. Naval Radiol. Def. Lab., San Francisco, 1947-49; resident physician Mpls. Gen. Hosp., 1949-50; sr. asst. surgeon Nat. Cancer Inst., USPHS, San Francisco, 1950-54; asst. research physician Cancer Research Inst., U. Calif., San Francisco, 1954-56; asst. prof. preventive medicine U. Calif. Sch. Medicine, San Francisco, 1956-60, assoc. prof., 1960-66, prof., 1966-91, chmn. dept. epidemiology and internat. health, 1978-88, prof. emeritus, 1991—; prof. epidemiology U. Calif. Sch. Pub. Health, Berkeley, 1981-91. Assoc. dir. G.W. Hooper Edn., U. Calif., San Francisco, 1970-74, acting dir., 1974-77, chmn. dept. epidemiology and internat. health, 1979-89; co-dir. Breast Screening Ctr. of No. Calif., Oakland, 1976-81; cons. Breast Cancer Task Force, Nat. Cancer Inst., Bethesda, Md., 1972-76; chmn. Biometry & Epidemiology Contract Rev. Com., Bethesda, 1977-81; bd. sci. counselors, divsn. cancer etiology Nat. Cancer Inst., Bethesda, 1982-86; scientific adv. com. Calif. State Tobacco-Related Disease Rsch. Program, 1991-93; cons. U. Crete Sch. Medicine, Heraklion, Greece, 1984. Contbr. articles to profl. jours. Eleanor Roosevelt Internat. Cancer fellow Am. Cancer Soc., Comitato Reserche Nucleari, Cassacia, Italy, 1962; U.S. Pub. Health Service Spl. fellow Galton Lab., U. London, 1969-70; recipient Alumni Achievement award Augustana Coll., Sioux Falls, S.D., 1979, Axion award Hellenic-Am. Profl. Soc. of Calif., San Francisco, 1984, Lewis C. Robbins award Soc. for Prospective Medicine, Indpls., 1985, Otto W. Sartorius, MD, award from Susan Love MD Breast Cancer Found., 2001. Mem. Am. Soc. Preventive Oncology (founding, pres. 1984-85, Disting. Achievement award 1992), Soc. for Prospective Medicine (founding), Am. Assn. Cancer Rsch., Am. Epidemiol. Soc., Am. Soc. Clin. Investigation, Am. Bd. Preventive Medicine (cert.). Achievements include research in breast cancer, med. oncology and hematology. Home: 335 Juanita Way San Francisco CA 94127-1657 Office: U Calif Sch Medicine Dept Epidemiology & Biostats Box 0560 MU420W San Francisco CA 94143-0001

PETRALIA, RONALD SEBASTIAN, entomologist, neurobiologist; b. Lawrence, Mass., Nov. 7, 1954; s. Samuel and Rosalie (Zanfagna) P. BS in Entomology summa cum laude, U. Mass., 1975; PhD in Entomology and Biology, Tex. A&M U., 1979. Rsch. asst. Tex. A&M U., College Station, 1975-79, rsch. assoc., 1979-80; asst. prof. biology St. Ambrose Coll., Davenport, Iowa, 1980-85; rsch. fellow dept. anatomy George Washington U., Washington, 1985-90; sr. staff fellow Nat. Inst. Deafness and Other Comm. Disorders, NIH, Bethesda, Md., 1991-97, staff scientist, 1997—. Presenter in field. Contbr. chpts. to books: Excitatory Amino Acids, 1992, The Mammalian Coclear Nuclei: Their Role in Neuroendocrine Function, 1996, The Ionotropic Glutamate Receptors, 1997, Ionotropic Glutamate to Receptors in the CNS, 1999, Handbook of Chemical Neuroanatomy: Glutamate, 2000; contbr. articles to profl. jours. Mem. AAAS, Chesapeake Soc. Microscopy (coun. mem., newsletter editor, past pres.), Soc. Neurosci., Entomol. Soc. Am., Microscopy Soc. Am., Assn. Rsch. Otolaryngology, Cambridge Entomol. Club, Sigma Xi. Roman Catholic. Home: 3 Pooks Hill Rd Apt 218 Bethesda MD 20814-5404 Office: NIDCD NIH Rm 50/4142 9000 Rockville Pike Bethesda MD 20892-8027 Business E-Mail: petralia@nidcd.nih.gov.

PETRANEK, STEPHEN LYNN, editor; b. Wash., Aug. 19, 1944; s. Chester J. and Mabel Oleta (Mercer) P.; m. Barbara Ergas, 1983. Student, U. Okla., Norman, 1962-63; BS, U. Md., 1970; postgrad., U. Mo., 1970-71. Editor-in-chief The Diamondback, U. Md., 1969-70; reporter Democrat and Chronicle, Rochester, NY, 1972, financial writer, 1972-73, asst. Sunday editor, 1973; editor Upstate mag., 1974—77; editor-in-chief Tropic Mag. The Miami Herald, 1977-78; dep. editor The Washington Post Mag., 1978-81, mng. editor, 1982-90; sr. editor LIFE mag., 1990-96; editor-in-chief This Old House mag., 1996—99, Discover mag., 1999—2006, editor-at-large, 2006—; group editor-in-chief Weider History Mags., 2006—. Author: newspaper series Decline and Fall of Stirling Homex, 1972. Recipient John Hancock award for fin. writing, 1972, Bus. Journalism award U. Mo., 1973, Frank Tripp Newswriting award, 1973; finalist Nat. Mag. award, 1997, 2000, 03. Mem. Sigma Delta Chi, Kappa Tau Alpha, Omicron Delta Kappa, Pi Delta Epsilon. Mem. United Ch. of Christ. Home: 38545 John Wolford Rd Waterford VA 20197 Office: 741 Miller Dr SE Ste D-2 Leesburg VA 20175 Office Phone: 703-779-8389. Business E-Mail: steve@weiderhistorygroup.com.

PETRASH, JEFFREY MICHAEL, lawyer; b. Cleve., Dec. 14, 1948; s. Robert Anthony and Naomi Marjorie (Close) P.; 1 child, Michael Stewart. AB, U. Mich., 1969, JD, 1973. Bar: Mich. 1974, D.C. 1975, Md. 1997. Assoc. Dickinson, Wright, McKean, Cudlip & Moon, Detroit, 1973-75, Hamel, Park, McCabe & Saunders, Washington, 1975-78; from assoc. to ptnr. Dickinson, Wright, Washington, 1978-99; sr. counsel Am. Gas Assn., Washington, 2000—. Served to capt. US Army, 1969—77. Mem. Soc. Barristers. Episcopalian. Avocation: sailing. Home: 6606 Hillandale Rd Bethesda MD 20815-6406 Office: 400 N Capitol St NW Washington DC 20001-1511 Office Phone: 202-824-7231. E-mail: jpetrash@aga.org.

PETRASICH, JOHN MORIS, lawyer; b. Long Beach, Calif., Oct. 13, 1945; s. Louis A. and Margaret A. (Moris) P.; children from previous marriage: Jason, Jacquelyn; m. Mary T. Nevin, Aug. 22, 1997. BA, U. So. Calif., 1967, JD, 1970. Bar: Calif. 1971, U.S. Dist. Ct. (cen. dist.) 1971, U.S. Ct. Appeals (9th cir.) 1973, U.S. Dist. Ct. (no. dist.) Calif. 1974, U.S. Ct. Appeals (ea. dist.) Calif. 1976. Assoc. Fulop, Rolson, Burns & McKittrick, Beverly Hills and Newport Beach, Calif., 1971-74, ptnr., 1975-82; ptnr., head litigation McKittrick, Jackson, DeMarco & Peckenpaugh, Newport Beach, 1983-93; shareholder, head litigation Jackson, DeMarco & Peckenpaugh, Newport Beach, 1993—; also bd. dirs. McKittrick, Jackson, DeMarco & Peckenpaugh, Newport Beach. Mem. editorial staff U. So. Calif. Law Rev., 1969-70. Mem. ABA, Beverly Hills Bar Assn., L.A. Bar Assn., Assn. Trial Lawyers Am., Orange County Bar Assn., Lawyers Club L.A., Order of Coif. Office: Jackson DeMarco Peckenpaugh PO Box 19704 Irvine CA 92623-9704 Business E-Mail: jpetrasich@jdplaw.com.

PETREN, CAROL ANN, lawyer, insurance company executive; m. Floyd Clarke. Grad. magna cum laude, Boston Coll.; JD, LLM, U. Mo. Sch. Law. Fed. prosecutor Jackson County, Kansas City, Mo.; asst. US atty. We. Dist. Mo.; counsel US Ho. Reps. Com. on Stds. of Ofcl. Conduct; mng. ptnr. Wilson, Elser, Moskowitz, Edelman & Dicker, Washington, 1994; dep. gen. counsel Sears, Roebuck and Co.; sr. v.p., dep. gen. counsel MCI, 2003—06; exec. v.p., gen. counsel CIGNA Corp., 2006—. Office: CIGNA Corp Two Liberty Pl 1601 Chestnut St Philadelphia PA 19192-1550 Office Phone: 215-761-1000. *

PETREQUIN, HARRY JOSEPH, JR., foreign service officer; b. Ste. Genevieve, Mo., July 1, 1929; s. Harry Joseph and Crescentia Ellen (Bechter) P.; m. Katharine McDonnell Drouin, Oct. 7, 1980; children: John Andrew, Marc Christopher, Paul Nicholas. AB, Westminster Coll., 1950; B of Fgn. Trade, Am. Grad. Sch. Internat. Mgmt., 1954; postgrad., Johns Hopkins U., 1960; MA, Tufts U., 1970. Joined U.S. Fgn. Svc., 1955; assigned AID and predecessor agys., 1955—; dep. dir. S.E. Asia Regional Econ. Devel. Office, Thailand, 1970-74; U.S. coord. Senegal River Basin Authority, Dakar, 1975-76; dir. ASEAN and South Pacific Affairs, 1977-80; dir. program devel. and evaluation staff Bur. Internat. Orgn. Affairs State Dept., 1980-81; dep. dir. AID Mission, Morocco, 1981-85; coord. AID Sr. Mgmt. Course, 1985-86, Indsl. Coll. of the Armed Forces, 1986-87; faculty dept. nat. security policy Nat. War Coll., Washington, 1987-89; internat. devel. cons. Black Mountain, NC, 1989—. Adj. prof. polit. sci. Warren Wilson Coll., Swannanoa, NC, 1993-94; faculty U. NC Coll. Srs., 1995—. Lt. (j.g.) USCGR, 1951-53, Comdr. Ready Res., 1973. Recipient Superior Honor award AID, 1979, State Dept. Superior Honor award, 1981, Comdrs. award for Civilian Svc., Dept. of the Army, 1989. Mem. Soc. Internt. Devel., World Federalist Assn. (nat. bd. dirs.), Am. Fgn. Svc. Assn., UN Assn. U.S., Acad. Polit. Sci., Cousteau Soc., Common Cause, Inst. Noetic Scis., World Future Soc., Amnesty Internat., Coast Guard Combat Vets Assn., Greenpeace, Vets. for Peace, The Land Inst., Phi Alpha Theta. Office Phone: 828-669-8404.

PETRI, THOMAS EVERT, congressman; b. Marinette, Wis., May 28, 1940; s. Robert and Marian (Humleker) Petri; m. Anne Neal, Mar. 26, 1983; 1 child, Alexandra. BA in Govt., Harvard U., 1962, JD, 1965. Bar: Wis. 1965. Law clk. to US Judge James Doyle US Dist. Ct. (we. dist.) Wis., Madison, 1965-66; vol. Peace Corps, Somalia, 1966-67; aide White House, Washington, 1969-70; dir. crime and drug studies Pres.'s Nat. Adv. Coun. on Exec. Orgn., 1969; lawyer pvt. practice, Fond du Lac, Wis., 1970-79; mem. Wis. State Senate, Madison, 1973-79, US Congress from 6th Wis. dist., 1979—, sr. mem. edn. and labor com., transp. and infrastructure com., ranking mem. on aviation subcom. Editor: Nat. Indsl. Policy: Solution or Illusion, 1984. Republican. Lutheran. Avocations: reading, swimming, hiking, bicycling, skiing. Office: US Ho Reps 2462 Rayburn Ho Office Bldg Washington DC 20515-0001 Office Phone: 202-225-2476.

PETRIASHVILI, MARINA, physician; arrived in US, 1997; d. Linette Tsertsvadze. MD, Tbilisi State Med. U., Georgia, 1983—89. Diplomate Tbilisi State Med. U., 1989, Ednl. Commn. for Foreign Med. Graduates Ednl. Commn. For Fgn. Med. Graduates, 1998, cert. Anesthesiology Residency NY U. Sch. of Medicine/NY, 2004, Fellowship in Cardiac Anesthesiology NY U. Sch. of Medicine, 2005, Am. Bd. of Anesthesiology Written Test Am. Bd. of Anesthesiology, 2004. Attending physician Rehab. Ctr. Kartli, Tbilisi, Georgia, 1990—93, Dimitrov Hosp. and Clinics Found., Tbilisi, Georgia, 1994—97; residency in surgery Albert Einstein Coll. of Medicine, Bronx, 2000—01; residency in anesthesiology NY U. Med. Ctr., NY, 2001—04; fellowship in cardiac anesthesiology NY U. Sch. of Medicine, NY, 2004—05; with Woodhull Med. and Mental Health Ctr., Bklyn. Active mem. Am. Soc. of Anesthesioligists, 2001; mem. Soc. of Cardiovasc. Anesthesiologists, 2004, Am. Soc. of Echocardiography, NY State Soc. of Anestheiologists, NY, 2001. Recipient Honors Diploma, Tbilisi State Med. U. Mem.: AMA (corr.). Home Phone: 718-803-8509; Office Phone: 212-263-5072. Personal E-mail: petrim02@hotmail.com.

PETRICK, ALFRED, JR., economist, educator; b. Mt. Vernon, NY, Dec. 30, 1926; s. Alfred and Ruth (Updike) P.; m. Ruth Goodridge, Jan. 2, 1956; children: Elizabeth, Andrew Wayne. BS, BA, Columbia U., 1952, MS, 1962; MBA, Denver U., 1966; PhD, U. Colo., 1969. Registered profl. engr., Colo. Sales engr. Ingersoll Rand Co., NYC, 1953-54; project engr. U.S. AEC, Grand Junction, Colo., 1954-57; mining engr. Reynolds Metals Co., Bauxite, Ark., 1957-61, Guyana, 1957-61; mineral economist U.S. Bur. Mines, Denver, 1963-70; Coulter prof. Colo. Sch. Mines, Golden, 1970-84, emeritus prof., 1984—; dir. Petrick Assocs., Evergreen, Colo., 1974—2004; ret., 2004. Author: Economics International Development, 1977, Economics of Minerals, 1980, Preparacion y Evaluacion, 1982. Mem. com. tech. aspects strategic materials Nat. Acad. Sci., Washington, 1973-76, mem. com. surface mining and reclamation, 1979. Served with USAF, 1945-47, PTO. Fulbright research scholar U. Otago, Dunedin, New Zealand, 1986; recipient Edn. award Instituto Para Functionarios De Las Industrias Minera y Siderurgica, Mexico City, 1981; recipient Service award Office Tech. Assessment, U.S. Congress, 1981. Mem. AIME (chmn. council econs. 1977-78, Henry Krumb lectr. 1986, service award), Profl. Engrs. Colo. Presbyterian. Home: 5544 S Hatch Dr Evergreen CO 80439-7233 Office: Colo Sch Mines Golden CO 80401 Personal E-mail: peta33@comcast.net.

PETRICK, ERNEST NICHOLAS, mechanical engineer, researcher; b. Pa., Apr. 9, 1922; s. Aurelius and Anna (Kaschak) P.; m. Magdalene Simcoe, June 13, 1946; children: Deborah Petrick Healey, Katherine, Denise, Victoria Petrick Kropp. BS in Mech. Engring, Carnegie Inst. Tech., 1943; MS, Purdue U., 1948, PhD, 1955. Registered profl. engr., Mich. Faculty Purdue U., 1946-53; dir. heat transfer research Curtiss-Wright Corp., Woodridge, NJ, 1953-56; chief advanced propulsion systems Curtiss-Wright Research divsn., Quehanna, Pa., 1957-60; chief research engr. Kelsey-Hayes Co., Detroit, 1960-65; chief scientist, tech. dir. U.S. Army Tank-Automotive Command, Warren, Mich., 1965-82; chief scientist, dir. engring. labs. Gen. Dynamics, 1982-87; engring. cons., 1987—; panel mem. combat vehicles NATO, 1973-82; mem. adv. bd. on basic combustion research NSF, 1973; chmn. advanced transp. systems com. White House Energy Project, 1973; mem. adv. com. NSF-RANN research program Drexel U. Coll. Engring., 1976-78; mem. Army Sci. Bd., 1983-89; cons. Air Force Studies Bd. NRC, 1991-93, cons. Def. Sci. Bd., 1994-95; cons. NAS, 1997—99, US Army Tank Automotive Rsch., Devel. & Engring. Ctr., 2001—03, Bd. Army Sci. and Tech. Rev. NAS Naval Studies Bd., 2003; adj. prof. engring. Wayne State U., Detroit, 1972-82, U. Mich., Ann Arbor, 1982-83; con. Coun. Environ. Quality, White House, 1973. Contbr. articles on transp., ground vehicles, propulsion and project mgmt. to profl. jours. Lt., chief engr. destroyer USNR, 1942—46, WWII. Recipient certificate of achievement U.S. Army, 1967, Outstanding Performance awards, 1970, 71, 76, 82, Outstanding Mech. Engring. award Purdue U., 1991; named Disting. Engring. Alumnus Purdue U., 1966. Mem. Soc. Automotive Engrs. (nat. dir. 1978-80), Am. Def. Preparedness Assn. (chmn. land warfare survivability divsn. 1990-95, Silver medal 1992, Recognition award 1992), Assn. U.S. Army, Sigma Xi, Pi Tau Sigma. Home: 1540 Stonehaven Rd Ann Arbor MI 48104-4150 Office: ENP Cons 1540 Stonehaven Rd Ann Arbor MI 48104

PETRICK, JOSEPH ANTHONY, small business owner, management consultant, educator; b. Pueblo, Colo., Dec. 31, 1946; s. Joseph John and Hermina Emma Petrick; m. Kimberly Marie Weber, Sept. 22, 1984. BA in Philosophy, Colo. State U., 1968; PhD, Pa. State U., 1972; MBA, U. of Cin., 1990. Cert. Human Resources Certification Inst., Wash., D.C., 1993. Asst. prof. of philosophy Coll. of Charleston, SC, 1972—75; assoc. prof. and head of philosophy dept. No. Ky. U., Highland Heights, Ky., 1975—82; asst. dean So. Ohio Coll., Fairfield, Ohio, 1982—84; head Dept. off-Campus Bus. Wilmington (Ohio) Coll., 1984—87; prof. U. of Cin., 1987—89; prof. of mgmt. Wright State U., Dayton, Ohio, 1989—. Prin., owner Orgnl. Ethics Assocs., Cin., 1992—, Performance Leadership Assocs., Cin., 1996—, Integrity Capacity Assocs., Cin., 2002—; bd. dirs. Human Resources Cert. Inst. Author: Total Quality in Managing Human Resources, 1995, Total Quality and Organization Development, 1997, Management Ethics: Integrity at Work, 1997, Managing Project Quality, 2002. Baldrige quality award examiner U.S. Dept. of Commerce, Washington, 1998—2000; examiner Ohio Quality Award for Excellence, Dayton, 1999—2000. Recipient Innovation in Bus. Edn. Group award, Midwestern Deans of U.S. Bus. Schs., 1998; fellow, Pa. State U., 1969—71, Woodrow Wilson Nat. Found., 1971—72, Malone Arabic Studies fellow, U.S. Arab Rels. Inst., 1995. Mem.: Acad. of Mgmt., Midwestern Soc. Human Resources and Indsl. Rels. (pres. 1996—97), U.S. Assn. Small Bus. and Entrepreneurship (v.p. individual entrepreneurship 1994—95), Am. Philos. Assn., Soc. Human Resource Mgmt., Sigma Iota Epsilon, Internat. Bus. Honor Soc. (pres. 2006), Beta Gamma Sigma. Democrat. Avocations: travel, reading, films, dance, golf. Home: 3505 Arborcrest Court Cincinnati OH 45236 Office: Wright State University 3640 Colonel Glenn Hwy Dayton OH 45435 Office Phone: 937-775-2428. E-mail: joseph.petrick@wright.edu.

PETRICK, MICHAEL JOSEPH, journalism educator; b. Antigo, Wis., Sept. 6, 1942; BS, U. Wis., Milw., 1965, MS, 1967; PhD, U. Wis., Madison, 1970. News editor Milw. South Times Star, 1966-67; disting. teaching fellow U. Wis., Madison, 1969-70; from asst. to assoc. prof. U. Md., College Park, 1970-78; copy editor Evening Star, Washington, 1974-75; chairperson dept. journalism Ctrl. Mich. U., Mt. Pleasant, 1978-84, prof., 1984-2000, prof. emeritus, 2000—. Writing and editing coach Ctrl. Mich. Newspapers, 1984-85; writing and reporting coach Greenville (Mich.) Daily News, 1997-99; chair bd. in control of student media Ctrl. Mich. U., 1997-99 Co-author: Using the Mass Media, 1975; contbr. articles to profl. jours Named to Ctrl. Mich. Jour. Hall of Fame, 2006. Mem. Md.-Del.-D.C. Press Assn. (chmn. freedom of info. com. 1972-73), Soc. Profl. Journalists (campus chpt. adviser 1970-99), Nat. Coun. Editl. Writers, Assn. for Edn. in Journalism and Mass Communication Office: PO Box 6 Mount Pleasant MI 48804-0006 E-mail: michael.petrick@cmich.edu.

PETRICOFF, M. HOWARD, lawyer, educator; b. Cin., Dec. 22, 1949; s. Herman and Neoma P.; m. Hanna Sue, Aug. 11, 1974; children: Nicholas, Eve. BS, Am. U., 1967-71; JD, U. Cin., 1971-74; M in Pub. Adminstrn., Harvard U., 1980-81. Bar: Ohio, U.S. Ct. Appeals (D.C. cir.) 1977, U.S. Ct. Appeals (10th cir.) 1985, U.S. Ct. Appeals (6th cir.) 1989, U.S. Supreme Ct. 1989. Asst. city law dir. City of Toledo (Ohio), 1975-77; asst. atty. gen. Ohio Atty. Gen. Office, Columbus, 1977-82; ptnr. Vorys, Sater, Seymour & Pease, Columbus, 1982—. Adj. prof. law Capital U. Law Sch., Columbus, 1991—. Contbr. articles to profl. jours. Reginald Heber Smith Found. fellow Washnigton, 1974-75. Mem. Ohio Bar Assn., Columbus Bar Assn., Ohio Oil and Gas Assn. Office: Vorys Sater Seymour & Pease PO Box 1008 52 E Gay St Columbus OH 43215-3161 Office Phone: 614-464-6400. Business E-Mail: mhpetricoff@vssp.com.

PETRIDES, GEORGE ATHAN, ecologist, educator; b. NYC, Aug. 1, 1916; s. George Athan and Grace Emeline (Ladd) P.; m. Miriam Clarissa Pasma, Nov. 30, 1940; children: George H., Olivia L., Lisa B. BS, George Washington U., 1938; MS, Cornell U., 1940; PhD, Ohio State U., 1948; postdoctoral fellow, U. Ga., 1963-64. Naturalist Nat. Park Service, Washington and Yosemite, Calif., 1938-43, Glacier Nat. Park, Mont., 1947, Mt. McKinley Nat. Park, Alaska, 1959; game technician W.Va. Conservation Commn., Charleston, 1941; instr. Am. U., 1942-43, Ohio State U., 1946-48; leader Tex. Coop. Wildlife Unit; assoc. prof. wildlife mgmt. Tex. A. and M. Coll., 1948-50; assoc. prof. wildlife mgmt., zool. and African studies Mich. State U., 1950-58, prof., 1958—; research prof. U. Pretoria, S. Africa, 1965; vis. prof. U. Kiel, Germany, 1967; vis. prof. wildlife mgmt. Kanha Nat. Park, India, 1983; del. sci. confs. Warsaw, 1960, Nairobi and Salisbury, 1963, Sao Paulo, Aberdeen, 1965, Lucerne, 1966, Varanasi, India, Nairobi, 1967, Oxford, Eng., Paris, 1968, Durban, 1971, Mexico City, 1971, 73, Banff, 1972, Nairobi, Moscow, The Hague, 1974, Johannesburg, 1977, Sydney, 1978, Kuala Lumpur, 1979, Cairns, Australia, Mogadishu, Somalia, Peshawar, Pakistan, 1980. Participant NSF Expdn., Antarctic, 1972, FAO mission to, Afghanistan, 1972, World Bank mission to, Malaysia, 1975 Author: Field Guide to Trees and Shrubs, 1958, 2d edit., 1972, Field Guide to Eastern Trees, 1988, 98, Field Guide to Western Trees, 1992, 98, First Guide to Trees, 1993, Trees of the California Sierra Nevada, 1996, Trees of the Pacific Northwest, 1998, Trees of the Rocky Mountains and Intermountain West, 2000, Trees of the American Southwest, 2000; editor wildlife mgmt. terrestrial sect. Biol. Abstracts, 1947-72; contbr. articles to biol. publs. Served to lt. USNR, 1943-46. Fulbright research awards in E. Africa Nat. Parks Kenya, 1953-54; Fulbright research awards in E. Africa Nat. Parks Kenya, Uganda, 1956-57; N.Y. Zool. Soc. grantee Ethiopia, Sudan, 1957; N.Y. Zool. Soc. grantee Thailand, 1977; Mich. State U. grantee Nigeria, 1962; Mich. State U. grantee Zambia, 1966; Mich. State U. grantee Kenya, 1969; Mich. State U. grantee Africa, 1970, 71, 73, 81; Mich. State U. grantee Greece, 1974, 83; Mich. State U. grantee Iran, 1974; Mich. State U. grantee Botswana, 1977; Mich. State U. grantee Papua New Guinea, Thailand, 1979; Iran Dept. Environment grantee, 1977; Smithsonian Instn. grantee India and Nepal, 1967, 68, 75, 77, 83, 85; World Wildlife Fund grantee W. Africa, 1968 Mem. Am. Ornithologists Union, Am. Soc. Mammalogists, Wildlife Soc. (exec. sec. 1953), Wilderness Soc., Am. Comm. Internat. Wildlife Protection, Ecol. Soc., Fauna Preservation Soc., E. African Wildlife Soc., Internat. Union Conservation Nature, Zool. Soc. So. Africa, Sigma Xi. Presbyterian. Home: 4895 Barton Rd Williamston MI 48895-9305 Office: Mich State U Dept Botany East Lansing MI 48824 E-mail: petrides@msu.edu.

PETRIE, BRUCE INGLIS, lawyer; b. Washington, Nov. 8, 1926; s. Robert Inglis and Marion (Douglas) P.; m. Beverly Ann Stevens, Nov. 3, 1950 (dec. Oct. 1993); children: Laurie Ann Roche, Bruce Inglis, Karen Elizabeth Medsger. BBA, U. Cin., 1948, JD, 1950. Bar: Ohio 1950, U.S. Dist. Ct. (so. dist.) Ohio 1951, U.S. Ct. Appeals (6th cir.) 1960, U.S. Supreme Ct. Assoc. Kunkel & Kunkel, Cin., 1950-51, Graydon, Head & Ritchey, 1951-57, ptnr., 1957—. Exec. prodr. (sch. video) Classical Quest, 2000; author: How To Get the Most Out of Your Lawyer, 2002; contbr. articles to legal jours. Pres. Charter Rsch. Inst., 2000—03; bd. edn. Indian Hill Exempted Village Sch. Dist., 1965—67, pres., 1967; adv. bd. William A. Mitchell Ctr., 1969—86; Green Areas adv. com. Village of Indian Hill, Ohio, 1969—80, chmn., 1976—80; active Ohio Ethics Com., 1974—75;

founder Parents as Tchrs. Metro Housing Authority Commn., 1991—; a prin. advocate merit selection judges Ohio; trustee, mem. bd. Seven Hills Neighborhood Houses' Inst. for Learning in Retirement; organizer Late Gt. Lakes Book Distbn. project, global vol. tchr. China, 2003—07; elder, trustee, deacon Knox Presbyn. Ch.; bd. dirs. Charter Com. Greater Cin., 1952—, Hamilton County Good Govt. League, Murray Seasongood Good Govt. Fund, 1975—, chmn., 1989—; bd. dirs. Nat. Civic League, Cin. Vol. Lawyers for Poor Found., Linton Music Series, Amernet Chamber Music Soc.; co-founder Sta. WGUC-FM; mem. WGUC-FM Cmty. Bd., 1974—, chmn., 1974—76. Recipient Pres.'s award U. Cin., 1976, Disting. Alumnus award, 1995. Fellow: Am. Bar Found.; mem.: ABA, Ohio State Bar Assn. Found. (Outstanding Rsch. in Law and Govt. award 1986, Charles P. Taft Civic Gumption award 1988, Ohio Bar medal 1988), Am. Law Inst., Nat. Civic League (coun. 1984—, Disting. Citizen award 1985), Am. Judicature Soc. (dir., Herbert Lincoln Harley award 1973), Cin. Bar Assn. (pres. 1981, Trustee's award 2000), Ohio Bar Assn., Cin. Country Club, Univ. Club, Cincinnatus Assn., Lit. Club, Order of Coif. Avocations: tennis, squash, woodworking, writing, horticulture. Home: 2787 Walsh Rd Cincinnati OH 45208-3428 Office: Graydon Head & Ritchey 1900 Fifth 3d Ctr 511 Walnut St Ste 1900 Cincinnati OH 45202-3157

PETRIE, DONALD JOSEPH, banker; b. NYC, Sept. 2, 1921; s. John and Elizabeth (Thomson) P.; m. Jane Adams, Aug. 27, 1949; children: R. Scott, Anne, Elizabeth, Douglas, Susan. BBA, Manhattan Coll., 1950. Personnel mgr. Otis Elevator Co., NYC, 1951-59; personnel dir. Brown Bros. Harriman & Co., NYC, 1959-68; exec. v.p. U.S. Trust Co., NYC, 1968-79; sr. v.p. Marine Midland Bank, NYC, 1979-86, Drake Beam Morin Inc., NYC, 1986-90; chmn., chief exec. officer Webster Corp., NYC, 1990—. Lectr. Baruch Sch. Bus., Coll. City N.Y., 1955-58; pres., chmn. exec. and fin. coms., dir. Webster Apts., N.Y.C., 1973—; adj. prof. mgmt. Hofstra U., Hempstead, N.Y., 1986-93. Author: Explaining Pay Policy, 1969, Handling Employee Questions About Pay, 1976. Capt. USAAF, 1942-46. Mem. N.Y.C. Partnership and C. of C. (chmn. mgmt. edn. and adv. com. 1964-98). Home: 11 Fairview Ave Great Neck NY 11023-1462 Office: 419 W 34th St New York NY 10001-1596 Office Phone: 212-967-9000.

PETRIE, FERDINAND RALPH, illustrator, artist; b. Hackensack, NJ, Sept. 17, 1925; s. Archibald John and Bessie (Rutherford) P.; m. Phyllis C. Haddow, Oct. 19, 1951; children: Beth, David. Advt. cert., Parson's Sch. Design, NYC, 1949; student, Art Students League, 1947-49, Famous Artists Course in Illustration, 1958-59. Illustrator J. Gans Assos., NYC, 1950-69. Free lance illustrator, artist, 1969—, owner, Petrie Gallery, Rockport, Mass., 1971-95; represented in permanent collections, U.S. Supreme Ct., Smithsonian Instn., Washington, Indpls. Mus. Art; designer U.S. commemorative stamp design, 2 Zaire commemorative stamps, 1980, USN, USCG, The Salvation Army; Author: Drawing Landscapes in Pencil, 1979; illustrator: The Drawing Book, 1980, The Color Book, 1981, The Alkyd Book, 1982, The Watercolorists Guide to Painting Trees, 1983, The Watercolorists Guide to Painting Skies, 1984; The Watercolorists Guide to Painting Water, 1985, Painting Nature in Watercolor, 1990. Served with U.S. Maritime Service, 1943-46. Mem. Artists Fellowship, Rockport Art Assn., Am. Artists Profl. League, N.J. Watercolor Soc. Presbyterian. Address: 51 Vreeland Ave Rutherford NJ 07070-2227

PETRIE, GEOFFREY MICHAEL, professional sports team executive, retired professional basketball player; b. Darby, Pa., Apr. 17, 1948; m. Anne-Marie Petrie; children: Mike, Anne-Marie, Susanne. Grad., Princeton U., NJ, 1970. Player Portland Trail Blazers, 1970—76, exec., 1976—89, sr. v.p. ops., 1989—93; v.p. basketball ops. Sacramento Kings, 1994—2006, pres. basketball ops., 2006—. Named NBA Rookie of Yr., 1971, NBA Exec. of Yr., The Sporting News, 1999, 2001; named to NBA All-Star Team, 1971, 74, NBA All-Rookie Team, 1971. Avocations: golf, tennis, guitar. Office: Sacramento Kings One Sports Pky Sacramento CA 95834 *

PETRIE, GREGORY STEVEN, lawyer; b. Seattle, Feb. 25, 1951; s. George C. and Pauline P.; m. Margaret Fuhrman, Oct. 6, 1979; children: Kathryn Jean, Thomas George. AB in Polit. Sci and Econs., UCLA, 1973; JD, Boston U., 1976. Bar: Wash. 1976, U.S. Dist. Ct. (we. dist.) Wash. 1976. Adminstr. Action/Peace Corps, Washington, 1973, Fed. Power Commn., Washington, 1974; assoc. Oles Morrison et al, Seattle, 1976-80; ptnr. Schwabe Williamson Ferguson & Burdell, Seattle, 1981-94; mng. shareholder Krutch Lindell Bingham Jones & Petrie, Seattle, 1994—. Mem. Seattle-King County Bar Assn., Profl. Liability Architects and Engrs., Wash. Athletic Club. Avocations: woodworking, skiing. Office: Krutch Lindell Bingham Jones & Petrie 1420 Fifth Ave Ste 3150 Seattle WA 98101 Home Phone: 206-632-4555; Office Phone: 206-682-1505. Business E-Mail: gsp@krutchlindell.com.

PETRIE, STEWART JUDSON, retired obstetrician, gynecologist; b. New Haven, July 15, 1923; s. Arthur Judson and Emma Robinson Petrie. BS, U. Conn., Storrs, 1943; MD, Temple U., Phila., 1950; postgrad., Yale U., New Haven, 1952—55. Diplomate Nat. Bd. Med. Examiners, Am. Bd. Ob-Gyn. Editor: Conn. Medicine; author: Letters and Journal of a Civil Surgeon, Capital of Libby Prison, Bloody Path to the Shenandoah. Comdr. US Power Squadron. Maj. USAF, 1942—85. Fellow: ACS, ACOG; mem.: New County Med. Assn. Avocations: writing, painting, boating. Home: 133 Linden Ave Branford CT 06450 E-mail: drpetrie1@aol.com.

PETRIE, WILLIAM MARSHALL, psychiatrist; b. Louisville, Oct. 19, 1946; s. Garner McReynolds and Claire (Samuels) P.; children: Christopher W., Ellen M., Shelley M.; m. Lori L. Molchin, Oct. 1, 1994; 1 child, Halle C. BA, Vanderbilt U., 1968, MD, 1972. Research psychiatrist NIMH, Rockville, Md., 1975-77; asst. prof. dept. psychiatry Vanderbilt Med. Ctr., Nashville, 1977-81, assoc. prof., 1981-82, assoc. clin. prof., 1982-87, clin. prof., 1992—; pvt. practice psychiatry Psychiat. Cons., P.C., Nashville, 1982—, pres., 1996—. Bd. dirs Psychiat. Solutions, Inc.; clin. instr. Georgetown U. Med. Ctr., 1975—77; cons. psychopharmacology rsch. br. NIMH, 1977—80; rschr. in geriatric psychopharmacology; med. dir. memory Study Ctr., 1987—; chmn. of psychiatry Parthenon Pavilion, 1994—96; bd. trustees Centennial Mutual Ctr., 1994—2000, vice-chmn. bd. trustees, 1998—2000; pres. Columbia Psychiat. Care Network, 1997—98, Psychiat. Cons., PC, 1999—2005. Mem. editl. bd. Gen. Hosp. Psychiatry, 1995—, Audio Digest Psychiatry, 1996-99; contbr. articles to profl. jours.; chpts. to books. Fellow Am. Psychiat. Assn. (disting. fellow, pres. mid. Tenn. dist. br. 1986-87); mem. AMA, Tenn. Med. Assn., Am. Assn. Geriatric Psychiatrists, Am. Coll. Psychiatrists, Tenn. Psychiat. Assn. (pres. 1999-2000). Democrat. Methodist. Office: Psychiat Cons PC 310 25th Ave N Nashville TN 37203-1515 Home Phone: 615-373-5033; Office Phone: 615-250-6780. Business E-Mail: wpetrie@psychiatricconsultants.com.

PETRIK, F. A., music educator; s. Frank P. Petrik and Anne R. Porter; m. Amanda F. Fleming, Aug. 15, 1998; children: Charles F., Cecelia A. BA in Music Edn., Mont. State U., Bozeman, 1999; MA in Ednl. Instrnl. Tech., Am. Intercontinental U., Atlanta, Ga., 2004. Cert. tchr. Oreg., 1999. Band dir. Portland Pub. Schs., Oreg., 1999—2002, Mt. Angel Pub. Schools, Oreg., Sherwood High Sch. Dist., Oreg. Musician Jazz Express Big Band, Portland, 2001—02, Keizer Cmty. Jazz Band, Keizer, Oreg. Vol. fire fighter Sourdough Fire Dept., Bozeman, 1994—95; youth adv. com. St. Paul Cath. Ch., Silverton, Oreg., 2005—06. Grantee Music Tech., Intel, 2001, New Music Instruments For Students, Mr. Holland's Opus Found., 2002. Mem.: Music Educator's Nat. Conf., Oreg. Music Educator's Assn. (licentiate). Conservative. Roman Catholic. Avocations: camping, soccer, fly fishing, mountain biking. Home: 216 N James St Silverton OR 97381 Office: Mt Angel Sch Dist 890 E Marquam St Mount Angel OR 97362 Home Phone: 503-873-2046; Office Phone: 503-625-8200. Personal E-mail: fmpetrik@msn.com. Business E-Mail: petrik_frank@mtangel.k12.or.us.

PETRIK, MICHAEL THOMAS, lawyer; b. Chgo., Jan. 13, 1957; s. Thomas J. and Bette J. (Sarich) P.; m. Susan Renée Prince, June 2, 1979; children: Michael Ray, Stephanie Renée. BS in Bus. Mgmt., Ea. Ill. U., 1979, BA in Econs., 1979; JD, Duke U., 1983. Bar: Ga. 1983, US Tax Ct. 1985. Assoc. Alston & Bird LLP, Atlanta, 1983—90, ptnr., 1991—, leader state and local tax group. Instr. constnl. law and tax, Atlanta Law Sch., 1984-92, state and local tax law, Ga. State U., 1992-98; tech. cons. Sales and Use Tax Alert, 1991-92. Edit. adv. bd.: State Income Tax Alert, 1991—, Ga. corr. State Tax Notes, Arlington, Va., 1990-97, interstate tax rep., 1996—, Corp. Bus. Taxation Monthly, 1999-; contbr. articles to profl. jours. Mem. emergency intervention svc. coun. United Way, Atlanta, 1984-90, bd. dirs. 1995-04; mem. Met. Atlanta Mentors' Coun., 1992-95, One-to-one Atlanta Leadership Coun., 1993-96; St. Joseph's Mercy Found. Leadership Coun., 2005-; bd. adv. United Way 211, 1992-03, chair; bd. advisors St. Pius Catholic HS, 2004-; Big Bros./Big Sisters, Atlanta, 2004-,2004-; United Way Pub. Policy Com.,2006-; United Way Cmty. Impact Coun., Atlanta, 2006-; active Vol. DeKalb, Atlanta, 1984-86; bd. dirs. Arrive Alive, Inc., Atlanta, 1987-91; bd. dirs. Duke Law Alumni Assn., 2005-; Delta Sigma Phi Found., 2006-; bd. trustees Brother Rice HS, Chgo., 2006-; trustee Lawyers Comm. Civil Rights, 2001-, Pub. Policy Com., 2007-; bd. of trustees Vasser Woolley Found., 2002-, Leadership Atlanta, 2001-, chair, 2004-05; adv. bd. The Salvation Army of Metro Atlanta, 2007-. Mem. KC, Ga. Bar Assn. (state coun. 1983—), Atlanta Bar Assn., Federalist Soc., St. Thomas More Soc., Serra Internat., Commerce Club, Delta Mu Delta, Omicron Delta Epsilon. Roman Catholic. Avocations: religion, literature, music. Office: Alston & Bird LLP 1201 W Peachtree St One Atlantic Ctr Atlanta GA 30309-3424 Office Phone: 404-881-7479. Office Fax: 404-253-8784. Business E-Mail: mike.petrik@alston.com.

PETRILLO, LEONARD PHILIP, lawyer, retired investment company executive; b. Toronto, Ont., Can., June 20, 1941; s. Philip and Bernice Petrillo; m. Linda née Hodgson; children: Larissa, Matthew, Stefanie, Ann-Marie, Karen. BSc, U. Toronto, 1964; LLB, Osgoode Hall Law Sch., Toronto, 1967. Bar: Ont. 1969. Ptnr. Robinson & Petrillo, 1969-79; corp. counsel Seel Enterprises Ltd., 1979-81; gen. counsel Toronto Stock Exch., 1981—84, v.p., gen. counsel, corp. sec., sec. to bd. dirs., 1984—2003; dir. OTG Fin. Inc., 2004—. Personal E-mail: leonard.petrillo@sympatico.ca.

PETRIN, HELEN FITE, lawyer, consultant, mediator; b. Bklyn., June 22, 1940; d. Clyde David and Connie Marie Keaton; m. Michael Richard Petrin, June 29, 1963; children: Jennifer Lee, Michael James, Daniel John. BS, Rider Coll. (now Rider U.), 1962, MA, 1980; postgrad., Glassboro Coll., NJ, 1981; JD, Widener U., 1987. Bar: Pa. 1989, N.J. 1990, U.S. Dist. N.J. 1990. Tchr. bus. edn. Pennsville (N.J.) Meml. High Sch., 1962-66; asst. prof. Salem Community Coll., Carney's Point, N.J., 1977-81; asst. prof. Brandywine Coll. Widener U., Wilmington, Del., 1981-87, asst. prof., adminstr., dir. paralegal program, 1987-88; dir. continuing legal edn. Widener U. Sch. Law, Brandywine, 1987-88; pvt. practice computer cons. Del., Pa., N.J., Del., Pa., N.J., 1988—; pvt. practice law Salem, N.J., 1989—; prosecutor Pilesgrove Township, N.J., 1990-91; dep. surrogate Salem County, N.J., 1991-2000. Word processing cons. New Castle County (Del.) Pers. Dept., 1983; mem. dist. I ethics com. N.J. Supreme Ct., 1993-96; instr. N.J. Inst. for CLE, 1995—; adv. com. on minority concerns Superior Ct. N.J. Vicinage 15, 1995—; judge mock trial N.J. State Bar, 1994—; mem. women's advocacy panel Salem C.C., 1998—. Pres. bd. Salem County YMCA, 1983; dir. mediator Salem County YMCA Mediation Svcs., 1995—2001; vol. atty. Phila. Vols. for Indigent Program, 1990—95, Camden Legal Svcs., Inc. for Salem County, 1990—2001; mem. Hope III com. (Home Ownership and Opportunity for People Everywhere), Salem, NJ, 1992—2001; vol. atty. Salem County N.J. Office Aging Sr. Law Day, 1991—2001; vol. dir. Guardianship Monitoring Program, 1993—2001; sec.-treas. Stand Up for Salem, Inc., 1997—2002; bd. dirs. Salem County YMCA, 1980—98, United Way Salem County, 1991—97, treas., 1994—95; bd. dirs. United Ways of Pa. & N.J., 1994—97, Stand Up for Salem, Inc., 1991—2002, Salem Main St. Program, 2000—03; bd. dirs., chair pers. com. Salem County Hist. Soc., 2002—06. Mem.: DAR (chpt. chaplain 2007), ABA (chmn. young lawyers econs. com. 1990—93, vice chmn. mktg. legal svcs. com. gen. practice sect. 1993—98), Salem County Bar Assn. (treas. 1991—92, sec. 1992—93, v.p., pres.-elect 1993—94, pres. 1994—95, dir. of Salem County, N.J. YMCA Family Ct. Mediation program 1995—2001), Phila. Bar Assn. (probate adv. panel 1992—94), Pa. Bar Assn., NJ State Bar Assn. (exec. com. young lawyers divsn. 1990—93, pro bono com. 1998—2000, fin. and ops. com. 2002—04, resolutions com. 2002—04, meeting arrangements and program com. 2002—04, nominations com. 2004—05, jud. and prosecutorial appointments com. 2005—, long term planning com. 2006—07, resolutions com. 2006—07), Salem County Hist. Soc. (bd. dirs. 2002—06, chmn. pers. com. 2002—06), Delta Pi Epsilon (sec. bd. dirs. 1980—82). Avocations: swimming, music, walking, reading. Home: PO Box 412 Woodstown NJ 08098-2722 Office: 51 Market St Salem NJ 08079-1909 Office Phone: 856-935-4950.

PETRINI, FABRIZIO, computer scientist, researcher; b. Foligno, Italy, May 26, 1964; m. Mariella DiGiacomo, June 22, 1997; 1 child, Alessandro DiGiacomo. Laurea in computer sci., U. Pisa, Italy, 1990, PhD in Computer Sci., 1997. Rsch. fellow Hewlett Packard Labs, Pisa, 1990-93, U. Oxford, U.K., 1999; mem. tech. staff Los Alamos (N.Mex.) Nat. Lab., 1999—2005; lab. fellow Applied Computer Sci. Group, Pacific N.W. Nat. Lab., Richland, Wash., 2006—. Grantee Enidata, 1990; Marie Curie fellowship European Cmty., 1997; recipient Excellence award Nat. Nuc. Security Agy., 2002, Def. Program award ASCI Q Integration Team, 2003. Mem. IEEE, Computer Soc. Office: Pacific Northwest Nat Lab Applied Computer Sci Group Richland WA 99352 Office Phone: 505-372-2874. Business E-Mail: fabrizio.petrini@pnl.gov.

PETRINO, BOBBY, professional football coach; b. Helena, Mont, Mar. 10, 1961; m. Becky Schaff; children: Kelsey, Nick, Bobby, Katie. BS in Math, Phys. Edn., Carroll U., 1983. Grad. asst. Carroll U., 1983—84, offensive coord., 1985—86; wide receiver, tight ends coach Weber State U., 1987—88; offensive coord. Idaho U., 1989—91; quarterbacks coach Ariz. State U., 1992—93; offensive coord. U. Nev., 1994, Utah State U., 1995—97, U. Louisville, 1998; quarterbacks coach, offensive coord. Jacksonville Jaguars, 1999—2001; offensive coord. Auburn U., 2002; head coach U. Louisville, 2002—07, Atlanta Falcons, Flowery Branch, Ga., 2007—. Office: Atlanta Falcons 4400 Falcon Pkwy Flowery Branch GA 30542 *

PETRINOVICH, LEWIS FRANKLIN, psychologist, educator; b. Wallace, Idaho, June 12, 1930; s. John F. and Ollie (Steward) Petrinovich. BS, U. Idaho, 1952; PhD, U. Calif., Berkeley, 1962. Asst. prof. San Francisco State Coll., 1957—63; from assoc. to prof. SUNY, Stony Brook, 1963-68; prof. U. Calif., Riverside, 1968-91, chmn. psychology, 1968-71, 86-89, prof. emeritus, 1991—. Bd. dirs. Eastman Med. Products, Cymed Corp. Author: Understanding Research in Social Sciences, 1975, Introduction to Statistics, 1976, Human Evolution, Reproduction and Morality, 1995, Living and Dying Well, 1996, Darwinian Dominion: Animal Welfare and Human Interests, 1999, The Cannibal Within, 2000; editor: Behavioral Development, 1981, Habituation, Sensitization and Behavior, 1984; cons. editor Behavioral and Neural Biology, 1972-90, Jour. Physiol. and Comparative Psychology, 1980-82, Jour. Comparative Psychology, 1983-90. Bd. dirs. Friends of Big Band Jazz, 2001—07. Fellow APA, Am. Psychol. Soc., Calif. Acad. Scis., Human Behavior and Evolution Soc., Western Psychol. Assn.; mem. Am. Ornithol. Union, Animal Behavior Soc., Sigma Xi Home: 415 Boynton Ave Berkeley CA 94707-1701 Office: U Calif Riverside Psychology Dept Riverside CA 92521-0001 Personal E-mail: lpetrin@aol.com.

PETRIS, ELLI, paralegal; b. Oceanside, NY, July 29, 1982; d. George and Anastasia Petris. BA in History and Polit. Sci., Molloy Coll., Rockville Ctr., NY, 2004; MA in Govt. and Politics, St. John's U., Jamaica, NY, 2006. Cert.: St. John's U. (in internat. law, diplomacy and pub. adminstrn.) 2006, Hofstra U., Hempstead, NY (in paralegal studies) 2007. Paralegal Law Office of John J. Budnick, Wartagh, NY, 1999—. Mem.: ASPA, Acad. Polit. Sci., Internat. Polit. Sci. Assn., Am. Polit. Sci. Assn., Am. Hist. Assn., Phi Alpha Theta. Home: 2438 Atlantic Blvd Wantagh NY 11793

PETRO, JIM (JAMES MICHAEL), former state attorney general; b. Cleve., Oct. 25, 1948; s. William John and Lila Helen (Janca) P.; m. Nancy Ellen Bero, Dec. 16, 1972; children: John Bero, Corbin Marie. BA, Denison U., 1970; JD, Case Western Res., 1973. Bar: Ohio 1973, U.S. Dist. Ct. (no. dist.) Ohio 1974, U.S. Ct. Appeals (6th cir.), U.S. Supreme Ct. Spl. asst. U.S. senator W.B. Saxbe, Cleve., 1972-73; asst. pros. atty. Franklin County, Ohio, 1973-74; asst. dir. law City of Cleve., 1974; ptnr. Petro & Troia, Cleve., 1974-84; dir. govt. affairs Standard Oil Co., Cleve., 1984-86; ptnr. Petro, Rademaker, Matty & McClelland, Cleve., 1986-93, Buckingham, Doolittle & Burroughs, Cleve., 1993-95; auditor State of Ohio, Columbus, 1995—2003, atty. gen., 2003—07. Mem. city coun. Rocky River, Ohio, 1977-79, dir. law, 1980; mem. Ohio Ho. of Reps., Columbus, 1981-84, 86-90; commr. Cuyahoga County, Ohio, 1991-95. Mem.: ABA, Ohio State Bar Assn., Cleve. Bar Assn. Republican. Methodist. *

PETROCELLI, DANIEL M., lawyer; b. East Orange, NJ; m. Alison Petrocelli; 4 children. BS cum laude, U. Calif., Los Angeles, 1976; JD magna cum laude, Southwestern U., 1980. Bar: Calif. 1981, US Ct. Appeals (9th cir.) 1981, US Dist. Ct. (ctrl. and no. districts.) Calif. 1981, US Supreme Ct. 1981, US Dist. Ct. Colo. 1998. Ptnr. (Century City office) O'Melveny & Myers LLP, LA, mem. policy com. Mem. The American Lawyer's Litigation Dept. of Yr.; nat. commentator on trials and other legal issues; spkr. to bus. groups, bar and judges associations, and citizen groups. Mem. Southwestern U. Law Review, 1978—79, editor-in-chief, 1979—80; author: Triumph of Justice: The Final Judgement on the Simpson Saga, 1998; contbr. articles to profl. jours. Named Litigator of Yr., Century City Bar Assn., honoree, Columbus Citizens Found., Alumnus of Yr., Southwestern U., Trial Lawyer of Yr., Malibu Bar Assn., San Diego Trial Lawyers Assn., So. Calif. Super Lawyer, LA Mag.; named one of Los Angeles' Top 50 Litigators, LA Bus. Jour., Lawyers of Yr., Calif. Lawyer. Mem.: Assn. of Bus. Trial Lawyers, State Bar Calif. (antitrust and unfair competition sects.), ABA (litigation sect. and corp. counsel com.), LA County Bar (antitrust and unfair competition sects.). Office: O'Melveny & Myers LLP 1999 Avenue of Stars 7th Fl Los Angeles CA 90067-6035 Office Phone: 310-246-6850. Office Fax: 310-246-6779. Business E-Mail: dpetrocelli@omm.com.

PETROFF, LAURA R., lawyer; b. Cleve., July 7, 1955; BA, Denison U., 1977; JD, Vanderbilt U., 1980. Bar: Ill. 1980, U.S. Dist. Ct. Ill. (No. dist.) 1980, Calif. 1986, U.S. Dist. Ct. Calif. (Ctrl. and No. dist.) 1986, U.S. Ct. Appeals (9th cir.). Ptnr. Winston & Strawn LLP, LA, 2000—, mng. ptnr. Chair, ptnr. compensation com. Winston & Strawn LLP, LA, mem. exec. com., mem. diversity com. Gen. counsel PIHRA Found.; founding mem. Women Rainmakers Roundtable. Mem.: ABA (bd. dirs. pub. counsel law ctr.), State Bar Calif., L.A. County Bar Assn. (co-chair edn. com. 1989—91, mem. exec.com. 1990—92). Office: Winston & Strawn LLP 333 S Grand Ave Los Angeles CA 90071-1543 Office Phone: 213-615-1736. Office Fax: 213-615-1750. E-mail: lpetroff@winston.com.

PETROKUBI, MARILYN, film company executive, producer, writer, researcher; d. Stephen Joseph and Mary L. (Butchkosky) P.; m. Robert A. Lieberman; 1 child, Matthew Alexander. BA, Upsala Coll., 1973; MLS, Rutgers U., 1974. Reference librarian Livingston (N.J.) Pub. Library, 1974-75, Phillipsburg (N.J.) Free Pub. Library, 1975-78; freelance researcher, producer, 1979—; pres., exec. producer TimeSteps Prodns., Inc., West Orange, N.J., 1987—. Library systems cons., 1979—. N.J. State Council on the Arts grantee, 1977. Mem. Media Comms. Assn. Internat., N.Y. Women in Film and TV. Avocations: gardening, hiking, skiing, ice skating, biking. Office: TimeSteps Prodns Inc 2 Glenside Dr West Orange NJ 07052-4709

PETRONE, JOHN R., retired music educator, composer; b. Youngstown, Ohio, Dec. 26, 1932; s. Angelo R. and Mary C. Petrone; m. Diane Rupple Petrone, Oct. 18, 1987; m. Margaret Adams Petrone, Apr. 12, 1958 (div. Feb. 20, 1986); children: Nicolette, Jennifer, John, Margaret, Michael, Susan. MusB, Youngstown Coll., 1958; MusM, Duquesne U., 1963; PhD in music composition, Conservatoire Musique La Lille, France, 1982. Cert. permanent tchg. cert. Ohio, 1980. Dir. music St. Mary's HS, Warren, Ohio, 1957—58; elem. music supr. Cath. Diocese of Youngstown (Ohio), 1958—60; music dir. Cardinal Mooney HS, Youngstown, Ohio, 1960—65; music dir., specialist Willoughby (Ohio) Eastlake Schs., 1965—84; ret. state of Ohio tchr., 1984; adj. faculty Ursuline Coll., Pepper Pike, Ohio, 1986—2005, ret., 2005. Composer (arranger and conductor): The Flight of Apollo Eleven, 1979; composer: (arranger, music dir.) Augustine, 1980, Mr. Jingeling, 1981, Care Bears, 1982; composer: NASA/Higbees Christmas show, 1983, (songs) Goin' Baroque, 1977, Haydn Seek, 1979, Disco-Tinued, 1979, Also Sprach Whatsisname. With spc. svcs. USAF, 1951—54, Korea. Recipient Outstanding Secondary Educator of Am., 1974, Martha Holden Jennings Scholar, 1975—76. Mem.: ASCAP, Am. Fedn. Musicians, Simfonia, Kappa Delta Pi, Phi Mu Alpha. Roman Catholic. Avocation: car racing. Home: 7325 Chardon Rd Kirtland OH 44094 Personal E-mail: j.r.petrone@adelphia.net.

PETRONELLA, MICHAEL A., publishing executive; b. NJ; BS in Acctg., Rider U., MBA. Joined as acct. Dow Jones & Co., 1974, sr. accountant, 1980—81, acctg. supr., 1981—84, acctg. mgr., 1984—88, budget dir., 1988—93, pres., Dow Jones Indexes/Ventures NYC, 1997—. Mem. supervisory bd. STOXX Ltd. Office: Dow Jones & Co 1 World Financial Ctr 200 Liberty St New York NY 10281

PETRONY, JOHN FRANCIS, lawyer; b. Youngstown, Ohio, May 26, 1968; s. Francis Leon and Dorothy Jane (Dubos) P.; m. Mari Michele Wren, July 29, 1995. BA in Polit. Sci. summa cum laude, Youngstown State U., 1990; JD, Ohio State U., 1993. Bar: Ohio 1993, U.S. Dist. Ct. (no. dist.) Ohio 1994. Assoc. atty. Harrington, Huxley, Smith, Mitchell & Reed, Youngstown, 1993—97; assoc. Nadler, Nadler & Burdman, Youngstown, 1997—2004, ptnr., 2004—05; sole practitioner Law Offices of John F. Petrony, LLC, Boardman, 2005—. Faculty mem. National Bus. Inst., 2001—02. Author: Choice of Business Entity in Ohio: How to do it Right. Downtown Youngstown Revitalization Com., 1998-. Mem.: ABA (bus. law sect, real property sect., com. partnerships and unincorporated bus. orgs., negotiated acquisitions com.), Ohio St. Bar Assn. (corp. law com., limited liability company subcommittee, real estate sect.). Republican. Roman Catholic. Avocations: golf, tennis, music. Home: 7395 Cobblers Run Youngstown OH 44514-5313 Office Phone: 330-744-0247, 330-758-2445. E-mail: john@petronylaw.com.

PETROPOULOS, EVANGELOS, former health institute director, educator, researcher; b. Athens, Greece, Jan. 14, 1935; arrived in U.S., 1965; s. Anastassios P. and Metaxia P. Petropoulos; m. Panayota E. Tzela, Nov.

12, 1964; children: Anna, Anastassios. MD, U. Athens, 1959, PhD in Exptl. Medicine, 1964; PhD in Endocrinology, U. Calif., San Francisco, 1970; MD (hon.), Med. U. Sofia, Bulgaria, 2003. Spl. NIH fellow U. Calif., San Francisco, 1968—73; attending physician in endocrinology Evangelisnos Med. Ctr., Athens, 1973—75; prof., head dept. physiology U. Zimbabwe Med. Sch., Harare, 1975—82, prof., dean, 1982—85, prof. physiology, 1986—88; dir. Inst. Internat. Health, prof. physiology Mich. State U., E. Lansing, 1988—2002, dir., prof. emeritus, 2003—. Mem. com. regional office Africa WHO, Brazzaville, Republic of the Congo, 1982—85; mem. com. Commonwealth Secretariat, London, 1984—85; cons. African health policies World Bank, Washington, 1991. Contbr. articles and monographs to profl. jours. Lt. Med. Corp. Greek Air Force, 1960—63. Grantee, NIH, 1968, 1972, 1994, 1996, 1999, 2001; Internat. fellow in health, Kellogg Found., 1986—90. Mem.: NY Acad. Scis., Am. Physiol. Soc. Christian Orthodox. Achievements include research in etiology of Balkan endemic nephropathy in Bulgaria, Serbia and Romania. Avocations: classical music, church chanting, farming, underwater fishing, history of medicine. Home: 11 Nichols Ln Peabody MA 01960 Office: Inst Internat Health Mich State U B-301 W Fee Hall East Lansing MI 48824-1315

PETROS, RAYMOND LOUIS, JR., lawyer; b. Pueblo, Colo., Sept. 19, 1950; BS, Colo. Coll., 1972; JD, U. Colo., 1975. Bar: Colo. 1975. Jud. clk. to Justice Paul V. Hodges Colo. Supreme Ct., Denver, 1975-77; assoc. Bermingham, White, Burke & Ipsen, Denver, 1977-78; from assoc. to ptnr. Hall & Evans, Denver, 1978-81; ptnr. Kirkland & Ellis, Denver, 1981-86; mem. Holme, Roberts & Owen, Denver, 1986-96, Petros & White, LLC, 1996—. Contbr. articles to profl. jours. Bd. dirs. Rocky Mountain Poison Control Found., Denver, 1988-94. Office: Petros & White LLC 730 Seventeenth St Ste 820 Denver CO 80202-3518

PETROSKEY, DALE ALAN, cultural organization administrator, former professional society administrator; b. Detroit, Aug. 17, 1955; s. Eugene Louis and Marie Therese (Boutain) P.; m. Ann Holiday Grover, Mar. 17, 1955; 3 children, Kathleen Mills, Frank, Claire. BA, Mich. State U., 1978. Asst. press sec. Mich. House Reps., Washington, 1978-81; press sec. to congressman Mark Siljander U.S. Ho. Reps., Washington, 1981, adminstrv. asst. to Bill Goodling, 1981-85; asst. press sec. White House, Washington, 1985-87; asst. sec. for pub. affairs Dept. Transp., Washington, 1987-88; sr. v.p. Nat. Geographic Soc., 1988-99; pres., coo Nat. Baseball Hall of Fame & Mus., Cooperstown, N.Y., 1999—. Founder Mayo Smith Soc., Mich. and Washington, 1983. Republican. Roman Catholic. Avocations: tennis, baseball, reading, travel. Office: Nat Baseball Hall of Fame & Museum PO Box 590 Cooperstown NY 13326-0001

PETROSKI, HENRY, engineering educator, writer; b. NYC, Feb. 6, 1942; s. Henry and Victoria Petroski; m. Catherine, July 15, 1966; children: Karen, Stephen. B Mech. Engring., Manhattan Coll., Riverdale, NY, 1963, DP (hon.), 2003; MS, U. Ill., 1964, PhD, 1968; DSc (hon.), Clarkson U., Potsdam, NY, 1990; DHL (hon.), Trinity Coll., Hartford, Conn., 1997; DSc (hon.), Valparaiso U., Ind., 1999. Registered profl. engr., Tex.; chartered engr., Inst. of Engrs. of Ireland. Instr. U. Ill., Urbana, 1965-68; asst. prof. U. Tex., Austin, 1968-74; engr. Argonne Nat. Lab., Ill., 1975-80; assoc. prof. civil engring. Duke U., Durham, NC, 1980-87, prof., 1987-93, Aleksandar S. Vesic prof., 1993—, prof. history, 1995—, chmn. dept. civil and environ. engring., 1991-2000, dir. grad. studies, 1981-86. Author: To Engineer is Human, 1985, Beyond Engineering, 1986, The Pencil, 1990, The Evolution of Useful Things, 1992, Design Paradigms, 1994 (Best Book award in engring., Am. Assn. U. Presses, 1994), Engineers of Dreams, 1995, Invention by Design, 1996, Remaking the World, 1997, The Book on the Bookshelf, 1999, Paperboy, 2002, Small Things Considered, 2003, Pushing the Limits, 2004, Success Through Failure, 2006, The Toothpick, 2007; writer: documentary To Engineer is Human, 1987, columnist: Am. Scientist, 1991—, ASEE Prism, 2000—. Fellow NEH, 1987-88, Nat. Humanities Ctr., 1987-88, Guggenheim fellow, 1990-91; recipient Outstanding Engring. Grad. award Manhattan Coll., 1992, Alumni award for disting. svc. Coll. Engring. U. Ill. at Urbana-Champaign, 1994, Washington award Western Soc. Engrs., 2006, Disting. Svc. award Engring. Alumni Assn. Duke U., 2007. Fellow ASCE (Civil Engring. History and Heritage award 1993), ASME (Ralph Coats Roe medal 1991), Am. Acad. Arts and Sci., Am. Philos. Soc., Inst. Engrs. Ireland, NAE, Soc. History Tech., The Moles (hon.), Sigma Xi, Tau Beta Pi. Office: Duke U Sch Engring PO Box 90287 Durham NC 27708-0287 Office Phone: 919-660-5203. Business E-Mail: petroski@duke.edu.

PETROSKI, JAMES, thermal engineer; s. Stanley and Virginia Petroski; m. Karen Petroski; children: Nathan, Diane, Kenneth. BS in Engring. Sci. & Mechanics, Ga. Inst. Tech., Atlanta, 1980; MS in Engring. Mechanics, Cleve. State U., 2005. Mech. engr. NASA, Cleve., 1989—96; sr. thermal engr. GE Lumination, Valley View, Ohio, 2000—. Cons. Design by Analysis, Parma, Ohio, 1997—99. Tchr. Ch., Middlefield, Ohio, 2000—07. Lt. USN, 1980—84, W.Coast. NROTC scholarship, USN, 1976—80. Mem.: ASME. Achievements include patents for heat dissipation system for high power LED system; LED flashlight with lens; LED extrusion light engine and connector; LED-based modular lamp; high power LED power pack for spot module illumination; night light for plumbing fixtures; zoomable spot module; magnetic attachment method for LED light engines. Office: GE Lumination 6180 Halle Dr Valley View OH 44125 Business E-Mail: james.petroski@ge.com.

PETROVIC, KIMBERLY ANN, nursing researcher, nursing educator; d. Joseph Felix and Janet Marie Petrovic. B in Biology, Wheaton Coll., Ill., 1994; M in Sociology, N.Mex. State U., Las Cruces, 1998; MSN, Vanderbilt U., Nashville, 2000; postgrad., U. Conn., Storrs, 2003—. RN Oreg., cert. gerontological nurse practitioner, Oreg. Grad. student rschr. Oreg. Health and Scis. U., Portland, 2000—02; unit mgr., supr. geriatrics Crestview, Portland, 2002—03; supr., weekend mgr. Harborside Healthcare, West Hartford, Conn., 2003—. Program dir. Ctr. on Aging and Human Devel. U. Conn., Storrs, 2003—05, instr. gerontology dept. human devel. and family studies, 2004—, instr., faculty mem. Sch. Nursing, 2005—; rsch. asst. Ctr. for Devel. Disabilities U. Conn. Health Ctr., Farmington, 2003—05; geriatrics rschr. Hartford Hosp., Conn., 2004—, rsch. mentor geriatric nursing, 2005—; presenter in field. Author: Nursing Care Management of Older Adults with HIV/AIDS and Chronic Depression, 2006; co-author (with others): Physician Attitudes and Practices on Providing Care To Individuals with Intellectual Disabilities: An Exploratory Study, 2004, Complementary and Alternative Medicine for Older Adults with Intellectual Disabilities, 2004, Cautious Optimism and the Care of Older Adults with Disabilities, 2004; co-author: Respite Care Manual, 2005, Adverse Events Associated with the Presence of Delirium in Hospitalized Older Adults, 2007, Medical Conditions and Medication Use in Adults with Down Syndrome: A descriptive Analysis, 2007; guest editor: Jour. Conn. State Med. Soc., 2004, reviewer: N.C.L.E.X. (Nursing) Questions, 2005—. Named to, Conn. Geriatric Edn. Consortium; recipient Nat. Rsch. Svc. award in geriatric nursing, NIH, 2000—02, Shelia Packard Nursing Rsch. award, 2006; rsch. fellow, U. Conn. Dept. Human Devel. and Family Studies, 2006, Pauline Toner grantee, U. Conn. Sch. Nursing, 2006. Mem.: Conn. Geriatrics Soc., Nat. Coun. on Family Rels., Gerontol. Soc. Am. (campus rep. U. Conn. 2003—04), Am. Geriatrics Soc., Sigma Theta Tau. Avocations: running, pilates, travel, windsurfing, writing. Office: U Conn Sch Nursing Dept Human Devel and Family Studies Storrs Mansfield CT 06269

PETROVICH, DOROTHY, elementary school educator; b. NJ, July 14, 1931; d. Nicholas and Freida (Kleva) Frantin; m. Walter Petrovich, Aug. 22, 1954; children: David, Amy. BS, Jersey City State Tchrs. Coll., 1953. Cert. Newspaper Inst. of Am., 1949, The Inst. Children's Lit., 1996. Tchr. Bd. Edn., Middletown, NJ, 1953-54; substitute tchr. various schs., 1954-70; remedial math. tchr. Monmouth Beach (N.J.) Bd. Edn., 1970-72, 1st-4th grade tchr., 1972-91, ret., 1991. Editorial asst. to Socialist Republic, winner writing awards, cons. to editorial bd. internat. mag. Mem. ACLU, NJ Edn. Assn., NEA, Monmouth Beach Edn. Assn. (sec.-treas.), Soc. Preservation Continued Homeownership. Home: 165 S Manor Ct Wall NJ 07719-3658 Personal E-mail: Dorpet247@aol.com.

PETROW, GEORGE J., lawyer; b. 1953; BA cum laude, U. Neb., Lincoln, 1976; JD, U. Utah, 1979. Bar: Calif. 1979, Utah 1980, Conn. 1983, NY 1988. Law clk. Hon. Bruce S. Jenkins, US Dist. Ct., Dist. of Utah, 1980—81; ptnr., securitization and structured fin. Sidley Austin LLP, NYC, 1997—, co-mng. ptnr. NYC office, mem. mgmt. and exec. coms. Exec. editor Utah Law Rev., 1978—79. Mem.: ABA. Office: Sidley Austin LLP 787 Seventh Ave New York NY 10019 Office Phone: 212-839-5300. Office Fax: 212-839-5599. Business E-Mail: gpetrow@sidley.com.

PETROWSKI, JOSEPH H., oil industry executive; BA in Econ. and Govt., Harvard Univ., 1976. Former pres., CEO Louis Dreyfus Energy Co. No. Am.; former exec. pres. Duke Louis Dreyfus; former pres., CEO Consolidated Natural Gas Energy Svcs.; mng. dir. JHP Assoc., LLP; pres., CEO Gulf Oil Partnership, Newton, Mass., 2005—. Contbr. articles to numerous profl. jours. Office: Gulf Oil Partnership Ste 300 275 Washington St Newton MA 02458-1646 *

PETRU, SUZANNE MITTON, retired health care finance executive; b. Shawano, Wis., Sept. 26, 1947; d. William Wallace and Gertrude Priscilla Mitton; m. W. James Petru, Jan. 2, 1987. BSBA, Northwestern U., 1970, MBA, 1971. CPA, Ill., Wis. Diplomate Am. Coll. Healthcare Execs. Sr. acct. Arthur Andersen & Co., Chgo., 1971-77; v.p. fin. Thorek Hosp. and Med. Ctr., Chgo., 1977-82; sec./treas. La Grange (Ill.) Meml. Health Sys., 1982-85; v.p. fin. La Grange Meml. Hosp., 1982-85; audit prin. Deloitte & Touche (formerly Touche Ross & Co.), Chgo., 1985-88; sr. v.p. fin., treas. SSM Health Care Sys., St. Louis, 1988-95; pres. healthcare divsn. Am. Home Assurance Co. (subs. Am. Internat. Group, Inc.), 1995-96; v.p., CFO, treas. Group Health Plan (subs. Coventry Corp.), 1996-98; v.p. Petru Enterprises, Petru Internat., 1998—; sr. v.p. fin., CFO Rockford (Ill.) Health Sys., 2000—05; ret., 2005. Mem. investment com. Sisters of Charity Healthcare Sys., Cin., 1993-96, mem. fin. com., 1994-96; mem. assoc. bd. La Grange Meml. Hosp., 1988-95; advisor Jr. Achievement, 1971-76. Fellow Healthcare Fin. Mgmt. Assn. (bd. dirs. 1989-91, principles and practices bd. 1992-95, nat. matrix 1985-86, 88-89, pres., pres.-elect, sec., bd. First Ill. chpt. 1979-86, compliance officers forum adv. coun. 1998—, Follmer Bronze award 1982, Reeves Silver award 1985, Muncie Gold award 1988, Alice V. Runyan chpt. 1988); mem. Fin. Execs. Inst., Country Club at Legends (adv. bd. 1991-93), St. Louis Club (house com. 1991-95). Republican. Presbyterian. Avocations: golf, travel. Home Phone: 727-596-9670. Personal E-mail: spetru@gboalliance.com.

PETRULIS, ALAN JOSEPH, artist; b. Quens, NY, June 20, 1954; s. Bernard and Julia Petrulis. BA, Queens Coll., 1977; MFA, Md. Inst. Art, Balt., 1979. Mgr. Eskell Lace Co., NYC, 1984—91, Dolphin Asset Mgmt. Corp., NYC, 2000—07. Dir. First St. Gallery, NYC, 1984—88. Represented in permanent collections Bklyn. Mus. Art, NY Hist. Soc., Mus. City NY, NY Transit Mus. Recipient Cannon prize, Nat. Acad. Design, NYC, 1984, Ralph Fabri prize, 1986. Mem.: NY-NJ Trail Conf., Met. Postcard Club (v.p. 2006—). Personal E-mail: ajpetrulis@hotmail.com.

PETRUS, ROBERT THOMAS, internet business owner, investor; b. Manchester, Conn., 1957; s. John Joseph and Geraldine Petrus; m. Laura Lee Waggoner, Nov. 22, 1986; children: Elizabeth Ashley, Nicholas Kent. BA with honors, Trinity Coll., Hartford, Conn., 1979. Mgmt. intern Aetna Life & Casualty Co., Hartford, 1979-82, sr. adminstr. data processing ops., 1982-85, cons. Tech. Ctr., 1985-90; pres. Omoo Distbn. Corp., Mansfield, Conn., 1990—; v.p. Cogitore, Inc., 1990—. Author: Get Organized!, 1991. Chmn. Conn. Youth for Pres. Ford, 1976; com. mem. Big Bros.-Big Sisters, Hartford, 1982-83; loaned exec. Greater Hartford United Way-Combined Health Appeals Campaign, 1985. Recipient ofcl. citation Conn. Ho. of Reps., 1985. Mem. Phi Beta Kappa, Pi Gamma Mu, Mu Alpha Theta. Republican. Avocations: photography, golf, skiing. Office: ODI-Omoo Distbn Inc 27 Wormwood Hill Rd Ste 101 Mansfield Center CT 06250-1135 Office Phone: 866-687-6857. Business E-Mail: robert.petrus@omoodistribution.com.

PETRUS, SALLY A., elementary school educator; b. Parma, Ohio, Sept. 20, 1965; d. Salvatore Charles Scherma and Carmie Lizzini-Scherma; m. Ronald M. Petrus, Oct. 13, 1990; children: triplets, Arianne Lee, Brianne Lynn, Carlianne Marie. BFA, Ohio U., Athens, 1987; MEd, Baldwin Wallace Coll., Berea, Ohio, 1991. Tchr. Parma City Sch. Dist., 1989—. Advisor student coun., Parma, 2004—, h.s. cheerleading, 1991—98. Recipient Cleve. Crystal Apple award, Cleve. Plain Dealer, 2001. Mem.: PTA (assoc.), Parma Edn. Assn. (assoc.), Nat. Tchrs. Assn. (assoc.). Home: 14572 Walking Stick Way Strongsville OH 44136 Office: Parma City Sch Dist 5210 Loya Pky Parma OH 44134 Home Phone: 440-878-8777; Office Phone: 440-885-2418. Personal E-mail: sallypabc@aol.com.

PETRUSH, JOHN JOSEPH, lawyer; b. Rochester, Pa., Oct. 15, 1942; s. Joseph Anthony and Helen Rosemarie (Klucarich) P.; children: John Joseph, Joshua Laurence. AB cum laude, Princeton U., 1964; LLB, Stanford U., 1967. Bar: Calif. 1967, Pa. 1970. Assoc. Bernard Petrie, San Francisco, 1967-68; law clk. to judge Common Pleas Ct. Beaver County, Pa., 1969; assoc. Buchanan, Ingersoll, Rodewald, Kyle & Buerger, Pitts., 1970-75; pvt. practice Beaver, Pa., 1976—. Mem. Beaver Town Coun., 1973-88; bd. dirs. Beaver County unit Am. Cancer Soc., 1976-90, United Way of Beaver County, 1986-92; trustee Beaver Area Sch. Dist. Edn. Found. With USMCR, 1961-63. Mem. ABA, ATLA, Pa. Bar Assn., Pa. Trial Lawyers Assn. (bd. govs. western chpt. 1984-90), Allegheny County Bar Assn., Beaver County Bar Assn. (treas. 1987-2002). Republican. Home: 331 Wilson Ave Beaver PA 15009-2323 Office: 348 College Ave Beaver PA 15009-2209 Office Phone: 724-775-8600. E-mail: john.j.petrush@verizon.net.

PETRUSKA, STEVEN C., construction executive; Grad. in Acctg., Ctrl. Mich. U., Mt. Pleasant, 1981. V.p. fin. South Tex. divsn. Pulte Homes Inc., 1984, pres. Las Vegas divsn., pres. SW region, area pres. Ariz. and Nev. ops., exec. v.p., COO Bloomfield Hills, Mich., 2004—. Dow Corning Exec.-in-Residence Ctrl. Mich. U., 2004—05. Office: Pulte Homes Inc 100 Bloomfield Hills Pky Ste 300 Bloomfield Hills MI 48304-2946 *

PETRUSKI, JENNIFER ANDREA, speech and language pathologist; b. Kingston, NY, Jan. 28, 1968; d. Andrew Francis and Judith (Cruger) Petruski. BS, SUNY, Buffalo, 1990, MSEd in Speech-Language Pathology, 1992. Cert. tchr. speech-hearing handicapped N.Y., lic. speech-lang. pathology N.Y., cert. of clin. competence. Speech-lang. pathologist Kingston City Schs., 1992—; clin. practicum supr. SUNY, New Paltz, 1996—. Cooperating tchr. SUNY, New Paltz, 1995—2004, Coll. St. Rose, 1997, 2004; ind. contr. speech svcs. Ulster County, 1997; summer sch. tchr. New Paltz Sch. Dist., 2002; student rev. team facilitator Kingston City Schs., NY, 2002—. Mem.: NY State Speech-Lang. and Hearing Assn., Am. Speech and Hearing Assn. (Continuing Edn. award 2004, 2006), Speech and Hearing Assn. Hudson Valley (corr. sec. 1995—2001, newsletter editor 1995—2002, membership com. 1995—2002, treas. 1997, pres. 1999—2000, nominating com. 1999—2000, membership chmn. 2000—02, legis. chmn. 2000—04, website adminstr. 2001—, historian 2001—, continuing edn. adminstr. 2002, program com. 2003, newsletter com. 2003—04), Bd. Regional Assn. Presidents (membership chair 2000—02, pub. info. chair 2003—04, Disting. Svc. award 2005). Home: PO Box 88 Hurley NY 12443 Personal E-mail: jpa1230@verizon.net. E-mail: jpetruski@aol.com.

PETRUZZELLI, JULIE A., lawyer; b. Glen Ridge, NJ, Apr. 18, 1957; BS in Chemistry/Biochemistry, Brown Univ., 1979; JD, Univ. Va., 1982. Bar: NY 1983, DC 1989, US Patent & Trademark Office. Ptnr. Venable LLP, Washington. Mem.: ABA, NY Bar Assn., Women's Bar Assn. DC, NY Patent, Trademark, and Copyright Law Assn., Am. Intellectual Property Law Assn. Office: Venable LLP 575 Seventh St NW Washington DC 20004 Office Phone: 202-344-4010. Office Fax: 202-344-8300. Business E-Mail: japetruzzelli@venable.com.

PETRUZZI, CHRISTOPHER ROBERT, business educator, consultant; b. Peoria, Ill., July 28, 1951; s. Benjamin Robert and Mary Katherine (Urban) P.; m. Georgina Sailer, June 20, 1992; children: Lillian Caroline, Vivian Audrey. BA, Wabash Coll., 1972; MBA, U. Chgo., 1974; PhD, U. So. Calif., 1983. Lectr. bus. U. Wis., Milw., 1975-77; cons. H.C. Wainwright, Boston, 1978-79; lectr. U. So. Calif., 1978-81; prof. bus. U. Pa., Phila., 1981-84; prof. acctg. NYU, 1984-89, Calif. State U., Fullerton, 1989—. Pres. ECON Investment Software, San Clemente, Calif., 1987-2000; pres. Smart Execution LLC, 2001-. Earhart fellow, 1972-73, U. Chgo. fellow, 1974-76. Libertarian. Christian. Office: Ste 302B 629 Camino de los Mares San Clemente CA 92673 Home: 1527 Via Tulipan San Clemente CA 92673 Personal E-mail: chris@smex.com.

PETRY, ALICE HALL, scholar, educator, writer; b. Hartford, Conn., July 8, 1951; d. James B. and Elizabeth K. Hall. BS with highest honors, U. Conn., 1973; MA, Conn. Coll., 1976; PhD, Brown U., 1979. Asst. prof. English RISD, Providence, 1980-86, assoc. prof., 1986-92, prof., 1992—, head dept. English, 1993-95; chair, prof. dept. English So. Ill. U., Edwardsville, 1995—2001. Lectr. ArtsAm. program USIA, Japan, 1991; vis. prof. U. Colo., Boulder, 1987. Author: Genius in His Way: The Art of Cable's Old Creole Days, 1988, Fitzgerald's Craft of Short Fiction: The Collected Stories, 1920-1935, 1991, Understanding Anne Tyler, 1990, Critical Essays on Anne Tyler, 1992, Critical Essays on Kate Chopin, 1996, On Harper Lee: Essays and Reflections, 2007. Am. Coun. Learned Socs. sr. postdoctoral fellow, 1987-88; Fulbright scholar, Brazil, 1985. Avocation: travel. Office: So Ill U Dept English Edwardsville IL 62026-1431 Office Phone: 618-692-2060. E-mail: apetry@siue.edu.

PETRY, DON D., educational association administrator; b. Grant City, Mo., Dec. 23, 1940; s. Harold and Mary R. (Barnett) P.; m. Peggy L. Luhrs, May 29, 1966; children: Clayton James, Heather Lynn. BSE, N.W. Mo. State U., 1962; MEd, U. Mo., 1966, EdD, 1969. Cert. elem. tchr., elem. prin., secondary prin., second English tchr., Mo. Elem. tchr. to HS prin. Rock Port Schs., Mo., 1961—66; instr. U. Mo., Columbia, 1966—69; assoc. dean adminstrn. to exec. v.p., prof. N.W. Mo. State U., Maryville, 1969—78; v.p. adminstrn., prof. to interim pres. CBN U., Virginia Beach, Va., 1978—84; founder, pres. Teled Internat., Virginia Beach, 1984; exec. dir. Nat. Coun. Pvt. Sch. Accreditation, Seattle. Cons. Oral Roberts U. Ednl. Fellowship and Internat. Christian Accrediting Assn., Tulsa, 1986—, Dominian Coll., Seattle, Graceland U., Ind.; adv., bd. dirs. Josue Internat. Ministries, El Salvador, 1991—; internat. vice chancellor Christian Faith U., Nigeria, 1989—; adj. prof. Oral Roberts U., Tulsa, 1990—. Author: Budgetary Guidelines for Higher Education, 1971. Mem. ASCD, Phi Delta Kappa (chpt. pres.), Rotary Club. Office: Nat Coun Pvt Sch Accreditation PO Box 13686 Seattle WA 98198-1010 Office Phone: 253-874-3408. Office Fax: 253-874-3409. E-mail: ncpsaexdr@aol.com. *

PETRYSHYN, WOLODYMYR V., retired mathematician; b. Murovane, Ukraine, Jan. 22, 1929; arrived in U.S.A., 1950; s. Vasyl and Maria Petryshyn; BA, Columbia U., 1953, MS, 1954, PhD, 1961. Postdoc. fellow NYU, 1961—64; assoc. prof. math. U. Chgo., 1964—67; prof. math. Rutgers U., New Brunswick, NJ, 1967—96, ret., 1996. Dir. Math.-Physics Sect. Shevchenko Sci. Soc., NYC. Author: Approximation-Solrability of Nonlinear Functional and Differential Equations, 1993, Generalized Topological Degree and Semilinear Equations, 1995, Development of Mathematical Sciences in Ukraine, 2004. Recipient M. Krylov award, Acad. Scis. Ukraine, 1992; grantee, NSF, 1964—86. Mem.: Ukrainian Acad. Sci. in Kiev. Achievements include first to establishing a new branch of mathematics, the A-proper mapping theory. Home: 10 Jackson Drive Cranford NJ 07016

PETT, JOHN LYMAN, banker; b. Erie, Pa., Dec. 7, 1948; s. Peter Paul and Dorothy (Rhoades) P. BS, Gannon U., 1971; MBA, DePaul U., 1977; postgrad., Harvard Bus. Sch., 1989. Asst dir. acctg. and adminstrn. Continental Can Co., Chgo., 1974-77; comml. v.p. and lending officer Mfrs. & Traders Trust Co., Buffalo, 1977-79, unit mgr. Mid. Market Lending, 1979-84, exec. v.p., chief credit officer, 1984—. Mem., cons. Erie County Fiscal Res. Com., Buffalo, 1984-86. Capt. USMC, 1971-74. Mem. Robert Morris Assocs., Am. Bankers Assocs., Wanakah Country Club (Hamburg, N.Y.). Republican. Roman Catholic. Avocations: golf, running, reading.

PETTENGILL, GORDON H(EMENWAY), physicist, researcher; b. Providence, Feb. 10, 1926; s. Rodney Gordon and Frances (Hemenway) P.; m. Pamela Anne Wolfenden, Oct. 28, 1967; children: Mark Robert, Rebecca Jane. BS, MIT, 1948; PhD, U. Calif., Berkeley, 1955. Staff mem. Lincoln Lab. MIT, Lexington, 1954-63, 65-68, prof. planetary physics, dept. earth, atmospheric and planetary scis. Cambridge, 1971—2001, dir. Ctr. Space Rsch., 1984-90; assoc. dir. Arecibo (P.R.) Obs., 1963-65, dir., 1968-71. Served with inf., Signal Corps AUS, 1944-46. Decorated Combat Inf. badge; recipient Magellanic Premium, Am. Philos. Soc., 1994. Fellow Am. Geophys. Union (Whipple award 1995, Charles A. Whitten award 1997); mem. AAAS, Am. Phys. Soc., Am. Astron. Soc., Internat. Astron. Union, Internat. Radio Sci. Union, Nat. Acad. Sci., Am. Acad. Arts and Sci. Achievements include pioneering several techniques in radar astronomy for describing properties of planets and satellites; discovering 59-day rotational period of planet Mercury. Office: MIT 77 Massachusetts Ave Rm 37-582D Cambridge MA 02139-4307

PETTERCHAK, JANICE A., writer; b. Springfield, Ill., Sept. 15, 1942; d. Emil H. and Vera C. (Einhoff) Stukenberg; m. John J. Petterchak, Oct. 5, 1963; children: John A., Julie Gilmour, James. AA in Liberal Arts, Springfield Coll., Ill., 1962; BS, U. Ill., 1972, MA in History, 1982. Supr. hist. markers Ill. State Hist. Soc., Springfield, 1973-74, asst. exec. dir., 1985-87; curator photographs Ill. State Hist. Libr., Springfield, 1974-79, assoc. editor, 1979-83, rep. local history svcs., 1983-85, libr. dir., 1987-95. Author: Mapping a Life's Journey: The Legacy of Andrew McNally III, 1995, Patrick O'Malley: A Journey with Family and Friends, 1996, Jack Brickhouse: A Voice For All Seasons, 1996, Roads Traveled:The Eugene & Kathryn Simonds Story, 1997, John Thomas Trutter: A Profile of Legacy and Leadership, 1997, Books That Stand the Test of Time: The Story of Bound to Stay Bound Books 1920 to 1998, Taming the Upper Mississippi, 2000; A Legacy of Style: The Story of Shelby Williams Industries, 2000, To Share: The Heritage, Legend and Legacy of Nathan Cummings, 2000, Out To Sea Again: A Naval Armed Guard in World War II, 2002, Lone Scout: W.D. Boyce and American Boy Scouting, 2003, Where Eagles Soar: A Brief History of Community Banking in Illinois, 2004, Historic Illinois, 2005, International Union of Operating Engineers Local 965 AFL-CIO 75th Anniversary 1931-2006; editor: Illinois History: An Annotated Bibliography, 1995; assoc. editor Ill. Hist. Jour.; contbr. articles to profl. jours. Grantee, NEH, 1987—95. Mem. Ill. State Hist. Soc.,

Sangamon County Hist. Soc. (bd. dirs. 1991-94, 99-2002, 04-, v.p. 1996-97, pres. 1995-96), U. Ill. Alumni Assn. Home: 11381 Mallard Dr Rochester IL 62563-8011 Business E-Mail: petterchak@biogwriter.com.

PETTERSEN, KEVIN WILL, investment company executive; b. Yonkers, NY, July 4, 1956; s. Kjell Will and Marilyn Ann (Stevens) Pettersen; m. Mary Elizabeth Murphy, Aug. 30, 1981; children: Kelly, Elizabeth, Erin. Diploma academia, Chaminade, Mineola, NY, 1974; BA in Econs., SUNY, Stony Brook, 1978. Buyer JC Penney Co., Inc., NYC, 1979-82; nat. sales mgr. Randa Corp., Inc., NYC, 1982-83; dir. sales Wemco, Inc., NYC, 1983-86; mng. dir., sr. v.p. D.H. Blair & Co., Inc., NYC, 1986—89; exec. v.p. Brean Murray, Foster Securities, Inc., NYC, 1989—90; v.p., br. mgr., corp. officer A.G. Edwards and Sons, Inc., Huntington, NY, 1990—2006; pres. Harborview Fin. Advisors, Inc., 2006—; br. mgr., registered prin. Raymond James Fin. Svcs., 2006—. Mem. pres. coun. A. G. Edwards, mem. Million Dollar Club, mem. chmn.'s coun., 1998; mem. exec. coun. Oppenheimer Funds Group. Active Oyster Bay Supr.'s Adv. Com. Crime, 1993—95; basketball coach girls team Cath. Youth Orgn., 1998—2007; del. Rep. Planning Com.; bd. dirs. Harbour Green L.I. Assn., 1990—94, pres., 1991. Recipient Outstanding Character award, Chaminade, 1974, Coach of Yr., Cath. Youth Orgn., 2007. Mem.: Chaminade Wall St. Assn., Monarch Soc., St. Rose of Lima Father's Guild, Soc. Friendly Sons of St. Patrick, Chaminade Torch Club, Green Harbour Beach Club (bd. dirs. 1994—98, treas. 1999). Republican. Roman Catholic. Avocations: golf, skiing, boating. Home: 85 Biltmore Blvd Massapequa NY 11758-8142 Office: Raymond James Fin Svcs Inc 5510 Merrick Rd Massapequa NY 11758 Office Phone: 516-795-5500.

PETTERSEN, KJELL WILL, securities trader, consultant; b. Oslo, June 19, 1927; came to US, 1946, naturalized, 1957; s. Jens Will and Ragna O. (Wickstrom) P.; m. Marilyn Ann Stevens, Aug. 16, 1952; children: Thomas W., Maureen, Kevin W., Maryann, Kathleen. Student, Zion Theol. Sch., 1945—49, NY Inst. Finance, 1955—56. Mgr. A.M. Kidder & Co., NYC, 1954-64; sr. v.p., sec., dir. Halle & Stieglitz, Fillor Bullard Co., Inc., 1964-73; sr. v.p., dir. mktg. Parrish Securities, Inc., NYC, 1973-74; cons. Loeb, Rhoades & Co., NYC, 1974-79; mng. dir. Prudential Securities, NYC, 1979-89; pres. Arbitration Recovery Cons., Marco, Fla., 1992-93; vice chmn. Noddings Investment Group, Inc., Oakbrook Terrace, Ill., 1993-95; mem. City Coun., Marco Island, Fla., 1997—2002, chmn., 2001—02. Dir. Ski for Light Inc., Mpls., Creative Arts Rehab. Ctr. Inc., NYC. Dem. candidate NY State Assembly, Nassau County, 1962; past dir. Guadalupe Ctr., Marco YMCA; pres. Quest for Peace Internat.; co-chmn. Marco Island Celebration 2000. Mem. Nat. Assn. Security Dealers (bd. arbitrators), NY C. of C., Norwegian-Am. C. of C. (dir. Guadalupe Ctr.), Scandinavian Found., Bankers Club of Am., Norwegian Club (NYC), Rotary. Home: 350 Rockhill Ct Marco Island FL 34145-3860 Personal E-mail: marcokjell@aol.com.

PETTERSEN, SUZANN, professional golfer; b. Oslo, Apr. 7, 1981; Profl. golfer, 2000—; mem. Evian Ladies European Tour, 2001—02, LPGA, 2003—. Mem. European team Solheim Cup, 2002, 03, 05. Named Rookie of Yr., Ladies European Tour, 2001. Achievements include winning LPGA tour events including the Michelob Ultra Open, 2007, McDonald's LPGA Championship, 2007; winner, French Open, 2001, and the SAS Masters, 2007, on the Ladies European Tour; winner, World Amateur Championship, 2000; winner, British Girls Championship, 1999; winner, Norwegian Amateur Championship, 1996-2000. Avocation: skiing. Mailing: HNP AS Huysman Nystuen & Ptnrs Gladengveien 3b 0661 Oslo Norway *

PETTERSEN, THOMAS MORGAN, accountant, corporate financial executive; b. Poughkeepsie, NY, Nov. 9, 1950; s. Olsen Thomas and Reva Frances (Palmer) P. BS, U. Albany, 1973. CPA NY. Sr. acct. Arthur Andersen and Co., NYC, 1973-76; sr. ops. auditor Gulf and Western Inc., NYC, 1977, fin. analyst, 1978; adminstr. auditing NBC, NYC, 1979, mgr. auditing Burbank, Calif., 1980, dir. auditing, 1981-88, dir. acctg. systems and ops. analysis, 1988-90; v.p. fin. and adminstrn. Data Dimensions, Inc., Culver City, Calif., 1991-92; cons. Westwood One, Inc., Culver City, 1992-93; CFO Computer Image Sys., Inc., Torrance, Calif., 1993-97; dir. corp. fin. DeCrane Aircraft Holdings, Inc., El Segundo, Calif., 1997-2000; bus. cons., 2000—. Mem. AICPA, Fin. Execs. Internat. Republican. Roman Catholic. Avocations: sports, travel. Home: 217 1st Pl Manhattan Beach CA 90266-6503

PETTEWAY, SAMUEL BRUCE, college president; b. Fayetteville, NC, July 18, 1924; s. Walter Bernard and Margaret Maysie (Cole) P.; m. Eleanor Glenn Sugg, Nov. 27, 1948; children— Margaret Petteway Small, Samuel Bruce. BS, N.C. State U., 1949, MEd, 1966, EdD, 1968. Gen. mgr. Homeowners Ins. and Realty Co., 1960-63; engring. tech. dept. chmn., dean occupational and transfer programs, dir. evening programs Lenoir County Community Coll., 1963-68; pres. Coll. of the Albemarle, Elizabeth City, NC, 1968-75, N.C. Wesleyan Coll., Rocky Mount, 1975-86; br. mgr. Sherwin Williams, 1953—60; first class radio engr. Radio WFTC-AM, 1949—53. Prof. Va. Poly. Inst. and State U., 1973-75, East Carolina U., 1994-99; pres. Philanthropic Cons., Inc., Kinston, N.C., 1986-96; sec. Coll. Mgmt. Svcs., Inc., Raleigh, N.C., 1989; lic. amateur radio operator, 1992—. Pres. chpt. Am. Cancer Soc., 1960-61, Boys' Club Lenoir County, 1987-91, Westminster Homeowners Assn., 1997; bd. dirs. Rocky Mount Acad., 1979-80, Triangle East, Inc., 1985-86, Cypress Glen Retirement Home, chmn. 1996; chmn. deferred giving com. N.C. Meth. Found., 1979-86; chmn. coun. on ministries 1st United Meth. Ch., Rocky Mount, 1980-81, Westminster United Meth. Ch., 1989-90, chmn. bd. trustees, 1994-99, chmn. adminstrv. bd., 2001-03; chmn. bd. trustees Art Edn. Found., 1980; mem. Nash County Bd. Health, 1985-86; bd. trustees United Meth. Retirement Homes, Inc., 1996-99; treas. Meth. Home for Children, 1997-2002. With USN, 1943—46, with USNR, 1946—51. Named Tar Heel of Week News and Observer, 1975, Today's Outstanding N.C. Citizen WNCT-TV, 1975; NSF fellow U. Ill., 1963 Mem. Nat. Assn. for Hosp. Devel., N.C. Assn. Colls. and Univs., N.C. Conf. United Meth. Ch. (chmn. bd. trustees 1973-79), Nat. Soc. Fund Raising Execs. (cert.), Rocky Mount C. of C. (bd. dirs. 1980-84), Rotary (scholarship com. dist. 7730 1995-2004), Phi Kappa Phi, Theta Alpha Phi. Clubs: Benvenue Country, Galaxy Social; Kinston Country. Lodges: Rotary (pres. 1980-81, bd. dirs. Kinston chpt. 1988-92). Republican. Office: 708 Westminster Ln Kinston NC 28501-2770 Personal E-mail: bpetteway@suddenlink.net.

PETTIBONE, PETER JOHN, lawyer; b. Schenectady, NY, Dec. 11, 1939; s. George Howard and Caryl Grey (Ketchum) P.; m. Jean Kellogg, Apr. 23, 1966; children: Stephen, Victoria. AB summa cum laude, Princeton U., 1961; JD, Harvard U., 1964; LLM, NYU, 1971. Bar: Pa. 1965, D.C. 1965, N.Y. 1968, U.S. Supreme Ct. 1974, Russia (fgn. legal cons.) 1995. Lectr. Heidelberg (Fed. Republic Germany) U., 1965-67; assoc. Cravath, Swaine & Moore, NYC, 1967-74, Lord Day & Lord, Barrett Smith, NYC, 1974-76, ptnr. NYC and Washington, 1976-94, Patterson, Belknap, Webb & Tyler LLP, NYC and Moscow, 1994-2000, Hogan & Hartson LLP, NYC and Moscow, 2000—. Pres. 1158 Fifth Ave. Corp., N.Y.C., 1991-94; pres. North Ferry Co., Shelter Island, N.Y., 1987-90; bd. dirs., vice-chmn. N.Y. State Facilities Devel. Corp., N.Y.C., 1983-89. Editor USSR Legal Materials, Columbia U., 1990-92. Trustee, treas. Hosp. Chaplaincy Inc., N.Y.C., 1980-86, Civitas, N.Y.C., 1984-92; mem. Coun. Fgn. Rels., 1993—; trustee Union Chapel, Shelter Island, N.Y., 1990—, CEC Internat. Ptnrs., 1996-2002; bd. dirs., vice chmn. Geonomics Inst., Middlebury, Vt., 1991-98; mem. vestry Ch. of Heavenly Rest, N.Y.C., 1987-93; mem. Nat. Adv. Coun. Harriman Inst. Columbia U., 1996—; mem. Russia com. Episcopal Diocese of N.Y.; bd. dirs. Transatlantic Ptnrs. Against AIDS. Capt. U.S. Army, 1965-67, Heidelberg, Germany. Mem. ABA, Assn. Bar City NY (chmn. com. on CIS affairs 1991-94), US-USSR Trade and Econ. Coun. Inc. (US co-chmn. legal com. 1980-92), US-Russia Bus. Coun. (bd. dirs.), Soc. of Cin., Anglers Club NYC, NY Yacht Club, Shelter Island Yacht Club, Moscow Country Club, Amateur Ski Club NY (pres. 1980-82), Canterbury Choral Soc. (pres. 1983-84), Internat. Tax and Investment Ctr. (bd. dirs.), Phi Beta Kappa. Episcopalian. Home: 1158 5th Ave New York NY 10029-6917 also: 10 Wesley Ave Shelter Island Heights NY 11965 Office: Hogan & Hartson LLP 875 3rd Ave New York NY 10022 Office Phone: 212-918-3510. Business E-Mail: pjpettibone@hhlaw.com.

PETTIETTE, ALISON YVONNE, lawyer; b. Brockton, Mass., Aug. 16, 1952; Student, Sorbonne, Paris, 1971—72; MA, Rice U., 1974; JD, Bates Coll., 1978. Bar: Tex. 79, U.S. Dist. Ct. (so. dist.) Tex. 80, U.S. Ct. Appeals (5th cir.) 81. Ptnr. Harvill & Hardy, Houston, 1983—84; assoc. O'Quinn & Hagans, Houston, 1984—86, Jones & Granger, Houston, 1986—88; pvt. practice Houston, 1988—. Editor: Houston Law Rev. U. Houston, 1976—78. Exercise instr. YWCA, Houston, 1976—81, U. St. Thomas, Houston. Named NDEA fellow, Rice U., Houston, 1972—74, Woodfow Wilson scholar, Tulane U., New Orleans, 1972. Mem.: ATLA, ABA, Houston Trial Lawyers Assn., Tex. Trial Lawyers Assn., Phi Delta Phi, Phi Beta Kappa. Office Phone: 713-630-0270, 713-446-4823. Personal E-mail: aypettiette@sbcglobal.net.

PETTIGREW, L. EUDORA, retired academic administrator; b. Hopkinsville, Ky., Mar. 1, 1928; d. Warren Cicero and Corrye Lee (Newell) Williams; children: Peter W. Woodard, Jonathan R. (dec.). MusB, W.Va. State Coll., 1950; MA, So. Ill. U., 1964, PhD, 1966; PhD honoris causa, U. Pretoria, South Africa, 2002, Holy Family Coll., 2002, Western Conn. State U., 2004. Music/English instr. Swift Meml. Jr. Coll., Rogersville, Tenn., 1950-51; music instr., librarian Western Ky. Vocat. Sch., Paducah, 1951-52; music/English instr. Voorhees Coll., Denmark, SC, 1954-55; dir. music and recreation therapy W.Ky. State Psychiatric Hosp., Hopkinsville, 1956-61; research fellow Rehab. Inst., So. Ill. U., Carbondale, 1961-63, instr., resident counselor, 1963-66, coordinator undergrad. ednl. psychology, 1963-66, acting chmn. ednl. psychology, tchr. corps instr., 1966; asst. prof. to assoc. prof. dept. psychology U. Bridgeport, Conn., 1966-70; prof., chmn. dept. urban and met. studies Coll. Urban Devel. Mich. State U., East Lansing, 1974-80; assoc. provost, prof. U. Del., Newark, 1981-86; pres. SUNY Coll. at Old Westbury, 1986-98. Cons. for rsch. and evaluation Hall Neighborhood House Day Care Tng. Project, Bridgeport, 1966-68, U.S. Ea. Regional Lab., Edn. Devel. Ctr., Newton, Mass., 1967-69; coordinator for edn. devel., 1968-69; cons. Bridgeport Public Schs. lang. devel. project, 1967-68, 70; Lansing Model Cities Agy., Day Care Program, 1971; U. Pitts., 1973, 74, Leadership Program, U. Mich. and Wayne State U., 1975, Wayne County Pub. Health Nurses Assn., 1976, Ill. State Bd. Edn., 1976-77; assoc. prof. U. Bridgeport, 1970, Ctr. for Urban Affairs and Coll. of Edn., Mich. State U., East Lansing, 1970-73; program devel. specialist Lansing Public Schs. Tchr. Corps program, 1971-73; coord. workshop Conflict Resolution The Woman's Role in Our World, 4th Internat. UN Conf. on Women, Beijing, China, 1995; lectr. in field; condr. workshops in field; guest spkr. Internat. Conf. on The New Role of Higher Edn. in the Context of an Ind. Palestinian State, An-Najah Nat. U., Nablus, Palestine, 1996; mem. exec. com. UN Non-Govtl. Orgn., Dept. Pub. Info., 2004—. Tv/radio appearances on: Black Women in Edn, Channel 23, WKAR, East Lansing, 1973, Black Women and Equality, Channel 2, Detroit, 1974, Women and Careers, Channel 7, Detroit, 1974, Black Women and Work: Integration in Schools, WITL Radio, Lansing, 1974, others; editor: Universities and Their Role in World Peace, 2003; contbr. articles to profl. jours. Mem. exec. com. UN Non Govtl. Orgns. Dept. Public Info., 2004. Recipient Diana award Lansing YWCA, 1977, Outstanding Profl. Achievement award, 1987, award L.I. Ctr. for Bus. and Profl. Women, 1988, Educator of Yr. 100 Black Men of L.I., 1988, Black Women's Agenda award, 1988, Woman of Yr. Nassau/Suffolk Coun. of Adminstrv. Women in Edn., 1989, Disting. Ednl. Leadership award L.I. Women's Coun. for Equal Edn. Tng. and Employment, 1989, L.I. Disting. Leadership award L.I. Bus. News, 1990, Disting. Black Women in Edn. award Nat. Coun. Negro Women, 1991; named Outstanding Black Educator, NAACP, 1968, Outstanding Woman Educator, Mich. Women's Lawyers Assn. and Mich. Trial Lawyers Assn., 1975, Disting. Alumna, Nat. Assn. for Equal Opportunity in Higher Edn., 1990, Woman of Yr., Nassau County League of Women Voters, 1991, Disting. Alumna So. Ill. U., 1997, N.Y. State Senate resolution of commendation, 1998; Elected to Achievers Hall of Fame: Long Island Bus. and Profl. Women's Orgn., 2001 Mem. AAAS, Nat. Assn. Acad. Affairs Adminstrs., Internat. Assn. Univ. Pres. (exec. com., spl. adviser to pres.), Phi Delta Kappa.

PETTIGREW, RODERIC I., federal agency administrator, radiologist, researcher; BS in Physics cum laude, Morehouse Coll., 1972; MS in Nuc. Medicine and Engring., Rensselaer Poly. Inst., 1973; PhD in Applied Radiation Physics, MIT, 1977; MD, U. Miami, 1979. Intern and resident internal medicine Emory U.; resident nuc. medicine U. Calif., San Diego; clin. rsch. scientist Picker Internat.; Robert Wood Johnson Found. fellow Emory U., 1985; prof. radiology, medicine (cardiology) and bioengineering Emory U. Sch. Medicine, Atlanta, dir. Ctr. for MR Rsch.; dir. Nat. Inst. Biomedical Imaging and Bioengineering NIH, Bethesda, Md., 2002—. Named Most Disting. Alumnus, U. Miami, 1990; recipient Benjamin E. Mays Award, 1989; Merrill scholar, Morehouse Coll., Whitaker Harvard-MIT Health Sci. scholar, MIT. Fellow: Am. Inst. Med. and Biomedical Engring., Internat. Soc. Magnetic Resonance in Medicine, Am. Coll. Cardiology, Am. Heart Assn.; mem.: Phi Beta Kappa. Achievements include research in dynamic three-dimensional imaging of the heart using magnetic resonance; co-developer first computer software package specifically designed for cardiac imaging using MRI. Office: Nat Inst Biomedical Imaging and Bioengineering 6707 Democracy Blvd Bethesda MD 20892 Office Phone: 301-496-8859. Office Fax: 301-480-0679. E-mail: pettigrr@mail.nih.gov.

PETTIGREW, THOMAS FRASER, social psychologist, educator; b. Richmond, Va., Mar. 14, 1931; s. Joseph Crane and Janet (Gibb) Pettigrew; m. Ann Hallman, Feb. 25, 1956; 1 child, Mark Fraser. AB in Psychology, U. Va., 1952; MA in Social Psychology, Harvard U., 1955, PhD, 1956; DHL (hon.), Governor's State U., 1979. Rsch. assoc. Inst. Social Rsch., U. Natal, Republic South Africa, 1956; asst. prof. psychology U. N.C., 1956-57; asst. prof. social psychology Harvard U., Cambridge, Mass., 1957-62, lectr., 1962-64, assoc. prof., 1964-68, prof., 1968-74, prof. social psychology and sociology, 1974-80; prof. social psychology U. Calif., Santa Cruz, 1980-94, rsch. prof. social psychology, 1994—; prof. social psychology U. Amsterdam, 1986-91. Adj. fellow Joint Ctr. Polit. and Econ. Studies, Washington, 1982—; adv. bd. women's studies program Princeton (N.J.) U., 1985-2001; vis. prof. Westfaelishe Wilhelms-U., Germany, 1993, Philipps U., Germany, 2000, 01, 04, 06, Schiller U., Germany, 2002; disting. vis. prof. Flinders U., Australia, 1997; sr. fellow Rsch. Inst. for the Comparative Study of Race and Ethnicity, Stanford U., 2001-02, mem. German govt. adv. com. Intercultural Conflicts and Social Integration, 2003-2006 Author: (with E.Q. Campbell) Christians in Racial Crisis: A Study of the Little Rock Ministry, 1959, A Profile of the Negro American, 1964, Racially Separate or Together?, 1971; (with Frederickson, Knobol, Glazer and Veda) Prejudice, 1982; (with Alston) Tom Bradley's Campaigns for Governor: The Dilemma of Race and Political Strategies, 1988, How to Think Like a Social Scientist, 1996; editor: Racial Discrimination in the United States, 1975, The Sociology of Race Relations: Reflection and Reform, 1980; (with C. Stephan & W. Stephan) The Future of Social Psychology: Defining the Relationship Between Sociology and Psychology, 1991; mem. editorial bd. Jour. Social Issues, 1959-64, Social Psychology Quarterly, 1977-80; assoc. editor Am. Sociol. Rev, 1963-65; adv. bd. Integrated Edn, 1963-84, Phylon, 1965-93, Edn. and Urban Society, 1968-90, Race, 1972-74, Ethnic and Racial Studies, 1978-95, Rev. of Personality and Social Psychology, 1980-85, Cmty. and Applied Social Psychology, 1989-2004, Individual and Politics, 1989-93, Jour. Ethnic and Migration Studies, 1994—, 21st Century Afro Rev., 1994—; contbr. articles to profl. jours. Chmn. Episcopal presiding Bishop's Adv. Com. on Race Relations, 1961-63; v.p. Episcopal Soc. Cultural and Racial Unity, 1962-63; mem. Mass. Gov.'s Adv. Com. on Civil Rights, 1962-64; social sci. cons. U.S. Commn. Civil Rights, 1966-71; mem. White House Task Force on Edn., 1967; mem. nat. task force on desegregation policies Edn. Commn. of States, 1977-79; trustee Ella Lyman Cabot Trust, Boston, 1977-79; Emerson Book Award com. United Chpts. Phi Beta Kappa, 1971-73; com. status black Ams. NRC, 1985-88. Guggenheim fellow, 1967-68, Sr. Scientist fellow NATO, 1974, Ctr. Advanced Study in Behavioral Scis. fellow, 1975-76, Sydney Spivack fellow Am. Sociol. Assn., 1978, Netherlands Inst. Advanced Study fellow, 1984-85, Bellagio (Italy) Study Ctr. resident fellow, Rockefeller Found., 1991; Fulbright New Century scholar, 2003-04; recipient Kurt Lewin Meml. award Soc. for Psychol. Study Social Issues, 1987, (with Martin) Gordon Allport Intergroup Rels. Rsch. prize, 1988, Faculty Rsch. award U. Calif., Santa Cruz, 1988, (with Tropp) Gordon Allport Intergroup Rels. Rsch. prize, 2003. Fellow APA (Weiss meml. lectr., 2003), Am. Sociol. Assn. (coun. 1979-82); mem. Soc. Psychol. Study Social Issues (coun. 1962-66, pres. 1967-68, Disting. Svc. award 1998), Soc. Exptl. Social Psychology (Disting. Scientist award 2002), European Assn. Social Psychology. Home: 524 Van Ness Ave Santa Cruz CA 95060-3556

PETTIJOHN, FRED PHILLIPS, retired publishing executive; b. Balt., May 11, 1917; s. Fred and Adelaide Josephine (Phillips) P.; m. Elaine Wilson, Dec. 7, 1946; children: Fred Phillips, Mark Clay. BAE, U. Fla., Gainesville, 1941. Sports editor Tallahassee Democrat, 1946-53; with Fort Lauderdale News, 1953-82, exec. editor, 1960-68, gen. mgr., 1968-77, editl. dir., from 1977; 1st v.p. Gore Newspapers Co., from 1960; now cons. Bd. dirs. Salvation Army, 1975-79, v.p., 1979; bd. dirs. Fla. Council 100, 1976-78. With AUS, 1943—45. Recipient Disting. Service award Fla. Press Assn., 1976, Disting. Alumnus award U. Fla., 1977; inducted into Fla. Newspaper Hall of Fame, 1990. Mem. Fla. Press Assn. (pres. 1963-64, 69-70), AP Mng. Editors (bd. dirs. 1964-66), So. Newspaper Pubs. Assn., Lauderdale Yacht Club, Tower Club, Sigma Delta Chi, Theta Chi. Democrat. Presbyterian. Home: 1564 Marion Ave Tallahassee FL 32303-5831

PETTINELLA, EDWARD, real estate company executive; Degree, State U., Geneseo; MBA, Syracuse U., NY. With Rochester (N.Y.) Cmty. Savings Bank, 1980—97; pres. N.Y. Divsn. Charter One Bank, 1997—2001; exec. v.p. Charter One Fin., Inc., 1997—2001, Home Properties, Rochester, 2001—04, CEO, 2004—. Bd. dir. Home Properties, State U. Geneseo, Geneseo Found.; bd. dir. Sch. Bus. Syracuse U. Bd. dir. United Way, Rochester, YMCA, Rochester. Office: Home Properties 850 Clinton Square Rochester NY 14604

PETTINELLA, NICHOLAS ANTHONY, corporate financial executive; b. Little Falls, NY, Sept. 9, 1942; s. Nicholas and Rose (Zuccaro) P.; m. Nancy C. Whitehouse, Oct. 28, 1978; children: Albert J., Michael A. BS, Bentley Coll., 1968; MBA, Babson Coll., 1975; postgrad., Harvard U., 1979, Stanford U., 1983. CPA. Mass. auditor Coopers & Lybrand, Boston, 1970-76; treas. Courier Corp., Lowell, Mass., 1976-80; controller corp. ops. Digital Equipment Corp., Maynard, Mass., 1980-81; dir. fin. Intermetrics, Inc., Burlington, Mass., 1981-83, sr. v.p. fin., chief fin. officer, treas., 1983-98; sr. v.p. fin., treas. Averstar, Inc., Burlington, 1999-2000; v.p., CFO IronBridge Networks, Inc., Lexington, Mass., 2000—01; CFO ideaLogix, Inc., Framingham, Mass., 2001—02, Accordare, Arlington, Mass., 2002—04; exec. v.p., CFO Harmony Line, Inc., Cambridge, Mass., 2004—. Bd. dirs. The Computer Mus., Boston, treas. 1988-98, bd. overseers 1997-99, Mus. Scis., Boston, 1999-2003. Chmn. fin. com. Town of Ashland, Mass., 1980-82. Served with U.S. Army, 1964-66. Mem. Fin. Execs. Inst., AICPA, Inst. Mgmt. Accts., Mass. Soc. CPAs, Treas. Club Boston, Pacioli Soc. Roman Catholic. Home: 141 South St Ashland MA 01721-2263

PETTIS, PATRICIA AMANDA, secondary school educator, farmer; b. Red Wing, Minn., Jan. 28, 1967; d. Albert A. and Marilyn June (MacAdams) Berg; m. Pettis Steven Mark, Sept. 5, 1992; children: Steven Joseph, Nathan Carl, Allie Amanda, Christopher Mark, Matthew Albert. BS in Edn., St. Cloud State U., Minn., 1990. English instr. LeSueur-Henderson H.S., Minn., 1997—98, Waterville Elysian Morristown Sch. Dist., Waterville, Minn., 1998—. Declamation head coach LeSueur-Henderson H.S., 1997—98; yearbook advisor WEM H.S., Waterville, 1998—2002, lit. mag. advisor, 1998—2003, class advisor, 1998—2006, nat. honor soc. advisor, 2000—. Sunday sch. educator St. Peters Cath. Ch., St. Peter, Minn. Mem.: Minn. Edn. Assn. (assoc.). Avocations: running, gardening, coaching and playing sports. Home: 46364 327th Ave Kasota MN 56050 Office: Waterville-Elysian-Morristown HS 500 East Paquin St Waterville MN 56096 Home Phone: 507-931-1268.

PETTIS-ROBERSON, SHIRLEY MCCUMBER, retired congresswoman; b. Mountain View, Calif. d. Harold Oliver and Dorothy Susan (O'Neil) McCumber; m. John J. McNulty (dec.); m. Jerry L. Pettis (dec. Feb. 1975); children: Peter Dwight Pettis, Deborah Pettis Moyer; m. Ben Roberson, Feb. 6, 1988. Student, Andrews U., Berrien Springs, Mich., 1942—43, student, 1945, U. Calif., Berkeley, 1944—45; PhD (hon.), Loma Linda U., Calif., 2002. Mgr. Audio-Digest Found., LA, Glendale, 1958—61; sec. treas. Pettis, Inc., Hollywood, Calif., 1958-68; mem. U.S. Congress, Calif., 1975—79. Pres. Women's Rsch. Edn. Inst., 1979—80; bd. dirs. Lumbermens Mut. Ins. Co., Kemper Corp., Am. Motors, Am. Mfg. Co. Mem. Former Mems. Congress, 1988—, Pres.'s Commn. Arms Control Disarmament, 1982—85, Commn. Presdl. Scholars, 1990—93; chair bd. Loma Linda U. Children's Hosp. Found.; trustee U. Redlands, Calif., 1980—83, Loma Linda U. Med. Ctr., Calif., 1990—95, bd. mem. Mem.: Morningside Country Club (Rancho Mirage, Calif.).

PETTIT, DONALD R., astronaut, flight engineer, researcher; b. Silverton, Oreg., Apr. 20, 1955; married; 2 children. BSChemE, Oreg. State U., 1978; PhD in Chemical Engring., U. Ariz., 1983. Staff scientist Los Alamos Nat. Lab., Los Alamos, N.Mex., 1984—96, mem. synthesis group, slated with assembling the technology to return to the moon and explore Mars, 1990, mem. Space Station Freedom Redesign Team, 1993; mission specialist, Lyndon B. Johnson Space Ctr. with technical duties in the Astronaut Office Computer Support Branch NASA, Houston, 1996—. Projects included: Reduced gravity fluid flow and materials processing experiments aboard the NASA KC-135 airplane, atmospheric spectroscopy measurements on noctolucent clouds seeded from sounding rocket payloads, volcano fumarole gas sampling on active volcanos, investigated problems in the detonation physics applied to weapons systems; completed first space flight as NASA ISS science officer and flight engineer aboard the International Space Station, Expedition-6 (launched in the STS-113 Space Shuttle Endeavour and returned to Earth on Soyuz TMA-1), Nov. 23, 2002 to May 3, 2003, logged over 161 days in space and 2 EVAs (spacewalks) totalling 13 hours and 17 minutes. During the 5 1/2 months aboard the ISS, the crew worked with numerous US and Russian science experiments. Office: NASA Lyndon B Johnson Space Ctr Houston TX 77058

PETTIT, ERIN, glaciologist; Grad. student in Geophysics, U. Wash. Lead scientist Girls on Ice, 1999—; glaciologist U. Wash., instr., Exploration Seminar, 2005—; tchr. Portland State U., 2006—. Lead scientist studying glaciers and ice sheets in Antarctica, Wash., Alaska, 1999—; program co-instr. North Cascades Inst., 2000—. Recipient Women of Discovery,

Earth award, Wings WorldQuest, 2007. Achievements include research in dynamics of ice flow with focus on the West Antarctic Ice Sheet; dynamic behaviors of ice divide, the movement of glaciers, and the formation of glacial ice cliffs; encouraging high school girls the opportunity to study the scientific method while gaining mountaineering and wilderness skills through the Girls on Ice program; with team camped beneath Blood Falls on Taylor Glacier (Antarctica), trekking up the Taylor Glacier, boring holes in the ice to place instruments to measure the strains & stresses in frozen ice. *

PETTIT, FREDERICK SIDNEY, metallurgical engineering educator, department chairman; b. Wilkes Barre, Pa., Mar. 10, 1930; s. Edwin Humes and Edith Mae (Barnecut) P.; m. Lou-Jean Mary Corso, Aug. 30, 1958; children: Frederick N., Theodore E., John C., Charles A. B in Engring., Yale U., 1952, M in Engring., 1960, D in Engring., 1962. Jr. engr. Westinghouse Electric Corp., Pitts., 1952-54; engr. Avco-Lycoming, Stratford, Conn., 1957-58; postdoctoral student Max Planck Inst. Phys. Chemistry, Gottingen, Fed. Republic Germany, 1962-63; sr. staff scientist Pratt & Whitney Aircraft Co., East Hartford, Conn., 1963-79; prof. metall.-material engring. dept., chmn. U. Pitts., Pa., 1979-88, prof., 1988—2006, prof. emeritus, 2006—, Harry S. Tack prof. materials engring., 1992—2006; mem. adv. bd. Jour. Oxidation of Metals, Plenum Press, N.Y., 1975—. 1st lt USMC, 1954-57. Fellow, NSF, 1962—63. Mem. Metall. Soc. (program dir. 1982-83), Electrochem. Soc. (sec.-treas. high temperature materials div. 1979-83), Am. Soc. Metals, Materials Rsch. Soc. Roman Catholic. Home: 201 Ennerdale Dr Pittsburgh PA 15237-4026 Office: U Pitts 848 Benedum Hall Pittsburgh PA 15261-2208 Business E-Mail: pettit@engr.pitt.edu.

PETTIT, GEORGE ROBERT, chemist, educator, cancer researcher; b. Long Branch, NJ, June 8, 1929; s. George Robert and Florence Elizabeth (Seymour) P.; m. Margaret Jean Benger, June 20, 1953; children: William Edward, Margaret Sharon, Robin Kathleen, Lynn Benger, George Robert III. BS, Wash. State U., 1952; MS, Wayne State U., 1954, PhD, 1956. Tchg. asst. Wash. State U., 1950-52, lecture demonstrator, 1952; rsch. chemist E.I. duPont de Nemours and Co., 1953; grad. tchg. asst. Wayne State U., 1952-53, rsch. fellow, 1954-56; sr. rsch. chemist Norwich Eaton Pharms., Inc., 1956-57; asst. prof. chemistry U. Maine, 1957-61, assoc. prof. chemistry, 1961-65, prof. chemistry, 1965; vis. prof. chemistry Stanford U., 1965; prof. chemistry Ariz. State U., 1965—, chmn. organic chemistry divsn., 1966-68, disting. rsch. prof., 1978-79, Dalton prof. medicinal chemistry and rsch., 1986—, Regent's prof. chemistry, 1990—. Vis. prof. So. African, Univs., 1978; dir. Cancer Rsch. Lab., 1974-75, 2005, Cancer Rsch. Inst., 1975-2005; co-dir. Ariz. Prostate Cancer Task Force, 2000-05; lectr. various colls. and univs.; cons. in field. Contbr. articles to profl. jours. Mem. adv. bd. Wash. State U. Found., 1981—85. With Res. USAF, 1949—53. Recipient Alumni Achievement award, Wash. State U., 1984. Fellow: Am. Inst. Chemists (Pioneer award 1989, Ariz. Gov.'s Excellence award 1993); mem.: Am. Soc. Oncology, Am. Assn. Cancer Rsch., Am. Soc. Pharmacognosy (Rsch. Achievement award 1995), Chem. Soc. London, Am. Chem. Soc. (mem. awards com. 1968—71, Guenther award in chemistry of natural products 1998), Phi Lambda Upsilon, Sigma Xi. Office: Ariz State U Dept Chemistry and Biochemistry Tempe AZ 85287-2404

PETTIT, GHERY DEWITT, retired veterinary medicine educator; b. Oakland, Calif., Sept. 6, 1926; s. Hermon DeWitt Pettit and Marion Esther (St. John) Menzies; m. Frances Marie Seitz, July 5, 1948; children: Ghery St. John, Paul Michael. BS in Animal Sci., U. Calif., Davis, 1948, BS in Vet. Sci., 1951, DVM, 1953. Charter diplomate Am. Coll. Vet. Surgeons. Asst. prof. vet. surgery U. Calif., Davis, 1953-61; prof. vet. surgery Wash. State U., Pullman, 1961-91, prof. emeritus, 1991—. Mem. Wash. State Vet. Bd. Govs., 1981—88, chmn., 1987; vis. fellow Sydney U., Australia, 1977. Author/editor: Intervertebral Disc Protrusion in the Dog, 1966; co-author: Centennial History of the Washington State University College of Veterinary Medicine, 1999; cons. editoral bd. Jour. Small Animal Practice, Eng., 1970-88; mem. editoral bd. Compendium on C.E., Lawrenceville, N.J., 1983-86, editoral rev. bd. Jour. Vet. Surgery, Phila., 1984-86, editor 1987-92; contbr. articles to profl. jours., chpts. to books. Elder Presbyn. Ch., Pullman, 1967—. With USN, 1944—46. Recipient Norden Disting. Tchr. award Wash. State U. Class 1971, Faculty of Yr. award Wash. State U. Student Com., 1985. Mem.: AVMA, Am. Coll. Vet. Surgeons (recorder 1970—77, pres., chmn. bd. dirs. 1978—80), Kiwanis Internat., Am. Legion, Phi Kappa Sigma (chpt. advisor 1981—, internat. 2d v.p. 1993—98, internat. pres. 1998—2000, Alumnus of Yr. award 2006), Phi Zeta, Sigma Xi. Republican. Avocations: camping, sailing.

PETTIT, GHERY ST. JOHN, electronics engineer; b. Woodland, Calif., Apr. 6, 1952; s. Ghery DeWitt and Frances Marie (Seitz) P.; m. Marilyn Jo Van Hoose, July 28, 1973; children: Ghery Christopher, Heather Kathleen. BS in Electrical Engring., Wash. State U., 1975. Cert. EMC engr., NARTE, EIT Wash., Colo. Nuclear engr. Mare Island Naval Shipyard, Vallejo, Calif., 1975-76; electronics engr. Naval Electronic Systems Engring. Ctr., Vallejo, 1976-79; sr. engr. Martin Marietta Denver Aerospace, 1979-83; staff engr. Tandem Computers Inc., Santa Clara, Calif., 1983-90, mgr. electromagnetic capability Cupertino, Calif., 1990-91, electromagnetic compatibility lead engr., 1991-95; electromagnetic compatibility engr. Intel Corp., Hillsboro, Oreg., 1995-96, Dupont, Wash., 1996—. Mem. U.S. tech. adv. group subcom. I, Spl. Com. on Radio Frequency Interferences subcom. Internat. Electrotechnical Commn.; mem. CISPR SC I, WG2, WG3 and WG4. Asst. cubmaster Boy Scouts Am., San Jose, Calif., 1985-86, cubmaster, 1986-88, ast. scoutmaster, 1988-90, scoutmaster, 1990-93. Mem. IEEE (sr.), Nat. Rsch. Coun. (bd. assessment of NIST programs 1999—2005), EMC Soc. (bd. dirs. 1999-2004, 2006—, v.p. commn. svcs. 2003—), Electromagnetic Capability Soc. (sec.-treas. Littleton, Colo. chpt. 1983, sec. Santa Clara Valley chpt. 1985-87, vice chmn. 1987-89, chmn. 1989-91, sec. Santa Clara Valley sect. 1991-92, treas. 1992-93, vice chmn. 1993-94, chmn. 1994-95), IEEE Electromagetic Capability Soc. (chmn. Seattle chpt. 1997-2000). Republican. Presbyterian. Avocations: flying, amateur radio, sailing. Office: Intel Corp 2800 Center Dr Dupont WA 98327-9773 Business E-Mail: ghery.pettit@intel.com.

PETTIT, JOHN DOUGLAS, JR., management educator; b. Alice, Tex, Aug. 19, 1940; s. John Douglas and Vivian Iola (Beaman) P.; m. Suzanne McLeod, Aug. 23, 1964; children: Melanie Ann Wilson, David Bryant. BBA, U. North Tex., 1962, MBA, 1964; PhD, La. State U., 1969. Instr. mgmt. Miss. State U., Starkville, Miss., 1964-65; grad. asst. La. State U., Baton Rouge, 1965-67, instr. mgmt., 1967-68; asst. prof. bus. Tex. Tech. U., Lubbock, Tex., 1968-69; assoc. prof. mgmt. U. North Tex., Denton, Tex., 1969-78, prof. mgmt., 1978-95; chair excellence in free enterprise Austin Peay State U., Clarksville, Tenn., 1995-96; interim chair and prof. dept. info. and decision scis. U. Tex., El Paso, Tex., 2000-2001, vis. prof. Dept. Mktg. and Mgmt., 2005—, interim chmn., 2005—06. Bd. dirs. Capital Instnl. Svcs., Dallas and NYC, mem. audit com., 2003—; cons. various orgns., 1969—98; mgr., co-owner Pettit's Cleaners/Hatters, Alice, 1992—96; vis. prof. mgmt. Wichita (Kans.) State U., 1994—95; vis. prof. Ecole Superieure de Commerce et de Mgmt., Poitier and Tours, France, 2002—03, U. Kuopio, Finland, 2003—04. Kuopio, Finland, 2002, Co-author: Business Communication: Theory and Application, 7th edit. 1993, Report Writing for Business, 10th edit. 1998, Lesikar's Basic Business Communication, 8th edit. 1999; mem. editl. bd. Organl. Comm. Abstracts, 1980-85; mem. editl. bd. Jour. Bus. Comm., 1987-90, mng. editor, 1990-94. Mem. choir Trinity Presbyn. Ch., Denton, 1985-2006; docent, Bass Performance Hall, Ft. Worth, 2006, usher, 2006; trainer, Metroport Meals on Wheels, Argyle, Tex., 2002-, driver, 2002-; actor, singer Denton Cmty. Theater Summer Prodn., 1988-95. Recipient Master's Degree award Chgo. Bd. Trade, 1963. Fellow Assn. Bus. Comm. (pres., 1st v.p., exec. dir., 1990-94); mem. Southwestern Fedn. Adminstrv. Disciplines (pres., v.p.), Acad. Mgmt., Denton Country Club (bd. dirs.), Blue Key Nat. Hon. Fraternity, Beta Gamma Sigma (hon.), Phi Kappa Phi (hon.), Delta Sigma Pi. Presbyterian. Avocations: music, tennis. Home: 9122 David Fort Rd Argyle TX 76226-2953 Business E-Mail: jpettit@utep.edu.

PETTIT, JOHN W., health facility administrator; b. Detroit, Mar. 6, 1942; s. John W. and Clara (Schartz) P.; m. Kathleen Endres, Aug. 8, 1970; children: Julie, Andrew, Michael. BBA, U. Notre Dame, 1964; MBA, Mich. State U., 1974. CPA, Mich.; CFP, 2001. Acct. Ernst & Ernst, Detroit, 1964-67; chief acct. Detroit Inst. Tech., Detroit, 1967-69; controller, dir. adminstrn. & fin. Mich. Cancer Found., Detroit, 1969-80; chief adminstrv. officer Dana-Farber Cancer Inst., Boston, 1980-94; exec. v.p., chief oper. officer John Wayne Cancer Inst., Santa Monica, Calif., 1995-97; fin. cons. LA, 1998—. Grant reviewer Nat. Cancer Inst., Bethesda, Md., 1979-94. Pres. advanced mgmt. program Mich. State U., 1978-79; mem. adv. bd. Arthritis Found. So. Calif. chpt., 1999—2004; mem. Town Meeting, Wellesley, Mass., 1991-94. Mem.: AICPA, Fin. Planning Assn. Avocations: sailing, woodworking, photography, music. Office: 21031 Ventura Blvd Ste 705 Woodland Hills CA 91364 Office Phone: 818-226-3838. E-mail: jwpettit@yahoo.com.

PETTIT, LAWRENCE KAY, university president; b. Lewistown, Mont., May 2, 1937; s. George Edwin and Dorothy Bertha (Brown) P.; m. Sharon Lee Anderson, June 21, 1961 (div. Oct. 1976); children: Jennifer Anna, Matthew Anderson, Allison Carol, Edward McLean; m. Elizabeth DuBois Medley, July 11, 1980 (div. Dec. 1998). BA cum laude, U. Mont., 1959; AM, Washington U., St. Louis, 1962; PhD, U. Wis., 1965. Legis. asst. US Senate, 1959-60, 62; asst. & assoc. prof. dept. polit. sci. Pa. State U., 1964-67; assoc. dir. fed. rels. Am. Council Edn., Washington, 1967-69; chmn. dept. polit. sci. Mont. State U., 1969-72; adminstrv. asst. to gov. State of Mont., 1973; chancellor Mont. Univ. System, Helena, 1973-79; pvt. practice ednl. cons. Mont., 1979-81; dep. commr. for acad. affairs Tex. Coordinating Bd. for Higher Edn., 1981-83; chancellor Univ. System of South Tex., 1983-86; chancellor (now pres.) So. Ill. U., Carbondale, Edwardsville, 1986-91, Disting. svc. prof., 1991-92; pres. Indiana U. Pa., 1992—2003, ret., 2003. Mem. adv. bd. S & T Bancorp., 1997-2003; mem. regional adv. bd. Nat. City Bank, 1997-99; bd. dirs. Ind. Healthcare Corp., 1992-2007. Author: (with H. Albinski) European Political Processes, 2d edit., 1974, (with E. Keynes) Legislative Process in the U.S. Senate, 1969, (with S. Kirkpatrick) Social Psychology of Political Life, 1972, (with J. Goetz and S. Thomas) Legislative Process in Montana, 1975; mem. editl. bd. Ednl. Record, 1985-98. Mem. adv. bd. Leadership Ctr. Ams., 1988-90, Ill. Coalition, 1989-92; dem. primary candidate for 2d dist. US Ho. of Reps., Mont., 1980; mem. Ill. Gov.'s Com. on Sci. and Tech., 1986-90; bd. dirs. Tex. Guaranteed Student Loan Corp., 1985-86, Reschini Found., 2003-07; chmn. Ill.-Niigata Commn. on Edn. and Econ. Devel., 1990-92; chair bd. dirs. Nat. Environ. Edn. and Tng. Ctr., 1994-04; mem. adv. bd. Princeton Rev., 2003-04. U. Wis. fellow 1962-63, Vilas fellow U. Wis., 1963-64. Mem. AAUP (pres. Mont. conf. 1971-72), Nat. Assn. Sys. Heads (pres. 1989), Am. Coun. on Edn. (chmn. leadership commn. 1989-90, sr. fellow 1991-92), Am. Assn. Higher Edn., Am. Assn. State Colls. and Univs. (Disting. Svc. award 1991), Newcomen Soc., Duquesne Club Pitts., World Affairs Coun. Pitts., Pa. Soc. (life), Rotary (Paul Harris fellow), Ind. C. of C. (bd. dirs. 1992-03), Sigma Chi (Significant Sig award 1988), Phi Kappa Phi. Episcopalian. Home: 2567 Overlook Blvd Helena MT 59601 Office Phone: 724-388-2543. Personal E-mail: lpettit@bresnan.net.

PETTITT, JAY S., architect, consultant; b. Redford, Mich., Jan. 6, 1926; s. Jay S. and Florence Marian (Newman) P.; m. Ruth Elizabeth Voigt, June 21, 1947; children— J. Stuart, Laura Ellen, Patricia Lynn, Carol Ann B.Arch., U. Mich., 1951. Registered architect, Mich. Draftsman Frank J. Stepnoski and Son, Fond du Lac, Wis., 1951; project architect Albert Kahn Assocs., Inc., Detroit, 1951-62, chief archtl. devel., 1962-67, v.p., 1967-88, dir. architecture, 1975-88; archtl. cons. Beulah, Mich., 1988—. Active Jr. Athletic Assn., Redford, Mich., 1959-63; com. chmn. Boy Scouts Am., 1960-65; supr. Benzonia Twp. Served with U.S. Army. 1943-46, ETO. Fellow AIA; mem. Mich. Soc. Architects (pres. 1967), Am. Arbitration Assn., Am. Assn. Hosp. Planning, Engring. Soc. Detroit, U. Mich. Pres.' Club Avocations: sailing, skiing. Office Phone: 231-882-4040. Personal E-mail: jaypettitt@bignetnorth.net.

PETTITTE, ANDREW EUGENE (ANDY PETTITTE), professional baseball player; b. Baton Rouge, June 15, 1972; m. Laura Pettitte, Jan. 9, 1993; children: Joshua Blake, Jared, Lexy Grace, Luke Jackson. Student, San Jacinto Coll., Tex. Pitcher NY Yankees, Bronx, 1995—2003, 2007—, Houston Astros, 2004—06. Co-author (with Bob Reccord, Mark Tabb): (autobiography) Strike Zone: Targeting a Life of Integrity & Purity, 2005. Mem. World Series championship team, 1996, 1998, 1999, 2000; named to Am. League All Star team, 1996, 2001 Office: Yankee Stadium E 161st St and River Ave Bronx NY 10451 Office Phone: 718-293-4300. *

PETTY, ELIZABETH MARIE, geneticist; b. Chgo., July 13, 1959; d. Ralph David and Joyce Elizabeth (Carlson) P.; life ptnr. Karen Kay Milner, Dec. 15, 1985. BA, Clarke Coll., 1981; MD, U. Wis., 1986. Diplomate Nat. Bd. Med. Examiners, Am. Bd. Pediats., Am. Bd. Med. Genetics, Molecular Genetics and Clin. Genetics. Pediat. intern and resident U. Wis., Madison, 1986-89; genetics fellow Yale U., New Haven, 1989-93; assoc. prof. U. Mich., Ann Arbor, 1994—, med. dir. genetic counseling program, 1996—, dir. med. genetics outpatient clinic, 1996—, assoc. dean student programs Med. Sch., 2006—. Expert witness DNA testing in State of Ohio and Mich., 1995—; presenter regional, nat. and internat. confs. on genetics, 1991—. Contbr. chpt. to books, articles, editls. to profl. jours.; peer reviewer various jours., 1994—. Participant Gay and Lesbian Health Group, Ann Arbor, 1994—; apptd. to State of Mich.'s Gov.'s Commn. on Genetic Privacy and Progress, 1997-98. Recipient Clin. Investigator award NIH-NCI, 1995-2000, RO1 award, 1997—, Am. Cancer Rsch. Fund award, 1997-98, U. Mich. award for Disting. Pub. Svc., 2000, Breast Cancer award Dept. Def., 2001, 06. Fellow Am. Soc. Human Genetics, Am. Coll. Med. Genetics; mem. AMA, Am. Acad. Scis., European Soc. Human Genetics, Human Genome Orgn., Alpha Omega Alpha. Democrat. Roman Catholic. Avocations: flute, photography. Office: U Mich 5220 MSRB III Ann Arbor MI 48109-0640

PETTY, GEORGE OLIVER, lawyer; b. LA, Mar. 31, 1939; s. Hugh Morton and May (Johnson) P.; m. Sandra Diane Kilpatrick, July 14, 1962; children: Ross Morton, Alison Lee, Christopher Henry. AB, U. Calif., Berkeley, 1961; LLB, U. Calif., 1964. Bar: Calif. 1965, Eng. and Wales 1986, U.S. Supreme Ct. 1976. Atty. Huovinen & White, Oakland, Calif., 1967-69; counsel Bechtel Power Corp., San Francisco, 1969-83; prin. counsel Bechtel Ltd., London, 1983-86; gen. counsel Sun-Diamond Growers of Calif., Pleasanton, Calif., 1987-95; pvt. practice, 1995—96; gen. counsel Tone Bros. Inc., 1997—. Leader Arlington Ave. Utilities Undergrounding Com., 1987—2001. Capt. US Army, 1965—67. Mem. Calif. State Bar Assn., Alameda County Bar Assn., Eng. and Wales Bar Assn., Middle Temple Inn. Office: ABF NAm Holdings Inc 8 California St 600 San Francisco CA 94111 Home Phone: 510-528-1690; Office Phone: 415-477-2800. Personal E-mail: gopetty@aol.com.

PETTY, M. S. MARTY, publisher; b. St. Louis, Mo., Dec. 17, 1952; married; 2 children. BA in Journalism, Univ. Mo., 1975; MS in Mgmt., Hartford Grad. Ctr. (Rensselaer), 1989. Asst. mng. editor Kansas City Star and Times; mng. editor Hartford (Conn.) Courant, 1983—89, de. exec. editor, assoc. pub., 1989, sr. v.p., gen. mgr.; pub., CEO Hartford (Conn.) Courant, 1997—2000; exec. v.p. St. Petersburg (Fla.) Times, 2000—, pub., 2004—. Trustee Poynter Inst. for Media Studies, Tampa Bay Newspapers Inc.; juror Pulitzer Prize awards; pres. Soc. of Newspaper Design, 1985; bd. dir. Wm. Randolph Hearst Found. journalism bd., 1987—89. Trustee Congressional Quarterly, Governing Mag., Fla. Trend Mag. Named a Woman of Distinction, Girl Scouts of Suncoast Coun., 2004; named Bus. Woman of Yr., Women's Coun., St. Petersburg Area C. of C., 2005. Mem.: Nat. Assn. Minority Media Executives, Newspaper Assn. Am. (diversity bd.), Am. Press Inst. (adv. bd.), Florida Press Assn. (bd. dir.). Office: St Petersburg Times 490 1st Ave S Saint Petersburg FL 33701

PETTY, MARGARET, elementary school educator; BA in Elem. Edn., Incarnate Word Coll., San Antonio; MS in Spl. Edn./Learning Disabilities, Ala. A&M Univ., Huntsville. Cert. Nat. Bd. Tchg. Standards, 2004. Lead tchr., spl. edn. Rainbow Elem. Sch., Madison, Ala., Liberty Mid. Sch., Madison, Ala. Nominee Disney Am. Tchr. award, 2002; named Ala. Elem. Tchr. of Yr., 2006, Ala. Tchr. of Yr., 2006. Office: Rainbow Elem Sch 50 Nance Rd Madison AL 35758 Office Phone: 256-830-4673. Business E-Mail: mpetty@madisoncity.k12.al.us, Mpetty@ALSDE.edu. *

PETTY, MARGE D., state senator; b. Ft. Wayne, Ind., Feb. 26, 1946; children: Brandon, Megan. BS, Tex. Christian U., 1968; MEd, Kans. U., 1978; JD, Washburn U. Sch. Law, 1990. Tchr., 1968-69; mgmt. consultant, 1981—94; health educator, 1978-81; mem. City Council of Topeka, 1985-89; dep. mayor Topeka, 1986; mem. Kans. Senate, 1989—2000; dir. pub. affairs and consumer protection Kans. Corp. Commn., 2003—. Mem. Topeka Metro. Ballet, Chamber of Commerce, Mulvane Art Ctr. Episcopalian. Home: PO Box 4262 Topeka KS 66604 Address: 1500 SW Arrowhead Rd Topeka KS 66604-4027

PETTY, MARSHA, chemistry educator; BA cum laude, Ouachita Baptist Univ., Arkadelphia, MA, 1977; postgrad. study, Henderson State Univ., Hendrix Coll., Univ. Ctrl. Ark. Tchr., 1976—; chemistry tchr. Ark. H.S., Texarkana, 1993—. Named Ark. H.S. Tchr. of Yr., Rotary Club, 2005, Ark. Tchr. of Yr., 2006. Mem.: Nat. Sci. Tchr. Assn. Office: Ark High Sch 3512 Grand Ave Texarkana AR 71854 *

PETTY, MARTY, publishing executive; m. Mark Petty; children: Lindsay, Skip. BJ, U. Mo., 1975; MS in Mgmt., Harvard Grad. Ctr., 1989. Asst. mng. editor Kansas City Star and Times; mng. editor The Hartford Courant, 1983-86, v.p., dep. exec. editor, 1986-89, assoc. pub. for projects and planning, 1989, sr. v.p., gen. mgr., pub., CEO, 1997—2000; exec. v.p. St. Petersburg Times, Fla., 2000—, pub. Fla., 2004—. Bd. dirs. St. Petersburg Times, Tampa, Fla.; chmn. Barnes Scholarship com. St. Petersburg Times Fund; trustee Poynter Inst. Media Studies, Congl. Quarterly, Governing mag., Fla. Trend mag., Tampa Bay Newspapers, Inc. Editor The Electronic Times, 1991-92. Mem. journalism bd. Wm. Randolph Hearst Found., 1987-89; mem. CEO adv. bd. Greater Hartford Arts Coun.; pres. bd. Camp Courant; bd. dirs. Hartford Courant Found., Hartford Hosp. Holding Co.; mem. The MetroHartford Growth Couns. millennium mgmt. com.; bd. dirs. Tampa Bay Partnership, Leadership Fla.; trustee Jr. Achievement, Acad. Prep, Kids Voting USA; mem. pres.'s coun. Eckerd Coll. Named a Woman of Distinction, Girl Scouts of Suncoast Coun., 2004; named Disting. Bus. Woman of Yr., St. Petersburg Area C. of C., 2005. Mem. Newspaper Assn. of Am. (Ptnrs. 2000 com., Copyright Clearance Ctr. adv. bd.), Soc. Newspaper Design (pres. 1985, active cons.), Am. Soc. Newspaper Editors, Am. Press Inst. (adv. bd.), AP Mng. Editors, Poynter Inst., Fla. Press Assn. (bd. dirs.), Nat. Assn. Minority Media Execs. Office: St Petersburg Times 490 1st Ave S Saint Petersburg FL 33701-1121 Office Phone: 727-893-8792. Office Fax: 727-892-2328. E-mail: mpetty@sptimes.com. *

PETTY, RICHARD, retired race car driver; b. Level Cross, NC, July 2, 1937; s. Lee and Elizabeth T. P.; m. Lynda Owens, 1958; children: Kyle, Sharon, Lisa, Rebecca. Auto racer, 35 years; ret., 1992; owner Car # 43. Actor(voice): (films) Cars, 2006. Mem. Pres.'s Coun. Fitness and Sport. Recipient Myers Bros. award Nat. Motorsports Press Assn., 1961, 67, 71; Excellence award NASCAR, 1987; named Grand Nat. Rookie of Year, 1959; Most Popular Driver in Grand Nat., 1962, 64, 68, 70, 74, 75, 76, 77, 78; Martini & Rossi Am. Driver of Year, 1971; Driver of Year Nat. Motorsport Press Assn., 1974-75; Driver of Quarter Century, 1991; inducted into N.C. Athletic Hall of Fame, 1973. Mem. Nat. Assn. Stock Car Auto Racing (7 time champion; Winston Cup grand nat. champion 1964, 67, 71, 72, 74, 75, 79) Achievements include entered 1015 Grand Nat. Races, winner 200, 1958-86, with 55 Superspeedway wins; winner Daytona 500, 1964, 66, 71, 73, 74, 79, 81; 1000th career Winston Cup start June 15, 1986 at Mich. Internat. Speedway; 500th consecutive start on Aug. 21, 1988 in Champion Spark Plug 500. Address: Petty Enterprises Inc 311 Branson Mill Rd Randleman NC 27317-8008

PETTY, THOMAS LEE, internist, educator; b. Boulder, Colo., Dec. 24, 1932; s. Roy Stone and and Eleanor Marie (Kudrna) P.; m. Carol Lee Piepho, Aug. 7, 1954; children: Caryn, Thomas, John. BA, U. Colo., 1955, MD, 1958. Intern Phila. Gen. Hosp., 1958-59; resident U. Mich., 1959-60, U. Colo., Denver, 1960-62, pulmonary fellow, 1962-63, chief resident medicine, 1963-64, instr. medicine, 1962-64, asst. prof., 1964-68, assoc. prof., 1968-74, prof. medicine, 1974—; pres. Presbyn./St. Luke's Ctr. for Health Scis. Edn., 1989-95; practice medicine, specializing in internal medicine, pulmonary medicine Denver, 1962—; prof. medicine Rush Univ., 1992—. Cons. Kindred Hosp., 1991-. Author: For Those Who Live and Breathe, 1967, 2d edit., 1972, Intensive and Rehabilitative Respiratory Care, 1971, 3d edit., 1982, Chronic Obstructive Pulmonary Disease, 1978, 2d edit., 1985, Principles and Practice of Pulmonary Rehabilitation, 1993, Enjoying Life With COPD, 1995, 3d edit., Pulmonary Disorders of the Elderly, 2007, others; contbr. articles to profl. jours. NIH and Found. grantee, 1966-88. Master ACP, Am. Coll. Chest Physicians (master, pres. 1982); mem. Assn. Am. Physicians, Assn. of Pulmonary Program Dirs. (founding pres. 1983-84, chmn. nat. lung health edn. program 1995—, co-chmn. 2000-04), Am. Bd. Internal Medicine (bd. govs. 1986-92), Am. Thoracic Soc. (Disting. Achievement award 1995), Phi Beta Kappa, Phi Delta Theta, Alpha Omega Alpha, Phi Rho Sigma (pres. 1976-78). Home: 1940 Grape St Denver CO 80220-1353 Office: 899 Logan St Ste 103 Denver CO 80203 Home Phone: 303-717-0325. Personal E-mail: tlpdoc@aol.com.

PETTY, TOM (THOMAS EARL PETTY), musician, composer; b. Gainesville, Fla., Oct. 20, 1950; s. Earl and Katherine Petty; m. Jane Benyo, 1974 (div. Sept. 9, 1996); children: Adria, Kim; m. Dana York, June 3, 2001. With band the Sundowners (1964) which later was called the Epics (1965-69) and Mudcrutch (1970-74), Gainesville, Fla.; songwriter, musician for Leon Russell, 1974—75; leader Tom Petty and the Heartbreakers, 1975—; toured the world with Bob Dylan, 1986; toured Am. with Georgia Satellites and Del Fuegos (Rock 'n' Roll Caravan tour), 1987. Albums: (with the Heartbreakers) Tom Petty and the Heartbreakers, 1976, You're Gonna Get It, 1978, Damn the Torpedoes, 1979, Hard Promises, 1981, Long After Dark, 1982, Southern Accents, 1985, Pack Up the Plantation-Live!, 1986, Let Me Up (I've Had Enough), 1987, Into the Great Wide Open, 1991 (Grammy nomination for Best Rock Performance by a Duo or Group with Vocal, 1992), Tom Petty and the Heartbreakers' Greatest Hits, 1993, Playback, 1995, She's The One (soundtrack), 1996, Echo, 1999 (Grammy nomination for Best Rock Album, 2000), Anthology: through the Years, 2000, The Last DJ, 2002, Live at the Olympic: The Last DJ and More, 2003; (with The Traveling Wilburys) Traveling Wilburys Vol. 1, 1989 (Grammy Award for Best Rock Performance by a Duo or Group with Vocal, 1990, Grammy nomination for Album of Yr., 1990), Traveling Wilburys Vol. 3, 1990; (solo albums) Full Moon Fever, 1989 (Grammy nomination for Album of Yr., 1990), Wildflowers, 1994 (Grammy nomination for Best Rock Album, 1996), Highway Companion, 2006; hit singles include Breakdown, 1978, Here Comes My Girl, 1979, Refugee, 1979, (duet with Stevie Nicks) Stop Dragging My Heart Around, 1981, The Waiting, 1981, You Got Lucky, 1982, Don't Come Around Here No More, 1985, Jammin' Me, 1987, Free Fallin', 1989, Running Down A Dream, 1989, I Won't Back Down, 1989, Into the Great Wide Open, Learning to Fly, 1991, Mary Jane's Last Dance, 1993, You Don't Know How It Feels, 1994, You Wreck Me, 1994, Walls, 1996, Free Girl Now, 1999, Swingin', 1999; Songs appear in films: Fast Times at Ridgemont High, 1982, Streets of Fire, 1984, The Silence of the Lambs, 1991, She's the One, 1996, Jerry Maguire, 1996; Actor (films) Made in Heaven, 1987, The Postman, 1997; (TV appearances) The Simpsons, 2002 (voice only), King of the Hill (voice only), 2005; host (radio show) Bried Treasure, 2005- Grammy nomination for Best Rock Performance by a Duo or Group with Vocal (with Stevie Nicks for Stop Draggin' My Heart Around), 1982, Grammy nomination for Best Rock Song (Learning to Fly), 1992, Grammy nomination for Best Rock Performance by a Duo or Group with Vocal (with Bob Dylan, Roger McGuinn, Neil Young, Eric Clapton, and George Harrison for My Back Pages), 1994, Grammy nomination for Best Rock Song (with the Heartbreakers for Room At The Top), 2000, Grammy Award for Best Male Rock Vocal Performance (for You Don't Know Hot It Feels), 1996, MTV Video Music Award for Best Male Video (with the Heartbreakers for Mary Jane's Last Dance), 1994, Video Vanguard Award, MTV Video Music Awards, 1994, MTV Video Music Award for Best Male Video (for You Don't Know How It Feels), 1995, Songwriter Award, ASCAP, 1990, Golden Note Award, ASCAP, 1996, Nat. Veteran's Foundation Special Award of Recognition, 1995, UCLA George & Ira Gershwin Award, 1996, Bill Graham Lifetime Achievement Award, CA Music Awards, 1998, Hollywood Walk of Fame Star (with the Heartbreakers), 1999, inducted, Rock & Roll Hall of Fame (with the Heartbreakers), 2002, Legend Award, Radio Music Awards, 2003, Century award, Billboard Music Awards, 2005. Office: Warner Bros Records 3300 Warner Blvd Burbank CA 91505-4694

PETTY, WILLIE CLIFFORD, musician, composer, educator; b. Eufaula, Ala., Sept. 24, 1967; s. Willie Edward and Arrie Pearl Petty; 1 child, LaKeyla Tarshay Jones-Petty. M in Music Edn. summa cum laude, Ala. State U., Montgomery, 1999; degree, Ala. State U., 1991. Cert. profl. educator Ala. Music educator, fine arts chmn. St. Jude HS, Montgomery, Ala., 1991—2000; pastoral musician, composer-in-residence Resurrection Cath. Missions, Montgomery, 1993—2005; composer, rec. artist World Libr. Publs., Franklin Park, Ill., 2002—. Composer: Come Magnify The Lord With Me, Glory To God, If Today You Hear His Voice, Have Mercy on Us for We Have Sinned, Mass of the Holy Spirit, Let the Children Come to Me, Everytime I Feel the Spirit; prodr.: (rec.) I Can Not Tell It All; singer: (recs.) Testify, Barbara Frost & Friends, (rec.) In Spirit and Truth. Mem. Montgomery AIDS Outreach, 1996—2004; bd. mem. The Greater Montgomery AIDS Task Force, 2000; mem. Look Up Ministries, Dothan, Ala., 2000. Named Tchr. of Yr., Ala. Dem. Party, 1999—2000; named one of Outstanding Coll. Students of Am., 1986—91; named to Who's Who in Am. Colls. and Univs., 1986—91; scholar, Pressor Found., 1989—90. Mem.: Nat. Assn. Pastoral Musicians (assoc.), Ala. Vocal Assn. (assoc.), ASCAP (assoc.), Music Educators Nat. Conf. (assoc.), Phi Kappa Lambda, Alpha Kappa Mu, Phi Eta Sigma. Democrat. Roman Catholic. Avocation: Aikido. Home: 1941 Green Acres Ct Montgomery AL 36106 Office: Resurrection Cath Missions 2815 Forbes Dr Montgomery AL 36110 Home Phone: 334-396-9965; Office Phone: 334-230-1916. Office Fax: 334-265-8081; Home Fax: 334-396-9965. Personal E-mail: wcliffordpetty@bellsouth.net. E-mail: cpetty@rcmsouth.org.

PETTYJOHN, SHIRLEY ELLIS, lawyer, real estate company executive; b. Liberty, Ky., Aug. 16, 1935; d. Wesley Barker and Ada Lou (Bryant) Ellis; m. Flem D. Pettyjohn, Sept. 24, 1955; children: Deena Renee, Ellisa Denise. BS in Commerce, U. Louisville, 1974, JD, 1977. Bar: Ky. 1978, Ind. 1988; lic. real estate broker, Ky., Ind.; cert. mediator. Pres. Universal Devel. Corp., 1984—, Pettyjohn Inc., Ky. and Ind., 1967—, Ind. Mediation Svcs., Inc., 1990—, Ky. Mediation Svcs., Inc., 1991—; v.p. Continental Investments Corp., 1986—; sr. ptnr. Pettyjohn & Assocs., Attys., 1987—. Editor Law-Hers Jour. Vice chmn. Louisville and Jefferson County Planning Commn., 1971-75; mem. Gov.'s Conf. on Edn., 1977, jud. nominee, 1981, Met. Louisville Women's Polit. Caucus, Bluegrass State Skills Corp., 1992-96, Ky. Opera Assn. Guild; elected mem. Ky. State Dem. Exec. Com., 1988-92; del. Nat. Dem. Conv. and Dem. Nat. Platform Com., 1988; bd. dirs. Ky. Dem. Hdqs., Inc., 1988-92, Pegasus Rising, Inc.; chmn. Okolona Libr. Task Force; mem. Clinton-Gore Nat. Steering Com., 1995; hon. mem. Gore 2000 Presdl. Campaign Com. Recipient Mayor's Cert. Recognition, 1974, Mayor's Fleur de lis award, 1969-73, Excellence in Writing award Arts Club Louisville, 1986, 87, 93, 99; inducted into Casey County Alumni Hall of Fame, 1997. Mem. ABA, NAFE, Nat. Assn. Adminstrv. Law Judges, Ky. Bar Assn., Louisville Bar Assn., Women Lawyers Assn. of Jefferson County, Am. Judicature Soc., Clark County Bar Assn., Ind. Bar Assn., Ind. Assn. Mediators, Am. Inst. Planners, Women's C. of C. of Ky. (past bd. dirs., chmn. legis. com.), Am. Legion (aux.), Fraternal Order Police Assn. (award 1982), Louisville Legal Secs. (past pres., editor Law-Hers Jour.), Coun. of Women Pres. (past pres., Woman of Achievement award 1974), Louisville Visual Arts Assn. (past bd. dirs.), Louisville Ballet Guild (chair audience devel. 1989-91), Fern Creek Woman's Club, Ky. Fedn. Women's Clubs, Gen. Fedn. Women's Clubs, Dem. Leadership Coun., Casey County Alumni Assn. (pres. 1998-2000), Poplar Level Area Bus. Assn., Jefferson County Dem. Women's Club (past v.p.), Nat. Fedn. Dem. Women's Clubs, Spirit of 46th Club, Mose Green Club, North End Club, 12th Ward Club, S. End Club, 3rd Ward Club, Highland Pk. Club, Grass Roots Club, Harry S. Truman Club, Beargrass Club, Arts Club of Louisville (past pres.), Sigma Delta Kappa (life), Chi Thi Theta, Century 2000 Democrat Club, Honorable Order Ky. Cols., Honorable Admiral Ky. Dept. Natural Resources. Home: 6924 Norlynn Dr Louisville KY 40228-1471 Office: 6922 Norylnn Dr Louisville KY 40228 Office Phone: 502-231-5580.

PETZ, EDWIN V., real estate company executive, lawyer; b. Beatrice, Nebr., May 14, 1935; s. Virgil Leonard and Ruth Elenor (Thomsen) P.; m. Daphne Cross, May 17, 1958 (div. June 1964); 1 dau., Katherine J.; m. Anne Higgins, Dec. 3, 1964 (div. Sept. 1993); 1 son, W. Christopher; m. Louise Loosli, Jan. 9, 1997. BA, Principia Coll., Elsah, Ill., 1955; JD, Harvard U., 1958. Bar: N.Y. 1959, Mass. 1976. Assoc. Chadbourne, Parke, Whiteside & Wolff, NYC, 1958-62; asst. gen. counsel Martin Marietta Corp., Bethesda, Md., 1963-64, 1965-75; gen. atty. sec. Bunker-Ramo Corp., Oakbrook, Ill., 1964-65; asst. gen. counsel United Brands Co., NYC, 1975-82, v.p., gen. counsel, sec., 1982-84; sr. v.p., gen. counsel Milstein Properties Corp., 1985—2003; sr. v.p., gen counsel The Milstein Group Inc., 1992—; sr. v.p., gen. counsel Ogden CAP Properties, LLC, 2003—. Mem. ABA, Assn. of Bar of City N.Y. Clubs: University (N.Y.C.). Republican. Episcopalian. Office: Ogden CAP Properties LLC 390 Park Ave New York NY 10022

PETZ, THOMAS JOSEPH, internist; b. Detroit, Feb. 10, 1930; s. Arthur J. and Marie (McCarthy) P.; m. Catherine Crowe, June 13, 1959; children: Thomas Jr., William, David, John, Catherine. BS, U. Detroit, 1951; MD, Wayne State U., Detroit, 1955. Diplomate Am. Bd. Internal Medicine and Pulmonary Disease. Intern Harper Hosp., Detroit, 1955-56, resident, 1958-59, 60-62, U. Calif., San Francisco, 1959-60; clin. instr. Wayne State U., Detroit, 1962-72, assoc. prof., 1972-76, clin. assoc. prof., 1976-95, clin. prof., 1996-97, prof. emeritus, 1997—; pvt. practice pulmonary disease and internal medicine Detroit, 1962-72, St. Clair Shores, Mich., 1977-96; med.-legal cons. Northville, Mich., 1996—. Chief pulmonary Wayne State U., Detroit, 1974-76, Harper Hosp., Detroit, 1972-79; dir. med. intensive care unit Harper Hosp., Detroit, 1977-83; chmn. dept. medicine Bon Secours Hosp., Grosse Pointe, Mich., 1984-86; chmn. Gen. Motors human rsch. com., 1995. Bd. govs. Wayne State Sch. of Medicine Alumni Assn., Detroit, 1981-85. Fellow Detroit Acad. Medicine (pres. 1982-83), Am. Coll. Chest Physicians, Detroit Med. Acad.; mem. Am. Coll. Physicians, Found. of Southeast Mich., 1992- (pres.2006-), Detroit Med. Club. Republican. Roman Catholic. Avocations: golf, skiing. Office Phone: 586-771-0700.

PETZAL, DAVID ELIAS, editor, writer; b. NYC, Oct. 21, 1941; s. Henry and Aline Born (Bixer) P.; m. Arlene Anne Taylor, May 29, 1974. BA, Colgate U., 1963. Editor Maco Publs., NYC, 1964—69; mng. editor Davis Publs., NYC, 1969—70; features editor Hearst Publs., NYC, 1970—72; mng. editor CBS Publs., NYC, 1972—79, editor, 1979—83, exec. editor, 1983—2001, Field & Stream Mag., NYC, 1983—2001, mng. editor, 2001—03, dep. editor, 2002—. Author: The .22 Rifle, 1972; editor: The Experts Book of the Shooting Sports, 1972, The Experts Book of Upland Game and Waterfowl Hunting, 1975, The Experts Book of Big-Game Hunting in North America, 1976, The Ency. of Sporting Firearms, 1991. Office: Bonnier Corp 19th Fl 2 Park Ave New York NY 10016-5602 Office Phone: 212-779-5287. Business E-Mail: david.petzal@bonniercorp.com.

PETZOLD, CAROL STOKER, state legislator; b. St. Louis, July 28; d. Harold William and Mabel Lucille (Wilson) Stoker; m. Walter John Petzold, June 27, 1959; children: Ann, Ruth, David. BS, Valparaiso U., Ind., 1959. Tchr. Parkwood Elem. Sch., Kensington, Md., 1960-62; legis. aide Md. Gen. Assembly, Annapolis, 1975-79; legis. asst. Montgomery County Bd. Edn., Rockville, Md., 1980; cmty. sch. coord. Parkland Jr. H.S., Rockville, 1981-87; mem. Md. Ho. of Dels., Annapolis, 1987—2007, mem. constl. and adminstrv. law com., 1987-93, mem. judiciary com., 1994—2006, chair subcom. on criminal justice, 2003—06, vice chair Montgomery County del., 1995—2006, dep. majority whip, 1999—2002. Mem. spl. com. drug and alcohol abuse Md. Ho. Dels., 1999—07, chair, 2007-; mem. transp. planning bd. Nat. Capitol Region, 1989—07; vice chmn. assembly on fed. issues Nat. Conf. State Legislatures, 1996-97, chair adv. com. on energy, 1997-99, chair energy and transp. com., 1998-99, pres. women's legis. network, 2004-05, chair transp. com., 2004-05; mem. State Adv. Coun. Adminstrv. Hearings, 1996-2007, chair, 1990-2001. Editor Child Care Sampler, 1974, Stoker Family Cookbook, 1976, Stoker Family History, 2007. Pres. Montgomery Child Care Assn., 1976-78; mem. Md. State Scholarship Bd., 1978-87, chmn. 1985-87; chmn. Legis. Com. Montgomery County Commn. for Children and Youth, 1979-84; mem., v.p. Luth. Social Services Nat. Capitol Area, Washington, 1980-86; mem. exec. com. coun. Montgomery United Way, 1981-2000. Named Mother of Yr., March of Dimes, 2000; named one of Top 100 Md. Women, Daily Record, 2002, 2004; recipient Statewide award, Gov.'s Adv. Bd. on Homelessness, 1994, recognized for outstanding commitment to children, US Dept. HEW, 1980, Award of Excellence, MADD, 2002, Disting. Legislator award, 2003, Impaired Driving Coalition, 2003, Legis. award, Md. Network Against Domestic Violence, 2003. Mem.: AAUW (honoree Kensington br. 1971, 2002, honoree Md. divsn. 1981), Women Legislators of Md., Md. Women Legislators Caucus (exec. com. 2003—04), Women's Polit. Caucus (chmn. Montgomery County 1981—83). Democrat. Lutheran.

PETZOLD, LINDA RUTH, computer scientist, educator, researcher; b. Chgo., Sept. 11, 1954; d. Carl George and Donna Elaine (Webb) P.; m. John Andrew Emerick, Aug. 9, 1978; 1 child, Matthew Ryan. BA in Computer Sci. and Math., U. Ill., 1974, PhD in Computer Sci., 1978. Rschr. Sandia Nat. Labs., Livermore, Calif., 1978-85; group leader Lawrence Livermore Nat. Lab., 1985-91; adj. prof. U. Ill., Urbana-Champaign, 1986—93; prof. computer sci., fellow Minn. Supercomputer Inst. U. Minn., Mpls., 1991—97; prof., dir. Computational Sci. Engring. Program U. Calif., Santa Barbara, 1997—, chair Dept. Computer Sci., 2003—. Author: Numerical Solution of Initial-Value Problems in Differential-Algebraic Equations, 1989. Recipient Dahlquist Prize, 1999. Mem. NAE, Soc. for Indsl. and Applied Math. (coun. 1987-93, v.p. for publs. 1993—, mng. editor Jour. Sci. Computing 1989-93), Assn. for Computing Machinery (sec.-treas. spl. interest group for numerical analysis 1986-89). Office: U Minn Dept Computer Sci 200 Union St SE Rm 4213 Minneapolis MN 55455-0154

PEURA, DAVID, medical educator; b. Lynn, Mass., June 15, 1946; m. Kristin Pattee, Jan. 25, 1969; children: Jessica, Brian. MD, U. Vt., Burlington, 1971. Diplomate Am. Bd. Internal Medicine, 1977. Prof. medicine U. Va. Health Sys., Charlottesville, 1996—. Master: Am. Coll. Gastroent.; mem.: Americian Gastroent. Assn. (pres. 2005—06). Office: Univ Va PO Box 800708 HSC UVa Charlottesville VA 22908-0708 Office Phone: 434-924-0316. Business E-Mail: dap8v@virginia.edu.

PEVEAR, ROBERTA CHARLOTTE, retired state legislator; b. Bethel, Maine, July 4, 1930; d. Frank Albert Sr. and Thirza Estella (Hickford) Gibson; m. Edward Gordon Pevear, Aug. 21, 1971. Diploma in Comml. Art, Gould Acad., 1947. Sec. Wilner Wood Products, South Paris, Maine, 1947-50; sec. export dept. Whitaker Cable, North Kansas City, Mo., 1951-56; sec. br. and dist. Anheuser-Busch, Inc., Kansas City, Mo., 1957-59; legal sec. Johnson & Johnson, New Brunswick, NJ, 1960-65, St. John, Ronder & Bell, Kingston, NY, 1966; sec., adminstrv. asst. Sears-Roebuck & Co., Overland Park, Kans., 1967-70, Exeter, NH, 1971-77; salesman Avon Products, Hampton Falls, NH, 1978-86; mem. ho. reps. State of N.H., 1979-88, ret., 1988. Commr. Rockingham Planning Commn., N.H., 1979-88, N.H. Planning Com., 1985-88; clk. Environment and Agrl. Com. N.H. Ho. Reps., 1983-88; del. mem. Rockingham County, 1979-88, exec. bd., 1984-88; chmn. Rockingham County Home, 1987-88. Civil Def. dir., Hampton Falls, NH, 1980—88. Recipient Community Citizen award Hampton Falls Grange, 1982, Seacoast Retired Sr. Service award, 1985. Mem. Nat. Order Women Legislators, N.H. Order of Women Legislators, DAR. Avocations: writing, genealogy, travel.

PEVEC, ANTHONY EDWARD, bishop; b. Cleve., Apr. 16, 1925; s. Anton and Frances Darovec P. MA, John Carroll U., Cleve., 1956; PhD, Western Res. U., Cleve., 1964. Ordained priest Roman Cath. Ch., 1950. Assoc. pastor St. Mary Church, Elyria, Ohio, 1950—52, St. Lawrence Ch., Cleve., 1952—53; rector-prin. Borromeo Sem. HS, Wickliffe, Ohio, 1953—75; adminstrv. bd. Nat. Cath. Edn. Assn., 1972—75; pastor St. Vitus Ch., Cleve., 1975—79; rector-pres. Borromeo Coll., Wickliffe, 1979—82; aux. bishop Diocese of Cleve., 1982—. Mem. v.p. Slovenian-Am. Heritage Found., Cleve., 1975—. Named Man of Yr., Fedn. Slovenian Nat. Homes, Cleve., 1985, Cath. Man of Yr., KC, 1998, Man of Yr., Pioneer Assn., 2001, Cathedral Latin Alumni Assn., 2003; named to Hall of Fame, St. Vitus Alumni Assn., 1989, Wickliffe Hall of Fame, 2000; recipient honoree, Heritage Found., Cleve., 1982, Alumni medal, John Carroll U., 2004. Mem.: KC (state chaplain 2003—05), Cath. Order Foresters (state chaplain 2000—04), U.S. Cath. Conf. (nat. adv. coun. 1996—97), Nat. Conf. Cath. Bishops (com. on vocations 1984—86, com. on pro-life activities 1990—92, com. on priestly formation 1993—95, com. on sci. and human values 1993—96). Democrat. Roman Catholic. Avocations: reading, music. Home and Office: Diocese of Cleveland 28700 Euclid Ave Wickliffe OH 44092-2527 Home Phone: 440-944-1400. Business E-Mail: bpaepevec@dioceseofcleveland.org. *Ultimately I must always remember that the Lord is totally in control of my life, no matter how complicated it may seem to be. I am here to do the Lord's will, and wherever I go I come to do His will.*

PEW, JOHN GLENN, JR., lawyer; b. Dallas, Apr. 18, 1932; s. John Glenn Sr. and Roberta (Haughton) P. BA, U. Tex., 1954, LLB, 1955. Bar: Tex. 1955, U.S. Dist. Ct. (no. dist.) Tex. 1959, U.S. Supreme Ct. 1959, U.S. Ct. Appeals (5th cir.) 1961, U.S. Ct. Appeals (10th cir.) 1982. Ptnr. Jackson Walker LLP, Dallas, 1964—. With USNR, 1955-58. Mem.: Order of Coif, Phi Beta Kappa. Republican. Presbyterian. Office: Jackson Walker LLP 901 Main St Ste 6000 Dallas TX 75202-3797 Office Phone: 214-953-6000. E-mail: jpew@jw.com.

PEW, ROBERT ANDERSON, retired real estate and equipment leasing corporation officer; b. Phila., Aug. 22, 1936; s. Arthur Edmund and Mary Elizabeth (Elliott) P.; children from previous marriage: Robert Anderson (dec.), James Cunningham, Glenn Edgar, Joan Elliott; m. Daria S. Decerio, June 19, 1993; 1 child, Richard Westerman. Student, Princeton U., 1954-56; BS, Temple U., 1959; MS in Mgmt. (Alfred P. Sloan fellow), MIT, 1970; LLD (hon.), Widener U., 1982; DPS (hon.), Temple U., 1983; LHD (hon.), Gettysburg Coll., 1984. Ops. asst. prodn. div. Sun Oil Co., Premont, Tex., 1959-60, ops. asst. prodn. div. Morgan City, La., auditor internal audit dept. Phila., 1960-65, staff asst. treasury dept., 1965-69, asst. to exec. v.p. corp. projects group, 1970-71, sec.-treas., mgr. financial control of products group, 1971-74, corp. sec., 1974-77; pres. Helios Capital Corp., 1977-96; CEO Radnor Corp., 1995-96; bd. dirs. Glenmede Corp., Phila., chmn., 1997—2004. Bd. dirs. Sun Co., Inc., Phila., Pew Charitable Trusts, Phila., Glenmede Trust Co. N.A., Phila. Trustee Children's Hosp., Phila., vice chmn., 1991—. Served Pa. Air N.G., 1956—59. Recipient R. Kelso Carter award Widener U., 1971 Mem. Aircraft Owners and Pilots Assn. (trustee, chmn. 1974-77, 85-2002, vice-chmn. 1979-85), Am. Hosp. Assn. (hon.), Coll. Physicians Phila., Union League Club, Harbor Club (pres. 1992-96), Phila. Aviation Country Club, Merion Cricket Club, N.E. Harbor Fleet, Seal Harbor Yacht Club. Republican. Presbyterian. Home: 916 Muirfield Rd Bryn Mawr PA 19010-1921 E-mail: dungarnem@aol.com.

PEWITT, JAMES DUDLEY, retired academic administrator; b. Franklin, Tenn., July 28, 1930; s. James Isaac and Eleanor (Dudley) P.; m. Betty Louise Hightower, Oct. 31, 1952; children: Ransom D., James P., Thomas E. Student, Vanderbilt U., 1948-51; MBA, MS, U.S.C., 1964, D in Bus. Adminstrn., 1967. Commd. lt. USAF, 1952, advanced through grades to col., 1969; AMC test pilot, 1958—62; spl. asst. for econ. analysis Office of Sec. of Air Force, 1967; exec. to asst. sec. Air Force for Fin. Mgmt. Nat. War Coll., 1971; asst. Da Nang Air Base, Vietnam, 1972; dep. comdr. for ops. Vietnam, 1972; vice comdr. Gunfighters, 1972; chief linebacker ops. Staff of Dir. of Ops., Vietnam, 1972; dir. mgmt. analysis USAF, 1973, ret., 1973; dir. grad. sch. bus. U. Ala., Birmingham, 1973-74, asst. v.p. ops. and planning, 1974-77, v.p. adminstrn., 1977-84, sr. v.p. adminstrn., 1984-90, Disting. prof., 1990—94, emeritus, 1994—. Bd. dir. Birmingham Cable Communications, Allied Products Co. Mem. Birmingham Airport Authority, 1986-93; chmn. bd. So. Mus. of Flight, 1993-2005; faculty rep. Sun Belt Conf., 1983-90, pres., 1989-90; mem. NCAA Coun., 1990-94. Decorated D.F.C. with 3 oak leaf clusters, Bronze Star, Legion of Merit with 2 oak leaf clusters, Air medal with 11 oak leaf clusters, 10 other awards and fgn. decorations; named to Ala, Aviation Hall of Fame, 2003. Mem. Birmingham C. of C. (bd. dirs. 1977-84, pres. 1983, chmn. 1984), Birmingham Country Club, Skull & Dagger, Phi Kappa Phi, Beta Gamma Sigma, Sigma Xi, Omicron Delta Kappa, Kappa Alpha, Order of Daedalians, Order of Quiet Birdmen. Avocations: flying, golf. Personal E-mail: dpewitt@aol.com.

PEYREFITTE, ASHTON GEORGE, JR., meteorologist, educator; b. New Orleans, Oct. 5, 1942; s. Ashton Gonzalo Peyrefitte and Melba Catherine Parpal. BS, Fla. State U., Tallahassee, 1967, MS, 1969; PhD, U. Utah, Salt Lake City, 1986. Mem. faculty St. Aloysius H.S., New Orleans, 1964—65; rsch. asst. Fla. State U., Tallahassee, 1967—70; instr. U. Lowell, Mass., 1971—72, SUNY, Oneonta, 1972—80; assoc. instr. U. Utah, Salt Lake City, 1980—81; assoc. prof. meteorology Plymouth State U., NH, 1985—2000, faculty emeritus; asst. prof. meteorology Ctrl. Mich. U., Mt. Pleasant, 2000—. Contbr. articles to profl. jours. Named Outstanding Tchg. Asst., U. Utah, 1981; fellow, NSF, 1969. Mem.: Nat. Weather Assn., Am. Meteorol. Soc. (banquet held in honor 2006). Office: Central Mich Univ Dept Geography 296A Dow Science Mount Pleasant MI 48859

PEYTON, JOHN, mayor; b. July 28, 1964; m. Kathryn Pearson; 1 child, John Conner. Grad. Exec. Edn. Program, Harvard Bus. Sch.; BA, Mercer U., 1986. V.p. Gate Petroleum Co., Fla.; mayor City of Jacksonville, Fla., 2003—. Mem. Harry S. Truman Scholarship Found., 2007—. Past pres. Greenscape of Jacksonville, 1998—99; chmn. Jacksonville Symphony Assn.; mem. St. John's Episcopal Ch.; bd. mem. Jacksonville Transp. Authority, 1996—99, chmn., 1999—2003. Recipient James Patterson Pageturner award, 2005, Children's Champion award, Episcopal Children's Services, 2005. Republican. *

PEZESHK, VIOLET, psychologist, educator; d. Mohammad and Gowhar Pezeshk; children: Jhanna Shaghaghi, Natasha Shaghaghi. PhD, Alliant Internat. U., 2000. Cert. hypnotherapist Calif.; DV specialist Minn., 1998. Mem. adj. faculty Dept. Clin. Psychology and MFT Alliant Internat. U., San Diego, 2001—; clin. psychologist Palomar Family Counseling, Escondido, Calif., 2003—04. Program dir. St. Clare's Home, Escondido, 2002—03. Author: (self-help book) Psychological Development of Children from Birth to Adolescence, (children's novel) Ziba, editor weekly clin. article for mag.; exhibitions include Peace on Earth. Mem.: APA (assoc.). Home Phone: 760-717-7557; Office Phone: 858-635-4754. Personal E-mail: drpezeshk@yahoo.com.

PEZICK, PATRICIA, music educator; b. Upper Darby, Pa., Mar. 20, 1954; d. Robert Thomas Pezick and Gloria Jean Christie; m. Robert James McCarthy; children: Maura McCarthy, Colin McCarthy. BS in Music Edn., West Chester U., 1976; M in Music Edn., Temple U., 1981. Cert. Orff-Schulwerk levels I and II. Tchr. 8th grade music Phoenixville Sch. Dist., Pa., 1976—77; tchr. music William Penn Sch. Dist., Lansdowne, Pa., 1977—80; grad. asst. Temple U., Phila., 1980—81; dir. choral, tchr. gen. music., coord. music curriculum Germantown Acad., Ft. Washington, Pa., 1983—, dir. musical, 2002—03; real estate agt. Prudential, Fox and Roach, Blue Bell, Pa., 2007—. Music prof. Chestnut Hill Coll., Phila., 1992; ch. organist in field. Edward R. Kast grantee, Germantown Acad., 1987, 1989, 2003, 2005. Mem.: Music Educators Nat. Conf., Am. Choral Dirs. Assn. Democrat. Roman Catholic. Avocations: reading, travel, exercise, musical theatre. Home: 883 Crestline Dr Blue Bell PA 19422 Office: 340 Morris Rd Fort Washington PA 19034 Office Phone: 215-646-3300 x233. Business E-Mail: pat.pezick@prufaxroach.com.

PEZZELLA, JERRY JAMES, JR., investment and real estate company executive; b. Chesapeake, Va., Sept. 30, 1937; s. Jerry James, Sr. and Mabel (Aydlett) Pezzella; m. Carolyn Blades; children: James M., Stanley J., Julie Pezzella Scanlon. BS, U. Richmond, 1963; MBA, U. Pa., 1964. Asst. v.p. Va. Nat. Bank (now Bank of Am.), Norfolk, 1964-68; chmn. bd., pres. First Am. Investment Corp., First Ga. Investment Corp., Atlanta, 1968-74; v.p. Great Am. Investment Corp., Atlanta, 1974-78; sr. exec. v.p., 1984-85; exec. v.p. Equity Fin. & Mgmt. Co., Chgo., 1978-99; pres., chmn. bd. First Capital Fin. Corp., Chgo., 1983-85; pres. GAFGI Holdings Inc., Chgo., 1983-98; chmn. bd. 1st Property Mgmt. Corp., 1990-92; dir., fin. officer, treas. Bear Paw Svc. Dist., 2002—. Instr. fin. Old Dominion U., 1965—67, Ga. State U., 1970—73; adj. prof. U. Richmond, 1975—77; real estate cons., 1997—2001; bd. dirs. Great Am. Mgmt. and Investment, Inc. Mem. exec. com. Nat. Multi Housing Coun., 1991—93, bd. dirs., 1992—94. Mem.: Met. Club (Chgo.). Home: 1240 Village Rd Murphy NC 28906-1763

PEZZULLO, RALPH MICHAEL, writer, playwright; b. NYC, Dec. 27, 1954; s. Lawrence Anthony Pezzullo and Josephine DeMattia; m. Alice Palmisano, Aug. 8, 1980 (div. Jan. 1994); children: John Lawrence, Michael Richard; m. Jessica Rae Pezzullo, May 19, 1994; children: Francesca Sophia, Alessandra Sabina. M in Pub. and Internat. Affairs, George Washington U., 1975. Grants specialist Nat. Endowment Arts, Washington, 1975—79. Author: At the Fall of Somoza, 1994, Eve Missing, 2003, Jawbreaker, 2005, Plunging Into Haiti, 2006, (plays) From Behind the Moon, 1984, The Tail of the Tiger, 1985, Eating the Shadow, 1990, Wilderness of Mirrors, 1994, Hide Mother in My Heart, 1996, Gauquin's Parrot, 1997, Spain, 1998, Stakes, 1999, Okeechobee Split, 2000, Murder Sketched Gently, 2000, (radio drama/series) The Life and Times of Swamp Fox, 1985. Recipient Spl. citation Kesselring award, 1986, Screenwriting award, Writer's Guild Am. E. Found., 1987, award, Ctr. Theater, 1994, Douglas Dillon prize, 2006; Playwriting fellow, Jerome Found., 1997, 1998, 1999, 2001. Mem.: PEN USA, Writer's Guild Am., Pvt. Eye Writers Am., Mystery Writers Am., Author's League Am., Art Student's League, Dramatists Guild. Avocations: painting, sports. Home: 10055 Reevesbury Dr Beverly Hills CA 90210 E-mail: pezzullo@mindspring.com, ralph@ralphpezzullo.com.

PEZZUTO, JOHN MICHAEL, dean, pharmacology educator; b. Hammonton, NJ, Aug. 29, 1950; s. Michael L. and Elizabeth (Brown) P.; m. Mimi Faith Rotstein, Aug. 29, 1986; children: John-Henry Albert, Elisabeth Lee, Michael Joseph Ivan; 1 child from previous marriage, Jennifer Anne. AB, Rutgers U., 1973; PhD, Coll. Medicine & DentistryN.J., 1977. Postdoctoral assoc. MIT, Cambridge, 1977-79; instr. chemistry U. Va., Charlottesville, 1979-80; asst. prof. U. Ill.-Chgo., 1980-84, assoc. prof., 1984-91, prof., 1991—2002, Disting. Univ. prof., 2002; dean Purdue U., Coll. Pharmacy, Nursing and Health Scis., West Lafayette, Ind., 2002—06, prof. medicinal chemistry and molecular pharmacology, 2002—06; founding dean, prof. chemistry Coll. Pharmacy, U. Hawaii, Hilo, 2006—. Assoc. dir. U. Ill. Cancer Ctr, 1991-95, dep. dir., 2000-02; interim head dept. med. chemistry and pharmacognosy, U. Ill., Chgo., 1992-95, 2000-01, head, 2001-02; dir. program for collaborative rsch. in pharm. scis. U. Ill., Chgo., 1995-98; pres., co-founder Internat. Therapeutics Inc., River Forest, Ill., 1996—; assoc. dean for rsch. and grad. edn. U. Ill., Chgo., 1998-2002. Editor-in-chief Internat. Jour. Pharmacognosy, 1991-95, Combinatory Chemistry and High Throughput Screening, 1996-97, Pharmaceutical Biology, 1997—; editor: Biotechnology and Pharmacy; contbr. articles to profl. jours. NIH fellow, 1977-80, Rsch. fellow Alexander von Humboldt Found., 1990-91; NIH Rsch. Career Devel. awardee, 1984-89, grantee NAt. Cancer Inst., 1984—, Nat. Inst. Dental Rsch., 1984-85. Mem. AAAS, Am. Chem. Soc., Am. Soc. Pharmacognosy, Am. Assn. Cancer Rsch., N.Y. Acad. Scis., Am. Soc. Biol. Chemists. Office: Univ Hawaii at Hilo Coll Pharmacy 60 Nowelo St Ste 101 Hilo HI 96720-4091 Office Phone: 808-443-5900. Business E-Mail: pezzuto@hawaii.edu.

PEZZUTTI, SANTO COSTANTE, advertising executive, art director; b. Udine, Italy, June 2, 1922; s. August and Libera Pezzutti; m. Gertrude Eleanor Doherty, June 15, 1957; children: Carol, Diane, Lynn, Paul. Student, Newark Sch. Fine and Indsl. Arts, Franklyn Sch. Profl. Arts, NYC, 1941—42, Art Students League, 1945. Art dir. Smart Balance Foods, Cresskill, NJ; exec. art dir. Dancer Fitzgerald Sample, NYC, 1958—78. Watercolor tchr. Summit Art Ctr., NJ, 1997. One-man shows include Phoenix Gallery, NYC, 1985, Monmouth U., Long Branch, NJ, 1995; contbr. illustrations, watercolor to books; one-man shows include Olympics Program, Atlanta, Carlmore Gallery, NY. Recipient 1st prize, Monmouth Arts Coun., Monmouth Mus., 2000. Mem.: Guild Creative Art (judge, 1st prize 2005), Art Alliance-Monmouth (judge), NJ Watercolor Soc. (judge, 1st prize silvermedal 1987), Monmouth Boat Club. Avocations: sailing, golf. Home and Studio: 50 Conover Ln Red Bank NJ 07701 Office Phone: 732-842-5810.

PFAFF, JUDY, artist; b. London, 1946. Student Wayne State U., 1965-66, So. Ill. U., 1968-69; B.F.A., Washington U.-St. Louis, 1971; postgrad. Yale U., 1970, M.F.A., 1973. Prof. arts, Columbia U., 1992-94, Milton Avery Disting. prof. art, Bard Coll., 1989, 91, 94- One-woman exhbns. include: Webb and Parsons Gallery, New Canaan, Conn., 1974, Artists Space N.Y., 1975, Theatre Gallery, U. So. Fla., Tampa, 1977, Los Angeles Contemporary Exhbn., 1978, Holly Solomon Gallery, N.Y., 1980, Daniel Weinberg Gallery, Los Angeles, 1984, Wacoal, Japan, 1985, Holly Solomon Gallery, 1986, Nat. Mus. Women in the Arts, Washington, 1989, Cleve. Ctr. for Contemporary Art., Cleve., 1990, Fabric Workshop, N.Y., 1991, Rotunda Gallery, N.Y., 1993; group exhbns. include: Whitney Mus. Am. Art, 1975, Hallwalls Gallery, Buffalo, 1976, Art Mus., U. Calif.-Santa Barbara, 1979, Neuberger Mus., SUNY-Purchase, 1979, Contemporary Arts Mus., Houston, 1980, Contemporary Arts Ctr., Cin., 1980, Mus. Modern Art, N.Y.C., 1984, Venice Biennale, 1984, Rotunda Gallery, Bklyn., 1984, Bklyn. Mus., 1985, WHitney Mus. Am. Art., N.Y., 1988, Internat. Art Projects, Asia, 1990, Mis. Modern Art., 1989, Inst. Contemporary Art, Phila., 1991, Cultural Space, N.Y., 1992, Henie-Onstad Art Ctr., Norway, 1992, Whitney Mus. Am. Art at Champion, Stamford, Conn., 1993, Drawing Ctr., N.Y., 1993; commd. work Spokane City Hall, 1984. Nat. Endowment Arts grantee, 1979; Named a Guggenheim fellow, 1983, MacArthur Fellow, 2004; Award of Merit Medal for Sculpture, Am. Acad. of Arts and Letters, 2002. Office: Bard Coll PO Box 5000 Annandale On Hudson NY 12504-5000 E-mail: pfaff@bard.edu.

PFAFF, LAURA KING, auction house executive; b. San Francisco; m. Rick Pfaff. BA in English, U. So. Calif., LA, 1976. Acct. exec. The Pacific Group, San Francisco, 1986—90; pres. Laura King & Co., San Francisco, 1990—94; sr. v.p., regional dir. Christie's, San Francisco, 1994—2001; chmn. Bonhams & Butterfields, San Francisco, 2001—. Bd. mem. San Francisco Symphony, No. Calif. Cancer Ctr., Calif. Pacific Med. Ctr., Fort Mason Found.; former bd. mem. San Francisco C. of C. Office: Bonhams & Butterfields 220 San Bruno Ave San Francisco CA 94103 Office Phone: 415-861-7500.

PFAFF, ROBERT JAMES, retired lawyer; b. Pitts., Jan. 12, 1943; s. William Michael and Elizabeth (Ludwig) P.; m. Carol Pillich, June 18, 1977. BS in Edn., Slippery Rock U., Pa., 1965; JD, Duquesne U., Pitts., 1973. Bar: Pa. 1973, US Dist. Ct. (we. dist.) Pa. 1973, US Supreme Ct. 1980. Tchr. secondary schs., Norwin and Jeanette, Pa., 1965-66; suit group supr. Liberty Mut. Ins. Co., Pitts., 1966-70; assoc. Egler, McGregor & Reinstadtler, Pitts., 1973-76; ptnr. Leopold, Eberhardt & Pfaff, Altoona, Pa., 1976-80; sr. ptnr. Meyer, Darragh, Buckler, Bebenek & Eck, Pitts., 1980-84, Pfaff, McIntyre, Dugas, Hartye & Schmitt, Hollidaysburg, Pa., 1984—2001, Thomson, Rhodes & Cowie, Pitts., 2001—05; ret., 2005. Mem. Def. Rsch. Inst., Pa. Bar Assn., Allegheny County Bar Assn., Pa. Assn. Mut. Ins. Cos. (claims com.), Pa. Def. Inst. Republican. Roman Catholic. Avocations: golf, music, licensed pilot. Home: 701 Cambridge Dr Presto PA 15142-1142

PFAFF, WILLIAM WALLACE, medical educator; b. Rochester, NY, Aug. 14, 1930; s. Norman Joseph and Eleanor Blakesley (Wells) P.; m. Patricia Ann Clark; children: Nancy, Karen, Margaret, Mary Catherine. AB, Harvard U., 1952; MD, SUNY, 1956. Intern U. Chgo., 1956-58; sr. asst. surgeon NIH, Bethesda, Md., 1958-60; resident Stanford U. Med. Ctr., Palo Alto, Calif., 1960-65; asst. prof. U. Fla., Gainesville, 1965-68, assoc. prof., 1968-71, prof. surgery, 1971-95, prof. emeritus, adj. prof., 1995—, dir. organ transplant programs, 1971-95. Bd. dirs. United Network for Organ Sharing, Richmond, Va., pres. elect, 1997-98, pres., 1998-99; pres., com. chmn. Southeastern Organ Procurement Found., Richmond, 1973-95. Fellow Am. Coll. Surgeons; mem. Am. Surg. Assn., Am. Soc. Transplant Surgeons, So. Surg. Assn., Transplantation Soc., Alachua County Med. Soc. (pres. 1977-78). Home: 2445 NW 15th Pl Gainesville FL 32605-5148 Office: U Fla Dept Surgery PO Box 100286 Gainesville FL 32610-0286 Home Phone: 352-378-2240; Office Phone: 352-265-0606. Personal E-mail: puffer12@aol.com. Business E-Mail: pfaff@surgery.ufl.edu.

PFAFFENROTH, PETER ALBERT, lawyer; b. Mineola, NY, Mar. 29, 1941; s. Albert and Genevieve Astrid (Anderson) P.; m. Sara Ann Beekey, June 26, 1966; children: Elizabeth Cartwright, Peter Cyrus, Catherine Genevieve. BS in Engring., Princeton U., 1963, Diploma in European Civilization, 1963; JD, U. Mich., 1966; LLM in Taxation, NYU, 1972, LLM in Corp., 1976, LLM in Internat. Law, 1998. Bar: N.J. 1966, U.S. Dist. Ct. (N.J. dist.) 1966. With Daimler-Benz, Stuttgart, Fed. Republic Germany, 1961, B.P. Benzin & Petroleum, Hamburg, Fed. Republic Germany, 1962, Office of Internat. Affairs, U.S. Treasury Dept., Washington, 1963, Office of Export Control, U.S. Commerce Dept., Washington, 1964, Commrs. Office, U.S. Patent Office, Washington, 1965; atty. McCarter & English, Newark, 1966-68, Kentz & Gilson, Esqs., Summit, NJ, 1968-69; corp. counsel Tex. Plastics, Maine Sugar Industries, Robbinsville, NJ, 1969-70; atty. c/o Lewis Stein, Esq., Netcong, NJ, 1970-71; pvt. practice Chester, NJ, 1971—. Avocations: antiques, foreign languages, travel, wine.

PFALTZ, HUGO MENZEL, JR., lawyer; b. Newark, Sept. 23, 1931; s. Hugo M. and Mary E. (Horr) Pfaltz; m. Marilyn M. Muir, Sept. 29, 1956; children: Elizabeth W., William M., Robert L. BA, Hamilton Coll., 1953; JD, Harvard U., 1960; LLM, NYU, 1965. Bar: N.J. 1960, U.S. Dist. Ct. N.J. 1960, U.S. Supreme Ct. 1977. Assoc. McCarter & English, Newark, 1960—61, Bourne & Noll, Summit, NJ, 1961—74; sole practice Summit, 1974—82; ptnr. Pfaltz & Woller, 1983—. Mem. Battleship N.J. Commn., 1985—, NJ Law Revision Commn., 1986—2003. Assoc. editor N.J. Law Jour., 1966—2002, editor, 1984—86. Chmn. Summit Rep. City Com., 1966; mem. N.J. Constl. Conv., 1966, N.J. Assembly, 1968—72. Served to lt. USNR, 1953—62. Mem.: ABA, Summit Bar Assn., Union County Bar Assn., N.J. Bar Assn., Summit Tennis Club, Beacon Hill Club (Summit), Baltusrol Club (Springfield, N.J.), Univ. Club (Washington), Univ Club (N.Y.C.). Home: 118 Prospect St Summit NJ 07901-2472 Office: 382 Springfield Ave Summit NJ 07901-2707 Home Phone: 908-273-5000; Office Phone: 908-273-1974. Personal E-mail: hugopf@aol.com.

PFANNER, HELMUT FRANZ, German language educator; b. Hohenweiler, Vorarlberg, Austria, Nov. 8, 1933; came to U.S., 1957; s. Georg Franz and Luise (Huber) P.; m. Rosemary Griffin, Mar. 16, 1959 (div. 1964); 1 child, Renate; m. Beverly Louise Radcliffe, Sept. 16, 1966 (div. 1988); children: Heidi, Eric, Marta; m. Nasy Inthisone, Dec. 27, 1995; children: Franz, Maximilian. Grad., Tchr. Tng. Coll., Feldkirch, Austria, 1952; student, Kans. U., 1957—58, Stanford U., 1959—64. Cert. elem. and secondary sch. tchr. Tchr. Volksschule Seewald, Fontanella, Vorarlberg, 1952-53, Volksschule Hohenweiler, 1953-57; English tchr. Hauptschule Belruptstrasse, Bregenz, Austria, 1958-59; German instr. U. Wash., Seattle, 1964-67; asst. prof. U. Va., Charlottesville, 1967-69; assoc. prof. U. N.H., Durham, 1969-79; vis. prof. Purdue U., West Lafayette, Ind., 1979-82; prof. German U. N.H., Durham, 1982-86; prof. German, dept. chmn. U. Nebr., Lincoln, 1986-90; prof. German Vanderbilt U., Nashville, 1999—2005, dept. chmn., 1990-93, prof. emeritus, 2005—. Dir. Summer Inst. German Lang. and Culture, U. Calif., Santa Barbara, 1992-99. Author: Hanns Johst, Vom Expr. z. Nationalsozial, 1970, Oskar Maria Graf. eine kritische Bibliogr., 1976, Exile in New York: German and Austrian Writers after 1933, 1983; co-editor: O.M. Graf: Beschreibung eines Volksschriftstellers, 1974, O.M. Graf in seinen Briefen, 1984; editor: Exile across Cultures, 1986, Oskar Maria Graf: Reden und Aufsätze aus dem Exil, 1989, Karl Jakob Hirsch: Quintessenz meines Lebens, 1990, World War II and the Exiles: A Literary Response, 1991, Karl Jakob Hirsch: Manhattan Serenade, 2001, Alfred Döblin, Briefe II, 2001. Fulbright scholar Kans. U., 1957-58, German Acad. Exch. scholar, 1963-64; Am. Philos. Soc. grantee, 1969, 73, Alexander von Humboldt fellow, 1972-73, 77-78, Am. Coun. Learned Socs. fellow, 1976-77, NEH fellow, 1996-97. Mem. MLA, PEN German Writers Abroad (Am. sec.-treas. 1979-2002), Internat. Assn. Germanic Studies, Am. Assn. Tchrs. German, German Studies Assn., Internat. Soc. for Exile Studies. Avocations: reading, skiing, tennis, music, travel. Office: Vanderbilt U Dept Germanic Slavic Langs PO Box 1567 Sta B Nashville TN 37235-1567 E-mail: h.pfanner@gmx.at.

PFANTZ, CRAIG D., farmer; b. Marshalltown, Iowa, Aug. 26, 1952; s. Verne C. Pfantz and Helen J. Riemenschneider; m. Mary Lynn Kenkel, Aug. 12, 1978; children: Ryan, Ashley, Brett. BS, Iowa State U., Ames, 1977. Farmer, State Center, Iowa, 1977—. Mem. deans adv. coun. Iowa State U., Ames, 2000—04. Mayor City of State Center, 2002—06, mem. coun., 1994—2002; bd. dirs. State Center Main St., 2000—04. Mem.: Iowa Barn Found. (bd. dirs.), Lions Club (pres. 1998—2000). Avocation: barn restoration.

PFARR, JOHN S., lawyer; BA, Harvard U., 1963; JD cum laude, U. Mich. Law Sch., 1969. Co-founder, prin. Biltmore Wealth Strategies Grp., Inc., Strategic Philanthropy, LLC, Profls. Back Office, LLC, Warwick, RI, 1999—; ptnr. estate planning grp. Graves & Rethore, P.C., Essex, Conn. Adj. prof. Mich. State U. Acad. Multidisciplinary Practice; faculty mem. Esperti Peterson Inst. Advanced Estate Planning Studies Prof. Mem.: RI Bar Assn. (mem. probate and trust com.), Planned Giving Coun. RI, Nat. Network Estate Planning Attys. Mailing: Graves & Rethore PC 37 Sunset Ter Essex CT 06426-1024 Office Phone: 860-767-6555. Office Fax: 860-767-3068. E-mail: jsp@gravesandrethore.com. *

PFAU, GEORGE HAROLD, JR., investment advisor; b. Milw., May 7, 1924; s. George Harold and Elisabeth C. (Hunter) P.; m. Anne Elizabeth Mayhew (dec.); 1 child, George Harold III; children by previous marriage: Mary D., Peter W., Elizabeth C.; m. Susan Colomb, Jan., 3, 2005. BS, Yale U., 1948. Tchr. Thacker Sch., 1948-49; with Fleishhacker Paper Box Co., San Francisco, 1952-54; salesman A.G. Becker & Co., San Francisco, 1954-55; v.p., sec., dir. Carl W. Stern & Co., San Francisco, 1955-57; with White Weld & Co. Inc., San Francisco, 1957-78; 1st v.p. corp. fin. dept. Blyth Eastman Dillon, San Francisco, 1978-79; sr. v.p. UBS Fin. Svcs., San Francisco, 1979—. Bd. dirs. 1 A Dist. Arg. Assn. Bd. dirs. The Guardsmen, 1966-67, Pathfinder Fund, 1974-82, San Francisco Zool. Soc., 1979-80; trustee Thacher Sch., Ojai, Calif., 1967-76, Town Sch., San Francisco, 1966-70; pres. Planned Parenthood San Francisco-Alameda County, 1968-69, bd. dirs., 1965—; chmn. Lincoln Club of No. Calif, 1993-95, mem., 1982—; chmn. Citizens for Better San Francisco. With C.E., 1942-44; with Am. Field Svc., 1944-45. Mem. Kappa Beta Phi, San Francisco Bond Club, Bohemian Club (San Francisco), Calif. Tennis Club, Villa Taverna. Office: UBS Fin Svcs 555 California St Fl 32D San Francisco CA 94104-1502 Home Phone: 415-931-3307. E-mail: george.ptau@ubs.com.

PFAU, JAMES MICHAEL, lawyer; b. Milw., Aug. 22, 1958; s. Raymond Aloysius and Patricia Ann (Foley) P.; children: Gretchen Canright, Anna Katharine. BS in Journalism with distinction, Northwestern U., 1979; JD magna cum laude, U. Mich., 1983. Bar: Minn. 1983, U.S. Dist. Ct. Minn. 1983. Ptnr. Faegre & Benson, Mpls., 1983—. Contbr. articles to profl. jours. Bd. dirs. St. Anthony Pk. Cmty. Coun., St. Paul, 1989-92. Mem. Minn. State Bar Assn. Episcopalian. Home: 2140 Fairmount Ave Saint Paul MN 55105 Office: Faegre and Benson LLP 90 S 7th St Ste 2200 Minneapolis MN 55402-3901 Office Phone: 612-766-8616. E-mail: jpfau@faegre.com.

PFAU, RICHARD ANTHONY, university president; b. NYC, Feb. 19, 1942; s. Hugo and Irene Beatrice P.; m. Nancy Ann DiPace, Sept. 12, 1964; children: Bradley Madison, Aleksandra Nicole. AB, Hamilton Coll., 1964; MA, U. Va., 1973, PhD, 1975. Systems analyst Equitable Life Ins. Co., NYC, 1964-66; asst. prof. history Dickinson Coll., Carlisle, Pa., 1975-80; assoc. prof., assoc. dean U. Miami, Coral Gables, Fla., 1980-85; dean of faculty, provost Emory (Va.) and Henry Coll., 1985-93; pres. Ill. Coll., Jacksonville, Ill., 1993—2002, Averett U., Danville, Va., 2002—. Author: No Sacrifice Too Great: The Life of Lewis L. Strauss, 1985. Contbr. articles, book revs. to profl. publs. Vestryman St. Thomas Episc. Ch., Abingdon, Va., Epis. Ch. Epiphany, Denville, Va.; chmn., sec.-treas., exec. com., bd. dirs. Va. Found. for Humanities and Pub. Policy; mem. bd. trustees Carlisle Sch., Martinsville, Va.; mem. adv. bd. Salvation Army, Jacksonville, Ill. Capt. USAF, 1966-71. DuPont fellow, 1974-75; Hoover fellow, 1982. Mem. Danville Golf Club, Danville Rotary Club, Omicron Delta Kappa, Alpha Psi Omega, Pi Delta Epsilon. Home: 500 Hawthorne Drive Danville VA 24541 Office: Averett Univ Pres Office 420 West Main Street Danville VA 24541

PFEFFER, CYNTHIA ROBERTA, psychiatrist, educator; b. Newark, May 22, 1943; d. Edward I. and Ann Pfeffer. BA, Douglas Coll., 1964; MD, NYU, 1968. Assoc. dir. child psychiatry inpatient unit Albert Einstein Coll. Medicine, Bronx, NY, 1973-79; chief child psychiatry inpatient unit N.Y. Hosp. Cornell Med. Ctr., White Plains, NY, 1979-95; assoc. prof. clin. psychiatry Weill Med. Coll. Cornell U., NYC, 1984—. Prof. psychiatry Cornell U. Med. Coll., 1989—; pres. N.Y. Coun. on Child and Adolescent Psychiatry, N.Y.C., 1989—; dir. childhood bereavement program Weill Med. Coll. Cornell U., 1999—. Author: The Suicidal Child, 1986, Difficult Moments in Child Psychotherapy, 1988; editor: Youth Suicide: Perspectives on Risk and Prevention, 1989, Intense Stress and Mental Disturbance in Children, 1996; co-editor: Neurologic Disorders: Developmental and Behavioral Sequelae for Child and Adolescent Psychiatric Clinics of North America, 1999. Recipient Erwin Stengel award Internat. Assn. Suicide Prevention, 1987, Wilford Hulse award N.Y. Coun. on Child & Adolescent Psychiatry, 1989, Sigmund Freud award Am. Soc. Psychoanalytic Physicians, 1994. Fellow Am. Psychiat. Assn., Am. Acad. Child and Adolescent Psychiatry (councillor-at-large 1989—, Norbert Rieger award 1988), Am. Psychopathological Assn.; mem. Am. Assn. Suicidology (pres. 1987, Young Contbrs. award 1981, 82). Office: NY Hosp Westchester Div 21 Bloomingdale Rd White Plains NY 10605-1504 also: 1100 Madison Ave New York NY 10028-0327 Office Phone: 914-997-5849, 212-717-2334. Business E-Mail: cpfeffer@med.cornell.edu.

PFEFFER, DAVID H., lawyer; b. NYC, Mar. 15, 1935; B. Chem. Engring., CCNY, 1956; JD, NYU, 1961, LL.M. in Trade Regulation, 1967. Bar: N.Y. 1961. With patent dept. U.S. Rubber Co., Wayne, NJ, 1957-61; assoc. Watson, Leavenworth, Kelton & Taggart, NYC, 1961-63, Morgan & Finnegan, LLP, NYC, 1963-70, prin., 1971—. Village prosecutor Roslyn Harbor, N.Y., 1976-78, village justice, 1979-2003; panel of arbitrators Am. Arbitration Assn, Ctr. Dispute Resolution, NY Civil Ct., Nat. Arbitration Forum, CPI Inst. Dispute Resolution. Mem. ABA (litigation sect.), N.Y. State Bar Assn., Assn. Bar City N.Y., Am. Intellectual Property Law Assn. (com. alt. dispute resolution), N.Y. Intellectual Property Law Assn. (com. on alt. dispute resolution), Order of Coif. Office: Morgan & Finnegan LLP 3 World Financial Ctr New York NY 10281-2101 Office Phone: 212-415-8700. E-mail: dpfeffer@morganfinnegan.com.

PFEFFER, JEFFREY, business educator; b. St. Louis, July 23, 1946; s. Newton Stuart and Shirlee (Krisman) P.; m. Kathleen Frances Fowler, July 23, 1986. BS, MS, Carnegie Mellon U., 1968; PhD, Stanford U., 1972. Tech. staff Rsch. Analysis Corp., McLean, Va., 1968-69; asst. prof. U. Ill., Champaign, 1971-73; from asst. prof. to assoc. prof. U. Calif., Berkeley, 1973-79; prof. Grad. Sch. Bus., Stanford (Calif.) U., 1979—. Dir. SonoSite, Inc., Audible Magic, Inc.; vis. prof. Harvard U. Sch. Bus., Boston, 1981—82, London Bus. Sch., 2005, IESE, Barcelona, 2006, Singapore Mgmt. U., 2006. Author: The External Control of Organizations, 1978, Organizational Design, 1978, Power in Organizations, 1981, Organizations and Organization Theory, 1982 (Terry Book award 1984), Managing with Power, 1992, Competitive Advantage Through People, 1994, New Directions for Organization Theory, 1997, The Human Equation, 1998, The Knowing-Doing Gap, 1999, Hidden Value, 2000, Hard Facts, Dangerous Half-Truths, and Total Nonsense, 2006, What Were They Thinking?, 2007; monthly columnist (mag.) Bus. 2.0. Bd. dir. San Francisco Playhouse. Fellow Acad. Mgmt. (bd. govs. 1984-86, New Concept award 1979, Richard D. Irwin award for scholarly contbns. to mgmt. 1989); mem. Labor and Employment Rels. Assn. Jewish. Avocations: cooking, music. Home: 425 Moseley Rd Hillsborough CA 94010-6715 Office: Stanford U Grad Sch Bus Stanford CA 94305 Home Phone: 650-340-7331; Office Phone: 650-723-2915. E-mail: pfeffer_jeffrey@gsb.stanford.edu.

PFEFFER, PATRICK, architect; PhD, U. Paris, 1984—90. Dir. Alcatel, Petaluma, Calif., 1996—2000, Gluon Networks, Petaluma, 2000—03; chief network arch. Detecon, San Mateo, Calif., 2003—. Contbr. scientific papers. Achievements include patents for pattern matching. Office: Detecon Inc 400 S El Camino Real Ste 500 San Mateo CA 94402 Home Phone: 707-762-4311.

PFEFFER, PHILIP ELLIOT, biophysicist; b. NYC, Apr. 8, 1941; s. Charles and Della (Smith) P.; m. Judith Stadlen, Dec. 22, 1962; children: Charles, Ari, Shira. AB, Hunter Coll., 1962; MS, Rutgers U., 1964, PhD, 1966. Rsch. asst. dept. chemistry Rutgers U., New Brunswick, NJ, 1964-66; rsch. fellow dept. chemistry U. Chgo., 1966-68; rsch. scientist Ea. Regional Rsch. Ctr. USDA, Phila., 1968-88, rsch. leader Ea. Regional Rsch. Ctr., 1976-88, lead scientist Ea. Regional Rsch. Ctr., 1988—. Editor-at-large Marcel Dekker, N.Y.C., 1990—; adj. prof. dept. biosci. and biotech. Drexel U., Phila., 1996—; vis. prof. U. Bordeaux, France, 1998. Editor: Nuclear Magnetic Resonance in Agriculture, 1989, Nuclear Magnetic Resonance in Plant Biology, 1996; mem. editl. bd. Jour. Carbohydrate Chemistry, 1985—, Jour. Magnetic Resonance Analysis; contbr. articles to profl. jours. including Plant Physiology, Carbohydrate Rsch., Biochemica Acta, Biophysica, Jour. Magnetic Resonance. Recipient Bond award Am. Oil Chemists Soc., 1976, Fed. Svcs. award Phila. Fed. Assn., 1979, Science and Edn. award USDA, 1982; fellow Orgn. for Econ. Cooperation and Devel., 1989; Agrl. Rsch. Svc. rsch. fellow, 1989; vis. scientist grantee Centre d'Etudes Nucleaires de Grenoble, 1986, Oxford U., 1989; Nat. Rsch. Initiative grantee, 1997, 2002. Mem. AAAS, Internat. Soc. for Magnetic Resonance, Am. Chem. Soc. (Phila. sect. Scientist of Yr. 1982), Soc. for Applied Spectroscopy. Achievements include patents and publs. concerning use of alpha-anions; discovery of deuterium isotope shift NMR method for determining carbohydrate structures; development of P-31 NMR in vivo methodology for studying metal ion transport and C-13 NMR for studying plant/microbe interactions in nitrogen fixing plant nodules and symbiotic mycorrhizae. Office: USDA 600 E Mermaid Ln Wyndmoor PA 19038-8598

PFEFFER, ROBERT, chemical engineer, academic administrator, educator; b. Vienna, Nov. 26, 1935; arrived in U.S., 1938, naturalized, 1944; s. Joseph and Gisela (Aberbach) P.; m. Marcia Borenstein, Dec. 24, 1960; children: Michael, Jacqueline. B in Chem. Engring., NYU, 1956, M in Chem. Engring., 1958, D in Engring. Sci., 1962. Mem. faculty CCNY, 1957-92, asst. prof. chem. engring., 1962-66, assoc. prof., 1966-71, prof., 1971-92, chmn. dept. chem. engring., 1973-87, Herbert Kayser prof., 1980-92, dean grad. studies and rsch., dep. provost, 1987-88, provost, v.p. acad. affairs, 1988-92; v.p. rsch. and grad. studies, prof. chem. engring. N.J. Inst. Tech., Newark, 1992-97, Disting. prof. chem. engring., 1997—. Vis. prof. Imperial Coll., London, 1969; Fulbright scholar Technion-Israel Inst.

Tech., 1976-77; cons. in field. Contbr. articles to tech. publs. Fulbright Hays scholar, 1976-77; DuPont faculty fellow, 1962; NASA faculty fellow, 1964-65 Mem. AIChE (Particle Tech. Forum Nat. award 1995, Thomas Baron Nat. award 2000), Am. Soc. Engring. Edn., Sigma Xi, Tau Beta Pi, Phi Lambda Upsilon. Jewish. Office: NJIT University Heights Newark NJ 07102 Home Phone: 480-502-9177; Office Phone: 973-642-7496. Business E-Mail: pfeffer@njit.edu.

PFEFFERBAUM, BETTY JANE, psychiatrist, educator; b. Seattle, Sept. 7, 1946; d. Lois (Yager) P.; m. Richard L. Van Horn, May 29, 1988. BA, Pomona Coll., 1968; MD, U. Calif., San Francisco, 1972; JD, U. Okla., Norman, 1993. Bar: Okla. 1993; diplomate Am. Bd. Psychiatry and Neurology with subspecialty in child psychiatry. Intern pediatrics Martin Luther King Jr. Gen. Hosp., Compton, Calif., 1972-73; resident in psychiatry Neuro Psychiat. Inst., UCLA, 1973-76, fellow in child psychiatry, 1975-77; pvt. practice psychiatry, LA, 1977-78; prof. U. Tex. Med. Sch., Houston, 1978-89; v.p. for edn. U. Tex. Health Sci. Ctr., Houston, 1987-89; prof., chief child sect. dept. psychiatry U. Okla. Health Scis. Ctr., Oklahoma City, 1989-96, chair dept. psychiatry, 1996—; adj. prof. Oklahoma City U. Sch. Law, 1994-95. Mem. Okla. Indigent Def. Sys. Bd., 1992-93, Okla. Bd. Mental Health and Substance Abuse Svcs., 1993-99. Contbr. articles to profl. jours. Grad. Leadership Tex., 1988, Leadership Okla., 1995. Fellow Am. Psychiat. Assn., Am. Acad. Child and Adolescent Psychiatry, Group for Advancement Psychiatry; mem. ABA, Order of Coif, Phi Beta Kappa, Pi Mu Epsilon. Jewish. Office: U Okla Health Scis Ctr William Pavilion Rm 3470 920 S L Young Blvd PO Box 26901 Oklahoma City OK 73104-5020 Home: 2517 Stratton Dr Edmond OK 73013 Office Phone: 405-271-5121. Business E-Mail: betty-pfefferbaum@ouhsc.edu.

PFEIFER, EDWARD C., secondary school educator; s. Clarence Ray Pfeifer; m. Deboarh L. Allen, July 28, 1984; 1 child, Jennifer M. BA, Boise State U., Idaho, 1986. Educator Marsing Sch. Dist., Idaho, 1987—. Councilperson Marsing City Coun., Idaho, 2004—. Home Phone: 208-896-6002; Office Phone: 208-896-4111.

PFEIFER, PAUL E., state supreme court justice; b. Bucyrus, Ohio, Oct. 15, 1942; m. Julia Pfeifer; 3 children. BA, Ohio State U., 1963, JD, 1966. Asst. atty. gen. State of Ohio, 1967-70; mem. Ohio Ho. of Reps., 1971-72; asst. prosecuting atty. Crawford County, 1973-76; mem. Ohio Senate, 1976-92, minority floor leader, 1983-84, asst. pres. pro-tempore, 1985-86; ptnr. Cory, Brown & Pfeifer, 1973-92; justice Ohio Supreme Ct., 1992—. Chmn. jud. com. Ohio Senate, 10 yrs. Mem. Grace United Meth. Ch., Bucyrus. Office: Supreme Court of Ohio 65 S Front St Columbus OH 43215-3431 Office Phone: 614-387-9020.

PFEIFER, POLLY LEE, elementary school educator; d. Gerald Edward and Nancy Lee Pfeifer. BA in Edn., Coll. Saint Benedict, St. Joseph, Minn., 1987; MA in Edn., St. Mary's U., Winona, Minn., 1994; student in Libr. Media Scis., Mankato State U., Minn., 2006—. Cert. tchr. Minn., 1987. Tchr. sci. Minnetonka (Minn.) Pub. Schs., 1987—. Mem.: NEA, Minn. Ednl. Media Orgn., Nat. Assn. Sci. Tchrs., Minnetonka (Minn.) Tchrs. Assn. (v.p. 1996). Roman Cath. Avocations: reading, basketball, golf. Office: Minnetonka Mid Sch West 6421 Hazeltina Blvd Excelsior MN 55331

PFEIFER, SAMANTHA M., obstetrician, gynecologist; d. C. Edward and Joan Balise Pfeifer; children: Alice Gwathmey Matthai, Charlotte Rose Matthai. AB, Bryn Mawr Coll., Pa., 1982; MD, U. Pa., Phila., 1986. Cert. Am. Bd. of Ob-gyn., 1994, infertility and reproductive endocrinology Am. Bd. of Ob-gyn., 1997. Assoc. prof. ob-gyn. U. Pa., Phila., 1993—. Mentor coll. students. Mem.: Am. Soc. Reproductive Medicine, North Am. Soc. Pediatric and Adolescent Gynecology (assoc.). Office: Univ Pa Med Ctr 3701 Market St 8th Fl Philadelphia PA 19104 Home Phone: 610-949-0161; Office Phone: 215-662-6315.

PFEIFER, TRACY M., plastic surgeon; b. Yonkers, NY, Dec. 20, 1960; d. Adrienne K and William A Pfeifer. BA, Rutgers U., 1982—84; MS, Calif. State U., Los Angeles, 1984—85; MD, U. of Medicine and Dentistry of NJ, 1987—91. Bd. cert. Am. Bd. of Plastic Surgery, 2001, Am. Bd. of Surgery, 1999. Plastic surgeon, pvt. practice Pfeifer Plastic Surgery, PLLC, NYC, 1999—. Fellow: Am. Coll. Surgeons; mem.: Am. Soc. Aesthetic Plastic Surgery, Am. Soc. Plastic Surgeons, NY Regional Soc. of Plastic Surgeons (exec. bd. mem. 2000—). Office: Pfeifer Plastic Surgery PLLC 565 Park Ave New York NY 10021 Home Phone: 212-996-7636; Office Phone: 212-860-0670. Office Fax: 212-593-8823. E-mail: tpfeifer@drpfeifer.com.

PFEIFFER, ERIC ARMIN, psychiatrist, gerontologist, writer; b. Rauental, Germany, Sept. 15, 1935; came to U.S., 1952; naturalized, 1957; s. Fritz and Emma (Saborowski) P.; m. Natasha Maria Emerson, Mar. 21, 1964; children: Eric Alexander, Michael David, Mark Armin. AB, Washington U., 1956, MD, 1960. Intern Albert Einstein Coll. Medicine, Bronx, NY, 1960-61; resident in psychiatry U. Rochester, NY, 1961-64; practice medicine specializing in psychiatry Durham, NC, 1966-76, Denver, 1976-78; asst. prof. Duke U., Durham, 1966-69, assoc. prof., 1969-72, prof., 1973-76, project dir., 1971-76, assoc. dir., 1974-76; dir. Davis Inst. Care and Study Aging, Denver, 1976-77; prof. psychiatry U. Colo., Denver, 1976-78; prof. psychiatry, chief div. geriatric psychiatry U. South Fla. Coll. Medicine, Tampa, 1978—, dir. Suncoast Gerontology Ctr., 1980—. Chief psychiatry svc. Tampa VA Med. Ctr., 1979-80; cons. in field; chmn. bd. Social Systems, Inc., 1975-76; chmn. com. on mental health and mental illness of elderly HEW, 1976-77. Author: Disordered Behavior, 1968, (with E.W. Busse) Behavior and Adaptation in Late Life, 1970, 3d edit., 1977, Successful Aging, 1974, Multidimensional Functional Assessment, 1977, Alzheimer's Disease, 1989. With USPHS, 1964-66. Markle Found. scholar acad. medicine, 1968-73; Eric Pfeiffer Chair in Alzheimer's Disease Rsch. named in his honor, U. S. Fla., 1985. Fellow Gerontol. Soc. (chmn. clin. medicine sect. 1975-76), Am. Psychiat. Assn.; mem. Am. Geriatrics Soc. (Allen Gold medal 1977), So. Psychiat. Soc., Phi Beta Kappa. Office: 12901 Bruce B Downs Blvd Tampa FL 33612-4742 Office Phone: 813-974-4355. E-mail: epfeiffe@hsc.usf.edu.

PFEIFFER, GARY M., chemicals executive; b. Richmond, Va., Oct. 24, 1949; m. Lear Strange; 2 children. BA in Polit. Sci., Coll. William and Mary, MBA. From mem. staff to sr. v.p., CFO DuPont, Wilmington, Del., 1974-97, sr. v.p., CFO, 1997—.

PFEIFFER, JANE CAHILL, former broadcasting company executive, consultant; b. Sept. 29, 1932; d. John Joseph and Helen (Reilly) Cahill; m. Ralph A. Pfeiffer, Jr., June 3, 1975. BA, U. Md., 1954; postgrad., Cath. U. Am., 1956—57; LHD (hon.), Pace Coll., 1978, U. Md., 1979; LHD (hon.), Manhattanville Coll., 1979, Amherst U., 1980, Babson Coll., 1981, U. Notre Dame, 1991; LHD (hon.), Bryant Coll., 1995, St. Thomas Aquinas Coll., 2006. With IBM Corp., Armonk, NY, 1955-76, sec. mgmt. rev. com., 1970, dir. comm., 1971, v.p. comm. and govt. rels., 1972-76, bus. cons., 1976-78; chmn. NBC, Inc., NYC, 1978-80; bus. cons., 1980—. Sr. advisor The Conf. Bd., 1991. Pres.'s adv. com. White House Fellows, 1966, Pres.'s Gen. Adv. Commn. on Arms Control and Disarmament, 1977-80, Pres.'s Commn. Mil. Compensation; trustee Rockefeller Found., U. Md., Carnegie Hall, 1981-1986, U. Notre Dame; bd. dirs. Catholic Univ. of Am., 1973-1978, Rockefeller Found., 1973-1985, White House Fellows, 1976-1981, Kettering Found., 1975-1979. Recipient Achievement award Kappa Kappa Gamma, 1974-80, Eleanor Roosevelt Humanitarian award NY League for Hard of Hearing, 1980, Disting. Alumna award U. Md., 1975, Humanitarian award NOW, 1980, Centennial Alumna medallion U. Md., 1988; White House fellow, Washington, 1966, Making Waves award, Greatest 50 Women in Radio and Television-AWRT, 2002. Mem. Coun. Fgn. Rels., Overseas Devel. Coun., Econ. of N.Y. Club. Office: C/O Jonathan L Smith Chesapeake Asset Mgmt LLC 1 Rockefeller Plz Rm 1210 New York NY 10020-2002 Home: Johns Island 1050 Beach Rd Apt 1G Vero Beach FL 32963-3413 Office Phone: 212-218-4044.

PFEIFFER, LEONARD, IV, executive recruiter, consultant; s. Leonard Jr. and Felicia Pfeiffer; m. Anna. BA, MBA, Harvard U. Mktg. mgr. Am. Express, NYC, 1970-72; project dir. S.T.I., NYC and San Francisco, 1972-74; v.p. R. Olivier & Assocs., NYC, 1974-76, A. Kane & Assoc., NYC, 1976-78; v.p., mng. dir. Korn/Ferry Internat., Washington and NYC, 1978-98; sr. ptnr., group leader Heidrick & Struggles, Washington, 1998—2001; pres. Leonard Pfeiffer & Co., Washington, 2001—. Bd. dirs. Cmty. Found., Washington, 1982-84, Nat. Ctr. for Missing Children, 1989—, Nat. Blood Found., 1995-97, Nat. Bldg. Mus., 1998-2001; founding mem. jr. bd. dirs. Washington Opera, 1983-93; men's com. Project Hope; devel. com. Nat. Head Injury Found., Choral Arts Soc., Nat. Symphony Orch. Lt. U.S. Army, 1968-70. Schepp Found. scholar, 1968-70. Mem. Am. Soc. Assn. Execs., Greater Washington Soc. Assn. Execs., Congl. Country Club, Harvard Club (activities com., admissions com. N.Y.C. chpt. 1975-81, 1st v.p. bd. dirs. Washington chpt. 1985-87). Avocations: water and snow skiing, power and sail boating, tennis. Office: Leonard Pfeiffer & Co 1319 F St NW Ste 800 Washington DC 20004-1140 Office Phone: 202-737-6327. Business E-Mail: lp@pfeiffercompany.com.

PFEIFFER, MARGARET KOLODNY, lawyer; b. Elkin, NC, Oct. 7, 1944; d. Isadore Harold and Mary Elizabeth Kolodny; m. Carl Frederick Pfeiffer II, Sept. 2, 1968. BA, Duke U., 1967; JD, Rutgers U., 1974. Bar: NJ 1974, NY 1976, DC 1981, US Supreme Ct. 1979. Law clk. to Hon. F.L. Van Dusen U.S. Ct. Appeals 3d cir., Phila., 1974-75; assoc. Sullivan & Cromwell, NYC and Washington, 1975-82, ptnr. litigation, antitrust, intellectual property, internat. trade and investment practice area, criminal def. and investigations, 1982—. Contbr. articles to profl. jours. Trustee Nat. Law Ctr. on Homelessness and Poverty. Mem. ABA, Internat. Bar Assn., DC Bar Assn., NY State Bar Assn., Assn. of Bar of City of NY, Am. Soc. of Internat. Law. Avocations: gardening, reading, music. Office: Sullivan & Cromwell 1701 Pennsylvania Ave NW Washington DC 20006-5866 Office Phone: 202-956-7540. Business E-Mail: pfeifferm@sullcrom.com.

PFEIFFER, MARY LOUISE, artist, educator; b. Troy, Ohio, Feb. 14, 1944; d. John Edward Dunnick and Helen Elizabeth Johnson-Dunnick; children: William G. II, Scott Edward. AS magna cum laude, Tidewater Coll., Virginia Beach, Va., 1976; BA, Fla. Internat. U., Miami, 1986, MA in Religious Studies, 2004; LLM, St. Thomas U. Sch. Law, Miami, 2002. Owner, operator Pfeiffer Originals, Art Glass Designs, Miami, 1976—; adj. prof. dept. religious studies Fla. Internat. U., 2002—, prof. Honors Coll., 2005—. Author: (technical textbook) Basic Radiography. Acting chmn. Navy Relief Soc., Meridian, Miss., 1968—69; pres., sec.-treas. Officers' Wives Club, 1968—69; POW-MIA com. NAS Oceana, Virginia Beach, 1970—75; hospitality coord. Performing Arts Cmty. and Edn., Miami, 1982—84; mem. steering com. 5th-7th tribal symposia St. Thomas U. Sch. of Law, 2002—06. Recipient Alumni Assn. Torch award, Fla. Internat. U. Alumni Assn., 2000, Outstanding Svc. award dept. religious studies, Fla. Internat. U., 2000, 2002. Fellow: The Honors Coll. (faculty); mem.: Phi Theta Kappa, Theta Alpha Kappa. Avocations: swimming, sailing, golf, travel. Home: 19160 NE 19 Pl North Miami Beach FL 33179-4316 Office: Florida Internat U UP Campus 11200 SW 8th St DM 233 Miami FL 33199 Home Phone: 305-936-1494; Office Phone: 305-348-4100. Office Fax: 305-348-2118. Business E-Mail: pfeiffer@fiu.edu.

PFEIFFER, MICHELLE, actress; b. Santa Ana, Calif., Apr. 29, 1957; d. Dick and Donna P.; m. Peter Horton, 1981 (div. 1988); 1 adopted child, Claudia Rose; m. David Kelley, Nov. 13, 1993, 1 child. Student, Golden West Coll., Whitley Coll. Actress: (feature films) Falling in Love Again, 1980, Hollywood Knights, 1980, Charlie Chan and the Curse of the Dragon Queen, 1981, Grease II, 1982, Scarface, 1983, Ladyhawke, 1985, Into the Night, 1985, Sweet Liberty, 1986, Amazon Women on the Moon, 1987, Witches of Eastwick, 1987, Married to the Mob, 1988, Tequila Sunrise, 1988, Dangerous Liaisons, 1988 (Acad. award nominee for best supporting actress, 1989, BAFTA award, 1990), The Fabulous Baker Boys, 1989 (L.A. Film Critics Assn. award for best actress, 1989, D.W. Griffith award Nat. Bd. Rev., 1989, N.Y. Film Critics award, 1989, Nat. Soc. Film Critics award for best actress, 1990, Golden Globe award for best actress drama, 1990, Acad. award nominee for best actress, 1990), The Russia House, 1990, Frankie & Johnny, 1991, Love Field, 1992 (Acad. award nominee for best actress, 1993), Batman Returns, 1992, The Age of Innocence, 1993, Wolf, 1994, Dangerous Minds, 1995, Up Close and Personal, 1996, To Gillian on her 37th Birthday, 1996, One Fine Day, 1996, A Thousand Acres, 1997, The Prince of Egypt (voice), 1998, The Story of Us, 1998, A Midsummer Night's Dream, 1999, Deep End of the Ocean, 1999, What Lies Beneath, 2000, I Am Sam, 2001, White Oleander, 2002, Sinbad: Legend of the Seven Seas (voice), 2003, I Could Never Be Your Women, 2007, Hairspray, 2007, Stardust, 2007; (TV movies) The Solitary Man, 1979, Callie and Son, 1981, The Children Nobody Wanted, 1981, Splendor in the Grass, 1981, One Too Many, 1983, Tales from the Hollywood Hills: Natica Jackson, 1987, Power, Passion and Murder, 1987; (TV series) Delta House, 1979, B.A.D. Cats, 1980; prodr: (films) A Thousand Acres, 1997; exec. prodr.: (films) One Fine Day, 1996. Named Woman of the Yr., Harvard's Hasty Pudding Theater Club, 1995; recipient Crystal award, Women in Film, 1993. *

PFEIFFER, PHILIP JOHN, lawyer; b. Houston, Aug. 16, 1947; BS, Sam Houston State U., 1969; JD, So. Meth. U., 1972. Bar: Tex. 1972. Ptnr. Fulbright & Jaworski LLP, 1979—, former ptnr.-in-charge San Antonio office San Antonio. Editor-in-chief Employment Discrimination Law (Second Supplement to Lindemann and Grossman). Named a Tex. Super Lawyer, Tex. Monthly Mag., 2003, 2004, 2005, 2006. Fellow Am. Coll. Labor and Employment Lawyers; mem. ABA, State Bar Tex., San Antonio Bar Assn., San Antonio Bar Found., Tex. Bar Found., Order of Coif, Phi Alpha Delta. Office: Fulbright & Jaworski LLP 300 Convent St Ste 2200 San Antonio TX 78205-3792 Office Phone: 210-270-7117. Office Fax: 210-270-7205. Business E-Mail: ppfeiffer@fulbright.com.

PFEIFFER, SOPHIA DOUGLASS, retired state legislator, lawyer; b. NYC, Aug. 10, 1918; d. Franklin Chamberlin and Sophie Douglass (White) Wells; m. Timothy Adams Pfeiffer, June 7, 1941; children: Timothy Franklin, Penelope Mesereau Keenan, Sophie Douglass. AB, Vassar Coll., 1939; JD, Northeastern U., 1975. Bar: R.I. 1975, U.S. Ct. Appeals (1st cir.) 1980, U.S. Supreme Ct. 1979. Editl. rschr. Time, Inc., NYC, 1940-41; writer Officer War Info., Washington, 1941-43, NYC, 1943-45; editl. staff Nat. Geog. Mag., Washington, 1958-59, 68-70; editor Turkish Jour. Pediatrics, Ankara, 1961-63; staff atty. R.I. Supreme Ct., Providence, 1975-76, chief staff atty., 1977-86; mem. Maine Ho. Reps., 1990-94; lectr. U. So. Maine, 1995. Bd. dirs. Death and Dying project. Contbr. in field. Chair bioethics study League Women Voters; pres. Karachi (Pakistan) Am. Sch., 1955-56; chair Brunswick Village Rev. Bd., 1986-89; trustee Brunswick Sewer Dist., 2000-05, bd. dirs. Coll. Guild, 2003-06. Home: 15 Franklin St Brunswick ME 04011-2101

PFEIFFER, STEVEN BERNARD, lawyer; b. Orange, NJ, Jan. 19, 1947; s. Bernard Victor and Elizabeth Sophia (Bissell) P.; m. Kristin Reagan, June 27, 1970; children: Victoria Pfeiffer Metz, Rachel Catherine, Emily Dorothea, Stephanie Kristin Bissell, Andrew Steven Bernard. BA in Govt., Wesleyan U., 1969; BA in Jurisprudence, Oxford U., 1971, MA, 1983; MA in African Studies, U. London, 1973; JD, Yale U., New Haven, Conn., 1976. Bar: NJ 1976, DC 1978. Assoc. Fulbright & Jaworski, Houston, London, 1976—83, ptnr. London, Washington, 1983—, ptnr.-in-charge London, 1983—86, 1989—2002, head internat. dept., 1989—2003, ptnr.-in-charge Washington office, 1998—2002, chmn. exec. com., 2003—. Bd. dirs. The Africa Am. Inst., NYC, Project HOPE, Washington, Barloworld Ltd., Johannesburg, Iridium Holdings LLC, Washington, NAACP Legal Defense and Ednl. Fund, NYC. Contbr. articles to profl. jours. Alumni-elected trustee Wesleyan U., Middletown, Conn., 1976-79, charter trustee, 1980-92, vice chmn. bd. trustees, 1986-87, chmn. bd. trustees, 1987-92, chmn. emeritus, 1992—; trustee St. Andrews Sch., Middletown, Del., 1995—. With USN, 1969, 72-74; asst. cinceur plans officer, Office of CNO, Washington, 1972-73; spl. asst. to Sec. of Navy, Washington, 1973-74. Rhodes scholar, 1969-72; Thomas Watson Travel fellow, The Watson Found., 1969. Mem. ABA, NJ State Bar Assn., Am. Soc. Internat. Law, Internat. Bar Assn. (past chmn. sect. energy and natural resources law 1992-94), Naval Res. Assn., Internat. Inst. Strategic Studies (London), Coun. Fgn. Rels. NY. Avocations: tennis, history, fishing, books. Office: Fulbright & Jaworski LLP Market Sq 801 Pennsylvania Ave NW Washington DC 20004-2623 Office Phone: 202-662-4585. Office Fax: 202-662-4643. Business E-Mail: spfeiffer@fulbright.com.

PFEIFFER, WILLIAM SANBORN, education educator, writer; b. Akron, Ohio, July 29, 1947; s. Harold Arthur and Jean Sanborn Pfeiffer; m. Evelyn Hepp Pfeiffer, July 17, 1976; children: Zachary Paul, Kathryn Blaire. BA in English, Amherst Coll., 1969; MA in English, Kent State U., 1973, PhD in English, 1975. Dept. head Southern Poly State U., Marietta, Ga., 1989—97, assoc. dean, arts and sci., 2000, v.p. acad. affairs, 2001—03; founding provost Ramapo Coll., Mahwah, NJ, 2003—04, interim pres., 2004—05, provost, interim CIO, 2005—06; pres. Warren Wilson Coll., Asheville, NC, 2006—. Author: (book) Technical Communication: A Practical Approach, 6th edit., 2006; author: (with Steven B. Zwickel) Pocket Guide to Technical Presentations and Professional Speaking, 2006; author: Technical Writing: A Practical Approach, 2004; author: (with J. Boogerd) Pocket Guide to Technical Communication, 4th edit., 2007; author: Pocket Guide to Public Speaking, 2002; author: (with C.H. Keller Jr.) Proposal Writing: The Art of Friendly and Winning Persuasion, 2000; author: Proposal Writing: The Art of Friendly Persuasion, 1989; contbr. articles to profl. jours. Avocations: jogging, hiking, travel, fly fishing. Home: 106 North Lane Swannanoa NC 28778 Office: Warren Wilson Coll PO Box 9000 Asheville NC 28815 Office Phone: 828-771-2070.

PFEIFLER, BRIAN C., financial planner; s. Brian D. Pfeifler; m. Emilia Helena Fanjul, Mar. 23, 2002. Grad., Amherst Coll., Mass. Joined Morgan Stanley, 1989, mng. dir. pvt. wealth mgmt. group NYC, 2002—. Bd. dirs. Concert Artists Guild, NYC. Named one of Top 100 Fin. Advisors, Barron's Mag., 2005, Top Advisors Under 40, On Wall St. Mag., 2006. Office: Morgan Stanley 1221 Ave of the Americas New York NY 10020 *

PFEISTER, RAYMOND LYNN, diversified financial services company executive; b. Cape Girardeau, Mo., May 31, 1946; s. Herman Joe and Imogene Elsie (Groseclose) P.; m. Susan Jane Selby, July 1, 1969; children: Joseph Robert, John Charles. BS, U. Ill., 1969, MBA, 1971; PhD, CUNY, 1978. Sales analyst Koppers Co., Magnolia, Ark., 1969-70; instr. bus. U. Ill., Urbana, 1971; spl. agt. Prudential Ins. Co. Am., Champaign, Ill., 1971, divsn. mgr. Balt., 1971-74, mktg. specialist, mgr. group pension Newark and NYC, 1974; account exec. Alexander & Alexander Inc., NYC, 1974-76, asst. v.p., 1976-78, v.p., 1978-80, Johnson & Higgins, NYC, 1980-83; founder, chmn. bd., CEO Pfeister Barter Inc., NY Reciprocal Trade Exch., 1979-87; founder, chmn., pres. Pfeister Corp., Wilmington, Del., 1977—; co-founder, pres., treas. Chattan Group, Ltd., NYC, 1983—; co-founder, pres., CEO Sheffield Assocs., Ltd., NYC, 1985—; co-owner Ceramic Design Ltd., Greenwich, Conn., 1987—2006; vice chmn. Fred Alger Mgmt., NYC, 1987—; chmn. bd. Pfeister Capital Mgmt., Bronxville, NY, 2006—. Bd. dirs. U.S. Ceramic Tile Corp., Canton, Ohio, London Pacific Life Ins. Co., Calif.; lectr., cons. in field. Author: The Strategic Planning Process for Alexander & Alexander Services, Inc. and Subsidiaries, 1980; contbg. author: The Practice of Planning—Strategic, Administrative and Operational, 1981. Pres. Jr. Achievement, Denver, 1963-64; active boy Scouts Am., 1964—, United Fund, 1973. Mem. APA, Acad. Mgmt., Nat. Eagle Scout Assn., Soc. Am. Foresters, Forest Products Rsch. Soc., Nat. Life Underwriters Assn., Nat. MBA Assn., U. Ill. Alumni Assn. (life, v.p. 1974—), Siwanoy Country Club, Campfire Club Am., Union League Club, Sigma Iota Epsilon. Office Phone: 914-337-1877. Personal E-mail: raypfeister@yahoo.com.

PFENDER, EMIL, mechanical engineering educator; b. Stuttgart, Germany, May 25, 1925; came to U.S., 1964, naturalized, 1969; s. Vinzenz and Anna Maria (Dreher) P.; m. Maria Katharina Staiger, Oct. 22, 1954; children: Roland, Norbert, Corinne. Student, U. Tuebingen, Germany, 1947-49; diploma in physics, U. Stuttgart, Germany, 1953, D Ing. in Elec. Engring., 1959. Assoc. prof. mech. engring. U. Minn., Mpls., 1964-67, prof., 1967—2000, prof. emeritus, 2000—. Contbr. articles to profl. jours.; patentee in field. Fellow: ASME; mem.: NAE. Home: 1947 Bidwell St Saint Paul MN 55118-4417 Office: U Minn Dept Mech Engring 111 Church St SE Minneapolis MN 55455-0150 Office Phone: 612-625-6012. Business E-Mail: pfender@tc.umn.edu.

PFENING, FREDERIC DENVER, III, manufacturing executive; b. Columbus, Ohio, July 28, 1949; s. Frederic Denver Jr. and Lelia (Bucher) P.; m. Cynthia Gordon, July 1, 1978 (div. 1999); children: Lesley, Frederic Denver IV; m. Janet Evans, 1999. BA, Ohio Wesleyan U., 1971; MA, Ohio State U., Columbus, 1976. Various positions Fred. D. Pfening Co., Columbus, 1976-88, pres., 1988—. Bd. dirs. Friends of Ohio State U. Librs., 1988-94, 98—, pres. 2004-, Columbus State C.C. Devel. Found., 1991-99, Hist. Sites Found., Baraboo, Wis., 1984-2004, pres., 1987-91. Mem. Am. Soc. Bakery Engrs., Orgn. Am. Historians, Bakery Equipment Mfrs. Assn. (bd. dirs. 1985-91), Young Pres.'s Orgn., World's Pres.'s Orgn., Circus Hist. Soc. (pres. 1986-89, mng. editor Bandwagon Jour.), Rotary. Office: 1075 W 5th Ave Columbus OH 43212-2629 Home Phone: 614-451-2939; Office Phone: 614-294-5361 ext 102. Business E-Mail: fpfening@pfening.com.

PFENNIG, DENNIS JOSEPH, secondary school educator; b. Bklyn., Jan. 21, 1941; s. Joseph Raymond Pfennig and Geraldine Helen Kenney Pfennig. BA, St. John's U., Jamaica, NY, 1962; MA, Niagara U., NY, 1963; PhD, U. Ga., Athens, 1975. Tchr. social studies Msgr. McClancy H.S., Jackson Heights, NY, 1963—67, Wantagh H.S., NY, 1967—68, Hayfield Secondary Sch., Fairfax County, Va., 1970—80, chair social studies, 1980—2000; ret., 2000. Pres. Springfield Village Homeowners Assn., Va., 2002—; mem. Adv. Social Svcs. Bd., Fairfax County, 2001—03. Named Outstanding Tchr.-Historian, Fairfax County Pub. Schs., 1988; fellow, Niagara U., 1962—63, U. Ga., 1968—70, 1973—74; grantee, NEH, 1985; scholar, La Salle Acad., 1954—58; Fulbright scholar, 1982. Mem.: So. Hist. Assn. (parliamentarian 1993—). Democrat. Roman Catholic. Avocations: reading, travel, exercise. Personal E-mail: denroi@aol.com.

PFEUFFER, ROBERT JOHN, musician; b. Cleve., Dec. 25, 1925; s. Henry Vincent and Elmo Alice (Burger) P.; m. Betty June Weller, Sept. 21, 1946; children— Barbara (Mrs. Steven Mosley), Jeanne, Susan, Catherine. B.Mus. in Edn, U. Mich., 1950, M.Mus. in Edn, 1951. Contrabassoonist, bassoonist Detroit Symphony Orch., 1951-61, Phila. Orch., 1962-91; instr. bassoon Wayne State U., 1957-61, New Sch. Music, Phila., 1969—; prin.

bassoon Lynchburg Symphony, 1994—, Roanoke Opera, 1996—, Milford Cmty. Band, Del. Served with AUS, 1942-44. Mem. U.S. Power Squadron, Kappa Kappa Psi, Pi Mu Alpha. Roman Catholic. Home: 6 Sharp Ln Camden Wyoming DE 19934-4526

PFIFFNER, JAMES PRICE, political science professor; b. Stevens Point, Wis., June 24, 1946; s. James Sturtevant and Alice Price Pfiffner; m. Debra Ann Jones, Aug. 11, 1979; children: Megan Cyr, Katherine Courtney, Morgan Meehan. BA in Polit. Sci., U. Wis., 1968, MA in Polit. Sci., 1972, PhD in Polit. Sci., 1975. Tchg. asst. U. Wis., Madison, 1971-74; rsch. fellow Brookings Inst., Washington, 1974-75; asst. prof. U. Calif., Riverside, 1975-78, Calif. State U., Fullerton, 1978-80, assoc. prof. polit. sci., 1980-84, John Brown Mason prof., 1983-84; spl. asst. to dir. Office Pers. Mgmt., Washington, 1980-81; assoc. prof. govt. and pub. policy George Mason U., Fairfax, Va., 1984-87, prof., 1987—, univ. prof., 2003—. Author: The President, the Budget, and Congress: Impoundment and the 1974 Budget Act, 1979, The Strategic Presidency: Hitting the Ground Running, 1988, 2d edit., 1996, The Modern Presidency, 1998, 5th edit., 2007, The Character Factor: How We Judge America's Presidents, 2004; editor: The President and Economic Policy, 1986, The Managerial Presidency, 1991, 2d edit., 1999, Governance and American Politics: Classic and Current Perspectives, 1995; co-editor: The Presidency in Transition, 1989, The Presidency and the Gulf War, 1993, Understanding the Presidency, 1997, 4th edit., 2007, The Future of Merit, 2000. With U.S. Army, 1969-70, Vietnam. Decorated Army Commendation medal for Valor, Vietnam/Cambodia, 1970; Brookings Instn. fellow, 1974-75, vis. scholar, 1983, 97; Nat. Assn. Sch. Pub. Affairs and Adminstrn. faculty fellow, 1980-81; S. T. Lee Professorial fellow Sch. for Advanced Study, U. London, 2007. Mem. Nat. Acad. Pub. Adminstrn., Cosmos Club. Office: George Mason U Sch Pub Policy 3C6 Fairfax VA 22030-4444 Office Phone: 703-993-1417. Business E-Mail: pfiffner@gmu.edu.

PFIFFNER, PATRICK MEEHAN, musician, educator; b. Stevens Point, Wis., Mar. 19, 1948; s. James Sturtevant and Alice Mary (Price) Pfiffner; m. Linda Sue Ridenour, Aug. 6, 1972; children: James Stanley, Jeffrey Allen. MusB, San Diego State U., 1976, MusM, 1977. Extra percussionist/timpanist San Diego Symphony, 1972—; percussionist Nederlander Orgn., San Diego, 1976—; resident drummer/percussionist/contractor Starlight Light Opera, San Diego, 1981—; extra percussionist/timpanist San Diego Opera, 1982—; prin. percussionist/timpanist San Diego Chamber Orch., 1985—; prof. music Point Loma Nazarene U., San Diego. Percussionist Sammy Davis, Bob Hope, George Burns, Mickey Rooney, Robert Goulet, Andre Bocelli, Johnny Mathis, Milton Berle, 1981—; dir. Grand Pacific Band, 1986—, Grossmont Coll. concert and jazz bands, 1979—86, Heartland Youth Orch., 1983—84. Author: The Ancestors of Patrick Meehan Pfiffner, 2002; contbr. articles to profl. jours.; performer: (CD) Those Hollywood Marches, with Lalo Shifrin, 1990, Russian CD, San Diego Chamber Orch., 1989, French CD, 1991, Berlioz: Symphonie Fantastique, San Diego Symphony Orch., Malcolm Arnold CD, 1992, Magnification CD, Rock Group Yes, 2001, nat. tours Broadway shows, including Beauty and the Beast, Hello Dolly, King and I, Ragtime, The Producers, Hairspray, others. Musician 2d class USN, 1967—71, USS Little Rock, Mediterranean Sea. Mem.: ASCAP, Percussive Arts Soc., Am. Fedn. Musicians Local 325. Avocations: long distance running, genealogy. Home: 13138 Beechtree St Lakeside CA 92040-3307 Office: Pt Loma Nazarene U 3900 Lomaland Dr San Diego CA 92106 Personal E-mail: patpfiffner@cox.net.

PFISTER, MARC, consumer products company executive, physician, researcher; s. Erwin and Gertrud Pfister; m. Susanna Pfister, Sept. 9, 1999; 1 child, Ayo Marc Lewis. BS, U. Berne, 1983, MD, 1988; diploma in Pub. Health, U. Basel, Switzerland, 1991. Cert. in strategic mktg. U. Berkeley, San Francisco, 2001. Clin. fellow Hosp. Interlaken, Berne, 1992—94; rsch. fellow U. Hosp. Berne, 1994, med. officer, clin. fellow, 1995—99; clin. rsch. post doctoral fellow U. Calif., San Francisco, 1999—2002; assoc. dir. Sanofi Aventis Pharm., Bridgewater, NJ, 2002—04; global head, exec. dir. Bristol-Myers-Squibb, Princeton, NJ, 2004—. Founder Modeling And Simulation Applications in Clin. Pharmatherapy Orgn., co-chair. Contbr. articles to profl. jours.; section editor JCP. Fellow: Am. Coll. Clin. Pharm.; mem.: Am. Soc. Nephrology (1st prize 1998), Am. Soc. Hypertension. Achievements include design of new methods for decision making; novel computer models for clinical research. Avocations: piano, jazz, classical music. Office: Bristol-Myers-Squibb Rsch Inst PO Box 4000 Rt 206 Princeton NJ 08540 Office Phone: 609-252-5322. Office Fax: 609-252-7822. Personal E-mail: mpfistersf@cs.com.

PFISTER, RAYMOND LAWRENCE, otolaryngologist; b. Newport, Ky., Apr. 13, 1925; s. Frederick Charles Pfister and Goldie Furnish; m. Barbara Schlenck, May 31, 1946; children: Debbie, Robyn, Holly, Michael. MD, U. Cin., 1948; postgrad., Harvard U., 1950. Asst. for otolaryngology Cin. Gen. Hosp., 1952—73; chief of staff Naples Cmty. Hosp., Fla., 1988—90, chmn. bd. dirs., 1990. Capt. USAF, 1952—54. Fellow: Am. Coll. Surgeons, Am. Bd. Head and Neck Surgery; mem.: Naples Yacht Club (commodore). Republican. Episcopalian. Avocations: sailing, horse racing. Home: 1325 7th St S Naples FL 34102 Personal E-mail: pfis13@aol.com.

PFLANZE, OTTO PAUL, history professor; b. Maryville, Tenn., Apr. 2, 1918; s. Otto Paul and Katrine (Mills) P.; m. Hertha Maria Haberlander, Feb. 20, 1951; children: Stephen, Charles, Katrine. BA, Maryville Coll., 1940; MA, Yale U., 1942, PhD, 1950. Historian Dept. State, 1948-49; instr. N.Y. U., 1950-51; asst. prof. U. Mass., 1952-58, U. Ill., 1958-61; prof. history U. Minn., 1961-76, Ind. U., 1977-86, emeritus, 1986; Stevenson Prof. of History Bard Coll., Annandale On Hudson, NY, 1987-92, emeritus, 1992. Chmn. Conf. Group Central European History, 1978; mem. exam. bd., grad. record exam Ednl. Testing Service, 1972-76; mem. Inst. Advanced Study, 1970-71, mem. Historisches Kolleg, Munich, 1980-81. Author: Bismarck and the Development of Germany: Vol. 1.-The Period of Unification, 1815-1871, 1963 (Biennal Book award Phi Alpha Theta), rev. edit., 1990, Vol. 2-The Period of Consolidation, 1871-1880, 1990, Vol. 3-The Period of Fortification, 1880-1898, 1990 (3 vols. collectively named Most Outstanding Book in History, Govt. & Polit. Sci. by Assn. Am. Pubs., 1991); translated as Bd. I-Bismarck, Der Reichsgründer, 1997, Bd II-Bismarck, Der Reichskanzler, 1998 (Einhard prize 1999); co-author: A History of the Western World: Modern Times, 3d edit, 1975; editor: Innenpolitische Probleme des Bismarck-Reiches, 1983; co-editor: Documents on German Foreign Policy, 1918-1945, Vols. I-III, 1949-50; editor Am. Hist. Rev., 1976-85; mem. editl. bd. Jour. Modern History, 1971-73, Central European History, 1972-74. Served to 1st lt. U.S. Army, 1942-46. Fulbright research fellow, 1955-57; fellow Am. Council Learned Socs., 1951-52; fellow Guggenheim Found., 1966-67; fellow Nat. Endowment Humanities, 1975-76; fellow Internat. Research and Exchanges Bd., 1976; fellow Thyssen Stiftung, Essen, 1986; recipient Humanities award McKnight Found., 1962. Mem. Am. Hist. Assn., German Studies Assn.

PFLUM, BARBARA ANN, retired allergist; b. Cin., Jan. 10, 1943; d. James Frederick and Betty Mae (Doherty) P.; m. Makram I. Gobrail, Oct. 20, 1973; children: Christina, James. BS, Coll. Mt. St. Vincent, 1967; MD, Georgetown U., 1971; MS, Coll. Mt. St. Joseph, 1993. Cons. Children's Med. Ctr., Dayton, Ohio, 1975—2006, dir. allergy clinic, 1983-89; dir. allergy divsn. Hopeland Splty. Clinic, Dayton, 1998-2000; ret., 2006. Fellow Am. Acad. Pediatrics, Am. Acad. Allergy and Immunology, Am. Coll. Allergy and Immunology; mem. Ohio Soc. Allergy and Immunology, Western Ohio Pediatric Soc. (pres. 1985-86) Roman Catholic. Home Phone: 937-293-2079. Personal E-mail: bapflum@hotmail.com.

PFLUM, WILLIAM JOHN, physician; b. NYC, July 30, 1924; s. Peter Arthur and Caroline (Schmidt) P.; m. Roseann Sarah Stubing, Oct. 13, 1956; children: Carol Jean, Jeanine, Suzanne, Denise, Peter. BS, Georgetown U., 1947; MD, Loyola U., Chgo., 1951. Diplomate Am. Bd. Allergy & Immunology. Intern St. Vincent's Hosp, NYC, 1951-52; resident in internal medicine NYU div. Goldwater Meml. Hosp., NYC, 1952-53; resident in allergy Inst. Allergy Roosevelt Hosp., NYC, 1956; attending internist allergy & immunology Overlook Hosp., Summit, NJ, 1958—. Assoc. attending Inst. Allergy, Immunology and Infectious Diseases, Roosevelt Hosp., N.Y.C., 1957-92; pvt. practice medicine, specializing in allergy and immunology, Summit, 1957-92; ret.; cons. in field. With USAAF, 1943—45, ETO. Decorated Purple Heart, air medal with two clusters, POW medal. Fellow Am. Acad. Allergy, Am. Coll. Allergists, Am. Assn. Clin. Immunology and Allergy; mem. Summit Med. Soc., Am. Assn. Clin. Immunology and Allergy (pres. Mid-Atlantic region 1975-76), Disabled Am. Vets., Mil. Order Purple Heart, Am. Ex-Prisoners of War, 8th Air Force Hist. Soc., World Marathon Runners Assn., Robert A. Cooke Allergy Alumni Assn. Achievements include completion of 26 consecutive Boston Marathons, 1971-1996 with Am. Med. Athletic Assn. Home: 1104 Presa Pl Lady Lake FL 32159 Home Phone: 352-205-8186.

PFOUTS, RALPH WILLIAM, economist, consultant; b. Atchison, Kans., Sept. 9, 1920; s. Ralph Ulysses and Alice (Oldham) P.; m. Jane Hoyer, Jan. 31, 1945 (dec. Nov. 1982); children: James William, Susan Jane Pfouts Portman, Thomas Robert (dec.), Elizabeth Ann Pfouts Klenowski; m. Lois Bateson, Dec. 21, 1984 (div.); m. Felicia Sprincenatu, 1993 (div.); m. June St. James, July 14, 2001 BA, U. Kans., 1942, MA, 1947; PhD, U. N.C., 1952. Rsch. asst., instr. econs. U. Kans., Lawrence, 1946—47; instr. U. N.C., Chapel Hill, 1947—50, lectr. econs., 1950—52, assoc. prof. econs., 1952—58, prof. econs., 1958—87; pvt. practice Chapel Hill, 1987—2005, Boise, Idaho, 2005—. Vis. prof. U. Leeds, 1983; vis. rsch. scholar Internat. Inst. for Applied Sys. Analysis, Laxenberg, Austria, 1983; prof. Ctrl. European U., Prague, 1991; chmn. grad. studies dept. econs. Sch. Bus. Adminstrn. U. N.C., Chapel Hill, 1957-62, chmn. dept. econs. Sch. Bus. Adminstrn., 1962-68 Author: Elementary Economics-A Mathematical Approach, 1972; editor: So. Econ. Jour, 1955-75; editor, contbr.: Techniques of Urban Economic Analysis, 1960, Essays in Economics and Econometrics, 1960; mem. editl. bd. Metroeconomica, 1961-80, Atlantic Econ. Jour, 1973—; contbr. articles to profl. jours Served as deck officer USNR, 1943-46 Social Sci. Rsch. Coun. fellow U. Cambridge, 1953-54; Ford Found. Faculty Rsch. fellow, 1962-63 Mem. AAAS, Am. Statis. Assn., N.C. Statis. Assn. (past pres.), Am. Econ. Assn., So. Econ. Assn. (past pres.), Atlantic Econ. Soc. (v.p. 1973-76, pres. 1977-78), Population Assn. Am., Econometric Soc., Math. Assn. Am., Phi Beta Kappa, Pi Sigma Alpha, Alpha Kappa Psi, Omicron Delta Epsilon Home and Office: 2308 W Norcrest Dr Boise ID 83705 Office Phone: 208-331-1234. Personal E-mail: rwpfouts@msn.com.

PFUND, RANDY (RANDELL PFUND), professional sports team executive; b. Oak Park, Ill., Dec. 29, 1951; Student, Wheaton Coll. Tchr., coach Glenbard South HS, Ill.; asst. coach, dir. booster orgn. Westmont Coll., Santa Barbara, Calif.; asst. coach LA Lakers, 1985—92, head coach, 1992—94; gen. mgr. Miami Heat, Fla., 1994—. Office: Miami Heat AmericanAirlines Arena 601 Biscayne Blvd Miami FL 33132 *

PHADKE, ARUN G., engineering educator; b. Gwalior, M.P., India, Aug. 27, 1938; came to U.S., 1959; s. Gajanan G. and Indira G. Phadke; m. Kusum K. Joglekar, Sept. 14, 1964; 1 child, Ajit A. BS, Agra U., India, 1955; B in Tech. with honors, Indian Inst. Tech., 1959; MS, Ill. Inst. Tech., 1961; PhD, U. Wis., 1964. Systems engr. Allis Chalmers, Milw., 1963-67; asst. prof. elec. engr. dept. U. Wis., Madison, 1967-69; cons. engr. Am. Elec. Power Svc. Corp., NYC, 1969-82; univ. disting. prof. Va. Poly Inst. & State U., Blacksburg, 1982—, 2000—. Cons. various electric utilities, equipment mfrs., 1980—. Co-author: Computer Relaying for Power Systems, 1988; patentee in field. Disting. Svc. citation, 1987, Centennial medal U. Wis., 1991. Fellow IEEE (chmn. power sys. relaying com., outstanding educator Power Engring. Soc. 1991, Millennium medal, Halperin award); mem. Edison Elec. Inst. (outstanding educator 1986), Conf. Internat. Grand Reseaux Electrique (chmn. working groups), Nat. Acad. Engring. Avocations: painting, tailoring. Office: Va Poly Inst & State U Elec Engring Dept 426 Whittemore Hall Blacksburg VA 24061-0111 E-mail: aphadke@vt.edu.

PHAIR, JOSEPH BASCHON, lawyer; b. NYC, Apr. 29, 1947; s. James Francis and Mary Elizabeth Phair; m. Bonnie Jean Hobbs, Sept. 04, 1971; children: Kelly I., Joseph B., Sean P. BA, U. San Francisco, 1970, JD, 1973. Bar: Calif., U.S. Dist. Ct. (no. dist.) Calif., U.S. Ct. Appeals (9th cir.). Assoc. Berry, Davis & McInerney, Oakland, Calif., 1974-76, Bronson, Bronson & McKinnon, San Francisco, 1976-79; staff atty. Varian Assocs., Inc., Palo Alto, Calif., 1979-83, corp. counsel, 1983-86, sr. corp. counsel, 1986-87, assoc. gen. counsel, 1987-90, v.p., gen. counsel, 1990-91, v.p., gen. counsel, sec., 1991-99; v.p. adminstrn., gen. counsel, sec. Varian Med. Sys., Inc., Palo Alto, Calif., 1999—2005. Mem. devel. bd. St. Vincent de Paul Devel. Coun., San Francisco, 1992—; mem. athletic devel. bd., U. San Francisco, 1999-, mem. athletic adv. bd., 2004-07. Mem. Bay Area Gen. Counsel, Silicon Valley Assn. Gen. Counsel, The Olympic Culb. Roman Catholic. Business E-Mail: joseph.phair@varian.com.

PHAIR, LIZ, vocalist; b. Cin., Apr. 17, 1967; d. John and Nancy Phair; m. Jim Staskouskas, 1995 (div. 2001) 1 child, James Nicholas Staskouskas Diploma, Oberlin Coll., 1990. Freelance artist, 1990; singer, songwriter, 1992—. Albums include: Exile in Guyville (name Album of Yr. Village Voice), 1993, Whip-Smart, 1994, Whitechocolatespaceegg, 1998, Liz Phair, 2003, Everything to Me, 2005; Actor (films) Cherish, 2002, Seeing Other People, 2004; (TV appearances) America Dreams, 2004 Named Best New Female Vocalist Rolling Stone Critic's Poll. Office: Matador Records 625 Broadway New York NY 10012-2611

PHALEN, ROBERT FRANKLYNN, environmental scientist; b. Fairview, Okla., Oct. 18, 1940; married, 1966; 2 children. B in Physics, San Diego State U., 1964, M in Physics, 1966; PhD in Biophysics, U. Rochester, 1971. Engring. aide advanced space systems dept. Gen. Dynamics/Astronautics, San Diego, 1962-63; asst. to radiation safety officer, lab. teaching asst. San Diego State U., 1964-66, instr. physics dept., 1966; mem. summer faculty biology dept. Rochester (N.Y.) Inst. Tech., 1970-72; rsch. assoc. aerosol physics dept. Lovelace Found. for Med. Edn. and Rsch., Albuquerque, 1972-74; from adj. asst. prof. to assoc. prof. in residence dept. community and environ. medicine U. Calif., Irvine, 1974-84, prof., dir. Air Pollution Health Effects Lab., 1985—, faculty Ctr. for Occupl. Environ. Health, 1985—. Editor Aerosol Sci. and Tech., mem. editl. bd., 2002-05; reviewer Am. Rev. Respiratory Disease, Applied Indsl. Hygiene, Bull. Math. Biology, Exptl. Lung Rsch., Jour. Toxicology and Environ. Health, Jour. Toxicology and Applied Pharmacology, Jour. Aerosol Sci., Sci., Toxicol. Scis.; reviewer, mem. editl. bd. Fundamental and Applied Toxicology, 1986-92, Inhalation Toxicology, 1988-04, Jour. Aerosol Medicine, 1988-98; mem. safety and occupl. health study sect. NIH, 1988-01, mem. spl. study sects., 1980, 81, chmn. spl. study sects., 1982-84, 87, 88, 92, mem. site visit teams, 1980-01; mem. expert panel on sulfur oxides EPA, mem. inhalation toxicology divsn. peer rev. panel, 1982, session chmn., 1983, participant workshop on non-oncogenic lung disease, 1984, mem. grants rsch. sci. rev. panel on health rsch., EPA advisor, 1985-88, 93-98, 03; mem. com. animal models testing interventions against aerosol agts. Nat. Acad. Sci., 2005-06; mem. task group on respiratory tract kinetic model Nat. Coun. Radiation Protection, 1978-97; mem. adv. panel on asbestos APHA, 1978; chmn. atmospheric sampling com. Am. Coun. Govtl. Indsl. Hygienists, 1982-92; chmn. NIOSH spl. study sect., 1983; panelist workshop NHLBI, 1982; sci. advisor Prentice Day Sch., 1986-04; dir. four internat. confs. on health effects of particulate air pollution; dir. internat. conf. on inhaled aerosol doses. Author: Inhalation Studies: Foundations and Techniques, 1984, The Particulate Air Pollution Controversy, 2002, (with others) Advances in Air Sampling, 1988, Concepts in Inhalation Toxicology, 1989, Deposition, Retention and Dosimetry of Inhaled Radioactive Substances, 1997; editor: Methods in Inhalation Toxicology, 1997; contbr. numerous articles to profl. jours. Am. Legion scholar. Fellow Acad. Toxicol. Scis.; mem. Am. Assn. Aerosol Rsch. (charter, chmn. ann. meeting 1985), Am. Conf. Govtl. Indsl. Hygienists, Am. Indsl. Hygiene Assn. (jour. reviewer, chmn. ann. conf. 1981, 85, 86), Brit. Occupl. Hygiene Soc., Internat. Soc. Aerosols in Medicine, So. Calif. Acad. Scis., Soc. for Aerosol Rsch., Health Physics Soc., Internat. Hormesis Soc. (charter), Soc. Toxicology, Career Achievement award 2000). Achievements include research in nasal, tracheobronchial and pulmonary transport of inhaled deposited particles and effects of pollutant exposure on transport kinetcs, laboratory simulation and characterization of airborne environmental pollutants, respiratory tract deposition and clearance models for inhaled particles, including species comparisons and body size effects, behavior of highly-concentrated aerosols with respect to deposition in the respiratory tract. Office: U Calif Air Pollution Health Effects Lab Cmty & Environ Medicine Irvine CA 92697-1825 Business E-Mail: rfphalen@uci.edu.

PHAM, CHRISTOPHER HOANG, electrical engineer, educator; naturalized; s. Le Pham and Nhung Thi Hoang; m. Vivian Trang Nguyen; children: Christopher Jr. HuyVu, Ariel ThuyTien, Elise CatTien. MSEE, San Jose State U., 1995, BSEE, 1994; postgrad., U. Calif., Davis, 1998—2000. Tech. support Hewlett Packard, Mountain View, Calif., 1987—88, NovTek Inc., San Jose, 1989—90; assoc. design engr. Ancot Corp., Menlo Park, Calif., 1990—92; devel. engr. and nuclear scientist Quantrads Sensors Corp., Santa Clara, Calif., 1993—94; sofware devel. & performance engr. Adaptec Inc., Milpitas, Calif., 1994—95; software devel. engr. Credence Systems Inc., Fremont, Calif., 1995—96; mem. of tech. staff SUN Microsystems Inc., Menlo Park, Calif., 1997—98; sr. software engr. Cisco Systems Inc., San Jose, Calif., 1998—2000, software mgr. I and II, 2000—01, engring. mgr. III, 2002—; engring. mgr. III, adj. prof. SJSU. Adj. prof. Evergreen Valley Coll., San Jose, 1998—2000, San Jose State U., 1995—. Contbr. articles to profl. jours. Pres.-elect VACETS, San Jose, 2006—, bd. dirs., 2006—. Recipient Asian Am. Engr. of the Yr. award, CIE-USA, 2005. Master: IEEE (sr.). Republican. Achievements include patents for technologies. Avocations: travel, language art. Home: SJSU EE Dept One Washington Sq San Jose CA 95192-0084 Office: Cisco Systems Inc 170 West Tasman Dr San Jose CA 95134 Home Phone: 408-332-1091; Office Phone: 408-525-8047. Personal E-mail: phamc@email.sjsu.edu. Business E-Mail: chpham@cisco.com.

PHAM, DAVID LAN, secondary school educator, writer; b. Binh Chuan, Thudaumot, Vietnam, Feb. 1, 1940; s. Khoai Van Pham and Chuc Thi Le; m. Tam Thi Nguyen, Nov. 22, 1965; children: Albert, Elizabeth, Wellington, An, Victoria. BEd, Faculty of Pedagogy, Saigon Vietnam, 1963; BA in History, Faculty of Letters, Saigon Vietnam, 1965; M in Libr. Sci, Faculty of Pedagogy, Saigon Vietnam, 1973. Tchr., chief libr. Ly Thuong Kiet Comprehensive H.S., Hoc Mon, Gia Dinh, Vietnam, 1963—75; social svcs. coord. Cath. Social Svcs. Refugee Resettlement Program, Bayou La Batre, Ala., 1987—96. Advisor Binh Duong Bo De Sch., 1968—75; advisor Binh Duong Confedn, Vietnamienne du Travail, 1968—75; vis. Thailand for Libr. Sci. Observation, 1973; advisor, founder Mutual Assistance Assn., Bayou La Batre, Ala., 1988—89. Columnist Thoi Bao Daily, Saigon, Vietnam, 1963—64, columnist Point South, Mobile, Ala., 1991—94; columnist: Binh Duong News, 2000— (award of apperciation, 2003); editor: (Bulletin) Bulletin Tin Viet, Dac San Que Huong, 1987—96; author: Two Hamlets in Nam Bo, 1999, Earthy Life, 2001, Vietnam History Dictionary, 2002, International Politico - Cultural Influences on Vietnam in the 20th Century, 2004. Gen. sec. Assn. Vietnamese Tchrs. of History and Geography, 1967—69, Viet. Libr. Assn, 1973—74; founder Tutorial Program, Bayou La Batre, Ala., 1992—96. Buddhist. Avocations: reading, travel, walking, writing, zen. Home: 1341 Leith Dr Toledo OH 43614 E-mail: davidlanpham@hotmail.com.

PHAM, KINH DINH, electrical engineer, executive, educator; came to U.S., 1974; s. Nhuong D. and Phuong T. (Tran) P.; m. Ngan-Lien T. Nguyen, May 27, 1985; children: Larissa, Galen. BS with honors, Portland State U., 1979; MSEE, U. Portland, 1982; postgrad., Portland State U., 1988-90. Registered profl. engr., Oreg., Calif., Ariz., Fla., Wash., Mass., Conn., RI, Tex., Colo. Elec. engr. Irvington-Moore, Tigard, Oreg., 1979-80, Elcon Assocs., Inc., Beaverton, Oreg., 1980-87, from sr. elec. engr., assoc. ptnr., 1987-96, v.p., 1996—, also bd. dirs. Adj. prof. Portland (Oreg.) C.C., 1982-2003, George Fox U., 2005—; mem. adv. bd. Mass Transit System Compatibility, 1994. Co-author: FE/EIT Exam: Electrical Engineering Review and Study Guide, 2000, Electrical Engineering Professional Engineer License Exam Review Handbook, 2001; pub.: Research and Education and Association, 2000; cons. tech. editor Rsch. and Edn. Assn., 1998—; contbr. articles to profl. jours. Recipient Cert. Appreciation, Am. Pub. Transit Assn. and Transit Industry, 1987. Sr. mem. IEEE, Industry Applications, Power Engring. and Vehicular Tech. Soc.; mem N.Y. Acad. Scis., Mass Transit Sys. Compatibility Adv. Bd, Eta Kappa Nu. Buddhist. Avocations: reading, travel, antiques, music. Office: Elcon Assocs Inc 12670 NW Barnes Rd Portland OR 97229-9001 Office Phone: 503-644-2490 x119. Personal E-mail: kinhpham@comcast.net. Business E-Mail: kpham@elconassoc.com.

PHAM, LEE, literature and language professor, consultant; s. Doanh Manh Pham and Hong Thi Phan; m. Vanlan Doan, Apr. 10, 1962; children: Mylinh, Julie, Linh Xuan, Joanne, Linh Trong, Vanlinh Pyle. BA, Nat. U. Saigon, Vietnam, 1961; diploma, U. Sydney, 1972; MEd, U. Houston, 1984, EdD, 1989. Tchr. English Chu Van An H.S., Saigon, Vietnam, 1961—75, Houston Ind. Sch. Dist., 1985—93; instr. US citizenship Inst. R & D, Houston, 2003—05; reader sat essay NCS Pearson Ednl. Measurement, Bloomington, Minn., 2005—. Cons. Radio Free Asia, Washington, DC, DC, 2003—; adj. faculty English as 2d lang. San Jacinto Coll. South Campus, Houston, 2004—05, Cy-Fair Coll. Fairbanks Ctr., Houston, 2006—. Author of poems; translator: (radio broadcasting program) News Reports & Interviews; art photography, Landscapes. Scholar, Australian Govt., 1971; Fulbright Grad. Study grantee, US Govt. Inst. Internat. Edn., 1975. Mem.: ATPE. Buddhism. Avocations: travel, photography, poetry. Home Phone: 281-286-9086.

PHAM, SI MAI, cardiothoracic surgeon; b. Ninh Hoa, Khanh Hoa, Vietnam, Oct. 6, 1955; arrived in US, 1975; s. Tro Pham and Nhung Thi Mai; m. Marie Christine Pham, Sept. 9, 1987; children: Benjamin Bartley, Anthony Ninh, Vivienne Elisabeth, Victoria B.H. Student, U. Saigon Sch. Pharmacy, Vietnam, 1973-75; BS in Chem. magna cum laude, Lebanon Valley Coll., Annville, Pa., 1979; MD, U. Pitts., 1983; D (hon.), U. Morón, 2002. Diplomate, surg. critical care Am. Bd. Surgery, Am. Bd. Thoracic Surgery. Intern, resident gen. surgery U. Pitts., 1983-86, rsch. fellow, cardiothoracic surgery, 1986-87, sr. and chief resident gen. surgery, 1987-89, resident cardiothoracic surgery, 1989-92, asst. prof. surgery, Sch. Medicine, 1992—98, dir. adult cardiac transplant program, Sch. Medicine, 1993-97, assoc. dir. heart transplant and artificial heart program, 1997-98, dir. cardiothoracic transplant rsch., 1997-98; dir. extracorporeal membrane oxygenation svc. Presbyn. U. Hosp., Pitts., 1993-98; dir. cardiopulmonary transplantation and artifical heart program, divsn. cardiothoracic surgery U. Miami Sch. Medicine, 1998—; assoc. prof. surgery U. Miami Sch. Medicine, 1998—2002, prof., 2002—. Prof. surgery U. Miami Sch. Medicine, 2002—; reviewer various med. jours. Contbr. articles to profl.

jours., chapters to books, scientific papers. Recipient Am. Chem. award, 1979, Radiology award U. Pitts., 1983, Dalsemer rsch. scholar award Am. Lung Assn., 1997-99; ACS Faculty fellowship award, 1994-96; grantee Children's Hosp. Pitts., 1987, Am. Heart Assn., 1987-89, 94-96, 96-99, Thoracic Surgery Found., 1996-97, 97-98, Am. Lung Assn., 1997—, Presbyn. U. Hosp., 1987-89, NIH, 1999—, Vietnamese Am. Med. Rsch. Found. sci. award, 2005. Fellow Am. Coll. Surgeons, Am. Heart Assoc. (cmty. bd. mem.); mem. Am. Soc. Artificial Internal Organs, Internat. Soc. Heart and Lung Transplantation, Soc. Critical Care Medicine, Am. Assn. Advancement of Sci., Am. Soc. Transplant Surgeons, Soc. Thoracic Surgeons, Am. Assn. Thoracic Surgery, Extracorporeal Life Support Organization, Assn. for Acad. Surgery, Phi Alpha Epsilon, Transplant Found. South Fla. (adv. bd. mem.). Avocations: reading, gardening. Home: 13250 SW 67th Ave Miami FL 33156-6929 Office: U Miami Sch Medicine Highland Profl bldg 1801 NW 9th Ave Ste 5th Fl Miami FL 33136 Office Phone: 305-355-5070. Business E-Mail: spham@med.miami.edu.

PHAN, CHARLES, chef; b. Da Lat, Vietnam, 1962; arrived in San Francisco, 1977; Grad., U. Calif. Berkeley. With family garment bus., Berkeley, Calif.; co-owner, exec. chef The Slanted Door, San Francisco, 1995—. Named Rising Star Chef, San Francisco Chronicle, 1997, Best Chef: Calif., James Beard Found., 2004. Office: The Slanted Door 1 Ferry Bldg #3 San Francisco CA 94111 Office Phone: 415-861-8032. Office Fax: 415-861-8329. *

PHAN, PHILLIP HIN CHOI, business educator, consultant; b. Singapore, Feb. 23, 1963; arrived in US, 1982; s. Bryan K. and Rosaline (Teo) Phan; m. Soo-Hoon Lee, Feb. 13, 1988. BBA with distinction, U. Hawaii, 1984; PhD, U. Wash., 1992. Cost contr. Westin Hotels & Resorts, Dallas and Singapore, 1984—88; assoc. prof. York U., Toronto, 1992—2000; cons. World Bank, 1998—2001, OECD, 1998—2000; Bruggeman prof. Rensselaer Poly. Inst., Troy, NY, 1998—; Bosch public policy fellow Am. Acad. Berlin, 2006—07. Asst. prof. CUNY, 1997; vis. prof. Nat. U. Singapore, 1998—2003, Singapore Mgmt. U., 2003—, Thammasat U., Thailand, 1997; Haniel Found. vis. prof. Humboldt U., Germany, 2004—05; ptnr. Core Competence Cons., Inc., Toronto, 1993—98; dir. Blood Trac Sys. Internat., Edmonton, 1996—98; mem. multi-nat. enterprises and investment com. Can. Coun. Internat. Bus., 1993—2000. Mem. editl. bd. Jour. Bus. Venturing, 1998—, Acad. Mgmt. Jour., 2002—, Jour. Fin. Stability, 2003—, Jour. Tech. Transfer, 2003—; co-editor: Asia Pacific Jour. Mgmt., 1999—2001. Named MBA Educator of the Yr., RPI, 2004; recipient Endowment Excellence award, Boeing Corp., 1992, Schulich Sch. Faculty Rsch. award, 1996; Rsch. grantee, Social Scis. and Humanities Rsch. Coun. Can., 1997, John Broadbent Rsch. Fund, 2000—, Kauffman Entrepeneur Found., 2002, Edna G. Benson fellow, 1992, Michael G. Foster fellow, 1992, Bosch Pub. Policy fellow, Am. Acad. in Berlin, 2006—07, George W. Tyler scholar, 1992. Mem.: Acad. Internat. Bus. (mem. senatorial com.), Inst. Mgmt. Scis., Acad. Mgmt. Republican. Avocations: reading, bicycling, tennis, scuba diving. Office: Lally Sch M&T 110 8th St Troy NY 12180-3522 Home: 250 S President St # 900 Baltimore MD 21202 Office Phone: 518-276-2319. E-mail: pphan@rpi.edu.

PHAN, RICHARD MAN, chemist; b. Saigon, Vietnam, July 30, 1970; came to U.S., 1993; s. Hong Van Phan and Tan Thi Nguyen; m. Ha Ngan Phung. BS, U. Utah, 1998, PhD, 2003. Project scientist Battelle, Dugway, Utah, 2003—04; sr. scientist Geomet Techs., Dugway, 2004—. NIH fellow, 2000. Mem. Golden Key Nat. Honor Soc. Office: Dugway Proving Ground PO Box 247 Dugway UT 84022 Home Phone: 435-833-9582; Office Phone: 435-831-7332. E-mail: phanmr@yahoo.com.

PHANG, MAY, music educator; MusB with honors, McGill U., Montreal, Can., 1992, MusM, 1994; D of Musical Arts, Temple U., 2004. Grad. asst. McGill U., 1992—94; instr. secondary piano Temple U., 1994—97; instr. piano Manayunk Cmty. Ctr. for the Arts, 1997, Settlement Music Sch., 1997; pianist, cello auditions Curtis Inst. Music, 1998; pianist Drexel U., 1999—2000; asst. prof. piano Carroll Coll., Wis., 2000—03; faculty piano Wis. Conservatory Music, Wis., 2001—03; asst. prof. piano DePauw U., Ind., 2003—. Guest artist Montreal Internat. Music Camp, Canada, 2002; faculty New Eng. Music Camp, 2000—01, Adult Chamber Music Workshop, Milw., 2002—03. Singer: DePauw Symphony Orch., MIMC Orch., Wis. Wind Orch., Ambler Symphony Orch., Phila. Orch., Singapore Symphony Orch., Temple U. Chamber Orch., Orch. Symphonique de Trois-Rivières, Banff Festival Chamber Players, Montreal Symphony Orch., McGill Symphony Orch., Temple U. Symphony Orch. Juror Piano Arts Wis. Competition, Wis., 2003; juror, clinician Carroll HS Piano Competition and Masterclass, 2003; juror Waukesha Symphony Concerto Competition, 2001, 2003, Polish Fest Chopin PIano Competition, Milw., 2001—02. Recipient 1st pl., Chopin Young Pianists Competition, Buffalo, 1990, Montreal Classical Music Festival, 1990—91, Concours d'orchestre Symphonique de Montréal, 1991, Can. Music Competition, 1991, Prix du Cercle du cent Associés, 1993, Concours d'orchestre Symphonique de Trois-Rivières, 1994, 2d pl., Pontoise Internat. Young Artists Competition, 1995; Clara Lichtenstein fellow, McGill U., 1992, Maureen Forrester-Montreal Musicians Guild scholar, 1991, Russel Conwell fellow, Temple U., 1994—96, Herbert A. Morse scholar, 1993. Mem.: Coll. Music Soc., Ind. Music Tchrs. Assn. (chair collaborative arts), Music Tchrs. Nat. Assn., Phi Kappa Lambda Soc. Office: Depauw Univ 313 S Locust St Greencastle IN 46135 Office Phone: 765-658-4403. Business E-Mail: mphang@depauw.edu.

PHARES, ALAIN JOSEPH, physicist, researcher; b. Beirut, Apr. 20, 1942; came to U.S., 1975, naturalized, 1982; s. Joseph Michel and Renee Cecile (Dommmar) P.; m. Claude Tawa, July 27, 1968; children— Caroline, Denis, Pascal. BS in Engring., St. Joseph U., 1964; Docteur-es-Sciences, U. Paris, 1971; PhD, Harvard U., 1973. Research fellow Nat. Council Sci. Research, Lebanon, 1973-75; assoc. prof. Lebanese U., 1973-75; research fellow Internat. Centre Theoretical Physics, Trieste, Italy, 1974, Harvard U., 1975-76; vis. asst. prof. U. Mont., 1976-77; asst. prof. physics Villanova U., Pa., 1977-79, assoc. prof. Pa., 1979-82, prof. Pa., 1982—, chmn. dept. Pa., 1981-91, dir. secondary sch. sci. Pa., 1981-94. Contbr. articles to profl. jours. Fellow, IAEA, 1974; grantee, NSF, 1991—98, PSC, 1991—, SDSC, 2002—03; French Govt. fellow, 1964—66. Mem. Am. Phys. Soc., Internat. Assn. Math. and Computers in Simulation, Sigma Xi Office: Villanova U Dept Physics Villanova PA 19085 Home Phone: 610-687-6358; Office Phone: 610-519-4889. Business E-Mail: alain.phares@villanova.edu.

PHARES, JAMES KENNETH, retired electronics engineer; b. Elkins, W.Va., Feb. 19, 1925; s. Dewey Paul and Cora Belle (Yokum) Phares; m. Lorna Jean Gibson, June 12, 1950; 1 child, Michael. BS in Electronics Engring., Davis and Elkins Coll., 1957. Comm. technician W.Va. State Police, Elkins, 1947—57; electronics engr. Goodyear Aerospace, Akron, Ohio, 1957—87; part-time instr. Goodyear Tech. Coll., Akron, 1967—97; ret., 1997. Author: Hunter-Killer Group WWII Anti-Submarine Warfare, 2006. With USN, 1943—46. Achievements include patents for money changing device; power control system. Avocations: amateur radio, astronomy, writing. Home: 610 Deborah Dr Akron OH 44319

PHARIS, RUTH MCCALISTER, retired bank executive; b. San Diego, Feb. 13, 1934; d. William L. and Mary E. (Beuk) McC.; m. E. Edwin Pharis, Mar. 14, 1953; children: Beth, Tracey, Todd. Grad., Del Mar Coll., Corpus Christi, Tex., 1979. Asst. cashier Parkdale State Bank, Corpus Christi, 1970-72, asst. v.p., 1972-76, v.p., 1976-79, Cullen Center Bank & Trust, Houston, 1979-81, sr. v.p., 1982-93; dir. human resources Scooter Store, Inc., New Braunfels, Tex., 2001—03. Instr. Am. Inst. Banking, 1977—79. Mem. adv. coun. Houston C.C. Mem. Human Resource Mgmt. Assn., Bank Adminstrn. Inst. (v.p. Coastal Bend chpt. 1979), Nat. Assn. Bank Women (ednl. chmn. Coastal Bend group), Am. Inst. Banking (rep.), Tex. Bankers Assn. (coun. 1983-84, instr.), Coastal Bend Personnel Soc. (v.p.), Houston Personnel Assn., New Braunfels (Tex.) Rep. Women (pres. 1999-2002), Corpus Christi C. of C. (mem. women's com. 1976-79), Order Eastern Star. Republican. Baptist. Home: 2779 Morning Star New Braunfels TX 78132-4722 Personal E-mail: rpharis@satx.rr.com.

PHELAN, DAVID C., lawyer; b. 1957; BA, Hamilton Coll., 1979; MA, Brown U., 1982; JD magna cum laude, Tulane U., 1985. Bar: NY 1987, Mass. 1995. Sr. ptnr. Wilmer Culter Pickering Hale and Dorr LLp, Boston; exec. v.p. and gen. counsel State Street Corp., Boston. Mem.: Mass. Bar Assn., NY Bar Assn. Office: State Street Corp 225 Franklin St Boston MA 02110

PHELAN, JOHN C., lawyer; b. NYC, Mar. 5, 1956; BA cum laude, Williams Coll., 1978; JD, Boston Univ., 1981. Bar: Mass. 1981, NY 1984. Ptnr., chmn. Real Estate Fin. practice group DLA Piper Rudnick Gray Cary, NYC. Faculty mem. NYU Real Estate Inst., 1989—93. Mem.: ABA, NY State Bar Assn. Office: DLA Piper Rudnick Gray Cary 1251 Ave of the Americas New York NY 10020-1104 Office Phone: 212-835-6140. Office Fax: 212-835-6001. Business E-Mail: john.phelan@dlapiper.com.

PHELAN, MARILYN ELIZABETH, law educator; b. Lubbock, Tex., July 12, 1938; m. Harold L. Phelan, Sept. 1, 1960; children: Pat, Scott, Kimberly. BA, Tex. Tech U., 1959, MBA, 1967, PhD, 1971; JD, U. Tex., 1972. Bar: Tex. 1961; CPA. Assoc. prof. Tex. Tech U., Lubbock, 1971-77, prof. law, 1977—, Paul Whitfield Horn prof. law, 1993—. Author: Law of Cultural Property, 1998, Nonprofit Enterprises--Corporations, Trusts, and Associations, 2000, Representing Tax Exempt Organizations, 2001, Museum Law., 2001, Nonprofit Organizations, 2003, 2007. Mem. ABA, AICPA, Nat. Conf. Commrs. Uniform State Laws, Am. Law Inst., State Bar Tex., Internat. Coun. Mus. (legal affairs com. mem.). Office: Tex Tech Univ Sch Law 18th & Hartford Sts Lubbock TX 79409 Home Phone: 806-783-8556; Office Phone: 806-742-3787 ext 251. Business E-Mail: marilyn.phelan@ttu.edu.

PHELAN, MARTHA ARMSTRONG, retired realtor; b. Shelby, Ohio, July 26, 1927; d. George Woodburn and Anna Louise (Wood) A.; m. Vincent Roche Phelan, Aug. 9, 1952 (dec. July 2000); children: Elizabeth Ann Riley, David Woodburn, Anne Louise. BA, Oberlin Coll., 1949; studied, Katherine Gibbs Secretarial Sch., 1950. Sec. U.S. Govt., Washington, 1950-52; adminstrv. officer Com. for Free Asia, NYC, 1952-53; legal sec. Atty. V.R. Phelan, Shelby, Ohio, 1975-79; realtor Mattox Realtors, Mansfield, Ohio, 1976-93, Hancock Agy., Shelby, Ohio, 1993—2006; ret., 2006. Precinct committeeman Rep. Orgn., Shelby, 1965—; poll worker Richland County Bd. Elections, Shelby, 1960—; mem. exec. com. Richland County Reps., Mansfield, 1965—; mem. Kingwood Ctr. Gardens; elder Presbyn. Ch., mem. choir, pres. Presbyn. Women, 2002—. Mem. Shelby Garden Club (pres. 1997-99), Shelby Women's Club (sec. 1990-01), Presyn. Choir 45 yrs., ch. session 7 yrs., Pres. Presbyn. Women 20 yrs. Republican. Presbyterian. Avocations: gardening, reading, creative arts and crafts, swimming, music. Home: 26 Woodland Rd Shelby OH 44875

PHELAN, ROBIN ERIC, lawyer; b. Steubenville, Ohio, Dec. 28, 1945; s. Edward John and Dorothy (Borkowski) P.; m. JoAnn Keach, June 27, 1970 (dec. May 18, 1994); children: Travis McCoy, Tiffany Marie, Trevor Monroe; m. Melinda Jo Ricketts, May 27, 1995; 1 child, Taezja Monet. BSBA, Ohio State U., 1967, JD, 1970. Bar: Tex. 1971, U.S. Ct. Appeals (5th cir.) 1981, U.S. Ct. Appeals (11th cir.) 1981, U.S. Ct. Appeals (6th cir.) 1986, U.S. Ct. Appeals (10th cir.) 1988, U.S. Supreme Ct. Ptnr. Haynes and Boone, Dallas, 1970—. Co-author: Bankruptcy Practice and Strategy, 1987, Cowans Bankruptcy Law and Practice, 1987, Annual Survey of Bankruptcy Law, 1988, Bankruptcy Litigation Manual; contbr. articles to profl. jours. Mem. ABA (chmn. insolvency and secured transactions com. internat. law sect.), Internat. Bar Assn., Internat. Insolvency Inst. (bd. dirs.), Am. Bankruptcy Inst. (dir., past pres.), Am. Coll. Bankruptcy, State Bar Tex. (chmn. bankruptcy law com. sect. bus. law 1989-91), Dallas Bar Assn. Roman Catholic. Avocation: athletics. Home: 4214 Woodfin Dr Dallas TX 75220-6416 Office Phone: 214-651-5612. Business E-Mail: robin.phelan@haynesboone.com.

PHELAN, THOMAS, clergyman, academic administrator, educator; b. Albany, NY, Apr. 11, 1925; s. Thomas William and Helen (Rausch) P. AB NY State Regents scholar 1942, President's medal 1945, Coll. Holy Cross, Worcester, Mass., 1945; S.T.L., Catholic U. Am., 1951; postgrad., Oxford U., Eng., 1958-59, 69-70. Ordained priest Roman Cath. Ch., 1951; pastor, tchr., adminstr. Diocese of Albany, 1951-58; resident Cath. chaplain Rensselaer Poly. Inst., Troy, NY, 1959-72, prof. history, 1972—, dean Sch. Humanities and Social Scis., 1972-95, inst. historian, inst. dean, sr. adviser to pres., 1995—. Chmn. architecture and bldg. commn. Diocese Albany, 1968-2003; cons. in field. Author: Hudson Mohawk Gateway, 1985, 2001, Achieving the Impossible, 1995; author monographs, articles, revs. in field. Treas. The Rensselaer Newman Found., 1962-2002; pres. Hudson-Mohawk Indsl. Gateway, 1971-84, bd. dirs. exec. com. 1984—; mem. WMHT Ednl. Telecomm. Bd., 1966-77, 84-90, chmn. 1973-77; chmn. Troy Hist. Dist. and Landmarks Rev. Commn., 1975-86, chmn. hist. adv. com., 1987-2003; v.p. Preservation League N.Y. State, 1979-82, mem. trustees coun., 1982-87, 89—, pres. 1987-89; sec. and bd. dirs. Ptnrs. for Sacred Places, 1989—; bd. dirs. Hall of History Found., 1983-87; trustee Troy Pub. Libr., 1992—. With USN, 1943-46. Recipient Paul J. Hallinan award Nat. Newman Chaplains Assn., 1967, Ann. award Albany Arts League, 1977, Disting. Cmty. Svc. award Rensselaer Poly. Inst., 1979, Edward Fox Demers medal Alumni Assn. Rensselaer Poly. Inst., 1986, Disting. Svc. award Hudson-Mohawk Consortium of Colls. and Univs., 1988; named Acad. Laureate of the SUNY Found. at Albany, 1988; Danforth Found. fellow, 1969-70; grantee Homeland Found., 1958-59, Dorothy Thomas Found., 1969-70. Fellow Soc. Arts, Religion and Contemporary Culture; mem. Ch. Soc. Coll. Work (dir., exec. com. 1970—), Am. Conf. Acad. Deans, Liturgical Conf., Soc. Indsl. Archaeology, Assn. Internat. pour l'Etudes des Religions Prehistoriques et Ethnologiques, Cath. Campus Ministry Assn., Cath. Art Assn., Assn. for Religion and the Intellectual Life (bd. dirs. 1987—), Soc. History of Tech. Clubs: Ft. Orange, Troy Country; Squadron A (N.Y.C.). Office: Rensselaer Poly Inst Troy NY 12180 Business E-Mail: phelan@rpl.edu. *Service and community building have motivated most of my business and personal actions. I received these values from my parents and from the church. I work to make positive contributions towards a world in which there is more justice and consequent hope of peace.*

PHELIZON, JEAN FRANCOIS, finance company executive; b. Paris, Apr. 28, 1946; s. Christian and Anne (Camuset) P.; m. Isabelle Delatour, July 3, 1971; children: Camille, Constance, Charlotte. MBA and MS, Paris U., 1970, PhD in Econ. Sci., 1975. Contr. Flat Glass div. St. Gobain, Paris, 1979; CFO St. Gobain Spain, Madrid, 1983-85; CFO paper wood div. St. Gobain, Paris, 1985-89; CEO, Lembacel, Lyon, France, 1988-89; CFO, Compagnie St. Gobain, Paris, 1989-2000, sr. v.p., 1998—; pres., CEO, Saint-Gobain Corp., 2000—; CEO, Certain Teed, 2000—04. Editor: Economica, 1970, 4th edit. 1998, Masson, 1981, 2d edit. 1984, Citic (China), 2003, 04, Praeger, 2006. Dir. French-Am. C. of C., Nat. Assn. Mfrs. Decorated chevalier Order of Merit, Legion of Honor. Home: 1315 Wrenfield Way Villanova PA 19085 Office: SG Corp PO Box 860 750 E Swedesford Rd Valley Forge PA 19482 E-mail: jfp@sgcna.com.

PHELPS, ARTHUR VAN RENSSELAER, physicist, consultant; b. Dover, NH, July 20, 1923; s. George Osborne and Helen (Ketchum) P.; m. Gertrude Kanzius, July 21, 1956 (dec. Jan. 3, 2003); children: Wayne Edward, Joan Susan. ScD in Physics, MIT, 1951. Cons. physicist rsch. labs. Westinghouse Elec. Corp., Pitts., 1951-70; sr. rsch. scientist Nat. Bur. Standards, Boulder, Colo., 1970-88; fellow Joint Inst. Lab. Astrophysics U. Colo., Boulder, 1970-88, adjoint fellow, 1988—, chmn., 1979-81. Chmn. Gordon Rsch. Conf., Plasma Chemistry, 1990. Recipient Silver Medal award Dept. Commerce, 1978. Fellow Am. Phys. Soc. (Will Allis prize 1990). Achievements include patent for Schulz-Phelps ionization gauge; research on electron and atomic collision processes involving low energy electrons, molecules, ions, metastable atoms and resonance radiation; on laser processes and modeling; on gaseous electronics. Office: U Colo JILA Campus Box 440 Boulder CO 80309-0440 Home: 1331 E Hecla Dr Unit 247 Louisville CO 80027-2341

PHELPS, ASHTON, JR., newspaper publisher; b. New Orleans, Nov. 4, 1945; s. Ashton Sr. and Jane Cary (George) Phelps; m. Suzanne Dupuy Phelps; children: Cary Clifton, Mary Louise, Sanders. BA, Yale U., 1967; JD, Tulane U., 1970. Trainee Times-Picayune Pub. Corp., New Orleans, 1970—71, asst. to pub., 1971—79, pres., pub., 1979—97, pub., 1997—. Chmn. Audit Com. of Associated Press, 1986—90, mem. nominating com., 1996—2002; bd. dirs. Bur. Govtl. Rsch., New Orleans, 1973—89, Xavier U. La., New Orleans, 1974—82, Internat. House, New Orleans, 1981—83, Coun. for Better La., 1982—85, Ochsner Found. Hosp., New Orleans, 1982—, Pub. Affairs Rsch. Coun., New Orleans, 1982—85, 2000—, La. Children's Mus., New Orleans, 1983—90, Yale Alumni Assn. La., 1985, Newspaper Advt. Bur. Future of Advt. Com., 1986—89, Met. Area Com., New Orleans, UNCF, 2004—. Mem.: La. Press Assn. (bd. dirs. 1984—93, v.p. 1989—90, pres. 1991—92), So. Newspaper Pubs. Assn. (bd. dirs. 1982—85, found. bd. dirs. 1982—83, pres. 1990—91). Avocation: tennis. Office: The Times-Picayune 3800 Howard Ave New Orleans LA 70125-1429

PHELPS, BARTON CHASE, architect, educator; b. Bklyn., June 27, 1946; s. Julian Orville and Elizabeth Willis (Faulk) P.; m. Karen Joy Simonson; 1 child, Charlotte Simonson Phelps. BA in Art with honors, Williams Coll., 1968; MArch, Yale U., 1973. Registered architect, Calif. With Colin St. John Wilson & Ptnrs., London, 1972-73, Frank O. Gehry and Assocs., Inc., Santa Monica, Calif., 1973-76, Charles Moore/Urban Innovations Group, LA, 1976-78; dir. architecture Urban Innovations Group, LA, 1980-84; prin. Barton Phelps & Assocs., LA, 1984—; asst. prof. architecture Rice U. Sch. of Architecture, Houston, 1977-79; asst. dean Grad. Sch. Architecture and Urban Planning, UCLA, 1980-83; prof. architecture Sch. Arts and Architecture UCLA, 1979—2001. Faculty mem. Nat. Endowment Arts, Mayors Inst. for City Design, 1990, 92, 98. Author, editor Architecture California, 1988-92, mem. editl. bd., 1998; editor: Views From the River, 1998; mem. editl. bd. Archtl. Record, 1998-2000. Mem. design review com. U. Calif., Santa Barbara, Calif., 2000—06; jury mem. US Presdl. Design Awards, 2000, Nat. AIA Honor Awards, 2003; mem. mayor's advisory panel Cultural Affairs Commn., LA, 2001—06; mem. architectural advisory bd. for oversees bldg. ops. US State Dept., 2005—06; bd. dirs. U. Elem. Sch. UCLA, 2000—06. Fellow Graham Found. for Advanced Studies in the Fine Arts, 1989, 96, Nat. Endowment for the Arts, 1990, 98. Mem. AIA (Coll. of Fellows, chair nat. com. on design, design excellence program USGSA, recipient design awards for L.A. Pub. Libr., Los Feliz, Woodland Hills, Will & Ariel Durant Branch, Cabrillo Marine Aquarium, Royce Hall at UCLA, Arroyo House, Kranz House, Sinquefield Ho., North Range Clark Libr. UCLA, L.A. Dept. Water and Power Ctrl. Dist. Hdqrs., North Hollywood Pump Sta., East Bldg. Seeds U. Elem. Sch., UCLA, Inst. Honor for Collaborative Design, Games XXIII Olympiad L.A. 1984), L.A. Conservancy (bd. dirs.). Democrat. Home: 10256 Lelia Ln Los Angeles CA 90077-3144 Office: Barton Phelps & Assocs 5514 Wilshire Blvd Los Angeles CA 90036-3829 Office Phone: 323-934-8615. Personal E-mail: bpala@aol.com. Business E-Mail: bphelps@bpala.com.

PHELPS, BONNIE NOREEN, retired secondary school educator; d. Norton Robert and Joyce Madelaine Phelps. B, U. Colo., 1966; M, Rivier Coll., 1974. Cert. tchr. NH, 1974. Sr. English tchr. Nashua HS North, NH, 1966—2007; ret., 2007. Running start faculty mem. NH Cmty. Tech. Coll., Claremont, 2000—; mem. faculty leadership com. High North Site Coun., 2005. Author: (poetry) The 14th (Illiand Lit. Presdl. Lit. award and hon. award, 1994), Hurricane Bonnie in POETRY'S ELITE Poetry.com, (poem) Sibilance (semifinalist N.Am. Open Poetry contest, 1993); poetry project: The Ripple Effect (performed by Nashua Symphony), 2006—07. Judge Yankee Pen Poetry Contest, Boston Writing Project in Nantucket, 2004; vol. Penguin Plunge Spl. Olympics, NH, 2005. Recipient Creative Comms. Poetic Achievement award, Nashua H.S. Nortn, 2005. Mem.: Am. Fedn. Tchrs., Nat. Coun. Tchrs. English (assoc.), Poetry Soc. N.H. (corr.; sec. of round robins 1987—88). Independent. Avocations: reading, writing, research on alternative health.

PHELPS, CHARLES ELLIOTT, economics professor, director; b. NYC, Apr. 20, 1943; s. McKinnie L. and Carolyn (McCleery) P.; m. Dale L. King, Sept. 2, 1967; children: Darin H., Teresa A. BA in Math., Pomona Coll., 1965; MBA in Hosp. Adminstrn., U. Chgo., 1968, PhD in Bus Economics, 1973. Rsch assoc., Ctr. for Health Adminstrn. Studies U. Chgo., 1969—71; rsch. economist, economics dept. RAND Corp., Santa Monica, Calif., 1971—79, dir., regulatory policies and institutions program, sr. staff economist, faculty mem., RAND Grad. Inst., 1979—84; prof. polit. sci. & econs. U. Rochester, NY, 1984—, dir., pub. policy analysis program NY, 1984—89, faculty mem., Rochester Ctr. for Economics Rsch. NY, 1984—, prof., cmty. and preventative medicine, Sch. Medicine and Dentistry NY, 1989—, chair, cmty. and preventative medicine, Sch. Medicine and Dentistry NY, 1989—94, provost NY, 1994—. Cons. JUREcon, Inc., LA, 1977-86; pvt. cons., Rochester, NY, 1986-; dir., pub. policy analysis program, U. Rochester, 1984-89, chair, health and soc. com., 1984-94, mem. academic computing exec. com., 1988-94, mem. exec. com. and informal exec. com., Sch. Medicine and Dentistry, 1989-94, chair, dept. cmty. and preventive medicine, 1989-94, chair, faculty adv. com. for presdl. search, 1993; mem. Nat. Adv. bd. Leonard Davis Inst. Health Economics, U. Pa., 1988-93; commr. Rochester Health Commn., 1995-2000; bd. trustee, Ctr. for Governmental Rsch., 1998-99; mem. Nat. Adv. Commn. for Digital Strategies, Libr. Congress, 2001-02; mem. report review com., NRC, 2002-. Co-editor Transforming Ideas: Selected Profiles in University of Rochester Research and Scholarship, 2000; Author Health Economics, 1st edit 1992, 2nd edit. 1997, 3rd edit., 2002; mem. editl. bd. Journal Health Economics, Journal Risk and Uncertainty, 1990-2000; founding assoc. editor, Economic Bulletin, 2000; contbr. articles to profl. jours. Mem. Greater Rochester Fights Back Against Drugs, 1990—91. Assoc. Nat. Bur. for Econ. Rsch.; mem. Inst. Medicine(mem. com. on med. technologies, 1985-86, com. for priority setting in med. tech., 1989-90, com. on Gulf War illnesses, 1999-2000), Am. Econ. Assn., Nat. Acad. Social Ins., Soc. for Med. Decision Making (trustee 1990-92), Assn. for Pub. Policy Analysis and Mgmt.(sec. 1980-91), Agy. for Health Care Policy and Rsch. (health care tech. study sect 1990-94). Avocations: photography, archery, astronomy, canoeing, woodworking. Office: Office of the Provost U Rochester 200 Wallis Hall Rochester NY 14627-0001 Home Phone: 585-381-2429; Office Phone: 585-275-5931. Office Fax: 585-461-1046. Business E-Mail: charles.phelps@rochester.edu.

PHELPS, CONNIE LEA, psychology and special education educator; b. Sioux City, Iowa, Aug. 4, 1953; d. Robert William and Carol Lea (Yaryan) Rice; m. Ronald Wayne Phelps, May 31, 1975. Diploma fgn. missions with honors Moody Bible Inst., 1977; BS in Bibl. Studies, Dallas Bible Coll.,

1981; MEd in Elem. Edn., East Tex. State U., 1982; EdD in Elem. Edn. U. Ark., 1987; MS in Spl. and Gifted Edn., Emporia State U., 2002. Tchr. Pleasant Wood Christian Sch., Dallas, 1979-82, Beverly Hills Christian Sch., Dallas, 1982-83; tchr., elem. coordinator Three Lakes Christian Sch., Troy, Mont., 1983-85; grad. asst. U. Ark., 1985-87; sub. tchr. Wichita Pub. Schs., 1999; gifted facilitator Truesdell Mid. Sch., 1999-2004, West HS, 2001-04, Kelly Elem. and Cleve. Traditional Magnet, 2001-03; asst. prof. psychology and spl. edn. Emporia State U., 2004-; Missionary appointee Alaska Bible Coll., Glennallen; with SEND Internat., 1987-90; advisor Educators Mus. Adv. Coun., Dallas, 1981-83; adj. faculty Baker U., Wichita, 1999-2004, Wichita State U., 2002-04; dir. gifted program Emporia State U., 2004-. Presenter in field. Contbr. articles to profl. jours. Active Dallas Mus. Fine Arts, 1980-82. Mem. AAUW, World Coun. for Gifted and Talented Children, Nat. Assn. for Gifted Children (counseling and guidance divsn. sec., curriculum studies divsn., computers and tech. divsn., rsch. divsn.), Assn. for the Edn. Gifted Underachieving Students, Supporting Emotional Needs of the Gifted, Mid-Am. Medieval Assn., Kans. Assn. for the Gifted, Talented and Creative (historian, bd. mem.), Tex. Assn. for the Gifted and Talented, Tex. State Tchrs. Assn., Poets Roundtable Ark., Mont. Assn. Tchrs. English and Lang. Arts, Phi Delta Kappa (chpt. mem. liaison, Flint Hills chpt. pres.). Home: 1737 Rural St Emporia KS 66801-5549 Home Phone: 620-340-0142; Office Phone: 620-341-5817. Office Fax: 620-341-5801.

PHELPS, DANIEL CHRISTOPHER, information scientist, researcher; b. Somerville, NJ, Oct. 7, 1969; s. Robert Scott Phelps and Eleanor Isabelle Jaeger, Ernest Jaeger (Stepfather); m. Gianna Lynne McDevitt, Sept. 2, 1992; children: Daniel Christopher Phelps, II, Katharine Amanda, John Robert. AS in Emergency Med. Svc., Tallahassee CC, 1990; BA in Spanish, Fla. State U., Tallahassee, 1997, MS in Info. Studies, 1998, PhD, 2005. Cert. paramedic Fla., 1989, respiratory therapist Fla., 1995. From tchg. asst. to mem. faculty Coll. Info. Fla. State U., Panama City, Fla., 1998—2002, mem. faculty Coll. Info., 2002—07; mem. tech. staff Software Engring. Inst., Carnegie Mellon U., Pitts., 2007—. V.p. Tallahassee Info. Sys. Security Assn., Tallahassee, 2003—04; rschr. Info. Tech. Process Inst., Eugene, Oreg., 2005—. Contbr. articles to profl. jours. Mem.: IEEE, Assn. Info. Sys., Assn. Computing Machinery. Office: Carnegie Mellon U Software Engring Inst 4500 5th Ave Pittsburgh PA 15213 Office Phone: 412-268-6617. Business E-Mail: dphelps@cert.org, dphelps@cmu.edu.

PHELPS, DAVID DWAIN, state agency administrator, former congressman; b. Eldorado, Ill., Oct. 26, 1947; m. Leslie Phelps; 4 children. BS, So. Ill. U. Mem. Ill. Ho. of Reps. from 118th dist., 1985-98; mem., 106th Congress from 19th Ill. dist., 1999—2003; mem. agr. com.; mem. small bus.; asst. sec. Ill. Dept. Transp., Springfield, Ill., 2003—. Mem. Transp. and Motor Vehicles, Appropriations I, Energy, Environ. and Natural Resources, Edn. Appropriations, Human Svcs., Elem. and Secondary Edn., Counties and Twp., Econ. Devel. Coms. Ill. Ho. of Reps., vice chmn. Coal Devel. and Mktg., Econ. and Urban Devel. Coms., chmn. Health Care Com. Democrat. Office: Ill Dept Transp 2300 S Dirksen Pkwy Rm 300 Springfield IL 62764

PHELPS, EDMUND STROTHER, economics professor; b. Evanston, Ill., July 26, 1933; s. Edmund Strother and Florence Esther (Stone) P.; m. Viviana Regina Montdor, Oct. 1, 1974. BA, Amherst Coll., 1955, DLitt (hon.), 1985; MA, Yale U., 1956, PhD, 1959. Economist Rand Corp., Santa Monica, Calif., 1959-60; asst. prof. Yale U., Cowles Found., 1960-62, assoc. prof., 1963-66; vis. assoc. prof. M.I.T., 1962-63; prof. econs. U. Pa., Phila., 1966-71, Columbia U., 1971-78, 79-82, McVickar prof. polit. economy, 1982—; scholar Russell Sage Found., 1993-94; prof. NYU, 1978-79. Fellow Ctr. for Advanced Study in Behavioral Scis., 1969-70; sr. advisor Brookings Inst., 1976—; econ. advisor European Bank for Reconstrn. and Devel., 1991-94; mem. econ. policy panel Observatoire Francais des Conjonctures Economiques, 1991—. Author: numerous books including Golden Rules of Economic Growth, 1966, Microeconomic Foundations of Employment and Inflation Theory, 1970, Economic Justice, 1973, Studies in Macroeconomic Theory, Vol. I, 1979, Vol. II, 1980, Political Economy, 1985, The Slump in Europe, 1988, Structural Slumps, 1994, Rewarding Work, 1997. Recipient Kenan Enterprise award, William R. Kenan Charitable Trust, 1996, Nobel prize in Economics, Nobel Found., 2006; fellow Social Sci. Rsch. Coun., 1966; Guggenheim fellow, 1978. Fellow: AAAS, Econometric Soc., Am. Econ. Assn. (disting. exec. com. 1976—78, v.p. 1983); mem.: Nat. Acad. Scis., Phi Beta Kappa. Home: 45 E 89th St New York NY 10128-1251 Office: Columbia Univ Dept Economics Rm 1004 New York NY 10027 *

PHELPS, JAMES FRANKLIN, retired county official; b. Mobile, Ala., May 29, 1940; s. James Carlton and Ela Kate (Hendrix) Phelps; m. Florence Annette Coley, June 30, 1972; children: Brant Michael, Kenneth Coley. Student, U. Ala., Mobile, 1962-63. Auditor Tax Collector's Office, Mobile, 1971-82, chief clk., 1983-86, chief adminstr., 1987-89; adminstr. collection divsn. Mobile County Revenue Commrs. Office, Mobile, 1989-96, adminstr., 1997—2002; ret., 2002. Republican. Baptist. Avocations: golf, woodworking, collecting and building die-cast model cars. Home: 9121 Howells Ferry Rd Semmes AL 36575-7207 E-mail: car57man@aol.com.

PHELPS, JUDSON HEWETT, health facility administrator, marketing professional; b. Evanston, Ill., Oct. 18, 1942; s. Sidney Norman and Mary Schuyler (Coons) Phelps; m. Barbara Ann Ray, Dec. 21, 1963; children: Wyeth Hewett, Christopher Ashley, Whitney Magee. BA, Williams Coll., 1964; MS, Springfield Coll., 1993. Lic. alchohol, drug counselor. Asst. brand mgr. Procter & Gamble Co., Cin., 1968—70; brand mgr. Memorex, Santa Clara, Calif., 1970—72; product mgr. Chesebrough Ponds Inc., Greenwich, Conn., 1972—76; v.p. mktg. L'Oreal subs. Cosmair Inc., NYC, 1976—77; v.p. sales Bio Products, Inc., Norwalk, Conn., 1978, exec. v.p., 1979, pres., 1980—86; corp. v.p. Ketchum & Co. parent co. Bio Products, Norwalk, 1982—86; mng. dir. Dameon Ptnrs. Inc., Wilton, Conn., 1987—88; pres. Theracom Corp., Rye, NY, 1988—89; v.p. Promotion Info. Bur., Norwalk, 1990; prin. Daniel Adams Co., Danbury, Conn., 1991—92; clin. coord., addictions therapist, counselor Ctr., Bridgeport, Conn., 1993—97; program dir. Gosnold-Thorne Counseling, Hyannis, 1998—. Adj. faculty Housatonic Cmty. Tech. Coll., Bridgeport, 1995—97. Family counselor Caregivers, Assn. Religious Communities, Danbury, Conn., 1975—79; leader, treas. Ridgefield Emmaus Teenage Christian Retreats, Conn., 1983—92; pres. Camp Dudley (YMCA) Alumni Assn., Westport, NY, 1974—79; chmn. Ridgefield Alcohol and Drug Use Commn., 1992—97. Lt. USNR, 1964—68. Home: 53 Gingerbread Ln Yarmouth Port MA 02675-1110 Office Phone: 508-375-6805.

PHELPS, MICHAEL, Olympic swimmer; b. Balt., June 30, 1985; Student, U. Mich. Mem. US Men's Olympic Swim Team, Sydney, 2000, Athens, 2004, Team Speedo, 2001—. Hon. bd. mem. Pathfinders for Autism. Named Swimmer of Yr., 2001, 2003, Am. Internat. Athlete of Yr., 2004, Sportsman of Yr., US Olympic Com., 2004; recipient Sullivan award, 2004. Achievements include holding World Record in 200m butterfly, 200m individual medley, 200m freestyle, 400m individual medley and 800m freestyle relay; holds American Records in 200m fly, 200m freestyle, 200m IM, 400m IM, 400m freestyle, 800m freestyle; only swimmer in history to set 5 world records in one international meet; became the youngest world record holder in modern history at age 15, Sydney Olympic games, 2000; being first male swimmer to break two world records in separate events in the same day; ten time world champion with 27 national titles; won gold medal, 200m IM, 400m IM, 100m butterfly, 200m butterfly, 4x200m free relay, 400m MR, Bronze medal, 200m freestyle, 4x100m free, Athens Olympic games, 2004; tied World Record with 8 medals in single Olympic games, Athens, 2004; won three gold medals at both the 2006 Pan Pacific Games and 2005 US Nationals; won five gold medals and one silver at the 2005 World Championships; won gold medals in 100m and 200m butterfly, 200m freestyle, 200m and 400m individual medley and 400m and 800m freestyle relay at the 2007 World Championships, becoming the only swimmer to win 7 in one world championship. Office: USA Swimming 1 Olympic Plaza Colorado Springs CO 80909 Mailing: PO Box 1734 Olney MD 20830-1734 *

PHELPS, MICHAEL EDWARD, biophysics professor; b. Cleve., Aug. 24, 1939; s. Earl E. and Regina Bridget (Hines) P.; m. Patricia Emory, May 15, 1969; children: Patrick, Kaitlin. BA in Chemistry and Math., Western Wash. State U., 1965; PhD in Chemistry, Washington U., St. Louis, 1970. Asst. prof. Washington U. Sch. Medicine and Engring., 1970-73, assoc. prof., 1973-75; assoc. prof. dept. radiology U. Pa., Phila., 1975-76; prof. radiological sciences UCLA, 1976—92, prof. biomathematics, 1980—84, chief divsn. biophysics, 1981—84, Jennifer Jones Simon prof., 1983—86, Norton Simon prof., 1996—, chief div. nuclear medicine, 1984—92, dir. Crump Inst. for Biol. Imaging, 1989—, chmn., dept. molecular and med. pharmacology, 1992—, chief, divsn. nuclear medicine, dept. molecular and med. pharmacology, 1992—2000; assoc. dir. UCLA/DOE Lab. Structural Biology and Molecular Medicine, 1984—2002; dir. UCLA/DOE Inst. Molecular Medicine, 2002—. Mem. study sect. NIH, Bethesda, Md., 1974-78. Author: Reconstruction Tomography in Diagnostic Radiology and Nuclear Medicine, 1977, Physics in Nuclear Medicine, 1980, 1987, 2002, Principles of Tracer Kinetics, 1983, PET: Molecular Imaging and its Biological Applications, 2004; contbr. articles to profl. jours. Recipient Von Hevesy Found. award, 1975,George Von Hevesy prize Von Hevesy Found., Zurich, 1978, 82, Oldendorf award, Soc. for Computerized Tomography and Neurological Imaging, 1981, S. Weir Mitchell award, Am. Acad. of Neuology, 1981, Ernest O. Lawrence award US Dept. Energy, 1984, Spec. award for Individual Distinction, Am. Nuclear Soc., 1984, Landauer Mem. award, Am. Assn. for Physicists in Medicine, 1988, Robert J. and Claire Pasarow Found. award, 1992, Disting. Scientists award, Inst. for Clin. PET, 1995, Enrico Fermi Presdl. award, 1999, Charles F. Kettering prize, GM Cancer Rsch. Found., 2001; holder Norton Simon endowed chair, 1983-; named Disting. Alumnus Western Wash. State U., 1980 Fellow Am. Heart Assn.; mem. ACP (Richard and Hinda Rosenthal award 1987), Inst. Medicine NAS (elected), Nat. Acad. Scis. (elected 1999), Soc. Nuclear Medicine (Paul Aebersold award 1983, Ted Block Mem. award, 1989), Internat. Soc. Cerebral Blood Flow and Metabolism (Cert. Excellence award 1979), NY Acad. Scis. (Sarah L. Poiley award 1984), Soc. Neuroscis. Roman Catholic. Business E-Mail: mphelps@mednet.ucla.edu.

PHELPS, ROBERT FREDERICK, JR., lawyer; b. Evanston, Ill., Aug. 20, 1956; s. Robert F. and Hanna (Kulej) P.; m. Joan Ann Brisky, Oct. 6, 1984; children: Jennifer Katherine, William Robert. BA, Trinity Coll., 1978; JD cum laude, U. Mich., 1981; LLM, NYU, 1987. Bar: Conn. 1981, U.S. Tax Ct. 1987. Atty. Cummings & Lockwood, Stamford, Conn., 1981—87, Day, Berry & Howard, Stamford, 1987—91; mng. dir. J.P. Morgan, NYC, 1991—. Cons. Conn. Safe Deposit Assn., 1983-87; mem. Fairfield County Estate Planning Coun., 1987-98; mem. coun. Conn. Tax and Estate Planning, 1990-92, Denver Estate Planning, Rocky Mountain Estate Planning, 2000—, Valley Estate Planners, Ariz., 2004—, Ctrl. Ariz. Estate Planning Coun., 2004— Contbr. articles to profl. jours. Bd. dirs. Greenwich Coun. on Youth and Drugs, Inc., 1985-89, Ctrl. City Opera House Assn., Denver, 2002—; elder Noroton Presbyn. Ch., Darien, Conn., 1990-93; mem. Rep. Town Meeting, Darien, 1992-95; res. elder Highland Park Presbyn. Ch., 1998-2002; mem. adv. bd. So. Meth. U. Cox Sch. Bus., 2000-02. Mem. ABA (real property and probate sect., tax sect., lectr. tax sect. fall meeting 2000), Conn. Bar Assn. (estates sect., tax and real property sects.), Middlesex Club, Denver Country Club, Phi Beta Kappa. Republican. Avocation: tennis. Home: 5495 Preserve Dr Greenwood Village CO 80121 Office: JP Morgan 370 17th St Ste 3200 Denver CO 80202 Office Phone: 303-607-7715. Business E-Mail: robert.phelps@jpmorgan.com.

PHEMISTER, ROBERT DAVID, veterinary medical educator; b. Framingham, Mass., July 15, 1936; s. Robert Irving and Georgia Nora Phemister; m. Ann Christine Lyon, June 14, 1960; children: Katherine, David, Susan. D.V.M., Cornell U., 1960; PhD, Colo. State U., Ft. Collins, 1967. Diplomate: Am. Coll. Vet. Pathologists. Research assoc. U. Calif., Davis, 1960-61, vis. rsch. pathologist, 1974-75; staff scientist Armed Forces Inst. Pathology, Washington, 1962-64; sect. leader to dir. collaborative radiol. health lab. Colo. State U., 1964-77; mem. faculty Coll. Vet. Medicine and Biomed. Scis., 1968-85, prof. vet. pathology, 1973-85, assoc. dean, 1976-77, assoc. dir. expt. sta., 1977-85, dean, 1977-85, interim acad. v.p. Univ., 1982, interim pres. Univ., 1983-84, spl. counselor to pres., 1984-85; vis. prof. Colo. State U., 1995-96; prof. vet. pathology Cornell U., 1985-99, dean and prof. emeritus, 1999—, dean Coll. Vet. Medicine, 1985-95. Cons. Miss. State U., 1977-81; commr. Colo. Advanced Tech. Inst., 1983-84; mem. governing bd. N.Y. Sea Grant Inst., 1985-95, vice chmn., 1990-92; mem. vet. medicine adv. com. FDA, 1984-88; mem. joint coun. on food and agrl. scis. USDA, 1988-92, mem. exec. com., 1989-92; chmn. Zweig Meml. Fund for Equine Rsch., 1985-95; mem. adv. panel for vet. medicine Pew Health Professions Commn., 1991-93. Author papers in field. Served to comdr. USPHS, 1960-68. Named Disting. Practitioner Nat. Acad. Practice, 1985, Honor Alumnus, Colo. State U., 1989; recipient Charles A. Lory award and Disting. Univ. Leadership award Colo. State U., 1984, Regional Health Adminstr.'s award, 1985. Mem. AVMA (coun. on edn. 1985-91, adv. bd. vet. specialities 1985-89), Assn. Am. Vet. Med. Colls. (pres. 1982-83), Colo. Vet. Med. Assn. (Disting. Svc. award 1985), N.Y. State Vet. Med. Soc. (Centennial award 1990), Sigma Xi, Phi Zeta, Phi Kappa Phi, Gamma Sigma Delta (Merit award for Adminstrn. 1995). Home: 3136 Rock Park Dr Fort Collins CO 80528

PHIBBS, CLIFFORD MATTHEW, surgeon, educator; b. Bemidji, Minn., Feb. 20, 1930; s. Clifford Matthew and Dorothy Jean (Wright) P.; m. Patricia Jean Palmer, June 27, 1953; children— Wayne Robert, Marc Stuart, Nancy Louise BS, Wash. State U., Pullman, 1952; MD, U. Wash., Seattle, 1955; MS, U. Minn., 1960. Diplomate Am. Bd. Surgery. Intern Ancker Hosp., St. Paul, 1955—56; resident in surgery U. Minn. Hosps., 1956—60; practice medicine specializing in surgery Oxboro Clinic, Mpls., 1962—, pres., 1985—; cons. to health risk mgmt. corps., 1994—. Mem. Children's Hosp. Ctr., Northwestern-Abbott Hosp., Fairview-Southdale Hosp., Fairview Ridges Hosp.; clin. asst. prof. U. Minn., Mpls., 1975-78, clin. assoc. prof. surgery, 1978—; med. dir. Minn. Protective Life Ins. Co. Contbr. articles to med. jours. Bd. dirs. Bloomington Bd. Edn., Minn., 1974—, treas., 1976, sec., 1977-78, chmn., 1981-83; mem. adv. com. jr. coll. study City of Bloomington, 1964-66, mem. cmty. facilities com., 1966-67, advisor youth study commn., 1966-68; vice chmn. bd. Hillcrest Meth. Ch., 1970-71; mem. Bloomington Adv. and Rsch. Coun., 1969-71; bd. dirs. Bloomington Symphony Orch., 1976—, Wash. State U. Found., trustee, 1990—; dir. bd. mgmt. Minnesota Valley YMCA, 1970-75; bd. govs. Mpls. Met. YMCA, 1970—; bd. dirs. Bloomington Heart-Health Found., 1989—, Martin Luther Manor, 1989; pres. Oxboro Clinics, 1985—; bd. dirs. Bloomington History Clock Tower Assn., 1990—; bd. dirs. Fairview Hosp. Clinic, 1994—, Bloomington Sister city Orgn., 1999-, Bloomington Cmty. Found., 1997-, Bloomington Health Adv. Bd., 2000-, MMA Minority and Cross-Cult. Affairs Com., 2000-, Com. on Cult. Competence Minnesota Med. Assn., 1986. Capt. MC, US Army, 1960-62. Mem. ACS, AMA (Physician Recognition awards 1969, 73, 76, 79, 82, 85, 88, 91, 94), Assn. Surg. Edn., Royal Soc. Medicine, Am. Coll. Sports Medicine, Minn. Med. Assn. (del. 1991-94), Minn. Surg. Soc., Mpls. Surg. Soc., Hennepin County Med. Soc., Pan-Pacific Surg. Assn., Jaycees, Bloomington C. of C. (chmn. bd. 1984, chmn. 1985-86), Bloomington Adv. Bd. health, Bloomington Sister City Bd., Bloomington Cmty. Found. (bd. dirs. 1996-). Home: 9613 Upton Rd Minneapolis MN 55431-2454 Office: 600 W 98th St Minneapolis MN 55420-4773 Personal E-mail: kphiibs@aol.com.

PHILANDER, SAMUEL GEORGE HARKER, oceanographer; b. Cape Town, South Africa, July 25, 1942; came to the U.S., 1963; s. Peter and Alice (Harker) P.; m. Hilda Teresa Storari, Sept. 16, 1967; 1 child, Rodrigo. BS, U. Cape Town, 1963; PhD, Harvard U., 1970. Sr. rsch. oceanographer GFDL/NOAA, Princeton, NJ, 1978-89; prof. dept. geoscis. Princeton U., 1990—, chmn., 1994—, Knox Taylor prof. geosciences. Author: El Niño, La Niña and the Southern Oscillation, 1990, Is The Temperature Rising? The Uncertain Science of Global Warming, 1998, Our Affair with El Niño, 2004. Recipient Gold medal U.S. Dept. Commerce, 1985. Fellow Am. Meteorol. Soc. (Sverdrup Gold medal 1985), Am. Geophys. Union, Am. Acad. Arts and Scis.; mem. NAS. Office Phone: 609-258-5683. Business E-Mail: gphlder@princeton.edu.

PHILBIN, ANN, art facility director; b. Boston, Mar. 21, 1952; d. Richard Moore and Ann Theresa (Muller) Philbin BA in art history, BFA in painting, U. NH, 1976; MA in mus. studies/arts adminstrn., NYU, 1982. Rschr. Frick Art Reference Libr., NYC, 1977-79; asst. to dir., program coord. Artists Space, NYC, 1979-80; asst. curatorial coord. The New Mus., NYC, 1980-81; curator Ian Woodner Family Collection, NYC, 1981-83; asst. dir. Grace Borgenicht Gallery, NYC, 1983-85; dir. Curt Marcus Gallery, NYC, 1985-88; account dir., dir. Art Against AIDS Livet Reichard Inc., NYC, 1988-90; dir. The Drawing Ctr., NYC, 1990—99, UCLA Hammer Museum, LA, 1999—. Bd. dirs. Elizabeth Streb, Ringside, NY, 1990, HIV Law Project, N.YC, 1993; founding mem. Women's Action Coalition, NYC, 1991. Recipient Best Monographic Mus. Show Nationally Award for exhibition Lee Bontecou: A Retrospective, Internat. Assn. Art Critics/USA, 2004. Address: UCLA Hammer Museum 10899 Wilshire Blvd at Westwood Blvd Los Angeles CA 90024

PHILBIN, JACK, communications executive; b. 1976; m. Lindsay Philbin; 1 child, Sierra. BA, Boston Coll.; student, Northwestern U. Kellogg Sch. Mgmgt. Co-founder & pres. Vibes Media, Chgo., 1998—. Named one of 40 Under 40, Crain's Chgo. Bus., 2006. Office: Vibes Media 19th Fl 205 W Wacker Dr Chicago IL 60606 Office Phone: 312-753-6330. Office Fax: 312-753-6332. E-mail: contact@vibes.com.

PHILBIN, PATRICK FRANCIS, lawyer, former federal agency administrator; b. 1967; BA summa cum laude, Yale U., 1989; JD magna cum laude, Harvard U., 1992; Diploma in Legal Studies, Cambridge U., 1995. Bar: Mass. 1995, DC 1997. Law clk. for Hon. Laurence H. Silberman US Ct. Appeals (DC Cir.), 1992—93; law clk. for Justice Clarence Thomas US Supreme Ct., 1993—94; assoc. Kirlmand & Ellis LLP, Washington, 1995—98, ptnr., 1998—2001, 2006—; dep. asst. atty. gen. Office Legal Counsel US Dept. Justice, Washington, 2001—03, assoc. dep. atty. gen., 2003—05. Spkr. in field. Recipient Exceptional Civilian Svc. Award, Office Sec. Def., 2002, Atty. Gen.'s Award for Excellence in Furthering the Interests of US Nat. Security, US Dept. Justice, 2004. Office: Kirkland & Ellis LLP 655 Fifteenth St, NW Washington DC 20005-5793 Office Phone: 202-879-5030. Office Fax: 202-879-5200. E-mail: pphilbin@kirkland.com. *

PHILBIN, REGIS (FRANCIS XAVIER), television personality; b. NYC, Aug. 25, 1931; s. Frank and Florence P.; m. Kay Faylan, 1957 (div. 1968); children: Amy, Danny; m. Joy Senese, Mar. 1, 1970; children: Joanna, Jennifer. Student, U. Notre Dame. Hollywood stagehand, NBC page The Tonight Show; truck driver, newswriter, sportscaster. Co-host The Joey Bishop Show, 1967-69, host Sta. KABC A.M. LA., 1975-83, Sta. WABC TV Morning Show, 1983-88 (with Kathy Lee Gifford in 1985); co-host (syndicated show) Live! With Regis and Kathie Lee, 1988-2000, Live! With Regis and Kelly, 2001—, exec. prodr., 2001—, Miss Am. Pageant, 1991, 92, 95; host, Who Wants to be a Millionaire, 1999-2002; co-author: Cooking with Regis and Kathie Lee, 1993, Entertaining with Regis and Kathie Lee, 1994; host (TV show) America's Got Talent, 2006-; author: I'm Only One Man, 1995, Who Wants to Be Me?, 2003; TV appearances include The Danny Thomas Hour, 1968, Get Smart, 1968, The Big Valley, 1968, Rowan & Martin's Laugh-In, 1968, Love, American Style, 1969, 71, That Girl, 1970, The Silent Force, 1970, The Jimmy Stewart Show, 1972, The Neighbors, 1975, The San Pedro Beach Bums, 1977, CHiPs, 1978, Lucan, 1978, Fantasy Island, 1979, 83, Ryan's Hope, 1987, 1988, Mad About You, 1993, Seinfeld, 1994, The Larry Sanders Show, 1994, The Cosby Mysteries, 1995, Hope & Gloria, 1995, The Fresh Prince of Bel-Air, 1996, Life's Work, 1996, Spin City, 1997, 99, 2000, Diagnosis Murder, 1998, Caroline in the City, 1998, The Simpsons, 1998, Becker, 2001, One Life to Live, 2002, Hope and Faith, 2003, 2005, 2006 The Apprentice, 2004, Extreme Makeover: Home Edition, 2004, Less Than Perfect, 2005; TV Film appearances SST:Death Flight, 1977, Mad Bull, 1977, Mirror, Mirror, 1979, Perry Mason: The Case of the Telltale Talk Show Host, 1993; Film appearances include The Bad News Bears Go To Japan, 1978, The Emperor's New Clothes, 1993, The Man Who Loved Women, 1983, Night and the City, 1992, Dudley Do-Right, 1999, Little Nicky, 2000, People I Know, 2002, Cheaper by the Dozen, 2003, The Breakup Artist, 2004, Miss Congeniality 2: Armed and Fabulous, 2005; (voice roles) Happily Ever After: Fairy Tales for Every Child, 1995, Mother Goose: A Rappin' and Rhymin' Special, 1997, Hercules, 1998, Family Guy, 2002, Pinocchio, 2002, Lilo & Stitch: The Series, 2004; albums It's Time For Regis!, 1968, When You're Smiling, 2004; host Walt Disney World Very Merry Christmas Parade, 1991, 1992, Walt Disney World Christmas Day Parade, 2002-05, Walt Disney World Happy Easter Parade, 1992, New Year's Rockin' Eve 2005, Fox New Year's Eve Live 2006. Named Personality of Yr., TV Guide, 2001; named one of 100 Most Powerful Celebrities, Forbes.com, 2007; named to Guinness Book of World Records for the most hours on camera, 2004, Acad. TV Arts & Sciences Hall of Fame, 2006, Broadcasting Hall of Fame, Nat. Assn. Broadcasters, 2006; recipient Four Daytime Emmy awards, Broadcasting & Cable Lifetime Achievement award, Crystal Apple award for contributions to the NY TV industry, Mayor Rudolph Giuliani, Star on Hollywood Walk of Fame, 2003. Achievements include setting Guinness World Record in 2004 for Most Hours on Camera (15,188 hours). Office: Regis & Kelly 7 Lincoln Sq New York NY 10023-5900

PHILIP, A. G. DAVIS, astronomer, educator, editor; b. NYC, Jan. 9, 1929; s. Van Ness and Lillian (Davis) P.; m. Kristina Drobavicius, Apr. 25, 1964; 1 dau., Kristina Elizabeth Elanor. BS, Union Coll., 1951; MS, N.Mex. State U., 1959; PhD, Case Inst. Tech., 1964. Tchr. physics, math. and chemistry Brooks Sch., 1954-59; instr. Case Inst. Tech., 1962-64; asst. prof. astronomy U. N.Mex., 1964-66, SUNY-Albany, 1966-67, assoc. prof., 1967-76, mem. exec. com. Arts and Scis. Coun., 1975-76; rsch. prof. astronomy Union Coll., Schenectady, NY, 1976—, astronomer Dudley Obs., 1967-81, Frank L. Fullam chair astronomy, 1980-81, editor Dudley Obs. Reports, 1977-81; astronomer Van Vleck Obs. Wesleyan U., 1982-94; editor contbns. VVObs., 1982-94; pres. Inst. for Space Observation, 1986—. Guest Acad. Scis. Lithuania, 1973, 76, 79, 86, 03, Stellar Data Ctr., Strasbourg, France, 1978, 79, 80, 82, 85, 86; vis. astronomer Moletai Obs., 1988, 94, 99, 00, Vatican Advanced Tech. Telescope, 1996—, CASLEO, Argentina, 2000—; bd. dirs., sec.-treas. N.Y. Astron. Corp., 1969-01; pres., treas. L. Davis Press, Inc., 1982—; trustee, chmn. Grants award com. Fund Astrophys. Rsch., 1985—; dir. Shapley Vis. Lectureships Program, 1994-05; rsch. bd. advisors Am. Biog. Inst., 1996-. Exhibited: 2d Ann. Photography Regional, Albany, 1980; author: (with M. Cullen and R.E. White) UBV Color - Magnitude Diagrams of Galactic Globular Clusters, 1976; (with A. Robucci, M. Frame, K.W. Philip) Mm, Fractal Series, Vol. 1,

Midgets on the Spike, 1991; editor: The Evolution of Population II Stars, 1972, (with D.S. Hayes) Multicolor Photometry and the Theoretical HR Diagram, 1975, (with M.F. Mc Carthy) Galactic Structure in the Direction of the Galactic Polar Caps, 1977, (with D. H. DeVorkin In Memory of Henry Norris Russell, 1977, (with Hayes) The HR Diagram, 1978, Problems in Calibration of Multicolor Systems, 1979, (with M.F. McCarthy and G.V. Coyne) Spectral Classification of the Future, 1979, X-Ray Symposium, 1981, (with Hayes) Astrophysical Parameters for Globular Clusters, 1981, (with A.R. Upgren) The Nearby Stars and the Stellar Luminosity Function, 1983, (with Hayes and L. Pasinetti) Calibration of Fundamental Stellar Quantities, 1985, (with D.W. Latham) Stellar Radial Velocities, Horizontal-Branch and UV-Bright Stars, 1985, Spectroscopic and Photometric Classification of Population II Stars, 1986, (with J. Grindley) IAU Symposium No. 126, Globular Cluster Systems in Galaxies, 1987, (with Hayes and Liebert) IAU Colloquium No. 95, The Second Conference on Faint Blue Stars, (with Hayes and Adelman) New Directions in Spectrophotometry, 1988, Calibration of Stellar Ages, 1988, (with A.R. Upgren) Star Catalogues; A Centennial Tribute to A.N. Vyssotsky, 1989, (with P. Lu) The Gravitational Force Perpendicular to the Galactic Plane, 1989, (with D.S. Hayes and S.J. Adelman) CCDs in Astronomy. II. Precision Photometry: Astrophysics of the Galaxy, 1991, (with Robucci, Frame and Philip K.) Midgets on the Spike, vol. I, 1991, (with A.R. Upgren) Objective-Prism and Other Surveys, 1991, N.Y. State Astronomy, 1992, (with B. Hauck and A.R. Upgren) Workshop on Databases for Galactic Structure, 1993, (with K.A. Janes and A.R. Upgren) IAU Symposium No. 167, New Developments in Array Technology and Applications, 1995, (with V. Straizys) Photometric Systems and Standard Stars, 1996, 30 Years of Astronomy at Van Vleck Observatory, 1997, (with Peter Boyce) Electronic Publishing: Now and the Future, 1997, (with J. Liebert and R. Saffer) The Third Conference on Faint Blue Stars, 1997, (with W. van Alterna and A. Upgren) Anni Mirabiles: A Symposium Celebrating the 90th Birthday of Dorrit Hottleit, 1999, The Kth Reunion, 2000, (with R.A. Koopmann) The Starry Universe: The Cecilia Payne-Gaposchkin Centenary, 2001, (with R.O. Gray and C. Corbally) The Garrison Festschrift, 2003, (with J. Sudzius and V. Straizys) Stellar Photometry: Past, Present and Future, 2003, (with William van Altena and Rebecca Koopmann) The Hottleit Centennial: A Year of Celebration, 2006; mem. editl. bd., 1994—, co-editor, 1998—, Baltic Astronomy, Astrometric and Photometric Group, Wesleyan U., 1997-03; lectr. tours (with K.W. Philip) An Introduction to the Mandelbrot Set, 1988-91; contbr. chpts. to books, articles to profl. jours.; worked with Dr. Irving Langmuir on "The Pathology of Science", 1950—. Served with AUS, 1951-53. Yale U. vis. fellow, 1976; rsch. grantee Rsch. Corp., NSF, NASA, Nat. Rsch. Lab., NAS, Am. Astron. Soc. Fellow AAAS, Royal Astron. Soc., Am. Phys. Soc.; mem. Am. Astron. Soc. (Harlow Shapley lectr. 1974—, auditor 1977, 79-85), Am. Math. Soc., Can. Astron. Soc., Internat. Astron. Union (chmn., sec. various coms. and commns., pres. commn. 30 1982-85, chmn. working group on spectroscopic and photometric data 1985-94, chmn. sci. organizing com. symposium # 167, mem. working group on pub. 2000-), N.Y. Acad. Scis., Astron. Soc. Pacific, Astron. Soc. N.Y. (sec.-treas. 1969-2001, editor newsletter 1974-2001), Capital Computer Club (bd. dirs. 1990—, v.p. 1993—), H. Rider Haggard Soc., Sigma Xi. Achievements include being 1st U.S. observer Soviet 6M telescope, 1980. Home: 1125 Oxford Pl Schenectady NY 12308-2913 Office: Union Coll Physics Dept Schenectady NY 12308

PHILIP, PETER VAN NESS, former trust company executive; b. NYC, Feb. 23, 1925; s. Van Ness and Lilian (Davis) P.; m. Sabina FitzGibbon, May 3, 1952; children: William Van Ness, Thomas Winslow, Peter Sandys. AB, Yale U., 1945; MBA, NYU, 1950. With Price, Waterhouse & Co., NYC, 1947-52; W.H. Morton & Co., Inc., NYC, 1952-73; pres., CEO Equitable Securities, Morton & Co., Inc., 1970-73; sr. v.p., dir. White Weld & Co., Inc., NYC, 1974-76; v.p. Morgan Guaranty Trust Co., NYC, 1977-88, ret. With 86th inf. div. AUS, 1943-45. Decorated Purple Heart, Bronze Star. Mem.: Racquet and Tennis (N.Y.C.); Links; Yale (N.Y.C.), Downtown Assn. (N.Y.C.), Bond (N.Y.C.); Bedford ((N.Y.); Golf and Tennis; Ekwanok (Manchester, Vt.). Home: Box 395 740 Guard Hill Rd Bedford NY 10506-1042

PHILIPP, KARLA ANN, music educator, conductor, musician; b. Milw., Sept. 12, 1955; d. John William and Catherine Ann Philipp. MusB, U. Ariz., 1977; MusM, Memphis State U., 1979. Tchr. itinerant strings Memphis City Schs., 1979—; condr. youth string ensemble and youth sinfonia Memphis Youth Symphony, 1997—. Sect. bass player Tucson Symphony Orch., 1977—78, Memphis Symphony Orch., 1979—89; prin. bass Jackson Symphony Orch., 1989—; note reading tchr., condr. Am. Suzuki Inst., Stevens Point, Wis., 1993—2005; dir. orch. Intermountain Suzuki String Inst., Salt Lake City, 2001—04; notereading tchr., dir. orch. Suzuki Inst. U. Memphis, 2005—, dir. orch. Summer String Camp, 2006—; presenter in field. Mem. Integrity, Memphis, 2003—. Recipient award for tchr. excellence, Rotary Club, Memphis, 1998, Outstanding Tchr. award, Tenn. Gov.'s Sch. for Arts, 1991, 1994, 1995; grantee, Rotary Club, Memphi, 1991, 1997; Haldeman scholar, U. Ariz. Sch. Music, 1974—78. Mem.: Internat. Soc. Bassists, Suzuki Assn. of Ams., West Tenn. Sch. Band and Orch. Assn., Tenn. Music Educators Assn., Music Educators Nat. Conf., Am. String Tchrs. Assn. (west Tenn v.p. 1993—95), Am. Fedn. Musicians Local 71. Episcopalian. Avocations: reading, travel. Office: Ridgeway High Sch 2009 Ridgeway Rd Memphis TN 38119 Home Phone: 901-761-7542; Office Phone: 901-416-8820. Personal E-mail: philippbass@aol.com.

PHILIPP, PETER ERIC, investment company executive, educator; s. Alexander and Beate Philipp. MBA, U. Calif., Berkeley, 1995. CFA CFA Inst., 1994. Asst. v.p. Wells Fargo & Co., San Francisco, 1989—95; mgmt. cons. Accenture, San Francisco, 1995—99; mng. dir. IncuBay, LLC, San Francisco, 1999—2001; founder Achex, Inc., San Francisco, 1999—2001; wealth mgr. Cambridge Investment Rsch., Inc., San Francisco, 2001—. Educator U.Calif. Berkeley Ext., 2006—. Bd. mem. Project Open Hand, San Francisco, 2007. Office: Cambridge Investment Research Inc 155 Montgomery St Ste 1001 San Francisco CA 94104 Office Phone: 415-677-9300.

PHILIPPON, MARC JOSEPH, orthopaedic surgeon; b. Quebec City, Can., May 9, 1965; arrived in U.S., 1990; s. Pontien Aderville and Micheline (Lortie) P.; m. Senenne Catalina Reid, Mar. 25, 1995; children: Michèle, Marc-Christophe, Mia-Véronique. BA with honors, Fla. Atlantic U., 1987; MD, McMaster U., Hamilton, Ont., Can., 1990. Lic. physician, Fla., Pa.; diplomate Am. Bd. Orthopaedic Surgery. Orthopaedic surgeon Holy Cross Hosp., Ft. Lauderdale, Fla., 1995—, chief orthopaedic surgery, 2000-01; chief orthopaedic surgeon humanitarian mission to Ukraine Kiev Orthopaedic Inst., 1997; orthopaedic surgeon Broward Gen. Hosp., Ft. Lauderdale, 1998—2002; dir. sports medicine/hip disorders dept. orthopaedic surgery U. Pitts. Med. Ctr.; dir. fellowship program U. Pitts. Med. Ctr. for Sports Medicine, dir. hip arthroscopy fellowship, dir. golf medicine program, dir. Fla. site. Cons. Howmedica Inc., Rutherford, N.J., 1996-97, Smith & Nephew Inc., Memphis, 1998-99; clin. adv. bd. Oratec Interventions, Inc., Menlo Park, Calif., 1998-2002; cons. Zimmer (Bristol-Myers Squibb); lectr. in field. Contbr. chapters to books, articles to profl. jours. Bd. dirs. Svc. Agy. for Sr. Citizens, Ft. Lauderdale, 1996-2000. Farquharson scholar Can. Med. Rsch. Coun., 1989. Fellow Internat. Coll. Surgeons, Am. Acad. Orthopaedic Surgeons; mem. AMA, Fla. Med. Assn., Phi Kappa Phi. Roman Catholic. Achievements include invention of orthopaedic surgery instrument and devices. Avocations: skiing, tennis, sailing, hockey, soccer. Office: 181 W Meadow Dr Ste 400 Vail CO 81657 Office Phone: 970-476-1100.

PHILIPPON, THOMAS, finance educator; b. Vincennes, May 17, 1974; s. Jean-Claude and Christiane Philippon; m. Marie Rutkoski. PhD in Econs., MIT, Cambridge, Mass., 2003. Asst. prof. of fin. NYU, NYC, 2003—. Author: (book) Le Capitalisme d'Heritiers. Office Phone: 212-998-0490.

PHILIPPS, EDWARD WILLIAM, former banker, real estate appraiser; b. NYC, Dec. 19, 1938; s. Edward Charles and Eleanor Elizabeth (Eisenger) P.; m. Diane Rose DiCuffa, June 12, 1960; children: James Michael, Robert Christopher. Appraiser Dry Dock Savs., NYC, 1956-70, Nat. Bank of West, White Plains, NY, 1970-72, Aires Real Estate, Yonkers, NY, 1972-74; sr. v.p. Am. Savs. Bank (merger Empire Savs. Bank), NYC, 1974-92; self employed real estate appraiser Yonkers, 1992-93; sr. v.p., chief lending officer LaJolla (Conn.) Bank, 1993-99; cons., 1999—. Mem. mortgage com. Cmty. Preservation Corp., N.Y.C., 1990-92. Mem. Am. Inst. Real Estate Appraisers, Homebuilders Assn. Fairfield County (bd. dirs.). Avocations: wood working, fishing. Home and Office: 261 Kimball Ave Yonkers NY 10704-3030 E-mail: ephilipp@optonline.net.

PHILIPS, LAURA ALMA, former pharmaceutical executive; b. San Francisco, Sept. 4, 1957; d. Irving and Mary Elizabeth (Gray) P.; m. Mark Maroncelli, Jule 29, 1979 (div. 1989); m. John Arnold Elliott, May 5, 1994. BA, Williams Coll., 1979; PhD, U. Calif., Berkeley, 1985; MBA, Cornell U., 1997. Postdoctoral fellow U. Chgo., 1985-87; asst. prof. Cornell U., Ithaca, NY, 1987-94; fellow, Office Senator Joseph Lieberman US Senate, Washington, 1994; fellow Office Sci. & Tech. Policy The White House, Washington, 1995; sr. policy adv. to sec. US Dept. Commerce, Washington, 1994—96; mgr. strategic analysis Corning Inc., NY, 1997—2002; v.p., program mgmt. AMDeC Found., 2002—03; COO, acting CFO NexGenix Pharmaceuticals, 2003—06. Cons. in field, Ithaca, 1996-97; bd. dirs., Delcath Systems, Inc. 2007- Contbr. articles to profl. jours. Bd. dirs. Boyce Thompson Inst., Planned Parenthood NY, 2003- Democrat.

PHILIPS, SUZANNE MARGUERITE See CASEY, SUE

PHILIPSBORN, JOHN TIMOTHY, lawyer, writer; b. Paris, Oct. 19, 1949; s. John David and Helen (Worth) P. AB, Bowdoin Coll., 1971; MEd, Antioch Coll., 1975; JD, U. Calif., Davis, 1978. Bar: Calif. 1978, U.S. Dist. Ct. (no., ctrl. and ea. dists.) Calif. 1978, U.S. Ct. Appeals (9th cir.) 1985, U.S. Supreme Ct. 1985; cert-specialist in criminal law State of Calif. VISTA vol. Office of Gov. State of Mont., Helena, 1972-73; cons. U.S. Govt., Denver, 1974; lectr. Antioch New Eng. Grad. Sch., Keene, N.H., 1973-75, U. N.H., Durham, 1973-75; ptnr. Philipsborn & Cohn, San Jose, Calif., 1978-80; atty., supr. Defenders Inc., San Diego, 1980-83; assoc. Garry, Dreyfus & McTernan, San Francisco, 1983-87; pvt. practice San Francisco, 1987—. Cons. Nicaraguan ct. evaluation projects, 1987-88, UN Internat. Tribunal, 1995—; coord. Internat. Conf. Adversarial Sys., Lisbon, Portugal, 1990; mem. adj. faculty New Coll. Law, San Francisco, 1991—; legal asst. project refugee camps S.E. Asia, 1992, legal edn. projects, Cambodia, 1995, Pakistan, 2001; cons. on continuing edn. of bar, 1995—; judge pro tem San Francisco Superior Ct., 2004-. Bd. editors Champion, Forum; contbr. articles to profl. jours., chpts. to book. Founder trial program San Francisco Schs., 1986; bd. dirs. Calif. Indian Legal Svcs., 1990-96. Recipient Excellence in Svcs. to the Poor award, 1984, Amicus Curiae Work award, Calif. Attys. Criminal Justice, 2003, 2004, Spirit award, Continuing Edn. Bar, 2006; Fullbright scholar, Portugal, 1989. Mem.: Calif. Attys. for Criminal Justice (assoc. editor jour. 1987—, co-chmn. govtl. misconduct com. 1989—92, bd. govs. 1989—94, chmn. Amicus Curiae com. 1992—, bd. govs. 2003—06), Calif. State Bar (evaluation panel criminal law specialists 1986—, com. on continuing edn. of bar 1991—94, criminal law subcom. state bd. legal specialists 1995—96), Nat. Assn. Criminal Def. Lawyers (assoc.; co-chmn. death penalty impact litig. group 1989, vice chmn. task force on emerging democracies 1990—91, co-chmn. govtl. misconduct com. 1990—92). Office: Civic Ctr Bldg 507 Polk St Ste 250 San Francisco CA 94102-3375 Office Phone: 415-771-3801.

PHILLABAUM, LESLIE ERVIN, publisher; b. Cortland, NY, June 1, 1936; s. Vern Arthur and Beatrice Elizabeth (Butterfield) Phillabaum; m. Roberta Kimbrough Swarr, Mar. 17, 1962; children: Diane Melissa, Scott Christopher. BS, Pa. State U., 1958, MA, 1963. Editor Pa. State U. Press, 1961-63; editor-in-chief U. N.C. Press, 1963-70; assoc. dir., editor La. State U. Press, Baton Rouge, 1970-75, dir., 1975—2003, emeritus dir., 2003—. Served to 1st lt. US Army, 1959—61. Mem.: Assn. Am. Univ. Presses (dir. 1978—80, 1983—86, pres. 1984—85), Acacia, Alpha Kappa Psi, Omicron Delta Kappa. Democrat. Home: 769 Castle Kirk Dr Baton Rouge LA 70808-6018

PHILLIP, CYNTHIA A., librarian; BA in Elem. Edn. and Remedial Reading, Capital U., Columbus, Ohio, 1978; MLS in Libr. and Info. Sci., Western Mich. U., Kalamazoo, 1985, MA in Ednl. Leadership, 1998. Reading tchr., 7th grade Sylvania City Schools, Ohio, 1978—81; substitute tchr. Three Rivers Cmty. Schools, 1981—85; elem. sch. libr. media specialist Van Buren Pub. Schools, Belleville, Mich., 1985—86, Grand Haven Area Pub. Schools, Mich., 1986—, coord. libr. services k-12, 1995—2000, asst. prin., 1998—2000, dept. head, cataloger, 2000—03; ednl. instl. specialist IBM, 1992—94. Pres. United Meth. Women, Ch. of Dunes, 2000; chair prog. resources United Meth. Women, Grand Rapids Dist., 2003—. Grantee Governor Engler's Next Day Grant, 1998, Tech. Challenge grant, 1999, Northshore Cmty. Found. grant, 2002, 2004. Mem.: Mich. Reading Assn., Mich. Assn. for Computer Users in Learning, Internat. Soc. Tech. in Edn., Assn. Supervision and Curriculum, Mich. Assn. for Media in Edn. (newsletter co-editor 1993—98, region 7 rep. 1994—98, pres.-elect, pres., past pres. 1999—2001, webmaster 2002—03, mktg. chair 2003—, Ruby Brown award 1992), AASL (mem. tchg. for learning task force 2000—03, mem. leadership forum planning com. 2002—03, chair affiliate assembly 2003, co-chair conf. prog. com. 2004—, pres. 2006—07, mem. exec. com., bd. dirs.), ALA (coun. mem. at large 2003—05, mem. membership com. 2004), Kappa Alpha Pi. Office: AASL 50 E Huron St Chicago IL 60611-2795 Office Phone: 312-280-4382. Office Fax: 312-280-5276. Business E-Mail: cphillip_56@yahoo.com. *

PHILLIPPE, RYAN, actor; b. New Castle, Del., Sept. 10, 1974; s. Richard and Susan Phillippe; m. Reese Witherspoon, June 5, 1999 (separated); children: Ava Elizabeth, Deacon. Student, New Castle Bapt. Acad., 1992. Co-founder Lucid Films. Actor: (films) Crimson Tide, 1995, Invader, 1996, White Squall, 1996, Nowhere, 1996, Little Boy Blue, 1997, I Saw What You Did Last Summer, 1997, Homegrown, 1998, 54, 1998, Playing by Heart, 1998, Cruel Intentions, 1999, The Way of the Gun, 2000, Antitrust, 2001, Gosford Park, 2001, Igby Goes Down, 2002, The I Inside, 2003, Crash, 2004, Five Fingers, 2005, Chaos, 2005, Flags of Our Fathers, 2006, Breach, 2007; (TV series) One Life to Live, 1992—93; (TV miniseries) The Secrets of Lake Success, 1993, (TV appearances) A Perry Mason Mystery: The Case of the Grimacing Governor, 1994, Matlock, 1994, Due South, 1994, Chicago Hope, 1996, The Outer Limits, 1996, (voice only) King of the Hill, 2000. Office: c/o William Morris Agy Attn: John Fogelman 151 El Camino Dr Beverly Hills CA 90212 *

PHILLIPS, ANTHONY GEORGE, neurobiology researcher; b. Barrow, Cumbria, Eng., Jan. 30, 1943; came to Can., 1953; s. George William and Mabel Lilian (Wood) P. BA, U. Western Ont., London, Can., 1966, MA, 1967, PhD, 1970. Asst. prof. psychobiology U. B.C., Vancouver, Canada, 1970-75, assoc. prof., 1975-80, prof., 1980—, head dept. psychology, 1994-99, prof. dept. psychiatry, 1999—, dir. U. B.C. Inst. Mental Health. Founder Quadra Logic Tech., Inc., Vancouver. Contbr. numerous papers to sci. jours. Chair inst. adv. bd. CIHR Inst. for Neurosci. Mental Health & Addiction, 2001—; bd. dirs. Tibetian Refuge Aid Soc., 1980—; chmn. Can.-India Village Aid, Vancouver, 1981—86, 2003—05. Recipient Killam Rsch. prize Can. Coun., 1977, D.O. Hebb award Can. Psychol. Assn.; Steacie fellow Nat. Scis. and Engring. Rsch. Coun. Can., 1980. Fellow Royal Soc. Can.; mem. Soc. Neurosci., Can. Soc. for Neurosci., Can. Coll. Neuropsychopharmacology. Office: U BC Dept Psych 2255 Wesbrook Mall Vancouver BC Canada V6T 1Z4 Office Phone: 604-822-4624. Business E-Mail: aphillips@psych.ubc.ca.

PHILLIPS, BARNET, IV, lawyer; b. NYC, July 5, 1948; s. Barnet III and Isabelle (Auriema) P.; m. Sharon Walsted Packey, Jan. 2, 1981; children: Victoria Ilonka, Caroline Walsted. BA, Yale U., 1970; JD, Fordham U., 1973; LLM, NYU, 1977. Bar: NY 1974. Assoc. Hughes Hubbard & Reed, NYC, 1973—76, Skadden, Arps, Slate, Meagher & Flom, NYC, 1977—81, ptnr., 1981—. Adj. assoc. prof. Fordham U., NYC, 1987-88; head Real Estate Investment Trust Practice Group, 2006-. Co-author: Structuring Corporate Acquisitions--Tax Aspects; articles editor: The Tax Lawyer, 1989-91. Bd. dirs Student/Sponsor Partnership, NYC, 1990-95; bd. cons. Portsmouth Abbey Sch., RI, 1991-96, chmn., 1997-2002; bd. trustees Saint Thomas More, the Cath. Chapel & Ctr. Yale U., New Haven, Conn., 2004—. Republican. Avocations: skiing, opera, triathlons. Home: 6 Hycliff Rd Greenwich CT 06831-3223 Office: Skadden Arps Slate Meagher & Flom Four Times Square 42nd Flr New York NY 10036-6522 Office Phone: 212-735-2220. Business E-Mail: bphillip@skadden.com.

PHILLIPS, BETTY LOU (ELIZABETH LOUISE PHILLIPS), writer, interior designer; b. Cleve. d. Michael N. and Elizabeth D. (Materna) Suvak; m. John S. Phillips, Jan. 27, 1963 (div. Jan. 1981); children: Bruce, Bryce, Brian; m. John D.C. Roach, Aug. 28, 1982. BS, Syracuse U., 1960; postgrad. in English, Case We. Res. U., 1963—64. Cert. elem. and spl. edn. tchr., NY; cert. interior designer, Calif. Tchr. pub. schs., Shaker Heights, Ohio, 1960—66. Sportswriter Cleve. Press, 1976-77; spl. features editor Pro Quarterback Mag., NYC, 1976-79; bd. dirs. Cast Specialties Inc., Cleve., 1960-2007. Author: Chris Evert: First Lady of Tennis, 1977, Picture Story of Dorothy Hamill, 1978 (ALA Booklist selection), American Quarter Horse, 1979, Earl Campbell: Houston Oiler Superstar, 1979, Picture Story of Nancy Lopez, 1980 (ALA Notable book), Go! Fight! Win! The NCA Guide for Cheerleaders, 1981 (ALA Booklist), Something for Nothing, 1981, Brush Up on Your Hair, 1981 (ALA Booklist), Texas.The Lone Star State, 1989, Provençal Interiors-French Country Style in America, 1998, French by Design, 2000, French Influences, 2001, Villa Décor: Decidedly French and Italian Style, 2002 (Foreword Mag. Best Non-Fiction Book, 2003), Unmistakably French, 2003, Emily Goes Wild, 2003 (Tex. Inst. Letters Best Children's Book, 2004), Secrets of French Design, 2004, The French Connection, 2005, Emily Works Out, 2005, Emily's Manners, 2005, Inspirations From France & Italy, 2007, The French Room, 2008; contbr. articles popular mags. Mem.: Am. Soc. Interior Designers (profl. mem., cert.), Soc. Children's Book Writers, Delta Delta Delta. Republican. Roman Catholic. Home: 4278 Bordeaux Ave Dallas TX 75205-3718

PHILLIPS, CARLY, writer; b. Mount Vernon, NY, July 7, 1965; d. Leonard Robert and Arlene Weinberg; m. Phillip Drogin, Mar. 23, 1965; children: Jaclyn Lindsay, Jennifer Ashley. BA, Brandeis U., Waltham, MA, 1987; JD, Boston U, 1990. Bar: N.Y. 1991, Conn. 1991. Author: (novels) The Bachelor, 2002 (NY Times Bestseller List, Reading with Ripa Nationally Televised Bookclub, 2002), The Playboy, 2003 (NY Times Bestseller List, 2003), The Heartbreaker, 2004 (NY Times Extended Bestseller List), Summer Lovin', 2005 (NY Times Extended Bestseller List), Hot Number, 2005, Cross My Heart, 2006, Hot Item, 2006 (NY Times Extended Bestseller List). Mem.: Novelists, Inc., Romance Writers of Am. Office: PO Box 483 Purchase NY 10577 E-mail: carlyphillips@optonline.net.

PHILLIPS, CAROLINE L., lab administrator; b. Washington, Oct. 7, 1955; d. Elinor and Frank duBose Phillips; m. Raymond L. Baumler, Oct. 1, 1983; 1 child, Irene Caroline Baumler. MS, Va. Commonwealth U., Richmond, 1981. Computer programmer/analyst Nat. Inst. Aging, Bethesda, Md., 1986—2000, info. tech. specialist data mgmt., 2001—. Vol. Sunday sch. tchr. Seven Locks Bapt. Ch., Potomac, Md., 2001—06; mem. Heritage Cir. Children Christian Children's Fund, Richmond, Va., 2005—06. Named Sec.'s Employee of the Month, Nat. Inst. Aging, 1989, 1996; recipient NIA Group award for publ. of a resource data book, 1990, Pub. Health Svc. On-the-Spot award, NIH/Nat. Inst. Aging, 1992, 1998, 1999, NIH award of Merit, 1994. Mem.: Psi Chi. Achievements include development of specifications for database of neuropsychological tests for a large epidemiologic study in Iceland; data management for a large epidemiologic sstudy of elderly people in Italy. Avocations: drawing, painting, jogging, swimming, music. Home Phone: 301-279-5965; Office Phone: 301-496-1178.

PHILLIPS, CARTER GLASGOW, lawyer; b. Canton, Ohio, Sept. 11, 1952; s. Max Dean and Virginia Scott (Carter) P.; m. Sue Jane Henry, June 5, 1976; children: Jessica, Ryan. BA summa cum laude, Ohio State U., 1973; MA, Northwestern U., 1975, JD magna cum laude, 1977. Bar: Ill. 1977, DC 1979, US Dist. Ct. (no. dist.) Ill., US Dist. Ct. (DC dist.), US Ct. Appeals (1st, 2d, 3d, 4th, 5th, 6th, 7th, 8th, 9th, 10th, 11th, DC and Fed. cirs.), US Supreme Ct. Law clk. to hon. Judge Robert Sprecher US Ct. Appeals (7th cir.), Chgo., 1977—78; law clk. to chief Justice Warren E. Burger US Supreme Ct., Washington, 1978—79; asst. prof. law U. Ill., Champaign, 1979—81; asst. solicitor gen. US Dept. Justice, Washington, 1981—84; ptnr. Sidley & Austin, Washington, 1984—. Mng. ptnr. DC office, mem. mgmt. com. Sidley Austin Brown & Wood LLP, Washington, 1995—; chmn. dean's adv. bd. Northwestern U. Law Sch., 2002—04, mem. dean's adv. bd., 2002—; chmn. Fed. Cir. Adv. Coun., U.S. Ct. Appeals, 2003—05, mem., 2003—; adj. prof. law Northwestern U. Law Sch., 2006—; pres., master Edward Coke Appellate Inn of Ct.; mem. adv. bd. Coll. Arts and Scis., Ohio State U. Contbr. articles to profl. jours. Bd. advs. Georgetown Univ. Law Ctr.'s Supreme Ct. Inst., Nat. Youth Leadership Forum on Law; bd. trustees Supreme Ct. Hist. Soc., Fed. City Coun.; bd. dir. Inst. Judicial Adminstrn., NYU Sch. Law; mem. adv. com. US Ct. Appeals, Fed. Cir. Named one of Top 45 Lawyers Under 45, Am. Lawyer Mag., 1995, 100 Best Lawyers in Am., Nat. Law Jour., 1995, 100 Most Influential Lawyers, 2006, Top 10 Newsmakers of 2006, IP Law and Bus., Best Appellate Lawyers in Am., 2007; recipient Alumni Merit Award, Northwestern U., 1998, Alumni Svc. Award, 2006, Rex Lee Advocacy award, 2001. Fellow: Am. Coll. Trial Lawyers; mem.: Am. Acad. Appellate Lawyers, Am. Law Inst., Order of the Coif, Phi Beta Kappa. Republican. Episcopalian. Office: Sidley Austin LLP 1501 K St NW Fl 10 Washington DC 20005-3705 Home Phone: 703-734-0985; Office Phone: 202-736-8270. E-mail: cphillips@sidley.com.

PHILLIPS, CARYL, writer; b. St. Kitts, West Indies, Mar. 13, 1958; BA with honors, The Queen's Coll., Oxford, Eng., 1979; AM (hon.), Amherst Coll., Mass., 1995; DUniv (hon.), Leeds Metro. U., 1997; D (hon.), U. York, 2003; DLitt (hon.), U. Leeds, 2003; AM (hon.), Yale U., 2006. Writer in residence Factory Arts Ctr. Arts Coun. Great Britain, London, 1980-82; writer in residence U. Mysore, India, 1987, U. Stockholm, 1989; vis. writer Amherst Coll., 1990-92, writer in residence, 1992—98, co-dir. creative writing ctr., 1994-97, prof. English, writer-in-residence, 1994-98; prof. English, Henry R. Luce prof. migration and social order Barnard Coll., Columbia U., NYC, 1998—2005, dir. Initiatives in the Humanities, 2003—05; prof. English Yale U., 2005—. Vis. lectr. U. Ghana, 1990, U. Poznan, 1991; vis. writer Humber Coll., 1992, 93; writer-in-residence Nat. Inst. Edn., Singapore, 1994; vis. prof. English NYU, 1993; vis. prof.

humanities U. W.I., 1999—2000; mem. arts coun. Gt. Britain Drama Panel, 1982—85; mem. prodn. bd. Brit. Film Inst., 1985—88, Bush Theatre, 1985—89; mem. Caribbean Writer bd. U.S. V.I., 1989—; hon. sr. mem. U. Kent, 1988—; cons. editor Faber & Faber, Inc., 1992—94, Caribbean series editor, 1996—2000; participant, keynote spkr 12 ann. confs. German-speaking countries New Lits. in English, Giessen, Germany, 1989; resident writer Hull (Engl.) Internat. Lit. Festival, 1992; instr. writing Arvon Found., summers, 1983—; reader, lectr. in field. Author: The Final Passage, 1985 (Malcolm X prize for lit., 1985), A State of Independence, 1986, The European Tribe, 1987 (Martin Luther King Meml. prize, 1987), Higher Ground, 1989, Cambridge, 1991, Crossing the River, 1993 (James Tait Black meml. prize), The Nature of Blood, 1997, The Atlantic Sound, 2000, A New World Order: Selected Essays, 2001, A Distant Shore, 2003 (PEN/Faulkner Award for Fiction nominee, 2004, Commonwealth Writers prize, 2004, Hurston/Wright Legacy award finalist, Nat. Book Cir. Critics finalist in fiction), Dancing in the Dark, 2005 (PEN Beyon the Margins prize, 06), Foreigners, 2007; editor: Extravagant Strangers: A Literature of Belonging, 1997, The Right Set: A Tennis Anthology, 1999; author: (plays) Strange Fruit, 1980, Where There Is Darkness, 1982, The Shelter, 1983, Rough Crossings, 2007, (TV documentary screenplays) Welcome to Birmingham, 1983, The Hope and Glory, 1984, Lost in Music, 1984, The Record, 1985, Darker Than Blue: Curtis Mayfield, 1995, BBC Profile Spl. Caryl Phillips Interviews Chinua Achebe, 2003, South Bank Show: Caryl Phillips, ITV, 2003, (films) Playing Away, 1986, The Final Passage, 1996, The Mystic Masseur, 2001 (Mar Del Plata Film Festival Silver Ombu for Best Screenplay), (radio plays) The Wasted Years, 1984 (Best Radio Play of Yr. award BBC, 1984), Crossing the River, 1985, The Prince of Africa, 1987, Writing Fiction, 1991, A Kind of Home: James Baldwin in Paris, BBC Radio 4, 2004, Hotel Cristobel, 2005, (radio documentaries) St. Kitts (Pride of Place), 1983, Sport and the Black Community, 1984, No Complaints: James Baldwin at Sixty, 1985, Archive Hour: I Too am America BBC Radio, 2003; contbr. (documentary programs) Bookmark, 1984, Black on Black, London Weekend TV, 1983, others; contbr. articles to periodicals. Recipient Young Writer of Yr. award, London Sunday Times, 1992, award, Lannan Lit., 1994, Caribbean Am. Heritage award for outstanding contbn. to lit., 2004; fellow, Guggenheim, 1992, 50th Anniversary, Brit. Coun., 1984, Royal Soc. Lit., 2000; Mel and Lois Tukman fellow, N.Y. Pub. Libr. Ctr. for Scholars and Writers, 2003, hon. fellow, The Queen's Coll. Oxford, 2006. Address: care G Garrett AP Watt Ltd 20 John St London WC1N 2DR England Office: Yale U English Dept 315 Linsly Chittenden Hall 63 High St New Haven CT 06520 Business E-Mail: Ggarrett@apwatt.co.uk.

PHILLIPS, CHANDLER ALLEN, biomedical engineer, human factors engineer; b. LA, Dec. 21, 1942; s. Chandler A. and Ann P.; m. Jane Draper, Feb. 14, 1980. AB in Biol. Scis., Stanford U., 1965; MD, U. So. Calif., 1969; AB in Classical Langs., Wright State U., 1982; PhD (hon.), U. Human Studies, Las Vegas, 1985. Registered profl. engr., Ohio, Calif. Rsch. physician U. Dayton, Ohio, 1972-74; asst. prof. physiology Wright State U., Dayton, 1975-79, assoc. prof. biomed. engring., 1979-84, prof. biomed. engring., 1984-91, prof. biomed. and human factors engring., 1991—99, prof. biomed. indsl. and human factors engring., 1999—. Author: Functional Electrical Rehabilitation, 1991, Human Factors Engineering, 2000; sr. editor: Mechanics of Skeletal and Cardiac Muscle, 1983, Effective Extremity Prostheses, 1989; regional editor Auto Medica, 1997-03; mem. editl. bd. Jour. Biomechanics, 1984-87, Jour. Clin. Engring., 1984-98, Auto Medica, 1988-97, Prosthetics-Orthotics Engring., 1995-98, Frontiers in Bioscience, 2003-. Amateur radio operator W65WV. Capt. USAF, 1970—72. Fellow: IEEE (Harry Rowe Mimno award 1984), Aerospace Med. Assn. (John Paul Stapp award 2002), Am. Inst. Med. and Biol. Engring., Am. Acad. Neurologic Orthopedic Surgeons (hon.). Avocations: commercial-instrument pilot, fishing, classical philology. Office: Dept Biomed Indsl Human Factors Engring Wright State U Dayton OH 45435 Home Phone: 937-849-9277; Office Phone: 937-775-5044.

PHILLIPS, CHARLES DAVID, gerontologist, researcher, medical educator; b. Abilene, Tex., Nov. 3, 1948; s. Willie Everette and Mary Charlene Phillips; m. Catherine Hawes, June 2, 1978; 1 child, Anna Michelle Tankersley. BA, Tarleton State U., Stephenville, Tex., 1971; MPH, U. NC, Chapel Hill, 1987; PhD, U. Tex., Austin, Tex., 1979. Asst. prof., dept. polit. sci. U. N.C., Chapel Hill, 1980—87; rsch. scientist RTI Internat., Rsch. Triangle Park, NC, 1988—96; dir. Myers Rsch. Inst., Beachwood, Ohio, 1996—2000; prof. dept. health policy and mgmt. Sch. Rural Pub. Health, Coll. Sta., Tex., dir. health svcs. rsch. program, 2000—01, head doctoral studies, 2001—. Mem. grad. faculty Tex. A&M U., 2000—. Mem. editl. bd.: The Gerontologist, 2000—; contbr. articles to profl. jours. Named Gerontologist of Yr., U. Tex., Houston Ctr. Aging, 2001; named to Rschr. Honor Roll, Nat. Citizens Coalition Nursing Home Reform, 2000; recipient Pub. Svc. award, 2005, Disting. Alumni award, Tarleton State U., 2006. Fellow: Gerontol. Soc. Am., interRAI; mem.: APHA, AcademyHealth, Delta Omega. Democrat. Office: Sch Rural Pub Health TAMUSHSC 1266 Tamu College Station TX 77843 Office Phone: 979-458-0080. Business E-Mail: phillipscd@tamhsc.edu.

PHILLIPS, CHARLES E., JR., computer software company executive; BS in Computer Sci., USAF Acad.; MBA in Fin., Hampton U., Va.; JD, NY Law Sch. CFA; bar: Ga., DC. Prin. Morgan Stanley & Co., Inc., 1994—95, mng. dir., 1995—2003; exec. v.p. strategy, partnerships & bus. devel. Oracle Corp., Redwood City, Calif., 2003—04, pres., 2004—, co-pres. PeopleSoft Calif., 2004. Bd. dirs. Oracle Corp., 2004—, Viacom Corp., Morgan Stanley, 2006—. Trustee Joint Ctr. for Polit. and Econ. Studies, Washington, NY Law Sch., bd. dirs., Jazz at Lincoln Ctr., NYC. Capt. USMC. Named one of 50 Black Profls. on Wall Street, Black Enterprise Mag., 50 Who Matter Now, Business 2.0, 2007. Office: Oracle Corp 500 Oracle Pky Redwood City CA 94065 Office Phone: 650-506-7000. Office Fax: 650-506-7200. *

PHILLIPS, CHARLES FRANKLIN, JR., retired economist; b. Geneva, NY, Nov. 5, 1934; s. Charles Franklin and Evelyn (Minard) P.; m. Marjorie Hancock, June 22, 1957; children: Charles Franklin, Susan Hancock, Anne Davis. BA, U. N.H., 1956; PhD, Harvard U., 1960. Asst. prof. econs. Washington and Lee U., Lexington, Va., 1959-63, assoc. prof., 1963-66, prof., 1966—2003, Robert G. Brown prof., 1979—2003; ret., 2003. Mem. adv. bd. Shenandoah Valley area, First Union, 1971—; econ. cons. pub. utilities. Author: Competition in the Synthetic Rubber Industry, 1963, The Economics of Regulation, 1965, rev. edit., 1969, The Regulation of Public Utilities, 1984, 3d edit., 1993; editor: Competition and Monopoly in the Domestic Telecommunications Industry, 1974, Competition and Regulation-Some Economic Concepts, 1976, Expanding Economic Concepts of Regulation in Health, Postal and Telecommunications Services, 1977, Regulation, Competition and Deregulation-An Economic Grab Bag, 1978, Regulation and the Future Economic Environment-Air to Ground, 1980. Mem. city coun. Lexington, 1969-71, mayor, 1971-88; mem. Va. Rep. Ctrl. Com., 1974-76, 77-96; trustee Hebron Acad., Maine, 1971-82; mem. Presbyn. Ch., 1959—, elder, 1993-98, trustee, 1994—; mem. Commn. on Rev. of Nat. Policy Toward Gambling, 1972-76; chmn. Valley Program for Aging Svcs., 1993-95, treas., 1996-99; bd. dirs. Rockbridge Area Presbyn. Home, 1973—, Nat. Regulatory Rsch. Inst., 1992-95, Stonewall Jackson Found., 1997-2000, 2001—, treas., 2003-04, pres, 2004—; pres. United Way of Lexington-Rockbridge County, 1996-98, crusade chmn., 1999; pres. Hist. Lexington Found., 1997-2000. Recipient award McKinsey Found., 1962, J. Rhoads Foster award, 1995. Mem. Am. Econ. Assn. (Disting. Mem. award transp. and pub. utility group 1997),, So. Econ. Assn., Am. Mktg. Assn., Kiwanis, Phi Beta Kappa, Omicron Delta Epsilon (pres. 1976-77, 78-79, 96-97, Outstanding Regional Dir. award 1971). Home: 414 Morningside Dr Lexington VA 24450-2739 Home Phone: 540-463-5409. Business E-Mail: phillipscf@wlu.edu.

PHILLIPS, DAVID P., grocery company executive; CFO Publix Super Markets, Lakeland, Fla., 1999—, treas. Office: Publix Super Markets PO Box 407 Lakeland FL 33802-0407 Office Phone: 863-688-1188. *

PHILLIPS, DOROTHY K., lawyer; BS, U. Pa.; MA, NYU; JD, Villanova Law Sch., 1978. Bar: Pa. 1978, NJ 1978, US Dist. Ct. (ea. dist.) Pa., US Dist. Ct. NJ, US Ct. Appeals (3d cir.), US Supreme Ct. Lectr. Marriage Coun. Phila., U. Pa., Hahnemann Med. Sch., Phila., 1970-75; atty. Adler, Barish, Daniels, Levin & Creskoff, Phila., 1978-79, Astor, Weiss & Newman, Phila., 1979-80; ptnr. Romisher & Phillips. P.C., Phila., 1981-86; prin. Dorothy K. Phillips & Assocs., LLC, 1986—. Judge Reimel Moot Ct. Competition, Villanova Law Sch., 1986; faculty Pa. Bar Inst., CLE Temple U. Sch. Law, 1987-89, Nat. Bus. Inst., lectr. 1998, 2000, 01, 03, 04. Author: The Legal Intelligencer, The Phila. Lawyer, 1998; family law columnist: Pa. Law Weekly, 2005-06; contbr. articles to profl. jours. Named a Super Lawyer Phila. Mag., 2005, 06, 07; named one of Top 50 Lawyers Phila. Mag., 2006; featured in Wall St. Jour., Phila. Inquirer, Phila. Bus. Jour., Harper's Bazaar, WPVI-ABC6, KYW-CBS3, WCAU-NBC10, FOX Phila., CN8. Mem.: ATLA, ABA, Lawyers Club, Montgomery County Bar Assn., Phila. Trial Lawyers Assn., Phila. Bar Assn. Custody Rules Drafting Com. (Supreme Ct. Pa., faculty), NJ State Bar Assn., Pa. Bar Assn., Pa. Trial Lawyers Assn. Business E-Mail: dkp@dkphillipslaw.com.

PHILLIPS, EARL NORFLEET, JR., diplomat, financial services executive; b. High Point, NC, 1940; s. Earl Norfleet Phillips and Lillian Jordan; m. Sarah Boyle, Oct. 19, 1971; children: Courtney Dorsett, Jordan Norfleet. BSBA, U. N.C., 1962; MBA, Harvard U., 1965. Security analyst Wertheim & Co., NYC, 1965-67; exec. v.p. Factors Inc., High Point, 1967-71, First Factors Corp., High Point, 1972-81, pres., 1982-98; chmn. GE Capital First Factors, High Point, 1998-2000; pres. Phillips Interests, 2000—; U.S. amb. to Eastern Caribbean, 2002—03. Bd. dirs. Oakdale Cotton Mills, N.C. Enterprise Corp., Culp Inc. Mem. nat. adv. coun. SBA, 1988—91; trustee High Point Regional Hosp., Asian Inst. Tech., Bangkok; former mem. Piedmont Triad Airport Authority; trustee U. N.C., Chapel Hill, 1983—91, chmn. bd., 1989—91, mem. endowment bd., 1985—2001; mem. U. N.C. Found., 1987—91; bd. govs. U. N.C. Sys., 1995—99; mem. N.C. Econ. Devel. Bd., Raleigh, 1984—91; bd. dirs. N.C. Citizens for Bus. and Industry, chmn., 1999—2000. Named Young Man of Yr., High Point Jaycees, 1971, High Point Citizen of Yr., 2000; named one of Five Outstanding Young Men, N.C. Jaycees, 1971; recipient Global Leadership award, Kenan-Flagler Bus. Sch., U. N.C., 2001, Disting. Alumnus award, U. N.C. Alumni Assn., 2002. Mem. Nat. Comml. Fin. Assn. (bd. dirs.), The Brook, High Point C.C. Club, String and Splinter Club, Linville Golf Club, Gorgons Head Lodge. Office: Phillips Interests Box 830 101 S Main St High Point NC 27261 Office Phone: 336-882-6431. E-mail: philphillips@northstate.net.

PHILLIPS, EDWARD JOHN, consulting firm executive; s. Harold E. and Mary C. P.; m. Kathleen A. Everett, July 23, 1960; children: Elizabeth J., Edward J. B of Mech. Engring., Villanova U., 1973; MBA, Widener U., 1975. Registered profl. engr., Ill., Pa., Ohio; chartered engr., U.K. Tech. ops. mgr. Motorola, Inc., Franklin Park, Ill., 1976-81; v.p. engring. Rival Mfg. Co., Kansas City, Mo., 1981-82; prin., sr. cons. Richard Muther & Assocs., Kansas City, 1982-85; chmn. KANDE, Inc., Overland Park, Kans., 1983-86; pres., CEO Sims Cons. Group Inc., Lancaster, Ohio, 1986—; chmn. bd. dirs., pres. Sims Consulting Group, Lancaster, Ohio. Bd. dirs. KANDE, Inc., Wilmington, Del. Author: Manufacturing Plant Layout, 1997; contbr. articles to profl. jours. Recipient Profl. Achievement award, Villanova U., 2006. Mem. NSPE, ASME (chmn. material handling divsn. 1989-91, internat. mgmt. com. 1977), MIMechE, Soc. Mfg. Engrs., Tau Beta Pi, Pi Tau Sigma. Office: Sims Cons Group Inc PO Box 968 Lancaster OH 43130-0968

PHILLIPS, ELIZABETH JASON, lawyer, state agency administrator; b. Boston, Sept. 3, 1936; d. Richard Eliot and Elizabeth Harding (McClure) Jason; m. William Morris Phillips, Jr., Mar. 2, 1991; children: Meredith Rowe, william Morris III, Eleanor Anne, Robert J., Lee B. Stewart. BA in History, U. Mass., 1958; MEd, U. Hartford, 1969; JD, Western New Eng. Coll., Springfield, Mass., 1977. Bar: Mass. 1977, U.S. Dist. Ct. Mass. 1978, Va. 1981, U.S. Dist. Ct. (ea. dist.) Va. 1981, U.S. Dist. Ct. DC 1981, U.S. Dist. Ct. (we. dist.) Va. 1982, U.S. Ct. Appeals (4th cir.) 1982, U.S. Supreme Ct. 1984. Ptnr. Thompson & Stewart, Ludlow, Mass., 1977-80; adminstr. Office Atty. Gen., Commonwealth of Va., Richmond, 1980-82, asst. atty. gen., 1982-84; dep. Commr. Indsl. Commn. Va., 1984-91; dep. commr., mgr. dispute resolution divsn. Va. Workers' Compensation Commn., Richmond, 1991—2001. Trustee Gloucester County Libr., 2002, sec.; Trustee Ludlow Hosp., 1979—80. Mem.: ABA, Va. Exec. Inst., Va. Assn. Adminstrv. Law Judges and Hearing Officers (pres-elect 1999), Va. Bar Assn., Richmond Bar Assn., Ludlow C. of C. (pres. 1980). Episcopalian. Home: Cedar Shade 3859 Raymond Walker Rd Hayes VA 23072-4620 Personal E-mail: ephil75441@aol.com.

PHILLIPS, ELVIN WILLIS, lawyer; b. Tampa, Fla., Feb. 27, 1949; s. Claude Everett and Elizabeth (Willis) P.; m. Sharon Gayle Alexander, June 20, 1970; children: Natasha Hope, Tanya Joy, Trey Alexander. BA, U. Fla., 1971; MA, We. Carolina U., 1974, EdS, 1975; JD, Stetson U., 1980. Bar: Fla. 1980, U.S. Dist. Ct. (mid. dist.) Fla. 1981, U.S. Ct. Appeals (11th cir.) 1988. Tchr. Monroe County Schs., Key West, Fla., 1970—73; asst. prin. Habersham County Schs., Clarksville, Ga., 1973—77; assoc. Dixon, Lawson & Brown, Tampa, 1980—81, Yado, Keel, Nelson et al, Tampa, 1981; ptnr. Lawson, McWhirter, Grandoff & Reeves, Tampa, 1981—88, Williams, Parker, Harrison, Dietz & Getzen, Sarasota, Fla., 1988—. Leadership Devel. Program fellow Southern Regional Coun., Atlanta, 1975. Mem. ABA (forum com. constrn. industry 1989-96), Assn. Legal Adminstrs., Fla. Bar (chmn. 1991-92, vice chmn. 1990-91, mem. benefits com.), Sarasota County Bar Assn., Phi Kappa Phi, Phi Alpha Delta, Phi Delta Kappa. Democrat. Baptist. Home: 3310 Del Prado Ct Tampa FL 33614-2721 Office: Williams Parker Harrison Dietz & Getzen 200 S Orange Ave Sarasota FL 34236-6802 Office Phone: 941-329-6633. Business E-Mail: ephillips@williamsparker.com.

PHILLIPS, ERNIE HOWARD, music educator; b. Gainesville, Ga., Apr. 5, 1957; s. Ernest Cecil and Charlotte (Inez) Phillips; m. Connie Harrison, June 5, 1982; children: Matthew, Ryan, Hamilton. MusB, U. Ga., 1979, M in Music Edn., 1981. Asst. band dir. East Hall HS, Gainesville, 1981—88; band dir., fine arts dept. head West Hall HS, Gainesville, 1988—. Guest honor band condr. U. Ga. Music Festival, 1998, Ga. Music Educators In-Svc. Conf., 1998; guest condr. U. Ga. Redcoat Band, 2001. Musician (prin. tubist): Gainesville Symphony Orch., 1982—, North Winds Symphonic Band, 1985—. Dir. Soc. Preservation and Encouragement Barber Shop Quartet Singing in Am., Gainesville, 1983—95; donor U. Ga. Scholarship Fund, Athens, 1993—; bass sect. mem. Lakewood Baptist Worship Choir, Gainesville, 1984—. Recipient Legion of Honor award, John Philip Sousa Found., 2001. Mem.: Ga. Music Educators Assn. (9th dist. instrumental chmn. 2005—), Nat. Band Assn., Music Educators Nat. Conf., U. Ga. Alumni Soc., Phi Beta Mu. Baptist. Home: 5024 Jay Creek Rd Oakwood GA 30566 Office: West Hall HS 5500 McEver Rd Oakwood GA 30566 Office Phone: 770-967-9826 ext 250. Business E-Mail: ernie.phillips@hallco.org.

PHILLIPS, EUAN HYWEL, publishing executive; b. Chipstead, Surrey, Eng., Mar. 31, 1928; s. Edgar Aneurin and Elsie Llewella (Davies) P.; m. Margaret June Savage, June 12, 1954; children: David John, Janet Margaret. BA, Emmanuel Coll., Cambridge, Eng., 1949, MA, 1965. Cost acct. J. Lyons & Co. Ltd., London, 1950-53; dispatch mgr. Pickerings Produce Canners Ltd., Manchester, Eng., 1953-56; mgmt. cons. P.A. Mgmt. Cons. Ltd., London, 1956-65; mng. dir. Unwin Bros. Ltd., Old Woking, England, 1965-73; univ. printer designate Cambridge U. Press, England, 1973-74, univ. printer, 1974-76, dir. Am. br. NYC, 1977-82; exec. dir. Assn. Am. U. Presses, 1987-90. Gov. Guildford Sch. Art, 1966-69, Cambridge Coll. Arts and Tech., 1974-76; dir. East Asian History of Sci., Inc., 1978-81 Contbr. to scholarly pub. With Royal Navy, 1946-48. Mem. Brit. Printing Industries Fedn. (coun. 1966-73, pres. Home Counties Alliance 1970-71), Troupers Light Opera Co., Connestee Falls Golf Assn. (pres. 1996-97), Connestee Falls Property Owners Assn. (bd. dirs. 2001—04). Home: 2637 Connestee Trl Brevard NC 28712

PHILLIPS, FLOYD LEIGH, plastic surgeon; b. Wilson, NC, Sept. 16, 1957; s. Floyd Leigh and Josephine Okey Phillips Jr.; m. Christi Candler, Sept. 16, 2001; 1 child, Ryleigh. BS, NC State U., Raleigh, 1979; MD, Bowman Gray Sch. Med., Winston-Salem, NC, 1984. Diplomate Am. Bd. Plastic Surgeons. Pvt. practice, 1990—. Fellow: Am. Coll. Surgeons; mem.: AMA, Fla. Soc. Plastic Surgeons. Presbyterian. Avocations: fishing, kayaking, triathlons. Office: 2855 University Dr #400 Pompano Beach FL 33065

PHILLIPS, FREDERICK FALLEY, architect; b. Evanston, Ill., June 18, 1946; s. David Cook and Katharine Edith (Falley) P.; m. Gay Fraker, 1983 (div. 1993); m. Linda Gardner, 2002; children: Daniel Gardner, Alice Katharine. BA, Lake Forest Coll., 1969; MArch, U. Pa., 1973. Registered architect, Ill., Wis. Intern Harry Weese & Assocs., 1974, 75; architect pvt. practice, Chgo., 1976-81; pres. Frederick Phillips and Assocs., Chgo., 1981—. Bd. dirs. Landmarks Preservation Coun., 1981-85, Chgo. Acad. Sci., 1988-97, Friends of Ceuros de Escazu, Costa Rica, 1992-95, Project Rush Chgo., 2001--; mem. aux. bd. Chgo. Architecture Found., 1975-89. Recipient award Townhouse for Logan Sq. Competition, AIA and Econ. Redevel. Corp. Logan Sq., 1980, Gold medal award Willow St. Houses, Ill. Ind. Masonry Coun., 1981, Silver award for pvt. residence, 1989, Gold medal award pvt. residence, 1994, Three Record Houses awards Archtl. Record, 1990, 95, award 2d Compact House Design Competition, 1990, award of exellence for pvt. residence AIA/Nat. Concrete Masonry Assn., 1992, 98, award pvt. residence Am. Wood Coun., 1993, Honorable mention-Best in Am. Living award Profl. Builders Mag., 1995, Builder's Choice award pvt. residence, Builder Mag., 1996, Jury's Choice award pvt. residence Chgo. Athenaeum, 1996, 2001, Am. Architecture award Chgo. Athenaeum, 2001, Grand award Residential Architecture Mag., 2003, award Custom Builder Mag., 2003, award Am. Inst. Steel Construction, 2004. Fellow AIA (chmn. task group mfg. housing Nat. Com. Design 1994-96, mem. awards task group 1998-01, chmn. 2000-01, Disting. Bldg. award for Willow St. Houses, Chgo. chpt. 1982, for Pinewood Farm 1983, for Pvt. Residences 1990, 92, 98, for Tower House, 2001, Housing Com. award 2006); mem. Chgo. Archtl. Club, Racquet Club (bd. govs. 1983-89), Arts Club, Cliff Dwellers Club (bd. govs. 1985-88). Office: Frederick F Phillips & Assocs 1456 N Dayton St Ste 200 Chicago IL 60622-2636

PHILLIPS, GARY STEPHEN, lawyer; b. Far Rockaway, NY, June 26, 1957; s. Lawrence and Ilene (Kaufman) P.; m. Debbie J. Kanner, Mar. 27, 1983; children: Joshua Charles, Allison Ilyse. BA with high honors, U. Fla., 1978, JD with honors, 1981. Bar: Fla. 1982, U.S. Dist. Ct. (so. dist.) Fla. 1982, U.S. Ct. Appeals (11th cir.) 1982, U.S. Supreme Ct. 1986. With Sparber, Shevin, Shapo & Heilbronner, Miami, Fla., 1981-87; pvt. practice law Miami, 1987-90; with Buchanan Ingersoll P.C., Miami, 1990-95, Phillips, Eisinger & Brown, P.A., Hollywood, Fla., 1996—2005, Phillips, Cantor & Berlowitz, 2006. Contbr. editor U. Fla. Law Rev., 1980-81. Named one of Leading Fla. Attys.-Comml. Litig., Best of the Bar, South Fla. Bus. Jour., 2003, Top Lawyers, South Fla. Legal Guide, 2003—06, States Legal Leaders, Fla. Legal Elite, 2005—06, Fla. Super Lawyers, 2006. Mem.: ABA, North Dade Bar Assn. (treas. 1992), Dade County Bar Assn., Fla. Bar Assn. (litig., real property, probate and trust law sects.), Am. Judicature Soc., Omicron Delta Epsilon, B'nai B'rith, Omicron Delta Kappa, Phi Beta Kappa. Democrat. Jewish. Office: 4000 Hollywood Blvd Ste 375 Hollywood FL 33021-6782

PHILLIPS, GENEVA FICKER, academic editor; b. Staunton, Ill., Aug. 1, 1920; d. Arthur Edwin and Lillian Agnes (Woods) Ficker; m. James Emerson Phillips, Jr., June 6, 1955 (dec. 1979). BS in Journalism, U. Ill., 1942; MA in English Lit., UCLA, 1953. Copy desk Chgo. Jour. Commerce, 1942-43; editl. asst. patents Radio Rsch. Lab. Harvard U., Cambridge, Mass., 1943-45; asst. editor adminstrv. publs. U. Ill., Urbana, 1946-47; editl. asst. Quar. of Film, Radio and TV UCLA, 1952-53; mng. editor The Works of John Dryden, Dept. English UCLA, 1964—2002. Bd. dirs. Univ. Religious Conf., L.A., 1979—. UCLA teaching fellow, 1950-53, grad. fellow 1954-55. Mem. Assn. Acad. Women UCLA, Friends of Huntington Libr., Friends of UCLA Libr., Friends of Ctr. for Medieval and Renaissance Studies, Samuel Johnson Soc. So. Calif., Assocs. U. Calif. Press, Conf. Christianity and Lit., Soc. Mayflower Descendants. Lutheran. Home: 213 First Anita Dr Los Angeles CA 90049-3815 Office: UCLA Dept English 2225 Rolfe Hall Los Angeles CA 90024

PHILLIPS, GERALD BAER, internal medicine scientist, educator; b. Bethlehem, Pa., Mar. 20, 1925; s. Abel H. and Cecilia (Blum) P.; m. Maria Bonzi Lewis, July 15, 1970; children: Abigail, Elizabeth. AB, Princeton U., 1946; MD, Harvard U., 1948. Diplomate Am. Bd. Internal Medicine. Intern Presbyn. Hosp., NYC, 1948-50; rsch. fellow Thorndike Meml. Lab., Med. Sch. Harvard U., Boston, 1950-53; vis. fellow biochemistry Columbia U. Coll. Physicians and Surgeons, NYC, 1954-56, from assoc. in medicine to assoc. prof., 1956-73, prof., 1973—. Sr. attending physician St. Lukes-Roosevelt Hosp.; attending physician NY-Presbyn. Hosp. Sr. asst. surgeon USPHS, 1952-54. Mem.: Am. Soc. for Biochemistry and Molecular Biology, Am. Soc. for Clin. Investigation, Alpha Omega Alpha. Home: 196 E 75th St New York NY 10021-3257 Office: 1000 10th Ave New York NY 10019-1147 E-mail: gbp1@columbia.edu. *I attribute any success I may have had to heredity and luck.*

PHILLIPS, GLYNDA ANN, editor; b. Riverside, Calif. d. Henry Grady and Patricia (Loflin) P. BA in English, Millsaps Coll., Jackson, Miss., 1977; MS in Comms., Miss. Coll., Clinton, 1996; postgrad., Inst. Children's Lit., West Redding, Conn., 1998—2002. News editor The Magee Courier, Miss., 1981-84; editor Miss. Farm Country mag., Jackson, 1984—. Contbr. articles to profl. jours. Recipient first place personal column Nat. Fedn. Press Women, 1984, first place personal column Miss. Press Women's Assn., 1984, 1st Pl. award Miss. Press Women's Assn., 1984, Best Media Campaign award AFBF Info. Contest, 1996, Excellence and Pres.'s award AFBF Pub. Rels. and Info. Program, 2006, Pub. Rels. Info. award Excellence, 2007.

PHILLIPS, HARVEY G., musician, performing arts educator; b. Aurora, Mo., Dec. 2, 1929; s. Jesse E. and Lottie A. (Chapman) P.; m. Carol A. Dorvel, Feb. 22, 1954; children: Jesse E., Harvey G., Thomas A. Student, U. Mo., 1947-48, Juilliard Sch. Music, 1950-54, Manhattan Sch. Music, 1956-58; MusD (hon.), New England Conservatory of Mu, 1971; HHD (hon.), U. Mo., Columbia, 1987. Founder, v.p. Mentor Music, Inc., NYC, 1958—79; v.p. Wilder Music, Inc., NYC, 1964-77, Magellan Music, Inc., NYC, 1971—, Peaslee Music Inc., 1971—; established faculty position Aspen Sch. Music, summer 1962, U. Wis., summer 1963, Hartt Sch. Music, Hartford, Conn., 1962-64, Mannes Sch. Music, NYC, 1964-65; exec. v.p.

Orch. USA, NYC, 1962-65; exec. v.p., pers. mgr., tubist Symphony of the Air N.Y.C., 1957-66; v.p. Brass Artists, Inc., NYC, 1964—; adminstrv. asst. to Julius Bloom, Rutgers U., New Brunswick, NJ, 1966-67; v.p. fin. affairs New Eng. Conservatory of Music, Boston, 1967-71; mem. faculty Sch. Music, Ind. U., Bloomington, 1971-94, disting. prof. music, trustee, 1979, disting. prof. emeritus, 1994. Adv. bd. Am. Brass Chamber Music, Inc., 1971—; chmn. bd. Summit Brass/Keystone Brass Inst., 1985—92, Rafael Mendez Brass Inst., 1993—; cons. Margun Music, Inc., 1977—; bd. dirs. Summit Brass. Brass coach Festival at Sandpoint, Idaho, 1986-94; mem. faculty Joven Orch., Spain, 1987-94, Festival Casal Orch., San Juan, P.R., 1964-76; dir. 1st Internat. Tuba Symposium Workshop, Ind. U., 1973, Brass-Wind Music Studios, Carnegie Hall, N.Y.C., 1961-67; tubist, King Bros. Circus Band, 1947, Ringling Bros. & Barnum & Bailey Circus Band, 1948-50, N.Y.C. Ballet Orch., 1951-71, N.Y.C. Opera Orch., 1951-62, Voice of Firestone Orch., 1951-53, Sauter-Finegan Orch., 1952-53, Band of Am., 1952-54, NBC Opera Orch., 1956-65, Bell Tel. Hour Orch., 1956-66, Goldman Band, 1957-62; founding mem., tubist N.Y. Brass Quintet, 1954-67; condr., co-prodr. Burke-Phillips All Star Concert Band, 1960-62; co-founder, tubist Matteson-Phillips Tubajazz Consort, 1976—; founding mem. TubaShop Quartet, 1996—; rec. artist Crest Records, 1958-78—; originator Octubafest, TubaChristmas, Tubasantas, Tubajazz, TubaEaster, Tubacompany, Summertubafest; exec. editor Instrumentalist mag., 1986-96, bd. advisors, 1996—. Founder, pres. Harvey Phillips Found., Inc., N.Y.C., 1977—; bd. dirs. Mid-Am. Festival of the Arts, 1982-90, Bloomington Area Arts Coun., 1983-90; judge 1st Internt. tuba competition of CIEM Internat. Competition for Musical Performers, Geneva, 1991. Served with U.S. Army Field Band, 1955-56. Recipient Disting. Svc. to Music award Kappa Kappa Psi, 1978, Cmty. Svc. award City of Bloomington, 1978, Nat. Assn. Jazz Educators award, 1977, 78, Nat. Music Conf. award, 1977, T.U.B.A. award, 1978, MI Hummel The Tuba Player award, 1990, Disting. Achievement award Ednl. Press Assn. Am., 1991, Mentor Ideal award Assn. Concert Bands, 1994, Lifetime Achievement award United Music Instruments, 1995, Sudler award medal of the Order of Merit Sousa Found., 1995, Summit Brass Outstanding Svc. and Support Internat. Brassfest, 1995, Orpheus award Phi Mu Alpha Sinfonia, 1997; elected to Acad. Wind and Percussion Arts Nat. Band Assn., 1995; recipient Edwin Franko Goldman citation Am. Bandmasters Assn., 1996, Devel. of Mus. Artistry and Opportunities for Future Generations award Colonial Euphonium Tuba Inst., 1998, Lifetime Achievement award Rafael Mendez Brass Inst., 1998, Platinum Piston Lifetime Achievement award, U. Ga., 1999; Legion of Hon., Goldman Meml. Band, 2002; Harvey Phillips Day proclaimed New England Conservatory Music, 1971, Harvey Phillips Day proclaimed Marionville, Mo. Bicentennial, 1976, Harvey Phillips Weekend Gov. of Mo., 1982; named hon. mem. U.S. Army Band Pershings Own, 1984. Mem. Am. Fedn. Musicians, Tubists Universal Brotherhood Assn. (bd. advs. 1973—, pres. 1984-87, hon.), Hoagy Carmichael Jazz Soc. (founder, acting pres. 1983—), Tau Beta Sigma, Phi Mu Alpha Sinfonia (Orpheus award 1997), Kappa Gamma Psi. Home and Office: Tubaranch 4769 S Harrell Rd Bloomington IN 47401-9028 Office: Sch of Music Ind U Bloomington IN 47405 Business E-Mail: philliph@indiana.edu. *The role of a performer and teacher is to give, to share skills and knowledge. My primary goal in life is to create new opportunities in the music profession, to develop, expand, and preserve the music arts.*

PHILLIPS, HOWARD WILLIAM, investment banker; b. NYC, May 16, 1930; s. Louis and Helen (Klein) P.; children: Jan Davis, Richard Louis; m. Carol Napack, June 9, 1985. BA, Dartmouth Coll., Hanover, NH, 1951, MBA, 1952; JD, Harvard U., Cambridge, Mass., 1957. Bar: NY 1957. Assoc. Cahill, Gordon, Reindel & Ohl, NYC, 1957-64; v.p., gen. counsel McCall Corp., NYC, 1964-68, sr. v.p., 1968-69; ptnr. Oppenheimer & Co., NYC, 1969-81; chmn. Holmes, Phillips & Co., NYC, 1981-83; dir. corp. fin. D.H. Blair Investment Banking Corp., 1983-95. Bd. dirs. Pioneer Behavioral Health, Boston; pres. Asolo Theatre Co., Sarasota, Fla., 2004-06. Served to lt. (j.g.) USNR, 1952-54. Mem. Easthampton Tennis Club (NY), Longboat Key Club (Sarasota), Sara Bay Country Club (Sarasota). Home: Box 2047 3 Cove Hollow Farm Rd East Hampton NY 11937 Office: 500 S Palm Ave PHT Sarasota FL 34236 Office Phone: 941-365-1995.

PHILLIPS, J. HARRISON, III, lawyer; b. Lewes, Del., Mar. 9, 1941; AA, Ea. Coll., 1962; LLB, Mt. Vernon Sch. Law, 1965. Bar: Md. 1972, U.S. Supreme Ct. 1976, U.S. Dist. Ct. Md. 1980. Law clk., Balt. County, 1967—70; asst. states atty. Worcester County, 1972—77; former prosecutor Md.; pvt. practice. Bd. dirs. Md. Criminal Def. Attys.; legal com. Nat. Orgn. Reform Marijuana Laws. Recipient Vol. of Yr. award, Md. Vol. Lawyers Svc., 2001. Mem.: Comml. Law League Am., Md. Criminal Def. Attys. Assn., Nat. Dist. Attys. Assn., Assn. Trial Lawyers Am., Md. Trial Lawyers Assn., Md. State Bar Assn., Worcester County Bar Assn., Nat. Assn. Criminal Def. Lawyers (life). Office: 115-72nd St Ocean City MD 21842 Office Phone: 410-524-1944. Office Fax: 410-524-9240. E-mail: phillips@ezy.net.

PHILLIPS, JAMES CHARLES, physicist, researcher; b. New Orleans, Mar. 9, 1933; s. William D. and Juanita (Hahn) P.; m. Joanna Vandenberg, Mar. 1, 1996. BA, U. Chgo., 1952, BS, 1953, MS, 1955, PhD, 1956. Mem. tech. staff Bell Labs., 1956-58; NSF fellow U. Calif. at Berkeley, 1958-59, Cambridge (Eng.) U., 1959-60; faculty U. Chgo., 1960-68, prof. physics, 1965-68; mem. tech. staff Bell Labs., 1968-96; cons. Bell Labs., Lucent Tech., 1996—. Sloan fellow, 1962-66; Guggenheim fellow, 1967. Fellow Am. Phys. Soc. (Buckley prize 1972), Minerals, Metals and Materials Soc. (William Hume-Rothery award 1992); mem. NAS. Home: 204 Springfield Ave Summit NJ 07901-3909

PHILLIPS, JAMES D., retired diplomat; b. Peoria, Ill., Feb. 23, 1933; s. James D. and Ehila (Hardy) P.; m. Rosemary Leeds, Mar. 30, 1957 (div. Dec. 1981); children: Michael, Madolyn, Catherine; m. Lucie Gallistel, Jan. 7, 1984; stepchildren: Charles, David BA, Wichita State U., 1956, MA, 1957; cert., U. Vienna, Austria, 1956; postgrad., Cornell U., 1958-61. Joined fgn. svc. Dept. State, 1961; served at Am. embassy Paris, before 1975; Am. Consulate Zaire, before 1975; Dept. State Washington, before 1975; dep. chief of mission Am. Embassy, Luxembourg, 1975-78, charge d'affaires The Gambia, 1978—80; student Nat. War Coll., Washington, 1980-81; office dir. Dept. State, Washington, 1981-84; consul gen. Am. Consulate, Casablanca, Morocco, 1984-86; US Amb. to Burundi, 1986-90; US Amb. Republic of the Congo, 1990-93; diplomat in residence The Carter Ctr., Atlanta, 1993-94; ret., 1994; pres. Dan Phillips & Assoc., Arlington, Va., 1994—2006. Contbr. articles to profl. jours. Former bd. dirs. H.M. Salaam Found., Jane Goodall Inst., 1994-2000. With U.S. Army, 1953-55. Mem.: Chevy Chase Club. Avocations: golf, tennis, skiing. Home: 3607 Military Rd Arlington VA 22207-4829 Office: 1101 30th St NW Ste 200 Washington DC 20007-3769

PHILLIPS, JAMES DICKSON, JR., retired federal judge; b. Scotland County, NC, Sept. 23, 1922; s. James Dickson and Helen (Shepherd) Phillips; m. Jean Duff Nunalee, July 16, 1960; children: Evelyn, James Dickson III, Elizabeth Duff, Ida Wills. BS cum laude, Davidson Coll., 1943; JD, U. N.C., 1948. Bar: N.C. 1948. Asst. dir. Inst. Govt., Chapel Hill, NC, 1948—49; ptnr. Phillips & McCoy, Laurinburg, NC, 1949—55, Sanford, Phillips, McCoy & Weaver, Fayetteville, NC, 1955—60; from asst. prof. to prof. law U. N.C., 1960—78, dean Sch. Law, 1964—74; judge US Ct. Appeals (4th Cir.), 1978—94, sr. judge, 1994—. Vice-chmn. N.C. Cts. Commn.; chmn. N.C. Bd. Ethics, 1977—78. With US Army, 1943—46. Decorated Bronze Arrowhead, Bronze Star, Purple Heart; recipient John J. Parker Meml. award, Thomas Jefferson award, Disting. Alumnus award, U. N.C., 1993. Mem.: Am. Law Inst. Democrat. Presbyterian.

PHILLIPS, JAMES EDGAR, lawyer; b. NYC, Aug. 30, 1949; s. Jack Louis Phillips and Jacqueline (Kasper) Ehrman; children: Zachary J., Mark H. BA, Boston U., 1971; JD, Case Western Reserve U., 1975. Bar: Ohio 1975, US Supreme Ct. 1977, US Dist. Ct. (so. dist.) 1978, US Ct. Appeals (6th cir.) 1981, US Dist. Ct. (no. dist.) 1982, US Ct. Appeals (7th cir.) 2001. Asst. prosecutor Franklin County Prosecutor Office, Columbus, Ohio, 1975-77, sr. asst. prosecutor, 1977-79; assoc. Vorys, Sater, Seymour & Pease, Columbus, 1979-84, ptnr., 1984—; spl. prosecutor State of Ohio, 1993—. Gen. counsel Nat. Fraternal Order of Police, Washington, 1987-2002, Conrail Police #1, US Postal Police #2; mem. Bd. Profl. Law Enforcement Certification; mem. Wong Sun Soc., 1997—; adj. prof. Ohio State U. Moritz Sch. Law, 2005—. Author: Civil Recovery in Ohio, 1986, Collective Bargaining in the Pub. Sector, 1988; editor Bar Briefs; contbr. articles Jours., 1987-89. Pres. bd. dir. Ohio Ctr. for Law-Related Edn., 1985—95; bd. dirs. Schottenstein Stores Corp., 2002—, Alvis House, 2005—06. Fellow Ohio Bar Found., Columbus Bar Found., Ohio Bar Assn. (chmn. com. law-related edn. 1982-86), Columbus Bar Assn., Sixth Cir. Jud. Conf. (life); Ohio Assn. Criminal Defense Lawyers (bd. dirs., treas.). Avocations: travel, photography. Office: Vorys Sater Seymour & Pease PO Box 1008 52 E Gay St Columbus OH 43216-1008 Office Phone: 614-464-5610. Business E-Mail: phillips@vssp.com.

PHILLIPS, JAMES HAROLD, retired lawyer; b. Dec. 18, 1934; s. Frank Carroll and Mabel Lorraine (James) Phillips; m. Jean Keir Woodruff, Oct. 2, 1959 (dec.); children: Susan, John(dec.), Sara, Jamie. BSEE, Rose-Hulman Inst. Tech., 1960; JD, George Washington U., 1967. Bar: Ariz. 68, U.S. Dist. Ct. Ariz. 68, U.S. Patent Office 68, U.S. Supreme Ct. 72, U.S. Ct. Customs & Patent Appeals 74, Tex. 80, U.S. Ct. Appeals (fed. cir.) 82. Patent atty. GE, 1967—68; ptnr. Drummond, Cahill & Phillips, Phoenix, 1968—73; asst. patent counsel NCR Corp., Dayton, Ohio, 1973—76; sr. profl. atty. Sun Co. Inc., Dallas, 1976—84; ptnr. Cates & Phillips, Phoenix, 1984—88; asst. patent counsel Bull HN Info. Sys., Phoenix, 1988—95; patent cons. Bull NH Info. Sys., Phoenix, 2000—05; counsel Squire, Sanders and Dempsey, Phoenix, 1995—2000, ret., 2000. Author: Paderewski Discovers America, 2006; contbr. articles to profl. jours. Charter mem. Phoenix Symphony Coun.; pres. AMICA-Tex. chpt. With USN, 1952—55. Mem.: Tex. Bar Assn., Ariz. Bar Assn. (chmn. patent, trademark and copyright sect. 1985—86). Personal E-mail: speedyjim@cox.net.

PHILLIPS, JANET COLLEEN, retired educational association administrator, editor; b. Pittsfield, Ill., Apr. 29, 1933; d. Roy Lynn and Catherine Amelia (Wills) Barker; m. David Lee Phillips, Feb 7, 1954; children—Clay Cullen, Sean Vincent. BS, U. Ill, 1954. Reporter Quincy (Ill.) Herald Whig, 1951, 52, soc. editor, 1953; editorial asst. Pub. Info. Office U. Ill.-Urbana, 1953-54, asst. editor libr., 1954-61; asst. editor Assn. for Libr. and Info. Sci. Edn., State College, Pa., 1960-61, mng. editor, 1961-89, exec. sec., 1970-89; adminstrv. dir. Interlibr. Delivery Svc. of Pa., 1990-99; ret. Mem. Palmer Mus. Arts, State Coll. Cmty. Theatre, Mt. Nittany Med. Ctr. Aux. Mem. Assn. for Libr. and Info. Sci. Edn., Embroiderer's Guild Am., Pa. State Blue Golf Course Club, Univ. Women's Club (Pa. State), Ctr. Hills Country Club, Am. Wine Soc., Cmty. Acad. Lifelong Learning, Delta Zeta. Presbyterian. Avocations: travel, golf, sewing, needlecraft. Address: 471 Park Ln State College PA 16803-3208 E-mail: janph2@aol.com.

PHILLIPS, JILL META, writer, critic, astrologer; b. Detroit, Oct. 22, 1952; d. Leyson Kirk and Leona Anna (Rasmussen) P. Student pub. schs., Calif. Lit. counselor Book Builders, Charter Oak, Calif., 1966-77; pres. Moon Dance Astro Graphics, Covina, Calif., 1994—. Author: (with Leona Phillips) A Directory of American Film Scholars, 1975, The Good Morning Cookbook, 1976, G.B. Shaw: A Review of the Literature, 1976, T.E. Lawrence: Portrait of the Artist as Hero, 1977, The Archaeology of the Collective East, 1977, The Occult, 1977, D.H. Lawrence: A Review of the Literature and Biographies, 1978, Film Appreciation: A College Guide Book, 1979, Annus Mirabilis: Europe in the Dark and Middle Centuries, 1979, (with Leona Rasmussen Phillips) The Dark Frame: Occult Cinema, 1979, Misfit: The Films of Montgomery Clift, 1979, Butterflies in the Mind: A Précis of Dreams and Dreamers, 1980; The Rain Maiden: A Novel of History, 1987, Walford's Oak: A Novel, 1990, The Fate Weaver: A Novel in Two Centuries, 1991, Saturn Falls: A Novel of the Apocalypse, 1993, Birthday Secrets, 1998, Your Luck is in the Stars, 2000; columnist Dell Horoscope Mag., Astrology Your Daily Horoscope Mag., 1998—; contbr. book revs. to New Guard mag., 1974-76; contbr. numerous articles to profl. jours. including Dell Horoscope, Midnight Horoscope, Astrology-Your Daily Horoscope, Am. Astrology. Mem. Young Ams. for Freedom, Am. Conservative Union, Elmer Bernstein's Film Music Collection, Ghost Club London, Count Dracula Soc., Dracula Soc. London, Richard III Soc. Republican. Personal E-mail: queenofwands52@aol.com.

PHILLIPS, JOHN A(TLAS), III, geneticist, educator; b. Sanford, NC, Jan. 24, 1944; s. John A. and Rachael (Sloan) P.; m. Gretchen Lynch, Aug. 1, 1965; children: Jennifer Allene, John Atlas IV, Charles Andrew, James William. Student, U. N.C., 1962-65; MD, Wake Forest U., 1969. Diplomate Am. Bd. Pediatrics, Am. Bd. Med. Genetics. Intern Children's Hosp. Med. Ctr., Boston, 1969-70, jr. resident, 1970-71, sr. resident, 1973-74, chief resident, 1974-75; asst. prof. Johns Hopkins U., Balt., 1978-82, assoc. prof., 1982-84; prof. pediatrics Vanderbilt U., Nashville, 1984—, prof. biochemistry, 1986—, David T. Karzon chair genetics, 1992—. Bd. sci. counselors Nat. Inst. Child Health, Washington, 1984-88; counsilor Ctr. Study Polymorphisme Humain, Paris, 1988—; mem. adv. com. Ctr. Reproductive Biology, Nashville, 1990-94; bd. dirs. March of Dimes Birth Defects Found., Nashville, 1986—; mem. adv. bd. Nat. Neurofibromatosis Found., Tenn., 1990—; mem. Tenn. Genetics Adv. Com., Nashville, 1984—. Contbr. to profl. publs. Lt. comdr. USNR, 1971-73. Recipient Sidney Farber award Children's Hosp., Boston, 1975, E Mead Johnson award Mead Johnson Co., 1984; Pediatric Postdoctoral fellow Johns Hopkins U. Sch. Medicine, 1975-77. Mem. Am. Soc. Clin. Investigation, Soc. Pediatric Rsch., Am. Coll. Med. Genetics (founding, bd. dirs. 1995—), Phi Beta Kappa, Alpha Omega Alpha. Achievements include discovery of cause of hemoglobin H disease in Black Americans; chromosomal location of multiple genes in humans; improved diagnoses of cystic fibrosis, hemophilia, inborn metabolic errors, familial neurodegenerative diseases, familial pulmonary hypertension, familial pulmonary fibrosis. Office: Vanderbilt U Sch Medicine Divsn Med Genetics DD 2205 Nashville TN 37232-0001 Office Phone: 615-322-7601.

PHILLIPS, JOHN BOMAR, lawyer; b. Murfreesboro, Tenn., Jan. 28, 1947; s. John Bomar Sr. and Betty Blanche (Primm) P.; m. Ellen Elizabeth Ellis, Aug. 9, 1969; children: John Bomar III, Anna Carroll, Ellis Elizabeth. BS, David Lipscomb Coll., 1969; JD, U. Tenn., 1974. Bar: Tenn. 1974, U.S. Dist. Ct. (ea. dist.) Tenn. 1975, U.S. Ct. Appeals (6th cir.) 1980. Assoc. Stophel, Caldwell & Heggie, Chattanooga, 1974-79; ptnr. Caldwell, Heggie & Helton, Chattanooga, 1979-91, Miller & Martin, Chattanooga, 1991—2005, mng. ptnr., 1997—2002, of counsel, 2005—; v.p and deputy gen. counsel labor and employment Coca-Cola Enterprises Inc., 2005—. Author: Tennessee Employment Law, 1989, 3d edit., 2000, Employment Law Desk Book for Tennessee Employers, 1989; editor: Tennessee Employment Law Letter, 1986—; host Danger Zones Video Tng. Series for Suprs., 1998—; mem. nat. moot ct. team U. Tenn. Law Rev. Pres. Chattanooga State Coll. Found., 1992-94, Boys Club of Chattanooga, 1983-84; sec. Tenn. Aquarium, 1989-2004. chair, 2005—; chmn. Chattanooga Conv. and Visitors Bur., 1996-97; bd. dirs. Vol. Comty. Sch., Chattanooga, 1980-85, Coun. for Alcohol and Drug Abuse, Chattanooga, 1981-83, Creative Discovery Mus., 1994-99, Girls Prep. Sch., 1997-2002, Allied Arts of Gtr. Chattahooga, 1997-2002; mem. Hamilton County Juvenile Ct. Commn., 1995-99. Fellow Tenn. Bar Found., Chattanooga Bar Found.; mem. ABA (labor law sect.), Tenn. Bar Assn. (chair labor law sect. 1992-93, Justice Joseph W. Henry award 1986-87), Chattanooga Bar Assn. (bd. govs. 1978-79), Chattanooga C. of C. (bd. dirs. 1998-2001), Order of Coif, Fairyland Country Club (Lookout Mountain, Tenn.), Walden Club (bd. govs. 1992-95), Mountain City Club, Kiwanis (pres. Chattanooga 1986-87). Episcopal. Avocations: reading, writing. Home: 1107 E Brow Rd Lookout Mountain TN 37350-1015 Office: Miller & Martin 832 Georgia Ave Ste 1000 Chattanooga TN 37402-2289 also: Cola Cola Enterprises Inc 2500 Windy Ridge Pkwy Atlanta GA 30339 Office Phone: 423-785-8325. E-mail: jphillips@millermartin.com, johnphillips@na.cokecce.com.

PHILLIPS, JOHN C., lawyer; b. Staten Island, NY, June 6, 1948; s. John D. G. and Eleanor (Stier) P.; m. Karen Francis McKenna, June 5, 1971; children: James, Thomas, Robert. AB in Govt., Cornell U., 1970; MA in Polit. Sci., Rutgers U., 1972, JD, 1975. Bar: NJ 1975, US Dist. Ct. NJ 1975, NY 1982, US Supreme Ct. 1985, US Ct. Appeals (3d cir.) 1985, Fla. 1988. Assoc. Carpenter, Bennett & Morrisey, Newark, 1975-79, Buttermore, Mullen & Jeremiah, Westfield, NJ, 1979-80; mng. ptnr. Buttermore, Mullen, Jeremiah & Phillips, Westfield, 1981-85, 87-2001; mem. DeVos, Phillips & Co. PC, 1986-87; of counsel Price, Meese, Shulman & D'Arminio, Woodcliff Lake, NJ, 2001—04; assoc. Sills Cummis Epstein and Gross, Newark, 2004—05, of counsel, 2005—. Trustee, dir. Animal Care Fund Inc., East Smithfield, Pa., 1983-98. Author: (with others) New Jersey Transactions, Zoning and Planning, 1993. Dir., coach Police Athletic League, Berkeley Heights, NJ, 1967—99; dir. Youth Soccer Club, Berkeley Heights, 1983—94; mem. Berkeley Heights Twp. Com., 1985—87, dep. mayor, 1986, 1987; Twp. atty. Berkeley Heights, 1989, 1991, 1994—2002; planning bd. atty. Twp. Warren, 1987—2001, Borough Alpine, 2007—; mem. NJ Hotel and Multiple Dwelling Safety Bd., 1988—, vice chmn., 1998—; mem. Rep. Mcpl. Com., 1985—2000, vice chmn., 1990—92, 1998—2000, mem. dist. XII ethics com., 1993—97, dist. XII fee arbitration com., 1998—2002, dist. VA fee arbitration, 2007—; mem. Kappa Alpha Lit. Soc., 1967—; trustee Kappa Alpha Assn., 1974—90; v.p. Kappa Alpha Assn. Found., 1978—87, vice-chmn., 1983, chmn., 1984. Recipient award for Assistance and Dedication to youth, Police Athletic League, Berkeley Heights, 1975, Dedicated Svc. award Berkeley Heights Twp. Com., 1983. Mem.: ABA, Inst. of Mcpl. Attys., Fedn. of Planning Ofcls., Urban Land Inst., Union County Bar Assn., N.J. State Bar Assn., Canoe Brook Country Club, Jaycees (sec. New Providence-Berkeley Heights chpt. 1982, Jaycee of Yr. 1982). Republican. Methodist. Home: 56 Emerson Ln Berkeley Heights NJ 07922-2414 Office: Sills Cummis Epstein and Gross One Riverfront Plz Newark NJ 07102 Home Phone: 908-322-5768; Office Phone: 973-643-5767. Business E-Mail: jphillips@sillscummis.com.

PHILLIPS, JOHN EDWARD, zoologist, educator; b. Montréal, Que., Can., Dec. 20, 1934; s. William Charles and Violet Mildred (Lewis) P.; m. Eleanor Mae Richardson, Sept. 8, 1956; children: Heather Anne, Jayne Elizabeth, Jonathan David, Catherine Melinda, Wendy Susannah. BSc with honors, Dalhousie U., Halifax, NS, 1956, MSc, 1957; PhD, Cambridge U., Eng., 1961. Asst. prof. Dalhousie U., Halifax, N.S., 1960-64; assoc. prof. U. B.C., Vancouver, Canada, 1964-71, prof., 1971—, head dept. zoology, 1991-96. Vis. rschr. Cambridge (Eng.) U., 1972, 76, 81; chair grant selection com. Nat. Rsch. Coun. Can., Ottawa, Ont., 1969-71; mem. coun. Nat. Sci. and Engring. Rsch. Coun., Ottawa, 1983-87. Mem. editorial bd.: Can. Jour. Zoology, 1971-75, Am. Jour. Physiology, 1978-93, Jour. Experimental Biology, 1981-85, Am. Zool., 1996-01; contbr. articles to profl. jours. Mem. grant selection com. Can. Cystic Fibrosis Found., Toronto, 1989-91; active Vancouver Bach Choir. Named to James chair St. Francis Xavier U., Antigonish, N.S., 1993; recipient Killam Rsch. prize U. B.C. Fellow Royal Soc. Can.; mem. Can. Soc. Zoologists (sec. 1972-76, v.p. 1976-78, pres. 1979, Fry medal 2000), Am. Soc. Zoologists (exec. 1983-85, chair divsn. comp. physiol. biochemistry 1983-85). Avocations: music, singing. Home: 12908 22 B Ave White Rock BC Canada V4A 6Z3 Office: U BC Dept Zoology Vancouver BC Canada V6T 1Z4 Personal E-mail: jephillips@telus.net.

PHILLIPS, JOHN MICHAEL, lawyer; b. Mobile, Ala., Feb. 4, 1975; s. John Urquhart and Mary Catherine Phillips. BA, U. Ala., Tuscaloosa, 1997, JD, 2000. Bar: Ala. 2000, Fla. 2001, Ga. 2002. Atty. Dore, Lanier & Phillips, Jacksonville, Fla., 2001—. Vice chmn. Spina Bifida Assn., Jacksonville, Fla., 2003—07. Mem.: Spl. Needs of Children Com., Jud. Rels. Com., Jacksonville Quarterback Club (sec. bd. dirs. 2003—). Achievements include research in dangerous instrumentality law evolution and impact. Avocations: travel, bicycling, sports. Office: Dore Lanier 76 S Laura St Ste 1701 Jacksonville FL 32202 Home Phone: 904-726-8898; Office Phone: 904-358-7881. Office Fax: 904-358-7899. Business E-Mail: jmphillips@dorelaw.com.

PHILLIPS, JOHN P(AUL), retired neurosurgeon; b. Danville, Ark., Oct. 14, 1932; s. Brewer William Ashley and Wave Audrey (Page) P.; m. June Helen Dunbar, Dec. 14, 1963; children: Todd Eustace, Timothy John Colin, Tyler William Ashley. AB cum laude, Hendrix Coll., 1953; MD, U. Tenn., 1956. Diplomate Am. Bd. Neurol. Surgeons. Intern Charity Hosp. La., New Orleans, 1957; resident surgery U. Tenn. Hosps., 1958; resident neurol. surgery U. Tenn. Med. Units, 1958-62; practice medicine, specializing in neurol. surgery Salinas, Calif., 1962-93; ret., 1993. Chief of staff, chief of surgery Salinas Valley Meml. Hosp.; mem. staffs Community Hosp. Monterey Peninsula, U. Calif. Hosp., San Francisco; asst. clin. prof. U. Calif., 1962—. Commd. Ky. col. Mem. AMA, ACS, Internat. Coll. Surgery, Harvey Cushing Soc., Congress Neurol. Surgery, Western Neurosurg. Assn., San Francisco Neurol. Soc., Pan Pacific Surg. Assn., Stanford U. Faculty Club (emeritus), Alpha Omega Alpha, Phi Chi, Alpha Chi. Office Phone: 831-484-1253.

PHILLIPS, JOHN R., lawyer; b. Leechburg, Pa., Dec. 15, 1942; BA, U. Notre Dame, 1966; JD, U. Calif. Law Sch. (Boalt Hall), 1969. Bar: Calif. 1970, U.S. Supreme Ct. 1992, DC 1993, U.S. Dist. Ct. DC 1993. Assoc. O'Melveny & Meyers, LA; ptnr. Phillips & Cohen, LLP, Washington, 1988—. Co-founder, dir. Ctr. Law in the Pub. Interest, LA, 1971—88; mem. 9th cir. jud. conf., 1989—92; appointee Commn. White House Fellowships, 1997—2001; spkr. in field. Mem. bd. editors: Calif. Law Rev., 1968—69; contbr. articles to profl. jours. Named one of 100 Most Influential Lawyers, Nat. Law Jour., 1997, 2000, 2006. Mem.: Taxpayers Against Fraud Assn. (founder, bd. dirs., Lifetime Achievement Award 2005). Office: Phillips & Cohen LLP 2000 Massachusetts Ave NW First Fl Washington DC 20036 Office Phone: 202-833-4567. Office Fax: 202-883-1815. *

PHILLIPS, JOHN ROBERT, political scientist, educator; b. Henderson, Ky., Dec. 16, 1942; s. Leander Armstead and Ann Reid (Brown) P. Diploma, Lang. Inst., Chateauroux, France, 1966; BA, Centre Coll., Danville, Ky., 1969; MA, Western Ky. U., Bowling Green, 1973. Instr. Drury Coll., Springfield, Mo., 1971-73, Western Ky. U., Bowling Green, 1975-79; asst. prof. Thiel Coll., Greenville, Pa., 1979-83, scholar-in-residence, 1983-85; pvt. cons., 1985—; adj. prof. Lockyear Coll., Evansville, Ind., 1987-88, prof. adminstrv. and social scis., 1988-91, acad. dean, 1988-90, v.p. acad. affairs, dean coll., 1990-91, Helen Hoffman disting. svc. prof., 1990-91; exec. dir. Henderson County Human Rels. Commn., 1991-93; dean acad. affairs, prof. political studies/govt. Springfield (Ill.) Coll., 1993-97, acting pres., 1996-97, provost, dean coll., 1997-98, prof. polit. and social scis., 1998—, Rose and H. Paul LaFata Endowed Chair for Disting. Tchg., 2003. Adj. prof. pub. adminstrn. Ind. State U., Terre Haute, 1991-92; field investigator on religion and culture in ancient city of Taxila, Pakistan, 1968, on indsl. pollution of hist. bldgs. and monuments, France, Italy, Austria, 1969; rschr. on nationalism, Scotland, 1972, 2002, on local

Scottish govt. and urban deves., 1993; participant in internat. confs. on The Future of a United Germany, 1991; mem. adv. coun. St. John's Hosp. Sch. Respiratory Therapy, 1993-97, Ursuline Acad Sch. Bd., v.p., 1995-97, pres., 1997-99, Cen. Ill. Fgn. Lang. and Internat. Studies Consortium, 1993—, chmn., 1994-96; cons.-evaluator Higher Learning Commn., North Ctrl. Assn. Colls. and Schs., 1999—. Mem. editl. bd.: Jour. Urban Affairs, 1985—89, book rev. editor: Pub. Voices, 2003, manuscript referee: Pub. Adminstrn. Rev., 1985—87, asst. editor: Pub. Voices, 2001—03; contbr. articles to profl. jours. Policy advisor Lt. Gov.'s Office, Frankfort, Ky., 1985-86; cons. Commn. on Ky.'s Future, Frankfort, 1985-87; mem. Bd. Cath. Edn., Diocese of Springfield, 1994-97; trustee Springfield Coll., 1996-97, commn. on human sexuality Episcopal Diocese of Springfield, 1997-98; bd. dirs. Liturgical Arts Festival of Springfield, 1998-2001. With USAF, 1963-68. Recipient Outstanding Tchg. in Polit. Sci. award, Am. Polit. Sci. Assn. and Pi Sigma Alpha, 2003, Most Inspirational Tchr. award, Western Ill. U., 2002. Mem. Am. Polit. Sci. Assn. (Leon Weaver Award com. 1990-93), Am. Soc. Pub. Adminstrn. (publs. com. 1984-88, 92-95), Urban Affairs Assn. (publs. com. 1985-89, nominating com. 1984-85, 88-89), Pi Sigma Alpha, Alpha Sigma Lambda. Democrat. Episcopalian. Home: 2605 Delaware Dr Springfield IL 62702-1213 Office: Springfield College L-106 Becker Libr 1500 N 5th St Springfield IL 62702-2643 Business E-Mail: jphillips@sci.edu.

PHILLIPS, JOSEPH BRANTLEY, JR., lawyer; b. Greenville, SC, Dec. 5, 1931; BS in Bus. Adminstrn., U. S.C., 1954, JD, 1955. Bar: SC 1955. Assoc. Leatherwood, Walker, Todd & Mann, Greenville, 1958-63, ptnr., 1963—2006; ret. Chmn. bd. deacons Presbyn. Ch., 1970-71, pres. Men of Ch., 1968-69, chmn. Christian Svc. Ctr., 1972-73; bd. dirs. Greenville Urban Ministry, 1978. Mem. ABA, S.C. Bar Assn., Greenville Bar Assn., Greenville Young Lawyers Club (pres. 1961-62), Lawyers Pilots Bar Assn., Kiwanis (pres. 1973). Clubs: Greenville Country (pres. 1977). Home: 207 Butler Springs Rd Greenville SC 29615-2261 Office: PO Box 87 Greenville SC 29602-0087

PHILLIPS, JOSEPH DANIEL, geophysicist, oceanographer; b. Woodbury, NJ, Sept. 11, 1938; s. Joseph Francis and Katherine Cecilia (Browne) P.; m. Gwendolyn Williams, 1961; children: Julia Kear, Stephanie Morgan, Joseph Williams. BA, Rutgers U., 1961; MS in Engring., Princeton U., 1963, MA, 1964, PhD, 1966. Engr. trainee Mobil Oil Co., NYC, 1957, N.Y. Shipbuilding Corp., Camden, NJ, 1958-60; engr. mgmt. trainee N.J. Bell Tel. Co., Newark/Camden, NJ, 1961; rsch. asst. Princeton (N.J.) U., 1962-65; asst. scientist Woods Hole (Mass.) Oceanographic Inst., 1965-68, assoc. scientist, 1968-77; staff rsch. scientist MIT, Cambridge, 1977-79; sr. rsch. scientist U. Tex., Austin, 1978-96; chief scientist World Geoscience Corp., Houston, 1996-1999; chief scientist, dir. tech. svcs. Fugro Airborne Surveys, Houston, 1999-2000; chief scientist, dir. tech. svs. Integrated Geophysics Corp., Houston, 2000. Cons. Mobil Oil Corp., Dallas, 1969, Exxon Corp., Houston, 1977, Bell Tel. Labs., Whippany/Murray Hill, N.J., 1976-78; vis. scholar U. Cambridge, Eng., 1974-75; adj. prof./instr. marine geophysics, seismics and geomagnetism, oceanography, acoustics and potential fields, faculty advisor MIT, Woods Hole Oceanographic Inst., U. Tex., 1968-96; cons. airborne/marine archeology Nat. Underwater and Marine Archeologic Agy., 1997, 98, 2003-. Contbr. articles to Jour. Geophys. Rsch. Sci., Geol. Soc. Am., Am. Petroleum Geologist, Ency. Brittanica. Fellow Explorers Club; mem. Am. Soc. Naval Engrs., Am. Geophys. Union, Soc. Exploration Geophysicists, AAAS, Marine Lodge, Phi Beta Kappa, Sigma Xi. Achievements include design of phase lock-in amplifiers for rock magnetometers; USN multi-beam sonar for seafloor geology; acoustically navigated vehicles for seafloor studies; vertical seismic profiling aboard deep ocean drilling project ships; aeromagnetic/electromagnetic detection of archeologic and groundwater salinity contamination sites, pipeline and wellhead surveying; multichannel acoustic seismo-acoustic reflection profile imaging of ocean watermasses; T-phase transmission studies; oceanic ridge and trench seismicity. Home: 3805 Gaines Ranch Austin TX 78735 Personal E-mail: joephillipsD@sbcglobal.net.

PHILLIPS, JOSEPH MICHAEL, historian, writer; b. Jacksonville, NC, June 17, 1960; s. Joseph Touart Phillips and Marie Louise Touzet; m. Samantha Jo Shub, Nov. 10, 1965; 1 child, Dominic Shehan. B. U. Tex., Arlington, 1983; M. U. Calif., Riverside, 1994; PhD, U. Tex., Austin, 2002. Reporter Cleburne Times-Review, Tex., 1983, Mesquite News, Tex., 1983, Irving Daily News, Tex., 1983—84, Ft. Worth Star-Telegram, 1984—90; rschr. Ctr. Am. History, Austin, 2003—05; adj. prof. U. Tex., Austin, 2004—. Author: (historical book) White Metropolis: Race, Ethnicity and Religion in Dallas, 1841 - 2001. Youth facilitator Bastrop Family Crisis Ctr., Tex., 2003—03; vol. United Way First Call for Help, Victorville, Calif., 1994—95; publicity chair Bastrop County Dem. Club, 2000—01. Recipient Outstanding Continuing Coverage Edn. award, Tex. State Tchrs. Assn., 1986, Ann. Faculty Appreciation award, U. Tex., Svcs. Students with Disabilities Office, 2002—03; fellow, U. Tex. History Dept., 1999—2000, 2000—01; Clara Driscoll fellow, Daus. of Tex. Revolution, 1997. Mem.: Am. Hist. Assn. Liberal. Home: 604 Laurel St Bastrop TX 78602 Home Phone: 512-303-4637. Personal E-mail: mphillips3925!@earthlink.net.

PHILLIPS, JOSEPH MICHAEL, neurosurgeon; b. Louisville, Feb. 3, 1952; s. Joseph Hugh and Nellie Juanita Phillips; m. Jeanne Marie Rivers, Nov. 29, 1982 (dec. Nov. 18, 2000); m. Judy Camille Belcuore, July 29, 2001; 1 child, Michael Thomas. BS, U. Notre Dame, Ind., 1974; PhD, NYU, 1981; MD, New U. Sch. Medicine, NYC, 1981. Resident in neurol. surgery Mass. Gen. Hosp., Boston, 1981—87; assoc. prof. surgery Dartmouth Med. Sch., Hanover, NH, 1988—2000; neurol. surgeon Upper Valley Neurology Neurosurgery, Lebanon, NH, 2000—. Mem.: Am. Assn. Neurol. Surgeons. Office: Upper Valley Neurology Neurosurgery 106 Hanover St Lebanon NH 03766 Home Phone: 802-649-8297; Office Phone: 603-448-0447. Business E-Mail: phillipsj@uvnn.com.

PHILLIPS, JOSHUA, pediatrician; b. Cleveland, Miss., Aug. 6, 1976; s. Barbara Brown Oltremari and Jack Franklin Phillips. MD, U. Miss., Jackson, 2002. Resident U. Miss. Med. Ctr., Jackson, 2002—06, chief resident pediat., 2006—07. Missionary to Kenya Pinelake Bapt. Ch., Brandon, Miss., 2006—06. Mem.: Am. Acad. Pediat. (assoc.), AMA (assoc.). R-Liberal. Baptist. Avocations: travel, running. Home: 104 Stonecastle Ct Brandon MS 39047 Office: Univ Miss Med Ctr 2500 North State St Jackson MS 39216 Home Phone: 601-992-9311; Office Phone: 601-984-1000. Personal E-mail: jfphillips@medicine.umsmed.edu.

PHILLIPS, JOY LAMBERT, lawyer, banker; b. Ft. Bragg, NC, Sept. 25, 1955; d. Jurloew Lambert and Mary Carolyn (Gregory) Trivette; m. Frank Warren Phillips, May 10, 1975. AA, N.E. Miss. Jr. Coll., Booneville, 1974; BA, U. Miss., 1976, JD, 1980. Bar: Miss. 1980. Assoc. Daniel, Coker, Horton & Bell, P.A., Jackson, Miss., 1980-85; sr. v.p., asst. gen. counsel Deposit Guaranty Nat. Bank, Jackson, 1985—98; gen. counsel Hancock Bank, Gulfport, Miss., 1999—. Seminar speaker, 1990-91. Treas., Miss. Opera Guild, Jackson, 1990-92; mentor Miss. Coll. Sch. Law, Jackson, 1989-92. Mem. ABA, Miss. Bar Assn. (pres. 2005-06), Hinds County Bar Assn., Harrison County Bar Assn., Miss. Women Lawyers (pres. 1989-90), Jackson Young Lawyers, Kiwanis (dir. 1991-93, pres. 1966). Avocations: reading, walking, dogs, biking. Home: PO Box 819 Gulfport MS 39502-0819 Office: Hancock Bank One Hancock Plz Gulfport MS 39501 Home Phone: 228-044-6044; Office Phone: 228-563-5755. E-mail: joy_phillips@hancockbank.com.

PHILLIPS, JOYCE MARTHA, human resources executive; b. Bridgeport, Conn., Dec. 18, 1952; d. Stephen and Shirley B. (Howard) Tabory; m. Glenn L. Phillips, July 14, 1974. BA in English, Fairfield U., Conn., 1974; MS in Indsl. Rels., U. New Haven, 1982. Tchr. English and Reading Fairfield Woods Jr. High Sch., 1975; asst. to v.p. mktg. Bunker Ramo Corp., Trumbull, Conn., 1975-76; rep. in investor rels. Gen. Electric Co., Fairfield, 1976-77, specialist in manpower rels., 1977-79, specialist in employee benefits Bridgeport, Conn., 1979-80, specialist in employee rels., orgn. and staffing, 1980-84; mgr. hdqrs. personnel and office svcs. Armtek Corp., New Haven, 1984-87, dir. compensation and benefits, 1987-89; v.p. human resources (div. sr. human resources officer) Citibank, NYC, 1989-91, v.p. compensation global fin., 1991-95; sr. v.p. human resources Barclays Bank/BZW, NYC, 1995-96; mng. dir., global head of human resources CIBC World Markets, NYC, 1996-99; evp and mng. dir. global human resources CIBC, NYC, 1999—. Counsel Fairfield U. Alumni Adv. Coun. Avocations: tennis, piano, dance, boating.

PHILLIPS, JULIA MAE, physicist; b. Freeport, Ill., Aug. 17, 1954; d. Spencer Kleckner and Marjorie Ann (Figi) Phillips. BS, Coll. William and Mary, Williamsburg, Va., 1976; PhD, Yale U., New Haven, Conn., 1981, postgrad., 2004. Mem. tech. staff AT&T Bell Labs., Murray Hill, 1981-88, supr. thin film rsch. group, 1988-95; dept. mgr. materials process computation and modeling dept. Sandia Nat. Labs., Albuquerque, 1995-2000, dep. dir. materials and process scis. ctr., 2000-01, dir. phys. and chem. sci. ctr., 2001—. Program mgr. Consortium Superconducting Elecs., 1989-92; mem. com. on condensed matter and materials physics NRC, 1996-99, mem. solid state scis. com., 1998-2001, mem. nat. materials adv. bd., 1999-2004, chair, 2002-2004, mem. com. on materials rsch. for def.-afternext, 1999-2002; vice chair Solid State Scis. com., 1999-2001, mem. bd. on physics and astronomy, 2000-06; mem. adv. com. math. and phys. scis. NSF, 2000-03. Editor: Heteroepitaxy on Silicon Technology, 1987, Epitaxial Oxide Thin Films and Heterostructures, 1994; prin. editor Jour. Materials Rsch., 1990-2005; mem. editl. bd. Applied Physics Letters and Jour. Applied Physics, 1992-94, Applied Physics Revs., 1998-2001; contbr. articles to profl. jours. Recipient Horizon award, U.S. Dept. Labor Women's Bur., 2002, Wilbur Cross medal, Nat. Acad. Engring., 2004. Fellow Am. Acad. Arts and Scis., Am. Phys. Soc. (exec. com. divsn. materials physics 1997-2000, exec. com. condensed matter physics, 2005—), AAAS (coun. 2003-06); mem. NAE, Materials Rsch. Soc. (sec. 1987-89, councillor 1991-93, 2d v.p. 1993, 1st v.p. 1994, pres. 1995), Fedn. Materials Soc. (exec. com. 1997), Sigma Xi, Phi Beta Kappa.

PHILLIPS, JULIEANNE APPLESON, history professor; b. Cleve., Jan. 15, 1952; d. Nick Appleson and Patricia Kepic (Appleson) Zajac; m. William Harold Phillips, July 2, 1977; children: Kristen Ann, Amy Lynn. AA, Cuyahoga C.C., Parma, Ohio, 1987; BA in History, Baldwin-Wallace Coll., Berea, Ohio, 1989; MA in History, Cleve. State U., 1990; PhD in Am. History, Case Western Res. U., 1996. Cert. history secondary edn. Ohio. Grant coord. Dayton-Tchg. Am. History, 2003—05; asst. prof. Urbana U., Ohio, 2005—. Author: (ency.) U.S. Aging Policy Interest Groups Institutional Profiles, (Web project) The History Place, (Web resource) Workshop for Teachers: Celebrating the 150th Anniversary of the Women's Rights Movement 1848-1998, (tchg. resource) Dayton Public Schools Social Studies Instructional Guide, (ency.) Encyclopedia of New England Culture, The Eleanor Roosevelt Encyclopedia, Organizing Black America, African American Women in the United States, The Historical Encyclopedia of World Slavery; contbr. articles and revs. to profl. jours. Judge Nat. Spelling Bee, Dayton, 2005, Nat. History Day, Cleve, 1986—2005; dir. Women Historians of Western Ohio, Dayton, 2000—05; independent evaluator Fairfield City and Northwest Sch. Dist. Tchg. Am. History Grant Miami U.-Hamilton, Hamilton, Ohio, 2006; moderator, steering com. mem. Buckeye Coun. for History Edn., 2006; panelist numerous profl. confs.; mem. Coord. Coun. Women in History; advisor, Urbana U. chpt. Phi Alpha Theta, 2005—. Recipient Elizabeth S. Magee Doctoral fellowship, Case Western Res. U., 1990—95, U.S. Achievement Acad. All Am. scholarship, U.S. Achievement Acad., 1989, Nat. Collegiate Edn. award, Nat. Collegiate Edn., 1989; fellow, Ohio Bd. of Regents, 1989—91. Mem.: Ohio Acad. of History (assoc.), Nat. Coun. for History Edn. (assoc.), Orgn. of Am. Historians (assoc.), Am. Hist. Assn. (assoc.). Office: Urbana Univ 579 College Way Urbana OH 43078 Home Phone: 937-335-2725; Office Phone: 937-484-1265. Business E-Mail: jphillips@urbana.edu.

PHILLIPS, KAREN BORLAUG, economist, rail transportation executive; b. Long Beach, Calif., Oct. 1, 1956; d. Paul Vincent and Wilma Borlaug. Student, Cath. U. P.R., 1973-74; BA, BS, U. N.D., 1977; postgrad., George Washington U., 1978-80. Rsch. asst. rsch. and spl. programs adminstrn. U.S. Dept. Transp., Washington, 1977—78, economist, office of sec., 1978—82; profl. staff mem. (majority) Com. Commerce Sci., Transp. U.S. Senate, Washington, 1982—85, tax economist (minority) com. on fin., 1985—87, chief economist (majority) senate com. on fin., 1987—88; commr. Interstate Commerce Commn., Washington, 1988—94; v.p. legis. Assn. Am. Railroads, Washington, 1994—95, sr. v.p. policy, legis. and comm., 1995—98; pres. Policy & Advocacy Assocs., Alexandria, Va., 1998—2000; v.p. N. Am. govt. affairs Can. Nat. Ry. Co., Washington, 2000—. Contbr. articles to profl. jours. Recipient award for Meritorious Achievement, Sec. Transp., 1980, Spl. Achievement awards, 1978, 80, Outstanding Performance awards, 1978, 80, 81. Mem. Am. Econ. Assn., Women's Transp. Seminar (Woman of Yr. award 1994), Transp. Rsch. Forum, Assn. Transp. Law Profls., Tax Coalition, Can.-Am. Bus. Coun. (bd. dirs.) Can.-Am. Border Trade Alliance, Blue Key, Phi Beta Kappa, Omicron Delta Epsilon. Republican. Lutheran. Office: Can Nat Rlwy Co Ste 500 601 Pennsylvania Ave NW Washington DC 20004 Home Phone: 703-548-7144; Office Phone: 202-347-7816. Personal E-mail: karen.phillips@cn.ca.

PHILLIPS, KAREN DIANE, surgeon; b. Dayton, Ohio, Jan. 11, 1968; d. Charles Joseph and Theresa Olwen Muscato; m. Ian Daniel Same, Sept. 24, 1999; children: Luke Daniel, Mason Charles. BS in Chemistry, Mary Washington U., Fredericksburg, Va., 1990; MD, Med. U. Ohio, Toledo, 1995. Diplomate Am. Bd. Surgery, 2001. Chief resident U. SC, Columbia, 1995—2000; intern, resident U. SC, Richland Meml. Hosp. and the Dorn Vets. Adminstrn. Hosp., 1996—2000; gen. surgeon Alamogordo Surg. Assocs., Alamogordo, N.Mex., 2001—04, So. Surg. Group, Lexington, SC, 2004—. Fellow: ACS; mem.: AMA, Soc. S.C. Surgeons, So. Med. Assn., Am. Soc. Breast Surgeons. Office: So Surg Group 2728 Sunset Blvd West Columbia SC 29169 Home: 1149 Katy Meadow Ct Fairborn OH 45324 Home Phone: 937-318-4063; Office Phone: 803-767-3814. Home Fax: 803-251-3382. Personal E-mail: kphillipsmd@hotmail.com.

PHILLIPS, KATHLEEN GAY, small business owner; b. Clarkston, Wash., Nov. 7, 1952; d. Cecil Martin Phillips and Nellie Florance Robertson; 1 child, John Cecil Dickeson-Phillips. Student, Lewis & Clark State Coll., 1973, Walla Walla C.C., 1990—91, Lewis & Clark State Coll., 1992; grad., H&R Tax Course, 2003. Cert. notary State of Idaho. Accounts clk. Lewis Clark State Coll., Lewiston, Idaho, 1975; co-founder Christina's Creations, Altus, Okla., 1982—, Funmates, Lewiston, 1982; dir. TK Springer, Inc., 1981; asst. mgr. Circle Drive Mobile Home Park, 1982—87. Surveyor Consumer Mail Panel, Palatine, Ill., 2000; restorer Gray Hut Apt. - Hist. Baughman House, Lewiston, 1993—99; rep. Western Modern Jewelry and Jewelry by Kathleen G. Phillips; history cons. Corps. Engrs. at Clarkston. With Medic Alert, 1979—; established Memory Walk & Safe Return, Alzheimer's Assn., 2005; worked with Gov. Kerathoun, Senator Craig, Senator Crapio, House of Rep. Helen Cheenawith, CL Otter. Pvt. US Army, 1991, Gulf War, with USNR. Recipient Oldest Tree award, Pks. & Recreation Bd., 1999. Mem.: Idaho Hist. Soc., Lewiston C. of C., The Planetary Soc., Clan Donald U.S. A., Am. Legion, Order of Ea. Star (life), Pi Beta Lambda. Methodist. Avocations: needlecrafts, painting, archaeology. E-mail: johndickeson@msn.com.

PHILLIPS, KEITH WENDALL, minister; b. Portland, Oreg., Oct. 21, 1946; s. Frank Clark and Velma Georgina (Black) P.; m. Mary Katherine Garland, July 16, 1973; children: Joshua, Paul, David. BA, UCLA, 1968; MDiv, Fuller Theology Sem., 1971, D. of Ministries, 1972; LHD (hon.), John Brown U., 1990; LHD (hon.), Sterling Coll., 2002. Dir. Youth For Christ Clubs, LA, 1965-71; pres. World Impact, LA, 1971—. Commencement speaker Tabor Coll., 1969, 91, John Brown U., 1990, Sterling Coll., 2002. Author: Everybody's Afraid in the Ghetto, 1973, They Dare to Love the Ghetto, 1975, The Making of a Disciple, 1981, No Quick Fix, 1985, Out of Ashes, 1996. Chmn. L.A. Mayor's Prayer Breakfast Com., 1985—; bd. dirs. Christian Cmty. Devel. Assn., 1992—; founder/coord. Crowns of Beauty Confs.; spkr. Promise Keeper. Named Disting. Staley lectr., 1969. Mem. Evangelistic Com. of Newark (pres. 1976—), World Impact of Can. (pres. 1978—), The Oaks (pres. 1985—), Faith Works (pres. 1987—) Baptist. Office: World Impact 2001 S Vermont Ave Los Angeles CA 90007-1279 *Our knowledge of God's Word outruns our obedience. The challenge for Christians is to live what we know.*

PHILLIPS, LARRY ARTHUR, artist; b. Syracuse, NY, Mar. 6, 1951; s. Arthur Foster and Vivian Phillips. Cork Gallery, Lincoln Ctr., NYC, 1990. Mem.: Ward-Nasse Gallery, Intuit the Ctr. for Intuitive and Outsider Art, Christians in Visual Arts. Home: 709 S West St Apt 4 Syracuse NY 13202

PHILLIPS, LARRY EDWARD, lawyer; b. Pitts., July 5, 1942; s. Jack F. and Jean H. (Houghtelin) P.; m. Karla Ann Hennings, June 5, 1976; 1 child, Andrew H.; 1 stepchild, John W. Dean IV. BA, Hamilton Coll., Clinton, NY, 1964; JD, U. Mich., 1967. Bar: Pa. 1967, Fla. 2004, US Dist. Ct. (we. dist.) Pa. 1967, US Tax Ct. 1969. Assoc. Buchanan Ingersoll & Rooney PC, Pitts., 1967—73, shareholder, 1973. Mem. ABA (sect. taxation, com. on corp. tax and sect. real property, probate and trust law), Am. Coll. Tax Counsel, Pa. Bar Assn., Fla. Bar, Tax Mgmt. Inc. (adv. bd.), Pitts. Tax Club, Allegheny County Bar Assn., Collier County Bar Assn., Duquesne Club. Republican. Presbyterian. Office: Buchanan Ingersoll & Rooney PC One Oxford Ctr 301 Grant St Fl 20 Pittsburgh PA 15219-1410 Office Phone: 412-562-8846. Business E-Mail: larry.phillips@bipc.com.

PHILLIPS, LEO HAROLD, JR., lawyer; b. Jan. 10, 1945; s. Leo Harold and Martha C. (Oberg) P.; m. Patricia Margaret Halcomb, Sept. 3, 1983. BA summa cum laude, Hillsdale Coll., 1967; MA, U. Mich., 1968, JD cum laude, 1973; LLM magna cum laude, Free U. of Brussels, 1974. Bar: Mich. 1974, NY 1975, US Supreme Ct. 1977, DC 1979. Fgn. lectr. Pusan Nat. U., Korea, 1969-70; assoc. Alexander & Green, NYC, 1974-77; counsel Overseas Pvt. Investment Corp., Washington, 1977-80, sr. counsel, 1980-82, asst. gen. counsel, 1982-85, Manor Care, Inc., Gaithersburg, Md., 1985-91, asst. sec., 1988-99, assoc. gen. counsel, 1991-99, v.p., 1996-99. Vol. Peace Corps, Pusan, Korea, 1968-71; mem. program for sr. mgrs. in govt. Harvard U., Cambridge, Mass., 1982. Contbr. articles to legal jours. Chmn. legal affairs com. Essex Condominium Assn., Washington, 1979-81; mem. fin. com., bd. trustees Miami City Ballet, 2001-06; deacon Chevy Chase Presbyn. Ch., Washington, 1984-87, moderator, 1985-87, supt. ch. sch., elder, trustee, 1987-90, pres., 1988-90, mem. nominating com., 1995-96; trustee, sec.-treas., Independence Grove, 2006—; trustee Scholastic Achievement Found. Palm Beach County, 2007-; pres. men's club, Delray Beach Presbyn. Ch., Fla., 2007—. Recipient Alumni Achievement award Hillsdale Coll., 1980; Meritorious Honor award Overseas Pvt. Investment Corp., 1981, Superior Achievement award, 1984. Mem. ABA (internat. fin. transactions com., vice-chmn. com. internat. ins. Law), Am. Soc. Internat. Law (Jessup Internat. Law moot ct. judge semi-final rounds 1978-83, chair corp. counsel com. 1993-97), Internat. Law Assn. (Am. br.; com. sec. 1982), DC Bar, NY State Bar Assn., Royal Asiatic Soc. (Korea br.), State Bar Mich., Washington Fgn. Law Soc. (sec.-treas. 1980-81, bd. dirs., program coord. 1981-82, v.p. 1982-83, pres.-elect 1983-84, pres. 1984-85, chmn. nominating com. 1986, 88), Washington Internat. Trade Assn. (bd. dirs. 1984-87), Assn. Bar City NY, Hillsdale Coll. Alumni Assn. (co-chmn. Washington area 1977-90), Univ. Club (NYC), Rotary (Delray Beach treas. 2003-2004, pres.-elect 2004-05, pres. 2005-06, asst. dist. gov. 2006-), Beach Property Owners Assn.(trustee 2006—).

PHILLIPS, M. IAN, physiologist, educator; b. London, July 30, 1938; arrived in US, 1967; s. Robert Leonard and Winifred Maud (Wheatley) Phillips; m. Blanca Aguiar, Nov. 29, 2004; m. Kate Phillips (div.). BSc with honors, U. Exeter, Eng., 1962; PhD, U. Birmingham, Eng., 1967, DSc, 1985. Vis. asst. prof. U. Mich., Ann Arbor, 1967—69; fellow Calif. Inst. Tech., Pasadena, 1969—70; prof. U. Iowa, Iowa City, 1970—80; chmn., prof. U. Fla., Gainesville, 1980—2003; v.p. rsch. U. South Fla., Tampa, 2003—06; Norris prof. Keck Grad. Inst., Claremont, Calif., 2006—. Program dir. neuro. NSF, Washington, 1990; chmn. cardiovascular study sect. NIH, Washington, 1992—94. Editor: Regulatory Peptides, 1990—2006, Gene Therapy, 2002, 3d edit., 2005, Antisense Therapeutics; co-author: Principles of Hormone & Behavior, 2005; author: (plays) Rembrandt. Bd. dirs. Moffit Cancer Ctr., Tampa, Fla., 2003—06. Recipient Lucian award, McGill U., Can., 1989, Frank Annunzio award, Christopher Columbus Fedn., 2002, Merit award, NIH, 1995—2006. Fellow: Am. Heart Assn. Achievements include discovery of brain peptides in hypertension; research in gene therapy for hypertension, stem cell rsch. on heart failure. Office: Keck Grad Inst 535 Watson Dr Claremont CA 91711 Home: 616 McKenna St Claremont CA 91711 Home Phone: 727-507-1190; Office Phone: 909-607-7487.

PHILLIPS, MARION GRUMMAN, civic volunteer, writer; b. NYC, Feb. 11, 1922; d. Leroy Randle and Rose Marion (Werther) Grumman; m. Ellis Laurimore Phillips, Jr., June 13, 1942; children: Valerie Rose (Mrs. Adrian Parsegian), Elise Marion (Mrs. Edward E. Watts III), Ellis Laurimore III, Kathryn Noel Phillips, Cynthia Louise (Mrs. Charles Prosser). Student, Mt. Holyoke Coll., 1940-42; BA, Adelphi U., 1981. Civic vol. Mary C. Wheeler Sch., 1964-68, Historic Ithaca, Inc., 1972-76, Ellis L. Phillips Found., 1960-91. Bd. dirs. North Shore Jr. League, 1960-61, 64-65, 68-69, Family Svc. Assn. Nassau County, 1963-69, Homemaker Svc. Assn. Nassau County, 1959, 61. Author: (light verse) A Foot in the Door, 1965, The Whale-Going, Going, Gone, 1977, Doctors Make Me Sick (So I Cured Myself of Arthritis), 1979; editor: (with Valerie Phillips Parsegian) Richard and Rhoda, Letters from the Civil War, 1982, Wooden Shoes the story of my Grandfather's Grandfather (F.M. Sisson), 1990, Irish Eyes, family hist. of McTarsneys and Sissons, 1990, The Log Chapel, A History of the Congregational Community Church, Rockwood, Maine, 1999; editor Jr. League Shore Lines, 1960-61, The Werthers in America-Four Generations and their Descendants, 1987; A B-Tour of Britain, 1986; contbr. articles on fund raising to mags. Mem. New Eng. Hist. Geneal. Soc., N.Y. Geneal. Biographical Soc., Hannah Adams Womens Club, PEO Sisterhood, Medfield Garden Club. Congregationalist. Mailing: 10 Longwood Dr # 203 Westwood MA 02090

PHILLIPS, MARJORIE SHAW, pharmacist, educator; b. Coral Gables, Fla. d. Howard Albert and Ricki Rose Shaw; m. William G. Phillips, Aug. 25, 1985. BS in Pharm., U. Fla., Gainesville, 1982, MS in Pharm., 1984. Pharmacy coord. medication safety and clin. rsch. Med. Coll. Ga. Health Sys., Augusta, Ga., 2004—; clin. prof. pharmacy practice U. Ga. Coll. Pharmacy, 2005—. Mem. safe medication use expert com. US Pharmacopeia, Rockville, Md., 2000—, vice chair safe medication use expert com., 2005—; vice chair human assurance com. Med. Coll. Ga., Augusta, 2001—, mem. human assurance com., 1992—, adj. asst. prof. dept. pharmacology, 2006—; pharmacist investigational drug svc. & med use improvement Med. Coll. Ga. Health Sys., 1991—2004, pharmacist, 1990—91; pharmacist quality assurance Meml. Hosp. Ormond Beach, Fla., 1985—90; pharmacy supr. fiscal affairs Shands Hosp., U. Fla., Gainesville, 1984—85. Contbr. articles to profl. jours., chapters to books. Recipient Forerunner award, Fla. Soc. Heath Sys. Pharmacists, 1988. Fellow: Am. Soc. Health-Sys. Pharmacists (chair ho. del. 2003—06, bd. dirs. 2002—06); mem.: Am. Soc. Cons. Pharmacists, Ga. Soc. Health-Sys. Pharmacists (pres. 1995—96, Pharmacist Yr. 1997). Office: Medical College of Georgia Health System Pharmacy 1120 Fifteenth Street BI-2101 Augusta GA 30912-5600 Office Phone: 706-721-0802. Business E-Mail: mphillip@mcg.edu.

PHILLIPS, MATTHEW TODD, history educator; b. Pitts., June 25, 1981; s. Henry Walter and Doreen Elaine Phillips; m. Sara Klingensmith, June 11, 2005. BA, Thiel Coll., Greenville, Pa., 2003; MA, Kent State U., Ohio, 2005. Tchg. asst. dept. history Kent State U., 2003—. Mem.: Soc. Historians Am. Fgn. Rels., Am. Hist. Assn., Alpha Chi, Phi Alpha Theta. Office: Dept History Kent State U 305 Bowman Hall PO Box 5190 Kent OH 44240 Home Phone: 724-859-1594.

PHILLIPS, MICHELLE GILLIAM, actress, writer; b. Long Beach, Calif., June 4, 1944; d. Gardner Burnett and Joyce Leon (Poole) Gilliam; m. John Phillips, Dec. 31, 1962 (div. 1970); children: Gilliam Chynna Phillips, Austin D. Hines, Aron S. Wilson. Grad. high sch., Ft. Jones, Calif. Model Francis Gill Agy., NYC, 1962-64; singer Mamas and Papas, 1965-69. Guest appearances in TV shows include Vega$, 1980, The Fall Guy, 1983, Santa Barbara, 1984, Murder, She Wrote, 1984, Scene of the Crime, 1985, Alfred Hitchcock Presents, 1985, T.J. Hooker, 1985, Star Trek: The Next Generation, 1988, Herman's Head, 1994, Diagnsos Murder, 1994, 99, Burke's Law, 1994, Lois & Clark: The New Adventures of Superman, 1995, Too Something, 1996, Beverly Hills, 90210, 1997, 98, Pauly, 1997, The Magnificent Seven, 1998, 99, 2000, The Love Boat: The Next Wave, 1998, Rude Awakening, 1999, Providence, 1999, Twice in a Lifetime, 2000; appeared in tv movies The Death Squad, 1974, The California Kid, 1974, The Useres, 1978, Moonlight, 1982, Murder Me, Murder You, 1983, Secrets of a Married Man, 1984, Covenant, 1985, Paint Me a Murder, 1985, Stark: Mirror Image, 1986, Assault and Matrimony, 1987, Mike Hammer: Murder Takes All, 1989, Trenchcoat in Paradise, 1989, Appearances, 1990, Rubdown, 1993, Rock 'n' Roll Revolution: The British Invade America, 1995, 919 Fifth Avenue, 1995, No One Would Tell, 1996, Pretty Poison, 1996, Sweetwater, 1999; appeared in feature films Monterey Pop, 1969, The Last Movie, 1971, Dillinger, 1973, Valentino, 1977, Bloodline, 1979, The Man with Bogart's Face, 1980, Savage Harvest, 1981, American Anthem, 1986, Let It Ride, 1989, Flashing on the Sixties: A Tribal Document, 1990, Scissors, 1991, Army of One, 1993, Anna Petrovic, You Rock!, 1998, Lost in the Pershing Point Hotel, 2000, TV series Aspen, 1977, The French Atlantic Affair, 1979, Hotel, 1983, Knots Landing, 1979, Second Chances, 1993, Malibu Shores, 1996, Knots Landing: Back to the Cul-de-Sac, 1997; author: California Dreamin', 1986, Monday Monday (Grammy award). Recipient medal of Honor for Stop War Toys Campaign Alliance for Survival, 1987, Soap Opera Awards for Best Villainess, 1990.

PHILLIPS, OLIVER, tropical forest ecologist, researcher; BA in Natural Scis., U. Cambridge, Eng., 1987, MA in Natural Scis., 1991; PhD in Population Biology, Washington U., St. Louis, 1993. NERC Rsch. fellow U. Leeds, England, 1996-99, lectr., 1999—2003, reader in tropical ecology, 2003—06, prof. tropical ecology, 2006—. Rsch. assoc. Mo. Bot. Garden, 1997—. Recipient Edmund H. Fulling award Soc. Econ. Botany, 1992. Mem. Soc. for Econ. Botany (mem. coun. 1996-99), Assn. Trop. Biology, Brit. Ecol. Soc. (Founder's Prize, 2004). Office: U Leeds Geography Sch Earth & Biosphere Inst Leeds LS2 9JT England Office Phone: 44 113 343 6832. Business E-Mail: o.phillips@leeds.ac.uk.

PHILLIPS, OLIVERIO MICHELSEN, retired chemical engineer; b. Fusagasuga, Colombia, June 6, 1928; s. Oliverio M. and Yolanda V. (Villaveces) P.; m. Yolanda M. Villaveces, Mar. 25, 1950; children: Jorge, Gustavo, Yolanda, Roberto, Francis, Alberto, Jose, Carolina. BS, MIT, 1948, MS, 1950, DSc, 1957. Indsl. cons., Bogota, 1968-95; cons. UN OAS, NYC, Washington, 1972-76; pres. Corp. Nal. Investigacion Forestal, Bogota, 1978-81; project mgr. Arinco S.A., Bogota, 1982-87, gen. mgr., 1987-92; ret., 1997. Bd. dirs. Corp. Financ. Popular, Bogota, 1968-71, Colciencias, Bogota, 1969-77, Ingeominas, Bogota, 1976-82. Mem. Inst. Colombiano de Normas Tecnicas, Inst. Investigaciones Tecnologicas (bd. dirs. 1983-87), Fedesarrollo (bd. dirs. 1969-95), Cooperacion Tecnica Internat. (bd. dirs. 1992-95), MIT Club (pres. 1966-68), Soc. Colombiana de Ciencias Quimicas (pres. 1962), N.Y. Acad. Scis. Roman Catholic. Avocations: music, reading, walking. Home: 6804 Chesterbrook Ct Apt 304 Raleigh NC 27615-7815 E-mail: ophillm@earthlink.net.

PHILLIPS, PAMELA KIM, lawyer; b. San Diego, Feb. 23, 1958; d. John Gerald and Nancy Kimiko (Tabuchi) Phillips; m. R. Richard Zanghetti, Sept. 16, 1989. BA cum laude, The Am. U., 1978; JD, Georgetown U., 1982. Bar: N.Y. 1983, U.S. Dist. Ct. (so. dist.) N.Y. 1983, Fla. 1994, U.S. Dist. Ct. (mid. dist.) Fla. 1994. Assoc. Curtis, Mallet-Prevost, Colt & Mosle, NYC, 1982-84, LeBoeuf, Lamb, Greene & MacRae, NYC, 1984-90, ptnr., 1991—. Mng. editor The Tax Lawyer, Georgetown U. Law Sch., Washington, 1980-81. Mem. coun. The Fresh Air Fund, 1991-94, Youth Leadership Jacksonville, 1999—; bd. dirs. Jacksonville Zool. Soc., Inc., 1996—, sec., 1997—; pres. First Coast Venture Capital Group, Inc., 1996-98. Am. Univ. scholar, Washington, 1976-78. Mem. ABA, Bar Assn. City N.Y. (sec. young lawyers com. 1987-89, chmn. 1989-91, second century com. 1990-93, banking law com. 1991-94), Jacksonville Bar Assn., River Club. Democrat. Roman Catholic. Avocations: tennis, travel. Home: 109 Carriage Lamp Way Ponte Vedra Beach FL 32082-1903 Office: LeBoeuf Lamb Greene & MacRae 125 W 55th St New York NY 10019-5369 also: 50 N Laura St Ste 2800 Jacksonville FL 32202-3656 Office Phone: 904-354-8000. E-mail: pamela.phillips@LLgm.com.

PHILLIPS, PATRICIA JEANNE, retired school system administrator; b. Amarillo, Tex., Jan. 13, 1935; d. William Macon and Mary Ann (Cawthon) Patrick; m. William Henry Phillips, June 22, 1962; 1 child, Mary Jeanne. BA, Millsaps Coll., 1954; MA, Vanderbilt/Peabody U., 1957; EdD, U. So. Miss., 1978. Tchr. Jackson Pub. Schs., Miss., 1954—73, prin., 1973—75, asst. prin., 1975—77; dir. ednl. program Eden Prairie # 272, Minn., 1977-80; dir. elem. edn. Meridian Pub. Schs., Miss., 1980—91, asst. supt. curriculum, 1991; ret., 1991. Part-time prof. Miss. Coll., Clinton, 1977, Miss. State U., Meridian, 1981—2002; cons. in field. Co-author: (testing practice) Test Taking Tactics, 1987; developer: tng. materials Best Practices; contbr. articles to profl. jours. Bd. dirs. Meridian Art Mus.; pres. Meridian Symphony Orch., 1987, 2000—; v.p. Meridian Coun. Arts, 1986. Named Boss of the Yr., Meridian Secretarial Assn., 1985, Art Educator of the Yr., Meridian Coun. Arts, 1991; recipient Excellence award, Pub. Edn. Forum, 1993. Mem.: Miss. ASCD, ASCD, Miss. Assn. Women (pres.), Rotary, Fidelis Beta (pres.-elect 2006, pres. 2007), Alpha Delta Kappa Gamma (pres. 1962), Phi Delta Kappa (pres. 1986—87), Phi Kappa Alpha. Republican. Methodist. Achievements include development of tng. materials Best Practices, Brain Growth: Applications for the Classroom. Avocations: grant writing, computers, golf, heirloom sewing. Home: 8450 SE 168th Kittredge Loop The Villages FL 32162-2851 Personal E-mail: jeannephill@embarqmail.com.

PHILLIPS, PAUL DAVID, JR., lawyer; b. Ft. Leavenworth, Kans., Oct. 16, 1950; s. Paul David Sr. and Rita Anne (Ruzicka) P.; m. Susan Zimmerman, May 25, 1974; children: Katherine, Helen, Alice, Mark. Student, Cambridge U., Eng., 1971-72; BA magna cum laude, Harvard U., 1973; JD, Yale U., 1976; postgrad., U. Sorbonne, 1976-77. Bar: Colo. 1977, US Dist. Ct. Colo. 1977, US Ct. Appeals (DC, 5th, and 10th cirs.) 1977, US Ct. Appeals (9th cir. & various other cts.), US Supreme Ct. Assoc. U.S. Customs, Washington, 1974, Holland & Hart, Denver, 1975, 77-83, ptnr., 1983—, chmn. environ law group, 1986; chmn. natural resources dept. Bogle & Gates, Seattle, 1990; ptnr. Holland & Hart, Denver. Founding editor Natural Resources and Environ.(ABA's natural resources sect.mag.), issues editor Environ. permitting (Negotiating the Maze), contbr. artical to profl. jour. Named The Best Lawyers in Am., Who's Who in Am. Mem. Colo. Bar Assn., Denver Bar Assn., Colo. Waste Soc., Colo. Mining Assn., Rocky Mountain Mineral Law Found. Avocations: running, skiing. Office: Holland & Hart 555 17th St Ste 3200 Denver CO 80202-3979 Office Phone: 303-295-8131. Office Fax: 303-713-6270. Business E-Mail: pphillips@hollandhart.com.

PHILLIPS, PETER CHARLES BONEST, economist, educator, researcher; b. Weymouth, Dorset, Eng., Mar. 23, 1948; came to U.S., 1980; s. Charles Bonest and Gladys Eileen (Lade) P.; m. Emily Dowdell Birdling, Feb. 10, 1971 (div. 1980); 1 child, Daniel Lade; m. Deborah Jane Blood, June 13, 1981; children: Justin Bonest, Lara Kimberley. BA, Auckland U., New Zealand, 1969, MA, 1971; PhD, London U., 1974; MA (hon.), Yale U., 1979. Teaching fellow U. Auckland, 1969-70, jr. lectr., 1970-71; lectr. in econs. U. Essex, Colchester, Eng., 1972-76; prof. econs. U. Birmingham, Eng., 1976-79, Yale U., New Haven, Conn., 1979-85, Stanley Resor prof. econs., 1985-89, Sterling prof. econs., 1989—; Alumni disting. prof. econs. U. Auckland, 1991—; pres. Predicta Software Inc., Madison, Conn., 1994—. Vis. scholar Ecole Polytechnique, Paris, 1977; univ. vis. prof. Monash U., Melbourne, Australia, 1986; vis. prof. Inst. Advanced Studes, Vienna, Austria, 1989; disting. visitor London Sch. Econs., 1989. Editor Econometric Theory jour., 1985; joint editor Asia Pacific Economic Review, 1995—; contbr. over 180 articles, book revs., notes to profl. jours. Recipient award for promotion of sci. Japan Soc., 1983, New Zealand medal Sci. and Tech., 1998, Plura Scripsit, 1997, Plurima Scripsit Econometric Theory award, 2000, Nzier Qantas Economist of Yr., 2000; Commonwealth Grants Com. scholar, Eng., 1971, Guggenheim fellow, N.Y., 1984-85. Fellow Am. Acad. Arts & Scis., Royal Soc. New Zealand (hon.), Econometric Soc., Jour. Econometrics, Am. Statis. Soc.; mem. Inst. Math. Stats., Modsim Soc. (Biennial Medal, 2003). Avocations: running, building, poetry, reading, native plant restoration. Office: Cowles Found PO Box 208281 New Haven CT 06520-8281 Home: PO Box 208281 New Haven CT 06520-8281 E-mail: peter.phillips@yale.edu.

PHILLIPS, PHILIP EDWARD, English professor; b. Fayetteville, Ark., Feb. 7, 1969; s. Carl M. P. and Peggy Sue P.; m. Sharmila Patel; 1 child: Edward. BA, Belmont U., Nashville, 1990; Cert. Langue Français Moyen 1, U. Cath. de l'Ouest, Angers, France, 1989; MA, Vanderbilt U., Nashville, 1992, PhD, 1996. Tchg. fellow Vanderbilt U., Nashville, 1991-96, lectr. in English, 1996—97; upper sch. tchr. in English and French Battle Ground Acad., 1997—99; asst. prof. English Mid. Tenn. State U., 1999—2004, assoc. prof., dept. English, 2004—, dir. grad. admissions. Author: John Milton's Epic Invocations, 2000; co-editor: New Directions in Boethian Studies, 2007; contbr. articles to Medieval English Studies, revs. to EMLS, Byron Jour., Carmina Philosophiae, poems to Vanderbilt Rev. Mem. Medieval Acad., MLA, Milton Soc. Am., Internat. Boethius Soc. (rec. sec. 1995—, editor newsletter, 1995, co-editor Carmina Philosophiae 1996-), Heights Nat. Alumni Assn. (bd. dirs. 1990—), Poe Found., Poe Studies Assn. Democrat. Episcopalian. Avocations: Tae Kwon Do, music, travel. Home: PO Box 246 Franklin TN 37065-0246 Office: Middle Tenn State U Dept English Box 70 Murfreesboro TN 37132 Home Phone: 615-591-4808; Office Phone: 615-898-2699. Office Fax: 615-898-5098. Business E-Mail: pphillip@mtsu.edu.

PHILLIPS, RENEÉ, writer; b. Freeport, NY; Student, Art Students League, 1979, Am. Art Sch., 1979, Fashion Inst. Tech., 1980, New Sch. for Social Rsch., 1980. Dir., founder Artopia, not-for-profit art orgn., NYC, 1980-84; pub., editor-in-chief Manhattan Arts Internat., NYC, 1983—2000; editor-in-chief www.Manhattan Arts.com. Juror Excellence in Arts Awards, 1988, N.Y. Lung Assn. Ann. Exhbn., 1990, Manhattan Arts Internat. Ann. Internat. Art Competition, 1992—; juror, co-curator Redefining Visionary Art, Doma Gallery, N.Y.C., 1989; curator Synthesis of Painting and Sculpture exhbn. 1st Women's Bank, N.Y.C., 1984, Salute to Liberty internat. art exhbn., N.Y.C., 1986, HerStory exhbns., 1999-2007, Small Works, 2004-05, The Healing Power of Art, 2002-04; editor-in-chief www.ManhattanArts.com; curator I Love Manhattan, N.Y.C., 2003, The Healing Power of Art, N.Y.C., 2003-05; bd. dirs., v.p. Women's Studio Ctr., L.I., N.Y., 2003—; spkr., lectr. in field. Author: The Complete Guide to New York Art Galleries, 1995-2006, Presentation Power Tools for Fine Artists, 1998, 2d edit., 2000, 3d edit., 2002, Success Now! for Artists: A Motivational Guide, 1998, 2d edit., 2003 Recipient award of merit Muscular Dystrophy Assn., 1986, award for outstanding contbns. to arts Mayor of N.Y.C., 1987. Mem. Internat. Assn. Art Critics, N.Y. Artists Equity (former bd. dirs.). Office: Manhattan Arts Internat 200 E 72nd St New York NY 10021-4537 Office Phone: 212-472-1660. Business E-Mail: info@ManhattanArts.com.

PHILLIPS, RICHARD A., retired literature and language educator; b. Chester, Pa., June 6, 1949; s. Albert Phillips and Florence (Dunn) P. BS, Cheyney U., Pa., 1971. Cert. tchr., Del. Tchr. Colonial Sch. Dist., New Castle, Del., 1971-87, 1991—2005, HighCroft Sch., Williamstown, Mass., 1986; exec. dir. Sylvan Learning Ctrs., Wilmington, Del., 1987-90; ret., 2005. Cmty. rels. vol. PAWS for People, Elkton, Md., bd. mem. Mem.: NEA, Del. State Edn. Assn. Retired (bd. dirs. 2006—, chmn. publicity 2000—06), New Castle County Edn. Assn. (bd. dir. 1991—2005, v.p. 1998—2005), Colonial Edn. Assn. (exec. com. 1971—84), Nat. Coun. Tchrs. English.

PHILLIPS, ROBERT, engineering educator, researcher; BS, U. Minn., 1986; PhD, Wash. U., 1989. Clark Millikan vis. asst. prof. Caltech, 1997—2000, prof. mech. engrng. and applied physics, 2000—. Contbr. articles to profl. jour. Recipient Pioneer award, NIH, 2004. Achievements include research in exploring nanoscale mechanics in biol. systems; the way DNA binding proteins that control gene expression expert mechanical forces on DNA resulting in the formation of loops. Office: Calif Inst Tech 159 Broad MC 128-95 Office 221 Steele 1200 E Calif Blvd Pasadena CA 91125 Office Phone: 626-395-3374. Office Fax: 626-583-4963. Business E-Mail: phillips@aero.caltech.edu. *

PHILLIPS, ROBERT ALEXANDER BELL, management consultant; b. London, Mar. 20, 1955; Canada; s. Robert Howard Daniel and Tanyss Bell Phillips; m. Brenda Marie Kieran, Oct. 27, 1986; children: Robert David Richard Kieran, Genevieve Tanyss Pride Kieran. MBA, Simon Fraser U., Vancouver, BC Can., 1994. V.p., dir. Elkhart Bell Internat., Calgary, Alberta, Canada, 1990—. Recipient ABEX award for Business Excellence. Fellow: Can. Securities Inst. Home: 2708 Signal Hill Dr SW Calgary AB Canada T3H 2L6 Office: Elkhart Bell International 2708 Signal Hill Dr SW Calgary AB Canada T3H 2L6 Home Phone: 403.680.5960. Personal E-mail: bobphillips.elkhart@hotmail.com.

PHILLIPS, ROBERT JAMES, JR., lawyer, corporate financial executive; b. Houston, 1955; s. Robert James. BBA, So. Meth. U., 1976, JD, 1980. Bar: Tex. 1980. Vp., gen. counsel Aegis Shipping Ltd., London, 1980-81; assoc. Bishop, Larrimore, Lamsens & Brown, 1981-82; pres. Phillips Devel. Corp., Ft. Worth, 1982—; pvt. practice Ft. Worth, 1982—87; assoc. Haynes and Boone, Ft. Worth, 1988-89; sr. v.p. Am. Real Estate Group, 1989-93, Am. Savs. Bank, N.A., New West Fed. Savs. and Loan Assn., 1989-93, Am. Savs. Bank, Ft. Worth, 1991-92; chmn., CEO creative risk control Environ. Risk Mgmt. Inc., Ft. Worth, 1992-94; chmn., CEO Pangburn Candy Co., 1996-99; exec. v.p. Ancor Holdings, 1999—2002; chmn., CEO Am. Staff Resources Corp., 1999—2004; pres. InterProm Capital L.L.C., 2003—04, Fund Corp., Inc., 2004—. Bd. dirs. Tex. Heritage, Inc. Bd. dirs., exec. com. Ft. Worth Ballet Assn., 1984-85, Van Cliburn Found.; v.p. planning, bd. dirs., exec. com. Ft. Worth Symphony Orch., 1984-85; bd. dirs. Mus. Modern Art, 1986; bd. dirs., exec. com., chmn. investment com. Tex. Boys Choir, 1983-85. Mem. ABA, Tex. Bar Assn., Ft. Worth Bd. Realtors, Phi Delta Phi, Kappa Sigma, Beta Gamma Sigma.

PHILLIPS, ROGER, retired steel company executive; b. Ottawa, Ont., Can., Dec. 17, 1939; s. Norman William Frederick and Elizabeth (Marshall) P.; m. Katherine Ann Wilson, June 9, 1962; 1 child, Andrée Claire. BSc, McGill U., Montreal, Can., 1960. V.p. mill products Alcan Can. Products Ltd., Toronto, Ont., 1969-70, exec. v.p., 1971-75; pres. Alcan Smelters and Chems. Ltd., Montreal, Que., 1976-79; v.p. tech. Alcan Aluminium Ltd., Montreal, 1980-81; pres. Alcan Internat. Ltd., Montreal, 1980-81; pres., CEO IPSCO Inc., Regina, Sask., Canada, 1982—2001. Sr. mem. Conf. Bd., Inc., NY, 1987—2002; bd. dirs. Toronto Dominion Bank, Can. Pacific Rlwy., Imperial Oil Ltd.; hon. dir. IPSCO Inc.; dir. Cleveland-Cliffs Inc. Bd. dirs. Conf. Bd. of Can., 1984-87; chmn. Coun. for Can. Unity, 1987-88. Fellow Inst. Physics UK (chartered physicist); mem. Can. Assn. Physicists, Am. Iron and Steel Inst. (bd. dirs. 1984-2001), Sask. C. of C. (bd. dirs. 1984-), Que. C. of C. (pres. 1981), Order of Can. (officer 1999), St. Denis Club, Univ. Club (Montreal), Calgary Petroleum Club. Home: 3220 Albert St Regina SK Canada S4S 3N9 Office: IPSCO Inc Armour Rd Regina SK Canada S4P 3C7 E-mail: rphillips@ipsco.com.

PHILLIPS, RONALD FRANK, academic administrator; b. Houston, Nov. 25, 1934; s. Franklin Jackson and Maudie Ethel (Merrill) P.; m. Jamie Jo Bottoms, Apr. 5, 1957 (dec. Sept. 1996); children: Barbara Celeste Phillips Oliveira, Joel Jackson, Phil Edward. BS, Abilene Christian U., 1955; JD, U. Tex., 1965. Bar: Tex. 1965, Calif. 1972. Bldg. contractor Phillips Homes, Abilene, Tex., 1955-56; br. mgr. Phillips Weatherstripping Co., Midland and Austin, Tex., 1957-65; corp. staff atty. McWood Corp., Abilene, 1965-67; sole practice law Abilene, 1967-70; mem. adj. faculty Abilene Christian U., 1967-70; prof. law Pepperdine U., Malibu, Calif., 1970—, dean Sch. Law, 1970-97, dean emeritus, 1997—, vice chancellor, 1995—. Mem. Nat. Conf. Commrs. on Uniform State Laws, 1988—2003. Deacon North A and Tenn. Ch. of Christ, Midland, 1959-62; deacon Highland Ch. of Christ, Abilene, 1965-70; elder Malibu Ch. of Christ, 1978-95; mgr., coach Little League Baseball, Abilene, Huntington Beach and Malibu, 1968-78, 90-95; coach Youth Soccer, Huntington Beach, Westlake Village and Malibu, 1972-80, 85-86, 91. Recipient Alumni citation Abilene Christian U., 1974 Fellow Am. Bar Found. (life); mem. ABA, State Bar Tex., State Bar Calif., Christian Legal Soc., L.A. Bar Assn., Assn. Am. Law Schs. (chmn. sect. on adminstrn. law schs. 1982, com. on cts. 1985-87), Am. Law Inst. Republican. Office: Pepperdine U 24255 Pacific Coast Hwy Malibu CA 90263-4951 Business E-Mail: ronald.phillips@pepperdine.edu.

PHILLIPS, RONALD LEWIS, plant geneticist, educator; b. Huntington County, Ind., Jan. 1, 1940; s. Philemon Lewis and Louise Alpha (Walker) P.; m. Judith Lee Lind, Aug. 19, 1962; children: Brett, Angela. BS in Crop Sci., Purdue U., 1961, MS in Plant Breeding and Genetics, 1963, Doctorate (hon.), 2000; PhD in Genetics, U. Minn., 1966; postgrad., Cornell U., 1966-67. Rsch. and tchg. asst. Purdue U., 1961—62; rsch. asst. U. Minn., St. Paul, 1962—66, rsch. assoc., 1967—68, asst. prof., 1968—72, assoc. prof., 1972—76, prof. genetics and plant breeding, 1976—93, Regents prof., 1993—, McKnight presdl. chair in genomics, 2000—. Vis. prof., Italy, 1981, Canada, 83, China, 86, Japan, 90, Morocco, 96; program dir. Competetive Rsch. Grants Office USDA, Washington, 1979, chief scientist, 1996—98, mem. adv. grant panels, NSF, DOE; chmn. Gordon Conf. on Plant Cell and Tissue Culture, 1985; mem. sci. adv. coun. U. Calif. Plant Gene Expression Ctr., Berkeley, 1986—93, chair, 1992—93; program adv. com. Palm Oil Rsch. Inst. Malaysia, 1992—2001; non-resident fellow Noble Found., 2001—06; sci. adv. bd. Donald Danforth Plant Sci. Ctr., St. Louis, 2000—; sci. liaison officer Internat. Rice Rsch. Inst. USAID, 2000—03, bd. trustees, 2004—, mem. adv. grant panels; dir. Plant Molecular Genetics Inst., 1991—94; trustee Biol. Stain Commn.; mem. Nat. Plant Genetic Resources Bd.; dir. Ctr. Microbial and Plant Genomics U. Minn., 2000—05. Co-editor: Cytogenetics, 1977, Molecular Genetic Modification of Eucaryotes, 1977, Molecular Biology of Plants, 1979, The Plant Seed: Development, Preservation and Germination, 1979, Genetic Improvement of Crops: Emergent Techniques, 1980, DNA-Based Markers in Plants, 1994, 2d edit., 2001; assoc. editor Genetics, 1978—81, Can. Jour. Genetics and Cytology and Genome, 1985—90, mem. editl. bd. Maydica, 1978—, In Vitro Cellular and Devel. Biology, 1988—92, Cell Culture and Somatic Cell Genetics of Plants, 1983—91, Jour. of the Oil Palm, 1994—, Proc. NAS, 1996—98; contbr. chpts. to Maize Beeding and Genetics, 1978, Staining Procedures, 1981, Chromosome Structure and Function, 1987, Corn and Corn Improvement, 1988, Plant Transposable Elements, 1988, Chromosome Engring. in Plants, 1991, Maize Handbook, 1994, sci. articles to profl. jours. Mem. chmn. coun. on ministries, lay leader Unitd Meth. Ch., 1968, dir. project AgGrad, 1983—; Cub Scout Pack co-chmn. Boy Scouts Am., 1976-77; judge Minn. Regional and State Sci. Fair, 1970-80. Recipient Purdue Agrl. Alumni Achievement award, 1961, Purdue Disting. Agrl. Alumni award, 1993; NSF fellow, 1961; NIH fellow, 1966-67; recipient Northrup King Oustanding Faculty Performance award, 1985, DeKalb Genetics Crop Sci. Disting. Career award, 1997. Fellow: AAAS (program com. 2003—06, chair sect. O, Wolf Agr. prize 2007), Crop Sci. Soc. Am. (awards com., divsn. chmn., bd. rep. 1988—91, pres.-elect 1998—99, pres. 1999—2000, past pres. 2000—01, Rsch. award 1988), Am. Soc. Agronomy (Caleb-Dorr award); mem.: NAS (chair sect. 62 1999—2002, nominating com. 2002), Am. Soc. Agronomy (award student sect.), Genetics Soc. Am., Sigma Xi, Alpha Zeta, Gamma Sigma Delta (award of merit 1994), Gamma Alpha (nat. treas.). Office: U Minn Dpt Agronomy-Plant Genetics Saint Paul MN 55108 Business E-Mail: phill005@umn.edu.

PHILLIPS, RUTH ANN, retired secondary school educator; b. Greensboro, NC, Nov. 26, 1948; d. Paul Frank and Agnes Elizabeth (Butler) P. AB, Elon Coll., 1971. Cert. health and phys. edn. tchr., N.C. Tchr. health and phys. edn., chmn. dept. Sellars-Gunn Jr. H.S., Burlington, NC, 1972-81, coach tennis, basketball, softball, 1973-81; tchr., coach varsity softball, chmn. health and phys. edn. Walter M. Williams Sr. H.S., Burlington, 1981—2001, ret., 2001. Participant Summer Nat. Sr. Olympic Games, 2007—. Named Tchr. of Yr., Sellars-Gunn Jr. High Sch., 1975, Secondary Phys. Edn. Tchr. of Yr., N.C., 1998, Eight Who Make A Difference, Homer Thompson Meml., 2001. Mem.: Why Nots Sr. Softball Team, State Employees Assn. NC, N.C. Assn. Educators, Sr. Games. Democrat. Methodist. Avocations: racquetball, softball. Home: 2027 S Mebane St Burlington NC 27215-7617

PHILLIPS, RUTHANNE, special education administrator; d. George and Margaret Ann Mitro. BA in Psychology, cum laude, Wittenberg U., Springfield, Ohio, 1979; MS in Spl. Edn., Calif. Luth. U., Thousand Oaks, 1983; MA in Ednl. Leadership, Calif. State U., LA, 2004. Multiple subjects tchg. credential Calif., learning handicapped specialist tchg. credential Calif., severely handicapped specialist tchg. credential Calif., resource specialist cert. of competence Calif., adminstrv. svcs. credential Calif., computers in edn. cert. Calif. Luth. Coll., child mental health specialist Calif. Luth. Coll. and Camarillo State Hosp., specially designed acad. instrn. in English Calif. Grad. student asst. Camarillo State Hosp. and Devel. Ctr., Calif., 1979—80, tchg. asst., 1980—81, spl. edn. tchr.,

1981—96, Calif. Dept. Youth Authority at Fred C. Nelles Sch., Whittier, 1996—97, LA County Office Edn. Divsn. Spl. Edn. at High Desert Prin.'s Adminstrv. Unit, Palmdale, 1999—2000; spl. edn. resource specialist tchr. LA County Office Edn. Divsn. Juvenile Cts. and Cmty. Schs. at Pacific Lodge Boys Home, Woodland Hills, 1997—99; spl. edn. program specialist Antelope Valley Spl. Edn. Local Plan Area, Palmdale, 2000—07; spl. edn. program specialist moderate/severe disabilities Palmdale Sch. Dist., 2007—. Mem. Calif. Svcs. Tech. Assistance and Tng. Region 11 Coordinating Coun., LA, 2000—07, sec., 2001—02, chairperson, 2002—04; mem. adv. bd. Antelope Valley Family Focus Resource and Empowerment Ctr., Palmdale, 2003—05; mem. Calif. Sys. Pers. Devel. Adv. Coun., Sacramento, 2003—05, Pacific Lodge Sch. Site Coun., Woodland Hills, 1997—99; campus adv. bd. Chapman U., Antelope Valley, Palmdale, 2001—03; bd. dirs. Very Spl. Arts of Calif., Sacramento, 2006—07. Mem. Friends of the Acton-Agua Dulce Libr., Acton, Calif., 2005—, Friends of Acton Park, Calif., 2005—; liturgy coord. St. Mary's Acton-Agua Dulce Mission, Acton, 2002—, historian, 2000—, lector, 2000—; religious edn. tchr. St. Mary's Acton-Aqua Duice Mission, 2001—03; asst. religious edn. coord. St. Mary's Acton-Agua Dulce Mission, Acton, 2004—05; literacy tutor Camarillo, 1992—97, Acton and Palmdale, 2002—. Recipient Wittenberg Alumni scholarship, Wittenberg U., 1975—79. Mem.: ASCD, CEC, Autism Soc. Am., Internat. Reading Assn., L.A. County Adminstrs. of Spl. Edn., Assn. Calif. Sch. Adminstrs., Antelope Valley Astronomy Club, Psi Chi, Alpha Xi Delta (Zeta chpt. historian 1978—79). Democrat. Roman Catholic. Avocations: scrapbooking, cardmaking, reading, travel, collecting 1st editions by Stephen King and Dean Koontz. Office: Palmdale Sch Dist Spl Edn and Student Svcs 39139 10th St E Palmdale CA 93550

PHILLIPS, SHAY E., pharmacist, educator; d. W. and G. Phillips. BS, Valdosta State U., Ga., 1998; PharmD, Fla. A&M U., Tallahassee, 2002. Cert. pharmacotherapy specialist Bd. Pharm. Specialties, 2006. Resident Tampa Gen. Hosp., Fla., 2003; asst. prof. pharmacy practice sch. pharmacy Hampton U., Va., 2003—. Recipient Preceptor of the Yr. award, Hampton U. Sch. Pharmacy, 2006. Mem.: Am. Colls. Clin. Pharmacy, Am. Assn. Colls. Pharmacy, Va. Soc. Health Sys. Pharmacist, Delta Sigma Theta. Personal E-mail: phillipsshay@hotmail.com.

PHILLIPS, SIDNEY FREDERICK, gastroenterologist, educator; b. Melbourne, Australia, Sept. 4, 1933; s. Clifford and Eileen Frances (Fitch) P.; m. Decima Honora Jones, Mar. 29, 1957; children: Penelope Jane, Nichola Margaret, David Sidney. M.B.BS, U. Melbourne, 1956, MD, 1961. Resident med. officer Royal Melbourne Hosp., 1957-61, asst. sub-dean clin. sch., 1961-62; research asso. Central Middlesex Hosp., London, 1962-63; rsch. assoc. Mayo Clinic, Rochester, Minn., 1963-66, cons. in gastroenterology, 1966-2000; prof. medicine Mayo Med. Sch., 1976-2000, prof. medicine emeritus, 2000—, dir. gastroenterology rsch. unit, 1977-94; program dir. Mayo Gen. Clin. Rsch. Ctr., 1974-87; dir. Mayo Digestive Diseases Core Ctr., 1984-90; Karl F. and Marjory Hasselman prof. rsch., 1994-2000. Editor: Digestive Diseases and Sciences, 1977-82, Gastroenterology International, 1990-95; sr. assoc. editor: Gastroenterology, 1991-96; contbr. chpts. to books, articles to profl. jours. Fellow ACP, Royal Coll. Physicians, Royal Australian Coll. Physicians; mem. Am. Motility Soc. (pres. 1994-96), Am. Soc. Clin. Investigation (emeritus), Gastroenterology Soc. Australia (hon.), Am. Gastroenterology Assn. Assn. Am. Physicians, Brit. Soc. Gastroenterology (hon.). Office: St Mary's Hosp Gastroenterology Unit 200 1st St SW Rochester MN 55905-0001 Home: Dakota on the Park 209 8th St E #411 Saint Paul MN 55101-3389 Personal E-mail: decimasidney@aol.com.

PHILLIPS, STACY D., lawyer; b. NYC, Sept. 5, 1958; d. Gerald F. and Francine Anne (Kantor) Phillips. AB, Dartmouth Coll., 1980; JD, Columbia U., 1983. Cert.: Family Law Specialist, bar: Calif. 1984, US Dist. Ct. Ctrl. and So. Districts Calif., US Ct. Appeals 9th Cir. Law clk. to Hon. Edward Rafeedie US Dist. Ct., LA, 1983-84; assoc. Wyman, Bautzer, Rothman, Kuchel & Silbert, LA, 1984-85, Jaffe & Clemens, Beverly Hills, Calif., 1986—90; founding ptnr. Mannis & Phillips, LA, 1995—2000, Phillips Lerner, Lauzon & Tamra LLP, LA, 2000—. Guest commentator various TV programs including Good Morning America, Hard Copy, Inside Edition; contbr. Divorce Mag., adv. bd.; bd. dirs. Legal Momentum (previously NOW Legal Def. and Edn. Fund); co-chair Calif. Leadership Coun. Bd. dirs. Vista del Mar Child and Family Services, Levitt & Quinn Family Law Ctr., Bnai Zion Found. Inc.; bd. trustees Alternative Living for the Aging. Named one of 50 Most Powerful Women in LA Law, LA Bus. Jour., 1998, Top 20 Attorneys Under 40 Years Old, LA Daily Jour., 1998, Top 50 Women Litigators in Calif., 2003; recipient Women of Action Award, Israel Cancer Rsch. Fund, 2000, Women of Achievement Award, Bnai Zion Found. Inc., 2001, Women Who Make a Difference Award, LA Bus. Jour., 2001, Patricia McClure Award, Asthma & Allergy Found. Am., 2001, Women of Achievement Award in Family Law and Mediation, Century City C. of C., 2001, 2002; grantee Policy Study Internship, Dartmouth U., 1978—78. Mem.: Beverly Hills Bar Assn. (mem. family law sect., mem. alternative dispute resolutions com.), LA Bar Assn. (mem. family law sect.), State Bar Calif. (mem. child custody and visitation com.), ABA (mem. family law sect.), Chancery Club of LA. Avocations: cooking, tennis. Office: 2029 Century Park E Ste 1200 Los Angeles CA 90067 Office Phone: 310-277-7117. Business E-Mail: sdpdissoqueen@plljlaw.com.

PHILLIPS, STANLEY DAVIS, ambassador; b. High Point, N.C. Attended, Moscow State U.; grad., U. N.C., Chapel Hill. Former chmn., CEO Phillips Industries, Inc.; former ptnr. Market Square Partnership; sec. commerce State of NC, 1993—97; chmn. NC Econ. Develop. Bd., 1998—2002; bd. mem. NC Dept. Transp.; US amb. to Estonia US Dept. State, Tallinn, 2007—. Chmn. Piedmont Triad Partnership, Econ. Develop. Corp. of High Point. Chair World Games of Special Olympics, 1999; bd. mem. Smithsonian Inst., Duke U., Wake Forest U. Med. Ctr. Office: Am Embassy 4530 Tallinn Pl Washington DC 20521 *

PHILLIPS, STEVE, electronics executive; arrived in US, 2001; BSc with honors in Electronic Engring., U. Essex, Eng.; postgraduate diploma in Mgmt. Studies, Thames Valley U., Eng. Various leadership positions Thorn EMI, 1984—96; info. tech. dir. European foods divsn. Diageo, 1996—99; v.p. info. tech. to sr. v.p., chief info. officer Gateway, Dublin, 1999—2003, sr. v.p., chief info. officer, 2003—04, Memec, 2004—05, Avnet, Inc., Phoenix, 2005—. Bd. dirs. Ariz. Tech. Coun., 2007—. Named one of Top 100 Chief Info. Officers, eWeek, 2007. Fellow: Instn. Elec. Engrs. Office: Avnet Inc 2211 S 47th St Phoenix AZ 85034-6403 Office Phone: 480-643-2000. *

PHILLIPS, STONE (LESTER STOCKTON PHILLIPS), newscaster; b. Texas City, Tex., Dec. 2, 1954; m. Debra Phillips; 1 child, Streeter. BA in Philosophy with honors, Yale U., 1977. Past prodr., reporter WXIA-TV, Atlanta; formerly with documentary unit Close-Up ABC News, assignment editor Washington, 1979—81, gen. assignment corr., 1982—86, corr. 20/20, 1986—92; prin. anchor Dateline NBC-TV, NYC, 1992—2007; contbg. corr. MSNBC. Past remedial-reading tchr. Fulton County Juvenile Ct., Atlanta; substitute host Good Morning America, 1986; guest sports anchor World News Sunday, 1986; past substitute anchor NBC Nightly News, Today, Meet the Press. Named to Scholar Athlete Hall of Fame, Nat. Football Found.; recipient F. Gordon Brown award for Outstanding Acad. & Athletic Leadership, Yale U., 1976, 3 Nat. Headliner awards for Outstanding Journalism, Overseas Press Club award, Nat. Assn. Black Journalists award, AMA award, Am. Psychol. Assn. award, B'nai B'rith award; NCAA Post-Grad. scholar. *

PHILLIPS, SUSAN MEREDITH, academic administrator, economist; b. Richmond, Va., Dec. 23, 1944; d. William G. and Nancy (Meredith) Phillips. BA in Math., Agnes Scott Coll., 1967; MS in Fin. and Ins., La. State U., 1971, PhD in Fin. and Economics, 1973. Asst. prof. La. State U., 1973—74, U. Iowa, 1974—78; econ. fellow Directorate of Econ. and Policy Rsch., SEC, 1976—78; assoc. prof. fin. dept. U. Iowa, 1978—83, assoc. v.p. fin. & univ. services, 1979—81; commr. Commodity Futures Trading Commn., 1981—83, chmn., 1983—87; prof. fin. dept., v.p. fin. and univ. svcs. U. Iowa, Iowa City, 1987—91; bd. govs. Fed. Res. Sys., Washington, 1991—98; dean Sch. of Bus., prof. fin. dept. George Washington U., Washington, 1998—. Trustee Fin. Acctg. Found., Norwalk, 2006—; bd. dirs. Chgo. Bd. Options Exch., Nat. Futures Assn., Kroger Co., State Farm Mutual Auto. Co. Co-author (with J. Richard Zecher): The SEC and the Public Interest; contbr. articles to profl. jours. Fellow Brookings Econ. Policy fellow, 1976—77. Office: George Washington U Sch Bus Ste 660 2201 G St NW Washington DC 20052 Business E-Mail: gwsbdean@gwu.edu.

PHILLIPS, THEODORE LOCKE, radiologist, educator; b. Phila., June 4, 1933; s. Harry Webster and Margaret Amy (Locke) Phillips; m. Joan Cappello, June 23, 1956; children: Margaret, John, Sally. BSc, Dickinson Coll., 1955; MD, U. Pa., 1959. Intern Western Res. U., Cleve., 1960; resident in therapeutic radiology U. Calif., San Francisco, 1963, clin. instr., 1963—65, asst. prof. radiation oncology, 1965—68, assoc. prof., 1968—70, prof., 1970—, chmn. dept. radiation oncology, 1973—98. Rsch. radiobiologist U.S. Naval Radiologic Def. Lab., San Francisco, 1963—65; rsch. physician Lawrence Berkeley Lab. Contbr. numerous articles to profl. publs. With USNR, 1963—65. Grantee, Nat. Cancer Inst., 1970—99. Mem.: Inst. Medicine, No. Calif. Radiation Oncology Assn., Radium Soc., Radiation Rsch. Soc. (pres. 1977), Am. Coll. Radiology, Calif. Med. Assn., Am. Assn. Cancer Rsch., N.Am. Hyperthermia Soc. (pres. 1994), Radiol. Soc. N.Am., Am. Soc. Clin. Oncology, Am. Soc. Therapeutic Radiology and Oncology (pres. 1984), Alpha Omega Alpha, Phi Beta Kappa. Republican. Office: U Calif San Francisco Dept Radiation Oncology 1600 Divisidero St ste H1031 San Francisco CA 94143-1708

PHILLIPS, THOMAS EDWORTH, JR., financial advisor, investment management consultant; b. Danville, Va., July 7, 1944; s. Thomas Edworth Sr. and Jean (Worley) P.; m. Claudia Mitchell, July 23, 1966; children: Kelly Marie, Melissa Joyce. BS in Econs., Va. Tech., 1966; cert. in investments, N.Y. Inst. Fin., 1969; MS in Bus., Va. Commonwealth U., 1973; postgrad., U. Pa., 1989. Cert. investment mgmt. analyst; registered investment adviser. Edn. coord. Prince William County Schs., Manassas, Va., 1966-67; investment broker Conrad and Co., Richmond, Va., 1967-68; investment exec. UBS Paine Webber, Inc., Richmond, 1968—, divisional v.p., 1980-99, sr. v.p. and prime cons., 2000—; registered prin. NY Stock Exch., Nat. Assn. Securities Dealers, 1987—. Access program nat. com. UBS Paine Webber, N.Y.C., Inc., 1989-90, mem. dir.'s coun., 1987-88, managed accounts nat. adv. bd., 1991-93; mem. mut. fund Nat. Adv. Coun., 1996—, pres.' council, 1997—; bd. dirs. Madison Group, Inc., Richmond, Meadowbrook Assocs., Inc., Richmond; speaker in field. Bd. dirs. Va. Non-Profit Housing Coalition, pres., 1992—; chmn. bd. deacons. Mt. Olivet Ch., Hanover, Va., 1984-85; trustee Hanover Acad., Ashland, Va., 1980-84; pres. alumni bd. Va. Commonwealth U., Richmond, 2003-05. Rotary Found. fellow, 1989. Mem. Investment Mgmt. Cons. Assn., Capital Soc., Va. Tech. Alumni Assn., Va. Commonwealth U. Alumni Assn., Rotary, Bull and Bear Club, Omicron Delta Epsilon. Avocations: horses, tennis, golf. Office: UBS PRIME Consulting Group 1021 E Cary St Ste 1800 Richmond VA 23219-4000 Home: 13464 Lakeview Farms Pl Ashland VA 23005 Office Phone: 804-775-1501. Business E-Mail: tom.phillips@ubs.com.

PHILLIPS, THOMAS J., JR., accountant, educator; b. Shreveport, La., May 8, 1954; s. Thomas J. and Elma S. Phillips; m. Myla D. Davis, Feb. 4, 1955; children: Trenton J., Tyler J. BS, U. La. Lafayette, 1975; MS, La. State U., Baton Rouge, 1977; PhD, Ga. State U., Atlanta, 1984. CPA La., 1979. Acct., cons., expert witness Various, Lafayette, Baton Rouge, Shreveport, and New Orleans, La., 1973—2006; instr. Acctg. Dept. Southeastern La. U., Hammond, 1979—80; tchg. fellow Ga. State U., 1980—81; asst. prof., assoc. prof. La. State U. Shreveport, 1984—87; asst. prof., assoc. prof., prof. La. Tech U., Ruston, 1987—95, dir. and KPMG prof., 1995—. Contbr. articles to academic and profl. jours. Recipient Outstanding Contbr. Award, Inst. Internal Auditors, 1988; fellow Ctrl. Bank Endowed Prof., La. Tech U., 1995—2000, KPMG Endowed Prof., 2000—. Mem.: AICPA, Inst. Mgmt. Accts. (Merit Cert. for Article 1993—94), Am. Acctg. Assn., Soc. La. CPA (pres. Shreveport chpt. 1991—92, Outstanding Educator award 1990). Mem. Ch. Of Christ. Avocations: travel, fishing. Office: La Tech U Railroad Ave 123 CAB Ruston LA 71272 Home Phone: 318-255-1405.

PHILLIPS, THOMAS JOHN, lawyer; b. Mpls., Nov. 24, 1948; BA, U. Minn., 1970; JD, U. Utah, 1973; LLM in Taxation, NYU, 1974. Bar: Wis. 1974. Ptnr. Quarles & Brady, Milw., 1991—. Co-author: Wisconsin Limited Liability Company Forms and Practice Manual, 1999. Mem. ABA (corp. tax com. tax sect.), Wis. Bar Assn., Profl. Inst. Taxation, Mil. Tax Club, North Shore Country Club, Order of Coif. Avocations: gardening, golf, hockey, jogging, racquetball. Office: 411 E Wisconsin Ave Ste 2040 Milwaukee WI 53202-4497 Home Phone: 262-241-5314; Office Phone: 414-277-5831. Business E-Mail: tjp@quarles.com.

PHILLIPS, THOMAS ROYAL, lawyer, former state supreme court chief justice; b. Dallas, Oct. 23, 1949; s. George S. and Marguerite (Andrews) P.; m. Lyn Bracewell, June 26, 1982; 1 son, Daniel Austin Phillips; 1 stepson, Thomas R. Kirkham. BA, Baylor U., 1971; JD, Harvard U., 1974; LLD (hon.), Tex. Tech. U., 1997; DHL (hon.), St. Edwards U., 1998. Bar: Tex. 1974; cert. in civil trial law Tex. Bd. Legal Specialization. Briefing atty. Supreme Ct. Tex., Austin, 1974-75; assoc. Baker Botts LLP, Houston, 1975-81, ptnr. Austin, 2005—; judge 280th Dist. Ct., Houston, 1981-88; chief justice Supreme Ct. Tex., Austin, 1988—2004; Spurgeon E. Bell disting. vis. prof. South Tex. Coll. Law, Houston, 2004—05; disting. prof. Sch. Law So. Meth. U., Dallas, 2004. Com. on fed.-state rels. Jud. Conf. U.S., 1990-96, Conf. Chief Justice, 1988—, pres. 1997-98; chair Tex. Jud. Dists. Bd., 1988-2004; mem. Tex. Jud. Coun., 1988-2004, chair, 1998-2004; mem. State Judges Mass Tort Litig. Com., 1991-96, Carter-Baker Commn. Fed. Election Reform, 2005; bd. dirs. Elmo B. Hunter Citizens Ctr. for Jud. Selection, 1992-94, Ctr. Am. Internat. Law., South Tex. Coll. Law; chair Nat. Mass Tort Conf. Planning Com., 1993-94; jud. bd. commn. Instns. of Democracy, Annenberg Found., 2003-04; mem. major infractions com. Divsn. 1 NCAA, 2006—; bd. dirs. Inst. Jud. Adminstrn. Bd. adv. Ctr. for Pub. Policy Dispute Resolution, U. Tex. Law Sch., 1993—; planning com. Tex. Hist. Commn., 2005-; adv. dir. Austin Habitat for Humanity, 1993-96; bd. dirs. Bastrop County Hist. Soc., 2005-. Recipient Outstanding Young Lawyer award Houston Young Lawyers Assn., 1986, Outstanding Tex. Leader award John Ben Sheppard Pub. Leadership Forum, 1989, award of excellence in govt. Tex. C. of C., 1992, Disting. Svc. award Nat. Ctr. for State Cts., 1999, Rosewood Gavel award St. Mary's U. Sch. Law, 2002, Price Daniel award for disting. pub. svc. Baylor U., 2004, Champion Children award Dallas (Tex.) CASA, 2004, Professionalism in Law award Burton Found., 2004, Harry L. Carrico award for Judicial Innovation Nat. Ctr. for State Cts., 2005; named Appellate Judge of Yr., Tex. Assn. Civil Trial and Appellate Specialists, 1992-93, Disting. Alumnus, Baylor U., 1998. Mem. ABA (task force lawyers polit. contbns. 1997-98, com. on 21st Century judiciary, 2002-03), Am. Law Inst. (advisor Fed. Jud. Code Project 1996-2001), Nat. Ctr. for State Cts. (chair, bd. dirs. 1997-98), State Bar Tex. (chmn. pattern jury charges IV com. 1985-87, vice chmn. adminstrn. justice com. 1986-87), Am. Judicature Soc. (bd. dirs. 1989-95, 99-2005, exec. bd. 1995-96), Tex. Philol. Soc., Houston Philol. Soc., Houston Bar Assn., Travis County Bar Assn., Bastrop County Bar Assn., Order of Coif (hon.). Republican. Episcopalian. Office: Baker Botts LLP 1500 San Jacinto Ctr 98 San Jacinto Blvd Austin TX 78701 Office Phone: 512-322-2565. Personal E-mail: cj@tomphillips.com. Business E-Mail: tom.phillips@bakerbotts.com.

PHILLIPS, THOMAS WADE, judge, lawyer; b. Oneida, Tenn., July 6, 1943; s. W.T. and Lucille (Lewallen) P.; m. Dorothy Mills, Jan. 2, 1971; children: Lori Ann, Wade Thomas. BA, Berea Coll., Ky., 1965; JD, Vanderbilt U., 1969; LLM in Labor Law, George Washington U., 1973. Bar: Tenn. 1969, U.S. Supreme Ct. 1972, U.S. Ct. Appeals (6th cir.) 1980. Assoc., ptnr. Baker, Worthington, Crosley, Stansberry & Wolfe, Huntsville, Tenn., 1973—77; ptnr. Phillips & Williams, P.C., Oneida, Tenn., 1977—91; U.S. magistrate judge ea. dist., Tenn., 1991—2002, U.S. dist. judge Tenn., 2002—. County atty. Scott County, Huntsville, 1976-91; city atty. Town of Oneida, 1978-91. Capt. JAGC, U.S. Army, 1969-73. Mem. ABA, Tenn. Bar Assn. (ho. of dels. 1989-91), Scott County Bar Assn. Office: US District Court Howard H Baker Jr Courtho 800 Market St Knoxville TN 37902-2327

PHILLIPS, TIKERA MONIQUE, elementary school educator; d. Tina E. Phillips. MS in Elem. Edn., LI U., Brookville, NY, 1995—2004. Customer rels. coord. Cablevision/Lightpath, Jericho, NY, 2000—04; tchr. Allen Christian Sch., Jamaica, NY, 2004—. Tutor First Bapt. Ch. Westbury, NY, 1998—2005. Baptist. Home Phone: 516-608-0027.

PHILLIPS, TODD, film director, film producer; b. Bklyn., 1970; Attended, NYU. Director, prodr.: (films) Hated, 1994; Frat House, 1998; Bittersweet Motel, 2000; dir., writer, actor Road Trip, 2000; dir., prodr., writer, actor Old School, 2003; dir., writer Starsky & Hutch, 2004; dir., prodr., writer: School for Scoundrels, 2006; exec. prodr.: (films) All the King's Men, 2006; actor: (TV series) Film School, 2004.

PHILLIPS, VICKI L., school system administrator; b. Marion, Ind., Jan. 15, 1958; d. Denver Phillips and Vivian (Burnette) Fuqua. BS in Edn., Western Ky. U., 1980, MA in Psychology, 1987; doctoral student, U. Ky., 1988—; EdD in instrnl. leadership, U. of Lincoln, Eng., 2002. Dir. devel. tng. dept. Panorama, Bowling Green, Ky., 1978—80; tchr. learning and behavior disorders Simpson County Bd. Edn., 1981—85; exceptional child cons. Ky. Dept. Edn. Office Edn. for Exceptional Children, 1986—90; chief exec. asst. to edn. commr. Ky. Dept. of Edn., 1986—93; dep. dir./chief of staff Nat. Alliance for Restructuring Edn., Wash., DC, 1993—95; dir. Greater Phila. First Partnership for Reform; exec. dir. Children Achieving Challenge, 1995—98; supt. Sch. Dist. of Lancaster, 1998—2003; sec. of edn. Pa. Dept. Edn., Harrisburg, 2003—04; supt. Portland Pub. Schools, Oreg., 2004—. Mem. ASCD, Nat. Coun. for Exceptional Children, Coun. for Behavior Disorders, Nat. Assn. for Sch. Psychologists, Ky. Assn. Sch. Adminstrs., Ky. Assn. for Psychology in the Schs., Ky. Assn. for Family-Based Svcs., Ky. Families for Family-Based Svcs., Ky. Families as Allies. Office: 501 N Dixon St Portland OR 97227-1804 *

PHILLIPS, VIRGINIA, retired federal employee; b. Glenmora, La., July 22, 1933; d. Leon Bunyan Phillips and Linnie Scott Rountree. BS, La. State U., Baton Rouge, 1953. Cert. tchr. La. Tchr. Hermansville HS, Hermansville, Mich., 1953—54, Washougal HS, Wash., 1955—56, El Dorado County HS, Placerville, Calif., 1956—57; sec. USAID, Tripoli, Libya, 1957—59, Seoul, Republic of Korea, 1959—61; sec. various law firms, temp. employment agys. Washington, 1963—69; fed. employee, 1969—94; ret. Dept. interior tutor Washington Pub. Schs., 1988—90. Bd. mem. Glenmora Cemetery Assn., 2003—05, pres., 2005; civilian rev. bd. Selective Svc. Sys., Washington, 1981—94; driving instr. AARP, Alexandria, La., 2002—; bd. dirs. Marlyn Condo., Washington, 1986—88, Westchester Corp., Washington, 1992—93. Mem.: DAR, Nat. Assn. Ret. Fed. Employees (contbr. to Retirement Life mag.), First Families Tenn., Sovereign Colonial Soc. Americans of Royal Descent, Colonial Order of Crown, Plantagenet Soc., Soc. Descendants Knights of Most Noble Order of Garter, Magna Charta Dames, First Families Miss., United Daus. Confederacy, Sons and Daus. of Pilgrims. Democrat. Avocations: genealogy, writing, photography. Home: 1016 A Nye Dr Alexandria LA 71303-5758

PHILLIPS, WADE, professional football coach; b. Orange, Tex., June 21, 1947; s. Oail Andrew (Bum) and Helen Phillips; m. Laurie Phillips; children: Tracey, Wesley. Student, U. Houston, 1965—68. Asst. football coach U. Houston, 1969; football coach Orange (Tex.) High Sch., 1970-72, Okla. State U., 1973-74, U. Kans., 1975; linebacker coach Houston Oilers, 1976, defensive line coach, 1977-80; defensive coord. New Orleans Saints, 1981-85, Phila. Eagles, 1986-88, Denver Broncos, 1989-93, head coach, 1993-94, Buffalo Bills, 1998—2000; def. coord. Atlanta Falcons, 2001—04, interim head coach, 2003—04; def. coord. San Diego Chargers, 2004—07; head coach Dallas Cowboys, 2007—. Office: Dallas Cowboys One Cowboys Pkwy Irving TX 75063 *

PHILLIPS, WALTER MILLS, III, psychologist, educator; b. NYC, Sept. 29, 1947; s. Walter Mills and Grace Mary (Mullen) P.; m. Anne Marie Boyle, July 3, 1971; children: Jonathan, Elizabeth. BS, Fordham U., 1970; MA, U. S.D., 1973, PhD, 1975. Lic. clin. psychologist, Conn.; diplomate Am. Coll. Forensic Examiners, Am. Bd. Disability Evaluators, Am. Bd. Disability Analysts; cert. sr. disability analyst. Adolescent resident counselor Hawthorne (N.Y.) Cedar Knolls Sch., 1970—71; NIMH tng. fellow, 1971—75; clin. psychology intern Inst. of Living, Hartford, Conn., 1974—75, clin. staff psychologist, 1975—79, sr. staff psychologist, 1979—82, asst. dir. dept. clin. psychology, 1980—82, dir. clin. psychology tng., 1980—82; co-dir. outpatient psychiatry U. Conn., Farmington, 1982—88; asst. prof. psychiatry, dir. psychiatry evaluation svc. U. Conn. Health Ctr., 1982—88, dir. Anxiety Rsch. and Treatment Ctr., 1985—88; pvt. practice psychotherapy Hartford, 1976—; dir. adolescent/young adult svc. Grandview Psychiat. Resource Ctr., Waterbury, Conn., 1988—90; dir. psychology Waterbury Hosp., 1990—98; pvt. practice clin. psychology Waterbury and Middlebury, Conn., 1990—. Asst. clin. prof. psychiatry Sch. Medicine Yale U., New Haven, Conn., 1988—; mem. psychology exec. com. Sch. Medicine Yale U., New Haven, 1990-98. Contbr. articles to profl. jours. Bd. dirs. Mem. APA, Am. Psychotherapy Assn. (diplomate), Conn. Psychol. Assn., Soc. Psychotherapy Rsch., Soc. Personality Assessment, Conn. Hosp. Assn. (chmn., dir. psychology conf. 1992-96), N.Y. Acad. Scis., Sigma Xi. Office: 415 Middlebury Rd Middlebury CT 06762 Office Phone: 203-758-8333. Business E-Mail: phillips.walter@comcast.net.

PHILLIPS, WALTER RAY, law educator; b. Democrat, NC, Mar. 19, 1932; s. Walter Yancey and Bonnie (Wilson) P.; m. Patricia Ann Jones, Aug. 28, 1954; children: Bonnie Ann, Rebecca Lee. AB, U. N.C., 1954; LL.B., Emory U., 1957, LL.M., 1962, JD, 1970; postgrad., Yale U., 1965-66. Bar: Ga. 1957, Fla. 1958, Tex. 1969, Mo. 2001, U.S. Supreme Ct. 1962. With firm Jones, Adams, Paine & Foster, West Palm Beach, Fla., 1957-58; law clk. to chief judge U.S. Dist. Ct., Atlanta, 1958-59; with firm Powell, Goldstein, Frazer & Murphy, Atlanta, 1959-60; bankruptcy judge U.S. Cts., Atlanta, 1960-64; prof. law U. N.D., 1964-65; teaching fellow Yale U., 1965-66; prof. law Fla. State U., 1966-68, Tex. Tech. U., Lubbock, 1968-71; Disting. vis. prof. law Baylor U., 1971; atty. Commn. on Bankruptcy Laws of U.S., Washington, 1971-72; dep. dir., adminstrv. officer, 1972-73; prof. Sch. Law, U. Ga., 1973-2000, assoc. dean, 1975-83, acting dean, 1976, Joseph Henry Lumpkin prof., 1977-94, also dir. univ's self. study, 1978, Herman E. Talmadge prof., 1994-2000. Chapman disting. vis. prof. law U. Okla., 1985-86; vis. prof. law U. Okla., 1990, U. Mo., Columbia, 1993, 94, 2001—; reporter Gov.'s Legislation for Ga., 1973; v.p., dir. Killearn Estates, Inc.; mem. Conf. on Consumer Fin. Law; prof.

London Law Consortium, 1999. Author: Florida Law and Practice, 1960, Encyclopedia of Georgia Law, 1962, Seminar for Newly Appointed Referees in Bankruptcy, 1964, Damages: Cases and Materials, 1967, (with James William Moore) Debtors' and Creditors' Rights, Cases and Material, 1966, 5th edit., 1979, The Law of Debtor Relief, 1969, 2d edit., 1972, supplement, 1975, (with James William Moore) Rule 6, Moore's Federal Practice, 1969, Adjustment of Debts for Individuals, 1979, 2d edit., 1981, supplement, 1982, 84, 85, Liquidation Under the Bankruptcy Code, 3d edit., 1988, supplement, 1989, 90, 91, 92, 93, 94, Cases and Materials on Corporate Reorganization, 1983, 3d edit., 1986, 4th edit., 1988, 5th edit., 1990, 7th edit., 1996, 8th edit., 1998, Family Farmer and Adjustment of Individual Debts, 1987, supplement, 1988, 89, 90, 91, 92, 93, 94, A Primer of Chapters 12 and 13 of the Bankruptcy Code, 1995. Bd. dirs. Lubbock Day Nurseries, 1969, pres., 1970-71. Served with USAF, 1950. Mem. ATLA, ABA (consumer bankruptcy com. 1973—, chmn. 1986-90), Fed. Bar Assn., Fla. Bar Assn., Tex. Bar Assn., Western Circuit Bar Assn., Ga. Bar Assn. (vice chmn. publs. com. 1977-89, com. on profl. responsibility 1983—2002), Mo. Bar Assn., Am. Judicature Soc., Phi Alpha Delta (chief tribune) Baptist. Home: 3800 Wakefield Dr Columbia MO 65203-5630 Office Phone: 573-882-0270. Business E-Mail: phillipswr@missouri.edu.

PHILLIPS, WANDA CHARITY, secondary school educator, writer; b. Gettysburg, Pa., Apr. 1, 1947; d. Roy Homer and Frances Marie (White) Kuykendall; m. James E. Phillips; children: Jenny, Peter, Micah. BS in Secondary Edn., Shippensburg U., Pa., 1968; cert. elem. edn., Grand Canyon Coll., 1973; MA in Adminstrn., No. Ariz. U., Flagstaff, 1993; EdD, George Fox U., Newberg, Oreg., 2007. Tchr. Littlestown H.S., Pa., 1969, Phoenix Indian Sch., 1971-72, Peoria Sch. Dist., Ariz., 1973—99; author ISHA Enterprises, Inc., Scottsdale, Ariz., 1985—. Ednl. seminar presenter ISHA Enterprises, Scottsdale, Ariz., 1986—, Assn. Christian Sch. Internat., Calif., 1988—. Author: Easy Grammar, 1986, Daily Grams: Guided Review Aiding Mastery Skills, 1986, Daily Grams: Guided Review Aiding Mastery Skills for Grade 3, 2003, Grade 4, 2003, Grade 5, 2003, Easy Writing, 1991, Daily Grams: Guided Teaching and Review for Grade 2, 2006, Easy Grammar, Grades 5 and 6, 1994 (children's book) My Mother Doesn't Like to Cook, 1993, Easy Grammar Plus, 1995, Easy Grammar: Grades 4 and 5, 1996, Easy Grammar: Grades 3 and 4, 1998, Grades 3, 4, 5, 6, 2006, Daily Grams: Grades 3, 4, 5, 6, and 7, 2002. Raspberry Cottage Tearoom Ministries. Mem.: Nat. Trust for Hist. Preservation, Paradise Valley Women's Club. Office: ISHA Enterprises Inc Easy Grammar Systems PO Box 25970 Scottsdale AZ 85255 Office Phone: 480-502-9454. E-mail: info@easygrammar.com.

PHILLIPS, WARREN G., secondary school educator; b. Weymouth, Mass., Feb. 1, 1954; s. Joseph Phillips and Eleanore Jorgensen; m. Karen E. Friberg, Feb. 14, 1976; children: Jefrey, Kristin. BA in Earth Sci. and Geography, Bridgewater State U., Mass., 1975; MA in Phys. Sci., Bridgewater State U., 1989, MEd in Instructional Tech., 2002. Cert. nat. bd. cert. middle sch. sci., geography and history tchr. Sci. tchr. Plymouth Pub. Schs., Mass., 1975—. Founder Helping Others While Learning. Contbg. author Explorer Science Series, 2002, Exemplary Science in Grades 5-8; contbr. Sing-A-Long Sci. CDs. Organizer Halifax Millennium Trail, Halifax, Mass.; outdoor edn. initiator, organizer Camp Bournedale, Heifer Internat. Named Tchr. of the Yr., Time/Chevrolet, 2002, Mid. Sch. Tchr. of Yr., Disney, 2004, USA Today Tchr., 2006; recipient Above and Beyond award, Mass. Software Internet Coun., 2002, 2003, Presdl. Svc. award, 2006; fellow, Earthwatch, 2007. Mem.: Nat. Sci. Ednl. Leadership Assn., Mass. Assn. Sci. Tchrs., Mass. Computer Users in Edn., Mass. Assn. Sci. Suprs., Nat. Sci. Tchrs. Assn. Avocations: gardening, woodworking, bicycling, soccer, basketball. Office: Plymouth Pub Schs 117 Long Pond Rd Plymouth MA 02360 Office Phone: 508-830-4450. Business E-Mail: a1science@yahoo.com.

PHILLIPS, WARREN HENRY, publishing executive; b. June 28, 1926; s. Abraham and Juliette (Rosenberg) P.; m. Barbara Anne Thomas, June 16, 1951; children: Lisa, Leslie, Nina. AB, Queens Coll., 1947, LHD (hon.), 1987; JD (hon.), U. Portland, 1973; LHD (hon.), Pace U., 1982, L.I. U., 1987. Copyreader Wall St. Jour., 1947-48, fgn. corr. Germany, 1949-50, chief London bur., 1950-51, fgn. editor, 1951-53, news editor, 1953-54, mng. editor Midwest edit., 1954-57, mng. editor, 1957-65, pub., 1975-88; exec. editor Dow Jones & Co., 1965-70, v.p., gen. mgr., 1970-71, exec. v.p., 1972, editl. dir., 1971-88, pres., 1972-79, CEO, 1975-90, also bd. dirs., past chmn., 1977-91; co-pub. Bridge Works Pub. Co., 1992—. Copyreader European edit. Stars and Stripes, 1949; pres. Am. Coun. Edn. for Journalism, 1971-73; mem. Pulitzer Prize Bd., 1977-87; adj. faculty Grad. Sch. Journalism, Columbia U., 1992, John F. Kennedy Sch. Govt., Harvard Univ., 1992. Author: (with Robert Keatley) China: Behind the Mask, 1973. Trustee Columbia U., 1980-93, trustee emeritus, 1993—; mem. vis. com. John F. Kennedy Sch. Govt., Harvard U., 1984-90, 92-97; corp. adv. bd. Queens Coll., 1986-90, found. bd. trustees, 1990-97, trustee emeritus, 1997—; bd. dirs. PBS, 1991-97. Named one of 10 Outstanding Young Men in U.S., U.S. Jaycees, 1958; inductee Info. Industry Assn.'s Hall of Fame, 1984. Mem. Am. Newspaper Pubs. Assn. (bd. dirs. 1976-84), Am. Soc. Newspaper Editors (pres. 1975-76), Bridgehampton Club, River Club. Office: Bridge Works Publ PO Box 1798 Bridgehampton NY 11932-1798

PHILLIPS, WILLIAM, real estate company executive; BA, U. Tex., Austin, 1973. Real estate broker Ga., 2007. Pres. The W G Phillips Co., Newnan, Ga., 1994—. V.p. San Antonio Housing Authority, 2003—05. Home Phone: 770-298-9220. Business E-Mail: billphillips@wgphillips.com.

PHILLIPS, WILLIAM AULT, pediatric dentist; b. Louisville, June 28, 1946; s. Clyde Custer, II, and Geraldine (Ault) P.; m. Karen Walters, June 28, 1969 (div.); children: Taylor Brett, Hayden Reign. DMD, U. Ky., 1971; MSD, Boston U., 1973; MS in Bus. Mktg. Webster U., 1993, MBA, 1994, JD, LaSalle U., 1996. Diplomate Am. Acad. Pediatric Dentistry; Am. Bd. Pediatric Dentistry (chmn. 1988). Pvt. practice pediatric dentistry, Louisville, 1973—; clin. instr. U. Louisville, 1973-78. Trustee Coun. Retarded Citizens, 1978-81; dir. Community Coordinated Child Care, 1980—. Fellow Am. Acad. Pediatric Dentistry, Am. Soc. Dentistry for Children, Acad. of Gen. Dentistry, Pierre Fauchard Acad. Republican. Presbyterian. Avocations: riding Harley Davidsons, sailing, water skiing, traveling, running. Office: 1001 Dupont Sq N Louisville KY 40207-4612 Home: 1408 Mockingbird Valley Grn Louisville KY 40207-1364

PHILLIPS, WILLIAM DANIEL, physicist; b. Wilkes-Barre, Pa., Nov. 5, 1948; s. William Cornelius and Mary Catherine (Savine) Phillips. BS, Juniata Coll., Huntingdon, Pa., 1970; PhD, MIT, 1976. Rsch. asst. MIT, Cambridge, 1970—76, Chaim Weizmann fellow, 1976—78; physicist Nat. Inst. Standards and Tech., Gaithersburg, Md., 1978—90, group leader, 1990—95, fellow, 1995—. Vis. prof. Ecole Normale Superieure, Paris, 1989—90; disting. prof. physics U. Md., College Park, 1991—. Editor (author): Laser Manipulation of Atoms and Ions, 1992; contbr. articles to profl. jours. Co-recipient Nobel Prize for physics, 1997, Schawlow prize in laser sci., APS, 1998; named Outstanding Young Scientist, Md. Acad. Sci., 1982; recipient Sci. Achievement award, Wash. Acad. Scis., 1982, Silver medal, Dept. Commerce, 1983, Gold medal, US Dept. Commerce, 1993, Pa. Soc., 1999, Albert A. Michelson medal, Franklin Inst., 1996. Fellow: Am. Acad. Arts and Scis., Am. Phys. Soc.; mem.: NAS, Pontifical Acad. Sci. (apptd. academician 2004), Optical Soc. Am. (hon.), Optical Soc. Am. (hon.), Soc. Physics Students, Sigma Xi. Achievements include demonstrated laser cooling of atomic beams; electromagnetic trapping of neutral atoms; discovery of sub-doppler laser cooling; produced sub-microkelvin 3D kinetic temperatures. Office: Nat Inst Stds & Tech 216 B123 100 Bureau Dr Stop 8424 Gaithersburg MD 20899-0003 Business E-Mail: william.phillips@nist.gov.

PHILLIPS, WILLIAM E., advertising agency executive; b. Chgo., Jan. 7, 1930; s. William E. and Alice N. Phillips; children: Michael, Tom, Sarah; m. Barbara Smith, Nov. 27, 1997. BS, Cornell U., 1951; MBA, Northwestern U., 1955. Brand mgr. Procter & Gamble, Cin., 1955-59; with Ogilvy & Mather, NYC, 1959-90; CEO Ogilvy Group, 1981-88; exec. in residence, prof. Johnson Grad. Sch. Mgmt. Cornell U., 1989-90. Bd. dirs. Gen. Housewares, Sun Glass Hut, Inc., Alliance Nat. Office Ctrs. Chmn. emeritus Outward Bound Internat.; chair Outdoor Edn., Cornell U., 1990—; co-chair Cayuga Soc. for Planned Giving at Cornell U.; trustee emeritus Cornell U.; trustee Internat. Tennis Hall of Fame, Newport, R.I., Florence Griswold Mus., Old Lyme, Conn., 1991—; active in Dem. politics. Lt. (j.g.) USN, 1951-54, Korea/Pacific/Mediterranean. Recipient Disting. Svc. award, Singapore Outward Bound, 1997, Kurt Hahn award, Outward Bound, 1998, Rhodes Exemplary Alumni Svc. award, Cornell U., 2001. Mem. Old Lyme Country Club, Am. Alpine Club, Explorers Club, Cornell Club, Univ. Club, Naval Mil. Club (London), Achilles Club N.Y.C. (bd. dirs.). Avocations: skiing, tennis, bicycling. Home: 200 N Cove Rd Old Saybrook CT 06475-2537 Business E-Mail: bill.phillips@ogilvy.com.

PHILLIPS, WILLIAM ROBERT, physician; b. Wash., Apr. 26, 1950; BA, U. Wash., 1971, MD, MPH, U. Wash., 1975. Diplomate Nat. Bd. Med. Examiners, Am. Bd. Family Practice, Am. Bd. Preventive Medicine; lic. physician and surgeon, Wash. Resident family practice Providence Med. Ctr., Seattle, 1975-78; resident preventive medicine U. Wash. Sch. Pub. Health & Cmty. Medicine, Seattle, 1976-79; vis. prof. U. Auckland, New Zealand, 1979, U. Tasmania, Hobart, Australia, 1979, U. Zimbabwe, Harare, 1993; clin. prof. family medicine U. Wash., Seattle, 1994—. Chief staff Ballard Cmty. Hosp., Seattle, 1985, chief family practice, 1984. Sr. assoc. editor Annals of Family Medicine, 2001—; Contbr. articles to profl. jours. Bd. trustees Ballard Cmty. Hosp., Seattle, 1985. Recipient USPHS primary care policy fellowship, 1995; named Family Physician of the Yr. Wash. Acad. Family Physicians, 1999. Fellow Am. Acad. Family Physicians (Mead Johnson award 1976, Warner-Chilcott award 1979), Wash. Acad. Family Physicians (Family Physician of Yr. 1999), Am. Coll. Preventive Medicine; mem. N.Am. Primary Care Rsch. Group (pres., rsch. awards), Soc. Tchrs. of Family Medicine. Office: Univ Washington Dept Family Medicine Box 356390 Seattle WA 98195-6390

PHILLIPS, WINFRED MARSHALL, academic administrator, mechanical engineer, educator, biomedical researcher; b. Richmond, Va., Oct. 7, 1940; s. Claude Marshall and Gladys Marian (Barden) P.; children: Stephen, Sean. BSME, Va. Poly. Inst., 1963; MA in Engring., U. Va., 1966, DSc, 1968. Mech. engr. U.S. Naval Weapons Lab., Dahlgren, Va., 1963; NSF trainee, tchg. and rsch. asst. dept. aerospace engring. U. Va., Charlottesville, 1963—67, rsch. scientist, 1966—67; asst. prof. dept. aerospace engring. Pa. State U., University Park, 1968-74, from assoc. prof. to prof., 1974—80, assoc. dean rsch. Coll. Engring., 1979—80; head Sch. Mech. Engring. Purdue U., West Lafayette, Ind., 1980-88; dean Coll. Engring. U. Fla., Gainesville, 1988-99, assoc. v.p. engring., 1989—99, v.p. rsch. and Don and Ruth Eckis prof. biomed. engring., 1999—. Bd. dir. Wachovia Bank, Gainesville; vis. prof. U. Paris, 1976—77; adv. com. Nimbus Corp., 1985—90, Hong Kong U. Sci. and Tech., 1990—93, AvMed Inc.; co-founder, v.p. CEO Inc., 1990—; acad. adv. coun. Indsl. Rsch. Inst., 1990—93; exec. com. Accreditation Bd. on Engring. and Tech., 1991—96; sci. adv. com. Electric Power Rsch. Inst., 1994—99; vice-chmn. Southeastern Coalition for Minorities in Engring., 1995—2000, chmn., 2001—04, chair Washington Accord, 2007—; internat. revs. for univs. in Saudi Arabia, Russia, Netherlands, Kuwait, Mexico, China, France Accreditation Bd. on Engring. and Tech., 1995—; bd. dirs Oak Ridge Associated Univs., 2002—05, bd. dirs., 2007—, chair coun., mem. exec. com., 2002—; mem. U.S. Pres.'s Commn. on Nat. Medal of Sci., 2003—. Sect. editor Am. Soc. Artificial Internal Organs Jour., 1985-99; contbr. over 175 articles to profl. jours., chpts. to books. Mem. Ind. Boiler and Pressure Vessel Code Bd., 1981—88; bd. dirs. Ctrl. Pa. Heart Assn., 1974—80, U. Fla. Found., 1989—91, 1995—2001. Named Disting. Hoosier Ind., 1987, Sagamore of the Wabash, 1988; recipient Career Rsch. award, NIH, 1974—78, NIH Surgery and Bioengring. Study sect., 1988—91, Fla. High Tech. and Industry Coun., 1990—94, Nat. Engring. award, Am. Assn. Engr. Socs., 2000, Linton Grinter award, 2000, Global Messenger award, Southeastern Consortium for Minorities in Engring., 2003. Fellow AAAS, AIAA, ASEE (vice chair 2001-02, chmn. bd. 2002—, Lamme award 2003), ASME (sr. v.p. edn. 1986-88, bd. dirs. 1995-2000, pres. 1998-99, Dedicated Svc. award 2001, Ralph Coates Roe medal 2005), NY Acad. Scis., Am. Astron. Soc., Am. Inst. Med. and Biol. Engring. (founding fellow, chair coll. fellows 1994-95, pres. 1996-97), Am. Soc. Engring. Edn. (past chmn. long range planning soc. awards 1990-92, vice chmn. engring. deans coun. 1991-93, chair 1993—, bd. dirs. 1994-98, 1st v.p. 1994-95, pres. 1996-97), Royal Soc. Arts, Biomed. Engring. Soc., Am. Soc. Artificial Internal Organs (trustee 1982-90, sec.-treas. 1986-87, pres. 1988-89, adv. bd. 1998—); mem. Nat. Assn. State Univs. and Land-Grant Colls. (com. quality of engring. edn.), Univ. Programs in Computer-Aided Engring., Design and Mfg. (bd. dirs. 1985-91), Am. Phys. Soc., Internat. Soc. Biotheology, Fla. Engring. Soc., Cosmos Club, Fla. Blue Key, Rotary (pres. Lafayette 1987-88), Sigma Xi, Phi Kappa Phi, Phi Tau Sigma, Sigma Gamma Tau, Tau Beta Pi (eminent engr.). Achievements include research in artificial heart pumps; reentry aerodynamics; blood rheology; modeling blood flow; fluid dynamics of artificial hearts; use of smooth blood contacting surface; prosthetic valve fluid dynamics; laser Doppler studies of unsteady biofluid dynamics. Home: 4140 NW 44th Ave Gainesville FL 32606-4518 Office: U Fla Rsch and Grad Programs 223 Grinter Hall Gainesville FL 32611 Office Phone: 352-392-9271. Business E-Mail: wphil@ufl.edu.

PHILLIPS, WINIFRED PATRICIA, composer; b. Mobile, Ala., Apr. 13, 1972; d. Winifred Waldron Phillips. BA summa cum laude in Comms., Kean U., 1994. Composer, prodr., actress, writer Nat. Pub. Radio, Washington, 1992—2002; composer, prodr., actress, writer Radio Tales XM Satellite Radio Dramas, Washington, 2002—; owner music and audio prodn. co. Gens. Prodns.; composer Take Two Interactive, NYC, 2005—06, Activision, Santa Monica, Calif., 2006—07. Composer Sony Computer Entertainment Am., Santa Monica, Calif., 2004. Composer, prodr., actress, writer (National Public Radio dramas) Generations Radio Theater Presents: Radio Tales, 1996—2002, (radio dramas) Radio Tales, XM Satellite Radio, 2002—, composer, prodr., actress (radio drama) The Odyssey Trilogy, 2003, Arabian Nights Trilogy, 2003, The Gift of the Magi, 1996, The Yellow Wallpaper, 1996, The Fall of the House of Usher, 1998, Sleepy Hollow, 1998, The Time Machine, 1999, Gulliver's Travels, 1999, The Mummy, 1999, The Island of Doctor Moreau, 2000, Dr. Jekyll and Mr. Hyde, 2000, Journey to the Center of the Earth, 2000, The Pit and the Pendulum, 2000, The Hunchback of Notre-Dame, 2001, Jason and The Argonauts, 2001, War of the Worlds, 2001, Phantom of the Opera, 2001, Beowulf, 2001, Twenty Thousand Leagues Under the Sea, 2001, The Invisible Man, 2001, The Lost World, 2002, composer, actress, author (radio musicals) Celtic Hero, 2000; composer, actress, author: radio musicals Lord of the Celts, 1998; author: (short stories) Breaking Point, 1991, Celtic Beauty for Sword and Sorceress 20 book anthology, 2003, (radio drama script) Light of Truth, 1985; composer: (video games) God of War, 2004, Charlie and the Chocolate Factory, 2005, The Da Vinci Code, 2006, Shrek the Third, 2007; singer, musician: Best of the Best: A Tribute to Game Music, 2007, Go Mario! (Super Mario Brothers), 2007, composer, singer, musician: God of War Video Game Soundtrack, 2004. Recipient GRACIE award for best nat./network drama series, Am. Women in Radio and TV, 2001, 2003, 2004, N.Y. Festivals award, Internat. Radio Festivals, 1997, AUDIE Honors award, Audio Pubs. Assn., 1999, GOLDEN REEL Merit award, Nat. Fedn. Cmty. Broadcasters, 2001, GRACIE award for outstanding achievement by an actress, Am. Women in Radio and TV, 1998, N.Y. Festivals award, Internat. Radio Festivals, 2001, N.Y. Festivals World medal, 2004, Outstanding Achievement in Original Music Composition for Videogame, Acad. Interactive Arts Sci., 2005, Best Original Score of Yr. awrd, Game Zone, 2005, Best Original Music award, Game Spot, 2005, Best Original Score award, IGN PS2, 2005, Music of Yr., Game Audio Network Guild, 2005, Best Interactive Score, 2005, Best Cinematic/Cut Scene Audio, 2005, Audio of Yr., 2005; grantee Endowment grantee, Wallace - Reader's Digest Funds, 1996—2002, NEA, 1996—2002, Durkin Hayes Publ., 1998. Mem.: SAG, BMI, NARAS, Game Audio Network Guild, Ind. Game Developers Assn., Am. Fedn. Musicians. Avocations: reading, Web design, computer art, travel. Business E-Mail: phillips@radiotales.com.

PHILLIPS, ZAIGA ALKSNIS, pediatrician; b. Riga, Latvia, Sept. 13, 1934; arrived in US, 1949; d. Adolfs and Alma (Ozols) Alksnis; (div. 1972); children: Albert L., Lisa K., Sintija. BS, U. Wash., 1956, MD, 1959. Fellow Colo. Med. Ctr., Denver, 1961-62; sch. physician Bellevue and Issaquah (Wash.) Sch. Dists., 1970-77; pvt. practice Bellevue, 1977—; staff pediatrician Overlake Med. Ctr., 1977—, Childrens Hosp. and Med. Ctr., Seattle, 1977—, Evergreen Med. Ctr., 1977—. Attending physician Allergy Clinic, Childrens Hosp., Seattle, 1988-2005; cons. and contact to pediatricians in Latvia, 1988—; team mem. to Latvia, Healing the Children Contact with Latvia, 1993-97; bd. mem. Bellevue's Stay in Sch. Program, 1994-97. Mem. Am. Latvian Assn., 1972—, Wash. Latvian Assn., Seattle, 1972—; pres. Latvian Sorority Gundega, Seattle, 1990-93; bd. dirs. Sister Cities Assn., Bellevue, 1992-98, Wash. Asthma Allergy Found. Am., 1992-99. Recipient Recognition award, City of Liepaja, 1995, Latvian Assn. Am., 2003, Recognition cross, Pres. of Latvia, 2005. Fellow Am. Acad. Pediat.; mem. Am. Latvian Physicians Assn. (bd. dirs. 1998—), Wash. State and Puget Sound Pediatric Assn. Office: Pediatric Assn 2700 Northup Way Bellevue WA 98004-1463 Office Phone: 425-827-4600. Personal E-mail: zap@u.washington.edu. Business E-Mail: zphillips@peds-associates.com.

PHILLIPSON, DONALD E., lawyer; b. Denver, July 22, 1942; BS, Stanford U., 1964, JD, 1968; MS, U. Calif., Berkeley, 1965. Former mem. Davis, Graham & Stubbs, Denver; now cons., writer. Mem. Nat. Soccer Hall of Fame (builder). Office: 14325 Braun Rd Golden CO 80401-1431 Office Phone: 303-279-1577.

PHILLIS, JOHN WHITFIELD, physiologist, educator; b. Port of Spain, Trinidad, Apr. 1, 1936; came to U.S., 1981; s. Ernest and Sarah Anne (Glover) P.; m. Pamela Julie Popple, 1958 (div. 1968); children: David, Simon, Susan; m. Shane Beverly Wright, Jan. 24, 1969. B in Vet. Sci., Sydney U., Australia, 1958, D in Vet. Sci., 1976; PhD, Australian Nat. U., 1961; DSc, Monash U., Australia, 1970. Sr. lectr. Monash U., 1963-69; vis. prof. Ind. U., Indpls., 1969; prof. physiology, assoc. dean rsch. U. Man., Winnipeg, Canada, 1970-73; prof., chmn. dept. physiology U. Sask., Saskatoon, Canada, 1973-81, asst. dean rsch., 1973-75; prof. physiology Wayne State U., Detroit, 1981—2004, prof. emeritus, 2004—, chmn. dept. physiology, 1981-97; courtesy prof. U. Fla., Gainsville, 2004—. Mem. scholarship and grants com. Can. Med. Rsch. Coun., Ottawa, Ont., 1973-79, rsch. prof., 1980; mem. sci. adv. bd. Dystonia Med. Rsch. Found., Beverly Hills, Calif., 1980-85, Curtis Rsch. Inst., Risingsun, Ohio, 1998-2000; mem. sci. adv. panel World Soc. for Protection of Animals, 1982-98; Wellcome vis. prof. Tulane U., 1986; mem. acad. scholars Wayne State U., 1995. Author: Pharmacology of Synapses, 1970; editor: Veterinary Physiology, 1976, Physiology and Pharmacology of Adenosine Derivatives, 1983, Adenosine and Adenine Nucleotides as Regulators of Cellular Function, 1991, The Regulation of Cerebral Blood Flow, 1993, Novel Therapies for CNS Injuries: Rationales and Results, 1996; editor Can. Jour. Physiology and Pharmacology, 1978-81, Progress in Neurobiology, 1973-97. Mem. grants com. Am. Heart Assn. of Mich., 1985-90, mem. rsch. coun., 1991-92, mem. rsch. forum com., 1991-96, chair, 1992-93; mem. Brain/Stroke Consortium Study Group, Am. Heart Assn., 1998. Wellcome fellow London, 1961-62; Can. Med. Rsch. Coun. grantee, 1970-81; NIH grantee, 1983-2000. Mem. Brit. Pharmacol. Soc., Am. Physiol. Soc., Soc. Neurosci., Internat. Brain Rsch. Orgn. Office: Wayne State U Sch Medicine Dept Physiology 540 E Canfield Ave Detroit MI 48201-1928 Personal E-mail: jphillis@med.wayne.edu.

PHILLIS, MARILYN HUGHEY, artist; b. Kent, Ohio; d. Paul Jones and Helen Margaret Hughey; m. Richard Waring Phillis, Mar. 19, 1949; children: Diane E., Hugh R., Randall W Student, Kent State U., 1945; BS, Ohio State U., 1949. Chemist Battelle Meml. Inst., Columbus, Ohio, 1949—53; illustrator periodical We. Res. Hist. Mag., Garrettsville, Ohio, 1974—79; illustrator book AAUW, Piqua, Ohio, 1976; instr. art Edison State C.C., Piqua, 1976; instr. watermedia Springfield Mus. Art, Ohio, 1976—84. Juror art exhbns. state and nat. art groups, 1980—; instr. painting state and nat. orgns., 1980—; lectr. art healing Wheeling Jesuit Coll., W.Va., 1994—96; founder, coord. Nat. Creativity Seminar, Stretching Boundaries for Creative People, 1993, 1995, 1997, 1999, 2002, 07. Author: Watermedia Techniques for Releasing the Creative Spirit, 1992; contbr. chapters to books, articles and illustrations to profl. jours.; one-woman shows include Stifel Fine Art Ctr., Wheeling, Springfield Art Mus., Zanesville Art Ctr., Ohio, Ohio U., Lancaster, Ohio U. East St. Clairsville, Cleve. Inst. Music, Columbus Mus. Art, Cheekwood Mus. Art, Bot. Hall, Nashville, Idaho Falls Art Ctr., Monroe C.C., Mich., exhibitions include Butler Mus. Am. Art, Youngstown, Ohio, Taiwan Art Edn. Inst., Taipei, 1994, Represented in permanent collections Ohio U., Lancaster and St. Clairsville, W.Va. No. CC, Wheeling, Springfield Mus. Art, Ohio, Heritage Hall mus., Talladega, Ala., Ohio Watercolor Soc., W.Va. Women Artists, U. Charleston, Monroe C.C., Mich., also corp. collections. Co-chmn. Cmty. Health and Humor Program, Wheeling, 1992 Recipient First awards Watercolor West, Riverside, Calif., 1990, Hudson Soc. award Nat. Collage Soc., 1995, Art Masters award Am. Artist Mag., 1996; named to Hall of Fame, Kent, Ohio, 2000, Hall of Fame, Wheeling, 2000 Mem. Internat. Soc. Study of Subtle Energies and Energy Medicine (art cons. sci. jour. 1992-2006, art and healing workshop 1995), Am. Watercolor Soc. (dir. 1991-93, newsletter editor 1992—,chmn. Jury of Awards, 2003, Osborne award 1975), Soc. Layerists in Multi-Media (nat. v.p. 1988-93), Ohio Watercolor Soc. (sec. 1979-82, v.p. 1982-89, pres. 1990-96, Gold medal, Best of Show 1993), Nat. Watercolor Soc. (chmn. selection jury 2001), Internat. Noetic Sci., Western Ohio Watercolor Soc. (pres. 1979-80, 2d award 1982), Allied Artists NY, W.Va. Watercolor Soc. (1st award 1993), Ky. Watercolor Soc., Ga. Watercolor Soc., So. Watercolor Soc. (pres. 1997-98, Silver award 1999) Avocations: hiking, reading, genealogy, music, travel. Home and Office: Phillis Studio 72 Stamm Cir Wheeling WV 26003-5549 E-mail: mhphillis@aol.com.

PHILOGENE, BERNARD J. R., academic administrator, science educator; b. Beau-Bassin, Mauritius, May 4, 1940; came to Can., 1961; s. Raymond Pierre and Simone Marie (Ruffier) P.; m. Hélène Marie Lebreux, July 7, 1964; children: Simone, Catherine. BS, U. Montreal, 1964; MS, McGill U., 1966; PhD, U. Wis., 1970; DSc (hon.), Compiègne, 1995; DSc (hon.), U. de Pau, France, 2005. Rsch. officer Can. Forestry Svc., Que., 1966—70, rsch. scientist Que., 1970—71; asst. prof. U. B.C., Vancouver, 1971-74; asst. prof., assoc. prof., then prof. entomology U. Ottawa, Canada, 1974—2005, vice dean sci. and engring., 1982—85, dean faculty of sci., 1986—90, acad. vice rector, 1990—97, acting dean, 1985—86, prof. emeritus, 2005—; pres. Can. Consortium of Sci. Socs., 1992—94.

Cons. OAS, Washington, 1979-80, Agence de Coop. Culture & Tech., Paris, 1982-83, Can. Internat. Devel. Agy., Ottawa, 1983-85, UN Environ. Program, Geneva, Switzerland, 1985-86, Internat. Devel. Research Ctr., Ottawa, 1985—. Mem. Ont. Pesticide Adv. Com., 1987-91. Decorated commandeur de l'Ordre des Palmes Académiques (France); knight of merit Order of St. John of Jerusalem. Fellow Entomol. Soc. Can. (bd. dirs. 1977-80); mem. Am. Inst. Biol. Scis., Entomol. Soc. Am., Can. Pest Mgmt. Soc., Assn. Can.-Française Advancement Sci. (bd. dirs. 1984-86), Internat. Soc. Chem. Ecology, Entomol. Soc. of Can. (Gold Medal 2000). Office: U Ottawa PO Box 450 30 Marie Curie St Ottawa ON Canada K1N 6N5 Home Phone: 613-742-1827; Office Phone: 613-562-5800. E-mail: bphilog@uottawa.ca.

PHILP, RICHARD NILSON, writer, editor, journalist, historian; b. Plainfield, NJ, July 7, 1943; s. Lester Perry and Gladys Emma Linea (Nilson) P. BA in English and Theater cum laude, U. N.C., 1965; MFA in Theater Lit. and Playwriting, Yale U., 1968. Lectr. Yale U., Princeton U., Fordham U., Juilliard, U. Utah, U. Wyo., others; faculty Summer Dance Festival U. Wyo., 1995-97. Author 8 plays, produced 1963-72; author: To Move, To Learn, 1973, Danseur: The Male in Ballet, 1977, Romeo and Juliet, Romeos Dancing, Shakespeare Without Words, 2003, Vladimir Malakov, 2003, Dracula the Ballet, 2004, Peter Pan: A Ballet Scenario, 2005, Alice in Wonderland: A Ballet Scenario, 2005, Village, A Biocentennial Celebration of the Village of Catskill, 2006; editor and contbg. author: Memoirs of a Dancer: Shadows, Dreams, Memories, 1979, The Gospel According to Dance, 1980, Alvin Ailey American Dance Theater, 1993, Passion & Line, 1997; exec. editor: Dance Books, 1981-86; founding bd. dirs. World Dance Alliance, 1993; chmn. Dance Mag. Prize for Reportage, Video Danse, 1992, 93, 96, 99; mng. editor Dance Mag., 1970-88, editor-in-chief, 1989—99, exec. editor, 2000-02, editor-in-chief emeritus, 2002-; assoc. editor Critics Choice, 1969-70, After Dark, Magazine of Entertainment, 1970-75; contbr. monthly column Kickoff, 1989—2002; contbr. articles to profl. jours. Treas. Dance Mag. Found., 1984-93; co-chmn. internat. adv. bd. Jackson Ballet Competition, Miss., 1989-2004; selection com. ann. Astaire awards Dance Mag., 1989-2005; bd. dirs. Israel Dance Collection Libr., 1989—95, Joffrey Ballet Sch., 1994—, Video Danse, Paris, Lively Art Christ Ch. Episcopal, Hudson, NY; treas., bd. dirs. Beattie-Powers Pl., 2006; adv. bd. Juilliard Sch., 1994—; bd. advisors Thomas Cole's Cedar Grove, 1999—; docent Thomas Cole's Cedar Grove, 2001—; active Catskill Bicentennial Com., 2006; historian Catskill Village, 2006—. Recipient Spl. citation Soc. Illustrators, Bronze medal 28th Internat. Film and TV Fest, NYC, 1985, Silver medal Chgo. Internat. Film Festival, 1985, TV Documentary Writing award Am. Film Festival, 1986, Nijinsky award, 1994, Ellen Rettus Planning Achievement award for cmty. svc., 2006. Mem. Catskill Writers Group (founder 1978), Devon Beekeepers Assn. (Eng.), Mountain Beekeepers Assn. Home and Office: 166 Bridge St Catskill NY 12414-1404 Home: The Towers Apt 22 33-15 80th St Jackson Heights NY 11372 Office Phone: 518-943-5308. Personal E-mail: richardphilp@mhcable.com.

PHILPOTT, HARRY MELVIN, former university president; b. Bassett, Va., May 6, 1917; s. Benjamin Cabell and Daisy (Hundley) P.; m. Pauline Breck Moran, Sept. 15, 1943; children: Harry Melvin, Jean Todd, Benjamin Cabell II, Virginia Lee. AB, Washington and Lee U., 1938, LL.D., 1966; PhD, Yale U., 1947; D.D., Stetson U., 1960; LL.D., U. Fla., 1969, U. Ala., 1970; H.H.D., Samford U., 1978, Montevallo U., 1980, Auburn U., 1981. Ordained to ministry Bapt. Ch., 1942; dir. religious activities Washington and Lee U., 1938-40; prof. religion U. Fla., 1947-52, v.p., 1957-65; dean, head dept. religion and philosophy Stephens Coll., 1952-57; pres. Auburn U., 1965-80. Mem. Regional Edn. Bd., 1966-82, vice chmn., 1973-75; chmn. Ala. Edn. Study Commn., 1967-69; pres. Southeastern Conf., 1972-74. Served to 1st lt. Chaplains Corps., USNR, 1943-46. Mem. Nat. Assn. State Univs. and Land-Grant Colls. (chmn. council presidents 1972-73, exec. com. 1973-78, pres. 1976-77), Fla. Blue Key, Kappa Alpha, Omicron Delta Kappa, Kappa Delta Pi, Phi Kappa Phi, Phi Beta Kappa. Home: PO Box 3037 Auburn AL 36831-3037

PHILPOTT, JONATHAN M., surgeon; b. Honolulu, Mar. 6, 1967; m. Elizabeth Etheridge, July 10, 1993; children: Mary Chandler, Sarah Morgan, William Mendel, Katherine L. Student, Oxford U., Eng., 1988; BA in Philosophy and History, Hampden-Sydney Coll., Va., 1990; MD, Ea. Va. Med. Sch., Norfolk, 1994. Diplomate Am. Bd. Thoracic Surgery, Am. Bd. Surgery, lic. NC, Pa., Va., Ind., Ohio. EMT Davis Ambulance Inc., Farmville, Va., 1988—90; intern in gen. surgery Pitt County Mem. Hosp., U. Med. Ctr. Ea. NC, Greenville, 1994—95, resident in gen. surgery, 1995—99, chief resident, 1999—2000; fellow in trauma surgery and critical care Hosp. U. Pa., Phila., 2000—02; fellow in cardiothoracic surgery Med. Coll. Ba., Richmond, 2002—04; fellow in trauma surgery and surgery critical care Hops. U. Pa., 2000—02; fellow in cardiothoracic surgery Med. Coll. Va., 2002—04; cardiothoracic and vascular surgeon Ind./Ohio Heart, Ft. Wayne, Ind., 2004—. Rsch. fellow in cardiovasc. physiology E. Carolina U. Sch. Medicine, Greenville, 1996—97; lectr. in field. Contbr. articles to profl. jours. Recipient Ray D. Minges award, E. Carolina U., Dept. Surgery, 1999; grantee, E. Carolina U., 1996—97, Am. Heart Assn., NC, 1997. Mem.: Luth. Hosp. Med. Dir. for Lung Volume Reduction Surgery, Ind. State Med. Soc., Internat. Soc. Heart and Lung Transplantation, Internat. Soc. Vascular Surgery, Assn. Acad. Surgery, Soc. Critical Care Medicine, Ea. Assn. Trauma, Soc. Thoracic Surgery, Am. Coll. Surgery, Alpha Omega Alpha. Avocations: fly fishing, scuba diving, golf. Home: 11023 Sycamore Hills Dr Fort Wayne IN 46814 Office: Ind/Ohio Heart 7910 W Jefferson Blvd Ste 102 Fort Wayne IN 46804

PHILPOTT, LARRY LA FAYETTE, retired horn player; b. Alma, Ark., Apr. 5, 1937; s. Lester and Rena (Owens) P.; m. Elise Robichaud, Nov. 24, 1962 (div. June 1975); children: Daniel, Stacy; m. Anne Sokol, Feb. 14, 1984. BS, Ga. So. Coll., 1962; MusM, Butler U., 1972. Instr. in horn Butler U., De Pauw U.; dir. music Cedarcrest Sch., Marysville, Wash., 1991—2007; instr. horn Western Wash. U., Dept Music, Bellingham, 1995-98. Mem., N.C. Symphony, 1960, Savannah (Ga.) Symphony, L'Orchestre Symphonique de Quebec, Que., Can., 1962-64, prin. horn player, Indpls. Symphony Orch., 1964-89, Flagstaff Summer Festival, 1968-; artist in-residence Ind.-Purdue Indpls.; appeared with, Am. Shakespeare Theatre, summer 1965, Charlottetown Festival, summers 1967-68, Flagstaff Summer Festival, 1968-85, Marrowstone Music Festival, 1985—. Served with USN, 1956-60. Mem. Music Educators Nat. Conf., Am. Fedn. Musicians, Internat. Conf. Symphony and Opera Musicians, Internat. Horn Soc., Coll. Music Soc., Phi Mu Alpha Sinfonia. Home: 8 Calahara Way Hot Springs Village AR 71909 Personal E-mail: larryphilpott@hotmail.com.

PHILSON, RICHARD MICHAEL, academic administrator; b. Lakeland, Fla., Aug. 27, 1950; s. Glenn McRae and Jeane Baker Philson; children: Matthew Chou, Renee Yu. BA, Wash. U., St. Louis, 1972; MA, U. Wis., Madison, 1977, U. Hawaii, Honolulu, 1983; PhD, U. Mich., Ann Arbor, 1999. Trainer/prodr. ednl. media U. South Pacific, Suva, Fiji, 1977—79; rsch. intern East-West Ctr., Honolulu, 1981—83; English faculty Chiang Mai U., Thailand, 1983—84; English instr. Tunghai U., Taichung, Taiwan, 1984—86, Myongji U., Seoul, 1987—88; pres. Plumeria's of Hawaii, Honolulu, 1986—87; pub. info. officer U. Hawaii, Honolulu, 1988—90; recruiting/mktg. officer Edmonds C.C., Kobe, Japan, 1990—91; instr./eap coord. Minn. State U., Akita, Japan, 1991—95; rsch. asst. U. Mich., Ann Arbor, 1995—99; pres. Kanda Inst. of Fgn. Languages, Tokyo, 1999—2001; exec. dir., internat. edn. Wichita State U., Kans., 2001—07; exec. dir. internat. program Old Dominion U., Va., 2007—. U. Hawaii working com. Govs. Congress on Hawaii's Internat. Role, Honolulu, 1988; organizing com. mem. Akita Internat. Fair, 1991—92; pres. Akita Faculty Assn. Minn. State U., 1993—95. Author: (handbook) Quality Standard Guidelines for Electronically Delivered Instruction, (booklet) Visions: Toward the 21st Century; contbr. chapters to books, articles to profl. jours. Mem. Com. Fgn. Rels., 2003—, Global Learning Ctr., Wichita, 2003—. Mem.: Assn. Internat. Educators (subcom. info. mgmt. 2005—), Chinese-Am. Soc. Ann Arbor (bd. dirs. 1999—2000), Rotary Club (internat. com. planning mem. 1990). Independent. Avocations: tennis, travel, glass-blowing.

PHIPARD, NANCY MIDWOOD, retired special education educator, poet; b. Boston, Jan. 31, 1929; d. William Henry and Jean Estelle (Dubbs) McAdams; m. Kenneth E. Brown, June 17, 1949 (div.); children: Christopher M. Brown, Jennifer Progodich, Michael H. Brown, Jeffrey D. Brown; m. Arnold J. Midwood, Jr., July 2, 1980 (dec.); m. Harvey F. Phipard, Jan. 14, 1998 (dec.). Student, Mt. Holyoke Coll., 1946-48; BA, Wellesley Coll., 1973; MEd, Boston Coll., 1975. Dir. confs. and insvc. tng., chmn. bd. Mass. Assn. for Children with Learning Disabilities, Waltham and Framingham, 1969-75; chmn. core edn. teams, cons. to spl. programs, grant writer Needham (Mass.) Pub. Schs., 1974-79; ret., 1979; pres., feature writer S.D. Assocs., Inc., Wellesley, Mass., 1980-81; dir. pub. rels., women's career conf. Babson Coll., Wellesley, 1982. Mem. program evaluation team Mass. Dept. Edn., Quincy, 1978. Author (as Nancy Brown, with Louis Dickstein): Psychological Reports, 1974; author: (poems) Portraits of a Life, 1996, Fields of Gold, 1996, Ever-Flowing Stream, 1997, Best Poems of 1998, 2002, Colors of the Past, 2000, Echoes of Yesteryear, 2000, America at the Millennium, The Best Poems and Poets of the 20th Century, 2000, Memories of Tomorrow, 2000, Journey to Infinity, 2000, Theatre of the Mind, 2003 (The Best Poems and Poets of 2003, 2004, The Best Poems and Poets of 2004, 2005). Bd. dirs., fundraiser Hospice Palm Beach (Fla.) County S., 1993—97; bd. dirs. La Coqueille Villas, Inc., Manalapan, Fla., 1994—98; bd. dirs., chair cmty. rels. Lincoln Child Ctr., Oakland, Calif., 1983—85; docent Calif. Hist. Soc., San Francisco, 1982—87. Recipient Editor's Choice award, Internat. Libr. Poetry, 1996, 1998, 2000, 2003, The Best Poems and Poets of 2003, 2004, 2005. Mem.: Internat. Soc. Poets (disting. mem.), Phi Beta Kappa. Avocations: tennis, travel, duplicate bridge.

PHIPPS, BENJAMIN KIMBALL, II, lawyer; b. Boston, Jan. 16, 1933; s. Benjamin Kimball and Bertha Elizabeth (Forsyth) P.; m. Phyllis Jarrett Anderson, Jan. 10, 1962; children: Lisa Jarrett, Christina Caroline. BS in Commerce, U. Va., 1955, LLB, 1958. Bar: Fla. 1964, U.S. Dist. Ct. (no. dist.) Fla., U.S. Claims Ct., U.S. Ct. Appeals (5th and 11th cirs.), U.S. Tax Ct.; cert. Inst. Profls. in Taxation, 2004. Pvt. practice, Tallahassee, 1965—. Counsel tax com. Fla. Ho. of Reps., 1966-72, counsel to spkr., 1973-74, mem. adv. com. fin. & tax com., 1983-84; mem. Legis. Task Force Taxpayers' Bill Rights, 1989-91; elected dir. Fla. Coun. Property Tax Lawyers, 2003 Contbr. articles to profl. jours.; columnist Tallahassee Democrat. Chmn. Hist. Tallahassee Preservation Bd., 1970-91; mem. Tallahassee Trust for Hist. Preservation, 1997—, treas., 1998—. Served to capt., U.S. Army, 1958-64. Mem. ABA (tax sect. state and local tax com.), Tallahassee Bar Assn., Fla. Bar Assn. (treas., vice chmn., chmn. tax sect. 1985-86, editl. bd. Fla. Bar Jour. News, chmn. 1975-76), Inst. Profls. Taxation, Gov.'s Club, Univ. Ctr. Club, Cosmos Club, Exch. Club, Tiger Bay Club (dir.), Fla. Econ. Club, St. Andrews Soc. (pres. 1978-79), Sigma Alpha Epsilon, Phi Alpha Delta, Pi Delta Epsilon. Republican. Episcopalian. Office: PO Box 1351 Tallahassee FL 32302-1351 Office Phone: 850-222-7000. Business E-Mail: bkp@thephippsfirm.com.

PHIPPS, JOHN RANDOLPH, retired army officer; b. Kansas, Ill, May 16, 1919; s. Charles Winslow and Kelsey Ethel (Torrence) P.; m. Pauline M. Prunty, Feb. 8, 1946; children: Charles W., Kelsey J. Phipps-Selander. BS in Econs. with honors, U. Ill., 1941; M.P.A., Sangamon State U., 1976; A course, Command and Gen. Staff Coll., 1959, nuclear weapons employment course, 1962; course, U.S. Army War Coll., 1973, U.S. Nat. Def. U., 1978. Owner, operator chain shoe stores in, Ill., 1946-70; commd. 2d lt. F.A. U.S. Army, 1941, advanced through grades to capt., 1943; service in Philippines and Japan; discharged as maj., 1946; organizer, comdr. Co. E, 130th Inf., Ill.; N.G., Mattoon, 1947, comdg. officer 2d Bn., 130th Inf., 1951, lt. col. 2d Bn., 130th Inf., 1951; called to fed. service, 1952; adv. (29th Regt., 9th Republic of Korea Div.), 1952-53; comdr. officer 1st Bn., 130th Inf., Ill. N.G., 1954, col., 1959; comdg. officer 2d Brigade, 33d Div., 1963-67; asst. div. comdr. 33d Inf. Div., 1967, brig. gen., 1967; comdr. 33d Inf. Brigade, Chgo., 1967-70, Ill. Emergency Ops. Hdqrs., 1970, asst. adj. gen. Ill., 1970-77, acting adj. gen., 1977-78, adj. gen., 1978, promoted to maj. gen., 1978, now maj. gen. ret. Decorated Silver Star, Bronze Star, Disting. Service medal, Combat Infantry Badge, Army Disting. Service medal Ill., various Philippine and Korean decorations; State of Ill. Long and Honorable Service medal. Mem. VFW, Adj. Gens. Assn. U.S., N.G. Assn. U.S., N.G. Assn. Ill., Am. Legion, Amvets. Home: 100 Wabash Ave Mattoon IL 61938-4524

PHIPPS, LYNNE BRYAN, interior architect, educator, minister; b. Chapel Hill, NC, Sept. 23, 1964; d. Floyd Talmadge and Sandra Patricia (McLester) Bryan. BFA, R.I. Sch. Design, 1986, B in Interior Architecture, 1987; cert. in parent edn., Wheelock Coll., Boston, 1989; MDiv, Andover Newton Theol. Sem., 1997. Ordained to ministry UCC Ch., 1997. Apprentice Thompson Ventulett Stainback, Atlanta, 1983-85; jr. designer Flansberg & Assocs., Boston, 1985—86; sr. designer Andrew Samataro & Assocs., Boston, 1986-87; prin. Innovative Designs, Duxbury, Mass., 1987—97; prin. Design One Consortium LLC, 2001—. Parent educator Families First, Cambridge, Mass.; guest lectr., jurist Auburn (Ala.) U., 1988, R.I. Sch. Design, Providence, 1990; guest jurist U. Memphis, 1995; assoc. prof. Mass. Bay C.C., Wellesley, 1997-2000; mem. adv. bd. U. R.I. Chamberlyne Sch. Design Alumni Coun., 1996—; guest lectr. Architectural and Family Issues; mem. adv. bd. Sch. Design IDA Coll., Newton, Mass. Youth min. St. Andrew's Episcopal Ch., Hanover, Mass., 1992—95; youth and family min. St. Stephen's Episcopal Ch., Cohasset, Mass., 1993—96; pastor Kingston Congl. Ch. UCC, 1997—2001. Mem. AIA (assoc.), Internat. Interior Design Assn., Internat. Platform Assn. Avocations: sailing, tennis, antique boats. Office: Design One Consortium LLC 422D South Rd Wakefield RI 02879

PHIPPS, PETER A., psychology professor; b. Charlottesville, Va., Dec. 27, 1956; adopted s. John Akers and s. Pauline Chunn Phipps; m. Suzanne Petri, June 1, 1991; 1 child, Aidan Thomas. BSW, Va. Commonwealth U., 1982; MA, Marymount U., 1990; MS, Lehigh U., 1992; PhD, Saybrook Grad. Sch., 1999. Asst. prof. Sullivan County C.C., Loch Sheldrake, NY, 1999—2002; dept. head Dutchess C.C., Poughkeepsie, NY, 2002—. Psychologist, Va., 1982—90, Burlington, NC, 1994—99; vis. instr. Lehigh U., 1990—93; adj. lectr. Allentown Coll., 1991—93; adj. instr. Durham Tech. C.C., 1996—97. Com. mem. PTA, Poughkeepsie, 2003—. Sgt. US Army, 1975—79. Mem.: APA, Delta Epsilon Sigma. Democrat. Achievements include research in Developmental paths for psychotherapists; Health care in a rural county. Avocations: bicycling, reading, painting, hiking. Office: Dutchess C C 53 Pendell Rd Poughkeepsie NY 12601 Home Phone: 845-471-15010; Office Phone: 845-431-8341. Office Fax: 845-431-89921. E-mail: phipps@sunydutchess.edu.

PHIPPS, ROBERT LEE, information technology manager; b. Oxnard, Calif., Mar. 16, 1963; m. Beatriz Phipps, Sept. 9, 1995; children: Cynthia, Stephanie. AS in Engring., Ventura Coll., Calif., 1983—93; BS in Computer Sci., Calif. State Poly. U., Pomona, 1984—89, MBA, 1993—2003. Cert. computing profl. Inst. Cert. Computing Profls., 1995, info. security mgr. Info. Systems Audit & Control Assn., 2005; wilderness 1st responder Wilderness Med. Assocs., 2006. Computer programmer Wilsey Foods, Industry, Calif., 1987—90; programmer-analyst Sirena Swimwear, El Monte, Calif., 1990—92; sr. programmer analyst Disney Consumer Products, Burbank, Calif., 1992—95, info. tech. mgr. Glendale, Calif., 1995—. Bd. mem., dir. mem. svcs. Inst. Cert. Computing Profls., Chgo., 1998—99. Team mem. Cmty. Emergency Response Team, Pomona, Calif., 2005—07. Mem.: ISACA, Am. Inst. Aeronautics & Astonautics (life), Air Force Assn. (life), Planetary Soc., MENSA, Toastmasters Internat. (Advanced Toastmasters Gold award 2003). Avocations: aerospace, hiking, scouting. Office: Disney Consumer Products 1101 Flower St Glendale CA 91201 Business E-Mail: robert.phipps@disney.com.

PHOCAS, GEORGE J., lawyer; b. NYC, Dec. 1, 1927; m. Katrin Gorny, Feb. 26, 1966; 1 child, George Alexander. AB, U. Chgo., 1950, JD, 1953. Bar: N.Y. 1955, U.S. Supreme Ct. 1962. Assoc. Sullivan & Cromwell, NYC, 1953-56; counsel Creole Petroleum Corp., Caracas, Venezuela, 1956-60; internat. negotiator Standard Oil Co. N.J. (Exxon), 1960-63; sr. ptnr. Casey, Lane & Mittendorf, London, 1963-72, counsel, 1972-76. Exec. v.p. Occidental Petroleum Corp., Los Angeles, 1972-74; adv., U.S. del. UN, ECAFE, Teheran, 1963 Trustee Assn. Naval Aviation, Washington, Owl's Head Aviation Mus., Maine; mem. vis. bd. U. Chgo. Law Sch.; bd. visitors U. Chgo. Law Sch. Capt., Infantry U.S. Army Mem. ABA, Law Soc. London, Brit. Inst. Comparative Law, Am. Soc. Internat. Law, Assn. Bar City N.Y.; Clubs: Boodles (London), Met. (N.Y.C.). Home: 29 Duchess of Bedford Walk London W87 QH England Address: Burnt Island Spruce Head ME 04859

PHOENIX, G. KEITH, lawyer; b. Centralia, Ill., Aug. 13, 1946; BA in Liberal Arts, So. Ill. U., 1968; JD, St. Louis U., 1973. Bar: Mo. 74, U.S. Dist. Ct. (so. dist.) Ill. 75, U.S. Ct. Appeals (7th and 8th cirs.) 82. Assoc. Coburn, Croft & Shepherd & Putzell, St. Louis, 1974—79; sr. counsel, pres. Sandberg, Phoenix & von Gontard, St. Louis, 1979—. Legal cons. Am. Acad. Pedist. Contbr. articles on med./legal topics to profl. jours. Mem. bd. trustees St. Louis U., 2005—. 1st lt. US Army, 1968—71, Vietnam. Decorated Bronze Star with cluster, Air medal with cluster, Vietnam medal; named one of Mo. and Kans. Civil Litig. Super Lawyers, 2005; named to Best Lawyers in Am., 2003, 2004, 2005, 2006. Mem.: Product Liability Adv. Coun., Am. Bd. Trial Advocacy (past pres.), Lawyer's Assn. (past pres.), St. Louis Bar Assn., Mo. Bar Assn., Ill. Bar Assn. (Named One of the Top Trial Lawyers in Am. 2002, 2003). Office: Sandberg Phoenix & von Gontard One City Centre 1500 Saint Louis MO 63101-1880 Office Phone: 314-231-3332. Business E-Mail: kphoenix@spvg.com.

PHOENIX, JOAQUIN RAPHAEL, actor; b. San Juan, Oct. 28, 1974; s. John Bottom and Arlyn Dunetz. Actor: (TV films) Backwards: The Riddle of Dyslexia, 1984, Kids Don't Tell, 1985, Secret Witness, 1988; (TV series) Morningstar/Eveningstar, 1986; (films) SpaceCamp, 1986, Russkies, 1987, Parenthood, 1989, Walking the Dog, 1991, To Die For, 1995, Inventing the Abbotts, 1997, U Turn, 1997, Return to Paradise, 1998, Clay Pigeons, 1998, 8MM, 1999, The Yards, 2000, Gladiator, 2000, Quills, 2000, Buffalo Soldiers, 2001, Signs, 2002, It's All About Love, 2003, (voice) Brother Bear, 2003, The Village, 2004, Ladder 49, 2004, Hotel Rwanda, 2004, Walk the Line, 2005 (Best Performance by an Actor in a Motion Picture-Musical or Comedy, Hollywood Fgn. Press Assn. (Golden Globe award), 2006). Office: Iris Burton Agy 1450 Belfast Dr Los Angeles CA 90069

PHOMMAHAXAY, PHANTHONG, ambassador; b. Vientiane, Laos, Mar. 2, 1941; m. Amphanh Luangrath; 4 children. Grad. in fgn. affairs, Centre Nat. d'Etudes Politiques Administratives et Juriques, Vientiane, Laos; diploma of fgn. affairs, London. With Lao Min. of Fgn. Affairs, Vientiane, 1962—, embassy attache Beijing, 1965—68, head passport sect., head polit. sect. Vientiane, 1968—73, 2d sec., 1st sec. and chargé d'affaires Lao embassy Paris, 1974—78, dir. NGO sect., dept. internat. orgns. Vientiane, 1978—80, 1st sec., dept. head mission Bangkok, 1980—84, dep. dir. gen., dir. gen. press dept. Vientiane, 1984—90, amb. to Indonesia, 1990—94, dir. gen. Asia Pacific and Africa dept. Vientiane, 1994—95, amb. to Australia and N.Z., 1995—98, amb. to Germany, the Netherlands, Switzerland and Austria, 1998—2001, amb. to US Washington, 2001—. Avocations: reading, golf. Office: Embassy of the Laos 2222 S St NW Washington DC 20008 E-mail: laoemb@verizon.net.

PHUNG, NGUYEN DINH, medical educator; b. Ninh Binh, Vietnam, Sept. 25, 1950; came to U.S., 1975; s. Thu Dinh Nguyen and Minh Tuyet Le; m. Thuy Thanh Tran, Sept. 25, 1974; children: The-Ngoc, Khoi-Nguyen, Thien Huong. MD, Saigon Med. Sch., 1973. Diplomate Am. Bd. Internal Medicine, Am. Bd. Allergy and Immunology. Clin. instr. medicine, staff physician U. Okla. Health Scis. Ctr. & Vets. Hosp., Oklahoma City, 1982-84; clin. asst. prof. medicine U. Tex. Med. Sch., Houston, 1989—. Co-author: Practical Allergy & Immunology, 1983; contbr. articles to profl. jours. Mem. ACP, Am. Acad. Allergy and Immunology. Avocations: writing, music. Office: Allergy and Asthma Clinic 2905 Milam St Houston TX 77006-3609

PI, EDMOND HSIN-TUNG, psychiatry educator; MD, Cath. U. Coll. Medicine, 1972. Cert. Am. Bd. Psychiatry and Neurology. Chief resident U. Ky. Med. Ctr., Lexington, 1977-78; instr. psychiatry U. So. Calif. Sch. Medicine, LA, 1978-80, asst. prof., 1980-83; assoc. prof. Med. Coll. Pa., Phila., 1983-85, U. So. Calif. Sch. Medicine, 1985-88, prof. clin. psychiatry, 1988—98; prof. Charles R. Drew U. Medicine and Sci., 1998—2003; clin. prof. psychiatry Sch. Medicine, UCLA, 1999—2005; prof. clin. psychiatry Sch. Medicine, U. So. Calif., 2005—, assoc. chair for clin. affairs, dept. psychiatry, 2006—. Asst. dir. psychopharmacology U. So. Calif. Sch. Medicine, 1978-80; asst. dir. adult psychiat. clinic L.A. County and U. So. Calif. Med. Ctr., 1980-83; dir. adult psychiat. clinic Med. Coll. Pa., Phila., 1983-85; dir. Adult Psychiat. Inpatient Svcs., L.A. County and U. So. Calif. Med. Ctr., 1985-91, dir. Adult Psychiat. Outpatient Svcs., 1995-97; dir. transcultural psychiatry U. So. Calif. Sch. Medicine, 1991-98; med. dir. State of Calif. Dept. Mental Health, 1997-98; dir. Consultation and Liaison Svcs., L.A. County and U. So. Calif. Med. Ctr., 1998; exec. vice-chmn., assoc. ctr. dir. Augustus F. Hawkins Mental Health Ctr., Martin Luther King. Jr./Charles R. Drew U. Med. Ctr., 1998-2003; dir. psychiat. inpatient svc. Harbor/UCLA Med. Ctr., 2003-05; dir. psychiat. consultation and liaison svcs. L.A. (Calif.) County and U. So. Calif. Med. Ctr., 2005—, assoc. chair clin. affairs, 2006—. Author: Reactions to Psychotropic Medications, 1987, (book chpts.) Transcultural Psychiatry, Clinical Psychopharmacology, 1985—; contbr. articles to profl. jours. Mem. Calif. Gov.'s Com. Employment of Disabled Persons, Sacramento, 1993—; bd. dirs. Chinese Bus. Assn., LA, 1990—92, Com. of 100, NYC, 1993—98, San Gabriel chpt. ARC, Calif., 1994—97, Mental Health Assn., LA County, Calif., 1995—97, 1998—2001. Vis. scholar Com. on Scholarly Comm. with People's Republic of China U.S. Nat. Acad. Scis., Washington, 1987-88; Treval fellow Am. Coll. Neuropsychopharmacology, 1982. Fellow Am. Psychiat. Assn. (chair com. Asian-Am. psychiatrists 1998-2000), Am. Soc. Social Psychiatry, Pacific Rim Coll. Psychiatry (treas. 1991-97), Am. Coll. Psychiatrists; mem. Soc. Study Psychiatry and Culture, Pacific Rim Assn. Clin. Pharmogenetics, Assn. Chinese Am. Psychiatrists (pres. 1995—). Avocations: photography, writing, travel, tennis, media communications. Office: LAC & USC Med Ctr Dept Psychiatry 2020 Zonal Ave IRD 13 Los Angeles CA 90033 Office Phone: 323-226-7975. Business E-Mail: ehpi@usc.edu.

PIANALTO, SANDRA, bank executive; b. Valli del Pasubio, Italy, Aug. 4, 1954; B in Economics, U. Akron, 1976; M in Economics, George Washington U., 1985; LHD (hon.), U. Akron, Baldwin-Wallace Coll., Kent State U., Ursuline Coll.; D of Bus. Adminstrn. (hon.), Cleve. State U. Economist bd. govs. Fed. Reserve Sys.; staff mem. budget com. U.S. Ho. of Reps.; economist rsch. dept. Fed. Res. Bank Cleve., 1983—84, asst. v.p.

pub. affairs, 1984—88, v.p., sec. bd. dirs., 1988—93, first v.p., COO, 1993—2003, pres., 2003—. Bd. dirs. Cleve. Found., Gr. Cleve. Partnership, U. Hosp. Health Sys., United Way Svcs. Cleve., Rock and Roll Hall of Fame and Mus., N.E. Ohio Coun. Higher Edn., Cath. Diocese Cleve. Found., Ohio Bus. Alliance for Higher Edn. and Economy. Office: Fed Res Bank Cleve PO Box 6387 Cleveland OH 44101-1387 Office Phone: 216-579-2000. *

PIANKA, GEORGE, orthopedic surgeon; arrived in US, 1964; s. Antoni and Aleksandra Pianka; m. Audrone Julia Raskys, Aug. 16, 1986; children: George, John Paul, Mark, Matthew. BS, Cornell U., Ithaca, NY, 1980; MD, U. Conn., Farmington, 1984. Intern Lenox Hill Hosp., NYC, 1984, resident orthopedics, 1985—89, attending physician orthopedics, 1990; fellow hand surgery Hosp. for Joint Diseases, NYC, 1989—90; attending physician orthopedics Phelps Meml. Hosp., Sleepy Hollow, NY, 1995. Contbr. chapters to books. Recipient Resident Tchg. award, Lenox Hill Orthopedic Dept., 1995, 2000. Fellow: Am. Soc. for Surgery of Hand, Am. Acad. Orthopedic Surgeons; mem.: NY Soc. for Surgery of Hand. Avocations: tennis, fishing, skiing. Office: Hudson Valley Bone and Joint Surgeons 24 Saw Mill River Rd Hawthorne NY 10532 also: 73 E 71st St New York NY 10021 Personal E-mail: sylviadrpianka@hotmail.com.

PIANKO, THEODORE A., lawyer; b. Dennville, NJ, Sept. 5, 1955; s. Theodore and Pasqualina (Liguori) Pianko; m. Beatriz Maria Olivera (div. Dec. 1985); m. Kathryn Anne Lindley, Feb. 18, 1990; children: Matthew James, Samuel Wahoo, Zoe Wahoo. BA, SUNY, 1975; JD, U. Mich., 1978. Bar: Mich. 1978, Ill. 1979, Calif. 1980. Atty. Ford Motor Co., Dearborn, Mich., 1978-80; assoc. Lillick McHose & Charles, LA, 1980-83; ptnr. Sidley & Austin, LA, 1983-94, Christie, Parker & Hale, Newport Beach, Calif., 1994—2006. Home: 60/11 Moo 4 Chernstalay Thalang Phuket 83110 Thailand Home Phone: 66-84-8501304; Office Phone: 66-76-271906.

PIANO, RENZO, architect; b. Genoa, Italy, Sept. 14, 1937; m. Magda Arduino, 1962; m. Emilia Rossato, 1992; children: Carlo, Matteo, Lia, Giorgio Anthony. Dip.Arch., Poly. of Milan, 1964; PhD in Fine Arts (hon.), Pratt Inst., NY, 2002. Worked with Franco Albini, Milan, 1962-64, E. Piano, Genoa, 1964-65, Z.S. Makowsky, London, 1965-70; ptnr. Piano and Rogers Architects, London, Paris and Genoa, 1970—, Piano and Rice, Genoa, Paris and London, 1977—93, Renzo Piano Building Workshop, Genoa, Paris and London, 1994—. Lectr. Poly. of Milan, 1965-68; vis. lectr. Columbia U., NYC, 1967, U. Pa., Phila., 1967, U. Bucharest, Romania, 1968, Poly. of Delft, Netherlands, 1969, Unesco, Paris, 1973, Oslo Sch. Architecture, 1976; prof. architecture Archtl. Assn. Sch., London, 1971, Poly. Cen. London, 1971, created with Harvard U., Architecture Workshop Found., 2001-. Prin. works include Italian Industry Pavilion, Expo '70, Japan, 1970, Fitzroy St. Comml. Ctr., Cambridge, UK, 1970, B&B Italia Offices, Como, 1971, Universal Oil Products U.K. Head Office and UOP Fragrances Ltd. Lab., Tadworth, Surrey, 1972, Aston Martin Lagonda Ltd. Offices, Showroom, Restaurant, etc., London, 1973, PATScentre, Cambridge, 1975, Inst. de Recherche et de Coordination Acoustique, Paris, 1977, Centre Beaubourg, Paris, 1977, Kronenbourg factory, Strasbourg, 1978, Quartiere Il Rigo housing estate, Corciano, Perugia, Italy, 1978-82, Civic Ctr. and Libr., Loano, Savona, Italy, 1980, Nationalgalerie extensions & housing, West Berlin, 1981, De Menil Collection bldg., Houston, 1981-83, Bance Agricola Comml. bldg., Reggio Emilia, Italy, 1981-83, IBM travelling exhbn. pavilions, 1982, Palazzo a Vela conversion, 1982, Centocelle/Torrespaccata Bus. Ctr., Rome, 1982, Banca Agricola Comml. br. bldg., Modena, Italy, 1982, 5 Met. Rwy. Stas., Genoa, 1983, Il Prometeo music rsch. lab., Venice, 1984, Centre Georges Pompidou cinema extensions, Paris, 1984, Comml. Ctr. office bldgs., Naples, Italy, 1984, Kenya Energy Tech. Inst., Nairobi, 1984, Leisure Ctr., Cremona, Italy, 1984, Columbus Expedition 500th Anniversary designs, Genoa, 1984, Office Bldg. for Lowara factory, Vicenza, Italy, 1985, Mus. for Menil Collection, Houston, 1986, Hdqs. for Light Metals Exptl. Inst., Novara, Italy, 1987, Nicola Football stadium, Bari, Italy, 1990, Bercy Comml. Ctr., Paris, 1990, IRCAM Extension, Paris, 1990, Cruise Ships for P&O, USA, 1990, Housing City of Paris, 1991, Thomson factories, Guyancourt, France, 1991, Underground stas. for Ansaldo, Genoa, Italy, 1991, Hdqrs. Credito Indsl. Sardo, Cagliari, Italy, 1992, Kansai Internat. Airport, Osaka, 1994, Lingotto Congress-Concert Hall, Turin, Italy, 1994, Renzo Piano Bldg. Workshop Office, Genoa, 1994, Cy Twombly Pavilion, Houston, 1995, Meridien Hotel at Lingotto and Bus. Ctr., Torino, Italy, 1995, Hdqs. Harbour Authorities, Genoa, 1995, Cinema, Offices, Contemporary Art Mus., Congress Ctr., Landscape, Cité Internat., Lyon, France, 1996, I Portici (Shopping St. at Lingotto), Turin, 1996, Ushibuka Bridge, Kumamoto, Japan, 1997, Mus. Sci. and Tech., Amsterdam, The Netherlands, 1997, Mus. Beyeler Found., Riehen, Basel, Switzerland, 1997, Mercedes Benz Design Ctr., Stuttgart, Germany, 1998, Lodi (Italy) Bank Hdqs., 1998, NY Times Bldg., NYC, 2000; Renovation and expansion of the Calif. Acad. Sciences, 2000, Morgan Pierpont Library, NYC, 2000, U. of Mich. Law Sch., 2002, Morgan Libr. and Mus., 2006, numerous others; exhbns. include Triennale, Milan, 1967, Archtl. Assn., London, 1970, Musée des Arts Decoratifs, Paris, 1973, IBM Travelling Exhbn. in Europe, 1986, Columbus Internat. Exposition, Aquarium and Congress Hall, Genoa, 1992, Out of the blue, Kunst-und Ausstellungshalle, Bonn, Germany, 1997, Out of the blue, Villa Pignatelli, Naples, Italy, 1997, Out of the blue, Gallery MA, Tokyo, 1998, Renzo Piano: The architect's studio, La. Mus. of Modern Art, Humlebaek Copenhagen, Denmark, 2003. Recipient 1st prize Place Beaubourg Competition, Paris, 1971, Auguste Perret prize Internat. Union Architects, 1978, Compasso d'Oro award, Milan, 1981, Arnold W. Brunner Memorial Prize in Architecture Am. Acad. of Arts and Letters, 1994, Erasmus prize, Netherlands, 1995, Art pirze Akademie Künste, Berlin, 1995, Premio Capo Circeo, 1996, Diploma European award for steel structures for elevated heliport structure at Lingotto (Italy), 1997, Pritzker Arch. prize, The White House, 1998, Wexner Prize, Wexner Ctr. for the Arts, 2001, Médaille D'Or, International Union of Architects, Berlin, 2002, Michelangelo Antonioni for the Arts, Rome Auditorium, Italy, 2002, Gold medal Italian Architecture, Milan, 2003, Bus. Cultural award, Italy-Am. C. of C., NY, 2003, McKim prize, Am. Acad. in Rome, 2005; decorated officer Nat. Order Legion of Honor (France), 2000; named one of 100 Most Influential People, Time Mag., 2006. Fellow: Am. Inst. Architects (hon.). Office: Atelier Piano 34 rue des Archives 75004 Paris France also: Studio Renzo Piano Via Rubens 29 16158 Genoa Italy E-mail: italy@rpbw.com, france@rpbw.com.

PIASSICK, JOEL BERNARD, lawyer; b. Atlanta, June 2, 1940; s. Louis S. and Sarah (Freeman) P.; m. Karen Pevow, Aug. 11, 1963; children: Joan, Louis. BA in Polit. Sci., Tulane U., 1962; LLB, U. Va., 1965. Bar: Va. 1965, Ga. 1966, Colo. 1999. Ptnr. Smith, Gambrell & Russell, Atlanta, 1967-90; ptnr., of counsel Kilpatrick Stockton LLP, Atlanta, 1990—; exec. v.p. Harbert Mgmt. Corp, Birmingham, Ala., 1998—. Fellow Am. Coll. Bankruptcy. Office: Harbert Mgmt Corp 1 Riverchase Pkwy S Birmingham AL 35244 E-mail: jpiassick@kilstock.com.

PIAZZA, MIKE (MICHAEL JOSEPH PIAZZA), professional baseball player; b. Norristown, Pa., Sept. 4, 1968; m. Alicia Rickter, 2005. Student, Miami-Dade C.C. Catcher LA Dodgers, 1992—97, Fla. Marlins, 1998, NY Mets, 1998—2005, San Diego Padres, 2006, Oakland Athletics, 2006—. Named Nat. League Rookie Player of Yr., Sporting News, 1993, Nat. League Rookie of Yr., Baseball Writers' Assn., 1993; named to Nat. League All-Star Team, 1993—2002, 2004, 2005, Slugger Team, Nat. League, 1993. Achievements include setting the Major League record for home runs by a catcher, 2004. Office: Oakland Athletics 7000 Coliseum Way Oakland CA 94621 *

PICADIO, ANTHONY PETER, lawyer; b. Latrobe, Pa., Dec. 7, 1941; s. Peter J. and Elsie M. (Caldarelli) P.; m. Lynette Norton. BA, U. Pitts., 1965, JD, 1970. Bar: Pa. 1970, U.S. Dist. Ct. (we. dist.) Pa. 1970, U.S. Ct. Appeals (3d cir.) 1971, U.S. Supreme Ct. 1998. Asst. atty. gen. Dept. Environ Protection Commonwealth Pa., 1970-72; ptnr. Reding, Blackstone, Rea & Sell, Pitts., 1972-75, Tucker, Arensberg, P.C., Pitts., 1975-85; founder, sr. ptnr. practice in bus. litigation and environ. law Picadio, Sneath, Miller & Norton, Pitts., 1985—. Mem.: Order of Coif. Office: Picadio Sneath Miller & Norton PC US Steel Tower 600 Grant St Ste 4710 Pittsburgh PA 15219-2703 Office Phone: 412-288-4000. E-mail: picadio@psmn.com.

PICARELLO, ANTHONY, JR., lawyer; b. 1969; AB, Harvard U.; AM, U. Chgo.; JD, U. Va. Bar: Va., DC. Clerk Fed. Dist. Ct., Portland, Maine; assoc. Covington & Burling, Washington; v.p., gen. counsel The Becket Fund for Religious Freedom, Washington. Named one of Litigation's Rising Stars, The Am. Lawyer, 2007. Office: The Becket Fund 1350 Conn Ave NW Ste 605 Washington DC 20036 *

PICASSO, PALOMA, fashion designer; b. Paris, Apr. 19, 1949; d. Pable Picasso and Françoise Gilot; m. Rafael Lopez-Cambil, 1978. Student, U. Sorbonne, Paris; studied jewellry design and fabrication. Designer jewellery Yves St. Laurent, 1969, Zolotas, 1971; founder Paloma Picasso Botique, Paris, Japan, Hong Kong. Designed costumes and sets for L'Interprétation, 1975, Success, 1978; creations designed by her for Paloma Picasso brand include: jewellery for Tiffany & Co., 1980; fragrances Paloma Picasso, 1984, Minotaure, 1992; cosmetics for L'Oréal; women's accessories for Lopez-Cambil Ltd., 1987; hosiery and eyewear for Carrera; bone china, crystal, silverware and tiles for Villeroy & Boch; home linens for Martex; fabrics and wallcoverings for Motif; appeared in film Immoral Tales, 1974. Office: Lopez-Cambil Ltd 37 W 57th St Fl 12 New York NY 10019-3411 also: Nourithe Serraf Martine Herbin 13 cité de Pusy 75017 Paris France

PICCIANO, ANTHONY GERADE, academic administrator; b. NYC, Aug. 19, 1947; s. Amadeo John and Philomena Mary Picciano; m. Elaine A. Nawalsky, May 7, 1999; children: Michael Amadeo, Dawn Marie. BA in Polit. Sci., Hunter Coll., NYC, 1970; MPA, Bernard Baruch Coll., NYC, 1975; PhD in Edn. Leadership, Fordham U., NYC, 1986. Asst. v.p. SUNY, New Paltz, 1977—79; dean adminstrn. Coll. SI, NYC, 1979—85; v.p., dep. to pres. Hunter Coll., NYC, 1985—89, prof., 1989—. Co-founder CUNY Online, NYC, 1998—; founding mem. Alfred P. Sloan Consortium, Needham, Mass., 2001—, bd. dirs.; mem. Am. del. 10th Sino-Am. Conf. Edn., Beijing and Taiyuan, China, 2005—06; mem. del. 9th Sino-Am. Conf. on Edn., NYC; cons. in field. Author: (book) Blended Learning: Research Perspectives, Education Leadership and Planning for Technology 4th Edition, Data Driven Decision Making for Effective School Lesdership, Education Research Primer, Computers in the Schools, Distance Learning: Making Connections across Virtual Space and Time; dir.: (multimedia program) The Five Points: A Multimedia Program in Social History. Elected commr. Bd. Fire Commrs., Pocantico Hills, NY, 2000—06; advisor, cons. Mt. St. Mary Coll., Newburgh, 1978—88; elected trustee bd. edn. Pocantico Hills Bd. Edn., Sleepy Hollow, 1976—85. Fellow, CUNY. Mem.: ASCD, Alfred P. Sloan Consortium (bd. dirs. 2001—06), Internat. Soc. Tech. Edn., Nat. Geog. Soc., Mus. Natural History. Roman Catholic. Avocations: reading, hiking, opera, golf, boating. Office: Hunter College 695 Park Ave New York NY 10021 E-mail: anthony.picciano@hunter.cuny.edu.

PICCININI, ROBERT M. (BOB PICCININI), grocery store chain executive; s. Mike Piccinini. Head, real estate dept. Save Mart Supermarkets, Modesto, Calif., 1971, pres., 1981, owner, 1985—, CEO, chmn. Former owner Fresno Giants. Mailing: Save Mart Supermarkets PO Box 4278 Modesto CA 95352-4278 Office: Save Mart Supermarkets 1800 Standiford Ave Modesto CA 95350

PICCININO, ROCCO MICHAEL, librarian; b. Phila., Aug. 21, 1949; s. Rocco Anthony and Ida Marie (Minicozzi) P. BA in History magna cum laude, LaSalle Coll., 1971; postgrad., U. NC, 1971—73; MSLS, Drexel U., 1981. Ednl. resources specialist CC of Phila., 1973-74; asst./assoc. libr. United Engrs. & Constructors Inc. (A Raytheon Co.) Libr., Phila., 1974-81, head libr. Boston, 1981-84; asst./assoc. dir. Wentworth Inst. of Tech. Libr., Boston, 1984-89; sci. libr. Smith Coll. Librs., Northampton, Mass., 1989-91, coord. br. libr. svcs., sci. libr., 1991—2006, assoc. dir. br. libr., head young sci. libr., 2007—. Mem. ALA (Assn. Coll. Rsch. Librs. divsn. instruction sect. policy com. 2002-04, nom. com. 2005-07, sci. and tech. sect. coun., co-chair coll. libr. discussion group 1998-02, forum for sci. and tech. libr. rsch. 2000-02, comparison of sci. and tech. com. 2002-04, conf. program planning com. 2003-05, nominating com. 2004—06, info. literacy com. 2006-), Libr. Adminstrn. and Mgmt. Assn. (bldg. and equipment sect., bldgs. for coll. and univ. librs. com., 2000-02, sys. and svcs. sect. program com. 2004-), Libr. and Info. Tech. Assn., Spl. Librs. Assn. (sci.-tech. divsn., Boston chpt. adv. coun. 1996-04, chair We. Outreach 1996-2004, nominating com. 2004-05), IEEE (libr. adv. coun. 2002-03), Phi Alpha Theta, Beta Phi Mu. Democrat. Roman Catholic. Avocations: travel, bicycling, reading, films. Home: 104 Woods Rd Northampton MA 01062-3507 Office: Smith Coll Young Sci Libr Northampton MA 01063-0001 Office Phone: 413-585-2951. Business E-Mail: rpiccini@email.smith.edu.

PICCO, STEVEN JOSEPH, lawyer; b. NYC, Sept. 9, 1948; s. Carl and Constance (Speers) Picco; m. Ada T. Ryan, July 15, 1972; children: Christopher, Timothy, Kaitlin. BS, Rider Coll., 1970; JD, Seton Hall U., South Orange, NJ, 1975. Bar: NJ 1975, US Dist. Ct. NJ 1975, US Ct. Appeals (3d cir.) 1975. Data processing programmer-sys. engring. NJ Dept. Labor and Industry, Trenton, 1970—75; project specialist NJ Dept. Environ. Protection, Trenton, 1975—76, dir. regulatory and govtl. affairs, 1976—78, acting dep. commr., 1979—80, asst. commr., 1979—81, NJ Dept. Energy, Newark, 1978—79; ptnr. Greenstone & Sokol, Trenton, 1981—87, Picco Mack Herbert Kennedy Jaffe & Yoskin, Trenton, 1988—97, Reed Smith LLP, Princeton, NJ, 1997—. Bd. dirs. Mercer County C. of C., Robert Wood Johnson U. Hosp. at Hamilton; mem. N.J. Seed., Am. Heart Assn., Heritage Bd. Avocations: golf, reading, community volunteer work. Office: Reed Smith LLP Princeton Forrestal Village 136 Main St Ste 250 Princeton NJ 08540 Office Phone: 609-514-5970. Business E-Mail: spicco@reedsmith.com.

PICHASKE, DAVID RICHARD, language educator; b. Kenmore, NY, Sept. 2, 1943; s. Donald Richard Pichaske and Martha Theresa Schisa; m. Elaine Ezekian (div.); children: Stephen Geoffrey, Kristin Diane; m. Michelle Lynn Payne, Sept. 3, 1991. BA, Wittenberg U., 1965; PhD, Ohio U., 1969. Asst. to assoc. prof. Bradley Polytech. Inst., Peoria, Ill., 1969—; assoc. to prof. S.W. Minn. State U., Marshall, 1980—. Sr. Fulbright lectr. U. Lodz, Poland, 1989—91, U. Latvia, Riga, 1996—97, Mongolian Nat. U., 2003. Author: Beowulf to Beatles: Approaches to Poetry, 1972, Writing Sense: A Handbook of Composition, 1975, A Generation in Motion: Popular Music and Culture in the Sixties, 1979, Chaucer's Literary Pilgrimage: Movement in the Canterbury Tales, 1977, Beowulf to Beatles and Beyond: The Varieites of Poetry, 1981, The Poetry of Rock, 1981, The Jubilee Diary: April 10, 1980-April 19, 1981, 1982, Visiting the Father and Other Poems, 1987, Late Harvest: Rural American Writing, 1992, Poland in Transition: 1989-91, 1994, Southwest Minnesota: The Land and the People, 2000, UBO3: A Season in Outer Mongolia, 2003, Hallelujah Anyway!, 2004, The Father Poems, 2005; co-author (with Joseph Amato and Richard Davies): A Place Called Home, 2003; author: Rooted: Seven Midwest Writers of Place, 2006. Recipient Minn. Book award, Minn. Humanities Commn., 2003. Mem.: Jour. Popular Music and Soc. (adv. editor 1995—), Minn. Machinery Mus. (bd. dirs. 2003—). Office: Southwest Minn State Univ Marshall MN 56258 Home: 10489 810th Ave Granite Falls MN 56241-4024 Office Phone: 507-537-6463. Personal E-mail: pichasked@hotmail.com.

PICK, JAMES BLOCK, business professor, writer; b. Chgo., July 29, 1943; s. Grant Julius and Helen (Block) Pick. BA, Northwestern U., 1966; MS in Edn., No. Ill. U., 1969; PhD, U. Calif., Irvine, 1974. Cert. computer profl. Asst. rsch. statistician, lectr. Grad. Sch. Mgmt., U. Calif., Riverside, 1975-91, dir. computing, 1984-91; co-dir. U.S.-Mex. Database Project, 1988-91; assoc. prof. mgmt. and bus., dir. info. mgmt. program U. Redlands, Calif., 1991-95, 99-01, prof. bus., 1995—, chair dept. mgmt. and bus., 1995-97, 98-99, chair faculty assembly Sch. Bus., 2001—04. Vis. prof. U. Iberoam., Mexico City, 1997, Mexico City, 2001; cons. internat. divsn. U.S. Census Bur., 1978; mem. Univ. Commons. Bd., 1982—86; mem. nat. curriculum task force IS, 1997; mem. U. Commn. Future Bus. Programs, 1998—2000; pres. Orange County chpt. Assn. Sys. Mgmt., 1978—79; mem. bd. govs. PCCLAS, Assn. Borderlands Studies, 1989—92, v.p., 2000—01, pres., 2002—; bd. profls. advisors demographic analysis U. Calif, Irvine, 2002—03; mem. exec. coun. Info. Resources Mgmt. Assn., 2003—; vis. rschr. Ctr. for Rsch. on Immigration, Population, and Pub. Policy U. Calif., Irvine, 2005; external faculty rsch. assoc. CRITO, U. Calif., Irvine, 2006—. Author: Geothermal Energy Development, 1982, MicroManual, 1986, Computer Systems in Business, 1986, Atlas of Mexico, 1989, The Mexico Handbook, 1994, Mexico Megacity, 1997, Mexico and Mexico City in the World Economy, 2001, Geographic Systems in Business, 2004, Exploring the Urban Community: A GIS Approach, 2005, GeoBusiness: GIS in the Digital Firm, 2007; mem. editl. bd. Jour. Borderlands Studies, 1999—, Jour. Info. Tech. Cases and Applications, 2002—, Frontera Norte, 2006—; mem. editl. bd.: Jour. Info. Tech. for Devel., 2007—; condr. rsch. info. sys., population, environ. studies; contbr. articles to profl. jours. Trustee Newport Harbor Art Mus., 1981—87, 1988—96, Berkeley Art Mus. and Pacific Film Archives, 2003—; mem. acquisitions com. Newport Harbor Art Mus., 1987—91, v.p., 1991—96; trustee, chmn. collection com. Orange County Mus. Art, 1996—; mem. com. Block Mus., 1999—2001, mem. bd. advisors, 2006—. Recipient Thunderbird award, Bus. Assn. L.Am. Studies, 1993, Outstanding Alumnus award, No. Ill. U., 2004; Ford Found. grantee, 1998—99, Sr. Fulbright scholar, 2001. Mem.: AAAS, Assn. for Info. Sys., Assn. Am. Geographers, Sociedad de Demografia Mexicana, Internat. Union Sci. Study Population, Population Assn. Am., Am. Statis. Assn., Am. Sociol. Assn., Assn. for Info. Systems, Assn. Computing Machinery, Standard Club (Chgo.). Office: U Redlands Sch Bus 1200 E Colton Ave Redlands CA 92374-3755 Business E-Mail: james_pick@redlands.edu.

PICKEL, ALAN SCOTT, lawyer; b. Cleve., Sept. 28, 1965; BS, Syracuse U., 1987, JD cum laude, 1990. Bar: Conn. 1990, N.Y. 1991, U.S. Dist. (ea. and so. dists.) N.Y. 1991, U.S. Dist. Ct. Conn. 1991. Assoc. Law Office of Jeffrey S. Stephens, Greenwich, Conn., 1990—91, Cooper Liebowitz Royster & Wright, Elmsford, NY and Stamford, Conn, 1991—93, Piazza Melmed & Berkowitz, Stamford, 1993—96; ptnr. Piazza & Melmed, Stamford, 1996—98, Piazza & Pickel, Stamford, 1998—2003, Law Offices of Alan Scott Pickel, Stamford, 2003—. Andrews scholar, 1988—90. Mem. ATLA, Conn. Trial Lawyers Assn., Conn. Bar Assn., N.Y. Bar Assn., Westchester County Bar Assn., Stamford/Norwalk Bar Assn. Office: Law Offices Alan Scott Pickel 1700 Bedford St Stamford CT 06905 Office Phone: 203-348-4100. Business E-Mail: apickel@alanpickel.com.

PICKELMAN, JOHN E., academic administrator; b. Saginaw, Mich., Oct. 29, 1945; s. Edwin John and Betty Joan (Kingham) P.; m. Dianna Joan Green, June 24, 1967 (div. Aug. 1975); children: Jason, Matthew; m. Barbara Ellen Wiersema, July 11, 1981. AB in English, Albion Coll., Mich., 1967; MA in Edn., U. Mo., Kansas City, 1970; PhD in Ednl. Adminstrn., U. Tex., Austin, 1976. Assoc. dean students William Jewell Coll., Liberty, Mo., 1967—71; dir. residence life Tex. Luth. Coll., Seguin, 1971—74; asst. to chancellor Dallas County CC Dist., 1975—78; v.p. student svcs. Brookhaven Coll., Farmers Branch, Tex., 1978—81, v.p. instrn., 1981—83; pres. Galveston Coll., Tex., 1983—91; chancellor North Harris Montgomery CC Dist., Houston, 1991—. Adj. prof. CC Leadership Prog. U. Tex., Austin. Author monographs, articles in profl. jours. Campaign chmn. United Way, Galveston, 1988; chmn. Galveston Hist. Found., 1983—; bd. dirs. Ronald McDonald House, Galveston, 1990. Named one of Outstanding Young Men in Am., 1979; named Outstanding CC Chief Exec. Officer, 1988, Disting. Grad. Coll. Edn., U. Tex., 1990, Citizen of Yr., Houston C. of C., 2001; recipient Internat. Leadership award, Nat. Inst. Staff and Orgnl. Devel., 2001, Aldine Scholarship Found. Cmty. Star award, 2005, John Pickelman Leadership North Houston Fellow award, 2005. Mem. Assn. Tex. Colls. and Univs. (pres. 1990-91, bd. dirs.), So. Assn. Colls. and Schs. (chmn. re-accreditation coms. 1978, vice chmn. 2006, chmn. 2007, Commn. Colls. James T. Rogers Meritorious Svc. award 2004), Galveston Rotary (bd. dirs. 1983—), Tex. Pub. Cmty./Jr. Coll. Assn. (exec. com. 1986-88), Tex. Assn. CCs (chmn. bd. dirs. 2005-07), Phi Theta Kappa (Shirley B. Gordon award of Distinction for Chief Exec. Officers 2005), Phi Delta Kappa. Avocations: gourmet cooking, golf, fishing, boating. Office: N Harris Montgomery CC Dist 5000 Research Forest Dr The Woodlands TX 77381-4356 Office Phone: 832-813-6500. E-mail: john.pickelman@nhmccd.edu. *

PICKENPAUGH, THOMAS EDWARD, archaeologist, anthropologist; b. St. Clairsville, Ohio, Feb. 8, 1945; s. Douglas Giffin and Betty June (Brown) P. BA, Kent State U., 1970, MA, 1971; ABD, Cath. U., 1980. Anthropologist, instr. sociology and anthropology Wheeling Coll., W.Va., 1972-73; anthropologist, instr., asst. prof. anthropology Ohio U.-Ea., 1972-74, 78, archaeologist, asst. prof. anthropology St. Clairsville, 1986-95; mus. technician US Dept. Interior, Nat. Pk. Svc., Washington, 1983; mus. technican Nat. Mus. Natural History, Smithsonian Instn., Washington, 1984-87; mus. specialist, loan officer USN, Naval Hist. Ctr., Washington, 1987—. Dir. archaeol. excavations Brokaw Village Site, St. Clairsville, Ohio, 1972-74, 76-78, 82, 86-96, 98, mem. archaeol. staff Thunderbird Site, Front Royal, Va., Savannah River, Ga., SC, Richard B. Russell Dam Project, 1980, El Mirador Site, Guatemala, 1980, Louis Berger Internat. Project, Trenton, NJ, 1983-84, Sully Plantation, Loudon County, Va., 1984, Fells Point Project, Balt., 1984, exhibited rsch. on Symbols of Rank and Power, Ohio U. Eastern Art Gall., 1998, others. Author: Dominant Predators and Paramount Leaders: Symbols of Rank and Power in Traditional Cultures, 2005; rsch. exhibition: Martin Luther King Meml. Libr., 2003—04; rsch. exhbn. Bead Mus., Washington, 2004—; contbr. articles to profl. jours. Rsch. grantee US Dept. Interior, Nat. Pk. Svc., 1978-79, Nat. Geog. Soc., 1992-93. Mem. AAAS, Am. Anthropol. Assn., Washington Assn. Profl. Anthropologists, Anthropol. Soc. Washington, Am. Assn. Museums, Internat. Platform Assn. Achievements include rsch. on prehistoric Am. Indians and the symbols of rank and power in traditional cultures, evidencce for Late Archaic in uplands of eastern Ohio, geographical range of Hamilton Incurvate triangle in area. Home: # 201 12512 Village Square Ter Rockville MD 20852-1954 Office: Naval Hist Ctr Washington Navy Yard 805 Kidder Breeze SE Washington DC 20374-5060 Home Phone: 301-881-5488; Office Phone: 202-433-7886. Business E-mail: thomas.pickenpaugh@navy.mil.

PICKENS, ALEXANDER LEGRAND, retired education educator; b. Waco, Tex., Aug. 30, 1921; s. Alex LeGrand and Elma L. (Johnson) P.; m. Frances M. Jenkins, Aug. 20, 1955. BA, So. Meth. U., 1950; MA, North Tex. U., Denton, 1952; EdD, Columbia U., 1959. Tchr. art public schs., Dallas, 1950-53, Elizabeth, N.J., 1953-54; instr. Coll. Architecture and Design U. Mich., 1954-59; assoc. prof. dept. art U. Ga., Athens, 1959-62; assoc. prof. Coll. Edn. U. Hawaii, Honolulu, 1962-68, prof. edn.,

1969—2001, chmn. doctoral studies curriculum instrn. Coll. Edn., 1984-89, asst. to dean for alumni affairs coll. devel., 1989-01, ret., 2001, emeritus prof., 2002—. Dir. children's classes Ft. Worth Children's Mus., 1951-53; head art Nat. Music Camp, Interlochen, Mich., summers, 1957-58, U. Oreg., Portland, summers 1959-60, 62; cons. youth art activities Foremost Dairies, Honolulu, 1964-74; cons. art films United World Films, 1970-75; art edn. cons. Honolulu Paper Co., 1970-76, Kamehameha Sch., Bishop Estate, 1978-95. Exhibited ceramics, Wichita Internat. Exhbn., Syracuse (N.Y.) Nat. Exhbn., St. Louis Mus., Dallas Mus., San Antonio Mus., Detroit Art Inst., Hawaii Craftsmen, also others; editorial bd.: Arts and Activities mag, 1955-82; editor: U. Hawaii Ednl. Perspectives, 1964-99; contbr. articles to profl. jours. Mem. adult com. Dallas County chpt. Jr. ARC, 1951-53; mem. exec. com. Dallas Crafts Guild, 1950-53; v.p., publicity chmn. U. Ga. Cmty. Concert Assn., 1960-62, program chmn. Gov.'s Commn. Observing 150 Yrs. Pub. Edn. in Hawaii, 1990-91; bd. dirs. Honolulu Theatre for Youth, 1998-2003; bd. dirs. Honolulu Symphony, 1998—; bd. dirs. Chamber Music Hawaii, 2003—. Served with USAAF. Recipient award merit Tex. State Fair, 1957, All-Am. award Ednl. Press Assn. Am., 1968, 70, 72, 75, 79, Regents' medal for tchg. U. Hawaii, 1989, Gov.'s Commn. Observance of 150 Yrs. Pub. Edn., 1990-91. Mem. AAUP, NEA, Internat. Soc. Edn., Nat. Art Edn. Assn., Coun. for Advancement and Support of Edn., Assn. Fundraising Profls., Nat. Planned Giving Coun., Hawaii Planned Giving Coun., Phi Delta Kappa, Kappa Delta Pi. Address: 1471 Kalaepohaku St Honolulu HI 96816-1804 Personal E-mail: apickens@hawaii.rr.com.

PICKENS, BOONE (T. BOONE PICKENS, THOMAS BOONE PICKENS JR.), oil industry executive; b. Holdenville, Okla., May 22, 1928; s. Thomas Boone Pickens and Grace Molonson; m. Lynn O'Brien, 1949 (div. 1971); 4 children; m. Beatrice Louise Carr, Apr. 21, 1972 (div.); 1 adopted child; m. Nelda Cain, 1999. BS in Geology, Okla. State U., 1951. Geologist Phillips Petroleum Co., 1951-54; consulting geologist, 1954-56; with Petroleum Exploration, Inc., 1956, Altair Oil & Gas Co.; chmn. bd., pres., dir. Mesa Petroleum Co., Inc., 1964-85; gen. ptnr., CEO Mesa Ltd. Partnership, 1985—96; founder BP Capital Mgmt., 1996—, Mesa Water, 1999—. Mem. Nat. Petroleum Council, 1970-; founder, chmn. United Shareholders Assn., Washington. Author: Boone, 1987, The Luckiest Guy in the World, 2000. Adviser Nat. Campaign for Drug Free Am. Named one of Forbes' Richest Americans, 2006. Office: BP Capital 8117 Preston Rd Ste 260 Dallas TX 75225 *

PICKENS, FRANCES JENKINS, artist, educator; b. Dodd's, Tex., Feb. 26, 1927; d. John Morgan and Mary (Burton) Jenkins; m. Alexander Pickens, Aug. 20, 1955. BA, U. of North Tex., 1947, MA, 1954; MEd, U. Hawaii, 1976. Tchr. art pub. schs., Dallas, 1948-55, Dearborn, Mich., 1955-58, White Plains, N.Y., 1958-59, Athens, Ga., 1960-62; gallery lectr. Honolulu Acad. Arts, 1962—63; tchr. art Punahou Sch., Honolulu, 1963-65, The Kamehameha Schs., Honolulu, 1965-85; jewelry and metal artist Honolulu, 1963—. Instr. jewelry U. Hawaii, Honolulu, 1967, 75, 77. Exhibited works in shows at Mus. of Contemporary Crafts, N.Y., Schmuckmuseum, Germany, Renwick Gallery, Washington, Wichita Nat., Women in Design Internat., Mich. Influence, 1981, Materials Hard and Soft, United States Metal, Hawaii Craftsmen Ann., Artists of Hawaii, 1965— (Disting. Artist 1991), East-West Ctr. Gallery, 2003, retrospective Honolulu Acad. Arts, 2001, KDA Gallery, Honolulu, 2005; represented in permanent collection at Acad. of Arts, The Contemporary Mus., Honolulu, Hawaii State Art Mus., Renwick Gallery, Washington, Wichita Art Assn., Kans.; photographs of work included in Goldsmith's Jour., Jewelry, Contemporary Design and Technique, Jewelry/Metalwork Survey, The Metalsmith's Book of Boxes and Lockets; contbr. articles to Arts and Activities mag., Sch. Arts, Ornament mag. Chmn. state crafts State Fair Tex., Dallas, 1954; Crafts Symposium planning com. Hawaii State Found. Culture and Arts, Honolulu, 1968-69; workshop for instrs. U.S. Army Arts and Crafts, Ft. Shafter, 1975. Named Distinguished Artist of Hawaii, Honolulu Acad. Arts, 1991. Mem. Soc. N.Am. Goldsmiths, Dallas Craft Guild, Hawai Craftsmen (charter, v.p., pres.), Renwick Alliance. Avocations: travel, jewelry, metalwork. Home: 1471 Kalaepohaku St Honolulu HI 96816-1804

PICKENS, JAMES T., JR., actor; b. Cleve., Oct. 26, 1954; m. Gina Pickens; 2 children. Actor: (films) F/X, 1986, Trespass, 1992, Menace II Society, 1993, Hostile Intentions, 1994, Jimmy Hollywood, 1994, Dead Presidents, 1995, Nixon, 1995, Power 98, 1996, Sleepers, 1996, Ghosts of Mississippi, 1996, Gridlock'd, 1997, Rocketman, 1997, Sphere, 1998, Bulworth, 1998, How Stella Got Her Groove Back, 1998, Liberty Heights, 1999, Traffic, 2000, Home Room, 2002, White Rush, 2003, Venom, 2005; (TV series) Roseanne, 1990—96, Beverly Hills, 90210, 1991—92, The Practice, 1997—2000, The X-Files, 1998—2002, Grey's Anatomy, 2005— (Outstanding Performance by an Ensemble in a Drama Series, SAG, 2007); (TV films) Exclusive, 1992, Sodbusters, 1994, A Child's Cry for Help, 1994, Lily in Winter, 1994, Trial by Fire, 1995, Sharon's Secret, 1995, Bloodhound, 1996, The Uninvited, 1996, Little Girl Fly Away, 1998, A Slight Case of Murder, 1999. Avocation: horseback riding. Mailing: Grey's Anatomy Los Feliz Tower 4th Fl 4151 Prospect Ave Los Angeles CA 90027 *

PICKENS, ROBERT BRUCE, retired accountant; b. Uniontown, Pa., May 20, 1926; s. Joseph Abraham and Margaret Gertrude (Brown) P.; m. Mary Ellen Evans, Sept. 9, 1950; children: Laura Gail Martin, Rachel Diane Rosen, David Bruce. BS in Bus. Adminstrn, Waynesburg Coll., 1950. C.P.A., Pa., Ill., Ind. Vice pres. Home Bottle Gas Corp., Uniontown, 1950-51; jr. accountant to sr. accountant Tenney & Co., Uniontown, 1951-56; mgr. Hosp. Service Assn. Western Pa., Pitts., 1956-57; auditor U. Pitts., 1957-58; sr. accountant Eugene A. Conniff Co., Pitts., 1958-59; mgr. Sheppard & Co., Pitts., 1959-63; supr. Alexander Grant & Co., Chgo., 1963-65; asst. to treas. CTS Corp., Elkhart, Ind., 1965, gen. auditor, controller, chief acctg. officer, 1966-81; ret., 1981; self-employed as acct., 1981-86; sec., controller, chief acctg. officer SEA Group, Inc. and SEA-ILAN, Inc., 1987-88; pvt. cons., 1989—; ret., 1999. Mem. Bower Hill Civic League, 1956-62; active Boy Scouts Am., 1938-62. Served to cpl. USAAC, 1944-45; USAF Res., 1947-50. Mem. AICPA, Pa. Inst. CPAs, Ill. CPA Soc., Ind. CPA Soc. Republican. Presbyn. (elder, trustee 1959-61, treas. 1960-61). Home: 73 Rogers Rd Carmel IN 46032-1467

PICKENS, SCOTT E., lawyer; b. Rochester, NY, June 27, 1956; BS with distinction, Cornell Univ., 1978, JD cum laude, 1981. Bar: DC 1981, US Ct. of Fed. Claims, US Ct. Appeals (Fed. cir.). Law clk. Judge John H. Pratt, US Dist Ct., DC Dist., 1981—82; ptnr. Miller & Chevalier Chartered, Washington; ptnr., leader Govt. Contracts & Govt. Disputes practice Pillsbury Winthrop Shaw Pittman, Washington. Editor: Cornell Law Rev. Mem.: ABA (vice chmn. E-Commerce com.), Bd. of Contract Appeals Bar Assn., Nat. Contract Mgmt. Assn., Nat. Def. Indsl. Assn., Fed. Cir. Bar Assn., DC Bar Assn. Office: Scott E Pickens Of Pillsbury Winthrop 2300 N St Nw Washington DC 20037-1122 Office Phone: 202-775-9843. Office Fax: 202-833-8491. E-mail: scott.pickens@pillsburylaw.com.

PICKER, RANDAL C., law educator; b. 1959; BA in Econs., U. Chgo., 1980, MA in Econs., 1982, JD, 1985. Bar: Ill. 1986, US Ct. Appeals 5th Cir., US Ct. Appeals 7th Cir. Law clk. to Hon. Richard Posner US Ct. Appeals 7th Cir., 1985—86; assoc. Sidley & Austin, Chgo., 1986—89, counsel, 1993—99; asst. prof. U. Chgo. Law Sch., 1989—93, prof., 1993—97, Paul and Theo Leffman prof. comml. law, 1998—, academic assoc. dean, 1994—96, dir. Olin Program in Law & Economics, 1999—2001. Commr. Nat. Conf. Commissioners on Uniform State Laws, 1991—; sr. fellow The Computation Inst. of U. Chgo. & Argonne Nat. Lab., 2000—. Co-author (with D. Baird & R. Gertner): Game Theory and the Law, 1994; co-author: (with D. Baird & T. Jackson) Security Interests in Personal Property: Cases, Problems and Materials, 2002. Mem.: ABA, Nat. Bankruptcy Conf., Am. Assn. Law Schools, Am. Bankruptcy Inst., Am. Law & Economics Assn. Office: U Chgo Law Sch 1111 E 60th St Chicago IL 60637 Office Phone: 773-702-0864. E-mail: r-picker@uchicago.edu.

PICKER, SEBASTIÁN, artist; Exhibitions include Gallery 355, Boston, 1976—77, 1980, Ctr. Culturel de Villeparisis, Paris, 1978, Kunstamt Kreutzberg, Berlin, 1979, Galería Skandia, Bogotá, Colombia, 1979, Galería D'Art Mestral, L'Escala, Spain, 1983, Cleveland Mus. Contemporary Art, 1986, Mass. Coll. Art, Boston, 1987, The Space, 1987, 1991, Bunker Hill Cmty. Coll., 1988, Optica Gallery, Montreal, 1990, Artists Found., Boston, 1990, Red Mesa, Gallup, N.Mex., 1993, Mills Gallery, Boston Ctr. for Arts, 1994, Crashing Thunder Gallery, Gallup, N.Mex., 1996, Meredith Kelly, Santa Fe, 1996—97, Arden Gallery, Boston, 1995, 1997, 2000, 2002, 2004—05, Brewster Arts, NY, 1998, Art Miami, 1999—2000, Turner Carroll Gallery, Santa Fe, 1999—2000, Museo Carlos Cruz Diez, Caracas, Venezuela, 2000, Arte Am., Miami, 2004—06, Brea Gallery, LA, 2005, Museo Raúl Anguiano, Guadalajara, 2006, Mason Murer Fine Art, Atlanta, 2006, Galería Pablo Guerrero, Guadalajara, 2006, Museo de Arrte Contemporáneo, Jorge Chávez Carrillo, Colima, Mex., 2007, Represented in permanent collections Fundació Vila Casas, Barcelona, Mus. Latin Am. Art, Longbeach, Calif., El Museo Cultural de Santa Fe, Albuquerque Mus. Recipient First prize, Macworld Art Contest, 1985; grantee Barcelona Sister City Travel Grant, Boston, 1984, Mass. Coun. on Arts and Humanities Grant, 1988, Mass. Artist Fellowship Prog., 1991. Office: Arden Gallery 129 Newbury St Boston MA 02116

PICKERELL, JAMES HOWARD, photojournalist; b. Dayton, Ohio, June 9, 1936; s. Howard and Frances (Harrison) P.; m. Mary Louise Fisher, June 26, 1965; children: Cheryl Elizabeth, Stacy Rae. Student, Ohio U., 1954-56; BA, UCLA, 1963. Comml. photographer, 1963—; ind. photographer Vietnam, 1963-67. Author: Vietnam in the Mud, 1966, Marketing Photography in the Digital Environment, 1994, Negotiating Stock Photo Prices, 5th edit., 2001; writer, pub.: newsletter Selling Stock. With USN, 1956-60. Mem. Nat. Press Photographers Assn. (1st Pl. Spot News award 1965), Am. Soc. Mag. Photographers (nat. bd. 1987-89), Profl. Photographers Assn., Beta Theta Pi. Address: 8104 Cindy Ln Bethesda MD 20817-6915 Home Phone: 301-365-1127; Office Phone: 301-251-0720. Personal E-mail: jim@chd.com.

PICKERING, CHIP (CHARLES WILLIS PICKERING JR.), congressman; b. Laurel, Miss., Aug. 10, 1963; m. Leisha Jane Prather; 5 children. BA in Bus. Adminstrn., U. Miss., 1986; MBA, Baylor U., Waco, Tex., 1989. Presdl. appointee USDA, 1989—90; legis. asst. Staff of US Senator Trent Lott, Miss., 1992—96; mem. US Congress from 3rd Miss. dist., 1997—. Co-chmn. Miss. for Bush, 2000, 04; mem. energy and commerce com. US Congress, asst. minority whip. Republican. Office: US House Reps 229 Cannon House Office Bldg Washington DC 20515-0001 Office Phone: 202-225-5031. Office Fax: 202-225-5797. *

PICKERING, JAMES HENRY, III, academic administrator, educator; b. NYC, July 11, 1937; s. James H. and Anita (Felber) P.; m. Patricia Paterson, Aug. 18, 1962; children: David Scott, Susan Elizabeth. BA, Williams Coll., 1959; MA, Northwestern U., 1960, PhD, 1964. Instr. English Northwestern U., 1963-65; mem. faculty Mich. State U., East Lansing, 1965-81, prof. English, 1972-81, grad. and assoc. chmn. dept., 1968-75, dir. Honors Coll., 1975-81; dean Coll. Humanities and Fine Arts U. Houston, 1981-90, sr. v.p., provost, 1990-92, pres., 1992-95; historian laureate Estes Park, Colo., 2006. Author: The Spy, 1971, The Harper Reader, 1971, Fiction 100, 1974, 1978, 1982, 1985, 1988, 1992, 1995, 1998, 2001, 2004, 2007, The World Turned Upside Down: Prose and Poetry of the American Revolution, 1975, The Spy Unmasked, 1975, The City in American Literature, 1977, Concise Companion to Literature, 1981, Literature, 1982, 86, 90, 94, 97, Mountaineering in Colorado, 1987, Wild Life on the Rockies, 1988, A Mountain Boyhood, 1988, The Spell of the Rockies, 1989, Purpose and Process, 1989, Poetry, 1990, In Beaver World, 1990, Rocky Mountain Wonderland, 1991, A Summer Vacation in the Parks and Mountains of Colorado, 1992, Fiction 50, 1993, Knocking Round the Rockies, 1994, Drama, 1994, Frederick Chapin's Colorado, 1995; This Blue Hollow: Estes Park, The Early Years, 1859-1915, 1999, Mr. Stanley of Estes Park, 2000, In the Vale of Elkanah, 2003, 07, The Ways of the Mountains, 2003, Early Estes Park Historical Narratives, 4 vols., 2004, America's Switzerland: Estes Park and Rocky Mountain National Park, The Growth Years, 2005, Enos Mill's Colorado, 2005, Estes Park and Rocky Mountain National Park, Then and Now, 2006, Rocky Mountain Celts, 2006. Historian laureate Town of Estes Park. Mem. Coll. English Assn. (pres. 1980-81), Phi Beta Kappa, Phi Kappa Phi, Omicron Delta Kappa. Office: U Houston Dept English Houston TX 77204-0001 Personal E-mail: jhpick@earthlink.net.

PICKERING, LAUREL, public health service officer; BA, SUNY Albany; MPH, Emory U. Rschr. Columbia U., Emory U., CDC; asst. to George Pataki NY State Assembly; exec. dir. NY Bus. Group on Health, NYC, 1996—. Chmn. bd. dirs. HealthPass, NYC; mem. purchaser adv. coun. Nat. Com. Quality Assurance; bd. dirs. Nat. Bus. Coalition on Health; mem. Educator Support Network. Named one of 40 Under 40, Crain's NY Bus., 2007. Office: NY Bus Group Health Ste 2705 61 Broadway New York NY 10006 Office Phone: 212-252-7440 ext. 224. E-mail: laurel@nybgh.org. *

PICKERING, THOMAS REEVE, retired aerospace transportation executive, diplomat; b. Orange, NJ, Nov. 5, 1931; s. Hamilton R. and Sarah C. (Chasteney) P.; m. Alice J. Stover, Nov. 24, 1955; children: Timothy R., Margaret S. AB, Bowdoin Coll., 1953; MA, Fletcher Sch. Law and Diplomacy, 1954, U. Melbourne, Australia, 1956. Joined U.S. Fgn. Svc., 1959; fgn. affairs officer ACDA, 1961; polit. adviser U.S. del. 18 Nation Disarmament Conf., Geneva, 1962-64; consul Zanzibar, 1965-67; counselor of embassy, dep. chief mission Am. Embassy, Dar es Salaam, Tanzania, 1967-69; dep. dir. Bur. Politico-Mil. Affairs, State Dept., 1969-73; spl. asst. to Sec. of State, 1973-74; exec. sec. Dept. State, 1973-74; U.S. amb. to Jordan, 1974-78; asst. sec. for Bur. Oceans, Internat. Environ. and Sci. Affairs, Washington, 1978-81; U.S. amb. to Nigeria, 1981-83; U.S. amb. to El Salvador, 1983-85; U.S. amb. to Israel, 1985-88; U.S. permanent rep. to UN, 1989-92; U.S. amb. to India, 1992-93; U.S. amb. to Russia, 1993-96; pres. Eurasia Found., 1996-97; undersec. of state for polit. affairs Dept. of State, Washington, 1997—2000; sr. v.p. internat. relations Boeing Co., 2001—06; ret., 2006; vice chmn. Hills and Co. Served to lt. comdr. USNR, 1956-59. Mem. Council Fgn. Relations, Internat. Inst. Strategic Studies, Phi Beta Kappa. Office Phone: 202-822-4712. Business E-Mail: thomas.r.pickering@boeing.com. E-mail: tpickering@hillsandco.com.

PICKETT, A. DEAN, lawyer; b. Casper, Wyo., June 25, 1949; s. A. Foy and Esther L. Pickett; m. Lucinda M. Wayne, July 3, 1971; children: Amanda M. Pickett-Williams, Gregory D. Allen-Pickett. BA, No. Ariz. U., Flagstaff, 1971; JD, U. Ariz., Tucson, 1974. Bar: Ariz. 1974, Wash. 1975, Colo. 1999. Ptnr. Mangum, Wall, Stoops & Warden, PLLC, Flagstaff, 1980—. Trustee Mus. No. Ariz., Flagstaff, 1982—2001, pres., 1999—2001. Lt. USN, 1974—78. Decorated Navy Achievement medal USN. Mem.: Nat. Assn. Coll. & Univ. Attys., Nat. Sch. Boards Assn. Coun. Sch. Attys. (vice chair 2007—, dir. 2002—). Presbyterian. Avocation: travel. Office: Mangum Wall Stoops & Warden PLLC 100 North Elden St Flagstaff AZ 86001

PICKETT, ALICIA EULISS, environmental scientist; b. Charlotte, NC, Sept. 29, 1969; d. Ronald Dean and Linda (Rowe) Euliss; m. Jordan Lee Pickett, Aug. 29, 1992; 1 child, Morgan Alizabeth. MS in Pub. Health, Walden U., Balt., 2006; BS in Environ. Health, Western Carolina U., NC, 1991. Registered environ. health specialist NEHA, sanitarian State of NC, cert. food safety profl. NEHA, pool & spa operator NSPF. Environ. health specialist US Pub. Health Svc., Fairbanks, Alaska, 1990, Brunswick Co. Health Dept., Bolivia, NC, 1992—95; instr. Cape Fear C.C., Wilmington, NC, 1995—; environ. health program specialist New Hanover Co. Health Dept., Wilmington, 1995—. Named NC Environ. Health Rookie of Yr., RS Bd., 1994. Mem.: APHA, Nat. Environ. Health Assn. Avocations: gardening, running. Home: 716 N Green Tee Rd Hampstead NC 28443 Office: New Hanover County Health Dept Environ Health Svcs 230 Mkt Pl Dr Ste 140 Wilmington NC 28403 Business E-Mail: apickett@nhcgov.com.

PICKETT, BETTY HORENSTEIN, psychologist; b. Providence, Feb. 15, 1926; d. Isadore Samuel and Etta Lillian (Morrison) Horenstein; m. James McPherson Pickett, Mar. 10, 1952. AB magna cum laude, Brown U., 1945, ScM, 1947, PhD, 1949. Asst. prof. psychology U. Minn., Duluth, 1949-51; asst. prof. U. Nebr., 1951; lectr. U. Conn., 1952; profl. assoc. psychol. scis. Bio-Scis. Info. Exch., Smithsonian Instn., Washington, 1953-58; exec. sec. behavioral scis. study sect. exptl. psychology study sect. div. research grants NIH, Bethesda, Md., 1958-61; rsch. cons. to mental health unit HEW, Boston, 1962-63; exec. sec. rsch. career program NIMH, 1963-66, chief cognition and learning sect. div. extramural research program, 1966-68, dep. dir., 1968-74, dir. div. spl. mental health programs, 1974-75, acting dir. div. extramural rsch. program, 1975-77; assoc. dir. extramural and collaborative rsch. program Nat. Inst. Aging, 1977-79; dep. dir. Nat. Inst. Child Health and Human Devel., Bethesda, Md., 1979-81, acting dir., 1981-82, dir. Div. Rsch. Resources, 1982-88. Mem. health scientist adminstr. panel CSC Bd. Examiners, 1970—76, 1981—88; mem. coun. on grad. edn. Brown U. Grad. Sch., 1989—91. Contbr. articles to profl. jours. Mem. APA, Am. Psychol Soc., Psychonomic Soc., Assn. Women in Sci., AAAS, Phi Beta Kappa, Sigma Xi. Home: 656 Morgan Bay Rd Surry ME 04684-0198

PICKETT, CECIL B., pharmaceutical executive; BS in Biology, Calif. State U., Hayward; PhD in Cell Biology, UCLA. Held various positions including rsch. fellow, biochemical regulation; assoc. dir. to dir., dept. molecular pharmacology & biochemistry Merck Rsch. Labs.; exec. dir., rsch. Merck Frosst Ctr. for Therapeutic Rsch., Montreal, Canada, v.p.; joined advancing to exec. v.p. discovery rsch. Schering-Plough Rsch. Inst., Schering-Plough Corp., Kenilworth, NJ, 1993—2002, pres., 2002—, sr. v.p., 2002—. Spkr. in field; mem. sci. bd. FDA; adv. com. to dir. NIH; nat. cancer policy bd. Inst. Medicine; disting. lectr. Jonsson Comprehensive Cancer Ctr., U. Calif., LA, 1995. Contbr. articles to profl. jours.; various editl bds.: med. jours. and rsch. orgns. Mem. vol. bd. dir. NJ Performing Arts Ctr. Named one of Leading Women and Minority Scientists, NY Acad. Sciences, 2005; recipient Scholarly Achievement and Acad. Dist., UCLA Alumni Assn., 1976, Robert A. Scala award, Rutgers U. and Univ. Medicine and Dentistry NJ, 1993, CIIT Ctr. for Health Rsch. Founders' award, 2001; scholar Macy scholar, Marine Biol. Labs, 1978. Mem.: AAAS, Inst. Medicine, Am. Assn. Cancer Rsch., Am. Soc. Biochemistry and Molecular Biology, Am. Soc. Cell Biology.

PICKETT, CECIL BRUCE, cell biologist; b. Canton, Ill., Oct. 5, 1945; married; two children. BS, Calif. State U., 1971; PhD, UCLA, 1976. Fellow in cell biology UCLA, 1976-78; with Merck Sharp & Dohme Rsch. Labs., 1978—93; exec. v.p. discovery rsch. Schering-Plough Rsch. Inst., Kenilworth, NJ, 1993—2002, pres., 2002—; sr. v.p. Schering Corp., 2004—; pres. SPRI, 2004—. Macy scholar Marine Biol. Lab, Woods Hole, Mass., 1978; vis. asst. prof. Coll. Medicine Howard U., Washington, 1978-83; adj. assoc. prof. N.J. Sch. Medicine & Dentistry, 1985-88; assoc. prof. U. Montreal, 1989; adj. prof. McGill U., 1990; disting. lecturer, Jonsson Comprehensive Cancer Ctr., UCLA, 1995; mem. sci. adv. bd. FDA; member, mem. GM Adv. Council, Cancer Rsch. Found., 2004. Recipient Robert A. Scala Award and Lectureship in Toxicology, Rutgers U. & U. Medicine & Dentistry of NJ, 1993, Founders award, CIIT Centers for Health Research, 2001. Mem. AAAS, IOM, NAS, Am. Soc. Biochemistry & Molecular Biology, Am. Assn. Cancer Rsch., Am. Soc. Cell Biology, Am. Assn. Advancement Sci.; mem. adv. com. to dir. NIH.

PICKETT, DONN PHILIP, lawyer; b. Chgo., May 3, 1952; s. Philip Gordon and Gloria Joan (Hansen) P.; m. Janet Benson, Aug. 25, 1973; children: Jessica Kelly, William Benson. BA magna cum laude, Carleton Coll., Minn., 1973; JD, Yale U., 1976. Bar: Calif. 1976, US Dist. Ct. (no. dist.) Calif. 1976, US Dist. Ct. (ctrl. dist.) Calif. 1980, US Dist. Ct. (ea. dist.) Calif. 1983, US Ct. Appeals (9th cir.) Calif. 1979, US Ct. Appeals (5th cir.) Tex. 1994, US Supreme Ct. 1991, US Dist. Ct. Ariz. 1997, US Dist. Ct. Colo. 1997, US Ct. Appeals (fed. cir.) 1997, US Ct. Appeals (11th cir.) 1998, US Ct. Appeals (1st cir.) 2006. Assoc. McCutchen, Doyle, Brown & Enersen, San Francisco, 1976-83, ptnr., 1983—2002, chair, 2001—02; ptnr. Bingham McCutchen LLP, San Francisco, 2002—, vice chmn., 2002—. Mem. U.S. Dist. Ct. Civil Justice Reform Act adv. group, 1995-99; bd. dirs. Equal Justice Works, 2005—, Legal Aid Soc., San Francisco, 2006—. Bd. dirs. Bay Area Coun., 2003—. Mem. ABA (chmn. civil practice com. antitrust sect. 2001-04, vice chmn. trial practice com. 2004-), State Bar Calif. (com. on adminstrn. of justice 1988-91, vice chmn. 1992-93, chmn. 1993-94, legis. chmn. 1994-96), San Francisco Bar Assn. (judiciary com. 1988-92, exec. com. conf. of dels. 1993-96, 2000, bd. dirs. 1997-99), Phi Beta Kappa. Office: Bingham McCutchen LLP 3 Embarcadero Ctr San Francisco CA 94111 Home Phone: 415-435-2313; Office Phone: 415-393-2082. Business E-Mail: donn.pickett@bingham.com.

PICKETT, EUGENIA V., social worker; b. Balt., Mar. 26, 1938; d. Robert Thomas and Eugenia King Valdivia; children: Jennifer Pickett Connoley, Juliana Ewing Harris; 1 stepchild, Jennifer Greenwald. BS, Towson U., 1959; MA, Antioch U., 1975. Diplomate psychotherapy Nat. Bd. Med. Psychotherapy; LCSW MD, cert. group psychotherapy Am. Group Psychotherapy Assn. Educator Balt. City Pub. Schs., 1960—69; staff coord. Greenmount Ave. Medical, Mental Health Clinic, Balt., 1970—76; psychiat. social worker pvt. practice, Balt., 1976—. Educator women's studies, childhood edn. Balt. C.C., Essex, 1978—79; primary trainer Assn. Music, Imagery, Salina, Kans., 1979—2003; cons. Ctr. Living Head Trauma, Balt., 1986—91; primary trainer Creative Therapies Inst., Massapeagua, NY, 1991—2003. Editor: Women: A Journal of Liberation, Journal of the Association for Music and Imagery. Mem. Balt. Def. Com., 1960; mem., pub. spkr. Women's Consciousness Raising Group, Balt., 1965—72; staff counselor, therapist Women's Growth Ctr., Balt., 1970—84; educator, meditation instr. Lotus Garden Buddhist Ctr., Stanley, Va., Balt. Shambhala Ctr., Balt., 1976—. Mem.: Md. Soc. Clin. Social Workers (sec. 1999—2002). Buddhist. Office: 500 W U Pkwy 1H Baltimore MD 21210-3236 Office Phone: 410-243-7300. Business E-Mail: epicdharma@aol.com.

PICKETT, JAMES V., food service executive; Chmn. Pickett Realty Advisors, Inc., Dublin, Ohio; pres., CEO of various companies generally known as Pickett Companies, 1969—; vice-chmn. Banc On Capital Corp., 1993—99; prin. Stonehedge Fin. Holding, Inc., 1999—2004. Bd. dir. Wendy's Internat., Inc., Dublin, 1982—2006, chmn. bd. dirs., 2006—. Mailing: Wendy's Internat Inc One Dave Thomas Blvd Dublin OH 43017

PICKETT, JUSTUS CUNNINGHAM, medical association administrator; BA, W.Va. U., 1954, BS, 1956; MD, Med. Coll. Va., 1958. Diplomate Am. Bd. of Orthop. Surgery, 1967. Surg. intern Med. Coll. Va. Hosps., 1958—59, resident, 1959—62, chief resident in orthop., 1961—63; pres.

Calif. Med. Assn., Sacramento, 1999—2000, chair bd. trustees, 2000—. Polit. cons. Calif. Med. Assn., Sacramento. Pres. Rotary Club of Napa, Calif. Ret. col. USAF, 1982—93. Recipient MacClaggen award, Calif. Med. Assn., 2005. Fellow: ACS, Am. Acad. of Orthop. Surgeons; mem.: Calif. Orthop. Assn., Western Orthop. Assn. Episcopalian. Office: JC Pickett MD Inc 3260 Beard Rd Napa CA 94558 Home Phone: 707-963-5880; Office Phone: 707-255-8877.

PICKETT, OWEN BRADFORD, lawyer, former congressman; b. Richmond, Va., Aug. 31, 1930; BS, Va. Poly. Inst., 1952; JD, U. Richmond, Va., 1955. CPA Va.; bar: Va. 1955, D.C. 1962. Pvt. practice, Virginia Beach, Va., 1964—86; mem. Va. Ho. of Dels., Richmond, 1972—86, US Congress from 2d Va. dist., Washington, 1987—2001; of counsel Troutman, Sanders, LLP, Virginia Beach, 2001—. Chmn. Va. Dem. State Ctrl. Com., 1980—82. Mem.: AICPA, ABA, DC Bar Assn., Va. Bar Assn. Democrat. Baptist. Office: Troutman Sanders LLP Ste 2000 222 Ctrl Pk Dr Virginia Beach VA 23462 Home Phone: 757-481-0979; Office Phone: 757-687-7525. Personal E-mail: obpickett@msn.com. Business E-Mail: owen.pickett@troutmansanders.com.

PICKETT, SANDRA, archivist, information scientist; BS, U. Tex.; MA, U. Houston. Councilwoman City of Liberty, Tex., 1974—98, mayor pro tem, 1976—98; commr., chair Tex. State Libr. & Archives Commn., Austin, 1995—. Past chmn. Liberty County Hist. Commn.; past dir., pres. Preservation Tex.; mem. Nat. Mus. & Libr. Svcs. Bd., Washington, 2004—. Named Citizen of Yr., C. of C., 1981; recipient John Ben Shepperd Leadership award, Tex. Hist. Commn., 1993; Paul Harris fellow, Rotary Internat., 1998. Mem.: Atascosito Hist. Soc. (pres.). Mailing: PO Box 19191 Liberty TX 77575 Office: Tex State Libr and Archives Commn PO Box 12927 Austin TX 78711 *

PICKETT, STEPHEN ALAN, hospital administrator; b. Ft. Wayne, Ala., Dec. 22, 1953; s. James Benjamin Pickett and Dorothy Jane (Howell) Pickett Fancher; m. Neil Annette Horsley, Mar. 5, 1977; children: Stefanie Leigh, Allison Marie. BBA, U. Montevallo, 1976; MPH, Tulane U., 1995. CPA, Ala. Sr. acct. Ernst & Whinney, Birmingham, Ala., 1976-78; contr. East End Meml. Hosp., Birmingham, 1978, v.p. fin., 1979-84, W. Va. U. Hosps., Morgantown, 1985-87, exec. v.p., adminstr., 1987-91; adminstr., COO Tulane U. Hosp. and Clinic, New Orleans, 1991-95, CEO, 1995—2004; CFO, UAB Health System, Birmingham, Ala., 2004—. Bd. dirs. Met. Hosp. Coun., 1991—, Associated Hosp. Svcs., 1991—. Active sustaining mem. campaign BSA, 1978; mem. Jefferson County Rep. Exec. Com., Birmingham, 1982, First Bapt. Ch. New Orlean (fin. com. 1993—). Fellow Healthcare Fin. Mgmt. Assn.; mem. AICPA, Ala. Soc. CPAs, U. Montevallo Alumni Assn. (life), Alpha Tau Omega Alumni Assn., Rotary. Baptist. Office: Chief Fin Officer UAB Health Sys 500 22d St S Ste 408 Birmingham AL 35233 Office Phone: 205-975-5412. Business E-Mail: spickett@uabmc.edu.

PICKETT, STEPHEN WESLEY, academic administrator, consultant; b. Billings, Mont., May 27, 1956; s. Wesley William and Carol Ann (Bollum) P. BA, Houston Bapt. U., 1980; MS, U. North Tex., 1988. Cert. elem. tchr., rehab. counselor, Tex. Hosp. tchr. Houston Ind. Sch. Dist., 1981-85; asst. to assoc. dean of students U. North Tex., Denton, 1988-90, asst. coord. disabled student svcs., Office Student Devel., 1990-91, dir. Office Disability Accommodation, 1991—2001, univ. mentor/advisor, 1992—2001; dir. disability svcs. U. Oreg., Eugene, 2002—. Assoc. dir. office of acad. advising U. Oreg., 2002—. Co-author: curriculum guide The Newspaper as a Student Communicator, 1982 (Exxon Found.'s Impact Two award). Chair Mayor's Com. on Employment of Persons with Disabilities, Denton, 1990; mem. coun.-at-large Sam Houston Area Coun. Boy Scouts Am., Houston, 1975—; grad. Denton C. of C. Leadership Program, 1992; pub. rels. chair leadership Denton Steering Com., 1993-94; mem. ad. bd. city of Denton Transit, 1990-2001; exec. bd. Svc. provision for Aging Needs, a United Way Agy., 1997-2001; mem. U. of North Tex. Adv. Bd. for ADA Access, 1992-2001, co-chair UNT ADA adv. com., 2000-01; mem. budget com. Denton County United Way, 1998-2001. Recipient Cmty. Svc. award U. North Tex., 1992, award for svcs. to persons with disabilities North Tex. Rehab. Assn., 1993, Disting. Alumnus award Houston Bapt. U., 1994, Outstanding Alumnus award Ctr. for Rehab. Studies, U. North Tex., 1995. Mem. Assn. Higher Edn. and Disability, Nat. Assn. Student Pers. Adminstrs., Tex. Assn. Coll. and Univ. Student Pers. Adminstrs. (chair multicultural com. 1994-95, v.p. 1995-96, co-chair endowment found. com. 1996-97), Tex. Assn. Higher Edn. and Disabilities (sec. 1998-99, conf. co-chair 1999). Presbyterian. Avocations: reading, travel, stamp collecting/philately. Office: U Oreg Disability Svc 164 Oregon Hall 5278 U Oreg Eugene OR 97403-5278 Business E-Mail: spickett@uoregon.edu.

PICKFORD, ROLLIN, JR., artist; b. Fresno, Calif., May 23, 1912; s. Rollin A. and Ruth (Lingby) P.; m. Gladys Burns Hall, June 30, 1940 (div. 1947); children— Jeffrey, James L.; m. 2d Glenna Ruth Pipes, Jan. 28, 1949; children— Joel, Melissa. Lower Div. Cert., Calif. State U.-Fresno, 1931: B.A. in Graphic Arts, Stanford U., 1933. Artist, Fresno Photoengraving, 1936-41, Display Advt., Inc., Fresno, 1941-74; painter, Fresno, 1946—; art instr. Calif. State U., Fresno, 1948-62. Contbr. article in field to various publs. Art com. mem. City of Fresno, 1965—. Recipient 167 awards including 1st prize (purchase), Watercolor U.S.A., Springfield, Mo., 1962, Calif. State Fair, 1963; Sweepstakes, Best of Show, All-Calif. Invitational, Laguna Beach, 1960; commd. by UN to paint UN Bldg. in N.Y.C. for UNICEF Greeting card. Mem. Calif. Nat. Watercolor Soc., West Coast Watercolor Soc., Carmel Art Assn., Watercolor USA Honor Soc. Democrat.

PICKHOLTZ, RAYMOND LEE, electrical engineering educator, consultant; b. NYC, Apr. 12, 1932; s. Isidore and Rose (Turkish) P.; m. Eda Rebecca Mittler, June 30, 1957; children: Robin, Andrew, Julie. BEE, CUNY, 1954, MEE, 1958; PhD, Poly. U. N.Y., 1966. Research engr. RCA Labs., Princeton, NJ, 1954-57, ITT Labs., Nutley, NJ, 1957-61; assoc. prof. Poly. Inst. Bklyn., 1962-71; prof. elec. engring., chmn. dept. George Washington U., Washington, 1977-80, prof., 1971—; pres. Telecommunication Assocs., Fairfax, Va., 1963—; cons. Inst. Def. Analyses, 1971-90, IBM Research, Yorktown Heights, NY, 1968-72; del. Union Radio Scientifique, Geneva, 1979—, vice chmn., 1987; del. NRC, Washington, 1980-83; cons. Motorola, CBC, NAB, USADR, Lucent, Verizon, 1996—. Vis. prof. U. Que., 1977; vis. scholar U. Calif., 1983; chmn. U.S. Nat. Commn. C, Union Radio Sci. Internat., 1990-92; mem. sci. and indsl. adv. bd. Telecom. Inst. Ont., Can. and Inst. Nacionale de la Recherches Scientique; vice chair, wireless panel World Tech. Evaluation Ctr. Editor: book series Computer Science Press, 1979—; IEEE Trans., 1975-80; editor-in-chief Jour. of Comms. and Networks, 2005—; author: Local Area and Multiple Access Networks, 1986; contbr. articles to profl. jours.; patentee in field. Recipient rsch. award RCA Labs., 1955; rsch. grantee Office of Naval Research, Washington, 1982, E-Systems, Falls Church, Va., 1983-96, MCI, Falls Church, Va., Instelsat, Washington, Nortel Networks, 1996—, DARPA, NSF, 1999—. Fellow IEEE (bd. govs. 1979-82, digital comm. com., Centennial medal 1984), AAAS, Washington Acad. Scis.; mem. IEEE Comm. Soc. (v.p. 1986-88, pres. 1990-92, Donald W. McLellan award, 1994, Erskine fellow New Zealand 1997, Third Millennium medal 2000, ACM MSWIN prize paper award, 1999, Best paper of 1999 in Jour. of Comms. and Networks, 2000, gen. chair, Infocom, Kobe, Japan 1997, gen. chair, ACM Mobicom Y2K, Boston, 2000), Math. Assn. Am., Cosmos Club, Sigma Xi, Eta Kappa Nu. Home: 3613 Glenbrook Rd Fairfax VA 22031-3210 Office: George Washington U Dept Elec Computer Engring Washington DC 20052-0001

PICKLE, GEORGE EDWARD, lawyer; b. New Orleans, Nov. 22, 1950; s. George E. Sr. and Virginia (Crowe) P.; m. Karen Lyle, Sept. 18, 1976; children: George E. III, Lauren M. Student, Rhodes Coll., 1968-70; BA, Millsaps Coll., 1972; JD, Georgetown U., 1975. Bar: Miss. 1975, U.S. Ct. Claims 1979, U.S. Tax Ct. 1979, U.S. Ct. Mil. Appeals 1976, U.S. Ct. Appeals (D.C. cir.) 1979, U.S. Supreme Ct. 1979, U.S. Dist. Ct. (so. dist.) Miss. 1980, U.S. Ct. Appeals (5th cir.) 1980, La. 1982, U.S. Dist. Ct. (ea. dist.) La. 1982, U.S. Dist. Ct. (mid. dist.) La. 1985, Tex. 1986., U.S. Dist. Ct. (so. dist.) Tex. 1986, U.S. Dist. Ct. (we. dist.) La. 1988. Law clk.to presiding justice U.S. Ct. Appeals (5th cir.), Askerman, Miss., 1975-76; assoc. Upshaw & Ladner, Jackson, Miss., 1980-82, Barham & Churchill, New Orleans, 1982-85; sr. atty. litigation, energy, environ., admiralty and products Shell Oil Co., Houston, 1985-96, assoc. general counsel, 1997—. Contbr. law rev., 1975; co-author, editor: Syllabus on Environmental Law, 1986. Bd. dirs. Tex. Civil Justice League, 1996—, Product Liability Advisory Coun., 1997—, bd. chair, 2006-07; bd. dirs. Am. Trust Reform Assn., 2004-, Civil Justice Assn. Calif., 2004-; chair operating Com. Civil Justice Reform Group, 1994—, Lawyers for Civil Justice Class Action Task Force, 2001-, bd. dirs., 2004-; sr. warden Episcopal Ch. of the Good Shepherd, Kingwood, Tex., 1991, dir. capital fund corp., 1988, lay eucharistic min., 1986-99; del. Tex. Senatorial and State Rep. convs., 1988-92; mem. exec. and vacancy coms. Rep. Party Harris County, 1990-96, chmn. precinct, 1990-96; mem. Georgetown U. Barristers Coun., 1973-75; referee N.W. Aquatic League, 1990-97; pres. Bear Br. Swim Team, 1991-93; Lt. cmdr. (head environ. litigation) USNR, 1976-79. Southwestern Scholar Rhodes Coll., Memphis, 1968. Mem. ABA (chmn. legis. jud. and govt. com. 2002-, vice chmn. young lawyers div. com. on environ. law, exec. editor Am. Criminal Law Rev. 1973-75, award for Profl. Merit 1976), Def. Rsch. Inst., Miss. Bar Assn. (elections com. 1982), La. Bar Assn., Tex. Bar Assn., Internat. Assn. Defence Coun. (vice chmn., sec. corp coun. 1991—, chair com. legis., judical & govt. affiars, 2003-), Alpha Tau Omega, Phi Alpha Theta, Omicron Delta Kappa, Pi Kappa Delta. Republican. Avocations: golf, water-skiing. Home: 3507 Tree Ln Humble TX 77339-2639 Business E-Mail: ed.pickle@shell.com.

PICKLE, JERRY RICHARD, lawyer; b. Paris, Tex., Feb. 2, 1947; s. Joseph Rambert and Martha Marie (Biggers) P.; m. Helen Leigh Russell, May 3, 1975; children: Jonathan Russell, Stephen Richard (dec.), Sarah Elizabeth. BA in History, U. Houston, 1969, JD, 1971. Bar: Tex. 1972, U.S. Dist. Ct. (no. dist.) Tex. 1974. Mem. Luna, Ballard & Pickle, Garland, Tex., 1972-74; assoc. Hightower & Alexander, Dallas, 1974-76, Cuba & Johnson, Temple, Tex., 1976-77; sr. corp. counsel Scott & White Clinic, Temple, 1977—. Asst. prof. Tex. A&M U. Coll. of Medicine, Temple, 1986—. Contbr. articles to profl. jours. V.p. The Caring House, Temple, 1989; v.p. Tex. divsn. Am. Cancer Soc., Temple, 1976—77; adv. bd. R.R. & Pioneer Mus., Temple, 1982—84; hist. preservation bd. City of Temple, 1979—90; chmn. Bell County Hist. Commn., 1980—82; bd. dirs. Bell County Mus., 1992—96, Temple Coord. Child Care Coun., 1991—93, Sr. Citizens Activities Ctr., Temple, 1993—94, pres., 1992—96; bd. dirs. Temple Cultural Activities Ctr., 1992—98, 2001—, pres., 1994—95; chair Heart o'Tex. Coun., Chisholm Trl. Dist., Boy Scouts Am., 1987—88; mem. U. N.C.-Chapel Hill Parents Coun., 2001—05; trustee Temple Ind. Sch. Dist., 2005—, sec., 2006—07, v.p., 2007—; dir. Temple Edn. Found., 2007—, Tax Appraised Bd. Bell County, Tex., 2006—. Mem.: ABA, Temple C. of C. (bd. dirs. 1983—85, 1988—90), Coun. Med. Group Practice Attys. (chair 2001—02), Am. Health Lawyers Assn. (chair tchg. hosp. and acad. med. ctrs. 1997—99), Bell-Lampasas-Mills Counties Young Lawyers Assn. (pres. 1980—81), Bell-Lampasas-Mills Counties Bar Assn. (bd. dirs. 1985—90, pres. 1988—89), State Bar Coll., Tex. Bar Found., Tex. Young Lawyers Assn., State Bar Tex. (health law sect. councilman 1980—84, chmn. 1983—84), Jaycees (chpt. dir. 1977—78), Rotary (chpt. dir. 1981—85, 1986—87). Democrat. Episcopalian. Avocations: reading, golf, music. Office: Scott & White Clinic 2401 S 31st St Temple TX 76508-0001 Office Phone: 254-724-3001. Office Fax: 254-724-4501. Business E-Mail: jpickle@swmail.sw.org.

PICKLE, ROBERT DOUGLAS, lawyer, apparel executive; b. Knoxville, Tenn., May 22, 1937; s. Robert Lee and Beatrice Jewel (Douglas) P.; m. Rosemary Elaine Noser, May 9, 1964. AA summa cum laude, Schreiner Mil. Coll., Kerrville, Tex., 1957; BSBA magna cum laude, U. Tenn., 1959, JD, 1961; graduate (hon.), Nat. Def. U., 1979, US Army JAG Sch., US Army Logistics Mgmt. Sch.; graduate, US Army Inf. Sch., Army Command-Gen. Staff Coll. Bar: Tenn. 1961, Mo. 1964, U.S. Ct. Mil. Appeals 1962, U.S. Supreme Ct. 1970. Atty. Brown Shoe Co., Inc., St. Louis, 1963-69, asst. sec., atty., 1969-74, sec., gen. counsel, 1974-85; v.p., gen. counsel, corp. sec. Brown Shoe Co., Inc. (formerly Brown Group, Inc.), St. Louis, 1985—. Indiv. mobilization augmentee, asst. army judge adv. gen. civil law The Pentagon, Washington, 1984-89. Provisional judge Municipal Ct., Clayton, Mo., summer 1972; chmn. Clayton Region attys. sect., profl. div. United Fund Greater St. Louis Campaign, 1972-73, team capt., 1974-78; chmn. City of Clayton Parks and Recreation Commn., 1985-87; liaison admissions officer, regional and state coordinator U.S. Mil. Acad., 1980—. Col. JAGC, U.S. Army, 1961-63. Decorated Meritorious Svc. medal; 1st U. Tenn. Law Coll. John W Green law scholar; recipient Cold War Recognition cert. Sec. Def. Fellow Harry S. Truman Meml. Library; mem. ABA, Tenn. Bar Assn., Mo. Bar Assn., St. Louis County Bar Assn., Bar Assn. Met. St. Louis, St. Louis Bar Found. (bd. dirs. 1979-81), Am. Corp. Counsel Assn., Am. Soc. Corp. Secs. (treas. St. Louis regional group 1976-77, sec. 1977-78, v.p. 1978-79, pres., mem. Quarter-Century Club 1979-80), U. Tenn. Gen. Alumni Assn. (pres., bd. dirs. St. Louis chpt. 1974-76, 80-84, bd. govs. 1982-89), U.S. Trademark Assn. (bd. dirs. 1978-82), Tenn. Soc. St. Louis (bd. dirs. 1980-88, treas., sec., v.p. 1984-87, pres. 1987-88), Smithsonian Nat. Assocs., World Affairs Coun. St. Louis, Inc., Am. Legion, University Club (v.p., sec. St. Louis chpt. 1976-81, bd. dirs. 1976-81), Stadium Club, West Point Soc. St. Louis (hon. mem., bd. dirs. 1992—), Conf. Bd. (coun. chief legal officers), Fontbonne Coll. Pres.'s Assocs. (O'Hara and Tower Socs), St. Louis U. Billiken Club, St. Louis U. DuBourg Soc. (hon. v.p.). Republican. Presbyterian. Avocations: reading, sports. Home: 214 Topton Way Saint Louis MO 63105-3638 Office: Brown Shoe Co Inc 8300 Maryland Ave Saint Louis MO 63105-3645 E-mail: rpickle@brownshoe.com.

PICKNICK, KEVIN M., commodities trader; b. Kansas City, Kans., Aug. 9, 1973; s. Glen M. and Beverly D. Picknick. B in Bus. Admin., Pitts. State U., Kans., 1995, fin. degree, mgmt. degree, Pitts. State U., Kans., 1995. Grain mcht. United Plains Ag, Sharon Springs, Kans., 2005—. Home: 427 N Ferlen Ave PO Box 325 Sharon Springs KS 67758 Home Phone: 785-821-3585. Personal E-mail: kpicknick@hotmail.com.

PICKREL, PAUL, language educator; b. Gilson, Ill., Feb. 2, 1917; s. Clayton and Inez (Murphy) P. AB, Knox Coll., 1938; MA, Yale U., 1942, PhD, 1944. Instr. English Lafayette Coll., 1941-42; instr. Yale U., 1943-45, asst. prof., 1945-50, lectr. English, 1954-66, chmn. Scholar of House Program, 1959-60, 61-66; fellow Morse Coll., 1962-66; adviser John Hay fellows, 1959-66; vis. prof. English Smith Coll., Northampton, Mass., 1966-67, prof., 1967-87, prof. emeritus, 1987—, chmn. dept., 1972-75, 81-82. Author: (novel) The Moving Stairs, 1948; also essays on fiction, numerous book revs.; mng. editor: Yale Rev., 1949-66; chief book critic: Harper's mag., 1954-65. Mem. Aurelian Honor Soc., Elizabethan Club (New Haven), Faculty Club (Northampton), Phi Beta Kappa.

PICKTON, ROBERT (BOB) J., information technology executive; b. Akron, Ohio, July 14, 1947; BS, Miami Univ.; MBA, Pepperdine Univ. V.p. & chief info. officer EHS Healthcare, Oakbrook, Ill., Mose Cone Health Sys., Greensboro, NC; sr. v.p. & chief info. officer Baylor Health Care Sys., Dallas, 1995—. Charter mem. Coll. Healthcare Info. Mgmt. Exec.; founding mem. HLT Standards Group. Office: SVP & CIO Baylor Health Care Sys 3500 Gaston Ave Dallas TX 75246 Business E-Mail: bobp@baylorhealth.edu.

PICÓN, CARLOS ARTURO, curator; b. San Juan, Aug. 31, 1954; s. Rafael Picón-Villariny and Hazel Gomez. BA in Classical & Near Ea. Archaelogy with honors, Haverford Coll., Bryn Mawr, Pa., 1972—76; MPhil in Classical Archaelogy, Oxford U., Eng., 1976—78, DPhil in Classical Archaelogy, 1978—83; attended, Yale U., 1973, U. Pa., 1975. Libr. & rsch. asst. dept. classical archaelogy Bryn Mawr Coll., 1973—76; from intern to curator primitive arts Met. Mus. Art, NYC, 1974; rsch. fellowship Haverford Coll., 1976; jr. rsch. fellow Christ Ch., Oxford, 1978—83; asst. curator Ashmole Archive, Kings Coll., London, 1984—86; curator we. antiquities San Antonio Mus. Art, 1986—90; curator-in-charge dept. Greek & Roman Art Met. Mus. Art, NYC, 1990—. Greek archaeology tutor Oxford U., 1978—83; advisor, collaborator British Mus., 1981—83; cons. antiquarian booksellers cons. Sims, Reed & Fog, London, 1984—86; organizer Appeal in Aid King's Coll. London & Sotheby's, 1985—86; vis. scholar dept. classics U. Tex., Austin, 1987—90; cons. curator Edward & Betty Marcus Found., Dallas, 1988—90. Contbr. articles to profl. jours. Trustee Corning Mus. Glass, 1995—; council of advisors Inst. Classical Architecture & Classical Am., NYC, 2003—. Numerous travel & rsch. grants, Lancely Green Fund & Harmsworth Trust, Meyerstein Fund, Craven Com., Arnold Fund, Christ Ch., 1977—83. Mem.: Archaelogical Inst. Am., German Archaelogical Inst. (cooresponding mem. 1995). Home: 169 E 78th St New York NY 10021 Office: Met Mus Art 1000 Fifth Ave New York NY 10028

PICONE-ZOCCHIA, JOANNE, educational consultant, writer; b. Bklyn., June 4, 1955; d. John D. and Anna G. Picone; m. Louis Zocchia, Jr, Aug. 13, 1983; children: Jonathon Louis Zocchia, Vanessa Anne Zocchia. MA, NY U., NYC, 1979. Cert. Ctr. Study of Expertise in Tchg. and Learning NYC, 2001. Tchr. West Islip Union Free Sch. Dist., NY, 1977—98, staff developer, 1998—2001; ednl. cons. Learner-Centered Initiatives, Ltd., Sea Cliff, 1995—, program dir., ptnr., 2005—. Fellow, Ctr. Study of Expertise in Tchg. and Learning, 1995—2005. Avocations: travel, theater, writing. Home: 85 Washington St Babylon NY 11702 Office: Learner Centered Initiatives Ltd 20 Elm Pl Sea Cliff NY 11579 Home Phone: 631-422-5425; Office Phone: 516-671-2991. Personal E-mail: jopiz@aol.com.

PICOTTE, LEONARD FRANCIS, naval officer; b. Calumet, Mich., Dec. 8, 1939; s. Irving René and Maria (Tamborino) P.; m. Sandra Lees Whiteley, July 14, 1984; children from previous marriage: Mary Elizabeth, Lance, Michael. BS in Econs. cum laude, U. No. Mich., 1963; MA in Polit. Sci., San Diego State U., 1975; grad. with distinction, Armed Forces Staff Coll., Norfolk, Va., 1976; M in Strategic Studies, Naval War Coll., Newport, RI, 1985. Commd. ensign USN, 1963, advanced through grades to rear adm., 1991; comdg. officer USS Marathon, Vietnam, 1971-73; exec. officer USS Point Defiance, San Diego, 1976-78; exec. officer, officer in charge Surface Warfare Officers' Sch., Coronado, Calif., 1978-80; exec. officer Naval Sta., San Diego, 1980; comdg. officer USS Alamo, San Diego, 1980-82; surface warfare detailer Bur. Naval Pers., Washington, 1982-84; comdg. officer USS Duluth, San Diego, 1986-88; 1st comdg. officer USS Wasp, 1988-90; insp. gen. Comdr. in Chief, U.S. Atlantic Command, Comdr. in Chief, U.S. Atlantic Fleet, Norfolk, 1990-92; comdr. Amphibious Group Two, Norfolk, 1992-95; ret., 1995; v.p. expeditionary warfare programs Am. Sys. Corp., Chesapeake, Va., 1995—2006; pvt. practice Chesapeake, Va., 2006—. Decorated Legion of Merit (2); recipient Disting. Svc. medal. Mem. Surface Navy Assn., USS Wasp Assn. (hon.), Army and Navy Club, Town Point Club, Hampton Roads Coun. Navy League Republican. Roman Catholic. Avocations: hunting, reading, gardening, chess. Home: 897 Brooklyn Plantation Prospect VA 23960 Address: Lighthouse Ln Calais ME 04619 Home Phone: 434-574-6371. Personal E-mail: lfpicotte@verizon.net.

PICOTTE, SUSAN CARROLL, lawyer; b. Brighton, Mass., Sept. 2, 1954; d. John Dennis, Jr., and Patricia (Curran) Carroll; m. William Burgess Picotte, Aug. 12, 1978; children: David Hunter, Philip Burgess. BA in Econs. magna cum laude, Russell Sage Coll., 1976; JD, Union U., Albany, N.Y., 1979. Bar: N.Y. 1980, U.S. Dist. Ct. (no. dist.) N.Y. 1980, U.S. Dist. Ct. (we. dist.) N.Y. 1985, U.S. Supreme Ct. 1988. With O'Connell & Aronowitz, P.C., Albany, 1978-79; assoc. firm Cooper, Erving & Savage, Albany, 1979-82, ptnr., 1983-86; ptnr. Cooper, Erving, Savage, Nolan & Heller, LLP, 1987-2001, Cooper, Erving & Savage LLP, 2002—. Mem. Albany Law Rev., 1977-78. Bd. dirs., 1st v.p. Coun. Cmty. Svcs. N.E. N.Y., Albany, 1980-86; trustee Shaker Heritage Soc., 1983-86; mem. Jr. League Troy, Inc., 1981-86; bd. dirs. Univ. Found. Albany, Inc., 1987-91; trustee Emma Willard Sch., 1990-95. Fellow N.Y. State Bar Found.; mem. ABA, N.Y. State Bar Assn. (ho. dels. 1992-96, nominating com. 1996—98), Albany County Bar Assn. (dir. 1983-94, sec. 1989-90, treas. 1990-91, v.p. 1991-92, pres. elect 1992-93, pres. 1993-94), N.Y. State Women's Bar Assn., Albany County Bar Found. (bd. dirs. 1995-2004), Emma Willard Sch. Alumnae Assn. (dir. 1982-88, v.p. 1988-90, pres. 1990-92), Albany Roundtable (dir. chpt. 1990—2006), Estate Planning Coun. Ea. N.Y. Inc. (bd. dirs. 2006—), Schuyler Meadows Club (bd. govs. 1993-96), Phi Kappa Phi. Roman Catholic. Office: 39 N Pearl St Albany NY 12207-2785 Business E-Mail: spicotte@coopererving.com.

PICOULT, JODI, writer; b. LI, NY; m. Tim Van Leer; 3 children. BA, Princeton Univ; MEd, Harvard Univ. Technical writer; textbook editor; English tchr. Author: (novels) Songs of the Humpback Whale, 1992, Harvesting the Heart, 1993, Picture Perfect, 1995, Mercy, 1996, The Pact, 1998, Keeping Faith, 1999, Plain Truth, 1999, Salem Falls, 2001, Perfect Match, 2002, Second Glance, 2003, My Sister's Keeper, 2004 (Publishers Weekly Bestseller, 2005), Vanishing Acts, 2005 (Publishers Weekly Bestseller, 2005), The Tenth Circle, 2006, Nineteen Minutes, 2007, (comic books) Wonder Woman Series, 2007. Avocation: ice hockey. Office: PO Box 508 Etna NH 03750 Business E-Mail: jodi@jodipicoult.com. *

PICOWER, WARREN MICHAEL, editor; b. NYC, Aug. 21, 1934; s. Abraham and Nell (Bloom) P.; divorced; children: Jenny Emelia, Eve Julie. BA, Queens Coll., 1956; MA, New Sch. for Social Rsch., 1978; PsyD in Psychology, Heed U., LA, 1982. Editorial asst. Newsweek mag., NYC, 1956-59; assoc. editor Zimmerman Pub. Co., NYC, 1961-63; assoc., mng. editor Fawcett Pubs., NYC, 1963, 64-65; mng. editor Tuesday Publs., NYC, 1965-67, exec. editor, v.p., 1967-73; sr. editor King Features Syndicate, NYC, 1974-78; mng. editor Food & Wine Mag., NYC, 1978-93; consulting editor Travel Holiday Mag., NYC, 1993-94; mng. editor Zagat Survey restaurant and hotel guides, NYC, 1994-97; sr. project editor Money Mag., NYC, 1997-98. Cons. in field. Contbr. articles to profl. jours.

PICRAUX, SAMUEL THOMAS, physicist, researcher; b. St. Charles, Mo., Mar. 3, 1943; s. Samuel F. and Jeannette D. Picraux; m. Danice R. Kent, July 12, 1970; children: Jeanine, Laura, Samantha. BS in Elec. Engring., U. Mo., 1965; postgrad., Cambridge U., Eng., 1965-66; MS in Engring. Sci., Calif. Inst. Tech., 1967, PhD in Engring. Sci. and Physics, 1969. Mem. tech. staff Sandia Nat. Labs., Albuquerque, 1969-72, div. supr., 1972-86, dept. mgr., 1986-96, dir., 1996-2001; prof. materials engring., exec. dir. materials rsch. Ariz. State U., 2001—05; chief scientist Ctr. Integrated Nanotech., Los Alamos Nat. Lab., 2005—. Mem. solid state scis. com. NRC, 1996-98; vis. scientist dept. physics Aarhus U., Denmark, 1975; NATO lectr., 1979, 81, 83, 86.; NSF lectr. 1976, 81. Author: Materials Analysis by Ion Channeling, 1982; editor: Applications of Ion Beams to Metals, 1974, Metastable Materials Formation by Ion Implantation, 1982, Surface Alloying by Ion Electron and Laser Beams, 1986, Beam-Solid Interactions and Transient Processes, 1987; editor Nuclear Instruments and Methods International Jour. B, 1983-91; contbr. numerous articles to profl. jours. Recipient Ernest Orlando Lawrence Meml. award U.S. Dept. Energy, 1990, 3 Basic Energy Scis. Outstanding Rsch. awards U.S. Dept. Energy, 1985, 92, 94, Mo. Honor award disting. svc. in engring., 2006; Fulbright fellow, 1965-66. Fellow AAAS, Am. Phys. Soc. (chmn. materials physics divsn. 1990); mem. IEEE (sr.), Am. Vacuum Soc., Materials Rsch. Soc. (pres. 1993). Office: Los Alamos Nat Lab Ctr Integrated Nanotech MST-CINT MSK771 Los Alamos NM 87545 Home Phone: 505-232-2977; Office Phone: 505-665-8554. Business E-Mail: picraux@lanl.gov.

PIDDOCK, JAMES ANTHONY, actor; b. Rochester, Kent, Eng., Apr. 8, 1956; came to U.S., 1981; s. Charles Frederick and Celia Mary (O'Callahan) P. BA in English, London U., 1977. Dir., tchr. drama The Drama Studio, Berkeley, London, Calif., 1980-81. Actor: (films) Lethal Weapon 2, 1989, Multiplicity, 1996, Independence Day, 1996, Best in Show, 2000, Austin Powers: Goldmember, 2002, A Mighty Wind, 2003, Love for Rent, 2005, Garfield: A Tale of Two Kitties, 2006, (TV films) A Mom for Christmas, 1990, The Women of Windsor, 1992, Mermaid Chronicles Part 1: She Creature, 2001, (TV miniseries) From the Earth to the Moon, 1998; actor, writer: (films) Traces of Red, 1992; writer: (films) One Good Turn, 1996, The Man, 2005; co-prodr.: (films) A Different Loyalty, 2004; exec prodr.: (TV series) Too Much Sun, 2000; Broadway theater Noises Off, 1983 (N.Y. Drama Desk award), Present Laughter, 1982, Design for Living, 1985; off-Broadway The Box's Own Story 1983; theatre The Caretaker, 1988, How the Other Half Loves, 1988; TV guest appearances include The Tracey Ullman Show, 1987, Coach, 1990, 91, Murder She Wrote, 1993, Mad About You, 1994-96, Angel, 2000, Yes, Dear, 2001, Friends, 2001, The Drew Carey Show, 2002, ER, 2002, Crossing Jordan, 2003, Lost, 2005. Avocations: soccer, baseball. Office: Harry Gold Assocs 3500 W Olive Ave Ste 1400 Burbank CA 91505-4659

PIDGEON, JOHN ANDERSON, headmaster; b. Lawrence, Mass., Dec. 20, 1924; s. Alfred H. and Nora (Regan) P.; children: John Anderson, Regan S., Kelly; m. Barbara Hafer, May 1986. Grad., Phillips Acad., 1943; BA, Bowdoin Coll., 1949; Ed.D., Bethany Coll., 1973; D.Litt., Washington and Jefferson Coll., 1979. Instr. Latin, adminstrv. asst. to headmaster Deerfield Acad., 1949-57; headmaster Kiskiminetas Springs Sch., Saltsburg, Pa., 1957—2004. Dir. Saltburg Savs. & Trust. Trustee Winchester-Thurston Sch.; vol. swimming coach Ind. U., Pa. Served as ensign USNR, 1943-46. Mem. New Eng. Swimming Coaches Assn. (pres. 1956-57), Cum Laude Soc., Delta Upsilon. Home and Office: 157 Greenview Dr Indiana PA 15701 Office Phone: 724-349-2151.

PIDOT, WHITNEY DEAN, lawyer; b. NYC, Mar. 2, 1944; s. George B. and Virginia (Ulrich) P.; m. Jeanne Stoddard, April 23, 1973; children: Whitney Dean Jr., Philip Martin, Seth Thayer. AB magna cum laude, Harvard U., 1966; JD, MBA, Columbia U., 1970. Bar: NY 1971. Ptnr. Shearman & Sterling, NYC, 1970, global mng. ptnr., 1998—2002, mem. exec. goup, 1998—2003, Asia mng. ptnr., 2001—03, of counsel, 2004—; chair, CEO Goelet Co. LLC, 2004—. Mem. adv. bd. Barclays Bank N.Y., 1989-92, Molecular Tool, Inc. (biotech.) Balt., 1991-96, Equine Genetic Rsch. Ptnrs., Balt., 1991-95; trustee, vice chair Winthrop Univ. Hosp., Mineola, NY. Mayor, Village of Matinecock, Locust Valley, N.Y., 1977-92; vice chmn. North Shore Mayors Com., Long Island, N.Y., 1980-92; bd. dirs. Nassau County (N.Y.) Village Officials Assn., 1978-80; commr. Locust Valley Fire Dist., 1979-93. Mem. N.Y. Bar Assn., Piping Rock Club (pres. 1988-94), Union Club N.Y.C., Phi Delta Phi. Republican. Home: Matinecock Farms PO Box 653 Locust Valley NY 11560 Office: Shearman & Sterling 599 Lexington Ave Ste C-2 New York NY 10022-6030 also: Geolet Co LLC 425 Park Ave New York NY 10022 Business E-Mail: wpidot@shearman.com.

PIECUCH, DIANE MARIE, music educator; b. Ironwood, Mich., Mar. 25, 1950; d. John H. Meyer and Betty E. Meyer-Lundberg. MusB, Mich. State U., East Lansing, 1972; MusM, George Mason U., Fairfax, Va., 1998. Cert. Orff Schulwerk George Mason U., 1988. Music tchr. Loudoun County Pub. Schs., Sterling, Va., 1972—75, Fairfax County Pub. Schs., Alexandria, Va., 1975—77, 1986—. V.p. PQ Prodns., Alexandria, 1977—96. Composer: (multiple songs) For Corporations And School. Min. of cmty. care St. John's Luth. Ch., Alexandria, 2005—06. Recipient Supts. award, Sch. Bd., 1991—92. Mem.: Fairfax Gen. Music Educators Assn. (assoc.; pres. 1995—97), Am. Orff Schulwerk Assn (assoc.; social chmn. 1989—91). R-Consevative. Lutheran. Avocation: jogging. Home: 6543 Kelsey Point Cir Alexandria VA 22315 Office: Rose Hill Elementary Sch 6301 Rose Hill Dr Alexandria VA 22310 Home Phone: 703-971-2370; Office Phone: 703-313-4200. Personal E-mail: dpq@cox.net. E-mail: diane.piecuch@fcps.edu.

PIEGARI, JAMES A., psychologist; b. Bklyn., Aug. 4, 1951; s. Vincent and Olympia Piegari. BS in Psychology, Georgetown U., 1972; MA in Clin. Psychology, St. John's U., 1975; MA in Psychology, Rutgers U., 1995, New Sch. Social Rsch., 1995; PhD in Psychology, Saybrook Grad. Sch. and Rsch. Ctr., 1999. Lic. psychologist NY, cert. sch. psychologist NY. Ops. rsch. analyst USPHS Hosp., SI, NY, 1976—78; applied behavioral scis. specialist United Cerebral Palsy Assns. NY State, SI, 1978—80, Terence Cardinal Cooke Health Care Ctr., NYC, 1980—2001, psychologist, 2002—; pvt. practice psychologist SI, 2002—. Mem. publs. com. Flower Hosp., NYC, 1980—81; cons. Vietnamese refugee program Mission of Immaculate Virgin, Mt. Loretto, SI, 1986—96; assoc. prof. Mercy Coll., Arthur Kill Correctional Facility, SI, 1989—90; supt. provider psychol. svcs. NYC Dept. Edn., 2002—; cert. mediator S.I. Cmty. Dispute Resolution Ctr.; mem. alumni admissions program Georgetown U. Contbr. articles to profl. jour., chapters to books. Mem. health and hosps. com. NYC Cmty. Bd., SI, NY, 1979—80; charter mem. Friends of South Beach Psychiat. Ctr., SI, NY, 1980—81, bd. dirs., 1980—81, chmn. mental health symposium com., 1980—81; mem. appellate divsn. panel mental health profl. psychologist Supreme Ct., NY. Recipient Employee Recogition award, Terence Cardinal Cooke Health Care Ctr., 2001. Mem.: APA, NY State Psychol. Assn. Avocations: Civil War antiques, photography, travel, motorcycle touring. Home and Office: 7 Azalea Ct Staten Island NY 10309

PIEKARSKI, VICTOR J., lawyer; b. Lawrence, Mass., Feb. 20, 1950; BA cum laude, Boston Coll., 1971; MBA, U. Chgo., 1978; JD cum laude, Northwestern U., 1974. Bar: Ill. 1974, U.S. Ct. Appeals (7th cir.) 1977, U.S. Supreme Ct. 1978. Ptnr. Querrey & Harrow Ltd., Chgo., to 1997, O'Hagan, Smith and Amundsen, LLC, Chgo., 1997—. Mem. ABA, Def. Rsch. Inst. Office: O'Hagan Smith and Amundsen LLC 150 N Michigan Ave Ste 3300 Chicago IL 60601-7586 E-mail: vpiekarski@osalaw.com.

PIEN, GRACE, medical educator; d. Shui-hsien and Arlene C. Pien. MD, Columbia U., NYC, 1994; MS, U. Pa., Phila., 2004. Asst. prof. medicine U. Pa. Sch. Medicine, Phila., 2002—. Office: Hosp Univ Pa Sleep Medicine Divsn 3624 Market St Ste 205 Philadelphia PA 19104 Office Phone: 215-662-7772. Office Fax: 215-662-7749.

PIEN, HOWARD, pharmaceutical executive; b. 1958; BS, MIT; MBA, Carnegie Mellon U. With Abbott Laboratories, Merck; v.p. & dir. product mktg.-US SmithKline Beecham, 1992—93, v.p. & dir. new product devel.-US, 1991—92, v.p. & dir. mktg.-US, 1993—95, mng. dir. & sr. v.p.-UK, 1995—97, sr. v.p. & dir.-North Asia, 1997; pres. pharm. internat. GlaxoSmithKline, 2001—03; CEO & dir. Chiron Corp., Emeryville, Calif., 2003—, chmn., 2004—. Office: Chiron Corp 4560 Horton St Emeryville CA 94608-2916

PIENE, CHLOE, artist, filmmaker; BA in Art History, Columbia U., NYC, 1993. Exhibitions include Me & More, Kunstmuseum, Luzern, 2003, Whitney Biennial, Whitney Mus. Am. Art, NY, 2004, Spirit, Galerie Nathalie Obadia, Paris, 2004, Videodrome II, Bates Coll. Mus. Art, 2004, Boys Will Be Boys?, Mus. Contemporary Art, Denver, 2005, Getting Emotional, 2005, Mus. Contemporary Art, Denver, 2005, Chloe Piene Galleries Nathalie Obadia, Sandroni Rey Gallery, LA, Klemens Gasser and Tanja Grunert, NYC. Syrian Orthodox. Avocation: golf. Studio: 66 Washington Ave 3rd Fl Brooklyn NY 11205 Business E-Mail: cpstudio@verizon.net.

PIEPER, DAROLD D., lawyer; b. Vallejo, Calif., Dec. 30, 1944; s. Walter A. H. and Vera Mae (Ellis) P.; m. Barbara Gillis, Dec. 20, 1969; 1 child, Christopher Radcliffe. AB, UCLA, 1967; JD, USC, 1970. Bar: Calif. 1971. Ops. rsch. analyst Naval Weapons Ctr., China Lake, Calif., 1966-69; assoc. Richards, Watson & Gershon, LA, 1970-76, ptnr., 1976—2005; gen. counsel Foothill Transit, 2000—, Greater L.A. County Vector Control Dist., 2001—05, Tri-City Mental Health Ctr., 2003—; spl. counsel L.A. Unified Sch. Dist., 2000—04; city atty. City of Vista, Calif., 2005—. Spl. counsel L.A. County Transp. Commn., 1984-93, L.A. County Met. Transp. Authority, 1993-94; commr. L.A. County Delinquency and Crime Commn., 1983-94, pres., 1987-94; chmn. L.A. County Delinquency Prevention Planning Coun., 1987-90. Contbr. articles to profl. jours. Peace officer Pasadena (Calif.) Police Res. Unit, 1972-87, dep. comdr., 1979-81, comdr., 1982-84; chmn. pub. safety commn. City of La Canada Flintridge, Calif., 1977-82, commr. 1977-88; bd. dirs. La Canada Flintridge Coordinating Council, 1975-82, pres. 1977-78; exec. dir. Cityhood Action Com., 1975-76; chmn. Youth Opportunities United, Inc., 1990-96, vice-chmn. 1988-89, bd. dirs. 1988-96; mem. L.A. County Justice Systems Adv. Group, 1987-92; trustee Lanterman Hist. Mus. Found., 1989-94, Calif. City Mgmt. Found., 1992—. Recipient commendation for Community Service, L.A. County Bd. Suprs., 1978, Commendation for Svc. to Youth, 1996. Mem. ABA, Calif. Bar Assn., L.A. County Bar Assn., San Diego County Bar Assn., City Attys. Assn. San Diego County (v.p. 2006, pres. 2007), La Canada Flintridge C. of C. and Cmty. Assn. (pres. 1981, bd. dirs. 1976-83), Peace Officers Assn., L.A. County, UCLA Alumni Assn. (life), U. So. Calif. Law Alumni Assn. Office Phone: 760-795-6042.

PIEPER, MICHAEL JOSEPH, television producer, actor, talk show host; b. Detroit, July 12, 1958; s. Frank John Pieper and Marie Yolanda Dansereau; m. Barbara Marie Michalik (div. Feb. 1990); children: Melanie Lynn, Heather Irene. Student, Marygrove Coll., 1976—78, Specs Howard Sch. Broadcast Arts, 1988. Ordained min. Universal Life Ch., 2000. Owner, prodr. Quixote Video, Huntington Beach, Calif., 1981—. Actor (TV series) T-bone Playhouse, 1981—82, actor, co-prodr. comedy soap opera, Daze of Our Wives, 1982—85; performer: (TV series) game show, Out-patient Bonanza, 1984—85; actor: (radio series) Proceed With Caution, 1985—86; (TV films) Streetlevel, 1983, The Banana Republic, 1983; actor, co-prodr. (TV films) Bartolo's Cafe, 1984, The Paper, 1992, host, co-prodr. (talk show) Forum, 1983—85, host Detroit Metro Magazine, 1985, songwriter Feathersong, 1996; songwriter: Legacy, 2006. Mem.: Internat. Platform Assn. (life). Avocations: singing, painting, photography, metaphysics. Home and Office: 6372 Walt St Westminster CA 92683-3614 Office Phone: 714-893-2720. Personal E-mail: magikrhino@gmail.com.

PIEPER, PATRICIA RITA, artist; b. Paterson, NJ, Jan. 28, 1923; d. Francis William and Barbara Margaret (Ludwig) Farabaugh; m. George F. Pieper, July 1, 1941 (dec. May 3, 1981); 1 child, Patricia Lynn; m. Russell W. Watson, Dec. 9, 1989. Student, Baron von Palm, 1937-39, Deal Conservatory, NJ, 1939-40, Utah State U., 1950-52; student Baron von Palm, 1937—39, student Deal (N.J.) Conservatory, 1939—40, student Utah State U., 1950—52. One-woman shows include Charles Russell Mus., Great Falls, Mont., 1955, Fisher Gallery, Washington, 1966, Tampa City Libr., 1977-81, 83, 84, Ctr. Pl. Art Ctr., Brandon, Fla., 1985; exhibited in group shows Davidson Art Gallery, Middletown, Conn., 1968, Helena (Mont.) Hist. Mus., 1955, Dept. Commerce Alaska Statehood Show, 1959, Joslyn Mus., Omaha, 1961, Denver Mus. Natural History, 1955, St. Joseph's Hosp. Gallery, 1980, 82, 84-86; represented in pvt. collections. Pres. Bell Lake Assn., 1976-78, 79; mem. Pasco County (Fla.) Water Adv. Coun., 1978—, chmn., 1979-82, 83-84, 86-88, 92—; gov.'s appointee to S.W. Fla. Water Mgmt. Dist., Hillsborough River Basin Bd., 1981-82, 84-87, sec., 1988-91, vice chmn., 1992; active Save Our Rivers program, 1982-84, 85-86, 92—; ad hoc chmn., 1991-92; mem. adv. bd. Fla. Suncoast Expwy., 1988-90; pres. Bell Lake Assn., 1986, 87; mem. adv. bd. Tampa YMCA, 1979-80. Winner photog. competition Gen. Tel. Co. of Fla., 1979; recipient Outstanding Svc. award Bell Lake Assn., 1987, Meml. award Land O'Lake Bd. of Realtors, 1989, Appreciation award Southwest Fla. Water Mgmt. Dist., 1993, finalist, Awds. of Excellence, Photographers winner in top 100 out of 8,000 Nat. Wildlife Fedn. competition, 1986, 1st place photography MacDill AFB, 1991. Mem. VFW (life), Nat. League Am. Pen Women (v.p. Tampa 1976-78, Woman of Yr. award 1977-78), Tampa Art Mus., Ret. Officer's Wives Assn., Land O'Lakes C. of C. (bd. dirs. 1981-82, Outstanding Svc. award 1980), Fla. Geneal. Soc., West State Archaeol. Soc. (distaff mem.), Ret. Officer's Assn., Lutz Club, Land O'Lakes Women's Club, Moose. Home: 3304 E Derry Dr Sebastian FL 32958-8577 *I believe that those of us born with the gift of creativity are truly blessed. It is our duty to make the most of, and be worthy of that gift. And if we work hard and sincerely apply ourselves a chosen few will become immortal through the beauty we leave behind for others to enjoy. As an artist and photographer I am truly blessed.*

PIEPGRAS, DAVID G., neurosurgeon, educator; b. Luverne, Minn., 1940; MD, U. Minn., 1965. Diplomate Am. Bd. Neurol. Surgery. Intern Mary Hitchcock Hosp., Hanover, Minn., 1965—66; resident in surgery Hennepin County Gen. Hosp., Mpls., 1969—70; resident in neurol. surgery Mayo Grad. Sch. Medicine, Rochester, 1970—74; staff St. Mary's Hosp., Rochester, 1974—, Rochester Meth. Hosp., 1974—; staff cons. dept. neurosurgery Mayo Clinic, Rochester, 1974—, prof. neurol. surgery. Bd. dirs. Am. Bd. Neurol. Surgery, 2002—. Fellow: ACS; mem.: AMA, Congress of Neurol. Surgeons, Am. Acad. Neurol. Surgeons. Office: Mayo Clinic Dept Neurol Surgery Rochester MN 55905-0001

PIEPHO, LEE (EDWARD LEE PIEPHO), humanities educator; b. Detroit, Jan. 10, 1942; s. Edward Ernest and Dolores Faye (Dowis) P.; m. Susan Brand, June 13, 1964. AB, Kenyon Coll., 1964; MA, Columbia U., 1966; PhD, U. Va., 1972. Instr. Sweet Briar Coll., Va., 1969—72, asst. prof., 1972—78, assoc. prof., 1978—83, prof., 1983—94, Shallenberger Brown prof., 1994—2006, rsch. prof., 2006—, dept. chmn., 2000—01, coord. European civilization program, 1986—89. Author: Holofernes' Mantuan, 2001; translator, editor: Adulescentia: The Eclogues of Mantuan, 1989; contbr. articles to profl. jours. Fellow, SIMRS, 1979, NEH, 1985, 1997; Dulin fellow, Folger Shakespeare Libr., 1989—90, Mednick fellow, 1996. Mem. Internat. Assn. for Neo-Latin Studies, Modern Lang. Assn. Am., Renaissance Soc. Am. Avocations: golf, tennis, scuba diving. Home: 137 Woodland Rd Sweet Briar VA 24595 Office: Sweet Briar Coll Dept English Sweet Briar VA 24595 Business E-Mail: lpiepho@sbc.edu.

PIEPHO, ROBERT WALTER, pharmacy educator, researcher; b. Chgo., July 31, 1942; s. Walter August and Irene Elizabeth (Huybrecht) Apfel; m. Mary Lee Wilson, Dec. 10, 1981. BS in Pharmacy, U. Ill.-Chgo., 1965; PhD in Pharmacology, Loyola U., Maywood, Ill., 1972. Registered pharmacist, Ill., Mo. Assoc. prof. U. Nebr. Med. Ctr., Omaha, 1970-78; prof. pharmacy, assoc. dean Sch. Pharmacy U. Colo., Denver, 1978-86; prof. pharmacol., dean U. Mo. Sch. Pharmacy, Kansas City, 1986—. Contbr. articles to profl. jours., chpts. to books. Pres. Club Monaco Homeowners Assn., Denver, 1980-82. Named Outstanding Tchr. U. Nebr. Coll. Pharmacy, 1975; recipient Arthur Hassan Colo. Pharmacal Assn., 1983, Excellence in Teaching U. Colo. Med. Sch., 1983 Fellow Am. Coll. Clin. Pharmacology (regent 1983-88, 91-96, pres. 1998-2000); mem. Am. Soc. Hosp. Pharmacists, Am. Soc. Pharmacology and Exptl. Therapeutics, Rho Chi Roman Catholic. Office: U Mo Sch Pharmacy 2464 Charlotte St Kansas City MO 64108-2718 Office Phone: 816-235-1609. Business E-Mail: piephor@umkc.edu.

PIERANGELI, SILVIA SUSANA, medical educator, consultant; b. Buenos Aires, Oct. 10, 1955; d. Hector Raul Pierangeli and Nelida Susana Vega de Pierangeli; m. Alvaro Schleh, Jan. 16, 2003; children: Maria Cecilia Miranda, Maria Eugenia Miranda. PhD, U. of Louisville, 1990. Lab. dir. Coll. of Am. Pathologists. Rsch. assoc. U. of Louisville, 1990—96; prof. Morehouse Sch. of Medicine, Atlanta, 1996—2006, U. Tex. Med. Br., Galveston, 2006—. Tech. dir. Louisville APL Diagnostics, Inc, Doraville, Ga., 1993—. Contbr. scientific papers to profl. publs. Recipient Fulbright scholarship, USIA, 1985—88. Mem.: Am. Coll. of Rheumatology. Achievements include research in Mechanisms of thrombosis induced by antiphospholipid antibodies in the antiphospholipid syndrome; discovery of better antigen for detection of antiphospholipid antibodies; development of better laboratory assay for diagnosis of antiphospholipid syndrome. Office Phone: 409-772-0222. Business E-Mail: sspieran@utmb.edu.

PIERARD, RICHARD VICTOR, history educator; b. Chgo., May 29, 1934; s. John Perkins and Diana Florence (Russell) P.; m. Charlene Burdett, June 15, 1957; children: David, Cynthia. BA, Calif. State U., LA, 1958, MA, 1959; PhD, U. Iowa, 1964. Prof. history Ind. State U., Terre Haute, 1964-2000, emeritus, 2000—. Vis. prof. Greenville (Ill.) Coll., 1972-73, Free Theol. Acad., Seeheim, Fed. Republic Germany, 1971, 78, Regent Coll., Vancouver, B.C., Can., 1975, Trinity Evang. Div. Sch., Deerfield, Ill., 1982, No. Bapt. Theol. Sem., Lombard, Ill., 1987, Fuller Theol. Sem., Pasadena, Calif., 1988, 91, Moscow Theol. Sem., 1997, 99, 2001, 2003, Gordon Coll., Wenham, Mass., 2000-2001; scholar-in-residence Gordon Coll., 2000—; Fulbright prof. U. Frankfurt, Fed. Republic Germany, 1984-85; Fulbright prof. U. Halle, German Dem. Republic, 1989-90; pres. Greater Terre Haute Ch. Fedn., 1987-88; del. Lausanne II Congress on World Evang., Manila, Philippines, 1989; mem. Bapt. Heritage & Identity Study Commn., Bapt. World Alliance, 1990. Author: The Unequal Yoke: Evangelical Christianity and Political Conservatism, 1970, Bibliography on the Religious Right in America, 1986; co-author: Twilight of the Saints: Biblical Christianity and Civil Religion, 1978, Civil Religion and the Presidency, 1988, Two Kingdoms: The Church and Culture through the Ages, 1993, The Revolution of the Candles: Christians in the Revolution of the German Democratic Republic, 1996, The New Millennium Manual, 1999; contbr. articles to religious and hist. publs. Del. White House Conf. on Librs., Washington, 1979, Ind. Dem. Party Convention, Indpls., 1980, 88; precinct committeeman Dem. Party, Terre Haute, 1978-80, 90—; mem. Ind. Gov.'s Adv. Com. on Librs., 1980-81. With U.S. Army, 1954-56. Recipient Terre award for cmty. svc., Terre Haute, Ind., 1991; Fulbright scholar U. Hamburg (Fed. Republic Germany), 1962-63; rsch. fellow U. Aberdeen (Scotland), 1978; Chavanne scholar Baylor U., 1988. Mem. Conf. on Faith and History (sec.-treas. 1967—), Evang. Theol. Soc. (pres. 1985), Am. Hist. Assn., Am. Soc. Ch. History, Ind. Assn. Historians, Am. Soc. Missiology, Internat. Assn. Mission Studies, Soc. for Encouragement and Preservation of Barbershop Quartet Singing in Am., Am. Bapt. Hist. Soc. (bd. mgrs. 1993—). Democrat. Home: 11 Pine Rd Beverly MA 01915 Personal E-mail: charrichp@aol.com.

PIERCE, ALLAN DALE, engineering educator, researcher, editor; b. Clarinda, Iowa, Dec. 18, 1936; s. Franklin Dale and Ruth Pauline (Wright) P.; m. Penelope Claffey, Oct. 27, 1961; children: Jennifer Irene, Bradford Loren. BS, N.Mex. Coll. Agrl. and Mechanic Arts, 1957; PhD, MIT, 1962. Registered profl. engr., Mass. Staff rschr. Rand Corp., Santa Monica, Calif., 1961-63; sr. staff scientist Avco Corp., Wilmington, Mass., 1963-66; asst. prof. MIT, Cambridge, 1966-68, assoc. prof., 1968-73; prof. mech. engring. Ga. Inst. Tech., Atlanta, 1973-76, Regent's prof., 1976-88; Leonhard chair in engring. Pa. State U., University Park, 1988-93; chmn. dept aerospace and mech. engring. Boston U., 1993-99, prof., 1993—. Vis. prof. Max Planck Inst., Goettingen, Fed. Republic Germany, 1976-77; vis. scientist Woods Hole Oceanographic Inst., 2002-03, adj. scientist, 2003-; cons. in field. Author: Acoustics: An Introduction to Its Physical Principles and Applications, 1981; editor phys. acoustics monograph series, 1988-97; editor Jour. Computation Acoustics, 1992-99; contbr. articles to profl. jours. Recipient Sr. U.S. Scientist award Alexander von Humboldt Found., 1976, Cert. of Recognition Nat. Aeronautics and Space Adminstrn., 1984, Per Bruel Gold medal for noise control and acoustics ASME, 1995; NSF fellow, 1957-60, Shell Oil fellow, 1960-61, Faculty fellow U.S. Dept. Transp., 1979-80. Fellow Acoustical Soc. Am. (editor-in-chief 1999—, Silver medal 1991, Rossing prize in acoustics edn. 2004, Gold medal 2005), ASME (Rayleigh lectr. 1992, Per Bruel Gold medal 1995, chair Noise Control and Acoustics Divsn. 1999-2000); mem. IEEE, AIAA. Home: PO Box 339 East Sandwich MA 02537-0339 Office: Boston U Dept Aerospace & Mech Engring 110 Cummington St Boston MA 02215-2407 Business E-Mail: adp@bu.edu.

PIERCE, CAROLE JEAN, artist; b. Dallas, Sept. 7, 1950; d. Bertrum Robert and Dorothy Lillian (Meyer) Brownie; m. Lee Pierce, Mar. 13, 1970; 1 child, Brandon. BFA in Painting and Printmaking, So. Meth. U., 1972; MFA in Printmaking, Calif. Coll. Arts & Crafts, 1994. Advt. prodn. Zale Corp., Dallas, 1972; mgr. direct mail Halle Bros., Cleve., 1973-75; advt. art dir. Sanger Harris, Dallas, 1975-79; photography coord. Neiman Marcus, Horchow Collection, Dallas, 1979-81; freelance art & photography coord. San Francisco, 1982-83; writer, researcher Culinary Historians Boston, 1983-85; researcher for curator N.Y. Pub. Libr., NYC, 1985-87; tchr., artist Kala Inst., Berkeley, Calif., 1987—. Guest instr. art history San Francisco State U., 2001; instr. independent studies Calif. Coll. of Arts and Crafts, Oakland, 1999; pvt. printmaking instr. for Mrs. Ann Getty, San Francisco, 98. Solo exhbns. include Joan Roebuck Gallery, Lafayette, Calif., 1994, Calif. Coll. Arts and Crafts, 1994, Shidoni Contemporary Gallery, Tesuque, N. Mex., 1995, Carole Pierce-Bill Weaver Painting and Sculpture, 1995, Draighead Green Gallery, Dallas, 1996, numerous others to Diane Nelson Fine Art, Laguna Beach, Calif., 2002; group exhbns. include Kala Inst., Berkeley, Calif., 1989, 92, Accurate Art Gallery, Sacramento, 1989, Matrix Gallery, Sacramento, 1989, Gallery House, Palo Alto, Calif., 1989, Orange County Ctr. Contemporary Art, Santa Ana, 1989, Coll. San Mateo, Calif., 1990, Pacific Art League, Palo Alto, 1990, Ford Aerospace Corp., San Jose, Calif., 1990, San Diego Art Inst., 1992, Shidoni Contemporary Gallery, 1993, U. Oreg., Eugene, 1994, Berkeley (Calif.) Art Ctr. Assn., 1994, Osaka (Japan) Found. Culture, 1994, Columbia (Mo.) Coll., 1995, Southwest Tex. State U., San Marcos, 1995, Amador County Arts Coun., Sutter Creek, Calif., 1995, Triton Mus. Arts Biennial Print and Drawing Competition and Exhbn., 1995, Gallery Route One, Point Reyes Calif., 1995, Mus. Moderna Art, N.Y.C., 1995, Barrett House Galleries, Dutchess County Art Assn., Poughkeepsie, N.Y., 1995, Pro Arts, Oakland, Calif., 1996, The Haggin Mus., Stockton, Calif., 1996, U. Hawaii, Hilo, 1996, The Munson Gallery, Santa Fe, N.Mex., 1998, numerous others to Craighead Green Gallery, Dallas, Tex., 2002, Michael Martin Galleries, San Francisco, 2003, and others; represented in permanent collections U.S. Embassy Nairobe, Kenya, Havana, Cuba, Harvard U., Sandoz Pharm.,

Fidelity Securities, Goldman Sachs Internat. Collection, Indsl. Light and Magic, Morgan Libr., N.Y.C., numerous pvt. collections. Vol. Mus. Modern Art, San Francisco; art coord. children's program, 1988-90. Recipient Monoprint award Pacific Art League, Palo Alto, Calif., 1990; juror award Hill Country Arts Found., Austin, Tex., 1991, 1st pl. award Calif. Coll. Arts & Crafts, Oakland, 1993, Berkeley Art Ctr. Assn. 10th Ann. Nat. Juried Exhbn., 1994, Monoprint award Nat. Acad. Design, N.Y.C. Mem. Am. Inst. Wine & Food, Internat. Wine & Food Soc., L.A. Printmakers Soc. (Monoprint award 1990). Avocations: reading, swimming, yoga, travel. Home: PO Box 1032 Ross CA 94957-1032 Studio: #2 Bridge Ave San Anselmo CA 94960

PIERCE, CHARLES ELIOT, JR., library director, educator; b. Springfield, Mass., Dec. 25, 1941; s. C. Eliot and Dora Mason (Redway) P.; m. Barbara G. Hanson, Oct. 18, 1969; children: Sheila H., Charles Eliot III BA, Harvard U., 1964, MAT., 1966, PhD, 1970. Prof. English Vassar Coll., Poughkeepsie, NY, 1970-87; dir. Pierpont Morgan Library, NYC, 1987—. Mem. vis. com. Vassar Coll. Art Gallery, Sherman Fairchild Found. Author: (literary criticism) The Religious Life of Samuel Johnson, 1983 Mem. Art Mus. Dirs., Johnsonians, Century Assn., Grolier Club, Walpole Soc., Knickerbocker Club. Episcopalian. Office: Pierpont Morgan Libr 29 E 36th St New York NY 10016-3490 Office Phone: 212-590-0305. Business E-Mail: cpierce@morganlibrary.org.

PIERCE, CHESTER MIDDLEBROOK, retired psychiatrist, educator; b. Glen Cove, NY, Mar. 4, 1927; s. Samuel Riley and Hettie Elenor (Armstrong) P.; m. Jocelyn Patricia Blanchet, June 15, 1949; children: Diane Blanchet, Deirdre Anona. AB, Harvard U., 1948, MD, 1952; ScD (hon.), Westfield Coll., 1977, Tufts U., 1984; D in Engring. Tech. (hon.), Wentworth Inst. Tech., 1997. Instr. psychiatry U. Cin., 1957-60; asst. prof. psychiatry U. Okla., 1960-62, prof., 1965-69; prof. edn. and psychiatry Harvard U., 1969—; pres. Am. Bd. Psychiatry and Neurology, 1977-78; ret., 1997. Mem. Polar Rsch. Bd.; cons. USAF. Author publs. on sleep disturbances, media, polar medicine, sports medicine, racism; mem. editl. bds. Advisor Children's TV Workshop; chmn. Child Devel. Assn. Consortium; bd. dirs. Action Children's TV. With M.C. USNR, 1953-55. Fellow: Brit. Royal Coll. Psychiatrists (hon.), Royal Australian and New Zealand Coll. Psychiatrists (hon.); mem.: Am. Acad. Arts and Scis., Am. Orthopsychiat. Assn. (pres. 1983—84), Black Psychiatrists Am. (chmn.), Inst. Medicine of NAS. Democrat. Home: 17 Prince St Jamaica Plain MA 02130-2725 Office Phone: 617-495-4929.

PIERCE, CHRISTOPHER A., neuropsychologist, consultant; PhD, U. Ala., 2000. Lic. psychologist Colo., 2002. Resident Rehab. Inst. Mich., Detroit, 2000—02; clin. neuropsychologist Neuropsychol. Cons., LLC, Boulder, Colo., 2002—. Mem.: Nat. Acad. Neuropsychology, Internat. Neuropsychological Soc., APA. Office: 1919 14th St # 812 Boulder CO 80302-5310

PIERCE, DANIEL THORNTON, physicist; b. LA, July 16, 1940; s. Daniel Gordon Pierce and Celia Francis Thornton Thayer; m. Barbara Harrison, Nov. 19, 1988; children: Jed, Maia, Stephen. BS, Stanford U., 1962, PhD in Applied Physics, 1970; MA, Wesleyan U., Middletown, Conn., 1966. NSF rsch. asst. materials sci. dept. Stanford U., 1961; lectr in physics U.S. Peace Corps, Kathmandu, Nepal, 1962-64; rsch. asst. Wesleyan U., 1964-66, Stanford Electronics Lab., 1966-70, rsch. assoc., 1970-71; rsch. staff Solid State Physics Lab., Swiss Fed. Inst. Tech., 1971-75; physicist Nat. Inst. Standards and Tech. (formerly Nat. Bur Standards), Gaithersburg, Md., 1975—, fellow, 1994—. Contbr. chpts. to books, numerous articles to profl. jours. Trustee Unitarian Ch. of Rockville, Md., 1994-96 Recipient IR-100 award R&D Mag., 1980, 85, Gold medal Dept. Commerce, 1987, William P. Schlichter award Nat. Inst. Standards and Tech., 1992. Fellow Am. Phys. Soc. (exec. com. Materials Physics Divsn. 1998-2001), Am. Vacuum Soc. (surface sci. exec. com. 1984-88, Gaede-Langmuir prize 1994). Achievements include patents for source of spin polarized electrons, absorbed current and low energy spin polarization detectors; development of scanning electron microscopy with polarization analysis. Office: Nat Inst Standards and Tech Mail Stop 6202 Bldg 216 Rm A223 Gaithersburg MD 20899-6202 Office Phone: 301-975-3711. Business E-Mail: daniel.pierce@nist.gov.

PIERCE, DANNY PARCEL, artist, educator; b. Woodlake, Calif., Sept. 10, 1920; s. Frank Lester and Letitia Frances (Parcel) P.; m. Julia Ann Rasmussen, July 19, 1943; children: Julia Ann, Mary L., Danny L., Duane Nels. Student, Art Ctr. Sch., LA, 1939, Chouinards Art Inst., 1940-41, 46-47, Am. Art Sch., NYC, 1947-48, Bklyn. Mus. Art Sch., 1950-53; BFA, U. Alaska, 1963. Instr. Hunter Coll., NYC, 1952-53, Burnley Sch. Art, Seattle, 1954-58, Seattle U., 1956-59; publ. Red Door Studio Press, Kent, Wash., 1959—; artist-in-res. U. Alaska, College, 1959-63; asst. prof. U. Wisc., Milw., 1964; head art dept. Cornish Sch. Allied Arts, Seattle, 1964-65; prof. art U. Wisc., Milw., 1965-84, prof. emeritus, 1984—. One-man shows include Contemporaries Gallery, N.Y.C., 1953, Handforth Gallery, Tacoma, Washington, 1958, U. Alaska, College, 1959, 63, 73, 74, Gonzaga U., Bradley Galleries, Milw., 1966, 68, 70, 72, 74, 76, 78-80, 82, Martin-Zambito Gallery, Seattle, 1997, 2002, Apple Blossom Time, 2000, Centennial Gallery, Kent, Wash., 2003, 04; father/son exhbn., 2002, Martin-Zambito Gallery, Seattle, 1999, 2007; represented in permanent collections Bibliothèque Nationale, Paris, Mus. Modern Art, N.Y.C., Libr. Congress, Washington, Smithsonian Instn., Washington, Seattle Art Mus., U. Washington Henry Art Gallery, Bklyn. Mus., Princeton U., U. Alaska, U. So. Calif., William and Mary Coll., Oostduinkerke (Belgium) Nat. Fishing Mus., Nat. Mus. Sweden, Stockholm, Johnson Wax Found., Racine, Wisc., Gen. Mills Collection Art, Mpls., Huntington Libr., San Marino, Calif., various pvt. collections; pub. 27 ltd. edit. books, 1959-98. Recipient Best Oil Landscape award Conn. Acad. Fine Arts, Hartford, 1st Prize oil Kohler Gallery, Seattle, 1974, others; chosen one of twelve artists to represent State Wash. Expo 70, Osaka, Japan, rep. U.S. Internat. São Paulo Biannual Art Exhbn.; established archives at Golda Meier Libr., U. Wis.-Mils. Mem. Artist Equity Assn. (charter, pres. Seattle chpt. 1958), Am. Colorprint Soc., Internat. Arts and Letters (life). Office: Red Door Studio 404 Summit Ave N Kent WA 98030-4712 Office Phone: 253-859-1504.

PIERCE, DAVID, information technology executive; With New World Pictures, New World Home Entertainment; sr. v.p. Columbia Tristar Home Video, 1989—94; exec. v.p., gen. mgr. Sony Wonder; pres., CEO Atari, Inc., NYC, 2006—. Office: Atari Inc 417 Fifth Ave New York NY 10016-2204

PIERCE, DAVID HYDE, actor; b. Albany, NY, Apr. 3, 1959; BA in theatre & English, Yale U., 1981. Appeared in plays Beyond Therapy, 1982, Holiday, 1982, Summer, 1983, That's It, Folks! 1983, Candida, 1984, The Seagull, 1984, The Grand Hysteric, 1984, The Three Zeks, 1984, Tartuffe, 1984, Donuts, 1985, Hamlet, 1986, The Author's Voice, 1987, The Maderati, 1987, Camille, 1987, The Cherry Orchard, 1988, Zero Positive, 1988, Much Ado About Nothing, 1988, The Heidi Chronicles, 1989, Elliot Loves, 1990, It's Only a Play, 1991, Monty Python's Spamalot, 2005, Curtains, 2006 (Tony award best performance by a leading actor in a musical, 2007); films include Bright Lights, Big City, 1988, Crossing Delancey, 1988, Rocket Gibraltar, 1988, The Fisher King, 1991, Little Man Tate, 1991, Sleepless in Seattle, 1993, Addams Family Values, 1993, Wolf, 1994, Nixon, 1995, Hercules, 1998, A Bug's Life, 1998, Jackie's Back!, 1999, Mating Habits of the Earthbound Human, 1999, Isn't She Great, 2000, Chain of Fools, 2000, Wet, Hot, American Summer, 2001, Osmosis Jones, 2001; TV series include The Powers That Be, 1993, Frasier, 1993-2004 (seven Am. Comedy awards), Laud Weiner, 2001, Full Frontal, 2002, Treasure Planet (voice), 2002, Down with Love, 2003. Recipient Emmy award, 1995, 1998, 1999, 2004, SAG Award, 1996, 2000, Q Award 1994, 95, 96, 98, TV Guide award, 2000, TV Critics Assn. award 1997, 1998. Am. Comedy award 1995-2000. *

PIERCE, DONALD FAY, lawyer; b. Bexley, Miss., Aug. 28, 1930; s. Percy O. and Lavada S. (Stringfellow) Pierce; m. Norma Faye Scribner, June 5, 1954; children: Kathryn Pierce Tuttle, D. F. Jr., John S., Jeff G. BS, U. Ala., 1956, JD, 1958. Bar: Ala. 1958, U.S. Ct. Appeals (5th cir.) 1958, U.S. Dist. Ct. (no., mid. and so. dists.) Ala. 1958, U.S. Ct. Appeals (11th cir.) 1982. Law clk. to presiding judge U.S. Dist. Ct. (so. dist.) Ala., 1958—59; ptnr. Hand, Arendall, Bedsole, Greaves & Johnston, Mobile, Ala., 1964—91, Pierce, Carr, Alford, Ledyard & Latta, P.C., 1991—; pvt. practice; of counsel Butler Pappas LLP. Mem. Products Liability Adv. Coun., 1990—; bd. overseers Vanderbilt Cancer Ctr., 1994—. Contbr. articles to profl. jours. Trustee UMS Prep Sch., 1980—87. 1st lt. US Army, 1951—53. Mem.: Def. Research Inst. (pres. 1987, chmn. 1988), Def. Counsel Trial Acad. (bd. dir. 1983—84), Internat. Assn. Def. Counsel, Am. Acad. Hosp. Attys., Fedn. Ins. and Corp. Counsel, Ala. Def. Lawyers Assn. (past pres.). Baptist. Home: 4452 Winnie Way Mobile AL 36608-2221 Office: Butler Pappas LLP 1110 Montlimar Dr Ste 1050 Mobile AL 36608 Office Phone: 251-338-1313. Business E-Mail: d.pierce@butlerpappas.com.

PIERCE, DONALD SHELTON, retired orthopedic surgeon, educator; b. Castine, Maine, May 21, 1930; s. Frederick Ernest and Jeannie (Emmet) P.; m. Janet Ten Broeck, Dec. 29, 1956; children: Donald Shelton, Stanton ten Broeck, Frederick Ernest, Jennifer Emmet. AB cum laude, Harvard U., 1953, MD, 1957. Diplomate Am. Bd. Spine Surgery, Am. Bd. Orthop. Surgery; lic. lay eucharistic minister Episcopal Ch., 2004. Intern U. Hosp., Cleve., 1957-58, resident, 1958-62; rsch. assoc. biomechanics lab. U. Calif., San Francisco, 1962-64; practice medicine specializing in orthopedic surgery San Francisco, 1962-64; instr. orthopedic surgery U. Calif. Med. Sch., San Francisco, 1962-64, Harvard Med. Sch., 1964-66; clin. and rsch. assoc. J.P. Kennedy Jr. Meml. Hosp., Brighton, Mass., 1964-66; clin. assoc. in orthopedics Harvard Med. Sch., 1966-67, clin. asst. prof. orthopaedic surgery, 1979-87, clin. assoc. prof., 1987-2000; ret., 2000; sr. orthopedic surgeon Mass. Gen. Hosp., Boston. Chief dept. rehab. medicine Mass. Gen. Hosp., Boston, 1965-72, assoc. orthopedic surgeon, 1969—, vis. orthopedic surgeon, 1969—; lectr. dept. mech. engring. MIT, 1970-72. Co-author: Amputees and Their Porstheses, 1971; author: The Total Care of Spinal Cord Injuries, 1977; contbr. articles in field to profl. jours. Pres. Wellesley (Mass.) Friendly Aid Assn., 1965-67, dir., 1967-70; dir. Family Svc. Counseling Region West, Wellesley, 1965-67; mem. exec. com., task force chmn. Mass. Rehab. Planning Commn., 1966-68; pres. Maine Ret. Skippers Race, 2003-05; co-chmn. capital campaign com. Trinity Espic. Ch., Maine. With USAF, 1951-52. Fellow ACS, Am. Acad. Orthopedic Surgeons, Royal Soc. Health, Pan Am. Med. Assn., Soc. Internat. Chirurgerie, Ortopaedie et Traumatologie; mem. NAS (mem. skeletal com. 1965-68, mem. subcom. basic projects, mem. com. prosthetics R & D 1966-68), NRC (musculoskeletal com., mem. subcom. basic projects, mem. com. prosthetics R & D), Othopedic Rsch. Soc., Am. Orthopaedic Assn., Cervical Spine Rsch. Soc. (pres. 1986), Fedn. Spine Assns. (pres. 1987), N.E. Med. Assn. (pres.), Ezekiel Hersey Coun., Harvard Med. Sch. (mem. Dean's Coun.). Personal E-mail: treetops-1@comcast.net.

PIERCE, FRANK POWELL, lawyer, judge; b. San Antonio, Dec. 28, 1953; s. Arnold Leigh and Marie Pierce; m. Ernestine Pierce; 4 children. BA in Polit. Sci., U. Houston, 1977; JD, Tex. So. U., 1980. Bar: Tex. 1980, U.S. Dist. Ct. (so. and we. dists.) Tex. 1982, U.S. Ct. Appeals (5th cir.) 1982, U.S. Supreme Ct. 1984. Atty. Bexar County Legal Aid, San Antonio, 1980-83; asst. city atty. City of San Antonio, 1983-87; judge County Ct. at Law No. 2, San Antonio, 1987—; asst. atty. gen., 1993—2001; judge Child Support Ct. 2, Harris County, 2001—. Mem. Bexar County Bail Bond Bd., 1987-88; mem. faculty St. Philip's Coll., part-time; adj. prof. South Tex. Coll. Law. Mem. speaker's bur. San Antonio Literacy Coun., 1988, mediation bd. Bexar County, 1989—; deacon Mt. Zion 1st Bapt. Ch., San Antonio; alumnus Leadership San Antonio; mem. minority recruitment task force Dental Sch., U. Tex. Health Sci. Ctr.; mem. Palmer Drug Abuse Bd., 1987—; bd. mgrs. Alamo br. YMCA, San Antonio; bd. dirs. Halfway House San Antonio, 1989; city councilman, San Antonio, 1991-93. Named Black Achiever in Govt., Iota Phi Lamda, 1984; recipient Citizen of Yr. award Omega Psi Phi, 1987, Man of Yr. award Mission Lodge, San Antonio, 1988. Mem. Tex. Bar Assn. Office: Family Law Ctr Ct Two 1115 Congress Ste 411 Houston TX 77002 Office Phone: 713-755-2910.

PIERCE, HILDA (HILDA HERTA HARMEL), painter; b. Vienna; arrived in U.S., 1940; m. Herman J. Slutzky; 1 child, Diana Rubin Daly (dec.). Student, Art Inst. Chgo.; studied with Oskar Kokoschka, Salzburg, Austria. Art tchr. Highland Park (Ill.) Art Ctr., Sandburg Village Art Workshop, Chgo., Old Town Art Ctr., Chgo.; owner, operator Hilda Pierce Art Gallery, Laguna Beach, Calif., 1981-85. Guest lectr. maj. art mus. and art tours, Carribean cruises South America, Argentina, Brazil, Israel, Egypt, France, Switzerland, Austria, Italy, Mex., San Diego, China, India, 1998—2002, Russian river cruise and major art mus., St. Petersburg, Moscow, 1994; lectr., Mexico, 1994—2007, U. Calif. Geisel Libr., San Diego, 2003—07; founder, chmn. Art Encounters, San Diego. One-woman shows include Fairweather Hardin Gallery, Chgo., Sherman Art Gallery, Marshall Field Gallery, exhibited in group shows at Old Orchard Art Festival, Skokie, Ill., Union League Club, Chgo., North Shore Art League, Winnetka, Ill., Art Inst. Chgo., Represented in permanent collections U. Calif. San Diego Art Libr., La Jolla, Carnival Cruise Lines megaliner M.S. Fantasy, megaliner M.S. Imagination, Rebecca and John Moores Cancer Ctr., U. Calif. San Diego, U. Calif. San Diego Geisel Libr.; featured (video) Survivors of the Shoah, Stephen Spielberg Found., 1996; author: Hilda: A True Story of Terror, Tears and Triumph, 2007; contbr. articles to profl. jours. and periodicals. Recipient Outstanding Achievement in Art award, Chgo. Immigrants Svc. League, 1964. Office Phone: 858-558-7556. Personal E-mail: hildapierce@aol.com. *An artist's most precious quality is curiosity. It has kept me young for many years, kept me searching, experimenting and never being complacent, in my life and my work.*

PIERCE, JAMES CLARENCE, surgeon, educator; b. Huron, SD, Aug. 5, 1929; s. Henry Montraville and Carrie Bernice (Matson) P.; m. Carol Sue Wilson, 1967; children: Henry MacDonald, Richard Matson, Elizabeth Gail. BA, Carleton Coll., 1951; MD, Harvard U., 1955; MS, U. Minn., 1963, PhD in Surgery, 1966. Diplomate Am. Bd. Surgery. Surg. intern Peter Bent Brigham Hosp., Boston, 1955-56; surg. fellow U. Minn., 1959-66; instr. surgery Med. Coll. Va., Richmond, 1966, prof. surgery and microbiology, 1972-75; dir. Tissue Typing Lab., 1969-75; attending surgeon, dir. surg. research, dir. transplantation service St. Luke's Hosp. Center, NYC, 1975-78; prof. surgery Columbia U., 1976, Ailsa Mellon Bruce prof. surgery, 1977-78; clin. prof. surgery Pa. State U. and, 1979-88; chmn. dept. surgery Geisinger Med. Center, Danville, Pa., 1979-90, chmn. emeritus, 1990—. Clin. prof. surgery Jefferson U., 1990—. Contbr. articles to profl. jours. Elder Presbyn. Ch. With M.C., USAF, 1957-59. NIH fellow, 1963-65; Royal Soc. Medicine Found. travelling fellow, 1971; James IV Assn. Surg. traveller, 1978 Mem. ACS (pres. Ctrl. Pa. chpt. 1981-82), Transplant Soc., Am. Soc. Transplant Surgeons, Ea. Surg. Soc., N.Y. Clin. Soc., Soc. Univ. Surgeons, Sigma Xi. Republican. Home: 1906 Red Ln Danville PA 17821-8415

PIERCE, JEAN LOIS, elementary school educator; b. Wackesha, Wis., Aug. 20, 1919; d. Louis Thieleman and Else Marg (Bagle) Knocke; children: Daniel Knocke, Caterine Susan. BA in Classical Humanities, U. Wis., Madison, 1946; MA in Latin and Spanish, Wayne State, Detroit. Tchr. Lamphere Jr. High, Madison, Mich.; tchr., dept. head Derby Jr. High., Birmingham, Mich. Writer Majorca Daily Bulletin, Palma de Mallorca, Spain, 1983—95, Island Life Mag., Palma de Mallorca, 2003—; jib sheet Detroit Yacht Club, Detroit, 2002. Author various poetry publ. Organizer Christian Sci. Ch., Palma de Mallorea, 1970—93. Mem.: Mich. Assn. Retired Sch. Personnel, Delta Kappa Gamma. Avocations: reading, boating, travel. Home: 1721 Millard Madison Heights MI 48071

PIERCE, JERRY EARL, publishing executive; b. Hindsdale, Ill., Aug. 3, 1941; s. Earl and Adeline A. (Zaranski) P.; m. Carol Louise Martin, Aug. 15, 1964; children: Patricia, Barbara, Linda. Bradley. BS, U. Ill., 1964. With R.R. Donnelley & Sons, Chgo., 1964-70, Western Pub. Co., Racine, Wis., 1970—, nat. pubs. acct. exec., 1975—. Chair bd. Pierce Sale Co., Inc., Restaurant Equipment World, Inc., Heat Transfer Engring. Inc.; chmn. bd. Tech Industries & Millwork, Inc., 1989-93; pres. B.J. Installation Co., Inc., 1989-91, ROI World Equipment, 1993—; v.p., sec. Savers Clubs Am., Inc.; v.p. Pierce Aviation, 2000—; chmn. adv. bd. Greater Winter Park, Bankfirst Bank, Winter Park, Fla. Chmn. Leadership Trust of Nat. Fedn. Ind. Bus. 1st lt. US Army, 1968—70. Mem.: Nat. Fed. Ind. Bus. Fla. (chmn. safe trust, Small Bus. Person of Year 2006), Goldenrod C. of C. (bd. dirs.), Nat. Bus. Aviation Assn., Food Equipment Distbrs. Assn. (bd. dirs. 1997—98), Food Svc. Cons. Soc., Cleve. Advt. Club, Interlachen Country Club (treas. Winter Pk., Fla.), Ctrl. Fla. Veterans Mem. Found. (bd. dirs.), Ctrl. Fla. Vets. Inc. (pres.). Republican. Episcopalian. Achievements include patents for refrigeration-to-water utility cost control system; invention of E-Commerce business model. Home: 2639 Ultra Vista Dr Maitland FL 32751 Office: 2413 N Forsyth Rd Orlando FL 32807-6455

PIERCE, JESSE R., lawyer; b. Waco, Tex., Feb. 16, 1949; BA, Austin Coll., Sherman, Tex., 1971; JD, U. Tex. Law Sch., 1974. Bar: US Supreme Ct., US Ct. Appeals (5th cir.), US Ct. Appeals (8th cir.), US Ct. Appeals (10th cir.), US Ct. Appeals (11th cir.), US Dist. Ct. (ea. dist.) Tex., US Dist. Ct. (no. dist.) Tex., US Dist. Ct. (so. dist.) Tex., US Dist. Ct. (we. dist.) Tex., cert.: Tex. Bd. Legal Specialization (Civil Trial Law). Ptnr. Clements, O'Neill, Pierce, Wilson & Fulkerson, Houston, Howrey LLP, 2005—06, King & Spalding, Houston, 2006—. Named Tex. Super Lawyer, Law & Politics, 2006, Tex. Monthly mag., 2006; named one of 500 Best Lawyers in Am., Law Dragon mag., 2005. Mem.: State Bar of Tex., Houston Bar Assn., ABA, Order of Coif. Office: King & Spalding 1100 Louisiana Ste 4000 Houston TX 77002-5213 Office Phone: 713-751-3235. Office Fax: 713-751-3290. *

PIERCE, JINA, curator, artist; d. Clair Yoder and Faye Brenneman; children: Jordan Devin, Riley Nate. BA in English, Fresno U., Calif., 1987. Exec. dir., founder Tri Lakes Ctr. Arts, Palmer Lake, Colo., 1997—2000; curator visual arts Sangre de Cristo Arts Ctr., Pueblo, Colo., 2000—. Bd. dirs. Colo. State Fair Art Show, Pueblo; prin. Big Think Art, Pueblo; dir. CSU Gallery. Mennonite. Office: Sangre de Cristo Art Ctr 210 N Santa Fe Pueblo CO 81003

PIERCE, JOHN CHARLES, singer; s. Charles David and Sally Emrich Pierce; m. Alice Katherine Obery, Aug. 11, 1981; children: Melissa Jean, Nathaniel David. MusM, U. Ill., Champaign-Urbana, 1976—82. Heldentenor Brandenburg State Theater, Cottbus, Germany, 1992—2002; asst. prof. music U. Mich., Ann Arbor, 2004—; freelance singer Dortmund, Germany, Darmstadt, Germany, Innsbruck, Austria, Chemnitz, Germany. Singer: (musical) West Side Story, (musicals) Otello, Laca, Hoffmann, Samson, Cavaradossi, Florestan. Choir, soloist First Presbyn. Ch., Saline, Mich., 2004—06. Finalist Regional award, Met. Opera Auditions, 1990; recipient Wagner prize, Liederkranz Competition, NYC, 1992, Max Gruenebaum award, City Cottbus, Germany, 2000. Mem.: Nat. Assn. Tchrs. Singing, Mich. Chpt. (pres. 2006—), Intern. Hans von Buelow Assn. (hon.). Office: Univ Mich Baits Dr Ann Arbor MI Home Phone: 734-944-2344; Office Phone: 734-764-8180. Business E-Mail: jcpierce@umich.edu.

PIERCE, JOHN GERALD (JERRY), lawyer; b. Winter Haven, Fla., Jan. 12, 1937; s. Francis E. and Margaret (Butler) P.; m. Kathleen E., Dec. 1, 1989; children: Kathleen M. Cooke, Nancy A., John Gerald Jr., Michael J. BChemE, U. Fla., Gainesville, 1959, JD with honors, 1965. Bar: Fla. 1966, US Dist. Ct. (mid. dist.) Fla. 1966, US Ct. Appeals (11th cir.) 1983. Assoc. Anderson & Rush, Dean & Lowndes, Orlando, Fla., 1966—68, Arnold, Matheny & Eagen, Orlando, 1968—70; ptnr. Pierce, Lewis & Dolan, Orlando, 1970—74; pvt. practice Orlando, 1974—2002; prin., owner Pierce & Assocs. PL, Orlando, 2003—. Served to 1st lt. US Army, 1959—65. Named Businessman of Yr., Nat. Rep. Congl. Com., 2004. Mem. ABA, Fla. Bar Assn., Orange County Bar Assn. Republican. Roman Catholic. Avocations: golf, boating, skiing. Home: 605 Fox Valley Dr Longwood FL 32779-2417 Office: 800 N Ferncreek Ave Orlando FL 32803-4127 Office Phone: 407-898-4848.

PIERCE, JOHN RANDALL, medical inspector, pediatrician; b. Nashville, May 9, 1947; MD, U. Tenn., 1971. Cert. Pediatrics, 1977, Neonatal-Perinatal Medicine, 1981. Chief Dept. Pediatrics, residency program dir. U.S. Army Med. Corps.; dep. comdr. clin. svcs., dir. med. edn. Walter Reed Army Med. Ctr.; cons. pediatrics US Surgeon Gen.; dep. med. inspector Veterans Health Adminstrn., US Dept. Veterans Affairs, Washington, 2002—04, med. inspector, 2004—. Asst. prof. pediatrics Uniformed Svcs. U. of Health Scis.; historian Walter Reed Soc. Co-author: Yellow Jack: How Yellow Fever Ravaged America and Walter Reed Discovered Its Deadly Secrets, 2005; contbr. articles to profl. jours. Col. med. corps US Army. Decorated Legion of Merit, Meritorious Svc. Medal, Joint Svc. Commendation Medal, Army Commendation Medal, Army Achievement Medal, Order of Mil. Med. Merit Surgeon Gen. Fellow: Am. Acad. Pediatrics. Office: US Dept Vet Affairs Vets Health Adminstrn 810 Vermont Ave NW Washington DC 20420 Office Phone: 202-273-5400.

PIERCE, JOHN THOMAS, physician, industrial hygienist, clinical toxicologist; b. Coffeyville, Kans., Mar. 15, 1949; s. John Gordon and Mary Ellen (McGrath) P.; m. Janet D. Brousseau, Aug. 7, 1981. MPH, U. Okla., 1977, PhD, 1978; MBBS, Internat. U. Health Scis., West Indies, 2004. Assoc. prof. U. North Ala., Florence, 1981-88; assoc. prof., dir. environ. and occupational health Va. Commonwealth U., Richmond, 1988-90; prof., chair dept. industrl. hygiene Cen. Mo. State U., Warrensburg, 1990-92; dir. Field Svcs. divsn. U. Kans. Med. Ctr., Kansas City, 1992—. Author: Industrial Hygiene Program Management, 1999; editor Applied Occupational and Environ. Hygiene, Hospital Safari, 2005 Capt. USNR, 1968-2000. Mem. VFW, Am. Acad. Indsl. Hygiene (local treas. 1993), Am. Acad. Clin. Toxicology, Am. Chem. Soc. (local treas. 1984-87), Am. Coll. Occupl. Environ. Medicine, Am. Bd. Toxicology, Am. Coll. Toxicology, Rotary (Paul Harris fellow), Am. Legion, Vietnam Vets. Am., Cath. War Vets., Sigma Xi, Phi Kappa Phi. Democrat. Roman Catholic.

PIERCE, LAWRENCE WARREN, retired federal judge; b. Phila., Dec. 31, 1924; s. Harold Ernest and Leora (Bellinger) Pierce; m. Wilma Taylor, 1948 (dec. May 1978); m. Cynthia Straker, July 8, 1979; children: Warren Wood, Michael Lawrence, Mark Taylor. BS, St. Joseph's U., Phila., 1948, DHL, 1967; JD, Fordham U., 1951, LLD, 1982, Fairfield U., 1972, Hamilton Coll., 1987, St. John's U., 1990. Bar: N.Y. 1951, U.S. Supreme Ct. 1968. Civil law practice, NYC, 1951—61; asst. dist. atty. Kings County, NYC, 1954—61; dep. police commr. NYC, 1961—63; dir. N.Y. State Divsn. for Youth, Albany, 1963—66; chmn. N.Y. State Narcotic Addiction Control Commn., 1966—70; vis. prof. criminal justice SUNY, Albany, 1970—71; dist. judge U.S. Dist. Ct., So. Dist. N.Y., 1971—81; judge U.S. Fgn. Intelligence Surveillance Ct., Washington, 1979—81; cir. judge U.S. Ct. Appeals 2d Cir., 1981—95; ret., 1995. Dir. Cambodian ct. tng. project

Internat. Human Rights Law Group, 1995. Past bd. dirs. CARE, Havens Fund Soc., Lincoln Hall for Boys, S-R and S.A.R., N.Y. chpts., Cath. Interracial Coun., Practising Law Inst. Mem.: ABA (com. on corr. svc. and facilities 1970—71, alt. observer U.S. Mission to UN 1988—90, site evaluation com., sec. legal edn. 1996—98), Spl. Com. Army Confinement Facilties (Office of Sec. of Army 1970), Urban League, Nat. Bar Assn., Am. Law Inst., Coun. Fgn. Rels.

PIERCE, LISA MARGARET, telecommunications industry executive, marketing professional, educator; b. Nyack, NY, June 2, 1957; d. William and Elizabeth Pierce. BA with honors, Gordon Coll., Wenham, Mass., 1978; MBA, Atkinson Sch., Salem, Oreg., 1982. Campaign mgr. Carter/Mondale, Manchester, Mass., 1976; investigator Dept. Social Svcs., Nyack, 1977-78; paralegal Beverly, Mass., 1978-79; campaign mgr. Reagan Presdl. Primary, Rockland County, NY, 1980; cons. Sidereal, Portland, Oreg., 1981-82; performance analyst Dept. Social Svcs., Pomona, NY, 1982; market analyst Momentum Techs., Parsippany, NJ, 1983; cons. Booz Allen & Hamilton, Florham Park, NJ, 1984, Deloitte-Touche, Morristown, NJ, 1985; market rschr., forecaster AT&T, Bedminster, NJ, 1985-87, asst. pvt. line product mgr., 1987-89, Integrated Svcs. Digital Network product mgr., 1989-93; dir. Telecom. Rsch. Assocs., St. Marys, Kans., 1994—98; v.p., rsch. fellow Giga Info. Group/Forrester Rsch., Cambridge, Mass., 1998—. Panelist, contbr. TeleCom. Assn., San Diego and Seattle, Internat. Comm. Assn., Atlanta, Ea. Comm. Forum, NY, Nat. Engrng. Consortium, Chgo., Super Comm., Soc. Telecom. Consultants, MPLS Forum, Mid Atlantic Venture Assn., GSA Fed. Telecom. Svc. Forums, VoiceCon, EVDO Forum, others; contbr. NY State ISDN/Internat User's Group; feature commentator AP Adio, Nat. Pub. Radio (All Things Considered and MarketWatch), Pub. Broadcasting Svc. Nightly Bus. Report, MSNBC, CNN and CNBC, Radio Wall Street, CBS Evening News Columnist Network World, 2001—02, Bus. Comm. Rev., 2002—. Named one of Top 10 Most Influential IT Analysts, Tech. Mktg. Mag., 2002, 2003; grantee in field. Mem.: IEEE. Home Phone: 941-539-6670. Personal E-mail: lmpierce@att.net. Business E-Mail: lpierce@forrester.com.

PIERCE, MARY, professional tennis player; b. Montreal, Que., Can., Jan. 15, 1975; d. Jim and Yannick Pierce. Profl. Tennis Player, 1989—. Victories include Comeback Player of the Yr., 1997, Australian Open (singles), 1995, French Open (singles & doubles), 2000, Wimbledon (doubles), 2005; 17 WTA Career Singles Titles, 10 WTA Career Doubles Titles. Office: IMG Ctr 1360 E 9th St Ste 100 Cleveland OH 44114

PIERCE, MARY E., retired elementary school educator, public relations consultant; b. Chgo. d. Henry Harris and Eva Irene (Hanes) P. BE, Chgo. Tchrs. Coll., 1944. One room sch. tchr. Will County, Monee, Ill.; tchr. 5th grade Peotone (Ill.) Sch. Dist.; tchr. elem. and jr. h.s. Steger (Ill.) Sch. Dist., chair lang. arts dept.; ret., 1979; chair sch. improvement plan; pub. rels. cons. Former pres. Steger Edn. Assn.; chmn. bd. dirs. #194 Employee Credit Union, Steger, 1972-95. Village clk. Village of Richton Park, 1992—; pres. Friends of Libr., Richton Park, 1980-2007, v.p.; bd. dirs. So. Suburban Cancer Soc., Tinley Pk., Ill., 1994—, S.E. Chpt. Ill. Credit Union, Calumet City, Ill., 1994-95. Recipient Cmty. Svc. award Cook County Sheriff's Office, Chgo., Merit award S.E. chpt. Ill. Credit Union League. Mem. Delta Kappa Gamma Soc. (Lambda State Beta Beta chpt. treas. 1979-2003). Avocation: golf. Home: 22147 Karlov Ave Richton Park IL 60471-1227

PIERCE, MICHAEL NORMAN, internist; b. NYC, May 1, 1955; s. Samuel and Ingeborg Pierce. BA in Biology, SUNY, Binghamton, 1977; MD, U. Vt., 1982. Diplomate Am. Bd. Internal Medicine. Intern, gen. surg. resident L.A. County/U. So. Calif. Med. Ctr., LA, 1982—84; intern, resident in internal medicine Calif.-Pacific Med. Ctr., San Francisco, 1985—88; attending physician St. Francis Meml. Hosp., San Francisco, 1989—96, Montefiore Med. Ctr., East Elmhurst, NY, 1997—98, St. Barnabas Hosp./CHS/HHC, East Elmhurst, 1998—2001; asst. attending physician St. Luke's Roosevelt Hosp. Ctr., NYC, 2002—05, assoc. attending physician, 2005; dir. HIV medicine and internal medicine attending All Med Med. and Rehab. NY, 2006. Chair Spring conf. St. Luke's Roosevelt Hosp. Ctr., 2003; judge, mem. abstract rev. bd. for resident's poster competition NY Downstate ACP-ASIM sci. meetings, 1997—2007; asst. attending physician St. Luke's Roosevelt Hosp. Ctr., NYC, 2002—04, mem. CME med. bd. com., 2002—05, key faculty, internal medicine residency program; asst. clin. prof. medicine Columbia U. Coll. Physicians and Surgeons, NYC, 2002—05; active HIV mgmt. preceptorship program Johns Hopkins U. Sch. Medicine, Balt., 2001; mem. Infectious Disease Soc. Am., Infectious Disease Soc. Am. HIV Med. Assn.; HIV med. specialist State of NY; prin. investigator Pfizer clin. trial of Maravaroc. Mem. editl. bd. Johns Hopkins U. Sch. Medicine Advanced Studies in Medicine, 2002—. Recipient Physician's Recognition award, AMA, 1991—; Pharm. Mfrs. Assn. grantee, 1979. Fellow: ACP (com. on med. students 2001—), Soc. Gen. Internal Medicine; mem.: AMA, N.Y. County Med. Soc., Med. Soc. State N.Y. (surveyor-reviewer hosp. CME programs 1998—, mem. com. on edn.). Office Phone: 718-292-0100. E-mail: mnpny@aol.com.

PIERCE, MILDRED LOUISE, librarian; b. Fulton County, Ga., Nov. 30, 1928; d. John Oliver Pierce and Florence Idella (Carr) Sansted; m. Harry Eugene Springer, Oct. 17, 1967; 1 child, Jesse Ladd. BS in Edn., SUNY, Geneseo, 1951; MA in Librarianship, U. Denver, 1955. Lic. Episcopalian lay reader, lay preacher. Libr. asst. SUNY, New Paltz, 1951; elem. libr. Hastings Pub. Schs., Hastings-on-the-Hudson, NY, 1951; libr. grad. student aide Denver Pub. Libr., 1954—55; children's bookmobile libr. Alexander Mitchell Pub. Libr., Aberdeen, SD, 1955—56; libr. Mineral County Sch. Dist., Hawthorne, Nev., 1956—64; adult edn. tchr. Clark County Sch. Dist., Las Vegas, 1964—65; tech. libr. RADSAFE, Reynolds Elec. and Engrng. Co., Mercury, Nev., 1965—67; reference cons. Mother Lode Libr. Sys., Auburn, Calif., 1967—68; dir. Tech. Info. Svc., Hawthorne, 1976—; dep. gen. conv., commn. liturgy and music Domestic and Fgn. Missionary Soc. of Protestant in the Episcopal Ch. of U.S.A., 2003. Author: Nevada Rockfinder, 1970; columnist An Ounce of Prevention, 1973—75; editor: Wordwebs, 1979—81. Founder, trustee Walker-Wassuk Arts Alliance, Hawthorne, 1977; founder trustee Preservation Mineral County Courthouse and Flag Chowder and Marching Soc., 1982; pres. Desert Dance Arts Theater, 1989—; candidate Nev. Senate, 1976, Nev. Assembly, 1978, 1980; gen. conv. dep. Episcopal Ch., 2003, mem. commn. on liturgy and music, 2004—. Mem.: NEA, ALA, States Assn., Am. Assn. Sch. Libr., Mineral County Tchrs. Assn., Nev. State Tchrs. Assn., Nev. Alliance for the Arts, Mineral County Coun. on Alcohol and Drug Abuse, Kappa Delta Pi. Republican. Episcopalian. Home: 674 I St PO Box 1721 Hawthorne NV 89415-1721 Office: Tech Info Svc PO Box 1721 Hawthorne NV 89415-1721 E-mail: tis@sisna.com.

PIERCE, MORTON ALLEN, lawyer; b. Liberec, Czechoslovakia, June 25, 1948; m. Nancy Washor, Dec. 14, 1975 (dec.); children: Matthew J., Nicholas L. BA, Yale Coll., 1970; JD, U. Pa., 1974; postgrad., Oxford U., 1974-75. Bar: N.Y. 1975. Assoc. Reid & Priest, NYC, 1975-83, ptnr., 1983-86, Dewey Ballantine, NYC, 1986—, vice-chmn., 2002—03, co-chmn., 2003—05, chmn., 2005—. Mem. mgmt. com. 1988—, chmn. corp. dept., 1999—, chmn., mergers and acquisitions group, 1990—, mem. exec. com., 2001—. Contbr. articles to profl. jours. Mem. ABA (chmn. subcom. on internat. securities matters 1985-91, adv. com. to fed. regulation of securities com. 1991-2000, task force on rev. of the fed. securities law 1991-2000), Assn. of the Bar of the City of N.Y. (securities law com. 1988-91, chmn. subcom. on securities and exch. commn. enforcement matters 1990-91), Internat. Bar Assn. (com. on securities transactions), Legal Aid Soc. (bd. dirs.), Gordon A. Rich Found. (bd. dirs.). Home: 188 E 76th St New York NY 10021-2826 Office: Dewey Ballantine LLP 1301 Ave Of The Americas New York NY 10019-6022 Office Phone: 212-259-6640. Office Fax: 212-259-6333. Business E-Mail: mpierce@dbllp.com.

PIERCE, NAOMI ELLEN, biology professor, researcher; b. Denver, Oct. 19, 1954; d. Arthur Preble and Ruiko (Ishizaka) P; m. Andrew James Berry, Mar. 9, 1996; children: Kate Clark Berry, Megan Elizabeth Berry. BS, Yale U., 1976; PhD, Harvard U., 1983. Fulbright postdoctoral fellow Griffith U., Brisbane, Australia, 1983-84; rsch. lectr. Christ Ch., U. Oxford, Eng., 1984-86; asst. prof. Princeton U., N.J., 1986-91; Sydney A. and John H. Hessel prof. biology, curator lepidoptera Harvard U. and Harvard Mus. Comparative Zoology, Cambridge, Mass., 1991—. Contbr. articles to profl. jours. MacArthur Found. fellow, Chgo., 1988-93. Fellow Harvard Soc. of Fellows (sr.). Office: Harvard U 26 Oxford St Cambridge MA 02138-2902

PIERCE, PATRICIA ANN, retired university administrator; b. Harriman, Tenn., Feb. 13, 1949; d. Fred Ernest and Lela Nora (Jones) P.; m. Jacky Albert Goss, Sept. 21, 1991; children: Wesley Matthew Goss, James Michael Goss. BS, U. Tenn., 1973; cert., Bryn Mawr Coll., 1991. Cert. secondary edn. tchr., Tenn.; cert. diversity trainer. Field rep. Tenn. Human Rights Commn., Nashville, 1973-76, compliance dir., 1976-78; assoc. dir.Opportunity Devel. Ctr. Vanderbilt U., Nashville, 1978-81, dir., 1981—2007. Cons. Pierce Consulting, Nashville, 1985—; presenter in field. Contbr. articles to profl. jours. Chair Mayor's Adv. Com. for People with Disabilities, Nashville, 1988-89; pres. bd. dirs. League for Hearing Impaired, Nashville, 1994-95, Nashville YWCA, 1996-98; spkr. Nat. Intramural Recreation Sports Assn., Nashville, 1994; del. People to People Internat. Learning Disability Del., Beijing, 1995; nongovtl. rep. NGO Forum, 4th World Conf. on Women, Beijing, 1995; People to People Internat. del. to Cuba, 2003; active Gov. Adv. Com. on Equal Employment Opportunity, 1992-96; mem. Leadership Nashville, 2003; commr. Tenn. Human Rights Commn., 2005—; bd. dirs. Internat. ATHENA, 2004—. Recipient Jean Harris award Rotary 1998, Mary Jane Werthern award Vanderbilt 1997, Nashville ATHENA award, 2003, Excellence and Equity award Tenn. Econ. Coun., 2006; named to Leadership America 2000; inducted in Acad. of Women of Achievement, 2002. Mem.: Women in Higher Edn. in Tenn. (historian 1999—, pres.), CABLE Profl. Womens Networking Orgn. (pres. 1991—92, historian 2000—, Promote Women award 1993), Am. Coun. Edn. (state facilitator 1994—95, bd. mem. 1994—, mem. Tenn. planning com., Outstandging Contbns. cert. 1995), Internat. Assn. Higher Edn. and Disability (pres. 1988—89, Ronald Blosser Dedicated Svc. award 1989), Internat. Women's Forum, Women's Polit. Caucus (v.p. 2001—02), Women in Numbers (bd. mem. 2000—, pres. 2003). Avocations: hiking, tennis, photography. Home: 954 Caney Creek Rd Harriman TN 37748 E-mail: ppierce954@comcast.net.

PIERCE, PAUL ANTHONY, professional basketball player; b. Oakland, Calif., Oct. 13, 1977; s. Lorraine Hosey. Student in Crime and Delinquency Studies, U. Kans., Lawrence, 1995—98. Forward-guard Boston Celtics, 1998—. Mem. USA Basketball Men's Sr. Nat. Team, 2002, 2006—. Founder The Truth Fund, 2002—. Named to All-Rookie First Team, NBA, 1999, Ea. Conf. All-Star Team, 2002—06; recipient Home Team Cmty. Svc. award, 2002. Achievements include leading the NBA in scoring (2144 points), 2001-02. Avocation: music. Office: Boston Celtics 226 Causeway St 4th Fl Boston MA 02114-4720

PIERCE, PHILIP SARGENT, clinical psychologist; b. Medford, Mass., Aug. 25, 1941; s. Elmer Grandville and Pauline Dudley Pierce; m. Rae Foster, Oct. 10, 1967; children: Jennifer, Jessica, John, Jill. BA, U. Maine, 1963; MA, U. N.H., 1965; PhD, U. S.C., 1971. Lic. psychologist, Maine. Clin. psychologist Pineland Ctr., Pownal, Maine, 1965-77, Togus (Maine) Vets. Med. and Regional Office Ctr., 1977-83, sr. psychologist, 1983—, acting chief mental health svc., 2003. Vis. prof. psychology U. So. Maine, Portland, 1971-72; asst. prof. psychology St. Joseph's Coll., North Windham, Maine, 1972-78, U. Maine, Augusta, 1977-78; clin. assoc. psychology U. Maine, Orono, 1981—; lectr. on psychology grad. program in sch. and health psychology U. New Eng., Biddeford Pool, Maine; adj. clin. faculty mem. Antioch New Eng. Grad. Sch., 1996-2000; cons., spkr., presenter in field; northeastern regional exam. coord. Am. Bd. Clin. Psychology, 1993-95, nat. credential rev. officer, 1995-97; mem. Am. Bd. Profl. Psychology, Inc. Contbr. numerous articles to profl. jours. Trustee Falmouth Congl. Ch., 1981-84, chmn. bd. trustees, 1983-84, sec. mem. giving and investments subcom., 1982-84, mem. Christian enlistment com., 1985-88, chmn., 1987-88, mem. nominations com., 1989-92, chmn. ch. coun., 1990-93, mem. bylaws com., 1994-97; bd. dirs. Falmouth Little League, 1984-90, coach, 1983-85, treas., 1984-90, umpire, 1983-93; bd. dirs. Maine Running Hall of Fame, 1994—, vice chmn., 1995-96, chmn., 1996-2004; bd. dirs. Maine Sports Hall of Fame, 1994—2004, 1st v.p., 1995-2001, chmn. honors and selection com., 1996-2002, pres. 2001-02. With U.S. Army, 1966 Fellow APA (divsn. newsletter editor 1981-84, exec. bd. 1981-82, pres. 1985-86, chmn. fellow com. 1990-96, coun. of reps. 1977-79, coun. liaison to Maine Psychol. Assn. 1995-97, coun. reps. for Maine and Vt., 1998-2001, chmn. rural caucus), Maine Psychol. Assn. (newsletter editor 1971-74, mem. exec. bd. 1971-88, pres. 1975-77, chmn. ethics com. 1992-98, policy coun. 1992-2002), Am. Psychol. Soc., Acad. Clin. Psychology (bd. dirs. 1993-2002, v.p. 1998-2002); mem. AAAS, N.Y. Acad. Sci., Assn. VA Lead Psychologists (chmn. gero-psychology task force 1983-84, chmn. APA-VA interaction task force 1984-85), Soc. Maine Psychologists (chmn. continuing edn. com. 1990-92, 98-2000, pres. 1992-94, treas. 1994-98), Maine Soc. Forensic Psychologists, Maine Track Club (sec. 1985-86, v.p. 1986-87, pres. 1987-88, race dir. 1984-2006). Democrat. Avocation: long distance running. Home: 79 Waites Landing Rd Falmouth ME 04105 E-mail: philip.pierce@med.va.gov.

PIERCE, PONCHITTA ANN, TV host, television producer, journalist, writer, consultant; b. Chgo., Aug. 5, 1942; d. Alfred Leonard and Nora (Vincent) P. Student, Cambridge U., Eng., summer 1962; BA in Journalism cum laude, U. So. Calif., 1964; DHL, Franklin Pierce Coll., 1986. Asst. editor Ebony mag., 1964-65, assoc. editor, 1965-67; editor Ebony mag. (N.Y.C. office), 1967-68; chief N.Y.C. editl. bur. Johnson Pub. Co., 1967-68; corr. news divsn. CBS, NYC, 1968-71; contbg. editor McCall's mag., 1971-77; editl. cons. Philps Stokes Fund, 1971-78; staff writer Reader's Digest, 1976-77, roving editor, 1977-80; co-prodr., host Today in New York, Sta. WNBC-TV, NYC, 1982-87; freelance writer, TV broadcaster, media cons. Co-host Sunday WNBC-TV, 1973—77, The Prime of Your Life, 1977—80; author: Status of American Women Journalists on Magazines, 1968, History of the Phelps Stokes Fund 1911-1972; contbg. editor: Earth Times Monthly, 2002. Del. to WHO Conf., Geneva, 1973; bd. dirs. Morris-Jumel Mansion, Housing Enterprise for the Less Privileged, Third St. Music Sch. Settlement, Inner-City Scholarship Fund, Sta. WNET-TV; active Columbia Presbyn. Health Scis. Adv. Coun.; bd. dirs. U. So. Calif. Ctr. on Pub. Diplomacy, Cuban Artists Fund. Recipient Penney-Mo. mag. award excellence women's journalism, 1967; John Russwurm award NYC Urban League, 1968; AMITA Nat. Achievement award in comm., 1974 Mem. NATAS, Women in Comm. (Woman Behind the News award 1969, Nat. Headliner award 1970), Fgn. Policy Assn. (mem. bd. govs., bd. dirs.), Women's Fgn. Policy Group, Coun. on Fgn. Rels., Calif. Scholarship Fedn. (life), Econs. Club N.Y., Lotos Club, Nat. Honor Soc., Mortar Bd.

PIERCE, RICHARD HARRY, oceanographer; PhD in Chem. Oceanography, U. R.I., 1973. Sr. scientist, dir. Ctr. for Eco-Toxicology, Mote Marine Lab., Sarasota, Fla. Office: Mote Marine Lab 1600 Ken Thompson Pkwy Sarasota FL 34236-1096 E-mail: rich@mote.org.

PIERCE, ROGER ARNOLD, II, pharmacist, director; b. Dover, NH, July 30, 1948; s. Roger A. Pierce and Helen A. Simmons; m. Doris M. Phaneuf, July 9, 1977; children: Michael R., Jennifer C. BA in Zoology, U. NH, Durham, 1971; BS in Pharmacy, U. RI, Kingston, 1973—76; MS in Health Svcs. Adminstrn., Ctrl. Mich. U., Mt. Pleasant, 1987—88. Registered pharmacist Maine, 2007, NH, 2007, RI, 2007. Pharm. mfr. sales rep. Eli Lilly Co., Harford, Conn., 1976—77; retail pharmacist State Pharmacy, Inc., Manchester, NH, 1977—80; hosp. staff pharmacist Dept. Vet. Affairs Med. Ctr., Manchester, 1980—82, Salem, 1982—85, pharmacy mgmt. trainee, hosp. staff pharmacist Richmond, 1985—87, asst. chief pharmacy svc., 1987—89, chief pharmacy svc. Long Beach, Calif., 1994—97, chief support svcs. health care grp., 1997—99; assoc. chief pharmacy svc. Edward Hines, Jr. Va. Hosp., Hines, Ill., 1989—92; regional clin. pharmacy mgr. Dept. Veterans Affairs Ctrl. Region Office, Ann Arbor, Mich., 1992—94; dir. Dept. Vet. Affairs. Consol. Mail Outpatient Pharmacy, LA, 1999—2005, Dept. Vet. Affairs Consol. Mail Outpatient Pharmacy, Tucson, 2005—. Chmn. pharmacy & nursing com. Va. Med. Ctr., Salem, 1985—87; pres. ctrl. Va. chpt. Fed. Pharmacist Assn., Richmond, 1986—88; clin. practitioner tchr. VCU Med. Coll. Va. Sch. Pharmacy, Richmond, 1988—89; chmn. lic. pharmacist profl. standards bd. Edward Hines Jr. Hosp., 1990—92; affiliate asst. prof., dept. of pharmacy practice Purdue U., Chgo., 1990—92; clin. asst. prof. pharmacy practice U. Ill., Chgo., 1990—93; chmn. vet. affairs ctrl. region lic. pharmacists profl. standards bd. Edward Hines, Jr. Hosp., Hines, 1991—92; cons. to bd. dirs. Vet. Affairs Ctrl. Region Consol. Mail Outpatient Pharmacy Establishment Project, Leavenworth, Kans., 1992—94; adj. asst. prof. pharmacy practice U. So. Calif. Sch. Pharmacy, 1995—2005; chariman vets. integrated svc. netowrk 22 licensed pharmacist profl. standards bd. Veterans Integrated Svc. Network, LA, 1999—2005; chmn. nat. vet. affairs cmop pharmacy technicans profl. standards bd. Nat. Vet. Affairs Consol. Mail Outpatient Pharmacy Network, Leavenworth, Kans., 2005—; mem. Nat. Vet. Affairs Licensed Pharmacist Profl. Standards Bd., DC, 2006—. Contbr. articles to profl. jours. Recipient Superior Performance award, 1984, Past Pres. award, Ctrl. Va. Chpt. Fed. Pharmacists Assn., 1989, Exceptional Performance award, 1989, Spl. Contbn. award, 1990, Dirs. Commendation Exceptional Performance award, 1991, Spl. Contbn. award, 1991, Outstanding Performance award, 1991, 1993, Superior Performance award, 1995—96, Spl. Contbn. award, 1998, 2000, 2002—03, 2006, Nat. Va. Hammer award, 1999, Superior Performance award, 2004, Exec. Career Field Performance award, 2005—06. Mem.: Assn. Mil. Surgeons of US, Fed. Pharmacists Assn., Mich. Chpt., Am. Pharmacists Assn., Fed. Pharmacists Assn. (pres. ctrl. Va. chpt. 1986—88, Past Pres. award 1989), Am. Soc. Health-Sys. Pharmacists, Leadership Va. Alumni Assn. (life), Nat. Ski Patrol (patrolman 1970—76), Kappa Psi Pharm. Frat. Avocations: hiking, hunting, fishing, golf, skiing. Office: Vet Affairs Consolidated Mail Outpatient Pharmacy 3675 E Britannia Dr Tucson AZ 85706-5041 Home Phone: 520-721-3284. Office Fax: 520-209-3040. Business E-Mail: roger.pierce@va.gov.

PIERCE, RUDOLPH F., lawyer; b. Boston, Aug. 12, 1942; s. Fred D. and Edna M. (Owens) P.; m. Mildred C. Pierce, Apr. 29, 2000; children from previous marriage: Kristen, Khari. BA, Hampton Inst., 1967; JD, Harvard U., 1970. Bar: Mass. 1970, DC 2002. Ptnr. Crane, Inker & Oteri, Boston, 1972-75, Keating, Perretta & Pierce, Boston, 1975-76; magistrate U.S. Dist. Ct. Mass., Boston, 1976-79; justice Mass. Superior Ct., Boston, 1979-85; ptnr. LeBoeuf, Lamb, Leiby & MacRae, Boston; dir., bus. & securities litig. Goulston & Storrs, Boston & Washington. Chmn. bd. dir. Nat. Inst. Trial Advocacy. Contbr. articles to profl. jours. Trustee Children's Hosp., Boston, 1986—, Inst. Healthcare Improvement; past chmn. New Eng. Aquarium. Fellow Am. Coll. Trial Lawyers; mem. Internat. Acad. Trial Lawyers, ABA, Mass. Bar Assn. (bd. dels.), Boston Bar Assn. (pres. 1989-90). Office: Goulston & Storrs Ste 1100 2001 K St NW Washington DC 20006 Office Phone: 202-721-1153. Business E-Mail: rpierce@goulstonstorrs.com.

PIERCE, SHAYN, biomedical engineer, educator; PhD in Biomedical Engrng., U. Va., 2002. Asst. prof. biomedical engrng. U. Va. Contbr. articles to profl. jours. Named one of Top 100 Young Innovators, MIT Tech. Review, 2004; recipient Rita Shaffer Young Investigator award, Biomedical Engrng. Soc., 2004. Office: U Va Dept Biomedical Engrng Box 800759 Health System Rm 2324 Charlottesville VA 22908

PIERCE, SHELBY CRAWFORD, oil industry executive, consultant; b. May 26, 1932; s. William Shelby and Iris Mae (Smith) Pierce; m. Marguerite Ann Grado, Apr. 2, 1954; children: Cynthia Dawn, Melissa Carol. BSEE, Lamar U., Beaumont, Tex., 1956; grad. program for sr. execs., MIT, 1980. With Amoco Oil Co., Texas City Refinery, 1956—, elec. engr., elec. foreman, area foreman, 1956—60, zone supr., gen. foreman, maintenance, 1961—67, oper. supt., 1967—69, coord. results mgmt., 1969—72; dir. results mgmt. Amoco Oil Co. Corp. Hdqs., Chgo., 1972-75; mgr. ops. Amoco Oil Co., Whiting (Ind.) Refinery, 1975—76, asst. refinery mgr., 1977-79; dir. crude replacement program Amoco Oil Co. Corp. Hdqs., Chgo., 1979-81, mgr. corp. refining and transp. engring., 1981—91, gen. mgr. engring. and constrn., 1992, v.p. internat. bus. devel., 1993-94, ret., 1994. Pres., dir. Amoco Eurasia Oil Co., Amoco Mex. Oil Co., Amoco India, Inc., Amoco Tech. Assistance Co., Trinidad; chmn., dir. Amoco Orient Oil Co.; v.p. Amoco Corp. Devel. Co., Latin Am., 1994; pres. Pierce Cons. Svc., 1995—; CEO, pres. Environ. Constrn. Co., 1996—98; mem. steering com. contractor safety U.S. Dept. Labor, 1989. Trustee Lamar U. Found., 1994—. Mem.: AIChE (mem. exec. bd. 1985—89, chmn. engrng. constrn. contracting divsn. 1988, Divsn. Man of Yr. award 1995), N.W. Ind. Bus. Roundtable (organizer and user coun. chmn. 1986, chmn. exec. bd. 1986—87), The Bus. Roundtable (constrn. com., adv. bd., chmn. constrn. cost effectiveness task force 1992—94), Constrn. Industry Inst. (chmn. Bus. Roundtable coun., mem. strategic planning com. 1991—93), Flossmoor Country Club, Sigma Tau. Republican. Methodist. Home and Office: 1715 Brookwood Dr Flossmoor IL 60422-1823 Office Phone: 708-798-4498. Office Fax: 708-957-4995. Business E-Mail: shelbypierce@msn.com.

PIERCE, STEPHEN D., oceanographer, researcher; s. Norton T. and Alice Davis Pierce; m. Anne E. Minnich, Dec. 31, 1994. PhD, Oreg. State U., Corvallis, 1998. Rsch. assoc. Oreg. State U., Corvallis, 1998—. Contbr. articles to profl. jours. Mem.: Am. Geophys. Union.

PIERCE, SUSAN RESNECK, academic administrator, literature educator, consultant; b. Janesville, Wis., Feb. 6, 1943; d. Elliott Jack and Dory (Block) Resneck; 1 child, Alexandra Siegel. BA, Wellesley Coll., 1965; MA, U. Chgo., 1966; PhD, U. Wis., 1972. Lectr. U. Wis., Rock County, 1970-71; from asst. prof. to prof. English Ithaca (N.Y.) Coll., 1973-82, chmn. dept., 1976-79; program officer Nat. Endowment for Humanities, 1982-83, asst. dir., 1983-84; dean Henry Kendall Coll. Arts and Scis. U. Tulsa, 1984-90; v.p. acad. affairs, prof. English Lewis and Clark Coll., Portland, Oreg., 1990-92; pres. U. Puget Sound, Tacoma, 1992—2003, Boca Raton Comty. Hosp. Found., 2004—05; pvt. practice, 2005—; sr. cons. Academic Search, 2006—. Vis. assoc. prof. Princeton (N.J.) U., 1979; bd. dirs. Janet Elson Scholarship Fund, 1984-1990, Tulsa Edn. Fund, Phillips Petroleum Scholarship Fund, 1985-90, Okla. Math. & Sci. High Sch., 1984-90, Hillcrest Med. Ctr., 1988-90, Portland Opera, 1990-92, St. Joseph's Hosp., 1992—, Seattle Symphony, 1993—; cons. U. Oreg., 1985, Drury Coll., Springfield, Mo., 1986; mem. Middle States and N. Cen. Accreditation Bds.; mem. adv. com. Fed. Women's Program, NEH, 1982-83; participant Summit Meeting on Higher Edn., Dept. Edn., Washington, 1985; speaker, participant numerous ednl. meetings, sems., commencements; chair Frederick Ness Book Award Com. Assn. Am. Colls., 1986; mem. award selection com. Dana Found., 1986, 87; mem. Acad.

Affairs Council, Univ. Senate, dir. tchr. edn., chmn. adv. group for tchr. preparation, ex-officio mem. all Coll. Arts and Scis. coms. and Faculty Council on Internat. Studies, all U. Tulsa; bd. dirs. Am. Conf. Acad. Deans; bd. trustees Hillcrest Med. Ctr.; participant Aspen Inst. Md. 1999, Annapolis Group Media Roundtable, 1996, Harvard Seminar, 1992; former bd. dirs. Assn. Am. Colls. and Univs., 1989-92, Am. Conf. of Academic Deans, 1988-91, Am. Assn. Colls., 1989-92. Author: The Moral of the Story, 1982, also numerous essays, jour. articles, book sects., book revs.; co-editor: Approaches to Teaching "Invisible Man"; reader profl. jours. Bd. dirs. Arts and Humanities Coun., Tulsa, 1984-90, Mizener Pk., 2004-; trustee Hillcrest Hosp., Tulsa, 1986-90; mem. cultural series com., community rels. com. Jewish Fedn., Tulsa, 1986-90; bd. dirs. Tulsa chpt. NCCJ, 1986-90, Kemper Mus. 1996—, Seattle Symphony, 1993-96, St. Joseph Hosp., 1992-93, Portland Opera, 1990-92, Ctr. for Arts, Boca Raton, 2004—. Recipient Best Essay award Arix. Quar., 1979, Excellence in Teaching award N.Y. State Edn. Council, 1982, Superior Group Service award NEH, 1984, other teaching awards; Dana scholar, Ithaca Coll., 1980-81; Dana Research fellow, Ithaca Coll., 82-83; grantee Inst. for Ednl. Affairs, 1980, Ford Found., 1987, NEH, 1989. Mem. MLA (adv. com. on job market 1973-74), South Ctrl. MLA, NIH (subcom. on college drinking), Assn. Governing Bds. (coun. of pres.), Nat. Inst. on Alcohol Abuse (presl. advisory group), Soc. for Values in Higher Edn., Assn. Am. Colls. (bd. dirs.), Am. Conf. Acad. Deans (bd. dirs. 1988-91), Coun. of Presidents, Assn. Governing Bds., The Annapolis Group (mem. exec. com.), Phi Beta Kappa, Phi Kappa Phi, Phi Gamma Kappa. Office Phone: 561-212-5103. Business E-Mail: srpconsulting@adelphia.net.

PIERCE, TAMORA, writer; b. South Connellsville, Pa., Dec. 13, 1954; d. Wayne Franklin Pierce and Jacqueline Sparks; m. Timothy Erving Liebe, Dec. 14, 1985. BA, U. Pa., 1977. Data collector Office Assessment, Kingston, NY, 1976—77; sec. Office Town Assessor, Hardenburgh and Denning, 1977—78; housemother McAuley Home for Girls, Buhl, Idaho, 1978—79; lit. agt. asst. Harold Ober Assocs., NYC, 1979—83; sec. Chase Manhattan Bank, NYC, 1983—89, Joseph Conklin, NYC, 1990—92; freelance writer NYC, 1992—. Author: Alanna: The First Adventure, 1983, In the Hand of the Goddess, 1984, The Woman Who Rides Like A Man, 1986, Lioness Rampant, 1988, Wild Magic, 1992, Wolf-Speaker, 1994, The Emperor Mage, 1995, The Realms of the Gods, 1996, Sandry's Book, 1997, Tris's Book, 1998, Daja's Book, 1998, Briar's Book, 1999, First Test, 1999, Plain Magic in Flights of Fantasy, 1999, Magic Steps, 2000, Page, 2000, Testing in Lost and Found, 2000, Street Magic, 2001, Squire, 2001, Folquin's Folly in Disney Adventures, 2001, Elder Brother in Half Human, 2001, Cold Fire, 2002, Lady Knight, 2002, Shatterglass, 2003, Trickster's Choice, 2003, Trickster's Queen, 2004, The Will Of The Empress, 2005, The Hidden Girl in Dreams and Visions, 2006, Huntress in Firebirds Rising, 2006, Terrier in 2006, 2006; co-author: White Tiger, 2007, Melting Stones, 2007; contbr. articles to profl. jours. and the Ultimate Book Guide; narrator, dir. (CD) Full Cast Audio Books; co-editor: Young Warriors, 2005, Student of Ostriches in Young Warriors, 2005. Mem. Greenpeace, 2001, World Wildlife Fedn., 1998—, Internat. Wolf Ctr., Ely, Minn., 1998—, N.Y. Ctr. Wildlife Conservation, NYC, 1997—. Recipient Edward E. Smith Meml. Skylark award, Boskone 42, 2005, Lit. Lights award, Boston Pub. Libr., 2006. Mem.: ACLU, Soc. Childrens Book Writers and Illustrators, Sci. Fiction and Fantasy Writers Am., The Authors Guild, Amnesty Internat. Avocations: audio theatre and books, military and civil history, wildlife, gemology. Personal E-mail: tampierce@aol.com.

PIERCE, THRESIA KORTE (TISH PIERCE), primary school educator; b. Maize, Kans. d. Herman and Marie Adeline (Lubbers) Korte; children: Judith, John, Mark. BS, Friends U., 1955; MS, U. Nev., Las Vegas, 1978. Cert. tchr., Nev., Nev. Life Ins. lic. Office worker Internat. Trust Co., Denver, Colo., 1951, Motor Equipment Co., Wichita, Kans., 1952-53; tchr. Wichita Pub. Schs., 1960-69, Clark County Sch. Dist., Las Vegas, Nev., 1970-2000. Author short stories; contbr. articles to profl. jours. Senator Clark County Edn. Assn., Clark County Classroom Tchrs. Nominee Wichita Women of Yr., 1967. Mem. NEA, Epsilon Sigma Delta (v.p. 1962). bd. dirs. Kansas Newman U., Wichita, 1966-68. Home: Bldg 6 Unit 1106 1600 S Valley View Blvd Las Vegas NV 89102-0547

PIERCE, WILLIAM SCHULER, cardiac surgeon; b. Wilkes-Barre, Pa., Jan. 12, 1937; s. William Harold and Doris Louis (Schuler) P.; m. Peggy Jayne Stone, June 12, 1965; children: William Stone, Jonathan Drew. BS, Lehigh U., 1958; MD, U. Pa., 1962. Intern U. Pa., 1962—63; resident in surgery Hosp. U. Pa., 1963—70; asst. prof. M.S. Hershey Med. Ctr., Pa. State U. Coll. Medicine, Hershey, 1970—73, assoc. prof., 1973—77, prof. surgery, 1977—, chief divsn. cardiothoracic surgery, 1991—95; assoc. chmn. dept. surgery, dir. rsch., dept. surgery, 1995—97. Contbr. over 300 articles to profl. jours. With USPHS, 1965—67. Fellow: ACS; mem.: AAAS, AMA, Soc. Clin. Surgery., Am. Surg. Assn., Soc. Univ. Surgeons, So. Pa. Assn. Thoracic Surgery, Inst. Medicine, Assn. Acad. Surgery, Am. Heart Assn., Soc. Vascular Surgery, Am. Soc. Artificial Internal Organs, Internat. Cardiovascular Soc. Achievements include invention of inventor cardiac valve, blood pump. Office: Milton S Hershey Med Ctr PO Box 850 Hershey PA 17033-0850 Office Phone: 717-531-8328. Business E-Mail: wpierce@psu.edu.

PIERCY, GORDON CLAYTON, bank executive, educator; b. Takoma Park, Md., Nov. 23, 1944; s. Gordon Clayton and Dorothy Florence (Brummer) Piercy; m. Roberta Margaret Walton, 1985; children: Elizabeth Anne, Kenneth Charles, Virginia Walton, Zachary Taylor Walton. BS, Syracuse U., 1966; MBA, Pace U., 1973. Mgmt. trainee Suburban Bank, Bethesda, Md., 1962-66; mktg. planning assoc. Chemical Bank, NYC, 1966-70; sr. market devel. officer Seattle-First Nat. Bank, 1970-74; product expansion adminstr., mktg. planning mgr. VISA, Inc., San Francisco, 1974-76; v.p., dir. mktg. Wash. Mutual Bank, Seattle, 1976-82; v.p., mktg. dir. First Interstate Bank Wash. N.A., Seattle, 1983-86; sr. v.p. mktg., dir. Puget Sound Nat. Bank, Tacoma, 1986-92; sr. v.p., dir. mktg. and sales Key Bank, Tacoma, 1993-94; dir. corp. sales KIRO-TV, Seattle, 1994; sr. v.p., dir. mktg. and sales Pacific N.W. Bancorp, 1994—2004; pres. Whidbey Western R.R., 1995—; prin. Whidbey Mktg., 2004—; mktg. instr. Embry-Riddle U., Oak Harbor, Wash., 2005—. Bd. dirs., treas. Whidbey Gen. Hosp. Found.; trustee Skagit Valley Coll. Mem.: Motorcar Operators West, S.W. Railcar Ltd. (mem. exec. com.), Island County Econ. Devel. Assn. (bd. dirs.), Pacific Railcar Operators, Mktg. Comm. Exec. Internat., Ctrl Whidbey Lions, Delta Mu Delta, Alpha Kappa Psi, Sigma Nu (treas.). Episcopalian. Home and Office: 750 N Snowberry Ln Coupeville WA 98239-3110 Office Phone: 360-678-4488.

PIERCY, MARGE, poet, writer; b. Detroit, Mar. 31, 1936; d. Robert Douglas and Bert Bernice (Bunnin) Piercy; m. Ira Wood, 1982. AB, U. Mich., 1957; MA, Northwestern U., 1958; DHL (hon.), Hebrew Union Coll., 2004, Union Coll., 2004, Eastern Conn. State U., 2005. Instr. Gary ext. Ind. U., 1960—62; poet-in-residence U. Kans., 1971; disting. vis. lectr. Thomas Jefferson Coll., Grand Valley State Colls., 1975, 1976, 1978, 1980; vis. faculty Women's Writers Conf., Cazenovia Coll., NY; Elliston poetry fellow U. Cin., 1986. DeRoy Disting. vis. prof. U. Mich., 1992; editor Leapfrog Press, 1997—; poetry editor Lillith, 1999—; fiction editor Seattle Rev., 2003. Author: Breaking Camp, 1968, Hard Loving, 1969, Going Down Fast, 1969, Dance the Eagle to Sleep, 1970, Small Changes, 1973, To Be of Use, 1973, Living in the Open, 1976, Woman on the Edge of Time, 1976, The High Cost of Living, 1978, Vida, 1980, The Moon is Always Female, 1980, Braided Lives, 1982, Circles on the Water, 1982, Tri-Colored Blocks for a Quilt, Essays, 1982, Stone, Paper, Knife, 1983, My Mother's Body, 1985, Gone to Soldiers, 1988, Available Light, 1988 (May Sarton award 1991), Summer People, 1989, He, She and It, 1991, Body of Glass, 1991 (Arthur C. Clarke award 1993), Mars and Her Children, 1992, The Longings of Women, 1994, Eight Chambers of the Heart, 1995, City of Darkness, City of Light, 1996, What Are Big Girls Made Of?, 1997 (Notable Book award ALA 1997), Storm Tide, 1998, The Art of Blessing the Day, 1999, Early Grrrl, 1999, Three Women, 1999, Sleeping With Cats, A Memoir, 2002, expanded edit., 2005, Colors Passing Through Us, 2003, Third Child, 2003, Sex Wars: A Novel of the Turbulent Post-Civil War Period, 2005, The Crooked Inheritance, 2006, Pesach for the Rest of Us, 2007; co-author: (with Ira Wood) So You Want to Write: How to Master the Craft of Writing Fiction and the Personal Narrative, 2001, 2d edit., 2005; (CD) Louder: We Can't Heed You Yet, 2004; author of poetry (17 vols.). Cons. N.Y. State Coun. on Arts, 1971, Mass. Found. for Humanities and Coun. on Arts, 1974; mem. Writer Bd., 1985-86; bd. dirs. Transition House, Mass. Found. Humanities and Pub. Policy, 1978-85, Am. ha-Yam, 1988-98, v.p., 1995-96; gov.'s appointee to Mass. Cultural Coun., 1990-91, Mass. Coun. on Arts and Humanities, 1986-89; artistic adv. bd. ALEPH Alliance for Jewish Renewal, Am. Poetry Ctr., 1988—; lit. adv. panel poetry NEA, 1989, mem. fiction and creative nonfiction panel, 2007; mem. adv. bd. Carrie A. Seaman Animal Shelter. Recipient Borenstone Mountain Poetry award, 1968, 74, Lit. award Gov. Mass. Commn. on Status of Women, 1974, Nat. Endowment of Arts award, 1978, Carolyn Kizer Poetry prize, 1986, 90, Shaeffer-Eaton-PEN New Eng. award, 1989, Golden Rose Poetry prize, 1990, Brit ha-Dorot award The Shalom Ctr., 1992, Notable Book award, 1997, Paterson poetry prize, 2000. Mem.: ARS, NOW, PEN, Am. Poetry Soc., Nat. Writers Union, Authors League, Authors Guild, Lower Cape Rose Soc., New Eng. Rose Soc., Mass. Audubon Soc., Citizens for the Preservation of Wellfleet, New Eng. Poetry Club. Address: PO Box 1473 Wellfleet MA 02667-1473 Personal E-mail: hagolem@c4.net.

PIERLUISI, PEDRO R., lawyer; b. San Juan, PR, Apr. 26, 1959; s. Jorge A. and Doris (Urrutia) Pierluisi; m. María Elena Carrión; children: Anthony, Michael, Jacqueline, Rafael. BA, Tulane U., 1981; JD, George Washington U., 1984. Bar: D.C. 1984, U.S. Dist. Ct. D.C. 1985, U.S. Ct. Appeals (D.C. cir.) 1985, P.R. 1990, U.S. Dist. Ct. P.R. 1990, U.S. Supreme Ct. 1990, U.S. Ct. Appeals (1st cir.) 1993. Assoc. Verner, Liipfert, Bernhard, McPherson & Hand, Washington, 1984—85, Cole, Corette & Abrutyn, Washington, 1985—90; ptnr. Pierluisi Pierluisi & Mayol-Bianchi, San Juan, 1990—93; atty. gen. Govt. of P.R., 1993—96; ptnr. O'Neill & Borges, San Juan, 1997—. Mem.: ABA (house dels. 1995—96, standing com. on substance abuse 1995—98, coordinating com. on gun violence 1998—2001, state membership chmn. 2000—03), Am. Arbitration Assn. (arbitrator), Internat. Ctr. Dispute Resolution (arbitrator), George Washington U. Internat. Law Soc. (pres. 1982—83), Nat. Assn. Attys. Gen. (chair ea. region 1996), Jose Jaime Pierluisi Found. (pres. 2003—06), Puerto Rico Homebuilders Assn. (bd. dirs. 1999—2003), Phi Alpha Delta (hon.; Munoz chpt.). Avocation: jogging. Office: O'Neill & Borges 250 Ave Munoz Rivera Am Internat Plz San Juan PR 00918-1808 Office Phone: 787-282-5706. E-mail: pedro.pierluisi@oneillborges.com.

PIERMATTI, JACK, dentist; b. Paterson, NJ, Sept. 25, 1953; s. Matthew and Viola Piermatti; m. Carol Ann Nakashian, July 30, 1978; children: Laura Ann, Valerie Jacqueline, John Michael. BS, Fairleigh Dickinson U., 1975, DMD, 1979. Cert. N.J. State Bd. Dentistry, 1979, diplomate Internat. Congress Oral Implantologists, 1997, Am. Bd. Oral Implantology, 1999, Am. Bd. Prosthodontics, 2004. Gen. practice resident St. Joseph's Hosp., Paterson, NJ, 1979—80; prosthodontics resident UMDNJ, Newark, 2001—04; pvt. practice, 1980—. Fellow, Acad. General Dentistry, 1997, Am. Acad. Implant Dentistry, 2000. Office: Dental Arts South Jersey PC 1001 Laurel Oak Rd Ste C-1 Voorhees NJ 08043 Office Phone: 856-783-5777. E-mail: jpiermatti@yahoo.com.

PIERNO, ANTHONY ROBERT, lawyer; s. Anthony M. and Mary Jane (Saporita) P.; m. Beverly Jean Kohn; children: Kathryn Ann, Robert Lawrence, Linda Jean Derengowski, Diane Marie Leonard. BA with highest honors, Whittier Coll., 1954; JD, Stanford U., 1959; LLD (hon.), Whittier Coll., 2000. Bar: Calif. 1960, D.C. 1979, Tex. 1994. Assoc. Adams, Duque & Hazeltine, LA; ptnr. Poindexter & Barger, LA; chief dep. commr. State of Calif., 1967-69, commr. of corps., 1969-71; ptnr. Wyman, Bautzer, Rothman & Kuchel, Beverly Hills, Calif.; sr. ptnr. Memel, Jacobs, Pierno & Gersh, LA, 1976-86, Pillsbury, Madison & Sutro, LA, 1986-89; sr. v.p., gen. counsel MAXXAM, Inc., L.A. and Houston, 1989-97. Author: Corporate Disaggregation, 1982; editor Stanford U. Law Rev. Trustee Whittier Coll., 1977-2000, chmn. bd. trustees, 1994-2000, chmn. presdl. selection com., 1989-90; chmn. Marymount Coll., Palos Verdes, Calif., 1989-92, trustee, 1976-93; past mem. Los Angeles County Children's Svcs. Commn. With US Army, 1954-56. Recipient Emcalian award Marymount Palos Verdes Coll., 1983, Whittier Coll. Lancer Soc. Lifetime Achievement award, 1984—, Lifetime Svc. award, 2004. Mem. ABA, LA County Bar Assn., State Bar Calif. (chmn. com. on corps. 1971-75, advisor to com. on corps. 1975-76, mem. exec. com. bus. law sect. 1976-80, chmn. spl. com. on franchise law), Calif. Club (LA), Am. Inns of Ct. Republican. Roman Catholic. Office: 92 Avenida Lirio Blanco Rancho Mirage CA 92270 E-mail: arplaw@msn.com.

PIEROG, MARGAUX MARIE, food service executive, restaurant manager; BS, Cornell U., Ithaca, NY, 2002. Cert. sommelier. Sommelier Culinary Adventures, Costa Mesa, Calif., 1998—2002. Asst. editor: Know Vino. Officer Delta Gamma Alumni Chpt., Newport Beach, Calif., 2003—05; profl. du vin Chaine des Rotisseurs, Orange County, Calif., 1999—2005; alumni asst. interviewer Cornell CAAN. Mem.: Mensa. Home Phone: 949-922-0634.

PIERONI, ROBERT EDWARD, internist, educator, military officer; b. Portland, Maine, June 20, 1937; s. Ansel Kirby and Agnes Mary (Dumais) P.; m. Dorothy Louise McDonnell, Oct. 3, 1970; children: Michelle Kirby, Robert Francis. BS, Boston Coll., 1959; MD, Pa. State U., 1971. Diplomate Am. Bd. Internal Medicine, Am. Bd. Family Practice, Am. Bd. Allergy and Immunology, Am. Bd. Quality Assurance, Am. Bd. Geriatric Medicine. Chemist Mass. Dept. Pub. Health, Boston, 1962-71, sr. bacteriologist, 1971-74; asst. prof. internal medicine U. Ala., Tuscaloosa, 1974-76, assoc. prof. dept. internal medicine and family practice, 1976-81, prof. internal medicine and family practice, 1981—; enlisted U.S. Army, 1961, advanced through grades to col., 1981. Prior cons. VA Hosp., Tuscaloosa, T. Hardin Med. Facility and Partlow State Hosp., Tuscaloosa, 1974—; cons. FDA, Dept. Def. Contbr. articles to profl. jours., chapters to books. Decorated Bronze Star, 1991, Commendation for Valor; recipient Golden Stethoscope award, 1982, Faculty Recognition award, 1986, Ala. Golden Eagle Humanitarian award Ala. Sr. Citizens Hall of Fame, 1988 and Physicians award, 1998, Wright A. Garner scientist award Ala. Acad. Sci., 1997, Designator A Proficiency award Army Surgeon Gen., 2001. Mem. AMA, ACP, Am. Coll. Allergy, Asthma and Immunology, Am. Geriatric Soc., Gerontol. Soc. Am., Am. Acad. Family Physicians, Physicians for Human Rights, VFW, Am. Legion. Democrat. Roman Catholic. Avocations: mountain trekking, scuba diving, studying medical and military history, reading. Home: 398 Riverdale Dr Tuscaloosa AL 35406-1814 Office: U Ala Dept Internal Medicine PO Box 870326 Tuscaloosa AL 35487-0001 Office Phone: 205-348-1287. Personal E-mail: dp398@comcast.net.

PIERRE, PERCY ANTHONY, engineering educator; b. Donaldsville, La., Jan. 3, 1939; s. Percy John and Rosa (Villavaso) P.; m. Olga A. Markham, Aug. 8, 1965; children: Kristin Clare, Allison Celeste. BSEE, U. Notre Dame, 1961, MSEE, 1963, D of Engring. (hon.), 1977; PhD in Elec. Engring, Johns Hopkins U., 1967; postgrad., U. Mich., 1968; DSc (hon.), Rensselear Poly. Inst. Asst. prof. elec. engring. So. U., 1963; instr. Johns Hopkins U., Balt., 1963-64; instr. physics Morgan State Coll., 1964-66; instr. info. and control engring. U. Mich., Ann Arbor, 1967-68; instr. systems engring. UCLA, 1968-69; research engr. in communications RAND Corp., 1968-71; White House fellow, spl. asst. Office of Pres., 1969-70; dean Sch. Engring., Howard U., Washington, 1971-77; program officer for engring. edn. Alfred P. Sloan Found., 1973-75; asst. sec. for research, devel. and acquisition U.S. Dept. Army, 1977-81; engring. mgmt. cons., 1981-83; pres. Prairie View (Tex.) Agrl. and Mech. U. System, 1983-89, Honeywell prof. elec. engring., 1989-90; v.p. rsch. and grad. studies Mich. State U., East Lansing, 1990-95, prof. elec. enging., 1995—. Dir. engring. coll. council Am. Soc. for Engring. Edn., 1973-75; mem. sci. adv. group Def. Communications Agy., 1974-75; mem. adv. panel Office Exptl. Research and Devel. Incentives, NSF, 1973-74; mem. Commn. Scholars To Rev. Grad. Programs, Ill. Bd. Higher Edn., 1972-74; mem. panel on role U.S. engring. sch. in fgn. tech. assistance, 1972, co-chmn. symposium on minorities in engring., 1973; mem. rev. panel for Inst. for Applied Tech., Nat. Bur. Standards, 1973-77; chmn. com. on minorities Nat. Acad. Engring., 1976-77; cons. to dir. Energy Rsch. and Devel. Adminstrn., 1976-77; mem. Army Sci. Bd., 1984; mem. adv. bd. Sch. Engring., Johns Hopkins U., 1981-84; cons. Office Sec. Def., 1981-84; mem. adv. bd. Lincoln Labs., MIT. Contbr. articles on communications theory to profl. publs. Trustee U. Notre Dame, 1974-77, 81—; trustee, mem. exec. com. Nat. Fund for Minority Engring. Students, 1976-77; bd. dirs. The Hitachi Found., 1987, Ctr. for Naval Analysis, 1986, Assn. Tex. Colls. and Univs.; pres. Southwest Athletic Conf., 1985-87, bd. dirs. CMS Corp., 1990—, Defense Sci., 1992-94, Old Kent Fin. Corp., 1993—, bd. trustee Aerospace Corp., 1991—. Recipient Disting. Civilian Service award Dept. Army, 1981; award of merit from Senator Proxmire, 1979. Mem. IEEE (sr. mem.; Edison award com. 1978-80), Sigma Xi, Tau Beta Pi. Home: 2445 Emerald Lake Dr East Lansing MI 48823-7256 Office: Mich State U 3224 Engineering East Lansing MI 48824-1226 Business E-Mail: pierre@msu.edu.

PIERRE, SAMUEL J., engineering educator; b. Haiti, Oct. 5, 1955; BEng. in Civil Engring., Ecole Polytechnique of Montreal, 1981; BSc in Math. and Computer sci., U. Que., Montreal, 1984, MSc in Math. and Computer Sci., 1985; MSc in Econs., U. Montreal, 1987; PhD in Elec. Engring., Ecole Polytechnique of Montreal, 1991. Registered profl. engr., Order of Engrs. of Que. Full prof. Ecole Polytechnique of Montreal, 1998—. Dir. Mobile Computing and Networking Rsch. Lab., Montreal, 1999—, Mobile Computing and Networking Rsch. Group, Montreal, 2003—; NSERC/Ericsson indsl. rsch. chair in next-generation mobile networking sys. Ecole Polytechnique of Montreal, 2002—. Recipient Sligos-Avignon award for the best rsch. paper, Ninth Internat. Conf. on Expert Sys. and their Applications, 1989, Disting. Paper award, OPNETWORK, 2003, 2005. Fellow: Engring. Inst. Can.; mem.: IEEE, Assn. for Computing Machinery, IEEE Computer Soc., IEEE Comm. Soc. Achievements include patents pending for Mobile Computing Systems. Office: Ecole Polytechnique of Montreal PO Box 6079 Station Centre-ville Quebec Montreal Canada H3C 3A7 Home Phone: (450) 629-1536. Office Fax: (514) 340-5159. Business E-Mail: samuel.pierre@polymtl.ca.

PIERSKALLA, WILLIAM PETER, dean, finance, engineering educator; b. St. Cloud, Minn., Oct. 22, 1934; s. Aloys R. and Hilda A. Pierskalla; m. Carol Spargo. Children: Nicholas, William, Michael. AB in Econs., Harvard U., 1956, MBA, 1958; MS in Math., U. Pitts., 1962; PhD in Ops. Rsch., Stanford U., 1965; MA, U. Pa., 1978. Assoc. prof. Case Western Res. U., Cleve., 1965-68, So. Meth. U., Dallas, 1968-70; prof. dept. indsl. engring. and mgmt. scis. Northwestern U., Evanston, Ill., 1970-78; exec. dir. Leonard Davis Inst. U. Pa., Phila., 1978-83, prof., chmn. health care sys. dept., 1982-90, prof. decision sci. and systems engring., dep. dean acad. affairs Wharton Sch., 1983-89, Ronald A. Rosenfield prof., 1986-93; dir. Huntsman Ctr. Global Competition and Leadership U. Pa. Wharton Sch., 1989-91; John E. Anderson prof. UCLA, 1993—99, dean John E. Anderson Grad Sch. Mgmt., 1993-97, disting. prof. to disting. prof. emeritus, 1999—. Cons. HHS, Bethesda, Md., 1974-87, MDAX, Chgo., 1985-91, MEDICUS, Evanston, 1970-75, Sisters of Charity, Dayton, Ohio, 1982-83, Project Hope, 1990; bd. dirs., chmn. The Bush Found.; bd. dirs. No. Wilderness Adventures, Informs. Contbr. articles to various publs. Mem. adv. bd. Lehigh U., 1986-93, U. So. Calif. Bus. Sch., 1987-93; regent St. Mary's Coll., 1998-2001, Hong Kong U. Sci. and Tech., 1992-2005. Recipient Harold Larnder Meml. prize Can. Oper. Rsch. Soc., 1993; grantee NSF, 1970-83, HHS, Washington, 1973-82, Office Naval Rsch., Arlington, Va., 1974-77. Fellow Inst. Ops. Rsch. and Mgmt. Scis. (v.p. publs. 2000-03); Mem. Ops. Rsch. Soc. Am. (pres. 1982-83, editor 1979-82, Kimball Disting. Svc. medal 1989), Inst. Mgmt. Scis. (assoc. editor 1970-77), Internat. Fedn. Operational Rsch. Socs. (pres. 1989-91), NAE, Omega Rho. Office: UCLA Anderson Grad Sch Mgmt 110 Westwood Plz Box 951481 Los Angeles CA 90095-1481 E-mail: william.pierskalla@anderson.ucla.edu. *

PIERSOL, ALLAN GERALD, mechanical engineer; b. Pitts., June 2, 1930; s. Robert James and Irene Laticia (Dematty) Piersol; m. Gertrud Teresia Moller, June 8, 1958; children: Allan Gerald Jr., Marie Theresa, John Robert. BS in Engring. Physics, U. Ill., 1952; MS in Engring., U. Calif., 1961. Lic. profl. engr., Calif. Rsch. engr. Douglas Aircraft Co., Santa Monica, Calif., 1952-59; mem. tech. staff Ramo Wooldridge Corp., Canoga Park, Calif., 1959-63; v.p. Measurement Analysis Corp., Santa Monica, Calif., 1963-71; prin. scientist Bolt Beranek and Newman, Inc., Conoga Park, 1971-85; sr. scientist Astron Corp., Santa Monica, 1985-88; owner Piersol Engring., Woodland Hills, Calif., 1988—. Lectr. U. So. Calif., LA, 1965—95; adj. lectr. Loyola Marymount U., LA, 2006—. Co-author: (book) Measurement and Analysis of Random Data, 1966, Random Data: Analysis and Measurement Procedures, 1971, 2000, Engineering Applications of Correletion and Spectral Analysis, 1980, 1993, Shock and Vibration Handbook, 2002. Mem.: ASME, Acoustical Soc. Am., Inst. Environ. Scis. and Tech. (Irwin Vigness Meml. award 1991). Achievements include patents for method and apparatus for determining terrain surface profiles. Home: 23021 Brenford St Woodland Hills CA 91364-4830 Office: Piersol Engring Co 23021 Brenford St Woodland Hills CA 91364-4830 Office Phone: 818-591-2119. Personal E-mail: apiersol@pacbell.net.

PIERSOL, LAWRENCE L., federal judge; b. Spirit Mound Township, SD, Oct. 21, 1940; s. Ralph Nelson and Mildred Alice (Millette) P.; m. Catherine Anne Vogt, June 30, 1962; children: Leah C., William M., Elizabeth J. BA, U. S.D., 1962, JD summa cum laude, 1965. Bar: S.D. 1965, U.S. Ct. Mil. Appeals, 1965, U.S. Dist. Ct. S.D. 1968, U.S. Supreme Ct. 1972, U.S. Dist. Ct. Wyo. 1980, U.S. Dist. Ct. Nebr. 1986, U.S. Dist. Ct. Mont. 1988. Ptnr. Davenport, Evans, Hurwitz & Smith, Sioux Falls, SD, 1968-93; judge U.S. Dist. Ct. SD, Sioux Falls, 1993—, chief judge, 1999—2005. Mem. budget com. Jud. Conf. U.S., 1996-2003, chair economy subcom., 2001-03; chmn. tribal ct. com., security com. 8th Cir. Jud. Coun.; editor-in-chief Law Rev.; mem. Judl. Conf. US, 2005-, exec. com., 2006-. Majority leader S.D. Ho. of Reps., Pierre, 1973-74, minority whip, 1971-72; del. Dem. Nat. Conv., 1972, 76, 80; S.D. mem. del. select commn. Dem. Nat. Com., 1971-75. Mem. ABA, State Bar S.D., Fed. Judges Assn. (bd. dirs., pres.). Avocations: reading, running, painting, sailing. Office: US Dist Ct 400 S Phillips Ave Sioux Falls SD 57104-6824 Home Phone: 605-338-7245; Office Phone: 605-330-6640.

PIERSON, AL See PIZZAMIGLIO, ALBERT

PIERSON, DAVID JOHN, medical educator; b. Portland, Oreg., Aug. 22, 1943; s. John Martin Pierson and Clara Jane Chapman; m. Dona L Kienle, Apr. 13, 1968; children: Christine, Erika. BA, Oreg. State U., Corvallis, 1965; MD, Johns Hopkins, Balt., 1969. Diplomate in internal medicine, pulmonary medicine, critical care medicine Am. Bd. Internal Medicine. Prof. medicine U. Wash., Seattle, 1976—; editor in chief, respiratory care

Am. Assn. for Respiratory Care, Dallas, 1997—; editor, critical care alert Thomson Healthcare, Atlanta, 1993—. Chair, critical care policy and test writing com. Am. Bd. Internal Medicine, Phila., 1999—2003. Color photography, 2 Solo Exhibits; numerous permanent installations. Vol., com. mem., officer Am. Lung Assn. Wash., Seattle, 1982—2006. Maj. US Army, 1974—76, Germany. Named to Pulmonary Hall of Fame, Am. Lung Assn. Wash., 2003; recipient Jimmy A Young medal (Lifetime Achievement award), Am. Assn. for Respiratory Care, 2005. Fellow: ACP, Am. Coll. Chest Physicians, Am. Assn. for Respiratory Care (life). Avocations: photography, music. Office: Harborview Med Ctr 325 Ninth Ave Box 359762 Seattle WA 98104 Business E-Mail: djp@u.washington.edu.

PIERSON, EDWARD SAMUEL, engineering educator, consultant; b. Syracuse, NY, June 27, 1937; s. Theodore and Marjorie O. (Bronner) P.; m. Elaine M. Grauer, June 6, 1971; 1 child, Alan. BS in Elec. Engring., Syracuse U., 1958; SM, MIT, 1960, ScD, 1964. Asst. prof., fellow MIT, 1965-66; assoc. prof., assoc. dept. head U. Ill., Chgo., 1966-75; program mgr. Argonne Nat. Labs., Ill., 1975-82; head dept. engring. Purdue U. Calumet, Hammond, Ind., 1982-95, spl. asst. to chancellor for environ. programs, 1995—2005. Cons. Argonne Nat. Lab., 1972-75, 82-93, Solmecs Corp., 1982-88, HMJ Corp., Washington, 1983-88, LM Mfg., 1994—. Contbr. articles to profl. jours. NSF fellow, 1958-60 Mem. IEEE, ASME, Am. Soc. Engring. Edn. Office: Purdue Univ Calumet Hammond IN 46323 Home Phone: 773-327-9188; Office Phone: 219-989-2467. E-mail: pierson@calumet.purdue.edu.

PIERSON, GREY, lawyer; b. Abilene, Tex., Dec. 31, 1950; s. Don and Annette (Grubbs) P. Student in history Baylor U., 1971, JD, 1974; student in internat. law Coll. William and Mary, Exeter, Eng., summer 1973. Bar: Tex. 1974, U.S. Dist. Ct. (no. dist.) Tex. 1974, U.S. Ct. Appeals (5th cir.) 1983, U.S. Supreme Ct. 1984. Assoc. Law Office of Tom Sneed, Odessa, Tex., 1974-76, Duke, Duke, & Jelinek, Arlington, Tex., 1976-78; ptnr. Duke & Pierson, Arlington, 1978-79, Pierson & Galyen, Arlington, 1983-88, Pierson, Baker & Ray, 1988-95, Pierson & Behr, 1995—; sole practice, Arlington, 1979-83; gen. counsel Mercer Internat. Transp., Ft. Worth, 1979-84; sr. legal adviser Dominica Caribbean Freeport Authority, Roseau, W.I., 1979; ptnr. Sta. KVMX-FM, Eastland, Tex., 1981-86. Contbr. articles to City Digest mag., 1979-80. Pres. Eastland Youth Council, 1967, Arlington Community Theatre, 1979; mem. Tarrant 2000 Commn. on Civil Justice, 1988; chmn. Tarrant County Rep. Jud. Recruitment Com., 1988; del. Rep. Nat. Conv., New Orleans, 1988. Recipient Disting. Svc. award Nat. Assn. Disabled Ams., Washington, 1982. Home: 301 W Abram St Arlington TX 76010

PIERSON, JACK, artist; b. Plymouth, Mass., 1960; BFA, Mass. Coll. Art, Boston. One-man shows include, Simon Watson, NY, 1990, Pat Hearn Gallery, NY, 1991, Richerd Kuhlenschmidt Gallery, LA, 1991, 1992, Tom Cugliani Gallery, NY, 1992, White Columns, NY, 1992, Jack Hanley Gallery, San Francisco, 1993, Regen Projects, LA, 1994, Edward Hopper & Jack Pierson: Am. Dreaming, Whitney Mus. Am. Art, NY, 1994, Luhring Augustine Gallery, NY, 1994, 1996, Fine Arts Work Ctr., Provincetown, Mass., 1994, Tex, Gallery, Houston, 1995, Mus. Contemporary Art, Chgo., 1995, Parco Gallery, Tokyo, 1995, White Cube, London, 1996, Galerie Philippe Rizzo, Paris, 1996, Taka Ishii Gallery, Tokyo, 1995, Pay Me In Coke, 1998, An Artifical Night, Ginza Art Space, Tokyo, 1998, exhibited in group shows at The Moderns, Feature, NY, 1995, Whitney Biennial, Whitney Mus. Am. Art, 1995, 2004, Defining the Nineties, Mus. Contemporary Art, Miami, 1996. Mailing: c/o Cheim & Read Gallery 547 West 25th St New York NY 10001

PIERSON, RICHARD NORRIS, JR., medical educator; b. NYC, Sept. 22, 1929; s. Richard Norris and Dorothy (Stewart) Pierson; m. Alice Roberts, Aug. 26, 1974; children from previous marriage: Richard N., Olivia Tiffany, Alexandra de Forest, Cordelia S.C. stepchildren: Alice W. Dunn, Eric C.W. Dunn. BA, Princeton U., 1951; MD, Columbia U., 1955. Diplomate Am. Bd. Internal Medicine, Am. Bd. Nuclear Medicine. Resident St. Luke's Roosevelt Hosp., NYC, 1955—61, assoc. dir., 1961—65, dir. div. nuclear medicine, 1965—89, dir. body composition unit, 1965—2003, attending physician, 1975—; prof. clin. medicine Columbia U., 1980—; dir. medicine Hackensack Hosp., 1973—74; staff assoc. Brookhaven Nat. Lab., 1970—2002; rsch. scholar Lawrence Radiation Lab., Berkeley, Calif., 1970—71. Bioengring. inst. Columbia U., 1976—, chmn., 1989—94. Editor: Quantitative Radiocardiography, 1975; contbr. articles to profl. jours. Warden St. Paul's Ch., 1980—82; bd. dirs. Englewood Health Dept., NJ, 1966—74, Empire Blue Cross/Blue Shield, NY, 1978—91, v.p. NY, 1990—91. NIH grantee, 1973—76, 1986—99, John A. Hartford grantee, 1967—70. Fellow: ACP, N.Y. Acad. Medicine; mem.: AAAS, N.Y. County Med. Soc. (pres. 1978—79), Soc. Nuclear Medicine (greater N.Y. area pres. 1982—83, del. to AMA 1991—2001, trustee 1991—, Berson-Yalow award 1995), Alliance for Continuing Med. Edn. (pres. 1987—89), Am. Med. Rev. Rsch. Ctr. (N.Y. State del. to AMA 1978—90, pres. 1985—89), Am. Bur. Med. Advancement in China (pres. 1979—87), N.Y. County Health Svc. Rev. Orgn. (chmn. 1980—82), Am. Inst. Nutrition, Am. Physiol. Soc., P&S Alumni Assn. (pres. 1989—91), Englewood Field Club, Century Club. Home: 60 Lincoln St Englewood NJ 07631-3117 Office: St Lukes Roosevelt Hosp Ctr 1111 Amsterdam Ave New York NY 10025-1716 Home Phone: 201-569-3562; Office Phone: 212-523-3385. Business E-Mail: RNP1@columbia.edu.

PIERSON, ROBERT DAVID, investor; b. Orange, NJ, Mar. 5, 1935; s. Carleton Wellington and Muriel Browning (Potter) Pierson; m. Virginia Duncan Knight, Apr. 30, 1960; children: Lisa Boles, Alexandra Mead, Robert Wellington. BA, Lehigh U., 1957. Exec. asst. 1st Nat. City Bank N.Y., NYC, 1958-61; asst. to pres. Cooper Labs. Inc., NYC, 1961-65; dir. mktg. svcs. Arbrook divsn. Johnson & Johnson, Somerville, NJ, 1965-69; v.p. Klemtner Advt. Inc., NYC, 1969-71; sr. v.p. Bowery Savs. Bank, NYC, 1972-80; vice chmn., dir. Carteret Bancorp, Inc., Wilmington, Del., 1980-90; pres. No. Divsn. Collective Bank, 1990-96, Collective Fin. Svcs., Inc., Harbor Mortgage Co. divsn. Collective Bank, Montclair, NJ, 1997-98; pvt. investor, 1998—. Mem. town coun. Twp. of Mendham, NJ, 1992—, mayor, 1995—96, 2003—04. With USCG, 1958—59. Mem.: Morristown Club, Morris County Golf Club. Republican. Presbyterian. Home: Green Hills Rd Mendham NJ 07945-3305

PIERSON, STUART F., lawyer; b. Washington, June 25, 1943; s. W. Theodore and Barbara F. Pierson; m. Jennifer M. Pierson, June 20, 1987; children: Stuart, Jr., Sean, Jody Skye, Emily J.; m. Carole S. (div. 1985). BA cum laude, Hobart Coll., 1965; diploma, L.S. ID, 1968. Bar: D.C. 1969, N.Y. 1984, U.S. Supreme Ct. 1974. Atty. U.S. Dept. Justice Civil Rights Divsn., Washington, 1968—71, AUSA WD Washington, Washington, 1971—73, Spec. AUSA WD, Washington, 1974, Verner Liipfert, Washington, 1975—88, Davis Wright, Washington, 1988—96, Levine Pierson, Washington, 1996—98; atty., white collar crime practice Troutman Sanders LLP, Washington, 1998—. Office: Troutman Sanders LLP Ste 1000 401 9th St NW Washington DC 20004-2134 Office Phone: 202-274-2897. Office Fax: 202-654-5622. E-mail: stuart.pierson@troutmansanders.com.

PIERSON, WILLIAM GEORGE, lawyer; b. Pontiac, Mich., Oct. 13, 1951; s. Robert D. and Elizabeth C. (Brode) P.; m. Mary K. Grossa, Sept. 25, 1986; children: Megan Ewing, Robert John. BBA, Cen. Mich. U., 1973; JD, Detroit Coll. Law, 1980. Bar: Mich. 1980, U.S. Dist. Ct. (ea. dist.) Mich. 1982, U.S. Supreme Ct. 1985. Sr. assoc. Kohl, Secrest, Wardle, Lynch, Clark & Hampton, Farmington Hills, Mich., 1980-89, Schwartz & Jalkanen, Southfield, Mich., 1989-90; sole practice Howell, Mich., 1991-99; counsel Oakland County Corp., Pontiac, Mich., 1999—. Mem. ABA (pub. law sect.), Mich. Bar Assn. (negligence sect., elected to rep. assembly 1999—), Oakland County Bar Assn (dist. ct. com. 1983-84, cir. ct. com. 1984-85, 2006—, negligence com. 1987-2005, chair negligence com. 2002, med.-legal com. 1989-96, pub. adv. com. on jud. candidates 2002-05). Avocations: golf, skiing, boating, camping. Home: 2153 Ridge Rd White Lake MI 48383-1742 Office: Oakland County Dept Corp Counsel 1200 N Telegraph Rd Dept 419 Pontiac MI 48341-0419 Office Phone: 248-858-0456. Personal E-mail: megrob@comcast.net. Business E-Mail: piersonw@oakgov.com.

PIESTER, DAVID L(EE), magistrate judge; b. Lincoln City, Nebr., Nov. 18, 1947; s. George Piester; married; children. BS, U. Nebr., 1969, JD, 1972. Bar: Nebr. 1972, U.S. Dist. Ct. Nebr. 1972, U.S. Ct. Appeals (8th cir.) 1976, U.S. Supreme Ct. 1979. Staff atty. Legal Svcs. S.E. Nebr., Lincoln, 1972-73, exec. dir., 1973-79; asst. U.S. atty. Dept. Justice, Lincoln, 1979-81; magistrate judge U.S. Dist. Ct. Nebr., Lincoln, 1981—. Cons. Legal Services Corp., Nat. Legal Aid and Defender Assn., 1974-77. Mem. Lincoln Human rights commn., 1978-79. Mem. Nebr. State Bar Assn., Fed. Magistrate Judges Assn., Lincoln Bar Assn., Eighth Cir. Jud. Coun. (ex officio 1993-96). Office: US Dist Ct 100 Centennial Mall North 566 Fed Bldg Lincoln NE 68508

PIETRINI, ANDREW GABRIEL, automotive aftermarket executive; b. Bryn Mawr, Pa., Feb. 27, 1937; s. Bernard and Irene (Norcini) P.; m. Pam Mari, Sept. 29, 1962; children: Darrin, Wayne BS, Villanova U., 1958. C.P.A., Pa. Jr. acct. Fernald & Co., Phila., 1958-60; sr. acct. O & W Audit Co., Narberth, Pa., 1960-62; asst. sec. James Talcott, Inc., NYC, 1962-68; pres. UIS, Inc., NYC, 1968—, dir., 1972—, chmn., CEO, pres., 1986—. Bd. dirs. Lebensfeld Found., N.Y.C., 1979— Mem. Am. Inst. C.P.A.s, Fin. Execs. Inst. Republican. Roman Catholic. Avocations: sailing, golf. Office: UIS Inc 15 Exchange Pl Ste 1120 Jersey City NJ 07302-3912

PIETROFESA, JOHN JOSEPH, psychologist, educator; b. NYC, Sept. 12, 1940; s. Louis John and Margaret P.; m. Cathy Marks, June 22, 1985; children: John, Paul, Maria, Dolores. EdB cum laude, U. Miami, 1961; MEd, 1963, Ed.D., 1967. Diplomate Am. Bd. Sexology; cert. cognitive behavior therapist, forensic counselor, sex therapist; lic. psychologist, social worker. Counselor Dade County (Fla.) pub. schs., 1965-67; prof. edn. Wayne State U., Detroit, 1967—; div. head theoret. and behavioral founds., 1977-83; dept. chair counselor edn., 1999—. Cons. Nat. Football League, 2003—; cons. to various schs., hosps. and univs. Author: The Authentic Counselor, 1971, 2nd edit., 1980, School Counselor as Professional, 1971, Counseling and Guidance in the Twentieth Century, 1971, Elementary School Guidance and Counseling, 1973, Career Development, 1975, Career Education, 1976, College Student Development, 1977, Counseling: Theory Research and Practice, 1978, Guidance: An Introduction, 1980, Counseling: An Introduction, 1984; mem. editl. bd. Counseling and Values, 1972-75. 1st lt. Mil. Police Corps, AUS, 1963-65. Mem. APA, ACA, Mich. Counseling ASsn., Assn. Counselor Edn. and Supervision, Phi Delta Kappa. Home: PO Box 99 Bloomfield Hills MI 48303-0099 Office: Wayne State U 321 Education Detroit MI 48202 Home Phone: 248-646-0821; Office Phone: 248-642-6066.

PIETRUSKI, JOHN MICHAEL, JR., pharmaceutical executive; b. Sayreville, NJ, Mar. 12, 1933; m. Roberta Jeanne Talbot, July 3, 1954; children: Glenn David, Clifford John, Susan Jane. BS with honors, Rutgers U., 1954; LLD (hon.), Concordia Coll., 1993. With Proctor and Gamble Co., 1954-63; pres. med. products div. C.R. Bard, Inc., 1963-77; with Sterling Drug, Inc., NYC, 1977-88; pres. Pharm. Group, 1977-81, corp. exec. v.p., 1981-83, pres., COO, 1983-85, chmn., CEO, 1985-88; pres. Dansara Cons., 1988—; chmn. Encysive Pharms., Inc., 1990—. Bd. dirs. PDI, Inc., Xylos Corp., Trial Card, Inc. 1st lt. US Army, 1955—57. Mem.: Union League Club (N.Y.C.), Phi Beta Kappa. Home: 27 Paddock Ln Colts Neck NJ 07722-1266 Office: One Penn Plaza Ste 3408 New York NY 10119 Office Phone: 212-268-5510. Personal E-mail: jmpco4@aol.com.

PIETRZEN, JULIE LYNN, lawyer; b. Southfield, Mich., Mar. 13, 1974; d. Eugene Victor Pietrzen and Joan Diane Bragg. BA, Albion Coll., Albion, Mich., 1996; JD, Case Western Res. U., Cleve., 2004. LCSW Mich. Patient advocate L&S Assocs., Inc., Haslett, Mich., 1996—97; program coord. YWCA of Western Wayne County, Mich., 1997—2000; atty. Frantz Ward LLP, Cleve., 2004—. Mem.: Cuyahoga County Bar Assn., Cleve. Bar Assn., Ohio State Bar Assn., Phi Delta Phi (province pres. 2004—, Balfour scholar 2003, Grad. of the Yr. 2004). Democrat. Avocations: volleyball, reading, writing, skiing. Office: Frantz Ward LLP 127 Public Sq 2500 Key Center Cleveland OH 44114

PIETZSCH, MICHAEL EDWARD, lawyer; b. Burlington, Iowa, Aug. 1, 1949; s. Walter E. and Leanna (Moore) P.; m. Ellen G. Hart; children: Christine E., Catherine M. AB, Stanford U., 1971; JD, U. Chgo., 1974. Bar: Ill. 1974, Ariz. 1976. Ptnr. McCabe & Pietzsch, Phoenix, 1975-90, Pietzsch & Williams, Phoenix, 1990-95, Polese, Pietzsch, Williams & Nolan, Phoenix, 1995—. Contbr. articles to profl. jours.; speaker at profl. confs. Del. White House Conf. Small Bus., Washington, 1986, White House Savs. Summit, 1998; chmn. bd. trustees Ariz. Sci. Ctr., 1994-98; pres. The Group, Inc., 1995-98. Fellow Am. Coll. Tax Counsel, Am. Coun. on Tax Policy, Am. Coll. Employee Benefits Counsel; mem. ABA (chmn. personal svc. orgns. com. tax sect. 1986-90), Stanford Phoenix Club (pres. 1982-84). Office: 2702 N Third St Ste 3000 Phoenix AZ 85004 Office Phone: 602-604-6250. E-mail: pietzsch@ppwn.com.

PIFER, SCOTT THOMAS, mathematics educator; b. Canton, Ohio, Mar. 13, 1980; s. Thomas Henry and Constance Marie Pifer. BS in Secondary Edn. in Math., Walsh U., North Canton, Ohio, 2003. Lic. tchr. Mass., 2004. Mem. golf course grounds crew Glenmoor Country Club, Canton, Ohio, 1997—2003; tchr. math. H.S. Quincy Pub. Schs., Quincy, Mass., 2003—. Mem.: Nat. Coun. Tchrs. Math. (assoc.). Home Phone: 781-857-2386; Office Phone: 617-984-8574. Personal E-mail: pife40@hotmail.com.

PIGA, STEPHEN MULRY, retired lawyer; b. Bklyn., Apr. 9, 1929; s. Stephen Paul and Ella (Mulry) P.; married, Feb. 23, 1952 (div.); children: Maureen, Stephen, Susan, Elizabeth; m. Emilie Halliday, Aug. 1, 1975 (dec. Aug. 2003); 1 dau., Margaret. AB, Princeton U., 1950; LLB, Columbia U., 1955. Bar: N.J. 1955, N.Y. 1956. Assoc. White & Case, NYC, 1955-63, ptnr., 1964-92; ret., 1992. Lectr. Practicing Law Inst. N.Y. and various insts., bar assns. Served to capt. USMCR, 1951-53. Mem. ABA, N.Y. State Bar Assn. (exec. com. tax sect. 1981-89, chmn. employee benefits com.), Assn. of Bar of City N.Y., N.J. Bar Assn., Am. Contract Bridge League (life master), Profl. Bowlers' Assn. Am., High Mt. Golf Club. Republican. Avocations: fishing, golf, bowling, bridge.

PIGFORD, THOMAS HARRINGTON, nuclear engineering educator; b. Meridian, Miss., Apr. 21, 1922; s. Lamar and Zula Vivian (Harrington) P.; m. Catherine Kennedy Cathey, Dec. 31, 1948 (dec. 1992); children: Cynthia Pigford Naylor, Julie Earnest; m. Elizabeth Hood Weekes, Nov. 12, 1994. BS in Chem. Engring., Ga. Inst. Tech., 1943; S.M. in Chem. Engring., M.I.T., 1948, Sc.D. in Chem. Engring., 1952. Asst. prof. chem. engring., dir. Sch. Engring. Practice, M.I.T., 1950-52, asst. prof. nuclear and chem. engring., 1952-55, assoc. prof., 1955-57; head engring., dir. nuclear reactor projects and asst. dir. research lab. Gen. Atomic Co., La Jolla, Calif., 1957-59; prof. nuclear engring., chmn. dept. nuclear engring. U. Calif., Berkeley, 1959—; sr. rsch. scientist Lawrence Berkeley Lab., 1959—. Mem. panel Nat. Atomic Safety Licensing Bd. AEC-Nuclear Regulatory Commn., 1963-77; mem. Pres.'s Commn. on accident at 3-Mile Island, 1979; mem. bd. radioactive waste mgmt. and energy engring. bd., NAS-NAE, chmn. waste isolation systems panel, waste isolation pilot plant panel, fusion hybrid panel, separations and transmutations panel, transmutation of military plutonium panel, panel on health standard for radioactive waste disposal, chmn. adv. coun. Inst. Nuclear Power Op.; mem. Sec. of Energy's expert cons. group on Chernobyl accident; chmn. nuclear oversight com. Sacramento Mcpl. Utility Dist.; chmn. nuclear safety com. Gulf States Utilities Co.; mem. expert cons. group Swedish Nuclear Power Inspectorate; mem. peer rev. group for waste isolation pilot plant; mem. corp. rev. com. Oak Ridge Nat. Lab; lectr. Taiwan Nat. Sci. Found., 1990; vis. prof. Kyoto U., 1975, Kuwait U., 1976; cons. in field. Author: (with Manson Benedict) Nuclear Chemical Engineering, 1958, 2d edit., 1981; contbr. numerous articles to profl. jours.; patentee in field. Served with USNR, 1944-46. Recipient John Wesley Powell award U.S. Geol. Survey, 1981; named Outstanding Young Man of Greater Boston, Boston Jaycees, 1955; E. I. DuPont DeNemours rsch. fellow, 1948-50; Berkeley citation U. Calif., 1987; Japan Soc. for Promotion Sci. fellow, 1974-75; grantee NSF, 1960-75, EPA, 1973-78, Dept. Energy, 1979-92, Ford Found., 1974-75, Electric Power Rsch. Inst., 1974-75, Mitsubishi Metals Corp., 1989-90; named to Ga. Tech. Hall of Fame, 1995. Fellow Am. Nuclear Soc. (bd. dirs., Arthur H. Compton award 1971); mem. AIME, NAE, Am. Chem. Soc., Am. Inst. Chem. Engrs. (Robert E. Wilson award 1980, Service to Society award 1985), Atomic Indsl. Forum (dir.), Sigma Xi, Phi Kappa Phi, Tau Beta Pi. Home: 166 Alpine Ter Oakland CA 94618-1823 Office: U Calif Dept Nuclear Engring Berkeley CA 94720-0001 Office Phone: 510-652-0393. Business E-Mail: pigford@nuc.berkeley.edu.

PIGMAN, JACK RICHARD, lawyer; b. Fostoria, Ohio, June 5, 1944; s. Jack R. and A. Ada (McDevitt) P.; m. Judy Lynn Price, June 19, 1968 (div. 1983); m. Carolyn Ruth Parker, May 31, 1986; children: Shaeney E. Pigman Craig, J. Ryan Pigman, Adam Parker. BA, U. Notre Dame, 1966; JD cum laude, Ohio State U., 1969. Bar: Ohio 1969, U.S. Ct. Mil. Appeals 1970. Law clk. Ohio Supreme Ct., Columbus, 1969-70; assoc. Wright, Harlor, Morris & Arnold, Columbus, 1970, 74-76; ptnr. Porter, Wright, Morris & Arthur and predecessor firms, Columbus, 1977—. Spkr. in field. Trustee Dublin Arts Coun., 2001—06, pres., 2005, 06; trustee Ctr. for New Directions, 1990-96, treas., 1996; trustee United Cerebral Palsy of Columbus and Franklin County, 1976-82, pres., 1980; trustee Columbus Met. Club, 1980-87, pres., 1985-86; trustee Brass Band of Columbus. 2007-. Capt. JAG US Army, 1970—74. Named to Best Lawyers in Am., Ohio Super Lawyers, 2004—07, Chambers USA, 2004—07. Mem. Ohio State Bar Assn., Columbus Bar Assn. (chmn. bankruptcy com. 1982-84). Republican. Avocations: tennis, reading, cooking, photography. Office: Porter Wright Morris & Arthur LLP 41 S High St Ste 2800 Columbus OH 43215-6194 Office Phone: 614-227-2119. Business E-Mail: jpigman@porterwright.com.

PIGNATELLI, DEBORA BECKER, state official; b. Hoboken, NJ, Oct. 25, 1947; d. Edward and Frances (Fishman) Becker; m. Michael Albert Pignatelli, Aug. 22, 1971; children: Adam Becker, Benjamin Becker. AA, Vt. Coll., 1967; BA, U. Denver, 1969. Exec. dir. Girl's Club Greater Nashua, NH, 1975-77; dir. tenant svcs. Nashua Housing Authority, 1979-80; vocat. counselor Comprehensive Rehab. Assocs., Bedford, NH, 1982-85; specialist job placement Crawford & Co., Bedford, 1985-87; mem. N.H. Ho. of Reps., Concord, 1986—91, mem. appropriations com., 1986-91, asst. minority leader, 1989—91; mem. N.H. Senate, Concord, 1992—2003, v.p. policy, Dem. whip, chair judiciary com., mem. capital budget com., chair enrolled bills com., long range capital budget overview com.; elected mem. N.H. Govs. Exec. Coun., 2005—. Del. Am. Coun. Young Polit. Leaders, Germany, 1987. Asst. coach Little League Baseball, Nashua, 1987—90; del. Dem. Nat. Conv., 1988, Gore del., 2000; mem. steering com. Gephardt for Pres. campaign, NH, 1987—88; bd. dirs. Sky Meadow Condominium Assn. Named one of 10 Most Powerful Women in NH, NH Editions mag., 1995; recipient Meritorious Svc. award, NH Women's Lobby, 1997, John F. Kennedy award, Hillsborough County Dems., 2001, Anita and Norman Freedman award, N.H. Dems., 2004, William Paine Domestic Violence award, 2005. Mem.: Women's Lobby, N.H. Children's Lobby. Jewish. Avocations: skiing, swimming, boating. Home: 22 Appletree Grn Nashua NH 03062-2252 Office Phone: 603-271-3632.

PIGOTT, CHARLES MCGEE, transportation equipment manufacturing executive; b. Seattle, Apr. 21, 1929; s. Paul and Theiline (McGee) P.; m. Yvonne Flood, Apr. 18, 1953. BS, Stanford U., 1951. With PACCAR Inc, Seattle, 1959—, exec. v.p., 1962-65, pres., 1965-86, chmn., pres., 1986-87, chmn., chief exec. officer, 1987-97, also bd. dirs., chmn. emeritus, 1997—. Pres. Nat. Boy Scouts Am., 1986-88, mem. exec. bd. Mem. Bus. Council. Office: Paccar Inc 777 106th Ave NE Bellevue WA 98004-5017

PIGOTT, EUGENE F., JR., state appeals court judge; b. Rochester, NY, Sept. 27, 1946; m. Peggy Pigott; 2 children. BA, LeMoyne Coll., 1968; JD, SUNY Buffalo Sch. Law, 1973. Bar: NY 1974. Atty. Offermann, Fallon, Mahoney & Adner, Buffalo, 1974—82; Erie County atty., 1982—86; chief trial counsel Offermann, Cassano, Pigott & Greco, 1986; judge NY State Supreme Ct., 1997—98; justice Appellate Divsn., 4th Dept., 1998—2000, presiding justice, 2000—06; assoc. judge NY State Ct. Appeals, 2006—. Office: State of NY Court of Appeals 20 Eagle St Albany NY 12207-1095 *

PIGOTT, JOHN DOWLING, geologist, geophysicist, geochemist, educator, consultant; b. Gorman, Tex., Feb. 2, 1951; s. Edwin Albert and Emma Jane (Poe) P.; m. Kulwadee Lawwongngam, May 28, 1994. BA in Zoology, U. Tex., 1974, BS in Geology, 1974, MA in Geology, 1977; PhD in Geology, Northwestern U., 1981. Ordained deacon Roman Cath. Ch., 2002, ordained Theravada Buddhist monk 2002. Geologist Amoco Internat., Chgo., 1978-80, sr. petroleum geologist Houston, 1980-81; asst., then assoc. prof. U. Okla., Norman, 1981—. Vis. prof. Mus. Natural History, Paris, 1988, Sun Yat Sen U., Kaohsiung, Taiwan, 1991; rsch. dir. 5 nation Red Sea-Gulf of Aden seismic stratigraphy and basis analysis industry consortium, 1992—; internat. energy cons., 1981—; instr. I.H.R.D.C., Boston, 1987-91, O.G.C.I., Tulsa, 1991—; energy advisor Ministry of Oil and Mineral Resources, Republic of Yemen, 1996—2000; advisor Prime Min. Rep. Yemen, 1998-2000; energy advisor Empresa Colombiana de Patroleos, Colombia, 2001, Petroleos de Venezuela, 2001-02. Mem. editl. bd. Geotectonica et Metallogenin Jour., 1992—2000. Mem. Am. Assn. Petroleum Geologists, Soc. Exploration Geophysicists, Soc. Petroleum Engrs., Geol. Soc. Am., Indonesian Petroleum Assn., Sigma Xi. Theravada Buddhist. Achievements include discovering relationship between global CO_2 and natural tectonic cycles on the scale of millions of years showing previous greenhouse times during the Phanerozoic, processing first three-dimensional amplitude variation with offset seismic survey to quantify rocks, fluids, and pressures in rocks, processing and displaying first ground penetrating radar survey as a seismic section for ultrahigh resolution sequence stratigraphy, developing tectonic subsidence analysis as a practical tool for investigating the comparative anatomy of a sedimentary basins, their tectonic history, and evolving hydrocarbon potential, and constructing first paleo-heatflow maps of the Red Sea for the past 25 ma. Office: U Okla Sch Geology & Geophysics 100 E Boyd St Norman OK 73019-1000 Office Phone: 405-325-3253.

PIGOTT, MARK C., automotive executive; BS in Indsl. Engring., Stanford U., Calif., MBA. V.p. Paccar Inc., Bellevue, Wash., 1988—89, sr. v.p., 1990—93, exec. v.p., 1993—95, bd. dirs., 1994—, vice chmn., 1995—96, chmn., CEO, 1997—. Mem. exec. com. Washington Roundtable. Named a Top CEO, Instl. Investor mag., 2005; named Mgr. of Yr., Truck & Off-Hwy. Ledger, 2004. Office: PACCAR PO Box 1518 Bellevue WA 98009 Office Phone: 425-468-7400. Office Fax: 425-468-8216. *

PIKAS, CHRISTINA KIRK, librarian, researcher; b. Wilmington, Del., Sept. 26, 1972; d. Howard Eliason and Gail Foster Kirk; m. Mark Michael Pikas, Oct. 24, 1998. B in Physics, U. Md., 1995, MLS, 2002. Libr. ASRC Aerospace, Ft. Meade, Md., 2003—03, The Johns Hopkins U. Applied Physics Lab., Laurel, Md., 2003—. Asst. editor: SciTech News, 2004—06. Lt. USN, 1995—99. Mem.: Am. Soc. for Info. Sci. and Tech., Spl. Librs. Assn., Phi Kappa Phi. Office: JHU Applied Physics Lab 11100 Johns Hopkins Rd Laurel MD 20723-6099 Home Phone: 301-498-9009; Office Phone: 240-228-4812. Business E-Mail: christina.pikas@jhuapl.edu.

PIKE, ANASTASIA, music educator, artist; BA in US Social and Cultural History, U. Md., College Park, 2001, MusB in Performance Harp, 2001, MA in Music History and Lit., 2003; M of Ch. Music Piano and Choral Conducting, Pensacola Theol. Sem., Pensacola, Fla., 2004; PhD in Musicology, Claremont Grad. U., Calif., 2007—; MusM in Performance Harp, Johns Hopkins U. Peabody Inst., Balt., 2007. Pvt. music instr., Ft. Meade, Md., 1991—; performing artist, 1988—; prof. music Patrick Henry Coll., Purcellville, Va., 2005—. Pianist Heritage Cmty. Ch., Severn, Md., 1996—. Grad. Musicology Assistantship, Johns Hopkins U., Peabody Inst., 2006—07, Grad. grant, 2007—, Grad. fellow, Claremont Grad. U., 2007—. Mem.: Soc. Am. Music, Am. Harp Soc., Am. String Tchrs. Assn., Am. Musicological Soc., Phi Alpha Theta Nat. History Honor Soc., Omicron Delta Kappa Nat. Leadership Honor Soc., Nat. Soc. of Collegiate Scholars, Golden Key Internat. Honor Soc., Pi Gamma Mu Internat. Social Sci. Honor Soc. Home Phone: 443-454-3756.

PIKE, GEORGE HAROLD, JR., religious organization administrator, clergyman; b. Summit, NJ, Jan. 14, 1933; s. George Harold and Ann Aurelia (Brewer) P.; m. Pauline Elizabeth Blair, Aug. 27, 1955; children: Elizabeth, George 3d, James. BA, Trinity Coll., Hartford, Conn., 1954; MDiv, Dubuque Theol. Sem., Iowa, 1957; DDiv (hon.), U. Dubuque, 1998. Ordained to ministry Presbyn. Ch. USA., 1957. Pastor 1st PResbyn. Ch., Kasson, Minn., 1956-59, 3d Presbyn. Ch., Dubuque, 1959-64; sr. pastor Presbyn. Ch., Bettendorf, Iowa, 1964-68, 1st Presbyn. Ch., Vancouver, Wash., 1968-78, Cranford, NJ, 1978-88; exec. chair Presbyn. Ch. USA, Louisville, 1988-93; interim pastor 2d Presbyn. Ch., Kansas City, Mo., 1993-95; dir. sem. devel. U. Dubuque, Iowa, 1995-98; retired, 1998; interim pastor Valley Presbyn. Ch., Green Valley, Ariz., 2000. Mem. exec. com. Consultation on Ch. Union, Princeton, 1980-89, pres., 1984-88. Dir. Bettendorf Bd. Edn., 1964-68, pres. 1967-68; bd. dirs. Southwest Wash. Hosps., Vancouver, 1969-78. Named Citizen of Yr., Jaycees, Bettendorf, 1967, Citizen of Yr., B'nai B'rith, Cranford, 1988; named to Honorable Order of Ky. Cols., 1989 Presbyterian. Avocations: golf, photography. Home: 928 W Union Bell Dr Green Valley AZ 85614-5928 Personal E-mail: Ghpike@aol.com.

PIKE, JOHN NAZARIAN, optical engineering consultant; b. Boston, Feb. 13, 1929; s. Arthur Thorndike and Sarah Lucy (Nazarian) Pike; m. Margaretta May Horner, Dec. 28, 1957; 1 child, Susan Horner; 1 child, Sally Katharine. AB, Princeton U., 1951; PhD in Physics and Optics, U. Rochester, 1958. Staff scientist Parma Rsch. Ctr., Union Carbide Corp., Ohio, 1956—63; mem. physics faculty Baldwin-Wallace Coll., Berea, Ohio, 1961-63; sr. scientist Tarrytown (N.Y.) Tech. Ctr., Union Carbide Corp., 1963-85; pres. J.J. Pike & Co., Pleasantville, NY, 1986—2006. Cons. indsl. optical instrumentation design Tenn. Sci., USAF. Mem. nat. com. for planned giving United Way of Am., 1997—2001; bd. dir. United Way of Westchester and Putnam, NY, 1979—85, 1995—, chmn., 1996—98, 1999—2000, 2003; bd. dirs. United Way of N.Y. State, 1999—2004, 2006—. Recipient Harold J. Marshall citation Cmty. Svc, United Way No. Westchester, 1976, Cmty. Svc. award, Union Carbide Corp., 1982, Spirit of Westchester and Putnam Vol. Leadership award, United Way Westchester and Putnam, 2001. Mem.: Sigma Xi, Phi Beta Kappa. Achievements include patents in field. Home and Office: 71 Cedar Ave Pleasantville NY 10570-1932

PIKE, JUDITH ROBYN, lawyer; b. Newton, July 23, 1959; d. Burton M. and Doris (Weingard) P.; m. Richard A. Miller, July 7, 1990. BA summa cum laude, Tufts U., 1981; JD, U. Pa., 1984. Bar: Mass. 1985, U.S. Dist. Ct. Mass. 1985. Assoc. Rackemann, Sawyer & Brewster, Boston, 1984-86, McDermott & Rizzo, Boston, 1986-90, Kirkpatrick & Lockhart, Boston, 1990—93; founder Law Office Judith R. Pike, Wellesley, Mass., 1993—. Named one of top Boston lawyers, Boston Mag., 2004. Mem.: Wellesley C. of C. (women's bus. network), Mass. Conveyancers Assn., ABA, Mass. Bar Assn., Boston Uncommon (women's accappella quintet) (dir.). Avocations: music, piano. Office: 462 Washington St Wellesley MA 02482 Office Phone: 781-237-2727. Office Fax: 781-237-2737. Business E-Mail: judy@judithpikelaw.com.

PIKE, KERMIT JEROME, cultural organization administrator; b. East Cleveland, June 19, 1941; s. Frank James and Pauline Frances (Prijatel) P.; m. Joyce Rita Massillo, June 27, 1964; children: Christopher James, Laura Elizabeth. BA, Case Western Res. U., 1963, MA, 1965. Rsch. asst. Western Res. Hist. Soc., Cleve., 1965-66, curator manuscripts, 1966-72, chief libr., 1969-75, dir. libr., 1976—2002, COO, 1997—, capital campaign mgr., 2006—. Adj. prof. history, libr. sci. Case Western Res. U., 1975-84. Author: Guide to the Manuscripts and Archives, 1972, Guide to Shaker Manuscripts, 1974; editor: Guide to Jewish History Sources, 1983; Compiler: Guide to Major Manuscript Collections, 1987. Mem. Super Sesquicentennial Com., Cleve., 1971, Cleve. Bicentennial History Com., 1992—96, Ohio Preservation Coun., 1997—, Ohio Hist. Records Adv. Bd., 2002—; chmn. Family Heritage Adv. Bd., Numa Corp., 1995—99; chmn. vis. com. on humanities and arts Cleve. State U., 1980—82; trustee Nationalities Svc. Ctr., Cleve., 1978—86. Recipient Achievement award No. Ohio Live, Cleve., 1987; Spl. Recognition award Gov. Richard F. Celeste of Ohio, 1990. Mem. Soc. Ohio Archivists (co-founder 1968, pres. 1971-72), Black History Archives (founder 1970), Orgn. Am. Historians, Soc. Am. Archivists, Manuscripts Soc., Midwest Archives Conf., Ohio Geneal. Soc., Early Settlers Assn. of the Western Res., Rowfant Club, Lake County Farmers' Conservation Club, Lambda Chi Alpha. Roman Catholic. Office: Western Res Hist Soc 10825 East Blvd Cleveland OH 44106-1777 Office Phone: 216-721-5722. Business E-Mail: kermit@wrhs.org.

PIKE, LARRY SAMUEL, lawyer; b. Savannah, Ga., Feb. 23, 1939; s. Abram and Ida (Feinberg) P.; m. Bonnie Jo Haykin, June 21, 1959; children: Douglas, Stacey, Scott. BA, Emory U., 1960, LLB, 1963; postgrad., Leeds U., Eng., 1960-61. Assoc. L. Jack Swertfeger Jr. Atty., Decatur, Ga., 1963-65; ptnr. Swertfeger, Scott, Pike & Simmons, Decatur, 1966-75, Simmons, Pike & Warren, Decatur, 1975-76, Lefkoff, Pike & Sims, Atlanta, 1976-85, Branch, Pike & Ganz, Atlanta, 1985-95, Holland & Knight LLP, Atlanta, 1995—. Pres. Ansley Park Civic Assn., Atlanta, 1977-79, Northshore Homeowners Assn., Tybee Island, Ga., 1992-95, The Temple, Atlanta, 1979-81, trustee, 1977—, Am. Cancer Soc., DeKalb County, Ga. unit, 1970-71, crusade chmn., 1969-70; trustee Ansley Park Beautification Found., Inc., Atlanta, 1984—, treas., 2000-06, v.p. 2006—; trustee The Temple Endowment Fund, Atlanta, 1979-87, Atlanta Jewish Cmty. Ctr., 1973-76; bd. overseers Hebrew Union Coll., Cin., 1987-93; alumni coun. Emory U., Atlanta, 1966-72; bd. trustees Union of Am. Hebrew Congregations, 1991-99; mem. Rabbinical Placement Commn., 1994-2000; mem. St. Joseph's Hosp. Leadership Coun., 2003—; mem. planned giving adv. bd. Cmty. Found. Greater Atlanta, 2005—; mem. gift planning adv. coun. Emory U., 2006—. Editor-in-chief law jour. and newspaper; contbr. articles to profl. jours. Named Outstanding Young Man of Yr., North DeKalb Jaycees, 1968, Super Lawyer, Atlanta Mag.; named one of Legal Elite, Ga. Trend mag.; Fulbright fellow, 1960—61. Mem. ABA, State Bar Ga. (exec. coun. Young Lawyers sect. 1968-72), Atlanta Bar Assn., Decatur-DeKalb Bar Assn. (sec. 1965-66), Atlanta Legal Aid Soc. (pres. 1974-75, past bd. dirs.), Atlanta Tax Forum, Lawyers Club Atlanta, B'nai B'rith (pres. Atlanta lodge 1970-71, Ga. pres. 1974-75, dist. 5 bd. govs. 1973-76, chair Youth Orgn. Bd. 1971-73), Bryan Soc., Phi Beta Kappa, Omicron Delta Kappa. Office: Holland & Knight LLP 2000 One Atlantic Ctr Atlanta GA 30309 Business E-Mail: larry.pike@hklaw.com.

PIKE, RALPH WEBSTER, chemical engineer, educator, academic administrator; b. Tampa, Fla., Nov. 10, 1935; s. Ralph Webster and Macey (Adams) P.; m. Patricia Jennings, Aug. 23, 1958. B in Chem. Engring., Ga. Inst. Tech., 1957, PhD, 1962. Rsch. chem. engr. Exxon R & D Co., Baytown, Tex., 1962—64; Paul M. Horton prof. chem. engring. and sys. sci. La. State U., Baton Rouge, 1964—, assoc. vice chancellor rsch., 1967—96, dir. La. Mineral Inst., 1979—, dean engring., 1999—2001. Cons. to chem. and petroleum refining industry, fed. govt. and State of La., 1964—. Author: Formulation and Optimization of Mathematical Models, 1970, Optimization for Engineering Systems, 1986, Optimizacion en Ingenieria, 1989. Active various civic, ch. and cmty. orgns., Baton Rouge, 1964—. 2d lt. U.S. Army, 1958-60. Recipient more than 100 rsch. grants, including NASA, NSF, Dept. Interior, Dept. Def., EPA, NOAA, state agys. and pvt. industry, 1964—. Fellow AIChE (chmn. nat. program com. 1984, local sect. 1985); mem. Am. Chem. Soc. (Charles E. Coates Mem. Award, 1994), Sigma Xi. Democrat. Methodist. Avocation: skiing. Home: 6063 Hibiscus Dr Baton Rouge LA 70808-8844 Office: La State U 1139 Energy Coast and Environment Bldg Baton Rouge LA 70803-0001 Office Phone: 225-578-3428. Business E-Mail: pike@lsu.edu.

PIKE, ROBERT WILLIAM, insurance company executive, lawyer; b. Lorain, Ohio, July 25, 1941; s. Edward and Catherine (Stack) P.; m. Linda L. Feitz, Dec. 26, 1964; children: Catherine, Robert, Richard. BA, Bowling Green State U., 1963; JD, U. Toledo, 1966. Bar: Ohio 1966, Ill. 1973. Ptnr. Cubbon & Rice Law Firm, Toledo, 1968-72; asst. counsel Allstate Ins. Co., Northbrook, Ill., 1972-74, assoc. counsel, 1974-76, asst. sec., asst. gen. counsel, 1976-77, asst. v.p., asst. gen. counsel, 1977-78, v.p., asst. gen. counsel, 1978-86, sr. v.p., sec., gen. counsel, bd. dirs., 1987-99, exec. v.p., 1999—. Bd. dirs. Allstate subs. Mem. bd. overseers Inst. for Civil Justice. Served to capt. inf. U.S. Army, 1966-68. Mem. ABA, Ill. Bar Assn., Ohio Bar Assn., Property Casualty Insurers Assn. Am. (bd. dirs., exec. com.), Ivanhoe (Ill.) Club. Roman Catholic. Home: 1795 W North Pond Ln Lake Forest IL 60045- Office: Allstate Ins Co 2775 Sanders Rd Ste F8 Northbrook IL 60062-6127

PIKE, THOMAS HARRISON, plant chemist; b. West Palm Beach, Florida, Oct. 9, 1950; s. Rufus Draper and Dora Marie (Thomason) P.; m. Julie Lynn (Simpson), Aug. 19, 1972; one child, Thomas Simpson. BS, Baylor Univ., 1972; MS, Calif. State U., 2001. Sci. instr. Valliant Pub. Sch., Okla., 1975—76; sch. adminstr. Swink Pub. Sch., Okla., 1976—81; plant chemist Western Farmers Electric Coop., Ft. Towson, Okla., 1981—2004; tech. editor Penn Well Pub., 2004—. Instr. dept. sci. and engring., Eastern Okla. State Coll., 1997—; mem. adv. bd. Kiamichi Vo-Tech. Sch., Idabel, Okla., 1985-87; tech. editor Penn Well Pub. Mem. adv. bd. Kiamichi Vo-Tech. Sch., Idabel, Okla., 1997—. Mem. ASME (co-chmn. task force, 1988-90); ASTM; Nat. Assn. Corrosion Engr. Achievements include rsch. in corrosion control of condensers, case history of turbine problems, improving boiler efficiency, preservation of turbines during extended outages, metal oxide transport, and water clarification; two patents in chemical process control technology. Home: R R 1 Box 299 Garvin OK 74736-9755 Office: Western Farmers Electric Coop PO Box 219 Fort Towson OK 74735-0219 Business E-Mail: t_pike@wfec.com.

PIKE, WILLIAM EDWARD, retired investment company executive; b. Ft. Collins, Colo., Jan. 25, 1929; s. Harry H. and Alice Francis (Swinscoe) P.; m. Catherine Broward Crawford, June 26, 1965; children: Elizabeth Catherine, Robert Crawford, Daniel William. Student, U. Colo., 1947-48; BS, U.S. Naval Acad., 1952; MBA, Harvard, 1960. Commd. ensign USN, 1952, advanced through grades to lt., 1958; ret., 1958; asst. treas. Morgan Guaranty Trust Co., NYC, 1962-64, asst. v.p., 1964-66, v.p., 1966-71, sr. v.p., 1971-74, chmn. credit policy com., 1974-86; exec. v.p. J.P. Morgan & Co. Inc., 1986-89; corp. dir., trustee, pvt. investor. Mem. Harvard Club N.Y.C. Clubs: Country (New Canaan, Conn.). Episcopalian. Home: Indian Waters Dr New Canaan CT 06840 Office: 36 Grove St New Canaan CT 06840-5329

PIKITCH, ELLEN KAREN, science educator; d. Benjamin and Ruth Pikitch; m. Allen Saul Zwickler, May 24, 1997; children: Adam Craig Zwickler, Randi Beth Zwickler; 1 child from previous marriage, Scott Merritt Emlen. BS, MA, CUNY, NYC, 1977; MS, Ind. U., Bloomington, 1982, PhD, 1983. Asst. prof. Oreg. State U., Newport, 1983—87, Sch. Fisheries, U. Wash., Seattle, 1987—90, assoc. prof., 1990—96, assoc. dir. rsch., dir. fisheries rsch. inst., 1992—96; dir. fisheries programs Wildlife Conservation Soc., NYC, 1996—98, dir. marine conservation programs, 1998—2002, dir. ocean strategy, 2002—03; exec. dir. Pew Inst. for Ocean Sci., NYC, 2003—; prof. U. Miami Rosenstiel Sch., Fla., 2003—. Mem. Pres. Clinton's Panel on Ocean Exploration, 2000—01; mem. sturgeon specialist group Internat. Union for the Conservation of Nature, 2002—; task force mem. Millennium Project Task Force on Environ. Sustainability, 2003—05; conservation com. mem. Sea Change Investment Fund, San Francisco, 2005—; co-founder Caviar Emptor Campaign, lead scientist. Contbr. articles to profl. jours. Named one of, Outstanding Young Women Am., 1986; recipient Nehemiah Gittleson award, City Coll., CUNY, 1977, Kenyon prize for Excellence in Pure and Applied Math., 1977, Emerging Scholar award, Phi Kappa Phi, Oreg. State U. Chpt., 1987, Disting. Svc. award, Coll. Ocean and Fisheries Sci., U. Wash., 1992, Silver Anvil award, Pub. Rels. Soc. Am., 2004; Breckenridge fellow, Ind. U., 1982, Eigenmann fellow, 1982—83, Pew fellow in marine conservation, 2000—04. Mem.: AAAS, Soc. for Conservation Biology, Am. Fisheries Soc. Achievements include research in fisheries management and ocean conservation. Office: Pew Institute for Ocean Science 126 East 56th St Mezzanine New York NY 10022 Home Phone: 917-209-3185; Office Phone: 212-756-0042. Business E-Mail: epikitch@miami.edu.

PILAFIAN, AUDREY KALENIAN, music educator; b. Chgo., Sept. 19, 1929; d. Hagop and Adrine Kalenian; m. Harry Pilafian, Sept. 10, 1949; children: Martin, Jack David, Robert John, Mary Katherine. Student, Northwestern U., 1947—49; MusB, U. Miami, 1951, MEd in Supervision and Adminstrn., 1972. Cert. supr./adminstr., gifted edn., music edn., elem. edn. tchr. Fla. Elem. sch. tchr. Miami/Dade Pub. Schs., 1962—76, gifted students tchr., 1976—92; adj. supr. Fla. Internat. U., Miami, 1994—. Musician U. Miami Symphony Orch., Coral Gables, Fla., 1953—56; pvt. cello tchr., Miami, 1970—; cellist Chamber Music Prof. Agy., Miami, 1995—2007. Vol. co-dir. strings ensemble Leewood Elem. Sch., Miami, 1992—2005; state bd. mem. Odyssey of the Mind, Inc., Fla., 1983—98; supt. Sunday Sch. St. Mary Armenian Ch., Hollywood, Fla., 1953—2007. Named Dade County Tchr. of Yr., Fla. Fedn. Woman's Clubs, 1968; recipient Pontifical Blessing Encyclical, His Holiness Karenkin I, Catholicos of all Armenians, 1998. Mem.: Phi Delta Kappa (tchr.), Sigma Alpha Iota (musician/performer, editor, historian), Alpha Delta Kappa (internat. chmn. Fine Arts Grants Bd. 1991—97, internat. music chmn. 2005). Avocations: cello, chamber music, amateur radio, travel, camping. Home and Studio: 9940 SW 60 St Miami FL 33173 Office Phone: 305-271-2512.

PILAND, NEILL FINNES, health services economist, researcher, educator; b. Pomona, Calif., Nov. 6, 1943; s. Finnes Elmer and Sylvia Beatrice (Renick) PiL.; m. Diane Lynn Fiedor, Aug. 12, 1977; children: Evan Neill, Spencer Lowell, Arden Geneva. BA, UCLA, 1965, MPH, 1970, PhD, 1979; MA, U. Calif., Davis, 1966. Rsch. assoc. Sch. Pub. Health UCLA, 1971-73, sr. rsch. assoc., 1973; health economist Stanford Rsch. Inst., Menlo Park, Calif., 1973-77, asst. mgr. health svcs. rsch., 1974-77; dir. health ctr. study Jicarilla Apache Tribe, Dulce, N.Mex., 1978-82; dir. health systems evaluation program Lovelace Med. Found., Albuquerque, 1982-83, dir. health svcs. rsch. and edn., 1983-91; dir. Ctr. Health & Population Rsch., Albuquerque, 1991-94, Lovelace Inst. for Health and Population Rsch., Albuquerque, 1994-96; rsch. dir. Ctr. Rsch. Med. Group Mgmt. Assn., Englewood, Colo., 1996—2002; prof. and dir. Inst. Rural Health, Idaho State U., Pocatello, 2002—, rsch. prof., 2005—; clin. assoc. prof. U. Colo. Sch. Medicine; rsch. prof. U. Denver; dir. policy and rsch. Colo. Health Inst., Denver, 2004—05; rsch. prof. Inst. Rural Health Idaho State U., 2005—. Clin. asst. prof. medicine U. N.Mex., Albuquerque, 1981, clin. assoc. prof., 1994—; vis. prof. U. N.H., Durham, 1989-90; mem. commn. tobacco control, Idaho, 2003-04 Co-author: Strategic Nursing Management: Power and Responsibility in a New Era; mem. editorial bd. Jour. Managerial Issues, 1991—; co-editor: Physician Profiling: A Sourcebook for Adminstrators, Chart Accounts for Healthcare Organizations, Reinventing Medical Practice; contbr. over 100 articles to profl. jours. Mem. rsch. com. N.Mex. HealthNet, 1986-88; chair econ. issues N.Mex. Com. on Pub. Health Impact of Smoking, 1988; bd. dirs. Am. Geriat. and Gerontology, 1984-87, Healthcare for Homeless, 1988-92; mem. exec. coun. N.Mex. ASSIST Com., 1992—, sci. adv. com. N.Mex. ASSIST Project, 1992—; mem. steering com. Group Practice Improvement Network, 1996—; mem. workgroup smoking control Colo. Dept. Health and Environment, 1999-2002; scholarship interviewer NHSC, 2003-04; mem. Idaho State Commn. Tobacco Control, 2004—; bd. dirs. Vets. Med. Rsch. Found., 2002—. Recipient traineeship, USPHS, 1968-70. Mem. APHA, Am. Econ. Assn., Soc. Rsch. Adminstrs., Assn. Health Svcs. Rsch. Avocations: tennis, hockey, hiking, biking. Home: 2 Rice Ave Pocatello ID 83201 Office: Inst Rural Health Idaho State U Graveley Hall 205 Campus Box 8174 Pocatello ID 83209-8174 Office Phone: 208-282-5021. Business E-Mail: pilaneil@isu.edu.

PILAR, L. PRUDENCIO R., financial services executive; b. Bacarra, Philippines, Sept. 12, 1943; came to U.S., 1977; s. Francisco and Maria (Raralio) P.; m. Vivien Ruth Narciso, Aug. 20, 1967; children: Prudencio Rex Jr., Diogene Ruthard, Keith N., Xydia Vida Ruth N., Benedict. BS in Edn., No. Luzon Tchrs. Coll., Laoag City, Philippines, 1964; MA in Adminstrn. and Supervision, No. Luzon Tchrs. Coll., 1972. CLU, ChFC. Prin., tchr. Bur. of Pub. Schs., Solsona, Philippines, 1964-77; agt. The Equitable, Honolulu, 1978-95; pres. Pilar Fin. & Tax Strategies, Inc., Honolulu, 1995—. Pres. St. Anthony Sch. Parent-Tchrs. Guild, Honolulu, 1987, 88, 89, 94. Fellow Life Underwriter Tng. Coun.; mem. Internat. Assn. for Fin. Planning, Nat. Assn. Life Underwriters, Diocesan Congress of Filipino Cath. Clubs, Oahu Coun. Filipino Cath. Clubs, KC. Democrat. Roman Catholic. Avocation: giving seminars. Office: Pilar Fin Svcs 1580 Nobrega St Honolulu HI 96819-3747

PILARCZYK, DANIEL EDWARD, archbishop; b. Dayton, Ohio, Aug. 12, 1934; s. Daniel Joseph and Frieda S. (Hilgefort) Pilarczyk. Student, St. Gregory Sem., Cin., 1948—53; PhB, Pontifical Urban U., Rome, 1955, PhL, 1956, STB, 1958, STL, 1960, STD, 1961; MA, Xavier U., 1965; PhD, U. Cin., 1969; LLD (hon.), Xavier U., 1975, Calumet Coll., 1982, U. Dayton, 1990, Marquette U., 1990, Thomas More Coll., 1991, Coll. Mt. St. Joseph, 1994, Hebrew Union Coll., 1997. Ordained priest Roman Catholic Ch., 1959. Asst. chancellor Archdiocese of Cin., 1961—63; synodal judge Archdiocesan Tribunal, 1971—82; faculty Athenaeum of Ohio, St. Gregory Sem., 1963—74; v.p. Athenaeum of Ohio, 1968—74, trustee, 1974—; rector St. Gregory Sem., 1968—74; archdiocesan dir. ednl. services, 1974—82; aux. bishop of Cin., 1974—82; vicar gen., 1974—82; archbishop of Cin., 1982—. V.p. Nat. Conf. Cath. Bishops, 1986—89, pres., 1989—92, chmn. com. on doctrine, 1996—2000; U.S. rep. Episc. bd. Internat. Commn. on English in Liturgy, 1987—97, chmn., 1991—97; jt. com. Orthodox and Cath. Bishops, 2002. Author: Praepositini Cancellarii de Sacramentis et de Novissimis, 1964—65, Twelve Tough Issues, 1988, We Believe, 1989, Living in the Lord, 1990, The Parish: Where God's People Live, 1991, Forgiveness, 1992, What Must I Do?, 1993, Our Priests: Who They Are and What They Do, 1994, Sacraments, 1994, Bringing Forth Justice, 1996, 1999, Thinking Catholic, 1998, Practicing Catholic, 1999, Believing Catholic, 2000, Live Letters, 2001, Twelve Tough Issues and More, 2002, Being Catholic, 2006, When God Speaks, 2006. Trustee Cath. Health Assn., 1982—85, Cath. U. Am., 1983—91, 1997—2000, Pontifical Coll. Josephinum, 1983—92. Ohio Classical Conf. scholar, Athens, 1966. Mem.: Am. Philol. Assn. Roman Catholic. Home and Office: 100 E Eighth St Cincinnati OH 45202-2129 Office Phone: 513-421-3131.

PILATI, STEFANO, apparel designer; b. Milan; Intern Nino Cerruti; menswear asst. Giorgio Armani, 1993—95; with fabric and rsch. devel. Prada, 1995—98, asst. designer Miu Miu womenswear and menswear, 1998—2000; design dir. Yves St. Laurent, 2000—04; creative dir. Yves St. Laurent Rive Gauche, 2004—. Office: Yves Saint Laurent 3 E 57th St New York NY 10022-2557

PILBEAM, DAVID ROGER, paleoanthropology educator; b. Brighton, Sussex, Eng., Nov. 21, 1940; came to U.S., 1968; s. Ernest Winton and Edith (Clack) P.; m. Maryellen Ruvolo, Dec. 18, 1982; 1 child, Katharine Alexandra. BA, Cambridge U., 1962, MA, 1966; PhD, Yale U., 1967; MA (hon.), Harvard U., 1982. Demonstrator in anthropology Cambridge U., Eng., 1965-68; asst. prof. anthropology Yale U., 1968-70, assoc. prof., 1970-74, prof., 1974-81, prof. anthropology, geology and geophysics, 1974-81, prof. anthropology, 1981-90; dean undergrad. edn. Harvard U., Cambridge, Mass., 1987—92, 1996—97, Henry Ford II prof. social sci., 1990—, sr. advisor to dean Harvard Coll., interim dean Faculty Arts and Scis., 2007; dir. Peabody Mus., 1990, curator paleoanthropology. Author: Evolution of Man, 1970, Ascent of Man, 1972; co-author: Human Biology, 3d edit., 1988; co-editor: Cambridge Encyclopedia of Human Evolution, 1992. Fellow Am. Anthropol. Assn.; mem. Am. Acad. Arts and Scis., Nat. Acad. Scis. (fgn. assoc.). Office: Harvard U Peabody Mus 11 Divinity Ave Cambridge MA 02138-2019 E-mail: pilbeam@fas.harvard.edu. *

PILCHER, CARL B., astrobiologist; BS in Chemistry, Poly. Inst. Bklyn., 1968; PhD in Chemistry, MIT, Cambridge, 1973; M of Pub. Affairs in Internat. Rels., Princeton U., NJ, 1987. Mem. faculty dept. physics and astronomy U. Hawaii Inst. Astronomy, 1973—85; chief Mission from Planet Earth Study Office NASA, dir. sci. Office of Exploration, spl. asst. exploration Office of Space Sci. and Applications, chief Advanced Studies Br. in Solar Sys. Exploration Divsn., asst. assoc. adminstr. strategic and internat. planning Office of Space Sci., bd. dirs. Office of Space Sci., spl. asst. astrobiology, 2001, sci. prog. dir. Solar Sys. Exploration Washington, 2001—05, sr. scientist astrobiology Office of Space Sci., 2005—; dir. NASA Astrobiology Inst., 2006—. Mem. Galileo Solid State Imaging Team NASA, 1977—; guest prof. U. Vienna, Austria, 1983—84; mid-career fellow Princeton U. Woodrow Wilson Sch. Pub. and Internat. Affairs, 1985. Contbr. articles to profl. jours. Grantee MacArthur Found. fellowship, Internat. Peace and Security. Office: Office of Space Sci Code SZ NASA Hdqs 300 E St NW Washington DC 20546 E-mail: Carl.B.Pilcher@nasa.gov.

PILCHER, CHRISTIE W., retired special education educator; b. Jackson, Tenn., Dec. 17, 1944; d. Charles Arthur Sr. and Ruby Mazie (Pope) Walker; m. David Wayne Pilcher, Mar. 20, 1966 (div. 1974); children: David Andrew, Clayton Everett. Student, Mercer U., 1962-63; BA, North Ga. Coll., 1966; MEd, Ga. State U., 1976. Tchr. reading US Army Edn. Ctr., Munich, 1967; tchr. K.G. US Dependent Sch., Munich, 1967-68; tchr. Ga. Acad. for the Blind, Macon, 1974-79; tchr. for visually impaired Bibb County Bd. Edn., Macon, 1979-91, spl. edn. K.G., 1991-94; tchr. visually impaired Troup County Bd. Edn., LaGrange, Ga., 1994—2000, Bartow

County Sch. Sys., Cartersville, Ga., 2000—01; tchr. spl. needs kindergarten Bibb County Bd. Edn., Macon, 2001—02, 2004—05, tchr. mildly intellectually disabled, 2004—05; ret., 2005. Parent advisor Ga. Parent Infant Network for Ednl. Svc., Clarkston, 1985—2004; tchr. summer program Ga. Bapt. Children's Home, Baxley, 1991. Vol. Ga. Radio Reading Svc., 2003—; mem. choir Mt. Zion Bapt. Ch., 2004—, Sunday sch. tchr., 2004—. Avocations: painting, reading, baking, travel, gardening. Home: 939 Clairmont Pl Macon GA 31204-1099 Personal E-mail: christiep@bellsouth.net.

PILCHER, JAMES BROWNIE, lawyer; b. Shreveport, La., May 19, 1929; s. James Reece and Martha Mae (Brown) P.; m. Lorene Pilcher; children: Lydia, Martha, Bradley. BA, La. State U., 1952; JD summa cum laude, John Marshall Law Sch., 1955; postgrad., Emory U., 1957. Bar: Ga. 1955. Legal aide to Spkr. of Ho. of Reps., Ga., 1961-64; assoc. city atty. City of Atlanta, 1964-69; pvt. practice law Atlanta, 1969—. Exec. com. Dem. Exec. Com. of Fulton County, Ga., 1974-86; bd. dirs. Whitehead Boys Club, 1961-89; trustee Ga. Inst. Continuing Legal Edn., 1988-89; pres. Atlanta Jaycees, 1961-62. Fellow, Lawyers Found. Ga., 1996—. Mem. ABA, Ga. Assn. Criminal Def. Lawyers (pres. 1980-82), State Bar Ga. (chmn. 1988-89, gen. practice and trial sect., chmn. criminal law sect. 1986-87), Atlanta Bar Assn., Ga. Trial Lawyers Assn. (life), Ga. Claimants Attys. Assn. (pres. 1983-84), NACDL (bd. dirs. 1980-85), Ga. Inst. Trial Advocacy (bd. dirs. 1986-89), South Fulton Bar Assn. (pres. 1987-88), Trial Lawyers for Pub. Justice (life), Atlanta Consumer Bankruptcy Attys. Group (life, pres. 2001-03), Kiwanis (Peachtree, Atlanta pres. 1983-84, gov. Ga. dist. 1992-93), Sierra Club Am. (life), Barristers Club of Emory U. Law Sch. Presbyterian. Home and Office: 1195 W Wesley Rd NW Atlanta GA 30327-1407 Personal E-mail: pilchers@comcast.net.

PILCHER, JAMES ERIC, physicist; b. Toronto, Ontario, Canada, Apr. 23, 1942; came to US 1965; s. Francis Eric and Isabel (Brand) P.; m. Carla Grosso, Aug. 31, 1970; children: Marc R., Daniel E., Erica M. BASc, U. Toronto, 1964, MSc, 1966; PhD, Princeton U., 1968. Rsch. assc. Princeton U., Princeton, NJ, 1968-69; vis. scientist CERN, Geneva, 1969-70, sci. assoc., 1979—80; asst. prof. Harvard U., Cambridge, Mass., 1970-72; asst./assoc. prof. U. Chgo., 1972-79, prof., 1979—, dir. Enrico Fermi Inst., 2001—. Member Physics Adv. Com., SSC, Dallas, 1990-. Author numerous articles to profl. jours. Fellow Alfred P. Sloan Found., 1972—76. Fellow Am. Phys. Soc. Achievements include discovery that there are exactly 3 families of light neutrinos. Office: University of Chicago EFI Box 47 5640 S Ellis Ave Chicago IL 60637 Office Phone: 773-702-7443. Office Fax: 773-702-1914. E-mail: j-pilcher@uchicago.edu. *

PILCHER, WEBSTER HOTCHKISS, neurosurgeon; b. Niagara Falls, NY, Sept. 6, 1950; s. Edward Barron and Priscilla Bernice Pilcher; m. Allyson Kerr Pilcher, June 27, 1971; children: Webster, Elisabeth, Bradford. AB, Colgate U., Hamilton, NY, 1972; DDS, Columbia U., NYC, 1977; MD, PhD, U. Rochester, NY, 1983. Diplomate Am. Bd. Neurosurgeons, 1995. Intern U. Rochester Med. Ctr., 1983—84, resident, 1984—89, asst. prof. neurosurg., 1990—95, assoc. prof. neurosurg., 1995—2002, prof., chmn. neurosurg., 2002—. Contbr. articles to profl. jours. Fellow, U. Wash., Seattle, 1989—90. Mem.: Am. Assn. Neurosurgeons, Neurosurg. Soc. Am. Episcopalian. Office: U Rochester Med Ctr Dept Neurosurg 601 Elmwood Ave Rochester NY 14642

PILDES, RICHARD H., law educator; AB, Princeton U., 1980; JD, Harvard Law Sch., 1983. Bar: Mass. 1987. Law clk. to Judge Abner Mikva US Ct. Appeals DC Cir., 1983—84; law clk. to Justice Thurgood Marshall US Supreme Ct., 1984—85; assoc. Foley, Hoag & Eliot, Boston, 1986—87; asst. prof. U. Mich. Law Sch., 1988—93, prof., 1993—2000, NYU Sch. Law, 2000—, Sudler Family prof. constl. law. Vis. prof. U. Chgo. Law Sch., 1997, NYU Sch. Law, 1999—2000, Harvard Law Sch., 2004; sr. fellow Program in Ethics & the Professors Harvard U., 1998—99. Author (with others): The Law of Democracy: Legal Structure of the Political Process, 2001. Carnegie scholar, 2004. Office: NYU Sch Law Vanderbilt Hall Rm 507 40 Washington Sq S New York NY 10012-1099 Office Phone: 212-998-6377. E-mail: rick.pildes@nyu.edu.

PILEGGI, DOMINIC F., state senator; b. Chester, Pa., Dec. 15, 1957; s. Francis and Mary Pileggi; m. Diana Pileggi; children: Elisa, Gabrielle, Michael. BA in Econs., St. Joseph's U., 1979; JD, Villanova Sch. of Law, 1982. Mayor City of Chester, Pa., 1998—2002; mem. Pa. Senate from 9th Dist., 2002—, majority leader, 2007—. Dir. Chester-Upland Sch. Dist.; city councilman, dir. pub. safety, 1994—98; ptnr. Law Firm of Pileggi & Pileggi. Bd. dirs. J. Lewis Crozer Libr., 1989—; mem. Chester Salvation Army Bd. of Advisors; mem., chmn. of exec. com. Rep. Party; bd. dirs. Del. County Indsl. Devel. Corp. Recipient T.M. Thomas Achievement award, 2001, Rev. Jesse F. Anderson award, 2002. Mem.: Rotary Club of Chester (past pres., Rotarian of Yr. 1995). Republican. Office: State House 459 Capitol Bldg Senate Box 203009 Harrisburg PA 17120-3009 E-mail: dpileggi@pasen.gov.

PILEGGI, DOMINIC J., electronics executive; BA, Rutgers U. Sales & mgmt. positions Thomas & Betts, Memphis, 1979—88, pres. electronics, 1988—94, pres. elec. products group, 1994—95; sr. exec. positions with Casco Plastic, Inc., Jordan Telecommunications, 1995—98; pres. EMS div. Viasystems Inc., 1998—2000; sr. v.p. Thomas & Betts, Memphis, 2000—02, group pres. electrical, 2000—03, pres., COO, 2003—04, pres., CEO, 2004—05, chmn., CEO, 2006—. Office: Thomas & Betts 8155 T&B Blvd Memphis TN 38125 Office Phone: 901-252-8000. *

PILEGGI, JENNIFER WENDY, transportation services executive; b. NYC, July 27, 1964; d. Jerome E. Rosenfeld. BA in Art History, cum laude, Yale U., 1986; JD, NYU, 1990. Bar: Calif. 1990. Assoc. Heller, Ehrman, White & McAuliffe, San Francisco, Marron, Reid & Sheehy, San Francisco; joined CNF Inc., Palo Alto, Calif., 1996; corp. counsel Menlo Worldwide Logistics subs., Redwood City, Calif., 1996—99, v.p., corp. counsel, 1999—2003, Menlo Worldwide subs., Redwood City, Calif., 2003—04; sr. v.p., gen. counsel, corp. sec. Con-way Inc. (formerly CNF Inc.), 2004—. Mem.: ABA, Calif. State Bar Assn. Office: CNF Inc 2855 Campus Dr Ste 300 San Mateo CA 94403 Office Phone: 650-378-5200. Office Fax: 650-357-9160. *

PILE-SPELLMAN, JOHN MARTIN, radiology and neurosurgery educator; b. Sioux City, Iowa, Jan. 12, 1951; s. George Geneser and Mary Carol (Dwight) Spellman; m. Eliza R. Pile, June 2, 1973; children: Megan, Katherine, Julian. BS, U. S.D., 1976; MD, Tufts U., 1978. Diplomate Am. Bd. Radiology. Resident radiology Mass. Gen. Hosp., Boston, 1980-83, fellow neuroradiology, 1983-85; interventional fellow neuroradiology NYU Med., NYC, 1986; prof. radiology and neurosurgery Med. Sch. Columbia U., NYC; attending radiologist, neurosurgeon Columbia U., NYC; radiologist Columbia Presbyn. Med. Ctr. Hosp., NYC, 1992—. Adj. prof. radiology and neurosurgery Med. Sch. Cornell U.; vice chmn. radiology for rsch. Columbia U.; attending radiologist and neurosurgeon N.Y. Hosp., N.Y.C., 1997—; dir. Internat. MRI. Mem. Soc. Cardiovasc. Radiology, Alpha Omega Alpha. Avocations: sailing, drawing. Office: CPMC Milstein Hosp 8 South Knuckle 177 Fort Washington Ave New York NY 10032-3713 Office Phone: 212-305-6515. Business E-Mail: jp59@columbia.edu.

PILGERAM, LAURENCE OSCAR, biochemist; b. Great Falls, Mont., June 23, 1924; s. John Rudolph and Bertha Roslyn (Phillips) P.; m. Cynthia Ann Moore, Apr. 16, 1971; children: Karl Erich, Kurt John. AA, U. Calif., Berkeley, 1948, BA, 1949, PhD, 1953. Instr. dept. physiology U. Ill. Profl. Coll., Chgo., 1954-55; asst. prof. dept. biochemistry Stanford (Calif.) U. Sch. Medicine, 1955-57; dir. arteriosclerosis rsch. lab. U. Minn. Sch. Medicine, Mpls., 1957-65, Santa Barbara, Calif., 1965-71; dir. coagulation lab., assoc. dir. Cerebrovascular Rsch. Ctr., Baylor Coll. Medicine, Tex. Med. Ctr., Houston, 1971-75; dir. Thrombosis Control Labs., Palo Alto, Calif., 1975-79, Santa Barbara, 1979—; prof. dept. molecular biology U. Calif., Santa Barbara, 2004—. Cons. NIH, Bio-Sci. Labs., FDA; del. Coun. on Thrombosis and Coun. on Strokes, Am. Heart Assn. Assembly. Co-editor: Nutrition and Thrombosis for the Nat. Dairy Coun., 1973; contbr. sci. articles to profl. jours. Recipient CIBA award, London, 1958, Karl Thomae award, Germany, 1973; NIH grantee, 1954-75; Life Ins. Med. Rsch. Fund fellow, 1952-54. Mem. Am. Soc. for Biochemistry and Molecular Biology. Office: PO Box 1583 Goleta PO Santa Barbara CA 93116 Office Phone: 805-967-5994. Business E-Mail: pilgeram@lifesci.ucsb.edu.

PILGRAM, SUZANNE, artist, art educator; b. Montclair, NJ, Feb. 25, 1945; d. Hans J. and Florence Ketchum Pilgram; m. Hassan Ghavam, Sept. 3, 1973. BA in Art, Am. U., 1967, MFA in Painting, 1970. Artist, clk. US Com. for UNICEF Children's Culture Ctr., 1970—73; prof. Coll. Translation, Tehran, Iran, 1973—80, Farah Pahlavi U., Tehran, 1977—78, Trenton State Coll., NJ, 1983; assoc. prof. Georgian Court U., Lakewood, NJ, 1981—. Printmaking coun. NJ Exhibit Intolerance, 2006—; lectr., presenter in field. One-woman shows include Phoenix Gallery, NYC, 2007, exhibitions include Columbia U., 2001, Trenton Artists Workshop, 2004, Phoenix Gallery, NYC, 2004—06. Grantee Fulbright-Hayes Group Projects Abroad, U.S. State Dept., Jamaica, 1983, Faculty Rsch. grant, Georgian Ct. U., 2004; Art fellow, Womens Studio Workshop, 2007. Mem.: Trenton Artists Workshop, N.J. Project (Grant 1987—). Avocation: gardening. Home: 9 Robin Rd Howell NJ 07731 Office: Georgian Ct Univ 900 Lakewood Ave Lakewood NJ 08701 Office Phone: 732-987-2330. Business E-Mail: pilgrams@georgian.edu.

PILGRIM, LONNIE (BO PILGRIM), food products executive; b. May 8, 1928; married. Ptnr. Pilgrim's Pride Corp., Pittsburg, Tex., 1953-68, CEO, 1968—98, chmn., CEO, 1998—2004, chmn., 2004—. Chmn. First State Bank Pitts. Served with U.S. Armed Forces, 1951-53. Office: Pilgrim's Pride Corp 4845 US Hwy 271 N Pittsburg TX 75686 Mailing: Pilgrim's Pride Corp PO Box 93 Pittsburg TX 75686-0093 *

PILIBOSIAN, MICHELE MASON, lawyer; b. Metairie, La., Nov. 5, 1970; BA, U. Tex., Austin, 1992; JD cum laude, U. Houston Law Sch., 1998. Bar: Tex. 1998, US Dist. Ct. (ea., no. and so. dists. Tex.) 1999, US Supreme Ct. 2003, US Dist. Ct. (we. dist. Tex.) 2003. Assoc. Baker Hostetler, LLP, Houston, 1998—2007, ptnr., 2007—. Candidates editor: Houston Jour. Internat. Law. Named a Rising Star, Tex. Super Lawyers mag., 2006. Mem.: Houston Young Lawyers Assn., Houston Bar Assn., Jr. League Houston. Office: Baker Hostetler 1000 Louisiana St Ste 2000 Houston TX 77002 Office Phone: 713-646-1333. E-mail: mpilibosian@bakerlaw.com.

PILISUK, MARC, psychology educator; b. NYC, Jan. 19, 1934; s. Louis and Charlotte (Feferholtz) P.; m. Phyllis E. Kamen, June 16, 1956; children: Tammy, Jeff. BA, Queens Coll., 1955; MA, U. Mich., 1956, PhD, 1961. Asst. prof., assoc. rsch. psychologist U. Mich., Ann Arbor, 1961-65, founder teach-in, 1965; assoc. prof. Purdue U., West Lafayette, Ind., 1965-67; prof.-in-residence U. Calif., Berkeley, 1967-77, prof. cmty. psychology Davis, 1977—. Vis. prof. U. Calif., Wright Inst., 1991—93; cons. Ctr. for Self Help Rsch., Berkeley, Calif., 1991—93; prof. psychology Saybrook Grad. Sch. & Rsch. Ctr., San Francisco, 1993—. Author: (textbooks) International Conflict and Social Policy, 1972, The Healing Web: Social Networks and Human Survival, 1986; editor: The Triple Revolution, 1969, Poor Americans, 1970, Triple Revolution Emerging, 1972, How We Lost the War on Poverty, 1973. Grantee, NSF, 1962—66;, NIMH fellow, 1959—60, tng. grantee, Nat. Inst. Alcoholism and Drug Abuse, 1973—77. Fellow: APA (pres. divsn. peace psychology 1996—97, cadre experts on violence, Presdl. award 2005, Lifetime Contbn. award 2005), Am. Orthopsychiat. Assn., Soc. for Psychol. Study Social Issues (coun., Sage award 2004—05); mem.: ACLU, APHA, Faculty for Human Rights in C.Am., Psychologists for Social Responsibility (steering com., Disting. Svc. award 2001, Anthony Marsalla Peace and Justice award 2006), Am. Soc. on Aging, Soc. for Cmty. Rsch. and Action. Business E-Mail: mpilisuk@saybrook.edu.

PILLA, ANTHONY MICHAEL, bishop; b. Cleve., Nov. 12, 1932; s. George and Libera (Nista) P. Student, St. Gregory Coll. Sem., 1952—53, Borromeo Coll. Sem., 1955, St. Mary Sem., 1943, student, 1956—59; BA in Philosophy, John Carroll U., Cleve., 1961, MA in History, 1967. Ordained priest Roman Cath. Ch., 1959. Assoc. St. Bartholomew Parish, Middleburg Heights, Ohio, 1959—60; prof. Borromeo Sem., Wickliffe, Ohio, 1960—72, rector-pres., 1972—75; mem. Diocese Cleve. Liturgical Commn., 1964—69, asst. dir., 1969—72; sec. for svcs. to clergy and religious pers. Diocese Cleve., 1975—79; titular bishop Scardona; and aux. bishop of Cleve. and vicar Eastern region Diocese of Cleve., 1979—80, apostolic adminstr., 1980—; bishop Cleve., 1981—; pres. Nat. Conf. Cath. Bishops, 1995—98. Trustee Borromeo Sem., 1975—79, Cath. U., 1981—84; trustee, mem. bd. overseers St. Mary Sem., 1975—79; mem. adv. bd. permanent diaconate program Diocese of Cleve., 1975—79, hospitalization and ins. bd., 1979. Bd. dirs. NCCJ, 1986—. Mem.: Greater Cleve. Roundtable (trustee 1981—), Cath. Conf. Ohio, Nat. Conf. Cath. Bishops, U.S. Cath. Conf., Nat. Cath. Edn. Assn. (dir. 1972—75). Home and Office: Chancery Office Diocese of Cleveland 1027 Superior Ave E Ste 300 Cleveland OH 44114-2503

PILLAI, PRAGASH, communications executive; b. 1973; BSEE, U. Mo., Columbia. V.p., Advanced Engring. Digital Video Charter Comm. Named one of 40 Executives Under 40, Multichannel News, 2006; recipient Young Engr. award, Soc. Cable Telecomm. Engineers, 2003, Cable's Next Generation of Innovators award, Multichannel News, 2004, Pacesetter award, Comm. Engring. & Design, 2004. Mem.: Inst. Elec. Electronics Engineers (vice chmn. 2003, young Engr. award for St. Louis 2002). Office: Charter Communications Inc 12405 Powerscourt Dr Ste 100 Saint Louis MO 63131-3660 Office Phone: 314-965-0555. Office Fax: 314-965-9745.

PILLANS, CHARLES PALMER, III, lawyer; b. Orlando, Fla., Feb. 22, 1940; s. Charles Palmer Jr. and Helen (Scarborough) P.; m. Judith Hart, July 6, 1963; children: Charles Palmer IV, Helen Hart. BA, U. Fla., Gainesville, 1962, JD, 1966. Bar: Fla. 1967, US Dist. Ct. (mid. dist.) Fla. 1967, US Ct. Appeals (2d cir.) 1968, US Supreme Ct. 1971, US Ct. Appeals (3d cir.) 1976, US Ct. Appeals (5th and 11th cirs.) 1981. Asst. state atty. 4th jud. cir., Jacksonville, 1970-72; asst. gen. counsel City of Jacksonville, 1972; assoc. Bedell, Bedell, Dittmar, Smith & Zehmer, Jacksonville, Fla., 1966-70; ptnr. Bedell, Dittmar, DeVault Pillans & Coxe, P.A., Jacksonville, 1972—. Mem. Fla. Bd. Bar Examiners, Tallahassee, 1979-84, chmn., 1983-84, Jud. Nominating Commn., 1988-92, chmn., 1990-91, 1st Dist. Ct. Appeal, Tallahassee, 1988-92, chmn., 1990-91, Supreme Ct. com. on standard jury instructions in civil cases, 1998—. Master Chester Bedell Inn of Ct.; fellow Am. Coll. Trial Lawyers, ABA; mem. Am. Bar Found., Fla. Bar Assn. (chmn. profl. ethics com. 1998-2002, chmn. 1998-99), Am. Bd. Trial Advocates (assoc.). Methodist. Home: 10 Buckthorne Dr Amelia Island FL 32034-6518 Office: Bedell Dittmar DeVault Pillans & Coxe PA Bedell Bldg 101 E Adams St Jacksonville FL 32202-3303 Office Phone: 904-353-0211. Business E-Mail: cpp@bedellfirm.com.

PILLAY, ANAND, education educator, researcher; b. London, Eng., May 7, 1951; s. Vallaithan and Patricia O'Leary; m. Margit Messmer, July 9, 1993; children: Kalyan, Bhanu; m. Bronislava Jedrusik, July 26, 1978 (div. Mar. 1992); 1 child, Anusha. BA, U. Oxford, 1973; MSc, U. London, 1974, PhD, 1977. Rschr. CNRS, Paris, 1978—81; temp. lectr. U. Manchester, 1981—82; vis. lectr. U. McGill, 1982—83; assoc. prof. U. Notre Dame, 1983—86, 1986—88, prof., 1988—96, U. Ill., 1996—2005; prof., Marie Curie chair Leeds U., England, 2005—. Org. Math. Sci. Rsch. Inst., 1998. Contbr. scientific papers; author: (book) An Introduction to Stability Theory, 1983; author: (edited with Ali Nesin) The Model Theory of Groups, 1989; author: (with D. Marker and M. Messmer) Model Theory of Fields; author: Geometric Stability Theory, 1996; author: (edited with D. Haskell and C. Steinhorn) Model theory, Algebra and Geometry, 2000. Sitar player WEFT radio, 1997—2003. Recipient Humboldt prize, Humboldt Found., 2001; grant, NSF, 1983—2003, Rsch. grant, 2001—. Mem.: Assn. Symbolic Logic, Am. Math. Soc., Socialist Forum. Office: Sch Math Leeds Univ Leeds LS2 9JT England Office Phone: 44 113 363 5171.

PILLAY, GAUTAM, chemical engineer, chemist, academic administrator; b. Buffalo, Jan. 28, 1967; s. Sivasankara K. K. and Revathi (Krishnamurthy) Pillay; m. Amy Matthews, 2004. BS, N.Mex. State U., Las Cruces, 1988; PhD, Tex. A&M U., 1993. Grad. rschr., staff mem. Los Alamos Nat. Lab., 1984-87, mem. tech. staff, 1997—2001; grad. rschr. Tex. A&M U., College Station, 1988-92; rsch. engr. Pacific N.W. Lab., Richland, Wash., 1992-95, sr. rsch. engr., 1995-97; adj. faculty Wash. State U., Richland, 1993-97; exec. dir. Inland N.W. Rsch. Alliance, Idaho Falls, Idaho, 2001—04; v.p. rsch. S.D. Sch. Mines and Tech., Rapid City, 2004—. Contbr. articles to profl. jours. Recipient Fed. Lab. Consortium award for excellence in tech. transfer, 1997; NSF Grad. Rsch. fellow, 1988—91. Mem.: AIChE (symposium chair), N.Y. Acad. Scis., Am. Nuc. Soc., Am. Chem. Soc., Electrochemical Soc. (symposium chair 1993—, mem. exec. com. 1994—, pres. Pacific N.W. sect. 1996—97, v.p. IE & EE divsn. 2002—04, pres. 2004—), Phi Kappa Phi, Alpha Chi, Omega Chi Epsilon, Tau Beta Pi. Avocations: general aviation, musician. Office: SD Sch Mines and Tech 501 E Saint Joseph St Rapid City SD 57701 Office Phone: 605-394-2493. E-mail: gautam.pillay@sdsmt.edu.

PILLER, CHARLES LEON, journalist; b. Chgo., Jan. 9, 1955; s. Jack H. and Alice (Shakow) P.; m. Surry Piller Bunnell, Aug. 21, 1984; 1 child, Nathan Bunnell Piller. BA, Lone Mountain Coll., 1977. Editor, writer U. Calif., San Francisco, 1982-89; sr. editor Macworld mag., San Francisco, 1990-96; exec. editor PC World Mag., San Francisco, 1996—97; tech. writer L.A. Times, 1996—2002, science writer computer tech. and biology, 2002—. Chair Ctr. Pub. Integrity, Washington, 1988—, also bd. dirs.; cons. US Senate, Washington, 1989-92. Author: Gene Wars, 1988, The Fail-Safe Society, 1991; contbr. numerous articles to newspapers and mags. Recipient of the John Swett Journalism award, 1993, Benjamin Fine Journalism award, 1995, Runner-Up Lincoln Steffens Journalism award, 1994, Am. Soc. of Business Press Editors (various awards). Office: LA Times 202 W First St Los Angeles CA 90012 Office Fax: 213-237-4712. Business E-Mail: charles.piller@latimes.com.

PILLING, DONALD L., management consultant, retired military officer; b. NYC, June 4, 1943; m. Barbara Orbon; children: Kathleen, Jennifer. Grad., US Naval Acad., 1965; PhD, U. Cambridge, 1970. Commd. ensign USN, Washington, 1965, advanced thru grades to admiral, 1997, ret., 2000; fed. exec. fellow Brookings Instn., 1985—86; dir. Navy Five-Year Def. Plan, Office Chief Naval Ops. USN, 1986—88; mem. staff. NSC, 1989—92; dir. programming, Office Chief of Naval Ops. USN, 1993—95, comdr. SIXTH Fleet/Naval Striking & Support Forces, So. Europe Gaeta, Italy, 1995—96, dep. chief naval ops. resources, warfare requirements & assessments Washington, 1996—97, vice chief naval ops., 1997—2000; pres., CEO LMI, McLean, Va., 2002—. Mem. bd. Naval War Coll., Applied Physics Laboratory; Applied Physics Laboratory Nat. Def. Industrial Assn. Author: Competition in Defense Procurement, 1989. Decorated Def. Disting. Svc. medal (2), Disting. Svc. medal Legion, Meritorious Svc. medal, Legion of Merit, Meritorious Svc. medal, Navy Commendation medal, Navy Achievement medal. Fellow: Nat. Acad. Pub. Adminstrn.; mem.: White House Fellows Commn., Coun. Fgn. Rels., Def. Sci. Bd. Office: LMI 2000 Corporate Ridge Mc Lean VA 22102 *

PILLIOD, JAMES P., state legislator, physician; b. NYC, Aug. 9, 1930; s. James J. and Mary Alice (Phillips) P.; m. Judith Bean. BA, Yale U., 1952; MD, Duke U., 1960. Diplomate Am. Bd. Pediatrics. Staff physician Lake Regional Gen. Hosp., 1964—; mem. N.H. Ho. of Reps., Concord, 1996—. Lt. (j.g.) USN. Diplomate Acad. of Pediatrics; mem. AMA (past del.), N.H. Med. Soc. (past pres.), N.H. Hosp. Assn. (Physician Staff Mem. of Yr. 1988), N.H. Pediat. Soc. (Pub. Servant of Yr. 1997). Office: NH State Legis State House Concord NH 03301

PILLOT, GENE MERRILL, retired school system administrator; b. Canton, Ohio, Apr. 13, 1930; s. John D. Pillot and Vera R. Granstaff; m. Beverly Ann Shaw, June 4, 1982; children: Vera Kathleen Martin, Michael Gene, Patrick Merrill. BS in Math., Ohio State U., 1952; MEd in Adminstrn. and Supvervision, Kent State U., 1957; EdD in Adminstrn. and Supervision, U. Fla., 1970. Asst. prin. North Royalton (Ohio) High Sch., 1959-61, prin., 1961-63; asst. prin. Sarasota (Fla.) Sr. High Sch., 1963-64, prin., 1964-68; dir. staff development Sarasota Dist. Schs., 1968-70, asst. supt., 1970-71, supt., 1971-80; dir. human resources Sarasota Meml Hosp., 1980-83; owner, broker Pillot Realty, Sarasota, 1986-90; commr. Sarasota City, 1989-2001, vice mayor, 1992-93, 96-97, 99-2000, mayor, 1993-94, 97-98, 2000-2001. Prof. Am. Assn. Sch. Adminstrs., Nat. Acad. Sch. Execs., 1969-73; adj. prof. U. South Fla., Tampa, 1978-81; pvt. cons. edn. orgns., 1969-76. Author (chpt.) Differentiated Staffing, Strategies for D.S., 1971; contbr. articles to profl. jours. Trustee Fla. Sch. Deaf/Blind, St. Augustine, 1980—89, chmn. bd. trustees, 1986—89; active Civil Svc. Bd., Sarasota, 1984—89; mem. adv. bd. Cath. Social Svcs., 1987—89; bd. dirs. Riverview Found., 1985—94, Girls Club, Sarasota, 1985—89, Hospice Found., Sarasota Opera Assn., Sarasota Mil. Acad., 2001—. Mem.: Phi Delta Kappa (Educator of Yr. 1980). Republican. Roman Catholic. Avocations: genealogy, ballroom dancing. Home: 10060 Cherry Hills Avenue Cir Bradenton FL 34202 E-mail: gpillot@aol.com.

PILLSBURY, GEORGE STURGIS, retired investment advisor; b. Crystal Bay, Minn., July 17, 1921; s. John S. and Eleanor (Lawler) P.; m. Sally Whitney, Jan. 4, 1947; children: Charles Alfred, George Sturgis, Sarah Kimball, Katharine Whitney. BA, Yale U., 1943. Mem. Lafayette Club, Woodhill Club, Minnetonka Yacht Club, Mpls. Club, River Club (NYC). Home: 1300 Bracketts Point Rd Wayzata MN 55391-9393 Office: 601 Carlson Pkwy Ste 800 Minnetonka MN 55305 Home Phone: 952-473-9634; Office Phone: 952-405-7945. Personal E-mail: gspbury@aol.com.

PILLSBURY, HAROLD CROCKETT, III, otolaryngologist; b. Balt., Dec. 5, 1947; m. Carol Higgins Pillsbury; children: Matthew, Benjamin, Thomas. BA, George Washington U., Washington, 1970, MD, 1972. Diplomate Nat. Bd. Med. Examiners, Am. Bd. Otolaryngology; lic. Conn., N.C. Resident gen. surgery U. N.C., Chapel Hill, 1972-73, resident otolaryngology, 1973-76; fellow Kantonsspital, Zurich, Switzerland, 1977; asst. prof. otolaryngology Yale U., New Haven, Conn., 1977-81, assoc. prof. otolayngology, 1981-82; assoc. prof. surgery, otolayngology, head and neck surgery U. N.C. Sch. Medicine, Chapel Hill, 1982-86, prof. surgery, otolaryngology, head and neck surgery, 1986—, Thomas J. Dark Disting. Prof., 1991—. Civilian cons. USAF Surgeon Gen. for Otolaryngology-Head and Neck Surgery, 1993; hon. guest lectr. Alpha Omega Alpha Induction Ceremonies, U. N.C., Chapel Hill, 1990, 91, Sch. of Medicine Commencement Ceremony, U. N.C., 1990. Alpha Omega

Alpha Induction Ceremonies, U. W. Va., 1991; Boies lectr. and prof. U. Minn. Dept. Otolaryngology, 1992, Whitehead lectr. Whitehead Med. Soc., U. N.C., 1994. Countbr. numerous articles to profl. jours. Recipient John A Kirchner Tchg. award, 1980, Disting. Alumni Achievement award George Washington U., 2006. Mem. Am. Acad. Otolaryngology-Head and Neck Surgery (pres. 1998-99, Honor award 1985, Disting. Svc. award 1994, Harris Mosher award 1986), Am. Bd. Otolaryngology (bd. dirs., past pres., current pres. bd. dirs.), Am. Laryngol., Rhinol. and Otol. Soc. (pres. 2007), Am. Laryngol. Assn. (pres. 2000-01), Soc. Univ. Otolaryngologists (pres. 1997-98), Alpha Omega Alpha. Office: U NC Dept Otolaryngology Head & Neck Surgery 1115 Bioinformatics Bldg 130 Mason Farm Rd CB # 7070 Chapel Hill NC 27599-7070 Office Phone: 919-966-8926.

PILNICK, GARY H., food products executive, lawyer; b. Forest Hills, NY, Sept. 17, 1964; m. Helen Pilnick. Grad., Lafayette Coll., 1986; law degree with honors, Duke U., 1989. Atty. Jenner and Block, Chgo., 1989—95; v.p., chief corp. counsel Specialty Foods Corp., 1995—97; chief counsel corp. devel. and fin. Sara Lee Corp., 1997—99; v.p., chief counsel Sara Lee Branded Apparel, 1999—2000; v.p., dep. gen. counsel, asst. sec. Kellogg Co., 2000—03, sr. v.p., gen. counsel corp. devel., sec., 2003—. Office: Kellogg Co Box 3599 1 Kellogg Sq Battle Creek MI 49016-3599 E-mail: gary.pilnick@kellogg.com. *

PILOUS, BETTY SCHEIBEL, medical/surgical nurse; b. Cleve., July 30, 1948; d. Raymond W. and Dorothy E. (Groth) S.; m. Lee Alan Pilous, Sept. 11, 1970; 1 child. Diploma in nursing, Huron Rd. Hosp., Cleve., 1970; BSBA, St. Joseph's Coll., 1989, MHSA, 1996. RN, Ohio; CPHQ. Nurse Huron Rd. Hosp., Cleve., 1970-71, Hillcrest Hosp., Cleve., 1974-77; head nurse, relief supr. Oak Park Hosp., Oakwood, Ohio, 1977-81; head nurse med.-surg. Bedford Hosp., Ohio, 1981-87; dir. inpatient svcs. Meridia Euclid Hosp., Euclid, Ohio, 1987-93. Coord. hosp. info. system for nursing, chair nurse practice com., los com. nursing liaison; DON, Manor Care, Willoughby, Ohio; team leader referral/assessment Hospice Western Res.; dir. clin. svcs. Total Health, 1998, dir. HCQIP, Ohio, 1999, dir. Post Acute Svcs., 2001-; dir. cmty.based svcs. Ohio KePRO, 2005—. Former instr. ARC; chair nurse practice com. Am. Heart Assn.; mem. nursing standards com. Cmty. Hosp. of Bedford; mem. health and safety com. Twinsburg Schs., Ohio, 1984, mem. curriculum com., 1981-83; chairperson standards com. Cmty. Hosp. of Bedford; former counselor jr. high youth 1st Congl. Ch., Twinsburg; past chair adv. bd. chairperson Brecksville Rainbown Assembly for Girls, 1992; mem. Twinsburg Libr. Levy Com., 1991; mem. Gov.'s Task Force on Compassionate Care, 2003-04. Recipient Paradiam award, 1991. Mem. Ohio Citizen League Nursing Nurse Execs. Network (former sec.), Ohio Hosp. Assn., Ohio Orgn. Nurse Execs., Ohio Directors of Nursing Assocs. Long Term Care, Nat. League Nursing, Southeast Cleve. Mid Mgrs. Ohio Orgn. Nurse Exec., Acad. Med.-Surg. Nursing (charter mem.), Networking Group Nurse Mgrs. (initiated), Order Eastern Star, Sigma Theta Tau, Iota Psi. Avocations: hiking, helping children. Office Phone: 216-447-9604. Personal E-mail: bpilous@aol.com.

PILSON, MICHAEL EDWARD QUINTON, oceanography educator; b. Ottawa, Ont., Can., Oct. 25, 1933; came to U.S., 1958; s. Edward Charles and Frances Amelia (Ferguson) P.; m. Joan Elaine Johnstone, July 6, 1957; children: Diana Jane, John Edward Quinton. BSc, Bishops U., Lennoxville, Que., Can.; MSc, McGill U., Montreal, Que., Can., 1958; PhD, U. Calif., San Diego, 1964. Chemist Windsor Mills (Can.) Paper Co., 1954-55; asst. chemist Macdonald Coll. of McGill U., 1955-58; biologist Zool. Soc. San Diego, 1963-66; asst. prof. U. R.I., Narragansett, 1966-71, assoc. prof., 1971-78, prof., 1978-2000, prof. emeritus, 2000—. Dir. Marine Ecosystems Rsch. Lab., Narragansett, 1976-97. Contbr. articles to profl. and popular jours.; author chpts. for 6 books, 1 textbook. Grantee NSF, NOAA, EPA, NIH. Mem. AAAS, AGU, ASLO, Oceanography Soc., Am. Soc. Mammalogists, Saunderstown Yacht Club (bd. govs. 1974-87, commodore 1985-87), Brome Cougar Spotters (pres. emeritus). Home: PO Box 27 Saunderstown RI 02874-0027 Office: U RI Grad Sch Oceanography Narragansett RI 02882 Office Phone: 401-874-6104. E-mail: pilson@gso.uri.edu.

PILZ, ALFRED NORMAN, manufacturing executive; b. Evergreen Park, Ill., Oct. 12, 1931; s. Alfred and Erma Louise (Deane) P.; m. Constance Ney, Nov. 1957; children: Kerry, Kurt, Stephen, Matthew. BS, Ill. Inst. Tech., 1953; MBA, Harvard U., 1960. Registered profl. engr., Mass. Indsl. engr. Harnischfeger Corp., Milw., 1956-58; cons. Arthur D. Little Co., Cambridge, Mass., 1959-60; asst. to exec. v.p., mgr. prodn. engring. Nat. Forge Co., Irvine, Pa., 1960-62; mgmt. cons. McKinsey & Co., NYC and Cleve., 1962-67; pres., gen. mgr. Ajax Iron Works div. Cooper Industries, Corry, Pa., 1967-72; pres., chief exec. officer WDP, Inc., 1972-79, Swank Refractories Co., Johnstown, Pa., 1972-77, Hyde Park (Pa.) Foundry & Machine Co., 1974-79, Shepard-Niles Corp., Montour Falls, NY, 1979-82, Acco Babcock Materials Handling, Frederick, Md., 1982-85; ptnr. Fagan and Co., Ligonier, Pa. Bd. dirs. Acco Babcock, Inc., Babcock Internat., Chemung Foundry, Parnell Precision Products Co., Carre-Orban and Partners, Liberty Mut. Ins. Co., Ind. Steel and Engring. Corp., Bedford Crane Co., Shepard Niles Corp., Marine Bank, WDP, Inc., Ligonier Valley (Pa.) R.R. Soc.; chmn. Parnell Precision Products, 1980-82, Ind. Steeland Engring., Bedford Crane Co., 1981-82, pres., chmn., CEO, Greenway Products. With USN, 1948—56, Korea. Mem.: Ligonier Railroad Assn. (bd. dirs.), Ligonier Railroad Hist. Soc., Petroleum Equipment Supplies Assn., Modern Railroad Industry Assn., Conveyor Equipment Mfg. Assn., Hoist Mfrs. Assn., Crane Mfrs. Assn., Ligonier Railroad Hist. Soc., Ft. Ligonier Assn., Navy League, Tin Can Sailors Assn., Nat. Trust Soc., Auburn-Cord-Duesenberg Club, HYP (Pitts.). Home: 139 Ramsey Rd Ligonier PA 15658-2204 Office: 223 E Main St Ligonier PA 15658-1347 Personal E-mail: greenwayproducts@verizon.net.

PIMLEY, KIM JENSEN, financial training consultant; b. Abington, Pa., Apr. 29, 1960; d. Alvin Christian Jensen and Helen Marie (Kairis) Meinken; m. Michael St. John Pimley, Nov. 10, 1988; 1 child, Oliver Jensen Pimley. BA, Emory U., 1982, MA magna cum laude, 1982; postgrad., U. Chgo., 1985—. Mgr. tng. ops. Continental Bank, Chgo., 1986-88, mgr. coll. rels., 1988-90; mgr. client svcs. The Globecon Group, NYC, 1990-92; prin. Pimley & Pimley, Inc., Princeton, NJ, 1992-93; pres. P&P Tng. Resources, Inc., Princeton, 1993—. Owner Jr. League Designer Showhouse, 1997. Contbr. poetry to various jours. Trustee Dem. Com., 1997—; chmn. silent auction Princeton Friends Sch., 2002-04; trustee Opera Festival NJ, 2000-03; bd. dirs., v.p. fin. Jewish Ctr. Princeton, 1999—, pres. 2004-05; NJ bd. dir. Am. Jewish Com., 2007-; bd. dirs. Princeton Healthcare Sys. Found., 2005—, United Jewish Fedn., Princeton, Mercer, Bucks, 2006; co-chmn. Nov. Night, 2006. Scholarship U. Chgo., 1984. Mem. ACLU (NJ bd. dirs.), Princeton Cmty. Dem. Orgn. (treas.), Oxford & Cambridge Club, Nassau Club. Office: P&P Tng Resources Inc 117 Library Pl Princeton NJ 08540-3019

PIMM, STUART L., ecology educator; b. Derbyshire, Eng., Feb. 27, 1949; naturalized, U.S. m. Julia Killeffer, June 2, 1990; 2 children. BA second class honors, Oxford, Eng., 1971; PhD, New Mex. State Univ., 1974. Asst. prof. Clemson Univ., SC, 1974—75, Tex. Tech Univ., Lubbock, 1975—79, assoc. prof., 1979—82; assoc. prof. ecology and evolutionary biology Univ. Tenn., Knoxville, 1982—86, prof., 1986—99, Columbia Univ., NYC, 1999—2002; Doris Duke chair of conservation ecology Duke Univ., NC, 2002—. Vis. prof. Griffith Univ., Queensland, Australia, 1983—84, Inst. for Nonlinear Sci., Univ. Calif., San Diego, 1987, Sch. of Ecosystem Mgmt., Univ. New Eng., Australia, 1987, Ctr. for Population Biology, Imperial Coll., Silwood Park, England, 1990, Mammal Rsch. Inst., Pretoria, South Africa, 1996, Pretoria, 2000; sr. vis. scholar Nat. Rsch. Coun., 1995; disting. assoc. in rsch. Bernice P. Bishop Mus., Honolulu, 1997—. Contbr. articles to profl. journals. Named one of world's most highly cited scientists, Inst. Sci. Info., 2002; recipient Pew Fellowship, 1993—96, Kemp prize for disting. ecologists, 1994, Aldo Leopold Leadership Fellow, 1999. Fellow: Am. Acad. Arts & Sci. Office: Nicholas Sch Environ and Earth Sci Duke Univ Box 90328 Durham NC 27708 Office Phone: 919-613-8000. Office Fax: 919-684-8741.

PINAC, ANDRÉ LOUIS, III, obstetrician, gynecologist; b. New Orleans, Dec. 8, 1955; s. André Louis Jr. and Patricia Elaine (Ledet) P.; 1 child, Amy Elizabeth. BS, U. Southwestern La., 1977; MD, La. State U., New Orleans, 1981. Diplomate Am. Bd. Ob-Gyn. Resident ob-gyn La. State U. Affiliated Hosps., New Orleans, Lafayette, Lake Charles and Baton Rouge, 1981-85; practice medicine specializing in ob-gyn Opelousas, La., 1985—; chief of staff Doctor's Hosp. Opelousas, 1993-94. Participant Cmty. Health Fair, Opelousas, 1987—; bd. dirs. Drs. Hosp. of Opelousas. Safety officer St. Landry Parish; bd. dirs. Little League, 1992-94. Named Duke at Mardi Gras Festival, Opelousas Garden Club, 1994, King Mardi Gras Ball Masque King Orme, 1999. Fellow Am. Coll. Ob-Gyn; mem. AMA, So. Med. Assn., La. State Med. Soc., St. Landry Parish Med. Soc., Opelousas Cath. Soccer Assn. (pres. 1991-93), Alpha Phi Alpha (life), Sigma Alpha Epsilon. Roman Catholic. Avocations: golf, jogging, swimming, basketball, trivia. Office: 816 Cresswell Ln Ste 1 Opelousas LA 70570-5881 Office Phone: 337-942-2112. Personal E-mail: alp3md@aol.com.

PINAUD, RAPHAEL, research scientist; s. Luiz Fernando and Sandra Maria Pinaud; m. Liisa Anne Tremere, Nov. 21, 2002; 1 child, Daniel. BS, Fed. U. Rio de Janeiro, 1999; MS, Dalhousie U., Halifax, Canada, 2001; PhD, Oreg. Health & Sci. U., Portland, 2005; postgrad., Duke U. Med. Ctr., Durham, NC, 2007. Grad. rsch. asst. Dalhousie U., Halifax, Nova Scotia, Canada, 1999—2001; grad. rsch. assoc. Oreg. Health & Sci. U., 2002—05; rsch. assoc. Duke U. Med. Ctr., 2006—07; head lab, asst. prof. brain and cognitive scis. U. Rochester, NY, 2007—. Editor: (book) Plasticity in the Visual System: From Genes to Circuits, Immediate Early Genes in Sensory Processing, Cognitive Performance and Neurological Disorders; contbr. chapters to books. Recipient The Neuron award, Soc. Neurosci., 2003, Eli Lilly award, 2003, N.L. Tartar award, Oreg. Health & Sci. U. Rsch. Found., 2004, award, Can. Insts. Health Rsch., Govt. of Can., 2006; fellow, Fed. U. Rio de Janeiro, 1997, NRC Brazil, 1997—99, U. Toronto Hosp. Sick Children, 2005—06; scholar, U. Toronto, 2006; Izaak Walton Killam Meml. scholar, Killam Trustees, Dalhousie U., 1999—2001. Mem.: Brazilian Soc. Neurosci. and Behavior, Iberoamerican Neurosci. Soc., Molecular and Cellular Cognition Soc., Internat. Brain Rsch. Orgn., Soc. Neurosci.

PINCHAK, ANN SIMCHA, lawyer; b. Waco, Tex., Sept. 6, 1957; d. Louis E. and Alice (Wright) P.; m. Richard Tomlinson, July 1, 1983; children: Will Tomlinson, David Tomlinson. BA, Rice U., 1979; student, U. Houston Coll. Law, 1982. Bar: Tex. 1982, U.S. Dist. Ct. (so. dist.) 1991, U.S. Ct. Appeals (5th cir.) 1988. Atty. East Tex. Legal Svcs., Tyler, 1982—84, Nelkin & Nelkin, Houston, 1984—85, Immigration Law, Houston, 1985—96, Pinchak and Assocs., Houston, 1996—2004; assoc. Quan, Burdette & Perez PC, Houston, 2004—. Lectr. Houston and Tex. chpt. Am. Immigration Law Assn., 1991—; pro bono asylum YMCA Internat. Svc. Houston, 1985-96; Coliason-Houston sect. Tex. Am. Immigration Law Assn., Houston, 1993-94. Contbr. articles to profl. jours. V.p. Hadassah, Houston, 1989-90; frequent spkr. bus. immigration, bus. immigration issues. Mem. Am. Immigration Law Assn., Nat. Access to Healthcare Coalition, State Bar Tex.

PINCHOT, BRONSON, actor; b. NYC, 1959; s. Rosina Pinchot. BA with honors, Yale U., 1981. Ind. actor, 1981—. Appeared in TV series including Sara, 1985, Perfect Strangers, 1986-93, The Trouble With Larry, 1993, Bruno the Kid, 1996, (voice) Dumb and Dumber, 1993, Step by Step, 1997-98, Meego, 1997; other TV appearances include George Burns Comedy Week, Amazing Stories, Saturday Night Live; films include Risky Business, 1983, The Flamingo Kid, 1984, Beverly Hills Cop, 1984, After Hours, 1985, Hot Resort, 1986, Second Sight, 1989, Blame It on the Bellboy, 1992, True Romance, 1993, Beverly Hills Cop III, 1994, It's My Party, 1995, The First Wives Club, 1996, Courage Under Fire, 1996, Stinkers, 1997, All New Adventures of Laurel and Hardy: For Love or Mummy, 1998, (voice) Quest for Camelot, 1998, The Virtuoso, 1999, Out of the Cold, 1999; (TV movies) Jury Duty, 1989, Merry Christmas George Bailey, 1997; (TV miniseries) The Langoliers, 1995; appeared in Broadway play Zoya's Apartment, 1990; appeared in off-Broadway prodn. Poor Little Lambs; other regional stage appearances in Distracted, 2007. *

PINCHUK, NICHOLAS THOMAS, manufacturing executive; b. Troy, NY, Oct. 11, 1946; s. Nicholas Thomas and Mildred Frances Pinchuk; m. Lee Joyce Pinchuk, Aug. 8, 1970; children: Madeline Pinchuk Boehning, Tanya, Thomas. BSEE, Rensselaer Poly. Inst., Troy, 1968, MEE, 1969; MBA, Harvard U., Cambridge, Mass., 1976. Various fin. and engring. mgmt. positions Ford Motor Co., 1972—83; v.p., CFO Carrier Internat. Corp., Syracuse, NY, 1985-86; v.p. strategic planning Carrier Corp. (subs. of United Techs. Corp.), Syracuse, 1986-87, pres. Asia-Pacific Ops. Singapore, 1987-97, pres. global refrigeration ops.; sr. v.p., pres. Worldwide Comml. and Indsl. Group Snap-On, Inc., 2002—07, pres., COO, bd. dirs., 2007—. Mem. mgmt. adv. bd. Syracuse U., 1997; bd. dirs. Columbus McKinnon Corp., 2007-. 1st lt. US Army, 1970—71, Vietnam. Mem. Am. Soc. Refrigeration and Air Conditioning Engrs. Office: Snap-On Inc PO Box 1410 Kenosha WI 53141-1410 Office Phone: 262-656-5200. *

PINCKNEY, CHARLES COTESWORTH, lawyer; b. Richmond, Va., Oct. 23, 1939; s. Thomas and Charlotte (Kent) P.; m. Helen Raney, Aug. 13, 1966; children: Sarah Whitley, Thomas. BA, Yale U., 1961; LLB, U. Va., 1967. Bar: Va. 1967. Assoc. Mays, Valentine, Davenport & Moore, Richmond, 1967-72; ptnr. Mays & Valentine, LLP, Richmond, 1972-2000, Troutman Sanders LLP, Richmond, 2001—. Bd. dirs. Sweet Briar Coll., 1996-2000; pres. Sheltering Arms Hosp., Richmond, 1986-87, bd. dirs., 1970-99, 2004-; trustee William H.-John G.-Emma Scott Found., 1974-, sec., 1994-99, v.p., 1999-2004, pres. 2005-; campaign chmn. United Way Svcs., 1998, bd. dirs., 1997-. Lt. (j.g.) USNR, 1961-63. Mem. Va. Bar Assn., Country Club of Va., Commonwealth Club (bd. govs. 1986-92, pres. 1991-92), Richmond German (pres. 1996-98, sec.-treas. 2006-), Soc. of Cin. Republican. Episcopalian. Home: 2 Roslyn Rd Richmond VA 23226-1610 Office: Troutman Sanders LLP 1001 Haxall Pt PO Box 1122 Richmond VA 23218-1122 Home Phone: 804-288-3367; Office Phone: 804-697-1383. E-mail: cotes.pinckney@troutmansanders.com.

PINCKNEY, NEAL T., psychologist, retired educator; b. NYC, July 26, 1935; s. Leo Allen and Jean P.; children: Andrew Allen, Jennifer Elizabeth, Matthew Ian. Cert. polit. social and hist. issues, King's Coll., U. Durham, 1957; AB, U. So. Calif., 1958, postgrad., 1958—61; PhD, Oxford U., 1966; postgrad., U. Vienna, U. Hiroshima, Stanford U. Mem. Pub. Welfare Commn., LA County, 1958—60; tchr. pub. schs., LA, 1960—61; tchr., counselor Las Vegas, 1961—62; adminstr. therapist psychiat. clinic, 1962—63; educator, dir. guidance svc. Dept. Def. Overseas Dep. Schs., Eng. and Japan, 1963—67; pvt. practice clin. psychology, 1967—87; lectr. Calif. State U., Sacramento, 1967—68, asst. prof., 1968—71, assoc. prof., 1971—77, prof. psychology and edn., 1977—87, prof. emeritus, 1987—, chmn. dept. behavioral scis., 1980—82, prof. counseling psychology, coord. grad. studies, dept. adminstrn., counseling and policy studies, 1992—; founder, clin. dir. Healing Heart Found., 1993—. Vis. prof. U. Calif.-Davis, 1979—; psychologist, instr. enforcement psychology and human rels. Calif. Hwy. Patrol, 1967-80; dir. Univ. Software Evaluation Project, 1987; tech. cons., adv. Ministry Edn. and Culture, Govt. Brazil, Brasilia, 1974-76; cons. psychologist Calif. Med. Facility, Vacaville, various law enforcement agys.; prof. U. Hawaii, lectr. U. Hawaii, Leeward CC, 1992-93; mem. profl. treatment team Preventive Medicine Rsch. Inst.-Ornish Residential Retreat for Reversing Heart Disease, 1996; sponsor, builder Makaha Chartres Labyrinth; webmaster Healing Heart Website, moderator, sponsor internet discussion group; dir. Judge Rotenberg Ednl. Ctr., 2004-06. Author: Healthy Heart Handbook, 1994, Law and Ethics in Counseling and Psychotherapy, A Casebook, 1961, 86; pub. USER, a Software Report Card, 1987; editor: Incite Newsletter of Hawaii Portable Computer Users Assn., 1987-88; editor: Ency. of Psychology, 2d edit. Served with 3d Armored Divsn. U.S. Army, 1954-55. Queen's scholar Eng., 1956-57; scholar Dept. State Fgn. Svc. Inst., 1974; fellow Ford Found., 1960-61. Mem. APA, Brit. Psychol. Assn., Japanese Psychol. Assn., Brazilian Psychol. Assn., Am. Ednl. Rsch. Assn., Am. Assn. Counseling and Devel., Am. Radio Relay League (life), Hawaii Personal Computer Users Group (pres. 1989-91, sys. operator Electronic Bulletin Bd. Svc.), Quarter Century Wireless Assn. (life), Vegetarian Soc. of Hawaii (bd. dirs.), No. Calif. DX Club, Hawaii DX Assn., Phi Delta Kappa, Delta Phi Epsilon, Commonwealth Club San Francisco, Oxonian Club Tokyo, Toastmasters (area gov. 1962-63), Mason Home: Ste 1601 1650 Ala Moana Blvd Honolulu HI 96815-1411 Business E-Mail: heart@kumu.org. *Those who rush through life are merely hurrying toward their death. When one pauses to savor its many subtle varieties one begins to gain some insight and to be in awe of the wonder of it all. Then we begin to place ourselves in perspective and everything has meaning.*

PINCOMB, JESSICA, information technology executive; b. 1975; V.p. sales Computer Assocs.; dir. bus. & mktg. NY Metro dist. Microsoft Corp., 2004—. Named one of 40 Under 40, Crain's NY Bus., 2007. Office: Microsoft Corp 6th Fl 1290 Ave of the Americas New York NY 10104 Office Phone: 212-245-2100. Office Fax: 212-245-3290. *

PINCUS, HOWARD J., geologist, engineer, educator; b. NYC, June 24, 1922; s. Otto Max and Gertrude (Jankowsky) Pincus; m. Maud Lydia Roback, Sept. 6, 1953; children: Glenn David, Philip Ethan. BS, CCNY, 1942; PhD, Columbia U., 1949. Cert. profl. geol. scientist Ind., 1964, profl. engr. Wis., 1981, profl. geolist Am. Inst. Profl. Geologists, 1981. Rsch. assoc. Lamont Geol. Obs., Columbia U., 1949-51; geologist Ohio Dept. Natural Resources, summers 1950-61; faculty Ohio State U., 1949-67, from instr. to assoc. prof., 1949-59, prof., 1959-67, chmn. dept. geology, 1960-65; rsch. geologist U.S. Bur. Mines, 1963—67, geologist, rsch. supr., 1967-68; prof. geol. sci. and civil engring. U. Wis., Milw., 1968-87, prof. emeritus, 1987—, dean Coll. Letters and Sci., 1969-72; cons. geology and rock mechanics, 1954-67, 68—. Sr. postdoctoral fellow NSF, 1962; mem. U.S. nat. com. tunneling tech. NAE, 1972—74; mem. U.S. nat. com. rock mechanics NAS/NAE, 1975—78, 1980—89, chmn., 1985—87; mem. U.S. com. Inaternat. Assn. Engring. Geology/NAS, chmn., 1987—90. Tech. editor: Geotechnical Testing Jour., 1992—95; mem. editl. bd. Geotechnical Testing Jour., 1996—2007. Served to 1st lt. C.E. US Army, 1942—46. Recipient award for tchg. excellence, U. Wis.-Milw. Alumni Assn., 1978. Fellow: AAAS, ASTM (Frank W. Reinhart award 1987, Merit award 1989), Geol. Soc. Am. (chmn. engring. geology divsn. 1973—74); mem.: Am. Inst. Profl. Geologists (pres. Ohio sect. 1965—66), Assn. Engring. Geologists, Am. Rock Mechanics Assn., Internat. Soc. Rock Mechanics, Internat. Assn. Engring. Geology, Soc. Mining Engrs., Geol. Soc. Am., Am. Geophysical Union, Sigma Xi, Phi Beta Kappa (pres. Ohio State U. chpt. 1959—60, pres. U. Wis.-Milw. chpt. 1975—77). Home and Office: 17523 Plaza Marlena San Diego CA 92128-1807 Personal E-mail: hpincus@san.rr.com.

PINCUS, LIONEL I., financial executive, entrepreneur; b. Phila., Mar. 2, 1931; s. Henry and Theresa Celia (Levit) P.; m. Suzanne Storrs Poulton (dec.). BA, U. Pa., 1953; MBA, Columbia U., 1956. Assoc. gen. ptnr. Ladenburg, Thalmann & Co., NYC, 1955-63; pres. Lionel I. Pincus & Co., Inc., NYC, 1964-66; pres., CEO E.M. Warburg & Co., Inc., NYC, 1966-70; chmn., CEO E.M. Warburg, Pincus & Co., LLC, 1970—. Trustee NY Presbyn. Hosp.; trustee, chmn. emeritus Columbia U.; trustee Sch. Am. Ballet, German Marshall Fund USA, 1982-88; mem. bd. overseers Columbia Grad. Sch. Bus.; bd. dirs. Am. Mus. Natural History, Nat. Park Found., 1995-01; mem. Partnership for NYC. Mem. Coun. Fgn. Rels., Nat. Venture Capital Assn. (Lifetime award), World Wildlife Fund (nat. coun.), Nat. Golf Links Am. Club, Meadow Club. Office: EM Warburg Pincus & Co LLC 466 Lexington Ave Fl 10 New York NY 10017-3147

PINCUS, ROBERT LAWRENCE, art critic, historian; b. Bridgeport, Conn., June 5, 1953; s. Jules Robert and Carol Sylvia (Rosen) P.; m. Georgianna Manly, June 20, 1981; 1 child, Matthew Manly. BA, U. Calif., Irvine, 1976; MA, U. So. Calif., 1980, PhD, 1987. Instr. writing and Am. studies U. So. Calif., LA, 1978-83; art critic L.A. Times, 1981-85, San Diego Union, 1985-92, San Diego Union-Tribune, 1992—. Vis. prof. art history San Diego State U., 1985-86, 92, lectr. U. San Diego, 1998-. Author: On A Scale That Competes with the World: The Art of Edward and Nancy Reddin Kienholz, 1990; co-author West Coast Duchamp, 1991, But Is It Art: The Spirit of Art as Activism, 1994, Paradise, 1994, Anne Mudge: Traces, 1996, Introduction to W.D.'s Midnight Carnival, 1988, Kitchen: Liza Lou, 1996, Manuel Neri: Early Work, 1953-78, 97, Gordas: Paintings and Installations by Tania Candiani, 2002, Defining of Vision: The Museum of Photographic Arts, 2007; contbr. reviewer, Artweek, 79; corr. editor, Art in America, 1988-. Recipient Ring Truth Prizes, Best Art Story, 1986, 1987, 1988, Chem. Bank award for Disting. Newspaper Art Criticism, 1994, Mo. Lifestyles Journalism award, 2001, Best Critical Writing award, San Diego Press Club, 1994, 2004, 2006. Mem. Internat. Assn. Art Critics, Coll. Art Assn. Democrat. Office: San Diego Union Tribune PO Box 120191 350 Camino De La Reina San Diego CA 92108-3003 Office Phone: 619-293-1831. Business E-Mail: robert.pincus@uniontrib.com.

PINCUS, THEODORE HENRY, public relations executive; b. Chgo., Sept. 15, 1933; s. Jacob T. and J. (Engel) Pincus; m. Sharon Barr, Jan. 16, 1988; children: Laura, Mark, Susan, Anne, Jennifer. BS in Journalism, Ind. U., 1955. Free-lance bus. writer, 1955—58; sr. exec. Harshe Rotman & Druck, Chgo., 1958—62; owner Theodore Pincus & Assocs., Chgo., 1962—, prin., owner, 2003—; chmn., CEO Fin. Rels. Bd., Inc., Chgo., 1965—98; vice chmn. BSMG Worldwide divsn. Interpub. Group, NYC, 1998—2001; fin. columnist Chgo. Sun Times, 2002—; sr. ptnr. Stevens Gould & Pincus, 2007—. Pub. affairs advisor to Nelson Rockefeller, NYC, 1960, NYC, 68; advisor U.S. Info. Agy., 1993—; adj. prof. fin. MBA Sch., DePaul U., 2002—; former mem. adv. bd. NASDAQ, USIA; ind. comm. cons., 2003—. Author: Giveaway Day, 1977, On the Offensive, 2001; contbr. artcles to profl. jours. including Wall St. Jour., Fortune and N.Y. Times; author: Read at Your Own Risk, 2007. Active presdl. nomination campaigns; vice-chmn. Midwest Region Am. Jewish Com.; mem. adv. bd. Ind. U. Bus. Sch., The Ill. Coalition. With USAF, 1955—57. Named Entrepreneur of Yr., Ernst and Young Merrill Lynch, 1998; recipient numerous nat. awards for profl. excellence in investor rels. and corp. pub. rels., including Silver Anvil award, Pub. Rels. Soc. Am., 1966, Civic Achievement award, Am. Jewish Com., 1993, Pub. Rels. Profl. of Yr., Pub. Rels. Soc. Am., 2002. Mem.: Nat. Investor Rels. Inst. (founding), Young Pres.'s Orgn., Union League, Standard Club. Office: 400 E Ohio St Chicago IL 60611-3322 Office Phone: 312-321-1202.

PINCUS, WALTER HASKELL, news editor; b. Bklyn., Dec. 24, 1932; s. Jonas and Clare (Glassman) Pincus; m. Betty Meskin, Sept. 12, 1954; 1 child, Andrew John; m. Ann Witsell Terry, May 1, 1965; children: Ward Haskell, Adam Witsell, Cornelia Battle Terry. BA, Yale U., 1954; JD, Georgetown U., 2001. With Wall St. Jour., 1957—58; cons. Senate Fgn.

Rels. Com., 1962-63; spl. writer Washington Evening Star, 1963-66; editor, reporter Washington Post, 1966-69; chief cons. Symington subcom. Senate Fgn. Relations Com., 1969-70; assoc. editor New Republic, 1972-74, exec. editor, 1974-75; spl. writer Washington Post, 1975—; cons. NBC News, 1971-79, CBS News, 1979-86, NBC News, 1987-88, Washington Post Co., 1989—. Vis. lectr. Yale U., 1988, 2002, Stanford U., 2003—. Trustee Shakespeare Theater, 1988—, co-chmn. edn. com., 1989—91, chmn. nominating com., 1992—96, mem. exec. com., 1992—. With US Army, 1955—57. Co-recipient Pulitzer prize, 2001; recipient Page One award, 1960, George Orwell award, 1977, George Polk award, 1978, Emmy award, 1981, Stewart Alsop award, 1999. Mem.: Coun. Fgn. Rels., Yale Club Washington. Home: 3202 Klingle Rd NW Washington DC 20008-3403 Office: Washington Post 1150 15th St NW Washington DC 20071-0001 Office Phone: 202-334-7429. E-mail: pincusw@washpost.com.

PINCZOWER, KENNETH EPHRAIM, lawyer; s. Joachim and Dinah Pinczower; m. Julie Pinczower; children: Devorah, David C., Chana, Fayga Tziporah, Samuel Joseph, Sarah. BA, Queens Coll., 1985; postgrad., Rabbinical Sem. Am., NYC, 1983-86; JD, Benjamin N. Cardozo Sch. Law, 1989. Bar: N.Y. 1990, N.J. 1990, DC 1991, Fla. 1993, U.S. Dist. Ct. (so. and ea. dists.) N.Y. 1990, U.S. Dist. Ct. N.J. 1990, U.S. Ct. Appeals (2d cir.) 2004, U.S. Supreme Ct. 2004. Auditor Seidman & Seidman/B.D.O., NYC, 1986-87; summer assoc. U.S. Attys. Office, So. Dist. N.Y., NYC, 1988; Alexander jud. fellow U.S. Dist. Judge, So. Dist. N.Y., NYC, 1987-88; asst. corp. counsel N.Y.C. Law Dept., 1989-95; atty. Barron, McDonald, Carroll & Cohen, NYC, 1995—. Editor: Cardozo Arts & Entertainment Law Jour., 1988—89. Com. mem. Nat. Conf. Synagogue Youth, 1991—; vol. instr. Jewish Edn. Program, NYC, 1983—86; instr. Aish Ha Torah, 1994—98; Shulchan Aruch Sar Eleph Machon Yerushalayim, 2000—; Talmud assoc. Mesorah Heritage Found., 1993—; chmn. Torah Chesed Fund Yeshiva U., 1993—. Avocations: talmudic law, tennis, basketball. Home: 725 W 231st St Bronx NY 10463 Office: Barron McDonald et al 1 Whitehall St New York NY 10004-2109 Office Phone: 212-510-9221. Personal E-mail: kejewels@aol.com. Business E-Mail: pinczok@nationwide.com.

PINCZUK, ARON, physicist; b. San Martin, Argentina, Feb. 15, 1939; s. Faiwel and Ester (Wejeman) P.; m. Gladys Norma Teitelman, June 14, 1962; children: Ana Gabriela, Guillermo Fabian. Licenciado, U. Buenos Aires, Argentina, 1962; PhD, U. Pa., 1969; D (hon.), U Autonoma, Madrid, 1997. Staff mem. Nat. Rsch. Coun., Argentina, 1971-76; head physics dept. Faculty of Scis., U. Buenos Aires, Argentina, 1974; vis. scientist Max Planck Inst., Stuttgart, Germany, 1976, IBM Rsch., Yorktown Heights, NY, 1976-77; staff mem. Bell Labs., Murray Hill, NJ, 1978—; prof. Columbia U., NYC, 1998—. Sec. Argentina Phys. Soc., Buenos Aires, 1972-75; editor Solid State Communications, 1989-92, assoc. editor in chief, 1992-2004, editor in chief, 2005—. Contbr. over 200 articles to profl. jours. and numerous chpts. to books. Recipient Oliver E. Buckley Condensed-Matter Physics prize Am. Physical Soc., 1994. Fellow: AAAS, Am. Phys. Soc.; mem.: Optical Soc. Am., Materials Rsch. Soc. Achievements include use and devel. novel optical methods in studies of structural phase transitions, semiconductor interfaces and interactions of free electrons in semiconductors; discovered novel phenomena in studies of quantum electron fluids. Office: Columbia U Dept Physics and Applied Physics New York NY 10027 Office Phone: 212-854-9632. Business E-Mail: aron@phys.columbia.edu.

PINDER, GEORGE FRANCIS, engineering educator, research scientist; b. Windsor, Ont., Can., Feb. 6, 1942; s. Percy Samuel and Stella Marie P.; m. Phyllis Marie Charlton, Sept. 14, 1963; children— Wendy Marie, Justin George. B.Sc., U. Western Ont., 1965; PhD, U. Ill., 1968. Research hydrologist U.S. Geol. Survey, 1968-72; mem. faculty dept. civil engring. Princeton U., 1972-89, prof., 1972-89, chmn. dept., from 1980, dir. water resources program, 1972-80; dean Coll. Engring. and Math. U. Vt., Burlington, 1989-96, dir. Rsch. Ctr. for Groundwater Remediation Design, 1993—, disting. prof. Coll. Engring. and Math., 2005—. Recipient O.E. Meinzer award Geol. Soc. Am., 1975, WUC medal, 1992; U. Vt. Univ. scholar, 1993. Fellow: Wessex Inst., Am. Geophys. Union (Robert E. Horton award 1969); mem.: ASCE (Julian Hinds medal 2002), Vt. Acad. Sci. and Engring. Home: 188 Bishop Rd Shelburne VT 05482-6933 Office: U Vt Coll Engring And Math Burlington VT 05405-0001

PINDLE, ARTHUR JACKSON, JR., philosopher, researcher; b. Macon, Ga., May 26, 1942; s. Arthur Jackson Sr. and Beatrice Rosetta (Williams) P.; 1 child, Zhinga D. BS in Physics, Morehouse Coll., 1964; MA in Philosophy, Yale U., 1973, MPhil, 1974, PhD in Philosophy, 1978. Physicist IBM, Inc., Poughkeepsie, NY, 1964, Naval Ordinance Station, Indian Head, Md., 1966-69, Satellite Experiment Lab, Suitland, Md., 1970-71; philosophy prof. Fayetteville (N.C.) State U., 1976-83; pres. HRG, Inc., New Orleans, 1983—; dir. rsch. NITRT, Inc., New Orleans, 1993—; pres. Grael Electronics, Inc., 1998; prof. philosophy Spelman Coll., 2006. Mem. bd. advs. Inst. Philosoph. Rsch., Boulder, Colo., 1980-83. Contbr. articles to profl. jours.; patentee personal computer console. Mem. Dem. Nat. Com., 1993-98. Avocations: yoga, chess. Home: 250 10th St NE Apt 3402 Atlanta GA 30309 Personal E-mail: apindle@netscape.net.

PINDYCK, BRUCE EBEN, lawyer, corporate financial executive; b. NYC, Sept. 21, 1945; s. Sylvester and Lillian (Breslow) P.; m. Mary Ellen Schwartz, Aug. 18, 1968; children: Ashley Beth, Eben Spencer, Blake Michael Lawrence. AB, Columbia U., 1967, JD, 1970, MBA, 1971. Bar: N.Y. 1971, Wis. 1987. Assoc. Olwine, Connelly, Chase, O'Donnell & Weyher, NYC, 1971-80; asst. gen. counsel Peat, Marwick, Mitchell & Co., NYC, 1980-82; ptnr. Hollyer, Jones, Pindyck, Brady & Chira, NYC, 1983-87; pres., CEO Meridian Industries, Inc., Milw., 1985—, also chmn. bd. dirs.; CEO Majilite Corp., Dracut, Mass., 1987—, also chmn. bd. dirs. Mem. capital campaign com. Columbia U., 1984-87. Mem. bd. visitors Columbia Coll., 2001—; bd. dirs. Harambee Cmty. Sch., 1991—96, Milw. Ballet Co., 1993—97, Milw. Pub. Mus., 1994—98, The Private Bank, Milw., 2005—, Jr. Achievement, 2005—. Mem. Columbia Coll. Alumni Assn. (regional dir. 1988-94, v.p. 1994-98, exec. com., 1994-98), World Pres.'s Orgn. Office: 100 E Wisconsin Ave Milwaukee WI 53202-4107 Home Phone: 414-352-9196; Office Phone: 414-224-0610. E-mail: bpindyck@meridiancompanies.com.

PINDYCK, FRANK, surgeon; b. NY, June 8, 1940; s. Sylvester and Lillian Pindyck; m. Suzanne Hock, Mar. 18, 1972; children: Lindsay Jane, Jennifer Sarah, Stephanie Lyn Pindyck-Constantino. AB, Princeton U., NJ, 1962; MD, SUNY, 1966. Diplomate Am. Bd. Surgery, 1977. Intern SUNY King County Med. Ctr., NYC; resident Mt. Sinai Hosp., NYC; attending surgeon Huntington Hosp., NY, 1974—2000, chief of surgery NY, 1993—2000; chief surgery VA Hosp., White River Junction, Vt., 2001—; assoc. prof. surgery Dartmouth Med. Sch., Hanover, NH, 2001—. Capt. USAF, 1968—70, Vietnam. Decorated Air Medal with oak leaf cluster USAF. Fellow: ACS; mem.: New Eng. Surg. Soc. Home Phone: 802-457-9138; Office Phone: 802-295-9363 x 5290. Personal E-mail: frank.pindyck@med.va.gov.

PINE, WILLIAM CHARLES, foundation executive; b. Canton, Ill., Nov. 4, 1912; s. William Charles and Katherine Pauline (Prichard) P.; m. Virginia Rae Keeley, June 14, 1945; children: William Charles, Barry Scott, Nancy Katherine Pine McMahon. BS, Monmouth Coll., Ill., 1939; DHL (hon.), Southwestern at Memphis, 1961; Dr.Laws (hon.), Mercy Coll. Detroit, 1966. Asst. dir. admissions Monmouth Coll., 1939-42; spl. agt. FBI, 1942-45; assoc. dir. Am. City Bur., NYC and Chgo., 1945-47; dir. pub. relations Lake Forest (Ill.) Coll., 1947-48, v.p., 1948-51; dir. scholarship prog. Ford Motor Co. Fund., Dearborn, Mich., 1951-72, asst. dir., 1972-75; prog. dir. The Collins Found., Portland, Oreg., 1976-79, exec. v.p., 1979-97; sr. cons. Providence St. Vincent Med. Found., 1997—. Contbr. articles to profl. jours. Mem. Historic Records Adv. Bd., Salem, Oreg., 1984-87. Mem. Soc. Former Spl. Agts. of FBI. Avocations: reading, mail order bus. Office: Providence St Vincent Med Fund 9205 SW Barnes Rd Portland OR 97225-6603 Office Phone: 503-216-2198.

PINEDA, ANSELMO, neurosurgery educator; b. Lima, Peru, Apr. 3, 1923; s. Anselmo Vicente and Juana (Munayco)P.; m. Monique Yvonne Martin, Mar. 15, 1955; children: Patricia M., Richard A., Gilbert V., Katherine A. MD, San Marcos U., Lima, 1951; MS, Northwestern U., 1962. Diplomate Am. Bd. Neurol. Surgery. Rotating intern Loayza Hosp., Lima, 1950—51; head histology sect. Leprosy dept. Ministry Pub. Health, Lima, 1951; asst. pathologist Nat. Inst. Neoplastic Diseases, 1952; vol. asst. lab. normal and path. histology nervous sys. San Marcos U. Sch. Medicine, 1953; rotating intern gen. surgery Chgo., 1955; jr. asst. resident neurosurgery U. Chgo., 1955—56, sr. asst. resident neurosurgery, 1956—57, chief resident neurosurgery, 1957—58; assoc. instr. neurosurgery U. Tex., 1958—61; assoc. neurosurgeon John Sealy Hosp., Galveston, Tex., 1960—61, attending neurosurgeon, 1961; acting chief neurosurgery VA Hosp., Long Beach, Calif., 1962—63; asst. clin. prof. dept. neurobiology UCLA, 1963—82, assoc. clin. prof. divsn. neurobiology/neurosurgery, 1982—. Cons. VA Hosp., Long Beach, 1966-67; chmn. Neurosurg. Peruvian American Found. NIH spl. fellow in Neuroanatomy Northwestern U., 1961-62. Fellow ACS, Am. Coll. Angiology, Royal Soc. Medicine; mem. AAUP, AAAS, AMA, Congress of Neurol. Surgeons, World Med. Assn., Am. Assn. Neurol. Surgeons, Calif. Med. Assn., Orange County Med. Assn., Am. Acad. Neurology, Am. Assn. Neuropathologists, Internat. Coll. Surgeons, Am. Assn. Anatomists, Am. Assn. Trauma, Am. Soc. Stereotaxic and Functional Neurosurgery, N.Y. Acad. Scis., Internat. Assn. Study Pain, U. Chgo. Surg. Soc., L.A. Surg. Soc., Sigma Xi. Office: 5267 Warner Ave Ste 301 Huntington Beach CA 92649 Office Phone: 562-787-2641. Personal E-mail: ap92649@aol.com.

PINELESS, HAL STEVEN, neurologist; b. Chgo., Oct. 19, 1954; s. William and Sophie (Lubnicka) P.; m. Edy Dianne Rudnick, Mar. 10, 1985; children: Adam, Emily. BS in Zoology, U. Ill., 1976; DO, Chgo. Coll. Osteo. Medicine, 1981. Diplomate Am. Osteo. Bd. Neurology and Psychiatry. Intern Chgo. Osteo. Hosp., 1981-82; resident Loyola U. Med. Ctr./Hines (Ill.) VA Ctr., 1982-85; asst. prof. neurology Chgo. Coll. Osteo. Medicine, 1985-86; pvt. practice Winter Park, Fla., 1986—. Pres. med. staff Fla. Hosp. East Orlando, 1990-93, bd. trustees, 1990-94; clin. asst. prof. medicine Fla. State U. Coll. Medicine, 2006—. Contbr. articles to profl. jours and newspapers. Mem. Am. Osteo. Assn., Am. Acad. Neurology, Am. Coll. Neuropsychiatrists, Nat. Headache Found., Chgo. Coll. of Osteopathic Alumni Assn. (pres. 2000-03). Avocations: golf, swimming, computers, photography. Office: 1890 State Rd 436 Ste 255 Winter Park FL 32792-2285 Office Phone: 407-657-7900.

PINES, ALEXANDER, chemistry educator, researcher, consultant; b. Tel Aviv, June 22, 1945; came to US, 1968. US citizen in 1981. s. Michael and Neima (Ratner) P.; m. Ayala Malach, Aug. 31, 1967 (div. 1983); children: Itai, Shani; m. Ditsa Kafry, May 5, 1983; children: Noami, Jonathan, Talia. BSc, Hebrew U., Jerusalem, 1967; PhD in Chemical Physics, MIT, 1972; D (hon.), U. Paris "Pierre et Marie Curie", 1999, U. Rome "La Sapienza", 2001. Asst. prof. chemistry U. Calif., Berkeley, 1972-75, assoc. prof., 1975-80, prof., 1980—, Pres.'s chair, 1993-97, Chandellor's rsch. prof., 1997-99, Miller rsch. prof., 1998-99, Glenn T. Seaborg prof. chemistry, 1999—. Faculty sr. scientist materials scis. div. Lawrence Berkeley Nat. Lab., 1975—; cons. Mobil Oil Co., Princeton, N.J., 1980-84, Shell Oil Co., Houston, 1981—; chmn. Bytel Corp., Berkeley, Calif., 1981-85; vis. prof. Weizmann Inst. Sci., 1982; adv. prof. East China Normal U., Shanghai, People's Rep. of China, 1985; sci. dir. Nalorac, Martinez, Calif., 1986-92; Joliot-Curie prof. Ecole Superieure de Physique et Chemie, Paris, 1987; Walter J. Chute Disting. lectr. Dalhousie U., 1989, Charles A. McDowell lectr. U. B.C., 1989, E. Leon Watkins lectr. Wichita State U., 1990; Hinshelwood lectr., U. Oxford, 1990, A.R. Gordon Disting. lectr. U. Toronto, 1990, Venable lectr. U. N.C., 1990, Max Born lectr. Hebrew U. of Jerusalem, 1990; William Draper Harkins lectr. U. Chgo., 1991, Kolthoff lectr. U. Minn., 1991; Md.-Grace lectr. U. Md., 1992; mem. adv bd. Nat. High Magnetic Field Lab., Inst. Theoretical Physics, U. Calif. Santa Barbara, Ctr. Pure and Applied Math. U. Calif., Berkeley; mem. adv. panel chem. Nat. Sci. Found.; Randolph T. Major Disting. Lectr. U. Conn., 1992; mem. bd. sci. govs. Weizemann Inst. Sci., 1997—; Peter Smith lectr. Duke U., 1993, Arthur William Davidson lect. U. Kansas, 1992, Arthur Birch lect. Australian Nat. U., 1993, Richard C. Lord Meml. lectr. MIT, 1993, Steacie lectr. Nat. Rsch. Coun. Can., 1993, Morris Loeb lectr. Harvard U., 1994, Jesse Boot Found. lectr., U. Nottingham, 1994, Frontiers in Chemistry lectr. Tex. A&M U., 1995, Bergman lectr. Weizmann Inst. Sci., 1995, faculty rsch. lectr. U. Calif., Berkeley, 1996, Raymond & Beverly Sackler lectr. Tel Aviv U., 1996; Priestley lectr. Pa. State U., 1997; Amy Mellon lectr. Purdue U., 1997; Rsch. frontiers chemistry lectr. U. Iowa, 1998, Moses Gomberg lectr. U. Mich., 1998, J and N Max T. Rogers, Mich. State U., 1998, Frontiers in Chemistry lectr., Wayne State U., 1998, Lord Todd Prof., Cambridge U., 1999, Abbot lectr., U. N.D., 2000, John D. Roberts lectr., Calif. Tech. U., 2000, Willard lectr., U. Wis., 2000, Cliford lectr., U. Pitts., 2000, William Lloyd Evan lectr. Ohio State U., 2000, Jacob Bigeleisen lectr. Stony Brook U., 2001, Laird lectr. U. B.C., 2001; Alan S. Tetelman fellow Yale U., 2001, Regitze Vold Meml. lectr. U. Calif., San Diego, 2001, Sammet guest prof. Goëethe U., Frankfurt, 2001. Editor Molecular Physics, 1987-91; mem. bd. editors Chem. Physics, Chem. Physics Letters, Nmr: Basic Principles and Progress, Advances in Magnetic Resonance, Accounts Chemistry Research, Concepts in Magnetic Reson; adv. editor Oxford U. Press; contbr. articles to profl. jours.; patentee in field. Recipient Strait award North Calif. Spectroscopy Soc., Outstanding Achievement award U.S. Dept. of Energy, 1983, 87, 89, 97, 98, R & D 100 awards, 1987, 89, Disting. Teaching award U. Calif., Ernest O. Lawrence award, 1988, Pitts. Spectroscopy award, 1989, Wolf prize in chemistry, Wolf Found., Israel, 1991, Donald Noyce Undergrad. Teaching award U. Calif., 1992, Robert Foster Cherry award for Great Tchrs. Baylor U., 1995, F.A. Cotton Medal for Excellence in Chemical Rsch., 1998, Dickson prize Carnegie Mellon U., 2001; Guggenheim fellow, 1988, Christensen fellow St. Catherine's Coll., Oxford, 1990; named in honor of his 50th birthday, Ampere Advanced Inst., Varenna, Italy; named to Scientific American 50 List, 2002. Fellow Am. Phys. Soc. (chmn. divsn. chem. physics), Inst. Physics; foreign fellow Royal Soc.; mem. NAS, Am. Chem. Soc. (mem. exec. com. divsn. phys. chemistry, Nobel Signature award in Graduate Edu. 1982, Baekeland Medal for Pure Chemistry, 1985, Harrison Howe award 1991, Centennial Spkr., Jour. Physical Chemistry, 1997, Langmuir award in Chemical Physics, 1998, Remsen award (Md. sect.) 2000, Dickson prize 2001), Royal Soc. Chemistry (Bourke lectr., Bourke Medal, 1988, Centenary lectr. and medal 1994), Internat. Soc. Magnetic Resonance (v.p., pres. 1993-96), Lawrence Hall Sci. Outreach Com. Achievements include pioneering contributions to the development of nuclear magnetic resonance (NMR) spectroscopy; his techniques are widely used in chemistry and materials science. Office: U Calif Chemistry Dept D64A Hildebrand Hill Berkeley CA 94720-0001 Office Phone: 510-642-1220. Office Fax: 510-486-5744. Business E-Mail: pines@berkeley.edu.

PINES, BURTON YALE, media executive; b. Chgo., Apr. 6, 1940; s. Hyman and Mary Pines. BA, U. Wis., 1961, MA, 1963, PhD, 1967. Instr. U. Wis., Madison, 1962-65; corr., bur. chief Time mag., Bonn, Saigon and Vienna, 1966-73, editor NYC, 1973-81; sr. v.p. Heritage Found., Washington, 1981-92; chmn. Nat. Ctr. for Pub. Policy Rsch., Washington, 1982-94; co-founder, exec. v.p. COO NET Polit. Newstalk Network (later known as America's Voice Cable TV Network), Washington, 1992-95; pres., CEO Booknet Cable TV Network, NYC, 1995—; exec. editor Internet ops. GOP Nat. Conv., 2000; sr. v.p. Nat. Exec. Svc. Corps, 2005—. Author: Back to Basics, 1982, Out of Focus, 1994; editor: Mandate for Leadership II, 1984, Mandate for Leadership III, 1988. Recipient Page One award N.Y. Newspaper Guild, 1976, 77, 78, Freedom's Found. award, 1983. Jewish. Office: BookNet 150 W 51st St Ste 1804 New York NY 10019-6848

PINES, WAYNE LLOYD, public relations executive; b. Washington, Dec. 31, 1943; s. Jerome Martin and Ethel (Schnall) Pines; m. Nancy Freitag, Apr. 16, 1966 (div. 2003); children: Noah Morris, Jesse Mireth; m. Carol Cole Kleinman, Jan. 7, 2007. BA, Rutgers U., 1965; postgrad., George Washington U., 1969—71. Reporter, city editor Middletown Times Herald-Record, NY, 1965—68; copy editor Reuters News, 1968—69; assoc. editor FDC Reports, Washington, 1969—72; chief consumer edn. and info. FDA, also editor, 1972—74, dep. asst. commr. for pub. affairs, chief press rels. Rockville, Md., 1975—79, assoc. commr. pub. affairs, 1978—82; exec. editor Product Safety Letter and Devices and Diagnostics Letter, Washington, 1974—75; spl. asst. to dir. NIMH, 1982—83; sr. v.p., sr. counselor Burson-Marsteller, 1983—97, exec. v.p., dir. med. issues, 1987—93; pres. regulatory svc. APCO Worldwide, Washington, 1993—; sr. counselor Grey Healthcare Group, 1993—2004; mng. dir. Comms. Ptnr. and Assoc., 1999—2005; exec. v.p. Garden City Group, 1996—2006; pres. Bio-pharm. Forum George Washington U., 2002—04. Adj. prof. Washington Pub. Affairs Ctr., U. So. Calif., 1980—81; instr. NYU Sch. Continuing Edn., 1982—84, Profl. Devel. Inst., 1983—85; columnist Med. Advt. News, 1985—90, WebMD, 1999—2001; chmn. Therametrix, Inc., 1999—2001; ethics bd. Patient Channel, 2002—; bd. dirs. Scolr Pharma Inc., Medstar Rsch. Inst., FDA Alumni Assn., FDA Alliance. Author: The Sermons of Jerome Martin Pines, 1978, FDA Advertising and Promotion Manual, 1992, When Lightning Strikes: A How-to Crisis Manual, 1994, A Practical Guide to Food and Drug Law and Regulation, 1998, How to Work with the FDA, 2001, Crisis Communication in Healthcare: A Delicate Balance, 2002, A Framework for Pharmaceutical Risk Management, 2003, Making Your Case to the FDA, 2005, FDA Advisory Committees Perils and Profits, 2005, DTC Advertising and Promotion: The Changing Environment, 2005, FDA: A Century of Consumer Protection, 2006, Communicatiing in a Healthcare Crisis, 2006; contbr. articles to profl. jours. Home: 5610 Wisconsin Ave Apt 908 Chevy Chase MD 20815 Office: APCO Worldwide 700 12th St NW Washington DC 20005 Home Phone: 301-654-2675.

PINGPANK, ROBERT CHARLES, retired mathematics educator; b. Waterbury, Conn., May 27, 1937; s. Henry Frederick and Mabel Jenny Pingpank; life ptnr. Richard Thomas Nolan, Sept. 14, 1955. BS, Trinity Coll., Hartford, Conn., 1959; MEd, U. of Hartford, 1964; CAS, Hartford Sem., 1970. Cert. secondary sch. adminstr. Conn., 1964. Math. tchr. Thomaston H.S., Thomaston, Conn., 1959—65, 1990—94, math. dept. head, 1967—90; tchr. Hamden Pub. Schs., Hamden, Conn., 1965—66, Cheshire Acad., Cheshire, Conn., 1966—67; adj. lectr. in math. Mattatuck C.C., Waterbury, Conn., 1970—80. V.p. The Litchfield Inst., Inc., Litchfield, Conn., 1984—96; guest spkr. Sr. Lifestyles radio program, 2005; guest lectr. Fla. Atlantic U., 2006. Author (with Richard T. Nolan): Soul Mates: More Than Partners, 2004. Active Compass of Lake Worth, Fla., 2004—; soc. of regents Cathedral of St. John the Divine, NYC, 2002—; mem. Integrity-Palm Beach, Lake Worth, Fla., 2001—; treas. St. Paul's Episcopal Ch., Bantam, Conn., 1975—87, asst. treas., 1987—94; mem. Lambda Legal, NYC, 2002—; notary pub. State of Fla., 1988—. Fellow: McCook Fellows Soc. Trinity Coll.; mem.: NEA, Harwood Soc. Cheshire Acad., Yale Legacy Ptnrs., Assn. Tchrs. Math. in Conn., Conn. Edn. Assn., Thomaston Edn. Assn. (treas.), Soc. Torch NYU, Cathedral Founders Soc. Wash. Nat. Cathedral. Independent. Episcopalian. Avocations: automobiles (history, design, mechanical, costs), Cavalier King Charles Spaniels. Home: 2527 Egret Lake Dr West Palm Beach FL 33413-2161 Home Phone: 561-642-8423. Personal E-mail: litchinst@aol.com.

PINGREE, BRUCE DOUGLAS, lawyer; b. Salt Lake City, June 6, 1947; s. Howard W. and Lois (Ivie) P.; m. Lorraine Bertelli, Oct. 11, 1981; children: Christian James, Matthew David, Alexandra Elizabeth, Meredith Gillian, Lauren Ashley, Geoffrey Nicholas. BA in Philosophy, U. Utah, 1970, JD, 1973. Bar: Ariz. 1973, Tex. 1990. Prnr. Snell & Wilmer, Phoenix, 1973—89; shareholder Johnson & Gibbs, Dallas, 1989—93; ptnr. Gardere & Wynne, Dallas, 1993—95, Baker Botts, LLP, Dallas, 1995—. Lectr. in field. Contbr. articles to profl. jours. Served to capt. USAR Fellow Am. Coll. Employee Benefit Counsel, Inc. (charter); mem. ABA (tax sect., past chair employee benefits com., past vice chair, past chmn. various subcoms., 1993-94, chair joint com. on employee benefits 1994-95), Tex. State Bar Assn. (chair, tax sect. benefits and compensation com. 2000), Dallas Bar Assn. (chair employee benefits sect. 2001-2002), S.W. Benefits Conf., Nat. Assn. Stock Plan Profls., Order of Coif. Episcopalian. Office: Baker & Botts LLP 2001 Ross Ave Ste 600 Dallas TX 75201-2900 Home: 4218 Rosa Ct Dallas TX 75220 Office Phone: 214-953-6878. Business E-Mail: bruce.pingree@bakerbotts.com.

PING-ROBBINS, NANCY REGAN, musician, writer, artist; b. Nashville, Dec. 19, 1939; d. Charles Augustus and Ruby Phyllis (Perdue) Regan; m. Robert Leroy Ping, June 19, 1959 (div. 1980); children: Robert Alan, Michael Regan, Bryan Edward; m. William Edward Robbins, Jr., Mar. 14, 1981. BMusic, Ind. U., 1964; MA, U. No. Colo., 1972; PhD, U. Colo., 1979. Pvt. instr. piano and flute, 1960—; organist Armed Forces Chapels, Frankfurt, Kaiserslautern, Germany, 1962-66; staff pianist US Armed Forces Spl. Svcs. Theater, Frankfurt, 1963-65; music tchr. Fayetteville Pub. Schs., Ind., 1966-67, Stratton Pub. Schs., Colo., 1967-70; instr. piano, staff piano accompanist U. No. Colo., Greeley, 1970-72; instr. music history U. Colo., Boulder, 1974; instr., asst. prof. music U. NC, Wilmington, 1974-79; assoc. prof. music, coord. music Shaw U., Raleigh, NC, 1979-87; dir. Atlantic CC Com. Arts Sch., 1987-88. Profl. harpsichord accompanist Internat. Inst. in Early Music, 1983; adj. prof. Atlantic Christian Coll. (now Barton Coll.), 1987—88, assoc. prof., 1987—95; mem., pianist Chekker Duo, 1996—2003, 2006—07. Recs. include: Early Popular Music on Piano/Harpsichord, 1984, Christmas at the Piano, 1997, En Blanc et Noir, 2001; author: The Piano Trio in the Twentieth Century, 1984, Scott Joplin: A Guide to Research, 1998, (memoir) Why the Circle Broke, 2006, (novel) Rachel's Choices, 2006; editor, compiler: The Music of Gustave Blessner, 1985; music reviewer: News and Observer, Raleigh, 1981-96, head music critic, 1989-95; artist: (painting) The White Show, Visual Arts Exch., Raleigh, NC, 2007; contbr. articles to profl. jours. Sec. Bach Festival Com., Raleigh, 1984; dir. music Bailey United Meth. Ch., N.C., 2000—. John H. Edwards fellow Ind. U., 1961; U. Colo. grad fellow, 1972-74; Mellon Found. grantee, 1982; N.C. Arts Coun. grantee, 1985; NEH summer seminar fellow, 1984. Mem. Am. Musicol. Soc. (sec.-treas. chpt. 1981-83), Soc. for Ethnomusicology (chmn. regional chpt. 1983-84), Wilson Piano Tchrs. Assn. (pres. 1988-90, 95-98), Soc. Am. Music (formerly Sonneck Soc., program com. 1999), Alpha Lambda Delta, Pi Kappa Lambda, Sigma Alpha Iota.

PINGS, ANTHONY CLAUDE, architect; b. Fresno, Calif., Dec. 16, 1951; s. Clarence Hubert and Mary (Murray) P.; m. Carole Clements, June 25, 1983; children, Adam Reed, Rebecca Mary. AA, Fresno City Coll., 1972; BArch, Calif. Poly. State U., San Luis Obispo, 1976. Lic. architect, Calif.; cert. Nat. Council Archtl. Registration Bds. Architect Aubrey Moore Jr., Fresno, 1976-81; architect, prin. Pings & Assocs., Fresno, 1981-83, 86—, Pings-Taylor Assocs., Fresno, 1983-85. Prin. works include Gollaher Profl. Office (Masonry Merit award 1985, Best Office Bldg. award 1986), Fresno Imaging Ctr. (Best Instnl. Project award 1986, Nat. Healthcare award Modern Health Care mag. 1986), Orthopedic Facility (award of honor Masonry Inst. 1987, award of merit San Joaquin chpt. AIA 1987),

Modesto Imaging Ctr. (award of merit San Joaquin chpt. AIA 1991), Peachwood Med. Ctr. (award of merit San Joaquin chpt. AIA). Mem. Calif. Indsl. Tech. Edn. Consortium Calif. State Dept. Edn., 1983, 84. Recipient Excellence in Bus. award Fresno, 1999. Mem. AIA (bd. dirs. Calif. chpt. 1983-84, v.p. San Joaquin chpt. 1982, pres. 1983, Calif. Coun. evaluation team 1983, team leader Coalinga Emergency Design Assistance team), Fresno Arts (bd. dirs., counsel 1989—, pres. 1990-93), Fig Gardens Home Owners Assn. (bd. dir. 1991—, pres. 1994—). Republican. Home: 4350 N Safford Ave Fresno CA 93704-3509

PINHEIRO, GERMANIA ARAUJO, physician, researcher; d. Francisco Arruda and Maria da Conceicao Pinheiro; m. Vinicius Cavalcanti Antao, June 23, 2003; 1 child, Sophie Pinheiro Cavalcanti. MD, Petropolis Sch. of Medicine, Brazil, 1992; MSc, Fluminense Fed. U., Brazil, 1998; PhD, Sao Paulo U., Brazil, 2003. Cert. Pulmonologist Rio de Janeiro State U., 1996, Occupl. Medicine Specialist Gama Filho U., 1998. Assoc. prof. of pulmonology Rio de Janeiro State U., Rio de Janeiro, Rio de Janeiro, 1996—2003; prof. occupl. medicine Gama Filho U., Rio de Janeiro, 1996—2003; pulmonologist Rio de Janeiro State Office for Justice and the Interior, Rio de Janeiro, 1998—2002; mem. State Tech. Commn. of Occupl. Lung Diseases - Rio de Janeiro State Office for Health, Rio de Janeiro, 1998—2003; physician Brazilian Army Ctrl. Hosp., Rio de Janeiro, 1997—99; adj. asst. prof. W.Va. U., Morgantown, W.Va., 2003—; epidemic intelligence svc. officer Nat. Inst. Occupl. Health/Ctrs. for Disease Control & Prevention, Morgantown, 2003—05, sr. svc. fellow, 2005—. Grantee Bronze Sponsorship, European Respiratory Soc., 2002. Mem.: European Respiratory Soc., Am. Thoracic Soc. Office: Nat Inst Occupl Health Ctrs for Disease Control & Prevention 1095 Willodale Rd Morgantown WV 26505 Home Phone: 304-598-7303; Office Phone: 304-285-6095. Office Fax: 304-285-6111. Personal E-mail: ghp6@cdc.gov.

PINICK, SARIAH KAY, music educator; d. Thomas Keith and Patricia Irene Pinick. MA in Music, U.Mo., Kansas City, 2003; MusB in Voice Performance magna cum laude, U.Mo., Columbia, 2000. Voice instr. Music Arts Inst., Independence, Mo., 2000—; adj. prof. in voice Blue River C.C., Independence, 2000—. Singer: (voice recital) Compositions of African American Women Composers, (opera singers competition) Ctr. for Contemporary Opera Internat. Opera Singers Competition (Semi-Finalist, 2004). Music ministry Anchor Point Bapt. Ch., Independence, 2004—06. Recipient Excellence in Music award, Pi Kappa Lambda, 1997, 1998. Mem.: Music Teachers Nat. Assn. (assoc.), Nat. Assn. of Teachers of Singing (assoc.), Pi Kappa Lambda (assoc.), Sigma Alpha Iota (life; v.p. 2005—06, Highest Scholastic Average award 2000). Avocations: travel, reading, cross stitch, piano. Office: Music Arts Inst 1010 S Pearl St Independence MO 64050 Home Phone: 816-721-4850; Office Phone: 816-836-1998.

PINIELLA, LOU (LOUIS VICTOR PINIELLA), professional baseball team manager; b. Tampa, Fla., Aug. 28, 1943; m. Anita Garcia, Apr. 12, 1967; children: Lou, Kristi, Derrick. Student, U. Tampa. Outfielder various minor-league teams, 1962-68, Cleve. Indians, 1968, Kans. City Royals, 1969-73, NY Yankees, 1974-84, coach, 1984-85, mgr., 1985-87, 1988, gen. mgr., 1987-88, spl. adv., TV announcer, 1989; mgr. Cin. Reds, 1990-92, Seattle Mariners, 1992—2002, Tampa Bay Devil Rays, 2003—05, Chgo. Cubs, 2006—; baseball analyst ESPN, 2005—06. Named Am. League Rookie of the Yr Baseball Writers Assoc of Amer, 1969; Named to Am. League All-Star Team, 1972; Named Am. League Mgr. of the Yr, 1995, 2001; recipient Ellis Island Medal of Honor, 1990 Achievements include winning two World Series while playing for the NY Yankees, 1977-78. Office: Chgo Cubs Wrigley Field 1060 W Addison St Chicago IL 60613 *

PINK, MICHAEL, performing company executive; b. York, Eng. Trained as classical dancer, Royal Ballet Sch. Dancer English Nat. Ballet, 1975—85; founding dir. Ballet Ctrl., London, 1987—91; assoc. dir. Northern Ballet, 1988; artistic dir. Milw. Ballet. Internat. tchr. Norwegian Nat. Ballet, Aterballetto, Balleto di Toscanna Italy, The Hartford Ballet, Rozas Dance Co., London Contemporary Dance Co., White Oaks Dance Project, Ballet Rambert, English Nat. Ballet, Phoenix Dance Co., London Ballet. Recipient First Pl. in inaugural, Ursula Moreton Choreographic Competition, First Pl., Royal Soc. of Arts Competition. Office: Milwaukee Ballet 504 W National Ave Milwaukee WI 53204 E-mail: michael@milwaukeeballet.org. *

PINK, (ALECIA B. MOORE), singer; b. Doylestown, Pa., Sept. 8, 1979; m. Carey Hart, Jan. 7, 2006. With Arista Records, 2001—. Singer: (albums) Can't Take Me Home, 2000, M!ssundaztood, 2001, Try This, 2003, I'm Not Dead, 2006, (songs) There U Go, 2000, Most Girls, 2000, (with Mya, Lil' Kim, Christina Aguilera) Lady Marmalade, 2001 (Grammy award Song Yr., 2002, 2 MTV Video Music awards, 2001), You Make Me Sick, 2001, Get the Party Started, 2001 (2 MTV Video Music Awards, 2002), Don't Let Me Get Me, 2002, Just Like a Pill, 2002, Family Portrait, 2002, Feel Good Time, 2003, Trouble, 2003 (Grammy award, Best Female Rock Performance, 2004), God is a DJ, 2003, Stupid Girls, 2006 (MTV Video Music award for Best Pop Video, 2006); actor: (films) Rollerball, 2002, Charlie's Angels: Full Throttle, 2003. Named one of 100 Sexiest Artists, VH1, 2002; recipient World Music award for Best Am. Pop Female Artist, 2003. Office: Box #390 5701 E Circle Dr Cicero NY 13039

PINKEL, DONALD PAUL, pediatrician; b. Buffalo, Sept. 7, 1926; s. Lawrence William and Ann (Richardson) P.; m. Marita Donovan, Dec. 26, 1949 (div. 1981); children: Rebecca, Nancy, Christopher, Mary, Thomas, Anne, Sara, John, Ruth; m. Cathryn Barbara Howarth, May 16, 1981; 1 child, Michael. BS, Canisius Coll., 1947; MD, U. Buffalo, 1951. Diplomate Am. Bd. Pediatrics, Pediatric Hematology and Oncology, Nat. Bd. Med. Examiners. From intern to resident to chief resident Children's Hosp., Buffalo, 1951-54; research fellow Children's Hosp. Med. Ctr., Boston, 1955-56; chief. of pediatrics Roswell Park Meml. Inst., Buffalo, 1956-61; founding dir. St. Jude Children's Rsch. Hosp., Memphis, 1961-73; chmn. pediatrics Med. Coll. Wis., Milw., 1974-78; pediatrician-in-chief Milw. Children's Hosp., 1974-78; founding dir. Midwest Children's Cancer Ctr., Milw., 1974; chief. of pediatrics City of Hope Med. Ctr., Duarte, Calif., 1978-82; chmn. pediatrics Temple U. Sch. Medicine, Phila., 1982-85; prof., Kana Rsch. chair, dir. pediatric leukemia program M.D. Anderson Cancer Ctr. U. Tex., Houston, 1985-93; prof. pediat. U. Tex. Med. Sch., Houston, 1985-99; prof. emeritus U. Tex.-M.D. Anderson Cancer Ctr., Houston, 1994—. Clin. prof. pediats. U. So. Calif., LA, 2002—; adj. prof. biol. scis. Calif. Polytechnic State U., San Luis Obispo, Calif., 2001—. Contbr. articles to profl. jours. Bd. dirs. Lee County Coop. Clinic, Mariana, Ark., 1972-74. Served with USN, 1944-45, served to 1st lt. U.S. Army, 1954-55. Recipient Albert Lasker award for Med. Rsch., Lasker Found., 1972, Windermere Lectureship Brit. Pediatric Assn., 1974, David Karnofsky award Am. Soc. Clin. Oncology, 1978, Zimmerman prize for Cancer Rsch. Zimmerman Found., 1979, Charles Kettering prize Gen. Motors Cancer Rsch., 1986, Clin. Rsch. award Am. Cancer Soc., 1988, Return of the Child award Leukemia Soc. Am., 1992, Pollin prize in pediat. rsch. N.Y. Presbyn. Hosp., 2003. Mem. Am. Soc. Clin. Oncology, Am. Pediat. Soc., Am. Assn. Cancer Rsch., Soc. Exptl. Biology and Medicine, Am. Soc. Hematology. Democrat. Roman Catholic. Avocations: swimming, sailing. Home: 275 Marlene Dr San Luis Obispo CA 93405 E-mail: donpinkel@yahoo.com.

PINKEL, GARY, university football coach; b. Akron, Oh., Apr. 27, 1952; m. Vicki Pinkel; children: Erin, Geoff, Blake. BS in Edn., Kent St. Univ., 1973, grad. studies, Bowling Green. Grad. asst. Kent St. Univ., 1974—75; wide receivers coach Bowling Green St. Univ., 1976—78; quarterbacks coach Washington Univ., 1979—83, offensive coord., 1984—90; head coach Toledo, 1991—2000, Univ. Mo., 2001—. Named to Kent St. Hall of Fame, 1997. *

PINKER, STEVEN A., psychologist, educator; b. Montreal, Que., Can., Sept. 18, 1954; arrived in US, 1976; s. Harry and Roslyn (Wiesenfeld) P. BA in Exptl. Psychology, McGill U., Montreal, 1976; PhD, Harvard U., 1979; DSc (hon.), McGill U., 1999; DPhil (hon.), Tel Aviv. U., 2003, U. Newcastle, 2005; DUniv (hon.), U. Surrey, 2003. Postdoctoral fellow Center for Cognitive Sci., MIT; asst. prof., dept. of psychology Harvard U., Cambridge, Mass., 1980-81, Stanford U., Palo Alto, Calif., 1981-82, MIT, Cambridge, 1982—85, assoc. prof., dept. of brain and cognitive sci., 1985—89; co-dir. Center for Cognitive Sci., MIT, 1985—94; prof., dept. of brain and cogniive sci. MIT; dir. McDonnell-Pew Center for Cognitive Neuroscience, MIT, 1994—99; Peter de Florez prof. MIT, Cambridge, 2000—03; Johnstone Family prof. of psychol. Harvard U., 2003—. Cons. Cognitive and Instructional Scis. Group, Xerox Corp. Palo Alto Rsch. Centers, 1981—82; vis. scholar, dept. of psychology Harvard Univ., 1987—88; vis. scholar, cognitive devel. unit Med. Rsch Coun., London, 1988; vis. scholar, dept. of psychology and linguistics Univ. Calif., Santa Barbara, 1995—96; hon. vis. prof., dept. of psychology Univ. of Auckland, New Zealand, 2001—04; inst. advisor Allen Inst. for Brain Sci., Seattle; spkr. in field. Author: Language Learnability and Language Development, 1984, Learnability and Cognition, 1989, The Language Instinct, 1994, How the Mind Works, 1997 (LA Times Science Book Prize, 1998, finalist for Pullitzer prize, 1998), Words and Rules, 1999, The Blank Slate, 2002 (finalist for Pulitzer prize, 2003); assoc. editor Cognition, 1984—; advisor, Am. Heritage Dictionary; serves on several advisory and editorial bds., contbr. articles to sci. jours. and chapters in books. Recipient Troland Rsch. award NAS, 1993, Golden Plate award, Am. Acad. of Achievement, 1999, Henry Dale prize Royal Instn. Gt. Britain, 2004, Henry Dale prize Royal Instn. of Gt. Britain, 2004; named Humanist Laureate Internat. Acad. Humanism, 2001, Humanist of Yr., Am. Humanist Assn., 2006. Fellow AAAS, APA (Disting. Early Career award 1984, Boyd McCandless award 1986, William James Book prize 1995, 99, 2003, Eleanor Maccoby Book prize 2003), Am. Acad. Arts and Scis., Linguistics Soc. Am. (Linguistics, Lang. and Pub. Svcs. award 1997), Am. Psychol. Soc. Office: Dept Psychology Harvard Univ William James Hall 970 33 Kirkland St Cambridge MA 02138 Office Phone: 617-495-0831. Office Fax: 617-495-3278. Business E-Mail: pinker@wjh.harvard.edu.

PINKERTON, A. LOUISE, vocalist, music educator; d. John W. and Jane R. Pinkerton; m. Royce F. Blackburn, Aug. 12, 2000; 1 child, Grace S. Blackburn. MusB, Ind. U., 2001; MusM, U. N.D., 2003. Music instr. Mayville State U., ND, 2002—04, Minn. State U., Moorhead, 2004—; lectr. music U. N.D., Grand Forks, 2005—. Intern Nat. Symphony Orch. John F. Kennedy Ctr. Performing Arts, Washington, 2001; publicity coord. Met. Opera Nat. Coun. Auditions, Grand Forks, 2005—; presenter in field. Singer: (opera) Fargo-Moorhead Opera, (musical) Crimson Creek Players, (performances) Opera in the Ozarks, (performance) Contemporary Opera Lab; presenter (report) SAI Philanthropies, Inc: Kennedy Center Internship. Recipient Dist. Winner and Regional Finalist, Met. Opera Nat. Coun. Auditions, 2002—04, Vivian Menees Nelson award, Nat. Fedn. Music Clubs, 2004, semi-finalist, William C. Byrd Young Artist awards, 2006. Mem.: Nat. Assn. Tchrs. Singing, Pi Kappa Lambda, Sigma Alpha Iota (province officer 2000—03, nat. arts assoc. com. mem. 2006—, Province Leadership award). Avocation: ballroom dance. Home Phone: 701-775-0108. Personal E-mail: louise_pinkerton@hotmail.com.

PINKERTON, RICHARD LADOYT, retired management educator; b. Huron, SD, Mar. 5, 1933; s. Abner Pyle and Orral Claudine (Arneson) P.; m. Sandra Louise Lee, Aug. 28, 1965 (div. 1992); children: Elizabeth, Patricia. BA, U. Mich., 1955; MBA, Case Western Res. U., 1962; PhD, U. Wis., 1969. Sr. market rsch. analyst Harris-Intertype Corp., Cleve., 1957-61; mgr. sales devel. Triax Corp., Cleve., 1962-64; coord. mktg. program Mgmt. Inst., U. Wis., 1964-67; dir. exec. programs Mgmt. Inst., U. Wis. (Grad. Sch. Bus.), also asst. prof. mktg., 1969-74; prof. mgmt., dean Grad. Sch. Adminstrn., Capital U., Columbus, Ohio, 1974-86; prof. mgmt., dir. Univ. Bus. Ctr., Craig Sch. Bus. Calif. State U., Fresno, 1986-89, prof. mktg., 1989-2000, chmn. mktg. and logistics dept., 1996-2000, dir. London semester, prof. emeritus, mem. bd., 2000—. Adj. prof. Case Western Res. U., 2004-; trustee Ohio Coun. Econ. Edn., 1976-87; cons. to govt. and industry, 1960—. Co-author: The Purchasing Manager's Guide to Strategic Proactive Procurement, 1996; contbr. articles to profl. jours. Bd. govs. Hannah Neil Home for Children, Columbus, 1975—78; mem. indsl. and cmty. devel. comm. City of Strongsville, Ohio; bd. dirs. The Fresno Townhouse Assn., 1992—2001. Officer USAF, 1955—57, lt. col. USAF, 1957—78. La Verne Noyes scholar, 1952—55, Nat. Assn. Purchasing Mgmt. fellow, 1967—68. Mem.: Am. Mktg. Assn. (chpt. pres. 1972—73), Nat. Assn. Purchasing Mgmt. (chmn. acad. planning 1979—84, rsch. symposium 1992), Nat. Assn. Contract Mgmt. (chmn. validation cert. com. 1990), Air Force Assn., Res. Officers Assn., Marines Meml. Club, Columbia Hills Country Club, Phi Gamma Delta, Alpha Kappa Psi, Beta Gamma Sigma. Home: 18487 Woodside Crossing South Strongsville OH 44149-6891 Home Phone: 440-846-1430; Office Phone: 440-846-1430.

PINKERTON, ROBERT BRUCE, mechanical engineer; b. Detroit, Feb. 10, 1941; s. George Fulwell and Janet Lois (Hedke) P.; m. Barbara Ann Bandfield, Aug. 13, 1966; 1 child, Robert Brent. BSME, Detroit Inst. Tech., 1965; MA in Engring., Chrysler Inst. Engring., 1967; JD, Wayne State U., 1976. From mech. engr. to emissions and fuel economy planning specialist Chrysler Engring. Office Chrysler Corp., Highland Park, Mich., 1967-80; dir. engring. Replacement div. TRW, Inc., Cleve., 1980-83; v.p. engring. TRW Automotive Aftermarket Group, 1983-86; v.p. engring. and rsch. Blackstone Corp., Jamestown, NY, 1986-89, pres., CEO, 1989-90, Athena Corp., Beaufort, SC, 1990—, Cedar Crest Corp., Beaufort, SC, 1990—; chmn., CEO Beaufort Land Co., 1998—. Bd. dirs. VRI, LLC, Coastal Banking Co., Inc., Low Country Nat. Bank, Village Renaissance, Inc., Carpenters Hall, Coastal Banking Co., Inc.; chmn. redevelopment commn. City Beaufort, 2004—. Mem. exec. com. Beaufort Schs. Oversight Com., 1995-99, Pvt. Industry Coun., 1996-99. Mem.: Greater Beaufort C. of C. (bd. dirs. 1997—98), Beaufort Roundtable (pres. 2000—02), Rotary (asst. dist. gov. 1997—98). Episcopalian. Home: PO Box 2417 Beaufort SC 29901-2417 Office: PO Box 2115 1203 Boundary St Beaufort SC 29902 Business E-Mail: rbp@athenacorp.com.

PINKETT, RANDAL D., entrepreneur; m. Zahara Pinkett. BSEE, Rutgers U., New Brunswick, NJ, 1994; MSc in Computer Sci., U. Oxford, Eng., 1996; MSEE, MBA, MIT, Cambridge, 1998, PhD in Media Arts and Scis., 2001. Mem. tech. staff Global Wireless Products Grp. Lucent Technologies, Piscataway, NJ, 1997—98; founder, pres., CEO MBS Ednl. Svcs. & Tng., LLC, East Windsor, NJ, 1997—2000; co-founder, dir. tech. Inner City Consulting Grp., Kansas City, Mo., 2000—01; founder, pres., CEO BCT Ptnrs., LLC, Newark, 2001—. Vice-chairperson bd. dirs. NJ Pub. Policy Rsch. Inst.; bd. dirs. Nonprofit Tech. Enterprise Network; bd. advs. Cmty. Tech. Ctrs.' Network. Named one of 30 Leaders for the Future, Black Enterprise Mag., 2000, Ebony Mag., 2001, 2007 People to Watch, Sunday Star-Ledger, NJ; recipient NJ Martin Luther King Commemorative Commn. Triumph award, 2001, MOBE Innovators and Influencers of the Internet award, 2002; grantee Next Generation Leadership fellowship, Rockefeller Found., 2003, Achievements Leadership NJ fellowship, 2004. Mem.: Nat. Black MBA Assn., Nat. Soc. Black Engrs., Assn. Am. Rhodes Scholars. Avocations: movies, music, exercise, travel. Office: BCT Ptnrs 105 Lock St Newark NJ 07103 *

PINKETT-SMITH, JADA, actress; b. Balt., Sept. 18, 1971; m. Will Smith, Dec. 31, 1997; 2 children. Actor: (films) Menace II Society, 1993, The Inkwell, 1994, Jason's Lyric, 1994, A Low Down Dirty Shame, 1994, Demon Knight, 1995, The Nutty Professor, 1996, Set It Off, 1996, Blossoms and Veils, 1997 (also exec. prodr.), Scream 2, 1997, Woo, 1998, Return to Paradise, 1998, Bamboozled, 2000, Kingdom Come, 2001, Ali, 2001, The Matrix Reloaded, 2003, The Matrix Revolutions, 2003, Collateral, 2004, (voice) Madagascar, 2005, Reign Over Me, 2007, (TV films) If These Walls Could Talk, 1996, Maniac Magee, 2003, (TV series) A Different World, 1992-93, exec. prodr. All of Us, 2003-; exec. prodr. (films) The Seat Filler, 2004; author (children's book): Girls Hold Up This World, 2004 (NY Times Bestseller list, NAACP Image award for outstanding lit. work-children's 2006). *

PINKHAM, FREDERICK OLIVER, foundation executive, consultant; b. Ann Arbor, Mich., June 16, 1920; s. Frederick Oliver and Leah Winifred (Hallett) P.; m. Helen Kostia, June 20, 1943; children: Peter James, Gail Louise, Steven Howard. AB, Kalamazoo Coll., Mich., 1942, LLD (hon.), 1958; MA, Stanford U., Calif., 1947, EdD, 1950; LLD (hon.), Lawrence U., Appleton, Wis., 1957; DSc (hon.), Ripon Coll., Wis., 1990. Tchr., counselor Sequoia Union H.S., Redwood City, Calif., 1947-49; rschr. Stanford Consultation Svc., 1949-50; asst. to pres. George Washington U., 1950-51; exec. sec. Nat. Commn. on Accrediting, 1951-55; pres. Ripon Coll., 1955-66; dir. The Yardstick Project, Cleve., 1966-67; sr. v.p., dir. Western Pub. Co., 1967-70; founder, pres. Edn. Mgmt. Svcs., Inc., 1970-76; asst. adminstr. for population and humanitarian affairs AID, Dept. State, 1976-77; chmn., pres. Population Crisis Com., 1977-87; assoc. dir. Inst. for Population and Resource Studies, Stanford U., 1987-90; program officer David and Lucile Packard Found., Los Altos, Calif., 1988-92; cons. for population David and Lucille Packard Found., 1993-99; cons. True North Found., Portland, Oreg., 1993-97, Compton Found., Menlo Park, Calif., 1993-97, Mgmt. Scis. for Health, 1995-97, Poptech, Washington, 1995. V.p., dir. rsch. Ednl. Recs. Bur., Darien, Conn., 1970-72; founder, pres. Edn. Mgmt. Svcs., Inc., 1970-76; v.p., co-founder World Bus. Coun., 1970-77; pres. Capital Higher Edn. Svc., 1975-76; pres., dir. The Omni Group, 1977-83; treas., co-founder Monterey Peninsula coll. Found., 1994-2000, 02-; cons. Program for the Topical Prevention of Conception and Disease Chgo. Rush U., 1999-2003. Chmn. Wis. adv. com. Nat. Commn. on Civil Rights; bd. visitors Air U.; pres. Wis. Found. of Ind. Colls.; chmn. Assn. colls. Midwest, Midwest Coll. Coun.; sec., trustee, mem. exec. com. Young Pres.'s Found.; chmn. task force on fgn. assistance Pres.'s Pvt. Sector Survey on Cost Control (Grace Comm.); chmn. bd. Global Tomorrow Coalition, 1985-89; bd. dirs. Internat. Human Assistance Programs, NYC, 1984-87, Mineral Fibre Internat. and Kings Mills Internat., 1986-90, Mgmt. Scis. for Health, 1997-2000, Skyline Crest Assn., 2002—; v.p. Big Sur Land Trust, 1990-2000; founder, pres. Inst. Reproductive Health, Calif., 2000—. Served with AUS, 1942-45, ETO. Decorated Bronze Star, Purple Heart. Mem. Young Pres. Orgn. (sec., dir., exec. com.), Soc. Internat. Devel., Nat. Heritage Soc. (watchkeeper, bd. govs.), Old Capital Club Monterey, Calif. (gov.). Home and Office: 8 Skyline Crst Monterey CA 93940-4111 E-mail: fpinkham@aol.com.

PINKINS, TONYA, actress; b. Chicago, May 30, 1962; m. Ron Brawer, Feb. 12, 1987 (div. 1987); 2 children; 4 children. Attended, Northwestern U., Summer Theater Inst., Chicago, 1978; student, Carnegie Mellon U., 1980—81; BA, Columbia Coll., Chicago, 1996; student, Calif. Western Law Sch., San Diego. Private acting instr. Montclair School of Dance, 1993; visual arts instr., 6th to 8th grades LAUSD, 2000—01; private coach voice, music performance, acting, 2002. Playwriting com. Playwrights' Preview Prodn., 1986—88; instr. cold reading Univ. Calif., San Diego, 2000. Actor: (Broadway plays) Merrily We Roll Along, 1981, Jelly's Last Jam, 1992 (Tony award best featured actress in a musical, 1992, Drama Desk award best featured actress in a musical, 1992, Clarence Derwent award, 1992, Outer Critics Circle award best featured actress in a musical, 1993), Chronicle of a Death Foretold, 1995, Play On!, 1997 (Tony nom. best actress in a musical, 1997), The Wild Party, 2000, Caroline, Or Change, 2004— (Tony nom. best actress in a musical, 2004, Obie award best perf., 2004), Radio Golf, 2007—, (Off Broadway plays) Little Shop of Horrors, 1983, A...My Name Alice, 1985, Just Say No, 1988, Believin'/Psychoneurotic Fantasies, 1990, The Caucasian Chalk Circle, 1990, The Merry Wives of Windsor, 1994, The Vagina Monologues, 2000, The House of Flowers, 2003; (plays) Stealin', Joe Turner's Come and Gone, 1989, The Piano Lesson, 1989, Approximating Mother, 1991, No Niggers, No Jews, No Dogs, 2000, Thoroughly Modern Millie, 2000; (TV series) As the World Turns, 1983—86, University Hospital, 1994, All My Children, 1991—95, 2003—; (TV films) American Dream, 1981, Rage of Angels: The Story Continues, 1986, Strapped, 1993, Against Their Will: Women in Prison, 1994, (TV Guest appearances) Crime Story, 1986, The Cosby Show, 1990, Law & Order, 1990, The Guardian, 2002; (films) Beat Street, 1984, See No Evil, Hear No Evil, 1989, Above the Rim, 1994, Love Hurts, 2002, Romance & Cigarettes, 2005, Premium, 2006; voice (audio books) The Women of Brewster Place, 1992, The Book of Virtues I and II, 1993, The Moral Compass, 1995, Chocolate for a Woman's Soul, 1997, The Silent Cradle, 1998; author: (book) Get Over Yourself: How to Drop the Drama and Claim the Life You Deserve, 2006; singer: (albums) Live @ Joe's Pub. Achievements include co-founder of OPERATION Z: zero tolerance of violence against women and children. *

PINKNEY, D. TIMOTHY, investment company executive; b. Long Beach, Calif., June 6, 1948; s. Robert Patten and Mary (Chernus) P.; m. Nancy Dianne Fisher, Aug. 21, 1971; 1 child, Heather Anne. BA, Calif. Luth. U., 1970; MA, Pepperdine U., 1976. CFP. Membership mgr. Seattle C. of C., 1977—79; v.p. mktg. John L. Scott Investment, Bellevue, Wash., 1980—81, SRH Fin., Bellevue, 1981—82, Foster Investment Co., Bellevue, 1982—83; pres., CEO Profitment Fin. Planning, Bellevue, 1983—88, Sheppard & Assocs. Personal Fin. Advs., Bellevue, 1988—91; mgr. and v.p. asset mgmt. div. U.S. Bank, Tacoma, 1991—92; v.p., Calif. and Nev. mgr. trust and investment mgmt. U.S. Bank of Calif., Sacramento, 1992—96; prin. The Savant Group, Citrus Heights, Calif., 1996—; founder, CEO Wealth Link Enterprises. Invited spkr. Russian Parliament, 1992. Author: book, video and cassete series Pathways to Wealth, Yes IRA's Still Make Cent$?, 1988. Co-chmn. Fin. Independence Week, Western Wash., 1987; bd. dirs. Traveler's Aid Soc., A United Way Agy., Seattle, 1988, pacesetter United Way, 1988-91; alumni class steward Calif. Luth. U., 1992-2003; chmn. Friends Scouting, 1994, chmn. bd. 1999, v.p. finance, 1997-98, Golden Empire Coun. Boy Scouts Am., 1999-2005; chmn. investment com. Calif. State U. Sacramento Found., 1998-99; bd. dirs. McClellan Aviation Mus., 2000-04, YMCA Found, 2002—, Aerospace Mus. Calif., 2004-06; pres. Sacramento Rotary Found., 2000-2002. Lt. USN, 1970-77, comdr. USNR, ret., 1992. Selected as Jr. Officer of Yr., USNR, 1984, 85; Career Achievement award Calif. Luth. U., 2002; Recipient Silver Beaver award, Boy Scouts of Am., 2003, Rotary Fellow, Sacramento, 2004. Mem. Nat. Spkrs. Assn. (bd. dirs. N.W. chpt. 1992), Internat. Assn. Fin. Planning (chmn. West Region 1987-90, pres. Western Wash. chpt. 1986-87), Seattle Soc. Fin. Planners (bd. dirs. 1985-86), Inst. CFPs, Real Estate Securities and Syndication Inst. (v.p. 1980-83), East King County and Pierce County Estate Planning Coun., Seattle Res. Officer Assn. (pres., v.p. 1983-85), Puget Sound Naval Res. Assn. (v.p. 1985-90), Naval Order of US, Sacramento Rotary (chmn. edn. com. 1994, bd. dirs. 2005-07), Sacramento Rotary Found. (pres. 2000-2002, bd. dirs. 1996-2005), Seattle Rotary (bd. dirs., chmn. membership devel. com.). Avocations: flying gliders, giant pumpkin growing and sculpting, photography. Home Phone: 916-632-9834; Office Phone: 916-721-1400. Personal E-mail: tpinkney@starstream.net. Business E-Mail: tpinkney@thesavantgroup.com.

PINKWATER, JULIE, publishing executive; B, Boston U. With Sotheby's Internat. Realty, Network TV Assn; with advertising agency McCaffrey & McCall, Penchina Selkowitz, McCann Erickson; mgr. position Ladies Home Jour.; beauty dir. Allure; advertising dir. More, 1998—2000, pub., 2000—01, Fitness Mag., G&J USA, NY, 2001—04; v.p., pub. Ladies Home Jour., NY, 2004—. Office: Ladies Home Jour 125 Park Ave 20th Floor New York NY 10017-5529 Office Phone: 212-551-7153. Office Fax: 212-455-1313. E-mail: julie.pinkwater@meredith.com. *

PINN, VIVIAN W., federal agency administrator, pathologist; b. Halifax, Va., 1941; BA, Wellesley Coll., 1963; MD, U. Va., 1967. Intern in pathology Mass. Gen. Hosp., Boston, 1967-68, rschr. in pathology, 1968-70; asst. pathologist Tufts U. New England Med. Ctr. Hosp., 1970-77, pathologist, 1977-82; from asst. to assoc. prof. pathology Tufts U., 1971-82, asst. dean student affairs, 1974-82; prof., dept. chair pathology Howard U., 1982-91; first dir. Office Rsch. on Women's Health, NIH, Bethesda, Md., 1991—, assoc. dir. rsch. women's health, 1994—, dir. Office Women's Health Rsch. Pres. Nat. Med. Assn., 1989—90. Office: NIH Office Rsch on Women's Health 9000 Rockville Pike Bldg 1 Rm 201 Bethesda MD 20892 Office Phone: 301-402-1770.

PINNA, GRAZIANO, biologist, researcher; b. Oristano, Sardinia, Italy, Feb. 18, 1968; arrived in US, 2001, permanent resident, 2004; s. Michele Pinna and Luigina Vaccargiu. PhD in Biol. Scis., U. Cagliari, Italy, 1995; M in Neuroendocrinology, Free U., Berlin, 1996, PhD in Med. Scis., 2001. Cert. specialist in pharmacology Free U., Berlin, 2000. Rschr. Schering AG, Berlin, 1993-94; rsch. scientist Free U., Berlin, 1994-2001; rsch. asst. prof. U. Ill., Chgo., 2001. Vis. scholar U. Ill., Chgo., 1997-98; cons. U. Naples (Italy) Federico II, 1997-98; advisor Clarke Inst. Psychiatry, Toronto, Can., 1998-99, Columbia U., N.Y.C., 1999-2000, Tonji Med. Sch., Wuhan, China, 2000-2001. Contbr. articles to profl. jours. Active Donazioni Latino Am., Italy, 1997-2001, AIDS-Hilfe, Berlin, 2000. Grantee Comett-European Cmty., Brussels, 1993, U. Cagliari, 1994, Deutsche Forschungsgemeinschaft, Germany, 1994, 97-2001, Regione Sardegna, Sardinia, Italy, 1996, Human Frontiers Sci. Program Orgn., Strasbourg, France, 1998, UIC Chgo., NIH. Mem. German Assn. for Neurowissenschaft, Soc. for Neurosci., Soc. for Women's Health Rsch. Roman Catholic. Achievements include invention of methods for thyroid hormones extraction and quantification in CNS; discovery of existance and physiological role of thyroid hormones in the human and rodent brain; discovery of physiological role for endogenous neurosteroids in the rodent brain. Office: Psychiatric Inst U Ill Chgo-Dept Psychiatry 1601 W Taylor St Chicago IL 60612 Office Phone: 312-355-1464. Business E-Mail: gpinna@psych.uic.edu.

PINNELL, SHELDON RICHARD, dermatologist, researcher, retired educator; b. Dayton, Ohio, Feb. 3, 1937; s. Jacob and Nevella P.; m. Doren Madey, 1983; children: Kevin, Alden, Tyson. AB, Duke U., 1959; MD, Yale U., 1963. Intern in medicine U. Minn. Hosp., Mpls., 1963-65; resident in dermatology Harvard U., Boston, 1968-71; prof. medicine Duke U. Med. Ctr., Durham, N.C., 1978—, chief div. dermatology, 1982-97, asst. prof. biochemistry, 1988—, J. Lamar Callaway prof. dermatology, 1989—2002, prof. emeritus, 2002—. Founding scientist Fibrogen, 1994—, SkinCeuticals, 1997—, SkinResearch, 2002—04, Skin Sci. Inst., 2004—. Contbr. over 200 articles to profl. jours. Achievements include eight patents in field. Office: Duke U Med Ctr PO Box 3135 Durham NC 27710-0001 Business E-Mail: pinne002@mc.duke.edu.

PINNELL-STEPHENS, JUNE ALICIA, information broker, consultant, librarian; b. Dayton, Ohio, June 11, 1948; d. Earl Emery and Helen Marie (Fedash) Pinnell; m. Dennis James Stephens, Jan. 3, 1982. BA, Pomona Coll., 1971; MLS, U. Wash., 1972. Cert. libr., Wash.; cert. tchr., Alaska. Children's libr. King County Libr. System, Seattle, 1972-76; coord. children's svcs. Bellingham (Wash.) Pub. Libr., 1976-80; libr. Mat-Su Community Coll., Palmer, Alaska, 1980-82; newsroom libr. Daily News-Miner, Fairbanks, Alaska, 1982-83; prin. Borealis Rsch., Fairbanks, 1983-85; sr. rsch. assoc. ASK* Info. Search, Fairbanks, 1985-87; prin. Profl. Info. Resources, Fairbanks, 1987-89; collection devel. libr. Fairbanks North Star Borough Pub. Libr., Fairbanks, 1988—. Mem. adj. faculty Western Wash. U., Bellingham, 1978-79; instr. U. Alaska, Palmer, Kodiak, Fairbanks, 1980-81, 84; chmn. Alaska We the People Project, Fairbanks, 1984-89; cons. N.W. Arctic Sch. Dist., Kotzebue, Alaska, 1985-87. Contbr. articles to profl. jours.; editor: AkLA Intellectual Freedom Manual, 1985. Mem. library com. Mayor's Transition Task Force, Fairbanks, 1985; del. Dem. Dist. Conv., Fairbanks, 1986, 90; mem. gov.'s celebration commn. U.S. Constl. Bicentennial 1986-89; bd. dirs. Fairbanks Symphony Assn. Mem. ALA (chmn. Wash. membership com. 1979-80, mem. exec. bd. 2005-), Alaska Libr. Assn. (chmn. IFC 1984-85, 90—, v.p., pres. 1985-87), Wash. Libr. Assn. (chmn. children's and young adults svcs. interest group 1976-78, 2d v.p. 1979-80), Pacific N.W. Libr. Assn. (chmn. intellectual freedom interest group 1986-88, sec. 1988-90, 1st v.p., pres.-elect 1991-92, pres. 1992-93), Alaska Civil Liberties Union (bd. dirs. 1987-92), Dance Omnium (bd. dirs. 1989-92). Avocations: scottish highland dance and music, gardening, boating, cooking. Address: ALA 50 E Huron Chicago IL 60611

PINNEY, THOMAS CLIVE, retired English language educator; b. Ottawa, Kans., Apr. 23, 1932; s. John James and Lorene Maude (Owen) P.; m. Sherrill Marie Ohman, Sept. 1, 1956; children— Anne, Jane, Sarah. BA, Beloit Coll., Wis., 1954; PhD, Yale U., 1960. Instr. Hamilton Coll., Clinton, NY, 1957-61; instr. English Yale U., New Haven, 1961-62; asst. prof. to prof., chmn. dept. English Pomona Coll., Claremont, Calif., 1962-97; ret., 1997. Editor: Essays of George Eliot, 1963, Selected Writings of Thomas Babington Macaulay, 1972, Letters of Macaulay, 1974-81, Kipling's India, 1986, A History of Wine in America, 1989, Kipling's Something of Myself, 1990, Letters of Rudyard Kipling, 1990,-2004 The Vineyards and Wine Cellars of California, 1994, The Wine of Santa Cruz Island, 1994, A History of Wine in America: From Prohibition to the Present, 2005. Guggenheim fellow, 1966, 84,Recipient Disting. Svc. citation Beloit Coll., 1984; fellow NEH, 1980; grantee Am. Coun. Learned Socs., 1974, 84, Am. Philos. Soc., 1968, 82, 94. Mem. MLA, Elizabethan Club (New Haven), Zamorano Club (L.A.), Phi Beta Kappa. Office: Pomona Coll Dept English Claremont CA 91711 Home: 890 E Harrison Ave 32 Pomona CA 91767

PINO, RICHARD EDMUND, corporate financial executive; b. Bklyn., Feb. 1, 1966; s. Edward James Pino and Sherry Sue Harris. BA in Econs., St. Francis Coll., 1989; MBA in Corp. Fin., Adelphi U., 1993; attended, Walden U., 1997. Paper specialist Merrill Lynch Capital Markets, 1988—89; fin. analyst TimeWarner, 1990—91; contr. Veronis, Suhler & Assocs., 1993—96; asst. contr. MediaLink Worldwide, 1996—97; dir. Global Media Advisors, 1997—99; v.p. fin. and adminstrn. Eagle Comm., 1999—2000; CFO Ocean Records, 2000—01, Frontline Communication Internat., 2001—05, Relegance Inc., 2005—. Bd. dirs., chmn. audit com. St. Christopher's Inc., Dobbs Ferry, NY, 1994—; bd. dirs., treas. Co-Operation Ireland, NYC, 1994—. Mem.: Nat. Assn. Credit Mgrs., Bus. Coun. NY State Inc., Fin. Exec. Network Group. Office Phone: 212-594-4404. Business E-Mail: rpino@att.net.

PINOVER, EUGENE ALFRED, lawyer; b. NYC, Jan. 8, 1948; s. Maurice Alfred and Harriet (Ortner) P.; m. Diana Elzey, Feb. 14, 1974; children: Julia, Benjamin, Hannah. BA cum laude, Dartmouth Coll., 1969; JD cum laude, NYU, 1973. Bar: N.Y. 1974, U.S. Dist. Ct. (so. and ea. dists.) N.Y. 1974. Ptnr., chair Real Estate Dept. Willkie Farr & Gallagher LLP, NYC. Office: Willkie Farr & Gallagher 787 7th Ave Lbby 2 New York NY 10019-6099 Business E-Mail: epinover@willkie.com.

PINSKY, ROY DAVID, lawyer; b. Syracuse, NY, Feb. 1, 1948; s. Norman M. and Rose C. Pinsky; m. Stephanie V. Pinsky, June 9, 1968; children: Alissa Jill, Todd Justin. BS, Syracuse U., 1969, JD, 1971. Bar: NY 1972, Fla. 1981. Ptnr. Pinsky, Canter and Pinsky, Syracuse, 1972, Pinsky and Pliskin, Syracuse, 1972-88, Pinsky & Skandalis, 1988—. Spl. cons. Syracuse Bd. Edn., 1972-74; mem. atty. grievance com. Fifth Jud. Dist. Contbr. articles to profl. jours. Bd. dirs. Young Israel-Shaarei Torah of Syracuse; trustee Jewish Home of Ctrl. NY Served with US Army, 1969-75. Mem. NY State Bar Assn., Fla. Bar Assn., Onondaga County Bar Assn., Transp. Lawyers Assn. (past trustee), Def. Rsch. Inst., Can. Transport Lawyers Assn., Conf. Freight Counsel, Syracuse U. Sch. Mgmt. Alumni Assn. (past. nat. pres.). Home: 4623 Glencliffe Rd Manlius NY 13104-2378 Office: PO Box 250 5790 Widewaters Pkwy Syracuse NY 13214-0250 Office Phone: 315-446-2384. Business E-Mail: rpinsky@pinskyskandalis.com.

PINSON, CHARLES WRIGHT, surgeon, educator, academic administrator; b. Albuquerque, May 29, 1952; s. Ernest Alexander and Jean Elizabeth Pinson. Student, Miami U., Oxford, Ohio, 1970-72; BA, U. Colo., Boulder, 1974, MBA, 1976; MD, Vanderbilt U., 1980. Diplomate Am. Bd. Surgery, Am. Bd. Surg. Critical Care, Nat. Bd. Med. Examiners. Resident in gen. surgery Oreg. Health Sci. U., Portland, 1980-86; fellow gastrointestinal surgery Lahey Clinic, Burlington, Mass., 1986-87; fellow transplant surgery Harvard U., Boston, 1987-88; dir. liver transplant program VA Western region, Portland, 1989-90, Oreg. Health Sci. U., Portland, 1988-90; interim chmn. dept. surgery Vanderbilt U., Nashville, 1993-95, chief divsn. hepatobiliary surgery and liver transplantation, 1990—2004, vice-chmn. dept. surgery, 1995-2001; dir. Vanderbilt Transplant Ctr., Nashville, 1993—; chmn. med. bd. Vanderbilt U. Med. Ctr., Nashville, 1997-99; chief of staff Vanderbilt U. Hosp., Nashville, 1997—2004; H. William Scott prof., chmn. dept. surgery Vanderbilt U., Nashville, 2001—04; chief med. officer, assoc. vice chancellor for clin. affairs Vanderbilt U. Med. Ctr., Nashville, 2004—. Adv. bd. Pacific N.W. Transplant Bank, Portland, 1989—90, Tenn. Donor Svcs., Nashville, 1991—, sec., 2003—. Mem. editl. bd. Annals Surgery, Jour. Gastrointestinal Surgery, Liver Transplantation, HPB; contbr. articles to profl. jours., chapters to books. Chair liver and intestine allocation com. United Network Organ Sharing, 2003—05; bd. dirs. ARC, Nashville, 1992—94, Am. Liver Found., 1992—96, Ronald McDonald House, 2002—, United Network Organ Sharing, 2000—02, Hosp. Hospitality House, Nashville, 2005—. Fellow, Am. Heart Assn., 1983—84. Mem.: Internat. Hepatopancreatobiliary Assn. (mem. sci. com. 2000—03, mem. exec. com. 2003—, treas. 2004—), Internat. Liver Transplantation Soc., Soc. Surgery Alimentary Tract, Assn. Acad. Surgery, N. Pacific Surg. Assn. (mem. sci. program 1990—92), Western Surg. Assn., So. Surg. Assn., Am. Surg. Assn., So. Med. Assn. (chmn. sect. surgery 1997—2001), Am. Physiologic Soc., Am. Hepatopancreatobiliary Assn. (mem. exec. com. 1997—, treas. 1999—2003, pres. elect 2001—03, pres. 2003—05), Am. Gastroent. Assn., Am. Soc. Study Liver Diseases, Am. Soc. Transplant Surgeons, Soc. Surg. Oncology, Halsted Soc., Soc. Univ. Surgeons, Phi Beta Kappa, Sigma Xi, Alpha Omega Alpha. Office: Vanderbilt U Med Ctr Ste 3810 TVC Nashville TN 37232-5545

PINSON, LARRY LEE, pharmacist, state agency administrator; b. Van Nuys, Calif., Dec. 5, 1947; s. Leland J. and Audrey M. (Frett) Pinson; m. Margaret K. Pinson, Mar. 18, 1972; children: Scott C., Kelly E. Student, U. Calif., Davis, 1967—69; AA, Am. River Coll., Sacramento, 1969; PharmD, U. Calif., San Francisco, 1973. Lic. pharmacist Calif., Nev. Staff pharmacist/asst. dir. pharm. svcs. St. Mary's Hosp., Reno, 1973-77; chief pharmacist May Ang Base USAF, 1973-77; mng. pharmacist Scolari's Food & Drug, Reno, 2001—05; exec. sec. Nev. State Bd. Pharmacy, 2005—, pres., 1996—2004, exec. sec., 2005—; pharm., therapeutics com. State Nev., 2004—. Cons. pharmacist Physicians Hosp., 1974—93, Reno Med. Plz., 1973—, Rural Calif. Hosp. Assn., 1973—74, Ford Ctr. Foot Surgery, 1980—; pharmacy coord. Intensive Pharm. Svcs., 1986—87; cons. Calif. Dept. Health & Corrections, Susanville, 1975—76, Nev. Med. Care Adv. Bd., Carson City, 1984—87; provider, reviewer Nev. State Bd. Pharmacy, Reno, 1975—84; instr. Nev. CC, 1974—76; adj. prof. Idaho State U., Pocatello, 1989—. Co-author: Care of Hickman Catheter, 1984. Softball coach Reno/Sparks Recreation Dept., 1973—92; bd. dirs. Am. Cancer Soc., 1986—90; mem. State of Nev. Pharmaceutics and Therapy Com., 2004—, Nev. Arthritis Found.; cubmaster Pack 153 Boy Scouts Am., Verdi, Nev., scoutmaster com. chmn. Reno troop 1, 1988—92. Named Pharmacist of the Yr., Nev. Pharm. Alliance, 1999; recipient Bowl of Hygeia award, Nev. Pharmacists Assn. and A. H. Robbins Co., 1984. Mem.: Greater Nev. Heatlh Sys. Agy., Nev. Profl. Stds. Rev. Orgn., Nev. Pharmacists Assn. (pres. 1981—82), Am. Pharm. Assn., Nat. Assn. Bds. Pharmacy, Kappa Psi. Avocations: skiing, fishing, backpacking, softball, golf. Home: PO Box 478 Verdi NV 89439-0478 Office: 555 Double Eagle Ct Ste 1100 Reno NV 89521 Office Phone: 775-850-1440. Personal E-mail: Rx2005@aol.com.

PINSON, WILLIAM MEREDITH, JR., pastor, writer, administrator; b. Ft. Worth, Aug. 3, 1934; s. William Meredith and Ila Lee (Jones) P.; m. Bobbie Ruth Judd, June 4, 1955; children: Meredith Pinson Creasey, Allison Pinson Hopgood. BA, U. N. Tex., 1955; BD, Southwestern Bapt. Theol. Sem., Ft. Worth, 1959, ThD, 1963. MDiv, 1973; LittD (hon.), Calif. Bapt. Coll., Riverside, 1978; DD (hon.), U. Mary Hardin-Baylor, Belton, Tex., 1984; LHD (hon.), Howard Payne U., Brownwood, Tex., 1986; LittD (hon.), Dallas Bapt. U., 1990; LLD (hon.), Hardin Simmons U., 1999. Ordained to ministry Bapt. Ch., 1955. Assoc. sec. Christian Life Commn., Dallas, 1957-63; prof. Christian ethics Southwestern Bapt. Theol. Sem., Ft. Worth, 1963-75; pastor First Bapt. Ch., Wichita Falls, Tex., 1975-77; pres. Golden Gate Bapt. Theol. Sem., Mill Valley, Calif., 1977-82; vol. dir. Tex. Bapt. Heritage Ctr., 2000—; disting. prof. Dallas Bapt. U., 2001—; disting. vis. prof. Baylor U., 2001—. Exec. dir. Bapt. Gen. Conv. Tex., 1982—2000, exec. dir. emeritus, 2000—; chmn. program com. Christian Life Commn. So. Bapt. Conv., spl. rschr. for home mission bd., nat. task force planned growth in giving, 1984—94, stewardship commn., 1986—96; bd. dirs. T.B. Maston Found.; adj. prof. Southwestern Bapt. Theol. Sem., 1976—77; chmn. study commn. freedom, justice and peace Bapt. World Alliance, 1975—80, study commn. on ethics, 1990—95, commn. on racism, 1992—, com. on polity and heritage, 2000—05; v.p. Bapt. Gen. Conv. Tex., 1972—73, state missions commn., 1976—77, vice chmn. urban strategy com., chmn. order of bus. com., 1976, chmn. steering com. Good News Tex., 1976—77, chmn. resolutions com.; spkr. in field; bd. dirs., chair centennial com. Baylor U. Health Care Sys., 2002—. Contbr. articles to profl. jours., chapters to books. Adv. bd. Bapt. History and Heritage Soc., 2002—; mem. adv. com. Sch. Leadership Dallas Bapt. U., 2003—. Named Lilly Found. scholar Southwestern Bapt. Theol. Sem., 1960-62; recipient Disting. Alumni award Southwestern Bapt. Theol. Sem., 1979, U. North Tex., 1980, Mosaic Missions award Home Mission Bd., 1984, Parabolani award Tex. Bapt. Men, 1999, Spirit of Excellence award Houston Bapt. U., 2000, Tex. Bapt. Missions award State Missions Commn., 2000, Pioneer award Tex. Bapt. Missions Found., 2001, W. Winfred Moore award for lifetime achievement in ministry Baylor U., 2001, Officers' award Bapt. History and Heritage Soc., 2003, Elder Statesman award Independence. Assn., 2005. Mem. So. Bapt. Assn. Colls. and Schs., So. Bapt. Assn. of State Exec. Dirs. (pres. 1996-97). Baptist. Avocations: travel, reading. Office: Bapt Gen Conv Tex 333 N Washington Ave Dallas TX 75246-1782 Home Phone: 972-298-7371; Office Phone: 214-370-9471. Office Fax: 214-370-0228. Business E-Mail: william.pinson@bgct.org.

PINSTRUP-ANDERSEN, PER, economist, educator; b. Bislev, Denmark, Apr. 7, 1939; came to U.S., 1965; s. Marinus and Alma (Pinstrup) Andersen; m. Birgit Lund, June 19, 1965; 1 child: Tina. BS, Royal Vet. and Agrl. U., Copenhagen, 1965; MS, Okla. State U., 1967, PhD, 1969; Dr. Tech. Scis. (hon.), Swiss Fed. Inst. Tech., 1996; DSc (hon.), Tamil Nadu U., 1999, Animal Scis. U., 1999; LLD, U. Aberdeen, 1999; Dr. Agr. and Environment (hon.), Wageningen U., The Netherlands, 2000. Agrl. economist Centro Internacional de Agricultura Tropical, Cali, Colombia, 1969-72, head econ. unit, 1972-76; dir. agro.-econ. div. Internat. Fertilizer Devel. Ctr., Florence, Ala., 1976-77; sr. rsch. fellow, assoc. prof. Econ. Inst. Royal Vet. and Agrl. U., Copenhagen, 1977-80, prof. devel. econs., 2003—; rsch. fellow Internat. Food Policy Rsch. Inst., Washington, 1980, dir. food consumption and nutrition divsn., 1980-87, dir. gen., 1992—2002; dir. food and nutrition policy program, prof. food econs. Cornell U., Ithaca, NY, 1987-92, prof. applied econs. and mgmt., 2003—, H.E. Babcock prof. food, nutrition and pub. policy, 2003—; disting prof. Wageningen U., 2000—. Cons. The World Bank, Washington, 1978-92, Can. Internat. Devel. Agy., 1982-83, 86, UNICEF, N.Y.C.; cons. subcom. on nutrition UN, Rome, 1980-87; chmn. CGIAR Sci. Coun., 2004—. Author: more than 400 publs. including, The World Food and Agricultural Situation, 1978, Agricultural Research and Economic Development, 1979, The Role of Fertilizer in World Food Supply, 1980, Agricultural Research and Technology in Economic Development, 1982; editor: (with Magaret Biswas) Nutrition and Development, 1985, Food Subsidies in Developing Countries: Costs, Benefits, and Policy Options, 1988, Macroeconomic Policy Reforms, Poverty, and Nutrition: Analytical Methodologies, 1990, The Political Economy of Food and Nutrition Policies, 1993, (with David Pelletier and Harold Alderman) Child Growth and Nutrition in Developing Countries: Priorities for Action, 1995, Seed of Contention, 2001, The Unfinished Agenda, 2002; mem. editl. bd. coms. of several jours With Danish Army, 1958-59. Recipient cert. of appreciation People to People, 1967, competition prize Nordic Soc. agrl. Rschrs. and Norsk Hydro, 1979, cert. of merit Gamma Sigma Delta, 1991, Disting. Alumnus award U. Colo., 1993, Disting. Alumni award Okla. State U., 1998, World Food prize World Food Found., 2001; fellow Ford Found., 1965-66, Kellogg gravel fellow, 1979. Mem. AAAS (chair sect. on agr. 2004), AAEA (pres. 2005-), Am. Assn. Agrl. Econs. (PhD Thesis award 1970, Outstanding Jour. Article award 1977, bd. dirs. 1996-99), Internat. Assn. Agrl. Econs., Columbian Nat. Orgn. Profls. in Agr. (hon., Charles Black award 1998, Agronomprisen 2000, World Food prize 2001, Rosenhjaerprisen, 2002). Office: Cornell U Divsn of Nutrition 305 Savage Hall Ithaca NY 14853 Office Phone: 607-255-9429. Business E-Mail: pp94@cornell.edu.

PINTER, GABRIEL GEORGE, retired physiology educator; b. Bekes, Hungary, June 23, 1925; came to U.S., 1958; s. Lajos and Regina (Szilagyi-Farkas) Pinter; m. Berit Helgesen, Dec. 19, 1958 (dec. May 1980); children: Renee Astrid, Eva Ingelill; m. Vera Lederer Dallos, May 24, 1984. MD, U. Sch. Medicine, Budapest, Hungary, 1951. Asst. prof. U. Sch. Medicine, Budapest, Hungary, 1951-56; rsch. assoc. U. Inst. Med. Rsch., Oslo, Norway, 1957-58; asst. prof. U. Tenn., Memphis, 1958-61; from asst. prof. to prof. U. Md., Balt., 1961-92; retired. Vis. prof. King's Coll., London, 1990-94. Contbr. articles to profl. jours.; translator (with wife) philos. and lit. works into Hungarian. Recipient A.V. Humboldt prize, Germany, 1980; Swedish Royal Med. Soc. fellow, Uppsala, 1972. Mem. Am. Physiol. Soc., Physiol. Soc. Gt. Brit., Scandinavian Physiol. Soc., European Soc. Microcirculation. Personal E-mail: ggvp@comcast.net.

PINTO, MARIE MALANIA, academic administrator, consultant; b. Tulare, Calif., Aug. 30, 1963; d. Joe Martin and Marie Inez Simoes; m. Joe John Pinto, Dec. 30, 1953; children: Jonathon Joseph, Jameson Jesse, Andrew Clayton, Jordan Michael. B in Bus. Mgmt., U. Phoenix, 2000, MBA, 2002; M in Ednl. Adminstrn., Calif. State U., Fresno, 2003. Cert. vocat. instr. Calif., 1996, adminstrv. svcs. credential 2003. Dept. mgr. Gottschalks, Visalia, Calif., 1984—91, tng. mgr., 1989—91, asst. buyer Fresno, 1991—94, asst. store mgr. Santa Maria, 1994—95; vocat. instr. Tulare Adult Sch., 1996—2002, work experience coord., 1999—2002, adminstrv. intern, 2002—03, asst. dir., 2003—. Staff devel. trainer, cons. Marie Pinto & Associates, Visalia, 1998—. Cons., vol. Visalia C. of C. Recipient School-to-Career Partnership award, Tulare County Office Edn., 2001. Mem.: Calif. Coun. Adult Educators (pres.-elect ctrl. sect.), Tng. and Employment Assn. Tulare County (v.p.), Assn. Calif. Sch. Adminstrs., Calif. Tchrs. Assn., Tulare Soroptimist, Tulare C. of C. Democrat. Roman Catholic. Avocations: aerobics, travel, reading, entertaining, volunteer work. Home: 5548 W Vine Ct Visalia CA 93291 Office: Tulare Adult Sch 575 W Maple Tulare CA 93274 Office Phone: 559-686-0225. Personal E-mail: jjpmmp98@aol.com. Business E-Mail: marie.pinto@tulare.k12.ca.us.

PINTO, MARK R., manufacturing executive; B, Rensselear Poly. Inst., Troy, NY; M, PhD, Stanford U., Calif. V.p., gen. mgr. network product IC divsn., chief tech. officer Bell Labs. and Lucent Microelectronics Group (later Agere Systems); sr. v.p., chief tech. officer, gen. mgr. New Bus. and New Products Group Applied Materials, Inc., 2004—, chmn. Venture Investment Com. Adj. prof. Yale U., New Haven. Contbr. articles to sci. jours. Named a Bell Labs fellow. Fellow: IEEE. Achievements include patents in field. Office: Applied Materials Inc PO Box 58039 Santa Clara CA 95052-8039 Office Phone: 408-727-5555. *

PINTO, ROSALIND, retired secondary school educator, volunteer; b. NYC; d. Barney and Jenny Abrams; m. Jesse E. Pinto (dec.); children: Francine, Jerry, Evelyn. BA in Polit. Sci. cum laude, Hunter Coll.; MA in Polit. Sci., History, Columbia U.; postgrad., Queens Coll., LaGuardia C.C. Lic. social studies tchr. jr. HS, NY, per diem substitute; cert. secondary sch. social studies grades 7-12, NY. Substitute tchr., 1956-79, 90, 91—; tchr. social studies I.S. 126Q, LI, NY, 1969-88, Jr. HS 217 Briarwood, NYC, 1988-89; ret., 1989; part-time cluster tchr. social studies and communication arts Pub. Sch. 140, Bronx, NY, 1990-92; substitute tchr. I.S. 227Q, 1992-93. Participant seminars and workshops. Author curriculum materials; contbr. study guide for regent's competency test, 1990; author numerous poems; contbr. articles to profl. jours. Enrollment asst. Insight Heart Team, 1989; vol. receptionist Whitney Mus., NYC; mem. com. on pub. transp. Cmty. Bd. 6, Queens, 1990—96, mem. com. on history, 1990—, chmn. beautification com., 1992—, mem. com. on planning and zoning, 1996—, mem. com. on environ. sanitation, 1999—; mem. Forest Hills Action League, 1999; advocate Census 2000 participation; active Gt. Smokies Song Chase Warren-Wilson Coll., NC, 1992; mem. Queens Hist. Soc., Forest Hills Van Ct. Homeowners Assn.; bd. dirs. Ctrl. Queens Hist. Soc.; past mem. Rego Park Coalition Against Crime; mem. Forest Hills Civic Assn., 1996—97; vol. local polit. campaigns. Recipient Project award, Beautification Com., 1995, Women's History Month Rosemary Gunning award, Queens Borough Pres., 2000, Editor's Choice award, Best Poems and Poets, 2001, 2002, 2004, 2005, 2007, Poet Merit award, Poetry Conv., 2002—03, 2005, 2006, 2007, Poetry Divsn. award, Noble House, 2006, Appreciation Cert., Night Out Against Crime, 2002, 2003, 2004, 2007, NY State Senate, 2004—05. Fellow: Mcpl. Art Soc. (hon. mention design 2000 award); mem.: NAFE, Internat. Soc. Poets (life; adv. panel, Internat. Poet of Merit award 1993, 2000, Editor's Choice award 2001), Ctr. for Sci. in the Pub. Interest, Robert F. Kennedy Dem. Assn. (bd. dirs., RFK Assn. cert. of appreciation for dedication 2005), Hunter Coll. HS Alumni Assn., Hunter Coll. Alumni Assn., Columbia U. Grad. Sch. Arts and Scis. Alumni Assn., NY Insight Alumni Assn. Avocations: poetry, reading, walking, art shows, plays. *Loving people and having faith in them and the possibility of happy outcomes is the greatest motivation toward achievement of goals.*

PIOMBINO, NICHOLAS, psychotherapist; b. NYC, Oct. 5, 1942; s. Nicholas Bruce and Ruth Mary (Rothbart) P. BA with honors, CCNY, 1964; MSW, Fordham U., 1971; cert. in adult psychoanalysis and psychotherapy, Postgrad. Ctr. Mental Health, NYC, 1982. Diplomate in clin. social work; cert. psychotherapist, social worker, N.Y. Social worker Manhattan State Hosp., NYC, 1971-73; pvt. practice psychotherapy NYC, 1976—; sch. social worker N.Y.C. Bd. Edn., 1974—2001; staff psychotherapist Postgrad. Ctr. Mental Health, 1978-86; supr., mem. faculty Psychoanalytic Inst. N.Y. Counseling and Guidance Svc., NYC, 1987—. Author: Poems, 1988, Light Street, 1996, Theoretical Objects, 1999, Fait Accompli, 2007, Free Fall, 2007, (essays) The Boundary of Blur, 1993, The Boundary of Theory, 2000, Hegelian Honeymoon, 2004, numerous poems; contbr. articles to profl. jours.; Exhibited in group shows at Maryann Boesky Gallery, 2001, Harvard Dudley House, 2005, PS 122, 2006. Mem. Postgrad. Psychoanalytic Soc., Soc. Clin. Social Work Psychotherapists. Office: 680 W End Ave New York NY 10025-6815 Home: 44 Prospect Park W Apt F2 Brooklyn NY 11215-2344 Office Phone: 212-316-1871. E-mail: nickpoetique@earthlink.net.

PIONK, JEROME LEE, federal official; b. Watertown, SD, Aug. 31, 1950; s. Jerome Ambrose and Helen Emeline Pionk; m. Song Yo Kim; children: Jerome, Angela Pionk Curtis. BS, SUNY, Albany, 1984; MA, Liberty U., 1991; grad., Command and Gen. Staff Coll., 1997; PhD, North Ctrl. U., Prescott, Ariz., 2007. Cert. counselor. Enlisted man U.S. Army, 1970, advanced through grades to sgt. maj., 1989, recruiter Minn., Republic of Korea, 1970—75; retention and recruiting staff specialist Army Enlistment Eligibility Activity, St. Louis, 1984—87; dir. theater army retention 8th Army, Seoul, 1987—92; sr. retention policy advisor Hdqs. Dept. Army, Washington, 1992—2000; ret., 2000; sr. def. analyst, rschr. Dept. Def. (Resource Cons. Inc.), Washington, 2000—03; rsch. analyst SAIC, 2003—04; chief recruiting incentives br. U.S. Army G-1, Pentagon, 2004—. Prof. Am. Mil. U., 2000—; exec. dir. Nat. Assn. Recruiters and Career Counselors, Washington, 1983—; bd. dirs. Ctr. Mil. Sociol. Studies. Author: Prairie Vignettes, 1999, History of Military Retention, 2001. Decorated Legion of Merit; recipient Olympic honor award Seoul Olympic Organizing Com., 1988, Order of Horatio Gates, Army Adj. Gen.'s Assn., 1992. Mem. VFW (life), DAV (life), Assn. Mil. Recruiters and Counselors, Am. Vets. (life), Am. Legion. Republican. Avocations: skydiving, travel, writing, fencing, automobile racing. Office: Army Office Human Resource Mgmt 300 Army Pentagon Washington DC 20310 Home: 12241 Tilney Ct Woodbridge VA 22192-6611 Personal E-mail: ngob1@aol.com.

PIONTKOWSKI, STEPHEN ROBERT, environmental services administrator; BS in Environ. and Hazardous Waste Mgmt., U. Findlay, Ohio, 1996; MS in Environ. Health, East Tenn. State U., Johnson City, 1999. Registered environ. health specialist Nat. Environ. Health Assn., 2004, cert. child passenger safety technician SafeKids, 2003, ServSafe instr. Nat. Restaurant Assn., 2001, pool operator Nat. Swimming Pool Found., 2000. Tech. svcs. asst. Willamette Industries, Inc., Kingsport, Tex., 1999; svc. unit environ. health officer Indina Health Svc., Bemidji, Minn., 2000—02, Indian Health Svc., San Carlos, Ariz., 2002—. Soccer coach AYSO, Johnson City, 1996—2000, soccer coach, referee Globe, Ariz., 2002—07; adult mentor Life Teen, St. Phillips, Bemidji, 2000—02, Life Teen, Holy Angels Ch., Globe, 2002—06. Lt. comdr. USPHS, 2000. Decorated Achievement medal USPHS; recipient Exceptional Performance award, Phoenix Area Indian Health Svc., 2006. Mem.: KC (Fourth Degree 2003), APHA, Alpha Sigma Phi.

PIORKOWSKI, JOSEPH D., JR., lawyer, physician, educator, military officer; b. Chester, Pa., Nov. 21, 1956; s. Joseph D. Piorkowski and Elizabeth C. Bell; m. Marjorie Eldridge, Aug. 4, 1984; childre, Joseph and Alexandra. BA cum laude, Hofstra U., 1976; DO, Phila. Coll. Osteo. Medicine, 1980; JD magna cum laude, Georgetown U., 1988; MPH, Johns Hopkins U., 1992. Diplomate Am. Bd. Preventive Medicine, Am. Bd. Legal Medicine, Am. Osteo. Bd. Family Practice, Nat. Bd. Examiners for Osteo. Physicians and Surgeons; lic. physician, Md., D.C.; bar: Md., D.C., Tex., U.S. Dist. Ct. D.C., U.S. Dist. Ct. Md., U.S. Ct. Appeals (4th and D.C. cirs.); cert. instr. advanced trauma life support; cert. advanced cardiac life support. Commd. ensign USN, 1977, advanced through grades to capt., 1996, flight surgeon fighter squadron 31/carrier air wing THREE, staff physician U.S.S. Kennedy, substance abuse coord., 1982-84, flight surgeon Naval Air Facility, peer review coord. Navy Med. Clinics Washington, 1984-88, head Naval Air Facility Med. Clin., 1986-88; intern in psychiatry Nat. Naval Med. Ctr., Bethesda, Md., 1980-81; law clk. to Hon. Oliver Gasch US Dist. Ct. DC, 1988-89; ptnr. Williams & Connolly, Washington, 1997—2000, Shook, Hardy & Bacon, Washington, 2001—04; prin. Piorkowski Law Firm, PC, Washington, 2004—. Instr. Mil. Tng. Network, Dept. Def., 1986—; adj. prof. law Georgetown U. Law Ctr., Washington, 1992—, clin. asst. prof. dept. surgery Georgetown U. Med. Ctr., 1995-2004 Contbr. articles to profl. jours. Coach Great Falls Youth Basketball, 2005—07; leader Daily Bread Food Pantry McLean Bible Ch. Decorated Meritorious Svc. medal; named one of 75 Best Lawyers in Washington, Washingtonian mag., 2002; acad. honors scholar, Hofstra U., 1976. Fellow Am. Coll. Preventive Medicine, Am. Coll. Legal Medicine, Aerospace Med. Assn. (assoc.); mem. ABA (litigation sect.), Soc. of U.S. Naval Flight Surgeons, Internat. Soc. Pharmacoepidemiology, Regulatory Affairs Profl. Soc., Assn. of Mil. Surgeons of U.S., Am. Osteo. Assn., Am. Coll. Family Practitioners, Internat. Assn. Defense Counsel, Order of Coif, Delta Omega, Psi Chi. Office: Piorkowski Law Firm 910 17th St NW Ste 800 Washington DC 20006 Home Phone: 703-757-7560; Office Phone: 202-223-5535. Business E-Mail: JPiorkowski@lawdoc1.com.

PIOT, PETER, international organization administrator; b. Leuven, Feb. 17, 1949; m. Greet Kimzeke, 1975; 2 children. MD, U. Ghent, 1974; PhD in Microbiology, U. Antwerp, 1981, PhD (hon.), 1997, Free U., 1995; DSc (hon.), U. West Indies, 2005. Sr. fellow microbiology and infectious diseases U. Washington, 1978—79; prof. microbiology Inst. Tropical Medicine, 1980—92; prof. pub. health Free U., Brussels, 1989—94; assoc. dir. Global Program AIDS/WHO, Geneva, 1995; exec. dir. Joint UN Program on HIV/AIDS, Geneva, 1995—; under sec.-gen. UN, 2002—. Dir. WHO Collaborating Ctr. AIDS, Antwerp, Project SIDA, Kinshasa; assoc. prof. U. Nairobi, STD/AIDS Project, Kenya; co-discoverer Ebola virus; Socrates chair, European Acad., Yuste, Spain, 2004; bd. Internat. AIDS Vaccine Initiative, King Boudouin Found. Editor: (with others) Chlamydial Infection, 1982, (with J.M. Mann) AIDS and HIV Infection in the Tropics, 1988, (with P. Lamptey) Handbook on AIDS Prevention in Africa, 1990, 2d edit. 1991, (with others) Basic Laboratory Procedures in Clinical Bacteriology, 1991; co-author: AIDS in Africa: A Handbook for Physicians, 1992, Reproductive Tract Infections in Women, 1992, (with K.K. Holmes)Sexually Transmitted Diseases, 1999, (with M. Carael) L'Epidemie de Sida et la Mondialisation des Risques, 2005. Knighted baron King Albert II, 1995; decorated officier l'Ordre Nat. du Léopard (Zaïre), comdr. l'Ordre du Lion (Sénégal), Nat. Order Burkina Faso and Madagascar; NATO fellow, 1978-79; recipient Kerkheer prize Medicine, 1989, Health award Flemish Cmty., 1990, AMICOM award Medicine, 1991, H. Breurs prize, 1992, A. Jauniaux prize, 1992, van Thiel award, 1993, Glaxo award infectious diseases, 1995, Nelson Mandela award, 2001, Gold medal Royal Acad. Arts and Scis., Belgium, 2002, E. Calderone medal Columbia U., 2003, Vlerick award, Belgium, 2004, Congl. Achievement award, Philippines, 2005, Grand Ofcl. Order Infante Don Enrique, Portugal, 2005, Acad. Alliance Found. Global Health Leadership award, NY, 2005; named Outstanding Physician, AMA, Chgo., 2004. Fellow Royal Coll. Physicians (London); mem. Royal Acad. Medicine, Royal Acad. Overseas Scis., Internat. AIDS Soc. (pres. 1992), Inst. Medicine, other European, US, and African socs. Achievements include co-discovering the Ebola virus. Office: UNAIDS 20 Ave Appla CH-1211 Geneva 27 Switzerland Office Fax: 22 7914179. Business E-Mail: executivedirector@unaids.org.

PIOT, PHILIPPE REGIS-GUY, educator, researcher; b. Saint-Tropez, France, Nov. 21, 1972; s. Roger Rene-Denis Piot and Laurette Therese Porro; m. Yin-e Sun, Sept. 23, 1973; 1 child, Julie Florence. PhD, U. Joseph Fourier, Grnoble, France. Rsch. assoc. Fermi Nat. Accelerator Lab., Batavia, Ill., 2002—05; assoc. prof. No. Ill. U., DeKalb, 2005—. Rsch. assoc. Deutsches Elektronen-Synchrotron, Hamburg, Germany, 1999—2002. Office: Northern Illinois University Faraday Building Dekalb IL 60115 Office Phone: 815-753-6468. Personal E-mail: philippe.piot@gmail.com. Business E-Mail: piot@nicadd.niu.edu.

PIOU-BREWER, MAGALIE, psychotherapist, educator, small business owner; b. Arthabaska, Que., Can., Apr. 26, 1971; d. Edouard Louis and Jacqueline Dorcal Piou; m. Michael Alexander Brewer, July 21, 2003; 1 child, Anya Lilly Brewer. Student, Cath. U., Leuven, Belgium, 1991—92; BA in Comm., Loyola Coll., Balt., 1993, MS in Pastoral Counseling, 2000; PhD in Clinical Psychology, George Washington U., 2004. Lic. counselor. Assoc. dir. admissions Loyola Coll., Balt., 1994—2001; child psychotherapist Stevenson Psychol. Svcs., Columbia, Md., 2001—03; clin. dir. Bridgeway Counseling Svcs., Columbia, 2004—; exec. dir. MPB Group, Inc., Columbia, 2004—. Adj. asst. prof. Loyola Coll. Grad. Ctr., Columbia, 2005—; spkr. in field. Acad. fellow, George Washington U., 2000—03, Maternal/Child Health grant, Kennedy Kreiger Inst., Balt., 2003. Mem.: APA, Am. Counselors Assn., Am. Mental Health Counselors Assn. Avocations: reading, travel. Office: MPB Group Inc 9650 Santiago Rd Ste 11 Columbia MD 21045 Office Phone: 410-730-2385.

PIOVEZAHN, ALESSANDRO R., public information officer, marketing professional, consultant; b. Rio de Janeiro, July 22, 1972; m. Raquel D. Muller. Degree in Mktg., ESPM, São Paulo, 1992. Cert. strategic marketing techniqûes Funserv, 1992. Mktg. cons. McDonald's, Foz do Iguaçu, Brazil, 1994—99; mktg. dir. USAdvertising, Danbury, Conn., 2000—06; pub. info. officer World Sports Alliance, NY, 2006. Cons. in field. Author: Positive Vibrations Always. Gen. dir. Positive Vibrations Always Found., New Fairfiled, Conn., 2000—07. Recipient Best Website of Yr. award, Intern, Assn. Websdevelopers and Creative Consultants, 2001. Achievements include first to participate activly in the photosharing and community industry interacting with the user base via website; development of the first humanitarian web portal focused on the discimitaion of information about the United Nations 8 millenium development goals; the first community and family oriented website in the community/blogs related industry. Office: World Sports Alliance 866 United Nations Plz New York NY 10017 Home Phone: 646-312-0867; Office Phone: 616-712-0183. Business E-Mail: alex@wsaigo.org.

PIPCHICK, MARGARET HOPKINS, advance practice psychiatric nurse, marriage and family therapist; m. Robert Pipchick; children: Christine, Kevin. BSN, Seton Hall U., 1968; MA, NYU, 1974; grad., Blanton Peale Grad. Inst., NYC, 1981; PhD, The Union Inst., 2001. Cert. traumatologist Green Cross. Various staff positions hosps., NY, NJ; teaching asst. Seton Hall U., South Orange, NJ, 1971-72; staff therapist, faculty Blanton-Peale Counseling Ctr., Cranford, NJ, 1974-90; pvt. practice individual, couple and family therapy Cranford, 1981—. Adj. faculty Fairleigh Dickenson U., Teaneck, NJ, 1989-93, Kean Coll., 1994, 95. Drew U., 2003. Contbr. chpt. to Founds. Psychiat. Mental Health Nursing. Mem. ANA, NJ State Nurses Assn., Am. Assn. Marriage and Family Therapists, Soc. Advanced Practice Psychiatric Nurses (pres.), Sigma Theta Tau. Office Phone: 908-272-9088.

PIPER, ADDISON LEWIS, securities executive; b. Mpls., Oct. 10, 1946; s. Harry Cushing and Virginia (Lewis) P.; m. Louise Wakefield (div.); children: Gretchen, Tad, William; m. Cynthia Schuneman, Nov. 14, 1979; children: Elisabeth LaBelle, Richard LaBelle. BA in Econs., Williams Coll., 1968; MBA, Stanford U., 1972. Mktg. cons. Earl Savage and Co., Mpls., 1968-69; mem. capital market dept. Piper and Jaffray, Mpls., 1969-70; asst. syndicate mgr. Piper, Jaffray and Hopwood, Mpls., 1972-73, v.p., 1973-79, dir. trading, 1973-77, dir. sales, 1977-79, exec. v.p., dir. mktg., 1979-83, chief exec. officer, chmn. mgmt. com., 1983—, chmn. bd. dirs., 1988—2003; vice chmn., dir. Piper Jaffray Cos. (spun off from U.S. Bancorp), Mpls., 2003—. Adv. com. N.Y. Stock Exch., 1966-90; bd. dirs. Allina Health Systems, Greenspring Corp., Mpls., Minn. Bus. Partnership, Mpls., Abbott Northwestern Hosp., Mpls.; trustee CARE Found., Mpls. Fin. chmn. Senator Durenberger Fin. Com., Mpls., 1980-88; chmn. Minn. Pub. Radio, 1985-95. Mem. Securities Industry Assn. (bd. govs. 1986-90, tax policy com.), Country Club of the Rockies (Colo.), Mpls. Club, Ventana Canyon (Tucson), Woodhill Country Club (Wayzata). Republican. Episcopalian. Avocations: skiing, golf, hunting, tennis, horseback riding. Office: Piper Jaffray Cos J1012058 800 Nicollet Mall Ste 800 Minneapolis MN 55402-7020

PIPER, ADRIAN MARGARET SMITH, philosopher, artist, educator; b. NYC, Sept. 20, 1948; d. Daniel Robert and Olive Xavier (Smith) P.; m. Jeffrey Ernest Evans, June 27, 1982 (div. 1987). AA, Sch. Visual Arts, 1969; BA in Philosophy, CCNY, 1974; MA, Harvard U., 1977, PhD, 1981; student, U. Heidelberg, Germany, 1977-78; LHD (hon.), Calif. Inst. Arts, 1992, Mass. Coll. Art, 1994. Asst. prof. U. Mich., Ann Arbor, 1979-86; Mellon rsch. fellow Stanford (Calif.) U., 1982-84; assoc. prof. Georgetown U., Washington, 1986-88, U. Calif., San Diego, 1988; prof. philosophy Wellesley (Mass.) Coll., 1990—. Disting. scholar Getty Rsch. Inst., 1998—; speaker, lectr. on both philosophy and art. Artist: one-woman exhbns. include N.Y. Cultural Ctr., N.Y.C., 1971, Montclair (N.J.) State Coll., 1976, Wadsworth Atheneum, Hartford, Conn., 1980, Nexus COntemporary Art Ctr., Atlanta, 1987, The Alternative Mus., N.Y.C., 1987, Goldie Paley Gallery, Phila., 1989, Power Plant Gallery, Toronto, 1990, Lowe Art Mus., Coral Gables, Fla., 1990-91, Santa Monica (Calif.) Mus. Contemporary Art, 1991, John Weber Gallery, N.Y.C., 1989, 90, 91, 92, Whitney Mus. Am. Art, N.Y.C., 1990, Hirschorn Mus., Washington, 1991, Ikon Gallery, Birmingham, Eng., 1991, Cornerhouse, Manchester, Eng., 1992, Cartwright Hall, Bradford, Eng., 1992, Kunstverein, Munich, Germany, 1992, Indpls. Ctr. Contemporary Art, 1992, Manasterio de Santa Clara, Moguer, Spain, 1992, Grey Art Gallery, N.Y.C., 1992, Paula Cooper Art Galler, 1992, 94; group exhbns. include Paula Cooper Gallery, 1969, Dwan Gallery, N.Y.C., 1969, 70, Seattle Art Mus., 1969, Stadtisches Mus., Leverkusen, Germany, 1969, Kunsthalle Berne, Berne, Switzerland, 1969, N.Y. Cultural Ctr., 1970, Allen Mus., Oberlin, Ohio, 1970, Mus. Modern Art, N.Y.C., 1970, 88, 91, Musee d'Art Moderne, Paris, 1971, 77, 89, Inhibodress Gallery, New South Wales, Australia, 1972, Calif. Inst. Arts, Valencia, 1973, Samuel S. Fleischer Art Meml., Phila., 1974, Mus. Contemporary Art, Chgo., 1975, Newberger Mus., Purchase, N.Y., 1978, Mass. Coll. Art, Boston, 1979, Artemesia Gallery, Chgo., 1979, A.I.R. Gallery, N.Y.C., 1980, Inst. Contemporary Arts, London, 1980, The New Mus., N.Y.C., 1981, 83, 85, Kenkeleba Gallery, N.Y.C., 1983, The Studio Mus. Harlem, N.Y.C., 1985, 89, Mus. Moderner Kunst, Vienna, Austria, 1985, Intar Gallery, N.Y.C., 1988, Whitney Mus. Downtown, N.Y.C., 1988, Art Gallery Ont., Toronto, 1988, Long Beach (Calif.) Art Mus., 1989, Simon Watson Gallery, N.Y.C., 1990, Feigen Gallery, Chgo., 1990, Barbara Krakow Gallery, Boston, 1990, Milw. Art Mus., 1990, Contemporary Arts Ctr., Houston, 1991, John Weber Gallery, 1991, Anne Plumb Gallery, N.Y.C., 1991, Hirschorn Mus., 1991, The Albuquerque Mus. Art, 1991, The Toledo Mus. Art, 1991, Denver Art Mus., Fukui Fine Arts Mus., Fukyuiken, Japan, 1992-93, N.J. State Mus., Trenton, 1992-93, Philippe Staib Gallery, N.Y.C., 1992, New Loom House, London, 1992, Espace-Lyonnais D'Art Contemporain, Lyon, France, 1993, Am. Acad. Inst. Arts and Letters, N.Y.C., 1993; permanent collections include Met. Mus. Art, Whitney Mus., L.A. Mus. Contemporary Art, San Francisco Mus. Modern Art, The Bklyn. Mus., Denver Art Mus., Kunstmuseum Berne, Musee d'Art Moderne, The Mus. Contemporary Art, Chgo., The Wadsworth Atheneum, Met. Mus. Art; art performances include RISD, 1973, The Whitney Mus. Am. Art, 1975, Kurfurstendamm, Berlin, 1977, Hauptstrasse, Heidelburg, Germany, 1978, Allen Meml. Mus., Oberlin, Ohio, 1980, Contemporary Art Inst. Detroit, 1980, San Francisco Art Inst., 1985, Calif. Inst. Art, 1984, The Studio Mus. Harlem, 1988; performances on video, 1987—; contbr. articles to profl. jours. Recipient N.Y. State Coun. on Arts award, 1989, Visual Arts award, 1990, Skowhegan medal for sculptural installation, 1995, Dance Theatre Workshop award for New Genres, 2000; NEH Travel fellow, 1979, NEA Visual Artists' fellow, 1979, 82, Andrew Mellon Postdoctoral fellow, 1982-84, Woodrow Wilson Internat. Scholars fellow, 1988-89, Guggenheim Meml. fellow, 1989, non-resident fellow N.Y. Inst. for Humanities, NYU, 1996—, Wissanschftskolleg zu Berlin Inst. Adv. Study fellow, 2005-; NEA Artists Forums grantee, 1987; rsch. fellowship NEH, 1998, Getty Rsch. Inst. Disting. scholarship, 1998-99, Internat. Forschungszentrum Kulturwissenschaften fellow Vienna, fellow Wissenschetskolleg zu Berlin Inst. Advanced Study, 2005-. Mem. AAUP, Am. Philos. Assn. (mem. ea. divsn.), Am. Soc. Polit. and Legal Philosophy, N.Am. Kant. Soc. Avocations: Medieval and Renaissance music, fiction, poetry, yoga, German. Office: Adrian Piper Rsch Archives Postfach 54 02 04 D-10042 Berlin Germany Office Phone: 49-30-308-253-18. E-mail: contact@adrianpiper.com, contack@adrianpiper.com.

PIPER, DON COURTNEY, political scientist, educator; b. Washington, July 29, 1932; s. Don Carlos and Alice (Courtney) Piper; m. Rowena Inez Wise, July 6, 1956; children: Sharon, Valarie. BA, U. Md., 1954, MA, 1958; PhD (James B. Duke fellow), Duke U., 1961. Research assoc. Duke U., 1961-62; exec. sec. Commonwealth-Studies Center, 1962-64; asst. prof. dept. govt. and politics U. Md., College Park, 1964-67, assoc. prof., 1967-69, prof., 1969-97, prof. emeritus, 1997—, head dept. govt. and politics, 1968-74, dir. grad. studies dept., 1982-95, mem. coun. of system faculty, 1989-90; chmn. faculty council College Park Faculty Assembly, 1974-75, chmn. campus senate, 1975-77, 89-90, univ. marshal, 1981-97, mem. Athletic Council, 1986-93, mem. senate ad hoc com. on undergrad. edn., 1986-88, chmn. chancellor's ad hoc com. on campus ceremonies, 1986-87, chmn. acad. com. of Athletic Council, 1986-89; chmn. campaign for College Park, 1988-89; chmn. retention review com. U. Md., 1990-91, chmn. budget and facilities com. athletic coun., 1991-93, chmn. senate com. on programs courses and curriculi, 1991-93, co-chair Mid. States self-study exec. com., 1995-97; tchg. fellow Lilly Ctr. for Tchg. Excellence, 1994—95. Rsch. asst. Am. Coun. Edn., 1966—68; mem. faculty adv. com., mem. adv. com. Md. State Bd. Higher Edn., 1977—82. Author: International Law of Great Lakes, 1967; co-author: International Law Standard and Commonwealth Developments, 1966, De Lege Pactorum, 1970, Foreign Policy Analysis, 1975; editor (with R. Taylor Cole): Post-Primary Education and Political and Economic Development, 1964; editor, author (with Ronald Terchek): Interaction: Foreign Policy and Public Policy, 1983; bd. editors World Affairs, 1971—94, mem. editl. adv. com. Internat. Legal Materials, 1977—78. Served to 1st lt. USAF, 1955—58. Mem.: Phi Beta Kappa (pres. Gamma chpt. 1978—79), Pi Sigma Alpha, Omicron Delta Kappa (faculty advisor 1990—97), Phi Kappa Phi (chpt. pres. 1982—83). Methodist. Home: 6312 Oakview Ct Hillsborough NC 27278

PIPER, ERVIN LEONARD, retired information technology manager, consultant; b. Cleve., Mar. 31, 1923; s. Edgar Ervin and Gertrude Eva Piper; m. Virginia Piper; children: Dale, Bruce. BS in Physics, Case Inst. Tech., Cleve., 1949; MS in Nuc. Physics, U. Ill., Champaign, 1951. Rsch. scientist Union Carbide Corp., Parma, Ohio, 1951—55, group leader, 1955—60, devel. divsn. mgr. lab Fostoria, Ohio, 1962—65, group leader Parma Rsch. Ctr., 1965—81; group leader Advanced Materials Lab, Lawrenceburg, Tenn., 1960—62; tech. mgr. Dylon Industries, Cleve., 1981—92, cons., 1992—96, ret., 1996. Contbr. chapters to books, scientific papers. Sgt. Signal Corps, 1943—46, PTO. Mem.: Carbide Ret. Corps.

PIPER, GEORGE CHILTON, lawyer; b. Lexington, Ky., Feb. 23, 1939; s. Lewis Allie and Anna (Zink) Piper; children: Jennifer A., Geoffrey C. AB, Harvard U., 1960; JD, U. Ky., 1967; MPH, Harvard Sch. Pub. Health, 1984. Ptnr. Martin, Ockerman & Brabart, Lexington, 1966—91; founding ptnr. Piper, Wellman & Bowers, Lexington, 1991—. Gen. counsel Planned Parenthood of Bluegrass, Inc., Lexington, 1971—2004. Sgt. E-4 US Army, 1961—64. Recipient Samdperil Essay award, Harvard Sch. Pub. Health, 1984. Office Phone: 859-231-1012. Office Fax: 859-231-1015. Business E-Mail: pwb@pwblaw.net.

PIPER, JAMI KATHLEEN, music educator, composer, musician; b. Oakland, Calif., Dec. 31, 1955; d. Barry Eugene Piper and Margaret Letitia (Weis) Smythe; children: Stephanie June Hauck, Matthew Lewis Hook. MusB, U. Pacific, Stockton, Calif., 1976; MFA, Mills Coll., Oakland, Calif., 1987; postgrad., U. Colo., Boulder. Cert. pre-sch. through 12 tchg. credential in music U. Colo., Boulder, 1997, nat. certified tchr. of music in piano Nat. Music Tchrs. Assn. Piano accompanist, soloist contracted, Calif., 1962—; piano tchr. self employed, Calif., 1976—94, 2004—, Colo., 1996—2002; adj. educator Music Tchr. Assn. Calif., Calif., 1989—, Music Tchr. Nat. Assn., Colo., 1994—2002; vocal, instrumental music tchr. Boulder Valley Sch., Colo., 1995—2002; gen. music, theory, and history tchr. Boulder Arts Acad., Colo., 1995—98; piano accompanist, soloist contracted, Colo., 1995—2002. V.p., treas. Music Tchr. Assn. Calif., Alameda County, 1990—92, pres., 1992—94; v.p. Boulder Area Music Tchr. Assn., Colo., 1994—95; chair of auditions Colo. Music Tchr. Assn., Colo., 1996—98; Am. advisor Kitumusote, Tanzania, 2005. Composer: (hymn) Benediction, 1986, Give Him the Praise, 1986, God Almighty, God of Love, 1987; musician: (solo concert debut U.S.) Oakland, Calif., 1973, (solo concert debut Europe) Mendemblik, Noord-Holland, 1988; arranger: Doulos, 1986, performer, co-arranger, project cons.: albums Look into the Word. Pres. Daughters of the King, Prince of Peace Chpt., Fair Oaks, Calif., 2006—. Named Artist of the Session, Festival Noord Holland; recipient Mary M. Henry prize, Mills Coll., Oakland, Calif., 1985—87; scholar, State of Calif., 1973—76; Music grant, U. Pacific, Stockton, Calif., 1973—76. Mem.: Calif. Assn. Profl. Music Tchrs. (pres. Sacramento chpt. 2007—), Nat. Music Tchr. Assn., Music Tchr. Assn. Calif., Pi Lambda Theta, Kappa Delta Pi. Democrat. Episcopalian. Achievements include world premier performance of "Awaken", by Ken McCaw. Avocations: sewing, gardening, ballet, figure skating. Home and Office: 5643 Chris Ann Ct Sacramento CA 95841-2800 Personal E-mail: jkpmuses@comcast.net.

PIPER, JOHN RICHARD, political science professor; b. Sewickley, Pa., Oct. 2, 1946; s. John Hubert and Carol Elizabeth (Coleman) P.; m. Hoa Thuy Pham, June 6, 1970; 1 child, Carolyn Hoa. BA, Pa. State U., 1968; MA, Cornell U., 1971, PhD, 1972. Prof. polit. sci. Blackburn Coll., Carlinville, Ill., 1972-76; asst. prof. polit. sci. U. Tampa (Fla.), 1976-80, assoc. prof. polit. sci., 1980-83; prof. polit. sci. U. Tampa, Fla., 1983—, chmn. dept. history, polit. sci. and sociology Fla., 1990-96; dir. honors program, 1996—. Author: Ideologies and Institutions: American Conservative and Liberal Governance Prescriptions Since 1933, 1997, The Major Nation-States in the European Union, 2005; contbr. articles to profl. jours. V.p. Fla. Collegiate Honors Coun., 1998—99, pres., 1999—2000; mem. Tampa Bay Com. Fgn. Rels., 1990—. Recipient Outstanding Educator award Blackburn Coll., 1974, Louise Loy Hunter award U. Tampa, 1981, award for teaching excellence Sears Roebuck Found., 1990; Fulbright-Hays grantee, 1988. Mem.: Am. Polit. Sci. Assn., Pi Kappa Phi, Phi Beta

Kappa, Omicron Delta Kappa. Democrat. Avocations: travel, swimming, reading. Office: Univ of Tampa 401 W Kennedy Blvd Tampa FL 33606-1490 Business E-Mail: rpiper@ut.edu.

PIPER, KATHLEEN, former political organization administrator; b. Ida County, Iowa; d. Pat and Rita Donahey McGuire; m. James Carl Piper, 1971; 2 children. Student, U. Iowa, Morningside Coll., Mt. Marty Coll. Co-owner Pied Piper Flower Shop, Yankton, S.D., 1986; vice chair Yankton County Dem. Com., 1980-95, state ctrl. committeewoman, 1995—; commr. Yankton County, 1986—, chair, 1996; state ctrl. com. S.D. Dem. Party, 1989-99, exec. bd., 1992-99, chairwoman, 1996-99. Mem. health care adv. com. Senator Tom Daschle, 1991—. Del. Nat. Dem. Conv., N.Y.C., 1992; mem. Gold adv. coun. appointed by Gov., 1993-95; participant Pres. Clinton and Hillary Rodham-Clinton's Health Care Initiative Rev., White House, 1993, Gt. Plains Rural Health Summit, 1994, Pres., Clinton and SBA Chief Roundtable Discussion Small Bus. and Health Care Reform, Washington, 1994; appointed del. White House Conf. Small Bus., 1994. Recipient Woman of Yr. award Ed Yankton Daily Press and Dakota, 1986, Emerging Leader for S.D. award Sioux Falls Argus Leader, 1990. Mem. S.D. County Commr. Assn. (exec. bd. 1992-94). Roman Catholic. Home: PO Box 737 Sioux Falls SD 57101-0737 also: 4412 Woolworth Ave Omaha NE 68105-1757

PIPER, LLOYD LLEWELLYN, II, engineer, government and service industry executive; b. Wareham, Mass., Apr. 28, 1944; s. Lloyd Llewellyn and Mary Elizabeth (Brown) P.; m. Jane Melonie Scruggs, Apr. 30, 1965; 1 child, Michael Wayne. BSEE, Tex. A&M U., 1966; MS in Indsl. Engring, U. Houston, 1973. Registered profl. engr., Tex.; diplomate hazardous waste mgmt. Am. Acad. Environ. Engrs. With Houston Lighting & Power Co., 1965—74; project mgr. Dow Chem. Engring. & Constrn Svcs., Houston, 1974—78, Ortloff Corp., Houston, 1978, mgr. engring., 1979—80, v.p., 1980—83; pres., CEO Plantech Engrs. & Constructors, Inc. subs. Dillingham Constrn. Corp., Houston, 1983—86; pres. Delta Plantech Co., Houston, 1985—86; dir. on-site tech. devel. Chem. Waste Mgmt., Inc., Oak Brook, Ill., 1986—88, mgr. projects Houston, 1988—94, dir. facility devel., 1994—95; asst. mgr. Richland Ops. U.S. Dept. Energy, Wash., 1995—96, dep. mgr., 1996—99, adminstr., 1999—2002, asst. mgr., 2002—03; dep. mgr. Carlsbad Field Office, U.S. Dept. Energy, 2003—. Bd. dirs., pres. Harris County Water Control and Improvement Dist., 1973—83; bd. dirs. Environ. Sci. and Tech. Found., 1997—99, United Way, 1998—2003, exec. com., 1998—2001, treas., 2000—01; bd. dirs. United Way of Carlsbad, 2004—, Ponderosa Joint Powers Agy. Harris County, 1977—83, pres., 1977—83; pres. bus. and industry adv. coun. North Harris Montgomery C. C. Dist., 1991—92. Contbr. articles to profl. jours. Recipient Disting. Svc. award Engrs. Coun. Houston, 1970; named Tex. Young Engr. of Yr., 1976, Nat. Young Engr. of Yr., 1976. Mem. IEEE (Outstanding Svc. award Houston sect. 1974), NSPE (chpt. pres. 1978, nat. chmn. engrs. in industry divsn. 1977, nat. v.p. 1977, chmn. nat. polit. action com. 1979-82, vice chmn. nat. engrs. week 1988-92, nat. trustee edn. found. 1988-90), Phi Kappa Phi, Tau Beta Pi. Office: Dept Energy PO Box 3090 Carlsbad NM 88221-0550 Home: PO Box 5342 Carlsbad NM 88221

PIPER, MARK HARRY, retired banker; b. Flint, Mich., Apr. 17, 1931; s. James U. and Dorothy (Weed) P.; m. Wanda L. Hubbard, June 20, 1953; children: Mark T., Kathryn L. BS, St. John's Mil. Acad., 1949; AB with distinction and honors in Econs, U. Mich., 1953, JD cum laude, 1956. Bar: Mich. 1956. With Clark, Klein, Winter, Parsons & Prewitt, Detroit, 1956-57, Genesee Mchts. Bank & Trust Co., Flint, 1957-88, v.p., sr. trust officer, 1966-72, sr. v.p., 1972-88, NBD Genesee Bank (formerly United Mich. Corp.), 1985-88, cashier, sec. bd. dirs., 1985-88. Adj. instr. bus. adminstrn. U. Mich., Flint, 1976-80; interim co-pension officer Detroit Conf. United Meth. Ch, 1993-99; pres. Flint Estate Planning Coun., 1969-70; mem. Flint citizens adv. coun. U. Mich., 1974-82; vice chmn., 1975-82. Bd. dir. Retirement Homes of Detroit Ann. Conf. Meth. Ch., 1964-76, vice chmn. profl. ministry and support, 1975, mem. bd. support systems, 1975, coun. fin. and adminstrn., 1976-84, chmn. coun. fin. and adminstrn., 1980-84; bd. dirs. United Meth. Devel. Fund, 1986-90; gen. bd. pensions United Meth. Ch., 1988-96, mem. investment com., gen. bd. pensions, 1988-00; mem. investment com. United Meth. Found. of Detroit. Conf. of United Meth. Ch., 1993-2004, interim exec. dir., 2004; trustee Flint YMCA Boysfarm Found., 1964-78, chmn., 1976-78; bd. mgmt. Flint YMCA Boysfarm, 1968-74; mem. Detroit Conf. Bd. P. United Meth. Ch., 1968-76, chmn., 1972-75, 88-02, mem., 1986-02; bd. dirs. U. Mich. Devel. Coun., 1980-82; bd. dirs., asst. treas., sec.-treas. Flint Area Young Life Found., 1979-2006, Mich. Area Young Life Com., 1980-88; bd. dirs., vice chmn. The Crim Road Race Inc., 1985-87; bd. mem. Stewardship Found. Mich., 2002-06. Mem. Mich. Bar Assn., Genesee County Bar Assn., Inst. Continuing Legal Edn., U. Mich.-Flint Club (bd. dirs., pres. 1973-74), Rotary Club. also: PO Box 3121 Estes Park CO 80517-3121 Personal E-mail: MHPiper3@aol.com.

PIPER, ROBERT JOHNSTON, retired architect, urban planner; b. Byron, Ill., Feb. 2, 1926; s. Leo Edward and Helen Anna (Johnston) P.; m. Carol Jane White, June 23, 1951; children— Christopher White, Brian Douglas, Eric Johnston. BS in Archtl. Engring, U. Ill., 1951; M. City and Regional Planning, Cornell U., 1953. Architect, planner Orput & Assos., Rockford, Ill., 1953-61; dir. profl. services AIA, Washington, 1961-67; partner, v.p. Perkins & Will, Chgo., 1967-74; dep. dir. Northeastern Ill. Planning Commn., Chgo., 1974-76; asso. Metz, Train, Olson & Youngren, Inc., Chgo., 1976-79; dir. community devel. City of Highland Park, Ill., 1980-91; ret., 1991; coord. Chgo. '93 and Chgo. Design Consortium Chgo. Cultural Ctr., 1992—. Pres. Landmarks Preservation Council Ill., Chgo., 1976-80 Author: Careers in Architecture, vocat. guidance manuals, 1967, 71, 75, 80, 85, 93; author, editor: Architect's Handbook of Professional Practice, 7th edit., 1963; prin. works include Regional Open Space Plan, Northeastern Ill., Spring Valley Operations Breakthrough Housing Complex, Kalamazoo, CBD Streetscape and Skokie Corridor Master Plan, Highland Park. Trustee Village of Winnetka, Ill., 1978-83; mem. Potomac Planning Task Force Dept. Interior, 1967-68, Commn. on Fed. Procurement, Washington, 1970-71; mem. nat. advisory bd. cmty. characteristics HEW, 1970-78; mem. Burnham Plan 1909 Centennial Com., 1999—. Served with USNR, 1944-46, PTO. Fellow AIA (mem. Task Force Future of Inst. 1974-75, various coms., pres. AIA Ill. coun. 1986, Disting. Achievement awards AIA Ill., AIA Chgo. 1993), Am. Inst. Cert. Planners; mem. Lambda Alpha (Chgo. Chpt. Mem. of Yr. award 1999, Daniel H. Burnham Disting. Svc. award, 2004). Episcopalian. Home: 1132 Oak St Winnetka IL 60093-2132 Personal E-mail: piper1132@comcast.net.

PIPER, THOMAS LAURENCE, III, banker; b. Washington, June 20, 1941; s. Thomas Laurence and Edna (Milewski) P.; m. Ann Runnette, Apr. 8, 1967; children: Thomas Laurence IV, Andrew Kerr. Student, U. Va., 1959—61. Assoc. Hodgdon & Co., Inc., Washington, 1962-65; sr. v.p., dir. Hayden Stone Inc., NYC, 1966-73; mng. dir. New Court Securities Corp., NYC, 1974-81, Dillon, Read & Co., Inc., NYC, 1981—97, UBS Warburg LLC, 1997—2000, Citigroup Pvt. Bank, 2000—03; sr. advisor The Nassau Group, 2003—04; sr. v.p. W.P. Stewart Asset Mgmt. (NA), Inc., 2005—. Chmn. fund dir. New Canaan chpt. ARC, 1978; bd. dirs. Manhattan coun. Boy Scouts Am., Waveny Care Ctr., New Canaan, Our Lady Queen of Angels, Manhattan; vice-chmn. adv. bd. U. Va. Art Mus., Charlottesville. Mem.: Bond Club NY, Investment Assn. NY (pres. 1974), Quail Valley Club, Red Stick Golf Club, Blind Brook Club, Country Club of New Canaan, Brook Club (N.Y.C.), Racquet and Tennis Club (N.Y.C.). Home: 14 Westmere Ave Norwalk CT 06853 Office Phone: 212-702-3248. Business E-Mail: tom@wpstewart.com. E-mail: tpiper3@optonline.net.

PIPER, THOMAS SAMUEL, minister, consultant; b. Racine, Wis., Feb. 26, 1932; s. Wallace William and Margaret Alice (Lahr) P.; m. Mary Alice Smith, Mar. 12, 1955 (dec. Feb. 2004); children: Daniel Thomas, David Michael, Grace Susan Piper Gonzales; m. Margaret Jean Brice, Nov. 5, 2005. BS, Lawrence U., 1954; ThM, Dallas Theol. Sem., 1969. Ordained to ministry Christian Ch., 1982. Mng. editor Good News Broadcaster mag., Lincoln, Nebr., 1969-82; pastor adminstrn. and edn. Faith Bible Ch., Sterling, Va., 1982-86; pres., cons. Ministries in Sync, Sterling, 1986—. Mem. writers conf. faculty Mt. Hermon (Calif.) Christian Conf., 1978-80, Christian Writers Inst., Wheaton, Ill., 1980; mem. pres.'s coun. Loudon County, Good News Jail and Prison Ministry, Arlington, Va., 1984-86; pres. local chpt. Christian Ministries Mgmt. Assn., Washington, 1987-88; mem. Christian Mgmt. Assn., 1989-90, Nat. Assn. Ch. Bus. Adminstrs., 1986-90. Contbr. articles to profl. jours. Coord. studies on uncomprised living program Christ Cmty. Ch., Ashburn, Va., 2000-01, cons., 2000-02; active McLean Bible Ch., 1995—; team leader, coach hosp./home visitation McLean (Va.) Bible Ch., 1996-99. With USN, 1956-58. Inductee Washington Park H.S. Hall of Fame, 2001. Mem. Voice of Bibl. Reconciliation (bd. dirs. 1991-93), Dallas Theol. Sem. Assn. (pres. local chpt. 1991-93), Internat. Assn. Bus. Communicators (life, pres. local chpt. 1977-79), Nat. Found., Inc. (donor advised fund adv. 1990-1995), Christian Cmty. Found. (donor advised fund adv. 1996-2001), Greater Washington Christian Edn. Assn. (cons. 1997-2002, program chmn., coord. 1997-2001, exec. editor 1998-2002, dir. conv. 1999-2002, bd. dirs. 1999-2002, chmn. planning com. 1999-2002, adminstrv. chmn., coord. 2001-02), Charities Support Found. (donor advised fund advisor 2002-06). Republican. Home and Office: Ministries in Sync 1307 E Holly Ave Sterling VA 20164-2614 Office Phone: 703-430-4097. Personal E-mail: tpiper@aol.com. *The strategic result of our calling today is helping churches in a me-centered high-tech age to synchronize their ministries to produce a pleasing and efficacious impact before a watching world.*

PIPER, WILLIAM HOWARD, bank executive; b. Flint, Mich., Oct. 15, 1933; s. James Underhill P. and Dorothy K. (Weed) Cooper; m. Joyce Rae Foster, June 6, 1959; children: Karen Elizabeth, William Howard, James Raymond. BA, Yale U., 1955. With NBD Genesee Bank, Flint, 1955—, pres., chief exec. officer, dir., 1985-90; sr. v.p. NBD Bancorp, 1990—; head of E. Mich. Banks, 1990—. Bd. dirs. U.S. Sugar Corp. Vice chmn., trustee emeritus McLaren Gen. Hosp., Flint, 1974—; trustee, vice chmn. Mott Found., 1985—; mem. adv. bd. Profl., Corp. Flint campus U. Mich., 1982—; dir. YWCA Found.; mem. Greater Flint Community Found.; mem. exec. com. Gen. Motors Inst. Bus. and Industry Ctr.; bd. dirs. Flint Inst. Music, 1983—, Flint Exec. Svc. Corp., 1985-87, Flint Coll. and Cultural Devel. Ctr.; sec., treas. Genesee Area Focus Coun. Mem. Flint C. of C. (dir. 1983-87) Clubs: Flint Golf, Univ. Republican. Methodist. Office: NBD Bank PO Box 331041 Detroit MI 48232-7041 also: Mott Found 503 S Saginaw St Ste 1200 Flint MI 48502

PIPERNO, DOLORES, research scientist; BS in Med. Tech., Rutgers U., 1971; MA in Anthropology, Temple U., 1979, PhD in Anthropology, 1983. Staff scientist Smithsonian Tropical Rsch. Inst., Balboa, Panama, CTPA dir. Panama. Mem.: NAS. Office: Smithsonian Tropical Rsch Inst Box 08943-03092 Balboa Ancon Panama Mailing: Unit 0948 Apo AA 34002-0948 Office Phone: 507 212 8101. Office Fax: 507 212 8154. E-mail: pipernod@si.edu.

PIPES, DORIS PERRY, secondary school educator, consultant; b. Tyrone, NY, Dec. 21, 1923; d. Raymond James and Mildred (Wood) Perry; m. Vernon Thomas Pipes, 1951 (div. 1965); 1 child, Vernon Thomas, Jr. AA, Cerritos Coll., 1962; BA, U. Calif., Fullerton, 1964; MA, U. Calif., LA, 1972. Cert. secondary sch. tchr. Coord. spl. programs, dept. chair program Pioneer High Sch., Whittier, Calif., 1964-65, dir. reading program, coord. tchr. tng., dept. head, 1966-67; instr. grad. sch. Whittier Coll., 1967-71; tchg. cons., classroom materials cons. Scholastic Mag., NYC, 1969-73; resource splst. Calif. High Sch., Whittier, 1973-90, cons. math dept., 1988-90; ret., 1990. Vis. guest lectr., dir. elem. reading clinic Loyola U., L.A., 1967-70; cons. Inglewood High Sch., 1971-72; adminstr. field testing parallel tests in Spanish and English, 1971, 77; reading tchr. Whittier Adult Sch., 1962-66. Contbr. article to jour. Mem. PTA Calif. High Sch., 1964-90 Recipient PTA award, 1989; named Outstanding Secondary Sch. Reading Program Nat. Assn. Secondary Sch. Prins., 1972, Outstanding Secondary Educator of Yr. Outstanding Secondary Educators, 1973. Mem. Internat. Reading Assn. (pres. Rio Hondo coun. 1967), Calif. Tchrs. Assn. (chair), Calif. High Sch. Tchrs. Assn., Alpah Gamma Sigma. Avocations: travel, reading, gardening. Home: 1581 Northwood Rd Apt 274H Seal Beach CA 90740

PIPES, GARY DALE, biochemist; s. Thomas Wesley and Martha Mae Pipes; m. Jacqueline Moore, Nov. 6, 1999. BS, Calif. State U., L.A., 1986; MS, CalTech, Pasadena, Calif., 1989. Sr. assoc. scientist Amgen Inc, Thousand Oaks, Calif., 1989—. Contbr. articles to profl. jours. Libertarian. Achievements include patents for LC/MS method and refolding of IgG's. Avocations: culinary arts, travel, computer science. Office: Amgen Inc One-Amgen Center Dr 8-1C Thousand Oaks CA 91320 Office Phone: 805-447-4950 18054474950.

PIPES, PAUL RAY, county commissioner; b. Truscott, Tex., Oct. 1, 1928; s. David and Maggie (Brown) Pipes; m. Linda Mullins, Dec. 17, 1961; children: Dana, Tricia. BBA, Sam Houston U., Huntsville, Tex., 1956, MEd, 1971. Acct. Pan Am. Petroleum Corp., Thibodaux, La., 1956-61; bus. tchr. Brenham H.S., Tex., 1962-90; county commr. Washington County, Brenham, 1991-98. With US Army, 1951-53, Korea. Decorated Def. Disting. Svc. medal. Republican. Methodist. Avocations: gardening, nature study. Home: 2106 Jane Ln Brenham TX 77833-5331

PIPES, ROBERT BYRON, mechanical engineer, educator; b. Shreveport, La., Aug. 14, 1941; s. Walter H. and Mattye Mae (Wilson) P.; m. Ruth Ellen Franz, June 27, 1964; children: Christopher Franz, Mark Robert. BS, La. Poly. Inst., 1964, MS, 1965; MSE, MA, Princeton U., 1969; PhD, U. Tex., 1972. Registered profl. engr., Del. Sr. structures engr. Gen. Dynamics Corp., 1969-72; asst. prof. mech. engring. Drexel U., 1972-74; assoc. prof. mech. and aerospace engring. U. Del., 1974-80, prof., 1980-91, also dir. Center Composite Materials, 1978-85, dean Coll. Engring., 1985-91, provost, v.p. acad. affairs, 1991-93; pres. Rensselaer Polytech. Inst., NY, 1993-98; disting. vis. scientist Coll. William and Mary, 1998—2001; Goodyear prof. polymer engring. U. Akron, Ohio, 2001—04; John C. Bray disting. prof. engring. Purdue U., 2004—. Cons. in field; com. mem. NRC. Author: Experimental Mechanics of Fiber Reinforced Composite Materials, 1982, Characterization of Advanced Composite Materials, 1987, 3d edit., 2002; series editor 12 vols. Composite Materials; contbr. articles to profl. jours. Bd. dirs. Omnova Solutions, Inc., Fairlawn, Ohio, 1993—2005. Recipient Gustus Larson award, ASME, 1987. Mem. ASME (Gustus Larson award 1983), Soc. Mfg. Engrs., Soc. Advancement of Material and Processing Engring., Nat. Acad. Engring. (elected 1987), Swedish Acad. Engring., Am. Soc. Composites, AIAA, SME, Sigma Xi, Tau Beta Pi, Pi Tau Sigma, Omicron Delta Kappa. Methodist. Achievements include pioneering work in the field of composite materials. Home and Office: 4509 Sugar Maple Dr Lafayette IN 47905 Office Phone: 765-494-5767. E-mail: bpipes@purdue.edu.

PIPES, SALLY C., think-tank executive; Asst. dir. Fraser Inst., Vancouver, B.C., Canada, 1974—91; pres., CEO Pacific Rsch. Inst. for Pub. Policy, San Francisco, 1991—. Co-author (with Spencer Star): Income and Taxation in Canada, (with Michael Walker) 7 editions of Tax Facts; has appeared nationally on TV programs such as 20/20 and Politically Incorrect, Dateline, Inside Politics and PBS's Think Tank; regularly asked to comment on timely issues by radio and print journalists; opinion editls. have been published in various newspapers including San Francisco Chronicle, L.A. Times, Investor's Business Daily, L.A. Daily News, The Orange County Register; writes a bi-monthly column in Chief Executive mag. Bd. dirs. Fin. Instns. Commn. (B.C.), 1980-84 (vice chmn. 1982-84, chmn. 1989-); mem. Vancouver City Planning Commn., 1982-84; trustee St. Luke's Hosp. Found. in San Francisco; bd. dirs. Ind. Women's Forum; mem. bd. advisors Western Jour. Ctr. and Citizens for Term Limits, San Francisco Lawyers chpt. of the Federalist Soc.; commr. Calif. Commn. on Transp. Investment, 1996; bd. govs. Donner-Can. Found. Mem. Mont Pelerin Soc., Nat. Assn. Bus. Economists, Can. Assn. for Bus. Econs. (pres. 2 terms), Assn. Profl. Economists of B.C. Office: Pacific Rsch Inst Pub Policy 755 Sansome St Ste 450 San Francisco CA 94111-1709 Office Phone: 415-955-6100.

PIPKIN, JAMES HAROLD, JR., lawyer; b. Houston, Jan. 3, 1939; s. James Harold and Zenda Marie (Lewis) P. BA, Princeton U., 1960; JD, Harvard U., 1963; Diploma in Law, Oxford U., Eng., 1965. Bar: D.C. 1964, U.S. Supreme Ct. 1969, D.C. Ct. Appeals, 1972. Law ck. to assoc. justice U.S. Supreme Ct., Washington, 1963-64; assoc. Steptoe and Johnson, Washington, 1965-70, ptnr., 1971-93; counselor to The Sec. of the Interior U.S. Dept. of the Interior, 1993-98; U.S. spl. negotiator for Pacific Salmon, Dept. of State, 1994-2001; rank of amb. Dept. of State, 1995-96; dir. office policy analysis U.S. Dept. Interior, 1998-2001; fgn. affairs officer U.S. State Dept., 2001—02. Counsel Friends of Music, Smithsonian Inst., Washington, 1984-88; mem. Nat. Arbitration Panel, 1983-94. Author or co-author: The English Country House: A Grand Tour, 1985, The Country House Garden: A Grand Tour, 1987, Places of Tranquility, 1990; contbr. photographs and articles to mags. including House & Garden, Smithsonian mag., The Mag. Antiques, Archtl. Digest. Grand officier Confrérie des Chevaliers du Tastevin, 1989—. Mem. ABA, D.C. Bar Assn., Met. Club. Home: 6109 Davenport Ter Bethesda MD 20817-5827

PIPKIN, MARVIN GRADY, lawyer; b. San Angelo, Tex., Nov. 15, 1949; s. Raymond Grady and Lillie Marie (Smith) P.; m. Dru Cheatham, July 24, 1971; children: Lacey Elizabeth, Matthew Todd. BBA, U. Tex., 1971, JD, 1974. Bar: Tex. 1974, U.S. Dist. Ct. (we. dist.) Tex. 1979, U.S. Ct. Appeals (5th cir.) 1983. Assoc. Green & Kaufman, San Antonio, 1974-79, ptnr., 1979-82, Kendrick & Pipkin, San Antonio, 1982-93, Drought & Pipkin L.L.P., San Antonio, 1993-98, Pipkin, Oliver & Bradley, LLP, San Antonio, 1998—. Mem. coms. on ethics and admissions Tex. Supreme Ct., admissions com.; adv. dir. Trinity Nat. Bank, San Antonio, 1983; bd. dirs. Allied Am. Bank, San Antonio, First Interstate Bank, San Antonio. Bd. dirs. Monte Vista Hist. Assn., San Antonio, 1975-78. Named Tex. Super Lawyer, Tex. Monthly, 2005; named one of Best Lawyers in Am., 2003—07, San Antonio's Best Attys., Scene San Antonio, 2004—07, Best Lawyers in Am., 2005—07. Fellow Tex. Bar Found., San Antonio Bar Found.; mem. ABA, Tex. Assn. Def. Counsel, Tex. Bar Assn., Tex. Assn. Bank Counsel, San Antonio Bar Assn., Tex. Wildlife Assn. (dir. 1998-05). Republican. Methodist. Avocations: sports, outdoor activities. Office: Pipkin Oliver & Bradley LLP 1020 NE 600 P 410 #810 San Antonio TX 78209 Home Phone: 210-824-8005; Office Phone: 210-820-0082. E-mail: mpipkin@pobllp.com.

PIPPEN, JENNIFER LYNN, therapist, consultant; b. Hinsdale, Ill., Nov. 10, 1975; d. Randy Lynn and Mary Hoekstra Pippen. BA summa cum laude, North Ctrl. Coll., Ill., 1998; M in Counseling Psychology cum laude, Trinity Grad. Sch., Ill., 2002. Lic. profl. counselor Ill., 2002, clin. profl. counselor 2005. Intern therapist Cath. Charities, Waukegan, Ill., 2001—02; therapist Maine Ctr., Park Ridge, Ill., 2002—. Missionary The Navigators, 1998—99; vol. West Suburban Humane Soc., Downers Grove, Ill., 2004. Mem.: ACA, Psi Chi. Avocations: piano, cross stitch. Office: Maine Ctr 819 Busse Hwy Park Ridge IL 60068 Home Phone: 630-759-5307; Office Phone: 847-696-1570 326.

PIPPEN, SCOTTIE, professional basketball player; b. Hamburg, Ark., Sept. 25, 1965; Student, U. Ctrl. Ark., 1983—87. With Seattle Super Sonics, 1987; guard/forward Chgo. Bulls, 1987—98, 2003—04, Houston Rockets, 1998—99, Portland Trailblazers, Oreg., 1999—2003. Player U.S. Olympic Basketball Team, 1988, 92; former analyst TNT. Named NBA All-Star Most Valuable Player, 1994, One of the 50 greatest players in NBA history, 1996; named to All-NBA team, 1992—98, NBA All-Star Team, 1990, 1992—97, NBA All-Defensive Team, 1991—2000. Achievements include mem. NBA Champion Chicago Bulls, 1991-1993, 1996-1998; mem. Gold medal U.S. Olympic Basketball Team, 1988, 1992. *

PIPPENGER, NICHOLAS JOHN, mathematician, researcher, computer scientist, educator; b. Abington, Pa., Mar. 14, 1947; s. Robert and Mary Emma Pippenger; m. Maria Margaret Klawe, May 12, 1980; children: Janek Evan Klawe, Sasha Kathleen. BS, Shimer Coll., 1965, MIT, 1967, MS, 1969, PhD, 1974. Mem. tech. staff Charles Stark Draper Lab., Cambridge, Mass., 1969—73; mem. rsch. staff IBM Corp., Yorktown Heights, NY, 1973—80, San Jose, Calif., 1980—87, fellow, 1987—89; prof. U. BC, Vancouver, Canada, 1988—2000, Princeton U., NJ, 2003—06, Harvey Mudd Coll, Claremont, Calif., 2006—; rsch. chair U. BC, Vancouver, 2000—03. Fellow: IEEE, Assn. Computing Machinery, Acad. Sci., Royal Soc. Can.; mem.: Math. Assn. of Am., Am. Math. Soc., Soc. Indsl. and Applied Math. Office: Harvey Mudd Coll Dept Math 1250 N Dartmouth Ave Claremont CA 91711 Home Phone: 909-624-1770. Business E-Mail: njp@math.hmc.edu.

PIPPERT, THOMAS W., lawyer; b. Cin., 1950; BA magna cum laude, Harvard U., 1972, JD cum laude, 1975. Bar: NY 1976, US Dist. Ct. (so. and ea. dist.) NY, US Ct. Appeals (2nd, 3rd & fed. cir.), US Ct. Appeals (ea. dist.) Wis. Atty. Patterson, Belknap, Webb & Tyler, NYC, ptnr. Mem. Phi Beta Kappa. Office: Patterson Belknap Webb & Tyler 1133 Ave of Americas New York NY 10036 Office Phone: 212-336-2555. Office Fax: 212-336-7893. Business E-Mail: twpippert@pbwt.com.

PIPPI, MIKE, entertainment management; b. Portland, Oreg., Apr. 20, 1947; BA, Lewis and Clark Coll., 1969. Founder, exec. dir. Frohman Acad. for Musical Theatre Edn., Carmel, Calif., 1982—91; producing dir. Am. Musical Theatre Festival, Monterey, Calif., 1985—91; co-founder, dir. internat. rels. Acad. Russian TV, Moscow, 1992—95; dir. spl. projects Turner Internat. Broadcasting, Moscow, 1993—95; global dir., artist recruitment and tng. Walt Disney Feature Animation, Burbank, Calif., 1996—98; exec. dir. Regional Arts and Culture Coun., Portland, Oreg., 1999—2000; dir. creative industries studies Portland (Oreg.) State U., 2000—04; exec. dir. Healthy Eating Lifestyle Principles, Inc., Monterey, Calif., 2005—. Mem. nat. policy bd. Ams. for The Arts, Washington, 1999-2001; Am. agent Russian Ministry of Culture, Moscow, 1987-92; vice chair cultural affairs St. Petersburg and L.A. Sister City Coms., 1991-95; founding trustee Nat. Alliance Musical Theatre Prodrs., N.Y.C., 1986-91. Avocations: writing, humanitarian programs, foreign affairs. Home: PO Box 22962 Carmel CA 93922-0962 Office Phone: 831-372-3616. Personal E-mail: pippihome@aol.com.

PIPPIN, M. LENNY, food products executive; m. Judy Pippin. BA, Fla. Atlantic U. CEO Albert Fischer, N.A., Dallas; pres., CEO Lykes Bros. Inc., Tampa, Fla., 1997-99, The Schwan Food Co., Marshall, Minn., 1999—. Office: The Schwan Food Co 115 W College Dr Marshall MN 56258 Office Fax: 507-537-8226.

PIPPIN, ROBERT B., philosopher, educator; b. 1948; BA with honors, Trinity Coll., Hartford, Conn., 1970; MA, Penn. State Univ., 1972, PhD in Philosophy, 1974. Asst. prof. New Coll., Sarasota, Fla., 1974—75, Univ. Calif., San Diego, 1975—81, assoc. prof., 1981—89, prof., 1989, 1989—92, dept. chair, 1990—92; prof. Univ. Chgo., 1992—, Raymond W. and Martha Hilpert Gruner disting. svc. prof. Author: Hegel's Idealism, 1989, Modernism as a Philosophical Problem, 1991. Recipient Disting. Achievement award, Andrew Mellon Found., 2001. Fellow: Am. Acad. Arts & Scis. Office: Dept Philosophy Univ Chgo 1115 E 58th St Chicago IL 60637 Office Phone: 773-702-5453. Business E-Mail: r-pippin@uchicago.edu. *

PIRAINO, THOMAS ANTHONY, JR., lawyer; b. Cleve., July 12, 1949; s. Thomas Anthony and Margaret (Stephens) P.; m. Barbara McWilliams, Sept. 4, 1976; children: Margaret, Ann, Mary. BA in History, magna cum laude, Allegheny Coll., 1971; JD, Cornell U., 1974. Bar: Ohio 1974. Assoc. counsel Parker-Hannifin Corp., Cleve., 1981-84, asst. gen. counsel, 1984-98, v.p., gen. counsel, sec., 1998—. Contbr. articles to legal jours. Mem. ABA, Ohio Bar Assn., Am. Corp. Counsel (sec. 1985—), Am. Soc. Corp. Secs. (past pres., Ohio chapter.) Avocations: tennis, jogging. Office: Parker Hannifin Corp 6035 Parkland Blvd Cleveland OH 44124-4141 *

PIRCHER, LEO JOSEPH, lawyer, director; b. Berkeley, Calif., Jan. 4, 1933; s. Leo Charles and Christine (Moore) P.; m. Phyllis McConnell, Aug. 4, 1956 (div. Apr. 1981); children: Christopher, David, Eric; m. Nina Silverman, June 14, 1987. BS, U. Calif., Berkeley, 1954, JD, 1957. Bar: Calif. 1958, (N.Y.) 1985, cert.: Calif. Bd. Legal Specialization (cert. specialist taxation law). Assoc. Lawler, Felix & Hall, L.A., 1957-62, ptnr., 1962-65, sr. ptnr., 1965-83, Pircher, Nichols & Meeks, L.A., 1983—. Adj. prof. Loyola U. Law Sch., LA, 1959—61; corp. sec. Am. Metal Bearing Co., Gardena, Calif., 1975—; dir. Varco Internat., Inc., Orange, Calif.; spkr. various law schs. and bar assns. edn. programs. Author (with others): (novels) Definition and Utility of Leases, 1968. Chmn. pub. fin. and taxation sect. Calif. Town Hall, LA, 1970—71. Mem.: ABA, Nat. Assn. Real Estate Investment Trusts Inc. (cert. specialist taxation law), L.A. County Bar Assn. (exec. com. comml. law sect.), N.Y. State Bar, Calif. State Bar, Regency (L.A.). Republican. Office: Pircher Nichols & Meeks Ste 1700 1925 Century Park E Los Angeles CA 90067-6022 Home Phone: 310-274-2455; Office Phone: 310-201-8901. Personal E-mail: lpircher@pircher.com.

PIRIE, ROBERT BURNS, JR., defense analyst; b. San Diego, Sept. 10, 1933; s. Robert Burns and Gertrude May (Freeman) P.; m. Joan Adams, Dec. 23, 1960; children: John Winthrop, Carl Joseph Emil, Susan Gilman. Student, Princeton U., 1950-51; BS, U.S. Naval Acad., 1955; BA, Magdalen Coll., Oxford U., 1959, MA, 1963. Commd. ensign U.S. Navy, 1955, advanced through grades to comdr., 1969; comdg. officer (U.S.S. Skipjack), 1969-72; dep. asst. dir. Congl. Budget Office, 1975-77; prin. dep. asst. sec. for manpower, res. affairs and logistics Dept. Def., Washington, 1977-79, asst. sec., 1979-81; mgmt. cons., 1981—; def. analyst Ctr. for Naval Analyses, Alexandria, Va., 1981-83; asst. v.p. Inst. for Def. Analyses, Alexandria, 1983-86, v.p., 1986-87; exec. v.p. Essex Corp., Alexandria, 1987, pres., 1987-88; sr. economist Rand Corp., Washington, 1989; dir. strategic studies group U.S. Naval War Coll., 1989-92; v.p. Ctr. Naval Analyses, Alexandria, 1992-94; asst. sec. of Navy for Installations and Environ. USN, Washington, 1994-2000, undersec. of Navy, 2000—01; sr. fellow Ctr. for Naval Analysis, 2001—. Chmn. bd. advisors Nat. Infrastructure Inst., 2004—. Vestryman St. John's Episcopal Ch., Chevy Chase, Md., 1973-76, 81, jr. warden, 1982-84, sr. warden, 1984-87; trustee U.S. Naval Acad. Found., 1980-94. Rhodes scholar, 1956 Mem. U.S. Naval Inst., U.S. Naval Acad. Alumni Assn. (trustee 1967-70), Vincent's Club, Cosmos Club. Home: 4405 Stanford St Chevy Chase MD 20815-5207 Personal E-mail: rpirie@aol.com.

PIRKEY, LOUIS THOMAS, lawyer; b. Ft. Worth, Dec. 6, 1937; s. Louis F. and Juanita (Copeland) P.; m. Jewell Katherine Buchanan, Oct. 19, 1940; children— Julia Hope, Jeffry Thomas. B.S.Ch.E., U. Tex., 1960; J.D. with honors, George Washington U., 1964. Bar: Tex. 1964, U.S. Supreme Ct. 1981, U.S. Ct. Appeals (5th and 11th cirs.), U.S. Dist. Ct. (we., so. and ea. dists.) Tex. Mem. Arnold, White & Durkee, Houston, 1964—, 1969—; chmn. intellectual property law sect. State Bar of Tex., 1982-83; mem. U.S. delegation Diplomatic Conf. on Rev. of Paris Conv., 1982. Fellow Tex. Bar Found.; mem. U.S. Trademark Assn. (dir.), ABA (chmn. Fed. trademark legislation com. 1972-74), Am. Patent Law Assn., Houston Bar Assn., Houston Patent Law Assn., Travis County Bar Assn., Licensing Execs. Soc., Interam. Assn. for Protection of Intellectual Property, Internat. Assn. Protection of Intellectual Property, Order of Coif, Phi Alpha Delta. Clubs: Headliners, Capital, Westwood Country (Austin); Univ. (Houston). Office: 600 Congress Ave Ste 2300 Austin TX 78701-2977

PIRKL, JAMES JOSEPH, industrial designer, educator, writer; b. Nyack, NY, Dec. 27, 1930; s. James and Ida Bertha (Gigrich) Pirkl; m. Sarah B. W. Woolsey, June 8, 1974; children: Theo, James, Philip. Cert. in advt. design, Pratt Inst., 1951, B in Indsl. Design cum laude, 1958. Design staff GM, Warren, Mich., 1958-65, sr. designer, 1961-64, asst. chief designer, 1964-65; instr. indsl. design Center Creative Studies, Detroit, 1963-65; faculty dept. design Syracuse (N.Y.) U., 1965-92, assoc. prof., 1969-73, prof. indsl. design, 1974-92, prof. emeritus, 1992—, coord. indsl. design program, 1979-84, chmn. dept. design, 1985-91; exec. council chmn. Sch. Art, 1976-78, 80-81; sr. rsch. fellow All-U. Gerontology Ctr., 1990-92. Prin. James J. Pirkl/Design, 1965—; cons. GE, 1967—70, N.Y. State Coun. Arts, 1968—69, Loretto Geriatric Ctr., Pulos Design Assocs., 1972—80, Fed. Prison Industries, 1974, Xerox Corp., 1975, Am. Soc. Aging, 1995, Ford Motor Design Ctr., 1992, Arthritis Found., 1993—96, Age Wave, Inc., 1993—96, GE Appliances, 1994, ProMatura Group, 1994—98, universal kitchen product R.I. Sch. Design, 1996—98, Boeing Co., 2004; chmn. accreditation coun. Design Found., 1982—84; designer, project dir. Transgenerational House, 2000—03; exec. dir. Transgenerational Design Matters, 2004—; lectr. in field. Author: Trangenerational Design: Products for an Aging Population, 1994; co-author: Guidelines and Strategies for Designing Transgenerational Products, 1988; co-designer GM Futurama Exhbn., N.Y. World's Fair, 1964—65; contbr. articles to profl. jours. Design mem. Everson Mus. Art, 1977—85; chmn. planning commn. Town of Cazenovia, 1988—93; mem. exhbns. com. Syracuse Cultural Resources Coun., 1992—93; coord. Tylenol/Arthritis Found. Student Design Awards Program, 1993—95; mem. senate Syracuse U., 1973—80, mem. adv. bd. SEARS Project, 1989—91, chmn. chancellor's citation, 1988—92. With SeaBees USN, 1951—55. Recipient Gold Indsl. Design Excellence award, Indsl. Designers Soc. Am. and Bus. Week Mag., 1994. Fellow: Indsl. Designers Soc. Am. (nat. bd. dirs. 1977—81, chmn. Ctrl. N.Y. chpt. 1977—81, v.p. Mid-East region 1978—81, chmn. NASAD liaison com. 1984—88, archives com. 1988—92, U.S. rep., del. Internat. Congress Socs. Indsl. Design 1989, chmn. universal design com. 1991—94, Edn. award 2001); mem.: Author's Guild, Am. Soc. Aging (contbr. articles to jour.), Nat. Ctr. Barrier Free Environment (adv. task force 1981), Human Factors Soc. (life), Nat. Assn. Schs. Art and Design (accreditation evaluator 1985—95), The Design Found. (chmn. accreditation coun. 1982). Achievements include patents for 4-way refrigerator handle. Home: 2007 Quail Run Dr NE Albuquerque NM 87122 Business E-Mail: jjp@transgenerational.org.

PIRKLE, EARL CHARNELL, retired geologist; b. nr. Buckhead, Ga., Jan. 8, 1922; s. Early Charnell and Eva Lee (Collins) P.; m. Valda Nell Armistead, July 9, 1942; children: Betty Jean, William A., Fredric L. AB, Emory U., 1943; MS, 1947; postgrad., U. Tenn., 1947-50; PhD, U. Cin., 1956. Certified profl. geologist. Prodn. coordinator, research crystallographer Pan-Electronics Labs., Inc., Atlanta, 1942-45; instr. geology U. Tenn., 1947-50; mem. faculty dept. phys. scis. and geology U. Fla., Gainesville, 1950-93, prof. emeritus, 1993—, prof., 1963—, chmn. dept. phys. scis., 1972-79; dir. Phys. Scis., 1979-82. Cons. in field; vis. prof. geology Emory U., summers 1959-65; rsch. cons. Fla. Dept. Nat. Resources Bur. Geology, 1950-70. Author: Natural Regions of the United States, 1977, 4th edit., 1985; Editor: Physical Science- Our Environment, 1968, Our Physical Environment, 1980; Contbr. articles to profl. jours. Served with AUS, 1945-46. Fellow Geol. Soc. Am., Soc. Econ. Geologists; mem. Am. Assn. Petroleum Geologists, Am. Soc. Mining, Metall. and Petroleum Engrs., Fla. Acad. Scis., Southeastern Geol. Soc., Phi Beta Kappa, Sigma Gamma Epsilon, Gamma Theta Epsilon, Sigma Chi. Democrat. Methodist.

PIRKLE, GEORGE EMORY, photographer, instructional media producer; b. Sept. 3, 1947; s. George Washington and Glanna Adeline (Palmer) P.; m. Karen Leigh Horn, Oct. 20, 1973; 1 child, Charity Caroline. Student, North Ga. Coll., 1965-66; BA in Journalism, U. Ga., 1969, MA, 1971. Radio announcer, sportscaster various radio stations, North Ga. area, 1968-70; TV prodr., dir. Instructional Resources Ctr., Athens, Ga., 1969-70; info. officer Southeastern Signal Sch., U.S. Army, 1971; prodr., dir. DA MoPic Svc. Continental Army Command Network and Signal Corps TV Divsn., 1972-73; pub. info. officer Ga. Dept. Revenue, Atlanta, 1973-78; coord. TV prodn. svcs. So. Co. Svcs., Inc., Birmingham, Ala., 1978-88; exec. v.p. Mgmt. and Human Devel. Assocs., Inc., Birmingham, Ala., 1984-86; prodr. Prodn. Works, Birmingham, Ala., 1984-88. Actor for various radio and TV commercials, corp. TV programs, radio dramas, stage plays, 1968—; owner Talking Rock Prodns., Cumming, Ga., 1989—; instr. Cliff Osmond Acting Program, 1989-92. Editor monthly newsletter Ga. Revenews, 1973-78; editor, dir. Bankers TV Network, 1990-92; writer, prodr., dir., exec. prodr. more than 500 corp. and pub. svc. TV and film programs; exec. prodr. videotape for Birmingham Film Coun., 1985; prodr., dir. Highway in Crisis, 1986; writer, prodr., dir. campaign film Birmingham Area United Way, 1981, 86, 87; writer, prodr., narrator, 1987 campaign film; anchor This Week in Banking, 1990-92. Master of ceremonies, gov.'s vet. awards presentation World Peace Luncheon, 1981, 82, 84, Birmingham; bd. directors Birmingham Internat. Ednl. Film Festival, 1987—91; dir., campaign film United Way, Pensacola, 1989; chmn. Sadie award com.; dir. student video competition; comml. acting instr. elan/Casablancas Modeling/Career Ctr., 1988—92; mem. tech. steering com. Forsyth Bd. Edn., 1995; bd. dirs. United Way of Forsyth County, 1995—2004; vol. Am. Cancer Soc. Relay for Life, 1996—2002; permanent mem. allocations com. United Way Forsyth County, 2000—04, v.p. allocations, 2003; chair Forsyth County Bd. Ethics, 2002—; mem. Comms. com. Birmingham Area couns. Boy Scouts Am., 1983—85, City Parks Recreation Bd., 1996—; mem. adv. bd. Sawnee Mtn. Preserve. 1st lt. US Army, 1971—73. Recipient So. Superlative Outstanding employee award, So. Co. Svcs., 1986, Battles award 1988, various others. Mem.: So. Electric Sys. Visual Comms. Subcom. (founding), Internat. TV Assn. (charter pres. Birmingham chapter 1984—85, pres. pro tem 1984, editor newsletter Freeze Frame), Hist. Soc. Forsyth County (pres. 1996), Ga. Hist. Soc., Rotary Club (Paul Harris fellow 2001), Cumming/Forsyth C. of C. (Bus. Mem. of the Yr. 2002). Avocations: photography, astronomy, genealogy, history, archaeology. Home Phone: 770-887-8849. E-mail: trvideo@bellsouth.net.

PIRODSKY, DONALD MAX, psychiatrist, educator; b. Freeport, NY, Feb. 2, 1945; s. Max and Doris Geilhard (Biedermann) P.; m. Gail Giufre Pallotta, Jan. 4, 1997; children: Laura Anne, Jason Donald. BA, Hofstra U., Hempstead, NY, 1966; MD, SUNY, Syracuse, 1970. Diplomate Am. Bd. Psychiatry and Neurology, Nat. Bd. Med. Examiners. Intern Northwestern U. Med. Ctr., Chgo., 1970-71; resident in psychiatry Strong Meml. Hosp., Rochester, NY, 1973-74, U. Ariz. Med. Ctr., Tucson, 1974-76; instr. psychiatry SUNY Health Sci. Ctr., Syracuse, 1976-78, attending psychiatrist, 1976-91, asst. prof. psychiatry, 1978-85, mem. exec. com. of med. coll. assembly, 1979-82, clin. assoc. prof., 1985—2006, adj. attending psychiatrist, 1991—2006; pvt. practice Syracuse and Fayetteville, NY, 1976—2006, Canastota, NY, 2006—; staff psychiatrist, dir. consultation/liaison svc. Syracuse VA Med. Ctr., 1976-87, chmn. pharmacy rev. and therapeutic agts. com., 1980-86. Psychiat. cons. Ariz. Sch. Deaf and Blind, Tucson, 1975-76, Syracuse Devel. Ctr., 1977-2006, Rochester Sch. Deaf, 1978-81; ex-officio mem. Family Counseling Agy., Tucson, 1975-76; adj. attending psychiatrist SUNY Health Sci. Ctr., Syracuse, 1991-2006. Author: Primer of Clinical Psychopharmacology: A Practical Guide, 1981, (with Jerry S. Cohn) Clinical Primer of Psychopharmacology: A Practical Guide, 2d edit., 1992; contbr. articles to profl. jours., chpts. to med. books. Lt. comdr. USPHS, 1971-73. Fellow Am. Psychiat. Assn. (Disting., mem. cen. NY dist. br.); mem. Am. Psychosomatic Soc., Am. Assn. Mental Retardation, Med. Soc. State of NY, NY State Psychiat. Assn., Onondaga County Med. Soc. Episcopalian. Avocations: sports, collecting baseball cards and other sports memorabilia. Office Phone: 315-247-9681.

PIROK, EDWARD WARREN, lawyer, consultant; b. Chgo., June 2, 1947; s. Edward Warren and Elinor Jean Pirok; m. Christine Merk, Jan. 23, 1972; children: Edward, Christopher, Jennifer, Elizabeth. BS, Ill. Inst. Tech., 1970; JD, Loyola U., 1973. Bar: N.Y. 1988, Ill. 1973, U.S. Supreme Ct., U.S. Ct. Appeals (2d and 7th cirs.) U.S. Dist. Ct. (so. and ea. dists.) N.Y., U.S. Dist. Ct. (no. dist.) Ill. Trial atty. Burlington No., Inc., Chgo., 1975-77; asst. gen. counsel Regional Transp. Authority, Chgo., 1977-82; gen. counsel Metra, The N.E. Ill. R.R. Corp., Chgo., 1982-87; trial atty. Metro-North Commuter R.R., NYC, 1987-89; of counsel Peltz & Walker, NYC, 1990-93; ptnr. Frank & Pirok, Ltd., Chgo., 1999—. 1st lt. Ill. Army N.G. Mem. ATLA, Ill. Trial Lawyers Assn. Roman Catholic. Avocations: golf, tennis. Office: Frank & Pirok Ltd 734 N Wells St Chicago IL 60610 Home: 299 Mallard Point Lake Barrington IL 60010-1783 Office Phone: 312-654-9020. E-mail: epirok@frank-pirok.com.

PIROZZI, MILDRED JEAN, retired nursing administrator; b. Syracuse, NY, Jan. 22, 1943; d. Alfred George and Mildred Erma (Tripp) Farmer; m. Robert T. Pirozzi, Jan. 25, 1969; children: Matthew Robert, Michael Thomas. Diploma, Gen. Hosp. Syracuse, 1963; BS, SUNY, Utica, 1983. RN, N.Y. Med., surg. staff nurse Gen. Hosp. Syracuse, 1963-64; staff nurse ICU U. Rochester Strong Meml. Hosp., N.Y., 1964-65; nurse ICU Upstate Med. Ctr. U. Hosp., Syracuse, 1965-69, rschr. anesthesia Upstate Med. Ctr., 1969-70; nurse recovery room Highland Hosp., Rochester, 1970-71; nurse orthopedic unit Auburn (N.Y.) Meml. Hosp., 1978-80; home dialysis tng. unit nurse SUNY Health Sci. Ctr., Syracuse, 1980-88; with home dialysis tng. unit U. Dialysis Ctr., Syracuse, 1988-91; home program coord. St. Joseph's Hops. Health Ctr., 1991—96, hemodialysis, 1996—2000, charge nurse hemodialysis, 2000—01, coord. self care/home hemo, 2001—04, charge nurse hemo, 2004—05; ret., 2005. Chmn. com. profl. edn. Ctrl. N.Y. chpt. Nat. Kidney Found., Syracuse, 1986-91. Co-author: Hemodialysis Training Manual for Patients and Partners, 1981, CAPD Training Manual for Patients, 1982. Mem. folk ensemble St. Joseph's Ch., 1984—. Recipient Above and Beyond award Nat. Kidney Found., 1991. Mem. Am. Nephrology Nurses Assn. (pub. rels. com. 1988-91, sec., treas., pres. ctrl. N.Y. chpt. 1984-93, 96-98, N.E. regional sec. 1987-89, N.E. regional officer 2003-05, legis. rep. 1991-95). Roman Catholic. Avocations: sewing, crafts, gardening, sports, music. Home: 4699 Howlett Hill Rd Marcellus NY 13108-9762 E-mail: rpirozzi@twcny.rr.com.

PIRRO, ALFRED ANTHONY, JR., emergency physician; b. Stamford, Conn., May 17, 1961; s. Alfred Anthony, Sr. and Frances (Battaglia) Pirro. BA in Natural Scis., Johns Hopkins U., Balt., 1983; MD, U. Conn., Storrs, 1987. Diplomate Am. Bd. Anesthesiology, Am. Bd. Critical Care Medicine. Resident in surgery Hosp. of St. Raphael, New Haven, 1987-90; fellow in neurosurgery Hartford Hosp., Conn., 1991-92, resident in anesthesiology, 1992-95, critical care fellow, 1995-97, staff anesthesiologist, 1997-99; emergency medicine physician Windham Hosp., Willamantic, Conn., 1991—; instr. anesthesiology John Dempsey Hosp.-U. Conn. Sch. Medicine, Hartford, 1997-99; owner Hosp. Physician Specialists, Elkton, Md.; med. dir. hospitalist program Union Hosp. Cecil County, Elkton, 2004—, chmn. dept. hospitalist medicine, 2007—. Chmn. critical care, chmn. med. records com. Union Hosp. Cecil County, 2002—, mem. med. exec. com., 2007—. Advisor Lally for Congress campaign, Mineola, NY, 1994. Scholar, Pitney Bowes, 1979; Beneficial-Hodson scholar, Johns Hopkins U., 1979. Mem.: AMA, Soc. Critical Care Medicine, Md. State Med. Soc. Republican. Office Phone: 443-350-4544. Personal E-mail: aapjrmd@aol.com.

PIRRO, JEANINE FERRIS, prosecutor; b. Elmira, NY, June 2, 1951; d. Leo and Esther Ferris; m. Albert J. Pirro, Aug. 23, 1975; children: Christi, Alexander. BA, U. Buffalo, 1972; JD, Albany Law Sch., 1975. Bar: N.Y. 1975. Legis. aide N.Y. State Senate, Albany, 1973-75; asst. dist. atty. Westchester County Dist. Atty. Office, White Plains, N.Y., 1975-78, chief Victim Witness Unit, 1978-79, chief domestic violence/child abuse bur., 1978-90, dist. atty., 1994—; county judge Westchester County, White Plains, 1990-93. Author, To Punish and Protect, 2003, 2d edit. 2004; contbr. articles to profl. jours. Chair Gov. Pataki's N.Y. State Commn. on Domestic Violence Fatalities Rev. Bd., 1996; bd. dirs. My Sister's Place, 1990—; bd. vis. Pace U. Sch. Law, 1994— Mem. N.Y. State Dist. Attys. Assn. (pres. 1999-2000), Nat. Mus. Women's History (bd. adv.). Republican. Roman Catholic. Office: Westchester County Dist Atty County Courthouse 111 Dr ML King Jr Blvd White Plains NY 10601-2507 *

PIRRUNG, MICHAEL CRAIG, chemistry professor, consultant; b. Cin., July 31, 1955; s. Joey Matthew and Grace (Fielman) P. BA, U. Tex., 1975; PhD, U. Calif., Berkeley, 1980. NSF postdoctoral fellow Columbia U., NYC, 1980-81; asst. prof. Stanford (Calif.) U., 1981-89; sr. scientist Affymax Rsch. Inst., Palo Alto, Calif., 1989; assoc. prof. Duke U., Durham, N.C., 1989-94, prof., 1994—. Dir. Duke U. program in biol. chemistry, 1994—, dir. biotechnology for bus., 1993—; cons. Am. Cyanamid, 1992—, Wyeth-Ayerst, 1995—, Chroma Xome 1995—; sci. advisor Affymax Rsch. Inst., 1991—. Recipient Newcomb Cleveland prize AAAS, 1991, Intellectual Property Owners Disting. Inventor award, 1993, Outstanding Young Tex. Ex., U. Tex. Ex-Students Assn., 1995. Fellow AAAS, John Simon Guggenheim Mem. Found.; mem. Am. Chem. Soc., Am. Soc. Plant Phys. Achievements include invention of DNA chips; research on mechanism of ethylene biosynthesis. Office: Duke U Dept Chemistry PM Gross Lab PO Box 90346 Durham NC 27708-0346

PIRSCH, CAROL MCBRIDE, retired county official, state senator, community relations manager; b. Omaha, Dec. 27, 1936; d. Lyle Erwin and Hilfrie Louise (Lebeck) McBride; m. Allen I. Pirsch, Mar. 28, 1954 (dec.); children: Pennie Elizabeth, Pamela Elaine, Patrice Eileen, Phyllis Erika, Peter Allen, Perry Andrew. Student, U. Miami, Oxford, Ohio, U. Nebr., Omaha. Former mem. data processing staff Omaha (Nebr.) Pub. Schs.; former mem. wage practices dept. Western Electric Co., Omaha; former legal sec. Omaha; former office mgr. Pirsch Food Brokerage Co., Inc., Omaha; former employment supr., mgr. pub. policy U.S. West Comm., Omaha; mem. Nebr. Senate, 1979-97; commr. Douglas County, 1997—2005, chair, 1999, 2004, vice chair, 2001, 2003. Founder, 1st pres., bd. dirs. Nebr. Coalition for Victims of Crime (Lifetime award 2002); bd. dirs. Centris Fed. Credit Union, 1st v.p., 2003—. Mem. Omaha Douglas County Bldg. Commn., 1997—2003, sec., 2000—03; cmty. cons. Omaha Jr. League, 2002—. Recipient Golden Elephant award, Kuhle award, 1986, Nebr. Coalition for Victims of Crime, Outstanding Legis. Efforts award YWCA, 1989, Breaking the Rule of Thumb award Nebr. Domestic Violence Sexual Assault Coalition, 1989, Cert. of Appreciation award U.S. Dept. Justice, 1988, Partnership award N.E. Credit Union League, 1995, Wings award LWV Greater Omaha, 1995, N.E. VFW Spl. Recognition award for Exceptional Svc., 1995, Victim Rights Week Recognition award, 1995, Victim Adv. Lifetime Achievement award, 2002; Crime Victims Adv. award Nebr. Atty. Gen., 1995. Mem. VASA, Nat. Orgn. Victim Assistance (Outstanding Legis. Leadership award 1981), Freedom Found., Douglas County Hist. Soc., Nebr. Taxpayers Assn., Keystone Citizen Patrol (Comm. Network of Citizen Patrols award, 1995), Audubon Soc., N.W. Cmty. Club, Keystone Task Force (Keystoner of the month, 1987, Queen Keystone, 2002), Omaha Bus. and Profl. Rep. Women.

PISANI, ANTHONY MICHAEL, architect; b. Cambridge, Mass., May 18, 1943; s. Anthony Joseph and Josephine Ann (Tortorella) P.; m. Emilia D'Agostino, Aug. 27, 1967; children: Emiliabianca, Giancarlo Diploma, Mus. Sch., 1966; BFA, Tufts U., 1966; MArch., Harvard U., 1971. Registered architect, Mass., Calif., Maine, Mich., N.Y., N.H., Tex., Vt. Project architect Kallmann & McKinell, Architects, Boston, 1971-73, Charles G. Hilgenhurst & Assocs., Boston, 1973-74, Desmond & Lord, Architects, Boston, 1974-77; pres. Anthony M. Pisani & Assocs., Architects, Boston, 1978—. Instr. design Boston Archtl. Center, 1971-74; vice-chmn. Boston Landmarks Commn., 1987-95. Major works in Eastern U.S., Ireland, Can., Mex., P.R., Japan; contbr. articles to profl. jours. Mem. Boston Zoning Bd. Appeal, 1998—. Mem. AIA, Boston Soc. Architects, Constrn. Specifications Inst., Urban Land Inst., Nat. Council Archtl. Registration Bds., Soc. Archtl. Historians Home: 95 Robinwood Ave Boston MA 02130-2110 Office: 374 Congress St Boston MA 02210-1807 Home Phone: 617-522-6692; Office Phone: 617-423-1022. E-mail: apisani@pisani.com.

PISANO, A. ROBERT, former actors guild executive, former film company executive; b. San Jose, Calif., Mar. 3, 1943; s. Anthony Edward and Carmen Jeanne (Morisoli) P.; m. Carolyn Joan Pollock, May 5, 1979; children: Catherine J., Anthony Daniel, Elizabeth A., Alexandra N. BA in Pub. Administrn., San Jose State U., 1965; JD, U. Calif.-Berkeley, 1968. Bar: Calif. Assoc. O'Melveny & Myers, LA, 1968-75, ptnr., 1976-85, 92-93; exec. v.p. office of chmn., gen. counsel Paramount Pictures, LA, 1985-91; exec. v.p. Metro-Goldwyn-Mayer Inc., Santa Monica, Calif., 1993-96; vice chmn. Metro-Goldwyn-Mayer, Inc., 1997-99; nat. exec. dir., CEO SAG, LA, 2001—05; pres., COO Motion Picture Assn. Am., 2005—. Bd. dirs. Resources Global Profls., 2002—, Fin. Planning Assn. Group of Funds, 2002—; cons. in field. Office: Motion Picture Assn Am 15503 Ventura Blvd Encino CA 91436

PISCHINGER, FRANZ FELIX, engineer, researcher, engineering educator; b. Waidhofen, Austria, July 18, 1930; s. Franz and Karoline (Bentz) P.; m. Elfriede Pischinger-Goessler, 1957 (2001); children: Gerhard, Martin, Stefan, Thomas, Alice; m. Elisabeth Pischinger-Froehlich, 2003. Diploma in Engring., Tech. U., Graz, Austria, 1952, DR in Internal Combustion Engines, 1954, Habilitation degree, 1958, Dr (hon.), 1994. Asst. Tech. U., Graz, 1953-58; head rsch. dept. Inst. Internal Combustion Engines (AVL), Graz, 1958-62; leading positions in rsch., devel. Kloeckner-Humboldt-Deutz AG, Cologne, Germany, 1962-70; dir. Inst. Applied Thermodynamics RWTH, Aachen, Germany, 1970-97; CEO FEV Motorentechnik, Aachen, Germany, 1978—2003, chmn. bd. Germany, 2003—; v.p. Deutsche Forschungsgemeinschaft, Bonn-Bad Godesberg, Germany, 1984—90; hon. prof. Dalian U., China, 2005. Exec. bd. mem. Coun. Tech. Scis. Union German Acad. Scis. Humanities. Contbr. articles to profl. jours. Decorated Ehrenring Sub asupiciis praesidentis republicae (Austria), 1954, Bundesverdienstkreuz 1st class (Germany), 1978; recipient Herbert Akroyd Stuard award Inst. Mech. Engrs., 1962, Carl-Engler-Medaille DGMK, Deutsche Wissenschaftliche Gesellschaft Erdöl, Erdgas Kohle, Hamburg, 1990, Austrian cross of Honor for Sci. and Art First Class, 1998, Hon. Prof., Dalian U. Tech., China, 2005. Fellow Soc.

Automotive Engrs. U.S.A.; mem. ASME Internat. (Soichiro Honda medal 2000), NAE (USA) (fgn. assoc.), Verein Deutscher Ingenieure (medal of honor 1993, decoration of honor 1997), Deutsche Gesellschaft Mineralöl-wissenschaft U. Kohlechemie, Rheinisch-Westfälische Akademie Wissenschaften, Aachen-Frankenburg Club, Rotary. Office: FEV Motorentechnik Neuenhofstrasse 181 52078 Aachen Germany

PISCHKE, FRANK JOHN, retired otolaryngologist; b. Chgo., July 7, 1936; s. Frank Joseph Pischke and Edith Jeanette Godar; m. Elsa Mendez, Aug. 21, 1965; children: Andrew, Rebecca. BS in Biology, Rockhurst U., Kansas City, Mo., 1958; MD, Kans. U., Lawrence, 1962. Diplomate Am. Bd. Otolaryngology. Asst. prof. Kans. U. Med. Ctr., Kansas City, 1969—84, Mercer Med. Sch., Macon, Ga., 1985—2001; ret., 2001. Sr. surgeon USPHS, 1962—65. Recipient Eagle Scout, Boys Scout Am., 1953. Fellow: Am. Coll. Surgeons, Am. Acad. Otolaryn.; mem.: AMA, Am. Acad. Otolaryn. Allergy. Avocations: singing, bicycling, rowing, skiing, reading. Home: PO Box 3093 Holiday Island AR 72631

PISCHKE, VAIL W., lawyer, judge; AB, LLB, JD, U. Notre Dame. Pres., chmn. bd., gen. counsel Met. Bank, Washington; developer, owner Nationally franchised hotels and motels, Shopping Ctr.; judge State of Va.; pvt. practice Falls Church, Va. Commr. chancery Cir. County Fairfax County, vol. judge pro tem; mem. Alcohol Safety Action Project Adv. Com. Va.; presenter, moderator state-wide Va. Jud. Seminars; legal advisor various ch. denominations in No. Va. and Washington; counsel, legal advisor Prison Fellowship; gen. counsel Christian Fellowship Ch. Past pres., v.p., chmn. bd. elders, gen. counsel, chmn. bd. trustees Our Savior Luth. Ch., Arlington, Va.; past pres., v.p., chmn. bd. elders, gen. counsel, trustee St. Paul's Luth. Ch., Falls Church; pres. Luth. Ch., Arlington, Va.; past pres. Fairfax chpt. Am. Cancer Soc., Va. Soc. Crippled Children and Adults; past dir. Salvation Army; past pres. Longfellow H.S. PTA, Fairfax County, Va.; past pres., v.p. McLean Sr. H.S. PTA, Fairfax County; past bd. dirs. Juvenile Detention Commn. No. Va., No. Va. Family Bd., No. Va. YMCA; bd. dirs. Washington United Givers Fund. Recipient Cert. Outstanding Svc., Va. Supreme Ct. Appeals. Mem. Assn. Dist. Ct. Judges in Va. (hon. life), Falls Church Bar Assn. (past pres., v.p., sec.), No. Va. Trial Lawyers Assn. (past parliamentarian, bd. dirs.), Va. Judges Assn. (life), Falls Church Rotary (past pres., v.p.), Nat. PTA (life). Home: 2043 Reynolds St Falls Church VA 22043-1634

PISCHL, ADOLPH JOHN, school administrator; b. East Orange, NJ, Mar. 28, 1920; s. Adolph and Anna (Ellerman) P.; m. Tennessee Wild, Sept. 9, 1947; 1 child, Sallyann. Certificate, Drake Coll., 1940. With Juilliard Sch. Music, NYC, 1962-86, asst. concert mgr., 1962-66; dir. pub. relations Juilliard Sch. Music, NYC, 1966-68; concert mgr. Juilliard Sch. Music, NYC, 1966-86; adminstr. Sch. Strings, NYC, 1987-88. With The Dance Mart, NYC, 1950-2005, pub. dir. Am. Dance Festival, Conn. Coll., 1964-68; mgr. Betty Jones Dances I Dance, 1966-68, Ruth Currier Dance Co., 1966-68, Anna Sokolow Dance Co., 1966-68, Julliard Sch. Bookstore, 1971-86. Founder, editor: Dance Perspectives, 1958-64, Dance Data, 1977; editor: Juilliard News Bull. and Rev. Ann, 1964-85; pub.: Dance Horizons, 1965-86 (Dance mag. award 1999); Contbr. articles to dance mags. Bd. dirs. Dance Notation Bur.; sec. bd. dirs. Walter W. Naumburg Found., Inc. With AUS, 1940-46. Home: 603 Valley View Pompton Plains NJ 07444 Personal E-mail: ajpischl@aeitv.net.

PISCITELLI, EMILE JAMES, philosopher, educator; s. Emil James and Maria Piscitelli; children: Niccola, Domenic. BA in Philosophy, St. Charles Sem., Phila., 1962; M in Theology, Harvard U., Cambridge, Mass., 1972; PhD, Georgetown U., Washington, 1976. Asst. prof. philos. theology Trinity Coll., Washington, 1967—72; prof. philosophy No. Va. CC, Annandale, 1973—. Vis. prof. philosophy Georgetown U., Washington, 1987. Author: In Praise of Love: A Conversation with Plato's Symposium, 2006; actor: (films) Xscape. Scholar, Diocese of Allentown, Pa., 1962—68. Democrat. Home: 4168 Elizabeth Ln Annandale VA 22003 Office Phone: 703-323-3358. Personal E-mail: thelogos@aol.com.

PISCITELLI, FELICIA ANN, librarian, musician, musicologist; b. Tinker Air Force Base, Oklahoma City, Okla., Sept. 21, 1956; d. Domenic Ralph and Frankie Lee Piscitelli. BA in Fine Arts, U. N.Mex, 1979, MusM, 1983; MLS, U. Ariz., 1990. Piano tchr., Albuquerque, 1982—84; libr. tech. asst. U. N.Mex, Albuquerque, 1984—89; original cataloger, assoc. prof. Tex. A&M U., College Station, 1991—, asst. dir. cataloging, 2004—. Contbr. articles to profl. jours., chapters to books (Walter Gerboth award music bibliography, 1994);, author program notes musical concerts. Part-time organist St. Thomas Aquinas Cath. Ch., College Station, 1993—2005. Grantee Hymnody Am. Protestantism Project, Inst. Study Am. Evangelicalism, 1998. Mem.: Am. Guild Organists, Music Libr. Assn., Brazos Valley Chorale, Sigma Alpha Iota (life). Roman Catholic. Avocations: music, travel, languages. Office: Tex A&M U Sterling C Evans Libr Cataloging College Station TX 77843-5000 Home Phone: 979-693-8688; Office Phone: 979-845-5453. Office Fax: 979-862-1166. Business E-Mail: f-piscitelli@tamu.edu.

PISHCHALNIKOV, YURI A., researcher; b. Kemerovo, Russia, Apr. 26, 1967; m. Irina V. Pishchalnikova. PhD, Moscow State U., 1997. Jr. rschr. Dept. of Acoustics, Physics Faculty, Moscow State U., 1997—98, sr. rschr., 1998—2003; rsch. fellow Dept. of Anatomy and Cell Biology, Ind. U., 2003—04, rsch. assoc., 2004—. Article reviewer Acoustical Soc. of Am., Jour. Sound and Vibration Jour., Experiments in Fluids. Contbr. articles to profl. jours. Recipient Best Abstract prize, 2006; Joint stipend, Acoustical Soc. Am. and Russian Acoustical Soc., 1995, George Soros Doctoral Fellowship award, Internat. Soros Sci. Edn. Program, 1995, 1996, fellowship, Ind. U., Sch. of Medicine, Indpls., 2000—01, 2003—04, Vis. Support Program award, US Office of Naval Rsch. Internat. Field Office, London, 2004, Rsch. grant, NIH, 2004—. Mem.: Am. Urol. Assn., Internat. Soc. Therapeutic Ultrasound, Acoustical Soc. Am. (mem. biomedical ultrasound tech. com. 2006—). Office: Ind U Dept Anatomy 635 Barnhill Dr MS-5055 Indianapolis IN 46202 Office Phone: 317-274-0548. Office Fax: 317-278-2040. E-mail: yura@anatomy.iupui.edu.

PISTER, KARL STARK, engineering educator; b. Stockton, Calif., June 27, 1925; s. Edwin LeRoy and Mary Kimball (Smith) P.; m. Rita Olsen, Nov. 18, 1950; children: Francis, Therese, Anita, Jacinta, Claire, Kristofer. BS with honors, U. Calif., Berkeley, 1945, MS, 1948; PhD, U. Ill., 1952; D of Pub. Policy (hon.), U. Fla., 2004; LHD (hon.), U. Colo., 2005. Instr. theoretical and applied mechanics U. Ill., 1949-52; faculty U. Calif., Berkeley, 1952-62, prof. engring. scis., 1962-96, Roy W. Carlson prof. engring., 1985-90, dean Coll. Engring., 1980-90, Roy W. Carlson prof. emeritus, chancellor Santa Cruz, 1991-96, pres., chancellor emeritus, 1996—, sr. assoc. to pres. Oakland, 1996-99, v.p. ednl. outreach, 1999-2000. Richard Merton guest prof. U. Stuttgart, Germany, 1978; cons. to govt. and industry; bd. dirs. Monterey Bay Aquarium Rsch. Inst.; trustee Am. U. Armenia, Grad. Theol. Union, Berkeley; chmn. bd. Calif. Coun. Sci. and Tech.; bd. dirs. Ctr. Future Tchg. and Learning. Contbr. articles to profl. jours.; mem. editl. bd. Jour. Optimization Theory and Applications, 1982, Ency. Phys. Sci. and Tech. With USNR, WWII. Fulbright scholar, Ireland, 1965, West Germany, 1973; recipient Wason Rsch. medal Am. Concrete Inst., 1960, Vincent Bendix Minorities in Engring. award Am. Soc. for Engring. Edn., 1988, Lamme medal, 1993, Alumni Honor award U. Ill. Coll. Engring., 1982, Disting. Engring. Alumnus award U. Calif. Berkeley Coll. Engring., 1992, Berkeley medal, 1996, U. Calif. Presdl. medal, 2000, World Tech. Network award for policy, World Tech. Coun., London, 2002 Alumnus of Yr. award Calif. Alumni Assn., Berkeley, 2006, Clark Kerr award U. Calif. Berkeley, 2007. Fellow: AAAS, ASME (Applied Mechanics award 1999, Internat. Pres.'s award 2000), Am. Acad. Arts and Scis., Am. Acad. Mechanics, Calif. Acad. Sci. (hon.); mem.: ASCE, NAE. Office: U Calif Dept Civil & Environ Engr Berkeley CA 94720 Office Phone: 510-642-3066. Business E-Mail: pister@ce.berkeley.edu.

PISTOLE, JOHN S., federal agency administrator; b. 1956; married; 2 children. Grad., Ind. U. Law Sch., 1981. Pvt. practice, Anderson, Ind., 1981—83; spl. agent Mpls. divsn. FBI, 1983—85, spl. agent NY divsn., 1985—90, supr. organized crime sect. Wash., 1990—94, field supr. white collar crime and civil rights squad, undercover coord. Indpls., 1994—99, asst. spl. agent in charge Boston, 1999—2001, inspector Wash., 2001—02, dep. asst. dir. counterterrorism divsn., 2002—03, asst. dir. counterterrorism divsn., 2003, exec. asst. dir., counterterrorism and counterintelligence, 2003—04, dep. dir., 2004—. Instr. Internat. Law Enforcement Acad., Budapest, Hungary, 1995—96; FBI rep. state dept. delegation, Sofia, Bulgaria; dir. Blue Team info. soc. working group, 2001. Office: FBI J Edgar Hoover Bldg 935 Pennsylvania Ave NW Washington DC 20535-0001

PISTOLE, THOMAS GORDON, microbiology professor, researcher, department chairman; b. Detroit, Sept. 17, 1942; s. Leotis Merton Pistole and Lillian Nell (Bosley) Besser; m. Donna Dulcie Straw, Sept. 11, 1965; children: James Alexander, Jennifer Katharine. PhB, Wayne State U., 1964, MS, 1966; PhD, U. Utah, 1969. Postdoctoral fellow U.S. Army, Frederick, Md., 1969-70; research assoc. U. Minn., Mpls., 1970-71; asst. prof. U. NH, Durham, 1971-77, assoc. prof., 1977-83, prof., 1983—, chmn., 1983-92, dist. prof., 2006, co-dir. discovery program undergrad. edn., 2007—. Vis. scientist Weizmann Inst., Rehovot, Israel, 1979; vis. prof. U. Edinburgh, Scotland, 1986; faculty fellow Office of V.P. for Acad. Affairs U. N.H., 1996-99; mem. ad hoc study sect. U.S. Dept. Agr., 2002. Co-editor: Biomedical Application of the Horseshoe Crab, 1979; mem. editl bd.: Jour. Invertebrate Pathology, 1988—90. NRC fellow, 1969-70; NIH sr. internat. fellow, 1986; grantee NIH, 1975-77, 89-93, 96-2006, NSF, 1981-84. Mem.: Soc. for Leukocyte Biology, Am. Assn. Immunologists, Am. Soc. for Microbiology. Avocations: singing, collecting old sheet music, walking, cooking. Office: U NH Rudman Hall Dept Microbiology Durham NH 03824-2617 Home Phone: 603-868-5766; Office Phone: 603-862-0111. Business E-Mail: thomas.pistole@unh.edu.

PISTORIUS, GEORGE, language educator, educator; b. Prague, Czechoslovakia, Mar. 19, 1922; came to U.S., 1958, naturalized, 1964; s. Theodor and Blazena (Jiranek) P.; m. Marie Skokan, June 30, 1945; 1 dau., Erika. Student, Charles U., Prague, 1945-48; postgrad., Université de Paris, 1948-50; certificats d'etudes superieures, Université de Strasbourg, France, 1950, 51; PhD, U. Pa., 1963. Asst. dept. comparative lit. Charles U., 1946-48; instr. Lafayette Coll., Easton, Pa., 1958-61, asst. prof. French, 1961-63; asso. prof. Williams Coll., 1963-68, prof. Romanic langs., 1968-92, chmn. dept., 1971-82, prof. emeritus, 1992—. Instr. French, Colby Coll. Summer Sch. Lang., 1959-65 Author: Bibliography of the works of F.X. Salda, 1948, Destin de la culture francaise dans une democratie populaire, 1957, L'Image de l'Allemagne dans le roman francais entre les deux guerres (1919-1939), 1964, Marcel Proust und Deutschland, Eine Bibliographie, 1981, 2d edit. 2002, André Gide und Deutschland: Eine internationale Bibliographie, 1990. Home: 54 Cluett Dr Williamstown MA 01267-2805

PISZEL, ANTHONY S. (BUDDY PISZEL), finance company executive; BA in Econs., Rutgers U., NJ; MBA in Acctg., Golden Gate U., San Francisco. Practice fellow Fin. Acctg. Stds. Bd., 1988—90; audit ptnr. Deloitte & Touche, 1990—93; CFO individual life ins. Prudential Fin. Inc., 1993—95, CFO inst. life ins., 1995—97, corp. v.p., 1997—98, sr. v.p., contr., 1998—2004; exec. v.p., CFO Health Net Inc., Woodland Hills, Calif., 2004—06, Fed. Home Loan Mortgage Corp., 2006—. Bd. dirs., chmn. audit com. RehabCare Group Inc. Mem.: AICPA, NJ State Soc. CPAs. Office: Fed Home Loan Mortgage Corp 8200 Jones Branch Dr Mc Lean VA 22102-3110 Office Phone: 703-903-2000. *

PITARO, THOMAS F., lawyer; b. Stockton, Mass., May 15, 1944; BS high honors, Calif. State U., LA, 1971; JD, UCLA, 1974. Bar: Nev. 1974. Pvt. practice, Las Vegas. Named one of Best Criminal Defense Attys., Las Vegas Review-Jour., 1999; recipient Justinian Award, Nev. Soc. of Italian-Am. Lawyers. Fellow: Am. Coll. Trial Lawyers; mem.: Nat. Assn. Criminal Defense Lawyers, Nev. Assn. Criminal Justice, State Bar Nev., Beta Gamma Sigma. Office: 330 S Third St, Ste 860 Las Vegas NV 89101 Office Phone: 702-382-9221. Office Fax: 702-382-9961. E-mail: notguilty@pitaro.net. *

PITCHER, GRIFFITH FONTAINE, lawyer; b. Balt., Nov. 1, 1937; s. William Henry and Virginia Griffith (Stein) P.; children; Virginia T. Pitcher Ballinger, L. Brooke Pitcher Fick, William T.B., Margaret W. Pitcher Saylors. BA, Johns Hopkins U., 1960; JD, U. Va., 1963. Bar: Ala. 1963, Fla. 1971, Ga. 1996. Assoc. Bradley, Arant, Rose & White, Birmingham, Ala., 1963-71; mem. Van den Berg, Gay & Burke, Orlando, Fla., 1971-76, Mahoney, Hadlow & Adams, Jacksonville, Fla., 1976-82; ptnr. Squire, Sanders & Dempsey, Miami, Fla., 1982-93; of counsel Mershon, Sawyer, Johnston, Dunwoody & Cole, Miami, Fla., 1994-95, Chamberlain, Hrdlicka, White, Williams & Martin, Atlanta, 1996—2002, Seyfarth Shaw LLP, Atlanta, 2002—. Contbr. articles to profl. jours. Vice chmn. Winter Park (Fla.) Planning & Zoning Bd., 1974-75. With Army N.G., 1961-64. Fellow: Am. Coll. Bond Counsel (founding fellow, past treas., past dir.); mem.: Ala. State Bar Assn., Ga. State Bar, Fla. Bar, Nat. Assn. Bond Lawyers, Order of Coif, Delta Phi. Republican. Personal E-mail: grifpitcher@charter.net.

PITCHUMONI, CAPECOMORIN SANKAR, gastroenterologist, educator; b. Madura, India, Jan. 20, 1938; came to U.S., 1967; s. Sankara and Jaya (Lekshmi) Iyer; m. Prema Iyer, Nov. 11, 1964; children: Sheila, Shoba, Suresh. Student, St. Xavier Coll., India, 1953-55; MB BS, Trivandrum Med. Coll., India, 1959, MD, 1965. Intern Med. Coll., Trivandurm, India, 1961-63; resident in gastroenterology Yale U., 1967-69; N.Y. Med. Coll., 1969-72; practice medicine specializing in gastroenterology NYC, 1972—; asst. prof. medicine Kottayam Med. Coll., India, 1967, N.Y. Med. Coll., 1972-75, assoc. prof., 1975-80, prof. clin. medicine, 1980-85, prof. medicine, 1985—, assoc. prof. preventive and social medicine, 1975-86, prof. community and preventive medicine, 1986—; chief sect. gastroenterology Our Lady of Mercy Med. Ctr., NYC, 1980—, assoc. dir. medicine, 1985—, program dir. internal medicine, 1987—, dir. medicine, 1992, chmn. emeritus dept. medicine, 2002—; chief divsn. gastroenterology St. Peters U. Hosp., New Brunswick, NJ, 2002—. Contbg. author med. textbooks; contbr. articles to profl. jours. Recipient Om Prakash award Indian Soc. Gastroenterology, 1976, Outstanding Scientist of Yr. award MV Spltys., Madras, 1994, Oration award Thangavelu Endowment, 1994. Master Am. Coll. Gastroenterology (gov. 1996-2000); fellow Royal Coll. Physicians and Surgeons Can., Am. Coll. Nutrition, Am. Gastroent. Assn.; mem. Assn. Physicians India, India Soc. Gastroenterology (life), Am. Inst. Nutrition, Gastrointestinal Endoscopy, Am. Soc. for Clin. Nutrition. Hindu. Home: 1 Nevius Pl Somerset NJ 08873 Office: St Peters U Hosp New Brunswick NJ Personal E-mail: drpitchumoni@gmail.com.

PITCOCK, JAMES KENT, otolaryngologist; b. Tachikawa AFB, Japan, Nov. 18, 1951; s. James Kenneth and Helen (Robertson) P.; m. Cynthia H. Zipperly. Student, U. Houston, 1974; MD, Baylor U., 1979. Diplomate Am. Bd. Otolaryngology. Resident in gen. surgery Baylor Coll. Medicine, Houston, 1979-81, resident in otolaryngology, head and neck surgery, 1981-84; clinician Kelsey-Seybold Clinic, P.A., Houston, 1984-85; lectr. head and neck surgery Inst. Laryngology and Otology, U. London, 1985-86; instr., fellow head and neck surgery U. Chgo., 1986-88; asst. prof. dept. otolaryngology, head and neck surgery, chief div. head and neck surgical oncology U. Calif.-Irvine Med. Ctr., Orange, 1988-92. Dir. head and neck oncology clin. and rsch. program Clin. Cancer Ctr. U. Calif., Irvine. Author: Oral and Maxillofacial Trauma, 1989, Musculocutaneous Flap Reconstruction of the Head and Neck, 1989, Surgery of the Skull Base, 1989. Fellow Am. Acad. Otolaryngology, Head and Neck Surgery; mem. Am. Rhinologic Soc. Office: Premier Med Grp 3701 Dauphin St Mobile AL 36608-1756 Home Phone: 251-343-9445; Office Phone: 251-341-3368. E-mail: jkpmobal@aol.com.

PITEGOFF, PETER ROBERT, dean, law educator; b. NYC, Mar. 6, 1953; s. Joseph and Libbie (Shapiro) P.; m. Ann Casady, Mar. 22, 1986; children: Maxwell Jacob, Elias Samuel. AB, Brown U., 1975; JD, NYU, 1981. Bar: Mass 1981, NY 1988; cert. tchr., RI. Tchr. Hope High Sch., Providence, 1974-75; community organizer Nat. Assn. for So. Poor, Petersburg, Va., 1975-76, Citizens Action League, Oakland, Calif., 1976-78; gen. counsel ICA Group, Boston, 1981-88; ptnr. Arrington & Pitegoff, Somerville, Mass., 1986-88; assoc. prof. U. Buffalo Law Sch., SUNY, 1988—94, prof., 1994—2005, vice dean academic affairs, 1998—2005; dean, prof. U. Maine Sch. Law, Portland, 2005—. Adj. asst. prof. law NYU, 1986-88; instr. Harvard Law Sch., 1985; cons. in field, 1978—; legal counsel cmty. devel. worker purchases of bus. corp. fin. dem. corp. structures child care policy and welfare policy. Contbr. to profl. publs. Root-Tilden scholarship NYU, 1978; grantee Pub. Interest Law Found., NYC, 1981. Democrat. Jewish. Avocations: athletics, travel, music. Office: U Maine Sch Law 246 Deering Ave Portland ME 04102 Office Phone: 207-780-4344. E-mail: pitegoff@usm.maine.edu. *

PITERNICK, ANNE BREARLEY, librarian, educator; b. Blackburn, Eng., Oct. 13, 1926; arrived in Can., 1956, naturalized, 1965; d. Walter and Ellen (Harris) Clayton; m. Neil Brearley, 1956 (div. 1971); m. George Piternick, May 6, 1971. BA, U. Manchester, Eng., 1948, F.L.A., 1983. Mem. library staff U. B.C., Vancouver, Can., 1956-66, head sci. div., 1960-61, head social scis. div., 1965-66, prof. Sch. Library, Archival and Info. Studies, 1966-91, prof. emerita, 1991—, assoc. dean Faculty of Arts, 1985-90. Pres. Can. Assn. Spl. Librs. Info. Svcs., 1969-70, Can. Libr. Assn., 1976-77; organizer Confs. on Can. Bibliography, 1974, 81; mem. Nat. Com. Bibliog. Svcs. Can., 1975-80, chmn. com. on bibliography and info. services social scis. and humanities, 1981-84; adv. bd. Nat. Libr. Can., 1978-84; adv. acad. panel Social Scis. and Humanities Rsch. Coun., 1981-84; mem. Nat. Adv. Com. Culture Stats., 1985-90; pres. adv. com. on campus enhancement U. BC, 2001-. Contbr. articles to profl. jours. Bd. dirs. Vancouver Friends of Chamber Music, 2001—. Recipient Queen's Silver Jubilee medal, 1977, award for Spl. Librarianship Can. Assn. Spl. Librs. and Info. Svcs., 1987, 75th Anniversary medal U.B.C., 1990, Can. 125 medal, 1993; fellow Coun. on Libr. Resources, 1980. Fellow Libr. Assn.; mem. Assn. Profs. Emeriti U. B.C. (pres. 2003-04), Coll. and Univs. Retiree Assns. Can. (bd. dirs. 2005-07) Achievements include research in electronic info. svcs. and scholarly comm. Home: 1849 W 63rd Ave Vancouver BC Canada V6P 2H9 Personal E-mail: annebp@interchange.ubc.ca.

PITINO, RICK, men's college basketball coach; b. NYC, Sept. 18, 1952; m. Joanne Pitino; children: Michael, Christopher, Richard, Ryan, Jacqueline. Grad., U. Mass., 1974. Grad. asst. U. Hawaii, 1974, asst. coach, 1975-76, Syracuse U., 1976-78; head coach Boston U., 1978-83; asst. coach NY Knicks, 1983-85, head coach, 1987-89, Providence U., 1985—87, U. Ky., Lexington, 1989-97; head coach, pres. Boston Celtics, 1997—2001; head coach U. Louisville, 2001—. Author: (with Bill Reynolds) Born to Coach: A Season with the New York Knicks, 1988, Success is a Choice, 1997, Lead to Succeed, 2000, (with Dick Weiss) Full Court Pressure: A Year in Kentucky Basketball, 1992. Named New Eng. Coach of Yr., 1979, 1983, Coll. Coach of Yr., The Sporting News, 1987; named to NYC Hall of Fame, 2006. Achievements include leading the Kentucky Wildcats to the 1996 NCAA Championship as head coach. Office: Mens Basketball Athletics Dept U Louisville Louisville KY 40292 Office Phone: 502-852-6651. E-mail: rick.pitino@louisville.edu. *

PITKIN, EDWARD THADDEUS, aerospace engineer, consultant; b. Putnam, Conn., Dec. 14, 1930; s. Thaddeus Eugene and Florence Mabel (Brown) P.; m. Clara Lucy Modliszewski, June 13, 1953; children— Gayle Linda, Dale Edward. BS, U. Conn., 1952; MS (Guggenheim fellow), Princeton, 1953; PhD (NASA fellow), UCLA, 1964. Project engr. Astro Div. Marquardt Co., Los Angeles, 1956-59, mgr. space propulsion, 1959-61; engring. cons. Los Angeles, 1961-64; asso. prof. aerospace engring. U. Conn., Storrs, 1964-70, prof. mech. and aerospace engring., 1970-90, prof. emeritus, 1990—; cons. engr., 1990—; asst. dean U. Conn., Storrs, 1977-87. Contbr. articles to profl. jours. Served as lt. USAF, 1953-55. Assoc. fellow AIAA Home: 115 Brookside Ln Mansfield Center CT 06250-1001 Office: U Conn Dept Mech Engring U-139 191 Auditorium Rd Storrs Mansfield CT 06269-3139

PITKIN, HOWARD F., state agency administrator; With Office of State Comptr., Conn., Conn. Dept. Banking, Hartford, 1977—, dir. bank exam. divsn., 1989—2000, adminstr. depository instns., 2000, chief. adminstrn., 2004—06, acting bank commr., 2006—07, bank commr., 2007—. Bd. mgrs. Downtown Hartford YMCA. Recipient Disting. Mgr. of Yr. award, State of Conn., 2000. Office: Conn Dept Banking 260 Constitution Plz Hartford CT 06103-1800 Office Phone: 860-240-8299. Office Fax: 860-240-8178. E-mail: howard.pitkin@ct.gov.

PITKIN, MARK, research scientist; PhD, Ctrl. Inst. Prosthetic Rsch., Moscow. Dir. foot biomechanics lab. Albrecht Ctr. Prosthetics and Rehab., St. Petersburg, 1983—89; rsch. assoc. prof. Tufts U. Sch. Medicine, Boston; dir. Ctr. for Human Performance, New Eng. Sinai Hosp., Stoughton, Mass. Founder, dir. Internat. Inst. Prosthetic Rehab. of Landmine Survivors, Boston; co-founder, pres. Internat. Standing Amputee Ice Hockey Fedn., 2004—06. Achievements include research in rolling joint prosthetic technology. Office: Tufts U Sch Medicine 150 York St Stoughton MA 02072 Office Phone: 781-297-1204.

PITKIN, ROY MACBETH, retired obstetrician, educator; b. Anthon, Iowa, May 24, 1934; s. Roy and Pauline Allie (McBeath) Pitkin; m. Marcia Alice Jenkins, Aug. 17, 1957; children: Barbara, Robert Macbeth, Kathryn, William Charles. BA with highest distinction, U. Iowa, 1956, MD, 1959. Diplomate Am. Bd. Ob-Gyn. Intern King County Hosp., Seattle, 1959—60; resident in ob-gyn U. Iowa Hosps. and Clinics, Iowa City, 1960—63; asst. prof. ob-gyn U. Ill., 1965—68; assoc. prof. ob-gyn U. Iowa, Iowa City, 1968—72, prof., 1972—87, head dept. ob-gyn, 1977—87; prof. UCLA, 1987—97, head dept. ob-gyn., 1987—95, prof. emeritus, 1997—. Mem. residency rev. com. ob-gyn., 1981—87; chmn., 1985—87. Author: The Green Journal 50 Years On, 2003; co-editor: The Best of After Office Hours, 2003; editor-in-chief Year Book of Obstetrics and Gynecology, 1975—86, Clinical Obstetrics and Gynecology, 1979—2000; editor: Obstetrics and Gynecology, 1985—2001; editor emeritus Obstetrics and Gynecology, 2001; contbr. articles to med. jours. Served to lt. comdr. M.C. USNR, 1963—65. Recipient NIH career awardee, 1972—77, Disting. Alumni Achievement award, U. Iowa, 2002. Fellow: Royal Ob-Gyn. (ad eundem); mem.: Coun. Sci. Editors (Dist. Svc. award 2002), Inst. Medicine, NAS, Soc. Perinatal Obstetricians (pres. 1978—79), Soc. Gynecol. Investigation (pres. 1985—86), German Soc.

Gyn-Ob. (hon.), Ctrl. Asn. Ob-Gyn., Am. Gyn-Ob. Soc. (pres. 1994—95), Am. Coll. Ob-Gyns., AMA (Goldberger award in clin. nutrition 1982). Presbyterian. Home: 78900 Rancho La Quinta Dr La Quinta CA 92253-6252 E-mail: r.pitkin@earthlink.net.

PITKO, PAMELA ANN, physical education educator, coach; b. Concordia, Kans., Sept. 17, 1966; d. Clifford Clinton, Jr. and Carolyn Williams; m. Bill L. Pitko, Aug. 3, 1991; children: Haley, Cotton. BS in Edn., Emporia State U., Kans., 1990, MS, 1991. Tchr. phys. edn. Madison Jr. and Sr. H.S., Kans., 1992—93, Eureka Jr. and Sr. H.S., 1993—. Mem. leadership team Eureka Jr. and Sr. H.S., 2002—, dept. chair, 1998—. Mem.: Kans. Assn. Health, Phys. Edn., Recreation and Dance. Republican. Roman Catholic. Avocations: exercise, reading. Office: Eureka Jr and Sr HS 815 N Jefferson St Eureka KS 67045-2403 Home: 509 E 3rd St Eureka KS 67045 Office Phone: 620-583-7428.

PITLUK, ELLEN EIDELBACH, lawyer, mediator; d. Mark Adrian and Baylor Merle Eidelbach; m. Lee Dean Pitluk, Feb. 1, 1985; children: Jessie, Mason. BA in Journalism, Tex. A&M U., College Station, 1981; JD, St. Mary's U., San Antonio, 2002, postgrad. Bar: Tex. 2003, U.S. Dist. Ct. (we. dist.) Tex. 2003. Grad. recruiter Trinity U., Dept. Health Care Adminstrn., San Antonio, 1990—94, 1997—99; rsch. asst. St. Mary's U., Sch. Law, 2000; law clk. Walsh, Anderson, Brown,. Schulze & Aldridge, 2001; law clk. hon. Frank Montalvo 288th Jud. Dist. Ct., Bexar County, 2002; atty., mediator pvt. practice, San Antonio, 2003—. Contbr. articles to profl. jours.; author of poems. Mem.: ABA, San Antonio Bar Assn., San Antonio Bar Found., Coll. State Bar Tex., State Bar Tex. Office: PO Box 780895 San Antonio TX 78278

PITMAN, ANGELIA DEE, web site design company executive; d. Emery Emil Pitman and Carolyn Ernestine Brackin; m. William Curtis Ladnier, May 2, 2006. MA ABT, U. NC, Chapel Hill, 1990—91. Website mgr. Am. Soc. Reproductive Medicine, Birmingham, Ala., 1993—. News reader Ala. Radio Reading Svc. for Visually Impaired, Birmingham, 2000—06. Home Phone: 205-688-0234.

PITMAN, GERALD H., plastic surgeon; AB, Williams Coll.; MD, U. Pa. Diplomate Am. Bd. Plastic Surgery. Resident in surgery Columbia divsn. NY Presbyn. Hosp., NYC; resident in plastic surgery NYU Med. Ctr., fellow in microsurgery, attending plastic surgeon, Tisch Hosp./Manhattan Eye, Ear and Throat Hosp. Clin. prof. surgery NYU Sch. Medicine; lectr. in field. Author: Liposuction and Aesthetic Surgery, 1993; contbr. numerous articles to profl. jours. Fellow: ACS, NY Acad. Medicine; mem.: NY State and County Med. Socs., NY Regional Soc. Plastic and Reconstructive Surgeons, NE Soc. Plastic Surgeons, Am. Soc. Aesthetic Plastic Surgery, Am. Soc. Plastic Surgeons. Achievements include pioneering the use of power-assisted liposuction and considered one the best in the world for this procedure. Avocations: boating, fishing, skiing, triathlons. Office: 170 E 73rd St New York NY 10021 Office Phone: 212-517-2600. Office Fax: 212-628-0774. Business E-Mail: info@drpitman.com.

PITMAN, JIM, professional sports team executive; m. Linda Pitman; children: Amy, Kyle. Grad. in Acctg., U. Ill., 1987. With audit divsn. Arthur Andersen, Phoenix, 1987—92; asst. contr. to corp. contr., v.p. fin. Phoenix Suns, 1992—99, exec. v.p. fin. and adminstrn., 1999—. Treas. Phoenix Suns Charities; bd. mem. US Airways Ctr. Edn. Found., Valley of the Sun YMCA. Avocations: basketball, softball, golf. Office: Phoenix Suns 201 E Jefferson St Phoenix AZ 85004 *

PITMAN, LAVERN FRANK, librarian; b. Poynette, Wis., June 8, 1943; s. George and Carolyn (Hutchinson) P.; m. Rosa Papist, Sept. 8, 1973 (dec. Oct. 1996); 1 child, Christina. BA, Wis. State U., 1965; MSLS, Catholic U. Am., 1973; MA, Frostburg State U., 1985. Cataloger copyright office Libr. Congress, Washington, 1966-71, Spanish/Italian cataloger shared divsn., 1971-79; libr. Frostburg (Md.) State U., 1980-98. Author: The Family of John and Deborah Flick Meyers, 1989, The Robertsons: A Norwegian Family in America, 1993; co-author: A Century of Commitment: Frostburg State University, 1997; editor: Civil War Diary of Jesse Meyers, Co. I, 23d Regiment, Wisconsin Volunteer Infantry, 2002. Historic Interpreter, Mt. Vernon, 1999-2004; curator Wayside Found., 1999-2000; libr. Md. Bur. Mines, 2000-02; trustee Shenandoah County Pub. Libr., Va., 2004—. Mem. Geneal. Soc. Allegany County, Geneal. Soc. Wis., State Hist. Soc. Wis., Frostburg Mus. Assn., Strasburg Mus., Norwegian-Am. Geneal. Ctr. and Naeseth Libr., Sons of Norway, Vesterheim Norwegian-Am. Mus., Clan Rose Soc. Am.

PITMAN-GELLES, BONNIE LOUISE, museum administrator, educator; b. Stamford, Ct., Apr. 24, 1946; d. Benjamin Pitman and Margaret (Hackett) Perry; m. George Gelles, Jan. 1, 1976 (div. 1985); 1 child, David Alexander. AB, Pine Manor Coll., 1966; BA cum laude, Sweet Briar Coll., 1968; MA, Tulane U., 1971. Curator of edn. Winnipeg Art Gallery, Canada, 1968-71, New Orleans Mus. Art, 1971-75; faculty New Orleans Ctr. for Creative Arts, 1975-76; cons. Nat. Endowment for Arts, Washington, 1976-80, panelist Arts in Edn., 1978-84; cons. NEH, Washington, 1977-79, panelist, 1978-79; market rep. Parker Bros., Inc., Salem, N.Y., 1980; cons. Bklyn Ednl. Cultural Alliance, 1980-81, Lincoln Ctr., NYC, 1980-81; assoc. dir. Seattle Art Mus., 1981—, acting dir., 1986-87; mem. faculty mus. mgmt. program U. Colo., Boulder, 1986; dep. dir. U. Art Mus. U. Calif., Berkeley, 1990—95; exec. dir. Bay Area Discovery Mus., Sausalito, Calif., 1995; dep. dir. Dallas Mus. of Art. Mem. nat. adv. com. Getty Ctr. for Edn. in the Arts, 1988—; cons. numerous mus. Author: Watermelon, 1973, Pumpkins into Coaches: Handbook on Youth Education in Museums, 1977, Museums as Educational Instruments, 1980, Museums, Magic and Children, 1981, Taking a Closer Look: Evaluation in Art Museums, 1992, Excellence and Equity: Education & The Public Dimension of Museums, Presence of Mind: Museums and the Spirit of Learning, 1999; editor: Southeast Regional Resource Book for Museums, 1973; numerous articles in field. Panelist Office of Edn., Washington, 1976-77, Nat. Mus. Act, Washington, 1975-7; assoc. mem. bd. dirs. Children's Hosp., Seattle; Sausalito C. of C. Recipient Leadership Tomorrow award United Way, C. of C., 1985, Disting. Svc. award Music & Art Found., Seattle, 1988; named to Centennial Honor Roll, Am. Assn. Museums, 2006. Am. Assn. Mus. (councilor at large 1976-79, 85-88, chmn. edn. com. 1976-80, v.p. 1979-80, 88-92), Internat. Com. Mus. (accreditation commr. 1985—, exec. com. 1977-83), Nat. Hist. Trust, Western Mus. Assn. (Director's Chair award 1992), Phi Beta Kappa, Delta Kappa Phi. Democrat. Avocation: sailing. *

PITOCCO, BARBARA MARY, psychotherapist, social worker; b. Milw., Wis., Dec. 23, 1947; d. Kenneth Paul and Elaine Helen Vogt; m. Joseph M. Pitocco, Nov. 18, 1990; children: David, Jerremy. BA, Marquette U., Milw., 1970; MSW, Fordham U., NYC, 1973. LCSW bd. cert. diplomate clin. social work NJ. Psychotherapist, dir. children's svc., vol. coord. Mid. Bergen Mental Health Ctr. (formerly Ctrl. Bergen Mental Health Ctr.), Paramus, NJ, 1973—81; sch. social worker Ft. Lee Bd. Edn., NJ, 1989—; pvt. practice psychotherapist Lodi, NJ, 1975—. Bd. mem., sec. Paramus Cath. Parent's Coun., 1999—2002; pres. Don Bosco H.S. Mother's Guild, 1998—99. Mem.: Acad. Cert. Social Workers, Nat. Assn. Social Workers. Avocations: gardening, knitting, hiking. Office: 375 Union St Lodi NJ 07644

PITOFSKY, ROBERT, federal agency administrator, law educator; b. Paterson, NJ, Dec. 27, 1929; s. Morris and Sadye (Katz) P.; m. Sally Levy, June 4, 1961; children: Alexander, David, Elizabeth. BA, NYU, 1951; LLB, Columbia U., 1954; LLD (hon.), Georgetown U., 1989, Nyenrode U., Netherlands, 2002. Bar: N.Y. 1956, D.C. 1973, U.S. Supreme Ct. 1972. Atty. Dept. Justice, Washington, 1956-57; assoc. Dewey, Ballantine, Bushby, Palmer & Wood, NYC, 1957-64; prof. law NYU, 1964-70; dir. Bur. Consumer Protection, FTC, 1970-73; prof. law Georgetown U. Law Ctr., Washington, 1973—83, 1989—, dean, exec. v.p. law ctr. affairs, 1983-89; commr. FTC, Washington, 1978-81, chmn., 1995-2001; of counsel Arnold & Porter, Washington, 1973-78, 81-95, 01—. Guest scholar Brookings Instn., Washington, 1989-90; vis. prof. law Harvard Law Sch., 1975-76, Columbia Law Sch., 2005; faculty mem. Salzburg (Austria) Seminar in Am. Studies, 1975; chmn. Def. Sci. Bd. task force on antitrust aspects of def. industry downsizing, 1994. Co-author: Cases on Antitrust Law, 1967, Cases on Trade Regulation, 5th edit. 2003; co-editor: Revitalizing Antitrust in Its Second Century, 1991; contbr. articles on consumer protection and antitrust to profl. publs. Served with U.S. Army, 1954-56. Recipient Disting. Service award FTC, 1972, Hart Pub. Svc. award Cons. Fedn. Am., 2001, Kirkpatrick Lifetime Achievement award FTC, 2002; named One of Ten Outstanding Mid-Career Law Profs. Time Mag., 1977, Disting. Columbia Law Grad. in Tchg., 2005. Mem. ABA (coun. antitrust sect. 1986-89), Am. Acad. Arts and Scis., Am. Law Inst., Assn. Am. Law Schs., Columbia U. Ctr. for Law Econ. Studies (adv. bd. 1975-95). Democrat. Jewish. Office Phone: 202-942-5662. Business E-Mail: Pitofsky@law.georgetown.edu.

PITONIAK, SCOTT MICHAEL, sportswriter; b. Rome, NY, Apr. 10, 1955; s. Andrew Edward and Edna (Holloway) Pitoniak; m. Beth Pitoniak; children: Amy Leigh, Christopher Drew. BS in Pub. Comm. magna cum laude, Syracuse U., 1977. Baseball writer Evening Times, Little Falls, N.Y., 1977; sportswriter Daily Sentinel, Rome, N.Y., 1977; sportswriter, columnist Observer-Dispatch, Utica, N.Y., 1978-84; pro football writer Dem. & Chronicle, Rochester, N.Y., 1985-90, sports projects writer, 1990—. Voter Heisman Trophy Award, 1981—; corr. Gannett News Svc., 1982—, Sporting News, 1982—; journalism prof. St. John Fisher Coll., 1995—. Author: (book) The Buffalo Bills Official Trivia Book, 1989, 1991; co-author: Silver Seasons: The Story of the Rochester Red Wings, 1996, Playing Write Field, 1997, Baseball in Rochester, 2003, Syracuse University Football, 2003, Buffalo Bills: The Good, the Bad, the Ugly, 2007, Slices of Orang, 2005, Tales from the Buffalo Bills, 2006; contbr. articles to mags., newspapers, news svcs. including Sporting News, USA Today, Washington Post, Phila. Inquirer, AP, UPI, others; co-host (TV series) Time Warner Comm., 1994—96. Vol. Alzheimer's Assn., Rochester, 1991—. Named one of Am.'s Top 10 Sports Columnist, APSE, 2000, torchbearer, Winter Olympics, 2002; named to Rochester Sports Walk of Fame, 1999, Syracuse U. Journalism Hall of Fame, 2000; recipient Disting. Health Journalism award Gold medal 1st Pl. newspaper divsn., 1991, 1st Pl. sports, N.Y. State AP Writing Contest, 1995, 2d Pl. features, 1993, 2d Pl. sports, 1991, 1997, 2d Pl. columns, 2001, Best of Gannett award, 1996—98, others; scholar Regents. Mem.: Basketball Writers Am., Coll. Football Writers Assn. Am. (bd. dirs.), Profl. Football Writers Am. (1st Pl. enterprise reporting 1999, 1st Pl. columns 2000, 2d Pl. columns, hon. mention columns 2004), Phi Kappa Phi, Kappa Tau Alpha. Roman Catholic. Avocations: reading, sports memorabilia collecting, volunteering, coaching youth sports, baseball. Office: Gannett Rochester Newspapers 55 Exchange Blvd Rochester NY 14614-2001 Home Phone: 585-227-5409; Office Phone: 585-258-2455. Business E-Mail: spitoniak@aol.com.

PITOT, HENRY CLEMENT, III, pathologist, educator; b. NYC, May 12, 1930; s. Henry Clement and Bertha (Lowe) Pitot; m. Julie S. Schutten, July 29, 1954; children: Bertha, Anita, Jeanne, Catherine, Henry, Michelle, Lisa, Patrice. BS in Chemistry, Va. Mil. Inst., 1951; MD, Tulane U., 1955, PhD in Biochemistry, 1959, DSc (hon.), 1995. Instr. pathology Med. Sch. Tulane U., New Orleans, 1955-59; postdoctoral fellow McArdle Lab. U. Wis., Madison, 1959-60, mem. faculty Med. Sch., 1960—, prof. pathology and oncology, 1966-99, prof. emeritus, 1999—; chmn. dept. pathology, 1968-71, acting dean Med. Sch., 1971-73, dir. McArdle Lab., 1973-91. Recipient Borden Undergrad. Rsch. award, 1955, Leaderle Faculty award, 1962, Career Devel. award, Nat. Cancer Inst., NIH, 1965, Parke-Davis award, 1968, Noble Found. Rsch. award, 1984, Esther Langer award, U. Chgo., 1984, Hilldale award, U. Wis., 1991, Founders award, Chem. Industry Inst. Toxicology, 1993, Midwest Regional chpt. Soc. Toxicology award, 1996, Emeritus Faculty award, U. Wis. Med. Sch., 2001, Disting. Lifetime Toxicology award, Soc. Toxicology, 2003, Gold-headed Cane award, Am. Soc. Investigative Pathology, 2005, Lifetime Disting. Alumnus award, Tulane Med. Sch., 2005, Disting. Svc. award, Assn. Pathology Chairs, 2005. Fellow: AAAS, N.Y. Acad. Scis.; mem.: Soc. Toxicologic Pathologists, Soc. Toxicology, Soc. Surg. Oncology (Lucy J. Wortham award 1981), Soc. Exptl. Biology and Medicine (pres. 1991—93), Am. Soc. Investigative Pathology (pres. 1976—77), Am. Cancer Soc. (life), Japanese Cancer Soc. (hon.), Am. Chem. Soc., Am. Soc. Biochemistry and Molecular Biology, Am. Assn. Cancer Rsch., Am. Soc. Cell Biology. Roman Catholic. Home: 314 Robin Pkwy Madison WI 53705-4931 Office: U Wis McArdle Lab Cancer Rsch 1400 University Ave Madison WI 53706-1599 Office Phone: 608-262-3247. Business E-Mail: pitot@oncology.wisc.edu. *Where and who we are today is the result of those whom we have met and known and loved until now.*

PITSCHMANN, LOUIS A., librarian, dean, educator; m. Lillian A. Clark. BA, Gannon U., 1967; MA in German Lit., Pa. State U., 1969; PhD in Germanic Languages and Lit., U. Chgo., 1975, MLS, 1977. Freelance abstractor AMA, 1977—79; head Icelandic Cataloging Project Cornell U. Librs., Ithaca, 1977—80, borrowing libr., 1980—82, assoc. acquisitions libr., 1982—83, dep. collections libr., North European studies libr., 1983—86; assoc. dir. collection devel. and mgmt. U. Wis., Madison, 1986—2001; dean librs. U. Ala., Tuscaloosa, 2001—. Instr. German U. Notre Dame, Ind., 1969—72; lectr. German language U. Chgo., 1975; adj. asst. prof. Cornell U., 1979; adj. faculty mem. U. Wis., Madison, 1991, Madison, 93, Madison, 95, Madison, 96; prof. libr. and info. studies, adj. prof. German U. Ala., 2001—; spkr. in field. Contbr. articles to profl. jours. George C. Marshall Fellow, Arnamagnaean Inst., U. Copenhagen, 1973, 1974. Mem.: ALA, Assn. Coll. and Rsch. Librs., Medieval Acad. Am. Office: U Ala 201 Amelia Gayle Gorgas Libr Box 870266 Tuscaloosa AL 35487-0266 Office Phone: 205-348-7561. Office Fax: 205-348-8833. E-mail: lpitschm@ua.edu. *

PITT, BERTRAM, cardiologist, educator, consultant; b. Kew Gardens, NY, Apr. 27, 1932; s. David and Shirley (Blum) P., m. Elaine Liberstein, Aug. 10, 1962; children: Geoffrey, Jessica, Jillian BA, Cornell U., 1953; MD, U. Basel, Switzerland, 1959. Diplomate Am. Bd. Internal Medicine, Am. Bd. Cardiology. Intern Beth Israel Hosp., NYC, 1959-60, resident Boston, 1960-63; fellow in cardiology Johns Hopkins U., Balt., 1966-67, from instr. to assoc. prof., 1967-77; prof. medicine, dir. div. cardiology U. Mich., Ann Arbor, 1977-91, prof. medicine Sch. Medicine, 1991—2005, prof. medicine emeritus Sch. Medicine, 2005—. Author: Atlas of Cardiovascular Nuclear Medicine, 1977; editor: Cardiovascular Nuclear Medicine, 1974; co-editor: Clinical Trials in Cardiology, 1997, Current Controlled Trials in Cardiovascular Medicine, 1999—. Served to capt. U.S. Army, 1963-65. Mem. ACP, Am. Coll. Cardiology, Am. Soc. Clin. Investigation, Assn. Am. Physicians, Am. Physiol. Soc., Am. Heart Assn. (James. B. Herrick award 2005), Assn. Univ. Cardiologists, Am. Coll. Chest Physicians, Johns Hopkins U. Soc. Scholars. Home: 24 Ridgeway St Ann Arbor MI 48104-1739 Office: U Mich Divsn Cardiology 1500 E Medical Center Dr Ann Arbor MI 48109-0005 Office Phone: 734-709-9894. Business E-Mail: bpitt@umich.edu.

PITT, BRAD, actor; b. Shawnee, Okla., Dec. 18, 1963; s. Bill and Jane Pitt; m. Jennifer Aniston, July 29, 2000 (div. Oct. 2, 2005);(adoptive children with Angelina Jolie) Maddox Chivan Jolie-Pitt, Zahara Marley Jolie-Pitt, Pax Thien Jolie-Pitt; (one child with Angelina Jolie) Shiloh Nouvel Jolie-Pitt Actor: (films) No Man's Land, 1987, Less Than Zero, 1987, Cutting Glass, 1989, Happy Together, 1990, Across the Tracks, 1991, Thelma and Louise, 1991, Johnny Suede, 1991, Contact, 1992, Cool World, 1992, A River Runs Through It, 1992, Kalifornia, 1993, Tprue Romance, 1993, The Favor, 1994, Interview with the Vampire, 1994, Legends of the Fall, 1994, 12 Monkeys, 1995 (Golden Globe award for best supporting actor, 1996, Acad. award nominee for Best Supporting Actor 1996), Sleepers, 1996, Seven Years in Tibet, 1997, The Devil's Own, 1997, Dark Side of the Sun, 1997, Meet Joe Black, 1998, Fight Club, 1999, Snatch, 2000, The Mexican, 2001, Spy Game, 2001, Ocean's Eleven, 2001, Full Frontal, 2002, Confessions of a Dangerous Mind, 2002, (voice only) Sinbad: Legend of the Seven Seas, 2003, Troy, 2004, Ocean's Twelve, 2004, Mr. & Mrs. Smith, 2005, Babel, 2006, Ocean's Thirteen, 2007; (TV movies) A Stoning in Fulham County, 1988, Too Young to Die, 1990; (TV series), Another World, 1987, Glory Days, 1990; (TV appearances) Growing Pains, 1987, 1989, Dallas, 1987, 1988, 21 Jump Street, 1988, Head of the Class, 1989, Freddy's Nightmares, 1989, thirtysomething, 1989, Tales from the Crypt, 1992, Friends, 2001, King of the Hill (voice only), 2003, Getaway, 2005; prodr.: (films) The Departed, 2006, Running with Scissors, 2006; exec. prodr.: God Grew Tired of Us: The Story of Lost Boys of Sudan, 2004. Named one of 50 Most Powerful People in Hollywood, Premiere mag., 2004—06, Barbara Walters-10 Most Fascinating People of 2006, The World's Most Influential People, TIME mag., 2007, The 100 Most Powerful Celebrities, Forbes.com, 2007; recipient Favorite Leading Man, People's Choice Awards, 2006. Office: Creative Artists Agy care Kevin Huvane 9830 Wilshire Blvd Beverly Hills CA 90212-1825 *

PITT, GEORGE, lawyer, investment banker; b. Chgo., July 21, 1938; s. Cornelius George and Anastasia (Geocaris) P.; m. Barbara Lynn Goodrich, Dec. 21, 1963 (div. Apr. 1990); children: Elizabeth Nanette, Margaret Leigh; m. Pamela Ann Pittsford, May 19, 1990. BA, Northwestern U., 1960, JD, 1963; grad. (hon.), US Army Intelligence Sch., Ft. Holabird, Md., 1964; Leading Strategic Change course, U. Va., 1999. Bar: Ill. 1963. Assoc. Chapman and Cutler, Chgo., 1963-67; ptnr. Borge and Pitt, and predecessor, 1968-87, Katten Muchin & Zavis, Chgo., 1987-97; sr. mng. dir. Banc One Capital Markets, Inc. (formerly First Chgo. Capital Markets, Inc.), 1998-2000; mng. dir. UBS Fin. Svcs. Inc. (formerly UBS PaineWebber Inc.), Chgo., 2000—. Conf. chmn. Bond Buyer's 3d Ann. Midwest Pub. Fin. Conf., 1994; conf. co-chmn. Bond Buyer's 8th Ann. Midwest Pub. Fin. Conf., 1999. Notes and comments editor Northwestern U. Law Rev., 1962-63. 1st lt. AUS, 1964. Fellow: Am. Coll. Bond Counsel; mem.: Ill. State Bar Assn., Univ. Club. Chgo., Phi Gamma Delta, Phi Delta Phi, Eta Sigma Phi. Home: 345 E Ohio St Apt 4810 Chicago IL 60611 Business E-Mail: george.pitt@ubs.com.

PITT, HARVEY LLOYD, risk management consultant, former federal agency administrator; b. Bklyn., Feb. 28, 1945; s. Morris Jacob and Sara (Sapir) P.; m. Saree Ruffin, Jan. 7, 1984; children: Robert Garrett, Sara Dillard; children from previous marriage: Emily Laura, Jonathan Bradley. BA, CUNY, 1965; JD with honors (Univ. scholar), St. John's U., NYC, 1968; LLD (hon.), St. John's U., 2002. Bar: N.Y. 1969, U.S. Supreme Ct. 1972, D.C. 1979. With SEC, Washington, 1968-78, legal asst. to commr., 1969; editor Instl. Investor Study, 1970-71; spl. counsel Office Gen. Counsel, Washington, 1971-72, chief counsel div. market regulation, 1972-73, exec. asst. to chmn., 1973-75, gen. counsel, 1975-78; ptnr. Fried, Frank, Harris, Shriver & Jacobson, Washington, 1978—2001; chmn. SEC, Washington, 2001—03; CEO Kalorama Ptnrs., LLC, 2003—. Adj. prof. law George Washington U. Nat. Law Ctr., 1974-82, U. Pa. Law Sch., 1983-84, vis. practitioner, 1984, Georgetown U. Law Ctr., 1976-84; comml. arbitrator Am. Arbitration Assn. Contbr. articles to profl. jours. V.p. Glen Haven Civic Assn., Silver Spring, Md., 1972-73, pres., 1974. Recipient Learned Hand award Inst. for Human Rels., 1988, Presdl. medal, Bklyn. Coll., 2003. Mem. ABA (past chmn. subcom. SEC practice and enforcement, past co-chmn. subcom. state takeover laws), Fed. Bar Assn. (Outstanding Young Lawyer award 1975), Adminstrv. Conf. U.S., Am. Law Inst. (project advisor on restatement law on corp. governance), Delta Sigma Rho, Tau Kappa Alpha, Phi Delta Phi. Office: Kalorama Ptnrs LLC Ste 800 1130 Connecticut Ave NW Washington DC 20036-3915 Office Phone: 202-721-0000. Business E-Mail: harvey@kaloramapartners.com.

PITT, HENRY ANTHONY, surgeon, researcher, medical educator; b. Elizabeth, NJ, Mar. 23, 1945; m. Elizabeth Jane Chambliss, June 21, 1969; children: Laura Elizabeth Teufel, David Andrew, Susan Clare. AB, Cornell U., 1967, MD, 1971. Diplomate Am. Bd. Surgery. Resident Johns Hopkins Hosp., Balt., 1971—73, 1975—78; asst. prof. surgery U. Calif., LA, 1979—85; prof. surgery Johns Hopkins U., Balt., 1985—97, Med. Coll. Wis., Milw., 1997—2004, Ind. U., Indpls., 2004—. Coach Little League Baseball, Pacific Palisades, Calif., 1980—84. Lt. comdr. USN, 1973—75. Named Aprahamian Tchr. of Yr., Med. Coll. Wis., Surgery, 2002, Hon. Prof., Tongi Med. Coll., Wuhan, China, 2006; recipient Letter in Baseball, Cornell U., 1967, Shipley award, So. Surg. Assn., 1989. Fellow: Royal Coll. Surgeons, Edinburgh (hon.); mem.: Internat. Hepato-Pancreato-Biliary Assn. (life; pres. 2004—06), Soc. Surgery Alimentary Tract (life; v.p. 2004—05), Am. Surg. Assn. (life; fellowship com. 2001—), Am. Hepato-Pancreato-Biliary Assn. (life; pres. 1999—2001), Soc. Clin. Surgery (life; pres. 1998—2000), Soc. U. Surgeons (life; sec. 1985—86), Alpha Omega Alpha (life; pres. 1970—71). Achievements include research in gallstone pathogenesis. Avocation: golf. Office: Indiana University 535 Barnhill Drive RT 130D Indianapolis IN 46202 Home Phone: 317-923-7488; Office Phone: 317-274-2304. Office Fax: 317-274-4554. Business E-Mail: hapitt@iupui.edu.

PITT, WILLIAM ALEXANDER, cardiologist; b. July 17, 1942; came to U.S., 1970; s. Reginald William and Una Sylvia (Alexander) P.; m. Judith Mae Wilson, May 21, 1965; children: William Matthew, Joanne Katharine. MD, U. B.C., Vancouver, 1967. Diplomate Royal Coll. Physicians Can. Intern Mercy Hosp., San Diego, 1967-68, resident, 1970-71, assoc. dir. cardiology, 1972-92; resident Vancouver Gen. Hosp., 1968-70, U. Calif., San Diego, 1971-72; with So. Calif. Cardiology Med. Group, San Diego, 1984—; pvt. practice Clin. Cons. Cardiology. Bd. trustees San Diego Found. for Med. Care, 1983-89, 91—, pres., chmn. bd. trustees, 1986-88, med. dir., 1991-96; trustee Pacific Found. for Med. Care, 1996—, med. dir., 1996—; bd. dirs. Mut. Assn. for Profl. Services, Phila., 1984-92; pres. Alternet Med. Svcs., Inc., 1992-95; pres. and med. dir. San Diego IPA, 1995-2005. Fellow Royal Coll. Physicians Can., Am. Coll. Cardiology (assoc.); mem. AMA, Am. Heart Assn., Calif. Med. Assn., San Diego County Med. Soc., San Diego County Heart Assn. (bd. dirs. 1982-88). Episcopalian. Office: So Calif Cardiology Med Group 6386 Alvarado Ct Ste 101 San Diego CA 92120-4906 Home Phone: 619-670-8308; Office Phone: 619-265-1237. Personal E-mail: wmapitt@aol.com.

PITTELKO, ROGER DEAN, clergyman, theology studies educator; b. Elk Reno, Okla., Aug. 18, 1932; s. Elmer Henry and Lydia Caroline (Nieman) Pittelko. AA, Concordia Coll., 1952; BA, Concordia Sem., St. Louis, 1954, MDiv, 1957, STM, 1958; postgrad., Chgo. Luth. Theol. Sem., 1959-61; ThD, Am. Div. Sch., Pineland, Fla., 1968; DMin, Faith Evang. Luth. Sem., Tacoma, 1983. Ordained to ministry Luth. Ch., 1958. Vicar St. John Luth. Ch., SI, NY, 1955—56, asst. pastor New Orleans, 1958-59; pastor Concordia Luth. Ch., Berwyn, Ill., 1959-63, Luth. Ch. Holy Spirit, Elk Grove Village, Ill., 1962—87; chmn. Commn. on Worship, Luth. Ch.-Mo. Synod, 1982—92, chmn. commn. worship, 1994—98, asst. bishop Midwest region English dist., 1983, pres., bishop English dist., 1987-97, 3d v.p., 1997—2001; prof. pastoral theology Concordia Theol. Sem., Ft. Wayne, Ind., 1997—2003; pastor Trinity Luth. Ch., Villa Park, Ill., 2003—05, Grace English Luth. Ch., Chgo., 2005—. Author: Guide to

Introducing Lutheran Worship; contbr. articles to jours. Mem.: Luth. Acad. for Scholarship, Concordia Hist. Inst., Itasca Country Club (Ill.), Maywood Sportsmans Club (Ill.). Republican. Lutheran. Office: Trinity Luth Ch 300 S Ardmore Ave Villa Park IL 60181-2699 Office Phone: 630-834-3440. Personal E-mail: emep@juno.com.

PITTELKOW, MARK ROBERT, physician, dermatologist, educator, medical researcher; b. Milw., Dec. 16, 1952; s. Robert Bernard and Barbara Jean (Thomas) P.; m. Gail L. Gamble, Nov. 26, 1977; children: Thomas, Cameron, Robert. BA, Northwestern U., 1975; MD, Mayo Med. Sch., 1979. Intern then resident Mayo Grad. Sch., 1979-84, post-doctoral exptl. pathology, 1981-83; from asst. to assoc. prof. dermatology Mayo Med. Sch., Rochester, Minn., 1984-95, prof. dermatology, 1995—, assoc. prof. biochemistry and molecular biology, 1992—. Cons. Mayo Clinic/Found., Rochester, 1984— Fellow Am. Acad. Dermatology; mem. AAAS, Am. Dermatol. Assn., Soc. Investigative Dermatology, Am. Burn Assn., Am. Soc. Cell Biology, N.Y. Acad. Scis., Chi Psi. Achievements include discovery of skin and epidermal growth control; autocrine growth factor production; growth and differentiation of keratinocytes. Home: 721 12th Ave SW Rochester MN 55902-2027 Office: Mayo Clinic 200 1st St SW Rochester MN 55905-0002 Office Phone: 507-284-2555. Business E-Mail: pittelkow.mark@mayo.edu.

PITTET, MIKAEL J., research scientist, director; b. Lausanne, Vaud, Switzerland, May 23, 1975; s. Marc-Henri and Jocelyne Pittet; m. Sylvie S. Zoëll, Sept. 8, 2002; 1 child, Antoine M. B in Biology, U. Lausanne, Switzerland, 0997, PhD, 2001. Postdoctoral fellow, tumor immunology Ludwig Inst. Cancer Rsch., Lausanne, 2001—03; postdoctoral fellow, immuno-imaging Ctr. Molecular Imaging Rsch., Boston, 2003—04, instr. radiology, 2004—06, asst. prof. radiology, 2006—. Contbr. articles to profl. jours. Fellow, Swiss Nat. Fund, Bern, Switzerland, 2002, Human Frontier Sci. Program Orgn., 2003. Mem.: Am.Assn. Cancer Rsch., Soc. Molecular Imaging, Dana Farber Harvard Cancer Inst. Avocations: sailing, photography, movies. Office: Ctr Molecualr Imaging Rsch Bldg 149 13th St Charlestown MA 02129

PITTMAN, AMANDA NELSON, music educator; d. General Lee and Amanda Hopkins Nelson; m. Marvin Benjamin Pittman, 1964; 1 child, Marvin Benjamin Jr. BMus, U. So. Calif., LA, 1948, MMus, 1961, DMA, 2003. Gen. tchg. credential in elem. edn. Calif. Tchr. elem. edn. Ft. Worth Schs., 1949—51; tchr. elem. music L.A. City Schs., 1957—64, Montgomery County Schs., Rockville, Md., 1964—66, L.A. City Schs., 1966—75, Beverly Hills Unified Schs., Calif., 1975—90, L.A. City Schs., 1990—91, Clark County Sch. Dist., Las Vegas, Nev., 1992—98, L.A. City Schs., 1999—. Instr. music edn. Pepperdine U., LA, 1967—70, U. So. Calif., LA, 1975—77, Calif. State U., LA, 2002—03. Adminstrv. officer USAFR, March AFB, Calif., 1959—64. Capt. USAF, 1951—56. Mem.: Calif. Music Educators Assn., L.A. City Elem. Schs. Music Assn. (v.p. 2004—06), Internat. Assn. for Jazz Edn., Music Educators Nat. Conf. (presenter 1960—2006), Women in Mil. Svc. for Am. Found. (charter mem.). Home: 8957 Haas Ave Los Angeles CA 90047

PITTMAN, CATHERINE SYLVIA, secondary school educator; b. Brunswick, Ga., Apr. 24, 1962; m. David Pittman; children: Drew, Meghan. BS, Ga. So. Coll., 1984, MEd, 1989, EdS, 1993. Tchr. grade 7,8 Risley Middle Sch., Glynn County, 1985-89; tchr. grades 9-12 Brunswick High Sch., Glynn County, 1989—. Named Ga. Tchr. of Yr., 1995, 1996, Milken Family Found. Nat. Educator, 1995; recipient YMCA Tribute to Women's Leaders, 1999. Mem. Glynn County Assn. of Educators, Ga. Assn. of Educators, Nat. Edn. Assn., Ga. Council of Social Studies, So. Assn. of Student Councils, Nat. Assn. of Student Activity Advisors. Office: Brunswick High Sch 3920 Habersham St Brunswick GA 31520-2799 E-mail: cpittman@glynn.k12.ga.us. *

PITTMAN, CONSTANCE SHEN, endocrinologist, educator; b. Nanking, China, Jan. 2, 1929; arrived in US, 1946; d. Leo F.-Z. and Pao Kong (Yang) Shen; m. James Allen Pittman, Jr., Feb. 19, 1955; children: James Clinton, John Merrill. AB in Chemistry, Wellesley Coll., 1951; MD, Harvard U., 1955. Diplomate Am. Bd. Internal Medicine, sub-bd. Endocrinology. Intern Baltimore City Hosp., 1955-56; resident U. Ala., Birmingham, 1956-57; instr. in medicine U. Ala. Med. Ctr., Birmingham, 1957—59, fellow dept. pharmacology, 1957-59, from asst. prof. to assoc. prof., 1959-70, prof., 1970—. Prof. medicine Georgetown U., Washington, 1972—73; mem. diabetes and metabolism tng. com. NIH, Bethesda, Md., 1972—76, mem. nat. arthritis, metabolism and digestive disease coun., 1975—78, mem. gen. clin. rsch. ctrs. com., 1979—83, 1987—90; bd. dirs., mem., exec. dir. Internat. Coun. for Control of Iodine Deficiency Diseases, 1994—; mem. Iodine Deficiency Disorders Elimination Steering Com. Kiwanis Internat., 2002—. Interim editor: ICCIDD Newsletter, 2004—06. Master ACP; mem. Assn. Am. Physicians, Am. Soc. for Clin. Investigation, Endocrine Soc. (coun., 1978-79, pres. women's caucus 1978-79), Am. Thyroid Assn. (pres. 1990-91), Kiwanis (mem. iodine deficiency disorders steering com.). Achievements include research in activation and metabolism of thyroid hormone; kinetics of thyroxine conversion to triiodothyrine in health and disease states; control of iodine deficiency disorders. Emails. Office: UAB Div Endocrinology/Metab Lab Med Ctr Birmingham AL 35294-0001 Office Phone: 205-934-0800. Business E-Mail: cpittman@uab.edu.

PITTMAN, HARRISON M., lawyer, educator; JD, U. Ark., LLM in Agrl. Law. Ben J. Altheimer disting. professorship for agrl. law William H. Bowen Sch. Law, U. Ark., Little Rock; rsch. asst. prof. law, interim co-dir. National Agrl. Law Ctr., U. Ark., Fayetteville, 2006—. Spkr. in field. Contbr. articles to profl. jours. Mem.: ABA (mem. Agrl. Com.), Ark. Bar Assn., Am. Agrl. Law Assn. Office: Nat Agrl Law Ctr U Ark Sch Law 1 University of Arkansas Fayetteville AR 72701 Office Phone: 479-575-7640. E-mail: hmpittm@uark.edu.

PITTMAN, JAMES ALLEN, JR., endocrinologist, educator; b. Orlando, Fla., Apr. 12, 1927; s. James Allen and Jean C. (Garretson) Pittman; m. Constance Ming-Chung Shen, Feb. 19, 1955; children: James Clinton, John Merrill. BS, Davidson Coll., 1948, DSc (hon.), 1981; MD, Harvard, 1952; DSc (hon.), U. Ala., Birmingham, 1984, Chung Shan Med U., Taichung, Taiwan, 2005. Intern, asst. resident medicine Mass. Gen. Hosp., Boston, 1952—54; tchg. fellow medicine Harvard U., 1953—54; clin. assoc. NIH, Bethesda, Md., 1954—56; instr. medicine George Washington U., 1955—56; chief resident U. Ala. Med. Ctr., Birmingham, 1956—58, instr. medicine, 1956—59, asst. prof., 1959—62, assoc. prof., 1962—64, prof. medicine, 1964—92, dir. endocrinology and metabolism divsn., 1962—71, co-chmn. dept. medicine, 1969—71, also prof., physiology and biophysics, 1967—92, dean, 1973—92, Disting. prof., 1992—. Mem. endocrinology study sect. NIH, 1963—67; mem. nat. adv. rsch. resources coun. NIH, 1991—95; asst. chief med. dir. rsch. and edn. in medicine U.S. VA, 1971—73; prof. medicine Georgetown U. Med. Sch., Washington, 1971—73; mem. grad. med. edn. nat. adv. com. HEW, 1976—78; mem. HHS Coun. on Grad. Med. Edn., 1986—90; hon. prof. Chung Shan Med. and Dental Coll., Taiwan, 1994; sr. advisor Internat. Coun. on Ctrl. of Iodine Deficiency Diseases, 1994—96. Author: Diagnosis and Treatment of Thyroid Diseases, 1963; contbr. articles in field to profl. jours. Master: Am. Coll. Endocrinology; fellow: AAAS; mem.: ACP, Stearman Restorers Assn., Hist. Sci. Soc., Am. Soc. for the History of Medicine, So. Soc. Clin. Investigation (Founder's medal 1993), Am. Fedn. Clin. Rsch. (pres. So. sect., nat. coun. 1962—66), Am. Chem. Soc., Am. Diabetes Assn., Am. Ornithologists Union (life), NY Acad. Scis. (life), Endocrine Soc. Ecuador (hon.), Soc. Nuc. Medicine, Am. Thyroid Assn., Am. Assn. Clin. Endocrinologists, Endocrine Soc., Assn. Am. Physicians, Inst. Medicine of NAS, Harvard U. Med. Alumni Assn. (pres. 1986—88), Wilson Ornithol. Club (life), Alpha Omega Alpha, Phi Beta Kappa, Omicron Delta Kappa. Office: U Ala Sch Med Pittman CAMS 1924 7th Ave S Birmingham AL 35294-0007 Office Phone: 205-934-3414. Personal E-mail: japdoc@msn.com. Business E-Mail: japdoc@uab.edu. *I hope that each time I meet a person, both of us leave the encounter the better for it.*

PITTMAN, JAMES MORRIS (JACK PITTMAN), cartoonist, illustrator, character designer, consultant; b. Sanford, NC, Oct. 22, 1952; s. James Berdine and Merry Louise (Thomas) P.; m. Patricia Lynne Smith, Nov. 27, 1977; children: Jay Scott, Jonathan Patrick, Joy Elizabeth. B of Environ. Design in Arch. with honors, N.C. State U., 1974. Sports and editl. cartoonist, illustrator, courtroom artist The News and Observer, Raleigh, NC, 1974-83; freelance cartoonist, illustrator Raleigh, 1983—. Adj. prof. Meredith Coll., Raleigh, 1993-94; advtsg. illustrator for Am. Express, Coca-Cola, Procter & Gamble, GMC, Palace Entertainment, Kellogg's, Wendy's, Carolina Hurricanes, NHL, Ericsson, Inc., Gatorade, GlaxoSmithKline, Nortel Networks. Illustrator: (book) A Dust of Snow, 1980, Are You Smart, Or What?, 2001, If You're So Smart, Prove It!, 2007, Darren Dwayne DeBakey and His Amazing Inventions, mags. include Nat. Geographic World, Wildlife in NC, Reader's Digest, (CD-ROM) Heavenword Children's Bible, 1997, The Birth of Kidd Millennium, 2001, (comic strip) Kidd Millennium, 2001-05; permanent collections include The Internat. Mus. of Cartoon Art, N.C. Mus. History, 2002-03, NC Wildlife Resources Commn. Offices, NC State U. Centennial Campus, 2006—. Deacon So. Bapt. Ch. Recipient various ADDY awards Triangle Advtsg. Fedn., 1983-97, 69th Exhbn. Merit; Best in Mag. Illustration award. Mem. Nat. Cartoonists Soc. (Best in Advt. and Illustration award Reuben divsn. 1995, 98, 2004), Raleigh Civitan Club. Mem. So. Bapt. Ch. Avocations: percussion, computers. Home: PO Box 10711 Raleigh NC 27605-0711 Office: J Pittman Illustrator 1740 Brooks Ave Raleigh NC 27607-6618 Office Phone: 919-785-1966. E-mail: jptoonist@aol.com, jack@jackpittman.net.

PITTMAN, JONATHAN, computer scientist; b. Newport News, Va., July 17, 1980; s. Sylvia Pittman. BS in Computer Sci., Miss. State U., 2006. Cert. info. assurance prof. Miss. State U., 2006. Sys. adminstr. Inst. for Neurocognitive Sci. and Tech., Starkville, Miss., 2004—. Sgt. N.G. US Army. Decorated Longevity medal US Army, Miss. War medal, Commendation medal, Army Reserves Components Achievement medal, Bronze Star, Good Conduct medal, Global War on Terrorism Svc. medal, Nat. Def. Svc. medal, Emergency Svc. medal, Achievement medal Army, Humanitarian Svc. medal US Army, Iraq Campaign medal; recipient 1st pl., Miss. Coll. Comptuer Programing Competition, 1998, Pearl River CC Comptuer Programing Competition, 2000, Miss. Gulf Coast CC Comptuer Programing Competition, 2002, 3rd pl., U. NC SE Collegiate Cyber Def. Competition, Charlotte, 2007; scholar for svc., NSF, 2006. Mem.: IEEE, Assn. for Computing Machinery, VFW (life). Home Phone: 662-323-0952.

PITTMAN, LISA, lawyer; b. Limestone, Maine, Jan. 4, 1959; d. William Franklin and Rowena Paradis (Umphrey) P.; 1 child, Graham Edward Paradis. BA with highest honors, U. Fla., 1980, MA, 1981, JD, 1984; LLM with highest honors, George Washington U., 1988. Bar: Fla. 1984, D.C. 1993, U.S Supreme Ct. 1993. Spl. asst. to gen. counsel Nat. Oceanic and Atmospheric Adminstrn., Washington, 1984-85, atty., advisor, 1985-87; minority counsel Com. on Mcht. Marine & Fisheries, Ho. of Reps., Washington, 1987-95; dep. chief counsel Com. on Resources, U.S. Ho. of Reps., Washington, 1995-2001, chief counsel, 2001—02, chief counsel, dep. staff dir., 2002. Contbr. articles to profl. jour. *

PITTMAN, MIA N., educational association administrator, entrepreneur; BA, U. Pa.; MBA in Fin., Temple U. With CoreStates Fin. Corp.; with venture capital arm The Reinvestment Fund, Phila.; v.p. comml. lending Progress Fin. Corp.; founder, pres., CEO Start Smart Inc., Upper Darby, Pa. Named one of 40 Under 40, Phila. Bus. Jour., 2006. Office: Start Smart Inc 202 Long Lane - 1st Fl Upper Darby PA 19082 Office Phone: 484-461-3025. Office Fax: 484-461-3562.

PITTMAN, R. ALLEN, federal agency administrator; Grad., U. Ark., 1974. Co-founder U.S. Oncology, Inc., chief adminstrv. officer, exec. v.p. human resources, 1993—2001, exec. v.p. exec. svcs., exec. dir., 2002—04; asst. sec. human resources & adminstrn. US Dept. Vets. Affairs, Washington, 2004—. Decorated Navy Commendation Medal with Combat V. Office: US Dept Veterans Affairs 810 Vermont Ave NW Washington DC 20420

PITTMAN, ROBERT TURNER, retired newspaper editor; b. Gates, NC, Sept. 24, 1929; s. Thomas Everett and Lillian (Turner) P.; m. Ruth Fike, Aug. 25, 1956; children— Laura Emily, Mary Ann, Lillian Elizabeth. BA, Washington and Lee U., 1951; MA, U. N.C., 1957. Reporter Times Dispatch, Richmond, Va., 1951; editor, pub. Daily Ranger, Glendive, Mont., 1957-58; writer editorials Times Union, Jacksonville, Fla., 1958-63; editorial editor Times, St. Petersburg, Fla., 1963-92; dir. Times Pub. Co., 1968-92. Trustee Poynter Inst. Media Studies, St. Petersburg, 1978-92. Editor: (jour.) Masthead, 1980—81. Active St. Petersburg Charter Revision Com., 1992-93; dir. Fla. Bar Found., 1994-96. Lt. (j.g.) USNR, 1951-55. Recipient Pinellas Civil Liberties award, 1993; U. N.C.-Chapel Hill scholarship established in honor, 1994, Liberty Bell award St. Petersburg Bar Assn., 1995. Mem. Nat. Conf. Editl. Writers (pres. 1978, life), Nat. Conf. Editl. Writers Found. Inc. (pres. 1984) Methodist. Home: 736 18th Ave NE Saint Petersburg FL 33704-4608

PITTMAN, ROBERT WARREN, investor; b. Jackson, Miss., Dec. 28, 1953; s. Warren E. and Lanita (Hurdle) P.; m. Sandra Hill, July 27, 1979; 1 child, Robert Thomas; m. Veronique Choa, Nov. 28, 1997; children: Andrew Forest, Lucy Li. Student, Millsaps Coll., 1971-72, Oakland U., 1972-73, U. Pitts., 1973-74; AMP, Harvard U., 1984-85. Disc. jockey Sta. WJDX-FM, Jackson, Miss., 1970-72, Sta. WRIT, Milw., 1972; research dir. Sta. WDRQ, Detroit, 1972-73; program dir. Sta. WPEZ, Pitts., 1973-74, Stas. WMAQ-WKQX NBC, Chgo., 1974-77, Sta. WNBC, NYC, 1977-79; exec. producer Album Tracks, NBC TV, NYC, 1977-78; dir., v.p., then sr. v.p. MTV Networks, NYC, 1979-82, exec. v.p., COO, 1983-85, pres., CEO, 1985-86, Quantum Media, Inc., NYC, 1987-89; exec. advisor Warner Communications, Inc., NYC, 1989-90; pres., chief exec. officer Time Warner Enterprises, NYC, 1990-95; CEO, Six Flags Entertainment, 1991-95; mng. ptnr., CEO, Century 21 Real Estate, 1995-96; pres., CEO Am. On-Line Networks, 1996-97; pres., COO Am. On-Line, Inc., 1997-2001; CO-COO AOL Time Warner, 2001, COO, 2002—; ptnr. Pilot Group, 2003—. Bd. dirs. Spot Runner, 2006—, Cendant Corp. Bd. dirs. Elec. Arts, N.Y.C. Ballet, N.Y. Shakespeare Festival, chmn., 1987—94; bd. dir., vice-chmn. Robin Hood Found.; bd. dir. Alliance Lupus Rsch. Recipient Program Mgr. of Yr. Billboard, 1977, Program Dir. of Yr. Hall Radio Report, 1978, Entrepreneur award White House SB Conf., 1986, Golden Plate award Am. Acad. Achievement, 1990, medal of Excellence Miss. U. Women, 1992, Vision award Retinitis Pigmentosa International, 1992, Lifetime Achievement Internat. Monitor award Internat. Teleproduction Soc., 1993, Gold Medal award Internat. Radio of TV Soc., 2002, Cablevision Mags. 20/20 Vision award, Pres. award Bank St. Coll. Edn.; named Innovator of Yr. Performance Mag., 1981, Humanitarian of Yr., AMC, 1984, Time Mag. Man of Yr. runner-up, 1984, Esquire Mag. Under 40 Leadership, 1985; named one of Pioneers of New Am. Start-Up, Success mag., One of Five Original Thinkers of 80s, Life Mag., 1990, 8 of 50 Most Influential Baby Boomers, Life Mag., 1996, Bus. Week's Top 25 Exec. of 1998, one of 50 Pioneers and Visionaries of TV, 2002; inducted Broadcast & Cable Hall of Fame, 1999. Methodist. Office: Pilot Group LLC 745 Fifth Ave 24th Fl New York NY 10151

PITTMAN, ROY CLINTON, JR., neurosurgeon, theologian, lawyer, philosopher; b. Florence, SC, Oct. 12, 1931; s. Roy Clinton and Edna Hester (Altman) P.; m. Therese Huguette Lamarche Pittman, Apr. 1958 (div. May 1976); 1 stepdaughter, Michele Lois Young; children: Charlotte Elisabeth, Clinton Christopher, Russell Roy; m. Jeanne Elmore Waters Pittman, Oct. 10, 1976. BS magna cum laude, Wofford Coll., Spartanburg, SC, 1952; MD, Med. U. S.C., Charleston, 1956; JD, Washburn U. Coll. Law, Topeka, Kans., 1991; MDiv with honors, Emory U. Candler Sch. Theology, Atlanta, 1995; DSc (hon.), The London Inst., 1973. Diplomate Am. Bd. Neurol. and Orthopedic Surgery; ordained to ministry Ea. Orthodox Ch., 2000; bar: Fla. 1992, U.S. Dist. Ct. (mid. dist.) Fla. 1992. Intern U.S. Naval Hosp., Newport, RI, 1956-57; resident in neurology U.S. Naval Hosp.-Nat. Naval Med. Ctr., Bethesda, Md., 1957-58; neurologist East Coast Neuropsychiat. Ctr.-U.S. Naval Hosp., Phila., 1958-59, head neurology br., 1959; resident in neurosurgery Jefferson Med. Coll. Hosp., Phila., 1959-61, chief resident, 1961-62; resident in gen. surgery Hahnemann Med. Coll. Hosp., Phila., 1962-63; pvt. practice neurol. surgery Morton Plant and Mease Hosps., Clearwater-Dunedin, Fla., 1963-82, Cmty. Hosp. of New Port Richey, New Port Richey, Fla., 1978-88; pvt. practice legal medicine, med. jurisprudence & bioethics Pittman Profl. Assn., Clearwater, Fla., 1995-98, Tarpon Springs, Fla., 1995-98; pres., gen. counsel The Quintessential Corp., Tarpon Springs, 1998-2000; founder, prior Trinity House Retreat, Greek Orthodox Monastery of the Holy Trinity, 2001—. Protestant chaplain Morton Plant/Mease Countryside Hosp., Clearwater, Fla., 1997-98. Contbr. articles to profl. jours. Pres. St. Petersburg (Fla.) Coll. Alumni Assn., 1973-75. Lt. MC, USN, 1956-59, lt. comdr., 1962. Recipient Top Paper Bioethics and The Law award Washburn U. Coll. Law, Topeka, Kans., 1990, Top paper Comparative Civil Law award Cumberland Sch. Law and U. Heidelberg Germany Faculty of Law, 1990; endowed Jeanne Pittman ann. Bioethics and the Law Top Paper award Washburn U. Coll. Law, Topeka, 1995. Fellow Internat. Coll. Angiology, Royal Soc. Health, Internat. Coll. Surgeons, Am. Coll. Legal Medicine; mem. AMA, Congress Neurol. Surgeons, Fla. Med. Assn., Fla. Bar, Phi Beta Kappa, Phi Delta Phi. Jeffersonian Democrat. Avocations: stamp collecting/philately, anthropology, travel.

PITTMAN, VIRGIL, federal judge; b. Enterprise, Ala., Mar. 28, 1916; s. Walter Oscar and Annie Lee (Logan) P.; m. Floy Lasseter, 1944 (dec.) 2000; children— Karen Pittman Gordy, Walter Lee; m. Lily Davis Verneuille, Mar. 15, 2002. BS, U. Ala., 1939, LL.B., 1940. Bar: Ala. bar 1940. Spl. agt. FBI, 1940-44; practice law Gadsden, Ala., 1946-51; judge Ala. Circuit Ct., Circuit 16, 1951-66; U.S. dist. judge Middle and So. Dist. Ala., 1966-71; chief judge U.S. Dist. Ct. for Ala. So. Dist., 1971-81, sr. judge, 1981—. Lectr. bus. law, econs. and polit. sci. U. Ala. Center, Gadsden, 1948-66 Author: Circuit Court Proceedings in Acquisition of a Tract of Right of Way, 1959, A Judge Looks at Right of Way Condemnation Proceedings, 1960, Technical Pitfalls in Right of Way Proceedings, 1961. Mem. Ala. Bd. Edn., 1951; bd. trustees, life trustee Samford U, 1975-; past bd. dirs., chmn. bd. Bapt. Oaks. Lt. (j.g.) USN, 1944-46, USS Wharton, Pacific Supply Corp. Mem. Ala. State Bar, Etowah County Bar Assn. (pres. 1949), Omicron Delta Kappa. Democrat. Baptist. Office: US Dist Ct 113 Saint Joseph St Mobile AL 36602

PITTMAN, WILLIAM CLAUDE, electrical engineer; b. Pontotoc, Miss., Apr. 22, 1921; s. William Claude and Maude Ella (Bennett) P.; m. Eloise Savage, Apr. 20, 1952; children: Patricia A. Pittman Ready, William Claude III, Thomas Allen. BSEE, Miss. State Coll., 1951, MSEE, 1957. From electronic engr. to supr. elec. engring. dept. U.S. Army Labs., Redstone Arsenal, Ala., 1951-59; supr. electronic engr. to aero. engring. supr. NASA/Marshall Space Flight Ctr., 1960; electronic engr. Army Missile Labs., 1962-82; program mgr. Army Labs. and R&D Ctr., Redstone Arsenal, 1982-99; vol. cons. Army Aviation and Missile Rsch., Devel. and Engring. Ctr., 1999—. Organizer numerous sci. and tech. confs. Author patents, reports, papers Sgt. USMC, 1940-46, PTO. Recipient Medal of Honor, DAR, Meritorious Civilian Svc. award Dept. Army, 1993. Fellow AIAA (assoc.; chmn. Miss.-Ala. chpt. 1981-82, Martin Schilling award 1980); mem. IEEE (sr. life), First Marine Div. Assn., DAV, IRE (chmn. Huntsville sect. 1957-58), Madison Hist. Soc., SAR (pres. Tenn. Valley chpt. 1984-85, Ala. Soc. 1990-91, Cert. 1991, Patriot medal), Tau Beta Pi, Phi Kappa Phi, Kappa Mu Epsilon. Avocations: history, genealogy. Home: 704 Desoto Rd SE Huntsville AL 35801-2032 Office: US Army Aviation Missile Command Huntsville AL 35898-5000 Office Phone: 256-876-1778. Personal E-mail: bill.pittman@amrdec.army.mi, wcpittman@comcast.net.

PITTONI, LUKE M., lawyer; b. Rockville, NY, May 14, 1945; s. Mario and Grace (Henjes) P.; m. Mary Jo Rocque, July 8, 1972; children: Elizabeth, Katherine, Ellen. BA in Econs., Holy Cross Coll., 1967; JD, Fordham U., 1971. Bar: N.Y. 1972, U.S. Ct. Appeals (2d. cir.) 1975, U.S. Dist. Ct. (so. and ea. dists.) N.Y. 1975, U.S. Supreme Ct. 1976, U.S. Dist. Ct. Conn. 1977, Conn. 1986. Assoc. Martin, Clearwater & Bell, NYC, 1972-75; trial atty. Anthony L. Schiavetti, NYC, 1975-78; assoc. Alexander & Green, NYC, 1978-79; ptnr. Heidell, Pittoni, Murphy & Bach, P.C., NYC, 1979—. Mem. ABA, Conn. Bar Assn., N.Y. State Bar Assn., Am. Bd. Profl. Liability Attys., Am. Bd. Trial Advocates (past pres. NYC chpt.), N.Y. State Med. Def. Lawyers Assn.(founder, past pres.), N.Y. State Med. Def. Bar Assn. (founder, pres. 1995-97), Def. Rsch. Inst., Internat. Assn. Def. Counsel. Home: 283 Quarry Rd Stamford CT 06903-5011 Office: Heidell Pittoni Murphy & Bach 99 Park Ave Fl 7 New York NY 10016-1506 Office Phone: 212-286-8585. Personal E-mail: lpittoni@hpmb.com.

PITTS, ALLIE FAYE, retired elementary school educator; d. Buck William and Lizzie Faye Hillyer; m. Jesse James Pitts (dec.); children: Joe, Margaret Evans. BS, Samuel Huston Coll., Austin, Tex., 1944; MS, Prairie View U., Tex., 1950. Tchr. Berclair Sch. Sys., Tex., 1936, Refugio Sch. Dist., Tex., 1939—40, Corpus Christi Sch. Dist., Tex., 1944—80, elem. counselor, 1970—80, ret., 1980. Sec. Mt. Zion Dist. Bd., Cuero, Tex., 1996—2006. Named Zeta of the Yr., Zeta Phi Beta Sorority, Inc., 1965, Woman of the Yr. in Bus., Delta Sigma Theta Sorority, 1975, Woman of the Yr., Bus. and Profl. Women, 1975; named to Tex. Black Women Hall of Fame, Mus. African Am. Life and Culture, 1986; recipient Svc. in Edn. award, Cap. City Creative Sch., 1980, Appreciation award, Deb Mothers Club, 2000. Mem.: NAACP (life; mem. exec. bd. 1986—2006, named Torch Bearer 2001), Ret. Tchrs. Assn. (assoc.; sec. 2001—06), Ladies Camellia Social Club (life; pres. 1956—2006, treas. 1956—2006, v.p. 1956—2006, 50 Yr. Svc. award 2006), Zeta Phi Beta Sorority, Inc. (life; pres. 1945—2005, treas. 1945—2005, v.p. 1945—2005, palimentarian 1945—2005, 60 Years Svc. award 2005). Democrat. Baptist. Avocation: travel. Home Phone: 361-853-4104.

PITTS, ANDREW J., lawyer; b. Rochester, NY, Nov. 11, 1966; BA, Trinity Coll., 1988; JD summa cum laude, Boston Univ., 1994, MBA, 1995. Bar: NY 1995. Assoc. Cravath Swaine & Moore LLP, NYC, 1995—2003, ptnr., corp., 2003—. Notes editor Boston Law Rev. Recipient Alumni Achievement award, Boston Univ. Office: Cravath Swaine & Moore LLP Worldwide Plz 825 Eighth Ave New York NY 10019-7475 Office Phone: 212-474-1620. Office Fax: 212-474-3700. Business E-Mail: apitts@cravath.com.

PITTS, BEVERLEY J., academic administrator; m. William Pitts; 2 children. BA in English, Anderson U., 1968; MA in Journalism, Ball State U., 1971, EdD in Higher Edn., 1981. Chair, dept. comm. Anderson U., 1980—85; coord., News Editl. Sequence Ball State U., 1985—88, dir. grad. studies in journalism, 1985—88, dir. gen. studies, 1988—90, dir. academic assessment and general studies, 1990, asst. provost, exec. dir.

rsch. and undergraduate curriculum, 1990—92, acting provost, 1994, 2001, acting supr. for information technology, 2000—01, assoc. provost, 1993—2002, provost, v.p. for academic affairs, 2002, acting pres., 2004; pres. U. Indpls., 2005—. Instr. english Anderson U., 1977—80, advisor student publs., 1977—85, asst. prof. comm., 1980—85; assoc. prof. journalism Ball State U., 1985—90, prof. journalism, 1991—. Staff writer, researcher, comm. cons. Nat. Football League Players Assn., Washington, DC (Nat. Football League Players Assn. award of Excellence, 2000); contbr. articles to profl. jours. and newspapers; book review editor College Media Review, 1982—85; design editor College Media Review, 1985—86; reviewer Journalism Educator, 1990—99, grant reviewer Nat. Endowment for the Humanities, 1990, co-publisher (textbook) The Process of Media Writing, 1997, editl. bd. mem. Perspectives, Journal of the Association of General and Liberal Studies, 1997—2001, co-founder Ind. Teachers of Writing, 1981, pres., 1982—83, program chair, fall conf., 1982. Bd. dir. Family Svcs. of Delaware County, 1999—2002, Lyn St. James Found., 2000—02, Cmty. Alliance to Promote Edn., 2001—03, Delaware County CofC, 2003—, Sagamore Inst., 2004—, Ind. Youth Inst., 2000—, chair, 2005; bd. dir. Muncie Rotary Club, 2000—04, sec., 2000—01, pres.-elect, 2001—02, pres., 2002—03; mem. Cmty. Found. Muncie, Ind. Humanities Coun.; bd. dir. pres. Prof. Garfield Found., 2004—; bd. dir. Delaware County Cmty. Found., 2000—, vice-chair, 2003—04, chair-elect, 2005; and several others. Recipient Anderson U. Outstanding Alumni award, 1999, Ball State U. Alumni award, 2000, Woman of Acheivement in Edn. award, Women in Communication; Ottoway Fellowship for Advanced Study, Am. Press Inst., Reston, Va., Ottoway Newspaper Found., 1986, Am. Press Inst. Fellowship for Advanced Study for Journalism Educators, 1987, Fellowship, Think Tank, Coll. of Scis. and Humanities, Ball State U., 1988, Fulbright Scholarship to study in Germany, 1994. Mem.: Assn. for General and Liberal Studies (nat. bd. dir. 1989—94, pres. 1993—94), Assn. for Edn. in Journalism and Mass Comm., Am. Conf. Academic Deans, Am. Assn. U. Adminstrators, Am. Assn. Higher Edn., Nat. Football League Players Assn. (cons. 1984—), Profl. Atheletes Found. (bd. dir. 1990—2004), Sigma Delta Chi. Office: U Indpls 1400 East Hanna Ave Indianapolis IN 46227-3697 Office Phone: 317-788-3211.

PITTS, EDGAR THURLOW, writer, retired educator; b. Rockport, Maine, Sept. 5, 1919; s. George Edgar and Mildred Nettie (Thurlow) Pitts; m. Elizabeth Knowlton, Dec. 21, 1942 (dec. May 1993); 1 child, Nathan Thurlow. BA with hons. in Math., U. Maine, 1942; diploma, U.S. Naval Acad., 1943; MEd in Adminstrn., U. Maine, 1953. Cert. tchr., prin., supt. schs. Maine. Math. tchr./prin. Stonington (Maine) H.S., 1946—53; prin. Ellsworth (Maine) H.S., 1953—70; supervising prin. Five Towns Sch. Dist., Western Hancock County, Maine, 1970—73; pvt. math. tchr. Eastern Maine, 1974—82. Co-author: Deer Isle Remembered, 1989, Stonington Past and Present, 1997; author: Long Ago and Far Away, 1936-45, 2d edit., 2001. Founder, chmn. Acad. Recognition Commn., State of Maine, 1959—63; various ad hoc com. chairs state, regional and local edn., Maine, 1960—98; past pres., exec. com. Main Tchrs. Assn. Lt. USNR, 1942—46. Mem.: NEA, Maine Edn. Assn. (life), Am. Legion (post comdr. 1997—2000), Masons, Phi Beta Kappa. Republican. Avocations: stamp collecting/philately, local and regional history, e-mail. Home: PO Box 14 Thurlow's Hill Stonington ME 04681 Office: Polaris Press PO Box 14 Stonington ME 04681 Office Phone: 207-367-2483.

PITTS, GARY BENJAMIN, lawyer; b. Miss., Aug. 23, 1952; s. Dextar Derwood and Eva Margaret (Bush) Pitts; m. Nicole Palmer; children: Andrew Ross, Caitlan Taylor, Austin Palmer, Chloe Nicole. Student, U. Miss., Oxford, 1970-71, Charleston Coll., SC, 1971-73; BA, McGill U., Montreal, Que., Can., 1973-74; JD, Tulane U., New Orleans, 1979. Bar: Tex. 1979, U.S. Ct. Appeals (5th cir.) 1980, U.S. Supreme Ct. 1983. Assoc. Julian & Seele, Houston, 1979-84, Ogletree, Pitts & Collard, Houston, 1984-85; ptnr. Pitts & Collard LLP, Houston and Dallas, 1985-96; owner Pitts & Assocs., Houston, 1996—. Capt. USNG, 1975-87. Office: Pitts & Assocs 8866 Gulf Fwy Ste 117 Houston TX 77017-6528 Office Phone: 713-910-0555. E-mail: defensebasecomp@aol.com.

PITTS, GREGORY SCOTT, corporate financial executive; s. Richard Alton Pitts and Shirley Virginia Healy. BS, US Mil. Acad., West Point, NY, 1983. Gen. mgr. ITW, Paslode Fla., Plant City, 1992—95; bus. devel. mgr. Oracle Software, Tampa, 1995—97; regional sales mgr. PeopleSoft, Tampa, 1997—2000; bus. devel. exec. Deloitte & Touche, Tampa, 2000—. Maj US Army, 1983—92, Korea, Okla., BC. Mem.: Mensa (assoc.). Independent. Avocations: music, travel, reading, sailing. Home Phone: 813-643-9237.

PITTS, JAMES ATWATER, finance company executive; b. Greenwich, Conn., Apr. 8, 1940; s. Jeremiah Patrick and Mary Louise (McGregor) P.; m. Noreen Mary Kiggins, July 20, 1963; children: Paul, Andrew, Sarah. BBA with honors, Niagara U., 1962; MBA, U. Conn., 1971; student in Advanced Mgmt. Program, Harvard Bus. Sch., Cambridge, Mass., 1985. CPA, N.Y. Staff acct. Price Waterhouse, Stamford, Conn., 1962; tax specialist Deloitte Haskins & Sells, Rochester, NY, 1965-68; div. contr. Xerox Corp., Stamford, 1968-76; asst. corp. contr. Digital Equipment Corp., Maynard, Mass., 1976-81; v.p., corp. contr. Data Gen. Corp., Westboro, Mass., 1981-86; exec. v.p. fin. adminstrn. and strategic planning Cullinet Software, Inc., Westwood, 1986-88; v.p., chief fin. officer Bain & Co. Inc., Boston, 1988-91; sr. v.p. fin. and adminstrn., treas., CFO Clean Harbors Inc., 1992-96; v.p. for fin. and adminstrn. The Boston Found., 1996—2004, chief investment officer, 2004, treas., 2004; ret., 2004. Bd. dirs. Wainright Bank & Trust Co., 2005—, mem. audit com., 2005—, mem. exec. com., 2005—. Chmn. Sudbury Town Fin. Com., Mass., 1984; v.p., mem. exec. com. Children's Mus. Boston, 1984-96; bd. dirs. Mus. Wharf Inc., 1988-96, Lake Winniepesaukee Assn., Wolfeboro, NH; chmn. Sudbury Long Range Capital Expenditures Com., 1981; trustee Lake Regional Conservation Trust, Meridith, NH; pres. Springfield Point Assn., 2000-. With US Army, 1963-64, USAR, 1965-90, Desert Storm, 1991. Decorated Meritorious Svc. medal, 1991; recipient Internat. Exec. Mgmt. award Internat. Mgmt. Inst. U. Geneva, 1980. Mem. AICPAs, Conn. CPA Soc., N.Y. Soc. CPAs, Fin. Execs. Inst., Harvard Bus. Sch. Assn. Boston (bd. govs. 1992-96, alumni treas. 2005—, audit com.), Nat. Assn. Corp. Dirs. (bd. dirs. New Eng. chpt. 2005-, chair audit com. New Eng. chpt., 2005-), Harvard Bus. Sch. Alumni Assn. (treas. 2005-), Res. Officers Assn. (life), Soc. Mil. Compts., Bald Peak Colony Club, Officers Club Mailing: 139A Charles St 222 Boston MA 02114 Home Phone: 617-227-5544. Personal E-mail: jamesapitts@aol.com.

PITTS, JAMES T., lawyer; b. Mar. 21, 1949; BA, Hendrix Coll., 1970; JD, Univ. Ark., 1973; LLM, Georgetown Univ., 1984. Bar: Ark. 1973, DC 1986. Acting Securities Commr. State of Ark.; staff mem. House Commerce, Consumer and Monetary Affairs Subcom.; various positions to asst. dir. Securities/Corporate Practices Divsn., Office of Comptroller US Treasury Dept.; ptnr. Winston & Strawn, Washington, 1987—2002; ptnr., transp. law Venable LLP, Washington, 2002—. Office: Venable LLP 575 Seventh St NW Washington DC 20004 Office Phone: 202-344-4687. Office Fax: 202-344-8300. Business E-Mail: jtpitts@venable.com.

PITTS, JOSEPH R. (JOE PITTS), congressman; b. Lexington, Ky., Oct. 10, 1939; s. Joseph S. and Pearl Jackson Pitts; m. Virginia Pratt, 1961; children: Karen R., Carol J., Daniel J. AB in Philos. and Religion, Asbury Coll., Wilmore, Ky., 1961; MEd in Comprehensive Sci., West Chester U., Pa., 1972. Tchr. math., sci., english and phys. ed. Mortonsville Elem. Sch., Versailles, Ky., 1962—63; tchr. math. and sci. Great Valley HS, Malvern, Pa., 1969—72; mem. Pa. State Ho. Reps. from Dist. 158, 1973—97; owner, operator landscape nursery, Unionville, Pa., 1974—90; mem. US Congress from 16th Pa. dist., 1997—, mem. energy and commerce com., 2001—. Transp. com. State of Pa., 1977-80, appropriations com., 1979-82, rep. policy com., chmn. labor rels. com., transp. and joint legis. budget and fin. coms., chmn. rep. appropriations com., 1989. 2nd lt. to capt. USAF, 1963—69. Decorated Air medal with five oak leaf clusters; recipient Pub. Servant award Chester-Del. Pomona Grange, 1980, Cmty. Leadership award Pa. for Biblical Morality, 1984, Disting. Govt. Svc. award Am. Mushroom Inst., 1985, Defender of Life award Pro Life Coalition S.E. Pa., 1985, William Penn award Pa. FACTS, 1985, Small Bus. Champion award Small Bus. Survival Com., 1999-2003, Best and Brightest award Am. Conservative Union, 2000, Friend of the Shareholder award Am. Shareholders Assn., 2000-2003, Taxpayer's Friend award Nat. Taxpayer's Union, 2000-2003, Silver Eagle award Pakistani Assn. N.Am., 2001. Mem.: NRA, Brandywine Valley Assn., VFW Post 5467, Rotary. Republican. Office: PO Box 837 Unionville PA 19375 Office Phone: 202-225-2411, 610-444-4581. Office Fax: 610-444-5750. *

PITTS, LEONARD GARVEY, JR., columnist, writer; b. Orange, Calif., Oct. 11, 1957; s. Leonard Garvey and Agnes (Rowan) P.; m. Marilyn Vernice Pickens, June 27, 1981; children: Markise Pickens, Monique Pickens; (stepchildren) Marlon, Leonard, Onjél. BA English, U. So. Calif., 1977. Editor, writer Soul Mag., LA, 1976-80; writer KFWB Radio, LA, 1980-83; editor Radioscope, LA, 1983-86; writer Westwood One Inc., Culver City, Calif., 1989-91; columnist, writer Miami (Fla.) Herald, 1991—. Writer, co-producer (broadcast) King: From Atlanta to the Mountaintop, 1986 (CEBA award 1987), (documentary) Young Black Men: A Lost Generation?, 1990 (Armstrong award 1991); writer, producer (documentary) Who We Are, 1988 (CEBA award 1989). Recipient Internat. Radio Festival award, 1991, Nat. Headliner award Arts criticsm, 1991, Pulitzer Prize for commentary, 2004. Mem. Fla. Soc. Newspaper Editors (award arts criticism), Nat. Headliners, Am. Assn. Sunday and Feature Editors (award arts criticism 1991), Nat. Assn. of Black Journalists (Award of Execllence in commentary 1994, 95). Democrat. Baptist. Avocations: computer strategy games, reading. Office: Miami Herald One Herald Plaza Miami FL 33132

PITTS, MELISSA DAWN, underwriter; b. Carthage, Ill., Mar. 11, 1977; d. John Christopher and Janice LaVonne Train; m. Marcus Anthony Pitts, May 30, 2004. B in Bus., Pacific Luth. U., Parkland, Wash., 2000, M in Bus., 2006. Cert. sales Omega, 2001. Loan officer Rainier Pacific, Federal Way, Wash., 2000—01; comml. underwriting specialist Travelers Bond, Federal Way, 2001—. Mentor Big Sisters Am., Tacoma, 2001—03; vol. Girl Scouts Fostering a Future, Kent, Wash. Mem.: Seattle Surety Assn., Mensa, Plus Bus. Club, Beta Gamma Sigma. Democrat. Avocations: reading, rollerskating, exercise. Office: Travelers Bond 33650 S 336th St Ste 200 Federal Way WA 98003

PITYNSKI, ANDRZEJ PIOTR, sculptor; b. Ulanow, Poland, Mar. 15, 1947; naturalized citizen, 1987; s. Aleksander and Stefania (Krupa) P.; m. Christina Teresa Gacek, Aug. 6, 1976; 1 child, Alexander Mark. MFA in Sculpture, Acad. Fine Arts, Cracow, Poland, 1974; postgrad., Art Students League, NYC, 1975. Cert. tchr., N.J.; supr. modeling, mold, enlarging, resin crafts. Supr. and instr. sculpture Tech. Inst. of Sculpture - Johnson Atelier, Mercerville, NJ, 1979—; instr. sculpture Rider U., Lawrenceville, NJ, 1992—97, Rutgers U., NJ, 1998—2002. Asst. to sculptor Alexander Ettl, Sculpture House, N.Y., 1975-79 Bronze/granite monumental sculptures include Shield of Honor, Ulanow, Poland, 2004, Count J. Tarnowski, Tarnobrzeg, Poland, 2003, General Kosciuszko, St. Petersburg, Fla., 2002, Sarmatian - Spirit of Freedom, Hamilton, N.J., 2001, Flame of Freedom, Balt., 2000, Blue Army-1998, Warsaw, Poland, Katyn-1940, Jersey City, N.J., 1991-92, Pope John Paul II, Manhattan, N.Y., 1991, Ulanow, Poland, 1989, General Anders, Doylestown, Pa., 1995, Father J. Popieluszko, Trenton, N.J., 1987, Avenger, Doylestown, Pa., 1987, Portrait Bust M Curie, 1986, Bayonne, N.J.; aluminum sculpture Partisans II, Hamilton, N.J., 1999, Partisans, Boston, 1983, Ignacy Paderewski, Cracow, Poland, 1973; one-man show at Hamilton, N.J., 2000, N.Y., 2001; exhbn. Mus. of Polish Army, Warsaw, 1995, Contemporary Artists Guild, Lever House, N.Y., 1991—, Zacheta Nat. Art Gallery, Warsaw, 1991, Fedn. Internat. De La Medaille/Brit. Mus., London, 1992, Cast Iron Gallery, Soho, N.Y., 1992, Alt. Ext. Gallery, Phila., 1992, Audubon Exhibits-54th Ann. Exhbn., Fed. Hall, N.Y.C., others. Recipient Polonia Restituta Cross, R.P. London, 1989, Gold Order of Merit, Rep. of Poland, 1990, Cultural award Am. Inst. Polish Culture, Washington, 1992; named Comdr. Order Merit of Republic of Poland, 1996, The Monuments Conservancy's Perennial Wisdom award-medal, N.Y.C., 1999, Honorary Citizen of Balt., 2001. Fellow Nat. Sculpture Soc.; mem. Allied Artists of Am. (Silver medal of honor 1985, Elliot Liskin Meml. award 1989, Mems. and Assocs. award 1994), Audubon Artists (Gold Medal of Honor 1996, Silver Medal of Honor 1997, 98), Contemporary Artists Guild, Am. Medallic Sculpture Assn. Republican. Roman Catholic. Avocations: horse jumping, hunting, Judo. Office: PO Box 220380 Brooklyn NY 11222 Office Phone: 609-510-8926. E-mail: andrewpitynski@comcast.net.

PITZ, ROBERT WENDELL, professor mechanical engineering; b. Aurora, Ill., Nov. 24, 1950; s. Wendell Edward and Anne (Benson) P.; m. Carol Elizabeth Armes; children: Matthew Robert, Anna Elizabeth BSME, Purdue U., 1973; MSME, U. Calif., Berkeley, 1976, PhDME, 1981. Staff scientist GE R&D, Schenectady, N.Y., 1981-86; asst. prof. Mech. Engring. Vanderbilt U., Nashville, 1986-89, assoc. prof. Mech. Engring., 1989—94, prof., 1994—. Contbr. articles to profl. jours. Recipient Presdl. Young Investigator NSF, 1987. Fellow Am. Assn. Mech. Engrs. (faculty advisor 1986); mem. AIAA, Optical Soc. Am., Am. Phys. Soc Office: Vanderbilt U Mech Engring PO Box 1592 Nashville TN 37202-0054 Office Phone: 615-322-0209.

PITZNER, RICHARD WILLIAM, lawyer; b. Fond du Lac, Wis., Sept. 19, 1946; s. Robert J. and Almira (Wurtz) P.; m. Georgene J. Thuerwachter, July 6, 1968 (div. 1991); children: Christie, Kyle; m. Ricki L. Mundstock, Jan. 4, 1998. BBA, U. Wis., 1968, MBA, 1969, JD, 1972. Bar: Wis. 1972, U.S. Dist. Ct. (we. dist.) Wis. 1972, U.S. Tax Ct. Ptnr. Murphy & Desmond, Madison, Wis., 1972—. Tchr. U. Wis., Madison, 1975-78. Named to Best Lawyers in Am., Super Lawyers in Wis. Mem. ABA, AICPA, Nat. Assn. Accts., Wis. Inst. CPAs, State Bar Wis., Wis. Inst. CPAs, Kensington Golf and Country Club, Nakoma Golf Club, Order of Coif, Beta Gamma Sigma. Avocations: golf, swimming. Home: 3123 Harlan Circle Madison WI 53711 Office: Murphy & Desmond 2 E Mifflin St Madison WI 53703-2889 Office Phone: 608-268-5568. Business E-Mail: rpitzner@murphydesmond.com.

PIUCCI, VIRGINIO LOUIS, academic administrator; b. Peekskill, NY, Nov. 1, 1925; s. Virginio and Marguerita (DiGregorio) P.; m. Elizabeth Logan, Mar. 25, 1951; children: Stephen, Mark, Matthew, Anthony, Andrew. BE, SUNY, New Paltz, 1949; MA, Columbus U., 1951; EdD, U. Fla., Gainesville, 1955; PhD (hon.), Internat. U., Vienna, Austria, 1999. Tchr. Suffern, NYC, 1949-51; instr. SUNY, Oneonta, 1951-52, assoc. prof., 1955-56, prof. edn. Oswego, dir. edn., 1962-65; dean profl. studies, prof. R.I. Coll., Providence, 1966-70; v.p. rsch. and innovation Govs. State U., University Park, Ill., 1971-77, v.p. Inst. Rsch. and Planning, 1977-82, v.p. adminstrv. planning, prof. pub. adminstrn., 1982-92, v.p. emeritus, 1992—. Hon. prof. pedadogy Moscow External U. for Humanities; founder, pres. emeritus European-Am. U. Forum, West Ga. tech. Coll., Waco, Ga. Decorated knight Order of Merit (Italy); recipient Univ. medallion U. Sassari, Italy; U. Fla. fellow. Mem. Am. Assn. Univ. Adminstrs. (Eileen M. Tosney award for excellence in practice of higher edn. adminstrn. 1992). Democrat. Roman Catholic. Avocations: reading, politics, baseball. Home and Office: 22460 Lakeshore Dr Richton Park IL 60471-1607 Fax: 708-748-9760. E-mail: vpivcci@aol.com.

PIUZE, MICHAEL JOSEPH, lawyer; b. Worcester, Mass., July 31, 1944; s. Albert Charles Piuze and Pauline (Sadick); m. Marnie Smart, Apr. 24, 1971; children: Nicole, Stephanie, Kate. BA, Lake Forest Coll., 1967; JD, U. Tex., Austin, 1971. Bar: Calif. 1972. Atty. Gilbert, Kelly, Crowley & Jennett, LA, 1972—75; sr. mem. Law Offices Michael J. Piuze, LA, 1973—. Named LA Trial Lawyer of Yr., 1996, Southern Calif. Trial Lawyer of Yr., 1998, Calif. Lawyer of Yr., 2001, Winningest Lawyer in US, Nat. Law Jour., 2001, 2002; named one of Best Lawyers in Am., 1993—2006, Top 10 Super Lawyers, LA Mag., 2004, Top 100 LA County Super Lawyers, 2004, 2005, 2006, Top 100 Calif. Atty., Daily Jour., 2000—06, Top 10 Litigators, Nat. Law Jour., 2003. Mem.: LA Trial Lawyers Assn., Calif. Trial Lawyers Assn., Assn. Trial Lawyers Am. Office: 11755 Wilshire Blvd Ste 1170 Los Angeles CA 90025 Office Phone: 310-312-1102. Office Fax: 310-473-0708. Business E-Mail: mpiuze@mjplaw.net.

PIVEN, FRANCES FOX, political scientist, educator; b. Calgary, Alta., Can., Oct. 10, 1932; arrived in U.S., 1933, naturalized, 1953; d. Albert and Rachel (Paperny) F.; 1 dau., Sarah. BA, U. Chgo., 1953, MA, 1956, PhD, 1962; L.H.D. (hon.), Adelphi U., 1985. Mem. faculty Columbia, 1966-72; prof. polit. sci. Boston U., 1972-82, Grad. Ctr., CUNY, 1982—. Co-author: Regulating the Poor: The Functions of Public Welfare, 1971, 2d edit., 1993, The Politics of Turmoil: Essays on Poverty, Race and the Urban Crisis, 1974, Poor People's Movements, 1977, New Class War, 1982, The Mean Season, 1987, Why Americans Don't Vote, 1988; editor: Labor Parties in Post Industrial Societies, 1992, The Breaking of the American Social Compact, 1997, Why Americans Still Don't Vote, 2000, Work, Welfare and Politics, 2002, The War at Home, 2004, Challenging Authority, 2006. Recipient C. Wright Mills award Soc. Study Social Problems, 1971, Fulbright Disting. Lectureship award U. Bologna, 1990, President's award APHA, 1993, Annual award Nat. Assn. Sec. of State, 1994, Lifetime Achievement award Pol. Sociology Am. Sociological Assn., 1995, Disting. Career award, 2000, Pub. Understanding of Sociology award, 2003; Guggenheim fellow, 1973-74; Am. Coun. Learned Socs. awardee, 1982. Mem. ACLU, Am. Polit. Sci. Assn. (v.p. 1981-82), Soc. Study Social Problems (pres. 1980-81, Lee founders award 1992), Am. Sociol. Assn. (pres. 2006-). Home: PO Box N Millerton NY 12546-0651 Office: CUNY Grad Sch 365 5th Ave New York NY 10016-4309 Business E-Mail: ffox-piven@gc.cuny.edu.

PIVEN, JEREMY, actor; b. New York, New York, July 26, 1965; s. Byrne and Joyce Piven. Student, Drake U. Actor: (films) Lucas, 1986, One Crazy Summer, 1986, Say Anything, 1989, Elvis Stories, 1989, The Grifters, 1990, White Palace, 1990, The Player, 1992, Body Chemistry II: The Voice of a Stranger, 1992, Bob Roberts, 1992, Singles, 1992, There Goes the Neighborhood, 1992, Judgement Night, 1993, Twenty Bucks, 1993, Car 54, Where Are You?, 1994, Floundering, 1994, PCU, 1994, Twogether, 1994, The Ticket, 1994, Miami Rhapsody, 1995, Dr. Jekyll and Ms. Hyde, 1995, Heat, 1995, Larger Than Life, 1996, Layin' Low, 1996, E=mc—2, 1996, Just Write, 1997, Grosse Pointe Blank, 1997, Livers Ain't Cheap, 1997, Kiss the Girls, 1997, Phoenix, 1998, Very Bad Things, 1998, Music From Another Room, 1998, Red Letters, 2000, The Crew, 2000, The Family Man, 2000, Rush Hour 2, 2001, Serendipity, 2001, Black Hawk Down, 2001, Highway, 2002, Me and Daphne, 2002, Old School, 2003, Runaway Jury, 2003, Scary Movie 3, Chasing Liberty, 2004, Two for the Money, 2005, Keeping Up with the Steins, 2006, Smokin' Aces, 2006, (voice) Cars, 2006,: (TV films) 12:01, 1993, Don King: Only in America, 1997, Partners, 1999; (TV series) Carol & Company, 1990, Rugrats (voice), 1991, The Larry Sanders Show, 1992—93, Pride and Joy, 1995, Ellen, 1995—98, Cupid, 1998, Entourage, 2004— (Emmy award for Outstanding Supporting Actor in a comedy series, 2006); (Broadway plays) Fat Pig, 2004. *

PIVEN, PETER ANTHONY, architect, management consultant; b. Bklyn., Jan. 3, 1939; s. William Meyer and Sylvia Lee (Greenberg) P.; m. Caroline Cooper, July 9, 1961; children: Leslie Ann, Joshua Lawrence. AB, Colgate U., Hamilton, NY, 1960; MArch, U. Pa., Phila., 1963; MS, Columbia U., NYC, 1964. Diplomate: cert. Nat. Coun. Archtl. Registration Bds.; registered arch., NY, Pa., NJ. Arch. Westermann-Miller Assocs., NYC, 1964-66, Bernard Rothzeid, A.I.A., NYC, 1967-68; v.p. Caudill Rowlett Scott, NYC, 1968-72; prin. Geddes Brecher Qualls Cunningham, Phila., 1972-87; pres. The Coxe Group, Inc., Phila., 1980-90, dir., prin. cons., 1980—. Adj. prof. U. Pa. Grad. Sch. Fine Arts, 1989—, Rensselaer Poly. Inst. Sch. Architecture, 1994—; vis. instr. Harvard U. Grad. Sch. Design.; lectr. U. Pa. Sch. Design, 2005; mem. 14th edit. com. Architects Handbook Profl. Practice. Author: Compensation Management: A Guideline for Small Firms, 1982, Architect's Essentials of Ownership Transition, 2002; co-author: Success Strategies for Design Professionals, 1987, Architect's Essentials of Starting a Design Firm, 2003; contbg. editor: Archtl. Record and Design Intelligence; author (contbg.): Architects Handbook of Professional Practice, 1994, 2001, Architects Handbook of Professional Practice Update, 2004, 2005, 2006. Mem. NYC Cmty. Planning Bd., 1969-72. Fellow AIA (chmn. fin. mgmt. com. 1976-80, chmn. Fellows Jury 1998, mem. conv. task force 1998, mem. Nat. Ethics Coun. 1998-2004, chmn. 2004, pres. Phila. chpt. 1980); mem. Phila. C. of C. (dir. 1980-81), The Carpenters Co. of City and County of Phila. (mng. com. 1989-91). Home: Apt 10 201 Queen St Philadelphia PA 19147 Office: The Coxe Group Inc 1218 3rd Ave Seattle WA 98101-3097 Home Phone: 215-952-2780. Business E-Mail: ppiven@coxegroup.com.

PIVER, M. STEVEN, gynecologic oncologist; b. Washington, Sept. 29, 1934; s. Harry Samuel and Sonia (Bard) P.; m. Susan Myers, June 25, 1958; children: Debra Ellen, Carolyn Jan, Kenneth Stuart. BS, Gettysburg Coll., 1957; MD, Temple U., 1961. Diplomate Am. Bd. Ob-Gyn, Am. Coll. Surgeons. Intern Nazareth Hosp., Phila., 1961—62; resident Johns Hopkins U. Hosp., Balt., 1962; resident ob-gyn. Pa. Hosp. U. Pa., Phila., 1965—68; fellow gynecologic oncology Hosp. Tumor Inst. U. Tex., Houston, 1968—70; asst. prof. gynecologic oncology UNC Sch. Medicine, 1970—71; assoc. chief gynecologic oncology Roswell Park Cancer Inst., Buffalo, 1972—83, founder, dir. Gilda Radner Familial Ovarian Cancer Registry, 1981—, chief gynecologic oncology, 1984—97; clin. prof., dir. divsn. gynecologic oncology SUNY, Buffalo, 1986—87, prof. gynecology, 1998—, chair emeritus gynecologic oncology, 1998—. Cons., editor Yearbook of Cancer, 1972-88; assoc. editor Nat. Cancer Inst., PDQ, 1984—; mem. editl. bd. The Female Patient, 1989—, Oncology Reports, 1993—; author: Ovarian Malignancies: Clinical Care of Adults and Adolescents, 1983, Gilda's Disease: Sharing Personal Experiences and a Medical Perspective on Ovarian Cancer, 1996, Myths and Facts About Ovarian Cancer, 1997; editor: Ovarian Malignancies: Diagnostic and Therapeutic Advances, 1987, Manual of Gynecologic Oncology/Gynecology, 1989, Conversations About Cancer, 1990, Handbook of Gynecologic Oncology, 1995; contbr. more than 300 articles to profl. jours. Bd. dirs. United Way Buffalo Erie County, 1986-91; chmn. bd. trustees D'Youville Coll., Buffalo, 1989—; pres. Friends Night People, Buffalo, 1988-97. Capt. USAF, 1962-64. Hon. fellow Phi Beta Kappa, Gettysburg Coll., 1956, Tex. Assn. Obstetricians Gynecologists, 1983, Alpha Omega Alpha, Temple U. Sch. Medicine, 1995; named Citizen Yr., Buffalo News, 1989; recipient YMCA Leadership award Buffalo YMCA, 1990, Brotherhood/Sisterhood Award Medicine (Western NY Region), NCCJ, 1991, St. Marguerite D'Youville Coll. Cmty. Svc. award, 1992. Fellow ACS, Am. Coll. Obstetricians and Gynecologists; mem. Am. Soc. Clin. Oncology, Soc. Gynecologic Oncologists, Soc. Surg. Oncology, Am. Radium Soc., Phi Beta Kappa, Alpha Omega Alpha. Achievements include documentation of hydroxyurea as a radiation sensitizer in cervix cancer that significantly improves cure rate and that ovarian cancer can be inherited; patent for method of enhancing the efficacy of anti-tumor agents. Home: 315 Lincoln Pky Buffalo NY 14216-3127 Office: Sisters Hosp 2157 Main St Buffalo NY 14214-2692 Business E-Mail: mpiver@chsbuffalo.org.

PIWNICA-WORMS, HELEN M., cell biologist, educator; BA, St. Olaf Coll.; PhD in Microbiology, Immunology, Duke Univ.; postdoctoral study, Dana-Farber Cancer Inst. Faculty Tufts Univ. Med. Sch., Harvard Med. Sch.; staff Beth Israel Hosp., Boston; prof. cell biology, physiology, internal medicine Washington Univ., St. Louis; and investigator Howard Hughes Med. Inst., 1994—. Former investigator Am. Heart Assn. Fellow: Am. Acad. Arts & Scis. Office: 554 McDonnell Med Sci Bldg Box 8228 Washington Univ Saint Louis MO 63110 Office Phone: 314-362-6834. Business E-Mail: hpiwnica@cellbiology.wustl.edu. *

PIXLEY, CARL PRESTON, mathematician; b. Omaha, Nov. 3, 1942; s. William Robert and Lillus Marie (Petty) Pixley; m. Cynthia Marie Nardone, Dec. 21, 1968; children: Laura Elizabeth, Margaret Marie. BS in Math., U. Omaha, 1966; MS in Math., Rutgers U., New Brunswick, NJ, 1968; PhD in Math., SUNY, Binghamton, 1972. Instr. U. Tex., Austin, 1972-73, asst. prof., 1974-77; assoc. prof. S.W. Tex. State U., San Marcos, 1978-81; sr. rsch. scientist Burroughs Corp., Austin, 1981-82, mgr., 1986-88; sr. mem. tech. staff Microelectronics and Computer Tech. Corp., Austin, 1988-92; mgr. adv. design verification tech. Motorola Inc., Austin, Tex., 1992—2001; sr. dir. Synopsys Inc., 2001—. Lectr. in field; invited spkr. Schloss Dagstahl workshop logic representations, Germany, 1996, DIMACS workshop, New Brunswick, NJ, 1996, Internat. Test Conf., Washington, 1996, Applied Math. Colloquium U. Ariz., 1996, formal verification in industry workshops, 1998, Concurrent Sys. Design Conf., Aizu, Japan, 1998, Internat. Test Conf. Roundtable on microprocessor verification, Washington, 1998, Internat. Symposium Quality Electronic Design, 2001, High Level Design Validation and Test, Memocode, 2004, 06, IEE EDA Forum, 2004, Savaut Soc., 2006, MTV, 2006, FMCAD, 2006, FMCAB, Memocode, MTV, 2006, others; invited panelist Design Automation Conf., 2003; bd. dirs. Accellera; organizer tutorial ASICON, 2003. Author: Constraint Based Verification, 2005; contbr. articles to profl. publs. Mem. IEEE, Am. Math. Soc., Math. Assn. Am. Methodist. Achievements include co-invention of Pixley-Roy Space; patents in field; research in infinite dimensional spaces, symbolic model checking, constraint-based verification, sequential equivalence, transaction to RTL equivalence. Office: Synopsys 2025 NW Cornelius Pass Rd Hillsboro OR 97124 Home: 16670 NW Mission Oaks Dr Beaverton OR 97006-8410 Office Phone: 503-547-6405.

PIZER, HOWARD CHARLES, sports and entertainment executive; b. Chgo., Oct. 23, 1941; s. Edwin and Estyr (Seeder) P.; m. Sheila Graff, June 14, 1964; children: Jacqueline, Rachel. BBA, U. Wis., 1963; JD magna cum laude, Northwestern U., 1966. Assoc. McDermott, Will & Emery, Chgo., 1966-72; ptnr. Katten, Muchin, Zavis, Chgo., 1972-74; exec. v.p., gen. counsel Balcor Co., Skokie, Ill., 1975-80; exec. v.p. Chgo. White Sox, Chgo., 1981—. Exec. v.p. United Ctr. Joint Venture. Past pres. Chgo. Spl. Olympics; bd. dirs. Chgo. Conv. and Tourism Bur., Inc., 1983—, Spl. Children's Charities, 1984—, Chgo. Baseball Cancer Charities, 1983—, Near West Side Cmty. Devel. Corp. Mem. Chgo. Bar Assn., Standard Club Chgo., Briarwood County. Home: 300 Euclid Ave Winnetka IL 60093-3606 Office: Chgo White Sox 333 W 35th St Chicago IL 60616-3651

PIZITZ, RICHARD ALAN, retail executive, real estate company officer; b. Birmingham, Ala., Feb. 24, 1930; s. Isadore and Hortense (Hirsch) P.; m. Joan Black; children: Richard Alan Jr., Jill Carole, Susan Lyn. BA, Washington & Lee U., 1951; MBA, Harvard U., 1953. Mdse. mgr. Pizitz Dept. Stores, Birmingham, 1953-59, v.p., 1959-66, pres., 1966-86, chmn. bd., 1986-87; chmn. Pizitz Mgmt. Group, Birmingham, 1987—. Pres. United Way, Birmingham, 1988, Ala. Commn. on Higher Edn., 1987-95; pres. Better Bus. Bur., Birmingham, 1962; mem. Ala adv. commn. U.S. Commn. on Civil Rights, 1985. Recipient Erskine Ramsay award, 1974; named Mktg. Man of Yr., Am. Mktg. Assn., 1966, Man of Yr., Young Men's Bus. Club, 1970. Mem. Ala. Commn. on Higher Edn., Birmingham C. of C. (pres. 1970), Ala. Retail Assn. (pres. 1965). Avocations: flying, skiing, tennis, scuba diving. Office: Pizitz Mgmt Group 2140 11th Ave S Ste 318 Birmingham AL 35205-2850 Address: 2936 Redmont Park Ln Birmingham AL 35205-2136

PIZZAGALLI, JAMES, construction executive; b. Burlington, Vt., Nov. 23, 1944; s. Angelo and Theresa (Moalli) P.; m. Judy Rock, June 21, 1969; 1 child, Michael. BS, U. Vt., 1966; JD, Boston U., 1969. Treas. Pizzagalli Constrn. Co., Burlington, Vt., 1969-76, v.p., 1976-91, chmn., CEO, 1991-98, co-chmn., 1998—. Dir. Chittenden Corp., Burlington, 1982—, AGC Edn. Found., Washington, 1992-2004, Shelburne (Vt.) Mus., 1983-92, 2000—; life dir. Assn. Gen. Contractors, Washington, 1976—, atty.-at law. Trustee U. Vt., 2000—05. Mem.: The Moles, Ethan Allen Club. Republican. Roman Catholic. Home: 3393 Harbor Rd Shelburne VT 05482-7611 Office: Pizzagalli Constrn Co PO Box 2009 South Burlington VT 05407 E-mail: jpizzagalli@pizzagalli.com.

PIZZAMIGLIO, ALBERT THEODORE (AL PIERSON), conductor; b. Ill. m. Nancy Alice Gilman, Mar. 27, 1978; five children. Studied music theory and composition; BA, MA, Ill. State U.; advanced music studies, U. Ill. Condr. Al Pierson Big Band U.S.A., 1975-89, Guy Lombardo's Royal Canadians, Aubrey, Tex., 1989—. Nat. youth music dir. Am. Inst. of Cooperation; co-host, owner TV show, Bloomington, Ill.; tchr. high sch. and coll. Musician, composer, arranger, vocalist, band leader; founder Al Pierson & Big Band U.S.A. (Best New Dance Band in the Country 1975, America's Number One Dance Band 1977), performed for fourteen yrs. at numerous famous ballrooms in the midwest and many prestigious pvt. parties, on twenty internat. dance tours including Europe, the Orient, the Middle East, the Caribbean, Mexico, Hawaii, Alaska and Tahiti; released 15 albums; recorded Guy Lombardo music album, 2000, now with Guy Lombardo's Royal Canadians performing throughout the continental U.S. and Can. and 44 other fgn. countries; condr. PBS TV series (past three yrs. and continuing), 1977, PBS TV spls., 1994, 95, 96, 97, 2000, Presdl. Inauguration Festivities, 1994. Mem. Pres. George Bush Inauguration, 2004, Pres. Bill Clinton's Inauguration, 1992. Recipient Superman award for helping save 32 lives in snowstorm, 1997, 98, 99, Ill. State U. Disting. Alumni award, 2004; inducted into Ballroom Dancers' Hall of Fame, 1976; named amb. Music for World pres. Ill. State U., 1998. Office: Gilman Inc Artists Mgmt RR 1 Aubrey TX 76227-9801 Personal E-mail: apglo@aol.com.

PIZZINGRILLI, KIM, state official; BBA in Econs., U. Pitts., Johnstown, 1981; M Govtl. Adminstrn., U. Pa., 1988. Auditor, acct., and asst. dir. bur. of audits Pa. Treasury Dept., 1981-87; sr. regulatory analyst Pa. Ind. Regulatory Rev. Commn., 1987-95; spl. asst. to sec. Dept. of State, Harrisburg, Pa., 1995-96, dep. sec. regulatory programs, 1996-98, acting sec., 1998-99, sec. of the commonwealth, 1999—2002; commr. Pa. Pub. Utility Comm., 2002—. Mem. Bd. of Property, Bd. of Fin. and Revenue, State of Pa.; mem. Pa. State Athletic Commn., Pa. State Nav. Commn. for the Delaware River and its Navigable Tributaries, mem. Pa. Mcpl. Retirement Bd.; keeper Great Seal of the Commonwealth. Mem. Nat. Assn. Sec. of State, Women Exec. in State Govt. Republican. Office: Pennsylvania Pub Utility Commn PO Box 3265 Harrisburg PA 17105-3265

PIZZO, PHILIP A., pediatrician, educator, dean; b. NYC, Dec. 6, 1944; BA, Fordham U., 1966; MD, U. Rochester, 1970. Diplomate Am. Bd. Pediat., Am. Bd. Hematology/Oncology. Intern Children's Hosp. Med. Ctr., Boston, 1970-71, jr. asst. resident, 1971-72, sr. resident, 1972-73; tchg. fellow Harvard U. Sch. Medicine, Boston, 1972-73; clin. assoc. Pediatric Oncology Br. of Nat. Cancer Inst., 1973-75, investigator, 1975-76, sr. investigator, 1976-80; head infectious disease sect. Pediatric Br. of Nat. Cancer Inst., 1980-96, chief pediat., 1982-96; sci. dir. divsn. clin. scis. Nat. Cancer Inst., 1994-96; prof. pediat. Sch. Medicine, Uniformed Svcs. U. Health Sci., 1987-96; Thomas Morgan Rotch prof., chmn. dept. pediat. Harvard U. Sch. Medicine, Boston, 1996—2001; dean Stanford U. Sch. Medicine, 2001—. Mem. clin. rsch. subpanel of Nat. Cancer Inst., 1978-81, infectious disease clin. ctr., NIH, 1978-96, transfusion com., 1984-87, pediatric core com., pediatric AIDS clin. trials group, 1988-94, sec. HIV task force, 1988; mem. sci. adv. bd. Children's Hospice Internat., 1988-94, AIDS program Nat. Inst. Allergy and Infectious Diseases, 1988-89; mem. clin. rsch. subcom. AIDS Rsch. Adv. Com., 1990-94; physician-in-chief, chmn. dept. medicine Children's Hosp., Boston, 1996—, Myron Karon Meml. lectr., 1986, Melissa Anne Krinsky Meml. lectr., 1989. Mem. AAAS, Inst. Medicine of NAS, Am. Soc. Hematology, Am. Fedn. for Clin. Rsch., Am. Soc. for Clin. Investigation, Am. Soc. Clin. Oncology (bd. dirs. 1996-1999), Elizabeth Glaser Pediatric AIDS Found. (bd. dirs. 1996-1999), Infectious Disease Soc. Am., Infectious Disease Soc. Am., Internat. Immunocompromised Host Soc., IDSA (bd. dirs. 1996—). Office: Stanford U Sch Med 300 Pasteur Dr. Ste M121 Palo Alto CA 94305 Office Phone: 650-724-5688. E-mail: philip.pizzo@stanford.edu.

PIZZO, SALVATORE VINCENT, pathologist; b. Phila., June 22, 1944; s. George J. Pizzo and Aida (Alcaro) Lepore; m. Carol Ann Kurkowski, Dec. 28, 1968 (div. 1987); children: Steven, David, Susan. PhD, Duke U., 1972; BS, St. Joseph's Coll., 1966; MD, Duke U., 1973. Asst. prof. Duke U. Med. Ctr., Durham, NC, 1976-80, assoc. prof., 1980-85, prof., 1985—, dir. med. scientist tng. program, 1987—, chmn., 1991—. Mem., chmn. program rev. com. NIH, Bethesda, Md., 1986-90; vice chmn. Gordon Conf. Proteases, Holderness, N.H., 1990, chmn., 1992-96; cons. in field, 1980—; mem. Cellular and Molecular Basis of Disease Rev. Com., 1990-96. Contbr. articles to profl. jours. Grantee NIH, 1976—, Am. Cancer Soc., 1976—; Disting. Faculty award, Duke U., 2004, Dean's award for excellence in mentoring, 2004; named one of the top 150 cited authors for jours. in the life sciences. Fellow AAAS; mem. Am. Heart Assn. (exec. com. Thrombosis coun. 1990, 92), Am. Chem. Soc., Am. Assn. Pathologists (program com. 1985-88, long range planning com. 1990-92), Am. Soc. Biological Chemists, Alpha Sigma Nu, Phi Beta Kappa, Alpha Omega Alpha, Sigma Xi. Achievements include patents in field; research in lipoproteins in coagulation and fibronolysis, a link to atherosclerosis, anticoagulation drug development; identification of ATP synthase as the target for Angiostatin action. Office: Duke U Med Ctr PO Box 3712 Durham NC 27710-0001 Office Phone: 919-684-3528. Business E-Mail: pizzo001@mc.duke.edu.

PIZZUTI, RONALD A., real estate developer; m. Ann Pizzuti; 3 children. BS, Kent State U., 1962. Chmn., CEO Pizzuti Cos., Columbus, Ohio, 1976—. Mem. Ohio Arts & Sports Facilities Commn.; bd. trustees Kenyon Coll.; chair bd. trustees Kent State U.; bd. dir. Kent State Found. Named one of Top 200 Collectors, ARTnews Mag., 2003—06; recipient Shining Stars of Seminole County. Lifetime Achievement award, 2002. Mem.: Columbus C. of C. (exec. com.). Avocation: Collecting modern and contemporary art. Office: Pizzuti Cos Ste 800 Two Miranova Pl Columbus OH 43215 Business E-Mail: rpizzuti@pizzuti.com.

PJESIVAC-GRBOVIC, JELENA, computer scientist, researcher; BS in Computer Sci., Ramapo Coll. NJ, Mahwah, 2003, BS in Physics, 2003; MS in Computer Sci., U. Tenn., Knoxville, 2006. Web developer, asst. sys. adminstr. Ramapo Coll. NJ, 1999—2003; rsch. asst. math. modeling and analysis group Los Alamos Nat. Lab., N.Mex., 2001—03; grad. rsch. asst. Innovative Computing Lab., Knoxville, 2003—. Grad. student senator U. Tenn., 2004—; intern engring. Google Inc., Mountain View, Calif., 2005, 06. Recipient Outstanding Academic Achievements Computer Sci. award, Ramapo Coll. NJ, 2003, Outstanding Academic Achievements Physics award, 2003, Outstanding Oral Presentation and Poster award, Los Alamos Student Rsch. Symposium, 2003, HPC Sys. Software award, Internat. Supercomputer Conf., 2004, Extraordinary Profl. Promise citation, U. Tenn., Knoxville, 2006; scholar, Am. Fedn. Tchrs., 2003; Hilton A. Smith Grad. fellowship, U. Tenn., Knoxville, 2003—04. Mem.: IEEE, Computing Rsch. Assn., Warsaw, Assn. Computing Machinery. Achievements include research in performance analysis and optimizations of MPI collective operations; multiscale model of avascular tumor growth. Office: Innovative Computing Lab 1122 Volunteer Blvd Ste 413 Knoxville TN 37996 Home: 3500 Sutherland Ave Apt C106 Knoxville TN 37919 Office Phone: 865-974-6722.

PLACE, MARY KAY, actress; b. Tulsa, Okla., Sept. 23, 1947; d. Bradley E. Place. Grad., U. Tulsa, 1969. Actor: (films) Bound for Glory, 1976, New York, New York, 1977, More American Graffiti, 1979, Starting Over, 1979, Private Benjamin, 1980, Act of Love, 1980, Modern Problems, 1981, Waltz Across Texas, 1980, The Big Chill, 1983, Smooth Talk, 1985, A New Life, 1987, Bright Angel, 1991, Captain Ron, 1992, Samantha, 1992, Teresa's Tattoo, 1994, Citizen Ruth, 1996, Manny & Lo, 1996, Eye of God, 1997, The Rainmaker, 1997, Naturally Native, 1998, How to Make the Cruelest Month, 1998, Pecker, 1998, Judgment Day: The Ellie Nesler Story, 1999, Being John Malkovich, 1999, Girl, Interrupted, 1999, Committed, 2000, My First Mister, 2001, Nailed, 2001, Safety of Objects, 2001, Human Nature, 2001, Sweet Home Alabama, 2002, Junk, 2002, Latter Days, 2003, Nobody Knows Anything, 2003, Evergreen, 2004, Death in Texas, 2004, Killer Diller, 2004, Silver City, 2004, Lonesome Jim, 2005, Nine Lives, 2005, Grace Is Gone, 2007; (TV films) The Girl Who Spelled Freedom, 1986, Out on the Edge, 1989, Traitor in My House, 1990, Crazy from the Heart, 1991, Just My Imagination, 1992, My Very Best Friend, 1996, For My Daughter's Honor, 1996, Love in Another Town, 1997, Point Last Seen, 1998; (TV series) Mary Hartman, Mary Hartman, 1976—77 (Emmy award, 1977), Fernwood Forever, 1977—78, My So-Called Life, 1994—95, Big Love, 2006—. (TV appearances) All in the Family, 1973, Temperatures Rising, 1973, thirtysomthing, 1990, Chicago Hope, 1995, The Wild Thornberry's, 2000, Leep Years, 2001, Citizen Baines, 2001, Undeclared, 2002, Law & Order: Special Victims Unit, 2002, The Handler, 2004, King of the Hill, 2004, The West Wing, 2004, Jack & Bobby, 2005, Numb3rs, 2006, Grey's Anatomy, 2006; dir.: (TV episodes) Baby Boom, 1988, Dream On, 1990, Friends, 1995, Arli$$, 1996, The Minor Accomplishments of Jackie Woodman, 2006; screenwriter (TV episodes) Mary Tyler Moore, 1970, Paul Sand in Friends and Lovers, 1974, M*A*S*H, 1973—74; singer: (albums) Aimin' to Please, Tonite! At the Capri Lounge, Loretta Haggers, 1976, Almost Crown. *

PLACENTI, FRANK MICHAEL, lawyer; b. Columbus, Ohio, Sept. 2, 1953; s. Anthony Joseph and Evelyn (Piteo) P.; m. Tobi M. Placenti, Apr. 29, 1971. BA cum laude, Ohio State U., 1975, JD summa cum laude, 1979. Bar: Ariz. 1979, U.S. Dist. Ct. Ariz. 1979, U.S. Ct. Appeals (9th cir.) 1979. Group co-dir. transactions and corp. governance Bryan Cave LLP, Phoenix. Judge pro tem Maricopa County Superior Ct., 1985—. Chmn. Super Bowl Kick-Off Luncheon, 1996, NBA All Star Kick-Off Luncheonj, 1995, Phoenix C. of C., 1991—92, Boys & Girls Clubs Met. Phoenix, 1992—93; chmn. bd. dirs. Phoenix Children's Hosp. Found., 2005—. James K. Barton Meml. scholar Ohio State U., 1977-79; named one of Outstanding Young Men in Am., 1981. Mem. ABA (litigation, communication law and young lawyers sects.), Maricopa County Bar (chmn. com., lectr. on litigation 1985-86), Greater Phoenix Leadership, Phoenix C. of C., Order of Coif, Phi Kappa Theta, Phi Kappa Tau, Phi Eta Sigma. Avocations: golf, travel, wine. Office: Bryan Cave LLP 1 Renaissance Sq Two N Ctrl Ave, Ste 2200 Phoenix AZ 85004 Office Phone: 602-364-7451. E-mail: fmplacenti@bryancave.com.

PLACK, VERNON C., financial analyst, investment advisor; BS, U.S. Military Acad., West Point; MBA, Campbell Univ. Cert. CFA. Investment rep. Alex Brown, Balt.; security analyst bank & thrift industry Johnston, Lemon & Co., Washington; security analyst positions through sr. analyst specialty fin. BB&T Capital Markets, Richmond, Va., sr. mng. dir., dir. rsch. Named #1 earnings estimator in fin. & #3 overall, Forbes Mag., 2007. Mem.: CFA Inst., Richmond Soc. Fin. Analysts (past pres.). Office: BB&T Capital Markets 909 E Main St Richmond VA 23219 *

PLACKE, JAMES ANTHONY, retired diplomat; b. Grand Island, Nebr., June 14, 1935; s. Gerhard F. and Florence E. (McCormick) P.; m. Mary Sabina Shea, July 25, 1959; children— Elizabeth, Stephen, Carolyn B.Sc., U. Nebr., 1957, MA, 1959. Commd. fgn. service officer Dept. State, 1958; econ. counselor Am. Embassy, Tripoli, Libya, 1970-71, Ottawa, 1977-79; fgn. service insp. Dept. State, Washington, 1971-73, dir. office food policy, 1974-76; minister Am. Embassy, Jiddah, Saudi Arabia, 1979-82; dep. asst. sec. Nr. Eastern and South Asian Affairs Bur., Dept. State, Washington, 1982-85; pvt. practice, 1986—90; dir. Cambridge Energy Rsch. Assoc., 1991-2000, sr. assoc., 2001—. Del. UN World Food Conf., 1974; mem. econ. expert working group Iraq Study Group, 2006. Recipient Meritorious Honor award Dept. State, 1969, 71; Presdl. Meritorious Service award, 1985 Office: Ste 201 1150 Connecticut Ave NW Washington DC 20036-4104 Office Phone: 202-463-8222.

PLAEGER, FREDERICK JOSEPH, II, lawyer; b. New Orleans, Sept. 10, 1953; s. Edgar Leonard and Bernice Virginia (Schiwetz) P.; m. Kathleen Helen Dickson, Nov. 19, 1977; children: Douglas A., Catherine E. BS, La. State U., 1976, JD, 1977. Bar: La. 1978, Tex. 1999, U.S. Dist. Ct. (ea. dist.) La. 1978, U.S. Ct. Appeals (5th cir.) 1981, U.S. Supreme Ct. 1989. Law clk. U.S. Dist. Ct. (ea. dist.) La., New Orleans, 1977-79; assoc. Milling, Benson, Woodward, Hillyer, Pierson & Miller, New Orleans, 1979-85, ptnr., 1985-89; v.p., gen. counsel, corp. sec. La. Land and Exploration Co., New Orleans, 1989-97; v.p., gen. counsel Burlington Resources Inc., Houston, 1997—2006; sr. v.p., gen. counsel EOG Resources, 2007—. Selected mem. Met. Area Com. Leadership Forum, 1986; bd. dirs. Soc. Environ. Edn., La. Nature and Sci. Ctr., 1992—94; trustee Houston Ballet, 2001—; bd. dirs. New Orleans Speech and Hearing Ctr., 1985—91, pres., 1988—90; bd. dirs. Children's Oncology Svcs. La. (Ronald McDonald Ho. of New Orleans), 1987—90. Recipient Service to Mankind award Sertoma, 1989; named Tex. Super Lawyer, Tex. Monthly Mag., 2004, 05, 06, 07. Mem.: ABA, Tex. Gen. Counsel Forum (pres. Houston chpt. 2005—06, statewide chmn. 2006—07), Am. Corp. Counsel Assn. (bd. dir. New Orleans chpt. 1995—98), La. Bar Assn., Inst. Energy Law (adv. bd. 2001—, exec. com. 2002—, chmn. 2005—), Houston City Club. Republican. Roman Catholic. Avocations: computers, fishing. Home: 5105 Longmont Dr Houston TX 77056-2417

PLAGER, S. JAY, federal judge; s. A. L. and Clara L. Plager; children: Anna Katherine, David Alan, Daniel Tyler. AB, U. N.C., 1952; JD, U. Fla., 1958; LLM, Columbia U., 1961. Bar: Fla. 1958, Ill. 1964. Asst. prof. law U. Fla., 1958—62, assoc. prof., 1962—64; assoc. prof. law U. Ill., Champaign-Urbana, 1964—65, prof., 1965—77; dir. Office Environ. and Planning Studies, 1972—74, 1975—77; dean, prof. law Ind. U. Sch. Law, Bloomington, 1977—84, prof. law, 1984—90; counselor to undersec. US Dept. Health and Human Svcs., 1986—87; assoc. dir. Office of Mgmt. and Budget Exec. Office of the Pres., 1987—88, adminstr. info. and regulatory affairs, 1988—89; cir. judge US Ct. Appeals (fed. cir.), 1989—2000, sr. judge, 2000—. Vis. rsch. prof. law U. Wis., 1967—68; vis. scholar Stanford U., 1984—85. Author (with others): Water Law and Administration, 1968; author: Social Justice Through Law-New Approaches in the Law of Property, 1970; author: (with others) Florida Water Law, 1980. Chmn. Gainesville (Fla.) Planning Commn., 1962—63; active Urbana Plan Commn., 1966—70, nat. air pollution manpower devel. adv. com., 1971—75; cons. Ill. Inst. for Environ. Quality, US EPA; chmn. Ill. Task Force on Noise, 1972—76; vice chmn. Nat. Commn. on Jud. Discipline and Removal, 1991—93; budget com. Jud. Conf. US Cts., 1996—2003. With USN, 1948—70. Office: US Ct Appeals for Fed Cir The National Courts Bldg 717 Madison Pl NW Washington DC 20439-0002 *

PLAINE, DANIEL J., lawyer; b. Washington, Aug. 23, 1943; s. Herzel H.E. and Norma (Stein) P.; m. Susan Ambrose, Oct. 5, 1985; children: Caroline, Meredith. BA magna cum laude, Williams Coll., 1965; LLB in Internat. Law, Cambridge U., Eng., 1967; JD, Yale U., 1970. Bar: DC 1970, US Dist. Ct. DC 1970, US Ct. Appeals (DC cir.) 1970, US Ct. Appeals (fed. cir.), 1985, US Supreme Ct., 1974. Ptnr. Steptoe & Johnson, Washington, 1970—95, Gibson, Dunn & Crutcher, Washington, 1995—. Marshall scholar, 1967. Mem. ABA, Am. Soc. Internat. Law, Washington Inst. Internat. Law, Phi Beta Kappa. Office: Gibson Dunn & Crutcher LLP 1050 Connecticut Ave NW Ste 200 Washington DC 20036-5306 Office Phone: 202-955-8286. E-mail: dplaine@gibsondunn.com.

PLAINE, LLOYD LEVA, lawyer; b. Washington, Nov. 3, 1947; d. Marx and Shirley P. Leva; m. James W. Hill. BA, U. Pa., 1969; postgrad., Harvard U.; JD, Georgetown U., 1975. Bar: DC 1975. Legis. asst. to US Rep. Sidney Yates, 1971-72; with Sutherland, Asbill & Brennan, Washington, 1975-82, ptnr., 1982—. Fellow Am. Bar Found., Am. Coll. Trust and Estate Counsel (past regent), Am. Coll. Tax Counsel; mem. ABA (past chmn. real property, probate and trust law sect., past coun. sect. of taxation). Office: Sutherland Asbill & Brennan Ste 6 1275 Pennsylvania Ave NW Washington DC 20004-2415 Office Phone: 202-383-0155.

PLAMANN, ALFRED A., wholesale distribution executive; Pres., CEO Cert. Grocers Calif., Unified We. Grocers Inc., Commerce, Calif., 2000—. Office: Unified Western Grocers Inc 5200 Sheila St City Of Commerce CA 90040 *

PLAME, VALERIE ELISE, former intelligence agent; b. Anchorage, Aug. 13, 1963; d. Samuel D. and Diane E. Plame; m. Joseph Charles Wilson IV, Apr. 3, 1998; children: Trevor Rolph, Samantha Finnell Diana. BA in Internat. Rels., Penn. State U., 1985; MA, London Sch. Econs., Coll. Europe, Belgium, 1995. Classified officer CIA, 1985—2003. Became the subject of a widespread government controversy when members of the Bush administration were accused of leaking her identity as an undercover CIA agent to members of the media; filed lawsuit against members of the Bush administration in 2006. *

PLANCHON, HARRY PETER, JR., research development manager; b. Aurora, Mo., Aug. 28, 1941; s. Harry P. and Ruth Arminta (Eden) P.; m. Virginia Grace Sapp, June 13, 1964; children: Benjamin John, Matthew Brian. BSME, U. Mo., 1964; MS in Nuclear Engring., U. Ill., 1971, PhD in Nuclear Engring., 1974; MBA, U. Chgo., 1990. Cert. profl. engr. Rsch. assoc., asst. prof. U. Ill. Nuclear Engring. Dept., Urbana, 1970-74; sr. engr., mgr. Clinch River Breeder Reactor Plant Systems Westinghouse Advanced Reaction Div., Madison, Pa., 1974-84; mgr. reactor analysis Exptl. Breeder Reacter Div., Argonne (Ill.) Nat. Lab., 1984-90; assoc. dir. Reacter Analysis Div., Argonne Nat. Lab., 1990-91; assoc. dir. ENG divsn. Argonne Nat. Lab., Idaho Falls, Idaho, 1991-2000, dir. nuclear tech. divsn., 2000—. Contbr. articles to profl. jours. Lt. USN, 1964-70. Fellow Am. Nuc. Soc. (Seaborg medal 1996); mem. Am. Soc. Mech. Engrs., Beta Gamma Sigma,

Tau Beta Pi, Pi Mu Epsilon, Pi Tau Sigma. Presbyterian. Avocations: hiking, skiing, photography, golf, reading. Office: Argonne National Laboratory PO Box 1625 Idaho Falls ID 83403-1625

PLANE, DONALD RAY, retired management science educator; b. Evansville, Ind., July 17, 1938; s. Edward L. and Margaret I. Plane; m. Rosemary Bieber, Sept. 4, 1961; children: Brian Russell, Dennis Lowell, Margaret Diane. ME, U. Cin., 1961; MBA (NDEA fellow), Ind. U., 1963, DBA (NDEA fellow), 1965. Instr. econs. U.S. Air Force Acad., 1965-67, asst. prof. econs., 1967-68; assoc. prof. mgmt. sci. U. Colo., Boulder, 1968-72, prof. mgmt. sci. and info. systems, 1972-84, head div. mgmt. sci., 1976-84; prof. mgmt. sci. Crummer Grad. Sch. Bus., Rollins Coll., Winter Park, Fla., 1984-2000, faculty pres. Crummer Grad. Sch. Bus., 1992-93, prof. emeritus, 2000—. Vis. Fulbright prof. mgmt. sci. U. Nairobi, 1978-79; cons. in field. Co-author: (with E.B. Oppermann) Business and Economic Statistics, 3d edit., 1986; (with J. Dinkel, G. Kochenberger) Management Science: Text and Applications, 1978, Quantitative Tools for Decision Support Using IFPS, 1986, Management Science: A Spreadsheet Approach for Windows, 1996. Served with USAF, 1965-68. Ford Found. fellow, 1965 Achievements include research, publs. in field. Home: 322 Bellingrath Ter Deland FL 32724

PLANITZER, RUSSELL E., computer company executive; b. 1944; Student, U.S. Naval Acad, 1966, Harvard U., 1974; MBA, Harvard Bus. Sch. Chmn. bd. dirs. Computervision Corp., Bedford, Mass., 1974—; gen. ptnr. J.H. Whitney & Co., NYC, 1981—93; chmn. bd. dirs., CFO DR Holdings Inc. of Del., 1990—; CEO Computervision (formerly Prime Computer); mng. prin. Lazard Tech. Ptnrs. Bd. dirs. Kubi Software, GGN, Tazz Software, Interwise, NetByTel, New River, Pass Key.com and Quantum Bridge Named CEO of Year, D.H. Brown Assocs., 1995. Office: Lazard Tech Partners 48th Floor 30 Rockefeller Plz New York NY 10020 Office Phone: 212-632-6000. Office Fax: 212-332-8677.

PLANK, KEVIN A., apparel executive; s. William and Jayne Plank; m. Desiree Jacqueline Guerzon, Mar. 2003; 1 child, James. Grad., U. of Md.: Coll. Park, 1997. Spl. teams capt. Md. Football Team; founder, CEO, chmn. Under Armour Inc., 1996—. Bd. trustees U. of Md. Named Entrepreneur of Year award Md. mfg. category, Ernst & Young, 2003. Office: Under Armour Inc Investor Relations 1020 Hull St Baltimore MD 21230-2080 Office Phone: 617-587-8911. *

PLANK, RAYMOND, energy executive; b. Mpls., May 29, 1922; s. Raby and Maude (Howe) P.; children:Katherine, Michael, Pamela, Roger, Dana. BA, Yale U., 1944. Founder, partner Plank & Somekawa (accounting), 1946-53; founder, pres. Apache Corp., Houston, 1954—79, CEO, 1966—2002, chmn., 1979—. Former dir. St. Paul Securities, Inc. Former chmn. U. Minn. Found.; chmn. Ucross Found.; trustee Com. for Econ. Develop., Washington. Served to 1st lt., bomber pilot USAAF, World War II So. Pacific. Mem. Beta Theta Pi. Clubs: Minneapolis, Woodhill Country. Republican. Office: Apache Corp 1 Post Oak Central Houston TX 77056 *

PLANK, ROGER B., energy executive; BA, Colgate Univ.; MBA, Univ. St. Thomas. With Apache Corp., Houston, 1981—, v.p., CFO, 1997-2000, exec. v.p., CFO, 2000—. Bd. dir. Parker Drilling Co.; past pres. Tex. Independent Producers & Royalty Owners Assn.; dir. Okla. Independent Petroleum Assn., Domestic Petroleum Council. Bd. mem. Alley Theatre, Houston, Ucross Found. Office: Apache Corp 2000 Post Oak Blvd Ste 100 Houston TX 77056-4400 *

PLANT, ALBIN MACDONOUGH, lawyer; b. Balt., July 30, 1937; s. Albin Joseph and Ruth E. (Frech) P.; m. Anne Warwick Brown, June 17, 1961; children: Katherine, Albin MacDonough Jr., Elizabeth Ashby. BA, Princeton U., NJ, 1959; LLB, U. Va., Charlottesville, 1963; MLA, Johns Hopkins U., Balt., 1978. Bar: Md. 1963, U.S. Dist. Ct. Md. 1963, U.S. Ct. Appeals 1970. Assoc. Semmes, Bowen & Semmes, Balt., 1963-71, ptnr., 1971-91, Stewart, Plant & Blumenthal, Balt., 1991—. Bd. dir. T. Rowe Price Savs. Bank; adj. prof. law U. Balt., 1979, U. Md., 1979—83, 1984—85. Bd. dir. Am. Horticulture Soc., Balt. Choral Arts Soc. Mem.: Am. Coll. Trust and Estate Counsel, Am. Bar Found. (life), Wednesday Law Club, Md. Club (bd. dir.), Lawyers Roundtable. Democrat. Office: 7 St Paul St Baltimore MD 21202-1626 Office Phone: 410-347-0511. Business E-Mail: amplant@spblaw.com.

PLANT, JACKSON VAUGHN, minister; s. Harry Jackson and Caroline Plant. Ordained pastor Ch. of God, 2006. Founder, pastor For This Time Ministries, Glen Burnie, Md., 1999—. With USN, 1988. Mem.: Alpha Tau Omega (life; v.p. 1984—85). Republican. Home Phone: 410-761-1091; Office Phone: 410-761-1091. Business E-Mail: jplant@jacksonplant.com.

PLANT, JOHN CHARLES, automotive executive; b. West Bromwich, West Midlands, Eng., Aug. 1, 1953; s. John and Florence (Harrison) P.; m. Christine Ann; children: Alexa Jayne, John Alexander. B in Commerce, Econs., Acctg. and Law, Birmingham U., Eng., 1974. Auditor Touche Ross, Birmingham, 1974-77; financier Lucas Auto Ltd., Birmingham, 1977—, Burnley, England, 1983—; mng. dir. Lucas Varity Elec. and Electronics, 1991—97; pres. Lucas Varity Automotive, 1999; pres., CEO TRW Chassis; gen. mgr. TRW Automotive, exec. v.p., 1999—2001, co-CEO, pres., CEO Livonia, Mich., 2001—. Bd. dirs. Martin Currie Portfolio Investment Trust PLC. Fellow Inst. Chartered Accts. in Eng. and Wales (mng. dir., FCA award 1981). Avocation: tennis. Office: TRW Automotive 12025 Tech Center Dr Livonia MI 48150 *

PLANT, ROBERT ANTHONY, singer, composer; b. Bromwich, Staffordshire, Eng., Aug. 20, 1948; Previously sang with rock groups Band of Joy and Alexis Korner, singer, composer Led Zeppelin, 1968—80, world-wide concert tours, performed (films) The Song Remains the Same, 1976; composer: (songs) Black Dog, Stairway to Heaven, D'Yer Mak'Er; albums include (with Led Zeppelin) Led Zeppelin, Led Zeppelin II, 1969, Led Zeppelin III, 1970, Led Zeppelin IV, Houses of the Holy, 1973, Physical Graffiti, 1975, The Song Remains the Same, Presence, 1976, In Through the Out Door, 1979, albums include (with Led Zepplin) Coda, 1982, solo albums include Pictures at Eleven, 1982, The Principle of Moments, Shaken N' Stirred, 1985, Now and Zen, 1988, Manic Nirvana, 1990, Fate of Nations, 29 Palms/Whole Lotta Love, 1994, No Quarter: Jimmy Page & Robert Plant Unledded, 1994, Walking into Calrksdale, 1998, Dreamland, 2002, albums (with the Honeydrippers) The Honeydrippers, Vol. I, 1985, performed at LIVE AID in Phila., with Jimmy Page and John Paul Jones, 1985; contbr. soundtrack to movie Wayne's World 2. Named to Rock and Roll Hall of Fame, 1995; recipient Grammy nomination (Best Hard Rock Performance) for "Calling to You", 1994, Grammy, 1999, Polar Music prize, Royal Swedish Acad. Music, 2006. Office: care Atlantic Rec Corp 1290 Avenue Of The Americas New York NY 10104-0101

PLANTS, WALTER DALE, retired elementary school educator, minister; b. Middlefield, Ohio, June 8, 1942; s. William E. and Hazel A. Plants; m. Sarah A. Gaddis, July 5, 1962; children: Dale Anthony, Jeanette Marie. BD, Azusa Pacific U., 1967; MEd, U. Nev., 1970. Cert. elem. tchr., ednl. adminstr. Elem. tchr. Churchill County Sch. Dist., Fallon, Nev., 1967—69, 1970—72, elem tchr., 1988—2001; grad. asst. U. Nev., Reno, 1969-70; tchr. Kingman (Ariz.) Elem. Sch. Dist. #4, 1972-77; head sci. program E. C. Best Elem. Sch., Fallon, 1988—2001; ret., 2007. Adj. instr. Ariz. State U., Tempe, 1973-77; cons. sci. Ariz. State Dept. Edn., 1975-77. Bd. dirs. Solar Energy Commn. Mohave County, Ariz., 1974; coord. County Sci. Fair, 1988-93; active Western Regional Sci. Fair Com.; sci. fair coord. Churchill County, 1989-94; mem. com. Regional Sci. Fair, 1992-94; min. non-demonimational ch., 1969-2005. HEW fellow, 1969; NSF grantee, 1973; AIMS Found. scholar, 1988; recipient Ariz. State PTA award, 1977, Ruth Neldon award Ariz. State Dept., 1977, Conservation award Big Sandy Natural Resources Conservation Dist. Ariz., 1976, Community Builder Svc. award Masons, Fallon, 1991, Disting. Leadership award, 1991-93; named State Tchr. of Yr. Nev. PTA, 1991, Conservation Tchr. of Yr., 1991; named to Congl. Select Edn. panel U.S. Congress, 1993. Mem. NEA, AAAS, Nat. Sci. Tchrs. Assn., Nat. Coun. Tchrs. Math., Internat. Reading Assn., Churchill County Edn. Assn. (Tchr. of Yr. 1989), Internat. Platform Assn., Nat. Arbor Day Found., World Wildlife Fund, Nat. Parks and Conservation Assn., Nat. Audubon Soc., Nev. State Tchrs. of Yr. Assn. (pres. 1994-96, pres. 1996-97), Phi Delta Kappa. Personal E-mail: wpla@charter.net.

PLAPINGER, WILLIAM A., lawyer; b. Washington, July 23, 1952; s. Jerome S. and Alice E. Plapinger; m. Kathleen J. Murray, Oct. 11, 1982; children: Alexander S., Elizabeth L., Thomas A. Student, Westfield Coll., U. London, 1972—73; AB, Vassar Coll., 1974; JD, NYU, 1978. Bar: NY 1979, US Dist. Ct. (ea. dist.) NY 1979, US Dist. Ct. (so. dist.) NY 1979, US Supreme Ct. 1983. Assoc. Sullivan & Cromwell, NY, 1976—86, ptnr., 1986—87, London, 1987—, mng. ptnr. London office, coord. European offices, 1995—, coord. European offices, 2000—. Trustee Vassar Coll., Poughkeepsie, 1996—, chair bd. trustees, 2006—; trustee Am. Sch., London, 1996—. Mem.: India Ho., Queenwood Golf Club, Vineyard Golf Club, Links Club. Office: Sullivan & Cromwell LLP 1 New Fetter Ln London EC4A 1AN England Mailing: 125 Broad St 32nd Fl New York NY 10004-2498 Office Phone: 44 0 20 7959 8900. Business E-Mail: plapingerw@sullcrom.com.

PLAPP, BRYCE VERNON, biochemistry educator; b. DeKalb, Ill., Sept. 11, 1939; s. Vernon Edgar and Eleanor Barbara (Kautz) P.; m. Rosemary Kuhn, June 13, 1962; children— Brendan Bryce, Laurel Andrea BS, Mich. State U., East Lansing, 1961; PhD, U. Calif.-Berkeley, 1966. Research assoc. J.W. Goethe U., Frankfurt/Main, Germany, 1966-68; research assoc. Rockefeller U., NYC, 1968-70; faculty U. Iowa, Iowa City, 1970—, prof. biochemistry, 1979—. Contbr. articles to profl. jours.; mem. editorial bd. Archives Biochemistry and Biophysics. Am. Cancer Soc. fellow, 1966-68 Mem. Am. Soc. for Biochemistry and Molecular Biology, Am. Chem. Soc., Sigma Xi Avocations: travel, sports. Office: Univ Iowa Dept Biochemistry 4-712 Iowa City IA 52242 Office Phone: 319-335-7909. E-mail: bv-plapp@uiowa.edu.

PLASIL, FRANZ, physicist; b. Prague, Czechoslovakia, May 17, 1939; came to U.S., 1960; s. Frank and Eva (Wenger) P.; m. Catherine Logan, Feb. 15, 1964 (div. Sept. 1979); two children: Maia, David; m. Carol Baratz, Apr. 12, 1980. BS, Queen Mary Coll., U. London, 1960; PhD, U. Calif., Berkeley, 1964. Chemist Lawrence Berkeley (Calif.) Lab., 1964-65; rsch. assoc. Brookhaven Nat. Lab., Upton, NY, 1965-67; rsch. staff physics div. Oak Ridge (Tenn.) Nat. Lab., 1967-78, group leader physics div., 1978-86, sect. head physics div., 1986-99; fellow U. Tenn.-Battelle, 1999—2002; hon. rsch. prof. dept. physics and astronomy U. Tenn., Knoxville, 2002—. Contbr. articles to Annals of Physics, Phys. Rev., Phys. Rev. Letters, Nuc. Phys., Phys. Letters. Recipient Alexander von Humboldt award 1985, E. Mach medal of honor Acad. of Sci. of the Czech Republic, 1998. Fellow Am. Phys. Soc. Achievements include rsch. in fission-imposed limits on the stability of rotating nuclei and rsch. in nucleus-nucleus collisions at ultrarelativistic energies. Home: 964 W Outer Dr Oak Ridge TN 37830-8607 Personal E-mail: plasil@comcast.net.

PLASKACZ, EDWARD JOHN, computer scientist, engineer, mathematics professor; s. John T. and Pauline H. Plaskacz; m. Elizabeth Ellen Prindiville, July 14, 1990. BS, Ill. Inst. Tech., Chgo., 1981, MS, 1982; PhD, Northwestern U., 1990. Engr. in tng. City of Chgo. Dept. of Water, 1979-81; engring. intern Sargent & Lundy Engrs., Chgo., 1981-82, engring. analyst, 1982-85; rsch. asst. Northwestern U., Evanston, Ill., 1985-90; computational scientist Argonne Nat. Lab., Ill., 1990—2003; math. instr. William Rainey Harper Coll., Palatine, Ill., 2003—. Contbr. numerous articles to profl. jours. Recipient Letter of Commendation Chgo. Dept. Water, 1980, Clinton Strycker award Ill. Inst. Tech., 1981, Atanasoff award Second Symposium on Parallel Computational Methods for Large-Scale Structural Analysis and Design, 1993, Exceptional Performance award Argonne Nat. Lab., 1995, 97. Mem. Sigma Xi, Tau Beta Pi, Chi Epsilon. Office: 1029 W Stearns Rd No 157 Bartlett IL 60103 Personal E-mail: eplaskacz@email.msn.com.

PLASKETT, THOMAS GEORGE, transportation executive, director; b. Raytown, Mo., Dec. 24, 1943; s. Warren E. and Frances S. P.; m. Linda Lee Maxey, June 8, 1968; children: Kimberly, Keith. B in Indsl. Engring., Kettering U.; MBA, Harvard U. Supr. indsl. engring. GM, Flint, Mich., 1968, supt. indsl. engring., 1969-73, sr. staff asst., treas. NYC, 1973; asst. contr. Am. Airlines, NYC, 1974, v.p. mktg. adminstrn., 1975-76, sr. v.p. fin., 1976-80, sr. v.p. mktg. Dallas, 1980—86; pres., CEO Continental Airlines Inc., Houston, until 1988; chmn., CEO, pres. Pan Am Corp., NYC, 1988—91; chmn. Fox Run Capital Assocs., 1991—; dir., interim pres., CEO, acting CFO Greyhound Lines, Inc., Dallas, 1994-95, chmn., 1995—99; vice-chmn. Legend Airlines, Dallas, 1997—2001, exec. v.p., 1999—2001; pres., CEO Probex Corp., Dallas, 1999—2000, chmn., 1999—2000. Bd. dirs. Radioshack Corp., Ft. Worth, Novell, Inc. 2002-2006, non-exec. chmn., 2006-, Waltham, Mass., Provo, Utah, Alcon Inc., Ft. Worth. Avocations: golf, skiing, squash. Office: PO Box 141111 Irving TX 75014-1111 Office Phone: 972-333-4751. Business E-Mail: tom@foxruncapital.com.

PLATAU, GERARD OSCAR, chemist, consultant; b. Potsdam, Germany, June 29, 1926; s. Martin and Ottilie Platau; m. Caroline (Freeman) Platau, May 27, 1961; 1 child, Steven. BA, Bklyn Coll., 1946; MS, Purdue U., 1948, PhD, 1950. From dept. mgr. to mng. ed. Chem. Abstracts Svc., Columbus, Ohio, 1961—79, sr. advisor, 1979—90; cons. Columbus, 1990—2004, Clearwater, Fla., 2004—. Conf. chmn. CODATA, Paris, 1987—90. Contbr. articles to profl. jours. Bd. dir. Upper Arlington Civic Orgn., Upper Arlington, Ohio, 1974—76. Fellow, Nat. Fedn. of Abstracting & Info. Svc., 1991. Mem.: Am. Soc. Info. Sci. & Tech. (dir. 1966—80, parliamentarian 1985—, Watson Davis award 1980), Am. Chem. Soc., The Ohio State U. Alumni Assn. Methodist. Avocations: travel, photography. Home: 2773 Via Cipriani Unit 1310B Clearwater FL 33764 Personal E-mail: gplatau@aol.com.

PLATE, THOMAS GORDON, columnist, educator; b. NYC, May 17, 1944; s. John William and Irene (Henry) P.; m. Andrea I. Margolis, Sept. 22, 1979; 1 child, Ashley Alexandra. AB, Amherst Coll., 1966; MPA, Princeton U., 1968. Writer Newsweek, NYC, 1968-70; editor Newsday, LI, N.Y., 1970-72; sr. editor N.Y. Mag., NYC, 1972-75; editor edit. page L.A. Herald Examiner, 1978-82; sr. editor Time Mag., NYC, 1982-83; editor in chief Family Weekly, NYC, 1984-85; editor edit. pages N.Y. Newsday, NYC, 1986-89, L.A. Times, 1989-95, Times Op-Ed Page columnist, contbg. editor, 1995—. Adj. prof. UCLA Pub. Policy Sch. and Letters and Scis.; mem. founders bd. UCLA Sch. Pub. Policy; founder Asia Pacific Media Network; participant World Econ. Forum, Davos. Author: Understanding Doomsday, 1971, Crime Pays!, 1975, Secret Police, 1981; co-author: Commissioner, 1978. Recipient Best Deadline Writing award Am. Soc. Newspaper Editors, 1981, Best Edit. awards L.A. Press Club, 1979, 80, 81, Best Edit. award Calif. Newspaper Pubs. Assn., 1991, 92, 94; media fellow Stanford U. Mem. Pacific Coun. on Internat. Rels., Century Assn. (N.Y.C.), Phi Beta Kappa. Avocations: tennis, photography, travel. Office: LA Times 405 Hilgard Ave Los Angeles CA 90095-9000

PLATER, WILLIAM MARMADUKE, literature and language professor, academic administrator; b. East St. Louis, Ill., July 26, 1945; s. Everett Marmaduke and Marguerite (McBride) P.; m. Gail Maxwell, Oct. 16, 1971; children: Elizabeth Rachel, David Matthew. BA in English, U. Ill., 1967, MA in English, 1969, PhD in English, 1973. Asst. dean U. Ill., Urbana, 1969—72, 1973—74, asst. dir. Unit One, 1971—72, acting dir. Unit One, 1972—73, asst. dir. Humanities, 1974—77, assoc. dir. humanities, 1977—83, assoc. coordinator interdisciplinary programs, 1977-83; prof. English, dean Ind. U., Indpls., 1983—87; dean faculties Ind. U.-Purdue U., 1987—2006, exec. vice chancellor, 1988—2006, acting chancellor, 2003, chancellor's prof. philanthropic studies, pub. affairs, English and Informatics, dir. internat. cmty. devel., 2006—. Bd. dirs. Met. Indpls. Pub. Broadcasting, Inc., 2001—; vis. scholar Carnegie Found. for the Advancement Tchg., Palo Alto, 2007; cons. in field. Author: The Grim Phoenix: Reconstructing Thomas Pynchon, 1978, Public Work and the Academy: An Academic Administrator's Guide to Civic Engagement and Service-Learning, 2004, also articles, revs., poetry. Bd. dirs. U. Ill. YMCA, Urbana, 1982—83, Metro. Interfaith Campus Ministry, Indpls., 1984—86; trustee Ind. Com. for Humanities, 1986—92, 2003—, bd. dirs., 1986—92, exec. com., 1988—92; bd. dirs. Ind. Repertory Theatre, 1987—93, Children's Mus., 1992—2001, exec. com., 1994—2001; bd. trustees Coun. for Adult and Experiential Learning, 1995—, chair, 2005—07; bd. dirs. Herron Gallery Contemporary Art, 1987—93; coun. academic affairs Nat. Assn. State U. and Land-Grant Colls., 1996—2006; bd. dirs. Midwest Univs. Consortium for Internat. Activities, Inc., 1996—98; bd. govs. Ind. U. Ctr. on Philanthropy, 1997—2006; bd. dirs. Metro. Indpls. Pub. Broadcasting, Inc., 2001—; adv. com. for tomorrow's Ind. Ind. State Mus., 2001—04; nat. adv. com. on cmty. engagement Carnegie Found. for Advancement Tchg., 2006—; chair accreditation team Western Assn. Schs. and Colls., 2006, 2007. Recipient Program Innovation prize Am. Acad. Ednl. Devel., 1982, Pres. Medallion for Svc. Pres. Ind. U., 1988, Maynard K. Hine Svc. award Ind. U. Alumni Assn., 2004. Mem.: NAACP (life). Home: 6477 Oxbow Way Indianapolis IN 46220 Home Phone: 317-251-1340; Office Phone: 317-274-4500. E-mail: wplater@iupui.edu.

PLATH, KATHRIN, biology professor, biomedical researcher; b. Germany; MS in Biochemistry, Humboldt U., 1994; PhD in cell biology, Humboldt U. to Berlin, 1999, Harvard Med. Sch.; post-doctoral tng. fellow, U. of Calif. Post-doctoral rschr. Whitehead Inst., 2003—06; asst. prof., rschr. Inst. for Stem Cell Biology and Medicine, UCLA, 2006—. Contbr. Named a spl. fellow, Leukemia and Lymphoma Soc., 2004—; fellow O'Donnel Post-Doctoral, Life Sciences Rsch. Found., 2001—04. Office: Dept of Biol Chemistry UCLA Sch of Medicine PO Box 951737 Los Angeles CA 90095 Office Phone: 310-206-8688. E-mail: kplath@mednet.ucla.edu. *

PLATIS, CHRIS STEVEN, adult education educator; b. East Chicago, Ind., May 21, 1926; s. Sam and Myra (Theodore) P.; m. Jeanette Brown. BS in Phys. Edn., Ind. U., 1955, MS in Edn., 1964, postgrad., 1965—68. Gen. foreman Cast Armor, Inc., East Chicago, 1951—53; tchr. East Chgo. and Ind. Pub. Schs., 1955—. Asst. sports editor East Chgo. Calumet News, 1973-78; asst. dir. No. Ind. State Sports Mus., 1984-95, 96, 97, 98, 00. Appearances include (films) A Bridge Too Far, The Longest Day, Bridge at Remagan, D-Day, The Battle of the Bulge; author: Teaching Kids of Tomorrow, 1978, Are Teachers Adequate for Today's Students?, 1997. Master Boy Scouts Am., East Chicago, 1965-87; asst. recreational dir. North Twp., Northern Ind., 1993; All-Pacific Army, Football, Basketball, Track, 1946. With U.S. Army, 1944-46. Named to East Chgo. Hall of Fame All Am. Amateur Baseball Congress, 1955, 56, 57, Ind. Amateur Baseball Hall of Fame, 1962, US Masters Track and Field All Am., 1995-98 (ranked 8 times # 1 and 2 in the country in masters track and field, 8 times ranked # 1 and 2 in the world in masters track and field, 1996-98, 10 nat. sr. Olympic medals), 35 (20 gold) individual Ind. Hoosier State Games Regional Medals, 35 (20 gold) individual Ind. Hoosier State Games Final Medals, 1996, 97, 98, 2000, 01, 2 Alltime State Records; Nat. Sr. Olympic track and field qualifier, 1997-99; 90 Yr. Greatest Athletes in East Chgo.'s History, Individual and Team Records Baseball Hall of Fame Archives, Cooperstown, NY, 2003; mem. team won 53 league championships, 54 playoff championships, 41 Ind. State baseball championships, 7 world regional titles, 2 runner-up world championships, Nat. C.I.O. baseball championship, 1950, 1949 Big Ten Baseball Champions, Ind. U.; conf. baseball champions, 1942-44; all-conf. team, 1942-44, capt., 1942-44; named Most Valuable Player, Best Infielder award, Batting Champ, All-Star Team, 1950; Ind. State Jr. Legion champions, all-state, Midwest All-Star team, 1942, Ind.-Ill. Bi-State champions, 1950, Most Valuable, Batting Champion, Best Infielder award, 1950; career and team records in Baseball Hall of Fame Archives, 2003; named Northwest Ind. Intriguing Family of Yr., 2002; recipient 15 league batting titles, 11 MVP awards, 22 times Ind. All State in Baseball, 21 times League Mgr. of Yr., Nat./European Tchr. of Yr., 1984, Life Time Achievement award Ind. U., 2007. Fellow VFW (charter mem. World War II Meml. 1998), Am. Legion, Normandy Invasion Club, Nat. Assn. of Basketball Coaches, Nat. Wildlife Assn. Republican. Avocations: reading, writing, baseball, tennis, golf. Home: 920 Troon Ct Schererville IN 46375

PLATIS, JAMES GEORGE, secondary school educator; b. Detroit, Mar. 23, 1927; s. Sam and Myra (Theodore) P.; m. Mary Lou Campbell, Aug. 16, 1974. BS in Physical Edn., Ind. U., 1955, MS in Edn., 1965; postgrad., Ind. State U., Terre Haute, 1967. Cert. physical edn. tchr., Ind. Foreman Cast Armor, Inc., East Chicago, Ind., 1951-53, Youngstown Sheet & Tube, East Chicago, 1953-54; dir., tchr. East Chicago Pub. Schs., 1955—. Sports editor East Chicago Globe/Calumet News, 1973-78, Herald Newspapers, Merrillville, Ind., 1973-78; asst. dir. No. Ind. State Sports Mus., 1984-99. Contbr. articles to newspapers, jours. Founder East Chicago Hall of Fame, 1975, Little Olympics, East Chicago, 1956; pres. Ind. Am. Amateur Baseball Congress, 1954-57, commr., 1984-98; dir. No. Ind. State Sports Mus., 1988-00. With AUS, 1945-47, ETO. Named to Ind. Amateur Baseball Hall of Fame, 1962, East Chicago Hall of Fame, 1976, All-Am. Amateur Baseball Congress, 1955, 56, The Athletic Congress Masters All-Am., 1986-98, 99, 2000, 2001-02; selected to 90 Yr. Greatest Athletes in East Chicago History, Nat. Athletic Congress, 1990; named Amateur Coach of Yr., US Baseball Fedn. Ind., 1990, Amateur Runner-up Coach of Yr., 1988; recipient 53 World and 61 Nat. No. 1 track rankings, Athletic Congress Masters, 1989-98, 2000, 2001-02, 16 League Batting Titles, 12 MV League Players awards; Ind. Jr. Legion State Champions, All-State Batting Champions, MVP in tournament, Conf. Baseball Champions, 1943, 44, 45, All-Conf. Team, 1944-45, Conf. Batting Champion, 1944, Team Cptn., 1945, All-Midwest team, Best Outfielder, 1944; 23 times Ind. all-state team; Ind. Nat. Baseball State Champions; mem. team won 53 League Championships, 54 Playoff championships, 41 Ind. State Baseball Championships, 5 Ind. State Champions Runner Up, 7 World Regional Titles, 5 World Finalists, 2 runner-up World Champions, Big Ten baseball champions Ind. U., 1949, Best Outfielder Congress All-State team, Ill., Ind. Bi-State Champions, 1950; Nat. C.I.O. Baseball Championship, 1951, 12 Times League Mgr. Of The Year, 1982-96; Big Ten Baseball Champions, Ind. U., 1949; named Athlete of Yr. Ind. Masters Track and Field, 1992, World Sr. Olympic Masters Track & Field Champion, Spain, 6 gold medals, named Best Performer, 3 Masters Track & Field World Records, 1992, Fla. Masters Track and Field Athlete of Yr., 1994-98; recipient 74 State Ind. Track and Field Individual Gold medals, 1983-99, 2000-02, 84 Ind. state regional individual gold medals, 1983-98, 2000-02, 322 All Am. Masters Track and Field Certs., 1986-99, 2000-02, 39 Ill. Grand Prix individual titles, 1989-92, 45 Mid-West Track and Field individual titles, 1989-92, 5 gold medals, silver medal World Sr. Olympic Masters Track & Field, 1996, Ga., 5 Masters Track & Field World Records, 1997, 2 Masters Track & Field World Records, 1998, Nat. Senior Olympics Qualifer, 1991,

93, 95, 97, 99, 2001, 03, 4 Gold medals, 2 World Records Nat. Sr. Olympics, 1999-2001, 7 gold medals World Sr. Olympic Masters Track and Field, Sydney, Australia, 2000, 5 World Records, selected Best Performer; named Internat. Man of the Yr. in Edn., 1991-92, 93, Profl. of the Yr. in Edn., 1991, Master Track and Field All-Am., 1986-2003, Northwest Ind. Intriguing Family of the Yr., 2002, 8 Decades of Baseball, Individual & Team Records in Baseball Hall of Fame, Cooperstown, NY, 2003, Youth award Chgo. Profl. Pitch & Hit Club, 2005. Fellow Nat. Assn. Basketball Coaches, Am. Assn. Health, Phys. Edn. and Recreation; mem. Athletic Dirs. Assn. Sportswriters Guild, VFW, Am. Legion, WWII Meml. (82nd Airborne Divsn., 1st Inf. Divsn. 1998), Mens Club Ind. U., Lifetime Achievment award, Ind. U., 2007. Republican. Avocations: reading, running, baseball, writing.

PLATNICK, NORMAN I., curator, entomologist; b. Bluefield, W.Va., Dec. 30, 1951; s. Philip and Fannie (Kascenewsky) P.; m. Nancy Stewart Price, June 14, 1970; 1 child, William Durin. BS in Biology, Concord Coll., 1968; MS in Zoology, Mich. State U., 1970; PhD in Biology, Harvard U., 1973. Asst. curator Am. Mus. Natural History, NYC, 1973-77, assoc. curator, 1977-82, curator, 1982-98, chmn. dept. entomology, 1987-94, Peter J. Solomon Family curator, 1998—; program dir. biotic surveys and inventories NSF, 2002—03. Sci. attaché Consulate of Gondwana, N.Y.C., 1976—. Author: The World Spider Catalog; co-author: Systematics and Biogeography, 1981; co-editor: Advances in Cladistics, 1983. V.p. Ctr. Internat. de Documentation Arachnologie, 1986-89 (pres. 1995-98). Fellow Willi Hennig Soc. (founder, pres. 1990-92); mem. Am. Arachnological Soc. (charter, membership sec. 1976—2002). Office: Am Mus Natural History Central Pk W At 79th St W New York NY 10024 Office Phone: 212-769-5612. Business E-Mail: platnick@amnh.org.

PLATSOUCAS, CHRIS DIMITRIOS, immunologist; b. Athens, Greece, Apr. 17, 1951; came to U.S., 1973; s. Dimitrios Evagelos and Maria (Tsonidis) P.; m. Emilia L. Oleszak, Oct. 18, 1985. BS, Patras U., Greece, 1973; postgrad., Purdue U., 1974; PhD, MIT, 1978. Rsch. fellow/assoc. Meml. Sloan-Kettering Cancer Ctr., NYC, 1978—81, asst. mem., 1982—85, asst. prof., 1981-85, head lab. biol. response modifiers, 1981-85; assoc. prof. dept. immunology M.D. Anderson Cancer Ctr., Houston, 1985-89, prof., dep. chmn., 1989-93, Ashbel Smith professorship, 1991-92, H.L. and O. Stringer professorship in cancer rsch., 1992-93; L.H. Carnell prof. dept. microbiology, immunology Temple U. Sch. Medicine, Phila., 1993—2007, chmn. dept. microbiology and immunology, 1993—2006; acting dean Coll. Sci. and Tech. Temple U., Phila., 1998-2000, dean Coll. Sci. and Tech., 2000—04, Old Dominion U., Norfolk, Va., 2007—. Biotech. cons., sci. reviewer study sects. NIH, Bethesda, Md., 1982—. Contbr. numerous articles to profl. jours. Nat. Rsch. Svc. award NIH, 1978-79; grantee NIH, Am. Cancer Soc., State of Tex., many others. Mem. Am. Assn. Immunologists, Am. Soc. Hematology, Am. Assn. Biochem & Molecular Biology, Soc. Investigative Pathology, Am. Assn. Cancer Rsch. Greek Orthodox. Achievements include patents in field; research on human T cell immunology, on T-cell antigen receptors, on tumor-infiltrating lymphocytes in malignant melanoma and ovarian carcinoma, on organ transplantation, on chronic rejection, on AIDS, on multiple sclerosis, schlerodema, osteoarthritis, and other autoimmune diseases. Office: Old Dominion Univ Office of Dean, Coll Sci 4600 Elkhorn Ave OCNPS Rm 143 Norfolk VA 23529 Home Phone: 215-300-8610; Office Phone: 757-683-3277. Business E-Mail: cplatsoucas@odu.edu.

PLATT, FRANKLIN DEWITT, retired history professor; b. Marion, La., Nov. 15, 1932; s. Robert Baxter and Ethel Estelle (White) P.; m. Dixie Ferguson, Aug. 4, 1956; 1 dau. Dixie. BA, La. State U., 1955; Rockefeller Bros. Theol. fellow, Union Theol. Sem., 1955-56; A.M., Washington U., St. Louis, 1963, PhD, 1969. Instr. dept. humanities Mich. State U., East Lansing, 1964-69, asst. prof., 1969-72, assoc. prof., 1972-77, prof., 1977-89, asst. chmn. dept. humanities, 1971-78, chmn., 1978-80, prof. history, 1989-96, prof. emeritus, 1997—. Co-author: The Western Humanities, 1991 (named Best Coll. Textbook Bookbuilders West 1998), Readings in the Western Humanities, 1994. Served with USNR, 1956-60. also: 5190 Far Oak Cir Sarasota FL 34238-3303 Address: 1134 Southlawn Ave East Lansing MI 48823 Business E-Mail: plattf@msu.edu.

PLATT, JAN KAMINIS, former county official; b. St. Petersburg, Fla., Sept. 27, 1936; d. Peter Clifton and Adele (Diamond) Kaminis; m. William R. Platt, Feb. 8, 1963; 1 child, Kevin Peter. BA, Fla. State U., 1958; postgrad., U. Fla. Law Sch., 1958-59, U. Va., 1962, Vanderbilt U., 1964. Pub. sch. tchr. Hillsborough County, Tampa, Fla., 1959-60; field dir. Girl Scouts Suncoast Coun., Tampa, 1960-62; city councilman Tampa City Coun., 1974-78; county commr. Hillsborough County, 1978—94, country commr., 1996—2004; chmn. Hillsborough County Bd. County Commrs., 1980-81, 83-84, 98-99, ret., 1994, re-elected, 1996, chmn., 1998-99, County Charter Rev. Bd., 2005—06; cp-chair Countrywide Cultural Plan, 2006—. Chmn. Tampa Bay Regional Planning Coun., 1982, West Coast Regional Water Supply Authority, Tampa, 1985, Hillsborough County Coun. Govts., 1976, 79, Agy. Bay Mgmt., Hills Environ. Protection Commn., Sunshine Amendment Drive 7th Congrl. Dist., Tampa, 1976, Cmty. Action Agy., Tampa, 1981, 83-84,chmn. pro tem Tampa Charter Revision Commn., 1975, chmn. Prison Sitting Task Force, Tampa, 1983, Tampa Housing Study Com., 1983, Met. Planning Orgn., Tampa, 1984, Bd. Tax Adjustment, Tampa, 1984, chmn. Hartline, 2002-03, Friendship Trailbridge Oversight Com., 2002-03, Tampa Bay Water, 2003-04; appointee Constn. Revision Commn., Fla., 1977, HRS Dist. IV Adv. Coun., Fla.; mem. Hillsborough County Expy. Authority, Taxicab Commn., Ch. Hills Cmty. Youth Coun.; vice chmn. steering com. Nat. Counties Environ. Task Force; pres. Suncoast Girl Scout Coun., 1973-74, Ch. Head Start Cmty. Found., 2005-07; chmn. County Charter Rev. Bd., 2005-07. Bd. dirs. March of Dimes, Tampa, The Fla. Orch., Tampa, Tampa Bay Sierra, Tampa Audubon; trustee Hillsborough County Hosp. Authority, Tampa, 1984-94; pres. Citizens Alert, Tampa, Bay View Garden Club, Rose Garden Cir., 2007; v.p. Hillsborough County Bar Aux.; adv. bd. Northside Cmty. Mental Health Ctr.: Access House, Tampa; active Arts Coun. Tampa-Hillsborough County, 1983-85, 96-2001, Drug Abuse Coordinating Coun. Orgn., Tampa, Bd. Criminal Justice, Tampa, Fla. Coun. on Aging, Inebriate Task Force, Tampa, Tampa Downtown Devel. Authority Task Force, Tampa Sports Authority, Tampa Area Mental Health Bd., Children's Study Commn., Manahill Area Agy. on Aging, Tampa, Athena Soc., Tampa Area Com. Fgn. Affairs, LWV; v.p. Life Enrichment Ctr.; bd. dirs. Arts Coun.; exec. com. Tampa Performing Arts Ctr., chmn. charter rev. bd.; co-founder, v.p. Ylor Fresh Market; pres. Keep Hillsborough Beautiful, 2007-, Waverly Homeowners Assn., 2007-; mem. Com. of 100. Recipient Athena award, Women in Comm., 1976, Spessard Holland Meml. award, Tampa Bay Com. for Good Govt., 1979, First Lady of Yr. award, Beta Sigma Phi, 1980, First Ann. Humanitarian award, Nat. Orgn. of Prevention of Animal Suffering, 1981, Women Helping Women award, Soroptimist Internat. Tampa, 1983, Good Govt. award, Tampa Jaycees, 1983, LWV, 1983, John Books Meml. award, Fla. Audubon Soc., 1989, Girl Scout Woman of Distinction award, 1996, Girl Scout Thanks award, 1996, Libery Bell award, Hillsborough County Bar Assn., 2000, Black Bear award, Suncoast and Tampa Bay Groups of the Sierra Club, 2001, Eliza Wolff award, Tampa United Meth. Ctrs., Outstanding Leadership in Local Environ. Protection, Fla. Local Environ. Resource Agys., 2002, Lifetime Achievement award for outstanding leadership in local environ. protection, 2004, Communicator of Yr., Tampa Ednl. Cable Consortium, 2005, Disting. Alumna award, Fla. State U., 2005, Tampa Bay Ethics award, Tampa U. Ctr. Ethics, 2005, Dan Hanson Conservationist Yr., Frank Sargenat Fishing Expo, 2006, Zonta Status of Women award, 2006. Mem. Am. Judicature Soc., State Assn. County Commrs. Fla. (at-large dir.), AAUW (bd. dirs.), Mortar Board (Disting. Liftetime Mem. award 2006), Garnet Key, Phi Beta Kappa (past pres. local alumni), Phi Kappa Phi. Democrat. Episcopalian. Home: 3531 Village Way Tampa FL 33629-8914

PLATT, JEFFREY LOUIS, surgeon, director, immunologist, educator, pediatric nephrologist; b. New Rochelle, NY, Mar. 21, 1949; s. Charles Alfred and Paula Platt; m. Agnes M. Schipper. BA in Politics with honors, NYU, 1971; postgrad., Columbia U., 1971-73; MD, U. So. Calif., 1977. Diplomate Am. Bd. Pediatrics, Nat. Bd. Med. Examiners. Intern in pediatrics Children's Hosp. L.A., 1977-78, resident, 1978-79, Della M. Mudd resident, 1979-80; med. fellow in pediatric nephrology U. Minn., Mpls., 1980-85, instr. dept. pediatrics, 1985-86, asst. prof., 1986-88, assoc. prof. pediatrics and cell biology and neuroanatomy, 1988-92; prof. surgery, pediatrics and immunology depts. Duke U., Durham, NC, 1992—98, Dorothy W. and Joseph W. Beard prof. exptl. surgery, 1994—98; prof. surgery immunology and pediatrics Mayo Clinic, Rochester, Minn., 1998—, dir. transplantation biology, vice chair surgery rsch., 2006—. Mem. editl. bd.: Transplantation, Transplant Immunology, Xenotransplantation, Jour. Immunology, Cellular Immunology; mem. editl. bd. Human Immunology, editor Innate Immunity; contbr. over 500 articles to med. jours.; author: 4 books. Recipient Clinician-Scientist award Am. Heart Assn., 1983-88, Established Investigator award Am. Heart Assn., 1988-93, Inst. Medicine of NAS. Mem. AAAS, NIH (Merit award), Assn. Am. Physicians, Am. Heart Assn (coun. kidney in cardiovasc. disease, coun. basic sci.), Internat. Soc. Nephrology, Am. Assn. Immunologists, Am. Fedn. Clin. Rsch., Am. Soc. Nephrology, Am. Assn. Pathologists, Soc. for Devel. Biology, Clin. Immunology Soc., Soc. Pediatric Rsch., Soc. Glycobiology, Soc. Exptl. Biology and Medicine, Alpha Omega Alpha. Office: Mayo Found Medical Scis Bldg Rm 2 Rochester MN 55905-0001 Business E-Mail: platt.jeffrey@mayo.edu.

PLATT, JONATHAN JAMES, lawyer; b. Southampton, NY, Aug. 3, 1950; s. William Bangs Jr. and Edith Elizabeth (Guldi) P.; m. Linda Lee Tiska, Sept. 23, 1978. BS in Fgn. Svc., Georgetown U., 1972; JD, Fordham U., 1976. Bar: N.Y. 1977, U.S. Dist. Ct. (ea. dist.) N.Y. 1988, U.S. Ct. Appeals (2d cir.) 1988. Assoc. William B. Platt, Jr., Southampton, 1977-78; ptnr. Platt & Platt, Southampton, 1978-80, Platt, Platt & Platt, Southampton, 1980-2000; pvt. practice Southampton, 2001—. Counsel Elks, Southampton, 1983—. Mem. ABA (gen. practice sect., probate and trust sect., real property sect., 1985—, sect. of law practice mgmt. 1993—), N.Y. State Bar Assn. (real property sect., trusts and estates law, gen. practice sect. 1977—, invited participant statewide conf. solo and small firm practitioners 1991), Suffolk County Bar Assn. (real property com., solo and small firm task force 1992-97, Pres.' award of merit 1994), Elks (hon., exalted ruler 1982-83, hon. life, dist. govt. rels. chmn. 1991-94, esquire to dist. dep. 1993-94). Republican. Roman Catholic. Avocations: photography, videography, golf, scuba diving. Office: 99 Sanford Pl Southampton NY 11968-3338 Home Phone: 631-283-9031; Office Phone: 631-283-0099. E-mail: jplattesq@aol.com.

PLATT, JOSEPH BEAVEN, former college president; b. Portland, Oreg., Aug. 12, 1915; s. William Bradbury and Mary (Beaven) P.; m. Jean Ferguson Rusk, Feb. 9, 1946; children: Ann Ferguson Walker, Elizabeth Beaven Garrow. BA, U. Rochester, 1937; PhD, Cornell U., 1942; LLD, U. So. Calif., 1969, Claremont McKenna Coll., 1982; DSc, Harvey Mudd Coll., 1981. Instr. physics U. Rochester, NY, 1941-43, from asst. prof. to prof., 1946-56, assoc. chmn. dept. physics, 1954-56; staff mem. Radiation Lab. MIT, Cambridge, 1943-46; founding pres. Harvey Mudd Coll., Claremont, Calif., 1956-76; pres. Claremont Grad. U., 1976-81. Trustee Aerospace Corp., 1972-85, Consortium for Advancement of Pvt. Higher Edn., 1985-92; chief physics br. AEC, 1949-51; cons. US Office Ordnance Rsch., NSF, 1953-56; mem. com. on sci. in UNESCO, NAS-NRC, 1960-62, mem. com. on internat. orgns. and programs, 1962-64, sci. advisor US Del., UNESCO Gen. Conf., Paris, 1960, alt. del., 1962, chmn. Subcom. on Sino-Am. Sci. Cooperation, 1965-79; mem. panel on internat. sci. Pres.'s Sci. Adv. Com., 1961; trustee Analytic Svcs., Inc., 1958-89, chmn., 1961-89; mem. adv. com. on sci. edn. NSF, 1965-70, 72-76, chmn., 1969-70, 73-74, 74-75; bd. dirs. Lincoln Found., 1979-85, Bell & Howell Corp., 1978-88, Am. Mut. Fund, 1981-88, DeVry, Inc., 1984-87, Sigma Rsch., 1983-87, Jacobs Engring. Co., 1978-86. Author: Harvey Mudd College: The First Twenty Years, 1994. Trustee China Found. for Promotion of Edn. and Culture, 1966—, Carnegie Found. for Advancement Tchg., 1970-78, Ancient Bibl. Manuscript Ctr., 1980-2005; chmn. select com. Master Plan for Higher Edn. Calif., 1971-73; mem. Carnegie Coun. for Policy Studies in Higher Edn., 1975-80. Fellow Am. Phys. Soc.; mem. IEEE, Automobile Club So. Calif. (bd. dirs. 1973-90, chmn. bd. dirs. 1986-87), Calif. Club, Sunset Club, Twilight Club, Cosmos Club, Bohemian Club, Phi Beta Kappa, Sigma Xi, Phi Kappa Phi. Home: 452 W 11th St Claremont CA 91711-3833 Business E-Mail: joseph_platt@hmc.edu.

PLATT, LESLIE A., lawyer; b. Bronx, NY, Aug. 7, 1944; s. Harold and Ann (Bienstock) P.; m. Marcia Ellin Berman, Aug., 1969; 1 son, Bill Lawrence. BA, George Washington U., 1966; JD, NYU, 1969. Bar: N.Y. 1970, U.S. Dist. Ct. D.C. 1972. Atty. advisor Office Gen. Counsel HUD, Washington, 1971-72, legis. atty., 1972-75, asst. gen. counsel for legis. svcs., 1975-78, assoc. gen. counsel for legis., 1978-80; dep. gen. counsel-legal counsel HEW (HHS 1980) Office Gen. Counsel, Washington, 1980-81, legal counsel and staff dir. White House Agent Orange group, 1980-81; pvt. practice Washington, 1982-91; exec. asst. to dir. NIH, 1991-92; exec. v.p., COO, gen. counsel The Inst. for Genomic Rsch., Gaithersburg, Md., 1992-95; sr. v.p. strategic devel., gen. counsel Am. Type Culture Collection, Manassas, Va., 1996-98; prin. assurance and adv. bus. practice Ernst & Young LLP, McLean, Va., 1999—2004; counsel Pillbury Winthrop Shaw Pittman, LLP, Washington, 2007—. Pres, dir. Found. for Genetic Medicine, Inc., 1997—2004; adj. prof. George Mason U., 2005—. Patentee in field. Chmn. cmty. adv. bd. Fairfax Hosp. Assn. Cameron Glen Facility; chair steering com. Reston/Herndon Bus.-H.S. Partnership; mem. Loudoun County Sci. and Tech. Cabinet, 2002—04, chair, 2006—; bd. dirs. No. Va. Tech. Coun., 2002—05. Recipient Disting. Svc. award HUD, 1978. Mem. ABA, Fed. Bar Assn., Am. Jud. Soc., Fed. Sr. Exec. Svc. (charter), Internat. Bar Assn. Home: 11901 Triple Crown Rd Reston VA 20191-3015 Office: Pillsbury Winthrop Shaw Pittman LLP 2300 N St NW Washington DC 20037 Office Phone: 202-663-8308. Business E-Mail: leslie.platt@pillsburylaw.com.

PLATT, NICHOLAS, retired ambassador; b. NYC, Mar. 10, 1936; s. Geoffrey and Helen (Choate) P.; m. Sheila Maynard, June 28, 1957; children: Adam, Oliver, Nicholas. BA cum laude, Harvard U., 1957; MA, Johns Hopkins U., 1959. Commd. fgn. svc. officer Dept. State, 1959; vice consul Windsor, Ont., Canada, 1959-61; Chinese lang. trainee, 1962-63; polit. officer consulate gen. Hong Kong, 1964-68; chief Asian Communist areas divsn. Bur. Intelligence and Rsch., Dept. State, Washington, 1969, chief North Asia div., 1970, dept. dir. Exec. Secretariat staff, 1971, dir. staff, 1972-73; chief polit. sect. U.S. Liaison Office, Peking, China, 1973-74; 1st sec. Am. embassy, Tokyo, 1974-77; dir. Office of Japanese Affairs, Dept. State, 1977-78; mem. staff Nat. Security Council, White House, 1978-79; dep. asst. sec. for internat. security affairs Dept. Def., 1980-81; dep. asst. sec. for internat. orgn. affairs Dept. State, 1981-82; amb. Lusaka, Zambia, 1982-84; exec. sec., spl. asst. to sec. state Dept. State, 1985-87; amb. to The Philippines Am. Embassy, Manila, 1987-91, amb. to Pakistan, 1991-92; pres. Asia Soc., NYC, 1992—2004, pres. emeritus, 2004—. Bd. dirs. Fiduciary Trust Internat. Recipient Meritorious award exemplary achievement pub. adminstrn. William A. Jump Found., 1973, Disting. Civilian Svc. medal Dept. Def., 1981, Presdl. Merit award, 1985, 87, Disting. Honor award U.S. Dept. State, 1987, 91, Wilbur Carr award, 1992. Mem. N.Y. Coun. Fgn. Rels., Met. Club (Washington), Century Club, Union Club. Home: 131 E 69th St New York NY 10021-5158

PLATT, NINA, law librarian; d. Harlan and Ethel (Byron) Thorlacius; m. Vernon Platt, Dec. 21, 1984. BS, U. ND, Grand Forks, 1980; Ms of Libr. and Info. Sci., Dominican U., River Forest, Ill., 1997. Libr. dir. Carnegie Libr., Devils Lake, ND, 1982—85; tech. svcs. mgr. Dorsey & Whitney, Mpls., 1986—95; systems libr. Minn. Office of Atty. Gen., St. Paul, 1995—97; dir. of libr. services Faegre & Benson LLP, Mpls., 1998—. Cons. Nina Platt & Associates, Prior Lake, Minn., 1993—98. Contbr. textbook Knowledge Management for the Information Professional, articles to profl. jours. and web sites. Mem.: Minn. Law Libr. Assn. (Law Librarianship award 2003), Spl. Libraries Assn. (Innovations in Tech. award 2003), Minn. Assn. Law Libraries, Am. Assn. Law Libraries (exec. bd. mem. 2002—), Minn. Libr. Assn. (assoc.), Hekla Club (pres. 1996—97). Achievements include development of Minnesota's appellate court opinions archive. Avocations: motorcycling, gardening. Office: Faegre & Benson LLP 2200 Wells Fargo Ctr 90 S 7th St Minneapolis MN 55402 Business E-Mail: nplatt@faegre.com.

PLATT, OLIVER, actor; b. Windsor, Ont., Can., Jan. 12, 1960; s. Nicholas Platt and Sheila Maynard; m. Camilla Campbell, 1993; children: Lily, George, Claire. Attended, Tufts U. Actor: (films) Crusoe, 1988, Married to the Mob, 1988, Working Girl, 1988, Flatliners, 1990, Postcards from the Edge, 1990, Beethoven, 1992, Diggstown, 1992, Benny & Joon, 1993, Indecent Proposal, 1993, The Temp, 1993, The Three Musketeers, 1993, Tall Tale, 1995, Funny Bones, 1995, Executive Decision, 1996, A Time to Kill, 1996, Venice, 1997, Bulworth, 1997, Dangerous Beauty, 1998, Doctor Dolittle, 1998, A Small Miracle, 1998, The Impostors, 1998, Simon Birch, 1998, Three to Tango, 1999, Gun Shy, 1999, Lake Placid, 1999, Bicentennial Man, 1999, Gun Shy, 2000, Ready to Rumble, 2000, Don't Say a Word, 2001, Liberty Stands Still, 2002, ZigZag, 2002, Ash Wednesday, 2002, Pieces of April, 2003, Hope Springs, 2003, Kinsey, 2004, Loverboy, 2005, The Ice Harvest, 2005, Casonova, 2005, The Ten, 2007, (TV films) The Infiltrator, 1995, Cinderelmo, 1999, (TV series) Deadline, 2000-01, Queens Supreme, 2003, Huff, 2004-, (Broadway plays) Shining City, 2006; assoc. prodr. (film) Big Night, 1996. Office: c/o William Morris Agy 151 S El Camino Dr Beverly Hills CA 90212-2704 *

PLATT, RORIN MORSE, history professor, historian; s. Sam and Murl Virginia Platt; m. Liudmila Fedorovna Konovalova, Mar. 12, 2004; 1 child, Vladimir Alekandrovich Konovalov. Attended, Georgetown U., DC, 1973, U. Va., 1981; BA, U. NC, Chapel Hill, 1976; MA, U. NC, Greensboro, 1979; PhD, U. Md., College Park, 1989. Grad. asst. British history U. NC, Greensboro, 1977—78, instr. US history, 1978—79; tchg. asst. U. Tenn., Knoxville, 1979—80; chmn. dept. history St. Stephen's Sch., Alexandria, Va., 1980—87; adj. asst. prof. history U. Md., Catonsville, 1989—90; vis. asst. prof. history U. Tenn., Chattanooga, 1990—91, adj. prof. history & polit. sci., 1991—95; history tchr., class dean McCallie Sch., Chattanooga, 1992—95; headmaster St. Timothy's-Hale Sch., Raleigh, NC, 1995—96; adj. prof. history & politics Meredith Coll., Raleigh, 1997—98; lectr. history Peace Coll., Raleigh, 1998—99; lead tchr., dir. summer history program Woodberry Forest Sch., Va., 1999—2000; vis. asst. prof. history Peace Coll., Raleigh, 1999—2001; assoc. prof. history Campbell U., Buies Creek, NC, 2001—. Varsity tennis & squash coach St. Stephen's Sch., 1980—87; ap reader, cons. US history Coll. Bd., NYC, 1992—99, faculty cons., ap European history, 1999—; mem. vis. evaluation com. SACS/VAIS, Woodberry, Va., 1996—96; policy expert in intelligence gathering and covert ops. Heritage Found., DC, 2000—07; mem. NC Hwy. Hist. Marker Adv. Com., Raleigh, 2004—; editl. bd. Brill Publishing's History Internat. Rels., Diplomacy & Intelligence, Netherlands, 2007—. Author: (books) Virginia in Foreign Affairs, 1933-1941, Wings of Redemption: Col. Earl L. Cole and the 385th Bombardment Group, Eighth Air Force, 1943-1945; contbr. articles to profl. jours., books and newspapers. Mem. Am. Diplomacy Publishers, 2000—07, book rev. editor, 1999—2006, bd. dirs., 2000—. Mellon Rsch. fellow, Va. Hist. Soc., 1990. Mem.: Raleigh History Club, Phi Alpha Theta (assoc.). Episcopalian. Avocations: tennis, squash, reading, travel, jogging. Office: Campbell Univ PO Box 356 Buies Creek NC 27506 Office Fax: 910-814-4311. Business E-Mail: platt@campbell.edu.

PLATT, THOMAS COLLIER, JR., federal judge; b. NYC, May 29, 1925; s. Thomas Collier and Louise Platt; m. Ann Byrd Symington, June 25, 1948; children: Ann Byrd, Charles Collier, Thomas Collier, III, Elizabeth Louise. BA, Yale U., 1947, LL.B., 1950. Bar: N.Y. 1950. Assoc. Root, Ballantine, Harlan, Bushby & Palmer, NYC, 1950-53; asst. U.S. atty. Bklyn., 1953-56; assoc. Bleakley, Platt, Schmidt, Hart & Fritz, NYC, 1956-60, ptnr., 1960-74; judge U.S. Dist. Ct. (ea. dist.) N.Y., 1974—, chief judge Bklyn., 1988-95. Former dir. Phoenix Mut. Life Ins. Co., RAC Corp., McIntyre Aviation, Inc.; atty. Village of Laurel Hollow, N.Y., 1958-74; acting police justice Village of Lloyd Harbor, N.Y., 1958-63 Alt. del. Republican Nat. Conv., 1964, 68, 72; del. N.Y. State Rep. Conv., 1966; trustee Brooks Sch., North Andover, Mass., 1968-82, pres., 1970-74. Served with USN, 1943-46 Mem. Fed. Judges Assn. (sec., bd. dirs. 1982-91). Clubs: Phelps Assn. (New Haven) (bd. govs. 1960-98); Cold Spring Harbor Beach (N.Y.) (bd. mgrs. 1964-70); Yale of N.Y.C. Episcopalian. Office: US Dist Ct PO Box 9014 Central Islip NY 11722-9014 Office Phone: 631-712-5600.

PLATT, THOMAS E., lawyer; b. Everett, Wash., May 12, 1949; BA summa cum laude, Harvard U., 1971, JD cum laude, 1974. Bar: Wash. 1974. Counsel US Senate Com., 1974—76; mem. Perkins & Coie, Seattle, ptnr. Past pres. (bd.dir.) Bus. Volunteers for Arts; mem. (bd. trustees) Seattle Repertory Theatre; chair of Pers. Com. St. Mark's Cathedral. Recipient Best Lawyers in Am. Mem.: ABA, Steering Com., Pacific Coast Labor Law Conf. (past chair), King County Bar Assn. (past pres., (bd.trustees)), Phi Beta Kappa. Office: Perkins & Coie 1201 3rd Ave Ste 4800 Seattle WA 98101-3029 Office Phone: 206-359-8475. Office Fax: 206-359-9000. Business E-Mail: tplatt@perkinscoie.com.

PLATT, WARREN E., lawyer; b. McNary, Ariz., Aug. 5, 1943; BA, Mich. State U., 1965; JD, U. Ariz., 1969. Bar: Ariz. 1969, Calif. 1991, Texas 1993. Atty. Snell & Wilmer, Phoenix. Mng. editor Ariz. Law Rev., 1968—69. Fellow Am. Coll. Trial Lawyers; mem. Blue Key, Order of Coif, Phi Alpha Delta Office: Snell & Wilmer One Arizona Ctr Phoenix AZ 85004-0001 also: 6000 Anton Blvd Ste 1400 Costa Mesa CA 92626 Office Phone: 602-382-6292, 714-427-7475. Business E-Mail: wplatt@swlaw.com.

PLATT, WILLIAM HENRY, judge; b. Allentown, Pa., Jan. 25, 1940; s. Henry and Genevieve (McElroy) P.; m. Maureen Hart, Nov. 29, 1969; children: Meredith H., William H., James H. AB, Dickinson Coll., 1961; JD, U. Pa., 1964. Bar: Pa. 1967, U.S. Supreme Ct. 1971. Ptnr. Yarus and Platt, Allentown, 1967-77; asst. pub. defender Lehigh County (Pa.), 1972-75, chief pub. defender, 1975-76, dist. atty., 1976-91; ptnr. Eckert, Seamans, Cherin & Mellott, 1991-95; city solicitor City of Allentown, 1994-95; judge Ct. Common Pleas of Lehigh County, Allentown, 1996—, pres. judge, 2002—07. Mem. criminal procedural rules com. Supreme Ct. Pa., 1982-92, chmn., 1986-92; mem. Gov.'s Trial Ct. Nominating Commn. Lehigh County, 1984-87; mem. Pa. Commn. on Crime and Delinquency Victim Services Adv. Com., 1983-91. Served with M.P., U.S. Army, 1964-66. Mem.: ABA, Pa. Conf. of State Trial Judges (edn. com. 1997—2002, chmn. criminal law sect. 2001—), Pa. Bar Inst. (bd. dirs. 1989—2000, exec. com. 1994—2000, pres. 1997—98, hon. life dir.), Pa. Assn. Dist. Attys. (exec. com. 1980—86, pres. 1983—84, chmn.

1986—87, tng. inst. mem. 1986—91), Nat. Assn. Dist. Attys. (state dir. 1982—84), Lehigh County Bar Assn. (bd. dirs. 2007—), Pa. Bar Assn. Office: Lehigh County Courthouse 455 W Hamilton St Allentown PA 18101-1614 Office Phone: 610-782-3393.

PLATTNER, MARC FLOREA, foundation administrator, editor; b. NYC, May 8, 1945; s. Irving Herman and Claire Yvette (Bakst) P.; m. Jacqueline Suzanne Stark, Sept. 19, 1976; children: David Marshall, Laura Wolcott. AB summa cum laude, Yale U., 1966; PhD in Govt., Cornell U., 1974. Mng. editor The Pub. Interest, NYC, 1971-75; program officer The Twentieth Century Fund, NYC, 1975-81; adviser econ. and social affairs US Mission to UN, NYC, 1981-83; fellow Nat. Humanities Ctr., Rsch. Triangle Pk., NC, 1983-84; dir. program Nat. Endowment Democracy, Washington, 1984-89, counselor, 1989—2002, v.p. rsch. studies, 2002—; editor Jour. Democracy, 1989—; dir. Internat. Forum Dem. Studies, 1994—. Adj. prof., Touro Coll., N.Y.C., 1973-75; cons. Exec. Coun. on Fgn. Diplomats, Armonk, N.Y., 1984-90; vis prof. Robert Schuman Ctr. Adv. Studies European U. Inst., Florence, Italy, 2002-03. Author: Rousseau's State of Nature, 1979; editor: Human Rights in Our Time, 1984; co-editor: The Global Resurgence of Democracy, 1993, Capitalism, Socialism and Democracy Revisited, 1993, Nationalism, Ethnic Conflict, and Democracy, 1994, Democratization in Africa, 1999, The Democratic Invention, 2000, The Global Divergence of Democracies, 2001, Islam and Democracy in the Middle East, 2003, World Religions and Democracy, 2005; contbr. numerous articles to various publs. Dir. issues rsch., Moynihan for Senate campaign, N.Y.C., 1976. Herbert H. Lehman fellow, 1966-70; Earhart Found. fellow, 1970-71. Mem. Am. Polit. Sci. Assn., Coun. on Foreign Relations, Phi Beta Kappa. Office: Nat Endowment Democracy 1025 F St NW 8th Fl Washington DC 20004 Business E-Mail: marc@ned.org.

PLATTNER, RICHARD SERBER, lawyer; b. NYC, Aug. 10, 1952; s. Milton and Sallee Sarah (Serber) P.; m. Susan M. Madden, June 4, 1976 (div. June 1979); m. Susan K. Morris, Mar. 30, 1983; children: Samuel Morris, Katherine Elise. BA cum laude, Mich. State U., 1973; JD, Ariz. State U., 1977. Bar: Ariz. 1977, U.S. Dist. Ct. Ariz. 1977, U.S. Ct. Appeals (9th cir.) 1987; cert. specialist personal injury and wrongful death. Assoc. Wolfe & Harris, Pa., 1977-79, Monbleau, Vermeire & Turley, Phoenix, 1979-81, Phillips & Lyon, Phoenix, 1981; sole practice Phoenix, 1982-91; ptnr. Plattner Verderame, P.C., 1991—. Posse comdr. Maricopa County Sheriff Exec. Posse, 1986-87; judge pro tem Maricopa County Superior Ct., 1986-2003, Ariz. Ct. Appeals, 1993. Editor: Trial Judges of Maricopa County, 1985; co-editor Jury Verdict Research newsletter, 1982-83. Mem. ATLA (sustaining mem., mem. Leader's Forum), Am. Bd. Trial Advs. (assoc. 1997—), Ariz. Trial Lawyers Assn. (life mem., editor Ariz. Appellate Highlights, 1985—, bd. dirs., 1987—, pres. 1991), Ariz. Bar Assn. (mem. civil practice and procedure com. 1988-99, civil jury instrn. com. 1991), Maricopa County Bar Assn., Phoenix Trial Lawyers Assn. (bd. dirs. 1983-95, pres. 1986-87), Ariz. Bus. and Profl. Assn. (pres. 1984-86). Office: PO Box 36570 Phoenix AZ 85067-6570 Office Phone: 602-266-2002, 877-805-4529. Business E-Mail: rplattner@plattner-verderame.com.

PLATTS, HOWARD GREGORY, cultural organization administrator, not-for-profit fundraiser, director; b. Aug. 14, 1947; s. Thayer Horton and Anne Elizabeth (Gregory) P.; m. Elizabeth Hertzler Murray, June 7, 1969; children: James Thayer, Christopher Wilke. AB, Harvard U., 1969; M. Pub. and Pvt. Mgmt., Yale U., 1980. Tchr. Potomac Sch., McLean, Va., 1969-72; investment officer First Am. Bank, Washington, 1972-78; fin. analyst Yale U., New Haven, 1979; fin. asst. to pres. Nat. Geog. Soc., Washington, 1980-82, asst. treas., 1982-91, sr. v.p., treas., 1992—. Trustee Nat. Presbyn. Sch., Washington, 1988-91, Decatur House, Washington, 1994-2004, Ctr. for the Study of the Presidency, Washington, 2004—; chmn., trustee regional blood svcs. ARC, Balt., 1992-2000; treas., bd. dirs. Friends of Fort Dupont, Washington, 1995-2002; governing bd. St. Albans Sch., Washington, 1997-2003 Trustee Westmoreland Congl. Ch., 1988-91. Mem. Washington Soc. Investment Analysts (pres., bd. dirs. 1985-91). Home: 5302 Portsmouth Rd Bethesda MD 20816-2929 Office: Nat Geog Soc 1145 17th St NW Washington DC 20036-4701 Office Phone: 202-857-7417. Business E-Mail: platts@aya.yale.edu.

PLATTS, TODD RUSSELL, congressman, state legislator; b. York, Pa., Mar. 5, 1962; m. Leslie Platts; 2 children. BS summa cum laude in Pub. Adminstrn., Shippensburg U. Pa., 1984; JD cum laude, Pepperdine U. Sch. Law, Malibu, Calif., 1991. Atty. Barley, Snyder, Senft & Cohen; mem. Pa. State Ho. Reps. from Dist. 196, 1993-2001, US Congress from 19th Pa. dist., 2001—, mem. transp. and infrastructure com., mem. edn. and labor com., ranking mem. healthy families and cmtys. subcommittee, mem. oversight and govt. reform com. Mem. aging and youth edn. com. State of Pa., 1993. Republican. Episcopalian. Office: US House Reps 1032 Longworth House Office Bldg Washington DC 20515 Office Phone: 202-225-5836. Office Fax: 202-226-1000. *

PLATTS-MILLS, THOMAS ALEXANDER E., immunologist, educator, researcher; b. Colchester, Essex, Eng., Nov. 22, 1941; came to U.S., 1982; s. John Faithful F. and Janet Katherine (Cree) P.-M.; m. Roberta Rosenstock, Apr. 9, 1970; children: Eliza, Timothy, James, Oliver. BA, Balliol Coll., Eng., 1963; MB, BChir, Oxford U., 1967; PhD, London U., 1982. Registrar in medicine Bury St. Edmunds, and New Market, Suffolk, England, 1968-71; fellow in medicine Johns Hopkins U., Balt., 1971-74; staff mem. Med. Rsch. Coun., England, 1976-82; hon. cons. physician Northwick Park Hosp., London, 1978-82; prof. medicine, head divsn. allergy and clin. immunology U. Va., Charlottesville, 1982—, dir. Asthma and Allergic Diseases Ctr., 1994. Mem. immunological scis. study sect. NIH, 1988. Editl. bd. Am. Jour. Respiratory Critical Care Medicine, Clin. and Exptl. Immunology, Clin. Allergy, Jour. Immunological Methods; contbr. articles to profl. jours. Grantee NIH. Fellow Royal Coll. Physicians, Am. Acad. Allergy; mem. Assn. Am. Physicians, Am. Acad. Allergy, Asthma and Immunology (v.p. 2004—2005, pres.-elect, 2005-2006, pres. 2006-), Southeastern Allergy Assn. (Hal Davidson award 1986, pres. 1987-88), Brit. Soc. Allergy and Clin. Immunology. Office: U Va Dept Medicine PO Box 800225 Charlottesville VA 22908-0225 E-mail: tap2z@virginia.edu.

PLATUS, LIBBY, journalist, art educator, sculptor, artist; b. LA, Aug. 18, 1939; d. Benjamin Lyon and Gertrude Goldman; children: Julie Linda, Diana Lisa. BA, UCLA, 1961. Interviewer, writer Restaurant Hospitality Mag., 2005—07; restaurant reviewer; writer Moving Pictures Mag., 2006—07, Cheers Mag., 2007, Valley Mag., 2007, Trains Mag., 2007. Lectr., condr. workshops numerous internat., nat., regional meetings and meetings in all 50 states, World Craft Conf., Kyoto, 1978, Vienna, 80, Glasgow Sch. Art, Scotland, 1980, 84, Loughborough Coll. Art., England, 1980, 84, RI Sch. Design, 1982, Parsons Sch. Design, NYC, 1982, Arrowmont, Gatlinburg, Tenn., 1978, Gatlinburg, 83, Gatlinburg, 87, Konstfackakolan, Sweden, 1984, Goldsmith's Coll., England, 1984, Taldeteo Linen Koneakoulo, Finland, 1984, Fairbanks Art Assn., Alaska, 1985, 95, 97, 2000, 04, Savannah Coll. Art and Design, Ga., 1987, 89, 90, 92, 94, 99, E. NC U., Greenville, 1989, Greenville, 92, Greenville, 97, Greenville, 2000, Greenville, 02, Navajo CC, Shiprock Reservation, N.Mex., 1992, World Wildfowl Carving Exhbn., Ward Found., Md., 1990, Kansas City Art Inst., 1990, 92, So. Ute Tribal Hdqrs., Ignacio, Colo., 1993, U. Western Sydney Design Dept., 1993, Sydney Coll. Art, 1993, Victorian Coll. Art, Melbourne, Australia, 1993, U. S. Australia, Underdale, Australia, 1993, Australian Nat. U., Canberra, 1993, Walariki Poly. Coll., Rotorua, New Zealand, 1993, Actearoa Inst., South Auckland, New Zealand, 1993, numerous others; cons. Millstream Arts Festival Coll. St. Benedict, St. Joseph, Minn., 1992, Mountain State Art and Crafts Festival, Cedar Lakes, W.Va., 1992, Grand Junction area C. of C., Home Based Bus. Trade Fair, Colo., 1992, Yavapai Coll. Creative Comm. Convergence, Sedona, Ariz., 1995; judge regional exhbn. Fairbanks Art Assn., 1984, Mont. Food and Gift Show Made in Mont. Program, Mont. Dept. Commerce, Great Falls, 1999, Art Harvest Jr. League Clearwater-Dunedin, Fla., 2000, Greater Gulf Coast Art Festival, Pensacola, Fla., 1999; judge culinary competition Western Food Svc. and Hospitality Expo., LA, 2001; panel moderator Calif. Restaurant Assn., Western Food Svc. and Hospitality Expo., LA, 2004; juror Millstream Arts Festival, Coll. St. Benedict, St. Joseph, 1992; participant Charmin Care TV comml., 1989. Exhibited in group shows at Richmond Designer Craftsmen, Calif., 1971, Crocker Gallery, Sacramento, 1973, Comsky Gallery, Beverly Hills, Calif., 1973, Galeria del Sol, Santa Barbara, Calif., 1973, Laguna Beach Mus. Art, Calif., 1973, Riverside Art Ctr., 1974, Calif. State U., Northridge, 1974, Fullerton, 1974, Calif. Design, LA, 1976, Cleve. Mus. Art, 1977, Represented in permanent collections Tex. Christian U., Faberge Hdqrs., NYC, pub. and pvt. collections, prin. works include Big Canyon Country Club, Newport Beach, Calif., Carolando Hyatt Hotel, Victorville, Calif., Blue Cross So. Calif., LA. Mem., mem. citizens adv. commn. LA Olympics Cultural and Fine Arts Commn., 1980—84; adv. bd. Crafts Report Edn. Fund, 1985—86; participant Rotary Internat. Group Study Exch., Bangalore, India, 1998. Named winner, Tex. Christian U. Nat. Invitational Fiberwork Competition, 1977; recipient Graphic Achievement award, Fox River Paper Corp., 1974. Mem.: Artists Equity (adv. bd. L.A. chpt. 1981—87). Home and Office: PO Box 55026 Sherman Oaks CA 91413-0026 Office Phone: 818-906-3989. E-mail: libbyplatus@earthlink.net.

PLATUSICH, CHRISTIAN MICHAEL, underwriter; b. Elmira, NY, Mar. 7, 1980; s. Bruce and Catherine Platusich. BS in Marine Transp., US Mcht. Marine Acad., Kings Point, NY, 2002. Cert. dynamic positioning operator Nautical Inst., 2004. Underwriter offshore energy XL Ins., NYC, 1995—. Lt. USNR, 2002, officer USCG, 2003—05. Mem.: Am. Marine Ins. Forum. Office: XL Ins Marine and Offshore Energy 99 Park Ave 3rd Fl New York NY 10016-1501 Home Phone: 570-337-5206; Office Phone: 212-894-9229. Personal E-mail: chris_platusich@yahoo.com.

PLAUCHE, NANCY CAROLINE, retired counselor; b. Lima, Ohio, Oct. 31, 1938; d. Willis Sylvanis and Mabel Louise (Neiswander) Siferd; m. Jack Plauche (div. 1979); children: Michel, Jacqueline, Jon. BFA, Ohio U., 1960; MS, Nova U., Ft. Lauderdale, Fla., 1984; PhD, The Union Inst., Cin., 1989. Counselor Pinellas county Schs., St. Petersburg, Fla., 1980—2002; smoke stopper's instr. Nat. Ctr. for Health Promotion/Morton Plant Hosp., Clearwater, Fla., 1986-92; ret., 2002. Co-dir. Counseling & Profl. Cons. Svcs., St. Petersburg, 1984-88. Co-author: All About Me, 1985, Safer Parenting, 1985; contbr. articles to profl. jours. Mem. Dem. Exec. Com., Wood City W.Va., 1977-79; sustainor Jr. League St. Petersburg. Mem. APA, So. Assn. Coll. Counselors, Am. Psychol. Soc., Am. Arbitration Assn., People to People Internat., Fla. Counseling Assn., Fla. Sch. Counselors Assn., Clearwater Area Panhellenic Assn. Democrat. Avocations: painting, drawing, travel, cultural exchange.

PLAUD, JOSEPH JULIAN, psychology educator; b. Worcester, Mass., Mar. 25, 1965; s. Henry Emile and Barbara Ann (Perry) P.; m. Christine Marie Therlault, Mar. 14, 1987 (div. Mar. 1990); 1 child, Brianna Marie; m. Deborah Muench, Jan. 30, 1999. BA summa cum laude, Clark U., 1987; PhD in Psychology, U. Maine, 1993. Lic. clin. psychologist, Mass.; bd. cert. behavior analyst Behavior Analyst Cert. Bd. Psychology resident U. Miss. Med. Ctr., Jackson, 1992-93; asst. prof. psychology U. ND, Grand Forks, 1993-97; dir. rsch., webmaster Cambridge Ctr. for Behavioral Studies, Mass., 1999—2003; pres. Franklin D. Roosevelt Am. Heritage Ctr., Inc. Cons. ND Devel. Ctr., Grafton, 1994—, State of NH, 1999—; forensic cons., 1993—; vis. scholar Brown U., 1998—; COO New Sch. for Learning Scis.; forensic psychology cons. Applied Behavioral Cons., Inc. Author: From Behavior Theory to Behavior Therapy, 1997; editor-in-chief Jour. Behavioral Analysis and Therapy, Jour. Sexual Offender Civil Commitment: Science and the Law; contbr. articles to profl. jours. Pres. Franklin D. Roosevelt Am. Heritage Ctr., Inc. Lt. comdr. Med. Svc. Corps, USNR, 2002. Fellow APA, Behavior Therapy and Rsch. Soc. (clin.); mem. AAAS, Assn. for Advancement of Behavior Therapy, Am. Psychol. Soc., Phi Beta Kappa, Psi Chi. Democrat. Roman Catholic. Home: 44 Hickory Ln Whitinsville MA 01588-1356 E-mail: plaud@fdrheritage.org.

PLAUT, JONATHAN VICTOR, rabbi; b. Chgo., Oct. 7, 1942; s. W. Gunther and Elizabeth (Strauss) P.; m. Carol Ann Fainstein, July 5, 1965; children: Daniel Abraham, Deborah Maxine. BA, Macalester Coll., St. Paul, Minn., 1964; postgrad., Hebrew Union Coll., Jerusalem, 1967-68; BHL, Hebrew Union Coll., Cin., 1968, MA, 1970, DHL, 1977, DD (hon.), 1995. Ordained rabbi, 1970. Rabbi Congregation Beth-El, Windsor, Ont., Canada, 1970-84; sr. rabbi Temple Emanu-El, San Jose, Calif., 1985-93; dir. comty. outreach and involvement Jewish Fed. of Met. Detroit, 1993-95; pres. JVP Fund Raising Cons., Inc., Farmington Hills, Mich., 1994—. Lectr. Assumption Coll. Sch., 1972-84, St. Clair Coll., 1982-84, U. Windsor, Ont., Can., 1984; adj. asst. prof. Santa Clara U., 1985-93; adj. prof. U. Detroit Mercy, 2002—; vis. Rabbinic scholar Temple Beth El, 1993—95; pres. JVP Fund Raising Cons., 1994—; rabbi emeritus Congregation Beth El, Traverse City, Mich., 1999—2004; rabbi Temple Beth Israel, Jackson, Mich., 2000—. Contbg. author: Reform Judaism in America: A Biographical Dictionary and Sourcebook, 1993; editor: Through the Sound of Many Voices, 1982, Jour. Can. Jewish Hist. Soc., 1976-83, The Jews of Windsor 1790-1990: A Historical Chronicle, 2007, One Voice: The Selected Sermons of W. Gunther Plaut, 2007, The Plaut Family Tracing the Legacy, 2007, also articles; host weekly program Religious Scope, Sta. CBET-TV, Religion in News, Sta. CKWW, 1971-84. Pres. Jewish Nat. Fund Windsor, 1978-81, chmn. bd. dirs., 1981-84; chmn. United Jewish Appeal Windsor, 1981-83, State of Israel Bonds, Windsor, 1980; nat. bd. dirs. Jewish Nat. Fund Can., 1972-84; pres. Reform Rabbis of Can., 1982-84; bd. dirs. Can. Jewish Congress, 1978-84, Jewish Family Svc. Santa Clara County, 1987-90, Jewish Fedn. Greater San Jose, 1986-93; chaplain San Jose Fire Dept., 1987-93; mem. exec. cabinet United Jewish Appeal, Windsor, 1971-84, mem. nat. rabbinic cabinet, 1993-95; mem. exec. com. Windsor Jewish Community Coun., 1970-84, chmn. 1975-84; mem. adv. coun. Riverview unit Windsor Hosp. Ctr., 1972-81; pres. Credit Counselling Svc. Met. Windsor, 1977-79. Honoree Jewish Nat. Fund, 1985. Mem. NCCJ, Can. Jewish Congress (nat. exec. bd. 1978-84), Can. Jewish Hist. Soc. (nat. v.p. 1974-84), Calif. Bd. Rabbis, Rabbinic Assn. Greater San Jose (chmn. 1986-87), Ctrl. Conf. Am. Rabbis, Nat. Assn. Temple Educators. Home and Office: 30208 Kingsway Dr Farmington Hills MI 48331-1648 Office Phone: 248-505-8888. Fax: 248-788-4144. Personal E-mail: jvplaut@earthlink.net.

PLAUTZ, KIMBERLY ANN, music educator; d. Chuck and Sue Siedschlag; m. Dan Plautz, 2002. BA, Lakeland Coll., Sheboygan, Wis., 1991; MS in Edn., Concordia U., Mequon, Wis., 2000. Cert. tchr. Wis. Band tchr. Sheboygan Area Schs., 1992—, St. Mary's Springs HS, Fond du Lac, Wis., 1991—92. Master adjudicator Wis. Sch. Music Assn., Waunakee, 1994—. Performer Kiel Mcpl. Band, Wis., 1989—. Mem.: Wis. Youth Band Directors Assn. (webmaster 2006—). Avocations: travel, animal rescue.

PLAVE, LEE JONATHAN, lawyer; s. Seymour and Matty P.; m. Ilene P. BA, Clark U., 1980; JD cum laude, NY Law Sch., 1983. Bar: NY 1983, DC 1987. Atty., Used Car Rule program advisor FTC, Washington, 1983—87; assoc. to ptnr. Brownstein & Zeidman, P.C., Washington, 1987—96; ptnr. DLA Piper (formerly Piper Rudnick), Washington, 1996—2007; ptnr., chmn. Domain Name practice group DLA Piper, Washington, 2005—07; ptnr. Plave Koch PKC, Va., 2007—. Assoc. editor NY Law Sch. Jour. Internat. and Comparative Law, 1982-83; contbr. articles to profl. jours. Mem. ABA, Internat. Bar Assn., Va State Bar Assn., DC Bar Assn., NY State Bar Assn., Internat. Franchise Assn. Jewish. Avocations: ice hockey, stamp collecting/philately, politics. Office: Plave Koch PLC 11250 Roger Bacon Dr Ste 5 Reston VA 20190 Office Phone: 703-774-1203. Office Fax: 703-774-1201. Business E-Mail: lplave@plavekoch.com.

PLAVINSKAYA, ANNA DMITRIEVNA, artist; b. Moscow, Nov. 26, 1960; came to U.S., 1989, naturalized, 1995; d. Dmitri Petrovich and Nina Nicolaevna; m. Gennady Ioffe, Jan 9, 1988 (div. July 1993). Diploma in Costume Design, Theatrical Art Coll., Moscow, 1976-80. Costume designer Evgeny Vahtangov Theater, Moscow, 1980-82; artist freelance Moscow, 1983-89; art restorer pvt. studio, NYC, 1990-93; artist freelance NYC, 1993—. Exhibited in group shows at Gallery Moscow Artists, 1983, Ctrl. Exhbn. Hall, Moscow, 1984, 88, Kuznetzky Most Gallery, Moscow, 1985, Tbilisi Acad. Art, Georgia, 1986, Tallinna Moepaevad '87, Tallinn, Estonia, 1987, Remizovo St. Gallery, Moscow, 1988, Pushkin Sq. Gallery, Moscow, 1988, Textile Art Ctr., Chgo., 1991, Russian Nobility Assn., NYC, 1991, 11th Cleve. Internat. Drawing Biennale, Middlesbrough, Eng., 1993 (2d prize), BWA Gallery, Wroclaw, Poland, 1994, BWA Gallery, Lublin, Poland, 1994, Elblag (Poland) Gallery, 1994, Tatraniska Gallery, Poprad, Tatry, Slovakia, 1994, State Gallery, Ostrova, Czech Republic, 1994, Port Royal Mus. Gallery, Naples, Fla., 1994, Art Addiction Gallery, Stockholm, 1996-98 (cert. merit 1997), Art Addiction Gallery, Venice, Italy, 1998, Internat. Platform Assn., 1998, (1st place, Best of Show), 1999 (1st place award), Le Salon, Paris, 2000, 02-04, 06 (Bronze medal 2000), Salon Internat. Beziers, 2001-04, 06, 07 (Bronze medal 2001, Prix de La Societe Des Beaux Arts 2002), Salon D'Automne Internat., Luneville, France, 2001, 04, 14e annee Europ'Art Geneve Palexpo, Switzerland, 2005; represented in permanent collections Cleve. Contemporary Art Collection, Middlesbrough, Eng., Zimmerli Art Mus., Norton and Nancy Dodge Collection, NJ. Mem.: Nat. Fedn. French Culture. Russian Orthodox. Avocations: fashion design, antique textile restoration, tennis. Home: 815 W 181st St Apt 3E New York NY 10033-4530 Office Phone: 212-795-4258. Personal E-mail: annaplavinskaya@hotmail.com.

PLAX, KAREN ANN, lawyer; b. St. Louis, June 29, 1946; d. George J. and Evelyn G. Zell; m. Stephen E. Plax, Dec. 19, 1968; 1 child, Jonathan. BA magna cum laude, U. Mo., St. Louis, 1969; JD with distinction, U. Mo., Kansas City, 1976. Bar: Mo. 1976, U.S. Supreme Ct. 1980. Atty. Thayer, Gum & Wickert, Grandview, Mo., 1976-84, Plax & Cochet, Kansas City, Mo., 1984-87; pvt. practice Kansas City, 1987—. Chair divsn. 3, region IV Mo. Supreme Ct. Com. to review ethical conduct of attys., 1997—2006; pres. Collaborative Law Inst. Mo., 2003—05, v.p., 2006—07. Author: Missouri Bar Practical Skills, 1998; asst. editor: Racial Integration in the Inner Suburb, 1970; contbr. articles to profl. jours. Recipient Pub. Svc. award U. Mo. Kansas City Law Found., 1998, Woman of Yr. award Assn. Women Lawyers of Greater Kansas City, 1999; named Family Law Practioner of Yr., Mo. Bar, 2005 Fellow: Am. Acad. Matrimonial Lawyers (pres. Mo. chpt. 1999—2001); mem.: ABA (family law sect. 1976—), Mo. Bar Family Law (legis. chair 1997—98, v.p. 1999—2000, Spl. Commendation for Legis. Role in Family Law 1998), Kansas City Met. Bar Assn. Office: Ste 300 1310 Carondelet Dr Kansas City MO 64114-4803 Office Phone: 816-942-1900. Personal E-mail: kaplax@swbell.net.

PLAYER, THELMA B., librarian; b. Owosso, Mich. d. Walter B. and Grace (Willoughby) Player. BA, Western Mich. U., 1954. Reference asst. USAF Aero Chart and Info. Ctr., Washington, 1954-57; reference libr. USN Hydrographic Office, Suitland, Md., 1957-58, asst. libr., 1958-59; tech. libr.br. head USN Spl. Project Office, Washington, 1959-68, Strategic Sys. Project Office, Washington, 1969-76. Mem. ALA, AAUW, English Speaking Union, Spl. Librs. Assn., Nat. Geneal. Socl, Internat. Soc. Brit. Genealogy and Family History, Ohio Geneal. Soc. Royal Oak Found., Daus of Union Vets. of Civil War, David Ackerman Descs. Episcopalian. Home: 730 24th St NW Washington DC 20037-2519

PLAYFAIR, JIM, professional hockey coach; b. Vanderhoof, BC, Can., May 22, 1964; m. Roxanne Playfair; children: Dylan, Jackson, Austyn. Defenseman Portland Winter Hawks, 1981—83, Calgary Wranglers, 1983—84, Edmonton Oilers, 1984, Nova-Scotia Oilers, 1984—87, Saginaw Hawks, 1987—89, Chgo. Blackhawks, 1987—89, Indpls. Ice, 1989—92; head coach Dayton Bombers (ECHL), 1993—96, Michigan K-Wings (IHL), 1996—98, Saint John Flames (AHL), 2000—02; asst. coach Calgary Flames, 2003—06, head coach, 2006—07, assoc. coach, 2007—. Recipient Minor Profl. Coach of Yr., The Hockey News, 2001. Achievements include being the head coach of Calder Cup Champion Saint John Flames, 2001. Office: Calgary Flames PO Box 1540 Stn M Calgary AB Canada T2P 3B9 *

PLAZEK, DONALD JOHN, materials scientist, educator; b. Milw., Jan. 12, 1931; s. Stanley and Marian (Parker) Plazek; m. Patricia Lenore Filkins, Oct. 29, 1955; children: Mary, Joseph, Caroline, Daniel, John, David, Anne. BS in Chemistry, U. Wis., 1953, PhD in Phys. Chemistry, 1957. Postdoctoral rsch. fellow U. Wis., Madison, 1957-58; fellow Mellon Inst., Pitts., 1958-67; assoc. prof. materials engrng. U. Pitts., 1967-74, prof., 1974-93, prof. emeritus, 1993—. Adj. prof. chemistry Carnegie-Mellon U., Pitts., 1987—. Mem. adv. bd. Jour. Polymer Sci., 1991—98; assoc. editor: Rubber Chemistry and Tech., 1993—97; contbr. scientific papers to profl. jours. Fellow, Brit. Rsch. Coun., 1976—77, Japan Soc. Promotion Sci., 1987—88, Polymer and Materials Sci. Engring., 2006. Fellow: Am. Phys. Soc.; mem.: Soc. Rheology (Bingham medal 1995), Am. Chem. Soc. (George Stafford Whitby award for disting. tchg. and rsch. Rubber divsn. 1993). Avocations: tennis, tropical fish, mushrooms. Office: U Pitts Dept Mech Engring and Materials Sci Dept Pittsburgh PA 15261-0001 Home Phone: 412-766-0247; Office Phone: 412-648-8427. Business E-Mail: plazek@engr.pitt.edu.

PLEASANT, JAMES SCOTT, lawyer; b. Anniston, Ala., July 14, 1943; s. James C. and Barbara (Scott) P.; m. Susan M. Pleasant, May 17, 1966; children: Deborah Kaye, Carol Ann, Julie Ruth. BS, Oreg. State U., 1965; JD summa cum laude, Williamette U., 1972. Bar: Tex. 1972, U.S. Dist. Ct. (no. dist.) Tex. 1973, U.S. Ct. Appeals (5th cir.) 1975, U.S. Supreme Ct. 1977. Ptnr. Gardere Wynne Sewell, LLP, Dallas, 1972—. Mem. Smithsonian Assn., Washington, 1985—, Dallas Mus. of Art, 1987—. Capt. U.S. Army, 1966-69, Vietnam. Mem. ABA (partnership law sect. 1969—), Tex. Bar Assn. (partnership law sect. 1989—), Vietnam Pilots Assn., Dustoff Assn. Office: Gardere Wynne Sewell LLP 1601 Elm St Ste 3000 Dallas TX 75201-4761 Office Phone: 214-999-4690. E-mail: pleja@gardere.com.

PLEASANTS, JULIAN MCIVER, history educator, summer school director; b. Pinehurst, NC, Nov. 12, 1938; s. James McIver and Jean (McIver) P.; m. Donna Marie Bishop, Feb. 28, 1987. BA, Davidson Coll., Chapel Hill, NC, 1960; MA, U. NC, 1962, PhD, 1971. Asst. prof. Western Carolina U., Cullowhee, NC, 1966-67; from asst. prof to prof. U. Fla., Gainesville, 1969—. Instr. Converse Coll., Spartanburg, SC, 1962; dir. summer sch. U. New Orleans, U. Fla., 1976-97, dir., proctor oral history program, 1996-; cons. Documentary on Frank P. Graham, 1991. Author: Frank P. Graham and The Senate Election of 1950 in North Carolina, 1990 (Best Book in NC History 1991), Buncombe Bob: The Life and Times of Robert Rice Reynolds, 2001, Orange Journalism: Voices From Florida Newspapers, 2003, Hanging Chads: The Inside Story of the 2000 Presidential Recount in Florida, 2004, Gator Tales: An Oral History of the University of Florida. Dir. Upward Bound program, Gainesville, 1971. 1st lt. US Army, 1962-64. Rotary Internat. fellow, 1965-66, fellow Archie K. Davis Found., 1990-91; recipient award of merit City of Innsbruck, Austria, 1985, 91; named one of 10 Outstanding Profs., Interfraternity Coun.-Omicron Delta Kappa, 1972; named Most Inspiring Prof. U. Fla.,

1989. Mem. Fla. Hist. Assn., So. Hist. Assn., Golden Key (hon.), Phi Alpha Theta. Avocations: reading, walking, travel. Home: 9424 SW 21st Ave Gainesville FL 32607-3243 Office: U Fla History Dept 4103 Turlington Hall Gainesville FL 32611 Business E-Mail: jpleasan@history.ufl.edu.

PLEAU, LAWRENCE WINSLOW, professional sports team executive; b. Boston, June 29, 1947; s. Ernest and Norma (Knowles) Pl.; m. Wendy Sargent MacDougall, May 3, 1969; children, Steven Lawrence, Shannon Lynn. Grad. high sch. Player Montreal Canadiens, 1969-72, N.Eng. Whalers, Hartford, Conn., 1972-79; asst. coach Hartford Whalers, 1979-80, coach, gen. mgr., 1980-83, asst. gen. mgr., 1983-84, coach, 1988-89; coach, gen. mgr. Binghamton Whalers, NY, 1984-88; asst. gen. mgr. player devel. NY Rangers, 1989, asst. gen. mgr., v.p. player personnel; gen. mgr. St. Louis Blues, 1997—. Player U.S. Olympic Hockey Team, Grenoble, France, 1968, U.S. Nat. Hockey Team, Stockholm, 1969, U.S.A. Hockey Team, Providence, 1976; radio, TV commentator, ESPN, Hartford, 1979-80; owner Bridge Marina Inc. With U.S. Army, 1967-69. Mem. All-Star Teams, 1973, 74, 75; named Coach of Yr. Am. Hockey League, 1986-87, Exec. of Yr., The Sporting News, 1999-2000. Democrat. Achievements include being a member of Stanley Cup Champion Montreal Canadiens, 1971. Avocations: deep sea fishing, golf, tennis. Office: St Louis Blues Hockey Club Savvis Ctr 1401 Clark Ave Saint Louis MO 63103

PLEICONES, COSTA M., state supreme court justice; b. Greenville, SC, Feb. 29, 1944; s. Mike and Lecha Pleicones; m. Donna Singletary; 2 children. BA in English, Wofford Coll., 1965; JD, U. SC, 1968. Bar: S.C. 1968. Pub. defender Richland County, SC; atty. Lewis, Babcock, Pleicones and Hawkins; municipal judge City of Columbia, SC; county atty. Richland County, SC; resident cir. ct. judge 5th Judicial Cir., 1991—2000; assoc. justice SC Supreme Ct., 2000—. With JAG US Army, 1968—73, with USAR, 1973—99. Office: 1231 Gervais St Columbia SC 29201-3206 also: PO Box 11330 Columbia SC 29211 *

PLEINTA, TOD ALGIERS, philosopher, educator; s. Terry Lynn and Vicki Ann Brown. AA in Journalism, Kaskaskia Coll., Centralia, Ill., 1983; BA in Philosophy, Monmouth Coll., Ill., 1988; MA in Philosophy, So. Ill. U., Edwardsville, 1992. Prof. Kaskaskia Coll., Vandalia, 1991—95; with Manpower, Vandolia, 1995—2000; supr. Print Shop, Anna, Ill., 2001—03; psycho-social rehab. tchr. Union County Counseling Svcs., Anna, Ill., 2003—04; prof. Shawnee Coll., Anna, Ill., 2006—07. Contbr. articles to profl. jours.; author: Creo-Individualism, 1992. Avocations: magic, carpentry, guitar. Home: 116 Washington St Apt 414 Anna IL 62906

PLEITEZ, CONCEPCION MARIA, elementary school educator; d. Isaac and Luar Salledo Ramos; children: Nruai Sopia, Sarah Marina, Cristina. BA, Calif. State U., LA, 1996; postgrad., Calif. Poly. U., Pomona, 1997—2005. Receptionist Mather, Annigian & Minto, West Covina, Calif., 1979—80; legal asst. Gloria Lorez-Hickson, Esquire, LA, 1980—81, Moseley & Carroll, El Monte, Calif., 1981—85; legal asst., office mgr. Richard F. Hernandez, Esquire, West Covina, Calif., 1985—96; elem. sch. tchr. Hacienda-La Puente Sch. Dist., La Puente, Calif., 1996—. Sch. site rep. HLPTA, Industry, Calif., 2003—, bargaining team mem., 2005—, bd. dirs. Author: (childrens book) If I Could Go to the Moon, 2007, Jaine and the Birds, 2007. Simultaneous interpreter Faith Cmty. Ch., West Covina, 2001—. Recipient Who award, CTA Orange Svc. Ctr. Coun., 2006. Mem.: Calif. State U. LA Alumni, Golden Key. Republican. Office: Wing Lane Elem Sch 16605 Wing Ln La Puente CA 91744

PLEPLER, RICHARD L., broadcast executive; b. Manchester, Conn., Dec. 17, 1958; s. Sanford Jay and Constance (Federman) Plepler. BA in Govt., Franklin and Marshall Coll., 1981. Spl. asst. spl. projects Office US Senator Christopher J. Dodd, Washington, 1981-84; pres. RLP Inc., NYC, 1985-92; sr. v.p. corp. comm. HBO Inc., NYC, 1992—97, exec. v.p. corp. comm., 1997—2002, exec. v.p., 2002—07, co-pres., 2007—. Office: HBO 1100 Avenue of the Americas New York NY 10036

PLESS, LAURANCE DAVIDSON, lawyer; b. Jacksonville, Fla., Dec. 22, 1952; s. James William Pless, III and Anne (Dodson) Martin; m. Dana Halberg, June 20, 1980; children: Anna Amesbury, William Davidson, Deane Ahlgren. AB cum laude with distinction in History, Duke U., 1975; JD, U. NC, Chapel Hill, 1980. Bar: Ga. 1980, US Supreme Ct. 2001. Assoc. Neely & Player, P.C., Atlanta, 1980-86, ptnr., 1986-92, Welch Spell P.C., Atlanta, 1992—2007, Spell Pless Davis Sauro, PC, Atlanta, 2007—. Contbr. articles to profl. jours.; mem. staff: NC Law Rev. Vol. Lawyers Found., Atlanta, 1980—92; trustee Asheville Sch., 2002—, chmn. trustees com., 2004—, vice chmn. bd. dirs., 2005—; bd. dirs. Christian Coun. Met. Atlanta, 1999—2002; me. bd. visitors U. NC, Chapel Hill, 2001—05. Named a Ga. Superlawyer, Atlanta Mag., 2004, 2007. Mem.: ABA (bus. law sect., mem. com. negoatiated acquisitions 2004—), State Bar Ga. (mem. bus. law sect., mem. corp. code revision com. 2007—), Lawyers Club (bd. dirs. bus. and fin. law sect. 1999—2006, mem. exec. com. ADC Hawat Ball 2005), Lake Rabun Assn., Capital City Club. Democrat. Episcopalian. Avocations: hiking, tennis, canoeing. Home: 25 Palisades Rd NE Atlanta GA 30309-1530 Office: 1170 Peachtree St NE Ste 1750 Atlanta GA 30309-7675 Personal E-mail: larry.pless@spellpless.com.

PLETCHER, CAROL H., chemicals executive; m. Wayne Pletcher. B in Chemistry, Juniata Coll., Huntingdon, Pa.; M in Phys. Chemistry, U. Mich.; PhD, Coll. Biol. Sciences, U. Minn. Sr. scientist Cargill, Inc., 1983—89, mgr., 1989—92, dir., 1992—93, asst. v.p., 1993—99, v.p., 1999—2001, chief innovation officer, 2001—. Mem. Coll. Biol. Sciences Alumni Soc. Bd. U. Minn., mem.steering com. for Cargill, Inc.; established with husband Pletcher Fellowship, Coll. Biol. Sciences, U. Minn. Named one of 25 Masters of Innovation, BusinessWeek; recipient Outstanding Achievement award, Coll. Biol. Sciences, U. Minn., 2003; Fellowship, Am. Assn. of U. Women. Mem.: Minn. High Tech Assn. (bd. dir. 2006—). Office: Cargill Inc PO Box 9300 Minneapolis MN 55440-9300

PLETCHER, ELDON, retired cartoonist; b. Goshen, Ind., Sept. 10, 1922; s. Arthur and Dora (Cripe) P.; m. Barbara Jeanne Jones, Jan. 29, 1948; children— Thomas Lee, Ellen Irene. Student, Chgo. Acad. Fine Arts, 1941-42, U. Aberdeen, Scotland, 1945, John Herron Art Sch., Indpls., 1946-47. Editl. cartoonist Sioux City Jour., Iowa, 1949-66, The Times-Picayune, 1966-85; free-lance gag cartoonist Sat. Eve. Post, Rotarian, Nat. Enquirer, other publs. Rep. permanent exhbns., Syracuse U., U. South Miss., U. Cin., Boston Mus. Art, Harry S. Truman Library, Lyndon B. Johnson Library, Wichita State U., John F. Kennedy Libr., Richard M. Nixon Libr., U. Mo.; cartoons appeared in The Continental Edit. of Yank (Army Weekly). Served with AUS, 1943-46. Recipient Christopher award, 1955, Freedoms Found. award, 12 years Mem. VFW, Assn. Am. Editorial Cartoonists. Democrat. Presbyterian. Personal E-mail: epletch@aol.com.

PLETSCH, MARIE ELEANOR, plastic surgeon; b. Walkerton, Ont., Can., May 3, 1938; came to U.S. 1962; d. Ernest John and Olive Wilhemina (Hossfeld) P.; m. Ludwig Philip Breiling, Aug. 25, 1967; children: John, Michael, Anne. MD, U. Toronto, 1962. Diplomate Am. Bd. Plastic Surgery. Intern Cook County Hosp., Chgo., 1962-63, resident, gen. surgery, 1963-64, St. Mary's Hosp., San Francisco, 1964-66; resident in plastic surgery St. Francis Hosp., San Francisco, 1966-69; practice med. specializing in plastic surgery Santa Cruz, Calif., 1969—; Monterey, Calif., 1990—; adminstr. Plasticenter, Inc., Santa Cruz, 1976-88, med. dir., 1987-88. Mem. AMA, Am. Soc. Plastic and Reconstructive Surgeons, Calif. Soc. Plastic Surgeons (mem. coun. 1986-89, sec. 1989-93, v.p. 1994-95, pres. elect 1995-96, pres. 1996-97), Am. Soc. Aesthetic Plastic Surgeons, Calif. Med. Assn., Assn. Calif. Surgery Ctrs. (pres. 1988-92), Santa Cruz County Med. Soc. (bd. govs. 1983-88, 1992-94), Santa Cruz Surgery Ctr. (bd. dirs. 1988-93, 2004—). Roman Catholic. Office: Santa Cruz Can Am Med Group 1669 Dominican Way Santa Cruz CA 95065-1523: 24571 Silver Cloud Ct Monterey CA 93940 Office Phone: 831-462-1000. Personal E-mail: pletsch@pacbell.net.

PLETZ, THOMAS GREGORY, lawyer; b. Toledo, Oct. 3, 1943; s. Francis G. and Virginia (Connell) P.; m. Carol Elizabeth Connolly, June 27, 1969; children: Anne M., John F. BA, U. Notre Dame, 1965; JD, U. Toledo, 1971. Bar: Ohio 1971, U.S. Ct. Appeals (6th cir.) 1978, U.S. Supreme Ct. 1985. Ct. bailiff Lucas County Common Pleas Ct., Toledo, 1967-71; jud. clk. U.S. Dist. Ct. (no. dist.) Ohio, Toledo, 1971-72; assoc. Shumaker, Loop & Kendrick, Toledo, 1972-76, litigation ptnr., 1976—. Acting judge Sylvania (Ohio) Mcpl. Ct., 1990—; mem. Ohio Bar Bd. Examiners, 1993-2003, chmn., 1996-99. Active Toledo Parish Coun., 1987-2003; mem. Nat. Conf. Bar Examiners Com., 1996-2001. With USNR, 1965-92; ret. CDR. Recipient Toledo Jr. Bar award, 1995. Mem. ABA, Ohio State Bar Assn., Toledo Bar Assn. (trustee 1981-93), Diocesan Attys. Bar Assn., 6th Cir. Jud. Conf. (life). Roman Catholic. Office: Shumaker Loop & Kendrick 1000 Jackson St Toledo OH 43604-1573 Office Phone: 419-321-1231. Business E-Mail: tpletz@slk-law.com.

PLEUGER, GUENTER, diplomat; b. Wismar, Germany, Mar. 25, 1941; m. Gabriella Mebus-Pleuger; 2 children. Student in Law and Polit. sci., U. of Colgne and U. of Bonn, 1960—64; PhD in Law, 1966; student, Ecol Nationale d'Administration, Paris, 1966—67. Fgn. svc. trainee consulate gen., Bonn and Liverpool, U.K., 1969—70; first sec. Permanent Mission of Fed. Republic of German to UN, NYC, 1970—74; with European Communities Divsn., Federal Fgn. Office, 1974—77; embassy spokesman and head of press divsn. German Embassy, New Delhi, 1977—79; policy planning staff Federal Fgn. Office, Bonn, 1980—85; dir. in charge of Public Info and Liaison with polit. parties Federal Fgn. Min. Office, Bonn, 1985—88; min.-counsellor for polit. affairs German Embassy, Washington, 1988—93; head of directorate for UN Affairs and coord. for human rights issues Federal Fgn. Office, Bonn, 1993—95, head of directorate gen. for UN Affairs, Human Rights and Humanitarian Aid, 1995—98, dir. gen., UN Affairs, Human Rights, Humanitarian Aid and Global Issues, 1998, polit. dir. Bonn, 1998—99, state sec. Berlin, 1999—2002; perm. rep. of Germany UN, NYC, 2002—04.

PLEVAN, BETTINA B., lawyer; b. Oceanside, NY, Nov. 21, 1945; BA, Wellesley Coll., 1967; JD magna cum laude, Boston U., 1970. Bar: NY 1971, US Dist. Ct., (Ea. dist.)NY, US Ct. Appeals, (2nd cir.), 1975, US Supreme Ct. 1977, US Ct. Appeals (DC cir.), 1977, US Ct. Appeals, (3rd. cir.), 1978, US Dist. Ct. (So. dist.) NY, 1979, US Tax Ct., 1979, US Ct. Appeals, (5th. cir.), 1982, US Ct. Appeals (9th cir.), US Dist. Ct. (No. dist.) NY, 1983, US Ct. Appeals, (4th cir.), 1986, US Dist. Ct. (We. dist.) NY, 1993, US Ct. Appeals, (6th cir.). Editor Boston U. law Review, 1968—70; mem. Proskauer Rose LLP (formerly Proskauer Rose Goetz & Mendelsohn), NYC, 1974—. Pres. Fed. Bar Coun., 1996—98, pres. emeritus, 1998—. Named one of The Best Lawyers in NY, NY mag., The 50 Most Influential Women Lawyers in Am., Nat. Law Jour., 2007. Fellow: Am. Acad. Appellate Lawyers, Am. Coll. Trial Lawyers; mem.: ABA (mem. Ho. Delegates 1986—91, bd. govs. 2006—), NY County Lawyers Assn., NY State Bar Assn., Assn. Bar of the City NY (mem., com. on state courts of superior jurisdiction 1975—78, chair 1978—81, mem. exec. com. 1981—85, chair coun. on jud. adminstrn. 1985—88, mem., long range planning com. 1988—90, chair 1992—95). Office: Proskauer Rose LLP 1585 Broadway Fl 27 New York NY 10036-8299 E-mail: bplevan@proskauer.com. *

PLEW, PAUL TIMOTHY, music educator, dean; s. Harlow Nelson and Dorothy Amelia Plew; m. Pamela Jean Smith, July 24, 1970; children: Paul Timothy, Janelle Jean Sonnenburg, Jason David. BS in Music, Bapt. Bible Coll., 1970; MusM, Pacific Luth. U., 1979; EdD, Nova Southeastern U., 1996. Prof. NW Bapt. Sem., Master's Sem.; dean of music dept. Master's Coll., Santa Clarita, Calif., 1979—; min. music Santa Clarita Bapt. Ch., 1990—. Regional pres. Choral Conductor's Guild, LA; co-founder So. Calif. Christian Coll. Music Faculty Conferences; choral adjudicator and clinician. Dir.: (numerous professional choral recordings);, singer various oratorio performances; condr.: Carnegie Hall, 2003, 2007. Named Amb. of Goodwill for Israel, Min. Tourism, Jerusalem, 2001, 2005. Mem.: Nat. Assn. Ch. Musicians (past pres.), Nat. Assn. Schs. Music, Santa Clarita Choral Music Educators Assn. (founder), Am. Choral Dirs. Assn. Achievements include research in musicology and hymnology. Office: Master's Coll 21726 Placerita Canyon Rd Santa Clarita CA 91321 Office Phone: 800-568-6248 ext 3181.

PLICHTA, THOMAS EDWARD, software engineering company executive; b. Milw., Oct. 26, 1945; s. Edward Stanley and Dorothy Barbara (Kaczmarek) P.; m. Regina Christine Gasperi, Feb. 13, 1970; children: David Michael, Amanda Stephanie BA, Marquette U., 1969; MA, Calif. State U., 1996. Capt. USN, 1969-96; prin. engr. Northrop Grumman, Charleston, SC, 1996—. Mem. Navy League, K. of C. Republican. Roman Catholic. Avocations: computers, electronics, amateur radio. Home: 2920 Sugarbush Way Charleston SC 29414-6718 Office Phone: 843-744-7520. Personal E-mail: tomplichta@comcast.net.

PLIMPTON, MARTHA, actress; Represented by Internat. Creative Mgmt., Beverly Hills, Calif. Actress (films) The River Rat, 1984, The Goonies, 1985, The Mosquito Coast, 1986, Shy People, 1987, Stars and Bars, 1988, Running on Empty, 1988, Another Woman, 1988, Parenthood, 1989, Silence Like Glass, 1989, Stanley & Iris, 1990, Daybreak, 1993, Josh and S.A.M., 1993, The Beans of Egypt, 1994, Mrs. Parker and the Vicious Circle, 1994, Beautiful Girls, 1996, Eye of God, 1997, (plays) Hobson's Choice, 2002 (Obie Award, 2002), The False Servant, 2005, Hurlyburly, 2005, Shining City, 2006, The Coast of Utopia, 2006 (Outer Critics Cir. award outstanding featured actress in a play, 2007, Drama Desk award outstanding featured actress in a play, 2007). *

PLIMPTON, THOMAS E., automotive executive; BS in Acctg., U. Kans.; MBA, Rockhurst Coll. Asst. gen. mgr. Peterbilt, Newark, Calif., gen. mgr., 1992—96; with Foden Truck Co. PACCAR Inc., England, exec. v.p. Bellevue, Wash., 1998—2002, pres., 2002—. Dir. PACCAR Fin. Corp. Avocations: golf, college football, basketball, reading. Office: Paccar Inc 777 106th Ave Bellevue WA 98004 Mailing: Paccar Inc PO Box 1518 Bellevue WA 98009 *

PLINE, JENNIFER ALICE, trust company executive; BA, Boston Coll., 1982, MBA, 1987. Chartered fin. analyst CFA Inst., 1990, chartered investment counselor Investment Counsel Assn. Am., 1990. Dir. client svc. Standish Mellon Asset Mgmt., Boston, 1987—2005; v.p. trusts Harvard Mgmt. Co., Boston, 2005—. Mem. adv. bd. Fin. Dept. Boston (Mass.) Coll., 2002—06. Mem. com. fgn. rels. City Boston; trustee Beth Israel Hosp., Needham, Mass., 2005—06; chmn.'s account exec. United Way Mass. Bay, Boston, 2004—06; mem. adv. bd. Horizons for Homeless Children, Boston, 2003—06. Office: Harvard Management Company 600 Atlantic Avenue Boston MA 02210 Office Phone: 617-720-6766.

PLISCHKE, LE MOYNE WILFRED, chemist, researcher; b. Greensburg, Pa., Dec. 11, 1922; s. Fred and Ruth Naomi (Rumbaugh) P.; m. Joan Harper, Mar. 11, 1966. BS, Waynesburg Coll., 1948; MS, W.Va. U., 1952. Rsch. chemist U.S. Naval Ordinance Test Sta., China Lake, Calif., 1952-53; asst. prof. chemistry Commonwealth U., Richmond, Va., 1953-54; rsch. chemist E.I. du Pont, Gibbstown, N.J., 1955-57, Monsanto Chem. Co., Pensacola, Fla., 1957—. Mem.: Am. Chem. Soc. Achievements include 18 U.S. patents and 51 foreign patents in field. Home: 2100 Club House Dr Lillian AL 36549-5402 Office: Monsanto Co The Chem Group PO Box 97 Gonzalez FL 32560-0097 E-mail: plis123@gulftel.com.

PLISHNER, MICHAEL JON, lawyer; b. Rockville Center, NY, Jan. 22, 1948; s. Meyer J. and Lillian (Gold) P.; m. Rosalind F. Schein, Jan. 26, 1969; children: Aaron, Alexander, Elias. BA summa cum laude, Yale U., 1969, JD, 1972. Bar: Calif. 1972, U.S. Dist. Ct. (no. dist.) Calif. 1972, U.S. Ct. Appeals (9th cir.) 1972. Assoc. McCutchen, Doyle, Brown & Enersen, San Francisco, 1972-79, ptnr., 1979—2001, Bingham McCutchen, San Francisco, 2001—, dep. chmn. litig. practice group. Mem. Phi Beta Kappa. Office: Bingham McCutchen LLP 3 Embarcadero Ctr San Francisco CA 94111-4003 Office Phone: 415-393-2240. Business E-Mail: michael.plishner@bingham.com.

PLISKOW, VITA SARI, anesthesiologist; b. Tel Aviv, Sept. 13, 1942; arrived in Can., 1951; came to U.S., 1967; d. Henry Norman and Renee (Mushkatel) Stahl; m. Raymond Joel Pliskow, June 30, 1968; children: Tia, Kami. MD, U. B.C., Vancouver, 1967. Diplomate Am. Bd. Anesthesiology. Ptnr. Olympic Anesthesia, Bremerton, Wash., 1971-84, pres., anesthesiologist, 1974-84; co-founder Olympic Ambulatory Surgery Ctr., Bremerton, 1977-83; ptnr., anesthesiologist Allenmore Anesthesia Assocs., Tacoma, 1983—. Staff anesthesiologist Harrison Meml. Hosp., Bremerton, 1971-95, Allenmore Hosp., Tacoma, 1983—. Trustee Tacoma Youth Symphony Assn., 1994—; active Nat. Coun. Jewish Women, 1972—. Fellow Am. Coll. Anesthesiologists, Am. Coll. Chest Physicians; mem. Am. Soc. Anesthesiologists (del. Wash. State 1987—), Wash. State Med. Assn. (del. Pierce County 1993-94), Wash. State Soc. Anesthesiologists (pres. 1985-87), Pierce County Med. Soc. (sec.-treas. 1992). Avocations: classical music, opera, singing (mezzo soprano). Office: PO Box 65274 University Place WA 98464-1274

PLITT, JEANNE GIVEN, librarian; b. Whitehall, NY, Aug. 27, 1927; d. Charles Russell and Anna Marie (Noyes) Given; m. Ferdinand Charles Plitt Jr., Jan. 19, 1952; children: Christine Marie, Charles Randolph. Student, St. Lawrence U., 1945—47; AB, U. Md., 1940; postgrad., Am. U., 1960—61; MLS, Cath. U. Am., 1968. Libr. asst. spl. services divsn. US Army, 1949—51; tchr. secondary various secondary schs., Md. and Va., 1951—67; from reference libr. to asst. dir. Alexandria (Va.) Libr., 1967—70, dir., 1970—. Chmn. librs.' tech. com. Coun. Govts., Washington, 1971—72, Washington, 1980—81. Chmn. No. Va. Libr. Networking Com.; active Little Theatre Group, Alexandria, Alexandria's Ams. with Disabilities Act Com. Recipient Alexandria Pub. Svc. award, 1964, 1974, Recognition award, Am. Assn. Ret. Persons, 1990. Mem.: PTA, ALA, Alexandria Hist. Soc. (bd. dirs. 1974—), Manuscript Soc., Va. Libr. Assn. (legis. com. 1988—), Cath. U. Alumni Assn., Urban League, U. Md. Alumni Assn., Alexandria Assn., Zonta (sec. local chpt. 1972—73, bd. dirs. 1988—), Vernon Country Club. Roman Catholic. Office: Alexandria Libr 5005 Duke St Alexandria VA 22304-2903

PLOG, STEPHEN E., anthropologist, educator; PhD, U. Mich., Ann Arbor, 1977. Commonwealth prof. dept. anthropology U. Va., Charlottesville. Contbr. articles to profl. jours., chapters to books; author: Stylistic Variation in Prehistoric Ceramics: Design Analysis in the American Southwest, 1980, Spatial Organization and Exchange: Archaeological Survey on Northern Black Mesa, 1986. Mem.: NAS. Office: Dept Anthropology U Va PO Box 400120 Brooks Hall 308 Charlottesville VA 22904-4120 Office Phone: 434-924-3535, 434-924-7044. E-mail: sep6n@virginia.edu.

PLOMP, TEUNIS (TONY PLOMP), minister; b. Rotterdam, Netherlands, Jan. 28, 1938; arrived in Can., 1951; s. Teunis and Cornelia (Pietersma) P.; m. Margaret Louise Bone, July 21, 1962; children: Jennifer Anne, Deborah Adele. BA, U. B.C., Vancouver, Can., 1960; BD, Knox Coll., Toronto, Ont., Can., 1963, DD (hon.), 1988. Ordained to ministry Presbyn. Ch., 1963. Min. Goforth Meml. Presbyn. Ch., Saskatoon, Sask., Canada, 1963-68, Richmond (B.C.) Presbyn. Ch., 1968—2004. Clerk Presbytery of Westminster, Vancouver, 1969-2003; moderator 113th Gen. Assembly Presbyn. Ch. Can., 1987-88, dep. clk., 1988—; chaplain New Haven Correctional Centre, Burnaby, B.C., 1973-99. Contbr. mag. column You Were Asking, 1982-2002. Presbyterian. Avocations: record collecting, bicycling, swimming. Personal E-mail: tony_plomp@telus.net.

PLONSEY, ROBERT, electrical and biomedical engineer; b. NYC, July 17, 1924; s. Louis B. and Betty (Vinograd) P.; m. Vivian V. Vucker, Oct. 1, 1948; 1 child, Daniel. BEE, Cooper Union, 1943; MSEE, NYU, 1948; PhD, U. Calif., Berkeley, 1955; postgrad. med. sch., Case Western Res. U., 1969-71; D of Technol. Scis., Slovak Acad. Scis., 1995. Registered profl. engr., Ohio. Asst. prof. elec. engring. U. Calif., Berkeley, 1955-57, Case Inst. Tech., Cleve., 1957-60, assoc. prof., 1960-66, prof., 1966-68, dir. bioengring. group, 1962-68; prof. biomed. engring. Sch. Engring. and Sch. Medicine Case Western Res. U., 1968-83, chmn. dept., 1976-80; vis. prof. biomed. engring. Duke U., Durham, NC, 1980-81, prof., 1983-96, prof. biomed. engring., Hudson prof. engring., 1990-93, Pfizer-Inc.-Edmond T. Pratt Jr. Univ. prof. biomed. engring., 1993-96, Pfizer-Inc.-Edmond T. Pratt Jr. Univ. prof. emeritus, 1996—. Mem. biomed. fellowships rev. com. NIH, 1966-70; mem. tng. com. Engrs. in Medicine and Biology, 1972-73, cons., 1974-96; cons. NSF, 1973-93; mem. internat. sci. adv. com. Ragnar Granit Inst., Tampere (Finland) U. Tech., 1992—; ad hoc mem. sci. adv. com. Whitaker Found., 1989-91. Author: (with R. Collin) Principles and Applications of Electromagnetic Fields, 1961, Bioelectric Phenomena, 1969, (with J. Liebman and P. Gillette) Pediatric Electrocardiography, 1982, (with T. Pilkington) Engineering Contributions to Biophysical Electrocardiography, 1982, (with J. Liebman and Y. Rudy) Pediatric and Fundamental Electrocardiography, (with R.C. Barr) Bioelectricity: A Quantitative Approach, 1988, 3d edit., 2007, (with J. Malmivuo) Bioelectromagnetism, 1995; mem. editl. bd. Trans. IEEE, Biomed. Engring, 1965-70; assoc. editor, 1977-79; mem. editl. bd. TIT Jour. 1971-81, Electrocardiology Jour., 1974—, Med. and Biol. Engring. and Computing, 1987— Critical Revs. in Biomed. Engring., 1994— procs. editor Engring. in Medicine and Biology, 17th Ann., Conf., 1965. Mem. com. on electrocardiography Am. Heart Assn., 1976-82; v.p. Your Schs., Cleveland Heights, Ohio, 1968-69, 73-75; provisional trustee Am. Bd. Clin. Engrs., 1973-74, pres. 1975, trustee, 1976-85. With AUS, 1944-46. Recipient sr. postdoctoral award NIH, 1980-81, Merit award Internat. Union Phys. and Engring. Scis. in Medicine, 1997, Ragnan Granit prize, 2003. Fellow AAAS, IEEE (chmn. Cleve. chpt. group on biomed. electronics 1962-63, chmn. publs. com. group on engring. in medicine and biology 1968-70, v.p. adminstrv. com. 1970-72, pres. 1973-74, chmn. fellows com. Engring. in Medicine and Biology Soc. 1986-88, 2000, v.p. tech. and conf. activities 1991, William S. Morlock award 1979, Centennial medal 1984, co-program chair ann. conf., Paris 1992, chmn. awards com. 1996, Millennium medal 2000, Ragnar Granit prize 2004); mem. AAUP, NAE (bioengring. peer com. 1988-91, 2001-04, chair 1990-91, 2003-04, nominating com. 1991-92, mem. com. 1992-94, program adv. com. 1996-98, NRC postdoctoral rsch. associateships evaluation panel 1987-90, Russ prize com. 2000-03), Internat. Acad. Med. and Biol. Engring. (founding mem. 1997), Am. Inst. Med. and Biol. Engring. (founding fellow 1992—), Alliance for Engring. in Medicine and Biology (treas. 1976-78), Biomed. Engring. Soc. (bd. dirs. 1975-78, 79-83, pres. 1981-82, chmn. affiliations com. 1987-89, ALZA Disting. lectr. 1988, Disting. Svc. award, 2004), Am. Physiol. Soc., Am. Soc. Engring. Edn. (bd. dirs. biomed. engring. divsn. 1978-83, chmn. 1982-83, Pilkington Outstanding Educator award, 2002). Office: Duke U Box 90281 Dept Biomed Engring Durham NC 27708-0281 Office Phone: 919-660-3131. Business E-Mail: robert.plonsey@duke.edu.

External recognition of success is not nearly so important as the inner awareness of coming to full grips with life, to be fully involved, bending all strengths to fulfill one's goals and philosophies. And of all involvements, those with people are most meaningful (to be aware of and share the feelings of colleagues, students, friends, and family—and to enrich these relationships)—and for me most difficult.

PLOSSER, CHARLES IRVING, bank executive, economics professor; b. Birmingham, Ala., Sept. 19, 1948; s. George Gray and Dorothy (Irving) P.; m. Janet Schwert, June 26, 1976; children: Matthew, Kevin, Allison. B.E. cum laude, Vanderbilt U., 1970; MBA, U. Chgo., 1972, PhD, 1976. Cons. Citicorp Realty Cons., NYC, 1972-73; lectr. Grad. Sch. Bus., U. Chgo., 1975-76; asst. prof. Grad. Sch. Bus. Stanford U., Calif., 1976-78; asst. prof. econs. W.E. Simon Grad. Sch. Bus., U. Rochester, NY, 1978-82, assoc. prof., 1982-86, prof., 1986-89, Fred H. Gowen prof. econs., 1989-92, John M. Olin Disting. prof. econs. and pub. policy, 1992—2006, acting dean, 1990-91, 92-93, dean, 1993—2003; pres. Fed. Res. Bank, Phila., 2006—. Chmn. bd. Consortium for Grad. Study in Mgmt., 1995-97; bd. dirs. ViaHealth, Inc., 1995-2000, Rochester Gas & Electric Corp, RGS Energy Group, 1996-2002, dir. adv. bd., 2002-05; bd. dirs. Grad. Mgmt. Admission Coun., 1997-2003, chmn. bd., 2002-03; rsch. assoc. Nat. Bur. Econ. Rsch. Editor, Jour. Monetary Econs., 1983-2006, Carnegie-Rochester Conference Series on Public Policy, 1989—; contbr. articles to profl. jours. 1st lt., U.S. Army, 1972-73. NSF research grantee, 1982, 84. Mem. Am. Econs. Assn., Econometrics Soc., Am. Fin. Assn., Tau Beta Pi, Beta Gamma Sigma. Office: Fed Res Bank Phila Ten Independence Mall Philadelphia PA 19106-1574

PLOTCH, WALTER, management consultant, fund raising counselor; b. NYC, July 19, 1932; s. Harry and Belle (Lebowsky) P.; m. Yvette Gabrielle Lambert, Mar. 20, 1957; children: Allison, Jennifer, Adrienne. AB, Queens Coll., 1957; MA, Harvard U., 1959; postgrad., 1959-62. Analyst L.F. Rothschild & Co., NYC and Boston, 1962-64; cmty. cons., 1964-65; edn. dir. New Eng. Anti-Defamation League, 1965-68; nat. edn. dir., 1968-76; v.p. Brakeley, John Price Jones Inc., NYC, 1976-79; sr. v.p., dir., 1979-89; sr. v.p. The Oram Group, Inc., NYC, 1989-92; exec. v.p.; pres., CEO Walter Plotch Assocs., Inc., Croton-On-Hudson, NY, 1992—2005. Mem. faculty Grad. Sch. Mgmt. and Urban Affairs, New Sch. U.; lectr. Harvard U. Grad. Sch. Edn.; cons. Harcourt, Brace, Plenum Pubs. Co-editor: Pluralism in a Democratic Society, 1977; gen. editor: The Job Corps Intergroup RElations Series, 1974; contbr. articles to profl. jours.; contbg. editor mag., Jour. Sponsored Rsch. Bd. dirs. Schizophrenia Found., 1975-90; nat. bd. dirs. NCCJ, 1980-84, Nat. Charitable Info Bur.,mem. exec. com. 1986-94. Served with USCGR, 1953-55, Korea. Grantee U.S. Office Edn., Dept. Labor, N.Y. Coun. Humanities; tchg. fellow Harvard U., 1959-61. Mem. Princeton Club, Phi Alpha Theta. Democrat. Jewish. Office: 39 Furnace Dock Rd Croton On Hudson NY 10520-1406

PLOTKIN, ALLEN, aerospace engineer, educator; b. NYC, May 4, 1942; s. Oscar and Claire (Chasick) P.; m. Selena Berman, Dec. 18, 1966; children: Samantha Rose, Jennifer Anne. BS, Columbia U., 1963, MS, 1964; PhD, Stanford U., 1968. Asst. prof. aerospace engring. U. Md., College Park, 1968-72, assoc. prof., 1972-77, prof., 1977-85; prof. dept. aerospace engring. San Diego State U., 1985—, chmn. dept., 1985-90, 93-96. Vis. assoc. Calif. Inst. Tech., Pasadena, 1975-76; cons. Naval Surface Weapons Ctr., White Oak, Md., 1981-84. Co-author: Low-Speed Aerodynamics, 1991, 2d edit., 2001. Recipient Engring. Sci. award Washington Acad. Scis., 1981; rsch. grantee NASA, NSF; NASA-Am. Soc. Engring. Edn. summer faculty fellow, 1969, 70. Fellow AIAA (assoc., assoc. editor jour. 1986—, Young Engr.-Scientist award Nat. Capital sect. 1976, Sustained Svc. award 2003, J. Leland Atwood award, 2005), ASME; mem. Soc. Naval Architects and Marine Engrs., Am. Soc. Engring. Edn., Aerospace Dept. Chairmen's Assn. (chmn. 1989-90), Sigma Xi, Tau Beta Pi. Democrat. Jewish. Avocations: jogging, reading, country music. Home: 17364 St Andrews Dr Poway CA 92064-1231 Office: San Diego State U Dept Aerospace Engring San Diego CA 92182 Office Phone: 619-594-7019.

PLOTKIN, HORACIO, pediatric endocrinologist, orthopedic surgeon, educator; b. Buenos Aires, Dec. 23, 1964; arrived in US, 2002; m. Carola Rabuffetti, Mar. 23, 1999; children: Sophie Adele, Lucas Jay, Olivia Robin. BS, J.J. Urquiza, Buenos Aires, 1981; MD, U. Buenos Aires, 1987. Resident in pediats. T. Alvarez Hosp., Buenos Aires, 1988—92; fellow in pediat. endocrinology J.P. Garrahan Hosp., Buenos Aires, 1991—92; fellow in metabolic bone diseases IDIM, Buenos Aires, 1992—96; fellow in endocrinology Yale U., New Haven, 1996—97; fellow in pediat. metabolic bone diseases McGill U., Montreal, Que., Canada, 1997—2002; asst. prof. pediats. U. Nebr. Med. Ctr., Omaha, 2002—07, asst. prof. orthop. surgery, 2002—07, assoc. prof. pediats., 2007—, assoc. prof. orthop. surgery, 2007—; dir. Metabolic Bone Diseases Clinic Children's Hosp., Omaha, 2002—, dir. Osteogenesiss Imperfecta Clinic, 2002—. Contbr. articles and cartoons to humorous publs. Named Home Town Hero, City of Omaha, 2005. Fellow: Am. Acad. of Pediats.; mem.: Endocrine Soc., Internat. Bone and Mineral Soc., Am. Soc. for Bone and Mineral Rsch. Office: Univ Nebr Med Ctr 985456 Nebraska Medical Center Omaha NE 68198-5456 Office Phone: 402-559-4056. Office Fax: 402-559-4001.

PLOTKIN, IRVING H. (IRVING HERMAN PLOTKIN), economist, consultant; b. Bklyn., July 19, 1941; s. Samuel H. and Dorothy (Falick) P.; m. Janet V. Bufe, July 26, 1969; children: Aaron Jacob, Joshua Benjamin. BS in Econs., U. Pa., 1963; PhD in Math. Econs., MIT, 1968. Corp. planning analyst Mobil Oil Co., NYC, 1962-63, Mobil Oil Italiana, Genoa, Italy, 1965; ind. cons. econs. and ops. rsch. to banks, mut. funds, ins. cos., govt. agys. Cambridge, Mass., 1965-68; sr. economist Arthur D. Little, Inc., Cambridge, 1968—2002. Dir. regulation and econs., 1974-2002, v.p., 1979-2002; bd. dirs. Arthur D. Little Valuation, Inc.; trustee Arthur D. Little, Inc., ESOP, 1988-2002; mgr. dir. tax svc. PricewaterhouseCoopers LLP, Boston, 2002—; instr. fin. and computer scis. MIT, 1965-68; lectr. maj. univs. U.S. and abroad; expert witness U.S. Ho. of Reps. and Senate coms., U.S. Ct. Claims, U.S. Tax Ct. I.C.C., FTC, Fed. Martime Commn., Fed. Dist. Cts., Fed. Res. Bd., other fed. and state govt. agys., 1967—. NASA fellow, 1963-66, NSF fellow, 1967, Am. Bankers Assn. fellow, 1968. Mem. Am. Econ. Assn., Econometric Soc., Am. Fin. Assn., Beta Gamma Sigma, Pi Gamma Mu, Tau Delta Phi (chpt. pres. 1962-63). Home: Apt 910 975 Memorial Dr Cambridge MA 02138-5754 Office: 125 High St Boston MA 02110 Office Phone: 617-530-5332. Business E-Mail: irving.h.plotkin@us.pwc.com.

PLOTKIN, LOREN H., lawyer; b. Bklyn., Feb. 8, 1943; s. Arthur and Betty Ann (Strugatz); m. Carol Baxter, Aug. 25, 1990; children: Lily, Kate. BA, Harpur Coll., SUNY, Binghamton, 1963; JD, St. John's U., NYC, 1966. Bar: N.Y. 1966, U.S. Dist. Ct. (so. and ea. dists.) N.Y. 1972, U.S. Tax Ct. 1976. Law asst. appellate divsn., first dept. N.Y. State Supreme Ct.; ptnr. Lans Feinberg & Cohen, NYC, 1969-81; mem. Levine & Thall, P.C., NYC, 1981-84, Levine Thall and Plotkin, N.Y.C., 1984-96, Levine Thall, Plotkin & Menin, L.L.P., NYC, 1996-99, Levine, Plotkin & Menin, L.L.P., NYC, 2000—. Lectr. on entertainment law. Notes and comments editor St. John's U. Law Rev., 1965-66. Home: 34 Lawrence Ln Palisades NY 10964-1604 Office: Levine Plotkin & Menin LLP 1740 Broadway Fl 22 New York NY 10019-4315

PLOTKIN, MANUEL D., management consultant, educator, former corporate executive, former government official; s. Jacob and Bella (Katz) P.; m. Diane Fern Weiss, Dec. 17, 1967; 1 child, Lori Ann. BS with honors, Northwestern U., 1948; MBA, U. Chgo., 1949. Price economist, survey coordinator U.S. Bur. Labor Statistics, Washington, 1949-51, Chgo., 1951-53; sr. economist Sears Roebuck & Co., Chgo., 1953-61, mgr. market research, 1961-66, chief economist, mgr. mktg. rsch., 1966-73, dir. corp. planning and research, 1973-77, exec. corp. planner, 1979-80; dir. U.S. Bur. Census, Washington, 1977-79; v.p., dir. group practice Divsn. Mgmt. Cons. Austin Co., Evanston, Ill., 1981-85; pres. M.D. Plotkin Research & Planning Co., Chgo., 1985—. Tchr. statistics Ind. U., 1953-54; tchr. econs. Wilson Jr. Coll., Chgo., 1954-55; tchr. quantitative methods and managerial econs. Northwestern U., 1955-63; tchr. mktg. rsch. and mktg. mgmt. DePaul U., Chgo., 1992-95; mem. Conf. Bd. Mktg. Rsch. Adv. Coun., 1968-77, chmn.-elect, 1977; chmn. adv. com. U.S. Census Bur., 1974-75; trustee Mktg. Sci. Inst., 1968-77; mem. Nat. Commn. Employment and Unemployment Stats., 1978-79, Adv. Coun. Edn. Stats., 1977-79, Interagy. Com. Population Rsch., 1977-79; mem. adv. coun. Kellstadt Ctr., DePaul U., 1987-92; trustee U.S. Travel Data Ctr., 1977-79. Contbr. articles to profl. jours. Served with AUS, 1943-46, ETO. Decorated Bronze Star medal with oak leaf cluster. Mem. Am. Mktg. Assn. (pres. Chgo. 1968-69, nat. dir. 1969-70, nat. v.p. mktg. rsch. 1970-72, nat. v.p. mktg. mgmt. 1981-83, pres., CEO 1985-86), Am. Statis. Assn. (pres. Chgo. 1966-67, Forecasting award 1963), Am. Econ. Assn., Nat. Assn. Bus. Economists, Planning Execs. Inst., World Future Soc., Midwest Planning Assn., U. Ill. Businessmen Rsch. Adv. Group, Chgo. Assn. Commerce and Industry, Beta Gamma Sigma, Alpha Sigma Lambda, Delta Mu Delta. Home and Office: 2650 N Lakeview Ste 3910 Chicago IL 60614-1831

PLOTKIN, STANLEY ALAN, virologist; b. NYC, May 12, 1932; s. Joseph and Lee (Fishbein) P.; m. Susan Lannon, Nov. 24, 1979; children: Michael, Alec. BA, NYU, 1952; MD, SUNY, NYC, 1956; MA (hon.), U. Pa., 1974; D honoris causa, U. Rouen, 2006. Diplomate Am. Bd. Pediat., Am. Acad. Pediat. Intern Cleve. Met. Gen. Hosp., 1956-57; resident pediat. Phila. Children's Hosp., 1961—62, dir. divsn. infectious diseases, sr. physician, 1969—90; registrar Hosp. for Sick Children, London, 1962-63; assoc. mem. Wistar Inst., Phila., 1963-74, prof. virology, 1974—; asst. prof. pediat. U. Pa., Phila., 1966-71, assoc. prof., 1971-74, prof., 1974-91; prof. emeritus, 1991—; assoc. chmn. dept. pediat. U. Pa., Phila., 1986-88; med. and sci. dir. Pasteur-Mérieux-Connaught Labs. (now Sanofi-Pasteur), Marnes-la-Coquette, France, 1991-97; advisor to pres. Sanofi Pasteur, Swiftwater, Pa., 1997—. Adj. prof. internat. health Johns Hopkins U., Balt., 2000—. Assoc. editor: Am. Jour. Epidemiology, 1967-87, Proc. Soc. Exptl. Biology and Medicine, 1968-85, Pediatric Infectious Disease jour., 1982-87, Vaccine jour., 1983—, Biologicals, 2000—, Human Vaccines, 2005—, Clin. Vaccine Immunology, 2006—, Clin. Infectious Diseases, 2007—. Served as med. officer USPHS, 1957-60. Decorated Legion of Honor (France); named Disting. Physician, Pediat. Infectious Diseases Soc., 1993, Disting. Alumnus, Children's Hosp., Phila., 2001; recipient Bruce medal, ACP, 1987, Clin. Virology award, Pan Am. Group Rapid Viral Diagnosis, 1995, Gold medal, Sabin Found., 2002, Children's Hosp., Phila., 2006, Fleming award, Infectious Diseases Soc. Am., 2004, Marshall award, European Soc. Pediat. Infectious Diseases, 2006, medal, Fondation Mérieux; grantee, Joseph P. Kennedy Found., 1964—66, Hartford Found., 1971—73, NIH, 1973—. Fellow: AAAS; mem.: NAS (Inst. of Medicine), French Acad. Medicine (foreign mem.), World Soc. Pediat. Infectious Diseases (pres. 2003—06), Am. Acad. Pediat. (chmn. infectious diseases com. 1987—90), Am. Soc. Microbiology, Am. Epidemiology Soc., Am. Pediat. Soc., Soc. Pediat. Rsch., Hungarian Soc. Microbiology (hon.). Achievements include pioneering work on vaccine strains for protection against polio, rabies, rubella, rotavirus and cytomegalovirus. Office Phone: 215-297-9321. Personal E-mail: stanley.plotkin@sanofipasteur.com.

PLOTKIN-SPOTTS, SHARON LEE, protective services official, educator; b. Miami Beach, Fla., Feb. 9, 1963; d. Herbert Levin and Esther Evelyn Levin-Passero; m. David Jacob Plotkin (div.); children: Alexandra Faye Plotkin, Andi Raye Plotkin; m. Richard A. Spott, Jr., Sept. 15, 2006. AA, Broward CC, Pembroke Pines, Fla., 1983; BS, Fla. Internat. U., Miami, 1985, MS, 1990. Counselor Jewish Cmty. Ctr., Miami, 1982—88; co-owner Ralph Rottens Not Pound, Miami Lakes, Fla., 1989—95; crime scene investigator North Miami Police Dept., Fla., 1995—. Advisor William Turner Tech. HS, Miami, 2003—06; pub. spkr., trainer various colls. and HS, Fla., 2004—; adj. faculty mem. Am. Intercontinental, Weston, Fla., 2005—. Co-author: Crime Scene Children, 2006. Vol. Camilos House, Miami, 2005—. Acad. grantee, Fla. Internat., 1986. Mem.: S. Fla. Forensic Assn., Assn. Bloodstain Pattern Analysts, Internat. Assn. Identification. Republican. Jewish. Avocations: reading, music, travel. Office: North Miami Police 700 NE 124 St North Miami FL 33161 Office Phone: 305-218-6949. Personal E-mail: slplotkin@bellsouth.net.

PLOTNICK, HARVEY BARRY, publishing executive; b. Detroit, Aug. 5, 1941; s. Isadore and Esther (Sher) Plotnick; m. Susan Regnery, Aug. 16, 1964 (div. Apr. 1977); children: Andrew, Alice; m. Elizabeth Allen, May 2, 1982; children: Teresa, Samuel. BA, U. Chgo., 1963. Editor Contemporary Books, Inc., Chgo., 1964-66, pres., pub., 1966—94; pres., CEO Paradigm Holdings, Inc., Chgo., 1994—. CEO Molecular Electronics Corpn., 2000. Trustee U. Chgo., 1994—, bd. gov., Argonne Nat. Lab., 2001—. Named one of Top 200 Collectors, ARTnews mag., 2005—06. Avocations: collecting old master prints, collecting Islamic ceramics. Office: Paradigm Holdings Inc 2 Prudential Plz Ste 3150 Chicago IL 60601-6790 Office Phone: 312-819-4015. E-mail: harvey1844@aol.com.

PLOTNICK, PAUL WILLIAM, lawyer; s. Sam and Mary P.; m. Eleanor Levy, Jan. 18, 1970; 1 child, Sarah Jennie. BA, So. Ill. U., 1969; JD, DePaul U., 1974. Bar: Ill. 1974., U.S. Dist. Ct. (no. dist.) Ill. 1974, U.S. Ct. Appeals (7th cir.) 1974, U.S. Tax Ct. 1975, U.S. Supreme Ct. 1977. Tchr. Chgo. Pub. Schs., 1969-74; pvt. practice Chgo., 1974-75; pres. Paul W. Plotnick, Ltd., Skokie, Ill., 1979—; asst. pub. defender Cook County Pub. Defender's Office, Chgo., 1975-79. Felony asst. Cook County Pub. Defender's Office, 2d dist., Ill., 1976-79. Contbr. articles, poem to profl. publs. Pres. Budlong Woods Civic Group, Chgo., 1982—83; candidate for judge Circuit Ct. Cook County, 1998—2000, 2002—. Staff sgt. US Army, 1969. Named Man of the Yr. Midwest Fedn. Men's Clubs, 1995; recipient Disting. Svc. award Chgo. Vol. Legal Svcs., 1995. Mem. ABA, Ill. State Bar Assn., Chgo. Bar Assn., N.W. Suburban Bar Assn., North Suburban Bar Assn. (bd. dirs. 2003-2006), Kiwanis (pres. Skokie Valley chpt. 1989-90, 2005-2007, Disting. Sec. award 1987, Disting. Pres. award 1991, Lay Person of the Yr. I.I. Dist. divsn. 7, Diamond Hixson fellow), Beth Hillel Men's Club (pres. 1991-93), Decalogue Soc., Phi Kappa Phi (DePaul U. chpt. Disting. Alumnus). Office: 9933 Lawler Ave Ste 312 Skokie IL 60077-3706 Office Phone: 847-675-2660. E-mail: 9933312@sbcglobal-.net.

PLOTNICK, ROBERT DAVID, economic consultant, educator; b. Washington, Aug. 3, 1949; s. Theodore and Jean (Hirshfeld) P.; m. Gay Lee (Jensen), Dec. 22, 1972. BA, Princeton U., 1971; MA, U. Calif., Berkeley, 1973, PhD, 1976. Rsch. assoc. Inst. Rsch. on Poverty, Madison, Wis., 1973—75; asst. prof. Bates Coll., Lewiston, Maine, 1975—77, Dartmouth Coll., Hanover, NH, 1977—84; assoc. prof. U. Wash., Seattle, 1984—90, prof., 1990, assoc. dean, 1990—95, acting dean, 1994—95. Vis. scholar Russell Sage Found., 1990, U. NSW, 1997, London Sch. Econs., 2004; rsch. affiliate Inst. Rsch. Poverty, 1989—, Nat. Poverty Ctr., 2004—, West Coast Poverty Ctr., 2005—; chmn. Population Leadership Program, 1999—2005; dir. Ctr. for Studies in Demography and Ecology, 1997—2002; adj. fellow Pub. Policy Inst Calif., 1998—2000; cons. Wash. Dept. Social and Health Svcs., Olympia, 1984—86, 1990—96, 2000; cons. in field. Author: Progress Against Poverty, 1975; contbr. articles to profl. journals. Recipient Teaching Excellence Award U. Wash., 1985, 89. Mem. Am. Econ. Assn., Assn. Policy Analysis and Mgmt., Population Assn. Am. Avocations: hiking, birdwatching. Office: U Wash Evans Sch Pub Affairs PO Box 353055 Seattle WA 98195-3055 Office Phone: 206-685-2055. Business E-Mail: plotnick@u.washington.edu.

PLOTNIK, ARTHUR, writer, columnist; b. White Plains, NY, Oct. 1, 1937; s. Michael and Annabelle P.; m. Meta Von Borstel, Sept. 6, 1960 (div. 1979); children: Julia Nicole, Katya Michelle.; m. Mary Phelan, Dec. 2, 1983. BA, State U. N.Y., Binghamton, 1960; MA, U. Iowa, 1961; MS in L.S, Columbia U., 1966. Gen. reporter, reviewer Albany (N.Y.) Times Union, 1963-64; freelance writer, 1964-66; editor Librarians Office, Library of Congress, 1966-69; assoc. editor Wilson Library Bull., Bronx, NY, 1969-74; editor-in-chief Am. Libraries, Chgo., 1975-89; assoc. pub. ALA, 1989-97; editl. dir. ALA Editions, 1993-97; writer, 1997—. Adj. instr. journalism Columbia Coll., Chgo., 1988-89; speaker in field. Author: The Elements of Editing: A Modern Guide for Editors and Journalists, 1982, Jacob Shallus, Calligrapher of the Constitution, 1987, Honk If You're a Writer, 1992, The Elements of Expression, 1996, 2d edit., 2006, The Urban Tree Book, 2000, The Elements of Authorship (reprint of Honk if You're a Writer), 2000, Spunk & Bite: A Writer's Guild to Punchier, More Engaging Language and Style, 2005, gen. articles, fiction and poetry; contbg. editor: The Writer, 2000—; mem. editl. bd.:, 2007—; exec. prodr.: Libr. Video mag., 1986—91; columnist: Editorial Eye, 1995—2001; contbr. articles to profl. jours. Bd. dirs. Am. Book Awards, 1979-82; bd. advs. Univ. Press of Am., 1982—1997. Served with USAR, 1962-67. Fellow Iowa Writers Workshop Creative Writing, 1961; recipient award Ednl. Press Assn. Am., 1973 (3), 77, 82, 83; cert. of excellence Internat. Reading Assn., 1970, First Pl. award Verbatim essay competition, 1986, award Am. Soc. Bus. Press Editors, 1987, First Pl. award poetry competition Irish-Am. Heritage Ctr., Chgo., 2005. Mem. ALA, ACLU, Treekeepers (Openlands Project). Home and Office: 2120 W Pensacola Ave Chicago IL 60618-1718 also: N E Pub Assocs Literary Agents PO Box 5 Chester CT 06412-0005

PLOTT, CHARLES RAYMOND, economics educator; b. Frederick, Okla., July 8, 1938; s. James Charles and Flossie Ann (Bowman) P.; m. Marianna Brown Cloninger, May 30, 1961; children: Rebecca Ann, Charles Hugh. BS in Prodn. Mgmt., Okla. State U., 1961, MS in Economics, 1964; PhD in Economics, U. Va., 1965; LHD (hon.), Purdue U., 1995; degree (hon.), L'université Pierre Mendès France, Grenoble, 1996. Asst. prof. economics Purdue U., 1965—67, assoc. prof. economics, 1968-70; Edward S. Harkness prof. econs. and polit. sci. Calif. Inst. Tech., Pasadena, 1971—, dir. Program for Study of Enterprise and Pub. Policy, 1979—, dir. Lab. for Exptl. Econs. and Polit. Sci., 1987—. Prin. investigator, NSF, 1972-; mem. Environ. Quality Lab., Calif. Inst. Tech., 1972, Resources for the Future, 1973; vis. prof. law U. So. Calif. Law Ctr., 1976; vis. prof. Stanford U., 1968-69, U. Chgo., 1980; Hooker Disting. prof., McMaster U., 1983; chmn. review bd. Calif. Inst. Tech.; mem. bd. on behavioral, cognitive and sensory scis., NRC Commn. on Behavioral and Social Scis. and Edn., 1997-2003; bd. dir. Lee Pharm., 1978-95. Author works in fields of econs., polit. sci., philosophy, exptl. methods, math. methods; contbr. articles to profl. jours.; mem. editl. bd. Social Sci. Rsch., 1976-77, Pub. Choice, 1973-90, Jour. Econ. Behavior, 1983-85, Econ. Theory, 1994-. Named to Coll. Bus. Hall of Fame Okla. State U., 1988; Ford Found. fellow, 1968, Guggenheim fellow, 1981-82, fellow Ctr. for Advanced Studies in Behavioral Scis., 1981-82, sr. rsch. fellow, Inst. for Policy Reform, 1992-93; Fulbright Scholar, 2006; NSF grantee, 1972, 74, 78, 79, 80, 83, 86, 88, 92, 95, 98, 2000; recipient Jour. of Finance Markets award, 1994, Best Paper award, 2003, GSAM Quant Best Paper prize, Review of Finance, 2004, Economic Inquiry 2006 Best Article award, GAIM Rsch. Paper of Yr. 2006 award. Fellow Am. Acad. Arts and Scis., Econometric Soc.; mem. Am. Econ. Assn., Econ. Sci. Assn. (pres. 1987-88), So. Econ. Assn. (mem. exec. com. 1977-78, v.p. 1985-87, pres. 1989-90, Georgescu-Roegen prize, 1995), Pub. Choice Soc. (pres. 1977-78), Western Econ. Assn. Internat. (v.p. 1996-97, pres. 1998-99), Consortium of Social Scis. Assns. (bd. dir. 1996-98), Royal Econ. Assn., Am. Polit. Sci. Assn., Econs. Sci. Assn. (pres. 1987-88), Mont Pelerin Soc., Pub. Choice Soc. (pres. 1976-78), The Mont Pèlerin Soc., NAS. Office: Calif Inst Tech Divsn Humanities & Social Scis 337 Baxter Hall MC 228-77 Pasadena CA 91125 Office Phone: 626-395-4209. Office Fax: 626-793-8580. Business E-Mail: cplott@hss.caltech.edu. *

PLOTTEL, GLORIA SUSANNE STONE, marketing professional; b. NYC, Feb. 16, 1966; d. Leroy Saul and Karen Lila Stone; m. Philip Benjamin Plottel, June 9, 1996. BA cum laude Univ. Profs. Program, Boston U., 1988; MS in Forest Resources Mgmt, SUNY, Syracuse, 1992; MBA, NYU, 2002. Mgr. dept. geography Boston U., 1989-90; tchg. asst. coll. environ. sci. and forestry SUNY, Syracuse, 1990-92; asst. acct. exec. Lowe and Ptnrs./SMS, NYC, 1993-95; asst. mgr. Champion Internat. Corp., Stamford, Conn., 1995-97; mktg. mgr. Bus. New Haven, 1997-98; prin. GSP Mktg., 2002—. Cons. Mass. Dept. Environ. Mgmt., Boston, 1993, No. Forest Lands Coun., Concord, N.H., 1993. Screenwriter: Seasoned Trails, 1989. Mem. exec. bd. U. Profs. Program, Boston U., 1997—; bd. mem. YMCA-YWCA Camping Svcs. of Greater NY, 1998—2003. SUNY internat. conf. grantee, 1991. Avocations: hiking, camping, swimming.

PLOTTEL, JEANINE PARISIER, foreign language educator; b. Paris, Sept. 21, 1934; came to U.S., 1943; m. Roland Plottel, 1956; children: Claudia S., Michael E., Philip B. Baccalauréat lettres, Lycée Français de N.Y., 1952; BA with honors, Barnard Coll., 1954; MA, Columbia U., 1955, PhD with distinction, 1959. Lectr. dept. French and Romance philology Columbia U., NYC, 1955-59; rsch. assoc. fgn. lang. program MLA of Am., NYC, 1959-60; lectr. dept. romance langs. CUNY, NYC, 1960; asst. prof. div. humanities Julliard Sch. Music, NYC, 1960-65; dir. lang. labs. Hunter Coll. CUNY, NYC, 1965-69; asst. prof. dept. romance langs. Hunter Coll. CUNY, NYC, 1965-69, assoc. prof. dept. romance langs., 1969-81, prof. dept. romance langs., 1981—2000, assoc. prof. French doctoral program grad. sch., univ. ctr., 1980-81, prof. French doctoral program grad. sch., univ. ctr., 1981—2000, prof. emeritus, 2000—. Exec. dir. AAVP NY state conf., 2002-07; mem. president's adv. coun. Barnard Coll., 2006-; dept. Romance langs. CUNY. Author: Les Dialogues de Paul Valéry, 1960; pub., editor N.Y. Literary Forum, 1978-88; contbr. articles to profl. jours., chpts. to books. Pres. Maurice I. Parisier Found., Inc.; alumni trustee Barnard Coll., 2007; bd. trustees Barvard Coll., 2007-. Named Officer des Palmes Acad., 1999; recipient NEH fellowship, 1979; grantee N.Y. Coun. for the Humanities, 1986, Helena Rubenstein Found., 1986, Florence J. Gould Found., 1986, 88, N.Y. Times Found., 1986. Mem. AAUP (exec. dir. N.Y. State Conf. 2002-06), Maison Française (bd. dirs. Columbia U.), Peyre Inst., CUNY, Soc. French Am. Cultural Svcs. & Ednl. Aid, Hunter Coll. Art Galleries, Inst. French Studies. Home: 50 E 77th St Apt 14A New York NY 10021-1836 Office: Hunter Coll-CUNY 695 Park Ave New York NY 10021-5024 Personal E-mail: plottel1@att.net.

PLOTZ, CHARLES MINDELL, physician, educator; b. NYC, Dec. 6, 1921; s. Isaac and Rose (Bluestone) P.; m. Lucille Weckstein, Aug. 5, 1945; children: Richard, Thomas, Robert. BA, Columbia U., 1941, D.Sc., 1951; MD, L.I. Coll. Medicine, 1944. Diplomate: Am. Bd. Internal Medicine. Intern New Haven Hosp., 1944-45; resident internal medicine Kings County Hosp., 1945-46, Maimonides Hosp., 1948-49; postdoctoral research fellow USPHS, Columbia Coll. Phys. and Surgs., 1949-50; practice medicine, specializing in internal medicine Bklyn., 1950—; chief Arthritis Clinic, attending physician Kings County Hosp. Center, 1950-85; chief L.I. Coll. Hosp. (Arthritis Clinic), 1950-65; asst. attending physician Mt. Sinai Hosp., 1955—; chief Mt. Sinai Hosp. (Arthritis Clinic), 1955-65, Arthritis Clinic, State U., Hosp., 1967-85; asst. physician Columbia-Presbyn. Med. Center, 1949-71; attending physician Bklyn. State Hosp.; dir. ambulatory care Bklyn. Hosp.Ctr., 1991-93; emeritus prof. medicine SUNY, 1991—; professorial lectr. Mt. Sinai Sch. Medicine, 1992—; emeritus prof. in medicine SUNY, 1991—. Cons. physician Peninsula Gen. Hosp., Jamaica Hosp.; cons. on rheumatology VA Hosp., Bklyn., L.I. Coll. Hosp.; cons. family practice Luth. Med. Ctr.; vis. cons. internal medicine Jewish Gen. Hosp., Mont., Que., Can., 1965; cons. internal medicine Avicenna Hosp. and Wazir Akbar Hosp., Kabul, Afganistan, 1965; prof. medicine, dir. continuing edn., chmn. dept. family practice SUNY Downstate Med. Ctr., 1967-91, prof. emeritus medicine and family practice, 1991—; Fulbright lectr. U. Paris, 1984, 91; professorial lectr. Mt. Sinai Sch. Medicine, 1992—. Editorial adv. bd.: Pakistan Med. Forum; editor-in-chief: Clin. Rheumatology in Practice, 1981—; editor-in-chief: Advances in Rheumatology, 1986—, Rheuma21st.com, 1998—. Mem. nat. bd. govs. Arthritis Found., 1964-82, bd. govs. N.Y. chpt., 1965—, v.p., 1971-83, trustee, 1977-82, N.Y. chpt. sr. v.p., 1977-82, vice chmn. bd. trustees, 1983-85, 87—, pres., 1985-87; trustee Leo N. Levi Meml. Nat. Arthritis Hosp., Alumni Fund-Alumni Assn. SUNY Downstate Med. Center, Bklyn. Inst. Arts and Scis., Bklyn. Bot. Garden; mem. adv. bd. MEDICO, corp. mem., 1977—; treas. Internat. League Against Rheumatism, 1981-89; trustee Internat. League Against Rheumatism Trust, 1981-89. Served to capt. AUS, 1946-48. WHO fellow U. Negev, 1974; master Am. Coll. Rheumatology, 1991—; recipient Gold medal Am. Coll. Rheumatology, 1992. Master Am. Coll. Rheumatology (Gold medal 1992), fellow ACP, Am. Acad. Family Physicians (charter), N.Y. Acad. Medicine (chmn. edn. com. 1976-78); mem. AMA, (N.Y. chpt.), AAUP, Internat. Soc. for Rheumatic Therapy (chmn. 1987-89), Am. Fedn. Clin. Rsch., Am. Rheumatism Assn. (past sec.-treas.), N.Y. Rheumatism Assn. (past pres., exec. com.), Harvey Soc., (N.Y. chpt.), Kings County med. socs., Bklyn. socs. internal medicine, Soc. Tchrs. Family Medicine, N.Y. State Acads. Family Physicians, Soc. Urban Physicians, Mystery Writers Am., Sigma Xi, Alpha Omega Alpha; hon. mem. Rheumatology Soc. France, Rheumatology Soc. Japan, Rheumatology Soc. Mex., Rheumatology Soc. Brazil, Rheumatology Soc. Yugoslavia, Rheumatology Soc. Norway, Rheumatology Soc. Egypt, Med. Soc. Czechoslovakia, Cosmos Club, Heights Casino Club. Home: 184 Columbia Hts Brooklyn NY 11201-2105 also: 450 Clarkson Ave Brooklyn NY 11203-2056 E-mail: rheuma21st@aol.com.

PLOUGH, ALONZO L., city health department administrator; BA in Biology, San Diego State U., 1973; MA in Sociology, Cornell U., 1975; MPH, Yale U. Sch. Medicine, 1977; PhD in Anthropology, Cornell U., 1978. Lectr., health policy and mgmt. Harvard U. Sch. Pub. Health, Cambridge, Mass., 1985—95; dep. commr., dir., pub. health Boston Dept. Health and Hosps., 1989—95; assoc. prof., health svcs. U. Wash. Sch. Pub. Health and Cmty. Medicine, 1995—; dir., health officer Seattle-King Co. Health Dept., 1995—. Mem., scientific adv. com. Nat. Ctr. for Health Statistics. Bd. dirs. Am. Lung Assn. of Wash., United Way of King Co., Wash. Dental Found.; chair, bd. Edn. Devel. Ctr., Inc.; chair, adv. com. King Co. Health Action Plan. Mem.: Nat. Assn. of City and County Health Officials. Office: Seattle-King Co Health Dept 999 Third Ave Ste 1200 Seattle WA 98104

PLOURD, CHRISTOPHER JOHN, lawyer, consultant; b. 1955; BA, Butler U., Indpls., 1977; JD, Thomas Jefferson Coll. Law, San Diego, 1980. Bar: Calif. 1981, US Dist. Ct. (so. dist. Calif.) 1981, cert.: State Bar Calif. (criminal law) 1991, bar: US Dist. Ct. (dist. Ariz.) 1995. Atty. Plourd, Blume, Scoville, Strickland & Breeze, P.C., El Centro, Calif., 1980—82; asst. pub. defender Imperial County Pub. Defenders Office, El Centro, 1983—86; staff atty. Defenders Inc., 1986—88; prin. Law Office of Christopher J. Plourd, San Diego, 1988—. Forensic sci. evidence cons. Mem.: San Diego Lawyers Club, Calif. Pub. Defenders Assn., NY Acad. Scis., Calif. Attys. for Criminal Justice, San Diego County Bar Assn., Am. Soc. Forensic Odontology, AAAS, Am. Acad. Forensic Scis. Office: Law Office of Christopher J Plourd 1168 Union St Ste 303 San Diego CA 92101 Office Phone: 619-615-6200. Office Fax: 619-615-6204. E-mail: dnacjp@flash.net.

PLOVNICK, MARK STEPHEN, business educator; b. NYC, June 8, 1946; s. Jacob and Dorothy Edith (Berger) Plovnick; m. Daisy Shulan Chan, Mar. 13, 1982. BSME, Union Coll., 1968; BA in Econs., Union Coll., 1968; MS in Mgmt., MIT, 1970, PhD in Mgmt., 1975. Instr., rschr. MIT, Cambridge, 1970—76; asst. prof. Clark Univ., Worcester, Mass., 1976—79, assoc. prof., 1979—89, chmn. dept. mgmt., 1979—82, assoc. dean Grad. Sch. Mgmt., 1982—89; prof. and dean Eberhardt Sch. Bus. U. Pacific, Stockton, Calif., 1989—. Cons. to various orgns., 1970—; dir. Devel. Rsch. Assocs., Reston, Va., 1979—82; adj. assoc. prof. U. Mass. Med. Sch., Worcester, Mass., 1982—89; adj. asst. prof. Boston Univ. Sch. Medicine, 1974—75; clin. instr. Harvard Med. Sch., Boston, 1977—78. Author: 5 books; contbr. numerous articles to profl. jours. Mem. Civil Svc. Commn., San Joaquin County, 1989—94; mem. gen. plan action team City of Stockton, 2004—; editl. bd. Comstock's Mag., 2006—; bd. dirs. United Way, 1991—94, Goodwill Industries, 1992—, Stockton Symphony, 1995—2001, Stockton Rotary Endowment, 2005—, No. Calif. World Trade Ctr., 2006—, Bank of Agrl. and Commerce, 2006—. Mem.: Greater Stockton C. of C. (bd. dirs. 1990—94, 2006—), Calif. Partnership for San Joaquin Valley, Yosemite Club (bd. dirs. 2004—). Office: U Pacific Eberhardt Sch Bus Stockton CA 95211-0001 E-mail: mplovnic@pacific.edu.

PLOWDEN, DAVID, photographer; b. Boston, Oct. 9, 1932; s. Roger and Mary Russell (Butler) P.; m. Pleasance Coggeshall, June 20, 1962 (div. 1976); children: John, Daniel; m. Sandra Oakes Schoellkopf, July 8th, 1977; children: Philip, Karen. BA Econs., Yale U., 1955; pvt. studies with Minor White, Rochester, NY, 1959-60. Asst. O. Winston Link Studio, NYC, 1958-59, George Meluso Studio, NYC, 1960-62; photographer, writer, 1962—. Assoc. prof. Inst. Design, Ill. Inst. Tech., Chgo., 1978-86; lectr. U. Iowa Sch. Journalism, 1985-88; vis. prof. Grand Valley State Univ., 1988-90, 91—; artist-in-residence U. Balt., 1990-91. Author and photographer: Farewell to Steam, 1968, Lincoln and His America, 1970 (Benjamin Barondess award 1971), The Hand of Man on America, 1971, 2d edit, 1974, The Floor of the Sky: the Great Plains, 1972, Bridges: the Spans of North America, 1974, 2d edit. 1984, 3d edit., 2002, Commonplace, 1974, Tugboat, 1976 (notable Children's books ALA 1976, Children's Book Showcase 1976), Steel, 1981, An American Chronology, 1982 (Notable Books ALA 1982, Booklist's Best of the 80s 1989), Industrial Landscape, 1985, A Time of Trains, 1987, A Sense of Place, 1988, End of an Era: The Last of the Great Lakes Steamboats, 1992, Small Town America, 1994, Imprints: The Photographs of David Plowden, 1997, David Plowden: The American Barn, 2003, A Handful of Dust, 2006, David Plowden: Vanishing Point Fifty Years of Photography, 2007; co-author, photographer, Nantucket, 1970, Cape May to Montauk, 1973, Desert and Plains, the Mountains and the River, 1975, The Iron Road, 1978 (notable children's books 1978, Honor list Horn Books 1979), Wayne County: the Aesthetic Heritage of a Rural Area, 1979; introduction The Gallery of World Photography/the Country, 1983; commd. illustrator Gems, 1967, The Freeway in the City, 1968, America the Vanishing, 1969, New Jersey, 1977, North Dakota, 1977, Vermont, 1979, New York, 1981, A Place of Sense, 1988; contbr. articles to numerous jours. including Time, Newsweek, Life, Audubon, Fortune, Smithsonian, Camera Arts, Lenswork; one-man shows include Columbia U., 1965, Smithsonian Instn., 1970-71, 75-76, 81, 89, Internat. Ctr. Photography, NY, 1976, Witkin Gallery, NYC, 1979, Cin. Art Acad., 1979, Gilbert Gallery, Chgo., 1980-81, Chgo. Ctr. Contemporary Photography, 1982, Fed. Hall Mus., NYC, 1982, Calif. Mus. Photography, Riverside, 1982-83, Chgo. Hist. Soc., 1985, Martin Gallery, Washington, 1987, Kunstmuseum, Luzern, Switzerland, 1987, Burchfield Ctr., Buffalo, 1987-88, Iowa State Mus., Des Moines, 1988-89, Catherine Edelman Gallery, Chgo., 1990, Grand Valley State U., 1993, Ewing Gallery, Washington, 1994, Beinecke Rare Book and Manuscript Lib. Yale U., 1997, Albright-Knox Art Gallery, 1997, Mus. Contemporary Photography, Chgo., 1998, Albin O. Kuhn Libr. & Gallery, U. Md., Balt., 1998, Tatar/Alexander Photogallery, Toronto, 1999, Lawrence Miller Gallery, NYC, 2000, The Chgo. Cultural Ctr., 2002, Peter Fetterman Gallery Photog. Works of Art, Santa Monica, Calif., 2004-05, Copia, Napa, Calif., 2004, Catherine Edelman Gallery, Chgo., 2007; exhibited in group shows at Met. Mus. Art, NYC, 1967, Kodak Gallery, NYC, 1976, Currier Gallery Art, Manchester, NH, 1978, Whitney Mus., 1979, Art Inst. Chgo., 1983-87, Witkin Gallery, NYC, 1988, Davenport (Iowa) Mus. Art, 1992, Mus. Contemporary Photography, Chgo., 1996, 98-99, City, 2000, Fay Gold Gallery, Atlanta, 2003-04, Catherine Edelman Gallery, Chgo., 2007; represented in permanent collections Albright-Knox Gallery, Art Inst. Chgo., Calif. Mus. Photography, Ctr. Creative Photography, Chgo. Hist. Soc., Libr. Congress, Smithsonian Instn., U. Md., J.B. Speed Mus., Iowa Humanities Bd., Iowa State Hist. Dept., Burchfield Art Ctr., Buffalo and Erie County Hist. Soc., Internat. Mus. Photography George Eastman House, Internat. Ctr. Photography, Ekstrom Libr. U. Louisville, Beinecke Rare Book and Mauscript Libr., Yale U., 1995—, Mus. Contemporary Photography, Chicy, Bayly Mus. U. Va., Charlottesville. John Simon Guggenheim fellow, 1968; grantee N.Y. State Coun. Arts, 1966, 87, Smithsonian Inst., 1970-71, Dept. Transp. and Smithsonian Inst., 1975-76, H. E. Butt Found., 1977, United Bd. Homeland Ministries, 1976, Chgo. Hist. Soc., 1980-84, Seymour H. Knox Found., 1987, Baird Found., 1987, State Hist. Soc. Iowa, 1987-88, Iowa Humanities Bd., 1987-88; recipient R.R. History award, 1989, Honored Imagemaker, Soc. for Photographic Edn., 2002; subjectof PBS documentary: David Plowden: Light, Shadow & Form, 2000. Mem. Am. Soc. Media Photographers. Home and Office: 609 Cherry St Winnetka IL 60093-2614 Office Phone: 847-446-2793. Home Fax: 847-446-2795. Personal E-mail: david@davidplowden.com.

PLOWMAN, JACK WESLEY, lawyer; b. Blairsville, Pa., Sept. 12, 1929; s. Ralph Waldo, Sr., and Ethel Beatrice (Nicely) P.; m. Barbara Ellen Brown, Apr. 5, 1952; children: Linda Ellen, Judith Lynn AB, U. Pitts., 1951, LL.B. with honors, 1956. Bar: Pa. 1956, U.S. Dist. Ct. (we. dist.) Pa. 1956, U.S. Ct. Appeals 1960, U.S. Supreme Ct. 1978. Assoc. Campbell, Houck & Thomas, Pitts., 1956-57; ptnr. Rose, Houston, Cooper & Schmidt, Pitts., 1957-63, Plowman & Spiegel, Pitts., 1963-2000; of counsel Bentz Law Firm, P.C., Pitts., 2000—. Adj. prof. emeritus Duquesne U. Sch. Law, 1963—80, 1983—2002. Editor-in-chief Pitts. Legal Jour., 1971—81, U. Pitts. Law Rev., 1955—56. Bd. dir. United Meth. Pub. House, 1984-96, Ward Home for Children, United Meth. Ch. Union, 1977-83, Wesley Inst., 1977-81, Neighborhood Legal Svcs. Assn., 1969-74; chancellor emeritus Western Pa. Ann. Conf., United Meth. Ch. Capt. JAG, USAFR, 1979-2000. Fellow Am. Bar Found. (life mem.), Am. Coll. Trial Lawyers, Allegheny County Bar Found. (trustee, sec.); mem. ABA, Pa. Bar Assn. (house del., 1982-88), Allegheny County Bar Assn. (pres. 1982), Pa. Bar Inst. (bd. dir. 1988-92), Am. Law Inst., Supreme Ct. Pa. Hist. Soc. (trustee, pres.). Republican. Office: Washington Ctr Bldg 680 Washington Rd Pittsburgh PA 15228 Home: 706 Bower Hill Rd Pittsburgh PA 15243-2040 Office Phone: 412-563-4500. E-mail: jplowman@bentzlaw.com.

PLUM, FRED, neurologist; b. Atlantic City, Jan. 10, 1924; s. Fred and Frances (Alexander) Plum; m. Susan Butler, Apr. 23, 1990; children from previous marriage: Michael, Christopher, Carol. BA, Dartmouth Coll., 1944, postgrad., 1944—45; MD, Cornell U., 1947; MD (hon.), Karolinska Inst., Stockholm, 1982; DSc (hon.), L.I. U., 1990. Resident N.Y. Hosp., 1947—50, fellow, 1950—53. Instr. neurology Sch. Medicine Cornell U., 1950—53, Anne Parrish Titzell prof. neurology, 1963—98, univ. prof., 1998—, chmn. dept. neurology, 1963—98; head neurology sect. U.S. Naval Hosp., St. Albans, NY, 1951—53; from asst. prof. to prof. neurology Sch. Medicine U. Wash., 1953—63; vis. scientist U. Lund, Sweden, 1970—71; vis. physician Rockefeller U. Hosp., 1975—85; assoc. neurosci. rsch. program MIT and Rockefeller U., 1977—87; mem. neurology study sect. NIH, 1964—68; nat. adv. coun. Nat. Inst. Neurol., Communicative Disorders and Stroke, 1984—86; founding mem. McKnight Endowment Fund for Neurosci., 1986, pres., 1986—90. Author (with J.B. Posner): Diagnosis of Stupor and Coma, 1966; author: 3d edit., 1982, Clinical Management of Seizures, 1976, 2d edit., 1983; author: (with others) Cecil Essentials of Medicine, 1986, 3d edit., 1995; editor, contbg. author: Cecil's Textbook of Medicine, 1968, chief editor neurology sect.: Contemporary Neurology series, 1980—96, founding editor: Vols. 1-40, 1966—93, Brain Dysfunction in Metabolic Disorders, 1974, mem. editl. bd.: Archives Neurology, 1958—68, chief editor:, 1972—76; editor: Annals of Neurology, 1977—85; founding editor:, 1986—; editor: Neurology Alert, 1981—; contbr. articles to sci. and profl. jours. Mem.: NAS, Assn. Am. Physicians, Assn. Rsch. Nervous Mental Diseases (pres. 1973, 1987), Am. Soc. Clin. Investigation, Soc. Neurosci., Am. Acad. Neurology (past mem. coun.), Am. Neurol. Assn. (v.p. 1974—75, pres. 1976—77, Jacoby award 1984), Inst. of Medicine, Am. Acad. Arts and Scis., Can., Brit., French, Itatlian, Swiss neurol. socs. (hon.), Alpha Omega Alpha. Achievements include research in conciousness, coma and stroke. Office: Weill-Cornell U Med Coll 525 E 68th St # A565 New York NY 10021-4870 Business E-Mail: frp2007@mail.cornell.edu.

PLUMB, CHARLES SUMNER, III, lawyer; b. Columbus, Ohio, Mar. 27, 1957; s. Charles Sumner II and Elaine Marcene (Wharton) P.; m. Kathleen Kendall Barry, Aug. 16, 1980; children: Joseph Quinn, Nora Kendall. BBA, So. Meth. U., 1979; JD, Ohio State U., 1982. Bar: Okla. 1982, U.S. Dist. Ct. (no., ea., and we. dists.) Okla. 1982, U.S. Ct. Appeals (10th cir.) 1982. Ptnr. Doerner, Saunders, Daniel & Andersen, Tulsa, 1982—. Editor Okla. Employment Law Letter, Tulsa, 1992—; articles editor Ohio State U. Law Jour., 1980-82. Office: Doerner Saunders Daniel & Andersen 320 S Boston Ave Ste 500 Tulsa OK 74103-3725 Office Phone: 918-591-5279. Business E-Mail: cplumb@dsda.com.

PLUMERI, JOSEPH JAMES, II, financial executive; b. Trenton, NJ, July 7, 1943; s. Samuel J. and Josephine (Vaccaro) Plumeri; m. Nancy Plumeri, June 18, 1966; children: Christian, Jay Michael, Leslie. BA in History, Coll. of William and Mary, 1966; postgrad., N.Y. Law Sch., 1967-69. Trainee Carter Berlind & Weill, NYC, 1968-69; stockbroker CBWL-Hayden Stone, NYC, 1968-73; br. mgr. Shearson Hayden Stone, Fort Lauderdale, Fla., 1973-74, exec. v.p. western region San Francisco, 1974-81; sr. exec. v.p. Shearson Lehman Hutton, NYC, 1981—, dir. mktg. and nat. sales, 1981-89, dir. domestic br. div., 1990-94; vice chmn., group CEO Travelers Group, Inc., NYC, 1994-2000; chmn., CEO Willis Group, Ltd., Jacksonville, Fla., 2000—, bd. mem., 2001—. Bd. visitors Coll. William & Mary, trustee endowment assn.; bd. visitors Nat. Ctr. on Addiction and Substance Abuse. Mem.: Columbus (N.Y.C.). Avocations: golf, reading. Office: Willis Group Ltd 3000 Bayport Dr Ste 300 Tampa FL 33607 Home: 455 Long Ln Far Hills NJ 07931-2742

PLUMEZ, JEAN PAUL, advertising executive, consultant; b. NYC, Oct. 31, 1939; s. Jean Paul and Marie Antoinette (Compagne) P.; m. Jacqueline Hornor, Feb. 20, 1965; children: Jean Paul, Nicole. BS in Chem. Engring., Bucknell U., 1962, BA in Chemistry, 1962; MBA, U. Pa., 1968. Product engr. Mobil Oil Co., Paulsboro, NJ, 1965-66; account mgr. Dancer Fitzgerald, Sample, Inc., NYC, 1968-86, exec. v.p., 1979-86; pres. Leadership on Paper, Larchmont, NY, 1986—; founding ptnr. The Right Direction, 1987—. Capt. Signal Corps U.S. Army, 1962-64. Mem. Alpha Chi Sigma, Beta Gamma Sigma, Kappa Delta Rho Clubs: Larchmont Yacht, Wharton of N.Y., Princeton of N.Y. Home and Office: 90 Beechtree Dr Larchmont NY 10538-1202 Home Phone: 914-833-0332; Office Phone: 914-833-0332. Personal E-mail: jplumez@aol.com.

PLUMMER, AHMED, professional football player; b. Wyoming, Ohio, Mar. 26, 1976; Studied Bus. and Human Resources, The Ohio State Univ. Cornerback San Francisco 49ers. Named to All-Madden Team, 2001, All-Rookie Team, Football News, 2000.

PLUMMER, CHRISTOPHER (ORME) (ARTHUR PLUMMER), actor; b. Toronto, Ont., Can., Dec. 13, 1929; s. John and Isabella Mary (Abbott) P.; m. Tammy Grimes, Aug. 19, 1956 (div. 1960); 1 child, Amanda; m. Particia Audrew Lewis, May 4, 1962 (div. 1967); m. Elaine Taylor, 1970. Student pub. and pvt. schs., Can.; pupil, Iris Warren, C. Herbertcasari; LLD (hon.), U. We. Ont., 2004; DFA (hon.), NY Julliard Sch.; PhD (hon.), U. Toronto, Ryerson and Western Ont. Stage debut in The Rivals with Can. Repertory Theatre, 1950; Broadway debut in Starcross Story, 1954, J.B.; London debut in Becket, 1961; leading actor Cymbeline, Am. Shakespeare Theatre, Stratford, Conn., 1955, Royal Shakespeare Co., London and Stratford, Avon, Eng., 1961-62, Stratford (Ont.) Shakespeare Festival, 1956, 57, 58, 60, 62, 67, Nat. Theatre Co., London; radio roles include Shakespeare, Canada; plays include Home is the Hero, 1954, Twelfth Night, 1954, 70-71, Dark is Light Enough, The Lark, Julius Caesar, The Tempest, 1955, (rearranger with Sir Neville Mariner) Henry VI, 1956, Hamlet, 1957, Winter's Tale, 1958, Much Ado About Nothing, 1958, J.B., 1958, King John, 1960, Romeo and Juliet, 1960, Richard III, 1961, Arturo Ui, 1963, The Royal Hunt of the Sun, 1965, Antony and Cleopatra, 1967, Danton's Death, 1971, Amphitryon 38, 1971, The Constant Wife, The Dark is Light Enough (Theatre World award), Medea, The Lark; (musicals) Cyrano, 1973 (Tony award for Best Actor in a Musical, 1974), The Good Doctor, 1973, Love and Master Will, 1975; performer (with Sir Neville Mariner and rearranged by Michael Lankester) A Midsummer's Night's Dream; Othello, 1982, Macbeth, 1988, No Man's Land, 1993, Barrymore, 1996 (Tony award for best actor in a play, 1997, Drama Desk, Outer Critics Cr. award, Edwin Booth award, Boston Critics' award, Chgo.'s Jefferson award, LA Ovation award best actor 1997-98), King Lear, 2004 (Tony nom. best actor in a play, 2004), Inherit the Wind, 2007; made TV debut 1953; TV prodns. include Little Moon of Alban, Johnny Belinda, 1958, Cyrano de Bergerac, 1962, Oedipus Rex, After the Fall, 1974, The Doll's House, The Prince and the Pauper, Prisoner of Zenda, Hamlet at Elsinore, BBC, 1964, Time Remembered, Capt. Brassbound's Conversion, The Shadow Box, 1981, The Thornbirds, 1983, Little Gloria-Happy at Last, A Hazard of Hearts, 1987, Crossings, 1986, Danielle Steele's Secrets, 1992, Liar's Edge, 1992, On Golden Pond, 2001, Night Flight, 2002; star TV series The Moneychangers, 1977, Harrison Bergeron, 1995, We the Jury, 1996, The Conspiracy of Fear, 1996; made film debut in 1957; films include Stage Struck, 1957, Wind Across the Everglades, 1958, The Fall of the Roman Empire, 1963, Inside Daisy Clover, 1965, Sound of Music (Acad. award), 1965, Triple Cross, 1967, Nobody Runs Forever, 1969, The Battle of Britain, 1969, The Royal Hunt of the Sun, 1969, Lock up your Daughters, 1969, The Phyx, 1970, Waterloo, 1971, The Man Who Would Be King, 1975, The Return of the Pink Panther, 1975, Conduct Unbecoming, 1975, International Velvet, 1978, Murder By Decree, 1979, Starcrash, 1979, The Silent Partner, 1979, Hanover Street, 1979, Somewhere in Time, 1980, Eyewitness, 1981, The Disappearance, 1981, The Amateur, 1982, Dreamscape, 1984, Ordeal by Innocence, 1984, Lily in Love, 1985, The Boss' Wife, 1986, The Boy In Blue, 1986, An American Tail, 1986 (voice), Souvenir, 1987, Dragnet, 1987, Light Years (voice), 1988, Where the Heart Is, 1989, Fire Head, 1991, Star Trek: VI: The Undiscovered Country, 1991, Rock a Doodle, 1992 (voice), Malcolm X, 1992, Wolf, 1994, Dolores Claiborne, 1994, Twelve Monkeys, 1995, Skeletons, 1996, The Arrow, 1997, Hidden Agenda, 1998, The Clown at Midnight, 1998, Winchell (TV), 1998, Blackheart, The Insider (Boston, LA, Chgo., Las Vegas and Nat. Critics's awards), 1999, All the Fine Lines, 1999, Celebrate the Century (TV mini-series), 1999, The Dinosaur Hunter, 2000, Dracula 2000, Nuremberg (TV mini-series), 2000, American Tragedy (TV mini-series, Golden Globe nomination), 2000, A Beautiful Mind, 2001, Nicholas Nickleby, 2002, Ararat, 2002, Blizzard, 2003, Cold Creek Manor, 2003, National Treasure, 2004, Alexander, 2004, Tma, 2005, (TV) Our Fathers (Emmy Nomination), 2005, Must Love Dogs, 2005, Four Minute Mile (TV), 2005, Syriana, 2005, The New World, 2005, Inside Man, 2006, The Lake House, 2006, Rick Burns documentary film on Eugene O'Neil, and The Man in the Chair. Decorated companion Order of Can., 1968; recipient Theatre World award, 1955, Evening Std. Theatre award, 1961, Delia Austrian medal, 1973, 2 Drama Desk awards, 1973, 82, Antoinette Perry award, 1974, Emmy award Nat. Acad. TV Arts and Scis., 1977, Genie award, Can., 1980, Golden Badge of Honor, Austria, 1982, Maple Leaf award Nat. Acad. Arts and Letters, many honors Eng., Austria, Can., Two Tony awards (seven nominations), Two Emmy awards (six nominations), Gt. Britain's Evening Std. award, Can.'s Genie award, Gov. Gen's Lifetime Achievement award, 2001, William Shakespeare award (Will award) classical theatre, Nat. Bd. Rev. Career Achievement award, NY., Jason Robard's award excellence in memory great friend, 2002; inducted in Am.'s Theatre's Hall of Fame, 1986, Can.'s Walk of Fame, 1997. Office: c/o Lou Pitt The Pitt Group 9465 Wilshire Blvd Ste 480 Beverly Hills CA 90212-2612 *

PLUMMER, DARIA MARIE, elementary school educator; b. Boston, Jan. 3, 1944; d. Agostino and Marie Montanari; m. Peter A. Plummer, July 8, 1967; 1 child, Katherine Adams. BA, U. Mass., Amherst, 1966; MA, U. Conn., Storrs, 1971. Cert. elem. edn. Conn., 1967, reading cons. Conn., 1971. Tchr. Kingston Pub. Schs., Mass., 1966—67, South Windsor Pub. Schs., Conn., 1967—. Sec. South Windsor Dem. Town Com., 2005—07; mem. Interfaith Coun., South Windsor, 1968—70; bd. mem. Hartford Region YWCA, 1975—81. Named Tchr. of Yr., South Windsor Pub. Schs., 2004; recipient Celebration of Excellence award, Conn. State Dept. Edn., 2001, Cmty. Svc. Leadership award, South Windsor Bd. Edn., 2007. Mem.: ASCD, NEA (life; dir. Washington chpt. 1994—96, Found. award for Tchg. Excellence 2002), Delta Kappa Gamma, Phi Delta Kappa, Conn. Edn. Assn. (life; v.p. 1990—94, pres. 1996—2000, John Rogers Human and Civil Rights award 2007). Avocations: reading, cooking, theater. Home: 235 Orchard Hill Dr South Windsor CT 06074 Office: Wapping Elem Sch 91 Ayers Rd South Windsor CT 06074 Home Phone: 860-432-8403.

PLUMMER, DIRK ARNOLD, chemical, electrical, and electronics engineer; b. Stamford, Conn., Apr. 18, 1930; s. Charles Arnold Plummer and Edwina Woodling Johnson; m. Janis Susan Lowery Stuart, Feb. 18, 1967 (div. 1973); 1 child, Julie. SBChemE, MIT, 1952; BSEE, U. Calif., Berkeley, 1961; MSEE, Monmouth U., 1995. Registered profl. engr., Conn., N.J.; cert. nondestructive test examiner of inspectors for radiography, magnetic particle, liquid penetrant and ultrasonic testing methods; cert. comml. pilot. Chem. engr. Foster Wheeler Corp., NYC, 1952; engr. The M.W. Kellogg Co., NYC, 1954; project engr. Am. Machine & Fdry. Co., Greenwich, Conn., 1955-56; devel. engr. Aerojet-Gen. Corp., Azusa, Sacramento, San Ramon, Calif., 1956-61; sr. mem. tech. staff Aerospace Comm. & Controls Divsn. RCA, Burlington, Mass., 1961-62; engr. Elec. Boat Div. Gen. Dynamics Corp., Groton, Conn., 1963; electronics engr. U.S. Civil Svc., various locations, 1963-88; constrn. inspector Bd. Chosen Freeholders, Freehold, NJ, 1994; pvt. practice Sea Bright, NJ, 1988—. Contbr. articles to profl. jours. Archtl. control officer Sea Bright Village Assn., 1991. 1st lt. US Army, 1952-54; col. USAR ret. Recipient Meritorious Svc. medal Pres. of U.S., 1982, Cert. Commendable Svc. Def. Supply Agy., 1972. Mem. AAAS, NSPE, ASCE, ASME, AIChE (profl. devel. officer 1990), IEEE (chmn. nuc. and plasma sci. chpt. 1990), Am. Phys. Soc., Am. Math. Soc., Math Assn. Am., Internat. Soc. Logistics, Am. Chem. Soc. Home and Office: 45 Village Rd Sea Bright NJ 07760-2233 Office Phone: 732-219-9553. Business E-Mail: dap@alum.mit.edu.

PLUMMER, E. WARD, physics professor; b. Astoria, Oregon, Oct. 30, 1940; married; 2 children. BA summa cum laude in Physics and Math., Lewis and Clark Coll., 1962; PhD in Physics, Cornell U., 1968. NRC postdoctoral fellow Nat. Bur. Standards, 1967—70, asst. sect. chief for surface physics Far Ultraviolet Sect., 1970—73; assoc. prof. physics U. Pa., 1973—77, prof., 1977—88, William Smith prof. physics, 1988—92; disting. prof. physics U. Tenn., 1992—; disting. scientist Oak Ridge Nat. Lab., 1992—; dir. Tenn. Advanced Materials Lab., 2001—. Dir. Lab. Rsch. Structure of Matter, 1990—92; vis. disting. scientist Oak Ridge Nat. Lab., 1992; mem. basic energy sci. adv. com. Dept. Energy, 2001—04; mem. exec. adv. bd. U. Pa. Materials Rsch. Sci. and Engring. Ctr., 2003—. Contbr. articles to sci. jours.; consulting editor: Chem. Physics, mem. editl. bd.: Phys. Rev. B, 1986—89, mem. editl. adv. bd.: Langmuir, 1989—93, mem. adv. editl. bd.: Chem. Physics Letters, 1991—94. Recipient Medard W. Welch award, Sci. and Tech. Soc., 2001. Fellow: NAS (mem. solid state sci. com. 1986—89). Office: Dept Physics and Astronomy U Tenn 201 South Coll Knoxville TN 37996-1200 E-mail: eplummer@utk.edu.

PLUMMER, JAKE (JASON STEVEN PLUMMER), professional football player; b. Boise, Idaho, Dec. 19, 1974; Grad., Ariz. State U., 1997. Quarterback Ariz. Cardinals, Phoenix, 1997—2002, Denver Broncos, 2003—07, Tampa Bay Buccaneers, Fla., 2007—. Founder The Jake Plummer Found., 1999—. Named to Am. Football Conf. Pro-Bowl Team, 2005. *

PLUMMER, JAMES D., electrical engineering educator; BS in elec. engring., UCLA, 1966; MS in elec. engring., Stanford U., 1967, PhD in elec. engring., 1971. Rsch. assoc. Stanford U., 1971—74, sr. rsch. assoc., 1974—78, assoc. dir. integrated circuits lab., 1974—84, dir., 1984—93, assoc. prof. elec. engring., 1978—83, prof., 1983—, John M. Fluke Prof. Elec. Engring., 1988—, prof. (by courtesy) materials sci. and engring., 1996—, sr. assoc. dean. Sch. Engring., 1993—96, dean, 1999—, chmn. elec. engring. dept., 1997—99, Frederick Emmons Terman Prof. Engring., 1999—, dir. Stanford Nanofabrication Facility, 1994—2000; nat. dir. NSF Nat. Nanofabrication Users Network, 1995—2000. Cons. to numerous semiconductor and other companies, 1970—; mem. bd. dirs. Internat. Rectifier, 1995—; mem. Cypress Semiconductor Tech. Adv. Bd., 1995-; Herbert H. Johnson lectr. in materials sci. and engring. Cornell U., 1998. Author, co-author of over 300 publs.; patentee in field. Recipient Outstanding Paper Award, Internat. Solid-State Circuits Conf., 1970, 1976, 1978, Outstanding Svc. Award, Elec. Engring. Dept., Stanford U., 1988, 2 Inventor Recognition Awards, Semiconductor Rsch. Corp., Tau Beta Pi Undergrad. Tchg. Award, Sch. Engring., Stanford U., 1992, Best Tchr. Award, Soc. Women Engineers, 1995, J.J. Ebbers award, IEEE, 2003, Aldert Van der Ziel award, 2003, Jacob Millman award, McGraw/Hill, 2004. Fellow: IEEE (Third Millenium Medal 2000); mem.: NAE, Materials Rsch. Soc., Am. Phys. Soc., Electrochem. Soc. (Solid State Sci. and Tech. Award 1991), Sigma Xi, Tau Beta Pi. Office: Stanford U Sch Engring 380 Panama Mall, 214 Terman Stanford CA 94305-4027

PLUMMER, LEONARD NIEL, geochemist; b. Lexington, Ky., Aug. 13, 1945; s. Leonard Niel and Marjorie Sidney Wiest Plummer; m. Phyllis C. Mohney, Aug. 21, 1945; children: Philip Niel, Michael Ross, Rebecca Wiest Weaver, Kathryn Elizabeth Cartwright. BA, U. Ky., Lexington, 1967, MS, 1969; PhD, Northwestern U., Evanston, Ill., 1972. Asst. prof. SUNY, Buffalo, 1972—74; hydrologist U.S. Geol. Survey, Reston, Va., 1974—92, sr. rsch. scientist, 1992—. Contbr. articles to sci. publs. Recipient Meritorious Svc. award, U.S. Dept. Interior, 1987, Disting. Svc. award, 1996, Spl. Recognition award, Assn. Ground Water Scientists and Engineers, Nat. Water Well Assn., 1990. Fellow: Geol. Soc. Am. (O.E. Meinzer award 1993); mem.: Geochemical Soc., Am. Chem. Soc., Am. Geophys. Union, Sigma Xi. Achievements include development of geochemical models for simulation of water-rock reactions; ground-water dating with chlorofluorocarbons; research in hydrochemistry of major US aquifers; contaminants in ground water such as arsenic, perchlorate, volatile organic carbon compounds; co-development of concept of stoichiometric saturation in solid-solution - aqueous solution reactions; solubility of calcium carbonate in water; application of environmental tracers to interpretation of groundwater age studies with sulfur hexafluoride, tritium/helium-3, and others. Avocation: violin.

PLUMMER, ORA BEATRICE, nursing educator, consultant; b. Mexia, Tex., May 25, 1940; d. Macie Idella (Echols); children: Kimberly, Kevin, Cheryl. BSN, U. N.Mex., 1961; MS in Nursing Edn., UCLA, 1966. Nurse's aide Bataan Meml. Meth. Hosp., Albuquerque, 1958—60, staff nurse, 1961—62, 1967—68; staff nurse, charge nurse, relief supr. Hollywood Cmty. Hosp., Calif., 1962—64; instr. U. N.Mex. Coll. Nursing, Albuquerque, 1968—69; sr. instr. U. Colo. Sch. Nursing, Denver, 1971—74, asst. prof., 1974—76; staff assoc. III We. Interstate Commn. for Higher Edn., Boulder, Colo., 1976—78; DON Garden Manor Nursing Home, Lakewood, Colo., 1978—79, nurse surveyor, cons., 1979—87; ednl. coord. Colo. Dept. Health, Denver, 1987—96. Active in faculty devel. Colo. Cluster of Schs.; bd. dirs. Domestic Violence Initiative. Contbr. articles to profl. jours. Mem. adv. bd. Affiliated Children's and Family Svcs., 1977; mem. Colo. Instnl. Child Abuse and Neglect Adv. Com., 1984-92; trustee Colo. Acad., 1990-96; mem. planning com. State Wide Conf. on Black Health Concerns, 1977; mem. staff devel. com. Western Interstate Commn. for Higher Edn., 1978, mem. minority affairs com., 1978, mem. coordinating com. for baccalaureate program, 1971-76; active in minority affairs, U. Colo. Med. Ctr., 1971-72; mem. ednl. resources com., pub. rels. com., rev. com. for reappointment, promotion and tenure U. Colo. Sch. Nursing, 1971-76, mem. regulatory tng. com., 1989-93; mem. gerontol. adv. com. Met. State Coll., 1989-94; mem. expert panel long term care tng. manual Health Care Financing Adminstrn., Balt., 1989; mem. employee diversity com. Colo. Dept. Health, 1989-96; mem. Nurse Del. to Cuba, 2000. Nominee Nightingale award, Colo., 2003. Avocations: public speaking, teaching, coaching mentoring, consultation. Office: 4300 Cherry Creek South Dr Denver CO 80246-1523

PLUMMER, WILLIAM B., publishing executive; BS, MIT, MS in Aeronautics and Astronautics; MBA, Stanford U. V.p. equity capital group GE Capital Corp., 1995—97; treas. Mead Corp., 1997—98, vice pres. corp. strategy and planning, 1998—2000, pres. Gilbert Paper Div., 2000; v.p., treas. Alcoa Inc., 2000—06; exec. v.p., CFO Dow Jones & Co, NYC, 2006—. Bd. dirs. John Wiley & Sons, Inc., 2003—. Office: Dow Jones & Co 1 World Financial Ctr 200 Liberty St New York NY 10281

PLUMMER, WILLIAM TORSCH, optical physicist; s. William Edwin and Margaret Fairchild (Torsch) P.; m. Susan Bowman White, Sept. 9, 1961; children: Kathryn, Hilleary. BA, Johns Hopkins U., 1960, PhD, 1965. Lens designer Muffoletto Optical Co., Towson, Md., 1963-69; sr. dir. optical engring. Polaroid Corp., Cambridge, Mass., 1969—2001; pres. WTP Optics, Inc., Concord, Mass., 2002—. Asst. prof. astronomy U. Mass., Amherst, 1967-69; vis. prof. Tufts U., Medford, Mass., 1984-88; sr. lectr. MIT, 1991—. Capt. signal corps USAR, 1965—67. Recipient David Richardson medal, 1980, Joseph Fraunhofer award, 1997, Robert M. Burley prize, 1997, Steve Benton Meml. award, 2006. Fellow SPIE, Nat. Speleological Soc., Optical Soc. Am.; mem. Nat. Acad. Engring., Phi Beta Kappa. Achievements include central optical and opto-mechanical developments in Polaroid SX-70 folding SLR camera, model 600 LMS camera, spectra camera, captiva camera, and in laser-based printing devices; implemented new concepts for precision in high-volume manufacture; 96 US patents in field for optical, mechanical, electronic, and chemical inventions. Home: 129 Arena Ter Concord MA 01742-4413 Personal E-mail: plummew@yahoo.com.

PLUMPTRE, TIM, think-tank executive; BA with honors, U. Toronto, Can., 1965; MSc in Econs., London Sch. Econs., 1966; cert. in Mgmt. Studies, Oxford U., Eng., 1973. Founder, pres. Inst. On Governance, Ottawa, Canada, 1990—. Adj. prof. Sch. Pub. Policy and Adminstrn. Carleton U.; spkr. in field; cons. in field. Author: Beyond the Bottom Line: Management in Government, 1988. Office: Inst Governance 122 Clarence St Ottawa ON Canada K1N 5P6

PLUNKET, DANIEL CLARK, pediatrician, educator; b. Birmingham, Ala., May 7, 1929; s. Henry Clark and Carolyn Clark (Langford) P.; m. Lillian C. Barrington, Dec. 31, 1971; children: Dennis, Beth, Ann, Brenda, Scott. BS, Emory U., 1949, MD, 1952. Diplomate Am. Bd. Pediat. Intern Med. Coll. Va. Hosp., Richmond, 1952-53, resident in pediatrics, 1953-54, Tripler Army Med. Center, Honolulu, 1958-59, Walter Reed Army Inst., 1962-64; pediatrician, pediatric hematologist/oncologist acad. medicine, chief pediatric service William Beaumont Gen. Hosp., El Paso, Tex., 1959-62; commd. 1st lt. U.S. Army, 1955, advanced through grades to col., 1967; asst. chief dept. pediatrics Letterman Army Med. Center, San Francisco, 1964-65; chmn. dept. pediatrics Fitzsimons Army Med. Center, Denver, 1965-75; prof. pediat. U. Okla. Coll. Medicine, Tulsa, 1975-2000; sr. assoc. dean for clin. affairs U. Okla. Health Scis. Ctr., Tulsa, 1993-2000; chmn. dept. pediat. U. Okla. Coll. Medicine, Tulsa, 1975-96, now prof. pediat. Clin. prof. pediatrics U. Colo., Denver, 1974-75. Mem. adv. chmn. March of Dimes, Tulsa chpt., 1975-92; bd. dirs. ARC, Tulsa chpt., 1981—. Decorated Legion of Merit; Walter Reed Inst. Research fellow hematology and research, 1962-64 Mem. AMA, Acad. Pediatrics, Am. Pediatric Soc., Am. Soc. Hematology. Episcopalian. Home: 2436 E 33rd St Tulsa OK 74105-2316 Office Phone: 918-749-6729. Personal E-mail: dan5729@aol.com.

PLUNKETT, STEVEN R., radiologist; b. Atlanta, Ga., Feb. 1, 1952; married; 4 children. BS in Biology, Fla. State U., Tallahassee, Fla., 1974; MD, Med. Coll. Ga., 1978. Cert. Am. Bd. Radiology, lic. NC, 1979, SC, 1988. Postdoctoral tng. Wake Forest U./Baptist Med. Ctr., Winston-Salem, NC, 1978—82; resident NC Baptist Hosp., Winston-Salem, NC, 1978—82; clin. instr., radiation therapy Bowman-Gray Sch. Medicine, Winston-Salem, NC, 1982—83; staff mem. Southeast Radiation Oncology Group, P.A., Charlotte, NC, 1983—; pres., med. dir. Matthews Radiation Oncology Ctr., Matthews, NC, 1990—. Lectr., 2nd and 4th yr. med. students, 1981—83; mem. home care adv. com. Presbyn. Hosp., 1984—85, mem. profl. continuing edn. com., 1985, mem. spkr. bur., 1984—99, mem. cancer care com., mem. oncology com., mem. steering com. for cancer symposium, mem. steering com., Campaign for Caring, 1991—92, med. dir., inpatient hospice unit, 1991—92, mem. planning com. for cancer symposium, 1998; presenter in field. Contbr. articles to profl. jours., columns in newspapers. Mem. stewardship com. First Presbyn. Ch., Winston-Salem, NC, 1982—83, bd. deacon, 1982—83; bd. dir. CanCare, 1990, The Bridge Youth Ministries, 1993—97; mem. exec. com. Charlotte Chpt., World Christian Tng. Ctr.; bd. trustee Charlotte Christian Sch., 1993—97; treas. Carolina Youth Commn., 1997—2006, bd. dir., 1997—2006. Mem.: AMA, Am. Cancer Soc. ((Forsyth County Unit) med. dir. 1982, (Forsyth County Unit) pres.-elect 1982, (Forsyth County Unit) pres. 1982—83, (Mecklenburg County Unit) bd. dir. 1984, (Mecklenburg County Unit) mem. exec. com. 1986—88, profl. edn. com. 1986—88, (Mecklenburg County Unit) pub, edn. com. 1986—88), NC Med. Soc. (alternate del. 1997), Piedmont Oncology Assn. (mem. exec. com. 1983—84, co-chmn. radiation oncology com. 1983—84), Am. Soc. Therapeutic Radiology and Oncology, Am. Soc. Clin. Oncology, Am. Coll. Radiology, State, County, Med. Soc., CARROS (pres. 1992—93), S.E. Cancer Control Consortium (v.p. 1991—92), Gynecologic Oncology Group. Avocations: photography, reading, golf, hunting. Address: Matthews Radiation Oncology Ctr 1400 Matthews Township Pkwy Matthews NC 28105 Office: Southeast Radiation Oncology Group PA 200 Queens Rd Ste 400 Charlotte NC 28204 Office Phone: 704-845-8800, 704-333-7376. *

PLUSQUELLIC, DONALD L., mayor; b. Akron, Ohio, July 3, 1949; m. Mary Plusquellic; children: Dave, Michelle. BS, Bowling Green State U., 1972; JD, U. Akron, 1981. Councilman Akron City Council, 1973-81, councilman-at-large, 1982-86, council pres., 1984-86; mayor City of Akron, 1987—. Trustee U.S. Conf. of Mayors; mem task force for funding homeland security in US cities US Dept Homeland Security, 2006—. Office: Office of the Mayor 200 Municipal Bldg 166 S High St Akron OH 44308-1626 *

PNEUMAN, LINDA JACKSON, retired physician; b. Memphis, July 9, 1938; d. John Thomas Jackson, Jr. and Winnie Griffin Jackson; m. Gerald Warnick Pneuman, June 16, 1978 (dec.); m. Terry Robert Cobb, Nov. 8, 1957 (div. 1974); children: Kimberly Winn Kirby, Elizabeth Lankford Fredricksmeyer. BS magna cum laude, U. Memphis, 1961; MD, Meharry Med. Coll., Nashville, 1976. Tchr. chemistry and biology St Mary's Episcopal Sch., Memphis, 1960—62; rsch. asst. Vanderbilt U. Psychopharmacology Rsch. Ctr., Nashville, 1966—67; intern, resident St. Joseph's Hosp., Denver, 1976—77; physician Denver U. Student Health Svc., Denver, 1977—81, US Dept. Def., Bad Aibling, Bavaria, Germany, 1978—79, U. Colo. Student Health Svc., Boulder, 1981—88, Calif. State U., Chico, Calif., 1988—2002; ret. Chair quality assurance U. Colo. Student Health Svc., Boulder, 1985—88; chair human subjects com. U. Colo., Boulder, 1986—88; chair quality assurace Calif. State U., Chico Student Health Svc., 1988—97, acting dir., 2000—01; chief clin. medicine Calif. State U. Chico, 1997—2001. Vol. naturalist City of Boulder Open Space and Mountain Parks, 2005—06; bd. mem. Boulder Valley Women's Clinic, 1986—88; fund raiser Friendship Bridge, Evergreen, Colo., 2005—06. Outstanding Student scholar, Hill Family Found., 1974, 1975. Mem.: Alpha Omega Alpha (life). Democrat. Episcopalian. Home: 205 Devon Pl Boulder CO 80302 Home Phone: 303-440-0565. Personal E-mail: lpneuman@csuchico.edu.

PNIAKOWSKI, ANDREW FRANK, structural engineer; b. Grodno, Poland, Aug. 18, 1930; s. Josef Leon and Janina (Kodzynski) Pniakowski; m. Margaret M. Czajkowski, Aug. 15, 1957; 1 child, Mary. Diploma Engr., Politechnika Warszawska, 1952. Registered profl. engr., Ont., Mass., Maine, N.H. Bridge design and field engr. Govt. of Poland, Ministry of R.R., Warsaw, 1952—57; bridge design engr. Dept. Hwys. of Ont., Toronto, Canada, 1958—66; sr. structural engr. Sverdrup & Parcel Assocs., Inc., Boston, 1967—71; chief structural engr. Louis Berger & Assocs., Inc., Needham, Mass., 1972—96; cons. engr. in transp., bridges, hwys., railroads, pub. bldgs., others. Mem.: Assn. Profl. Engrs. of Province of Ont., Prestressed Concrete Inst., Am. Concrete Inst., Am. Inst. Steel Constrn. Roman Catholic.

PNUELI, AMIR, computer science educator; b. Nahalal, Israel, Apr. 22, 1941; married; 3 children. BSc in Math., Technion U.; PhD in Applied Math., Weizmann Inst. Sci., 1967; doctorate (hon.), U. Uppsala, 1997, U. Joseph Fourier, 1998, Carl von Ossietzky U., 2000. Fellow Stanford U., Watson Rsch. Ctr., Yorktown; prof. computer sci. Weizmann Inst. Sci., Rehovot, Israel, sr. rschr., prof., 1981—99, head Minerva Ctr. Verification of Reactive Systems, 1998; prof. computer sci. NYU, 1999—. Co-founder Mini-Systems, 1971; founder, chmn. dept. computer sci. Tel-Aviv U., 1973; co-founder AdCad. Author (with Z. Manna): The Temporal Logic of Reactive and Concurrent Systems: Specification, 1991, Temporal Verification of Reactive Systems: Safety, 1995. Recipient A.M. Turing award, Assn. Computing Machinery, 1996, Israel Prize in Exact Sciences, 2000. Mem.: NAE, Israeli Acad. Arts and Scis. Achievements include seminal work introducing temporal logic into computing science; outstanding contributions to program and system verification. Office: Computer Sci Dept Courant Inst Math Sci NYU 251 Mercer St New York NY 10012 Office Phone: 212-998-3225. Business E-Mail: amir@cs.nyu.edu.

POA, LI, cardiac surgeon; b. Taipei, Taiwan, Oct. 11, 1964; s. David Shan-Ping and Cheng Fan Poa; m. Hyunah Lee Poa, Aug. 19, 1990; children: Christina, Philip, Katie. BA, Northwestern U., Evanston, Ill., 1986, MD, 1989, M, 1988. Diplomate Am. Bd. Surgeons. Intern Albert Einstein Med. Ctr., Phila., 1989-90, resident surgery, 1990-94; resident cardiothoracic surgery UCLA Med. Ctr., 1994-96, chief cardiothoracic surgery, 1994-96; pvt. practice Inglewood, Calif., 1996—. Mem. ACS, AMA, Soc. Thoracic Surgeons. Office: 61-182 CHS 10833 Le Conte Ave Los Angeles CA 90095-3075 also: Daniel Freeman Med Ctr 301 N Prairie Ave Ste 505 Inglewood CA 90301-4512 Address: 1430 Esplanade Chico CA 95926-3366 Office Phone: 530-894-3278.

POAD, FLORA VIRGINIA, retired librarian, retired elementary school educator; b. Roanoke, Va., Oct. 8, 1921; d. Thomas Franklin and Ethlind (Wertz) Huff; m. Stanley Theodore Benton, Dec. 24, 1942 (div. Oct. 1983); children: Peggy, Betty, Mary Jo, Lucy; m. James Joseph Poad, June 6, 1986. Student, Radford Coll., 1939—41, Ohio U., 1956—57; BS in Edn., Ohio No. U., 1960; MA in LS, U. Toledo, 1964; postgrad., Kent State U., 1964—66, postgrad., 1971. Reference asst. Roanoke Pub. Libr., 1939-42; catalog asst. Univ. Libr., Emory U., Atlanta, 1942; sec. ARC, Atlanta, 1943; catalog asst. Pickerington (Ohio) Pub. Libr., 1950-51; tchr. Celina (Ohio) Pub. Schs., 1957-62; tchr., libr. Toledo Pub. Schs., 1962-64; libr. supr. Oregon (Ohio) Pub. Schs., 1964-85; instr. U. Toledo, 1970, reference libr., 1971-86; tchr. Sylvan Learning Ctr., Toledo, 1985-92; ret., 1992. Evaluation team Ohio Dept. Edn., Columbus, 1973; rep. Ohio Gov.'s Conf. on Librs., Columbus, 1974; chmn., adv. bd. libr. sci. dept. Cmty.-Tech. Coll., 1965-69; v.p., pres. Ohio Assn. Sch. Librs., 1971-73. Vol. Am. Cancer Soc., Toledo, 1946—48, 1986—87, Mobile Meals, Toledo, 1986—93, Helping Hands, Toledo, 1994—; vol. libr. Otterbein Portage Valley, 1999—2003; bulletin editor Ohio Assn. Sch. Librs., 1968—71, pres., 1971—72. Martha Holden Jennings scholar, 1976—. Mem. Nat. Honor Soc., Delta Kappa Gamma, Pi Lambda Theta, Kappa Delta Pi, Phi Kappa Phi. Avocations: reading, walking, crafts.

POBLETE, J. VICENTE, medical director; b. Manilla, Philippines, Apr. 2, 1962; s. Vicente Ferrer and Evangelista Pascual Poblete; m. Maria Nenita Tanquintic, Apr. 11, 1962; children: Jose Vicente, Jose Miguel, Alexandria Nicole. MD, U. Va., 1987. Diplomate Ohio, 1995. Pvt. practice Accentuate Within, Avon Lake, Ohio, 1999—; med. dir. Cmty. Health Partners Wound Care Ctr., Lorain, Ohio. Mem.: Am. Soc. for Aesthetic Plastic Surgery (life). Office: Accentuate Within 32730 Walker Rd Ste F-1 Avon Lake OH 44012 Office Phone: 440-930-8187.

POCALYKO, MICHAEL NICHOLAS, investment banker, venture capitalist; b. Fountain Hill, Pa., Dec. 24, 1954; s. Walter and Anna Margaret (Pagats) P.; m. Barbara Wilson Snelbaker, Dec. 26, 1976; children: James Kenneth, Kathryn Laura. AB, Muhlenberg Coll., 1976; MPA, Harvard U., 1985; MBA, U. Pa., 1995. Commd. ensign USN, 1976, advanced through grades to comdr., 1992; aviation detachment officer in charge USS Pharris, 1983-84; mem. strategic concepts group Office of Chief of Naval Ops., Washington, 1985-86, spl. asst. to dep. chief of naval ops., 1986-87; aviation detachment officer in charge USS Boone, 1988-90; with Office of Sec. of Navy, Washington, 1990-92; sr. fellow Atlantic Coun. U.S., Washington, 1992-93; with Office of Sec. Def., Washington, 1993—95; founder, prin. M.N. Pocalyko Investment Bankers, 1995—97; mng. dir., CEO Monticello Capital, 1997—, corp. dir., chmn., 1997—. Audit com. chmn. Challenger Corp., 2002—; chmn. Advanced Environ. Resources Inc., 2003—, Erdevel Europa S.à r.l., 2003—, Erdevel Water Sys. S.r.l., 2004—; trustee Fairleigh Dickinson U., 2000—06; dir. Envambien, S.A., 2007—. Co-editor, contbr.: A John Hawkes Symposium: Design and Debris, 1977; contbr.: Reconstituting America's Defense, 1992; rapporteur: The Future of Russian-American Relations in a Pluralistic World, 1992, The Future of Ukrainian-American Relations in a Pluralistic World, 1992; co-author: The NATO Infrastructure Program, 1993; author: The New Trade Order, 1994, Trends in the International Business Competition Environment, 2001; contbr. articles, essays, op-eds to profl. publs., books, newspapers. Apptd. Fairfax County Industrial Devel. Authority, 1999—2000; apptd. mem. exec. coun. Boy Scouts Am. Nat. Capital Area Coun., 2002—; apptd. mem. Va. Commonwealth Competition Coun., 2000—03; mem. Fairfax County Rep. Com., 1996—2004, Va. Ho. Delegates 36th dist. Rep. Com., 1996—2001, chmn., 2001—06. Recipient Eagle Scout award, 1968, Vincent Astor Found. award U.S. Naval Inst., 1983, Lamb award, Evangelical Lutheran Ch. Am., 1998, Silver Beaver award, Boy Scouts Am., 2002; decorated Navy Commendation Medal, Navy Achievement Medal, Meritorious Svc. Medal (3 awards), 16 other decorations. Mem. U.S. Naval Inst., Internat. Inst. Strategic Studies, Coun. on Fgn. Rels., Assn. Naval Aviation, Muhlenberg Coll. Alumni Assn. (exec. coun. 1986-90, chmn. com. 1986-90), Metropolitan Club (New York), Tower Club (Tysons Corner Va.), Am. Legion, V.F.W., Masons, Sovereign Military Order Temple Jerusalem (gran officier), Military Order Foreign Wars, Military Order Carabao, Sigma Phi Epsilon, Sigma Tau Delta. Republican. Lutheran. Avocations: fly fishing, horseback riding. Office: Monticello Capital One Fountain Sq Reston Town Ctr 11911 Freedom Dr Ste 710 Reston VA 20190-5629 Office Phone: 703-674-0500. Business E-Mail: pocalyko@monticellocapital.com.

POCHI, PETER ERNEST, physician; b. Boston, Mar. 8, 1929; s. Anesti and Alice (Peterson) P.; m. Barbara Orlob, June 11, 1955; children: Alan, Rena. AB cum laude, Harvard Coll., 1950; MD, Boston U., 1955. Diplomate Am. Bd. Dermatology. Intern Boston City Hosp., 1955-56, vis. dermatologist, 1978-91, assoc. dir., 1967-74, 78-84, acting chief dermatology, 1984-85; resident in dermatology Boston U. Hosp., 1958-61, vis. dermatologist, 1977-91, acting chief dermatology, 1984-85; assoc. in medicine Peter Bent Brigham Hosp., Boston, 1972-78; sr. cons. in dermatology Lemuel Shattuck Hosp., Boston, 1975-91; Herbert Mescon prof. dermatology Sch. Medicine, Boston U., 1988-91, prof. emeritus, 1991—, interim chmn. dept. dermatology, 1984-85. Cons. med. service in dermatology Boston VA Hosp., 1978-82; lectr. dermatology Sch. Medicine, Tufts U., 1980-91; assoc. staff New Eng. Med. Ctr. Hosp., 1981-91. Assoc. editor Jour. Investigative Dermatology, 1968-73; contbg. editor Year Book of Dermatology, 1983-90; mem. editl. bd. Archives of Dermatology, 1979-84, Jour. Am. Acad. Dermatology, 1981-90; hon. editor Acta Dermatovenerologica Albanica, 2004—; contbr. articles to med. jours bd. dirs. Cmty. Music Ctr., 1973-77, 97-2003, corp. mem., 1994-97, 2005—; governing bd. Boston Musical Theater, 2000-03. With USN, 1956-58. USPHS fellow, 1960-62, 62-63; USPHS grantee, 1965-84 Fellow Am. Acad. Dermatology (bd. dirs. 1981-85); mem. Am. Fedn. Clin. Rsch., AMA, Boston Dermatol. Club (sec.-treas. 1967-69), Boston U. Sch. Medicine Alumni Assn. (pres. 1979-80), Boston U. Nat. Alumni Coun., Dermatology Found., Evans Med. Found. (dir., sec.), Internat. Soc. Dermatology, Mass. Acad. Dermatology, Mass. Med. Soc. (chmn. sect. dermatology 1977-78), New Eng. Dermatol. Soc., Soc. Investigative Dermatology (bd. dirs. 1976-81, v.p. 1986-87), Am. Acne and Rosacea Soc. Home: 333 Commonwealth Ave Boston MA 02115-1933 E-mail: pepderm@bu.edu.

POCHICK, FRANCIS EDWARD, financial consultant; b. Metuchen, NJ, May 28, 1931; s. Frank Stephen and Bertha Barbara Pochick; m. Shirley Ann Elliott, Feb. 16, 1957; children: Bonnie Lynn, Keith Francis. Student, Rutgers U., 1949-50, 54-55. Agt. New Eng. Mut. Life. Ins. Co., Newark and New Brunswick, NJ, 1958-61, Lambert M. Huppeler Co., Inc., NYC, 1962-64, cons., 1964, sr. cons. employee benefits, 1967-87; fin. cons.

Francis E. Pochick Assocs., NYC, 1987—. Mem. adv. bd. Mercer Fund, Cmty. Found. N.J., 1986—, Rec. for the Blind, Princeton, 1989, charitable devel. officer Nat. Found., Inc., 1992, Nat. Coun. on The Aging, Planned Giving Coun. 1994; mem. com. bd. dirs. health Princeton Coun. Planned Giving, 1993; v.p. The Benefits Planning Co., Ltd., Charlottesville, Va., 1995. With USMC, 1951-54. Mem. Am. Soc. Pension Actuaries, Nat. Assn. Life Underwriters, Fin. Planning Assn., Estate Planning Coun., Nat. Assn. Philanthropic Planners, Lions, Glenmore Country Club. Home: 1451 Bremerton Ln Keswick VA 22947-9147 Office: PO Box 518 Keswick VA 22947-0518 also: No Jersey Br 30 Two Bridges Rd Fairfield NJ 07004-1550 Office Phone: 434-295-7173. Personal E-mail: blmccann118@aol.com. Business E-Mail: fepassoc@earthlink.net.

POCHINI, JUDY HAY, interior designer, writer, editor; b. Phoenix, Mar. 16, 1932; d. Cecil Clifford and Nadine Mary (Larimer) Cook; m. Gordon Eugene Hay, June 5, 1971 (dec. 1974); m. Robert Frank Pochini, Sept. 18, 1983 (dec. 1995). BA, U. Calif., Santa Barbara, 1953; MA in Journalism, U. Calif., Berkeley, 1965. Exec. sec. Mobil Oil Corp., Mpls., 1958-60, Kaiser Aluminum & Chem. Corp., Oakland, Calif., 1960-64; asst. trade publ. editor Sunset mag., Menlo Park, Calif., 1966-68, trade publ. editor, 1968-73; owner, home furnishings editor Lifestyle West, Walnut Creek, Calif., 1974-79; interior designer Berman's Drexel-Heritage, Oakland, 1979-85, Suburban House Drexel-Heritage, Concord, Calif., 1986-87; ptnr., interior designer Judy Hay Interiors, Lafayette and Santa Barbara, Calif., 1987-95, owner, 1995—. Mem. nat. consumer action panel Carpet & Rug Industry, Dalton, Ga., 1973-75; cons. in field. Contbr. articles to profl. jours. Mem. AAUW (pres. 2002-04), Internat. Furnishings and Design Assn., Women in Comms. Inc., U. Calif. Santa Barbara Alumni Assn. (music affiliates bd.), Chi Omega. Democrat. Mem. Unity Ch. Office: 1026 Coast Village Rd 140 Santa Barbara CA 93108

POCKRASS, JOSEPH CRAIG, music educator; b. NYC, May 21, 1971; s. Arlen Stuart and Evelyn Leona Pockrass; m. Jessica Ann Hegele, July 30, 1995; children: David Stuart, Benjamin Thomas, Anna Elizabeth. BS, Ball State U., 1994. Lic. tchg. K-12 gen., instrumental, and choral music Ind., 2002. Choral/computer tchr. Twin Lakes Sch. Corp., Monticello, Ind., 1994—95; spl. edn. asst. Wash. Twp. Schs., Indpls., 1995—96; choral/drama tchr. Durham Pub. Schs., N.C., 1996—97; elem. gen. music tchr. Chapel Hill-Carrboro City Schs., N.C., 1997—2001; elem. gen./instrumental music tchr. Indpls. Pub. Schs., 2001—. Piano/voice tchr. Ashley Arts Music Sch., Durham, 1998—2000; piano tchr. Meridian Music, Carmel, Ind., 2001—. Finalist Tchr. of Yr., Elizabeth Blaker Sch. 55, 2004; named, Sch. 55, 2006. Mem.: Ind. State Tchrs. Assn., MENC. Achievements include conducted the first VH1 Save the Music Celebration Concert for the Indpls. Pub. Sch. Dist. Home: 27 Hampshire Ct Noblesville IN 46062 Office: Eliza Blaker School 55 1349 East 54th St Indianapolis IN 46220 Home Phone: 317-877-1903. Personal E-mail: jpock@aol.com. Business E-Mail: pockrasj@ips.k12.in.us.

POCOCK, EMIL, history professor; b. NYC, 1946; m. Ann Higginbotham, 1988. BA in Am. Studies, U. Md., College Park, Md., 1968; PhD in History and Am. Studies, Ind. U., Bloomington, 1984. Editor Office Chief Mil. History, Washington, 1968—69, NY Times, NYC, 1969—73, Macmillan, NYC, 1973—75; instr. history U. Ga., Athens, 1984—86; asst. prof. to prof. history Ea. Conn. State U., Willimantic, Conn., 1986—. Mem.: Internat. Coun. Shopping Ctrs., Am. Studies Assn., Orgn. Am. Historians. Avocation: radio amateur. Office: Ea Conn State Univ 83 Windham St Willimantic CT 06226 Office Phone: 860-465-4611. Business E-Mail: pocock@easternct.edu.

POCOCK, J. MICHAEL, communications executive; B in Telecomm., U. Ky., Lexington. Various sr. mgmt. pos., consumer products divsn. GE Co., Fairfield, Conn.; mem. mgmt. team Epson Am., Torrance, Calif.; variuos sr. mgmt. pos. Murata Bus. Systems, Dallas; variuos sr. mgmt. positions including pres., CEO Quadmark Ltd. Xerox Corp., Rochester, NY, 1992—94; v.p., gen. mgr. Digital Equipment Corp., Acton, Mass., 1994—96; v.p., gen. mgr. N.Am. sales Compaq Computer Corp., Houston, 1996—99, gen. mgr. comml. products computer group, 1999, v.p. corp. strategy; pres., CEO Polaroid Corp., Waltham, Mass., 2003—06; sr. v.p., gen. mgr. Linksys Cisco Systems, Inc., Irvine, Calif., 2006—. Office: Linksys 121 Theory Dr Irvine CA 92617

POCOSKI, DAVID JOHN, cardiologist; b. Waterbury, Conn., July 15, 1945; s. Edward J. and Stella E. (Kolpa) Pocoski; m. Madelyn M. Pocoski, Sept. 25, 1971; 1 child, Sarah C. BS, U. Conn., Storrs, 1967; MD magna cum laude, Upstate Med. Ctr., Syracuse, NY, 1971. From intern to fellow in cardiology U. Rochester, NY; founder, pres. Osler Clinic of Medicine, Melbourne, Fla.; chief of staff, dir. cardiac rehab. Sea Pines Rehab. Hosp.; chmn. dept. cardiology Holmes Regional Med. Ctr., Melbourne. Commr. Holy Name Jesus Cath. Ch. Maj. USAF, 1974-76. Recipient Outstanding Scientist of the 20th Century award. Fellow Am. Coll. Cardiology; mem. AMA, Alpha Omega Alpha, Phi Beta Kappa. Republican. Roman Catholic. Avocations: music, art, running, community service. Home: 930 S Harbor City Blvd Melbourne FL 32901-1963 Office: Chmn Dept Cardiology Holmes Regional Med Ctr Melbourne FL 32901 Office Phone: 321-725-5050. Personal E-mail: fdhp93a@aol.com.

POCRASS, RICHARD DALE, management consultant; b. Meadville, Pa., Mar. 7, 1940; s. Irving F. and Roslyn (Sperber) P.; m. Rena Levy, Feb. 3, 1968; children: Michael B., S. Douglas. BS in Math., U. Pitts., 1962, MBA in Fin., 1964. EDP sales mgr. NCR Corp., Pitts., 1962-67, retail mktg. mgr. LA, 1972-74; v.p., dir. Nanoseconds Sys., Fairfield, Conn., 1967-69, dir., 1968-72; v.p. gen. mgr. Hart Jewelry Co., Warren, Ohio, 1969-71, dir., 1981-84; mktg. mgr. Data Source Corps subs. Hercules, Inc., El Segundo, 1974-75; pres. Webster-Pocrass & O'Neil (name changed to Pocrass Assocs. 1981), LA, 1976—, Health Tech. Inc. Pub. CEO, chmn. bd. dirs. Chocolates a la Carte, Valencia, Calif. Author: The Recruitment Letter; author (with Maronde) Drug Abuse Study for Hoffman LaRoche, 1980. Bd. dirs. West Valley Little League, U.S. Pastry Alliance, Providence Holly Cross Med. Ctr. Found., L.A. Mission Coll. Found., Western Overseas, Inc., Long Beach, Calif. Mem. Am. Mktg. Assn. L.A. Spkrs. Bur., Soc. for Human Resource Mgmt., L.A. Area C. of C., Bank Mktg. Assn., Retail Controllers Assn., Calif. Exec. Recruiters Assn., Pers. and Indsl. Rels. Assn., Internat. Platform Assn., Rotary. Republican. Jewish. Home: 18815 Paseo Nuevo Dr Tarzana CA 91356-5136 Office: 28455 Livingston Ave Valencia CA 91355-4173 Office Phone: 661-257-3700. Personal E-mail: rick@candymaker.com.

PODBERESKY, SAMUEL, lawyer; b. Cremona, Italy, Mar. 16, 1946; came to U.S., 1947; s. Noah and Mina (Milikowsky) P.; m. Rosita Rubinstein, March 8, 1970; children: Daniel J., Michael J. BS in Aeronautical Engring., U. Md., 1967; JD, U. Md., Balt., 1971. Bar: Md. 1972. Flight test engr. Vertol div. Boeing Co., Phila., 1967-68; regulatory atty. FAA, Washington, 1971-78; dep. asst. gen. counsel U.S. Dept. Transp., Washington, 1978-86, asst. gen. counsel aviation enforcement and proceedings, 1986—. Author: Never the Last Road, 2003. Office: US Dept Transp 1200 New Jersey Ave SE Washington DC 20590-0001

PODBILSKI, LISA LYN, Mandarin Chinese educator; b. Waukegan, Ill., June 10, 1974; d. C. Keith and Gloria Ogle; m. David Paul Podbilski, Sept. 17, 1999; children: Victoria Ione, Denon James. BA in East Asian Lang. and Culture, Mich. State U., East Lansing, 1997. Tchr. Mandarin Chinese Indian Trail Acad., Kenosha, Wis., 2000—03, Berkeley Prep. Sch., Tampa, Fla., 2003—. Tutor, Fla., 2005—. Sec., treas. Kenosha County/Huairou County Sister City Coun., Kenosha, 2001—03. Home Phone: 813-960-5268; Office Phone: 813-885-1673. Personal E-mail: oulisha@hotmail.com.

PODBOY, ALVIN MICHAEL, JR., law librarian, director; b. Cleve., Feb. 10, 1947; s. Alvin Michael and Josephine Esther (Nagode) P.; m. Mary Ann Gloria Esposito, Aug. 21, 1971; children: Allison Marie, Melissa Ann. AB cum laude, Ohio U., 1969; JD, Case Western Res. U., 1972, MLS, 1977. Bar: Ohio 1972, US Dist. Ct. (no. dist.) Ohio 1973, US Supreme Ct. 1992. Assoc. Joseph T. Svete Co. LPA, Chardon, Ohio, 1972-76; dir. pub. svcs. Case Western Res. Sch. Law Libr., Cleve., 1974-77, assoc. law libr., 1977-78; libr. Baker & Hostetler, LLP, Cleve., 1978-88, dir. librs., 1988—. Instr. Notre Dame Coll. of Ohio, Cleve., 1991-2002, Ursuline Coll., Cleve., 2003—, Am. Inst. Paralegal Studies, Cleve., 1991-96. Mem. (editl. adv. bd.) Law Tech. News, 1999—, Practice Innovations, 2001—. Bd. overseers Case Western Res. U., 1981-87, vis. com. sch. libr. sci., 1980-86, Westlaw adv. bd., 1987-92, bd. govs. law sch. alumni assn., 1992-95, West's Legal Directory Ohio Adv. Panel, 1990-91; adv. com. West's Info. Innovators Inst., 1995-97; chmn. Case Western Res. Libr. Sch. Alumni Fund, 1979-80; Rep. precinct committeeman Cuyahoga County, Cleve., 1981-95, exec. com., 1984-87; Rep. precinct committeeman Portage County, Aurora, 2004—; treas. Aurora Meml. Libr. Trust, 2004-; 2nd vice comdr. Aurora Am. Legion Post 803, 2006-. 1st lt. USAF, 1972. Mem.: ABA, Arnold Air Soc., Case Western Res. U. Libr. Sch. Alumni Assn. (pres. 1981), Ohio Regional Assn. Law Librs. (pres. 1985), Am. Assn. Law Librs. (chmn. pvt. law librs. spl. interest sect. 1994—95, exec. bd. 2001—04, cert.), Cleve. Bar Assn., Ohio State Bar Assn. (chmn. librs. com. 1989—91), Phi Alpha Theta, Pi Gamma Mu. Roman Catholic. Avocation: alpine skiing. Home: 417 East Parkway Blvd Aurora OH 44202 Office: Baker & Hostetler LLP 3200 National City Ctr Cleveland OH 44114-3485 Home Phone: 330-995-7643; Office Phone: 216-861-7101. Business E-Mail: apodboy@bakerlaw.com.

PODD, ANN, newspaper editor; b. Buffalo, Jan. 15, 1954; d. Edward and Florence (Bojan) P.; m. Timothy Murray, 1980; children: Laura, Gregory. AB, Syracuse U., 1976; MBA, SUNY, Buffalo, 1981. Reporter AP, 1977, Buffalo Courier-Express, 1977-80, bus. editor, 1980-82, Bergen (N.J.) Record, 1982-88, N.Y. Daily News, 1988-90, assoc. editor, 1990-92, assoc. editor, dir. human resources, 1992-93; dep. spot news editor Wall St. Jour., NYC, 1994, spot news editor, 1994—2000, nat. TV editor, 2000—03, day editor, 2003—05; Hong Kong mng. editor Wall St. Jour. Asia, Hong Kong, 2005—. Office: Wall Stret Journal 25/F Central Plaza 18 Harbour Rd Hong Kong Hong Kong

PODESTA, JOHN DAVID, law educator, former White House chief of staff; b. Chgo., Jan. 8, 1949; s. John David, Sr. and Mary (Kokoris) Podesta; m. Mary Spieczny, Nov. 4, 1978; children: Megan Rouse, Mae, Gabriel. BS, Knox Coll., 1971; JD, Georgetown U., 1976. Bar: DC 1976. Trial atty. Dept. of Justice, Washington, 1976-77; spl. asst. to dir. ACTION, Washington, 1978-79; counsel Senate Judiciary Com., Washington, 1979-81; chief minority counsel Senate Judiciary Subcom., Washington, 1981-86; chief counsel Senate Agr. Com., Washington, 1987-88; pres., gen. counsel Podesta Assocs., Inc., Washington, 1988-93; asst. to pres., staff sec. The White House, Washington, 1993-95, asst. to pres., dep. chief of staff, 1997-98, chief of staff to Pres., 1998—2001; pres., CEO Ctr. Am. Progress, Washington, 2001—. Vis. prof. law Georgetown U. Law Ctr., Washington, 1983, Washington, 1995—97, Washington, 1998—2000, Washington, 2001—; chair US Senate subcom., Task Force Privacy and Tech., Washington, 1991; mem. coun. Adminstrv. Conf. US, Washington, 1993—95; mem. Com. Protecting and Reducing Govt. Secrecy, Washington, 1995. Author: Protecting Electronic Messaging, 1990. Fellow: Natural Resources Def. Coun. (sr.); mem.: ABA (coun., sec. individual rights and responsibilities 1994—, chair 2002—03), DC Bar (chair adminstrv. law sect. 1982—83), League Conservation Voters (bd. dirs. 2001—). Democrat. Office: Ctr Am Progress 1333 H St NW 10th Fl Washington DC 20005 also: Georgetown U Law Ctr 574 McDonough Hall Washington DC 20001-2075

PODESTA, ROGER E., lawyer; b. Aug. 10, 1947; BA, Columbia U., 1969; JD, Harvard U., 1973. Bar: NY 1973. Law clk. to Hon. Wilfred Feinberg US Ct. Appeals (2nd cir.), 1973-74; ptnr., head Product Liability Practice Debevoise & Plimpton LLP, NYC. Case and comments editor: Harvard Law Rev., 1972-73. Mem. ABA, Phi Beta Kappa. Office: Debevoise & Plimpton LLP 919 Third Ave New York NY 10022 Office Fax: 212-909-6836. E-mail: repodesta@debevoise.com.

PODGOR, ELLEN SUE, law educator; b. Bklyn., Jan. 30, 1952; d. Benjamin and Yetta (Shilensky) Podgor. BS magna cum laude, Syracuse U., 1973; JD, Ind. U., Indpls., 1976; MBA, U. Chgo., 1987; LLM, Temple U., 1989. Bar: Ind. 1976, N.Y. 1984, Pa. 1987. Dep. prosecutor Lake County Prosecutor's Office, Crown Point, Ind., 1976-78; ptnr. Nicholls & Podgor, Crown Point, 1978-87; instr. Temple U. Sch. Law, 1987-89; assoc. prof. law St. Thomas U., Miami, Fla., 1989-91, Ga. State U., Atlanta, 1991—2006. Vis. scholar Yale Law Sch., 1998; vis. prof. U. Ga., 2000; John S. Stone vis. endowed chair U. Ala., 2001; vis. prof. George Washington U., 2003; Culvenhouses chair Stetson U. Coll. Law, 2005—06. Author (with Israel): White Collar Crime in a Nutshell; author: (with Israel, Borman, Henning) White Collar Crime: Law and Practice; author: (with Wise and Clark) International Criminal Law: Cases and Materials, Understanding International Criminal Law; author: (with Henning, Taslitz, Garcia) Criminal Law: Concepts and Practice; assoc. editor Ind. Law Rev., 1975—78; contbr. articles to profl. jours. Del. Ind. Dem. Conv., 1982. Mem.: NACDL (bd. dirs.), ABA, Ind. Bar Assn., Am. Law Inst, Am. Bd. Criminal Lawyers (hon.). Democrat. Jewish. Office: Stetson Univ Coll Law 1401 61st St Gulfport FL 33707 Business E-Mail: epodgor@law.stetson.edu.

PODGORNY, GEORGE, emergency physician; b. Tehran, Iran, Mar. 17, 1934; s. Emanuel and Helen (Parsian) P.; came to U.S., 1954, naturalized, 1973. B.S., Maryville Coll., 1958; postgrad. Bowman Gray Sch. Medicine, 1958; M.D., Wake Forest U., 1962; m. Ernestine Koury, Oct. 20, 1962; children: Adele, Emanuel II, George, Gregory. Intern in surgery N.C. Bapt. Hosp., Winston-Salem, 1962-63, chief resident in gen. surgery, 1966-67, in cardiothoracic surgery, 1967-69; sr. med. examiner Forsyth County, N.C., 1972—; dir. dept. emergency medicine Forsyth Meml. Hosp., Winston-Salem, 1974-80; sec.-treas. Forsyth Emergency Services, Winston-Salem, 1970-80; clin. prof. emergency medicine East Carolina U. Sch. Medicine, Greenville, 1984—, chmn. residency rev. com. on emergency medicine, 1980-88; mem. Accreditation Coun. for Grad. Med. Edn. Dir. Emergency Med. Svcs. Project Region II of N.C., 1975—; chmn. bd. trustees Emergency Medicine Found.; chmn. residency rev. com. emergency medicine Accreditation Coun. Grad. Med. Edn.; founder Western Piedmont Emergency Med. Svcs. Coun., 1973; mem. N.C. Emergency Med. Svcs. Adv. Coun., 1976-81; assoc. prof. clin. surgery Bowman Gray Sch. Medicine, Wake Forest U., Winston-Salem, 1979—. Bd. dirs. Piedmont Health Systems Agy., 1975-84; trustee Forsyth County Hosp., Authority, 1974-75; bd. dirs. N.C. Health Coordinating Coun., 1975-82, Medic Alert Found. Internat. Fellow Internat. Coll. Surgeons, Internat. Coll. Angiology, Royal Soc. Health (Great Britain), Royal Soc. Medicine, Southeastern Surg. Congress; mem. Am. Coll. Emergency Physicians (charter, pres. 1978-79), AMA, (chmn. coun. of sect. emergency medicine 1978-90, alt. del. for Am. Coll. Emergency Physicians, 1990—), Am. Bd. Emergency Medicine (pres. 1976-81). Contbr. articles to profl. publs. on trauma, snake bite and history of medicine; editorial bd. Annals of Emergency Medicine, Med. Meetings. Home and Office: 2115 Georgia Ave Winston Salem NC 27104-1917 Office Phone: 336-727-1161.

PODGORSAK, ERVIN B., medical physicist, educator, administrator; b. Vienna, Sept. 28, 1943; arrived in Slovenia, 1946, came to U.S., 1968, Can., 1973; s. Franc and Gabriella Podgorsak; m. Mariana Ambrozic, Oct. 23, 1965; children: Matthew, Gregor. Dipl.Ing. in Physics, U. Ljubljana, Slovenia, 1968; MSc in Physics, U. Wis., 1970, PhD in Physics, 1973. Diplomate Am. Bd. Med. Physics. Rsch. asst. U. Ljubljana, 1965-68, U. Wis., Madison, 1968-73; postdoctoral fellow U. Toronto, Ont., Canada, 1973-74; asst. prof. McGill U., Montreal, Que., Canada, 1975-79, assoc. prof., 1980-84, prof. med. physics, 1985—, dir. med. physics unit, 1991—; dir. dept. med. physics Montreal Gen. Hosp., 1979—. Hon. vis. prof. U. Ljubljana, 1995—; presenter in field. Author Radiation Physics for Medical Physicists, 2005; editor Review of Radiation Oncology Physics: A Handbook for Teachers and Students, 2005; contbr. numerous articles to sci. jours., chpts. to books. Recipient (with C. Zankowski) Sylvia Fedoruk prize in Med. Physics, 1997, (with C. Zankowski) Farrington Daniels award in Med. Physics, 1997, Agora Award, Le Palais des Congres, Montreal, 1998. Fellow Can. Coll. Physicists in Medicine (bd. dirs. 1981-89, v.p. 1984-87, pres. 1987-89), Am. Assn. Physicists in Medicine (bd. dirs. 1990-93, assoc. editor Med. Physics Jour. 1989-2005, radiother. com. 1994-96, Lifetime Achievement in Med. Physics award Upstate NY chpt. 2005, William D. Coolidge award 2006), Am. Coll. Med. Physics (bd. chancellors 1997-99); mem. Can. Assn. Physicists, Can. Orgn. Med. Physics, Can. Assn. Radiation Oncologists, Can. Radiation Protection Assn., Internat. Stereotactic Radiosurgery Soc. (bd. dirs. 1991-95) Home: 1540 croissant Seville Brossard PQ Canada J4X 1J4 Office: Montreal Gen Hosp Dept Med Physics 1650 Cedar Ave Montreal PQ Canada H3G 1A4 Office Phone: 514-934-8052. E-mail: epodgorsak@medphys.mcgill.ca.

PODHORETZ, JOHN, editor, writer; b. NYC, Apr. 18, 1961; s. Norman Podhoretz and Midge (Decter); m. Ayala Cohen, Oct. 13, 2002. AB, U. Chgo., 1982. Former researcher, reporter Time; exec. editor news Insight Mag., Washington, 1985-87; contbg. editor U.S. News and World Report, Washington, 1987-88; speechwriter to Pres. Ronald Reagan and George H. W. Bush White House, Washington, 1988-89; spl. asst. to William Bennett Office of Nat. Drug Control Policy, 1989; asst. mng. editor Washington Times, 1989-91; sr. fellow Hudson Inst., 1991-94; contbr. FOX News Channel, 1997—. TV critic N.Y. Post, 1994-95, editor editl. page, columnist 1997—; co-founder, former dep. dir. The Weekly Std., 1995-97, currently contbg. editor; weekly columnist National Review Online; cons. editor Regan Books; co-founder White House Writers Group; author Hell of a Ride: Backstage at the White House Follies 1989-1993, 1992, Bush Country: How Dubya Became a Great President While Driving Liberals Insane, 2004; cons. (TV) West Wing. Recipient J.C. Penney/Mo. award for excellence in feature sects., 1990. Jewish. Achievements include Five-time winner on Jeopardy!. Office: FOX News Channel 1211 Ave of Americas New York NY 10036

PODHURST, AARON SAMUEL, lawyer; b. NYC, Apr. 29, 1936; s. Louis and Rae (Pomerantz) P.; m. Dorothy Ellen Podhurst, Sept. 7, 1958; children: Karen Beth Dern, Laura Koffsky, Julie Weinberg. BBA, U. Mich., 1957; JD, Columbia U., 1960. Bar: Fla., 1961, N.Y., 1961. Assoc. Nichols, Gaither, Miami, 1962—67; founding ptnr. Podhurst, Orseck P.A., Miami, 1967—. Vice pres. Miami Coalition for Safe Cmty., 1994—; mem. Orange Bowl Com., Miami, 1996—. Recipient Nat. Medallion award NCCJ, 1994; Harlan Fiske Stone scholar, 1960. Mem. ABA (aviation com.), Internat. Acad. Trial Lawyers (pres. 1990), Acad. Fla. Trial Lawyers (pres. 1978, aviation com.), Am. Coll. Trial Lawyers, Assn. Trial Lawyers Am. (bd. govs., aviation com.), Internat. Soc. Barristers, Inner Cir. of Advocates. Office: Podhurst Orseck PA 25 W Flagler St Ste 800 Miami FL 33130-1712 Home Phone: 305-663-7331; Office Phone: 305-358-2800. Business E-Mail: info@podhurst.com.

PODICHETTY, VINOD KUMAR, medical researcher; arrived in U.S., 2000; s. Haricharan and Vasantha Podichetty. MBBS, Maharastra Inst. Med. Sci. & Rsch., India, 1998; MS, Cleve. State U., 2002; cert. in Protection of Human Research Subjects, U. Miami, 2002. Diplomate Indian Med. Coun., 1999. Staff physician Aware Hosps., Hyderabad, Andhra Pradesh, India, 1998; chief med. officer Aware Cancer Rsch. Inst., Hyderabad, Andhra Pradesh, India, 1999—2000; rsch. asst. Cleve. (Ohio) Clinic Found., 2000—02; coord., rsch. assoc. Cleve. Clinic Fla., Weston, Fla., 2003—04, project dir., 2004—; project lead U. Hosp. West Eng., Bristol, England, 1999. Co-director, spine symposium Cleve. Clinic Fla., Weston, Fla., 2003; dir. Primary Health Care Ctr. - Pulse Polio Program, Latur, Maharastra, India, 1997. Contbr. articles to profl. jours. Grantee, Pharm. Industry, 2002—05; scholar, Dept. Health Scis. Cleve. State U., 2000—02. Mem.: Am. Med. Writers Assn., Assn. Clin. Rsch. Profls., Am. Coll. Health Assn., Indian Soc. Human Genetics, Indian Med. Coun., Nat. Assn. Spine Specialists, N.Am. Spine Soc., Indian Student Orgn. (pres. 2002), Continuing Med. Edn. Com. Achievements include research in effectiveness of calcitonin nasal spray in the treatment of lumbar canal stenosis; thoracic microendoscopic discectomy; chronic non-malignant musculoskeletal pain in older adult: clinical issues and opioid intervention; age-based comparative outcomes of elderly patients receiving lumbar decompression surgery; ASA class, not age, predicts complications after minimally invasive spine surgery. Home Phone: 305-816-0184; Office Phone: 954-659-5630.

PODOLNY, JOEL M., dean, management educator; AB magna cum laude, Harvard U., 1986, AM, 1989, PhD in Sociology, 1991. Asst. prof. orgnl. behavior Stanford U., 1991—95, assoc. prof., 1995—96, assoc. prof. strategic mgmt. and orgnl. behavior, 1996—99, prof., 1999—2000, William R. Timken prof. orgnl. behavior and strategic mgmt., 2000—02, sr. assoc. dean for academic affairs, 2000—02; prof. sociology and bus. adminstrn. Harvard U., Cambridge, 2002—05, Novartis prof. leadership and mgmt.; dir. rsch. Harvard Bus. Sch., Cambridge, 2003—05; dean, William S. Beinecke prof. mgmt. Yale Sch. Mgmt., New Haven, 2005—. Author: Status Signals: A Sociological Study of Market Competition, 2005; co-author: Strategic Management, 2001; cons. editor American Journal of Sociology, 1992—94, mem. editl. bd. Administrative Science Quarterly, 1999—2000; mem. editl. bd. American Sociological Review, 2005; assoc. editor Industrial and Corporate Change, 1999—; contbr. articles to profl. jours. Bd. mem. Greenwich Assocs. Mem.: Am. Sociol. Assn. Office: Yale Sch Mgmt Box 208200 New Haven CT 06520-8200 Office Phone: 203-432-6035. Office Fax: 203-432-5092. Business E-Mail: joel.podolny@yale.edu.

PODRATZ, KARL C., gynecologic surgeon, oncologist, educator; b. New Ulm, Minn., Feb. 7, 1943; s. Clarence F. and Elsa (Sievert) P.; m. Roxann Rochford; 1 child, Scott Karl. BA, U. Minn., 1966; MD in Medicine, St. Louis U., 1974, PhD in Biochemistry, 1974. Resident in ob-gyn. U. Chgo., 1974-77; gynecologic oncology fellow Mayo Clinic, Rochester, Minn., 1977-79, gynecologic surgeon/oncologist, 1979—, chmn. dept. ob-gyn., 1986-2000, Joseph and Barbara Atkins prof. surgery, 1990—. Dir. gynecologic oncology tng. program Mayo Clinic, Rochester, 1985—. Assoc. editor Evidence Based Obstet Gynecology; editor Gynecologic Oncology. Chair exec. com. Gynecol. Cancer Found., 2003-. Fellow ACS; mem. Soc. Gynecologic Oncology (pres. 1998-99), Cen. Assn. Ob-Gyn. (pres. 1997, past sec.-treas. 1987-95), Soc. Gynegol. Surgeons (pres. 2005-), Western Assn. Gynecologic Oncologists (past pres. 1991). Avocations: downhill skiing, golf, gardening, cooking, travel. Office: Mayo Clinic 200 1st St SW Rochester MN 55905-0002 Business E-Mail: podratz.karl@mayo.edu. *

PODWALL, KATHRYN STANLEY, biology professor; b. Chgo., Oct. 14; d. Frank and Marie C. Stanley. BS, U. Ill.; MA, NYU. Prof. biology Nassau C.C., Garden City, NY. Developmental reviewer West Ednl. Pub., Amesbury, Mass. and Highland Park, Ill., 1989, 91-92; reviewer AAAS, Washington, 1970—; exec. bd., advisor Women's Faculty Assn., Nassau C.C., 1990—, pres, 2000-2002; lectr. in field. Author: Tested Studies for Laboratory Teaching, vol. 5, 1993; editor: (books and cassettes) Rhyming Simon Books and Cassettes, 1990, Sight Reading Syncopation, 1998, Today's Way To Play the Standards, 2000, Today's Way To Play the Classics, 2000, (book and CD) Cartoons & Car Tunes, 2001, Cartoons & Kid Tunes, 2002, Cartoons and Christmas Tunes, 2003, Rhythms and Blues, 2006, 50 Jazz Duets, 2006. Recipient L.I. Alzheimer's Found. Svc. award, 2002, Excellence award, Nat. Inst. for Staff and Orgnl. Devel., 2003, Chancellor's award excellence in tchg., SUNY, 2004. Mem. AAUW, Am. Assn. for Women in Cmty. Colls., Nat. Assn. Biology Tchrs. (life), Nat. Sci. Tchrs. Assn. (life), Soc. for Coll. Sci. Tchrs., Met. Assn. Coll. and Univ. Biologists, Nat. Cathedral Assn., N.Y. Acad. of Scis., Friends of Archives (charter), Xerces Soc., Southampton Colonial Soc., LaSalle County Hist. Soc. (life), Garden City Hist. Soc. (life), Soroptimists (bd. dirs. dist. 1 1994-96, club pres. 1992-94, Nassau County Pres. award 2001), U. Ill. Alumni Assn. (life). Avocations: travel, gardening, zoological pursuits. Office: Nassau Community College One Education Dr Garden City NY 11530 Office Phone: 516-572-7575. Business E-Mail: podwalk@ncc.edu.

POE, DAVID RUSSELL, lawyer; b. Columbia, Mo., Sept. 4, 1948; s. Russell Warren and Chloe Ardith (Prichard) P.; m. Constance Elizabeth Vaught, Aug. 3, 1974; children: Meghan Elizabeth, Michael Lewis. BS in Mechanical and Aerospace Engring., U. Mo., 1970; JD, Duke U., 1974. Bar: NY 1975, NC 1977, US Supreme Ct. 1985, DC 1991, US Ct. Appeals (1st, 2d, 4th, 6th and DC cirs.), US Dist. Ct. (so., ea. dists.) NY, US Dist. Ct. (ea. dist.) NC. Network engr. Southwestern Bell Telephone Co., St. Louis, 1970-71; assoc. LeBoeuf, Lamb, Leiby & MacRae, NYC, 1974-82, ptnr., 1983-89, Washington, 1989-93, LeBoeuf, Lamb, Greene & MacRae, LLP, Washington, 1994—, chmn. hydroelectric practice. Adj. faculty Columbus Sch. Law, Cath. U. Am., 1992-98. Vestry St. Paul's Ch., Englewood, NJ, 1986-89; legal advisor First Presbyn. Pre-Sch. and Kindergarten, Englewood, 1984-88; vestry St. John's Ch., McLean, Va., 1996-97, 1999-2001, jr. warden, 2000-01. Mem. ABA (pub. utility sect., chmn. adminstrv. law com. 1988-89, chmn. cable TV com. 1989-92, mem. coun. 1990-93, chmn. publs. com. 1993-95, chmn. ann. mtg. 1997, vice-chair 2001-02, chair-elect 2002-03, sect. chair 2003-04, sect. delegate to House of Delegates 2005-), Fed. Comm. Bar Assn., Fed. Energy Bar Assn. (vice chmn. jud. rev. com. 1994-95, chmn. 1995-96). Office: LeBoeuf Lamb Greene MacRae LLP Ste 1200 1875 Connecticut Ave NW Washington DC 20009-5728 Office Phone: 202-986-8039. Office Fax: 202-956-3237. Business E-Mail: dpoe@llgm.com.

POE, GEORGE WILKINSON, literature and language professor; b. Greenville, SC, Mar. 28, 1952; s. Frank Swift and Rosalie (Haynes) P.; m. Sylviane Rosello, Jan. 8, 1977. BA with high honors in French, Davidson Coll., NC, 1974; postgraduate student, U. Paris IV, 1974—75; MA, Middlebury Coll., Vt., 1975; PhD, Duke U., 1981. Part-time instr. French Duke U., Durham, NC, 1976—78; instr. to asst. prof. Davidson Coll., 1978—82; asst. prof. Hanover Coll., 1982—87, Sewanee: The U. of the South, Tenn., 1987—90, assoc. prof., 1990—97, dept. chair, 1994—2000, prof. French and French Studies, 1997—. Faculty dir. Jr. Yr. in France Davidson Coll., 1979-81; study abroad dir. dept. French Hanover Coll., 1982-87, U. South, 1989, dir. Sewanee in France summer prog., 1989; Camargo scholar in residence, vis. prog. dir., 1995. Author: The Rococo & 18th Century French Literature, 1987; co-editor: The French Novel, 1995; editl. bd. Synthesis: An Interdisciplinarhy Jour., 1994; contbr. articles and revs. to profl. jours. Alumni coord. meml. fund Ghigo-Embry-Meeks Fund Davidson Coll., 1987. Recipient US Prof. of Yr. award, Carnegie Found. for Advancement of Tchg. and Coun. for Advancement and Support of Edn., 2006; Camargo Found. grant, 1992. Mem. MLA (del. nat. assembly 1988-91), Soc. Marivaux (adminstrv. adv. bd. 1989), Am. Assn. Tchrs. French, Am. Soc. 18th Century Studies, Tenn. Fgn. Lang. Tchg. Assn., South Atlantic MLA. Avocations: theater, cinema, travel, golf. Office: Dept French and French Studies Sewanee The U of the South 735 University Ave Sewanee TN 37383 Office Phone: 931-598-1522. E-mail: gpoe@sewanee.edu.

POE, LAURA, nursing educator, administrator; b. Salt Lake City, July 20, 1962; d. William D. and Laree Jardine (Birch) P. Grad., Utah Tech. Coll., 1980; A degree, Brigham Young U., 1984, B, 1986, MS, 1988. Asst. dir. Divsn. Occupl. and Profl. Licensing Utah Bd. Nursing, exec. dir. Author: (with others) Geri-Assistant Care Manual; contbr. articles to profl. jours. Mem. Utah Nurses Assn. (del., chair govt. rels. com.), Nightingale Soc., Phi Kappa Phi, Sigma Theta Tau.

POE, LUKE HARVEY, JR., lawyer; b. Richmond, Va., Jan. 29, 1916; s. Luke Harvey and Alice Morris (Reddy) Poe; m. Josephine Jaster, Mar. 20, 1998. BS in Math, U. Va., 1938, JD, 1941; postgrad. (Rhodes scholar), Oxford U., Eng., 1939; D.Phil., Christ Ch., 1957. Bar: Va. bar 1940, D.C. bar and D.C. Ct. Appeals bar 1967, U.S. Supreme Ct. bar 1969, Md. bar 1974. Assoc. Cravath, Swaine & Moore, NYC, 1941—42; tutor St. John's Coll., Annapolis, Md., 1946—50, asst. dean, 1947—49, tenure tutor, 1953—60, dir. physics and chemistry lab., 1959—60; asst. chmn. Nat. Citizens Com. for Kennedy and Johnson and chmn. Citizens Com., Pres.'s Inaugural Com., 1960—61; asst. to chmn. bd. Aerojet-Gen. Corp., El Monte, Calif., 1961—63; divsn. pres. Internat. Tech. Assistance and Devel. Co., Washington, 1963—66; ptnr. Howard, Poe & Bastian, Washington, 1966—83; pvt. practice law, 1983—. Bd. dirs. First Am. Bank of Md.; cons. Dept. Transp., Dept. State, NEH; lectr. War Coll. of USAF, Gen. Studies program U. Va.; seminar leader Aspen Inst. Humanistic Studies; guest panelist Panel on Sci. and Tech. of Com. on Sci. and Astronautics, U.S. Ho. of Reps., 1970; pres. bd. dirs. Watergate East, Inc., 1976-79, 90-92; organizer U. Va. Unified Liberal Arts Program, 1988—. Author: The Combat History of the Battleship U.S.S. Mississippi, 1947, The Transition From Natural Law to Natural Rights, 1957; (with others) lab. manuals Einstein's Theory of Relativity, 1957, Electro-Magnetic Theory, 1959; editor: (with others) Va. Mag., 1936-38, U. Va. Law Rev., 1940-41. Dean's adv. coun. Lehigh U., 1962-65, mem. Seminar on Sci., Tech. and Pub. Policy, Brookings Instn., 1964-66; coun. on trends and perspectives U.S. C. of C., 1966-69; chmn. bd. Bristol Property Mgmt. and Svcs., Inc., 1967-88; chmn. Annapolis Bd. Zoning Appeals, 1966-75; mem. Annapolis Mayor's Task Force, 1967-74, Md. Gov.'s Commn. on Capital City, 1970-76. Lt. comdr. USNR, 1942-46. Decorated Jhalavada Order of Durbargadh, Dhrangadhara. Mem. Am. Law Inst., AAUP, Raven Soc. (pres.), Soc. of Cincinnati, Sr. Common Room and High Table (Christ Church), Met. Club (Washington), Travellers Club (London), Brook Club (N.Y.C.), New Providence Club (Annapolis), Vincent's Club (Oxford), Phi Beta Kappa, Phi Delta Phi. Episcopalian. Home: 139 Market St Annapolis MD 21401-2628 also: 2500 Virginia Ave NW Washington DC 20037-1901 Office Phone: 202-337-3080. Personal E-mail: lharveypoe@aol.com.

POE, MYA, communications executive, director; b. Cin., Feb. 15, 1970; d. Nancy J. Green and Marvin Richard Poe. PhD, U. Mass., Amherst, 2005. Profl. writer, 1993—96; lectr. MIT, Cambridge, 2000—05, dir. tech. commn., 2005—. Mem.: Nat. Coun. Tchrs. English. D-Liberal. Avocations: travel, dressage. Office: MIT 77 Massachusetts Ave Bldg 14N-229B Cambridge MA 02139 Home Phone: 401-617-9744; Office Phone: 617-253-3039.

POE, RANDALL ELLSWORTH, public relations executive, author; b. Colorado Springs, Colo., Nov. 2, 1935; s. Everett E. and Emilie (Hamburger) P.; m. M. Catherine Ferguson, June 12, 1959 (div. July 1988); 1 child, Andrea Catherine. BA in Journalism, U. Calif., San Jose, 1958. Exec. dir. The Conf. Bd., NYC, 1961-68, news dir., 1968-74, news dir./media mgr., 1974-88, dir. comm., exec. dir., 1988—. Contbr. articles to maj. mags., chapters to books; columnist bus. pubs. Office: The Conf Bd 845 3rd Ave 2nd Fl New York NY 10022-6601

POE, ROBERT ALAN, lawyer; b. Bracken County, Ky., Apr. 25, 1951; Student, U. Ky.; BA, Centre Coll., 1973; JD, U. Va., 1976. Bar: Colo. 1976. Mem. Holland & Hart, Denver, 1976—. Adj. prof. taxation U. Denver, 1986-88. Articles editor Va. Law Rev., 1974-76. Mem. ABA, Order of Coif, Phi Beta Kappa. Office: Holland & Hart 8390 E Crescent Pkwy Ste 400 Greenwood Village CO 80111-2822 Home Phone: 303-766-7694; Office Phone: 303-290-1616. E-mail: apoe@hollandhart.com.

POE, TED, congressman, former judge; b. Temple, Tex., Oct. 13, 1948; m. Carol Poe. BA in Polit. Sci., Abilene Christian U., 1970; JD, U. Houston Law Ctr., 1973. Asst. dist. atty. Harris County, Tex., 1973—81, criminal ct. judge Tex., 1981—2003; mem. US Congress from 2nd Tex. dist., 2005—, mem. transp. and infrastructure com., mem. internat. rels. com., mem. small bus. com., founder Victims' Rights Caucus. Instr. U. Houston, FBI Nat. Acad., Quantico, Va., US Mil. Acad., West Point. Bd. mem. Nat. Children's Alliance; past bd. mem. Children's Assessment Ctr. Houston, CASA Child Advocates, Child Abuse Prevention Coun., Parents of Murdered Children, MADD, Drug Abuse Resistance Edn., Roseate Women's Ctr. for Abused Women, Abilene Christian U. Served Res. C-130 Unit USAF, 1970—76. Named Outstanding Nat. Victim Adv., Nat. Victim Ctr., Outstanding Judge, Found. for Improvement of Justice, Outstanding Instr., Tex. Dist. Atty. Assn., Best Judge, Kans. Peace Officers Assn., Outstanding Dist. Judge, Houston Police Officers Assn., Harris County Dep. Sheriffs Assn., Outstanding Young Lawyer, Houston Bar Assn.; recipient Spirit of Enterprise award, US C. of C., Congl. Partnership award, S.E. Tex. Regional Planning Commn., 2006, Social Change award, Tex. Assn. Against Sexual Assault, Morton Bard award, Nat. Orgn. Victims Assistance. Republican. Christian. Office: US Ho Reps 1605 Longworth Ho Office Bldg Washington DC 20515-4302 Office Phone: 202-225-6565. *

POE, TERRY LYNN, music educator; b. Asheboro, NC, Mar. 30, 1952; s. George McLamb and Christine Teague Poe. B in music edn., Wake Forest U., 1970—74. Assoc. dir. Raleigh Boychoir, Raleigh, NC, 1974—94; chapel organist St. Mary's Coll., Raleigh, 1979—84; church organist Trinity U. Meth. Ch., Raleigh, NC, 1976—; choral music tchr. Wake County Pub. Schools, 1974—. Mentor coord. Carroll Mid. Sch., Raleigh, NC, 1995—, fine arts chmn., 1979—, beta club coun. chmn., 1994—. Mem. Wake County Exec. PTA Coun., 1988—89, Boy Scouts Am., 1965—70. Mem.: Am. Guild Organists, Nat. Edn. Assn. Democrat. Bapt. Avocation: flying. Home: 704 Hampstead Pl Raleigh NC 27610 Office: Carroll Mid Sch 4520 Six Forks Rd Raleigh NC 27609 Personal E-mail: terrylpoe@aol.com.

POEHLEIN, GARY WAYNE, retired chemical engineering professor; b. Tell City, Ind., Oct. 17, 1936; s. Oscar Raymond and Eva Lee (Dickman) P.; m. Sharon Eileen Wood., Jan. 1, 1958; children: Steven Ray, Timothy Wayne, Valorie Ann, Sandra Lee. BSChemE, Purdue U., 1958, MSChemE, 1961, PhD, 1966. Design engr. Proctor & Gamble, Cin., 1958-61; from asst. prof. to assoc. prof. Lehigh U., Bethlehem, Pa., 1965-75, prof. chem. engring., 1975-78, co-dir. emulsion polymers inst., 1973-78; dir. sch. chem. engring. Ga. Inst. Tech., Atlanta, 1978-86, assoc. v.p. rsch., dean grad. studies, 1986-91, v.p. interdisciplinary programs, prof. chem. engring., 1991-95; prof. chem. engring., 1978-96; dir. Chem. and Transport Systems Divsn. NSF, 1996-2000; ret., 2000. Bd. dirs. Flexible Products Co., Marietta, Ga.; interim chair chem. engring. dept., vis. prof. Lehigh U., 2001—02. Contbr. over 100 articles to tech. publs. Mem. sch. bd. Bethlehem Area Sch. Dist., 1969-75. Recipient Honor Scroll award Phila. br. Am. Inst. Chemists, 1977, Mac Pruitt award Coun. for Chem. Rsch., 1989. Fellow AIChE. Avocations: woodworking, sailing. Home: 407 S Henry St Alexandria VA 22314-5901 Personal E-mail: gspoehlein@aol.com.

POEHLER, AMY, comedienne, actress; b. Burlington, Mass., Sept. 16, 1971; m. Will Arnett, Aug. 29, 2003. Grad., Boston Coll. Cast mem. Second City, Chicago, 1993—96, Upright Citizen's Brigade, 1996—, Saturday Night Live, 2001—. Actor: (films) Saving Manhattan, 1998, Tomorrow Night, 1998, Deuce Bigalow: Male Gigolo, 1999, The Devil and Daniel Webster, 2001, Wet Hot American Summer, 2001, Martin & Orloff, 2002, Mean Girls, 2004, Envy, 2004, Southland Tales, 2006, Man of the Year, 2006, Blades of Glory, 2007; actor, writer, prodr. (films) Wild Girls Gone, 2005, actor, writer (TV series) Upright Citizens Brigade, 1998—2000, appearances include Late Night with Conan O'Brien, 1998—2000, Apt. 2F, 1997, Spin City, 1998, Undeclared, 2002, Arrested Development, 2004. Office: Saturday Night Live NBC Studios 30 Rockefeller Plz New York NY 10112 *

POEHLING, KATHERINE, pediatrician; d. Gary Poehling; m. Timothy Peters, May 4, 1996; children: Jennifer Peters children: Robert Peters. MD, Wake Forest Sch. of Medicine, Winston-Salem, NC, 1995; MPH, Vanderbilt U. Sch. of Medicine, Nashville, Tenn., 2001. Lic. Med. Tenn. State Bd. of Med. Examiners, 1999, cert. Bd. Am. Acad. Pediat., 1998. Fellow Vanderbilt U., Nashville, 1999—2002, asst. prof. of pediat., 2002—07; assoc. prof. pediats. Wake Forest U. Med. Ctr., Winston-Salem, NC, 2007—. Mem. NC Med. Bd., 2007. Fellow: Am. Acad. Pediat.; mem.: Soc. Pediatric Rsch., Ambulatory Pediat. Assn., Infectious Disease Soc. Am., Alpha Omega Alpha. Achievements include research in Clin. rsch. on pediat. respiratory infections.

POEHLMANN, CARL JOHN, agricultural researcher; b. Jamestown, Mo., Jan. 29, 1950; s. Edwin and Lucille P.; m. Linda Kay Garner, Dec. 29, 1973; children: Anthony, Kimberly. BS, U. Mo., 1972, MS, 1978. Farmer, Jamestown, Mo., 1972-73; vocat. agrl. tchr. Linn (Mo.) Pub. Schs., 1973-75, Columbia (Mo.) Pub. Schs., 1975-78; dir., mgr. agronomy rsch. ctr. U. Mo., Columbia, 1978-2000; dir. MOAES Field Ops., 2000—06; asst. dir. Mo. Agrl. Rsch. Sta., 2006—. Mem. Am. Soc. Agronomy (div. A-7 chair 1985-86, bd. mem. 1991-94, cert. crop advisor 1993—), Crop Sci. Soc. Am., Soil Sci. Soc. Am., Internat. Assn. Mechanization Field Experiments, Users and Screeners Assn. (fed. excess personal property). Mem. Christian Ch. (Disciples Of Christ). Office: MU Field Ops 3600 New Haven Rd Columbia MO 65201-9608 Business E-Mail: poehlmannc@missouri.edu.

POEHNER, RAYMOND GLENN, retired bank executive; b. Cleve., Oct. 2, 1923; s. Raymond Frank and Winifred (Kirchbaum) P.; m. Frances E. Dunaway Gillespie, Jan. 4, 1958 (dec. 1993); children: R. David, Jacqueline Diane, Leslie Marie, Jon Anthony, Rebecca Glen; stepchildren: Bruce Gillespie, Tony Gillespie. Student, pub. schs., Chgo. and Cleve. Enlisted USN, 1941, advanced through grades to chief petty officer, 1957, ret., 1965; with Security Pacific Nat. Bank, San Diego, 1966-80, loan officer, 1971-74, credit card officer, 1975-80, asst. br. mgr., 1974-80, asst. mgr.; ret., 1980. Mem. VFW, U.S. Naval Inst. (assoc.), Fla. Sheriff's Assn., Am. Biog. Soc. (nat. bd. advisors), R.I. Rsch. (cert. assoc.), Fleet Res. Assn., Rep. Legion of Merit, Nat. Geographic Soc., Nat. Assn. Civilian Conservation Corps Alumni, Optimist Club (dir. 1978), Fraternal Order Police (booster Fla. chpt.). Republican.

POESCH, JESSIE JEAN, art historian; b. Postville, Iowa, May 19, 1922; parents: Edward H. and Vina (Meier) P. BA, Antioch Coll., Yellow Springs, Ohio, 1944; MA, U. Del., Newark, 1956; PhD, U. Pa., Phila., 1966. Relief worker Am. Friends Svc. Com., France, Germany, Phila., 1946—54; curatorial asst. H.F. DuPont Winterthur Mus., Del., 1956-58; from asst. prof. to prof. art history Tulane U., New Orleans, 1963-92, Maxine and Ford Graham chair in fine arts, 1988-92. Guest curator Painting in the South, Va. Mus. Fine Arts, Richmond, 1980-84, Jefferson's America and Napoleon's France, New Orleans Mus. Art, 2003; curator Newcomb Pottery: An Enterprise for So. Women, 1895-1940, Newcomb Coll. Tulane U. and Smithsonian Instn. traveling exhbn. svc., 1980-87. Author: Titian Ramsay Peale, 1799-1885, and His Journals of the Wilkes Expedition, 1961, The Art of the Old South: Painting, Sculpture, Architecture and the Products of Craftsmen, 1560-1860, 1983, (with John Cuthbert) David Hunter Strother: One of the Best Draughtsmen the Country Possesses, 1997; (book/exhbn. catalogue) The Early Furniture of Louisiana, 1972, Newcomb Pottery: An Enterprise for Southern Women 1895-1940, 1984, Will Henry Stevens, 1987; editor: (with Barbara Bacot) Louisiana Buildings 1720-1948, 1997, (with Nancy E. Green) Arthur Wesley Dow and American Arts and Crafts, 1999, Newcomb Pottery and Crafts, 2003, Printmaking in New Orleans, 2006; also numerous articles and book revs. Fellow U. Del., 1954-56; Fulbright scholar U. London, 1960-62; NEH grantee, London, 1969-70. Mem. Soc. Archtl. Historians (bd. dirs. 1986-89), Coll. Art Assn., Am. Antiquarian Soc., La. Endowment for the Humanities (bd. dirs. 1984-90, La. Humanist of Yr. 1992), Victorian Soc. Am. (bd. dirs. 1988-92). Office: Tulane U Dept Newcomb Art New Orleans LA 70118 Office Phone: 504-314-2225. Business E-Mail: jpoesch@tulane.edu.

POETTCKER, HENRY, retired academic administrator; b. Rudnerweide, Russia, Mar. 27, 1925; s. John and Margaretha (Voth) P.; m. Aganetha Baergen, July 4, 1946; children: Victoria, Ronald, Martin. AB, Bethel Coll., North Newton, Kans., 1950; BD, Mennonite Bibl. Sem., Chgo., 1953; ThD, Princeton Theol. Sem., 1961, converted PhD, 1973. Ordained to ministry Mennonite Ch., 1948; instr. Can. Mennonite Bible Coll., Winnipeg, Man., 1954-59, pres., 1959—78, Mennonite Bibl. Sem., Elkhart, Ind., 1979—90, assoc. for devel., 1991-93. Interim dean Bluffton Coll., Ohio, 1965-66; vis. lectr. Taiwan Theol. Coll. and Tainan Theol. Coll., Taiwan, 1973-74. Editor: (with Rudy A. Regehr) Call to Faithfulness, 1972, Alumni Bull. Can. Mennonite Bible Coll, 1960-73. Pres. Gen. Conf. Mennonite Ch., Newton, Kans., 1968-74. Home: 301-475 Lindenwood Dr E Winnipeg MB Canada R3P2P3 Personal E-mail: henr2502@mts.net. *The secret of happiness lies not in doing what one likes, but in liking what one does.*

POGGIO, TOMASO ARMANDO, physicist, educator, computer scientist, researcher; b. Genoa, Italy, Sept. 11, 1947; came to U.S., 1981; s. Angelo and Maria Adele (Moro) P.; m. Barbara Venturini-Guerrini, July 29, 1972; children: Martino, Allegra. D in Physics summa cum laude, U. Genoa, 1971. Researcher Max Planck Inst., Federal Republic of Germany, 1971-82; assoc. prof. to prof. MIT, Cambridge, 1982-88, Uncas and Helen Whitaker prof., dept. brain and cognitive scis., 1988—. Corp. fellow Thinking Machines Corp., Cambridge, 1985—; adv. bd. MIT/Bradford Press series on Computational Models of Cognition and Perception, 1984, VNY Sci. Press series of monographs in neuroinformatics and robotics, 1984; Eugene McDermott Chair, McGovern Inst. for Brain Rsch., 2002. Assoc. editor Sys. and Control Letters, 1984; mem. editl. bd. Synapse, 1986, Visual Neurosci., 1987, Neural Computation, 1988, Network, 1989, others; adv. bd. Jour. Math. Biology, 1977, Lecture Notes in Biomathematics, 1979; contbr. over 200 sci. papers to profl. publs. Recipient Cassa di Risparmio of Genoa award, 1966, Otto-Hahn-Medaille award Max-Planck Soc., 1979, Columbus prize Instituto Internazionale delle Communicazioni Genoa, 1982, Premio Luigi Carlo Rossi award (with V. Torre) Elsag Elettronica, Italy, 1984, Max-Planck-Forschungs Preis Alexander von Humboldt-Stiftung, 1992, At&T New Rsch. Fund Award, 1996, MIT 50K Entrepreneurship Competition Award, Imagen, 1997, Gabor Award, Internat. Neural Network Soc., 2003; Angelo delle Riccia grad. fellow, 1969-70, fellow CNR Lab. Biophysics and Cybernetics, Italy, 1971. Fellow: Am. Assn. Artificial Intelligence, Am. Acad. Arts and Scis.; mem.: IEEE, Soc. for Neuroscience, Italian Acad. Scis. (foreign mem.), Istituto Lombardo dell' Academia di Scienze e Lettere (foreign mem.), Optical Soc. Am., Am. Math. Soc. Office: MIT 77 Massachusetts Ave Cambridge MA 02139

POGO, GUSTAVE JAVIER, cardiothoracic surgeon, educator; b. Buenos Aires, Feb. 7, 1957; came to US, 1964; s. Angel Oscar and Beatriz (Garcia-Tuñon) P.; m. Janis Teitler, Feb. 17, 1983; children: Michael Tyler, Katherine Elizabeth. BA cum laude, NYU, 1979, MD, 1983. Cert. Am. Bd. Surgery, Am. Bd. Thoracic Surgery. Intern gen. surgery North Shore Univ. Hosp., Manhasset, NY, 1983—84, resident cardiothoracic surgery, 1984—88, mem. provisional surg. staff, 1991—94, asst. attending surgeon to sr. attending surgeon, 1994—; resident cardiothoracic surgery Mt. Sinai Med. Ctr., NYC, 1988—91; adj. assoc. prof. surgery NYU Sch. Medicine. Contbr. articles to profl. jours. Fellow ACS, Am. Coll. Chest Physicians, Am. Coll. Cardiology; mem. Soc. Thoracic Surgery. Office: North Shore Univ Hosp 300 Community Dr Manhasset NY 11030-3801 Office Phone: 516-562-4970. Office Fax: 516-562-3787.

POGUE, DAVID, journalist; m. Jennifer Pogue; 3 children. BA in Music summa cum laude, Yale Univ., 1985. Writer, Desktop Critic column Macworld mag., 1988—2000; personal-tech. columnist NY Times, NYC, 2000—. Conductor, synthesizer programmer, arranger (Broadway plays); author: (computer books) Macs for Dummies, 1992, The iMac for Dummies, 1999, The iBook for Dummies, 1999, PalmPilot: The Ultimate Guide, 1998, Switching to the Mac: The Missing Manual, 2003, Mac OS X: The Missing Manual, 2005; co-author (with Adam Engst): Crossing Platforms, 1999; co-author: (with Joe Schorr) Macworld Mac Secrets, 2001; co-author: (with Scott Speck) (music books) Opera for Dummies, 1997, Classical Music for Dummies, 1997; author: (humor books) The Microsloth Joke Book, 1997, The Great Macintosh Easter Egg Hunt, 1998; editor: Tales from the Tech Line, 1998; author: Magic for Dummies, 1998, (novels) Hard Drive, 1995; tech. corr. CBS News Sunday Morning, 2000—(Bus. Emmy award, 2004). Mem.: Internat. Brotherhood of Magicians. Avocations: magic, music. Office: Technology Columnist NY Times 229 W 43rd St New York NY 10036

POGUE, DONALD CARL, federal judge; m. Susan Bucknell, 1971; 2 children. BA, Dartmouth Coll., 1969; MA, JD, Yale U., 1974. Bar: Conn. 1974. Pvt. practice, 1974-75; ptnr. Kestell, Pogue & Gould, 1976-89; commr. Conn. Commn. Hosps. and Health Care, 1989-94; judge Conn. Superior Ct., 1994-95, U.S. Ct. Internat. Trade, NYC, 1995—. Office: US Ct Internat Trade One Federal Plz New York NY 10278-0001

POGUE, JOHN MARSHALL, physician; b. Washington, Sept. 21, 1945; s. L(loyd) Welch and Mary Ellen (Edgerton) P. *His father and mother are his guiding lights. Ancestor William Bradford "was the first American citizen of the English race who bore rule by the free choice of his brethren," the first American historian, and thus the Father of American History. Ancestor Hannah (Bradford) Ripley (Governor William Bradford's granddaughter) was America's first Physician of her gender. His uncle, Massachusetts Institute of Technology Institute Professor Harold Eugene Edgerton, enhanced his interest in Science. He worked with Harold on ultrahigh-speed photography in Harold's Stroboscopic Light Laboratory and on sonar probes. The difficult Harold did at once; the impossible took a little longer.* AB with honors, Princeton U.; MD, Georgetown U. Diplomate Nat. Bd. Med. Examiners. Intern, resident Georgetown U. Hosp., Washington; editor, author Bradford Jour., 1983—; historian Gov. Bradford Compact,

1996—, surgeon, 1999—, v.p., 2005—. Spkr. and lectr. in field of cardiology. *He is a Fellow of six Scientific and Learned Societies, and he is active in numerous Cardiology Societies. He received Honors in various Medical School courses, having ranked within the top 5% of the entire Medical School class in those courses. As a premedical student at Princeton University, he achieved high academic distinction climaxed by his ranking within the top 2% of his class of 789 students in the junior year - the year that is particularly important for premedical students. He also received a Letter of Individual Commendation for his scholarship from the Dean of the College at Princeton.* Author: Herbert Martin Giffin, M.D., A Role Model Physician and a Doctor's Doctor: From Princeton to Johns Hopkins, Mayo Clinic, USN, and Yater Clinic, 2000, Sir William Osler, M.D., The Preeminent Physician: From McGill to the University of Pennsylvania, Johns Hopkins, and Oxford, 2004; designer Ofcl. Gov. William Bradford Flag, 1987 (New Constellation award Nat. Flag Found., 1996), Ofcl. Order of Descs. of Colonial Physicians and Chirurgiens Flag, 2005; editor, contbr.: Pogue/Pollock/Polk Genealogy as Mirrored in History, From Scotland to Northern Ireland/Ulster, Ohio, and Westward, 1990 (recipient 5 First Pl. Genealogy awards, recipient 2 Meritorious History awards), assoc. editor: Hereditary Soc. Blue Book, 1997—, 1998, 1999, 2000; dir.(of film): Hugo Victor Rizzoli, Preeminent Neurosurgeon, A.B. and M.D., Johns Hopkins, Neurosurg. Tng. at Johns Hopkins Hosp., 2005; contbr. articles on cardiology to med. jours. Fellow Royal Soc. Medicine, Royal Microscopical Soc. Oxford, Royal Statis. Soc., Royal Geog. Soc., Royal Soc. Arts, Internat. Soc. Holter and Noninvasive Electrocardiology; mem. Am. Heart Assn. (coun. clin. cardiology, coun. basic cardiovasc. scis.), AMA, Royal Soc. Medicine (cardiology sect., cardiothoracic sect.), European Soc. Cardiology, Laennec Cardiovasc. Sound Soc., Am. Soc. Echocardiography (coun. cardiac sonography, coun. intraoperative echocardiography), Internat. Soc. Cardiovasc. Ultrasound, Internat. Cardiac Doppler Soc., Internat. Soc. Electrocardiology (Glasgow U.), Internat. Soc. Holter and Noninvasive Electrocardiology, Internat. Acad. Cardiovasc. Scis., Can., Soc. Cardiovasc. Magnetic Resonance, Capital Area Heart Failure Soc. (founding mem. 2002), Heart Failure Soc. Am., Heart Valve Soc. Am. (cardiac imaging coun.), Internat. Soc. Cardiovasc. Pharmacotherapy, Switzerland, Internat. Soc. Heart Rsch., Can., Cardiac Muscle Soc., World Heart Fedn., Switzerland, European Assn. Cardiovasc. Prevention and Rehab., European Microscopy Soc. (Netherlands), Friends Nat. Libr. Medicine (founding mem. 1988), Friends McGill U. Osler Med. Libr., Friends Oxford U. Mus. History Sci., Ashmolean Natural History Soc. Oxford, Oxford Hist. Soc., Internat. Shakespeare Assn. (Stratford-upon-Avon), Princeton U. Alumni Assn., Princeton Tigertones Alumni, DC Soc. Mayflower Descs. (surgeon 1998-), Order Descs. Colonial Physicians and Chirurgiens (surgeon gen. 1994-2000, 2006-, chmn. hon. membership com. 1994-, v.p. gen. 2000-03, pres. gen. 2003-06, hon. pres. gen. life, 2006—), Nat. Gavel Soc., Hereditary Order of Descs. of Colonial Govs. (rec. sec. gen. 2005-), Provincial Families Md., Kenwood Citizens Assn., RSM Music Soc./Royal Soc. Medicine Music Club, Royal Soc. Medicine Book Club, Princeton U. Club, Washington, Oxford Bibliographical Soc. of Oxford U. Bodleian Libr. Avocations: classical music, reading. Home and Office: 5204 Kenwood Ave Chevy Chase MD 20815-6604

POGUE, RICHARD WELCH, lawyer; b. Cambridge, Mass., Apr. 26, 1928; s. Lloyd Welch and Mary Ellen (Edgarton) P.; m. Patricia Ruth Raney, July 10, 1954; children: Mark, Tracy, David. BA, Cornell U., 1950; JD, Mich. Law Sch., 1953. Bar: Mich. 1953, Ohio 1957, U.S. Dist. Ct. (no. dist.) Ohio 1960, U.S. Ct. Appeals (6th cir.) 1972, U.S. Ct. Appeals (D.C. and 9th cirs.) 1979. Assoc. Jones, Day, Reavis & Pogue, Cleve., 1957-60, ptnr., 1961—94, mng. ptnr., 1984-92, sr. ptnr., 1993-94, cons., 2004—; sr. advisor Dix & Eaton, Cleve., 1994—2003. Vis. prof. Mich. Law Sch., 1993-95; bd. dirs. Rotek Inc., Aurora, Ohio Chmn. Cleve. Found., 1985-89, Greater Cleve. Roundtable, 1986-89, Greater Cleve. Growth Assn., 1991-93, Univ. Hosps., 1994-99, United Way Cleve., 1989, Kulas Found., 1998—, Bus. Vol. United, 1998-2001, Nat. Inventors Hall of Fame, 1996—, Newcomen Soc. U.S., Phila., 2000-05, pres. coun. found., 2001-06; mem. commn. higher edn. and econ. Gov., 2003-04; mem. Adminstrv. Conf. U.S., 1974-80; vice chmn. Cleve. Tomorrow, 1988-93; trustee Case Western Res. U., 1989-2003, U. Akron, 2004—; active Coun. Fgn. Rels., 1989—, Am./EC Assn. Bus. Adv. Coun., 1988-93; trustee Rock and Roll Hall of Fame and Mus., 1986-99; co-chmn. 1996 Cleve. Bicentennial Commn., interim chmn. Cleve. Inst. Music, 1994; chmn. dean's adv. coun. U. Mich. Law Sch., 2006—. Capt. U.S. Army, 1954-57. Recipient Outstanding Alumnus award U. Mich. Club, Cleve., 1983, Torch of Liberty award Anti-Defamation League, 1989, Leadership Cleve. Vol. of Yr. award, 1990, 1st Econ. Devel. Workshop award Nat. Coun. on Urban Econ. Devel., 1992, Humanitarian award Nat. Conf. Christians and Jews, 1992; named Cleve. Bus. Exec. of Yr., 2000, Cleve. United Way Vol. of Yr., 2002. Mem. ABA (chmn. antitrust sect. 1983-84), Ohio State Bar Assn. (chmn. antitrust sect. 1969-73). Clubs: Bohemian (San Francisco), Soc., Union (Cleve.). Republican. Mem. United Ch. of Christ. Office: Jones Day North Point 901 Lakeside Ave Cleveland OH 44114-1190 Office Phone: 216-586-7300. Office Fax: 216-586-7960. Business E-Mail: rwpogue@jonesday.com.

POGUE, VELVIE ANNE, nephrologist, educator; d. Henry Robinson and Maggie Mandigo; m. Alfred Robert Ashford; children: Alfred C. Ashford III, Adrienne Ashford. BS, So. U., Baton Rouge, 1970; MD, Harvard U., 1974. Diplomate Am. Bd. Internal Medicine, 1978, nephrology Am. Bd. Internal Medicine, 1980. Intern in internal medicine Harlem Hosp. Ctr., NYC, 1974—75, resident in internal medicine, 1975—77, fellow in clin. nephrology, 1977—79, attending physician, 1979—, chief divsn. nephrology, 1990—; assoc. prof. clin. medicine Coll. Physicians and Surgeons, Columbia U., NYC, 2002—. Rschr. African Am. Study of Kidney Disease and Hypertension, NYC. Named to America's Leading Black Doctors, Black Enterprise Mag., 2001. Mem.: Am. Heart Assn., Nat. Kidney Found., Internat. Soc. Hypertension in Blacks, Nat. Med. Assn., Am. Soc. Nephrology. Achievements include research in complications of hypertension, including hypertensive renal disease in blacks; impact of changes in blood pressure staging on recognized severity of hypertension. Office: Harlem Hospital Center 506 Lenox Ave New York NY 10037 Business E-Mail: vap1@columbia.edu.

POGUE, WILLIAM REID, retired astronaut, foundation administrator, aerospace scientist, consultant; b. Okemah, Okla., Jan. 23, 1930; s. Alex W. and Margaret (McDow) P.; m. Jean Ann Pogue; children: William Richard, Layna Sue, Thomas Reid. BS in Secondary Edn., Okla. Bapt. U., 1951, D.Sc. (hon.), 1974; MS in Math., Okla. State U., 1960. Commd. 2d lt. USAF, 1952, advanced through grades to col., 1973; combat fighter pilot Korea, 1953; gunnery instr. Luke AFB, Ariz., 1954; mem. acrobatic team USAF Thunderbirds, Luke AFB and Nellis AFB, Nev., 1955-57; asst. prof. math. USAF Acad., 1960-63; exchange test pilot Brit. Royal Aircraft Establishment, Ministry Aviation, Farnborough, Eng., 1964-65; instr. USAF Aerospace Research Pilots Sch., Edwards AFB, Calif., 1965-66; astronaut NASA Manned Spacecraft Center, Houston, 1966-75; pilot 3d manned visit to Skylab space sta.; ret. Decorated Air medal with oak leaf cluster, D.S.M.; named to Five Civilized Tribes Hall of Fame, Choctaw descent; recipient Distinguished Service medal NASA, Collier trophy Nat. Aero. Assn.; Robert H. Goddard medal Nat. Space Club; Gen. Thomas D. White USAF Space Trophy Nat. Geog. Soc.; Halley Astronautics award, 1975; de la Vaalx medal Fedn. Aeronautique Internat., 1974; V.M. Komarov diploma, 1974; inducted into Okla. Aviation and Space Hall of Fame, 1980, U.S. Astronaut Hall of Fame, 1997. Fellow Acad. Arts and Scis. of Okla. State U., Am. Astron. Soc.; mem. Soc. Exptl. Test Pilots, Explorers Club, Sigma Xi, Pi Mu Epsilon. Baptist (deacon). Home: 4 Cromer Dr Bella Vista AR 72715-5318 E-mail: wrpogue@arkansas.net.

POHAN, ARMAND, transportation executive, professional hockey club executive, lawyer; b. Langley Field, Va., Apr. 28, 1944; s. Armen and Helen (Turner) P.; m. Margaret A. Neigel, Dec. 18, 1976; children: Andrew Stephen, Alicia Margaret, Amanda Turner AB, Harvard U., 1964, JD, 1967. Bar: N.J. 1967. Assoc. McCarter & English, Newark, 1968-70; asst. prosecutor Hudson County, N.J., 1970-72; assoc. McCarter & English, 1973-76, ptnr., 1976-77; v.p. A-P-A Transport Corp., North Bergen, N.J., 1977-83, pres., 1983—, Colo. Rockies Hockey Club, Denver, 1978-81; chmn. bd. dirs. NY Waterway, 2001—. Mem. Fort Lee Bd. Adjustment, N.J., 1977-78; mem. Fort Lee Planning Bd., 1979, 2002—, borough atty., Fort Lee, 1973-76, councilman, 2003—; bd. govs. Nat. Hockey League, 1978-81; trustee Bede Sch., Englewood, N.J., 1984-90; trustee Dwight-Englewood Sch., 1984-92, pres., 1985-92; trustee Fontainebleau Assn., 2002—, treas., 2003—. Mem. N.J. Bar Assn. Office: NY Waterway 115 River Rd Ste 120 Edgewater NJ 07020 Office Phone: 201-313-2162. E-mail: apohan@aol.com.

POHL, FREDERIK, freelance/self-employed writer; b. NYC, Nov. 26, 1919; s. Fred George and Anna Jane (Mason) P.; m. Carol Ulf, Sept. 15, 1953 (div. 1981); children— Ann, Karen, Frederik, Kathy; m. Elizabeth Anne Hull, July 27, 1984 Editor Popular Pubs., NYC, 1939-43; editor Popular Sci., NYC, 1946-49; freelance writer NYC, 1950-60, 80—; editor Galaxy Pubs., NYC, 1961-69, Bantam Books, NYC, 1973-80. Author: Man Plus, 1977 (Nebula award), Gateway, 1978 (Nebula, Hugo, Campbell awards, Prix Apollo award), Jem, 1979 (Am. Book award), The Years of the City (Campbell award 1985), Chasing Science, 2000, The Boy Who Would Live Forever, 2004, Platnum Pohl, 2005 Served to sgt. USAAF, 1943-45; Italy Recipient Popular Culture Assn. award, 1982 Fellow AAAS; mem. Sci. Fiction Writers of Am. (pres. 1974-76, Grand Master award 1993), World Sci. Fiction (pres. 1980-82), Authors Guild, Astron. Soc. Pacific. Democrat. Unitarian Universalist. Home: 855 Harvard Dr Palatine IL 60067-7026

POHL, GUNTHER ERICH, retired library administrator; b. Berlin, July 22, 1925; came to US, 1927; s. Erich Ernst and Martha (Seidel) P.; m. Dorothy Edna Beck, Aug. 21, 1949; children: Christine, Louise, Elizabeth, Ronald BA, NYU, 1947, MA, 1950; MLS., Columbia U., 1951. Librarian local history and genealogy divsn. N.Y. Pub. Libr., NYC, 1948-69, chief local history and genealogy divsn., 1969-85, ret., 1985. Compiler: N.Y. State Biography and Portrait Index. Fellow N.Y. Geneal. and Biog. Soc.; mem. ALA (chmn. genealogy com. 1971-73, 76-78, History sect. award 1996), N.Y. Geneal. and Biog. Soc. (libr., trustee 1982-92), Sigma Phi Epsilon (trustee local chpt. 1978—). Republican. Avocations: stamps, opera, collecting new yorkiana. Home: 134 Lowry Ln Wilmore KY 40390

POHL, KATHLEEN SHARON, editor; b. Sandusky, Mich., Apr. 7, 1951; d. Gerald Arthur and Elizabeth Louise (Neukamm) P.; m. Bruce Mark Allen Reynolds, June 11, 1982. BA in Spanish, Valparaiso U., 1973; MA in English, No. Mich. U., 1975. Producer, dir. fine arts Sta. WNMU-FM, Marquette, Mich., 1981-82; instr. communications Waukesha County (Wis.) Tech. Inst., 1983; editor Ideals mag., Milw., 1983-85; editor, mng. editor Raintree Pubs., Milw., 1985-87; mng. editor, now exec. editor Country Woman mag., Greendale, Wis., 1987—; exec. editor Country Handcrafts mag., Greendale, 1990-93, Taste of Home Mag., Greendale, Wis., 1993—; editor Talk About Pets, Greendale, 1994-95. Author nature book series, 1985-87; sr. editor: Country Woman Christmas Book, 1996—; mng. editor: Irwin the Sock (Chgo. Book Clinic award 1988); exec. editor Taste of Home's Quick Cooking Mag., 1998—, Down the Aisle Countr Style, 2000, Taste of Home's Light & Tasty Mag., 2000—. Mem. Nat. Mus. of Women in Arts, Alpha Lambda Delta (hon.). Home: N54 W26326 Lisbon Rd Sussex WI 53089-4249 Office: Country Woman Mag 5400 S 60th St Greendale WI 53129-1404

POHL, PAUL MICHAEL, lawyer; b. Erie, Pa., July 17, 1948; s. Joseph Paul and Mary (Strenio) P.; m. Kaya Lynn Gavriloff, Aug. 13, 1970; children: Thomas Michael, Mary Elizabeth, Michael David. AB, Princeton U., 1970; JD, U. Pitts., 1975. Bar: Pa. 1975, Ohio 1976, U.S. Dist. Ct. (we. dist.) Pa. 1975, U.S. Dist. Ct. (no. dist.) Ohio 1976, U.S. Ct. Appeals (5th cir.) 1980, U.S. Ct. Appeals (11th cir.) 1983, U.S. Ct. Appeals (1st, 3d and 6th cir.) 1993, U.S. Ct. Appeals (D.C. cir.) 1995. Reporter Erie Daily Times, 1970-71; law clk. to presiding justice Pa. Supreme Ct., 1975-76; assoc. Jones, Day, Reavis & Pogue (now Jones Day), Cleve., 1976-82, ptnr., 1982—. Guest mem. faculty Sch. Law, Hofstra U., Hempstead, N.Y., 1982, 84; mem. trial advocacy program Sch. Law, Emory U., Atlanta, 1983—; bd. dirs. JURA Corp., Erie, Lord Corp., Cary, N.C.; mem. CLE bd. Supreme Ct. of Pa. Co-author: Conflicts of Interest—A Trial Lawyers Guide, 1984. Bd. dirs. Franciscan U., Steubenville, Ohio, 1991—, vice chmn., 1994—; bd. dirs. Gannon U., Erie; chmn. bd. dirs. Seton Hill Coll., Greensburg, Pa., 1997—; mem. supervisory bd. Found. Maria Thron, Gaming, Austria, 1996—. With USMC, 1971-72. Named one of Cleve.'s 78 Most Interesting People, Cleve. mag., 1978. Mem. Cleve. Bar Assn. (mem. com. task force on violent crime 1983). Roman Catholic. Office: Jones Day Reavis & Pogue 500 Grant St Pittsburgh PA 15219-2502 also: Jones Day Reavis & Pogue 901 Lakeside Ave E Cleveland OH 44114-1116

POHL, ROBERT OTTO, physics professor; b. Gottingen, Germany, Dec. 17, 1929; came to U.S., 1958; s. Robert Wichard and Auguste Eleonore (Madelung) P.; m. Karin Ursula Koehler, May 6, 1961; children: Helen M., Robert S., Otto C. Vordiplom, U. Freiburg, Fed. Rep. Germany, 1951; diploma, U. Erlangen, Fed. Rep. Germany, 1955, Dr. rer. nat., 1957. Asst. U. Erlangen, 1957-58; rsch. assoc. Cornell U., Ithaca, NY, 1958-60, asst. prof., 1960-63, assoc. prof., 1963-68, prof., 1968-2000, Goldwin Smith prof. physics emeritus, 2000—. Vis. prof. Tech. Hochschule Stuttgart, 1966-67, Tech. U. Munchen, 1973-74, Konstanz U., Regensburg U., 1987-88, all Fed. Republic Germany; vis. scientist Nuc. Research Ctr., Juelich, Fed. Rep. Germany, 1980-81, Hahn-Meitner Inst., Berlin, 1995. Contbr. articles on solid state physics to profl. jours. Recipient Sr. Scientist award Alexander von Humboldt Found., 1980; Guggenheim Found. fellow, 1973, Erskine fellow U. Canterbury, New Zealand, 1988. Fellow AAAS, Am. Inst. Physics (O.E. Buckley award 1985); mem. NAS, Internat. Thermal Conductivity Confs. Office: Cornell U Physics Dept Ithaca NY 14853-2501 Home Phone: 607-533-4742; Office Phone: 607-255-3303. Business E-Mail: pohl@ccmr.cornell.edu.

POHLAD, CARL R., bank executive, professional sports team executive; b. West Des Moines, Iowa, Aug. 23, 1915; m. Eloise Pohlad (dec. 2003); 3 children. Student, Gonzaga U. With MEI Diversified, Inc., Mpls., 1959—, chmn. bd., 1976—94; pres. Marquette Bank Mpls., N.A., pres., dir., Bank Shares, Inc.; owner Minn. Twins, 1985—. Bd. dirs. Meth. Hosp. Adminstrv. Group, T.G.I. Friday's, Tex. Air Corp., Ea. Airlines, Continental Airlines, Inc., Carlson Cos. Inc. Named one of Forbes' Richest Americans, 2006. Address: MN Twins Hubert H Humphrey Metrodome 34 Kirby Puckett Pl Minneapolis MN 55415-1523

POHLAD, ROBERT C., consumer products company executive; Dir. Mesaba Holdings Inc.; v.p. N.W. area Pepsi-Cola Bottling Group; pres. Pohlad Cos., 1987—2000; CEO PepsiAmericas, 2000—, vice chmn., 2001—02, chmn., 2002—. Office: PepsiAmericas 4000 Dain Rauscher Plaza 60 S Sixth St Minneapolis MN 55402 *

POHLHAUS, TESS, theater educator; d. Irene and Mark Pohlhaus. BA, Washington Coll., Chestertown, Md., 2003. Cert. secondary tchr. Md. Theatre tchr. Rising Sun HS, North East, Md., 2003—. Actor: Romeo and Juliet, 2004, Twelfth Night, 2005, Measure for Measure, 2006, (European premiere) Father Joy, 2006. Avocations: music, acting. Office Phone: 410-658-9115.

POHLMAN, CRAIG STEVEN, application developer; s. Keith Charles Pohlman and Juley Ann Hoover. BS in Computer Sci., Rose-Hulman Inst. Tech., Terre Haute, Ind., 2000. Scoreboard graphics operator Phoenix Suns, US Airways Ctr., 1998—, Glendale Arena, Ariz., 2003—06; software engr. Lockheed Martin, Goodyear, Ariz., 2000—. Coach MATHCOUNTS, Goodyear, 2000—; camp counselor, vol. Am. Cancer Soc., Phoenix, 2002—. Recipient Pres.'s Vol. Svc. award, USA Freedom Corp., 2004—07. Avocations: skiing, travel, video games. Home: 1909 E Laguna Dr Tempe AZ 85282-5912 Personal E-mail: pohlmacs@gmail.com.

POHOST, GERALD MICHAEL, cardiologist, medical educator; b. Washington, Oct. 27, 1941; married; 3 children. BS, George Washington U., 1963; MD, U. Md., 1967. Diplomate Am. Bd. Internal Medicine, Am. Bd. Cardiovascular Disease, Am. Bd. Nuclear Medicine. Intern Montefiore Hosp. & Med. Ctr., Bronx, N.Y., 1967-68, asst. resident, 1968-69; sr. resident Jacobi Hosp. Albert Einstein Coll. Medicine, Bronx, 1969-70; cardiology resident Montefiore Hosp. & Med. Ctr.; clin. & rsch. fellow in medicine Mass. Gen. Hosp., Boston, 1971-73; rsch. fellow in medicine Harvard Med. Sch., Boston, 1971-73, instr. medicine, 1974-77, asst. prof., assoc. prof. medicine, 1977-83; with dept. radiology Mass. Gen. Hosp., Boston, 1977-83, asst. gen. med. svcs., 1978-82; prof. medicine, radiology U. Ala., Birmingham, 1983—, Mary Gertrude Waters chair cardiovascular medicine divsn. cardiovascular disease, 1991—, prof. cardiovascular medicine, 1991—, dir. Ctr. for NMR R&D; prof. medicine Univ. So. Calif., head, divsn. cardiovascular medicine, Keck Sch. Medicine, 2002—06; sr. v.p., med. officer Salick Cardiovascular Ctrs., LA, 2006—. Cons. nuclear medicine radiology dept. Mass. Gen. Hosp., 1977-83; dir. ctr. NMR R&D U. Ala. Hosp., Birmingham, 1986—. Sr. editor: Noninvasive Cardiac Imaging, 1983, New Concepts in Cardiac Imaging, 1985, 86, 87, 88, 89, The Principles and Practice of Cardiovascular Imaging, 1991; contbr. more than 400 articles, reviews, book chpts., editls. to profl. jours.; nat. and internat. spkr. in field; mem. editl. bd. Circulation, Jour. Magnetic Resonance in Medicine, Am. Jour. Cardiology, Internat. Jour. Cardiology, NMR in BioMedicine, Coronary Artery Disease, others; editor Jour. Cardiovasc. Magnetic Resonance, 1998—; editor-in-chief Jour. Cardiovascular Magnetic Resonance, 1999—; rsch. interests in radionuclide and nuclear magnetic resonance studies of the heart, myocardial metabolism, cardiac pathophysiology. SCOR grant NIH, 1990—, tng. grant, 1992—, Dept. Energy grant, 1992—, Nat. Ctr. Rsch. Resources, 1992—. Fellow Am. Coll. Cardiology (editl. bd. jour., chmn. cardiac imaging com. 1982-88, current procedural terminology com. 1988-94, gov. rels. com. 1989-95, trustee 1994-99); mem. AMA (chmn. panel nuclear magnetic resonance imaging 1985-88), Am. Fedn. Clin. Rsch., Am. Soc. Clin. Investigations, Am. Assn. Profs., Am. Heart Assn. (fellow coun. clin. cardiology 1975—, Mass. affiliate 1975-83, established investigator 1979-84, Richard and Hinda Rosenthal award for excellence in clin. investigation 1985, chmn. advanced cardiac tech. com. of coun. on clin. cardiology 1981-86, exec. com. 1981-95, 98—2000, Ala. affiliate 1983—2000, long range planning com. 1986-89, chmn. 1989-91, vice chmn. exec. com. coun. clin. cardiology 1989-91, nominating com. 1989-91, chmn. 1993-95, budget com. 1989-91, chmn. exec. com. 1991-93, immediate past chmn. 1994, rsch. com. fellow subgroup A 1988-91), Soc. Nuclear Medicine (coun. nuclear Cardiology 1990-92), Soc. for Cardiovasc. Magnetic Resonance (pres. 1995-98, founder 1995, exec. com. 1995-99, trustees, 1995), Soc. Magnetic Resonance in Medicine (exec. com. 1987—, sci. program com. 1988-89, pres. 1986-87), Nat. Heart, Lung and Blood Inst. (program project rev. com. A 1984-88, cardiovascular and renal study sect. 1991-94, radiol. study sect. 1994-99), So. Med. Assn., NIH Reviewers Res., U.S. Nuclear Regulatory Commn. (adv. com. 1984-93), Assn. Univ. Cardiologists, Assn. Profs. Cardiology (sec. treas. 1995-96), Sigma Xi. Home: 612 N Las Palmas Ave Los Angeles CA 90004-1020 Office: Salick Cardiovascular Ctrs 8900 Wilshire Blvd Beverly Hills CA 90211 Office Phone: 310-967-3300. *

POIAN, EDWARD LICIO, historian; b. Trieste, Friuli-Venezia Giulia, Italy, June 10, 1946; arrived in U.S., 1954, naturalized, 1960; s. Angelo Del Picollo and Zaira (de Bourbon-Comelli) Poian; m. Maria del Carmen Lopez Clinton, Nov. 22, 1969 (div. Mar. 1980); children: Jeanne Marie, Nicole Anna; m. Nancy Flynn, Sept. 18, 1982. AS, U.S. Govt. Inst., 1965; BS, Mercy Coll., Dobbs Ferry, NY, 1988; MS, LI U., Bklyn., 1989; PhD, U. Ariz., Tucson, 1992. Chief exec. Budget Fin. Inc., Pittsfield, Mass., 1968-70; acting postmaster U.S. Postal Svc., Chappaqua, 1971-80; v.p. Lehman Bros Khun Loeb, NYC, 1980-83; CEO Cosmopolitan Armaments, NYC, 1983-90; intern The UN Univ., 1989-90; prof. history Mercy Coll., Dobbs Ferry, N.Y., 1991—, prof. history and polit. sci., 1991—. Cons. in field; intern UN U., 1990. Author: On the Outside Looking In, 1972, Peace and Regional Security Through Education in Africa, 1992, Problems in Coordination Among Western Donor Governments in Relations to Multilateral and Social Programmes of the United Nations System, 1990; contbr. articles to profl. jours. Rector, CEO Internat. Ednl. Rsch. Found., Inc., Yonkers, NY, 1991—; trustee archeology dept. U. Trieste, 1986—; dir. history and govt. assn. Mercy Coll., 1988. With USCG, 1963—67, served to capt. USCG Res., 1968—98. Decorated Knight of Malta Cross of Gregory the Great Vatican City; recipient UN award, 1988. Fellow: World Assn. Former UN Interns and Fellows; mem.: VFW, Naval War Coll. Alumni Assn., Am. Soc. Polit. Sci., Yonker Hist. Soc., Mil. Officers Assn. Am., U.S. Naval Inst. (life), Navy League (N.Y. chpt.) (life), Fleet Res. Assn. (life), Am. Legion (life), Phi Gamma Mu, Phi Alpha Theta. Republican. Roman Catholic. Avocations: archaeology, historical research, art collector, philanthropy. Office: Mercy Coll Dept History and Polit Sci 555 Broadway Dobbs Ferry NY 10522-1134 Home: PO Box 50 Hastings On Hudson NY 10706 Office Phone: 914-693-4500. Personal E-mail: doctorpoian@email.com.

POILE, DAVID ROBERT, professional sports team executive; b. Toronto, Ont., Can., Feb. 14, 1949; s. Norman Robert (dec.) and Margaret (Elizabeth) P.; m. Elizabeth Ramey, July 4, 1971; children: Brian Robert, Lauren Elizabeth. BS, Northeastern U., 1971. Asst. mgr. Atlanta Flames, 1971-80, Calgary Flames, Alta., Can., 1980-82; gen. mgr., v.p. Washington Capitals, Landover, Md., 1982-95; exec. v.p., gen. mgr. Nashville Predators, Nashville, 1997—. Named NHL Exec. of Yr., Sporting News, 2007. Office: Nashville Predators Nashville Arena 501 Broadway Nashville TN 37203-3932

POINAR, GEORGE ORLO, JR., entomologist, science educator; b. Spokane, Wash., Apr. 25, 1936; s. George O. and Helen Louise (Ladd) P.; m. Eva I. Hecht; children: Hendrik, Maya; m. 2d, Roberta Theresa Heil; 1 child, Gregory. BS, Cornell U., 1958, MS, 1960, PhD, 1962. Prof. dept. entomology U. Calif., Berkeley, 1964—95; courtesy prof. dept. zoology Oreg. State U., Corvallis, 1995—. Author: Entomogenous Nematodes, 1975, Nematodes for Biological Control of Insects, 1979, The Natural History of Nematodes, 1983, co-author (with Roberta Poinar) The Quest for Life in Amber, (with Roberta Poinar) The Amber Forest, (with R. Milki) Lebanese Amber, 2001, (with G.M. Thomas) Diagnostic Manual for the Identification of Insect Pathogens, 1978, (with G.M. Thomas) Laboratory Guide to Insect Pathogens and Parasites, 1984, (with Hans-Börje Jansson) Diseases of Nematodes, Vols. 1, 2, 1988. Grantee NATO, NSF, NIH,

1962-72. Avocations: photography, piano, tennis. Office: Oreg State Univ Dept Zoology Corvallis OR 97331 Home Phone: 541-752-0917; Office Phone: 541-737-5366. Business E-Mail: poinarg@science.oregonstate.edu.

POINDEXTER, WILLIAM MERSEREAU, lawyer; b. LA, June 16, 1925; s. Robert Wade and Irene M. Poindexter; m. Jani Jennifer Wohlgemuth, Feb. 14, 2000; children: James Wade, David Graham, Honour Hélené, Timothy John, Cory Todd, E. W. Greg. BA, Yale U., 1946; postgrad., U. Chgo., 1946-47; LL.B., U. Calif., Berkeley, 1949. Bar: Calif. 1952. Practiced in, San Francisco, 1952-54, Los Angeles, 1954—; mem. firm Poindexter & Doutre, Inc., 1964—. Pres. Consol. Brazing & Mfg. Co., Riverside, Calif., 1949—52. Pres. South Pasadena-San Marino YMCA, Calif., 1963; mem. San Marino Sch. Bd., 1965—69, pres., 1967, Conf. Ins. Counsel, 1975. With USMCR, 1943. Fellow: Am. Coll. Trust and Estate Counsel; mem.: ABA, State Bar Calif., Los Angeles County Bar Assn., Calif. Lincoln clubs (LA downtown chpt. chmn. 1997—2003), Yale Club (pres. So. Calif. chpt. 1961). Republican. Presbyterian. Office: 1 Wilshire Bldg Ste 2420 Los Angeles CA 90017 Office Phone: 213-628-8297.

POINSETTE, DONALD EUGENE, engineering executive, management consultant; b. Ft. Wayne, Ind., Aug. 17, 1914; s. Eugene Joseph and Julia Anna (Wyss) P.; m. Anne Katherine Farrell, Apr. 15, 1939 (dec.); children: Donald J., Eugene J., Leo J., Sharon Poinsette Smith, Irene Poinsette Snyder, Cynthia Poinsette West, Maryanne Poinsette Stohler, Philip J. Student, Purdue U., 1934, Ind. U., 1935-37, 64. With GE Corp., RCA, Stewart Warner Corp., 1937-39; metall. rsch. and field sales cons. P.R. Mallory Corp., 1939-49; dist. sales mgr. Derringer Metall. Corp., Chgo., 1949-50; plant engr. Cornell-Dubilier Electric Corp., Indpls., 1950-53; with Jenn-Air Corp., Indpls., 1953-74, purchasing dir., 1953-71, mgr. value engrng. and quality control, 1969-74; bus. mgmt. cons. Mays and Assocs., Indpls., 1974-76. Pres. Marian Coll. Parents Club, Indpls., 1969-70; com. mem. Boy Scouts Am.; nat. trustee Xavier U., 1972-73, Dad's Club, Cin.; mem. Triad choral groups. Recipient Testimonial Golden Anniversary award Purdue U., 1987; named to U.S. Finder's List, Nat. Engrs. Register, 1956, Army Navy E award for excellence in engrng. and prodn., 1944. Mem. Nat. Assn. Purchasing Mgmt., Indpls. Purchasing Mgmt. Assn., Soc. Am. Value Engrs. (cert. value specialist, sec.-treas. Ctrl. Ind. chpt. 1972-73), Soc. Ret. Execs. Indpls., Ind. U. Alumni Assn., Purdue U. Alumni Assn., Columbian (pres. 1972-73), Internat. Platform Assn., Tau Kappa Epsilon, K.C. (4 deg.). Home: 8480 Craig St Apt 131 Indianapolis IN 46250-4561

POINTER, SAM CLYDE, JR., retired federal judge, lawyer; b. Birmingham, Ala., Nov. 15, 1934; s. Sam Clyde and Elizabeth Inzer (Brown) P.; m. Paula Purse, Oct. 18, 1958; children: Minge, Sam Clyde III. AB, Vanderbilt U., 1955; JD, U. Ala., 1957; LL.M., NYU, 1958. Bar: Ala. 1957. Ptnr. Brown, Pointer & Pointer, 1958-70; judge U.S. Dist. Ct. (no. dist.) Ala., Birmingham, 1970-2000, chief judge, 1982-99; judge Temp. Emergency Ct. Appeals, 1980-87; mem. Jud. Panel Multi-dist. Litigation, 1980-87; ptnr. Lightfoot, Franklin & White, 2000—. Mem. Jud. Conf. U.S., 1987-90; mem. Jud. Coun. 11th Cir., 1987-90, mem. standing com. on rules, 1988-90, chmn. adv. com. on civil rules, 1990-93. Bd. editors: Manual for Complex Litigation, 1979-91. Mem. ABA, Ala. Bar Assn., Birmingham Bar Assn., Am. Law Inst., Am. Judicature Soc., Farrah Order of Jurisprudence, Phi Beta Kappa. Episcopalian. Office: Lightfoot Franklin & White The Clark Bldg 400 N 20th St Birmingham AL 35203 E-mail: spointer@lfwlaw.com.

POIRIER, LOUIS JOSEPH, neurology educator; b. Montreal, Que., Can., Dec. 30, 1918; s. Gustave Joseph and Calixta (Brault) P.; m. Liliane Archambault, June 11, 1947; children: Guy, Michel, Louise, Esther. BSc, U. Montreal, 1942, MD, 1947; PhD, U. Mich., 1950; D (hon.), U. Rennes, France, 1973. Asst. prof. U. Montreal, 1950-55, assoc. prof., 1955-58, prof. faculty of medicine, 1958-65; chmn. dept. anatomy Faculty of Medicine, Laval U., Cité Universitaire, Que., 1970-78, prof. exptl. neurology, 1970-83; dir. Centre de Rsch. in Neurobiology, Laval U. and Hosp. de l'Enfant-Jesus, 1977-85, prof. emeritus, 1985—. Editor: Advances in Neurology, vol. 24, 1979; contbr. articles to profl. jours. Pres. Que. Health Scis. Research Council, 1978-81. Decorated officer Order of Can.; recipient Que. sci. award, 1975; Killam commemorative scholar, 1977, 78 Mem. AAAS, Royal Soc. Belgium (hon.), Neurol. Soc. France (hon.), Am. Assn. Anatomists, Am. Physiol. Soc., Soc. for Neuroscis., Internat. Brain Research Orgn., Can. Med. Assn. (emeritus). Address: 603 Chemin Caron Lac Simon Montpellier PQ Canada J0V 1M0

POITIER, CONSTANCE RENA, music specialist, educator; b. Quincy, Fla., June 1, 1955; d. Leroy Cornelius and Dorothy Louise Parker Harris; m. James Poitier, July 22, 1995; children: Carla Felicia DuPont, Carl Franklin DuPont, Jr. BA, Bethune-Cookman Coll., 1977; ME, Fla. Atlantic U., 1984; edn. specialist magna cum laude, Nova U., 2004. Nat. bd. cert. tchr. 2004, cert. nat. bd. cert. minority recruiter. Choral dir., gen. music Roosevelt Jr. H.S., West Palm Beach, Fla., 1977-81; drama coach Jupiter (Fla.) H.S., 1985; music specialist Roosevelt Elem., 1981-86, Riverview (Fla.) Elem., 1986-96; min. of music Spring Hill Bapt. Ch., Tampa, Fla., 1994-96; choral dir. Atlantic H.S., Port Orange, Fla., 1996-97; choral dir. Daytona Beach Gospel Choir Daytona Beach Bapt. Ch., Fla., 1996—; music specialist Palm Terrace Elem., Daytona Beach, Fla., 1997—, Bonner Elem., 2004—; asst. to the choral dir. Bethune Cookman Coll., 2003; proprietor Poitier Fin. Svcs. Choral dir. Progress M&E Bapt. State Conv., 1973-76; choral dir., pianist 1st Bapt. Ch. College Hill, Tampa, 1986-96; choir cons., guest dir., clinician for choral workshops; concert and rec. artist; pvt. instr., voice and piano; choral festival judge; gospel music workshop clinician. Author: My Book of Poems, 1996. Fellow NEA, NAACP, Am. Choral Dirs., Westside Bus. and Profls., Fla. Vocal Assn., Fla. Music Educators Assn., Fla. Music Educators Nat. Conf., Zeta Phi Beta. Home: 3801 Birch Mtn Rd Port Orange FL 32129 Office: Bonner Elem Sch George Ingram Blvd Daytona Beach FL 32114-1253 E-mail: connie8082@bellsouth.net.

POITIER, SIDNEY, actor, film director; b. Miami, Fla., Feb. 20, 1927; Grew up on Cat Island, The Bahamas. At age 15 moved to Miami, and at age 16 to NYC. s. Reginald and Evelyn (Outten) Poitier; m. Juanita Hardy, Apr. 29, 1950 (div. 1965); children: Beverly, Pamela, Sherri, Gina; m. Joanna Shimkus, Jan. 23, 1976; children: Anika, Sydney. Student, The Bahamas. Accepted to Am. Negro Theatre, NYC, on second audition and made debut in Days of Our Youth, 1945. Amb. to Japan from the Bahamas, 1997; bd. dirs. Walt Disney Co., 1994—2003. Performer: (Broadway plays) Lysistrata, 1946; Anna Lucasta, 1974; A Raisin in the Sun, 1959—60 (Tony Award nomination for best actor in a play, 1960); dir.: Carry Me Back to Morningside Heights, 1968; actor: (films) No Way Out, 1950, Cry, the Beloved Country, 1951, Red Ball Express, 1952, Go, Man, Go!, 1954, Blackboard Jungle, 1955, Good-bye, My Lady, 1956, Edge of the City, 1957, Something of Value, 1957, Band of Angels, 1957, The Mark of the Hawk, 1958, The Defiant Ones, 1958 (Acad. award nomination for best actor in a leading role, 1959), Virgin Island, 1958, Porgy and Bess, 1959, All the Young Men, 1960, A Raisin in the Sun, 1961, Paris Blues, 1961, Pressure Point, 1962, Lilies of the Field, 1963 (Acad. Award for best actor in a leading role, 1964, Golden Globe Award for best motion picture actor - drama, 1964), The Long Ships, 1963, The Bedford Incident, 1965, The Greatest Story Ever Told, 1965, A Patch of Blue, 1965, The Slender Thread, 1965, Duel at Diablo, 1966, To Sir, with Love, 1967, In the Heat of the Night, 1967, Guess Who's Coming to Dinner, 1967, The Lost Man, 1969, The Call Me Mister Tibbs!, 1970, Brother John, 1971, The Organization, 1971, The Wilby Conspiracy, 1975, Shoot to Kill, 1988, Little Nikita, 1988, Sneakers, 1992, The Jackal, 1997; (TV films) Separate but Equal, 1991 (Emmy Award nomination for outstanding lead actor in a miniseries or special, 1991), Children of the Dust, 1995, To Sir, with Love II, 1996, Mandela and de Klerk, 1997 (Emmy Award nomination for outstanding lead actor in a miniseries or special, 1997), David and Lisa, 1998, The Simple Life of Noah Dearborn, 1999, The Last Brickmaker in America, 2001; actor, prodr. (TV films) East of Eden, 1999, actor, dir. (films) Buck and the Preacher, 1972, A Warm December, 1973, Uptown Saturday Night, 1974, Let's Do It Again, 1975, A Piece of the Action, 1977, actor, writer (story) For Love of Ivy, 1968; dir.: (films) Stir Crazy, 1980, Hanky Panky, 1982, Fast Forward, 1985, Ghost Dad, 1990; author: (autobiography) This Life, 1980, The Measure of a Man: A Spiritual Autobiography, 2000. Served 1267th Med. Deatchment US Army, 1944—45, veteran's hosp., LI. Decorated Hon. Knight Comdr. Order Brit. Empire; recipient Golden Globe Award for World Film Favorite - Male, 1969, Cecil B. DeMille Award, Golden Globe Awards, 1982, Lifetime Achievement Award, Am. Film Inst., 1992, Kennedy Ctr. Honors, 1995, Lifetime Achievement Award, Screen Actors Guild, 2000, Hall of Fame Award, NAACP, 2001, Hon. Award, Acad. Awards, 2002, Star on Hollywood Walk of Fame. Achievements include First black person to win an Acad. Award for a leading role, 1964. *

POJETA, JOHN, JR., geologist, researcher; b. NYC, Sept. 9, 1935; s. John and Emilie (Pilat) P.; m. Mary Louise Eberz, June 23, 1957; children: Kim Louise, John Martin. BS, Capital U., Columbus, Ohio, 1957; MS, U. Cin., 1961, PhD, 1963. Teaching fellow U. Cin., 1957-63; geologist U.S. Geol. Survey, 1963—, chief lower paleozoic studies unit, 1969-74, chief br. paleontology and stratigraphy, 1989-94. Assoc. prof., lectr. George Washington U., 1965-74; research assoc. Smithsonian Instn., 1969—; U.S. Geol. Survey-Australian Bur. Mineral Resources exchange scientist, 1974-75 Author papers in field. Pres. Potomac Woods Citizens Assn.; mem. area 4 coun. Montgomery County (Md.) Bd. Edn.; mem. bd. Citizens for Good Govt.; trustee Paleontol. Rsch. Instn., 1976—85, 1999—, v.p., 1978—79, pres., 1980—82. Fellow: AAAS (coun.), Geol. Soc. Am. (sr.); mem.: Australasian Paleontologists, Paleontol. Soc. (sec. 1982—88, pres. 1989—90, bus. mgr. spl. studies 1989—). Home: 1492 Dunster Ln Rockville MD 20854-6119 Office: US Geol Survey Smithsonian Instn Rm E-308 MRC121 Mus Natural History Washington DC 20560-0137 Office Phone: 202-633-1347. Business E-Mail: pojetaj@si.edu.

POKORNY, JAN HIRD, architect, educator; b. Brno, Czechoslovakia, May 25, 1914; came to U.S., 1940, naturalized, 1945; s. Jaroslav and Theresia (Harrer) P.; m. Marise Angelucci, 1967; 1 son, Stefan Alexander. Engr.-Architect, Tech. U., Prague, 1937; MS in Architecture, Columbia U., 1941. Gen. practice architecture, Prague, 1938-39; designer Winn-Roensch & Brezner, Detroit, 1942, Leo Bauer, Detroit, 1942-44, Skidmore, Owings & Merrill, NYC, 1944-45; CEO Jan Hird Pokorny (architect), NYC, 1945-71, 77—; partner Pokorny & Pertz, 1971-77. Assoc. prof. Columbia Sch. Architecture, 1958-74, dir. evening program in architecture, 1957-73, prof. architecture Grad. Sch. Architecture, Planning and Preservation, 1974-82, prof. emeritus, 1982—; architect mem. Art Commn. City N.Y., 1973-77, James William Kideney award N.Y. State Assn. of Architects, 1992. Contbr. articles to profl. jours.; prin. works include: Taylor Meml. Library and Reeves Student Union Bldg. at Centenary Coll. for Women, Hackettstown, N.J., Lewisohn Hall at Columbia U., (with Damaz and Weigel) Student Union Bldg., Adminstrn. Bldg., Library and Fine Arts Bldg. at N.Y. State U., Stony Brook, (with David Todd Assts.) master plan Library, Auditorium and renovated Music Bldg., Speech and Theatre Bldg., Lehman Coll.-City U. N.Y.; housing at Grasslands Westchester Med. Ctr. and housing for Urban Devel. Corp., in Middletown, Elmira and Wayne County, N.Y., Corp. offices for Samuel H. Kress Found., Ambassador's Offices U.S. Mission to UN, Offices John and Marry R. Markle Found.; restoration of: Schermerhorn Row Block, South St., Seaport, N.Y.C., Monsignor McGolrick Park Shelter, Bklyn., Sloppy Louie's Restaurant, South St., Seaport, N.Y.C., Shellens Gallery of Bklyn. History, Bklyn. Hist. Soc., Firemen's Meml., N.Y.C., Church of Incarnation, N.Y.C., Morris-Jumel Mansion, N.Y.C., Century Club Facade, N.Y.C. Bd. dirs. Am. Fund Czechoslovak Refugees, 1959—, sec., 1964-71, chmn., 1971—; trustee Grand Central Terminal Trust Fund, NYC; v.p. Fine Arts Fedn. NYC, pres. Bohemian Benevolent and Literary Assn., NYC, 1987—; landmark commr. NYC, 1996-. Recipient Ethnic New Yorker award by Mayor of N.Y., 1985, Lifetime Preservation award Columbia Alumni, 1990, Felber Gold medal Czech Tech. U., 1991, James William Kideney award, AIA, 1992, award for Morris-Jumel restoration N.Y.C. Landmarks Commn., 1993, "Quintessential Architect" AIA NY State Fellows award, 2000. Fellow AIA (awards of merit 1955, 61,74, N.Y. state assn. award 1975, Bard award 1985, Arthur Ross award); mem. Nat. Acad. Design. Clubs: Century Assn. Office: Jan Hird Pokorny Associates Inc 39 W 37th St New York NY 10018-6217 Office Phone: 212-759-6462. Office Fax: 212-759-6540. E-mail: pokorny@jhpokorny.com.

POKORNY, JOSEPH WENCESLAUS, III, engineer; b. Park Ridge, Ill., July 11, 1979; s. Joseph Wenceslaus Pokorny, Jr. and Marlene Pokorny. BS, U. Ill., Champaign, 2001, MS, 2003. Tchg. asst. U. Ill., Champaign, 2001—03; application support engr. The MathWorks, Inc., Natick, Mass., 2003—04, tng. engr., 2004—. Presenter in field. Recipient Lincoln Arc Welding award, James F. Lincoln Arc Welding Found., 2001. Mem.: IEEE. Democrat. Roman Catholic. Avocations: sports, fishing, travel. Home: Apt 4403 195 Binney St Cambridge MA 02142 Office: The MathWorks Inc 3 Apple Hill Dr Natick MA 01760

POKOTILOW, MANNY DAVID, lawyer, educator; b. Patterson, NJ, June 26, 1938; s. Samuel Morris and Ruth (Fuchs) P.; children: Mali, Charyse, Mona, Andrew. BEE, Newark Coll. Engring., 1960; LLB, Am. U., Washington, DC, 1964. Bar: Pa. 1964, US Supreme Ct. 1969. Examiner Patent Office, Washington, 1960-64; ptnr. Caesar, Rivise, Bernstein, Cohen & Pokotilow Ltd., Phila., 1965—. Lectr. Pa. Bar Inst., various trade assns., expert witness on protection of computer software, patents, trademarks, trade secrets and copyrights; faculty Temple U. Sch. Law, 1985-94; mem. Pa. Bar Inst. Intellectual Property com. Vol. Support Ctr. for Child Advs., Phila., 1979—; bd. dirs., organizer Phila. Bar Assn. 10k Race, Phila., 1980-, Packard Press Road Run Grand Prix, 1986; bd. dirs. Hist. Soc. U.S. Dist. Ct. (ea. dist.) Pa., 1989-, v.p. 1998-2002, pres. 2002-03. Recipient Chair award for vol. excellence Am. Diabetes Assn., 1991; honored by Support Ctr. for Child Advs., 1992 and Am. Diabetes Assn., 1997; named to Million Dollar Club, Am. Diabetes Assn., 2002; named one of Best Lawyers in Greater Phila. area Phila. Mag., 1999, Best Lawyers in Am., 2006, 07; named to Top Tier of Am. Leading Lawyers for Bus., 2003-04. Fellow Am. Acad. Trial Lawyers; mem. ABA (chmn. proprietary rights in software com., coun. sci. and tech. sect. 1989—), IEEE, Assn. Trial Lawyers Am., Phila. Bar Assn. (bd. govs. 1982-84, chmn. sports and recreation com. 1977—, hon. trustee campaign for qualified judges 1993), Phila. Patent Law Assn. (bd. govs. 1982-84, chmn. fed. practice and procedure com. 1983-88), Phila. Trial Lawyers (chmn. fed. cts. com. 1994-98), Lawyers Club Phila. (bd. govs. 1984-94, chmn. publicity 1994-98), Pa. Trial Lawyers, Tau Epsilon Rho (vice chancellor Phila. grad. chpt. 1986-88, chancellor 1988-90). Office: Caesar Rivise Bernstein Cohen & Pokotilow Ltd 1635 Market St Fl 12 Philadelphia PA 19103-2212 Home Phone: 610-664-8411; Office Phone: 215-567-2010. Business E-Mail: mpokotilow@crbcp.com.

POKRAS, SHEILA FRANCES, retired judge; b. Newark, Aug. 5, 1935; m. Norman M. Pokras, 1954; children: Allison, Andrea, Larry. Student, Beaver Coll., 1953-54; BS in Edn., Temple U., 1957; JD cum laude, Pepperdine U., 1969. Bar: Calif. 1970, U.S. Dist. Ct. D.C. 1970, U.S. Dist. Ct. Calif. 1970, U.S. Supreme Ct. 1975. Tchr. elem. and secondary schs., Phila. and Newark, 1957-59; pvt. practice law Long Beach, Calif., 1970-78; city councilwoman Lakewood, Calif., 1972-76; judge Long Beach Mcpl. Ct., 1978-80, L.A. Superior Ct., 1980-98; ret., 1998. Supervising judge, 1986; del. Calif. State Dem. Cen. Com., 1975, Calif. State Conv., 1975; mem. Com. on Gender Bias in Calif. Courts, 1986-89 Advisor Jr. League, 1980-85; mem. early childhood adv. bd. Long Beach City Coll.; bd. dirs. Long Beach Alcoholism Coun., 1979-80, Boys and Girls Club Am., 1981-89, Long Beach Symphony, 1985, Jewish Community Fedn., 1982-86, past mem. community rels. com.; active Nat. Women's Polit. Caucus, LWV. Named Woman of Yr., NOW, Long Beach, 1984; recipient Torch of Liberty award, B'nai B'rith Anti-Defamation League, 1974; honoree, Nat. Conf. Christians and Jews, 1986. Mem. ABA, AAUW, Nat. Assn. Women Judges (dist. supr. 1986), Calif. Bar Assn. (judges div.), Calif. Judges Assn. (mem. ann. seminar com. 1981-89), Mcpl. Cts. Judges Assn. (mem. Marshall com. 1979-80), L.A. County Bar Assn. (judges div., mem. arbitration com.), Women Lawyers Assn., L.A. (judges sect.), Women Lawyers Assn. Long Beach, Long Beach Legal Aid Found. (v.p. 1976-78), Long Beach Bar Assn. (active various coms., bd. govs. 1977-78, Judge of Yr. 1987), Long Beach C. of C. (bd. dirs.). Avocations: swimming, golf, jogging, classical music, movies.

POKROSS, DAVID R., JR., lawyer; b. Dayton, Ohio, 1945; AB magna cum laude, Harvard U., 1966, JD cum laude, 1969. Bar: Mass. 1969. Mem. Palmer & Dodge, Boston; ptnr. Edwards Angell Palmer & Dodge, Boston. Trustee & Chmn. Plimoth Plantation; Former Trustee Ctr. Blood Rsch. Mem.: Am. Bar Assn., Mass. Bar Assn., Boston Bar Assn. Office: Edwards Angell Palmer & Dodge 111 Huntington Ave Boston MA 02199-7613 Office Phone: 617-239-0827, 617-239-0287. Office Fax: 617-316-8428, 617-227-4420. Business E-Mail: dpokross@eapdlaw.com.

POLAK, ELIJAH, engineering educator, computer scientist; b. Bialystok, Poland, Aug. 11, 1931; came to US, 1958, naturalized, 1977; s. Isaac and Fruma (Friedman) P.; m. Virginia Ann Gray, June 11, 1961; children: Oren, Sharon. BSEE, U. Melbourne, Australia, 1957; MSEE, U. Calif., Berkeley, 1959, PhD in Elec. Engring., 1961. Instrument engr. ICIANZ, Melbourne, Australia, 1956-57; summer student IBM Rsch. Labs., San Jose, Calif., 1959-60; vis. asst. prof. MIT, fall 1964; assoc. dept. elec. engring. and computer scis. U. Calif., Berkeley, 1958-61, asst. prof. elec. engring. and computer scis., 1961-66, assoc. prof., 1966-69, prof., 1969-94, prof. grad. Sch., 1994—. Author: (with L.A. Zadeh) System Theory, 1969, (with E. Wong) Notes for a First Course on Linear Systems, 1970, (with others) Theory of Optimal Control and Mathematical Programming, 1970, Computational Methods in Optimization, 1971, Optimization: Algorithms and Consistent Approximations, 1997. Guggenheim fellow, 1968; UK Sci. Rsch. Coun. Sr. fellow, 1972, 76, 79, 82 Fellow IEEE; mem. Soc. Indsl. and Applied Math. (assoc. editor Jour. Theory and Applications Optimization 1972—), Soc. Math. Programming. Jewish. Avocation: cross country skiing. Home: 38 Fairlawn Dr Berkeley CA 94708-2106 Office: U Calif Dept Elec Engring Cp S Berkeley CA 94720-0001 Office Phone: 510-642-2644. Business E-Mail: polak@eecs.berkeley.edu.

POLAK, EMIL JOSEPH, history professor, researcher; b. Bay Shore, NY, Aug. 16, 1936; s. Emil Frank and Mary Rose (Comitsky) Polak; m. Patricia Faith Leuzzi, Aug. 3, 1968. AB cum laude, U. Albany, 1957; AM, Columbia U., 1958, PhD, 1970. Lectr. Bklyn. Coll., 1961—65; instr. St. John's U., Jamaica, NY, 1965—66; lectr. S.I. C.C., 1966—67; instr. CCNY, 1967—70; asst. prof. Queensborough CC, Bayside, NY, 1970—76, assoc. prof., 1977—81, prof. dept. history, 1982—. Author: A Textual Study of Jacques de Dinant's Summa dictaminis, 1975, Medieval and Renaissance Letter Treatises and Form Letters: A Census of Manuscripts Found in Eastern Europe and the Former U.S.S.R., 1993, Medieval and Renaissance Letter Treatises and Form Letters: A Census of Manuscripts Found in Part of Western Europe, Japan and the United States of America, 1994; editor: A Medievalist's Odyssey: Helene Wieruszowski Scholar, 2004. Recipient Performance Excellence award, Queensborough CC, 2000, Excellence in Faculty scholarship award, 2002; fellow, Am. Acad. Rome, 1963, CUNY Rsch. Found., 1977—2007, Internat. Rsch. Exchanges Bd., 1978, 1981, 1996; grantee, Am. Coun. Learned Socs./USSR Acad. Scis., 1981, Gladys Krieble Delmas Found., 1995, NEH, 1997, Renaissance Soc. Am., 2000. Mem.: L.I. Maritime Mus., Internat. Soc. Classical Tradition, Medieval Latin Studies Group, Medieval Club N.Y., Am. Assn. Neo-Latin Studies, Early Book Soc., Internat. Assn. Neo-Latin Studies, Soc. Fellows Am. Acad. Rome, Am. Soc. History of Rhetoric, Internat. Soc. History of Rhetoric, Am. Hist. Assn., Medieval Acad. Am., Renaissance Soc. Am., Am. Phil. Assn., Bohemia Hist. Soc., Bayport Heritage Assn., Sayville Hist. Soc., Columbia U. Grad. Sch. Arts and Scis. Alumni Assn., U. Albany Alumni Assn., Pi Gamma Mu, Kappa Phi Kappa. Avocations: travel, theater, films. Office: Queensborough CC Dept History 222-05 56 Ave Oakland Gardens NY 11364-1497 Office Phone: 718-631-6291. Office Fax: 718-631-6372.

POLAK, JONATHAN GARLAND, lawyer; b. Phila., Dec. 8, 1968; s. Joseph John Jr. and Doris Evelyn Polak; m. Rebecca Claffey, Aug. 19, 1995; children: Elizabeth, Caroline, Andrew. BS, So. Meth. U., Dallas, 1991, JD, 1994. Assoc. Arter & Hadden, LLP, Dallas, 1994—96, Calhoun & Stacy, PC, Dallas, 1996—99; ptnr. Dann Pecar Newman & Kleinman, PC, Indpls., 2000—06, Sommer Barnard, PC, Indpls., 2006—. Chmn. bd. dirs. N Power Ind., Inc., Indps., 2003—. Mem.: 7th Cir. Bar Assn. Office: Sommer Barnard PC 1 Indiana Sq Ste 3500 Indianapolis IN 46204

POLAK, LORI LYN, medical products executive; b. Phila., Nov. 11, 1968; d. Robert Edwin Zarzycki and Marcia Lynn Rawson; m. Timothy Lee Polak, Sept. 21, 2001; 1 child, Katherine Grace. BA, Temple U., Phila., 1996; MBA, Drexel U., Phila., 2006. Bus. devel. analyst OmniCare Clin. Rsch., Blue Bell, Pa., 1998—99; proposal mgr. Parexel Internat., Media, Pa., 1999—2000; clin. sourcing project mgr. Johnson & Johnson, Raritan, NJ, 2000—. Cons. Rsch. Pharm. Svcs., Blue Bell, 2000—02. Recipient Productivity award, Johnson & Johnson, 2007. Mem.: Pharm. Outsourcing Mgmt. Assn., Drug Info. Assn., Beta Gamma Sigma. Republican. Episcopalian. Office: Johnson & Johnson 920 Route 202 South Raritan NJ 08869 Home Phone: 908-996-3389; Office Phone: 908-218-7543. Personal E-mail: tlp05663@earthlink.net. Business E-Mail: lpolak1@prdus.jnj.com.

POLAK, VIVIAN LOUISE, lawyer; b. NYC, Nov. 1, 1952; d. Henri and Greta Etty (Querido) P. BA cum laude, Barnard Coll., 1974; JD, Harvard U., 1977. Bar: NY 1978, DC 1978, US Dist. Ct. (ea. and so. dists.) NY 1978. Assoc. Donovan, Leisure, Newton and Irvine, NYC, 1977-86; ptnr. LeBoeuf, Lamb, Greene & MacRae, NYC, 1986—. Editor-in-chief Alley Way Newsletter (inside look new media law. NY law jour.), 2000—01; co-editor-in-chief Start-Up and Emerging Co. Strategist Am. Lawyer Media, 2001—03. Contbr. articles to profl. jours. Mem. NY State Bar Assn. (sec. antitrust sect. 1991-92, mem. exec. com. 1992-95, chmn. internat. trade com. 1985-90), Assn. Bar City NY (com. copyright & lit. property) 1987-1988. Office: LeBoeuf Lamb Greene and MacRae 125 W 55th St New York NY 10019 Office Phone: 212-424-8289. Office Fax: 212-649-9474. E-mail: vpolak@llgm.com.

POLAKIEWICZ, LEONARD ANTHONY, foreign language and literature educator; b. Kiev, Ukraine, Mar. 30, 1938; came to the U.S., 1950; s. Wladyslaw and Aniela (Ossowska) P.; m. Marianne Helen Swanson, Sept. 7, 1963; children: Barbara, Kathryn, Janet. BS in Russian with distinction, U. Minn., 1964, BA in Internat. Rels., 1964; MA in Russian, U. Wis., 1968; cert. Russian area studies, 1969; PhD in Slavic Langs./Lit., U. Wis., 1978; diploma in Polish Curriculum and Instrn., Curie-Sklodowska U., Lublin, Poland, 1981. Instr. U. Minn., Mpls., 1970-78, asst. prof., 1978—90, assoc. prof., 1990—, Morse Alumni disting. teaching assoc. prof. Slavic langs. and literatures, dir. Inst. Langs., 1991-93, chair Slavic dept., 1993—97, 1999—2000, 2006—. Vis. asst. prof. U. London, 1984; dir. U. Minn. Polish

Lang. Program, Curie-Sklodowska U., Lublin, Poland, summers 1984-89, dir. Russian Faculty Exch., Herzen Pedagogical U., St. Petersburg, Russia, 1993—; mem. selection com. Fulbright Tchr. Exch. Program, USIA, 1989, Title VI Dept. Edn., 1990, NEH Tchr.- Scholar Program, 1994; reviewer divn. ednl. programs NEH, 1990, translation program, 1993, 94; mem. rev. bd. Ctr. Applied Linguistics Polish Proficiency Test, 1990; mem. exec. com. Coun. on Internat. Edn., N.Y.C., 1991-94; mem. Russian Lang. Program Acad. Policy Com. CIEE, N.Y.C., 1994-2002; mem. nat. task force Polish Studies in Am., Ind. U., 1995-96; project dir. Nat. Coun. Orgns. of Less Commonly Taught Langs. Polish Lang. Learning Framework, 1995-2001; Polish examiner Yale U. Ctr. Lang. Study, 2006—; dir. U. Minn. Curie Sklodowska U. Faculty Exch., 1988—, U. Minn. Cath. U. of Lublin Faculty Exch., 1995-2001; coord. Def. Lang. Inst. Polish Proficiency Testing, 1998; apptd. adv. bd. Am. U. Poland, 2004—; mem. nat. screening com. Fulbright-Hays Program, US Dept. State, 2006; mem. rev. panel Boren fellowship, Nat. Security Edn. Program, 2007. Author: Supplemental Materials for First Year Polish, 1991, Supplemental Materials for Fifteen Modern Polish Short Stories, 1994, Directory of US Institutions of Higher Education and Faculty Offering Instruction in Polish Language, Literature and Culture, 1996-97, Intermediate Polish: A Cultural Reader with Exercises, 1999, (with Joanna Radwanska Williams and Waldemar Walczynski) Polish Language Learning Framework, 2002; assoc. editor Slavic and East European Jour., 1988-94; mem. editl. bd. The Learning and Tchg. of Slavic Langs. and Cultures: Toward the 21st Century, 1996-2000; reviewer Choice Mag., Modern Lang. Jour., Canadian Slavonic Papers, Slavic and East European Jour., Soviet and Post-Soviet Rev. Bd. dirs. Immigration Hist. Rsch. Ctr., Mpls., 1984-89, Am. Univ. in Poland, 2004—; co-founder Polish-Am. Cultural Inst., Mpls., 1986; vice-chair Polish Am. Congress' Commn. Edn., 1987; mem. gov.'s Commn. on Ea. Europe, St. Paul, 1991. With U.S. Army, 1961-63. Ford Found. fellow, 1964-65, NDEA fellow, Title IV, 1966-68; grantee Kościuszko Found., 1981, Coun. for European Studies grantee Columbia U., 1981, 84, 86, Rsch. Assoc. grantee Russian and East European Ctr., U. Ill., 1982, 83, 84, Wasie Found. grantee, 1983, IREX Collaborative Activities and New Exchs. grantee, 1984, Ireland Travel grantee Trinity Coll., Dublin, 1984, Bush Found. Rsch. grantee, 1986-87, grantee U.S. Dept. Edn., 1988-91; Fulbright-Hays Group Projects Abroad grantee for Poland, 1989, USIA U. Linkage grantee for Poland, 1989-93, IREX Short Term Travel grantee, 1995, USIA Coll. and Univ. Affiliations grantee for Poland, 1995-2000; recipient Polanie Club of the Twin Cities Merit award, 1982, Curie-Sklodowska U. medal for acad. linkage devel., 1992, Cavalier's Cross of Order of Merit of Republic of Poland, 1999, Disting Svc. award Herzen Pedagogical U., St. Petersburg, Russia, 2002, Pres.'s Outstanding Svc. award, 2003, A. Ronald Walton award Nat. Coun. Less Commonly Taught Langs., 2006. Mem. AAUP, Am. Assn. for the Advancement Slavic Studies, Am. Assn. Tchrs. Slavic and East European Langs. and Lits. (com. on testing and profl. devel. 1997—, Excellence in Tchg. in U.S. award 1994), Internat. Czeslaw Milosz Soc. (pres. 1984-85), N.Am. Chekhov Soc., Am. Coun. Tchrs. of Russian, Polish Inst. Arts & Scis. Am. (N.Y.C., Waclaw Lednicki Humanities award com. 1996), Assn. Literary Scholars & Critics, Soc. of Lovers of the Russian Book, Irish Assn. of Russian and East European Studies, Polish Tchrs. Assn. of Am., Polish Studies Assn. (mem. biannual prize jury 1998), Bristol Group Internat. Assn. Tchrs. Polish, U. Minn. Acad. Disting. Tchrs., The Australia and New Zealand Slavists' Assn. Roman Catholic. Avocations: reading, philatelics, genealogy, touring, gardening. Home: 466 Oak Creek Dr S Vadnais Heights MN 55127-7008 Office Phone: 612-625-1384. Business E-Mail: polak001@tc.umn.edu.

POLAKOFF, ABE, baritone; b. Bucharest, Rumania; s. Sam and Mary P. Ousherenkova; children: David Fred, Mark Evan, Robert Ira; m. Judyth Kanner, Dec. 5, 1992. Civil engring. student, CCNY; profl. tng. program, Am. Theater Wing, 1952-54; student, N.Y. Coll. Music, 1955-57. Dir. Island Opera Players; opera lectr. Arts Couns. (municipalities and schs.); cantor Progressive Shaari Zedek synagogue, Bklyn., 1972-77, Temple Emanuel, Denver, 1984-94. Debuts include Marcello in La Boheme, Milan, Florence, 1960; leading baritone Zurich Opera, 1961-63, numerous appearances with N.Y. Met. Opera, City Opera N.Y., Phila. Lyric Opera, Pitts. Opera, Seattle Opera, Berlin Deutsche Opera, Frankfurt Opera, Cinn. Opera, Hamburg, Munich Staatsoper, Stuttgart Staatsoper, The Netherlands Opera, Cin. Opera, Kansas City Lyric Opera, Canadian Opera Co., others; soloist with Mex. State Symphony Orch., Kalamazoo Symphony Orch., Winston-Salem (N.C.) Symphony, numerous concert and recital appearances Sgt. U.S. Army, 1943-46. 1st prize winner Am. Theatre Wing Vocal Profl. Scholarship award, 1954, 1st prize winner Am. Opera Auditions, 1960, Silver medal Vercelli (Italy) Internat. singing contest, 1960; Rockefeller Found. grantee, 1961-62; Bayreuth Festival Masterclass scholar. Mem. Cen. Opera Service, Am. Guild Musical Artists, Actors Equity Assn. Address: 11132 76th Ave Apt 7H Forest Hills NY 11375-6409 E-mail: judyth@nvbb.net.

POLAMALU, TROY, professional football player; b. Garden Grove, Calif., Apr. 19, 1981; Grad., U. So. Calif., 2003. Safety Pitts. Steelers, 2003—. Named to NFL Pro-Bowl Team, 2004, 2005, NFL All-Pro Team, 2005. Office: c/o Pittsburgh Steelers 3400 S Water St Pittsburgh PA 15203

POLAN, MARY LAKE, obstetrics and gynecology educator; b. Las Vegas, N.Mex., July 17, 1943; Student, Smith Coll., Paris, 1963—64; BA cum laude, Conn. Coll., 1965; PhD in Biophysics and Biochemistry, Yale U., 1965—70, MD, 1972—75. Diplomate Am. Bd. Ob-Gyn., Am. Bd. Reproductive Endocrinology, Nat. Bd. Med. Examiners. Clin. clk. in ob-gyn. and pediat. Radcliffe Infirmary, Oxford (Eng.) U. Med. Sch., 1974; instr. Pahlavi U., Shiraz, Iran, 1978; postdoctoral fellow dept. biology, NIH postdoctoral fellow Yale U., New Haven, 1970—72, resident dept. ob-gyn. Sch. Medicine, 1975—78, fellow in oncology, then fellow in endocrinology-infertility, 1978—80, asst. instr., then lectr. molecular biophysics-biochemistry, 1970—72, instr., then asst. prof. ob-gyn., 1978—79, 1980—85, assoc. prof., 1985—90; Katharine Dexter McCormick and Stanley McCormick Meml. prof. Stanford (Calif.) Sch. Medicine, 1990—, chair dept. gynecology and obstetrics, 1990—. Vis. prof. Hunan Med. Coll., Changsha, China, 1986; mem. med. bd. Yale-China Assn., 1987—90; liaison com. on ethics in modern world Conn. Coll., New London, 1988—90; mem. med. adv. bd. Ova-Med Corp., Palo Alto, Calif., 1992—95, Vivus, Menlo Park, Calif., 1993—97; bd. dirs. Metra Biosys., Mountain View, Quidel, San Diego, 1993—, Am. Home Products, Madison, NJ, 1994, Adiana Inc., Redwood City, Calif., 2002—; mem. reproductive endocrinology study sect. NIH, 1989—90, co-chmn. task force on opportunities for rsch. on woman's health, 1991, mem. dir. panel on clin. rsch., 1995—98; mem. sci. adv. bd. Apop Corp., Princeton, NJ, 2003—; mem. health adv. bd. DuPont, Wilmington, Del., 2003—. Author: Second Seed, 1987; guest editor: Seminars in Reproductive Endocrinology, 1984, Infertility and Reproductive Medicine Clinics of North America: GnRH Analogues, Vol. 4, 1993; editor, with DeCherney: Surgery in Reproductive Endocrinology, 1987;; editor: (with DeCherney, S. Boyers and R. Lee) Decision Making in Infertility; ad hoc reviewer: Jour. Clin. Endocrinology and Metabolism, Fertility and Sterility, Ob-Gyn., others; contbr. chapters to books, articles to med. jours.; editl. bd. Jour. Women's Health, Rodale Health Bd. Adv., 1993—2002. Mem. bd. trustees Conn. Coll., New London, 2000—. Fellow, NSRA, 1981—82; grantee, NIRA, 1982—85, HD, 1985—90, NRSA, 1987—88, Johnson & Johnson, 1993—96; scholar, Assn. Acad. Health Ctrs., 1993—96. Fellow: ACOG (PROLOG task force for reproductive endocrinology and infertility 1988—89, rep. to CREOG coun. 1994—97); mem.: Bay Area Reproductive Endocrine Soc., San Francisco Gynecologic Soc., Inst. Medicine (com. on rsch. capabilities of acad. depts. ob-gyn. 1990—91, bd. on health scis. policy 1992—96, membership com. 1996—98, chair membership com. 1998—2001, mem. governing coun. 2002—05, coun. liaison to food and nutrition bd. 2002—, coun. mem. 2006—), Am. Gynecologic and Obstetric Soc., Soc. for Reproductive Endocrinologists, Soc. for Gynecologic Investigation, Am. Fertility Soc., Phi Beta Kappa. Achievements include patents for methods of diagnosing and treating urinary incontinence relating to collagen proteolysis in pelvic supporting tissue, US patent number 6,420,119; issued July 2002. Office: Stanford U Sch Medicine Dept Gyn OB 300 Pasteur Dr HH333 Stanford CA 94305-5317 Office Phone: 650-723-5533. Office Fax: 650-723-7737. E-mail: polan@stanford.edu. *

POLANCO, PLACIDO ENRIQUE, professional baseball player; b. Santo Domingo, Dominican Republic, Oct. 10, 1975; m. Lily Polanco; children: Aide Rose, Ishmael. Student, Miami-Dade Wolfson CC, Fla. Draft pick St. Louis Cardinals, 1994, player, 1998—2002, Phila. Phillies, 2002—05, Detroit Tigers, 2005—. Mem. Dominican Republic Team World Baseball Classic, 2006. Named Am. League Championship Series MVP, 2006; named to Am. League All-Star Team, 2007; recipient Stockton/Broeg award, Baseball Writers' Assn. of Am., St. Louis chpt., 2000, 2001. Avocation: golf. Mailing: Detroit Tigers Comerica Park 2100 Woodward Ave Detroit MI 48201 *

POLANSKI, ROMAN, film director, writer, actor; b. Paris, Aug. 18, 1933; s. Ryszard and Bule (Katz-Przedborska) P.; m. Barbara Lass (div.); m. Sharon Tate (dec.); m. Emmanuelle Seigner. Student, Art Sch., Cracow, State Film Coll., Lodz. Appeared in (children's radio show) The Merry Gang, (stage prodn.) Son of the Regiment; dir.: (films) Two Men and a Wardrobe, 1958, When Angels Fall, 1958, Le Gros et le Maigre, 1960, Knife in the Water, 1962 (Venice Film Festival award), The Mammals, 1963 (Tours Film Festival award), Repulsion, 1965 (Berlin Film Festival award), Cul-de-Sac, 1966 (Berlin Film Festival award), The Vampire Killers, 1967, Rosemary's Baby, 1968, Macbeth, 1971, What?, 1972, Chinatown, 1974 (Best Dir. award Soc. Film and TV Arts, Priz Raoul-Levy, 1975), The Tenant, 1976, Tess, 1980 (Cesar award), Pirates, 1986, Bitter Moon, 1994, Death and the Maiden, 1994, The Ninth Gate, 1999, The Pianist, 2002 (Best Dir. Acad. award, 2003, Best Film, British Acad. Film Award (BAFTA), 2003, The David Lean Award for Achievement in Direction, 2003, 2003), Oliver Twist, 2005; dir., co-writer (films) Frantic, 1988; actor: (on stage) The Metamorphosis, 1988; (films) A Generation, The End of the Night, See You Tomorrow, The Innocent Sorcerers, Two Men and a Wardrobe, The Vampire Killers, What?, The Magic Christian and Andy Warhol's Death, Back in the U.S.S.R., A Pure Formality, Chinatown, The Tennant; actor, dir.: (plays) Amadeus; Warsaw, 1981; Paris, 1982; Amadeus/Italy, 1999; dir.: (Operas) Lulu, 1974, Rigoletto, 1976; (Operas, (musical comedy) Tales of Hoffman, Master Class, 1996—97; (Operas) Tanz der Vampire, 1997, 2000; author: (autobiography) Roman, 1984. Recipient Lifetime Achievement award, European Film Awards, 2006. Office: ICM 8942 Wilshire Blvd Beverly Hills CA 90211-1934

POLANSKY, LARRY PAUL, legal association administrator; b. Blkyn., July 24, 1932; s. Harry and Ida (Gershgom) P.; m. Eunice Kathryn Neun; children: Steven, Harriet, Bruce. BS in Acctg., Temple U., 1958, JD, 1973. Bar: Pa. 1973, U.S. Dist. Ct. (ea. dist.) Pa. 1973, U.S. Ct. Appeals (3d cir.) 1973, D.C. 1978, U.S. Supreme Ct. 1980. Acct., systems analyst City of Phila., 1956-63; data processing mgr. Jefferson Med. Coll. and Hosp., Phila., 1963-65; systems engr. IBM Corp., Phila., 1965-67; dep. ct. adminstr. Common Pleas Cts. of Phila., 1967-76; dep. state ct. adminstr. Pa. Supreme Ct., Phila., 1976-78; exec. officer D.C. Cts., Washington, 1979-90. Presdl. appt. to bd. dirs. State Justice Inst., 1985-89; bd. dirs. Search Group, Inc. Author: A Primer for the Technologically Challenged Judge, 1995; contbr. articles to profl. jours. Elected supervisor, Kidder Twp., 2003-; served as cpl. U.S. Army, 1951-53, Korea. Fellow Inst. for Ct. Mgmt., Denver, 1984; recipient Reardon award Nat. Ctr. for State Cts., 1982, Disting. Svc. award Nat. Ctr. for State Cts., 1986, Justice Tom C. Clark award Nat. Conf. of Metro. Cts., 1991, award of merit Nat. Assn. Ct. Mgmt., 1996. Mem. ABA (jud. adminstrn. divsn., chmn. tech. com. 1991-93, 95, exec. com. lawyers conf. 1985-98, chmn. 1991-92, JAD coun. 1994-97), Conf. State Ct. Adminstrn. (bd. dirs. 1980-86, pres. 1984-85). Republican. Jewish. Avocations: tennis, skiing, computers, golf. Home and Office: PO Box 752 Lake Harmony PA 18624-0752 Home Phone: 570-722-9288; Office Phone: 570-722-9288. E-mail: polanskyl@aol.com.

POLANSKY, MARK L., astronaut; b. Paterson, NJ, June 2, 1956; s. Irving and Edith Polansky; m. Lisa Ristow; 1 child. BS in aero. and astronautical engring., MS in aero. and astronautical engring., Purdue U., West Lafayette, Ind., 1978. Commd. 2d lt. USAF, 1978, student pilot Vance AFB, Okla., 1978—80, pilot F-15 Langley AFB, Va., 1980—83; pilot F-5E aggressor pilot for tng. Clark AFB, Philippines, 1983—86; trainee Test Pilot Sch. USAF, Edwards AFB, Calif., 1986—87; test pilot USAF, Eglin AFB, Fla., 1987—92; aerospace engr., rsch. pilot NASA Johnson Space Ctr., Houston, 1992—96, astronaut, 1996—. Pilot STS-98 (Atlantis), 2001; chief CAPCOM Branch, 2002; chief instructor astronaut NASA, 2003—04, chief of the Return Flight and Orbiter Repair Branches; comdr. STS-116 Mission (Discovery), 2006. Recipient Flying Tng. award, USAF, 1980, Air Force Meritorious Svc. medal, Air Force Commendation medal with two Oak Leaf Clusters. Mem.: Aircraft Owners and Pilots Assn., AIAA, Soc. Exptl. Test Pilots. Achievements include 5000 flight hours in 3 different aircraft; 1 space mission, over 309 hours in space. Avocations: ice hockey, snowskiing, light aircraft flying, music, art. Office: NASA Astronaut Office Johnson Space Ctr Houston TX 77058 *

POLANYI, JOHN CHARLES, chemist, educator; b. Berlin, Jan. 23, 1929; s. Michael and Magda Elizabeth (Kemeny) Polanyi; m. Anne Ferrar Davidson, 1958; 2 children. BSc, Manchester U., Eng., 1949, MSc, 1950, PhD, 1952, DSc, 1964; DSc (hon.), U. Waterloo, 1970, Meml. U., 1976, McMaster U., 1977, Carleton U., 1981, Harvard U., 1982, Rensselaer U., Brock U., 1984, Lethbridge U., Sherbrooke U., Laval U., Victoria U., Ottawa U., 1987, Manchester U. and York U., Eng., 1988, U. Montreal, Acadia U., 1989, Weizmann Inst., Israel, 1989, U. Bari, Italy, 1990, U. B.C., 1990, McGill U., 1990, Queen's U., 1992, Free U. Berlin, 1993, Laurentian U., 1995, U. Toronto, 1995, U. Liverpool, 1995; LLD (hon.), Trent U., 1977, Dalhousie U., 1983, St. Francis-Xavier U., 1984, Concordia U., 1990, Calgary U., 1994. Mem. faculty dept. chemistry U. Toronto, Ont., Canada, 1956—, prof., 1962—. William D. Harkins lectr. U. Chgo., 1970; Reilly lectr. U. Notre Dame, 1970; Purve lectr. McGill U., 1971; F.J. Toole lectr. U. N.B., 1974; Philips lectr. Haverford Coll., 1974; Kistiakowsky lectr. Harvard U., 1975; Camille and Henry Dreyfus lectr. U. Kans., 1975; J.W.T. Spinks lectr. U. Sask., Canada, 1976; Laird lectr. U. We. Ont., 1976; CIL Disting. lectr. Simon Fraser U., 1977; Gucker lectr. Ind. U., 1977; Jacob Bronowski Meml. lectr. U. Toronto, 1978; Hutchinson lectr. Rochester (N.Y.) U., 1979; Priestley lectr. Pa. State U., 1980; Barré lectr. U. Montreal, 1982; Sherman Fairchild disting. scholar Calif. Inst. Tech., 1982; Chute lectr. Dalhousie U., 1983; Redman lectr. McMaster U., 1983; Wiegand lectr. U. Toronto, 1984; Edward U. Condon lectr. U. Colo., 1984; John A. Allan lectr. U. Alta., 1984; John E. Willard lectr. U. Wis., 1984; Owen Holmes lectr. U. Lethbridge, 1985; Walker-Ames prof. U. Wash., 1986; John W. Cowper disting. vis. lectr. SUNY, Buffalo, 1986; vis. prof. chemistry Tex. A&M U., 1986; Disting. vis. spkr. U. Calgary, 1987; Morino lectr. U. Japan, 1987; J.T. Wilson lectr. Ont. Scil. Ctr., 1987; Welsh lectr. U. toronto, 1987; Spiers Meml. lectr. Faraday divsn. Royal Soc. Chemistry, 1987; Polanyi lectr. Internat. Union Pure and Applied Chemistry, 1988; W.B. Lewis lectr. Atomic Energy of Can. Ltd., 1988; Consol. Bathurst vis. lectr. Concordia U., 1988; Priestman lectr. U. N.B., 1988; Killam lectr. U. Windsor, 1988; Herzberg lectr. Carleton U., 1988; Falconbridge lectr. Laurentian U., 1988; DuPont lectr. Ind. U., 1989; Luther lectr. U. Regina, 1989; Franklin lectr. Rice U., 1990; Laurier lectr. Wilfred Laurier U., 1990; Pratt lectr. U. Va., 1990; Goodrich lectr. Case Western Reserve U., 1990; Phillips lectr. U. Pitts., 1991; Albert Noyes lectr. U. Tex., 1992; John and Lois Dove Meml. lectr. U. Toronto, 1992; Fritz London lectr. Duke U., 1993; Castle lectr. U. South Fla., 1993; Linus Pauling lectr. Calif. Inst. Tech., 1994; Hagey lectr. U. Waterloo, 1995; Larkin Stuart lectr. U. Toronto, 1995; Hungerford lectr. York Club, 1995; disting. lectr. ser. Meml. U., 1995; John C. Polanyi Nobel Laureate lectr. U. Toronto, 1995; Floyd E. Bartell Meml. lectr. U. Mich., 1996; Christian Culture award lectr. Assumption U., 1996; Liversidge lectr. U. Sydney, 1996; disting. scientist lectr. Apotex, Inc., 1996; mem. sci. adv. bd. Max Planck Inst. Quantum Optics, Germany, 1982—92; mem. nat. adv. bd. on Sci. and Tech., 1987—89; hon. cons. Inst. Molecular Sci., Okazaki, Japan, 1989—94; bd. dirs. Steacie Inst. Molecular Scis., Ottawa, Ont.; founding mem., pres. Can. Com. of Sci. and Scholars; Beam Disting. vis. prof. U. Iowa, 1992; Charles M. and Martha Hitchcock prof. U. Calif., Berkeley, 1994; Young Meml. visitor Royal Mil. Coll., 1994; mem. Bd. of Premier's Coun., 1994; co-chair Internat. Consultative Group on Improving UN Rapid Reaction Capability. Editor (with F.G. Griffiths): The Dangers of Nuclear War, 1979; contbr. articles to jours., mags., newspapers; prodr. (film) Concepts in Reaction Dynamics, 1970. Mem. Queen's Privy Coun. for Can., 1992; founding mem. Can. Pugwash Com., 1960; Can. Ctr. for Arms Control and Disarmament. Decorated Officer Order of Can., Companion, knight Grand Cross Order St. John of Jerusalem; co-recipient (with N. Bartlett) Steacie prize, 1965, Wolf prize in chemistry, Wolf Found., 1982; recipient Marlow medal, Faraday Soc., 1962, Centenary medal, Chem. Soc. Gt. Brit., 1965, Norandaaward, Chem. Inst. Can., 1967, award, Brit. Chem. Soc., 1971, Mack award and lectureship, Ohio State U., 1969, medal, Chem. Inst. Can., 1976, Remsen award and lectureship, Am. Chem. Soc., 1978, Nobel prize in Chemistry, 1986, Izaak Walton Killam Meml. prize, 1988, C. Polanyi award, Can. Soc. Chemistry, 1992, Floyd E. Bartell Meml. lectureship, U. Mich., 1996, Liversidge lectureship, U. Sydney, 1996, Christian Culture award and lectureship, Assumption U., 1996; fellow Sloan Found., 1959—63, Guggenheim, 1979—80, Geoffrey Frew, 1996, Disting. Anniversary, Australian Nat. U., 1996. Fellow: Royal Soc. Chemisry (Michael Polanyi medal 1989), Royal Soc. Edinburgh, Royal Soc. Can. (founding mem., pres., com. on scholarly freedom, Marshall Tory medal 1977), Trinity Coll., U. Toronto (hon.), Royal Soc. London (Royal medal 1989, Bakerian lectureship and award 1994), Chem. Inst. Can. (hon.); mem.: NAS (fgn. mem.), Croation Acad. Scis. and Arts, Russian Acad. Scis. (foreign mem.), Pontifical Acad. Scis. (Rome), Am. Acad. Arts and Scis. (mem. com. on internat. security studies, hon. fgn.). Office: U Toronto Dept Chemistry Rm 262 80 St George St Toronto ON Canada M5S 3H6

POLASCIK, MARY ANN, ophthalmologist; b. Elkhorn, W.Va., Dec. 28, 1940; d. Michael and Elizabeth (Halko) Polascik; m. Joseph Elie, Oct. 2, 1973; 1 dau., Laura Elizabeth Polascik Jr. BA, Rutgers U., 1967; MD, Pritzker Sch. Medicine, 1971. Jr. pharmacologist Ciba Pharm Co., Summit, NJ, 1961-67; intern Billings Hosp., Chgo., 1971-72; resident in ophthalmology U. Chgo. Hosp., 1972-75; practice medicine specializing in ophthalmology Dixon, Ill., 1975—2005. Pres. McNichols Clinic, Ltd.; cons. ophthalmology, Jack Mabley Devel. Ctr., 1976-93; mem. staff Katherine Shaw Bethea Hosp, 1975-2005. Bd. dirs. Sinnossippi Mental Health Ctr., 1977-82, Dixon Cmty. Trust Mental Health Ctr., 1989—. Mem. Am. Acad. Ophthalmology, Alpha Sigma Lambda, Galena Territory Club. Roman Catholic.

POLASEK, EDWARD JOHN, retired electrical engineer, consultant; b. Cudahy, Wis., Oct. 12, 1927; s. John Vincent and Mary Ann (Totka) P.; m. Alice S. Nee (Harnecki), Aug. 18, 1948. BSEE, Marquette U., 1948. Registered profl. engr., Wis., Fla. Cons. engr. Eau Claire, Wis., Gainesville, Fla., 1955-60, various countries, Korea, Vietnam, Nicaragua, 1960-72; v.p., dir. Finley Engring. Co., Eau Claire, 1972-78; pres. Chippewa Devel. Co., Eau Claire, 1978-82; planning engr. Harza Engring. Co. in Cairo, Egypt and Dominican Rep., 1982-86; cons. engr. Gainesville, 1986-99; ret. Cons. Lake Altoona Rehab. Dist., Eau Claire, 1974. Author: Planning Methods, 1982, Feasibility Study, 1984; editor: Field Engineer's Handbook, 1982. Chmn. Eau Claire chpt. Am. Cancer Soc.; master gardner U. Fla. Ext. Svc., Gainesville, 1990. With USN, 1944-46, PTO. Mem. Nat. Soc. Profl. Engrs. (pres. 1956), IEEE, Audobon Soc., Tau Beta Pi, Eta Kappa Nu. Avocations: mycology, fishing, art. Address: 3532 Hwy 51 N Woodruff WI 54568 E-mail: polasek@gru.net.

POLATSCH, BERNARD, obstetrician, gynecologist; b. NYC, Aug. 13, 1937; s. Irving William and Rose Polatsch; m. Iris Abrahamson, May 15, 2005; 1 child, Daniel Barret. BA, NYU, Bronx, 1958; MD, U. Buffalo, 1962. Ob-gyn. pvt. practice, Hicksville, NY, 1969—. Sr. attending North Shore U. Hosp., Plainview, NY, 1969—. Capt. USAF, 1963—65. Fellow: Am. Coll. Surgeons, Am. Coll. Ob-gyn. Office: 400 S Oyster Bay Rd Ste 204 Hicksville NY 11801

POLATTY, ROSE JACKSON, civic worker; b. Atlanta, Sept. 17, 1922; d. James Wilmot and Esther Ann (Sweeny) Jackson; m. George Junius Polatty,Nov. 27, 1942; children: George Junius, Robert Wilmot, Rose Crystal, Richard James. AB in Journalism, U. Ga., 1943; postgrad., Oglethorpe U., 1962-63, Ga. State U., 1963. Active U. Ga. Alumni Soc.; pres. Class of 1943 Alumni, 1948-58; bd. mgr., 1966-69; v.p., 1971-73; chmn. seminar, 1971; exec. sec. Atlanta Boy Choir, 1968-69; bd. dirs. Atlanta Arts Coun., 1968-69; adv. com. Kennesaw Coll. on Wheels, 1974-78; bicentennial chmn. City of Roswell (Ga.), 1975-76; sec. hist. preservation commn., 1978-82; chmn., 1983-84. Active Ga. Trust Hist. Preservation, Ga. Conservancy. Mem. adminstrv. bd., chmn. altar guild, Roswell United Meth. Ch., 1977-89. Recipient Recognition award Nat. 4-H Alumni, 1959, Svc. award City of Roswell, 1976, Cmty. Svc. award Roswell Optimist Club, 1977, Roswell Jaycees Leadership award, 1977, Cmty. Svc. award Zion Bapt. Ch., 1977, Vol. award Friends Roswell Libr., 2000. Mem. Roswell Hist. Soc. (charter 1971), Atlanta Symphony Assocs., Colonial Dames XVII Century (charter Nicholas Wallingford chpt. 1979, v.p. 1980-81, pres. 1982-83), U.D.C. (Phillips Legion chpt.), Altanta Audubon Soc., High Mus. Art (charter), PEO (chpt. AA, Ga., charter 1977), DAR (Joseph Habersham chpt.), Roswell Women's (charter 1948, pres. 1966-68), Roswell Garden (charter 1951, pres. 1975-77), N. Fulton Coun. Garden Clubs (charter 1975, pres. 1975-77), Kappa Delta,Delta Omicron, Phi Beta Kappa, Phi Kappa Phi, Kappa Delta Pi. Home: 889 Mimosa Blvd Roswell GA 30075-4436 Personal E-mail: rosejp@aol.com.

POLAY, BRUCE, musician, conductor, educator; b. Bklyn., Mar. 22, 1949; s. Benjamin and Joan Polay; m. Louise Phillips, Dec. 17, 1983; children: Elizabeth Louise, Bruce Adam, Rachel Joanne, Jacob Benjamin, Julia Christine. MusB, U. So. Calif., 1971; MA, Calif. State U., 1977; DMA, Ariz. State U., 1989. Music dir. So. Calif. Philharm., Long Beach, 1971-81; grad. asst. in theory and orch., asst. condr. univ. symphony Ariz. State U., Tempe, 1981-83; condr. Phoenix Symphony Guild Youth Orch., 1981-83; music dir. Knox-Galesburg (Ill.) Symphony, 1983—; prof. music Knox Coll., Galesburg, 1983—, chair music dept., 2001—05. Guest condr. in Belarus, Italy, Eng., Mexico, Romania, Russia, Ukraine, Spain; bd. dirs. Ill. Coun. of Orchs., 1992—; mem. adv. bd. Found. for New Music, 1996—; bd. advisors Barlow Endowment for Music Composition; mem. music program adv. panel Ill. Arts Coun., 2004—. Orchestral compositions include Enconium, 1986, Perspectives, 1989, Concerto for Tenor Trombone, 1990, Tranquil Cycle for Tenor and Orch., 1992, Cathedral Images, 1993, Bondi's Journey: An Orchestral Rhapsody on Jewish Themes, 1994, Pictures For an Exhibition Piano, 1995, Anniversary Mourning for a cappella choir, 1996, Sandburg Cycle for Soprano, Tenor and Piano, 2000, Semi-Suite for Vin, Cello and Piano, 2001, Golden Oldie for Orchestra, 2001, Elegy for Violin and Small Orchestra, 2002, Suite of Preludes for Organ, 2002, Illumination for Orchestra, 2003, Suite on Catalonian

Folksongs for String Orchestra, 2004, 3 Violin Duets on Catalonian Folksongs, 2005, 5 novelettes for harp and string orchestra, 2006, Sparkle for Orchestra, 2007. Recipient Ill. Condr. of Yr. award Ill. Coun. Orchs., 1997, 2004, Exceptional Achievement award Knox Coll., 1999, 2004, Programming of the Yr. award, 2006; named Ill. Orchestra of Yr. Knox-Galesburg Symphony, 1986, 2003. Mem. ASCAP, Am. Music Ctr., Phi Kappa Phi. Mem. Lds Ch. Avocations: body surfing, reading, American history. Home: 1577 N Cherry St Galesburg IL 61401-1820 Office: Knox Coll Campus Box 5 Galesburg IL 61401-4999 Home Phone: 309-337-3720; Office Phone: 309-341-7208. Business E-Mail: bpolay@knox.edu.

POLCHINSKI, JOSEPH G., physicist, science educator; Prof. physics U. Calif., Santa Barbara. Author: String Theory: An Introduction to the Bosonic String, 1998, String Theory: Superstring Theory and Beyond, 1998. Recipient Dannie Heineman prize for Math. Physics, Am. Phys. Soc., 2007. Mem.: NAS, Kavli Inst. for Theoretical Physics. Achievements include research in D-branes in theoretical physics and their importance in String Theory. Office: Univ Calif Kavli Inst Theoretical Physics Santa Barbara CA 93106-4030 Office Phone: 805-893-3126. Office Fax: 805-893-2431. E-mail: joep@itp.ucsb.edu. *

POLCZYNSKI, ERIC JAMES, pharmacist; b. Natrona Heights, Pa., Aug. 27, 1971; s. James Frances and Vida Elizabeth Polczynski; m. Evette Polczynski, Feb. 19, 1996; children: Colton, Beatrice. BS in Pharmacy, U. Pitts., 1994. Registered pharmacist Pa. Clin. pharmacist Tuba City Med. Ctr., Indian Health Svc., USPHS, Ariz., 1994—97, Shipprock Med. Ctr., Indian Health Svc., USPHS, 1997—2001; asst. chief pharmacist Dulce Health Ctr., Indian Health Svc., USPHS, N.Mex., 2001—. Lt. comdr. USPHS, 1994—. Mem.: AMSUS, APHA. Democrat. Avocations: mountain climbing, skiing, hiking, mountain biking. Office: Dulce Health Ctr Pharmacy Dept 12000 Stone Lake Rd Dulce NM 87528

POLDEN, DONALD, dean, law educator; BBA, George Washington U.; JD cum laude, Ind. U. Sch. Law. Law clerk for Hon. William C. Hanson, Chief Justice U.S. Dist. Ct. for So. Dist. Iowa, 1975—76; of counsel Hawkins and Norris, 1978—90; prof. law Drake U. Sch. Law, 1976—93; assoc. dean U. Memphis Sch. Law, 1991—93, dean, prof law, 1993—2003, Santa Clara U. Sch. Law, 2003—. Vis. prof. U. Louisville Sch. Law, 1984. Co-author: Employment relationships: law and practice, 1998; contbr. articles to law jours. Fellow: Coll. Labor and Employment Lawyers; mem.: Am. Law Inst. (elected mem. 1993), ABA (life). Office: Santa Clara U Sch Law El Camino Real Santa Clara CA 95053 Office Phone: 408-554-4362. E-mail: dpolden@scu.edu.

POLEBAUM, MARK NEAL, lawyer; b. Lowell, Mass., May 1, 1952; s. Eugene Harvey and Phyllis Diane (Sherman) P.; m. Diane M. Buhl, June 6, 1982; children: Katherine Elizabeth, Jessica Leigh, Michael William. BA, Middlebury Coll., 1974; JD, NYU, 1978. Bar: Mass. 1979, U.S. Dist. Ct. Mass. 1979. Law clk. Chief Judge John C. Godbold, U.S. Ct. Appeals (5th cir.), Montgomery, Ala., 1978-79; assoc. Hale and Dorr, Boston, 1979-83, jr. ptnr., 1983-86, sr. ptnr., 1986—2004; ptnr., co-chmn. Bankruptcy & Comml. dept. Wilmer Cutler Pickering Hale & Dorr, Boston, 2004—. Counsel bondholders com. in out of ct. restructuring of Swan Brewery, Inc.; counsel bondholders com. in chpt. 11 reorgn. of EUA Power Corp. Editor (rsch.): NYU Law Rev.; contbr. articles to profl. jours. Mem. appropriations com., City of Lexington, Mass., 1984-88. Watson Found. fellow, 1974-75; named Mass. Super Lawyer, Boston Mag., 2004; Pro Bono Turnaround award, Turnaround Mgmt. Assn. Fellow Am. Coll. Bankruptcy; mem. ABA (corp., banking and bus. law sects., ad hoc subcom. on scope of uniform comml. code), Am. Bankruptcy Inst., Mass. Bar Assn., Phi Beta Kappa, Order of the Coif. Office: Wilmer Cutler Pickering Hale & Dorr 60 State St Boston MA 02109-1816 Office Phone: 617-526-6792. Office Fax: 617-526-5000. Business E-Mail: mark.polebaum@wilmerhale.com.

POLEDNA, MATHIAS, video artist; b. Vienna, 1965; arrived in LA, 2000; Student, U. Applied Arts, U. Vienna, Austria. Prin. works include Produktion Pop (with Martin Beck and Jon Savage), 1996, Fondazione, Generali Found., Vienna, Austria, 1998, Actualite, 2001, Sufferers' Version, 2004, exhibitions include Zones of Disturbance, Graz, Austria, 1997, Grazer Kunstverein, 2001, Richard Telles Fine Art, LA, 2002, 2005, 2007, Mus. Modern Art Found., Vienna, Austria, 2003, 2006, MUMOK, Vienna, 2003, Galerie Meyer Kainer, 2004, 2007, Witte de With Ctr. Contemporary Art, Netherlands, 2006, exhibited in group shows at Martin-Gropius-Bau, Berlin, 2004, Stedelijk Mus. Post CS, Amsterdam, Netherlands, 2004, Tate, Liverpool, Eng., 2004, Haus der Kunst, Munich, 2005, Atelier Augarten, Wien, Austria, 2005, Lisson Gallery, London, 2005, Whitney Mus. Am. Art, 2006, Galerie Daniel Buchholz, Cologne, Germany, 2007, Hammer Mus., LA, 2007. Mailing: c/o Richard Telles Fine Art 7380 Beverly Blvd Los Angeles CA 90036

POLEMITOU, OLGA ANDREA, accountant; b. Nicosia, Cyprus, June 28, 1950; d. Takis and Georgia (Nicolaou) Chrysanthou. BA with honors, U. London, 1971; PhD, Ind. U., Bloomington, 1981. CPA Ind. Asst. productivity officer Internat. Labor Office/Cyprus Productivity Ctr., Nicosia, 1971-74; cons. Arthur Young & Co., NYC, 1981; mgr. Coopers & Lybrand, Newark, 1981-83; dir. Bell Atlantic, Reston, Va., 1983-97; v.p. corp. auditing Columbia Energy Group, Herndon, 1997—2000; pres., CEO Aristion, Inc., Reston, Va., 2000—. Chairperson adv. coun. Extended Day Care Cmty. Edn., West Windsor Plainsboro, NJ, 1987—88. Contbr. articles to profl. jours. Bus. cons. project bus. Jr. Achievement, Indpls., 1984—85. Mem.: AICPAs, NAFE, Princeton Network Profl. Women, Va. Soc. CPAs, N.J. Soc. CPAs (sec. mem. in industry com.), Ind. CPA Soc., Nat. Trust Hist. Preservation. Avocations: water-skiing, tennis. Home: PO Box 2744 Reston VA 20195-0744 Office: 11921 Freedom Dr Ste 550 Reston VA 20190 Business E-Mail: opolemitou@aristion.com.

POLEN-DORN, LINDA FRANCES, communications executive; b. Cleve., Mar. 23, 1945; d. Stanley and Mildred (Kain) Neuger; m. Samuel O. Dorn; children: Lanelle, Brian, Adam, Dawn. BA cum laude, U. Miami, 1967; MBA, Nova Southeastern U., 1993. Reporter Miami News, Del., 1966-67, Miamian Mag., 1967—68; dir. pub. rels. Muscular Dystrophy Assn., Miami, 1968—72; cons., adv. and pub. rels. Ft. Lauderdale, 1974—77; pub. rels. writer J. Cory and Assocs., Ft. Lauderdale, 1978—79; account supr. Maizner & Franklin, Ft. Lauderdale, 1979—86; v.p. mktg., comm. Glendale Fed. Bank, 1986—95; prod. mktg. mgr. Ryder Sys., Inc., Miami, 1995—2003; cons. Southeastern Consulting Group, LLC, Ft. Lauderdale, 2004—. Active Symphony of Ams. Soc., Ft. Lauderdale, 2004—, Symphony Soc. Ft. Lauderdale, 1987-2003—. Mem. Internat. Assn. Bus. Communicators, Am. Mktg. Assn., Broward C. of C. (vice chmn. govt. affairs 1984-85). Avocation: travel.

POLENZ, JOANNA MAGDA, psychiatrist; b. Cracow, Poland, Oct. 20, 1936; came to U.S., 1961; d. Mieczyslaw and Nusia (Goldberger) Uberall; m. Daryl Louis Polenz, July 8, 1962 (div. 1991); children: Teresa Ann, Daryl Philip, Elizabeth Sophia. MD, U. Sydney, Australia, 1960; MPH, Columbia U., 1992. Diplomate Am. Bd. Psychiatry and Neurology. Intern Bklyn. Hosp., 1961-62; resident in psychiatry Mt. Sinai Med. Ctr., NYC, 1962-65, ednl. fellow, 1965-66, rsch. assoc., 1966-67; med. dir. Tappan Zee clin. Phelps Meml. Hosp., Tarrytown, NY, 1968-71, dir. dept. psychiatry, 1972-77; sr. attending psychiatrist Meml. Hosp. Ctr., 1972-93; pvt. practice Briarcliff Manor, NY, 1971-91; physician Joint Commn. Accreditation of Healthcare Orgns., Oakbrook Terrace, Ill., 1993—2004; pres. Sch. of Health.com, NYC, 1998—; assoc. dir. adminstrn. N.Y.C. Health and Hosp. Corp., 2004—. Lectr. in field. Author: In Defense of Marriage, 1981; (with other) Test Your Marriage IQ, 1984, Test Your Success IQ, 1985, The Last Sick Generation, 2000; contbr. articles to profl. jours.; numerous TV appearances including Phil Donahue, 1988, Oprah Winfrey 1984. Grant Found. grantee, 1970. Fellow Am. Psychiat. Assn. (disting. life); mem. AMA, Westchester Psychiat. Assn. (sec. 1982-85, chmn. fellowship com. 1989-98). Avocations: travel, international affairs. Home and Office: SchoolofHealth.com 123 E 75th St Ste 10B New York NY 10021 Office Phone: 212-426-5605. Office Fax: 212-828-2507. Business E-Mail: jpolenz@nyc.rr.com.

POLESKIE, STEPHEN FRANCIS, retired art educator, artist, writer, publisher; b. Pringle, Pa., June 3, 1938; s. Stephen Francis and Antoinette Elizabeth (Chludzinski) P.; m. Jeanne Mackin, 1979. BS, Wilkes Coll., 1959; postgrad., New Sch. for Social Research, 1961. Owner Chiron Press, NYC, 1961-68; instr. Sch. Visual Arts, NYC, 1968; prof. art Cornell U., Ithaca, NY, 1969-2001, prof. emeritus, 2001—. Vis. critic Pratt Graphic Arts Center, N.Y.C., 1965-68; vis. artist Colgate U., Hamilton, N.Y., 1973, USSR, 1979, Escuela de Bellas Artes, Honduras, 1980, Loughborough Coll. Art and Design, Eng., 1989; vis. prof. U. Calif., Berkeley, 1976; reviewer in field. Contbr. short stories to mags. and book; one-man shows include Louis K. Meisel Gallery, N.Y.C., 1978-80, Galerie Kupinski, Stuttgart, Germany, 1979, Palace of Culture and Sci., Warsaw, Poland, 1979, Sky Art Presentation, MIT, 1981, Am. Ctr., Belgrade, 1981, William and Mary Coll., 1983, McPherson Art Gallery, Victoria, B.C., Can., 1984, Studio D'Ars, Milan, 1985, Gallery Flaviana, Locarno, Switzerland, 1985, Il Salatto Gallery, Como, Italy, 1985, Galleria Schneider, Rome, 1987, Mus. Sztuki Lodz, Poland, 1987, Alternative Mus., Lido di Spina, Italy, 1987, Galerie Klaus Lea, Munich, 1987, Patricia Carega Gallery, Washington, 1988, Nine Columns Gallery, Palermo, Italy, 1988, John Hansard Gallery, Southampton, Eng., 1989, Quai Art Gallery, Isle of Wight, Eng., 1989, Lee Art Gallery, Clemson (S.C.) U., 1990, Apogeeairway, N.Y.C., 1991, Nine Columns Gallery, Brescia, Italy, 1991, Glenn Curtiss Mus., Hammondsport, N.Y., 1993, Caproni Mus., Trento, Italy, 1995, Temple U., Rome, 1995, Gallery Modern Art, Maribor, Slovenia, 1995, Palazzo Communale, Todi, Italy, 1995, Upstairs Gallery, Ithaca, NY, 2006, Palazzo Della Pretura, Piacenza, Italy, Internat. Art Ctr., Kyoto, Japan, 2006, Terrain Gallery, NYC; represented in collections at Met. Mus., N.Y.C., Mus. Modern Art, N.Y.C., Victoria and Albert Mus., London, Whitney Mus., N.Y.C., Walker Art Ctr., Mpls., Tate Gallery, London, Fort Worth Art Center, Nat. Collection, Washington, State Mus., Lodz, Poland, others; pub. Onager Edits., 2004, publ. The Balloonist The Story of T.S. C. Lowe, 2005. Am. Fedn. of Arts grantee, 1965; Carnegie Found. grantee, 1967; Nat. Endowment for Arts grantee, 1973; N.Y. State Council on Arts grantee, 1973; Creative Artists Public Service Program grantee, 1978; Best Found. grantee, 1985 Home: PO Box 849 Ithaca NY 14851-0849 Office Phone: 877-275-6388. Personal E-mail: onageredítions@aol.com.

POLEVOY, NANCY TALLY, lawyer, social worker, genealogist; b. NYC, May 27, 1944; d. Charles H. and Bernice M. (Gang) Tally; m. Martin D. Polevoy, Mar. 19, 1967; children: Jason Tally, John Gerald. Student, Mt. Holyoke Coll., 1962—64; BA, Barnard Coll., 1966; MSW, Columbia U., 1968, JD, 1986. Bar: N.Y. 1987. Caseworker unmarried mothers' svc. Louise Wise Svcs., NYC, 1967, caseworker adoption dept., 1969-71; caseworker Youth Consultation Svc., NYC, 1968-69; asst. rsch. scientist, psychiat. social worker NYU Med. ctr., NYC, 1973-81; adv. ct. apptd. spl. advs. Manhattan Family Ct., NYC, 1981-82; cons. social work, 1981-86; matrimonial assoc. Ballon, Stoll & Itzler, 1987, Herzfeld & Rubin, P.C., 1987-88; practice NYC. Contbr. articles to profl. jours. Mem. parents' adv. bd. Riverdale Country Sch., 1988—93; mem. outreach bd. Manhattan divsn. United Jewish Appeal Fedn., 1990—94, exec. bd. Manhattan divsn., 1992—94, mem. met. campaign cabinet, 1994—95, mem. task force aging, 2004—; trustee Jewish Assn. Svcs. to Aged, 1996—, v.p., 1999—2003; bd. dirs. Ctr. Jewish History, 1996—; archives com. Ctrl. Synagogue, 1991—2005, chair, 1994—2005; trustee Am. Jewish Hist. Soc., 1992—, asst. treas., 1995—98, v.p., 1998—2003, 2005—. Recipient French Govt. prize, 1963, honor for lifetime cmty. svc., United Jewish Appeal Fedn. N.Y., 2003. Mem.: NASW, Acad. Cert. Social Workers, N.Y. State Bar Assn., Assn. Bar City of N.Y., Barnard Coll. Alumni Assn. (v.p. 1966, class pres. 1966 1996—). Home and Office: 1155 Park Ave New York NY 10128-1209

POLEWAY, CHRISTOPHER J., former publishing executive; b. Bklyn., 1958; m. Poleway; 2 children. BA, St. Bonaventure Univ., Olean, NY; MBA, Fordham Univ. Mgr. fin. sys. HBO, 1982—88; gen. mgr. Corp. Fin. Reporting, 1988—91; Circulation Planning Mgr. Fortune, 1991—92, asst, bus. mgr., 1992—94, advertising bus. mgr., 1994—97, dir. of fin. and op., 1997—99, v.p. and gen. mgr., 1999—2000, chief op. officer, 2000—01; pres. Fortune/Money Group, 2001—07.

POLFLIET, SARAH JEAN, physician; b. Austin, Minn., July 4, 1975; d. Richard John and Charlotte Bertha Polfliet. BS in Physiology, U. Calif., Santa Barbara, 1998; MD, U. Va., Charlottesville, 2002; MD in Psychiat., Law, U. Calif., San Francisco, 2006. DEA Certification Med. Bd. of Calif., 2003, lic. MD Med. Bd. of Calif., 2003. Sec. in cmty. rels. U. Calif., 1997—98, asst. instr. of biology lab., 1998, resident physician San Francisco, 2002—06; physician Schuman-Liles Cmty. Psychiatry Clinic, Oakland, Calif., 2003—06; pvt. practice in psychiat. and psychopharmacology, San Francisco, 2006—; chief resident intensive svcs. Langley Ptnr. Psychiat. Inst., 2006. Rsch. asst. U. Va., Dept. of Psychiatry, Charlottesville, Va., 1999; co-leader for long-term women's depression group U. Calif., San Francisco, 2004—, psychiatry physician, women's mood and hormone clinic, 2004—05, jr. attending, 2005—, rsch. co-investigator, dept. psychiatry, 2005—; psychiatry physician, women's high-risk obstetric clinic San Francisco Gen. Hosp., 2004—05. Contbr. numerous articles and presentation to profl. jours. and confs.; author: Where Do Seagulls Go at Night, 2003. Vol. for cmty. outreach program St. Thomas Aquinas Ch., Charlottesville, Va., 1998—2002; vol. Magic Cir. Protective Shelters, Charlottesville, Va., 1999—2002; med. student selection com. U. of Va., Sch. of Medicine, 2001—02; vol. spkr. Med. Youth Soc., San Francisco, 2003—06; vol. St. Elizabeth's Ho. for Battered Women, 2006—. Recipient Julius R. Krevans award for Clin. Excellence, U. Calif., San Francisco, 2003, Pathology Honors, U. Va., Sch. of Medicine, 1999—2000, Edwin Alston award, U. Calif. San Francisco Psychiatric Residency Program, 2006; Bowman's scholarship, U. Va., Sch. of Medicine, 1999—2000, Forensic Fellow, U. Calif. San Francisco, Psychiatry and Law Program, 2006—07. Fellow: Am. Psychiat. Assn. (hon.); mem.: Am. Assn. Psychiat. and Law, U. Calif., Santa Barbara, Alumni Assn. (hon.), Alpha Omega Alpha (hon.), Assn. Women Psychiatrists (hon.), No. Calif. Psychiat. Assn. (hon.), U. Va., Sch. of Medicine, Alumni Assn. (hon.). Achievements include research in evaluating training of psychiatry residents about neuroleptic medications; rural suicide outreach programs in Virginia, including composition of suicide outreach survey and meta-analysis of data to further assist tele-psychiatry program.

POLHAMUS, BARBARA, nutritionist, educator; d. Helen and Leslie Polhamus. PhD, MPH, U. N.C., Chapel Hill, 1991—97. Registered dietitian Am. Dietetic Assn., 1982. Nutrition dir. Dorchester Ho. Multi-Svc. Ctr., Mass., 1982—84; nutrition dir., maternal and child health Mass. Dept. Pub. Health, Boston, 1984—91; rsch. assoc. U. N.C., Chapel Hill, 1998—2000; nutritionist CDC, Nat. Ctr. for Chronic Disease Prevention and Health Promotion, Divsn. Nutrition and Phys. Activity, Atlanta, 2000—. Tech. cons., Ukraine micronutrient survey CDC, Atlanta, 2002. Contbr. chapters to books, articles to profl. jours., sci. material for web sites. Recipient award of Excellence Pub. Health Tng. and Nutrition Team award, 2005; fellow, Dannon Inst., 1998; grantee, Inst. Nutrition, 1994. Mem.: APHA (elected sect. mem. 2002—04). Liberal. Avocations: yoga, hiking, travel. Office: CDC 4770 Buford Hwy NE MS K-25 Atlanta GA 30341 Personal E-mail: bfp9@cdc.gov.

POLI, KENNETH JOSEPH, editor, writer, photographer; b. Bklyn., June 8, 1921; s. Joseph H. and Irene (Seeman) P.; m. Virginia Osk, Dec. 14, 1946; 1 child, Bruce. Student, Goddard Coll., 1938-40. Writer, photographer North Atlantic Area Office ARC, NYC, 1946-49. Editorial cons., 1965— Author Critical Focus Column, 1972-83; editor: External House Mags., Internat. Nickel Co., N.Y.C., 1949-53, Leica Photography mag., E. Leitz, Inc., N.Y.C., 1953-65; assoc. editor Popular Photography mag., Ziff-Davis Pub. Co., N.Y.C., 1965-68, sr. editor, 1968-1970, editor, 1970-83, cons. 1983-87; cons. editor Photography Ann., 35-mm Photography, Photography Directory and Buying Guide, 1970-83; contbr. articles to photog. jours. and encys. With inf. U.S. Army, 1942-45, PTO. Decorated Purple Heart medals, Bronze Star. Mem. Am. Photog. Hist. Soc., Photographic Adminstrs., Circle of Confusion, Mensa. Home and Office: Apt 6167 1 Jefferson Ferry Dr South Setauket NY 11720-4727

POLICANO, ANDREW J., dean, finance educator; b. July 4, 1949; m. Pamela Z. Policano; children: Emily, Keith. BS in math., SUNY, Stony Brook, 1971; MA in economics, Brown U., 1973, PhD in economics, 1976. Asst. prof. U. Iowa, Iowa City, 1975-79, assoc. prof. dept. economics, 1979-81, prof., chair dept. economics, 1984-87, sr. assoc. dean academic affairs, 1987-88; prof. dept. economics Fordham U., NYC, 1981-84, asst. chair, dir. grad. studies, 1982-83; rsch. assoc. Ctr. for Study of Futures Markets Columbia U., NYC, 1982-86; dean divsn. social & behavioral sci. SUNY, Stony Brook, 1988-91; dean Sch. Bus., U. Wis., Madison, 1991—2001, Kuechenmeister Prof. Bus., 2001—04; dean Pual Merage Sch. Bus., U. Calif., Irvine, 2004—, prof. economics/pub. policy, 2004—. Guest prof. Inst. Advanced Studies, Vienna, Austria, 1985; dir. Nat. Guardian Life, Madison, 1991-2004, PIC Wis., 1995-2002, Badger Meter, 1997—; mem. Wis. Glass Ceiling Commn., 1995-2000. Recipient Disting. Alumnus award SUNY, Stony Brook, 1994. Mem. Assn. to Advance Collegiate Schools of Bus. (bd. dirs., 1997-98). Office: U Calif Paul Merage Sch Bus 350 SB Irvine CA 92697-3125 Office Phone: 949-824-8470. Business E-Mail: dean@merage.uci.edu.

POLICINSKI, CHRIS, food products executive; BA, Univ. Notre Dame, 1980; MBA, NYU. Mgmt. positions with Pillsbury Co., Kraft Gen. Foods; v.p. strategy, bus. & internat. develop. Land O'Lakes Inc., Arden Hills, Minn., 1997—99, exec. v.p. COO dairy foods value added group, 1999—2002, exec. v.p., COO dairy foods, 2002—05, pres., CEO, 2005—. Bd. dirs. Grocery Manufacturers Am.; bd. dir. Nat. Milk Prod. Fedn., Nat. Coun. Farmer Cooperatives. Bd. dirs. Greater Twin Cities United Way, Minn. Bus. Partnership; trustee Grad. Inst. Cooperative Leadership. Office: Land O'Lakes Inc 4001 Lexington Ave N Saint Paul MN 55126-2998 Mailing: Land O'Lakes Inc PO Box 64101 Saint Paul MN 55164-0101

POLICINSKI, EUGENE FRANCIS, syndicated columnist, editor, radio and television personality, producer; b. South Bend, Ind., Aug. 31, 1950; s. E.T. and Margaret C. (O'Neill) P.; m. Kathleen Beta O'Donnell Powell, Aug. 19, 1972; children: Ryan, David. Degree in Journalism and Polit. Sci., Ball State U., 1972; student, Nashville Sch. Law, 2005—07. Corr. Gannett News Svc., Washington, 1979-82; Wash. editor USA Today, Arlington, Va., 1982-83, page one editor, 1983-85, mng. editor sports, 1989—96; spl. asst. to chmn./CEO Freedom Forum, Arlington, Va., 1996-98; Wash. editor Freedom Forum website, 1998-99; dep. dir. First Amendment Ctr., Nashville, 1999—2004, exec. dir., 2004—; v.p., 2006—. Host, commentator USA Today Sky Radio, Arlington, 1992—95; host Newseum Radio, 1998—2001; adj. faculty Winthrop U., 1999—; exec. prodr. Speaking Freely (PBS), 2001—05; host Freedom SIngs, 2003—. Founding editor USA Today Baseball Weekly, 1991. Bd. advisors Ctr. Study Sport in Soc., 1995—; trustee US Sports Acad., 1997—2006, Watkins Coll. Art and Design, 2001—04; dir. J-IDEAS program Ball State U., 2003—04. Named one of 100 Most Important People in Sports Sporting News, 1992-93, 95, Sports Person of Yr., U.S. Sports Acad., 1996; named to Journalism Hall of Fame, Ball State U., 1989, Alumni of Yr., 1996. Mem. NATAS (gov. 2004), Am. Soc. Newspaper Editors, Soc. Profl. Journalists, Assn. Educators in Journalism and Mass Comms. Avocations: sailing, bicycling, golf. Office: First Amendment Center Office of Exec Dir 1207 18th Ave S Nashville TN 37212-2807 Home Phone: 615-460-9314; Office Phone: 615-727-1600. Business E-Mail: gpolicinski@fac.org.

POLICY, CARMEN A., professional sports team executive; b. Youngstown, Ohio, Jan. 26, 1943; s. Albert and Ruby (Tisone) P.; m. Aug. 8, 1964 (div. Mar. 1989); children: James, Daniel, Edward, Kerry, Kathy; m. Gail Marie Moretti, June 27, 1991. Grad., Youngstown State U., 1963; JD, Georgetown U., 1966. Bar: Ohio 1966, Va. 1966, D.C. 1966. Assoc. Nadler & Nadler, Youngstown, 1966-68; asst. prosecutor City of Youngstown, 1968-69; ptnr. Flask & Policy, Weimer & White, Youngstown, 1969-90; spl. counsel to atty. gen. State of Ohio, 1970-91; v.p., gen. counsel San Francisco 49ers, NFL, 1983-90, pres., 1990-99; pres., CEO & co-owner Cleve. Browns, 1998—2004, consultant, 2004—. Mem. various coms. NFL, 1990—; bd. dirs. World League Am. Football, N.Y.C., 1991—. Com. mem. various charities, Youngstown, 1969-90, San Francisco, 1990—. Mem. Va. Bar Assn., Ohio Bar Assn., D.C. Bar Assn. Roman Catholic. Avocations: scuba diving, hiking.

POLICY, VINCENT MARK, lawyer; b. Warren, Ohio, Mar. 29, 1948; s. Vincent James and Anna Marie (Berardi) P.; m. Katherine Anne Veazey; children: Nicholas, Katherine Nicole. BA, U. Md., 1970; JD, Georgetown U., 1973. Bar: N.Y. 1974, D.C. 1975, U.S. Supreme Ct. 1977. Assoc. Cahill Gordon & Reindel, Washington and NYC, 1973-78, Hogan & Hartson, Washington, 1978-85; prin. Pohoryles & Greenstein PC, Washington, 1985-89, Greenstein, Delorme & Luchs, P.C., Washington, 1989—. Author: Speedy Trial, A Constitutional Right in Search of Definition, 1973. Mem. D.C. Bar Assn. (chmn. rental housing com. 1985-88), D.C. Assn. Realtors (speaker 1984—), Apt. and Office Bldg. Assn. (lectr. 1985—), Greater Washington Bd. Trade (subcom. on initiatives, econ. growth com.), D.C. Builders Assn. (legis. affairs com.), Phi Beta Kappa, Omicron Delta Kappa. Lodges: KC. Democrat. Roman Catholic. Avocation: sailing. Office: Greenstein DeLorme & Luchs 1620 L St NW Ste 900 Washington DC 20036-5613

POLILLO, RONALD R., federal official; b. Honolulu, Mar. 25, 1949; s. John F. and Dolores T. Polillo; m. Marion E. Lapworth, June 16, 1983; m. Karen E. Rickards, Sept. 18, 1971 (div. Feb. 21, 1981); children: William Thomas Schweitzer, Albert M., Mazie L. Alimenti, Kimberly A., Jennifer L. BS in Math. Scis., Fla. Inst. Tech., 1972; M in Aviation Mgmt., Embry Riddle Aero. U., 1984. Mathematician U.S. Army Ft. Belvoir, Ft. Belvoir, Va., 1974—75; mathematician, divsn. mgr. FAA, WJH Technical Center, NJ, 1975—96, aviation security lab facility mgr., 2000—01, security integrated product team lead Washington, 1996—2000; transp. security lab facility mgr. Transp. Security Adminstrn., WJH Technical Center, 2001—04; v.p. homeland security and defense Hi-Tec Systems, Inc., Egg Harbor Township, NJ, 2004—. Contbr. articles to profl. jours. Hon. comdr. USAF 105th Aeroport Squadron, McGuire AFB, NJ, 2001—03; pres. Jersey Cape Region, Antique Automobile Club Am., Ocean City, NJ, 1983—86. Recipient Outstanding Performance awards, U.S. Govt., 1975—2004; scholar, Rotary Club, 1967. Mem.: NRA (life), Air Traffic Control Assn. (assoc.), Game Preserve Estell Manor (chmn. membership com., co-chair of arrangements committe 2002—06), North Am. Hunting Club (life), Pi Kappa Alpha (chief justice and steward 1968—72). Republican. Roman Catholic. Avocations: hunting, fishing, shooting sports, antique car restoration, travel. Home: 6140 Robin Dr Mays Landing NJ

08330 Office: Hi-Tec Systems Inc Ste 108 500 Scarborough Dr Egg Harbor Township NJ 08234 Home Phone: 609-625-4918; Office Phone: 609-272-1515. Office Fax: 609-272-1888; Home Fax: 609-272-1888. Business E-Mail: ron.polillo@hitecsystems.com.

POLIMENI, JOHN MATTHEW, economics professor; b. Schenectady, NY, Nov. 21, 1972; s. John Joseph and Catherine Marie Polimeni. BS in Math., Rensselaer Poly. Inst., 1994; MA in Econs., SUNY, Albany, 1996; PhD in Ecol. Econs., Rensselaer Poly. Inst., 2002. Cert. graduate studies in Econs. NY State Public Svc. Commn. Asst. prof. econs. Albany (N.Y.) Coll. Pharmacy, 2004—. Hon. mem. Scientific Coun. Romanian Nat. Acad. Sci., 2006—. Contbr. Young Faculty Rsch. award, Rensselaer Polytech. Inst., 2004. Fellow Internat. Congress Chemistry and Environ.; mem. Acad. Political Sci., Am. Assn. Advancement of Sci., Am. Econ. Assn., Am. Health Econs. Assn. (charter mem.), Am. Statistical Assn., European Soc. Ecol. Econs., Game Theory Soc., Global Health Edn. Consortium, Internat. Assn. Energy Econs., Internat. Health Econ. Assn., Internat. Soc. Ecol. Econ., Internat. Studies Assn., Soc. European Anthropology, Soc. Industrial and Applied Maths., US Assn. Energy Econs., US SOc. Ecol. Econs. (charter mem.). Presbyterian. Office: Albany Coll Pharmacy 106 New Scotland Ave Albany NY 12208

POLIMENI, REBECCA H., special education educator; b. Albertson, NY, Dec. 13, 1973; d. Vincent and Joan M Polimeni. BA in psychology, Hofstra U., 1995—97; MA in spl. edn., Columbia U., 1999—2001. Tchr. asst. Devel. Disabilities Inst., Young Autism Program, Smithtown, NY, 1997—98; home tutor and parent trainer Pvt. Practice, NY, 1997—; tchr. cons. Autism Help Ctr., Medford, NY, 2000—01; program coord. Devel. Disabilities Inst., Young Autism Program, Ronkonkoma, NY, 2001—03; behavior cons. LI Devel. Cons., Lake Grove, NY, 2003—; behavior consultation Pvt. Practice, NY, 2004—. Staff devel. spkr. LI Devel. Consulting and Pvt. Practice, 2003—. Recipient Adele Leonard Endowed Prize for excellence in Linguistics, Hofstra U., 1997, Provost's Scholar, Hosftra U., 1997, Dean's List, Hofstra U., 1995—97; Academic scholarship, 1995. Mem.: Counsel for Exceptional Children, Psi Chi Nat. Honor Soc., Golden Key Nat. Honor Soc. Independent. Avocations: travel, writing, music, outdoor activities, exercise. Home Phone: 516-922-9462. Personal E-mail: autad@cs.com.

POLIN, ALAN JAY, lawyer; b. NYC, Sept. 5, 1953; s. Mortin and Eleanor (Clarke) P.; m. Sharon Lynn Hirschfeld, Oct. 10, 1976; children: Jay Michael, Meryl Beth. Student, Cornell U., 1971—74; BA cum laude, Seton Hall U., 1978; JD, Nova U., 1981. Bar: Fla. 1981, N.Y. 1990; lic. athlete agt. Fla., life, health and variable annuities agt. Fla., mortgage broker Fla. Assoc. Berryhill, Avery, Williams & Jordan, Esq., Ft. Lauderdale, Fla., 1981-82, Greenspoon & Marder, P.A., Miami, Fla., 1982-83; pvt. practice Ft. Lauderdale, 1983-86; ptnr. Mousaw, Vigdor, Reeves & Hess, Ft. Lauderdale, 1986-90; pvt. practice Coral Springs, Fla., 1990—. Adj. faculty mem. Nova U; mem. grievance com. Fla. Bar, 1989-92, vice chair, 1990-91, chair, 1991-92. Chmn. Broward County Crct. Ct. Handbook, 1988; contbr. chpt. to Bridge the Gap Attorney's Handbook, 1987. Vice chmn. Fla. Intergovtl. Fin. Commn., 2001—02; mem. exec. com. Broward County Dem., 1989—96; vice mayor City of Coral Springs, 1994—96, 2002—04, commr., 1991—2004; chmn. Fla. Intergovtl. Fin. Commn., 2002—04; commr. Town of Hillsboro Beach, 2006—; dir. Temple Beth Am., Margate, Fla., 1991—93; bd. dirs. Fla. Regional Bd. of Anti-Defamation League, 1994—, Children's Cardiac Rsch. Found., Inc., 1996—2007, The Irving Fryer Found., Inc., 1995—96, Am. Heart Assn., 1997—, Jr. Achievement So. Fla., 2001—04; bd. dirs. cmty. redevelopment agy. City of Coral Springs, 2004—06. Recipient Am. Jurisprudence award Nova U. Law Ctr., 1981, Disting. Pub. Svc. award, Anti-Defamation League, 2000. Mem. Fla. Bar Assn. (bd. govs. young lawyers divsn. 1987-89), Broward County Bar Assn. (exec. com. young lawyers sect. 1986-87), North Broward Assn. Realtors, Inc. (affiliate, std. contract forms com. 1989-95, atty./realtor rels. com. 1989-91), Kiwanis (Key Club advisor 1990-91). Office: 3300 University Dr Ste 304 Coral Springs FL 33065-4132 Business E-Mail: alanpolin@polinlaw.com.

POLIN, JANE L., foundation official; b. NYC, Sept. 30, 1958; BA, Wesleyan U., Middletown, Conn., 1980; MBA, Columbia U., 1988. Asst. dir. ann. giving Wesleyan U., 1980—82; centennial fund assoc. Met. Opera Assn., NYC, 1982—84; devel. officer Columbia U., NYC, 1984—88; program mgr., comptr. GE Fund, Fairfield, Conn., 1988—99; v.p. cmty. devel. and corp. affairs Sperry & Hutchinson, Inc., 1999—2000, philanthropic advisor, 2001—; bd. dirs. Fred Friendly Seminars, 2005—. Panelist arts-in-edn. Nat. Endowment for Arts, Washington, 1989—90, 1994—95, NEH, 1997; adv. bd. mem. ARC, 1991—99, United Way Am., 1991—99, Inst. for Internat. Econs., 1995—99, Young Audiences, NYC, 1991—2000, mem. Advt. Coun., 1998—2003; judge Frances Hesselbein Cmty. Innovation Fellows Program, 2001—02, Peter F. Drucker Award for Nonprofit Innovation, 1996—2000. Mem.: Alpha Delta Phi. Home and Office: 67 Riverside Dr Apt 7D New York NY 10024-6136 Fax: 212-873-1568. Personal E-mail: janepolin@aol.com.

POLINER, GARY A., corporate financial executive; Joined as atty. Northwestern Mutual Life Ins. Co., Milw., 1977, sr. v.p., CFO, sr. v.p., CFO, chief investment officer, 2007—. Office: Northwestern Mutual 720 E Wisconsin Ave Milwaukee WI 53202-4797 *

POLINER, JASON M., lawyer; b. NYC, Oct. 1, 1954; BA, SUNY, Binghamton, 1976; JD, SUNY, Buffalo, 1979. Bar: NY 1980, US Dist. Ct. So. & Ea. Districts NY 1992. Ptnr. Wilson, Elser, Moskowitz, Edelman & Dicker LLP, NYC, Albany. Office: Wilson Elser Moskowitz Edelman & Dicker LLP 23rd Fl 150 E 42nd St New York NY 10017-5639 Office Phone: 212-490-3000 ext. 2204. Office Fax: 212-490-3038. Business E-Mail: polinerj@wemed.com.

POLING, KERMIT WILLIAM, minister; b. Elkins, W.Va., Oct. 1, 1941; s. Durward Willis and Della Mae (Boyles) P.; m. Patricia Ann Groves, June 12, 1965; children: David Edward Elson, Mikael Erik. Diploma in Bible, Am. Bible Sch., 1966; BA in Bible, Reed Coll. Religion, 1968; AA, W.Va. U., 1970; ThD, Zion Theol. Sem., 1971; postgrad., Wesley Theol. Sem., 1974; LLD, Geneva Theol. Coll., 1980; DSL (hon.), Berean Christian Coll., 1981; postgrad., Mansfield Coll., U. Oxford, Eng., 1986, Mansfield Coll., U. Oxford, 1990, postgrad., 1991; D Ecumenical Rsch., St. Ephrem's Inst. for Oriental Studies, 1989; BRE, Am. Bible Coll., 1991; M of Herbology, Emerison Coll., 1994. Ordained to ministry United Meth. Ch., 1967. Pastor Parkersburg-Crossroads (W.Va.) Cir., 1967-70; asst. sec. W.Va. Ann. Conf., 1967-69; pastor Hope-Halleck Morgantown Cir., 1970-76, Trinity-Warren Grafton (W.Va.) Charge, 1976-83, 1st Trinity Pennsboro (W.Va.) Charge, 1983-97, South Parkersburg United Meth. Ch., 1997—2004. Editor local ch. news; instr. Bible Bodkin Bible Inst., 1975-75, United Meth. Lay Acad., 1992—2004; mem. staff Taylor County Coop. Parish, 1976-83; coord. Hughes River Coop. Parish, 1983-86; mem. chaplains com. Grafton City Hosp., 1976-82; mem. coun. Ctr. d'Etudes et d'Action Oecumeniques, 1972-74; bishop in Partibus of Tayma. Author: A Crown of Thorns, 1963, A Silver Message, 1964, History of the Halleck Church, 1970, Eastern Rite Catholicism, 1971, From Brahmin to Bishop, 1976, Cult and Occult: Data and Doctrine, 1978, The Value of Religious Education in Ancient Traditional Churches, 1993, Anniversary History of Trinity Church, Pennsboro, 1997; editor: Jane's Heirs; contbr. articles and poems to religious jours. Decorated Royal Afghanistan Order of Crown of Amanullah, Royal Order of the Golden Eagle of Napoca, Byzantine Order of Leo the Armenian, Order of Polonia Resitutia, Mystical Order of St. Peter, knight Grand Cross of the Order of St. Dennis of Zante, companion Naval Order of U.S.; recipient Good Citizenship award Doddridge County, 1954, Silver medal Ordre Universel du Merit Humain, Geneva, 1973, Commendation for Outstanding Achievement in Ministry, Ohio Ho. of Reps., 1988; recipient U.S. Heritage award, 2002; named Chief of Dynastic Ho. of Polanie-Patrikios, 1988, Prince of the Holy Roman Empire, 2005. Mem. SAR, Assn. Bible Tchrs. (founder), Internat. Platform Assn., Naval Order U.S., Sovereign Order St. John Jerusalem, Ritchie County Ministerial Assn. (pres. 1984-97), Order Sacred Cup, Knights of Malta, Order of the Crown of Lauriers. Home: 101 E Myles Ave Pennsboro WV 26415

POLINSKY, JANET NABOICHECK, retired state official, retired state legislator; b. Hartford, Conn., Dec. 6, 1930; d. Louis H. and Lillian S. Naboicheck; m. Hubert N. Polinsky, Sept. 21, 1958 (div.); children: Gerald, David, Beth. BA, U. Conn., 1953; postgrad., Harvard Bus. Sch., 1954. Mem. Waterford 2d Charter Commn. (Conn.), 1967-68, Waterford Conservation Commn., 1968-69; Waterford rep. Town Meeting, 1969-71, S.E. Conn. Regional Planning Agy., 1971-73; mem. Waterford Planning and Zoning Commn., 1970-76, chmn., 1973-76; mem. Waterford Dem. Town Com., 1976-92. Del. State Dem. Conv., 1976, 78, 80, 82, 84, 86, 90, 92; mem. Conn. Ho. of Reps. from 38th Dist., 1977-82, asst. majority leader, 1981-83, chmn. appropriations com., 1983-85, 87-89, ranking mem., 1985-87, minority whip, 1985-86, dep. spkr., 1989-92; dep. commr. dept. adminstrv. svcs. State of Conn., 1993-94, chmn., 1994-95, asst. sec. of state, 1995, commr. utilities ctrl. auth., 1995-97. Trustee Eugene O'Neill Meml. Theatre Ctr., 1973—76, 1981—92; corporator Lawrence and Meml. Hosps., 1987—88; mem. New Eng. Bd. Higher Edn., 1981—83; mem. fiscal affairs com. Ea. Conf. Coun. State Govts., 1983—88; mem. Limoge Village Bd., 2000—02; sec. Cascades Master bd., 2000—07, 2002—07. Named Woman of Yr., Waterford Jr. Women's Club, 1977, Nehantic Women's Bus. and Profl. Club, 1979, Legislator of Yr., Conn. Libr. Assn., 1980. Mem. Order of Women Legislators, Delta Kappa Gamma (hon.). Home: 7141 Haviland Cir Boynton Beach FL 33437-6463 Personal E-mail: naboi1@aol.com.

POLIS, MICHAEL PHILIP, engineering educator; b. NYC, Oct. 24, 1943; s. Max and Sylvia (Goldner) P.; m. Claudette Martin, May 28, 1966; children: Melanie Bobby, Martin Pascal, Karine Melissa. BSEE, U. Fla., 1966; MSEE, Purdue U., West Lafayette, Ind., 1968, PhD, 1972. Grad. instr. elec. engring. Purdue U., West Lafayette, 1966-71; postdoctoral fellow Ecole Polytechnique, Montreal, 1972-73, asst. prof. elec. engring., 1973-74, assoc. prof., 1974-82, prof., 1982-83; program dir. sys. theory NSF, Washington, 1983-87; chmn. dept. elec. and computer engring. Wayne State U., Detroit, 1987-93; dean Sch. Engring. and Computer Sci. Oakland U., Rochester, Mich., 1993-2001, prof. elec. and systems engring., 2001—. Expert witness various law firms, 1989—; cons. Mich. Bell-Ameritech, Detroit, 1989-95, ICAM Technologies, Inc., Montreal, 1981-83; vis. rsch. assoc. LAAS, Toulouse, France, 1978. Contbr. articles to profl. jours. Mem. IEEE (sr.), IEEE Control Sys. Soc. (bd. govs. 1993-95, 98-2000, Best Paper Trans. on Automatic Control 1974-75, Disting. Mem. 1993, v.p. mem. activities 1990-91, assoc. editor 1981-82). Office: Oakland Univ Sch Engring & Computer Sci Rochester MI 48309-4778 Home Phone: 313-886-5089; Office Phone: 248-370-2743.

POLISH, SHELDON S., lawyer; b. Cleve., Feb. 14, 1943; BS in Acctg., Ohio State U., 1965; JD, Cleve. State U., 1969. CPA Fla., 1974; bar: Ohio 1969, Fla. 1974. Dir. tax., office mng. ptnr. Ernst & Young, Ft. Lauderdale, Fla.; shareholder, chmn. Ft. Lauderdale tax dept. Greenberg Traurig, P.A.; shareholder Berger Singerman, Ft. Lauderdale, Fla., 2003—. Named one of Top 100 Attys., Worth mag., 2005, Top Lawyers in Tax, Estates and Trusts, South Fla. Legal Guide, 2005—07; recipient Pres.'s award for Outstanding Svc. to the Jewish Fedn., Cmty. Svc. award, Jewish Cmty. Ctr., Esther Lowenthal Cmty. Svc. award, Jewish Fedn. Young Leadership award. Mem.: Fla. Inst. CPA, AICPA, Fla. Bar Assn., ABA, Greater Ft. Lauderdale Tax Coun. Office: Berger Singerman 350 E Las Olas Blvd Ste 1000 Fort Lauderdale FL 33301 Office Phone: 957-712-5132. E-mail: spolish@bergersingerman.com.

POLISI, JOSEPH WILLIAM, academic administrator; b. NYC, Dec. 30, 1947; m. Elizabeth Polisi; 3 children. BA in Polit. Sci., U. Conn., 1969; MA in Internat. Relations, Tufts U., 1970, MusM, 1973, M of Mus. Arts, 1975; DMA, Yale U., 1980; DHL (hon.), Ursinus Coll., Collegetown, Pa., 1986; MusD (hon.), Curtis Inst. Music, 1990; DMA, New England Conservatory Music, 2001; DHL (hon.), Juilliard Sch., 2005; DFA (hon.), Fordham U., Bronx, NY, 2006. Exec. officer Yale Sch. of Music, New Haven, 1976-80; dean of faculty Manhattan Sch. of Music, NYC, 1980-83; dean Coll. Conservatory of Music U. Cin., 1983-84; pres. The Juilliard Sch., NYC, 1984—. Spkr. in field. Performances as bassoonist throughout the U.S.; contbr. articles to various publs. in U.S. and France; author: The Artist as Citizen, 2005. Dir. Edward John Noble Foundation, Irene Diamond Fund. Named Educator of Yr., Musical Am. Internat. Dir. Performing Arts, 2005. Mem.: Royal Acad. Music London (hon.). Office: Juilliard Sch Office of Pres 60 Lincoln Center Plz New York NY 10023-6588

POLITAN, NICHOLAS H., lawyer; b. 1961; BA, Duke U., 1983; JD, Stanford U., 1986. Bar: Calif. 1986, D.C. 1999, N.Y. 2000. Ptnr. Bingham McCutchen LLP, NYC, co-chmn. project fin. practice group. Mem.: ABA-comml. fin. svc. com. Office: Gibson Dunn & Cratcher 200 Park Ave New York NY 10166-0193 Office Phone: 212-705-7726, 212-351-2616. Office Fax: 212-752-5378. Business E-Mail: nick.politan@bingham.com, npolitan@gibsondunn.com.

POLITE, EVELYN C., retired elementary school educator, evangelist; b. Pineland, SC, Dec. 25, 1937; d. Martin and Mary Brantley Coger; m. Horace Polite, Jan. 1, 1958 (dec. Jan. 1987); children: Horace Lenton, Tracy Polite Floyd. BS, Allen U., 1960; M in Elem. Edn., Armstrong-Savannah (Ga.) State U., 1976; cert. specialist of arts in theology, Zoe U., Jacksonville, Fla., 2000; PhD in Christian Counseling, Zoe U., 2001. Tchr. math. Beaufort County Bd. Edn., Bluffton, SC, 1960—61, Florence County Bd. Edn., Florence, SC, 1961—63, Jasper County Bd. Edn., Ridgeland, SC, 1963—64, 1991—92, Savannah Pub. Schs., 1964—90; math. tutor Dept. Family and Children, Savannah, 1992—94; ret., 1994. Test-item writer Ednl. Testing Svc., Princeton, NJ, 1990; dir. Widows Harvest Ministries, Savannah, Ga.; care and counseling min. Coastal Cathedral Ch. of God. Pres. 42d St Civic Club, Savannah, 2000—03; exec. v.p. Cuyler-Brownsville Neighborhood Orgn., Savannah, 2001—02; chmn. bd. dirs. House of Hope Cmty. Outreach Ctr. Recipient Outstanding Tchr. award, Math.-Sci. Roundtable, Atlanta, 1990. Mem. Ch. Of God. Avocations: world missions, travel, physical fitness, reading Christian literature. Office: Coastal Cathedral Ch of God 2208 E DeRenne Ave Savannah GA 31406 Home: 33 Wild Heron Villas Rd Savannah GA 31419-8981 Office Phone: 912-354-5225. Personal E-mail: evelyn33@bellsouth.net.

POLITI, BETH KUKKONEN, publishing services company executive; b. Englewood, NJ, Sept. 18, 1949; d. Andrew and Beatrice G. (Druskin) Kukkonen; m. Joseph Politi, Oct. 21, 1982; children: Andrew, Joseph. BS in Mktg., Miami U., Oxford, Ohio, 1971. Media buyer Schwab, Beatty & Porter, Inc., 1971-72; media planner Adler, Schwartz & Connes, 1972-73; media buyer/planner Schwab Beatty divsn. Marstellar, 1973-74; dir. insert advt. Benjamin Co., Inc., Elmsford, N.Y., 1975-78, prodn. mgr., 1978-80, v.p. client svcs., 1980-83, editor supr., 1979-83; v.p. Bergen County Profl. Svcs., Ft. Lee, NJ, 1983—2007; pres. MarketValue Appraisal Svcs, Inc., 2007—. Assoc. pub. Benjamin Co., Inc., 1981—83; freelance proofreader Montage Media, Mahwah, NJ, 1999—2003. Trustee bd. edn. Pascack Valley Regional HS Dist., 1999—; v.p. Pascack Valley Regional H.S. Dist., 2002—06, pres., 2006—; dist. fee artibration com. Office of Atty. Ethics of Supreme Ct. NJ, 2001—05, ethics com., 2006—; tax assessor Borough Bogota, NJ, 2004—; del. exec. com. Bergen County Sch. Bd. Assn., 2003—, v.p. exec. com., 2005—06, pres., 2006—. Home: 4 Smoke Rise Ct Montvale NJ 07645-1139

POLITZ, NYLE ANTHONY, lawyer; b. Lake Charles, La., May 7, 1953; s. Henry Anthony and Jane Marie (Simoneaux) P.; m. Teresa; children: Brandon, Jared, Caroline. Student, La. State U., Shreveport, 1971-72, U. Guadalajara, 1972, La. State U., 1972-74, JD, 1977. Bar: La. 1978, U.S. Dist. Ct. (ea., mid. and we. dists.) La. 1978, U.S. Ct. Appeals (5th cir.) 1979. Assoc. Booth, Lockard, Jack, Pleasant & LeSage, Shreveport, La., 1978-79; ptnr. Booth, Lockard, Politz, LeSage & D'Anna, L.L.C., Shreveport, 1979-96; assoc. Pendley Law Firm, Plaquemine, La., 1996-98; ptnr. Jones, Odom, Davis & Politz, LLP, Shreveport, 1998—. Lectr. La. State U., Shreveport, Shreveport Police Acad. Resolutions com. La. Dem. Party, 1980; bd. dirs. Liberty Bank & Trust, Greenwood, La., 1980-86. Mem.: ABA, Shreveport Bar Assn. (exec. com. 1983—85, 1993—94, bd. dirs. pro bono project, chmn. 1993—94), La. Assn. Justice (bd. govs. 1983—94), La. State Bar Assn. (ho. of dels. 1986—98, 2000—), Am. Assn. Justice, KC. Democrat. Roman Catholic. Avocations: whitetail deer and wild turkey hunting, golf. Office: Jones Odom et al PO Box 1320 Shreveport LA 71164-1320 Office Phone: 318-221-1600. Business E-Mail: nyle.politz@jodplaw.com.

POLITZER, HUGH DAVID, physicist, educator; b. NYC, Aug. 31, 1949; s. Alan A. and Valerie T. (Diamant) P. BS, U. Mich., 1969; PhD, Harvard U., 1974. Jr. fellow Harvard U. Soc. Fellows, 1974-77; mem. faculty Calif. Inst. Tech., 1977—, prof. theoretical physics, 1979—, exec. officer for physics, 1986-88. Recipient J.J. Sakurai prize, 1986; fellow NSF, 1969-74, Sloan Found., 1977-81, Woodrow Wilson grad. fellow, 1969-74, Guggenheim fellow, 1997-98; co-recipient High Energy and Particle Physics prize European Phys. Soc., 2003, Nobel Prize in Physics, 2004. Mem. Phi Beta Kappa. Achievements include discovery of asymptotic freedom in the theory of the strong interaction. Office: Calif Inst Tech High Energy Physics 1201 E California Blvd Mail Code 452-48 Pasadena CA 91106-3368 Business E-Mail: politzer@theory.caltech.edu.

POLK, DAVID BRENT, pediatrician, educator; BS in Chemistry and Biology summa cum laude, Ouachita U., 1980; MD, U. Ark., Little Rock, 1984. Diplomate Am. Bd. of Pediat., 1999. Dean's prof. of pediat. and cell and devel. biology Vanderbilt U., Nashville, 1990—. Office: Vanderbilt University 2215 Garland Ave MRBIV 1025 Nashville TN 37232 Office Phone: 615-322-7449. Office Fax: 615-343-5323. E-mail: d-brent.polk@vanderbilt.edu.

POLK, DENNIS, electronics executive; BS acctg., Santa Clara Univ. CPA. Audit mgr. Grant Thornton LLP; fin. mgmt. positions from corp. contr. to sr. v.p., CFO Savoir Technology Group Inc., 1995—2000; v.p. fin. DoveBid Inc., 2000—01; sr. v.p. corp. fin., CFO SYNNEX Corp., Fremont, Calif., 2002—06, CFO, COO, 2006—07, COO, 2007—. Office: SYNNEX Corp 44201 Nobel Dr Fremont CA 94538-3178 *

POLK, GEORGE WASHINGTON, telecommunications executive, entrepreneur; b. Washington, Apr. 21, 1963; s. William Roe and Ann (Cross) P. BA, Harvard U., 1985. Fin. analyst Merrill Lynch Capital Mkts., NYC, 1986-87, asst. to chmn., 1987-88; v.p., corp. devel. Wave Systems Corp., NYC, 1988-90; pres. EP Systems Corp., Rolling Meadows, Ill., 1990-93; sr. v.p., internat. networks Geotek Comm., Montvale, N.J., 1994-98; pres. Global Wireless Holdings (Latin Am.), London, 1998-2000; CEO & founder The Cloud Inc., 2003—. Dir. Colourpath Ltd., London, 1993—. Bd. govs. Middle East Inst., Washington, 1997—; mem. nominating com. George Polk Awards, N.Y.C., 1992—; mem. Coun. on Fgn. Rels. Fellow Royal Geographic Soc., Royal Inst. Internat. Affairs; mem. Internat. Mobile Telecomm. Assn. (vice chmn. 1996-97), Global Tech. Pioneer, World Econ. Forum. Office: The Cloud Networks Ltd 54 bartholomew close London ec1a 7ry England Office Phone: +44 (0)20 7710 6500, 44-720 7225 2800.

POLK, JAMES RAY, journalist; b. Oaktown, Ind., Sept. 12, 1937; s. Raymond S. and Oeta (Fleener) P.; m. Bonnie Becker, Nov. 4, 1962; children: Geoffrey, Amy; m. Cara Bryn Saylor, June 21, 1980; 1 child, Abigail. BA, Ind. U., 1962. With A.P., Indpls., 1962-65, Milw., 1965, Madison, Wis., 1966-67, Washington, 1967-71; investigative reporter Washington Star, 1971-75; correspondent NBC News, Washington, 1975-92; sr. producer CNN Spl. Assignment, 1992—. Pres. Investigative Reporters and Editors, Inc., 1978-80, chmn. bd., 1980-82, nat. coll. chmn., 1983-90. With U.S. Navy, 1955-58. Named to Ind. Journalism Hall of Fame, 1994; recipient Pub. Affairs Reporting award, Am. Polit. Sci. Assn., 1961, Raymond Clapper Meml. award, 1972, 1974, Pulitzer prize for nat. reporting on Watergate, 1974, Sigma Delta Chi award, 1974, Nat. Headliner awards, 2d pl. award TV documentary, 1996, 2003, investigative reporting, 1993, Emmy award for coverage of Oklahoma City bombing, 1996, Ind. U. Disting. Alumni award. Mem. Phi Kappa Psi. Office: CNN Center Atlanta GA 30303

POLK, MALCOLM, chemistry professor; b. Chgo., Feb. 2, 1938; s. Andrew and Irene Mosley; 1 child, Irene. BS in Chemistry, U. Ill., 1960; PhD in Chemistry, U. Pa., 1964. Chemist E.I. DuPont, Wilmington, Del., 1965—67, 1968—72; assoc. prof. Prairie View (Tex.) Coll., 1967—68; polymer chemist U.S. Dept. Interior, Washington, 1982—83; assoc. prof., then prof. Atlanta U., 1973—85, Ga. Inst. Tech., Atlanta, 1984—2003, prof. emeritus, 2003—. Dir. Polymer Rsch. Ctr., Atlanta, 1980—84; mem. com. on liquid crystalline polymers NRC, 1987—89; leader conf. in field. Contbr. chapters to books. Grantee, Polymer Rsch. Ctr., Office Naval Rsch., 1980—84, Nat. Textile Ctr., 1992—95, NIH/MBS, 1978—81. Mem.: Nat. Orgn. Profl. Advancement of Black Chemists and Chem. Engrs. (Outstanding Tchr. award 1990), Fiber Soc., Am. Chem. Soc., Phi Lambda Upsilon. Achievements include invention of multidimentional crosslinear rigid-rod benzobistzole polymer fibers. Avocations: ancient history, travel, cycling, reading, playing cards. Office: Ga Inst Tech Atlanta GA 30332 Office Phone: 404-894-2490. Office Fax: 404-894-8780. E-mail: malcolmp@bellsouth.net.

POLK, MILBRY CATHERINE, writer; b. Oxford, Eng., Feb. 24, 1954; came to U.S., 1956; d. William Roe Polk and Joan Alison Cooledge; m. Phillip Allen Bauman, Sept. 29, 1984; children: Adelaide Elisabeth, Milbry Catherine, Mary Harding. Student, U. London, 1972; BA in Anthropology with honors, Harvard U., 1976. Edn. and spl. projects staff Am. Mus. Natural History, NYC, 1977-79; expedition leader, photographer Nat. Geog. Soc. Exploration of Egyptian Western Desert, Egypt, 1979; staff writer 10964, Palisades, N.Y., 1990—; founder, dir. Virtual Xplorations Web Site, Palisades, 1996—2000. Dir. Wings Trust 1992-2005, Wings WorldQuest, 2004—; comml. photographer; Film Festival; lectr. in field. Founder, asst. dir. and programmer Margaret Mead Film Festival, 1977-79; asst. prodr. (film) Margaret Mead, Portrait of a Friend, 1979, dir. (film retrospective for Mus. of Am. Indian) The Ancestors, 1979; script cons. (feature film) Rollover, 1979; rschr. (TV series) Legacy, 1982; dir. Leathercraft Mus. Project, 1983; project dir., photographer, illustrations editor: The History of Arabian Transportation, 1984-87; founder, dir. Palisades Art Fair, 1989-93; founder, dir. Women Explorers: An Oral History Project, 1991-95; contbr. articles and photographs to mags.; author: Egyptian Mummies, 1997, New Mothers Book, 1987, The Egyptian Door, 1976, Women of Discovery, 2001 (Outstanding Book award Lit. Jour.), Tales Told of the Explorers Club, 2003; author (sch. curriculum) Man Eating Tigers of Sundarbans, 1996; exhibited in group shows at Ceres Gallery, N.Y., 1990-95, Somerstown Gallery, 1991, Schoolhouse, 1991,

Nat. Arts Club, 1988-91, Palisades Art Fair, 1989-93, Thomsen Gallery, 1989-91, The Cathedral of St. John the Divine, 1989, Rockland Ctr. for the Arts, 1988, Wadsworth Athenaeum, Hartford, Conn., 1983, Foto Gallery, N.Y., 1980; editor: Series 6 Biographies of Women Explorers, 2004, Looting of the Baghdad Museum, 2005; contbr. editor, Explorer's Jour., 1999—; prodr.: Wings World Quest, 2003-07 (Women of Discovery award). Founder, trustee Wings World Quest; mem. journalism adv. com. George Polk Awards; mem. bd. visitors N.Y. Acad. Medicine, 1996-00; founder, bd. dirs. InterCulture, Inc., Ft. Worth; bd. dirs. Children's Shakespeare Theatre; exec. coun. N.Y. Hall of Sci.; judge Wesport Youth Festival, Explorers Club; event prodr. Wings Women Discovery awards; mem. Students on Ice-Internat. Polar Year Arctic Youth Expedition, 2007-. Named Outstanding Woman of Yr. 1986, Am. Film Festival; grantee N.Y. State Coun. on Arts, 1979; subject CBS News Documentary They Also Dared, 1996, Gracie Allen award, 21 Leaders of 21st Century award Women's ENews.org, 2003, Womens Environ. Leadership award Unity Coll., 2007. Fellow Royal Can. Geog. Soc., Explorers Club, Soc. Woman Geographers (spl. events com. 1990-93, nat. coun. 1993-96); mem. Nat. Arts Club (bd. govs.), S.Am. Explorers Club, Dutch Treat Club, Piermont Rowing Club (bd. dirs.), Masters Rowing Assoc., Radcliffe Club N.Y. Episcopalian. Home and Office: Wings WorldQuest PO Box 52 Palisades NY 10964-0052 Business E-Mail: milbry@post.harvard.edu. *

POLK, WILLIAM ROE, historian; b. Ft. Worth, Tex., Mar. 7, 1929; m. Joan Alison Cooledge, Dec. 1950; children: Milbry Catherine Polk, Alison Elizabeth Polk; m. Ann Borders Cross, June 9, 1962 (div. Oct. 1979); children: George Washington Polk, Eliza Polk; m. Baroness Elisabeth von Oppenheimer, Dec. 29, 1981. BA with honors, Harvard U., 1951, PhD, 1958; BA with honors, Oxford, Eng., 1955, MA, 1959; LLD (hon.), Lake Forest Coll., 1967. Asst. prof. Harvard Univ., 1956-62; fgn. svc. res. officer class 1, mem. policy planning coun. U.S. State Dept., 1961-65; prof. U. Chgo., 1965-73; pres. Adlai Stevenson Inst., Chgo., 1967-72; sr. dir. W.P. Carey Found.; chmn. EP Systems, NYC, 1990-93, Chaika Oil Co., London and Moscow, 1993-95. Bd. dirs. Hyde Park Bank, Chgo., Microform Data Systems, Arlington Books, Cambridge, Naftex Ltd., Harris & Harris, Morrison Internat. Ltd., The Salzburg Seminar; cons. Aetna Life and Casualty, Time Inc., TWA, Crocker Nat. Bank, Wheelabrator Frye Inc., Fuller Petroleum, GTE, Teledyne, J. Henry Schroder, U.K., Power Corp., Can., Allianz Versicherungs A.G., Germany, Volkswagen A.G., Germany, Flughafen Frankfurt Main A.G., Germany, Louis Féraud & Cie, France, UN Stockholm and Vancouver Confs. on the Environment; lectr. in field. Author: What the Arabs Think, 1952, Backdrop to Tragedy, 1957, The Opening of South Lebanon, 1963, The United States and the Arab World, 1965, The United States and the Arab World, 3rd edit., 1975, Passing Brave, 1973, 1974, The Golden Ode, 1974, 1977, 1993, The Elusive Peace, 1979, The Arab World, 1980, The Arab World Today, 1991, The Vence Partitas, 1992, Neighbors and Strangers: The Fundamentals of Foreign Affairs, 1997, Polk's Folly: An American Family History, 2000, 2001, Understanding Iraq, 2005, 2006, The Birth of America, 2006, 2007, Violent Politics: Insurgency, Guerilla Warfare and Terrorists, 2007; author: (with George McGovern) Out of Iraq: A Practical Plan for Withdrawal Now, 2006; editor: The Civilization of Islam, 1962, 1975, The Developmental Revolution, 1963, The Beginnings of Modernization in the Middle East, 1968; contbr. articles to books and profl. jours. including Fgn. Affairs, N.Y. Rev. Books, The Atlantic, Harper's. Bd. dirs. YMCA C.C., The Middle East Inst. Recipient Medal of Honor, Kingdom of Afghanistan, 1967; fellow Rockefeller Found., 1951-55, Ford Found., 1954, Guggenheim Found., 1961. Mem. The Century Assn., Coun. on Fgn. Rels., Middle East Studies Assn. (bd. dirs.), Soc. of the Cin. Democrat. Avocations: exploration, tennis, sailing, gardening. Home: 669 Chemin de la Sine F-06140 Vence France E-mail: williamrpolk@post.harvard.edu.

POLL, MARTIN HARVEY, film producer; b. NYC. BS, Wharton Sch. Bus. U. Pa., 1943. Exec. producer Theatre Network TV Inc., NYC, 1953; pres. Gold Medal Studios, Bronx, N.Y., 1954-62; ind. producer, 1962—. (Named Hon. Commr. Motion Picture Arts N.Y.C. 1958, recipient David Di Donatello Best Film Producer award Pres. Italy 1968, N.Y. Film Critics award 1968, Hollywood Fgn. Press Assn. Golden Globe award 1968, Brit. Acad. award 1968); films include Love is a Ball, 1962, Sylvia, 1964, The Appointment, 1968, The Lion in Winter, 1968 (Best Picture award), The Magic Garden of Stanley Sweetheart, 1970, Night Watch, 1972, The Man Who Loved Cat Dancing, 1973, Love and Death, 1975, The Sailor Who Fell From Grace with The Sea, 1976, The Dain Curse, Somebody Killed Her Husband, 1978, Nighthawks, 1981, Arthur the King, 1984, Gimme An F, 1984, Haunted Summer, 1987, My Heroes Have Always Been Cowboys, 1991, (TV miniseries) Diana—Her True Story, 1993. Served with AUS, 1944-47. Mem. Producers Guild of Am., Acad. Motion Picture Arts and Scis., Cinema Circulus, Friends of Library U. So. Calif.

POLL, ROBERT EUGENE, JR., bank executive; b. Urbana, Ill., Apr. 16, 1948; s. Robert E. Sr. and Dorothy (Baker) P.; children: Alexandra, Bianca; m. Caroline Vaughan, Sept. 20, 2003. BA, Kenyon Coll., 1970; MBA, Ind. U., 1972. V.p. Chase Manhattan Bank, NYC, 1972-78; assoc. Lazard Freres & Co., NYC, 1978-82, mng. dir., mgr. mcpl. divsn., 1985-98; gen. ptnr. William Blair & Co., Chgo., 1982-84; sr. mng. dir. Poll Financial, LLC, 1998—; co-chmn. Chief Consol. Mining Co., 2002; pres., CEO Bernard Techs., Inc., 2002; mng. dir., chief investment officer Castleton Ptnrs., 2005—06. Adv. bd. Pub. Fin. Inst., N.Y.C., 1976, Worldvest. Trustee Citizens Budget Commn.; chmn. Ind. U. Bus. Conf. Mem. N.Y. Acad. Sci., Tavern Club (Chgo.), N.Y. Athletic Club, Ind. U. Kelley Sch. Bus. Alumni Assn. (dir.). Home: Apt 13A 350 Central Park W New York NY 10025-6503 Office Phone: 212-280-3950. Personal E-mail: rppollfin@att.net. Business E-Mail: rpoll@pollfinancial.com.

POLLACE, PAMELA L., public relations executive; b. San Jose, Calif., May 1953. BA, U. Santa Clara, 1975. Acct. mgr. mktg. comm. Oxbridge, Inc.; acct. supr. Burson Marsteller; spokesperson, mgr., dir. Intel Corp, Santa Clara, Calif., 1987-96, v.p., dir. worldwide press rels., 1996—2000; v.p. dir. corp. comms. Intel Corp., Santa Clara, Calif., 2000—. Office: Intel Corp Worldwide Press Rels PO Box 58119 Santa Clara CA 95052-8119

POLLACK, GERALD ALEXANDER, economist, educator, federal agency administrator; b. Vienna, Jan. 14, 1929; came to US 1938, naturalized 1944; s. Stephen J. and Tini (Herschel) P.; m. Patricia E. Sisterson; children: Nora P. Silverman, Carol A. BA, Swathmore Coll., Pa., 1951; MA, MPA, Princeton U., 1953, PhD, 1958. Corp. economist Leeds & Northrup Co., Phila., 1958-62; officer in charge internat. payments U.S. Dept. State, Washington, 1962-63; internat. economist Joint Econ. Com. of Congress, Washington, 1963-65; chief economist Office Spl. Rep. for Trade Negotiations, 1964; dep. asst. sec. U.S. Dept. Commerce, Washington, 1965-68; v.p. Loeb, Rhoades & Co., NYC, 1968-69, Bendix Corp., Southfield, Mich., 1969-70, Citibank, NYC, 1970-71; internat. economist Exxon Corp., NYC, 1971-86; v.p., chief economist Overseas Shipholding Group, NYC, 1986-89; assoc. prof. fin. Pace U., NYC, 1990-94; assoc. dir. for internat. econs. Bur. Econ. Analysis, U.S. Dept. Commerce, 1994-99. Contbr. articles to profl. jours. Bd. dirs. Jamaica Estates Assn., 1976-80, Oakwood Friends Sch., Poughkeepsie, N.Y., 1979-89; trustee Lindley Murray Fund, 1990-94; mem. Greenwich Dem. Town Com., 1992-94, 2001—; clk. Flushing Monthly Meeting Soc. of Friends, 1990-94; mem. Greenwich Rep. Town Meeting, 1999-2003; bd. mem. Greenwich Forum on War and Peace, 2006-. With US Army, 1953—55. Mem.: Violoncello Soc., Coun. on Fgn. Rels., Fairfield County Symphony Soc., Phi Beta Kappa. Democrat. Mem. Soc. Of Friends. Avocations: cello, classical music, photography, hiking, bicycling. Personal E-mail: gapollack@hotmail.com.

POLLACK, GERALD LESLIE, physicist, researcher, educator; b. Bklyn., July 8, 1933; s. Herman and Jennie (Tenenbaum) P.; m. Antoinette Amparo Velasquez, Dec. 22, 1958; children: Harvey Anton, Samuela Juliet, Margolita Mia, Violet Amata. BS, Bklyn. Coll., 1954; Fulbright scholar, U. Gottingen, 1954-55; MS, Calif. Inst. Tech., 1957, PhD, 1962. Physics student trainee Nat. Bur. Standards, Washington, 1954-58, solid state physicist, 1961-65, cons. Boulder, Colo., 1965-70; assoc. prof. dept. physics Mich. State U., East Lansing, 1965-69, prof., 1969—2005, prof. emeritus, 2005—; cons. NRC, Ill. Dept. Nuclear Safety; physicist Naval Med. Rsch. Inst., Bethesda, Md., summer 1979. Physicist USAF Sch. Aerospace Medicine, San Antonio, Tex., summer 1987; adj. prof. Dept. Physics, Colo. Sch. Mines, Golden, 2005-06. Co-author (with D.R. Stump): Electromagnetism, 2002; contbr. articles to profl. jours. Fellow Am. Phys. Soc.; mem. Am. Assn. Physics Tchrs. Business E-Mail: pollack@msu.edu.

POLLACK, HENRY CLINTON, III, pediatric emergency physician; b. NYC, Oct. 10, 1969; s. Henry Clinton Pollack, Jr. and Wendy Elaine Reilly; m. Susan Germaine Lozier, May 28, 2000; 1 child, Dahlia Lozier. BA, Brown U., Providence, 1987—92; MD, Boston U., 1996—2000. Lic. pediatrics Am. Bd. Pediat., 2003, pediatric emergency medicine Am. Bd. Pediat., 2006. Resident Children's Hosp., Oakland, Calif., 2000—03; fellow Montefiore Med. Ctr., Bronx, NY, 2003—06; attending physician Children's Hosp. Ctrl. Calif., Madera, Calif., 2006—. Mem.: Am. Coll. Emergency Physicians, Am. Acad. Pediat. D-Liberal. Avocations: travel, skiing, poetry. Office: Childrens Hosp Cttl Calif 9300 Valley Childrens Pl Madera CA 93636 Home Phone: 559-877-3335.

POLLACK, IAN FREDRIC, physician, researcher; b. Holliswood, NY, Aug. 26, 1960; s. Jonah and Roberta Minnie (Wainick) P.; m. Constance Shenk, Aug. 15, 1982; children: Benjamin Nathan, Andrew Maxwell. BS magna cum laude, Emory U., 1980; MD, Johns Hopkins U., 1984. Intern in surgery U. Pitts., 1984-85, resident in neurosurgery, 1985-91, postgrad. fellow dept. neurobiology, 1988-90, asst. prof. dept. neurosurgery, 1990-96, assoc. prof., 1996—99, prof., 1999—, Walter Dandy prof., 2001—, co-dir. Brain Tumor Ctr., 1996—. Chmn. brain tumor strategy group. Contbr. articles to New Eng. Jour. Medicine, Cancer Rsch., Exptl. Neurology, Jour. Neurosurgery, Cancer, Jour. Neurosurgery Rsch., Neurosurgery, Brain Rsch., others. Van Wagenen fellow Am. Assn. Neurol. Surgeons, 1991; recipient Resident Rsch. award ACS, 1990, Pitts. Neurosci. Soc., 1989, Preuss award Am. Assn. Neurol. Surgeons and Congress Neurological Surgeons Joint Sect. on Tumors, 1989, Young Clinician Investigator award Am. Assn. Neurol. Surgeons, 1992. Mem. AAAS, Congress of Neurol. Surgeons, Phi Beta Kappa, Alpha Omega Alpha. Achievements include research in the growth factor response properties of human brain tumor cells in culture, the role of selective inhibitors on tumor growth in culture, molecular markers of brain tumor prognosis and immunotherapeutic strategies for brain tumors. Office: U Pitts Dept Neurosurgery 9402 Presbyn Univ Hosp 230 Lothrop St Pittsburgh PA 15213-2536 also: Childrens Hosp Pitts Dept Neurosurgery 3705 5th Ave Pittsburgh PA 15213-2583 E-mail: ian.pollack@chp.edu.

POLLACK, IRWIN WILLIAM, psychiatrist, educator; b. Phila., Aug. 14, 1927; s. Nathan and Rose (Bergman) P.; m. Barbara Jean Callaway, Oct. 9, 1988; children from previous marriage: Nathaniel Edward, Joshua Frank, Jonathan Daniel AB, Temple U., 1950; MA, Columbia U., 1951; student, U. Pa., 1951—52; MD, U. Vt., 1956. Diplomate: Am. Bd. Psychiatry and Neurology. Intern Grad. Hosp. U. Pa., 1956—57; asst. resident psychiatry Henry Phipps Psychiat. Clinic (John Hopkins Hosp.), 1957—60; chief resident psychiatry Johns Hopkins Hosp., 1960—61, adminstr. psychosomatic clinic, psychiat. liaison svc., 1961—64; psychiatrist-in-chief Sinai Hosp., Balt., 1964—69; mem. faculty psychiatry Coll. Medicine and Dentistry N.J. (Rutgers Med. Sch.), 1968—87, 1987—, clin. prof. psychiatry, 1998. Assoc. prof. psychiatry, 1968-70, prof. psychiatry, 1979-99, emeritus prof. psychiatry 1999-, chmn. dept. Univ. Medicine and Dentistry N.J.; prof. neurology, dir. Ctr. for Cognitive Rehab.; exec. dir. Coll. Medicine and Dentistry (Cmty. Mental Health Ctr.), 1970-77 Served with USNR, 1945-46 Fellow Am. Psychiat. Assn. (life); mem. N.J. Psychiat. Assn., Am. Psychosomatic Soc., Am. Congress Rehab. Medicine, Alpha Omega Alpha Achievements include spl. research or problems of time and space perception, psychology of phys. disability, doctor-patient relationships, cognitive retraining of brain-injured persons. Home: 1499 W Shore Rd West Danville VT 05873 E-mail: iwpollack@aol.com.

POLLACK, JEFFREY LEE, restaurateur; b. San Francisco, May 1, 1945; s. Albert and Loretta (Popper) P.; m. Patricia Bowdle Connell, Feb. 20, 1983; children: Lizabeth Ann, Hilary Margaret, Nicholas Albert. BA, San Jose State U. Owner, surety underwriter North Beach Bonding Co., San Francisco, 1968-75; proprietor Old Waldorf, San Francisco, 1974-80, Punchline, 1978-80, Julius' Castle, San Francisco, 1980—2006, New Joe's, San Francisco, 1984-99, Shadows, San Francisco, 1985-95, Iron Horse, 1986-92, Pollack Group, San Francisco, 1985—, Nick's Lighthouse Restaurant, San Francisco, 1991—, Original Joe's # 2, 1992-95, O'Connell's, 1994-96, Dalla Torre, 1996—2006. Mem. Downtown Assn. (bd. dirs. 1987—, v.p. 1992), Union Sq. Assn., North Beach C. of C. (bd. dirs. 1989, v.p. 1992), Port Tenants Assn., Fisherman Wharf Assn., Commonwealth Club. Democrat. Avocations: classic car collecting, movies. Office: Pollack Group Ltd 5 Fishermans Wharf San Francisco CA 94133

POLLACK, JOE, retired columnist, critic, writer; b. Bklyn., Feb. 3, 1931; s. Samuel H. and Anna (Weisman) P.; m. Joan Henriksen, Mar. 6, 1952 (div. 1964); children: Wendy, Dara, Sharon; m. Carol Atchison, Dec. 1, 1964 (dec. 1993); m. Ann Lemons, Nov. 20, 1994. BJ, U. Mo., 1952. Sports writer St. Louis Globe-Democrat, 1955-61; dir. pub. rels. St. Louis Football Cardinals, 1961-72; critic, columnist St. Louis Post-Dispatch, 1972-95. Critic Sta. KSDK-TV, St. Louis, 1973-88, Sta. KMOV-TV, St. Louis, 1988-92; commentator Sta. KMOX, St. Louis, 1960-85, Sta. KWMU, St. Louis, 1994—. Author: Joe Pollack's Guide to St. Louis Restaurants, 1988, updated, 1992, (with Ann Lemons Pollack) Beyond Toasted Ravioli, 1998, Beyond Gooey Butter Cake, 2001, The Great St. Louis Eats Book, 2005; contbr. numerous articles to mags. Mem. Am. Theatre Critics Assn., Profl. Football Writers Assn., Am. Soc. Profl. Journalists. Home: 7417 Oxford Dr Saint Louis MO 63105-2915 Office Phone: 314-862-3321. Personal E-mail: jpalfood@aol.com.

POLLACK, MARSHA, secondary school educator; d. Harry and Rose Grunberg; m. Bertram Pollack, July 14, 1944; 1 child, Meredith Pollack-Richman. BA, Bklyn Coll., 1968, MS, 1973; Specialist Diploma in Adminstrn. and Supervision, Queens Coll., 2003. Cert. tchr. Nat. Bd. Profl. Tchg. Standards, 2001. Tchr. N.Y.C. Dept. of Edn., Bklyn. and Queens, 1968—2002, asst. prin. Queens, 2002—03, tchr./coach/staff devel., 2003—. L.E.A.D. tchr. N.Y.C. Dept. of Edn., 1998—2002, nat. staff devel., 2000; profl. devel. Jericho Mid. Sch., 2003; lesson plan-abstract evaluator Internat. Reading Assn., 2003—05. CAL grantee, Chase Manhattan, 2001. Mem.: Am. Fedn. Tchrs., Nat. Coun. Tchrs. English, Phi Delta Kappa, Internat. Reading Assn., ASCD. Avocations: law, educational research, writing. Home Phone: 718-479-0894; Office Phone: 718-831-4000. Office Fax: 718-831-4008. Personal E-mail: bjpmhp@aol.com. Business E-Mail: mpollac2@nycboe.net.

POLLACK, MARTHA E., dean, computer science and engineering educator; AB summa cum laude, Dartmouth Coll., 1979; MS in Engring., U. Pa., 1984, PhD in Computer and Info. Sci., 1986. Sr. rschr., computer scientist Artificial Intelligence Ctr., SRI Internat.; prof. Dept. Computer Sci. and Intelligent Sys. Program U. Pitts.; joined Coll. Engring. U. Mich., Ann Arbor, 2000, assoc. chair computer sci. and engring., 2004—, dean Sch. Info., 2007—. Program chair for the 15th Internat. Joint Conf. on Artificial Intelligence. Contbr. articles to profl. jours. Recipient Chancellor's Disting. Rsch. Award, U. Pitts., 2000, Sarah Goddard Power Award, 2007. Fellow: Michigan Soc. Fellows, Am. Assn. Artificial Intelligence (Computers and Thought Award 1991); mem.: NSF (Young Investigator's Award 1992), Computing Rsch. Assn. (bd. dirs.). Office: U Mich Sch Info 1085 S University Ave 304 West Hall Ann Arbor MI 48109-1107 Office Phone: 734-615-8048. E-mail: pollackm@umich.edu. *

POLLACK, MARTIN D., lawyer; b. Newark, July 24, 1951; BA, MA, Johns Hopkins U., 1973; JD, U. Pa., 1976; LLM, NYU Sch. Law, 1979. Bar: NJ 1976, US Dist. Ct. NJ 1976, NY 1977, US Tax Ct. 1978. Ptnr., co-head tax dept. Weil, Gotshal & Manges LLP, NYC, 1995—. Assoc. adj. prof. NYU Sch. Continuing Edn., 1983—, assoc. adj. prof. tax law NYU Sch. Law, 1989—; lectr. Real Estate Inst., 1979-83; lectr. in field; mem. adv. bd. Tax Mgmt. US Income. Mem. U. Pa. Law Review 1975-1976; mem. adv. bd. Equipment Leasing newsletter.; Contbr. articles to profl. jours. Mem. ABA, NY State Bar Assn. (mem. tax sect.), NJ State Bar Assn. (mem. tax sect.), Phi Beta Kappa. Office: Weil Gotshal & Manges LLP 767 5th Ave New York NY 10153 Office Phone: 212-310-8461. Office Fax: 212-310-8007. Business E-Mail: martin.pollack@weil.com.

POLLACK, MICHAEL, lawyer; b. NYC, July 14, 1946; s. Irving and Bertha (Horowitz) P.; m. Barbara Linda Shore, Aug. 23, 1970; children: Matthew, Ilana. BEng, Cooper Union, 1967; MS, U. Pa., 1970; JD, Temple U., 1974. Bar: Pa. 1974, U.S. Dist. Ct. (ea. dist.) Pa. 1974, N.Y. 2000. Rsch. scientist Pa. Rsch. Assocs., Phila., 1968-69; engr. GE Co., Valley Forge, Pa., 1969-70, Burroughs Corp., Great Valley, Pa., 1970-71; assoc. Blank, Rome, Comisky & McCauley, Phila., 1974-82, ptnr., mgr. dept. real estate, 1982—. Lectr., course planner Pa. Bar Inst., Phila. Mem. ABA, Pa. Bar Assn., Phila. Bar Assn., Internat. Assn. Attys. and Execs. in Corp. Real Estate (bd. dirs.), Eta Kappa Nu, Tau Beta Pi. Republican. Avocations: music, tennis. Office: Blank Rome LLP 1 Logan Sq Philadelphia PA 19103-6998 Home Phone: 610-527-9655; Office Phone: 215-569-5670. E-mail: pollack@blankrome.com.

POLLACK, MICHAEL BRUCE, lawyer; b. Phila., Mar. 27, 1958; s. Solomon Robert and Ethel (Sutow) Pollack; m. Deborah Ann Moses, Aug. 15, 1982; children: Jennifer Cara, Benjamin Philip. BS in economics, U. Pa., 1980; postgrad., U. Pa. Law Sch., 1982-83; JD, Boston U., 1983. Bar: Pa., 1983, US Dist. Ct. Ea. Dist. Pa., 1984. Ptnr., Phila. office Reed Smith Shaw & McClay (now Reed Smith LLP), 1983—, dir. strategic planning, mem. exec. com. & mgmt. com. 1st v.p., sec. W.P. Carey & Co., Inc., NYC, 1987. Bd. dirs. Temple Sinai. Mem. ABA, Pa. Bar Assn., Beta Alpha Psi. Republican. Jewish. Avocation: golf. Office: Reed Smith LLP 2500 One Liberty Pl 1650 Market St Philadelphia PA 19103-7301 Office Phone: 215-851-8182. Office Fax: 215-851-1420. Business E-Mail: mpollack@reedsmith.com.

POLLACK, RHODA-GALE, theater educator, director; b. Pitts., Dec. 30, 1937; d. Jacob Allen and Jessie (Sapolaky) Klein; m. Sanford S. Pollack, Dec. 25, 1957; 1 child, Jessica. BFA in Drama, Carnegie Mellon U., 1958; MA in Drama, San Francisco State U., 1966; PhD in Drama, Stanford U., 1971. Prodr., dir. Ariz. Playmakers, Phoenix, 1959-61; freelance dir., 1959—; costume designer, 1960—; costumer U. Calif.-Berkeley, 1963-64; lectr. Mills Coll., Oakland, Calif., 1965-76; assoc. prof. theatre U. Wis.-Parkside, Kenosha, 1976-86, chmn. fine arts div., 1980-86; dean, prof. theatre Coll. Fine Arts Wichita State U., 1986-92; dean, prof. Coll. Fine Arts U. Ky., 1992-98, prof. dept. theatre, 1998—; mem. adv. coun. Sta. WGTD-FM, Kenosha, 1980-84; mem. Racine Arts Coun., 1983-86; mem. dance and theatre panel Wis. Arts Bd., Madison, 1984. Dir. 46 prodns., costume designer 45 prodns. Author: George S. Kaufman (Twayne's United States Authors Series), 1988, A Sampler of Plays by Women, Peter Lang, 1990; contbr. articles to profl. jours. Active bd. dirs. Lexington Philharm, 1993—2002, Lexington Arts and Cultural Coun., 1992—2002, Internat. Council Fine Arts Deans (pres. 1992-94). Avocations: flower gardening; cooking; moviegoing. Office: U Ky Coll Fine Arts 109 Fine Arts Bldg Lexington KY 40506-0001 Office Phone: 859-257-7018. Business E-Mail: rgpoll01@uky.edu.

POLLACK, ROBERT ELLIOT, biologist, educator, writer; b. Bklyn., Sept. 2, 1940; s. Ephraim Hyman and Molly (Pollack) P.; m. Amy Louise Steinberg, Dec. 23, 1961; 1 child, Marya BA in Physics, Columbia U., 1961; PhD in Biology, Brandeis U., 1966. Asst. prof. pathology Med. Sch. NYU, NYC, 1969-70; sr. scientist Cold Spring Harbor Lab., NY, 1971-75; prof. microbiology Med. Sch., SUNY-Stony Brook, 1975-78; prof. biol. sci. Columbia U., NYC, 1978—; dean Columbia Coll., NYC, 1982-89. Bd. dirs., chmn. sci. adv. bd. Tapestry Pharms., 1994-; instr. Pratt Archtl. Sch., Bklyn., 1970; lectr. psychiatry Ctr. for Psychoanalytic Tng., Columbia U., 1999—, dir. Ctr. for the Study of Sci. and Religion, 1999—; vis. prof. pharmacology Albert Einstein Coll. Medicine, Bronx, N.Y., 1977-92; dean's disting. lectr. in Humanities, Columbia Med. Sch., 2000; lectr. Rosenthal Colloquium, March of Dimes, 1989; McGregory lectr. Colgate U., 1979; du Vigneaud lectr. Med. Sch., Cornell U., 1983. Co-editor: Readings in Mammalian Cell Culture, 1973, 3d rev. edit., 1981, Signs of Life, 1984 (translations in 7 langs., Lionel Trilling award 1995), The Missing Moment, 1999, The Faith of Biology and the Biology of Faith, 2000; mng. editor BBA Revs. on Cancer, 1980-86; contbr. numerous rsch. articles on molecular cell biology to profl. jours. Trustee N.Y. Found., 1988-96, Brandeis U., 1989-94, Solomon Schechter Sch. of N.Y.C., 1996-98; fellow World Econ. Forum, 1995—; bd. overseers List Coll. of the Jewish theol. Sem. of Am., 1996-99; pres. Jewish Campus Life Fund, Columbia U., 1997-2001. Recipient Rsch. Career Devel. award NIH, 1974, Alexander Hamilton medal, 1989, Lionel Trilling award Columbia U., 1995; NIH spl. fellow Weizmann Inst., Rehovot, Israel, 1970-71; grantee Nat. Cancer Inst., NIH, 1968-92, Am. Cancer Soc., 1985-94; John Simon Guggenheim fellow, 1993. Fellow AAAS; mem. N.Y. Acad. Scis., Am. Soc. Microbiology. Office: Columbia U Fairchild Hall 1212 Amsterdam Ave # Mc2419 New York NY 10027-7003 Office Phone: 212-854-2409. Business E-Mail: pollack@columbia.edu.

POLLACK, ROBERT HARVEY, psychology professor; b. NYC, June 26, 1927; s. Solomon and Bertha (Levy) P.; m. Martha Dee Katz, Aug. 20, 1948; children: Jonathan Keith, Lance Michael, Scott Evan. BS, CCNY, 1948; MS, Clark U., Worcester, Mass., 1950, PhD, 1953. Lectr. U. Sydney, Australia, 1953-61; spl. rsch. fellow Columbia U., NYC, 1960-61; chief div. cognitive devel. Inst. Juvenile Rsch., Chgo., 1961-63, dep. dir. rsch., 1963-69; from clin. asst. prof. to clin. assoc. prof. rsch. U. Ill. Coll. Medicine, Chgo., 1962-67; prof. psychology U. Ga., Athens, 1969-96, chair grad. program. exptl. psychology, 1970-78, chair grad. study com., 1978-86; prof. emeritus, 1996—; chair grad. program in life-span psychology U. Ga., Athens, 1988-96. Editor: The Experimental Psychology of Alfred Binet, 1969; contbr. over 100 articles and chpts. to profl. publs. Cpl. U.S. Army, 1945-46. Grantee Nat. Inst. Child Health and Human Devel., 1965, 67, 72, 78. Fellow AAAS, Am. Psychol. Assn.; mem. Am. Assn. Sex Edn., Counsellors and Therapists, Gerontol. Soc. Am., Australian Psychol. Soc., Soc. for Researching Child Devel., Soc. for Sci. Study Sex, Sigma Xi. Democrat. Avocations: travel, stamp collecting/philately, opera, military history. Office: U Ga Dept Psychology Athens GA 30602 Office Phone: 706-542-3084. Business E-Mail: bpollack@uga.edu.

POLLACK, ROBERT WILLIAM, psychiatrist, corporate financial executive; b. NYC, May 22, 1947; s. George and Esther P.; m. Pam Gregory, Sept. 15, 1984; 1 child, Jessie. BS in Biology, Yale U., New Haven, Conn.,

1969; MD, SUNY Downstate Med. Ctr., Bklyn., 1973. Diplomate Am. Bd. Psychiatry and Neurology. Tng. resident U. Fla., 1973-76, chief resident dept. psychiatry, 1975-76, asst. prof. dept. psychiatry Gainesville, 1976-77; clin. asst. prof. dept. psychiatry Shands Hosp., Gainesville, 1977—; chief dept. psychiatry Fla. Hosp., Orlando, 1983, 84; clin. dir. assessment and evaluation team West Lake Hosp., Longwood, Fla., 1984-87, clin. dir. intensive evaluation unit, 1987-89; med. dir. Fla. Psychiat. Assocs., Winter Park, 1989-92, Fla. Psychiat. Mgmt., Winter Park, 1990-97; corp. med. dir. FPM Behavioral Health, 1993-97; co-founder Profl. Quality Analysts, Inc., Casselberry, Fla., 1997—2001; CEO VShift, Orlando, Fla., 2002—03; CMIO Ctrl. Fla. Healthcare Coalition, 2003—05; pres. Matrix Network Tech. Group, Orlando, 2003—04, Quantum Delta Enterprises, Orlando, 2004, Nexia Strategy Corp., Orlando, 2005; exec. v.p. analysis AQMI Strategy, Orlando, 2006; exec. v.p. strategic planning PaySource USA, Dayton and Orlando, 2007—. Med. dir. consultation, liaison svc. and spl. med. unit Winter Park Meml. Hosp., 1992; integrated surveyor Jt. Commn. for Accreditation of Healthcare Orgns., 1998—2000, sentinel event, 1999—2000; pres., CEO The Rondo Group, Longwood, Fla., 2000—; CEO Cory Marvin Erving Found, 2001—05; chief med. info. officer Ctrl. Fla. Healthcare Coalition, 2003—; bd. dirs. Analytic Data Systems, Inc., Teknovation; chmn. Bd. Living Hope Ministries, 2004—06; gen. ptnr. Erving Pollack Joint Venture Group, BOD Teknovation Review Bd. Contbr. 4 articles to profl. jours.; author sci. reports. Chmn. Retinitis Pigmentosa Casino Night, Orlando, 1988-92; bd. dirs. Tennis with a Different Swing, Orlando, 1988-92; mem. Seminole County Assn. on Domestic Violence, 1998-; chmn. Living Hope Internat. Ministries, 2005-. Recipient Quality Achievement award, Ctrl. Fla. Healthcare Coalition, 2003. Mem. US Blind Golfers Assn. (chairperson nat. championships 1998, 99, 2000, vice-chmn. nat. championship com., 1991-92, chair 48th ann. championship com., 1992-93), Alaqua Country Club (bd. dirs.). Methodist. Achievements include introduction of use of computerized topographical brain mapping as a diagnostic tool in central Florida; development of Data Portals, wireless/web-based data acquisition system. Avocations: golf, winemaking. Office: PaySource USA 7680 Universal Blvd Ste 680 Orlando FL 32819 Office Phone: 407-345-8430. Business E-Mail: robert.pollack@paysourceinc.com.

POLLACK, RONALD FRANK, healthcare organization executive, lawyer; b. NYC, Feb. 21, 1944; s. Max Louis and Hanna Esther (Borchardt) Pollack Baruch; m. Rebecca Lucy Bolling, Jan. 8, 1972; children: Sarah Shoshana, Abraham Max, Martin Landrum. BA, Queens Coll., 1965; JD, NYU, 1968. Bar: N.Y. 1968, D.C. 1978, U.S. Ct. Appeals (D.C. cir) 1970, U.S. Ct. Appeals (5th cir.) 1971, U.S. Ct. Appeals (6th cir.) 1974, U.S. Supreme Ct. 1973. Atty. Ctr. on Social Welfare Policy and Law, NYC, 1968-73; founder, exec. dir. Food Research and Action Ctr., NYC, 1970-80; dean Antioch Sch. Law, Washington, 1980-83; exec. dir. Families U.S.A., Washington, 1983—. Sec. treas., bd. dirs. Food Research and Action Ctr., Washington, 1980—; mem. civil legal services D.C. Jud. Conf. Com., 1980-83; appointee Pres.'s Adv. Commn. on Consumer Protection and Quality in the Health Care Industry, 1997-98. Author: If We Had Ham, We Could Have Ham and Eggs...If We Had Eggs: A Study of the National School Breakfast Program, 1972, Out to Lunch: A Study of USDA's Child Care Feeding and Summer Feeding Programs, 1974; co-author: On the Other Side of Easy Street: Myths and Facts About the Economics of Old Age, 1987. Treas. Jewish Fund for Justice, 1985-88, bd. dirs., 1985-93; bd. dirs. Am. Jewish World Service, Self-Help Community Services, 1974-77; mem. domestic adv. bd., project rev. bd. U.S.A. for Africa/Hands Across Am., 1986-88; v.p. of bd. dirs. Burgundy Farm Country Day Sch., 1988-90, pres. 1990-91; bd. dirs. Americans for Health, 1986-91. Arthur Garfield Hays Civil Liberties fellow, 1967-68; research fellow Legal Services Corp., Washington, 1978-80 Office: Families USA 1201 New York Ave Washington DC 20005

POLLACK, SEYMOUR VICTOR, computer science educator; b. Bklyn., Aug. 3, 1933; s. Max and Sylvia (Harrison) P.; m. Sydell Altman, Jan. 23, 1955; children: Mark, Sherie. BChemE, Pratt Inst., 1954; MChemE, Bklyn. Poly. Inst., 1960. Lic. chem. engr., Ohio. Engr. Schwarz Labs., Mt. Vernon, NY, 1954-55; design engr. Curtiss-Wright, Wood-Ridge, NJ, 1955-57, Fairchild Engines, Deer Park, NY, 1957-59, GE, Evendale, Ohio, 1959-62; rsch. assoc. U. Cin., 1962-66; prof. computer sci. Washington U., St. Louis, 1966-95, prof. emeritus, 1995—. Cons. Mo. Auto Club, St. Louis, 1969-82, United Van Lines, Fenton, Mo., 1984-86, Computer Sci. Accreditation Bd., N.Y.C., 1985-93. Author: Structured Fortran, 1982, UCSD Pascal, 1984, Studies in Computer Science, 1983, The DOS Book, 1985, Turbo Pascal Programming, 1991; cons. editor Holt Rinehart & Winston, N.Y.C., 1979-86. Bd. dirs. Hillel orgn., Washington U., 1983-84. Recipient Alumni Achievement award Pratt Inst., 1966, Outstanding Teaching award Burlington Northern Found., 1987. Mem. Assn. for Computing Machinery, Am. Assn. for Engring. Edn. Jewish. Avocations: trombone, walking, classical and jazz piano, jogging. Office: Washington U PO Box 1045 Saint Louis MO 63188-1045 Business E-Mail: svp@cse.wustl.edu.

POLLACK, STANLEY P., lawyer; b. NYC, Apr. 23, 1928; s. Isidor and Anna (Shulman) P.; m. Susan Aronowitz, June 16, 1974; 1 child, Jane. BA, NYU, 1948; JD, Harvard U., 1951; LLM in Taxation, NYU, 1959. Bar: N.Y. 1951, U.S. Dist. Ct. (so. dist.) N.Y. 1955. Sole practice, NYC, 1955-61; v.p., gen. counsel James Talcott, Inc., NYC, 1961-73; sr. exec. v.p. Rosenthal & Rosenthal Inc., NYC, 1973—. Served to j.g. lt. USNR, 1951-54. Mem. Bklyn. Bar Assn. (banking com., bankruptcy com.), Fed. Bar Council, Assn. Comml. Fin. Attys.'s (pres. 1968), Factors Chain Internat. Clubs: Harvard (N.Y.C.). Home: 6 Peter Cooper Rd New York NY 10010-6701 Office: Rosenthal & Rosenthal Inc 1370 Broadway # 2 New York NY 10018-7302

POLLACK, STEPHEN J., investment company executive, stockbroker; b. NYC, Aug. 25, 1937; s. Harold S. and Gladys H. P. BS in Econs., U. Pa., 1960; grad., Wharton Sch. Bus., Manhattan, NY. V.p. retail sales Drexel Burnham Lambert, NYC, 1960-77; 1st v.p. investments Dean Witter Reynolds Inc., NYC, 1978-98; 1st v.p., fin. advisor Morgan Stanley, NYC, 1998—, v.p., fin. advisor, 2001—03; with Pollack Asset Mmgt., 2004—06; sr. v.p. investments Lempert Bros. Internat. USA, NYC, 2006—. Pres. B'nai B'rith Gotham, NYC; exec. v.p. Cosmopolitan League City of Hope; v.p. cir. mem. Whitney Mus., NYC; treas. Sutton Pl. Synagogue, pres. Havurah Group. With USAR, 1966. Recipient Double Chai Citation, State of Israel Bonds, 1984, Appreciation award City of Hope, 1984, Kiter Key Club award Franklin Funds, Million Dollar Club Svc. award, B'nai B'rith Internat. award. Mem. NASD, Securities Investor Protection Corp., Internat. Assn. Fin. Planners, Assn. Investment Brokers (bd. dirs.), Youngmen's Philanthropic League (bd. dirs.), Internat. Study Rsch. Inst., Exec. Forum, Fin. Investment Analysts Group, Fin. Analysts-Money Mgrs. Soc., Town Club, Atrium Club, Schuylkill Country Club, Wharton Sch. Club, U. Pa. Club, Yale Club, East River Tennis Club, Fresh Meadow Country Club, Matterhorn Sports Club, East Side Rep. Club, Knickerbokker Rep. Club, Berks County Tennis Club, Penn. Club (charter), Friars Club. Home: 245 E 40th St Apt 14E New York NY 10016-1714 Office: Lempert Bros Internat USA Rockefeller Ctr 27th Fl 1270 Ave of the Americas New York NY 10020 Personal E-mail: stephenpollack12@yahoo.com.

POLLACK, SYDNEY, film director; b. Lafayette, Ind., July 1, 1934; s. David and Rebecca (Miller) P.; m. Claire Griswold, Sept. 22, 1958; children: Steven, Rebecca, Rachel. Grad., Neighborhood Playhouse Theatre Sch., NYC, 1954. Asst. to Sanford Meisner, Neighborhood Playhouse Theatre, 1954, instr. acting, 1954-60. Exec. dir. West Coast br. The Actors Studio. Appeared in Broadway prodns.: The Dark Is Light Enough, 1954, A Stone For Danny Fisher, 1955; appeared on live TV programs: Alcoa Presents, others; toured in Stalag 17; dir. TV programs: The Chrysler Theatre, Ben Casey, 1962-63, Something About Lee Wiley, 1963-64; dir: (films) The Slender Thread, 1965, This Property is Condemned, 1966, The Scalphunters, 1968, Castle Keep, 1969, Jeremiah Johnson, 1972, Three Days of the Condor, 1975, The Electric Horseman, 1979, The Firm, 1993; dir., prodr. They Shoot Horses, Don't They?, 1969, The Way We Were, 1973, The Yakuza, 1975, Bobby Deerfield, 1977, Absence of Malice, 1981, Out of Africa, 1985 (Academy Award for Best Picture and Dir.), Havana, 1990, The Firm, 1993, Sabrina, 1995; prodr. Songwriter, 1984, Bright Lights, Big City, 1988, The Fabulous Baker Boys, 1989, Presumed Innocent, 1990, Sliding Doors, 1998, Cold Mountain, 2003; prodr.: Breaking and Entering, 2006; exec. prodr.: Honeysuckle Rose, 1980, White Palace, 1990, King Ralph, 1991, Dead Again, 1991, Leaving Normal, 1992, Searching for Bobby Fischer, 1993, Flesh and Bone, 1992, Sense and Sensibility, 1995, Sliding Doors, 1997, Up At the Villa, 1998, The Talented Mr. Ripley, 1998, For Love of the Game, 1998, The Talented Mr. Ripley, 1999, Blow Dry, 2001, Birthday Girl, 2001, Iris, 2001, Heaven, 2002, The Quiet American, 2002, In the Name of Love, 2003, Forty Shades of Blue, 2005, Catch a Fire, 2006; (actor) The Player, 1992, Death Becomes Her, 1992, Husbands and Wives, 1992, The Firm, 1993, Eyes Wide Shut, 1997, Civil Action, 1998, (voice) The Majestic, 2001, Changing Lanes, 2002, Avenue Montaigne, 2006, (TV) Mad About You, 1998, Eyes Wide Shut, 1999; dir., prodr., actor: Tootsie, 1982, Random Hearts, 1999, The Interpreter, 2005; TV appearances include Playhouse 90, 1959, Alfred Hitchcock Presents, 1960, The Deputy, 1961, Ben Casey, 1962, (voice) Frasier, 1994, Mad About You, 1998, Will & Grace, 2000, 01, 02, Just Shoot Me!, 2000, (voice) King of the Hill, 2000, Served with U.S. Army, 1957-59. Recipient Acad. award for best dir. and best picture, 1986; John Huston award Directors Guild Am., 2000. also: Deloitte & Touche 350 S Grand Ave Los Angeles CA 90071-3406 Office: Artists Mgmt Group 9465 Wilshire Blvd Ste 519 Beverly Hills CA 90212-2604 *

POLLAK, KEVIN, actor; b. San Francisco, Oct. 30, 1957; m. Lucy Webb, 1995. Appeared in films Avalon, 1990, L.A. Story, 1992, Another You, 1991, Ricochet, 1991, A Few Good Men, 1992, Indian Summer, 1993, The Opposite Sex (And How to Live With Them), 1993, Grumpy Old Men, 1993, Clean Slate, 1994, Miami Rhapsody, 1995, The Usual Suspects, 1995, Canadian Bacon, 1995, Casino, 1995, Grumpier Old Men, 1995, House Arrest, 1996, Apt Pupil, 1997, Cannes Man, 1996, Truth or Consequences N.M., 1997, The Sex Monster, 1998, She's All That, 1999, End of Days, 1999, Deterrence, 1999, Deal of a Lifetime, 1999, The Whole Nine Yards, 2000, Steal This Movie!, 2000, The Wedding Planner, 2001, 3000 Miles to Graceland, 2001, Dr. Dolittle 2, 2001, Stolen Summer, 2002, Juwanna Mann, 2002, Mother Ghost, 2002, The Santa Clause 2, 2002, Rolling Kansas, 2003, Blizzard, 2003, Seven Times Lucky, 2004, The Whole Ten Yards, 2004, Our Time is Up, 2004, Hostage, 2005, Niagara Motel, 2005, The Santa Clause 3: The Escape Clause, 2006; appeared on TV in The Don's Analyst, 1997, Salute to Martin Scorsese, 1997, Ruby Bridges, 1998, From the Earth to the Moon, 1998, Capitol Law, 2006, others, (TV series) Work with Me, 1999, Movie Lover's Road Trip, 2003, Celebrity Poker Showdown, 2003. *

POLLAK, LISA, radio producer; Grad., U. Mich., 1990. Reporter News & Observer, Raleigh, NC, Charlotte (NC) Observer; columnist Balt. Sun, 1997—2004. Prodr.: This American Life, 2004—. Recipient Pulitzer prize for feature writing, 1997. Office: This American Life WBEZ Radio 848 E Grand Ave Chicago IL 60611

POLLAK, LOUIS HEILPRIN, judge, educator; b. NYC, Dec. 7, 1922; s. Walter and Marion (Heilprin) P.; m. Katherine Weiss, July 25, 1952; children: Nancy, Elizabeth, Susan, Sarah, Deborah. AB, Harvard U., 1943; LLB, Yale U., 1948; LLD (hon.), Wilkes U., 2002, Columbia U., 2004, Roger Williams U., 2005. Bar: N.Y. 1949, Conn. 1956, Pa. 1976. Law clk. to Justice Rutledge U.S. Supreme Ct., 1948-49; with Paul, Weiss, Rifkind, Wharton & Garrison, NYC, 1949-51; spl. asst. to Amb. Philip C. Jessup State Dept., 1951-53; asst. counsel Amalgmated Clothing Workers Am., 1954-55; mem. faculty Yale Law Sch., 1955-74, dean, 1965-70; Greenfield prof. U. Pa., 1974-78, dean Law Sch., 1975-78, lectr., 1980—; judge U.S. Dist Ct. (ea. dist.) Pa., Phila., 1978—, now sr. judge. Vis. lectr. Howard U. Sch. Law, 1953; vis. prof. U. Mich. Law Sch., 1961, Columbia Law Sch., 1962. Author: The Constitution and the Supreme Court: A Documentary History, 1966. Mem. New Haven Bd. Edn., 1962-68; chmn. Conn. adv. com. U.S. Civil Rights Commn., 1962-63; mem. bd. NAACP Legal Def. Fund, 1960-78, v.p., 1971-78. Served with AUS, 1943-46. Mem.: ABA (chmn. sect. individual rights 1970—71, Spirit of Excellence award 2003), Am. Law Inst. (coun. 1978—), Am. Acad. Polit. and Social Sci. (bd. dirs. 2001—), Am. Philos. Soc., Am. Acad. Arts and Scis., Assn. Bar City N.Y., Phila. Bar Assn., Fed. Bar Assn. Office: US Dist Ct 16613 US Courthouse 601 Market St Philadelphia PA 19106-1713 Office Phone: 215-597-9590.

POLLAK, MARK, lawyer; b. Paris, July 16, 1947; came to U.S., 1955; s. Joseph and Zofia (Berkowitz) P.; m. Joanne Elizabeth Harris, Dec. 26, 1976; children: Joshua David, Jonathan Stephen, Benjamin Eric, Rebecca Lynn. BA, Bklyn. Coll., 1968; MA in City Planning, U. Pa., 1972, JD, 1972. Bar: Md. 1972. Assoc. Piper & Marbury, Balt., 1972-81, ptnr., 1981-99, Wilmer, Cutler & Pickering, Washington, 1999—2004, Wilmer Cutler Pickering Hale and Dorr LLP, Washington, 2004—07, Ballard Spahr Andrews & Ingersoll, LLP, Balt., 2007—. Bd. dirs. Jack Kent Cook Found. Author: Sports Leagues and Teams--An Encyclopedia 1871 to 1996, 1997. Bd. dirs. Balt. Children's Mus., Downtown Partnership of Balt., Inc. Mem. ABA, Md. Bar Assn., Am. Coll. Real Estate Lawyers, Am. Planning Assn., Nat. Assn. Bond Lawyers. Office: Ballard Spahr Andrews & Ingersoll LLP 300 E Lombard Baltimore MD 21202-3268 Home Phone: 410-366-0925; Office Phone: 410-528-5563. Business E-Mail: pollakm@ballardspahr.com.

POLLAK, RAYMOND, general and transplant surgeon; b. Johannesburg, Nov. 12, 1950; came to U.S., 1977; MB BCh, U. Witwatersrand, Johannesburg, 1973. Diplomate Am. Bd. Surgery. Rotating intern Gen. Hosp., Johannesburg, 1974; intern in surgery U. Ill. Hosps. and Clinics, Chgo., 1977-78, resident in surgery; immunology and transplant fellow U. Ill., Chgo., 1982-84, assoc. prof. surgery, chief divsn. transplant dept. surgery, 1988-98, prof. surgery dept., surgeon, 1995—, chief divsn. transplant Peoria, 2000—05; dir. Clinical Trials Dept. Edward Hosp., Naperville, Ill., 2005—. Fellow ACS, Royal Coll. Surgeons Edinburgh. Office: Edward Hosp Clinical Trials Dept 801 S Washington St Naperville IL 60540 Office Phone: 630-527-5672. Business E-Mail: rpollak@edward.org.

POLLAK, WILLIAM L., newspaper publishing executive; AB cum laude, Harvard U., 1978, MBA, 1982. Exec. v.p. sales The New York Times, exec. v.p. circulation, 1994—98; pres. & CEO Am. Lawyer Media, 1998—. Dir. ProBono.Net; chmn. graduate bd. dir. The Harvard Crimson. Office: Am Lawyer Media 345 Park Ave So New York NY 10010 *

POLLAN, STEPHEN MICHAEL, lawyer, writer, life coach, finance expert; b. NYC, May 19, 1929; m. Corinne Staller; children: Michael, Lori, Tracy, Dana. LLB, Bklyn. Law Sch., 1951; BBS, LI U., 1985. Bar: NY 1951. Asst. prof. Marymount Coll., 1960-70; pres. Royal Bus. Funds AMEX, 1970-76; sr. real estate cons. Nat. Westminster Bank, 1976-78; asst. prof. fin. C.W. Post Coll., LI U. Sch. Bus., 1994-96; prin. Stephen M. Pollan, P.C., NYC, 1980—; pvt. practice NYC, 2006—. Mem. President's Commn. on Small Bus. Co-author: Die Broke, Live Rich, Lifescripts, 1996, Second Acts, 2003, It's All in Your Head, 2006, Lifelines, 2007, other personal fin. books; contbr. numerous articles to nat. bus. publs. Pres. Gay Head Cmty. Coun., 1975; vice chmn. UN Com. for UN Day, 1971-72. Mem. Nat. Assn. Small Bus. Investment Cos. (regional pres. 1975, bd. govs.). Home: 1095 Park Ave New York NY 10128-1154 Office: 400 Park Ave Ste 1420 New York NY 10022 Office Phone: 212-688-8333. Business E-Mail: stephen@stephenpollan.com.

POLLARD, DANIEL L., financial analyst; s. Alan Payson Pollard and Hinda Leah Greyser. BA, U. Mass., Boston, 1990; JD, Harvard U., Cambridge, Mass., 1994. Bar: Mass. 1995. Mgmt., program analyst, office student fin. assistance and direct loans US Dept. Edn., Washington, 1996—99, policy, legislative analyst, 1999—2004, sr. portfolio analyst, 2004—. Contbr. articles to profl. jours. Mem.: Toastmasters (FSA pres. 2006—07, area gov. 2007—). Achievements include knowledge of the facets of student loan programs - legislation, policy, budget, operations, systems, data mining, and portfolio assessment - has provided a resource for study groups and committees. Office: US Dept Edn 830 First St NE Washington DC 20202 Home Phone: 703-527-7559.

POLLARD, DENNIS BERNARD, lawyer, educator; b. Phila., May 12, 1968; BS in Psychology, Pa. State U., 1990; JD, Ohio State U., 1993; postgrad., U. Mich., 1996. Bar: Ohio 1993, U.S. Dist. Ct. (no. dist.) Ohio 1994, U.S. Ct. Appeals (6th cir.) 1994. Staff atty. The Legal Aid Soc. Cleve., 1993-95; atty. student affairs, student life Pa. State U., 1995-96; acad. adminstrv. intern U. Mich. Law Sch., Ann Arbor, 1996-97; asst. dean student affairs U. Tenn. Coll. Law, Knoxville, 1997-98; program dir. tenants' rights unit Tenants' Action Group of Phila., 1998-99, dir. devel., legis. affairs and special projects, 1999—2001. Pres. Pollard Enterprises, LLC, 1993—. Mem. ABA, Ohio State Bar Assn., Assn. Fundraising Profls., African-Am. C. of C. Pa., N.J., Del., Phi Delta Phi. Avocation: biking.

POLLARD, FRED DON, finance company executive, director; b. Proctorsville, Vt., Sept. 15, 1931; s. Bryant Frank and Millie Viola (Brobst) P.; m. Sandra Jean Norton, Oct. 19, 1957; children: Fred Don, Bruce Gardiner, Mark Bryant. BA, Dartmouth Coll., 1953, MBA, 1954. CPA, N.Y. Staff auditor Touche, Niven, Bailey & Smart, Chgo., 1954-55, 57-58; with Hertz Corp., Chgo., 1958-60, London, 1960-62, Paris, 1962-64, NYC, 1964-65; European controller Avis Rent A Car, London, 1965-69, internat. treas., 1969-71, asst. v.p., dir. fin. Garden City, NY, 1971-72, asst. treas., 1972-75; treas. Garcia Corp., Teaneck, NJ, 1975-78; v.p. fin., treas. Augsbury Orgn., Inc., Ogdensburg, NY, 1978-79, sr. v.p. fin., treas., 1979-83; pres. Corp. Fin. Assocs. No. N.Y., Canton, 1983—, Agrl. Processing Corp., Canton, 1983—; pres. and treas. AG Pro Ltd., Massena, NY, 1998—. Vis. lectr. sch. of mgmt. Clarkson U., Potsdam, 1986-87, dept. econs. St. Lawrence U., Canton, N.Y., 1987-88; cons. Whalen, Davey & Looney LLP, 1990-2000. Served with U.S. Army, 1955-57. Mem. N.Y. State Soc. CPAs, Am. Inst. CPAs., St. Lawrence county C. of C. (bd. dirs. 1997—). Lodges: Masons; Shriners. Presbyterian. Home: Old Stone House 1129 County Route 25 Canton NY 13617-6539 Office: 24 Commerce Dr Massena NY 13662 Office Phone: 315-764-5611. Business E-Mail: president@agprosoy.com.

POLLARD, HARVEY B., medical educator, neuroscientist; b. San Antonio, May 26, 1943; BA in Biology, Rice U., 1964; MS in Biochemistry, U. Chgo., 1969, MD, 1969, PhD, 1973. Rsch. assoc. NIH-Nat. Inst. Arthritis and Metabolic Diseases, Bethesda, Md., 1969-71, sr. investigator, 1972-74, 1977-79, sect. chief, 1979-81; lab. chief Nat. Inst. Diabetes, Digestive and Kidney Diseases, Bethesda, 1981-96; prof., chair dept. anatomy, physiology and genetics Uniformed Svcs. U. Sch. Medicine, Bethesda, 1997—. Contbr. over 275 articles to profl. jours. With USPHS, 1969-96. Recipient Commendation medal USPHS, 1982, Alumni award for Disting. Svc., U. Chigo. Alumni Assn., 1989, NIH Inventor's award, 1991. Mem. Biophys. Soc., Soc. for Neurosci., Am. Soc. for Pharmacology and Exptl. Therapeutics, Soc. for Cell Biology, Endocrine Soc., Am. Coll. Psychoneuropharmacology, Am. Soc. for Biochemistry and Molecular Biology, Am. Assn. Anatomists., Am. Physiol. Soc., Institute of Medicine of Washington, D.C. Office: USU Sch Med Dept Anatomy Physiology and Genetics Bethesda MD 20814-4712 E-mail: hpollard@usuhs.mil.

POLLARD, HENRY, arbitrator, mediator; b. NYC, Jan. 10, 1931; s. Charles and Sarah (Lanster) P.; m. Adele Ruth Brodie, June 16, 1954; children: Paul A., Lydia S. AB, CCNY, 1953; JD, Columbia U., 1954. Bar: N.Y. 1954, Calif. 1962. Assoc. Sullivan & Cromwell, NYC, 1954, 56-61; ptnr. Kaplan, LIvingston, Goodwin, Berkowitz & Selvin, Beverly Hills, Calif., 1962-81, Pollard, Bauman, Slome & McIntosh, Beverly Hills, 1981-87, Seyfarth, Shaw, LA, 1987-95; of counsel Oberstein, Kibre & Horwitz, LA, 1995-99. Arbitrator/mediator, mem. large complex case program Am. Arbitration Assn.; arbitrator/mediator, N.Y. Stock Exch., Am. Stock Exch., Pacific Stock Exch., L.A. County Dispute Resolution Svcs.; settlement officer Beverly Hills Mcpl. Ct., L.A. County Superior Ct. Editor Columbia U. Law Rev., 1953-54. Served with U.S. Army, 1954-56. Harlan Fiske Stone scholar, 1953-54. Mem. ABA, Calif. Bar Assn., Beverly Hills Bar Assn. Home Phone: 310-457-4420; Office Phone: 310-457-1713. Office Fax: 310-457-1713. Business E-Mail: adrpollard@aol.com.

POLLARD, HERSCHEL NEWTON, artist, psychologist; s. Herschel Newton and Lora Frances Pollard; m. Luz Mariela Gomez Bolanos, Oct. 10, 1997; m. Margaret Lila Kathleen Innes, 1962 (div. 1972); children: Steven Morton, Christopher Charles, Charles William, Heather Dianne, Herschel Newton. BA, Vanderbilt U., 1960; postgrad., Ga. State U., 1963—63, U. of Tenn., 1963—64, Vanderbilt Divinity Sch., 1963—64; PhD, Vanderbilt U., 1972; postgrad., Chattanooga State Tech. Coll., 1992—94. Lic. clin. psychology Tenn., forensic psychology Tenn., clin./cons. psychology Miss., Ark., Alaska, Fla. Counselor InterUniversity Psychol. and Counseling Ctr., Nashville, 1964—72; prof. Grad. Sch. Murray State U., Ky., 1967—69; adj. prof. St. Thomas Aquinas Coll., Nashville, 1970—71; intern Nashville Cmty. Mental Health Ctr., 1971—72; pvt. practice psychologist Memphis, 1972—74; clin. dir. NW Miss. Regional Mental Health Sys., Clarkesdale, Miss., 1975—76; dir. Kuskokwim Mental Health Svcs., Aniak, Alaska, 1976—77; clin. dir. Anchorage Cmty. Mental Health Svcs., 1977—78; pvt. practice psychologist Naples, Fla., 1979—86, Chattanooga, 1986—90; owner, dir. Montlake Studios, Chattanooga, 1990—; instr. Von Liebig Ctr. for the Arts, Naples, 1990—2003, Art League of Bonita Springs, Fla., 1995—98, Cape Coral Arts Studio, Fla., 2002—04, Visual Arts Ctr., Punta Gorda, Fla., 2003—07; pres. Art Inst. of Fla., Inc., Punta Gorda, 2006—. Contbg rschr. Pres.'s Commn. to Investigate Civil Disturbances, Nashville, 1970; mem. Pres.'s Commn. on Mental Health, Washington, 1976—78; instr. Visual Arts Ctr., Punta Gorda, Fla., 2002—; founder Nat. Aviation Art Exhbn., Nat. Air Show, Punta Gorda, 2006. Author, dir., prodr.: (films) Dealing with Conflict (1st award Religion and Ethics Divsn., EFLA Am. Film Festival, 1964); author: (biographical commentary and docudrama) Vincent van Gogh: Love, God and Art, (rsch. monograph) The Re-emergence of a Noteworthy Baroque Painting, (drama) The Madman of Arles, (book) Pollard's Brief Handbook for Painters, (novels) Wait for the Thunder, (biography) The Art of Frances Morton Pollard, (ednl. audiovisual) The Nineteen Friends of Robbie McNee (Excellence award Ednl. Film Libr. Assn., 1964), (film) Turning Point, 1971; designer, pub. Pollard's Infinite Palette; exhibitions include Von Liebig Ctr. for the Arts, Naples, Cape Coral Arts Studio, Naples Nat. Art Festival, Mus. of the Everglades, Robb and Stucky Atrium, Ft. Myers, Fla., No. Trust, Naples, Impac U., Punta Gorda, Goff Gallery, Visual Arts Ctr., Ave Maria U., Naples, 1st Cmty. Nat. Bank, Port Charlotte, Preseller Gallery, Punta Gorda, Alla Prima Pastel Invitational, Naples, The 2005 H. Pollard Retrospective Exhibit, Art and Humanities Gallery, Port Charlotte, Parthenon Mus., Nashville, Hunter Mus., Chattanooga, Larson Gallery, Northern Trust, Naples, Parthenon Mus., Nashville, others, Represented in permanent collections Portrait of Sir Denis Mahon, Nat. Gallery, Gt. Britain, The Entombment of Christ, Ave Maria U. Mus., Naples. Rep. SW Fla. Arts Coun., Ft. Myers, Fla., 2003—04; originator children's art exhbn. Early Edn. Project, 2003; bd. dirs. Early Edn. Project

Policy Coun., Punta Gorda, 2002—03; pres. Von Liebig Ctr. for the Arts, Naples, 2003—04, Ctr. for the Visual Arts, Punta Gorda, 2005; bd. dirs. Charlotte Artists Guild, 2004—05, pres., 2005—. Lt. (j.g.) USN, 1960—62. Named Artist of Month, Charlotte County Bd. Commrs., 2005; recipient Mitchell scholarship, Vanderbilt U., 1956—60, Tchg. fellowship, NIMH, 1964—72, 1st Prize, 2003 Plein Aire Festival, 2003, 1st Award, Visual Art Ctr., 2004, 1st Judge's award, Charlotte Nat. Art Competition, 2004, 1st Prize, Tenn. State Fair Art Competition, 1965, 1st Award, Collier County Fair Art Competition, 1970, Bowles award for portraiture, 2005, 1st award comml. aviation divsn., Nat. Aviation Art Exhbn., others. Mem.: APA (licentiate), Charlotte Artists Guild (pres. 2005—), Naples Art Assn. (pres. 2003—04), Am. Numis. Assn. Achievements include development of The Pollard Pain Scale; design of Pollard's Infinite Palette. Avocations: Pre-Columbian archaeology, coin collecting/numismatics, ceramics, psychology of art, art. Office: CESA Pub 179 Maria Ct Punta Gorda FL 33950 Personal E-mail: hnpollard@aol.com. E-mail: artinstituteoffl@aol.com.

POLLARD, MARCUS, professional football player; b. Valley, Ala., Feb. 8, 1972; m. Amani Pollard; children: Myles, Micah. Attended, Bradley Univ. Tight end Indianapolis Colts, 1996—2004, Detroit Lions, 2005—. Founder TRUST 81 charity. Office: Detroit Lions Inc 222 Republic Dr Allen Park MI 48101

POLLARD, MICHAEL ROSS, lawyer, health science association administrator; b. Flint, Mich., Apr. 14, 1947; s. Gail Winton Pollard and Evelyn Georgeanna (LeMire) Goplen; m. Penelope Brigham, Aug. 22, 1970. AB in Polit. Sci., U. Mich., 1969; JD, Harvard U., 1972, MPH, 1974. Bar: Mass. 1972, D.C. 1975. Profl. assoc. for program devel. Nat. Acad. Scis. Inst. Medicine, Washington, 1974-77, dir. law and ethics div., 1977-78; atty. advisor Office of Policy Planning, FTC, Washington, 1978-81, asst. dir. Bur. Consumer Protection, 1981-83; dir. Office of Policy Analysis, Pharm. Mfrs. Assn., Washington, 1983-88; exec. dir. Am. Pharm. Inst., Washington, 1988-89; counsel Michaels, Wishner & Bonner, P.C., Washington, 1988-89, ptnr., 1989—2000; cons. fed. policy and regulation Medco Health Solutions, Inc., 2000—. Cons. Nat. Ctr. for Health Svcs. Rsch., Rockville, Md., 1975-80, Office Tech. Assessment U.S. Congress, 1984-95; dir. Inst. for Health Policy Solutions, 1992—. Contbr. articles to profl. jours. Treas. Nat. Leadership Coalition on AIDS, 1988-93; treas. and dir.-at-large Nat. Commn. on Cert. of Physician Assts., 1991-97, James B. Angell scholar U. Mich., 1967, 68, 69; docent Hendricks Hill Mus., 2001—; vis. com. Harvard U. Sch. Pub. Health, 2002—; mem. nat. adv. com. Calif. Health Benefits Rev. Program, 2004—; pres. Southport Island Assn., 2006—. Mem. Rotary Internat., Phi Beta Kappa, Pi Sigma Alpha. Democrat. Avocations: running, bicycling, gardening, drawing, architecture. Home: 7300 Maple Ave Chevy Chase MD 20815-5108 also: 29 Paradise Lane Southport ME 04576 Office Phone: 202-639-1884.

POLLARD, MORRIS, microbiologist, educator; b. Hartford, Conn., May 24, 1916; s. Harry and Sarah (Hoffman) P.; m. Mildred Klein, Dec. 29, 1938 (dec. 2001); children: Harvey, Carol, Jonathan. D.V.M., Ohio State U., 1938; MS, Va. Poly. Inst., 1939; PhD (Nat. Found. Infantile Paralysis fellow), U. Calif.-Berkeley, 1950; DSc (hon.), Miami U., Ohio, 1981. Mem. staff Animal Disease Sta., Nat. Agrl. Research Center, Beltsville, Md., 1939-42; asst. prof. preventive medicine Med. br. U. Tex., Galveston, 1946-48, assoc. prof., 1948-50, prof., 1950-61; prof. biology U. Notre Dame, Ind., 1961-66, prof., chmn. microbiology, 1966-81, prof. emeritus, 1981—, 2001—, dir. Lobund Lab., 1961-85, Coleman dir. Lobund Lab., 1985—, Coleman Found. prof., 1985—2001. Vis. prof. Fed. U. Rio de Janeiro, Brazil, 1977; vis. prof. Katholieke U., Leuven, Belgium, 1981; mem. tng. grant com. NIH, 1965-70; mem. adv. bd. Inst. Lab. Animal Resources NRC, 1965-68; mem. adv. com. microbiology Office Naval Research, 1966-68, chmn., 1968-70; cons. U. Tex., M.D. Anderson Hosp. and Tumor Inst., 1958-66; mem. colon cancer com. Nat. Cancer Inst., 1972-76, chmn. tumor immunology com., 1976-79; mem. com. cancer cause and prevention NIH, 1979-81; program rev. com. Argonne Nat. Lab, 1979-85, chmn., 1983-85; lectr. Found. Microbiology, 1978 Editor: Perspectives in Virology Vol. I to XI, 1959-80; contbr. articles to profl. jours. Served from 1st lt. to lt. col. Vet. Corps, AUS, 1942-46. Recipient Disting. Alumnus award Ohio State U., 1979, Army Commendation medal, Presdl. citation, Hope award Am. Cancer Soc., 2000; named Hon. Alumnus U. Notre Dame, 1989; McLaughlin Faculty fellow Cambridge U., 1956; Raine Found. prof. U. Western Australia, 1975; vis. scientist Chinese Acad. Med. Scis., 1979, 81; hon. prof. Chinese Acad. Med. Scis., 1982. Mem. Am. Acad. Microbiology (charter), Brazilian Acad. Scis., Soc. Exptl. Biology and Medicine, Am. Soc. Microbiology (Acad. Sci. Achievement award 1990), Am. Soc. Investigative Pathology, Am. Assn. Cancer Rsch., Am. Soc. Lab. Animal Sci., Am. Soc. Virology, Assn. Gnotobiotics (pres.), Internat. Commn. Lab. Animal Sci., AAAS, Internat. Assn. Gnotobiology (pres.), Internat. Assn. Gnotobiotics (hon. pres. 1987), Sigma Xi, Phi Delta Epsilon (hon.), Phi Zeta (hon.). Office: Lobund Lab U Notre Dame Notre Dame IN 46556 Home: 1025 Park Pl Apt 137 Mishawaka IN 46545-3537 Office Phone: 574-631-7564.

POLLARD, OVERTON PRICE, retired lawyer; b. Ashland, Va., Mar. 26, 1933; s. James Madison and Annie Elizabeth (Hutchinson) Pollard; m. Anne Aloysia Meyer, Oct. 1, 1960; children: Mary O., Price, John, Anne, Charles, Andrew, David. AB in Econs., Washington and Lee U., 1954, JD, 1957. Bar: Va. Claims supr. Travelers Ins. Co., Richmond, Va., 1964-67; asst. atty. gen. State of Va., Richmond, 1967, 70-72; spl. asst. Va. Supreme Ct., Richmond, 1968-70; exec. dir. Pub. Defender Commn., Richmond, 1972—2003; ptnr. Pollard & Boice and predecessor firms, Richmond, 1972-87. Bd. govs. Va. Criminal Law Sect., Richmond, 1970—72; pres. Met. Legal Aid, Richmond, 1978; chair sr. lawyers sect. Va. State Bar, 1999—2000. Del. State Dem. Conv., Richmond, 1985; mem. Va. Commn. Family Violence Prevention, 1995; bd. dirs. Henrico County Housing Corp., 1999. With USN, 1957—59. Recipient Svc. award, Criminal Law Bd. of Govs. Pub. Defender Study, 1971, Outstanding Svc. award, Pub. Defender Commn., 1998, Carrico Professionalism award, Va. State Bar Criminal Law Sect., 2005. Fellow: ABA Found., Va. Law Found.; mem.: ABA, Va. Bar Assn. (Pro Bono Publico award 1995, Walker award 2005), Nat. Legal Aid and Defender Assn. (Reginald Heber Smith award 1991), Richmond Bar Assn., Va. Bar Assn. (chmn. criminal law sect. 1991—93). Democrat. Baptist. Avocation: fishing. Home: 7726 Sweetbriar Rd Richmond VA 23229-6622

POLLARD, SAMUEL D., film producer, director and editor; BA, Baruch Coll., 1973. Prof. Kanbar Inst. Film & TV, NYC. Mem., adv. com. Nat. Endowment for Humanities, Nat. Endowment for Arts, Ind. TV Svc. Editor: (TV series) Vegetable Soup, 3-2-1 Contact, Children's Television Workshop (Emmy award, 1989, 1991), (documentaries) Just Crazy About Horses, 1978, Style Wars, 1983, Distant Harmony, 1987, Depression, 1988, Mo'Better Blues, 1990, Jungle Fever, 1991, Juice, 1992, Surviving the Game, 1994, Clockers, 1995, Girl 6, 1996, Bamboozled, 2000, Twelve Disciples of Nelson Mandela, 2005; editor, prodr. (documentaries) Four Little Girls, 1997, American Roots Music, 2001, When the Levees Broke: A Requiem in Four Acts, 2006 (George Polk award for Documentary TV, 2006); prodr.: (documentaries) Goin' Back to T-Town, 1993, Jim Brown: All American, 2002, The Rise and Fall of Jim Crow, 2002 (George Peabody award, 2003), The Blues, 2003, Spike Lee Presents Mike Tyson (Emmy award), The Mystery of Love, 2006; exec. prodr.: I'll Make Me a World, 1999 (George Peabody award, 2000), Brother Outsider: The Life of Bayard Rustin, 2003, Bragging Rights, 2006; prodr., dir. (documentaries) Eyes on the Prize II, 1990 (Emmy award, 1987). *

POLLARD, THOMAS DEAN, cell biologist, educator; b. Pasadena, Calif., July 7, 1942; s. Dean Randall and Florence Alma (Dierker) Pollard; m. Patricia Elizabeth Snowden, Feb. 7, 1964; children: Katherine, Daniel. BA cum laude, Pomona Coll., Claremont, Calif., 1964; MD cum laude, Harvard Med. Sch., 1968. Intern Mass. Gen. Hosp., Boston, 1968—69; staff assoc. lab. biochemistry Nat. Heart and Lung Inst., Bethesda, Md., 1969—72; asst. prof. anatomy Harvard Med. Sch., Boston, 1972—75, assoc. prof., 1975—78; Bayard Halsted prof., dir. dept. cell biology and anatomy Johns Hopkins U. Sch. Medicine, Balt., 1977—96; pres. Salk Inst. Biol. Studies, La Jolla, Calif., 1996—2000, prof., 1996—2001, U. Calif., San Diego, 1996—2001; Eugene Higgins prof. molecular, cellular and devel. biology and cell biology Yale U., New Haven, 2001—06, prof. cell biology, 2002—, prof. molecular biophysics and biochemistry, 2003—, Sterling prof. molecular, cellular and devel. biology and cell biology, 2006—. Vis. scientist Med. Rsch. Coun. Lab. Molecular Biology, Cambridge, England, 1984; mem. NRC Commn. Life Sci., 1990—97, chair, 1993—97; mem. coun. NIH Nat. Inst. Gen. Med. Sci.; adj. prof. biology, bioengineering and chemistry and biochemistry U. Calif., San Diego, 1997—2001; chair dept. molecular, cellular and devel. biology Yale U., 2004—. Contbr. articles to profl. jours.; mem. editl. bd.: Cell Biology - Internat. Reports, 1976—81, Jour. Cell Biology, 1977—82, Jour. Submicroscopic Cytology, 1978—82, Cell Motility and the Cytoskeleton, 1980—94, Jour. Muscle Rsch. and Cell Motility, 1980—88, Microscopy Rsch. and Technique, 1981—93, Current Opinion in Cell Biology, 1988—, Current Biology, 1991—, Protein Profile, 1994—97, Trends in Biochemical Scis., 1995—, Procs. NAS, 1996—98, assoc. editor: Molecular Biology of the Cell, 1991—. Co-recipient Lewis S. Rosentiel Disting. Work in Basic Med. Rsch. award, Brandeis U., 1996, Gairdner award for Achievement in Med. Rsch., Gaidner Found., 2006; recipient Rsch. Career Devel. award, US Pub. Health Svc., 1974—78, MERIT award, Nat. Inst. Gen. Med. Sci., 1988—98; Winston Churchill Overseas fellowship, Churchill Coll., UK, 1984, Guggenheim fellowship, 1994. Fellow: Am. Acad. Microbiol., AAAS (bd. dirs. 2006—), Inst. Medicine, Biophys. Soc. (mem. coun. 1977—80, pres. 1992—93, Pub. Svc. award 1997), NAS, Am. Acad. Arts & Scis.; mem.: Am. Soc. Biochemistry and Molecular Biology, Marine Biol. Lab. (trustee 1991—97), Am. Soc. Cell Biology (mem. exec. com. 1976—77, mem. coun. 1976—79, pres. 1987—88, K.R. Porter lectr. 1989, E.B. Wilson medal 2004). Achievements include patents in field. Office: Dept Molecular Cellular and Devel Biology Yale U PO Box 208103 New Haven CT 06520-8103 E-mail: thomas.pollard@yale.edu.

POLLARD, VERONICA, automotive executive; m. Joel Dreyfuss; 1 child, Justin. Student, U. Wis.; Bachelor's Degree, Boston U.; Master's Degree, Columbia U. First grade tchr., NY; mgr. internat. affairs Cosmo Pub. Rels. Corp., Tokyo; staff writer San Francisco Chronicle; asst. dir. pub. affairs Newsweek Mag.; publicist ABC TV Network, mgr. bus. info.; dir. corp. comm. Capital Cities/ABC, Inc.; v.p. corp. pub. rels. ABC; v.p., external affairs Toyota Motor Corp. Services N.Am., 1998—2002; group v.p. corp. comm. Toyota Motor N.Am., Inc., 2002—. Bd. dirs. Granite Broadcasting Corp.; mem. individual investor adv. com. N.Y. Stock Exch. Former dir. Nat. YMCA of the U.S.A., YMCA Greater N.Y.; trustee Mus. for African Art, NY; active YMCA; hon. bd. mem. West Side YMCA, NY, 1990—98, bd. chair; dir. The Doe Fund, NY. Mem.: Women's Forum. Office: Toyota Motor NAm Ste 4900 Nine West 57th St New York NY 10019

POLLARO, PAUL PHILIP, artist; b. NYC, Aug. 2, 1921; s. Charles and Maria (Aprile) P.; m. Jo Ann Stover, July 16, 1962 (div. Nov. 1979); children: Lauren, Paul Jr.; m. Laura Clayton, Apr. 2, 1985. Student, Art Students League, 1945-48, Pratt Graphic Ctr., 1972. Instr. painting The New Sch. of Social Rsch., NYC, 1964-69; vis. artist Notre Dame U., South Bend, Ind., 1965-67; asst. prof. art, chmn. art dept. Wagner Coll., Staten Island, NY, 1970-73; asst. dir. The MacDowell Colony, Peterborough, NH, 1973-76; pvt. practice Hancock, NH, 1976—. One-man shows include Jersey City Mus., NJ, 1966 (2d prize), S.I. Mus. Art, NY, 1973, Manchester Inst. Arts and Scis., Manchester, NH, 1970-85, Chryser Mus., Norfolk, Va., 1991, others. Sgt. U.S. Army, 1942-45, PTO. Tiffany Found. grantee, NYC, 1967, N. State Coun. Arts grantee, 1985; MacDowell Colony fellow, 1965-69. Roman Catholic. Home: Norway Hill Hancock NH 03449

POLLET, SUSAN L., lawyer; b. Manhasset, NY, Dec. 17, 1954; d. Myron J. and Barbara Audrey (Kananack) Feldman; m. Richard Pollet, June 30, 1985; children: Katharine Ann, Eve Whitney. BS in Consumer Econ. and Pub. Policy, Cornell U., 1976; JD, Emory U., 1979. Bar: Ga. 1979, N.Y. 1980. Legal asst. ICC Industries, Inc., NYC, 1979; lawyer Dwyer, Peltz & Walker, NYC, 1980-82, Acito & Klein P.C., NYC, 1982-84; supervising atty. litigation Long Island Lighting Co., Hicksville, N.Y., 1984-86; part-time county atty. Putnam County Dept. of Social Svcs., 1994-97; assoc. ct. atty. Westchester County Family Ct., NY, 1997—2004; exec. dir. PACE Women's Justice Ctr., 2004—05; counsel, dir. Parent Edn. and Awareness Program of O.C.A., 2005—. Adj. prof. Mercy Coll., N.Y., 1991-97; pvt. practice, 1988-97; law guardian for children, 1988-97. Contbr. articles to profl. jours. Legal facilitator P.E.A.C.E. Program; former mem. 9th Jud. Dist. Task Force; mem. 9th Jud. Dist. Gender Fairness Com., 2004—, State Family Violence Task Force, 2004—; nominating com. Temple Bethel, 1999—2001; bd. dirs. Chappaqua Children's Workshop, 1991—92, Pleasantville Children's Ctr., 1988—89; amb. Cornell Alumni Admissions, 1991—2003. Mem.: Women's Bar Assn. of the State of N.Y. (state dir. 1997—2005, co-chair legis. com. 1999—2001, v.p. 2001—02, co-chair legal rights children com. 2002—05, co-chair domestic violence com. 2005—), Westchester County Bar Assn. (family ct. com. 1991—92), Westchester Women's Bar Assn. (v.p. 1993—95, pres. 1995—97, chair archives and historian com. 2001—, co-chair subcom. women and politics 2002—03), Westchester Children's Assn. (bd. dirs. 2000—04, Gagliardi award com. 2005—). Avocations: reading, art, hiking, writing. Home: 67 Ludlow Dr Chappaqua NY 10514-1222 Office Phone: 646-483-3536. Personal E-mail: susanpollet@aol.com. Business E-Mail: spollet@courts.state.ny.us.

POLLEY, HARVEY LEE, retired missionary, math and science educator; b. Wapato, Wash., Aug. 14, 1924; s. Edward Prestley and Alda June Polley; m. Corinne Weber; children: Catherine, David, Corinne, Robert. BA, Whitworth Coll., 1951; postgrad., East Wash. Coll., 1953, Berkeley Bapt. Div. Sch., 1958—59; MEd, Ctrl. Wash. Coll., 1958; postgrad., Ecole d'Adminstrn. des Affaires Africaines, Brussels, 1959—60. Tchr. Quincy Pub. Schs., Wash., 1953—57, N.W. Christian Schs., Spokane, 1958; missionary Am. Bapt. Fgn. Missionary Soc., Democratic Republic of Congo, 1958—89; tchr. Evang. Pedagogical Inst., Kimpese, Democratic Republic of Congo, 1961—69, asst. legal rep., dir., prin., supt., 1969—72; dir. BIM Hostel, Kinshasa, Democratic Republic of Congo, 1972—73; mem. staff Ctr. Agrl. Devel. Lusekele, Democratic Republic of Congo, 1975—85, dir., 1976—79, 1983—85, Plateau Bateke Devel. Program, Kinshasa, 1985—89; ret., 1989. Author: Mpila Kele, a rural development guide written in the Kituba lang., 1989. Mem. Coun. Elders, Kimpese, 1969-72; pres. bd. adminstrn. Vanga (Zaire) Hosp., 1981-83; mem. exec com. Nat. Human Nutrition Planning Coun. Govt. Zaire-USAID, Kikwit, 1983-85. With U.S. Army, 1946-47, USAF, 51-53. Home: 2405 W Johannsen Rd Spokane WA 99208-9616

POLLEY, RICHARD DONALD, microbiologist, chemist; b. Bklyn., Feb. 23, 1937; s. George Weston and Evelyn (Tuttle) P.; m. Linda R. Radford, Sept. 21, 1991; children from previous marriage: Gordon MacHeath, Jennifer Elizabeth, Tabitha Isabelle, Sean Sullivan. Student, Trinity Coll., 1954-57; BS, Hofstra U., 1960. Lic. nuclear radiation tech. U.S. Govt., 2003. Asst. advt. mgr. tech. Sun Chem. Corp., 1961-63; tech. advt. mgr. Celanese Plastics Co., Newark, 1963-67; account dir. McCann Indsl. Tech. Sci. Mktg., NYC, 1967-68, v.p., gen. mgr. Miami, 1968-70; pres. Intercapital Belgium S.A., Brussels, Nassau, Bahamas, Panama City, Panama, 1970-72; cons. Nuclear Regulatory Commn., Atomic City, Idaho, 1975—76; founder, pres., tech. dir. Iodinamics Corp., Lancaster, Pa., El Paso, Tex., El Paso, Tex., 1973-76; founder, CEO, COO, tech. dir., bd. dirs., chmn. Hydrodine Corp., Miami, 1976—2002, chmn., CEO, tech. dir., 1986—2002, also bd. dirs. Founder, chmn. CEO, COO, tech. dir. Polymorphic Polymers Corp., Miami, 1978—90; founder, COO, tech. dir., CEO, bd. dirs. Omnidine Corp., Miami, 1980—98, bd. dirs.; pres., tech. dir. Skin Care Labs., Inc., Miami, Fla., 1979—90; tech. dir. Hydrodine Biotech (Far East) Ltd., Bangkok, Thailand, Hong Kong, Singapore and Kuala Lumpur, 1989—98; CEO, tech. dir. Polllabs., Sao Paulo, Brazil, 1990—2000; tech. dir. Ecology Tech. do Brasil, Sao Paulo, 1993—2000; tech. dir., environ. and agrl. mgr. Environ. Tech. do Brasil, Sao Paulo, 1995—; chief internat. tech. dir. environ. microbiology Gen. Environ. Sci. Corp., Solon, Ohio, 1993—2000; chmn., co-founder Peer Group Influencers Ltd., London, Miami, 1988—98; v.p., bd. dirs. Internat. Airlines, Long Beach, Calif., 1984—2000; COO, tech. dir. Swiver Corp., Miami, 1994—2002; tech. dir. chief scientist Infinity Techs., Ltd., Panama City, 1996—98; founder, bd. dirs., CEO, pres., tech. dir. PolleyTech Corp., Pembroke Pines, Fla., 1998—; overseas dir. field Iodine Deficiency Disease med. demonstration projects Beth Israel Hosp., Harvard U. Med. Sch., 1977—88; lectr. Harvard Bus. Sch., 1980; cons. water disinfection control, water environments Pan Am. Health Orgn., others; med. and tech. dir. Enzymes Brasil, Ltd., Sao Paulo, 2001—, med. mgr., tech. dir., Guayaquil, Ecuador, 2001—; chmn. med./sci. adv. bd., found. tech. dir. RAH Med. Rsch. Found., Napa Valley, Calif., 2001—; cons. IGFA Wetlands Project, 2001—; founder, CEO, COO, chmn. bd. dirs. Xurex Nano-Coatings Corp., Davie, Fla., 2005—. Mem. editl. adv. bd. Chem. Week, 1988; contbr. articles to profl. jours.; patentee. Mem. cmty. bd. Am. Heart Assn., Am. Stroke Assn., Broward County, PR. Recipient R. Buckminster Fuller Home of the Future award for paints and water system, 1976. Mem. AAAS, NRA, Am. Concrete Inst., N.Y. Acad. Scis., Internat. Iodine Inst. (chmn. bd. and tech. dir. 1976—), Associaçao de Ciencia e Tecnologia Ambiental (bd. dirs. Sao Paulo 1993—), The Nature Conservancy, World Wildlife Fund, Sierra Club, Audubon Soc., Wilderness Soc., Defenders of Wildlife, Environ. Defense Org., Fla. Wildlife Fedn., Internat. Game Fish Assn., others. Achievements include patents for farm, industrial, commercial, medical, environmental and household protective coatings and water treatment devices, nuclear industries; fields of medicine, environmental protection, agriculture and enzymes soil road building, asphalt and soil enzymes roads, lagoons, aquaculture, ponds; drinking water reservoirs, hazardous waste containment area soil reservoirs; soil aircraft landing strips; coinventor, foundational nano-molecular protective coatings. Office: Xurex Nano-Coatings Corp 531 Gallatin Place NW Albuquerque NM 87121 E-mail: rpolley@xurex.com.

POLLEY, SARAH, actress; b. Toronto, Canada, Jan. 8, 1979; d. Michael and Diane Polley; m. David Wharnsby. Attended, Canadian Film Centre. Actor: (films) One Magic Christmas, 1985, Confidential, 1986, Prettykill, 1987, The Big Town, 1987, Blue Monkey, 1987, The Adventures of Baron Munchausen, 1988, Babar: The Movie, 1989, Exotica, 1994, Children First, 1996, Joe's So Mean to Josephine, 1996, The Sweet Hereafter, 1997, The Hanging Garden, 1997, The Planet of Junior Brown, 1997, Jerry and Tom, 1998, Last Night, 1998, Guinevere, 1999, eXistenZ, 1999, Go, 1999, The Life Before This, 1999, This Might Be Good, 2000, The Weight of Water, 2000, Love Come Down, 2000, No Such Thing, 2001, The I Inside, 2003, My Life Without Me, 2003, Dermott's Quest, 2003, Luck, 2003, Dawn of the Dead, 2004, Sugar, 2004, Siblings, 2004, Don't Come Knocking, 2005, The Secret Life of Words, 2005, Beowulf & Grendel, 2005; (TV series) Road to Avonlea, 1990—96, (TV appearances) Night Heat, 1985, Friday the 13th, 1987, Ramona, 1988, Slings and Arrows, 2006; dir.: (films) The Best Day of My Life, 1999, All I Want for Christmas, 2002; dir., writer (films) I Shout Love, 2001, Away from Her, 2006, dir., prodr.,writer Don't Think Twice, 1999. Office: Celai Chassels Gary Goddard & Associates 10 Mary St Toronto M4Y 1P9 Canada *

POLLICK, G. DAVID, academic administrator, philosopher; b. Kansas City, Mo., Oct. 13, 1947; children: Dayna, Landon; m. Karen Bentley Pollick, 2002. BA in Philosophy, U. San Diego, 1971; PhL in Philosophy, St. Paul U., Ont., Can., 1973; MA in Philosophy, U. Ottawa, Can., 1973, PhD in Philosophy, 1981. Lecturer, philosophy U. San Diego, San Diego, 1972-73; tchr.-counselor, neurologically and physically handicapped Aseltine Sch. Neurol. Handicapped, 1972-73; dir. heroin rehab. ctr. Imperial County Diversion Program, El Centro, Calif., 1973-74; tchr.-counselor, emotionally handicapped Finley Elem Sch, Holtville, Calif., 1974-75; lecturer, philosophy U. Ottawa, Ottawa, Ont, Canada, 1975-77; asst. prof. philosophy, dept. chrm., acad. coordinator St. John's U., Collegeville, Minn., 1977-84; assoc. prof., dean coll. arts and scis. Seattle U., 1984—89; acting pres., provost, v.p. for acad. affairs SUNY, Cortland, 1989—93; co-CEO, pres. Art Inst. Chgo., Sch. Art Inst. Chgo., 1993—95; pres. Lebanon Valley Coll., Annville, Pa., 1996—2004, Birmingham So. Coll., 2004—. Pres. Big South Conf., 2004—. Author: The Work of Roman Ingarden, 1977, (with others) The Aesthetics of Roman Ingarden, 1982; co-editor Supplementary Volume on Aesthetics, 1977. With USN, 1966—68. Fellow philosophy and fine arts, Inst. Ecumenical and Culture Rsch., 1976-77; Koscjusko Found. award, 1978. Avocations: sculpture, art history, archaeology. Office: Birmingham-Southern Coll 900 Arkadelphia Rd Birmingham AL 35254 Office Phone: 717-867-6100. *

POLLIHAN, THOMAS HENRY, lawyer; b. St. Louis, Nov. 15, 1949; s. C.H. and Patricia Ann (O'Brien) P.; m. Donna M. Bickhaus, Aug. 25, 1973; 1 child, Emily Christine. BA in Sociology, Quincy U., 1972; JD, U. Notre Dame, 1975; Exec. Masters in Internat. Bus., St. Louis U., 1992. Bar: Mo. 1975, Ill. 1976. Jud. law clk. to judge Mo. Ct. of Appeals, St. Louis, 1975-76; from assoc. to ptnr. Greenfield, Davidson, Mandelstamm & Voorhees, St. Louis, 1976-82; asst. gen. counsel Kellwood Co., St. Louis, 1982-89, gen. counsel, sec., 1989—, v.p., 1993—2002, sr. v.p., 2002—05, exec. v.p., 2005—. Adj. prof. St. Louis U. Cook Sch. Bus., 2001—04. Trustee Quincy (Ill.) U., 1987-93, 97-2004, pres. alumni bd., 1986-87, Quincy (Ill.) U. Found., 1993-94, 97-; dir., sec. New Piasa Chautauqua, Ill., 1996-97. Named Quincy U. Alumnus of Yr., 1997. Mem. Bar Assn. Met. St. Louis. Roman Catholic. Avocations: soccer, bicycling. Office: Kellwood Co 600 Kellwood Pkwy Ste 300 Chesterfield MO 63017-5897 Home: 2080 Key Harbour Dr Lake Saint Louis MO 63367 Office Phone: 314-576-3312. Business E-Mail: tom.pollihan@kellwood.com. *

POLLIN, BURTON RALPH, language educator; b. Worcester, Mass. s. Louis and Rae (Cohen) P.; m. Alice Pollin, Jan. 30, 1944; children: Diana Claire, Myles Clement. BA, CCNY, 1936; PhD, Columbia U., 1962. Tchr. English NYC Bd. Edn., 1936-62, chmn. dept. English, 1956-62; lectr. English CUNY, 1957-62, assoc. prof. to full prof., 1962-73, prof. emeritus, 1973—. Lectr. on Poe NY State Coun. Humanities, 1996—99, 2003—05. Author: Education and Enlightenment in the Works of William Godwin, 1962, Godwin Criticism: A Synoptic Bibliography, 1967, Dictionary of Names and Titles in Poe's Collected Works, 1968, Discoveries in Poe, 1970, Benjamin Constant's Translation of Godwin's Political Justice, 1972, The Music for Shelley's Poems: An Annotated Bibliography of 1309 Compositions, 1974, Poe, Creator of Words, 1974, The Imaginary Voyages, vol. 1 of Collected Writings of...Poe, 1994, Word Index to Poe's Fiction, 1982, The Brevities of Poe, vol. 2 of Collected Writings of Poe, 1985, Poe's Writings in the Broadway Jour., vols. 3-4 of Collected Writings, 1986, Insights and Outlooks: Essays on Great Writers, 1986, Images of Poe's Works: A Comprehensive Descriptive Catalogue of Illustrations, 1989, The German Face of Poe (with Thomas Hansen), 1995, Poe's Writings in the Southern Literary Messenger, vol. 5 of Collected Writings of Poe (with J.V. Ridgely), 1986, Poe's Seductive Influence on Great Writers, 2004; adv. bd. editors Poe Studies, 1980—, Poe Rev., 2000-04; contbr. over 200 articles to profl. jours. Founder, continuing bd. dirs. Bronxville Beautification Coun., 1980—; active Friends of NY Pub. Libr., Carnegie Hall, Libr. of Bronxville, Eastchester Arts Coun., Columbia U. Libr. Friends, Supporters of Guggenheim Found.; bd. trustees Poe Mus., Richmond, Va. Recipient Poe award, Bronx County Hist. Soc., 2001, Rotary Club award, 2002, Alice and Burton Pollin for effective beautification of Bronxville, 2002; fellow John Hay Whitney, 1947; grantee Am. Philos. Soc., US, 1964—65, London, 1965, 1968, NY State U. Rsch. Found., 1966, Carl and Lily Pforzheimer, 1966, 1969, SUNY, 1967—73, Am. Coun. Learned Socs., 1968, 1975, 1984, Guggenheim Found., 1973—74, CUNY Rsch. Found., 1973, 1980, 1986, NEH, 1983—84, Lectureship on Poe, NY State Humanities Coun., 1996—99, 2003—05. Mem. MLA (life), Poe Studies Assn. (hon., life), Am. Lit. Assn. Avocations: literary research, piano playing, travel, environmentalism. Home: 3 Stoneleigh Plz Apt 4D Bronxville NY 10708-2638

POLLINGER, WILLIAM JOSHUA, lawyer; b. Passaic, NJ, Dec. 14, 1944; s. Irving R. and Ethel (Groudan) P.; m. Helen Rizzo, May 30, 1977; children: Samantha, Zachary. BA, Rutgers U., 1966; JD, Am. U., 1969. Bar: N.J. 1969, U.S. Dist. Ct. N.J. 1969, N.Y. 1981, U.S. Supreme Ct. 1982, U.S. Ct. Appeals (3d cir.) 1986; cert. Civil Trial Atty. N.J. Supreme Ct., 1983; masters level cert. U.S.A. Track and Field Ofcl. Assoc. Krieger & Klein, Passaic, 1969-75; ptnr. Delorenzo & Pollinger, Hackensack, NJ, 1975-84; pres. William J. Pollinger, P.A., Hackensack, 1984-88, Pollinger, Fearns & Kemezis, P.A., 1988-90, Pollinger & Fearns, P.A., Hackensack, 1990-92, William J. Pollinger P.A., Hackensack, NJ, 1992—. Mem. Bergen County Ethics Com., NJ, 1984—88; lectr. ins. N.J.-ICLE, 1998—. Arbitrator Better Bus. Bur. of Bergen and Rockland Counties, Paramus, N.J., 1983-89, Am. Arbitration Assn., 1983—. Assoc. of Yr. award Builders Assn. No. N.J., Paramus, 1981. Master: Justice Robert L. Clifford Am. Inn of Ct.; mem.: ATLA, Def. Rsch. Inst., Am. Arbitration Assn., Trial Attys. N.J., Bergen County Bar Assn., N.J. State Bar Assn. (ins. law com.), Grand Lodge Free and Accepted Masons (past master), Phi Delta Phi. Avocation: track and field officiating. Office: 302 Union St Hackensack NJ 07601-4303 Office Phone: 201-487-5666.

POLLIO, RALPH THOMAS, managing editor, writer, magazine publishing consultant; b. Bronx, N.Y., Nov. 1, 1948; s. Thomas and Dolores (Miccioli) P.; m. Rita Lucia Napolitano, Sept. 29, 1974 (div. 1991); 1 child, Christopher. BCE, Manhattan Coll., 1978; postgrad., Columbia U., 1988—. Founding pub., editor, owner Ea. Basketball Publs., Franklin Square, N.Y., 1975-88; cons., ptnr., founder Ea. Basketball Mag., Rochester, Mich., 1988—; founding pub., owner, editor High School News, 1984, EB News, 1981; mng. editor Harman Consumer Group, Woodbury, N.Y. Contbr. articles to mags. and profl. jours., 1985—. Sgt. U.S. Army N.G., 1969-74. Mem. U.S. Basketball Writers Assn. (1st Place award for best mag. feature 1984), ASCE, Soc. Profl. Journalists, Sigma Delta Chi, Internat. Soc. Philos. Enquiry, World Lit. Acad., Mag. Pubs. Assn., Am. Soc. Mag. Editors, Mensa, and numerous other high IQ socs. Roman Catholic. Clubs: N.Y. Road Runners (N.Y.C.), Dix Hills Runners. Avocations: working out, listening to jazz, gourmet cooking, reading, film. Home: 1201 Hempstead Ave Malverne NY 11565-1213 Office Phone: 516-682-3715. Business E-Mail: rpollio@harman.com.

POLLITT, BYRON H., JR., retail executive; BS in Bus. Econs., U. Calif.; MBA, Harvard U. Mgmt. cons. McKinsey & Co.; v.p. corp. ops. planning Walt Disney Co., 1990—92, v.p. bus. planning, 1992—94, CFO, 1994—95, sr. v.p., CFO Disneyland Resorts, 1995—99, exec. v.p., CFO Walt Disney Pks. and Resorts, 1999—2003; exec. v.p., CFO Gap, Inc., San Francisco, 2003—07; CFO Visa Inc., Foster City, Calif., 2007—. Bd. mem. ARC Bay Area Chpt. Office: Visa Inc 900 Metro Ctr Blvd Foster City CA 94404 Office Phone: 650-952-4400. *

POLLITT, JEROME JORDAN, art historian, educator; b. Fair Lawn, NJ, Nov. 26, 1934; s. John Kendall and Doris B. (Jordan) P.; m. Susan Baker Matheson, Feb. 10, 1977. BA, Yale U., 1957; PhD, Columbia U., 1963. Instr. history of art Yale U., New Haven, 1962-64, asst. prof., 1964-68, assoc. prof., 1969-73, prof., 1973-98, prof. emeritus, 1998—, chmn. dept. classics, 1975-77, chmn. dept. history of art, 1981-84, dean, 1986-91. Author: Art and Experience in Classical Greece, 1972, The Ancient View of Greek Art, 1975, Art in the Hellenistic Age, 1986, The Art of Greece: Sources and Documents, 1990, Personal Styles in Greek Sculpture, 1996; editor-in-chief: Am. Jour. Archaeology, 1973-77; contbr. articles to profl. jours. Mem. Archaeol. Inst. Am., Coll. Art Assn. Home: 48 Dillon Rd Woodbridge CT 06525-1219 Office: Dept Art History Yale U PO Box 208272 New Haven CT 06520-8272 Business E-Mail: Jerome.Pollitt@yale.edu.

POLLOCK, ALEXANDER JOHN, banker; b. Indpls., Jan. 28, 1943; s. Alex S. and Doris L. (VanHorn) P.; m. Anne M. Fryfogle, Jan. 27, 1968; children: Elizabeth, Alexander, Evelyn, James. BA, Williams Coll., 1965; MA, U. Chgo., 1966; M.P.A., Princeton U., 1969. Instr. philosophy Lake Forest Coll., Ill., 1967; with internat. banking dept. Continental Ill. Nat. Bank, Chgo., 1969-77, v.p., 1977-82, sr. v.p., 1982-85; prin. Nolan Norton & Co., Chgo., 1985-86; chief fin. officer Marine Corp., Milw., 1986; pres. Marine Bank N.A., Milw., 1987; pres., CEO Cmty. Fed. Savs., St. Louis, 1988-90; vis. scholar Fed. Res. Bank of St. Louis, 1991; pres., CEO Fed. Home Loan Bank Chgo., 1991—2004; fellow Am. Enterprise Inst. Pub. Policy Rsch., Washington, 2004—. Bd. dirs. Gt. Lakes Higher Edn. Corp., Allied Capital Corp., Chgo. Merc. Exch.; past pres. Internat. Union for Housing Fin. Trustee Ill. Coun. on Econ. Edn.; chmn. bd. dirs. Great Books Found. Mem.: Union League Club, Univ. Club, Phi Beta Kappa. Office: Am Enterprise Inst 1150 Seventeenth St NW Washington DC 20036 Office Phone: 202-862-7190. Business E-Mail: apollock@aei.org. *Omnia superans vi rationis et arte loquendi.*

POLLOCK, BRUCE GODFREY, psychiatrist, educator; b. Toronto, Ont., Can., Aug. 18, 1952; s. Ira Justus and Sheila Joy (Godfrey) P.; m. Judith Arluk, May 18, 1982; children: Debra, Ariel. BS, U. Toronto, 1975, MD, 1979; PhD, U. Pitts., 1987. Chief resident Clarke Inst. Psychiatry, Toronto, 1982-83; fellow U. Pitts., 1983-84, asst. prof. dept. psychiatry, 1984-90, assoc. dir. clin. pharmacology dept. psychiatry, 1987-95, assoc. prof. depts. psychiatry and pharmacology, 1990-96, dir. geriat. psychopharm. dept. psychiatry and pharmacology, 1995—, prof. depts. psychiatry, pharmacology and pharm. scis., 1997—, chief acad. divsn. geriatrics and neuropsychiatry, 2001, Sandra A. Rotman chair neuropsychiatry, 2005—; head divsn. geriatric psychiatry U. Toronto, 2005—. Contbr. chapters to books, articles to profl. jours. Centennial fellow Med. Rsch. Coun. of Can., Ottawa, 1983, Merck fellow geriatric clin. pharmacology, Am. Fedn. for Aging Rsch., N.Y.C., 1988; recipient Gerat. Mental Health award NIMH, Bethesda, Md., 1992, Ind. Scientist award, 1997, Sr. Investigation Award, Am. Assoc. for Geniatric Psychiatry, Bethesda, Md., 2003. Fellow Royal Coll. Physicians Can., Am. Psychiat. Assn. (disting.). Home: 7032 Meade St Pittsburgh PA 15208-2429 Office: Rotman Rsch Inst Baycrest 3560 Bathurst St Toronto Canada M6A 2E1 Home Phone: 412-243-5415.

POLLOCK, EARL EDWARD, lawyer; b. Decatur, Nebr., Feb. 24, 1928; s. Herman and Della (Rosenthal) P.; m. Betty Sokol, Sept. 8, 1951; children: Stephen, Della, Naomi. BA, U. Minn., 1948; JD, Northwestern U., 1953; LLD (hon.), Morningside Coll., 1995. Bar: D.C. 1955, Va. 1955, Ill. 1959, U.S. Supreme Ct. 1960. Law clk., chief justices Vinson and Warren, U.S. Supreme Ct. Washington, 1953-55; atty. antitrust div. Dept. Justice, Washington, 1955-56, asst. to solicitor gen., 1956-59; ptnr. Sonnenschein Nath & Rosenthal, Chgo., 1959—. Life trustee Loyola U., Chgo., Northwestern Meml. Hosp.; pres. Fla. West Coast Symphony, Sarasota, 2004-05. Mem. Chgo. Bar Assn. (chmn. antitrust law com. 1967-68), ABA (chmn. antitrust law sect. 1979-80), Alumni Assn. Northwestern U. Sch. Law (pres. 1974-75, svc. award 1976). Office: Sonnenschein Nath 233 S Wacker Dr Ste 8000 Chicago IL 60606-6491

POLLOCK, ELLEN JOAN, editor; b. Mar. 4, 1955; Reporter Am. Lawyer mag., NYC; editor Manhattan Lawyer; with Wall St. Jour., 1989—2007, legal issues editor, 1989, sr. writer, dep. page one editor; exec. editor BusinessWeek, 2007—. Author: Turks and Brahmins: Upheaval at Milbank, Tweed Wall Street's Gentlemen Take Off Their Gloves, 1990, The Pretender: How Martin Frankel Fooled the Financial World and Led the Feds on One of the Most Publicized Manhunts in History, 2002. Office: BusinessWeek 43rd Fl McGraw-Hill Bldg 1221 Ave of Americas New York NY 10020

POLLOCK, JEFFREY, neuroscientist, radiologist; b. Birmingham, Ala., Sept. 3, 1975; s. William James and Barbara Pollock; m. Erika Grote, July 1, 2000; 1 child, Emily Rebecca. MD, U. South Ala., Mobile, Ala., 2001. Lic. Ala., 2001. Fellow neuroradiology Wake Forest U., Winston Salem, NC, 2006—. Office: Wake Forest Univ Bapt Med Radiology Dept Med Ctr Blvd Winston Salem NC 27157 Home Phone: 336-721-2130; Office Phone: 336-655-0188. Business E-Mail: jpollock@wfubmc.edu.

POLLOCK, JEFREY IAN, pollster, political consultant; b. Phila., Oct. 26, 1971; s. Jay Leonard P. and Joy Eileen Kliener. BA, U. Pa., 1993; MPA, Columbia U., 1997. Pres. Global Strategy Group, NYC, 1995—; adj. prof. Columbia U. Sch. Internat. Pub. Affairs, NYC, 1998—. Named a Rising Star, Campaigns and Elections mag., 1998; named one of 40 Under 40, Crain's NY Bus., 2007. Democrat. Jewish. Office: Global Strategy Group 5th Fl 895 Broadway New York NY 10003 Office Phone: 212-260-8813. Office Fax: 212-260-9058. E-mail: jpollock@globalstrategygroup.com. *

POLLOCK, JOHN PHLEGER, lawyer; b. Sacramento, Apr. 28, 1920; s. George Gordon and Irma (Phleger) P.; m. Juanita Irene Gossman, Oct. 26, 1945; children: Linda Pollock Harrison, Madeline Pollock Chiotti, John, Gordon. AB, Stanford U., 1942; JD, Harvard U., 1948. Bar: Calif. 1949, U.S. Supreme Ct. 1954. Ptnr. Musick, Peeler & Garrett, LA, 1953-60, Pollock, Williams & Berwanger, LA, 1960-80, Rodi, Pollock, Pettker, Christian & Pramov, LA, 1980—89, of counsel, 1989—. Contbr. articles to profl. publs. Trustee Pitzer Coll., Claremont, Calif., 1968-76, Fletcher Jones Found., 1969—, Good Hope Med. Found., 1980-2006, Pacific Legal Found., 1981-91; pres. LA area coun., Boy Scouts Am., 1970. Fellow Am. Coll. Trial Lawyers; mem. ABA, LA County Bar Assn. (trustee 1964-66). Home: 30602 Paseo Del Valle Laguna Niguel CA 92677-2317 Office: 444 S Flower St Ste 1700 Los Angeles CA 90071-2918 Home Phone: 949-495-2948; Office Phone: 213-895-4900. Personal E-mail: phleger1@msn.com.

POLLOCK, KAREN ANNE, computer analyst; b. Elmhurst, Ill., Sept. 6, 1961; d. Michael Paul and Dorothy Rosella (Foskett) Pollock. BS, Elmhurst Coll., 1984; MS, North Ctrl. Coll., 1993. Formatter Nat. Data Corp., Lombard, Ill., 1985; computer specialist Dept. VA, Hines, Ill., 1985—. Lutheran. Avocations: cross-stitch, mystery books, bowling, bicycling, softball.

POLLOCK, LAWRENCE I., retail executive, investment company executive; BS, Ohio State Univ. Pres., COO Zale Corp., 1994—96; exec. v.p., COO Home Place Inc., 1997—98, pres., CEO, 1998—99; pres. Cole Nat. Corp., 2000—03, pres., CEO, 2003—04; pres., mng. ptnr. Lucky Stars Partners LLC, 2004—; bd. dir. Borders Group Inc., 1995—, non-exec. chmn., 2006—. Pres. Bellefaire JCB; trustee Musical Arts Assn. (Cleveland Orch.), Nat. Conf. for Cmty. & Justice No. Ohio region, WVIZ/PBS & 90.3 WCPN ideastream. Office: Borders Group Inc Bd Directors 100 Phoenix Dr Ann Arbor MI 48108 *

POLLOCK, PAUL JAMES, lawyer; b. NYC, July 11, 1960; s. Edmund and Gertrude (Weissman) P.; m. Linda Susan Chinman, Sept. 17, 1988. AB, Colgate U., 1982; JD, Fordham U., 1985. Bar: N.Y. 1986. Assoc. Willkie Farr & Gallagher, NYC, 1986-88, Brown, Raysman & Millstein, NYC, 1988; ptnr. Piper Rudnick LLP, 1996, Katten Muchin Zavis Rosenman, NYC. Mem. ABA, Assn. Bar City of N.Y., Team Redline Club (pres.). Democrat. Office: Katten Muchin Zavis Rosenman 575 Madison Ave New York NY 10022 Office Phone: 212-940-8555. Office Fax: 212-940-8776. E-mail: paul.pollock@kmzr.com.

POLLOCK, R. JEFFREY, lawyer; b. San Francisco, Jan. 5, 1946; BA, DePauw U., 1968; MT, Harvard U., 1971; JD, Northeastern U., 1976. Bar: Ohio 1976, Mich. 2002. Asst. sec. dept. community devel. Commonwealth of Mass., 1972—73; assoc. Burke, Haber & Berick, Cleve., 1976—84, ptnr., 1984—90; atty. McDonald, Hopkins LLC, prin., 1990—; gen. counsel Metaldyne Corp., 2001—05. Mem. ABA, Ohio State Bar Assn., Cleve. Bar Assn. Office: McDonald Hopkins LLC 600 Superior Ave E Ste 2100 Cleveland OH 44114-2653 Home Phone: 216-321-2565; Office Phone: 216-348-5400. E-mail: jpollock@mcdonaldhopkins.com.

POLLOCK, ROBERT B., insurance company executive; BBA, Univ. Wis., Madison, 1976. Actuary CUNA Mutual Ins. Co., 1974—81; staff actuary through sr. v.p. Assurant Employee Benefits, 1981—93; pres., CEO Assurant Employee benefits, 1993—99; exec. v.p., CFO Assurant Inc., 1999—2005, pres., COO, 2005—06, pres., CEO, 2006—07, on adminstrv. leave, 2007—. Past chmn., disability ins. com. Health Ins. Assn. Am. Fellow: Soc. of Actuaries; mem.: Am. Acad. of Actuaries. Office: Assurant Inc 1 Chase Manhattan Plz New York NY 10005 *

POLLOCK, ROBERT ELWOOD, nuclear scientist; b. Regina, Sask., Can., Mar. 2, 1936; s. Elwood Thomas and Harriet Lillian (Rooney) Pollock; m. Jean Elizabeth Virtue, Sept. 12, 1959; children: Bryan Thomas, Heather Lynn, Jeffrey Parker, Jennifer Lee. BSc (hon.), U. Man., Can., 1957; MA, Princeton U., 1959, PhD, 1963. Instr. Princeton (N.J.) U., 1961—63, asst. prof., 1964—69, rsch. physicist, 1969—70; Nat. Rsch. Coun. Can. postdoctoral fellow Harwell, England, 1963—64; assoc. prof. Ind. U., Bloomington, 1970—73, prof., 1973—84, disting. prof., 1984—2001, prof. emeritus, 2001—, dir. Cyclotron Facility, 1973—79, mem. nuc. sci. adv. com., 1977—80. Recipient Alexander von Humboldt Sr. U.S. Scientist award, 1985—88. Fellow: Am. Phys. Soc. (Bonner prize 1992). Home: 2811 Dale Ct Bloomington IN 47401-2414 Office: Ind U Swain Hall Dept Physics Bloomington IN 47405

POLLOCK, STEWART GLASSON, lawyer, state supreme court justice; b. East Orange, NJ, Dec. 21, 1932; BA, Hamilton Coll., 1954, LLD (hon.), 1995; LLB, NYU, 1957; LLM, U. Va., 1988. Bar: NJ 1958. Asst. U.S. atty., Newark, 1958-60; ptnr. Schenck, Price, Smith & King, Morristown, NJ, 1960-74, 76-78; commr. N.J. Dept. Pub. Utilities; counsel to gov. State of N.J., Trenton, 1978-79; assoc. justice N.J. Supreme Ct., Morristown, 1979-99; of counsel Riker Danzig Hyland & Perretti, Morristown, 1999—. Mem. NJ Commn. on Investigation, 1976-78; chmn. commn. on the rules of profl. conduct NJ Supreme Ct., 2000—; co-chmn. Govs. Judicial Adv. Panel. Contbr. articles to profl. jours. Fellow Am. Coll. Comml. Arbitrators; mem. ABA (chmn. appellate judges conf. 1991-92), N.J. Bar Assn. (trustee 1973-78), Am. Judicature Soc. (dir. 1984-88), Morris County Bar Assn. (pres. 1973). Office: Riker Danzig Scherer Hyland & Perretti LLP Hdqs Plz 1 Speedwell Ave Morristown NJ 07962-1981 Business E-Mail: spollock@riker.com.

POLLOCK, TRESA M., engineering educator; BS, Purdue U., 1984; PhD in Materials Sci. and Engring., MIT, 1989. With Gen. Electric Aircraft Engines, 1989—91; prof. Dept. of Materials Sci. and Engring. Carnegie Mellon U., 1991—99, U. Mich., Ann Arbor, L.H. and F.E. Van Vlack prof. materials sci. and engring. Bd. dirs. TMS. Assoc. editor Metallurgical and Materials Transactions; contbr. articles to profl. jours. Recipient Bradley Stoughton Award, Carnegie Mellon Ladd Rschr. Award, Nat. Young Investigator Award, NSF. Fellow: ASM Internat. (chair Structural Materials Div., Internat. Rsch. Silver Medal Award); mem.: NAE. Office: U Mich 2022 Gerstacker 2300 Hayward St Ann Arbor MI 48109 Office Phone: 734-615-5150. Office Fax: 734-763-4788. E-mail: tresap@engin.umich.edu.

POLLOCK-O'BRIEN, LOUISE MARY, public relations executive; b. Tarentum, Pa., Mar. 14, 1948; d. Louis P. and Amelia M. (Ballay) Pollock; m. Vincent Miles O'Brien. BS, Ind. U. of Pa., 1970. Tchr. Archbishop Wood H.S., Warminster, Pa., 1970-75; spokesperson, publicist Calif. Olive Industry, Fresno, 1976-78; account exec. Ketchum Pub. Rels., NYC, 1979-81, account supr., 1982-83, v.p., 1984, v.p., group mgr., 1985-88, sr. v.p., group mgr., 1988-89, assoc. dir., dir. food mktg., sr. v.p., 1990-91; chmn. Aronow & Pollock Comm., Inc., NYC, 1991—2004; pres. Pollock Comm. Inc., NYC, 2004—. Mem. pub. rels. adv. com. Mayor's Vol. Action Com., N.Y.C., 1986; mem. food svc. adv. bd. L.I. City Coll., Bklyn., 1987-88. V.p., fundraiser West 76th St. Block Assn., N.Y.C., 1982. Mem. Internat. Foodservice Editl. Coun. (v.p., bd. dirs. 1984-85). Avocations: watercolor painting, skiing. Office: Pollock Comm Inc 665 Broadway New York NY 10012-4408 Office Phone: 212-941-1414. E-mail: lpollock@pollock-pr.com.

POLMAN, JERRY R., choral director, singer; s. Roy L. and Judy J. Polman; m. Renee L. Jeandell, Dec. 13, 2003. MusB in Music Edn., Grace Coll., Winona Lake, Ind., 2004. Choral dir. Ctrl. Noble Cmty. Sch. Corp., Albion, Ind., 2004—; dir. Warsaw Cmty. Choir, Ind., 2005—. Musical dir. Pleasantview Bible Ch., Warsaw, 2006—07. Mem.: Nat. Assn. Tchrs. Singing (assoc.). Home Phone: 574-269-4478.

POLON, IRA H., lawyer; b. NYC, Mar. 9, 1943; BA, Lehigh U., 1965; LLB, Columbia U., 1968. Bar: N.Y. 1968, D.C. 1971, U.S. Ct. Appeals (D.C. cir.) 1972. Ptnr. Dickstein Shapiro Morin & Oshinsky LLP, Washington. Mem. ABA (mem. corporation, banking and bus. law sect.), D.C. Bar, N.Y. State Bar Assn., Bar Assn. D.C.

POLONSKY, ARTHUR, artist, educator; b. Lynn, Mass., June 6, 1925; s. Benjamin and Celia (Hurwitz) P.; children: Eli, D.L., Gabriel. Diploma with highest honors, Sch. Mus. Fine Arts, Boston, 1948. Instr. painting dept. Sch. Mus. Fine Arts, Boston, 1950-60; asst. prof. dept. fine arts Brandeis U., 1954-65; assoc. prof. Boston U., 1965-90, prof. emeritus, 1990—. One-man shows include Boris Mirski Gallery, Boston, 1950, 1954, 1956, 1964, Durlacher Gallery, NYC, 1965, Mickelson Gallery, Washington, 1966, 1974, Boston Pub. Libr., 1969, 1990, 1993, 1996, 1999, Boston Ctr. for Arts, 1983, Starr Gallery, Boston, 1987, Fitchburg Art Mus., 1990, Kantar Fine Arts, Newton, Mass., 2002, St. Botolph Club Gallery, Boston, 2004—05, exhibited in group shows at Met. Mus., NYC, 1950, The Salon Des Jeunes Peintres, Paris, 1950, Stedelijk Mus., Amsterdam, The Netherlands, 1950, Carnegie Internat. Expn., 1951, Boston Arts Festival, 1954—55, 1985, Inst. Contemporary Art, Boston, 1960, Boston Mus. Fine Arts, 1976, Expressionism in Boston, Decordova Mus., Lincoln, Mass., 1986, Palais Univ. de Strasbourg, France, 1992, Boston's Honored Artists, Danforth Mus., Framingham, Mass., 1995, 2007, DeCordova Mus., Lincoln, Mass., 2002, Sagendorph Gallery, Keene State Coll., Keene, NH, 2003, Francesca Anderson Gallery, Lexington, Mass., 2004, Represented in permanent collections Mus. Fine Arts, Boston, Fogg Mus., Harvard U., Addison Gallery of Am. Art, Andover, Mass., Stedelijk Mus., Amsterdam, Walker Art Ctr., Mpls., Zimmerli Art Mus., Rutgers U., New Brunswick, NJ, Honolulu Acad. Arts, DeCordova Mus., Lincoln, Mass., High Mus. Art, Atlanta, The Danforth Mus., Framingham, Mass. Recipient Louis Comfort Tiffany award for painting, 1951, 1st prize Boston Arts Festival, 1954; European travelling fellow Sch. Mus. Fine Art, Boston, 1948-50; named Copley Master, Copley Soc. Boston, 1986. Mem. Artists Equity Assn., Inc. (founding, former dir. New Eng. chpt.). Address: 364 Cabot St Newtonville MA 02460-2252 Office Phone: 617-969-6789.

POLOZOLA, FRANK JOSEPH, federal judge; b. Baton Rouge, Jan. 15, 1942; s. Steve A. Sr. and Caroline C. (Lucito) P.; m. Linda Kay White, June 9, 1962; children: Gregory Dean, Sheri Elizabeth, Gordon Damian. Student bus. adminstrn., La. State U., 1959-62, JD, 1965. Bar: La. 1965. Law clk. to US Dist. Ct. Judge E. Gordon West, 1965-66; assoc. Seale, Smith & Phelps, Baton Rouge, 1966-68, ptnr., 1968-73; part-time magistrate US Dist. Ct. (Mid. Dist.) La., Baton Rouge, 1972-73, magistrate, 1973-80, judge, 1980—, chief judge, 1998—2005. Adj. prof. Law Ctr., La. State U., 1977-95. Bd. dirs. Cath. HS. Mem. La. Bar Assn., Baton Rouge Bar Assn., Fed. Judges Assn., 5th Cir. Dist. Judges Assn., La. State U. L Club, KC, Wex Malone Inns of Ct., Omicron Delta Kappa. Roman Catholic. Office: US Dist Ct Russell B Long Fed Bldg & US Courthouse 777 Florida St Ste 313 Baton Rouge LA 70801-1717

POLSBY, ALLEN ISAAC, retired lawyer; b. New Haven, Nov. 4, 1937; s. Daniel II and Edythe (Woolf) P.; m. Gail Kissling, Aug. 30, 1963; children: Daniel Laurence, Abigail Starr. AB, Brown U., Providence, 1959; JD, George Wash. U., Washington, DC, 1962. Bar: DC 1962, US Ct. Appeals (DC cir.) 1963, US Supreme Ct. 1979. Assoc., Denning & Wohlstetter, Washington, 1962-63; trial atty. CAB, 1963-66; asst. counsel research, tech. programs subcom. Com. on Govt. Ops., US Ho. of Reps., 1966; atty. Office Gen. Counsel, HUD, Washington, 1966-2003, acting gen. counsel, 1996, assoc. gen. counsel legis. and regulations, 1996-2000, assoc. gen. counsel appeals, 2000-03.

POLSBY, DANIEL D., dean, law educator; b. Norwich, Conn., Mar. 14, 1945; BA, Oakland U., 1964; JD magna cum laude, U. Minn., 1971. Bar: Minn. 1971, D.C. 1972, Ill. 1977, N.Y. 1982. Law clk. to Judge Harold Leventhal U.S. Ct. Appeals (D.C. cir.), 1971-72; assoc. Wilmer, Cutler & Pickering, Washington, 1972-74; legal adviser to commr. FCC, Washington, 1974-76; asst. prof. law Northwestern U., Chgo., 1976-78, assoc. prof., 1978-79, prof., 1979—99, Kirkland & Ellis prof., 1990—99; prof. law George Mason U., Sch. Law, 1999—, assoc. dean, 1999—2004, acting dean, 2004—05, dean, 2005—. Vis. prof. Cornell U., 1981-82, U. Mich., 1982, U. So. Calif., 1990, Chgo. corr., The Economist, 1990-1994, legal. Author: The False Promise of Gun Control, 1994. Mem. ABA, ALI, Order of Coif. Office: George Mason U Sch Law 3301 Fairfax Dr Arlington VA 22201-4426 Office Phone: 703-993-8087. E-mail: polsby@gmu.edu. *

POLSBY, GAIL K., psychotherapist; b. Washington, Jan. 13, 1939; d. Thomas Edward and Elise Wildman (Hammer) Kissling; m. Allen I. Polsby, Aug. 30, 1963; children: Daniel, Abigail. BA, U. Md., 1960; MSW, Cath. U., DC, 1963. Mem. faculty Washington Sch. Psychiatry, 1967—2001, bd. dirs., 1993—, chmn. bd. dirs., 2001—07; pvt. practice psychotherapy, Chevy Chase, Md., 1969—; cons. doctoral program Clin. Social Work Inst., Washington, 1999—2003. Sec., bd. dirs. Washington Sch. Psychiatry, 1995—2001, chair faculty coun. Editor quar. newspaper Washington Sch. Psychiatry News, 1997-2005. Mem. Am. Group Psychotherapy Assn., Nat. Fedn. Clin. Social Workers. Avocations: hiking, biking. Home: 5651 Bent Branch Rd Bethesda MD 20816-1049

POLSHEK, JAMES STEWART, architect; b. Akron, Ohio, Feb. 11, 1930; s. Alex and Pearl (Beyer) P.; m. Ellyn May Margolis, June 29, 1952; children: Peter, Jennifer. BS, Case Western Res. U., 1951; MArch, Yale U., 1955. With I.M. Pei & Assocs., NYC, 1955-56, Ulrich Frazen & Assocs., NYC, 1957-60; with Westermann & Miller & Assocs., NYC, 1960-61; pvt. practice architecture NYC, 1962-80; dean Sch. Architecture and Planning, spl. advisor to pres. for design and planning Columbia U., NYC, 1972-87; prin. James Stewart Polshek & Ptnrs., NYC, 1980—. Trustee Mcpl. Art Soc., NYC Fulbright fellow, 1956-57 FAIA (1st. v.p. 1971, pres.-elect 1972) Clubs: Yale of NY, Century Assn., AAAL, 2005. Achievements include design of of William J. Clinton Presdl. Ctr., Little Rock, Ark., 2004. Office: Polshek Ptnrshp Arch LLP 320 W 13th St New York NY 10014 Office Phone: 212-807-7171. Office Fax: 212-807-5917.

POLSKY, CYNTHIA HAZEN, artist, art collector, philanthropist; b. NYC, Feb. 16, 1939; m. Leon B. Polsky; 2 children. BA, Marymount Coll., 1978; MBA, Fordham U., 1981. Art collector arts of S.E. Asia and India, 20th century Am. and European paintings, sculpture and 19th and 20th century decorative arts; one-woman shows include U.S. galleries and mus., Represented in permanent collections Corcoran Mus., Washington, DC, Fogg Mus., Cambridge, Mass., Johnson Mus., Cornell U., Ithaca, NY, NY Acad. Scis. and Rockefeller U., NYC. Trustee Met. Mus. Art, NYC, mem. acquisitions com., mem. exec. com., chmn. membership com.; hon. life trustee Asia Soc., Storm King Art Ctr., Mountainville, NY; trustee Pierpont Morgan Libr., NYC; mem. Bryant Park Art Commn.; mem. exec. com. Rockefeller U. Coun.; mem. collector's com. Nat. Gallery Art. Office: 667 Madison Ave New York NY 10021 Office Phone: 212-751-4917.

POLSKY, DONALD PERRY, architect; b. Milw., Sept. 30, 1928; s. Lew and Dorothy (Geisenfeld) P.; m. Corinne Shirley Neer, Aug. 25, 1957; children: Jeffrey David, Debra Lynn. BArch, U. Nebr., Lincoln, 1951; postgrad., U. So. Calif., 1956, U. Calif., Los Angeles, 1957, U. Nebr., Omaha, 1964, U. Ill., 1965. Project architect Richard Neutra, Architect, Los Angeles, 1953-56, Daniel Dworsky, Architect, Los Angeles, 1956; prin. Polsky, AIA & Assocs., Los Angeles, 1956-62, Omaha, 1964—; dir. dept. architecture MCA, Inc., Universal City, Calif., 1962-64. Adj. prof. Coll. Arch., U. Nebr., 1998—99. Prin. works include Mills residence, 1958, apt. bldgs., 1960, Polsky residence, 1961, Milder residence, 1965. Chmn. Design Control I480 Study Mayor's Riverfront Devel., Omaha, 1969, 71; pres. Swanson Sch. Community Club, Omaha, 1972; mem. Mayor's Adv. Panel Design Services, Omaha, 1974; vice chmn. Omaha Zoning Bd. Appeals, 1976; dir. Siena/Francis House. Recipient archtl. awards Canyon Crier Newspaper, Los Angeles, 1960, House and Home Mag., Life Mag., AIA, Santa Barbara, Calif., 1962. Fellow AIA (pres. Omaha chpt. 1968); mem. Nebr. Soc. Archs. (pres. 1975, awards 1964, 68, 87, 91, 93, 94, 95, 97, 01, Firm of Yr. 1997, Harry F. Cunningham Gold medal 2002). Home: 10010 Frederick St Omaha NE 68124-2651 Office Phone: 402-391-7176 ext. 15.

POLSON, SHAWN WILLIAM, microbiologist, molecular biologist; b. Augusta, Ga., Jan. 4, 1977; m. Sara Catherine James. BS in Biology, U. SC, Aiken, 1999; MS in Microbiology, Clemson U., SC, 2002; PhD in Marine Biomedicine and Environ. Sci., Med. U. SC, Charleston, 2002—. Tchg. and lab. asst. U. SC, Aiken, 1998—99; grad. rsch. asst. Clemson U., 1999—2000, grad. tchg. asst., 2000—02; molecular biologist NOAA/Nat. Ocean Svc., JHT Inc. Contract, Charleston, 2003—. Prodn. editor Procs. Eighth Symposium on the Natural History the Bahamas, San Salvador, 1999—2001; sci. party mem., r/v melville Intergovernmental Oceanog. Commn. NW Pacific Cruise, Honolulu, 2002. Decorated ROTC medal The DAR, The Mil. Order World Wars, Medal The Ret. Officers Assn.; recipient Citizenship award, Am. Legion, 1991, Scholastic Excellence medal, 1995, AP Scholar with Distinction, Coll. Bd., 1995, Cert. Achievement, NOAA's Nat. Ocean Svc., 2004. Mem.: Coral Disease and Health Consortium, Internat. Soc. for Reef Studies, Am. Soc. for Microbiology, Sigma Xi (assoc.), Mensa, Gamma Beta Phi, Omicron Delta Kappa. Avocations: carpentry, hiking, fishing, gardening, travel. Office: Hollings Marine Lab 331 Ft Johnson Rd Charleston SC 29412 Office Phone: 843-225-5343.

POLSTER, JAMES, writer, film producer; b. Cleve., Sept. 14, 1947; s. Harold and Ethel Polster; m. Carol Pulitzer, Oct. 29, 1982; 1 child, Nick. BS, Tulane U., 1969; MA, Columbia U., 1973; EdM, Harvard U., 1982. Free lance journalist L.A. Times, San Francisco Examiner, Boston Globe, others, 1977-89; screenwriter Columbia/Tri-Star, Hollywood, Calif., 1988; prodr. Columbia Pictures, Burbank, Calif., 1991-95, NBC, Burbank, 1991-95. Advisor Indira Ghandi, New Delhi, 1979; spokesman Save the Rain Forest, 1987; lectr. in field. Author: A Guest in the Jungle, 1987 (MacDowell award 1988), Brown, 1995 (Critics Choice award 1995, Publishers Weekly Best Book of the Yr., Cable Radio Network Best Book of the Yr.); prodr. moves: Hart to Hart, others. Named to Shaker Heights (Ohio) Hall of Fame, 1996; recipient New Orleans Press Club awards, 1980, 81, Spl. Jury prize Internat. Film Festival, 1987; Wurlitzer Found. fellow, 1988; Calif. Arts Coun. grantee, 1995. Fellow Explorers Club; mem. Internat. Soc. Philos. Inquiry, Writers Guild Am., Vintage Auto Racing Assn., Fgn. Corr. Club (hon.), London Press Club (hon.). Avocations: auto racing, bobsled racing, hydroplane racing, drums.

POLSTON, MARK FRANKLIN, minister; b. Indpls., Feb. 9, 1960; s. Albert Franklin and Mildred (Wiggington) P.; m. Lisa Kaye Polston, July 21, 1984; children: Jordan Franklin, Jonathan Mark. AS, Somerset CC, Ky., 1981; BS, Campbellsville Coll., 1984; JD, Ind. Sch. Law, 1995. Real estate agt. Homestead Real Estate, Somerset, 1978-89; pastor Trace Fork Separate Bapt. Ch., Liberty, Ky., 1979-81, Calvary Separate Bapt. Ch., Nancy, Ky., 1980-84, Harmony Separate Bapt. Ch., Jacksonville, Fla., 1984-85, Fairview Separate Bapt. Ch., Russell Springs, Ky., 1985-89, Calvary Separate Bapt. Ch., Nancy, Ky., 1989-91, Edinburgh (Ind.) Separate Bapt. Ch., 1991; sales rep. Sentry Ins., Somerset, 1989-91; dep. atty. gen. Ind. Atty. Gen., Indpls., 1992—. Clk. Gen. Assn. Separate Bapt., 1988-96; bd. dirs. Separate Bapt. Missions., Inc., 1988-92; adj. prof. Ind. Vocat. Tech. Coll., Indpls., 1993-95. Office: Ind Atty Gen 402 W Washington St Indianapolis IN 46204-2739 Address: Edinburgh Separate Bapt Ch 905 S Main St Edinburgh IN 46124-1311

POLSTRA, LARRY JOHN, lawyer; b. Lafayette, Ind., June 28, 1945; s. John Edward and Elizabeth (Vandergraff) P.; m. Joan Marie Blair Rozier, Sept. 2, 1972 (dec.); 1 stepchild, Shawn M. Rozier; m. Barbara Dominy, Mar. 18, 1988; stepchildren: Tobi Shawn Hoff, Teri Lane Kelly. BS in Bus. Mgmt., Bob Jones U., 1968; JD, Atlanta Law Sch., 1976, LLM, 1977. Bar: Ga. 1976, U.S. Dist. Ct. (no. dist.) Ga. 1976, U.S. Ct. Appeals (11th cir.) 1990, U.S. Supreme Ct. 1994. Mktg. dir. N.Am. Security, Atlanta, 1972-73; acctg. supr. Allstate Ins. Co., Atlanta, 1973-76; sole practice Atlanta, 1976-77; ptnr. Law Smith (formerly Smith & Polstra), Atlanta, 1977-94, of counsel, 1995, England & McKnight, 1996-97, Gary Martin Hays and Assoc., PC (formerly Hays & Maysilles, PC), 1997—. Arbitrator Fulton County Superior Ct., Atlanta, 1986. Served to 1st lt. USMC, 1968-71, Vietnam. Mem. ATLA, Atlanta Bar Assn., Ga. Assn. Trial Lawyers, Ga. Assn. Criminal Def. Lawyers, Marine Corps Assn. Ga. Lawyers. Avocation: golf. Home: 2597 Regency Dr E Tucker GA 30084-2326 Office: 3098 Breckinridge Blvd Duluth GA 30096 Office Phone: 770-934-8000. Personal E-mail: lpolstra@aol.com.

POLT, MICHAEL C., ambassador; b. Austria; married; 2 children. M in Pub. Adminstrn., U. Tenn. Various sr. level positions including dep. dir. for European security and arms control issues US Dept. State, Washington; dep. chief of mission U.S. Embassy, Bern, Switzerland, U.S. Embassy Bonn and U.S. Embassy Berlin, Germany, 1998—2001; prin. dep. asst. to sec. of state, bur. legis. affairs US Dept. State, Washington, 2002—04, US amb. to Serbia and Montenegro Belgrade, 2004—06, US amb. to Serbia, 2006—. Minister-counselor Sr. Fgn. Svc. U.S. Recipient Presdl. Meritorious Svc. award, Thomas Jefferson award for Svc. to U.S. Citizens Overseas, Am. Citizens Abroad. Office: DOS Amb 5070 Belgrade Pl Washington DC 20521-5070 *

POLTRACK, DAVID F., broadcast executive, marketing educator; b. June 3, 1945; BA in History magna cum laude, U. Notre Dame; MBA in Mktg., NYU. With media dept. Ted Bates Advt., until 1969; mgr. mktg. svcs., then dir. rsch. & sales promotion, dir. mktg. info., dir. mktg. svcs., dir. advt. CBS TV, NYC, 1969-79, v.p. mktg. svcs. network sales, 1979-82, v.p. rsch., 1982-87, v.p. mktg. CBS Mktg. Div., 1987-88, sr. v.p. planning & rsch., 1988—94, exec. v.p. rsch. and planning, 1994—2006; pres. CBS Vision, 2006—; exec. v.p., chief rsch. officer CBS Corp., 2006—. Adj. prof. mktg. Columbia U.; adj. prof. TV mgmt. Leonard Stern Sch. Bus., NYU. Author: Television Marketing: Network, Local and Cable, 1983; contbr. articles to profl. jours. Recipient Hugh Malcolm Beville Jr. award, Nat. Assn. Broadcasters & Broadcast Edn. Assn., 1994. Mem.: Mktg. Rsch. Coun. (past pres.), Internat. Radio and TV Found. (former bd. mem.), Advt. Rsch. Found. (past chmn.), Nat. Assn. TV Arts and Scis., Advt. Rsch. Coun. (v.p.), Mktg. Sci. Inst. (trustee, mem. exec. com.), Media Rating Coun. (past chair). Office: CBS Corp 530 W 57th St New York NY 10019 also: Coulmbia Bus Sch 3022 Broadway New York NY 10027 also: Leonard Stern Sch Bus Kaufman Mgmt Ctr 44 W 4th St, Ste 9-181A New York NY 10012 Office Phone: 212-854-7903, 212-854-7647, 212-998-0500, 212-995-4006. E-mail: dfp6@columbia.edu, dpoltrac@stern.nyu.edu.

POLUS GERSTNER, LILLIAN, educational association administrator, director; b. Nashville, Tenn., Oct. 10, 1951; d. Moses and Rosalie Polus; m. Alan Ira Gerstner, Dec. 12, 1976; children: Michael Jacob Gerstner, Lisa Faye Gerstner. BS, Northwestern U., Evanston, Ill., 1973. Cert. tchr. secondary sch. State Bd. Edn., Ill., 1973. Adminstrv. asst. Blau Bishop & Assocs., Chgo., 1973—80; bookseller Waldenbooks, Skokie, Ill., 1986—91; site dir. Holocaust Meml. Found. Ill., Skokie, 1991—. Dir. Holocaust Expression Theatre, B'nai B'rith Youth Orgn., Great Midwest Region, Ill., 1998—2004; spkr. and presenter in field. Author: (plays) Pages of Testimony, 2003; editor (compiler): Books on the Holocaust for Young Readers, Bibliography & Videography for the Study of the Holocaust, (films) Films on the Holocaust for Young Viewers. Lerner fellow, Jewish Found. Righteous, 2001. Mem.: Northwestern Alumni Club Chgo. (v.p. 1989—91, pres. 1991—93, sec. 1987—89, treas. 1985—87), Assn. Holocaust Orgns. (dir. 1998—2000). Jewish. Avocations: travel, reading. Home: 10018 La Crosse Avenue Skokie IL 60077-1008 Office: Holocaust Memorial Foundation of IL 4255 Main Street Skokie IL 60076-2063 Home Phone: 847-675-2334; Office Phone: 847-677-4640. Personal E-mail: lilliangerstner@mac.com. Business E-Mail: lgerstner@hmfi.org.

POLVERINI, PETER J., dean, dental educator; m. Carol Polverini. B in biology, Marquette U., 1969, DDS Dental-Oral Pathology, 1973; DMS, Harvard U. Cert. in oral and maxillofacial pathology Harvard U. Asst. prof. dept. diagnostic and surgical sciences U. Pittsburgh Sch. Dental Medicine, 1977—81; various positions Northwestern U. Med. and Dental Sch., 1981—92; prof. dentistry and chief oral and maxillofacial pathology U. Mich. Sch. Dentistry, 1992—95, chair dept. oral medicine, pathology, and surgery, 1995—96, chair dept. oral medicine, pathology, and oncology, 1996—2000, Donald A. Kerr Endowed Collegiate Prof., 1996—2000; dean U. Minn. Sch. Dentistry, 2000—03, U. Mich. Sch. Dentistry, 2003—. Mem. editl. bd. Lab. Investigation, Jour. Oral Pathology and Medicine; assoc. editor Angiogenesis. Address: U Mich Sch Dentistry 1011 N Univ Ave Ann Arbor MI 48109-1078

POLYAKOV, ALEXANDER M., physics professor; b. Moscow, Sept. 27, 1945; arrived in US, 1989; s. Mark and Ada (Pevzner) P.; m. Daria Makogonenko, June 22, 1981; children: Dimitry, Alex. PhD, Landau Inst., Moscow, 1969. Sr. rschr. Landau Inst., Moscow, 1969-89; Joseph Henry prof. physics Princeton U., 1989—. Author: Gauge Fields and Strings, 1987; co-author (with A. A. Belavin and A.B. Zamolodchikov): Infinite conformal symmetry in two-dimensional quantum field theory, 1984. Recipient Heineman medal Am. Phys. Soc., 1985, Dirac medal Inst. for Theoretical Physics, Trieste, Italy, 1986, Lorentz medal Royal Acad. Netherlands, Amsterdam, 1994, Niels Bohr medal UNESCO, 1998, Pomeranchyk prize, Moscow, 2004. Fellow: Am. Acad. Arts and Scis.; mem.: NAS, French Acad. Scis., Russian Acad. Scis. Office: Dept Physics Princeton Univ PO Box 708 Princeton NJ 08542

POLYAKOV, YURIY SERGEYEVICH, engineer, researcher; b. Moscow, Sept. 3, 1980; s. Sergey Vladimirovich Polyakov and Lyubov Ivanovna Polyakova. BS in Computer Info. Systems summa cum laude, Excelsior Coll., Albany, NY, 2002; MS in Computer Sci., NJ Inst. Tech., Newark, 2003; PhD in Chem. Engring., Moscow State U. Environ. Engring., 2004. MCSE, cert. computing profl. Rsch. asst. Moscow State U. Environ. Engring., 1997—98; field engr. Cross Country Land Svcs., Leavenworth, Wash., 1998—99, network adminstr., software engr., 1999—2001; network engr., software engr. Envision Technologies Inc., Wenatchee, 2001—02; rschr., engring. cons. US Poly Rsch., Ashland, Pa., 2002—. Contbr. articles to profl. jours., chapters to books. Recipient Young Scientist award, Moscow Mayor's Office, 2005. Mem.: AIChE, North Am. Membrane Soc., Am. Filtration Soc. Achievements include patents pending for Hollow Fiber Membrane Adsorber and Process for the Use Thereof; research in the theory of novel filtration processes; study of nonuniform particle deposition on the inner and outer surfaces of ultrafiltration and microfiltration membranes; mathematical modeling of coupled turbulent heat and mass transfer with chemical conversions; development of approximate method for nonlinear differential and integrodifferential equations; phenomenological analysis of natural time and space series with stochastically varying components; development of feedback algorithm for switch location with application to network design. Office: USPolyResearch 906 Spruce St Ashland PA 17921 Office Phone: 570-875-3353. Business E-Mail: ypolyakov@uspolyresearch.com.

POLYDORIDES, ALEXANDROS DEMETRIOS, pathologist; s. Nicos Demetrios and Georgia Kontogiannopoulou Polydorides. AB summa cum laude, Princeton U., NJ, 1995; PhD, Rockefeller U., NYC, 2002; MD, Cornell U., NYC, 2003. Lic. MD Dept. of Pub. Health, State of Conn., 2006. Resident, anatomic pathology and chief resident NY Presbyn. Hosp. Weill Cornell Med. Ctr., NYC, 2003—06; fellow oncologic pathology Meml. Sloan Kettering Cancer Ctr., NYC, 2006—. Recipient Disting. Housestaff award, NY Weill Cornell Med. Ctr. Alumni Coun., 2006, Outstanding Lab. Work award, Princeton U., Dept. of Physics, 1993, Paul E. Strandjord Young Investigator award, Acad. of Clin. Lab. Physicians and Scientists, 2005, Herman L. Jacobius Prize in Pathology, Weill Med. Coll. of Cornell U., 2003, McGraw Hill award, 1996, George Khoury '65 Sr. Prize for Academic Excellence, Princeton U., Dept. of Molecular Biology, 1995; Dwight P. Green scholarship, Princeton U., 1991—93, Samuel Bayard Dod scholarship, 1993—95, grant, Hellenic Med. Soc. of NY, 2001. Fellow: Am. Soc. Clinical Pathology, Coll. of Am. Pathologists; mem.: Acad. of Clin. Lab. Physician and Scientists (assoc.), NY Path. Soc. (assoc.), US and Can. Acad. of Pathology (assoc.), Phi Beta Kappa, Sigma Xi. Home: Apt 20-O 1233 York Ave New York NY 10021-6306 Office: Meml Sloan-Kettering Cancer Ctr Dept Pathology 1275 York Ave New York NY 10021

POLZONETTI, PIERPAOLO, musicologist, music educator; b. Italy, June 27, 1969; s. Claudio and Fernanda Polzonetti; m. Lena Rose Magee, June 2, 2001. PhD, Cornell U., Ithaca, NY, 2003. Asst. prof. U. NC, Greensboro, 2003—06, U. Notre Dame, 2006—. Author: Tartini e la Musica Secondo Natura, 2001 (Internat. prize in musicology Petrassi Inst. Latina); contbr. articles to profl. jours. Recipient Alfred Einstein award, 2004, Am. Musicological Soc. Achievements include development of gastromusicology, semiotics of food in opera and opera buffa and the American Revolution. Home Phone: 574-234-2370; Office Phone: 574-631-0391. Business E-Mail: ppolzone@nd.edu.

POMBO, RICHARD WILLIAM, former congressman, rancher, farmer; b. Tracy, Calif., Jan. 8, 1961; s. Ralph and Onita Pombo; m. Annette Rina Cole, 1983; children: Richie, Rina, Rachel. Student, Calif. State U., Pomona, 1979—82. Councilman City of Tracy, 1991-92; mayor pro-tem Tracy City Coun., 1992; mem. US Congress from 11th Calif. dist., 1993—2007; mem. agrl. com., resources com., transp. and infrastructure com., chmn. subcom. on livestock and horticulture. Chmn. Pvt. Property Rights Task Force, 1993-94, Endangered Species Act Task Force, 1995-96; co-chmn. Spkr.'s Environ. Task Force, 1996. Author (with Joseph Farah) This Land Is Our Land: How to End the War on Private Property, 1996 Co-founder San Joaquin County Citizen's Land Alliance, Calif., 1986—; active San Joaquin County Econ. Devel. Assn., Tracy Bus. Improvement Dist., City Coun. (vice chmn. Cmty. Devel. Agy., Cmty. Parks Com., and Waste Mgmt. Com.), San Joaquin County Rep. Ctrl. Com. Mem. Rotary Club. Republican. Roman Catholic. *

POMERANTZ, CHARLOTTE, writer; b. Bklyn., July 24, 1930; d. Abraham L. and Phyllis (Cohen) P.; m. Carl Marzani, Nov. 12, 1966; children: Gabrielle Rose, Daniel Avram. BA, Sarah Lawrence Coll., 1953. Children's books include The Bear Who Couldn't Sleep, 1965, The Moon Pony, 1967, Ask the Windy Sea, 1968, Why You Look Like You Whereas I Look Like Me, 1968, The Day They Parachuted Cats on Borneo, 1971 (chosen for Internat. Year of the Child 1977-78), The Princess and the Admiral, 1974 (Jane Addams Children's Book award), The Piggy in the Puddle, 1974 (Featured on Reading Rainbow in Claymation, 1992, NYT Outstanding Picture Book of the Year award 1974), The Ballad of the Long Tailed Rat, 1975, Detective Poufy's First Case, 1976, The Mango Tooth, 1977 (Jr. Literary Guild Selection), The Downtown Fairy Godmother, 1978, The Tamarindo Puppy and Other Poems, 1980 (an ALA Notable Book), Noah's and Namah's Ark, 1980, If I Had a Paka, 1982 (Jane Addams Honor award 1983), Buffy and Albert, 1982, Posy, 1983 (1984 Christopher award), Whiff, Sniff, Nibble and Chew, 1984, Where's the Bear?, 1984, The Half-Birthday Party (Jr. Literary Guild Selection), 1984, All Asleep, 1984, One Duck, Another Duck, 1984, How Many Trucks Can a Tow Truck Tow? (Children's Book of the Year Libr. of Congress 1991) 1987, Timothy Tall Feather, 1987, The Chalk Doll (Top 10 Picture Books of 1989 Boston Globe, Parents Choice award, 1990) 1989, Flap Your Wings and Try, 1989, Serena Katz, 1992, The Outside Dog (One of 100 Books Recommended by the N.Y. Pub. Libr., 1993, ALA Notable) 1993, Halfway to Your House, 1993, Here Comes Henny (based on the wordplay of James Joyce), 1994, Mangaboom, 1997, You're Not My Best Friend Anymore, 1998 (Jr. Libr. Guild Selection 1998), The Birthday Letters, 2000, The Mousery, 2000 (Christopher award), (book of poems) Thunderboom!, 2005; co-author, lyricist play Eureka!, 1997; author radio play Whiff Sniff Nibble and Chew, 1997; contbr. stories to mags.; spl. editl. asst.: Einstein on Peace, 1960; editor: A Quarter Century of Un-Americana, 1963. Address: 260 W 21st St New York NY 10011-3447

POMERANTZ, FREDERICK J., lawyer; b. Apr. 3, 1952; BA magna cum laude, CUNY, 1973; MA, Cornell U., 1975; JD, Bklyn. Law Sch., 1979. Bar: NY 1980, US Dist. Ct. Ea. Dist. NY, US Dist. Ct. So. Dist. NY, US Supreme Ct. Ptnr. fin. institutions practice group Wilson, Elser, Moskowitz, Edelman & Dicker LLP, NYC. Mem.: Fedn. Regulatory Counsel Inc., NY State Bar Assn. (torts, ins. & compensation law sect., chmn. com. govtl. rels.), Assn. of the Bar of the City of NY, Phi Beta Kappa. Office: Wilson Elser Moskowitz Edelman & Dicker LLP 23rd Fl 150 E 42nd St New York NY 10017-5639 Office Phone: 212-490-3000 ext. 2109. Office Fax: 212-490-3038. Business E-Mail: pomerantzf@wemed.com.

POMERANTZ, MARTIN, chemistry educator, researcher; b. NYC, May 3, 1939; s. Harry and Pauline (Sietz) P.; m. Maxine Miller, June 4, 1961; children: Lee Allan, Wendy Jane, Heidi Lauren. BS, CCNY, 1959; MS, Yale U., 1961, PhD, 1964. NSF postdoctoral fellow U. Wis.-Madison, 1963-64; asst. prof. Case Western Res. U., Cleve., 1964-69; assoc. prof. chemistry Yeshiva U., NYC, 1969-74, prof., 1974-76, chmn. dept., 1971-72, 73-76; prof. chemistry U. Tex.-Arlington, 1976—; co-dir. Ctr. for Advanced Polymer Rsch., 1988-91; dir. Ctr. for Advanced Polymer Rsch., 1991—; vis. assoc. prof. U. Wis.-Madison, 1972; vis. prof. Columbia U., NYC, 1970-75, Ben Gurion U. of the Negev, Beer Sheva, Israel, summers 1981, 85; program officer NSF, 2005—07. Contbr. articles to sci. jours. Fellow Alfred P. Sloan Found., 1971-76, NSF and Sterling, 1962-63, Leeds and Northrup Found., 1960-62, Woodrow Wilson fellow, 1959-60; grantee NSF, Robert A. Welch Found., Def. Adv. Rsch. Projects Agy., Air Force Office Sci. Rsch., Dept. Energy, Petroleum Rsch. Fund, Tex. Advanced Tech. program, Tex. Advanced Rsch. program, Disting. Record of Rsch. award U. Tex., Arlington, 1997, also others. Mem. Am. Chem. Soc. (Wilfred T. Doherty award Dallas-Fort Worth sect. 1997), Phi Beta Kappa, Sigma Xi. Achievements include research in synthesis, reactions and properties of organo lambda-5-phosphazenes, reactions of carbenes with other molecules, with themselves and with diazo precursors; design, synthesis and study of electronically conducting polymers with enhanced properties, synthesis and study of electroluminescent (light emitting) polymers, synthesis and study of potentially planar bithiophenes, preparation and study of polymeric ionic self-assembled monolayers (ISAMs), non-linear optical materials. Home: 5521 Williamstown Rd Dallas TX 75230-2127 Office: U Tex Dept Chemistry-Biochemistry PO Box 19065 Arlington TX 76019-0065 Office Phone: 817-272-3811. Business E-Mail: pomerantz@uta.edu.

POMERANTZ, MARTIN ARTHUR, astronomer, educator, physicist; b. Bklyn., Dec. 17, 1916; AB, Syracuse U., 1937; MS, U. Pa., 1939; PhD, Temple U., 1951; Fil. Dr. (hon.), U. Uppsala, Sweden, 1967; ScD (hon.), Swarthmore Coll., 1973; DSc (hon.), U. Del., 2001, Syracuse U., 2007. Rsch. asst. Bartol Rsch. Found., 1938—41, rsch. fellow, 1941—43, physicist, 1943—59, dir., 1959—85, pres., 1985—87; v.p. The Franklin Inst., 1967—85, exec. v.p., 1985—87, Bartol prof., 1968—89; prof. emeritus U. Del., 1990—, pres. emeritus, 1987—. Fulbright scholar, vis. prof. Muslim U., Aligarh, India, 1952—53; leader Nat. Geog. Soc. expeditions, 1948—59; chmn. U.S. Com. for Internat. Yrs. of the Quiet Sun Nat. Acad. Scis., 1962—66, mem. Com. on Polar Rsch., 1959—71, mem. Space Sci. Bd., 1963—70, mem. Geophysics Rsch. Bd., 1959—73; v.p. Com for Internat. Yrs. of the Quiet Sun Internat. Coun. Sci. Unions, v.p. Com. Internat. Geophysique, 1962—66; mem. Com. on Solar-Terrestrial Rsch. Nat. Acad. Scis., 1981—86; vis. prof. astronomy Swarthmore Coll., 1961, 64, 67; vis. prof. U. Tokyo, 1983, Potchefstroom U., South Africa, 1987; Sigma Xi nat. lectr., 68; OAS vis. prof., 73. Editor: Jour. of the Franklin Inst.; mem. editl. bd.: Space Sci. Revs.,: Antarctic Rsch. Series. Recipient Centennial Gold medal, Syracuse U., 1970, Prix de la Belgica, Acad. Royal des Scis., des Lettres et des Beaux Arts de Belgique, 1985, Disting. Pub. Svc. award, NSF, 1987, medal for disting. sci. achievement, NASA, 1990. Fellow: AAAS, Am. Geophys. Union, Am. Phys. Soc.; mem.: Am. Polar Soc. (hon.), Rotary Internat., Cosmos Club, Explorers Club, Sigma Pi Sigma (hon.). Home: 100 Deer Valley Rd Apt GE San Rafael CA 94903 Personal E-mail: mapomeratz@sbcglobal.net.

POMERANTZ, MARVIN, thoracic surgeon; b. Suffern, NY, June 16, 1934; s. Julius and Sophie (Luksin) Pomerantz; m. Margaret Twigg, Feb. 26, 1966; children: Ben, Julie. AB, Colgate U., 1955; MD, U. Rochester, 1959. Diplomate Nat. Bd. Med. Examiners, Am. Bd. Surgery, Am. Bd. Thoracic Surgery (bd. dirs. 1989-95). Intern Duke U. Med. Ctr., Durham, NC, 1959—60, resident, 1960—61, instr. surgery, 1966—67; asst. prof. surgery U. Colo. Med. Sch., Denver, 1967—71, assoc. prof. surgery, 1971—74, assoc. clin. prof. surgery, 1974—93, prof. surgery, chief gen. thoracic surgery, 1992—; chief thoracic and cardiovascular surgery Denver Gen. Hosp., 1967—73, asst. dir. surgery, 1967—70, assoc.dir. surgery, 1970—73; pvt. practice Arapahoe CV Assocs., Denver, 1974—92; prof., chief gen. thoracic surgery sect. U. Colo. Health Sci. Ctr., 1992—; resident Duke U. Med. Ctr., Durham, NC, 1963—67. Clin. assoc. surgery br. NCI, 1961—63; mem. staff Univ. Hosp., Denver, Denver Gen. Hosp., Rose Med. Ctr., Denver, Denver VA Med. Ctr., Children's Hosp., Denver, U. Coll. Health Sci. Ctr., 1992—, bd. dirs., 1990—96; vice chmn. Am. Bd. Thoracic Surgery, 1995—97, chmn., 1997—99. Guest editor Chest Surgery Clinics N.Am., 1993; contbr. numerous articles to profl. publs., chapters to books. Master: AMA; fellow: ACS, Am. Coll. Chest Surgeons; mem.: Soc. Vascular Surgeons, Soc. Thoracic Surgeons (nomenclature/coding com. 1991—95, standards and ethics com., govt. rels. com., chmn. program com. 1994—95), Rocky Mtgn. Traumatologic Soc., rgery Soc., Internat. Cardiovascular Soc., Denver Acad. Surgery (pres. 1980), Colo. Med. Soc., Am. Heart Assn. (bd. dirs. Colo. chpt. 1993), Am. Assn. Thoracic Surgeons (program com. 1991), Western Thoracic Surg. Assn. (v.p. 1992, pres. 1993—94, counselor-at-large 1988—90). Office: UCHSC Divsn CTS 4200 E 9th Ave # C310 Denver CO 80262-0001

POMERANTZ, MARVIN ALVIN, manufacturing executive; b. Des Moines, Aug. 6, 1930; s. Alex and Minnie (Landy) P.; m. Rose Lee Lipsey, Nov. 12, 1950; children: Sandy Pomerantz, Marcie Morrison, Vickie Ginsberg, Lori Long. BS in Commerce, U. Iowa, 1952. Exec. v.p. Midwest Bag Co., Des Moines, 1952-60; founder, pres., gen. mgr. Gt. Plains Bag Corp., Des Moines, 1961-75; v.p. Continental Can Co. Inc., Greenwich, Conn., 1971-75; v.p., gen. mgr. Forest Products Brown Systems Operation (div. Continental Can Co. Inc.), Greenwich, Conn., 1975-77; pres. Diversified Group Internat. Harvester, Chgo., 1980-81, ex. v.p., 1981-82; pres., chmn., chief exec. officer The Mid-Am. Group, Des Moines, 1981—; chmn., chief exec. officer Gaylord Container Corp., Deerfield, Ill., 1986—2002. Mem. Greater Des Moines Commn.; trustee Drake U., 1978—; pres. Iowa State Bd. Regents, 1987-93, 95-96; mem. U.S. Olympic Budget and Audit Commn., Colorado Springs., Colo., 1989-92. Republican. Office: The Mid-Am Group 4700 Westown Pkwy Ste 303 West Des Moines IA 50266-6718 Office Phone: 515-224-3610.

POMERANTZ, WENDY JANE, pediatrician, educator; d. Martin and Maxine Pomerantz. BA in Biochemistry summa cum laude, U. Tex., Austin, 1988; MD, U. Tex. SW Med. Sch., Dallas, 1992; MS in Epidemiology, U. Cin., 1998. Bd. cert. pediat. Am. Bd. Pediat., 1995, bd. cert. pediat. emergency medicine Am. Bd. Pediat., 1998. Internship pediats. Children's Hosp. Dallas, 1992—95, residency pediats., 1992—95, fellowship, 1995—98; assoc. prof. clin. pediat. Cin. Children's Hosp., U. Cin., 1998—; affiliated faculty Ctr. Epidemiology and Biostatistics Cin. Children's Hosp., 2002—. Development EMS Telemetry Protocols Children's Med. Ctr., Dallas; co-coordinator Injury Prevention & Advocacy Course Curriculum, 2002—; designer Children for Injury Free Coalition for Kids Website, 2003, content provider, 03; with Rebound Basketball Ednl. Program, 2004—. Co-dir. Injury Free Coalition for Kids in Cin., 2000—06; mem. Cin. Youth Collaborative Mentoring Program, 1997—98, Am. Red Cross Med. Assistance Team, 2000—; chariperson Ohio Emergency Med. Svcs. for Children Com., 2006; mem. Cin. Safe Kids Coalition, 1999—, chair, pub. policy com., 1999—2002; mem. Mt. Lookout Civic Club, 1999—2003; coach St. Mary's Girls Basketball, 2000—03; playground devel. Cin. Recreation Commn., 2001—06; advisor Avondale Cincy After Sch. Program, 2004—; co-dir. Safety Resources Ctr., 2004—. Recipient Nat. Merit Scholarship, 1984, Presdl. Endowed Scholarship, 1984, Panhellenic Merit Scholarship, 1986, SW Med. Found. Scholarship, 1988, Pediat. House Officers Rsch. award, 1995, Divisional Tchg. award, Cin. Children's Hosp., 1998—99, Physician's Recognition award, AMA, 1999—2000, Divisional Tchg. award, Cin. Children's Hosp., 2000—01, 2003—04, Presdl. Partnership award, Cin. Recreation Commn., 2006; Grad. scholar, U. Cin., 1996—98. Fellow: Am. Acad. Pediat. (sect. injury and poision prevention, newsletter editor 2002—06); mem.: AMA, APHA, Soc. Academic Emergency Medicine, Emergency Med. Com., Ohio Chapter, Am. Acad. Pediat. (chair, pediat. emergency medicine com. 2006—), Tex. Med. Assn., Ambulatory Pediatric Assn., Cin. Safe Kids Coalition (pub. policy chair 1999—2002), Am. Red Cross Med. Assistance Team. Avocations: travel, golf, needlepoint. Office: Cincinnati Childrens Hospital Divsn Emergency Medicine 3333 Burnet Avenue MLC 2008 Cincinnati OH 45229 Home Phone: 513-321-4482; Office Phone: 513-636-7966.

POMERANZ, FELIX, accounting educator; b. Vienna, Mar. 28, 1926; s. Joseph and Irene (Meninger) P.; m. Rita Lewin, June 14, 1953; children: Jeffrey Arthur, Andrew Joseph. BBA, CCNY, 1948; MS, Columbia U., NYC, 1949; PhD, U. Birmingham, Eng., 1992. Diplomate Am. Bd. Forensic Acctg.; CPA, NY, Va., La., NC; cert. computer profl., fraud examiner, govt. fin. mgr. Audit staff Coopers & Lybrand, CPAs, NYC, 1949-56; mgr. Marks, Grey & Shron (now Ernst & Young, CPA's), NYC, 1956-58; asst. chief auditor Am.-Standard, NYC, 1958-62; mgr. systems Westvaco Corp., NYC, 1962-66; dir. operational auditing Coopers & Lybrand, CPAs, NYC, 1966-68, ptnr., 1968-85; disting. lectr./dir. Ctr. for Acctg., Auditing, Tax Studies Fla. Internat. U., Miami, 1985-93, prof. acctg., 1993—2002, assoc. dir. sch. acctg., 1993—99, affil. faculty dept. religious studies, 1996—2002, prof. emeritus, 2003—. Author: Managing Capital Budget Projects, 1984; The Successful Audit: New Ways to Reduce Risk Exposure and Increase Efficiency, 1992; co-author: Pensions-An Accounting and Management Guide, 1976; Auditing in the Public Sector: Efficiency, Economy, and Program Results, 1976; Comparative International Auditing Standards, 1985; contbr. articles to profl. jours. Emeritus trustee Nat. Ctr. for Automated Info. Rsch.; founding mem. Ctr. for Study of Islam and Democracy; founder Afghan Inst. Accts.; mem. rev. panel Inst. Chartered Fin. Analysts of India Jour. Audit Practice. 1st lt. AUS, 1944-46, 51-52. Recipient Spear Safer Harmon faculty fellow Coll. Bus. Administrn., 1987, Outstanding Svc. award, 1998, Matriculation Merit award, 2000. Mem. AICPA, NY State Soc. CPA, Assn. Sys. Mgmt., Acad. Acctg. Historians, Assn. Govt. Accts., NY Acad. Scis., Am. Acctg. Assn., Inter-Am. Acctg. Assn., Assn. Cert. Fraud Examiners, Beta Gamma Sigma, Beta Alpha Psi (Most Disting. and Most Outstanding Prof. awards 1993, Most Supportive Prof. award 2002), Alpha Kappa Psi (Dr. Felix Pomeranz Faculty of Yr. award, Endless Work award, Loyal Mem. award 2006). Home: 250 Jacaranda Dr Apt 406 Fort Lauderdale FL 33324-2532 Office: Fla Internat U Sch Acctg University Park Miami FL 33199-0001 Personal E-mail: pomeranzf@bellsouth.net. Business E-Mail: pomeranf@fiu.edu.

POMERANZ, KENNETH L., history professor; PhD, Yale U., 1988. UCI Chancellor's prof. history U. Calif., Irvine. Author: The Making of a Hinterland: State, Society and Economy in Inland North China, 1853-1937, 1993; author: (with Steven Topik) The World that Trade Created: Society, Culture and the World Economy, 1400 to the Present, 1999; author: The Great Divergence: China, Europe and the Making of teh World Economy, 2000. Fellow: Am. Acad. Arts and Sciences. Office: Dept History Univ California Irvine 200H Murray Krieger Hall Irvine CA 92697-3275 Office Phone: 949-824-5169. Office Fax: 949-824-2865. E-mail: klpomera@uci.edu.

POMERENE, JAMES HERBERT, retired computer engineer; b. Yonkers, NY, June 22, 1920; s. Joel Pomerene and Elsie Bower; m. Edythe R. Schwenn, Dec. 1, 1944; children: James Bennett, Katherine Ellen, Andrew Thomas Stewart. BSEE, Northwestern U., 1942; postgrad., Princeton U., 1950. Elec. engr. Hazeltine Corp., Little Neck, NY, 1942-46; mem. staff electronic computer project Inst. for Advanced Study, Princeton, NJ, 1946-51, chief engr., 1951-56; sr. engr. IBM Corp., Poughkeepsie, NY, 1956-67, sr. staff mem. Armonk, NY, 1967-76. Cons. in field. Patentee in field. IBM fellow T.J. Watson Rsch. Ctr., 1976—. Fellow IEEE (Computer Pioneer award Computer Soc. 1986, Edison medal 1993, Eckert-Mauchly award 2006); mem. NAE, Sigma Xi, Tau Beta Pi. Episcopalian. Home: 403 Bedford Rd N Chappaqua NY 10514-2207 Personal E-mail: jhpomerene@aol.com.

POMEROY, CLAIRE, dean; m. William Preston Robertson. MD, U. Mich. Coll. Medicine; MBA, U. Ky. Resident in internal medicine and infectious disease U. Minn., fellow internal medicine and infectious diseases, faculty mem., established HIV clinic at Mpls. Veterans' Adminstrn. Med. Ctr.; chief divsn. infectious diseases U. Ky. Coll. Medicine, asst. dean clin. affairs, assoc. dean rsch. informatics, prof.; exec. assoc. dean U. Calif. Davis Sch. Medicine, 2003, prof. infectious diseases and microbiology and immunology, vice chancellor human health sciences, 2005—, dean, 2005—. Faculty senate coun. U. Ky.; reviewer Nat. Institutes of Health, Dept. Veterans' Affairs. Bd. trustee U. Ky. Office: Office of Dean UC Davis Health System 2315 Stockton Blvd Sacramento CA 95817 Office Phone: 916-734-3578. E-mail: cpomeroy@ucdavis.edu.

POMEROY, EARL RALPH, congressman, retired commissioner; b. Valley City, ND, Sept. 2, 1952; s. Ralph and Myrtle Pomeroy; 2 children. Student, Valley City State U.; BA in Polit. Sci., U. ND, 1974, JD, 1979. Bar: ND 1979. Atty. Sproul, Lenaburg, Fitzner and Walker, Valley City, 1979-84; mem. ND State Ho. Reps., 1980—84; ins. commr. State of ND, Valley City, 1984-92; mem. US Congress from ND (at large), 1993—, mem. ways and means com., mem. agr. com., co-chair Ho. Dem. Social Security Task Force, co-chair Rural Health Care Coalition. Recipient Found. award Rotary, 1975, Rural Health Champions Legis. award Nat. Rural Health Assn. 2004; named Outstanding Young North Dakotan ND Jaycees, 1982. Mem. Nat. Assn. of Ins. Commrs. (chmn. midwest zone 1987-88, exec. com. 1987-88), Phi Beta Kappa. Democrat. Presbyterian. Office: US House Reps 1501 Longworth House Office Bldg Washington DC 20515 Office Phone: 202-225-2611. Office Fax: 202-226-0893. *

POMEROY, GREGG JOSEPH, lawyer; b. Flushing, NY, June 22, 1948; s. George Bart and Dianne (Marshall) P.; m. Deborah Christina Pomeroy, Feb. 16, 1985 (div.); children: Christopher William, Glenn David; m. Suzanne R. Pomeroy, July 25, 1992; children: Adam Barton, Sarah Nicole. BA, U. Fla., 1971; JD, Samford U., 1974. Bar: Fla. 1974, U.S. Dist. Ct. Fla. 1974, U.S. Ct. Appeals (11th cir.) 1974; cert. cir. ct. and county ct. mediator. Asst. pub. defender 17th Jud. Cir., Ft. Lauderdale, Fla., 1974-75; ptnr. Pomeroy, Pomeroy & Pomeroy, Ft. Lauderdale, 1976-86, Pomeroy & Pomeroy, P.A., Ft. Lauderdale, 1987-96; pvt. practice Fort Lauderdale, 1996—. Served to specialist class 4 USNG, 1970-76. Mem. ABA, Def. Research Inst., NRA, Coral Ridge Power Squadron, Harleys Owners Group. Clubs: Boat U.S., NRA. Roman Catholic. Avocations: boating, motorcycling. Home Phone: 561-965-1116; Office Phone: 954-725-2626. E-mail: pomeroylaw@aol.com.

POMEROY, JOHN J., lawyer, insurance company executive; b. Brockton, Mass., Sept. 25, 1948; BS, Boston Coll., 1970; JD, Duke U., 1973. Bar: Conn. 1973. Sr. v.p., gen. counsel, sec. Affiliated FM Insurance Co., Arkwright Mutual Insurance Co., Appalachian Insurance Co., Factory Mutual Insurance Co., Johnston, RI. Mem.: ABA, Federation of Insurance and Corp. Counsel, Conn. Bar Assn. Office: Factory Mutual Insurance Co 1301 Atwood Ave PO Box 7500 Johnston RI 02919 *

POMEROY, LEE HARRIS, architect; b. NYC, Nov. 19, 1932; s. Alfred and Florence Pomeroy; m. Sarah Pomeroy; children: Jordana, Jeremy, Alexandra. BArch, Rensselaer Poly. Inst., 1955; MArch, Yale U., 1961. Registered arch., NY, Conn., Mass., Vt., NJ, Fla., Pa., Maine, Nat. Coun. of Registrators Bd. Arch. William Tabler, NYC, 1958-59, The Archs. Collaborative, Cambridge, Mass., 1959-60; pres. Lee Harris Pomeroy Archs., NYC, 1965—. Prof. Sch. Architecture, CUNY, 1962-87; prin. solar rsch. group ECOSOL, Conn., Eng., Spain, 1965-84; dir. Project for Pub. Spaces, Inc., NYC, 1982-88; dean's adv. coun. Sch. Architecture, Resselaer Poly. Inst., 1991—, adv. to pres., 1994-98. Prin. works include Swiss Bank Tower and Saks Fifth Ave. ext., NYC (Arthur Ross award 1991), Teda Conv. Ctr., Tianjin, China, Binhai Convention Ctr. Hotel, Teda; restoration of Plaza Hotel, NY, Sch. Art and Dance City Coll., NYC, 1989, New Rochelle Pub. Libr., 1980 (Design award AIA-ALA 1980, NY State AIA and Urban Design awards 1980), Dutchess County Jail, Poughkeepsie, NY (Design award AIA-ALA 1981), HBO Satellite Comm. Ctr., 1983 (NY State AIA design award 1984), Manitou Sta. planned cmty., 1973 (AIA and Progressive Architecture awards 1973), Henry St. studios artists housing (Progressive Architecture mag. design award 1963, AIA design award 1975), Bedford Mews housing (AIA, Owens Corning energy conservation and Record Homes design awards 1980), Fulton Mall, Bklyn., 1985 (City Club NYC Bard award for design 1985), Trinity Ch. Bridge (Design award AIA 1991), Hotel Usixtu, Prague, Czech Republic, Lally Sch. of Mgmt. and Tech., Rensselaer Poly. Inst., Troy, NY, Reconstrn. of Union Square Subway, 2001, MOMA, Bleeker St. and Dekalb Ave. Stas., Cosco Housing, Shanghai, Jin Ling Hotel on Hynan Island, Parish House, St. James Ch. Restoration, NYC, Skill City, Bangelore, India, Hiline Housing and Hotel, NY. Mem. Cmty. Bd. 5, Midtown Manhattan, NYC, 1980-91; bd. dirs. Bellview Assn., with Bellview Med. Ctr., NYC, 1992—; trustee, v.p. Putnam County Hist. Soc. and Foundry Mus., 1990-2000. 1st lt. USA Signal Corp., 1955-57. Recipient Mcpl. Arts Soc. award, NYC, 1982; Nat. Endowment for Arts grantee, NYC, 1983. Fellow AIA (bd. dirs. 1979-81), Inst. of Urban Design; mem. Royal Inst. of British Archs., Mcpl. Arts Soc., Regional Plan Assn., Yale Club, Century Club, City Club NY (co-chmn. Bard award program for excellence in urban design 1988-90, 94). Avocations: tennis, photography, travel. Home: 285 Central Park W New York NY 10024-3006 Office: 462 Broadway Fl 3 New York NY 10013-2696 Office Phone: 212-334-2600. Business E-Mail: leepom@lhparch.com.

POMEROY, ROBERT CORTTIS, lawyer; b. Syracuse, NY, Sept. 17, 1943; s. Stuart E. and Elizabeth (Corttis) Pomeroy; m. Sandra Campbell; children: Lisa, Robert Jr., Heather. AB, Hamilton Coll., 1965; LLB, Harvard U., 1968. Bar: Mass. 1968, Fla. 1981. Assoc. Goodwin Procter LLP (formerly Goodwin, Procter & Hoar LLP), Boston, 1968-76, ptnr., 1977—2005, of counsel, 2005—. Mem.: Am. Coll. Trust and Estate Counsel. Avocations: skiing, golf, sailing. Home: 3 Pier 7 Charlestown MA 02129-4225 Office: Goodwin Procter LLP Exchange Pl Boston MA 02109-2881 Home Phone: 617-241-8807; Office Phone: 617-570-1150. Business E-Mail: rpomeroy@goodwinprocter.com.

POMES, STEPHEN VINCENT, school librarian; b. Houston, Sept. 9, 1963; s. Charles Patrick and Patricia Anne Pomes; life ptnr. Lisa Jean Winterburn. BA in History, U. New Orleans, 1988; M in Libr. and Info. Sci., La. State U., Baton Rouge, 1990. Br. libr. Jefferson Parish Libr., Metairie, La., 1990—92; regional tech. libr. US Dept. Interior, New Orleans, 1992—. Treas. SLA, LaSoMi Chpt., New Orleans, 2003. Author book reviews to profl. jours. and publs. Coun. mem. La. Fed. Depository Libr. Coun., Baton Rouge, 2005—; treas. Spl. Librs. Assn., New Orleans, 2003. Mem.: ALA, Spl. Libraries Assn. (pres. 2001—02, treas. 2004), La. Fed. Depository Coun. (coun. mem. 2005—), La. Libr. Assn. (webmaster 2005). Democrat. Roman Catholic. Avocations: reading, history. Office: US Dept Interior 1201 Elmwood Park Blvd New Orleans LA 70123 Home Phone: 504-468-9335; Office Phone: 504-736-2521. Office Fax: 504-736-2525. Business E-Mail: stephen.pomes@mms.gov.

POMFRET, BONNIE, music educator; d. Richard and Carolyn D. Pomfret; m. Arthur Lewis (div.); 1 child, Cara R. Lewis. State music exam., Musikhoschule Freiburg, Germany, 1977; MusM, Boston Conservatory, 1980; MusD, Ind. U., Bloomington, 1992. Assoc. prof. music Ill. State U., Normal, 1986—97; dir. vocal studies Emory U., Atlanta, 1997—2004; mem. music faculty Shorter Coll., Rome, Ga., 2004—06; dir. opera U. Ala., Birmingham, 2006—; music faculty Salve Regina U., Newport, RI, 2007—. Cons. in field; cert. and curriculum coord. McClosky Inst. Voice, Maynard, Mass., 1996—. Singer: (CD) De Toda La Eternidad, 2005. Fellow, NEH, NY and Bayreuth, 1994; Ambassadorial fellow, Rotary Internat., Rome and Berlin, 1980—81. Mem.: Coll. Music Soc., Nat. Assn. Tchrs. Singing, Pi Kappa Lambda. Avocations: walking, gardening, sewing, knitting.

POMFRET, DAVID B., medical educator, internist; b. Somerset, Mass., Nov. 22, 1937; s. David B. Pomfret and Rhea Chouinard; m. Anna Rafferty, Mar. 31, 1964; children: Mark, Bruce, Scott, Heidi. BS, Stonehill Coll., 1959; MD, Univ. Coll., Dublin, Ireland, 1964. Diplomate Am. Bd. Internal Medicine. Chief medicine Leonard Morse Hosp., Natick, Mass., 1968—71, chief staff, 1976—80; clin. prof. Tufts U., Boston, 1976—; prof. medicine Tumaini U., Moshi, Tanzania, 1996—2000. Author: Computer Science, 1998, Dispatches From Kilimanjaro, 2001. Fellow: ACP. Avocations: skiing, sailing, offshore racing. Home: 20 Grey Gull Rd Jamestown RI 02835-2808 Office: Kilimanjaro Christian Med Ctr Box 3010 Moshi Tanzania Office Phone: 401-423-0291. Personal E-mail: pomfret1@juno.com.

POMORSKI, STANISLAW, lawyer, educator; b. Lwow, Poland, Nov. 23, 1934; arrived in U.S., 1972, naturalized, 1983; s. Juliusz and Maria (Ziemba) Pomorski; m. Patricia Smith; children: Lukasz, Christopher, Maria. M.Law, U. Warsaw, 1956, D.Law, 1968. Law clk., 1958-61; pvt. practice law Warsaw, 1961-64; vis. scholar Harvard U. Law Sch., Cambridge, Mass., 1964-66; rsch. assoc. Polish Acad. Scis., 1966-72; mem. faculty Rutgers U. Law Sch., Camden, NJ, 1973—, prof. law, 1977-81, disting. prof. law, 1981—2006, disting. prof. law emeritus, 2006—. Fellow Soviet law U. Leyden, Netherlands, 1980—81; trustee Nat. Coun. Soviet and East European Rsch., Washington, 1988—94. Author: (book) American Common Law and the Principle Nullum Crimen Sine Lege, 2d edit., 1975, Restructuring the System of Ownership in the USSR, 1991, On Multiculturalism, Concepts of Crime and the De Minimis Defense, 1997, Justice in Siberia, 2001, Modern Russian Criminal Procedure: The Adversarial Principle and Guilty Plea, 2006. Fellow, Ford Found., 1972—73. Office: Rutgers U Law Sch 5th And Penn St Camden NJ 08102 Office Phone: 856-225-6395. Business E-Mail: pomorski@camden.rutgers.edu.

POMP, ALFONS, surgeon; b. Can., Nov. 2, 1954; m. Rachel Chartrand; children: Audrey Chartrand, Genevieve Chartrand. BSc, McGill U., Montreal, 1971—76; MD, Sherbrooke U., 1980. Cert. Am. Bd. Surgery, 1987. Fellow surg. nutrition and metabolism R.I. Hosp./Brown U., 1986—88; assoc. prof. surgery U. Montreal/Hotel Dieu Hosp. Montreal, 1988—99; assoc. prof., surgery Mount Sinai Med. Sch., NYC, 1999—2003; assoc. prof. Cornell Med. Coll., NYC, 2003—. Contbr. articles to profl. jours. Fellow: ACS. Office: Weill Med Coll Cornell 525 E 68th St Box 294 New York NY 10021 Office Phone: 212-746-5294. E-mail: alp2104@med.cornell.edu.

POMPADUR, I. MARTIN, communications executive; b. Bklyn, June 25, 1935; s. Jack and Florence (Raitbord) P.; m. Joan Lynn Krassner, Dec. 18, 1960 (div. 1986); children: F. Douglas (dec.), Jana Sue; m. Marian Hackett, Dec. 23, 1987 (div. 2003); 1 child, Chelsea Rae. BA, Williams Coll., 1955; LLB, U. Mich., 1958. Bar: Conn. 1958, NY 1961. Atty. ABC-TV Network, NYC, 1960-61, 61-66, chief adminstrv. officer, 1966-68, gen. mgr., 1968-70, v.p. broadcast div., 1970-72, corp. v.p., 1972; pres. ABC Leisure Group I, 1973-75, asst. to pres. parent co., 1975-76; also dir. parent co.; sr. v.p. Ziff Corp., 1977-78, pres., 1978-82; chmn., chief exec. officer GP Sta. Ptnr., 1982-96; mng. gen. ptnr. TV Sta. Ptnr., 1982-96; chmn., CEO PBTV, Inc., 1984-96; mng. gen. ptnr. Northeastern TV Investors Ltd. Partnership, 1984-96; prin. owner, sec. Caribbean Internat. News Corp., 1985—, also bd. dir.; CEO, COO RP Media Mgmt., Inc., 1986; CEO ML Media Ptnr., L.P., 1986—; CEO, COO RP Opportunity Mgmt., 1988—2002; CEO ML Media Opportunity Ptnr., L.P., 1988—2002; exec. v.p. News Corp.; pres. News Corp. Ea. Ctrl. Europe; chmn. News Corp. Europe, 2000—. Prin. shareholder Hispanic Media Inc., 1986-90; prin. shareholder, vice-chmn. Hunter Pub. L.P., 1986-94; co-trustee Lidan Trust, 1983—; atty. Young & Rubicam, Inc., advt. agy., NYC, summer 1961. Mem. Stamford bd. reps., chmn. legis. and rules com., 1959-60. Office: News Corp 4th Fl 1211 Ave of the Americas New York NY 10036 also: News Corp Europe 1 Virginia St 6th Fl London England

POMPAN, JACK MAURICE, management consultant; b. NYC, Jan. 23, 1926; s. Maurice A. and Helen (Schmidt) P. m. Esther Terri Scharaga, July 4, 1958; children: Neil Charles, Lori Beth. BS in Indsl. Mgmt., Ga. Inst. Tech., 1948; MBA with distinction, NYU, 1973, advanced profl. cert., 1978. Trainee to budget mgr. Redmond Co., Owosso, Mich., 1948—55; mgmt. cons. Coopers and Lybrand, NYC, 1955—60; contr. Hazel Bishop Inc., NYC, 1960—61; treas. Floyds Stores Inc., Valley Stream, NY, 1961—66; pres. Farmers Pantry Inc., Mamaroneck, NY, 1966—68; v.p. pub. divsn. Intext, Inc., NYC, 1968—74; prin. Baxter, Pompan & Storr, Mgmt. Cons., and predecessors, Greenwich and NYC, 1974—83, Jack M. Pompan, Mgmt. Cons., Rockville Centre, NY, 1983—92, Pompan & Co., Rockville Centre, 1992—; v.p. Eisner Computer Solutions, LLC, NYC, 1997—98. Adj. prof. Hofstra U., 1977, Roth Grad. Sch. Bus. Adminstrn., C.W. Post Ctr., L.I. U., 1974-79, NYU, 1982-89. Bus. and econs. editor Info. Please Almanac, 1978-82. Trustee edn. chmn., v.p. Ctrl. Synogogue, Rockville Centre, NY, 1983-86, pres. 1986-88; mem. Greater NY Coun., Union for Reform Judaism, 2004—. Lt. USNR, 1943-46, 51-53. Mem. Exec. Forum at NYU, Inst. Mgmt. Accts. (cert. merit 1953), Am. Jewish Com., Princeton Club N.Y. Office: 70-01 Maine Ave Rockville Centre NY 11570-3641 Office Phone: 516-678-5206. E-mail: jpompan@optonline.net.

POMPEO, ELLEN, actress; b. Everett, Mass., Nov. 10, 1969; Actor: (films) 8 1/2 x 11, 1999, Coming Soon, 1999, Eventual Wife, 2000, In the Weeds, 2000, Moonlight Mile, 2002, Catch Me If You Can, 2002, Daredevil, 2003, Old School, 2003, Undermind, 2003, Nobody's Perfect, 2004, Art Heist, 2004; (TV series) Grey's Anatomy, 2005— (Outstanding Performance by an Ensemble in a Drama Series, SAG, 2007), (TV appearances) Strangers with Candy, 1999, Law and Order, 1996, 2000, Get Real, 2000, Strong Medicine, 2001, The Job, 2001. Office: Creative Artists Agy 9830 Wilshire Blvd Beverly Hills CA 90212-1825

POMPER, PHILIP, historian, educator; b. Chgo., Apr. 18, 1936; s. Solomon and Rebecca (Fenigstein) P.; m. Alice N. Epstein, Aug. 27, 1961 (div.); children: Erica, Stephen, Karen; m. Emily Meyer, June 26, 1994 (dec. July 2003); m. Linda R. Shulsky, March 11, 2007. BA, U. Chgo., 1959, MA, 1961, PhD, 1965. Instr. history Wesleyan U., Middletown, Conn., 1964-65, asst. prof., 1965-71, assoc. prof., 1971-76, prof., 1976—, chmn. dept. history, 1981-84; William F. Armstrong prof. history, 1992—. Author: The Russian Revolutionary Intelligentsia, 1970, 2nd edit., 1993, Peter Lavrov and the Russian Revolutionary Movement, 1972, Sergei Nechaev, 1979 (Choice award 1979), The Structure of Mind in History: Five Major Figures in Psychohistory, 1985, Trotsky's Notebooks, 1933-35:

Writings on Lenin, Dialectics and Evolutionism, 1986, Lenin, Trotsky, and Stalin: The Intelligentsia and Power, 1990; assoc. editor History and Theory, 1991—; editor: World History: Ideologies, Structures, and Identities, 1998; co-editor: History and Theory, Contemporary Readings, 1998; co-editor: The Return of Science: Evolution, History and Theory, 2002; contbr. articles on Russian history and theory of history to profl. jours. Fellow, Ford Found., 1963—64, Social Scis. Rsch. Coun., 1968, Hoover Instn., 1987, Wilson Ctr., 1988; Russian Rsch. Ctr. scholar, 1987—. Mem.: Am. Assn. for Advancement of Slavic Studies, Conn. Acad. Arts and Scis. Home: 13 Red Orange Rd Middletown CT 06457-4916 Office: History Dept Wesleyan U Middletown CT 06459-0001 Business E-Mail: ppomper@wesleyan.edu.

POMRENZE, COLONEL, archivist, consultant; children: Hava Pomrenze LEvene, Jay, Debra Pomrenze Flegg, Haya Rochel, Davida Schlomit. BS, Ill. Inst. Tech., 1936; MA, U. Chgo., 1938, postgrad., 1938—40. Enlisted US Army, advanced through grades to col., ret.; cons. recs. mgmt. and archives. Disting. adj. prof. Am. U. Contbr. articles to profl. jours. Decorated Legion Merit, Army Commendation medal, Bronze Star. Fellow: Soc. Am. Archivists; mem.: Inst. Cert. Recs. Mgrs. (pres. bd. regents 1976). Home: 3333 Henry Hudson Lky Apt 4R Bronx NY 10463

PONCE, MARY HELEN, writer; d. Tranquilino Ponce and Vicenta Solis; children: Joseph, Anna, Mark, Ralph. BA, Calif. State U., Northridge, 1978, MA, 1980; PhD, U. N.Mex., Albuquerque, 1996. Asst. prof. Calif. State U., Northridge. Adj. faculty U. N.Mex., Albuquerque. Author: Taking Control, 1987, The Wedding, 1989, Hoyt Street: An Autobiography, 1993, Calle Hoyt: Recuredos de Una Juventud Chicana, 1995; contbr. articles to mags. Fellow, U. Calif., Santa Barbara. Mem.: San Francisco Art History Mus., Mex. Am. Polit. Assn. Avocations: gardening, hiking, writing.

PONCE DE LEON, MONICA, architect; BArch, U. Miami, Fla., 1989; MArch in Urban Design, Harvard U., Cambridge, Mass., 1991. Prin. arch. Office dA, Boston, 1991—; design instr. sch. architecture U. Miami, 1991—93; asst. prof. architecture Northeastern U., 1993—96; prof. grad. sch. design Harvard U., 1996—. Vis. prof. grad. sch. design Harvard U., 1994—96; vis. scholar sch. architecture U. Houston, 1995; vis. prof. RI Sch. Design, 1996, So. Calif. Inst. Architecture, 2002; Thomas W. Ventulett III Disting. chair archtl. design Ga. Inst. Tech., 2004—05. Mng. editor: Assemblage, 1993—95; prin. works include Roads Tower Apt. Bldg. (Arango Design award, 2002), Upper Crust (Honor award, Boston Soc. Archs., 2002), Papago Trail (Unbuilt Architecture award, Boston Soc. Archs., 2002), Tongxian Art (Design award in Architecture, 49th Progressive Architecture awards, 2002), Northeastern U. Multi-faith Spiritual Ctr. (Young Archs. Design award, Boston Soc. Archs., 1999, Design award of Merit, Internat. Assn. Lighting, 2000, Harleston Parker medal, 2002), Witte Arts Bldg. (Design Citation in Architecture, 50th Progressive Architecture awards, 2003), Intergenerational Learning Ctr. (Design Citation in Architecture, 52nd Ann. Progressive Architecture awards, 2005, Charter award for New Urbanism, Congress for the New Urbanism, 2005), exhibitions include Work of Monica Ponce de Leon & Nader Tehrani, Ariz. State U., 1996, Office dA: Obras de Arquitectura, U. Navarra, 1997, Zero Tolerances, Atlantic Contemporary Arts Ctr., 2002, Housing Patterns, U. Colo. Coll. Architecture and Planning, 2003, Recent Work, RI Sch. Design, 2004. Named one of Emerging Voices, Archtl. League NY, 2003; recipient Young Archs. award, 1997, Architecture award, AAAL, 2002. Office: Office dA 1920 Washington St #2 Boston MA 02118 Office Phone: 617-541-5540. Office Fax: 617-541-5535. E-mail: poncedeleon@officeda.com. *

POND, BYRON O., JR., retired manufacturing executive; b. 1936; BSBA, Wayne State U., 1961. With Fed. Mogul Corp., Detroit, 1958-68, Maremont Corp., Chgo., 1968-86, dir. sales exhaust systems div., 1970-74, corp. v.p., 1974-76, sr. v.p. nat. accounts, 1976-78, exec. v.p., 1978-79, pres., CEO, 1979—86; exec. v.p. Arvin Industries, Columbus, Ind., 1991—93, pres., CEO, 1993—96, chmn., 1996—99; pres. Amcast Industrial Corp., 2001—02, chmn., 2002—05, pres., CEO, 2004—05; interim CEO Cooper Tire & Rubber Co., Findlay, Ohio, 2006. Bd. dirs. Cooper Tire & Rubber Co., 1998—. Recipient Disting. Alumni award, Wayne St. U.

POND, PATRICIA BROWN, library and information scientist, educator; b. Mankato, Minn., Jan. 17, 1930; d. Patrick H. and Florence M. (Ruehle) Brown; m. Judson S. Pond, Aug. 24, 1959. BA, Coll. St. Catherine, St. Paul, 1952; MA, U. Minn., 1955; PhD, U. Chgo., 1982. Sch. libr., Minn., NYC, 1952-62; asst. prof. libr. sci. U. Minn., 1962-63; reference libr. U. Mont., 1963-65; asst. prof. U. Oreg., 1967-72, assoc. prof., 1972-77; prof., dept. chair, assoc. dean Sch. Libr. and Info. Sci. U. Pitts., 1977-85. Mem. ALA (life), Phi Beta Kappa, Beta Phi Mu, Delta Phi Lambda, Kappa Gamma Pi. Home: 15829 SW Village Cir Beaverton OR 97007-3532 Personal E-mail: ppond1@mindspring.com.

POND, THOMAS ALEXANDER, physics professor, academic administrator; b. LA, Dec. 4, 1924; s. Arthur Francis and Florence (Alexander) P.; m. Barbara Eileen Newman, Sept. 6, 1958; children: Arthur Phillip Ward, Florence Alexandra. AB, Princeton U., 1947, AM, 1949, PhD, 1953; DSc, SUNY, Stony Brook, 1998. Instr. physics Princeton U., 1951-53; asst. prof., then assoc. prof. physics Washington U., St. Louis, 1953-62; prof. physics SUNY, Stony Brook, 1962-81, prof. emeritus, 1982—, chmn. dept., 1962-68, exec. v.p., 1967-79, acting pres., 1970, 75, 78; prof. physics Rutgers U., New Brunswick, NJ, exec. v.p., chief acad. officer, 1982-91, exec. v.p., chief acad. officer emeritus, 1991—, acting pres., 1990, prof., 1991-97, prof. emeritus, 1997—; acting sr. v.p. for acad. affairs U. Medicine and Dentistry N.J., New Brunswick, 1998. Bd. dirs. Action Com. for L.I., 1978-80, Tri-State Regional Planning Commn., 1979-82; trustee Univs. Research Assn., 1985-87; bd. dirs. Fermilab, 1987-89. Served to ensign USNR, 1943-46. Fellow AAAS; mem. Am. Phys. Soc., Phi Beta Kappa, Sigma Xi. Home: 144 Fox Run Arlington VT 05250

PONDER, CATHERINE, clergywoman; b. Hartsville, SC, Feb. 14, 1927; d. Roy Charles and Kathleen (Parrish) Cook; 1 child, Richard. Student, Worth Bus. Coll., 1948; BS in Edn., Unity Ministerial Sch., 1956; doctorate (hon.), Unity Sch., 1976. Ordained to ministry Unity Sch. Christianity, 1958. Min. Unity Ch., Birmingham, Ala., 1958-61, founder, min. Austin, Tex., 1961-69, San Antonio, 1969-73, Palm Desert, Calif., 1973—. Author: (books) The Dynamic Laws of Prosperity, 1962, The Prosperity Secret of the Ages, 1964, The Dynamic Laws of Healing, 1966, The Healing Secret of the Ages, 1967, Pray and Grow Rich, 1968, The Millionaires of Genesis, 1976, The Millionaire Moses, 1977, The Millionaire Joshua, 1978, The Millionaire from Nazareth, 1979, The Secret of Unlimited Prosperity, 1981, Open Your Mind To Receive, 1983, Dare To Prosper!: The Prospering Power of Prayer, 1983, The Prospering Power of Love, 1984, Open Your Mind to Prosperity, 1984, The Dynamic Laws of Prayer, 1987, (memoir) Prosperity Love Story, From Rags to Enrichment, 2003. Office: 73-669 US Hwy 111 Palm Desert CA 92260-4033

PONDER, DAN E., JR., former state legislator, food service executive; b. Dothan, Ala., Sept. 13, 1954; s. Daniel E. and Josephine Beall Ponder; m. Mary Lou Ponder, 1978; children: Chatherine, Elizabeth. BS, Auburn Univ., 1976. Treas. and sec. Beall Peanut Co., Inc., 1976—85; pres. Ponder Enterprises, Inc., 1984—; chmn. Seminole County Bd. Commissioners, 1990—96; rep. dist. 160 Ga. Ho. of Reps, 1996—2001. Recipient Citizen of Yr., Seminole County, Profile in Courage award, John F. Kennedy Libr. Found., 2003. Mem.: Ind. Hardee's Franchisee Assn., Leadership Ga., Donaldsville Lions Club. Republican. Presbyterian. Mailing: PO Box 106 Donalsonville GA 31745 *

PONDER, HERMAN, geologist; b. Light, Ark., Jan. 31, 1928; s. Herman Cook and Sylvia Adell (Cameron) P.; m. Barbara Elaine Sando, May 10, 1947; children: Teresa Elaine, David Mark. BA, U. Mo., 1955, PhD, 1959. Rsch. engr. A.P. Green Refractories Co., Mexico, Mo., 1959-61, lab mgr., 1961-63; project engr. Colo. Sch. Mines Rsch. Inst., Golden, 1963—67, mngr. mining divsn., 1967—70, pres., 1970—85; v.p. Copper Range Co., White Pine, Mich., 1985—89; chmn. bd. dirs. Analytica, Inc., 1985—98. Served with USN, 1946-47. Recipient Disting. Alumnus award U. Mo., 1993. Home: 2725 E Papago Trl Sierra Vista AZ 85650-8112

PONDROM, LEE GIRARD, physicist, researcher; b. Dallas, Dec. 26, 1933; s. Levi Girard and Guinevere (Miller) P.; m. Cyrena Jo Norman, Aug. 25, 1961. BS, So. Meth. U., 1953; MS, U. Chgo., 1956, PhD, 1958. Instr., dept. physics Columbia U., NYC, 1960-63; assoc. prof. dept. physics U. Wis., Madison, 1963-69, prof. physics, 1969—, Robert Williams Wood prof., 1992—. Dept. chmn. U. Wis., 1997-2000; mem. high energy adv. com. Brookhaven Nat. Lab., 1973-75, chmn. Associated Universities, Inc., vis. com., 1987; mem. physics adv. com. Fermi Nat. Accelerator Lab., 1979-82, chmn., 1981-82; adv. com. for physics NSF, 1981-84; mem. high energy adv. panel (physics) U.S. Dept. Energy, 1981-84, 87-88, chmn. subcom. on detectors, 1987-88, mem. subpanel on future facilities, high energy physics, 1983, mem. subpanel on future modes of exptl. research in high energy physics, 1987; trustee Univs. Research Assn., 1973-76, 82-85; mem. sci. policy com. Stanford Linear Accelerator Ctr., 1984-88; mem. Internat. Com. Future Accelerators, 1984-90; chmn. Snowmass 1986 Summer Study on the SSC.; chmn. User's Orgn. for the SSC, 1987-89, mem. sci. policy com. SSC Lab., 1992; mem. CDRF awards com. to scientists in former Soviet Union, 1996. Contbr. articles to profl. jours. Served to 1st lt. USAF, 1958-60. J.S. Guggenheim Meml. fellow, 1971-72, Japan Soc. for Promotion of Sci. fellow; recipient Disting. Alumni award So. Meth. U., 1983, W.K.H. Panofsky award Am. Phys. Soc., 1994. Fellow Am. Phys. Soc. (chmn. div. particles and fields 1987, com. on status of women in physics 1989—, chmn. com. to award the Panofsky prize 1991); mem. AAAS, Phi Beta Kappa (pres. Wis. Alpha chpt. 1996-97). Episcopalian. Home: 210 Princeton Ave Madison WI 53726-4077 Office: U Wis Dept Physics Madison WI 53706 E-mail: pondrom@hep.wisc.edu. *I have been fortunate to pursue a career in research and teaching at a university and at various U.S. national laboratories, where the individual has much freedom to do whatever he or she wants. Close association with many colleagues and my work with younger people in physics have been sources of stimulation.*

PONEMAN, DANIEL BRUCE, lawyer; b. Toledo, Mar. 12, 1956; s. Meyer and Delores Suzanne (Shapiro) P.; m. Susan Anne Danoff, Aug. 12, 1984; children: Claire Gillian, Michael Bruder, William Meyer. AB in Govt. and Econs. magna cum laude, Harvard Coll., 1978; MLitt in Politics, Lincoln Coll., Oxford, Eng., 1981; JD cum laude, Harvard U., 1984. Bar: D.C. 1985, N.Y., 1985. Vis. fellow Internat. Inst. Strategic Studies, London, 1980-81; rsch. fellow ctr. sci. and internat. affairs Kennedy sch. govt. Harvard U., 1981-84; assoc. Covington & Burling, 1985-89; White House fellow U.S. Dept. of Energy, 1989-90; dir. def. policy and arms control NSC, Washington, 1990-93, spl. asst. to the Pres., sr. dir. nonproliferation and export controls, 1993-96; counsel Hogan & Hartson L.L.P., 1996-97, ptnr., 1999—2002; prin. The Scowcroft Group, 2001—. Author: Nuclear Power in the Developing World, 1982, Argentina: Democracy on Trial, 1987, Going Critical, 2003; contbr. articles to profl. jours. and newspapers including N.Y. Times, Washington Post, Wall Street Jour., L.A. Times, Boston Globe, Fin. Times. Mem. Commn. to Asses the Orgn. of Govt. to Combat the Proliferation of Weapons of Mass Distruction, 1997-99; mem. Pres.' Export Coun. Subcom. on Export Adminstrn. Grantee Corp. Pub. Broadcasting; Lord Crewe scholar. Mem. D.C. Bar, N.Y. Bar, Coun. Fgn. Rels., Phi Beta Kappa. Home: 1541 Forest Ln Mc Lean VA 22101 Office: The Scowcroft Group 900 17th St NW Ste 500 Washington DC 20006 Business E-Mail: poneman@scowcroft.com.

PONITZ, DAVID H., former academic administrator; b. Royal Oak, Mich., Jan. 21, 1931; s. Henry John and Jeanette (Bouwman) P.; m. Doris Jean Humes, Aug. 5, 1956; children: Catherine Anne, David Robinson. BA, U. Mich., 1952, MA, 1954; EdD, Harvard U., 1964; PhD (hon.), U. Dayton, 1996. Prin. Waldron (Mich.) Area Schs., 1956-58, supt., 1958-60; cons. Harvard U., Boston Sch. Survey, 1961-63; supt. Freeport (Ill.) Pub. Schs., 1962-65; pres. Freeport C.C., 1962-65, Washtenaw C.C., 1965-75, Sinclair C.C., 1975-97, pres. emeritus, 1997—. Cons. to cmty. colls.; chmn., pres. Ohi Advanced Tech. Ctr.; ednl. cons., 1997—. Mem. editl. adv. bd. Nations Schs., 1963-70; chmn. adv. bd. C.C. Rev., 1978-89. Past chmn. Dayton Mayor's Coun. on Econ. Devel., 1977-85; mem. Nat. Adv. Coun. on Nursing; former co-chair Performing Arts Edn. Task Force; bd. dirs. Alliance for Edn.; former campaign chmn. Ann Arbor and Dayton United Way; past vice chmn. Dayton Citizens Adv. Coun. for Desegregation Implementation; v.p. Miami Valley Rsch. Park; mem., past chmn. Area Progress Coun., Dayton; bd. dirs. Dayton Devel. Coun.; mem. F.S.B. bd. Citizens Fed. Banks, Universal Energy Systems Bd.; past chmn. Miami Valley Joint Labor/Mgmt. Profls., Area Progress Coun.; chmn. bd. dirs Ctr. Occupational R&D; bd. chair Wright Tech. Network; bd. dirs. Dean Family Funds; trustee Thomas B. Fordham Found., pres., 2006—; mem. Midwestern Higher Edn. Commn.; vice chair Miami Valley Rsch. Found.; past chmn. bd. dirs. League Innovation C.C.; bd. dirs. Miami Valley Regional Planning Commn.; chair found. bd. Mus. of USAF. Served with U.S. Army, 1954-56. Named Outstanding Alumnus, U. Mich., One of Top 100 Pres. in U.S. Coun. for Advancement and Support of Edn., Exec. of Yr., Bd. Realtors; named to Hall of Fame, Nat. Mgmt. Assn., 2001; recipient Presdl. medallion, Patron emeritus Horry-Georgetown Tech. Coll., Bogie Buster Red Jacket award, 1987, Thomas J. Peters award for Excellence, Assn. Cmty. and Jr. Colls., 1988, Marie N. Martin Chief Exec. Officer award, ACCT, 1989, The Living Legend award, Martin Luther King Jr. Holiday Celebration Com., 1991, Hon. Alumnus award, Sinclair, 1991, honor, India Found., 1992, Disting. Eagle Scout award, Nat. Eagle Scout Assn., 1993, Smitty award, Anti-Defamation award, Anti-Defamation League, 1996, Citizen Legion of Honor award, 1997, hon. award, Citizen Legion, 1997, Edn. award, Gov., 1999. Mem. Am. Assn. Cmty. and Jr. Colls. (nat. future commn., bd. dirs., chmn. 1988-89, Nat. Leadership award 2002), Ohio Tech. and C.C. Assn. (pres. 1979-80), Nat. Mgmt. Assn. (Hall of Fame award 2001), Rotary. Methodist. Office Phone: 937-434-6640. Business E-Mail: dponitzsinclair@woh.rr.com.

PONITZ, JOHN ALLAN, lawyer; b. Battle Creek, Mich., Sept. 7, 1949; m. Nancy J. Roberts, Aug. 14, 1971; children: Amy, Matthew, Julie. BA, Albion Coll., 1971; JD, Wayne State U., 1974. Bar: Mich. 1974, U.S. Dist. Ct. (ea. dist.) Mich. 1975, (we. dist.) Mich. 1986, U.S. Ct. Appeals (6th cir.) Mich. 1981, U.S. Supreme Ct. 1992. Assoc. McMachan & Kaichen, Birmingham, Mich., 1974—75; atty. Grand Trunk Western R.R., Detroit, 1975-80, sr. trial atty., 1980-89, gen. counsel, 1990-95; ptnr. Hopkins & Sutter, Detroit, 1995-2000, Maxwell, Ponitz & Sclawy, Troy, Mich., 2000—01; of counsel Fabrizio & Brook, P.C., Troy, 2002—03; gen. counsel A&M Hospitality, Southfield, Mich., 2002—. Served to capt. USAF, 1974-82. Mem.: Mich. Bar Assn., Oakland County Bar Assn. Lutheran. Avocation: golf. Office: A&M Hospitality 24725 Greenfield Rd Southfield MI 48075 Office Phone: 248-395-5250. Business E-Mail: jponitz@ponitzlaw.com.

PONKO, WILLIAM REUBEN, architect; b. Wausau, Wis., Apr. 4, 1948; s. Reuben Harrison and Ora Marie (Ranke) P.; m. Kathleen Ann Hilt, May 5, 1973; children: William Benjamin, Sarah Elizabeth. BArch magna cum laude, U. Notre Dame, 1971. Cert. Nat. Coun. Archtl. Registration Bds. V.p., arch., dir. ednl., instl. specialty Le Roy Troyer & Assocs. (now the Troyer Group), Mishawaka, Ind., 1971—; design instr. dept. arch. U. Notre Dame, 1976. Mem. Ind. State Bd. Registration for Architects, 1990—; mem. registration exam com. Nat. Coun. Archtl. Registration Bds., 1992—, vice chair 1996, chair 1997. Prin. archtl. works include: St. Peter Luth. Ch., Mishawaka, Ind., 1979, 4 brs. for South Bend Pub. Libr., 1983, Edward J. Funk & Sons office bldg. Taylor U., Upland, Ind., 1982, Taylor U. Lbir., carillon tower, 1985, Early Childhood Devel. Ctr. U. Notre Dame, 1994, Convents for Sisters of Holy Cross St. Mary's, Notre Dame, Ind., 1995. Mem. AIA (gold medal for exellence in archtl. edn. 1971), Ind. Soc. Archs. (Design Excellence award 1978, chpt. pres. 1985, Juliet Peddle award 2000). Office: The Troyer Group Inc 550 Union St Mishawaka IN 46544-2346

PONNAPALLI, RAMACHANDRA MURTY, retired statistician, researcher; b. Guntur, India, Mar. 15, 1933; s. Subrahmanyam and Lakshmikantamma Ponnapalli; m. Lalitha Konakanchi Ponnapalli, May 16, 1954; children: Vaniprasad, Sasikantha, Pardhasaradhi, Sailaja. BA wtih honors, Andhra U., India, 1953, MSc; PhD, U. Calif., Berkeley, 1964. Asst. prof. U. Alta., Edmonton, Canada, 1969—76, U. West Ont., London, Canada, 1976—78, U. Windsor, Canada, 1978—82; assoc. prof. SUNY, Utica, NY, 1984—88; sr. statistician FDA, Rockville, Md., 1988—2003; ret. Rsch. grant, Can. Govt., Edmonton, 1971—76. Mem.: Am. Statis. Assn. Avocation: bridge.

PONOROFF, LAWRENCE, dean, law educator, consultant; b. Chgo., Sept. 10, 1953; s. Charles Melvin and Jean Eileen (Kramer) P.; m. Monica J. Moses, July 25, 1981; children: Christopher J., Devon E., Laura J., Scott C. BA summa cum laude, Loyola U., Chgo., 1975; JD, Stanford U., 1978. Bar: Colo. 1978, Ohio 1988, US Dist. Ct. Colo., US Dist. Ct. (no. dist.) Ohio, US Ct. Appeals (10th cir.). Assoc. Holme Roberts & Owen, Denver, 1978-84, ptnr., 1984-86; asst. prof. law U. Toledo, 1986-88, assoc. prof. coll. of law, 1988-90, prof. law, assoc. dean academic affairs, 1990-92, prof., 1990-95, Tulane U. Sch. Law, New Orleans, 1995-00, J. Mitchell Franklin prof. pvt. and comml. law, 2000—, vice dean, 1998-2001, dean, 2001—. Vis. prof. Wayne State U. Law Sch., 1993, U. Mich. Law Sch., 1997; lectr. fed. juc. ctr.; cons. long range planning subcom. of com. on adminstrn. of bankruptcy sys. Jud. Conf. US, mem. adv. com. on bankruptcy rules, 2004—; dir. Am. Bd. Cert., 2000—06; bd. advisors editors Am. Bankruptcy Inst. Law Rev., 2000—03; bd. dirs. La. Supreme Ct. Hist. Soc.; exec. dir. For the Children Literacy Program. Co-author: (with S.E. Snyder) Commerical Bankruptcy Litigation, 1989; (with J. Dolan) Basic Concepts in Commercial Law, 1998; (with Epstein and Markell) Making and Doing Deals: Contracts in Context, 2002, 2d edit., 2006; (with J. Dolan and B. Markell) Core Concepts of Commercial Law: Past, Present and Future, 2004. Bd. dir. La. Supreme Ct. Hist. Soc. Recipient L. Hart Wright Tchg. award, U. Mich. Law Sch., Felix Frankfurter Tchg. award, Tulane U. Law Sch. Fellow Am. Coll. Bankruptcy, Am. Bar Found.; mem. ABA, Am. Bar Inst., Am. Law Inst., La. State Bar Assn. (bd. govs. 2001-03). Home: 6025 Pitt St New Orleans LA 70118-6010 Office: Tulane Law Sch 6329 Freret St New Orleans LA 70118 Office Phone: 504-865-5937. Business E-Mail: lponoroff@law.tulane.edu.

PONSETI, IGNACIO VIVES, orthopaedic surgery educator; b. Cuidadela, Balearic Islands, Spain, June 3, 1914; s. Miguel and Margarita (Vives) P.; 1 child, William Edward; m. Helena Percas, 1961. BS, U. Barcelona, 1930, MD, 1936, D honoris causa, 1984. Instr. dept. orthopaedic surgery State U. Iowa, 1944-57, prof., 1957—. Author papers and a book on cogenital and developmental skeletal deformities. Capt. M.C. Spanish Army, 1936-39. Recipient Kappa Delta award for orthopaedic rsch., 1955. Mem. Assn. Bone and Joint Surgeons, Am. Acad. Cerebral Palsy, Soc. Exptl. Biology and Medicine, Internat. Coll. Surgeons, N.Y. Acad. Sci., AMA (Ketoen gold medal 1960), Am. Acad. Orthopedic Surgeons, ACS, Am. Orthopedic Assn., Pediatric Orthopaedic Soc. (hon.), Iowa Med. Soc., Orthopedic Rsch. Soc. (Shands award 1975), Sigma Xi, Asociacion Argentina de Cirugia (hon.), Asociacion Balear de Cirugia (hon.), Sociedad de Cirujanos de Chile (hon.), Sociedad Espanola de Cirugia Ortopedica (hon.), Sociedad Brasilera de Ortopedia e Traumatologia (hon.). Home: 110 Oakridge Ave Iowa City IA 52246-2935 Office: Carver Pavilion U Iowa Hosps Iowa City IA 52242 Business E-Mail: ignacio-Ponseti@uiowa.edu.

PONT, JOHN, football coach, educator; b. Canton, Ohio, Nov. 13, 1927; s. Bautista and Susie (Sikurinec) P.; m. H. Sandra Stoutt, June 23, 1956; children: John W., Jennifer Ann, Jeffrey David. BS, Miami U., Oxford, Ohio, 1952, MS, 1956. Profl. football player, Canada, 1952—53; instr., coach freshman football and basketball Miami U., Oxford, 1953—55, asst. prof., head football coach, 1955—62; head football coach Yale U., 1963—65; prof., head football coach Ind. U., Bloomington, 1965—73; head coach Northwestern U., Evanston, Ill., 1973—77, athletic dir., 1974—79; head football coach, athletic dir. Hamilton, Ohio; head football coach, tennis coach, asst. athletic dir. Coll. Mt. St. Joseph, Cin.; head football coach Gakusei-Engo-Kai Inc., Tokyo; dir. football ops. Ohio Dominican U., Columbus, 2003—. Agt. Equitable Assurance Soc., U.S., 1981-82; v.p. Fin. Leasing Corp., 1983-85, Splty. Brush, Inc.; athletic dir. Jewish Community Center, Canton, 1953; v.p. NCAA Coun., 1979-80; mem. bd. dirs. Cin. chpt. Nat. Football Found. Hall Of Fame; pres. NFL Alumni-S.W. Ohio. Mem. Pres.'s Coun. on Phys. Fitness; chmn. Ind. Easter Seal, 1968-69, Ind. div. Cancer Crusade, 1969; bd. dirs. Multiple Sclerosis, N.E. Ill. counc. Boy Scouts Am., Boys Hope. Served with USN, 1945-47. Named Coach of Year Coaches Assn., 1967, Coach of Year Football Writers, 1967, Coach of Yr. Washington Touchdown Club, 1968, Coach of Yr. Walter Camp Found.; recipient Significant Sig award, 1968, Disting. Am. award Nat. Football Found., 1987, Lifetime Achievement award All Am. Football Found., 1997; charter mem. Miami U. Hall of Fame, 1968; elected Ind. Football Hall of Fame, 1984, Butler County Hall of Fame, 1986, Mid-Am. Conf. Hall of Fame, 1992, Ind. U. Sports Hall of Fame, 1992. Mem. Am. Football Coaches Assn. (chmn. ethics com.), Kusatsu City Football Assn. Japan (hon. chmn.), Am. Legion, Blue Key, Sigma Chi, Phi Epsilon Kappa, Omicron Delta Kappa. Republican. Home: 482 White Oak Dr Oxford OH 45056-9272 Personal E-mail: pont52@aol.com.

PONTAROLO, MICHAEL JOSEPH, lawyer; b. Walla Walla, Wash., Sept. 1, 1947; s. Albert and Alice Mary (Fazzari) P.; m. Elizabeth Louise Onley, July 18, 1970; children: Christie, Amy, Nick, Angela. BA, Gonzaga U., 1969, JD, 1973. Bar: Wash. 1973, US Dist. Ct. (ea. dist.) Wash. 1974. Assoc. Mullin & Etter, Spokane, Wash., 1973-74, William Iunker, Spokane, 1974-75, Delay, Curran & Boling, Spokane, 1975-77; prin. Delay, Curran, Thompson & Pontarolo, P.S., Spokane, 1977-97, Delay, Curran, Thompson, Pontarolo & Walker, Spokane, 1997—. Mem. Spokane County Med. Legal Com., 1987-88, 91; chmn. liaison com. Superior Ct., 1987-88, 94-97, chair, 1994-95, mem. arbitration bd., 1987-2002; mem. Bench Bar Com., 1987-88; bd. gov., nom. com., superior ct. judge adv. com. to Gov. Locke, Wa.; adj. prof. Gonzaga U. Sch. Law, 1987—, bd. advisors, 2000—, vice-chair strategic planning com., 2005-06. Bd. dir. Community Ctr. Found., Spokane, 1986-89; active Spokane C.C. Legal Secretary Adv. Com.; mem. adv. bd. Spokane C.C., 1992—. Recipient Cert. of Recognition, Superior Ct. Clk., Spokane, 1986; named one of Best Lawyers in Am., 2003-06. Mem.: ABA, ATLA, Wash. State Bar Assn. (bd. govs. 2003—06), Spokane County Bar Assn. (trustee 1984—86, sec.-treas. 1987—88, v.p. 1988—89, pres. 1989—90, membership com. chair 1992—93), Wash. State Trial Lawyers Assn. (v.p. east 1979—80, CLE program chmn. 1984, chair 1995—96, mem. awards com. 1995—99, roundtable co-chair 2006—07, Cert. of Appreciation 1982, 1990, 1992, Leadership award 1984), Wash. State Bar Assn. (spl. dist. counsel 1984—2003, interprofl. com. 1987—90, character and fitness com. 1991—94, com. chair 1993—94, mem. jud. recommendation com. 1994—98, co-chair jud.

recommendation com. 1996—, chair jud. recommendation com. 1997—98, consumer protection com. 2000—01, rules profl. conduct com. 2000—03, spl. disciplinary counsel 2001, ins. and litigation com. 2005—06, rules profl. conduct com. 2006—07, 2006—07). Alpha Sigma Nu. Office: Delay Curran Thompson Pontarolo & Walker PS 601 W Main Ave Ste 1212 Spokane WA 99201-0684 Office Phone: 509-455-9500. E-mail: mikep@dctpw.com.

PONTIUS, STANLEY N., bank holding company executive; b. Auburn, Ind., Aug. 26, 1946; s. Clayton and Frances (Beuret) P.; m. Cheryl Ann Dawson, Aug. 3, 1968; children: Jarrod B., Dorian K. BS, Ind. U., 1968; grad., Stonier Grad. Sch. of Banking, 1979. Bank One, 1968-91; dir., pres., COO 1st Fin. Bancorp, Hamilton, Ohio, 1991, dir., pres., CEO, 1992—2003, 1st Nat. Bank of Southwestern Ohio, Hamilton, 1991-97, chmn., CEO, 1997-98, chmn., 1998—2003. Bd. dirs. Health Alliance Greater Cin., Ohio Casualty Corp. (chmn., 1994-), Fort Hamilton Health Network (chmn.), Hamilton Cmty. Found. With U.S. Army, 1968-70. Mem. Am. Bankers Coun., Hamilton-Fairfield Arts Assn. Leadership Hamilton, Metropolitan Growth Alliance, "The Community Banker" magazine (adv. bd.).

PONT MARCHESE, MARISARA, former Puerto Rican government official; b. Río Piedras, PR, Oct. 29, 1941; d. Rafael Pont and Sara Marchese. BA in Humanities cum laude, U. P.R., 1962-63; MS in Libr. Sci., Columbia U., 1971. Asst. to libr. med. scis. campus U. P.R., Río Piedras, 1964-72; spl. aide to Pres. Senate Commonwealth of P.R., San Juan, 1972; dep. aide in mgmt. Office of Gov. of P.R., San Juan, 1973, exec. aide to dir. of communications, 1973-74, dir. communications, 1974-76; pres. Plus Image Devel. and Pub. Rels., San Juan, 1977-86, Comstat/Rowland Pub. Rels., San Juan, 1986—; lectr. U. PR, pres. Commn. of Transition, 2004—05; sec. state Commonwealth of P.R., San Juan, 2005. Mem. Assn. Profl. Pub. Rels. Practitioners of P.R. (pres. 1984-86), Pub. Rels. Soc. Am., Overseas Press Club P.R. (co-chmn. ann. award program 1981-89), P.R. Mfrs. Assn., P.R. C. of C. (pub. rels. award 1985), Bankers Club. Roman Catholic. Business E-Mail: marisarap@comstat-pr.com.

PONTUAL, ROMULO, broadcast executive; V.p. space tech. News Corp., 1996—98, sr. v.p., 1998—99, exec. v.p. news tech., 1999—2002, exec. v.p. TV platforms, 2002; with Hughes Electronics Corp.; exec. v.p., chief tech. officer DIRECTV Group, El Segundo, Calif., 2004—. Vice chmn. Innova S de RL, 2000; mem. mgmt. bd. Sky Brasil Servicos Ltd., 2001. Office: DIRECTV Group 2230 E Imperial Hwy El Segundo CA 90245 Office Phone: 310-964-5000. *

PONZI KAY, MARYLOU, human resources specialist; b. NYC, Oct. 14, 1950; d. Bruno and Constance Louise (DeLuca) P.; m. William J. Kay, Jr., Oct. 24, 1993. BA, SUNY, Geneseo, 1972; MA, U. Iowa, 1974, SUNY, Buffalo, 1979; cert. in advanced study in labor rels., N.Y. Inst. Tech., 1995. Cert. sr. profl. in human resources Soc. for Human Resources Mgmt. Cert. Inst., 2002. Pers. adminstr. Michelin Tire Corp., Lake Success, N.Y., 1978-83; tech. recruiter 1st Data Resources, Lake Success, N.Y., 1983-84; mgr. human resources Chem. Bank, Jericho, N.Y., 1984-87; pers. officer J.P. Morgan Inc., NYC, 1987-89; mgr. employment Am. Express Inc., NYC, 1989-92; dir. human resources RockBottom Stores, Inc., 1992-95; asst. dir. human resources Canon U.S.A., Lake Success, N.Y., 1995-97, dir. human resources, 1997-2000, dir. corp. human resources and devel., 2000; dir. human resources Esselte Ams., Melville, NY, 2000—02; v.p. global compensation benefits and svcs. Esselte Corp., 2002—05; v.p. human resources Smartmatic Corp., Boca Raton, Fla., 2005—07; v.p. human resources N.Am. and Caribbean Sol Melia, Miami, Fla., 2007—. Instr. French and Spanish, Amityville H.S. Adult Edn., 1986-96; adj. prof. human resources N.Y. Inst. Tech., 2000-05. Editor: New England Guide, 1982, Canada Guide, 1982. Pres. LeBourget Alliance, Amityville, N.Y., 1995-97; pres. bus. adv. coun. Adults and Children with Learning Disabilities, 1994-97, trustee, 1997-, bd. dir., 2005-06; sr. exec. orientation Miami C. of C., 2006. Mem. ASTD, Soc. Human Resources Mgmt., Human Resources Strategic Issues Coun., World at Work. Roman Catholic. Avocations: languages, travel, cooking, sports. Office: Sol Melia 800 Brickell Ave Miami FL 33131 Office Phone: 305-929-5201. Personal E-mail: mwk93@aol.com. Business E-Mail: maryloup@sol-group.com.

POOL, MARY JANE, writer, editor; d. Earl Lee and Dorothy (Matthews) P. Grad., St. de Chantal Acad., 1942; BA in Art with honors, Drury Coll., 1946; LHD (hon.), Drury U., 2002. Mem. staff Vogue mag., NYC, 1946-68, assoc. merchandising editor, 1948-57, promotion dir., 1958-66, exec. editor, 1966-68; editor House and Garden mag., 1969, editor-in-chief, 1970-80. Cons. Baker Furniture Co., 1981-94, Aves Advt., Inc., 1981-94, bd. dirs.; mem. bd. govs. Decorative Arts Trust; past mem. bd. govs. Fashion Group, Inc., N.Y.C Author: The Gardens of Venice, 1989, The Gardens of Florence, 1992, Gardens in the City-New York in Bloom, 1999; co-author: The Angel Tree, 1984, The Angel Tree—A Christmas Celebration, 1993, The Christmas Story, 2001, editor: 20th Century Decorating, Architecture, Gardens, Billy Baldwin Decorates, 26 Easy Little Gardens. Mem. bus. com. N.Y. Zool. Soc., 1979-86; trustee Drury Univ., 1971—; bd. dirs. Isabel O'Neil Found., 1978—. Recipient award Nat. Soc. Interior Designers, Disting. Alumni award Drury Coll., 1961, Edith Wharton Women of Achievement award, 1999; Pool Art Ctr. at Drury U opened 2004. Address: 1 E 66th St New York NY 10021-5854

POOL, PHILIP BEMIS, JR., investment banker; b. NYC, Apr. 11, 1954; s. Philip B. and Virginia Middleton (French) P.; m. Joan H. Barnes, May 19, 1978; children: Elliott Livingston, Victoria Middleton. BS in Commerce, U. Va., 1976; MBA, Columbia U., 1980. Asst. treas. The Bank of N.Y., NYC, 1976-78; v.p. Kidder Peabody & Co., Inc., NYC, 1980-85; mng. dir. Merrill Lynch & Co., NYC, 1985-94, Donaldson, Lufkin & Jenrette, NYC, 1994—2001, Willis Stein & Ptnrs., Locust Valley, NY, 2001—. Mem.: U. Va. Alumni Assn. (bd. mgrs.), Nat. Golf Links of Am., Racquet and Tennis Club, Lyford Cay Club, Meadow Brook Club, Piping Rock Club (gov. 1989—). Republican. Episcopalian. Avocations: golf, squash.

POOLE, DAVID P., lawyer, utilities executive; b. Houston, Mar. 13, 1962; s. Preston L. and Shari J. Poole; 1 child, Aubrey. BSc in Petroleum Engring., Tex. Tech. U., Lubbock, 1984, JD, 1988. Bar: Tex. 1988, DC 1989, US Dist. Ct. (no. dist. Tex.) 1988. Assoc. Worsham, Forsythe Woodridge, Dallas, 1988—97, ptnr., 1997—2002, mng. ptnr., 2001—02; ptnr., mng. ptnr. Hunton & Williams LLP, Dallas, 2002—04; assoc. gen. counsel, sr. v.p. TXU Corp., Dallas, 2004—06, gen. counsel, exec. v.p., 2006—; also chief legal officer TXU Power. Mem. exec. bd. Cir. 10 Coun. Boy Scouts of Am., Dallas, 2003—. Mem.: Dallas Bar Assn. (co- chair CLE Com. 2003—04). Office: TXU Corp 1601 Bryan 600 Dallas TX 75201 Office Phone: 214-812-6001. *

POOLE, EVA DURAINE, librarian; b. Farrell, Pa., Dec. 20, 1952; d. Leonard Milton and Polly Mae (Flint) Harris; m. Tommy Lynn Cole, May 15, 1970 (div. Sept. 1984); 1 child, Tommy Lynn Cole, Jr.; m. Earnest Theodore Poole, Sept. 22, 1990; 1 child, Aleece Remelle Poole. BA in LS, Tex. Woman's U., Denton, 1974, MLS, 1976; postgrad., U. Houston, 1989. Libr. asst. Emily Fowler Pub. Libr., Denton, Tex., 1970-74; children's libr. Houston Pub. Libr., 1974-75, 1st asst. libr., 1976-77; children's libr. Ector County Libr., Odessa, Tex., 1977-80; head pub. svcs. Lee Davis Libr. San Jacinto Coll., Pasadena, Tex., 1980-84; libr. dir. San Jacinto Coll. South, Houston, 1984-90; libr. svcs. mgr. Emily Fowler Pub. Libr., Denton, 1990-93, interim dir., 1993; dir. librs. Denton Pub. Librs., 1993—. Mem. Libr. Svcs. Constrn. Act Adv. Coun., 1994-97, Libr. Svcs. Tech. Act Adv. Coun., 1997-2000; mem. TEXSHARE adv. bd. Tex. State Libr. and Archives Commn., 1999-2005, chmn., 2003-2004; bd. dirs. Denton Area Tchrs. Credit Union, 2003-06, Denton Area Tchrs. Credit Union, 2007—; mem. adv. bd. U. North Tex. Sch. Libr. and Info. Sci., 2000—, chair, 2006-07; mem. members coun. Online Computer Libr. Ctr., 2004-07; mem. presdl. search adv. com. U. North Tex., 2005-06; mem. external constituent bd. Tex. Woman's U. Sch. Libr. and Info. Studies, 2005—. Bd. dirs. Amigos Libr. Svcs., 2000-03, Girl Scouts Cross Timbers Coun., 2002-04, United Way of Denton County, 2002—, exec. com., bd. pres., 2006-07, Friends of Librs. U.S.A., 2003-2007. Named to Outstanding Young Women of Am., 1991. Mem. ALA (chair Loleta Fyan jury com. 1999-2000) Allied Profl. Assn.(chmn. cert. pub. libr. adminstr. program 2005-06, mem. com. orgn., 2005-06), Pub. Libr. Assn. (mem. budget and fin. com. 1999-2002, chair budget and fin. com. 2001-2002, 2004-05, nat. conf. com. 2002-04, chair bylaws and orgn. 2002-03, mem. instnl. scholarships task force 2006, bd. dirs. 2007—), Libr. Adminstrn. and Mgmt. Assn. (program com. 1994-97, mem.-at-large bd. dirs. 2000-02, chair cultural diversity com. 2000-01, com. on orgn. 2002-05, rep. to Freedom to Read Found. 2002-03, strategic planning com. 2005-06), Tex. Libr. Assn. (pub. libr. divsn. sec. 1995-96, chair 1997-98, leadership devel. com. 1995-97, leadership devel. com. chair 1996-97, alumnae 1st class Tex. Accelerated Libr. Leaders 1994, legis. com. 1997-99, Dist. 7 coun. 1996-99, exec. bd. 1998-2000, 2002-05, ad hoc commn. on pub. lib. stds. com. chair 1998-2000, 2002 conf. local arrangements com. 2001-02, chair 2000 conf. program com. 1998-2000, chair awards com. 2001-02, pres.-elect 2002-03, pres. 2003-04, chair Tocker Found. com. 2006—), Pub. Libr. Adminstrs. North Tex. (vice chair 1994-95, chair 1995-96), Tex. Mcpl. Libr. Dirs. Assn. (pres. 1995-96, grantee 1993, Libr. of Yr. 1998), Denton Rotary Club (mem. bd. dirs., 2006—, pres.-elect, 2007—), Tex. Mcpl. League (bd. dirs. 1997-2000). Office: Denton Pub Libr 502 Oakland St Denton TX 76201 Home Phone: 940-484-8963; Office Phone: 940-349-8750. Business E-Mail: eva.poole@cityofdenton.com.

POOLE, KEITH T., political science professor; b. Newport, Oreg., 1947; m. Janice K. Poole, 1972. BS in Polit. Sci., Portland State U., 1972; MA in Polit. Sci., U. Rochester, 1975, PhD in Polit. Sci., 1978. Asst. prof. polit. sci. U. Oreg., 1978—82; postdoctoral fellow in polit. economy Carnegie-Mellon U., 1981—82; vis. prof. polit. sci. divsn. humanities and social sci. Calif. Inst. Tech., 1992, 1995; prof. Grad. Sch. Indsl. Adminstrn. Carnegie-Mellon U., 1982—2000; Kenneth L. Lay prof. polit. sci. U. Houston, 2000—04; fellow Ctr. Advanced Study in Behavioral Sciences, 2003—04; prof. polit. sci. U. Calif. San Diego, 2005—. Editl. bd. Social Sci. Quarterly, 1998—, American Jour. Polit. Sci., 1998—2002, Jour. Politics, 2001—04, Legislative Studies Quarterly, 2002—05. Author (with L. Harmon Zeigler): (books) Women, Public Opinion, and Politics: The Changing Political Attitudes of American Women, 1985; author: (with Howard Rosenthal) Congress: A Political-Economic History of Roll Call Voting, 1997; author: Spatial Models of Parliamentary Voting, 2005; author: (Nolan M. McCarty and Howard Rosenthal) Polarized America: The Dance of Ideology and Unequal Riches, 2006; author: (with Howard Rosental) Ideology and Congress, 2006; author: (with Nolan M. McCarty) (monograph) Income Redistribution and the Realignment of American Politics, 1997; contbr. articles to profl. journals. Recipient Warren E. Miller prize best article, 2001. Fellow: Am. Acad. Arts and Sciences. Office: Dept Political Science Univ Calif San Diego Social Sciences Bldg Rm 301 9500 Gilman Dr MC 0521 La Jolla CA 92093-0521 Office Phone: 858-534-1452. E-mail: kpoole@ucsd.edu.

POOLE, NANCY GEDDES, art gallery curator, writer; b. London, Ont., Can., May 10, 1930; d. John Hardy and Kathleen Edwards (Robinson) G.; m. William Robert Poole, Aug. 15, 1952; 1 child, Andrea Mary. BA, U. Western Ont., 1956, LLD, 1990. Owner, dir. Nancy Poole's Studio, Toronto, Ont., Canada, 1969-78; acting dir. London Regional Art Gallery, Ont., Canada, 1981—, exec. dir. Ont., 1985-89; dir. London Regional Art and Hist. Museums, Ont., Canada, 1989-95. Chair governing coun. Ont. Coll. Art, 1972-73; bd. dirs. Robarts Rsch. Inst., 1995. Author: The Art of London 1939-1980, 1984; editor Jack Chambers, 1978, The Collection, 1990. Bd. govs. U. Western Ont., 1974-85; bd. dirs. Western Area Youth Svcs., 1996; chair Western Area Youth Svcs. Found., 2004-06, Hazel Cryderman-Wees Found., 2004. Fellow Ont. Coll. Art. Mem.: Order of Can. Office: 420 Fanshawe Park Rd London ON Canada N5X 2S9

POOLE, RICHARD WILLIAM, economist; b. Oklahoma City, Dec. 4, 1927; s. William Robert and Lois (Spicer) Poole; m. Bertha Lynn Mehr, July 28, 1950; children: Richard William, Laura Lynne, Mark Stephen. BS, U. Okla., 1951, MBA, 1952; postgrad., George Washington U., 1957—58; PhD, Okla. State U., 1960. Rsch. analyst Okla. Gas & Electric Co., Oklahoma City, 1952- 54; mgr. sci. and mfg. devel. dept. Oklahoma City C. of C., 1954—57; mgr. Office of J.E. Webb, Washington, 1957-58; from instr. to prof. econs. Okla. State U., Stillwater, 1960-65, prof. econs., dean Coll. Bus. Adminstrn., 1965-72, v.p., prof. econs., 1972-88, Regents Disting. Svc. prof., prof. econs., 1988-93, emeritus v.p., dean, Regents Disting. Svc. prof./prof. econ., 1993—. Cons. to adminstr. NASA, Washington, 1961—69; adviser subcom. govt. rsch. U.S. Senate, 1966—69; lectr. Intermediate Sch. Banking, Ops. Mgmt. Sch., Okla. Bankers Assn., 1969—88; lectr. internat. off-campus programs Oklahoma City U., 1994—96. Author (with others): The Oklahoma Economy, 1963, County Building Block Data for Regional Analysis, 1965. Mem. Gov.'s Com. Devel. Ark.-Verdigris Waterway, 1970—71, Gov.'s Five-Yr. Econ. Devel. Plan, 1993; past v.p., bd. dirs., past chmn. Mid-Continent R & D Coun. 2d lt. arty. US Army, 1946—48. Named to Coll. Bus. Adminstrn. Hall of Fame, Okla. State U., 1993, Stillwater Hall of Fame, Payne county Hist. Soc. and Stillwater C. of C., 1996, Okla. Higher Edn. Hall of Fame, 1998; recipient Delta Sigma Pi Gold Key award, Coll. Bus. Adminstrn. U. Okla., 1951, Tchg. award on Am. free enterprise sys., Merrick Found., 1992, Disting. Alumni award, Okla. State U., 1995, Henry G. Bennett Disting. Svc. award, 1999. Mem.: Southwestern Bus. Adminstrn. Assn. (past pres.), Nat. Assn. State Univs. and Land Grant Colls. (past chmn. commn. edn. for bus. professions), Am. Assembly Collegiate Schs. Bus. (past bd. dirs.), Southwestern Econ. Assn. (past pres.), Stillwater C. of C. (past bd. dirs., pres.), Santa Fe Trail Assn. (bd. dirs. 2001—02), Okla. C. of C. (past bd. dirs.), Okla. Heritage Assn. (bd. dirs. 2000—05), Omicron Delta Kappa, Phi Eta Sigma, Phi Kappa Phi, Beta Gamma Sigma (past bd. dirs.). Home: 14901 N Pennsylvania Apt 336 Oklahoma City OK 73134

POOLE, ROGER CLIFF, retired academic administrator, finance educator, retired military officer; b. Fayetteville, NC, Dec. 31, 1936; married. BA, The Citadel, 1959, PhD (hon.) in Bus., 2005; MBA in Mgmt., U. SC, 1962, PhD in Fin., 1974; diploma, US Army War Coll., 1981. V.p. Investors Nat. Life Insurance Co., Inc, Columbia, SC, 1963—66; instr. fin. U. SC, 1969—70; asst. prof. fin. Va. Commonwealth U., Richmond, 1970—73, coord. of fin.; v.p. fin. and adminstrn., mem. bd. dirs. Century Construction Co. Inc., Richmond; sec., treas., mem. bd. dirs. Century Constructors of Virginia, Inc., 1973—76; asst. prof. fin. U. Richmond, 1976—79, assoc. dean, dir. of grad. studies Richard S. Reynolds Grad. Sch., 1979—83, assoc. prof. fin., 1983—85, prof. fin., 1985—88, dean E. Claiborne Robins Sch. Bus., 1988—93; v.p. academic affairs, dean The Citadel, Charleston, 1993—96, 1997—99, interim pres., 1996—97, 2005, 2006, BOV disting. fellow fin., 2005—. Dir. Transp., Troop Support & Energy Dept. Army Ops. Ctr., Desert Shield/Desert Storm. Ret. brigadier gen. USAR. Decorated Legion of Merit Award, Meritorious Svc. Medal with Oak Leaf Cluster, Army Commendation Medal with Oak Leaf Cluster, Army Reserve Components Achievement Medal with Two Oak Leaf Clusters, Nat. Defense Svc. Medal, Armed Forces Reserve Medal with 30-year Device, Army Svc. Ribbon, Army Reserve Components Overseas Training Ribbon with Numeral 3. Fellow: Southwestern Fin. Assn., Life Mgmt. Inst.; mem.: So. Risk and Insurance Assn., So. Econs. Assn., So. Fin. Assn., Soc. for Advancement of Mgmt., Fin. Execs. Inst., Acad. Internat. Bus., Am. Coll. Charter Life Underwriter, Order of St. Stanislaus. Office: The Citadel 171 Moultrie St Charleston SC 29409

POOLE, SCOTT, architect, educator; b. Jan. 1, 1951; MArch, U. Tex., 1983. Registered arch., Va. Instr. Va. Tech., Blacksburg, 1986—, prof. arch., dir. Sch. Arch. and Design, 2004—. Lectr. Yale U., U. Va., Sch. arch., Aarhus, Denmark; Gilmore vis. lectr. U. Calgary, 2000; vis. prof. Royal Danish Acad. Art, Copenhagen; workshop presenter Royal Inst. Tech., Stockholm. Recipient Tchg. Excellence award, Va. Tech. Coll. Arch. and Urban Studies, 2002; Fulbright scholar, Finland. Mem.: AIA. Office: Va Tech Sch Arch & Design 201 Cowgill Hall Blacksburg VA 24061 Business E-Mail: spoole@vt.edu.

POOLE, WILLIAM, bank executive; b. Wilmington, Del., June 19, 1937; s. William and Louise (Hiller) P.; m. Mary Lynne Ahroon, June 26, 1960 (div. May 1997); children: William, Lester Allen, Jonathan Carl; m. Geraldine S. Stroud, July 12, 1997. AB, Swarthmore Coll., 1959, LLD (hon.), 1989; MBA, U. Chgo., 1963, PhD, 1966. Asst. prof. polit. economy Johns Hopkins U., Balt., 1963-69; professorial lectr. Am. U., Washington, 1970-71; assoc. professorial lectr. George Washington U., Washington, 1971-73; professorial lectr. Georgetown U., Washington, 1972; vis. lectr. Harvard U., Cambridge, Mass., 1973, MIT, Cambridge, 1974, 77; Bank Mees and Hope vis. prof. econs. Erasmus U. Rotterdam, 1991; prof. econs. Brown U., Providence, 1974-98, dir. ctr. for study fin. markets and insts., 1987-92, chmn. econs. dept., 1981-82, 85-86; economist Fed. Res. Sys., Washington, 1964, 69-70, sr. economist, 1970-74; pres., CEO Fed. Res. Bank St. Louis, 1998—. Adviser Fed. Res. Bank, Boston, 1973-74, cons., 1974-81; vis. economist Res. Bank of Australia, 1980-81; mem. Coun. Econ. Advisers, 1982-85; adj. scholar Cato Inst., 1985-98. Author: (book) Principles of Economics, 1991; contbr. articles to profl. jours. Dir. United Way Gr. St. Louis; bd. trustees Webster U. Recipient Adam Smith award, Nat. Assn. Bus. Econs., 2006. Mem. Am. Econ. Assn., Western Econ. Assn. (mem. internat. exec. com. 1986-89, mem. nominating com. 1995). Office: Fed Res Bank St Louis PO Box 442 Saint Louis MO 63166-0442 Office Phone: 314-444-8301. E-mail: wpoole@stls.frb.org. *

POOLE, WILLIAM DANIEL, writer, editor; b. Statesville, NC, Nov. 3, 1932; s. William Oscar and Edna (Brewer) P.; m. Sandra Ball, June 14, 1980. BA, Wake Forest U., 1955. Reporter Norfolk (Va.) Virginian-Pilot, 1955-57, Washington Star, 1957-61, real estate editor, 1961-71, features editor, asst. mng. editor, 1971-81; v.p. Ins. Info. Inst., NYC, 1981-91; pub. Insurance Rev. mag., NYC, 1986-91. Contbr. articles to profl. jours. Mem. White House Corr. Assn., Nat. Assn. Real Estate Editors (pres. 1970-71), Newspaper Comics Coun. (chmn. 1975-77), Soc. Am. Travel Writers, Mystery Writers of Am., Ins. Mktg. Comms. Assn., Am. Assn. Sunday and Feature Editors, Amateur Comedy Club, Dutch Treat Club, The Players Club, Nat. Press Club (D.C.), Omicron Delta Kappa, Sigma Phi Epsilon. Republican. Baptist. Home: 139 E 63rd St New York NY 10021-7408

POOLER, ROSEMARY S., federal judge; b. 1938; BA, Bklyn. Coll., 1959; MA, U. Conn., 1961; JD, U. Mich. Law Sch., 1965; cert. in Sr. Mgmt. in Govt., Harvard U., 1978; degree (hon.), SUNY, Albany, 1986. With Crystal, Manes & Rifken, Syracuse, 1966—69, Michaels and Michaels, Syracuse, 1969—72; asst. corp. counsel Dir. of Consumer Affairs Unit, Syracuse, 1972—73; common counsel City of Syracuse Pub. Interest Rsch. Group, 1974—75; chmn., exec. dir. Consumer Protection Bd., 1975—80; commr. NY State Pub. Services Commn., 1981—86; staff dir. NY State Assembly, Com. on Corps., Authorities and Commns., 1987—94; judge Supreme Ct., 5th Jud. Dist., 1991—94; dist. judge US Dist. Ct. (no. dist.) N.Y., Syracuse, 1994—98; cir. judge US Ct. Appeals, (2nd cir.), 1998—. Vis. prof. Syracuse Univ. Coll. of Law, 1987—88; v.p. legal affairs Atlantic States Legal Found., 1989—90. Mem.: Assn. of Supreme Ct. Justices of the State of NY (sec. 1993—94), Women's Bar Assn. of the State of NY, NY State Bar Assn., Onondaga County Bar Assn. Office: Federal Bldg 100 S Clinton St Syracuse NY 13261-7395 also: 40 Foley Square New York NY 10007 *

POOLEY, JAMES HENRY, lawyer; b. Dayton, Ohio, Oct. 4, 1948; s. Howard Carl and Daisy Frances (Lindsley) P.; children by previous marriage: Jefferson Douglas, Christopher James; m. Laura-Jean Anderson, Oct. 13, 1984; 1 child, Catherine Lindsley. BA, Lafayette Coll., 1970; JD, Columbia U., 1973. Bar: Calif. 1973, U.S. Dist. Ct. (no. dist.) Calif. 1973, U.S. Ct. Appeals (9th cir.) 1974, U.S. Supreme Ct. 1977, U.S. Dist. Ct. (ctrl. dist.) Calif. 1978. Assoc. Wilson, Mosher & Sonsini, Palo Alto, Calif., 1973-78; ptnr. Mosher Pooley & Sullivan, Palo Alto, 1978-88, Graham and James LLP, 1988-93, Fish & Richardson, Menlo Park, Calif., 1993-98, Gray Cary Ware & Freidenrich LLP, Palo Alto, Calif., 1998—2002, Milbank, Tweed, Hadley & McCloy LLP, Palo Alto, Calif., 2002—06, Pooley & Oliver LLP, Palo Alto, Calif., 2006—07, Morrison & Foester LLP, Palo Alto, Calif., 2007—. Arbitrator, spl. master U.S. Dist. Ct. (no. dist.) Calif., Santa Clara Superior Ct., San Jose, 1979—; lectr. Practicing Law Inst., N.Y.C., 1983, 85-86, 88, 95, 97, 98, 99, Santa Clara U. Sch. Law, 1985-87, 98, U. Calif., Boalt Hall Sch. Law, 1997—. Author: Trade Secrets, 1982, Protecting Technology, 1983, Trying the High Technology Case, 1984, Trade Secrets: A Guide to Protecting Proprietary Business Information, 1989, Trade Secrets, 1997; co-author: Millennium Intelligence, 2000; editor, co-author: California Trade Secrets Law, 1996; contbr. articles to profl. jours.; editor-in-chief Trade Secret Law Reporter, 1984-85; bd. advisors Santa Clara Computer and High Tech. Law Jour., 1984—. Bd. advisors Berkeley Ctr. for Law and Tech., 1997—; chmn. Nat. Trade Secret Law Inst., 1994; pres. Am. Friends of the Acad. of St. Martin in the Fields, 1998—. Named Lawyer of Yr., Calif. Lawyer mag., 2003. Mem. Am. Intellectual Property Lawyers Assn. (chmn. trade secrets com. 1996-98, pres., 2007-), Am. Electronics Assn. (chmn. lawyers' com. 1981-82), Internat. Bar Assn., Union Internationale des Avocats. Office: Morrison & Foester LLP 755 Page Mill Rd Palo Alto CA 94304 E-mail: jpooley@mofo.com.

POON, ALAN MING WANG, sports association executive, director; s. Chung and Chai Poon; m. Grace Wong, 1980; 1 child, Arthur. MBA, Pacific We. U., 1984. Dir., sales mgr. Ed's News and Confectionery Ltd., Canada, 1984—87; dir., bus. mgr. Alanica Foodservices Ltd., Canada, 1988—94; product and export mgr. Hop Hing Group, Hong Kong, 1995—97; regional dir. Seawide Internat. Group, Hong Kong, 1997—2002; export mgr. Sunnyside Ltd., Hong Kong, 2002—05; regional dir. BTL Sports Inc., Toronto, Canada, 2005—. Part-time trainer BTL Sports Inc., 2005—. Author: Mechanic Tennis Training Program (cert. Hong Kong Tennis Assn., 2002). Recipient Quality Assurance Sys. award, Sunnyside Ltd., 2002. Fellow: Inst. Administrative Mgmt. (Internat. Essay Contest award 2000, Total Quality Management award 1992), Brit. Inst. Adminstrv. Mgmt. (hon. cert. 1982). Achievements include research in direct-mailing-orders as a marketing strategy. Office: BTL Sports Inc 4211 Sheppard Avenue East Unit A111 Toronto ON Canada M1S 5H5 Business E-Mail: btlsl2005@yahoo.ca.

POON, CHRISTINE A., pharmaceutical company executive; b. Cin., June 23, 1952; d. James and Virginaia Poon; m. Mike Tweedle. BS in Biology, Northwestern U., 1973; MS in Biology and Biochemistry, St. Louis U., 1973; MBA in Fin., Boston U., 1982. Various mgmt. positions Bristol-Myers Squibb, 1985—2000, v.p., sr. v.p. for Can. and L.Am. pharm. ops., pres., gen. mgr. Squibb Diagnostics' Can. operation, 1994, pres. Med. Devices, 1997—98, pres. internat. medicines, 1998—2000; co. group chmn. pharm. group Johnson & Johnson, New Brunswick, NJ, 2000—01, worldwide chmn. pharms. group, 2001—03, worldwide chmn.

medicines and nutritionals, 2003—, vice chmn., mem. exec. com., 2005—. Bd. dirs. Prudential Fin., Inc., 2006—; bd. adv. Healthcare Businesswomen's Assn. Bd. dirs. Fox Chase Cancer Ctr., Phila. Named Woman of Yr., Healthcare Businesswomen's Assn., 2004; named one of 50 Women to Watch, Wall St. Jour., 2005, 2006, Most Powerful Women, Forbes mag., 2005, 10 Most Powerful Women in NJ Bus., Star-Ledger, 2006, 50 Most Powerful Women in Bus., Fortune mag., 2006. Office: Johnson & Johnson 1 Johnson and Johnson Plaza New Brunswick NJ 08901 *

POON, PETER TIN-YAU, engineer, physicist; b. Hengyang, Hunan, China, May 31, 1944; came to U.S., 1967; s. Sam. Chak-Kwong and Lai (Yiu) P.; m. Mable Tsang, Apr. 13, 1974; children: Amy Wei-Ling, Brian Wing-Yan. *Parents, Sam Chak-Kwong and Lai (Yiu) Poon grew up in China. Father fought along side the Flying Tigers during World War II, and later became a US citizen. Wife, Mable, grew up in Hong Kong and completed her studies in Hawaii. She is an Office Manager, Human Resources Administration, California Institute of Technology. Daughter, Amy, completed her MD at University of California, San Francisco, and has completed her training as a chief resident at Stanford University Medical Center. Son, Brian, graduated from University of California, Berkeley, in Electrical Engineering-Computer Science, and has acquired experience as a professional in software engineering.* BS, U. Hong Kong, 1965; MA, Calif. State U., Long Beach, 1969; PhD, U. So. Calif., 1974. Tech. mgr. and sr. engr. advanced tech. and missions Jet Propulsion Lab./Calif. Inst. Tech., Pasadena, 1974—83; advisor Space Sta. Ada Task NASA, 1984—85, task leader software mgmt. and assurance program, software mgmt. stds., 1986—88, element mgr. software info. sys.; from multimission sys. mgr. to telecom. and mission sys. mgr. Cassini and Mars missions Jet Propulsion Lab., 1988—2001, telecom. and mission sys. mgr. global surveyor Mars Odyssey mission, 2001—, telecomm. and mission sys. mgr. Voyager Interstellar mission, telecom. and mission sys. mgr. Ulysses mission, telecom. and mission sys. mgr. European Very Long Baseline Interferometry Network Project, Space Geodesy Project, 2001—. Del. various confs.; US chmn., program mgmt. com., panel chair Internat. Software Engring. Stds. Symposium, UK, Canada, Brazil and US, 1992—99, Canada, 1992—99, Brazil, 1992—99, England, 1992—99, United States, 2000—; mem. Internat. Orgn. for Standardization in Info. Tech. Subcom. and US Tech. Adv. Group, 1995—2007. Mem. editl. bd.: Software Quality Profl., Am. Soc. for Quality, 1998—; contbr. articles to profl. jours. Active JPL steering com. United Way, Pasadena, Calif., 1998—2005. Recipient Group awards NASA, 1977-2006, Recognition cert. Inventions and Contbns. Bd., award from Mars Global Surveyor and Mars Odyssey, 2002. Mem. IEEE (exec. com. software engring. stds. 1993-2000), Arcadia Music Club (pres. 1994-95), Sigma Xi, Eta Kappa Nu, Phi Kappa Phi, Athenaeum. Avocations: music, hiking, theater. Office: Jet Propulsion Lab Calif Inst Tech 4800 Oak Grove Dr Pasadena CA 91109-8099 Business E-Mail: peter.t.poon@jpl.nasa.gov.

POONS, LARRY, artist; b. Tokyo, Oct. 1, 1937; came to U.S., 1938; Student, New Eng. Conservatory Music, 1955-57, Boston Mus. Fine Arts Sch., 1958. Mem. vis. faculty N.Y. Studio Sch., 1967. Lectr. in field. Author: The Structure of Color, 1971; exhibitions include Green Gallery, NYC, 1963—65, Art Inst. Chgo., 1966, Corcoran Gallery Art, Carnegie Inst., 1967, Leo Castelli Gallery, 1967—68, Documenta IV, Kassel, W. Germany, 1968, Whitney Mus. Am. Art, 1968, 1972, Lawrence Rubin Gallery, 1970—73, Whitney Biennial, 1973, Knoedler & Co., 1973—78, Knoedler Contemporary Art, N.Y.C., 1974—78, Andre Emmerlich Gallery, 1979—87, Albright-Knox Art Gallery, Buffalo, 1968, 1970, Pasadena Art Mus., 1969, Gallery 99, Bar Harbor Islands, Fla., 1981, Mus. Fine Arts, Boston, 1981—82, Galerie Montaigne, Paris, 1990, Helander Gallery, Palm Beach, Fla., 1990, Gallery Afinsa, Madrid, 1991, Salander-O'Reilly Galleries, N.Y.C., 1991—96, 1998, Frederick Spratt Gallery, San Jose, 1996—97, Ruth Bachofner Gallery, Santa Monica, 1996, Art Pub., Geneva, Switzerland, 1997, Claudia Carr Gallery, 1997, Larry Evan/James Willis and Frederick Spratt Gallery, San Francisco, 1997, exhibited in group shows at Matthew Mark, Pat Hearn, 1998, Sideshow 195, Bklyn., 1998, Art and the Am. Experience, Kalamazoo Inst. of the Arts, 1998, Staatliche Kunsthalle, Baden-Baden, Germany, 1999, Ameringe Howard Fine Art, N.Y.C., 2000, Bernard Jacobson, 2002, Jacobson Howard, NYC, 2003—04, Side Show Gallery, Bklyn., 2003, 2006, Studio 18 Gallery, NYC, 2004, Albright Knox, Buffalo, 2005, Represented in permanent collections Mus. Modern Art, N.Y.C., Allen Meml. Art Mus., Oberlin Coll., Cleve. Mus. Art, Hirschhorn Mus. and Sculpture Garden, Washington, Milw. Art Ctr., Solomon R. Guggenheim Mus., N.Y.C., Tate Gallery, London, Whitney Mus. Am. Art, Met. Mus. Art, Chgo. Art Inst., Denver Mus., Boston Mus. Fine Arts, Albright-Knox Art Gallery, Stedelijk Mus., Amsterdam, Woodward Found., Washington, David Mirvish Gallery, Toronto, Bernard Jacobson Gallery, London, one-man shows include Salander-O'Reilly Gallery, N.Y.C., 2001, Theo Waddington, Boca Raton, Fla., 2000, Galleria Metta, Madrid, 2000, Perrella Gallery, Johnstown, N.Y., 2000, Bernard Jacobson, 2002, Bernard Jacobson Gallery, London, 2004, 2007, Jacobson Howard Gallery, 2004—05, Side Show Gallery, Bklyn., 2005—06, Danese Gallery, NYC, 2007. Address: 831 Broadway New York NY 10003-4706

POOR, HAROLD VINCENT, electrical engineering educator; b. Columbus, Ga., Oct. 2, 1951; s. Harold Edgar and Virginia (Hardin) P.; m. Connie Irene Hazelwood, Sept. 1, 1973; children: Kristin Elizabeth, Lauren Alissa. BEE with highest honors, Auburn U., 1972; PhD, Princeton U., 1977. From asst. prof. to prof. U. Ill., Urbana, 1977—90; prof. dept. elec. engring. Princeton U., NJ, 1990—, George Van Ness Lothrop prof. engring., 2003—05, Michael Henry Strater univ. prof. elec. engring., 2005—, dir. Ctr. for Innovation in Engring. Edn., 2005—06, dean engring. and applied scis., 2006—. Acad. visitor Imperial Coll. London U., 1985, 2003; vis. prof. Newcastle (Australia) U., 1987, Stanford U., 2004; vis. scholar Harvard U., 2004; sr. vis. fellow Imperial Coll., London U., 1993; cons. in field. Author: An Introduction to Signal Detection and Estimation, 1988, 2d edit., 1994, Wireless Communication Systems: Advanced Techniques for Signal Reception, 2004, Wireless Networks: Multiuser Detection in Cross-Layer Design, 2005, MIMO Wireless Communications, 2007; co-editor: Wireless Communications: Signal Processing Perspectives, 1998; contbr. articles to profl. jours. Grantee NSF, Office Naval Rsch., Army Rsch. Office, Darpa, 1978—; recipient Dir.'s Disting. Tchg. scholars award NSF, Disting. Alumnus award Tau Beta Pi 2005; John Simon Guggenheim Meml. Found. fellow, 2002-04. Fellow IEEE (bd. dirs. 1991-92, pres. Info. Theory Soc. IEEE 1990, editor-in-chief IEEE Transaction Info. Theory, 2004-07, Disting. Mem. award Control Sys. Soc. 1994, Third Millennium medal 2000, Joint Paper award with IEEE com. soc., 2001, Grad. Tchg. award 2001, EAB Major Ednl. Innovation award, 2004, James H. Mulligan Jr. Edn. medal 2005), AAAS, Acoustical Soc. Am., Am. Soc. Engring. Edn. (Terman award 1992, Centennial cert. 1993), Inst. Math. Stats., Optical Soc. Am.; mem. NAE, Am. Acad. Arts and Scis., Cosmos Club (Washington). Office: Princeton Univ Sch Engring and Applied Sci Princeton NJ 08544-0001 Office Phone: 609-258-2260.

POOR, JANET MEAKIN, III, landscape designer; b. Cin., Nov. 27, 1929; d. Cyrus Lee and Helen Keats (Meakin) Lee-Hofer; m. Edward King Poor III, June 23, 1951; children: Edward King IV, Thomas Meakin. Student, Stephens Coll., 1947-48, U. Cinn., 1949-51, Triton Coll., 1973-76. Pres. Janet Meakin Poor Landscape Design, Winnetka, Ill., 1975—. Chmn. bd. dirs. Chgo. Botanic Garden. Author, editor: Plants That Merit Attention Vol. I: Trees, 1984, Vol. II: Shrubs; contbr. articles to profl. jours. Participant in long range planning City of Winnetka, 1978-82, archtl. and environ. bd., 1980-84, beautification commn., 1978-84, garden coun., 1978-82; adv. coun., Sec. of Agr. Nat. Arboretum, Washington; nat. adv. bd. Filoli, San Francisco; trustee Ctr. Plant Conservation at Mo. Bot. Garden, St. Louis, also mem. exec. com.; mem. adv. coun. The Garden Conservancy, 1989—, chmn. Open Days Program Garden Conservancy; trustee Winnetka Congl. Ch., 1978-80; bd. dirs. Lady Bird Johnson Wildflower Ctr., Austin, Tex., McKee Bot. Garden, Vero Beach, Fla. Recipient merit award Hadley Sch. Blind, 1972; named Vol. of Yr. Hadley Sch. Blind. Mem. Chgo. Hort. Soc. (chmn. bd. dirs. 1987-93, medal 1984, gold medal garden design, exec. com., chmn. rsch. com., women's bd., designer herb garden Farwell Gardens at Chgo. Botanic Garden, Hutchinson medal 1994), Am. Hort. Soc. (bd. dirs., Catherine H. Sweeney award 1985), Garden Club Am. (chmn. nat. plant exchange 1980-81, chmn. hort. com. 1981-83, bd. dirs., 1983-85, corresponding sec. 1985-87, Horticulture award Zone X1 1981, Creative Leadership award 1986), Fortnightly Club, Garden Guild (bd. dirs.), Garden Club Am. (v.p. 1987-89, medal awards chmn. 1991-93, Medal of Honor 1994). Republican. Avocations: gardening, writing, music, lecturing, horticulture research. Office Phone: 847-446-2898.

POOR, PETER VARNUM, television producer and director; b. NYC, May 17, 1926; s. Henry Varnum and Bessie Breuer (Freedman) P.; m. Eloise Marcovicci Miller, Sept. 27, 1950; children: Candida Eustacia, Anna Maria, Graham Varnum. BA, Harvard U., 1947; postgrad., Centro Sperimentale di Cinematografia, Rome, 1951-52. Prodn. asst. New World Films, NYC, 1948; editor, dir. Willard Pictures, NYC, 1948-51; film editor, dir. and producer CBS News-Airpower, 1954-57, 7 Lively Arts, 1957-58, Twentieth Century, 1958-66, 21st Century, 1966-69, 60 Minutes, 1970-71, CBS Reports, 1971-75; sr. producer NBC News, Monitor, First Camera, White Paper, 1977-87; freelance producer and dir. Crow House Prodns., NYC, 1988—. Instr. in TV journalism Fordham U., 1976-78; screening com. Fulbright Grants in Film, TV and Radio, 1965-67, chmn., 1967, 70; adj. assoc. history of documentary Columbia U. Grad. Sch. Journalism, 1987; adj. asst. prof. visual arts NYU, 1991-92. Producer-dir.: (TV documentary films) What's New at School, 1972, The IQ Myth, 1975, The Biggest Lump of Money in the World, 1985, The Japan They Don't Talk About, 1986, Nuclear Power in France, 1987, The Cronkite Report, 1993. Served with USAF, 1944-45. Recipient Emmy award Acad. TV Arts and Sci., 1961-62, 67, Lasker TV award Lasker Found., 1968-69, U.S. CEA Forum award, 1967, 87; hon. mention Robert Kennedy Journalism Award in TV, 1976; Fulbright scholar, 1951-52. Mem. Dirs. Guild Am. (coun. 1980-90), Film Editors Union, Writers Guild Am. East. Clubs: Phoenix S-K (Cambridge, Mass.). Avocations: bicycling, reading, photography, gardening. Home and Office: 1150 5th Ave New York NY 10128-0724 Office Phone: 212-722-3836. E-mail: p.poor@worldnet.att.net.

POORE, PAUL MICHAEL, school system administrator; b. Schenectady, NY, Apr. 20, 1951; s. Franklin Earl and Josephine Poore (Stepmother); m. Miriam Lee Boss, Nov. 10, 1979. BA, SUNY, Albany, 1973, MA, 1976; EdM in Counseling and Guidance, U. NH, Plymouth, 1989. Cert. guidance counselor NH, 2002; sch. adminstr. NY, 1990, permanent lic. secondary edn. NY, 1976. English tchr. Saratoga Springs H.S., NY, 1973—76, Am. Internat. Sch., Dusseldorf, Germany, 1976—77; supr. shareholder svcs. dept. Am. Funds Svc. Co., LA, 1977—80; tchr. Yoyogi Seminar Prep. Sch., Tokyo, 1980—83; English dept. chair Am. Cmty. Schs., Athens, Greece, 1983—85; counselor and English tchr. Can. Acad., Kobe, Japan, 1985—90; dir. Harare Internat. Sch., Zimbabwe, 1989—2007, Lincoln Sch., Kathmandu, Nepal, 1990—98; exec. dir. Assn. Am. Schs. in S.Am., Pembroke Pines, Fla., 2007—. Accreditation adviser Coun. Internat. Schs., Petersfield; presenter in field. Author: (ednl. rsch.) Culture: The Space Between the Bars, The Silence Between the Notes (Disting. Overseas Lecture, 2005); dir.: (dramatic prodn.) Our Town, (musical prodn.) Pippin, Fiddler on the Roof; actor: (dramatic prodn.) Wizard of Oz, Snow White, Cinderella, Caucasian Chalk Circle, The Most Happy Fella, A Resounding Tinkle, (children's theatre prodn.) Little Match Girl; musician: (musical prodn.) West Side Story. Recipient Internat. Supt. of the Yr., Assn. for the Advancement of Internat. Edn., 2005, Nat. Supt. of the Yr., Am. Assn. of Sch. Administrators, 2005, AAIE Disting. Overseas Lecture, Assn. for the Advancement of Internat. Edn., 2005, Overseas Schools Leadership Inst., U.S. Dept. of State, 2001, Disting. Prin. Nomination, Bd. of Directors, Lincoln Sch., Nepal, 1993, 1997, Furthering Artistic Talent in Nepal, Queen of Nepal, 1997, Ednl. Leadership Acad., Internat. Schools Services, 1996. Mem.: Acad. Internat. Sch. Heads (bd. mem. 2000—07, treas., exec. com. 2004—07), Assn. Internat. Schs. in Africa (treas. 1998—2007, bd. mem. 1998—2007), Signum Laudis, Phi Delta Kappa. Avocations: sailing, saxophone, travel. Office: Assn American Schools in S America 12333 NW 18th St Pembroke Pines FL 33026 Home Phone: 263-4744218; 1234 NW 168 Ave Pembroke Pines FL 33026 Home Phone: 263-4744218; Office Phone: 954-436-4034. Personal E-mail: pppoore@hotmail.com.

POORMAN, ROBERT LEWIS, retired academic administrator; b. Germantown, Ohio, Dec. 9, 1926; s. Dale Lowell and Bernice Velma (Krick) P.; m. Lois May Romer, Dec. 26, 1949; children: Paula Beth, Janice Marie, Mark Leon, John Alex, Lisa Ann, Daniel Romer. Student, Ohio Wesleyan U., 1944-45, U. Va., 1945-46; BSEd., Ohio State U., 1948, MA, 1950; postgrad., U. So. Calif., 1951-53; Ed.D. (Kellogg fellow 1960-62, Disting. Scholar Tuition grantee 1960-62), UCLA, 1964. Tchr., counselor, adminstr., secondary schs., Colo., Mo., Ariz., 1948-57; registrar Phoenix Coll., 1957-60; intern Bakersfield Coll., 1960-63, asst. to pres., 1963-64, asso. dean instrn., 1964-65, dean students, 1965-67; founding pres. Lincoln Land C.C., 1967-88, pres. emeritus; edn. cons. MARA of Malaysia, 1983; higher edn. cons. Springfield, Ill., 1988—; interim pres. Parkland Coll., Champaign, Ill., 1989-90. Vis. assoc. prof. Fla. Internat. U., 1994-95, Fulbright Sr. Specialist peer reviewer, 2007-; lectr. in field; cons. in field. Contbr. articles to profl. jours. Bd. dirs. (past) United Way of Springfield, bd. dirs. Urban League of Springfield, Good Will Industries of Springfield, Gov.'s Prayer Breakfast, Springfield Mental Health, Griffin H.S. Bd., Diocesan Sem.; mem. adv. bd. Sacred Heart Acad., Springfield Commn. on Internat. Visitors, Sister Cities Assn. With USNR, 1944—46. Recipient Midwest region CEO of Yr. Assn. C.C. Trustees, 1988, recognition Ill. C.C. Trustees Assn., 1988; named an Outstanding CEO for Ill. Cmty. Colls. U. Tex. Leadership Program, 1987; named a leader in shaping the century State Jour. Register, 1999; Phi Theta Kappa fellow, 1981; Fulbright Sr. scholar, Lithuania, 1993, Ukraine, 1996, China, 2000; Fulbright sr. specialist, Tanzania, 2003. Mem. Am. Assn. Cmty. and Jr. Colls., Ill. Coun. Pub. C.C. Pres. (sec. 1973-74, vice chmn. 1974-75, chmn. 1975-76), Coun. North Ctrl. Cmty. and Jr. Colls. (exec. bd. 1979-81), North Ctrl. Assn. (cons., evaluator 1984-88) Republican. Roman Catholic. Home and Office: 2324 Willemoore Ave Springfield IL 62704-4362 Home Phone: 217-546-1936. Home Fax: 217-793-6939. E-mail: rpoorman@att.net.

POOS, LAWRENCE RAYMOND, history educator; b. Eaton, Ohio, Feb. 8, 1954; s. Raymond Henry and Edna (Brower) P. AB, Harvard U., 1976; PhD, Cambridge U., Eng., 1984. Fellow Fitzwilliam Coll., Cambridge, 1980-83; prof. The Cath. U. of Am., Washington, 1983—; dean sch. of arts and scis. The Catholic U. of Am., Washington, 2002—. Author: A Rural Society After the Black Death, 1991, Lower Ecclesiastical Jurisdiction in Late Medieval England, 2001, (with L. Bonfield) Select Cases in Manorial Courts 1250-1550: Property and Family Law, 1998; editor: Continuity and Change, 1985-00; contbr. articles to scholarly jours. Fellow Royal Hist. Soc. (London). Avocations: exercise, travel, computers. Office: The Cath U of Am 620 Michigan Ave NE Washington DC 20064-0001 Home Phone: 202-544-4439; Office Phone: 202-319-5115. E-mail: poos@cua.edu.

POOVEY, MARK NIXON, lawyer; b. Durham, NC, Aug. 11, 1956; s. Jerry Postel and Ruth Eugenia (Royal) P.; m. Deborah Lou Best, Dec. 29, 1984. BA cum laude, Wake Forest U., 1978, JD cum laude, 1980. Bar: NC 1980, US Dist. Ct. We., Mid. and Ea. Districts NC 1980, US Ct Appeals 4th Cir. 1980. Ptnr. Martin & Poovey, Morganton, NC, 1980-83; with Womble, Carlyle, Sandridge & Rice PLLC, Winston-Salem, NC, 1983—, leader tech. and commerce practice group. Editor Wake Forest Law Rev., 1979. Mem. ABA, NC Bar Assn., Forsyth County Bar Assn. Republican. Baptist. Avocations: backpacking, photography, golf, snow skiing. Office: Womble Carlyle Sandridge & Rice PLLC PO Box 84 Winston Salem NC 27102 Office Phone: 336-721-3641. Office Fax: 336-733-8398. Business E-Mail: mpoovey@wcsr.com.

POPA, RADU D., law librarian; MA in Romance Langs. and Lit., U. Bucharest, Romania, 1972; MS in Libr. and Info. Sci. emphasis on Reference in Fgn. and Internat. Law, Columbia U., 1989. Libr. asst. NYU Law Sch. Libr., 1986—88, internat. and fgn. law specialist, 1988—89, reference libr., spl. collections, 1989—92, internat. and fgn. law reference libr., 1992, internat. law libr. & head spl. collections, 1993—94, assoc. dir., global libr. services, 1994—96, acting co-dir., 1994, assoc. dir. rsch. and online services, 1996—2003, acting dir., 2003—05, dir., asst. dean libr. svcs., 2005—. Lectr. in field. Editor: Albatross Publishing House, 1972—74; editl. dir. Tribuna Romaniei, Bucharest, Romania, 1974—85; author: Accidental Tourist on the New Frontier: An Introductory Guide to Global Legal Research, 1998; contbr. articles to profl. jour.; author: Bas-relief with Heroes, 1988, Poetry-A Scar on the Wall of Air, 1996, (introductory essay) Ut Musica Poesis, 2000, La Naissance: structures symboliques, 2001. Mem.: Romanian Writers Assn., Internat. Assn. Law Libraries, Am. Soc. Internat. Law, Am. Assn. Law Libraries (sec./treas., Fgn., Comparative and Internat. Law Spl. Interest Sect. 1995—97), ACORD (Assn. for Cooperative Ops. Rsch. and Develop.) (exec. v.p., NGO for advancement of rule of law in Romania 1997—2001, Order of Merit, rank of officer 2000). Fluent in French, Italian and Romanian; working knowledge of Spanish, German, Russsian and Latin. Office: NYU Law Library 40 Washington Sq South Rm 102 New York NY 10012 Home Phone: 212-876-7063; Office Phone: 212-998-6320. E-mail: radu.popa@nyu.edu.

POPAT, SAURIN RAJNIKANT, oncologist, surgeon; b. Kampala, Uganda, Aug. 19, 1969; s. Rajnirant Nagi and Bharti Rajnirant Popat; m. Katharine Elizabeth Herbert, Sept. 11, 1999; children: Alexander Shivam, Evan Kavi, Carys Meera Rose. BA, Queen's U., Kingston, Ont. Can., 1990; MD, U. Western Ont., 1992. Asst. prof. surgery U. Rochester, NY, 2000—04, asst. prof. otolarynology, 2004—06, asst. prof. oncology, 2003—06; asst. prof. surg. oncology Roswell Park Cancer Inst., Buffalo, 2006—07, assoc. prof. surg. oncology, 2007—. Dir. head and neck surg. oncology U. Rochester Med. Ctr., 2000—06; bd. dir. Univera Health, Buffalo, 2007—; self-employed med. legal cons., Rochester, 2002—06, Buffalo, 2006—. Contbr. scientific papers to profl. jours., chapters to books. Vo. physician med. aid mission U. Toronto, Thailand, 1996. Recipient Roundtree prize, U. Western Ont., 1990. Fellow: Am. Head and Neck Soc., Royal Coll Physicians and Surgeons Can., Am. Coll. Surgeons, Royal Coll. Surgeons Can., Royal Coll. Physicians. Avocations: hockey, golf. Office: Roswell Park Cancer Inst Elm and Carton Sts Buffalo NY 14263

POPE, ALEXANDER H., retired lawyer; b. NYC, June 4, 1929; s. Clifford H. and Sarah H. (Davis) P.; m. Katherine Mackinlay, Sept. 14, 1985; children by previous marriage: Stephen C., Virginia L., Daniel M. AB with honors, U. Chgo., 1948, JD, 1952. Bar: Ill. 1952, Republic of Korea 1953, Calif. 1955, U.S. Supreme Ct. 1970. Pvt. practice, LA, 1955-77, 87-96; assoc. David Ziskind, LA, 1955; ptnr. Shadle, Kennedy & Pope, LA, 1956, Fine & Pope, LA, 1957-59, 61-77; legis. sec. to gov. State of Calif., 1959-61; county assessor Los Angeles County, LA, 1978-86; ptnr. Mayer, Brown & Platt, LA, 1987-88, Barash & Hill, LA, 1989-92; of counsel Seyforth, Shaw, Fairweather & Geraldson, LA, 1993-96; exec. dir. Calif. citizens budget commn. Ctr. Govtl. Studies, Los Angeles, 1997-2000. Nat. bd. mem. Vols. for Stevenson, 1952; vice-chmn. L.A. County Dem. Cen. Com., 1958-59; pres. Westchester Mental Health Clinic, 1963; mem. Calif. Hwy. Commn., 1966-70; mem. L.A. Bd. Airport Commrs., 1973-77, v.p., 1973-75, pres., 1975-76; trustee, sec. L.A. Theatre Ctr., 1984-89; trustee Spring St. Found., 1990-2004. With US Army, 1952—54, Mo., Korea. Mem. ACLU, U. Chgo. Alumni Clubs Greater L.A. and San Francisco Bay area (pres. 1970-71), Population Connection, Ams. United for Seperation of Ch. and State, Sierra Club, Common Cause, Order of Coif, Phi Beta Kappa. Democrat. Unitarian. Home: 1155 Euclid Ave Berkeley CA 94708-1602 Personal E-mail: kandap@juno.com.

POPE, ANDREW, health science association administrator; Acting dir., sr. program officer Bd. on Neuroscience and Behavioral Health, Inst. of Med., 1998-99; dir. Bd. on Health Sciences Policy, Inst. of Medicine, 1999—; acting dir. Bd. on Neuroscience and Behavioral Health, Inst. of Med., 2003—. Office: Inst Medicine 500 5th St, NW Washington DC 20418-0007

POPE, ANDREW JACKSON, JR., (JACK), retired judge; b. Abilene, Tex., Apr. 18, 1913; s. Andrew Jackson and Ruth Adella (Taylor) Pope; m. Allene Esther Nichols, June 11, 1938; children: Andrew Jackson III, Walter Allen. BA, Abilene Christian U., Tex., 1934, LLD (hon.), 1980; LLB, U. Tex., 1937; LLD (hon.), Pepperdine U., Malibu, Calif., 1981, St. Mary's U., San Antonio, 1982, Okla. Christian U., Oklahoma City, 1983. Bar: Tex. 1937. Practice law, Corpus Christi, 1937-46; judge 94th Dist. Ct., Corpus Christi, 1946-50; justice Ct. Civil Appeals, San Antonio, 1950-65, Supreme Ct. Tex., Austin, 1965-82, chief justice, 1982-85; ret., 1985. Author: John Berry & His Children, 1988; chmn. bd. editors Appellate Procedures in Texas, 1974; contbr. articles to profl. jours. Pres. Met. YMCA, San Antonio, 1956—57; chmn. Tex. State Law Libr. Bd., 1973—80; trustee Abilene Christian U., 1954—. With USNR, 1944—46. Recipient Silver Beaver award, Alamo Coun. Boy Scouts Am., 1961, Disting. Eagle award, 1983, Rosewood Gavel award, 1962, Outstanding Alumnus award, Abilene Christian U., 1965, St. Thomas More award, St. Mary's U., San Antonio, 1982, Greenhill Jud. award, Mcpl. Judges Assn., 1980, citation, Houston Bar Found., 1985, award, San Antonio Bar Found., 1985, Disting. Jurist award, Jefferson County Bar, 1985, Oustanding Alumnus award, U. Tex. Law Alumni Assn., 1988, George Washington Honor medal, Freedom Found., 1988, Disting. Lawyer award, Travis County, 1992. Fellow: Tex. Bar Found. (Law Rev. award 1979—81); mem.: ABA, Tex. Ctr. for Legal Ethics and Professionalism (Outstanding Svc. award 2007), State Bar Tex., Tex. Supreme Ct. Hist. Soc. (v.p.), Tex. State Hist. Assn., Am. Judicature Soc., Tex. Philos. Soc., Bexar County Bar Assn., Travis County Bar Assn., Nueces County Bar Assn. (pres. 1946), State Bar Tex. (pres. jud. sect. 1962, Oustanding Fifty Yrs. Lawyer award 1994), Christian Chronicle Coun. (chmn.), KP (grand chancellor 1946), Masons, Sons Rep. of Tex., Austin Knife and Fork (pres. 1980), Order of Coif, Pi Sigma Alpha, Phi Delta Phi, Alpha Chi. Mem. Ch. Of Christ. Home: 2803 Stratford Dr Austin TX 78746-4626

POPE, C. LARRY, food products executive; BBA, Coll. William & Mary, 1975, EMBA, 1994. Controller Smithfield Foods Inc., Smithfield, Va., 1980—99, v.p. fin., 1999—2000, CFO, 2000—01, pres., COO, 2001—06, pres., CEO, 2006—. Bd. mem. Coll. William & Mary Bus. Sch. Found. Office: Smithfield Foods Inc 200 Commerce St Smithfield VA 23430-1204 *

POPE, CARL, environmental organization administrator; BA summa cum laude, Harvard U., 1967. Vol. Peace Corps, Barhi Barhi, India, 1967-69; assoc. conservation dir. Sierra Club, San Francisco, polit. dir., conservation dir., exec. dir., 1992—. Author: Sahib: An American Misadventure in India, 1971, Hazardous Waste in America, 1981; co-author (with Paul Rauber): Strategic Ignorance: Why the Bush Administration Is Recklessly Destroying a Century of Environmental Progress, 2004. Bd. dirs. Calif. League of

Conservation Voters, 1986-87, exec. dir., 1973-83; bd. dirs. Pub. Voice, 1989-92, Nat. Clean Air Coalition, Calif. Common Cause, 1976-78, Pub. Interest Econs., Inc., 1973-76; bd. dirs. Zero Population Growth, 1972-90, also polit. dir., 1970-73. Mem.: America Coming Together (treas.). Address: Sierra Club 85 2nd St Fl 2 San Francisco CA 94105-3456

POPE, CHARLES C., computer hardware company executive; BS in Acctg., U. Utah; MBA, Brigham Young U. With Hewlett Packard Co., Diasonics Corp.; dir. budgets and analysis Seagate Technology, Scotts Valley, Calif., 1985, dir. fin. for Thailand ops., v.p. fin. Far East ops., v.p. fin., treas. Scotts Valley; v.p., gen. mgr. Seagate Magnetics; sr. v.p. storage products Seagate Technologies, sr. v.p. fin., CFO, 1998—. Office: Seagate Tech PO Box 66360 Scotts Valley CA 95067-0360

POPE, DALE ALLEN, investment company executive; b. Racine, Wis., Apr. 11, 1953; s. Warren Edward and Ruth Ann (Adams) Pope; m. Colleen Rene Esson, Aug. 6, 1976; children: Shayna Rene, Justin Daniel, Evan Hunter. BBA, U. Wis., Eau Claire, 1975; postgrad., U. Wis., 1976-77. CLU. Estate and ins. planning cons., 1978-81; asst. v.p. Am. Bankers Life, Miami, Fla., 1981-82; pres. and COO IFS Capital Corp., North Palm Beach, Fla., 1982—87; founder, pres. and CEO Am. Capital Corp., Valley Forge, Pa., 1987—2001; dir. bus. devel. Pan-Am. Fin. Advisers, Valley Forge, 2001—03; pres. and CEO DP Properties, Inc., 2003—. Mem.: Nat. Assn. Securities Dealers, Inc. (dist. bus. conduct com. 1990—92, bd. arbitrators), Soc. Fin. Svc. Profls., Fin. Planning Assn. (bd. dirs. 2003, v.p. human resources), Rotary Club Wayne (past. pres., bd. dirs.), Rotary (dist. gov.'s rep. 1994—95, bd. dirs. 1996—97, asst. dist. gov. 1996—, Paul Harris fellow 1989). Avocations: golf, tennis, hunting, fishing. Office Phone: 610-909-3301. Personal E-mail: dpope53@comcast.net.

POPE, DEBORAH RENAYE, literature and language professor; BA in English, Bethany U., Scotts Valley, Calif., 1982; MA, Wheaton Coll., Ill., 1990. Instr. Seiwa Gakuen Sch., Kochi, Japan, 1990—91, Montreal Coll., Canada, 1991—92; coord. World Relief Corp., Wheaton, 1992—94; assoc. prof. Northwest U., Kirkland, Wash., 1994—. Office: Northwest Univ 5520 108th Ave NE Kirkland WA 98033 Home Phone: 425-889-5296.

POPE, EDDIE, professional soccer player; b. Greensboro, NC, Dec. 24, 1973; m. Corina Pope, 2000; 2 children. Attended, Univ. NC. Defender DC United, 1997—2002, NY NJ MetroStars, 2003—04, Real Salt Lake, 2005—. 80 caps, 8 goals U.S. Nat. Soccer team, 1996—; mem. U.S. World Cup team, 1998, 2002, 06. Named Major League Soccer Defender of the Yr., 1997; named to Major League Soccer All-Star team, 1997—2005, Major League Soccer All-Time Best XI, 2005. Mailing: US Soccer Fedn 1801 S Prairie Ave Chicago IL 60616

POPE, HARRISON GRAHAM, JR., psychiatrist, educator; b. Lynn, Mass., Dec. 26, 1947; s. H. Graham and Alice (Rider) P.; m. Mary M. Quinn, June 7, 1974; children: Kimberly, Hilary, Courtney. AB summa cum laude, Harvard U., 1969, MPH, 1972, MD, 1974. Diplomate Am. Bd. Psychiatry and Neurology. Resident in psychiatry McLean Hosp., Belmont, Mass., 1974-77, clin. rsch. fellow Mailman Rsch. Ctr., 1977-79, asst. psychiatrist, 1979-84, assoc. psychiatrist, 1984-92, psychiatrist, 1992—, chief biol. psychiatry lab., 1984—; Dupont-Warren rsch. fellow Harvard Med. Sch., Boston, 1976-77. Instr. psychiatry Harvard Med. Sch., Boston, 1977-82, asst. prof., 1982-85, assoc. prof., 1985-99, prof. 1999—; staff psychiatrist Hampstead (N.H.) Hosp., 1976-80; vis. fellow The Maudsley Hosp., London, 1977, Hôpital. Ste. Anne, Paris, 1977; mem. Am. Psychiat. Assn., 1976-80, adv. com. on schizophrenic, paranoid and affective disorders, 1979, adv. com. on preparation of DSM-III-R, 1984, task force on nomenclature and stats., 1979, 84. Author: Voices from the Drug Culture, 1971, The Road East, 1974, (with J.I. Hudson) New Hope for Binge Eaters: Advances in the Understanding and Treatment of Bulimia, 1984; co-editor: The Psychobiology of Bulimia, 1987, Use of Anticonvulsants in Psychiatry: Recent Advances, 1988, Psychology Astray: Fallacies in Studies of "Repressed Memory" and Childhood Trauma, 1997; The Adonis Complex: The Secret Crisis of Male Body Obsession, 2000; mem. editl. bd. European Psychiatry, Paris, 1984—, Internat. Jour. of Eating Disorders, 1984—, Jour. Clin. Psychiatry, 1993-; contbr. numerous articles to profl. jours. Named one of Outstanding Americans under 40 Esquire mag., 1984; fellow Scottish Rite Schizophrenia Program, No. Masonic Jurisdiction, 1977-81, Charles A. King Trust, Boston, 1977-79. Avocation: weightlifting. Office: McLean Hosp 115 Mill St Belmont MA 02478-1048

POPE, INGRID BLOOMQUIST, sculptor, poet, painter; b. Arvika, Sweden; became U.S. citizen. d. Oscar Emanuel and Gerda (Henningson) Brostrom; m. Howard Richard Bloomquist, Feb. 14, 1941 (dec. Nov. 1982); children: Dennis Howard, Diane Cecile Connelly, Laurel Ann Shields; m. Marvin Hoyle Pope, Mar. 9, 1985 (dec. June 1997). BA cum laude, Manhattanville Coll., 1979, MA in Humanities, 1981; MA in Religion, Yale U., 1984. Exhbns. include Manhattanville Coll., Purchase, N.Y., Yale Div. Sch., Ch. of Sweden in N.Y.C., First Ch. of Round Hill; author: (books) Musings, 1994, Hosannah, Help Please, 1999, Blessings, 2003. Past bd. dirs. N.Y.C. Mission Soc., Greenwich YWCA, Greenwich Chaplaincy, Greenwich Acad. Parents' Assn., past pres; past trustee First Ch. Round Hill, Greenwich; pres. Ch. Women United, Greenwich, 1989-91. Mem. AAUW, Nat. Assn. Pen Women, English Speaking Union, Nat. Wildflower Assn., Yale Club N.Y.C., Lakeview Club (Austin, Tex.), Acad. Am. Poets, Nat. Mus. of Women in Arts, Yale Alumnae Club (Austin and Greenwich, Conn.). *I need to share my feelings deep inside be it in verse or prose or form or line. I need to say it, do it, show, or write and so creatively I try to do my best. I lift up brush and paint a scene, I struggle with a stone or mold in clay or write my verse just as I do today.*

POPE, JACQUELINE PRIVETTE, music educator; b. Darlington, SC, Aug. 13, 1936; d. Leo Thomas Privette and Ophelia Mae Norris; m. George Wallace Kilpatriok (div.); children: George Ashley, Laurie Dawn, Andrew Wallace; m. James L. Pope, June 21, 1997. BA, Furman U., 1958; student, Bapt. Internat. Sem., 1960—61; studied with Powell Everhart, Atlanta, Ga., 1964—67, studied with Irene Harrower, 1972—74, studied with Claude Shirley, 1980—81; MusM in Voice Performance, Ga. State U., 1987; studied with Joseph Meeks, Kennesaw State U., 1995. Minister music and edn. Westminster (S.C.) Bapt. Ch., 1958—59; tchr. music Louisville (Ky.) City Schs., 1959—60, Jefferson County Schs., Louisville, 1961—62; substitute tchr. Houston (Tex.) City Schs., 1962—63; pvt. voice and piano tchr. Austell, Ga., 1964—; dir. music Southminster Presbyn. Ch., Marietta, Ga., 1983—91; music specialist Cobb County Pub. Schs., Marietta, 1987—98; chancel choir dir. Luth. Ch. Nativity, 1992—2005. Chmn. caring ministry Luth. Ch. Nativity, 1992—2004; dir. of music Cobb Children's Theater, 1972—82. Performer: (CD) Jacqueline P. Pope Sings for You. Mem.: Nat. Assn. Tchrs. Singing, Nat. Music Tchrs. Assn., Ga. Music Tchrs. Assn. (chmn. voice auditions 1980—81), South Cobb Arts Alliance, Alpha Delta Kappa (pres. 1999—2001, state pianist 2002—). Democrat. Lutheran. Avocations: gardening, painting. Home: 2565 Sloan St Austell GA 30106 Office Phone: 770-732-8666.

POPE, JOHN CHARLES, former airline company executive; b. Newark, Mar. 30, 1949; s. John Aris Coutant and Eleanor Laura (Hillman) P. BA, Yale U., New Haven, 1971; MBA, Harvard U., Cambridge, Mass., 1973. Dir. profit analysis and capital analysis GM, NYC, 1973-77; sr. v.p. fin., treas., CFO Am. Airlines, Inc., AMR Corp., Dallas-Fort Worth, 1977-88; exec. v.p., CFO UAL Corp., United Airlines (subs.), Chgo., 1988-91, pres., COO, 1991-94. Bd. dirs. Fed. Mogul Corp., Detroit, R.R. Donnelley & Sons, Chgo., Dollar Thrifty Automotive Group, Inc., Tulsa, CNF Inc., San Mateo, Calif., Dollar Thrifty Automotive Group, Inc., Tulsa, Fed. Mogul Corp., Detroit, Kraft Foods, Northfield, Ill., R.R. Donnelley, Chgo.; chmn. bd. Waste Mgmt., Houston; bd. trustees, treas. Shedd Aquarium, Chgo. Office Phone: 847-735-0112. *

POPE, JOHN EDWIN, editor, columnist; b. Athens, Ga., Apr. 11, 1928; s. Henry Louis and Rose (McAfee) P.; m. Eileen Pope; children: Shirley, Susan, Eddie, David. BA in Journalism, U. Ga., 1948. Sports editor Banner-Herald, Athens, Ga., 1943-48; So. sports editor UPI, Atlanta, 1948-50; sports writer Atlanta Constn., 1950-54; exec. sports editor Atlanta Jour., 1954-56; asst. sports editor Miami (Fla.) Herald, 1956-67, sports editor, 1967—2001. Author: Football's Greatest Coaches, 1956, Baseball's Greatest Managers, 1960, Encyclopedia of American Greyhound Racing, 1963, Ted Williams: The Golden Year, 1970, (with Norm Evans) On the Line, 1976, The Edwin Pope Collection, 1988; contbr. articles to popular mags. and Ency. Brittanica, World Book. Recipient Bill Corum Meml. award Thoroughbred Racing Assn., 1962, top sports column award Nat. Headliners Club, 1962, 79, 82, 86, Eclipse award Thoroughbred Racing Assn., 1976, 82, 86, Red Smith award AP Sports Editors, 1989; named to Internat. Churchmen's Sports Hall of Fame, 1976; recipient Knight-Ridder editl. excellence award, 1996, Nat. Sportswriters and Sportscasters Assn. Hall of Fame, 1995, Fla. Sports Hall of Fame, 1996, Bert McGrane award Coll. Football Hall of Fame, 2000, Dick McCann award NFL Pro Football Hall of Fame, 2002, A.J. Liebling award Boxing Writers Assn. Am., 2005; named Orange Bowl Hall of Hon., 2003. Mem. Profl. Football Writers Am. (pres. 1968-69), Football Writers Assn. Am., Golf Writers Am., Nat. Turf Writers, U.S. Tennis Writers. Presbyterian. Office: Miami Herald 235 Harbor Dr Key Biscayne FL 33149 Home Phone: 305-361-9786. Personal E-mail: edwinpope@aol.com. E-mail: epope@herald.com.

POPE, JOHN MARVIN, journalist; b. Hattiesburg, Miss., Nov. 5, 1948; s. Paul M. Jr. and Mary Lee (Scott) P.; m. Diana Pinckley, May 19, 1984. BA cum laude, U. Tex., 1970, MA, 1972. Copy editor The States-Item, New Orleans, 1972-73, reporter, 1973-80, The Times-Picayune, New Orleans, 1980-86, med.-health reporter, 1986—. Hearst Found. vis. fellow U. Tex., 2005. Co-author: American First Ladies: Their Lives and Their Legacy, 1996. Recipient Med. Writing award, La. State Med. Soc., 1990, 1998, 2005, Frank Allen award, La.-Miss. AP, 1989, Louise McFarland award for excellence in pub. health comm., La. Pub. Health Assn., 2003; fellow Knight Found., Ctrs. for Disease Control and Prevention, 2001; Knight Ctr. for Specialized Journalism fellow, 1999. Fellow Phi Beta Kappa; mem. Soc. Profl. Journalists, Nat. Assn. Sci. Writers, Investigative Reporters and Editors, Press Club New Orleans (4 1st pl. awards 1978-87, Alex Waller award 1987). Avocations: running, travel, aerobics. Office: The Times-Picayune 3800 Howard Ave New Orleans LA 70125-1429 Business E-Mail: jpope@timespicayune.com.

POPE, KATHERINE COLLINS, television executive; b. Glencoe, Ill., Oct. 15, 1972; d. Michael A. and Christine Pope; m. Richard A. Robbins, June 2, 2001. Grad., Sarah Lawrence Coll. Assoc. prodr. A&E; writer & prodr. documentaries CBS; writer & prodr. VH1, 1999—2000; mgr. primetime series NBC Studios, 2000—01, dir. primetime series, 2001—02, v.p. primetime series, 2002—04; v.p. drama devel. NBC Entertainment, 2003—04, exec. v.p., 2006—07; sr. v.p. drama series NBC Universal TV Studio (name changed to Universal Media Studios, 2007), 2004—06, pres., 2007—. Assoc. prodr. (TV series) Biography, writer & prodr. Behind the Music, 1999—2000. Named one of Women in Entertainment Power 100, Hollywood Reporter, 2006. Office: Universal Media Studios 3000 W Alameda Burbank CA 91523 E-mail: katherine.pope@nbcuni.com. *

POPE, KERIG RODGERS, retired magazine executive; b. Waukesha, Wis., Sept. 30, 1935; s. Kerig James Pope and Mildred (Offerman) Troemel; m. Claudia T. Koralewski, Nov. 1961 (div. 1975); children—Kerig William, Giles Thomas; m. Beth Leslie Kasik, May 24, 1980; children: Kolin Jared, Zoe Alissa. Grad., Art Inst. Chgo., 1958. Designer Jack Denst Wallpaper Designs, Chgo., 1958-60; designer Continental Casualty Ins. Co., Chgo., 1960-62, Leo Burnett Advt. Agy., Chgo., 1962-63; art dir. Mercury Records Corp., Chgo., 1963-66; mng. art dir. Playboy mag., Chgo., 1966—. Exhibited in group shows Whitney Mus. Am. Art, N.Y.C., 1969, Mus. Contemporary Art, Chgo., 1972, Bienal de Sao Paulo, Brazil, 1973, Museo de Arte Moderno, Mexico City, 1974, Nat. Collection Fine Arts, Washington, 1979, Moderno, Mexico City, 1974, Mus. Contemporary Art, Chgo., 1996; represented in permanent collections Nat. Collection Fine Arts, Washington, Mus. Contemporary Art, Chgo., Smart Mus., U. Chgo. Recipient silver medal Communigraphics, N.Y.C., 1971, gold medal, 1971, 72; award of excellence Soc. Publ. Designers, 1979, 4 awards of excellence Design Ann., 1984, Silver medal Illustrators 29, 1986, Silver medal Soc. of Illustrators, 1988. Mem.: Soc. Publ. Arts (3 Silver awards 1987), Soc. Typog. Arts (Silver medal 1998, Gold medal 1999, 2001), Art Dirs. Club N.Y., Soc. Illustrators (Gold medal 1981, 1984, Silver medal 1988, Gold medal 1991, Silver medal 1998, Gold medal 1999), Arts Club (Chgo.). Office: Playboy Enterprises Inc 680 N Lake Shore Dr Fl 15 Chicago IL 60611-4455

POPE, KITTY, library director; b. Canada; MLS, U. Western Ont. Asst. dir. & mgr. customer svcs. Calgary Pub. Libr., Alta., Canada, 2001—04; exec. dir. Alliance Libr. Sys., East Peoria, Ill., 2004—. Co-recipient Network Libr. of Yr. award, Libr. of Congress Nat. Libr. Svc. for the Blind & Physically Handicapped, 2005, 2006, Leadership Achievement award, Assn. Specialized & Coop. Librs. Agys., 2007, Libr. of the Future award for Alliance Second Life Libr. 2.0, ALA, 2007. Office: Alliance Libr Sys 600 High Point Lane East Peoria IL 61611 Office Phone: 309-694-9200 ext. 2101, 800-700-4857. Office Fax: 309-694-9230. E-mail: kpope@alliancelibrarysystem.com.

POPE, LISTON, JR., writer, journalist; b. New Haven, Dec. 26, 1943; s. Liston and Bennie (Purvis) P. BA in English, Duke U., 1965; postgrad., Sorbonne, Paris, 1965-70, U. Vienna, 1966-67. Probation officer Bronx (N.Y.) Supreme Ct., 1972-73; freelance journalist NYC, 1972—; war correspondent World Coun. of Chs., Beirut, 1978-79, Nat. Cath. News Svc., Managua, Nicaragua, 1983-84; radio prodr. Pacifica Radio, NYC, 1983-90; critic art/lit. Pacifica News, NYC, 1984-89; sr. editor N.A. Gilbert & Sons Publs., NYC, 1993—; pub. Mantis Press, NYC, 1995—. Press agent Liston Pope & Assocs., NYC, 1983—90; media dir. Casa Nicaragua, NYC, 1983—90. Author: Redemption: A Novel of War in Lebanon, 1994, Living Like the Saints: A Novel of Nicaragua, 1996, Floriane: Stages of Love, 1998, (plays) Somoza's Niece, 1987, Oratorio, 1987, Canto Epico, 1989, The Van Gogh Testament, 2005, (trilogy) Newell Gilbert's Boyhood: American Wine, Journey on the Needing, Infernal Innocence, 2006. Vis., supporting vol. Meml. Sloan-Kettering, 1972-78; recreation dir., tutor Cath. Guardian Group Home, 1975-90; life skills tchr. Harlem I Men's Shelter, N.Y.C., 1991-93; AIDS support worker St. Vincent's Supportive Care, Bellevue Visitation Program, Bellevue Pediatrics. Recipient Narrative Poetry award, NY Poetry Soc., 1972, Grand prize, Am. Poetry Assn., 1986. Home and Office: 126 W 73rd St Apt 11A New York NY 10023-3031 Office Phone: 212-874-6017. E-mail: liston4949@yahoo.com.

POPE, MARCIA L., lawyer; b. St. Petersburg, Fla., May 12, 1961; AB, Harvard Univ., 1983; JD, Univ. Va., 1986. Bar: Calif. 1986. Assoc. to ptnr., Employment & Labor practice Pillsbury Winthrop Shaw Pittman, San Francisco, 1986—, employment counsel. Office: Pillsbury Winthrop Shaw Pittman 50 Fremont St San Francisco CA 94105 Office Phone: 415-983-6487. Office Fax: 415-983-1200. Business E-Mail: marcia.pope@pillsburylaw.com.

POPE, MARK ANDREW, lawyer, academic administrator; b. Munster, Ind., May 22, 1952; s. Thomas A. and Eleanor E. (Miklos) P.; m. Julia Risk Pope, June 15, 1974; children: Brent Andrew, Bradley James. BA, Purdue U., 1974; JD cum laude, Ind. U., 1977. Bar: Ind. 1977, U.S. Dist. Ct. (so. dist.) Ind. 1977, U.S. Ct. Appeals (7th cir.) 1984. Assoc. Johnson & Weaver, Indpls., 1977-79, Rocap, Rocap, Reese & Young, Indpls., 1980-82, Dutton & Overman, Indpls., 1982-88, ptnr., 1988-89; asst. gen. counsel Lincoln Nat. Corp., Fort Wayne, Ind., 1989-91, sr. counsel, 1991-95, v.p. govt. rels., 1995-2001; dir. athletics Ind. U.-Purdue U., Ft. Wayne, 2001—. Bd. dirs. Ft. Wayne Bicentennial Coun.; pres., bd. dirs. ARCH, Inc., 1994-97. Bd. editors, devel. editor Ind. U. Law Rev., 1976-77 Mem. pres.'s coun. Purdue U., 1977—; applied econs. cons. Jr. Achievement, 1989—95; bd. dirs. Jr. Achievement of No. Ind., 1992—94; grad. Leadership Ft. Wayne, 1992; adv. coun. Ind. U. Bus. Sch., Purdue U., Ft. Wayne, 2000—02; trustee Allen County War Meml. Coliseum, 2002—; bd. mem. Ft. Wayne Urban League, 2006—; mem. parish coun. St. Elizabeth Ann Seton Ch., 1993—96, pres., 1993—95; bd. edn. mem. Bishop Luers HS, 2000—03, pres., 2002—03; mem. bd. trustees Allen County War Meml. Coliseum, 2002—; mem. bd. dirs. Ft. Wayne Urban League, 2006—. Named Disting. Hoosier, Gov. of Ind., 1974. Fellow Ind. Bar Found., Indpls. Bar Found. (disting.); mem. ABA (dist. rep. young lawyers divsn. 1981-83, dir. 1983-84, liaison coord. 1985-86, 87-88, exec. coun. 1981-88, cabinet 1982-88, gen. practice sect. coun. mem. 1986—, membership chmn. 1987-89, chmn. career and family com. 1990-92, dir. 1991-93), Indpls. Bar Assn. (v.p. 1983, chmn. young lawyers divsn. 1981), 500 Festival Assocs. (vice-chmn. of 500 festival parade 1985-89), Orchard Ridge Country Club (bd. dirs. 1995-2001, sec. 1996-97, pres. 1999-2001). Avocations: tennis, golf, running. Office: Ind U Purdue U at Ft Wayne Gates Sports Ctr 2101 E Coliseum Blvd Fort Wayne IN 46805-1499 Office Phone: 260-481-5443. Business E-Mail: popem@ipfw.edu.

POPE, MARTIN, chemist, educator; b. NYC, Aug. 22, 1918; s. Philip and Anna (Frimet) P.; m. Lillie Bellin, June 27, 1946; children: Miriam, Deborah Judith. BS in Chemistry, CCNY, 1939; PhD in Phys. Chemistry, Poly. Inst. Bklyn., 1950. Scientist Radiation Lab. Bklyn. Navy Yard, 1941—42; rsch. scientist Balco Rsch. Lab., Newark, 1946—47, tech. dir., 1951-56; sr. rsch. scientist NYU Radiation and Solid State Physics Lab., NYC, 1956-60, rsch. assoc. prof., 1960-65; assoc. prof. chemistry NYU, 1965—68, prof., 1968—88, prof. emeritus phys. chemistry, 1988—. Co-dir. NYU Radiation and Solid State Physics Lab., 1968—83, dir., 1983—88; vis. prof. U. Alexandria, Egypt, 1981. Contbr. articles to sci. jours., chapters to books; mem. editl. bd.: Molecular Crystals, 1965—97; co-author: Electronic Processes In Organic Crystals, 1982, Electronic Processes in Organic Crystals and Polymers, 1999. Pres. Ezra Jack Keats Found., NYC, 1983—. Pvt. to 1st lt. USAAF, 1942—46, WWII. Recipient Townsend Harris medalist, CUNY, 1996, Davy medal, Royal Soc., UK, 2006; grantee, Dept. Energy, 1958—88, NSF, 1960—75; honored at internat. conf., U. Rochester, 1998. Fellow: AAAS, NY Acad. Scis., Am. Phys. Soc.; mem.: Am. Chem. Soc., Sigma Xi. Achievements include patents in field. Avocation: mineralogy. Office: Dept Chemistry NYU New York NY 10003

POPE, MICHAEL ARTHUR, lawyer; b. Chgo., June 27, 1944; s. Arthur Wellington and Phyllis Anne (O'Connor) P.; m. Christine Collins, Nov. 19, 1966; children: Jennifer, Amy, Katherine. BS, Loyola U., Chgo., 1966; JD cum laude, Northwestern U., 1969. Bar: Ill. 1969, N.Y. 1985, U.S. Dist. Ct. (no. dist.) Ill. 1969, U.S. Ct. Appeals (7th cir.) 1970, U.S. Supreme Ct. 1980. Tchg. asst. U. Ill. Coll. Law, Champaign, 1969-70; assoc. Isham, Lincoln & Beale, Chgo., 1970-76; ptnr. Phelan, Pope & John, Ltd., Chgo., prin., 1976—95; capital ptnr. McDermott, Will & Emery, Chgo., 1995—. Adj. prof. law Chgo.-Kent Law Sch. Ill. Inst. Tech., 1982-85; chair bd. trustees Nat. Jud. Coll., 2002-03. Mem. ABA, Ill. Bar Assn., Chgo. Bar Assn., Am. Bd. Profl. Liability Attys. (pres. 1985-87), 7th Cir. Bar Assn. (pres. 2003-04), Internat. Assn. Def. Counsel (pres. 1993-94), Internat. Soc. Barristers, Am. Coll. Trial Lawyers, Internat. Acad. Trial Lawyers (bd. dirs. 1999-2004), Am. Law Inst., Econ. Club Chgo., The Chgo. Club, Skokie Country Club (Glencoe Ill.), East Bank Club (Chgo.). Office: McDermott Will & Emery 227 W Monroe St Chicago IL 60606-5096 Home Phone: 847-835-5340; Office Phone: 312-984-7780. E-mail: mpope@mwe.com.

POPE, ROBERT DANIEL, lawyer; b. Screven, Ga., Nov. 29, 1948; s. Robert Verlyn and Mae (McKey) P.; children: Robert Daniel Jr., Veronica Teres, Jonathan Chase, Byron Christopher, Jessica Victoria. BS in Criminal Justice magna cum laude, Valdosta Coll., Ga., 1975; JD, John Marshall Law Sch., Savannah, Ga., 1980. Bar: Ga. 1981, U.S. Dist. Ct. (no., mid. and so. dist.) Ga. 1983, U.S. Ct. Appeals Ga. 1982. Pvt. practice, Cartersville, 1981—. Mem. Valdosta Indigent Def. Atty. Panel, 1981-83, Bartow County Indigent Def. Panel, Cartersville, 1987-91, So. Dist. of Ga. Indigent Def. Panel, Brunswick, 1982-84; mem. Cobb County Cir. Defender's Panel for Indigent Criminal Def., Marietta, Ga., 1986— Recognized as one of most successful criminal def. lawyers Cobb County Cir. Defenders Office, 1994. Mem. Ga. Assn. Criminal Def. Lawyers, Ga. Bar Assn. (criminal law sect.), Am. Criminal Justice Orgn. (Valdosta chpt. pres. 1974-75). Home: 74 Spruce Ln SE Cartersville GA 30121-7643 Office: PO Box 1043 Acworth GA 30101

POPE, ROBERT DEAN, lawyer; b. Memphis, Mar. 10, 1945; s. Ben Duncan and Phyllis (Drenner) P.; m. Elizabeth Dante Cohen, June 26, 1971; 1 child, Justin Nicholas Nathanson. AB, Princeton U., 1967; Diploma in Hist. Studies, Cambridge U., 1971; JD, Yale U., 1972, PhD, 1976. Bar: Va. 1974, D.C. 1980. Assoc. Hunton & Williams, Richmond, Va., 1974-80, ptnr., 1980—. Mem. steering com. Bond Attys. Workshop, 1994—98; lectr. in law U. Va. Law Sch., 2000—02; advisor, com. on govtl. debt and fiscal policy Govt. Fin. Officers Assn., 1993—99; adj. prof. law William & Mary Law Sch., 2004—. Author: Making Good Disclosure: The Role and Responsibilities of State and Local Officials Under the Federal Securities Laws, 2001; co-author: Disclosure Rules of Counsel in State and Local Government Securities Offerings, 2d edit., 1994. Mem. adv. com. Va. Sec. of Health and Human Svcs. on Continuing Care Legislation, 1992-94; mem. Anthony Commn. on Pub. Fin.; adv. coun. dept. history Princeton U., 1987-91; mem. Mcpl. Securities Rulemaking Bd., 1996-99, vice chmn. 1998-99. Mem.: Nat. Council Cmty. Justice, Nat. Conf. Cmty. Justice (bd. dirs. Richmond), Yale Law Sch. Assn. (exec. com. 1985—88), Va. Bar Assn. (chmn. legal problems of elderly 1982—88), Am. Coll. Bond Counsel (bd. dir. 2003—, sec. 2004—06, treas. 2006—), Am. Acad. Hosp. Attys., Nat. Assn. Bond Lawyers (bd. dirs. 1982—89, treas. 1984—85, sec. 1985—86, pres. 1987—88, coordinating coun. 2005—, Bernard P. Friel medal for contbns. to pub.fin. 1994), Bond Club Va. (bd. dirs. 1990—98, v.p. 1993—94, pres. 1994—95), Phi Beta Kappa. Republican. Episcopalian. Avocations: history, golf, music, book reviews. Office: Hunton & Williams 951 E Byrd Richmond VA 23219-4074 Home: 9704 Old Country Trace Richmond VA 23238 Office Phone: 804-788-8438. Business E-Mail: dpope@hunton.com.

POPE, ROBERT E(UGENE), fraternal organization administrator; b. Wellington, Kans., Sept. 10, 1931; s. Samuel E. and Opal Irene (Davis) P. BSChemE with honors, U. Kans., 1952, MS, 1958. Registered profl. engr., Kans. Asst. instr. U. Kans., Lawrence, 1952-56; lab. technician Monsanto Co., St. Louis, 1952; project engr. Mallinckrodt, Inc., St. Louis, 1953-59; traveling sec. Theta Tau, St. Louis, 1959-62, exec. sec., 1963-84, exec. dir., 1984-96, exec. dir. emeritus, 1996—. Carillonneur, Grace United Meth. Ch., St. Louis, 1985—, chmn. adminstrv. coun., 1991-95, trustee, 1997-99; lay mem. Mo. Conf., United Meth. Ch., 2000-06; trustee Theta Tau Ednl. Found., 1997-2002; bd. dirs. St. Louis Cmty. Tower Bells, 2000—. Mem. Am. Soc. Assn. Execs. (life), Profl. Fraternity Execs. Assn. (charter), Profl. Fraternity Assn. (exec. sec. 1977-86, Disting. Svc. award 1995), Theta Tau

(Alumni Hall of Fame 1988, mem. bd. editors The Gear of Theta Tau 1993—2001, editor-in-chief 1996—2001), Tau Beta Pi, Phi Lambda Upsilon, Omicron Delta Kappa. Democrat. United Methodist. Avocations: physical fitness, sports, photography, stamp collecting/philately, writing. Home: 13 Sona Ln Saint Louis MO 63141-7742

POPE, STEPHEN BAILEY, mechanical engineer, educator; b. Nottingham, Eng., Nov. 26, 1949; came to U.S., 1977; s. Joseph Albert and Evelyn Alice (Gallagher) P.; m. Linda Ann Syatt, Aug. 16, 1979; children: Sarah Evelyn, Samuel Joseph. BS in Engring., Imperial Coll., London, 1971; MS, Imperial Coll., 1972, PhD, 1976; DSc in Engring., U. London, 1986. Rsch. asst. Imperial Coll., London, 1972-77; rsch. fellow Calif. Inst. Tech., Pasadena, 1977-78; asst. prof. MIT, Cambridge, Mass., 1978-81, assoc. prof., 1981, Cornell U., Ithaca, N.Y., 1982-87, prof. engring., 1987-98, Sibley Coll. prof. mech. engring., 1998—. Cons. GE, Schenectady, N.Y., 1984—, GM, Warren, Mich., 1985—, Allison Engine Co., Indpls., 1986—. Editor: Combustion Theory and Modelling; assoc. editor Physics of Fluid; contbr. articles to profl. jours. Overseas fellow Churchill Coll, Cambridge, Eng., 1989; awards NSF, Army Rsch. Office, Air Force Office Sci. Rsch., U.S. Dept. Energy. Fellow Royal Soc., Am. Phys. Soc., Combustion Inst., Am. Acad. Arts & Scis. Office: 254 Upson Hall Cornell U Ithaca NY 14853 Business E-Mail: pope@mae.cornell.edu. *

POPE, THADDEUS MASON, law educator; b. Pitts., Aug. 2, 1969; s. Lawrence Sheldon and Reina Gloria Pope; m. Linda Louise Bosse, May 2, 1998; 1 child, Phineas Lawrence. JD, MA, Georgetown U., 1997, PhD, 2003. Bar: Calif. 1999. Jud. law clk. U.S Ct. Appeals, (7th cir.), Milw., 1999—2000; atty. Arnold & Porter LLP, LA, 2000—05; prof. law U. Memphis, 2005—. Contbr. articles to profl. jours. Pro bono adv. medicaid benefits City of L.A., 2003—05. Recipient Wiley W. Manuel award, State Bar Calif., 2004, Hon. Benjamin Aranda III Outstanding Pub. Svc. award, L.A. County Bar Assn., 2005. Mem.: Kennedy Inst. Ethics, APHA, Am. Soc. Law, Medicine & Ethics. Office: U Memphis School Law 3715 Central Ave Memphis TN 38152 Office Phone: 901-678-1623. Office Fax: 901-202-7549. Business E-Mail: tmpope@memphis.edu.

POPE, W. ALAN, psychology professor, psychotherapist; b. Abilene, Tex., Aug. 7, 1958; s. Walter Steele and Ida Vickery Pope. PhD, Duquesne U., 2000. Computer programmer Household Fin. Corp., Prospect Heights, Ill., 1980—83; systems analyst Time-Life Inc., Chgo., 1983—84, Wash. Nat. Ins. Corp., Evanston, Ill., 1984—86; asst. prof. U. West Ga., Carrollton, 2001—; psychotherapist Ielase Inst., Pitts., 1993—96. Cognitive sci. rsch. asst. U. Del., 1988—91; cons. editor Janus Head: Jour. of Interdisciplinary Studies in Lit., Continental Philosophy, and the Arts, Pitts., 1999—; tchg. fellow Duquesne U., 1996—97. Author: From Child to Elder: Personal Transformation in Becoming an Orphan at Midlife, 2006; contbr. articles to profl. publs. Organizer Padmasambhava Buddhist Ctr., Carrollton, Ga., 2004—. Grant to study Japanese culture, Asian Studies Devel. Program, NEH, 2002. Mem.: APA, Soc. for Values in Higher Edn., Inst. Noetic Scis., Assn. Asian Studies, Internat. Network on Personal Meaning, Assn. Humanistic Psychology. Achievements include research in psychospiritual transformation. Home: 527 Roy North Rd Carrollton GA 30117 Office: U West Ga Dept Psychology Carrollton GA 30118 Home Phone: 770-830-8992; Office Phone: 678-839-0601. Personal E-mail: wapope@hotmail.edu. Business E-Mail: apope@westga.edu.

POPE, WILLIAM L., lawyer, judge; b. Brownsville, Tex., 1960; s. William E. and Maria Antonieta P.; m. Sandra Solis, May 16, 1992; children: Ana Lauren, William E.H. AA, Tex. Southmost Coll., 1980; postgrad., U. Tex., 1980-81, Tex. Christian U., 1982, Tex. Coll. Osteo. Medicine, 1982-83; JD, Baylor U., 1986; MD (hon.), Cosmopolitan U. & Rsch. Inst., Vina del Mar, Chile, 1998. Bar: Tex. 1986, US Dist. Ct. (so. dist.) Tex. 1988, US Supreme Ct. 1990, US Tax Ct. 2007. Assoc. Adams & Graham, Harlingen, Tex., 1986-91, ptnr., 1991—; mcpl. ct. judge City of La Feria, Tex., 1987—. Bd. trustees Episcopal Day Sch., Brownsville, Tex., 1999—2000. Mem.: Cameron County Bar Assn., Am. Coll. Legal Medicine, Tex. State Bar Assn. (mem. judiciary rels. com. 1999—2005). Mem. Ch. Of Christ. Office: Adams & Graham LLP PO Drawer 1429 Harlingen TX 78551-1429

POPEO, R. ROBERT, lawyer; b. Boston, Apr. 9, 1938; AB, Northeastern U., 1958; JD, Boston Coll., 1961. Bar: Mass. 1961, DC 1972. Law clerk US Dist. Ct. Mass., 1961-63; instr. Sch. Law Boston U., 1964-67; U.S Commr., 1967-71; asst. atty. gen. Commonwealth of Mass., 1970-74; chmn., pres. Mintz, Levin, Cohn, Ferris, Glovsky and Popeo, PC, Boston, 1989—, mem. policy com. Editor: Boston Coll. Indsl. and Comml. Law Rev., 1960—61; student editor Ann. Survey Mass. Law, 1960—61. Trustee Boston Coll.; mem. bd. overseers Boston Coll. Law Sch., Northeastern U.; mem. bd. advisors Boston Coll. Carroll Sch. Mgmt., Birmingham Bus. Sch.; mem. exec. comm. Mass. Bus. Round Table. Named one of top 100 Lawyers in Am., Nat. Law Jour. Fellow: Am. Coll. Trial Lawyers; mem.: ABA, Mass. Bar Assn., DC Bar Assn., Boston Bar Assn., Practising Law Inst. Office: Mintz Levin Cohn Ferris Glovsky & Popeo PC One Financial Center Boston MA 02111 Home Phone: 781-444-8013; Office Phone: 617-348-1716. Office Fax: 617-542-2241.

POPHAM, DAVID KENTNER, minister; b. Vernal, Utah, Jan. 16, 1963; s. Harmon Reeves and Geraldine Bailey Popham; m. Kerrie Ellen Shahan, June 4, 1988; children: Olivia, Jenna. BA, U. Cumberlnads, Williamsburg, Ky., 1985; MDiv, So. Bapt. Theol. Sem., Louisville, Ky., 1991. Minister Kingsbury Cmty. United Ch. of Christ, Vernal, Utah, 1997—2005; assoc. conf. minister Rocky Mountain Conf. United Ch. of Christ, Denver, 2005—. Homeless liasion Unitah Sch. Dist., Vernal, 2003—04; hospice chaplain Applegate Home Healthcare, Vernal, 2003—05. Mem.: So. Poverty Law Ctr., Soc. Bibl. Lit. Democrat. Avocations: reading, writing, hiking, films. Home: 2499 S Colorado Blvd #1201 Denver CO 80222 Office: Rochy Mountain Conf UCC 1140 W 5th Ave Denver CO 80204

POPKIN, ALICE BRANDEIS, lawyer; b. NYC; d. Jacob H. and Susan Brandeis Gilbert; m. Jordan J. Popkin; children: Susan Cahn, Anne, Louisa. AB magna cum laude, Radcliffe Coll., 1949; JD, Yale U., 1953. Bar: NY 1953, US Dist. Ct. (so. dist.) NY 1956, US Ct. Appeals (2nd cir.) 1959, US Supreme Ct. 1962, DC 1972, Mass. 1987. Assoc. Cahill Gordon & Reindel, 1953—61; dir. internat. programs Peace Corps, 1961—63; project co-dir. Georgetown Inst. Criminal Law and Procedure, 1967—72; spl. counsel Senate Sub-Com. to Investigate Juvenile Delinquency, 1972—74; atty., prof. Antioch Sch. Law, 1974—77; assoc. adminstr. EPA, 1977—79; pvt. practice cons. on internat. environ. issues, 1979—81; practicing atty., 1981—87; of counsel Toabe and Riley, Chatham, Mass., 1987—. Fellow Brandeis U.; trustee Radcliffe Coll.; active Chatham Harbor Mgmt. Com.; trustee Eldredge Pub. Libr., 1994—, pres. bd. trustees, 2005—. Mem. ABA, Mass. Bar Assn., Barnstable County Bar Assn., Estate Planning Coun. Cape Cod, Planned Giving Coun. Cape Cod. Office: Toabe & Riley Box 707 154 Crowell Rd Chatham MA 02633-2800 Personal E-mail: adee.abp@comcast.net.

POPKIN, BARRY MICHAEL, nutrition educator; b. Wis., May 23, 1944; s. Arnold Julius and Annie Cohen Popkin; m. Carol L. Council, June 12, 1981 (div. July 1986); 1 child, Matthew; ptnr. Anne-Linda Furstenberg, Jan. 1, 1987. BS, U. Wis., 1967, MS, 1969; PhD, Cornell U., 1974. Rsch. economist U. Wis., Ithaca, 1971-72; assoc. prof. Rockefeller Found., Manila, 1974-76; from asst. prof. to prof. nutrition U. N.C., Chapel Hill, adj. prof., Dept. of Economics; dir. UNC Interdisciplinary Obesity Ctr., Nutrition Transition Rsch. Program. Cons. Afro-Urban Inst., Milw., 1970, USAID, 1976, World Bank, Washington, 1991-97, Internat. Food Policy Rsch. Inst., Washington, 1998—; bd. trustees Pan Am. Health Edn. Found., Washington, 1990-96; bd. dirs. Dannon Found., N.Y.C., 1998—. Recipient Wis. King Christian IV award for civil rights, 1965, Bernard G. Greenberg Alumni Leadership Endowment Award, Sch. Pub. Health, 1992, Kellogg prize Soc. for Internat. Nutrition Rsch., 1998. Fellow Woodrow Wilson Found., Carolina Population Ctr.; mem. Internat. Union Nutritional Scis. (chair nutrition transition com. 1998), Am. Soc. Nutritional Scis., Population Assn. Am., Am. Econs. Assn., Lineberger Comprehensive Cancer Ctr., Delta Omega Hon. Pub. Health Soc., Phi Kappa Phi, Phi Eta Sigma. Office: Carolina Population Ctr U NC 123 W Franklin St Chapel Hill NC 27516-2524 Office Phone: 919-966-1732. Office Fax: 919-966-9159, 919-966-6638. E-mail: popkin@unc.edu. *

POPKIN, JOEL, economist, consultant; b. Trenton, NJ, July 6, 1932; s. Nathaniel Robert and Betty (Finkle) Popkin; m. Elizabeth Rose Alk, Oct. 17, 1968; children: Neil Robert, Sara Rachel. BS in Econs., U. Pa., 1954, PhD, 1965. Asst. economist Allied Chem. Co., NYC, 1957—59; lectr., rschr. U. Pa., Phila., Northwestern U., Evanston, Ill., George Washington U., Washington, 1960—64; econometrician Dept. Commerce, Washington, 1964—66; divsn. chief, asst. commr. US Bur. Labor Stats., Washington, 1966—73; sr. staff economist Pres.'s Coun. Econ. Advisors, Washington, 1973—74; dir., mem. rsch. staff Nat. Bur. Econ. Rsch., Washington, 1974—78; pres. Joel Popkin and Co., Washington, 1978—. Mem. visitors com. dept. U. Pa., 1987—2001. Lt. USAR, 1955—57. Recipient Julius Shiskin award for contbns. to econ. stats., 1994. Fellow: Am. Statis. Assn.; mem.: Internat. Assn. Rsch. on Income and Wealth, Nat. Assn. Bus. Economists, Conf. Bus. Economists (chmn. 1989), Am. Econ. Assn., Cosmos Club, Nat. Economists Club (chmn. bd., pres. 1978—80). Home: 6706 Loring Ct Bethesda MD 20817-3148 Office: 2001 L St NW Washington DC 20036-4970 Office Phone: 202-466-9063.

POPLAU, RONALD W., social studies educator; AA, St. Lawrence Coll., 1957; BA, St. Paul Sem., 1959; MA, Emporia State Univ., 1968. Dir., continuing edn. Ottawa Univ., 1976—; social sci. tchr. St. Paul, 1962—64, Brazil, 1964—65, Ward H.S., Kans. City, Kans., 1965—69, Shawnee Mission Sch. Dist., 1969—; now social sci. tchr. NW H.S., Shawnee Mission, Kans. Finalist Nat. Tchr. of Yr., 2006; named a US Army Outstanding Citizen, 1997; named Shawnee Citizen of Yr., 1994, Kans. Tchr. of Yr., 2006; named to Nat. Tchr. Hall of Fame, 1999; recipient Penney's Golden Rule award, 1993, Kiwanis John Trembly award, 1993, Kans. City Star Honor, 1994, Wooster Coll. Excellence in Tchg. award, 1997, Disney Teacher award, 2005. Office: Shawnee Mission Northwest HS 12701 W 67th St Shawnee KS 66216 Business E-Mail: nwpoplau@smsd.org. *

POPLAWSKI, NIKODEM J., physicist, researcher; b. Torun, Poland, Mar. 1, 1975; s. Bozena and Janusz Poplawski. MS, Warsaw U., Poland, 1999; PhD, Ind. U., Bloomington, 2004. Postdoctoral fellow, rsch. assoc. physics dept. Biocomplexity Inst., Ind. U., Bloomington, 2004—; fellow Inst. for Pure and Applied Math., U. Calif., LA, 2006. Mem.: Am. Phys. Soc. (assoc.), European Phys. Soc. (assoc.), Internat. Soc. on Gen. Relativity and Gravitation (assoc.). Office: Ind Univ Physics Dept 727 E 3rd St Bloomington IN 47405 Business E-Mail: nipoplaw@indiana.edu.

POPLER, KENNETH, behavioral health services administrator, psychologist; BA in Psychology, CUNY, 1967; MA in Psychology, New Sch. Social Rsch., NYC, 1969, PhD in Psychology, 1974; MBA, Wagner Coll., 1994. Diplomate Am. Bd. Profl. Psychology. Case worker N.Y.C. Dept. Social Svcs., 1967-70; intern Bklyn. Psychiat. Ctrs., 1970-72; sch. psychologist N.Y.C. Bd. Edn., 1972-73; psychologist Mid Nassau Cmty. Guidance Ctr., Hicksville, NY, 1973-77; dir. St. Mary Cmty. Mental Health Ctr., Hoboken, NJ, 1978-81; pres., CEO S.I. Mental Health Soc., Inc., 1981—. Asst. rsch. scientist N.Y. State Psychiat. Inst., NYC, 1971; psychometrician LI Jewish Hillside Med. Ctr., Queens, NY, 1972—73; vol. rsch. Manhattan Sch. Seriously Disturbed Children, NYC, 1972—73; instr. CUNY, Bklyn., 1972—73; sr. psychologist dir. psychol. svcs. HHC Gouverneur Hosp., NYC, 1973—78; pvt. practice, NYC, 1976—85; asst. clin. prof. psychiatry Mt. Sinai Med. Sch., NYC, 1978—95; apptg. by mayor N.Y.C. Bd. Health, 2003—. Apptd. by mayor N.Y.C. Cmty. Svcs. Bd., 1984—, chmn., 2003—; pres. Coalition Voluntary Mental Health Agys., Inc., 1991—94; sec. Head Start Sponsoring Bd. Coun., NYC, 1985—92; chmn. S.I. United Way Execs. Com., 1985, Mental Health Coun., SI, 1987—89. Mem.: Rotary. Office: SI Mental Health Soc Inc 669 Castleton Ave Staten Island NY 10301-2099

POPNIK, MARLENE ALITA, retired school librarian; b. Paterson, NJ, Aug. 31, 1942; d. Clarence L. and Katherine M. Borst; m. Joseph R. Popnik, Aug. 5, 1972. BS, SUNY, Geneseo, 1964. With Fonda-Fultonville Ctrl. Sch., 1964-65; libr. Spencerport (N.Y.) Ctrl. Sch., 1965-68, 69-72, U.S. Dependant Sch., Wethersfield, Eng., 1968-69, Susquehanna Twp. Schs., Harrisburg, Pa., 1973-2000; retired, 2000. Mem. ALA, Pa. Sch. Librs. Assn., Delta Kappa Gamma. Home: 6349 Mifflin Ave Harrisburg PA 17111-4266 E-mail: jomarlene@aol.com.

POPOFSKY, MARK S., lawyer; s. M. Laurence and Linda Seltzer Popofsky; m. Suzanne Yelen. BA, Brown U., Providence, 1990; JD, Harvard U., Cambridge, Mass., 1993. Bar: Calif. 1994, DC 1999. Law clk., to Judge D.W. Nelson US Ct. Appeals (9th cir.), Pasadena, Calif., 1993—94; atty. antitrust divsn. US Dept. Justice, 1994—97, sr. counsel, antitrust divsn., 1998—99; ptnr. Kaye Scholer LLP, 1999—. Office: Kaye Scholer LLP 901 15th St NW Washington DC 20005 Office Phone: 202-682-3500.

POPOFSKY, MELVIN LAURENCE, lawyer; b. Oskaloosa, Iowa, Feb. 16, 1936; s. Samuel and Fannye Charlotte (Rosenthal) P.; m. Linda Jane Seltzer, Nov. 25, 1962; children: Mark Samuel, Kaye Sylvia. BA in History summa cum laude, U. Iowa, 1958; BA in Jurisprudence (first class honors), Oxford U., Eng., 1960; LLB cum laude, Harvard U., 1962. Bar: Calif. 1962. Assoc. Heller, Ehrman, White & McAuliffe, San Francisco, 1962-69, ptnr., 1969—, mem. exec. com., 1980-93, co-chair, 1988-93. Contbr. articles to law jours. Bd. dirs. Mt. Zion Hosp., San Francisco, 1982-88, U.S. Dist. Ct. (no. dist.) Calif. Hist. Soc., 1988-2004, Jewish Home for Aged, San Francisco, 1989-96, Golden Gate U., 1997-2000, Jewish Cmty. Fedn., 1997-2001. Recipient Anti-Defamation League's Disting. Jurisprudence award, 2000; named State Bar of Calif. Antitrust Lawyer of the Yr., 2000, Best in Calif. Antitrust, 2005, Sr. Statesman Antitrust, Chambers, 2006; Rhodes scholar, 1958. Fellow Am. Bar Found., Am. Coll. Trial Lawyers; mem. ABA, Calif. Bar Assn., San Francisco Bar Assn., Bur. Nat. Affairs (adv. bd. antitrust sect.), Calif. Acad. Appellate Lawyers. Democrat. Jewish. Home: 1940 Broadway Apt 10 San Francisco CA 94109-2216 Office: Heller Ehrman 333 Bush St Ste 3000 San Francisco CA 94104-2834 Home Phone: 415-928-7780; Office Phone: 415-772-6310. Business E-Mail: lpopofsky@hewm.com.

POPOVA, NINA, dancer, choreographer, director; b. Novorossisk, USSR, 1922; Student in Paris, studied ballet with Olga Preobrajenska, Lubov Egorova, Anatole Vilzak, Anatole Oboukhov, Igor Schwezoff. Ballet debut with Ballet de la Jeunesse, Paris, London, 1937-39; soloist Original Ballet Russe, 1939-41, Ballet Theatre (now Am. Ballet), 1941-42, Ballet Russe de Monte Carlo, 1943, 47, Ballet Alicia Alonso, Cuba; faculty Sch. Performing Arts, NYC, 1954—; later artistic dir. Houston Ballet, 1975; tchr. Nat. Acad. Arts, Champaign, Ill., also NYC, 1975—, now Eglevsky Ballet Sch., L.I.; tchr. ballet Mexico City, Mex.; asst. choreographer mus. comedy Birmingham So. Coll., Ala., 1960; numerous appearances on Broadway stage, TV; former mem. regular cast Your Show of Shows; currently tchg. NYC. Address: 33 Adams St Sea Cliff NY 11579-1614

POPOVICH, GEORGE LEE, theater educator; s. George and Hazel Popovich; children: Wiley Thomas, Jennifer Lee. BA, Calif. State U., Fullerton, 1971, MA, 1975, U. Tex., El Paso, 1980; PhD, Ohio State U., Columbus, 1987. Cert. tchr. Calif. Dir. theater virtual theater lab Henry Ford CC, Dearborn, Mich., 1985—. Dir.: The Tempest, 2004 (Kennedy Center's Am. Coll. Theater Festival), The Skriker. Regional dir. Dads of Mich., Howell. Named one of Critics Picks, Detroit Free Press, 2006; recipient Innovation of Yr award, Liberal Arts Network Devel., 2007, League for Innovation in the C.C., 2007; grantee, Tech. Investment Fund, 1996, 1998, 2000, 2005. Mem.: Assn. Theater Higher Edn. Libertarian. Achievements include development of a system for incorporating 3D scenery and characters into live stage performances. Avocations: gardening, travel, videography, camping. Office: Henry Ford Cmty Coll 5101 Evergreen Rd Dearborn MI 48128 Home Phone: 734-775-1334; Office Phone: 313-845-6478. Business E-Mail: popovich@hfcc.net.

POPOVICH, GREGG, professional basketball coach; b. Chgo., Jan. 28, 1949; m. Erin Popovich; children: Micky, Jill. BA in Soviet Studies, USAF Acad., 1970; MA in Phys. Edn. & Sports Scis., U. Denver. Asst. coach USAF Acad., 1973—79; head coach Pomona-Pitzer Coll., Claremont, Calif., 1979—87; asst. coach San Antonio Spurs, 1988-92, gen. mgr., 1994—2002, exec. v.p. basketball ops., 1994—, head coach, 1996—; asst. coach Golden State Warriors, 1992—94. Asst. USA Men's Sr. Nat. Team, 2002—04. 2nd lt. USAF, 1970—75. Named NBA Coach of Yr., 2003; recipient Daily Point of Light award, Pres. George H.W. Bush, 1992. Achievements include winning NBA Championships as head coach of the San Antonio Spurs, 1999, 2003, 2005, 2007. Office: San Antonio Spurs One AT&T Ctr San Antonio TX 78219 *

POPOVICI, ADRIAN, law educator; b. Bucharest, Rumania, Sept. 6, 1942; came to Can., 1951; s. Adrian and Alice (Moruzi) P.; children—Adrian, Alexandra. BA, Stanislas Coll., Montreal, 1959; B.C.L., McGill U., 1962; D.E.S., U. Paris, 1965. Bar: Que. 1963. Prof. law U. Montreal, Que., Canada, 1968—. Author: L'Outrage au Tribunal, 1977, La Couleur du Mandat, 1995; editor: Problèmes de Droit Contemporain, 1974 Roman Catholic. Home: 5589 Canterbury Montreal PQ Canada H3T 1S8 Office: U Montreal Faculte de Droit CP 6128 Succursale A Montreal PQ Canada H3C 3J7 E-mail: adrian.popovici@umontreal.ca.

POPOVICS, SANDOR, civil engineer, educator, researcher; b. Budapest, Hungary, Dec. 24, 1921; came to U.S., 1957; s. Milan and Erzsebet (Droppa) P.; m. Lea M. Virtanen, Aug. 29, 1960; children: John, Lisa. 1st Degree in Civil Engring., Poly. U., Budapest, Hungary, 1944; Advanced Degree in Civil Engring., Poly. U., 1956; PhD, Purdue U., 1961. Registered profl. engr. Ariz., Pa. Rsch. engr. Met. Lab., Budapest, 1944-48; adj. prof. Tech. Coll., Budapest, 1949-52; rsch. engr., mgr. Inst. for Bldg. Scis., Budapest, 1949-56; grad. asst. Purdue U., Lafayette, Ind., 1957-59; prof. engring. Auburn (Ala.) U., 1959-69; prof. civil engring. No. Ariz. U., Flagstaff, 1968-76; prof. engring. King Abdulazziz U., Jeddah, Saudi Arabia, 1977-78; Samuel S. Baxter prof. civil engring. Drexel U., Phila., 1979-92, rsch. prof., 1992—. Pres. Optimum Engring. Rsch. Author: Fundamentals of Portland Cement Concrete, 1982, Concrete Materials, 2d edit., 1992, Strength and Related Properties of Concrete, 1998, over 300 tech. papers. Recipient numerous grants and awards. Fellow ASCE (life), Am. Concrete Inst.; mem. ASTM, Ala. Acad. Scis., Ariz. Acad. Scis., Sigma Xi, Chi Epsilon. Avocations: jogging, music, fine art. Home and Office: 283 Congress Ave Lansdowne PA 19050-1206 Office: Drexel U Dept Civil Archtl & Environ Engring 32nd and Chestnut Philadelphia PA 19104 Business E-Mail: popovics@coe.drexel.edu.

POPP, JOSEPH BRUCE, manufacturing executive; b. Chgo., July 9, 1919; s. Peter Leon and Anna (Chomyz) P.; m. Mabel Lydia Szymanski, Oct. 23, 1941 (dec. Mar. 1993); m. Elinor A. Maves, Jan. 27, 1996; children: Dianne, Lydia, Bruce, Anita, Gregory. Founder, owner Poultry Farm, Westville, Ind., 1941-48, Gary (Ind.) Undercoating Co., 1948-51; survey analyst George S. May Co., Chgo., 1952-54; gen. sales mgr. Maurey Instrument Corp., Chgo., 1958-64; founder, owner Joe Popp Sales Co., North Riverside, Ill., 1964-89, Chart Pool USA Inc., Portage, Ind., 1966—. Bd. dirs. YMCA Camp Tecumseh, Brookston, Ind., 1973—. Sgt. US Army, 1942—46. Mem. Nat. Fedn. of Ind. Bus., Greater Portage C. of C., The Gideons Internat., Nat. Inst. Animal Agr. Republican. Achievements include patents for Bloodhound Property Security System. Home: 1133 Lincoln St Hobart IN 46342-6039 Office: Chart Pool USA Inc 5695 Old Porter Rd Portage IN 46368-1194 Personal E-mail: bloodhoundidentification@yahoo.com.

POPP, LILIAN MUSTAKI, writer, educator; b. NYC; d. Peter and Mae Claire (Cary) Mustaki; m. Robert J. Popp. BA, Notre Dame Coll.; postgrad., Columbia U.; MS in Edn., Hunter Coll. Tchr. English McKee Vocat. and Tech. H.S., SI, NY, 1946-63, chmn. acad. studies, 1963-71; prin. William Howard Taft H.S., Bronx, NY, 1971-79; adj. prof. Wagner Coll., SI, 1960-85; instr. Richmond Coll., CUNY, 1968-70; prof. St. John's U., 1991-93. Mem. Cmty. Sch. Bd., 1980—93, chmn., 1989—90; examiner N.Y.C. Bd. Edn., 1960—85. Author, editor: Journeys in Science Fiction, 1961, Four Complete World Novels, 1961, Gertrude Lawrence as Mrs. A., 1961, Four Complete Modern Novels, 1962, Four Complete Heritage Novels, 1963, Four Complete Novels of Character and Courage, 1964; contbr. articles to profl. jours. Chmn. vols. N.Y.C. Child Abuse Prevention Program, 1984—86; regional dir., mem. exec. bd. March of Dimes; book discussion leader Snug Harbor Cultural Ctr., 1981—; pres. Com. for a Nuclear-Free Island, 1986—91; v.p. Staten Islanders Against Nuclear Weapons, 1991—95; pres. S.I. chpt. Brandeis U. Nat. Women's Com., 1996—99, leader News and Shmews; founder, pres. Coalition of S.I. Women's Orgns., 1996—; mem. edn. com. Staten Island Cmty. TV; mem. Libr. com. Staten Island Hist. Richmond Town; pres. Staten Island Youth Coun.; mem. libr. com. Coll. Staten Island; cmty. outreach chair Women for Women of Sierra Leone, 2001; bd. dirs. Staten Island Mental Health Soc., McKee HS Alumni and Friends Assn. Recipient Women Helping Women award Soroptimists, 1985, Thomas Wilson award for Substance Abuse Prevention, 1990, S.I. Advance Woman of Achievement award, 1994, Cmty. Hero award S.I. Register, 1996, Woman of Distinction award World of Women, 1998, Paul O'Dwyer Humanitarian award Staten Is. Dem. Assn., 1999; named Outstanding Woman, NY State Sen. Vincent J. Gentile, 1998, Women's History Month award NY City Coun. Spkr. Peter Vallone and Councilmen Jeremiah O'Donovan, Oddo and Fiala, 2001, Bus. and Profl. Women's Club S.I. award of distinction, 2004, Woman of Distinction award, Second Chance Gospel Choir, 2005, NAACP, Staten Island Br, William A. Morris Humanitarian award, 2005. Mem. AAUW (pres.), Belles Lettres Lit. Soc. (pres.), S.I. Hist. soc., NYC Assn. Tchrs. English (pres. 1967-71), Nat. Coun. Tchrs. English (bd. dirs. 1968-69), Acad. Pub. Edn., McKee Tchrs. Assn. (pres. 1969), HS Prins. Assn. (exec. bd.), Arista Hon. Soc. (hon.), Delta Kappa Gamma (pres. Alpha Beta chpt.), Phi Delta Kappa (v.p. 1990-92). Avocations: travel, reading, photography, jewelry making.

POPP, NATHANIEL, archbishop; b. Aurora, Ill., June 12, 1940; s. Joseph and Vera (Boytor) P. BA, St. Propcopius Coll., 1962; MDiv, Pontifical Gregorian U., Rome, 1966; PhD, U. Oradea, Romania, 2003. Ordained priest Romanian Greek Cath. Ch., 1966; consecrated bishop Romanian Orthodox Episcopate of Am., 1980; elevated to archbishop, 1999. Asst. pastor St. Michael Byz Ch., Aurora, 1967; parish priest Holy Cross Romanian Orthodox Ch., Hermitage, Pa., 1975-80; aux. bishop Romanian

Orthodox Episcopate of Am., Orthodox Ch. in Am., Jackson, Mich., 1980-84, ruling bishop Detroit, 1984—; mem. Holy Snyod Orthodox Ch. in Am., Syosset, NY, 1980—; Episcopal moderator Pastoral Life Ministries, O.C.A., 1991—2000. Bd. dirs. Moldovita Romanian Orthodox Ch., Hayward, Calif, 1982; tchr. summer youth programs Romanian Diocese; confessor to sisterhood Holy Transfiguration Monastery; rep. Conf. on Monasticism, Cairo, 1978; participant Monastic Consultation, Cairo, 1979, Seventh Assembly, Vancouver, Can., 1983; active mem. diocesan liturgical commn.; spkr., lectr. in field. Author: Holy Icons, 1969; editor newspaper Solia; contbr. numerous articles to profl. jours. Chmn. Romanian-Am. Heritage Ctr., Grass Lake, Mich.; organizer, chmn. Help for Romania Nat. Relief Fund and Help the Children of Romania Relief Fund; chmn. Congress of Romanian Ams., 1991—; mem. adv. bd. Orthodox Christian Laity, 1999—; pres. Ctr. for Orthodox Christian Studies, St. Andrew, Detroit, 2000; Dr. Honoris Causa, U. Oradea, Romania, 2003; chmn. bd Orthodox Witness, 2003-. Romanian Orthodox. Home and Office: Romanian Orthodox Episcopate Am 2535 Grey Tower Rd Jackson MI 49201-9120 also: PO Box 305 Grass Lake MI 49240-0309 Office Phone: 517-522-4800. E-mail: hgbnpopp@aol.com, nathaniel@roea.org.

POPPE, LAURIE CATHERINE, matrimonial lawyer, social worker, real estate executive; b. Fairfax, Va., Jan. 31, 1964; d. Loren Edward Brunner, Jr. and Elizabeth May Carper, Edward Monroe Peffly, Jr. (Stepfather); m. Christopher Carsten Poppe; 1 child, Sarah Elizabeth. A.Arch., No. Va. C.C., Annandale, 1985; AAS in Restaurant Mgmt., The Restaurant Sch., Phila., 1988; BA in Psychology, Rutgers U., New Brunswick, NJ, 1999; MSW, Rutgers U., 2005; JD, Rutgers U., Newark, 2005. Bar: N.J. 2005; LCSW N.J., 2005. Owner, mem. Dominion Properties, LLC, McLean, Va., 1994—; law clk. to Hon. Ann R. Bartlett, Superior Ct. NJ State Judiciary, Somerville, 2005—; with Norris, McLaughlin & Marcus, P.A., Bridgewater, NJ, 2006—. Scholarship founder for ind. rsch. Douglass Coll., Mabel Smith Honors Program, New Brunswick, 1999—2002. Grantee, Mabel Smith Honor Program, 1998. Mem.: AAUW, NASW, ABA, Somerset County Bar Assn., N.J. State Bar Assn., Psi Chi. Achievements include research in utilization of early intervention programs. Avocations: martial arts, singing, culinary arts, travel. Home Phone: 908-722-0700 ext. 4312; Office Phone: 908-722-0700 ext. 4312. Business E-Mail: lcpoppe@nmmlaw.com.

POPPE, PAMELA J., accountant; b. Breckenridge, Minn., Oct. 25, 1948; d. John T. and Anita Ruth (Knudsen) Sanker; m. James Wayne Kelly, May 10, 1969 (div. May 1993); children: Jamison Marc, Brian Lee m. James E. Poppe, Jan. 19, 2000. BA in Music Edn., Concordia Coll., Moorhead, Minn., 1969; BS in Indsl. Adminstrn., Iowa State U., 1980. CPA, Iowa. Band and choir tchr. Danube (Minn.) Ind. Schs., 1969-70; orch. tchr. Raleigh (N.C.) City Schs., 1972-73; French and English tchr. Bethel Acad., Kinston, N.C., 1974; jr. high sch. music tchr. Lenoir County Schs., Kinston, 1974-76; in-charge staff auditor McGladrey Pullen, Des Moines, 1980-82; with internal auditing dept. Am. Fed. Savs. & Loan, Des Moines, 1982-84; v.p. fin. Gentry, Ltd., Des Moines, 1984-89; dir. property mgmt. adminstrn. R&R Investors, Ltd., West Des Moines, Iowa, 1989—96; controller Venter Spooner Inc., Johnston, Iowa, 1997—2006; cons. RH Mgmt. Resources, Des Moines, 2006—07; acct. RSM McGladrey, Des Moines, 2007—. Mem. acct. adv. bd. Am. Inst. Bus., Des Moines, 1988-94. Chairperson Holy Trinity Luth. Ch., Ankeny, Iowa, 1991. Recipient Elijah Watts Sells award AICPA, 1980. Mem. Cert. Financial Mgrs. Assn., Iowa Timberline Users Group, Iowa Soc. CPAs, Mensa, Phi Beta Kappa. Avocations: reading, needlecrafts, quilting, dance, bicycling. Home: 909 SE Kensington Rd Ankeny IA 50021-3960 Office: 400 Locust St Ste 640 Des Moines IA 50309 Home Phone: 515-965-1265; Office Phone: 515-558-5547. Business E-Mail: pam.poppe@rsmi.com.

POPPEL, HARVEY LEE, management consultant, investment banker; b. Bklyn., Dec. 18, 1937; s. Frank M. and Fannie (Axenzow) P.; m. Emily A. Daigneault, Jan. 2, 1959; children: Marc F., Clinton S. BS, Rensselaer Poly. Inst., 1958, MS, 1959. Sr. info. systems analyst Westinghouse Electric Corp., Pitts., 1959-65; mgr. industry systems Western Union, Paramus, NJ, 1965-67; from assoc. to mem. operating coun. Booz, Allen & Hamilton, NYC, 1967-84; gen. ptnr. Poptech, LLC, Sarasota, Fla., 2003—. Bd. dirs. Larscom, Santa Clara, Calif., 1996-02; mng. dir. Broadview Assocs., Ft. Lee, 1984-96; mem. panel, lectr. on computers, comms. and info. industry; judge Entrepreneur of Yr., 1991, 93, 94, 95, 96; investor in start-ups. Co-author: Information Technology: The Trillion-Dollar Opportunity, 1987; contbr. articles to profl. jours. Mem. Aspen Inst. Fellows, Inst. Mgmt. Cons., Israel Cancer Assn. (exec. com.), Rep. Jewish Coalition, Palm Beach Civic Assn. (bd. dirs. 2006—)Road Runners Club, Banyan Golf Club, Marin Country Club, Breakers Ocean Club, Zeta Psi Office: 1391 6th St Sarasota FL 34236-4906 Personal E-mail: hpoppel@msn.com.

POPPEL, SETH RAPHAEL, entrepreneur; b. Bklyn., Mar. 17, 1944; s. Frank M. and Fritzi R. (Axenzow) P.; m. Danine Vokt, June 30, 1974; children: Clarysa, Jared, Stacy. BS magna cum laude, L.I. U., 1965; MBA, Columbia U., 1967. Asst. prof. L.I. U., Greenvale, N.Y., 1967-68; v.p. Synergistic Sys. Corp., NYC, 1968-77; v.p., dir. corp. planning Chase Manhattan Corp., NYC, 1977-90; owner, pres. Yearbook Libr., NYC, 1980—; chmn., pres. Am. Vision Ctrs., NYC, 1990-96. Owner harness horses Seth Poppel Stables, 1983—; founder, owner, operator Seth Poppel Yearbook Archives, 1986-2000. Recipient Claire F. Adler award in math., 1964-65, Mepham H.S. Hall of Fame award, 1993; E.I. DuPont fellow, 1965-67, Downie Muir fellow, 1965-66. Mem. U.S. Trotting Assn., Beta Gamma Sigma, Psi Chi, Omega Epsilon. Office Phone: 877-444-4724. Personal E-mail: sethpoppel@aol.com.

POPPENSIEK, GEORGE CHARLES, retired veterinary scientist, retired educator; b. NYC, June 18, 1918; s. George Frederick and Emily Amelia (Miller) P.; m. Edith M. Wallace, July 3, 1943; children: Neil Allen, Leslie Marion. Student, Cornell U., 1936-37, MS, 1951; student, U. Pa., 1937-42, V.MD, 1942. Diplomate Am. Bd. Microbiology, Am. Coll. Vet. Microbiology (charter), Am. Coll. Vet. Preventive Medicine (hon.). Asst. instr. medicine U. Pa. Sch. Vet. Medicine, 1943; asst. prof. vet. sci. U. Md., 1943-44; head dept. vet. virus vaccine prodn. Lederle Labs. div. Am. Cyanamid Co., 1944-49; dir. diagnostic lab. N.Y. State Coll. Vet. Medicine Cornell U., 1949-51, research assoc. Vet. Virus Research Inst., 1951-55; veterinarian Plum Island Animal Disease Ctr., animal disease and parasite research div. Agrl. Research Service, U.S. Dept. Agr., 1955-56, acting-in-charge diagnostic investigations, 1956-58, charge immunological investigations, 1958-59; dean and prof. microbiology N.Y. State Coll. Vet. Medicine, Cornell U., 1959-74, James Law prof. comparative medicine, 1974-88, dean emeritus, James Law prof. comparative medicine emeritus, 1988—; guest prof. U. Bern, Switzerland, 1975; ret., 1988. Exam. com. Nat. Bd. Vet. Med. Examiners, 1976-79; bd. dirs. Cornell Rsch. Found., 1963-74; chmn. bd. dirs. Cornell Veterinarian, Inc., 1976-86 Recipient Certificate of Merit award U.S. Dept. Agr., 1958; citation Sch. Vet. Med., U. Pa., 1978, Centennial medals U. Pa., 1984, Ohio State U., 1985; others. Fellow AAAS, Am. Acad. Microbiology (charter); mem. AVMA, Am. Soc. Virology (charter), NY State Vet. Med. Soc. (disting. life), Am. Bd. Microbiology, US Animal Health Assn., Assn. Am. Vet. Med. Colls. (pres. 1970-71), So. Tier Vet. Med. Assn., Am. Vet. Radiology Soc., Am. Soc. for Microbiology, NY Agrl. Soc. (life), Argentine Nat. Acad. Agronomy and Vet. Medicine (hon.), Soc. Polona Medicinae Veterinariae (hon.), Sigma Xi, Phi Kappa Phi, Alpha Psi, Omega Tau Sigma, Phi Zeta. Congregationalist. Home: 32 Horizon Dr Ithaca NY 14850-9769 Personal E-mail: poppensiek@clarityconnect.com.

POPPER, JOANNA, marketing executive, filmmaker; b. Chgo., Ill., Dec. 24, 1972; d. Frank James and Deborah Epstein Popper. BA, Northwestern U., 1994; MBA, U. Pa., Phila., 2000. Assoc. Chase Manhattan Bank, NY, Brazil, 1994—98; sr. assoc. strategy cons. McKinsey & Co, Miami, Fla.; sr. mktg. mgr. DHL Express, Plantation, 2002—06; dir. strategic mktg. Telemundo, Miami, 2006—. Director, interviewer: The ABC's of Eating Disorders. Women's and youth leadership leaders United Way, Miami, 2002—06; mentor Take Stock in Children, Miami, 2002—04; exec. com. Leadership Miami, 2005—06; young democrats fundraiser Democrats, Miami, 2004—06; bus. devel. dir. The Fla. Rm. Film Festival, Miami, Fla., 2004—05. Named one of Top 50 Savvy Singles, The New Times and Hope Ctr., 2006; recipient Up and Comer's award, South Fla. Bus. Jour., 2006. D-Liberal. Avocations: travel, reading, writing, fitness, entertaining. Home: 400 South Pointe Dr 1702 Miami Beach FL 33139 Home Phone: 305-607-7169.

POPPERS, PAUL JULES, anesthesiologist, educator; b. Enschede, Netherlands, June 30, 1929; came to U.S., 1958; naturalized, 1963; s. Meyer and Minca (Ginsburg) P.; m. Ann Feinberg, June 3, 1969; children: David Matthew, Jeremy Samuel. MD, U. Amsterdam, 1955. Diplomate Am. Bd. Anesthesiology. Instr. anesthesiology Columbia U., NYC, 1962-63, assoc., 1963-65, asst. prof. anesthesiology, 1965-71, assoc. prof. anesthesiology, 1971-74; prof., vice chmn. dept. anesthesiology NYU, 1974-79; prof., chmn. dept. anesthesiology Stony Brook U., NY, 1979—97, disting. prof., chmn. dept anesthesiology, 1997—2000, disting. prof. emeritus, 2000—. Cons. Brookdale Med. Ctr., Bklyn., 1975-2000, VA Med. Ctr., Northport, N.Y., 1979-2000, The N.Y. Hosp. Med. Ctr. of Queens (formerly Booth Meml. Hosp.), Flushing, N.Y., 1979-98, L.I. Jewish Med. Ctr., New Hyde Park, N.Y., 1980-98, Ea. L.I. Hosp., Greenport, N.Y., 1995-99, Am. Hosp. Paris, 1989-93; cons., lectr. USN, 1968-85 Author: Regional Anesthesia, 1977; editor: Beta Blockade and Anaesthesia, 1979; sect. editor Jour. Clin. Anesthesia, 1990-2000; mem. editl. bd. Internat. Jour. Clin. Monitoring and Computing, 1990-2000, Anaesthesiology Digest, 1991-94, Gynecologic and Obstetric Investigation, 1996-2001; contbr. over 200 articles to profl. jours. Rsch. fellow NIH, 1961; recipient medal Polish Acad. Scis., Poland, 1987, Univ. medal Jagiellonian U., Krakow, Poland, 1987, 1st Sci. award Post-grad. Assembly in Anesthesiology; named Hon. Prof. Anesthesiology, U. Leiden, The Netherlands, 1977. Fellow Am. Coll. Anesthesiology, Am. Coll. Ob-gyns., Royal Soc. Medicine, Post-grad. Assembly in Anesthesiology (hon. chmn. 1989-2005); mem. Am. Soc. Anesthesiologists, Assn. Univ. Anesthesiologists, Internat. Anesthesia Rsch. Soc., Soc. Obstetric Anesthesia and Perinatology, Am. Soc. Regional Anesthesia, Jerusalem Acad. Medicine, Am. Soc. Pharmacology and Exptl. Therapeutics, Fedn. Am. Soc. Exptl. Biology, Sigma Xi. Personal E-mail: paulpoppers@hotmail.com.

POPPITI, KIMBERLY D., performing arts educator; b. NY, July 20, 1968; d. Lawrence John and Patricia Elaine Poppiti; m. Glenn P. Warmuth; 1 child. BA, Stony Brook U., NY, 1991, MFA, 1994; PhD, NYU, 2003. Instr. drama, dance Dowling Coll., Oakdale, NY, 1998—2003, asst. prof. drama, dance, 2003—06, asst. prof. speech, media studies, drama, dance, 2006—, chair drama, dance, 2003—06, co-chair speech, media studies, drama, dance, 2006—. Dir. Dowling Coll. Student Theatre, 2003—. Contbr. articles to profl. jours. Mem.: La Leche League (leader 2006—), Am. Alliance for Theatre Educators. Avocations: horseback riding, martial arts, Karate. Office: Dowling Coll Idle Hour Blvd Rm 326 Oakdale NY 11769 Business E-Mail: poppitik@dowling.edu.

POPPLER, DORIS SWORDS, lawyer; b. Billings, Mont., Nov. 10, 1924; d. Lloyd William and Edna (Mowre) Swords; m. Louis E. Poppler, June 11, 1949; children: Louis William, Kristine, Mark J., Blaine, Claire, Arminda. Student, U. Minn., 1942-44; JD, Mont. State U., 1948. Bar: Mont. 1948, U.S. Dist. Ct. Mont. 1948, U.S. Ct. Appeals (9th cir.) 1990. Pvt. practice law, Billings, 1948-49; sec., treas. Wonderpark Corp., Billings, 1959-62; atty. Yellowstone County Attys. Office, Billings, 1972-75; ptnr. Poppler and Barz, Billings, 1972-79, Davidson, Veeder, Baugh, Broeder and Poppler, Billings, 1979-84, Davidson and Poppler, P.C., Billings, 1984-90; U.S. atty. Dist. of Mont., Billings, 1990-93; field rep. Nat. Indian Gaming Commn., Washington, 1993-2000. Pres. Jr. League, 1964-65; bd. dirs., pres. Yellowstone County Metre Bd., 1982; trustee Rocky Mt. Coll., 1984-90, mem. nat. adv. bd., 1993—; mem. Mont. Human Rights Commn., 1988-90; bd. dirs. Miss Mont. Pageant, 1995—; elected to Billings City Coun., Billings, Mont., 2002; elected dep. mayor coun. woman Ward4, 2002—. Recipient Mont. Salute to Women award, Mont. Woman of Achievent award, 1975, Disting. Svc. award Rocky Mt. Coll., 1990, Disting. Female Alumna award U. Montana Law Sch., 1996, 2004, Status Women award Zonta Club, 2004. Mem. AAUW, Mont. Bar Assn., Nat. Assn. Former U.S. Attys., Nat. Rep. Lawyers Assn., Internat. Women's Forum, Yellowstone County Bar Assn. (pres. 1990, Lifetime Achievement award 2004), Alpha Chi Omega. Republican.

POPRÁDY, GÉZA, librarian; b. Tök, Hungary, Mar. 19, 1940; s. Géza and Ilona (Lugmayer) P.; m. Maria Wéber, July 13, 1963; children: Géza, Judit, Peter. Student, Eötvös Lorand U., Budapest, Hungary, 1958-63. Cert. librarian, tchr. Librarian Architectural Info. Ctr., Budapest, 1963-64, Ctrl. Rsch. and Design Inst. for Silicate Industry, Budapest, 1964—83; head dept. Nat. Széchényi Library, Budapest, 1984-90, dep. dir.-gen., 1990-93, acting dir.-gen., 1993-94, dir.-gen., 1994-99, counsellor, 1999—. Author: (book) The Application of Technical Information, 1977, The Systematic Catalogue, 1981, Preservation of Library Materials, 2000, Trends of Librarianship (Handbook of Librarians), 2003; contbr. articles to profl. jours. Recipient Szabó Ervin medal Min. of Culture, 1989. Mem. Assn. Hungarian Librarians (sec.-gen. 1987-90, v.p. 1990-98, award 1988). Avocations: reading, gardening. Home: Árpád vezér u 27 H-2081 Piliscsaba Hungary Office: Nat Széchényi Library Budavári Palota F-épület 1827 Budapest Hungary E-mail: poprady@oszk.hu.

POPRAWA, ANDREW, diversified financial services company executive, accountant; b. Toronto, Ont., Can., Nov. 13, 1952; s. Mieczyslaw and Wanda P.; m. Rita Poprawa, Oct. 10, 1981; children: Alexandra, Jason. B in Commerce, U. Toronto, 1975. Chartered acct., Can., cert. govt. fin. mgr. CEO St. Stanislaus Credit Union, Toronto, 1980-82; dir. Toronto Ops. Office of Supt. of Fin. Instns., Canada, 1982—92; dir. Credit Unions and Cooperatives Ministry of Fin., Province of Ont., Toronto, 1992—93; pres., CEO Deposit Ins. Corp. of Ont., Toronto, 1993—. Mem. Toronto Bd. Trade; mem. governance com. Canadian Cooperative Assn.; mem. conf. bd. Can. Governance Adv. Com., Can. Nat. Award for Governance Pub. Sector. Mem.: Inst. Charter Accountants Ont., Lakeshore Yacht Club. Roman Catholic. Avocations: scuba diving, sailing, skiing, hockey. Office: Deposit Insurance Corp of Ontario 4711 Yonge St #700 Toronto ON Canada M2N 6K8 Home Phone: 905-624-2818; Office Phone: 416-325-9580. Business E-Mail: apoprawa@dico.com.

POPSON, LUCY (MARIA D. POPSON), elementary school educator; BS, Pacific Union Coll., MA in Edn. with Reading emphasis. Tchr. Walter Douglas Elem. Sch., Tucson, 1994—. Named Ariz. Tchr. of Yr., 2006. Office: Walter Douglas Elem Sch 3302 N Flowing Wells Tucson AZ 85705 Business E-Mail: popsonm@flowingwells.k12.az.us. *

PORCARO, MICHAEL FRANCIS, advertising executive; b. NYC, Apr. 3, 1948; s. Girolamo M. and Marianna (DePasquale) P.; m. Bonnie Kerr, Apr. 7, 1972; children: Sabrina, Jon. BA in English, Rockford Coll., Ill., 1969. Broadcaster Sta. KFQD-AM; KENI-AM/TV, Anchorage, 1970-71, Sta. KENI-AM/TV, Anchorage, 1972-73; v.p. ops. Cook Inlet Broadcasters, Anchorage, 1973-74; owner Audio Enterprises, Anchorage, 1974-75; asst. Alaska Pub. Broadcasting Commn., Anchorage, 1975-76, exec. dir., 1976-81; CEO, ptnr. Porcaro Blankenship Advt. Corp., Anchorage, 1981-97; CEO Porcaro Comms., Anchorage, 1997—; chmn. bd. Bernholz & Graham, Pub. Rels., 2001—07, NY, 2007; ptnr. Porcaro Vancouver Ad and Pub. Rels., 2003, Porcaro L.A. (Calif.) Ad and Pub. Rels., 2004—. Cons. Arco Alaska TV sta., Anchorage, 1981; expert witness U.S. Senate Subcom. on Telecom., Washington, 1978; chmn. citizens adv. com. dept. journalism U. Alaska, 1995-96; pub. rels. Bernholz & Graham, N.Y., 2007. Afternoon talk show host KENI, 2000—. Chmn. Municipality of Anchorage Urban Design Commn., 1990-93; mem. mayor's transition team Municipality of Anchorage, 1987-88; bd. dirs. Anchorage Glacier Pilots Baseball Club, 1987-88, Anchorage Mus. History and Art, Alaska Ctr. Internat. Bus., 1996, Commonwealth North, 1996-2000, Friends of Alaska Children's Trust, 1996-97, Anchorage Symphony Orch.; chmn. bd. dirs. Brother Francis Shelter for the Homeless, Anchorage, 1993-96; mem. mktg. com. gov.'s transition team, 1995; mem. United Way Anchorage Cabinet, 1996; bd. dirs. Alaska Spl. Olmpics, 2001, Anchorage Econ. Devel. Corp., 2001, Alaska Moving Image Preservation Assn., 2001. Recipient Silver Mike award Billboard mag., 1974, Bronze award N.Y. Film Critics, 1981, Best of North award Ad. Fedn. Alaska, 1982—, Addy award, 1985, 91, Grand Addy award 1990, Cable TV Mktg. award 1986; Paul Harris fellow. Mem. Advt. Fedn. Alaska, Anchorage C. of C. (bd. dirs.), Alaska Moving Image Preservation Assn. (bd. dirs. 2001). Republican. Roman Catholic. Avocations: softball, hockey, travel, exercise. Office: Porcaro Comm 433 W 9th Ave Anchorage AK 99501-3519 Office Phone: 907-276-4262. Personal E-mail: mike.porcaro@porcaro.ca.

PORCELLI, FRANK PAUL, lawyer; b. Wilmington, Del., Sept. 15, 1947; s. Attilio F. and Evelyn S. (Feingold) P.; m. Carol M. Stenger Porcelli, Sept. 29, 1972; children: Regan, Erik, Ryan. AB in English Lit., magna cum laude, Boston Coll., Chestnut Hill, Mass., 1968; JD, Harvard U., 1971; MS in Chemistry, Northeastern U., 1981. Bar: Mass. 1971, Del. 1972, U.S. Patent & Trademark Office. Assoc. Fish & Richardson, Boston, 1971-78, ptnr., 1979-94; prin. Fish & Richardson PC, Boston, 1995—, chmn. appellate practice group, 1996—. John A. Reilly visiting prof.-intellectual property law Harvard U. Law Sch., Cambridge, Mass., 1998—99, Cambridge, 2000—01, visiting prof.-law, 2001—02; instr.-biotech. litig. Patent Resources Group Continuing Legal Edn., 2000—. Co-author: (book chpt.) State Trademark & Unfair Competition Law, 1987; contbr. articles to profl. jours.; co-author (with John Dragseth): (casebook patent law) Patents-Hist. Perspective. Served to capt. U.S. Army Res., 1968-73. Named one of top Boston lawyers, Boston Mag., 2002. Mem.: Boston Patent Law Assn. (pres. 1990—91), Fed. Ct. Bar Assn., Am. Intellectual Property Law Assn. (chmn. chem. practice subcom. legis. 1987—89, chmn. chem. practice subcom. judicial & adminstrv. decisions 1989—91, chmn. spl. practice com. 1991—92), ABA. Avocations: golf, running, downhill skiing, history, watching college football and basketball. Office: Fish & Richardson PC 225 Franklin St Fl 32 Boston MA 02110-2809 Home Phone: 617-489-1118; Office Phone: 617-521-7808. Office Fax: 617-542-8906. Business E-Mail: porcelli@fr.com.

PORCELLO, LEONARD JOSEPH, engineering research and development executive; b. NYC, Mar. 1, 1934; s. Savior James and Mary Josephine (Bacchi) P.; m. Patricia Lucille Berger, July 7, 1962 (dec. Sept. 1991); children: John Joseph, Thomas Gregory; m. Victoria Roberta Smith, June 21, 1996. BA in Physics, Cornell U., 1955; MS in Physics, U. Mich., 1957, MSEE, 1959, PhD in Elec. Engring, 1963. Research asst. U. Mich., Ann Arbor, 1955-58, instr. elec. engring., 1958-61; research engr. Radar & Optics Lab., 1968-72; asso. dir. Willow Run Labs., 1970-72, asso. prof., 1969-72, prof., 1972-73, adj. prof., 1973-75. Dir. radar and optics divsn. Environ. Rsch. Inst. of Mich., Ann Arbor, 1973-76, v.p., 1973-76, trustee, 1975; asst. v.p., mgr. sensor sys. operation Sci. Applications Internat. Corp., Tucson, 1976-79, v.p., 1979-85, corp. v.p., 1985-87, mgr. def. sys. group, 1986-95, sr. v.p., 1987—, dep. mgr. tech. and advanced sys. sector, 1993-97, mgr. applied sys. group, 1995-2000, dep. mgr. space and tech. solutions sector, 1997-99; CFO, bd. dirs. TIAS ARMS, 2004—. Bd. dirs. Tucson Jr. Strings, 1977-79, chmn., 1978-79 Fellow IEEE; mem. Optical Soc. Am., AAAS, Sigma Xi, Eta Kappa Nu. Roman Catholic. Achievements include research on imaging radar, synthetic aperture radar systems and radar remote sensing. Home: 5072 Grandview Ave Yorba Linda CA 92886-4216 Office: Sci Applications Internat Corp Attn LJ Porcello PO Box 820 Yorba Linda CA 92885-0820 Office Phone: 714-695-1465. Business E-Mail: leonard.j.porcello@saic.com.

PORCHEA, SAMEANO FRANCISCO, educational association administrator, systems analyst; b. Hemingway, SC, Jan. 15, 1975; d. Samuel Levern and Joyce Claudette Porchea. BS in Edn., Francis Marion U., Florence, SC, 1996, MEd, 1998. Tchr. math. and sci. Florence Sch. Dist. 1, 1996—2002, chairperson math. dept., 2000—02; rsch. asst. Office Program Evaluation U. SC, Columbia, 2002—04, tchg. asst., 2004—; edn. assoc. (test developer) SC State Dept. Edn., Columbia, 2002—. Adj. prof. Florence Darlington Tech., 2000. Named Doctoral Student of Yr., U SC, Columbia, 2004, Tchr. of Yr., Henry N. Sneed Mid. Sch., Florence, 1998—99; James A. Stoddard fellow, U SC, Columbia, 2004. Mem.: Nat. Coun. Measurement in Edn., Am. Edn. Rsch. Assn., Am. Statis. Assn., SC Coun. Tchrs. Math., Nat. Coun. Tchrs. Math., SC Educators Practical Use of Rsch., Pi Mu Epsilon. Democrat. United Methodist. Avocations: data analysis, research in education, bowling, writing poems, buying gadgets. Home: PO Box 12343 Columbia SC 29201 Office: SC Dept Edn 1206-B Rutledge Bldg 1429 Senate St Columbia SC 29201 Office Phone: 803-737-4276. Office Fax: 803-734-8527. Business E-Mail: sporchea@ed.sc.gov.

PORCHER, ROBERT, restaurant manager, retired professional football player; b. 1969; Grad., South Carolina State U. Former profl. football player Detroit Lions; pres. Southern Hospitality Restaurant Grp., Detroit Football Classic L.L.C.; founder Porcher Cancer Relief Fund. Bd. mem. Super Bowl XL Host Com.; chmn. Cmty. Rels. Action Team; bd. mem. NFL Players Assn. Exec. Bd., Detroit Econ. Growth Corp. Hon. chairperson Detroit Tribute to Local Initiatives Support Corp. Silver Anniversary event; involved with The Heat and Warmth Fun, Police Athletic League, Skillman Found., Focus: HOPE. Named one of 40 Under 40, Crain's Detroit Bus., 2006. Office: Southern Hospitality Restaurant Group 243 W Congress Ste 1060 Detroit MI 48226 Office Phone: 313-963-1940. Office Fax: 313-963-1947.

PORDON, WILLIAM PHILIP, music educator; b. Buffalo, Aug. 4, 1925; s. William Peter Pordon and Victoria Regina (Valenches) Dobson; m. Eleanor Grace Haggett, Sept. 28, 1951; children: Judith, Dorothy, Gregory. MusB, Chgo. Conservatory of Music, 1950, MusM, 1951. Violinist Atlanta Symphony, 1951-55; music tchr. Augusta (Ga.) Pub. Schs., 1955-59; dir. music Wayland (Mass.) Pub. Schs., 1960-69; asst. prof. music edn. U. Lowell, Mass., 1969-85. Author: String Starter, 1983; author/composer: Midnight Tango, 1990. With U.S. Army, 1942-44, ETO. Recipient Lowell Mason award Mass. Music Educators Assn., 1981. Mem. Am. String Tchrs. Assn. (pres. San Diego sect. 1985—). Achievements include designed and implemented the Point Loma String Project at Point Loma Nazarene University for training string teachers. Avocation: oil and watercolor painting. Home: 3154 Old Heather Rd San Diego CA 92111-7714 E-mail: wpordon@aol.com.

PORDUM, FRANCIS J., former state legislator, educator, marketing professional; b. Lackawanna, NY; m. Rebecca Pordum; 1 child, Carolyn. BA, Colgate U., 1968; MEd, State U. Coll., Buffalo. Formerly tchr. and coach; mem. N.Y. State Assembly, 1983-96, mem. majority steering com., chmn. local govts. com., chmn. com. on state and local rels., chmn. ethics com.; v.p. mktg. and profl. svcs. Capitol Hill Mgmt. Svcs., Inc., Albany,

NY, 1997—. Former mem. banking com., corrections com., ins. com., racing and wagering com., transp. com., commn. on critical transp. choices and hazardous wastes and toxic substances N.Y. County. Legislator, Erie County. Recipient Pub. Servant of Yr. award Erie County Fedn. Sportsmen, 1983, Citizen of Yr. award Am.-Polish Eagle, 1984, Legislator Citation of Merit award Nat. Columbus Day Com., 1985, Friend of Edn. award Hamburg Tchrs. Assn., 1986, others. Mem. Profl. and Businessmen's Assn. Western N.Y., Chopin Singing Soc., Polish Am. Congress, Lackawanna Tchrs. Fedn. Address: 7476 Derby Rd Derby NY 14047-9687

POREMBKA, MICHAEL RICHARD, assistant principal, supervisor; b. Latrobe, Pa., Dec. 30, 1974; s. Richard D. and Carmella J. Porembka. BA in History Edn., St. Vincent Coll., Pa., 1997; MEd, Gannon U., Erie, Pa., 2002, Prin. Certification, 2004. Cert. Tchr. Pa., 1997, Administrv. Pa., 2002, Adminstrv. Prin. Pa., 2004, prin. cert. Gannon U., Pa., 2004. Tchr. Greater Latrobe (Pa.) Jr. HS, 1998—2006; social studies dept. coord. Greater Latrobe (Pa.) Sch. Dist., 2002—; asst. prin. Greater Latrobe (Pa.) Jr. HS, 2006—; sports/radio broadcaster WCNS Radio, Latrobe, Pa., 2001—. Track coach Greater Latrobe (Pa.) Jr. HS, 1997—2003, football coach, 1998—99, student assistance team mem., 2000—; strategic planning com. Greater Latrobe (Pa.) Sch. Dist., 2001—; asst. softball coach Greater Latrobe (Pa.) Sr. HS, 2005—06. Prodr.(co-host): (radio show) The Sunday Evening Polka Cafe; sports commentator (radio broadcast) Greater Latrobe High School Football on 1480 WCNS Radio. Platelet donor ARC, Greensburg, Pa., 1998—2006; com. mem. Westmoreland County Courthouse Com., Greensburg, Pa., 2005—06; lector St. Rose Roman Cath. Ch., Latrobe, Pa., 2002—06. Mem.: Nat. Assn. Secondary Sch. Principals (assoc.), Internat. Polka Assn. (assoc.), NEA (assoc.), Am. Greek Beneficial Soc. (assoc.), B.P.O. Elks (assoc.). Roman Catholic. Avocations: golf, cars, music. Office: Greater Latrobe Sch Dist 410 Main St Latrobe PA 15650 Office Phone: 724-539-4200.

PORFILIO, JOHN CARBONE, federal judge; b. Denver, Oct. 14, 1934; s. Edward Alphonso Porfilio and Caroline (Carbone) Moore; m. Joan West, Aug. 1, 1959 (div. 1983); children: Edward Miles, Joseph Arthur, Jeanne Kathrine; m. Theresa Louise Berger, Dec. 28, 1983; 1 stepchild, Katrina Ann Smith. Student, Stanford U., 1952—54; BA, U. Denver, 1956, LLB, 1959, LLD (hon.), 2000. Bar: Colo. 1959, US Supreme Ct. 1965. Asst. atty. gen. State of Colo., Denver, 1962—68, dep. atty. gen., 1968—72, atty. gen., 1972—74; US bankruptcy judge Dist. of Colo., Denver, 1975—82; judge US Dist. Ct. Colo., Denver, 1982—85, US Ct. Appeals (10th cir.), Denver, 1985—99, sr. judge, 1999—. Instr. Colo. Law Enforcement Acad., Denver, 1965—70, State Patrol Acad., Denver, 1968—70; guest lectr. U. Denver Coll. Law, 1978. Committeeman Arapahoe County Rep. Com., Aurora, Colo., 1968; mgr. Dunbar for Atty. Gen., Denver, 1970. Mem.: ABA. Roman Catholic. Office: US Ct Appeals Byron White US Courthouse 1825 Stout St Denver CO 80238 *

PORGES, AMELIA, lawyer; BA, Cornell U., 1973; MPP, Harvard U., 1980, JD cum laude, 1980. Bar: DC 1980, US Ct. Appeals, Fed. Cir., US Ct. Internat. Trade. Sr. counsel for dispute settlement, head enforcement, assoc. gen. counsel US Trade Rep., 1980—90, 1994—2000; sr. legal officer, counsellor for legal affairs Gen. Agreement on Tariffs and Trade; secretariat, 1990—94; of counsel Powell Goldstein Frazer & Murphy, Washington, 2000—02; counsel Sidney Austin LLP, Washington, 2002—. Vis. fellow Kyoto U. Faculty of Law, 1977—78; vis. lectr. Sophia U., Tokyo, 1985; adj. prof. Johns Hopkins U. Sch. Advanced Internat. Studies, 1999—; program co-chair Internat. Trade Update, Georgetown U. Law Ctr., 2002—. Author: Analytical Index/Guide to GATT Law and Practice, 1995; contbr. articles to profl. jours. Commr. Japan-US Friendship commn.; mem. US-Japan Conf. on Cultural and Ednl. Interchange, 2007—; mem. adv. bd. Stanford U. GATT Digital Archive, 2003—; mem. chpt. 19 panelists NAFTA, 2001—; bd. mem. Trade Policy Forum, 2005—. Fellow, Coun. on Fgn. Relations, Internat. Affairs, 1988—89; Fulbright fellow, 1985. Mem.: ABA (mem. internat. trade steering group 1994—), Am. Soc. Internat. Law (exec. coun. 1990—95, co-chair Internat. Econ. Law Interest Group 2007—). Office: Sidley Austin LLP 1501 K St NW Washington DC 20005 Office Phone: 202-736-8361. Office Fax: 202-736-8711. Business E-Mail: aporges@sidley.com.

PORIES, WALTER JULIUS, surgeon, educator; b. Munich, Jan. 18, 1930; s. Theodore Francis and Frances (Lowin) P.; m. Muriel Helen Aronson, Aug. 18, 1951; children: Susan E., Mary Jane, Carolyn A., Kathy G.; m. Mary Ann Rose McCarthy, June 4, 1977; children: Mary Lisa, Michael McCarthy. BA, Wesleyan U., Middletown, Conn., 1952; MD with honors, U. Rochester, 1955. Diplomate Am. Bd. Surgery, Am. Bd. Thoracic Surgery. Intern Strong Meml. Hosp., Rochester, NY, 1955—56, resident, 1958—62; chmn. dept. surgery Wright-Patterson AFB, Ohio, 1952—67; asst. prof. surgery and oncology U. Rochester, 1967—69; prof. surgery and assoc. chmn. dept. surgery Case Western Res. U., 1969—77; prof. surgery, biochemistry, exercise and sport medicine East Carolina U., Greenville, NC, 1977—, chmn. dept. surgery, 1977—96, chief Metabolic Inst., 2005—; chief surgery Pitt County Meml. Hosp., 1977—96, prof. surgery U. Health Scis. of Uniformed Svcs., 1982—; founder, assoc. dir. Rochester Cancer Ctr., 1967—69; founder, dir. Cleve. Cancer Ctr., 1972—77, Hospice of Cleve., 1975; founder, chmn. bd. Hospice of Greenville, 1981; med. dir. Home Health Care of Greenville, 1978—83; pres. Surg. Rev. Corp., Raleigh, 2003—. Founder, chmn. bd. Ctr. for Creative Living, 1985-91; pres., chmn. Echo Mgmt. Orgn., 1994—; vis. scholar NIH, 1996; sec. treas., pres. N.C. Med. Bd., 1997-2003. Author: Clinical Applications of Zinc Metabolism, 1974; editor: Operative Surgery series, vols. 1-4, 1979-83, Office Surgery for Family Physicians, 1985; editor in chief Current Surgery, 1990-2005; editor Nat. Curriculum for Residency in Surgery, 4th edit., 1988—. Bd. dirs. Boy Scouts Am., Cleve., 1974-77, Greenville Arts Mus., 1980-82; pres. Sequoiah, Inc., 1999—; bd. dirs. East Carolina U. Found., United Meth. Homes, 2003-. Maj. USAF, 1955-67; col. USAR, 1979-91, comdr. USAF Hosp., Durham, N.C.; activated Desert Shield, 1990. Decorated Legion of Merit; Thorndyke scholar, 1948-51; recipient McLester award USAF, 1966, Miss. Magnolia Cross, 1989, Presdl. citation for Desert Shield, 1994; named to Hon. Order of Ky. Cols., 1965. Fellow ACS, Am. Coll. Cardiology, Am. Coll. Chest Physicians; mem. Soc. for Vascular Surgery, Soc. Surg. Oncology, Soc. Univ. Surgeons, Am. Surg. Assn., Soc. Environ. Geochemistry (past pres.), Residency Rev. Com. for Surgery (vice-chair 1992-98), So. Surg. Assn., Soc. for Thoracic Surgery, Ea. Carolina Health Orgn. (pres., chmn. bd. 1994-99), Assn. Programs Dirs. in Surgery (pres. 1995-96), N.C. Surg. Assn. (pres. 1995-96), Am. Soc. Bariatic Surgery (pres. 2002), Sigma Xi (O. Max Gardner prize), Phi Kappa Phi. Home: Deep Sun Farm 7464 NC 43 N Macclesfield NC 27852 Office: East Carolina U Dept Surgery Greenville NC 27858 Home Phone: 252-752-4317; Office Phone: 252-744-3290. Personal E-mail: pories@aol.com.

PORILE, NORBERT THOMAS, chemistry professor; BA, U. Chgo., 1952, MS, 1954, PhD, 1957. Rsch. assoc. Brookhaven Nat. Lab., Upton, NY, 1957-59, assoc. chemist, 1959-63, chemist, 1963-64; vis. prof. chemistry McGill U., 1963-65; assoc. prof. chemistry Purdue U., West Lafayette, Ind., 1965-69, prof. chemistry, 1969—. Rsch. collaborator Brookhaven Nat. Lab., Argonne Nat. Lab., Los Alamos Sci. Lab., Lawrence Berkeley Lab.; vis. prof. Facultes des Scis., Orsay, France; fellow Soc. Promotion of Sci. in Japan, Inst. Nuclear Study, U. Kyoto, 1961. Editor: Radiochemistry of the Elements and Radiochemical Techniques, 1986-90. John Simon Guggenheim meml. fellow Institut de Physique Nucleaire Orsay, 1971-72; recipient F.D. Martin Undergrad. Teaching award, 1977; Von Humboldt Sr. U.S. Scientist award Philipps U., Marburg, W. Ger., 1982 Mem. Am. Chem. Soc., Am. Phys. Soc. Office: Purdue U Dept Chemistry Brown Lab Lafayette IN 47907 Office Phone: 765-494-5329.

PORITZ, DEBORAH TOBIAS, former state supreme court justice and attorney general; b. Bklyn., Oct. 26, 1936; m. Alan Poritz; children: Jonathan, Mark. BA, Bklyn. Coll., CUNY, 1958; JD, U. Penn., 1977. English tchr. Ursinus Coll., Collegeville, Pa., 1967—70; dep. atty. gen. NJ Dept. Law and Pub. Safety, 1977—81, asst. chief environ. protection section, 1981—84, dep. atty. gen. in charge of appeals, chief banking, ins. and pub. securities section, 1984—86, asst. atty. gen., dir. divsn. law, 1986—89; chief counsel to Gov. Thomas Kean State of NJ, Trenton, 1989—90; ptnr. Jamieson, Moore, Peskin & Spicer LLP, Princeton, NJ, 1990—94; atty. gen. State of NJ, Trenton, 1994—96; chief justice NJ Supreme Ct., Trenton, 1996—2006. Recipient Presdl. medal, Bklyn. Coll., 2000. *

POROMANSKA, MARGARITA KIRILOVA, science educator, environmental scientist; b. Gabrovo, Bulgaria, Nov. 3, 1960; arrived in U.S., 2000; d. Kiril Georgiev Poromanski and Liliana Dimitrova Ralcheva; 1 child, Viktor Dimitrov Arabadjiev. MSc in Biology/Zoology, U. Sofia, Bulgaria, 1983; MSc in Environ. Sci., Ctrl. European U., Budapest, Hungary, 2000. Cert. substitute tchr. Ill. Environ. sci. expert Union Nature Conservation, Sofia, Bulgaria, 1998—99, Pearson Custom Pub., Indpls., 2004—; instr. biology Coll. DuPage, Glen Ellyn, Ill., 2001—, Waubonsee CC, Sugar Grove, 2001—, Columbia Coll., Chgo., 2002—, Nat. Louis U., 2004—. Sci. and fgn. langs. tutor Ednl. Svcs. Glen Ellyn, Ill., 2001—, W. Suburban Ednl. Assocs., Naperville, Ill., 2002—; rsch. fellow Inst. Ecology Bulgarian Acad. Scis., Sofia, 1988—96; sr. reviewer AP Environ. Sci. Coll. Bd. Edn., 2006—. Author, editor: New Portals to Appreciating Our Global Environment, 2005. Judge science competition Malcolm X Coll., Chgo., 2004; sr. reviewer AP Course Audit in Environ. Sci. Coll. Bd. Edn., 2006—07. Grantee, Open Soc. Found., 1992; scholar, 1999, Carl-Duisberg Found., 1994. Mem.: NEA, Ill. Edn. Assn., Ctrl. European U. Alumni Assn. Avocations: hiking, bicycling, birdwatching. Home: 1662 Monticello Ct # C Wheaton IL 60187 Office: Coll DuPage Natural And Appied Sci Dept 425 Fawell Blvd Glen Ellyn IL 60137-6599 Personal E-mail: m_poromanska@yahoo.com.

POROSOFF, HAROLD, chemist, science administrator, research and development company executive; b. Bklyn., Apr. 3, 1946; s. Solomon and Ruth (Goldberg) P.; m. Leslie Pamela Freiman, May 19, 1948; children: Lauren, Stephen, Marc. BS, MIT, 1966; PhD, Brown U., 1970. Various rsch. and mgmt. positions fibers div. Am. Cyanamid Co., Stamford, Conn. and Milton, Fla., 1970-78, various mgmt. positions Shulton Rsch. div. Clifton, NJ, 1978-83, dir., 1983-88, v.p. R & D chem. rsch. divsn. Stamford, 1989-93; v.p. R & D Cytec Industries Inc., Stamford, 1993-95; v.p., chief tech. officer Cytec Industries, Inc., Stamford, 1995-98, cons., 1998—. Patentee in field. Chmn. Scarsdale Cable TV Commn. Mem. AAAS. Office: 22 Olmsted Rd Scarsdale NY 10583-2324 E-mail: hpphd@optonline.net.

POROTSKY, RICHARD D., JR., lawyer; b. Cin., Oct. 10, 1970; BS, Vanderbilt U., 1993, JD, 1996. Bar: Ohio 1996, US Dist. Ct. Southern Dist. Ohio 1996, US Ct. of Appeals Sixth Cir. 2000, Ky. 2004. Assoc. Dinsmore & Shohl LLP, Cin. Mentor, HOSTS Prog. Cin. Youth Collaborative; head coach, Youth Baseball White Oak Athletic Assn.; co-chair, Red Mass 2005 St. Thomas More Soc.; mem., pastoral coun., lector St. James Ch.; co-chair, coord. Holiday Giving Basket; mem. Western Econ. Coun. Named one of Ohio's Rising Stars, Super Lawyers, 2006. Mem.: ABA, Ohio State Bar Assn., Cin. Bar Assn. (Cmty. Svc. Com.). Office: Dinsmore & Shohl LLP 255 E Fifth St Ste 1900 Cincinnati OH 45202-4700 Office Phone: 513-977-8200. Office Fax: 513-977-8141.

PORT, LILLY BRUCK LIEB, retired advocate, columnist, commentator; b. Vienna, May 13, 1918; came to U.S., 1941, naturalized, 1944; d. Max and Sophie M. Hahn; m. Sandor Bruck, Mar. 7, 1943; 1 child, Sandra Lee (Mrs. John David Evans III); m. David L. Lieb, Dec. 7, 1985; m. Charles S. Port, Nov. 22, 1998. PhD in Econs., U. Vienna; postgrad., Sorbonne, Paris, Sch. of Econs., London, Sch. of Bus., Columbia U., 1941-42, Sch. of Social Work, NYU, 1964-66. Dir. consumer edn. Dept. Consumer Affairs, City of N.Y., 1969-78; project dir. Am. Coalition of Citizens with Disabilities, 1977-78; consumer advisor, broadcaster In Touch Networks, NYC, 1978-90; consumer affairs commentator Nat. Pub. Radio, 1980-82; ret. Author: Access, The Guide to a Better Life for Disabled Americans, 1978; contbr. articles to disability and rehab. to books, ency. and mag. Presid. Scarsdale Hadassah, 1960-68. Chmn. Westchester county, Bonds for Israel, 1960-68; trustee Kol AMI-JCC, White Plains, N.Y.; assoc. Jewish Mus.; sponsor Lilly Bruck Lieb Creative Writing Program, Purchase Coll., SUNY; mem. pres.'s coun. White Plains (N.Y.) Hosp. Recipient Woman of Yr. award Anti Defamation League, 1972. Democrat. Home: 25 Murray Hill Rd Scarsdale NY 10583-2829 Personal E-mail: lblone@aol.com.

PORT, P. ALLAN, lawyer; s. Paul Port; m. Peggy Port; children: Paul Hunter, Maggie. Grad., Yale U., 1964; JD, U. Tex., 1967. Law clk. to Judge J.C. Hutcheson Jr. U.S. Circuit Ct. of Appeals; assoc. Baker Botts; ptnr. Childress, Port & Crady; mng. ptnr. Seawell & Riggs (now Gardere Wynne Seawell); exec. v.p. Orillion USA, 2000—02; exec. v.p., gen. counsel Amegy Corp., 2002—. Office: Amegy Corp 4400 Post Oak Pkwy Houston TX 77027-7459 *

PORT, SIDNEY CHARLES, mathematician, educator; b. Chgo., Nov. 27, 1935; s. Isadore and Sarah (Landy) P.; m. Idelle Jackson, Mar. 24, 1957; children— Ethan, Jonathan, Daniel. AB, Northwestern U., 1957, MS, 1958, PhD, 1962. Staff mathematician Rand Corp., 1962-66; asso. prof. math. U. Calif. at Los Angeles, 1966-69, prof., 1969—. Author: (with P. Hoel and C. Stone) Probability, Statistics and Stochastic Processes, 1971, (with C. Stone) Brownian Motion and Classical Potential Theory, 1978, Theoretical Probability for Applications, 1993; contbr. articles to profl. jours. Fellow Inst. Math. Statistics; mem. Am. Math. Soc. Office: UCLA Dept Math Los Angeles CA 90024 Home: 680 Kingman Ave Santa Monica CA 90402 Home Phone: 310-454-0717; Office Phone: 310-825-4701.

PORTA, SIENA GILLANN, sculptor, educator; b. NYC, Nov. 5, 1951; d. Vincent Anthony Porta and Barbara Ann Gill Porta Hutchinson; m. Robert Christopher Dell, May 30, 1986; 1 child, Malcolm Vincent Dell. BS in Studio Arts, Bklyn. Coll., CUNY, 1977; MFA in Sculpture, Pa. State U., 1979. Sci. illustrator Columbia U./Lamont-Doherty Geol. Obs., Palisades, NY, 1980—87; scenic artist Saturday Night Live, NYC, 1986—89, Met. Opera, NYC, 1987—92; master scenic artist numerous Broadway prod., including Frankie and Johnny, Boiler Rm., Sorrows and Rejoicings, 1992—; adj. prof. contemporary arts Ramapo Coll., 2000—; adj. prof. art St. Thomas Aquinas, Sparkill, NY, 2000—; represented by Noho Gallery, NYC, 14 Sculptors Inc., NYC. Adj. prof. Bergen CC, Paramus, NJ, 1984—85; artist-in-residence Brisons Veor, Cornwall, England, 2003. One-woman shows include 14 Sculptors Gallery, NYC, 1984-85, 88, 90, Mid-Hudson Arts and Sci. Ctr., Poughkeepsie, NY, 1992-93, Dominican Coll., Blauvelt, NY, 1980, 2005, Noho Gallery, NYC, 2003, 2005; group shows at A.B. Condon Gallery, NYC, 1982-83, Terrain Gallery, NYC, 1984, Am. Cultural Ctr., Reykiavik, Iceland, 1988, Notre Dame U., South Bend, Ind., 1990, Lehigh U., Phila., Blue Hill Cult. Ctr., Pearl River, NY, 1995, Eighth Floor Gallery, NYC, 1996, NJ City U., Jersey City, Nassau C.C., Garden City, NY, The Interchurch Ctr., Riverside Dr., NY, 1998, Adelphi U., NY, 2000, St. Thomas Aquinas Coll., Sparkill, NY, 2000, Galleri Ofeigur, 2001, Noho Gallery, 2001-02, 04-05, Snaefelsness Regl. Museum, 2002, Hafnarborg Ctr. for Culture, Mus, 2002-03, Regional Mus. of Hornafjorduv, 2003, Rutgers U., 2003, 14 sculptors at McLevy Park Outdoor Installation, Bridgeport, Conn., 2004, 14 sculptures including The Lockwood Mathews Mansion Mus. Pk., Norwalk, Conn., 2005, N.J. City U., 2007. others; represented in collections at Fulbright Commn., Reykjavik, Bergen C.C., Paramus, NJ, 1988, St. Philip R.C. Ch., Norwalk, Conn., Jacob Riis Nat. Park US Embassy, Brisons Veor Trust Cornwall, Eng., Iceland, Hafnarborg Mus.; subject of video Me and The Mirror, 1990; contbr. articles to popular mag., Internat. Sculpture Ctr. Pa. State Arts Coun./Hershey Med. Coll. grantee, 1978-79; NY State Coun. on the Arts grantee, 1986; USIA-Ptnrs. of Ams. travel grant to St. Lucia, W.I., 1992, NY Fdn. for the Arts grantee, 2002.; artist resident Brisons Veor, Cornwall, Eng., 2003. Mem. Everyday Zen Ctr. of Prescott, Ariz. Home: PO Box 46 Palisades NY 10964-0046 Personal E-mail: sportaedu@aol.com.

PORTAL, GILBERT MARCEL ADRIEN, oil industry executive; b. Paris, Aug. 2, 1930; came to U.S., 1982; s. Emmanuel Jules and Henriette Josephine (Bonnard) P.; m. Monique Janine Adam, July 12, 1951; children: Dominique, Veronique, Marc-Emmanuel. Baccalaureate, Lycee Charlemagne U., Paris, 1949; Ingenieur Civil des Mines, Sch. of Mines, St. Etienne, 1955; diplome du C.P.A., Ctr. Advanced Bus., Paris, 1969; auditeur 30 eme session IHEDN, Higher Studies Nat. Defense, Paris, 1978. Geophysicist Societe Nationale Elf Aquitaine, Sahara, Algeria, 1957-63, exploration mgr. north sea, 1963-65, dep. exec. v.p. Europe, 1965-68, dep. exec. v.p. North and South Am., 1968-70, chief exec. officer Iraq, 1970-72, dir., chief exec. officer Gabon, Africa, 1972-76, dep. exec. v.p. hydrocarbons, 1976-78, exec. v.p. North Africa, Mid. East, Far East, 1978-82; pres. Elf Aquitaine Petroleum, Houston, 1982-89; chmn., chief exec. officer Elf Exploration, Inc., Houston, 1989-90; sec.-gen. European Petroleum Industry Assn., 1990-95; ptnr. G.M.H. Internat. Oil and Gas Consulting, Paris, 1995—; pres. internat. devel. Howard Energy Internat. LLC, 1999—2002. Served to lt. French Army, 1955-57. Decorated Legion of Honor (France), Nat. Merit Order (France); Equatorial Star (Gabon). Mem. Cercle Royal Gaulois Artistique et Littéraire. Roman Catholic. Office Phone: (33) 1 45 58 01 02. Business E-Mail: gmh@portal-consult.com.

PORTALE, ALFRED, chef, restaurant owner; b. 1958; married. Grad., Culinary Inst. Am., 1981. Exec. chef Gotham Bar and Grill, NYC, 1985—87, exec. chef, ptnr., 1987—; ptnr. One Fifth Avenue, NYC, 1992—. Mem. Singapore Airlines Internat. Chef Panel. Author: Gotham Bar and Grill Cookbook, 1998 (Julia Child Cookbook award, 1998), 12 Seasons Cookbook, 2001, Simple Pleasures, 2004. Named Best Chef in NY, 1993, Most Outstanding Chef in Nation, James Beard Found., 2006; named to Who's Who in Food & Beverage in Am., 1989; recipient Ivy award, Restaurants & Institutions mag., 1990. Office: Gotham Bar & Grill 12 E 12th St New York NY 10003-4498 *

PORTE, JOEL MILES, language educator; b. Bklyn., Nov. 13, 1933; s. Jacob I. and Frances (Derison) P.; m. Ilana D'Ancona, June 17, 1962 (div. 1977); 1 child, Susanna Maria; m. Helene Sophrin, Oct. 18, 1985. AB magna cum laude, CCNY, 1957; A.M., Harvard U., 1958, PhD, 1962. Instr. English Harvard U., Cambridge, Mass., 1962-64, asst. prof., 1964-68, assoc. prof., 1968-69, prof., 1969-82, Bernbaum prof. lit., 1982-87, chmn. dept. English and Am. Lit., 1985-87; Frederic J. Whiton prof. English Cornell U., Ithaca, NY, 1987-89, Ernest I. White prof. Am. Studies and Humane Letters, 1989—. Vis. lectr. Am. Studies Rsch. Ctr., Hyderabad, India, spring 1976. Author: Emerson and Thoreau: Transcendentalists in Conflict, 1966, The Romance in America: Studies in Cooper, Poe, Hawthorne, Melville and James, 1969, Representative Man: Ralph Waldo Emerson in His Time, 1979, In Respect to Egotism: Studies in American Romantic Writing, 1991; editor: Emerson in His Journals, 1982, Emerson: Prospect and Retrospect, 1982, Emerson: Essays and Lectures, 1983, New Essays on Portrait of a Lady, 1990, A Cambridge Companion to Ralph Waldo Emerson (with Saundra Morris), 1999, Emerson's Prose and Poetry: A Norton Critical Edit. (with Saundra Morris), 2001, Consciousness and Culture: Emerson and Thoreau Reviewed, 2004. Scholar in Residence, Rockefeller Found., Bellagio, Italy, 1979; fellow John Simon Guggenheim Found., 1981-82. Mem. Am. Lit. Assn., Phi Beta Kappa. Home: 14 Yardley Green Ithaca NY 14850-1237 Home Phone: 607-273-3576; Office Phone: 607-255-6806. E-mail: jp26@cornell.edu.

PORTELA, ANTONIO GOUVEA, retired mechanical engineer, researcher; b. Lisbon, Portugal, Jan. 26, 1918; s. Raul Lello Portella and Esther Gouvea Portela; married, Sept. 29, 1965; 2 children. Engr. degree, Inst. Superior Tecnico, Lisbon, 1960; prof. degree, Inst. Sup. Tecn., Lisbon, 1958. Cert. mech. engring. Contbr. articles to profl. jours. Mem. AAAS, ASME, Am. Nuclear Soc., N.Y. Acad. Scis., Academia de Engenharia of Portugal. Office: Inst Superior Tecnico Av Rovisco Paes Lisbon Portugal

PORTELL, KEITH S, application developer, consultant; s. Sherman Melvin and Caroline Margaret Portell; m. Claudia Kane Epting, July 14, 1996; children: Andrew Justin, Aaron Michael. BS in info sys. mgmt., U. Of Md. U. Coll., 1995—97; Database Systems Technologies Grad. Cert., U. of Md. U. Coll., 2001—03, MS in computer sys. mgmt., 2001—04. MCSE Microsoft, 1997, cert. Novell Master Network Engineer Novell, 1994. Supr. Six Flags Corp., Houston, 1982—88; sys. analyst Giant Food, Inc., Landover, Md., 1988—94; lan/wan engr. Bus. Network Assoc., Annapolis, Md., 1994—95; network adminstr. Micros Systems, Inc., Beltsville, Md., 1995; lead network engr. Zurich Personal Ins., Balt., 1996—97; meta data architect Mayo Clinic, Jacksonville, Fla., 1997—. Contbr. articles. Mgmt. dir. Jaycees, Annapolis, Md., 1996—98. Mem.: Health Data Warehousing Assn. (assoc.), Am. Med. Informatics Assn (assoc.). Independent. Christian. Achievements include invention of Medical Data Trust - Mayo Clinic. Avocations: travel, reading, computers. Home: 6935 La Loma Dr Jacksonville FL 32217 Office: Mayo Clinic 4500 San Pablo Rd #VAS153A Jacksonville FL 32224 Home Phone: 904-504-2745; Office Phone: 904-953-0416. Personal E-mail: keith@keithportell.net. Business E-Mail: portell.keith@mayo.edu.

PORTEOUS, G. THOMAS, JR., judge; b. 1946; BA, La. State U., 1968, JD, 1971. Spl. counsel, atty. gen., 1971-73; asst. dist. atty. Dist. Atty. Office Parish of Jefferson, 1973—84; ptnr. Edward, Porteous & Amato, Grenta, La., 1973-74, Edwards, Porteous & Lee, Grenta, 1974-76, Porteous, Lee & Mustakas, 1976-80, Porteous & Mustakas, Metairie, La., 1980-84; city atty. City of Harahan, La., 1982-84; dist. ct. judge divsn. A State of La., 1984-94; dist. judge U.S. Dist. Ct. (ea. dist.), La., 1994—. Mem. ABA, Fed. Bar Assn., La. State Bar Assn., 4th and 5th Cir. Judges Assn., Jefferson Bar Assn., Am. Judges Assn., La. Dist. Atty. Assn. Office: US Dist Ct E Dist 500 Poydras St Rm C-206 New Orleans LA 70130-3313 Office Phone: 504-589-7585.

PORTER, ANDREW CALVIN, dean, psychologist, educator; b. Huntington, Pa., July 10, 1942; s. Rutherford and Grace (Johnson) P.; children: Matthew, Anna, John, Joe, Kate. BS, Ind. State U., 1963; MS, U. Wis., 1965, PhD, 1967. Vis. asst. prof. Ind. State U., 1967; asst. prof. ednl. psychology Mich. State U., East Lansing, 1967—70, dir. office rsch. consultation, 1967—73, assoc. prof. ednl. psychology, 1970—74; vis. scholar Nat. Inst. Edn., Washington, 1973—74, chief measurement and methodology divsn., 1974—75; prof. ednl. psychology Mich. State U., East Lansing, 1974—88; assoc. dir. basic skills group Nat. Inst. Edn., Washington, 1975—76; dir. Sch. Advanced Studies Coll. Edn. Mich. State U., East Lansing, 1979—81, assoc. dean rsch. and grad. study Coll. Edn., 1981—85; Anderson-Bascom prof. edn., prof. ednl. psychology U. Wis., Madison, 1988—2003, dir. Wis. Ctr. Edn. Rsch., 1988—2003; Patricia and

Rodes Hart prof. ednl. leadership and policy Vanderbilt U., Nashville, 2003—07, dir. Learning Scis. Inst., 2003—07; dean Grad. Sch. Edn., U. Pa., 2007—. Mem adv. com. What Works Clearinghouse Inst. Edn. Scis., 2002-, steering com. math./sci. partnerships, Nat. Acad. Sci., 2003-2005, nat. assessment governing bd., 2004-; chmn. adv. coun. on edn. stats., U.S. Dept. Edn., 1994-2001; chair bd. Internat. Studies, Nat. Acad. Sci., Nat. Rsch. Coun., 1998-2001 Editor: (with A. Gamoran) Methodological Advances in Cross-National Surveys of Educational Achievement, 2002; mem. editl. bd. Tchrs. Coll. Record, 1995—, Am. Ednl. Rsch. Jour., 2004—. Bd. dirs. Madison Urban League, 1992-96. Recipient Disting. Alumni award, Ind. State U., 1994, Sch. Edn. Dean's Club Faculty Disting. Achievement Award, U. Wis.-Madison, 1996, Crystal Apple Award, Mich. State U., 2000, Alumni Achievement award, U. Wis., Madison, 2005. Mem. Am. Ednl. Rsch. Assn. (pres. 2001, Outstanding Reviewer award 2003), Nat. Coun. Edn. Measurement, Nat. Coun. Tchrs. Math., Nat. Acads. (lifetime nat. mem.), Nat. Acad. Edn. (v.p. 2005), Phi Delta Kappa (life). Office: U Pa Grad Sch Edn 3700 Walnut St Philadelphia PA 19104 Office Phone: 215-898-7014. E-mail: andyp@gse.upenn.edu. *

PORTER, BIGGS C., corporate financial executive; B in Acctg., Duke U.; M in Profl. Acctg., U. Tex., Austin. CPA. Audit prin. Arthur Young & Co.; corp. controller, asst. treas. Vought Aircraft; CFO integrated systems sector Northrop Grumman, CFO comml. aircraft divsn.; sr. v.p., corp. controller TXU Corp., Dallas; v.p., corp. controller Raytheon Co., Waltham, Mass., 2003—, acting CFO, 2005—06; CFO Tenet Healthcare Corp., Dallas, 2006—. Mem.: AICPA. Office: Tenet Healthcare Corp 13737 Noel Rd Dallas TX 75240 Office Phone: 781-522-3000. *

PORTER, BLAINE ROBERT MILTON, sociology professor, psychology professor; b. Morgan, Utah, Feb. 24, 1922; s. Brigham Ernest and Edna (Brough) P.; m. Elizabeth Taylor, Sept 27, 1943 (dec.); children: Claudia Jackson, Roger B., David T., Patricia A. Hintze, Corinna; m. Myrna Katherine Kennedy, Feb. 26, 1988. Student, Utah State U., 1940-41; BS, Brigham Young U., 1947, MA, 1949; PhD (Grant Found. fellow family life edn. 1951-52), Cornell U., 1952. Instr. sociology Iowa State Coll., 1949-51; asst. prof. sociology and child devel. Iowa State U., 1952-55; prof., chmn. dept. human devel. and family relationships Brigham Young U., 1955-65, dean Coll. Family Living, 1966-80, prof., 1980-87. Vis. prof. Fulbright rsch. scholar U. London, 1965-66; vis. prof. U. Wurzberg, 1980-81, 83; facilitator human rels. workshops for the Human Devel. Inst., Denver, 1988-90, pres., CEO Families for Children Internat., Inc., 2001—. Editor: The Latter-day Saint Family, 1963, rev. edit., 1966; editor quar. jour.: Family Perspective, 1966-82; contbr. articles to profl. jours. Pres. elect Iowa Coun. Family Rels., 1954-55; pres. Utah Coun. Family Rels. Coun., 1957-58; chmn. sect. marriage counseling Nat. Coun. Family Rels., 1958-59, bd. dirs., 1957-60, exec. com., 1958-72, pres., 1963-64; bd. dirs. Am. Family Soc., 1975-85. Pilot USAAF, 1942-45. Recipient Prof. of Yr. award Brigham Young U., 1964. Mem. Am. Home Econs. Assn. (vice chmn. sect. family relations and child devel. 1955-56), Am. Sociol. Assn. (sec. sect. on family 1964-67), Am. Assn. Marriage and Family Therapy, Am. Psychol. Assn., Soc. Research in Child Devel., Sigma Xi, Phi Kappa Phi (chpt. pres. 1969-71) Home: 1675 Pine Ln Provo UT 84604-2163 Office: 4505 HBLL Brigham Young U Provo UT 84602 Personal E-mail: porter22@comcast.net.

PORTER, BRUCE JACKMAN, computer engineer, application developer, portfolio manager, civil engineer; b. El Paso, Tex., Aug. 7, 1954; s. Covington Baskin and Carolyn Fee (Bruce) P.; m. Janette Anne Brown, Oct. 19, 1985; children: Laura, Holly, Travis. BS, US Mil. Acad., 1976; MS in Computer Sci., Stanford U., 1985, MS in Civil Engring., 1985; grad., U.S. Army War Coll., 1997. Engr. in tng., Pa. Commd. 1st lt. U.S. Army, 1979-80, advanced through grades to lt. col., 1993, co-commdr. 17th armored engr. bn. Ft. Hood, Tex., 1977-80, constrn. engr. Misawa, Japan, 1981-83, orgnl. evaluator Ft. Leavenworth, Kans., 1989-90, ops. officer 5th engr. combat bn. Saudi Arabia and Iraq, 1990-91; assoc. prof. mathematics U.S. Mil. Acad., West Point, NY, 1985-88; chief concepts officer USA Engr. Sch., Ft. Leonard Wood, Mo., 1991-93; logistics assistance officer 1st Cavalry Divsn., Ft. Hood, Tex., 1993-94; comdg. officer 20th Engr. Bn., 1st Cavalry Divsn., Ft. Hood, Tex., 1994-96; sr. engr. trainer Nat. Tng. Ctr., Ft. Irwin, Calif., 1997-98; cmdr., engr. brigade 4th Infantry Divn., Ft. Hood, Tex., 1998—99; exec. officer Army chief of staff for ops. Pentagon, Washington, 1999—2001; investment rep. Edward Jones & Co., Buellton, Calif., 2001—. Pioneer new courses in computer theory and discrete math. U.S. Mil. Acad., 1987-88; proponent Army Engr. Restructive Initiative, 1991-92; panel mem. Army Study Team for Battle Dynamics, 1992; mem. Summer Study for Chief of Staff of Army, 1992. Co-author: Army Keystone Operations Field Manual, 1993; pub. papers on combat engr. reorgn., 1991-92, 98. Decorated DSM, Bronze Star, Legion of Merit. Home: 345 Meadowlark Rd Santa Ynez CA 93460 Office: 175 H McMurray Rd Buellton CA 93427 Office Phone: 805-688-9079.

PORTER, CHARLES MICHAEL (MIKE PORTER), diversified financial services company executive; b. Danville, Ill., Jan. 11, 1957; s. Charles K. Jr. and Constance K. (Kinnaman) P.; m. Kathryn S. Klein, July 15, 1990; children: Eric J., Jerry D. AA, Danville Area C.C., 1986; BS in Accountancy, U. Ill., 1988, MS in Taxation, 1989. Owner C.M. Porter Realty, Danville, Ill., 1980-85; staff acct. Clifton Gunderson & Co., Danville, Ill., 1989; staff tax acct. McGladrey & Pullen, Peoria, Ill., 1989-91, Galesburg, Ill., 1991-95; dir. tax Dollar Gen. Corp., Goodlettsville, Tenn., 1995—2002; v.p., CFO Clear Check, Inc., Greenville, SC, 2002—06; pres., chmn. Rodeo Stockyard, Inc.; v.p., CFO Viking Master Builders LLC, Greenville, SC, 2007—; pres., CEO Profl. Bucking Bull Assocs., LLC, 2007—. Owner Thunder Run Ranch; sec. Viking Master Builders LLC, bd. dirs. Former bd. dirs., treas. Dollar Gen. Literacy Found. Mem. Tax Execs. Inst., Internat. Mass Retailers Assn. (former chmn. tax adv. com.), Profl. Rodeo Cowboys Assn. (assoc.), Southern Extreme Bull Riding Assn., U. Ill. Alumni Assn., Am. Bucking Bull Assn. Avocations: rodeo, stock and ranch horses, rodeo bull breeding. Office: Viking Master Builders 121 Interstate Blvd Ste 2B Greenville SC 29615 Business E-Mail: mike@rodeostockyard.com.

PORTER, CHARLES RALEIGH, JR., retired lawyer; b. Waco, Tex., Sept. 22, 1922; s. Charles Raleigh and Virginia Louise (Bowen) P.; m. Alice Mungall, Sept. 16, 1946; children: Charles Raleigh III, Melissa Ann, Alice Marguerite, Daniel Bowen. BBA, U. Tex., 1943, JD, 1949. Bar: Tex. 1948, U.S. Dist. Ct. (so. dist.) Tex. 1949, U.S. Ct. Appeals (5th cir.) 1955, U.S. Dist. Ct. (we. dist.) Tex. 1972, U.S. Dist. Ct. (no. dist.) Tex. 1977. Asst. Nueces County Attys. Office, Corpus Christi, Tex., 1949-50, Asst. Dist. Attys. Office, Corpus Christi, 1950-53; ptnr. Anderson & Porter, Corpus Christi, 1953-63, Sorrell, Anderson & Porter, 1964-68, Porter, Rogers, Dahlman & Gordon, 1969-92; ret., 1992. Mem. adv. bd. dirs. Frost Nat. Bank, San Antonio. Past mem. exec. bd. Perkins Sch. Theology, So. Meth. U.; past chairperson adminstrv. bd. First United Meth. Ch., Corpus Christi, Tex.; mem. chancellor's com. U. Tex.; past mem. adv. bd. U. Tex. Marine Sci. Inst.; mem. Dean's Roundtable, U. Tex. Sch. Law, 2001; Past mem. bd. dirs. Meth. Home, Waco. Lt. USNR, 1944—46. Mem.: Internat. Assn. Def. Counsel, Spanish Oaks Golf Club, Rockport Country Club, Scottish Rite, Masons. Home: 51 Blue Heron Dr Rockport TX 78382-3771 Personal E-mail: charlie_alice_allegro@yahoo.com.

PORTER, CHRIS, food products executive; With Burlington Industries, Greensboro, NC; head electronic bus. unit Sara Lee Corp., CFO European food divsn., v.p. bakery market expansion Chgo., 2004—. Named one of Top 40 Under 40, Crain's Chgo. Bus., 2006. Office: Sara Lee Corp 3500 Lacey Rd Downers Grove IL 60515 E-mail: cporter@saralee.com.

PORTER, DANIEL J., oil industry executive; B in Chem. Engring., U. Akron, Ohio. Mgmt. positions Std. Oil Ohio, BP/Amoco; regional pres. No. Gt. Plains Region, mgr. Mandan, ND refinery Tesoro Corp., 2001—02, pres. NW region Tesoro Refining and Mktg. Co., 2002—05, mgr. Anacortes refinery, 2002—05, sr. v.p. mktg., 2005—. Office: Tesoro Corp 300 Concord Plz San Antonio TX 78216-6999 Office Phone: 210-283-2000.

PORTER, DARWIN FRED, writer; b. Greensboro, NC, Sept. 13, 1937; s. Numie Rowan and Hazel Lee (Phillips) P. BA, U. Miami, 1959. Bur. chief Miami Herald, 1959-60; v.p. Haggart Assoc., NYC, 1961-64; editor, author Arthur Frommer Inc., NYC, 1964-67, Frommer/Pasmantier Pub. Corp., NYC, 1967-86, Prentice Hall Press, NYC, 1987-90, Simon & Schuster, NYC, 1991—. Author: Frommer Travel Guides to: England, 1964, Spain, 1966, Scandinavia, 1967, Los Angeles, 1969, London, 1970, Lisbon/Madrid, 1972, Paris, 1972, Morocco, 1974, Rome, 1974, Portugal, 1968, England, 1969, Italy, 1969, Germany, 1970, France, 1970, Caribbean, Bermuda, the Bahamas, 1980, Switzerland, 1984, Austria and Hungary, 1984, Bermuda and the Bahamas, 1985, Scotland and Wales, 1985, the Virgin Islands, 1991, Scotland, 1992, Jamaica/Barbados, 1992, Puerto Rico, 1992, the Caribbean, 1993, Bermuda, 1993, the Bahamas, 1993, Austria, 1993, Madrid & the Costa del Sol, 1993, San Francisco, 1996, California, 1996, Caribbean Cruises, 1996, Caribbean Ports of Call, 1996, Georgia and the Carolinas, 1996, Charleston and Savannah, 1996, Munich and The Bavarian Alps, 1996, Vienna & the Danube, 1996, Guide to Caribbean Cruises, 1997, Frommer's Europe, 1997, Frommer's Venice, 1997, Barcelona, Madrid & Seville, 1997, Frommer's Portable London, 1998, Frommer's Portable Bahamas, 1998, Frommer's Portable Paris, 1998, Frommer's Portable Berlin, 1999; author: Butterflies in Heat, 1976, Marika, 1977, Venus, 1982, Razzle-Dazzle, 1998, Blood Moon, 1998, Frommer's Sweden, 1999, Frommer's Denmark, 1999, Midnight in Savannah, 2000, Hollywood's Silent Closet, 2000, Frommer's Frankfurt, 2001, Frommer's Great Britain, 2001, Bahamas for Dummies, 2002, Caribbean for Dummies, 2002, Rhinestone Country, 2002, Frommer's Charleston, 2003, Frommer's Savannah, 2003, Frommer's Sicily, 2003, Frommer's Norway, 2003, France for Dummies, 2003, Frommer's Cayman Islands, 2003, Frommer's Dominican Republic, 2003, The Secret Life of Humphrey Bogart, 2003, Katharine the Great, 2004, Fommer's Europe By Rail, 2004, Howard Hughes: Hell's Angel, 2004, Frommer's Seville and Southern Spain, 2005, Frommer's Andalusia, 2005, Irreverent Paris, 2005, Brando Unzipped, 2006, Frommer's Tuscany Day by Day, 2006, Jacko: His Rise & Fall, 2007, Frommer's Dream Vacations, 2007. Recipient Silver award Internat. Film and TV Festival NY, 1977. Mem. Soc. Am. Travel Writers, Smithsonian Assoc., Nat. Trust for Hist. Preservation, Sigma Delta Chi. Home: 75 Saint Marks Pl Staten Island NY 10301-1606 Personal E-mail: porterandprince@hotmail.com.

PORTER, DAVID HUGH, musician, classicist, academic administrator, music educator; b. NYC, Oct. 29, 1935; s. Hugh B. and Ethel K. (Flentye) P.; m. Laudie Ernestine Dimmette, June 21, 1958 (dec. Nov., 1986); children: Hugh, Everett, Helen, David; m. Helen Louise Nelson, Aug. 24, 1987. BA with highest honors, Swarthmore Coll., 1958; PhD (Danforth Grad. fellow, Woodrow Wilson Grad. fellow), Princeton U., 1962; student, Phila. Conservatory Music, 1955-61. Instr. in classics and music Carleton Coll., Northfield, Minn., 1962-63, asst. prof., 1963-68, assoc. prof., 1968-73, prof., 1973-87, William H. Laird prof. liberal arts, 1974-87, pres. faculty, 1980-82, coll. pres., 1986-87; pres. Skidmore Coll., Saratoga Springs, NY, 1987—99, prof. classics, 1987—99; vis. prof. classics Williams Coll., Williamstown, Mass., 1999—, Harry C. Payne vis. prof. liberal arts, 2000—. Phi Beta Kappa vis. lectr., 1979-92, vis. scholar, 1994-95; vis. prof. classics Princeton U., 1986; recitalist, lectr., especially on contemporary music, at colls., univs. throughout U.S., U.K., on radio and TV; chmn. Hudson-Mohawk Assn., 1990-92, Inst. for Internat. Edn. of Students, 2004—. Author: Only Connect: Three Studies in Greek Tragedy, 1987, Horace's Poetic Journey: A Reading of Odes I-III, 1987, Virginia Woolf and Logan Pearsall Smith, 2002, Virginia Woolf and the Hogarth Press, 2004; editor: Carleton Remembered, 1909-86, 1987, The Not Quite Innocent Bystander: Writings of Edward Steuermann, 1989; contbr. articles to profl. jours. Rsch. fellow NEH, 1969-70, 83-84, Am. Coun. Learned Socs., 1976-77 Mem. Am. Philological Assn., Classical Assn. Atlantic States. Democrat. Mem. United Ch. Of Christ. Avocations: hiking, reading, collecting rugs and books. Home: 5 Birch Run Dr Saratoga Springs NY 12866-1023 E-mail: ddodger@skidmore.edu.

PORTER, DAVID LINDSEY, history and political science professor, writer; b. Holyoke, Mass., Feb. 18, 1941; s. Willis Hubert and Lora Frances (Bowen) P.; m. Marilyn Esther Platt, Nov. 28, 1970; children: Kevin, Andrea. BA magna cum laude, Franklin Coll., 1963; MA, Ohio U., 1965; PhD, Pa. State U., 1970. Asst. prof. history Rensselaer Poly. Inst., Troy, NY, 1970-75, co-dir. Am. studies program, 1972-74; ednl. adminstrv. asst. Civil Svc. Office State of N.Y., Troy, 1975-76; asst. prof. history William Penn U., Oskaloosa, Iowa, 1976-77, assoc. prof. history, 1977-82, prof. history and polit. sci., 1982-86, Louis Tuttle Shangle prof. history and polit. sci., 1986—, chmn. Sperry & Hutchinson Found. lectureship series, 1980-82, acting chair social and behavioral scis. divsn., 2000—01. Supr. legis. internship program Iowa Gen. Assembly, 1978—, records inventory project Mahaska County, 1978-79, internship program Washington Ctr., 1985—; active Franklin D. Roosevelt Meml. Commn.; chpt. adviser Phi Alpha Theta, 1977—. Author: The Seventy-sixth Congress and World War II, 1939-40, 1979, Congress and the Waning of the New Deal, 1980, Michael Jordan: A Biography, 2007; co-author: The San Diego Padres Encyclopedia, 2002; contbr. Dictionary of American Biography, 1981, 1988, 1994, 1995, Directory of Teaching Innovations in History, 1981, The Book of Lists #3, 1983, Biographical Dictionary of Internationalists, 1983, The Hero in Transition, 1983, Herbert Hoover and the Republican Era: A Reconsideration, 1984, The History of Mahaska County, Iowa, 1984, Franklin D. Roosevelt, His Life and Times: An Encyclopedic View, 1985, The Rating Game in American Politics: An Interdisciplinary Approach, 1987, Sport History, 1987, Book of Days, 1988, Sports Encyclopedia North America, 1988, The Harry S. Truman Encyclopedia, 1989, Encyclopedia of Major League Baseball Team Histories: The National League, 1991, Twentieth Century Sports Champions, 1992, Statesmen Who Changed the World, 1993, Ency. Modern Social Issues, 1996, Advanced Placement U.S. History 2, 1996, Encyclopedia of United States Popular Culture, 1997, Encyclopedia of Civil Rights, 1997, Encyclopedia of Propaganda, 1997, Total Padres, 1997, The Scribner Encyclopedia of American Lives, 1998, 1999, 2001, 2004, 2007, American National Biography, 1999, The Sixties in America, 1999, Racial and Ethnic Relations in America, 1999, History of Mahaska County, Iowa, 2000, Great Athletes, rev. edit., 2001, The Scribner Encyclopedia of American Lives, Sports Figures, 2002, Great Events: 1900-2001, rev. edit., 2002, The Scribner Encyclopedia of American Lives, The 1960's, 2003, Encyclopedia of U.S. History, 2003, Dictionary of American History, 3rd. edit., 2003, Encyclopedia of the Great Depression, 2003, Native Americans in Sports, 2004, The Fifties in America, 2005; contbr.: The Seventies in America, 2006; editor, contbr. Biographical Dictionary of American Sports: vols. Baseball, 1987, Football, 1987, Outdoor Sports, 1988, Basketball and Other Indoor Sports, 1989, 1989-92 Supplement for Baseball, Football, Basketball and Other Sports, 1992, 1992-95 Supplement for Baseball, Football, Basketball and Other Sports, 1995, African-American Sports Greats, 1995, Baseball, revised and expanded edit., 3 vols., 2000; Latino and African American Athletes Today, 2004, Basketball: A Biographical Dictionary, 2005, compiler A Cumulative Index to the Biographical Dictionary of American Sports, 1993, assoc. editor (with others) American National Biography, 24 vols., 1999; contbr. articles to profl. jours., local newspapers. Mem. Franklin D. Roosevelt Meml. Commn.; participant Green Bay Packers Project, 1992; historian United Meth. Ch.; official scorer Babe Ruth State Tournament, 2000, 03. Grantee NSF, 1967, NEH, 1974, Rensselaer Poly. Inst., 1974, Eleanor Roosevelt Inst., 1981, William Penn Univ., 1986, 89, 92; recipient Choice Outstanding Acad. Book awards, 1989. Mem. AAUP, Am. Hist. Assn., Orgn. Am. Historians, N.Am. Soc. for Sport History, Soc. History Am. Fgn. Rels., Ctr. for Study of the Presidency, Soc. Am. Baseball Rsch., Friends of the Nat. Baseball Hall of Fame, Popular Culture Assn., Profl. Football Rschrs. Assn., Coll. Football Rschrs. Assn., Coll. Football Hist. Soc., State Hist. Soc. Iowa, Mahaska County Hist. Soc. (v.p.), Iowa State UN Assn. (chmn. ann. assembly 1982, nat. soc. Disting. Svc. award 1981), Mahaska County UN Assn. (v.p.), Oskaloosa Babe Ruth League (bd. dirs.), Oskaloosa Cmty. Choir, Friends of Oskaloosa Pub. Libr. (mem. nominating com.), Friends of the Nat. Baseball Hall of Fame, Phi Alpha Theta, Kappa Delta Pi. Home: 2314 Ridgeway Ave Oskaloosa IA 52577-9109 Office: William Penn Univ Dept Social and Behavioral Scis Divsn Oskaloosa IA 52577-1757

PORTER, DIXIE LEE, retired insurance company executive, consultant; b. Bountiful, Utah, June 7, 1931; d. John Lloyd and Ida May (Robinson) Mathis. BS, U. Calif., Berkeley, 1956, MBA, 1957. CLU. Personnel aide City of Berkeley, 1957-59; employment supr. Kaiser Health Found., LA, 1959-60; personnel analyst UCLA, 1961-63; personnel mgr. Reuben H. Donnelley, Santa Monica, Calif., 1963-64; personnel officer Good Samaritan Hosp., San Jose, Calif., 1965-67; fgn. svc. officer AID, Saigon, Vietnam, 1967-71; gen. agt. Charter Life Ins. Co., LA, 1972-77, Kennesaw Life Ins. Co., Atlanta, 1978—, Phila. Life Ins. Co., San Francisco, 1978—; pres. Womens Ins. Enterprises, Ltd., 1976—; ret., 2007. Cons. in field. Co-chair Comprehensive Health Planning Commn. Santa Clara County, Calif., 1973-76; bd. dirs. Family Care, 1978-80, Aegis Health Corp., 1977-92, U. Calif. Sch. Bus. Adminstrn., Berkeley, 1974-76; task force on equal access to econ. power U.S. Nat. Womens Agenda, 1977—, Lake County Transp. Coun., 2000—. With USMC, 1950-52. Mem. AAUW, CLU Soc., U. Calif. Alumni Assn., U. Calif. Sch. Bus. Adminstrn. Alumni Assn., Bus. and Profl. Women, Prytanean Alumni, The Animal Soc. Los Gatos/Saratoga (pres. 1987-90), The Am. Legion, Beta Gamma Sigma, Phi Chi Theta. Republican. Episcopalian. Office Phone: 707-263-9271.

PORTER, DOUGLAS W., health products executive; V.p. transformation CIGNA HealthCare, 1999—2001, v.p. employer svcs., 2001—02; sr. v.p. client svcs. Express Scripts, Inc., 2002—04, sr. v.p. client and patient svcs., 2004—. Office: Express Scripts Inc 13900 Riverport Dr Maryland Heights MO 63043 Office Phone: 314-770-1666. *

PORTER, ELSA ALLGOOD, writer, educator; b. Amoy, China, Dec. 19, 1928; d. Roy and Petra (Johnsen) Allgood; m. Raeford B. Liles, Mar. 19, 1949 (div. 1959); children: Barbara, Janet; m. G. Hinckley Porter, Nov. 22, 1962; children: David, Brian, Wendy. BA, Birmingham-So. Coll., 1949; MA, U. Ala., 1959; M in Pub. Adminstrn., Harvard U., 1971; LHD (hon.), U. Ala., 1986. With HEW, Washington, 1960-73; with U.S. CSC, Washington, 1973-77; asst. sec. Dept. Commerce, Washington, 1977-81; disting. practitioner in residence Washington Pub. Affairs Ctr., U. So. Calif., Washington, 1982-84; v.p. R & D The Maccoby Group, Washington, 1990-96; sr. fellow Meridian Internat. Inst., 1990—. Chair comml. adv. subcom. NASA, 1997—2003. Fellow World Acad. Art & Scis., Nat. Acad. Pub. Adminstrs.; mem. Women's Nat. Dem. Club. Home: 2309 SW 1st Ave Apt 742 Portland OR 97201-5008

PORTER, ETHEL MAE, publishing executive; b. Phila., July 16, 1947; d. Everette Marmon and Ethel Mae Porter. BA in Econs., Mount Holyoke Coll., 1969; MA in Internat. Rels., Yale U., 1971, MPhil in Am. Studies, 1975, PhD in Am. Studies, 1978. Sr. account exec. CTB McGraw-Hill, Monterey, Calif., 2003—04; v.p. Riverside Pub., Itasca, Ill., 2004—. V.p. Harcourt Ednl. Measurement, San Antonio, 1984—2002. Former mem. San Antonio Libr. Found., San Antonio, Tex. Recipient Educator's Hall of Fame, Phi Delta Kappa, Inc.k Gamma Tau Chpt., 1998. Mem.: Nat. Assn. of Black Sch. Educators (life Policy Fellow, Inst. for Ednl. Leadership 1979-1980). Office: Riverside Pub 425 Spring Lake Dr Itasca IL 60143 Home Phone: 630-372-2541; Office Phone: 630-467-6516. Office Fax: 630-467-7150. Business E-Mail: ethel_porter@hmco.com.

PORTER, GEORGE HOMER, III, physician, medical foundation executive; b. Charlotte, NC, Sept. 7, 1933; s. George Homer Jr. and Sallie Mapp (Jacob) P.; m. Virginia Pillow, Apr. 5, 1958; 1 child, Virginia Mapp (dec.). AB magna cum laude, Duke U., 1954, MD with honors, 1958. Diplomate Am. Bd. Internal Medicine, Am. Bd. Hematology, Am. Bd. Med. Oncology. Intern internal medicine Duke U. Med. Ctr., Durham, NC, 1958-59; asst. resident medicine, instr. medicine Barnes Hosp., Washington U. Sch. Medicine, St. Louis, 1959-60; sr. resident physician The Peter Bent Brigham Hosp., Boston, 1960-61; clin. assoc. medicine, fellow hematology NIH, Bethesda, Md., 1961-64; staff hematologist-oncologist Ochsner Clinic, New Orleans, 1964—; chmn. emeritus, dept. hematology/oncology Ochsner Health Sys., New Orleans; trustee, mem. exec. com. Alton Ochsner Med. Found., New Orleans, 1973—, pres., chief exec. officer, 1980—2001; pres. Ochsner Clinic Found., New Orleans, 2001—. Prin. investigator Southeastern Cancer Study Group, 1973-78; bd. dirs. Eye, Ear, Nose and Throat Hosp., New Orleans, 1986—, Hibernia Corp., Hiberna Nat. Bank, New Orleans, 1980-92. Bd. dirs. Am. Cancer Soc., New Orleans, 1978-89, La. Cancer and Lung Trust Fund, 1980—, Leukemia Soc. Am., 1968-72, The Chamber, New Orleans, 1984-88, Bus. Task Force on Edn., New Orleans, 1985—, Bur. Govtl. Rsch., New Orleans, 1988—, Metrovision Partnership, New Orleans, 1990—. Named Tchr. of Yr., Alton Ochsner Med. Found., 1967. Fellow ACP (life), Internat. Soc. Hematology; mem. AMA, ABA (mem. sect. on med. schs.), AAAS, Internat. Assn. for Study Lung Cancer (founding), Am. Fedn. Clin. Rsch., Am. Hosp. Assn., Am. Assn. Clin. Oncology, Am. Assn. Hematology, Am. Soc. Internal Medicine, Internat. AIDS Soc., La. Med. Soc., Am. Cancer Soc., Orleans Med. Soc. Soc. Surg. Oncology, Am. Coll. Legal Medicine (assoc.-in-medicine, bd. trustees NO/AIDS Task Force, bd. dirs. Acad. Med. Ctr. Consortium), Internat. Soc. for AIDS Edn., Assn. for Health Care Rsch., Mensa, SAR, Royal Soc. St. George, Milton Soc., Confrerie chevaliers du Tastevin, New Orleans Country Club, Boston Club, Century Assn. (N.Y.C.), Pickwick Club, Phi Beta Kappa. Office: Ochsner Clinic Found 1516 Jefferson Hwy New Orleans LA 70121-2429 *

PORTER, GERALD JOSEPH, retired mathematician, educator; b. Elizabeth, NJ, Feb. 27, 1937; s. Fred and Tillie Florence (Friedman) P.; m. Judith Deborah Revitch, June 26, 1960; children: Daniel, Rebecca, Michael. AB, Princeton U., 1958; PhD, Cornell U., 1963; MA (hon.), U. Pa., 1971. Instr. MIT, Cambridge, 1963-65; asst. prof. math. U. Pa., Phila., 1965-69, assoc. prof., 1969-75, prof., 1975—2005, prof. emeritus, 2006—, chmn. undergrad. affairs dept. math., 1971-73, assoc. dean computing Sch. Arts and Scis., 1981-91, dir. Interactive Math. Text Project, 1991-96. Chair-elect faculty senate U. Pa., 1992-93, chair, 1993-94, past chair, 1994-95, 2001-02; prin. investigator NSF MACMATC Grant, 1997-2001; chair U. Pa. Social Responsibility Adv. Com., 2005-. Author: (with D.R. Hill) Interactive Linear Algebra, 1996. Mem. Dem. Com., Haverford Twp., Pa., 1976-82, ward leader, 1980-84, treas., 1984-87. Postdoctoral fellow Office Naval Rsch., 1965-66. Mem. Am. Math. Soc., Math. Assn. Am. (chmn. com. computers in math. edn. 1983-86, chmn. investment com. 1986-2003, bd. govs. 1980-83, 86-2002, mem. fin. com. 1986-2000, exec. com. 1992-2002, chmn. audit and budget com. 1988-90, 92, treas. 1992-2002, chair com. on profl. devel. 1995-2001, chair membership com. 2004—), Nat. Assn. Mathematicians. Democrat. Jewish. Home: 161 Whitemarsh Rd Ardmore PA 19003-1698 Office: U Pa 4N69 DRL 209 S 33rd St Philadelphia PA 19104-6395 Business E-Mail: gjporter@math.upenn.edu.

PORTER, GRANT A., investment banker; married. Natural resources group Lehman Brothers, Inc., NYC and London, 1985—2000, now vice chmn. NYC. Corp. trustee The Taft Sch., Watertown, Conn. Named a Top Dealmaker, Dealmaker mag., 2006. Office: Lehman Brothers Inc 745 Seventh Ave New York NY 10019 Office Phone: 212-526-2027. Office Fax: 212-520-0801. Business E-Mail: gporter@lehman.com. *

PORTER, HENRY HOMES, JR., investor; b. Chgo., Nov. 13, 1934; s. Henry H. and Mary (Kinney) P.; m. Louisa Catherine Perkins, June 10, 1961; children: Mary Porter Johnson, Catherine. AB, Yale U., 1956; MBA, Harvard U., 1962. With Gen. Mills, Inc., Mpls., 1962-76, asst. treas., 1964-67, treas., 1967-76, v.p. fin., treas., 1969-76; sr. v.p., chief fin. officer, dir. Brown & Williamson Industries, Inc., 1977-79, Batus, Inc., 1980; now ret. Chmn. bd. Active Ankle Systems, Inc.; bd. dirs. SEI Investment Co. Lt. (j.g.) USNR, 1957-60. Home: 8 Eaglehead Rd Manchester MA 01944-1549

PORTER, J. REID, lawyer; BA, U. Tex., Austin, 1999; JD, St. Mary's U. San Antonio, 2002. Bar: Tex. 2002. Jud. intern to Hon. Edward Prado US Dist. Ct. (we. dist. Tex.); assoc. Walters, Balido & Crain, Dallas. Life mem. Young Friends of the Ronald McDonald House Dallas. Named a Rising Star, Tex. Super Lawyers mag., 2006. Mem.: ABA, Dallas Assn. Young Lawyers, Dallas Bar Assn., Phi Delta Phi. Office: Walters Balido & Crain 900 Jackson St Founders Sq Ste 600 Dallas TX 75202 Office Phone: 214-347-8344. E-mail: reid.porter@wbclawfirm.com. *

PORTER, J. RIDGELY, III, lawyer; b. Va., Apr. 28, 1948; s. John R and Mary Manning (Barclay) P.; m. DeLane Williams, 1978; 1 child, Eleanor M. BA, U. Va., 1970; JD, Washington & Lee U., 1973. Law clerk to US judge, 1973-74; ptnr. Carr & Porter, 1974—2005; pvt. practice Law Offices J. Ridgely Porter, III, Orange, Va., 2006—. Pres. Va. Internat. Terminals, 1985—92; chmn. bd. Chesapeake Gen. Hosp., 1986—96; owner Cattle Farms. Mem.: ABA, Va. Bar Assn., Met. Club (DC). Episcopalian. Office Phone: 540-661-0361. Personal E-mail: ridgeporter@aol.com.

PORTER, JAMES KENNETH, retired judge; b. Newport, Tenn., Apr. 6, 1934; s. John Calhoun and Bessie Betis (Crouch) P.; m. Evelyn Janet Rhodes, Sept. 17, 1955; children: Jane Caroline, James Kenneth Jr. BS, U. Tenn., Knoxville, 1955, JD, 1957. Bar: Tenn. 1957, U.S. Dist. Ct. (ea. dist.) Tenn. 1958, U.S. Ct. Appeals (6th cir.) 1971. Ptnr. Porter, Porter & Dunn, Porter & Porter, Newport, 1957-74; state rep. Tenn. Gen. Assembly, Nashville, 1961-65, minority fl. leader, 1963-65; county atty. Cocke County, Tenn., 1961-63, commr. County Election Commn. Tenn., 1966-72, chmn. Tenn., 1968-70; mem. Tenn. Senate, Nashville, 1972-74; state cir. judge 4th Jud. Cir., Newport, 1974-93; ret., 1993; state presiding judge 4th Jud. Cir., Newport, 1984-86, 88-90, 1992-93; judgeship nominee U.S. Dist. Ct. (ea. dist.), Tenn., 1986; Tenn. Ct. Appeals nominee, 1990. Del. S.E. Law Rev. Conf., Durham, N.C., 1957, Nat. Conf. State Legislator Leaders, Boston, 1963; discussion leader Nat. Jud. Coll., Reno, 1981, faculty adviser, 1982; mem. Gov.'s Correction Overcrowding Commn., Nashville, 1985-86. Contbr. articles to U. Tenn. Law Rev., 1956-57, editor in chief, 1957. Active Farm Bur., 1962-82; mem. adv. coun., trustee Walters State Community Coll., Morristown, Tenn., 1975-86. Mem. ABA (Tenn. jud. del. 1984), Tenn. Jud. Conf. (v.p. 1980-81), Tenn. Trial Judges Assn. (bd. dirs. 1976-86, pres. 1982-85), Tenn. Bar Assn. (spl. trial counsel 1973-76), Cocke County Bar Assn., Smoky Mountain Country Club (bd. dirs. 1964-67, v.p. 1966-67), Order of Coif, Sigma Alpha Epsilon (Highest Effort Law award 1986), Phi Delta Phi. Republican. Baptist. Avocations: golf, gardening, guitar. Home: 306 North St Newport TN 37821-2413 Office: 106 S Mims Ave Newport TN 37821-3125 Personal E-mail: porterk@planetc.com, porterjk@gmail.com.

PORTER, JAMES MORRIS, retired judge; b. Cleve., Sept. 14, 1931; s. Emmett Thomas and Mary (Connell) P.; m. Helen Marie Adams, May 31, 1952; children: James E., Thomas W., William M., Daniel J. AB, John Carroll U., 1953; JD, U. Mich., 1957. Bar: Ohio 1957. Assoc. firm M.B. & H.H. Johnson, Cleve., 1957-62, McAfee, Hanning, Newcomer, Hazlett & Wheeler, Cleve., 1962-67; ptnr. firm Squire, Sanders & Dempsey, Cleve., 1967-92; judge Ohio Ct. Appeals, 8th Dist., Cleve., 1993-2000, Cuyahoga County Common Pleas Ct., Cleve., 2001. 1st lt. U.S. Army, 1953-55. Fellow Am. Coll. Trial Lawyers; mem. The Country Club (Cleve.). Republican. Roman Catholic.

PORTER, JEFFREY R., lawyer; b. 1963; m. Jill Porter; 2 children. BA with high honors in Polit. Sci., cum laude, Bates Coll., 1985; JD, Cornell U., 1988. Bar: Mass. 1988, US Dist. Ct. (Dist. Mass.). Ptnr., chair environ. law sect. Mintz, Levin, Cohn, Ferris, Glovsky & Popeo PC, Boston. Treas., bd. dirs. Boston Harbor Island Alliance; vice chmn., bd. trustees Nature Conservancy Mass. Chpt.; mem. dept. environ. protection Bur. Waste Site Clean Up Adv. Com. Mem.: AIM, NAIOP, ABA (environ., energy and resources sect., litig. sect.), Boston Bar Assn., Phi Beta Kappa. Office: Mintz Levin Cohn Ferris Glovsky & Popeo PC One Financial Center Boston MA 02111 Office Phone: 617-348-1711. Office Fax: 617-542-2241. Business E-Mail: jporter@mintz.com.

PORTER, JILL, journalist; b. Phila., Aug. 5, 1946; d. Sidney and Mae (Merion) Chalfin; m. Eric Porter, Mar. 7, 1970 (div. 1975); m. Fred Hamilton, Oct. 28, 1983; 1 child, Zachary. BA, Temple U., 1968. Pub. rels. Manning Smith P.R., Phila., 1968-69; reporter Norristown Times Herald, Norristown, Pa., 1969-72, The Trentonian, Trenton, NJ, 1972-75, The Phila. Daily News, Phila., 1975-79, columnist, 1979—. Instr. Temple U., 1976—80. Contbr. articles to numerous mags. Vol. Phila. Futures, 1994, 95, 96, Phila. Cares, 1997, Career Wardrobe, 2006. Recipient numerous journalism awards. Avocations: dance, biking, reading. Home: 134 Rolling Rd Bala Cynwyd PA 19004-2615 Office: Phila Media Holding LLC Phila Daily News 400 N Broad St Philadelphia PA 19130-4015 Office Phone: 215-854-5850. E-mail: porterj@phillynews.com.

PORTER, JIM, human resources specialist; m. Deb Porter; 4 children. Grad., Northwest Mo. State U. Various human resources positions Trane Co., La Crosse, Wis., Hoechst-Roussell Pharmaceuticals, Inc., Somerville, NJ, ELBA Corp., Denver; recruiter to sr. v.p. and chief adminstrn. officer Honeywell Internat., 1982—2003; sr. v.p. human resources Carlson Cos., Inc., Minnetonka, Minn., 2003—05, exec. v.p. human resources, 2005—. Office: Carlson Cos Inc 701 Carlson Pkwy Minnetonka MN 55305 Office Phone: 763-212-1000. Office Fax: 763-212-2219.

PORTER, JOHN E., lawyer; b. Cin., Oct. 23, 1958; s. Robert Carl Jr. and Joanne (Patterson) P.; children: Rebecca Sheyne, Robin Leigh. BSEE with distinction, Stanford U., 1980, JD, 1983. Bar: Calif. 1983, U.S. Ct. Appeals (9th cir.) 1983, U.S. Dist. Ct. (cen. dist.) Calif. 1984. Law clk. to Hon. Procter Hug U.S. Ct. Appeals, ninth cir., 1983—84; ptnr. Paul, Hastings, Janofsky & Walker LLP, LA, mem. policy com. Bd. visitors Stanford (Calif.) Law Sch., 1990-94. Mem. Stanford Law Soc. of So. Calif. (treas. 1990-95). Office: Paul Hastings Janofsky & Walker LLP 515 S Flower St Los Angeles CA 90071-2228 Office Phone: 213-683-6305. Office Fax: 213-996-3305. E-mail: johnporter@paulhastings.com.

PORTER, JOHN EDWARD, former congressman; b. Evanston, Ill., June 1, 1935; s. Harry H. and Beatrice V. P.; 5 children. Attended, MIT; BSBA, Northwestern U., 1958; JD with distinction, U. Mich., 1961; degree (hon.), Northwestern U., Tufts U., Mt. Sinai Sch. Medicine, Oreg. Health Scis. U., Howard U., Rush U. Bar: Ill. 1961, D.C. 2005, U.S. Supreme Ct. 1968. Former honor law grad. atty., appellate div. Dept. Justice, Washington; mem. Ill. Ho. of Reps., 1973—79, 96-106th Congresses from 10th Ill. Dist., Ill., 1980-2001; ptnr. Hogan & Hartson, Washington, 2001—. Founder, co-chmn. Congl. Human Rights Caucus; legis. sponsor Radio Free Asia; founder Congl. Coalition on Population and Devel.; chmn. Global Legislators Organized for a Balanced Environment; chmn. Commn. on Security and Cooperation in Europe; chmn. com. future roles acad. health ctrs. Inst. Medicine, NAS, chmn. com. on presdl. and fed. adv. com. sci. and tech.; co-chmn. Ctr. for Global Devel. Commn. on Weak States and Nat. Security Past editor: Mich. Law Rev. Bd. dirs., vice chair PBS, Rand Corp.; vice chair Rsch.! Am.; chair Found. for NIH; bd. dirs. Am. Heart Assn., Brookings Instn., Chgo. Botanic Gardens, Population Resource Ctr., Princeton, NJ; trustee emeritus John F. Kennedy Ctr. for Performing Arts. Recipient Best Legislator award League of Conservation Voters, 1973, Ind. Voters Ill., 1974, Chgo. Crime Commn., 1976, Lorax award Global Tomorrow Coalition, 1989, Spirit of Enterprise award U.S. C. of C., 1988, 89, 90, Golden Bulldog award Watchdogs of the Treasury, 12 times, Taxpayer's Friend award Nat. Taxpayers Union, Taxpayer Superhero award Grace Commn.'s Citizens Against Government Waste, Mary Wood Lasker award for pub. svc., Edwin C. Whitehead award Rsch! Am., Carter award Nat. Found. Infectious Diseases, Pub. Svc. award Fedn. Am. Socs. for Exptl. Biology, Svc award Am. Soc. Cell Biology, Disting. Pub. Svc. award Am. Soc. Microbiology, Pub. Svc. Excellence award Assn. Am. Med. Colls., Lifetime Achievement award Juvenile Diabetes Found., Decade of Brain award Nat. Found. Brain Rsch., Lifetime Achievement award Am. Psychiat. Assn. and Acad. Consortium, Dr. Nathan Davis award AMA, Morris K. Udall Pub. Svc. award Michael J. Fox Found., Pub. Health Continuum award Coalition for Health Funding, Beacon award Am. Soc. Assn. Execs., Henry M. Jackson Leadership award Union Couns. for Soviet Jewry, Anatoly Scharansky Freedom award Chgo. Action for Soviet Jewry, others. Mem.: Inter-Am. Dialogue, Coun. Fgn. Rels. Republican. Office: Hogan & Hartson 555 13th St NW Washington DC 20004 Home Phone: 708-684-0890; Office Phone: 202-637-5695. E-mail: jeporter@hhlaw.com.

PORTER, JOHN FRANCIS, III, banker; b. Wilmington, Del., Sept. 17, 1934; s. John Francis, Jr. and Eloise Wilhelmina (Berlinger) P.; m. Ann Mayfield, Sept. 8, 1956; children: Leslie Gibson, Nina Porter Winfield, Sophie Porter Rohrer. BA, U. Va., 1956; MBA, U. Del., 1965. With Del. Trust Co., Wilmington, 1958-97, asst. treas., 1960-66, sec., 1966-68, v.p., sec., 1968-72, sr. v.p., sec., 1972-75, exec. v.p., 1975-79, pres., 1979-88; chmn., chief exec. officer Del. Trust Co. (now Wachovia), 1988-97; vice chmn. BANKPAC, 1982-86, chmn., 1986-88, Del. Trust Capital Mgmt., 1988-97. Mem. Ct. on Judiciary Preliminary Investigatory Com., 1991-97. Mem. bank adv. bd. State of Del., 1969-71; mem. coun. banking State of Del., 1970-2005, chmn., 1976-2005; trustee Alfred I. duPont Testamentary Trust, 1995—; pres. Wilmington and Brandywine Cemetery, 1974—; bd. dirs., trustee, mem. fin. com. mem. exec. com., chmn. audit com. Christiana Care, 1985-99; bd. dirs. Penjerdel, 1989-97, state v.p., 1990-97; bd. gov. Winterthur Corp. Coun., 1989-95, chmn., 1993-95; bd. dirs. Winterthur Mus., 1993-95; bd. dirs. Nemours Found., 1995—, chmn., 2005—, The Glenmede Trust Co. N.A., 2000—. Capt. arty., U.S. Army, 1957. Mem. Am. Bankers Assn. (govt. rels. coun. 1984-88), Del. Bankers Assn. (pres. 1984-85, bd. dirs. 1981-87), Del. Bus. Roundtable (vice chmn. exec. coun. 1989-92, chmn. 1993-94), Wilmington Country Club (bd. dirs. 1970—, pres. 1973-74), Wilmington Club (bd. govs. 1980-89), Nassau Club, Wilmington Country Club (bd. dir.), Wilmington Club (bd. govs. 1980-89), Hole In The Wall Golf Club (Naples, Fla.), Naples Yacht Club. Office: The Nemours Found 1600 Rockland Rd Wilmington DE 19803-3607 Home Phone: 302-658-9482; Office Phone: 302-651-6048.

PORTER, JOHN WESTON, counselor, consultant, administrator; b. Fostoria, Ohio, Dec. 26, 1939; s. William Thomas and Ida Elizabeth (Carter) Porter. Student, U. Cin., 1958; BA, Heidelberg Coll., 1961; MA in Cmty. Psychology, U. DC, 1973, MA in Counseling, 1975; postgrad., Antioch Coll., Yellow Springs, Ohio, 1974, Frostburg U., Md., 1970, George Washington U., Washington, DC, 1968. Cert. Nat. Bd. Cert. Counselors, DC. Claims rep. Social Security Adminstrn., Cleve. and Akron, Ohio, 1961-62; office mgr. Phoenix Cos., Washington and LA, 1966-70; rschr. Frostburg U., U. DC, 1970-73; edn. and career devel. specialist DC Pub. Schs., 1973-79, career edn. unit, 1979-83, Career Assessment Ctr., 1983-85, asst. dir. guidance and counseling, 1985-95; mem. cmty. adv. coun. Washington Hosp. Ctr., 1987—. Counseling mentor DC Pub. Schs., 1998—2003; dir. Westport Consulting, 2001—; cons. DC Pub. Sch. HiScip program, New Couns. Mentor, 2001—02. Contbr. articles to profl. jours. Vice chmn. adv. coun. Group Health Assn., Washington, 1977—79, 1981—83; sec. Md.-DC Am. Coll. Testing Coun., 1987—88, vice chair, 1988—90, chair, 1990—91, mem. exec. com., 1991—; mem. adv. com. Children's Edn. Found., 1989—93, mem. fund raising com., 1989—, exec. bd., 1992—, asst. treas., 1992—93, treas., 1993—95; pres. N.E. Hill Found., 1990—92; mem. com. DC Career and Tech. Edn. Task Force, 2000; team chmn. Wilson HS, 2002, mem. student mgmt. task force, 2002—03, grant rev. panelist, 1998, 2002—03; mem. planning com. Friends of Turkey Thicket Rec. Ctr., 2005, cons., 2005—; treas. Tues. Evening Square Dance Group, 2006—. Lt. (j.g.) USN, 1962—66, lt. USNR. Recipient award, Ohio Acad. Sci., 1954—57, Cleve. Plain Dealer Operation Demonstrate, 1956, Svc. award, Heidleberg Coll. Publs., 1961, Recognition cert., DC Assn. Career Devel., 1975, 1976, DC City Coun., 1982, Children's Edn. Found., 1990, Recognition award Outstanding Contbn. to Guidance and Counseling, 1987, Commn. Svc. award, Advisory Neighborhood Commn., 2004, 2005. Mem.: ACA (counselor adv.-legis.), Coun. Accreditation Counseling and Related Ednl. Programs (site visit team 2000—), Assn. Counselor Edn. and Supervision, DC Career Devel. Assn. (exec. bd. 0983—1990, treas. 1983—86), DC Sch. Counselors Assn. (Outstanding Leadership award 1994), Nat. Career Devel. Assn. (assembly del. 1984, master career coun. 2003), Am. Sch. Counselors Assn. (chair rsch. com. 1990—91, career guidance com., leadership recognition cert. 1987), Am. Counseling Assn. (chmn. govt. rels. N. Atlantic region 1980—81, cert. Outstanding Contbn. in Govt. Rels. 1982, Recognition award 1987), DC Counseling Assn. (treas. 1975—77, exec. bd. 1975—80, sec. 1977—78, pres. 1979—80, trustee 1989—92, treas. 1991—92, trustee 2003—04, counselor adv.-legis., Mem. of the Yr. 1980, Outstanding Leadership award 1980), Phi Delta Kappa (edn. found. rep. 1993—95, v.p. membership 1995—96, pres. 1996—97, MACI project adv. coun. Hosp. Sick Children 1997—98, rev. panel DC vocat. edn. grants 1998, lic. profl. counselor, DC). Home: 821 Taylor St NE Washington DC 20017-2009 Personal E-mail: jw.wb.porter@erols.com.

PORTER, JOHN WILSON, educational association administrator, director; b. Ft. Wayne, Ind., Aug. 13, 1931; BA, Albion Coll., Mich., 1953, D (hon.) in Pub. Adminstrn., 1973; MA, Mich. State U., East Lansing, 1957, PhD, 1962, LLD (hon.), 1977, Cleary Coll., Howell, Mich., 1987, LLD, 1989; LHD, Adrian Coll., Mich., 1970, U. Detroit, 1979; LLD, Western Mich. U., Kalamazoo, 1971, Ea. Mich. U., Ypsilanti, 1975; HHD, Kalamazoo Coll., 1973, Detroit Coll. Bus., 1975, Madonna Coll., Livonia, Mich., 1977; DEd, Detroit Inst. Tech., 1978; AA, Schoolcraft Coll., Livonia, Mich., 1979; DBA, Lawrence Inst. Tech., 1988. Counselor Lansing Pub. Schs., Mich., 1953-58; cons. Mich. Dept. Pub. Instrn., 1958-61; dir. Mich. Higher Edn. Assistance Authority, 1961-65; assoc. supt. for higher edn. Mich. Dept. Edn., 1966-69, state supt. schs., 1969-79; pres. Ea. Mich. U., Ypsilanti, 1979-89; v.p. Nat. Bd. for Profl. Teaching Standards, 1989; gen. supt. Detroit Pub. Schs., 1989-91; CEO Urban Edn. Alliance, Inc., Ypsilanti, Mich., 1991—2003. Mem. numerous profl. commns. and bds., 1959—, including Commn. on Financing Postsecondary Edn., 1972-74, Commn. for Reform Secondary Edn., Kettering Found., 1972-75, Edn. Commn. of States, 1973-79, Nat. Commn. on Performance-Based Edn., 1974-76, Nat. Commn. on Manpower Policy, 1974-79, Mich. Employment and Tng. Svcs. Coun., 1976-79, Nat. Adv. Coun. on Social Security, 1977-79, Commn. on Ednl. Credit, Am. Coun. on Edn., 1977-80; task panel on mental health of family Commn. on Mental Health, 1977-80; mem. Nat. Coun. for Career Edn. (HEW), 1974-76; pres. bd. dirs. Chief State Sch. Officers, 1974-79; pres. Coun. Chief State Sch. Officers, 1977-78; bd. dirs. Comerica Bank, 1986-2002; former chmn. bd. Coll. Entrance Exam. Bd., 1984-86; apptd. by Gov. John Engler, Mich. Sch. Dist. Accountability Bd., 1999, Gov. Jennifer M. Granholm, Lt. Gov.'s Commn. on Higher Edn. and Econ. Growth, 2004. Author: Mich. Internat. Student Problem Inventory, 1962, Educational Leadership for the 21st Century, 2006. Mem. East Lansing Human Relations Commn., 1965-69, Mich. Martin Luther King, Jr. Holiday Commn., 1986-90, Gov. James Blanchard's Blue Ribbon Commn. on Welfare Reform, Nat. Measurement Coun., 1972-78, Mich. Sch. Dist. Accountability Bd., 1999, Catherine McAuley Health Systems Bd., 1990-2000, Lt. Gov.'s Commn. Higher Edn. and Econ. Growth, 2004; trustee East Lansing Edgewood United Ch., 1963-79, Nat. Urban League, 1973-79, Charles Stewart Mott Found., 1981—, Albion Coll., 1989-; bd. dirs. Mich. Congress Parents and Tchrs., 1958-68, Mich. Internat. Council, 1977—; chmn. Am. Assn. State Colls. and US Task Force on Excellence in Edn., 1983; mem. bd. overseers com. for Grad. Sch., Harvard U., 1980-88; mem. edn. com. NAACP; convener goal 6 Nat. Edn. Goals Panel, 1990-2000. Recipient numerous awards including Disting. Svc. award Mich. Congress Parents and Tchrs., 1963, Disting. Svc. award NAACP, Lansing, 1968; cert. of outstanding achievement Delta Kappa chpt. Phi Beta Sigma, 1970; award for disting. svc. Assn. Ind. Colls. and Univs. Mich., 1974; Disting. Alumni award Coll. Edn., Mich. State U., 1974; award for disting. svc. to edn Mich. State U., 1974; Disting. Alumni award, 1979; award for disting. svc. to edn. in Mich. Mich. Assn. Secondary Sch. Prins., 1974; Pres.'s award as disting. educator Nat. Alliance Black Sch. Educators, 1977; Marcus Foster Disting. Educator award, 1979; recognition award Mich. Ednl. Rsch. Assn., 1978; recognition award Mich. Assn. Secondary Sch. Prins., 1978; recognition award Mich. Assn. Intermediate Sch. Adminstrs., 1979; recognition award Mich. Assn. Sch. Adminstrs., 1979; Mich. Sch. Bus. Ofcls., 1979; resolution Mich. State Legislature, 1978; Anthony Wayne award Coll. Edn., Wayne State U., 1979; Educator of Decade award Mich. Assn. State and Fed. Program Specialists, 1979; Spirit of Detroit award Detroit City Coun., 1981; Disting. Svc. award Ypsilanti Area C. of C., 1988; Philip A. Hart award Mich. Women's Hall of Fame, 1988; Summit award Greater Detroit C. of C., 1991; Mich. State C. of C. award 1991; Olivet Coll. award for Leadership and Social Responsibility, 2001; Lifetime Achievement award Albion Coll., 2003; inducted Mich. Edn. Hall of Fame, 1992; John W. Porter Disting. Chair endowed at Eastern Mich. U., 1999; Coll. of Edn. bldg. at Ea. Mich. U. named for him, 1999; bestowed 1st ever John W. Porter Leadership award Detroit Pub. TV, 2006. Mem.: NAACP (life), Am. Assn. Sch. Adminstrs., Am. Assn. State Colls. and Univs. (pres.'s coun., chmn. task force on excellence in edn. 1983), Greater Detroit C. of C. (Summit award 1991), Mich. State C. of C. (Disting. Svc. and Leadership award 1991), Mich. PTA (hon. life), Ea. Mich. U. Alumni Assn. (disting. svc. award 1997), Tuskeegee Airmen (Disting. Svc. award 1991), Econ. Club (dir. 1979), Sigma Pi Phi, Phi Delta Kappa.

PORTER, JON CHRISTOPHER, SR., congressman; b. Ft. Dodge, Iowa, May 16, 1955; m. Laurie Porter; children: J. Christopher, Nicole. Student, Briar Cliff Coll. Electronic appliance repair-distbn. store mgr., 1978—81; agt. Farmers' Ins. Grp. Corp., 1982—88, dist. mgr., 1988—2000; mem. City Coun., Boulder City, Nev., 1983—93, mayor, 1987—91; mem. Nev. State Senate from dist. 1, 1995—2002, US Congress from 3rd Nev. dist., 2003—. Mem. U. Nev. Inst. for Ins. and Risk Mgmt., Las Vegas; Rep. majority whip US Congress, 1997, mem. ways and means com., mem. budget com. Chair bd. dirs. Las Vegas Events, pres., 1993-95; charter bd. dirs. So. Nev. Water Authority; bd. dirs. Las Vegas Conv. and Visitors Authority; bd. dirs. Nev. League of Cities; mem. civilian mil. coun. Nellis AFB. Named Elected Official of Yr., Nev. League of Cities, 1988; recipient Crystal Apple award, Clark County, Nev. Sch. Dist., 1998, Friend of the Shareholder award, Am. Shareholders Assn., 2004, Hero of the Taxpayer award, Americans for Tax Reform, 2004, Small Bus. Adv. award, Small Bus. Survival Com., 2004. Republican. Roman Cath. Office: US House Reps 218 Cannon House Office Bldg Washington DC 20515-2803 Office Phone: 202-225-3252. *

PORTER, JUDITH DEBORAH REVITCH, sociologist; b. Phila., Mar. 26, 1940; d. Eugene and Esther (Tulchinsky) Revitch; m. Gerald Joseph Porter, June 26, 1960; children: Daniel, Rebecca, Michael. Student, Vassar Coll., 1958-60; BA, Cornell U., 1962, MA, 1963; PhD, Harvard U., 1967. Lectr. Bryn Mawr (Pa.) Coll., 1966-67, asst. prof., 1967-73, assoc. prof., 1973-79, prof. sociology, 1979—, chair dept. sociology, 1987-93. Author: Black Child, White Child: The Development of Racial Attitudes, 1971; contbr. articles to profl. jours. Committeeperson Haverford Twp. Dem. Party, 1976-96; bd. dirs. Phila. AIDS Fund, 1992-98, Phila. Com. End Homelessness, 1984-, Women Against Abuse, 1995-; vice-chmn. exec. com. drugs and alcohol, Mayor, Phila.; vol. Congreso de Latinos Unidos, Inc., Greater Phila. Coalition Against Hunger. Recipient Shannon award NIMH, 1992-94; Ford Found. fellow, 1973-74; NSF fellow, 1967; NIDA grant Co-PI, 1998-2001. Mem. APHA, Am. Sociol. Assn., Phi Beta Kappa, Phi Kappa Phi. Jewish. Address: 161 Whitemarsh Rd Ardmore PA 19003-1634 Office: Bryn Mawr Coll Dept Sociology Bryn Mawr PA 19010 Business E-Mail: jporter@brynmawr.edu.

PORTER, LILIANA ALICIA, artist, photographer, painter, printmaker, filmmaker; b. Buenos Aires, Oct. 6, 1941; came to U.S., 1964, naturalized, 1982; d. Julio and Margarita (Galetar) P.; m. Luis Camnitzer, 1965 (div. 1978); m. Alan B. Wiener, May 28, 1980 (div. 1991). Grad., Nat. Sch. Fine Arts, Argentina, 1963. Co-dir., instr. Studio Camnitzer-Porter summer workshops, Lucca, Italy, 1974, 75, 76, 77; prof. art Queens Coll., CUNY, NYC, 1991—2007, ret., 2007. Adj. lectr. SUNY Coll., Old Westbury, N.Y., 1974-76, Purchase br., 1987; co-dir. Studio Porter-Wiener, N.Y.C., 1979-87. One-woman shows of prints/paintings/photographs include Galeria Artemultiple, Buenos Aires, Argentina, 1977, 78, Galleria Arte Comunale, Adro, Brescia, Italy, 1977, Hundred Acres Gallery, NYC, 1977, Mus. Modern Art, Cali, Colombia, 1978, Center for Interamerican Relations, NYC, 1980, Galeria Arte Nuevo, Buenos Aires, 1980, Barbara Toll Fine Arts, NYC, 1979, 81, 82, 84, Galerie Jolliet, Montreal, 1983, Museo de Arte Contemporaneo, Panama City, Panama, 1984, Dolan/Maxwell Gallery, Phila., 1985, U. Alta., Edmonton, 1985, Dolan/Maxwell Gallery, Phila., 1985, Galería Luigi Marrozzini, San Juan, PR, 1986, Galería-Taller, Museo de Arte Moderno, Cali, Colombia, 1987, The Space, Boston, 1988, Syracuse U., NY, 1990, Steinbaum-Krauss Gallery, NYC, 1993, Galeria Ruth Benzacar, Buenos Aires, 1994, U. Art Gallery, N.Mex. State U., Las Cruces, 1995, Monique Knowlton Gallery, 1996, Ruth Benzacar Gallery, NY, 1997, Mus. de Bellas Artes Juan Manuel Blanes, Montevideo, Uruguay, 1997, Espacio Mínimo, Murcia, Espana, 1998, 2000, Annina Nosei Gallery, NY, 1999, 2000, 02, 04, Artcore Gallery, Toronto, Can., 1999, Ruth Benzacar Gallery, Buenos Aires, 2000, Sicardi Gallery, Houston, 2000, 02, 06, Ctr. Photography, Woodstock, NY, 2000, Phoenix Mus., 2000, Galeria Espacio/Mimimo, Madrid, 2000, 03, 04, Brito-Cimino, Sao Paulo, Brazil, 2001, Casas Riegner Gallery, Miami, Fla., 2003, Hosfelt Gallery, San Francisco, 2003, 06, Centro Cultural Recoleta, Buenos Aires, 2003, Palacio Aguirre, Cartagena, Spain, 2004, Eli Marsh Gallery, Amherst Coll., Mass., 2004, Annina Nosei Gallery, NYC, 2004, Galeria Ruth Benzacar, Buenos Aires, 2005, Carrie Secrist Gallery, Chgo., 2005, Sala de Veronicas, Murcia, Spain, 2005, Galeria Petrus, San Juan, PR, 2005, Galeria Casas Riegner, Bogota, Colombia, 2005, Goya-Girl Contemporary, Balt., 2006, Hosfelt Gallery, NYC, 2007, Galleria Valentina Bonomo, Rome, 2007, Galeria Espacio Mimimo, Madrid, Spain, 2007; retrospective exhibits 1968-90 Fundacion San Telmo, Buenos Aires, 1990, Museo Nacional de Artes Plasticas, Montevideo, Uruguay, 1991, Centro de

Recepciones del Gobierno, San Juan, PR, 1991, Bronx Mus. Art, NYC, 1992, retrospective exhibit Archer Huntington Art Gallery U. Tex. Austin, 1993, Staller Ctr. for the Art SUNY at Stony Brook, NY, 1998, Centro Cultural Recoleta, Sala Cronopios, Buenos Aires, Argentina, 2003; exhibited in numerous group shows including most recently El Mus. del Barrio, NYC, 2000, Casa de America, Madrid, 2000, Contemporary Mus., Balt., 2000, NY, others, Mass. Coll. Art, Huntington Gallery, Boston, 2001, ARCO, Madrid, 2001, Centro Cultural Borges, Buenos Aires, 2001, Peter Lewis Theater, Guggenheim Mus., NY, 2001, Hosfelt Gallery, San Francisco, 2001, Fundacion Telefonica, Madrid, 2001, Fundacion Joan Miro, Barcelona, 2001, Carrie Secrist Gallery, Chgo., 2001, Contemporary Art Ctr., NY, 2001, The Mahady Contemporary Gallery at Marywood U., Scranton, Pa., 2002, Kunst Werke, Berlin, 2003; represented in permanent collections Mus. Phila., Mus. Modern Art, NYC, RCA Corp., NYC, NY Public Libr., NYC, La Biblioteque Nationale, Paris, France, Museo del Grabado, Buenos Aires, Museo Universitario, Mexico City, Mexico, Museo de Art Moderno, Cali, Colombia, Museo de Bellas Artes, Caracas, Venezuela, Met. Mus. Art, NYC, Daros Collection Zurich, Tate Modern, London. Recipient 1st prize Argentinian Art 78 Mus. Fine Arts, Buenos Aires, 1978, Grand Prix XI, Internat. Print Biennial, Cracow, Poland, 1986, 1st prize VII Latin Am. Print Biennial, San Juan, Puerto Rico, 1986; fellow Guggenheim Found., 1980-81, N.Y. Found. for the Arts, 1985, grantee, 1999. Studio: 720 Greenwich St 10G New York NY 10014 Personal E-mail: lilianaporter@gmail.com. E-mail: lilianaporter@earthlink.net.

PORTER, MARC BENNETT, auction house executive; b. July 30, 1960; BA, U. Pa., BS in Econs., 1982; JD, Yale U., New Haven, 1987. Various positions including assoc. in bus. devel. and mgr. estates and appraisals Christie's Fine Art Auctioneers, NYC, 1990—96, internat. bus. dir. 19th and 20th century art, 2000—03, internat. mng. dir., 2003—; pres. Christie's Am., 2004—. Office: Christies Fine Art Auctioneers 20 Rockefeller Plz New York NY 10020 Office Phone: 212-636-2372. Personal E-mail: MarcPorter@aol.com.

PORTER, MICHAEL E., competitive strategy educator; b. Ann Arbor, Mich., May 23, 1947; s. Howard Eugene and Stana (Vernerova) P. BS, Princeton U., 1969; MBA, Harvard U., 1971, PhD, 1973. Asst. prof. Grad. Sch. Bus., Harvard U., 1973-77, assoc. prof., 1977-82, prof., 1982—, C. Roland Christensen Prof. Bus. Admin., Bishop William Lawrence U. Prof., 2000—. Bd. dirs. Alpha-Beta Techs., Hyatt Mgmt. Co., Inforte, Corp.; bd. advisers, WebEx Communications Inc.; adviser to several fgn. govts., including Canada, India, Ireland, New Zealand, Portugal, the U.K. Author: Interbrand, Choice, Strategy and Bilateral Market Power, 1976, Competitive Strategy: Techniques for Analyzing Industries and Competitors, 1980 (Outstanding Acad. Book selection Choice mag. 1980-81), (with R.E. Caves and A.M. Spence) Competition in the Open Economy, 1980, Competitive Advantage: Techniques for Achieving and Sustaining Superior Performance, 1985, Competition in Global Industries, 1986, The Competitive Advantage of Nations, 1990; mem. editorial adv. bd. Long Range Planning, Antitrust Law and Econs. Rev. Mem. Presdl. Commn. on Indsl. Competitiveness, 1983, Gov's Council on Econ. Growth and Technology, Mass., 1991. Served to capt. AUS, 1969-76. Recipient David A. Wells Prize in Econs. Harvard U., 1973-74, McKinsey award for best article Harvard Bus. Rev., 1979, 87, Charles Coolidge Parlin award Am. Mktg. Assn., 1991, Adam Smith award, Nat. Assoc. Bus. Economists, 1997. Fellow Acad. Mgmt. (George R. Terry award 1985), Fin. analysts Fedn. (Graham and Dodd award 1980), Internat. Acad. Mgmt.; mem. Am. Mktg. Assn., Strategic Mgmt. Soc. Clubs: Cap and Gown. Republican. Office: Harvard Bus Sch Ludcke House 690 Soldiers Field Rd Boston MA 02163-1317 Office Phone: 617-495-6309. Office Fax: 617-547-8543. E-mail: mporter@hbs.edu. *My work has sought to make a positive impact on the ability of companies to compete effectively and on the ability of government to play a constructive role in that process. I have tried to bring a new level of sophistication to the understanding of competition by combining the tools of an economist with a strong awareness of and interest in the problems of the practicing manager. I have also sought to influence public policy by bringing to its formulation a closer awareness of the realities of competition than is embodied in contemporary economic theory.*

PORTER, MICHAEL PELL, lawyer; b. Indpls., Mar. 31, 1940; s. Harold Troxel and Mildred Maxine (Pell) P.; m. Alliene Laura Jenkins, Sept. 23, 1967 (div.); 1 child, Genevieve Natalie Porter Eason; m. Janet Kay Smith Hayes, Feb. 13, 1983 (div.). Student, DePauw U., Greencastle, Ind., 1957-58; BA, Tulane U., New Orleans, 1961, LLB, 1963. Bar: La. 1963, U.S. Ct. Mil. Appeals 1964, N.Y. 1969, Hawaii 1971. Clk. U.S. Ct. Appeals (5th cir.), New Orleans, 1963; assoc. Sullivan & Cromwell, NYC, 1968-71, Cades Schutte Fleming & Wright, Honolulu, 1971-74, ptnr., 1975-94; mem. faculty Addis Ababa (Ethiopia) U. Sch. Law, 1995-99; sr. regulatory advisor Egyptian Capital Market Authority, Cairo, 1999—2002; advisor capital market Palestinian Nat. Authority, 2002—03; lectr. Arab Acad. Banking and Fin. Scis., 2003; legal adv. Securities and Exch. Commn. Bangladesh, 2004—05. Legal advisor St. Matthews Anglican Ch., Addis Ababa, Ethiopia, 1995—99; cons, Rep. of Yemen, 1997; mem. deans coun. Law Sch. Tulane U., 1981—88; dep. vice chancellor Episcopal Diocese Hawaii, 1980—88, chancellor, 1988—94, Episcopal Ch., Micronesia, 1988—95; legal cons. Bangladesh SEC, 2004—05. Author: Hawaii Corporation Law & Practice, 1989; Hawaii reporter State Limited Partnership Laws, 1992-94. Bd. dirs. Jr. Achievement Hawaii, Inc., 1974-84, Inst. Human Svcs., Inc., 1980-88; donor Michael P. Porter Dean's Scholastic Award, U. Hawaii Law Sch., 1977—. With JAGC, U.S. Army, 1963-66, Vietnam. Fulbright scholar, 1997-99; Tulane U. fellow, 1981; lectorship named in his honor, Addis Abba, 1994-97; established Michael P. Porter Prizes on Ethnic Harmony and Religious Tolerance in a Dem. Soc. at Addis Ababa, 1995. Mem.: ABA, Hawaii Bar Assn. E-mail: porterconsultant@yahoo.com.

PORTER, NANCY LEFGREN, reading recovery educator; b. Council Bluffs, Iowa, Apr. 26, 1945; d. Elvin W. and Verna V. (Hansen) Lefgren; m. Eugene D. Porter, Apr. 3, 1965; children: Theresa McFarland-Porter, M.S., Dr. Tracy K.P. Gregg. BS, U. Iowa, 1976, completed devel. activities program, 1983, MS, 1992. Cert. Reading Recovery trained tchr., reading specialist, 1993. Tchr. Iowa City Sch. Dist., 1976-93, reading recovery Title I tchr., 1993—. Mem. After Sch. Tutoring Program, Iowa City; instr. U. Iowa, 1997. Author (curriculum) Lites and Shadows, 1993, reading curriculum, 1997 (Blue Ribbon award 1997); presenter (cmty. collaboration) NSCI At-Risk, 1994. Precinct chair Dem. Party, Johnson City, Iowa, 1990-96; exec. bd. LWV, 1989-90; WELCA chair Gloria Dei Luth. Ch. Women; mem. corp. bd. Alpha Xi Delta. Grantee K-3 At Risk Grant, 1992, State of Iowa, 1992-97; named Educator of Yr. East Ctrl. Uniserve Unit, 1992. Mem. Iowa State Edn. Assn. (exec. bd. 1993—, Friend of Edn. award 1997, student ISEA), Iowa City Edn. Assn. (pres. 1983-84, 97, govtl. affairs chair 1983—, Educator of Yr. 1992), Delta Kappa Gamma (pres. 1995-96), Pi Delta Kappa (program chair 1994-95). Democrat. Lutheran. Avocations: biking, camping, dance, reading, enjoying grandchildren. Home: 2519 Potomac Dr Iowa City IA 52245-4827

PORTER, PHILIP DREW, lawyer; b. Buffalo, Jan. 31, 1947; s. Verne William and Eleanor Marie Porter. BA, Canisius Coll., Buffalo, 1969; MEd, U. S.C., 1974, JD, 1982. Bar: DC 1982, Va. 1996. Tchr., guidance counselor, curriculum coord. Barnwell (S.C.) County Schs., 1969-76; coord. sec. curriculum Horry County Schs., Conway, SC, 1976-79; assoc. Shaw Pittman, Washington, 1982-86, Fenwick & West, LLP, Washington, 1986-96; ptnr. Hogan & Hartson, LLP, McLean, Va., 1996—, dir. intellectual property practice group. Mem. and chair steering com. D.C. Bar, Washington, 1994-97. Contbr. articles to profl. jours. Bd. advisors George Mason U. Internet Multimedia Ctr., Fairfax, Va., 1998-2000; mem. D.C. Computer Law Forum, 1992-96. Recipient Golden Achievement awards D.C. Bar, 1995, 96, Cert. of Appreciation, 1999, Appreciation award Century Club of George Mason U., 1998. Mem. Computer Law Assn. Office: Hogan and Hartson LLP 8300 Greensboro Dr Ste 1100 Mc Lean VA 22102 Business E-Mail: pdporter@hhlaw.com.

PORTER, PHILIP THOMAS, retired electrical engineer; b. Clinton, Ky., Mar. 18, 1930; s. Philip Henry and Ruth Frances (Pennebaker) P.; m. Louise Monroe Jett, July 3, 1957; children: Philip C., Sara Shelby Porter Taylor. BA in Physics, Vanderbilt U., 1952, MA in Physics, 1953. Mem. tech. staff Bell Telephone Labs., Murray Hill, NJ, 1953-62, Holmdel, NJ, 1962-70, supr., 1971-78, West Long Branch, NJ, 1979-83; dir. wireless and wireline network compatiblity studies Telcordia Tech., Red Bank, NJ, 1984-94; ret., 1994. U.S. del. Consultative Com. for Internat. Radio, Geneva, 1984-93. Contbg. author: Electronics Engineers' Handbook, 1982, History of Science and Technology in the Bell System, 1985, Digital Communications, 1986; patentee in field. Fellow IEEE. Unitarian Universalist. Avocations: group singing, bridge. Personal E-mail: pporter@triad.rr.com.

PORTER, PHILIP WAYLAND, geography educator; b. Hanover, NH, July 9, 1928; s. Wayland Robinson and Bertha Maria (LaPlante) P.; m. Patricia Elizabeth Garrigus, Sept. 5, 1950; children: Janet Elizabeth, Sara Louise, Alice Catherine. AB, Middlebury Coll., 1950; MA, Syracuse U., 1955; PhD, U. London, 1957. Instr. geography U. Minn., Mpls., 1957-58, asst. prof., 1958-64, assoc. prof., 1964-66, prof., 1966-2000, prof. emeritus, 2000—; assoc. to v.p. acad. affairs, also dir. Office Internat. Programs, 1979-83. Geography panel Com. on Space Programs for Earth Observations Nat. Acad. Scis., 1967-71; liaison officer Midwest Univs. Consortium for Internat. Activities, 1979-83 Author: (with Eric S. Sheppard) A World of Difference: Society, Nature, Development, 1998, Challenging Nature: Local Knowledge, Agroscience and Food Security in Tanga Region, Tanzania, 2006; contbr. articles to profl. jours. With AUS, 1952-54. Grantee Ctrl. Rsch. Fund, 1955-56, NSF, 1961-62, 78-80, 92-93, Social Sci. Rsch. Coun., 1966-67, Rockfeller Found., 1969, 71-73, Gen. Svc. Found., 1981-83, Exxon Edn. Found., 1983-84, Fulbright, 1992-93; Bush Sabbatical fellow, 1985-86. Mem. Assn. Am. Geographers (Lifetime Achievement award 2004), Phi Beta Kappa (alumni mem.). Home: 10 Burkehaven Terr Sunapee NH 03782-2402 Office: U Minn Dept Geography Minneapolis MN 55455 Personal E-mail: pwporter@verizon.net.

PORTER, RICHARD H., lawyer; b. NYC, Mar. 25, 1948; s. Hercules M. and Lottie M. (Thomas) P.; m. Yvonne F. Reid, May 28, 1971; 1 child, Reid Thomas. AB magna cum laude, Dartmouth Coll., 1969; JD, Yale U., 1972. Bar: Wis. 1972, U.S. Supreme Ct. Commd. 2d lt. U.S. Army, 1969, advanced through grades to capt., resigned, 1979; staff lawyer Judiciary Com. of House of Reps., 1974; ptnr. Foley & Lardner, Milw., 1979; sr. atty. Ameritech; arbitrator NY Stock Exch., Am. Arbitration Assn.; ptnr. Gonzalez Saggio & Harlan LLP. Mem. Phi Beta Kappa, Sigma Pi Phi, Alpha Phi Alpha, Wis. State Bar Assn., Milw. Bar Assn., Wis. Minority Lawyers Assn. (pres. 1984). Congregationalist. Office: Gonzalez Saggio & Harlan LLP 225 E Mich St 4th Fl Milwaukee WI 53202 Office Phone: 414-277-8500 Ext. 1107. Business E-Mail: richard_porter@gshllp.com.

PORTER, ROBERT CARL, JR., lawyer; b. Cin., Sept. 21, 1927; s. Robert Carl and Lavinia (Otte) P.; m. Joanne Patterson, July 5, 1952; children: Robert Carl III, David M., John E. BA with distinction, U. Mich., 1949; JD, Harvard U., 1952. Bar: Ohio 1952, U.S. Dist. Ct. (so. dist.) Ohio 1954, U.S. Ct. Appeals (6th cir.) 1954, U.S. Ct. Mil. Appeals 1956, U.S. Tax Ct. 1980, U.S. Supreme Ct. 1956. Ptnr. Porter & Porter, Cin., 1953-54; sole practice Cin., 1954-63; sr. ptnr. Porter & McKinney, Cin., 1963-88, Porter & Porter, Cin., 1989—. Dir. and officer numerous cos. Served with JAGC, USAF, 1952-53. Mem. ABA, Ohio State Bar Assn., Cin. Bar Assn., Cin. Country Club, Univ. Club, U. Mich. Club, Harvard Law Sch. Assn., Masons, Scottish Rite, Shriners, Phi Beta Kappa. Presbyterian. Home: 2365 Bedford Ave Cincinnati OH 45208-2656 Office: Porter & Porter 2100 4th and Vine Tower Cincinnati OH 45202 Home Phone: 513-871-5447; Office Phone: 513-621-3993. E-mail: rcpjr@porterlawoffices.com.

PORTER, ROGER BLAINE, federal official, educator; b. Provo, Utah, June 19, 1946; s. Blaine Robert and Elizabeth M. (Taylor) P.; m. Ann Robinson, Jan. 6, 1972; children: Robert Roger, Stacy Ann, David R., Rachel Elizabeth. BA in History and Polit. Sci., Brigham Young U., 1969; PhB, Oxford U., 1971; MA, PhD, Harvard U., 1978; PhD (hon.), Weber State U., 2003. Asst. dean, tutor in politics Queen's Coll., Oxford U., 1971-72; spl. asst. to pres. The White House, 1974-77; rsch. assoc. Kennedy Sch. Govt. and Grad. Sch. Bus., Harvard U., Cambridge, Mass., 1977-79, asst. prof. pub. policy, 1979-81, assoc. prof., 1981, prof. govt. and bus., 1985—; spl. asst. to Pres. of U.S., 1981-82; dep. asst. to Pres. of U.S., 1982-85; dir. White Ho. Office of Policy Devel., Washington, 1982-85; counselor to sec. U.S. Treasury, 1981-85; exec. sec. Nat. Productivity Adv. Com., 1981-85, Cabinet Coun. on Econ. Affairs, 1981-85, Econ. Policy Coun., 1985; asst. to U.S. Pres. for econ. and domestic policy, 1989-93. Exec. sec. Pres.'s Econ. Policy Bd., 1974—77; sr. scholar Woodrow Wilson Internat. Ctr. for Scholars, 1993—; dir. Ctr. for Bus. and Govt. Harvard U., 1995—2000, master Dunster House, 2001—; mem. Pres.'s Commn. on White House Fellowships, 1976—2001; bd. dirs. Zions Bancorp., Pactiv Corp., Nat. Life Ins. Co., Tenneco, Inc., Mutual of Am., Extra Space Storage, Packaging Corp. Am. Author: Presidential Decision Making, 1980, U.S.-USSR Grain Agreement, 1984, Efficiency, Equity, Legitimacy: The Multilateral Trading System at the Millenium, 2001; asst. editor: Public Policy, 1979—81. Mem. Utahns for Effective Govt., Salt Lake City, 1971-72; mem. Rep. Nat. Com. Econ. Adv. Com., 1977-81; trustee Gerald R. Ford Found.; mem. adv. bd. George Bush Sch. Govt. and Pub. Svc., Tex. A&M U. Rhodes scholar, 1969; Woodrow Wilson fellow, 1969; White House fellow, 1974; recipient spl. citation U.S. Sec. Treasury, 1977, Rolex Intercollegiate Tennis Achievement award, 1996; named One of 10 Outstanding Young Men in Am., 1981 Fellow Nat. Acad. Pub. Adminstrn.; mem. White House Hist. Assn. (bd. dirs. 1993—), Phi Kappa Phi, Pi Sigma Alpha, Phi Eta Sigma, Phi Alpha Theta. Republican. Mem. Lds Ch. Avocations: classical music, basketball, tennis, travel. Home: 12 Clifton St Belmont MA 02478-3363 Office: Harvard U Kennedy Sch Govt 79 JFK St Cambridge MA 02138-5801

PORTER, ROGER JOHN, research and development company executive, neurologist, pharmacologist; b. Pitts., Apr. 4, 1942; s. John Keaggy and Margaret (Parker) P.; m. Candace Marie Leland, Feb. 17, 1968; children: David, Stacey. BS, Eckerd Coll., 1964; MD, Duke U., 1968. Diplomate Nat. Bd. Med. Examiners, Am. Bd. Neurology, Am. Bd. Electroencephalography. Intern U. Calif., San Diego, 1968-69; resident in neurology U. Calif., San Francisco, 1971-74; fellow rsch. tng. program Duke U., Durham, NC, 1966-67; staff assoc. sect. epilepsy Nat. Inst. Neurol. Diseases and Stroke, NIH, Bethesda, Md., 1969-71; investigator U. Calif., San Francisco, 1972-73; sr. rsch. assoc. epilepsy br. neurol. disorders program Nat. Inst. Neurol. and Communicative Disorders and Stroke, NIH, Bethesda, 1974-78, asst. chief epilepsy br., 1977-79, acting chief, 1979-80, acting chief clin. epilepsy sect., IRP, 1979-84, chief epilepsy br. neurol. disorders program, 1980-84, chief med. neurology br. and clin. epilepsy sect. IRP, 1984-87; dep. dir. Nat. Inst. Neurol. Disorders and Stroke, NIH, Bethesda, 1987-92; v.p., clin. pharmacology Wyeth-Ayerst Rsch., Radnor, Pa., 1992-97, v.p. clin. rsch., 1997—99, v.p., dep. head clin. rsch., 1999—2002; cons., 2002—. Adj. prof. neurology U. Pa., 1993—; prof. neurology Uniformed Svcs. U. Health Scis., Bethesda, 1980-93, adj. prof. pharmacology, 1982—; cons.-lectr. neurology Nat. Naval Med. Ctr., Bethesda, 1978-93; chmn. White House Subcom. on Brain and Behavioral Scis., 1990-92; scholar-in-residence Assn. Am. Med. Colls., Washington, 1989-90; mem. NIMH/Nat. Inst. Neurol. Disorders and Stroke Coun. of Assembly of Scientists, 1983-86, pres., 1985-86; mem. pharmacy and therapeutics com. NIH, 1977-86, chmn., 1978; mem. instnl. rev. bd. human subjects Nat. Inst. Neurol. Disorders and Stroke, 1984-87, chmn., 1986-87. Mem. editl. bd. Acta Neurologica Scandanavica, 1991-97, Annals of Neurology, 1987-92, Epilepsia, 1982-86, Clin. Neuropharmacology, 1999-2001; contbr. articles to profl. jours., chpts. to books; author 13 books, writer, contbr. 5 motion pictures, 1 exhibit. Bd. trustees Eckerd Coll., 1994—97; commd. officer USPHS, 1969—92. Recipient MacArthur Outstanding Alumnus award Eckerd Coll., 1977, Fulbright Disting. Prof. award, 1985, Disting. Alumnus award Duke Duke U. Med. Ctr., 1989, USPHS Dist. Svc. Medal, 1991, USUHS Commendable Svc. Award, 2001. Fellow Coll. Physicians Phila. (trustee 2006—), Am. Acad. Neurology, Am. Neurol. Assn.; mem. Am. Electroencephalographic Soc., Am. Epilepsy Soc. (pres. 1989-90), Soc. Neurosci., Am. Soc. Clin. Pharmacology and Therapeutics, Am. Soc. Exptl. Neurol. Therapeutics (pres.-elect 2006), Internat. League Against Epilepsy (sec.-gen. 1989-93), Am. Soc. Pharmacology and Exptl. Therapeutics. Home and Office: 461 Timber Ln Devon PA 19333-1232 Office Phone: 610-989-3767. Business E-Mail: rjportermd@aol.com.

PORTER, STEPHEN CUMMINGS, geologist, educator; b. Santa Barbara, Calif., Apr. 18, 1934; s. Lawrence Johnson Porter Jr. and Frances (Cummings) Seger; m. Anne Mary Higgins, Apr. 2, 1959; children: John, Maria, Susannah. BS, Yale U., 1955, MS, 1958, PhD, 1962. Asst. prof. geology U. Wash., Seattle, 1962-66, assoc. prof., 1966-71, prof., 1971—2002, dir. Quaternary Research Ctr., 1982-98, prof. emeritus, 2002—. Bd. earth scis. Nat. Acad. Sci., Washington, 1983-85; adv. com. divsn. polar programs NSF, Washington, 1983-84; vis. fellow Clare Hall Cambridge (Eng.) U., 1980-81; guest prof. Chinese Acad. Scis., People's Republic of China, 1987—; v.p. Internat. Union Quaternary Rsch., 1992-95, pres., 1995-99. Co-author: Physical Geology, 1987, The Dynamic Earth, 1989, 5th edit., 2004, The Blue Planet, 1995, 2d edit., 1999, Environmental Geology, 1996, Dangerous Earth, 1997; editor: Late Quaternary Environments of the United States, 1983, Quaternary Rsch., 1976—2000; co-editor: The Quaternary Period in the U.S., 2004; assoc. editor Radiocarbon, 1982—89, Am. Jour. Sci., 1997—, mem. editl. bd. Quaternary Sci. Revs., 1988—, Quaternary Internat., 1989—2005. Served to lt. USNR, 1955-57. Recipient Benjamin Silliman prize Yale U., 1962; Willis M. Tale lectr. So. Meth. U., 1984, S.F. Emmons lectr. Colo. Sci. Soc., 1996; Fulbright Hays sr. rsch. fellow, New Zealand, 1973-74. Fellow Geol. Soc. Am. (Kirk Bryan award 2004, Disting. Career award 2005), Arctic Inst. N.Am. (bd. govs.), AAAS; mem. Am. Quaternary Assn. (coun., pres. 1992-94, Disting. Career award 2004). Avocations: photography, mountain climbing. Home: 18034 15th Ave NW Shoreline WA 98177-3305 Office: U Wash Dept Earth and Space Scis Seattle WA 98195-1310

PORTER, THOMAS W.B., lawyer; b. Ann Arbor, Mich., July 15, 1957; s. James Morris and Helen Marie (Adams) P.; m. Anne R.P. Ballew, Aug. 2, 1980; children: Devin B., Clare B., Keith B. BA, John Carroll U., 1977; JD, U. Mich., 1980. Bar: D.C. 1980, Mich. 1985, U.S. Ct. Claims 1980, U.S. Dist. Ct. (ea. dist.) Mich. 1985, U.S. Ct. Appeals (4th cir.) 1981, U.S. Ct. Appeals (fed. cir.) 1982, U.S. Ct. Appeals (6th cir.) 1986, U.S. Ct. Appeals (9th cir.) 1991, U.S. Ct. Appeals (7th cir.) 1992, U.S. Ct. Appeals (1st cir.) 1994. Trial atty. U.S. Dept. Justice Civil Div., Washington, 1980-85; assoc. Dykema Gossett PLLC, Detroit, 1985-87, ptnr., 1988-93, mem., 1994-98; gen. counsel Barton Malow Co., Southfield, Mich., 1997—98, v.p., gen. counsel, 1998—2001, sr. v.p., gen. counsel, 2001—04, exec. v.p., sec., chief legal officer, 2004—; chmn. United Integrity Assurance, Ltd., 2004—. Bd. dirs. Met. Affairs Coalition, 2004—, Design Build Inst. Am., 2005—, treas., 2007—. Recipient Spl. Achievement award U.S. Dept. Justice Civil Div., Washington, 1984. Mem. Fed. Bar Assn. (mem. chpt. exec. bd. 1992-95, program chair 1995-96, treas. 1996-97, sec. 1997-98, v.p. 1998-99, pres.-elect 1999-2000, pres. 2000-01). Office: Barton Malow Co 26500 American Dr Southfield MI 48034 Office Phone: 248-436-5040.

PORTER, THOMAS WILLIAM, III, lawyer; b. Dallas, Aug. 23, 1941; s. Thomas William and Ruth Mae (Campbell) P.; m. Sally Ann Shell, May 10, 1963 (div. July 1983); children: Elizabeth Elisse, Laura Christina; m. Patty Ann Sanders, Nov. 2, 1985. BBA in Fin., So. Meth. U., Dallas, 1963; LLB, Duke U., Durham, NC, 1966. Bar: Tex. 1966, U.S. Dist. Ct. (no. dist.) Tex. 1967, U.S. Dist. Ct. (so. dist.) Tex. 1975, U.S. Dist. Ct. (we. dist.) Tex. 1977, U.S. Ct. Appeals (5th cir.) 1977. Assoc. Jackson & Walker, Dallas, 1966-72; ptnr. Bracewell & Patterson, Houston, 1972-74, Foreman & Dyess, Houston, 1974-81; sr. ptnr. Porter & Hedges LLP, Houston, 1981—, chmn., 2000—. Bd. dirs. US Concrete, Helix Energy Solutions, Copano Energy. Life mem. bd. visitors Duke U. Law Sch.; trustee Tex. Heart Inst.; dir. Alley Theatre, Hobby Ctr. Performing Arts. Fellow: Tex. Bar Found.; mem.: ABA (fed. regulation of securities com. 1979—, com. on law firms 1981—), State Bar Tex. Assn. (coun. mem. sect. bus. law 1984—86, securities and investment banking com. 1976—), Coronado Club, River Oaks Country Club. Republican. Methodist. Office: Porter & Hedges LLP Reliant Energy Plz 36th Fl 1000 Main St Houston TX 77002-6336 Office Phone: 713-226-6635. Business E-Mail: bporter@porterhedges.com.

PORTER, VERNA LOUISE, lawyer; b. May 31, 1941; BA, Calif. State U., 1963; JD, Southwestern U., 1977. Bar: Calif. 1977, U.S. Dist. Ct. (ctrl. dist.) Calif. 1978, U.S. Ct. Appeals (9th cir.) 1978; cert. Dispute Resolutions Programs Act Mediator, L.A. County Bar Assn., 2005. Ptnr. Eisler & Porter, LA, 1978-79, mng. ptnr., 1979-86; pvt. practice, 1986—. Judge pro-tempore LA Mcpl. Ct., 1983—, LA Superior Ct., 1989—, Beverly HIlls Mcpl. Ct., 1992—; mem. subcom. landlord tenant law, State Calif., panelist conv.; mem. real property law sect. Calif. State Bar, 1983; mem. client rels. panel, vol. LA County Bar Dispute Resolution; ct. appointed arbitrator civil cases, fee arbitrator LA Superior Ct.; mem. BBB Abitrator Automobile Lemon Laws, 2000—. Editl. asst., contbr. Apt. Bus. Outlook, Real Property News, Apt. Age. Mem. adv. coun. Freddie Mac Vendor, 1995—; mem. World Affairs Coun. Mem. ABA, LA County Bar Assn. (client-rels. vol. dispute resolution fee arbitration 1981—; arbitrator lemon law claims), LA Trial Lawyers Assn., Wilshire Bar Assn. Women Lawyers' Assn., Landlord Trial Lawyers Assn. (founding, pres.), Da Camera Soc. Republican. Office: 2500 Wilshire Blvd Ste 1226 Los Angeles CA 90057-4365 Office Phone: 213-385-1568. Business E-Mail: vlporter@vlpesq.com.

PORTER, WALTER ARTHUR, retired judge; b. Dayton, Ohio, June 6, 1924; s. Claude and Estella (Raymond) P.; m. Patricia Reeves Higdon, Dec. 3, 1947; children— Scott Paul, David Bryant. BS in Engring, U. Cin., 1948, LL.B., 1949. Bar: Ohio 1949. Legal dep. Montgomery County Probate Ct., 1949-51; asst. pros. atty. Montgomery County, 1951-56; with Albert H. Scharrer (atty.), Dayton, 1956-61; mem. firm Smith & Schnacke, Dayton, 1962-85, pres., 1980-85; judge Montgomery County Common Pleas Ct., 1985-95; of counsel Thompson Hine & Flory, Dayton, 1996-2001. Served with inf. U.S. Army, 1943-45, ETO. Mem. ABA, Ohio Bar Assn. (pres. 1973-74), Dayton Bar Assn., Am. Coll. Trial Lawyers, Am. Coll. Probate Counsel, Phi Alpha Delta, Omicron Delta Kappa. Clubs: Mason. Democrat. Presbyterian. Home: 872 Timberlake Ct Kettering OH 45429-3494 Personal E-mail: wapphp@aol.com.

PORTER, WALTER THOMAS, JR., retired bank executive; b. Jan. 8, 1934; s. Walter Thomas and Mary Rebecca (Brookes) P.; m. Dixie Jo Thompson, Apr. 3, 1959; children: Kimberlee Paige, Douglas Thompson, Jane-Amy Elizabeth. BS, Rutgers U., 1954; MBA, U. Wash., 1959; PhD, Columbia U., 1964. CPA, Wash., N.Y. Staff cons. Touche Ross & Co., NYC, 1959-61, dir. edn., 1964-66; NDEA fellow Columbia U., 1961-64;

assoc. prof. U. Wash., 1966-70, prof., 1970-74; vis. prof. N. European Mgmt. Inst., Oslo, 1974-75; nat. dir. planning Touche Ross & Co., Seattle, 1975-78, dir. exec. fin. counseling, 1978-84; exec. v.p., mgr. pvt. banking Rainier Nat. Bank, 1984-87, exec. v.p., mgr. capital mgmt. and pvt. banking, 1987-88, vice-chmn., 1988—92, Security Pacific Bank Washington, 1989-92; exec. v.p., mgr. capital mgmt. group Bank of Am., Seattle, 1992-99; chmn. Porter Investments LLC, 1999—. Vis. lectr. taxation U. Wash., 1978—85; vis. lectr. strategic planning Nat. U. Ireland, 2003; bd. dirs. Coldstream Capital Mgmt., Bite, Inc. Author: The Bank of America Guide to Personal Financial Solutions, 2d edit., 1998, The Glory of Washington: The People and Events That Shaped the Husky Athletic Tradition, 2001, Husky Stadium: Great Games and Golden Moments, 2004, A Football Band of Brothers: Forging the University of Washington's First National Championship, 2007. Mem. Seattle adv. bd. Salvation Army, 1975-83, 89-97, pres., 1993-95; trustee Ryther Child Ctr., 1975-85, pres., 1979-81; trustee Lakeside Sch., 1977-87, pres., 1984-86; trustee Va. Mason Med. Ctr., 1986-97, chair bd. govs., 1994-96; chair Nat. Campaign for Student Athlete U. of Wash., 1995-2000, Mus. History and Industry, 1982-83, Olympic Park Inst., 1996-2001. With U.S. Army, 1955-57. Mem. Sand Point Country Club. Congregationalist.

PORTER, WAYNE RANDOLPH, dermatologist; b. Washington, Jan. 10, 1948; s. James Randolph and Betty Rose (Burgess) P. BS, MIT, 1970; MD, Duke U., 1973. Diplomate Am. Bd. Internal Medicine, Am. Bd. Dermatology. Intern U. Miami (Fla.) Affiliated Hosps., 1973-74; resident in internal medicine U. Miami Sch. Medicine, 1973-76, resident in dermatology, 1976-78, clin. instr., then asst. prof. dermatology (vol.), 1978-85, assoc. prof. (vol.), 1985—2005, prof., 2005—. Adj. prof. Barry U. Sch. Grad. Medicine, 2000—; practice medicine specializing in dermatology, North Miami Beach, 1978—; mem. staff U. Miami-Jackson Meml. Hosp. Mem. med. adv. bd. Dade-Broward chpt. Lupus Found. Am. Fellow Internat. Soc. for Dermatologic Surgery, Am. Acad. Dermatology, Am. Assn. Dermatologic Surgeons; mem. AMA, ACP, Internat. Soc. Pediat. Dermatology, Fla. Med. Assn., Fla. Dermatology Soc., Miami Dermatol. Soc. (pres.), Dade County Med. Assn., So. Med. Assn., Bath Club (Miami Beach), Coral Reef Yacht Club. Office: 909 N Miami Beach Blvd Miami FL 33162-3712 Home Phone: 305-285-8983; Office Phone: 305-949-4223. E-mail: wrpmd@bellsouth.net.

PORTER, WILLIAM LYMAN, architect, educator; b. Poughkeepsie, NY, Feb. 19, 1934; s. William Quincy and Lois (Brown) Porter; m. Lynn Rogers Porter; children: Quayny Lyman, Zoe Lynn, Eve Lyman. BA, Yale U., 1955, M.Arch., 1957; PhD, MIT, 1969. Designer, job capt. Louis I. Kahn (architect), Phila., 1960-62; urban designer, asst. chief of design Ciudad Guayana project Joint Center for Urban Studies of Harvard and MIT, Caracas, Venezuela, 1962-64; Mellon fellow dept. urban studies and planning MIT, 1964-65; Samuel Stouffer fellow Joint Center for Urban Studies, Harvard and MIT, 1966-67; asst. prof. urban design, depts. architecture and urban studies and planning MIT, 1968-70, assoc. prof. urban design, 1970-71, prof. architecture and planning, 1971—2004, Norman B. and Muriel Leventhal prof. architecture and planning, 1988—2004, prof. emeritus, 2004—, head. dept. architecture, 1987-91, dean Sch. Architecture and Planning, 1971-81; co-dir. Aga Khan Program for Islamic Architecture Harvard U.-MIT, 1979-85. Cons. in field; mem. Nat. Archtl. Accrediting Bd., 1978—80, pres., 1979; mem. Mass. Designer Selection Bd., 1978—79, chmn., 1979; mem. steering com. Aga Khan Award for Architecture, 1977—86, mem. master jury, 1989; prin. Four Architecture Inc., Boston, 1994—. Co-author: Excellence by Design: Transforming Workplace and Work Practice, 1999; co-founder, co-editor: Places: A Quar. Jour. Environ. Design, 1982—88, Facilities Engineering and Management Handbook: Commercial, Industrial and Institutional Buildings, 2000, Design Representation, 2003. Trustee Milton Acad., Mass., 1989—2001; mem. bd. overseers Coll. Fine Arts, U. Pa., 1984—90, Mus. Fine Arts, Boston, 1992—94. Fellow: AIA; mem.: Boston Soc. Archs. (dir. 1969—73, 1977—81), Harvard Musical Assn. (Boston), Phi Beta Kappa (hon.). Home: 17 Concord Ave Cambridge MA 02138-2321 Office: MIT Sch Architecture & Planning 77 Massachusetts Ave Cambridge MA 02139-4307 Business E-Mail: wlporter@mit.edu.

PORTER, WILMA JEAN, retired educational consultant; b. Sylacauga, Ala., May 30, 1931; d. Harrison Samuel and Blanche Leonard Butcher; m. Douglas Taylor Porter, Apr. 18, 1953; children: Daria Cecile, Blanche Evette, Douglas Vincent. BS, Tuskegee U., 1951; MS, Mich. State U., 1966; PhD, Iowa State U., 1980. Asst. dietitian Miss. State Tb Sanatorium, 1951-52; therapeutic dietitian dept. of hosp. City of N.Y., SI, 1952-53; libr. asst. Mississippi Valley State Coll., Itta Bena, Miss., 1963-65; asst. prof. Grambling (La.) State U., 1966-75, Howard U., Washington, 1976-80; country dir. U.S. Peace Corps, Tonga, 1980-82; asst. dir. internat. programs Ft. Valley (Ga.) Coll., 1983-84, dir. Inst. Advancement, 1984-88; dir. Sch. Home Econs., Tenn. Technol. U., Cookeville, 1989-96; ret., 1996. Project dir. Capitol Hill Health and Homemaker, Washington, 1982-83; interim dir. Inst. Advancement Alcorn State U., Lorman, Miss., 1988-89. Author lab. manual for quantity foods, 1977; editor: (cookbook) Some Christmas Foods and Their Origins from Around the World, 1983. Convenor Nat. Issues Forums, Ga. and Tenn., 1985-90; citizen participant Nat. Issues Forums Soviet Dialogue, Newport Beach, Calif., 1988; bd. dirs. Leadership Putnam, Cookeville, 1990-94; chmn. Tenn. Technol. U. campaign United Way, 1989; mem. devel. and planning com. Peach County Ft. Valley, 1985-87; mem. Peach County Heart Fund Dr., 1986-88; participant People to People Internat. to China; ct. apptd. spl. adv. for children vol. CASA N.E. La. Title III grantee U.S. Dept. Edn., 1986, 87; Tenn. Dept. Human Svcs. grantee, 1993, 94. Mem. AAUW (program chair 1991-92, pres. Cookeville br. 1993-94), Am. Family and Consumer Scis. Assn., Am. Dietetic Assn., La. Assn. Family and Consumer Scis., La. Dietetic Assn., CASA N.E. La. Democrat. Roman Catholic. Avocations: writing, vegetable and flower gardening. Home: 1415 ML King Jr Ave Grambling LA 71245

PORTERFIELD, CHRISTOPHER, magazine editor, writer; b. Weston, W.Va., Apr. 3, 1937; s. James Herman and Irene (Smith) P.; m. Stephanie Brown, Jan. 20, 1962; children: Christopher Brown, Tessa Louise, Kevin Stephenson. BA, Yale U., 1958; MA, Columbia U., 1965. Music critic Time mag., NYC, 1967-69, cultural correspondent London, 1969-72; exec. producer Daphne Prodns., NYC, 1974-79; sr. editor Time mag., NYC, 1980-93, asst. mng. editor, 1993-96; exec. editor, 1996—2003; contbr., 2003—. Co-Author: (with Dick Cavett) (books) Cavett, 1973, Eye on Cavett, 1983; contbr. articles to popular mags. and periodicals, 1975—. Mem. Writers Guild of Am. Avocations: reading, music, tennis. Home and Office: 315 Central Park W New York NY 10025-7664

PORTERFIELD, WILLIAM WENDELL, chemist, educator; b. Winchester, Va., Aug. 24, 1936; s. Donald Kennedy and Adelyn (Miller) P.; m. Dorothy Elizabeth Dail, Aug. 24, 1957; children: Allan Kennedy, Douglas Hunter. BS, U. N.C., 1957, PhD, 1962; MS, Calif. Inst. Tech., 1960. Sr. research chemist Hercules, Inc., Cumberland, Md., 1962-64; asst. prof. chemistry Hampden-Sydney Coll., Va., 1964-65, assoc. prof., 1965-68, prof. chemistry, 1968—, Charles Scott Venable prof. chemistry, 1989—, chmn. natural sci. div., 1973—77, chmn. dept. chemistry, 1982-85, 93-96, 2002—06. Vis. fellow U. Durham (U.K.), 1984 Author: Concepts of Chemistry, 1972, Inorganic Chemistry, 1984, 2d edit., 1993; contbr. articles to profl. jours. Mem. Am. Chem. Soc., Royal Chem. Soc. (London, Eng.), Phi Beta Kappa Home: PO Box 697 Hampden Sydney VA 23943 Office Phone: 434-223-6179. Business E-Mail: wporterfield@hsc.edu.

PORTERFIELD-PYATT, CHAUMONDE R., music educator, advocate; b. Visalia, Calif., Oct. 18, 1943; d. Roy E. and Zoisla Saladin; m. Melvin E. Pyatt, June 16, 1984; children: Michelle R. Pyatt children: Brian K. Porterfield, Erik D. Porterfield, Kevin G. Porterfield. AA, Coll. Sequoias, Visalia, Calif., 1963; post grad. with Stanley Glasser, U. London, 1981; BS, U. San Francisco, 1988; degree (hon.), Wessex Theology Coll. Cert. C.C. supr. Calif., 1988, C.C. instr. Calif., 1987, Wellstone Actions Adv. Campaign Mgmt. Sch., 2006. Prof. music Coll. Sequoias, Visalia, Calif., 1981—. Exec. dir. 49th Mozart Festival, 1982; guest soloist Grieg Piano Concerto, No. 1, Opus 16 Kings County Symphony, 1988; state legislative advocate Faculty Assn. Calif. Cmty. Colleges, 1994; conf. presenter Copyright Laws II, Lobbying 101: How to Stalk the Wild Legislator, 2002. Accompanist and singer: Desert Song, 1963, Music Man, 1963; performer (with Maestro Igor Stravinsky): Von Himmel Hoch and Symphony of Psalms, 1965; performer: (with Maestro Aaron Copland) Musica Viva with the San Francisco Symphony, 1966; performer: New J. S. Bach Chorales Premiere, 1988, recitals featuring Composers of Chopin, Rachminoff, Liszt, Debussy, J. S. Bach, and Beethoven, Piano Dedication Concert-Visalia United Methodist Church, 1984; singer: San Francisco Chorale, 1967; contbr. articles to profl. jours. Recipient cert. Appreciation, Fine Arts Divsn. Coll. Sequoias, 2000; Music fellow, Wessex Theol. Coll., Eng., 1989. Mem.: NEA, C.C. Assn. (advocacy chair 1994—, polit. action com. 1994—, lobbying com 1994—, legislation com. 1994—, exec. bd 1998—, advocate 1998—, bd. dir. dist D, W. H. O. award 2004), Coll. Sequoias Tchrs. Assn. (sec. 1989, state rep. 1998—, W. H. O. award 2004), Music Assn. Calif. Cmty. Colleges (legis. advocacy rep. 1984, exec. bd. 1984—), Am. Theatre Organ Soc., Am. Guild Organists (conf. presenter 1984), Calif. State Tchrs. State Coun. (higher edn. rep. 2001), Calif. Teachers Assn. (life; exec. bd. 1989, advocate 1998—, higher edn. dir. at large 2004, com. higher edn. 2004, state dir. 2004—), Calif. Scholastic Fedn. (life), Mu Phi Epsilon (pres. 1967). Achievements include Invited guest to sail on the QE2 from New York to Southampton, England; featuring piano artists Eugene Istomin, Peter Orth, Michael LaGrand, Leonard Pennario and Charles Strauss; Invited guest performer on Steinway pianos once belonging to Vladimir Horowitz, Van Cliburn and Ignace Paderewski. Office: Coll Sequoias 915 S Mooney Blvd Visalia CA 93277 Home Phone: 559-732-5267; Office Phone: 559-730-3810. Business E-Mail: chaumondep@cos.edu.

PORTES, FERNANDO A., project manager; b. Sabana de la Mar, Dominican Republic; came to U.S., 1995; s. Manuel Ulises Portes and Onfalia Antonia Pimentel Rodriguez. BS magna cum laude, U. Santo Domingo, Dominican Republic, 1986, BEng magna cum laude, 1988; MPS, MEng, Cornell U., 1991; MBA, Cath. U., Santo Domingo, 1995. Cert. quality engr., project mgmt. profl. Sr. quality engr., quality engr. supt. Baxter, Santo Domingo, 1989, 1992—95; project engr., sr. process engr., sr. procurement analyst Merck, 1990, 1995—2001; sourcing sys. mgr. J&J, Raritan, NJ, 2001—03; prin. project mgr. Wyeth, 2003—05; pres., founder Best Project Mgmt., 2005—; affiliate prof. Stevens Inst. Tech., 2005—. Mem. Merck Mgmt. Devel. Program, 1997-00. Pres. Merck Hispanic Orgn., West Point, 1998-99, treas., 2000-01. Mem. Project Mgmt. Inst. Democrat. Roman Catholic. Avocations: politics, current affairs, dance, history, sociology. Address: 380 Mountain Rd 1514 Union City NJ 07087 Home Phone: 201-864-3161; Office Phone: 201-617-9240. E-mail: portes@verizon.net.

PORTES, PEDRO RENÉ, psychology professor, department chairman; b. Havana, Cuba, June 19, 1950; arrived in U.S., 1961; s. Helio B. Portes and Eulalia D. Cortada; m. Patricia Ranagan, May 28, 1977; 1 child, André Sebastian. BS in Psychology, U. Iowa, Iowa City, 1972; MS in Psychology, Nova Southeastern U., Ft. Lauderdale, Fla, 1977; PhD in Ednl. Psychology, Fla. State U., Tallahassee, 1982. Lic. profl. counselor, psychologist. Asst. to full prof. Dept. Ednl. and Counseling Psychology Coll. Edn. U. Louisville, 1982—. Mental health counselor United Behavioral, Louisville, 1995; program evaluator Ohio Valley Ednl. Coop., Shelbyville, 1999—2003; pres. Ky. Specialists in Group Work, 1986. Editor: Journal of the Society for Accelerated Learning, 1992—98; author: Making Kids Smarter, 1998, Dismantling the Achievement Gap, 2005. Named Disting. Rschr., U. Louisville, 1998; Fulbright scholar, Peru, 1988, Colombia, 1996. Mem.: Ky. Counseling Assn., Am. Ednl. Rsch. Assn. (sec. 1999—2000, Rsch. award in Human Devel. 2005), Fulbright Assn. Avocations: tennis, chess, basketball, pool, ping pong/table tennis. Office: U Louisville 320 Edn Louisville KY 40292

PORTES, RICHARD DAVID, economics professor; b. Chgo., Dec. 10, 1941; s. Herbert and Abra (Halperin) P.; m. Barbara Diana Frank, 1963 (div. 2005); children: Jonathan, Alison; m. Helene Mireille Rey, 2006; child: Ana. BA summa cum laude, Yale U., 1962; MA, Balliol and Nuffield Colls., Oxford, 1965, DPhil, 1969; DSc honoris causa, U. Libre de Bruxelles, 2000, London Guildhall U., 2000. Official fellow Balliol Coll., 1965—69; asst. prof. econs. and internat. affairs Princeton U., 1969-72; prof. econs. U. London, 1972-94; head dept. econs. Birkbeck Coll., 1975-77, 80-83; pres. Ctr. for Econ. Policy Rsch., 1983—; dir. Ecole des Hautes Etudes, Paris, 1978—; prof. econs. London Bus. Sch., 1995—. Disting. Global vis. prof. U. Calif., Berkeley, 1999—2000; assoc. Nat. Bur. Econ. Rsch., Cambridge, Mass., 1980—; vis. prof. Harvard U., Cambridge, 1977—78; dir. European Corp. Governance Inst., 1999—2005; Joel Stern disting. vis. prof. internat. fin. Columbia Bus. Sch., 2003—04; mem. Group of Econ. Policy Advisors to Pres. of European Commn., 2001—. Editor, author: Planning and Market Relations, 1971, The Polish Crisis, 1981, Deficits and Detente, 1983, Threats to International Financial Stability, 1987, Global Macroeconomics, 1987, Blueprints for Exchange Rate Stability, 1989, Macroeconomic Policies in an Interdependent World, 1989, External Constraints on Macroeconomic Policy, 1991, The Path of Reform in Central and Eastern Europe, 1991, Economic Transformation in Central Europe, 1993, European Union Trade with Eastern Europe, 1995, Crisis? What Crisis? Orderly Workouts for Sovereign Debtors, 1995, Crises de la dette, 2003, European Government Markets, 2006, European Government Bond Markets, 2006, European Corporate Bond Markets, 2006; contbr. articles to profl. jours. Pres. Richard and Margaret Merrell Found. Decorated Comdr. Brit. Empire; Rhodes scholar; Guggenheim fellow, 1977-78. Mem. Coun. Royal Econ. Soc. (exec. com. 1987-92, sec.-gen. 1992—), Econ. Policy (bd. govs., sr. editor 1985—), Coun. on Fgn. Rels. Office: London Bus Sch Regents Pk London NW1 4SA England Business E-Mail: rportes@london.edu.

PORTIS, ALAN MARK, physicist, researcher; b. Chgo., July 17, 1926; s. Lyon and Ruth P.; m. Beverly Portis, Sept. 5, 1948; children: Jonathan, Stephen, Sara, Eliyahu. Ph.B., U. Chgo., 1948; AB, U. Calif., Berkeley, 1949, PhD, 1953. Mem. faculty U. Pitts., 1953-56, U. Calif.-Berkeley, 1956—, prof. physics, 1964-95, prof. emeritus, 1995—, asst. to chancellor for research, 1966-67, asso. dean grad. div., 1967-68, dir. Lawrence Hall Sci., 1969-72, univ. ombudsman, 1981-83, 92-94, assoc. dean Coll. Engring., 1983-87, 94-95. Author: Electromagnetic Fields/Sources and Media, 1978, Electrodynamics of High-Temperature Superconductors, 1993; contbg. author: Berkeley Physics Laboratory, 1964, 65, 66, 71. Fulbright fellow, 1961, 67, Guggenheim fellow, 1965, SERC sr. fellow, U.K., 1991-92. Fellow Am. Phys. Soc.; mem. Am. Assn. Physics Tchrs. (Robert Andrews Millikan award 1966). Personal E-mail: amportis@sbcglobal.net.

PORTIS, CHARLES MCCOLL, reporter, writer; b. El Dorado, Ark., Dec. 28, 1933; s. Samuel Palmer and Alice (Waddell) P. BA, U. Ark., 1958. Reporter The Comml. Appeal, Memphis, 1958, Ark. Gazette, Little Rock, 1959-60, N.Y. Herald Tribune, NYC, 1960-64. Author: Norwood, 1966, True Grit, 1968, The Dog of the South, 1979, Masters of Atlantis, 1985, Gringos, 1991. Sgt. USMC, 1952-55, Korea. Presbyterian. Home: 7417 Kingwood Rd Little Rock AR 72207-1734

PORTIS, CLINTON, professional football player; b. Laurel, MS, Sept. 1, 1981; Degree, U. Miami. Running back Denver (Colo.) Broncos, 2002—03, Washington Redskins, 2004—. Named NFL Offensive Rookie of the Yr., AP, 2002; named to NFL Pro-Bowl, 2003. Achievements include being a member of NCAA Champion Miami Hurricanes, 2001. Office: 21300 Redskins Park Dr Ashburn VA 20147

PORTLAND, RENE (MAUREEN PORTLAND), retired women's college basketball coach; b. 1953; d. Margaret Muth; m. John Portland; 1 adopted child, Delisa children: Christine, John Jr, Stephen. BA in Social Sci., Immaculata Coll., 1975. Asst. coach, women's basketball team Immaculata Coll., 1975—76; head coach St. Joseph's U., Phila., 1976—78, U. Colo., Boulder, 1978—80, Pa. State U., University Park, 1980—2007. Named Atlantic 10 Conf. Coach of Yr., 1983, Women's Basketball Coaches Assn. (WBCA) Coach of Yr., 1991, 2004, Converse/US Basketball Writers Assn. Nat. Coach of Yr., 1992, Newspaper Enterprise Assn. Nat. Coach of Yr., 1993, Big 10 Conf. Coach of Yr., 1994, 2000, USA Basketball's Developmental Coach of Yr., 1997, Women's Basketball Jour. Nat. Coach of Yr., 2000, IKON/WBCA Dist. 6 Coach of Yr., 2000, Big Ten Coach of Yr. (Coaches & Media), 2003, 2004, Renaissance Person of Yr., Pa. State U., 2005; named to Pa. Sports Hall of Fame, 2001, Mount Nittany Soc., 2002. Mem.: Women's Basketball Coaches Assn. (WBCA) (pres. 1989—90). Achievements include being a member of three consecutive national championship teams at Immaculata University, 1972-75; as a women's basketball coach, has won seven conference championships & eight conference tournament titles.

PORTMAN, GLENN ARTHUR, lawyer; b. Cleve., Dec. 26, 1949; s. Alvin B. and Lenore (Marsh) P.; m. Katherine Seaborn, Aug. 3, 1974 (div. 1984); m. Susan Newell, Jan. 3, 1987. BA in History, Case Western Res. U., 1968; JD, So. Meth. U., 1975. Bar: Tex. 1975, U.S. Dist. Ct. (no. dist.) Tex. 1975, U.S. Dist. Ct. (so. dist.) Tex. 1983, U.S. Dist. Ct. (we. and ea. dists.) Tex. 1988, Ct. of Appeals, Ffith Cir., 1998. Assoc. Johnson, Bromberg & Leeds, Dallas, 1975-80, ptnr., 1980-92, Arter, Hadden, Johnson & Bromberg, Dallas, 1992-95, Arter & Hadden LLP, Dallas, 1996—2003, Bennett, Weston & LaJone, PC, Dallas, 2003—. Chmn. bd. dirs. Physicians Regional Hosp., 1994-96; mem. exec. bd. So. Meth. U. Sch. Law, 1994—; lectr. bankruptcy topics South Tex. Coll. Law, State Bar Tex.; mem. vis. com. Coll. Arts and Scis., Case Western Res. U., 1999-2004. Asst. editor-in-chief Southwestern Law Jour., 1974-75; contbr. articles to profl. jours. Firm rep. United Way Met. Dallas, 1982-92; treas. Lake Highlands Square Homeowners Assn., 1990-93. Mem. ABA, Am. Bankruptcy Inst., State Bar Tex., Dallas Bar Assn., Turnaround Mgmt. Assn., So. Meth. U. Law Alumni Assn. (coun. bd. dirs., v.p. 1980-86, chmn. admissions com., chmn. class agt. program 1986-89, chmn. fund raising 1989-91), 500 Club Inc., Assemblage Club. Republican. Methodist. Office: 1750 Valley View Ln Ste 120 Dallas TX 75234 Home: 1306 Bradford Dr Coppell TX 75019 Office Phone: 214-691-1776 ext. 207. Office Fax: 214-393-4007. Personal E-mail: glennportman@tx.rr.com. Business E-Mail: gportman@bwlpc.com.

PORTMAN, JOHN C., JR., architect, developer; b. Walhalla, SC, Dec. 4, 1924; s. John Calvin and Edna (Rochester) P.; m. Joan Newton, Dec. 23, 1944; children: Michael Wayne, John Calvin III, Jae Phillip, Jeffrey Lin, Jana Lee, Jarel Penn. Midshipman, U.S. Naval Acad., 1944; BS in Architecture, Ga. Inst. Tech., 1950, DFA, 1993, Emory U., 1993, Atlanta Coll. Art, 1993. Diplomate: Registered architect, Ga. With Ketchum, Gina and Sharp, H.M. Heatly, Asso. (Architects), NYC and Atlanta, 1945-49, Stevens & Wilkinson, Atlanta, 1950-53; individual practice Atlanta, 1953-56; partner Edwards and Portman (Architects), Atlanta, 1956-68; prin. John Portman and Assocs., 1968—; CEO The Portman Holdings, Atlanta, chmn. bd. dirs., 1971—; chmn. bd. dirs., CEO, dir. AMERICAS-MART, Atlanta, 1957—. Bd. dirs. Nations Bank., Aaron Rents, Inc., 2006-; pres. Central Atlanta Progress, 1970-72. Prin. works include: The Regent Hotel, Marina Sq., both Singapore, Embarcadero Center, The Pan Pacific-San Francisco, San Francisco Fashion Ctr., Hyatt Regency O'Hare Hotel, Chgo., Peachtree Center, Atlanta; George W. Woodruff Phys. Edn. Ctr., R. Howard Dobbs Student Ctr., both Emory U., Atlanta, Atlanta Merchandise Mart, Atlanta Apparel Mart, Atlanta Decorative Arts Center, Atlanta Gift Mart, Inforum, One Peachtree Ctr., Kennedy Community Center and Middle Sch, Hyatt Regency Hotel, Westin Peachtree Plaza Hotel, Atlanta Marriott Marquis, Northpark Town Ctr., Riverwood, Greenbriar Shopping Ctr., Olympic Village Housing, all Atlanta, Blue Cross-Blue Shield Bldg, Chattanooga, Ft. Worth Nat. Bank Bldg. and Garage, Brussels Internat. Trade Mart, Dana Fine Arts Bldg. at Agnes Scott Coll, Decatur, Ga., Renaissance Center, Detroit, Bonaventure Hotel, Los Angeles, N.Y. Marriott Marquis, Rockefeller Ctr. renovation, N.Y.C., Shanghai Centre, Dream Lake Villas, Hangzhou Qiantang River City, Shandong Bldg., Guomai Bldg., BAODA Bldg., Senfuli Bldg., S Renzhill Complex, Peoples Republic of China, Capital Sq., Kuala Lumpur, Malaysia. Co-author: The Architect as Developer, 1990. Hon. counsul, Denmark; sponsor Atlanta Symphony; mem. nat. adv. bd. Ga. Inst. Tech. Found. Bd. Inc.; trustee Atlanta Arts Alliance, Nat. Jewish Hosp. and Research Center; Dean's adv. coun. Emory U. Sch. Bus.; dir. Atlanta C. of C. (named famous Georgian 1991). Served with USNR, 1942-44. Decorated knight Royal Order Knights of Dannebrog, Denmark; officer Royal Order of the Crown, Belgium; recipient Ivan Allen award N. Ga. chpt. AIA, 1964; award excellence Am. Inst. Steel Constrn., 1973; Design in Steel award Am. Iron and Steel Inst., 1975; medal for hotel design AIA, 1978; Silver medal for innovative design Ga. chpt. AIA, 1981, Community Devel. award Atlanta Bus. League, 1986, others; named Outstanding Young Man of Year, Ga. Jr. C. of C., 1959; Salesman of Year, Sales and Mktg. Execs., Atlanta, 1968; recipient Exceptional Achievement award Ga. Inst. Tech. Alumni Assn., 1985, Disting. Service award Empire Real Estate Bd., Atlanta, 1984, Martin Luther King Salute to Greatness, 1993, Disting. Community Svc. award Atlanta Urban League Inc., 1991, Disting Svc. award Atlanta Bus. League, 1991, Atlanta Downtown Partnership's Resurgens award Design of Peachtree Plz. Park, 1991, Altanta Downtown Partnership's Resurgens award Design of One Peachtree Ctr., 1993, Horatio Alger award Horatio Alger Assn., 1990, Nat. Home Furnishings Assn. Disting. Svc. award, 1990, Shaping the City award Atlanta Convention and Visitors Bureau, 1988, Trendsetter award Foodsvc. Cons. Soc. Internat., 1987, Torch of Liberty award Anti-Defamation League, 1994; named Man of Yr. Danish Am. Soc., 1986, Father of Yr. Southeast Father's Day Council, 1986; named to Bus. Hall of Fame Coll. Bus. Adminstrn. Ga. State U., 1987, Atlanta Bus. Chronicle, 1991, Atlanta Entrepreneurs Hall of Fame Atlanta Entrepreneurs Network, 1990; named Famous Georgian, Atlanta C. of C.; Paul Harris fellow Rotary Found. Rotary Internat., 1991. Fellow AIA (Atlanta Svc. to Profession award 1992); mem. Nat. Council Archtl. Registration Bds., Am. Inst. Interior Designers (hon.), Soc. Internat. Bus. Fellows (hon.), World Trade Club (founding), Ga. Archtl. and Engring. Soc., Atlanta Rotary Club, Atlanta Action Forum, Omicron Delta Kappa, Tau Sigma Delta Clubs: Commerce (bd. dirs.). Office: Portman Holdings LLC 303 Peachtree St NE Ste 4600 Atlanta GA 30308 Office Phone: 404-614-5252. Office Fax: 404-614-5400.

PORTMAN, NATALIE, actress; b. Jerusalem, June 9, 1981; d. Avner and Shelley Hershlag. BS in Psychology, Harvard U., 2003. Appeared in motion pictures including The Professional, 1994, Developing, 1995, Heat, 1995, Beautiful Girls, 1996, Everyone Says I Love You, 1996, Beautiful Girls, 1996, Mars Attacks!, 1996, Star Wars: Episode I-The Phantom Menace, 1999, Anywhere But Here, 1999, Where the Heart Is, 2000, Zoolander, 2001, Star Wars Episode II-Attack of the Clones, 2002, Cold Mountain, 2003, Garden State, 2004, True, 2004, Closer, 2004 (Golden Globe award for best supporting actress, 2005), Domino One, 2005, Star Wars: Episode III-Revenge of the Sith, 2005, Free Zone, 2005, V for

Vendetta, 2006, Paris, je t'aime, 2006; appeared in stage prodns. including Diary of Anne Frank, 1997 (Nominee Tony award), The Seagull, 2001. Office: Creative Artists Agy 9830 Wilshire Blvd Beverly Hills CA 90212 *

PORTMAN, ROBERT JONES, former federal official, former ambassador; b. Cin., Dec. 19, 1955; m. Jane D. Portman; children: Jed, Will, Sally BA, Dartmouth Coll., 1979; JD, U. Mich., 1984. Assoc. Patton Boggs LLP, Washington, 1984—86; ptnr. Graydon Head & Ritchey LLP, Cin., 1986-89, 1991—93; assoc. counsel to Pres. The White House, Washington, 1989—91, dep. asst. to Pres., dir. Office Legis. Affairs, 1989—91; mem. U.S. Del. to UN Subcom. on Human Rights, 1992, U.S. Congress from 2nd Ohio dist., 1993—2005; mem. ways & means com.; budget com.,ethics com., select com. on homeland security; chmn. Rep. leadership; US Trade Rep. Exec. Office of the Pres., Washington, 2005—06, dir. Office Mgmt. & Budget, 2006—07. Co-author (with Cheryl Bauer): Wisdom's Paradise: The Forgotten Shakers of Union Village, 2004. Bd. trustees Springer Sch., The United Way, Hyde Park Community United Meth. Ch.; founding trustee Cin.-China Sister City Com.; former bd. dirs. United Home Care; vice chmn. Hamilton County George Bush for Pres. Campaign, 1988, 92; chmn. Rep. Early Bird Campaign com., 1992; del. Rep. Nat. Conv., 1988, 92; active Hamilton County Rep. Party Exec. com., Hamilton County Rep. Party Fin. Com. Mem. Cin. World Trade Assn. Republican. *

PORTNEY, PAUL ROGERS, dean; BA in Econs. and Math., Alma Coll., Mich., 1967; PhD in Econs., Northwestern U., 1973. Chief economist White House Coun. on Environ. Quality, Washington, 1979-80; joined Resources for the Future, Washington, 1972—, head rsch. divisions, 1986—89, v.p., 1989-95, pres., CEO, 1995—2005; dean Eller Coll. Mgmt., U. Ariz., Tucson, 2005—, Halle chair in leadership, 2005—. Vis. prof. U. Calif., Berkeley, 1977—79, Princeton U., 1992—94. Office: U Ariz Eller Coll Mgmt McClelland Hall 1130 E Helen St Tucson AZ 85721-0108 Office Phone: 520-621-2125. Office Fax: 520-621-8105. E-mail: pportney@eller.arizona.edu.

PORTNOW, MARJORIE, painter; b. NYC, Sept. 30, 1942; d. Julius J. and Bessie M. (Aptaker) P. BA in Art History, Cae-Western Res. U., 1964; MFA in Painting summa cum laude, Bklyn. Coll., 1972; postgrad., Pratt Inst., 1964-65, Skowhegan Sch. Painting, 1965. Mem. faculty Vt. Studio Ctr., 1987—2005, Vt. Studio Sch., Johnson, 1987—95, U. Pa., Phila., 1988—91, Pa. Acad. Fine Arts, Phila., 1988—2003, Snowaggan Sch. Painting and Sculpture, 1989, U. Calif., Santa Cruz, 1991—93, Bklyn. Coll., 1994—96, Phila. Acad. Fine Arts, NY Studio Sch., NYC, 1994—95, Nat. Acad. Design, NYC, 2000—06. One-woman shows include Hollins U., Roanoke, Va., 2000, Peter Rose Gallery, NY, 2003, Oxbow Gallery, North Hampton, Mass., 2005, exhibited in group shows at curated by Graham Nichson, Olana, NY, 2000, fLizan Tops Gallery, East Hampton, NY, 2000, Julie Heller Gallery, Provincetown, Mass., 0201, Lower Manhattan Cultural Coun., NY, 2004, 2005, Sharon Arts Ctr., Peterborough, NH, 2005, exhibitions include Nat. Acad. Design, NY, 2005. Fellow, MacDowell Colony, 1971, 72, 75, Yaddo, 1972, 74, 77; Artists for Environment grantee 1972, Tiffany grantee, 1972-73, 78, Radcliffe Inst. grantee 1973-74, 74-75, 93, Ingram Merrill grantee 1975-76, Nat. Endowment for the Arts grantee, 1980, 94, N.Y. State Creative Artists Pub. Svc. grantee, 1981-82, N.Y. Found. for the Arts grantee, 1986, Radcliffe grantee, 1990, Fullbright grantee, 1993; named juror painting N.Y. Found. for the Arts, 1988. Mem.: Nat. Acad. Design. Office: National Acad Design 5 E 89th St New York NY 10128 Office Phone: 212-925-6321. Office Fax: 212-426-1711.

PORTNOY, ELLIOTT IVAN, lawyer; b. Morgantown, W.Va., Nov. 1, 1965; s. Donald Charles and Enid Joan (Pallant) Portnoy; m. Estee Renee Mermelstein, Sept. 6, 1992; children: Joshua Brandon, Noah Abraham, Daniela Faye. BA, Syracuse U., 1986; PhD in Politics, Oxford U., Eng., 1989; JD, Harvard U., 1992. Bar: Md. 1992, DC 1993. Staff asst., cons. dem. policy com. US Senate, Washington, 1985-88; ptnr. Arent Fox Kintner Plotkin & Kahn, Washington, 1992—2002, past head lobbying practice; ptnr. Sonnenschein Nath & Rosenthal LLP, Washington, 2002—, chmn., 2007—, chair firm pub. law & policy strategies group, 2002—06, mem. firm policy & planning com. Atty. Clinton-Gore presdl. transition, Washington, 1992-93. Author: Guide to Congress, 1991. Founder, pres. bd. dirs. Kids Enjoy Exercise Now Found., Washington, Oxford, 1987—; bd. dirs. Jewish Social Services Agy., Washington, 1996—; exec. com. Dem. Young Lawyers Com., Washington, 1996—. Rhodes scholar, Oxford U., 1986-89; named Washingtonian of the Yr., Washingtonian Mag., 1999. Mem.: ABA (vice chair legis. process & lobbying com.). Office: Sonnenschein Nath & Rosenthal LLP 7800 Sears Tower 233 So Wacker Dr Chicago IL 60606-6404 Office Phone: 202-408-6433. Office Fax: 202-408-6399. Business E-Mail: eportnoy@sonnenschein.com.

PORTNOY, JEFFREY STEVEN, lawyer; b. Bklyn., July 5, 1947; s. Bernard and Edna (Fure) Portnoy; m. Sandi Edelstein, Mar. 29, 1970; 1 child, Carrie Paige. AB in Polit sci., Syracuse U., 1969; JD, Duke U., 1972. Bar: Hawaii 72, U.S. Dist. Ct. Hawaii 72, U.S. Ct. Appeals (9th cir.) 73, U.S. Supreme Ct. 78, U.S. Dist. Ct. No. Mariana Islands 84. With Cades, Schutte, Fleming and Wright, Honolulu, 1972—78; ptnr. Cades Schutte, Honolulu, 1979—. Adj. prof. media law dept. journalism U. Hawaii, Honolulu, 1986—92; chmn. biden com. U.S. Dist. Ct., 1991—94. Former editor-in-chief: Hawaii Employment Law Letter. Pres., bd. dirs. Manoa Valley Theatre, Honolulu, 1980—97; mem. Honolulu Cmty. Media Coun., 1983—; chmn. Honolulu Neighborhood Commn., 1984—88, We The People; mem. Hawaii Bicentennial Commn.; pres., bd. dirs. Hawaii Internat. Film Festival. Recipient Freedom of Press award, Sigma Delta Chi, 1984. Mem.: Def. Rsch. Inst. (DRI Amb. award 1988, Exceptional Performance award 1991—92), Hawaii Def. Lawyers Assn. (lawyer del. 9th cir. jud. conf. 1989—91, assoc. pres. 1991—95, lawyer del. 9th cir. jud. conf. 2002—05), Hawaii State Bar Assn. (bd. dirs. 1990—93, del. to ABA House of Dels. 1994—96, pres.-elect 2006, rep. adv. bd. ninth cir., pres. 2007). Jewish. Home: 5111 Palaole Pl Honolulu HI 96821-1530 Office: Cades Schutte 1000 Bishop St Honolulu HI 96813 Office Phone: 808-521-9221. E-mail: jportnoy@cades.com.

PORTNOY, SARA S., lawyer; b. NYC, Jan. 11, 1926; d. Marcus and Gussie (Raphael) Spiro; m. Alexander Portnoy, Dec. 13, 1959 (dec. 1976); children: William, Lawrence. BA, Radcliffe Coll., 1946; LLB, Columbia U., 1949. Bar: N.Y. 1949, U.S. Dist. Ct. (so. dist.) N.Y. 1952, U.S. Dist. Ct. (ea. dist.) N.Y. 1975, U.S. Ct. Appeals (2d cir.) 1975, U.S. Supreme Ct. 1975. Assoc. Seligsberg, Friedman & Berliner, NYC, 1949-51; atty. AT&T, NYC, 1951-61; vol. atty. Legal Aid Soc. of Westchester, NY, 1966-74; assoc. Proskauer Rose Goetz & Mendelsohn, NYC, 1974-78, ptnr., 1978-94; ret., 1994. Mem. Commn. on Human Rights, White Plains, N.Y., 1973-78; mem. bd. visitors Columbia Law Sch., 1996-02; bd. dirs. Legal Aid Soc. of Westchester County, N.Y., 1975-83, Columbia Law Sch. Assn., 1990-94, Mosholu Montifiore Cmty. Ctr., 1998—; mem. Pres.'s Coun. Yaddo; dir. Muscular Dystrophy Assn., 2000-03. Mem. Assn. Bar City of NY (chair com. legal support staff 1994, mem. com. on homeless, sr. lawyers com., chair Pub. Svc. Network 2003-06), South Fork Country Club (dir. 1997-2006), The Children's Storefront (dir. 1998—), Legal Momentum (bd. legal advisors 2004—).

PORTOGHESE, PHILIP SALVATORE, medicinal chemist, educator; b. NYC, June 4, 1931; s. Philip A. and Constance (Antonelli) P.; m. Christine L. Phillips, June 11, 1960; children— Stephen, Stuart, Philip. BS, Columbia U., 1953, MS, 1958; PhD, U. Wis., 1961; Dr. honoris causa, U. Catania, Italy, 1986, Royal Danish Sch. Pharmacy, Copenhagen, 1992. Asst. prof. Coll. Pharmacy, U. Minn., Mpls., 1961-64, assoc. prof., 1964-69, prof. medicinal chemistry, 1969—, prof. pharmacology, 1987—, dir. grad. study in medicinal chemistry, 1974-86, head dept., 1974-83; disting. prof. medicinal chemistry, 2000. Cons. NIMH., 1971-72; mem. med. chemistry B sect. NIH, 1972-76; mem. pharmacology, substance abuse and environ. toxicology interdisciplinary cluster President's Biomed. Research Panel, 1975; mem. expert panel of Flavor and Extract Mfrs. Assn. of U.S., 1984—. Mem. editorial adv. bd. Jour. Med. Chemistry, 1969-71; editor-in-chief, 1972—; mem. editorial adv. bd. Med. Chem. series, 1972-77. US Army, 1954—56. Named Highly Cited Rschr., Inst. for Sci. Info., 2001; recipient Ernest H. Volwiler award (oustanding contbns. to pharm. scis., Am. Assn. Colls. Pharmacy, 1984, N.B. Eddy Meml. award, Coll. on Problems of Drug Dependency-NAS NRC, 1991, Recognition award, U. Wis., 1996, Merit award, NIH, 1997, Oak and the Tulip award, European Fedn. Medicinal Chemistry, 1999, Nauta award, Internat. Fedn. Medicinal Chemistry, 2006. Fellow AAAS, Acad. Pharm. Scis., Am. Assn. Pharm. Scientists (Rsch. Achievement award 1990); mem. Am. Chem. Soc. (Medicinal Chemistry award 1990, E.E. Smissman-Bristol-Meyers-Squibb award 1991, Alfred Burger award 2000, named to Hall of Fame 2007), Am. Soc. Pharm. Exptl. Therapeutics, Internat. Union Pure and Applied Chemistry (commn. on medicinal chemistry 1978-82, internat. com. med. chemistry 1982-85), Soc. Neurosci., Sigma Xi, Rho Chi (Lectr. award 1999), Phi Lambda Upsilon. Home: 17 Oriole Ln Saint Paul MN 55127-6334 Office: U Minn Coll of Pharmacy 308 Harvard St SE Minneapolis MN 55455-0353 Office Phone: 612-624-9174. Business E-Mail: porto001@umn.edu.

PORTOVELTSKY, SIMCHA, musician, cellist; b. St. Petersburg, Russia, Mar. 25, 1962; arrived in US, 1980, permanent resident, 1987; d. Abram Filat and Inna Lizaveta Portoveltsky. Student in Music, Julliard, NYC, 1980—83. With Syracuse Symphony Orchestra, NY, 1983—87, cellist 2nd chair NY, 1987—90; cellist Chgo. Symphony Orchestra, 1990—98; cellist 1st chair Dallas Symphony Orchestra, 1998—. Cello tchr. Meriks Sch. Music, Dallas, 1998—. Mem.: Tex. Internat. Music Assn., Freelance Musicians Assn. Jewish. Avocations: music, photography, sailing.

PORTS, JAMES FRANKLIN, federal agency administrator, former state legislator; b. Balt., Dec. 1, 1958; s. James Franklin and Dale (Ziegler) P.; m. Linda Lee Linton, 1980; children: Christopher James, Jonathan Russell, Kelsey Linton. AA, Essex C.C., Balt., 1989. Pipe fitter Harry Sparks Heating, 1977-78; fitter/installer Balt. Gas and Elec. Co., 1982-85, maint. technician, 1985-89, trainer, quality control inspector, 1989—; mem. Md. Ho. Delegates from Dist. 8, 1991—2002, constl. and adminstrv. law com., 1991-92, workers compensation work group, 1991-92, ways and means com., 1992—2002, subcom. on edn., 1993, subcom. on transp., subcom. on housing/social issues, 1994, spl. joint com. on transp., 1994, subcom. taxes and revenue, 1995; asst. sec. for adminstrn. Md. Dept. Transp., 2002—04, dep. sec., 2004—07; dep. adminstr. Nat. Hwy. Traffic Safety Adminstrn., US Dept. Transp., Washington, 2007—. Vice pres. N.E. Fullerton Cmty. Assn., 1986-90; mem. Taxpayers for Govt. Efficiency, 1989—; mem. Md. Rep. State Ctrl. Com., 1989-90. Recipient People Against Child Abuse award, Md. Sch. Blind award, Balt. County Police Dept. award, Expeditionary medal. Mem. VFW (comdr. 1991-92), Toastmasters, FOP, Phi Theta Kappa. Republican. Protestant. Office: Nat Hwy Traffic Safety Adminstrn US Dept Transp 400 7th St Washington DC 20590 *

PORZAK, GLENN E., lawyer; b. Ill., Aug. 22, 1948; m. Judy Lea McGinnis, Dec. 19, 1970; children: Lindsay and Austin. BA with distinction, U. Colo., 1970, JD, 1973. Bar: Colo. 1973. Assoc. Holme Roberts & Owen, Denver, 1973-80, ptnr., 1980-85, mng. ptnr. Boulder office, 1985-95; mng. ptnr. Porzak Browning & Bushong LLP, Boulder, 1996—. Bd. dirs. Wells Fargo Bank Boulder, Ctr. of Am. West, U. Colo. Mus., U. Colo., presdl. search com., 2005-06. Contbr. articles to profl. jours. Bd. dirs. Manor Vail Resorts Condominium Assn., 2001, pres., 2003—07; bd. dirs. U. Colo. Found., 2002—, vice chmn., 2004—06, chmn., 2006—. Named Disting. Alumnus U. Colo., 1991, U. Colo. Sch. Law, 2006. Fellow Explorers Club (bd. dirs. 1995-96, Citation of Merit 1998); mem. Am. Alpine Club (pres. 1988-91), Colo. Mtn. Club (pres. 1983, hon. mem. 1983—), Colo. Outward Bound (trustee 1992-2002, vice chmn. 1997-99, chmn. 1999-2001), Phi Beta Kappa. Achievements include reaching summit of Mt. Everest, climbing highest peak on all seven continents. Home: 405 Baseline Rd Boulder CO 80302 Office: Porzak Browning & Bushong 929 Pearl St Ste 300 Boulder CO 80302-5108 Office Phone: 303-443-6800. Business E-Mail: gporzak@pbblaw.com.

PORZIG, ULLRICH E., retail executive; m. Linda K. Porzig. With May Co., 1982—93, sr. v.p. fin., CFO Foley's, 1988—93; sr. v.p., CFO, treas. Payless ShoeSource, Inc., Topeka, 1986—88, 1996—, Petro Stopping Ctrs. L.P., 1993—96. Office: Payless ShoeSource Inc 3231 SE 6th Ave Topeka KS 66607-2207

POSADA, JORGE RAFAEL, professional baseball player; b. Santurce, PR, Aug. 17, 1971; s. Jorge Posada, Sr.; m. Laura Posada, Jan. 21, 2000; children: Jorge Jr., Paulina. AA, Calhoon CC, 1991. Draft pick NY Yankees, 1990, player, 1995—. Co-founder Jorge Posada Found., 2000—. Named to Am. League All-Star Team, 2000—03, 2007; recipient Louisville Silver Slugger award, 2000—03, Thurman Munson award, Assn. for Help of Retarded Children, 2001. Achievements include being a member of the World Series Champions, 1998, 99, 2000. Office: NY Yankees Yankee Stadium 161st St and River Ave Bronx NY 10451 *

POSAMENTIER, ALFRED STEVEN, mathematics professor, dean; b. NYC, Oct. 18, 1942; s. Ernest and Alice (Pisk) P.; children: Lisa Joan, David Richard. AB, Hunter Coll., 1964; MA, CCNY, 1966; postgrad., Yeshiva U., NYC, 1967-69; PhD, Fordham U., 1973; Nostrifizierung of Doctorate, U. Vienna, Austria, 1992. Tchr. math Theodore Roosevelt H.S., Bronx, NY, 1964-70; asst. prof. math. edn. CCNY, NYC, 1970-76, assoc. prof., 1977-80, prof., 1981—, dept. chmn. dept. secondary and continuing edn., 1974-80, chmn., 1980-86, dir. select program in sci. and engring., 1978—2002, dir. Germany/CCNY Exch. Program, 1985—, dir. Austria/CCNY Exch. Program, 1987—, dir. Czech Republic/CCNY Exch. Program, 1989—, dir. sci. lectr. program, 1981-94; assoc. dean Sch. Edn., CCNY, NYC, 1986-95, dep. dean, 1995-99, dean, 1999—; dir. initiatives program City Coll. UK, 1983—. Chmn. bd. dirs. Salvadori Ednl. Ctr. on Built Environ., 1988-99, 2005-; supr. math. and sci. Mamaroneck HS, NY, 1976-79; NSF math. devel. program for secondary sch. tchrs. math., NYC, 1978-82; project dir. numerous NSF sponsored math./sci. tchr. devel. insts., 1976-99; cons. NYC Bd. Edn., 1973-75, NYC Bd. Edn. Office of Evaluation, 1974-80, NYC Bd. Edn. Examiners, 1979-92, NYS Math Standards Comm., 2003-05, numerous others; coord. NSF NE Resource Ctr. Sci. and Engring., 1980-90; lectr. various confs.; vis. prof. U. Vienna, Austria, 1985, 87, 88, 90, Tech. U., Berlin, 1989, 95, U. Warsaw, 1988, Tech. U., Vienna, 1993-98, Pedgogical Inst., Vienna, 1993-99, Humboldt U., Berlin, 1996; dir. NYC Math. Project, 1994—, Math for the New Millennium Project, 1995-2000. Author: A Study Guide for the Scholastic Aptitude Test in Math., 1969, Challenging Problems in Geometry, 1970, 2nd edit., 1996, Challenging Problems in Algebra, 1970, Geometry, Its Elements and Structure, 1972, rev. edit., 1977, Geometric Constructions, 1973, Excursions in Advanced Euclidean Geometry, 1980, 2d edit., 1984, Teaching Secondary School Mathematics: Techniques and Enrichment Units, 1981, 7th edit., 2006, Uncommon Problems for Common Topics in Algebra, 1981, Unusual Problems for Usual Topics in Algebra, 1981, Math Motivators: Investigations in Pre-Algebra, 1982, Math Motivations: Investigations in Geometry, 1982, Using Computers in Mathematics, 1983, 2d edit., 1986, Math Motivators: Investigations in Algebra, 1983, Using Computers: Programming and Problem Solving, 1984, 2d edit., 1989, Advanced Geometric Constructions, 1988, Challenging Problems in Algebra, 1988, 2d edit., 1996, Arbeitsmaterialien: Mathematik, 1994, The Art of Problem Solving: A Resource for the Mathematics Teacher, 1996, Students! Get Ready for Mathematics for SAT-I: Problem Solving Strategies and Practice Tests, 1996, Teachers! Prepare Your Students for Mathematics for SAT-I: Methods and Problem-Solving Strategies, 1996, Deutsch-Englisch Mathematik Worterbuch, 1996, 2d edit., 2000, Tips for the Mathematics Teacher: Research-Based Strategies to help Students Learn, 1998, Problem-Solving Strategies for More Effective and Elegant Solutions: A Resource for the Mathematics Teacher, 1998, Making Pre-Algebra Come Alive, 2000, Making Algebra Come Alive, 2000, Making Geometry Come Alive, 2000, Advanced Euclidean Geometry: Excursions for Secondary Teachers and Students, 2002, Math Wonders: To Inspire Teachers and Students, 2003, Math Charmers: Tantalizing Tidbits for the Mind, 2003, Pi: A Biography of the World's Most Mysterious Number, 2004, What Successful Math Teachers Do, 7-12, 2005, What Successful Math Teachers Do, K-6, 2007; author: (with Dr. H.A. Hauptman Nobel Laureate) 101+ Great Ideas for Introducing Key Concepts in Mathematics, 2006; author: (6 textbook series) Progress in Mathematics, 2005—, Exemplary Practices for Secondary Math Teachers, 2007, The Fabulous Fibonacci Numbers, 2007; contbr. articles to profl. jours. and newspapers. Trustee Demarest Bd. Edn., 1977-80. Decorated Austrian Cross of Honor for Sci. and Art-First Class, 2004, Grand Medal of Honor, Austria, 1994; named Tchr. of Yr. CCNY Alumni Assn., 1993; hon. fellow U. South Bank, London, 1988, Ehrenbürger Vienna U. Tech., 2003; Fulbright scholar U. Vienna, 1990; recipient Medal of Distinction City of Vienna, 1996, Medal of Honor Technische Fachhochschule Berlin, 1996, 1000 Years Austria commemorative medal Govt. of Austria, 1997, Townsend Harris medal CCNY Alumni, 2006; Hon. Univ. Prof. of Austria, 1999; named to Hall of Fame, Hunter Coll., 2005. Mem. Math. Assn. Am., Nat. Coun. Tchrs. Math. (reviewer new publs., referee articles Math. Tchr. Jour.), Assn. Tchrs. Math. NY (exec. bd. 1966-67), Assn. Tchrs. Math. NY State, Assn. Tchrs. Math. NJ, Nat. Coun. Suprs. of Math. Home: 634 Caruso Ln Rivervale NJ 07675-6210 Home Phone: 201-664-1331; Office Phone: 212-650-5471. Personal E-mail: asp2@juno.com.

POSCH, ROBERT JOHN, JR., lawyer; b. Levittown, NY, Feb. 24, 1950; s. Robert John and Maryrose (Finnegan) P.; m. Mary Lou Collins, July 28, 1974; children: Judith Ann, Robert III, Eric, Ludmilla, Alex. BA, Manhattan Coll., 1972; JD, Hofstra U., 1975, MBA, 1981. Bar: N.Y. 1977, U.S. Ct. Appeals (2d cir.) 1977. From legal asst. to assoc. counsel Doubleday & Co., Inc., Garden City, NY, 1975—87; sec., counsel Doubleday Book & Music Clubs, Inc., Garden City, 1987-2000; v.p. legal postal and govt. affairs Doubleday Direct, Inc., Garden City, 2000—; sr. v.p. legal postal and govt. affairs BOOKSPAN, Garden City, 2000—, chief compliance officer, chief privacy officer, sec. Elected exec. bd. Better Bus. Bureau, 2003; instr. Nassau C.C., Hempstead, N.Y., 1984-92; mem. adv. bd. real estate symposium Hofstra U.; bd. dirs. Crossings, Inc.; v.p. Literary Express sect. Profl. Book Clubs Inc.; spkr. in field. Author: Direct Marketer's Legal Adviser, 1983, What Every Manager Needs to Know About Marketing and the Law, 1984, Marketing and the Law, 1988, Cumulative Supplement, 1989, 90; (with others) The Direct Marketing Handbook, 1984, 91; columnist: Direct Marketing, 1981—; contbr. articles to profl. jours. Mem. ABA, Am. Corp. Counsel Assn. (newsletter editor 1988-92, bd. dirs. Greater N.Y. chpt.), Postcom (bd. dirs., exec. com.), Direct Mktg. Assn. (privacy, use tax and legal lobbying groups, various coms. 1986—), Continuity Mailers Assn., Christian Legal Soc., Nassau Bar Assn. (com. mem. 1977—, AAP Postal Affairs), L.I. Assn., N.Y. State Bus. Coun., Alpha Mu Alpha, Beta Gamma Sigma. Republican. Achievements include design of a baseline negotiated service agreement for standard mail with United States Postal Service. Home: 3151 Grand Blvd Baldwin NY 11510-4826 Office: BOOKSPAN 401 Franklin Ave Ste 100 Garden City NY 11530-5945 Home Phone: 516-868-2699. Business E-Mail: robert.posch@bookspan.com.

POSEN, RICHARD L., lawyer; b. NYC, May 26, 1950; AB, Johns Hopkins U., 1972; JD, NYU, 1975. Bar: NY 1976. Ptnr. litig. dept. Willkie Farr & Gallagher LLP, NYC, mem. Exec. Com., 1995—. Articles editor Annual Survey Am. Law, 1974-75. Mem. Assn. Bar City NY, Fed. Bar Coun. Office: Willkie Farr & Gallagher LLP 787 7th Ave New York NY 10019-6018

POSEN, ZAC, apparel designer; b. NYC, Oct. 24, 1980; s. Stephen and Susan. Grad., Parsons Sch. Design, 1999, Ctrl. St. Martins Coll. Art and Design, London, 1999—2001. Intern NY Costume Inst., Met. Mus. Art, Nicole Miller, Tocca; founder, designer Outspoke LLC, NYC, 2001—. Named to, Crain's NY Bus. "40 under 40", 2004. Office: Outspoke LLC 13-17 Laight St New York NY 10013 Office Fax: 212-925-1264. Business E-Mail: info@zacposen.com. *

POSER, ERNEST GEORGE, psychologist, educator; b. Vienna, Mar. 2, 1921; emigrated to Can., 1942, naturalized, 1946; s. Paul and Blanche (Furst) P.; m. Maria Jutta Cahn, July 3, 1953; children: Yvonne, Carol, Michael. BA, Queen's U., Kingston, Ont., 1946, MA, 1949; PhD, U. London, 1952. Diplomate: Am. Bd. Profl. Psychologists; registered psychologist, B.C. Asst. prof. U. N.B., 1946-48; chief psychologist N.B. Dept. Health, 1952-54; prof. psychology McGill U., Montreal, 1954-83, assoc. prof. psychiatry Faculty Medicine, 1963-83; adj. prof. dept. psychology U. B.C., 1984-95; dir. behavior therapy unit Douglas Hosp. Center, Montreal, 1966-83. Author: Adaptive Learning: Behavior Modification with Children, 1973, Behavior Therapy in Clinical Practice, 1977. Chair World Views Collaborative, Vancouver, BC, 2004—. Hon. fellow Middlesex Hosp., London, 1964 Fellow Canadian Psychol. Assn., Am. Psychol. Assn. Personal E-mail: erjuposer@shaw.ca.

POSER, NORMAN STANLEY, law educator; b. London, May 28, 1928; came to U.S., 1939, naturalized, 1946; s. Jack and Margaret (Salomon) P.; m. Miriam Kugelman, Sept. 1, 1957 (div. 1979); children: Samuel Marc, Susan; m. Judith Eiseman Cohn, Aug. 11, 1985. AB cum laude, Harvard U., 1948, LLB cum laude, 1958. Bar: N.Y. 1958. Asso. Greenbaum, Wolff & Ernst, NYC, 1958-61; atty. SEC, Washington, 1961-64, asst. dir. div. trading and markets, 1964-67; asso. Rosenman, Colin, Kaye, Petschek, Freund & Emil, NYC, 1967-68; v.p. Am. Stock Exchange, NYC, 1968-72, sr. v.p., 1972-75, exec. v.p., 1975-80; adj. prof. law NYU, 1975-80; prof. law Bklyn. Law Sch., 1980—. Cons. World Bank, SEC, OAS, various stock exchs.; spl. counsel N.Y. Stock Exch., 1987—. Mem. adv. bd.: Regulation and Law Report, 1979-03, Rev. Securities and Commodities Regulation, 1975—; author: International Securities Regulation: London's "Big Bang" and the European Securities Markets, 1991, Broker-Dealer Law and Regulation, 1995, 2d edit., 1997, 3d edit. 2000, (with James A. Fanto) 4th edit., 2007, Escape: A Jewish Scandinavian Family in the Second World War, 2006. Served with U.S. Army, 1951-53. Mem. Am. Law Inst., ABA, N.Y.C. Bar Assn., Nat. Futures Assn. (arbitrator 1987—). Clubs: Harvard (N.Y.C.). Office: 250 Joralemon St Brooklyn NY 11201-3700 Office Phone: 718-780-7948. E-mail: norman.poser@brooklaw.edu.

POSES, FREDERIC M., engineering company executive; b. 1942; BBA in Fin., NYU, 1965. Vol. Peace Corps, 1967-69; various positions Allied Corp., 1969-85; pres. plastics and engineered materials divsn. AlliedSignal Inc., Morristown, NJ, 1985-86, pres. fibers divsn., 1986-88, exec. v.p., pres. engineered materials, 1988-98, pres. and COO, 1998-99; chmn. and CEO Am. Standard Cos., Piscataway, NJ, 2000—. Office: 1 Centennial Ave Piscataway NJ 08854-3921 *

POSEY, DOUGLAS HARRIS, pathologist; s. Douglas Harris and Reba Tucker Posey; m. Ashraf Mozayani, June 23, 2005; children: Vyllis Wells, Kimberly Dione, Lateesa. MD, Wayne State U., Detroit, 1976. Asst. prof.

MeHarry Med. Coll., Nashville, 1983—86; assoc. pathologist Ministry Health, Riyadh, Saudi Arabia, 1986—87, NW Mo. Pathologist MD, Inc., St. Joseph, 1987—88; asst. prof. pathology Howard U., Washington, 1989—90; assoc. dir. pathology lab. Heartland Health Sys., St. Joseph, 1990—98. Lt. comdr. USN, 1977—83. Decorated Viet Nam Commandation award US Army; fellow, Cook County Hosp., Chgo., 1988—89. Fellow: Am. Acad. Forensic Scis. (licentiate); mem.: Found. Ednl. Medicine (founder, pres. 2005). Achievements include design of automated blood alcohol. Home: 2921 Lenox Rd NE #411 Atlanta GA 30324 Office: Georgia Bureau of Investigation 3121 Panthersville Rd Decatur GA 30037 Home Phone: 713-254-5607; Office Phone: 404-270-8186. Home Fax: 404-816-4943. Personal E-mail: drdouglasposey@gmail.com.

POSEY, ELDON EUGENE, mathematician, educator; b. Oneida, Tenn., Jan. 25, 1921; s. Daniel M. and Eva (Owens) P.; m. Christine K. Johnson, Dec. 25, 1943; children: Margaret Posey McQuain, Daniel Marion. BS, East Tenn. State U., 1947; MA, U. Tenn., 1949, PhD, 1954. Instr. U. Tenn., 1954—55; asst. prof. W.Va. U., Morgantown, 1955—59; assoc. prof. Va. Poly. Inst., Blacksburg, 1959—61, prof., 1961—64; prof. math. U. NC, Greensboro, 1964—88, prof. emeritus, 1988—, head dept. math., 1964—80. Capt. USAAF, 1941—46. Decorated Air medal with 18 oak leaf clusters, DFC, Silver Star, Purple Heart, Bronze Star with 6 oak leaf clusters. Mem.: Math. Assn. Am., Am. Math. Soc., Pi Mu Epsilonf, Sigma Xi. Home and Office: 7 Dogwood Cir Blacksburg VA 24060-6298 Personal E-mail: eposey@bellsouth.net.

POSEY, PARKER, actress; b. Balt., Nov. 8, 1968; d. Chris Posey. Student, SUNY, Purchase. Actor (films) Joey Breaker, 1993, Description of a Struggle, 1993, The Wake, 1993, Sleepless in Seattle, 1993, Dazed & Confused, 1993, Coneheads, 1993, Flirt, 1993, Dead Connection, 1994, Opera No. 1, 1994, Iris, 1994, Mixed Nuts, 1994, Amateur, 1994, Sleep With Me, 1994, Drunks, 1995, Frisk, 1995, An Eviction Notice, 1995, Party Girl, 1995, Kicking and Screaming, 1995, The doom Generation, 1995, The Daytrippers, 1996, Basquiat, 1996, Waiting for Guffman, 1996, SubUrbia, 1997, The House of Yes, 1997, Clockwatchers, 1997, Henry Fool, 1997, What Rats Won't Do, 1998, You've Got Mail, 1998, The Misadventures of Margaret, 1998, The Venice Project, 1999, Dinner at Fred's, 1999, Scream 3, 2000, Best in Show, 2000, Josie and the Pussycats, 2001, The Anniversary Party, 2001, Personal Velocity: Three Portraits, 2002, The Sweetest Thing, 2002, The Event, 2003, A Mighty Wind, 2003, Laws of Attraction, 2004, The Sisters of Mercy, 2004, Blade: Trinity, The OH in Ohio, 2006, Superman Returns, 2006, For Your Consideration, 2006, Fay Grim, 2006, Broken English, 2007, Broken English, 2007; (TV series) As The World Turns, 1991-92; (TV films) First Love, Fatal Love, 1991, Tracey Takes on New York, 1993, Hell on Heels: The Battle of Mary Kay, 2002, Frankenstein, 2004; (TV miniseries) Armistead Maupin's Tales of the City, 1993, More Tales of the City, 1998, Further Tales of the City, 2001; (TV appearances) (voice only) Futurama, 2000, (voice only) The Simpsons, 2000, Will & Grace, 2001, Boston Legal, 2006; (stage) Hurlyburly, 2005, (Lucille Lortel awards, outstanding featured acress, 2005); screenwriter (with Rory Kelly) Dumb in Love, 1995; contributing editor, Open City literary mag. Recipient Spl. Jury prize Sundance Film Festival, 1997; named Queen of Indies by TIME Mag. Office: William Morris Agy 151 S El Camino Dr Beverly Hills CA 90212-2775 *

POSHARD, GLENN (GLENDAL W. POSHARD), academic administrator, former congressman; b. Herald, Ill., Oct. 31, 1945; BA, So. Ill. U., 1970, MS, 1974, PhD, 1984. Tchr. high sch., 1970—74; asst. dir. then dir. Ill. State Regional Edn. Svc. Ctr., 1974—84; mem. Ill. State Senate, 1984-88, 101st-105th Congresses from 22nd (now 19th) Ill. Dist., 1989-98; tchr., adminstr. John A. Logan Coll., Carterville, Ill.; vice chancellor for adminstrn. So. Ill. U., Carbondale, Ill., 1999—2003, chmn. bd. trustees, 2004—05, pres., 2006—. Founder The Poshard Found. for Abused Children. Served in US Army, 1962—65. Democrat. Office: So Ill U 1400 Douglas Dr Carbondale IL 62901 E-mail: poshard@notes.siu.edu.

POSIN, KATHRYN OLIVE, choreographer; b. Butte, Mont, Mar. 23, 1943; d. Daniel Q. and Frances (Schweitzer) P. BA in Dance, Bennington Coll., 1965; MFA in Interdisciplinary and World Dance, NYU, 1994; studies in composition, 1965-78, studies in ballet, 1965-90, studies in modern dance, 1967-80. Mem. dance co. Am. Dance Theater at Lincoln Ctr., 1965; dancer Anna Sokolow Dance Co., 1965-73; artistic dir. Kathryn Posin Dance Co., NYC, 1972-91; choreographer Eliot Feld Ballet, NYC, 1978, Netherlands Dance Theater, Den Hague, Switzerland, 1980, Alvin Ailey Am. Dance Theater, NYC, 1980; mem. dance faculty U. Wis., Milw., 1984-86, choreographer, 1984-88; tchr., choreographer UCLA, 1988-90, Trinity Coll., Hartford, Conn., 1990-91; tchr. world dance Gallatin Sch. of NYU, 2006—. Mem. dance faculty, choreographer U. Calif., Santa Barbara, 1986; tchr. dance technique and performance Tchr.'s Coll. Columbia U., spring 1990; tchr. composition and technique Nat. Inst. of Arts, Taiwan, 1991; tchr. world dance Gallatin Sch. NYU; founding chair Joffrey Ballet Sch., New Sch. U. BFA in Dance, 1998. Choreographer (performing cos./orgns.) Cherry Orchard, Lincoln Ctr., NYC, 1978, Alvin Ailey Am. Dance Theater, 1981, Netherlands Dans Theater 84182, Extemporary Dance Co. London, Balletmet, Columbus, Ohio, Milw. Ballet, 1991, 1993, 1995, 1996, Cin. Ballet, 1997, Kansas City Ballet, 2004, Louisville Ballet, 2004, (prin. works) Salvation, Off-Broadway, NYC, 1969, Waves, 1975 (Am. Dance Festival commn.), The Cherry Orchard, NY Shakespeare Festival, 1979, Mary Stuart, Acting Co., 1980, Shady Grove (grantee jt. program of Ohio Arts and Humanities Couns., 1991), The Tempest, Am. Shakespeare Festival, Stratford, Conn., 1982, Midsummer Night's Dream, Arena Stage, Washington, 1982, Boys From Syracuse, Am. Repertory Theater, Harvard U., 1983, The Paper Gramophone, Hartford Stage, 1989, Of Rage and Remembrance, 1990 (Premiere of Yr. in Music and Dance, Milw. Jour.), Stepping Stones, 1993 (co-recipient Meet the Composer/Choreographer award Milw. Ballet, 1993), many others; subject of documentary Kathy's Dance. Grantee Guggenheim Found., 1978, NY State Coun. on Arts, 1977, 79, 80, Jerome Robbins Found., 1972; grantee Nat. Endowment for Arts 1981, 82, 85-87, choreography fellow, 1995-96; Doris Humphrey fellow Am. Dance Festival, New London, Conn., 1968. Office: Kathryn Posin Dance Co 20 Bond St New York NY 10012-2406 Office Phone: 212-777-1515. Personal E-mail: Pozndance@aol.com.

POSITAN, WAYNE JOHN, lawyer; b. Newark, Sept. 11, 1948; BA in Govt. magna cum laude, Boston U., 1970; JD, NYU, 1974. Bar: NJ 1974, US Dist. Ct. NJ 1974, US Dist. Ct. (ea. dist.) NY 1987, US Dist. Ct. (so. dist.) NY 1989, US Ct. Appeals (3d cir.) 1981, US Supreme Ct. 1989. Assoc. Lum, Biunno & Tompkins, Newark, 1974-82; ptnr. Lum, Drasco & Positan, Roseland, NJ, 1982—; mng. ptnr. Lum Danzis, Roseland, NJ, 1990—. Author: (with others) Business Torts Litigation, 2005, Employment Litigation Handbook, 1998, Jury Instructions in Employment Litigation, 1994, 2d edit., 2005; assoc. editor Annual Survey of American Law, 1972-73; editor-in-chief N.J. Labor and Employment Law, 1998, 2d edit., 2005. Trustee Montclair State U., 1999-2006. Staff sgt. USAR, 1970-76. Mem. ABA (ho. of dels. 2003—, chmn. employment and labor law com. sect. litig. 1990-93, chmn. sect. litig. ann. meeting 1995-96, co-chair task force on merit selection of judges 1996-97, coun. mem. sect. litig. 1997-2000, chmn. commn. multijurisdictional practice 2000-02, dir. divsn. 2001-05, bd. govs. 2006—), NJ Bar Assn. (labor and employment sect. chmn. 1995-97, pres. 2006-07), Am. Inns of Ct. (master Sidney Reitman Laborand Employment 1993-2005), Confrerie de la Chaine des Rotisseurs (vice conseiller gastronomique Saddle River Valley chpt. 1987—), Essex Fells Country Club, Phi Sigma Delta. Republican. Presbyterian. Avocations: golf, photography, fishing. Office: Lum Drasco Positan LLC 103 Eisenhower Pky Roseland NJ 07068-1049 Office Phone: 973-228-6730. E-mail: wpositan@lumlaw.com.

POSKANZER, STEVEN GARY, academic administrator, lawyer; b. Cortland, NY, Sept. 1, 1958; s. Charles Newton and Joan Rae (Mamolen) P.; m. Jane Anne Nofer; children: Jill Madeline, Craig Robert. BA, Princeton U., 1980; JD, Harvard U., 1983. Assoc. Arent, Fox, Kintner, Plotkin & Kahn, Washington, 1983-85; asst. gen. counsel U. Penn., Philadelphia, Pa., 1985—88; assoc. gen. counsel U. Penn, Philadelphia, Pa., 1988—93; spl. asst. to provost Princeton U., 1991—92; exec. asst. to pres. U. Chgo., 1993-97; assoc. provost SUNY, Albany, 1997—98, sr. assoc. provost, 1998—2000, vice provost, 2000—01, interim pres. New Paltz, 2001—03, pres., 2003—. Author: Higher Education Law: The Faculty, 2001. Mem. Phi Beta Kappa, 1980. Office: SUNY New Paltz 75 S Manheim Blvd New Paltz NY 12561 Home: 29 Cedar Ridge Rd New Paltz NY 12561-2728 Office Phone: 845-257-3288.

POSLER, GERRY LYNN, agronomist, educator; b. Cainsville, Mo., July 24, 1942; s. Glen L. and Helen R. Posler; m. O. Shirley Weeda, June 23, 1963; children: Mark L., Steven C., Brian D. BS, U. Mo., 1964, MS, 1966; PhD, Iowa State U., 1969. Asst. prof. Western (Macomb) Ill. U., 1969-74; assoc. prof. Kans. State U., Manhattan, 1974-80, prof., 1980—, asst. dept. head, 1982-90, dept. head, 1990-98. Contbr. articles to profl. jours. and popular publs., abstracts, book reviews. Fellow Am. Soc. Agronomy, Crop Sci. Soc. Am.; mem. Am. Forage Grassland Coun., Crop Science Soc. Am. (C-3 div. chmn. 1991), Coun. Agrl. Science Tech. (Cornerstone club), Nat. Assn. Colls. Tchrs. Agr. (tchr. fellow award 1978, ensminger interstate dist. teaching award, 1987, north cen. region dir. 1989, v.p. 1990, pres. 1991; life mem.), Kans. Assn. Colls. Tchrs. Agr. (pres. 1983-85), Kans. Forage Grassland Coun. (bd. dirs. 1989-92), Gamma Sigma Delta (Outstanding Faculty award 1991, pres. 1987). Home: 3001 Montana Ct Manhattan KS 66502-2300 Office: Kans State U Dept Agronomy Throckmorton Plant Sci Ctr Manhattan KS 66506 E-mail: gposler@oznet.ksu.edu.

POSNER, ETHAN M., lawyer; b. Dec. 17, 1962; BA with high honors, Wesleyan U., 1984; JD magna cum laude, U. Mich., 1989. Bar: NY 1990, DC 1991. Adj. prof. law Georgetown U., Washington, 2001; health care mgmt. cons. APM, Inc.; law clk. for Judge Harrison L. Winter US Ct. Appeals (4th cir.); ptnr. Covington & Burling, Washignton, chmn., Health Care Practice Group; dep. assoc. atty. gen. US Dept. Justice, 1999—2001. Named one of Best Lawyers in Am., 2006, Litigation's Rising Stars, The Am. Lawyer, 2007. Mem.: ABA Litig. Sect. (co-chmn., antitrust class actions com.). Office: Covington & Burling 1201 Pennsylvania Ave NW Washington DC 20004-2401 Office Phone: 202-662-5317. Office Fax: 202-662-6291. Business E-Mail: eposner@cov.com.

POSNER, GARY HERBERT, chemist, educator; b. NYC, June 2, 1943; s. Joseph M. and Rose (Klein) P.; children: Joseph, Michael. BA, Brandeis U., 1965; MA, Harvard U., 1965, PhD, 1968. Asst. prof. Johns Hopkins U., Balt., 1969-74, assoc. prof., 1974-79, prof. dept. chemistry, 1979—, Scowe prof. chemistry, 1989—, prof. dept. environ. chemistry, 1982—, chmn. dept. of chemistry, 1987-90. Mem. medicinal chemistry study sect. NIH, 1986-89; cons. Batelle Meml. Inst., Columbus, Ohio, 1983, S.W. Rsch. Inst., San Antonio, Nova Pharm. Co., Balt.; mem. Fulbright-Hays Adv. Screening Com. in Chemistry, 1978-81; Michael vis. prof. Weizmann Inst. Sci., Rehovot, Israel, 1983; leader Round Table discussion Welch Found. Conf. Chem. Rsch., Houston, 1973, 83; Novartis Chemistry lectr., 2004-2005; lectr. in field. Author: Introduction to Organic Synthesis Using Organocopper Reagents, 1980; mem. editl. bd. Organic Reactions, 1976-89; exec. editor Tetrahedron Reports, 1996-2006. Named Chemist of Yr., State of Md., 1987; fellow Japan Soc. for Promotion Sci., 1991; recipient Johns Hopkins U. Disting. Tchng. award, 1994, merit award NIH, 2006. Mem. AAAS, AAUP, AAUP, Am. Chem. Soc. (A.C. Cope Sr. Scholar award 2004), Phi Beta Kappa Office: Johns Hopkins U Dept Chemistry 3300 N Charles St Baltimore MD 21218 E-mail: ghp@jhu.edu.

POSNER, JEROME BEEBE, neurologist, educator; b. Cin., Mar. 20, 1932; s. Philip and Rose (Goldberg) Posner; m. Gerta Grunen, Aug. 29, 1954; children: Roslyn, Joel, PJ. BS, U. Wash., 1951, MD, 1955. Internship King County Hosp., Seattle, 1955—56; asst. resident in neurology U. Wash. Affiliated Hosps., Seattle, 1956—59, fellow in neurology, 1958—59; spl. fellow NIH, U. Wash., 1961—63; instr. medicine U. Louisville Sch. Medicine, 1959—61; attending neurologist King County Hosp., 1962—63; asst. prof. neurology Cornell U. Med. Coll., NYC, 1963—67, assoc. prof., 1967—70, prof., 1970—, vice chmn. dept. neurology, 1978—87; asst. attending neurologist N.Y. Hosp., 1963—67, assoc. attending neurologist, 1967—70, attending neurologist, 1970—; assoc. Cotzias Lab. of Neuro-Oncology, Sloan Kettering Inst. Cancer Research, NYC, 1967—76, mem., 1976—; chief neuropsychiat. service, attending physician dept. medicine Meml. Hosp. for Cancer and Allied Diseases, 1967—75, attending physician, 1975—, chmn. dept. neurology, 1975—87, 1989—97, Cotzias chair neuro-oncology, 1986—; Evelyn Frew clin. rsch. prof. Am. Cancer Soc., 1996—2006. Mem. med. adv. bd. Burke Rehab. Ctr., White Plains, NY, 1973—2005; adj. prof., vis. physician Rockefeller U. and Hosp., NYC, 1973—75; mem. neurology B study sect. NIH, 1972—76; coun. mem. NINDS, 1998—2001. Author (with F. Plum): Diagnosis of Stupor and Coma, 3d edit., 1980; author: (with H. Gilbert and L. Weiss) Brain Metastasis, 1980, Neurologic Complications of Cancer, 1995; author: (with DeAngeles) Intracranial Tumor, 2002; mem. editl. bd.: Archives of Neurology, 1971—76, Annals of Neurology, 1976—80, Am. Jour. Medicine, 1978—93, Neurology, 1992—96; contbr. articles to profl. jours. Served with M.C. US Army, 1959—61. Fellow: AAAS; mem.: AMA, Am. Acad. Arts and Scis., Soc. Neuroscis., Inst. Medicine N.Y. Acad. Scis., Harvey Soc., Assn. Am. Physicians, Am. Physiol. Soc., Am. Neurol. Assn. (pres. 1997—99), Am. Fedn. Clin. Rsch., Am. Assn. Cancer Rsch., Am. Acad. Neurology (Farber Brain Tumor award 1988), Can. Neurol. Soc. (hon.), Alpha Omega Alpha. Office: Meml Sloan-Kettering Cancer 1275 York Ave New York NY 10021-6094 Home Phone: 212-753-7359; Office Phone: 212-639-7047. Business E-Mail: posnerj@mskcc.org.

POSNER, KATHY ROBIN, retired communications executive; b. Oceanside, NY, Nov. 3, 1952; d. Melvyn and Davonne Hope (Hansen) P. BA in Journalism, Econs., Manhattanville Coll., 1974. Corp. liaison Gulf States Mortgage, Atlanta, 1980-82; dir. promotion Gammon's of Chgo., 1982-83; coordinator trade show mktg. Destron, Chgo., 1983-84; pres. Postronics, Chgo., 1984-87; v.p. Martin E. Janis & Co., Inc., Chgo., 1987-90; chmn. Comm 2 Inc., Chgo., 1990—2005, ret., 2005. Editor: How to Maximize Your Profits, 1983; contbg. editor Internat. Backgammon Guide, 1974-84, Backgammon Times, 1981-84, Chgo. Advt. and Media; columnist Food Industry News. Bd. dirs. Chgo. Beautification Com., 1987, Concerned Citizens for Action, Chgo., 1987, Midwest Bd. Shaare Zedek, Med. Ctr. Jerusalem; mem. steering com. Better Boys Found.; campaign mgr. Brown for Alderman, Chgo., 1987; mem. bd. cons. Little City Found.; mem. benefit bd. C.A.U.S.E.S. Mem. NATAS, NOW, Women in Comm., Am. Soc. Profl. and Exec. Women, Women in Film-Chgo. (bd. dirs.), Mensa, Acad. Arts (v.p.), Ill. Restaurant Assn. (mem. adv. bd.), Chgo. Area Pub. Affairs Group, City Club Chgo. (bd. dirs.), Chgo. Legal Clinic (bd. dirs.). Republican. Jewish. Avocations: politics, reading. Home: 100 E Huron # 3505 Chicago IL 60611 Personal E-mail: kathyposner@aol.com.

POSNER, KENNETH, lighting designer; Ed., SUNY Purchase. Lighting design (Broadway plays) The Rose Tattoo, 1995, The Father, 1996, Getting Away with Murder, 1996, The Rehearsal, 1996, The Last Night of Ballyhoo, 1997, The Little Foxes, 1997, A View From the Bridge, 1997, Side Man, 1998 (Lucille Lortel award), Little Me, 1998, You're a Good Man, Charlie Brown, 1999, The Lion in Winter, 1999, Swing!, 1999, Uncle Vanya, 2000, The Adventures of Tom Sawyer, 2001, The Goat, or Who Is Sylvia?, 2002, The Smell of the Kill, 2002, The Man Who Had All the Luck, 2002, Hairspray, 2002, Imaginary Friends, 2002, Wicked, 2003, Oldest Living Confederate Widow Tells All, 2003, The Frogs, 2004, Little Women, 2005, Dirty Rotten Scoundrels, 2005, Glengarry Glen Ross, 2005, The Odd Couple, 2005, Lestat, 2006, The Coast of Utopia, 2006 (Drama Desk award outstanding lighting design, 2007, Tony award best lighting design of a play, 2007), The Pirate Queen, 2007, Legally Blonde, 2007, Grease, 2007, (Off-Broadway) The Wild Party, The Play About the Baby, tick, tick...BOOM!, The Waverly Gallery, Pride's Crossing, As Bees in Honey Drown, Cowgirls, The Food Chain, subUrbia. *

POSNER, LOUIS JOSEPH, lawyer, accountant; b. NYC, May 29, 1956; s. Alex Posner and Hilda G. (Gottlieb) Weinberg; m. Betty F. Osin, June 21, 1986; 1 child, Daniel. BS in Acctg., Drexel U., 1979; MS in Taxation, Pace U., 1985; JD, NY Law Sch., 1989. Bar: N.Y. 1990, DC 1991, U.S. Ct. Appeals (2d cir.) 1993, U.S. Supreme Ct. 1994. Auditor Arthur Andersen & Co., CPAs, Phila., 1979-81; tax sr. Kenneth Leventhal & Co., CPAs, NYC, 1981-82; tax mgr. Mann Judd Landau, CPAs, NYC, 1983-86; tax dir. Integrated Resources, Inc., NYC, 1986-89; pvt. practice NYC, 1989—. Instr. Nat. Bus. Inst., 2003—; spkr. in field. Prodr., dir. Your Legal Rights. Founder, exec. dir. Voter March, 2000—. Mem.: AICPA, ABA, Nat. Lawyers Guild, N.Y. State Bar Assn. (trusts estates sect.), Assn. Atty CPA's, N.Y. County Lawyers Assn. (trusts estates sect.), N.Y. State Soc. CPA's (tax. com. 1985—90, mem. faculty NYC chpt. Found. Acctg. Edn. 1989—90), Assn. Bar. City of N.Y., Mensa (coord. spl. interest group NYC chpt. 1978—99). Home: 160 E 48th St Apt 12T New York NY 10017-1225 Office: 305 Madison Ave Ste 1740 New York NY 10165 Office Phone: 212-490-4500. Business E-Mail: posner@lawfind.com.

POSNER, MICHAEL HOFFMAN, lawyer; b. Chgo., Nov. 19, 1950; s. Harry Randolph and Elizabeth (Hoffman) Posner; m. Deborah Korzenik, Dec. 12, 1986. Children: Alexander Posner, Hannah Posner, Daniel Posner. BA with honors, U. Mich., 1972; JD, U. Calif., Berkeley, 1975. Bar: Calif. 1975, Ill. 1976, US Dist Ct. No. Dist. Ill. 1976. Rsch. asst. Internat. Commn. Jurists, Geneva, 1974; assoc. Sonnenschein, Nath & Rosenthal, Chgo., 1975-78; exec. dir. Human Rights First, NYC, 1978—2005, pres., 2005—. Vis. lectr. Yale Law Sch., New Haven, 1981-84, Columbia Law Sch., NYC, 1984—; bd. dirs. Fair Labor Assn. Contbr. articles to profl. journals Mem.: Coun. Fgn. Rels., ABA. Democratic. Jewish. Avocations: tennis, skiing, hiking. Office: Human Rights First 333 7th Ave New York NY 10001-5004

POSNER, RICHARD ALLEN, federal judge; b. NYC, Jan. 11, 1939; s. Max and Blanche Posner; m. Charlene Ruth Horn, Aug. 13, 1962; children: Kenneth A., Eric A. AB, Yale U., 1959, LLD (hon.), 1996; LLB, Harvard U., 1962; LLD (hon.), Syracuse U., 1986; LLD (hon.), Georgetown U., 1992, U. Pa., 1997; LLD (hon.), Northwestern, 2001, Aristotle Univ. Thessaloniki, 2002; PhD (hon.), U. Ghent, 1995, Univ. Athens, 2002. Bar: NY 1963, US Supreme Ct. 1966. Law clk. to Hon. William J. Brennan Jr. US Supreme Ct., Washington, 1962—63; asst. to commr. FTC, Washington, 1963—65; asst. to solicitor gen. US Dept. Justice, Washington, 1965—67; gen. counsel Pres.'s Task Force on Comm. Policy, Washington, 1967—68; assoc. prof. Stanford U. Law Sch., Calif., 1968—69; prof. U. Chgo. Law Sch., 1969—78, Lee and Brena Freeman prof., 1978—81, sr. lectr., 1981—; judge US Ct. Appeals (7th cir.), Chgo., 1981—, chief judge, 1993—2000. Rsch. assoc. Nat. Bur. Econ. Rsch., Cambridge, Mass., 1971—81; pres. Lexecon Inc., Chgo., 1977—81. Author: Antitrust Law: An Economic Perspective, 1976, The Economics of Justice, 1981, The Problems of Jurisprudence, 1990, Cardozo: A Study in Reputation, 1990, Sex and Reason, 1990, Sex and Reason, 1992, The Essential Holmes, 1992, Overcoming Law, 1995, Aging and Old Age, 1995, The Federal Courts: Challenge and Reform, 1996, Law and Legal Theory in England and America, 1996, Law and Literature, revised and enlarged edit., 1998, The Problematics of Moral and Legal Theory, 1999, An Affair of State: The Investigation, Impeachment, and Trial of President Clinton, 1999, Frontiers of Legal Theory, 2001, Breaking the Deadlock: The 2000 Election, The Constitution, and the Courts, 2001, Antitrust Law, 2d edit., 2001, Public Intellectuals, 2001, Law, Pragmatism and Democracy, 2003, Catastrophe: Risk and Response, 2004, Preventing Surprise Attacks: Intelligence Reform in the Wake of 9/11, 2005, Uncertain Shield: The U.S. Intelligence System in the Throes of Reform, 2006—, Not a Suicide Pact: The Constitution in a Time of National Emergency, 2006—; author: (with William M. Landes) The Economic Structure of Tort Law, 1987, Economic Analysis of Law, 7th edit., 2007, The Economic Structure of Intellectual Property Law, 2003; author: (with Tomas J. Philipson) Private Choices and Public Health: The AIDS Epidemic in an Economic Perspective, 1993; pres. Harvard Law Rev., 1961—62; editor: Jour. Legal Studies, 1972—81, Am. Law and Econs. Rev., 1999—2005. Fellow: AAAS, Brit. Acad., Am. Law Inst.; mem.: Am. Law and Econ. Assn. (pres. 1995—96), Am. Econ. Assn., Century Assn. Office: US Ct Appeals 7th Cir 219 S Dearborn St Chicago IL 60604-1702 *

POSNER, SIDNEY, advertising executive; b. Syracuse, NY, Jan. 14, 1924; s. Harry and Fannie (Hoffman) P.; m. Miriam Frances Kaplowitz, June 8, 1952; children: Steven Charles, Peter Scott, Robert Keith. BS, Syracuse U., 1947. Asst. advt. mgr. Rudolph Bros., Syracuse, 1947-48; copy chief Kaletski Advt. Agy., Syracuse, 1948-50; promotion mgr. Photo Trade News, NYC, 1950-53; asst. to pres. Dobin Advt. Agy., NYC; pres. S. Posner & Co. Advt. Agy., NYC, 1955-59, Constellation Art Corp., 1959-76, Communicorp, NYC, 1959-76, Bus. Counselors Corp., NYC, 1959-76, Newmark, Posner & Mitchell Inc., NYC, 1959-92, Posner Comm. Inc., Boca Raton, Fla., 1993-94. Personal E-mail: sidandmimi@adelphia.net.

POSNER, SYLVIE PÉREZ, lawyer; d. Carlos Miguel Pérez and Emilia Inés Amezaga; m. Michael J. Posner, Aug. 23, 1987; 1 child, Christopher Barrett. BS, Fla. State U., Tallahassee, 1980; JD, U. Miami, Coral Gables, 1988. Bar: Fla. 1989, Fla. So. Dist. 1989, US Ct. Appeals, 11th Cir. 1989. Legislative aide Fla. Senate, Tallahassee, 1981—84; cert. legal intern Dade County Pub. Defender, Miami, 1986—87; rsch. asst. U. Miami Sch. Law, Coral Gables, Fla., 1987—88; law clk. Frumkes and Greene, P.A., Miami, Fla., 1987—88, U.S. Ct. Appeal (4th dist.) Fla., West Palm Beach, 1990—94; asst. atty. gen. Office Atty. Gen., 1994—2000; sr. staff atty. U.S. Ct. Appeals (4th dist.) Fla., West Palm Beach, 2000—05. Mem. Phi Alpha Delta Legal Frat., Coral Gables, Fla., 1985—88, Health and Law Soc., Coral Gables, Fla., 1985—88; participant Trial Advocacy Program, Nat. Inst. of Trial Advocacy, Coral Gables, Fla., 1987; mem. Appellate Law Sect., Fla. Bar, Fla., 1994—, Govt. Law Sect., Fla. Bar, Fla., Broward County Hispanic Bar Assn., Fort Lauderdale, Fla., 1998—2000, Fla. Assn. of Police Attorneys, Fla., 1994—2000; mem. appellate law clk. edn. com. Fla. Supreme Ct., 2002—05. Vol. lawyers program Fla. Bar, Miami, 1989—90; vol. tel. crisis counselor Switchboard of Miami, Inc., Miami, 1981—83; supporting mem. Norton Art Mus., West Palm Beach, Fla., 2003; mem. leadership coun. So. Poverty Law Ctr., 1999—; mem. Emily's List, Washington, DC, 2002; apptd. mem. Dade County Dem. Exec. Com., Miami, 1982—84; exec. v.p. Dade County Young Democrats, Miami, 1988—89; del., fla. dem. conv. Fla. Dem. Party, Orlando, Fla., 1988, del., state dem. conv. Miami, 1984. Nominee Outstanding Young Women of Am., Nat. Fedn. of Dem. Women, 1985, Assoc. Ed., Inter-American Law Review, U. Miami, 1985—88. Independent. Roman Catholic. Avocations: swimming, travel, reading, hiking, dancing. Personal E-mail: sylvieposner@yahoo.com.

POSNICK, JEFFREY CRAIG, plastic surgeon; b. Mpls., Mar. 1, 1952; s. Irving H. and Nan (Fine) P.; m. Patricia Joan Grundlegar, Jan. 7, 1989; children: Joshua, David. BA summa cum laude, U. Minn., 1973; DMD, Harvard U., 1977; MD, Vanderbilt U., 1979. Diplomate Am. Bd. Oral/Maxillofacial Surgery, Am. Bd. Plastic Surgery. Resident oral/maxillofacial surgery Vanderbilt U. Hosp., Nashville, 1977-79, resident gen. surgery, 1979-80, chief resident oral and maxillofacial surgery, 1980-81; resident gen. surgery Mass. Gen. Hosp., Boston, 1981-83; fellow pediatric craniofacial surgery U. Pa., Phila., 1983; resident plastic surgery Ea. Va. Sch. Medicine, Norfolk, 1984-86; dir. craniofacial surgery Hosp. for Sick Children, U. Toronto, Ont., Can., 1986-92; dir. Craniofacial Ctr. Georgetown Children's Med. Ctr., Georgetown U. Med. Ctr., Washington, 1992-98; dir. Posnick Ctr. for Facial Plastic Surgery, Chevy Chase, Md., 1998—; and clin. prof., plastic surgery, otolaryngology/head and neck surgery, oral and maxillofacial surgery and pediat. Georgetown Univ., Washington. Clin. prof. plastic surgery, pediats., otolaryngology/head and neck surgery, oral and maxillofacial surgery Georgetown U., 1998—. Author, editor: Craniofacial and Maxillofacial Surgery in Children and Young Adults, 2000; contbr. more than 200 articles to profl. jours. Rsch. grantee Med. Rsch. Coun. Can., 1990, Plastic Surg. Edn. Found., 1990, Saudi Arabia Edn. Found., 1992, Cleft Palate Found., 1995; named one of Top Doctors, Washingtonian mag., Best Dentists, Washingtonian mag. Fellow ACS, Royal Coll. Surgeons (Can.); mem. Internat. Soc. Craniofacial Surgeons, Am. Cleft Palate/Craniofacial Assn., Am. Assn. Plastic Surgery, Am. Assn. Asthetic Plastic Surgeons, Am. Soc. Plastic Surgery, Am. Soc. Oral and Maxillofaciail Surgery; Phi Beta Kappa. Avocations: collecting antiques, american history. Home: 10100 Counselman Rd Potomac MD 20854-5020 Office: Posnick Ctr Facial Plastic Surgery 5530 Wisconsin Ave Ste 1250 Chevy Chase MD 20815-4314 Fax: 301-986-1974. E-mail: jposnick@drposnick.com. *

POSPELOV, DMITRIY, transportation executive; BA, Moscow State Inst. Fgn. Langs., 1993. Transp. infrastructure specialist Oao Lukoil, Moscow, 2003—06; transp. infrastructure mgr. Getty Petroleum Mktg. Inc, Houston, 2006—.

POSPICHAL, MARCIE W., neuroscientist, psychologist, educator; b. Great Lakes, Ill., Feb. 22, 1959; BS in Psychology, Fla. So. Coll., 1985; MA in Psychology, Neurosci., Vanderbilt U., Nashville, 1990, PhD in Psychology, 1991. Tchg. asst. Vanderbilt U., Nashville, 1988—91, faculty lectr. dept. psychology, 1991—95, rsch. assoc. dept. psychology, 1991—97, editl. asst. Jour. Comparative Neurology, 1992—97, asst. dir. programs Ctr. for Molecular Neurosci., 1996—2001, coord. grad. studies Vanderbilt Brain Inst., 1997—2001, asst. dir. programs in neurosci. edn. Vanderbilt Brain Inst., 1999—2001; adj. instr. dept. psychology Fla. So. Coll., Lakeland, 2001—. Neurosci. cons. Bd. of Nat. Health Mus., 1999; lectr. in field; condr. seminars in field; mem. neurosci. coun. com. Vanderbilt U., Nashville, 1999—2001; Assoc. Vice-Chancellor's planning com. for the 2001 Consortium on Neurogenetics Vanderbilt Med. Ctr., 1999—2001, Vice-Chancellor's Com. on Cmty. Outreach, 1998—2001; mem. neurosci. PhD curriculum com. Vanderbilt U., 1997—2001; adj. mem. Ctr. for Molecular Neurosci. Faculty Recruitment Com., 1997—2001. Contbr. articles and abstracts to profl. jours. Vol. WDCN, Nashville, 1999; mem. Safe and Drug-Free Nashville Metro Schs. Com., 1997; vol. reader for the blind WPLN Listening Libr., Nashville, 1992—93. Co-recipient NSF grantee, 1999; recipient Rsch. Svc. award, Nat., 1995; fellow postdoctoral fellow, Vanderbilt U., 1996, 1993—94, 1991—92, grad. rsch. fellow, 1986—88, 1991; grantee Fight for Sight Postdoctoral Tng. grantee, 1992—93. Mem.: Internat. Brain Rsch. Orgn., Soc. for Neurosci. (com. on neurosci. liberacy 2001—), Assn. of Neurosci. Depts. and Programs. Achievements include research in neurotoxic and electrolytic stereotaxic brain lesioning in rodents; pressure injectin and iontophoretic application of tract tracing substances such as HRP and its conjugates in non-human primates; tract tracing using live slice tissue preparation in non-human primates. Office: thern Coll Dept Psychology Lakeland FL

POSPISIL, GEORGE CURTIS, health science administrator; b. Thomas, Okla., Aug. 8, 1945; s. George Frank and Zelpha Earline (Hensley) P.; children: Heather Elizabeth, Derek Curtis; m. Hoda Nasr, Aug. 24, 2002. Student, Wheaton Coll., 1963-64; BA, U. Okla., 1968; MA, 1971. Tchr. Peace Corps, Maseru, Lesotho, 1973-74; dir. health svcs. fin. project State of Wis., Madison, 1975-76; pub. health advisor USPHS, Rockville, Md., 1972-73, program/policy analyst, 1977—81, 1984—86, congl. liaison, 1989—99, clin. trials policy adv., 1998-2001, contract mgr., 1982-84, 2005—; dir. Svcs. Crime Victims/Witnesses Project, Tioga County, NY, 1986—; pub. health educator Office of the Sec., OHRP, HHS, 2001—04; health scientist Office of Rsch. Oversight, VA, Bedford, Mass., 2004—05; health sci. adminstr. NIH, Bethesda, Md., 2005—07. Guest lectr. U. Wis., Summer Inst., Carthage Coll.; analyst biomed. rsch. program NIH, 1989—; sci. editor The Johns Hopkins U. Krieger Mind/Brain Inst., 1993—95; pub. health analyst U.S. Dept. Health and Human Svcs., Office of Sec. Editor: Decde of the Brain, 1990, Maximizing Human Potential: Decade of the Brain, 1991. Mem. Rockville Humanities Commn., 1981-83; spokesperson Neighborhood Planning Com., 1980-82; coordinator mental health svcs. Cuban Refugee Project, Ft. McCoy, Wis., 1980; sec. cmty. adv. com. mental health program Montgomery House, 1982-86; rsch. and tng. adminstr. Cornell U., Ithaca, N.Y., 1986-89; bd. dirs. Family Svc. Montgomery County, 1984-86; legis fellow U.S. Senate Labor and Human Resources Com./Health Office, 1991; mem. county Spl. Olympics Com., 1982-86; mem. Citizens' Planning Subcom. Carroll County Md.; insp. gen. Civil Air Patrol; mem. adv. com. troop 321 Boy Scouts Am.; bd. dirs. Shepherd's Staff Cmty. Svc. program. Mem. Soc. Rsch. Adminstrs. Office: NIH Nat Inst on Drug Abuse 6101 Executive Blvd Bethesda MD 20892 Personal E-mail: pospisilg@nida.nih.gov.

POSPISIL, JOANN, historian, archivist; b. Schulenburg, Tex., Dec. 10, 1947; d. Edwin James and Jossie Annie (Mica) Krametbauer; m. Gerald Joseph Pospisil, Nov. 19, 1966; 1 child, Ryan Joseph. BA summa cum laude, U. Houston, 1992, MA, 1994. Cert. archivist Acad. Cert. Archivists, 2001. Sec. to v.p. Bohler Bros. of Am., Inc., Houston, 1972-75, asst. corp. sec., 1975-77; archival intern Sul Ross State U. Archives of the Big Bend, Alpine, Tex., 1993; rsch. asst. U. Houston Recovering U.S.-Hispanic Literary Heritage, 1993-94; archival technician Houston Acad. Medicine-Tex. Med. Ctr. Jesse H. Jones Libr., 1995-98; asst. archivist Baylor Coll. Medicine Archive, Houston, 1997—2004, archivist, 2004—. Task force mem., rsch. cons. Houston Urban Coun., 1993; contbg. historian Candelilla Wax Industry, Tex. Archeol. Rsch. Lab., 2004. Contbr. articles to profl. jours. Sec. handbook com. Clay Road Bapt. Parent-Tchr. Orgn., Houston, 1980-81; coord. Houston Police Dept., Houstonians on Watch, 1982-91; sec., membership chair, libr. aide Spring Branch Ind. Sch. Dist. Parent-Tchr. Assn., Houston, 1983-89; presenter geographical and cultural topics to classrooms in Spring Br. Elem. Sch., Northbrook H.S., Houston, 1985-95; interviewer oral history program Alliance Am. Quilts, 1999-; pres., pub. chair, sec. Spring Branch Addition Civic Assn. Inc., pres., 2005-07. treas. 2007—. Recipient Spanish award Houston C.C., 1985, Josephine Del Barto scholar U. Houston, 1989-90, Helen M. Douthitt scholarship in history, 1990-91; named Sadie Iola Daniels scholar Assn. for Study of African Am. Life and History, Washington, 1990. Mem. Ctr. for Big Bend Studies, Soc. Am. Archivists, Tex. Czech Geneal. Soc. (charter), Archvists Houston Area (charter), Soc. Southwest Archivists, Tex. Hist. Assn., West Tex. Hist. Assn. (life, bd. dirs. 2006—, local arrangements com., 2006, nominating com., 2007), Tex. Oral History Assn. (bd. dirs. 2005—, v.p. 2005-06, Cmty. award com. 2005—, pres. 2006-07, Lifetime Achievement award com., 2007—), Phi Kappa Phi, Phi Alpha Theta. Avocations: hiking, genealogy, whitewater rafting, reading non-fiction. Home: 9418 Railton St Houston TX 77080-1431 Office: Baylor Coll Medicine Archives One Baylor Plz BCMC 177A Mail Stop BCM 506 Houston TX 77030

POSPISIL, LEOPOLD JAROSLAV, anthropologist, law educator; b. Olomouc, Czechoslovakia, Apr. 26, 1923; came to U.S., 1949, naturalized, 1954; s. Leopold and Ludmila (Petrlak) P.; m. Zdenka Smyd, Jan. 31, 1945; children: Zdenka, Mira. Juris Universae Candidatus, Charles U., Prague, Czechoslovakia, 1947, JD, 1991; BA in Sociology, Willamette U., Salem, Oreg., 1950; MA in Anthropology, U. Oreg., 1952; PhD, Yale U., 1956; ScD (hon.), Willamette U., 1969; PhD (hon.), Charles U., Prague, Czech Rep., 1994. Instr. Yale U., New Haven, 1956-57, asst. prof., 1957-60; asst. curator Peabody Mus., 1956-65, assoc. prof., 1960-65, prof., curator, 1965-93, dir. divsn. anthropology, 1966-93; prof. anthropology, 1965-93; prof. and curator emeritus, 1993—. Dir. Peabody Mus. Anthropology divsn. Yale U., New Haven, 1966—93; Robert Merton Prof. Law U. Munich, Germany, 1978—79; vis. prof. Anthropology Charles U., Prague, Czech Republic, 1991—; vis. prof. Law Capetown U., South Africa, 1989; DFC prof. Law U. Munich, 1982. Author: Kapauku Papuans and Their Law, 1958, Kapauku Papuan Economy, 1963, Kapauku Papuans of West New Guinea, 1963, Anthropology of Law, 1971, Ethnology of Law, 1972, Anthropologie des Rechts, 1981, Sprache, Symbole und Symbolverwendungen in Ethnologie, Kulturanthropologie, Politik, Religion und Recht, 1993, Obernberg: Quantitative Analysis of a Tyrolean Economy, 1996, Etnologie Prava, 1997, Sociocultural Anthropology, 2004; contbr. articles to profl. jours. Guggenheim fellow, 1962, NSF fellow, 1962, 64-65, 67-71, NIMH fellow, 1973-79; Social Sci. Rsch. Coun. grantee, 1966. Fellow AAAS, N.Y. Acad. Scis., Am. Anthrop. Assn.; mem. NAS, Conn. Acad. Arts and Scis., Explorers Club, Czechoslovakian Acad. Arts and Scis. (past pres.), Coun. Free Czechoslovakia, Assn. for Polit. and Legal Anthropology (pres.-at-large), Assn. for Social Anthropology in Oceania, Soc. for Econ. Anthropology, Sigma Xi. Independent. Avocations: gardening, mountain climbing. Home: 554 Orange St New Haven CT 06511-3819 Office: 51 Hillhouse Ave New Haven CT 06520-3703 Office Phone: 203-432-3771. Personal E-mail: pospisil@sbcglobal.net. Business E-Mail: anthropology@yale.edu.

POSS, JEFFERY SCOTT, architect, educator; b. Harvey, Ill., May 20, 1956; m. Barbara Young Cook, May 1, 1999. BAS, U. Ill., 1978, MArch, 1980. Intern architect Charles Kober Assocs., Chgo., 1980-81, Skidmore, Owings and Merrill, Chgo., 1981; designer Newman/Lustig and Assocs., Chgo., 1983-84; design assoc. Kevin Roche John Dinkeloo and Assocs., Hamden, Conn., 1985-87; project architect and designer Tai Soo Kim Assocs., Hartford, Conn., 1987-89; pvt. practice Urbana, Ill., 1989—; assoc. prof. U. Ill. Sch. Arch., Champaign-Urbana, Ill., 1989—. Vis. prof. Glasgow Sch. Art, 1999, 2001; design cons. Isaksen Glerum Wachter Archs., P.C., Urbana, 2001—; invited juror, lectr. in field. Contbr. articles to profl. jours. Recipient 1st Alt. Paris prize, Nat. Inst. for Archtl. Edn., 1981, 1st pl., Champaign Pk. Dist./AIA, 1989, Nat. Design award, Concrete Steel Reinforcing Inst., 1992, 2d pl. WWII Meml., State of Md., 1996, Merit award, Saluda Shoals Amphitheater, State of N.C., 2001; 1st Pl. Francis J. Plym Traveling fellow, U. Ill., 2004. Mem. AIA (Excellence in Edn. Honors award 1993, Ctrl. Ill. award for design excellence, 1993, 97, 2000, 06, Small Project award 2007), Am. Soc. Archtl. Perspectives (Excellence in Graphic Representation Architecture award 1990, 93). Business E-Mail: poss@uiuc.edu.

POSS, STEPHEN DANIEL, lawyer; b. Buffalo, Jan. 13, 1955; s. Gilbert H. and Bernice L. (Lippman) Poss; m. Jane Fitz Simon, 1990. BA magna cum laude, Amherst Coll., 1978; JD, U. Chgo., 1981. Bar: N.Y. 1982, Mass. 1988; U.S. Dist. Ct. (so. dist.) N.Y. 1984, U.S. Dist. Ct. Mass. 1988; U.S. Tax Ct. 1983; U.S. Supreme Ct. 1986; U.S. Ct. Appeals (1st cir.) 1989, U.S. Ct. Appeals (fed. cir.) 1992. Assoc. Cravath, Swaine & Moore, NYC, 1981-87, Goodwin Procter LLP, Boston, 1988-89, ptnr., 1989—. Teaching asst. to prof. Henry Steele Commager, 1977; lectr. Mass. Continuing Legal Edn., 1987—, Mass. Bar Assn. Ednl. Seminars, 1992-94; seminar chmn. SEC Inst. II, 1998; lectr. Nasdaq Exec. Forum, 1998, 2001; mem. civil litigation curriculum com. Mass. Continuing Legal Edn., 1997—; lectr. SEC Inst., 1999-2001, mem. nat. adv. bd., 2001--; mem. Nasdaq Investor Rels. Forum, 2000. Advisor campaign Bill Guy for U.S. Senate from N.D., 1974, Quentick Burdick for U.S. Senate, N.D., 1976, Bill Bradley for U.S. Senate, N.J., 1978, Gary Hart for U.S. Senate, Colo., 1980, Jeff Bingaman for U.S. Senate, N.Mex., 1982; pro bono counsel to Dem. Nat. Com., 1986-87; bd. dirs. Internat. Forum, N.Y.C., 1984; counsel of N.Y. Law Assocs., N.Y.C., 1985; assoc. dir., bd. dirs. Mass. Audubon Soc., 1997-2000, adv. counsel, 2001—. John Woodruff Simpson fellow, 1978. Mem.: ABA (vice chair securities litigation subcom. bus. law sect. 2000—), SEC Inst., Inc. (nat. adv. bd. 2001—), Boston Bar Assn., Mass. Bar Assn. (vice chair bus. litigation com. 1992—94), Internat. Churchill Soc. Office: Goodwin Procter LLP Exchange Pl Boston MA 02109-2803 E-mail: sposs@goodwinprocter.com.

POSS, WILLIAM BRADLEY, physician; b. Kansas City, Kans., June 3, 1961; s. William Gary and Joan Marie Poss; m. Constance Helene Ide, May 28, 1983; children: William Matthew, Jeffrey Michael. BS, U. Kans., Lawrence, 1983; MD, U. Kans., Kansas City, 1987; MMM, U. So. Calif., LA, 2005. Diplomate Am. Bd. Pediats., Am. Bd. Pediat. Critical Care. Commd. ens. USN, 1987, advanced through grades to capt.; dir. pediat. intensive care unit Naval Med. Ctr. San Diego, 1996—99, chmn. dept. pediats., 1999—2001, dir. med. edn., 2002—05, attending physician, 1995—; amphibious task force surgeon Fleet Surg. Team ONE, 2001—02; fleet surgeon USN 3d Fleet, 2005—; commd. Attending physician Primary Children's Med. Ctr., Salt Lake City, 2001—; assoc. prof. Uniformed Svcs. U. Health Scis. Contbr. papers to profl. publs., chpts. to books. Decorated Meritorious Svc. medal USN, Global War on Terrorism Expeditionary medal; named Tchr. of Yr., Naval Med. Ctr. San Diego, 1998. Fellow: Am. Acad. Pediats.; mem.: Soc. Critical Care Medicine, Am. Coll. Physician Execs. (cert.), Am. Coll. Healthcare Execs. (cert.), Beta Gamma Sigma. Avocations: reading, music, running, travel, hiking. Office: USN Third Fleet 53690 Tomahawk Dr Ste 338 San Diego CA 92147-5000

POSSICK, PAUL AARON, dermatologist; b. Fitchburg, Mass., Apr. 22, 1937; s. Abraham and Jennie (Smith) Possick; m. Marjorie Eve Baer, June 18, 1961; children: Lisa, Marc. BS, Tufts U., Medford, Mass., 1960; MD, Tufts U., Boston, 1964. Diplomate Am. Bd. Dermatology, 1969. Dermatologist USPHS, Cin., 1968—70, Westwood Dermatology, NJ, 1971—. Office: Westwood Dermatology 390 Old Hook Rd Westwood NJ 07675

POST, AUGUST ALAN, retired economist, artist; b. Alhambra, Calif., Sept. 17, 1914; s. Edwin R. and Edna (Stickney) P.; m. Helen E. Wills, Nov. 21, 1940; 1 child, David Wills. AB, Occidental Coll., LA, 1938, LLD, 1974; student, Chouinard Inst. Art, 1938; MA, Princeton U., NJ, 1940; LLD, Golden Gate U., 1972, Claremont Grad. Sch., Calif., 1978. In banking bus., 1933-36; instr. econs. Occidental Coll., 1940-42; asst. prof. Am. U., 1943; economist Dept. State, 1944-45; rsch. dir. Utah Found., 1945-46; chief economist, adminstrv. analyst State of Calif., 1946-50, state legis. analyst, 1950-77. Cons. Com. Higher Edn. and State, 1964; mem. Nat. Com. Support of Pub. Schs., 1967; mem. nat. adv. panel Nat. Ctr. Higher Edn. Mgmt. Systems, 1971-72; chmn. Calif. Gov.'s Commn. on Govt. Reform, 1978; mem. faculty U. So. Calif. Grad. Sch. Pub. Adminstrn., 1978-80; Regents' prof. U. Calif., Davis, 1983, vis. prof., 1984-85; spl. cons. Touche Ross and Co., 1977-87; cons., interim exec. dir. Calif. Commn. for Rev. of Master Plan for Higher Edn., 1985; mem. adv. bd. Calif. Tomorrow nat. shows and one-man shows; dir. Crocker Art Gallery Assn., pres., 1966-67. Trustee U. Calif., Berkeley Art Mus., 1986-91; mem. adv. com. on future ops. Coun. State Govts., 1965; bd. mgrs., pres. YMCA; bd. dirs. Sacramento Civic Ballet Assn.; trustee Calif. Coll. Arts and Crafts, 1982-86; chmn. Calif. State Task Force on Water Future, 1981-82, Sacramento Regional Found., bd. dirs., 1983-91; bd. dirs. Calif. Mus. Assn., pres., 1976-77, Policy Analysis for Calif. Edn., 1985—, Senate Adv. Commn. on Control of Cost of State Govt., 1986—, Pub. Policy Inst. Calif., 1994-2004; co-chmn. Calif. Citizen's Budget Commn., 1992-99, chmn., 1999—; chmn. Citizen's Commn. on Ballot Initiatives, 1992—, Catalonia Sister State Task Force, 1988—, Commn. on Innovation, Calif. Cmty. Colls., 1992; chair Judicial Coun. Select Com. on Judicial Retirement, 1993—; mem. Supreme Ct. Select Com. Judicial Ethics, 1995-96; bd. dirs. Ctrl. Valley Found., 1994-99. With USNR, 1943-44. Mem. Nat. Acad. Pub. Adminstrn., Phi Beta Kappa, Kappa Sigma. Home: 1900 Rockwood Dr Sacramento CA 95864-1527 Personal E-mail: alanpost@sbcglobal.net.

POST, AVERY DENISON, retired church official; b. Norwich, Conn., July 29, 1924; s. John Palmer and Dorothy (Church) P.; m. Margaret Jane Rowland, June 8, 1946; children: Susan Post Ross, Jennifer C., Elizabeth Post Elliott, Anne Post Roy. BA, Ohio Wesleyan U., 1946; B.D., Yale U., 1949, S.T.M., 1952; L.H.D. (hon.), Lakeland Coll., Sheboygan, Wis., 1977; D.D. (hon.), Chgo. Theol. Sem., 1978, Middlebury Coll., Vt., 1978, Defiance Coll., Ohio, 1979; LL.D. (hon.), Heidelberg Coll., Ohio, 1982, Chapman Coll.; Litt.D. (hon.), Elmhurst Coll. Ordained to ministry, 1949; pastor chs. in Vt., Ohio, Conn. and N.Y., 1946-63; sr. minister Scarsdale (N.Y.) Congl. Ch., 1963-70; minister, pres. Mass. conf. United Ch. Christ, 1970-77; pres. United Ch. Christ, NYC, 1977-89; mem. central com. World Council Chs., 1978-91; exec. com., bd. govs. Nat. Council Chs., 1977-89. Moderator, planning com. 7th Gen. Assembly World Coun. Chs.; lectr. Bible Adelphi Coll., Garden City, N.Y., 1958-59; Luccock lectr. Yale U. Div. Sch., 1961; lectr. homiletics Union Sem., N.Y.C., 1967-69, bd. dirs., 1967-77; trustee Andover Newton Theol. Sem., 1970-80; del. numerous internat. ch. meetings; sr. fellow Hartford Sem., 1989-93. Bd. dirs. Bridges for Peace, 1990-94; exec. dir. Bangor Theol. Sem., Hanover, N.H., 1991-93. With USNR, 1943-45. Decorated Comdr.'s Cross (Federal Republic Germany), 1990; recipient 1st Ecumenical award Mass. Coun. Chs., 1976; Disting. Achievement award Ohio Wesleyan U., 1983 Mem. PTA (life), Randolph Mountain Club (N.H.), Phi Beta Kappa, Omicron Delta Kappa. Democrat. E-mail: avemarg@verizon.net.

POST, DAVID ALAN, broadcast executive; b. NYC, Oct. 20, 1941; s. Emil R. and Ruth (Rosen) P.; m. Arline Goldbrum, June 10, 1962 (div. 1981); children: Randee, Lori, Jill; m. Katlean de Monchy, Dec. 13, 1984; 1 dau., Emily Hart. Student, CCNY, 1959-61; grad., Fleigenheimer Ins. Inst., 1961, N.Y. Inst. Fin., 1968. Sales rep. Aetna Life Ins. Casualty, Hartford, Conn., 1961-63; sales mgr. Globe Rubber Products, Phila., 1963-67; ptnr. Zuckerman Smith and Co., NYC, 1968-71; dir. corp. fin. Andersen and Co., NYC, 1971-72; exec. v.p., dir. R.K. Pace Post Investment Bankers, NYC, 1973-76; chmn., chief exec. officer, founder Page Am. Group, Inc., Hackensack, N.J., 1976-86; co-founder, bd. dirs. Cellular Sys. Inc., 1991-92; chmn., founder Channel Am. TV Network, NYC, 1987-96; chmn., co-founder Can Do Woman TV & Other Media, NYC, 1996-2000; chmn., CEO UMagic Systems, Inc., an Internet Tech. Co., NYC, 2000—; chmn., exec. prodr. Can do Woman div. of Nextpert News, NYC, 2000—; exec. prodr. Nextpert News Network, 2002—; founder, exec. prodr. Two Minute TV Network, 2004—. Contbr. articles to INC. mag.; creator several TV series. Mem. Nat. Assn. TV Programming Execs. Republican. Jewish. Avocation: writing. Office: Nextpert News Network 350 Fifth Ave Ste 5600 New York NY 10118 Home: 35 Sutton Pl 15C New York NY 10022-2464 E-mail: david@nextpert.com.

POST, GAINES, JR., retired history professor, dean, academic administrator; b. Madison, Wis., Sept. 22, 1937; s. Gaines and Katherine (Rike) P.; m. Jean Wetherbee Bowers, July 19, 1969; children: Katherine Doris, Daniel Lawrence. BA, Cornell U., 1959, Oxford U., 1963; MA, Stanford U., 1964, PhD, 1969. Instr. Stanford U., 1966-69; asst. prof. history U. Tex., Austin, 1969-74, assoc. prof., 1974-83; dean faculty, sr. v.p. Claremont McKenna Coll., Calif., 1983-88, prof., 1988—99, emeritus prof., 1999—. Exec dir. Rockefeller Found. Commn. on Humanities, 1978-81. Author: The Civil Military Fabric of Weimar Foreign Policy, 1973, Dilemmas of Appeasement: British Deterrence and Defense, 1934-37, 1993, Memoirs of a Cold War Son, 2000; co-author The Humanities in American Life, 1980; editor: German Unification: Problems and Prospects, 1992. Mem. exec. com. Forming the Future Project, Austin Ind. Sch. Dist., 1982; mem. Tex. Com. for Humanities, 1981-83; mem. coun. Calif. Congl. Recognition Program, 1984-88, Calif. Coun. Humanities, 1995-2003. Rhodes scholar, 1961-63; Am. Coun. Learned Socs. fellow, 1982-83; Am. Philos. Soc. grantee, 1974.

POST, GLEN FLEMING, III, telecommunications industry executive; b. El Dorado, Ark., Oct. 4, 1952; s. Glen F. Jr. and Mary L. (Tubberville) P.; children: Brad, Luke, Matt. BS in Acctg., La. Tech. U., 1974, MBA, 1976. Pvt. practice tax acctg., 1974-76; with CenturyTel Inc., Monroe, La., 1976—, v.p., 1982—84, sr. v.p., treas., 1984-86, sr. v.p., CFO, 1986—88, exec. v.p. & COO, 1988—90, pres. & COO, 1990—92, vice chmn., pres., CEO, 1992—2003, chmn., CEO, 2003—. Bd. dir. Yelcot Telephone Co., No. La. Regions Bank. Mem. exec. cabinet Coll. Adminstrn. & Bus., La. Tech. Univ.; bd. dir. La. Tech. Univ. Found., La. Tech. Univ. Rsch. Found. Recipient Tower Medallion award, La. Tech. Univ., 1997, Lifetime Achievement award in bus., DeGree Enterprises, 2003. Mem. Am. Mgmt. Assn., STICC (subcom. acctg.), Beta Alpha Psi. Office: CenturyTel Inc 100 Century Tel Dr Monroe LA 71203 *

POST, JEFFREY H., insurance company executive; BBA, Univ. Wis., Madison. Chief actuary Fireman's Fund Ins. Co., 1994—96, CFO, 1996—2001, pres., CEO, 2001—04; pres., CEO, dir. CUNA Mutual Group, Madison, Wis., 2005—. Dir. Am. Ins. Assn. Fellow: Casualty Actuarial Soc.; mem.: Am. Acad. Actuaries. Office: CUNA Mutual Group 5910 Mineral Point Rd Madison WI 53705 *

POST, JOHN N., lawyer; b. 1940; BS, St. Peter's Coll., 1962; JD, Georgetown U., 1965. Bar: NJ, Dist. of Columbia. Co-founder, mng ptnr. Post, Polak, Goodsell, MacNeill & Strauchler, P.A. Jag Officer US Marine Corps. Office: Post Polak Goodsell MacNeill & Strauchler PA 425 Eagle Rock Ave Ste Roseland NJ 07068-1717 Office Phone: 973-228-9900. Office Fax: 973-994-1705. E-mail: jnp@ppgms.com. *

POST, MIKE, lighting designer; b. Suffern, NY, June 2, 1962; s. Dirck Hooper and Barbara Spence Post. AB, Ripon Coll., Wis., 1984; MFA in Theatre Design and Tech., U. Mont., Missoula, 1995. Asst. prodn. mgr./master electrician Ala. Shakespeare Festival, Montgomery, 1995—2004; asst. prof. lighting and sound U. So. Miss., Hattiesburg, 2004—. Assistant lighting design, Love Jerry, video design, Macbeth Military Base Tour with The Alabama Shakespeare Festival, lighting design, A Streetcar Named Desire with The Montana Rep, A Midsummer Night's Dream with Georgia Shakespeare. Office Phone: 601-266-5918. Business E-Mail: michael.post@usm.edu.

POST, PETER DAVID, lawyer; b. Reading, Pa., Jan. 2, 1947; s. Carl B. and Frances (Gaughan) P.; children: Michael, Elizabeth. BS, Pa. State U., 1968; JD, Harvard U., 1971. Bar: Pa. 1971, La. 1974, US. Ct. of Appeals (3rd, 4th, 6th, 10th 11th & dc cirs.), US Supreme Ct., All State and Fed. Cts. in Pa. Assoc. Reed, Smith, Shaw & McClay, Pitts., 1975-81, ptnr., 1982—, dept. head, 1992—2000; ptnr. Reed Smith LLP, Pitts. Commr. Upper St. Clair Township, Pa., 1991—94; editor-in-chief The Pa. Labor Letter, 1998—2002. Contbr. articles to profl. jour. With JAGC USN, 1971—75. Named The Best Lawyers in Am., Pa. Super Lawyers, Who's Who in America. Avocations: golf, skiing, fishing, cycling. Office: Reed Smith LLP 435 6th Ave Pittsburgh PA 15219-1886 Office Phone: 412-288-3070. Fax: 412-288-3063. Business E-Mail: ppost@reedsmith.com.

POST, PETER L., marketing executive, writer; m. Patricia C. Post; 2 children. BA, U. Penn., 1972; MFA, Pratt Inst. Reporter Valley Voice, Middlebury, Vt.; dir. comm. & publications Champlain Coll., 1979—84; pres., founder PostScript, Inc., Burlington, Vt., 1984—; dir. Emily Post Inst.; columnist, Etiquette At Work, Boston Sunday Globe, 2004—, NY Times Syndication Sales Corp., 2005—; columnist, Professional Courtesy, Men's Health, 2005—. Founder Emily Post Bus. Seminar Series. Co-author: (books) The Etiquette Advantage in Business, 1999; author: Essential Manners for Men, 2003, Essential Manners for Couples, 2005. Bd. mem. Wake Robin Retirement Comty., Vt. Office: PostScript Inc 444 S Union St Burlington VT 05401 Office Phone: 802-863-2568. Office Fax: 802-863-4179. E-mail: peter@postscriptinc.com.

POST, RICHARD BENNETT, retired human resources executive; b. Clyde, Ohio, July 5, 1936; s. Robert Irving and Elinor May (Bennett) P.; m. Nancy Jane Wardlow, Aug. 31, 1956; children: David Bennett, Todd McKinley, Amy Ellen, Brett Richard, Brina Marie. BS in Psychology, Iowa State U., Ames, 1958; student, Ohio U., Athens, 1954-56; postgrad., George Washington U., Washington, DC, 1959-60, So. Ill. U., Edwardsville, 1972-74. With US Civil Svc. Commn., 1958-79, chief evaluation divsn. St. Louis, 1967-71, chief staffing divsn., 1971-74, dep. reg. dir., 1974-79; dep. assoc. dir. staffing US Office Pers. Mgmt., Washington, 1979-81, assoc. dir. staffing, 1982-86, dir. Washington area svc. ctr., 1986-94; ret., 1994. Cert. lay spkr. United Meth. Ch., 1973—; treas. Meadows Homeowners Assn., 2000-07. Recipient Dirs.' Disting. Svc. award US Office Pers. Mgmt., 1986, Dirs.' citation for Exemplary Pub. Svc., 1994. Mem. AARP (pres. King George Area chpt. 2003-04, treas., 2005—), Sr. Execs. Assn. (life), Fed. Exec. Inst. Alumni Assn., Vienna Choral Soc. (pres. 1987-89), Masterworks Chorus, King George, Va. Avocations: woodworking, singing, gardening. Personal E-mail: Postrn@Worldskyline.com.

POST, ROBERT CHARLES, law educator; b. Bklyn., Oct. 17, 1947; s. Ted and Thelma (Feifel) P.; m. Fran Layton, Jan. 22, 1981; children: Alexander, Amelia. AB, Harvard U., 1969, PhD, 1980; JD, Yale U., 1977; LLD (hon.), Chgo.-Kent U., 1998. Bar: D.C. 1979, Calif. 1983. Law clk. to chief judge U.S. Ct. Appeals (D.C. cir.), 1977-78; law clk. to justice William Brennen Jr. U.S. Supreme Ct. D.C., 1978-79; assoc. Williams & Connelly, Washington, 1980-82; acting prof. law U. Calif., Berkeley, 1983-87, prof. law, 1987-94, Alexander F. and May T. Morrison prof. law, 1994—2003; David Boies prof. law Yale U., New Haven, 2003—. Author: Constitutional Domains, 1995; editor: Law and the Order of Culture, 1991, Censorship and Silencing: Practices of Cultural Regulation, 1998; co-editor: Race and Representation: Affirmative Action, 1998, Human Rights in Political Transistions: Gettysburg to Bosnia, 1999, Civil Society and Government, 2001; co-author: Prejudicial Appearances: the Logic of America Antidisaimation Law, 2001. Gen. counsel AAUP, 1992-94. Fellow Guggenheim Found., 1990-91, Am. Coun. Gen. Socs., 1990-91. Mem. AAUP, Am. Acad. Arts and Scis. Office: Yale Law Sch PO Box 208215 New Haven CT 06520 Office Phone: 203-432-4946. E-mail: robert.post@yale.edu.

POST, STEPHEN GARRARD, theologian, philosopher, educator; b. Bayshore, NY, May 6, 1951; s. Henry Albertson Van Zo and Marguerite Magee Post. MA in religious studies, U. Chgo., 1979; PhD in Ethics and Soc., U. Chgo., 1983. Prof. dept. humanities Marymount Coll., Tarrytown, NY, 1985—88; prof. dept. bioethics Sch. Medicine, Case Western Res. U., Cleve., 1988—. Mem. nat. ethics adv. bd. Alzheimer's Assn., Chgo., 1997—; bd. advisors John Templeton Found., Radnor, Pa., 1998—2002; pres. Inst. for Rsch. on Unltd. Love, Altruism, Compassion, Svc., Cleve., 2001—. Author: (book) The Moral Challenge of Alzheimer Disease, 2000; editor-in-chief (ency.) Ency. of Bioethics, 2003. Episcopalian. Avocations: sailing, gardening, writing. Office Phone: 216-368-6205.

POST, WILLIAM JOSEPH, utility executive; b. Salem, Ohio, Oct. 13, 1950; s. John Joseph and Barbara Louise (Walton) P.; m. Mary Kay Lane, May 2, 1987; children: Kathryn Leigh, Carly Nancy. BS, Ariz. State U., 1972. Budget mgr. Ariz. Pub. Svc., Phoenix, 1978-82, contr., 1982-85, v.p., contr., 1985-87, v.p. fin. and rates, 1987—; chmn., CEO Pinnacle West Capital Corp., 2001—. Mem. exec. com. Nuclear Energy Inst. Bd. dir. Tumbleweed, Phoenix, Tempe Leadership, 1987, YMCA, Phoenix, 1989. Staff sgt. U.S. Army, 1969-75. Republican. Presbyterian. Office: Pinnacle West Capital 400 N Fifth St Phoenix AZ 85004 Home: 4235 E Claremont St Paradise Valley AZ 85253-3948 *

POSTAER, LARRY, advertising executive; b. Chgo. Grad., U. Mo. Sch. Journalism, 1959. Catalog copywriter Sears; with Stern, Walters & Simmons, Chgo., 1962-64, creative dir., 1964-76; sr. v.p., group creative dir. Needham Harper & Steers, Chgo., 1976-81, exec. v.p., dir. creative svcs. LA, 1981-86; co-founder, exec. v.p., dir. creative svcs. Rubin Postaer and Assoc., Santa Monica, 1986—. Named Co-leader of Yr. for 1990, Western States Advt. Agys. Assn., 1991. Office: 2525 Colorado Ave Santa Monica CA 90404

POSTE, GEORGE HENRY, biology professor, former pharmaceutical company executive; b. Polegate, Sussex, Eng., Apr. 30, 1944; came to U.S., 1972; s. John H. and Kathleen B. (Brooke) P.; 1 child, Eleanor Kathy; m. Linda C. Suhler Lopez, Nov. 21, 1992; stepchildren: John Robert, Lisa Carolyn. DVM, U. Bristol, 1966, PhD, 1969, DSc, 1987, LLD (hon.), 1995. Lectr. U. London, 1969-72; assoc. prof. SUNY, Buffalo, 1972-76; prof. pathology Roswell Park Meml. Inst., Buffalo, 1976-80; v.p. rsch. SmithKline Beckman, Phila., 1980-82, v.p. R & D, 1982-86, v.p. worldwide rsch. and pre-clin. devel., 1987-88, pres. R & D, 1988-89; pres. R & D techs. SmithKline Beecham, King of Prussia, Pa., 1989-90, vice-chmn., exec. v.p. R & D, 1990-91, pres. and chmn. R & D, 1992-97; chief sci. and tech. officer SmithKline Beecham Corp. PLC, King of Prussia, Pa., 1997-99; CEO Health Tech. Networks, Scottsdale, Ariz., 2000—; non-exec. chmn. OrchidBioSciences Inc., Princeton, NJ, 2002—; Del E. Webb Disting. prof biology Ariz. State U., Tempe, 2003—, dir. Biodesign Inst., 2003—. Mem. pathology B study sect. NIH, Bethesda, Md., 1978-82; chmn. Gordon Conf., N.H., 1985-86, diaDeXus, 1997-2003, Cerebrus, 1997; pres. coun. U. Tex. M.D. Anderson Cancer Ctr.; bd. dirs. Monsanto, Exelixis, SmithKline Beecham Corp. PLC, Orchid BioSciences Inc., 2000-; mem. adv. coun. Beckman Ctr. for Molecular and Genetic Medicine, Stanford U.; mem. coun. Oxford Internat. Biomedical Centre; chmn. task force on bioterrorism, U.S. Dept. of Defense, 2001-04. Editor: Cell Surface Revs., New Horizons in Therapeutics, Cancer Metastasis Revs., Advanced Drug Delivery Revs., 15 books; contbr. articles to profl. jours. Mem. governing bd. UCLA Symposia, Life Sci. Rsch. Found.; mem. bd. Overseers Sch. Vet. Medicine, U. Penn., Gov.'s adv. com. Sci. and Tech., Pa.; mem. adv. bd. Natural Sci. Assn., U. Pa. Fleming fellow U. Oxford, Eng., 1995, Pitt fellow U. Cambridge, Eng., 1995; named Comdr. of British for svcs. in devel. of bioscis., 1999, Scientist of the Year, R&D mag., 2004. Fellow Royal Soc., Royal Coll. Vet. Surgeons, Royal Coll. Pathologists, Ins. Biology (London), Acad. Med. Scis. (London); mem. AAAS, Am. Soc. Cell Biology, Pathol. Soc., Nat. Assn. Biomed. Rsch. (bd. govs. 1984), Univ. Assn. Space Rsch. (mem. coun. 1984), Pharm. Mfrs. Assn. (former chmn. rsch. and devel. section 1988). Avocations: military history, foreign affairs, photography, auto racing. Office: Biodesign Inst Ariz State Univ PO Box 875001 Tempe AZ 85287-5001 Office Phone: 480-727-8662. Business E-Mail: george.poste@asu.edu.

POSTELL, SHAWN T., music educator, school disciplinarian; b. Columbus, Ohio, Dec. 23, 1963; s. Jack M. and Joan M. Postell; m. Teri I. Postell, Aug. 23, 1999. BA, U. Wis., Green Bay, 1988. Band dir. Hilbert Pub. Schs., Wis., 1988—, dean students, 2004—. Music dir., founder Bay City Swing, Green Bay, 1983—. Mng. dir., founder Hilbert Cmty. Theater, 1994—2004. Home: 5477 Gold Dust Dr De Pere WI 54115 Office: Hilbert HS 1139 W Milwaukee St Hilbert WI 54129

POSTELNEK, STEPHEN A., lawyer; b. NYC, Apr. 24, 1940; BSME, Columbia U., 1961; MSME, Poly. Inst. Bklyn., 1968; JD, St. John's U., 1974. Bar: NY 1975, US Supreme Ct., NY State & Fed. Courts. Design engr. Pratt and Whitney Aircraft Engring. Corp., East Hartford, Conn., Grumman Aerospace Corp., Bethpage, NY; ptnr. Wilson, Elser, Moskowitz, Edelman & Dicker LLP, NYC. Mem.: ABA, NY State Trial Lawyers Assn., Assn. of the Bar of the City of NY, St. Thomas More Inst. Legal Rsch., NY State Bar Assn. Office: Wilson Elser Moskowitz Edelman & Dicker LLP 23rd Fl 150 E 42nd St New York NY 10017-5639 Office Phone: 212-490-3000 ext. 2208. Office Fax: 212-490-3038. Business E-Mail: postelneks@wemed.com.

POSTIGLIONE, COREY M., artist, critic, art educator; b. Chgo., July 25, 1942; BA, U. Ill. Circle Campus; also with Martin Hurtig & Roland Ginzel; MA in 20th Century Art History, Sch. Art Inst. Chgo. Instr. painting Evanston Art Ctr., Ill., 1971—79, Ill. Inst. Tech., 1975—83, Columbia Coll., Chgo., 1979—89, Art Inst. Chgo., 1981—83, U. Ill., Chgo., 1983; instr. art history and criticism Columbia Coll., Chgo., 1990—, tenured prof., 1996—, instr., 2D design studio, 1999—. Asst. dir. Jan Cicero Gallery, Chgo., 1975—76; juror 38th Ann. Old Orchard Art Festival, 1995, 19th Elkhardt Regional, Midwest Mus. Am. Art, Elkhardt, Ind., 1997; judge Riverside Artfair '97, Riverside Art Ctr., Riverside, Ill., 1997; bd. dir. White Walls, 1992. Contbr. editor of reviews and articles The New Art Examiner, 1976—83, Dialogue mag., 1989—, Contbr. reviews and articles New Art Assn., 1975—76, C mag., contbr. editor ArtForum, 2003; contbr. catalogue essay for Liz Langer Retrospective, Artemisia Gallery, Chgo., catalogue essay for Alexandra Domowska for the Pougialis Exhbn., Columbia Coll. Chgo. Hokin Annex Gallery, catalogue essay for Karen Lebergott one-person exhbn., Columbia Gallery, catalogue essay for John Pillips, 2005; collections arranged, Art in Chgo., 1996, 1998, 2000, 2002, one-man shows include Evanston Art Ctr., Ill., 1972, Mayer Kaplan JCC, Skokie, Ill., 1973, Jan Cicero Gallery, Chgo., Ill., 1976, 1978, 1983, 1985, 1995, 1997, Columbia Coll. Gallery, Chgo., 1981, 1997—98, Passages, Oakton Cmty. Coll., 1998, A&D Gallery, Columbia Coll., Rivereast Art Ctr., Chgo., 2005, exhibitions include New Works on Paper, Jan Cicero Gallery, 1993, Labyrinth Series, Jan Cicero Gallery, 1993, Exquisite Corpse, Transmission Gallery, Glasgow, Scotland, 1994, Lakeside Views, Evanston Art Ctr., 1994, Brad Cooper Gallery, Tampa, Fla., 2003, and others, installation work, Blink, No. Ill. U. Gallery, Chgo., 2000. Recipient Third Prize (all show), Italian Am. Exhibit, 1981, Merit award, Evanston & Vicinity Exhbn., 1998. Mem.: Am. Abstracts Artists, NY, Chgo. Art Critics Assn. Home: 4508 N Monticello Chicago IL 60625 Office: Columbia Coll Dept Art & Design 623 S Wabash Rm 1004 Chicago IL 60625 Office Phone: 312-344-7190. Business E-Mail: cpostiglione@colum.edu, cpostiglione@popmail.colum.edu.

POSTLEWAITE, ANDREW WILLIAM, economics professor, department chairman; b. Harvey, Ill., Aug. 23, 1943; s. Edward Homer and Margaret (Hostetler) P.; children: Justin, Kevin. BA in Economics, Ill. Wesleyan U., 1965; MS in Math., DePaul U., 1969; PhD in Applied Math., Northwestern U., 1974; LHD (hon.), Wesleyan U., 2001. Lectr. DePaul U., Chgo., 1970—73; rsch. fellow CORE, Louvain, Belgium, 1973—74; asst. prof. econs. U. Ill., Urbana, 1974—76, assoc. prof. econs, 1976—80; prof. econs. U. Pa., Phila., 1980—82, prof. econs. fin., pub. mgmt., 1982—, chmn. dept. econs., 1982—87, 1990, Harry P. Kamen prof. economics. Bd. dirs. Nat. Bur. Econ. Rsch., Cambridge, Mass.; vis. asst. prof. U. Calif. San Diego, 1976; vis. prof. Princeton U., 1979—80, Stanford Bus. Sch., 1988—89, Calif. Inst. Tech., 2002, Harvard U., 2003, Yale U., 2004; cons. in field; assoc. editor Jour. Economic Theory, 1981—87, 2005—, Jour. Games and Economic Behavior, 1990—97, 2006—; co-editor Econometrica, 1997—2005; editor Internat. Economic Rev., 1996—98; editor Organization Theory and Allocation Processes sect. Fundamentals of Pure and Applied Economics, 1985—94. Contbr. articles to profl. jours. Coun. mem. Game Theory Soc., 2005—; bd. dirs. Nat. Bur. Economic Rsch., 1986—. Grantee NSF, 1975—. Fellow: Am. Acad. Arts and Sciences, Econometric Soc. (coun. mem. 2000—05); mem.: Am. Econ. Assn. (prize com. 2002—). Office: U Pa Dept Econs 3718 Locust Walk Philadelphia PA 19104-6209 Office Phone: 215-898-7350. Office Fax: 215-573-2057. E-mail: apostlew@con.sas.upenn.edu.

POSTMAN, ROBERT DEREK, dean, mathematics professor, writer; s. Benjamin and Edith Postman; m. Elizabeth Ann DelCorso, Aug. 6, 1965; children: Chad, Blaire, Ryan. BA, Kean Coll., 1966; MA, Columbia U., 1967, EdD, 1971. Faculty Hunter Coll., NYC, 1970—76, Tchrs. Coll. Columbia U., NYC, 1977—81; prof. math. and edn. Mercy Coll., Dobbs Ferry, NY, 1976—, chair dept., 1978—, dean grad. edn. programs, 1988—. Founder, head Urban Tchg. Acad.; math. cons. sch. dists. and state edn. depts.; cons. Psychol. Corp. Devel. of Calif.; bd. dirs. Westchester Com. Tech. and Disabled; presenter in field; lectr. in field. Author: SAT Mathematics, 2006, numerous other books, Mathematics on the Geoboard, 1974, Intermediate Mathematics, 1976, Growth in Mathematics, 1980, 1982, Collegiate Reading, 1985, High School Mathematics, 2 vols., 1988, Macmillian Mathematics, 1990, Mathematics Today, 1991, Consumer Mathematics, 1993, (series) Enrichment Mathematics, 1978, Computer Programming, 1983, Mathematics Unlimited, 1986, others, books on ACT, SAT and GRE; contbr. articles to profl. jours. Mem. Closter Bd. Edn., NJ, 1973—79; del. NJ Sch. Bds. Assn., NJ, 1974—77; coach, organizer Closter Recreation Commn.; coach Closter Comets soccer team, 1984—. With USAF, 1959—63. Full Grad. Doctoral fellow, Columbia U., 1966—71, NDEA fellow, 1966—70. Mem.: Assn. Mentally Ill Children Westchester (bd. dirs.), Assnq. Tchr. Educators (exec. bd.), NY Acad. Scis., Soc. Applied Learning Tech., Nat. Coun. Tchrs. Math., Phi Delta Kappa, Kappa Delta Pi. Roman Catholic. Home: 33 Julia St Closter NJ 07624-2417 Office: Mercy Coll 555 Broadway Dobbs Ferry NY 10522-1134

POSTOL, LAWRENCE PHILIP, lawyer; b. Bridgeport, Conn., Oct. 18, 1951; s. Sidney Samuel and Eunice Ruth (Schine) P.; m. Ellen Margaret Russell, Mar. 22, 1975; children: Raymond Russell, Stephan Russell, Carolyn Russell. BS, Cornell U., 1973, JD, 1976. Bar: Conn. 1976, D.C. 1977, U.S. Dist. Ct. D.C. 1977, U.S. Ct. Appeals (D.C. cir.) 1977, U.S. Supreme Ct. 1980, Va. 1982, U.S. Ct. Appeals (4th cir.) 1982, U.S. Dist. Ct. (ea. dist.) Va. 1985, U.S. Dist. Ct. Md. 1989, U.S. Dist. Ct. Conn. 1990. Assoc. Arent, Fox, Washington, 1976-80, Seyfarth, Shaw LLP, Washington, 1980-83, ptnr., 1985—; assoc. Jones, Day, Washington, 1983-85. Lectr. Loyola U., New Orleans, U. Cin., 1987-93; bd. advisers The Environ. Counselor Jour.; spl. counsel Greater Washington Bd. Trade, 1991-93. Author: Legal Guide to Handling Toxic Substances in the Workplace, 1990, Americans with Disabilities Act - A Compliance Manual for Employers, 1993. Jewish. Avocations: sports, soccer. Home: 6340 Chowning Pl Mc Lean VA 22101-4129 Office: Seyfarth Shaw LLP 815 Connecticut Ave NW Washington DC 20006-4004 Office Phone: 202-828-5385. Office Fax: 202-828-5393. Business E-Mail: lpostol@seyfarth.com.

POSTON, ANITA OWINGS, lawyer; b. Sylacauga, Ala., Sept. 24, 1949; d. John T. and Margaret Owings; m. Charles E. Poston, June 9, 1973; children: Charles Evans Jr., John W., Margaret Elizabeth. BA, U. Md., 1971; JD, Coll. William & Mary, 1974. Bar: Va. 1974. Atty. Vandeventer Black LLP, Norfolk, Va., 1974—. Substitute judge Norfolk (Va.) Gen. Dist. Cts., 1982-90; mem. Bar Examiners Bd.; mem. bd. visitors Coll. William and Mary. Mem. State Bd. C.C.s, Richmond, 1985-90, chmn. 1988-89; mem. Norfolk Sch. Bd., 1990-2002, chmn. 1998-2002; bd. dirs. WHRO Pub. Broadcasting, chair, 2002-04; bd. dirs. Access Coll. Found., Va. Symphony Orch., Towne Bank, Norfolk. Mem. ABA (law fellows), Va. Bar Assn. (pres. 2000), Norfolk-Portsmouth Bar Assn. (pres. 1998-99), Va. Law Fellows, Am. Inn of Ct. Office: Vandeventer Black LLP 500 World Trade Ctr Norfolk VA 23510-1679 Office Phone: 757-446-8600. Office Fax: 757-446-8670. Business E-Mail: aposton@vanblk.com.

POSTON, REBEKAH JANE, lawyer; b. Wabash, Ind., Apr. 20, 1948; d. Bob E. and April (Ogle) P. BS, U. Miami, 1970, JD, 1974. Bar: Fla. 1974, Ohio 1977, U.S. Dist. Ct. (so. and mid. dists.) Fla., U.S. Ct. Appeals (11th cir.). Asst. U.S. atty. U.S. Atty.'s Office, Miami, Fla., 1974—76; spl. atty. organized crime and racketeering sect. Strike Force, Cleve., 1976—78; ptnr. Fine, Jacobson, Schwartz, Nash & Block, Miami, 1978—94, Steel Hector & Davis, Miami, 1994—2006, Squire, Sanders & Dempsey LLP, Miami, 2006—. Adj. prof. U. Miami Law Sch., Coral Gables; mem. U.S. sentencing guidelines com. So. Dist. of Fla., Miami. Named one of Best Lawyers in Am., 2003—, Fla.'s Elite Lawyers, Fla. Trend mag., 2004—06; recipient Fla.'s Super Lawyer, Law and Politics, 2006—07. Mem. Fla. Bar Assn., Nat. Assn. Criminal Def. Attys., Nat. Directory Criminal Lawyers, Am. Immigration Lawyers Assn., Dade County Bar Assn. Democrat. Lutheran. Avocations: power boat racing, swimming. Home: 1541 Brickell Ave Apt 3706 Miami FL 33129-1229 Office: 200 SE 2nd St Miami FL 33131 Office Phone: 305-577-7022. Business E-Mail: rposton@ssd.com.

POSTON, WALKER SEWARD, II, medical educator, researcher; BA in Biol. Scis., U. Calif., Davis, 1983; PhD in Psychology, U. Calif., Santa Barbara, 1990; MPH, U. Tex., Houston, Health Sci. Ctr. Clin. psychology resident USAF Med. Ctr., Wright-PAtterson AFB, Ohio, 1989-90; dir. psychology svcs., asst. chief mental health svcs. 9th Med. Group, Beale AFB, 1990-92; fellow in behavioral medicine Wilford Hall Med. Ctr., 1992-93; chief health and rehab. psychology svc. Malcolm Grow Med. Ctr., 1993-95, faculty, 1993-95; clin. asst. prof. dept. med. and clin. psychology F. Edward Herbert Sch. Medicine, Bethesda, Md., 1993-95; asst. prof. medicine Baylor Coll. Medicine, Houston, 1995-99; assoc. prof. U. Mo., Kansas City, 1999—. Rsch. exch. scientist Karolinska Inst., Stockholm, Sweden, 1997, 98. Contbr. articles to profl. jours. Recipient Minority Scientist Devel. award Am. Heart Assn., 1995; U. Calif. Doctoral scholars fellow, 1984-85, 85-86, 86-87, 88-89, Clin. fellow Wilford Hall Med. Ctr., Lackland AFB, 1992-93; Nat. Merit scholar, 1979-80. Fellow, Am. Heart Assn., North Am. Assoc. for the Study of Obesity. Office: Univ Mo 5319 Holmes St Kansas City MO 64110-2437

POSUNKO, BARBARA, retired elementary school educator; b. Newark, July 17, 1938; d. Joseph and Mary (Prystauk) P. BA, Rutgers U., Newark, 1960; MA, Kean U., Union, NJ, 1973; teaching cert., Seton Hall U., Newark, 1966. Cert. elem. tchr., reading specialist, N.J. Social case worker Newark City Hosp., 1960-65; elem. tchr. Plainfield Bd. Edn., NJ, 1966; elem., jr. and sr. high sch. tchr. minimum basic skills and reading Sayreville Bd. Edn., NJ, 1966-82, tchr. Chpt. I and minimum basic skills, 1982-95, cooperating tchr. to student tchr., 1983, coord. testing, 1984-95; ret., 1995. Sch. coord. for congressionally mandated study of ednl. growth and opportunity, 1991-95; mem. numerous reading coms. Recipient Outstanding Tchr. award N.J. Gov.'s Tchr. Recognition Program, 1988. Mem. NEA, Internat. Reading Assn., N.J. Reading Assn., N.J. Edn. Assn. Home: 17 Drake Rd Mendham NJ 07945-1805

POSVAR, MILDRED MILLER, opera singer; b. Cleve. d. William and Elsa (Friedhofer) Mueller; m. Wesley W. Posvar, Apr. 30, 1950; children: Wesley, Margot Marina, Lisa Christina. Degree in Music (hon.), Cleve. Inst. Music, 1946; doctorate (hon.), Cleve. Ins. Music, 1983; diploma, New England Conservatory Music, 1948, doctorate (hon.), 1966; MusD (hon.), Bowling Green State U., 1960; doctorate (hon.), Washington Jefferson U., 1988. Founder Opera Theater of Pitts., 1978—; mem. music faculty Carnegie-Mellon U., 1996—. Operatic debut in Peter Grimes, Tanglewood, 1946; appeared N.E. Opera Theater, Stuttgart State Theater, Germany, 1949-50, Glyndebourne Opera, Edinburgh Festival; debut as Cherubino in Figaro, Met. Opera, 1951; 23 consecutive seasons Met. Opera; radio debut Bell Telephone Hour; TV debut Voice of Firestone, 1952; appeared in films including Merry Wives of Windsor (filmed in Vienna), 1964; Vienna State Opera debut, 1963, appearances with San Francisco, Chgo. Lyric, Cin. Zoo, San Antonio, Berlin, Munich, Frankfurt, Pasadena, Ft. Worth, Kansas City, Pitts., Tulsa and St. Paul operas. Bd. dirs. Gateway to Music. Recipient Frank Huntington Beebe award for study abroad, 1949, 50, Grand Prix du Disque, 1965, Outstanding Achievements in Music award Boston C. of C., 1959, Ohioana Career medal, 1985, Outstanding Achievement in Opera award, Slippery Rock U., 1985, YWCA Ann. Tribute to Women award, 1989, Keystone Salute award Pa. Fedn. Music Clubs, 1994; named one of outstanding women of Pitts., Pitts. Press-Pitts. Post-Gazette, 1968, Person of Yr. in Music, Pitts. Jaycees, 1980. Mem. Nat. Soc. Arts and Letters (pres. 1989-90, Gold medal 1984), Disting. Daus. Pa. (pres. 1991-93), Tuesday Mus. Club, Phi Beta Kappa, Phi Delta Gamma, Sigma Alpha Iota. Office: Opera Theater of Pittsburgh PO Box 110108 Pittsburgh PA 15232-0608

POTAMKIN, ROBERT, automotive executive; b. Mar. 12, 1946; m. Lexi Brockway. Grad., U. Pa., 1970, JD, 1972. CEO Potamkin Cos., Phila., 1972—; co-chmn. Potamkin Auto Group, Phila.; co-chmn., co-CEO Planet Automotive Group Inc., Miami, Fla.; bd. of overseers U. Pa. Law Sch. Million Dollar Roundtable United Way; co-founder Potamkin Prize for Alzheimer's Rsch. Mem.: World Presidents Orgn. Office: Potamkin Cos 130 Spruce St Apt 30B Philadelphia PA 19106-4325 also: Planet Automotive 2333 Ponce De Leon Blvd # 50 Coral Gables FL 33134-5418

POTASH, CHARLES, lawyer; b. May 31, 1932; BA in History with honors, U. Pa., 1953; JD, Temple U. Sch. Law, 1959. Bar: Pa. 1960, US Dist. Ct. (ea. dist.) 1972, US Ct. Appeals (3d cir.) 1981, Superior Ct. Pa. 1960, Supreme Ct. Pa. 1960, US Supreme Ct. 1982. Law clerk Justice Benjamin R. Jones, Supreme Ct. Pa., 1959—60; ptnr. Wisler, Pearlstine, Talone, Craig, Garrity & Potash, LLP, Blue Bell, Pa., 1960—2004, of counsel, 2004—; solicitor Methacton Sch. Dist. Authority, 1960—2004, Methacton Sch. Dist., 1960—94, North Penn Sch. Dist., 1960—96, Upper Perkiomen Sch. Dist., 1960—, Lower Providence Twp. Sewer Authority, 1962—85, North Penn Sch. Authority, 1967—2007, Lower Merion Sch. Dist., 1970—2001, Cheltenham Twp. Sch. Dist., 1970—, Springfield Twp. Sch. Dist., 1973—2004, Upper Dublin Sch. Dist., 1974—2000, Jenkintown Sch. Dist., 1983—2005, Norristown Area Sch. Dist., 1988—99, Abington Sch. Dist., 1992—, Upper Perkiomen Sch. Authority, 1967—2004, Cheltenham Sch. Dist. Authority, 1970—96. Rsch. editor Temple Law Quarterly, 1958—59. Bd. trustees Congregation Rodeph Shalom, Phila., 1980—87; mem. Selective Svc. Adminstrn., 1985—95; mem. bd. overseers Gratz Coll., 1994—98, mem. bd. regents, 1998—; mem. selection bd. 13th Congressional Dist. Svc. Acad., 1995—2004. 1st lt. US Army, 1953—56, Korea. Named solicitor emeritus, Jenkintown Sch. Dist. Bd. Dir., 2005. Mem.: ABA, Pa. Bar Assn., Phila. Bar Assn., Montgomery Bar Assn. (bd. dirs. 1971—75, chmn. jr. bar com., chmn. Am. citizenship com., chmn. mcpl. law com., mem. judiciary com.), Military Order Fgn. Wars, Brant Beach Yacht Club. Office: Wisler Pearlstine Talone Craig Garrity & Potash LLP 484 Norristown Rd Blue Bell PA 19422-2354

POTASH, JEREMY WARNER, public relations executive; b. Monrovia, Calif., June 30, 1946; d. Fenwick Bryson and Joan Antony (Blair) Warner; m. Stephen Jon Potash; 1 son, Aaron Warner. AA, Citrus Coll., 1965; BA, Pomona Coll., 1967. With Forbes Mag., NYC, 1967-69, JETRO, San Francisco, 1970-75; v.p., co-founder, pres. Potash & Co. Pub. Rels., Oakland, Calif., 1980—. Founding exec. dir. Calif.-Asia Bus. Coun., Alameda, 1991—; editor Cal-Asia Member Alert, 1991—; exec. dir. Customs Brokers and Forwarders Assn., San Francisco, 1990—; adv. bd. Asia Pacific Econ. Rev., 1996—; mem. No. Calif. Dist. Export Coun.,

2000—, Pacific Coun. Internat. Policy, 2000—; mem. adv. bd. Ctr. Pacific Rim U. San Francisco, 2005—; mem. adv. bd. China-Am. Bus. and Edn. Ctr., Calif. State U. East Bay, 2005. Editor: Southeast Asia Environmental Directory, 1994, Southeast Asia Infrastructure Directory, 1995-96. Co-founder J.L. Magnes docent program, 1980; pres. NorCal WAORT, 1985—86; bd. dirs. Judah L. Magnes Mus., Berkeley, 1981—94. Named Export Citizen of Yr., U.S. Dept. Commerce, 1998. Mem. Oakland Women's Lit. Soc., Book Club Calif. Office: Potash & Co Pub Rels 1050 Marina Village Pkwy Alameda CA 94501

POTASH, STEPHEN JON, public relations executive; b. Houston, Feb. 25, 1945; s. Melvin L. and Petrice (Edelstein) P.; m. Jeremy Warner, Oct. 19, 1969; 1 child, Aaron Warner. BA in Internat. Rels., Pomona Coll., 1967. Account exec. Charles von Loewenfeldt, Inc., San Francisco, 1969-74, v.p., 1974-80; founder, pres. Potash & Co., Pub. Rels., Oakland, Calif., 1980-87, 1990—. Exec. dir. Calif. Coun. Internat. Trade, 1970-87; v.p. corp. communications APL Ltd., Oakland, 1987-90; chmn. Potash & Co., Oakland, 1990-2007, dir., 1990-. Co-author (with Robert J. Chandler): Gold, Silk, Pioneers & Mail: The Story of Pacific Mail Steamship Company, 2007. Bd. dir. Calif. Coun. Internat. Trade, 1987-94, Calif.-Asia Bus. Coun., 1992—, Temple Sinai, Oakland, 1979-81; adv. com. Old Mint, San Francisco Mus., Clampers-Yerba Buena. Mem.: Pub. Rels. Soc. Am. E-mail: steve@potashco.com.

POTEMPA, KATHLEEN M., dean, nursing educator; b. Oct. 3, 1948; Diploma in nursing, Providence Hosp. Sch. Nursing, Southfield, Mich., 1970; BA in Psychology summa cum laude, U. Detroit, 1974; MS in Nursing, Rush U., 1978, D of Nursing Sci., 1986. Charge nurse coronary ICU Holy Cross Hosp., Ft. Lauderdale, Fla., 1970-71; staff nurse, charge nurse cardiovasc. ICU Henry Ford Hosp., Detroit, 1971-74; nurse practitioner Rush-Presbyn.-St. Luke's Med. Ctr., Chgo., 1974-75; nursing edn. coord. dept. nursing Michael Reese Hosp. and Med. Ctr., Chgo., 1975-77, nursing supr., 1977-78; asst. unit leader dept. gerontol. nursing Rush U. Coll. Nursing, Chgo., 1978-79, asst. chmn., 1979-80, assoc. chmn., asst. prof. gerontol. nursing, 1980-85, asst. prof. gerontol. nursing, 1985-86; asst. prof. nursing, dept. internal medicine, practitioner Rush Med. Coll., Rush U., 1987-88; asst. then assoc. prof. dept. med.-surg. nursing Coll. Nursing, U. Ill., Chgo., 1988—96, dir. tng., pre and postdoctoral fellowship instnl. rsch., 1992—94, exec. assoc. dean Coll. Nursing, 1994-95, interim dean Coll. Nursing, 1995-96; prof., dean Sch. Nursing Oreg. Health Scis. U., Portland, 1996—2006, v.p., 2002—06; dean, prof. nursing, Sch. Nursing U. Mich., Ann Arbor, 2006—. Rsch. assoc. Robert Wood Johnson Tchg. Nursing Home Project, VA Edward Hines Jr. Hosp., Hines, Ill., 1985-86, co-dir. Exercise Rsch. Lab., 1985-86; dir. nursing Johnston R. Bowman Health Ctr. for Elderly, Rush Presbyn. St. Luke's Med. Ctr., Chgo., 1980-85. Contbr. articles to profl. jours. Recipient Oreg. Med. Rsch. Found. Mentor award, 2002, Disting. Alumni award, Rush U., 2003. Fellow Am. Acad. Nursing; mem. ANA (coun. nurse rschrs.), Am. Soc. Hypertension, Gerontol. Soc. Am., Midwest Nursing Rsch. Soc., Heart Assn. Met. Chgo., Am. Heart Assn. Oreg., Ill. Coun. Nurse Rschrs., Am. Heart Assn. (coun. cardiovasc. nursing, coun. hypertension, coun. on strokes), Am. Assn. Coll. Nursing Bd. (sec. 2004), Sigma Theta Tau. Office: U Mich Sch Nursing 400 N Ingalls Rm 1320 Ann Arbor MI 48109

POTEMPA, PHILIP MATTHEW, journalist, columnist, communications educator; b. San Pierre, Ind., Aug. 13, 1970; s. Chester John and Peggy Louise Potempa. BA, Valparaiso U., 1992. Arts and entertainment reporter Vidette-Messenger Newspaper, Valparaiso, Ind., 1991-95, Times Newspaper N.W. Ind., Munster, 1995—; adj. prof. comms. Valparaiso U., 1997—. Arts and entertainment corr. South Bend (Ind.) Tribune, 1993—; prof. comm. Purdue U., Westville, Ind., 1998—; radio commentator WLJE-FM, Ind., 2002—; corr. Indpls. Star Newspaper, 2003—. Co-author: It's a Wonderful Life: A Memory Book, 2003; author: From the Farm, 2004. Bd. dirs. Ind. Journalism Hall of Fame. Recipient Reporting award, Hoosier State Press Assn., 1995, AP Mng. Editors, 1997. Mem.: Ind. Hist. Soc., Soc. Profl. Journalists (award 1996), Chgo. Headline Club (bd. dirs.). Republican. Roman Catholic. Avocation: collecting historical autographs. Office: Times Newspaper 601 W 45th St Munster IN 46321 Home: 104 W Eliza San Pierre IN 46374 Office Phone: 800-837-3232 3247. E-mail: ppotempa@NWITimes.com.

POTENTE, EUGENE, JR., interior designer; b. Kenosha, Wis., July 24, 1921; s. Eugene and Suzanne Marie (Schmit) P.; m. Joan Cioffe, Jan. 29, 1946; children: Eugene J., Peter Michael, John Francis, Suzanne Marie. PhB, Marquette U., 1943; postgrad., Stanford U., 1943, NY Sch. Interior Design, 1948; DFA, Carthage Coll., 1997; DLitt (hon.), Concordia U., 1997. Cert. lighting Nat. Coun. on Lighting Qualification. Founder, chmn. Studios of Potente, Inc., Kenosha, Wis., 1949—; pres., founder Archtl. Svcs. Assocs., Kenosha, 1978—, Bus. Leasing Svcs. of Wis. Inc., 1978—. Past nat. pres. Inter-Faith Forum on Religion, Art and Architecture; vice chm. Wis. State Capitol and Exec. Residence Bd., 1981—. Sec. Kenosha Symphony Assn., 1968-74; bd. dirs. Ctr. for Religion and the Arts, Wesley Theol. Sem., Washington, 1983-84. With US Army, 1943—46, WWII, ETO. Recipient Disting. Alumni award Marquette U., 1999; named to St. Catherine's HS Hall of Fame, 2002. Fellow Am. Soc. Interior Designers; Mem. Am. Soc. Interior Designers (treas., pres. Wis. chpt. 1985-86, 94-95, chmn. nat. pub. svc. 1986, Gold medal Wis. chpt. 2003), Interior Design Coalition Wis (pres 2003-04), Illuminating Engring. Soc. N.Am., Internat. Interior Design Assn., Elks, Am. Legion (life), Sigma Delta Chi. Roman Catholic. Home: 8609 2nd Ave Pleasant Prairie WI 53158-4720 Office: 914 60th St Kenosha WI 53140-4041 Personal E-mail: gpotente@wi.rr.com. Business E-Mail: eugene@potenteinc.com.

POTENZA, JOSEPH MICHAEL, lawyer; b. Stamford, Conn., June 27, 1947; s. Michael Joseph Sr. and Rose Elizabeth (Coppola) P.; m. Karen Louise Yankee, Jan. 28, 1978; children: Wendy Lynn, Chiara Micol. BSEE cum laude, Rochester Inst. Tech., 1970; JD, Georgetown U., 1975. Bar: Va. 1975, D.C. 1976, U.S. Dist. Ct. D.C., U.S. Ct. Appeals (fed. cir.), U.S. Ct. Appeals (6th cir.), U.S. Supreme Ct. Patent examiner U.S. Patent and Trademark Office, Arlington, Va., 1970-74, law clk. bd. appeals, 1974-75, law clk. to presiding judge 6th cir. U.S. Ct. Appeals, 1975-76; assoc. Banner, Birch, McKie & Beckett, Washington, 1976-80, ptnr., 1980—, Banner & Witcoff, Washington, 1995. Adj. prof. Georgetown U. Law Ctr., Washington, 1985—; faculty Nat. Inst. Trial Advocacy-Patent Inst., 1996—; task force on intangibles. Brookings Inst. Editor (monographs) Sorting Out Ownership Rights in Intellectual Property, 1980, Recent Developments in Licensing, 1981; co-author: Patent Trial Advocacy Casebook, 2006; contbg. author Patent Litigaton Strategies Handbook, Patent Misuse-The Critical Balance, A Patent Lawyer's View, Fed. Cir. Bar Jour., Vol. 15, 2005. Bd. dirs. Found. for a Creative Am., 1991—. Recipient Patent and Trademark Office Superior Performance award Dept. Commerce, 1973-75. Fellow Am. Bar Found.; mem. ABA (young lawyers divsn. exec. coun. 1979—, chmn. legis. action com. 1980—, chmn. patent trademark and copyright com. 1977—, house of dels. 1984-86, sci. and tech. sect., coun. mem. 1985—, membership chmn. 1985—, budget co-chmn. 1987—, budget officer 1988—, vice chmn. 1991—, chmn.-elect 1992-93, chmn. 1993, chmn. standing com. on pub. oversight, 1996-2005, spl. adv. on pub. oversight 2005-, fed. practice and procedure com. intellectual property law sect. 1995-96, spring CLE program 1997-98, chmn. summer CLE 1999, 2001, chair fed. practice and procedure com. div. chmn., divsn. VI IP law sec. 1995-97, sec. 2001-04, chmn. divsn. 108 patent sys. policy 2005-), IEEE, AAAS (nat. conf. lawyers and scientists), Am. Intellectual Property Law Assn. (chmn. unfair competition com. 1980-81), DC Bar Assn. (sec. patent, trademark, copyright sect.), Va. Bar Assn., Wash. Patent Lawyers Club (pres. 1988-89), Am. Inns of Ct. (founding mem. and exec. com. Giles S. Rich 1991—, v.p. 1997, pres. 1998-99), Phi Sigma Kappa, Alpha Sigma (pres. 1979-80), Tau Beta Pi. Office: Banner & Witcoff 1100 13th St Ste 1200 Washington DC 20005-4051 Home: 11990 Market St Reston VA 20190 Office Phone: 202-824-3000. Business E-Mail: jpotenza@bannerwitcoff.com.

POTENZA, VITO, lawyer; Degree in Polit. Sci. with honors (hon.), Union Coll., 1969; JD, Georgetown U. Law Ctr., 1975. Criminal def. lawyer (trial and appellate counsel) DC Pub. Defender Svc., 1975—80; staff attorney Nat. Security Agency (NSA), 1980—86, asst. gen. counsel for litigation, 1986—92, assoc. gen. counsel for adminstrn./litigation, 1992—93, dep. gen. counsel to prin. dep. gen. counsel, 1993—95, acting gen. counsel, 1995—. Recipient Meritorious Civilian Svc. award, 1992, Secretary of Defense medal for Meritorious Civilian Svc., Dept. Def., 2001, Presdl. Rank of Meritorious Exec., 2001; Thomas J. Watson Traveling Fellowship, 1969—70. Office: Nat Security Agency (NSA) Fort Meade MD 20755-6000 Office Phone: 301-688-6705. Office Fax: 301-688-4546.

POTERBA, JAMES MICHAEL, economist, educator; b. Flushing, NY, July 13, 1958; s. William Samuel and Margaret Mary (Toale) P.; m. Nancy Lin Rose, June 23, 1984; children: Matthew Robert, Timothy James, Margaret Rose. AB, Harvard U., 1980; MPhil, Oxford U., Eng., 1982, DPhil, 1983. From asst. to assoc. prof. MIT, Cambridge, Mass., 1983-88, prof., 1988—, Mitsui prof., 1996—, dept. head, 2006—. Dir. pub. econs. rsch. program Nat. Bur. Econ. Rsch., Cambridge, 1990—; fellow Ctr. Advanced Study in Behavioral Scis., 1993-94, Hoover Instn. Stanford U., 2000-01, mem. Pres. Adv. Panel on Fed. Tax Reform, 2005; trustee Coll. Retirement Equity Fund, 2006—. Editor: Economic Policy Responses to Global Warning, 1991, International Comparisons of Household Saving, 1994, Housing Markets in the United States and Japan, 1994, Empirical Foundations of Household Taxation, 1996, Fiscal Institutions and Fiscal Performance, 1999, Jour. Pub. Econs., 1998-2006; contbr. articles to profl. jours. Recipient award for Excellence in Sci. Reviewing NAS, 1999; Marshall scholar, 1980-83, Batterymarch fellow, 1986. Fellow: Ctr. Advanced Study in Behavioral Scis., Econometric Soc., Am. Acad. Arts and Scis.; mem.: Am. Fin. Assn. (dir. 1993—95), Nat. Tax Assn. (2d v.p.), Am. Econ. Assn. (exec. com. 2001—03), Phi Beta Kappa. Office: MIT 373 A Memorial Dr Rm E52-350 Cambridge MA 02142-1347 Home Phone: 617-489-4580; Office Phone: 617-253-6673. E-mail: poterba@mit.edu.

POTH, STEFAN MICHAEL, retired diversified financial services company executive; b. Detroit, Dec. 9, 1933; s. Stefan and Anna (Mayer) P.; m. Eileen T. McClimon, May 28, 1966; 1 child, Stefan Michael Jr. Cert. in acctg., Walsh Inst., Detroit, 1954. CPA Mich., cert. consumer credit exec. Sr. acct. Lybrand, Ross Bros. & Montgomery, Detroit, 1953-56, 58-61; with Ford Motor Credit Co., Dearborn, Mich., 1961-91, v.p. leasing truck and recreational products and tractor financing, 1973-77; v.p. cen. and western U.S. ops. Ford Motor Credit CO., Dearborn, 1977-79; v.p. mktg. and ops. svcs. Ford Motor Credit Co., Dearborn, 1979-85, v.p. bus. planning, 1985-90, v.p. credit policy, 1990-91. Bd. dirs. GE Credit Auto Resale Svcs., Inc.; adv. coun. Credit Rsch. Ctr., Krannert Grad. Sch. Mgmt., Purdue U., 1984—91. Chmn. adv. coun. Credit Rsch. Ctr. Krannert Grad. Sch. Mgmt., Purdue U., 1989-90; mem. bd. dirs. Internat. Credit Assoc., 1989-91. With AUS, 1956-58. Roman Catholic. Home: 7230 Mohansic Dr Bloomfield Hills MI 48301-3550

POTLURI, VENKATESWARA RAO, medical facility administrator; b. Krishna Dist., India, Jan. 1, 1955; came to U.S., 1983; s. Venkata Krishnaiah and Bulli Ademma (Koduru) P.; m. Padma Sree Peddu, Dec. 4, 1986; children: Vani, Vamsee Krishna, Varun. BSc, ANR Coll., Gudivada, India, 1975; MSc, AU Coll. Sci. and Tech., Waltair, India, 1977; MPhil, Delhi U., India, 1979, PhD, 1982. Diplomate Am. Bd. Med. Genetics, 1984. Postdoctoral fellow Mt. Sinai Med. Ctr., NYC, 1983-85, vis. asst. prof., 1985-87; lab. dir., adj. mem. med. staff Norwalk (Conn.) Hosp., 1987-98; lab. dir. Lab. Diagnostics (divsn. Cytogenetics), Norwalk, 1998—2001; lab dir. Ctr. for Genetic Svcs. Inc. (divsn. Lab. Corp. of Am.), Corpus Christi, Tex., 2001—03, Dynagene divsn. Lab. Corp. Am., Houston, 2003—. Fellow: Am. Coll. Med. Genetics (founding); mem.: Am. Soc. Human Genetics. Avocations: classical music, Telugu literature, home improvement. Home: 4018 Blue Bonnet Blvd Apt D Houston TX 77025 Office: Dynagene 7400 Fannin Ste 1200 Houston TX 77054

POTPARIC, ZORAN, plastic surgeon; b. Pljevlja, Montenegro, Nov. 7, 1951; married. MD, U. Sarajevo, 1976. Cert. Am. Bd. Plastic Surgery, 1999. Intern U. Med. Ctr., Sarajevo, Bosnia-Herzegovina, 1976—77, resident, 1980—84, asst. prof. surgery, 1984—91; resident dept. plastic surgery Jackson Meml. Hosp./U. Miami, Fla., 1995—97; fellow Ea. Va. Med. Sch., Norfolk, 1986, 1992—94, resident, 1994—95; fellow Providence Hosp., Southfield, Mich., 1991; assoc. prof. surgery La. State U. Med. Ctr., Shreveport, 1997—99; staff physician La. State U. Med. Ctr. Hosp., Shreveport, 1997—99, Imperial Point Med. Ctr., Ft. Lauderdale, Fla., 1999, Broward Gen. Med. Ctr., Ft. Lauderdale, 1999, Holy Cross Hosp., Ft. Lauderdale, 1999, North Ridge Hosp., Ft. Lauderdale, 1999, Meml. Regional Hosp., Hollywood, Fla., North Broward Med. Ctr., Ft. Lauderdale; pvt. practice surgeon Ft. Lauderdale, 1999—. Contbr. articles to med. jours., chapters to books. Mem.: AMA, Ft. Lauderdale Surg. Soc., Broward County Med. Assn., Fla. Med. Assn., So. Med. Assn., Am. Soc. Laser Surgery, Med. Soc. Va., D. Ralph Millard Plastic Surgery Soc., Plastic Surgery Rsch. Coun. Avocations: travel, skiing, history. Office: 935 Intracostal Dr Fort Lauderdale FL 33304 Office Phone: 954-567-1300. Office Fax: 954-567-1301. *

POTSIC, WILLIAM PAUL, otolaryngologist, educator; b. Berwyn, Ill., May 22, 1943; s. Andrew M. and Estella (Buschak) P.; m. Roberta I. Kite; children: Amie, Jordan. BS, U. Ill., 1965; MD cum laude, Emory U., 1969; postgrad., U. Pa.; M in Med. Mgmt., Tulane U., 1998. Intern, resident U. Chgo., 1969-74; practice medicine specializing in pediatric otolaryngology Phila., 1974—; staff Presbyn. Hosp., U. Pa. Hosp., Phila., Children's Seashore House, Phila.; prof. otorhinolaryngology and human comm. U. Pa., Phila., 1974-93, E. Mortimer Newlin prof., 1993—; dir. div. otorhinolaryngology and human comm. Children's Hosp., Phila., 1975—, pres. med. staff, 1982-84, med. dir. Cochlear Implant Program, 1991—, vice-chmn. clin. affairs dept. surgery, 1995—, dir. ambulatory surg. svcs., 1997—, dir. ctr. for childhood comm., 1999. Author: Surgical Pediatric Otolaryngology, 1997; contbr. articles to profl. jours. Recipient 1st prize for clin. rsch. Am. Acad. Ophthalmology and Otolaryngology, 1977, Sylvan E. Stool award for outstanding lifetime contbns. in ear nose and throat advances in children, Presdl. award Soc. Otorhinolaryngology and Head and Neck Nurses, 2002; NIH grantee. Mem. AMA, Am. Acad. Otolaryngology Head and Neck Surgery, Am. Laryngology, Otolgy and Rhinology Soc., Am. Coll. Physician Execs., Internat. Acad. Cosmetic Surgery, Pa. Med. Soc., Phila. Coll. Physicians, Phila. County Med. Soc., Phila. Laryngol. Soc. (treas. 1983), Phila. Pediatric Soc., Am. Laryngol. Assn. (Gabriel Tucker award 2005), Phila Laryngol. Soc. (pres. 1984), Phila. Soc. Facial Plastic Surgeons, Politzer Soc., Soc. Ear, Nose and Throat Advances in Children (pres. 1983), Am. Soc. Pediatric Otolaryngology (pres. 1991, Potsic Ann. award for basic sci. rsch.), Soc. Univ. Otolaryngologists, Am. Acad. Pediat., Alpha Omega Alpha, Phi Chi. Home: 1057 Beaumont Rd Berwyn PA 19312-2007 Office: Children's Hosp Phila 34th And Civic Center Blvd Philadelphia PA 19104 Office Phone: 215-590-3450. E-mail: potsic@email.chop.edu.

POTTASH, A. CARTER, psychiatrist, hospital executive; b. Phila., Nov. 30, 1948; s. R. Robert and Elizabeth (Braunschweig) P. BS with high honors, Trinity Coll., Hartford, Conn., 1970; MD, Yale U., 1974. Intern Tufts U. Sch. Medicine, Springfield, Mass., 1974-75; clin. fellow Yale-New Haven Hosp., 1977-78; fellow Yale U., New Haven, 1975-78; med. dir. Psychiatric Diagnostic Labs. Am., Summit, NJ, 1979-83. Lectr., cons. in field; vis. prof. St. Elizabeth Med. Ctr., Northeastern Ohio U. Coll Medicine, 1979; clin. prof. NYU, 1989—; pres. Fla. Consultation Svcs., P.A., West Palm Beach, 1992—, Psychiatric Assocs. N.J., P.A., Summit, N.J., 1978-93, Met. Med. Group P.C., N.Y.C., 1981-92, So. Fla. Med. Group P.A., Delray Beach, 1984-93, Stony Lodge Hosp., Inc. and Stony Lodge Med. Group P.C., Briarcliff Manor, N.Y., 1985—; Hampton Med. Group, P.A., Rancocas and Summit, N.J., 1986—; exec. med. dir. Fair Oaks Hosp., Summit, 1978-92, The Regent Hosp., N.Y.C., 1981-92, Lake Hosp of the Palm Beaches, Lake Worth, Fla., 1984-92, Fair Oaks Hosp. at Boca/Delray, Fla., 1984-92, Hampton Hosp., Rancocas, N.J., 1986-95—; chmn. Stony Lodge Hosp., Briarcliff Manor, N.Y., 1985—. Editor Psychiatry Letter, 1980-91; mem. editl. bd. Internat. Jour. Psychiatry in Medicine, 1978-87, The Psychiatric Hosp., 1982—, Jour. Nat. Assn. Pvt. Psychiatric Hosps., 1980-81, Fla. Psychiatry Newsletter, 1992—; reviewer Jour. Nervous and Mental Disorders, Alcoholism, Clin. and Exptl. Rsch., JAMA, Hosp. and Cmty. Psychiatry; contbr. articles to profl. jours. Mem. adv. bd. Mothers for More Halfway Houses, N.Y.C., 1986—; cons. com. on women and alcoholism Jr. League of N.Y.C., 1987; bd. dirs. Met. Soc. Arts, N.Y.C., 1984-87. Fellow Am. Coll. Clin. Pharmacology, Assn. Clin. Scientists, Nat. Acad. Clin. Biochemistry, Am. Psychiat. Assn. (disting. fellow), The Acad. Medicine N.J.; mem. AMA, Soc. Neurosci., Nat. Acad. Clin. Biochemistry, Palm Beach County Med. Soc., Am. Acad. Clin. Psychiatrists, Brit. Brain Rsch. Assn. (hon.), European Brain and Behavioral Soc. (hon.), Am. Soc. Addiction Medicine, Am. Academy of Addiction Psychiatry (founding mem. 1987), Fla. Med. Soc., Palm Beach County Psychiat. Soc., Med. Soc. State N.Y., Med. Soc. N.J., Union County Med. Soc., N.Y. Athletic Club, Canoe Brook Country Club, Beacon Hill Club, Phi Beta Kappa, Delta Phi Alpha. Office: PO Box 511 West Palm Beach FL 33402-0511 Office Phone: 561-837-2215.

POTTER, ALICE CATHERINE, medical technician; b. Oil City, Pa., June 24, 1928; d. Howard Taylor and Hilda Marian (Lewis) P. BA, U. Findlay, 1949; postgrad., Springfield City Hosp., Ohio, 1949-50. Registerd med. technologist Am. Soc. Clin. Pathologists; cert. clin. lab. scientist. Med. technologist Mercy Hosp., Springfield, 1950-54, Oil City Hosp., 1954-67; staff med. technologist Thomas Jefferson U. Hosp., Phila., 1968-83, sr. med. technologist, 1983—97, retired, 1997—2002. Vol. Acad. Natural Scis., Phila., 1995-2000 Mem. Am. Soc. Clin. Lab. Scientists, Pa. Soc. Clin. Lab. Scientists (membership chmn. Delaware Valley chpt. 1977-78, chmn. pub. rels. 1982-94, 96-97, bd. dirs. 1989-91, 97-98, 98-99, 99-2004, pres.-elect 1991-92, pres. 1992-93, Scrimshaw award 1992) Republican. Avocations: travel, needlecrafts. Home: 1701 Wallace St Philadelphia PA 19130-3312

POTTER, ALLAN L., lawyer; b. Corpus Christi, Tex., Apr. 27, 1947; s. C. Burtt and Marion J. Potter. Student, U. Tex., 1965-67; BA, Baylor U., 1969, JD, 1971. Bar: Tex. 1971, U.S. Ct. Appeals (5th cir.) 1972, U.S. Ct. Appeals (6th and 11th cirs.), U.S. Supreme Ct. 1975; cert. in bus. and consumer bankruptcy Tex. Bd. Legal Specialization. Law clk. 13th Ct. Appeals Tex., Corpus Christi, 1972-73; ptnr. Potter & Potter, Corpus Christi, 1973-91. Pvt. trustee U.S. Bankruptcy Ct., Corpus Christi, 1975-91. Chmn. Nueces County Dem. Com., Corpus Christi, 1982-86. Mem. Corpus Christi Bankruptcy Bar Assn. (pres. 1992-93). Baptist. Office: PO Box 3159 606 N Carancahua Ste 820 Corpus Christi TX 78463-3159

POTTER, BILL R., business executive; s. Billy Gene and Rachel Evelyn Potter; m. Diane S. Potter (div.); children: Gregory James, Alex Michael. BS in Fermentation Sci., U. Calif., Davis, 1976. Pres. Sawyer of Napa, Inc., Calif., 1976—92; v.p. Howes Leather Co., Inc., Quincy, Mass., 1992—95, Eagle Ottawa Leather Co., Grand Haven, Mich., 1995—97; CEO, pres. Robert Talbott, Inc., Monterey, Calif., 1998—, also bd. dirs. Mem.: Vistage Internat., Mensa. Avocations: motorcycling, travel.

POTTER, CALVIN J., retired library director; b. Sheboygan, Wis., Nov. 3, 1945; married. Student, U. Wis., Sheboygan; BA, Lakeland Coll., 1968; postgrad., U. Wis. Past Wis. state assemblyman dist. 26; with dist. 9 Wis. State Senate, 1990-98, chmn. edn. com.; asst. supt. Dept. Pub. Instrn., Madison, Wis., 1998—2003. Former tchr. Mem. Sheboygan County Hist. Soc. Mem. NEA, Wis. Edn. Assn., Izaak Walton League. Address: N6266 Rio Rd Sheboygan Falls WI 53085-2203

POTTER, CARYL A., III, lawyer; b. Norfolk, Va., Apr. 4, 1947; BA in sociology, Stanford U., 1972; JD, U. Mo., Columbia, 1973. Bar: DC 1978. Govt. contract practice, Washington, 1978—91; joined Sonnenschein Nath & Rosenthal LLP, Washington, 1991, now vice chmn. of firm, mem. policy & planning com., mem. & former head govt. contracts practice group. Capt. Judge Adv.'s Office USAF, 1973—78. Office: Sonnenschein Nath & Rosenthal LLP Ste 600, E Tower 1301 K St NW Washington DC 20015 Office Phone: 202-408-6340. Office Fax: 202-408-6399. Business E-Mail: cpotter@sonnenschein.com.

POTTER, DAVID B., lawyer; b. Nov. 1, 1954; BA, Southwest State U., 1977; JD magna cum laude, U. Minn., 1980. Bar: Minn. 1980. Ptnr., bus. litig. Oppenheimer Wolff & Donnelly LLP, Mpls., chmn., 2007—. Editor (note & comment): Minn. Law Rev.; contbr. articles to profl. jours. Mem.: Order of the Coif. Office: Oppenheimer Wolff & Donnelly LLP Plaza VII Ste 3300 45 S 7th St Minneapolis MN 55402 Office Phone: 612-607-7412. Office Fax: 612-607-7100. E-mail: dpotter@oppenheimer.com. *

POTTER, DAVID STONE, Greek and Latin educator; b. Cambridge, Mass., Mar. 15, 1957; s. Harold David and Elizabeth Fleming (Stone) P.; m. Ellen Ann Bauerle, Aug. 18, 1990; children: Claire Penelope, Natalie Sarah Ni Qing. BA, Harvard U., 1979; PhD, Oxford U., 1984. Vis. asst. prof. Greek and Latin Bryn Mawr (Pa.) Coll., 1984-86; asst. prof. Greek and Latin U. Mich., Ann Arbor, 1986-91, from assoc. to prof. Greek and Latin, 1991-96—, dir. Lloyd Hall Scholars program, 1999—2004. Author: Prophecy and History in the Crisis of the Roman Empire, 1990, Prophets and Emperors: Human and Divine Authority from Augustus to Theodosius, 1994, Literary Texts and the Roman Historian, 1999, Life Death and Entertainment in the Roman Empire, 1999, The Roman Empire at Bay AD 180-395, 2004, Companion to the Roman Empire, 2006, The Caesars, 2007, (weekly column) What Would the Romans Say, Chgo. Tribune, 2004-. Recipient Phi Beta Kappa award Harvard U., 1979, Conington prize Oxford U., 1988. Episc. Home: 2377 Timbercrest Ct Ann Arbor MI 48105-9269 Office: Univ Mich Dept Classical Studies Ann Arbor MI 48109-1003 Office Phone: 734-936-2249. E-mail: dsp@umich.edu.

POTTER, EMMA JOSEPHINE HILL, language educator; b. Hackensack, NJ, July 18, 1921; d. James Silas and Martha Loretta (Pyle) Hill; m. James H. Potter, Mar. 26, 1949. AB cum laude with honors in classics, Alfred U., 1943; AM, Johns Hopkins U., 1946. Tchr. Latin, Balt. County Pub. Schs., 1943-44; instr. French and Spanish, Balt. Poly. Inst., 1950-83, instr. Spanish adult edn. classes, 1946-48; treas. Bruno-Potter, Inc. Trustee James Harry Potter Gold Medal award of ASME. Donor commemorative plaque in honor of Martha Pyle Hill to Chenango County Coun. Arts, 1996. Mem. Internat. Platform Assn., Clan Hay Soc. Scotland (Am. br.), John Hopkins U. Faculty Club, Colonial Williamsburg Duke of Gloucester Soc. Democrat. Home: 419 3d Ave Avon By The Sea NJ 07717-1244

POTTER, FRED LEON, lawyer, retired insurance company executive; b. Kansas City, Dec. 15, 1948; s. Donald Warren and Olive Lucile (Ater) P.; m. Mertie Lorraine Scribner, June 13, 1970; children: Mark, Amy, Joy. BA, Harvard U., 1970, MBA, 1972; JD, U. Mich., 1975. Bar: N.H. 1975, U.S.

Dist. Ct. N.H. 1975. Atty. Sulloway, Hollis & Soden, Concord, NH, 1975-80, 96—; pres., gen. counsel Christian Mut. Life Ins. Co., Concord, NH, 1980-96. Ptnr., mgmt. cons. Potter-Brock Assn., Tucson, 1969-82; trustee Gordon-Conwell Theol. Seminar, South Hamilton, Mass., 1983—; bd. dirs. N.H. Savs. Bank Corp., Concord, 1987-90; exec. dir. N.H. Health Plan, 2002—, N.H. Vaccine Assn., 2002—. Clk. Concord Union Sch. Dist., 1978-84; deacon 1st Bapt. Ch., Concord, 1978-85; elder Grace Bible Fellowship, 1993—; coach Concord Little League, 1985-87, 90-93. Mem. ABA, N.H. Bar Assn. (treas. 1980-84, v.p. 1984-85, pres. 1986-87, Pres. Disting. Service award 1983), Merrimack County Bar Assn. (sec. 1976-80), Christian Legal Soc., Computer Law Assn., Order of Coif. Evangelical. Home: 4 Pond Place Ln Concord NH 03301-3033 Office: 9 Capitol St Concord NH 03301-6310 Home Phone: 603-228-1272; Office Phone: 603-223-2816. Business E-Mail: FPotter@sulloway.com.

POTTER, GEORGE KENNETH, artist; b. Bakersfield, Calif., Feb. 26, 1926; s. Howard Eugene and Edythe (Keast) P.; m. Heliodora Carneiro de Mendonca, July 30, 1954 (div. July 1956); 1 child, Helen Marcia Pessoa; m. Ruth Mary Griffen, Aug. 4, 1962 (div. July 1989); children: Katherine Anne Klein, Claire Lorraine, Cynthia Ann. Student, Acad. Art U., San Francisco, 1947—48, Jean Metzinger Acad. Frochot, Paris, 1950—52, Inst. Statale dei Belli Arti, Florence, Italy, 1951; BA magna cum laude, San Francisco State U., 1974. Tchr. pvt. watercolor workshops, San Francisco, Santa Fe, Hawaii, Italy, Adriatic, Sacramento Fine Arts Ctr., others; lectr. San Francisco State U.; instr. Acad. Art U., San Francisco; judge Vacaville 28th Ann., 2005, Calif. State Fair Art Exhbn., 1968. One-man shows include Rotunda Gallery, San Francisco, 1949, 52, Gallerie 8, Paris, 1952, Brazilian-Am. Inst., Rio de Janeiro, 1955, U. Santa Clara, Calif., 1958, Coll. Marin, Calif., 1958, Maxwell Galleries, San Francisco, 1958, 62, Rosacrucian Mus., San Jose, Calif., 1959, U. Calif.-Berkeley, 1959, Gallery 5, Santa Fe, 1960, Kaiser Art Ctr. Gallery, Oakland, Calif., 1980, Marin County Civic Ctr., San Rafael, Calif., 1985, NutTree Gallery, Vacaville, Calif., 1987, Foundry Gallery, Sacramento, 2003, 20th St. Gallery, Sacramento, 2005, New Artworks Fair Oaks, 2007, numerous others; competitive exhibitions include Am. Watercolor Soc., NYC, 1961, 74, 76, 79, 03, Calif. Watercolor Assn., 2004-07, Phelan Awards Competition San Francisco Mus. Art, 1949, Calif. Palace Legion Honor, 1958, 60, San Francisco, 1958, 60, 63, 75, Springville (Utah) Invitational, 1963, Jack London Invitational (award 1958), Oakland, Calif., 1957-65, Calif. State Fair (awards 1958, 72, award of excellence 2006) Sacramento, 1957-58, 61-68, 70-74, 76, 79, 86, 2006, Oakland Watercolor Ann., 1948, 52, Mother Lode Ann., Sonora, Calif., 1957-58, 63, 65, Kingsley Ann., E.B. Crocker Art Mus., Sacramento, 1948, 58, 61, 62, 64, 65, Marin Soc. Artists Ann., 1948-49, 58, 61, 65-73, 75, 77, 95-98, 04, 05, 06, Marin County Ann. (awards 1966, 67), 1962, 65-67, 70, 71, 76, Western Assn. Mus. Shows, 1964, 67, 74, 05, 06, No. Calif. Arts Ann., 1961, 68, 88, 97, 98, 03-06, Fukuoka (Japan) Invitational Exchange Show with Oakland, 1964, Soc. Western Artists Ann. at M.H. De Young Mus., San Francisco, 1956-64, Statewide Watercolor Show (award), Santa Cruz, 1958, Watercolor U.S.A., Springfield, Mo., 1973, 74, Royal Watercolor Soc. Invitational Exhbn., London, 1975, From London to Leeds Mus. Art, Eng., 1975, Palace of the Legion of Honor, San Francisco, A City Buys Art Invitational, 1967, San Francisco Art Festival, 1975, Palo Alto Cultural Ctr. (award 1977), 1977, Calif. Modernist Watercolors of 1950's, Pasadena Mus. Calif. Art, 2006; executed murals Moore Bus. Forms, Inc., Oakland, 1963, Town Hall, Corte Madera, Calif., Macy's of Calif., Sacramento, 1963, San Mateo, 1964, Stockton, 1965, stained glass dome for Hale Meml., Soc. Calif. Pioneers, San Francisco, 1974, Calif. Dept. Motor Vehicles, Oakland, 1975; stained glass and resin triptych U. Calif. at San Francisco Moffitt Hosp., 1976, Embassy Stes. Hotel, Sacramento (watercolor commn.), 2001, W. Robert Griswold, Jr., Tiburon, Calif. (sculpture commn.), 2002; represented in permanent collections including HUD San Francisco regional office, San Francisco Art Commn., San Diego Mus. Art; art dir. McCann-Erickson Advt. Inc., Rio de Janeiro, 1954-55, Johnson and Lewis Advt., San Francisco, 1957, Michelson Advt., Palo Alto, Calif., 1959-60; contbr. The Calif. Style-Watercolor Artists 1925-55 (McClelland and Last), 1985, The NY Art Rev., 1988, Watercolors Editions Limited, 1990, California Watercolors 1850-1970, McClelland and Last, 2002. Served with USMCR, 1944-46, PTO. Recipient Macy's Art award, San Francisco, 1958, 1st award Watercolor Delta Ann., Antioch, Calif., 1969, 1st award Alameda County Fair, 1974, 79, 85, Santa Rosa 12th Ann., 1975, Best of Show Calif. Arts League Open Exhibition, 1988, 98, First Popular award Calif. Arts League Open, 1989, 2d award Calif. Art League, 1997, 1st place award, 1997, 1st place award Marin Soc. Artists Ann. Open, 1997, Watercolor Artists Sacramento Horizons, 19th ann. Grumbacher award, 1997, Valley Sculpture Artists 1st Ann. Exhbn. Merit award, 1998-99, award of excellence Opus Magnum XI, 1998, Wash. 20th Ann. Exhbn., 1998, First award sculpture, 1997, First award 1999, Award of Merit No. Calif. Arts Annual Open, 1999, Florence Ferrario Meml. award, 1998, Award of Excellence League of Carmichael Artists Annual Open, 1999, Merit award 1998, 2d Sculpture award, 1st Mixed award Calif. Art League, 2000, First award Valley Sculpture Artists Members Show, 2000, 1st Watercolor award Watercolor Artists Sacramento Open, 2000, 1st Watercolor award, 1st Mixed award Calif. Arts. League Ann. Open, 2001, Merit award Sacramento Watercolor Artists Open, 2002, 1st Ann. Meml. award Valley Sculpture, 2003, award of merit No. Calif. Arts Open, 2003, 1st award and 1st Popular award, 2004, 1st Watercolor award, 2d Print award, 3d Mixed award Calif. Art League Open, 2004, Richeson Golden Watercolor award Calif. Art League, 2005, First Watercolor award, 2005, Best of Color Open Show, 2006, First Watercolor award No. Calif. Arts Member Show, 2005, Second Watercolor award, 2005, Judge's award Magnum Opus, Best of Color Sacramento Fine Arts Ctr., 2006, Haley Meml. award, 2005, Best of Show, Watercolor Artists Sacramento Open, 2005, 06, Best of Show, Watercolor Artists Sacramento Wash. Mem.'s Show, 2006, award of Excellence Watercolor Artists Sacramento Members Show, 2007, Best of Show Vacaville Art Fest, 2005, First award Marin Soc. Artists, 2006, Calif. State Fair award of excellence, 2006, 2d prize Vacaville Ann., 2006, others. Mem. Am. Watercolor Soc. (signature mem.), Calif. Watercolor Assn. (signature mem.), Marin Soc. Artists (life), No. Calif. Arts, Watercolor Artists Sacramento, Valley Sculpture Artists. Address: 4824 Skyway Dr Fair Oaks CA 95628-6520 Office Phone: 916-966-8248. Personal E-mail: kpotterart@yahoo.com.

POTTER, GEORGE WILLIAM, JR., mining executive; b. St. Louis, Aug. 5, 1930; s. George William and Fay Marguerite (Finch) P.; m. Emily Louise Withers, Feb. 11, 1956; 1 child, Anne Finch Russ. BA, U. Mo., Kansas City, 1952. Pres. Oritz Mines, Inc., Joplin, Mo., 1962—64, chmn. bd. dirs., 1964—87, Nancy Oil & Royalty Co., Joplin, 1981—86; pres., chmn. bd. dirs. Potter Industries, Inc., Joplin, 1981—90; chmn. bd. dirs. Cresset Corp., Joplin, 1986. One-man shows include Barn Gallery, Kansas City, Mo., 1974, Fountain Valley Sch., Colorado Springs, Colo., 1974, U. Leyden, The Netherlands, 1977, others; author books (under pseudonym E.L. Withers): The House on the Beach, 1957, The Salazar Grant, 1959, Diminishing Returns, 1960, Heir Apparent, 1961, The Birthday, 1962, Royal Blood, 1964; fgn. edits. include Brit., French, Italian, German, Scandinavian, Japanese. Founding bd. dirs. Winfred L. and Elizabeth C. Post Meml. Art Reference Libr., 1977-82, Kansas City Ballet, 1976-79; trustee Conservatory of Music, Kansas City, 1988-2001. Recipient Mo. Writers award, U. Mo., Columbia, 1967. Mem. Authors Guild, Nat. Trust for Hist. Preservation, Soc. Fellows Nelson Gallery Found. (coun. 1988-91), Kansas City Country Club. Home: 1239 W 61st Terr Kansas City MO 64113-1327

POTTER, HOLLIS GROMISCH, radiologist; b. NYC, 1958; MD, NY Med. Coll., 1985. Nat. Bd. of Med. Examiners 1985, diplomate Am. Bd. Radiology, Diagnostic Radiology 1990. Intern Danbury Hosp., 1985—86; resident No. Shore U. Hosp., Manhasset, NY, 1986—90; fellow skeletal radiology NY Hosp., Cornell U. Med. Coll., NY, NY, 1990—91; fellow musculoskeletal radiology Hosp. Spl. Surgery, NYC, 1990—91, attending radiologist, chief, divsn. of magnetic resonance imaging, co-dir. rsch., 1992—, assoc. scientist-rsch. divsn.; attending radiologist NY Presbyn. Hosp. Prof. radiology Weill Med. Coll., Cornell U.; spkr. in field. Contbr. scientific papers, chapters to books; reviewer: Jour. of Am. Acad. of Orthopaedic Surgeons, Jour. of Biomechanics, Radiology, Jour. of Orthopaedic Rsch., Jour. of Bone and Joint Surgery. Recipient Editor's Recognition award with Distinction, 1996, 1997. Mem.: Am. Orthopaedic Soc. for Sports Medicine, Soc. of Skeletal Radiology, Radiological Soc. of N.Am., Internat. Soc. for Magnetic Resonance in Medicine, AMA, Am. Coll. of Radiology, Am. Acad. of Orthopaedic Surgeons, ACL Study Group, NY Roentgen Soc., Am. Roentgen Ray Soc., Phi Beta Kappa, Alpha Omega Alpha. Office: Hosp for Spl Surgery 535 E 70th St New York NY 10021-4872 Office Phone: 212-606-1023. Business E-Mail: potterh@hss.edu.

POTTER, J. STEWART, property manager; b. Ft. Worth, July 8, 1943; s. Gerald Robert Potter and Marion June (Mustain) Tombler; m. Dianne Eileen Roberb, Dec. 31, 1970 (div. Aug. 1983); 1 child, Christopher Stewart; m. Deborah Ann Blevins, Oct. 20, 1991. AA, San Diego Mesa Coll., 1967. Cert. apt. mgr., apt. property supr., housing adminstr. Sales mgr. Sta. KJLM, La Jolla, Calif., 1964-67; mgr. inflight catering Host Internat., San Diego, 1967-69; lead aircraft refueler Lockheed Co., San Diego, 1969-70; property mgr. Internat. Devel. and Fin Corp., La Jolla, 1970-72; mgr. bus. property BWY Constn. Co., San Diego, 1972-73; mgr. residents Coldwell Banker, San Diego, 1973-74; mgr. Grove Investments, Carlsbad, Calif., 1974-76, Villa Granada, Villa Seville Properties Ltd., Don Cohn, Chula Vista, Calif., 1976-83; gen. mgr. AFL-CIO Bldg. Trades Corp., National City, Calif., 1983—2003; instr., Cert. Apt. Mgmt. San Diego Apt. Assn., 1995-98. Bd. dirs. San Diego County Apt. Assn., 1995-97, San Diego County Policy Panel Youth Access to Alcohol, 1994-2002, San Diego Crime Victims Fund, 1998-2003, Founding Families San Diego Hist. Soc. Mem. Am. Assn. Retired Persons, San Diego County Apt. Assn. (bd. dirs.), La Jolla Monday Night Club (treas. 1984-89), La Jolla Hist. Soc. Roman Catholic. Avocation: golf. Personal E-mail: jspotter@san.rr.com.

POTTER, JACK (JOHN E. POTTER), federal agency administrator; b. NYC, 1955; m. Maureen Potter; 2 children. B in Econs., Fordham U.; M in Mgmt., MIT. With US Postal Svc., 1977—, mgr. of Capital Metro ops., 1998—2000, sr. v.p. labor rels., 1998—99, sr. v.p. ops., 1999—2000, COO, 2000—01, postmaster gen., CEO, 2001—. Recipient Bd. Governors award, US Postal Svcs., 1999, Elmo R. Zumwalt Legacy award, Marrow Found., 2003, J. Edward Day award, Assn. Postal Commerce, 2003, Tom Tully award, Am. Bus. Media, 2006. Office: US Postal Svc 475 L'Enfant Plz Rm 10022 Washington DC 20260-0010 Business E-Mail: pmgceo@usps.gov.

POTTER, JAMES EARL, retired international hotel management company executive; b. Utica, NY, July 25, 1933; s. Earl Moses and Helen May Potter. BS in Hotel Mgmt. with distinction, Cornell U., 1954, postgrad., 1955-56. Owner, propr. Old Drovers Inn, Dover Plains, NY, 1956-89; various acctg. positions Inter-Continental Hotels Corp., NYC, 1960-62, fin. dir. for Asia and Pacific, 1963-69; v.p. Overseas Nat. Airways Hotels, NYC, 1969-71; sr. v.p. Inter-Continental Hotels Corp., NYC, 1972-89, London, 1990-92. Instr. acctg. Cornell U., Ithaca, N.Y., 1957-59. Author: A Room with a World View, 1996. Trustee Opera Co. Boston, 1978-85; mem. Cornell U. Coun., 1988-91; mem. patron com. Met. Opera, N.Y.C.; bd. dirs., mem. investment com., treas. Santa Fe Opera. Mem.: Culinary Inst. Am. (trustees com. on acad. policy 1980—90), Santa Fe Opera Found. (mem. fin. com. 2002—03, trustee), Cornell Hotel Soc., Santa Fe Opera Club (bd. dirs.), Cornell Club (N.Y.C.), Met. Opera Club (bd. dirs., pres.). Presbyterian. Avocation: opera.

POTTER, JAMES G., lawyer, food products executive; s. Maxine Potter. BS in Philosophy and Psychology, U. Chicago; JD, Harvard Law Sch. Assoc. Keck, Mahin & Cate, Morgan, Lewis and Bockius; chief legal officer Prudential Bank and Trust Co. & Prudential Savings Bank (subsidiaries of Prudential Insurance Co.), 1989—97; exec. v.p., gen. counsel, sec. Provident Mutual Life Insurance Co., 1997—2000; v.p., gen. counsel, sec. Del Monte Foods Co., 2001—02, sr. v.p., gen. counsel, sec., 2002—. Office: Del Monte Foods Co One Market St San Francisco CA 94105

POTTER, JOHN FRANCIS, oncologist, surgeon; b. NYC, July 26, 1925; s. John Albert and Isabelle Cecelia (Sullivan) P.; m. Tanya Agnes Kristof, Nov. 19, 1955; children: Tanya Jean, Miriam Isabelle, John Mark. MD, Georgetown Med. Sch., 1949. Intern Grasslands Hosp., Valhalla, NY, 1949-50, resident in surgery, 1949-50, Georgetown U. Hosp., Washington, 1953-56; sr. investigator Nat. Cancer Inst., Bethesda, Md., 1957-60; chief divsn. surg. oncology Georgetown Med. Ctr., Washington, 1960-85; instr, asst.prof., then assoc. prof. surgery Georgetown U. Sch. Medicine, 1957-64, prof., 1969—2000; dir. Vincent T. Lombardi Cancer Rsch. Ctr., Washington, 1967-87, U.S. Mil. Cancer Inst., Bethesda, Md., 2000—. Mem. U.S. Mil. Health Adv. Com.; presdl. apptd. mem. bd. regents Uniformed Svcs. U. of the Health Scis., 1999. Hon. prof. Universidad Cayetano Heredia, Lima, Peru, 1980. Lt. (j.g.) USNR, 1951-53. Recipient Pres.'s medal Georgetown U., 1991. Mem. Soc. Surg. Oncology (rep. adv. bd.), ACS, Assn. Am. Cancer Insts. (v.p. 1985-86, pres. 1986-87, bd. dirs. 1982, chmn. bd. dirs. 1987-88), So. Surg. Assn., Peruvian Cancer Soc. (hon.). Office: US Mil Cancer Inst Walter Reed Army Med Ctr Bldg # A109 6900 Georgia Ave NW Washington DC 20307 E-mail: john.potter.1@na.amedd.army.mil.

POTTER, JOHN LEITH, retired mechanical and aerospace engineer, retired educator, consultant; b. Metz, Mo., Feb. 5, 1923; s. Jay Francis Lee and Pearl Delores (Leeth) P.; m. Dorothy Jean Williams, Dec. 15, 1957; children: Stephen, Anne, Carol. BS in Aerospace Engring., U. Ala., Tuscaloosa, 1944, MS in Engring., 1949; MS in Engring. Mgmt., Vanderbilt U., 1976, PhD in Mech. Engring., 1974. Engr., educator various indsl., ednl. and govt. orgns., 1944-52; chief, flight and aerodyns. lab. Redstone Arsenal, Ala., 1952-56; mgr., div. chief, dep. tech. dir., sr. staff scientist Sverdrup Tech., Inc., Tullahoma, Tenn., 1956-83; research prof. Vanderbilt U., Nashville, 1983-92, prof. emeritus, 1992—; cons. engr. Nashville, 1983—. Convener NATO-AGARD, U.S. and Eng., 1980-82, mem. working group, 1984-88; mem. adv. com. Internat. Symposium on Rarefied Gasdynamics, 1970—; invited lectr. USSR Acad. Scis., 1967; mem. NRC com. on assessment nat. aeronautical wind tunnel facilities, 1987-88; mem. NASA working groups, 1987—; mem. Engring. Accreditation Commn., 1985-90. Editor: Rarefied Gas Dynamics, 1977. Contbr. articles to profl. publs., chpts. to books Chmn. bd. dirs. Coffee County Hist. Soc., Tenn., 1971-72; bd. dirs. Southeastern Amateur Athletic Union, 1972-73; pres. Tullahoma Swim Club, 1972-73. Recipient Outstanding Fellow award U. Ala. Aerospace Engring. Dept., 1987; elected 150th Anniversary Disting. Engring. Fellow U. Ala. Coll. Engring., 1988; USAF Arnold Engring. Devel. Ctr. fellow, 1993. Fellow AIAA (assoc. editor jour. 1970-73, publs. com. 1973-78, assoc. editor Progress in Astronautics and Aeronautics 1981-85, Gen. H.H. Arnold award Tenn. chpt. 1964); mem. U. Ala. Capstone Engring. Soc. (regional bd. dirs. 1972-77), Sigma Xi, Tau Beta Pi, Theta Tau, Pi Tau Sigma, Sigma Gamma Tau. Home: 400 University Park Dr Apt 394 Birmingham AL 35209

POTTER, MICHAEL J., retail stores executive; b. Oreg., 1960; BS, U. Oreg., 1983; MBA, Capital U., Ohio. CFO, sr. v.p. Consolidated Stores Corp. (now Big Lots), Columbus, Ohio, 1991—2000; pres., CEO Big Lots, Columbus, Ohio, 2000—. Office: Big Lots 300 Phillipi Rd Columbus OH 43228-5311

POTTER, MYRTLE S., research and development company executive; BA, U. Chgo. Various sales, marketing, and bus. positions Merck and Co., v.p. N.E. Region Bus. Group, 1993—96; v.p. strategy and econ. US Pharmaceuticals Group Bristol-Myers Squibb, 1996—97, group v.p. Worldwide Medicine Group, 1997—98, sr. v.p. sales, US Cardiovascular/Metabolics, 1998, pres. US Cardiovascular/Metabolics, 1998—2000; exec. v.p. Genetech, Inc., South San Francisco, 2000—01, exec. v.p. comml. ops., COO, 2001, president, commercial ops., co-chmn., product portfolio com., cons., 2004—. Bd. dirs. Calif. Healthcare Inst., 2001—, Amazon.com, 2004—. Named Top 50 Most Powerful Women In Business, Fortune, 2003, Most Powerful Black Executives in America, 15 Young Global Business Influentials, Time, Woman of Yr., Healthcare Bus. Women's Assn., 2000; named one of 50 Women to Watch, Wall St. Jour., 2005; recipient National Woman of Distinction Award, Girl Scouts of the USA, 2004. One of the architects of the Astra/Merck joint venture and led the work that set Prilosec on pace to be one of the biggest pharmaceutical products in the world; Won the Merck Chairman's Award for work on the Astra/Merck joint venture. Office: Genetech Inc 1 DNA Way South San Francisco CA 94080

POTTER, NICHOLAS F., lawyer; b. 1963; AB magna cum laude, Harvard U., 1985, JD, 1988. Bar: NY 1989. Counsel Skadden, Arps, Slate, Meagher & Flom LLP, NYC, London; mem. Debevoise & Plimpton LLP, NYC, 1998—, ptnr., co-head Insurance Industry Group, co-chair Pro Bono Com., mem. Mergers & Acquisitions Practice Group and Securities Practice Group. Mem.: ABA, Assn. Bar City NY. Office: Debevoise & Plimpton LLP 919 Third Ave New York NY 10022 Office Phone: 212-909-6459. E-mail: nfpotter@debevoise.com.

POTTER, ROBERT DANIEL, federal judge; b. Wilmington, NC, Apr. 4, 1923; s. Elisha Lindsey and Emma Louise (McLean) P.; m. Mary Catherine Neilson, Feb. 13, 1954; children: Robert Daniel Jr., Mary Louise, Catherine Ann. AB in Chemistry, Duke U., 1947, LLB, 1950; LLD (hon.), Sacred Heart Coll., Belmont, NC, 1982. Bar: NC 1951. Pvt. practice law, Charlotte, NC, 1951-81; dist. judge US Dist. Ct. (we. dist.) NC, 1981—2001, chief judge, 1984-91, now sr. judge, 1991—. Commr. Mecklenburg County, Charlotte, 1966-68. Served as 2d lt. U.S. Army, 1944-47, ETO. Mem. N.C. Bar Assn., Charlotte City Club. Republican. Roman Catholic. Home Phone: 704-366-5127; Office Phone: 704-552-7742.

POTTER, ROBERT JOSEPH, technical and business executive; b. NYC, Oct. 29, 1932; s Mack and Ida (Bernstein) P.; married; children: Diane Gail, Suzanne Lee, David Craig. BS cum laude, Lafayette Coll., 1954; MA in Physics, U. Rochester, 1957, PhD in Optics, 1960. Cons. ANPA Rsch. Inst., AEC Brookhaven Nat. Lab., RCA Labs., US Naval Rsch. Labs., 1952-60; mgr. optical physics and optical pattern recognition IBM Thomas J. Watson Research Center, Yorktown Heights, NY, 1960-65; assoc. dir. Applied Rsch. Lab., Xerox Corp., Rochester, NY, 1965-67; v.p. advanced engring. Xerox Corp., 1967-68, v.p. devel. and engring., 1968-69, v.p., gen. mgr. Spl. Products and Systems divsn. Stamford, Conn., Pasadena, Calif., 1969-71, v.p. info. tech. group Rochester, 1971-73, Dallas, 1973-75, pres. Office Sys. divsn., 1975-78; sr. v.p., chief tech. officer Internat. Harvester Co., Chgo., 1978-82; group v.p. integrated office sys. Nortel Networks, Richardson, Tex., 1984—87; pres., CEO Datapoint Corp., San Antonio, 1987—90, R.J. Potter Co., Dallas, 1990—. Bd. govs., vice chmn. IIT Rsch. Inst., 1999—2002; chmn. Tatum CIO Ptnrs., LLP, 2000—02; adv. dir. Am. Nat. Bank, 2002—05; mem. rsch. adv. bd. U. Tex., Dallas, 2003—07; bd. dirs. Zebra Techs., Cree, Inc., Molex Inc., Bradshaw Group, Speed FC. Contbr. articles to profl. jours. Life trustee Ill. Inst. Tech.; trustee Alliance Higher Edn. Recipient IBM Outstanding Tech. Contbn. award, 1964, Disting. Achievement award Soc. Mfg. Engrs., 1981; Kroner scholar Lafayette Coll., 1954; Disting. Rochester scholar U. Rochester, 1995. Fellow Optical Soc. Am., Am. Phys. Soc.; mem. Phi Beta Kappa, Sigma Xi. Office: R J Potter Co 5215 N O Connor Blvd Ste 360 Irving TX 75039-3739 Office Phone: 972-869-8270. Business E-Mail: RJPotter@RJPotter.com.

POTTER, SHARON LYNN, prosecutor; b. 1959; JD, Calif. We. Sch. Law, 1985. Bar: W. Va. 1985, US Dist. Ct. (so. dist.) W. Va. 1985, Pa. 1987. Asst. US atty. US Dept. Justice, Wheeling, W.Va., US atty., 2006—. Office: US Attys Office PO Box 591 Wheeling WV 26003-0011 Office Phone: 304-234-0100. Office Fax: 304-234-0110. *

POTTER, TANYA JEAN, lawyer; b. Washington, Oct. 30, 1956; d. John Francis and Tanya Agnes (Kristof) P.; m. Howard Bruce Adler; 1 child, Alexandra Potter Adler. BA, Georgetown U., 1978, JD, 1981. Bar: D.C. 1982, U.S. Ct. Appeals (D.C. cir.), U.S. Ct. Appeals (fed. cir.), U.S. Dist. Ct. (D.C. dist.), U.S. Ct. Internat. Trade. Assoc. Ragan and Mason, Washington, 1981-88; atty.-adviser Office of Chief Counsel for Import Adminstrn., U.S. Dept. Commerce, Washington, 1989-92. Mediator D.C. Superior Ct., 1982-84. Author: Practicing Before the Federal Maritime Commission, 1986, supplement, 1988, Preferentiality Under the Proposed Commerce Department Regulations, 1990, Oil Refining in U.S. Foreign-Trade Zones, 1990. Rep. Avenel Homeowners Adv. Coun., 1994-97; dir. Avenel Bd. Dirs., 1997, 98, 99-2001. Recipient Cmty. Svc. Recognition award ARC, Washington, 1986. Mem. ABA, Bar Assn. of D.C. (exec. coun. ad law sect. 1985-89). Avocations: sports, travel, visiting museums and art galleries.

POTTER, TOM, mayor; b. 1940; m. Karin Hansen; 4 children. BA, Univ. Portland. Lt. Portland Police Dept., Portland, Oreg., 1967—94; mayor City of Portland, 2004—. With Portland Police Sunshine Div.; chmn. Shepherd Legal Scholarship Fund Com.; interim exec. dir. Oregon Public Safety Training and Standards, 1997. Driver Meals on Wheels-Portland. Recipient World Mayor award, 2006. Mem.: Shepherd Legal Scholarship Fund Com., Parents of Friends, Lesbians & Gays. Office: Office of the Mayor Ste 340 1221 SW 4th Ave Portland OR 97204 Office Phone: 503-823-4120. Office Fax: 503-823-3588. *

POTTER, WILLIAM BARTLETT, diversified financial services company executive; b. Washington, Jan. 4, 1938; s. George Holland and Virginia (Bartlett) P.; m. Simone Robert, June 6, 1964; children: Eva Simone, William Bartlett. AB, Princeton U., 1960; MBA, Emory U., 1962. With Merc.-Safe Deposit & Trust Co., Balt., 1962—, asst. sec., asst. treas., 1964-66, asst. v.p., 1966-68, v.p., 1968-69, sr. v.p., 1969-76, exec. v.p., 1976, Preston Trucking Co., 1976-77, pres., 1977-86; chmn., pres. Preston Trucking, 1986-92; Preston Corp., 1986-93, chmn., 1994—. Home: 41880 RCR 44 Steamboat Springs CO 80487 Personal E-mail: will@wbpotter.family.com.

POTTER, WILLIAM GRAY, JR., university librarian; b. Duluth, Minn., Feb. 18, 1950; s. William Gray and Kathryn Martha (Scheuer) P.; m. Marsha Ann Munie, Sept. 23, 1982. BA in English, So. Ill. U., Edwardsville, 1973; MLS, U. Ill., Urbana-Champaign, 1975; MA in English, U. Ill., 1976, PhD in Libr. and Info. Sci., 1984. Libr. U. Wis.-Whitewater, 1975-78; asst. dir. gen. svcs. U. Ill.-Urbana, 1978-85; assoc. dean librs. Ariz. State U., Tempe, 1985-89; univ. libr., assoc. provost U. Ga., Athens, 1989—. Editor: Serials Automation, 1980, Libr. Trends, 1981, Info. Tech.

and Librs., 1984-89; Coll. and Rsch. Libr., 2002 -. Contbr. articles to profl. jours. Bd. dirs. Richard B. Russell Found., 1989— (sec., 1990—), ARL, 1996-99, SOLINET, 2001-03; trustee OCLC, 1994-2000. Recipient Hugh Atkinson Meml. award, 1997; Nix-Jones Outstanding Libr. Ga., 1998; LITA/Gaylord Award 2000; named Disting. Alumnus of Yr. So. Ill. U., Edwardsville, 2001. Mem. ALA, Libr. And Info. Tech. Assn. (pres. 1987), Assn. Coll. Rsch. Libr., Ga. Libr. Assn. Office: U Ga Librs U Ga Athens GA 30602-1641 Office Phone: 706-542-0621. Office Fax: 706-542-4144. Business E-Mail: wpotter@uga.edu. *

POTTER, WILLIAM JAMES, investment banker; b. Toronto, Aug. 11, 1948; s. William Wakely and Ruby Loretta (Skidmore) P.; m. Linda Lee, Nov. 25, 1972; children: Lisa Michelle, Meredith Lee, Andrew David. AB, Colgate U., 1970; MBA, Harvard U., 1974. With White Weld & Co., Inc., NYC, 1974-75, Toronto Dominion Bank, Toronto (Can.) and NY, 1975-78, group mgr. Toronto, 1979-82; 1st v.p. Barclays Bank PLC, NYC, 1982-84; mng. dir. Prudential-Bache Securities, Inc., NYC, 1984-89; pres. Ridgewood Capital Funding Inc., NYC, 1989—, Ridgewood Group Internat. Ltd., NYC, 1989—2004, Kingsdale Capital, Inc., 2004—06; chmn. R. Meredith & Co., Inc., 2004—. Advisor Ladenberg Thalman Internat., 1990—92, Laidlaw Holdings, Inc., 1992—93, Centennial Fund LLP, Canada; bd. dirs. Aberdeen Australian Equity Fund Inc., Md., Aberdeen Asia Pacific Income Fund Inc., Md., Aberdeen Asia Pacific Income Fund Ltd., New Zealand, Alexandria Bancorp, Canada, E.C. Power Inc., Aberdeen Commonwealth Fund Inc., Md., Voicenet Inc., Del., Power Air Corp., Simberi Gold Corp., Canada. Author: Finance for the Minerals Industry, 1985. Trustee Glen Ridge Ednl. Found, 1994—; advisor Nat. Cancer Resources Found., 2003—; bd. dirs. Glen Ridge (N.J.) Cmty. Fund, 1985—94. Mem.: Nat. Fgn. Trade Coun. (Washington, bd. dirs., chmn. fin. com., exec. com. 1983—), New England Club N.Y., Econ. Club N.Y., Buck Hill Country Club (Pa.), Glen Ridge Country Club (NJ), Nat. Club (Toronto), Williams Club (N.Y.C.), Harvard Club (N.Y.C.). Congregationalist. Avocations: golf, tennis. Office: Ridgewood Group Internat Inc 236 W 27th St Fl 3 New York NY 10001-5906 E-mail: wpotterrgi@aol.com.

POTTINGER, RONALD WAYNE, food products executive; s. Eugene A. and Reba R. Pottinger; m. Tamara Pottinger, July 16, 1985; 1 child, Nicole E. BA, Bellarmine, Louisville, 1980. Mem. sales/svc. staff IBM, Louisville, 1977—85; sales v.p. Blendex Co., Louisville, 1985—97, CEO, 1997—; pres. Pottinger Enterprises, Louisville, 2001—, HPP, Simpsonville, Ky., 2005—. Mem. Jeffersontown Chamber, Ky., 2006—. Custom Quality Svcs., Louisville, 2006—. Mem.: Inst. Food Technicians (assoc.). Avocation: boating. Office: Blendex Co 11208 Electron Dr Louisville KY 40299 Home Phone: 502-722-0562; Office Phone: 502-267-1003. Office Fax: 502-657-4352. E-mail: rpottinger@blendex.com.

POTTLE, STEVEN L., lawyer; b. Anchorage, Nov. 3, 1960; Student, Univ. of London, Japanese Bus. and Soc. Program, Tokyo; BBA, Univ. Wash., 1983; JD, Vanderbilt Univ., 1987. CPA; bar: Ga. 1987. Acct. Ernst & Whinney; ptnr., co-chmn., tech. group, chmn., corp. health care group Alston & Bird LLP, Atlanta. Office: Alston & Bird LLP One Atlantic Ctr 1201 W Peachtree St NW Atlanta GA 30309-3424 Office Phone: 404-881-7278. Office Fax: 404-881-7777. Business E-Mail: spottle@alston.com.

POTTORFF, JO ANN, state legislator; b. Wichita, Kans., Mar. 7, 1936; d. John Edward McCluggage and Helen Elizabeth (Alexander) Ryan; m. Gary Nial Pottorff; children: Michael Lee, Gregory Nial. BA, Kansas State U., 1957; MA, St. Louis U., 1969. Elem. tchr. Pub. Sch., Keats and St. George, 1957-59; cons., elem. specialist Mid Continent Regional Edn. Lab., Kansas City, Mo., 1971-73; cons. Poindexter Assocs., Wichita, 1975; campaign mgr. Garner Shriver Congl. Camp, Wichita, 1976; interim dir. Wichita Area Rape Ctr., 1977; conf. coord. Biomedical Synergistics Inst., Wichita, 1977-79; real estate sales asst. Chester Kappelman Group, Wichita, 1979-98, J.P. Weigard & Sons, Wichita, 1998—; state rep. State of Kans., Topeka, 1985—; regional dir. Women in Govt. Mem. exec. com. Nat. Conf. State Legis. Com. Mem. sch. bd. Wichita Pub. Schs., 1977-85; bd. dirs. Edn. Consol. and Improvement Act Adv. com., Kans. Found. for the Handicapped; mem. Children and Youth Adv. com. (bd. dirs.); active Leadership Kans.; chairperson women's network Nat. Conf., State Legislators; mem. Wichita Children's Home Bd.; vice chmn. Nat. Assessment Governing Bd.; chair edn. com. assembly on state issues Nat. Conf. State legislators. Recipient Disting. Svc. award Kans. Assn. Sch. Bds., 1983, Outstanding Svc. to Sch. Children of Nation award Coun. Urban Bds., 1984, awards Gov.'s Conf. for Prevention of Child Abuse and Neglect, Kans. Assn. Reading. Mem. Leadership Am. Alumnae (bd. dirs., sec) Found. for Agr. in Classroom (bd. dirs.), Jr. League, Vet. Aux. (pres.), Bd. Nat. State Art Agys., Rotary, Ky. Assn. Rehab. Facilities (Ann. award), Nat. Order Women in Legislature (past bd. dirs.), Nat. Conf. State Legislatures (chmn. edn. assembly state issues, exec. com.), Rotary, Chi Omega (pres.). Avocations: politics, travel. Office: Weigard 6530 E 13th St N Wichita KS 67206-1247

POTTRUCK, DAVID STEVEN, venture capitalist; b. 1948; m. Emily Pottruck; 2 children. BA, U. Pa., 1970, MBA with honors, 1972. With Arthur Young & Co., 1974-76, sr. cons.; with Citibank N.Am., 1976-81, v.p.; with Shearson/Am. Express, 1981-84, sr. v.p. consumer mktg. and advt.; with Charles Schwab & Co., San Francisco, 1984—; exec. v.p. mktg., br. adminstr. Charles Schwab and Co., Inc.; pres. Charles Schwab & Co., 1992—94; pres., COO The Charles Schwab Corp., 1994—98, pres., co-CEO, 1998—2003, pres., CEO, 2003—04; chmn., CEO Red Eagle Ventures Inc. (formerly Pottruck Group), 2004—. Apptd. commr. by Congress The Advisory Commn. on Internet Commerce; bd. dirs. Intel Corp., 1998—, US Trust Co., N.A., DoveBid, Inc.; chmn. Eos Airlines. Co-author: Clicks and Mortar: Passion Driven Growth in an Internet Driven World. Bd. dirs. US Ski and Snowboard Team Found.; pres. Pottruck Family Found.; trustee U. Penn. Named Exec. of the Year, San Francisco Bus. Times, CEO of the Year, Morningstar; named one of Top 15 CEOs, Worth mag.; recipient Torch of Liberty award, Anti-Defamation League, 2000. Office: Pottruck Family Foundation 1016 Lincoln Blvd #221 San Francisco CA 94129 *

POTTS, BARBARA JOYCE, retired historic site director; b. LA, Feb. 18, 1932; d. Theodore Thomas and Helen Mae (Kelley) Elledge; m. Donald A. Potts, Dec. 27, 1953; children: Tedd, Douglas, Dwight, Laura. AA, Graceland Coll., 1951; grad., Radiol. Tech. Sch., 1953; grad. program for sr. execs. in state and local govt., Harvard U., 1989. Radiol. technician Independence (Mo.) Sanitarium and Hosp., 1953, 58-59, Mercy Hosp., Balt., 1954-55; city coun. mem.-at-large City of Independence, 1978-82, mayor, 1982-90; exec. dir. Jackson County Hist. Soc., 1991-97; ret., 1997. Chmn. Mid-Am. Regional Coun., Kansas City, Mo., 1984-85; bd. dirs. Mo. Mcpl. League, Jefferson City, 1982-90, v.p., 1986-87, pres., 1987, 88; chmn. Mo. Commn. on Local Govt. Cooperation, 1985-90; bd. dirs., Mercantile Bank, 1989-98, chair ind. adv. bd., 1997-99; bd. dirs. Women's Found. of Greater Kansas City, 1997-2003; mem. chancellor's adv. bd. UMKC Women's Ctr., 1996-; mem. adv. bd. Comprehensive Mental Health Svcs., 1997-. Author: Independence, 1985. Mem. Mo. Gov.'s Conf. Edn., 1976, Independence Charter Rev. Bd., 1977; bd. dirs. Hope House Shelter Abused Women, Independence, 1982—, Vis. Nurses Assn., 1990-93, Truman Heartland Cmty. Found., 1990-2003, bd. chmn., 1997-99, Mid-Continent coun. U.S. Girl Scouts, 1991-95, Harry S. Truman Libr. Inst., 1995—, Truman Med. Ctr., 2001—, Coun. on Philanthropy, 2001-03, Leadership 20/20 Vision; adv. bd. Ewing M. Kauffman Fund, 2002-06, Greater Kansas City Cmty. Found., 1999-02, Salvation Army, 1999—; pres. Child Placement Svcs., Independence, 1972-89, Greater Kansas City region NCCJ, 1990-2004; bd. vis. UMKC Sch. Medicine, 2002—; trustee Independence Regional Health Ctr., 1982-90, 94-2001, Park Coll., 1989-99, 2004—, chmn. bd. trustees, 1995-99. Eye Found. Kansas City, 1997-99; mem. Nat. Women's Polit. Caucus, 1978—; mem. adv. bd. Greater Mo. Focus on Leadership, mem. steering com., 1989—. Recipient George Lehr Meml. award for cmty. svc., 1989, Woman of Achievement award Mid-Continent coun. Girl Scouts U.S.A., 1983, 75th Anniversary Women of Achievement award Mid-Continent coun. Girl Scouts, 1987, Jane Adams award Hope House, 1984, Cmty. Leadership award Comprehensive Mental Health Svcs., Inc., 1984, 90, Graceland Coll. Alumni Disting. Svc. award 1991, Disting. Citizen award Independence C. of C., 1993, Outstanding Cmty. Svc. award Jackson County Inter-Agy. Coun., 1994, Outstanding Cmty. Svc. award Cmty. Svcs. League, 1996, Jackson County Humanitarian of Yr. award, 1997, Disting. Citizen award, 1997, Paul Harris award Ind. Rotary Club, 1997, Outstanding Svc. award City of Independence Human Rels. Commn., 1999, Greater Kans. City Coun. Philanthropy Vol. of Yr. award, 2000; named Friend of Edn. Indpendence NEA, 1990. Mem.: LWV (Cmty. Svc. award 1990), Jackson County Hist. Soc., Nat. Trust for Hist. Preservation. Mem. Lds Ch. Home: 18508 E 30th Ter S Independence MO 64057-1904

POTTS, CHARLES AARON, management, publishing executive, writer; b. Idaho Falls, Aug. 28, 1943; s. Verl S. and Sarah (Gray) Potts; m. Judith Samimi, 1977 (div. 1986); children: Emily Karen, Natalie Larise; m. Ann Weatherill, June 19, 1988. BA in English, Idaho State U., Pocatello, 1965. Lic. real estate broker Wash. Pres. Walla Walla Rental Properties, 1984—86; dir. Washington Apt. Assocs., 1984—88; owner Palouse Mgmt., Inc., Walla Walla, Wash., 1979—. Founder, dir. Litmus Inc., 1967—77; founding editor COSMEP, Berkeley, Calif., 1968; host poetry radio program Oasis NPR-KUER, Salt Lake City, 1976—77; N.W. rep. Chinese Computer Comm., Inc., Lansing, Mich., 1988—94; pres. Tsunami Inc.; founder Temple Bookstore, 2002, Temple Sch. Poetry, 2002. Author: Blues from Thurston County, 1966, Burning Snake, 1967, The Litmus Papers, 1969, Little Lord Shiva, 1969, Blue Up the Nile, 1972, Waiting in Blood, 1973, The Trancermigracion of Menzu, 1973, The Golden Calf, 1975, Charlie Kiot, 1976, The Opium Must Go Thru, 1976, Valga Krusa, 1977, Rocky Mountain Man, 1978, A Rite to the Body, 1989, The Dictatorship of the Environment, 1991, Loading Las Vegas, 1991, How the South Finally Won the Civil War, 1995, 100 Years in Idaho, 1996, Lost River Mountain, 1999, Facist Haikus, 1999, Little Lord Shiva: The Berkeley Poems, 1968, 1999, Angio Gram, 2000, Nature Lovers, 2000, prophet/profit, 2001, Slash and Burn, 2001, Across the Pacific, 2002, Lucintite, 2002, Compostrella/Star Field, 2004, Kiot: The selected early poems of Charles Potts, 1963-1977, 2005, The Portable Potts, 2005, Greatest Hits, 2005, The Yellow Christ, 2007, Laffing Water, 2007; editor: Pacific Northwestern Spiritual Poetry, 1998, The Temple, 1997—2002, Walla Walla Poetry Party, 1990—2003; columnist (with Kyushu Gleaner): Japan's Political Choices, 1995—. Rep. to exec. com. 5th Congl. Dist., Wash. State Dems., 1993—95. Recipient Profl. Achievement award, Idaho State U., 1994. Mem.: Soc. Neurolinguistic Programming (master practitioner), Chinese Lang. Computer Soc., Pacific N.W. Booksellers Assn., Toastmasters, Fukuoka Internat. Forum, Italian Heritage Assn. (ice cream chair 1990, award 1993). Avocations: tennis, raspberries. Office: Palouse Mgmt Inc 129 E Alder St PO Box 1773 Walla Walla WA 99362-1962 Personal E-mail: potts@thetemplebookstore.com.

POTTS, DENNIS WALKER, lawyer; b. Santa Monica, Calif., Dec. 17, 1945; s. James Longworth and Donna (Neely) P.; children: Brandon Earl Woodward, Trevor Shipley. BA, U. Calif., Santa Barbara, 1967; JD, U. Calif., 1970. Bar: Hawaii 1971, Calif. 1971, U.S. Dist. Ct. Hawaii 1971, U.S. Ct. Appeals (9th cir.) 1973, U.S. Supreme Ct. 1978, U.S. Dist. Ct. (cen. dist.) Calif. 1983. Assoc. Chuck Mau, Honolulu, 1971-74; sole practice Honolulu, 1974—. Mem. litigation com. ACLU Hawaii, 1977-82; former mem. Hawaii Acad. Plaintiff's Attys. Disting. Svc. Cert. ACLU Hawaii. Fellow Internat. Napoleonic Soc.; mem. ATLA (sustaining), Consumer Lawyers Hawaii (treas., bd. govs.), Honolulu Club. Office: 2755 ASB Tower 1001 Bishop St Honolulu HI 96813-3429 Office Phone: 808-537-4575. Business E-Mail: dennispotts@hawaii.rr.com.

POTTS, GERALD NEAL, manufacturing executive; b. Franklin, NC, Apr. 10, 1933; s. Joseph Thomas and Virgie (Bryant) Potts; m. Ann Eliza Underwood, Dec. 21, 1956 (div. 1991); children: Catherine, Thomas, Alice. BS, U. N.C., 1954; grad., Advanced Mgmt. Program, Harvard, 1973. With Vulcan Mold & Iron Co., Chgo., 1957-59, sales engr., 1959-62, gen. sales mgr. Latrobe, Pa., 1963-65, v.p. sales, 1965-68; v.p. Vulcan, Inc., Latrobe, 1968-72, exec. v.p., 1972-73, pres., 1973-85, CEO, 1977-85, chmn., 1981-85; group exec. Teledyne Inc., 1985-92; pres. Woodings Verona Tool Works Inc., 1993-97; ret. Trustee Greater Latrobe Cmty. Chest, 1970—87, pres., 1978—79; bd. dirs. Latrobe Area Hosp., chmn., 1985—88; mem. adv. bd. U. Pitts., Greensburg, Pa., 1974—80; trustee Seton Hill Coll., Greensburg, 1974—80. With US Army, 1954—56. Mem.: Duquesne Club (Pa.), Chi Phi. Personal E-mail: jpotts1120@comcast.net.

POTTS, JOHN THOMAS, JR., physician, educator; b. Phila., Jan. 19, 1932; married; 3 children. BA, LaSalle Coll, Phila., 1953; MD, U. Pa., Phila., 1957; DSc, LaSalle U. From intern to asst. resident in medicine Mass. Gen. Hosp., Boston, 1957—59; resident Nat. Heart Inst., 1959—60; rsch. fellow in medicine Mass. Gen. Hosp., Boston, 1960—63; sr. research staff Nat. Heart Inst., 1963—66, head sect. polypeptide hormones, 1968—81; from asst. to assoc. prof. medicine Harvard U. Med. Sch., Boston, 1968—75, prof., 1975—; prof. medicine Harvard-MIT Divsn. Health Sci. and Tech., 1978—, Jackson prof. Clin. Medicine, 1981—96, disting. Jackson prof. clin. medicine, 1996—; chief endocrine unit Mass. Gen. Hosp., Boston, 1968—81, physician-in-chief, 1981—96, dir. rsch., 1995—2003. Recipient Andre Lichwitz prize, Endocrine Soc., 1968. Mem.: AAAS, Am. Soc. Bone and Mineral Rsch. (William F. Neumann award 1987), Am. Soc. Clin. Investigation, Assn. Am. Physicians, Endocrine Soc. (pres. 1987, Ernest Oppenheimer award 1968, Fred Konrad Koch award 1991), Inst. Medicine NAS. Office: Mass Gen Hosp 149 13th St Charlestown MA 02129-2020 Office Phone: 617-724-2167.

POTTS, KEVIN T., retired chemistry professor; b. Sydney, Oct. 26, 1928; married; children: Mary Ellen, Jeannette, Karen, Susan. BSc, U. Sydney, 1950, MSc, 1951; PhD in Organic Chemistry, Oxford U., Eng., 1954, DSc, 1973. Demonstrator chemistry U. Sydney, 1950, tchg. fellow, 1951; rsch. asst. organic chemistry Oxford U., 1951-54; scientist Med. Rsch. Coun. of Eng., 1954-56; rsch. asst. organic chemistry Harvard U., 1956-58; lectr. Adelaide, 1958-61; asso. prof. chemistry U. Louisville, 1961-65; assoc. prof. Rensselaer Poly. Inst., 1965-66, prof. chemistry, 1966-94; prof. emeritus Rensselaer Poly Inst., 1994—; chmn. dept. Rensselaer Poly. Inst., 1973-80. Contbr. articles in field organic chemistry to sci. jours. Grantee Nat. Cancer Inst., Nat. Heart Inst., Dept. Energy, NSF, Am. Chem. Soc.-Petroleum Rsch. Fund. Mem. AAAS, Am. Chem. Soc., Brit. Chem. Soc., Royal Soc. Chemistry. Home: 102 Pelican Cv Sneads Ferry NC 28460-9520 Office: Rennselaer Poly Inst Dept Chemistry 110 Eighth Troy NY 12180 E-mail: pottskt@charter.net.

POTTS, MARTHA WILBURN, elementary school educator; b. Richmond, Va., Dec. 22, 1970; d. Dennis John, Sr. and Margarite Reynolds Wilburn; m. Travis Stephen Potts, July 20, 1996; children: Dennis Stephen Donahue, Caroline Ryan Vallejo. BA in Mass Comm., Mary Baldwin Coll., Staunton, Va., 1991; MEdn, Va. Commonwealth U., Richmond, 1994. Tchr. Richmond City Pub. Schs., 1997—2004, Loudoun County Pub. Schs., Sterling, Va., 2004—. Dist. coord. We the People, the Citizen and the Constn., Richmond, 1994—2004. Avocations: travel, woodworking, reading. Home: 40545 Lovettsville Rd Lovettsville VA 20180-2346 Office: Countryside Elem Sch 20624 Countryside Blvd Sterling VA 20165 Home Phone: 540-822-4842; Office Phone: 703-444-8050. Home Fax: 540-822-4866. Personal E-mail: marthapotts1@yahoo.com. Business E-Mail: mpotts@loudoun.k12.va.us.

POTTS, RICHARD BRUCE, paleoanthropologist; b. Abington, Pa., Aug. 16, 1953; s. William Raymond and Ruth Hopkins (Bready) P. BA, Temple U., 1975; PhD, Harvard U., 1982. Curatorial asst. Peabody Mus. Harvard U., Cambridge, Mass., 1980-81; asst. prof. anthropology Yale U., New Haven, 1981-85; curator phys. anthropology Nat. Mus. Natural History Smithsonian Instn., Washington, 1985, head Human Origins Program. Curator phys. anthropology Yale U. Peabody Mus., New Haven, 1983-85; dir. human origins program Smithsonian Instn., Washington, 1985—; rsch. assoc. Nat. Mus. Kenya, Nairobi, 1984—; adj. prof. anthropology George Washington U., Washington, 1992—. Author: Early Hominid Activities at Olduvai, 1988, Humanity's Descent, 1996; co-author: Terrestrial Ecosystems Through Time, 1992. Sci. adv. coun. L.S.B. Leakey Found., Oakland, Calif., 1993—. Named Darwin Lectr. U. Ky., 1987. Mem. AAAS, Am. Assn. Phys. Anthropologists, Paleoanthropology Soc., Soc. Vertebrate Paleontology. Achievements include development of SEM method of identifying stone tool cut marks on bones, method of landscape-scale excavation of early human sites, hypothesis of variability selection. Office: Smithsonian Instn Human Origins Program NHB 351 Washington VA 20560-0112 E-mail: potts.rick@nmnh.si.edu.

POTTS, ROBERT LESLIE, academic administrator; b. Jan. 30, 1944; s. Frank Vines and Helen Ruth (Butler) Potts; m. Irene Elisabeth Johansson, Aug. 22, 1965; children: Julia Anna, Robert Leslie. BA, So. Coll., 1966; JD, U. Ala., 1969; LLM, Harvard U., 1971. Law clk. to chief judge U.S. Dist. Ct. (no. dist.) Ala., 1969—70; rschr. Herrick, Smith, Donald, Farley & Ketchum, Boston, 1970—71; lectr. Boston U., 1971, U. Ala., 1973—75, 1988; ptnr. Potts & Young, Florence, Ala., 1971—84; gen. counsel U. Ala. Sys., 1984—89; pres. U. North Ala., 1990—2004; chancellor ND Univ. Sys., 2004—. Mem. Nat. Adv. Com. on Instnl. Quality and Integrity, 1994—2001; com. on colls. So. Assn. Colls. and Schs., 2001—04; chmn. Nat. ROTC subcom. for Sec. of Army, 1999—2001; adv. com. rules of civil procedure Ala. Supreme Ct., 1973—88; chmn. Ala. Bd. Bar Examiners, 1983—86, Ala. Coun. Coll. and Univ. Pres., 2001—03, Nat. Conf. Bar Examiners, 1994—95. Contbr. numerous articles to profl. jours., edn. and schs. Trustee Ala. State U., 1976—79, Oakwood Coll., 1978—81; pres. Ala. Higher Edn. Loan Corp., 1988—93. Mem.: ABA (ho. of dels. 2001—03), ND State Bd. Career Technical Edn., Western Interstate commn. Higher Edn., Midwestern Higher Edn. Compact (commr.), Am. Assn. State Colls. and Univs. (bd. dirs. 2002—04), Ala. Bar Assn. (pres. young lawyers sect. 1979—80). Office: ND Univ Sys 600 E Blvd Ave Dept 215 Bismarck ND 58505-0230 Home Phone: 701-255-3054; Office Phone: 701-328-2963. Business E-Mail: robert.potts@ndus.nodak.edu.

POTTS, SANDRA, library director; d. Robert and Marilyn Canute; m. David Potts, June 26, 1983. Bachelor's degree, Coe Coll., 1969; MEd, Ctrl. Mich. U., 1975; MLS, Wayne State U., 1993. Elem. sch. tchr., Mich., 1970—74; libr. White Pine Libr. Coop., Saginaw, Mich., 1975—95; libr. dir. Northwood U., Midland, Mich., 1995—. Mem.: ALA, Midwest Archives, Mich. Libr. Assn., Alpha Xi Delta. Sentinal Party. Office: Northwood Univ Strosacker Library 4000 Whiting Dr Midland MI 48640 Home Phone: 989-799-4922; Office Phone: 989-837-4333.

POTTS, STEPHEN DEADERICK, lawyer; b. Memphis, Nov. 20, 1930; s. Ramsay Douglas and Anne (Van Dyke) P.; m. Irene Potter, Mar. 14, 1953; children: Lori Potts-Dupre, Stephen Deaderick Jr., Stacy Potts Krogh. AB, Vanderbilt U., 1952, LLB, 1954. Bar: Tenn. 1954, D.C. 1961. Assoc. Farris, Evans & Evans, Nashville, 1957-61; ptnr. Shaw, Pittman, Potts & Trowbridge, Washington, 1961-90; dir. U.S. Office Gov. Ethics, Washington, 1990-2000; chmn. bd. dirs. Ethics Resource Ctr., Washington, 2004—. Mem. Pres.'s Commn. on the Fed. Appt. Process, 1991-92, Pres.'s Coun. on Integrity and Efficiency, 1990-2000. Past pres. Washington Tennis Patrons Found., 1970—72; past. chmn. USTA Olympic com. 1st lt. US Army, 1954—57. Mem. ABA, U.S. Supreme Ct. Bar Assn., D.C. Bar Assn., Chevy Chase Club (bd. govs. 1982-86), Met. Club (bd. govs. 2000-04), Alibi Club, U.S. Tennis Assn. (bd. dirs., won 5 nat., 1 internat. father/son championships, twice ranked 1st in U.S.). Methodist. Office: Ethics Resource Ctr Ste 400 1747 Pennsylvania Ave Washington DC 20006 Home Phone: 301-907-9383; Office Phone: 202-872-4762. Business E-Mail: steve@ethics.org.

POTTS, TIMOTHY F., museum director; b. Australia; Dir. media and telecommunications, corp. fin. dept. Lehman Brothers, NYC, London; prof. U. Melbourne; dir. Nat. Gallery of Victoria, Australia, Kimbell Art Mus., Fort Worth, Tex., 1998—. Adj. prof. La Trobe U., Melbourne. Author: (monograph) Mesopotamia and the East: An Archaeological & Historical Study of Foreign Relations 3400-2000 BC, 1995; editor: Kimbell Art Museum: Handbook of the Collection, 2003; co-editor: Culture Through Objects: Ancient Near Eastern Studies in Honour of P. R. S. Moorey, 2003. Office: Kimbell Art Mus 3333 Camp Bowie Blvd Fort Worth TX 76107-2792

POTVIN, ALFRED RAOUL, engineering executive; b. 1942; m. Janet Holm, Mar. 20, 1965 BEE, Worcester Poly. Inst., 1964; MSEE, Stanford U., 1965, Engr. in EE, 1967; MS in Bioengring., U. Mich., 1970, MS in Psychology, 1970, PhD in Bioengring., 1971. Registered profl. engr., Tex. Asst. prof. elec. engring. U. Tex., Arlington, 1966—68, assoc. prof. biomed. engring. and elec. engring., 1971—76, prof., 1976—84, chmn. biomed. engring., 1972—84; dir. med. instrumentation sys. rsch. divsn. Eli Lilly & Co., Indpls., 1984—90, dir. tech. assessment and project mgmt., 1990—92, dir. engring., med. devices and diagnostics divsn., 1992—93; prof. elec. engring. Purdue Sch. Engring. and Tech., Ind. U.-Purdue U., Indpls., 1993—96; dean engring. and tech. Ind. U.-Purdue U., Indpls., 1993—95; pres. MEECO, Melbourne, Fla., 1996—. Faculty fellow, life scientist, cons. NASA, Houston, 1972-76, NASA and Moffett Field, 1974-76; clin. prof. biophysics U. Tex. Health Sci. Ctr., Dallas, 1967-84; mem. phys. med. device panel FDA, Washington, 1978-84; mem. adv. bd., reviewer Biomed. Engring. NSF, Washington, 1983-89, 92-97; founding dir. Ctr. Advanced Rehab. Engring., 1983-84, mem. adv. bd., 1984-88; mem. adv. bd. Engring. Rsch. Ctrs. NSF, Washington, 1988-92, Biomed. Engr. Worcester Polytech. Inst., Mass., 1987—. Coll. Engrs. Duke U., Durham, N.C., 1987-94, U. Calif., Berkeley, 1989-92, Coll. Engrs. U. Denver, 1990-93, Sch. Engr. and Tech. Ind. U.-Purdue U., Indpls, 1992-93, med. engring. Jet Propulsion Lab., Pasadena, Calif., 1989; chmn. NIH Resource Ctr. Case Western Res. U., Cleve., 1988-96; bd. advisors Sch. of Health and Rehab. Sci., U. Pitts., 1993-97; mem. adv. com. NIH, 1987-92, 93-95; bd. dirs. Biomed. Engring. Alliance for Engring. in Medicine and Biology. Author: (with W.W. Tourtellotte) Quantitative Examination of Neurologic Functions, 1985; editl. bd. IEEE Spectrum, 1987-90, 92-95, Biomed. Sci. and Tech., 1990-93; co-editor spl. issue on biosensors IEEE Trans. on Biomed. Engring., 1986, spl. issue on status and future directions in biomed. engring. Medicine and Biol. Mag., 1989; mem. editl. bd. Biomed. Sci. and Tech., 1990-92; mem. adv. bd. The Biomed. Engring. Handbook, 1995, 2000. Mem. Masthead Property Owners Assn., Indpls., 1984-96, Manasota Key Property Owners Assn., Englewood, Fla., 1985-98. Recipient Life Scientist award NASA, 1974, Hall of Achievement award U. Tex. at Arlington, 2006; spl. fellow NIH, 1968. Fellow: IEEE (gen. chmn. annual conf. 1872, pres. Engring. in Medicine and Biology Soc. 1983, re-elected 1984, chmn. health care engring. com. 1986, editl. bd. spectrum 1987—89, founding mem. steering com. symposium on computer based med. systems 1988—94, co-editor spl. issue Medicine and Biology 1989, editl. bd. spectrum 1992—94, internat. conf. com.

1993—95, Centennial award 1984), Biomed. Engring. Soc. (chmn. edn. and pub. affairs com. 1979—83), Assn. Advancement Med. Instrumentation, Am. Inst. Med. and Biol. Engring. (bd. dirs. 1991—94, v.p. pub. awareness 1993—94, founding fellow 1992, co-pres. world congress on med. biol. engring. in Chgo. in yr. 2000 1993—99, devel. com. 1996—99), Houston Soc. Engrs. in Medicine and Biology (Career Achievement award 1993); mem.: Ind. Elec. Mfg. Assn. (bd. dirs. 1993—96, Svc. to Industry award 1996), Assn. Advancement of Med. Instrumentation, Alliance Engrs. in Medicine and Biology (v.p. nat. affairs 1987—89, pres. 1989—92), Am. Soc. Engring. Edn. (chmn. biomed. engring. divsn. 1979—80), Presdl. Founders Worcester Poly. Inst., Appalachian Long Distance Hikers Assn., Appalachian Trail Club. Avocations: boating, hiking, travel, gourmet dining, skiing. Personal E-mail: arpotvin@gmail.com.

POTVIN, PIERRE, physiologist, educator; b. Quebec City, Can., Jan. 5, 1932; s. Rosario and Eva (Montreuil) P.; m. Louise Dube, Aug. 31, 1963; children: Aline, Bernard. BA, Laval U., 1950, MD, 1955; PhD, U. Toronto, 1962. Asst. prof. Faculty of Medicine Laval U., Quebec City, 1956-63, assoc. prof., 1963-68, prof., 1968-98, prof. emeritus, 1998—, vice dean exec., 1977-86, dean, 1986-94. V.p. Internat. Conf. of Deans of French-Speaking Faculties of Medicine, 1990-96, pres. evaluation coun., 1994—2006; hon. prof. Norman Bethune U. Med. Sci., Changchun, China, 1992. Assoc. editor Modern Medicine Can., 1958-61, Laval Med., 1962-70. Fellow Royal Coll. Physicians and Surgeons Can. (hon.), Ordre Nat. du Lion (officer), Senegal, Sahamatrei Order, Cambodia, Order Can., Ordre Nat. des Palmes académiques, Légion d'Honneur, France. Roman Catholic. Avocation: painting. Office: Laval U Faculty of Medicine Dept Anat & Physiology Quebec City PQ Canada G1K 7P4 Business E-Mail: pierre.potvin@phs.ulaval.ca.

POU, NELLIE, assemblywoman; Degree in Mcpl. Budget and Fin., Rutgers U. Assemblywoman N.J. Gen. Assembly, 1997—; assembly asst. minority leader, 2000—01; dep. spkr., 2002—. Mem. N.J. Dept. Health, Profl. Adv. Com., 1991—92, Passaic County Human Svcs. Adv. Coun., 1991—95, Passaic County-Bergen County HIV Health Svcs. Adv. Coun., 1993—97; chair Mayor's Health Planning Task Force, 1988—97; mem. Passaic County Planning and Policy Partnership Com., 1996—. Commr. Paterson Pub. Libr. Bd. Trustees, 1983—84; mem. N.J. Task Force on Child Abuse and Neglect, 1997—. Democrat. Office: 100 Hamilton Plz Ste 1403-05 Paterson NJ 07505 E-mail: AswPou@njleg.org.

POULET, ANNE LITLE, museum director, art historian; b. Wash., Pa., Mar. 20, 1942; d. John Francis and Ruth Virginia (Kurtz) Litle; m. Francois Poulet, May 20, 1967. BA cum laude, Sweet Briar Coll., Va., 1964; MA Inst. Fine Arts, NYU, 1970. Curator Dept. European Decorative Arts and Sculpture Mus. Fine Arts, Boston, 1980—99; curator European Decorative Arts and Sculpture emerita Russell B. & Andrée Beauchamp Stearns, 1999—; dir. Frick Collection, NYC, 2003—. Catalogue, vol. 5, Wrightsman Collection, Met. Mus. Art., NYC, 1967—72, exhibitions include Corot to Braque, Mus. Fine Arts, Boston, 1978—80; author: (exhibit catalogue) Corot to Braque, 1978—80; editor-in-chief Jour. Mus. Fine Arts, Boston, 1989—93; co-author: (catalogue) Clodion (1738-1814), 1992; author, guest curator Jean-Antoine Houdon (1741-1828): Sculptor of the Enlightenment, Nat. Gallery Art, Washington, DC, 2003; contbr. articles to profl. jours. Recipient Iris Fedn. award for decorative arts, 2000, Chevalier dans l'order des arts et des letres, France; grantee, Ford Found., 1965, Lamb Mellon, 1990, 1998, 2000—01; Kress fellowship, 1976. Fellow: Am. Acad. Arts & Sciences; mem.: Assn. Art Mus. Dir., Am. Fedn. Arts, Am. Assn. Mus., French Heritage Soc. (co-founder, former vice chmn. bd.). Office: The Frick Collection 1 E 70th St New York NY 10021-4967

POULEUR, HUBERT GUSTAVE, cardiologist, consultant; b. Bouffioulx, Belgium, June 6, 1948; m. Michelle Leonet, July 7, 1973; children: Anne-Catherine, Jean-Hubert. MD, U. Louvain, Belgium, 1973, PhD, 1980. Intern, resident, then fellow in internal medicine U. Louvain, Belgium, 1973-77; Pub. Health Service internat. research fellow U. Calif, San Diego, 1977-79; asst. prof. U. Louvain, Brussels, 1979-83, assoc. prof., 1983-91, prof., 1991-94; assoc. dir. clin. rsch. Pfizer Inc., Groton, Conn., 1993-95; v.p. cardiovascular clin. R&D Bristol-Myers Squibb, Princeton, NJ, 1996-2000; exec. dir. cardiovasc. and metabolic group Pfizer Inc., NYC, 2001—. Disting. clin. scientist Syntex Clin. Rsch., Palo Alto, Calif., Maidenhead, U.K., 1988-93. Contbr. numerous sci. articles to profl. jours. Recipient Damman prize Damman Found., 1977, Bekales prize Bekales Found., 1986; Squibb Cardiovascular fellow Belgian Soc. Cardiology, 1982. Fellow Am. Coll. Cardiology; mem. Am. Heart Assn. (fellow Coun. of Circulation, fellow Coun. Clin. Cardiology), Atlantic Salmon Fedn., Trout Unltd. Avocation: fly fishing. Home: 43 Woodlane Rd Lawrenceville NJ 08648-5544 E-mail: hubert.pouleur@pfizer.com.

POULIOT, ASSUNTA GALLUCCI, retired business school owner, director, consultant; b. West Warwick, RI, Aug. 14, 1937; d. Michael and Angelina (DeCesare) Gallucci; m. Joseph F. Pouliot Jr., July 4, 1961; children: Brenda, Mark, Jill, Michele. BS, U. RI, Kingston, 1959, MS, 1971. Bus. tchr. Cranston H.S., RI, 1959-61; bus. dept. chmn. Chariho Regional H.S., Wood River Junction, RI, 1961-73; instr. U. RI, 1973-78; founder, dir. Ocean State Bus. Inst., Wakefield, RI, 1977-95, fin. aid cons., 1995—2005, ednl. cons., 1996—2005. Dir. Fleet Nat. Bank, 1985-91; bd. mgrs. Bank of New Eng., 1984-85; commr. Accrediting Coun. Ind. Colls. and Schs., 1995-98, chair accreditation com. team visits, 1998-2001, intermediate rev. com., 2000-01, rev. bd., 2000—; spkr. in field including Glencoe/McGraw-Hill Pub. Co., 1995-2006. Ednl. author, Glencoe McGraw Hill Pub. Co., 1999-2002. Pres. St. Francis Women's Club, Wakefield, 1975; sec. St. Francis Parish Coun., Wakefield, 1980; mem. Econ. Devel. Commn., Wakefield, 1981-85; mem. South County Hosp. Corp., Wakefield, 1978-97; fin. dir. Bus. and Profl. Women's Club, Wakefield, 1982-84; chmn. Ladies Golf Charity, 1985-91; mem. Computer Info. Systems Com., Chariho Regional Career and Tech. Ctr. Mem. RI Bus. Edn. Assn. (newsletter editor 1979-81), New Eng. Bus. Coll. Assn. (sec. 1984-86, pres. 1985-87), RI Assn. Career and Tech. Schs. (treas., bd. dirs. 1979-95), Eastern Bus. Edn. Assn. (conf. leader), Nat. Bus. Edn. Assn. (conf. leader), Career Coll. Assn. (conv. speaker, pub. rels. com., govt. rels. com., membership com., key mem., nominating com., evaluator), Assn. Colls. and Schs. (commr. commn. on postsecondary schs. accreditation 1994-98), RI Women's Golf Assn., Am. Cancer Soc., U. RI Alumni Assn. (Excellence Bus. award 1992), Phi Kappa Phi, Delta Pi Epsilon (pres., newsletter editor). Clubs: Point Judith Country (past ladies golf chmn., RI Women's golf rep.). Roman Catholic. Avocations: golf, gardening. Home: 137 Kenyon Ave Wakefield RI 02879 Office: 15835 Sandy Point Dr Fort Myers FL 33917-5464 Personal E-mail: sjpouliot@aol.com.

POULOS, ANDREW, JR., protective services official, director; s. Andrew Poulos, Sr. and Susan Marie Poulos; m. Danielle Catherine Loblein, Mar. 5, 2005. Cert.: NJ Police Tng. Commn. (police officer), Del. Coun. Police Tng. 2001, Am. Coll. Forensic Examiners (in homeland security) 2006. Police officer first class Del. Dept. Pub. Safety, Dover, 2000—02; patrolman New Castle Police Dept., New Castle, Del., 2002—03; capt. Ft. Monmouth Police Dept., NJ, 2003—. Dir. Law Enforcement Tng. Solutions, Beachwood, NJ, 2005; exec. dir. Nat. Law Enforcement and Corrections Adv. Coun., Beachwood, 2006—07. Recipient J. Edgar Hoover Meml. Gold medal, Nat. Assn. Chiefs of Police, 2006. Mem.: Internat. Law Enforcement Educators and Trainers Assn., FBI Law Enforcement Exec. Devel. Assn., Internat. Assn. Chiefs of Police. Office: Fort Monmouth Police Dept 977 Murphy Dr Fort Monmouth NJ 08722 Office Phone: 732-532-1112. Office Fax: 732-532-5684; Home Fax: 877-892-6314. Personal E-mail: info@le-training.com. Business E-Mail: apoulos@fmpd.org.

POULOS, CHRISTOPHER, literature and language educator; s. Chris and Betty P. BA in Leadership Studies, Univ. Richmond; MA in Spanish Tchg., Columbia Univ. With Peace Corps, Honduras; Spanish tchr. Joel Barlow HS, Redding, Conn., 2000—. Adj. prof. Spanish Fairfield U. Named Conn. Tchr. of Yr., 2007. Office: Joel Barlow High Sch 100 Black Rock Turnpike Redding CT 06896 Business E-Mail: cpoulos@region9ps.org. *

POULOS, JAMES THOMAS, endocrinologist, educator; b. Lynn, Mass., Apr. 11, 1938; s. Thomas Dimitrios and Christine Julia (Zorzy) Poulos; m. Mary Margaret White, June 22, 1963; 1 child, Christopher Kreag. BS, Tufts U., 1959, MD, 1963. Diplomate Am. Bd. Internal Medicine, Am. Bd. Endocrinology and Metabolism. Intern New Eng. Med. Ctr., Boston, 1963—64, resident, 1964—65; resident and fellow in endocrinology U. Chgo., 1967—70; practice medicine specializing in endocrinology Lafayette, Ind., 1970—2004. Adj. prof. clin. pharmacology Purdue U., West Lafayette, Ind., 1976—95, pres. coun.; chmn. therapeutics com. Ind. Dept. Medicaid, 2002—; clin. faculty Ind. U. Sch. Medicine, mem. dean's search com., 1998, mem. therapeutics com., 2002—04; dir., pres. med. staff Lafayette Home Hosp., 1978—79; pres. Arnett HMO, 1986—97; bd. dirs. North Ctrl. Health Svc.; chmn. therapeutics com. State of Ind. Family and Social Svc. Adminstrn., 2002—; dir. regional diabetes ctr. Sisters of St. Francis Health Systems Inc., 1985—, Greater Lafayette Health Svc., 1985—, mem. mission com., 2005—; bd. dirs. GLHS Inc., 2005; mem. mission com. Sisters St. Francis Health Sys. Co-author: The Metabolic Influence of Progestins Advances in Metabolis Disorders, 1971; contbr. articles to profl. publ. Mem. Nat. Rep. Senatorial Com., Nat. Rep. Congrl. Com.; bd. dirs. Coalition Living Well After 50, 2007—. With M.C., US Army, 1965-67. Fellow ACP (councilor-at-large Ind. chpt.), Am. Coll. Endocrinology, Am. Assn. Clin. Endocrinologists; mem. AMA, Am. Diabetes Assn. (dir. Ind. chpt. 1980—, pres. 1986-88, 96-98, bd. dirs., com. profl. practice 1987-88, pres. 1994—), Endocrine Soc., Internat. Diabetes Fedn., Am. Lung Assn. (pres. West Ctrl. Ind. 1982-83), Lafayette C. of C, Nat. Lipid Assn., Ind. Endocrine Soc., Ind. Lipid Working Group, John Purdue Club. Home and Office: 1000 Windwood Ln West Lafayette IN 47906-4737 Office Phone: 765-743-1741. Personal E-mail: jpoulos@insightbb.com.

POULSEN, JENS KRISTIAN, ultrasonics researcher; b. Thisted, Denmark, Jan. 30, 1966; arrived in Can., 1998; s. Kjeld and Else Marianne Westergaard P. MSEE, Tech. U. Denmark, Lyngby, 1992. Rsch. asst. Radiometer, Copenhagen, 1988; instr. Tech. U. Denmark, 1988-89; rsch. asst. Jydsk Telefon, Aarhus, 1989, Skejby Sygehus, Aarhus, 1992-98; ultrasonics rschr. Toronto U., Ont., Can., 1998—. Computer cons. Medistim, Oslo, 1994-97. Inventor in field; contbr. articles to profl. jours. Mem. IEEE/Ultrasonics Ferroelectrics and Frequency Control (student mem.), IEEE/Engring. in Medicine and Biology Soc. (student mem.). Avocations: running, salsa dancing. Office: U Toronto Dept Med Biophys 2075 Bayview Ave Toronto ON Canada M4N 3M6

POULSON, RICHARD JASPER METCALFE, lawyer; b. Elizabeth City, NC, Sept. 4, 1938; s. Richard Jasper and Dorothy (Morse) P.; m. Anne Keenan, Dec. 21, 1963 (div. 1976); m. Anne Dare Wrenn, Sept. 25, 1993; children: Richard Hugh Hundley, Anna Blair Masters. BA, U. Va., 1960; JD, Am. U., 1968; ML in Taxation, Georgetown U., 1970. Bar: Va. 1968, D.C. 1969, U.S. Supreme Ct. 1976. V.p. Am. Security & Trust Co., Washington, 1968-70; assoc. Hogan & Hartson, Washington, 1970-73, ptnr., 1973-94, sr. ptnr. London, 1990-93; chmn. Rapidan Capital Ptnrs., 1994—; sr. mng. dir. The Appian Group, Washington, 1995-98; chmn. The Animex Group, Warsaw, 1998—; exec. v.p., sr. advisor to chmn. Smithfield Foods, Inc., NYC, 1998—. Adj. prof. Georgetown U. Law Ctr., 1971-76; lectr. Law and Fgn. Svc. Schs. Georgetown U.; internat. advisor in field; active Euro-Arab Conciliation and Arbitration Sys. Trustee, bd. mgrs. U. Va., Charlottesville, 1992—98, v.p., 1994—95, pres., 1995—97; dir., chmn. exec. com. Mary & Daniel Loughran Found., Washington, 1976—, pres., 2002—; chmn., dir. Montpelier Steeplechase Found., Orange, Va., 1991—98; chmn., trustee U.S. Rugby Football Found., Boston, 1988—2001. Mem. Law Soc. of Eng. and Wales, Metro. Club, Keswick Country Club, Columbia Country Club, Saratoga Golf and Polo Club, Commonwealth Club. Republican. Episcopalian. Avocations: horseback riding, hunting, steeplechase racing, thoroughbred breeding. Home: Hare Forest Farm PO Box 287 Orange VA 22960 Office: Smithfield Foods Inc 499 Park Ave 6th Fl New York NY 10022 Office Phone: 212-758-2100. Business E-Mail: dickpoulson@smithfieldfoods.com. *

POULTER, CHARLES DALE, chemist, educator, consultant; b. Monroe, La., Aug. 29, 1942; s. Erwin and Mary Helen Poulter; m. Susan Raetzsch, Aug. 24, 1964; children: Mary Christa, Gregory Thomas. BS, La. State U., Baton Rouge, 1964; PhD, U. Calif., Berkeley, 1967. NIH postdoctoral fellow UCLA, 1967-68; asst. prof. chemistry U. Utah, Salt Lake City, 1969-75, assoc. prof., 1975-78, prof., 1978-94, John A. Widtsoe prof. chemistry, 1994—, chair dept. chemistry, 1995-2000; editor-in-chief Jour. Organic Chemistry, 2001—. Fellow AAAS, Am. Acad. Arts and Scis.; mem. Am. Chem. Soc. (organic exec. com. 1983-86, biol. divsn. councillor 1993-98, chair organic divsn. 1998, Ernest Guenther award 1991, Utah award 1992, Arthur C. Cope scholar 1998, Repligen award 2002, James Flack Norris award 2004). Office: U Utah Dept Chemistry 340 S 1500 E Rm 2020 Salt Lake City UT 84112

POUMELE, CLAIRE TUIA, school system administrator; MA, U. Portland; PhD, Brigham Young U. Tchr. Leone HS, 1977—78; vice prin. Samoana HS, 1980—82, prin., 1987—88; established Tafuna HS, 1982—87; dep. dir. Secondary Div. Am. Samoa Dept. Edn., 1989, dep. dir. instructional svcs., 2005—07, acting dir. edn., 2006—07, dir. edn., 2007—. Office: Am Samoa Dept Edn Edn Bldg PO Box 186 Pago Pago AS 96799 *

POUND, FRANK R., JR., lawyer; b. Mayo, Fla., Nov. 3, 1933; s. Frank Reese and Elizabeth (Hart) P.; m. Betty Armstrong, Aug. 31, 1957; children: Tamara, Susan, Tracy, Brittain. BS, U. Fla., 1959, JD, 1961. Bar: Fla. 1962, U.S. Dist. Ct. (mid. dist.) Fla. 1962, U.S. Supreme Ct. 1969; cert. civil trial advocate; cert. civil trial lawyer; cert. mediator. Asst. county solicitor, Orlando, Fla., 1962-64; trial assoc. Crofton, et.al., Titusville, Fla., 1964-66; assoc. Howell, et.al., Rockledge, Fla., 1966-71; ptnr., pres. Lovering, Pound & Clifton, Cocoa, Fla., 1971—90; cir. judge 18th Jud. Cir. of Fla., 1991—98. Bd. dirs. Wuesthoff Health Sys., Inc., 2000—06. Chmn. Titusville Airport Authority, 1972, Sheriff's Civil Service Bd., Titusville, 1983-86, Coll. Leadership, Brevard 2000-02. Served to col. USMC res., 1952-84. Mem. Acad. Fla. Trial Lawyers, Fla. Bar Assn. (bd. govs. 1979-82), Brevard County Bar Assn. (pres. 1972-73). Lodges: Rotary (Cocoa) (pres. 1982-83), Carlton Am. Inn of Ct. (pres. 2005-06). Office Phone: 305-639-0505.

POUND, JOHN BENNETT, lawyer; b. Champaign, Ill., Nov. 17, 1946; s. William R. and Louise Catherine (Kelly) P.; m. Mary Ann Hanson, June 19, 1971; children: Meghan Elizabeth, Matthew Fitzgerald. BA, U. N. Mex., 1968; JD, Boston Coll., 1971. Bar: N. Mex. 1971, U.S. Dist. Ct. N. Mex. 1971, U.S. Ct. Appeals (10th cir.) 1972, U.S. Supreme Ct., 1993. Law clk. to Hon. Oliver Seth, US Ct. Appeals, 10th Cir., Santa Fe, 1971-72. Asst. counsel Supreme Ct. Disciplinary Bd., 1977-83, dist. rev. officer, 1984—; mem. Supreme Ct. Com. on Jud. Performance Evaluation, 1983-85; bd. dirs. Archdiocese Santa Fe Cath. Social Svcs., 1995—. Contbr. articles to profl. jours. Pres. bd. dirs. N.Mex. Ind. Coll. Fund, Santa Fe; chmn. N.Mex. Dem. Leadership Coun., 1991—; bd. dirs. Santa Fe Boys Club, 1989-92; rules com. N.Mex. Dem. Party, 1982—; v.p. Los Alamos Nat. Lab. Comm. Coun., 1985-90; fin. chmn. N.Mex. Clinton for Pres. campaign, 1992; co-chmn. Clinton-Gore Re-election Campaign, N.Mex., 1996, 2000; co-chmn. Gore for Pres., N.Mex., 2000; co-chmn. Kerry for Pres., N.Mex., 2004. Fellow Am. Bar Found., Am. Coll. Trial Lawyers, N.Mex. Bar Found.; mem. ABA, Am. Bd. Trial Advocates, N.Mex. Bar Assn. (health law sect. 1987—), Santa Fe County Bar Assn. Democrat. Roman Catholic. Avocations: history, languages, literature, swimming, baseball. Office: Long Pound Komer PA PO Box 5098 2200 Brothers Rd Santa Fe NM 87505-6903 Office Phone: 505-982-8405. Personal E-mail: lpk@nm.net, jmpound@comcast.net.

POUND, RICHARD WILLIAM DUNCAN, lawyer, accountant; b. St. Catharines, Ont., Can., Mar. 22, 1942; s. William Thomas and Jessie Edith Duncan (Thom) P.; m. Julie Houghton Keith, Nov. 4, 1977. B in Commerce, McGill U., Montreal, 1962, B in Civil Law, 1967; BA, Sir George Williams U. (now Concordia U.), Montreal, 1963; PhD (hon.), U.S. Sports Acad., 1989; LLD (hon.), U. Windsor, Can., 1997, U. We. Ont., 2004; DSA (hon.), Laurentian U., 2005; D (hon.), Beijing Sports U., 2006; LLD (hon.), Lakehead U., Can., 2007. Bar: called to Que. bar 1968, Ont. bar, 1980; chartered acct., 1964, F.C.A, 2001. Auditor Riddell, Stead, Graham & Hutchinson, Montreal, 1963-65; law clk., then atty. firm Laing, Weldon, Courtois, Clarkson, Parsons, Gonthier & Tétrault, Montreal, 1965-71; mem. firm Stikeman Elliott, Montreal, Toronto, Ottawa, Calgary, Vancouver, London, NYC, Sydney, 1972—. Lectr. taxation McGill U. Faculty Law; lectr. Que. Real Estate Assn.; mem. Ct. of Arbitration of Sport, Lausanne, 1991—; officer Order of Can., officer Ordre nat. du Quebec, Order of St. John of Jerusalem, Queen's Counsel, 1992. Author: Five Rings Over Korea, 1994, Chief Justice W.R. Jackett: By the Law of the Land, 1999, Stikeman Elliott The First Fifty Years, 2002, High Impact Quotations, 2004, Canadian Facts and Dates, 2004, Inside the Olympics, 2004, Inside Dope, 2006, Unlucky to the End, The Story of Janise Marie Gamble, 2007; editor-in-chief: Doing Business in Canada, 1987—, Canada Tax Cases, 1993—, Stikeman Income Tax Act (annotated); author: Pound's Tax Case Notes, 1988—, Legal Notes, CGA mag., 1986-03; mem. editl. bd. Can. Tax Svc., 1972-82. Pres. Can. Olympic Assn., 1977-82, sec., 1968-76, dir., 1968—; mem. Internat. Olympic Com., 1978—, exec. bd., 1983-87, 92-2000, v.p., 1987-91, 1996-2000; bd. govs. McGill U., 1986—, chmn., 1994-99, chancellor, 1999—; gov. Martlet Found.; former trustee Stanstead Wesleyan Coll.; chmn. McGill U. Athletic Bd.; chmn. McGill U. Fund Coun.; founding chmn., pres. World Anti-Doping Agy., 1999-. Decorated knight Mil. and Hospitaler Order of St. Lazarus of Jerusalem; named to Can. Swimming Hall of Fame, 1969, Sports Fedn. Can. Hall of Fame, 1976, Can. Olympic Order, 1995, Quebec Sports Hall of Fame, 2001, Gold Medallion award Internat. Swimming Hall of Fame, 2002, B.C. Swiming Hall of Fame, 2005; named one of 100 Most Influential People of 2005, Time mag. Fellow Order of Chartered Accts.; mem. Can. Bar Assn., Can. Tax Found., Internat. Fiscal Assn., Internat. Assn. Practicing Lawyers, Can. Squash Racquets Assn., Royal Life Savs. Soc., Alumni Assn. McGill U. (former pres.). Clubs: Montreal Amateur Athletic Assn. (pres. 1987-88), Club Atwater (Montreal); Jesters, Mt. Bruno Country. Home: 87 Arlington Ave Westmount PQ Canada H3Y 2W5 Office: Ste 4000 1155 Rene Levesque Blvd W Montreal PQ Canada H3B 3V2 Office Phone: 514-397-3037. Business E-Mail: rpound@stikeman.com.

POUND, ROBERT VIVIAN, physics professor; b. Ridgeway, Ont., Can., May 16, 1919; arrived in U.S., 1923, naturalized, 1932; s. Vivian Ellsworth and Gertrude C. (Prout) Pound; m. Betty Yde Andersen, June 20, 1941; 1 child, John Andrew. BA, U. Buffalo, 1941; AM (hon.), Harvard Coll., 1950; DSc (hon.), SUNY, Buffalo, 1994. Rsch. physicist Submarine Signal Co., 1941—42; staff mem. Radiation Lab. MIT, Cambridge, 1942—46; Soc. Fellows jr. fellow Harvard U., Cambridge, 1945—48; asst. prof. physics Harvard Coll., Cambridge, 1948—50, assoc. prof., 1950—56, prof., 1956—68; chmn. dept. physics, 1968—72; Mallinckrodt prof. physics, 1968—89; emeritus, 1989—; dir. Physics Lab. Harvard U., Cambridge, 1975—83. Fulbright rsch. scholar Oxford (Eng.) U., 1951; vis. rsch. fellow Merton Coll., 1980; Fulbright lectr., Paris, 58; vis. prof. Coll. de France, 1973; vis. fellow Joint Inst. Lab. Astrophysics, U. Colo., 1979—80; Zernike vis. prof. U. Groningen, The Netherlands, 1982; vis. sr. scientist Brookhaven Nat. Lab., 1986—87; vis. prof. U. Fla., 1987; W.G. Brickwedde lectr. Johns Hopkins U., Balt., 1992; Julian Mack lectr. U. Wis., 1992. Author, editor Mmicrowave Mixers, 1948; contbr. articles to profl. jours. Associated Univs., Inc., 1976—. Recipient B.J. Thompson Meml. award, Inst. Radio Engrs., 1948, Eddington medal, Royal Astron. Soc., 1965, Nat. medal Sci., Pres. U.S., 1990; fellow John Simon Guggenheim, 1957—58, 1972—73. Fellow: AAAS, Am. Acad. Arts and Scis., Am. Phys. Soc.; mem.: NAS, French Phys. Soc. (mem. coun. 1958—61), French Acad. Scis. (assoc.; fgn.), Sigma Xi, Phi Beta Kappa. E-mail: pound@fas.harvard.edu.

POUNDS, REGINA DOROTHEA, writer; arrived in U.S., 1980; d. Friedrich and Herta Klein; m. Wayne C. Pounds, June 21, 1968; 1 child, Louis C. Author: Theo's Ghost, 2000, Lord Eaglebeak, 2000, Leonora, 2002, Wild Violets, 2005; contbr. articles to pubs. Mem.: Defenders of Wildlife, World Wildlife Fund. Avocations: history, languages, poetry, art. Mailing: PO Box 414 Belleville IL 62222 Personal E-mail: oldberliner@yahoo.com.

POUNDS, WILLIAM FRANK, management educator; b. Fayette County, Pa., Apr. 9, 1928; s. Joseph Frank and Helen (Fry) P.; m. Helen Anne Means, Mar. 6, 1954; children: Thomas Mcclure, Julia Elizabeth. BSChemE, Carnegie Inst. Tech., 1950, MS in Math. Econs., 1959, PhD in Indsl. Adminstrn., 1964. Indsl. engr. Eastman Kodak Co., 1950-51, 55-57; cons. Pitts. Plate Glass Co., 1958-59, asst. to gen. mgr. Forbes finishes divsn., 1960—61; faculty Sloan Sch. Mgmt., MIT, 1966-98, prof. mgmt., 1966-98, dean, 1966-80; sr. adv. Rockefeller Family and Assocs., 1981-91. Bd. dirs. Idexx Labs., Inc., Mgmt. Scis. for Health, Inc.; bd. dir. Sunoco, Inc., 1973—2000, General Mills, Inc., 1979—91; trustee/vice chmn. Putnum Funds, 1974—2000. Chmn. bd. trustees Boston Mus. Fine Arts, 2000-03; trustee WGBH Ednl. Found., 2002—. Served as aviator lt. (j.g.) USNR, 1951-55. Fellow Am. Acad. Arts and Scis. Home: 83 Cambridge Pkwy # W1205 Cambridge MA 02142-1241

POUNDSTONE, SALLY HILL, library director; m. Robert Bruce Poundstone; children: Nancy Katrina, Holly Megan, Angus Bruce, Alice Heather. BA, U. Ky., 1954, MA in Libr. Sci., 1955. Asst. head ref. dept. Louisville Free Pub. Libr., 1955-59; libr. Folger Shakespeare Libr., Washington, 1959-60; chief acquisition dept. White Plains (N.Y.) Pub. Libr., 1960-62; libr. Bedford Hills (N.Y.) Pub. Elem. Sch., 1965-66; dir. Mamaroneck (N.Y.) Free Libr. and Emelin Theatre, 1966-87, Westport (Conn.) Pub. Libr., 1987-98; prin. SHP Libr. Consultants, 1998—. Instr. libr. sci. N.Y. U., 1968-69, Coll. of New Rochelle (N.Y.), 1970-71; adv. coun. mem. Pratt Inst. Grad Sch. of Libr. and Info. Sci., 1978-87; adminstrv. svcs. chmn. N.Y. Met. Ref. and Res. Libr. Agy., 1977-79, bd. trustees, 1979-88, 2d v.p. and chair, 1984-85, pres., 1985-88; planning and devel. com. mem. Bibliomation, Inc., 1988-90; chair Conn. State Adv. Coun. for Libr. Planning and Devel., 1988-90. Pres. Garden Club of Mamaroneck, 1969-70, Larchmont-Mamaroneck Film Coun., 1971-72; bd. dirs. Mamaroneck Hist. Soc., 1976-87, pres., 1976-77; vice chmn. Village of Upper Nyack Planning Bd., 1988-89; mem. leadership com. and task force Westchester 2,000, 1984-87; com. mem. Rotary Club of Westport, 1987—; active Downtown Westport Adv. Com., 1989-90, Rep. Town. Com., Weston, Conn., 1990-93, Westport Bridge and Traffic Com., 1990-97, Honorable Order of Ky. Cols., 1995—, United Way Profl. Adv. Com., 1994-97, Westport Telecomm. Com., 1994-96, and others; v.p., dir. Woodcock Nature Ctr., 1998—, pres., 2001—06; mem. Wilton Rep. Town Com., 2000—; mem. Planning and Zoning Bd. Commns., 2000—, sec., 2004-05, vice chair 2005-06, chair, 2006—. Mem. ALA, Conn. Libr. Assn.,

Fairfield Libr. Adminstrs. Group, Archons of Colophon, Pub. Libr. Dirs. Assn. Westchester County (various offices and chairs), N.Y. Libr. Assn. (sec. treas. adult librs. assn. 1970-72, pres. pub. librs. sect. 1981-82, chair planning com. 1984-85). Home and Office: 48 Sharp Hill Rd Wilton CT 06897-3531

POUNDSTONE, WILLIAM NICHOLAS, JR., writer; b. Morgantown, W.Va., Sept. 29, 1955; s. William Nicholas and Doris Mae (Jamison) P. Critic NY Times, NYC, 1992—, The Economist, London, 1996—. Author: Big Secrets, 1983, The Recursive Universe, 1984, Labyrinths of Reason, 1988, Prisoner's Dilemma, 1992, Carl Sagan: A Life in the Cosmos, 1999, How Would You Move Mount Fuji?, 2003, Fortune's Formula: The Untold Story of the Scientific Betting System that Beat the Casinos and Wall Street, 2005, Gaming the Vote: Why Elections Aren't Fair (And What We Can Do About It), 2007; co-producer Dave Bell Assocs., LA, 1993-94, producer, 1994-95. Mem. PEN, Writers Guild.

POURBAIX, ALEXANDER, energy executive; BA with distinction, U. Alta., LLB. Pres. energy TransCanada Corp., 1997—; chmn., dir. TransCanada Turbines Ltd. Mem. bd. mgmt. Alta. Econ. Devel. Authority; active Calgary Homeless Found.; bd. dirs. Jr. Achievement of So. Alta. Recipient Top 40 Under 40 award for leadership excellence, 2002—03. Office: TransCanada Corp 450 1st St SW Calgary AB Canada T2P 5H1 Office Phone: 403-920-2122. Business E-Mail: alex_pourbaix@transcanada.com.

POURCIAU, LESTER JOHN, JR., retired librarian; b. Baton Rouge, Sept. 6, 1936; s. Lester John and Pearlie M. (Hogan) Pourciau; 1 child, Lester John Thomas III. BA, La. State U., 1962, MS, 1964; PhD, Ind. U., 1975. Asst. ref. libr. U. S.C., Columbia, 1963—64; ref. libr. Florence County Pub. Libr., SC, 1964—65; coord. ref. svcs. U. Fla., Gainesville, 1966—67; dir. librs. U. Memphis, 1970—99, assoc. v.p. for acad. affairs, dir. librs., 1987—91. Chmn. coun. of head librarians State Univ. and C.C. System Tenn., 1980, 87, 97; acad. assoc. Atlantic Coun. of U.S., U. Memphis; fgn. expert, vis. lectr. Beijing U. of Posts & Telecomms., Beijing Normal U., Peking U., Renmen U., Qinghua U., Chingqing Inst. Posts & Telcomms., Guizhou Normal U., Republic of China, 1993, Beijing U. Posts and Telecom, 1993, Nanjing U. Posts and Telecom., Anhui Normal U., Beijing U. Posts and Telecom., 1994, People's Republic of China, 1994; cons. prof. Beijing U. Posts and Telecom., 1996—; participant 2d Internat. Conf. Crimea 95, Librs. and Assn. in the Transient World, Republic of Crimea; participant, dep. chair organizing com., 1996—; Peking U. Internat. Conf., Beijing, 1998. Contbr. articles to profl. jours. With USAF, 1955-59. Recipient Adminstrv. Staff award Memphis State U., 1981, Commendation Boy Scouts Am., 1985, Commendation Tenn. Sec. State, 1989, Honor award Tenn. Libr. Assn., 1990, Allen J. Hammond award for Disting. Svc. U. Memphis, 1999, SLIS Disting. Alumni award Ind. U., 1999, TRACES award U. Memphis Assn. Retirees, 2003; named Outstanding Alumnus, La. State U., 1988; named Libr. of Yr., Memphis Libr. Coun., 1989; fellow Higher Edn. Act Ind. U.; named to 30th Ann. Honor Roll. ALA Office Intellectual Freedom and Freedom to Read Found. U. Memphis, 1999. Mem.: ALA, Memphis Old Time Car Club (sec. 1981, pres. 1982, 1989), Mid-Am. Old Time Automobile Assn., Antique Automobile Club Am., Nat. Assn. Watch and Clock Collectors (chpt. pres. 1983, sec.-treas. 1988—89). Office: Memphis State U U Libr Memphis TN 38152-0001 Business E-Mail: pourciau@memphis.edu.

POUSADA, LIDIA, physician; b. Mt. Kisco, NY, July 21, 1957; d. Manuel and Maria Nieves (Mejuto) P.; m. Andrew Kemper Goodman, June 26, 1983 (div. Sept. 1986); 1 child, Sara Pousada Goodman; m. Wayne William Maibaum, Apr. 11, 1987 (div. July 1993); 1 child, Anna Pousada Maibaum; m. James Paul Kreindler, Mar. 2, 1996; 1 child, Victoria Pousada Kreindler. BS, CUNY, NYC, 1978; MD, N.Y. Med. Coll., 1980. Diplomate Am. Bd. Internal Medicine, Am. Bd. Geriatric Medicine. Student geriatric fellowship NYU Med. Sch., NYC, 1978-80; resident in internal medicine Montefiore Med. Ctr., Bronx, NY, 1980-83, dir. geriatric unit, 1986-89; with nat. health svc. North Cent. Bronx Hosp., 1983-84, Morris Heights Health Ctr., Bronx, 1985; instr. City Coll. Med. Sch., NYC, 1982-85, Albert Einstein Coll. Medicine, Bronx, 1983-84, 86-89, asst. prof. medicine, 1988-89; assoc. prof. clin. medicine N.Y. Med. Coll., 1993—; pvt. practice geriatric medicine, 2002—. Dir. geriatric cons. svc. Montefiore Med. Ctr., 1987—89, assoc. chief divsn. geriatrics, 1988—92; chief divsn. geriatrics and gerontology Sound Shore Med. Ctr., 1992—2002. Author: Geriatric Diagnostics, 1983, Emergency Medicine for the House Officer, 1986, 2d edit., 1995, Emergency Medicine for Nurses, 1989, Perioperative Medical Care of the Geriatric Patient, 1989, Case Studies in Emergency Medicine for the House Officer, 1993. Physician scholar Nat. Health Svc., 1978-80. Fellow ACP, Gerontol. Soc. Am., Am. Geriatric Soc.; mem. Physicians for Social Responsibility. Office: 141 North State Rd Briarcliff Manor NY 10510 Office Phone: 914-762-2900.

POUSCHINE, JOHN LAURENCE, private equity investment executive; b. Glen Cove, NY, Jan. 28, 1957; s. Ivan and Helen (Carlson) P.; m. Catherine Dana, Nov. 16, 1991; children: Alexander, Anna. BA, Princeton U., 1979; MBA, Harvard U., 1983. Officer's asst. JP Morgan, NYC, 1979-81; assoc. Prudential Securities, Inc., NYC, 1983-85; v.p. Bradford Ventures Ltd., NYC, 1985-88; sr. v.p. Electra Inc., NYC, 1989-96; mng. dir. Pouschine Cook Capital Mgmt., LLC, 1997—. Chmn. bd. dirs. A World of Tile, Denver, Doe & Ingalls Mgmt., Durham, NC, Latex Internat., Shelton, Conn., St. Clair Entertainment, L.A., Great Lakes Home Health Svcs., Jackson, Mich. Bd. dirs. Russian Children's Welfare Soc., N.Y.C. Mem. Bridgehampton Club, Nassau Club, Princeton Club of N.Y., Union Club. Avocation: sports. Office: Pouschine Cook Capital Mgmt 375 Park Ave Ste 3408 New York NY 10152 E-mail: jpouschine@pouschinecook.com.

POUSSAINT, ALVIN FRANCIS, psychiatrist, educator; b. NYC, May 15, 1934; s. Christopher Thomas and Harriet (Johnston) P. BA, Columbia U., 1956; MD, Cornell U., 1960; MS, UCLA, 1964. Intern UCLA Ctr. for Health Sci., 1960-61, resident in psychiatry Neuropsychiat. Inst., 1961-64, chief resident, 1964-65; So. field dir. Med. Com. Human Rights, Jackson, Miss., 1965-66; asst. prof. psychiatry Tufts U. Med. Sch., 1966-69; assoc. prof. psychiatry, assoc. dean students Harvard Med. Sch., 1969-75, 78—, prof. psychiatry, 1993—, dean students, 1975-78. Cons. HEW, 1969-73. Author numerous articles in field. Nat. treas. Black Acad. Arts and Letters, 1969-70, Med. Com. Human Rights, 1966—. Recipient Michael Schwerner award, 1968, Am. Black Achievement award in Bus. and the Professions Johnson Pub. Co., Inc., 1986, John Jay award for Disting. Profl. Achievement Columbia Coll., N.Y., 1987, Medgar Evers Medal of Honor Beverly Hills/Hollywood chpt. NAACP, Hollywood, Calif., 1988, and numerous hon. degrees. Fellow AAAS, Am. Orthopsychiatric Assn., Am. Psychiat. Assn. (mem. com. on Black Psychiatrists 1970-75); mem. Nat. Med. Assn., Am. Acad. of Child Psychiatry, Children's Longwood. Office: Judge Baker Ctr 53 Parker Hill Ave Boston MA 02120-3225

POUSSOT, BERNARD JEAN, pharmaceutical executive; m. Delphine Cecile Poussot, May 15, 1976; children: Rodolphe, Eve, Juliette. Grad., Ecole Superieure de Commerce de Paris, 1975. Deputy gen. mgr. Wyeth France, 1986, pres., gen. mgr., 1987—91; group v.p. Europe Wyeth-Ayerst Internat., Collegeville, Pa., 1991, exec. v.p., 1993, pres., 1996, pres. worldwide pharm. bus., 1997—2002; exec. v.p. Wyeth R & D Wyeth, Madison, NJ, 2002—07, pres., COO, vice chmn., bd. mem., 2007—. Mem.: PhRMA (chmn. internat. section 1999). Office: Wyeth Five Giralda Farms Madison NJ 07940-0874

POUTSMA, MARVIN L., retired chemical research administrator; b. Grand Rapids, Mich., Aug. 7, 1937; m. Yolanda Arco, July 20, 1968; children: John C., Julie A. BS, Calvin Coll., 1958; PhD, U. Ill., 1962. Staff scientist corp. rsch. Union Carbide, Tarrytown, N.Y., 1961-65, group leader corp. rsch., 1965-68, sr. scientist corp. rsch., 1968-73, sr. group leader corp. rsch., 1972-78; group leader chemistry divsn. Oak Ridge (Tenn.) Nat. Lab., 1978-80, sect. head chemistry divsn., 1980-83, dir. chemistry divsn., 1984-93, dir. chem. & analytical scis. divsn., 1994-2000, ret., 2000. Contbr. chpts. to books and articles to profl. jours. Fellow AAAS; mem. Am. Chem. Soc. Office: Oak Ridge Nat Lab PO Box 2008 Oak Ridge TN 37831-6197 Office Phone: 865-576-8339. Business E-Mail: poutsmaml@ornl.gov.

POUW, KING T., food products executive; MSE, Ruhr U., Bochum, Germany. With Kellogg Co., 1978, dir. ops. and tech. L.Am., 1995—98, v.p. global supply chain, ops. effectiveness, 1998—99, supply chain dir. Europe, 1999, v.p. supply chain Europe, sr. v.p. ops., 2000—01, exec. v.p. ops. and tech. Battle Creek, Mich., 2001; sr. v.p. bus. transformation ConAgra Foods, Inc., Omaha, 2006—. Office: ConAgra Foods Inc 1 ConAgra Dr Omaha NE 68102-5001 Office Phone: 402-595-4000. Office Fax: 402-595-4709. *

POUZILHAC, ALAIN DUPLESSIS DE, advertising executive; b. Sète, Herault, France, June 11, 1945; s. Pierre and Jeanine (Caffarel) de P.; m. Carole de Pouzilhac, Sept. 6, 1969; children: Edouard, Cedric, Philippine. Asst. account exec. Publicis, Paris, 1968; account supr. DDB, Paris, 1969—75; COO Havas Conseil, Neuilly, France, 1976-82, chmn., CEO, 1982-87, HDM, Neuilly and Puteaux, France, 1987-89, Eurocom, Neuilly, 1989—, EURO RSCG Worldwide, Neuilly, France, 1991, Havas Advt., 1996—2005, Havas, 2001—05, France 24, 2005—. Avocations: soccer, rugby. Home: 21 rue de Miromesnil 75008 Paris France Office: France 24 5 rue des Nations Unies 92455 Issy Les Moulineaux France Office Phone: 33 1 73 01 24 12. Business E-Mail: adepouzilhac@france24.com.

POVICH, DAVID, lawyer; b. Washington, June 8, 1935; s. Shirley Lewis and Ethyl (Friedman) Povich; m. Constance Enid Tobriner, June 14, 1959; children: Douglas, Johanna, Judtih, Andrew. BA, Yale U., 1958; LLB, Columbia U., 1962. Bar: D.C. 1962, U.S. Ct. Appeals (4th cir.) 1980, U.S. Tax Ct. 1981, U.S. Ct. Appeals (5th and 11th cirs.) 1984, U.S. Dist. Ct. Md., U.S. Ct. Appeals (3d cir.) 1997. Law clk. to assoc. judge D.C. Ct. Appeals, Washington, 1962-63; exec. com. Williams & Connolly, 1986-87, ptnr., 1963—2005, of counsel, 2006—. Bd. dirs., officer Lisner Home for Aged. Mem.: ABA, Barristers (exec. com. 1992—93), Bar Assn. D.C., D.C. Bar Assn. Office: Williams & Connolly 725 12th St NW Washington DC 20005-5901 Office Phone: 202-434-5071. E-mail: dpovich@wc.com.

POVICH, LYNN, journalist, Internet executive, editor; b. Washington, June 4, 1943; d. Shirley and Ethyl P.; m. Stephen B. Shepard, Sept. 16, 1979; children: Sarah, Ned. AB, Vassar Coll., 1965. Rschr., reporter, writer, editor, sr. editor Newsweek mag., NYC, 1965—91; editor-in-chief Working Woman mag., NYC, 1991—96; mng. editor, sr. exec. prodr. East coast programming MSNBC Interactive, Secaucus, NJ, 1996—2001. Editor: All Those Mornings at the Post, 2006. Bd. mem. Internat. Women's Media Found., 1998—, co-chair, 2002—05; vice chair, adv. com. women's rights divsn. Human Rights Watch, 2003—. Recipient Matrix award N.Y. Women in Comms., 1976; named to Acad. of Women Achievers YWCA, 1993. Mem.: Online News Assn. (founder).

POWDERLY, WILLIAM H., III, lawyer; b. Pitts., Feb. 23, 1930; BS, Georgetown U., 1953; LLB, U. Pitts., 1956. Bar: Pa. 1956. Ptnr. Reed Smith, LLP, Jones Day; of counsel Tucker Arensberg PC, Pitts. Office: Tucker Arensberg PC 1500 One PPG Pl Pittsburgh PA 15222 Office Phone: 412-594-3925. Business E-Mail: wpowderly@tuckerlaw.com.

POWE, NEIL RICHARD, physician, educator, epidemiologist, public health service officer; b. Phila., May 11, 1955; BA, Princeton U., 1976; MD, MPH, Harvard U., 1981; MBA, Wharton Grad. Sch., Phila., 1986. Intern, resident hosp. U. Pa., 1981-84, Robert Wood Johnson Clin. scholar; instr. Johns Hopkins U., Balt., 1986-88, asst. prof., 1988-94, assoc. prof., 1994-98, prof., 1998—. Dir. Welch Ctr. for Prevention, Epidemiology and Clin. Rsch., 1998—, Johns Hopkins Evidence Based Practice Ctr.; co-dir. Robert Wood Johnson Clin. Scholars Program. Contbr. articles to profl. jours. Assn. Health Svcs. Rsch. fellow, 1997. Fellow: ACP (tchg. and rsch. scholar); mem.: Inst. Medicine, Am. Soc. Clin. Investigation. Office: Johns Hopkins U 2-600 2024 E Monument St Baltimore MD 21287-0007 E-mail: npower@jhsph.edu.

POWELL, ADAM CLAYTON, engineering educator, consultant; b. NYC, 1970; PhD in Materials Engring., MIT, Cambridge, Mass., 1997. Metallurgist NIST, Gaithersburg, Md., 1997—99; asst. prof. MIT, Cambridge, Mass., 1999—2006; mng. engr. Veryst Engring. LLC, Needham, Mass., 2006—. Musician: (gospel choir director) Boston Temple Youth Gospel Choir. Achievements include development of Method for understanding pore structure formation in polymer membranes. Office: 47A Kearney Rd Needham MA 02494-2503 Office Phone: 781-433-0433. Business E-Mail: apowell@veryst.com.

POWELL, ALAN, engineering educator, research scientist; b. Buxton, Derbyshire, Eng., Feb. 17, 1928; arrived in U.S., 1956; s. Frank and Gwendolen Marie (Walker) P.; m. June Sinclair, Mar. 28, 1956. Student, Buxton Coll., 1939-45; diploma in aeros., Loughborough Coll., 1948; BSc in Engring. (hon.), London U., 1949; honors diploma 1st class, Loughborough Coll., 1949; DTech (hon.), Loughborough U. Tech., 1980; PhD, U. Southampton, 1953. Chartered engr. Engr. Percival Aircraft Co., Luton, Eng., 1949-51; from rsch. asst. to lectr. U. Southampton, Eng., 1951-56; rsch. fellow Calif. Inst. Tech., Pasadena, 1956-57; engr. Douglas Aircraft Co., 1956; assoc. prof. UCLA, 1957-62, prof. engring., 1962-65, head Aerosonics lab., 1957-65; assoc. tech. dir., head acoustics and vibration lab. David Taylor Model Basin, Dept. Navy, Washington, 1965-66, tech. dir., 1966-67, David Taylor Naval Ship Research & Devel. Center, Bethesda, Md., 1967-85; mem. Undersea Warfare Research & Devel. Council, 1966-76, chmn., 1971-72; mem. council on Fed. Labs., 1972-85; prof. mech. engring. U. Houston, 1985-2000, chmn., 1985-87, prof. emeritus, 2000—. Com. on hearing bioacoustics and biomechs. NAS-NRC, 1961-85, exec. coun., 1963-65, chmn., 1965-66, advisor, 1985-95, mem. naval studies bd. 1990-95; mem. various coms. Naval Studies Bd. and Marine Bd., 1990-96; advisor Chinese U. Devel. Project, 1989-91; cons. Douglas Aircraft Co., 1956-65, others; adv. coun. Internat. Towing Tank Conf., 1981-85; mem. advisor U.S.-Japan Program Natural Resources, 1987-90, mem. Marine Facilities Panel; gen. chmn. 3d advanced vehicles conf. AIAA and Soc. Naval Archs. and Marine Engrs., 1976; chmn. internat. conf. Computer Aided Design, Manufacture and Ops. in Marine and Offshore Industries, 1987-88; cons. Sci. Applications Internat., Inc., 1987-90; governing bd. Am. Inst. Physics, 1995-97. Contbr. articles to profl. jours. Recipient Navy Meritorious Civilian Service award, 1970; Brit. Empire scholar, 1945; named Meritorious Exec. Pres. of U.S., 1982; Capt. Robert Dexter Conrad gold medal for sci. achievement Sec. Navy, 1984; dedication spl. issue Internat. Jour. Aeroacoustics vol. 2 nos. 3/4, 2003. Fellow Royal Aero. Soc. London (Baden-Powell prize 1948, Wilbur Wright prize 1953), Acoustical Soc. Am. (biennial award 1962, assoc. editor Jour. 1962-67, chmn. edn. com. 1964-66, exec. coun. 1966-69, chmn. medals and awards com. 1978-81, v.p. elect 1981-82, v.p. 1982-83, pres. elect 1989-90, pres. 1990-91, past pres. 1991-92, Silver medal in engring. acoustics 1992, designated Nat. Spkr. in Engring. Acoustics 1994-98), Inst. Mech. Engrs., Inst. Acoustics (U.K.); mem. AIAA (assoc. fellow, Aeroacoustics award 1980), ASME (Rayleigh lectr. 1988, Per Brüel Gold medal 1991), Inst. Noise Control Engrs. (initial mem., dir. 1974-77, Disting. lectr. 1975, 83, v.p. 1981-84, bd. cert. 1993), Acoustics, Speech and Signal Processing Soc. (exec. com. 1969-72, awards com. 1971-73, bylaws com. chmn. 1973-75), Am. Soc. Naval Engrs. (life), Am. Acad. Mechanics, Tau Beta Pi (hon. life). Office: U Houston Dept Mech Engring Houston TX 77204-4006

POWELL, ALMA JOHNSON, writer, advocate, foundation administrator; b. Birmingham, Al., Oct. 27, 1937; d. Robert and Mildred Johnson; m. Colin L. Powell, Aug. 1962; children: Michael, Linda, Annemarie. BA, Fisk U., 1957; LHD (hon.), Emerson Coll., 1996. Audiologist Boston Guild Hard of Hearing, 1959—62. Author: (children's books) America's Promise, 2003, My Little Wagon, 2003. Chair nat. coun. Best Friends Found., 1989—2001; chair Alliance for Youth, 2004—. Named one of 100 Most Powerful Women in Wash., Washingtonian mag., 2001.

POWELL, ANNE ELIZABETH, editor-in-chief; b. Cheverly, Md., Nov. 11, 1951; d. Arthur Gorman and Barbara Anne (MacAran) P.; m. John Alan Ebeling Jr., 1972 (div. 1983). BS, U. Md., 1972. Reporter Fayetteville (N.C.) Times, 1973-75; home editor Columbus (Ga.) Ledger-Enquirer, 1976; assoc. editor Builder mag., Washington, 1977-78; architecture editor House Beautiful's Spl. Publs., NYC, 1979-81; editor Traditional Home mag., Des Moines, 1982-87, Mid-Atlantic Country mag., Alexandria, Va., 1987-89; editor in chief publs. Nat. Trust for Hist. Preservation, Washington, 1989-95; editor-in-chief Landscape Architecture Mag., Washington, 1995-98, Civil Engring. Mag., Washington, 1998—. Author: The New England Colonial, 1988. Mem. Nat. Press Club, Am. Soc. Mag. Editors. Home: 1105 Park St NE Washington DC 20002-6317 Office: American Society of Civil Engrs Civil Engring Mag 1801 Alexander Bell Dr Reston VA 20191-4344 Office Phone: 703-295-6213.

POWELL, ARDAL, music company executive, editor; b. Bournemouth, Dorset, England, Apr. 22, 1958; BA with honors, U. Cambridge, 1980, MA, 1989, PhD, 2004. Cert. Kononklijk Conservatorium, Den Haag, 1983. Pres. Folkers & Powell, Makers Hist. Flutes, Hudson, NY, 1983—. Editor: Traverso, Hist. Flute Newsletter, 1989—; translator: The Virtuoso Flute-Player by Johann George Tromlitz; author: (monograph) The Flute, The Keyed Flute by Johann George Tromlitz (; editor: The Baroque Flute Fingering Book by Margaret N. Neuhaus, (periodical collected reprint) Traverso: Historical Flute Newsletter, Volumes 1—10, 1989—98. Fellow, NEH, 1993—94. Mem.: Am. Musical Instrument Soc. (bd. govs. 2001—, Bessaraboff prize 2005), Nat. Flute Assn. (com. 1987), Juggler Meadow Morris Men. Avocation: sailing.

POWELL, BARRY BRUCE, classicist, educator; b. Sacramento, Apr. 30, 1942; s. Barrett Robert and Anita Louise (Burns) Powell; m. Patricia Ann Cox; children: Elena Melissa, Adam Vincent. BA in Classics, U. Calif., Berkeley, 1963, PhD, 1971; MA, Harvard U., 1965. Asst. prof. Northern Ariz. U., Flagstaff, 1970-73; from asst. prof. to prof. U. Wis., Madison, 1973—, chmn. dept. classics, 1985-92, chmn. program integrated liberal studies. Author: Composition by Theme in the Odyssey, 1973, Homer and the Origin of the Greek Alphabet, 1991, Classical Myth, 1995, 5th edit., 2007, New Companion to Homer, 1997, A Short Introduction to Classical Myth, 2001, Writing and the Origins of Greek Literature, 2002, Homer, 2003, 2d edit., 2007, Ramses in Nighttown, 2006, The War at Troy: A True History, 2006; author: (with Ian Morris) The Greeks: Society, Culture, History, 2004, numerous poems; writer screenplays; contbr. articles to profl. jours. Woodrow Wilson fellow, 1965. Mem.: Am. Acad. in Rome, Classical Assn. Midwest and South, Archeol. Inst. Am., Am. Sch. Classical Studies at Athens (mng. com.), Am. Philol. Assn., Phi Beta Kappa (former pres. Madison chpt.). Home: 1210 Sweetbriar Rd Madison WI 53705-2228 Office: Univ Wis Dept Classics Madison WI 53707 Home Phone: 608-233-5991; Office Phone: 608-262-2041. E-mail: bbpowell@wisc.edu.

POWELL, BAYARD LOWERY, oncologist, educator; b. Raleigh, NC, June 22, 1954; MD, U. N.C., 1980. Diplomate Am. Bd. Internal Medicine, Am. Bd. Med. Oncology. Intern, then resident in internal medicine N.C. Bapt. Hosp., Winston-Salem, 1980-83, mem. staff; fellow in hematologic oncology Bowman Gray Sch. Medicine, Winston-Salem, 1983-86, assoc. prof. hematologic oncology. Named one of NC's Best Doctors, Bus. NC mag., 2002. Mem. ACP, Am. Assn. for Cancer Rsch., Am. Soc. Hematology, Am. Soc. Clin. Oncology. Office: Bowman Gray Sch Medicine Cancer Ctr Wake Forest U Med Ctr Blvd Winston Salem NC 27157-0001 also: 2707 Buena Vista RD Winston Salem NC 27106 Office Phone: 336-716-4354. Business E-Mail: bpowell@wfubmc.edu. *

POWELL, BENJAMIN ALBOND, federal agency administrator, lawyer; b. Apr. 1967; BSE, U. Pa.; JD, Columbia U. Bar: 1999. Law clk. to Justice Byron R. White US Supreme Ct., law clk. to Justice John Paul Stevens; assoc. Kellogg, Huber, Hansen, Todd and Evans LLP; corp. counsel Vitria Tech., Inc.; program examiner State and USIA Branch Office of Mgmt. and Budget, Exec. Office of Pres., Washington; spl. asst. & assoc. counsel to Pres. The White House, Washington, 2002—06; gen. counsel Office Nat. Intelligence, Washington, 2006—. Captain USAF. Office: Office Nat Intelligence NEOB 725 17th St Washington DC 20500

POWELL, BILLY, musician; b. Corpus Christi, Tex., June 3, 1952; s. Donald and Marie Powell. Roadie with Lynyrd Skynyrd, 1970—72, keyboardist, 1972—77, 1987—; band mem. Alias, 1979, The Rossington-Collins Band, 1980—82, Allen Collins Band, 1983—85, Vision, 1985—87. Musician: (albums) Second Time Around, (with Lynyrd Skynyrd) Pronounced Leh-Nerd Skin-Nerd, 1973, Smokes, 1973, Second Helping, 1974, Nuthin' Fancy, 1975, Gimme Back My Bullets, 1976, One More from the Road, 1976, Street Survivors, 1977, Southern by the Grace of God, 1988, Lynyrd Skynyrd 1991, The Last Rebel, 1993, Endangered Species, 1994, Freebird: The Movie, 1996, Southern Nights, 1996, Twenty, 1997, Lyve, 1998, Edge of Forever, 1999, Universal Masters Collection, 1999, Christmas Time Again, 2000, Vicious Cycle, 2003, (with Alias) Contraband, 1979, (with the Rossington-Collins Band) Anytime, Anyplace, Anywhere, 1980, This is the Way, 1982, (with the Allen Collins Band) Here, There & Back, 1983. Named to Rock and Roll Hall of Fame, 2006. Office: Vector Mgmt PO Box Nashville TN 37212 also: Sanctuary Records 5226 Greens Dairy Rd Raleigh NC 27616-4612

POWELL, CARLETON D., federal judge; b. SC, 1939; BA, U. Va., 1961; LLB, U. Richmond, 1967. With IRS, 1967—70; trial atty. appellate sect., tax divsn. US Dept. Justice, Washington, 1970—77, sr. trial atty., 1977—80, reviewer, 1980—85; spl. trial judge US Tax Ct., Washington, 1985—. Commd. officer US Army, 1962—64. Mem.: Commonwealth VA Bar Assn. Office: US Tax Court 400 2nd St NW Washington DC 20217 *

POWELL, CAROLYN WILKERSON, retired music educator; b. Hamburg, Ark., Oct. 9, 1920; d. Claude Kelly and Mildred (Hall) Wilkerson; m. Charles Luke Powell, Dec. 12, 1923; children: Charles Luke Jr., James Davis, Mark Wilkerson, Robert Hall. AB, Ctrl. Meth. U., Fayette, Mo., 1942; MA in Tchg., U. NC, 1970. Life tchg. cert. Mo., cert. tchr. N.C. Choral dir. Maplewood-Richmond Heights Sch., St. Louis, 1943-45; pvt. piano tchr. Greensboro, NC, 1951-63; organist Presbyn. and Meth. chs., Greensboro, 1950-61; dir. ch. youth choirs, Greensboro, 1958-61; choral and humanities tchr. Page HS, Greensboro, 1963-67; choral dir. Githens Jr. HS, Durham, NC, 1967-80; ret., 1980. Chmn. Choral Festival N.C. Dist., 1968—78; accompanist, music dir. Altavista (Va.) Little Theatre, 1981—83. Den mother Boy Scouts Am., Greensboro, 1951—57; mem. Chapel Hill Preservation Soc., NC, 1985—; vol., chapel organist, pediat. tutor U. NC Hosps., Chapel Hill, 1984—89; mem. Chapel Hill Hist. Soc.;

Sunday and vacation schs. tchr., organist Grace Meth. Ch., Greensboro; organist St. Peter's Episcopal Ch., Altavista, 1981—83; organist Episcopal ch. svc. Carol Woods Retirement Cmty., Chapel Hill, 1999—. Mem.: AAUW, NEA, Classroom Tchrs. Assn., Am. Organists Guild, Music Educators Nat. Conf., Ackland Art Mus. Assn., Carolina Club, Nat. Federated Music Club Euterpe, Chapel Hill Country Club, Univ. Woman's Club, Delta Kappa Gamma. Avocations: reading, golf, needlecrafts, gardening, travel. Home: Apt 1113 750 Weaver Dairy Rd Chapel Hill NC 27514-1441

POWELL, COLIN LUTHER, former secretary of state, former Chairman of the Joint Chiefs of Staff; b. NYC, Apr. 5, 1937; s. Luther and Maud Ariel (McKoy) P.; m. Alma Vivian Johnson, Aug. 25, 1962; children: Michael, Linda, Annemarie. BS in Geology, CUNY, 1958; MBA, George Washington U., 1971; Grad., Nat. War Coll., 1976. Commd. 2d lt. U.S. Army, 1958; advanced through grades to gen., 1989; ret., 1993; asst. to dep. dir. Office Mgmt. & Budget, Washington, 1972—73; battalion comdr. Republic of Korea, 1973—74; comdr. 2d Brigade, 101st Airborne Div., Ft. Campbell, Ky., 1976—77; exec. asst. to sec. US Dept. Energy, Washington, 1979; sr. mil. asst. to dep. sec. US Dept. Def., Washington, 1979—81, asst. div. comdr. 4th Inf. Div. Ft. Carson, Colo., 1981—83, mil. asst. to sec. def. Washington, 1983—86; assigned to U.S. V Corps, Europe, 1986—87; dep. asst. to the Pres. for nat. security affairs NSC, Washington, 1987, asst. to Pres. for nat. security affairs, 1987—89; comdr.-in-chief US Forces Command, Ft. McPherson, Ga., 1989; chmn. Joint Chiefs of Staff The Pentagon, Washington, 1989—93; sec. US Dept. State, Washington, 2001—05; strategic limited ptnr. Kleiner Perkins Caufield & Byers, Menlo Park, Calif., 2005—. Founding chair America's Promise.; pub. spkr. addressing audiences across the country and abroad; mem. Wash. Baseball Club, 2005—. Author: (with Joseph E. Persico) My American Journey (autobiography), 1995. Decorated Legion of Merit (2), Bronze Star, Air medal, Purple Heart; named hon. knight comdr. Most Honorable Order of the Bath Queen Elizabeth II, 1993; recipient Presdl. Medal of Freedom (2), Ronald Reagan Freedom award, 1993, President's Citizens Medal, Congressional Gold Medal, Sec. of State Disting. Svc. Medal, Sec. of Energy Disting. Svc. Medal, Ellis Island Family Heritage award in Govt. Svc., Statue of Liberty-Ellis Island Found., Inc, 2005, Legion of Honor, France, 2006, several sch. and other inst. have been named in his honor; The White House fellow, 1972—73. Mem. Assn. U.S. Army. Republican. Episcopalian. Office: Kleiner Perkins Caulfield & Byers 909 N Washington St Ste 700 Alexandria VA 22314

POWELL, DAVID CHARLES, music educator, meteorologist; b. Keokuk, Iowa, May 14, 1926; s. Othello Dotson and Miriam Estella (Trittschuh) Powell; m. Judith Ann Ahrens, Feb. 2, 1950; children: Walter David, Katharine Elise. MusB, Ind. U., 1949, MusM, postgrad., Ind. U., 1951; BS, U. Utah, 1964, MA, 1968, PhD, 1974. Cert. music tchr. Instr. piano Ea. Ky. State Coll., Richmond, 1951—52; tchr. math. and music Darby (Mont.) Pub. Schs., 1953—56; pvt. piano instr. Whitefish, Mont., 1956—62; rsch. scientist, sr. scientist meteorology Battelle, Pacific NW Nat. Lab., Richland, Wash., 1968—88; pvt. piano instr. Richland, 1989—. Contbr. articles and papers to profl. publs. Cmty. educator classical music history, 1981—. With US Army, 1944—46, ETO. Grad. fellow, NASA, 1965—67. Mem.: Nat. Guild Piano Tchrs., Wash. State Music Tchrs. (treas., publicity com. 1989—91), Nat. Music Tchrs. Assn., Audubon Soc. (pres. lower Columbia Basin chpt. 1975—76). Episcopalian. Achievements include development of computer programs to model atmospheric conditions. Avocations: hiking, birdwatching, camping, travel, music. Home and Office: 2110 Hudson Ave Richland WA 99354 Office Phone: 509-946-4429. E-mail: res0szlg@verizon.net.

POWELL, DEBORAH ELIZABETH, pathologist, dean; b. Lynn, Mass., Nov. 28, 1939; MD, Tufts U., 1965. Diplomate Am. Bd. Pathology. Intern Georgetown Med. Ctr., Washington, 1965-66; resident in pathology NIH, Bethesda, Md., 1966-69; exec. dean, vice-chancellor clin. affairs U. Kans. Sch. Medicine, Kansas City, 1997—2002; dean, asst. v.p. for clin. scis. U. Minn. Med. Sch., Mpls., 2002—. Past pres. U.S. & Can. Acad. Pathology, Inc.; trustee Am. Bd. Pathology. Mem.: Am. Soc. Investigative Pathologists, Inst. Medicine, Coll. Am. Pathologists. Office: U Minn Med Sch Dean's Office MMC 293 Mayo 8293 420 Delaware St SE Minneapolis MN 55455 Home Phone: 952-546-1215. Business E-Mail: dpowell@umn.edu.

POWELL, DENNIS D., computer systems network executive; BBA in Acctg., Oreg. State U. Former sr. ptnr. Coopers & Lybrand LLP; v.p., corp. contr. Cisco Systems, Inc., San Jose, Calif., 1997—2002, sr. v.p. corp. fin., 2002—03, sr. v.p., CFO, 2003—. Mem. FDIC Adv. Com. on Banking Policy; expert witness on fin. reporting Senate Banking Com. and Ho. Fin. Subcom. Mem.: AICPA (task force for in-process R&D 2000), Fin. Execs. Internat. Office: Cisco Systems Inc 170 W Tasman Dr San Jose CA 95134 *

POWELL, DINA HABIB, federal agency administrator; b. Cairo, 1973; d. Onsi Habib and Hoda Soliman. BA, U. Tex. Mem. rels. coord. to rep. Dick Army U.S. Ho. of Reps., Washington; dir. congl. affairs, sr. adv. to chmn. of Rep. Nat. Com. Washington, 1999—2001; spl. asst. to pres. for presdl. personnel, Exec. Office of Pres. The White House, Washington, 2001—05; asst. sec. ednl. & cultural affairs US Dept. State, Washington, 2005—. Office: US Dept State 301 Fourth St SW Rm 800 Washington DC 20547 Office Phone: 202-203-5118. Office Fax: 202-203-7469.

POWELL, DON WATSON, gastroenterologist, educator; b. Gadsden, Ala., Aug. 29, 1938; s. Gordon C. and Ruth (Bennett) P.; m. Frances N. Rourke; children: Mary Paige, Drew Watson, Shawnne Margaret. BS with honors, Auburn U., 1960; MD with highest honors, Med. Coll. Ala., Birmingham, 1963. Diplomate Am. Bd. Internal Medicine, Am. Bd. Gastroenterology. Intern, resident P.B. Brigham Hosp., Boston, 1963-65; resident Yale U. Sch. Med., New Haven, 1968-69, spl. NIH fellow in physiology, 1969-71; asst. prof. medicine U. N.C., Chapel Hill, 1971-74, assoc. prof., 1974-78, prof., 1978-91; mem. external adv. bd., v.p. for rsch. U. Tex. Health Sci. Ctr., San Antonio, 2005—. Chief divsn. digestive diseases U. N.C., 1977-91, dir. Ctr. Gastrointestinal Biol. Diseases, 1985-91, assoc. chmn. clin. affairs dept. medicine, 1989-91; Edward Randall and Edward Randall, Jr. Disting. chmn. U. Tex. Med. Br., Galveston, 1991-02, prof. internal medicine, neurosci. and cell biology, 1991—, assoc. dean rsch., Sch. Medicine, 2002-06; program dir. Gen. Clin. Rsch. Ctr., 2003—; cons. WHO, Geneva, 1980-82, Burroughs-Wellcome, Inc., Research Triangle Pk., N.C., 1981-82, Hoffman-LaRoche, Inc., Nutley, N.J., 1982-93, Glaxo Smith Kline, Harlow, Eng., 2004-05;cons. Lexicon Genetics, The Woodlands, Tex., 2005—; mem. merit rev. bd. VA, 1977-80; mem. gen. medicine A-2 study sect. NIH, 1985-89, mem. Nat. Inst. Diabetes Digestive and Kidney Diseases Adv. Coun., 1994-97; coun., bd. rep. adv. com. to dir. NIH, 1996-97. Assoc. editor: Textbook of Gastroenterology, 4th edit., 2003, Atlas of Gastroenterology, 3d edit. 2003, Cecil Textbook of Medicine, 22d edit., 2004; mem. edit. bd. Am. Jour. Physiology, Gastrointestinal and Liver Physiology, 1979-97, Am. Jour. Med. Sci., 1984-92, Regulatory Peptide Letter, 1990—, Annals of Internal Medicine, 1993-96, Current Treatment Options in Gastro. 1998—; contbr. over 100 articles to profl. jours. Capt. M.C., U.S. Army, 1965-68. Recipient Rsch. Career Devel. award NIH, 1973-78, Merit award, 1987, Outstanding Physician of Yr. award Gulf Coast chpt. Crohn's Colitis Found. Am., 1994, John P. McGovern MD award in Oslerian Medicine, 2002, others. Master ACP (mem. med. knowledge self-assessment program VII gastroenterology com. 1983-85); fellow AAAS, mem. Am. Physiol. Soc., Am. Gastroenterol. Assn. (v.p. 1991-92, pres. 1993-94, coun. acad. rep. 1999—, Julius Friedenwald medal 2001, Mentored Rsch. award, 2005), Gastroenterology Rsch. Group (chmn. 1988-89), So. Soc. Clin. Investigation, Federated Socs. Gastroenterology and Hepatology (chmn. 1996-98, Assn. Am. Physicians, Am. Clin. and Climatol. Assn., Alpha Omega Alpha (bd. dirs. 2000—). Avocation: singing. Office: U Tex Med Br 4 106 McCullough 301 Univ Blvd Galveston TX 77555-0764 Office Phone: 409-772-5607. Business E-Mail: dpowell@utmb.edu.

POWELL, DONALD ASHMORE, clinical research psychologist; b. Spartanburg, SC, Oct. 29, 1938; s. Russell Kermit Powell and Mignon Kathlene Cox; m. Palmyra Langston, 1961 (div. 1972); children: Donald Langston, Donetta Plamyra, Ashley Preston, Stephanie Anne; m. Shirley L. Buchanan, Aug. 17, 1992 (dec. June 1998); m. Trisha Pope, May 18, 2002. BS, U. S.C., 1960, MA, 1962; PhD, Fla. State U., 1967. Rsch. psychologist Dorn VA Med. Ctr., Columbia, S.C., 1969—, acting dir. R&D, 1996-2000; prof. U. S.C. Sch. Medicine, Columbia, 1979—. Adj. prof. U. S.C., Columbia, 1969—; cons. U.S. Heart, Lung and Blood Inst., Bethesda, 1986—; program specialist VA Mental Health and Behavioral Scis., Washington, 1984-88. Author: (with others) Eyeblink Conditioning, 1999. Rsch. fellowship NIH, 1967-69; vis. scholar NIH, 1974; recipient Merit Rsch. award Dept. of Vet. Affairs, 1996—. Mem. Soc. for Neurosci., Am. Psychol. Soc., Pavlovian Soc. (Pavlovian Rsch. award 1991), Soc. for Neurosci. (pres. S.C. chpt. 1980-81, councilor 1982-85). Democrat. Avocations: running, reading. Office: Dorn VA Med Ctr 6439 Garners Ferry Rd Columbia SC 29209-1638 Office Phone: 803-695-6821. Business E-Mail: donnie.powell@med.va.gov.

POWELL, DONALD E., federal agency administrator; b. Perryton, Tex., May 2, 1941; m. Twanna C. Powell; 2 children. BS in Econs., West Tex. State U.; grad., Southwestern Sch. Banking, So. Meth. U. Loan officer, sec. First Fed. Savings & Loan, Amarillo, Tex., 1963—71; with Boatmen's First Nat. Bank, Amarillo, Tex., 1971—97, chmn., pres., CEO; pres., CEO First Nat. Bank Amarillo, Tex., 1997—2001; chmn. bd. FDIC, Washington, 2001—05; coord. Recovery & Rebuilding in the Gulf Coast Region US Dept. Homeland Security, 2005—. Active City of Amarillo Housing Bd., Franklin Lindsay Student Aid Fund, Cal Farley's Boys Ranch; adv. bd. mem. George Bush Sch. Govt. & Public Svc.; chmn. Amarillo C. of C.; chmn. bd. regents Tex. A&M U. Sys.; past bd. dirs. High Plains Bapt. Hosp., Harrington Regional Med. Ctr. Office: Coord Gulf Coast Rebuilding US Dept Homeland Security Washington DC 20528

POWELL, DURWOOD ROYCE, lawyer; b. Raleigh, NC, Nov. 21, 1951; s. Albert Royce and Powell; m. Leej Ida Copperfield, Mar. 1, 1980. BS, U. N.C., 1974, JD, 1979; LLM in Taxation, Emory U., 1985. Bar: N.C. 1979, U.S. Dist. Ct. (ea., mid. and we. dists.) N.C. 1981, U.S. Tax Ct. 1981, U.S. Ct. Appeals (4th cir.) 1984, U.S. Ct. Claims 1984, U.S. Supreme Ct. 1984, D.C. 1988, N.Y., 1989, U.S. Ct. Appeals (D.C. cir.) 1988, N.Y. 1989. Mgmt. analyst GAO, Norfolk, Va., 1974-76; tax staff Arthur Andersen & Co., Washington, 1979-80; assoc. Biggs, Meadows, Etheridge & Johnson, Rocky Mount, NC, 1980-82, Biggs Law Firm, Rocky Mount, 1982-83; ptnr. Maupin, Taylor, Ellis & Adams, Raleigh, NC, 1985—, also bd. dirs., 1985—. Adj. prof. corp. taxation Grad. Sch. Bus., U. N.C., Chapel Hill, 1989-92; faculty Duke U. Tax and Estate Planning Conf., 1991; mem. negotiation project Harvard U., Cambridge, Mass., 1992. Contbr. articles to profl. jours. Tax reform com. Duke U., Washington, 1988. Mem. ABA (tax, corp., banking and securities sects.), N.C. Bar Assn. (tax and corp. sects.), Phi Beta Kappa, Phi Eta Sigma. Home: 7616 Wingfoot Dr Raleigh NC 27615-5485 Office: Maupin Taylor Ellis & Adams 3200 Beech Leaf Ct Ste 500 Raleigh NC 27604-1064

POWELL, EARL ALEXANDER, III, art museum director; b. Spartanburg, SC, Oct. 24, 1943; s. Earl Alexander and Elizabeth (Duckworth) P.; m. Nancy Landry Powell, July 17, 1971; children: Cortney, Channing, Sumner. AB with honors, Williams Coll., 1966; AM, Harvard U., 1970, PhD, 1974; DFA (hon.), Williams Coll., 1993, Otis Parson Art Inst. Tchg. fellow in fine arts Harvard U., 1970-74; curator Michener Collection U. Tex., Austin, 1974-76, asst. prof. art history, 1974-76; mus. curator, sr. staff asst. to asst. dir. and chief curator Nat. Gallery Art, Washington, 1976-78, exec. curator, 1979-80; dir. L.A. County Mus. Art, 1980-92, Nat. Gallery Art, Washington, 1992—. Chmn. US Commn. Fine Arts; trustee Am. Fedn. Arts, Morris and Gwendolyn Cafritz Found., White House Hist. Assn., Nat. Trust Hist. Preservation, John F. Kennedy Ctr. for Performing Arts; mem. com. for preservation The White House; fed. coun. Arts and Humanities; fine arts adv. panel Fed. Res. Bd., Friends of Art and Preservation in Embassies; mem. Nat. Portrait Gallery Com.; mem. Pres.'s Com. on Arts and Humanities; mem. vis. com. Williams Coll. Mus. Art. Author: American Art at Harvard, 1973, Selections from the James Michener Collection, 1975, Abstract Expressionists and Imagists: A Retrospective View, 1976, Milton Avery, 1976, The James A. Michener Collection: Twentieth Century American Painting, catalogue raisonne, 1978, Thomas Cole monograph, 1990. Mem. Nat. Coun. on the Arts; mem. Pres.'s Com. on the Arts and Humanities. With U.S. Navy, 1966-69, comdr. Res., 1976-80. Decorated officier Arts and Letters,chevalier Legion of Honor; grand ofcl. Order of the Infante D. Henrique medal, 1995; recipient King Olav medal, 1978, Bicentennial medal Williams Coll., 1995; Harvard U. travelling fellow, 1973-74, Mexican Cultural award, 1996, commendatore dell'Ordine al Merito della Repubblica Italiana, 1998. Mem. Am. Acad. Arts and Scis., Walpole Soc., Assn. Art Mus. Dirs., Am. Philos. Soc., Friends of Art and Preservation in Embassies. Office: Nat Gallery Art 2000B S Club Dr Landover MD 20785 Office Phone: 202-842-6001.

POWELL, EDWARD A., JR., (NED POWELL), nonprofit organization executive; b. Richmond, Va. m. Diane Powell. BA, Washington and Lee U.; MBA, U. NC, 1978. Lic. real estate broker Va. Yeoman USN, Def. Intelligence Agy.; owner, mgr. Mechanism Design, Inc., 1989—97; asst. sec. fin. mgmt. US Dept. Veterans Affairs, 1998—2000, acting dep. sec., 2000—01; pres., CEO USO, Arlington, Va., 2002—. Former adj. prof. U. Richmond. Recipient Disting. Fed. Exec., Assn. Govt. Accountants, 2000. Mem.: World Pres. Orgn. Office: USO 2111 Wilson Blvd Ste 1200 Arlington VA 22201

POWELL, J. BRAXTON, state official; b. Suffolk, Va. m. Judy Scott; 2 children. BSBA in Fin., Va. Tech. With Va. Dept. Treas., 1983—, dep. state treas., state treas., 2006—. Bd. dir. Commonwealth Va. Treas. Bd., Va. Housing Devel. Authority. Mem.: Nat. Assn. State Treas. (so. regional v.p.). Office: State Treas 101 North 14th St Richmond VA 23219 Office Fax: 804-225-2142, 804-225-3187. *

POWELL, JAMES BOBBITT, health facility administrator, pathologist; b. Burlington, NC, Aug. 28, 1938; s. Thomas Edward and Sophia (Sharpe) P.; m. Pamela Oughton, Sept. 12, 1969 (div. Sept. 1979); 1 child, Daphne P. Markcrow; m. Anne Ellington, Oct. 20, 1984; children: James Bobbitt (dec.), John Banks, James Rosser, Helen Bobbitt. BA, Va. Mil. Inst., 1960; MD, Duke U., 1964. Diplomate Am. Bd. Pathology. Intern Duke U. Med. Ctr., Durham, NC, 1964-65; resident Cornell Med. Ctr., NYC, 1965-67, Englewood (N.J.) Hosp., 1967-69; founder Biomed Labs, Burlington, NC, 1969—; pres. Roche Biomed. Labs., 1982-95; pres., CEO Lab. Corp. Am. Holdings, 1995-97; CEO Tripath Imaging, Burlington, NC, 1997—2000. Bd. dirs. Mid-Carolina Bank, Living Microsystems, Warren Lee Co. Contbr. articles to sci. publs. Trustee Elon U., NC, 1979—, chmn. bd. trustees; bd. dirs. Alamance Found. Maj. M.C. US Army, 1969—72. Mem. Alamance Country Club. Republican. Methodist. Avocations: tennis, US military history. Office: 1573 York Pl Burlington NC 27215

POWELL, JAMES LAWRENCE, educational association administrator, museum director, geologist; b. Berea, Ky., July 17, 1936; s. Robert Lain and Lizena (Davis) P.; m. Joan Hartmann; children: Marla, Dirk, Joanna. AB, Berea Coll., 1958; PhD, MIT, 1962; DSc (hon.), Oberlin Coll., 1983; LHD (hon.), Tohoku Gakuin U., 1986; DSc (hon.), Beaver Coll., 1992. Asst. prof., assoc. prof., prof. Oberlin Coll., Ohio, 1962-83, chmn. geol. dept., 1965—73, v.p., provost, 1975—81, assoc. dean, 1973—75, acting pres., 1981—83; pres. Franklin and Marshall Coll., Lancaster, Pa., 1983-88, Reed Coll., Portland, Oreg., 1988-91; pres., chief exec. officer The Franklin Inst., Phila., 1991-94; pres., dir. Los Angeles County Mus. Natural History, LA, 1994—2001; exec. dir. Nat. Physical Sci. Consortium, LA, 2001—. Mem. Nat. Sci. Bd., 1986-98; adj. prof. Univ. So. Calif., 1995-2001 Author: Strontium Isotope Geology, 1972, Pathways to Leadership: Achieving and Sustaining Success: A Guide for Nonprofit Executives, 1995, Night Comes to the Coctzcems; Dinosaur Extinction and the Transformation of Modern Geology, 1998; Mysteries of Terra Firma: Age and Evolution of the Earth, 2001, Grand Canyon: Solving Earth's Grandest Puzzle, 2005. Fellow: Geol. Soc. Am.; mem.: Phi Beta Kappa, Phi Kappa Phi, Sigma Xi. Office: Nat Physical Science Consortium Ste 348 3716 S Hope Los Angeles CA 90007-4344 Business E-Mail: jpowell@usc.edu.

POWELL, JAMES MATTHEW, history professor; b. Cin., June 9, 1930; s. Matthew James and Mary Loretta (Weaver) P.; m. Judith Catherine Davidorf, May 29, 1954 (dec. 1992); children: James, Michael, Mark, Mary Helen, Miriam, John BA, Xavier U., Cin., 1953, MA, 1955; postgrad., U. Cin., 1955-57; PhD, Ind. U., 1960. Instr. Kent State U., Ohio, 1959-61; asst. prof. U. Ill., Urbana, 1961-65, Syracuse U., NY, 1965-67, assoc. prof. NY, 1967-72, prof. history NY, 1972—, dir. Ranke Cataloging Project NY, 1977—. Disting. vis. prof. medieval history Rutgers U., New Brunswick, 1996—97. Author: Medieval Monarchy and Trade, 1962, Civilization of the West, 1967, Anatomy of a Crusade, 1213-1221, 1986, 2d edit., 1990, Albertanus of Brescia: The Pursuit of Happiness in the Early Thirteenth Century, 1992, The Crusades, the Kingdom of Sicily, and the Mediterranean, 2007; translator: Liber Augustalis, 1971, The Deeds of Pope Innocent III, 2004, paperback edit., 2007; editor: Innocent III: Vicar of Christ or Lord of the World, 1963, revised and enlarged 2d edit., 1994, Medieval Studies, 1976, 2d edit., 1992; (with George G. Iggers) Leopold von Ranke and the Shaping of the Historical Discipline, 1989, Muslims Under Latin Rule, 1100-1300, 1990, (with Michael Gervers) Tolerance and Intolerance: Social Conflict in the Age of the Crusades, 2001; contbg. editor: New Catholic Encyclopedia, 2000—; cons. Ency. of the Crusades, 2000-06; contbr. articles to profl. jours. Grantee NEH, 1977-84, 84, Inst. for Advanced Study, Princeton, N.J., 1989-90, Progetto Radici, Brescia, Italy, 1994-95; Fritz Thyssen Stiftung, 1986, 89; recipient John Gilmary Shea prize Am. Cath. Hist. Assn., 1987. Fellow Royal Hist. Soc. (corr.); mem. Am. Hist. Assn., Am. Cath. Hist. Assn. (1st v.p. 2005, pres. 2006), Medieval Acad. Am., Soc. Italian Hist. Studies (coun. 1976-79, v.p. 1991-92, pres. 1993-95), Midwest Medieval Conf. (pres. 1965-66), Soc. Study of the Crusades and the Latin East (sec. 1989-95), Haskins Soc. Democrat. Roman Catholic. Office: Syracuse U Maxwell Sch Syracuse NY 13244-0001

POWELL, JEFFREY SCOTT, endocrinologist; s. Norman Emory and Barbara Ellen Powell; m. Ellen Lynn Rothbaum, June 11, 1995; children: Abigail, Ryan. BA cum laude in Biology, Harvard U., Cambridge, Mass., 1991; MD, Albert Einstein Coll., Bronx, NY, 1995. Diplomate Am. Bd. Internal Medicine. Intern to resident in internal medicine Columbia Med. Ctr., NYC, 1995—98; fellow in endocrinology Colubmia U., Coll. Physicians and Surgeons, NYC, 1998—2001; endocrinologist Mt. Kisco (N.Y.) Med. Group, 2001—. Chief divsn. endocrinology No. Westchester Hosp., Mt. Kisco, 2006—. Contbr. articles to profl. jours. Fellow: Am. Coll. Endocrinology; mem.: Am. Assn. Clin. Endocrinology, Alpha Omega Alpha. Office: Mt Kisco Med Group 90 S Bedford Rd Mount Kisco NY 10549 Office Phone: 914-241-1050. Office Fax: 914-242-2915. Personal E-mail: jpowell@mkmg.com.

POWELL, JERRY W., lawyer; b. Montgomery, Ala., Jan. 6, 1950; m. Carolyn Powell; children: Jennifer, Jeffrey. BA cum laude, Birmingham-So. Coll., 1972; JD, U. Ala., 1975. Bar: Ala. 1975, U.S. Dist. Ct. Ala. (No. and Mid. dist), U.S. Ct. Appeals (11th cir.). Law clk. No. Dist. Ala., 1975—76; gen. counsel, sec. Compass Bancshares, Inc., Birmingham, Ala. Mem. editl. bd.: Alabama Law Review, 1973—75. Mem.: ABA, Am. Soc. Corp. Secretaries, Am. Corp. Counsel Assn. (pres. Ala. chpt. 1984—85), Ala. State Bar Assn., Birmingham Bar Assn., Order of Coif (bench and bar). Office: Compass Bancshares Inc 15 S 20th St Birmingham AL 35233 Office Phone: 205-297-3960. Office Fax: 205-297-3043. Business E-Mail: jerry.powell@compassbank.com.

POWELL, JOHN, composer; b. Eng., Sept. 18, 1963; arrived in US, 1997; m. Melinda Lerner; 1 child. Student, Trinity Coll. Music, London. Band mem. The Fabulists; co-founder Independently Thinking Music, London, 1995; former mem. Media Ventures. Composer: (TV series) Stay Lucky, 1989, (TV films) High Incident, 1996, Human Bomb, 1998, (films) The Wild Heels, 1994, Mondokino, 1996, Face/Off, 1997 (ASCAP award), With Friends Like These..., 1998, Antz, 1998 (ASCAP award), Endurance, 1999, Forces of Nature, 1999, Chill Factor, 1999, The Road to El Dorado, 2000, Chicken Run, 2000 (ASCAP award), Just Visiting, 2001, Shrek, 2001 (Annie award for Music Score, 2001, ASCAP award), Evolution, 2001, Rat Race, 2001, I Am Sam, 2001, D-Tox, 2002, The Bourne Identity, 2002 (ASCAP award), Drumline, 2002, The Adventures of Pluto Nash, 2002, Two Weeks Notice, 2002, Stealing Sinatra, 2003, Agent Cody Banks, 2003, The Italian Job, 2003 (ASCAP award), Gigli, 2003, Paycheck, 2003, The Bourne Supremacy, 2004 (ASCAP award), Mr. 3000, 2004, Alfie, 2004, Be Cool, 2005, Robots, 2005 (ASCAP award), Mr. & Mrs. Smith, 2005 (ASCAP award), Ice Age: The Meltdown, 2006 (ASCAP award, Ivor Novello award, Brit. Acad. Composers & Songwriters, 2007), United 93, 2006, X-Men: The Last Stand, 2006 (ASCAP award), Happy Feet, 2006 (ASCAP award), Stop Loss, 2007. Office: c/o Kraft-Engel Mgmt Ste 200 15233 Ventura Blvd Sherman Oaks CA 91403 *

POWELL, JOYCE, educational association administrator, secondary school educator; Grad., Glassboro State Coll.; MA in Urban Edn. and Cmty. Affairs, William Paterson Coll., 1981. Tchr. Barse Elem. Sch., Vineland, NJ; tchr. computer math, English, vocational training, health, and US history Vineland HS South, Vineland, NJ, 1980—, chairperson Special Edn. Dept. Bd. dirs. Ednl. Improvement and Resource Ctr. (EIRC) South, NJ Tchg. and Learning Collaborative, Work Environment Coun.; mem. NJ Profl. Tchg. Standards Bd., Comprehensive Sys. Personnel Devel., NJ State Dept. Edn. Bd. dirs. Cumberland/Salem Counties Planned Parenthood; mem. Teen Pregnancy Coun. of Cumberland County, Alcohol and Drug Abuse Coun., Downe Township Zoning Bd. Recipient Gov.'s Tchr. Recognition Award, 1991; grantee NJ Devel. Disabilities Coun.; Eagleton Fellow, Rutgers U., Eagleton Sch. Politics, 1989. Mem.: NEA, NJ Edn. Assn. (NJEA) (chairperson Exceptional Child Com., former v.p., sec.-treas., pres.), Cumberland County Edn. Assn., Vineland Edn. Assn., So. NJ Regional Tchr. Ctr., Alpha Delta Kappa. Office: NJEA Box 1211 Trenton NJ 08607-1211 Office Phone: 609-559-4561. Office Fax: 609-599-1201. E-mail: joyce.powell@njea.org. *

POWELL, JULIE, writer; b. Austin, Tex. BA, Amherst Coll., Mass. Contbr. articles on food to numerous profl. jours. (James Beard award for food journalism, 2004); author: (novels) Julie and Julia: 365 Days, 524 Recipes, 1 Tiny Apartment Kitchen, 2005 (Quill award for Debut Author Yr., 2006). Office: c/o Author Mall Little Brown and Co 1271 Ave Americas New York NY 10020

POWELL, KATHLEEN LYNCH, lawyer, real estate executive; b. NYC, Dec. 30, 1949; d. Daniel Francis and Mary Margaret (Flynn) L.; m. P. Douglas Powell. BA in Math. cum laude, Coll. Mt. St. Vincent, Riverdale,

NY, 1970; postgrad., U. Pa., Phila., 1976-77; JD cum laude, U. Md., 1977; LLM in Taxation, NYU, 1991. Bar: Pa. 1977, NJ 1978, NY 1984, DC 1985, Conn. 1995, US Ct. Appeals (3d cir.) 1980, US Supreme Ct. 1981. Research analyst, claims rep. Social Security Adminstrn., Balt., 1973-76; assoc. Drinker, Biddle & Reath, Phila., 1977-84, ptnr., 1984-86; v.p., gen. counsel M. Alfieri Co., Inc., Edison, NJ, 1987-89; v.p., counsel BPG Properties, Ltd., Phila., 1992—. Instr. Inst. for Paralegal Tng., Phila. 1984—. Vol. atty. Support Ctr. for Child Advocates, Phila., 1979-86, Queen Village Neighbors Assn., Phila., 1984-86; pres. Soc. Hill Towers Buyers Assn., Phila., 1979-80; bd. dirs. Soc. Hill Civic Assn., 1980. Mem. ABA, Pa. Bar Assn., Phila. Bar Assn. (chair zoning and land use com. 1985-86), Conn. Bar Assn.

POWELL, KENDALL J., consumer products company executive; BA, Harvard Univ., 1976; MBA, Stanford Univ., 1979. Mktg. & mgmt. positions General Mills Inc., Mpls., 1979—90; v.p. mktg. dir. Cereal Partners Worldwide, 1990—96; pres. Yoplait USA divsn. General Mills Inc., Mpls., 1996—97, pres. Big G div., 1997—99, sr. v.p., 1998—2004; CEO Cereal Partners Worldwide, Morges, Switzerland, 1999—2004; exec. v.p. Meals, Pillsbury USA, Bakeries & Foodservice General Mills Inc., Mpls., 2004—05, exec. v.p., COO U.S. retail, 2005—06, pres., COO, 2006—. Bd. mem. Cereal Partners Worldwide. Bd. mem. Twin Cities United Way. Office: General Mills Inc 1 General Mills Blvd Minneapolis MN 55426 *

POWELL, KENNETH GRANT, aerospace engineering educator; b. Euclid, Ohio, July 3, 1960; s. Thomas Edward and Mary Catherine (Byrum) P.; m. Susanne Maria Krummel, Aug. 31, 1991; children: Jasmine Tara, Ryan Grant, Nicole Maia. SB in Math., MIT, 1982, SB in Aeronautics, 1982, SM in Aeronautics, 1984, ScD in Aeronautics, 1987. Asst. prof. dept. aerospace engrng. U. Mich., Ann Arbor, 1987-93, assoc. prof. dept. aerospace engrng., 1993-2000, prof. dept. aerospace engrng., 2000—02, Arthur F. Thurnau prof., 2002—. Lectr. Von Karman Inst. for Fluid Dynamics, Brussels, 1990, 96; cons. Ford Motors, Dearborn, Mich., 1992-95; cons. Detroit Edison, 1996-98; exec. dir. Francois-Xavier Bagnoud Prize Bd., 1998-2000. Named Presdl. Young investigator NSF, 1988; recipient Tchg. Excellence award U. Mich. Coll. Engring., 1992, Outstanding Tchg. award Tau Beta Pi, 1988, 99, 2005, Tchg. Excellence award Sigma Gamma Tau, 1989, 95. Fellow AIAA (assoc.); mem. Tau Beta Pi, Sigma Xi, Sigma Gamma Tau. Home: 5531 Spring Hill Dr Ann Arbor MI 48105-9552 Office: U Mich Dept of Aerospace Engring Ann Arbor MI 48109

POWELL, LARRY, communications educator; b. Greenville, Ala., May 14, 1948; s. A. Harold Powell and Virginia Brown; m. Clarine Thrower, Dec. 19, 1970. BA, Auburn U., Ala., 1970; MA, Auburn U., 1971; PhD, U. Fla., 1975. From asst. prof. to prof. Miss. State U., Starkvill, 1975—86; vcons. Kitchens, Powell & Kitchens, Orlando, Fla., 1987—96; owner Powell Cons., Orlando, 1996—98; prof., former chair U. Ala., Birmingham, 1998—. Vis. prof. Meisei U., Hino, Japan, 1984—85; prof. Ctrl. Fla. U., Orlando, 1996—98; media pollster Birmingham News, Birmingham, 2001—; cons. in field. Co-author: Political Campaign Communication, 2003, Interviewing: Situations and Content, 2005; contbr. articles to profl. jours.; co-author: Holy Murder: Abraham, Isaac, and the Rhetoric of Sacrifice, 2006. Polit. advisor Bus. Coun. of Ala., Montgomery, 1994—96, WVTM-TV/WBRC-TV, Birmingham, 2001—02. Named one of Top 100 Comm. Rschrs., Assn. of Comm. Adminstrs., 1998; recipient Miss. Jaycee Gov. award, 1986; Ala. Dept. Pub. Health grantee, 1999—2000. Master: So. States Comm. Assn. (life; chair polit. com. 1999—2000); mem.: Nat. Comm. Assn., Religious Comm. Assn. (life). Home: 328 Shadeswood Dr Hoover AL 35226 Office: Univ of Alabama Comm Studies Dept 901 S 15th St Birmingham AL 35294 Office Phone: 205-934-8784. Business E-Mail: lpowell@uab.edu.

POWELL, LEWIS FRANKLIN, III, lawyer; b. Richmond, Va., Sept. 14, 1952; s. Lewis F. Jr. and Josephine (Rucker) P.; m. Lisa T. LaFata; children: Emily, Hannah, Luke. BA, Washington & Lee U., 1974; JD, U. Va., 1978. Bar: Va. 1978, U.S. Dist. Ct. (ea. and we. dists.) Va. 1979, U.S. Ct. Appeals (4th cir.) 1979, U.S. Ct. Appeals (2d cir.) 1983, U.S. Ct. Appeals (11th cir.) 1992, U.S. Supreme Ct. 1985. Law clk. to judge U.S. Dist. Ct. (ea. dist.), Richmond, 1978-79; assoc. Hunton & Williams, Richmond, 1979—86, ptnr., 1986—. Pres. young lawyers conf. Va. State Bar, 1986-87. Bd. dirs. William Byrd Cmty. Ho., Richmond, 1982-87, Boys Club of Richmond, 1984-90, Maymont Found., Richmond, 1987-92, St. Christopher's Sch., Richmond, 1989-96. Mem. Richmond Bar Assn. (chmn. improvement justice com. 1982-83), 4th Cir. Jud. Conf., Am. Law Inst. Avocations: fly fishing, mountaineering, hiking. Office: Hunton & Williams Riverfront Plz East Tower 951 E Bird St Richmond VA 23219

POWELL, MARSHA, director, educator; BS in Math., SUNY, Cortland, 1978, MS in Math., 1992. Applications programmer Cornell U., Ithaca, NY, 1978—80; sr. systems analyst Cbord Group, Inc., Ithaca, 1980—82; prof., program chmn. Tompkins Cortland CC, Dryden, NY, 1982—; computer forensic examiner Broome County Govt. Security, Binghamton, NY, 2003—. Pres., chmn. Cayuga Chamber Orch., Ithaca, 1993—2003; patroller Nat. Ski Patrol, Cortland, 1993—2006. Recipient Incentive award for classroom rsch., Tompkins Cortland C.C., Coll. Tchg. Ctr., 1996, NY State Chancellor's award for excellence in tchg., NY State Dept. Edn., 2004. Mem.: High Tech. Crime Investigation Assn., Internat. Assn. Computer Investigative Specialists (cert.). Office: Tompkins Cortland CC 170 North St Dryden NY 13053

POWELL, MELCHIOR DANIEL, educational administrator, lawyer; b. NYC, July 7, 1935; children: Anthony, Vanessa. BS, NJ State U., 1957; MA, George Washington U., 1963; JD, U. Balt., 1966; PhD, U. Md., 1968. Bar: Md. 1966. Atty. City of Greenbelt, Md., 1966-67; dir. contract rsch. Nat. Assn. Counties, 1967-71; assoc. prof. urban affairs U. No. Colo., Greeley, 1971-72; dir. Appalachian region com. Office of Rsch. Mgmt., Washington, 1972-73; dean Grad. Ctr. Pub. Policy and Adminstrn. Calif. State U., Long Beach, 1973-92, prof. emeritus, 1992—. Exec. sect. We. Govtl. Rsch. Assn., 1992-95; vis. prof. Fla. Atlantic U., 1995-96; exec. dir., pres. So. Md. Higher Edn. Ctr., 1997—; cons. in field. Author: Education for the Future Pub. Svc., 1981, Achieving Closer Ties, 1984; contbr. articles to profl. jours. Mem. Mayor's Task Force City of Long Beach, 1978, mem. charter comm., 1979, bd. dirs. poverty program, 1980; mem. Calif. workers compensation rate setting commn., 1991, So. Md. Workforce Infrastructure Bd. Served to lt. (j.g.), U.S. Navy, 1959-63. Mem. Western Govt. Rsch. Assn. (pres. 1980-82, exec. sec. 1982-95), Am. Soc. Pub. Adminstrn. (pres. Md. chpt. 1972-73, program chmn. Nat. Conf. 1980, conf. chmn. 1986, 93, pres. L.A. Metro chpt. 1976-77, Dykstra award 1977, Will Baughman award 1982), Urban Affairs Assn. (pres. 1986-87), Internat. Assn. Schs. and Insts. of Adminstrn. (v.p. N.Am. 1989—, mem. bd. mgmt., 2001—, chair working group accountability, culture and trust, 2006-). Democrat. Roman Catholic. Home: 422 Overlook Dr Lusby MD 20657-3202 Office: SMHEC 44219 Airport Rd California MD 20619 Home Phone: 410-394-0211; Office Phone: 301-737-2500. Business E-Mail: mpowell@smhec.org.

POWELL, MICHAEL KEVIN, investment company executive, former federal official; b. Birmingham, Ala., Mar. 23, 1963; s. Colin and Alma Powell; m. Jane Knott; children: Bryan, Jeffrey. BA, Coll. William and Mary, 1985; JD, Georgetown U., 1993. Policy advisor to asst. sec. def. for internat. security affairs, Washington, 1988—90; law clk. to Hon. Harry T. Edwards U.S. Ct. Appeals (D.C. cir.), Washington, 1993—94; assoc. O'Melveny & Myers LLP, 1994—96; chief of staff divsn. antitrust U.S. Dept. Justice, Washington, 1996—97; commr. FCC, Washington, 1997—2001, chmn., 2001—05; sr. advisor Providence Equity Partners, Washington, 2005—. Formed cons. firm MK Powell Group, 2005—; bd. dirs. ObjectVideo Inc., 2005—. Bd. visitors Georgetown U. Law Ctr.; bd. dirs. U.S. Telecomm. Tng. Inst. Cavalry platoon leader, troop exec. US Army, 1985—88, Amberg, Germany. Recipient Freedom of Speech medal, Media Inst., 1999; Henry Crown fellow, Aspen Inst., 1999. Office: Providence Equity Partners Inc 1050 Connecticut Ave NW Ste 1250 Washington DC 20036

POWELL, NANCY JO, federal official, former ambassador; b. Cedar Falls, Iowa; BA, No. Iowa U., 1970. Dep. chief of mission US Embassy, Lome, Togo, 1990—92, consul gen. New Delhi, 1993—95, dep. chief of mission Khaka, Bangladesh, 1995—97; US amb. to Uganda US Dept. State, Kampala, 1997—99, prin. dep. asst. sec. for African affairs, 1999—2001, acting asst. sec. African affairs, 2001, US amb. to Ghana Accra, 2001—02, US amb. to Pakistan Islamabad, Pakistan, 2002—04, prin. dep. asst. sec. & acting asst. sec. for legis. affairs Washington, 2004—05, acting asst. sec. Bur. Internat. Narcotics and Law Enforcement Affairs, 2005, sr. coord. for Avian & Pandemic Influenza, 2005—06; nat. intelligence officer for South Asia, Nat. Intelligence Council Office Nat. Intelligence, Washington, 2006—. Office: Office of Dir Nat Intelligence NEOB 725 17th St Washington DC 20500

POWELL, NICHOLE LARAI, chemistry professor, researcher; arrived in US, 1999, permanent resident, 2002; d. Ripton Roy Powell and Grace Monica Clarke-Powell; 1 child, Maria-Cristina Pascoe. BS in Biochemistry with honors, U. West Indies, Mona, Jamaica, 1995; PhD in Chemistry, Ga. State U., Atlanta, 2003. Instr. Ga. State U., Atlanta, 2001—03; adj. instr. Ga. Perimeter Coll., Lawrenceville, Ga., 2003—05; asst. prof. Tuskegee U., Ala., 2004—. Chmn. academic affairs com. faculty senate Tuskegee U., 2005—. Mem.: Am. Chem. Soc. (sec. Auburn local sect. 2005, chmn. elect Auburn local sect. 2006, chair Auburn local sect. 2007), Am. Soc. Microbiology, Phi Beta Delta. Office: Tuskegee University 102 Armstrong Hall Tuskegee AL 36088 Home Phone: 678-423-4258; Office Phone: 334-724-4489. Business E-Mail: nlpowell@tuskegee.edu.

POWELL, RAYMOND WILLIAM, financial planner, school administrator; b. Waterbury, Conn., June 17, 1944; s. Don C. and Kathryn (Linhard) P.; m. Janet Yasinski, June 24, 1967; 1 child, Raymond Joseph. BS, So. Conn. State Coll., New Haven, 1966, MS, 1969; postgrad., U. Bridgeport, Conn. CFP; enrolled agt. CEO R.W. Powell Enterprises, Inc., fin. and tax cons., Prospect, Conn., 1972—; dir.-owner Powells Income Tax Svc., Watertown, 1972—, Powell's Acctg. Svc., 1975—, Powell's Fin. Planning Svc., 1977—; supt. of schs. Winchester, Conn., 1995—2001. Contbr. articles to profl. jours. Vice chmn. Watertown Town Coun., 1975-76. Mem. Nat. Assn. Enrolled Agts., Internat. Assn. Fin. Planners, Am. Soc. Tax Cons., Conn. Assn. Enrolled Agts. Democrat. Office: PO Box 7077 42 Waterbury Rd Prospect CT 06712-1238 Home Phone: 860-274-5880; Office Phone: 203-758-5700. Business E-Mail: powells.financial@snet.net.

POWELL, RICHARD GORDON, retired lawyer; b. Rochester, NY, Jan. 7, 1918; BS, Harvard U., 1938; LL.B., Columbia U., 1941. Bar: N.Y. 1941, U.S. Supreme Ct. 1955. Assoc. Sullivan & Cromwell, NYC, 1941-52, ptnr., 1952-85. Former mem. bd. mgrs. Englewood (N.J.) Community Chest; trustee, elder 1st Presbyterian Ch. Mem. ABA, Assn. Bar City of N.Y., Am. Law Inst. Home: 200 E 65th St # 33N New York NY 10021-4451

POWELL, ROBERT ELLIS, mathematics professor, dean; b. Lansing, Mich., Mar. 16, 1936; s. James Ellis and Mary Frances (Deming) P.; children: Carl Robert, Glenn Arthur, Charles Addison; m. Lisbeth Nilsen, Nov. 21, 1992. BA, Mich. State U., 1958, MA, 1959; PhD, Lehigh U., 1966. Instr. math. Lehigh U., 1964-66; asst. prof. math. U. Kans., Lawrence, 1966-69; vis. asst. research prof. U. Ky., Lexington, 1967-68; vis. asst. prof. math. Ind. U., Bloomington, summer 1969; assoc. prof. math. Kent State U., Ohio, 1969-74, prof. math., 1974-95, dean grad. coll., 1980-92, prof. math emeritus, dean emeritus grad. coll., 1995—; prof. math., dean grad. sch., dir. rsch. U. Scranton, Pa., 1995-2000. Mem. Ohio Bd. Regents' Adv. Com. on Grad. Study, 1980-92, chmn., 1983-84. Co-author: Summability Theory, 1973, rev. edit., 1988, Intuitive Calculus, 1973; contbr. numerous articles to profl. jours. Bd. dirs. Kent State U. Found., 1981-91. NSF summer grantee, 1964, 65; recipient Fulbright award, 1988. Mem. Midwestern Assn. Grad. Schs. (bd. dirs. 1988-92, chmn. 1990-91), Coun. Grad. Schs. (bd. dirs. 1990-91), Northea. Assn. Grad. Schs. (bd. dirs. 1998-2000). Home: 73 Concession Oak Dr Bluffton SC 29909

POWELL, RONALD ROWE, library science educator; b. Columbia, Mo., May 24, 1944; s. Hampstead Rowe and Elizabeth Floris (Sapp) P.; m. Jeanne Ann Branstetter, Jan. 28, 1967; children: Rebecca Lynn, Angela Leigh. AB, U. Mo., 1967; MS, Western Mich. U., 1968; PhD, U. Ill., 1976. Bibliographer U. Ill., Urbana, 1968-69, asst. circulation libr., 1969-71, rsch. asst., 1971-74, rsch. assoc., 1974-75; libr. dir. U. Charleston, W.Va., 1976-79; asst. prof. U. Mich., Ann Arbor, 1979-86; assoc. prof. U. Mo., Columbia, 1986-92, dir. grad. studies, 1987-90, chmn. Dept. Libr. Sci., 1990-92; prof. Wayne State U., Detroit, 1993—, interim dir., 1999. Editl. bd. Assn. Libr. & Info. Sci. Edn., Raleigh, 1984-88, dir., 1989-91; vis. prof. Universidade de Brasilia, Brazil, 1985; sec. Coll. Libr. Sect., Assn. for Coll. and Rsch. Libr., Chgo., 1982; sr. fellow Coun. Libr. Resources, Wash., 1982; guest lectr. Moscow State U. of Culture, 1996. Author: Basic Research Methods for Librarians, 1997, 4th edit., 2004; co-author: Success in Answering Reference Questions, 1987, Basic Reference Sources, 1990, The Next Library Leadership, 2003; co-editor: Topics in Library and Information Studies, 1989-2000, Qualitive Research in Information Management, 1992; co-editor Jour. Edn. for Libr. and Info. Sci., 1995-2001, Research Methods in Library and Information Studies, 2000—; mem. editl. bd. Jour. Academic Librarianship, 2000-02, Libr. and Info. Sci. Rsch., 2002—. Recipient Curator's scholarship U. Mo., Columbia, 1962. Mem. ALA (chmn. standing com. libr. edn. 1992-93, chair libr. rsch. round table 1996-1998), Assn. Coll. and Rsch. Libr., Assn. for Libr. and Info. Sci. Edn., Mich. Libr. Assn., Internat. Info. Acad., Beta Phi Mu. Avocations: music, reading, tennis. Home: 21529 Garrison St Dearborn MI 48124-2301 Office Phone: 313-577-6199. Business E-Mail: ad5328@wayne.edu.

POWELL, SCOTT C., bank executive; With Comml. Credit Co., 1988; dir. credit risk mgmt. Global Consumer Grp. Citigroup, Inc.; head retail lending Bank One Corp., 2003; co-CEO home fin. J.P. Morgan Chase & Co., head Chase auto and student fin., 2005—. Bd. trustees Phipps Houses. Office: JP Morgan Chase & Co 270 Park Ave New York NY 10017-2070

POWELL, SHIRLEY THERESSA, elementary school educator; b. Kingfisher, Okla., Sept. 28, 1949; d. Walter Charles and Alzadie Bessie Baker; m. Floyd Dean Powell, Feb. 22, 1969; children: Marc Len, Corey Lyndale, Ginger LaDean, Carmen LaShay. BA in Edn., Wichita State U., 1988; MA in Tchg., Friends U., Wichita, Kans., 1990. Cert. elem. tchr. Kans. State Dept. of Edn., 2004. 3d gr. tchr. Chisholm Trail Elem., Wichita, Kans., 1988—92, 4-5 gr. tchr., 1992—2002, 5th gr. tchr., 2002—. Team leader Chisholm Trail Elem., Wichita, Kans., 1995—2003, quality performance accreditation team, 1995—2003, yr. book advisor to students, 1996—, sch. store advisor to students, 1996—2003, career day amb. trainer, 1996—. Recipient Salute To Delta Gt. Tchrs. award, Delta Sigma Theta Sorority, Inc., 1992, Outstanding Svcs. to Children of Chisholm Trail Elem. award, Chisholm Trail Elem. Prin., 1993-94, Outstanding Tchr. of Yr. award, Wichita Assn. of Black Sch. Educators, 1995. Mem.: Links, Inc. (assoc.; fin. sec. 2004—, Wichita chpt.), Phi Delta Kappa (assoc.), Delta Sigma Theta (assoc.). Office: Chisholm Trail Elem Sch 6015 Independence Wichita KS 67219 Home Phone: 316-651-0147; Office Phone: 316-973-9452. Business E-Mail: spowell2@usd259.net.

POWELL, STEPHEN WALTER, judge; b. Hamilton, Ohio, Jan. 25, 1955; s. Walter E. and Bobbi M. (Powell) P.; m. Kathryn Powell; children: Eric R.W., S. Michael; stepchildren: Greggory A., Garrett A. BA, Heidelberg Coll., 1977; JD, U. Dayton, 1981. Bar: Ohio 1981, U.S. Dist. Ct. (so. dist.) Ohio 1982. Referee Common Pleas Ct., Juvenile, Domestic and Probate, Hamilton, 1984-88; ptnr. Powell, Napier, Carmella and Allen, Hamilton, 1986-91; judge Area II Ct., Butler County, Ohio, 1989-91; judge probate div. Butler County Common Pleas Ct., Hamilton, 1991-95; presiding judge Ohio Ct. Appeals, 12th Appellate Dist., Middletown, 1995-97, adminstrv. judge, 1997-98, presiding judge, 1999—, appellate judge, 1994—. Agt. Commonwealth Land Title, Louisville, 1988-90; parliamentarian Judges Assn. Ohio Ct. Appeals, 1995—. Sec. Butler County Rep. Cen. Com., 1982-88; trustee Union Twp., Butler County, West Chester, 1979-88; bd. dirs. United Way Hamilton Area, 1986-90., Ky. Col. Named Man of the Day Sta. WMOH, Hamilton, 1986; recipient Meritorious Svc. award Ohio Assn. Probate Judges, 1992, 93, 94. Mem. ABA, Ohio Bar Assn., Butler County Bar Assn., Common Pleas Judges Assn., Ohio Mcpl & County Ct. Judges Assn., Am. Judicature Soc., Cin. Bar Assn. Presbyterian. Office: Ohio Ct Appeals 12th Appellate Dist 1 City Centre Plz # 1009 Middletown OH 45042-1901 Home: 1001 Reinartz Blvd Middletown OH 45042-1924 Home Fax: 513-425-8751.

POWELL, THOMAS EDWARD, III, biological supply company executive, physician; b. Elon College, N.C., Aug. 1, 1936; s. Thomas Edward, Jr., and Sophia Maude (Sharpe) P.; m. Betty Durham Yeager, June 19, 1965; children: Frances Powell Barnes, Thomas Edward IV, Caroline Powell Rogers. AB in Biology, Va. Mil. Inst., 1957; MD, Duke U., 1961; MA, Harvard U., 1966. Surgeon USPHS, 1966-68; co-founder Biomed. Reference Labs., Inc., Burlington, N.C., 1969, exec. v.p., 1969-75, chmn. exec. com., 1979-82, also dir.; exec. v.p. Carolina Biol. Supply Co., Burlington, N.C., 1968-80, chmn., 1977-80, 94—, pres., 1980-94; pres. Wolfe Sales Corp., Burlington, 1980-84, Waubun Labs. Inc., Schriever, La., 1980—, Bobbitt Labs., Inc., Burlington, 1983-94; bd. mgrs. Wachovia Bank and Trust Co. N.A., Burlington. Contbr. articles to profl. jours. Bd. dirs. United Way Alamance County, Burlington, 1968—; bd. dirs. Elon Coll., N.C., 1968—, sec., 1975—; bd. dirs. Am. Cancer Soc., Burlington, 1971-81; bd. dirs. Burlington Day Sch., 1973—, pres., 1974-78, 80-84; bd. dirs. N.C. Citizens for Bus. and Industry, Raleigh, 1983-87, Nat. Found. for Study of Religion and Econs., Greensboro, 1984-88, Blue Ridge Sch., Dyke, Va., 1985-90. Served to capt. USAR, 1957-66. Recipient Citizens Service award Elon Coll. Alumni Assn., 1980. Mem. Assn. Biology Lab. Edn., N.C. Acad. Sci., Alamance-Caswell Med. Soc., N.C. Med. Soc., Assn. Venture Founders, Newcomen Soc. Democrat. Mem. United Ch. of Christ. Clubs: Alamance Country (Burlington); Capital City (Raleigh, N.C.); Congl. Country (Washington); N.C. Country (Pinehurst); Hope Valley Country (Durham, N.C.); Greensboro City.

POWELL, THOMAS ERVIN, financial consultant, small business owner; b. Trion, Ga., Mar. 19, 1947; s. Ervin and Myrtice (Wike) P.; m. Lana Lois Lang, June 20, 1976; children: Thomas Christopher, Alissa Lynne, Ashley Beth. BS, U. Ctrl. Fla., 1974, MS, 1977; postgrad. studies, U. Fla., 1979. CPA, Fla.; cert. internal auditor. Pub. acct. KPMG Peat Marwick, Orlando, Fla., 1974-75, Arthur Andersen & Co., Orlando, 1975-77; instr. acctg. U. Ctrl. Fla., Orlando, 1977-81; dir. Inst. Internal Auditors, Altamonte Springs, Fla., 1981-95; pres. The Powell Group, Inc., Windermere, Fla., 1996—; dir. of consulting Graham & Cottrill, PA, 1998-2000; COO, treas., exec. v.p. fin. and trust svcs. Investment Trust Co. Fla., Inc., Ocoee, 2000—03; spl. asst. to pres. Valencia CC, Orlando, Fla., 2003—05; treas. Holyland Expansive Ministers, Orlando, 2005—. Mem. accreditation com. Am. Assembly Collegiate Schs. Bus., 1992-93; adj. prof. Rollins Coll., Winter Park, Fla., 1999-2003. Author: Examination Writer's Guide, 1978, rev. edit., 1991, 96; mem. editl. bd. Issues in Acctg. Edn. Jour., 1995—. Vice chmn. audit bd. City of Orlando, 1990-95; treas. Christian Endowment Found., 1996-2003; chmn. Practice Advising Coun.; mem. Orlando/Orange County Airport Zoning Bd., 1997-2001; chmn. adv. coun. West Orange H.S., 1997-98; mem. West Orange H.S. Found.; mem. strategic dir. com. Orange County Pub. Schs., 1999-2003; bd. dirs. Goodwill Industries, 2003—. With USAF, 1967-71. Mem. AICPA, Am. Acctg. Assn. (profl. exam. com. 1986-89, 93-98, audit edn. conf. com. 1990-93, mem. profl. rels. com. 1997-98, v.p. profl. practices 1994-96, chmn. practice adv. coun. 1996-2000), Inst. Internal Auditors, Fla. Soc. CPAs (edn. com. 1990-93, legis. com. 1991), Beta Alpha Psi (adv. coun. 1993-95, Alumnus of Yr. U. Ctrl. Fla. 1992), Beta Gamma Sigma. Republican. Avocations: guitar, skiing, photography, singing, music. Home: 1938 Maple Leaf Dr Windermere FL 34786-8003 Office: 1938 Maple Leaf Dr Windermere FL 34786-8003 E-mail: tom@stringtherapy.com.

POWELL, VALERIE JEAN, elementary school educator; d. Travis and Wilma Looney; m. Craig Powell, July 26, 1981; children: Stephen C., Nicholas A. BS in Elem. and Early Childhood Edn., U. North Ala., Florence, 1979, MA in Early Childhood Edn., 1986. Cert. tchr. Nat. Bd. for Profl. Tchg. Stds., 2001. Kindergarten tchr. Morgan County Schs., Decatur, Ala., 1979—2006, reading coach, 2006—. Tchr.-in-residence Hands-on Activity Sci. Program, Huntsville, Ala., 1999—2000. Named Morgan County Tchr. of Yr., Morgan County Schs., 1999, Outstanding Educator, Girl Scouts Am., 1999, Outstanding Reading Tchr., Ala. Reading Assn., 2005. Mem.: Tennessee Valley Reading Coun. (pres. 2006—). Office: Morgan County Schools 1325 Point Mallard Pkwy Decatur AL 35601 Home Phone: 256-773-4831; Office Phone: 256-353-6442. Business E-Mail: vlpowell@morgank12.org.

POWELL, WILLIAM ARNOLD, JR., retired bank executive; b. Verbena, Ala., July 7, 1929; s. William Arnold and Sarah Frances (Baxter) Powell; m. Barbara Ann O'Donnell, June 16, 1956; children: William Arnold III, Barbara Calhoun, Susan Thomas, Patricia Crain. BSBA, U. Ala., 1953; grad., La. State U. Sch. Banking of South, 1966. With Am. South Bank, N.A., Birmingham, Ala., 1953—93, asst. v.p., 1966, v.p., 1967, v.p., br. supr., 1968—72, sr. v.p., br. supr., 1972—73, exec. v.p., 1973—79, pres., 1979—83, vice chmn. bd., 1983—93. also bd. dirs.; pres. AmSouth Bancorp., 1979—93; ret., 1993. Bd. dirs. AmSouth Bank, Fla. Bd. dirs. United Way Found.; past pres. United Way, campaign chmn., 1987; life mem. Birmingham Met. Devel. Bd.; bd. dirs. Warrior-Tombigbee Devel. Assn.; life trustee Ala. Ind. Colls.; pres.'s coun. U. Ala., Birmingham, life bd. visitors. Lt. US Army, 1954—56. Named William A. Powell, Jr. Endowed Professorship in his honor, U. Ala. Mem.: Met. Devel. Assn. (life; bd. dirs.), Birmingham Area C. of C. (life; bd. dirs.), Birmingham Country Club, The Club, Mountain Brook. Home: 2114 Hickory Ridge Cir Birmingham AL 35243-2925

POWELL, WILLIAM COUNCIL, SR., service company executive; b. Burlington, NC, Nov. 5, 1948; s. Thomas Edward Jr. and Annabelle (Council) P.; m. Jacqueline Garrison, July 3, 1976; children: William C. Jr., Ashley C. Student, U. S.C., 1968-69; BS, Va. Mil. Inst., 1971; MBA, Wake Forest U., 1974; postgrad., Elon Coll., 1972. Lic. pilot, real estate broker. NC adminstrv. assoc. Carolina Biol. Supply Co., Inc., Burlington, 1971—91; v.p. Bobbitt Labs., Burlington, 1974-77, pres., 1977—82; owner HEADS, Inc., Elon, NC, 1978—, pres., 1984—; owner Ashwil Acres Farm, Mebane, NC, 1981—2005. Pres. Granite Diagnostics, Inc., Burlington, 1981-84, UST Specialists Inc., 1991-2000, Burlington, Warren Land Co., 1994-2005, Merrymount Property Owners Assn., Inc., 1996-2000, Merrymount Boat Slip Assn., Inc., 1996-2005, Stratonet Inc., 1996-2001, Forest Realm, Inc., 2001—, Goat Island Maritime Inc.,

2001—, Powell Realm Inc., 2001—, Poignard Compact Inc., 2001-; owner Powell Real Estate, Burlington, 1979-2001; bd. dirs. Excalibur Lock Co., Inc., Waubun Labs, Inc., Schriever, La.; v.p. fin. Environ. Responsible Bus. Inc., 1992-97; mem. Babcock Sch. Alumni Coun. Wake Forest U., 1981-85; mgr. Macon Farm, 1992-95; chmn. bd. Ensci Corp., Inc., 1991-95, ptnr. Port Assocs., 1987-2002, Port Assocs. II, 1992-2002; chmn. bd. Netpath Inc., 1995-96, bd. dirs.; filed for election N.C. Senate, 2000, 02. Bd. advisors Elon Coll., NC, 1984-86, bd. visitors, 1987-92; bd. advisors Duke U. Marine Lab., Beaufort, NC, 1985-92; nat. adv. coun. Baruch Marine Inst., 1998-2006; adv. panel Air Quality Compliance Panel State of NC Dept. Environ. Health and Natural Resources, 1994-2006; guardian Boy Scouts Am., Burlington, 1985; trustee Dr. T.E. Powell Jr. Trust, 1989-95; v.p. fin. Cherokee coun. Boy Scouts of Am., 1990-92, exec. bd., 1990-94, exec. bd. Old N. State coun., 1994-95; active Front St. United Meth. Ch., Burlington, NC. Capt. USAR, 1971-79. Recipient Bill Fish Cert. State of S.C., 1983, 2 Bill Fish Certs. State of N.C., 1990, Sower's award Duke U., 1985, N.C. Gov.'s Cup for Billfishing, 1991, 3rd Pl., Big Rock Blue Marlin Tourn, 1998. Mem. NRA (life), Newcomen Soc. N.Am. (life), Billiard Congress Am., Am. Angus Assn., Billiard and Bowling Inst. Assn., NC Forestry Assn. (legis. affairs com. 1994—), N.C. Wildlife Habitat Found. (life), Ducks Unltd. (life sponsor, area chmn. 1985-87, 1997-2005), Safari Club Internat. (state pres. 1985-88, life), Aircraft Owners and Pilots Assn., Cessna Pilots Orgn., Atlantic Coast Conservation Assn. (life), Alamance Wildlife Club (bd. dirs. 1992-95, 2000-03, pres. 1999-2000), Rolls Royce Owners Club (life), N.Am. Hunting Club (life), Found. N.Am. Wild Sheep (life), Chaine des Rotisseurs (chevalier 1991), Brotherhood of the Knights of the Vine (master knight 1991), 10 Point Hunt Club, Am. Angus Assn., Nat. Wild Turkey Fedn., Quail Unltd. (life), NC Cattlemans Assn. (life), Nat. Cattlemans Assn., Inc., Internet Users Group Alamance, Ocean Green Assn., Debordieu Club, Nat. Soc. SAR, Sons Confederate Vets., Alamance County Cattleman's Assn., Citation Fishing Team (capt. 1979—), Alamance Country Club, Debordieu Beach Club. Home: 1109 W Front St Burlington NC 27215-3610 Office: Home Entertainment and Decor Sys Inc 945 E Haggard Ave Elon NC 27244 also: Netpath Inc 2260 S Church St Ste 601 Burlington NC 27215-5380 Office Phone: 336-584-0835. Personal E-mail: wcp@netpath.net.

POWELL, WINONA, music educator; b. Harrisonville, Mo., Feb. 1, 1928; d. Robert James and Naomi Noell Powell; m. Carlos Aguirre, Nov. 14, 1974 (div. Sept. 5, 1975). BA, U. Kansas City, Mo., 1956; MA, Vanderbilt U., Nashville, 1958; MusM, Northwestern U., Evanston, Ill., 1963; MEd, U. Ariz., Tucson, 1977. Tchr. music Kennett H.S., Mo., 1958—59, Kansas City Pub. Sch., 1959—62, Tucson Unified Sch. Dist., 1963—90. Family planning Peace Corps, Barahona, Dominican Republic, 1966—69; airline stewardess TWA, Kansas City, Mo., 1949—55. Vol. Project Hospitality/Salvation Army, Tucson, Neighborhood Watch, Tucson, 1984—86, Tucson Bot. Gardens, 1991—95; trustor U. Ariz. Music Dept. Scholarships; publicity chair Hemlock Soc., 1985—98. R-Consevative. Methodist. Avocations: exercise, swimming, dance, travel. Home: 602 N Avenida Alegre Tucson AZ 85745 Home Phone: 520-623-2384. Personal E-mail: winonapowell@juno.com.

POWELSON, GALE DAWN, elementary school educator; b. Defiance, Ohio, Jan. 19, 1953; d. Arlo Lee and Majorie May Wagner; m. Robert Louis Powelson, Aug. 16, 1974; children: Michelle Dawn Patrick, Matthew Robert. M in ednl. adminstr., Ind. U./Purdue U., 1995—96, BSc in elem. edn., 1990—94. Classroom tchr. Monroeville, 1995—96, Village Elem., Ft. Wayne, Ind., 1996—98, asst. prin., 1998—2000, elem. prin., 2000—04; classroom tchr. Meadowbrook Elem., New Haven, Ind., 2004—. Adj. prof. Ind. U./Purdue U., Ft. Wayne, Ind., 1998—. Mem.: Nat. Reading Recovery Coun. (assoc.), Assn. of Supervision and Curriculum Devel. (assoc.), Nat. Assn. of Elem. Principals (assoc.), Internat. Reading Assn. (assoc.; local ira officer 2004—05), Delta Kappa Gamma (assoc.), Ind. U./Purdue U. Ft. Wayne Alumni Assn. (life), Kappa Delta Phi (life; pres. 1999—). Catholic. Avocations: travel, horticulture. Home: 10711 State Rd 101 Monroeville IN 46773 Office: East Allen County Schools US 930 East New Haven IN 46774 Home Phone: 260-623-3558. Personal E-mail: GPOW1234@aol.com. Business E-Mail: gppowelson@eacs.k12.in.us.

POWER, A. KATHRYN, federal agency administrator; m. Brian Power; children: Matthew, Brendan. EdB, St. Joseph's Coll., Md.; MEd, Western Md. Coll.; postgrad. Harvard U. Tchr. various pub. schs.; computer sys. analyst US Dept. Def.; exec. dir. RI Coun. Cmty. Mental Health Centers, 1985—90; dir. RI Anti Drug Coalition, Gov.'s Drug Program, RI Office Substance Abuse, RI Dept. Mental Health, Retardation and Hospitals, 1993—2003, Ctr. for Mental Health Services, Substance Abuse and Mental Health Adminstrn., HHS, Rockville, Md., 2003—. Pres. Nat. Assn. State Mental Health Program Directors, 1997. Capt. USNR. Recipient Award for Disting. Svc., Sec. US HHS, 2005; fellow Toll fellow, Coun. State Legislators, 1991. Office: Ctr for Mental Health Services 5600 Fishers Ln Rockville MD 20857

POWER, FRANCIS WILLIAM, newspaper publisher; b. Webster, SD, Aug. 12, 1925; s. Frank B. and Esther C. (Fowler) P.; m. Margaret Jean Atkinson, Mar. 24, 1951; children: Patricia Ann, John Michael, Kerry Jean. BBA, U. N.Mex., 1948. Display advt. sales rep. The Register, Santa Ana, Calif., 1948-51; advt. mgr. Valley Morning Star, Harlingen, Tex., 1951-62; gen. mgr. Pampa (Tex.) Daily News, 1962-69; bus. mgr. Brownsville (Tex.) Herald, 1969-75; pub. The Lima (Ohio) News, 1975-91; v.p. Freedom Comm., Inc., until 1991; ret., 1991. Served with USNR, 1943-46. Mem.: Shawnee Country Club, Elks, Rotary. Roman Catholic. Office: Freedom Comm Inc 17666 Fitch Irvine CA 92614-6022

POWER, J.D., III, (JAMES DAVID POWER III), marketing executive; b. Worcester, Mass., May 30, 1931; m. Julie Power (dec. 2002); 4 children; m. Joan Power, 2003. BA in English, Coll. of the Holy Cross, Worcester, Mass., 1953; MBA, U. Penn., 1959; PhD (hon.), Coll. of the Holy Cross, Calif. Lutheran U., Calif. State U. Northridge, Coll. Misericordia. Financial analyst Ford; mktg. rsch. cons. Marplan GM; mktg. rsch. exec. J.I. Case; dir. corp. planning McCulloch Motors Inc., Los Angeles, Calif.; founder, pres. J.D. Power & Assocs., Calif., 1968—, chmn., 1996—. Adj. prof. mktg. Calif. State U. Northridge. Line officer duty U.S. Coast Guard, Arctic and Antarctica. Recipient Disting. Service Citation, Automotive Hall of Fame, 1992. Office: J D Power & Assocs 2625 Townsgate Rd Westlake Village CA 91361

POWER, JOHN BRUCE, lawyer; b. Glendale, Calif., Nov. 11, 1936; m. Sandra Garfield, Apr. 27, 1998; children by previous marriage: Grant, Mark, Boyd. AB magna cum laude, Occidental Coll., 1958; JD, NYU, 1961; postdoctoral, Columbia U., 1972. Bar: Calif. 1962. Assoc. O'Melveny & Myers, LA, 1961—70, ptnr., 1970—97, resident ptnr. Paris, 1973—75; Sheffelman disting. lectr. Sch. Law, U. Wash., Seattle, 1997. Mem. Social Svcs. Commn. City of L.A., 1993, pres., 1993; pres. circle, exec. com. Occidental Coll., 1979-82, 91-94, chair, 1993-94; adj. prof. UCLA Sch. Law, 1999; mem. Tri-Bar Opinion Com., 2005-. Contbr. articles to jours. Bd. dirs. Met. L.A. YMCA, 1988—, treas., 1998-2001; bd. mgrs. Stuart Ketchum Downtown YMCA, 1985-92, pres., 1989-90; mem. L.A. County Rep. Ctrl. Com., 1962-63; trustee Occidental Coll., 1992—, chmn., 2001-03, acting gen. counsel, 1998-2000. Recipient YMCA Golden Book of Disting. Svc. award, 2002, Alumni Seal award Occidental Coll., 2003; Root Tilden scholar. Fellow Am. Coll. Comml. Fin. Lawyers (bd. regents 1999-03); mem. ABA (comml. fin. svcs. com., com. legal opinions, vice chair 2005-07, chair 2007—, UCC com., bus. law sect.), Am. Bar Found., Calif. Bar Assn. (chmn. partnerships and unincorporated assns. com. 1982-83, chmn. uniform commn. code com. 1984-85, chmn. opinions com. 2000-04, exec. com. 1987-91, chmn. bus. law sect. 1990-91, chmn. coun. sect. chairs 1992-93, liaison to state bar commn. on future of legal profession and state bar 1993-95, advisor to exec. com. 1997—, Bus. Law Sect. Lifetime Achievement award 2004), L.A. County Bar Assn. (exec. com. comml. law and bankruptcy sect. 1970-73, 86-89), Internat. Bar Assn., Fin. Lawyers Conf. (bd. govs. 1982—, pres. 1984-85), Exec. Svc. Corps (sec. 1985-00, dir. 1994-2007, vice-chmn. 2000-07), Occidental Coll. Alumni Assn. (bd. govs. 1965-68, pres. 1967-68), Phi Beta Kappa (councilor 1982—, pres. 1990-92). Office: O Melveny & Myers 400 S Hope St Los Angeles CA 90071-2899 Personal E-mail: johnpower@earthlink.net.

POWER, JOSEPH ALOYSIUS, JR., lawyer; b. Oct. 15, 1952; s. Joseph Aloysius and Mary Ellen (Cavenaugh) Power; m. Susan Vohs, Apr. 26, 1980; children: Joseph Aloysius III, Michael Anthony, Ryan Patrick, James Ian. BA, U. Notre Dame, 1974; JD, Loyola U., Chgo., Ill., 1977. Bar: Ill. 1977, U.S. Dist. Ct. (no. dist.) Ill. 1977, U.S. Ct. Appeals (7th cir.) 1994, U.S. Supreme Ct. 1992. Assoc. John D. Hayes & Assocs., Chgo., 1977—84; ptnr. Hayes & Power, Chgo., 1984—91, Power, Rogers & Lavin, Chgo., 1991—93, Power, Rogers & Smith, Chgo., 1993—. Chmn. bd. dirs. Assn. of Trial Lawyers Assurance a mutual risk retention group, 1988—2000; author, lectr. Ill. Inst. Contg. Legal Edn., Springfield, Ill., 1983—89; bd. mgrs. Trial Lawyers for Pub. Justice, 1994—, v.p., 1996—97, pres.-elect, 1997—98, pres., 1998—99. Trustee Loyola U., Chgo., 2004—; bd. dir. Ill. Pub. Action, Chgo., 1987—93. Fellow: Inner Cir. of Advocates, Internat. Acad. Trial Lawyers, Am. Coll. Trial Lawyers; mem.: U.S. Sen. Judiciary Com. (chmn.'s adv. coun. 1994, Ill. Supreme Ct. rules com. 1995—2004, chmn. 1996—2001), ATLA, Ill. Bar Assn., Ill. Trial Lawyers Assn. (author, lectr. 1984—, bd. mgrs. 1984—, chmn. membership com. 1985—87, chmn. legis. com. 1987—89, 3d v.p. 1989—90, 2d v.p. 1990—91, pres. elect 1991—92, pres. 1992—93), Chgo. Bar Assn. (chmn. young lawyers sect. fed. trial bar advocacy program No. dist. Il 1984), ABA, Chgo. Athletic Assn. Democrat. Roman Catholic. Home: 344 W Wellington Ave Chicago IL 60657-5637 Office: Power Rogers & Smith Three First National Plaza 70 West Madison St Suite 5500 Chicago IL 60602 Office Phone: 312-236-9381. Business E-Mail: joepower@prslaw.com.

POWER, JOSEPH EDWARD, lawyer; b. Peoria, Ill., Dec. 2, 1938; s. Joseph Edward and Margaret Elizabeth (Birkett) P.; m. Camille June Repass, Aug. 1, 1964; children— Joseph Edward, David William, James Repass Student, Knox Coll., Galesburg, Ill., 1956-58; BA, U. Iowa, 1960, JD, 1964; CAP, The Am. Coll., Bryn Mawr, Pa., 2004. Bar: Iowa 1964. Law clk. to judge U.S. Dist. Ct., 1964-65; mem. Bradshaw, Fowler, Proctor & Fairgrave, P.C., Des Moines, 1965—2005, of counsel, 2005—. Trustee Am. Inst. Bus., 1987-2002, chmn., 1992-2002; bd. dir. Iowa Law Sch. Found., 1992-2004, Plymouth Ch. Found., 1991-99; bd. dir. Des Moines Cmty. Found., 1996—, sec.-treas., 2001—; bd. dir. Iowa Natural Heritage Found., 1995—, chmn., 2003-05; mem. Des Moines Civil War Roundtable. Fellow Am. Coll. Trust and Estate Counsel (state chair 1994-2000); mem. Iowa Bar Assn. (chmn. probate, property and trust law com. 1983-87), Polk County Bar Assn., Des Moines Estate Planners Forum (pres. 1982-83), Wakonda Club, Rotary Club. Mem.United Ch. Of Christ. Home: 1928 Elm Cr West Des Moines IA 50265 E-mail: jedwardpower@aol.com.

POWER, MARY ELEANOR, biology professor; BA magna cum laude, Brown Univ., 1971; MS, Boston Univ. Marine Biology Program, Woods Hole, Mass., 1974; PhD in Zoology, Univ. WAshington, Seattle, 1981. Asst. prof., zoology, integrative biology Univ. Calif., Berkeley, 1987—92, assoc. prof., integrative biology, 1992—96, prof., 1996—; faculty mgr. Angelo Coast Range Reserve, 1989—. Peer adv. bd. Inst. Ecosystem Studies, Millbrook, NY, 1996—99; sci. adv. bd. Nat. Ctr. for Ecological Analysis and Synthesis, 1996—98; peer rev. panel Grand Canyon Monitoring and Rsch. Ctr., 1998—99; group leader Presdl. Adv. Commn. Western Water Policy, 1997; bd. dir. Nature Conservancy, 1997—; dir. Calif. Biodiversity Ctr., 2001—. Fellow: Am. Acad. Arts & Scis.; mem.: Ecological Soc. Am. (chair, aquatic ecology sect. 1995—97), Phi Beta Kappa, Sigma Xi. Office: Dept Integrative Biology Univ Calif Berkeley CA 94720-3140 Office Phone: 510-643-7776. Business E-Mail: mepower@socrates.berkeley.edu, mepower@berkeley.edu. *

POWER, MARY SUSAN, political scientist, educator; b. Hazleton, Pa., July 5, 1935; d. Younger L. and Cleo (Brook) Power; 1 child, Catherine Laverne. BA, Wells Coll., 1957; postgrad., Exeter U., Eng., 1955-56, Yale U., 1958-59; MA, Stanford U., 1960; PhD, U. Ill., 1961. Asst. prof. Susquehanna (Pa.) U., 1961-64; assoc. prof. U. Ark., Fayetteville, 1965-68; assoc. prof. polit. sci. Ark. State U., State University, 1968-79, prof., 1979—2000, prof. emeritus, 2000—. Author: (book) Before the Convention, Religion and the Founding Fathers, 1984, Jacques Maritaln and the Quest for a New Commonwealth, 1992, Political Philosophy & Cultural Renewal: Collected Essays of Francis Wilson, 2001; columnist (newspaper) The Son, 2005—; contbr., articles to profl. jours. Mem. Fed. Edn. Commn. States, 1982—84; N.E. chair Arkansans for Progress, 1990—96; alt. del. Rep. Nat. Conv., 1972, 1976, 1988, del., 1992; mem. State com. Ark. Rep. Com., 1968—96, sec., 1978—80; mem. Craighead County Election Commn., 1986—88; chmn. Craighead County GOP, 1986—88, vice chmn., 1990—96, N.E. regional chmn., 1988—96; chmn. Craighead County Sheffield for Gov., 1990; mem. exec. com. Ark. Rep. Party, 1990—96, N.E. regional chair, 1988—96; treas. women's soc. Blessed Sacrament Ch., Jonesboro, 1996—2000, chmn. jubilee 2000; chair Silver Caths., 2002—; bd. dirs. Beacons and Bridges, 2005. Relm Found. fellow, 1960, NSF-Am. Polit. Sci. Assn. fellow, 1963, Nat. Def. Seminar fellow, Nat. War Coll., 1973, NEH fellow, 1978, Pres.'s fellow, Ark. State U., 1988—89. Mem.: AAUP (state sec. 1978—80, pres. 1983—90), So. Polit. Sci. Assn., Am. Polit. Sci. Assn., Ark. Polit. Sci. Assn. (bd. dirs., v.p. 1992—93, pres. 1993—94), Phi Kappa Phi (pres. 1991), Phi Gamma Mu (sec.-treas. 1990—2000), Phi Sigma Alpha. Republican. Roman Catholic. Personal E-mail: spower@fastdata.net.

POWER, PEGGY ANN, elementary school educator; b. Chgo., Sept. 17, 1973; d. Edward and Lois Power. BA, U. Ill., Chgo., 1994, MEd, 1996, postgrad., 2004—. Cert. elem. sch. tchr., Ill. Rsch. asst. U. Ill., Chgo., 1991-96; sales asst. Chgo. Bd. Trade, 1991-96; spl. edn. tchr. Gladstone Elem. Sch. Chgo. Bd. Edn., 1995—. Poet: Outstanding Poets of 1994, Best Poems of the 90's, 1992, Distinguished Poets of America, 1993. Active Wis. Dairy Coun., 1996—, Lawry's Menu for Success, Chgo., 1996—, After-Sch. Acad. Ctr., Chgo., 1996—; rep. Chgo. Tchr.'s Union, 1997—, bd. dirs., elem. v.p., 2004—, IFT/AFT del., 2004—. Recipient Gwendolyn Brookes Poet Laureat award, 1990; Baer-Darfler scholar Morgan Park Women's Assn., 1994-96; Marilyn Mucha fellow U. Ill., Chgo., 1995. Mem. ASCD, Coun. Exceptional Children, Nat. Coun. Tchrs. English, U. Ill. Chgo. Alumni Club, Pi Lambda Theta. Democrat. Roman Catholic. Avocations: Karate, poetry, pottery, kayaking. Home: Apt 407 710 Oakton St Evanston IL 60202-2927 Personal E-mail: peggypower@juno.com.

POWER, SAMANTHA J., public policy educator, writer; b. Dungarvan, Ireland, 1970; Grad., Yale U., Harvard U. Law Sch. Reporter covering wars in former Yugoslavia US News & World Report and Economist, 1993—96; polit. analyst Internat. Crisis Group; prof. practice in pub. policy, JFK Sch. Govt Harvard U., founding exec. dir. Carr Ctr. for Human Rights Policy Cambridge, 1998—2002. Author: A Problem from Hell, America and the Age of Genocide, 2003 (Pulitzer prize, 2003, Nat. Book Critics Cir. award gen. nonfiction, 2003, Artur Ross prize for best book in US fgn. policy, 2003); co-editor (with Graham Allison): Realizing Human Rights, 2000; contbr. articles to pubs. such as The New Yorker, NY Rev. Books, Washington Post, NY Times. Recipient Nat. Mag. award for best reporting, 2005. Office: Carr Ctr Human Rights Policy Harvard Univ - Rubenstein-217 79 John F Kennedy St Cambridge MA 02138 E-mail: samantha_power@harvard.edu.

POWER ANDERSON, VANESSA L., dean; d. Curtis and Betty M. Power; m. Myron R. Anderson. PhD, Va. Tech., Blacksburg, 2006. Gear up project dir. State Coun. Higher Edn. for Va., Richmond, 2001—02; sr. asst. dean Coll. William and Mary, Williamsburg, Va., 2002—04; asst. to the asst. provost and dir. Ctr. for Academic Enrichment and Excellence, Blacksburg, Va., 2004; grad. asst. Va. Tech., Blacksburg, 2004; interim asst. dean student life Metro State Coll. Denver, 2005; dean student svcs. Denver Sem., Littleton, Colo., 2005—. Grant reviewer US Dept. Edn., Washington, 1999. Bd. mem. Tech Fed. Credit Union Freedom First, Salem, Va., 1999—2003, Valdosta State U., Ga., 1998—2005; adv./affiliate ProLiteracy, Syracuse, NY, 2006. Mem.: Omicron Delta Kappa (nat. comm. on ext. 2001—02), Kappa Delta Pi (sec. Va. Tech. 2001—02), Kappa Omicron Nu, Sigma Gamma Rho (life; v.p. 2006). Home Phone: 303-337-2930; Office Phone: 303-762-6901. Personal E-mail: vpower@vt.edu.

POWERS, ANTHONY RICHARD, JR., educational sales professional; b. Chgo., June 14, 1942; s. Anthony Richard and Bernadine Rene (Schwenke) P.; m. Marianne Fugiel, Mar. 15, 1980; children: Kathleen Mary, Anthony Richard III. BA, Quincy Coll., 1964; MS, U. Notre Dame, 1974. Cert. tchr., Ill. Sci. tchr. St. Rene Sch., Chgo., 1964-70; sci. coord. Queen of All Saints Sch., Chgo., 1970-76; sci. and math. product mgr. Ideal Sch. Supply Co., Oak Lawn, Ill., 1976-79, customer svc. mgr., 1980-83, Midwest sales mgr., 1983-85; nat. sales mgr. Ednl. Teaching Aids, Vernon Hills, Ill., 1985-89, v.p., 1989-97; accounts mgr. Numerical Algorithms Group, Downers Grove, Ill., 1997-2001; midwest acct. mgr. Freedom Sci., Vernon Hills, Ill., 2001—, midwest regional mgr., 2001—04, Texthelp Sys., 2004—. Lectr., De Lourdes Coll., Des Plaines, Ill., 1970-78; sci. adviser, Archdiocese of Chgo., 1969-76. Author sci. edn. materials. Pres. Orchard Estates Condominium Assn., 1986-87; chmn. Vernon Hills Fire and Police Commn., 1995—. Mem. Northeastern Ill. Sci. Assn. (pres. 1970-75), U.S. Golf Assn., Internat. Brotherhood Magicians, K.C. Roman Catholic. Avocations: magic, music, golf. Home: 241 Tally Ho Dr Vernon Hills IL 60061-2900 Office: Texthelp Sys 241 Tally Ho Dr Vernon Hills IL 60061 Home Phone: 847-549-7528; Office Phone: 847-549-0344. Personal E-mail: arpnd74@aol.com. Business E-Mail: dpowers@texthelp.com.

POWERS, BRUCE RAYMOND, writer, language educator, consultant; b. Bklyn., Dec. 10, 1927; s. George Osborne and Gertrude Joan (Bangs) P.; m. Dolores Anne Dawson, July 25, 1969; children: Christopher, Patricia Student, U. Conn., 1947—49; AB, Brown U., 1951, MA, 1965; postgrad., U. Pa., 1961. Announcer, engr. Sta. WNLC, New London, Conn., 1946—47; tng. officer CIA, Dept. Def., 1951—55; TV sales/svc. rep. NBC, 1955; TV news writer and reporter Movietone News UP Assns., Inc., 1955—56; asst. to pres. Gotham-Vladimir Advt., Inc., 1956—57; asst. account exec. D'Arcy Advt. Co., 1957—58; asst. campaign dir. Cmty. Counseling Svcs., Inc., 1958—59; dir. fund-raising campaign Tamblyn & Brown, Inc., 1959—60; instr. Brown U., Providence, 1963—65, Ryerson Poly. Inst., Toronto, 1966, Nazareth Coll., Rochester, NY, 1966—67; asst. prof. English and comm. studies Niagara U., Lewiston, NY, 1967—86, chmn. permanent curriculum com. English dept., 1970—71, assoc. prof., 1986—92, prof., 1986—92, prof. emerito, 1992—; dir. Film Repertory Ctr., 1971—92, dir. comm. studies program, 1973—87. Prodr., mng. dir. Exptl. Film Retrospective, N.Y. State Coun. Arts, Buffalo, 1972; narrator (documentary) Niagara: Fading in the Mist, 1996; panelist, judge Artists Com. 2d World Festival Animated Films, Zagreb, Yugoslavia, 1974; lectr., vis. artist ARTPARK, Lewiston, 1975; project dir. Bicentennial Symposium, N.Y. State Am. Revolution Bicentennial Commn., Buffalo, 1975-76; rsch. assoc. Ctr. Culture and Tech., U. Toronto, 1977-81; keynote spkr. Dupont de Nemours & Co. Health and Safety Conf., Buffalo, 1990; ptnr. Moon Island Documentary Group, 1997—. Author: The Silent Foil, 2005; co-author: (with Marshall McLuhan) The Global Village, Oxford, 1989; editor The Film and Study Guide, 1973-74. Served with Underwater Demolition Teams, USNR, PTO, 1945-46 Scholar, Brown U., 1961—62. Mem. MLA, Underwater Demolitions Teams/Seal Assn. Va. Beach, Broadcast Edn. Assn., Soc. Cinema Studies, Am. Soc. Journalism Sch. Adminstrs., Assn. Edn. Journalism and Mass Comm., Internat. Exptl. Film Soc. (founding pres. 1971-73), Ariz. Sr. Acad. U. Ariz., We. N.Y. Audio-Visual Assn., N.Y. Coll. English Assn., Phi Beta Kappa Roman Catholic. Home: 915 Sun Valley St North Tonawanda NY 14120-1952 Home Phone: 716-694-4815.

POWERS, CHRISTOPHER SHERIDAN, science educator, web site designer; b. Denver, Aug. 10, 1971; s. Philip Stephen Powers and Janine Marie Harp; m. Mary Theresa Ciganek, July 28, 1994; 1 child, Myrrh Curie. BS, Oral Roberts U., Tulsa, Okla., 1994. Cert. tchr. Assn. Christian Schs. Internat., 2007. Sci. tchr. Christian Fellowship Sch., Lakewood, Colo., 1994—. Sci. tchr. adv. bd. mem. Current Sci. Mag., Lakewood, 2004—; presenter Colo. Sci. Conv., Denver, 2003. Author of poems, (dialogue) A Cost So Great (1st Pl. Nat. Original Dialogue Competition, 2006). Recipient Second Mile award, Christian Fellowship Sch., 1998, Exemplary Sch. Program award, Assn. Christian Schs. Internat., 2003. Mem.: Am. Inst. Biol. Scis. Conservative. Achievements include introduced a new type of volleyball serving style which has been widely adopted; design of volleyball coaching equipment made from PVC pipe; new junior volleyball cheer that has been widely adopted. Avocations: writing, volleyball, movies, chess, reading. Office: Faith Christian HS 4890 Carr St Arvada CO 80002 Home Phone: 720-320-3898. Personal E-mail: xrosein3@yahoo.com.

POWERS, CLAUDIA MCKENNA, state legislator; b. Key West, Fla., May 28, 1950; d. James Edward and Claudia (Antrim) McKenna; children: Gregory, Theodore, Matthew, Thurston. BA in Edn., U. Hawaii, 1972; MA, Columbia U., 1975. Cert. tchr., N.Y. Mem. Greenwich Rep. Town Meeting, Conn., 1979-93, sec. bldg. com., 1982-84, sec. legis. com., 1986—88, 1990—93; mem. Conn. Ho. of Reps., Hartford, 1993—, ranking mem. govt. adminstrn. and elections com., 1995-96, asst. minority leader, 1997-98, vice chmn. Rep. bill rev. com., 1997—2004, house minority whip, 1999—2003, dep. minority leader, 2003—06, mem. spl. com. of inquiry into impeachment of the gov., 2004, dep. minority leader at large, 2007—. Mem. editl. bd. Greenwich Mag., 1995-98. Conn. commr. Edn. Commn. of the States, 2000—, also mem. steering com.; campaign chmn. Greenwich Rep. Town Com., 1984, 85, chmn., 1986-90; sec. Rep. Round Table, Greenwich, 1988-90; bd. govs. Riverside Assn., Greenwich, 1987-91, sec., 1991-92; class mother Riverside Sch., Greenwich, 1984-90; mem. altar guild Christ Ch., Greenwich, 1990—, lay eucharistic min., 2004—; adminstrv. coord. Greenwich Teen Ctr., 1990-91; alt. del. Rep. Nat. Conv., New Orleans, 1984—, San Diego, 1996; v.p. LWV of Greenwich, 1990-91; bd. trustees Norwalk Maritime Ctr., 2001—; bd. dirs. Gov.'s Prevention Partnership, 2004—. Episcopalian. Home and Office: 15 Hendrie Ave Riverside CT 06878-1808

POWERS, DAVID LOUIS, lawyer; b. Bay City, Mich., Mar. 18, 1961; s. Earl Louis and Norma Beatrice (Ashcraft) P.; m. Cheryl Denise Wixson, June 1, 1991; children: Matthew Jacob, Michael Jonathan. BA, Alma Coll., 1983; JD, U. Detroit, 1986. Bar: Mich. 1986, US Dist. Ct. (ea. dist.) Mich. 1986, US Dist. Ct. (we. dist. 1987), US Ct. Appeals (6th cir.) 1990, US Supreme Ct. 2002. Ptnr. Lambert, Leser, Cook, Giunta & Smith, P.C., Bay City, Mich., 1986—2000, Smith, Martin, Powers & Knier, PC, Bay City, 2001—. Contbr. articles to profl. publs. Del. Bay County Rep. Conv., 1996-97; vol. Action Ctr. of Bay County, Inc., dir. 1990-92. Named

Superlawyer, Law and Politics Mag., 2006. Mem. Bay County Bar Assn. (pres. 2000-01), Bay Area Landlords and Bus. Owners Assn. (v.p. 1988-90, dir. 1990-97), Bay Area C. of C. (dir. 2005), Bay City Downtown Mgmt. Bd. (chmn. 2002-03), Save Our Shoreline (v.p. 2001-). Lutheran. Home: 861 S Linwood Beach Rd Linwood MI 48634-9511 Office: Smith Martin Powers & Knier PC 900 Washington Ave Bay City MI 48708 Office Phone: 989-892-3924.

POWERS, DAVID RICHARD, educational administrator; b. Cambridge Springs, Pa., Apr. 5, 1939; s. William Herman and Elouise Fancheon (Fink) Powers; m. Mary Julia Ferguson, June 11, 1960. Student, Pa. State U., 1957-60; BA, U. Pitts., 1963, MA, 1965, PhD, 1971. Dir. CAS advising ctr. U. Pitts., 1966-68, asst. dean faculty, 1968-70, asst. to chancellor, 1970-76, assoc. provost, 1976-78, vice provost, 1978-79; v.p. for acad. affairs George Mason U., Fairfax, Va., 1979-82; vice chancellor for acad. affairs W.Va. Bd. Regents, Charleston, 1982-88; exec. dir. Minn. Higher Edn. Coord. Bd., St. Paul, 1989-94, Nebr. Coord. Commn. Post-secondary Edn., Lincoln, 1994—2005, exec. dir. emeritus, 2005. Prin. author: Making Participatory Management Work, 1983, Higher Education in Partnership with Industry, 1988; contbr. articles to Ednl. Record, Adult Learning, Forum for Applied Rsch. on Pub. Policy. Founder mem. bd. trustees Western Govs. U. Grantee USOE Faculty Seminar, Taiwan, 1967, ARC Ctr. for Edn. & Rsch. with Industry Appalachian Regional Commn., 1983, Republic of China Sino-Am. Seminar, 1985; recipient Award for Acad. Quality W.Va. Coun. Faculty, 1986. Mem. State Higher Edn. Exec. Officers, Western Coop. Ednl. Telecomm., Civil Air Patrol, Pi Sigma Alpha. Avocation: boating. Home: 6513 Spencer Ln Clinton WA 98236 Office Phone: 360-341-1533. Personal E-mail: davidpowers@whidbey.com.

POWERS, EDWARD ALTON, minister, educator; b. Jamestown, NY, Oct. 26, 1927; s. Leslie Edgar and Mabelle Florence (Alton) P.; children: Randall Edward, Christopher Alan, Ann Lynn. BA, Coll. of Wooster, 1948; MDiv, Yale U., 1952; EdD, Columbia U., 1973. Ordained to ministry Congl. Ch., 1951. Pastor, Hamden, Conn., 1949-53, Pleasant Hill, Ohio, 1953-56; sec. dept. youth work Congl. Christian Ch. Bd. Home Missions, 1956-60; gen. sec. divsn. Christian edn., bd. home missions Congl. and Christian Chs., 1960-61; divsn. Christian edn., bd. homeland ministries United Ch. of Christ, 1962-73; gen. sec., divsn. evangelism, edn., ch. ext. United Ch. Bd. Homeland Ministries, 1973-79; mem. faculty Inst. Mgmt. Competency, Am. Mgmt. Assn., NYC, 1980-87; affiliate faculty Milano, New Sch. Mgmt. and Urban Policy, 1981—. Mem. program bd. divsn. edn. and ministry Nat. Coun. Chs., 1963-80; mem. edn. working group World Coun. Chs.; chmn. Peace Priority Team, United Ch. of Christ, 1970-75, adminstr., editor sexuality study, 1977; ptnr. Cane Powers Cons., and Powers, Wayno & Assocs., 1987-2003. Author: Journey Into Faith, 1964, Signs of Shalom, 1973, (with Rey O'Day) Theatre of the Spirit, 1980, In Essentials Unity, 1982, Youth in the Global Village, 1982; also articles. Home: 7 Gramercy Park W Apt 5B New York NY 10003-1759 Home Phone: 212-529-4081; Office Phone: 212-229-5400 ext. 1520. Personal E-mail: powersea@aol.com.

POWERS, ELIZABETH WHITMEL, lawyer; b. Charleston, SC, Dec. 16, 1949; d. Francis Persse and Jane Coleman Cotten (Wham) P.; m. John Campbell Henry, June 11, 1994 (dec. Jan. 1997); m. Henry C. B. Lindh, June 16, 2000. AB, Mt. Holyoke Coll., 1971; JD, U. S.C., 1978. Bar: SC 1978, NY 1979. Law clk. to justice S.C. Cir. Ct., Columbia; assoc. Reid & Priest, NYC, 1978—86, ptnr., 1986—97; of counsel LeBoeuf, Lamb, Greene & MacRae, NYC, 1997—2004, ptnr., 2004—. Exec. editor S.C. Law Rev., Columbia, 1977-78. Vol. N.Y. Jr. League, NYC, 1983—; bd. dirs. The Seamen's Ch. Inst., 1996—2006, sec., 1999—2006; trustee Ch. Club, 1991—94, 1997—2001, v.p., 1992—94. Mem.: Nat. Soc. Colonial Dames in State of N.Y. (pres. 1992—95), Nat. Soc. Colonial Dames of Am. (parliamentarian 1994—2000, regent Gunston Hall 2001—02), S.C. Bar Assn., ABA.

POWERS, HENRY MARTIN, JR., oil industry executive; b. Bath, Maine, July 18, 1932; s. Henry Martin and Eva (Saunders) Powers; m. Hepzibah Hinchey Reed, June 20, 1959; children: Henry Martin III, Carlton Reed. BS, Maine Maritime Acad., Castine, 1954. Marine engr. Am. Export Lines, NYC, 1954-58; staff engr. Bull & Roberts Inc., NYC, 1958-59; gen. sales mgr. Williams Bros., Inc., Portland, Maine, 1959-61; v.p. C. H. Sprague & Son Co., Boston, 1961-72, pres., 1972—, also chmn. bd. dirs.; chmn. bd. dirs. Sprague, Inc., Portsmouth, NH, 1999—. Chmn. Pease Devel. Authority, 1990—93; bd. dirs. Shanley Corp., Strawbery Banke Inc., 1st NH Banks, Seaward Constrn. Co., Santa Holding Co., Intelligent Controls, Environ. Resource Return. V.p. Seacoast United Fund, 1967—69; chmn. fuels, energy com. New Eng. Coun., 1974—75; pres. Portsmouth Coun., 1966—67; bd. visitors Maine Maritime Acad. Served to lt. USNR, 1956—58. Mem.: Mechanic Fire Soc., Navy League, Cumberland Club (Portland), Algonquin Club (Boston), Masons. Office: Sprague Inc 2 Intl Dr Ste 1 Portsmouth NH 03801-6810 Home: 100 Shepard's Cove Rd I-2 Kittery ME 03904 Office Phone: 603-431-1000. Personal E-mail: hpowers5@comcast.net.

POWERS, JAMES MATTHEW, neuropathologist, educator, researcher; b. Cleve., Sept. 15, 1943; s. Alfred Patrick and Margaret Anne (Gunther) P.; m. Karen P. Smith, 1983; children: Kristin, Scott, Conor. BS in Biology, Manhattan Coll., 1965; MD, Med. U. SC, Charleston, 1969. Diplomate in anatomic pathology and neuropathology Am. Bd. Pathology. Dir. electron micros. lab. VA Hosp., Charleston, 1973-76; asst. prof. pathology Med. U. SC, Charleston, 1973-76, assoc. prof. pathology, 1976-80, prof. pathology, 1980-88; vice chmn. dept. pathology Columbia Coll. Physicians and Surgeons, NYC, 1989-92; prof., dir. neuropathology U. Rochester, 1992—2005, assoc. chair of edn., 1994-97, dir. residency tng. program, 1994—2003, prof. pathology and lab. medicine. Sec. Biol. Stain Commn., 1994—2001. Author: (practice guidelines) Archives Pathology and Laboratory Medicine, 1995, Greenfield's Neuropathology, 2002; mem. editl. bd.: Human Pathology, 1991—2005, Brain Pathology, 1995—2000, Acta Neuropathologica, 1995—2005, Biotech. and Histochemistry, 1994—2001, Modern Pathology, 1996—2004, Neurology, 1999—2004, Am. Jour. Surg. Pathology, 1999—2005, Jour. Neuropath. Exptl. Neurology, 2000—06; contbr. chpt. to book, articles to profl. jours. Mem. Internat. Soc. Neuropathology (v.p. 1994-97), Am. Assn. Neuropathologists (pres. 1993, Moore award 1975, 76, 77, 81, Lifetime Achievement award for Meritorious Contbns. to Neuropathology 2007), US-Can. Acad. Pathology. Office: U Rochester Sch Medicine and Dentistry Box 626 601 Elmwood Ave Rochester NY 14642 Office Phone: 585-275-3201. Office Fax: 585-273-1027. E-mail: james_powers@urmc.rochester.edu. *

POWERS, JOHN T., JR., former mayor; Mayor City of Spokane, Wash., 2001—03. Bd. dirs. Assn. Wash. Cities, Inland Northwest Tech. Edn. Ctr., Spokane Regional Econ. Devel. Coun.; co-chair Spokane Task Force on Race Rels., U.S. Conf. Mayors; mem. Gas & Elec. Utility Restruction Task Force, Wash. State Competitiveness Coun., Assn. Northeast Wash. Mayors.

POWERS, LINDA SUE, biophysicist, educator, biomedical engineer; b. Pitts., Feb. 8, 1948; d. Luther Thurston and Helen Grace (Currence) Powers. BS in Physics and Chemistry, Va. Poly. Inst. and State U., 1970; MA in Physics, Harvard U., 1972, PhD in Biophysics, 1976. Mem. tech. staff AT&T Bell Labs., Murray Hill, N.J., 1976-88; dir. bio-catalysis sci. ctr., prof. chemistry & biochemistry Utah State U., Logan, 1988-91, prof. elec. engring., biol. & irrigation engring., 1991—2006; dir. Nat. Ctr. for the Design of Molecular Function, 1991—; Thomas R. Brown prof. bioengring., prof. elec. and computer engring. U. Ariz., Tucson, 2007—. Adj. prof. U. Pa. Med. Sch., Phila., 1978-2000; vis. fellow Princeton U., 1981-82. Mem. editl. corr. Comments Molecular Cellular Biophysics, 1980-89; editl. bd. Biophysics Jour., 1989-96, Am. Inst. of Physics Internat. Basic and Applied Biol. Physics, 1993—, Internat. Series Basic and Applied Biol. Physics, 1994-2003, Wiley Encyclopedia of Biomedical Engineering, 2002-05; contbr. numerous articles to profl. jours. and books. Recipient 1st U.S. Bioenergetics award, 1982, State of Utah Gov.'s medal for sci. and tech., 1994. Fellow Am. Phys. Soc. (divsn. biol. physics 1988-92, exec. bd. 1977-83, chmn. 1984-85), Am. Inst. Chemists, IEEE (steering com. 2002-03), AAAS, NAS (com. chem. and biol. terrorism, 1997-98, com. countering agr. bioterrorism 2001-02), Biophys. Soc., Soc. Applied Spectroscopy, Sigma Pi Sigma, Phi Lambda Upsilon. Avocations: breeding and showing horses, writing music, windsurfing, snowboarding. Office: Univ Ariz Dept Elec and Computer Engring PO Box 210104 Tucson AZ 85721-0104 Home Phone: 435-994-2111.

POWERS, MARY ELLEN, lawyer; b. Cleve., 1955; AB, Oberlin Coll., 1977; JD, Univ. Va., 1980. Bar: DC 1980, admitted to practice: US Dist. Ct. for DC 1981, US Ct. of Appeals, DC Cir. 1982, US Ct. of Appeals, Fifth Cir. 1987, US Supreme Ct. 1996. Ptnr.-in-charge DC office Jones Day, Washington. Mem.: Women's Bar Assn. (Star of the Bar 2004), DC Bar Assn. (pro bono com.). Office: Jones Day 51 Louisiana Ave Washington DC 20001-2113 Office Phone: 202-879-3870. Office Fax: 202-626-1700. Business E-Mail: mepowers@jonesday.com.

POWERS, MATTHEW DOUGLAS, lawyer; b. San Francisco, July 7, 1959; BS, Northwestern U., 1979; JD cum laude, Harvard Law Sch., 1982. Bar: Calif. 1982, Dist. Ariz., US Dist. Ct. (no. dist. Calif.) 1982, US Dist. Ct. (ctrl. dist. Calif.) 1983, US Ct. Appeals (9th cir.) 1983, US Dist. Ct. (ea. dist. Calif.) 1985, US Ct. Appeals (fed. cir.) 1986, US Supreme Ct. 1988, US Ct. Internat. Trade 1990, US Dist. Ct. (so. dist. Tex.) 1990, US Dist. Ct. (no. dist. Ind.) 1991, US Dist. Ct. (ea. dist. Mich.) 2003, US Ct. Appeals (2nd, 5th, and 7th cirs.) 1991, US Dist. Ct. (ea. dist. Mich.) 2003. Head, mng. ptnr., global patent litig. grp. Weil, Gotshal & Manges, LLP, Redwood City, Calif., mem. mgmt. com. Lectr. in field; tchr. patent litig. U. Calif. Boalt Hall Sch. Law, Berkeley; lectr. patent law Stanford U., Santa Clara U.; mem. adv. bd. Inst. Transitional Arbitration; mem. exec. com. Boalt Hall, Berkeley Ctr. for Law & Tech., Santa Clara U. Sch. Law, High Tech. Law Inst.; mem. No. Dist. Calif. Patent Rules Com., No. Dist. Calif. Patent Jury Instrn. Com.; chmn. Internat. Patent Law Subcommittee, 1989; mem. ICC Commn. on Intellectual and Indsl. Property, 1990. Editor-in-chief Intellectual Property & Tech. Law Jour., co-editor-in-chief Jour. of Propriety Rights, mem. editl. bd. Mealey's Litig. Reports: Intellectual Property, Internat. Litig. Quarterly, 1991, published (numerous articles). Mem. leadership coun. Am. Diabetes Assn., San Francisco; bd. dirs. Greater Bay Area Make-A-Wish Found.; mem. exec. com. Orientation in In USA Law Prog., U. Calif. Named a Leading Lawyer, PLC Which Lawyer?, 2006; named The "Go To" Patent Litigator in No. Calif., The Recorder, 2003, Father of Yr., Father's Day Coun. San Francisco, 2004, Trial Lawyer of Yr., Santa Clara County Trial Lawyers Assn., 2005, Calif. Lawyer Atty. of Yr. in Intellectual Property, Calif. Lawyer mag., 2005; named one of 8 Star Attys. in all fields in the US, Chambers Global Guide, 2001, Top 10 Attys. in Silicon Valley, The Lawyer (London), 2001, Top 100 Attys. in the World, 2001, 7 Top IP Trial Lawyers in the Country, IP Worldwide, 2002, Top 25 IP Lawyers in Calif., San Francisco Daily Jour., 2003, Top 25 Attys. in All Fields in the San Francisco Bay Area, San Francisco Chronicle, 2003, Top 45 Attys. Under 45, Am. Lawyer mag., 2003, Top 10 Trial Lawyers in Am., Nat. Law Jour., 2006. Mem.: ABA. Office: Weil Gothal & Manges LLP 201 Redwood Shores Pky Redwood City CA 94065 Office Phone: 650-802-3200. Office Fax: 650-802-3100. E-mail: matthew.powers@weil.com. *

POWERS, PAULINE SMITH, psychiatrist, educator, researcher; b. Sept. 23, 1941; m. Henry P. Powers; children: Jessica, Samantha. AB in Math., Washington U., 1963; MD, U. Iowa, Iowa City, 1971. Med. intern Emanuel Hosp., Portland, Oreg., 1971-72; psychiatry resident U. Iowa, Iowa City, 1972-74, U. Calif., Santa Barbara, 1974-75; from asst. prof. to assoc. prof. psychiatry Coll. Medicine U. So. Fla., Tampa, 1975-85, prof., 1985—, dir. eating disorder program, 1979—, dir. psychosomatic medicine divsn., 1979—. Author: Obesity: The Regulation of Weight, 1980; editor: The Current Treatment of Anorexia Nervosa and Bulimia, 1984; co-editor: (with J. Yager and P. Powers) Clinical Manual of Eating Disorders, 2007. Fellow: Am. Psychiat. Assn. (Rush Gold Outstanding Exhibit medal 1976, Dorfman Jour. Paper award 1987); mem.: Nat. Eating Disorders Assn. (pres.-elect 2003—05, pres. 2005—06, Lifetime Achievement award 2006), Acad. Eating Disorders (founding pres., Women Helping Women award 1995, Profl. Excellence award 1997, Outstanding Clinician award 2000). Office: U So Fla Coll Medicine Dept Psychiatry 3515 E Fletcher Ave Tampa FL 33613-4706 Home Phone: 813-971-5804; Office Phone: 813-974-2926. Business E-Mail: ppowers@health.usf.edu.

POWERS, RICHARD EDWARD, JR., lawyer; b. Evanston, Ill., July 20, 1952; s. Richard Edward and Helen Lufen Powers; m. Diane Wojda, Aug. 12, 1978. BS, Gonzaga U., 1974; JD, U. Notre Dame, 1977. Bar: Tex. 1977, DC 1979. Ptnr. Butler & Binion LLP, Washington, 1977-99, Dorsey & Whitney LLP, Washington, 1999—2005, Venable LLP, Washington, 2005—. Bd. regents Gonzaga Univ.; mem. Bretton Woods Com. Mem.: ABA, Internat. Bar Assn., Energy Bar Assn., DC Bar Assn., Tex. Bar Assn. Home: 5233 Elliott Rd Bethesda MD 20816-2910 Office: Venable LLP 575 7th St NW Washington DC 20004 Office Phone: 202-344-4360. Office Fax: 202-344-8300. Business E-Mail: repowers@venable.com.

POWERS, RICHARD GERARD, history educator; b. Rochester, NY, Jan. 26, 1949; s. Albert Dominic and Evelyn Rogers Powers; m. Patricia Marie Maslyn, May 29, 1971. BA in History, SUNY, Brockport, NY, 1971, postgrad., 1971—75. Tchr. US history, govt. and European history H.W. Schroeder H.S., Webster, NY, 1971—. Recipient Excellence Secondary Sch. Tchg. award, U. Rochester, 2000, Spl. Recognition award Excellence Tchg., Tufts U., 2000. Office: Webster Central School District 875 Ridge Road Webster NY 14580 Home Phone: 585-342-7456; Office Phone: 585-670-5000. Personal E-mail: gems158@aol.com. E-mail: dick_powers@websterschools.org.

POWERS, RICHARD S., writer, educator; b. Evanston, Ill., June 18, 1957; BA summa cum laude, U. Ill., 1978, MA, 1980. Computer programmer and freelance data processor, Boston, 1980; writer-in-residence U. Ill., 1992, Swanlund chair in English, 1996, profl. Ctr. Advanced Studies, 1999. Author: Three Farmers on Their Way to a Dance, 1986 (Book of Yr. Time mag., 1991), Prisoner's Dilemma, 1988, The Gold Bug Variations, 1991 (Book of Yr. Time mag., 1991), Operation Wandering Soul, 1993, Galatea 2.2, 1995, Gain, 1998 (Named one of best bus. books of 1998, James Fenimore Cooper prize Am. Soc. Historians, 1999), Plowing the Dark, 2000, The Time of Our Singing, 2003 (Pushcart prize, 2003, W.H. Smith Literary award, 2003), The Echo Maker, 2006 (Nat. Book award fiction, 2006). Named Author of Yr., Ill. Assn. Teachers English, 2001; named one of Five Writers of the Decade, Esquire mag., 1989; recipient Rosenthal award, Am. Acad. Arts and Letters, 1985, Lannan Literary award, 1999, Vursell award, Am. Acad. Arts and Letters, 2000, Corrington award literary excellence, Centenary Coll., 2001, Dos Passos prize lit., Longwood U., 2003, Amb. Book award, 2004; MacArthur fellow, 1989. Fellow: Am. Acad. Arts & Sci. Avocations: cello, guitar, clarinet, saxophone, reading. Office: Dept English Univ Illinois MC 718 608 South Wright St Urbana IL 61801 Office Phone: 217-333-2391. E-mail: rpowers@express.cities.uiuc.edu. *

POWERS, ROBERT DAVID, physician; b. Plainfield, NJ, Nov. 6, 1953; s. John B. and Marian E. (Kuhn) P.; m. Sally Ann Harmet, 1977; children: Alison, Elizabeth, Carolyn. BA, Amherst Coll., 1975; MD, U. Va., 1979; MPH, Yale U., 1999. Intern U. Minn., Mpls., 1979-81; resident U. Va., 1981—83, from asst. to assoc. prof., 1983—94, prof., 2006—; assoc. prof. U. Conn. Sch. Medicine, Farmington, 1994—99, chief emergency medicine, 1997—2005, vice chmn. dept. trauma and emergency medicine, 1997—2005, prof., 1999—. Fellow ACP. Office: U Va Sch Medicine Dept Emergency Medicine Charlottesville VA 22908 Business E-Mail: rdp5p@virginia.edu.

POWERS, ROBERT P., electric power industry executive; B in Biology, Tufts U., Medford, Mass., 1975; M in Radiol. Hygiene, U. NC, 1976. Cert. sr. reactor operator 1991. Radiation protection engr. Pacific Gas & Electric Co., San Francisco, 1982; sr. engr. radiation protection Diablo Canyon Nuc. Generating Sta., 1984, radiation protection mgr., 1987, dir. mech. maintenance, 1991, mgr. site svcs., 1992, mgr. quality svcs., 1993, mgr. ops. svcs., 1996, v.p., 1996; sr. v.p. nuc. generation Am. Electric Power Svc. Corp., 1998, exec. v.p. nuc. and tech. svcs., 2001—03, exec. v.p. generation, 2003, exec. v.p. AEP Utilities - East. Office: Am Electric Power Svc Corp 1 Riverside Plz Columbus OH 43215-2373 Office Phone: 614-716-1000. *

POWERS, RONALD GEORGE, management consultant; s. Lee Whitney and R. Anne Powers; m. Elizabeth Braislin McClellan, July 24, 1980. Chmn. Boardroom Advisors, Inc., Winter Park and Tampa, Fla., The Strategic Mgmt. Adv. Group, Inc., Winter Park and Tampa, Fla. Adviser to chief execs. of banks, corps. and govts. on strategic mgmt. issues, 1971—. Trustee Trinity Sch., Fla. Symphony Orch. Mem. Interlachen C. of C. Republican. Episcopalian. Home: PO Box 2174 Winter Park FL 32790-2174 Office: PO Box 1922 Winter Park FL 32790-1922 Office Phone: 407-491-1334. E-mail: boardroomadvisor@mindspring.com.

POWERS, ROSS, Olympic athlete; b. Bennington, Vt., Feb. 10, 1979; Mem. U.S. Snowboard Team; olympic gold medalist in halfpipe, 2002; founder Ross Powers Found., 2001. Named Nat. Champion, 1993, 1994, 1997, Grand Prix Champion, FIS World and Overall Champion, 1998, US Open title, 1998; recipient 2nd pl., 1992, 3rd pl., 1993, 1st pl., World Cup, 1995, 1996, 2nd pl., 1995, 3rd pl., 1995, 2nd pl., 1996, 3rd pl., 1996, 1st pl., World Championship, 1996, 2nd pl., World Cup, 1997, Bronze medal in Snowboarding (Halfpipe), Nagano Olympics, Japan, 1998, 1st pl., World Championship, 2000, Gold medal, NBC Gravity Games, 2000, TNT Winter Goodwill Games, 2000, Silver medal, ESPN X Games, 2000, Bronze medal, 2001, Gold medal in Snowboarding (Halfpipe), Olympic games, 2002. Office: The Ross Powers Found c/o Pete Carlisle P O Box 17574 Portland ME 04112

POWERS, SCOTT, television producer, actor; b. Chgo., Aug. 23, 1948; s. Raymond Alford and Ruby Marilyn (Ivacko) P. BS, Ithaca Coll., 1970; MBA, Fairleigh Dickinson U., 1971. Producer Young & Rubicam, Inc., NYC; account exec. Kelly, Nason, Inc., NYC; sr. account exec. Bozell & Jacobs, Inc., NYC; account supr. Foote, Cone & Belding, Inc., NYC; actor NYC, LA, 1982—; pres. Scott Powers Prodns., Inc., NYC, 1988—. Pres. CaribCom, Inc., NYC, 1996—. Author: Here's Looking At You!, 1997; contbr. articles to publs.; cartoonist Thankyounext, 1990—. Mem. Better Bus. Bur. NYC, 1991—, Knickerbocker Rep. Club, NYC, 1971—; bd. dirs. Profl. Comedians Assn., NYC, 1988-91, v.p., 1989-91; bd. dirs. One World Arts Found., 1992—; judge Internat. Film and TV Festivals, NYC, 1991—. Mem. AFTRA (bd. dirs. 1989-91), SAG, Actor's Equity Assn., NATAS (judge Emmys 1985—), NYC C.of C., Met. Club, NY Athletic Club, Players Club, Mensa, Intertel. Republican. Congregationalist. Avocations: skiing, sailing, tennis, squash, international river running. Home: 180 Central Park S New York NY 10019-1562 Office: Scott Powers Studios Inc 135 W 29th St Ste 404 New York NY 10001

POWERS, SUSAN J., information technology executive; BS in Math., Southern Ill. U.; MBA, Northern Ill. U. V.p. programs Ga. CIO Leadership Assn.; adv. bd. Tech. Assn. Ga., Travel Commerce; v.p. product mktg. Worldspan, 1993, v.p. sales and mktg., sr. v.p. worldwide e-commerce, chief info. officer and sr. v.p. worldwide product solutions. Editl. bd. Bus. Travel News, 2001—. Named Best Product Devel. or Engring. Exec., Am. Bus. Awards, 2003; named one of People of Yr., Travel Agent Mag., 1994, 2000, 100 Most Powerful Women in Travel, 2003; recipient Woman of Yr. Tech. award, (WIT) Women in Tech., 2003. Office: World Headquarters 300 Galleria Parkway Atlanta GA 30339 Office Phone: 770-563-7400.

POWERS, THOMAS LYNWOOD, professor, military reserve officer; b. Richmond, Va., Sept. 3, 1947; BA with honors, U. Richmond, 1969; PhD, U. Ga., 1978. Prof. history U. S.C., Sumter, 1979—. 1st lt. U.S. Army, 1972-74. Mem. Am. Hist. Assn., Orgn. Am. Historians,, Am. Soc. Mil. History, So. Hist. Assn., Soc. History Am. Fgn. Rels. Office: U SC 200 Miller Rd Sumter SC 29150-2498

POWERS, THOMAS MOORE, writer; b. NYC, Dec. 12, 1940; s. Joshua Bryant and Susan (Moore) P.; m. Candace Molloy, Aug. 21, 1965; children: Amanda, Susan, Cassandra. BA, Yale U., 1964. Reporter Rome (Italy) Daily American, 1965-67, U.P.I., NYC, 1967-70; freelance writer, 1970—; contbg. editor The Atlantic mag.; editor, founding ptnr. Steerforth Press, So. Royalton, Vt., 1993—. Author: Diana: The Making of a Terrorist, 1971, The War at Home, 1973, The Man Who Kept the Secrets: Richard Helms and the CIA, 1979, Thinking About the Next War, 1982, Total War: What It Is, How It Got That Way, 1988, Heisenberg's War: The Secret History of the German Bomb, 1993, The Confirmation, 2000, Intelligence Wars: American Secret History from Hitler to Al Qaeda, 2002. Recipient Pulitzer prize for nat. reporting, 1971 Mem. PEN Am. Center, Council on Fgn. Relations. Address: 106 Chelsea St South Royalton VT 05068-9800 also: Lit Rep Lynn Nesbit 445 Park Ave New York NY 10022-2606 Office Phone: 802-763-8585. E-mail: tom@steerforth.com.

POWERS, TIMOTHY EUGENE, lawyer; b. Waukegan, Aug. 3, 1955; s. Herman Eugene and Beryl Grace (Weiskittel) P.; m. Joni Grace Helm, Mar. 21, 1987. BA, UCLA, 1977; JD, So. Meth. U., 1980. Bar: Tex. 1980. Assoc. Passman & Jones, Dallas, 1980-82; ptnr. Haynes and Boone, Dallas, 1982—, chmn., Internat. Practice Group, bd. dir. Mem. adv. bd. Southwestern Legal Found. Internat. and Comparative Law Ctr., Richardson, Tex., 1982—. Soc. Internat. Bus. fellow, 1987—. Mem.: State Bar Tex., Internat. Bar Assn. (chmn. internat. bankruptcy cooperation sub-com. 1987—95, constitution com. 2002—, vice chmn. project fin. sub-com. 2003—05), Internat. Bar Found. (trustee 2003—), Inter-Pacific Bar Assn., Am. Law Inst. (adv. internat. insolvency project 1994—2000), Japan Am. Soc. of Dallas/Ft. Worth (pres. 1992—93, bd. dir. 1990—), Coun. on Fgn. Relations, Leadership Dallas, No. Tex. Commn., Dallas C. of C. (internat. forum), Tex. Assn. Bank Counsel, Dallas Bar Assn., Tex. Bar Assn. (chmn. Internat. Law Sect. 1987—88), ABA (internat. comml. transactions com. 1988—90, governing coun., Internat. Law Sect. 1990—93, chmn. internat. comml. transactions com. 1992—96, co-chmn. transnational legal practice com. 1999—2001, governing coun. 1999—2005, Internat. Law and Practice Sect., chmn. fgn. investment in US real estate com.), Phi Delta Phi. Republican. Roman Catholic. Office: Hayne and Boones LLLP 901 Main St Ste 3100 Dallas TX 75202-3789 Office Phone: 214-651-5610. Office Fax: 214-200-0610. Business E-Mail: timothy.powers@haynesboone.com.

POWERS, TIMOTHY H., electric power industry executive; Sr. positions ABB, Inc., BBC Brown Boveri, Inc.; sr. v.p., CFO Hubbell Inc., 1998—2001, pres., CEO, 2001—04, bd. dir., 2001—, chmn., pres., CEO, 2004—. Office: c/o Hubbell 584 Derby Milford Rd Orange CT 06477 *

POWERS, WILLIAM BRYAN, academic administrator; b. Indpls., Ind., July 2, 1960; s. Rosalie and Anthony William Powers; m. Sarah Jayne Young, Sept. 19, 1987; 1 child, Rosemary Clair. BA, Purdue U., 1978—82; JD, Ind. U. Sch. of Law, 1982—85; LLM, The John Marshall Law Sch., 1999—2002. Bar: Ind. 1988. Asst. cons. on legal edn. ABA, Indpls., 1986—96; assoc. dean for admission and student affairs The John Marshall Law Sch., Chgo., 1996—. Author: (book review) Jour. of Computer & Info. Law; co-editor: (book) Reflections of the Chairpersons; author: Rsch. Institutes of ABA Approved Law Schools; editor: Law Sch. Facilities Reference Book; author: A Study of Contemporary Law Sch. Curricula; contbr. articles Ind. Law Rev. Mem. Ill. Lawyers Assistance Program Oper. Com., Chgo., 2001—03. Mem.: Nat. Network of Law Sch. Officers, Midwest Assn. of Fin. Aid Advisors, Am. Assn. of Coll. Registrars and Admission Officers, Midwest Assn. of Law Sch. Admissions (treas. 2002—), Nat. Assn. for Law Placement, Chgo. Bar Assn., ABA (chair, student services com. 2000—02), Union League Club of Chgo. Avocations: travel, bridge. Office: The John Marshall Law Sch 315 S Plymouth Ct Chicago IL 60604 E-mail: 6powers@jmls.edu.

POWERS, WILLIAM CHARLES, JR., academic administrator, law educator; b. 1946; BA, U. Calif., Berkeley, 1967; JD, Harvard U., 1973. Bar: Wash. 1974, Tex. 1980. Law clk. to Hon. E. A. Wright U.S. Ct. Appeals (9th cir.), Seattle, 1973-74; asst. prof. Wash. U., Seattle, 1974-77, assoc. prof., 1977-78; prof. law U. Tex., Austin, 1978—, assoc. dean acad. affairs, 1984—87, 1994—95, univ. disting. prof. and Hines H. Baker and Thelma Kelly Baker chair in law, 1997—, John Jeffers Rsch. Chair in law, 2000—, dean Sch. Law, 2000—06, pres., 2006—. Chair Spl. Investigation Com. Enron Corp. Author: Texas Products Liability Law, 1992; co-author: Cases and Materials in Torts, 1998, Cases and Materials in Products Liability, 2002. Mem.: Am. Law Inst. Office: U Tex at Austin Office of Pres PO Box T Austin TX 78713-8920 Home: 3600 Murillo Cir Austin TX 78703 Home Phone: 512-472-7831; Office Phone: 512-232-1120. Office Fax: 512-471-6987. E-mail: wpowers@law.utexas.edu. *

POWERS, WILLIAM EDWARD, emergency physician, medical educator, flight surgeon; b. Atlanta, Sept. 16, 1957; s. Richard Candler and Olive Carol Osburn Powers; m. Nancy Carolyn Freeman, May 17, 1986; children: Nicole, Will. MS in Biomed. Engring., U. Ill., Chgo., 1981; MS in Aerospace Medicine, Wright State U., 1991; MD, Rush U., 1985; postgrad., U. Houston, 2001—03. Diplomate Am. Bd. Emergency Medicine, Am. Bd. Preventive Medicine. Intern in gen. surgery Orlando (Fla.) Regional Med. Ctr., 1985-86, resident in emergency medicine, 1986-88; resident in aerospace medicine Wright State U., Dayton, Ohio, 1989-91; biomed. engr., rsch. asst. U. Ill., Chgo., 1980-81; chief resident emergency medicine Orlando (Fla.) Regional Med. Ctr., 1987; assoc. dir. emergency medicine Kissimmee (Fla.) Meml. Hosp., 1988-89; asst. med. dir. Martin-Marietta Aerospace, Orlando, Fla., 1988-89; emergency med. physician, clin. instr. Wright State U. Med. Sch., Dayton, Ohio, 1989-91; med. officer, flight surgeon NASA Johnson Space Ctr., Houston, 1991-92; asst. med. dir. Cape Canaveral Hosp., Cocoa Beach, Fla., 1991-93, Twin Cities Hosp., Niceville, Fla., 1991-93; asst. prof. emergency medicine, rsch. dir. U. Tex. Med. Sch., Houston, 1993-95; asst. prof. family medicine, dir. urgent care U. Tex. Med. Br., Galveston, 1995-96; asst. prof. medicine Baylor Coll. Medicine, Houston, 1996—2001; med. dir. emergency dept. Meml. Hermann Hosp. S.E., 2002—03; flight surgeon U. Tex. Med. Branch, 2003—04, NASA, 2004—. Contbr. articles to profl. publs. Med. missionary Missionary Ventures, Honduras, 1995, 98. Fulbright scholar U. Vienna, Austria, 1996. Fellow Am. Coll. Emergency Physicians, Aerospace Med. Assn. (assoc. fellow). Avocations: flying, photography, piano, running. Office: Mail Code SD 2, 2101 NASA Pkwy Houston TX 77058 Office Phone: 281-483-4481. Personal E-mail: WEPowers@aol.com.

POWLEN, DAVID MICHAEL, investment banker, consultant; b. Logansport, Ind., May 28, 1953; s. Daniel Thomas and Bertha Frances (Cappa) P.; m. Miriam Lango, Apr. 23, 2005; 1 child, Brooks Ryan. JD, Harvard U., 1978, AB, 2005. Bar: Ind. 1978, NY 2004, Pa. 2005, U.S. Dist. Ct. (so. dist.) Ind. 1978, U.S. Ct. Appeals (7th cir.) 1985, Bus. Bankruptcy Law Am. Bd. Cert., 2001. Assoc. Barnes & Thornburg, Indpls., 1978-84, ptnr., 1985-01, chmn., adminstr. creditors rights dept.; mng. dir., mgr. restructuring group McDonald Investments Inc., Cleve., 2001—04; sr. v.p. Mesirow Fin. Cons., NYC, 2004—06; mng. dir. Western Res. Ptnrs., Phila., 2006—. Contbr. articles to profl. jours. Mem. ABA (bus. bankruptcy com., secured creditors and chpt. 11 subcom., comml. fin. svcs. com., creditors rights subcom.), Am. Bankruptcy Inst. (chmn. fin. advisors com.), Assn. Insolvency and Restructuring Advisors (cert. insolvency and restructuring advisor 2005-), Ind. Bar Assn. (chmn. bankruptcy and creditors rights sect. 1990-91), Indpls. Bar Assn. (chmn. edn. com. 1984, chmn. ct. liaison com. 1985, bankruptcy and comml. law sect.), Turnaround Mgmt. Assn. (bd. dirs. NE Ohio chpt. 2001-04), Harvard Club, Phi Beta Kappa. Office: Western Res Ptnrs Ste P108 2001 Hamilton St Philadelphia PA 19130 Office Phone: 317-727-2211, 215-563-6870. Business E-Mail: dpowlen@wesrespartners.com.

POWSNER, EDWARD RAPHAEL, physician; b. NYC, Mar. 17, 1926; m. Rhoda Lee Moscovitz, June 8, 1950; children: Seth, Rachel, Ethan, David. SB in Elec. Engring., MIT, 1948, SM in Biology, 1949; MD, Yale U., 1953; MS in Internal Medicine, Wayne State U., 1957; MHSA, U. Mich. Diplomate Am. Bd. Nuclear Medicine, Am. Bd. Pathology in clin. pathology and anatomic pathology, Am. Bd. Internal Medicine; lic. physician, Mich. Intern Wayne County Gen. Hosp., Eloise, Mich., 1953-54, resident internal medicine, 1954-55, Detroit Receiving Hosp., 1955-56; fellow in hematology Wayne State U. and Detroit Receiving Hosp., 1957-58; clin. investigator VA Hosp., Allen Park, Mich., 1958-61, chief nuclear medicine svc., 1961-78; dir. clin. labs. Mich. State U., East Lansing, 1978-81; staff pathologist Ingham Med. Ctr., Lansing, Mich., 1978-81; dir. nuclear medicine St. John Hosp., Detroit, 1982-95. Rsch. asst. biology MIT, 1948-49, 50; asst. instr. medicine Wayne State U. Coll. Medicine, 1954-56, instr., 1959-61; assoc. prof. pathology Wayne State U. Sch. Medicine, 1961-68, assoc. medicine, 1961, prof. pathology, 1968-78; prof. pathology Mich. State U., 1978-81, assoc. chairperson, 1980-81, clin. prof., 1981-82; chief clin. labs. Detroit Gen. Hosp., 1969-73; chief lab. svcs. Health Care Inst., Wayne State U., 1976-78; mem. adv. coun. Nuclear Medicine Tech. Cert. Bd., 1990-91. Bd. editors Am. Jour. Clin. Pathology, 1963-76, 83-88; author 2 textbooks, 11 chpts., 50 peer reviewed papers, 17 abstracts and other publs. With U.S. Army, 1944-47. Mem. AMA (sect. coun. on pathology), Am. Soc. Clin. Pathologists (rep. 1987-89, 93-2000, govt. rels. com. 1993-95, mem. coun. nuclear medicine 1978-82, chmn. 1982-84), Am. Coll. Nuclear Physicians, Am. Soc. Nuclear Cardiology, Coll. Am. Pathologists, Detroit Acad. Medicine, Mich. Soc. Pathologists, Mich. State Med. Soc., Soc. Nuclear Medicine, Washtenaw County Med. Soc., Sigma Xi, Tau Beta Pi. Office: Eastside Nuclear Medicine 2370 E Stadium Blvd #315 Ann Arbor MI 48104-4810

POWSNER, SETH M., psychiatrist, educator; s. Edward Raphael and Rhoda Lee (Moscovitz) P.; m. Elizabeth C. Yen, Aug. 18, 1985. BSEE, MIT, 1974; MD, Yale U., 1978. Cert. bd. cert. psychiatrist Amer Bd. of Psychiatry and Neurology, added qualifications in geriatric psychiatry Amer Bd. of Psychiatry and Neurology. Resident in psychiatry Michael Reese Hosp., Chgo., 1978—82, asst. dir. psychiat. tng., 1983-84; pvt. practice, specializing in psychiatry Chgo., 1982-86; unit chief Charter Barclay Hosp., Chgo., 1983-84; psychiatrist Ill. State Psychiat. Inst., Chgo., 1984-85; rsch. cons. U. Chgo. Med. Sch., Chgo., 1985-86; asst. prof. Yale Med. Sch., New Haven, 1986-92, assoc. prof. psychiatry, 1992—2005; chief psychiat. consultation svc. Yale-New Haven Hosp., 1994—2000, chief crisis intervention unit, 2000—; prof. psychiatry and surgery Yale Med. Sch., New Haven, 2006—. Contbr. articles to profl. jours. Recipient Biomed. Pilot Projects Initiative grant, Culpepper Found., 1998—99. Mem. AMA, IEEE, Am. Psychiat. Assn., Assn. for Computing Machinery. Achievements include patents for graphical summary of patient status. Avocations: skiing, skating. Office: Yale Univ Dept Psychiatry 20 York St Rm 2039 New Haven CT 06510-3202

POYADUE, FLORENE STEWART, nurse, foundation administrator; b. Lovejoy, Ill., Nov. 17, 1934; d. Charles Archibald and Florene (Walker) Stewart; m. Octave Anthony Poyadue, Sept. 30, 1956; children: Turhan Michael, Keith Matthew, Jill Alexandria, Dean Archibald. Diploma in nursing, St. Mary's Infirmary, St. Louis, 1955; BVE, San Jose State U., Calif., 1975; MA in Marriage, Family and Child Counseling, Santa Clara U., Calif., 1983, PhD (hon.) in Cmty. Svc., 1993. RN Calif. Staff nurse Charity Hosp., New Orleans, 1955—56; staff nurse, asst. head nurse, head nurse Providence Hosp., El Paso, Tex., 1957—65; staff nurse, supr. Muenchweiler Hosp., Germany, 1965—67; dir. nursing Rivera's Eastside Hosp., San Jose, 1968—69; program coord. Cubberly Adult Sch., Palo Alto, Calif., 1970—85; founder, CEO Parents Helping Friends, Inc., San Jose, 1976—98. Cons. FSP Enterprise, San Jose, 1998—2005; spkr., cons., presenter workshops in field. Co-author: The Parent to Parent Handbook, 2001; contbr. articles to profl. jours., chpts. to books; author: tng. manuals, course study materials, (poems) Moods in Poetry. Mem. adv. bd. Bridge Sch.; mem. PHP Cmty. Assocs. Bd. Named Doer, San Jose Mercury News, 1985; named to Hall of Fame, South Bay Black Cmty., 1999; recipient Earle Williams award, St. Mary's Infirmary, 1955, Golden Rule award, J. C. Penney, 1982, 1991, Citizen of Achievement award, AAUW, 1984, Svc. to Spl. Needs Families award, San Andreas Regional Ctr., 1984, Commendation, Bishop Diocese San Jose, 1985, Sen. Lloyd Bentson award, Surgeon Gen.'s Conf., 1987, Outstanding award, Santa Clara U., 1987, Ignatian award, 1988, Letter of Commendation, Calif. Gov. Deukmejian, 1989, Woman of Achievement award, San Jose Mercury News, Women's Fund, 1990, Inclusion award, State of Calif., 2000, Pope John 23d award, Italian Cath. Fedn., 2001, Infant Devel. Assn. State of Calif. award, 2003, numerous others; grantee Family of Achievement award, Joseph P. Kennedy Jr. Found., 1990. Mem.: South Bay Black Nurses Assn. (long range planning com. 1990—2003, Nurse of Yr.), Nat. Black Nurses Assn., St. John Vianney Sr. Club (mem. hospitality com.). Democrat. Roman Catholic. Avocations: bowling, dance, writing poetry, Scrabble. Office: Parents Helping Parents Inc 3041 Olcott St Santa Clara CA 95054-3222

POYDASHEFF, ROBERT STEPHEN, lawyer; b. NYC, Feb. 13, 1930; s. Stephen Alexander Poydasheff and Pauline M. Miller; m. Anastasia Catherine Latto, Aug. 29, 1954; children: Catherine Alexandra, Robert Stephen Jr. BA in Polit. Sci., The Citadel, 1954; JD, Tulane U., 1957; MA, Boston U., 1966; diploma, Command and Gen. Staff Coll., 1969, Army War Coll., 1976. Bar: S.C. 1958, Ga. 1979, US Supreme Ct. 1964, US Ct. Mil. Appeals, US Ct. Mil. Rev. 1964, US Dist. Ct. (fed. dist.) S.C. 1988, US Dist. Ct. (fed. and mid. dists.) Ga. 1987. Commd. 2d lt. U.S. Army, 1955, advanced through grades to col., 1975, ret., 1979; sr. v.p. SunTrust Bank of West Ga., Columbus, 1979-95; pvt. practice Columbus, 1995—. Instr. bus. law Am. U. Ext. Divsn., Ft. Benning, 1961-63; adj. prof. internat. law, Am. govt., and bus. law U. Md. Ext. Divsn., Berlin, 1964-67, Vietnam, 1967-68; adj. prof. Troy State U., Ft. Benning, Ga., 1976—; cons., exec. v.p. ATI-Allied Tech. Internat. Inc., Columbus, 1995—; past legal advisor to Sec. of Army and Sec. of Def. on mil. dependent sch. and labor rels. Contbr. commentaries, papers, and analyses to profl. jours. City councilor City of Columbus, 1996-2002; mayor of Columbus, Ga., 2003-07; bd. dir. Springer Opera House Assn., 1998—; trustee Ga. Coun. of Humanities, exec. com., 1998—; bd. edn. Ft. Benning Sch., 1976-79, chmn. pers. actions com., 1976-79; trustee Dr. Hosp., Columbia; bd. dirs. Columbus United Way, River Ctr. Performing Arts; past pres. Chattahoochee coun. Boy Scouts Am., Columbus; past pres. Chattahoochee Valley, Assn. of US Army, Anne Elizabeth Shepherd Home, Columbus Symphony, ARC; chmn. bd. dir. Leadership Morality Inst.; chmn. Civilian Mil. Coun., Ga. Govs. Commn. on Transp. Decorated Legion of Merit with 2 oak leaf clusters, Bronze Star, commendation medal with oak leaf cluster, Vietnam Svc. medal with four bronze stars, Order of St. George, Episcopal Ch., Inf. Order of St. Maurice; parachutist badge; badge of The Army secretariet; recipient Ga. Govs. medal for the humanities, Outstanding Civilian Svc. medal U.S. Army, 2004; St. Michael the Anchangel medal G. Orthodox Metropolis. Fellow Leadership Morality Inst.(chair of bd.); mem. Ga. Mcpl. Assn. (bd. dirs.), Columbus Bar Assn., C. of C. (mil. affairs com., bd. dirs.), Kiwanis, Masons (32 deg.), Phi Delta Phi, Pi Sigma Alpha. Republican. Episcopalian. Avocations: jogging, reading, gymnastics. Home: 6349 Mountainview Dr Columbus GA 31904-2213 Office: 944 2d Ave Columbus GA 31902 Office Phone: 706-317-3224. Personal E-mail: bobpoydasheff@bellsouth.net.

POYNER, KENNETH G., systems engineer, writer; b. Norfolk, Va., Jan. 13, 1956; s. Kenneth G. and Rosa B. Poyner; m. Karen C. Cohn, Oct. 15, 1977. BS, Excelsior Coll., NY, 1983. Cert. CISSP Internat. Info. Systems Security Certifications Consortium, 2002. Info. assurance mgr. Expeditionary Warfare Tng. Group, Atlantic, Norfolk, Va., 1998—. Author: (poetry collection) Cordwood, (collection) Sciences, Social. Mem.: IEEE, Mensa, Intertel. Avocations: literature, drama, powerlifting. Home: PO Box 14452 Norfolk VA 23518 Home Phone: 757-473-0846; Office Phone: 757-462-8172.

POZA, HUGO BERNARDO, aerospace company executive; b. Havana, Mar. 12, 1945; s. Hugo Ernesto and Carmen (Valle) P.; m. Mary Karen Connors, Jan. 21, 1967; children: Hugh Thomas, Sean Christopher, Vanessa Kristi. BS in Elec. Engring., U. Dayton, 1966; MS in Elec. Engring., Purdue U., 1967, PhD, 1971. Mem. tech. staff TRW Systems Group, Redondo Beach, Calif., 1971-73, dept. staff engr., 1973-75, sr. staff engr., 1975-77, asst. program mgr., 1977-80; mgr. mil. systems ops. Mil. Electronics Div. TRW, San Diego, 1981-84, v.p., gen. mgr. Mil. Electronics and Avonics Div., 1985—86; sr. v.p. M/A-COM Government Systems, 1986—88; v.p., gen. mgr., Avionics div. Lockheed Martin-Sanders, 1988—95, exec. v.p., 1995; v.p., aerospace electronic Lockheed Martin; v.p., gen. mgr., Strategic Systems div. Raytheon Co., Falls Church, Va., v.p., Homeland Security, 2002—. Mem. tech. adv. bd. Quest Tech. mag. Contbr. articles to profl. jours; patentee in field. Bd. dirs. Am. Martyrs Youth Group, 1975-78; bd. dirs. Manhattan Beach Single Young Adults, 1979-81; mem. Christian Family Movement, 1979-81, St. Gabriel's Youth Ministry, 1981—. Named one of 50 Most Important Hispanics in Tech. & Bus., Hispanic Engr. & Info. Tech. mag., 2005. Mem. IEEE, AIAA, World Affairs Council Los Angeles, Old Crows, Tau Beta Pi Clubs: Escondido, Tennis. Roman Catholic. Office: Raytheon Co 7700 Arlington Blvd Falls Church VA 22042 *I have always believed in giving all I have to anything I dedicate myself. I have strived to be the very best in all my endeavors, but never by stepping on someone else's pride. I am a positive thinker with a winning attitude. My success in life has been greatly due to the support of my family and my strong belief in the Lord.*

POZDRO, JOHN WALTER, retired music educator, composer; b. Chgo., Aug. 14, 1923; s. John and Rose Anna P.; m. Shirley Allison Winans, June 12, 1954; children— John Winans, Nancy Allison Thellman. Student, Am. Conservatory Music, Chgo., 1941-42; B.M. in Music, Northwestern U.-Evanston, Ill., 1948, M.M. in Music, 1949; PhD in Music, Eastman Sch. Music, 1958. Instr. Iowa State Tchrs. Coll., Cedar Falls, 1949-50; instr. to assoc. prof. U. Kans., Lawrence, 1950-64, prof. music, 1964-93, dir. theory and composition, 1961-88; ret., 1993; teaching fellow Eastman Sch. Music, Rochester, NY, 1956-57. Chmn. symposium com. U. Kans., Lawrence, 1958-69. Representative works include Third Symphony, 1960, Piano Sonata No. 4, 1976, Malooley & Fear Monster, 1977, Impressions, Winds, Piano, 1984, Tryptich for Carillon, 1996, the Spirit of Mt. Oread, 1989. Winds of Autumn, 1996. Served with U.S. Army, 1943-46. Recipient U. Calif. Berkeley medal for Disting. Svc., 1993; grantee Ford Found., 1960, Nat. Endowment Arts, 1976; nominated for Pulitzer prize in Music, 1960. Mem. ASCAP, Pi Kappa Lambda. Presbyterian. Avocations: golf, photography, writing. Home: 4700 Muirfield Dr Lawrence KS 66047-1820

POZEN, ROBERT CHARLES, investment company executive; b. NYC, Aug. 8, 1946; s. Morris and Miriam Pozen; m. Elizabeth Kelner, Apr. 11, 1976; children: Joanna, David. BA, Harvard U., 1968; JD, Yale U., 1972, JSD, 1973. Bar: N.Y. 1977, D.C. 1978, U.S. Supreme Ct., U.S. Ct. Appeals (4th, 5th, 7th and D.C. cirs.). Assoc. prof. law NYU, 1974-77; assoc. gen. counsel SEC, Washington, 1978-80; ptnr. Caplin & Drysdale, Washington, 1981-86; sr. v.p., gen. counsel, mng. dir. FMR Corp./Fidelity Investments, Boston, 1987—96; pres. Fidelity Mgmt. and Rsch. Co., Boston, 1997—2001; vice chmn. Fidelity Investments, Boston, 2001—02; secy. econ. affairs Commonwealth Mass., 2003; non-exec. chmn. Mass. Fin. Svcs. Investment Mgmt., Boston, 2004—. Mem. adv. bd. Securities Regulation Law Reporter Bur. Nat. Affairs, Washington, 1981; vis. lectr. Harvard Law Sch., Cambridge, Mass., 1986; mem. legal adv. com. N.Y. Stock Exchange, 1987; appt. mem., Commn. to Strengthen Social Security John Olin Visiting Prof., Harvard Law Sch, 2002-2003. Author: Financial Institutions: Investment Mgmt. Cases, Materials and Problems, 1977; contbr. articles to profl. jours. Mem. ABA (securities com. 1981—, employee retirement income secuity act 1985-86). Office: MFS 500 Boylston St Boston MA 02116-3470

POZEN, SHARIS ARNOLD, lawyer; b. Jefferson City, Mo., Jan. 31, 1964; d. John Burleigh and Mary Carolyn Arnold; m. Thorn Lord Pozen, Sept. 1, 1991; children: Hannah Carolyn, Grace Leigh. BA, Conn. Coll., 1986; JD, Washington U., 1989. Staff atty. U.S. FTC, Washington, 1989—93, asst. to dir. bur. of competition, 1993—94, atty. advisor, 1994; assoc. Hogan and Hartson LLP, Washington, 1995—99, counsel, 1999—2000, ptnr., 2000—. Editor: Market Power Handbook, 2003. Chair. bd dirs. The Ballet Studio, Washington, 2004—; vice chair membership Horace Mann PTA, Washington, 2005—. Mem.: ABA. Office: Hogan and Hartson LLP 555 13th St NW Washington DC 20004 Office Phone: 202-637-6948. Office Fax: 202-637-5910. Business E-Mail: sapozen@hhlaw.com.

POZNANSKI, ANDREW KAROL, pediatric radiologist; b. Czestochowa, Poland, Oct. 11, 1931; came to U.S., 1957, naturalized, 1964; s. Edmund Maurycy and Hanna Maria (Ceranka) P.; children: Diana Jean, Suzanne Christine. BSc, McGill U., 1952, MD CM, 1956. Diplomate: Am. Bd. Radiology, Royal Coll. Physicians and Surgeons Can. Intern Montreal (Que., Can.) Hosp., 1956-57; resident Henry Ford Hosp., Detroit, 1957-60, staff radiologist, 1960-68, U. Mich. Med. Center, Ann Arbor, 1968-79; co.-dir. pediatric radiology C.S. Mott Children's Hosp., Ann Arbor, 1971-79; radiologist-in-chief Children's Meml. Hosp., Chgo., 1979-99; prof. radiology U. Mich., 1971-79, Northwestern U. Med. Sch., 1979—. Bd. dirs. Nat. Coun. on Radiation Protection, 1983-90; mem. Internat. Commn. on Radiologic Protection, 1981-89; mem. adv. panel on radiologic devices FDA, 1975-77, chmn., 1976-77; trustee Am. Bd. Radiology, 1993-2003. Author: The Hand in Radiologic Diagnosis, 1974, 2d edit., 1983, Practical Approaches to Pediatric Radiology, 1976; co-author: Bone Displasias, An Atlas of Genetic Disorders of Skeletal Development, 2002 bd. editors: Skeletal Radiology, 1975-95, Radiographics, 1980-84, Pediatric Radiology, 1986-91. Mem.: AMA, Internat. Skeletal Soc. (founder, pres. 1992—94), John Caffey Soc., Radiol. Soc. N.Am., Soc. Pediatric Radiology (pres. 1980—81), Am. Roentgen Ray Soc. (pres. 1993—94), Polish Radiol. Soc. (hon.), Can. Assn. Radiologists (hon.), European Soc. Radiology (hon.), Alpha Omega Alpha. Home: 2400 N Lakeview Ave Chicago IL 60614-2747 Office: Childrens Meml Hosp 2300 N Childrens Plz Chicago IL 60614-3394 Office Phone: 773-880-3521. Business E-Mail: apoznanski@ameritech.net.

POZNER, LARRY S., lawyer, educator; b. Indpls., Nov. 13, 1947; BS in Bus. Adminstrn., U. Colo., 1969; JD, U. Calif., 1973. Bar: Colo. 1973. Dep. state pub. defender, 1973—77; pub. defender Colo. Springs, 1973—77, Denver, 1973—77; former lead counsel Broncos Football Club; former def. co-counsel Denver Broncos; ptnr. Reilly Pozner & Connelly, Denver. Adj. prof. law U. Denver, 1983—92, lectr., 1981—82, adj. asst. prof., 1982—85; with faculty Nat. Criminal Def. Coll., 1985—95; legal analyst NBC News, 1998—2000; lectr. in field. TV appearances include: NBC Nightly News; The Today Show; Rivera Live; Fox News; CNN; NPR; Court TV; co-author (with Roger Dodd): Cross Examination: Science & Techniques, 1993; contbr. articles to profl. jours. Mem.: Colo. Trial Lawyers Assn., ACLU Colo., Colo. Criminal Def. Bar (pres. 1985—86), Nat. Assn. Criminal Def. Lawyers (officer 1992, pres. 1998—99, immediate past pres. 1999—2000). Office: Reilly Pozner & Connelly The Kittredge Bldg 511 16th St Ste 700 Denver CO 80202 Office Phone: 303-893-6100. Office Fax: 303-893-6110. E-mail: lpozner@hrpwlaw.com.

POZZAN, TULLIO, medical educator; b. Venice, Italy, Feb. 22, 1949; s. Mario and Lucia (Velluti) P.; m. Silvia Panozzo, Sept. 16, 1978; 1 child, Lucia. MD, U. Padua, Italy, 1973. Lic. physician. Asst. prof. gen. pathology U. Padua Med. Sch., Italy, 1974—83, assoc. prof., 1983—86, prof., 1986—. Long term European Molecular Biology Orgn. fellow dept. biochemistry U. Cambridge, England, 1979—81; dept. chmn. U. Padua Med. Sch., 1992—2003. Editor: Jour. Neurochemistry, 1991; contbr. sci. articles to profl. jours. Mem. European Molecular Biology Orgn. (editor jour. 1991). Roman Catholic. Avocations: skiing, tennis, classical music. Home: V Conti 5 35131 Padua Italy Office: U Padova Dept Biomedical Scis Viale G Colombo 3 35121 Padua Italy

POZZATTI, RUDY OTTO, artist; b. Telluride, Colo., Jan. 14, 1925; s. Innocente and Mary L. (Mimiolla) P.; m. Dorothy I. Pozzatti, May 20, 1946; children: Valri Marie, Rudy Otto, Gina Maria, Mia Ines, Illica Lara. BFA, U. Colo., 1948, MFA, 1950, DHL, 1973. Mem. faculty dept. art U. Nebr., Lincoln, 1950-52, 53-56, Ind. U., Bloomington, 1956-91, prof. fine arts, 1964-91, disting. prof., 1975-91; ret., 1991; artist-in-residence Roswell Mus. and Art Ctr. One-man exhbns. include Cleve. Mus. Art, 1955, Whitney Mus. Am. Arts, NYC, 1961, Tyler Sch. Art, Rome, 1969, Sheldon Meml. Art Gallery U. Nebr., 1969, Mitchell Mus. Art, Mt. Vernon, Ill., 4 other sites, 1992-93, Ind. U. Art Mus., Bloomington, 2002, Evansville Mus. ARt, 2002; represented in permanent collections, Mus. Modern Art, NYC, Libr. Congress, Washington, Art Inst. Chgo., Cleve. Mus. Art. Served with AUS, 1943-46. Recipient George Norlin silver medal U. Colo., 1974; finalist Robert Foster Cherry award Baylor U., 2007; Fulbright grantee, 1952-53, 63-64, grantee US Dept. State, USSR, 1961, Yugoslavia, 1965, Brazil, 1974, Hungary, 1986; grantee Rockefeller Found., Bellagio, Italy, 1995; Guggenheim fellow, 1963-64; Fellow Ford Found., 1963, grantee, Japan, 1981. Mem. Soc. Am. Graphic Artists, Am. Color Print Soc., Coll. Art Assn. (bd. dirs.), Artists Equity Assn., Ind. Acad. (elected). Roman Catholic. Personal E-mail: rpozzatt@indiana.edu.

POZZO, RICCARDO, philosophy educator; b. Milan, June 7, 1959; s. Giancarlo and Carla (Rizzani) Pozzo; m. Annette Popel, Sept. 4, 1992; 1 child, Carlo. Laurea in Philosophy, U. Milan, 1983; Promotion in Philosophy, U. Saarland, Saarbrücken, 1988; Habilitation in Philosophy, U. Trier, 1995. Rsch. assoc. U. Saarland, 1984-85; fellow Deutscher akademischer Austauschdienst, 1985-97, Herzog August Bibliothek Wolfenbüttel, 1988-90, Alexander von Humboldt-Stiftung, 1990—98; h.s. tchr. Sch. Superintendency Lombardy, Milan, 1994-96; tchr. Cath. U. Am., Washington, 1996—2003, U. Verona, 2003—. Lectr. U. Trier, 1991—96. Author: Hagel: Introductio in Philosophiam, 1989, Kant und das Problem cinor Einloitung, 1989, El giro kantlano, Georg Friedrich Meiers Verhunftiehre, 2000; editor:

The Impact of Aristotellanism on Modern Philosophy, 2004, L'autore e i juol diritti, 2005, Aristotele nella società contemporanea, 2006; editor: (with Karl-Otto Apol) Zur Rekonstruktion der praktischen Philosophie, 1990; editor: (with Michael Oberhausen) Vorlesungsverzeichnisse der Universität Königsberg 1720-1804, 1999; editor: (with Michael Oberhausen and Heinrich P. Delfosse) Vernunftkritik und Aufklärung, 2001; editor: (with Heinrich P. Dolfosso and Clemens Schwaiger) Meier-Index: Vernunftleh, 2005; cons. editor: Longanesi Editore, 1988—89, Foltrinelli Editore, 1989—. Recipient 6th Study Tour of Japan, Japanese Ministry of Fgn. Affairs, 1984. Mem.: Soc. Filosofica Italiana (bd. dirs. 2005), Soc. Medieval and Renaissance Philosophy, Hegel Soc. N.Am., Italian Soc. Kant Studies, N.Am. Kant Soc., Alexander von Humboldt Assn. Italy (sec., bd. dirs. 2003—), Alexander von Humboldt Assn. Am. (bd. dirs. 2002—03), Am. Philos. Assn., Rotary Internat. (internat. dist. 2040 Milano Ovest sec. 2 2005—06). Roman Catholic. Avocation: contemporary literature. Office: via San Francesco 22 I-37129 Verona Italy Office Phone: +39/045/8028143. Business E-Mail: riccardo.pozzo@univr.it.

PRABHAKAR, KUMKUM, biology professor; naturalized, US, 1999; d. Dalip Singh and Meena Rani Cheema; m. Sunil Prabhakar, Mar. 1, 1979; children: Pankaj, Rahul. BSc with honors in Botany, U. Delhi, India, 1973, MSc in Botany, 1975, PhD in Botany, 1980. Rsch. assoc., dept. botany U. Delhi, 1981, sr. lectr. botany Maitreyi Coll., 1982—93; instr. biology Nassau C.C., Garden City, NY, 1995—2000, asst. prof. biology, 2000—05, assoc. prof. biology, 2005—. Overseas councillor, dept. botany The Botanica, Delhi, 1998—; advisor Kingsborough C.C., Bklyn., 2005—; chmn. gen. edn. natural sci. assessment com. Nassau C.C., 2001—; vis. prof. La Suerte Tropical Biology Sta.; cons. in field. Author: The Botany Notebook, Investigative Introductory Botany, 1st edit.; contbr. chapters to books, articles to profl. jours. Chmn. cmty. svc. com. Nassau C.C., 2005—06, presenter sr. ctrs. Spkrs. Bur., 1999. Recipient Excellence in Tchg. award, SUNY, Albany, 2002, Excellence award, Nat. Inst. Staff and Orgnl. Devel., 2007; grantee, NSF, 2005—. Mem.: NSTA (assoc.; presenter conf., San Diego 2002), ASCD (assoc.), Met. Assn. Coll. and U. Biologists (archivist 2000—), Bot. Soc. Am. (conf. presenter 2007), Nat. Assn. Biology Tchrs. (assoc.; Otto Burgdorf apprenticeship N.Y. chpt. 2001—03, nominee Biology Tchr. award 2006), Internat. Soc. Plant Morphologists (life; councillor 2005—), Women's Faculty Assn. at Nassau C.C. (pres. 2006—), Friends Hempstead Plains (sec. 1995—2005), Delta Kappa Gamma (assoc.; v.p. elect 2006—, Ruth and Williams scholarship 2006). Hindu. Avocations: yoga, cooking, gardening, travel. Office: Nassau Community College One Education Drive Garden City NY 11530 Home Phone: 516-378-6303; Office Phone: 516-572-8086. Business E-Mail: prabhak@ncc.edu.

PRABHU, KRISH ANANT, telecommunications industry executive, educator; b. Ankola, India, Aug. 2, 1954; came to U.S., 1975; s. Anant K. and Indira (Mahale) P.; m. Shuba George, June 14, 1980; 3 children. BSc with honors, Bangalore U., India, 1973; MSc, Indian Inst. Tech., Bombay, 1975; MSEE, U. Pitts., 1977, PhD, 1980. Mem. tech. staff Bell Labs., Holmdel, NJ, 1980-84; mem. tech. staff, also mgmt. positions Rockwell Internat., Richardson, Tex., 1984-92; v.p. R & D, Alcatel Network Systems, Richardson, 1992—95; pres. Alcatel Broadband Products, 1995—97; CEO Alcatel USA, Inc., 1997—99; COO Alcatel S.A., 1999—2001; venture ptnr. Morgenthaler Ventures, 2001—04; pres., CEO Tellabs, Inc., Naperville, Ill., 2004—. Adj. prof. U. Tex. at Dallas, Richardson, 1988—; mem. adv. coun. U. Tex., Arlington, 1992—. Contbr. articles to tech. jours. Mem. IEEE (sr.), NMA. Avocations: tennis, chess, reading. Office: Tellabs Inc One Tellabs Ctr 1415 W Diehl Rd Naperville IL 60563

PRABHU, VASANT M., corporate financial executive; Grad., Indian Inst. Tech., Bombay, India; MBA, U. Chgo. V.p., ptnr. N.Y. office Booz, Allen & Hamilton; with Pepsico Inc., U.S., Europe, Latin Am.; sr. v.p., CFO Pepsico Internat.; pres. info. and media group McGraw-Hill Cos., Inc., 1998—2000; exec. v.p., CFO Safeway Inc., 2000—03, Starwood Hotels & Resorts Worldwide Inc., 2003—. Office: Starwood Hotels & Resorts Worldwide Inc 1111 Westchester Ave White Plains NY 10604 *

PRABHU, VRUNDA P., mathematics professor; b. Bombay, Oct. 10, 1961; d. Sumati Prabhu; m. Shailesh Vengurlekar; 1 child, Sagar; 1 child, Natasha. BSc in Math. and Stats., U. Bombay, 1981, MSc in Math., 1983; PhD, U. Kans., Lawrence, 1993. Assoc. prof. William Woods U., Fulton, Mo., 1993—2002; assoc. prof. Bronx C.C. CUNY, NYC, 2002—. Active cmty. devel. tsunami affected regions, Tamil Nadu, India, 2005—06. Recipient award, War Trauma Found., 2005; grantee, NSF, 2002—06. Mem.: Am. Math. Soc. Achievements include design of FractionsGrid. Office: Bronx CC CUNY W181 University Ave Bronx NY 10453 Home Phone: 267-980-1650; Office Phone: 267-980-1650.

PRABHUDESAI, MUKUND M., pathology educator, health facility administrator, researcher, academic administrator; b. Lolyem, Goa, India, Mar. 17, 1942; came to U.S., 1967; s. Madhav R. and Kusum M. Prabhudesai; m. Sarita Mukund Usha, Feb. 1, 1972; 1 child, Nitin M. MB, BS (MD), G.S. Med., Bombay, 1967, postgrad., 1973-75. Diplomate Am. Bd. Pathology. Asst. pathologist Fordham Hosp., Bronx, NY, 1973-74, assoc. pathologist, 1974-76; assoc. dir. clin. pathology Lincoln Med., Bronx, 1976, dep. dir. pathology, 1977-79; chief pathology and lab. medicine svc., coord. R&D VA Med. Ctr., Danville, Ill., 1979—, dir. electron microscopy lab., 1987—. Senator U. Ill. Chgo.; co-investigator U. Ill. Coll. Medicine, Urbana-Champaign, clin. prof. pathology and internal medicine, 1982—. Contbr. articles to Am. Jour. Clin. Nutrition, Jour. AMA, Am. Jour. Clin. Pathology. Member Gifted Student Adv. Bd., Danville, 1984-86; v.p. Am. Cancer Soc. Vermilion County chpt., 1982, pres., 1986-88. VA rsch. grantee, 1980-82, 82-85, 83. Fellow Coll. Am. Pathology (inspector 1981-, Ill. state del. to C.A.P. Ho. Dels. 1992-, mem. reference com. 1993, chair, standard and integration com., 2000-); mem. AAAS, Am. Coll. Physician Execs., Ill. State Soc. Pathologists (bd. dirs. 1990-, chmn. membership com. 1990-). Achievements include development of cancer of bladder following portocarval shunting; research in adverse effects of alcohol on lung structure and metabolism; on effects of soy and bran on cholesterol, fish and coronary artery disease, endocrine response to soy protein, in induction and reversibility of atherosclerosis in trout, effects of ethanol on Vitamin A, lymphatics in atherosclerosis, iron in atherosclerosis, development of dermofluorometer for detection of P.V.D. Office: PO Box 3583 Placida FL 33946 Office Phone: 217-748-6272. E-mail: sarita@soltec.net, mdesaih@aol.com.

PRADA, MIUCCIA BIANCA, fashion designer; b. 1949; m. Patrizio Bertelli. PhD in Polit. sci.; student, mime performer, Teatro Piccolo, Milan, 1973—78. With family business Prada, Milan, 1978—. Introduced the following product lines to Prada: handbags, 1985, women's ready-to-wear, 1989, Miu Miu line, 1992, men's wear 1995; showed product line in NYC for the first time in 1994; opened boutique in London, 1994. Named one of Time Mag. 100 Most Influential People, 2005, the 30 Most Powerful Women in Europe, Wall St. Jour., 50 Women to Watch, 2005, Top 200 Collectors, ARTnews mag., 2005—06. Office: Prada SpA 2 Via Andrea Maffei 20154 Milan Italy Address: Prada ApA 30 Via Melzi D'Eril 20100 Milan Italy Office Phone: 02 54 67 01. *

PRADO, EDGAR, horse racing jockey; b. Lima, Peru, June 10, 1967; Horse racing jockey Breeder's Cup Series. Achievements include over 5,000 races won in career; winning Belmont Stakes, 2002, 2004; winning Kentucky Derby (riding Barbaro), 2006. Office: Breeders Cup PO Box 4230 Lexington KY 40544-4230

PRADO, EDWARD CHARLES, federal judge; b. San Antonio, June 7, 1947; s. Edward L. and Bertha (Cadena) P.; m. Maria Anita Jung, Nov. 10, 1973; 1 child, Edward C. AA, San Antonio Coll., 1967; BA, U. Tex., 1969, JD, 1972. Bar: Tex. 1972. Asst. dist. atty. Bexar County Dist. Atty.'s Office, San Antonio, 1972-76; asst. pub. defender US Pub. Defender's Office, San Antonio, 1976-80; judge US Dist. Ct. Tex., San Antonio, 1980; U.S. atty. US Dept. Justice, San Antonio, 1981—84; judge US Dist. Ct. (we. dist.) Tex., San Antonio, 1984—2003, US Ct. Appeals (5th cir.), San Antonio, 2003—. Served to capt. U.S. Army. Named Outstanding Young Lawyer of Bexar County, 1980. Mem. ABA, Tex. Bar Assn., San Antonio Bar Assn., San Antonio Young Lawyers Assn., Fed. Bar Assn. Republican. Roman Catholic. *

PRADOS, JOHN WILLIAM, retired engineering educator; b. Spring Hill, Tenn., Oct. 12, 1929; s. Gustave Olivier and Elizabeth Branham Prados; m. Ruth Lynn Baird, Sept. 2, 1951; children: Elizabeth Pauline Bowman, Laura Lynn, Anne Caroline Lynch. BS in Chem. engring., U. Miss., Oxford, Miss., 1947—51; PhD, U. Tenn., Knoxville, 1954—57, MS, 1953—54. Registered Profl. Engr., State Bd. of Archtl. and Engring. Examiners/Tenn., 1964. Asst. prof. chem. engring. U. Tenn., Knoxville, 1956—59, assoc. prof. chem. engring., 1959—64, prof. chem. engring., 1964—2001, assoc. dean engring., 1969—71, dean of admissions and records, 1971—73, acting chancellor, 1973—73, v.p. academic affairs, statewide sys., 1973—81, acting chancellor, martin campus Martin, 1979, v.p. academic affairs and rsch., statewide sys., 1981—88, v.p. emeritus, 1989—, univ. prof., 1989—2001, head, chem. engring. dept., 1990—93, univ. prof. emeritus, 2001. Cons. Nuc. Divsn., Union Carbide Corp., Oak Ridge, 1957—84, Martin Marietta Energy Sys., 1984—86; vice chmn. Engring. Accreditation Commn., Accreditation Bd. for Engring. and Tech., Inc., Baltimore, Md., 1981—84, chmn., 1984—85; commr. Commn. on Colleges, So. Assn. of Colleges and Schools, Decatur, Ga., 1986—92, exec. councillor, 1986—89; dir. Accreditation Bd. for Engring. and Tech., Inc., Baltimore, Md., 1988—93; sec. Accreditation Bd. for Engring. and Tech., Inc., Baltimore, Md., 1989—90, pres., 1991—92; trustee So. Assn. of Colleges and Schools, Decatur, Ga., 1995—98; editor, jour. of engring. edn. Am. Soc. for Engring. Edn., Washington, 1996—2001; trustee F. W. Olin Coll. of Engring., Needham, Mass., 2002—; sr. edn. assoc. NSF, Arlington, Va., 1994. First lt. USAF, 1951—53, Biloxi, Miss.; Albuquerque, N.Mex.; Limestone, Maine. Recipient L. E. Grinter Award for Contributions to Engring. Edn., Accreditation Bd. for Engring. and Tech., Inc., 1993, Alumni Outstanding Tchr., U. Tenn., 1967, Outstanding Engring. Alumnus, 1975, Faculty Macebearer, 1997—98, James T. Rogers Disting. Leadership award, So. Assn. Colls. and Schs., 2004. Fellow: Am. Inst. Chem. Engrs. (dir. 1975—77, treas. 1996—2001, Knoxville-Oak Ridge Chmn. Engr. of Yr. 1999, Knoxville-Oak Ridge Chem. Engr. of Yr. 1977), Am. Inst. of Chemists (life), Am. Soc. for Engring. Edn. (life Lifetime Achievement award 2007); mem.: Am. Chem. Soc., Tech. Soc. of Knoxville, Torch Club, Phi Kappa Phi (Disting. Mem. 1974), Tau Beta Pi (exec. coun. 1986—90), Sigma Xi, Sci. Rsch. Soc. (pres. 1983—84, treas. 1990—2002), Alpha Tau Omega. Roman Catholic. Home: 7021 Stagecoach Trail Knoxville TN 37909-1112 Office: 419 Dougherty Engineering Bldg 1512 Middle Dr Knoxville TN 37996-2200 Business E-Mail: jprados@utk.edu.

PRADZYNSKI, ANDRZEJ HENRYK, chemist; b. Plock, Poland, Jan. 1, 1924; arrived in U.S., 1969; s. Maurycy and Frania (Goldkind) Nejman; m. Halina Romana Bromberger, Apr. 1, 1946; children: Richard E. Neuman, Zgibniew Jacek. BS, U. Wroclaw, Poland, 1949, MS, 1951. Asst. prof. crystallography, chmn. dept. U. Wroclaw, 1948-51; sect. mgr. materials testing Inst. Aviation, Warsaw, Poland, 1951-57; adj. prof. Polish Acad. Scis., Warsaw, 1957-68; dept. dir. Atomic Energy Commn. Poland, Warsaw, 1959-68; rsch. assoc. IV nuclear reactor U. Tex., Austin, 1969-80; exec. v.p. Halinco Skin Care Products, Inc., Austin, 1980-2000. Cons. IAEA, Vienna, Austria, 1968-69. Author: Industrial Radiography (in Polish), 1957; also more than 30 articles in IAEA Conf. Procs., Nukleonika, ISA Trans., others. Mem. Am. Chem. Soc., N.Y. Acad. Scis. Achievements include patent for method and apparatus for collection and analysis of mercury in the atmosphere; developer method of photo-nuclear activation analysis of copper in ores and concentrates, synthetic standards for EDX-ray analysis, method of collection and analysis of mercury in air, method of nondestructive X-ray analysis of heavy metals in toys. Developed pre-concentration methods of trace elements in water for EDX-ray analysis.

PRAGER, DAVID ELLIS, lawyer; b. NYC, Apr. 29, 1954; s. Irwin Richard and Susan (Lasoff) P. BA summa cum laude, SUNY, Buffalo, 1981; JD, U. Penn., 1984. Bar: NY 1985, US Dist. Ct. (ea. dist.) NY 1988. Assoc. Poletti, Freidin, Prashker & Gartner, NYC, 1984, Kaye, Scholer, Fierman, Hays & Handler, NYC, 1985-91; ptnr. Phillips, Nizir, Benjamin, Krim & Ballon, LLP, NYC, 1991, Sills Cummis Epstein & Gross, Newark, Bond, Schoeneck & King, PLLC, NYC, 2007—. Contbr. articles to profl. jours. Bd. dirs. St. Bart's Players Theatrical Troupe, NYC, 1995—. Jewish. Avocations: acting, writing. Office: Bond Schoeneck & King PLLC 330 Madison Ave New York NY 10017-5001 Office Phone: 646-253-2330. Office Fax: 646-253-2301. Business E-Mail: dprager@bsk.com. *

PRAGER, KENNETH MICHAEL, pulmonologist, educator; b. Bklyn., Jan. 3, 1943; s. Max and Hilda Prager; m. Regene Eleanore Gronich, June 25, 1967; children: Karen Rachel Kramer, Joshua Harris, Tamar Anne, Benjamin Dov. BA, Columbia U., 1964; MD, Harvard U., 1968. Cert. ME in internal med. Am. Bd. Internal Med. Intern Columbia Presbyn. Med. Ctr., NYC, 1968—69, resident, 1971—72; chief med. resident Billings Hosp. U. of Chgo., 1972—73; from assoc. in medicine to clin. prof. Columbia Coll. of Physicians and Surgeons, NYC, 1973—99, clin. prof. of medicine, 1999—. Dir. of clin. ethics Columbia Presbyn. Med. Ctr., 1998—, chmn. of med. ethics com., 1994—. Co-author: Medical Ethics Issues in the Elderly, 2003; contbr. articles to profl. jours. and newspapers. Bd. dirs. Am. Coun. on Sci. and Health, NYC, 2001—; mem. Bd. of Health, Englewood, NJ, 1989—92; chmn. bd. dirs. Moriah Sch., Englewood, NJ, 1983—85. Asst. surgeon, acting med. dir. USPHS Indian Health Svc., 1969—71. Recipient Med. Housestaff Tchg. award, NY Presbyn. Hosp., Dept. Medicine, 1999—2000, Physician of Yr. award, Dept. Nursing, Columbia Presbyn. Med. Ctr., 2003, Alfred Markowitz Svc. award, NY Presbyn. Hosp., Soc. Practitioners, 2006, Leonard Tow Humanism in Medicine award, Columbia U. Coll. Physicians and Surgeons, 2006. Fellow: ACP; mem.: AMA, Am. soc. for bioethics and Humanities, Med. Soc. of the State of N.Y., Am. Coll. of Chest Physicians. Jewish. Home: 231 South Dwight Place Englewood NJ 07631 Office: Columbia Presbyterian Medical Center 161 Fort Washington Avenue New York NY 10032 Office Phone: 212-305-5535. Personal E-mail: kmp43@aol.com.

PRAGER, STEPHEN, chemistry professor; b. Darmstadt, Germany, July 20, 1928; came to U.S., 1941, naturalized, 1950; s. William and Gertrude Ann (Heyer) P.; m. Julianne Heller, June 7, 1948. B.Sc., Brown, 1947; PhD, Cornell, 1951. Mem. faculty U. Minn., Mpls., 1952—, assoc. prof. chemistry, 1956-62, prof., 1962-90, prof. emeritus, 1990—. Cons. Union Carbide Corp., Oak Ridge, 1954-74 Asso. editor: Jour. Phys. Chemistry, 1970-79. Fulbright scholar and Guggenheim fellow, 1958, 59; Fulbright lectr. and Guggenheim fellow, 1966-67 Mem.: Am. Phys. Soc., Am. Chem. Soc. Home: 3320 Dunlap St N Saint Paul MN 55112-3709 E-mail: psprager@cs.com.

PRAGER, SUSAN WESTERBERG, academic administrator, law educator; b. Sacramento, Dec. 14, 1942; d. Percy Foster Westerberg and Aileen M. (McKinley) P.; m. James Martin Prager, Dec. 14, 1973; children: McKinley Ann, Case Mahone. AB, Stanford U., 1964, MA, 1967; JD, UCLA, 1971. Bar: N.C. 1971, Calif. 1972. Atty. Powe, Porter & Alphin, Durham, NC, 1971-72; acting prof. law UCLA, 1972-77, prof. Sch. Law, 1977—, Arjay and Frances Fearing Miller prof. law, 1992-99, 2001—06, assoc. dean Sch. Law, 1979-82, dean, 1982-98; provost Dartmouth Coll., Hanover, NH, 1999—2001; pres. Occidental Coll., 2006—. Bd. dirs. Pacific Mut. Life Holding Co., Newport Beach, Calif. Editor-in-chief, UCLA Law Rev., 1970-71. Trustee Stanford U., 1976-80, 87-97. Mem. ABA (council of sect. on legal edn. and admissions to the bar 1983-85), Assn. Am. Law Schs. (pres. 1986), Order of Coif. Office: Occidental Coll / Office of Pres 3rd Fl, Coons Adminstn Bldg 1600 Campus Rd Los Angeles CA 90041-3314 E-mail: prager@law.ucla.edu. *

PRAHALAD, C.K., finance educator, corporate strategist; b. India; BS, U. Madras, 1960. Harvey C. Fruehauf prof. bus. adminstrn. & prof. corp. strategy and internat. bus. Stephen M. Ross Sch. Bus., U. Mich. Co-author: Competing for the Future, 1994, The Future of Competition: Co-Creating Unique Value with Customers, 2004, The Fortune at the Bottom of the Pyramid: Eradicating Poverty Through Profits, 2004; contbr. articles to profl. jours. Office: Stephen M Ross Sch Bus U Mich 701 Tappan St Ann Arbor MI 48109-1234 Office Phone: 734-763-5573. Office Fax: 734-936-8715. E-mail: ckp@umich.edu.

PRAHL, JOSEPH MARKEL, mechanical engineering educator; b. Beverly, Mass., Mar. 30, 1943; s. Frederick Adolph and Dorothy (Markel) P.; m. Rena Elizabeth Wadt, July 11, 1964 (div. June 1970); m. Lawanda McDuffie, July 15, 1977; children: Erika Elise, Meagan Michelle. BA, Harvard U., 1963, SM, PhD, Harvard U., 1968. Reg. profl. engr., Ohio. Asst. prof. Case Western Res. U., 1968-74, assoc. prof., 1974-85, prof., 1985—, chmn. dept. mech. and aerospace engring., 1992—. Payload specialist NASA-JSC, Houston, 1990-92. Contbr. articles to sci. jours. Recipient Abe Zarem Educator award, AIAA, 2006. Office: Dept Mech & Aerospace Engring Case Western Res U 10900 Euclid Ave Cleveland OH 44106-7222 Office Phone: 216-368-2941. E-mail: joseph.prahl@case.edu. *

PRAKAPAS, EUGENE JOSEPH, art gallery director; b. Lowell, Mass., July 29, 1932; s. Joseph S. Prakapas and Viola Schensnol; m. Dorothy A. Seitner, Dec. 1, 1971. BA, Yale U., 1953; MA, Oxford U., Balliol, 1959. Editor-in-chief, v.p. Trident Press and Pocket Books divsn. Simon & Schuster, Inc., NYC, 1960-70; co-dir. Carus Gallery, NYC, 1973-75; dir. Prakapas Gallery, NYC, 1976—. Vis. curator San Francisco Mus. Modern Art, 1986. Author: Bauhaus Photography, 1985. Lt. (s.g.) USNR, 1953-57. Fulbright fellow, 1957-59; Yale U. scholar, 1949-53. Mem. Art Dealers Assn. Am., Assn. Internat. Photography Art Dealers. Home Phone: 914-961-5091; Office Phone: 914-961-5091. Business E-Mail: eugeneprakapas@optonline.net.

PRAMMANASUDH, STACY, professional golfer; b. Enid, Okla., Sept. 23, 1979; m. Pete Upton, Jan. 24, 2004. Grad. in Exercise & Sports Sci., U. Tulsa, 2002. Mem. Futures Tour, 2002—03, LPGA, 2003—. Named a First-Team All-Am., 1999—2002; named Futures Tour Player of Yr., 2003; named an Acad. All-Am., 2000—02. Achievements include winning the 2005 Franklin American Mortgage Championship and the 2007 Fields Open in Hawaii on the LPGA Tour; winner, Frye Chevrolet Classic, 2003, and Lincoln Financial Futures Golf Classic, 2005, on the Futures Tour; winner, Stanford Pepsi Intercollegiate, 1999-2001. Avocations: yoga, gardening. Mailing: c/o LPGA 100 International Golf Dr Daytona Beach FL 32124-1092 *

PRANGE, ARTHUR JERGEN, JR., psychology and psychiatry professor, neuroscientist; b. Grand Rapids, Mich., Sept. 19, 1926; s. Arthur Jergen and Martha Frances (Elliott) P.; m. Sarah Elizabeth Bowen, Feb. 4, 1950; children— Christine Anne, Martha Louise, Laura Beth, David Elliott. BS, U. Mich., 1947, MD, 1950. Intern Wayne County Gen. Hosp., Eloise, Mich., 1950-51; resident in psychiatry U. NC, Chapel Hill, 1954-57, instr., 1957-60, asst. prof., 1960-64, asso. prof., 1964-68, prof. psychiatry, 1968-83, Boshamer prof. psychiatry, 1983—, acting chmn. dept. psychiatry, 1983-85, dir. NIMH Clin. Rsch. Ctr., 1979—. Vis. scientist Med. Rsch. Coun. Unit, Epson, Surrey, Eng., 1968-69; chmn. clin. projects rsch. rev. com. HEW, NIMH, 1975-76, chmn. bd. sci. counselors, 1986-87; mem. psychopharmacologic drugs adv. com. HEW, FDA, 1979-82. Editor: The Thyroid Axis, Drugs and Behavior, 74; Contbr. articles to med. jours. Recipient NIMH Career Devel. award 1961-69, Career Scientist award, 1969-95, Gold Medal award Soc. of Biol. Psychiatry, 1992, Exemplary Psychiatrist award Nat. Alliance for the Mentally Ill, 1997, Selo prize Nat. Alliance for Rsch. in Schizophrenia and Affective Disorders, 1997. Fellow Am. Psychiat. Assn. (life, Rsch. in Psychiatry award 1996), Am. Coll. Neuropsychopharmacology (life, pres. 1987, Hoch award 1995); mem. Internat. Soc. Psychoneuroendocrinology (founding mem.), NC Neuropsychiat. Assn., Collegium Internationale Neuropsychopharmacologicum, Royal Coll. Psychiatrists (London). Home: 6503 Meadowview Rd Hillsborough NC 27278-8314 Office: Univ NC Sch Medicine Dept Psychiatry Chapel Hill NC 27599-0001

PRANGE, HILMAR WALTER, neurology educator; b. Reichenbach, Germany, Aug. 4, 1944; s. Georg Friedrich Reinhold and Gertrud Wilhelmine (Mueller) P.; m. Carin Juliane Schroeter, Mar. 14, 1970; children: Klaus Richard, Juliane. MD, U. Rostock, Germany, 1969, lic. specialist neurology and psychiatry, 1974; Habilitation, Georg-August U., Goettingen, Germany, 1982. Medical diplomate. Med. resident Regional Hosp., Stralsund, Germany, 1969-71; med. asst. then psychiatrist Univ. Hosp., Rostock, 1971-75; asst. med. dir. Ev. Johannes Hosp., Bielefeld, Germany, 1975-76; head neurologic out-patient clinic Univ. Hosp., Goettingen, Germany, 1976-78, asst. med. dir. dept. neurology, 1979—87, dir. neurol. intensive care unit, 1987—. Mem. expert group German Ministry of Health. Author: Neurosyphilis, 1987, Infectious Diseases of the Central Nervous System, 1995; editor: CNS Barriers and Modern CSF Diagnostics, 1993, Systemic Infections Causing Bacterial CNS Diseases, 1997, Infectious Diseases of the Central Nervous System, 2001, Emergencies in Neurology, 2002, Neurological Intensive Medicine, 2004; contbr. articles to profl. jours. Grantee German Forschungsgemeinschaft, German Tech. Cooperation, German MS Soc. Mem.: EMEA, German Med. Assn. (mem. commn. drug security), European Neurol. Soc. Lutheran. Avocation: Cultural history, sports, jogging (marathons), swimming. Business E-Mail: hprange@gwdg.de.

PRANGE, ROY LEONARD, JR., lawyer; b. Chgo., Sept. 12, 1945; s. Roy Leonard and Marjorie Rose P.; m. Carol Lynn Poels, June 5, 1971; children: David, Ellen, Susan. BA, U. Iowa, 1967; MA, Ohio State U., 1968; JD, U. Wis.-Madison, 1975. Bar: Wis. 1975, U.S. Dist. Ct. (we. and ea. dists.) Wis. 1975, U.S. Ct. Appeals (7th cir.) 1978, U.S. Supreme Ct. 1978. Assoc. Ross & Stevens, S.C., Madison, Wis., 1975—79, ptnr., 1979—90, Quarles & Brady, LLP, Madison, 1990—. Lectr. bankruptcy, debtor-creditor rights, U. Wis., Madison, 1982—. Contbr. Wis. Lawyer's Desk Reference Manual, 1987, Comml. Litigation in Wis. Practice Handbook, 1995, West's Bankruptcy Exemption Manual, 1997—. 1st lt. U.S. Army, 1969-72. Fellow Am. Coll. Bankruptcy; mem. ABA, Wis. State Bar (dir. bankruptcy, insolvency, creditors rights sect. 1985-91, chair 1990-92, mem. continuing legal edn. com. 1990-95), Am. Bankruptcy Inst., Dickens Fellowship (v.p. 1980-84). Avocations: swimming, bicycling, scuba diving. Office: Quarles & Brady LLP PO Box 2113 33 E Main St Ste 900 Madison WI 53701-2113 Office Phone: 608-283-2485. Business E-Mail: rlp@quarles.com.

PRANSES, ANTHONY LOUIS, retired electric power industry executive; b. Claracq, France, May 3, 1920; s. Anthony Kasimer and Georgette (Pilon) F.; m. Margaret Louise Hamill, July 24, 1943; children— Anthony Randolph, Terry Jay, Renee Louise. Student, Sorbonne, Paris, France, 1937-39; BS in Metall. Engring, Carnegie Inst. Tech., 1942, grad. student, 1946-48. With Westinghouse Electric Corp., 1945-86, mgr. mfg. planning Lima, Ohio, 1954-57, plant mgr., 1958-59, mgr. mfg. services, 1959-72, mgr. mfg., 1972-80, cons., 1980-86. Joined Am. Youth Hostels, 1935, founder Pitts. council, 1947, pres. council, 1947-50, mem. nat. bd. dirs., 1954-72, Midwest regional v.p., 1957-59, nat. pres., 1959-62, pres. Lima council, 1962-75, 87-91, chmn. nat. bd. dirs., 1963-67. Served to capt., C.E. AUS, 1942- 45. Home: 6005 Poling Rd Lima OH 45807-9492 E-mail: pranses@wcoil.com.

PRASAD, AJAY KRISHNA, mechanical engineering educator; b. Shimoga, India, Sept. 2, 1961; s. Sira Gopal Krishna and Ramaa (Acharya) P.; m. Jyothi Ramprasad, July 1996. BTech, Indian Inst. Tech., 1983; MS, U. Miami, 1985; PhD, Stanford U., 1989. Asst. prof. U. Del., Newark, 1992-97, assoc. prof., 1997—. Contbr. articles to profl. jours. Avocations: reading, gardening, travel, woodworking. Home: 510 Briar Ln Newark DE 19711-3614 Office: Univ Del 120 Spencer Lab Newark DE 19716-3140

PRASAD, ANANDA SHIVA, medical educator; b. Buxar, Bihar, India, Jan. 1, 1928; came to U.S., 1952, naturalized, 1968. s. Radha Krishna and Mahesha (Kaur) Lall; m. Aryabala Ray, Jan. 6, 1952; children: Rita, Sheila, Ashok, Audrey. BSc, Patna Sci. Coll., India, 1946, MB, BChir, 1951; PhD, U. Minn., 1957; doctorate honoris causa, U. Claude Bernard of Lyon, 1999. Intern Patna Med. Coll. Hosp., 1951-52; resident St. Paul's Hosp., Dallas, 1952-53, U. Minn., 1953-56, VA Hosp., Mpls., 1956; instr. dept. medicine Univ. Hosp., U. Minn., Mpls., 1957-58; vis. assoc. prof. medicine Shiraz Med. Faculty, Nemazee Hosp., Shiraz, Iran, 1960; asst. prof. medicine and nutrition Vanderbilt U., 1961-63; mem. faculty, dir. div. hematology dept. medicine Wayne State U., Detroit, 1963-84, assoc. prof., 1964-68, prof., 1968-2000, dir. research dept. medicine, 1984-97, disting. prof., 2000—. Mem. staff Harper-Grace Hosp., VA Hosp., Allen Park, Mich.; mem. trace elements subcom. Food and Nutrition Bd., NRC-Nat. Acad. Scis., 1965-68; chmn. trace elements com. Internat. Union Nutritional Scis.; mem. Am. Bd. Nutrition; pres. Am. Coll. Nutrition, 1991-93. Author: Zinc Metabolism, 1966, Trace Elements in Human Health and Disease, 1976, Trace Elements and Iron in Human Metabolism, 1978, Zinc in Human Nutrition, 1979, Biochemistry of Zinc, 1993; editor: Clinical, Biochemical and Nutritional Aspects of Trace Elements, 1982, Am. Jour. Hematology, Jour. Trace Elements in Exptl. Medicine; editor: Zinc Metabolism, Current Aspects in Health and Disease, 1977; co-editor: Clinical Applications of Recent Advances in Zinc Metabolism, 1982, Zinc Deficiency in Human Subjects, 1983, Essential and Toxic Trace Elements in Human Health and Disease, 1988, Essential and Toxic Trace Elements in Human Health and Disease: An Update, 1993; Jour. Am. Coll. Nutrition; contbr. articles to profl. jours., also reviewer. Trustee Detroit Internat. Inst., Detroit Gen. Hosp. Rsch. Corp., 1969—72. Recipient Rsch. Recognition award Wayne State U., 1964, award Am. Coll. Nutrition, 1976, Disting. Faculty Fellowship award Wayne State U., 1986, Medal of Honor, City of Lyon, France, 1989, Pioneer in Sickle Cell Disease Rsch. award Nat. Heart Lung Blood Inst./NIH, 1997; Pfizer scholar, 1955-56, WCMS Spl. Recognition award for Profl. Ach., 1998, Klaus Schwartz medal Internat. Assn. Bioinorganic Scientists, 2001, Spl. Recognition award Am. Assn. Physicians India, 2001; inducted Heritage Hall Fame, Mich., 2003, Asian Acad. Hall Fame, 2007. Master ACP (Outstanding Rsch. Related to Medicine award 2007), Am. Coll. Nutrition; fellow AAAS, Am. Inst. Nutrition (trace elements panel), Internat. Soc. Hematology; mem. AMA (Goldberger award 1975), Internat. Soc. Trace Element Rsch. in Humans (pres. 1986-92, chmn. steering com. 1985-86, Raulin award 1989), Am. Soc. Clin. Nutrition (awards com. 1969-70), Am. Fedn. Clin. Rsch. (pres. Mich. 1969-70), Am. Physiol. Soc., Am. Soc. Clin. Investigation, Am. Soc. Hematology, Assn. Am. Physicians, European Acad. Scis., Arts and Humanities (corr.), Ctrl. Soc. Clin. Rsch., Soc. Exptl. Biology and Medicine (councillor Mich. 1967-71), Wayne State U. Acad. Scholars (pres.-elect 1997-98, pres. 1998-99), Wayne County Med. Soc., Internat. Soc. Internal Medicine, Am. Soc. Clin. Nutrition (Robert H. Herman award 1984), Nutrition Soc. India (Gopalan oration award 1988), Nat. Heart, Lung, Blood Inst. NIH (mem. coun. 2002-2004), Cosmos Club (Washington), Sigma Xi. Home: 4710 Cove Rd Orchard Lake MI 48323-3604 Office: Univ Health Ctr 5-C 4201 Saint Antoine St Detroit MI 48201-2153 Office Phone: 313-577-1597. Business E-Mail: prasada@karmanos.org.

PRASAD, NAVIN, ophthalmologist; MD, Darbhanga Med. Coll., India, 1990. Bd. Cert. Ophthalmology All India Inst. of Med. Scis., New Delhi, 1995, cert. U.S. Med. Lic. Exam Ednl. Commn. of Fgn. Med. Grads., 2004. Med. intern Darbhanga Med. Coll., Laheriasarai, India, 1990—91, sr. ho. officer, 1991—92; resident physician All India Inst. of Med. Scis., New Delhi, 1992—95, registrar, sr. resident, 1995—98; sr. ho. officer, ophthalmology James Cook U. Hosp., Middlesbrough, England, 2000—03; glaucoma fellow Mass. Eye & Ear Infirmary, Harvard Med. Sch., Boston, 2005—. Author: (internat. jour. article) Jour. of Cataract Refract Surgery, Eyenews, Eye, (poster in internat. conf.) Longterm intervisit intraocular pressure fluctuation following selective laser trabeculoplasty as primary therapy in open angle glaucoma. Perform cataract eye surgeries in eye camps Second Sight of UK, Bisalpur, India, 2002. Merit Scholarship, Govt. of India, 1981, 1983. Fellow: The Royal Coll. of Physicians and Surgeons of Glasgow (assoc.); mem.: The Assn. for Rsch. in Vision and Ophthalmology (assoc.), All India Ophthal. Soc. (life), Am. Acad. Ophthalmology (assoc.). Achievements include research in Study of corneal endothelial loss due to phacoemulsification in different types of anterior capsulotomies. Home Phone: 248-614-0025. Personal E-mail: india12@gmail.com.

PRASAD, NEIL A., telecommunications industry, computer company executive; arrived in US, 1988, naturalized, 2000; s. Ayilliyath and Annie Prasad; m. Caroline George, Dec. 27, 1992; children: Jake Joseph, Anya Joseph, Gino Joseph. BEE, Gujarat U., India, 1987; MSEE, U. Houston, 1991. Cert. profl. engr., Instn. Engrs., India, 1987, Nat. Soc. Profl. Engrs., Va., 1990, Tex. Soc. Profl. Engrs., 1991; in leadership excellence Toastmasters Internat., 2004. Software engr. Software Interfaces, Inc., Houston, 1991; sr. design engr. WilTel, Inc. Advanced Tech. Group, The Woodlands, Tex., 1991—95; sr. engr. MCI Telecom. Corp., Richardson, Tex., 1995—96; sr. mgr. Stratacom, Inc., San Jose, Calif., 1996, Cisco Sys., Inc., San Jose, Calif., 1996—; dir. IPDR.org, Nantucket, Mass., 2005—07; pres. CEO Abaeca Solutions, 2006—. Amb. ATM Forum, Mountain View, Calif., 1994—99; chmn., internet protocol network mgmt. group TeleManagement Forum, Morristown, NJ, 2000—06, dir., 2006—; divsn. gov. Toastmasters Internat., Mission Viejo, Calif., 2004—05; spkr., presenter in field. Contbr. articles to profl. jours. Vol. Cisco Emergency Response Team; coun. mem. Ascension Parish, San Jose, 2006—. Recipient Project Mgmt. and Tng. Excellence award, Wiltel Inc., 1995. Mem.: IEEE, Planetary Soc., Am. Physical Soc., Assn. Computing Mahinery, Instn. Engrs. (assoc.), Mensa, Toastmasters Internat. (named Disting. Toastmaster 2006, Humorous Speech Contest winner 2006). Roman Catholic. Achievements include development and industry demonstration of network management systems for data, voice, and video telecommunications services; leading strategic industry initiatives in the network management area; patents pending for innovations in network performance management. Avocations: marathon running, travel, literature, swimming, ice skating. Home: 822 Daffodil Way San Jose CA 95117 Office: Cisco Systems Inc 170 W Tasman Dr San Jose CA 95134 Home Phone: 408-307-0308; Office Phone: 408-525-7209. Personal E-mail: ap4411@yahoo.com.

PRASAD, PRIYA, engineer, researcher; Ford tech. fellow, mgr. safety rsch. dept. Ford Rsch. Lab., Dearborn, Mich. Recipient Henry Ford Award, First Recipient Nat. Award for Advancement of Motor Vehicle Rsch. and Devel. Mem.: NAE. Office: Ford Rsch Lab 2101 Village Rd Dearborn MI 48124

PRATER, EMMA LOU, retired academic administrator; b. Tyler, Tex., July 22, 1929; d. Roy Andrew and Alice Gay Wyatt; m. Kenneth L. Prater; children: Sherry S., Sandra C. AA, Tyler Jr. Coll., Tex., 1967; BS, Tex. A&M U., 1971, MS, 1982. With advt. sales and promotion Gen. Electric, Tyler, 1957—64; acct. Tyler (Tex.) Jr. Coll., 1964—77, dir. student activities, 1980—89; dir. acctg. Spring Ind. Sch. Dist., Houston, 1977—80; ret., 1989. Adv. Tex. State Govt. 600 Assn. Tex. Jr. Colls., 1989—2006; former pres. alumni bd. Nat. Jr. Coll. Cheerleader Assn., 1984; coach cheerleading Tyler Jr. Coll., 1969—89. Author: Cheerleading, 1984. Dir. adult 55+ Westwood Bapt. Ch. Recipient Black and Gold award, Tyler Jr. Coll., 1991. Mem.: Tyler Jr. Coll. Alumni Assn. Achievements include Emma Lou Prater Presdl. scholarship named in honor at Tyler Jr. Coll. Home: 509 Elmridge Tyler TX 75703 Business E-Mail: ret-epra@tjc.edu.

PRATER, MARK A., lawyer, accountant; b. 1959; BS with honors, Portland State Univ., 1981; JD, Willamette Univ., 1984; LLM, Univ. Fla., 1987. CPA Wash., 1986; bar: Oreg. 1984, Wash. 1984. Tax assoc. Touche Ross, Portland, Oreg., 1984—86; assoc. Dunn Carney Allen Higgins & Tongue, 1987—90; chief tax counsel Com. Fin., U.S. Senate, 1990—. Mem.: Oreg. Soc. CPA, Wash. Soc. CPA. Office: Committee on Finance Room 219 Senate Dirksen Office Building Washington DC 20510-6200

PRATER, MARY ANNE, special education educator, researcher; d. Herman Bates and Barbara M. Prater. MusB, U. Utah, Salt Lake City, 1975, MS, 1982; PhD, Utah State U., Logan, 1987. Asst. prof. So. Ill. U., Carbondale, 1987—90; prof., dept. chair, assoc. dean U. Hawaii at Manoa, Honolulu, 1990—2001; prof., dept. chair Brigham Young U., Provo, Utah, 2001—. Author: Developmental Disabilities in Children's Literature: Issues and Annotated Bibliography, 2000, Teaching Strategies for Students with Mild to Moderate Disabilities, 2007. Active Ch. of Jesus Christ of Latter-day Saints. Recipient Disting. Paper award, Hawaii Edn. Rsch. Assn., 1996, 2002, Spl. Recognition award, Devel. Disabilities Divsn. of the Coun. for Exceptional Children, 2000; Rsch. grantee, U.S. Dept. Edn., 1986—87, 2000—01, Pers. Preparation grantee, 1987—90, 2004—, Leadership Preparation grantee, 1996—2001, Post-Doctoral fellow, U. Ky., 1997. Mem.: ASCD, Coun. for Learning Disabilities, Am. Assn. Colls. Tchr. Edn., Coun. for Exceptional Children (various coms.). Office: Brigham Young University 340 MCKB Provo UT 84602 Home Phone: 801-377-1194.

PRATHER, DONNA LYNN, psychiatrist; b. Charlotte, NC, Nov. 4, 1946; d. James Boyd and Ann (Joyner) P. BA, Queens Coll., Charlotte, 1968; MD, U. N.C., 1978. Supr. Meckenburg County Dept. Social Svcs., Charlotte, 1971-74; family practice intern Charlotte Meml. Hosp., 1978-79, resident in family practice, 1979-81; fellow in family medicine U. N.C., Chapel Hill, 1981-82; resident in psychiatry N.C. Meml. Hosp., Chapel Hill, 1982-85; pvt. practice psychiatry Chapel Hill, NC, 1985—. Psychiatrist Person Counceling Ctr., Roxboro, N.C., 1983-92; med. dir. Orange-person-Chatam Mental Health Ctr., Chapel Hill, 1992—; clin. assoc. prof. U. N.C., Chapel Hill, 1985—. Mem. N.C. Psychiat. Assn., N.C. Med. Soc., Am. Psychiat. Assn., N.C. Psychiat. Assn. (chmn., com. for women 1990-91, ethics com. 1997-99). Avocation: music. Office: 200 N Greensboro St Ste D-7 Carrboro NC 27510 Office Phone: 919-929-6519.

PRATHER, GERALD LUTHER, management consultant, retired judge, military officer; b. LaGrange, Ga., Apr. 7, 1935; s. Luther Pate and Hazel Belle (McCullough) P.; m. Carolyn Pearson, Nov. 22, 1956; children: Dean Allen, Bryan Pate, Jeri Lynn, Angela BSE.E., Auburn U., 1966; MS in Mgmt., Air Force Inst. Tech., 1972; postgrad. advanced mgmt., U. Houston, 1978; grad., SQ Officer Sch., Maxwell AFB, 1963, ICAF, Washington, 1974, Ecumenical Ctr. Religion and Health, San Antonio, Tex., 2000. Enlisted USAF, 1954-56, commd. 2d lt., 1956, advanced through grades to maj. gen., 1981, various assignments as pilot, 1956-68, served in Vietnam, 1967-68, commdr. 1963d Comm. Squadron Chanute AFB, Ill., 1968-69, comdr. 1918th Comm. Squadron Scott AFB, Ill., 1969-70, dep. dir. comm.-electronics for 15th Air Force March AFB, Calif., 1970-72, chief comm. ops. div. hdqrs. Washington, 1972-75, comdr. strategic comm. div. Offutt AFB, Nebr., 1975-77, comdr. European Comm. Div. Ramstein AFB, W. Ger., 1977-80; dir. Command Control, Comm. & Computer Systems, Hdqrs. U.S. Readiness Command MacDill AFB, Fla., 1980-81; asst. chief of staff of Info. Systems Hdqrs. USAF, Washington, 1981-84, comdr. Air Force Comm. Command Scott AFB, Ill., 1984-86, ret., 1986; pvt. practice mgmt. cons. Del Rio, Tex., 1986-1997; Justice of the Peace Val Verde County, Tex., 1987-97. Lectr. in field; also air traffic controller, parachutist; bd. dir. Del Rio Internat. Airport. Speech writer Team America 1983 (Freedom Found. nat. award 1984). Scoutmaster Boy Scouts Am., Sacramento, 1963, chmn. com., 1964, cub master Auburn, Ala.; sponsor Explorer Troop, Boy Scouts Am., Scott AFB, Ill., 1969; chmn. Amistad Dist. Boy Scouts Am., 1988, Eagle Scout advancement, 1994—, Val Verde County United Way campaign, 1989, pres., bd. dirs., 1990; v.p. programs, exec. bd. BSA, 2005—; pastoral counselor St. James Ch., 2002, pastoral care specialist, 2002—; chaplain Val Verde Regional Hosp., 2002—, Juvenile Detention Ctr., 1998—. Decorated DSM with oak leaf cluster, Legion of Merit with one oak leaf cluster, DFC, Bronze Star with V device, Air medal with two oak leaf clusters, Republic of Vietnam Gallantry Cross with Palm; recipient Gen. Edwin W. Rawlings award Air Force Inst. Tech., 1972, Comdt.'s award, 1972, Order of the Sword, 1986, Silver Beaver award Boy Scouts Am., 2003, Eagle Scout award, 2006; Wilma E. West fellow Boy Scouts Am., 2005. Mem.: VFW (life), Del Rio C. of C. (v.p. 1989—90, bd. dir. 1990—99, v.p. 1991—92, pres. 1995—96, bd. dir. 1999—, life dir. 2005—), Air Force Assn. (Jimmy Doolittle award 1984), Telephone Pioneers of Am., Soc. Logistics Engrs., Justice of the Peace and Constables Assn., Soc. Am. Mil. Engrs., Air Traffic Control Assn., Armed Forces Comm.-Electronics Assn. (mem. com. 1981—82, chmn. ethics com. 1982—83, internat. v.p. 1982—84, assoc. dir. 1984—96, bd. dirs. 1999, Meritorious Gold medal 1976, 1983), Non-Commd. Officers Assn. (hon.), Air Force Sgts. Assn. (hon.), Army Airways Comm. Svc. Alumni Assn. (life; dir. 2000—, Life Achievement award 2003, Honor award 2003, Hall of Honor 2002, Life Achievement award 2003), Disabled Am. Vets. (life), Ret. Officers Assn. (life), Vietnam Vets. Am. (life), Del Rio Club, Lions (dir. 1989—94, v.p. 1994, Svc. award 1992—93, 2002—03, Helen Keller fellow 2004), Civitan, Am. Legion, Order of Daedalians (life). Avocations: singing, gardening, sketching, automotive mechanics, private pilot. Address: HC 1 Box 7 Del Rio TX 78840-9720 Office Phone: 830-774-4483.

PRATHER, JOHN GIDEON, lawyer; b. Somerset, Ky., Dec. 12, 1919; s. James Frederick and Josephine Linnwood (Collier) Prather; m. Marie Jeanette Moore, Oct. 1945; children: John G., Jerome Moore. BA, U. Ky., 1940, JD, 1947. Bar: Ky. 1947, U.S. Dist. Ct. (ea. dist.) Ky. 1950. Pros. atty., Somerset, 1950—63; commonwealth atty. 28th Jud. Dist., 1963—64; sole practice Somerset; sr. ptnr. Law Offices of John G. Prather, Somerset. Bd. dirs. First & Farmers Bank, Somerset. Served to lt. USN, 1942—46. Mem.: ABA (probate sect.), Def. Rsch. Inst., Ky. Bar Assn. (ethics com., com. on fees), Pulaski County Bar Assn., Odd Fellows, Shriners, Kiwanis. Democrat. Mem. Christian Ch. (Disciples Of Christ). Office: PO Box 616 Somerset KY 42502-0616 Office Phone: 606-679-1626.

PRATHER, KENNETH EARL, lawyer; b. Detroit, May 9, 1933; s. Earl and Agnes (Mesanko) P.; m. Shirley Armstrong, Dec. 26, 1955; children: Eric, Kimberly, Jon, Laura, Lisa; m. Jeanette M. Elder (dec. 2005), June 30, 1973; 1 child, Kenneth. PhB, U. Detroit, 1955, JD 1960. Bar: Mich. 1960. Assoc. Kenney, Radom, Rockwell & Kenney, Detroit, 1960-66; ptnr. Kenney, Kenney, Chapman & Prather, Detroit, 1966-76, Prather, Hilborn & Harrington, P.C., Detroit, 1982, Prather & Assocs., P.C., Detroit, 1982-2000; pvt. practice, Detroit, 1976-82, 82-2007; adj. prof. law U. Detroit. Fellow Am. Acad. Matrimonial Lawyers (bd. govs. 1988-89); mem. State Bar Mich. (chairperson family law sect. 1983-84), Detroit Athletic. Contbr. articles to legal jours. Home: 5 Stratford Pl Grosse Pointe MI 48230-1907 Office: 19838 Mack Ave Grosse Pointe Woods MI 48236 Office Phone: 313-884-5622. Personal E-mail: ken.prather@pratherfamilylaw.com.

PRATHER, LENORE LOVING, former state supreme court chief justice; b. West Point, Miss., Sept. 17, 1931; d. Byron Herald and Hattie Hearn (Morris) Loving; m. Robert Brooks Prather, May 30, 1957; children: Pamela, Valerie Jo, Malinda Wayne. BS, Miss. Univ. Women, 1953; JD, U. Miss., 1955; D (hon.), Miss. Univ. Women, 2003. Bar: Miss. 1955. Practice with B. H. Loving, West Point, 1955-60; sole practice, 1960-62, 65-71; assoc. practice, 1962-65; mcpl. judge City of West Point, 1965-71; chancery ct. judge 14th dist. State of Miss., Columbus, 1971-82, supreme ct. justice Jackson, 1982-92, presiding justice, 1993-97, chief justice, 1998-2001; interim pres. Miss. U. for Women, Columbus, Miss., 2001—02. V.p. Conf. Local Bar Assn., 1956-58; sec. Clay County Bar Assn., 1956-71 1st woman in Miss. to become chancery judge, 1971, and supreme ct. justice, 1982, and chief justice, 1998-2000; recipient Miss. Bar Found. Professionalism award, 2005; named Outstanding Miss. Woman, Pres.'s Commn. on Status of Women, 1986-87. Mem. Miss. State Bar Assn. (Jud. Excellence award 2000-01), DAR, Rotary, Pilot Club, Jr. Aux. Columbus Club. Episcopalian. Achievements include becoming the first female chancellor in Mississippi; the first female supreme court justice; the first female chief justice in Mississippi. Personal E-mail: lenorepr@bellsouth.com.

PRATHER, ROBERT CHARLES, SR., lawyer; b. Kansas City, Mo., Feb. 16, 1945; s. Charles William and Shirley Anne P.; m. Lana Jo Ball, Jan. 25, 1969; children: Robert Charles Jr., Lisa Michelle. BSc in Comm., U. Tex., 1967, JD, 1970; postgrad., U. Tasmania, Australia, 1968. Bar: Tex. 1971, U.S. Dist. Ct. (no. dist.) Tex. 1978, U.S. Ct. Appeals (5th and 11th cirs.) 1981, U.S. Supreme Ct. 1978. Staff atty., com. clk. Senator W.T. Moore State Affairs Com. Tex. State Senate, Austin, 1971; asst. dist. atty. Dallas, 1971-74; asst. atty. U.S. No. Dist. Tex., Dalls, 1974-80; econ. crime enforcement specialist U.S. Dept. Justice, Dallas, 1980-81; assoc. trial atty. Turner, Rodgers, Sailers, Jordan & Calloway, Dallas, 1981-83; ptnr., trial atty. Jordan, Dunlap, Prather & Harris LLP, Dallas, 1983—. Author: (with others) A Document Numbering System, 1981, Texas ADR Practice Guide West, 1995. Gen. counsel, bd. dirs. Childrens Cancer Fund Dallas, Inc., 1982-91; soccer coach YMCA, North Dallas C. of C., 1979-84. Recipient Spl. Achievement award U.S. Dept. Justice, Washington, 1976; Rotary Found. fellow, 1968. Mem. ABA, Dallas Bar Assn., Assn. Atty.-Mediators (pres. North Tex. chpt. 2003), Am. Arbitration Assn. (panel 1992—), Argyle Club (pres. Dallas), Park City Club (bd. dirs.), Rotary (parliamentarian, bd. dirs.), Phi Alpha Delta. Baptist. Office: Jordan Dunlap Prather & Harris LLP 8111 Preston Rd Ste 400 Dallas TX 75225-6373 Office Phone: 214-696-6060. Business E-Mail: prather@jdplegal.com.

PRATHER, SUSAN LYNN, public relations executive; b. Melrose Park, Ill. d. Horace Charles and Ruth Anna Paula (Backus) P.; divorced. BS, Ind. U., 1973, MS, 1975. Arts administr. Lyric Opera Chgo., 1975; jr. account exec. Morton H. Kaplan Assocs., Chgo., 1976-78, sr. account exec., 1978-81; account supr. Ketchum Pub. Relations, Chgo., 1981-83, v.p., 1983-87, v.p., group mgr., 1985-87; v.p., dir. pub. relations Cramer-Krasselt, Chgo., 1987-95, sr. v.p., dir. pub. rels., 1996—. Cons. Velamints, Foster Wheeler, Kellogg Co., Battle Creek, Mich., 1985—, Village of Rosemont, Ill., PrincCo Personal Comm., Sr. Friendlys, Anti-Cruelty Soc. Chgo., Ill. State Toll Hwy. Authority; founder, prin. pratherpr, 2003-. Singer various recitals; founder, dir. Chgo. Sports Hall of Fame, 1978-81. Mem. archives com. Chgo. Symphony Orch., 1986—, mem. long term planning com., 1987-89; mem. press advance team Papal Visit to Chgo., 1978; mem. White House Press Advance Team, Chgo., 1976-80. Mem. Pub. Rels. Soc. Am. (bd. dirs. Chgo. chpt. 1987—), Internat. Pub. Rels. Assn., Publicity Club (bd. dirs. 1986—, Merit award 1982, Golden Trumpet awards, Silver Trumpet awards), Bus. and Profl. Assn. Lutheran. Avocation: figure skating. Home: 155 N Harbor Dr Apt 2212 Chicago IL 60601-7321

PRATHER, WILLIAM C., III, lawyer, writer; b. Toledo, Ill., Feb. 20, 1921; s. Hollie Cartmill and Effie Fern (Deppen) P. *Grandfather, William C. Prather II, judge, States Attorney, hotelier and farmer in Cumberland County, Illinois, was direct descendant of John Prater, gentleman, Wiltshire 1492-1547.* BA, U. Ill., 1942, JD, 1947. Bar: Ill. 1947, U.S. Supreme Ct. 1978. Co-pres. student govt. U. Ill., 1942, asst. dean, 1942-43; atty. First Nat. Bank Chgo., 1947-51; asst. gen. counsel U.S. Savs. and Loan League, Chgo., 1951-59; gen. counsel U.S. League of Savs. Instns., Chgo., 1959-82, gen. counsel emeritus, 1982—; sole practice Cumberland County, Ill., 1981—. Sem. lectr. in law, banking. Editor: The Legal Bulletin, 1951-81, The Federal Guide, 1954-81; author: Savings Accounts, 8th edit., 1981; contbr. articles to publs. Lt. U.S. Armed Forces, 1943-45. Decorated Bronze Star. Mem. ABA, FBA, Internat. Bar Assn., Ill. Bar Assn., Chgo. Bar Assn., Union Internat. des Avocats, Nat. Lawyers Club Washington, Cosmos Club, Univ. Club Chgo., Kiwanis, Mattoon Golf and Country Club, Exeter and County Club (Eng.), Am. Club Riviera (France), Tennis Club de Beaulieu (France), Soc. Colonial Wars, St. Andrew's Soc., Am. Legion, Phi Delta Phi, Phi Gamma Delta, Phi Eta Sigma, Phi Alpha Chi.

PRATKANIS, ANTHONY RICHARD, social psychologist, educator; b. Portsmouth, Va., Apr. 2, 1957; s. Tony R. and Rosemarie (Gray) P. BS summa cum laude, Ea. Menonite Coll., 1979; MA, Ohio State U., 1981, PhD, 1984. Rsch. assoc. Ohio State U., Columbus, 1981-83; asst. prof. indsl. adminstrn. & psychology Carnegie Mellon, 1984—87; asst. prof., then assoc. prof. psychology U. Calif., Santa Cruz, 1987-95, prof., 1995—. Expert legal witness; reviewer acad. jours. Co-author: (with E. Aronson) The Age of Propaganda, 1992, (with D. Shadel) Weapons of Fraud, 2005; co-editor: (with A. Greenwald and S. Breckler) Attitude Structure and Function; contbr. articles to profl. papers, book chpts Postdoctor fellow Carnegie-Mellon U., Pitts., 1983-84; J.B. Smith scholar Ea. Mennonite Coll., Harristonburg, Va., 1975-79. Fellow APA, Soc. Personality and Social Psychology; mem. Midwestern Psychol. Assn., Soc. Exptl. Social Psychology. Democrat. Research includes attitudes, persuasion, social influence. Home: 166 Montclair Dr Santa Cruz CA 95060-1025 Office: U Calif Bd Psychology Santa Cruz CA 95064 Business E-Mail: peitho@cats.ucsc.edu.

PRATS, MICHAEL, petroleum engineer, educator; b. Tampa, Fla., Dec. 18, 1925; s. Miguel and Maria (Carbó) P.; m. Mary Blanche Flaherty, Apr. 7, 1951; children: Delicia Anne, Barbara Eileen, Teresa Kaye, Steven Michael. BS in Physics, U. Tex., 1949, MA in Physics, 1951. With Shell Devel. Co., Houston, 1950—, cons. rsch. engr., then sr. rsch. assoc., 1972-89; pres. Michael Prats & Assocs., Houston, 1989—. Cons. prof. petroleum engring. dept. Stanford U., 1997—99; adj. prof. dept. geosystems petroleum engring. U. Tex., Austin, 1991—2001; participant scientist exch. Royal/Dutch Shell Lab., Amsterdam, Netherlands, 1954, 55, Shell Internat. Petroleum, The Hague, Netherlands, 1981, Maraven, S.A., Caracas, Venezuela, 1981-83. Author: Thermal Recovery, 1982, Spanish transl., 1987; contbr. articles to profl. jours.; 23 patents in field. Served to staff sgt. USAAF, 1944-46, PTO. Recipient Disting. Svc. award Rep. Honduras, 1989, KAPITSA medal Acad. Natural Scis. (Moscow), 1995; named to

Internat. Hall of Fame, 1989. Mem.: NAE, AIME (hon.), Russian Acad. Nat. Scis. (fgn.), Acad. Engring. Armenia (fgn.), Assn. Petroleum Engrs. Mex., Can. Inst. Mining, Acad. Medicine, Engring. and Sci. of Tex., Mex. Nat. Acad. Engring. (corr.), Soc. Petroleum Engrs. (hon.; bd. dirs. 1976—79, sr. tech. editor 1987—90, Uren award 1974, Disting. Mem. award 1983, Enhanced Oil Recovery Pioneer 1986, Thermal Recovery Disting. Achievement award Thermal Ops. Symposium 1991, Anthony F. Lucas Gold medal 1993, Legend of Hydraulic Fracturing 2006), Pi Epsilon Tau (hon. diploma of honor 1986). Avocation: travel. Address: 2834 Bellefontaine St Houston TX 77025-1610 Personal E-mail: mikep@mprats.com.

PRATT, ALAN JOHN, business and marketing consultant; b. Eng., July 21, 1927; s. Alan Reginald and Ellen Gwendoline (Roff) P.; m. Asako Tsuneyoshi, May 1, 1961. BA in Engnrg., Watford Coll., 1948; MBA, Calif. We. U., 1974; PhD, DBA, 1976. Surveyor Air Registration Bd., Eng. and Hong Kong, 1957-63; pres. Eutectic of Japan, Tokyo, 1963-66; group v.p. Alexander Industries, 1966-69; dir. Far East Digital Equipment Corp., Japan, 1969—72; dir. for Japan Gen. Instrument Corp., 1972—75; exec. v.p. Klingelnberg Japan Ltd., Tokyo, 1975-79; mng. ptnr. Pratt and Assocs., Kailua-Kona, Hawaii, 1979—; pres. Astra-Pacific Internat., Inc., Kailua-Kona, 1978—87. Assoc. sr. cons. Adams-Boston Cons. Co., Tokyo, 1964-68; guest lectr. Japan-Am. Inst. Mgmt. Sci., Honolulu. pres. Kona Coffee Festival, 1984-86, Crime Stoppers West Hawaii, 1981-85, 92—, founder pres., 1992—; bd. dirs. Crime Stoppers Internat., chmn. conf., 1994, pres. 1997, 2001; pres. IQBiometrix Internat., Inc, 2000. Mem. Am. Mgmt. Assn., Inst. Quality Engrs., Soc. Mfg. Engrs., Am. C. of C. in Japan (chmn. programs com. 1972-74), Royal Aero Soc. Gt. Britain, Brit. Inst. Mgmt., Brit. Mgmt. Assn., Kona Coast C. of C. (chmn. programs and comms. com. 1980, pres. 1981-82, chmn. Japan-Asia-Australia tourist and trade rels. com. 1983-86), C. of C. of Hawaii (dir. 1981-83). Roman Catholic. Home and Office: PO Box 5186 Kailua Kona HI 96745-5186 E-mail: csipratt@aol.com.

PRATT, DANA JOSEPH, publishing consultant; b. Cambridge, Mass., Dec. 9, 1926; s. Carroll Cornelius and Marjory (Bates) P.; m. Therese Louis, July 14, 1957; children: Joseph Caldwell, Michael Louis, Benjamin Lyon B.Naval Sci., Tufts U., 1946, BA, 1948. Mgmt. trainee N.J. Bell Telephone Co., Newark, 1948-50; sales asst. Princeton U. Press, NJ, 1950-53; sales mgr. U. Ill. Press, Urbana, 1953-55; field cons. Franklin Book Programs, NYC, 1955-59; staff assoc. Am. Book Pubs. Council, NYC, 1959-62; exec. sec. Assn. Am. Univ. Presses, NYC, 1962-66; asst. dir. Yale U. Press, New Haven, 1966-78; dir. pub. Library of Congress, Washington, 1978-93. Co-founder Internat. Group Pub. Librs. Contbr. articles to profl. jours. Served as ensign USNR, comdg. officer PC 566, 1946-47 Recipient Award for Superior Svc. Libr. of Congress, 1993. Mem. Washington Book Pubs. (pres. 1984-85), Soc. for Scholarly Pub. (bd. dirs. 1982-86), Washington Map Soc., Washington Rare Book Group. Home and Office: The Towers 514E 4201 Cathedral Ave NW Washington DC 20016-4901 Office Phone: 202-237-1380. E-mail: danajpratt@msn.com.

PRATT, DAVID, lawyer; b. NYC, Mar. 25, 1964; BS magna cum laude in Acctg., SUNY, Albany, 1986; JD cum laude, Bklyn. Law Sch., 1991; LLM in Taxation, NYU, 1993. Bar: NY 1992, Fla. 1993, cert.: Fla. Bar Bd. Legal Specialization and Edn. (tax and wills and trusts and estates). CPA Arthur Andersen & Co., NYC; ptnr. Proskauer Rose, LLP, Boca Raton, Fla., 2005—. Adj. prof. U. Fla. Levin Coll. Law; faculty mem. Am. Law Inst.-ABA. Contbr. articles to profl. jours. Vice-chair bd. trustees Jewish Cmty. Found. of Jewish Fedn. of South Palm Beach County; mem. legal com. Jewish Nat. Fund; mem. exec. com. of profl. advs. Cmty. Found. Palm Beach and Martin Counties. Named one of Top 100 Attys., Worth mag., 2006. Fellow: Am. Coll. Trust and Estate Counsel; mem.: Boca Raton Estate Planning Coun., AICPA, NY State Bar Assn., Palm Beach County Bar Assn. Office: Proskauer Rose LLP 1 Boca Pl 2255 Glades Rd Ste 340 W Boca Raton FL 33431-7360 Office Phone: 561-995-4777. Office Fax: 561-241-7145. E-mail: dpratt@proskauer.com. *

PRATT, DONALD GEORGE, physician; b. Higgins, Tex., Oct. 19, 1946; s. George Horace and Esta Vici (Barker) P. BS in Biomed. Sci., West Tex. State U., 1970; MD, U. Tex., Galveston, 1974. Diplomate Am. Bd. Family Practice, Am. Bd. Radiology (Radiation Oncology). Intern Scott & White Meml. Hosp., Temple, Tex., 1974-75, resident in gen. surgery and pathology, 1975-77, physician, 1979-83; resident in family practice McLennan County Med. Edn. and Rsch. Found., Waco, Tex., 1977-79; physician Family Practice Assocs., El Paso, Tex., 1983; owner, pvt. contractor Minor Emergency Ctrs., Amarillo, Tex., 1983-85; resident in radiation therapy U. Tex., Galveston, 1985-88; ptnr. Cons. in Radiation Oncology, P.A., Amarillo, 1988—2003, pres., 1994—2003, Cons. in Radiation Oncology, 1994—2003; dir. dept. radiation oncology Harrington Cancer Ctr., Amarillo, 1994—2003, pres. staff, bd. dirs., 1995-99; prin. investigator Radiation Oncology Group, 1988-95; pres. of staff Harrington Cancer Ctr., 1995—99; ptnr. Cons. in Radiation Oncology, P.A., Amarillo, 1988—2003, pres., 1994—2003; cons. in radiation oncology, 1994—2003. Dir. Dept. Radiation Oncology Harrington Cancer Ctr., Amarillo, Tex., 1994—2003. Mem. AMA, Am. Soc. Therapeutic Radiology and Oncology, Tex. Med. Assn., Potter/Randall County Med. Soc., Tex. Radiol. Soc. Home: 261 S Timbercreek Dr Amarillo TX 79118-3751

PRATT, GEORGE CHENEY, law educator, retired judge; b. Corning, NY, May 22, 1928; s. George Wollage and Muriel (Cheney) Pratt; m. Carol June Hoffman, Aug. 16, 1952; children: George W., Lise M., Marcia Pratt Burke, William T. BA, Yale U., 1950, JD, 1953. Bar: N.Y. 1953, U.S. Supreme Ct. 1964, U.S. Ct. Appeals 1974. Law clk. to Charles W. Froessel (Judge of N.Y. Ct. Appeals), 1953—55; assoc. then ptnr. Sprague & Stern, Mineola, NY, 1956—60; ptnr. Andromidas, Pratt & Pitcher, Mineola, 1960—65, Pratt, Caemmerer & Cleary, Mineola, 1965—75; partner Farrell, Fritz, Pratt, Caemmerer & Cleary, 1975—76; judge U.S. Dist. Ct. (Ea. Dist. of N.Y.), 1976—82, U.S. Cir. Ct. Appeals for 2d cir. (Uniondale), NY, 1982—93; sr. circ. judge U.S. Cir. of Appeals for 2d Cir., NY, 1993—95; counsel Parnon & Pratt L.L.P., NYC, 1995—2000, Farrell Fritz PC, 2001—. Prof. Touro Law Sch., Huntington, NY, 1993—2003. Fellow: Coll. Comml. Arbitrators; mem.: ABA, Reins. and Ins. Arbitration Soc., Nassau County Bar Assn., N.Y. State Bar Assn. United Ch. Of Christ. Office: Farrell Fritz PC 1320 Reckson Plz Uniondale NY 11556 Office Phone: 516-227-0604. Business E-Mail: gpratt@farrellfritz.com.

PRATT, HARRY DAVIS, retired entomologist; b. North Adams, Mass., Apr. 13, 1915; s. Harry Edward and Ethel Mae (Davis) P.; m. Caroline Georgine Kreiss, Apr. 13, 1944 (dec. May 1951); children: Harry Davis Jr., Katherine Maria Pratt Garrison, George Kreiss; m. Dora Belle Ford, Nov. 29, 1952 (dec. July 1998). BS, Mass. State Coll., 1936, MS, 1938; PhD, U. Minn., St. Paul, 1941. Registered profl. entomologist. Asst. entomologist USPHS Malaria Control War Areas, San Juan, 1942-46; chief med. entomol. lab. USPHS Communicable Disease Ctr., Atlanta, 1946-53, chief insect rodent tr., 1953-63, chief Aedes aegypti control tng., 1964-68; chief insect rodent control tng. Environ. Control Agcy., Atlanta, 1968-72; cons., tchr., writer Atlanta, 1972—. Spl. cons. Econ. Coop. Administrn., Saigon, Vietnam, 1950, WHO, Geneva, 1966, Kuala Lumpur, Malaysia, 1969. Fellow Entomol. Soc. Am. (life); mem. Am. Mosquito Control Assn. (pres. 1967), Entol. Soc. Washington, Ga. Entomol. Soc. Mem. Christian Ch. (Disciples Of Christ). Home: 104 So Almond Dr Simpsonville SC 29681 Office Phone: 864-228-4941.

PRATT, JOHN PATRICK, lawyer; b. Managua, Nicaragua, Nov. 19, 1967; s. Alfred Sidney Pratt and Thelma Reyes; 1 child, Patrick Alexander. BA in Philosophy, Fla. State U., 1994; JD, Tulane U., 1997. Bar: Fla. 1998, D.C. 1999, U.S. Dist. Ct. (so. dist.) Fla. 1998, U.S. Ct. Appeals (11th cir.) 1998, U.S. Supreme Ct. 2001, U.S. Ct. Appeals (9th cir.) 2002, cert.: Fla. Bar (immigration and nationality law). Law clk. Office of Dist. Counsel IRS, St. Paul, 1995; law clk. Office of Asst. Chief Counsel U.S. Customs Svc., New Orleans, 1996-97; assoc. Zyne, Saleeby & Saleh, P.A., Miami, 1997-98, Montiel Davis & Woodward Kimber, P.A., Miami, 1998-2000, Leaf & Assocs., P.A., Miami, 2000-01, Kurzban, Kurzban, Weinger & Tetzeli, P.A., 2001—. Cons. Beacon Coun., Miami. Mem. ABA, Am. Immigration Lawyers Assn., Hispanic Nat. Bar Assn. Roman Catholic. Avocations: reading, tennis. Office: Kurzban Kurzban Weinger & Tetzeli PA 2650 SW 27 Ave Ste 200 Miami FL 33133 Office Phone: 305-444-0060. Personal E-mail: jpatrickpratt@aol.com. Business E-Mail: jpratt@kkwtlaw.com.

PRATT, JON, not-for-profit executive; JD, Antioch Sch. Law; MPA, Harvard U. Atty., lobbyist Minn. Pub. Interest Rsch. Group; regional dir. Youth Project; dir. Philanthropy Project; founder, exec. dir. Minn. Coun. Nonprofits, Saint Paul, 1987—. Adv. com. mem. Nat. Ctr. for Charitable Statistics, Johns Hopkins U. State of Sector Project. Contbg. editor Nonprofit Quarterly; contbr. articles to profl. jours. Mem.: Nat. Coun. Nonprofit Assns. (co-chair Pub. Policy Com.). Office: Minn Coun Nonprofits 2314 University Ave W #20 Saint Paul MN 55114 Office Phone: 651-642-1904. Office Fax: 651-642-1517.

PRATT, MURRAY LESTER, manufacturing executive; b. Mt. Holly, NJ, Mar. 11, 1956; 8. John N. and Mildred E. P.; m. Sharon Louise Busby, Aug. 13, 1988; children: Kevin Harrison, Brian Gavel, Melissa Anne, Heather Marie. BS in Indsl. Engring., Northwestern U., 1976; MS in Computer Sci., Ill. Inst. Tech., 1983. Sys. analyst Gen. Foods USA, Chgo., 1981—84, sys. specialist, 1984—87, mgr. computer integrated mfg., 1987—91; mgr. KF logistics sys. Kraft Foods, Northfield, Ill., 1991—99, mgr. supply chain optimization, 1999—2001, program mgr. collaborative planning, forecasting and replenishment and vendor mng. inventory, 2001—06, assoc. dir. customer supply chain integration, 2006—, assoc. dir. radio frequency identification, 2006—. Presbyterian. Avocations: current affairs, tennis, volleyball, hiking. Home: 2508 Violet Blvd Glenview IL 60026 Office: Kraft Foods Three Lakes Dr Northfield IL 60093-2753 Office Phone: 847-646-6779. Business E-Mail: mpratt@kraft.com.

PRATT, ROBERT CRANFORD, political scientist, educator; b. Montreal, Que., Can., Oct. 8, 1926; s. Robert Goodwin and Henrietta (Freeman) P.; m. Renate Hecht, July 15, 1956; children: Gerhard, Marcus, Anna. BA, McGill U., Montreal, 1947; postgrad., Inst. Science Politique, Paris, 1948; MPhil, Oxford U., Eng., 1952. Lectr. McGill U., 1952-54, 56-58, Makerere U., Uganda, 1954-56; rsch. officer Oxford Inst. Commonwealth Studies, 1958-60; prin. Univ. Coll., Dar-es-Salaam, Tanzania, 1961-65; chmn. internat. studies program U. Toronto, Ont., Can., 1966-71, prof. polit. sci., 1966—. Spl. asst. to pres., Tanzania, 1965, 69; rsch. fellow Internat. Devel. Rsch. Ctr., 1978; commonwealth vis. prof. U. London, 1979-80; dir. Rsch. Project on Western Mid. Powers and Global Poverty, 1985-89; vis. fellow Devel. Ctr. Orgn. for Econ. Cooperation and Devel., Paris, 1986-87. Author: (with Anthony Low) Buganda and British Overrule, 1960, The Critical Phase in Tanzania, Nyerere and the Emergence of a Socialist Strategy, 1976, Towards Socialism in Tanzania, 1979, (with Robert Matthews) Human Rights in Canadian Foreign Policy, 1988, Internationalism Under Strain: The North-South Policies of Canada, The Netherlands, Norway and Sweden, 1989; (with Roger Hutchinson) Christian Faith and Economic Justice: A Canadian Perspective, 1989); Middle Power Internationalism: The North-South Dimension, 1990, Canadian International Development Assistance Policies: An Appraisal, 1994, 2nd edit., 1996. Decorated officer Order of Can.; recipient Killam award Can. Coun., 1968, Ludwik and Estelle Jus Meml. Human Rights award, 1995; Rhodes scholar Oxford U., 1950. Fellow Royal Soc. Can.; mem. Can. Polit. Sci. Assn., Can. African Studies Assn. (past pres.), Can. Assn. for Study of Internat. Devel. (mem. exec. coun.), Ecumenical Forum Can. (past chmn.). New Democrat. Home: 205 Cottingham St Toronto ON Canada M4V 1C4 Business E-Mail: cranford.pratt@sympatico.ca.

PRATT, ROBERT WINDSOR, lawyer; b. Findlay, Ohio, Mar. 6, 1950; s. John Windsor and Isabelle (Vance) P.; m. Catherine Camak Baker, Sept. 3, 1977; children: Andrew Windsor, David Camak, James Robert. AB, Wittenberg U., Springfield, Ohio, 1972; JD, Yale U., 1975. Bar: Ill. 1975, U.S. Dist. Ct. (no. dist.) Ill. 1976, U.S. Dist. Ct. (we. dist.) Mich. 1995, U.S. Ct. Appeals (fed. cir.) 1984, U.S. Ct. Appeals (7th cir.) 1996, U.S. Ct. Appeals (D.C. cir.) 2004. Assoc. Keck, Mahin & Cate, Chgo., 1975—81, ptnr., 1981—97; pvt. practice Wilmette, Ill., 1998—99; sr. asst. atty. gen. Office Ill. Atty. Gen., 1999—2001, chief antitrust bur., 2001—. Bd. dirs. Chgo. region ARC, 1985-96, vice chmn., 1988-92, chmn., 1992-96, bd. dirs. Mid-Am. chpt., 1992-96. Mem. ABA, Yale Club (Chgo.). Office Phone: 312-814-3722. Business E-Mail: rpratt@atg.state.il.us.

PRATT, WILLIAM, lawyer; BA magna cum laude, Tulane U., 1974; JD with honors, Columbia U., 1977. Bar: Ill. 1977, NY 1990. Named one of Am. Leading Bus. Lawyers Litig./Gen. Cmml., Chambers USA, 2004—05. Fellow: Am. Coll. Trial Lawyers; mem.: Bd. Visitors Columbia Sch. Law, Phi Beta Kappa. Office: Kirkland & Ellis LLP Citigroup Ctr 153 E 53rd St New York NY 10022-4611 Office Phone: 212-446-4862. Office Fax: 212-446-4900. Business E-Mail: wpratt@kirkland.com.

PRATT, WILLIAM CROUCH, JR., literature and language professor, writer; b. Shawnee, Okla., Oct. 5, 1927; s. William Crouch and Irene (Johnston) P.; m. Anne Cullen Rich, Oct. 2, 1954; children: Catherine Cullen, William Stuart, Randall Johnston. BA, U. Okla., 1949; MA, Vanderbilt U., 1951, PhD, 1957. Rotary Internat. fellow U. Glasgow, Scotland, 1951-52; instr. English Vanderbilt U., 1955-57, Miami U., Oxford, Ohio, 1957-59, asst. prof., 1959-64, assoc. prof., dir. freshman English, 1964-68, prof., 1968—98; prof. emeritus Mami U., 1998—. Fulbright-Hays lectr. Am. lit., prof. Am. lit. Univ. Coll., Dublin, Ireland, 1975-76; resident scholar Miami U. European Ctr., Luxembourg, fall 1976; lectr. Yeats Internat. Summer Sch., Sligo, Ireland, 1979, 81, 82, 83, James Joyce Summer Sch., Dublin, 1996; writer-in-residence Tyrone Guthrie Ctr., County Monaghan, Ireland, summer 1992, 96; lectr. in mod. lit., Retirement Learning at Vanderbilt, Nashville, fall 2004, 05, 06, 07. Author: The Imagist Poem, 1963, rev. edit., 2001, The Fugitive Poets, 1965, rev. edit., 1991, The College Writer, 1969, College Days at Old Miami, 1984, The Influence of French Symbolism on Modern American Poetry, 1985, Miami Poets, 1988, Homage to Imagism, 1992, The Big Ballad Jamboree, 1996, Singing the Chaos: Madness and Wisdom in Modern Poetry, 1996, Miami University: A Personal History, 1998, Ezra Pound, Nature and Myth, 2002, Ezra Pound and the Making of Modernism, 2007, Ezra Pound, Language and Persona, 2007; contbr. essays, translations, poems, revs. to lit. jours., books. Served to lt. USNR, 1953-55. Mem.: Internat. Contemporary Lit. and Theatre Soc., Ezra Pound Internat. Conf. (sec. 1991—2005), Omicron Delta Kappa, Sigma Alpha Epsilon, Phi Beta Kappa. Republican. Home: 212 Oakhill Dr Oxford OH 45056-2710 Personal E-mail: wmcpratt@aol.com. *True happiness is to live in the understanding of what we love, the pursuit of what we believe in.*

PRATTE, GEOFFREY LYNN, lawyer, arbitrator; b. Bonne Terre, Mo., Sept. 14, 1940; s. Charles John and Ruth Jane (Thornton) P.; m. Gretchen Ann Westendorf, Mar. 15, 1969; children: Stephen Charles, Geoffrey Marc, Nicole Elizabeth, Gregory Lynn, Robert Wendell. BA in Philosophy, Kilroe Coll., 1963; MA in French, St. Louis U., 1967; JD, Wash. U., 1974. Bar: Mo. 1974, U.S. Dist. Ct. (ea. dist.) Mo. Tchr. Divine Heart Sem., Donaldson, Ind., 1963-65; analyst CIA, McLean, Va., 1967-71; assoc. Roberts & Roberts, Farmington, Mo., 1974-87; pvt. practice Farmington, Mo., 1987—; asst. pros. atty. St. Francois County, Farmington, Mo., 1987-93; city pros. atty. Bonne Terre, Mo., 1988—2003. Labor arbitrator Fed. Mediation and Conciliation Svc., Washington, 1988—. Bd. dirs. Terre du Lac Property Owners Assn., 1976-87. Mem.: KC, Order of the Coif. Roman Catholic. Avocations: jogging, gardening. Office: 205 E Liberty St Farmington MO 63640-3129 Office Phone: 573-756-8082.

PRATTE, ROBERT JOHN, lawyer; b. Victoria, BC, Can., Feb. 14, 1948; s. Arthur Louis Jr. and Marie Bertha (Latremouille) P.; children: Merie Elise, Jessica Louise, Allison Adele, Chelsea Nicole. BA, Northwestern U., 1970; JD, Tulane U., 1976. Bar: Minn. 1976, Ariz. 1997. Ptnr. Best & Flanagan, Mpls., 1976-84, Briggs & Morgan, Mpls., 1985—, head mortgage banking group. Editor: Mortgage Lending in Minnesota—A Desktop Reference Guide, 1990. Ex-officio mem. Wilderness Inquiry, Minn.; pres. Twin Cities Northwestern U. Alumni Assn., 1978; active Wayzata Cmty. Ch., Mpls. With US Coast Guard, 1971—73. Fellow Am. Coll. Mortgage Attys. (regent); mem. ABA, Minn. State Bar Assn., Hennepin County Bar Assn., Mortgage Bankers Assn. (mem. Legal Issues and Regulatory Compliance Com.) Avocations: fly fishing, wine collecting, cooking. Home: 19900 Manor Rd Excelsior MN 55331-9256 Office: Briggs & Morgan 80 S 8th St #2200 Minneapolis MN 55402-2157 Office Phone: 612-977-8537. Business E-Mail: rpratte@briggs.com. *Undertake with enthusiasm and pursue to completion the tasks that others are unwilling or unable to do. Never be satisfied with mediocrity. Surround yourself with those who are smarter than you; have the patience and judgement to let them succeed. Success can be measured by the hours you spend with your children--reading, fishing, and playing.*

PRATTER, MELVIN RICHARD, medical educator; MD, SUNY Buffalo Sch. Medicine, 1973. Cert. pulmonary and critical care Am. Bd. Internal Medicine, 1979. Prof. medicine Robert Wood Johnson Sch. Medicine, Camden, NJ. Achievements include research in etiology and treatment of cough and shortness of breath. Office: Cooper Health Sys Ste 312 3 Cooper Plz Camden NJ 08103 Home Phone: 610-359-1159; Office Phone: 856-342-2406. Office Fax: 856-541-3968. Business E-Mail: pratter-melvin@cooperhealth.edu.

PRATTIS, SUSAN MARIE, veterinarian, educator; BA, Amherst Coll.; VMD, U. Pa., 1985; PhD, NC State U., 1992; cert. in info. tech., Bay Path Coll., Longmeadow, Mass., 1994. Diplomate Am. Coll. Lab. Animal Medicine, lic. veterinarian Mass., Pa., NY. Instr. comparative medicine U. Chgo., 1992—94; clin. vet. Northwestern U., Chgo., 1994—95; adj., clin. asst. prof. Sch. Vet. Medicine Tufts U., North Medford, Mass., 1995—96; assoc. dir., lab. animal medicine Mass. Gen. Hosp., Boston, 1995—96; asst. prof. health Hampshire Coll., Amherst, Mass., 1997—2001; asst. prof. neurosci., honors prof. Yeshiva U., NYC, 2001—04; asst. prof. biology, honors prof. Adelphi U., Garden City, NY, 2004—. Cons. Spelman Coll.; owner Small Wonders Animal Healthcare, Easthampton, NY. Mem.: AAAS, Fed. Am. Soc. for Exptl. Biology, Am. Vet. Med. Assn. Home: 27 Hisgen Ave Easthampton MA 01027

PRATT-JOHNSON, YVONNE KAREN, education professor; b. Bklyn., Feb. 20, 1954; d. Cyril and Jennie Pratt; m. Raphael Nathaniel Johnson, Feb. 15, 1949; children: Jonathan Leslie Johnson, Michael Raphael Johnson. BA, Stony Brook U., NY, 1975; MS, Georgetown U., Washington, DC, 1977; MA, Columbia U., NYC, 1978, MEd, 1980, Ed.D, 1986. Prof. Borough of Manhattan CC of CUNY, NYC, 1978—2003; prof. edn. St. John's U., Queens, NY, 2003—. Tchr. trainer Hunter Coll. the CUNY, NYC, 1991—94. Recipient Excellence Award for Tchg. and Rsch., Nat. Inst. for Staff and Orgnl. Devel. Excellence; grantee The Rockefeller Fellow Award, Rockefeller Rsch. Found. Mem.: ASCD, Internat. Assn. Tchrs. English as a Fgn. Lang., Am. Ednl. Rsch. Assn. Avocation: travel. Home: 90 La Salle St 12F New York NY 10027 Office: St John's Univ 8000 Utopia Pky Jamaica NY 11439 Home Phone: 212-222-6769. Home Fax: 212-222-1823. Personal E-mail: yypj15@aol.com. E-mail: prattjoy@stjohns.edu.

PRAUSNITZ, JOHN MICHAEL, chemical engineer, educator; b. Berlin, Jan. 7, 1928; arrived in U.S., 1937, naturalized, 1944; s. Paul Georg and Susi Prausnitz; m. Susan Prausnitz, June 10, 1956; children: Stephanie, Mark Robert. B Chem. Engring., Cornell U., 1950; MS, U. Rochester, 1951; PhD, Princeton, 1955; Dr. Ing., U. L'Aquila, 1983, Tech. U. Berlin, 1989, U. Padova, 2004; DSc, Princeton U., 1995. Mem. faculty U. Calif., Berkeley, 1955—, prof. chem. engring., 1963—. Cons. to cyrogenic, polymer, petroleum and petrochem. industries; Miller rsch. prof., 1966, 78; sr. investigator Lawrence Berkeley Nat. Lab., Berkeley; Wilhelm lectr. Princeton U., 1980; W.K. Lewis lectr. MIT, 1993; Edward Mason lectr. Brown U., 1999; Danckwerts lectr. Royal Acad. Engring., London, 2000; hon. prof. Tech. U. Shanghai, 2001; Dodge lectr. Yale U., 2004. Author: (with others) Computer Calculations for Multicomponent Vapor-Liquid Equilibria, 1967, (Computer Calculations for High-Pressure Vapor-Liquid Equilibria, 1968, Molecular Thermodynamics of Fluid-Phase Equilibria, 1969, 2d edit., 1986, 3d edit., 1999, Regular and Related Solutions, 1970, Properties of Gases and Liquids, 3d edit., 1977, 4th edit., 1987, 5th edit., 2000, Computer Calculations for Multicomponent Vapor-Liquid and Liquid-Liquid Equilibria, 1980; contbr. to profl. jours. Recipient Alexander von Humboldt Sr. Scientist award, 1976, Carl von Linde Gold Meml. medal, German Inst. for Cryogenics, 1987, Solvay prize, Solvay Found. for Chem. Scis., 1990, Corcoran award, Am. Soc. for Engring. Edn., 1991, 1999, D.L. Katz award, Gas Processors Assn., 1992, Waterman award, Tech. U. Delft, 1998, Rossini award, Internat. Union of Pure and Applied Chemistry, 2002, Nat. medal of Sci., 2005; Guggenheim fellow, 1962, 1973, fellow, Inst. Advanced Study, Berlin, 1985, Christensen fellow, St. Catherine's Coll. Oxford U., 1994, Erskine fellow, U. Canterbury, Christchurch, New Zealand, 1996. Mem.: NAS, NAE, AIChE (Colburn award 1962, Walker award 1967, Inst. Lectr. award 1994), Am. Acad. Arts and Scis., Am. Chem. Soc. (E.V. Murphee award 1979, Petroleum Chemistry Rsch. award 1995). Office: U Calif 308 Gilman Hl Berkeley CA 94720-1462 Office Phone: 510-642-3592. Business E-Mail: prausnit@cchem.berkeley.edu.

PRAVEL, BERNARR ROE, lawyer; b. Feb. 10, 1924; BSChemE, Rice U., 1947; JD, George Washington U., 1951. Bar: D.C. 1951, Tex. 1951, U.S. Supreme Ct. 1951. Ptnr. Pravel, Hewitt firm, 1956—99; sr. counsel Akin, Gump, Houston, 1999—2002; ret., 2006. Patent editor George Washington U. Law Rev., 1950. Precinct chmn. Houston Rep. Com., 1972-74. Served to lt. (j.g.) USNR. Fellow Am. Bar Found., Tex. Bar Found.; mem. ABA (chair intellectual property sect. 1991-92), Tex. Bar Assn. (chmn. patent, trademark sect. 1968-69, bd. dirs. 1976-79, Outstanding Contbn. 1982), Nat. Coun. Patent Law (chmn. 1970-71), Am. Intellectual Property Law Assn. (pres. 1983-84), Houston Intellectual Property Law Assn. (pres. 1983-84, Outstanding Svc. award 1986), Order of Coif, Kiwanis, Tau Beta Pi. Home: 10806 Oak Hollow St Houston TX 77024-3017 Personal E-mail: bpravel@sbcglobal.net.

PRAY, LLOYD CHARLES, geologist, educator; b. Chgo., June 25, 1919; s. Allan Theron and Helen (Palmer) P.; m. Carrel Myers, Sept. 14, 1946; children: Lawrence Myers, John Allan, Kenneth Palmer, Douglas Carrel. BA magna cum laude, Carleton Coll., 1941; MS, Calif. Inst. Tech., 1943, PhD (NRC fellow 1946-49), 1952. Geologist Magnolia Petroleum Co., summer 1942, U.S. Geol. Survey, 1943-44; hydrographic officer USN, 1944-46; Geologist U.S. Geol. Survey, 1946-56 part time; instr. to assoc. prof. geology Calif. Inst. Tech., 1949-56; sr. research geologist Denver Research Ctr., Marathon Oil Co., 1956-62, research assoc., 1962-68; prof. geology U. Wis., Madison, 1968-88; emeritus prof. geology, 1989—. Short course vis. prof. U. Tex., Austin, 1964, U. Colo., 1967, U. Miami, 1971, U.

Alta., 1969, Colo. Sch. Mines, 1985; vis. scientist Imperial Coll. Sci. and Tech., London, 1977, U. Calif. Santa Cruz, 1987, Nat. Park Svc. Geology panel, 1993. Author articles sedimentary carbonates, the Permian Reef complex, stratigraphy and structural geology So. N.M. and W. Tex., porosity of carbonate facies, Calif. rare earth mineral deposits. Pres. Colo. Diabetes Assn., 1963-67, v.p., 1968; mem. adv. panel earth scis. NSF, 1973-76. Served as hydrographic officer USNR, 1944-46. Named Layman of Year Am. Diabetes Assn., 1968; recipient Disting. Teaching award U. Wis. Madison, 1988, Disting. Achievement citation Carleton Coll., 1991, Wallace Pratt Resources Stewardship award Guadalupe Mountains Nat. Pk., 1998. Fellow Geol. Soc. Am. (rsch. grants com. 1965-67, com. on nominations 1973, com.Penrose medal 1979-81); mem. Am. Assn. Petroleum Geologists (rsch. com. 1958-61, lectr. continuing edn. program 1966-69, continuing edn. com. 1978-80, Levorsen award 1966, Matson trophy 1967, Disting. lectr. 1986-87, 87-88, Disting. Educator award 1998), Soc. Sedimentary Geologists (hon. life mem. Permian Basin sect. 1977, hon. mem. internat. soc. 1982, sec.-treas. 1961-63, v.p. 1966-67, pres. 1969-70, Twenhofel award 1999), Am. Geol. Inst. (edn. com. 1966-68, ho. bd. dels. 1970-72), West Tex. Geol. Soc. (Disting. Svc. award 2005, Pioneer award 2006), Phi Beta Kappa. Office: Univ Wis Dept Geology Madison WI 53706

PRAY, RALPH EMERSON, metallurgical engineer; b. Troy, NY, May 12, 1926; s. George Emerson and Jansje Cornelius (Owejan) P.; m. Beverley Margaret Ramsey, May 10, 1959; children: Maxwell, Ross, Leslie, Marlene. Student, N.Mex. Inst. Mining & Tech., Socorro, 1953-56, U. N.Mex., Albuquerque, 1956; BS, U. Alaska, 1961; DSc, Colo. Sch. Mines, Golden, 1966. Electrician, miner, 1944—47; chief party, field courtographer planning survey dept. N.Mex State Hwy., 1949—50; engr.-in-charge Dept. Mines and Minerals, Ketchikan, Alaska, 1957-61; asst. mgr. mfg. rsch. Universal Atlas Cement div. U.S. Steel Corp., Gary, Ind., 1965-66; rsch. metallurgist Inland Steel Co., Hammond, Ind., 1966-67; owner, dir. Mineral Rsch. Lab., Monrovia, Calif., 1968—. Pres., Keystone Canyon Mining Co., Inc., Pasadena, Calif., 1972-79, U.S. Western Mines, 1973—, Silveroil Rsch. Inc., 1980-85, v.p. Mineral Drill Inc., 1981-90; pres., CEO Copper de Mex. S.A. de C.V.; prime contractor def. logistics agy. U.S. Dept. def., 1989-92; designer Vanavara Electrolytic Gold Refinery, Krasnoyarsk, Russia, 1995; owner Precision Plastics, 1973-82; bd. dirs. Bagdad-Chase Inc., 1972-75; ptnr. Mineral R&D Co., 1981-86; lectr. Purdue U., Hammond, Ind., 1966-67, Nat. Mining Seminar, Barstow (Calif.) Coll., 1969-70; guest lectr. Calif. State Poly. U., 1977-81, Western Placer Mining Conf., Reno, Nev., 1983, Dredging and Miner Conf., Reno, 1985, others; v.p. dir. Wilbur Foote Plastics, Pasadena, 1968-72; strategic minerals del. People to People, Rep. South Africa, 1983; expert witness, cons. Bur. Land Mgmt., U.S. Dept. of Interior, 2000-2002; hist. cons. gold mining History TV Channel, 1999; guest spkr. Greater L.A. County Svc. Clubs, 1980-81; workshop condr. King Abdullaziz U., Jeddah, Saudi Arabia, 2002; v.p., tech. dir. U.S. Mining and Minerals Corp., 2006. Author: Jingu, The Hidden Princess, 2002; guest editor Calif. Mining Jour., 1978—; contbr. articles to profl. jours.; contbr. author Bre-x Gold Today, Gone Tomorrow, 1997. Vol. Monrovia Police Dept.; city coord. Neighborhood Watch., 1990-99, Citizen Patrol, 1997-99. With U.S. Army, 1950-52. Recipient Disting. Svc. medal Monrovia Police Dept., 1998. Fellow Geol. Mining and Metall. Soc. India (life), Am. Inst. Chemists, South African Inst. Mining and Metallurgy; mem. Soc. Mining Engrs., Am. Chem. Soc., Am. Inst. Mining, Metall. and Petroleum Engrs., NSPE, Can. Inst. Mining and Metallurgy, Geol. Soc. South Africa, Soc. Mineral Analysts, Sigma Xi, Sigma Mu. Achievements include research on recovery of metals from refractory ores, benefication plant design, construction and operation, underground and surface mine development and operation, mine and process plant management; syndication of natural resource assets with finance sources; freelance fiction and nonfiction writer; patents for chemical processing and steel manufacture; measurement of residual mercury in ancient and modern mine wastes of Chile. Office: 805 S Shamrock Ave Monrovia CA 91016-3651 Office Phone: 626-357-6511.

PRAY, RALPH MARBLE, III, lawyer; b. San Diego, June 7, 1938; s. Ralph Marble, Jr. and Doris (Thomson) Pray; m. Karen L. Pray (div. May 1988); children: Matthew Thomson, Kristen Leigh; m. Sandra Anne Shaw, June 7, 1988. BS, U. Redlands, 1960; JD, U. Calif., San Francisco, 1967. Bar: Calif. 1967, US Dist. Ct. (so. dist.) Calif. 1968, US Supreme Ct. 1972, US Dist. Ct. (ea. dist.) Calif. 1985, US Dist. Ct. (ctrl. dist.) Calif. 1989, US Dist. Ct. (no. dist.) Calif. 1992. Assoc. Gray, Cary, Ware & Friedenrich and predecessor, San Diego, 1967-73, ptnr., 1973—; mem. mgmt. com. Gary, Cary, Ames & Frye, San Diego, 1975-80. Arbiter Superior Ct., San Diego, 1984—. Lt. USN, 1960—64. Mem.: NRA, SAR, ABA, Am. Arbitration Soc. (arbiter), Calif. Bar Assn., Thurston Soc., San Diego Zool. Soc., Ducks Unltd., Club of Coronado, Rotary, Order of Coif. Republican. Episcopalian. Home: 535 C Ave Coronado CA 92118-1824 Office: DLA Piper US LLP 4365 Exec Dr Ste 1100 San Diego CA 92121-2133 Office Phone: 858-638-6890.

PRAYSON, MICHAEL J., orthopedic surgeon, medical educator, director; b. Cleve. s. Richard A., Sr. and Karen A. Prayson; m. Elizabeth A. Eaton; children: Elise, Michelle, Eric. BS, Kent State U., Ohio, 1989; MD, Northeastern Ohio Univs. Coll. Medicine, Rootstown, 1989. Bd. Cert. in Orthopaedic Surgery Am. Bd. Orthopaedic Surgery, 1997. Orthopedic trauma fellow U. Pitts. Med. Ctr., 1994—95, asst. prof. orthopedic surgery, 1999—2004, U. Mo., Kansas City, Mo., 1995—98; asst. prof. orthopedic surgery, neoucom Akron Gen. Med. Ctr., 1998—99; assoc. prof. orthopedic surgery, dir. orthopedic trauma Wright State U. and Miami Valley Hosp., Dayton, 2004—. Orthopedic trauma dir. Miami Valley Hosp., Dayton, 2004—. Mem., chmn. bylaws com. Pa. Trauma Sys. Found., Harrisburg, 2000—03; mem. Wright State Physicians, Inc., Dayton, 2004—06. Fellow: Am. Acad. Orthopedic Surgery; mem.: Dayton Orthopedic Soc., Ohio Orthopedic Soc., Orthopedic Trauma Assn., Alpha Omega Alpha Honor Med. Soc. (life), Ohio Orthopedic Soc., Dayton Orthopedic Soc., Orthopedic Trauma Assn. Roman Catholic. Avocations: sports, outdoor activities, travel. Office: Dept Orthopedic Surgery 30 E Apple St Dayton OH 45409 Office Phone: 937-208-2741.

PREBLE, LAURENCE GEORGE, lawyer; b. Denver, Apr. 24, 1939; s. George Enos and Ruth (Jewett) Preble; m. Deborah Joan Horton, Aug. 24, 1963; children: Robin Lee, Randall Laurence. B in Petroleum Refining Engring., Colo. Sch. Mines, 1961; JD cum laude, Loyola U., Los Angeles, 1968. Bar: Calif. 1969, D.C. 1983, N.Y. 1987, U.S. Dist. Ct. (cen. dist.) Calif. 1969. Assoc. firm O'Melveny & Myers, Los Angeles, 1968-76, ptnr. LA, 1976—2000; dir. devel. KUD Internat. LLC, 2001—. Adj. prof. law Southwestern U., 1970-75, Loyola U. of L.A. Sch. Law, 1984-92, 99-2000, Fordham U. Sch. Law, 1992-98, Calif. Continuing Edn. of the Bar; lectr., author Practicing Law Inst. Trustee Harvey Mudd Coll., 1991-94, Citizens Bidget Commn. N.Y.C., 1994-98, Ho. Ear Inst., 1998—, vice-chmn., 2001—. Recipient Disting. Achievement medal, Colo. Sch. Mines, 1998. Mem. Los Angeles County Bar Assn. (chmn. real property sect. 1979-80, Outstanding Leadership award 1999), Assn. Bar City of N.Y. (real property sect. exec. com. 1993-96), N.Y. State Bar Assn. (exec. com. real property sect. 1996—), Calif. Bar Assn. (mem. exec. com. real property sect.), ABA, Am. Coll. Real Estate Lawyers (bd. govs. 1986—), Anglo-Am. Real Property Inst., La Canada-Flintridge C. of C. (pres. 1974-75), Loyola Law Sch. Alumni Assn. (pres. 1978). Office: KUD Internat LLC STE 950 100 Wilshire Blvd Santa Monica CA 90401-1145

PREBLE, ROBERT CURTIS, JR., insurance executive; b. Oak Park, Ill., Dec. 19, 1922; s. Robert Curtis and Dorothy (Seidel) P.; m. Lidia Blazik, May 29, 1963. BA, Amherst Coll., Mass., 1947; MBA, Harvard U., Cambridge, Mass., 1949, postgrad., 1971. CLU, Chartered Fin. Cons. Pvt. to 1st lt. US Army, 1943—46; 33d divsn. capt. Nat. Guard, Ill., 1950—53; asst. to gen. supt., asst. buyer Carson Pirie Scott & Co., Chgo., 1949—52; with sales dept. Northwestern Mut. Life Ins. Co., Chgo., 1952—53, Nat. Life Ins. Co., Chgo., 1953—59; prin. Preble Assocs., Chgo., 1959—; pres., treas. Savs. Plans Inc., Chgo., 1980—. Cons. Iowa Savs. & Loan League, 1959-82; consul of Colombia, 1981-86, Bolivia, 1965-70; bd. dirs., chmn. fin. com. Guardsman Life Ins. Co., 1962-74; chmn. exec. com. World Book Life Ins. Co., 1974-83; gov.'s adv. bd. Ill. Dept. Ins., 1965-70; dir. Scandia Savs. & Loan Assn., 1968-83, Chgo. Coun. on Fgn. Rels., 1971-77, Chgo. Estate Planning Coun., 1977-80. Dept. regional chmn. Dem. Nat. Fin. Com., 1952; bd. dirs. Sr. Ctrs. Met. Chgo., 1974—77, McCormick Theol. Sem., 1977—83; deacon 4th Presbyn. Ch. of Chgo., 1967—70. Recipient Svc. award, Chgo. coun. Boy Scouts Am.f, 1962; record holder, Ill. Masters Swimming, 2003. Mem. Soc. Fin. Svc. Profls. (past pres. Chgo. chpt., Huebner scholar 1991, Grauer award 1998), Million Dollar Roundtable (life), Nat. Assn. of Insurance and Fin. Advisors, Assn. for Advanced Life Underwriting (founding pres. 1957), Harvard Bus. Sch. Assn. (alumni coun. 1977-82), Harvard Alumni Assn. (dir. 1980-82), Inst. Internat. Edn. (midwest adv. bd., 1979-99), Found. Study Cycles (internat. adv. bd.), Soc. Colonial Wars (coun.), Mil. Order World Wars, Univ. Club (Lifetime Achievement award 2004), Chgo. Club, Harvard Bus. Sch. Club (past pres.), Amherst Club (past pres.), Oak Park Country Club, Spanish Wells Country Club, Chi Psi (past chmn. ednl. trust, pres. 1992-95, Svc. award 1986). Home: 4208 Fleet Landing Blvd Atlantic Beach FL 32233

PRECIADO, PAMELA, artist; b. Evanston, Ill., Aug. 30, 1944; d. John James and Lena Day (Stevenson) Wills; m. Harold Prediado, June 1969 (div. July 1984). Student, U. Kans., U. Ill., San Francisco Acad. Fine Art, Am. Acad. Art Chgo., Art Inst. Chg. Comml. portrait artist. Year of the Woman, Dem. and Rep. women of 104th Congress, Black Caucus of 104th Congress, portrait montage Dem. women running for office State of Ill., 1994, exhibitions include Wells Fargo Bank, San Francisco, Godfrey Gallery, Mark Hopkins Hotel, Joseph Alioto Gallery, Macy's Dept. Store, San Francisco, Represented in permanent collections Booth Fisheries of Consol. Foods Corp., DeKalb AgResearch Corp. Mem.: NAFE, LWV, Portrait Soc. Am., Am. Soc. Portrait Artists, Chgo. Artists Coalition, Palette and Chisel Acad. Fine Art. Democrat. Avocations: travel, teaching art, tennis. Studio: Fine Art and Portraiture 1838 N Hudson Ave Chicago IL 60614 Office Phone: 312-664-2506. E-mail: vince188@juno.com.

PRECKEL, PAUL VEITCH, agricultural economics educator, researcher; b. Cumberland, Md., 1954; s. Ralph Frederick and Margaret Preckel. BS in Math. Scis., Ohio State U., 1977; MS in Ops. Rsch., Stanford U., 1979, PhD in Ops. Rsch., 1983. Asst. prof. agrl. econs. Purdue U., West Lafayette, Ind., 1983-89, assoc. prof., 1989—94, prof., 1999—. Cons. Electric Power Rsch. Inst., Palo Alto, Calif., 1980-83, Control Analysis Corp., Palo Alto, 1980-81, Hudson Inst., Hudson-on-Croton, N.Y., 1982, World Bank, 2003-06. Contbr. articles and abstracts to profl. jours. Grad. engring. fellow Stanford U., 1977. Mem. Am. Agrl. Econs. Assn. (assoc. editor Jour. 1991-93, editor 2007—), Math. Programming Soc. Avocations: scuba diving, bicycling. Office: Purdue U 639 Krannert West Lafayette IN 47907

PREDDY, RAYMOND RANDALL, retired newspaper publisher, educator; b. Texarkana, Ark., Feb. 1, 1940; s. Raymond Watson and Dorothy Belle (Long) P.; m. Sarah Elizabeth Mitchell, Nov. 20, 1965; children: Lewis, Tiffany. BS, Northwestern U., 1961, MS in Journalism, 1962. Copy editor Louisville Courier-Jour., 1965-69; with Dayton (Ohio) Daily News, 1969-74, asst. city editor, 1971, met. editor, 1971-74; systems mgr. Dayton Newspapers, Inc., 1974-76; bus. mgr. Waco (Tex.) Tribune-Herald, 1976-77, asst. pub., 1977-78; pub. Waco Tribune-Herald, 1978-96. Part time journalism instr. Baylor U., Waco. Pres. Waco United Way, 1986, Waco Found., 1984-86, Waco Symphony Assn., 1985-86; moderator Grace Presbytery, 2005. Served with USN, 1962-65; capt. Res. (ret.) Named Tex. Newspaper Leader of 1994; recipient Pat Taggart award from Tex. Daily Newspaper Assn. Mem.: Rotary. Presbyterian. Personal E-mail: rrpreddy@aol.com.

PREDOCK, ANTOINE SAMUEL, architect, educator; b. Lebanon, Mo., June 24, 1936; s. Antoine Samuel and Ruth (Mayfield) P.; children: Hadrian, Jason. Student, U. N.Mex., 1957-61; BArch, Columbia U., NYC, 1962. Registered arch., N.Mex., Ariz., Calif., Nev., Wyo. Prin. Antoine Predock Arch. P.C., Albuquerque, 1967—; Kea Disting. prof. U. Md., 1981-82; lectr., exhibitor Centre Georges Pompidou, Paris, 1981; vis. prof. Ariz. State U., Tempe, 1982—; honor awards juror Nat. AIA awards, 1987; design critic in architecture Harvard U., fall 1987. Prin. works include Pima Cmty. Coll. Learning Ctr., Green Valley, Ariz. (Am. Architecture award, 2005), US Fed. Courthouse, El Paso, Tex. (GSA Design award, 2004), Shadow House, Santa Fe (Tucker Archtl. award, 2004, AIA/N.Mex. Honor award, 2004), Robert Hoag Rawlings Pub. Libr. (AIA Western Mountain Region Honor award, 2004), Spencer Theater for Performing Arts, Austin City Hall, Tex., Flint RiverQuarium, San Diego Padres Ballpark. Recipient numerous awards including Gran Premio, Bienal Internacional, Buenos Aires, 1989, 31st Progressive Architecture Competition citation, 1984, 85; Am. Acad. in Rome fellow, 1984-85. Fellow AIA (Gold Medal 2006). Home and Office: Antoine Predock Arch PC 300 12th St NW Albuquerque NM 87102-1818 Office Phone: 505-843-7390. Office Fax: 505-243-6254. *

PREECE, JENNIFER J., dean, information scientist, educator; BSc, U. Ulster, 1971; grad., Chelsea Coll., U. London, 1971; PhD, Open U., 1985. Tchr. Faraday Comprehensive Sch., England; head HS sci. The Study, Wimbledon, England, 1974; rschr., developer Computers in the Curriculum Project Chelsea Coll., U. London, England, 1975; lectr. biology and computing Barnfield Coll., England, 1977; course mgr. Open U., Milton Keynes, England, 1979—81, asst. prof. computer based edn., 1981—85, assoc. prof. computing, 1985—90, sr. assoc. prof., 1990, grad. tutor human-computer interaction, 1991—92; prof. info. sys. and human-computer interaction, dir. Ctr. for People and Sys. Interactions South Bank U., 1994—97; prof., chair Info. Sys. Dept. U. Md., Balt., 1997—2002, prof., 2002—05; prof., dean Coll. Info. Studies, U. Md., College Park, 2005—. Spkr. in field; vis. prof. U. Guelph, Ont., Canada, 1993—94, Ont., Canada, 1995; vis. scholar Va. Commonwealth U., Richmond, 1993—94; vis. prof. Waikato U., New Zealand, 2003. Co-author: Human-Computer Interaction: Selected Readings: A Reader, 1990, A Guide to Usability: Human Factors in Computing, 1993, Interaction Design: Beyond Human-Computer Interaction, 2007; author: Online Communities: Designing Usability and Supporting Sociability, 2000; contbr. articles to profl. jours. Grantee Erskine Fellowship, 2003. Office: Coll Info Studies Rm 4105 Hornbake Libr Bldg, S Wing U Md College Park College Park MD 20742-4345 Office Phone: 301-405-2036. E-mail: preece@umd.edu. *

PREECE, LYNN SYLVIA, lawyer; b. Birmingham, Eng., June 13, 1955; d. Norman and Sylvia Florence (James) Preece. LLB, Leeds U., Eng., 1976; postgrad., Washington U., St. Louis, 1978-79; JD, Loyola U., 1981. Bar: Ill., 1981. Assoc. Barnes Richardson, Chgo., 1980-86; from assoc. to ptnr. Burditt & Radzius, Chgo., 1986-88; ptnr. Katten Muchin & Zavis, Chgo., 1988-96, Baker & McKenzie, Chgo., 1996—. Adj. prof. John Marshall Law Sch., 1998—. Contbr. articles to profl. jours. Chair customs com. Chgo. Bar Assn., 1986-87, Am. Bar Sect. Internat. Law, Washington, 1993-95, practitioners workshop bd., 1995-97; sec., dir. Women in Internat. Trade, Chgo., 1986-89, British Am. C. of C., Chgo., 1990; dir. Chgo. Internat. Sch., 1994-96. Recipient Gold medal Duke of Edinurghs award Scheme, London, 1973. Mem.: ABA (program officer, coun. mem., newsletter editor 1996—98), Internat. Bar Assn., Ct. Internat. Trade Bar Assn. Avocation: gardening. Office: Baker & McKenzie Ste 3500 130 E Randolph Dr Chicago IL 60601-6342 Home Phone: 773-665-0243; Office Phone: 312-861-8022. E-mail: Lynn.S.Preece@Bakernet.com.

PREER, JOAN C., retired assistant principal, retired science educator; d. Clarence Norman and Mary Katherine Casey; m. Andrew Stephen Preer, Sr., May 14, 1965; 1 child, Andrew Stephen Jr. BS in Chemistry, Tenn. A&I State U., Nashville, 1964; M in Adminstrn., Roosevelt U., Chgo., 1980. Ill. tchg. cert. Type 03 Chgo. Pub. Schs., 1969, tchg. cert. grades 3-8 Chgo. Pub. Schs., 1973, gen. sci. endorsement Chgo. Pub. Schs., 1987, sci. tchr. leadership workshop cert. Ill. State Bd. Edn., 1992, adminstrv. cert. Type 75 Ill. State Bd. Edn., 1995. Sci. tchr. Beasley Academic Magnet Ctr., Chgo., 1979—90; sci. coord. Beasley Academic Magnet Sch., Chgo., 1990—96, asst. prin., 1995—2001; ret., 2001. Curriculum writer Bill Kurtis Prodns., Chgo., 1986—2000, Mus. Sci. and Industry, Chgo., 1993—94, Field Mus. Natural History, Chgo., 1995, Brookfield Zoo, Chgo., Argonne Nat. Labs., Chgo., Chgo. Bur. Sci., Chgo., Chgo. Zool. Soc., Chgo.; integrated math., sci. and tech. design team Ill. State U., Normal; middle level childhood sci. stds. com. Nat. Bd. for Profl. Tchg. Stds., 1991—93. Contbg. mem. Nat. Com. to Preserve Social Security and Medicare, 2003—06, Northshore Animal League, Chgo., 2000—06, S.W. Indian Children, 2000—06; active Habitat for Humanity, 2001—06; contbg ptnr. Trinity Broadcasting Network Ministries, Calif., 2001—06. Named Honors Sci. Tchr., Ill. State Bd. Edn.; recipient Golden Apple award, Golden Apple Found., 1988, Cert. Recognition For Excellence In Sci. and Math Tchg., Sigma Xi, 1989, Cert. Recognition For Excellence In Tchg., Ill. Fedn. Tchrs., 1989, Cert. Recognition For Contbns. To Leadership In Sci. Edn., Ill. State Bd. Edn., 1990, Cert. Recognition, Nat. Assn. Precollege Dirs. in Assn. with the AMOCO Corp. Mem.: Chgo. Prins. and Adminstrs. Assn., Ret. Tchrs. Chgo. (life). Achievements include development of a school-level assessment system. Avocations: designing computer programs, travel, designing clothing, designing educational games, writing stories for children. Home Phone: 773-875-8281.

PREGERSON, HARRY, federal judge; b. LA, Oct. 13, 1923; s. Abraham and Bessie (Rubin) P.; m. Bernardine Seyma Chapkis, June 28, 1947; children: Dean Douglas, Kathryn Ann. BA, UCLA, 1947; LL.B., U. Calif.-Berkeley, 1950. Bar: Calif. 1951. Pvt. practice, Los Angeles, 1951—53; Assoc. Morris D. Coppersmith, 1952; ptnr. Pregerson & Costley, Van Nuys, 1953—65; judge Los Angeles Mcpl. Ct., 1965—66, Los Angeles Superior Ct., 1966—67, US Dist. Ct. Central Dist. Calif., 1967—79, US Ct. Appeals (9th cir.), Woodland Hills, 1979—. Faculty mem., seminar for newly appointed distr. Judges Fed. Jud. Center, Washington, 1970—72; mem. faculty Am. Soc. Pub. Adminstrn., Inst. for Ct. Mgmt., Denver, 1973—; panelist LA chpt. FBA, 1989, Calif. Continuing Edn. of Bar, 9th Ann. Fed. Practice Inst., San Francisco, 1986, Internat. Acad. Trial Lawyers, LA, 1983; lectr. seminars for newly-appointed Fed. judges, 1970—71. Author: over 450 published legal opinions. Mem. Community Rels. Com., Jewish Fedn. Coun., 1984—, Temple Judea, Encino, 1955—; bd. trustees Devil Pups Inc., 1988—; adv. bd. Internat. Orphans Inc., 1966—, Jewish Big Brothers Assn., 1970, Salvation Army, LA Met. area, 1988—; worked with US Govt. Gen. Svcs. to establish the Bell Shelter for the homeless Child Day Care Ctr., the Food Partnership and Westwood Transitional Village; bd. dirs. Marine Corps Res. Toys for Tots Program, 1965—, Greater LA Partnership for the Homeless, 1988—. 1st lt. USMCR, 1944—46. Decorated Purple Heart, Medal of Valor Apache Tribe; recipient Promotion of Justice Civic award, City of San Fernando, 1965, award, San Fernando Valley Jewish Fedn. Coun., 1966, Profl. Achievement award, Los Angeles Athletic Club, 1980, Profl. Achievement award UCLA Alumni Assn., 1985, Louis D. Brandeis award, Am. Friends of Hebrew U., 1987, award of merit, Inner City Law Ctr., 1987, Appreciation award, Navajo Nation and USMC for Toys for Tots program, 1987, Humanitarian award, Los Angeles Fed. Exec. Bd., 1987—88, Grateful Acknowledgement award, Bet Tzedek Legal Svcs., 1988, Commendation award, Bd. Suprs. Los Angeles County, 1988, Others award, Salvation Army, 1988. Mem.: ABA, Marines Corps Res. Officers Assn., State Bar Calif., San Fernando Valley Bar Assn., L.A. County Bar Assn., Am. Legion (Van Nuys Post), DAV (Birmingham chpt.). Office: US Ct Appeals 9th Cir 21800 Oxnard St Ste 1140 Woodland Hills CA 91367-7919 *

PREHM, MARY ELIZABETH, elementary school educator; b. Mar. 4, 1948; BS, Murray State U., Ky., 1970, MA, 1972. 4th, 5th, & 7th grade tchr. Paris Spl. Sch. Dist., Tenn., 1970—73; bus. mgr., circulation mgr. Fulton Daily Leader, Ky., 1973—77; 7th grade lang. arts tchr. W.O. Inman Mid. Sch., 1977—. Named Young Woman of Yr., Henry County Jaycees, Tenn., 1990. Mem.: NEA, Tenn. Edn. Assn., Paris Assn. City Tchrs. Home: 3515 County Home Rd Paris TN 38242 Office: 400 Harrison Paris TN 38242

PREISER, WOLFGANG FRIEDRICH ERNST, architect, educator, consultant, researcher; b. Freiburg, Germany, June 26, 1941; came to U.S., 1967; s. Gerhard Friedrich and Ursula Helene (von Huelsen) P.; m. Cecilia M. Fenoglio, Feb. 16, 1985; children: Johanna, Timothy, Andreas, Nicholas. Student, Vienna Tech. U., 1963; diploma in Engring., Architecture, Inst. of Tech., 1967; M.Arch., Va. Poly. Inst. and State U., 1969; PhD in Man-Environ. Relations, Pa. State U., 1973. Architect, Germany, Austria, Eng., 1960-66; prof. architecture Va. Poly. Inst. and State U., Pa. State U., U. Ill., U. N.Mex., U. Cin., 1970—; research architect constrn. engring. research lab. U.S. Army, 1973-76; co-dir. Inst. Environ. Edn., U. N.Mex., 1976-86; dir. Ctr. for R & D, U. N.Mex., Albuquerque, 1986-90; dir. research Archtl. Research Cons. Inc., 1976—; pres. Planning Rsch. Inst., Albuquerque, 1980—90; prin. Preiser Cons., Cin., 1990—. Lectr. ednl., profl. and civic groups worldwide; v.p. faculty club U. N.Mex., 1976-78; pres. Internat. Club, Va. Poly. Inst. and State U., 1968-69; rschr. in field. Author: Improving Building Performance, 2003; co-author: Post-Occupancy Evaluation, 1988; contbr. articles to profl. jours., chapters to books; editor: Facility Programming, 1982, Programming the Built Environment, 1985, Building Evaluation, 1989, Pueblo Style and Regional Architecture, 1989, Design Intervention: Toward A More Humane Architecture, 1991, Professional Practice in Facility Programming, 1993, Design Review: Challenging Urban Aesthetic Control, 1994, New Direction in Urban Public Housing, 1998, Directions in Person-Environment Research and Practice, 1999, Universal Design Handbook, 2001, Japanese transl., 2001, Assessing Building Performance, 2005, Designing for Designers, 2007. Trustee Cin. Chamber Orch., 1992-98, v.p., 1995-98. Recipient Outstanding Svc. award Coll. Design, Arch., Art, and Planning U. Cinn., 2005, Career award Environ. Design Rsch. Assn., 1999, Ann. Rieveschl award, U. Cin., 1999, MCB Univ. Press (UK) award excellence, 1998, Faculty Devel. award rsch. U. Cin., 1992, Faculty Achievement award, 1995, Pogue/Wheeler Traveling award, 1993, Dean's Spl. award, 1994, Finland's Inst. Tech. award, 1966, awards Am. Iron and Steel Inst., 1968, Progressive Arch. Ann., 1985, 89, undergrad. teaching award U. Ill., 1976, hon. mention 1st Kyoto award Internat. Coun. of Soc. Indsl. Design, 1979; Fulbright fellow, 1967, 87, Ford Found. fellow, 1968, Nat. Endowment Arts fellow, 1979, 82; grad. fellow U. Cin., 1996 Mem.: NAS (chmn. com. on programming and post-occupancy evaluation, bldg. rsch. bd. 1985—86), Environ. Design Rsch. Assn. (vice chmn. 1974—76, sec. 1973—74, Lifetime Achievement award 2007), Soc. Human Ecology (pres. 1980—86), U. Cin. Grad. Fellows, Phi Kappa Phi. Office: Univ Cin Coll Daap Sch Arch Cincinnati OH 45221-0016 Office Phone: 513-556-6743. Business E-Mail: wolfgang.preiser@uc.edu.

PREISS, JACK, biochemistry professor; b. Bklyn., June 2, 1932; s. Erool and Gilda (Friedman) P.; m. Karen Sue; children: Jennifer Ellen, Jeremy Oscar, Jessica Michelle. BS in Chemistry, CCNY, 1953; PhD in Biochemistry, Duke U., 1957. Scientist NIH, Bethesda, Md., 1960-62; asst. prof. dept. biochemistry, biophysics U. Calif., Davis, 1962-65, assoc. prof., 1965-68, prof., 1968-85, chair dept. biochemistry, 1971-74, 77-81; prof. dept. biochemistry Mich. State U., East Lansing, 1985-2000, chair dept., 1985-89, Univ. Disting. Prof., 2001—. 16th loomis lectr. Iowa State U., 1997—98. Mem. editl. bd.: Jour. Bacteriology, 1969—74, Arch. Biochem. Biophysics, 1969—, Plant Physiology, 1969—74, 1977—80, assoc. editor:, 1980—92; editor, 1993—95, Jour. Biol. Chemistry, 1971—76, 1978—83, 1994—99, 2000—05, Plant Physiol. Biochemistry, 1997—2003. Recipient Camille and Henry Dreyfus Disting. scholar award Calif. State U., 1983, Alexander von Humboldt Stiftung Sr. US Scientist award, 1984, Merit award, Japanese Soc. Starch Sci., 1992, Disting. Faculty Mem. award Mich. Assn. Governing Bds. State Univ., 1997, Mich. Sci. of Yr. award Impressions 5 Mus., 1997, Pan-Am. Biochemistry and Molecular Biology award lectr. Spanish Biochem. Soc., 2000; Alsberg-Schoch Meml. lectr. Am. Assn. Cereal Chemists, 1990, Nat. Sci. Coun. lectr. Republic of China, 1988; Guggenheim Meml. fellow, 1969-70, Japan Soc. for Promotion of Sci. fellow, 1992-93; grantee NIH, 1963-97, NSF, 1978-89, Dept. Energy, 1993-2005, USDA, 1988—, US-Isreal Binat. Agrl. R & D Fund., 2005—. Mem. AAAS, Am. Chem. Soc. (Charles Pfizer award in enzyme chemistry 1971), Biochem. Soc., Am. Soc. Biol. Chemists and Molecular Biology, Am. Soc. Microbiologists, Am. Soc. Plant Physiologists, Soc. for Complex Carbohydrates, Protein Soc., Pan Am. Soc. Biochemistry and Molecular Biology (sec. gen., 1994-96, vice chmn. 1997-99, chmn. 2000-02, past chmn. 2003-05). Office: Mich State Univ Dept Of Biochemistry & Molecular Biology East Lansing MI 48824 Office Phone: 517-353-3137. Business E-Mail: preiss@msu.edu.

PREISTER, DONALD GEORGE, state legislator, greeting card manufacturer; b. Columbus, Nebr., Dec. 23, 1946; s. Maurice J. Preister and Leona T. (Dusel) Chereck. BS in Edn., U. Nebr., 1977. Unit dir. Boys' Clubs of Omaha, 1973-83; dep. city clk. City of Omaha, 1984-85; tchr. The Great Peace March, U.S., 1986; founder, owner Joy Creations, Co., Omaha, 1988—; mem. Nebr. Legislature from 5th dist., Lincoln, 1992—. Instr. Metro C.C., Omaha, 1979-80. Author: (sect.) Drug Abuse Prevention, 1977. Troop leader Boy Scouts Am., Omaha, 1973-83. Served with U.S. Army, 1966-68, Vietnam. Decorated Bronze Star. Mem. Vets. for Peace, Nebr. Sustainable Agr. Soc., Optimist. Democrat. Roman Catholic. Avocations: gardening, running, horses. Home: 4522 Borman St Omaha NE 68157-2318 Office: State Capitol Dist 5 Lincoln NE 68509

PRELUTSKY, JACK, author; b. Brooklyn, 1940; m. Carolynn Prelutsky. Children's poet laureate Poetry Found., 2006—. Author: The Bad Bear (transl.), 1967, A Gopher in the Gardens and Other Animal Poems, 1967, No End of Nonsense (transl.), 1968, Lazy Blackbird and Other Verses, 1969, Three Saxon Nobles and Other Verses, 1969, The Terrible Tiger, 1969, Toucans Two and Other Poems, 1971, Circus, 1974, The Pack Rat's Day and Other Poems, 1974, Nightmares: Poems to Trouble Your Sleep, 1976, It's Halloween Christmas, Thanksgiving, Valentine's Day, verse, 4 vols., 1977-83, The Snopp on the Sidewalk and Other Poems, 1977, The Mean Old Mean Hyena, 1978,The Queen of Eene, 1978, The Headless Horseman Rides Tonight: More Poems to Trouble Your Sleep, 1980, Rainy Day Saturday, 1980, Rolling Harvey Down the Hill, 1980, The Sheriff of Rottenshot, 1982, Kermit's Garden of Verses, 1982, The Bay Uggs Are Hatching, 1982, The Random House Book of Poetry for Children, 1983, It's Snowing! It's Snowing!, 1984, What I Did Last Summer, 1985, New Kid on the Block, 1984, My Parents Think I'm Sleeping, 1985, Ride a Pink Pelican, 1986, Tyrannosaurus Was a Beast, 1988, The Dragons Are Singing Tonight, The Beauty of the Beast. Address: care Greenwillow Books 1350 Avenue Of The Americas New York NY 10019-4702 *

PREM, F. HERBERT, JR., retired lawyer; b. NYC, Jan. 14, 1932; s. F. Herbert Prem Sr. and Sybil Gertrude (Nichols) Prem; m. Patricia Ryan, Nov. 18, 1978; children from previous marriage: Julia Nichols, F. Herbert III(dec.). AB, Yale U., 1953; JD, Harvard U., 1959. Bar: NY 1960. Assoc. Whitman and Ransom, NYC, 1959-66, ptnr., 1967-93, co-chmn. exec. com., 1988-92, chmn., 1993, Whitman Breed Abbott & Morgan LLP, NYC, 1993-99, of counsel, 2000; ret., 2000. Bd. dirs. Scoville Meml. Libr., treas., 2007—; bd. dirs. Salisbury Visiting Nurse Assn.; pres. Crescendo, Inc., 2005—06. Vol. atty. The Legal Aid Soc., NYC, 2000—03; vol. chaplain Sharon Hosp., Conn., 2003—05; bd. dirs. Bagaduce Music Lending Libr., Inc., 1988—95, pres., 1989—93; bd. dirs. The Health Care Chaplaincy, Inc., 1998—2004, Inter Faith Neighbors, Inc., 2001—03, Legal Aid Soc., NYC, 1969—73, Cmty. Action for Legal Svc., Inc., 1967—70, treas. Lt. j.g. USNR, 1953—56. Mem. ABA, Assn. Bar City NY (sec. 1967-69), NY State Bar Assn., Am. Law Inst. (life), Union Club, Yale Club. Episcopalian.

PREMA, NITYA, marriage and family therapist, artist; b. LA, June 15, 1941; d. James Nicholson and Phyllis Wickersham; children: Fritjof Swenson, Derek Swenson, Krista Mills. AS, Santa Rosa Jr. Coll., Calif., 1977; BA, Sonoma State U., Rohnert Park, Calif., 1980; MA, Profl. Sch. of Psychology, San Francisco, 1983. Lic. marriage and family therapist Bd. of Behavioral Sci., Calif., 1982; psychiat. technician, Bd. of Vocat. Nursing, 1979. Owner, designer and mfr. Nitya Visionary Designs and Gallery, Forestville and Sebastopol, Calif., 1982—92; therapist/social worker O'Connor Hosp. Vista's Program, San Jose, Calif., 1997—99; psychotherapist San Jose Jails/Mental Healtlh, Calif., 1998—2000; pvt. practice family therapist San Andreas and Visalia, Calif., 2000—. Spkr. Internat. Transpersonal Conf., Ireland, 1994; spkr.'s bur. Calif. Assn. of Marriage and Family Therapists, Santa Rosa, 1996. Author: The Spiral Labyrinth Journey: A Pilgrimage into Sacred Space. Activist Rainbow Labyrinth Journey. Named one of Am.'s Top Mental Health Profls. Mem.: Ebbets Pass Forest Watch, Brewster Kaleidoscope Soc. Achievements include design of magic wands, kaleidoscopes, glass and metal sculptures. Business E-Mail: artglasscopes@yahoo.com.

PREMACK, ANN J., writer; b. Shanghai, Jan. 5, 1929; interned in Japanese detention ctr., 1943-45; came to the U.S., 1945; d. John Joseph James and Mae Victoria Parker; m. David Premack, Oct. 26, 1951; children: Ben, Lisa, Tim. BS with distinction, U. Minn., Mpls., 1951. Author: Why Chimps Can Read, 1975; co-author (with D. Premack): The Mind of An Ape, 1983; co-editor: Causal Cognition: A Multidisciplinary Debate, 1995; co-author (with D. Premack): Original Intelligence: Unlocking the Mystery of Who We Are, 2003, French translation, 2003, Japanese translation, 2005; contbr. chapters to books, articles to profl. jours. Avocation: owning and running an avocado grove. Home: 6163 Heatherton Dr Somis CA 93066-9716 Personal E-mail: dpremack@aol.com, dpremack@msn.com.

PREMACK, DAVID, psychologist; b. Aberdeen, SD, Oct. 26, 1925; s. Leonard B. and Sonja (Liese) P.; m. Ann M. James, Oct. 26, 1951; children: Ben, Lisa, Timothy. BA magna cum laude, U. Minn., 1949, PhD, 1955. Rsch. assoc. Yerkes Labs. Primate Biology, Orange Park, Fla., 1955; rsch. assoc., asst. prof. psychology U. Mo., Columbia, 1956-58, assoc. prof., 1959-62, prof., 1963-64, U. Calif., Santa Barbara, 1965-75; vis. prof. Harvard U., 1970-71; prof. U. Pa., 1975—. Artist-in-residence Yaddo, Saratoga Springs, N.Y., 1955; fellow Van Leer Jerusalem Inst., 1980, Inst. for Advanced Study, Berlin, 1985-86; vis. scientist Japan Soc. for Promotion Sci., 1980; univ. rsch. lectr. U. Calif., Santa Barbara, 1973; mem. sci. gov. bd. Fyssen Found., Paris, 1989—; assoc. neurosci. rsch. program, La. Jolla, Calif., 1991—. Author: Intelligence in Ape and Man, 1976, (with Ann James Premack) The Mind of an Ape, 1983, Gavagai! Or the Future History of the Animal Language Controversy, 1986 (with Dan Sperber and Ann James Premack) Causal Cognition: A Multidisciplinary Debate, 1995, (with Ann James Premack) Original Intelligence: Unlocking the Mystery of Who We Are, 2003, French translation, 2003, Japanese translation, 2005; mem. editl. bd. Jour. Exptl. Psychology: Animal Processes, 1976—, Cognition, 1977—, Brain and Behavior Sci., 1978—, Jour. Cognitive Neurosci. Served with U.S. Army, 1943-46. Ford Found. tchg. intern, 1954; USPHS postdoctoral fellow, 1956-59; Social Sci. Rsch. Coun. fellow, summer 1963; Ctr. for Advanced Study in Behavioral Scis. fellow, 1972-73; Guggenheim fellow, 1979-80; grantee NSF, 1961—, USPHS, 1960-80; recipient Kenneth Craik Resch. award St. John's Coll.-Cambridge U., 1987, Internat. Sci. prize Fyssen Found., Paris, 1987. Fellow AAAS; mem. Am. Psychol. Soc. (William James fellow 2005), Soc. Exptl. Psychologists. Home Phone: 805-386-4278. Personal E-mail: dpremack@aol.com.

PREMCHAND, ARIGAPUDI, retired financial consultant; b. Kadavakollu, India, Aug. 22, 1933; arrived in U.S., 1970; s. Venkataramiah and Manikyamma Arigapudi; m. Rama Premchand, May 8, 1953; 2 children. Diploma in econ. adminstrn., Delhi Sch. Econs., 1954; MA, Andhra U., 1953; DLitt (hon.), Krishna Devaraya U., 2002. Lectr. Andhra (India) U., 1954—57; rsch. officer Union Min. Fin., Delhi, 1957—68; cons. Ford Found., 1968—70; economist to asst. dir. Internat. Monetary Fund, Washington, 1970—98; cons. Asian Devel. Bank, 1998—2003, World Bank, 1998—, Kennedy Sch., 1998—2004; ret., 2004. Author, editor: 12 books; contbr. chapters to books. Fellow, Indian Inst. Econs., 1960, Oxford U., 1980. Hindu. Avocations: reading, writing. Home: 5 Sonrisa Irvine CA 92620-7915 Home Fax: 714-669-9374. Personal E-mail: apremchand1@cox.net.

PREMO, PAUL MARK, oil industry executive; b. Syracuse, NY, Nov. 20, 1942; s. Matthias George and Kathryn (Whitbread) P.; m. Mary Catherine Hennessy, June 19, 1965; children: Deborah, Mark. BSChemE, Manhattan Coll., Riverdale, NY, 1964; MS in Chem. Engring., MIT, 1965. Chem. engr. Chevron Rsch., Richmond, Calif., 1965-69; fin. analyst Chevron Corp., San Francisco, 1969-72, coord., mgr. supply and distbn., 1972-79; mgr. petroleum regulations Chevron USA, San Francisco, 1979-81, sec.-treas., 1981-85, mgr. property tax adminstrn., 1985-86, mgr. natural gas regulatory affairs, 1986-92; exec. cons. Resource Mgmt. Internat., San Rafael, Calif., 1992-95; v.p. Foster Assoc., Inc., San Francisco, 1995—98; prin. Energy Econs. Consulting, Mill Valley, Calif., 1998—. Dir. Ky. Agrl. Energy Corp., Franklin. Trustee Calif. Tax Found., 1985-. Mem. Calif. State C. of C. (tax com.), Western Oil and Gas Assn., Am. Petroleum Inst. (property tax com.), Natural Gas Supply Assn., Inst. Property Taxation, Calif. Taxpayers Assn. (bd. dirs. 1985-), MIT Alumni Assn., Commonwealth (San Francisco), Sigma Xi, Tau Beta Pi. Avocations: investments, carpentry, travel. Home: 310 Hazel Ave Mill Valley CA 94941-5054 Personal E-mail: paulpremo@msn.com.

PRENDERGAST, KENNETH LEE MICHAEL, JR., career officer; b. Macdill Air Force Base, Fla., Sept. 16, 1956; s. Kenneth Lee and Pauline Ann (Hall) P.; m. Naomi Sue Kincade, Aug. 6, 1976; children: Melissa Ann, Robert Anthony. BA, Jacksonville State U., 1986; BS, U. N.Y., 1986; MA, U. Fla., 1990; MPA, Troy State U., 1997; M of Strategic Studies, U.S. Army War Coll., 2003. Enlisted US Army, 1978, commd. 2d lt. mil. police corps, 1982; advanced through ranks to col., 2003; exec. officer Company D 1st Bn., Ft. McClellan, Ala., 1983; aide de camp to dep. comdg. gen., M.P. sch. commandant Ft. McClellan, Ala., 1984-85; ops. tng. officer Provost Marshal's Office US Army WESTCOM, Ft. Shafter, Hawaii, 1987; co. commdr. mil. police US Army Support Commd., Ft. Shafter, 1988—89; ops. officer Provost Marshal's Office US Army Law Enforcement Command, Ft. Shafter, Hawaii, 1989; fgn. area officer US Embassy, Kinshasa, Zaire, 1991—92, U.S. Embassy, Yaounde, Cameroon, 1992—93; internat. officer instr. US Army Command and Gen. Staff Coll., Ft. Leavenworth, Kans., 1993; joint task force 161 and ARFOR plans officer Guantanamo Bay, Cuba, 1994; MP long range plans officer 89th Mil. Police Brigade, Ft. Hood, Tex., 1994-95; exec. officer 720th Mil. Police Battalion, Ft. Hood, 1995-96; Am. Polit. Sci. Assn. congrl. fellow Senator Bob Graham, Washington, 1996-97; chief of plans and ops. office Chief of Legis. Liaison Office of Sec., U.S. Army, Washington, 1997-98; dir. legis. strategy Washington, 1998-99; bn. comdr. 19th Mil. Police Bn., Seoul, Republic of Korea, 1999—2001; provost marshal and task force comdr., joint task force patriot Ft. George G. Meade, Md., 2001—02; provost marshal, dir. operational protection Third US Army, US Army Forces Ctrl. Command, and Coalition Forces Land Component Command, Camp Arifjan, Kuwait, 2003—05; brigade comdr. 202nd Mil. Police Group (CID), Seckenheim, Germany, 2005—07; provost marshall, dir. emergency svcs. US Army Europe, 7th Army, 2007—. Vol. coach youth football, soccer, baseball, 1974—; leader Boy Scouts Am., Ft. Hood, 1989—, mem. com., 1994-96. Decorated Legion of Merit (with two oak leaf clusters), Bronze Star Medal. Mem. VFW, Ret. Officers Assn., Korean-Am. Assn., Assn. U.S. Army, 720th Mil. Police Battalion Reunion Assn. (life), Mil. Police Regimental Assn. (life), Mil. Officers Assn. Am., Fgn. Area Officer Assn. (founding), U. Fla. Nat. Alumni Assn. (life), Jacksonville State U. Alumni Assn. (life), Am. Polit. Sci. Assn., Am. C. of C. in Korea, Harley Owners Group (life), Alpha Kappa Delta. Roman Catholic. Avocations: sailing, scuba diving, water-skiing, skydiving, foreign travel. Home and Office: CMR 435 Box 246 APO AE 09086 Business E-Mail: kenneth.prendergast@us.army.mil.

PRENDERGAST, SIR KIERAN, former international organization official; b. Campbeltown, Scotland, 1942; married; 4 children. BA, St. Patricks Coll., Strathfield, Sydney; MA, Salesian Coll. and St. Edmond Hall, Oxford. Posted NATO Dept. at the Fgn. Office, 1967—69, NATO in Nicosia, Cyprus, 1969—72; second sec. NATO, 1969—72, first sec. to desk officer, 1973—76; asst. pvt. sec. Sec. of State for Fgn.and Commonwealth Affairs, 1976—79; posted United Kingdom Mission to the UN, 1979—82; Counselor and Consul gen. Tel Aviv, 1982—86; high commr. to Zimbabwe, 1989—92, to Kenya, 1992—95; amb. to Turkey, 1995—97; Under-Sec.-Gen. for polit. affairs UN, 1997—2005. Office: UN Headquarters First Ave at 46th St New York NY 10017

PRENDERGAST, ROBERT ANTHONY, pathologist educator; b. Bklyn., Nov. 6, 1931; BA, Columbia U., 1953; MD, Boston U., 1957. Intern Bellevue Hosp., 1957-58; resident Boston City Hosp., 1958-59, Meml. Sloan-Kettering Hosp., 1959-61; vis. physician Rockefeller U., 1963-65, asst. prof., 1965-70, assoc. prof. opthamology, 1970-99; prof. ophthalmology and pathology Johns Hopkins U. Sch. Medicine, 1999—, prof. emeritus. Adj. sr. scientist Marine Biol. Lab., Woods Hole, Mass., 2006—, bd. dirs. Mem. Am. Assn. Immunology, Am. Soc. Exp. Pathology, H.G. Kunkel Soc., Assn. Vision & Ophthal., Pluto Club. Achievements include research in cellular immunology, ontogeny of the immune response, transplantation immunology, viral immunopathology, immunopathology of ocular inflammatory diseases. Office: Marine Biol Lab Woods Hole MA 02543 Home Phone: 508-457-1375. Business E-Mail: rprender@mbl.edu.

PRENDERGAST, WILLIAM JOHN, ophthalmologist; b. Portland, Oreg., June 12, 1942; s. William John and Marjorie (Scott) P.; m. Carolyn Grace Perkins, Aug. 17, 1963 (div. 1990); children: William John, Scott; m. Sherryl Irene Guenther, Aug. 25, 1991. BS, U. Oreg., Eugene, 1964; MD, U. Oreg., Portland, 1967. Diplomate Am. Bd. Ophthalmology. Resident in ophthalmology U. Oreg., Portland, 1970-73; pvt. practice specializing in ophthalmology Portland, 1973-82; physician, founder, ptnr. Eye Health NW (formerly Oreg. Med. Eye Clinic), Portland, 1983—; also bd. dirs.; founder, pres. (Focus Group) Inc. Focus Group Inc., Ophthalmic Clinic Networking Venture, Portland, 1992—. Clin. asst. prof. ophthalmology Oreg. Health Sci. U., 1985—; dir. Eye Health Ptnrs. Med. Optometric Managed Eye Care Venture, 1998. Vol. surgeon, Hosp. de la Familia, Nuevo Progreso, Guatamala, 2001-07, vol. surgeon N.W. Med. Teams, Oaxaca, Mexico, 1989-90. With USPHS, 1968-70. Fellow Am. Acad. Ophthalmology; mem. Met. Bus. Assn., Multnomah Athletic Club, Mazamas Mountaineering Club, Portland Yacht Club, Phi Beta Kappa, Alpha Omega Alpha. Avocations: sailing, mountain climbing. Office: Eye Health NW 1955 NW Northrup St Portland OR 97209-1614 Office Phone: 503-227-2020. Business E-Mail: prenderw@ehnpc.com.

PRENSKY, ARTHUR LAWRENCE, pediatric neurologist, educator; b. NYC, Aug. 31, 1930; s. Herman and Pearl (Newman) P.; m. Sheila Carr, Nov. 13, 1969. AB, Cornell U., 1951; MD, N.Y. U., 1955. Diplomate: Am. Bd. Psychiatry and Neurology. Intern Barnes Hosp., St. Louis, 1955-56; resident and research fellow in neurology Harvard U., Mass. Gen. Hosp., Boston, 1959-66; instr. neurology Harvard Med. Sch., 1966-67; mem. faculty Washington U. Sch. Medicine, St. Louis, 1967—, prof. pediatrics and neurology, to 1975, Allen P. and Josephine B. Green prof. pediatric neurology, 1975-2000, prof. emeritus of neurology, 2000—; pediatrician St. Louis Children's Hosp.; neurologist Barnes and Allied Hosps., Jewish Hosp., St. Louis. Author: (with others) Nutrition and the Developing Nervous System, 1975; editor: (with others) Neurological Pathophysiology, 2d edit, 1978, Advances in Neurology, 1976; mem. editorial bd. Pediatric Neurology, 1984-90, Jour. Child Neurology, 1985—. Served with USAF, 1957-59. Fellow Am. Acad. Neurology; mem. Am. Neurol. Assn., Am. Soc. Neurochemistry (mem. council 1973-77), Central Soc. Neurol. Rsch. (pres. 1977-78), Child Neurology Soc. (pres. 1979-80, Hower award 2000), Am. Pediatric Soc., Internat. Child Neurology Assn., Japanese Soc. Child Neurology, Profs. Child Neurology (pres. 1984-86) Home: 15 Monarch Hill Ct Chesterfield MO 63005-4004 Office: 1 Children's Pl Saint Louis MO 63110-1014 Office Phone: 314-454-6120. Business E-Mail: prenskya@neuro.wustl.edu.

PRENTKE, RICHARD OTTESEN, lawyer; b. Cleve., Sept. 8, 1945; s. Herbert E. and Melva B. P.; m. Susan Ottesen, June 9, 1974; children: Catherine, Elizabeth. BSE, Princeton U., 1967; JD, Harvard U., 1974. Assoc. Perkins Coie, Seattle, 1974-80, ptnr., 1981—, CFO, 1989-94. Author: School Construction Law Deskbook, 1989, rev. 2d edit. 1998; contbr. articles to profl. jours. Pres., trustee Seattle County Day Sch., 1990-95; trustee Pocock Rowing Found., 1996-02. Lt. USN, 1967—70. Fellow Leadership Tomorrow, Seattle, 1985-86. Mem. ABA, Wash. State Bar Assn. (mem. jud. screening com. 1985-91, chmn. 1987-91), Seattle-King County Bar Assn. (chmn. jud. task force 1990-93), Am. Arbitration Assn. (arbitrator 1988—), Princeton U. Rowing Assn. (pres. 1993-02, trustee 1976—), Rainier Club, Princeton Varsity Club (trustee 2003-), Princeton Varsity Club Wash. (trustee 1986-95, pres. 1990-92), Seattle Tennis Club. Avocations: art, carpentry, travel, rowing, sports. Office: Perkins Coie 1201 3rd Ave Fl 40 Seattle WA 98101-3029 Office Phone: 206-359-8888. Business E-Mail: rprentke@perkinscoie.com.

PRENZLOW, ELMER JOHN-CHARLES, JR., minister; b. Norfolk, Nebr., Apr. 4, 1929; s. Elmer Edward and Alvina C. (Henning) P.; m. Karen McHarg DeMoss, July 4, 1980; 1 child, Elmer Carl III. BA, Northwestern Coll., Watertown, Wis., 1950; BD in Theology, WELS Luth. Sem., Mequon, Wis., 1953; MA in English and Philosophy, U. Minn., 1961; MS in Edn. Psychology, U. Wis., 1969; PhD in Psychology and Criminal Justice, Walden U., 1975. Pastor St Paul's Lutheran Ch., Bloomer, Wis., 1953-62; chaplain, instr. U. Wis., Milw., 1962-79; dir. devel. and pub. relations Luth. Ch.-Mo. Synod, Southern Wis. Dist., Milw., 1979-82; major gifts counselor Luth. Ch.-Mo. Synod Internat. Hdqrs., St. Louis, 1982-88; dir. devel. and fin. resources Adult Christian Edn. Found. Bethel Series, Madison, Wis., 1988-89; world relief devel. counselor Luth. Ch.-Mo. Synod Internat. Hdqrs., St. Louis, 1989-94; v.p. major gifts Luth. Ch.-Mo. Synod Found., St. Louis, 1994-98; spl. asst. to pres. Luth. World Relief, NYC, 1998—. Vice chmn. Standing Com. Dept. Campus Ministry Luth. Coun. U.S.A., N.Y., 1964-83; chmn. Milw. Religious Counselors, 1965-72, dept. humanities Spencerian Bus. Coll., 1967-77; v.p. Patricia Stevens Career Coll., bd. dirs. 1978-91; spkr., lectr. in field. Contbr. articles to profl. jours. Mem. Wis. State Legis. Com for Kerner Report, Madison, 1968-69, Nat. Adv. Commn.U.S. Justice Dept. on Law Enforcement standards and goals, Washington, 1971-73, ad hoc com. for establishing U.S. Bur. Prisons Nat. Inst. for Corrections, Washington, 1973-75, 19th congr. dist. Wis. svc. acad. review bd., Milw., 1975-82; sub. pastor for vacations in North dist. of Lutheran Ch.-Mo. Synod, 1998-2004. Named Outstanding Prof. Spencerian Bus. Coll., Milw., 1972. Mem. Assn. of Luth. Devel. Execs., Optimists, Wis. Club, Lions Club. Republican. Avocations: travel, music, auto racing, golf, fishing. Home and Office: 15794 225th Ave Bloomer WI 54724-4741 Business E-Mail: revkaren@bloomer.net. *Nothing communicates to others what we believe more loudly and effectively than the measure of those principles they witness being personally carried out in our own lives!.*

PREONAS, GEORGE ELIAS, lawyer; b. Dayton, Ohio, Oct. 5, 1943; s. Louis D. and Mary (Drakos) P.; m. Aileen Strike, June 1, 1944; children: Annemarie, Michael, Stephen. BA, Stanford U., 1965; JD, U. Mich., 1968. Bar: Ill. 1968, Nev. 1969, Calif. 1974. Ptnr. Seyfarth, Shaw, Fairweather & Geraldson, LA, 1968—. Mem. ABA, L.A. County Bar Assn., Calif. Bar Assn., Ill. Bar Assn., Nev. Bar Assn. Office: Seyfarth Shaw 2029 Century Park E Ste 3300 Los Angeles CA 90067-3019

PREOVOLOS, PENELOPE ATHENE, lawyer; b. San Francisco, Sept. 16, 1955; d. James Peter and Lorraine Lucille (Tiscornia) P.; m. Richard Gonzalo Katerndahl, Mar. 24, 1984. AB with greatest distinction, U. Calif., Berkeley, 1976; JD cum laude, Harvard U., 1979. Bar: Calif. 1979, U.S. Dist. Ct. (no. dist.) Calif. 1979, U.S. Ct. Appeals (9th cir.) 1979. Law clk. to Hon. Charles M. Merrill U.S. Ct. Appeals (9th cir.), San Francisco, 1979-80; assoc. Morrison & Foerster, San Francisco, 1980-85, mng. ptnr. San Francisco office, 1995-96, ptnr. San Franciso, 1985—. Contbr. articles to profl. jours. Bd. dirs. San Francisco Neighborhood Legal Assistance Found., 1990—. Recipient Calif. leading antitrust lawyers, by Chambers USA, Best Lawyers Am., 2006, 2007. Mem. ABA (litig. and antitrust sect.), State Bar of Calif. (sec. antitrust and trade regulation law sect. 1993-94, chair 1994-95), Phi Beta Kappa, served 9th cir. adv. com. on rules of practice & Internal oper. procedures 1990-93. Democrat. Roman Catholic. Exec. editor Harvard Civil Rights — Civil Liberties Law Review, 1978-1979. Office: Morrison & Foerster 425 Market St Ste 3100 San Francisco CA 94105-2482 Office Phone: 415-268-7187. Office Fax: 415-268-7522. Business E-Mail: ppreovolos@mofo.com.

PRESANT, SANFORD CALVIN, lawyer, educator, writer, tax specialist; b. Buffalo, Nov. 15, 1952; s. Allen and Reeta Presant; children: Jarrett, Danny, Lauren; m. Nancy Loeb. BA, Cornell U., 1973; JD cum laude, SUNY, Buffalo, 1976; LLM in Taxation, Georgetown U., NYU, 1981. Bar: N.Y. 1977, D.C. 1977, U.S. Tax Ct. 1977, U.S. Ct. Claims 1978, Calif. 1992, U.S. Supreme Ct. 1982. Staff atty. SEC Options Task Force, Washington, 1976-78; assoc. Barrett Smith Schapiro, NYC, 1978-80, Trubin Sillcocks, NYC, 1980-81; ptnr. Carro, Spanbock, Fass, Geller, Kaster, NYC, 1981-86, Finley, Kumble, Wagner, Heine, Underberg, Manley, Myerson & Casey, NYC, 1987, Kaye, Scholer, Fierman, Hays & Handler, NYC, 1987-95, Battle Fowler LLP, LA, 1995-2000, Ernst & Young, LA, 2000; nat. dir. real estate tax strategies, opportunity funds Ernst & Young LLP, LA, 2000; ptnr. DLA Piper Rudnick Gray Cary US LLP, LA, 2005—. Adj. assoc. prof. real estate NYU, 1984-00; frequest lectr. in tax law; regular TV appearances Nightly Bus. Report, PBS, 1986-88; co-chmn. NYU Conf. Fed. Taxation Real Estate Trans., 1987, PLI Advanced Tax Planning Real Estate, 1987, PLI Ann. Real Estate Tax Forum, 1999—; program dir. Nareit Law and Acctg. Conf., 2003; conf. chmn. various confs. in field. Author: Realty Joint Ventures, 1980-86, Tax Sheltered Investments Handbook-Special Update on Tax Reform Act of 1984, Real Estate Syndication Handbook, 1986, The Tax Reform Act of 1986, 1987, Real Estate Syndication Tax Handbook, 1987, Understanding

Partnership Tax Allocations, 1987, The Final Partnership Nonrecourse Debt Allocation Regulations, 1987, Taxation of Real Estate Investments, 1987, Understanding Partnership Tax Allocations, 1987, Tax Aspects of Environmental (Superfund) Settlements, 1994, The Proposed Publicly Traded Partnership Regulations, 1995, (with others) Tax Aspects of Real Investments, 2002, Structuring Real Estate Private Equity Funds, 2005, Joint Ventures With Tax-Exempt Entities, 2005, others. Kripke Securities Law fellow NYU, 1976. Mem. ABA (nat. chmn. audit subcom. of tax sect. partnership com. 1984-86, partnership tax allocation subcom. chmn. 1986-90, nat. chmn. partnership com. 1992-94, chmn. task force publicly traded partnerships 1995—, others), N.Y. State Bar Assn. (tax sect. partnership com. 1980—), Assn. Bar City of N.Y. Republican. Jewish. Office: Real Estate Capital Markets DLA Piper Rudnick Gray Cary US LLP 1999 Avenue of the Stars Fourth Fl Los Angeles CA 90067-5403 Office Phone: 213-977-3303, 310-595-3190. Office Fax: 866-222-9401, 310-595-3490. Business E-Mail: sanford.presant@ey.com, susan.teague@dlapiper.com.

PRESBY, J. THOMAS, financial advisor, director, arbitrator; b. Newark, Feb. 15, 1940; s. George and Shirley (Kandel) P.; m. Elaine Merle Smith, Aug. 19, 1961; children: Philip, Terry, Mona. BSEE, Rutgers U., 1961; MBA in Indsl. Adminstrn., Carnegie-Mellon U., 1963. CPA, Ohio, N.Y. Ptnr. Touche Ross, NYC, 1972-76; regional ptnr. Touche Ross Internat., Paris, 1976-79, nat. dir. client svcs., 1979-81, exec. dir. internat., 1981-82, ptnr.-in-charge fin. svcs. ctr., 1982-90, mng. ptnr. Ea. Europe, Brussels, 1990-94, chief exec. officer Europe, Paris, 1991-95; COO Deloitte Touche Tohmatsu Internat., NYC, 1995—, dep. chmn., chief oper. officer, 1997, chief staff, mem. exec. group, 1999—2002. Mem. bus. adv. coun. Grad. Sch. Indsl. Adminstrn., Carnegie-Mellon U., Pitts., 1984-2001; trustee Rutgers U., New Brunswick, NJ, 1985-90; bd. dirs. Tiffany & Co., Amvescap PLC, Am. Eagle Outfitters, World Fuel Services, Turbochef Technologies, German Marshall Fund., First Solar Inc. Mem. AICPA, Ohio Soc. CPAs, N.Y. Soc. CPAs, Harmonie Club. Avocations: antique autos, racquetball, squash, motorcycling, fly fishing. Home: 6 Holton Ln Essex Fells NJ 07021-1709 Office: 655 Madison Ave Ste 2300 New York NY 10021 Office Phone: 646-358-3043. Personal E-mail: tom.presby@verizon.net.

PRESCOTT, BARBARA LODWICH, educational association administrator; b. Chgo., Aug. 15, 1951; d. Edward and Eugenia Lodwich; m. Warren Paul Prescott, Dec. 2, 1979; children: Warren Paul Jr., Ashley Elizabeth. BA, U. Ill., Chgo., 1973, MEd, 1981; MA, U. Wis., 1978; postgrad., Stanford U., 1983-87. Cert. tchr., learning handicapped specialist, cmty. coll. instr., Calif. Grad. rschr. U. Ill., Chgo., 1979-81; learning handicapped specialist St. Paulus Luth. Sch., San Francisco, 1981-83; grad. rsch. asst. Sch. Edn. Stanford (Calif.) U., 1983-87; learning handicapped specialist/lead therapist Gilroy Clinic Speech-Hearing-Learning Ctr., Crippled Children's Soc., Santa Clara, Calif., 1988-89; ednl. dir. Adolescent Intensive Resdl. Svc. Calif. Pacific Med. Ctr., San Francisco, 1989-95; exec. dir. Learning Profiles, South Lake Tahoe, Calif., 1995—. Instr. evening San Jose City Coll., 1988-92. Contbr. articles to profl. jours.; author: Proceedings of Internat. Congress of Linguistics, 1987; editor: Proceedings - Forum for Research on Language Issues, 1986; author videotape: Making a Difference in Language and Learning, 1989. Recipient Frederick Bork Teaching Trainee award San Francisco State U., 1983; Ill. State scholar, 1973. Mem. Calif. Assn. Pvt. Specialized Edn. and Svcs., Phi Delta Kappa (v.p. 1984-86), Pi Lambda Theta (sec. 1982-83), Phi Kappa Phi, Alpha Lambda Theta. Office Phone: 630-924-8052. E-mail: prescott4@netscape.com.

PRESCOTT, DARRELL, lawyer; b. Montpelier, Vt., May 17, 1949; AB magna cum laude, Harvard Univ., 1971, JD, 1975. Bar: NY 1976, US Dist. Ct. (so. & ea. NY) 1976, US Ct. Appeals (2d cir.) 1985, US Ct. Appeals (11th cir.) 1996, US Ct. Appeals (Fed. cir.) 2000, US Supreme Ct. 1996. Ptnr. Baker & McKenzie LLP, NYC. Contbr. articles to profl. jours.; co-editor: Joint Ventures in the Internat. Arena, ABA, 2003. Knox fellow. Fellow: Am. Bar Found. (sec., liaison officer 2005—06); mem.: ABA (programs officer, Sect. Internat. law, CLE award, Sect. Internat. Law 2004), Assn. Bar City of NY, Phi Beta Kappa. Office: Baker & McKenzie LLP 1114 Ave of the Americas New York NY 10036 Office Fax: 212-316-1637. E-mail: darrell.prescott@bakernet.com.

PRESCOTT, DAVID L. C., JR., music educator; s. David L. C. Prescott, Sr. and Lavina Hall Prescott. BS in Bus. Adminstrn., Old Dominion U., 1981, MusB in Music Edn., 1992, MS in Secondary Edn., Choral Conducting, 2002. Acct. W. E. Moulton, Jr. & Assocs., Portsmouth, Va., 1981—90; music specialist Tanners Creek Elem. Sch., Norfolk, Va., 1992—93; dir. choral activities Ocean Lakes H.S., Virginia Beach, Va., 1993—97, Kempsville H.S., Virginia Beach, Va., 1997—. Guest clinician, condr. Various Churches And Civic Choirs, Va., 1992—; dir. music Holland Rd. Bapt. Ch., Virginia Beach, 1983—97, Faith Wesleyan Ch., Norfolk, 1995—2005, Thalia United Meth. Ch., Virginia Beach, 2005—. King herod: (musical theatre) Jesus Christ Superstar; costumer (dramas and musical theatre works) A Man for All Seasons, Christ and St. Luke's Arts Guild, 2000, Our Town, Christ and St. Luke's Art Guild, 1999, Jesus Christ Superstar, Christ and St. Luke's Art Guild, 2001, Guys and Dolls, Wizard of Oz, Annie Get Your Gun, Mame, Pippin, Carousel Cinderella, Kempsville H.S., 1999—2005. Mem. bd. dirs. Virginia Beach Ballet, 1990—93. Named Kempsville H.S. Tchr. of Yr., 2007; recipient Award of Distinction - Choral Conducting, Fest. Music Competitions, 1999. Mem.: Music Educators Nat. Conf., Va. Music Educators Assn., Am. Choral Dir.'s Assn., Phi Mu Alpha Sinfonia. Wesleyan. Avocations: antiques, flower arranging. Office: Kempsville High School 5194 Chief Trail Virginia Beach VA 23464 Office Phone: 757-474-8400 ext. 58104. E-mail: dlpresco@vbschools.com.

PRESCOTT, EDWARD C., economist, educator; b. 1940; BA in Mathematics, Swarthmore Coll., 1962; MS in Operations Rsch., Case-Western Reserve U., 1963; PhD in Economics, Carnegie Mellon U., 1967. Lectr. U. Penn, 1966—67; asst. prof. Economics Dept. U. Penn., 1967—71; asst. prof. Grad. Sch. Indsl. Admin. Carnegie Mellon U., 1971—72, assoc. prof., 1972—75; vis. prof. Economics Norwegian Sch. Bus. and Economics, 1974—75; prof. Economics Grad. Sch. Indsl. Admin. Carnegie Mellon U., 1975—80; Ford vis. rsch. prof. U. Chgo., 1978—79; vis. prof. Economics Northwestern U., 1979—80; vis. prof. Finance Kellogg Grad. Sch. Mgmt. Northwestern U., 1980—82; sr. advisor rsch. dept. Fed. Reserve Bank, Mpls., 1980—2003; prof. Economics U. Minn., 1980—98, U. Chgo., 1998—99, U. Minn., 1999—2003; prof. dept. Economics Ariz. State U., 2003—; sr. monetary advisor Fed. Reserve Bank, Mpls., 2003—. Leader NBER/NSF Workshop in Indsl. Orgn., 1977—84; rsch. assoc. Nat. Bureau of Economic Rsch., 1988—; spkr. in field. Author (with S.L. Parente): Barriers to Riches, 2000; co-editor: Economic Theory, 1991; assoc. editor: Jour. Econometrics, 1976—82, Internat. Economic Review, 1980—90, Jour. Economic Theory, 1990—92; contbr. articles to profl. jours. Named Regents' Prof., U. Minn., 1996, McKnight Presidential Chair in Economics, 2003, W.P. Carey Chair, U. Ariz., 2003; recipient Erwin Plein Nemmers prize in Econ., Northwestern U., 2002, Laurea Honoris Causa in Economica, U. Rome, 2002, Nobel Prize for Econ. Sciences, 2004; fellow, Econometric Society, 1980, Am. Acad. Arts & Scis., 1992; Brookings Economic Policy Fellow, 1969—70, Guggenheim Fellow, 1974—75. Mem.: Soc. Advancement of Econ. Theory (pres. 1992—94), Soc. Econ. Dynamics and Control (pres. 1992—95). Office: Ariz State U Dept Econs Tempe AZ 85287-3806 *

PRESCOTT, JOHN MACK, biochemist, retired university administrator; b. San Marcos, Tex., Jan. 22, 1921; s. John Mack and Maude (Raborn) P.; m. Kathryn Ann Kelly, June 8, 1946; children: Stephen Michael, Donald Wyatt. BS in Chemistry, S.W. Tex. State Coll., 1941; MS in Biochemistry and Nutrition, Tex. A&M U., 1949; PhD in Biochemistry, U. Wis., 1952. Lab. asst. Dow Chem. Co., Freeport, Tex., 1942-43; faculty Tex. A&M U., College Station, 1946-49, 52-85, prof. biochemistry, 1959-85, dean Coll. Sci., 1970-77, v.p. for acad. affairs, 1977-81, dir. Inst. Occupational and Environ. Medicine, 1981-87, prof. med. biochemistry, 1981-85, prof. emeritus, 1985—, spl. asst. to dep. chancellor for biotech. devel., 1987-88; research asst. U. Wis.-Madison, 1949-51, U. Tex., Austin, 1951-52; vis. prof. Harvard Med. Sch., 1982. Contbr. articles profl. jours. Mem. Tex. Bd. Examiners in Basic Scis., 1974-79, mem. Tex. State Bd. Edn., 1984-88. Served to lt. USAAF, 1943-46; lt. col. USAF Res., 1946-68. Mem. Am. Soc. for Biochemistry and Molecular Biology, Soc. for Exptl. Biology and Medicine, Sigma Xi, Phi Lambda Upsilon. Home: 31 Forest Dr College Station TX 77840-2337

PRESCOTT, RICHARD CHAMBERS, writer; b. Houston, Apr. 1, 1952; s. Chambers Richard and Dorothy Mae (Bashara) P.; m. Sarah Elisabeth Grace, Oct. 13, 1981. Author: The Sage, 1975, Moonstar, 1975, Neuf Songes (Nine Dreams), 1976, 2d edit., 1991, The Carouse of Soma, 1977, Lions and Kings, 1977, Allah Wake Up, 1978, 2d edit., 1994, Night Reaper, 1979, Dragon Tales, 1983, Dragon Dreams, 1986, 2d edit., 1990, Dragon Prayers, 1988, 2d edit., 1990, Dragon Songs, 1988, 2nd edit., 1990, Dragon Maker, 1989, 2d edit., 1990, Dragon Thoughts, 1990, Tales of Recognition, 1991, Kings and Sages, 1991, Dragon Sight: A Cremation Poem, 1992, Three Waves, 1992, Years of Wonder, 1992, Dream Appearances, 1992, Remembrance Recognition and Return, 1992, Spare Advice, 1992, The Imperishable, 1993, The Dark Deitess, 1993, Disturbing Delights: Waves of The Great Goddess, 1993, The Immortal: Racopa and the Rooms of Light, 1993, Hanging Baskets, 1993, Writer's Block and Other Gray Matters, 1993, The Resurrection of Quantum Joe, 1993, The Horse and the Carriage, 1993, Kalee Bhava: The Goddess and Her Moods, 1995, The Skills of Kalee, 1995, Because of Atma, 1995, Measuring Sky Without Ground, 1996, The Goddess And The God Man, 1996, Kalee: The Allayer of Sorrows, 1996, Living Sakti, 1997, The Mirage and the Mirror, 1998, Inherent Solutions to Spiritual Obscurations, 1999, The Ancient Method, 1999, Quantum Kamakala, 2000; contbr. articles to profl. jours.

PRESKA, LORETTA A., federal judge; b. 1949; BA, Coll. of St. Rose, 1970; JD, Fordham U., 1973; LLM, NYU, 1978; LHD (hon.), Coll. of St. Rose, 1995. Assoc. Cahill, Gordon & Reindel, NYC, 1973-82; ptnr. Hertzog, Calamari & Gleason, NYC, 1982-92; fed. judge U.S. Dist. Ct. (So. Dist.), NY, 1992—. Mem. N.Y. State Bar Assn., N.Y. County Lawyers Assn., Fed. Bar Coun., Fordham Law Alumni Assn. (v.p.). Office: US Courthouse 500 Pearl St Rm 1320 New York NY 10007-1316

PRESKA, MARGARET LOUISE ROBINSON, historian, educational association administrator; b. Parma, NY, Jan. 23, 1938; d. Ralph Craven and Ellen Elvira (Niemi) Robinson; m. Daniel C. Preska, Jan. 24, 1959; children: Robert, William, Ellen Preska Steck. BS summa cum laude, SUNY, 1957; MA, Pa. State U., 1961; PhD, Claremont Grad. Sch., 1969. Instr. LaVerne (Calif.) Coll., 1968-75, asst. prof., asso. prof., acad. dean, 1972-75; instr. Starr King Sch. for Ministry, Berkeley, Calif., summer, 1975; v.p. acad. affairs, equal opportunity officer Minn. State U., Mankato, 1975-79, pres., 1979-92; project dir. Kaliningrad (Russia) Mil. Re-Tng., 1992-96; disting. svc. prof. Minn. State U. Sys., 1993—; pres. Inst. for Effective Tchg. Minn. State U., Winona, 1993—98; owner BuildaBikeInc.com, 2000—. Bd. dirs. XCEL Energy Co., Milkweed Edits.; pres. emerita Minn. State U., Mankato, 1992—; provost, CEO AbuDhabi Campus, Zayed U., United Arab Emirates, 1997-99. Pres. Pomona Valley chpt. UN Assn., 1968-69, Unitarian Soc. Pomona Valley, 1968-69, PTA Lincoln Elem. Sch., Pomona, 1973-74; pres., chmn. bd. Nat. Camp Fire Boys and Girls, 1984-88; mem. Pomona City Charter Revision Commn., 1972; chmn. The Fielding Inst., Santa Barbara, 1983-86; bd. dirs. Elderhostel Internat., 1983-87, Minn. Agrl. Interpretive Ctr. (Farmam.), 1983-92, Am. Assn. State Colls. and Univs., Moscow on the Mississippi - Minn. Meets the Soviet Union; nat. pres. Campfire, Inc., 1985-87; chmn. Gov.'s Coun. on Youth, Minn., 1983-86, Minn. Edn. Forum, 1984; mem. Gov.'s Commn. on Econ. Future of Minn., 1985—, NCAA Pres. Commn., 1986-92, NCAA Cost Cutting Commn., Minn. Brainpower Compact, 1985; commr. Great Lakes Govs.' Econ. Devel. Coun., 1986, Minn Gov.'s Commn. on Forestry. Carnegie Found. grantee Am. Coun. Edn. Deans Inst., 1974; recipient Outstanding Alumni award Pa. State, Outstanding Alumni award Claremont Grad. Sch., YWCA Leader award 1982, Exch. Club Book of Golden Deeds award, 1987; named One of top 100 alumni, SUNY, 1895-1985, 1985, Hall of Heritage award, 1988, Wohelo Camp Fire award, 1989. Fellow Fielding Inst.; mem. AAUW (pres. Mankato 1990-92), LWV, Women's Econ. Roundtable, St. Paul/Mpls. Com. on Fgn. Rels., Am. Assn. Univ. Adminstrs., Rotary, Horizon 100. Unitarian Universalist. Home: 10 Sumner Hls Mankato MN 56001-3931 E-mail: mpreska@hickorytech.net.

PRESKILL, JOHN PHILLIP, physics professor; b. Highland Park, Ill., Jan. 19, 1953; m. Roberta M. Gross, June 22, 1975; children: Carina Lou, Micaela Marie. AB in Physics, Princeton U., 1975; AM in Physics, Harvard U., 1976, PhD in Physics, 1980. Jr. fellow Harvard Soc. Fellows, 1980-81; asst. prof. physics Harvard U., Cambridge, Mass., 1981-82, assoc. prof., 1982-83; assoc. prof. theoretical physics Calif. Inst. Tech., Pasadena, 1983-90, prof., 1990—; dir. Inst. Quantum Info., 2000—; John D. MacArthur prof., 2002—; dir. Ctr. for Physics of Info., 2003—. Andrejewski lectr. Humbolt U., Berlin, 2001; Lorentz chair U. Leiden, 2002; Rouse Ball lectr. U. Cambridge, 2005. Recipient Presdl. Young Investigator award NSF, 1984-89; fellow NSF, 1975-78, Alfred P. Sloan Found., 1982-86. Fellow Am. Phys. Soc. Office: Calif Inst Tech 452-48 Div Physics Math & Astronomy Pasadena CA 91125-0001 Office Phone: 626-395-6691. Office Fax: 626-568-8473. E-mail: preskill@theory.caltech.edu, preskill@iqi.caltech.edu.

PRESLAR, LEN BROUGHTON, JR., hospital administrator; b. Concord, NC, Aug. 13, 1947; s. Len B. and Billie M. (James) P.; m. Joyce W. Whittington, July 11, 1971; children: Bradley E., Whitney A., Andrew C. BA, Wake Forest U., 1971; MBA, U. N.C., Greensboro, 1980. Admissions clk. N.C. Bapt. Hosp., Winston-Salem, 1969-71, systems analyst, 1971-72, budget mgr., 1973, contr., 1973-75, v.p. fin. mgmt., 1975-88, pres., chief exec. officer, 1988—. Bd. dirs. Univ. Healthsystem Consortium; bd. mgrs. Wachovia Bank; mem. owners and affiliate rels. com. Premier, Inc. Deacon local Bapt. ch. Fellow Hosp. Fin. Mgmt. Assn.; mem. N.C. Hosp. Assn. (bd. dirs.). Republican. Baptist. Avocations: gardening, golf. Office: NC Bapt Hosp Medical Center Blvd Winston Salem NC 27157-0001

PRESLEY, ARTHUR HENRY, writer, artist; b. Delano, Calif., June 1, 1953; s. James Hampton and Marjorie Joy (Quandt) P. AA, Bakersfield Coll., 1978; student, Brigham Young U., 1979—82, student, 1987—89. Asst. city planner City of Lindsay, Calif., 1988—89; freelance writer Bakersfield, 1995—. Contbr. poetry to Beneath the Harvest Moon, 1996, Best Poems of the '90s, 1996, Treasured Poems of America, 1998, CAMI Jour., 1995, Seasons of My Life, 2000, Theatre of the Mind, 2003, Labours of Love, 2005. Avocations: reading, music, astronomy, gardening, cooking.

PRESLEY, BRIAN, investment company executive; b. Evansville, Ind., Dec. 28, 1941; s. Harry and Ruth P.; m. Mary Nell Minyard, Aug. 17, 1972; children: Debra, Cynthia, David, Jeffrey, Clark, Gregory, Steven. BSBA, U. Evansville, 1963; MBA, Mich. State U., 1964; diploma, Wharton Sch., U. Pa., 1995. Market rsch. analyst Stanley Works, New Britain, Conn., 1964-68; tax shelter coord. F.I. Dupont, Memphis, 1968-73; v.p. Bullington Schas, Memphis, 1973-75; pres., mng. ptnr. Presley Assocs., Memphis, 1965-93; pres., CFO CSG, Inc., Memphis, 1975—. Gen. ptnr. various real estate and oil and gas partnerships, 1974-1986; pres. Cooper St. Group Securities, Inc., 1983-86; divsn. mgr. Advantage Capital Corp. (divsn. AIG Advisors, Inc.), 1986-89, reg. v.p., 1989, CEO 1990-94, mng. dir., mktg. strategist, 1995; pres. Presley Adv. Inc., 1995—, pub. Presley Adv. Letter; instr. fin. divsn. continuing edn. Memphis U. Bd. dirs. Apt. Coun. Tenn., 1980-86, sec.-treas., 1982-83; pres. Memphis Apt. Coun., 1983; mem., U. Evansville Nat. Alumni Bd., 1988-91; prodr. 2 daily radio stock market commentary shows, 1988; fin. commentator Sta. WEVU-TV (ABC), Ft. Myers/Naples, 1988-89; host syndicated radio show for sr. citizens, 1979-81; mem. found. bd. and fin. com. Fla. Gulf Coast U., 2001—. Mem. Leadership Charlotte; chmn. Charlotte County Econ. Devel. Coun., 1999-2002; pres. Enterprise Charlotte Found., 2002-06; chmn. Angels Found. Charlotte County, 2002-05; bd. dirs. Charlotte County Cmty. Found., 2005—; vice chmn. Charlotte Cmty. Found., 2007—. Recipient Richard L. McLaughlin award, Econ. Devel. Coun., Fla., 2002. Mem. Internat. Assn. Fin. Planners (broker dealer adv. coun. 1993-97), Admirals Club (life, bd. dirs.), Naples Jazz Soc. (chmn. bd. dirs. 1993-96), Naples Sailing and Yacht Club (bd. dirs.1991-96), Pi Sigma Epsilon, Beta Gamma Sigma, Tau Kappa Epsilon Alumni Assn. (pres. Memphis area 1979-80), Isles Yacht Club (bd. dirs. 2001-04). Presbyterian. Home and Office: Acorn Ranch 5161 Acorn Ranch Rd Punta Gorda FL 33982-9511 Office Phone: 941-505-9017. Business E-Mail: brian@presleyadvisoryinc.com.

PRESLEY, JAMES WRIGHT, writer, environmentalist; b. Nash, Tex., Jan. 13, 1930; s. James Alexander and Lola Opal (Wright) Presley; m. Fran Burton, Jan. 13, 1962; children: John Francis, Ann Burton. BA, East Tex. State Tchrs. Coll., 1950; MA, U. Tex., Austin, 1955, Mexico City Coll., 1955; PhD, U. Tex., Austin, 1991. Reporter Texarkana (Tex.-Ark.) Gazette, 1947—49; asst. news editor Amarillo (Tex.) Globe-Times, 1956; staff writer Shreveport (La.) Times, 1958—59; copy editor The Light, San Antonio, 1959—61, 1969; part-time news editor Texarkana Gazette, 1969—71; polit. cons. Texarkana, 1960—; freelance writer, 1961—. Contbg. editor, editl. adv. bd. Tex. Observer, Austin, 1960—80; mgmt. cons. Red River Regional Coun. Alcoholism, Texarkana, 1975; spkr. workshops, Tex. and Ark. Co-author: Center of the Storm, 1967, Please Doctor, Do Something!, 1972, Vitamin B6: The Doctor's Report, 1973, Public Defender, 1974, Human Life Styling, 1975, Food Power, 1978; author: A Saga of Wealth: Rise of the Texas Oilmen, 1978, Never in Doubt, 1981; featured interviewee PBS-TV Documentary series on Tex., 1986; featured interviewee: other documentaries. Co-founder, pres., etc. Texarkana Anti-Pollution Soc.; co-founder, bd. dirs., etc. Friends United for a Safe Environ., Tex.-Ark., 1988—; press aide Henry Gonzalez-for-Gov., San Antonio, 1958. Staff sgt. USAF, 1950—53. Recipient various news prizes, AP, various other news assns., 1969—71, Anson Jones award, Tex. Med. Assn., 1971, John H. McGinnis Meml. award, Southwest Rev., 1981. Mem.: Am. Med. Writers Assn., N.Y. Acad. Scis., Oral History Assn., Soc. Environ. Journalists, Internat. Soc. Fluoride Rsch., Am. Assn. History of Medicine. Democrat. Achievements include author history of diabetes mellitus in the U.S. (1880-1990), 1991, 2 vols; led numerous environmental campaigns. Avocations: book collecting, investigating unsolved cases, fencing, running. Home and Office: 417 W 27th St Texarkana TX 75503-4232

PRESLEY, JOHN WOODROW, academic administrator; b. Jonesboro, Ark., Mar. 24, 1948; s. Marvin Woodrow and Willa Louise (Taylor) P.; m. Katherine Bailey Harrison, Oct. 17, 1978. BSE, Ark. State U., 1970; MA, So. Ill. U., 1972, PhD, 1975; postgrad., Johns Hopkins U., 1976, U. Tex., 1980. From asst. prof. to prof., asst. v.p. acad. affairs Augusta State U., 1974—89; assoc. provost Lafayette Coll., 1989—92; dean Coll. of Arts, Scis. and Letters U. Mich., Dearborn, 1992-99; provost, v.p. acad. affairs SUNY at Oswego, 1999—2003; v.p. acad. affairs, provost Ill. State U., 2003—. Author and presenter in fields of modern lit. and higher edn. adminstrn. Author: The Robert Graves Letters and Manuscripts at Southern Illinois University, 1976. NDEA fellow, 1972. Office: Ill State Univ 410 Hovey Hall Normal IL 61790 Office Phone: 309-438-7018. E-mail: jwpresl@ilstu.edu.

PRESLEY, LISA MARIE, singer; b. Memphis, Tenn., Feb. 1, 1968; d. Elvis and Priscilla Presley; m. Danny Keough, Oct. 3, 1988 (div. 1994); children: Danielle Riley Keough, Benjamin Storm Keough; m. Michael Jackson, May 18, 1994 (div. Jan. 18, 1996); m. Nicholas Cage, Aug. 10, 2002 (div. May 16, 2004); m. Michael Lockwood, Jan. 22, 2006. Mgmt. Elvis Presley Trust; owner, chmn. bd. Elvis Presley Enterprises, Inc.; co-owner with mother Priscilla Elvis Presley's Memphis nightclub, operated by Presley Estate, 1997—2003. Singer: (albums) To Whom It May Concern, 2003 (cert. Gold), Lights Out, 2003, Now What, 2005; actor: (music video) You Are Not Alone, Michael Jackson, (car commercial), 1989; appeared on (cover of Vogue mag.), 1996, (cover of Vogue mag. with mother and daughter), 2004, featured in (TV) Elvis by the Presleys, 2005. Internat. spokesperson Citizens Commn. on Human Rights; co-founder (with Isaac Hayes) LEAP (Literacy, Edn., and Ability Program); involved with Fight for Kids. Office: Elvis Presley Enterprises Inc PO Box 16508 3734 Elvis Presley Blvd Memphis TN 38186-0508

PRESLEY, LUCINDA HANKS, art educator; d. Jack Holcomb and Jacquelyn Rayburn Hanks; children: Jacquelyn Elizabeth, John Talbot, Kathleen Hanks. B in Journalism, U. Tex., Austin, 1970; MA in Interdisciplinary Studies, U. Tex., Tyler, 1998. Artist-in-education Tyler Mus. Art, Tex., 1997—2000; dir. after-sch. programs Troup Elem. Sch., Tex., 1997—2004; coord. edn. and spl. programs Tyler Mus. Art, 2000—03; dir. sci., arts Discovery Sci. Pl., Tyler, 2003—, dir. spl. initiatives, 2007—; dir. edn., program Young Audiences NE Tex., Tyler, 2003—07. Cons., educator, arts integration programs Palestine Ind. Sch. Dist., Tex., 1981—94; docent tour coord. adult tours Mus. Fine Arts, Houston, 1977—80; mem. fine arts tng. cadre Tex. Edn. Agy. Region VII, Kilgore, 2003—; mem. ctr. for informal learning schs. initiative Exploratorium, San Francisco, 2003—; mem. Leadership Tex., 1996—; adj. instr. art Tyler Jr. Coll., 1999—. Pres. Palestine Jr. Svc. League, 1989—90. Fellow, Am. Assn. Mus., 1997. Mem.: Am. Assn. Mus., Tex. Art Educators Assn. Avocations: reading, painting, fiber arts design, piano. Office: Discovery Science Place 308 N Broadway Tyler TX 75702 Office Phone: 903-533-8011 26. Office Fax: 903-593-0300. E-mail: lucinda@discoverysciencepIace.com.

PRESLEY, PRISCILLA (PRICILLA ANN WAGNER, PRISCILLA BEAULIEU PRESLEY), actress; b. Bklyn., May 24, 1945; m. Elvis Presley, 1967 (div. 1973); 1 child, Lisa Marie; 1 child (with Marco Garibaldi), Navarone. Studied with Milton Katselas; student, Steven Peck Theatre Art Sch., Chuck Norris Karate Sch.; HHD (hon.), Rhodes Coll., Memphis, 1998. Co-owner Bis and Beau Boutique, 1973—76; co-executor, pres. Elvis Presley Enterprise, Inc. (acquired by CKX, Inc.), Memphis, 1979—2005, founder, 1980—2005, exec. cons., 2005—; bd. dir. CKX, Inc., Las Vegas, Nev., 2005—. Launched & developed internat. fragrance line, 1988—, Moments, 1990, Experiences, 1994, Indian Summer, 1996; designer of jewelry line; launched website, 2005—; bd. dir. Metro-Goldwyn-Mayer Inc., 2000—; lectr. SMART TALK. Appearances include (films) The Naked Gun: From the Files of Police Squad!, 1988, The Adventures of Ford Fairlaine, 1990, The Naked Gun 2 1/2, 1991, The Naked Gun 33 1/3: The Final Insult, 1994, (TV series) Those Amazing Animals, 1980-81, Dallas, 1983-88, Melrose Place, 1996, (TV movies) Love Is Forever, 1983, Breakfast With Einstein, 1998 (also exec. prodr.), Hayley Wagner, Star, 1999, After Dallas, 2002; exec. prodr. (TV movie) Elvis and Me, 1988, The Road to Graceland, 1998, Finding Graceland, 1998; co-prodr.(TV mini series) Elvis, 1990; host, Elvis: The Great Performances, 1992; featured in (TV) Elvis 85, 1984, Elvis: Life and Times, 1997, After Dallas, 2002, Elvis by the Presleys, 2005, (TV mini series) Between the Lines, 2004; guest appearances include The Fall Guy, 1983, Tales from the Crypt, 1993, Touched by an Angel, 1997, Spin City,

1999, After They Were Famous, 2002, Oprah Winfrey Show, 2005; author: Elvis and Me, 1987. Amb. Dream Found., 2000—; mem. Citizen's Commn. on Human Rights. Named one of 50 Most Beautiful People in the World, People Mag., 1992. Office: Paul Bloch & Michelle Bega c/o Rogers & Cowan 8687 Melrose Ave 7th Fl West Hollywood CA 90069 Address: Norman Brokaw c/o William Morris Agency 151 El Camino Beverly Hills CA 90212 Office Phone: 310-850-4206, 310-854-8100.

PRESNIAKOV, ALEXANDER, artist, sculptor, inventor, writer; b. San Francisco, June 28, 1963; s. Alexander Alexandervich and Nina (Hanova) P. Student, Acad. of Art Coll., San Francisco, 1979-82. Curator Gen. Svcs. Adminstrn., Washington, 1983; artist Washington, 1984-85, San Francisco, 1986—; pres. Multimedia Global Arts Inc., St. Petersburg, Russia, 2007—. Songwriter Hilltop Records, LA, 1996—, Amerecord, LA, 1996—, Premier Melodies, NYC Commd. to paint life-size portraits of Prince Charles, Princess Diana, Miss Dame Barbara Cartland, Amb. Gerald Posner Carmen, presdl. candidates for 1985 Polit. Conservative Action Conf., Sheraton Hotel, Washington, Pres. Ronald Reagan, San Francisco mayor Willie Brown; series Women in Love Cycle, 1986—; author: Eagle's Nest, 2001, Lords of Death, 2005, 8 others; screenwriter. Recipient Literary Excellence award Iliad Press, 1995; named Prof. and Corr. Academician Dept. Arts Accademia Internazionale, Italy. Mem. Internat. Soc. Poets (disting. mem., Hall of Fame 1997-98), Legion of Honor Mus., De Young Mus., Gallery Marabella (hon.). Republican. Russian Orthodox. Achievements include invention of Manshield Deflector; the Scrubber glove; artistic ideal ultrafictionilization used in all US govt. agencies. Avocations: tennis, golf, equestrian. Home and Studio: 499 33rd Ave Apt 206 San Francisco CA 94121 Office Phone: 415-572-9928. Personal E-mail: alexanderpresniakov@gmail.com.

PRESS, AIDA KABATZNICK, retired editor, poet, writer; b. Boston, Nov. 18, 1926; m. Newton Press, June 5, 1947; children: David, Dina Press Weber, Benjamin Presskreischer. BA, Radcliffe Coll., 1948. Reporter Waltham (Mass.) News-Tribune, 1960-63; freelance writer, 1960-63; editl. cons. Mass. Dept. Mental Health, Boston, 1966-72; Waltham/Watertown reporter Boston Herald Traveler, 1963-70; dir. news and publs. Harvard Grad. Sch. Design, Cambridge, Mass., 1972-78; publs. editor Radcliffe Coll., Cambridge, 1978-81, dir., editor of publs., 1981-83, editor Radcliffe Quar., 1971-93, dir. pub. info., 1983-93; cons. editor Regis Coll. Alumnae Mag., Weston, Mass., 1994. Editor emerita Radcliffe Quar., 1993—; contbr. articles to newspapers and mags. Recipient Publs. Distinction award Am. Alumni Coun., 1974, Top 5 coll. Mag., Coun. for Advancement and Support of Edn., 1984, Top 10 Univ Mags., 1991, Gold medal Coll. Mags., 1991, Alumnae Achievement award Radcliffe Coll., 1994, Radcliffe Coll. Presdl. Commendation, 1992. Mem. Phi Beta Kappa. Avocations: hiking, playing recorder.

PRESS, ANTHONY L., lawyer; BA in Economics and Polit. Sci., Yale U., 1981; JD, UCLA, 1986. Bar: Calif. 1986. Dep. gen. counsel Kolts Commn.; asst. to dep. gen. counsel Christopher Commn.; ptnr. Morrison & Foerster LLP, LA, chmn. litig. dept.-LA office, chmn. pro bono com., mng. ptnr.-Century City, CA office. Mem.: LA County Bar Assn., ABA (mem. litig. sect.). Office Phone: 213-892-5597. Office Fax: 213-892-5454. Business E-Mail: apress@mofo.com.

PRESS, BARRY HARRIS JAY, plastic surgeon; s. Robert Alfred and Phyllis Elaine (Rovner) P.; m. Cynthia Jane Witz, Aug. 11, 1973; children: Sarah Jane, Rachel Ann. BS in Microbiology with honors, U. Iowa, 1973, MD, 1977. Diplomate Am. Bd. Med. Examiners, Am. Bd. Surgery, Am. Bd. Plastic Surgery. Intern U. Minn. Hosps., 1977—78, resident otolaryngology, 1979—80, resident surgery, 1980—85; resident plastic surgery Med. Ctr. NYU, 1985—87; asst. prof. plastic surgery Stanford (Calif.) U. Sch. Medicine, 1987—94; assoc. chief plastic surgery, med. dir. Burn Ctr. Santa Clara Valley Med. Ctr., San Jose, Calif., 1987—95; assoc. prof. plastic surgery Stanford (Calif.) U. Sch. Medicine, 1994—95; surgeon, owner Plastic Surgeons Inst., Mountain View, Calif., 1995—99, Barry Press, M.D., San Jose, 1999—. Adj. clin. prof. plastic surgery Stanford U., 2006—. Contbr. chapters to books, articles to profl. jours. Fellow ACS; mem. AMA, Am. Soc. Plastic and Reconstructive Surgeons, Am. Burn Assn., Calif. Med. Assn., Santa Clara County Med. Assn., Calif. Soc. of Plastic Surgeons, Am. Soc. for Surgery of the Hand, San Jose Surg. Soc. Office: Barry Press MD Ste A 2550 Samaritan Dr San Jose CA 95124-4104 Office Phone: 408-356-1148. Office Fax: 408-356-1140. Business E-Mail: bpressmd@ix.netcom.com.

PRESS, CHARLES, retired political science professor; b. St. Louis, Sept. 12, 1922; s. Otto Ernst and Laura (Irion) P.; m. Nancy Miller, June 10, 1950; children: Edward Paul, William David, Thomas Leigh, Laura Mary. Student, Elmhurst Coll., Ill.; B of Journalism, U. Mo., 1948; MA, U. Minn., 1951, PhD, 1953. Faculty N.D. Agrl. Coll., 1954-56; dir. Grand Rapids Area Study, 1956-57; with Bur. Govt., U. Wis., 1957-58; faculty Mich. State U., East Lansing, 1958-91, prof. polit. sci., 1964-91; emeritus, 1991—; chmn. dept. Mich. State U., 1966-73. Cons. Mich. Constl. Conv., 1962-63; supr. Ingham County, 1966-72; tchr. summers, London; tchr. U. N.S.W., Sydney, Mich. State U. Author: Main Street Politics, 1962, (with Charles Adrian) The American Government Process, 1965, Governing Urban America, 1968, 5th edit., 1977, American Politics Reappraised, 1974, (with Kenneth VerBurg) States and Community Governments in a Federal System, 1979, 3d edit., 1991, American Policy Studies, 1981, The Political Cartoon, 1982, (with others) Michigan Political Atlas 1984, (with Kenneth VerBurg) American Politicians and Journalists, 1988, (with Kenneth VerBurg) Looking Over Sir Arthur's Shoulder, How Doyle Turned the Trick, 2004, Parodies and Pastiches Buzzing Around Sir Arthur Conan Doyle, 2006; (weekly newspaper column) The Pros and Cons of Politics. Sec. Ingham County Bd. Health, 1983-93; chmn., mem. East Lansing Bd. Rev., 1966-86; bd. dirs. Urban League, 1971-73; mem. East Lansing Housing and Urban Devel. Commn., 1988-93. Served with AUS, 1943-45. Recipient Disting. Prof. award Mich. State U., 1980, Alumni Merit award Elmhurst (Ill.) Coll., 1995. Mem. Am. Polit. Sci. Assn., Midwest Polit. Sci. Assn. (pres. 1974-75), So. Polit. Sci. Assn., Mich. Conf. Polit. Scientists (pres. 1972-73), Nat. Municipal League, B.S.I. Home: 987 Lantern Hill Dr East Lansing MI 48823-2831 Personal E-mail: pressc@msu.edu.

PRESS, FRANK, geophysicist; b. Bklyn., Dec. 4, 1924; s. Solomon and Dora (Steinholz) Press; m. Billie Kallick, June 9, 1946; children: William Henry, Paula Evelyn. BS, CCNY, 1944, LLD (hon.), 1972; MA, Columbia U., 1946, PhD, 1949; DSc (hon.), 28 univs. Rsch. assoc. Columbia U., 1946—49, instr. geology, 1949—51, asst. prof. geology, 1951—52, assoc. prof., 1952—55; prof. geophysics Calif. Inst. Tech., 1955—65, dir. seismol. lab., 1957—65; prof. geophysics, chmn. dept. earth and planetary scis. MIT, Cambridge, 1965—77, inst. prof., 1981; sci. advisor to pres., dir. Office Sci. and Tech. Policy, Washington, 1977—81; pres. NAS, 1981—93, pres. emeritus, 2000—; Cecil & Ida Green sr. fellow Carnegie Inst. of Washington, 1993—97; ptnr. Washington Adv. Group, 1996—. Mem. Pres.'s Sci. Adv. Com., 1961—64, Com. on Anticipated Advances in Sci. and Tech., 1974—76, Nat. Sci. Bd., 1970—76; mem. lunar and planetary missions bd. NASA; participant bilateral scis. agreement with Peoples Republic of China and USSR; mem. U.S. delegation to Nuc. Test Ban Negotiations, Geneva and Moscow; prof. emeritus MIT, 2000—. Author (with M. Ewing, W.s. Jardetsky): Propagation of Elastic Waves in Layered Media, 1957; author: (with R. Siever) Earth, 1986; author: Understanding Earth, 2003; author: (contbr.) articles to over 160 publs. Decorated cross of Merit Germany, Legion of Honor France; named Sherman Fairchild Disting. scholar, Calif. Inst. Tech., 1994, A.D. White prof., Cornell U.; recipient Columbia medal for Excellence, 1960, Pub. Svc. award, U.S. Dept. Interior, 1972, Gold medal, Royal Astron. Soc., 1972, Pub. Svc. medal, NASA, 1973, Japan prize, Sci. and Tech. Found. Japan, 1993, Pupin medal, Columbia U., 1993, Nat. medal of Sci., Pres. U.S., 1994, Philip Hauge Abelson prize, AAAS, 1995, Lomonosov Gold medal, Russian Acad. Sci., 1998. Mem.: NAS, Engring. Acad. Japan (fgn. assoc.), Acad.Scis. Russia (fgn. mem.), Royal Soc. U.K., French Acad. Scis., Am. Philos. Soc., Seismol. Soc. Am. (pres. 1963), Soc. Exploration Geophysicists, Am. Geophys. Union, Geol. Soc. Am. (councilor), Am. Acad. Arts and Scis. Office: Ste 616 South 2500 Virginia Ave Washington DC 20037-1901 Office Phone: 202-682-0164. Business E-Mail: fpress@nas.edu.

PRESS, FRED, artist; b. Boston, Oct. 14, 1919; s. Samuel and Rose Press; m. Alice Bernadette, Nov. 4, 1942; children: David, Peter, Christopher. Student, Vesper George Sch. Art, Boston, 1938-39. Founder, chief designer sculpture collection Contemporary Arts, Inc., Boston, 1937-62; tchr. Vesper George Sch. Art, Boston, 1945—50; chief designer, exec. v.p. sales agy. NYC, 1951—70; freelance in design field, 1970—85. Mem. Mass. Art Commn. One-man shows include Stuart Art Gallery, Boston, 1947, Jaffrey Civic Ctr., 1989, Granary Gallery, Martha's Vineyard, Mass., 1990, exhibited in group shows at NAD, N.Y.C., Delgado Mus. Art, New Orleans, Springfield Art League, Mass., Pan Am. Soc., Boston, Conn. Acad. Fine Arts, Allied Artists, N.Y., Vose Galleries, Boston, Boston Mus. Fine Arts, Silvermine Guild Artists, Conn., Mus. Contemporary Art, Boston, Ky. Derby Mus., Nat. Art League, Olin Art Ctr., Hoyt Inst. Fine Arts, Sharon Arts Ctr., Represented in permanent collections Worcester (Mass.) Art Mus., prin. works include 2 Bronze Reliefs, U.S. Navy Meml., Washington, individual pvt. collections; featured in Am. Artist Mag., Christian Sci. Monitor, Dance Mag.; author: (book) Sculpture at Your Fingertips, 1961; mng. editor: Ofcl. 6th Air Force Mag., 1944—45. Tech. sgt. USAF, 1942—45. Recipient ann. awards for soap sculpture, Proctor and Gamble Co., 1936—39, 1st prize for Slave sculpture, Delgado Mus. Art, 1946; scholar, HS Commerce. Home: 262 Hadley Rd Jaffrey NH 03452

PRESS, JIM (JAMES E. PRESS), automotive executive; b. Calif., Oct. 4, 1946; m. Linda Press; 4 children. BA in Bus. Adminstrn., Kans. State U., 1968. With Ford Motor Co., 1968—70; joined Toyota Motor Corp., Torrance, Calif., 1970; exec. v.p. Toyota Motor Sales, U.S.A., Inc., 1999—2005, COO, 1999—2005, pres., 2005—; mng. officer Toyota Motor Corp., 2003—, pres. Toyota North Am., 2006—. Bd. dirs. Toyota Motor Corp., 2007—. Avocations: boating, motorcycling, auto racing, skiing, scuba diving. Office: Toyota North America 9 W 57th St Ste 4900 New York NY 10019 *

PRESS, TERRY, marketing executive; children: Gracie, Ethan. Head mktg. DreamWorks SKG; head mktg. worldwide DreamWorks Animation, 2006—07. Faculty mem. UCLA Film Sch. Named one of 100 Most Powerful Women in Entertainment, Hollywood Reporter, 2005, 2006. Office: DreamWorks SKG 100 Universal City Plz # 5121 Universal City CA 91608 *

PRESS, WILLIAM HENRY, physicist, computer scientist; b. NYC, May 23, 1948; s. Frank and Billie (Kallick) P.; m. Margaret Ann Lauritsen, 1969 (div. 1982); 1 dau., Sara Linda; m. Jeffrey Foden Howell, Apr. 19, 1991; 1 son, James Howell. AB, Harvard Coll., 1969; MS, Calif. Inst. Tech., 1971, PhD, 1972. Asst. prof. theoretical physics Calif. Inst. Tech., 1973-74; asst. prof. physics Princeton (N.J.) U., NJ, 1974—76; prof. astronomy and physics Harvard U., Cambridge, Mass., 1976-98, chmn. dept. astronomy, 1982-85; dep. lab. dir. Los Alamos Nat. Lab., N.Mex., 1998—2004, sr. fellow, 2004—; Raymer prof. computer scis. and integrative biology U. Tex., Austin, 2007—. Mem. numerous adv. coms. and panels NSF, NASA, NAS, NRC; vis. mem. Inst. Advanced Study, 1983-94; mem. Def. Sci. Bd., 1985-89, sci. adv. com. Packard Found., 1988—, program com. Sloan Found., 1985-91; chmn. adv. bd. NSF Inst. Theoretical Physics, 1986-87; mem. Computer Sci. and Telecomm. Bd., 1991-96; U.S. del. IUPAP Gen. Assembly, 1996; cons. MITRE Corp., 1977—; trustee Inst. Def. Analysis, 1988—, exec. com., 1990—; chief naval ops. Exec. Panel, 1994-2000. Author: Numerical Recipes, 1986; contbr. articles to profl. jours. Sloan Found. research fellow, 1974-78 Fellow: Am. Phys. Soc., Am. Acad. Arts and Scis.; mem.: NAS, Coun. on Fgn. Rels., Assn. for Computing Machinery, Internat. Soc. Relativity and Gravitation, Internat. Astron. Union, Am. Astron. Soc. (Helen B. Warner prize 1981). Office: Los Alamos Nat Lab MS F 600 Los Alamos NM 87545-0001

PRESSEL, MORGAN, professional golfer; b. Tampa, Fla., May 13, 1988; d. Kathy (Krickstein) and Mike Pressel. Profl. golfer LPGA, 2006—. Mem. US Team PING Jr. Solheim Cup, 2002, 03, 05; mem. East Team Cannon Cup, 2002—04. Named Player of Yr., Am. Jr. Golf Assn., 2005; recipient Nancy Lopez award, 2006, CoURagE award, Birdies for Breast Cancer, 2006. Achievements include winning the North and South Women's Amateur, 2004, US Women's Amateur, 2005; became youngest (18 years, 10 months, 9 days) major champion in LPGA history on April 1, 2007 at the Kraft Nabisco Championship; youngest (12) to qualify for the US Women's Open, 2001; won 11 events on the American Junior Golf Association circuit. Avocations: photography, computers. Mailing: LPGA 100 International Golf Dr Daytona Beach FL 32124-1092 *

PRESSER, HARRIET BETTY, social studies educator; b. Bklyn., Aug. 29, 1936; d. Phillip Rubinoff and Rose (Gudowitz) Jabish; m. Neil Nathan Presser, Dec. 16, 1956 (div.); 1 child, Sheryl Lynn. BA, George Washington U., 1959; MA, U. N.C., 1962; PhD, U. Calif., Berkeley, 1969. Statistician Bur. Census, Washington, 1959; research assoc. Inst. Life Ins., NYC, 1962-64; lectr. demography U. Sussex, Brighton, England, 1967-68; staff assoc. Population Council, NYC, 1968-69; asst. prof. sociomed. scis. Columbia U., NYC, 1969-73, assoc. prof. sociomed. scis., 1973-76; prof. sociology U. Md., College Park, 1976—99, dir. Ctr. on Population, Gender, and Social Inequality, 1988—2001, disting. faculty rsch. fellow, 1993-94, disting. univ. prof., 1999—; fellow in residence Netherlands Inst. for Advanced Study in Humanities & Social Sci., Wassenaar, The Netherlands, 1994-95. Fellow-in-residence Ctr. for Advanced Study in the Behavioral Scis., Stanford, Calif., 1986-87, 91-92, 2003-04; scholar-in-residence Russell Sage Found., NYC, 1998, 99, 2000; resident scholar Bellagio Study and Conf. Ctr., Rockefeller Found., 2000; acad. visitor Gender Inst. London Sch. Econs and Polit. Scis., 2000; vis. scholar Max Planck Inst. for Demographic Rsch., Rostock, Germany, 2007. Editl. bd. Time and Soc., 1991-95, Social Forces, 1984-87, Signs, 1975-85, Applied Population and Policy, 2002-, Rose Monograph Series, 2003-05, Jour. of Marriage and the Family, 2003; assoc. editor Jour. Health and Social Behavior, 1975-78; co-editor (with Gita Sen) Women's Empowerment and Demographic Processes: Moving Beyond Cairo, 2000; author: Working in a 24/7 Economy: Challenges for Am. Families, 2003; editor: Population Studies and Demographic Change, Transaction Pubs., 2005-. Grantee NICHD, 1972-78, 83-88, Population Coun., 1976-79, NSF, 1982-83, 90-94, 2000-03, Rockefeller Found., 1983-85, 88-94, William and Flora Hewlett Found., 1989—06, Andrew W. Mellon Found., 1994-95, W.T. Grant Found., 1996-99, Russell Sage Found., 1976-79, 2003-04, Alfred P. Sloan Found., 2007—; recipient Rosabeth Moss Kanter award for excellence in work-family rsch., 2001, Lawrence R. Klein award, 2003, Disting. Sr. Scholar award AAUW Edn. Found., 2007. Fellow AAAS, Sociol. Rsch. Assn.; mem. APHA (coun. mem. population sect. 1976-79), Population Assn. Am. (bd. dirs. 1972-75, 2nd v.p. 1983, 1st v.p. 1985, pres.-elect 1988, pres. 1989), Am. Sociol. Assn. (coun. mem. at large 1990-93, chmn., coun. mem. population sect. 1978-83). Office: U Maryland Dept Sociology College Park MD 20742-0001

PRESSER, STANLEY, social sciences educator, researcher; b. Bklyn., Feb. 18, 1950; s. Sidney and Sydonia (Cohen) P.; m. Yan Yu; 1 child, Solomon Zhi-Qian. AB, Brown U., 1971; PhD, U. Mich., 1977. Rsch. investigator Survey Rsch. Ctr., U. Mich., 1977-78, head field office, 1981-83; rsch. assoc. Inst. Rsch. Social Sci., U. N.C., 1978-81; dir. Detroit Area Study, U. Mich., 1983-85; assoc. dir. sociology program NSF, 1985-87, dir., 1987-88; prof. sociology U. Md., 1989—; dir. Survey Rsch. Ctr., 1989-2000. Vis. prof. sociology U. Md., 1988-89; dir. joint U. Md. and U. Mich. program in Survey Methodology, 1992-96; bd. overseers Nat. Opinion Rsch. Ctr. Gen. Social Survey, 1984-85, 93-97; spl. cons. Nat. Econ. Rsch. Assocs., 1986-89; cons. U.S. Dept. Justice, 1995, Dept. Commerce, 1991, GAO, 1988-89, EEO Commn., 1985, NOAA, 1991-94, State of Alaska Atty. Gen., 1989-92; bd. dirs. Roper Ctr., Consortium Social Sci. Assns. Co-author: Questions and Answers in Attitude surveys, 1981, Survey Questions: Handcrafting the Standardized Questionaire, 1986, Valuing Oil Spill Prevention, 2004; editor Pub. Opinion Quar., 1993-97; co-editor: Sourcebook of Harris National Surveys, 1981, Survey Rsch. Methods, 1989, Methods for Testing and Evaluating Survey Questions, 2004; mem. editl. bd. Pub. Opinion Quar., 1983-87, Sociol. Methods and Rsch., 1980-83, Social Psychology Quar., 1979-82; contbr. articles to profl. jours. Fellow: Am. Statis. Assn.; mem.: Sociol. Rsch. Assn., Am. Sociol. Assn. (chair profl. ethics com. 1999—2001), Am. Assn. Pub. Opinion Rsch. (pres. 1993—94). Office: U of Md Sociology Dept College Park MD 20742-1315

PRESSER, STEPHEN BRUCE, lawyer, educator; b. Chattanooga, Aug. 10, 1946; s. Sidney and Estelle (Shapiro) P.; m. Carole Smith, June 18, 1968 (div. 1987); children: David Carter, Elisabeth Catherine; m. ArLynn Leiber, Dec. 13, 1987; children: Joseph Leiber, Eastman Leiber. AB, Harvard U., 1968, JD, 1971. Bar: Mass. 1971, DC 1972. Law clk. to Judge Malcolm Richard Wilkey U.S. Ct. Appeals (D.C. cir.), 1971-72; assoc. Wilmer, Cutler & Pickering, Washington, 1972-74; asst. prof. law Rutgers U., Camden, NJ, 1974-76; vis. assoc. prof. U. Va., 1976-77; prof. Northwestern U., Chgo., 1977—, class 1940 rsch. prof., 1992-93, Raoul Berger prof. legal history, 1992—, assoc. dean acad. affairs Sch. Law, 1982-85. Prof. bus. law Kellogg Sch. Mgmt., Northwestern U., Chgo., 1992—. Author: (with Jamil S. Zainaldin) Law and Jurisprudence in American History, 1980, 6th edit., 2006, Studies in the History of the United States Courts of the Third Circuit, 1983, The Original Misunderstanding: The English, The Americans and the Dialectic of Federalist Jurisprudence, 1991, Piercing the Corporate Veil, 1991, revised ann., (with Ralph Ferrara and Meredith Brown) Takeovers: A Strategist's Manual, 2d edit., 1993, Recapturing the Constitution, 1994, (with Douglas W. Kmiec, John Eastman and Raymond Marcin) The American Constitutional Order: History, Cases, and Philosophy, 1998, 2d edit., 2004, An Introduction to the Law of Business Organizations, 2005; assoc. articles editor Guide to American Law, 1985. Trustee Village Winnetka, Ill., 2000-04, police and fire commr., 2004-; mem. acad. adv. bd. Washington Legal Found. Recipient summer stipend NEH, 1975; Fulbright Sr. scholar Univ. Coll., London Sch. Econs. and Polit. Sci., 1983-84, Inst. Advanced Legal Studies, 1996; Adams fellow Inst. U.S. Studies, London, 1996; assoc. rsch. fellow Inst. U.S. Studies, 1999—. Mem. Am. Soc. Legal History (bd. dirs. 1979-82), Am. Law Inst., Univ. Club Chgo. (bd. dirs. 1997-99, sec. 1999), Legal Club Chgo., Reform Club (London), Mich. Shores Club (Wilmette). Office: Northwestern U Law Sch 357 E Chicago Ave Chicago IL 60611-3069 E-mail: s-presser@law.northwestern.edu.

PRESSLER, LARRY, former senator, lawyer; b. Humboldt, SD, Mar. 29, 1942; s. Antoine Lewis and Loretta Geneive (Claussen) P.; m. Harriet Dent, 1982; 1 child, Laura. BA, U. S.D., 1964; diploma (Rhodes scholar), Oxford U., Eng., 1965; MA in Govt., Harvard U., 1971, JD, 1971. Bar: N.Y., D.C. Fgn. svc. officer, 1971—74; mem. 94th-95th Congresses from 1st S.D. Dist., 1974-78, U.S. Senate from S.D., 1979-97; pres. Pressler and Assocs.; U.S. del. Inter-Parliamentary Union for 97th Congress; mem. bd. visitors all mil. svc. academies; chmn. commerce, sci. and transp. coms. U.S. Senate, 1995-96; founder telecomm. group Pressler & Assocs., Washington, 1997—. Prin. sponsor Telecomm. Act of 1996, Pressler Telecomm. Act; mem. fgn. rels. com., 1980-95; congl. del. to UN Gen. Assembly, 1986, 92; former bus. cons. McKinsey & Co.; former atty. U.S. State Dept. Legal Advisor's Office; sr. fellow U. Calif., L.A., 2000—; sr. ptnr. O'Connor and Hannan, 1997-2002; sr. advisor Solomon, Smith, Barney and Monitcello Capital; vis. prof. Fudan U., Shanghai, 2005; lectr. Am. govt. U.S. Naval Acad., 2005; vis. prof., Thomas Hawkins Johnson vis. scholar West Point Mil. Acad., 2006; disting. prof. St. John's U., Queens, NY, 2007; bd. mem., corp. exec. Infosys Techs., Bangalore, India; bd. dirs. Phila. Stock Exch. Author: U.S. Senators from the Prairie, 1982, Star Wars: The SDI Debates in Congress, 1986. 1st lt. U.S. Army, 1966-69, Vietnam. Mem. Am Assn. Rhodes Scholars, D.C. Bar Assn., N.Y. State Bar Assn., VFW, ABA, Century Club (N.Y.), Met. Club (Washington), St. Albans Tennis Club, Bohemian Club Calif., Cosmos Club, 25th Infantry Divsn. Assn., Phi Beta Kappa. Avocations: golf, tennis, rowing. Home Phone: 202-210-5330; Office Phone: 202-333-5856.

PRESSLEY, DELORIS N., literacy educator; b. Nesmith, SC, Aug. 14, 1950; d. Murray Vanderbilt Nesmith, Sr. and Blanche Lamar Nesmith; m. Booker Theodore Pressley, Mar. 5, 1976; children: Malcolm L., Marquis B. B in Elem. Edn., Allen U., 1972; MEd, U. S.C., 1976; postgrad., U. S.C., Francis Marion U., 1995. Cert. elem. edn. Part-time curriculum and instrn. facilitator Battery Park Elem. Sch., Nesmith, 2003—04, literacy coach, 2004—05, elem. edn. tchr., 2005. Chairperson Williamsburg County Sch. Dist. Tchr. Forum, Kingstree, SC, 2000—02; rep. Pee Dee Edn. Tchr. Forum, Florence, SC, 2000—02. Named Tchr. of Yr., Battery Pk. Elem. Sch., 1986, 2000, Williamsburg County Dist. Tchr. of Yr., 2000; recipient mini grant, Pee Dee Edn. Found., 1990, 1994; grantee, Ednl. Improvement Act, 1999. Mem.: NEA, S.C. Internat. Reading Assn., Nat. Coun. Tchrs. English, Internat. Reading Assn. Democrat. United Methodist. Avocations: reading, gardening. Home: 721 Nesmith Corner Rd Nesmith SC 29580 Office Phone: 843-558-5233.

PRESSLEY, FRED G., JR., lawyer; b. NYC, June 19, 1953; s. Fred G. Sr. and Frances (Sanders) P.; m. Cynthia Denise Hill, Sept. 5, 1981. BA cum laude, Union Coll., 1975; JD, Northwestern U., 1978. Bar: Ohio 1978, U.S. Dist. Ct. (so. dist.) Ohio 1979, U.S. Dist. Ct. (no. dist.) Ohio 1985, U.S. Dist. Ct. (ea. dist.) Wis. 1980, U.S. Ct. Appeals (6th cir.). Assoc. Porter, Wright, Morris & Arthur, Columbus, Ohio, 1978-85, ptnr., 1985—. Bd. dirs. Columbus Area Leadership Program, 1981-84, Franklin County Bd. Mental Retardation and Devel. Disabilities, Columbus, 1989-97, Union Coll., Schenectady, N.Y., 1992—. Recipient Civic Achievement award Ohio Ho. of Reps., 1988. Mem. ABA. Avocations: jogging, golf, basketball, history. Office: Porter Wright Morris & Arthur 41 S High St Ste 2800 Columbus OH 43215-6194

PRESSLY, THOMAS JAMES, history professor; b. Troy, Tenn., Jan. 18, 1919; s. James Wallace and Martha Belle (Bittick) P.; m. Lillian Cameron, Apr. 30, 1943; children: Thomas James II, Stephanie Suzuki. AB, Harvard U., 1940, AM, 1941, PhD, 1950; LLD (hon.), Whitman Coll., 1981. Instr. history Princeton (NJ) U., 1946-49; asst. prof. U. Wash., 1949-54, assoc. prof., 1954-60, prof., 1960-87, prof. emeritus, 1987—. Vis. assoc. prof. Princeton U., 1953-54, Johns Hopkins U., 1969-70. Author: Americans Interpret Their Civil War, 1954; editor: (with W. H. Scofield) Farm Real Estate Values in the United States, 1965, (with others) American Political Behavior, 1974, Diary of George Templeton Strong (abridged), 1988, (with Glenn M. Linden) Voices From the House Divided, 1995, (with Maclyn P. Burg) The Great War At Home and Abroad, 1999. With US Army, 1941—45. Ford Found. Faculty fellow, 1951-52; Ctr. for Advanced Study in Behavioral Scis. fellow, 1955-56. Mem. Am. Hist. Assn., So. Hist. Assn. (editl. bd. Jour. So. History 1973-77), Orgn. Am. Historians. Home and Office: 4545 E Laurel Dr NE Seattle WA 98105-3838 Home Phone: 206-525-4655.

PRESSMAN, EDWARD R., motion picture producer; b. NYC, Apr. 11, 1943; m. Annie McEnroe; 1 child. Grad., Stanford U.; student, London Sch. Econs. Co-founder Pressman-Williams Enterprises. Prodr.: (films) Out of It, 1969, The Revolutionary, 1970, Dealing: or the Berkeley to Boston Forty Brick Lost Bag Blues, 1972, Sisters, 1973, Phantom of the Paradise, 1974, Old Boyfriends, 1979, Heart Beat, 1980, The Hand, 1981, Conan the Destroyer, 1984, Plenty, 1985, Cherry 2000, 1987, Wall Street, 1987, Talk Radio, 1988, Blue Steel, 1990, Reversal of Fortune, 1990, Waiting for the Light, 1990, Homicide, 1991, Year of the Gun, 1991, Storyville, 1992, Bad Lieutenant, 1992, Hoffa, 1992, The Crow, 1994, Street Fighter, 1994, City Hall, 1996, The Island of Dr. Moreau, 1996, The Crow: City of Angels, 1996, The Blackout, 1997, Two Girls and a Guy, 1997, New Rose Hotel, 1998, Legionnaire, 1998, Endurance, 1999, The Crow: Salvation, 2000, The Beautiful Country, 2004, Undertow, 2004, The Crow: Wicked Player, 2005, Amazing Grace, 2006; exec. prodr.: Badlands, 1973, Despair, 1978, Paradise Alley, 1978, Victoria, 1979, The Boat, 1981, Conan the Barbarian, 1982, The Pirates of Penzance, 1983, Crimewave, 1985, Half Moon Street, 1986, True Stories, 1986, Flicks, 1987, Masters of the Universe, 1987, Good Morning Babylon, 1987, Walker, 1987, Paris By Night, 1988, Martians Go Home, 1990, To Sleep With Anger, 1990, Waiting for the Light, 1990, Iron Maze, 1991, Dream Lover, 1994, Judge Dredd, 1995, Black and White, 1999, After the Truth, 1999, The Endurance, 2000, Happy Times, 2000, Harvard Man, 2001, The Guys, 2002, The Cooler, 2003, Party Monster, 2003, The Hebrew Hammer, 2003, Owning Mahowny, 2003, Love Object, 2003, Rick, 2003, Never Die Alone, 2004, The King, 2005, Thank You for Smoking, 2005, Driving Lessons, 2006, Fur: An Imaginary Portrait of Diane Arbus, 2006. Office: Edward R Pressman Film Corp 445 N Bedford Dr Penthouse Beverly Hills CA 90210 *

PRESSMAN, JACOB, retired rabbi; b. Phila., Oct. 26, 1919; s. Solomon David and Dora (Levin) P.; m. Marjorie Steinberg, June 14, 1942; children: Daniel Joseph, Joel David, Judith Sharon. BA, U. Pa., 1940; MHL, Jewish Theol. Sem., 1944, Dr.Hebrew Letters, 1960, Dr. Humane Letters, 1979. Ordained rabbi, 1945. Rabbi Forest Hills Jewish Ctr., NYC, 1944-46, Congregation Sinai, LA, 1946-50, Temple Beth Am, LA, 1950—85; ret. Dir. Bonds of Israel, L.A., 1988-90, city chmn., 1990-91; vice chmn. bd. govs. L.A. Jewish Fedn. Coun., 1988—; founder U. Judaism, L.A. Hebrew High Sch., Herzl Sch., Camp Ramah at Ojai, Akiba Acad., Rabbi Jacob Pressman Acad. Author: Dear Friends, 2001, This Wild and Crazy World, 2001. Recipient Simon Greenberg award for Outstanding Achievement in Rabbinate, Ziegler Sch. Rabbinic Studies, U. Judaism, L.A., 2004. Mem. Rabbinical Assembly Western Region (pres. 1954-56), Bd. Rabbis So. Calif. (pres. 1958-61). Office Phone: 310-652-7353. E-mail: jpress6511@aol.com. *God is. God is good. His creation is good, and so, mankind, being of His creation is good. As an act of grace, God gives man the power to choose between good and evil in his ways, and with even greater grace gives man the awareness that he has this choice. Man is perfectible. His perfect stage, the Messianic era, is coming; but it will always be coming, never at a moment in time to arrive, but always inviting us to progress to newer and higher goals personally and as a society, each new mountaintop of human progress toward that nobler future merely opens our eyes to visions of even greater and more God-like human life.*

PRESSMAN, RONALD R., utilities executive; b. NYC, Apr. 11, 1958; m. Mary Pressman; 3 children. Grad., Hamilton College, NY, 1980. Gen. mgr. ctr. and ea. Europe GE, London, 1990—92; CEO GE Power Sys. Europe, 1992—95, CEO Power Sys. global mktg., 1995—96; pres., CEO GE Capital Real Estate, 1997; sr. v.p. GE Co., 2000—; pres., CEO G.E. Employers Reinsurance Co., 2000—. Bd. dirs. A Better Chance, Kansas City Civic Coun.; mem. exec. bd. Nat. Realty Com., Wharton Real Estate Bus. Sch. Recipient Crown American Golden Crown award, 1998, Fin. Svcs. Exec. of Yr., Comml. Property News. Office: GE Employers Reinsurance Co PO Box 2991 Shawnee Mission KS 66201-1391

PRESTAGE, JAMES JORDAN, university chancellor, consultant; b. Deweyville, Tex., Apr. 29, 1926; s. James J. and Mona (Wilkins) P.; m. Jewel Limar, Aug. 12, 1953; children— Terri, James Grady, Eric, Karen, Jay BS cum laude, So. U., Baton Rouge, 1950; MS, U. Iowa, 1955, PhD, 1959. Instr. biology Prairie View Coll., Tex., 1955-56; asst. prof. So. U., Baton Rouge, 1959, assoc. prof. biology, 1959-61, prof. biology, 1961—, dir. computer sci. ctr., 1968-71, 72-73, dean acad. affairs, v.p. acad. affairs, 1973-81, exec. v.p., 1981-82, chancellor, 1982-85, univ. disting. prof. emeritus, 1985—; univ. disting. prof. biology Dillard U., New Orleans, 1987—. Chair divsn. natural scis. Dillard U., 1990—97; asst. dir. La. Coordinating Council for Higher Edn., Baton Rouge, 1971—72; mem. commn. on scholars Ill. Bd. Higher Edn., 1975—82; mem. com. on off-campus instrn. La. Bd. Regents, 1975—; mem. La. Data Processing Coun., Baton Rouge, 1979—82; vis. prof. biology Dillard U., New Orleans; trustee Am. Coll. Testing Program, 1983—86; faculty assoc. Danforth Found., 1966—70; cons. in field. Mem. exec. bd. Istrouma council Boy Scouts Am.; vice chmn. bd. trustees Greater Mt. Carmel Baptist Ch., Baton Rouge; bd. dirs. Capital Area United Way, Baton Rouge. Served with USN, 1944-46, 50-52; ETO, Korea Named Most Outstanding Faculty Mem., So. U., 1966-67; Nat. Med. Fellowships fellow U. Iowa, Iowa City, 1956-59; NIH grantee, 1960-65 Mem. Conf. Acad. Deans So. States. NAACP, Sigma Xi, Alpha Chi, Alpha Phi Alpha (chpt. pres.), Sigma Pi Phi Democrat. Avocations: fishing, reading, gardening. Home: 2145 77th Ave Baton Rouge LA 70807-5508 Office: So Br PO Box 9222 Baton Rouge LA 70813

PRESTAGE, JEWEL LIMAR, political science professor; b. Hutton, La., Aug. 12, 1931; d. Brudis L. and Sallie Bell (Johnson) Limar; m. James J. Prestage, Aug. 12, 1953; children— Terri, James, Eric, Karen, Jay. BA, So. U., Baton Rouge, 1951; MA, U. Iowa, 1952, PhD, 1954; LHD (hon.), U. D.C., 1994, Loyola U., Chgo., 1999; LLD (hon.), Spelman Coll., 1999. Assoc. prof. polit. sci. Prairie View (Tex.) Coll., 1954-55, 56; assoc. prof. polit. sci. So. U., 1956-57, 58-62, prof., 1962—, chairperson dept., 1965-83, dean pub. policy and urban affairs, 1983-89, dist. prof. emeritus, dean emeritus pub. policy, 1989—; prof. polit. sci. Prairie View U., 1989-90, dean Benjamin Banneker Honors College, Prairie View (Tex.) Coll., 1990-98, prof. political sci., 1998—; disting. prof. emeritus polit. sci. Benjamin Banneker Honors Coll., 2000—. Chmn. La. adv. com. to U.S. Commn. on Civil Rights, 1975-85; mem., chmn. nat. adv. coun. on women's ednl. programs U.S. Dept. Edn., 1980-82; dist. vis. prof. U. Iowa, 1987-88. Author: (with M. Githens) A Portrait of Marginality: Political Behavior of the American Woman, 1976; contbr. articles to profl. jours. Rockefeller fellow, 1951-52; NSF fellow, 1964; Ford Found. postdoctoral fellow, 1969-70 Mem. NAACP, Am. Polit. Sci. Assn. (v.p. 1974-75, Frank Goodnow award 1998), So. Polit. Sci. Assn. (pres. 1975-76, Manning Daner award 1998), Nat. Conf. Black Polit. Scientists (pres. 1976-77), Nat. Assn. African Am. Honors Programs (pres. 1993-94), Am. Soc. for Pub. Adminstrn. (pres. La. chpt. 1988-89, nat. exec. coun. 1989-90), Policy Studies Orgn. (exec. coun. 2000), Links Inc., Alpha Kappa Alpha. Home: 11114 Wortham Blvd Houston TX 77065 Office: So Univ PO Box 125 Prairie View TX 77446-0125 *Commitments which guide my life are: (1) maximum development of personal potential through pursuit of excellence in all endeavors; (2) fair play, respect, compassion and quest of community in relations with fellow human beings; (3) utilization of personal talents in the interest of removing impediments to the good life "for all persons"; (4) pursuit of truth as the pervasive concern in academia; and (5) transmission of the above as priority goals to all with whom I have contact.*

PRESTBO, JOHN ANDREW, editor, writer, journalist; b. Northwood, ND, Sept. 26, 1941; s. Oscar Bernt and Jeanne (Schol) P.; m. Darlene Parrish, Aug. 14, 1965; children: Bradford Jonathan, Laura Christine. BS, Northwestern U., 1963, MS, 1964. Reporter, writer Wall Street Jour., Chgo., 1964-74, staff editor, Page 1 NYC, 1974-75, commodities editor, 1975-77, bur. chief Cleve., 1977-81, markets editor NYC, 1984—, editor Dow Jones Indexes, 1993—; v.p. editorial Dow Jones Radio 2, Inc., Princeton, NJ, 1981-83; exec. dir. Dow Jones Indexes, Princeton, 2006—. Author: Sleuthing, 1976; co-author: (with Frederick C. Klein) News and the Market, 1974, (with Douglas R. Sease) Barron's Guide to Making Investment Decisions, 1994, 2nd edit., 1998, The Wall Street Jour. Book of Internat. Investing, 1997; editor: This Abundant Land, 1975, Dow Jones Commodities Handbook, 1976-79, The Dow Jones Guide to the World Stock Market, 1994-98, The Market's Measure, 1999, Dow Jones Indexes, 2006—. Served with USAFR, 1966-73. Recipient Econ. Reporting award Ind. Natural Gas Assn., U. Mo., 1967; recipient Achievement-bur. writing award G.M. Loeb, 1968 Home: 14 Charleston Dr Skillman NJ 08558-1801 Office: 4300 Rte 1 Monmouth Junction NJ 08852 Home Phone: 908-874-6780; Office Phone: 609-520-7079. Business E-Mail: john.prestbo@dowjones.com.

PRESTI, SAM, professional sports team executive; b. Concord, Mass. Student, Va. Wesleyan Coll., Norfolk; BA in Comm., Politics and Law, Emerson Coll., Boston, 2000. Intern San Antonio Spurs, 2000—01, basketball spl. asst., 2001—02, asst. dir. scouting, 2002—03, dir. player pers., 2003—05, asst. gen. mgr., 2005—07, v.p., 2006—07; gen. mgr. Seattle SuperSonics, 2007—. Recipient Young Alumnus award, Emerson Coll., 2005. Office: Seattle SuperSonics 351 Elliott Ave W Ste 500 Seattle WA 98119 Office Phone: 206-281-5800. *

PRESTINE, JOAN SINGLETON, writer, educator, editor; b. Salt Lake City, Mar. 11, 1944; d. Herbert William and Frances Bowdidge Singleton; m. Douglas C. Prestine, Apr. 5, 1963; children: Scott, Deb, Jeffrey. BA, U. So. Calif., LA, 1965. Author, lectr., freelance editor Children's Picture Book, 1987—. Pub. cons., 1987—; lectr. Santa Monica Coll., Pierce Coll., West LA Coll., Ventura Coll., Coll. of Canyons, Moorpark Coll., Oxnard Coll., Learning Tree U., Arapahoe Coll., Colo. State U. Denver, U. Colo., Denver U., 1987—. Author: (picture books My Special Feelings series) I Want This and This and This, 1987, Love Me Anyway, 1987, My Parents Go On a Trip, 1987, Someone Special Died, 1987, Me First, 1987, Sometimes I'm Afraid, 1987, Match Who You Are With What You Do, 1987, How to Write Picture Books for Fun and Profit, 1987, Chipper Chipmunk Cruises, 1989, (picture books Kids Have Feelings Too series) Someone Special Died, 1993, 2003, Sometimes I Feel Awful, 1993, 2003, It's Hard to Share My Teacher, 1994, 2003, Mom and Dad Break Up, 1996, 2003, Moving Is Hard, 1997, 2003, (resource guides) Family Day Care Activities from A to Z, 1989, Earthquake Preparedness, 1990, Helping Children Cope with Death, 1993, Helping Children Understand Their Feelings, 1993, Helping Children Share Their Teacher, 1994, Helping Children Understand Divorce, 1996, Helping Children Cope With Moving, 1997, Easy Activities for Every Kid, 2001. Mem Jr. League LA, 1976—; chair St. Joseph Ctr., 1991—, vol. cir., 1996; pres. JLLA Sustainer, 2004—; founder Investments Plus, 1983, pres., 1983—1986, Rec. Sec., 1986—; Benefactor Huntington Libr.; bd. mem. Parrots Internat., 2005—; Leader Boy Scouts Am., 1972—1984, Girl Scouts Am., 1975—1980, Peterson Automotive Mus., Nat. Charity League, Checkered Flag 200, 2003—, Pres. Cir. Orthop. Hosp., 2004—; 11-99 Found., 2002—; with LA Conservancy. Named PTA Parent of Yr., Bellagio Rd. Sch., 1977, Parent of Yr., Parent Tchr. Student Assn., U. High Sch., 1983; recipient Parenting Shelf, Parents Choice Mag., 1994, Dir.'s award, Early Childhood News, 1997, Carolyn Helman Lichtenberg Crest award, 2002. Mem.: FOCAL, Westside Writer's Guild, Pubs. Mktg. Assn., Soc. Children's Book Writers and Illustrators, So. Calif. Children's Book Writers and Illustrators, Internat. Reading Assn., Childrens Author Network, Book Publicists of So. Calif., Authors Guild, Nat. Assn. Edn. of Young Children (life), Pi Beta Phi (alumni bd., pres. 1996—99, program chair 1993—96). Avocations: car rallies, reading, travel, walking. Office: 2070 South 7th Street, Suite E San Jose CA 95112 Personal E-mail: joanprestine@msn.com.

PRESTON, ANDREW JOSEPH, pharmacist, drug company executive; b. Bklyn., Apr. 19, 1922; s. Charles A. and Josephine (Rizzutto) Pumo; m. Martha Jeanne Happ, Oct. 10, 1953; children: Andrew Joseph Jr., Charles Richard, Carolyn Louise, Frank Arthur, Joanne Marie, Barbara Jeanne. BSc, St. John's U., 1943. Cert. bus. intermediary Internat. Bus. Brokers Assn. Mgr. Press Club, Bklyn. Nat. League Baseball Club, 1941-42; purchasing agt. Drug and Pharm. divsn. Intrassind, Inc., 1947; chief pharmacist Hendershot Pharmacy, Newton, NJ, 1949; agt. Bur. of Narcotics, U.S. Treasury Dept., 1948-49; owner Preston Drug & Surg. Co., Boonton, NJ, 1949-86; CEO Preston Pharmaceutics, Inc., Butler, NJ, 1970-80, Preston Bus. Cons., Inc., Kinnelon, NJ, 1987—. Commr. NJ State Bd. Pharmacy, 1970—72, pres., 1973; organizer State of NJ Drug Abuse Spkrs. Program, 1970—76; chmn. Morris County Drug Abuse Coun., 1969—70; lectr. drug abuse and narcotic addition various cmty. orgns., 1968—78; mem. adv. bd. Nat. Cmty. Bank, Boonton, 1973. Contbr. editls. to profl. jours. Chmn. bldg. fund com. Riverside Hosp., Boonton, 1963; mem. exec. com. Gov. Tom Kean Ann. Ball, 1985—86; chmn. Pharmacists of NJ for election of Pres. Ford, 1976, Pharmacists for Gov. Tom Kean, 1981—84, NJ Pharmacists for Reagan/Bush, 1984; mem. exec. com. Morris County Overall Econ. Devel. Com., 1976—82; chmn. Pharmacists for Fenwick, 1982; v.p. Kinnelon (NJ) Rep. Club, 1980; Rep. com. Kinnelon, 1990; mem. adv. com. to Congressman Dean Gallo on Pres. Clinton's Health Security Plan, 1994; mem. Morris County (NJ) Rep. Fin. Com., 1972; pres. Ronald Reagan NJ Re-Election Adv. Bd., 1984. Lt. (j.g.) USNR, 1943—46. Recipient Bowl Hygeia award, Robbins Co., 1969, Pres.'s award, E.R. Squibb, 1968, Square Club award, NJ Pharm., 1969, Andrew J. Preston award for Polit. Action established in his honor, 1999, Spl. NJ Pharmacists award for loyal svc., NJ Pharm. Assn., NJ Polit. Action Com., 2002. Mem.: VFW, Morris-Sussex Pharmacists Soc., Morris County Pharm. Assn., NJ Pub. Health Assn., Pharmacists Guild NJ, Pharmacists Guild Am. (pres. NY divsn. 1946—47), Inst. Bus. Appraisers, Internat. Bus. Brokers Assn., NJ Narcotic Enforcement Officers Assn., Internat. Narcotic Enforcement Officers Assn., Nat. Cmty. Pharmacists Assn., NJ Pharm. Assn. (econs. com. 1960—65, pres. 1967—68, Oscar Singer Meml. award 1987, William H. McNeil award 1994, Presdl. Citation award 2000, Spl. NJ Pharmacists award 2002), Am. Pharm. Assn., St. John's Alumni Assn., NJ Assn. Realtors, Nat. Assn. Realtors, Morris County Bd. Realtors, Am. Legion, Smoke Rise Club, KC (4th Degree 2005), Elks. Roman Catholic. Home and Office: 507 Pepperidge Tree Ln Kinnelon NJ 07405-2223 Home Phone: 973-838-4873; Office Phone: 973-838-5342.

PRESTON, BRETT JOSEPH, lawyer; b. Savannah, Ga., Nov. 9, 1962; s. Roland Leroy and Marsha Ann Preston; m. Amanda Preston; children: Alison, Grant, Natalie. BA, Duke U., Durham, NC, 1983; JD, Washington U., St. Louis, 1986. Atty. Shackleford, Farrior, Stallings & Evans, Tampa, Fla., 1986—91; shareholder Hill, Ward & Henderson, Tampa, 1991—. Mem.: Fla. Def. Lawyers Assn., Def. Rsch. Inst., Fedn. Def. & Corp. Counsel. Avocations: reading, sports, exercise. Home: 22 Spanish Main Tampa FL 33609 Office: Hill Ward & Henderson PO Box 2231 Tampa FL 33601

PRESTON, CHARLES GEORGE, lawyer; b. Nov. 11, 1940; s. Charles William and Gudveig Nicoline (Hoem) P.; m. Hilde Delphine van Stappen, Mar. 12, 1970; children: Charles William, Stephanie Delphine, Christina Nicoline. BA, U. Wash., 1963, MPA, 1968; JD, Columbia U., 1971. Bar: Wash. 1971, D.C. 1981, U.S. Dist. Ct. D.C. 1981, U.S. Dist. Ct. (we. dist.) Wash. 1971, U.S. Ct. Appeals (9th cir.) 1972, U.S. Ct. Appeals (4th cir.) 1979, U.s. Ct. Appeals (5th and D.C. cirs.) 1978, U.S. Ct. Appeals (2d cir.) 1980, U.S. Ct. Appeals (11th cir.) 1981, U.S. Supreme Ct. 1977, U.S. Ct. Claims 1982, U.S. Ct. Appeals (1st cir.) 1984, U.S. Ct. Appeals (3d, 6th and 7th cirs.) 1987, Va. 1987, U.S. Dist. Ct. (ea. dist.) Va. 1989, U.S. Dist. Ct. (we. dist.) Wash. 1971, U.S. Dist. Ct. (no. dist.) Calif. 1981, U.S. Bankruptcy Ct. Va. 1990. Assoc. Jones, Grey, Bayley & Olson, Seattle, 1971-72; atty., asst. counsel for litigation Officer of Solicitor U.S. Dept. Labor, Seattle, 1972-76, Washington, 1976-81; atty. Air Line Pilots Assn., Washington, 1981-82; mng. ptnr. MacNabb, Preston & Waxman, Washington, 1981-86, Preston & Preston, Great Falls, Va., 1986-95, Charles G. Preston, P.C., 1995—. Pres. Preston Group, Inc., 1989—98, Preston Funding LLC, 2006—; mgr. RE2I Realty, Inc., 2005—; lectr. in field. Mem. Wash. State Bar, D.C. Bar Assn., Va. Bar Assn., Tng. Law Inst. (pres. 1985-95), Gt. Falls Bus. and Profl. Assn. (pres. 1990), The Serbian Crown, Va. (pres. 1989-99). Office: Charles G Preston PC 774C Walker Rd Great Falls VA 22066-2639 Home Phone: 703-759-4343; Office Phone: 703-759-3300. E-mail: preston.law@verizon.net.

PRESTON, CHARLES MICHAEL, lawyer; b. Balt., Oct. 11, 1945; s. Carlton Edward and Jeannette Thorn (Baker) P.; m. Carol Ann Armacost, June 21, 1969 (div. Dec. 1978). BA, Western Md. Coll., 1967; JD, U. Balt., 1970. Bar: Md. 1970, U.S. Dist. Ct. Md. 1972, U.S. Supreme Ct. 1974, U.S. Dist. Ct. (trial bar) 1984. Law clk. to Hon. E.O. Weant, Jr., Westminster, Md., 1970-71; assoc. Hoffman & Hoffman, Westminster, 1972-75; ptnr. Hoffman, Hoffman & Preston, Westminster, 1976-77, Hoffman, Stoner & Preston, Westminster, 1978-79; ptnr., v.p. Stoner, Preston & Boswell Chartered, Westminster, 1980—. Rev. bd., panel mem. Atty. Grievance Commn., Annapolis, Md., 1978-95; mem. Md. Ct. Appeals Commn. on alternate dispute resolution, 1998-2000, adv. bd., Md. Mediation and Conflict Resolution Office (co-chair, Circuit Courts Com.), 2001-, Md. Ct. of Appeals Task Force on Professionalism, 2002-. Contbr. articles to profl. jours. Mem. Carroll County Gen. Hosp., Westminster, 1983—; trustee Raymond I. Richardson Found., Middleburg, Md., 1979-93; bd. dirs. Carroll County Agrl. Ctr., Westminster, 1975—; dir. N.W. dist. ARC, Balt., 1987-95; trustee Balt. Opera Co., 1998-2001. With U.S. Army, 1970-71. Fellow Md. Bar Found. (dir. 1998-, sec., treas. 2005-), Am. Bar Found.; mem. ABA (del. ho. of dels. 1997-00), Md. State Bar Assn. (treas. 1991-96, bd. govs. 1985-86, 91-00, pres.-elect 1997, pres. 98), Carroll County Bar Assn. (pres. 1985), Pro Bono Resource Ctr. Md. (bd. dirs. 1997-00), Elks. Presbyterian. Avocations: skiing, ice skating, woodworking, music, travel. Office: Stoner Preston & Boswell PO Box 389 188 E Main St Westminster MD 21157-5017

PRESTON, ELIZABETH A., psychologist; b. Missoula, Mont., May 9, 1957; d. Jay William and Elizabeth (Cummings) P.; children, Katherine Jennifer Lee, Jayson Douglas Lee. BA summa cum laude, U. Minn., 1979; PhD, Princeton U., 1984; Postdoctoral Cert., Calif. Sch. Profl. Psychology, 1988. Postdoctoral intern El Dorado County, Placerville, Calif., 1984-85, San Mateo (Calif.) County, 1985-87; adj. faculty Calif. Sch. Profl. Psychology, Berkeley, 1987; postdoctoral intern Kaiser Permanent, Santa Rosa, Calif., 1988-89; therapist Waldenhouse, Inc., San Francisco, 1989; clin. dir. Alinda Youth Svcs., Fairfield, Calif., 1990; therapist Kairos Unltd., Oakland, Calif.; pvt. practice Oakland, Calif., 1994—. Activist No. Calif. War Tax Resistors, Berkeley, 1991. NSF fellow, 1980-83; U. Mont. scholar, 1975-76, 77-78. Mem. Am. Psychol. Assn., Calif. Psychol. Assn., Phi Beta Kappa, Phi Kappa Phi. Office: 4100-10 Redwood Rd 126 Oakland CA 94619 Office Phone: 510-482-5344.

PRESTON, FORREST L., healthcare executive; Founder, chmn. Life Care Centers of Am., Cleveland, Tenn., 1970—. Office: Life Care Centers of Am PO Box 3480 3570 Keith St NW Cleveland TN 37320-3480

PRESTON, FRANCES WILLIAMS, music company executive; b. Nashville, Aug. 27, 1934; children: Kirk, David, Donald. Degree (hon.), Lincoln Coll., Ill., Berklee Sch. Music. With BMI (Broadcast Music Inc.), Nashville, 1958—, v.p., 1964-85, sr. v.p. performing rights NYC, 1985, exec. v.p., CEO, 1986, pres., CEO, 1986—2004, pres. emeritus, 2004—. Bd. dirs. Bionovo Inc., 2006—. Mem. Film, Entertainment and Music Commn. Adv. Council State of Tenn.; founding mem. bd. dirs. Leadership Nashville; past pres. bd. dirs. John Work Meml. Found.; chmn. bd. dirs. Country Music Found., Inc., 1983-85, trustee, past pres., chmn. bldg. com.; mem. Commn. on White House Record Library, Carter adminstrn., Pres.'s Panama Canal Study Com., Carter adminstrn.; bd. dirs. Rock & Roll Hall of Fame; mem. adminstrv. council Internat. Confedn. of Socs. of Authors and Composers; v.p. Nat. Music Council; past bd. dirs. Peabody Awards; hon. trustee Nat. Acad. Popular Music; pres. T.J. Martell Fedn. for Leukemia, Cancer and AIDS Rsch.; established Frances Williams Preston Rsch. Labs. for T.J. Martell Fedn., 1993; bd. dirs. R&B Found. Recipient achievement award Women's Equity Action League, spl. citation award NATAS, Golden Baton award Young Musicians Found., Humanitarian award Internat. Achievement in Arts award, 1995, Creative Achievement award Elaine Kaufman Cultural Ctr., 1996, Lester Sill Humanitarian award, 1996, Nat. Trustees award Grammys, 1998; named one of Am.'s 50 Most Powerful Women Ladies' Home Jour.; named to Country Music Hall of Fame. Mem. Country Music Assn. (life mem. bd. dirs., Irving Waugh Award of Excellence), Nashville Symphony Assn. (past sec., bd. dirs.), NARAS Found. (bd. dirs., pres.'s adv. bd.), Nashville Songwriters Assn. (life mem., bd. dirs.), Gospel Music Assn. (life mem. bd., past chmn., past pres.), Am. Women in Radio and TV (past nat. dir.). Clubs: (Friars Found. Applause award). Lodges: Rotary (1st woman mem. Nashville club), Friars. Presbyterian. Office: BMI 320 W 57th St Fl 3 New York NY 10019-3790

PRESTON, JEROME, JR., retired lawyer; b. SI, NY, Nov. 15, 1922; s. Jerome and Iva (Stone) P.; m. Dorothy Greeno McCann, Oct. 3, 1953; children: Richard M., Douglas J., David G. AB, Harvard U., 1947; LL.B., Yale U., 1950. Bar: Mass. 1951. Ptnr. Foley Hoag LLP, Boston, 1956—92, ret. sr. ptnr., 1992—. Trustee Eaton-Vance Income Fund of Boston, Inc., 1976-95. Trustee Univ. Hosp., 1956-96, overseer, 1996—; bd. dirs. Cambridge Sch. of Weston, 1973-78, pres., 1975-77; mem. Wellesley (Mass.) Planning Bd., 1962-70, chmn., 1966-68. Served to 1st lt. Signal Corps AUS, 1943-46. Mem. ABA, Mass. Bar Assn., Boston Bar Assn., Am. Law Inst., Handel and Haydn Soc. (pres. 1988-92, pres. emeritus 1992-, gov. 1988-92), Tavern Club. Democrat. Home: 1010 Memorial Dr Apt 2G Cambridge MA 02138-4853 Office: Foley Hoag LLP 155 Seaport Blvd Ste 1600 Boston MA 02210-4853 Home Phone: 617-661-9115; Office Phone: 617-832-1149. Personal E-mail: jprestonh@aol.com.

PRESTON, JOHN ELWOOD, lawyer; b. Celina, Ohio, Sept. 15, 1941; s. Homer Harlan and Nancy Alice (Boroff) P.; m. Alexandra Learned, Aug. 7, 1965. BA, Ohio U., 1962; LLB, George Washington U., Washington, 1965. Bar: D.C. 1967, Calif. 1973, U.S. Dist. Ct. D.C. 1967, U.S. Dist. Ct. (cen. dist.) Calif. 1984. Staff asst. Office of U.S. Senator Thomas H. Kuchel, Washington, 1964-66; atty., advisor Office of Gen. Counsel, GAO, Washington, 1966-71; mem. regulations study group Commn. on Govt. Procurement, Washington, 1970-71; div. counsel Litton Industries, Beverly Hills, Calif., 1971-79, group v.p., 1979-88, asst. gen. counsel, 1988-89, assoc. gen. counsel, 1989-90, v.p., assoc. gen. counsel, 1990-93, sr. v.p., gen. counsel, 1993—. Bd. dirs. Parks Jaeger Aerospace, Orlando, Fla., 1988-92; arbitrator Am. Arbitration Assn., L.A., 1986—. Contbr. articles to profl. jours. Mem. ABA (chmn. various coms.), Soc. Internat. Lawyers, Fed. Bar Assn., Nat. Contract Mgmt. Assn., Phi Alpha Delta. Avocations: golf, tennis, music, theater. Office: Litton Industries Inc 21240 Burbank Blvd Woodland Hills CA 91367-6675

PRESTON, JULIA, journalist; BA in Latin American Studies, Yale Univ., 1976. Latin Am. corr. Washington Post, 1986—92, U.N. corr., 1993—95; Mexico corr. The New York Times, 1995—2001, U.N. Bureau chief corr., 2002—03, dep. investigations ed., 2003—. Author: (Book) What Duarte Won, 1985, The Trial that Shook Cuba, 1989, The Battle for San Salvador, 1990, The Case of the Cesna 310: An Exchange, 1990, The Defeat of the Sandanistas, 1990. Recipient Robert F Kennedy award for Humanitarian Journalism, 1994, Maria Moors Cabot Prize for disting. coverage of Latin Am., 1997, Pulitzer Prize for Journalism, 1998. Office: The New York Times 229 W 43rd St New York NY 10036 Office Phone: 212-566-1251. Office Fax: 212-566-3690.

PRESTON, PAUL MICHAEL, anthropologist, writer; b. Joliet, Ill., Nov. 26, 1950; s. Michael J. Preston and Eleanor Frances Seely; life ptnr. Tim A. Lukaszewski, Dec. 10, 1980. BA, U. of Chgo., 1972, MA, 1973; MEd, U. of Ariz., 1977; PhD, U. of Calif., 1992. Cert. tchr. Ariz., 1977. Tchr. and dept. chair English, St. Rita Sch. for the Deaf, Cin., 1973—76; mem. faculty English and spl. edn. depts. Pima C.C. Dist., Tucson, 1976—80; dir. disabled student svcs. Calif. State U., Hayward, 1980—86; infant devel. specialist Children's Hosp., Oakland, Calif., 1987—90; med. anthropologist U. Calif., San Francisco, 1993—98; co-dir. Nat. Rsch. and Tng. Ctr. on Families with Disabilities, Berkeley, Calif., 1993—98; dir. Nat. Resource Ctr. for Parents with Disabilities, Berkeley, Calif., 1998—. Rschr. Nat. Inst. of Disability and Rehab. Rsch., Berkeley, 1999—, prin. investigator, 1994—98; chmn. rsch. design panel Nat. Rsch. and Tng. Ctr. for Families of Parents with Disabilities, 1993—99; fed. grant reviewer U.S. Dept. HSS, Cin., 1995—2002; adj. prof. Union Inst., Cin., 1995—2002. Author: Mother Father Deaf: Living between Sound and Silence. Harvard University Press, 1994, (monograph) National Information Packet for Deaf Parents and School Personnel, 2001; contbr. scientific papers. Emeritus bd. mem. Cmty. Resources for Ind. Living, Hayward, Calif., 1980—2002; bd. dirs. The Ed Roberts Campus, Berkeley, Calif., 1998—2002. Fellow, U. of Ariz., 1976—77, Regent's fellowship, U. of Calif. San Francisco, 1990—92, U. Dean's fellowship, 1986—90; scholar, NEH, 1968—73. Mem.: Soc. for Applied Anthropology, Nat. Assn. of the Deaf, Soc. for Med. Anthropology, Am. Anthropology Assn., Soc. for Disability Studies, Children of Deaf Adults Internat. (Lifetime Achievement award 2001). Independent. Avocations: backpacking, gardening, cooking, travel. Office: Through the Looking Glass 2198 Sixth Street Suite 100 Berkeley CA 94710-2204 Office Phone: 800-644-2666 x 104. E-mail: ppreston@lookingglass.org.

PRESTON, RICHARD MCKIM, lawyer; b. Balt., June 2, 1947; s. Wilbur Day Jr. and May Virginia (Honemann) P.; m. Trisa Jean Thompson, Apr. 28, 1961. BA, Washington & Lee U., 1969, JD cum laude, 1976; MA cum laude, Fairleigh Dickinson U., 1973. Assoc. vomBaur, Coburn, Simmons & Turtle, Washington, 1976-79, Seyfarth, Shaw, Washington, 1979-82, ptnr., 1982—. Mng. ptnr. Constrn. Group, 1987—; bd. govs. Washington Bldg. Congress, 1997—. Contbr. articles to profl. publs., chpt. to book. Bd. advisors Jubilee Support Found., Washington, 1989—; mem. Washington & Lee Law Coun., Lexington, Va., 1986-93. Mem. River Bend Golf and Country Club, Sankaty Head Golf Club, Metro. Club (D.C.). Office: Seyfarth Shaw 815 Connecticut Ave NW Washington DC 20006-4004 Home Phone: 703-250-5140; Office Phone: 202-828-5370. Business E-Mail: rpreston@seyfarth.com.

PRESTON, ROB, editor-in-chief; BA in journalism, St. Bonaventure U.; MA in econ., State U. NY at Binghamton. Past editl. mgmt. positions CommunicationsWeek Internat.; editor-in-chief Network Computing mag., 2002—06; past sr. mgmt. editor Info. Week mag., editor-in-chief, 2006—. Office: Info Week 600 Community Dr Manhasset NY 11030 Office Phone: 516-562-5692. Fax: 516-562-5036. E-mail: rpreston@cmp.com. *

PRESTON, SEYMOUR STOTLER, III, chemicals executive; b. Media, Pa., Sept. 11, 1933; s. Seymour Stotler and Mary Alicia (Harper) P.; m. Jean Ellen Holman, Sept. 8, 1956; children: Courtney J., Katherine E., Alicia D., Shelley S. BA, Williams Coll., 1956; MBA, Harvard Coll., 1958. With Pennwalt Corp., Phila., 1961-89, exec. v.p. in charge of chems. and equipment ops., worldwide, 1975-77, pres., COO, 1977-89; pres., CEO Elf Atochem N.Am., Inc. (formerly Atochem N.Am.), Phila., 1990-93. Chmn. AAC Engineered Sys. Inc., 1994-2003; bd. dirs. Scott Splty. Gases, Inc., Albermarle Corp., Tufco Techs., Inc., Ocean Power Tech. Inc.; non-exec. chmn. Ind. Publs., Inc., 2004—. Trustee Shipley Sch., Bryn Mawr, Pa., 1976-88, Phila. Orch. Assn., 1992-95; trustee Acad. Natural Scis., 1980—, chmn., 1995-2000, pres., CEO, 2000-02; bd. mgrs. Franklin Inst., Phila., 1980-92; bd. dirs. Lawrenceville (NJ) Sch., 1982-99, Wistar Inst., 1997—, Barra Found., 1998—, chmn., 2004—. 1st lt. USAF, 1958-61. Mem. Soc. for Chem. Industry, Greater Phila. C. of C. (bd. dirs. 1979-94), Radnor Hunt Club (Malvern, Pa.). Office Phone: 610-889-3980. Personal E-mail: spmillrace@aol.com.

PRESTON, STEPHEN W., lawyer; b. May 30, 1957; BA summa cum laude, Yale U., 1979; diploma with first class honors, Trinity Coll., Univ. Dublin, 1980; JD magna cum laude, Harvard U., 1983. Bar: DC 1983. Law clk. to Hon. Phyllis A. Kravitch U.S. Ct. Appeals (11th cir.), 1983—84; vis. fellow Ctr. for Law in Pub. Interest, Washington, 1984—85; ptnr. Wilmer, Cutler & Pickering, Washington, 1986—93; prin. dep. gen. counsel, acting gen. counsel Dept. of Def., 1993—95; dep. asst. atty. gen. Dept. of Justice, 1995—98; gen. counsel Dept. of Navy, 1998—2000; ptnr., vice-chmn. Def. Nat. Security & Govt. Contracts dept. Wilmer Cutler Pickering Hale & Dorr, Washington, 2001—. Editor: Harvard Law Rev. Recipient Disting. Pub. Svc. medal Dept. of Def., 1995, 2000, Dept. of Navy, 2000. Fellow: Am. Bar Found.; mem.: ABA (mem. standing com. on law, nat. security adv. com.), Council on Fgn. Rels., Phi Beta Kappa. Office: Wilmer Cutler Pickering Hale & Dorr LLP 1875 Pennsylvania Ave NW Washington DC 20006 Office Phone: 202-663-6900. Office Fax: 202-663-6363. Business E-Mail: stephen.preston@wilmerhale.com.

PRESTON, STEVEN C., federal agency administrator, former service company executive; b. Aug. 4, 1960; m. Molly Preston; 5 children. BA in Polit. Sci. with highest distinction, Northwestern U., 1982; MBA, U. Chgo., 1985; student, Ludwig Maximillian U., Munich, Germany. Investment banker Lehman Bros., 1985-93; sr. v.p., corp. treas. First Data Corp.; CFO The ServiceMaster Co., Downers Grove, Ill., 1997—2003, exec. v.p., 2003—06; adminstr. SBA, Washington, 2006—. Vice chmn. bd. visitors Northwestern U. Weinberg Coll. Arts & Sciences; bd. dirs. Hinsdale Hosp. Found; mem. adv. bd. Tri-Artisan Partners, Concentric Equity Partners. Office: SBA 409 3rd St SW Rm 7000 Washington DC 20416 *

PRESTON, THOMAS RONALD, language educator, researcher; b. Oct. 31, 1936; s. Thomas and Marie Katherine (Nettlow) P.; m. Mary Ruth Atkinson, June 4, 1960; children: Lorel, Mary, Thomas BA, U. Detroit, 1958; MA, Rice U., 1960, PhD, 1962. Asst. prof. English Duquesne U., Pitts., 1962-63; Asst. prof. English U. Fla., Gainseville, 1963-67; assoc. prof., chmn. dept. Loyola U., New Orleans, 1967-69; prof., chmn. dept. U. Tenn., Chattanooga, 1969-73, U. Wyo., Laramie, 1973-82; prof., dean arts and scis. U. North Tex., Denton, 1982-92, prof. English, 1992—. Chmn. Wyo. Council for Humanities, Laramie, 1976-77 Author: Not in Timon's Manner, 1975; editor U. Ga. edit. of Smollett's Humphry Clinker, 1990; contbr. articles on 18th century lit. to profl. jours. Recipient John W. Gardner award Rice U., 1962; George Duke Humphrey award U. Wyo., 1982; NEH grantee, 1979; Am. Council of Learned Socs. grantee, 1980 Mem. Am. Soc. for 18th Century Studies, South Ctrl. Soc. for 18th Century Studies (pres. 1986-87). Democrat. Anglican.

PRESTOWITZ, CLYDE VINCENT, JR., economist, researcher; b. Wilmington, Del., Sept. 6, 1941; s. Clyde Vincent and Lillian (Lang) Prestowitz; m. Carol Ann Jay, Mar. 29, 1964; children: Anne, Clyde, Brian. BA with honors, Swarthmore Coll., 1963; MA, U. Hawaii, 1965; MBA, U. Pa., 1980. Mgr. market devel. Scott Paper Co., Phila., 1968—72, dir. planning Europe Brussels, 1972—76; v.p. Japan Egon Zehnder Internat., Tokyo, 1976—78; dir. mktg. Am. Can Co., Greenwich, Conn., 1978—79; pres. Prestowitz Assocs., New Canaan, Conn., 1979—81; dep. asst. sec. internat. econ. policy U.S. Dept. Commerce, Washington, 1981—82, acting asst. sec. internat. econ. policy, 1982—83, counselor to sec., 1983—86; Wilson fellow, 1986—87; sr. assoc. Carnegie Endowment for Internat. Peace, Washington, 1987—89; founder, pres. Econ. Strategy Inst., Washington, 1989—. Vice-chmn. Pacific Basin Econ. Coun., 1989—; vice chmn., presdl. com. U.S./Pacific Trade and Investment Policy. Author: Trading Places: How We Are Giving Our Future to Japan and How to Reclaim It, 1993, Rogue Nation: American Unilateralism and the Failure of Good Intentions, 2003, Three Billion New Capitalists: The Great Shift of Wealth and Power to the East, 2005; co-author: The New North American Order, 1991, Future of the Auto Industry: It Can Compete, Can It Survive?, 1992, Powernomics: Economics and Strategy After the Cold War, 2000. Republican. Presbyterian. Office: Econ Strategy Inst 3050 K St NW Washington DC 20007 Office Phone: 202-295-4645. Office Fax: 202-339-0880. Business E-Mail: presto@econstrat.org.

PRETE, GAYLE COMPTON, advertising and marketing executive; b. Washington, Nov. 28, 1956; d. Walter Dale and Jeanne (Parker) C.; m. Lanny Ross Huff, May 22, 1982 (div. 2002); m. James G. Prete, May 30, 2005. B in Gen. Studies, U. Mich., 1978. Mgr. br. merchandising CBS Records, Chgo., 1978, local promotion, mktg. mgr. Indpls., Boston, NYC, 1978-81; spl. projects supr. Pickwick Internat. Musicland Group, Mpls., 1981-82; account exec. Campbell-Mithun Advt., Mpls., 1982-85; mktg. mgr., communications Universal Foods Corp., Milw., 1985-86; nat. advt. mgr. Thorobred Advt. Agy. (Jockey Internat., Inc.), Wis., 1986-88, dir. consumer and trade advt., 1988-89, v.p. advt., 1990-92; dir. mktg./advt. Allen-Edmonds Shoe Co., Port Washington, Wis., 1993-95; v.p., dir. Fin. Mktg. Plus Direct Mktg. Group, Libertyville, Ill., 1995-97; dir. mktg. & merchandising AR Accessories Group Inc., Milw., 1997-98; v.p. creative svcs. Tucker-Knapp Integrated Mktg. Comms., Schaumburg, Ill., 1998-2000; sr. mgr. creative svcs. Discover Fin. Svcs. (Morgan Stanley Dean Witter), Riverwoods, Ill., 2000—04, dir. mktg. prodn. svcs., 2004—07, dir. mktg. portfolio usage, 2007—. V.p., sec. Java Masters, Inc., 1992-2005. Mem. Traffic Audit Bur. for Media Measurement (bd. dirs. 1988-93), Assn. Nat. Advertisers (print adv. com., out of home advt. com. 1989-92), Union Park Lofts Bd. Mgrs. (treas., 2004-2007). Avocations: dance, gymnastics, conga drumming, autocross. Office: Discover Fin Svcs 2500 Lake Cook Rd 25 Deerfield IL 60015-3851 Personal E-mail: javanuts@aol.com. Business E-Mail: gayleprete@discoverfinancial.com.

PRETTYMAN, ALFRED EMERSON, language and behavioral science educator, publishing executive; b. Balt., Feb. 15, 1935; s. Edward Augusta and Helen P.; m. Julia Poussaint (div.); children: Meryl, Evan; m. Kathleen Conwell, Dec. 25, 1987 (dec.); m. Susan Stedman, Aug. 17, 1997. BS, Hamilton Coll., 1956; postgrad., Cornell U., 1959, U. Pacific. Coll. exec. editor Harper & Row Pub., NYC, 1966-70, sr. editor, trade, 1969-71; founder, pres. Emerson Hall Pub., NYC, 1971—80; asst. prof. Rutgers U., New Brunswick, NJ, 1972—80, Rockland C.C., SUNY, Suffern, NY, 1988—98; co-founder, pres. Pretty-Steady Prodns., NYC, 1992—; adj. faculty Ramapo (NJ) Coll., 1999—. Chair bd. The Nyack (NY) Ctr., 1996—98, exec. dir., 1999—2001; cons. N.E. Humanities, Washington, 1970—73, N.E. Arts, Washington, 1970—72; elector Nat. Medal Lit., NYC, 1980; co-chair lit. NY State Coun. Arts, 1970; judge Nat. Book Awards, NYC, 1980; bd. chair Ophelia J. Berry Fund, Pathways to Coll., 2003—. Editor: U.S.: National Civics in a Mosaic Democracy 1996, 98, U.S.: The Intercultural Nation, 1999; prodr. Ogun's Fire: The Sculpture of Melvin Edwards, 1993; contbr. chpts. to books; contbr. articles to profl. jours. Recipient Excellence In Comm. award Creative and Editl. Black Achievement, 1983. Mem.: Orgn. Am. Historians, Soc. for the Advancement of Am. Philosophy, Assn. Study Africana Philosophy (co-founder 1977, pres. 1977—79, 1997—99, 2004—06). Avocations: tennis, cooking, gardening, fly fishing, singing. Home and Office: 215 W 98th St Apt 12-b New York NY 10025-5635

PRETTYMAN, ELIJAH BARRETT, JR., lawyer; b. Washington, June 1, 1925; s. Elijah Barrett and Lucy Courtney (Hill) P.; m. Noreen Prettyman; children by previous marriage: Elijah Barrett III, Jill Savage Lukoschek. BA, Yale U., 1949; LLB, U. Va., 1953. Bar: Wash., D.C. 1954, U.S. Supreme Ct. 1957. Pvt. practice, Washington, 1955—; law clk. to Hon. Justices Jackson, Frankfurter and Harlan U.S. Supreme Ct., Washington, 1953-55; assoc. Hogan & Hartson, Washington, 1955—63, ptnr., 1964—2001, of counsel, 2002—; inspector gen. Dist. of Colo., Washington, 1998—99. Spl. asst. to Atty. Gen. U.S., 1963, White House, 1963-64; also Pres. rep. to Interagy. Com. on Transport Mergers; spl. cons. subcom. to investigate problems connected with refugees and escapees, U.S. Senate Judiciary Com., Vietnam, 1967-68; outside cons. to subcom. on oversight and investigations, Ho. of Reps. com. on internal and fgn. commerce, 1978; spl. cons. for ABSCAM investigation to Com. on Standards of Ofcl. Conduct, U.S. Ho. of Reps., 1980-81; trustee emeritus, past exec com. Am. U., Washington; past trustee, mem. exec. com. Washington Journalism Ctr.; past adv. com., Media Law Reporter. Author: Death and the Supreme Court, 1961 (Edgar Allan Poe award); Editor: (with William E. Jackson) The Supreme Court in the American System of Government (Justice Robert H. Jackson), 1955; contbr. articles to profl. jours. Past corp. mem. Salvation Army; past mem. adv. com. Procedures of Jud. Coun., DC; past mem. adv. bd. Inst. Comm. Law Studies, Cath. U.; bd. govs., St. Albans Sch., 1957-63, 65-72, chmn., 1965-67; past mem. nat. adv. com., Nat. Inst. for Citizen Edn. in Law; bd. dirs., past pres., exec. com. PEN/Faulkner Found.; v.p., past chmn. publ. com., exec. com. Supreme Ct. Hist. Soc.; bd. dirs. Robert H. Jackson Ctr., Jamestown, NY, 2006-; past internat. adv. group Toshiba Corp.; past commr. Supreme Ct. Jud. Fellows Commn., chmn., 2003-05. With AUS, 1943—45. Chmn. recipient Pub. Achievement award Common Cause, 1999, Disting. Pub. Svc. award DC, 1999, Justice Potter Stewart award Coun. for Ct. Excellence, 2000, Lifetime Achievement award Am. Law Magazine, 2007. Fellow: ABA; mem.: D.C. Cir. Hist. Soc. (pres. 2000—02, chmn. 2003—), Am. Acad. Appellate Lawyers (past pres.), Am. Judicature Soc. (past vice chair, exec. com.), Met. Washington Bd. Trade, DC Bar Assn. (bd. govs., Lawyer of Yr. award 1998), DC Bar (1st pres. 1972—73, bd. govs. 1973—74, jud. evaluation com.), DC Bar Found. (pres. 1983—84), Jud. Conf. DC Cir., Am. Coll. Trial Lawyers, Chevy Chase Club, Met. Club, Alfalfa Club, Barristers Club, Lawyers Club (past pres.). Methodist. Home: 2737 Devonshire Pl NW # 424 Washington DC 20008-5148 Office: Columbia Sq 555 13th St NW Washington DC 20004-1109 Office Phone: 202-637-5685. Business E-Mail: ebprettyman@hhlaw.com.

PRETTYMAN, JOHN A., English language educator; BA in English, Syracuse U., NY, 1984; MS in Edn., SUNY, Oswego, 1996. Adj. instr., tutor Onondaga CC, Syracuse, 1985—89, asst. prof., 1990—; English instr. Ednl. Opportunity Ctr. SUNY Morrisville, 1986—90; instr. Job Tng. Partnership Agy. Program, Syracuse, 1989—90. Recipient Employee Appreciation award, Onondaga CC, 2006. Mem.: Assn. Supervision and Curriculum Devel., Am. Civil Liberties Union, N.Y. State United Tchrs., Nat. Coun. Tchrs. English, Schomberg Ctr. for Rsch. in Black Culture, So. Poverty Law Ctr. Office: Onondaga CC 4941 Onondaga Rd Syracuse NY 13215-2099

PREUCIL, DORIS BOGEN, music educator; b. Milw., Dec. 10, 1932; d. Walter Leopold and Adele Anne (Jarvis) Bogen; m. William Warren Preucil, Sept. 4, 1954; children: William, Jr., Walter, Anne, Jeanne. MusB with distinction, Eastman Sch. Music, Rochester, NY, 1954; MusM, U. Iowa, 1968; studied with Shinichi Suzuki, Talent Edn. Inst., Japan, 1982. Violinist Rochester Philharm. Orch., 1952—54, Nat. Symphony Orch., Washington, 1954—56; freelance violinist & tchr. Iowa City, 1956—72; asst. prof. Western Ill. U., Macomb, 1972—76; founder, dir., master tchr. Preucil Sch. Music, Iowa City, 1975—97, dir. emerita, tchr., 1997—. Suzuki Professorial chair U. Wis., Stevens Point, 1986; hon. bd. mgrs. Eastman Sch. Music, Rochester, 2005—. Musician (1st violinist): Milw. Symphony, 1948—50, Rochester Philharm., 1952—54, Tri-City Symphony, 1958—72; concertmaster:, 1971—72; musician: Eastman Faculty Quartet, 1951—54, Lydian Trio, 1972—75, Preucil Family Players, 1975—84; author, editor: The Suzuki Viola Sch., 1976—, arranger: The Solo with Orchestra series 2004-. Trustee Nat. Guild Cmty. Schs. Arts, 1988—91; bd. dirs. Amateur Chamber Music Found., 1998—; elder, deacon 1st Presbyn. Ch., Iowa City, 1964—. Named Tchr. of the Yr., Iowa State Music Tchrs. Assn., 2005; recipient Lifetime Achievement award, Eastman Sch. Music, 2004. Mem.: Internat. Suzuki Assn. (founding bd. mem. 1983—95), Suzuki Assn. Am. (cert. tchr., trainer 1980—, pres. 1982—84, Disting. Svc. award 1992), Rotary (mem. music commn. 1989—). Avocations: music, reading, travel. Home: 317 Windsor Dr Iowa City IA 52245 Personal E-mail: wdpreucil@mchsi.com.

PREUS, DAVID WALTER, bishop, minister; b. Madison, Wis., May 28, 1922; s. Ove Jacob Hjort and Magdalene (Forde) P.; m. Ann Madsen, June 26, 1951; children: Martha, David, Stephen, Louise, Laura. BA, Luther Coll., Decorah, Iowa, 1943, DD (hon.), 1969; postgrad., U. Minn., 1946-47; BTh, Luther Sem., St. Paul, 1950; postgrad., Union Sem., 1951, Edinburgh U., 1951-52; LLD (hon.), Wagner Coll., 1973, Gettysburg Coll., 1976; DD (hon.), Pacific Luth. Coll., 1974, St. Olaf Coll., 1974, Dana Coll., 1979, Tex. Luth. Coll., 1994; LHD (hon.), Macalester Coll., 1976; DD (hon.), Luther Coll., 1969. Ordained to ministry Luth. Ch., 1950; asst. pastor First Luth. Ch., Brookings, SD, 1950-51; pastor Trinity Luth. Ch., Vermillion, SD, 1952-57; campus pastor U. Minn., Mpls., 1957-58; pastor Univ. Luth. Ch. of Hope, Mpls., 1958-73; v.p. Am. Luth. Ch., 1968-73, pres., presiding bishop, 1973-87; exec. dir. Global Mission Inst. Luther Northwestern Theol. Sem., St. Paul, 1988-94; Luccock vis. pastor Yale Div. Sch., 1969; chmn. bd. youth activity Am. Luth. Ch., 1960-68; mem. exec. com. Luth. Council U.S.A.; v.p. Luth. World Fedn., 1977-90; mem. cen. com. World Council Chs., 1973-75, 80-90; Luth. del. White House Conf. on Equal Opportunity Chmn. Greater Mpls. Fair Housing Com., Mpls. Council Chs., 1960-64; Mem. Mpls. Planning Commn., 1965-67; mem. Mpls. Sch. Bd., 1965-74, chmn., 1967-69; mem. Mpls. Bd. Estimate and Taxation, 1968-73, Mpls. Urban Coalition; sr. public adv. U.S. del. Madrid Conf. of Conf. on Security and Cooperation in Europe, 1980-81; bd. dirs. Mpls. Inst. Art, Walker Art Center, Hennepin County United Fund, Ams. for Childrens Relief, Luth. Student Found., Research Council of Gt. City Schs., Urban League, NAACP; bd. regents Augsburg Coll., Mpls. Served with Signal Corps AUS, 1943-46, PTO. Decorated comdr.'s cross Royal Norwegian Order St. Olav, Order of St. George 1st deg. Orthodox Ch. of Georgia (USSR), 1989; recipient Regents medal Augustana Coll., Sioux Falls, S.D., 1973, Torch of Liberty award Anti-Defamation League, 1973, St. Thomas Aquinas award St. Thomas U., Pax Christi award St. John's Univ/. Collegeville, Minn., 1997. Lutheran.

PREUSS, CHARLES FREDERICK, lawyer; b. Santa Barbara, Calif., Feb. 27, 1941; BA, Dartmouth Coll., 1962; JD, Stanford U., 1969. Bar: Calif. 1970. Atty. Bronson, Bronson & McKinnon, 1969—93; ptnr. Preuss Walker & Shanagher, San Francisco, 1993-98, Preuss, Shanagher, Zvoleff & Zimmer, San Francisco, 1998; mng. ptnr., head West Coast offices Drinker Biddle & Reath LLP, San Francisco, and ptnr., products liability practice group. Mem. Product Liability Adv. Coun., Inc., bd. dir., Def. Rsch. Inst., 1996-99. Mem. Am. Bd. Trial Advocates, Internat. Assn. Def. Counsel. Office: Drinker Biddle & Reath LLP 50 Fremont St San Francisco CA 94105-2235 Office Phone: 415-591-7566. Office Fax: 415-591-7510. Business E-Mail: charles.preuss@dbr.com.

PREUSS, DAPHNE, geneticist, biology professor; BS in Chemistry, U. Denver, 1985, BS in Natural Sciences, 1985; PhD in Genetics, MIT, 1990. Albert D. Lasker prof. molecular genetics & cell biology U. Chgo., 1995—; prin. investigator Howard Hughes Med. Inst., Chgo., 2000—06; co-founder Chromatin, Inc., Chgo., 2000, sr. v.p., 2007, chief sci. officer, 2007—, pres., 2007—. Bd. gov. Argonne Nat. Lab. Contbr. articles to profl. jours. Bd. govs. Argonne Nat. Labs., Chgo., 2003—. Named one of Discover 20 (List of 20 Promising Young Scientists), Discover Mag., 2000, 40 under 40, Chgo. Crain's Bus. Review, 2001; recipient Ammi Hyde award for Young Alumni Achievement, U. Denver, Women in Cell Biology Jr. award, Am. Soc. Cell Biology, Promega Early Career Life Scientist award, 2001; David and Lucille Packard fellow, Packard Found., 1997-2004, Searle Scholar. Mem.: NAS (lifetime nat. assoc.). Achievements include invention of chromosomes for plants; Chromatin's patented mini-chromosome technology. Office: Dept Molecular Genetics and Cell Biology U Chgo Ctr for Integrative Sci 929 E 57th St CIS W519 Chicago IL 60637 also: Chromatin Inc 2201 W Campbell Park Dr Ste #10 Chicago IL 60612 Office Phone: 773-702-1605, 312-455-1935. Office Fax: 773-702-6648, 312-563-9120. E-mail: dpreuss@midway.uchicago.edu.

PREUSS, ROGER EMIL, artist; b. Waterville, Minn., Jan. 29, 1922; s. Emil W. and Edna (Rosenau) P.; m. MarDee Ann Germundson, Dec. 31, 1954 (dec. Mar. 1981). Student, Mankato Comml. Coll., Mpls. Sch. Art. Emeritus instr. Mpls. Coll. Art and Design; emeritus Mpls. Inst. Arts Speakers Bur.; former judge Goodyear Nat. Conservation Awards Program; founder U.S. Fed. Roger Preuss Waterfowl Prodn. Area, LeSueur County, Minn., 1997; former advisor Wildlife Forever Nat. Fish-Art Contest. One-man shows include St. Paul Fine Art Galleries, 1959, Albert Lea Art Ctr., 1963, Hist. Soc. Mont., Helena, 1964, Brotherhood Fine Arts Ctr., 1965, Le Sueur County Hist. Soc. Mus., Elysian, Minn., 1976, Merrill's Gallery Fine Art, Taos, N.Mex., 1980; exhbns. include Mpls. Inst. Art Msa exhibit, 1946, Midwest Wildlife Conf. Exhbn., Kerr's Beverly Hills, Calif., 1947, Laguna Art Mus., Calif., 1947, Joslyn Meml. Mus., Omaha, 1948, Hollywood Fine Arts Center, 1948, Minn. Centennial, 1949, Federated Chaparral Authors, 1951, Nat. Wildlife Art, 1951-52, N.Am. Wildlife Art, dir. exposition, 1952, Ducks Unltd. Waterfowl exhibit, 1953-54, St. Paul Winter Carnival, 1954, St. Paul Gallery Art Mart, 1954, Harris Fine Arts Ctr., Provo, Utah, 1969, Galerie Internat., N.Y.C., 1972, Holy Land Conservation Fund, N.Y.C., 1976, Faribault Art Ctr., 1981, Wildlife Artists of the World Exhbn., Bend, Oreg., 1984, U. Art Mus., U. Minn., Mpls., 1990, Rochester Art Ctr., 1991, Minn. Hist. Soc.-Hill House, 1992, Bemidji Art Ctr., 1992, Jack London Ctr., Dawson City, Yukon Territory, Can., 1992, Weyerhaeuser Meml. Mus., Little Falls, Minn., 1995, Minn. Valley Nat. Wildlife Refuge Ctr., Bloomington, 1995, Sagebrush Artists Exhbn., Klamath Falls, Oreg., 1995, Smithsonian Inst., Blauvelt Art Mus.; represented in permanent collections: Demarest Meml. Mus., Hackensack, N.J., N.Y. Jour. Commerce, Mont. Hist. Soc., Inland Bird Banding Assn., Minn. Capitol Bldg., Mont. State U., Wildlife Am. Collection, LeSueur Hist. Soc., Voyageurs Nat. Park Interpretive Ctr., Krause-Hartig VFW Post, Mpls., Nat. Wildlife Fedn. Collection, Minn. Ceremonial House, U.S. Wildlife Svc. Fed. Bldg., Fort Snelling, Minn., Crater Lake Nat. Park Visitors Ctr., VA Hosp., Mpls., Luxton Collection, Banff, Alta., Can., Internat. Inst. Arts, Geneva, Mont. Capitol Bldg., People of Century-Goldblatt Collection, Lyons, Ill., Harlem Savings Collection, N.Y.C., Weisman Art Mus., Mpls., Minn. Vets. Home, Mpls., Roger Preuss Art Collection, Augustana Ctr. for Western Studies, Sioux Falls, S.D., Minn. Mus. Am. Art, St. Paul, U. Minn.

Art Mus., C.M. Russell Mus., Great Falls, Mont., Le Sueur County Courthouse, Le Center, Minn., others, numerous galleries and pvt. collections; designer: Fed. Duck Stamp, U.S. Dept. Interior, 1949, Commemorative Centennial Pheasant Stamp, 1981, Gold Waterfowl medallion Franklin Mint, 1983, Gold Stamp medallion Wildlife Mint, 1983, 40th Anniversary Commemorative Fed. Duck Stamp etching, 1989; panelist: Sportsman's Roundtable, Sta. WTCN-TV, Mpls. (emeritus), from 1953; author: Is Wildlife Art Recognized Fine Art?, 1986; contbr.: Christmas Echos, 1955, Wing Shooting, Trap & Skeet, 1955, Along the Trout Stream, 1979; contbr. Art Impressions mag., Can., Wildlife Art, U.S.; contbr. illustrations and articles in Nat. Wildlife; assoc. editor emeritus: Out-of-Doors mag.; compiler and artist: Outdoor Horizons, 1957, Twilight over the Wilderness, 1972, 75 limited edition prints Wildlife of America, from 1950; contbr. paintings and text Minnesota Today; creator paintings and text Preuss Wildlife Calendar; inventor: paintings and text Wildlife Am. Calendar; featured artist Art West, 1980-84, Wildlife Art; featured in films Your BFA- Care and Maintenance, Black Ducks Along the Border Former del. Nat. Wildlife Conf.; bd. dirs. emeritus Voyageurs Nat. Park Assn., Deep-Portage Conservation Found.; former bd. dirs. Wetlands for Wildlife U.S.A.; active Wildlife Am.; co-organizer, v.p., bd. dirs. Minn. Conservation Fedn., 1952-54; mem. U.S. Hospitalized Vets. Venison Program, 1957—; trustee Liberty Bell Edn. Found.; Waseca Arts Coun.; founder, dir. Roger Preuss Conservation Preserve for Study of Nature, 1990—; adv. Wildlife Forever. With USNR, WWII. Recipient Stamp Design award U.S. Fish and Wildlife Svc., 1994, Minn. Outdoor award, 1956, Patron of Conservation award, 1956, award for contbns. conservation Minn. Statehood Centennial Commn., 1958, 1st award Am. Indsl. Devel. Coun., citation of merit VFW, award of merit Mil. Order Cootie, 1963, merit award Minn. Waterfowl Assn., 1976, Silver medal Nat. SAR, 1978, Svcs. to Arts and Environ. award Faribault Art Ctr., 1981, Ptnrs. for Wildlife award U.S. Fish and Wildlife Svc., 1994; named Wildlife Conservationist of the Yr., Sears Found.-Nat. Wildlife Fedn. program, 1966, Am. Bicentennial Wildlife Artist, Am. Heritage Assn., 1976; hon. mem. Ont. Chippewa Nation of Can., 1957; named Knight of Mark Twain for contbns. to Am. art Mark Twain Soc., 1978; named to Water, Woods and Wildlife Hall of Fame, named Dean of Wildfowl Artists, 1981, Hon. Ky. Col.; recipient hon. degree U.S. Vets. Venison program, 1980, Western Am. award significant contbns. to preservation arts and history No. Prairie Plains, Augustana Coll. Ctr. for Western Studies, Sioux Falls, S.D., 1992, Pub. Svc. award U.S. Dept. Interior, 1996, Marshall award 2004; named creator first signed, numbered photolithographic modern print pub. in N.Am., 1959; documented Colorado Springs Fine Arts Ctr., 1993, colleague of Frederick R. Weisman Mus., Mpls., 1994; grantee NEH, 1995, Prairie Lakes Arts Coun., 1995. Fellow Internat. Inst. Arts (life), Nat. Wildlife Fedn. (past nat. wildlife week chmn. Minn.), Minn. Ducks Unltd. (bd. dirs. emeritus), Minn. Artists Assn. (v.p., bd. dirs. 1953-59), Minn. Mycol. Soc. (pres. emeritus, hon. life), Le Sueur County Hist. Soc. (hon. life), Minn. Conservation Fedn. (hon. life), Wildlife Artists World (charter, emeritus internat. v.p., chmn. fine arts bd.), Prairie Chicken Soc. (patron), Mission Oceanic Arctic, Minn. Press Club (emeritus), Silver Lake Sports (hon.), Wildlife Rehab. Ctr. Minn. Office: care Wildlife Am PO Box 580004-a Minneapolis MN 55458-0004 *With a modicum of natural skills in painting and writing, my basic goal throughout all my work has been to help people appreciate and understand nature. If I as a naturalist am a small voice for our world's waters, woods, and wildlife, if I have influenced many children and adults to become more environment conscious, if my art brings to others a measure of joy, then my best aspirations for my creations have been fulfilled.*

PREVATT, DAVID O., civil engineer, researcher; b. Nassau, Bahamas; m. Sandra Hadley. BSc with honours, U. West Indies, Trinidad, 1985; PhD in Civil Engring., Clemson U., SC, 1998. Registered civil engr., Bd. Engring. of Trinidad and Tobago, 2001, cert. profl. structural engr., Mass., 2003. Civil engr. designs engring. br. Min. of Works, Port-of-Spain, Trinidad and Tobago, 1985—90; rsch. asst. U. West Indies, St. Augustine, Trinidad and Tobago, 1990—93; sr. engr. Simpson Gumpertz & Heger Inc., Waltham, Mass., 1998—2004; asst. prof. Clemson U., 2004—07, U. Fla., Gainesville, 2007—. Recipient Herb Busching award, Roof Cons. Inst., 1997, award for faculty excellence, Clemson U., 2007; Kimley-Horn fellow, 1996, R.C. Edwards fellow, Clemson U., 1996, 1997. Mem.: ASCE (assoc. Exceed Tchg. fellow 2006), UK Wind Engring. Soc., Assn. Profl. Engrs. Trinidad and Tobago, Am. Assn. for Wind Engring., Chi Epsilon. Achievements include research in wind load studies on residential structures. Office Phone: 352-392-9537 x 1540. E-mail: dprev@ce.ufl.edu.

PREVE, ROBERTA JEAN, librarian, researcher; b. Wilmington, Del., Feb. 27, 1954; d. Burton Hugo Sanders and Betsy (Kan) Klein; m. Thomas Alan Preve, Sept. 23, 1978; children: Stephanie Jean, Melanie Marie. BA, U. NH, 1975; MLS, Simmons Coll., 1985. Rschr. U. N.H., Durham, 1974-75; rsch. asst. Eikonix Corp., Burlington, Mass., 1976-79; asst. cashier, credit dept. mgr. Dania (Fla.) Bank, 1980-83; rsch. assoc. Ctr. for Strategy Rsch., Cambridge, Mass., 1984-86; info. svcs. Braxton Assocs., Boston, 1986-87; mktg. adminstr. Summit Tech., Waltham, Mass., 1987-91; mgr. market rsch. AT&T Capital Corp., Framingham, Mass., 1991-95; mgr. Bus. Info. Ctr. Raytheon Co., Lexington, Mass., 1995—. Co-owner T&R Pest Mgmt., Attleboro, Mass., 1988—95. Mem. Spl. Librs. Assn., New England Online (dir., logistics chair 1986-90), Beta Phi Mu. Avocations: hiking, reading, needlecrafts, sports. Office: Raytheon Co 235 Presidental Way Woburn MA 01801 Office Phone: 339-645-8707. Business E-Mail: roberta_j_preve@raytheon.com.

PREVIDI, MICHAEL, meteorologist, research scientist; b. Englewood, NJ, Aug. 19, 1979; BS in Meteorology, Rutgers U., New Brunswick, NJ, 2001, PhD in Environ. Sci, 2006. Tchg. asst. Rutgers U., New Brunswick, NJ, 2001—02, grad. rsch. asst., 2002—06, postdoctoral assoc., 2006; postdoctoral rsch. scientist Lamont-Doherty Earth Obs. Columbia U., NYC, 2007—. Grantee Tchg. assistantship, Rutgers U. Dept. of Environ. Sci, 2001—02, Grad. Rsch. assistantship, Rutgers U. Dept. of Environ. Sci., 2002—05. Mem.: AAAS, Am. Meteorol. Soc., Am. Geophys. Union. Achievements include research in in atmospheric science. Avocation: basketball. Office: Columbia U Lamont Doherty Earth Obs 61 Route 9W Palisades NY 10964 Office Phone: 845-365-8631. Business E-Mail: mprevidi@ldeo.columbia.edu.

PREVIN, ANDRÉ (LUDWIG), composer, conductor, pianist; b. Berlin, Apr. 6, 1929; came to U.S., 1938, naturalized, 1943; s. Jack and Charlotte (Epstein) P.; m. Dory Previn, 1958 (div. 1965); m. Betty Bennett (div.); 2 children; m. Mia Farrow, Sept. 10, 1970 (div. 1979); children: Matthew and Sascha (twins), Fletcher, Lark, Daisy; m. Heather Hales, Jan. 1982 (div. 1999); 1 child, Lukas; m. Anne-Sophie Mutter, 2002-. Student, Berlin Conservatory, Paris Conservatory; privately with, Pierre Monteux, Mario Castelnuovo-Tedesco. Mem. faculty Guildhall Sch., London, Curtis Inst., Phila., Berkshire Music Ctr. Rec. artist classical music for RCA, EMI, Phillips, Telarc, Deutsche Gramophone, 1946—; composer (orchestra) Concerto for Cello, 1960, Concerto for Guitar Concerto, 1960, Principals, 1980, Reflections, 1981, Concerto for Piano, 1985 Honey and Rue, 1992, The Magic Number, 1995, Vocalise, 1994, Sallie Chisum Remembers Billy the Kid, 1995, Diversions, 1999, Violin Concerto (Anne-Sophie), 2001, Double Concerto for Violin, Double Bass and Orchestra, 2004; composer (chamber/solo) Two Little Serenades, 1970, Paraphase on a Theme of William Walton, 1973, Four Outings for Brass, 1974, Peaches, 1978, Matthew's Piano Book, 1979, Triolet for Brass, 1985, A Wedding Waltz, 1986, Variations on a Theme by Haydn, 1990, Cello Sonata, 1993, Sonata for Violin, Vineyard, 1994, Trio for Piano, Oboe, and Bassoon, 1994, Bassoon Sonata, 1997, Hoch soil Er Leben, 1997, Tango Song and Dance, 1998, String Quartet with Soprano, 2003; composer (vocal) Five Songs, 1977, Four Songs, 1994, Three Arias from the Streetcar Named Desire, 1998, Two Rememberances, 1995, Three Dickinson Songs, 1999, The Giraffes Go to Hamburg, 2000, String Quartet (with Soprano), 2003; composer (musicals) Coco, 1960, The Good Companions, 1964; composer (cadenzas) W.A. Mozart: Concerto for Flute and Harp, C major, K 299, W.A. Mozart: Piano Concerto No. 20, D minor, K 466 (3rd mvt.), W.A. Mozart: Piano Concerto No. 24, C minor, K 491 (1st mvt.); composer (movie scores) The Sun Comes Up, 1949 (also musical dir.), Scene of the Crime, 1949, Challenge to Lassie, 1949, Tension, 1950, The Outriders, 1950, Shadow on the Wall, 1950, Three Little Words, 1950 (also musical dir.), Dial 1119 (also musical dir.), 1950, Kim, 1950, Cause for Alarm!, 1951, The Girl Who Had Everything, 1953, Bad Day at Black Rock, 1955, It's Always Fair Weather, 1955 (also condr., music supervisor), Invitation to the Dance, 1956, The Catered Affair, 1956, The Fastest Gun Alive, 1956, Hot Summer Night, 1957, Designing Women, 1957, House of Numbers, 1957, Who Was That Lady?, 1960, The Subterraneans, 1960, Elmer Gantry, 1960, Pepe, 1960 (also condr.), All in a Night's Work, 1961, One, Two, Three, 1961 (also condr.), Four Horseman of the Apocalypse, 1962, Long Day's Journey Into Night, 1962, Two for the Seesaw, 1962, Irma la Douce, 1963(Academy award, 193), Dead Ringer, 1964, Goodbye Charlie, 1964, Kiss Me Stupid, 1964, Inside Daisy Clover, 1965, Harper, 1966, The Fortune Cookie, 1966, The Swinger, 1966, Throughly Modern Millie, 1967, Valley of the Dolls, 1967, Paint Your Wagon, 1969, Mrs. Pollifax-Spy, 1971, Bang Bang, 1973, (TV mini series) Jennie: Lady Randolph Churchill, 1974, Léon, 1994, (opera and TV) A Streetcar Named Desire, San Francisco Opera, 1998 (also condr.), Fight Club, 1999, Return to the Arena: The Making of Rollerball, 2000; musical dir. (films) Act of Violence, 1948, Big Jack, 1949, The Secret Garden, 1949, The Great Sinner, 1949, Border Incident, 1949, Small Town Girl, 1953, Kiss Me Kate, 1953, Give a Girl a Break, 1953, Invitation to the Dance, 1956; condr. (films) Malaya, 1949, Above and Beyond, 1952, The Way West, 1967, The Music Lovers, 1970, Jesus Christ Superstar, 1973, Elephant Man, 1980; musician (film) Young at Heart, 1954; condr., music supervisor Kismet, 1955, Silk Stockings, 1957, GiGi, 1958 (Academy award, 1958), Porgy and Bess, 1959 (Academy award, 1959), My Fair Lady, 1964 (Academy award, 1964); music supervisor, musical dir., Bells Are Ringing, 1960; condr., musical dir. Rollerball, 1975; musical dir. (TV) 26th Annual Academy Awards, 1954, 28th Annual Academy Awards, 1956, 32nd Annual Academy Awards, 1960, 33rd Annual Academy Awards, 1961; condr.-in-chief Houston Symphony, 1967-70; music dir. London Symphony Orch., 1969-79, condr. laureate 1993-, Royal Philharm. Orch., Eng., 1988-91 (also music dir. 1985-88); music dir. South Bank Music Festival, London, 1972-74, Pitts. Symphony, 1976-84, L.A. Philharm., 1985-89; composer (theatre) Every Good Boy Deserves Favour, 1976, Oslo Philharmonic, 2002-03; guest condr. maj. symphony orchs. and festivals in U.S. and Europe including: festivals in Salzburg, Edinburgh, Flanders, Vienna, Osaka, Prague, Berlin, Bergen; appears annually with Boston Symphony Orchestra, N.Y. Philharmonic, Vienna Philharmonic, and others; recordings include Andre Previn/Royal Philharmonic Orchestra Holst: The Planets, Andre Previn/Royal Philharmonic Orchestra Vaughan Williams: Symphony No. 2, Andre Previn/Los Angeles Philharmonic Orchestra Prokofiev: Alexander Nevsky & Lt. Kije, Andre Previn/Royal Philharmonic Orchestra Vaughan Williams: Symphony No. 5 & Tallis Fantasia, Andre Previn/Vienna Philharmonic Orchestra Strauss: Also sprach Zarathustra & Tod und Verklarung, Andre Previn/Los Angeles Philharmonic Orchestra Bartok: Concerto for Orchestra / Janacek: Sinfonietta, Andre Previn/Vienna Philharmonic Orchestra/Arleen Auger Strauss: Ein Heldenleben & Four Last Songs, Andre Previn/Royal Philharmonic Orchestra/Horacio Guiterrez Brahms: Piano Conc. No. 2 & Haydn Variations, Andre Previn/Vienna Philharmonic Orchestra Strauss: Alpine Symphony, Andre Previn/Los Angeles Philharmonic Orchestra Dvorak: Symphony No. 9 New World & Carnival Overture, Andre Previn/Royal Philharmonic Orchestra/Horacio Guiterrez Brahms: Piano Concerto No. 1 & Tragic Overture, Andre Previn/Vienna Philharmonic Orchestra/Franz Bartolomey Strauss: Don Juan & Don Quixote, Andre Previn/Vienna Philharmonic Orchestra The Essential Richard Strauss, Andre Previn/Joe Pass/Ray Brown After Hours: Jazz Standards, Andre Previn/Ray Brown/Mundell Lowe Uptown: Songs of Harold Arlen, Duke Ellington & others, Andre Previn/Mundell Lowe/Ray Brown Old Friends, Andre Previn Triple Play, Ludwig van Beethoven String Quartet op. 131(Version for String Orchestra) Wiener Philharmoniker André Previn, Richard Strauss Der Rosenkavalier Le Chevalier à la Rose Il cavaliere della rosa (Suite) Orchestermusik Orchestral Music aus/from Intermezzo Salome Capriccio Wiener Philharmoniker André Previn, 1993, Frédéric Chopin Klavierkonzert Piano Concerto Concerto pour Piano Concerto per pianoforte: No. 2 24 Préludes op. 28 Maria João Pires Royal Philharmonic Orchestra André Previn, 1994(Grand Prix du Disque Frédéric Chopin - Warsaw, 1995), Samuel Barber Violinkonzert Violin Concerto Concerto pour Violon op. 14 Gil Shaham London Symphony Orchestra André Previn, 1994 (Cannes Classical award, 1995), Carl Orff Carmina Burana, 1994, Jean Sibekius Violinkonzert Violin Concerto Concerto pour Violon Concerto per violino 2 Serenaden Serenades op. 69 Humoresque op. 87 No. 1, Anne-Sophie Mutter Staatskapelle Dresden André Previn, 1995 (Edison award, 1997), Serge Prokofiev Violinkonzerte Violin Concertos Concertos pour Violon Concerti per violino: Nos. 1 and 2 Sonate für Violine solo Sonata for Solo Violin op. 115, Gil Shaham London Symphony Orchestra André Previn, 1996 (Gran Premio del Disco "Ritmo" (Madrid), 1996, Grand Prix de la Nouvelle Académie, 1996), Erich Korngold Symphony op. 40 Much Ado about Nothing op. 11 (Suite for Chamber Orchestra) London Symphony Orchestra André Previn, 1997, Richard Strauss, Horn Concertos No. 1 and No. 2 Oboe Concerto Duet Concertino for Clariner and Bassoon with String Orchestra, George Gershwin Songbook, 1998, Duke Ellington We Got It Good and That Ain't Bad, An Ellington Songbook, André Previn A Streetcar Named Desire, 1998 (Echo award, 1999), Maurice Ravel L'Enfant et les Sorttilèges Ma Mère l'Oye, 1999, Anne-Sophie Mutter, Back to the Future, 2000, André Previn Diversions, 2001, Erich Korngold, 2002, Anne Sophie Mutter Tango Song and Dance, 2003, André Previn Violin Concerto & Bernstein Serenade, 2003 (Grammy award, 2005), Tchaikovsky-Korngold Violin Concertos; author: Music Face to Face, 1971, No Minor Chords, 1991; editor Orchestra, 1979, André Previn's Guide to Music, 1983, André Previn's Guide to the Orchestra: With Chapters on the Voice, Keyboards, Mechanical and Electronic Instruments, 1986. Served with AUS, 1950-51. Knighted (KBE), Her Majesty Queen Elizabeth II, 1996; recipient awards Nat. Grammophone Soc., Kennedy Ctr. Honoree, 1998, Glenn Gould prize, 2005; decorated Germany's Commander's Cross of the Order of Merit; named Musician of Yr., Musical America. Mem. Acad. Motion Picture Arts and Scis., Dramatists Guild, Brit. Composers Guild, Nat. Composers and Condrs. League, Degrees Curtis Inst., Royal Acad., Guild Hall Sch./Duquesne U. Office: care Columbia Artists 165 W 57th St New York NY 10019-2201

PREVITE, ROBERT (BOBBY), composer, musician; b. Niagara Falls, NY, July 16, 1959; s. Vincent James and Angela Previte; 1 child, Katherine. BA, SUNY, Buffalo. Musician, 1985—. Composer: The 23 Constellations of Joan Miró, 2002, Counterclockwise, 2003, The Coalition of the Willing, 2006, Dialed-In, 2006, The Separation, 2007. Recipient composition award, NEA, Jerome Found., 2005; fellow, MacDowell Colony, 1999, 2000, 2001, 2003, 2005. Mem.: ASCAP. E-mail: etiverp@rcn.com.

PREVITTI, JAMES P., real estate executive; Founder Forecast Group, Rancho Cucamonga, Calif., 1971—, pres., CEO, 1989—. Recipient Fair Housing award L.A. Times; named Builder of Yr., Real Estate Entrepreneur of Yr. Mem. Calif. Bldg. Industry Assn. (pres., Medal of Honor). Office: Forecast 3536 Concours Ste 320 Ontario CA 91764-5593

PREVOST, ROXANE LISE, music theory educator; d. Roger Andre and Lise Houle Prevost. BA, U. Guelph, Ont., 1992; MusB, U. Ottawa, 1997; MusM, U. Western Ont., 1999; PhD, SUNY at Buffalo, 2003. Tchg. asst. U. Western Ont., London, 1997—99, SUNY, Buffalo, 1999—2001, instr., 2001—02; asst. prof. dept. music U. Ottawa, 2003—. Chair music grad. symposium SUNY, Buffalo, 2002—03; presenter in field; publ. in field. Ont. Grad. scholar, Govt. Ont., 1997—99, Pres. scholar, U. Western Ont., 1997—99, Social Scis. and Humanities Rsch. Coun. of Can. Doctoral fellow, Govt. Can., 2002—03, Coll. of Arts and Scis. Dissertation fellow, SUNY at Buffalo, 2002—03. Mem.: Music Theory Soc. N.Y. State, Can. U. Music Soc., Soc. for Music Theory. Roman Catholic. Avocations: violin, piano. Office: U Ottawa Dept Music 50 University Ottawa ON K1N 6N5 Canada Home Phone: 613-789-1614. Personal E-mail: rprevost@uottawa.ca.

PREVOZNIK, MICHAEL E., lawyer; BS, U. Notre Dame, 1983; MBA, U. Chgo., 1985, JD magna cum laude, 1988. With Dechert, Price & Rhodes; chief legal compliance officer SBCL, 1994—96; v.p., chief legal compliance officer SmithKline Beecham Healthcare Svcs., 1996—98, v.p. compliance, 1998—99; v.p. legal Quest Diagnostics, NJ, 1999—2003, gen. counsel, 1999—, sr. v.p. legal & compliance, 2003—. Office: Quest Diagnostics 1290 Wall St W Lyndhurst NJ 07071 E-mail: Michael.E.Prevoznik@questdiagnostics.com. *

PREWITT, CHARLES THOMPSON, geochemist; b. Lexington, Ky., Mar. 3, 1933; s. John Burton and Margaret (Thompson) P.; m. Gretchen B. Hansen, Jan. 31, 1958; children: Daniel Hansen. SB, MIT, 1955, SM, 1960, PhD, 1962. Rsch. scientist E.I. DuPont De Nemours & Co. Inc., Wilmington, Del., 1962-69; assoc. prof. SUNY, Stony Brook, 1969-71, prof., 1971-86, chmn. dept. earth and space scis., 1977-80; dir. Geophys. Lab., Carnegie Inst. of Washington, 1986-98, mem. rsch. staff, 1998—2003; adj. prof. Dept. Geoscis. U. Ariz., Tucson, 2003—. Sec.-treas. U.S. Nat. Com. for Crystallography, Washington, 1983-85, 99—; gen. chmn. 14th Meeting of Internat. Mineral Assn., Stanford, Calif., 1986; chmn. NRC/NAS com. on physics and chemistry of earth materials, 1985-87; mem. bd. govs. Consortium for Advanced Radiation Svcs.; co-dir. NSF Ctr. for High Pressure Rsch., 1991—; disting. vis. prof. chemistry Ariz. State U., 1983. Editor: (jour.) Physics and Chemistry of Minerals, 1976-85; contbr. more than 190 articles to profl. jours. Bd. dirs. Internat. Ctr. for Diffraction Data, 1998-2002. Capt. USAR, 1956-65. NATO sr. postdoctoral fellow, 1975, Churchill overseas fellow, 1975, Japan Soc. for Promotion of Sci. fellow, 1983, Ernst Cloos Meml. scholar Johns Hopkins U., 2002-. Fellow AAAS, Mineral. Soc. Am. (pres. 1983-84, Roebling medal 2003), Am. Geophys. Union, Internat. Centre Diffraction Data; mem. Geol. Soc. Am., Am. Crystallographic Assn., Materials Rsch. Soc., Mineral. Soc. Gt. Britain and Ireland, Cosmos Club. Office: Dept Geosics Univ Arizona Tucson AZ 85721-0077 Office Phone: 520-621-9993.

PREWITT, JEAN, not-for-profit organization executive; Degree, Harvard U.; degree in law, Georgetown U. Formerly lawyer Donovan Leisure Newton & Irvine; sr. v.p., gen. counsel United Internat. Pictures, 1982—89; with Nat. Telecomm. and Info. Adminstrn. U.S. Dept. Commerce, 1989—94; prin. Podesta Assocs., Washington, 1994—99; pres. Ind. Film & TV Alliance, LA, 2000—01, CEO, 2001—; bd. mem. Film LA, 2006—. Pres. Casa De Los Amigos, LA, 2003—. Adv. bd. Friends of Cancer Rsch., Washington, 2003—. Office: 10850 Wilshire Blvd 9th Fl Los Angeles CA 90024-4321 Business E-Mail: jprewitt@ifta-online.org.

PREWITT, KENNETH, political science professor, foundation administrator; b. Alton, Ill., Mar. 16, 1936; s. Carl Kenneth and Louise (Carpenter) P.; children: Jennifer Ann, Geoffrey Douglas. BA, So. Meth. U., 1958; MA, Washington U., St. Louis, 1959; PhD, Stanford U., 1963. Prof. polit. sci. U. Chgo., 1964-80, chmn. dept. polit. sci., 1975-76; dir. Nat. Opinion Rsch. Ctr., 1976-79; pres. Social Sci. Rsch. Coun., NYC, 1979-85, 95-98; sr. v.p. Rockefeller Found., NYC, 1985-95; dir. U.S. Census Bur., Washington, 1998-2001; dean grad. faculty New Sch. U., NYC, 2001—02; Carnegie Prof. of Public Affairs School of International and Public Affairs, Columbia Univ., NYC, 2002—. Vis. scholar U. Nairobi, Kenya, 1968-71; bd. dirs. Washington U., So. Meth. U., Energy Found., Ctr. Advanced Study Behavioral Scis. Author: Political Socialization, 1969, Ruling Elites, 1973, Labryrinths of Democracy, 1973, Politics and Science in Census-Taking, 2003. Guggenheim fellow, 1983; fellow Center Advanced Study in Behavioral Scis., 1983; recipient Officer's Cross of Order of Merit, Rep. of Germany. Fellow AAAS, Am. Acad. Arts and Scis.; mem. Am. Polit. Sci. Assn., Coun. on Fgn. Rels. E-mail: kp2058@columbia.edu.

PREWITT, WILLIAM CHANDLER, finance company executive; b. Phila., Aug. 23, 1946; s. Richard Hickman and Jean Mary (Simpkins) Prewitt; m. Karen Ruth Padgett, May 15, 1971. BA in History, Transylvania Coll., 1968; cert., Coll. Fin. Planning, 1985; MS in Fin. Planning, Coll. for Fin. Planning, 1991. Dist. exec. Cen. N.C. Coun., Albemarle, 1971-74, Transatlantic Coun., Heidelburg, Fed. Republic Germany, 1974-78; field dir. Dutchess City Coun., Hyde Park, NY, 1978-80; prin. Prewitt Properties, Charleston, SC, 1980—, William C. Prewitt Cert. Fin. Planner, Charleston, SC, 1986—2004; owner Charleston Fin. Adv., LLC, 2005—; registered rep. First Investors Corp., Charleston, SC, 1982-83. Lectr. Coll. of Charleston, 1987—, Trident Tech. Coll., Charleston, 1987—, Charleston So. U. Sec. Hist. Ansonborough Neighborhood Assn., Charleston, 1987—90, v.p., 1999, pres., 1999—2000; v.p. Charleston Fgn. Affairs Forum, 2007—; treas. South Carolinians to Limit Congl. Terms, 1991—2000; deacon 1st Presbyn. Ch., Rockingham, NC, 1972—74; elder 1st Scots Ch., Charleston, 1990—93, meml. fund trustee, 1999—2000; pres. Christian Family Y, 1995—97, bd. dirs., 1991—99; exec. bd. Coastal Carolina Coun. Boy Scouts Am., 2001—04; mem. Moultrie State Fund Com., 2004—07. 1st lt. Res. USMC, 1968—71. Named One of 300 Best Fin. Advisors, Worth Mag., 1996, 1997, 1998, One of 120 Best Fin. Advisors for Drs., Med. Econs. Mag., 1998—2007. Mem.: SCV, SAR (treas. 1996—2003, chpt. pres. 2004—06), Nat. Assn. Personal Fin. Advisors (pres. region 1994—96, chmn. ethics and stds. com. 1996—99, nat. bd. dirs. 1996—99, chmn. compensation com. 1999—, Robert J. Underwood award 2005), Internat. Assn. Fin. Planners (registry 1986—92), Inst. Cert. Fin. Planners, S.C. Soc. Cert. Fin. Planners (pres. 1985—87, chmn. bd. dirs. 1988—90), St. David's Soc., Internat. Churchill Soc., Société Francaise (sec. 1999—2001, pres. 2001—02), Navy League (pres. 1992, chmn. bd. dirs. 1993, mem. Charleston Coun.), Carolina Yacht Club, Cruising Club Charleston (navigator 2003—04, vice comdr. 2004—05, comdr. 2005—06), Rotary (bd. dirs. 2000—02). Republican. Avocation: sailing, historic restorations. Home: 33 Hasell St Charleston SC 29401-1604 Office: 15 Broad St Charleston SC 29401-3030 Office Phone: 843-722-3331. Business E-Mail: bill@charlestonfinancial.net.

PREWOZNIK, JEROME FRANK, retired lawyer; b. Detroit, July 15, 1934; s. Frank Joseph and Loretta Ann (Parzych) Prewoznik; m. Marilyn Ruth Johnson, 1970; 1 child, Frank Joseph II. AB cum laude, U. Detroit, 1955; JD with distinction, U. Mich., 1958. Bar: Calif. 1959. Pvt. practice, Calif., 1960-91. Served in US Army, 1958—60. Mem.: State Bar Calif. Republican.

PREY, BARBARA ERNST, artist; b. NYC, Apr. 17, 1957; d. Herbert Henry and Margaret (Joubert) Ernst; m. Jeffrey Drew Prey, Jan. 11, 1986; children: Austin William Ernst Prey, Emily Elizabeth Prey. BA with honors, Williams Coll., 1979; MDiv, Harvard U., 1986. Sales staff Tiffany and Co., NYC, summer 1977; intern Met. Mus. Art, NYC, summer 1979; pers. asst. Prince Albercht Castell, Castell, Germany, 1980-81; with modern painting dept. Sotheby's Auction House, NYC, 1981-82; sales asst.

Marlborough Gallery, NYC, 1982; tchg. asst. Boston Coll., 1984, Harvard U., Cambridge, Mass., 1984-85; vis. lectr. Tainan (Taiwan) Coll. and Sem., 1986-87; artist Oyster Bay, NY, 1987—. Art juror Washington and Jefferson Coll., Washington, 1990; artist-in-residence Westminster Sch., Simsbury, Conn., 1998; lectr. Nat. Gallery Art, Washington, 2005; mem. chmn.'s coun. Heckscher Mus.; presenter in field. Exhibited in group shows at Mus. Fine Arts, Mus. Southwest, Midland, Tex., Nassau County, N.Y., 1988, Nat. Arts Club, NYC, 1988, Gallery One, Rockland, Maine, 1992, Williams Coll., Williamstown, Mass., 1993, Johnstown Art Mus., Pa., 1993, Blair Art Mus., Holidaysburg, Pa., 1993, Phila. Mus. Art Gallery, 1995, Westmoreland Mus. Am. Art, Greensburg, Pa., 1996 (Best in Show award), Farnsworth Mus. Art, Rockland, Maine, 1997, Guild Hall Mus., East Hampton, NY, 1998, Portland Mus. Art, Md., 1998, US Embassy, Prague, 2002, Heckscher Mus. Art, Huntington, NY, 2002, Guild Hall Mus., East Hampton, NY, 2002, 2004, Gilcrease Mus., Tulsa, 2002, Internat. Space Station, 2003, The White House, Collection of Pres. and Mrs. George Bush, 2003, 2004, Kennedy Space Ctr., 2003—06, US Embassy, Oslo, Prague, Liberia, Belarus, 2003, 2004, 2005, Minsk, 2004, Madrid, 2006, 2007, Paris, 2006, 2007, Vilnius, 2006, 2007, NASA Commn X-43.: Columbia Tribute, 2004, NASA Commn: Shuttle Discovery Relaunch, US Embassy, Paris, 2005, Mona Bismarck Found., 2007, Picturing Long Island, The Heckscher Mus., 2007, Kennedy Space Ctr., 2007, one-woman shows include Harvard-Yale-Princeton Club, Pitts., 1991, Jensen Fine Arts, NYC, 1999, 2001, Represented in permanent collections Pres. and Mrs. George Bush Farnsworth Mus. Art, Kennedy Space Ctr.; illustrator Boys Harbor Cookbook, 1988, A Dream Became You, A City Grows Up, 1991, (covers) NY Daily News, Am. Artist Mag., 1994, Barbara Ernst Prey: Watercolors, 1998, Internat. Art Newspaper, 2001, NY Post, 2001, (PBS) True North, 2001, (PBS) Metro Section, 2001, Arts and Antiques Mag., 2001, 2003, Barbara Ernst Prey: A Trace in the Mind, 2002, NY Times, 2002, 2003, 2004, 2005, Artwork in the American Embassy Prague, 2002, Artwork in the American Embassy Oslo, 2003, The Robb Report, 2003, White House Christmas Card, 2003, LA Times, 2004, The New Yorker, 2004, Larry King Live CNN, 2004, (PBS) WLIW-NY, 2005, 2006, Style Sect., Washington Post, 2005, NPR, 2005, Wall St. Jour., 2006, NY Sun, 2006, displayed 1997 Holiday Card on 80,000 screens worldwide Bloomberg Bus. News, featured on Fox TV News, 1999; contbr. to popular mags., local newspapers. Class agt. Williams Coll., Williamstown, Mass., 1981—91; active 1st Presby. Ch., Oyster Bay, NY. Fulbright scholar, Germany, 1979-80; grantee Roothbert Fund, Chataugua, N.Y., 1982-84; recipient Ch. History award Gordan-Conwell Sem., S. Hamilton, Mass., 1984, Henry Luce Found., Taiwan, 1986-87, Jean Thoburn award, 1994, Women of Distinction award, N.Y. State Senate, 2004, Women of Distinction award, Distinction Mag., 2005. Mem. Pitts. Watercolor Soc. (Jean Thoburn award 1994), Nat. Mus. Women in the Arts. Avocations: tennis, skiing, birdwatching, reading, squash. Home and Office: 22 Pearl St Oyster Bay NY 11771-2305 E-mail: bprey@optonline.net.

PREYSZ, LOUIS ROBERT FONSS, III, management consultant, educator; b. Quantico, Va., Aug. 1, 1944; s. Louis Robert Fonss, Jr. and Lucille (Parks) P.; m. Patricia Dianne Yelland; children: Louis Robert Fonss IV, Christine Elizabeth, Michael Anthony, Daniel Timothy. BA, U. Wis., 1968; MBA, U. Utah, 1973; postgrad., Rutgers U., 1983; grad., Command and Gen. Staff Coll., 1986. Tchg. and rsch. asst. U. Utah, Salt Lake City, 1972—73; mktg. and pers. officer Security 1st Nat. Bank of Sheboygan, Wis., 1973—76; mktg. dir. 1st Nat. Bank Rock Island, Ill., 1976—77; asst. v.p., mktg. sales mgr. 1st Nat. Bank Birmingham, Ala., 1977—78; v.p. mktg. mgr. Sun 1st Nat. Bank Orlando, Fla., 1978—80; adj. prof. Disney U., Orlando, 1978—79; pres. Preysz Assocs., Saint Augustine, Fla., 1980—. Assoc. prof. mgmt. and banking Flagler Coll., St. Augustine, Fla., 1982—; faculty U. Wis., Sheboygan, 1973-76, Fla. Inst. Tech., 1976-77, St. Ambrose Coll., Davenport, Iowa, 1976-77, U. Ctrl. Fla., 1979-81, Columbia (Mo.) Coll., 1981-82; mem. tng. and profl. devel. coun. Bank Mktg. Assn., 1976-78, chmn., 1978; mem. mktg. and pub. rels. com. Wis. Bankers Assn., 1975; v.p. Ala. Automated Clearing House Assn., 1977-78; spkr. in field; host to daily FM radio program Money Issues. Author: How to Introduce a New Service, 1976, Energy Efficiency Programs and Lending Practices for Florida's Financial Institutions, 1980, Credit Union Marketing, 1981, An Effective Management Structure for Multi-Bank Holding Companies, 1983, Credit Union Strategic Marketing, 1993; contbg. editor: Target Market, an Instructional Approach to Bank Cross Selling of Services, New Accounts Training Manual, 1977, Tested Techniques in Bank Marketing, 1977; contbg. author: Rapid Debt Reduction Strategies, 1990, The Debt Free Army, 1993; mem. editl rev. bd. SAM Advanced Mgmt. Jour.; contbg. reviewer Professional Selling in the Buyer's Era, Human Resource Management, 8th edit.; contbr. articles to mags. Bd. dirs. Cath. Charities Bur. Inc., 1988—89, v.p., 1989; bd. dirs. United Way St. Johns County, 1989—95, chmn., 1991—95; charter mem. U.S. Com. for Battle Normandy Mus., 1989, Nat. WWII Meml.; mem. Reagan Presdl. Libr., 1989, Rep. Presdl. Task Force, 1982—86, Rep. Nat. Com., 1980—89, 2000—, Rep. Nat. Com. Victory, 2000; charter mem. George W. Bush for Pres.; bd. dirs., treas., deacon Grace Cmty. Ch., 1996—99; fin. chair Billy Graham Crusade, Jacksonville Crusade. Capt. US Army, 1968—72, officer Florida Army N.G. Recipient Congrl. Order Merit, Rep. Congrl. Com., 2003. Fellow: Soc. Advancement Mgmt. Honor Soc. (internat. v.p., bd. dir., cons., Mgmt. Excellence award 1990); mem.: Disabled Am. Vets., Ronald Reagan Presdl. Libr., Friends of Collections Soc. Pres. Harrison Home, Mil. Officers Assn. Am., Nat. World War II Mus., Nat. Mus. US Army (charter), Civil War Preservation Trust, Civil War Soc., West Point Soc. North Fla. (hon.), U. Wis. Alumni Assn., U. Utah Alumni Assn., Nat. Guard Officers Assn. Fla., Nat. Guard Assn. U.S., US Holocaust Meml. Mus. (charter), Nat. Trust Hist. Preservation, St. Augustine Officers Club, US Army Hist. Found. (charter), Nat. D-Day Mus. (charter), Rotary (Paul Harris fellow), Sigma Beta Delta, Omicron Delta Kappa, Phi Gamma Delta. Republican. Mem. Christian Ch. Avocations: military history, exercise, civil war history, sports. Office: PO Box 1027 Saint Augustine FL 32085-1027 Office Phone: 904-819-6243. Personal E-mail: mosserrs@aol.com. Business E-Mail: preyszlr@flagler.edu.

PREZIOSO, GIOVANNI P., lawyer; b. Boston, 1957; AB in Hist. and Lit. magna cum laude, Harvard U., 1979, JD magna cum laude. Bar: DC 1982. Assoc. Cleary, Gottlieb, Steen & Hamilton, LLP, Washington, 1982—91, ptnr., 1991—2002, 2006—; gen. counsel, chief legal officer SEC, Washington, 2002—06. Mem.: ABA (chmn. fed. securities law subcommittee on mcpl. and govtl. obligations). Office: Cleary Gottlieb Steen & Hamilton LLP 2000 Pennsylvania Ave NW Washington DC 20006 Office Phone: 202-974-1650. Office Fax: 202-974-1999. E-mail: gprezioso@cgsh.com.

PRIBRAM, KARL HARRY, neuroscience and psychology educator, brain researcher; b. Feb. 25, 1919; BS, U. Chgo., 1938, MD, 1941; PhD in Psychology (hon.), U. Montreal, Can., 1992; PhD in Philosophy (hon.), U. Bremen, 1996. Diplomate Am. Bd. Neurol. Surgery, Am. Bd. Med. Psychotherapists. Lectr. Yale U., New Haven, 1951-58; dir. psychology Inst. of Living, Hartford, Conn., 1951-58; fellow Ctr. for Advanced Studies in Behavioral Sci., Stanford U., Calif., 1958-59, assoc. prof. Calif., 1959-62, NIH lifetime rsch. career prof. Calif., 1962-89, prof. emeritus Calif., 1989—; eminent scholar Radford U., Va., 1989—2006, prof. emeritus Va., 2006—. Vis. scholar, hon. lectr. MIT, 1954, Clark U., 1956, Harvard, 1956, Haverford Coll., 1961, U. So. Calif., 1961, U. Leningrad, 1962, U. Moscow, 1962, U. Alta., Can., 1968, Ctr. for Study Dem. Insts., 1967-75, U. Coll., London, 1972, U. Chgo., 1973, Menninger Sch. Psychiatry, 1973-76, Ohio State U., 1975; vis. lectr. Grass Found., 1977; Phillips lectr., Haverford Coll., 1979; Lashley lectr., Queens Coll., 1979; Hubert Humphrey lectr. Macalester Coll., 1981; lectr. Internat. Mgmt. Inst., Geneva, Switzerland, 1987, Inst. Med. Psychology, Naples, 1988; disting. lectr. Second Annual Symposium of the Mind, Arlington, Tex., 1988; disting. rsch. prof. Georgetown U., George Mason U., 2006—; hon. lectr. Sirius Seminaries, Paris, 1988, Bielfeld, Germany, 1990, numerous others. Author: Brain and Behavior, vol. 1-4, 1969, What Makes Man Human, 1971, Languages of the Brain: Experimental Paradoxes and Principles in Neuropsychology, 1971; The Neurosciences: Third Study Program, 1971, Brain and Perception: Holonomy and Structure in Figural Processing, 1991, Rethinking Neural Networks: Quantum Fields and Biological Data, 1993, Origins: Brain and Self Organization, 1994, Scale in Conscious Experience: Is the Brain Too Important to be Left to Specialists to Study?, 1995, Freud's Project Reassessed, 1976; editor, mem. consulting bd. Neuropsychologia, Jour. Math. Biology, Internat. Jour. Neurosci., Behavioral and Brain Scis., Jour. Mental Imagery, Jour. Human Movement Studies, Jour. Social and Biol. Structures, ReVision, STSM Quar., Indian Jour. Psychophysiology, Internat. Jour. Psychophysiology, Cognition and Brain Theory; contbr. over 400 articles to profl. jours. Recipient Lifetime Rsch. Career award in neurosci. NIH, 1962-89, Humanitarian award INTA, 1980, Realia honor Inst. Advanced Philosophic Rsch., 1986, 93, Outstanding Contbns. award Am. Bd. Med. Psychotherapists, Neural Network Leadership award Internat. Neural Network, 1996, Dagmar and Vaclev Havel prize, 1989. Fellow Am. Acad. Arts and Scis., NY Acad. Scis. (hon. life); mem. AAUP, AMA, AAAS, APA (pres. div. physiol. and comparative psychology 1967-68, pres. div. theoretical and philos. psychology 1979-80), Internat. Neuropsychol. Soc. (founding pres. 1967-69), Internat. Assn. Study of Pain, Soc. Exptl. Psychologists (Anderson Lifetime Achievement award 2005), Am. Psychol. Soc., Am. Psychopathological Assn. (Paul Hoch award 1975), Am. Acad. Psychoanalysis, Soc. Biol. psychiatry (Manfred Sakel award 1976), Soc. Clin. and Exptl. Hypnosis (Henry Guze award 1991), Soc. Neurosci., Sigma Xi. Home: PO Box 679 Warrenton VA 20188-0679 Business E-Mail: pribramk@georgetown.edu.

PRICE, ALFRED LEE, lawyer, mining executive; b. Little Rock, May 19, 1935; s. Dewey Ernest and Dorothy Ava (Cooper) P.; m. Magdalena Torres, June 20, 1958; children: Gregory L., Ana Maria. BA, Hendrix Coll., 1956; JD, Tulane U., 1967. Bar: La. 1967, Miss. 1974, D.C., U.S. Supreme Ct., 1980, U.S. Tax Ct., 1977, cert. arbitrator, mediator, Am. Arbitration Assn. and Better Bus. Bur., Nat. Arbitration Forum. Office mgr., dir. personnel Petroleum Helicopters Co., Lafayette, La. and New Orleans, 1956-67; atty. Offshore Navigation and Petroleum Helicopters Co., New Orleans, 1967-74; gen. counsel First Miss. Corp., Jackson, 1974-93, corp. sec., 1988-93; commr. Miss. Employment Commn., Jackson, 1994—2002. Arbitrator Am. Arbitration Assn., 1998—. Mem. Jackson C.of C., chmn. legislative com., 1991-94. Recipient Arbitrator of Yr., Better Bus. Bureau, 1998. Mem. ABA, La. Bar Assn., Miss. Bar Assn., Hinds County Bar Assn., Miss. Mfrs. Assn. (bd. dirs.), Miss. Econ. Coun. (chmn. tort reform com.), River Hills Club. Methodist.

PRICE, AMELIA RUTH, not-for-profit foundation president, artist, small business owner; b. Bklyn., Sept. 4, 1942; d. Dr. Alphonse Frederick Pagano and Adele Marie Savarese; 1 child, Ean James. BA, Georgian Ct. Coll., Lakewood, NJ, 1964; MA in Art Hist., Cath. U. of Am., Washington, DC, 1968. Cert. Permanent Certificate, Art State of NY Edn. Dept., 1971. Art tchr. Bd. Coop. Ednl. Svcs., Patchogue, NY, 1967—68; art director Roland Advt. Co., NYC, 1968—69; art dept. chair Bd. Coop. Ednl. Svcs. II, Deer Park, NY, 1969—78; v.p. Delicious Selections Ltd, White Plains, NY, 1981—95; pres., owner Parker Commodities Ltd, Kings Park, NY, 1995—; owner Bubbling Oaks Samoyeds, Commack, NY, 1974—. Co-founder bubbling oaks samoyeds kennels Bubbling Oaks Samoyeds, Commack, NY, 1974—2002. Samoyed Newsletter and other publs.featuring Samoyeds, 1999—; contbr. articles on Samoyeds and their care to various publs., 1999. Pres. Samoyed Club of Am. Edn. and Rsch. Found., Inc., Madison, Wis., 2001—, v.p., 1997—2001. Recipient #1 Samoyed Bitch, Kennel Rev., 1974, 1975, 1976, 1977, 1978, 1983, 1984, #3 Samoyed, Dogs in Canada, 1976, Top Winning Team, Orgn. for the Working Samoyed Inc., 1986, 1988. Mem.: Habour Lights Painter, Decorative Artists LI, Soc. Decorative Painters, Nat. Assn. Woman Bus. Owners (pub. affairs com. 2003—), Primitive and Aboriginal Dog Soc., Russia Primitive and Aboriginal Dog Soc., Suffolk County Kennel Club Inc. (chmn. hospitality 1989—99, bd. dirs. 1996—99), Westbury Kennel Assn. (chmn. of trophies 1985, chmn. judges' transport. 2000), Samoyed Club of America Inc. (pres. 1997—99, Top Winning Bitch 1975, 1976, 1985, Top Winning Team 1985, Top Winning Bitch 1986, Top Winning Team 1987). Home: 128 Cowie Rd Commack NY 11725

PRICE, ARDYTHE BERNADEANE, nurse; b. Two Hills, Alta., Can., Sept. 27, 1948; d. Peter Cecil and Doris Eunice Tym; children: Shelley, Steven. AS, Pacific Union Coll., 1972; BA in English, Loma Linda U., 1973. RN Calif. RN Agnews State Hosp., Santa Clara, Calif., 1975—80, Kaiser, San Jose, Calif., 1980—90, Fremont Riedout, 1991—92, Sierra Nursing Registry, various cities, Calif., 1992—2002, Res-Care/Sierra Nurses, Yuba City, Calif., 1995—2002; staff nurse RN Maxin Healthcare, Sacramento, 2007—. Rep. Calif. Nursing Assn., San Jose, Calif., 1974; various coms. and bds. Agnews State Hosp., San Jose, Calif., 1979—80; pvt. nurse, Yuba City, Calif. Vol. Salvation Army, Marysville, Calif., 1996; mem. Sutter County Dem. Ctrl. Com., Yuba City, Calif., 1996—; sec. Yuba Sutter Dem. Club, Yuba City, 2001—; bd. dirs. comms. Samaritan Village, Yuba City, Calif., 1996—. Mem.: Sutter County Dem. Women's Club, Women of the Moose (chmn. ednl. advancement 2004—05). Democrat. Seventh Day Adventist. Avocations: boating, camping, fishing. Home: 1445 Stabler Ln # 4 Yuba City CA 95993 Personal E-mail: ardytheprice@aol.com.

PRICE, B. BYRON, historian; BS, U.S. Mil. Acad., 1970; MA in Mus. Sci., Tex. Tech. U., 1977; postgrad., Am. U., Washington, 1975. Tchg. asst. Tex. Tech. U., Lubbock, 1975, rsch. coord. Ranching Heritage Ctr./Mus., 1976-77; curator of history Panhandle-Plains Hist. Mus., Canyon, Tex., 1977-82, exec. dir., 1982-86, Nat. Cowboy Hall of Fame and Western Heritage Ctr., Oklahoma City, 1987-96, Buffalo Bill Hist. Ctr., Cody, Wyo., 1996—. Lectr. in field; condr. seminars in field; cons. in field. Advisory editor: The Handbook of Texas, 1986-96; editl. bd. N.Mex. Hist. Rev., 1990-93, Jour. Ariz. History, 1993-95; assoc. editor The Ency. of the West, 1996; author: Cowboys of the American West, 1996, Crafting a Southwestern Masterpiece, 1986, Imagining the Open Range: Erwin E. Smith, Cowboy Photographer, 1997, Longhead: A Painter's Painter, 1991, The National Cowboy Hall of Fame Chuck Wagon Cook Book, 1995, She Doesn't Write Like a Woman: Mari Sandoz and the Cattlemen, 1996, Fine Art of the West, 2004; co-author: The Golden Spread: An Illustrated History of Amarillo and the Texas Panhandle, 1986; co-editor: Cowboy Justice, 1997, Adventuring with the Old-Timers: Trails Traveled and Tales Told, 1979; contbr. articles to profl. jours. Mem. tourism task force Okla. Dept. Commerce, 1987; mem. Okla. Film Adv. Commn., 1988-90; bd. dirs. Okla. Ctr. for the Book, 1990—; judge Arts for the Parks Ann. Exhbn., 1992-93; mem. cultural opportunities work group Okla. Futures, 1993; mem. Oklahoma City Conv. and Visitors Commn., 1996—. Recipient Gov.'s Arts award State of Okla., 1994. Mem. Tex. Assn. Mus. (exec. coun. 1985-86), Okla. Mus. Assn. (v.p. 1993-95), Mus. West Consortium (pres. 1996—), Western History Assn. (mem. program com. 1997), Am. Assn. Mus., Tex. State Hist. Assn., Western Writers of Am., Panhandle Plains Hist. Soc. Office: Buffalo Bill Hist Ctr 720 Sheridan Ave Cody WY 82414-3428

PRICE, BETTY JEANNE, chimes musician; b. Long Beach, Calif., June 12, 1942; d. Grant E. and Miriam A. (Francis) Sickles; m. Harvey H. Price, Aug. 6, 1975; children: Thomas Neil Gering, Timothy Ray(dec.), Pamela Kay(dec.). Degree in Acctg., Northland Pioneer Coll., Show Low, Ariz., 1977. Youth missionary Open Bible Standard Missions, Trinidad, 1958-59; typographer Joel H. Weldon & Assocs., Scottsdale, Ariz., 1980-89; exec. chief acct. Pubs. Devel. Corp., San Diego, 1991-93; coord. music and worship College Ave. Bapt. Ch., San Diego, 1994-95; ChoirChime soloist, 1986—; exec. acct. Advance Reprographics, San Diego, 1996—2003. Chime musician and writer. Author: 101 Ways to Fix Broccoli, 1994, ABC's of Abundant Living, 1995; contbg. author God's Vitamin C for the Spirit, 1995, BounceBook, 1997, You Can Bounce Back Too, 1998, Pathway of Love, One Man's Remarkable Journey, 2002, Breaking Free from Financial Bondage: A Guide to Living Debt Free, 2004; musical arranger: handbell/chime Classical Sounds, 2005, A Musical Tour Around the World, 2005, Music for Special Occasions, 2005, Sounds of Christmas, 2005, A Musical Christmas Story, 2005, Hymns of Faith, 2005; musician: (CD) Classical Chimes, 2005, Chimes of Faith, 2005, Christmas Chimes, 2005. Mem.: ASCAP, Am. Guild English Handbell Ringers. Business E-Mail: chimesoloist@aol.com.

PRICE, BRUCE DEITRICK, advertising executive, author; b. Norfolk, Va., June 20, 1941; s. Harry Borum Price and Sue Spalding Deitrick. BA with honors, Princeton U., 1963. Pres., editor Black Book, Inc., NYC, 1968-73; owner/creative dir. Word-Wise Advt., NYC, 1973—; owner, dir. Word-Wise Ednl. Services, NYC, 1984—. Author: Into the Unknown, 1969, Ralph, 1970, American Dreams, 1984; contbr. articles on language and education to profl. jours.; patentee kaleidoscopic toy. With U.S. Army, 1964-66. Mem. Am. Inst. Graphic Artists, Mensa, Ivy Club. Democrat. Avocations: painting, poetry, sports.

PRICE, CAROL LEAH, mathematics educator; BS in Secondary Math. Edn., La. State Univ.; MS, Univ. So. Miss., PhD In Ednl. Leadership. Tchr., 1986—; elem. sch. tchr. E. Baton Rouge Parish; math. tchr. Zachary (La.) H.S. Named La. Tchr. of Yr., 2007; recipient Presdl. Award for Excellence in Mathematics Tchg., 1998. Office: Zachary High Sch, 4100 Bronco Lane Zachary LA 70791 Business E-Mail: carol.price@zacharyschools.org. *

PRICE, CHARLES GOWER, music educator; b. Carmel, Calif., Dec. 21, 1939; s. Vivian Lawson and Josephine Potter Price; m. Susan Pasquarelli, Oct. 19, 1972; m. Sandra Shahan (div.); children: Alexis Claude Bercq, Shana Price Johnson, Meghan Price Kuhi. BA in Music with Honors, Stanford U., Calif., 1962, MA in Performance Practice Early Music, 1963, PhD in Musicology, 1967. Asst. prof. Calif. State Coll., San Bernardino, 1967—72, Swarthmore Coll., Calif., 1974—75; prof. music hist. West Chester U., Pa., 1990—2004; west coast rep. Jay A. Steele Agy., San Lorenzo, Calif., 1972—73; asst. prof. W.Va. U., Morgantown, W.Va., 1975—76; prof., dir. music program Bucks County C.c., Newtown, Pa., 1976—90; english and music tchr. Willis Jepson Jr. High Sch., Vacaville, Calif., 1973—74. Prof. emeritus West Chester U., 2004—. Editor: (musical edition) William Babell's 12 Sonantas For Violin Or Oboe With Basso Continuo; contbr. articles various profl. jours. Music in the arts com. Phila. Music Alliance, Phila., 1988—90; exec. bd. San Bernardino Allied Arts Coun., Calif., 1968—70; program com. San Bernardino Valley Concert Assn., 1968—70. Fellow Musicology fellowship, French Govt., 1963—64, NEH, 1977, 1984;, 1987. Mem.: Am. Musicological Soc. (pres., mid-atlantic chpt. 1988—92). Home Phone: 505-758-1853.

PRICE, CHARLES H., II, former ambassador; b. Kansas City, Mo., Apr. 1, 1931; s. Charles Harry and Virginia (Ogden) P.; m. Carol Ann Swanson, Jan. 10, 1969; children: Caroline Lee, Melissa Marie, Charles H., C. B., Pickette. Student, U. Mo., 1951-53; LLD (hon.), Westminster Coll., 1984, U. Mo., 1988; LHD (hon.), Baker U., 1991; DSc (hon.), U. Buckingham, Eng., 1993. Chmn. bd., dir. Price Candy Co., Kansas City, 1969-81, Am. Bancorp., Kansas City, 1973-81; chmn., chief exec. officer Am. Bank & Trust Co., Kansas City, 1973-81; Am. ambassador to Belgium Brussels, 1981-83; Am. ambassador to U.K. London, 1983-89. Chmn. bd. Americanc, Inc., St. Joseph, Mo., 1989—92, pres., CEO, 1990—92; chmn. bd. Merc. Bank Kansas City, Mo., 1992—96; bd. dirs. Palmer Capital Assocs., Ltd., London. Trustee Midwest Rsch. Inst., Kansas City, chmn., 1990-93. Hon. fellow Regent's Coll., London, 1986; recipient William Booth award Salvation Army, 1985, World Citizen of Yr. award Mayor of Kansas City, 1985, Trustee Citation award Midwest Rsch. Inst., 1987, Disting. Svc. award Internat. Rels. Coun., 1989, Mankind award Cystic Fibrosis Found., 1990, Gold Good Citizenship award SAR, 1991, Chancellor's medal U. Mo. Kansas City, 1992, William F. Yates medallion William Jewell Coll., 1996. Mem.: The Vintage Country Club, White's Club, Swinley Forest Club, Kansas City Country Club, Eldorado Country Club, Brook Club, Cypress Point Club, Los Angeles County Club, River Club, Sigma Alpha Epsilon. Republican. Episcopalian. Office: 1 W Armour Blvd Ste 300 Kansas City MO 64111-2087 Office Phone: 816-360-6175.

PRICE, CHARLES STEVEN, lawyer; b. Inglewood, Calif., June 10, 1955; s. Frank Dean Price and Ann (Rounds) Bolling; m. Sandra Helen Laney, Feb. 26, 1983; children: Katherine Laney, Courtney Ann, Diana Emily. BA, U. Calif., Santa Barbara, 1976; JD, U. Chgo., 1979. Bar: Ariz. 1980, U.S. Dist. Ariz. 1980, U.S. Ct. Appeals (9th cir.) 1982. Assoc. Brown & Bain P.A., Phoenix, 1979-85, ptnr., 1985-96, Allen & Price P.L.C., Phoenix, 1996-2000, Allen, Price, Padden & Sanders, PC, Phoenix, 2000—04, Mariscal Weeks McIntyre & Friedlander, Phoenix, 2005—. Office: Mariscal Weeks McIntyre & Friedlander 2901 N Central Ave Ste 200 Phoenix AZ 85012 Office Phone: 602-285-5042. Business E-Mail: Charles.price@mwmf.com.

PRICE, CLIFFORD WARREN, retired metallurgist, researcher; b. Denver, Apr. 22, 1935; s. Warren Wilson and Vivian Fredricka (Cady) P.; m. Carole Joyce Waterman, June 14, 1969; children: Carla Beth, Krista Lynn Price. MetE, Colo. Sch. Mines, 1957; MS, Ohio State U., 1970, PhD, 1975. Design engr. Sundstrand Aviation-Denver, 1957-60; materials specialist Denver Rsch. Inst., 1960-63; sr. metallurgist Rocky Flats div. Dow Chem. Co., Golden, Colo., 1963-66; staff metallurgist Battelle Columbus (Ohio) Labs., 1966-75; sr. scientist Owens-Corning Fiberglas, Granville, Ohio, 1975-80; metallurgist Lawrence Livermore (Calif.) Nat. Lab., 1980-93; retired, 1993. Contbr. articles to profl. jours. Battelle Columbus Labs. fellow, 1974-75. Mem. Metall. Soc. AIME, Microscopy Soc. Am. (treas. Denver 1961-62), Am. Soc. Metals Internat. Achievements include research on electron, scanning probe and optical microscopy, secondary ion mass spectroscopy, deformation, fracture and recrystallization mechanisms in metals, recrystallization kinetics. E-mail: clifford.price@comcast.net.

PRICE, DANIEL MARTIN, lawyer; b. St. Louis, Aug. 23, 1955; s. Albert and Edith S. (Werner) P.; m. Kim Ellen Heebner, July 15, 1984; children: Emma Rachel, Joseph Armin, Joshua Simon. BA, Haverford Coll., 1977; diploma in law, Cambridge U., 1979; JD, Harvard U., 1981. Bar: D.C. 1981, Pa. 1986, US Supreme Ct. 1999. Assoc. Drinker, Biddle & Reath, Phila., 1981-82, 86-89; dep. gen. counsel Office of U.S. Trade Rep., Washington, 1989-92; ptnr. Powell, Goldstein, Frazer & Murphy, Washington, 1992—2002; ptnr. and mem. exec. com. Sidley Austin Brown & Wood LLP, Washington, 2002—, and chair, Internat. Trade and Dispute Resolution practice. Atty., adviser Dept. State, Washington, 1982-84; dep. agt. U.S. Iran-U.S. Claims Tribunal, Hague, The Netherlands, 1984-86; lectr. Haverford Coll., 1982; mem. adv. bd. Can.-U.S. Law Inst., British Inst. of Internat and Comparative Law, European Inst., Georgetown Univ. Law Ctr. Inst. of Internat. Econ. Law. Articles editor Harvard Law Rev., 1980-81; contbr. articles to profl. jours. including Am. Jour. Internat. Law, Internat. Lawyer, Internat. Fin. Law Rev., Harvard Internat. Law Jour., others. Mem. Bush-Cheney Transition Team, 1999—2000. Am. Keasbey scholar Cambridge U., 1977-78. Mem. ABA, Internat. Bus. Forum (legal adv. bd. 1987-89), Am. Arbitration Assn. (panel arbitrators), Internat. C. of C. (arbitrator), Orgn. for Internat. Investment (counsel), Coun. on Fgn. Rels., Phi Beta Kappa., Internat. Ctr. for Settlement of Investment Disputes (mem. panel of arbirators), Dept. of State Adv. Com. on Intl. Econ. Policy.

Office: Sidley Austin Brown & Wood LLP 1501 K St NW Washington DC 20005 Office Phone: 202-736-8226. Office Fax: 202-736-8711. Business E-Mail: dmprice@sidley.com.

PRICE, DAVID CECIL LONG, physicist, researcher; b. London, Jan. 17, 1940; came to U.S., 1966; s. Cecil Long and Freda (Salusbury) P.; m. Marie-Louise Saboungi, Nov. 24, 1989; children: Morgan, Alkes. BA, Cambridge U., 1961, MA, 1962, PhD, 1966. Rsch. assoc. Brookhaven Nat. Lab., Upton, NY, 1966-68; mem. staff Argonne (Ill.) Nat. Lab., 1968—2001, dir. solid state sci. divsn., 1974-79, dir. intense pulsed neutron source program, 1979-81, sr. physicist, 1981—2001; exec. dir. high-flux isotope reactor Oak Ridge (Tenn.) Nat. Lab., 2004—05; dir. rsch. CRMHT, Orleans, France, 2001—04, 2005—. Vis. prof. Japanese Soc. Promotion Sci., 1977; disting. vis. prof.Grad. U. for Adv. Studies, Hayama, Japan, 2000; mem. panel research opportunities with low energy neutrons Nat. Acad. Scis., 1976-77; sr. sci. advisor physics panel Energy Research Adv. Bd., Dept. Energy, 1986-87. Editor: Neutron Scattering (Methods of Experimental Physics, vols. 23 A, B, C), 1986-87. Recipient U. Chgo. award for disting. performance at Argonne Nat. Lab., 1988, Warren prize Am. Cryst. Assn., 1997, Alexander von Humboldt Rsch. award, 1998. Fellow Am. Phys. Soc., Inst. Physics (U.K.). Office: CRMHT 45071 Orleans France Home Phone: 773-752-8283; Office Phone: 33-238-255531. E-mail: price@cnrs-orleans.fr.

PRICE, DAVID EUGENE, congressman, education educator; b. Johnson City, Tenn., Aug. 17, 1940; s. Albert Lee and Elna (Harrell) Price; m. Lisa Beth Kanwit, July 27, 1968; children: Karen Elizabeth, Michael Edmond. Student, Mars Hill Coll., NC, 1957—59; BA in Am. Hist. and Math., U. NC, 1961; BD in Theology, Yale U., 1964, PhD in Polit. Sci., 1969. Legis. aide Staff of US Senator Edward Lewis Bartlett of Alaska, 1963-67; prof. polit. sci. and pub. policy Duke U., Durham, NC, 1973-86; mem. US Congress from 4th NC dist., 1987—95, 1997—, mem. appropriations com., chmn. homeland security subcommittee, mem. democracy assistance commn., co-chair Dem. budget grp. Exec. dir. NC Dem. Party, Raleigh, 1979-80, chmn., 1983-84, mem. 1983—; staff dir. nat. com. on presdl. nomination Dem. Party, 1981-82 Author: Who Makes the Laws, 1972, Bringing Back the Parties, 1984, Policymaking in Congl. Coms., 1979, The Congressional Experience: A View From the Hill, 2000. Named a Champion of Sci., Sci. Coalition, 2002, 2004; recipient Engring. Deans Coun. award, Am. Soc. Engring. Edn., 2003, Charles Dick Medal of Merit, NC Nat Guard, Hubert H. Humphrey Pub. Svc. award, Am. Polit. Sci. Assn. Mem. Am. Polit. Sci. Assn., Soc. Values in Higher Edn., Phi Beta Kappa, Kiwanis. Democrat. Baptist. Avocations: jogging, music. Office: US House Reps 2162 Rayburn House Office Bldg Washington DC 20515-3304 Office Phone: 202-225-1784. Office Fax: 202-225-2014. *

PRICE, DAVID TAYLOR, college baseball player; b. Aug. 26, 1985; Student in Sociology, Vanderbilt U., Nashville, 2005—. Pitcher USA Baseball Nat. Team. Named a First Team All-Am., 2007; named Southeastern Conf. Pitcher of Yr., 2007, Roy F. Kramer Southeastern Conf. Athlete of Yr., 2007, Collegiate Baseball's Nat. Co-Player of Yr., 2007, Player of Yr., Am. Baseball Coaches Assn., 2007, Coll. Player of Yr., Baseball Am., 2007, CSTV, 2007; recipient Golden Spikes award, USA Baseball, 2007, Dick Howser Trophy (Player of Yr. award), Nat. Collegiate Baseball Writer's Assn., 2007. Achievements include becoming the first overall pick by the Tampa Bay Devil Rays in the 2007 Maj. League Baseball draft. Mailing: Vanderbilt Baseball Athletic Dept 2601 Jess Neely Dr Nashville TN 37212 *

PRICE, DEBORAH A., federal agency administrator; b. St. Louis; BA, U. Mo. Dir. Nat. Prayer Breakfast, 1984—85; scheduler for Sen. William L. Armstrong US Congress, dir. rsch. and adminstrn., Senate Rep. Com., policy adv. to Sen. Don Nickles; exec. dir., Sec. Commn. on Opportunity in Athletics US Dept. Edn., sr. adv. to dep. sec., chief of staff, Office of Fed. Student Aid, asst. dep. sec., Office of Safe and Drug-Free Schools, 2004—. Republican. Office: Office Safe and Drug-Free Schools US Dept Edn 400 Maryland Ave SW Rm 1E110 Washington DC 20202 Office Phone: 202-205-4169. E-mail: deborah.price@ed.gov. *

PRICE, DENNIS LEE, industrial engineer, educator; b. Taber, Alberta, Can., Oct. 24, 1930; s. Walter and Wilma Harlan (Nance) P.; m. Barbara Ann Shelton; children: Denice Lynn Price Tsugawa, Philip Walter. BA, Bob Jones U., 1952; BD, MA, Am. Bapt. Sem. of the West, Berkeley, Calif., 1955; MA, Calif. State U., Long Beach, 1967; PhD in Indsl. Engring., Tex. A&M U., 1974. Cert. product safety mgr., hazard control mgr., human factors profl. Clergyman Am. Bapt. Conv., Calif., 1953-66; tech. staff autonetics divsn. Rockwell Internat., Anaheim, Calif., 1966-69; sr. engr. Martin Marietta Aerospace, Orlando, Fla., 1969-72; rsch. assoc. Tex. A&M U., College Station, 1972-74; tchg. asst. Calif. State U., Long Beach, 1963-66; asst. prof. dept. indsl. engring. and ops. rsch. Va. Poly. Inst. and State U., Blacksburg, 1974-78, assoc. prof. dept. indsl. and systems engring., 1979—83, prof., 1984-95, prof. emeritus, 1996—, dir. safety projects office, 1975-95, coord. Human Factors Engring. Ctr., 1986-95. Expert witness in safety engring. and human factors, 1978—; mem. U.S. Nuclear Waste Tech. Rev. Bd., 1989-95; U.S. tech. adv. group Internat. Stds. Tech. Com. 159 Ergonomics, 1987-94; chmn. com. on transp. of hazardous materials NRC, 1981-87; chmn. group 3 coun. emerging issues subcom. Transp. Rsch. Bd., 1987-89; chmn. task force on pipeline safety NAS, 1986 Mem. editorial bd. Human Factors, Santa Monica, Calif., 1989-95; author: (with K.B. Johns, J.W. Bain) Transportation of Hazardous Materials, 1983, (with W. Hammer) Occupational Safety Management and Engineering, 2000; author: Why Christ is the Only Way, 2003, Death, That's Life, 2005; contbr. chpts. to books, articles to profl. jours.; reviewer in field. Recipient Disting. Svc. award Nat. Rsch. Coun. NAS, 1987, 89, Outstanding Svc. commendation Transp. Rsch. Bd. NAS, 1981, Jack A. Kraft Innovator award Human Factors and Ergonomics Soc., 1996, Best Book award San Diego Christian Writers Guild, 2004; grantee NIOSH, Va. Dept. Transp. and Safety, 1977-82, 86-87, IBM, 1981-84, USN Office of Naval Rsch., 1978-80, USN Naval Systems Weapons Command, 1978-79. Mem. Inst. Indsl. Engrs. (sr.), Am. Soc. Safety Engrs. (profl.), Human Factors Soc. (rep. to rev. panel Guideline for the Preparation of Material Safety Data Sheets), System Safety Soc. (Educator of Yr. 1993), Alpha Pi Mu. Avocation: flying. Home: 15204 Moonglow Dr Ramona CA 92065-4529 Office: Va Poly Inst and State Univ Dept Indsl and Sys Engring Blacksburg VA 24061

PRICE, DONALD DENNIS, neuroscientist, psychologist; b. Pasadena, Calif., Aug. 3, 1942; s. Donald Raymon and Geraldine Marie Price; m. Elizabeth Coleman, Aug. 2, 1997; 1 child, Amy Rose. BA, U. Calif., Davis, 1965, PhD, 1969. Post doctoral student UCLA, 1969—70; asst. prof. Med. Coll. of Va., 1971—74, prof., 1980—97; rsch. psychologist, physiologist NIH, 1975—79; prof. oral surgery and neuroscience U. Fla., Gainesville, 1997—. Contbr. articles to profl. jours. Recipient Founders award, Am. Acad. Pain Medicine, 2004, John Bonica award, Ea. Pain Soc., 2004; Rsch. grantee, NIH, 1971—74, 1981—84, 1987—. Mem.: Soc. for Neurosci., Internat. Assn. for the Study of Pain, Am. Pain Soc. (com. mem., Kerr award 2004). Achievements include development of pain measurement methods; discovery of neurons, pathways, and brain regions that process pain, mechanisms of pain relief by placebo/hypnosis; patents in field. Avocations: cartooning, philosophy. Office: Univ Fla PO Box 100416 1600 SW Archer Rd Gainesville FL 32610-0416 Home Phone: 352-331-1780; Office Phone: 352-846-2718. Office Fax: 352-846-0588. Business E-Mail: dprice@dental.ufl.edu.

PRICE, DONALD RAY, academic administrator, researcher, agricultural engineer; b. Rockville, Ind., July 20, 1939; s. Ernest M. and Violet Noreen (Measel) P.; m. Joyce Ann Gerald, Sept. 14, 1963; children: John Allen, Karen Sue, Kimberly Ann, Daniel Lee BS in Agrl. Engring., Purdue U., 1961, PhD in Agrl. Engring., 1971; MS in Agrl. Engring., Cornell U., 1963. Registered profl. engr., Fla. From asst. prof. to prof. Cornell U., Ithaca, N.Y., 1962-80, dir. energy programs, 1975-77, 78-80; program mgr. Dept. Energy, Washington, 1977-78, cons.; assoc. dean research U. Fla., Gainesville, 1980-83, dean Grad. Sch., 1983-84, v.p. rsch., 1984—; pres. U. Fla. Rsch. Found., Inc.; program dir. NSF, 2003—. Chmn. bd. dirs. Progress Research, Inc.; cons. to Pres. Carter, Washington, 1978; bd. dirs. Nat. Food and Engring. Council, Columbia, Mo., 1978-85, S.E. Healthcare Found., Gainesville, Fla., 1985 Contbr. numerous articles on engring. to profl. jours.; patentee mech. device Mem. Ithaca Sch. Bd., N.Y., 1979-80; elder Ch. of Christ, Gainesville, Fla., 1983—. Recipient citation Pres. Carter, 1979, Disting. Alumnus award Purdue U., 1990. Fellow Am. Soc. Agrl. Engrs. (dir. 1990, paper awards 1963, 77, 78, Young Engr. of Yr. award 1980); mem. Soc. Research Adminstrs., Nat. Assn. Univ. Research Adminstrs., S.E. Univ. Research Assn., Research Univs. Network Lodges: Rotary. Democrat. Avocations: tennis, jogging, woodworking. Office: NSF 4201 Wilson Blvd Arlington VA 22203 Home: 1505 Fort Clarke Blvd Apt 7105 Gainesville FL 32606-9104 E-mail: dprice@nsf.gov.

PRICE, EDGAR HILLEARY, JR., manufacturing executive, consultant; b. Jacksonville, Fla., Jan. 1, 1918; s. Edgar Hilleary and Mary Williams (Phillips) P.; m. Elise Ingram, June 24, 1947; 1 son, Jerald Steven. Student, U. Fla., 1937-38. Mgr. comml. flower farm, 1945-49, Fla. Gladiolus Growers Assn., 1949-55; exec. v.p. Tropicana Products, Inc., Bradenton, Fla., 1955-73, dir. div. govt. and industry regulations, to 1979; dir.; exec. v.p. Indsl. Glass Co., Inc., Bradenton, 1963-73; pres., chmn. bd. Price Co., Inc., Bradenton, cons., 1973—. Dir. emeritus F.P.L. Group, Inc.; past chmn. Fla. Citrus Commn., Fla. Gov.'s Freeze Damage Survey Team, Spl. Commn. for Study Abolition Death Penalty; bd. dirs. Fla. Power and Light Co., Fla. Fair Assn., Fla. Citrus Expn., Fla. Fruit and Vegetable Assn., G.T.E. Fla., Fla. Cyprus Gardens, Ellis Bank Co.; past chmn. Joint Citrus Legis. Com.; past mem. Fla. Plant Bd., Fla. Bd. Control, Fla. Legis. Coun.; exec. com. Growers and Shippers League Fla., Fla. Agrl. Council, Spl. Health Agrl. Research and Edn.; past pres., chmn. bd. Fla. Hort. Soc. Past chmn., commr. census 12th Jud. Circuit; mem. Gov. Fla. Com. Rehab. Handicapped, Fla. Commn. on Ethics, 1976-77, Pres. Carter Inaugural Fin. com., 1977, Ea. 5th Circuit U.S. Jud. Nominating Commn., 1977—, Fla. Senate from 36th Dist., 1958-66; past chmn. Manatee County Bd. Sch. Dist. Trustees, Local Housing Authority Bradenton, Bradenton Sub. Std. Housing Bd., Bradenton Charter Adv. Com.; del. Dem. Nat. Conv., 1960, dist. del., 1964; past trustee, mem. exec. com. Stetson U.; former trustee New Coll., Aurora Found. Served to 1st lt. USAAF, 1941-45. Named Boss of Yr., Nat. Secs. Assn., 1959, Man of Yr. for Fla. agr. Progressive Farmer mag., 1959; recipient merit award Am. Flag Assn., 1962, Gamma Sigma Delta, 1965, leadership award Fla. Agrl. Ext. Svc., 1963, Outstanding Senator award Fla. Radio Broadcasters, 1965, Allen Morris award s most valuable mem. Fla. Legislature, 1965, Most Valuable Mem. award Fla. Senate, St. Petersburg Times, 1965, Brotherhood award Sarasota chpt. NCCJ, 1966, Disting. Citizen award Manatee County, 1970, Disting. Alumnus award U. Fla., 1972, Svc. to Mankind award Sertoma Internat., 1976, Goodwill Disting. Citizen award, 1979, Crystal Shield award Salvation Army, 1996; inducted into Fla. Agrl. Hall of Fame, 1992, Tampa Bay Bus. Hall of Fame, 1992. Mem. Fla. C. of C. (bd. dirs. emeritus and past chmn.), Manatee C. of C. (past pres.), Fla. Hort. Soc. (past pres., chmn. bd.), Fla. Flower Assn., ARC Clara Barton Soc., Blue Key (hon.), Omicron Delta Kappa (hon.), Kiwanis (pres. 1955), Sigma Alpha Epsilon. Home: 3009 Riverview Blvd W Bradenton FL 34205-3420 Office: PO Box 9270 Bradenton FL 34206-9270 *The turning point in my life came at the age of 32 when I accepted Jesus Christ as my personal Lord and Saviour. I believe every person should live his life up to the fullest extent of his God-given talents and ability. I think we have a responsibility to "pay our dues" for the privilege of living in a free land by being actively involved in our government.*

PRICE, ELIZABETH ANNE, lawyer; b. Boston, Aug. 23, 1960; BA, George Washington U., 1983, JD with honors, 1986. Bar: Ga. 1986, U.S. Dist. Ct. (no. dist.) Ga. 1986, U.S. Ct. Appeals (11th cir.) 1986, U.S. Supreme Ct. 1995. Ptnr., litig., trial practice Alston & Bird LLP, Atlanta, 1986—. With U.S. Army, interrogator/Arabic linguist, 1978-81. Mem. State Bar Ga. (access to justice com., ct. futures com.), Atlanta Bar Assn. (bd. dirs. 1996—, pres.). Office: Alston & Bird 1 Atlantic Ctr 1201 W Peachtree St NW Atlanta GA 30309-3400 Office Phone: 404-881-7264. Business E-Mail: lprice@alston.com.

PRICE, ELY, dermatologist; b. NYC, Aug. 9, 1932; s. Jacob and Mary (Flattau) P.; m. Ilona Brodie, Apr. 30, 1989; children from previous marriage: Jeremy, Andrew. BS cum laude, CCNY, 1953; AM, Ind. U., 1956; MD, U. Lausanne, Switzerland, 1964. Diplomate Am. Bd. Dermatology. Intern Brookdale Hosp. Med. Ctr., Bklyn., 1964-65, resident internal medicine, 1965-66; fellow Mt. Sinai Hosp., NYC, 1965-66; resident in dermatology Kings County Hosp., Bklyn., 1966-69; practice dermatology Bay Ridge Skin and Cancer Dermatology, P.C., Bklyn., 1969—; attending-in-charge, head dermatology Maimonides Med. Ctr., Bklyn., 1985—; clin. assoc. prof. dermatology SUNY Sci. Ctr., Bklyn., 1985—. Cons. in medicine Luth. Med. Ctr., Bklyn., 1988—; cons. in dermatology Victory Med. Hosp., Bklyn., 1989—. Fellow ACP, Am. Acad. Dermatology, Am. Soc. Dermatol. Surgery, N.Y. Acad. Medicine. Avocation: golf. Office: Bay Ridge Skin & Cancer Dermatology PC 9921 4th Ave Brooklyn NY 11209-8347 Home: 5598 Vista Del Mando S Unit B Laguna Woods CA 92637-6923 E-mail: elyilona@aol.com.

PRICE, FRANK, motion picture and television company executive; b. Decatur, Ill., May 17, 1930; s. William F. and Winifred A. (Moran) P.; m. Katherine Huggins, May 15, 1965; children: Stephen, David, Roy, William. Student, Mich. State U., 1949-51, HHD (hon.), 2003. Writer, story editor CBS-TV, NYC, 1951-53, Columbia Pictures, Hollywood, Calif., 1953-57, NBC-TV, Hollywood, Calif., 1957-58; producer, writer ZIV-TV, Hollywood, Calif., 1958, Universal Television, Universal City, Calif., 1959-64, v.p., 1964-71, sr. v.p., 1971-73, exec. v.p. in charge of production, 1973-74, pres., 1974-78; v.p., dir. MCA, Inc., 1976-78; pres. Columbia Pictures Prodn., 1978-79; chmn., chief exec. officer Columbia Pictures, 1979-84, also bd. dirs.; chmn. MCA Motion Picture Group, 1984-86; chmn., chief exec. officer Price Entertainment Inc., 1987-90; chmn. Columbia Pictures, 1990-91; chmn., chief exec. officer Price Entertainment, 1991—; prodr. The Tuskegee Airmen, 1996. Trustee U. So. Calif., 1996—, chmn. bd. counselors Sch. of Cinema-TV, 1990—; mem. Nat. Coun. on the Arts, 2006—. With USN, 1948-49. Recipient Peabody award, 1996, NAACP Image award, 1996. Mem. Writers Guild Am. West, N.Y. State Soc. Cin. Office: Price Entertainment 620 Park Ave New York NY 10021

PRICE, GARY, librarian; m. Lisa Cohen, May 2007. BA, U. Kansas, Lawrence, Kansas, 1988; M in Libr. and Info. Sciences, Wayne State U., Detroit, Mich., 1996. Reference libr. George Washington U. (Va. campus), 1995—2001; founder, chief editor, compiler ResourceShelf, 2001—; news editor Search Engine Watch, 2004—06; founder, contbr., editor Docuticker, 2004—; libr., dir. online info. resources Ask.com (formerly called Ask Jeeves, Inc.), 2006—. Faculty mem. WebSearch U.; frequent spkr. at Search Engines Strategies, WebSearch U., Computers in Libraries, Internet Librarian and other industry conferences; info. rsch. cons. Co-author (with Chris Sherman): The Invisible Web, 2001; contbr. articles to Washington Post, Guardian & Chronicle of Higher Edn., Fast Facts, Speech and Transcript Ctr., News Ctr., Audio/Video News on World Wide Web, Congl. Rsch. Svc. Reports, Virtual Acquisition Shelf, & News Desk, others. Named one of Top Librarian Personalities on the Web, 2002; recipient Innovations in tech. award, Spl. Libraries Assn., 2002, Anges Henbry award, Spl. Libraries Assn. (News Divsn.), 2004, Alumnus of Yr., Wayne State U., 2004. Achievements include being a renowned expert in search, particularly structured data search. Office: Ask.com 555 12th St Ste 500 Oakland CA 94607 E-mail: gary.price@resourceshelf.com. *

PRICE, GLENDA DELORES, dean, college president; b. York, Pa., Oct. 10, 1939; d. William B. Price and Zelma E. Holmes McGeary. BS, Temple U., 1961, MEd, 1969, PhD, 1979. Clin. lab. specialist. Cytotechnologist Temple U. Hosp., Phila., 1961-67, prof. clin. lab. sci.; faculty Coll. Allied Health Professions, Temple U., Phila., 1967-79, asst. dean allied health, 1979-86; dean allied health Sch. Allied Health Professions, U. Conn., Storrs, 1986—; pres. Marygrove Coll., Detroit, 1998. Pres. Am. Soc. Clin. Lab. Contbr. over 20 articles to profl. jours., chpts. to books. Bd. trustees U. New Eng., Biddeford, Maine, 1989—; bd. dirs. Windham Hosp., Willimantic, Conn., 1989—, E. Hartford VNA, 1989—; allied health adv. Pew Health Prof. Commn., Durham, N.C., 1991—. Recipient Leadership award SUNY-Buffalo, 1982; named Mem. of the Yr., Pa. Soc. Med. Tech., 1979; decorated Legion of Honor, Chapel of Four Chaplains, 1977. Mem. Am. Soc. Allied Health Professions (sec. 1985-87), Am. Soc. Med. Tech. (pres. 1979-80), Alpha Kappa Alpha, Alpha Mu Tau, Alpha Eta, Phi Kappa Phi. Democrat. Baptist. Home and Office: U Conn 358 Mansfield Rd Storrs Mansfield CT 06269-9000

PRICE, GREGORY, environmentalist; s. Clarence James and Josephine Price. BS in Geography and Earth Sci., Ctrl. Mich. U., Mount Pleasant, 1992. Groundwater technician Huron Pines Resource Conservation and Devel., Inc., Grayling, Mich., 1995—99; registered environ. health specialist II Mid Mich. Dist. Health Dept., Ithaca, 1999—. Bd. Trustee's Academic scholar, Ctrl. Mich. U., 1988—89. Mem.: Nat. Environ. Health Assn. (licentiate; registered environ. health specialist/registered sanitarian). Avocations: camping, running, fishing, motorcycling, cross country skiing. Office: Mid Michigan District Health Dept 151 Commerce Dr Ithaca MI 48847 Home Phone: 989-875-1020; Office Phone: 989-875-1020. Personal E-mail: gprice@mmdhd.org.

PRICE, GRIFFITH BALEY, JR., lawyer; b. Lawrence, Kans., Aug. 15, 1942; s. Griffith Baley and Cora Lee (Beers) P.; m. Maria Helena Martin, June 29, 1968 (div.); children: Andrew Griffith, Alexandra Helena; m. Nancy Culver Rhodes, Aug. 17, 1997; children: Carolyn Rhodes, Sarah Culver. AB cum laude, Harvard U., Cambridge, Mass., 1964; LLB, NYU, 1967. Bar: NY 1967, DC 1991, US Ct. Appeals (6th cir.) 1975, US Ct. Appeals (2nd cir.) 1978, US Ct. Appeals (3d, 5th and 11th cirs.) 1981, US Ct. Appeals (1st cir.) 2002, US Ct. Appeals (fed. cir.) 1984, US Supreme Ct. 2001. Assoc. Dewey, Ballantine, Bushby, Palmer & Wood, NYC, 1967-75; ptnr. Milgrim Thomajan & Lee, NYC, 1976-86; of counsel, ptnr. Finnegan, Henderson, Farabow, Garrett & Dunner, LLP, Washington, 1987—. Adj. prof., lectr. George Washington U. Law Ctr., Washington, 1989—93; mem., chair pub. adv. com. US Patent and Trademark Office, 1999—2004; lectr., spkr. in field. Author: (with others, treatise) Milgrim on Trade Secrets, 1986; contbr. articles to profl. jours. Root-Tilden scholar NYU Law Sch., 1964-67. Fellow: Am. Intellectual Property Law Assn. (bd. dirs., com. chmn.); mem.: ABA (intellectual property sec., com. chmn.), Assn. Interamerican Indsl. Property, Fed. Cir. Bar Assn., Licensing Execs. Soc., Internat. Trademark Assn. (bd. dirs., com. chmn.), Cosmos Club, Nat. Press Club, Harvard Club (Washington), NY Athletic Club. Unitarian Universalist. Office: Finnegan Henderson Farabow Garrett & Dunner LLP 901 New York Ave NW Washington DC 20001-4413 Home Phone: 301-263-0853; Office Phone: 202-408-4000. Business E-Mail: gbprice@finnegan.com.

PRICE, HENRY ESCOE, broadcast executive; b. Jackson, Miss., Oct. 13, 1947; s. Henry E. Price Sr. and Alma Kate (Merrill) Noto; m. Maria Diane Harper, Apr. 8, 1972; children: Henry E. III, Norman Harper. BS in Radio, TV, Film, Journalism, U. So. Miss., 1972. Announcer, news dir. Sta. WROA Radio, Gulfport, Miss., 1967-69; comml. producer Sta. WJTV-TV, Jackson, Miss., 1969-73; prodn. mgr. Sta. WAAY-TV, Huntsville, Ala., 1973-77, Sta. WPEC-TV, West Palm Beach, Fla., 1977-79; dir. promotion Sta. WPTV-TV, Palm Beach, Fla., 1979-81; TV cons. Frank Magid Assoc., Marion, Iowa, 1981-83; dir. advt. and promotion Sta. WJLA-TV, Washington, 1983-84; v.p., dir. programming Sta. WUSA-TV, Gannett TV, Washington, 1984-88; pres., gen. mgr. Sta. WFMY-TV, Gannett TV, Greensboro, N.C., 1988-91, Sta. KARE-TV, Mpls., 1991-96; v.p., gen. mgr. Sta. WBBM-TV, CBS TV Stas., Chgo., 1996—2000; pres., gen. mgr. Sta. WXUU-TV, Winston-Salem, NC, 2000—; sr. fellow in TV, Northwestern U. Media Mgmt. Ctr. Pres. Carolina News Network, 1988-91; adj. faculty media mgmt. Ctr. Northwestern U., 2000—. Vice chair, bd. dirs. The Courage Ctr., Mpls.; regional dir. Nat. Conf.; mem. exec. com., bd. dirs. The Minn. Orch.; Pacesetter program chair Mpls. United Way Campaign; active Twin Cities Dunkers, Twin Cities Comm. Coun., 11 Who Care. Mem. Chgo. C. of C. (bd. dirs.), Ill. Broadcasters Assn. (bd. dirs.). Avocations: furniture design and construction, reading, walking, bicycling. Address: 700 Coliseum Dr Winston Salem NC 27106

PRICE, HILARY B., cartoonist; b. Dec. 4, 1969; life ptnr. Kerry LaBounty. BA, Stanford U., 1992. Advt. copywriter, 1992—95; syndicated cartoonist King Features Syndicate, 1995—. Author & artist (comic strips) Rhymes With Orange, 1995—. Mem.: Nat. Cartoonists Soc. (3rd v.p. 2007—09). Office: c/o King Features Syndicate 15th Fl 300 W 57th St New York NY 10019-5238 E-mail: hilary@rhymeswithorange.com. *

PRICE, ILENE ROSENBERG, lawyer; b. Jersey City, July 2, 1951; d. Irwin Daniel and Mildred (Riesberg) Rosenberg; m. Jeffrey Paul Price, Feb. 18, 1973. AB, U. Mich., 1972; JD, U. Pa., 1977. Bar: Pa. 1977, DC 1978, U.S. Dist. Ct. DC 1979, U.S. Ct. Appeals (D.C. cir.) 1979. Assoc. Haley, Bader & Potts, Washington, 1977-80; staff atty. Mut. Broadcasting System Inc., Arlington, Va., 1980-82, asst. gen. counsel, 1982-85; gen. counsel MultiComm Telecommunications Corp., Arlington, 1985-88; east coast counsel Westwood One, Inc., Arlington, 1988-91; gen. counsel Resource Dynamics Corp., Vienna, Va., 1991—2001; legal search cons. The McCormick Group, Arlington, 2001—03; gen. counsel Bluewave Resources, LLC, McLean, Va., 2003—. Mem. Fed. Communications Bar Assn., Wash. Met. Area Corp. Counsel Assn., Women's Bar Assn. D.C. (bd. dirs. 1984-87). Office: Bluewave Resources LLC Ste 310 6830 Elm St Mc Lean VA 22101 Home Phone: 703-893-6079; Office Phone: 703-448-3400. Business E-Mail: ileneprice@bwres.com.

PRICE, JAMES GORDON, physician, educator; b. Brush, Colo., June 20, 1926; s. John Hoover and Rachel Laurette (Dodds) Price; m. Janet Alice McSween, June 19, 1949; children: James Gordon II, Richard Christian, Mary Laurette, Janet Lynn. BA, U. Colo., 1948, MD, 1951. Diplomate charter Am. Bd. Family Practice. Intern Denver Gen. Hosp., 1951—52; practice medicine specializing in family medicine Brush Co., 1952—78; prof. family practice U. Kans. Med. Ctr., 1978—93; chmn. dept. U. Kans. Med. Center, 1982—90, exec. dean, 1990—93, prof. emeritus in family practice, 1993—. Dir., pres. Am. Bd. Family Practice, 1979; mem. Inst. Medicine of NAS, 1973—. Med. editor: Gen. Learning Corp., 1973—92, mem. editl. bd.: Med. World News, 1969—79; editor: Am. Acad. Family Physician Home Study Self Assessment Program, 1978—83; columnist: Your Family Physician, 1973—90. Trustee Family Health Found. Am., 1970—82; vol. physician St. Jude's Hosp., St. Lucia, West Indies, 1998—99. With USNR, 1943—46. Fellow: Am. Acad. Family Physicians (charter, pres. 1973); mem.: Phi Beta Kappa, Alpha Omega Alpha. Home: 12205 Mohawk Rd Shawnee Mission KS 66209-2137 Business E-Mail: jimtad@sbcglobal.net.

PRICE, JAMES TUCKER, lawyer; b. Springfield, Mo., June 22, 1955; s. Billy L. and Jeanne Adele Price; m. Francine Beth Warkow, June 8, 1980; children: Rachel Leah, Ashley Elizabeth. BJ, U. Mo., 1977; JD, Harvard U., 1980. Bar: Mo. 1980. Assoc. firm Spencer Fane Britt & Browne, Kansas City, 1980-86; ptnr. Spencer Fane Britt & Browne LLP, Kansas City, 1987—, chair environ. practice group, 1994—, mem. exec. com., 1997—. Mem. Brownfields Commn., Kansas City, 1999—; mem. steering com. Kansas City Bi-State Brownfields Initiative, 1997—. Contbr. to monographs, other legal publs. Mem. ABA (coun. sect. environ, energy and resources 1992-95, vice chmn. solid and hazardous waste com. 1985-90, chmn. 1990-92, chmn. brownfields task force 1995-97, vice chmn. environ. transactions and brownfield com. 1998-2000), Mo. Bar Assn., Kansas City Met. Bar Assn. (chmn. environ. law com. 1985-86), Greater Kansas City C. of C. (co-chair Brownfields Working Group, 1996-98, chmn. energy and environ. com. 1987-89). Office: Spencer Fane Britt & Browne LLP 1000 Walnut St Ste 1400 Kansas City MO 64106-2140 Office Phone: 816-292-8228. Business E-Mail: jprice@spencerfane.com.

PRICE, JASON TODD, director; s. Sam and Marietta Price. MA in History, Tex. Tech U., Lubbock, 2005. Tchg. asst. Tex. Tech U., Lubbock, 2002—04; adj. instr. history and devel. math Frank Phillips Coll., Borger, Tex., 2004—05, academic coord. Title IV, 2005—. Travel grantee, Tex. Tech History Dept., 2002, 2005. Mem.: Mensa. Home Phone: 806-273-2170.

PRICE, JOE D., pipeline developer; m. Etsuko Price. Founder Shin'enKan Found. for Japanese art, Corona del Mar, Calif. Bd. dir. Friends of Kebyar, 1983—. Named one of Top 200 Collectors, ARTnews Mag., 2004. Avocation: Collecting Edo-period Japanese art. Mailing: PO Box 1111 Bartlesville OK 74005 Office Phone: 949-759-8550.

PRICE, JOE L., bank executive; B in Acctg., U. NC, Charlotte, 1983. With PriceWaterhouse; mgmt. positions Bank of Am. Corp., Charlotte, NC, 1992—95, contr., 1995—97, gen. auditor, 1997—99, pres. consumer fin. group, 1999—2002, corp. strategy & consumer spl. assets exec., 2002—03, risk mgmt. exec. global corp. and investment banking, 2003—06, CFO, 2006—. Bd. dirs. Habitat for Humanity; mem. adv. bd. Belk Sch. Bus. U. NC. Office: Bank of Am Corp 100 N Tryon St Corp Ctr Charlotte NC 28255 *

PRICE, JOHN ALEY, lawyer; b. Maryville, Mo., Oct. 7, 1947; s. Donald Leroy and Julia Catherine (Aley) P.; m. Deborah Diadra Gunter, Aug. 12, 1995; children: Theodore John, Joseph Andrew. BS, N.W. Mo. State U., 1969; JD, U. Kans., 1972. Bar: Kans. 1972, N.C., 2006, U.S. Dist. Ct. Kans. 1972, U.S. Ct. Appeals (10th cir.) 1972, Tex. 1984, U.S. Ct. Appeals (5th cir.) 1984, U.S. Supreme Ct. 1987; cert. civil trial law Tex. Bd. Legal Specialization, pro bono atty. Tex., 1992. Law clk. U.S. Dist. Ct. Kans., Wichita, 1972-74; from assoc. to ptnr. Weeks, Thomas and Lysaught, Kansas City, Kans., 1974-82; ptnr. Winstead, Sechrest & Minick, Dallas, 1982-96, litigation sect. coord., 1990-92, intellectual property sect. litigation coord., 1993-95; gen. counsel Travelhost Inc., Dallas, 1996—, Club Co., Inc., 1999-2001. Pres. Umansys, Inc., Dallas, 2000—04; spl. prosecutor Leavenworth County Office Dist. Atty., 1970-71, Sedgwick County Offce Dist. Atty., Wichita, Kans., 1971-72. Author: Our Boundless Self (A Call to Awake), 1992, A Gathering of Light: Eternal Wisdom for a Time of Transformation, 1993; co-author: Soular Reunion: Journey to the Beloved, 1998; editor (mag.) Academic Analyst, 1968-69; assoc. editor U. Kans. Law Rev., 1971-72, Dallas Bus. Jour.; contbr. articles to profl. jours. Co-dir. Douglas County Legal Aid Soc., Lawrence, Kans., 1971-72; co-pres. Northwood Hills PTA, Dallas, 1984, Westwood Jr. H.S. PTA, 1989-90; founder New Frontiers Found., 1993; co-founder Wings of Spirit Found., 1994, dir., v.p. 1994—. Recipient Tex. Super Lawyer, Law and Politics and Tex. Monthly Mag., 2003, 2006. Mem. ABA, Kans. Bar Assn. (mem. task force for penal reform; Pres.'s Outstanding Svc. award 1981), Tex. Bar Assn., Pro Bono Coll., State Bar Tex., World Bus. Acad., Inst. Noetic Scis., UN Assn. (human rights com. Dallas chpt. 1991-93, bd. dirs. 1991-93), Campaign for the Earth (chpt. coord. Global Report 1991-92, coord. govt. and polit. area 1991-92), Blue Key, Order of Coif, Phi Delta Phi, Sigma Tau Gamma (v.p. 1968-69). Mem. Unity Ch. Office: Travelhost Inc 10701 N Stemmons Fwy Dallas TX 75220-2419 Office Phone: 972-556-0541. Personal E-mail: japrice@travelhost.com. *We create our reality every moment of existence. Our only limitations are those we choose to accept.*

PRICE, JOHN R., lawyer, educator; b. Indpls., Nov. 28, 1934; s. Carl Lee and Agnes I. P.; m. Suzanne A. Leslie, June 22, 1963; children: John D., Steven V. BA with high honors, U. Fla., 1958; LL.B. with honors, NYU, 1961. Bar: Wash. 1977, U.S. Ct. Appeals (9th cir.), U.S. Dist. Ct. (we. dist.) Wash. Assoc. McCutchen, Doyle, Brown & Enersen, San Francisco, 1961-69; prof. law U. Wash., Seattle, 1969-97, dean, 1982-88; of counsel Perkins Coie, Seattle, 1976—2004. Author: Contemporary Estate Planning, 1983, Price on Contemporary Estate Planning, 1992, 7th edit. (with Samuel A. Donaldson), 2007, Conflicts, Confidentiality and Other Ethical Issues, 2000, 2d edit., 2007. Served with U.S. Army, 1953-55 Root-Tilden fellow NYU Sch. Law, 1958-61 Fellow Am. Coll. Trust and Estate Counsel (former regent); mem. ABA, Am. Law Inst., Order of Coif, Phi Beta Kappa. Congregationalist. Home: 3794 NE 97th St Seattle WA 98115-2564 Office: 1201 3rd Ave Ste 4800 Seattle WA 98101-3099 E-mail: jprice@perkinscoie.com.

PRICE, JOHN RANDOLPH, writer; b. Alice, Tex., Feb. 12, 1932; s. John Randolph and Eva Mae (Boney) P.; m. Janis Bryant Price, June 20, 1953; children: Susan Lynn, Leslie Anne. BS, U. Houston, 1957; PhD (hon.), Emerson Inst., 2001; DHL (hon.), Holmes Inst., 2003. Dir. advt. Gates Radio Corp., Quincy, Ill., 1957-62; v.p. Sander Rodkin, Ltd., Chgo., 1962-64; exec. v.p. Stewart, Price, Tomlin, Inc., Chgo., 1964-67; v.p. Goodwin, Dannenbaum, Littman & Wingfield, Inc., Houston, 1967-70; pres. O'Neill, Price, Anderson, Fouchard, Inc., Houston, 1970-74, John Price & Co., Houston, 1974-79, Arnan, Inc., Austin, 1979-81; chmn. bd. The Quartus Found. Inc., Boerne, Tex., 1981—. Author: The Superbeings, 1981, The Manifestation Process, 1983, The Planetary Commission, 1984, Practical Spirituality, 1985, With Wings as Eagles, 1987, The Abundance Book, 1987, Prayer, Principles & Power, 1987, A Spiritual Philosophy for the New World, 1990, Empowerment, 1992, The Angels Within Us, 1993, Angel Energy, 1995, Living a Life of Joy, 1997, The Success Book, 1998, The Wellness Book, 1998, The Meditation Book, 1998, The Love Book, 1998, The Jesus Code, 2000, The Alchemist's Handbook, 2000, Removing the Masks That Bind Us, 2001, Nothing Is Too Good to Be True, 2003. Staff sgt. USAF, 1952-56. Recipient Joseph S. Cullinan award U. Houston, 1956, Grand Prix Best Consumer Mag. Advt. award, 1970. Mem. Internat. New Thought Alliance (Humanitarian award 1992, Joseph Murphy award 1994). Achievements include organizer of first annual World Peace day on December 31, 1986. Office: The Quartus Found Inc PO Box 1768 Boerne TX 78006-6768 Office Phone: 830-249-3985. Business E-Mail: quartus@quartus.org.

PRICE, JONATHAN G., geologist; b. Danville, Pa., Feb. 1, 1950; s. A. Barney and Flora (Best) P.; m. Elisabeth McKinley, June 3, 1972; children: Alexander D., Argenta M. BA in Geology and German, Lehigh U., 1972; MA, U. Calif., Berkeley, 1975, PhD, 1977. Cert. profl. geologist. Geologist Anaconda Copper Co., Yerington, Nev., 1974-75, U.S. Steel Corp., Salt Lake City, 1977, Corpus Christi, 1978-81; rsch. assoc. Bur. Econ. Geology, U. Tex., Austin, 1981-85, rsch. sci., 1984-88, program dir., 1987-88; dir. Tex. Mining & Mineral Resources Rsch. Inst., Austin, 1984-88; dir., state geologist Nev. Bur. Mines & Geology, U. Nev., Reno, 1988-92, 95—. Staff dir. Bd. on Earth Scis. & Resources Nat. Rsch. Coun., Washington, 1993-95; asst. prof. Bucknell U., Lewisburg, 1977-78; chair We. States Seismic Policy coun., 1998-2002. Author, editor: Igneous Geology of Trans-Pecos Texas, 1986. Vol. instr. CPR and first aid ARC, 1983-95, bd. dirs. Sierra Nev. chpt., 1991-92. German Acad. Exch. Svc. fellow U. Heidelberg, 1972-73; recipient Explorer award Am. Geol. Inst., 1995. Fellow Geol. Soc. Am., Soc. Econ. Geologists (nat. pres. 2003); mem. Am. Inst. Profl. Geologists (Nev. sect. pres. 1992, nat. pres. 1997, John T. Galey Sr. Meml. pub. Svc. award 1999), Assn. Am. State Geologists (pres. 2000-01), Mineral. Soc. Am., Phi Beta Kappa. Office: Nev Bur Mines & Geology UNR Ms 178 Reno NV 89557-0088 Office Phone: 775-784-6691 15. Business E-Mail: jprice@unr.edu.

PRICE, JOSEPH HUBBARD, lawyer; b. Montgomery, Ala., Jan. 31, 1939; s. Aaron Joseph and Minnie Jule (Reynolds) P.; m. Cynthia Winant Ramsey, Sept. 14, 1963 (div. 1980); children: Victoria Reynolds, Ramsey Winant; m. Courtney McFadden, Apr. 25, 1980. AB, U. Ala., 1961; LLB, Harvard U., 1964; postgrad., London Sch. Econs., 1964-65. Bar: Ala. 1964, D.C. 1968. Law clk. to justice Hugo L. Black U.S. Supreme Ct., Washington, 1967-68; assoc. Leva, Hawes, Symington, Martin & Oppenheimer, Washington, 1968-71; v.p. Overseas Pvt. Investment Corp., Washington, 1971-73; ptnr. Leva, Hawes, et. al., Washington, 1973-83; ptnr., internat. law Gibson, Dunn & Crutcher, Washington, 1983—2005. Capt. US Army, 1966—67, Vietnam. Decorated Bronze Star; Frank Knox Meml. fellow London Sch. Econs., 1964-65. Mem. ABA, Am. Soc. Internat. Law, Supreme Ct. Hist. Soc., Phi Beta Kappa, Met. Club. Office: Gibson Dunn & Crutcher 1050 Connecticut Ave NW Ste 900 Washington DC 20036-5306

PRICE, JOSEPH MAURICE, retired military officer; b. Shelbyville, Ill., Jan. 23, 1941; s. Maurice Ray and Naomi Aileene Price; m. Carole Lynn Hill, Oct. 31, 1964; children: Jennifer Lynn Shelton, Douglas Carl, Gregory Joseph. BS, Ill. Inst. Tech., Chgo., 1964; MS in Physics, Naval Post Grad. Sch., Monterey, Calif., 1976. Commd. ensign USN, 1964, advanced through grades to capt., 1986; program mgr. satellite comm. Space & Naval Warfare Systems Command, Arlington, Va., 1988—93; dep. dir. navy space systems Office of the Chief of Naval Ops., Arlington, 1993—94; ret. USN, 1994; C4, space, info. ops analyst Commn. on Roles and Missions of the Armed Forces, Arlington, 1994—95; dir. navy hdqs. support L-3 Comm./Titan Group, Arlington, 1997—. Elder Ch. of Christ, Dale City, Va., 1994—2006. Decorated Legion of Merit USN. Mem.: Armed Forces Comm. and Electronics Assn. Home: 6189 Rossiter Ct Manassas VA 20112 Office: L-3 Communications/Titan Group 2611 Jefferson Davis Highway Arlington VA 22202 Home Phone: 703-730-2855; Office Phone: 703-601-1285.

PRICE, JOSEPH MICHAEL, lawyer; b. St. Paul, Dec. 2, 1947; s. Leon and Rose (Kaufman) P.; m. Louise Rebecca Braunstein, Dec. 19, 1971; children: Lisa, Laurie, Julie. BA, U. Minn., 1969, JD, 1972. Bar: Minn. 1972, U.S. Dist. Ct. Minn. 1974. Ptnr. Faegre & Benson, Mpls., 1972—. Mem. Minn. Bar Assn., Hennepin County Bar Assn. Home: 4407 Country Club Rd Minneapolis MN 55424-1148 Office: Faegre & Benson 2200 Wells Fargo Ctr 90 S 7th St Ste 2200 Minneapolis MN 55402-3901 Office Phone: 612-766-8617. Business E-Mail: Jprice@faegre.com.

PRICE, JOSEPH STERLING, retired air force officer; b. Rockville Centre, NY, June 2, 1954; s. Harold Lloyd and Lola Peele (Talton) P.; m. Karen Lee Peters, Oct. 14, 1978. BS in Indsl. Mgmt., Ga. Inst. Tech., Atlanta, 1976; MS in Logistics Mgmt., Air Force Inst. Tech., 1980. Quality control chemist Jesco Lubricants Co., Atlanta, 1976; commd. 2d lt. USAF, 1976, advanced through grades to lt. col., 1992, ret., 2002. Mem. Ga. Tech. Alumni Assn., Nat. Eagle Scout Assn. (life), Nat. Def. Indsl. Assn. (life), Appalachian Trail Cons. (life), SCV, The Longstreet Soc., Am. Legion, Mil. Officers Assn. Am. (life). Avocations: hiking, history. Personal E-mail: jsterlingprice@hotmail.com.

PRICE, JUDITH HOLM, educational psychologist; b. Milw., Nov. 6, 1937; d. Paul James and Dorothy Ruth (Munton) Holm; m. Thomas Munro Price, Aug. 8, 1959; children: Scott Michael, Andrea Lynn. BA, Carroll Coll., 1959; MA, U. Iowa, 1973; PhD, U. Wyo., 1980. Nat. cert. sch. psychologist. Tchr. Waukesha Pub. Sch., Wis., 1959, Madison Pub. Sch., 1959-63; preschool assessment specialist Grant Wood Area Edn. Agy. 10, Cedar Rapids, Iowa, 1976-78; Ednl. Resource Ctr. facilitator Albany County Sch. Dist. 1, Laramie, Wyo., 1980-89, dir. spl. svc., 1989—93; acad. dean Brush Ranch Sch., Tererro, N.Mex., 1993—96; hist. home renovator Yerington, Nev., 1997—. Substitute tchr. Melbourne (Australia) Sch., 1978; temporary prof. U. Wyo., Laramie, 1981, 84; mem. computer conf. com. Wyo. Dept. Edn., Casper, 1984-85, com. for devel. spl. edn. database, 1987, task force cert. standards for early childhood spl. edn. tchr., 1988; speaker Wyo. Fedn. CEC, Riverton, 1986, task force on specific learning disability criteria, 1988; conf. mem. Council for Exceptional Children Software Conf., Washington, 1986; provider state-wide inservice Specific Learning Disability Criteria, 1988. Spl. edn. rules and regulations task force Wyo. Dept. Edn., 1990—92; mem. Wyo. gov. Early Intervention Coun., 1990—93; governing bd. pres. South Lyon Health Ctr., Inc., 2003—07; chmn. South Lyon Health Ctr., Inc. Found., 2007—. Mem. Nat. Assn. Sch. Psychologists (alt. del. 1983), Wyo. Sch. Psychoednl. Assn., Council for Exceptional Children (com. specific learning disability 1987-88, speaker 1988, pres. Frontier chpt. 1989), Assn. Curriculum Devel., N.Mex. Assn. Non-Pub. Sch., Phi Kappa Phi, Phi Delta Kappa, 2003. Avocations: computers, skiing, camping, travel. Office: The Nordyke House 727 State Route 339 Yerington NV 89447-9553

PRICE, LARA, professional sports team executive; Grad., Colo. State U., Ft. Collins. Dir. team svcs. Continental Basketball Assn.; mgr. team svcs. NBA; dir. mktg. Phila. 76ers, 1996—98, v.p. mktg., 1998—2001, sr. v.p. mktg., 2001—03, sr. v.p. bus. ops., 2003—. Mem. Phila. chpt. steering com. Nat. Sports Mktg. Network. Bd. dirs. Found. Melanoma Rsch. Office: Phila 76ers Wachovia Ctr 3601 S Broad St Philadelphia PA 19148 *

PRICE, (MARY VIOLET) LEONTYNE, retired concert and opera singer, soprano; b. Laurel, Miss., Feb. 10, 1927; d. James A. and Kate (Baker) Price; m. William Warfield, Aug. 31, 1952 (div. 1973). BA, Central State Coll., Wilberforce, Ohio, 1949, DMus, 1968; student, Juilliard Sch. Music, 1949-52; pupil, Florence Page Kimball; LHD, Dartmouth Coll., 1962, Fordham U., 1969, Yale U., 1979; MusD, Howard U., 1962; Dr. Humanities, Rust Coll., 1968. Singer: (Operas) (debut) in 4 Saints in 3 Acts, 1952, (appeared) Bess in Porgy and Bess, Vienna, Berlin, Paris, London, under auspices U.S. State Dept., N.Y.C. and U.S. tour, 1952—54; recitalist, soloist (symphonies) U.S., Can., Australia, Europe, 1954—, appeared concerts in India, 1956, 1964, soloist Hollywood Bowl, 1955—59, 1966, Berlin Festival, 1960, role as Mme. Lidoine in Dialogues des Carmelites, San Francisco Opera, 1957; singer: (Operas) NBC-TV, 1955—58, 1960, 1962, 1964, San Francisco Opera Co., 1957—59, 1960—61, 1963, 1965, 1967, 1968, 1971, as Aida at La Scala, 1957;: (Operas) Vienna Staatsoper, 1958, 1959—60, 1961, Berlin Opera, 1964, Rome Opera, 1966, 1968, (recital) Brussels Internat. Fair, auspices State Dept., 1958, Verona Opera Arena, 1958—59, Yugoslavia for, State Dept., 1958; rec. artist RCA-Victor, 1958—, appeared Covent Garden, London, 1958-59, 70, Chgo. Lyric Theatre, 1959, 60, 65, Oakland (Calif.) Symphony, 1980, soloist Salzburg Festival, 1959—63, appeared Tetro alla Scala, Milano, 1960-61, 63, 67, Met. Opera, N.Y.C., 1961-62, 64, 66, 75, 76, since resident mem., until 1985, soloist Salzburg Festival, 1950, 60, debut Teatre Dell'Opera, Rome, 1967, Teatro Colon, Buenos Aires, Argentina, 1969, Hamburg Opera, 1970, recordings A Christmas Offering with Karajani, God Bless America with Charles Gerhardt, Arias from Don Giovanni, Turandot, Aida, Emani, Messa di Requiem, Trovatore, Live at Ordway, The Prima Donna Collection, A Program of Song with D. Garvey, Right as the Rain with André Previn. Co-chmn. Rust Coll. Upward Thrust Campaign; trustee Internat. House.; hon. vice-chmn. U.S. com. UNESCO; Hon. bd. dirs. Campfire Girls. Decorated Order at Ment Italy; named Musician of Year, Mus. Am. mag., 1961; recipient Merit award for role of Tosca in NBC-TV Opera, Mademoiselle mag., 1955, 20 Grammy awards for classical vocal recs. Nat. Acad. Rec. Arts and Scis., citation YWCA, 1961, Spirit of Achievement award Albert Einstein Coll. Medicine, 1962, Presdl. medal of freedom, 1964, Springarn medal NAACP, 1965, Schwann Catalog award, 1968, Nat. Medal of Arts, 1985, Essence award, 1991, others. Fellow: Am. Acad. Arts and Sci.; mem.: AFTRA, Actors Equity Assn., Am. Guild Mus. Artists, Delta Sigma Theta, Sigma Alpha Iota. Inducted into Am. Classical Music Hall of Fame, 1998. Office: Price Enterprises 1133 Broadway Ste 920 New York NY 10010-7901

PRICE, LEW PAXTON, writer, engineer; b. Takoma Park, Md., Dec. 19, 1938; s. Raymond Miller and Clarene Pearl (Morris) P.; m. Sherrie Darlene Sellers, June 25, 1960 (div. Apr. 1979); children: Terilyn Ann, Heather Rae, Crystal Alene. BS, U.S. Air Force Acad., Colorado Springs, Colo., 1960. Hon. Ho-O Ryu Bushido 6th Dan Master. Electronics engr. Pacific Telephone, Sacramento, Calif., 1965-66, engrng. coord., bldgs., 1966-85; pres., design engr. Condor Aeroplane Works, Ltd., Sacramento, 1983-85; engrng. coord. Tuttle Engrng. and Constrn. Consultants, El Dorado Hills, Calif., 1989-92; scientist, flute design cons., writer, flutemaker Fair Oaks, Garden Valley, Calif., 1977—. Cons. flute design and physics. Author: The Cosmic Stradivarius, 1974, Aquarian Anastasis, 1975, The Music of Life, 1984, Dimensions in Astrology, 1986, Native North American Flutes, 1990, Secrets of the Flute (Math, Physics & Design), 1991, Creating & Using the Native American Love Flute, 1994, Creating & Using Grandfather's Flute, 1995, The Oldest Magic (Prehistory & Influence of Music), 1995, Creating & Using Older Native American Flutes, 1995, Creating & Using Smaller Native American Flutes, 1995, Creating & Using the Native American Concert Flute, 1996, More Secrets of the Flute, 1997, Creating and Using Larger Native American Flutes, 1998, Creating and Using the Largest Native American Flutes, 1998, Creating and Using Very Small Native American Flutes, 1998, Behind Light's Illusion (7-book series), 1999, 2000, 2001, Climbing on Course, 2003, (biography) When a Man is a Man, 2003; author, programmer: (computer program) Flute Design (Native American), 1996. Co-advisor Aviation Explorers, archery/space/sci. merit badge instr./examiner, Boy Scouts Am., North Highlands, Calif., 1968-70; panelist United Crusade, Sacramento, Calif., 1971; rifle/pistol/shotgun safety instr. NRA, Fair Oaks, Calif., 1970-72. Capt. USAF, 1960-65. Mem. No. Calif. Flute Circle (co-organizer 1996), Oreg. Native Am. Flute Circle (hon.). Avocations: flying, singing, flute, hiking, archery. Home and Office: PO Box 88 Garden Valley CA 95633-0088 Personal E-mail: lewprice@softcom.net.

PRICE, MARY KATHLEEN, law librarian, educator; b. Buffalo, Feb. 28, 1942; d. Donn Dale and Mary Elizabeth (Domedion) P. BA with honors, U. Fla., 1963; MS, Fla. State U., 1967; postgrad., Ala. Law Sch., Tuscaloosa, 1967-70; JD with honors, U. Ill., Champaign, 1973. Bar: Ill. 1973, U.S. Dist. Ct. (no. dist.) Ill. 1973. Tchr. Duval and Brevard County Schs., Jacksonville and Titusville, Fla., 1960-63; asst. law libr. U. Ala. Law Sch., Tuscaloosa, 1967-70, U. Ill., Champaign, 1970-73; assoc. Ross, Hardies & O'Keefe, Chgo., 1973-75; law libr., prof. law Duke U. Law Sch., Durham, NC, 1975-80; dir. law libr., prof. law U. Minn., Mpls., 1980-90, acting asst. v.p. acad. affairs, 1985-86; law libr. Libr. of Congress, 1988—94; dir. law libr., prof. law NYU Sch. Law, 1994—2003; assoc. dean libr. & tech., Clarence J. TeSelle prof. law Levin Coll. Law, U. Fla., Gainesville, 2003—. Mem. acad. adv. bd. Westlaw, St. Paul, 1984-87; vis. prof. law Uppsala U., 1987, 89. Recipient Law Librarianship award Minn. Assn. Law Libraries, 1984, Disting. Alumni award Fla. State U., 1987. Mem. Am. Assn. Law Librs. (pres. 1983-84), Commn. Legal Edn. Exchange with PRC (chmn. libr. subcom. 1984—), Assn. Am. Law Schs. (mem. accreditation com. 1983-87, exec. bd. 1988-90), Order of Coif. Democrat. Roman Catholic. Home: 7901 Takoma Ave Silver Spring MD 20910-5227 Office: Levin Coll Law U Fla Box 117628 Gainesville FL 32611 Office Phone: 352-273-0706. Office Fax: 352-392-5093. E-mail: pricek@law.ufl.edu.

PRICE, MARY SUE SWEENEY, museum director; d. William Robert Sweeney; m. Clement A. Price, 1988. BA in English, Allegheny Coll., 1973; D.H.C. (hon.), Caldwell Coll. With textbook pub. co., NYC; supr. pub. rels. Newark Mus., 1975, dep. dir., 1990—93, dir., 1993—. Past pres. ArtTable Inc.; v.p. ArtPrice NJ Inc.; bd. dirs. St. Vincent Acad., Newark Arts Coun. Mem.: Assn. Art Mus. Dirs., Am. Assn. Mus., NJ Assn. Mus. (bd. dirs.). Office: Newark Mus 49 Washington St Newark NJ 07102 Office Phone: 973-596-6550.

PRICE, MICHAEL F., money management executive; b. 1952; div., 3 sons. Grad., U. Okla., 1975. Rsch. asst., mgr., to CEO Heine Securities, Short Hills, NJ, 1975-97; CEO Franklin Mutual Advs. Inc. (formerly Heine Securities), Short Hills, NJ, 1997; pvt. investor, 1998—. Pres., chmn. bd. dirs. Franklin Mutual Series Fund Inc. Named one of Forbes' Richest Americans, 2006. Office: Franklin Mutual Advisers Inc 51 John F Kennedy Pkwy Short Hills NJ 07078-2702

PRICE, MICHAEL HOWARD, journalist, critic, composer; b. Amarillo, Tex., Sept. 14, 1947; s. John Andrew and Thelma Adeline (Wilson) P.; m. Christina Renteria, Aug. 31, 1980. BA in Journalism, West Tex. State U., 1970. Edn. writer Amarillo Globe-News, 1968-74, fin. editor, 1974-76, city editor, 1976-77; adminstr. Amarillo Coll., 1977-80; bur. chief Ft. Worth Star-Telegram, 1980-83, features editor, 1983-85, film critic, 1985-98; dir. motion picture programming Sundance Sq. Entertainment Dist., Ft. Worth, 1998—2002; critic-at-large Ft. Worth Bus. Press, 2002—. Cons. journalism West Tex. State U., Canyon, 1977-90, Tex. Tech U., Lubbock, 1982-85; dirs. The Harvey Awards comic-book profls. awards, 1990—; syndicated columnist N.Y. Times News Svc., 1990-98; critic-in-residence Sta. KRLD Newsradio, Dallas-Ft. Worth, 1998—; columnist Fangoria mag., 2002—. Author: (CD-ROMs) A Century of Fantastic Cinema, 1995, Silver Screen Sensations, 1996; (albums) Cognitive Dissonance, 1994, The Last Temptation of Price, 1995, R. Crumb—The Musical, 1995, Swingmasters Revue, 1995, Claus & Effect, 1996, Diddy Wah Diddy, 1997, Big Hoedown Tonight!, 1999, From Hell to Texas, 1999, Arghlebargle, 2001; (books) Forgotten Horrors: The Definitive Edition, 1999, Forgotten Horrors II, 2001, Hollywood and the Piano, 2001, Spawn of Skull Island, 2002, Human Monsters in the Movies, 1994, Krime Duzzin't Pay, 1995, The Guitar in Jazz, 1996, Stitches, 1996, Frights Genuine & Fancied, 1996; (novels) The Prowler, 1989, Carnival of Souls, 1991, Holiday for Screams, 1992, Lon Chaney, Jr.: A Critical Biography, 1997; co-author: The Big Book of Biker Flicks, 2002; screen actor: Ramming Speed, 1997, Southern Fried Homicide, 1998, Beauty & the Beasts, 1998, Vincent Price: A Critical Biography, 1998, It's Christmastime at the Movies, 1998. Creative dir. Tex. Gridiron Show, Fort Worth, 1984-85, 92-93; pres. Ft. Worth Film Festival, Inc., 1997—. Grad. fellow in journalism U. Mo., 1975; inducted into Tex. Tornados Blues Hall of Fame, 1995. Mem. ASCAP, Soc. Profl. Journalists (bd. dirs. 1992-94), Soc. Film Critics. *People who believe that writing is a glamour gig often ask, "How do you become a writer?" as if in search of some magical formula. The only answer is: "WRITE." For whatever purpose and however large or small a readership: WRITE.*

PRICE, MICHAEL J., investment banker; BS in Econs., U. Pa.; MBA, Harvard U. Mng. dir., telecom, tech. group Lazard, NYC, 1994—2005; sr. mng. dir., corp. adv. bus. Evercore Ptnrs., NYC, 2005—. Bd. overseers, Coll. Arts & Sci. Univ. Pa.; bd. dir. Rockefeller Univ. Coun. Recipient Rainmaker award, Dealmaker mag., 2006. Office: Evercore Ptnrs 43rd Fl 55 E 52nd St New York NY 10055 Office Phone: 212-857-3100. Office Fax: 212-857-3101. *

PRICE, MICHAEL WITWER, art gallery owner, lawyer; b. Bronxville, NY, Dec. 30, 1941; s. Will James and Jeanette Witwer Price; children: Freyzewd Negussie, Seth, Rachel, Lucero. BA, Yale U., 1964; MS in City Planning, MIT, 1970; JD, Boston U., 1983. Bar: Mass. 1983. Dir. legal and social svc. Am. Friends Svc. Com., East Jerusalem, 1972—75; asst. dir. admissions Yale U., New Haven, 1976—78; pvt. practice law Boston, 1983—90; counsel Mass. Dept. Pub. Health Hosps., Boston, 1990—94; arts coord. Internat. Inst., Boston, 1996—98; owner MPG Contemporary, Boston, 1998—. Co-author: Boston's Immigrants 1840-1925, 2000. Bd. dirs. West End Boys and Girls Club, Boston, 2004—. Mem.: St. Botulph Club. Avocations: sailing, reading. Home: 7 Westford St Boston MA 02134 Office: MPG Contemporary 450 Harrison Ave Boston MA 02118

PRICE, NELSON (JOHN NELSON PRICE), author, journalist; b. Augusta, Ga., May 7, 1957; s. John Paul and Joy Gertrude (Scheck) P. BA in Journalism and Psychology, Ind. U., 1978. City hall reporter Lawrence Jour.-World, Kans., 1978-79; fed. cts. reporter, social issues writer Ft. Wayne Jour.-Gazette, Ind., 1979-80; edn. writer Indpls. News, 1981-85; columnist, feature writer Indpls. Star-News, 1985—2002. Bd. dirs. The Sagamore, Indpls.; adj. prof. journalism Ind. U.-Purdue U., Indpls., 2003—. Author: Indiana Legends: Famous Hoosiers from Johnny Appleseed to David Letterman, hardcover 1997, softcover 2005, Indianapolis: Leading the Way, 2000, Legendary Hoosiers: Famous Folks from the State of Indiana, 2001, Indianapolis Then and Now, 2004; contbr. articles to profl. jours., chapters to books. Recipient Sagamore of the Wabash award Gov. Ind., 1995, 2002, Martin Luther King Jr. award Indpls. Edn. Assn., 1986, Best Sports Writing award Hoosier State Press Assn., 1994, Best Column award, 1994, Best Feature Story award, 1994, Best Personality Profile award, 1994. Mem. Soc. Profl. Journalists (awards), Mental Health Assn. Marion County (awards).

PRICE, PAUL BUFORD, physicist, researcher; b. Memphis, Nov. 8, 1932; s. Paul Buford and Eva (Dupuy) P.; m. JoAnn Margaret Baum, June 28, 1958; children— Paul Buford III, Heather Alynn, Pamela Margaret, Alison Gaynor. BS summa cum laude, Davidson Coll., NC, 1954, DSc (hon.), 1973; MS in Physics, U. Va., Charlottesville, 1956, PhD in Physics, 1958. Fulbright scholar U. Bristol, England, 1958-59, Tata Inst. Fundamental Rsch., Bombay, 1965—66; NSF postdoctoral fellow Cambridge U., England, 1959-60; physicist R&D Ctr., GE, Schenectady, 1960—69; prof. physics U. Calif., Berkeley, 1969—, Miller rsch. prof., 1972—73, chmn. dept. physics, 1987—91, McAdams prof. physics, 1990—92, dean phys. scis., 1992—2001, dir. Space Scis. Lab., 1979—85, prof. grad. sch. Dept. Physics, 2002—. Vis. adv. com. Bartol Rsch. Inst., Newark, Del., 1991-94; adv. bd. Indian Inst. Astrophysics, Bangalore, 1993-95; cons. to lunar sample analysis planning team NASA; space sci. bd. NAS, mem. polar rsch. bd., 1999-01; adj. prof. physics Rensselaer Poly. Inst., 1967-68; vis. prof. Tata Inst. Fundamental Rsch., Bombay, 1965-66, U. Rome, 1983, 92; sci. assoc. Ctr. d'Etude Rsch. Nuclear, 1984; rschr. in high-energy neutrino astrophysics, climatology, microbial life in extreme environs.; mem. U.S. Ice Core Working Group, 2002-04; sci. adv. bd. U. Vienna, Austria; adv. bd. libr. U. Calif., Berkeley, 2006—; bd. dirs. Terradex Corp., Walnut Creek, Calif.; univ. review leader in field. Author: (with others) Nuclear Tracks in Solids; Contbr. (with others) articles to profl. jours. Regional dir. Calif. Alliance Minority Participation, Berkeley, 1993-04; bd. dirs. Pk. Hills Homes Assn., Berkeley, 2002-05. Recipient Disting. Svc. award Am. Nuclear Soc., 1964, Indsl. Rsch. awards, 1964, 65, 71, E.O. Lawrence Meml. award AEC, 1971, medal for exceptional sci. achievement NASA, 1973; Sci. Symposium in honor of 65th birthday, Aug 23-24, 1997, Berkeley Leadership and Rsch. Distinction citation, 2002; John Simon Guggenheim fellow, 1976-77; named region of Antarctica after him, U.S. Bd. Geographic Names. Fellow: Am. Geophys. Union, Am. Phys. Soc., Indian Inst. Astrophysics (hon.); mem.: NAS (chmn. geophysics sect. 1981—84, sec. class phys.-math. scis. 1985—88, chmn. phys. and math. sci. class 1988—91), Bohemian Club. Achievements include discovery of nuclear tracks in solids; invention of nuclepore filters for microbiology; fission track geochronology; optical dust logger; biospectral logger; nine patents; invention of instrument for radon detection. Avocation: travel. Office: U Calif Dept Physics 335 Old LeConte Berkeley CA 94720 Home Phone: 510-548-5206; Office Phone: 510-642-4982. Business E-Mail: bprice@berkeley.edu.

PRICE, PAUL L., lawyer; b. Chgo., Apr. 21, 1945; s. Walter S. and Lillian (Czerepkowski) L.; m. Dianne L. Olech, June 3, 1967; children: Kristen, Kathryn. BBA, Loyola U., Chgo., 1967; JD with honors, Chgo. Kent IIT, 1971. Bar: Ill. 1971, U.S. Dist. Ct. (no. dist.) Ill., U.S. Ct. Appeals (7th cir.). Tax acct. Arthur Anderson & Co., Chgo., 1970—71; assoc. Doyle & Tarpey, Chgo., 1971—75, Gordon & Assocs., Chgo., 1975—76; from assoc. to ptnr. Pretzel & Stouffer, Chartered, Chgo., 1976—96; ptnr. Price, Tunney, Reiter, Chgo., 1996—2007, Hepler Broom LLC, 2007—. With USMC, 1969—70. Fellow: Am. Coll. Trial Lawyers; mem.: ABA, Ill. Inst. Tech.-Chgo. Kent Coll. Law Alumni Assn. (pres. 1989—90), Assn. Def. Trial Attys., Lawyers for Civil Justice (bd. dirs. 1999—2001), Def. Rsch. Inst. (bd. dirs. 1999—2001), Fedn. Def. and Corp. Counsel (pres. 1999—2000), Ill. Assn. Def. Trial Counsel (pres. 1990—91), Soc. Trial Lawyers, Ill. Bar Assn. Roman Catholic. Office: Hepler Bloom LLC 150 N Wacker Dr Ste 3100 Chicago IL 60606 Home Phone: 847-253-3896; Office Phone: 312-230-9100. Business E-Mail: plprice@heplerbroom.com.

PRICE, PETER WILFRID, ecology educator, researcher; b. London, Apr. 17, 1938; arrived in U.S., 1966; BSc with honors, U. Wales, Bangor, 1958-62; MSc, U. New Brunswick, Fredericton, 1964; PhD, Cornell U., 1970. Asst. prof. U. Ill., Urbana, 1971-75, assoc. prof., 1975-79; research ecologist Mus. No. Ariz., Flagstaff, 1979-80; assoc. prof. No. Ariz. U., 1980-85, prof. ecology, 1985-94, Regents' prof., 1994—2002, Regents' prof. emeritus, 2002—. Author: Evolutionary Biology of Parasites, 1980, Biological Evolution, 1996, Insect Ecology, 3d edit., 1997, Macroevolutionary Theory on Macroecological Patterns, 2003; editor: Evolutionary Strategies of Parasitic Insects, 1975, A New Ecology, 1984, Plant-Animal Interactions, 1991, Effects of Resource Distribution on Plant-Animal Interactions, 1992, The Ecology and Evolution of Gall-Forming Insects, 1994, Population Dynamics, 1995, Population Dynamics: New Approaches and Synthesis, 1995. Guggenheim fellow, 1977—78, Fulbright Sr. scholar, 1993—94. Fellow: NSF (panel mem. 1978—81, 1991—93), Entomol. Soc. Am. (Founders award 1993), Brit. Ecol. Soc., Ecol. Soc. Am. (bd. editors 1973—76), Royal Entomol. Soc. (hon.). Office: No Ariz U PO Box 5640 Flagstaff AZ 86011-5640

PRICE, REYNOLDS, writer, educator; b. Macon, NC, Feb. 1, 1933; s. William Solomon and Elizabeth (Rodwell) P. AB summa cum laude (Angier Duke scholar), Duke, 1955; BLitt (Rhodes scholar), Merton Coll., Oxford U., Eng., 1958; LittD, St. Andrews Presbyn. Coll., 1978, Wake Forest U., 1979, Washington and Lee U., 1991, Davidson Coll., 1992; LittD, Elon Coll., U. N.C., 2003. Mem. faculty English Duke U., 1958—; asst. prof., 1961-68; assoc. prof., 1968-72; prof., 1972-77; James B. Duke prof., 1977—; acting chmn., 1983; writer in residence U. N.C., Chapel Hill, 1965, U. Kans., 1967, 69, 80, U.N.C., Greensboro, 1971; Glasgow prof. Washington and Lee U., 1971; faculty Salzburg Seminar, 1977. Author: A Long and Happy Life, 1962, The Names and Faces of Heroes, 1963, A Generous Man, 1966, Love and Work, 1968, Permanent Errors, 1970, Things Themselves, 1972, The Surface of Earth, 1975, Early Dark, 1977, A Palpable God, 1978, The Source of Light, 1981, Vital Provisions, 1982, Private Contentment, 1984, Kate Vaiden, 1986, The Laws of Ice, 1986, A Common Room, 1987, Good Hearts, 1988, Clear Pictures, 1989, The Tongues of Angels, 1990, The Use of Fire, 1990, New Music, 1990, The Foreseeable Future, 1991, Conversations with Reynolds Price, 1991, Blue Calhoun, 1992, Full Moon, 1993, The Collected Stories, 1993, A Whole New Life, 1994, The Promise of Rest, 1995, Three Gospels, 1996, The Collected Poems, 1997, Roxanna Slade, 1998, Learning a Trade, 1998, Letter to a Man in the Fire, 1999, A Perfect Friend, 2000, Feasting the Heart, 2000, Noble Norfleet, 2002, The God Priest's Son, 2005. A Serious Way of Wondering, 2003, Recipient William Faulkner Found. award notable 1st novel, 1962, Sir Walter Raleigh award, 1962, 76, 81, 84, 86, award Nat. Assn. Ind. Schs., 1964, Roanoke-Chowan Poetry award, 1982; Guggenheim fellow, 1964-65; fellow Nat. Endowment for Arts, 1967-68, lit. adv. panel, 1973-76, chmn., 1976; recipient Nat. Inst. Arts and Letters award, 1971, Bellamann Found. award, 1972, Lillian Smith award, 1976, N.C. award, 1977, Nat. Book Critics Circle award, 1986, Elmer H. Bobst award, 1988, R. Hunt Parker award N.C. Lit. and Hist. Soc., 1991, Northcarolinana award, 1999, Caldwell award NC Humanities Coun., 2002. Mem. Am. Acad. Arts and Scis., Am. Acad. Arts and Letters, Phi Beta Kappa, Phi Delta Theta. Home: PO Box 99014 Durham NC 27708-9014 Office: care Harriet Wasserman Lit Agy Inc 137 E 36th St New York NY 10016-3528

PRICE, RICHARD EDWARD, lawyer; b. Stanford, Calif., Apr. 30, 1969; s. Richard Maxwell and Mary Frances Price; m. Brook Renee Gauntz, Sept. 14, 2002. BA, U. Mass., 1991; JD, George Washington U., 1994; LLM, Cambridge U., England, 1995. Bar: N.Y. 1995, Mass. 1995, D.C. 1996, U.S. Ct. Appeals (D.C. cir.) 1997. Atty. Koteen & Naftalin, L.L.P., Washington, 1996—99, Vinson & Elkins L.L.P., 1999—2005; sr. counsel One Comm. Corp., Rochester, NY, 2005—. Mem.: Federalist Soc., Fed. Comm. Bar Assn., Genesee Valley Club, Univ. Club (Washington), Golden Key, Pi Sigma Alpha. Office: One Comm Corp 100 Chestnut St Rochester NY 14604

PRICE, RICHARD GALEN, sound recording engineer, music producer, conductor; b. Ann Arbor, Mich., Jan. 31, 1956; s. Galen B. and Nina Ruth (Hudson) Price; m. Margaret Addison Bowles, July 6, 1985; 1 child, Hannah Leigh. MusB in Horn Performance, U. Mich., Ann Arbor, 1977; postgrad., The Juilliard Sch., NYC, 1977—79, Pierre Monteux Domaine Sch., Hancock, Maine, 1987. Hornist, founding mem. Borealis Wind Quintet, NYC, 1976—91; freelance musician various orgns., NYC, 1977—91; interim chair dir. and baritone soloist 2d Congl. Ch., Greenwich, Conn., 1988—95; pres., sr. prodr. Candlewood Digital LLC, New Fairfield, Conn., 2006—; music dir., conductor Danbury Concert Chorus, Conn., 2002—. Arranger: brass quintet music Carols for Brass, 1976—80. Bd. mem. Pro Arte Singers, New Canaan, Conn., 1995—97, Conn. Folklife Project, Danbury, 2005—. Nominee many Grammy nominations as prodr., engr., editor. Avocations: woodworking, boating, fishing. Home: 29 Lake Dr S New Fairfield CT 06812 Office: Candlewood Digital LLC 29 Lake Dr S New Fairfield CT 06812 Business E-Mail: richard@candlewooddigital.com.

PRICE, ROBERT, media and communications executive, investment banker, lawyer; b. NYC, Aug. 27, 1932; s. Solomon and Frances (Berger) P.; m. Margery Beth Wiener, Dec. 18, 1955 (div.); children: Eileen Marcia, Steven. AB, NYU, 1953; LLD, Columbia U., 1958. Bar: NY 1958, U.S. Dist. Ct. 1958, U.S. Ct. Appeals 1958, U.S. Supreme Ct. 1958, ICC: 1958, FCC: 1958, IRS: 1958. With R.H. Macy & Co., Inc., 1955-58; practiced in NYC, 1958—; law clk. to judge U.S. Dist. Ct. (so. dist.) N.Y., 1958-59; asst. U.S. atty. So. Dist. N.Y., 1959-60; ptnr. Kupferman & Price, 1960-65; dep. mayor NYC, 1965-66; exec. v.p., dir. Dreyfus Corp., NYC, 1966-69; v.p., investment officer Dreyfus Fund, until 1969; gen. ptnr. Lazard, Freres & Co., 1972-82; pres. N.Y. Law Jour., Nat. Law Jour.; pres., treas., dir. Price Comm. Corp., 1979—; chmn., pres., dir. PriCellular Corp., 1988-95; pres., dir. TLM Corp., 1989—2000. Mem. adv. com. Bankers Trust Co. N.Y.; dir. Holly Sugar Corp., Lane Bryant, Inc., Graphic Scanning Corp.; chmn. N.Y.C. Port Authority Negotiating Com. for World Trade Ctr., 1965-66; spl. counsel N.Y. State Joint Legis. Com. on Ct. Reorgn.; asst. counsel N.Y. State Joint Legis. Com. on N.Y. Banking Laws; mem. The N.Y. State Mcpl. Assistance Corp., 1996-2000; commr. N.Y. State Commn. of Investigations, N.Y.C., 2000—. Contbr. articles to profl. publs. Trustee CUNY, 1996-98; chmn. govt. and civil svc. divsn. United Jewish Appeal Greater NY, 1966; co-chmn. met. NY blood drive ARC, 1966; campaign mgr. John V. Lindsay, Campaigns for Congressman, NYC, 1958, 60, 62, 64, for Nelson A. Rockefeller Oreg. Rep. presdl. primary campaign, 1964, Lindsay campaign for mayor, NYC, 1965; del. NY Rep. State Conv., 1962, 66; del. Rep. Nat. Conv., 1988, 92, 96; lectr. Rep. Nat. Com., 1966; bd. dirs. Am. Friends Hebrew U.; past trustee Columbia U. Sch. Pharm. Scis. With US Army, 1953-55. Recipient Yeshiva U. Heritage award, Pub. Svc. award, Queens Catholic War Vets. Mem. ABA, FCC Bar Assn., Assn. Bar City NY, NY State Dist. Attys. Assn., Coun. Fgn. Rels., Columbia Law Sch. Alumni Assn. (dir.), Scribes, Tau Kappa Alpha. Home: 25 E 86th St New York NY 10028-0553 Office: Price Communications Corp 45 Rockefeller Plz Ste 3200 New York NY 10111-0100 Office Phone: 212-757-5600.

PRICE, ROBERT DEMILLE, lawyer; b. NYC, Oct. 11, 1915; s. Willard DeMille Price and Eugenia Reeve; m. Newell Potter, Aug. 15, 1940 (div. May 1946); 1 child, Jonathan; m. Ruth Bentley, July 5, 1946; children: Katharine, Susannah, Rebecca. AB in Econs. with honors, Cornell U., 1936; JD, Harvard U., 1940; MBA, Clark U., 1973. Bar: Mass. 1940, U.S. Dist. Ct. Mass. 1941, U.S. Ct. Appeals (1st cir.) 1976, U.S. Tax Ct. 1977, U.S. Supreme Ct. 1978. Assoc. Ropes & Gray, Boston, 1940-43, 1946-50; ptnr. Vaughan, Esty, Crotty & Mason, Worcester, Mass., 1950-53, Sibley, Blair & Mountain, Worcester, 1953-70, Corbin, Sarapas, Madaus & Arakelian, Worcester, 1970-73, Price & Madaus, Worcester, 1973-87; pres. Robert D. Price, PC, Holden, Mass., 1987—. Dir. Appian Way Pizza, Ltd., Worcester, 1951-61, Food Specialties, Inc., Worcester, 1951-61, James Monroe Wire and Cable Co., S. Lancaster, Mass., 1973—; mem. Fin. Com., Holden, 1989-95, conservation com., 1999-2003. Moderator (TV series) Am. Bar Assn. Jr. Bar Assn., 1947—50. Bd. dirs. Friends Gale Free Librs., Inc., Holden, 1988—; mem. adv. bd. Met. Dist. Commn., 1990—96; pres. Humanist Chaplaincy at Harvard, 1995—; bd. dirs., sec. Humanist Assn. Mass., 1979—, Am. Humanist Assn., 1991—94; trustee AHA Humanist Found., 1999—2003. Lt. USNR, 1943—50. Mem.: Worcester County Bar Assn., Mass. Bar Assn., Boston Athenaeum (propr. 1949—), Worcester Club (dir. 1953—56). Avocations: museum and art shows, photography, alpine climbing, sailing. Office: 11 Malden St Holden MA 01520-1826 Office Phone: 508-829-2717. Personal E-mail: rdp1915@yahoo.com.

PRICE, ROBERT EBEN, judge; b. Waco, Tex., Jan. 13, 1931; s. Robert Eben and Mary Hamilton (Barnett) P.; m. Ann Hodges, June 4, 1954; children— Eben, Mary, Ann, Emily. BA, So. Methodist U., 1952, JD, 1954, LL.M., 1972; postgrad., Air War Coll., 1976. Bar: Tex. 1954, U.S. Supreme Ct., U.S. Ct. Mil. Appeals, U.S. Ct. Claims, U.S. Dist. Ct. (no. dist.) Tex. 1954. Mem. firm Taylor, Mizell, Price, Corrigan & Smith, Dallas, 1956-86; judge Dallas County Probate Ct. No. 2, 1986—. Lectr. continuing legal edn. program U. Houston Law Found., 1993—; lectr. law So. Meth. U. Law Sch., 1973-74, faculty paralegal cert. program Sch. Continuing Edn., 1987-89; lectr. practice skills program State Bar Tex., 1974-78. Editor-in-chief: Southwestern Law Jour., 1953-54. Trustee and sec. St. Michael and All Angels Found., 1984-88; bd. dirs. Downtown Ministry, Diocese of Dallas Episcopal, 1986-88; chmn. legis. and legal awareness subcom., vice chmn. Tex. Gov.'s Com. on Employment of Handicapped, 1978-82. Served as legal officer USAF, 1954-56; col. JAGC Res. ret. Fellow: Tex. Bar Found., Am. Coll. Trust and Estate Counsel; mem.: ABA (nat. conf. spl. ct. judges com. on probate and surrogates cts. 1992—), Tex. Coll. Probate Judges (mem. faculty), State Bar Tex. (lectr. profl. devel. program 1988—), Dallas Bar Assn., Coll. State Bar Tex., Nat. Coll. Probate Judges, Phi Delta Theta, Phi Eta Sigma, Phi Alpha Delta. Episcopalian. Home: 4300 Arcady Ave Dallas TX 75205-3704 Office: Probate Ct 2 ste 211 509 Main St Dallas TX 75202-3508 Home Phone: 214-528-9518; Office Phone: 214-653-7138.

PRICE, ROBERT F., lawyer; BS in Acctg., Loyola Coll., 1969; JD, U. NC, 1974. Bar: Md. 1974. Asst. gen. counsel USF&G; mng. dir., gen. counsel Alex Brown & Sons, Inc.; sr. v.p., gen. counsel Legg Mason, Inc., Boston, 1998—. Mem. exec. com. compliance and legal divsn. Securities Industry Assn., mem. fed. regulation com.; mem. legal adv. bd. NASD; bd. dirs. St. Ignatious Loyola Acad. Office: Legg Mason Cds Inv Serv PO Box 55214 Boston MA 02205-5214 Office Phone: 410-539-0000. E-mail: rfprice@leggmason.com. *

PRICE, ROBERT IRA, coast guard officer; b. NYC, Sept. 22, 1921; s. Alfred and Mary Edna (Schweitzer) P.; m. Virginia Louise Miller, June 20, 1946; children: Andrea Jean, Keven Virginia. BBA, CCNY, 1942; BS, U.S. Coast Guard Acad., 1945; postgrad., M.I.T., 1950-53. Registered profl. engr., D.C. Commd. ensign U.S. Coast Guard, 1945, advanced through grades to vice adm., 1978; asst. chief Mcht. Marine Tech. Div., Washington, 1965-67; chief planning staff Office Mcht. Marine Safety, 1967-71; capt. Port of Phila., 1971-73; chief Office Marine Environ. Washington, 1974-76; comdr. 11th Coast Guard Dist. Long Beach, Calif., 1976-78; comdr. Atlantic Area and 3d Coast Guard Dist. NYC, 1978-81; ret., 1981; sr. v.p. J.J. Henry Co. (marine engrs.), NYC, 1981-86; maritime cons., 1986—. Prin. U.S. negotiator to tech. programs Intergovtl. Maritime Consultative Orgn., UN, 1962-71 Contbg. author: Ship Design and Construction, 1980; Contbr. articles to profl. jours. Decorated D.S.M. with gold star, Legion of Merit with gold star, Meritorious Service medal with gold star, Coast Guard Commendation medal. Fellow Royal Instn. Naval Architects, Soc. Naval Architects (Land medalist 1982); mem. Sigma Xi. Clubs: Propeller, Army Navy, N.Y. Yacht. Office Phone: 321-751-4666.

PRICE, ROBERT J., insurance company executive; BS, Pa. State U. CPA. Former audit ptnr. Price Waterhouse; various positions Aetna Inc., 1989—2000, sr. v.p., CFO, 1998—2000; pres., CEO CitiInsurance, 2000—01; sr. v.p., contr. The Hartford Fin. Svcs. Group, Inc., 2002—07. Bd. mem. Greater Hartford Arts Coun.; Bushnell Park Carousel Soc. Mem.: Conn. Soc. of Cert. Pub. Accountants, Am. Inst. Office: Hartford Fin Svcs Group Hartford Plaza 690 Asylum Ave Hartford CT 06115 *

PRICE, ROBERT STANLEY, lawyer; b. Phila., Jan. 21, 1937; s. Benjamin and Estelle B. (Muchnick) P.; m. Emilie W. Kirschbaum, June 27, 1965 (dec. Mar. 1998); children: Louise P. Kelly, Marianna R. BA, Kenyon Coll., 1958; LLB, Yale U., 1961. Bar: Pa. 1963, U.S. Dist. Ct. (ea. dist.) Pa. 1963, U.S. Ct. Appeals (3d cir.) 1963, N.Y. 1993. Assoc. Dechert, Price & Rhoads, Phila., 1961-63; asst tax atty. Smith, Kline & French, Phila., 1963-67; tax atty. Pa. Ctrl. Transp. Co., Phila., 1967-70; tax counsel IU Internat., Phila., 1970-72; ptnr. Townsend, Elliott & Munson, Phila., 1972-76, Pepper, Hamilton & Scheetz, Phila., 1977-86, Saul, Ewing, Remick & Saul, Phila., 1986-93; spl. cons. Saul, Ewing, Remick & Saul (now Saul Ewing LLP), Phila., 1994—2001. Ind. tax cons. Fischbein-Badillo-Wagner-Harding, NYC, 1998—2001, Mintz, Levin, Cohn, Ferris, Glovsky and Popeo, P.C., NYC, 2001—. Author: ABCs of Industrial Development Bonds, 1981, 5th edit., 1990; contbr. articles to profl. jours. Pres. Samuel Eells Lit. and Ednl. Found., 1980—2007. With US Army, 1961—62. Mem. ABA (tax exempt fin. com.), Pa. Bar, Phila. Bar Assn., N.Y. Bar, Racquet Club Phila. (v.p. 1987-88), Alpha Delta Phi (pres. 1975-78). Office: 3800 Centre Sq W Philadelphia PA 19102-2186 E-mail: rpricedj@verizon.net.

PRICE, ROBERT WILLIAM, school superintendent, consultant; b. Ogden, Utah, May 13, 1950; s. William Robert and Eileen Louise (Rabe) P.; m. Sally Sandman, Sept. 20, 1975; children: Geoffrey Thomas, Caitlin Elizabeth. BS in Child Devel., Calif. State U., Hayward, 1973, MS in Sch. Adminstrn., 1986; EdD, U. Pacific, 1998. Cert. elem. tchr., Calif. Tchr. Turlock (Calif.) Sch. Dist., 1974-81; asst. prin. Monte Vista Mid. Sch., Tracy, Calif., 1981-82, prin., 1982-87; asst. supt. instrn. Tracy Pub. Schs., 1987-90, 91-93, interim supt., 1990-91; supt. Empire Union Sch. Dist., Modesto, Calif., 1993—. Cons. Campfire, Tracy, 1983; founding mem. Tracy Exch. Club, 1985; co-founder Project Bus. & Edn. Together, Tracy, 1985; bd. dirs. Boys and Girls Club of Tracy, 1987-93. Recipient Adminstrv. Leadership award Calif. Media & Libr. Educators Assn., 1994. Mem. Assn. Calif. Sch. Adminstrs. (planning com. supts. symposium 1995—, v.p. programs Region 7 1994—), Calif. League Mid. Schs. (adv. panel Region 6 1993—, chair legis. action 1994-95, Region 6 Educator of Yr. 1991). Democrat. Office: Empire Union Sch Dist 116 N Mcclure Rd Modesto CA 95357-1329 E-mail: bprice@empire.k12.ca.us.

PRICE, STEVEN, venture capitalist, communications executive, lawyer; b. NYC, Feb. 14, 1962; s. Robert and Margery Price; m. Tina Gitlin, Mar. 16, 1991. BS magna cum laude, Brown U., 1984; JD, Columbia U. Sch. Law, 1989. Spl. asst. to US Amb. to the START Talks in Geneva US Dept. State, 1989—90; assoc. Davis Polk & Wardell, 1991; with mergers and acquisitions group Goldman, Sachs & Co.; COO PriCellular Corp., 1994—97, bd. dirs., 1996, pres., CEO, 1997—2001; deputy asst. sec. def. spectrum and command, control and communications policy US Dept. Def., 2001—03; pres., CEO LiveWire Capital, 2003—04; gen. partner Spectrum Equity Investors, 2004—. Dir. Met. Coun. Poverty, 1999—, UJA Fedn. NY, 2000—, US Nat. Archives Bd., 2003—; advisory bd. for computing and IT Brown U., 2003—; cons. Office Sec. Def. and Def. Sci. Bd., 2003—. Co-founder Brown U. Ctr. for Combat Casualty Recovery. Mem.: ABA, Bar Assn. Wash., DC, Assn. Bar NY, Phi Beta Kappa. Office: Spectrum Equity Investors One International Place Boston MA 02110 Office Phone: 617-464-4600. Office Fax: 617-464-4601. Business E-Mail: steven@spectrumequity.com.

PRICE, T. MICHAEL, bank executive; m. Heather Price; children: Olivia, Rebecca, Sydney, Natalie, Meredith. B, U. Utah, Salt Lake City, 1987; MBA, Cleve. State U., 1997. Various positions including br. mgr., comml. lender and regional br. exec. Nat. City Corp., 1987, head small bus. banking divsn., CEO Cin. and No. Ky. Region Nat. City Bank, sr. v.p. Bd. dirs. Greater Cin. Boy Scouts, Dan Beard Coun., Cin. Freestore Foodbank, Holocaust and Humanity Ctr., Cin. Opera, U. Cin. Econs. Devel. Ctr., Cin. Bus. Com. Office: Nat City Corp Nat City Ctr 1900 E Ninth St Cleveland OH 44114-3484 Office Phone: 216-222-2000. *

PRICE, THEODORA HADZISTELIOU, individual, child and family therapist; b. Athens, Greece, Oct. 1, 1938; arrived in U.S., 1967; d. Ioannis and Evangelia (Emmanuel) Hadzisteliou; m. David C. Long Price, Dec. 26, 1966 (div. 1989); children: Morgan N., Alkes D. L. Diploma in piano tchg., Nat. Conservatory, Athens, 1958; BA in History/Archaeology, U. Athens, 1961; DPhil, U. Oxford, Eng., 1966; MA in Clin. Social Work, U. Chgo., 1988. LCSW, bd. cert. diplomate in clin. social work. Mus. asst., resident tutor U. Sydney, Australia, 1966-67; instr. anthropology Adelphi U., NYC, 1967-68; archaeologist Hebrew Union Coll., Gezer, Israel, 1968; asst. prof. classical archaeology/art U. Chgo., 1968-70; jr. rsch. fellow Harvard Ctr. Hellenic Studies, Washington, 1970-71; clin. social worker Harbor Light Ctr., Salvation Army, Chgo., 1988-89; therapist Inst. Motivational Devel., Lombard, Ill., 1989-90; caseworker Jewish Family & Cmty. Svc., Chgo., 1989-90; staff therapist Family Svc. Ctrs. of South Cook County, Chicago Heights, 1990-91; pvt. practice child, adolescent, family therapy Bolingbrook, Ill., 1991—; dir. counseling svcs., clin. supr., psychotherapist Family Link, Inc., Chgo., 1993; staff therapist Cen. Bapt. Family Svcs., Gracell Rehab., Chgo., 1991, 91-92; casework supr., counselor Epilepsy Found. Greater Chgo., Chgo., 1992-93; therapist children, adolescents and families dept. foster care Cath. Charities, Chgo., 1993-94; individual and family therapist South Ctrl. Cmty. Svcs. Individual-Family Counseling Svcs., Chgo., 1994-97. Bd. dirs., counselor Naperville Sch. Gifted and Talented, 1982—84; lectr. in field. Author: (monograph) Kourotrophos, Cults and Representations of the Greek Nursing Deities, 1978; contbr. articles to profl. jours. Eleutherios Venizelos scholar, 1962—65, Meyerstein Traveling grantee, Oxford, Eng., 1963, 1964. Mem.: NASW, Am. Bd. Clin. Soc. Workers, Ill. Clin. Social Workers, Nat. Acad. Clin. Social Workers. Avocations: piano, Byzantine chanting, writing. Home and Office: 10 Pebble Ct Bolingbrook IL 60440-1557 Office Phone: 630-378-1187. *Nobody stands alone, for each of us partakes and contributes to universal energy and creation. Every thought or action has progressively timeless impact. Therefore, working in helping people is influencing the flow of creation.*

PRICE, THOMAS E., congressman; b. Lansing, Mich., Oct. 8, 1954; m. Elizabeth; 1 child, Robert. Bachelor's, MD, U. Mich. Intern in surgery Emory U. Affiliated Hosps., resident in orthop. surgery; founder Compass Orthop. (formerly North Fulton Orthop. Clinic); mem. Ga. Senate, Atlanta, 1996—2004, majority leader, 2002—03; mem. US Congress from 6th Ga. dist., 2005—; mem. Edn. and Workforce com., Fin. Svcs. com. Rep. health care task force Am. Legis. Enterprise Coun.; bd. dirs. Northside Bank. Mem. bd. dirs. North Metro YMCA; active Roswell Presbyn. Ch., Ga. Ensemble Theatre, Chattahoochee Nature Ctr. Mem. Rotary (bd. dirs.). Republican. Presbyterian. Office: US Ho Reps 506 Cannon Ho Office Bldg Washington DC 20515-1006 also: Dist Office Ste 50 3750 Roswell Rd Marietta GA 30062 Office Phone: 202-225-4501. Office Fax: 202-225-4656. *

PRICE, THOMAS FREDERICK, theater educator; b. Salt Lake City, June 19, 1937; s. Thomas William P. and Caryl Susan Brown; children: Devin, Jennifer. BA in Drama, Pomona Coll., Claremont, Calif., 1960; MA in Theatre, San Francisco State U., 1962; PhD in Drama, Stanford U., Calif., 1968; student, Columbia U. Rare Book Sch., NYC, 1983. Asst. prof. English U. of the Pacific, Stockton, Calif., 1968-70; asst. prof. drama U.S. Internat. U., Sch. Performing Arts, San Diego, 1970-74; archivist, curator The Philibrick Theatre Libr., Los Altos Hills, Calif., 1975-85; vis. prof. English Tianjin Normal U., China, 1985-87; adj. prof. English Sussex County CC, Newton, NJ, 1991; adj. prof. theatre So. Oreg. State U., Ashland, 1991-92; assoc. prof. English Tamkang U., Taipei, Taiwan, 1993—2004; adj. prof. U. Laverne, Calif., 2004—06; assoc. prof. fgn. langs. Huafan U., Taipei, Taiwan, 2007—. Ednl. broadcaster KPFA-FM, LA, 1959—62, KSRO-FM, Ashland, Oreg., 1990—92; dramaturge Caligula, Old Globe Theatre, San Diego, 1973; organizer Gordon Craig retrospective Stanford U. Dept Spl. Collections, 1985; dramaturge Mother Courage & Her Children, Spoon River Anthology, Allen Theatre, Claremont Coll., 2004—05. Author: Edward Gordon Craig Revisited, 1984, Edward Gordon Craig and the Theatre of the Imagination, 1985, Dramatic Structure and Meaning, 1992, rev. edit., 1999; editor: Critical Edition of the Jealous Wife and Polly Honeycombe by George Colman the Elder, 1997; contbr. articles to profl. jours. Recipient Taiwan Nat. Sci. Found. award, 1998, Disting. Tchr. award Tamkang U., 1998, 2000; Emma May Shiel fellow Stanford U. Mem.: Calif. Scholarship Fedn. Personal E-mail: ecripto@yahoo.com.

PRICE, THOMAS MUNRO, computer consultant; b. Madison, Wis., Oct. 2, 1937; s. John Edward and Georgia Winifred (Day) P.; m. Judith Ann Holm, Aug. 8, 1959; children: Scott Michael, Andrea Lynn. BS, Carroll Coll., Waukesha, Wis., 1959; MS, U. Wis., 1961, PhD, 1964. Prof. math. U. Iowa, 1964-77, U. Wyo., Laramie, 1978-79, computer user cons., 1979-85, MIS prof., 1985-89; computer cons., 1989—; home rebuilder Pecos, N.Mex., 1994-97; historic home renovator Yerington, Nev., 1997—. Contbr. articles to profl. jours. Mem.: Yerington Rotary (pres. 2006—07). Home: Nordyke House 727 State Rt 339 Yerington NV 89447

PRICE, TIMOTHY R., accountant; b. Reigate, Eng., Jan. 26, 1943; m. Frances Baird; 4 children. BA, U. Victoria, Can., 1964. Chartered acct. Touche Ross & Co., Montreal, 1965-69; pres., COO Mico Enterprises Ltd., 1970-80; pres., CEO Hees Internat. Bancorp Inc., Toronto, 1980-88, mng. ptnr., chmn., 1988—96; chmn. The Edper Group Ltd., Toronto, 1997, Trilon Fin. Corp., Toronto, 1997—2002, Brascan Fin. Corp., Toronto, 2002—04, Funds Mgmt. Brookfield Asset Mgmt. Inc., Toronto, 2005—. Bd. dirs. Astral Media Inc., Morguard REIT, Brookfield Homes Corp., Q9 Networks Inc.; chmn. Brascan Found., 1997—. Bd. dirs. St. Michael's Hosp. Found.; bd. govs. York U., Can.; chmn. Ctr. for Addiction and Mental Health Found. Office: Brookfield Asset Mgmt Inc PO Box 771 BCE Pl 181 Bay St Ste 300 Toronto ON Canada M5J 2T3 Office Phone: 416-363-9491.

PRICE, TOM, journalist; b. Pitts., May 26, 1946; s. H. Samuel and Anna Mae (Nicholson) P.; m. Susan Crites; 1 child, Julianna Margaret. BS in Journalism, Ohio U., 1968. Writer, editor Athens (Ohio) Messenger, 1968-73; freelance writer, 1973-75; politics writer Dayton (Ohio) Jour. Herald, 1975-82; corr. Washington bur. Cox Newspapers, Washington, 1982-96; freelance writer politics, govt., tech., bus. and edn., 1996—; Washington columnist Optics and Photonics News, 2002—; contbg. writer Congl. Quar. Rschr., 2004—. Author: Frommer's Washington, D.C. for Dummies, 2003, 4th edit., 2007, The Irreverent Guide to Washington, DC, 2005, 6th edit., 2007; co-author: (with Susan Crites Price) The Working Parents Help Book, 1994 (Parent's Choice award, Scholastic Book Club selection), rev. edit., 1996, (with Tony Hall) Changing the Face of Hunger, 2006, paperback edit., 2007; co-author Working Solutions Internet Column; nat. newspaper columnist Working Parents Lifeline, 1996-98. Mem.: Washington Ind. Writers, Am. Soc. Journalists and Authors. Presbyterian. Avocations: photography, hiking, travel, reading.

PRICE, TREVOR ROBERT PRYCE, psychiatrist, educator; b. Concord, NH, Nov. 29, 1943; BA, Yale U., 1965; MD, Columbia U., 1969. Diplomate Am. Bd. Psychiatry and Neurology (sr. examiner 1985—), with Geriatric Psychiatry, Am. Bd. Internal Medicine, Nat. Bd. Med. Examiners. Intern in medicine Med. Ctr. U. Calif., San Francisco, 1969-70; resident in internal medicine Med. Ctr. of U. Calif., San Francisco, 1972-74; resident in psychiatry Dartmouth Med. Sch., Hanover, N.H., 1974-77, asst. prof., assoc. prof. psychiatry and medicine, 1977-85; assoc. prof., prof. psychiatry U. Pa. Sch. Medicine, Phila., 1985—88; dir. psychiat. in-patient svcs. Hosp. of U. Pa., 1985-88; prof. psychiatry Med. Coll. Pa., Pitts., 1989-90, prof. psychiatry and medicine, 1991-95, 1993—2002; chmn. dept. psychiatry Med. Coll. Pa. and Hahnemann U., Pitts., 1989-95, sr. assoc. dean, 1993-95; pres., CEO Allegheny Neuropsychiat. Inst., Pitts., 1994—98, exec. dir., 1994—; chmn. dept. psychiatry Med. Coll. Pa. Hahnemann Sch. Medicine, Phila., 1995—2002; prof. psychiatry and med. Drexel U. Coll. Med., Phila., 2002—03, chmn. dept. psychiatry, 2002; pvt. practice Bryn Mawr, Pa., 2002—04; pres., treas. Price & Price Practices Psychiatry, PC, Bryn Mawr, 2003—. Bd. dirs. Coll. Health Consortium, Inc., Phila., Highland Dr. Rsch. and Edn. Found., Yale Club Pitts., Pitts. Psychoanalytic Found., Med. Coll. Pa. Hosp.; mem. blue ribbon bd. Alzheimer's Disease Alliance, Western Pa., 1989-97; mem. governing bd. Med. Coll. of Pa. Hosp., 1999-2002. Mem. editl. bd. Convulsive Therapy, 1984-94, Jour. Neuropsychiatry and Clin. Neurosci., 1992—, Allegheny Gen. Hosp. Jour. Neurosci., 1992-98, Seminars in Neuropsychiatry, 1995—; editl. reviewer 15 psychiat. and med. jours., 1978; contbr. chpts. to books and articles in profl. jours. Mem. N.H. Commn. on Laws Effecting Mental Health, 1974-75; bd. dirs. Advanced Studies Program, Friends of St. Paul's Sch., Concord, N.H., 1983-87. Recipient William C. Menninger award Ctrl. Neuropsychiat. Assn., 1977, Faculty Teaching award dept. psychiatry Dartmouth Med. Sch., 1984, Pres. award for Exceptional Achievement AHERF, 1994, numerous grants. Fellow: Am. Coll. Psychiatrists, Am. Neuropsychiat. Assn. (bd. dirs. 1993—95, exec. dir. 1995), Am. Psychiat. Assn. (disting. life fellow); mem.: Assn. Medicine and Psychiatry, Assn. Convulsive Therapy, Assn. Acad. Psychiatry, Am. Assn. Dirs. Psychiat. Residency Tng., Assn. for Acad. Psychiatry, Soc. Biol. Psychiatry, Am. Assn. Chairmen of Depts. Psychiatry, Pa. Psychiat. Assn., Columbia Club of Phila., Yale Club Phila., H-Y-P Club Pitts., Yale Club Pitts. Avocations: fly fishing, tennis, reading, piano, kayaking. Office: 950 Haverford Rd Ste 302 Bryn Mawr PA 19010 Office Phone: 610-527-5926. Personal E-mail: myTwins2@verizon.net. *Life at its best is being continually challenged and fully engaged, yet not self-absorbed.*

PRICE, WILLIAM CHARLIE, lawyer; b. Bristol, Va., Oct. 28, 1956; BA, Duke U., 1978; JD, Yale U., 1981. Bar: Calif. 1983. Law clk. to Hon. Stanley A. Weigel US Dist. Ct. (no. dist. Calif.), 1981—82; asst. US atty. major crimes unit and pub. fraud and corruption unit, Dist. Oreg. US Dept. Justice, 1985—88; ptnr. Quinn, Emanuel, Urquhart, Oliver & Hedges, LLP, LA, 1988—. Instr. Nat. Inst. Trial Advocacy. Named one of Top 10 Trial Lawyers in Am., Nat. Law Jour., 2004, 2006; recipient John Fletcher Caskey prize, 1981. Mem.: State Bar Calif., Phi Beta Kappa. Office: Quinn Emanuel Urquhart Oliver & Hedges LLP 865 S Figueroa St 10th Fl Los Angeles CA 90017 Office Phone: 213-443-3000. E-mail: williamprice@quinnemanuel.com. *

PRICE, WILLIAM JAMES, IV, investment banker; b. Balt., Oct. 6, 1924; s. William James 3d and Frances (Robbins) P.; m. Marjorie Beard, Dec. 6, 1952; children: Marjorie, Jonathan Robbins, William James V, Juliet Robbins. BS, Yale U., 1949. Propr. Price & Co., 1949-52; with Alex. Brown & Sons, Balt., 1952-98, gen. partner, 1959-84, mng. dir., 1984-89. Chmn. Sonitrol Security Svcs., Inc., NC. Trustee Union Meml. Hosp. Found., Washington Coll., St. Paul's Sch. and St. Paul's Sch. for Girls, Eugene B. Casey Found. With inf. AUS, 1943—46, ETO. Decorated Bronze Star, Purple Heart with oak leaf cluster, Combat Infantry badge. Mem.: Nat. Assn. Securities Dealers (bd. govs. 1964—66, vice chmn. 1966).

PRICE, WILLIAM RAY, JR., state supreme court justice; b. Fairfield, Iowa, Jan. 30, 1952; s. William Ray and Evelyn Jean (Darnell) P.; m. Susan Marie Trainor, Jan. 4, 1975; children: Emily Margret, William Joseph Dodds. BA with distinction, U. Iowa, 1974; postgrad., Yale U., 1974-75; JD cum laude, Washington and Lee U., 1978. Bar: Mo. 1978, U.S. Dist. Ct. (we. dist.) Mo. 1978, U.S. Ct. Claims 1978, U.S. Ct. Appeals (8th cir.) 1985. Assoc. Lathrop & Norquist, Kansas City, Mo., 1978-84, ptnr., 1984-92, chmn. bus. litigation sect., 1987-88, 90-92, exec. com., 1989-92; judge Mo. Supreme Ct., Jefferson City, 1992—, chief justice, 1999—2001. G.L.V. Zumwalt monitoring com. U.S. Dist. Ct. (we. dist.) Mo., Kansas City. Pres. Kansas City Bd. Police Commrs.; mem. Together Ctr. & Family Devel. Ctr., Kansas City; chmn. merit selection com. U.S. marshal Western Dist. of Mo., Kansas City; bd. dirs. Truman Med. Ctr., Kansas City. Rockefeller fellow, 1974-75; Burks scholar Washington & Lee U., 1976. Mem. Christian Ch. Office: Supreme Ct Mo PO Box 150 207 W High St Jefferson City MO 65102-0150 *

PRICE, WILLIAM WALLEY, JR., counselor, artist; b. Providence, May 21, 1957; s. William Walley and Betty Price; m. Danijela Milicevic, July 7, 2001. BFA in Illustration, RI Sch. Design, Providence, 1979, postgrad., 1999—2000. Counselor Amos Ho., Providence, 1988—. Tchr. art Amos Ho., 1988—97, carpenter, 1988—97, dir. men's shelter, 1988—95. Poet (collection of poetry fom various poets) Songs of Honour, (collection of poetry from various poets) Labours of Love, (collection of poetry) The Colors of Life (Editor's Choice award, 2003), A Surrender to the Moon (Editor's Choice award, 2005), (collection of poetry fom various poets) Great Poems of the Western World, (cd's (six in all) The Sound Of Poetry, photographer (collection of photography) Colours of the World, photography (collection of photographers) Internat. Libr. Photography (Best Photo's, 2005). Mem. ACLU, Providnce, RI, 2004—06, So. Poverty Law Ctr., Montegomery, Ala., 2002—06. Recipient First Black Eagle Scout, Boy Scouts of Am., 1975. Democrat. Achievements include design of public library bookmobile bus. Avocations: fishing, travel, computers. Home: 135 Providence St Providence RI 02907 Office: 415 Friendship St Providence RI 02907 Personal E-mail: williamprice388@hotmail.com.

PRICE BODAY, MARY KATHRYN, choreographer, small business owner, educator; b. Ft. Bragg, NC, May 20, 1945; d. Max Edward and Katharine (Jordan) Price; m. Les Boday (div. 1982); children: Shawn Leon Boday, Irmali Ferecho Boday; m. Richard A. Weil, May 1, 1986. BFA, U. Okla., 1968, MFA, 1970; studies with David Howard, 1972-74. Soloist dancer Mary Anthony Dance Co., NYC, 1971-74, Larry Richardson Dance Co., NYC, 1971-73; dancer Pearl Lang Dance Co., NYC, 1971-73, Gaku Dance Theater, NYC, 1972-74; ballet mistress and soloist dancer St. Gallen Ballet, Switzerland, 1974-75; dancer, tchr. Zurich Ballet, Switzerland, 1975-76; asst. prof. U. Ill., Champaign-Urbana, 1976-79; artist-in-residence Cornish Inst., Seattle, 1979-80; pres. The Dance Works, Inc., Seattle, 1981-90; dir. Seahurst Ballet, 1982-84; pres. The Dance Works, Inc., Erie, Pa., 1990-94; dir. dance dept., asst. prof. Mercyhurst Coll., Erie, Pa., 1990-94; dir. Peoria Ballet, 1994-99; asst. prof. Bradley U., Peoria, 1994—; dir. Ill. Ballet (formerly Ctrl. Ill. Ballet), 1999—; assoc. prof. Ann Lacy Sch. Am. Dance and Arts Mgmt., Oklahoma City U. Tchr. Harkness Ballet NY, Mary Anthony Dance Sch., Zurich Ballet, Nat. Acad. Arts Ill., Summer Dance lab., Kneeland Workshops, Port Townsend, Wash., 1968, Pa. Gov.'s Sch. of Arts, 1991, 92, 94, Dance Masters Am., 2006, Okla. Dance Masters, 2006; tchr., choreographer Jefferson HS Performing Arts, Portland; choreographer Mary K. Price Dance Co., U. Ill., Nat. Acad. Arts, Cornish Inst., Seahurst Ballet; tchr., co-dir. Kneeland Seminars, Las Vegas, Nev., Port Townsend, 1989, Port Townsend, 90, Oklahoma City U., 1990, Am. Coll. Dance Festival, 1991—93; tchr. David Howard summer workshop Mercyhurst Coll., 1992, Tulsa Ballet Theatre, 1993, 94; tchr. David Howard workshop Seattle tchrs., 1996, U. Ill., 1997, Western Mich. U., 1999; guest artist, asst. prof. Slippery Rock U., 1994; owner Dance Works, Peoria, Ill., 1994—; guest artist So. Ballet Theatre, 2000, 01, David Howard and Mary Price Boday Summer Intensives, Worcester, 2000—02, Mt. Hood Ballet Acad., 2002—03; lectr. Knox Coll., 2000—; assoc. prof. Oklahoma City U., 2005—; dir., workshop tchr. Ann Lacy Sch. Am. Dance and Arts Mgmt., 2006—07. Choreographer (ballets) Ballet Co. St. Gallen, 1988, The Nutcracker, Warner Theater Erie, Peoria Ballet, 1995, Texarkana Ballet, 2006, Gloria, Ill. Ballet with Bradley U. Chorale, 2002, Liebeslieder Waltzes, 2003, Carmina Burana, 2005, 30 Yr. Gala, 1995, Alice in Wonderland, 1996, Little Mermaid of Lake Peoria, 1997, Rudolph the Red Nose Reindeer, Ill. Ballet, Shrine Mosque, 2000, Evanston Dance Ctr., 2004, Rock Ballet, Peoria Civic Ctr. Theatre, The Lion, Witch, and Wardrobe, 2001, Sleeping Beauty, 2003, Hansel and Gretel, 2002, Power of Dance, 2002, Coppella, 2002, Nat. Ballet Panama, 2003, Mary & Friends, Seattle, 1990, co-choreographer (ballets) The Nutcracker Ballet, 1991—93, Coppella, 1993, The Little Mermaid of Lake Erie, Warner Theater, 1994, staged Swan Lake, 1999, 2004. Named one of Outstanding Young Women of Am., 1977, 25 Women in Leadership, Week TV, 2003; recipient Outstanding Dancer award, U. Okla., 1968. Office: Ann Lacy Sch Am Dance and Arts Mgmt Okla City Univ 2501 N Blackwelder Oklahoma City OK 73106 Office Phone: 405-208-5523. Business E-mail: mboday@okcu.edu.

PRICER, WAYNE FRANCIS, counseling consultant; b. Bogue, Kans., Feb. 11, 1935; s. William C. and Lena I. (Hecke) P.; m. Alice M. Fitzpatrick, July 25, 1964; children: Wayne F. Jr., Elizabeth Anne. AB, Ft. Hays State U., 1957; MEd, U. N.D., 1963; postgrad., Wayne State U. Nat. cert. counselor; nat. cert. career counselor; nat. cert. sch. counselor; lic. prof. counselor Mich.; master career counselor. Tchr. Bogue (Kans.) Grade Sch., 1958-62; counselor Lamphere High Sch., 1963-64, 69-75; asst. prin. Page Jr. High, Madison Heights, Mich., 1964-68, prin., 1968-69; adj. counselor Oakland Community Coll., Bloomfield Hills, Mich., 1969—; dir. guidance Lamphere Schs., Madison Heights, Mich., 1975-99; adj. prof. Oakland C.C., 1969—; counseling cons. Royal Oak, Mich., 1999—. Bd. dir., 2d v.p., v.p. Haviland Collectors Internat. Ednl. Found. Contbr. articles to prof. jours. Bd. dir., 2d v.p. Haviland Collectors Internat., 1997—99, Mich. Assn. Retired Sch. Personnel. Named Counselor of Yr. Oakland Counseling Assn., 1999, Lifetime Achievement awards MCDA, 1999, Lamphere Schs., 1999, MAMEG, 2000. Mem. ACA, Am. Mental Health Counselors Assn., Alliance Ret. Americans, Assn. Career and Tech. Edn., Assn. Counselor Edn. and Supervision, Am. Coll. Counselors Assn., Am. Fedn. Tchrs., Am. Sch. Coun. Assn., Assn. Adult Devel. and Aging, Assn. Assessment in Counseling, Lamphere Fedn. Teachers, Assn. Mich. Sch. Counselors, Mich. Assn. for Adult Devel. and Aging, Mich. Assn. Coll. Admission Counselors, Mich. Counseling Assn., Mich. Assn. Counselor Edn. and Supervision, Mich. Assn. Measurement and Evaluation in Guidance (former pres.), Mich. Assn. Specialists in Group Work, Mich. Career Devel. Assn. (treas. 1994-2000), Mich. Assn. Ret. Sch. Pers., Mich. Assn. Career and Tech. Edn., Mich. Mental Health Counselors Assn., Mich. Sch. Counselors Assn., Mich. Assn. Humanistic Edn. and Develop., Mich. Assn. Multi-Cultural Develop., Nat. Assn. Coll. Admission Counselors, Nat. Career Devel. Assn., Oakland Assn. Counseling and Devel. (former pres.), Mich. Fedn. Tchrs., Suburban Assn. of Retired Sch. Personnel, Mich. Coll. Counseling Assn., Assn. Mich. Sch. Counselors, Mich. Fedn. Tchrs., Phi Delta Kappa. Avocations: genealogy, photography. Office: 719 S Washington Ave Royal Oak MI 48067-3829 Office Phone: 248-246-2464. E-mail: wfpricer@aol.com.

PRICHARD, JOHN DAVID, minister; b. Burnwell, W.Va., July 19, 1948; s. Joseph and Agnes Arvada (Fisher) P.; m. Drema Kay Clark, Apr. 11, 1970; children: Angela Kay, John David II. AB, Nazarene Bible Coll., 1980; postgrad., U. Bibl. Studies, Bethany, Okla., 1989; BA in Biblical Studies, Am. Bible Coll. and Sem., 2000, postgrad., 2003, Masters Sem., Evansville, Ind., 2007. Ordained minister Ch. of the Nazarene, 1981. Pastor, zone youth dir. Dille (W.Va.) Ch. of the Nazarene, 1975-77; pastor Craigsville (W.Va.) Ch. of the Nazarene, 1980-82, Walton (W.Va.) Ch. of the Nazarene, 1982-84, Marion (Va.) Ch. of the Nazarene, 1984-88, Beckley (W.Va.) First Ch. of the Nazarene, 1988-95, Charleston (W.Va.) South Hills Ch. of the Nazarene, 1995—; rep. Nazarene Pub. House, Kansas City, Mo., 2007. Ch. planter Va. Dist., Wytheville, 1985-86; area coord. Va. Nazarene Dist., Marion, 1987-88; dist. adult dir. W.Va. South Dist., 1990-99; cafeteria mgr. W.Va. Dist. Campgrounds, 1990—2006; dist. coll. recruiter Nazarene Bible Coll., Colorado Springs, Colo., 1990—; small ch. growth trainer W.Va. South Dist. Ch. of the Nazarene; Sunday sch. chmn. W.Va. South Dist. Ch. of the Nazarene, 1999—20077. Chmn. Libr. Commn., Walton, W.Va., 1983-84; dir. Weekday Religious Edn. Program, Marion, 1985-86; co-chair Greater Beckley Area Crusade, 1993; mem. Beckley Ministerial Assn.; vol. hospice chaplain Raleigh County Hospice Group, 1993-95. With USN, 1966-70, Vietnam. Recipient Gt. Commn. Leadership award W.Va. South Dist., 1990, Second Mile award W.Va. South Sunday Sch. Ministries, 1998, W.Va. South Dist. Disting. Svc. award, 2006; named Alumnus of Yr., W.Va. South Dist., Nazarene Bible Coll., Colorado Springs, 1990. Mem. Am. Acad. Ministry. Democrat. Office: South Hills Ch of the Nazarene 1565 Smith Rd Charleston WV 25314-2326 E-mail: johnprichard@suddenlink.net.

PRICHARD, PETER S., newspaper editor; b. Auburn, Calif., Dec. 18, 1944; s. Jarvis B. and Floris C. (Smith) P.; m. Ann O'Donnell, Nov. 13, 1971; children: Oliver W., Lindsay M. AB, Dartmouth Coll., 1966. Wire editor Greenwich (Conn.) Time, 1970-72; reporter Democrat and Chronicle, Rochester, N.Y., 1972-75; assoc. news dir. WOKR TV, Rochester, N.Y., 1975-76; reporter Times Union, Rochester, 1976-78; asst. to chmn. communications Gannett Co. Inc., Rochester, 1980-82, dir. communications, Office of Chief Exec., 1980-82; columns editor USA Today, Washington, 1982-83, dep. assoc. editorial dir., 1983-84, assoc. editorial dir., 1984-86, mng. editor spl. projects, 1986-87, sr. editor, 1988, editor, sr. v.p., news, 1988—; sr. v.p. News Gannett Co. Inc., Washington, 1988—, chief news exec., 1990—. Author: The Making of McPaper: The Inside Story of USA Today, 1987 (Frank Luther Moh Rsch. award Kappa Tau Alpha 1987). Vice chmn., bd. trustees Washington Journalism Ctr., 1989—. With U.S. Army, 1967-69, Vietnam. Decorated Bronze Star. Mem. Nat. Press Club, Am. Soc. Newspaper Editors (Reston, Va.) (various coms. 1985—). Office: USA Today 7950 Jones Branch Dr Mc Lean VA 22108-0001

PRICHARD, VINCENT MARVIN, lawyer; b. Kirksville, Mo., July 16, 1946; s. George William and Mary Elizabeth (Love) P. BS, U. Colo., 1969; JD, U. Denver, 1974. Bar: Colo. 1975, U.S. Dist. Ct. Colo. 1975. Atty. Bur. Hearings and Appeals Social Security Adminstrn., Denver, 1975-79; asst. regional counsel Dept. Energy, Lakewood, Colo., 1979-82; atty. Fed. Legal Info. Through Electronics, Denver, 1982-93; info. tech. profl. U. Colo. Health Scis. Ctr., Denver, 1994-99; info. tech. mgr. Colo. Water Conservation Bd., Denver, 2000—04, ret., 2004. With U.S. Army, 1969-71. Mem. Colo. Bar Assn., 1st Jud. Dist. Bar Assn. Home: PO Box 3520 Evergreen CO 80437-3520

PRICKETT, DAVID CLINTON, physician; b. Fairmont, W.Va., Nov. 26, 1918; s. Clinton Everett and Mary Anna (Gottschalk) Prickett; m. Mary Ellen Holt, June 29, 1940 (dec. Feb. 1987); children: David C., Rebecca Ellen, William Radcliffe, Mary Anne, James Thomas, Sara Elizabeth; m. Pamela S. Blackstone, Nov. 17, 1991 (dec. Mar. 2002). Student, Fairmont State Coll., 1940—42; AB, W.Va. U., 1944; MD, U. Louisville, 1946; MPH, U. Pitts., 1955. Pres. Prickett Chem. Co., 1938-43; acct. W.Va. Conservation Commn. and Fed. Works Agy., 1941, 42; lab. asst., instr. chemistry W.Va. U., 1943; intern Louisville Gen. Hosp., 1947; surg. resident St. Joseph's Hosp., Parkersburg, W.Va., 1948-49; gen. practice W.Va., 1948-50, 55-61; mem. staff Fairmont (W.Va.) Gen. Hosp., 1955-60, Fairmont Emergency Hosp., 1955-60; physician USAF, N.Mex. and Calif., 1961-62, U.S. Army, Fort Ord, Calif., 1963-64; resident physician San Luis Obispo County Hosp., 1965-66; pvt. practice LA, 1967—; mem. staff St. Francis Hosp., LA, 1970-71; physician So. Calif. Edison Co., 1981-84. Physician Bethlehem Mines Corp., Idamay, W.Va., 1956; resident physician Sedgwick County Hosp., Wichita, Kans., 1964-65; med. dir. South Gate auto assembly plant GM, 1969-71; staff physician City of LA, 1971-76; relief med. practice Appalachia summer seasons, W.Va. and Ky., 1977, 86, 88-97. Author: The Newer Epidemiology, 1962, rev., 1990, Public Health, A Science Resolvable by Mathematics, 1965; contbr. articles to profl. jours. Sr. counsellor, US Commercial Travelers, Fairmont, W.Va., 1939-40; med. officer USPHS, Navajo Indian Reservation, Tohatchi (N.Mex.) Health Ctr., 1953-55, surgeon, res. officer, 1957-59; pres. W.Va. Pub. Health Assn., 1951-52; sec. indsl. and pub. health sect. W.Va. Med. Assn., 1956; W.Va. dist. 4 health officer; health officer Marion County, W.Va., 1951-53; dist. health officer Allegheny County, Pa., 1957; officer Aux. Civil Def. Police, W.Va., 1942; med. advisor Boy Scouts Am., W.Va., 1956-57, N.Mex., 1954; mem. Med. Rsv. Corps of LA, 2005—. 2d lt. AUS, 1943-46. Dr. Thomas Parran fellow U. Pitts. Sch. Pub. Health, 1955; named to Hon. Order Ky. Cols. Fellow APHA; mem. AMA, Am. Occupl. Med. Assn., Am. Acad. Family Physicians, Western Occupl. Med. Assn., Calif. Med. Assn., Los Angeles County Med. Assn., SR, W.Va., Am. Legion, Elks, Sierra Club Calif., Rio Hondo Symphony Guild, Phi Chi. Avocations: photography, auto repairs, amateur radio, square and round dancing, history. Address: PO Box 4032 Whittier CA 90607-4032 Office Phone: 626-330-4106.

PRIDE, BENJAMIN DAVID, sales executive; b. SI, NY, Sept. 20, 1952; s. Benjamin David and Evelyn Marie (Dann) Pride; m. Jane Jeanette Adams, Oct. 12, 2002; stepchildren: Emily Adams, Phillip Adams. BA, St. Francis Coll., Bklyn., 1974. Office mgr., prodn. estimator Leber Katz Ptnrs., NYC, 1975-76; prodn. estimator, media planner, out-of-home media buyer, sports buyer Dancer, Fitzgerald & Sample, NYC, 1976-81; v.p. sports and promotion Backer, Spielvogel, Bates Worldwide, NYC, 1981-95, Zenith Media, NYC, 1995-96; ptnr. Schineller & Pride, NYC, 1996-97; account exec. Newport Media, NYC, 1997-99; asst. mgr., sr. membership dir. UCC Total Home, Eatontown, NJ, 2001—03; advt. cons. Rosnik Pub., Inc., NYC, 2003—04; bus. devel. mgr. Securitas Security Svcs. USA, Inc., 2004—06; v.p. sales Classic Protection, Inc., NYC, 2006—. Divsn. capt. USCG Aux., 2000. Republican. Roman Catholic. Avocations: boating, fishing. Office Phone: 718-568-3590. Personal E-mail: bdpjjp@aol.com. Business E-Mail: benpride@classicprotection.com.

PRIDE, MIKE, editor; BA, U. South Fla. Sports writer Tampa (Fla.) Tribune; city editor Clearwater (Fla.) Sun, Tallahassee Democrat; mng. editor Concord (NH) Monitor, editor, 1983—. Mem. Pulitzer Prize Bd., 2000—, co-chmn., 2007—. Russian linguist US Army. Recipient Editor of Yr. award, Nat. Press Found., 1987, Yankee Quill award. Office: Monitor Pub Co PO Box 1177 Concord NH 03302-1177 Office Phone: 603-224-5301. Office Fax: 603-224-4287. *

PRIDHAM, THOMAS GRENVILLE, retired microbiologist; b. Chgo., Oct. 10, 1920; s. Grenville and Gladys Etheral (Sloss) P.; m. Phyllis Sue Hokamp, July 1, 1943 (dec. Feb. 1994); children: Pamela Sue, Thomas Foster, Grenville Thomas, Rolf Thomas, Montgomery Thomas; m. Edna Lee Boudreaux, Mar. 6, 1995 (dec. Apr. 2006). BS Chemistry, U. Ill., 1943, PhD Bacteriology, 1949. Instr. bacteriology U. Ill., Champaign-Urbana, 1947; rsch. microbiologist No. Regional Rsch. Lab., USDA, Peoria, Ill., 1948—51, No. Regional Rsch. Lab. USDA, Peoria, 1953—65, U.S. Indsl. Chem., Balt., 1951—52; supr. tech. ops. Acme Vitamins, Inc., Joliet, Ill., 1952—53; sr. rsch. biologist U.S. Borax Rsch. Corp., Anaheim, Calif., 1965—67; supervisory rsch. microbiologist No. Regional Rsch. Ctr. USDA, Peoria, 1967—81, head agrl. rsch. culture collection No. Regional Rsch. Lab., 1967—81; ret., 1991. Cons. Mycogen Corp., San Diego, 1985-87; U.S. sr. scientist Germany, Darmstadt, 1977 Contbg. author: Actinomycetales: The Boundary Microorganisms, 1974, Bergey's Manual of Determinative Bacteriology, 1974, Synopsis and Classification of Living Organisms, 1982; mem. editl. bd. Jour. Antibiotics, 1969-81; contbr. articles to Jour. Bacteriology, Applied Microbiology, Phytopathology, Actinomycetes, Mycologia, Devel. Indsl. Microbiology, Jour. Antibiotics, Internat. Bull. Bacteriological Nomenclature Taxonomy, Antibiotics Ann., Antimicrobial Agts., Chemotherapy, also others With USNR, 1943-45, with Rsch. Res., 1945-54, lt. ret. Fulbright scholar, Italy, 1952; grantee Soc. Am. Bacteriologists, 1957 Fellow: Am. Acad. Microbiology; mem.: Alexander von Humboldt Assn. Episcopalian. Achievements include patents in fermentative production of riboflavin and of antibiotics; research in microbial culture collection technology and management, systematics of streptomycetes, industrial microbiology. Home: 16645 S Pacific PO Box 1098 Sunset Beach CA 90742

PRIDMORE, ROY DAVIS, retired federal official; b. Gaffney, SC, May 18, 1925; s. Davis Bailey and Ethel (Hughes) P.; m. Doris Hedy Glatzl, July 16, 1960 (dec. Aug. 5, 2000); children: Lisa Ann, David Michael. Cert., Columbus U., Washington, 1949, Am. Inst., 1953, U.S. Dept. Agr. Grad. Sch., 1957. Pers. asst. Dept. Army, Fort Myer, Va., 1955-58; staff asst. D.C. Hwy. Dept., Washington, 1962-67; adminstrv. asst. Dept. Transp., Washington, 1958-62, adminstrv. officer, 1967-94, ret., 1994. Vice pres. Springboard Swim Club, Springfield, Va., 1984-85. Served with U.S. Army, 1946-47; mem. Res. (ret.) Decorated Legion of Merit. Democrat. Roman Catholic. Avocations: swimming, gardening.

PRIEBE, CEDRIC JOSEPH, JR., retired pediatric surgeon; b. NYC, Feb. 7, 1930; s. Cedric Joseph and Mary Martha (O'Beirne) P.; m. Cynthia Amelia Cali, June 11, 1955; children: Diane Marie, Janice Marie, Cedric Joseph III, Catherine Marie, Michael Stephen, Gregory Paul, Marta Marcella. BS cum laude, Fordham U., 1951; MD, Cornell U., 1955. Bd. cert. Am. Bd. Surgery, 1961, Pediat. Surgery, 1976, Pediat. Surgery, 1984, Pediat. Surgery, 1993, Pediat. Surgery, 2003. Resident surgery Roosevelt Hosp., NYC, 1955—60; resident pediat. surgery Ohio State U., Children's Hosp., Columbus, 1965—67; pediat. surgeon, asst. and assoc. prof. Roosevelt Hosp., Colombia U., NYC, 1967—79; chief pediat. surgery, prof. surgery La. State U., Charity Hosp., New Orleans, 1979—82; dir. surg. edn. Children's Hosp. New Orleans, 1979—82; chief pediat. surgery, prof. surgery SUNY, U. Hosp., Stony Brook, 1982—2007; adminstrv. vice chmn. dept. surgery Stony Brook Sch. Medicine, 2002—07, faculty senate, 1991—2007, mem. promotion and tenure com., 2001—07, exec.com., 1999—2007, pres., 2003—07; ret., 2007. Sr. clin. trainee in cancer control NIH, Washington, 1963—65. Editl. cons. Jour. Pediat. Surgery, Phila., 1994—; author: (with others) Neoplasia in Childhood, 1966; contbr. articles to profl. jours Maj. USAF, 1956—65. Mem.: ACS, Med. Soc. State N.Y., N.Y. Soc. Pediat. Surgery (v.p. 1976—78, pres. 1978—79, 1986—), Children's Oncology Group, Pediat. Oncology Group (cancer control com. 1992—2000), Am. Pediat. Surg. Assn. (membership com. 1990—93, by-laws com. 1993—95, cancer com. 1996—99), Am. Acad. Pediat. (surg. sect. publs. com. 1989—92, chair publs. com. 1992), Soc. for Surgery Alimentary Tract, Am. Burn Assn. Republican. Roman Catholic. Avocations: tennis, squash racquets, travel. Home: 9 Woodhull Cove Ln Setauket NY 11733-1643 Office: SUNY at Stony Brook HSC T 19 Stony Brook NY 11794-8191 Home Phone: 631-941-4291; Office Phone: 631-444-7950. Personal E-mail: priebe@optonline.net. Business E-Mail: cedric.priebe@stonybrook.edu, cjpriebe@notes.cc.sunysb.edu.

PRIEM, RICHARD GREGORY, writer, executive; b. Munich, Sept. 18, 1949; arrived in U.S., 1953; s. Richard Stanley and Elizabeth Teresa (Thompson) Priem; m. Janice Lynne Holland, July 27, 1976; children: Michael John, Matthew Warren(dec.), Kathryn Elizabeth Guthrie. BS in Radio-TV-Film, U. Tex., 1970; MEd in Ednl. Tech., U. Ga., 1979; postgrad., Coll. William and Mary, 1981-82. Cert. fraud examiner. Radio personality, sales exec. KOKE, Inc., Austin, Tex., 1968-73; numerous positions including asst. prof. dept. behavioral scis. and leadership U.S. Mil. Acad., anti-terorism staff officer and insp. gen. U.S. Army, 1973-94; dep. divsn. mgr. Sci. Applications Internat. Corp., Vienna, Va., 1994-97; asst. v.p. SAIC, 2003—. Cons. Dallas Cowboys Football Club, 1981; scouting coord. Army Football, 1983-85; cons. in field of anti-terrorism. Contbr. articles to profl. jours. Mem. Assn. Cert. Fraud Examiners, Internat. Soc. for Performance Improvement, Phi Kappa Phi, Kappa Delta Pi, Internat. Assn. Bomb Technicians and Investigators. Home: 13505 Trail Vista Ct NE Albuquerque NM 87111-9248 Personal E-mail: rpriem@earthlink.net.

PRIESAND, SALLY J., rabbi; b. Cleve., June 27, 1946; d. Irving Theodore and Rosetta Elizabeth (Welch) P. BA in English, U. Cin., 1968; B.Hebrew Letters, Hebrew Union Coll.-Jewish Inst. Religion, 1971, MA in Hebrew Letters, 1972; D.H.L. (hon.), Fla. Internat. U., 1973; DD (hon.), Hebrew Union Coll., 1997. Ordained rabbi 1972. Student rabbi Sinai Temple, Champaign, Ill., 1968, Congregation B'nai Israel, Hattiesburg, Miss., 1969-70, Congregation Shalom, Milw., 1970, Temple Beth Israel, Jackson, Mich., 1970-71; rabbinic intern Isaac M. Wise Temple, Cin., 1971-72; asst. rabbi Stephen Wise Free Synagogue, NYC, 1972-77, assoc. rabbi, 1977-79; rabbi Temple Beth El, Elizabeth, NJ, 1979-81, Monmouth Reform Temple, Tinton Falls, 1981—2006, rabbi emerita, 2006—; chaplain Lenox Hill Hosp., NYC, 1979-81. Author: Judaism and the New Woman, 1975. Mem. commn. on synagogue rels. Fedn. Jewish Philanthropies N.Y., 1972-79, mem. com. on aged commn. synagogue rels., 1972-75; mem. task force on equality of women in Judaism pub. affairs com. N.Y. Fedn. Reform Synagogues, 1972-75; mem. com. on resolutions Ctrl. Conf. Am. Rabbis, 1975-77, com. on cults, 1976-78, admissions com., 1983-89; chmn. Task Force on Women in Rabbinate, 1977-83, chmn. 1977-79, mem. exec. bd., 1977-79, com. on resolutions, 1989-92, chmn. com. conv. program, 1993-96; mem. joint commn. on Jewish edn. Ctrl. Conf. Am. Rabbis-Union Am. Hebrew Congregations, 1974-77; mem. task force on Jewish singles Commn. Synagugue Rels., 1975-77; mem. N.Y. Bd. Rabbis, 1975—, Shore Area Bd. Rabbis, 1981—; mem. interim steering com. Clergy and Laity Concerned, 1979-81; bd. dirs. NCCJ, N.Y.C., 1980-82, Jewish Fedn. Greater Monmouth County, trustee, 1988-2000, strategic planning comm., 1996—, hon. v.p., 2000—; trustee Planned Parenthood of Monmouth County, 1982-90, 2006—; v.p. Interfaith Neighbors, 1988-96, pres., 1997—; mem. UAHC-CCAR Joint Commn. on Synagogue Affiliation, 1992-2002; bd. govs. Hebrew Union Coll.-Jewish Inst. Religion, 1993-2005; trustee Union Am. Hebrew Congregations, 1994-98; mem. nat. clergy adv. bd. Planned Parenthood Fedn. Am., 2007—; bd. dirs. Ctr. Holocaust Studies, Brookdale C.C., 2006—, Jewish Heritage Mus. Monmouth County, 2007—. Cited by B'nai Brith Women, 1971; named Woman of Yr. Temple Israel, Columbus, Ohio, 1972, Woman of Yr. Ladies Aux. N.Y. chpt. Jewish War Vets., 1973, Woman for All Seasons N. L.I. region Women's Am. ORT, 1973, Extraordinary Women of Achievement NCCJ, 1978, Woman of Achievement Monmouth County Adv. Commn. on Status Women, 1988; recipient Quality of Life award Dist. One chpt. B'nai B'rith Women, 1973, Medallion Judaic Heritage Soc., 1978, Eleanor Roosevelt Humanities award Women's div. State of Israel Bonds, 1980, Rabbinical award Coun. Jewish Fedn., 1988, Woman of Leadership award Monmouth Coun. Girl Scouts U.S., 1991, The Woman Who Dares award Nat. Coun. Jewish Women, 1993, Women's Studies Disting. Alumnae award Friends of Women's Studies U. Cin., 1997; named to Alumni Hall of Fame, Fairview Park H.S., 2002. Mem. Hadassah (life), Ctrl. Conf. Am. Rabbis, NOW, Am. Jewish Congress, Am. Jewish Com., Assn. Reform Zionists Am., Jewish Women Internat. (life), Nat. Coun. Jewish Women, Women Reform Judaism (life), Jewish Peace Fellowship, Women's Rabbinic Network, Nat. Breast Cancer Coalition, HUC-JIR Rabbinic Alumni Assn. (sec., treas. 1997-99, v.p. 1999-2001, pres. 2001-03, past pres., 2003-05). Achievements include being the first US woman rabbi. Office: 332 Hance Ave Tinton Falls NJ 07724-2730 Home: 32 Fernwood Dr Ocean NJ 07712-8713 Office Phone: 732-493-4896. Business E-Mail: rsjp@optonline.net.

PRIEST, DANA, journalist; married; 2 children. BA, U. Calif., Santa Cruz. Intelligence reporter, Nat. News Desk Washington Post, 1987—. Author: The Mission: Waging War & Keeping Peace with America's Military, 2003 (Pulitzer prize finalist for gen. non-fiction, 2004). Recipient MacArthur Found. Rsch. & Writing grant, 2001, Gerald R. Ford prize for Disting. Reporting on Nat. Def., 2001, Excellence in Journalism award, State Dept., 2001, George Polk award for nat. reporting, 2006, Pulitzer Prize for beat reporting, 2006, Bob Considine award, Overseas Press Club, 2006. Office: Washington Post Nat News Desk 1150 15th St Washington DC 20071-0070 Office Phone: 202-334-4490. Office Fax: 202-496-3883. E-mail: priestd@washpost.com.

PRIEST, GEORGE L., law educator; b. 1947; BA, Yale U., 1969; JD, U. Chgo., 1973. Assoc. prof. U. Puget Sound, Tacoma, 1973-75; law and econ. fellow U. Chgo., 1975-77; prof. U. Buffalo, 1977-80, UCLA, 1980-81, Yale U., New Haven, 1981—, John M. Olin Prof. Law and Econs., 1986—, dir. John M. Olin Ctr. for Law, Econs. and Pub. Policy, 1986—. Dir. program in civil liability; John M. Olin prof. law and econs., 1986—. Mem. Pres.' Com. on Privatization, 1987-88. Office: PO Box 208215 New Haven CT 06520-8215 E-mail: george.priest@yale.edu.

PRIEST, JESSIE SHAW, media specialist; d. Shaw Wesley and Shaw McFadden (Teddie) James; m. David Priest, Dec. 27, 1972; children: David, LaDawndrea Catoria. Cert. edn. tchr. SC State Dept. of Edn., 1967. Reading tchr. Chavis Elem. Sch., Hemmingway, SC, 1967—70; elem. tchr., 1967—73; media specialist Planterville Elem. Sch., Georgetown, SC, 1970—2005. Home Phone: 843-546-0233.

PRIEST, MARSHALL FRANKLIN, III, cardiologist; b. Rio de Janeiro, Feb. 27, 1943; came to the U.S., 1945; s. Marshall Franklin Jr. and Eleanor Margaret (Harris) P.; m. Martha Prather, June 11, 1966; children: Paula Carol, Molly McCall, Marshall Franklin IV. BS, U. Tenn., 1965, MS, 1969, MD, 1973. Bd. cert. internal medicine and cardiovascular disease. Intern U. Tenn. Affiliated Hosp., Memphis, 1973-74, resident, 1974-76; cardiology fellow U. Ala. Hosps., Birmingham, 1976-78, instr. medicine and cardiology, 1978-79; cardiologist Boise (Idaho) Heart Clinic, 1979-94, Idaho Cardiology Assocs., Boise, 1994—. Clin. asst. prof. medicine U. Washington. Fellow Am. Coll. Cardiology, Am. Soc. Cardiac Angiography and Interventions; mem. Am. Heart Assn. (fellow coun. on clin. cardiology), Alpha Omega Alpha. Avocations: running, biking, backpacking, canoeing, climbing. Office: Idaho Cardiology Assocs 300 E Jefferson St Ste 201 Boise ID 83712-6221 *

PRIEST, SHARON DEVLIN, retired state official, not-for-profit developer; b. Montreal, Can. m. Bill Priest; one son Adam. Tax preparer, instr. H & R Block, Little Rock, 1976-78; owner, founder Devlin Co., Ark., 1983-86; account exec. Greater Little Rock C. of C., 1990-94; vice mayor Little Rock, 1989-90, mayor, 1991-92; Sec. of State State of Ark., 1994—2002; exec. dir. The Downtown Partnership, 2002—. Bd. dir. Invesco Inc., New Futures. Bd. dirs., past pres. Metroplan (Environ. Svc. Award 1982), YMCA, Southwest Hosp.; bd. dirs. Fed. Reserve Bank St. Louis; mem. Carter-Baker Commn. Fed. Election Reform Commn., Advt. and Promotion commn., Ark. Internat. Visitors Coun., Pulaski Are Transp. Svc. Policy Com., St. Theresa's Parish Coun., Exec. com. for Ark. Mcpl. League, Nat. League of Cities Trans. and Comm. Steering Com. and Policy Com., adv. bd. M.M. Cohn., Little Rock City Beautiful Commn., 1980-86, Carter Barker Election Reform Commn., 2005, BP Ind. Safety Panel, 2005-06; former bd. dir. Downtown Partnership, S.W. YMCA, 1984, 86, sec.; former mem. Cmty. Housing Resource Bd., 1984-86, Pub. Facilities Bd. S.W. Hosp., 1985-86, S.W. Merchants' Assn., 1985—, 2d v.p., 1985; chmn. Little Rock Arts and Humanities Promotion Commn.; led petition dr. for appropriation for Fourche Creek Plan 7A. Recipient of the Fighting Back Freedom Fighter Award, 1995; Environ. Svc. Award from the Little Rock Metroplan Comm., 1982. Mem. Leadership Inst. Alumni Assn. (4 Bernard de la Harpe Awards), Rotary. Achievements include being selected by Ark. Bus. as one of the Top 100 Women in Ark. Office: Downtown Partnership PO Box 1937 Little Rock AR 72203 Office Phone: 501-375-0121. Business E-Mail: spriest@downtownlr.com.

PRIESTLEY, JASON (JASON BRADFORD PRIESTLEY), actor; b. Vancouver, BC, Can., Aug. 28, 1969; m. Ashlee Petersen, Feb. 2, 1999 (div. Jan. 2, 2000); m. Naomi Lowde, May 14, 2005; 1 child. Driver Kelley Racing, 2002. Actor: (TV series) Sister Kate, 1989-90, Beverly Hills 90210, 1990-1998 (Golden Globe award nominee for best actor in a drama series 1993)(also dir. 15 episodes, 1993-97, prodr., dir. episodes in 1995-96; prodr. 58 episodes 1996-97, exec. prodr. 1997-98), Eek! The Cat(voice), 1992, Tru Calling, 2004-2005; (TV movies) Teen Angel, 1989, Choice of the Heart: The Margaret Sanger Story, 1995, Vanishing Point, 1997, Kiss Tomorrow Goodbye, 2000 (also exec. prodr., dir.), Teen Angel Returns, 1990, Common Ground, 2000, Homicide: The Movie, 2000, Warning: Parental Advisory, 2002, The True Meaning of Christmas Specials, 2002, I Want to Marry Ryan Banks, 2004, Sleep Murder, 2004, Murder at the Presidio, 2005, Colditz, 2005, Snow Wonder, 2005, Shades of Black: The Conrad Black Story, 2006, Subs, 2007, Luna: Spirit of the Whale, 2007; (films) The Boy Who Could Fly, 1986, Watchers, 1988, Nowhere To Run, 1989, Calendar Girl, 1993, Tombstone, 1993, Cold-Blooded, 1995, Love and Death on Long Island, 1997, Hacks, 1997, The Thin Pink Line, 1998, Conversations in Limbo, 1998, Choose Life, 1999, Dill Scallion, 1999, Standing On Fishes, 1999, Eye of the Beholder, 1999, Barenacked in America, 1999 (also prodr., dir.), The Highwayman, 2000 (also prodr.), Lion of Oz (voice), 2000, Herschel Hopper: New York Rabbit (voice), 2000, Zigs, 2001, The Fourth Angel, 2001, Cherish, 2002, Cover Story, 2002, Darkness Falling, 2002, Time of the Wolf, 2002, Fancy Dancing, 2002, Die, Mommie Die, 2003, Chicks with Sticks, 2004, Going the Distance, 2004, Hot Tamale, 2005, Made in Brooklyn, 2006; (TV mini series) Above and Beyond, 2006; guest appearances include Airwolf, 1987, 21 Jump Street, 1987, The Outer Limits, 1997 (also dir.), MacGyver, 1988, Quantum Leap, 1989, Superman, 1998, Grosse Point, 2001 (also dir.), Spin City, 2001 & 2003, 8 Simple Rules...for Dating My Teenage Daughter, 2002, 2003, Celebrities Uncensored, 2003, 04, American Idol, 2004, Overhaulin, 2004, What I Like About You, 2005, Hockeyville, 2006, Love Monkey, 2006, Without a Trace, 2006, Masters of Horror, 2006, Medium, 2007, (several episodes) Side Order of Life, 2007 Named one of the 50 Most Beautiful People in the World, People Mag., 1991, 1992, TV's 25 Greatest Teen Idols, TV Guide, 2005; won 1998 Grand-Am race, Mid-Ohio Sports Car Course. Avocations: hockey, race car driving. *

PRIEUR, C. JAMES, insurance company executive; BA, Coll. Militaire Royal de S. Jean, Quebec; MBA, Univ. We. Ontario, 1975. Equity analyst & portfolio mgr. Sun Life Fin. Inc., 1979—85, head Canadian private placements, 1985—88, v.p. securities investments Canada, 1988—91, v.p. investments Canada, 1991—92, v.p. investments U.S., 1992—97, sr. v.p., gen. mgr. U.S. ops., 1997—99, pres., COO, 1999—2006; CEO Conseco Inc., Carmel, Ind., 2006—. Bd. dir. LIRMA Internat. Inc. Office: Conseco Inc 11825 N Pennsylvania St Carmel IN 46032 *

PRILLELTENSKY, ISAAC, dean; b. Cordoba, Argentina, Sept. 18, 1959; s. Jacobo Prilleltensky and Betty Priyoltensky; m. Ora Rappoport, Dec. 14, 1982; 1 child, Matan. PhD, U. Man., Winnipeg, 1989. Prof. Peabody Coll., Vanderbilt U., Nashville, 2003—06; dean U. Miam, Sch. Edn., Coral Gables, 2006—. Fellow, APA, 1996. Office: U Miami Sch Edn PO Box 248065 Coral Gables FL 33124-2040 Office Phone: 305-284-3505. E-mail: isaacp@miami.edu.

PRIMEAU, KEITH, retired professional hockey player; b. Toronto, Nov. 24, 1971; m. Lisa Primeau; 4 children. Center Detroit Red Wings, 1990—96, Hartford Whalers, 1996—97, Carolina Hurricanes, 1997—99, Phila. Flyers, 2000—06. Mem. Team Can., Olympic Games, Nagano, Japan, 1998; player NHL All-Star Game, 1999, 2004. Office: c/o Phila Flyers 3601 S Broad St Philadelphia PA 19148

PRIMI, DON ALEXIS, advertising, public relations, rail transportation executive; b. NYC, Jan. 14, 1947; s. John Prosper, Sr. and Eileen Mary Primi. A in Advt., State U. N.Y., 1967; BS in Mktg. and Advt., Hofstra U., 1971; advanced astron. studies degree, Vanderbilt Mus. and Planetarium, 1967. Ordained priest Roman Cath. Ch., 2007. Gen. mgr. Recreational Pub. Corp.; pres., owner Fantasia Trains/REE R.R. Equipment Exchange, 1980, Don Primi Designs, 1984, Rail Industries, Rail Fin. Corp., 1987, Gold Coast Ltd./Royal Rail, 1987, Rail Enterprises, 1990, LPA North Am., 1992, Alexis Daniels, 1992, Salon Promotions, 1992, Trans Fla. Express, Inc., 2001. Cons. in field, ry. industry, brick and clay products industry; designer corp. identity programs. Recipient awards, Printing Industries Met. N.Y., Gold Boli advt. awards, Kimberly-Clark Graphic excellence awards, Astrophoto awards. Mem.: Astron Soc. L.I. (pres., pub. rels. dir.), Sales and Mktg. Execs., Nat. R.R. Assn. Passengers, R.R. Pub. Rels. Assn., Assn. Ry. Progress Inst., Rail Mktg. Club N.Y. Achievements include designs published in periodicals. Home: 4065 Old Settlement Rd Merritt Island FL 32952-6211 Office: 160 5th Ave New York NY 10010-7003 E-mail: dprail21@brevard.net.

PRIMM, EARL RUSSELL, III, publishing executive; b. Rhinelander, Wis., Oct. 24, 1958; s. Earl Russell and Betty Joan (Dennis) P. AB in Classics (hon.), Loyola U. Chgo., 1980; MA in Libr. Sci., U. Chgo., 1990. Asst. to edn. dir. J.G. Ferguson Pub. Co., Chgo., 1981-84; prodn. mgr. Joint Commn. on Accreditation of Hosps., Chgo., 1984-85; sr. editor J.G. Ferguson Pub. Co., Chgo., 1985-87; asst. editor U. Chgo. Press., 1987-88; editorial dir. J.G. Ferguson Pub. Co., Chgo., 1988-89; project mgr. Children's Press, Chgo., 1989-92; exec. editor Franklin Watts, Inc., Chgo., NYC, 1992-95; editl. dir. Grolier Children's Pub., Danbury, Conn., 1995-97; pres. Editl. Directions, Inc., Chgo., 1997—. Mem. adv. bd. U. Chgo. Pub. Program, 1990-2000; judge Lambda Lit. awards, Washington, 1994-2000; guest lectr. Sch. Edn. Harvard U., 2004. Editl. chief: Career Discovery Encyclopedia, 1990, Favorite Children's Authors and Illustrators, 2002; editor: Civil Rights Movement in America, 2nd edit., 1991, Extraordinary Hispanic Americans, 1991; editl. dir. The Child's World, 2002, Tradition Books, 2002. Mem. crisis counselor Nat. Runaway Switchboard, Chgo., 1985-88; Horizon's hotline counselor, Chgo., 1987-88; bd. dirs. Gerber/Hart Libr. and Archives, Chgo., 1992-94. Named Honors Sr. of Yr., Loyola U. Chgo., 1980; recipient Mertz Latin Scholarship key Loyola U. Chgo., 1980. Mem. Am. Libr. Assn. Democrat. Home: 1000 W Washington Blvd #147 Chicago IL 60607-2148 Office: 1000 W Washington Blvd # 203 Chicago IL 60607 Office Phone: 312-829-5456. E-mail: russell@editorialdirections.com.

PRIMM, RICHARD KIRBY, physician; b. Thomasville, NC, May 23, 1944; s. Richard Wesley and Gertrude (Berrier) P.; m. Sharon Kay Lucas, Dec. 28, 1968; children: Heather, Lucas. BA, Duke U., 1966; postgrad., Baylor U., 1966-67; MD, U. N.C., 1970. Intern internal medicine Vanderbilt U. Hosp., Nashville, 1970-71, resident in internal medicine, 1973-75, chief resident, 1975-76; fellow cardiovascular diseases U. Ala., Birmingham, 1976-78, chief fellow, instr. medicine, 1978-79; asst. prof. medicine Vanderbilt U. Sch. Medicine, Nashville, 1979-84; staff cardiologist Wenatchee (Wash.) Valley Clinic, 1984--. Clin. asst. prof. medicine U. Wash., Seattle, 1985-91, clin. assoc. prof. medicine, 1991-2003, clin. prof. medicine, 2003—; adminstrv. lead dept. cardiology Wenatchee Valley Clinic, 1987-91, 1997-2006. Contbr. articles to profl. jours. Capt. U.S. Army, 1971-73. Recipient Heusner Pupil award U. N.C., 1969, Hillman Teaching Excellence award Vanderbilt U., 1976. Fellow: Am. Coll. Cardiology (gov. Wash. chpt. 2002—05); mem.: AHA, Wash. Heart Assn. (trustee 1990—94), North Pacific Soc. Internal Medicine (pres. 2007), Physicians for Social Responsibility, Alpha Omega Alpha. Avocations: downhill skiing, backpacking. Office: Wenatchee Valley Med Ctr 820 N Chelan Ave Wenatchee WA 98801-2028 Home Phone: 509-662-3789; Office Phone: 509-663-8711. Business E-Mail: rprimm@wvclinic.com.

PRIMMER, LILLIAN JUANDA, science educator; d. Melvin Palmer and Amanda Severina (Olstad) Bekkum; m. Donald Gale Primmer, June 17, 1967; children: Donald Guy, Jacqueline Juanda Gruber. BS, U. Wis., 1990, MEd, 1993. Tchr. Clintonville Pub. Schs., Wis., 1990—96; part-time tchr. Christa McAulliffe Acad., Appleton, Wis., 2002, 2004. Part-time tchr. Enstein Acad., Green Bay, Wis., 1991; participant/tchr.-facilitator Sci. World, Drummond, Wis., 1994—99; pres. Wis. Elem. & Middle Level Sci. Tchrs., Wis., 1998—99. Merit badge counselor Boy Scouts/Girl Scouts, Clintonville, Wis., 1990—; hunter safety instr. Dept. Nat. Resources, Clintonville, 1994—; fundraiser, participating survivor Relay for Life, Clintonville, Viroqua. Recipient Disting. Tchr. Sci., Wis. Elem. Sci. Tchrs., 1995; grantee Earthwatch grant, Wis. Acad. Scis., Arts & Letters, 1994. Mem.: NSTA, Wis. Soc. Sci. Tchrs. (co-chair forum com., Outstanding Tchr. Sci. 1996). Avocations: hunting, fishing, camping, volleyball, knitting. Home: 69 Ninth St Clintonville WI 54929

PRIMO, DAVID MARTIN, political science professor; s. Mauro and Elda Primo; m. Neeta Primo. BA in Polit. Sci. and Econs., Brown U., Providence, 1998, MA in Polit. Sci., 1998; MA in Econs., Stanford U., Calif., 2001, PhD in Polit. Sci., 2002. Asst. prof. polit. sci. U. Rochester, NY, 2002—. Author: The Plane Truth: Airline Crashes, the Media, and Transportation Policy, 2003; contbr. articles to profl. jours. Named Undergraduate Prof. of Yr., U. Rochester Students' Assn., 2005; recipient Goergen award for Disting. Artistry in Undergraduate Edn., U. Rochester, 2005. Mem.: Phi Beta Kappa, Omicron Delta Epsilon. Office: Univ Rochester Political Science Dept Harkness Hall 333 Rochester NY 14627-0146 Office Phone: 585-273-4779.

PRIMO, JOAN ERWINA, retail and real estate consulting business owner; b. Detroit, Aug. 28, 1959; d. Joseph Carmen and Marie Ann (Nash) P.; m. David James Yared, Sept. 20, 1997; 1 son, Benjamin Primo Yared. BA, Wellesley Coll., 1981; MBA, Harvard U., 1985. Acct. exec. Michigan Bell, Detroit, 1981—82, AT&T Info. Sys., Southfield, Mich., 1983; planning analyst Gen. Motors, Detroit, 1984; v.p. Howard L. Green & Assocs., Troy, Mich., 1985—89; prin., founder Strategic Edge, Inc., Southfield, 1989—2006. Contbr. articles to profl. jours. Mem.: Internat. Coun. Shopping Ctrs. (faculty, seminar leader 1987—, Mich. state com. officer, rsch. adv. task force), Detroit Country Day Sch.-Lower Sch. Parents Assn. (bd. dirs. 2004—05, v.p. 2005—06, pres. 2006—07), Ivy Club Detroit (bd. dirs. 1994—99, sec. 1995—99), Harvard Bus. Sch. Club Detroit (bd. dirs. 1994—98, v.p. 1995—96, exec. v.p. 1996—97), Wellesley Club Southeastern Mich. (pres. 1994—98). Republican. Avocations: antiques, travel, theater, gourmet cooking. Home: 224 Woodwind Dr Bloomfield Hills MI 48304-2172 Office: The Strategic Edge 24333 Southfield Rd Ste 211 Southfield MI 48075-2849 Office Phone: 248-557-1664. Business E-Mail: jprimo@thestrategicedge.com.

PRIMO, QUINTIN E., III, real estate company executive; BS in Fin. with honors, Ind. U.; MBA, Harvard U. Former mng. dir. Q. Primo & Co., Inc.; CEO, co-founder, co-chmn. Capri Capital L.P., Chgo., 1992—. Chmn. Urban Family and Cmty. Ctrs.; chmn. Com. of 100 Ill. Pub. Policy Caucus. Mem.: Urban Land Inst., Pension Real Estate Assn., Real Estate Roundtable (dir.). Office: Capri Capital LP Ste 3430 875 N Michigan Ave Chicago IL 60611

PRIMOSCH, JAMES THOMAS, music educator, composer, musician; b. Cleve., Oct. 29, 1956; s. Edward Joseph and Rose Marie (Potochar) P.; m. Mary Marguerite Murphy, April 5, 1986. BA in Composition magna cum laude, Cleve. State U., 1978; MA in Composition, U. Pa., Phila., 1980; DMA in Composition awarded with distinction, Columbia U., NYC, 1988; studied piano privately with Lambert Orkis, Phila., 1978-80; studied composition with John Harbison, Tanglewood, 1984. Asst. prof. music U. Pa., 1988—94, assoc. prof. music, 1994—2001, prof. music, 2001—. Grad. assistantships Columbia-Princeton Electronic Music Ctr., 1982-84, 86-87, preceptorship Columbia U., 1984-85; residency Va. Ctr. Creative Arts, 1985, MacDowell Colony, 1988, Bellagio Conf. Ctr., 1992; regional vis. artist Am. Acad. in Rome, 1994; composer in residence Marlboro Music Festival, 1994. Composer more than 60 compositions and 26 published works; compositions performed by Chgo. Symphony Orch., LA Philharm., St. Paul Chamber Orch., Cleve. Chamber Symphony, NY New Music Ensemble; compositions performed at Carnegie Hall, Dorothy Chandler Pavilion, Town Hall, Weill (Carnegie) Recital Hall, others; reviewer High Performance Rev. Mag., 1987-95. Recipient 3rd prize, People's prize Internat. Gaudeamus Competition, The Netherlands, 1977, Helen L. Weiss prize U. Pa., 1979, David Halstead prize U. Penn., 1980, 3rd prize Shreveport Symphony Composer's Competition, 1980-81, John H. Bearns prize, 1981, 1st. prize Holtkamp Organ Composition Contest, 1982, Eda and Boris Rappoport prize Columbia U., 1984, Tanglewood prize in Composition Berkshire Music Ctr., 1984, Cleve. Arts prize, 1992, Elise Stoeger prize Chamber Music Soc. Lincoln Ctr., 1999; recipient Recognition award Mader Meml. Fund, 1980, BMI Student Composers award, 1982; New Music Consort Composition Contest winner, 1987, League of Composers ISCM winner, 1988; Fine Arts scholar Cleve. State U., 1974-78, scholar Cleve. Fortnightly Music Club, 1976-78, Arthur Loesser Meml. scholar, 1977-78, Yale Composer's Workshop at Norfolk, 1981, Columbia U. scholar, 1981-82, Charles Ives scholar Am. Acad. Inst. Arts & Letters, 1985; U. fellow U. Penn., 1978-79, Composers Conf. Johnson Vt., 1979-80, CBS Found. fellow U. Penn., 1979-80, Margaret Lee Crofts fellow Berkshire Music Ctr. Tanglewood, 1984, Guggenheim fellow, 1985, NEA, 1991-92, Goddard Lieberson fellow Am. Acad. Arts and Letters, 1993, Pew fellow in arts, 1996, Independence Found. Arts fellow, 2005; ASCAP Found. Young Composers grant, 1984, 82, Meet The Composer grant 1980, 82, 85, 87, 89-90, 94, 96-97, Am. Music Ctr. Copying Assistance grant, 1985, 90, Pa. Coun. on the Arts, 1990, 98, 02, Presser Found. grantee U. Pa. Mem. BMI, Pi Kappa Lambda. Roman Catholic. Avocation: reading.

PRIMPS, WILLIAM GUTHRIE, lawyer; b. Ossining, NY, Sept. 8, 1949; s. Richard Byrd and Mary Elizabeth (Guthrie) P.; m. Sophia Elizabeth Beutel, Aug. 25, 1973; children: Emily Ann, Elizabeth Armstrong, William Andrew. BA, Yale U., 1971; JD, Harvard U., 1974. Bar: N.Y., 1975. Assoc. LeBoeuf, Lamb, Leiby & MacRae LLP, NYC, 1974-82, ptnr., chmn. recruiting com., 1983—. Counsel to Bd. Zoning Appeals, Bronxville, 1988-89, chmn., 1989-91. Class coun. Yale U., New Haven, 1986-91; trustee Village of Bronxville, 1991-97, dep. mayor, 1995-97; deacon Reformed Ch. Bronxville, 1989-94, elder, 1998-2002; bd. dirs. Bronxville Sch. Fdn. 1998—, v.p., 2003—, Ivy Football Assn., 2003—, mem. adv. coun. Atlantic Legal Found. Inc., 2002-; counsel to ethics bd., Bronxville, 2004—. Mem. ABA, N.Y. State Bar Assn., Assn. Yale Alumni (class rep. 1986-91), Yale Club, Bronxville Field Club. Republican. Office: LeBoeuf Lamb Greene & MacRae 125 W 55th St New York NY 10019-5369 Office Phone: 212-424-8827. Office Fax: 212-424-8500. Business E-Mail: wprimps@llgm.com.

PRINA, L(OUIS) EDGAR, journalist; b. West New York, NJ, Oct. 7, 1917; s. Louis Edgar and Marion (Duggan) P.; m. Frances Lee Lorick, Feb. 14, 1947; 1 dau., Lee Lorick II. AB, Syracuse U., 1938, MA, 1940. Reporter Adirondack Daily Enterprise, 1938; telegraph editor Hornell Evening Tribune, NY, 1940—41; copy editor, asst. night city editor N.Y. Sun, NYC, 1946-48, Washington corr., 1948-50; nat. affairs writer Washington Star, 1950-66; mil. affairs writer/editor Copley News Svc., Washington, 1966-77, bur. chief, 1977-84, sr. corr., 1984-87; editor Navy mag., Washington, 1961-68; columnist Sea Power mag., 1968—. Author: The Political Virgin, 1958, Flew to South Pole for Overnight Visit, 1966. Served with USN, 1941-46, 51-53; capt. Res. (ret.). Recipient honorable mentionHeywood Broun award, 1956, Disting. Public Svc. award USN, 1965, Alfred Thayer Mahan award Navy League U.S., 1987, Copley Ring of Truth award, 1971, 74-76, 79, 80-81, Chancellor's Sr. Alumni award Syracuse U., 1998; nominated for Pulitzer Prize (twice). Mem. U.S. Naval Inst., Nat. Press Club (chmn. bd. govs.), White House Corrs. Assn., Explorers Club, Soc. Profl. Journalists (pres. Washington chpt., named to Hall of Fame 1999), Kappa Sigma, Phi Kappa Phi. Clubs: Gridiron, Chevy Chase, Met. of Washington. Roman Catholic. Home: 4813 Quebec St NW Washington DC 20016-3228 Office: The Metro Club Box 47 1700 H St NW Washington DC 20006-4689

PRINCE, ANDREW STEVEN, lawyer, retired government agency administrator; b. Bklyn., Oct. 9, 1943; s. Milton S. and Beatrice M. (Ratkin) P.; m. Rochelle Moskowitz, July 4, 1973; children: Brett, Kenneth. BS, U.S. Naval Acad., 1965; MBA, JD, Harvard U., 1974. Bar: N.Y. 1975, U.S. Supreme Ct. 1980. Assoc. firm Shearman & Sterling, NYC, 1974-81; dep. asst. sec. Navy Dept., Washington, 1981-86; exec. v.p., gen. counsel Urquhart and Co., Inc., McLean, Va., 1986-94; mng. dir. Nat. Capital Cos. LLC, Bethesda, Md., 1997-2000; mng. dir., COO HFS Capital LLC, McLean, Va., 2000—02; CEO, pres. Bretken Enterprises, 2002—03, Prince Strategic Group LC, McLean, Va., 2003—. Sec. Potash Import & Chem. Corp., N.Y.C., 1979-81; mem. panel of arbitrators Am. Arbitration Assn., N.Y.C., 1979- Bd. dirs. Harvard Coop. Soc., Cambridge, Mass., 1972-74; bd. dirs. USO, Washington, 1982-86, N.Y.C., 1979-81. Served with USN, 1965-70; capt. Res., ret Mem. Harvard Bus. Sch. Club, Washington, DC (bd. dir., pres.), Mil Order World Wars (judge adv.), Naval Acad. Alumni Assn., Naval Acad. Found. (dir.). Personal E-mail: aprince65@hotmail.com. Business E-Mail: aprince@princestrategic.com.

PRINCE, ANNA LOU, composer, music publisher, construction executive; b. Isabella, Tenn., May 28, 1935; d. Ulysses Gordon and Della Carrie (Hawkins) Prince; children: Sandra, Teresa, Vandi. Diploma, Carolina Sch. Broadcasting, 1966; Zion diploma, Israel Bible Sch., Jerusalem, 1970; diploma, S.W. Tech. Coll., 1970; student, United Christian Assn., 1976; MusD, London Inst. Applied Rsch., 1991; diplomatic diploma, Acad. Argentina de Diplomacia, 1993; PhD (hon.), Australian Inst. Coord. Rsch., Victoria, 1993; diploma of honors on internat. affairs, Inst. Des Affaires Internat., Paris, 1994. Lic. Bible tchr. United Christian Acad. Songwriter Hank Locklin Music Co., Nashville, 1963-70; entertainer 1982 World's Fair, Knoxville, Tenn., 1982; ptnr., owner Prince Wholesale Bait Co., Canton, NC, 1976-82, Grad Builders, Canton, 1982-86, Prince TV Co., Canton, 1986—. Music pub. Broadcast Music, Inc., Nashville, 1982—; mem. prodn. staff, talent coord. (TV series) Down Home, Down Under, 1989-90; host TV show Real Heros of Country Music in Nashville, 1997-2003. Songs recorded on RCA: I Feel a Cry Coming On, 1965 (#1 in Eng.), Best Part of Loving You, (#1 in Eng.), Anna, 1969 (Billboard 1970, recorded in Ireland 1974, hit in Europe and New Zealand); singer, composer I'm In Love With You, 1995; over 20 songs recorded to date; appeared Grand Ole Opry, 1970; exec. prodr., host TV talk show, Real Hereos of Country Music, 1989— (Emmy nomination 1997); author: The Strange Life of Anna Prince, 2006. Candidate for county commr. Dem. Party Macon County, NC, 1984; bd. dirs. Macon County Taxpayers Assn., Inc., 1984, v.p., 1984-86; bd. dirs. Head Start, Topton, NC, 1969-73; judge Emmy Awards, Am. Registrar Ohio Valley, 2002— Nominated Disting. Women NC, NC Coun. Coun. on Status of Women, 1984, Jefferson award WYFF TV and Am. Inst. for Pub. Svc., Outstanding Bus. Woman Small Bus. Adminstrn., 1984. Mem. BMI, Internat. Parliament Safety and Peace (life, dept. fgn. affairs, dep. mem. assembly), Nashville Songwriters Assn. Internat. (moderator, tchr. 1984-86), Country Music Assn., Reunion Profl. Entertainers, Fraternal Order Police, C. of C., Order of Knight of Templars (dame) Lofsensic Order (dame), Maison Internat. des Intellectuals. Democrat. Personal E-mail: docaprince@aol.com.

PRINCE, BART, architect; b. Albuquerque, June 24, 1947; BArch, Ariz. State U., Tempe. With Bruce Goff, 1970—72, George Wynn, Albuquerque, 1972—73; vis. instr. Sch. Architecture and Planning U. N.Mex., Albuquerque, 1980—81; prin. Bart Prince, Arch., Albuquerque. Vis. prof., Bruce Goff chair U. Okla. Sch. Architecture, Norman, 1992. Exhibitions include XIIe Biennale de Paris, 1982, Kans. State U. Sch. Architecture, 1982, Drawings by Ten N.Mex. Archs., U. N.Mex. Art Mus., Albuquerque, 1982, Bart Prince, Farish Gallery, Rice U., Houston, 1993, prin. works include Brad and June Prince Residence (Record House of Yr. award, 1989), Joe and Etsuko Price Residence (Record House of Yr. award, 1991). Office: 3501 Monte Vista NE Albuquerque NM 87106 Office Phone: 505-256-1961. Office Fax: 505-268-9045. E-mail: architect@bartprince.com. *

PRINCE, CHARLES O., III, (CHUCK PRINCE), diversified financial services company executive; b. Lynwood, Calif., Jan. 13, 1950; s. Charles Prince Jr.; m. Margaret L. Wolff, Sept. 20, 2003. BA, U. So. Calif., 1971, MA, JD, 1975; LLM, Georgetown U., 1983. Bar: Pa. 1975, Md. 1979, Minn. 1982. Atty. U.S. Steel Corp., 1975—79; gen. counsel Commercial Credit Co., 1979—86; exec. v.p., gen. counsel, sec. Traveler's Group, NYC, 1986-98; co-gen. counsel, sec. Citigroup (merger of Traveler's Group and Citibank), NYC, 1998—2000; chief admin. officer Citigroup, Inc., NYC, 2000, COO, 2001—02, CEO, 2003—, chmn., 2006—, chmn. & CEO, Global Corp. & Investment Bank Group, 2002—03. Mem. Coun. Fgn. Rels.; bd. dirs. Johnson & Johnson, New Brunswick, NJ, 2006—. Bd. dirs. United Negro Coll. Fund; trustee Columbia U., Juilliard Sch.; bd. mem. Joan & Sanford I. Weill Med. Coll., Cornell U. Office: Citigroup Inc 399 Park Ave New York NY 10022 also: Citigroup 153 E 53rd St New York NY 10043-0001 *

PRINCE, DANFORTH, publishing executive, journalist; b. Toledo, June 14, 1953; s. Edward Mitchell Prince and Elizabeth Jane Danforth. BA, Hamilton Coll., Clinton, NY, 1975. V.p., treas. Porter & Prince Corp., NYC, 1983—; pres., CEO, publ. Blood Moon Prodns. Ltd., NYC, 1997—; pres., CEO Ga. Lit. Assn., NYC, 1997—. Co-author, dir. rsch.: Europe & Caribbean Series of The Frommer Guides, 1983—; co-author: Blood Moon's Guide to Film, 2006. Mem.: North Am. Travel Journalists Assn. Office: Blood Moon Prodns Ltd 75 Saint Marks Pl Staten Island NY 10301 Office Phone: 718-556-9410. Office Fax: 718-816-4092. Personal E-mail: danforthprince@hotmail.com.

PRINCE, DAVID CANNON, lawyer; b. Hawkinsville, Ga., July 4, 1950; s. Carl Willis and Carobel (Cannon) Prince; m. Mary MacIntyre, June 30, 1973. BA in Econs., Clemson U., 1972; JD, St. John's U., Jamaica, NY, 1980. Bar: NY 1981, Ga. 1982, US Dist. Ct. (no. dist.) Ga. 1982. Atty. enforcement SEC, Atlanta, 1981-86; regional counsel Shearson Lehman Bros. Inc., Atlanta, 1986-92; gen. counsel Robinson-Humphrey Co., Inc., Atlanta, 1992—2001; chief legal officer SunTrust Capital Markets, Inc., 2001—06; gen. counsel Stephans Investment Mgmt. Group, LLC, Little Rock, 2006—. Capt. USAF, 1972—78. Mem.: ABA (co-chairperson young lawyers divsn. 1986—88). Democrat. Avocations: sailing, running. Office: Stephens Inc 111 Ctr St 23rd Fl Little Rock AR 72201 Office Phone: 501-377-2151.

PRINCE, GEORGE EDWARD, retired pediatrician; b. Erwin, NC, Nov. 25, 1921; s. Hugh Williamson and Helen Herman (Hood) P.; m. Millie Elizabeth Mann, Nov. 26, 1944; children: Helen Elizabeth, Millie Mann, Susan Hood, Mary Lois. MD, Duke U., 1944. Diplomate Am. Bd. Pediatrics, Am. Bd. Med. Examiners. Intern Boston Children's Hosp. Harvard Svc., Boston, 1944-45; resident pediatrics Children's Hosp., Louisville, 1945-47; instr. pediatrics U. Louisville, 1947; founder Gastonia (N.C.) Children's Clinic, 1947, pediatrician, 1947-86; pub. health physician Gaston County Health Dept., Gastonia, N.C., 1986-98, med. dir., 1995-98, ret., 1998. Chmn. bd. dirs. Carolina State Bank; bd. dirs. So. Nat. Bank, Gastonia, 1979-95, Hospice, Gastonia, 1987-92; organizer, dir. AIDS Adv. Coun., Gaston County, N.C., 1988-94; coord. N.C. chpt. Pediatric Rsch. in Office Setting, 1986-92. Contbr. articles to profl. jours. Mem. Gaston County Human Rels. Com., Gastonia, 1966; mem. Sch. Health Adv. Coun., Gaston County, 1980-97. Maj. USAF, 1955-57. Recipient Balthis Heart Assn. award, Gaston County, 1981, 1998, Good Amb. award, Health Dept., 1986, Family Adv. award, Commn. on the Family, Gaston County, 1995, commendation, City of Gastonia, 2001, Gaston County Bd. Commrs., 2001. Fellow Am. Acad. Pediatrics (pres. N.C. chpt. 1984-86); mem. AMA, N.C. Pediatric Soc. (hon., pres. 1970), N.C. Med. Soc., Gaston County Med. Soc. (pres. 1966), Rotary (pres. 1984), County Club (bd. dirs. 1975-76). Democrat. Methodist. Avocations: golf, skiing, sailing, bridge.

PRINCE, GREGORY SMITH, JR., retired college president; b. Washington, May 7, 1939; s. Gregory Smith and Margaret (Minor) P.; m. Toni Layton Brewer; children: Tara Wyndom, Gregory S. III. BA, Yale U., 1961, M in Philosophy, 1969, PhD, 1973; cert. in teaching English as a Second Language, Georgetown U., 1961; DHL (hon.), LLD (hon.), Amherst Coll., 1991. Instr. New Asia Coll., Kowloon, Hong Kong, 1961-62, Chinese U., Kowloon, 1962-63, Yale China Assn., Kowloon, 1961-63, Woodberry Forest (Va.) Sch., 1963-65; dean summer programs Dartmouth Coll., Hanover, NH, 1970-72, asst. dean faculty, 1972-78, assoc. dean faculty, 1978-89; pres. Hampshire Coll., Amherst, Mass., 1989—2005; sr. cons. Pathways to Coll., 2005—. Vice chair coun. on racial and ethnic justice ABA; bd. dirs. Mass Ventures. Producer: (film) A Way of Learning, 1988. Trustee Montshire Mus. Sci., Hanover, 1973-89, Washington Campus, 1978—; trustee, chmn. Univ. Press New England, Hanover, 1983-84; trustee, pres. Yale-China Assn., New Haven, 1969-84; bd. dirs. Five Colls., Inc., Amherst, 1989-2005; bd. dirs. Mass. Internat. Festival for Arts, 1994-98; chmn. bd. dirs. Assn. Ind. Colls. and Univs. Mass., 1994-95; chair commn. on accreditation Am. Coun. Edn.; bd. dirs. Mass. Nature Conservancy, 1996—; bd. dirs. Nat. Assn. Ind. Colls. and Univs., 1999-2001, Friendship House, 2002—. Coe fellow Stanford U., 1965, Woodrow Wilson fellow Yale U., 1966, NDEA fellow, 1967-70. Mem. Internat. Assn. of Chiefs Police Found. (bd. dirs. 1991-95), Nat. Assn. of Ind. Colls. and Univs. Democrat. Episcopalian. Office: Hampshire Coll 893 West St Amherst MA 01002-3372 Home: 24 Academy Rd Norwich VT 05055-9480

PRINCE, HAROLD, theatrical director, producer; b. NYC, Jan. 30, 1928; s. Milton A. and Blanche (Stern) P.; m. Judith Chaplin, Oct. 26, 1962; children: Charles, Daisy. AB, U. Pa., 1948, DFA (hon.), 1971; LittD, Emerson Coll., 1971. Chmn. Performing Arts Libr., NYC; participant, Voices of the Arts Kennedy Ctr. for Performing Arts, Washington, 2005. Co-prodr.: Pajama Game, 1954-56 (Antoinette Perry award), Damn Yankees, 1955-57 (Antoinette Perry award), New Girl in Town, 1957-58, West Side Story, 1957-59, A Swim in the Sea, 1958, Fiorello, 1959-61 (Antoinette Perry award, Pulitzer prize), Tenderloin, 1960-61, A Call on Kuprin, 1961, They Might Be Giants, London, 1961, Side by Side by Sondheim, 1977; prodr.: Take Her, She's Mine, 1961-62, A Funny Thing Happened on the Way to the Forum, 1962-64 (Antoinette Perry award), Fiddler on the Roof, 1964-72 (Antoinette Perry award), Poor Bitos, 1964, Flora the Red Menace, 1965; dir., prodr.: She Loves Me, 1963-64, London, 1964, Superman, 1966, Cabaret, 1966-69 (Antoinette Perry award 1968), Zorba, 1968-69, Company, 1970-72 (Antoinette Perry award 1972), A Little Night Music, 1973-74 (Antoinette Perry award 1975), Pacific Overtures, 1976, A Doll's Life, 1982; co-dir., prodr.: Follies, 1971-72 (Tony award for directing), Faust, 1990; co-prodr., dir.: Candide, 1974-75 (Tony award for directing), Merrily We Roll Along, 1981; dir.: A Family Affair, 1962, Baker Street, 1965, Great God Brown, 1972-73, The Visit, 1973-74, Love for Love, 1974-75, Ashmedai, 1976, Some of My Best Friends, 1977, On The Twentieth Century, 1978, La Fanciulla Del West, 1978, Evita, London, 1979, N.Y.C., 1980, L.A., 1982, Australia, 1980, Chgo., 1980, Detroit, 1982, Sweeney Todd, The Demon Barber of Fleet Street, Broadway, 1979, London, 1980, Silverlake, 1980, Willie Stark, 1981, Candide, 1982, 94, 97, Madama Butterfly, 1983, Turandot, 1983, Play Memory, 1984, End of the World, 1984, Grind, 1985, Cabaret Revival, 1987, Roza, 1987, Phantom of the Opera, London, 1986, N.Y.C., (Antoinette Perry award) 1988, Kiss of the Spider Woman, Toronto, 1992, London, 1992, N.Y.C., 1993, Show Boat, Toronto, 1993, N.Y.C., 1994 (Tony award for directing), La Fanciula del West, Don Giovanni, N.Y. City Opera, 1989, Faust, Met. Opera, 1990, The Petrified Prince, 1994, (off broadway) Diamonds, 1984; adapter, dir. (off broadway) Grandchild of Kings, 1992, Candide, Broadway, 1997, Parade, Broadway, 1998, Hollywood Arms, Broadway, 2002, Bounce, Chgo., Wash., 2003, The Phantom of the Opera, 2004, Fiddler on the Roof, 2004; co-prodr: (films) The Pajama Game, 1957, Damn Yankees, 1958; dir.: (films) Something for Everyone, 1970, A Little Night Music, 1978, 3Hree, Phila. & L.A. Mem. coun. Nat. Endowment Arts; pres. League N.Y. Theatres, 1964-66; chmn. Performing Arts Libr., N.Y.C. Recipient 20 Antoinette Perry (Tony) Meml. awards, Critics Circle awards, Pulitzer prize, 1961, Best Mus. awards London Evening Std., Kennedy Ctr. Honors, 1994, Spl. Tony award lifetime achievement in theatre, 2006. Office: Harold Prince 10 Rockefeller Plz Ste 1104 New York NY 10020-1903

PRINCE, KENNETH STEPHEN, lawyer; b. Newton, Mass., Jan. 28, 1950; s. Samuel and Edna L. Prince; m. Patricia Denning, Jan. 15, 1977 (dec. Nov. 1985); 1 child, Kenneth Stephen Jr.; m. Jane M. McCabe, Sept. 5, 1987; 1 child, Allison Pamela. BA, U. Pa., 1972; JD, Boston Coll., 1975. Bar: N.Y. 1976, Mass. 1975, U.S. Dist. Ct. (so. and ea. dists.) N.Y. 1978. Assoc. Shearman & Sterling, NYC, 1975-83, ptnr., 1984—, antitrust group practice leader, 1992—2003, 2005—. Mem. N.Y. Law Inst. (exec. com. 1984-96), Order of Coif. Home: 15 Dellwood Rd Darien CT 06820-2915 Office Phone: 212-848-4139. Business E-Mail: kprince@shearman.com.

PRINCE, LEAH FANCHON, lab administrator, executive secretary; b. Hartford, Conn., Aug. 12, 1939; d. Meyer and Annie (Forman) Berman; m. Herbert N. Prince, Jan. 30, 1955; children: Daniel L., Richard N., Robert G. Student, U. Conn., 1957—59, Rutgers U., 1962; BFA, Fairleigh Dickinson U., 1970; postgrad., Caldwell Coll. for Women, 1973—75, Parsons Sch. of Design, NYC, 1978. Cert. tchr. art, N.J. Tchr. art Caldwell-West Caldwell Pub. Schs., NJ, 1970—75; pres. Britannia Imports Ltd., Fairfield, NJ, 1979—89; tchr. religious studies Bohrer-Kaufman Hebrew Acad., Randolph, NJ, 1981—82; co-founder, corp. sec. Gibraltar Biol. Labs., Inc., Fairfield, 1970—; dir., co-founder Gibraltar Inst. for Rsch. and Tng., Fairfield, 1984—. Cons. Internat. Antiques and Fine Arts Industries, U.K., 1979-89; cons. in art exhibitry Passaic County Coll., Paterson, N.J., 1989-93; art curator Fairleigh Dickinson U., Rutherford, N.J., 1972-74; curator history of nursing 20th century Bloomfield (N.J.) Coll., 1990-91; lectr. Am. Soc. Microbiology, New Orleans, 1989; spkr. in field. Exhibited in group shows at Bloomfield Coll., NJ, 1990, Caldwell Women's Club, NJ, 1991, State Fedn. Women's Clubs Ann. Show, 1992 (1st pl. award 1992), Newark Art Mus., 1992, West Essex Art Assn., NJ, 1990, Somerset Art Assn., NJ, 1994, Mortimer Gallery, Gladstone, NJ, 1994 (1st pl. award 1998), Tewksbury Hist. Soc., 1994, 98, 2004 (1st pl. award 1994, 98, 2004), Tewksbury Hist. Soc., 2001-02, 04-06, (Juried Art award 2001-02, 04-06), Nat. Meeting Am. Pen Women, Calif., 2002, Washington, 2004 (1st pl. award); one-woman shows include Passaic County Coll., NJ, 1990, Caldwell Coll., 1990; author children's stories. Chair ann. juried art awards Arts Coun. of Essex Bd. Trustees, Montclair, N.J., 1984-90; chair fundraising Arts Coun. Essex County, N.J., 1989. Mem. AAUW, Soc. Childrens Book Writers and Illustrators, Somerset Art Assn., Nat. League Am. Pen Women (pres. N.J. br., Juried Art award 2001, 2004), Barnegat Light Yacht Club. Republican. Avocations: boating, tennis, opera, painting, travel. Home: 5 Standish Dr Mendham Twp Morristown NJ 07960-3224 Personal E-mail: herb/leah@aol.com.

PRINCE, M. DAVID (MORRIS DAVID PRINCE), retired electronics research and technical manager, computer graphics pioneer; b. Greensboro, N.C., Mar. 27, 1926; m. Fay Wright, June 8, 1947; children: Stephen, Nicholas, Timothy, Rebecca. BEE, Ga. Inst. Tech., 1946, MSEE, 1949. Project mgr. Ga. Tech. Engring. Expt. Sta., Atlanta, 1952-57; sr. tech. staff ITT Labs., Atlanta, 1957-59; rsch. lab. dir., sr. staff specialist Lockheed-Ga. Co., Marietta, 1959-90; ret. 1990. Prof. Ga. Inst. Tech., 1980-90, adj. prof., 1990—; cons. Sys. Cons. Assocs., Atlanta, 1970-; chmn. Electronics Automation Program, Computer-Aided Mfg. Internat., 1982-83; adj. prof. Ga. Tech. Coll. Computing, 1995—. Author: Interactive Graphics for Computer-Aided Design, 1971 (pioneer text CAD, translated to Japanese, Russian and Chinese langs.); contbr. articles to profl. jours.; patentee computers and electronics; invited worldwide speaker; co-inventor velocity modulation TV for enhancing picture detail utilized by manufacturers in an estimated 100 million TV sets. Advanced through grades to lt. USNR, 1944-48. Recipient NASA Group Achievement award, 1984. Named

Engr.-Scientist of Yr., Lockheed-Ga. Co., 1981; named to Ga. Inst. Tech. Engring. Hall of Fame, 2004. Fellow IEEE (life). Avocations: piano, astronomy, book collecting. Home and Office: 3747 Peachtree Rd NE Apt 401 Lenbrook Atlanta GA 30319 Office Phone: 404-262-4557. Personal E-mail: mdprince@mindspring.com.

PRINCE, THOMAS E., bank executive; b. 1947; With Security Pacific Corp., LA, 1968-92, sr. v.p., controller, 1984—92; exec. v.p., treas. Downey Savs Loan Assn., Newport Beach, Calif., 1992—2004, CFO, 1992—, COO, 2004—. Office: Downey Savs Loan Assn 3501 Jamboree Rd Ste 5000 Newport Beach CA 92660-2980 Mailing: Downey Savings Loan Assn PO Box 6000 Newport Beach CA 92658-6000 Office Phone: 949-509-4440. Office Fax: 949-854-8162.

PRINCE, THOMAS RICHARD, accountant, educator; b. New Albany, Miss., Dec. 7, 1934; s. James Thompson and Callie Florence (Howell) P.; m. Eleanor Carol Polkoff, July 14, 1962; children: Thomas Andrew, John Michael, Adrienne Carol. BS, Miss. State U., 1956, MS, 1957; PhD in Accountancy, U. Ill., 1962. CPA, Ill. Instr. U. Ill., 1960—62; mem. faculty Northwestern U. Kellogg Sch. Mgmt., Evanston, Ill., 1962—, prof. acctg. info. and mgmt., 1969—, chmn. dept. acctg. info. and mgmt., 1968—75, prof. health industry mgmt., 1990—; cons. in field. Dir. Applied Rsch. Sys., Inc. Author: Extension of the Boundaries of Accounting Theory, 1962, Information Systems for Management Planning and Control, 3d edit, 1975, Financial Reporting and Cost Control for Health Care Entities, 1992, Product Life-Cycle Costing and Management of Large-Scale Medical Systems Investments, 1997, Strategic Management for Health Care Entities: Creative Frameworks for Financial and Operational Analysis, 1998. Served to 1st lt. AUS, 1957-60. Mem. AICPA, INFORMS, AHA, HFMA, HIMMS, AUPHA, Am. Accounting Assn., Am. Econ. Assn., Fin. Execs. Inst., AAAS, Ill. Soc. CPA, Inst. Mgmt. Acct., Alpha Tau Omega, Phi Kappa Phi, Omicron Delta Kappa, Delta Sigma Pi, Beta Alpha Psi. Congregationalist. Home: 303 Richmond Rd Kenilworth IL 60043-1138 Office: Northwestern U Leverone Hl Evanston IL 60208-2002 Office Phone: 847-491-2669. Business E-Mail: t-prince@kellogg.northwestern.edu.

PRINCE, WILLIAM B., lawyer; b. Albuquerque, Feb. 7, 1949; BS cum laude, Brigham Young U., 1973; JD, U. Utah, 1978. Bar: Utah 1978. Ptnr. Holme Roberts & Owen, Salt Lake City; ptnr.-in-charge, co-chmn., environ., natural resources, energy practice Dorsey & Whitney LLP, Salt Lake City, 1996—. Mem. Office of Exception and Appeals Fed. Energy Adminstrn., 1974-75. Co-author: Utah Environmental and Land Use Permits Manual, 1981; assoc. editor Jour. Contemporary Law U. Utah, 1977-78. Mem. ABA (natural resources, energy and environ. law sect., chmn. hard minerals com. 1991—), Utah State Bar (past chmn. energy, natural resources and environ. law 1986-87), Northwest Mining Assn., Air and Waste Mgmt. Assn. (Rocky Mountain sect., treas. Great Basin chpt. 1991—). Office: Dorsey & Whitney LLP Ste 925 Wells Fargo Plz 170 S Main St Salt Lake City UT 84101-1655 Office Phone: 801-933-7370. Office Fax: 801-933-7373. Business E-Mail: prince.william@dorsey.com.

PRINCE, (PRINCE ROGERS NELSON), musician, actor; b. Mpls., June 7, 1958; s. John L. and Mattie D. (Shaw) Nelson; m. Mayte Garcia, 1996 (div., 2000); 1 son (dec.); m. Manuela Testolini, Dec. 31, 2001 (separated, 2006) Singer, songwriter, actor. Albums include For You, 1978, Dirty Mind, 1979, Controversy, 1981, 1999, 1983, film star and soundtrack Purple Rain, 1984 (Academy Award for best original score, 1984), Around the World in a Day, 1985 (Best Soul/Rhythm and Blues Album of the Yr., Downbeat readers poll, 1985), Parade, 1986, Chaos and Disorder, 1996, Sign O' the Times, 1987, Lovesexy, 1988, Batman: Motion Picture Soundtrack, 1989 (Soundtrack of Yr. award Playboy mag. readers' poll, Best Pop/Rock album Downbeat mag. readers' poll), (with the New Power Generation) Diamonds and Pearls, 1991, (symbol as title), 1992, Come, 1995, The Greatest Romance Ever Sold, 1999, 94 East, 2000, The Very Best of Prince, 2001, Beautiful Experience, 2001, The Rainbow Children, 2001, One Night Alone...Live!, 2002, N.E.W.S., 2003, Musicology, 2004, 3121, 2006, Planet Earth, 2007; films include Purple Rain, 1984, film star and soundtrack Under the Cherry Moon, 1986, film star and soundtrack Sign O' the Times, 1987; film appearance and soundtrack Graffiti Bridge, 1990 (ASCAP award for most performed songs from a motion picture, 1991); formerly mem. group Prince and the Revolution (Best Soul/Rhythm and Blues Group of Yr. Downbeat mag. readers poll 1985); composer Showgirls, 1995, Girl 6, 1996, The Gold Experience, 1995, Crystal Ball, 1998, Rave Un2 the Joy Fantastic, 1999, Bamboozled, 2000, Happy Feet, 2006 (The Sonf of the Heart, Best Original Song-Motion Picture, Golden Globe award, Hollywood Fgn. Press Assn., 2007). Recipient 3 Grammy awards, 1985, Am. Music Achievement award for infuence on look and sound of the 80's, NAACP Spl. Achievement award, 1997, Webby Lifetime Achievement award, Internat. Acad. Digital Arts and Sciences, 2006, Best Male R&B award, Black Entertainment TV (BET), 2006, Male Artist award, NAACP Image Awards, 2007; named Rhythm and Blues Musician of Yr. Down Beat mag. readers' poll, 1984, 1992; inducted Rock and Roll Hall of Fame, 2004. Office: Paisley Park Studios 7801 Audubon Rd Chanhassen MN 55317-8201

PRINCE CRYSTAL, CHRISTINA, minister, media specialist; b. Cheavy Conty, Tenn., July 31, 1957; d. Walter Lee and Rosie L. (Lemon) Webb; m. Jeffrey Small; 1 child, Jeffrey Gerell Small; m. Ronald E. Prince. AA, Christ is the Answer U., Fla., 1995, MDiv, 1997, ThD, LHD, Christ is the Answer U., Fla., 1999. Drug abuse counselor One Nation, LA, 1994; film prodr. P.A.T., Inc., Long Beach, Calif., 1997-00; radio broadcaster KTYM, Inglewood, Calif., 1997; TV co-host TVM Global Entertainment, Las Vegas, 1997; min. Christ is the Answer, Long Beach, 1998. Composer songs, author booklets. Chmn. Sea for Mothers, Van Nuys, Calif., 1997; human resources dir., Deliverance Crusade, Long Beach, 1998; family counselor, child abuse, One Nation, Hollywood, Calif., 1999; v.p. Working for the Needy, J.W. Bradley Assocs., 1991 (Best Youth Leader award 1999); dir. G.L.A.D. Team, Go Love and Do, Inc., 1989-99; dir. Indian Actors Workshop, Indian Rights Workshop, 1999 (Humanity award 2000). Recipient Best D.J. award, Casting Call, Inc., Hollywood, 1983, Inner City Hunger Relief achievement award, Cityfolks, Inc., L.A., 1994, Black Female Designers awrd, REGI Mag., Chgo., 1997. Mem. NAACP, Working Women Inc. Home: PO Box 6400 Long Beach CA 90806-0191

PRINCE-RAMUS, JOSHUA, architect; BA in Philosophy, Yale U., 1991; MArch, Harvard U., 1996. With Office Met. Architecture, 1996—2006; ptnr., founder Office Met. Architecture NYC, 2001—06; founder Ramus Ella Architects, 2006—. Partner-in-charge Mus. Plaza, Louisville, Dee and Charles Wyly Theater, Dallas, Annenberg Ctr. Info. Sci. and Tech., Pasadena, Calif. Office: Ramus Ella Architects PC 160 Varick St 10th Fl New York NY 10013 Office Phone: 646-230-6557, 646-230-6558. E-mail: jramus@rex-ny.com.

PRINCETON, JOY CAROL, retired nursing educator; b. St. Paul, Dec. 8, 1935; d. Eugene Russell Princeton and Margaret Edna Ehlers Princeton; children: Todd A. Myers, Michael D. Myers, Sarah C. Mooney. BSN, U. Colo., 1969, MSN, 1970, MA in Anthropology, 1975, PhD in Anthropology, 1977. RN Minn., Colo., N.C., Utah. Head nurse, obstetrics Abbott Hosp., Mpls., 1958—65; supr. obstetrics Boulder Meml. Hosp., Colo., 1965—68; asst. prof. U. Co. Sch. Nursing, Denver, 1970—73; assoc. prof. Duke U. Sch. Nursing, Durham, NC, 1978—81; prof. U. Utah Coll. Nursing, Salt Lake City, 1982—95; assoc. dir. U. Hosp., Salt Lake City, 1987—91. Mem. White House Com. on Children & Youth, Colo. Chpt., Denver, 1970—73; expert panel mem. Am. Acad. Nursing, Culturally Competent and Sensitive Health Care, Washington, 1991—93; cons. U. N.C. Med. Sch., Chapel Hill, NC, 1984—85, U. Rochester Sch. of Nursing, NY, 1988, NIH, Nat. Ctr. Nursing Rsch., 1988, U. Capetown Sch. Medicine, South Africa, 1990—91, HHS, PHS Divsn. Nursing, Rockville, Md., 1987—88, 1990—91, St. Louis U. Med. Ctr., 1990—91, Regis Coll. Sch. of Nursing, Denver, 1990—91; adv. Utah State Dept. Health, Salt Lake City, 1991—92; cons. in field, grad. student mentor, 1995—. Author: Maternity Nursing Today, 1973—77 (Am. Nurses Assn. Book of Yr., Parent/Child Nursing, 1973); mem. editl. bd.: Health Care for Women, 1984—94, Medical Anthro Quar., 1984—88, 1993—94, Scholarly Inquiry for Nursing Practice, 1985—90, Jour. Profl. Nursing, 1985—91, 1994—97, Jour. Nursing Edn., 1991—94, Nursing Outlook Jour., 1993—94; contbr. articles to profl. jours.; review panel mem. profl. jours., 1995—2006. Named Nurse of Yr., NC Nurses Assn., 1980; grantee, Dept. Health and Human Svcs., 1982—95; Edn1. grants, Dept. Health, Edn. and Welfare, U. Colo. Programs, 1970—73, grants for master's and doctoral edn., U.S. Pub. Health Svc., 1982—95. Fellow: Soc. Applied Anthropology, Am. Acad. Nursing. Democrat. Avocations: library work, hiking, camping, travel. Home: 2720 14th St Boulder CO 80304 Office Phone: 303-444-8163.

PRINCIPI, ANTHONY JOSEPH, pharmaceutical company executive, former secretary of veterans affairs; b. NYC, Apr. 16, 1944; s. Antonio Joseph and Theresa (Princiotta) P.; m. Elizabeth Ann Ahlering, June 26, 1971; children: Anthony, Ryan, John BS, U.S. Naval Acad., 1967; JD, Seton Hall U., 1975. Commd. 2d lt. U.S. Navy, 1967, advanced through grades to comdr., 1984, line officer Washington, 1967-72; atty. JAGC, San Diego, 1975-80; counsel Com. on Armed Service U.S. Senate, Washington, 1980-83, staff dir. Com. on Vet.'s Affairs, 1984—88; dep. adminstr. congl. & pub. affairs VA, Washington, 1983-84; dep. sec. US Dept. Veterans Affairs, Washington, 1989-90, acting sec., 1992—93, sec., 2001—05; ptnr. Luce, Forward, Hamilton & Scripps, San Diego, 1990-95; sr. v.p., CEO Lockheed Martin IMS Integrated Solutions Co., Santa Clara, Calif., 1995-2001; pres. QTC Medical Services, 2001; v.p. govt. rels. Pfizer Inc., Washington, 2005—. Chmn. Base Realignment & Closure (BRAC) Commn., 2005. Decorated Bronze Star with combat "V", Vietnamese Cross of Gallantry, Navy Commendation medal with combat "V" (3); recipient Meritorious Service medal VA, 1983 Mem. ABA (chmn. subcom. gen. practice sect. 1985—) Republican. Roman Catholic. Avocations: gardening, skiing. Office: Pfizer Inc 325 Seveth St NW Ste 120 Washington DC 20004

PRINDLE, WILLIAM ROSCOE, retired glass company executive; b. San Francisco, Dec. 19, 1926; s. Vivian Arthur and Harriette Alnora (Nickerson) P.; m. June Laverne Anderson, June 20, 1947; children—Carol Susan, William Alastair. BS, U. Calif., Berkeley, 1948, MS, 1950; Sc.D., M.I.T., 1955. Asst. tech. dir. Hazel-Atlas Glass Co., 1954-56; mgr. research Hazel-Atlas Glass div. Continental Can Co., Wheeling, W.Va., 1956-58, gen. mgr. research and devel., 1959-62; mgr. materials research Am. Optical Co., Southbridge, Mass., 1962-65; v.p. research Southbridge and Framingham, Mass., 1971-76; dir; research Ferro Corp., Cleve., 1966-67, v.p. research, 1967-71; exec. dir. Nat. Materials Adv. Bd., NRC-NAS, Washington, 1976-80; dir. adminstrv. and tech. svcs. R & D div. Corning Glass Works, NY, 1980-85, dir. materials rsch. 1985-87; assoc. dir. R & D, Engring. div. Corning Glass Works (now Corning, Inc.), NY, 1987-90; div. v.p., assoc. dir. tech. group Corning Inc., NY, 1990-92; ret. Pres. XII Internat. Glass Congress, 1980, Internat. Commn. on Glass, 1985-88. Served with U.S. Navy, 1944-46. Named Disting. Ceramist of New Eng., New Eng. sect. Am. Ceramic Soc., 1974, Toledo Glass and Ceramic award NW Ohio sect., 1986, Albert Victor Bleininger Meml. award Pitts. sect., 1989, Phoenix award as Glass Industry Man of Yr., 1983; Friedberg Meml. lecture Nat. Inst. Ceramic Engrs., 1990, Greaves-Walker award, 2004. Fellow Am. Ceramic Soc. (disting. life, pres. 1980-81), Soc. Glass Tech., Am. Soc. for Metals Internat.; mem. NAE, AAAS, World Acad. of Ceramics, Cosmos Club (Washington), Sigma Xi, Phi Gamma Delta. Home: 1556 Crestline Dr Santa Barbara CA 93105-4611 Personal E-mail: wprindle@aol.com.

PRINGLE, DAVID L., insurance company executive; BA in Ins. and Risk Mgmt., Miss. State U. Sales assoc. to state sales coord. AFLAC Inc., asst. agy. dir. West territory, dir. tng., sr. v.p. fed. rels. Sec., prin. fundraiser Aflac's Polit. Action Com. (Aflac PAC). Office: AFLAC Inc 1932 Wynnton Rd Columbus GA 31999 Office Phone: 706-323-3431. Office Fax: 706-324-6330. *

PRINGLE, LAURENCE PATRICK, writer; b. Rochester, NY, Nov. 26, 1935; s. Laurence Erin and Marleah Elizabeth (Rosehill) P.; m. Judith Malanowicz, June 23, 1962 (div. 1970); children: Heidi Elizabeth, Jeffrey Laurence, Sean Edmund; m. Alison Newhouse, July 14, 1971 (div. 1975); m. Susan Deborah Klein, Mar. 13, 1983; children: Jesse Erin, Rebecca Anne. BS in Wildlife Biology, Cornell U., 1958; MS in Wildlife Biology, U. Mass., 1961. Tchr. sci. Lima (N.Y.) Cen. Sch., 1961-62; editor Nature and Sci. mag. Am. Mus. Natural History, NYC, 1963-70; free-lance writer, 1970—. Writer-in-residence Kean College, Union, N.J., 1985-86. Author: (children's books) Dinosaurs and Their World, 1968, The Only Earth We Have, 1969, From Field to Forest, 1970, In a Beaver Valley, 1970, One Earth, Many People, 1971, Ecology: Science of Survival, 1971, Cockroaches: Here, There, Everywhere, 1971, From Pond to Prairie, 1972, This Is a River, 1972, Pests and People: The Search for Sensible Pest Control, 1972, Estuaries: Where Rivers Meet the Sea, 1973, Into the Woods: Exploring the Forest Ecosystem, 1973, Follow a Fisher, 1973, Twist, Wiggle and Squirm: A Book about Earthworms, 1973, Recycling Resources, 1974, Energy: Power for People, 1975, City and Suburb: Exploring an Ecosystem, 1975, Chains, Webs and Pyramids: The Flow of Energy in Nature, 1975, Water Plants, 1975, The Minnow Family: Chubs, Dace, Minnows and Shiners, 1976, Listen to the Crows, 1976, Our Hungry Earth: The World Food Crisis, 1976, Death is Natural, 1977, The Hidden World: Life Under a Rock, 1977, The Controversial Coyote: Predation, Politics and Ecology, 1977, The Gentle Desert: Exploring an Ecosystem, 1977, Animals and Their Niches: How Species Share Resources, 1977, The Economic Growth Debate: Are There Limits to Growth?, 1978, Dinosaurs and People: Fossils, Facts and Fantasies, 1978, Wild Foods, 1978, Nuclear Power: From Physics to Politics, 1979, Natural Fire: Its Ecology in Forests, 1979, Lives at Stake: The Science and Politics of Environmental Health, 1980, What Shall We Do with the Land?: Choices for America, 1981, Frost Hollows and Other Microclimates, 1981, Vampire Bats, 1982, Water: The Next Great Resource Battle, 1982, Radiation: Waves and Particles/Benefits and Risks, 1983, Wolfman: Exploring the World of Wolves, 1983, Feral: Tame Animals Gone Wild, 1983, The Earth Is Flat—and Other Great Mistakes, 1983, Being a Plant, 1983, Nuclear War: From Hiroshima to Nuclear Winter, 1985, Animals at Play, 1985, Here Come the Killer Bees, 1986, Throwing Things Away: From Middens to Resource Recovery, 1986, Restoring Our Earth, 1987, Home: How Animals Find Comfort and Safety, 1987, Rain of Troubles: The Science and Politics of Acid Rain, 1988, Living in a Risky World, 1989, Nuclear Energy: Troubled Past, Uncertain Future, 1989, Bearman: Exploring the World of Black Bears, 1989, The Animal Rights Controversy, 1989, Saving Our Wildlife, 1990, Global Warming: Assessing the Greenhouse Threat, 1990, The Golden Book of Insects and Spiders, 1990, Killer Bees (rev. edit.), 1991, Batman: Exploring the World of Bats, 1991, Living Treasure: Saving Earth's Threatened Biodiversity, 1991, Antarctica: The Last Unspoiled Continent, 1992, The Golden Book of Volcanoes, Earthquakes, and Powerful Storms, 1992, Chemical and Biological Warfare: The Cruelest Weapons, 1993, revised edit., 2000, Oil Spills: Damage, Recovery, and Prevention, 1993, Jackal Woman: Exploring the World of Jackals, 1993, Scorpion Man: Exploring the World of Scorpions, 1994, Dinosaurs! Strange and Wonderful, 1995, Vanishing Ozone: Protecting Earth from Ultraviolet Radiation, 1995, Coral Reefs: Earth's Undersea Treasures, 1995, Dolphin Man: Exploring the World of Dolphins, 1995, rev. edit., 2002, Fire in the Forest: A Cycle of Growth and Renewal, 1995, Taking Care of the Earth: Kids in Action, 1996, Smoking: A Risky Business, 1996, An Extraordinary Life: The Story of a Monarch Butterfly, 1997, Nature! Wild and Wonderful, 1997, Everybody Has a Bellybutton: Your Life Before You Were Born, 1997, Elephant Woman: Cynthia Moss Explores The World of Elephants, 1997, Drinking: A Risky Business, 1997, One Room School, 1998, Explore Your Senses: SIGHT, 1999, Explore Your Senses: HEARING, 1999, Explore Your Senses: TASTE, 1999, Explore Your Senses: TOUCH, 1999, Explore Your Senses: SMELL, 1999, BATS! Strange and Wonderful, 2000, The Environmental Movement: From Its Roots to the Challenges of a New Century, 2000, Sharks! Strange and Wonderful, 2001, Global Warming: The Threat of Earth's Changing Climate, 2001, A Dragon in the Sky: The Story of a Green Darner Dragonfly, 2001, Scholastic Encyclopedia of Animals, 2001, Strange Animals, New to Science, 2002, Crows! Strange and Wonderful, 2002, Dog of Discovery: A Newfoundland's Adventures with Lewis and Clark, 2002, Whales! Strange and Wonderful, 2003, Snakes! Strange and Wonderful, 2004, American Slave, American Hero: York of the Lewis and Clark Expedition, 2006, Penguins! Strange and Wonderful, 2007, (fiction) Jesse Builds a Road, 1989, Octopus Hug, 1993, Naming the Cat, 1997, Bear Hug, 2003, (adult books) Wild River, 1972, Rivers and Lakes, 1985. Recipient Spl. Conservation award, Nat. Wildlife Fedn., 1978, Eva L. Gordon award, Am. Nature Study Soc., 1983, Orbis Pictus award, Nat. Coun. Tchrs. English, 1998, Nonfiction award, Washington Post/Children's Book Guild, 1999, Lifetime Achievement prize for excellence in sci. books, AAAS, 2005; fellow, John Simon Guggenheim Meml. Found., 2006. Mem.: The Authors Guild. Home and Office: PO Box 252 West Nyack NY 10994-0252 Office Phone: 845-623-7275.

PRINGLE, LEWIS GORDON, marketing professional, educator; b. Lansing, Mich., Feb. 13, 1941; s. Gordon Henry and Lucile Roxana (Drake) P.; children: Lewis Gordon Jr., William Davis, Thomas Benjamin. BA, Harvard U., 1963; MS, MIT, 1965, PhD, 1969. V.p., dir. mktg. sci. BBDO, Inc., NYC, 1968—73; asst. prof. mktg. Carnegie-Mellon U., Pitts., 1973—74; exec. v.p., dir. rsch. svcs., corp. dir. BBDO, Inc., NYC, 1978—91; exec. v.p. BBDO Worldwide, 1986—91; chmn., CEO BBDO Europe, 1986—91, LG Pringle and Assocs., 1992—95; Joseph C. Seibert prof. mktg. Farmer Sch. Bus. Adminstrn., Miami U., Oxford, Ohio, 1995—2000. Bd. dirs. Yorktown U., prof.; mem. vis com. Sloan Sch. Mgmt., MIT. Assoc. editor Jour. Advt. Rsch.; mem. editl. bd. Jour. Mktg. Sci.; mem. editl. bd. Jour. Market Rsch.; contbr. numerous articles to Harvard Bus. Rev., Mktg. Scis., others. Active local Boy Scouts Am. Ford Found. fellow, 1967 Fellow Royal Statis. Soc.; mem. INFORMS (chmn. mktg. strategy com.), Market Rsch. Coun., Am. Psychol. Assn., European Soc. Mktg. and Opinion Rsch., Am. Mktg. Assn., Inst. Ops. Rsch. and Mgmt. Sci. Office: Silver Creek Farm 2858 N Stout Rd Liberty IN 47353 Business E-Mail: lewpring@hughes.net.

PRINGLE, ORAN ALLAN, mechanical and aerospace engineering educator; b. Lawrence, Kans., Sept. 14, 1923; s. Oran Allan and Mae (McClell) Pringle; m. Billie Hansen, June 25, 1947; children: Allan, Billie, James, Rebecca. BSME, U. Kan., 1947; MS, U. Wis., 1948, PhD, 1967. Registered profl. engr., Mo. Mech. engr. Black and Veatch (cons. engrs.), Kansas City, Mo., 1947-48; engr. Boeing Airplane Co., Wichita, 1952—; prof. U. Mo., Columbia, 1948—90, prof. emeritus, 1991—. Co-author: Engineering Metallurgy, 1957; contbr. articles to profl. lit. Bd. dirs. Untied Cerebral Palsy Boone County, Mo. With US Army, 1943—45. Ford Found. grantee. Mem.: ASME (chmn. fastening and joining com. design engring. divsn.), Sigma Xi. Home: 1820 University Ave Columbia MO 65201-6004 Office: Dept Mech and Aerospace Engring U Mo Columbia MO 65201

PRINGLE, PAUL C., lawyer; b. 1943; AB, Dartmouth Coll., 1965; JD, U. Mich., 1968. Bar: NY 1969, Calif. 1972. Ptnr. corp. securities Sidley Austin Brown & Wood LLP, San Francisco and LA. Office: Sidley Austin Brown & Wood Ste 2000 555 California St San Francisco CA 94104-1715 Office Phone: 415-772-1249. Office Fax: 415-772-7400. Business E-Mail: ppringle@sidley.com.

PRINGLE, ROBERT MAXWELL, diplomat; b. NYC, Nov. 12, 1936; s. Henry Fowles and Helena Huntington (Smith) Pringle; m. Barbara Ann Cade, Sept. 26, 1964; children: James Maxwell, Anne Elizabeth. BA, Harvard U., 1958; PhD, Cornell U., 1967. Dir. econ. policy staff Bur. African Affairs Dept. State, 1981-83; dep. chief mission Ouagadougou, Burkina Faso, 1983-85, Port Moresby, Papua New Guinea, 1985-87; ambassador to Mali, 1987-90; dir. cen. African affairs U.S. Dept. State, 1990-93; dir. ecology and terrestrial conservation U.S. Dept. of State, 1993-95; dir. sr. seminar U.S. Dept. State, 1995-96; dep. chief of mission Dept. State, Pretoria, 1996-99; prof. nat. security policy Nat. War Coll., 1999—2001. Author: Rajahs and Rebels: The Ibans of Sarawak Under Brooke Rule, 1970, Indonesia and the Philippines: American Interests in Island Southwest Asia, 1980, A Short History of Bali, 2004. Mem.: African Studies Assn., Assn. Asian Studies. Avocations: photography, gardening, scuba diving. Home: 216 Wolfe St Alexandria VA 22314-3858 Home Phone: 703-519-8252; Office Phone: 703-519-8252. E-mail: pringler@post.harvard.edu.

PRINN, RONALD G., atmospheric science educator; b. Hamilton, New Zealand, June 11, 1945; BSc, U. Auckland, New Zealand, 1967, MSc with 1st honors, 1968; ScD, MIT, 1971. Asst. prof. MIT, Cambridge, Mass., 1971-76, assoc. prof., 1976-82, prof., 1982-93, Tepco prof., 1993—, head dept. earth, atmospheric and planetary scis., 1998—2003. Chair com. on earth sci. NAS, Washington, 1982-84; chair Internat. Global Atmospheric Chemistry Project, Stockholm, 1988-95. Recipient Vernadsky Meml. lectr. Russian Acad. Sci., Moscow, 1984. Fellow Am. Geophys. Union (Macelwane medal 1981), AAAS (chmn. atmospheric and hydrospheric scis. 1999). Office: MIT Bldg 54-1312 Cambridge MA 02139 Business E-Mail: rprinn@mit.edu.

PRINS, HARALD EDWARD LAMBERT, anthropologist, educator; b. Alphen aan de Rijn, The Netherlands, Sept. 7, 1951; came to US, 1978; s. Adriaan Hendrik Johan and Pietertje Anna Catharina (Poorter) P.; m. Bunny McBride, Sept. 29, 1985. Doctorandus, U. Nijmegen, The Netherlands, 1976; cert. in advanced 16 mm filmmaking, Parsons Sch., NYC, 1980; PhD, New Sch. Social Rsch., NYC, 1988. Asst. prof. comparative hist. U. Nijmegen, 1976—78; dir. R & D Assn. Aroostook Indians, Houlton, Maine, 1981—82; staff anthropologist Aroostook Band of Micmacs, Presque Isle, Maine, 1982—90; mem. grad. faculty Kans State U., Manhattan, 1990—, prof. anthropology, 1996—, Coffman chair Univ. Disting. Tchg. Scholars, 2004—05, Univ. Disting. prof., 2005—. Vis. lectr. anthropology Bowdoin Coll., Brunswick, Maine, 1986—88; vis. asst. prof. Colby Coll., Waterville, Maine, 1988—89; adj. prof. U. Maine, Orono, 1989; expert witness on Indian rights US Congress, Washington, 1990; faculty adv. AISES, 1992—97, Native Am. Student Body, 1997—2001; internat. observer presdl. elections, Paraguay, 1993; expert witness Nfld. aboriginal landclaims Nfld. Fed. and Provincial Ct., Canada, 1998—; disting. lectr. U. Maine, Presque Isle, 2002; keynote spkr. High Plains Soc. Applied Anthropology, 2002, Northeastern Anthrop. Assn., 2003; plenary spkr. U. Nijmegen, Netherlands, 2003; prin. investigator Acadia Nat. Pk. Ethnohistory Project, Nat. Pks. Svc., 2003—07; guest curator mus. exhibit Smithsonian Instn., 2003—07. Co-prodr.: (documentaries) Our Lives in Our Hands, 1986, Oh, What a Blow that Phantom Gave Me!, 2003; mem. editl. bd. Maine Hist., 1992—, Am. Anthropologist, 1998—2002, Explorations in Media Ecology, 2005—; co-editor: American Beginnings, 1994; author: The Mi'kmaq: Resistance, Accommodation and Cultural Survival, 1996; editor: Am. Anthropologist, 1998—2002, Visual Anthropology Rev., 2000—04; co-author: Cultural Anthropology: The Human Challenge,

2005, 12th edit., 2007, Evolution and Prehistory: The Human Challenge, 2005; co-editor: 8th edit., 2007; co-author: The Essence of Anthropology, 2006; contbr. chapters to books, articles to profl. jours. Mem adv. bd. Salt Inst. Documentary Field Studies, Maine, 1990—; adv./rschr. land claims Miawpukek Band of Mikmaq, Conne River, Nfld., 1996—; cultural preservation adv. Plains Apache Tribe, Anadarko, Okla., 1993-97; fed. recognition and landclaims adv./rschr. Aroostook Band of Micmacs, Presque Isle, 1981-91. Named Kans. Prof. of Yr., Carnegie Found. for Advancement of Tchg. and Coun. for Advancement and Support of Edn., 2006; recipient Conoco Prize Outstanding Tchg., Kans. State U., 1993, Presdl. award Outstanding Tchg., 1999, John Culkin award Outstanding Practice in Media, 2004; grantee, NEH, 1989; Vera List fellow, 1978. Mem.: Soc. Anthropology of Lowland S.Am., Maine Hist. Soc., Soc. L.Am. Anthropology, Soc. Visual Anthropology (prog. editor 1995, bd. dirs. 1995—, pres. 2000—), Am. Anthrop. Assn. (jury Ethnographic Film Festival 1998). Avocations: hiking, sailing, drawing, photography, wildlife. Office: Dept Anthropology Kans State U 207 Waters Hall Manhattan KS 66506 Office Phone: 785-532-4966. E-mail: prins@ksu.edu.

PRINS, RICHARD T., lawyer; b. Grand Rapids, Mich., 1950; BA summa cum laude, Calvin Coll., 1972; JD cum laude, U. Mich., 1977. Bar: NY 1979. Ptnr., co-heads investment mgmt. matters, mergers and acquisitions, securities and general corporate matters Skadden, Arps, Slate, Meagher & Flom LLP, NYC. Office: Skadden Arps Slate Meagher & Flom LLP 4 Times Sq New York NY 10036 Office Phone: 212-735-2790. Office Fax: 917-777-2790. Business E-Mail: rprins@skadden.com.

PRINZ, JESSE J., philosophy educator; BA summa cum laude with honors in Philosophy, NYU, 1992; PhD with honors in Philosophy, Univ. Chgo., 1997. Postdoctoral fellow, dept. philosophy U. Md., College Park, 1997; asst. prof. Dept. Philosophy and Philosophy-Neuroscience=Psychology Prog., 1997—2002; rsch. fellow Sch. for Advanced Study, Univ. London, England, 2002; assoc. prof., dept. philosophy U. NC, Chapel Hill, 2003—. Vis. asst. prof., divsn. of the humanities Calif. Inst. Tech., 2001; vis. fellow Collegium Budapest, Hungary, 2003, Ecole Normale Superieure, Paris, 2005, Ctr. for Advanced Study in the Behavioral Sciences, Stanford, 2005—06. Author: Furnishing the Mind: Concepts and Their Perpetual Basis, 2002, Gut Reactions: A Perpetual Theory of Emotion, 2004; contbr. chapters to books, articles to profl. jours.; reviewer for several profl. publications and organizations, mem. editl. bd. Philosophical Psychology, 2002—03, Cognitive Science, 2003—04, European Review of Philosophy, 2005—, Philosophical Explorations, 2005—, Philosophy Compass, 2006—. Mem.: Soc. for Philosophy and Psychology (mem. exec. com. 2004—07, prog. dir. 2007, Stainton prize for Notable Achievement in Cognitive Sci. 2003), Aesthetics Soc. Am. (mem. prog. com. 2004—05), Internat. Soc. for Rsch. on Emotions (mem. exec. com. 2004—). Office: Dept Philosophy CB #3125 Caldwell Hall UNC/Chapel Hill Chapel Hill NC 27599-3125 Office Phone: 919-962-3323. Business E-Mail: jesse@subcortex.com.

PRINZ, RICHARD ALLEN, surgeon; MD, Loyola U., Chgo., 1972. Diplomate Am. Bd. Surgery, bd. dirs., 1994—. Intern Barnes Hosp., St. Louis, 1972-73, resident in surgery, 1973-74, Loyola U., Chgo., 1974-77, attending surgeon, 1980-93; staff Rush Presbyn.-St. Luke's Med. Ctr., Chgo., 1993—; Helen Shedd Keith prof., chmn. dept. gen. surgery Rush U., Chgo., 1993—. Mem. Am. Surg. Assn., Am. Assn. Endocrine Surgeons (pres. 1996), Midwest Surg. Assn. (pres. 1997), Western Surg. Assn. (treas. 1993-97, pres. 2002-), Chgo. Surg. Soc. (pres.-elect 2002-, pres. 2003). Office: Rush U 818 Profl Bldg 1725 W Harrison St Chicago IL 60612-3828 Office Phone: 312-942-6511. Business E-Mail: rprinz@rush.edu.

PRINZE, FREDDIE, JR., actor; b. LA, Mar. 8, 1976; m. Sarah Michelle Gellar, Sept. 1, 2002. Grad., La Cueva H.S., 1994. Actor: (TV series) Family Matters, 1994, ABC Afterschool Spl., 1996, Freddie, 2005—06; (films) To Gillian on Her 37th Birthday, 1996, The House of Yes, 1997, I Know What You Did Last Summer, 1997, I Still Know What You Did Last Summer, 1998, She's All That, 1999, Wing Commander, 1999, Boys and Girls, 2000, Head Over Heels, 2001, Summer Catch, 2001, Scooby-Doo, 2002, Scooby-Doo 2: Monsters Unleashed, 2004, (voice) Shark Bait, 2006, Brooklyn Rules, 2006, (voice) Happily N'Ever After, 2007. Office: c/o BWR Pub Rels 6th Fl West Tower 9100 Wilshire Blvd Beverly Hills CA 90212 *

PRIOR, CORNELIUS BERNARD, JR., utilities executive, financial consultant; b. Hartford, Conn., Feb. 26, 1934; s. Cornelius B. Sr. and Katherine (Daly) P.; m. Trudie Yolleck, 1993; children: Elizabeth, Michael, Sarah. AB, Holy Cross Coll., Worcester, Mass., 1956; LLB, Harvard U., Cambridge, Mass., 1962. Bar: NY 1963. Assoc. atty. Sullivan and Cromwell, NYC, 1963-68; gen. counsel Private Investment Co. for Asia, Tokyo, 1969-71; v.p. Drexel Firestone, NYC, 1971-75; sr. v.p. Blythe Eastman Dillon, NYC, 1975—78; mng. dir. Paine Webber, NYC, 1978—80, Kidder, Peabody and Co., NYC, 1980-87; chmn. & CEO Atlantic Tele-Network, Inc., St. Thomas, V.I. Bd. dirs. Atlantic Telenetwork Co., St. Thomas. Bd. dirs., trustee Holy Cross Coll.; mem. vis. com. Harvard Law Sch., dean's adv. coun.; trustee, chair capital campaigns Antilles Sch.; chmn. Caribbean Assn. of Nat. Telephone Orgns.; mem. adv. bd. Peter Gruber Found.; trustee, treas., mem. exec. com. Caribbean and C.Am. Action. Served to lt (j.g.) USN, 1956-59. Fulbright scholar, 1962—63. Mem.: Bar Assn. of NY, Univ. Club (NYC). Roman Catholic. Office: Atlantic TeleNetwork Inc PO Box 12030 St Thomas VI 00801 Office Phone: 340-774-2260. Business E-Mail: cbpriorjr@atni.com.

PRIOR, DAVID B., academic administrator; m. Anny Prior; children: Kylie, Jonathan. BA, Queen's U. Belfast, No. Ireland, 1964, PhD in Geomorphology, 1968. Freelance broadcaster BBC TV, 1963—64; lectr., sr. lectr. Queen's U. Belfast, Northern Ireland, 1966—78; vis. asst. prof. La. State U., 1968—69; vis. assoc. prof., Coastal Studies Inst., La. State U. 1977; assoc. rsch. prof. Coastal Studies Inst., La. State U., 1978—80, rsch. prof., 1980—85, prof. geology and geophysics dept., 1985—89; vis. assoc. prof. U. Manitoba, 1972; vis. prof. Clark U., Worcester, Mass., 1976—77; head Environ. Marine Geology Atlantic Geoscience Ctr., Canada, 1989—92; dir. Atlantic Geosci. Ctr. Bedford Inst. Oceanography, Halifax, 1992—96; dep. dean, assoc. dean rsch., assoc. dean solid earth sciences Tex. A&M U., College Station, Tex., 1996—97, prof. geology and geophysics, 1996—97, dean coll. geosciences, 1997—2003, interim exec. v.p., provost, 2002—03, provost, 2002—07; exec. vice chancellor academic affairs U. Tex. System, 2007—. With Brit. Royal Navy, 1959—64. Fellow: Geol. Soc. London. Office: 601 College St Austin TX 78701-2982 Office Phone: 512-499-4233. Office Fax: 512-499-4240. *

PRIOR, GARY L., lawyer; b. Niagara Falls, NY, June 26, 1943; s. Harold D. and Adeline Thelma (Lee) Prior; m. Nancy O'Shaughnessy, Aug. 23, 1975; children: Joseph Lee, Julia Elizabeth. BS, Tulane U., 1965; JD, U. Chgo., 1968. Bar: Ill. 1968, U.S. Dist. Ct. (no. dist.), Ill. 1968, U.S. Ct. Appeals (7th cir.) 1973, U.S. Ct. Appeals (3d cir.) 1974, U.S. Trial Bar 1983, U.S. Supreme Ct. 1989, U.S. Dist. Ct. (we. dist.) Wis. 1992, U.S. Dist. Ct. (ea. dist.) Wis. 1993, U.S. Dist. Ct. Minn. 1994, U.S. Ct. Appeals (fed. cir.) 2002. Assoc. Rooks, Pitts, and Poust, Chgo., 1968-71, McDermott, Will, and Emery, Chgo., 1971-74, ptnr., 1974—2002, dir. trial dept. tng., 1980-85, mem. securities approval com., 1986—94, mem. nominating com., chmn., 1988-89, partnership com., 1989-92, mem mgmt. com., 1991-93; of counsel Tabet, DiVito, and Rothstein, LLC, Chgo., 2002—03, ptnr., 2004—. Trustee Prior Family Charitable Found., Furry Friends Found. Mem.: Fed. Cir. Bar Assn., Ill. State Bar Assn., Ill. Appellate Lawyers Assn. Avocations: history, farming, scuba diving. Home: 2512 N Burling St Chicago IL 60614-2510 Office: Tabet DiVito & Rothstein The Rookery 209 S LaSalle Ste 700 Chicago IL 60604 Office Phone: 312-762-9472. Business E-Mail: gprior@tdrlawfirm.com.

PRIOR, JOHN THOMPSON, pathology educator; b. St. Albans, Vt., Oct. 8, 1917; s. Thomas William and Pauline Thompson Prior; m. Elizabeth Titus Troy, July 24, 1948; children: Anne, Polly, John Jr., Thomas, Jeffrey, Timothy. BS, U. Vt., 1939, MD, 1943. Diplomate Am. Bd. Pathology. Resident in pathology Binghamton (N.Y.) City Hosp., 1946-47; fellow in pathology Syracuse (N.Y.) U. Med. Coll., 1947-49; asst. prof. pathology SUNY, Syracuse, 1949-54, assoc. prof., 1954-63, prof., 1963-72, clin. prof. pathology, 1972—. Active ARC Blood Bank, Syracuse, 1966-70; pres. N.Y. State Assoc. Lab., Syracuse, 1959-60; med. dir. PSRO Ctrl. N.Y., Syracuse, 1983-84; mem. N.Y. State Hosp. Rev. & Planning Assn., Albany, 1980-82; bd. dirs. Am. Med. Peer Rev. Assn., 1985-90. Contbr. articles to profl. jours. Bd. dirs. Lung Assn. Ctrl. N.Y., Syracuse, 1994—. Col. M.C., U.S. Army, 1944-77. Decorated Bronze Star, Silver Star, Legion of Merit, Belgian Croix de Guerre; recipient William Hammond Citation, N.Y. State Jour. Medicine, N.Y.C., 1984, Disting. Alumnus award U. Vt., Burlington, 1994. Mem. Onondaga County Med. Soc. (pres. 1974, disting. svc. award 1981). Avocations: golf, tennis. Home: 4615 Pewter Ln Manlius NY 13104-9329

PRIOR, MARK, professional baseball player; b. San Diego, Calif., Sept. 7, 1980; Attended, Vanderbilt, 1998—99; MBA, U. So. Calif., 2001. Pitcher Chgo. Cubs, 2002—. Named to NL All-Star Team, 2003; recipient Golden Spikes award for Best Coll. Baseball Player, 2001. Office: Chgo Cubs Wrigley Field 1060 W Addison Chicago IL 60613

PRIOR, WILLIAM ALLEN, electronics company executive; b. Benton Harbor, Mich., Jan. 14, 1927; s. Allen Ames and Madeline Isabel (Taylor) P.; m. Nancy Norton Sayles, July 7, 1951 (div. Oct. 1971); children: Stephanie Sayles, Alexandra Taylor, Robert Eames, Eleanor Norton; m. Carol Luise Becker-Ehmck, Oct. 30, 1971; children: Michael Becker-Ehmck, Jeffrey Renner. AB in Physics, Harvard Coll., 1950, MBA, 1954. Salesman IBM, Mineola, L.I., NY, 1950-52; sales engr. Lincoln Electric Co., Cleve., 1954-57; ptnr. Hammond Kennedy & Co., NYC, 1957-66; v.p. The Singer Co., NYC, 1967-68; pres. Tansitor Electronics, Bennington, Vt., 1969-71, Aerotron Inc., Raleigh, NC, 1971-82; v.p. J. Lee Peeler & Co., Durham, NC, 1986-89; pres. Accudyne, Inc., Raleigh, 1990-99. Chmn. Royal Blue Capital, Inc., Raleigh; bd. dirs. NeoDyne, Inc., Raleigh. Cpl. USAAF, 1945-46, Germany. Mem. IEEE, North Ridge Country Club (Raleigh), Raleigh Racquet Club, Harvard Club of N.Y.C., 50 Group. Republican. Avocations: tennis, skiing, computer programming. Home: 329 Meeting House Cir Raleigh NC 27615-3133 Personal E-mail: wprior@mbal954.hbs.edu.

PRIORE, CHRISTOPHER ANSELMO, artist; b. Buffalo, Apr. 28, 1959; s. Robert Michael and Annetta Anselmo Priore. Studied, Tyler Sch. Art/Temple U., Rome, 1979—80; BFA, Carnegie Mellon U., Pitts., 1981. One-man shows include Pitts. Ctr. for the Arts, 1990, Scarfone/Hartley Gallery, U. Tampa, Fla., 1994, E.M. Donahue, NYC, 1997, Cardozo Gallery, Benjamin N. Cardozo Sch. Law, Yeshiva U., NYC, 2000, Museo ItaloAmericano, San Francisco, 2004, Italian Am. Mus., NYC, 2004, The McKinney Ave. Contemporary, Dallas, 2005, exhibited in group shows at Carnegie Mus. Art, Pitts., 1988, So. Alleghenies Mus. Art, Loretto, Pa., 1988, Albright-Knox Art Gallery, Buffalo, NY, 1990, Fukuya Art Gallery, Hiroshima, Japan, 1995, Kunstun Technik, Berlin, 1998, L Gallery, Moscow, 1998, Del. Ctr. for Contemp. Arts, Wilmington, 2003, Kim Foster Gallery, NYC, 2005, prin. works include "SKY", The Pitts. Children's Mus., 1988—98, "Rise!", MTA NYC Transit, 1997—98, Represented in permanent collections Singers Forum, NYC, Westinghouse Energy Ctr., Monroeville, Pa., Italian Am. Mus., N.Y.C. Grantee, Richard King Mellon Found., 1988, Eben Demarest Trust, 1988, 1991, N.Y. Found. Arts. Artist Sponsorship Program, 1997—98, 1999. Democrat. Roman Catholic. Avocations: weightlifting, swimming. Studio: 579 Fort Washington Ave Ste 3E New York NY 10033 Office Phone: 212-568-2836. E-mail: christopherpriore@earthlink.net.

PRIORE, LOUIS VINCENT, pharmacist; b. Buffalo, May 26, 1953; s. Vincent Mark and Jean Marie Priore. BS in Pharmacy, SUNY, Buffalo, 1977. Mem.: Fla. Soc. Health Sys. Pharmacists. Home: 4 Lake Vista Trail Apt 206 Port Saint Lucie FL 34952-6382

PRIORY, RICHARD BALDWIN, former electric power industry executive; b. Lakehurst, NJ, May 15, 1946; s. Joseph Albert Jr. and Betty (Baldwin) P.; m. Joan Ellen Rourke, May 30, 1968; children: Jennifer Joan, Richard Baldwin Jr. BSCE magna cum laude, W.Va. Inst. Tech., 1969; MS in Engring., Princeton U., 1973; grad. utility exec. program, U. Mich., 1982; grad. advanced mgmt. program, Harvard U., 1991. Registered profl. engr., N.C., S.C. Design engr., project engr. Union Carbide Corp., 1969-72; asst. prof. structural engring. U. N.C., Charlotte, 1973-76; design engr. Duke Power Co., Charlotte, N.C., 1976-78, prin. engr., 1978-81, mgr. project mgmt. divsn., 1981-84, v.p. design engring., 1984-88, sr. v.p. generation and info. svcs., 1988-91, exec. v.p. power generation group, 1991-94, pres., COO, 1994-97; chmn., CEO Duke Energy Corp. (formerly Duke Power Co.), Charlotte, 1997—2003. Bd. dirs. Duke Energy Corp., Dana Corp., EEI, AEIC; mem. Duke Fluor Daniel Mgmt. Com. Bd. visitors U. N.C., Charlotte; past chmn. bd. dirs. Charlotte-Mecklenburg Edn. Found.; pres., bd. trustees Discovery Place, Inc., 1992-93; past mem. Charlotte-Mecklenburg Pub. Broadcasting Found.; vice chmn. campaign drive United Way Ctrl. Carolinas, Inc., 1990; adv. coun. N.C. Alliance for Competitive Technologies. Mem. ASCE, Nat. Acad. Engring, Charlotte Engrs. Club. Avocation: golf.

PRISCHMANN GRYNIEWICZ, DEBORAH ANNE, voice educator, vocalist; d. Richard D. Prischmann and Carole Anne Frascone; m. Ronald Joseph Gryniewicz, Mar. 13, 1962. B in Music Edn., U. Ariz., 1979; MusM in Opera/Vocal Pedagogy, Temple U., 1985. Cert. N.J. Dept. Edn., 1984. Vocal solo artist Jubilant Voice Ministry, Doylestown, Pa., 1990—; dir., instr. Meadow Lark Vocal Studio, Doylestown, 1990—; vocalist in Voices of Pops Peter Nero and the Philly Pops, Phila., 2001—; prof. voice U. of the Arts, Phila., 2005—. Gen. music tchr. Lebanon (N.J.) Boro Sch., 1987—91; dir. music Washington's Crossing (Pa.) United Meth. Ch., 1987—88; youth chorus dir. Musical Arts Acad., Doylestown, 1997—99; musical vocal dir. Ctrl. Bucks West H.S., Doylestown, 1998—99; worship leader Doylestown United Meth. Ch., 1999—2001; vocal worship cons. Calvary Chapel, Chalfont, Pa., 2001—03; vocal clinician William Penn H.S., Newark, 2004—04. Composer: (solo debut vocal album) Light My Way, (vocal solo album) Deborah - Christmas at America's Keswick - live!, (solo vocal contemporary christian album) The Me God Sees, (solo contemporary christian album) The Way, The Truth, The Life. Dir. music Ctrl. Schwenkfelder Ch., Worcester, Pa., 1979—82. Finalist Outstanding Sr. award, U. Ariz., 1979; recipient Ruby Sword of Honor for outstanding leadership, Sigma Alpha Iota, 1979, Grad. Tchg. Assistantship, Temple U., 1980; Full Gen. Music scholar, U. Ariz., 1976. Mem.: ASCAP, Nat. Assn. Tchrs. Singing (vocal adjudicator 1992—93). Republican. Avocations: travel, equestrian, gardening, birdwatching. Office: University of the Arts 320 South Broad St Philadelphia PA 19102 Home Phone: 215-348-3598; Office Phone: 215-717-6000.

PRISCO, FRANK J., psychotherapist; b. NYC; s. Frank J. and Isabel (Gatano) P.; m. August Frances; children: Frank, Christian, Meredith. BS in History, NYU, 1964, MA in History and Psychology, 1972, PsyD in Psychoanalysis, 1980. Diplomate Am. Psychotherapy Assn., Am. Bd. Psychol. Specialties of Am. Coll. Forensic Examiners; cert. psychoanalyst, cert. med. hypnotherapist. Cons., staff therapist Creedmore Psychiat. Ctr.; faculty Psychanalytic Inst., LI; pvt. practice Ctr. for Modern Psychoanalytic Studies; instr. psychology N.Y.C. Bd. Edn. Trainer of trainers Conflict Mgrs. Program, N.Y.C.; discussion leader Gt. Books Found. Eucharistic min. Cath. Ch.; group leader Great Books Found. Recipient Soc. of Emil award, 1980. Mem. AAAS, Am. Psychol. Soc., Am. Assn. Guidance and Counseling, N.Y. Acad. Scis., Nat. Assn. Advancement Psychoanalysis, Am. Poetry Assn. (Poet Merit award 1988-90), Soc. Modern Psychoanalysis. Home: 14710 22ND Ave Whitestone NY 11357-3512 Home Phone: 718-445-5596; Office Phone: 212-752-0704.

PRISELAC, THOMAS M., health facility executive, educator; BA in Biology, Washington & Jefferson Coll.; MPH Health Svcs. Adminstrn. and Planning, U. Pitts. Asst. adminstr. Cedars-Sinai Med. Ctr., LA, 1979—81, assoc. adminstr., 1981—82, sr. assoc. adminstr., 1982—83, v.p. adminstrn., 1983—85, sr. v.p. ops., 1985—91, exec. v.p., COO, 1988—94, pres., CEO, 1994—. Adj. prof. UCLA Sch. Pub. Health; tchr., principles of orgn. leadership Master of Pub. Health for Health Professionals; past chmn. Coun. of Teaching Hosp. of Assn. of Am. Med. Coll.; chmn. Calif. Healthcare Assn., Healthcare Assn. of Southern Calif.; bd. dirs. Am. Hosp. Assn., VHA, Inc., Nat. Com. for Quality Healthcare, Calif. Healthcare Found.; lectr. in field. Bd. dirs. Blue Cross Calif. Office: Cedars Sinai Med Ctr 8700 Beverly Blvd Rm 2628 Los Angeles CA 90048 Address: UCLA Sch Pub Health Dept Health Services Box 951772 Los Angeles CA 90095-1772 Office Phone: 310-423-5711, 310-206-3435. Office Fax: 310-423-0120, 310-206-4722. Business E-Mail: tmp@cshs.org.

PRISING, JONAS, employment services executive; MBA, Stockholm Sch. Econs. Asia-Pacific regional mgr. AB Electrolux, Singapore, 1989—93, mng. dir. comml. cleaning equipment divsn. Paris, 1993—95, mng. dir. comml. cleaning equipment divsn., head global sales and mktg. for divsn. London, 1995—99; dir. global accounts Europe, Mid. East and Africa Manpower, Inc., London, 1999—2002, mng. dir. Italy Milan, 2002—05, exec. v.p., pres. N.Am. Milw., 2006—. Office: Manpower Inc 5301 N Ironwood Rd Milwaukee WI 53217 Office Phone: 414-961-1000. *

PRISINZANO, THOMAS EDWARD, chemistry professor, researcher; b. NYC, July 19, 1973; s. Paul Robert and Eileen Gilleece Prisinzano; m. Deanna Olech Olech, Sept. 30, 1973; children: Sara Marie, Joseph Paul. BS, U. Del., Newark, 1995; PhD, Va. Commonwealth U., Richmond, 2000. Grad. asst. Va. Commonwealth U., 1995—2000; asst. prof. U. Iowa, Iowa City, 2003—. Faculty mem. Ctr. Biocatalysis and Bioprocessing, Iowa City, 2003—, U. Iowa Pain Rsch. Program, 2003—. Co-author: (textbook) Comprehensive Medicinal Chemistry Second Edition. Recipient J. Doyle Smith award, Va. Commonwealth U., Sch. Pharmacy, 1998, Early Career Investigator award, Coll. Problems Drug Dependence, 2003, D. John Faulkner award, Am. Soc. Pharmacognosy, 2005, Travel award, Internat. Narcotics Rsch. Conf., 2005; fellow, Nat. Inst. Diabetes and Digestive and Kidney Diseases, 2000—03; grantee, Nat. Inst. Drug Abuse, 2005. Mem.: Internat. Narcotics Rsch. Conf., Soc. Neurosci., Am. Assn. Pharm. Scientists, Coll. Problems Drug Dependence, Am. Soc. Pharmacognosy, Am. Chem. Soc., Theta Xi (life). Roman Catholic. Achievements include patents pending for Novel Opioid Receptor Ligands; discovery of Novel Scaffold for Mu Opioid Receptor Ligands; Mu Opioid with Altered Receptor Regulation; research in Method for the Detection of Salvinorin A in Biological Fluids; patents pending for Novel Opiate Agonists That Do Not Promote Receptor Regulation as Analgesics with Limited Tolerance Liability. Office: U Iowa 115 S Grand Ave Iowa City IA 52242 Home Phone: 319-354-6421; Office Phone: 319-335-6920. Office Fax: 319-335-8766. E-mail: thomas-prisinzano@uiowa.edu.

PRISSEL, BARBARA ANN, paralegal, law educator; b. Plum City, Wis., July 7, 1946; d. John Henry and Mary Ann Louise (Dankers) Seipel; m. Stephen Joseph Prissel, Dec. 16, 1967; children: Angela, Benjamin. Grad. with honors, Mpls. Bus. Coll., 1966; at, Moraine Park Tech. Coll., 1983—. Cert. office tech. instr., interactive TV, adult edn. instr., adminstrv. profl. instr. Legal sec. Mott, Grose, Von Holtum & Hefferan, Mpls., 1966-67, Whelan, Morey & Morey Attys. at Law, Durand, Wis., 1967-70, Murry Law Office, River Falls, Wis., 1968-70, Potter, Wefel & Nettesheim, Wisconsin Rapids, Wis., 1970-71; paralegal Kilgore Law Office, Ripon, Wis., 1985—2004; sec. to adminstr. Moraine Park Tech. Coll., Fond du Lac, Wis., 1971—72. Chmn. legal adv. com. Moraine Park Tech. Coll., Fond du Lac, 1996-98, mem. adminstrv. assts. adv. com., 1984-86, mem. legal adv. commn. 1984-. Contbr. poems to newspapers. Ch. rep. Ch. Women United, Ripon, 1984-87; pianist Christian Women's Orgn., Ripon, 1985-95; pianist, organist Our Lady of Lake Ch., Green Lake, Wis., 1987—; piano instr. Mike's Music & Sound Inc., 2005-. Mem.: NAFE, Legal Profls. Assn. (East Ctrl. Wis. pres. 1994—95, sec. 1995—96, chmn. Day-In-Ct. 1999, NALS Fedn. liaison 2000—02, sec. 2001—02, state legal edn. task force 2003—04, v.p. 2003—04, pres. 2003—, v.p. East Ctrl. Wis. chpt. 2004—, chmn. ednl. liaison com., Legal award of Excellence 1995—96), Wis. Assn. Legal Profession (state legal ednl. liaison com. 1997—98, state legal edn. task force 2003—04, ann. meeting com. mem. 2005, mem. nominations and elections com. 2005—06, mem. com. 2007—, mktg. com. 2007—), Nat. Assn. Legal Profession, Nat. Women's History Mus. Roman Catholic. Avocations: teaching and playing piano, creative writing, cooking, swimming, exercising. Home: 129 Wolverton Ave Ripon WI 54971-1144

PRISTOOP, SIMON MORRIS, retired physicist, systems engineer, consultant; b. Balt., Mar. 8, 1933; s. Leon Pristoop and Gladys Marner; m. Maria del Carmen Carmona Santana, Nov. 29, 1986; children from previous marriage: Flora Gee, Robert Emmett, Gina Springmann, Steven. BS in Physics and Math., U. Md., College Park, 1954. Physicist Naval Ordnance Lab., White Oak, Md., 1954—56, Vitro Corp., Silver Spring, Md., 1956—58; engr. Melpar Corp., Falls Church, Va., 1958—60, Northrop Corp., Arlington, Va.; electronic systems engr. Westinghouse Corp., Friendship Airport, Md., 1960—64; cons. NASA, Greenbelt, Md., 1964; sr. engr., program mgr. Tracor Corp., Rockville, Md., 1965—69; program mgr. Latton Systems, College Park, Md., 1970—74; program mgr., sys. engr. Syscon Corp., Washington, 1975—89; program mgr. software Colsa Corp. Naval Base, PR, 1989—95; cons. Dynecorp, United Def., RI, 1995—96, Pa., 1996—98; ret. Contbr. scientific papers to profl. jours. Co-chair Home Rule Charter Campaign, Prince George County, 1960—62; chmn. Prince George Bd. Appeals, Md., 1971—74; candidate fed. congress Dem. Congl. Dist. 15, Fla., 2004; vice chair Brevard County Dem. Exec. Com., Fla., 2002—03, com. chair, 1999—. Mem.: Am. Civil Liberties Union, Moose Lodge. Democrat. Avocations: politics, jogging, weightlifting.

PRITCHARD, CLAUDIUS HORNBY, JR., retired university president; b. Charleston, W.Va., June 28, 1927; s. Claudius Hornby and Katherine (Ellison) P.; m. Marjorie Walker Pullen, Aug. 9, 1952; children: Virginia Aiken, Katherine Winston, Olivia Reynolds, Claudius V. BA, Hampden-Sydney Coll., 1950; MA, Longwood U., 1965; PhD, Fla. State U., 1971. Comml. loan teller Am. Nat. Bank and Trust Co., Danville, Va., 1950-53; asst. cashier Planters Bank & Trust Co., Farmville, Va., 1953-55; asst. to pres. Hampden-Sydney (Va.) Coll., 1955-57, bus. mgr. and treas., 1957-67, v.p. devel., 1967-71; sr. budget analyst-edn. State of Fla., Tallahassee, 1971-72; pres. Sullins Coll., Bristol, Va., 1972-76; v.p. adminstrn. Maryville U., St. Louis, 1976-77, pres., 1977-92, pres. emeritus, 1992—. Adv. dir. Commerce Bank of St. Louis, 1982—92. Author: Col. D. Wyatt Aiken (1828-1887) South Carolina's Militant Agrarian, 1970; contbr. articles to profl. jours. Mem. bd. visitors Charleston So. U., 1993—2005; chmn. Summerville Comml. Design Rev. Bd., 1999—; bd. dirs. West St.

Louis County YMCA, Chesterfield, Mo., 1985—92. With USNR, 1945—46. Fla. State U. fellow, 1969-70, Arthur Vining Davis fellow Am. Council on Edn., 1974; recipient Disting. Svc. award Charleston Southern U., 2000; named Citizen of Year Chesterfield, Md., 1986. Mem. AAUP, SCV, Am. Assn. Higher Edn., So. Hist. Assn., S.C. Hist. Soc., Mo. Colls. Fund (bd. dirs., chmn. 1987-88), Mil. Order of the Stars and Bars, Ind. Colls. and Univs. Mo., Chesterfield C. of C. (pres. 1987, Chesterfield Citizen of Yr. award 1986), Rotary. Republican. Presbyterian.

PRITCHARD, DALTON HAROLD, retired electronics executive; b. Crystal Springs, Miss., Sept. 1, 1921; s. Cecil Harold and Marvie Prudence (Lofton) P.; m. Caroline Ann Hnatuk, Apr. 27, 1947; 1 child, Mary Ann Pritchard Poole. BSE.E., Miss. State U., 1943; postgrad., Harvard, MIT Radar Sch., 1943-44. Mem. tech. staff RCA Labs., Riverhead, NY, 1946-50, mem. tech. staff Princeton, NJ, 1950-75, fellow tech. staff, 1975-87. Session chmn., mem. program com. Internat. Conf. on Consumer Electronics, Chgo., 1980-85 Contbr. articles to profl. jours.; patentee in field. Mem. N.J. Gov.'s Sci. Adv. Council, Princeton, 1981-85. Served to capt. U.S. Army Signal Corps Decorated Bronze Star; recipient Eduard Rhein prize Edward Rhein Found., Berlin, Fed. Republic of Germany, 1980; Disting. Engring. fellow Miss. State U., 1991. Fellow IEEE (Vladimir Zworykin award 1977, David Sarnoff award 1981), Soc. Info. Display, Nat. Assn. Engrs., Nat. Acad. Engring., Sigma Xi, Tau Beta Pi, Kappa Mu Epsilon Republican. Baptist. Avocations: amateur radio, tennis. Home: 3 Bent Tree Ln Hilton Head Island SC 29926-1906 Office Phone: 843-681-3904.

PRITCHARD, DAVID EDWARD, physics professor; b. NYC, Oct. 15, 1941; m. Andrea Hasler; children: Orion, Alexander. BS, Calif. Inst. Tech., 1962; PhD, Harvard U., 1968. Postdoctoral fellow MIT, Cambridge, Mass., 1968, instr., 1968-70, asst. prof., 1970-75, assoc. prof., 1975-80, prof., 1980—. Cecil and Ida Chair, 2001—. Vis. scientist Stanford Rsch. Inst., 1975; vis. prof. U. Paris Sud Orsay, 1983; disting. visitor Joint Inst. for Lab., Astrophysics, 1989, 98, mem. subpanel, 1990—94, chmn., 1994; co-chair First Quantum Electronic and Laser Sci. Conf., 1989; chair Internat. Conf. on Atomic Physics, 2002; Selby Travelling lectr. of Australia, 04. Div. assoc. editor Phys. Rev. Letters, 1983-88; contbr. articles to profl. jours. Polaroid fellow Harvard U., 1962-63, NSF predoctoral fellow, 1963-68. Fellow: AAAS, Optical Soc. Am. (bd. dirs. 1998—2001, Max Born award 2004), Am. Acad. Arts and Scis., Am. Phys. Soc. (disting. traveling lectr. laser sci. topical group 1992—94, rep. steering com. laser sci. topical group, rep. joint coun. on quantum electronics, Broida prize 1991, Centennial spkr. 1999, Schawlow prize 2003); mem.: NAS, Am. Assn. Physics Tchrs. (rsch. in physics edn. com.), Effective Educational Tech., Inc. (co-founder), Tiverton Yacht Club (R.I.). Avocations: sailing, carpentry. Home: 88 Washington Ave Cambridge MA 02140-2708 Office: MIT Rm 26-241 Dept Physics Cambridge MA 02139 Home Phone: 617-492-4872; Office Phone: 617-253-6812. Business E-Mail: dpritch@mit.edu.

PRITCHARD, ELSIE TOMLINSON, librarian; b. Dothan, Ala., Nov. 14, 1947; d. Eugene and Merle (Coleman) Tomlinson; m. Robert Donald Pritchard II, Dec. 23, 1966; children: Claire, Alison. BS, Old Dominion U., 1969; MLS, U. Pitts., 1972; MusM, Morehead State U., 1990. Tech. svcs. libr. Boston Conservatory, 1978-79; music cataloger Morehead (Ky.) State U., 1972-78, 82-86, acquisitions libr., 1986-92, asst. dir. Tech. Svcs., 1993—2005, dean libr. svc., 2005—. Elder Morehead Presbyn. Ch., 1982—. Mem. ALA, Ky. Libr. Assn., Assn. Coll. and Rsch. Libs. Office: Camden Carroll Libr Morehead St # U Morehead KY 40351

PRITCHARD, HUW OWEN, chemist, educator; b. Bangor, Wales, July 23, 1928; s. Owen and Lilian Venetia P.; m. Margaret Ramsden, Nov. 3, 1956; children— Karen, David. B.Sc., U. Manchester, 1948, M.Sc., 1949, PhD, 1951, D.Sc., 1964. Asst. lectr. chemistry Manchester (Eng.) U., 1951-54, lectr., 1954-65; prof. chemistry York U., Ont., Can., 1965-97, prof. emeritus Can., 1997—. Contbr. articles to profl. jours. Fellow: Royal Soc. Can. Office: Chemistry Dept York Univ Toronto ON Canada M3J 1P3 Business E-Mail: huw@yorku.ca.

PRITCHARD, JOHN F., lawyer; b. Libertyville, Ill., Jan. 20, 1943; BA, Yale U., 1965; JD, U. Calif., Berkeley, 1968. Bar: N.Y. 1970. Ptnr., leader Litigation practice Pillsbury Winthrop Shaw Pittman, NYC. Articles editor Calif. Law Review, 1966-68. Office: Pillsbury Winthrop Shaw Pittman 1540 Broadway New York NY 10036 Office Phone: 212-858-1620. Office Fax: 212-858-1500. Business E-Mail: john.pritchard@pillsburylaw.com.

PRITCHARD, JONATHAN K., geneticist, educator; BSc in Biology and Math., Pa. State U., 1994; PhD in Biol. Scis., Stanford U., Calif., 1998. Postdoctoral fellow dept. stats. U. Oxford, England, 1998—2001; asst. prof. dept. human genetics U. Chgo., 2001—05, prof., 2006—. Contbr. articles to sci. jours. Co-recipient Paper of Yr. award, Lancet, 2003; recipient Mitchell prize, Am. Statis. Assn. and Internat. Soc. Bayesian Analysis, 2002; Packard fellow, 2004, Alfred P. Sloan fellow, 2004. Office: Dept Human Genetics U Chgo 920 E 58th St CLSC 507 Chicago IL 60637 Office Phone: 773-834-5248. Office Fax: 773-834-0505. E-mail: pritch@uchicago.edu. *

PRITCHARD, KATHLEEN JO, not-for-profit association administrator; b. Milw., Feb. 6, 1951; d. Owen J. and Madelon (Coogan) P.; m. William A. Durkin Jr., Oct. 22, 1982; children: Elizabeth Durkin, Christine Durkin, W. Ryan Durkin. BA in Anthropology, U. Wis., Oshkosh, 1973; MA in Pub. Adminstrn., U. Wis., 1980; PhD in Polit. Sci., U. Wis., Milw., 1986. Rsch. analyst Wis. Coun. on Criminal Justice, Madison, 1974-77; planning analyst Wis. Dept. Health and Social Svcs., Madison, 1977-80; assoc. lectr. U. Wis., Milw., 1980-89; vis. asst. prof. Marquette U., Milw., 1986, 90-91; policy cons. dept. adminstrn. City of Milw., 1992; Outcomes Project dir. United Way of Greater Milw., 1992-96, dir. impact and evaluation, 1997—; chmn. United Way of Am. Forum on Outcomes II, 1997. Faculty advisor Model OAS, UN advisor, Milw., 1986-91; campus rep. spkr. Wis. Inst. for Study of War, Peace and Global Cooperation, Milw., 1989-90; mem. United Way Am. Task Force on Impact, 1995—; instr. Nat. Acad. Volunteerism, 1996. Contbr. articles to profl. jours., chpts. to books Dir. cmty impact United Way of Greater Milw., 1998; trustee Pub. Policy Forum, 2000—, NonProfit Mgmt. Fund, 2000—03, NonProfit Mgmt. Edn. Ctr., 2000—03; pres. Whitefish Bay Village, 2002—; dir. cmty. impact, product devel. United Way Am.; mem. exec. coun. Met. Milw. Sewerage Dist.; mem. Lakefront Devel. Com., 2004—; v.p., bd. dirs. North Shore Fire Dept., 2005—06, pres., bd. dirs., 2007—; pres. coun. Dominican HS; mem. exec. steering com. Partnership for Healthy Milw., 2001—04; bd. dirs. Counseling Ctr. of Greater Milw., 2004—. Recipient Alice Paul Dissertation award Women's Caucus for Polit. Sci., 1984; Grad. Sch. fellow U. Wis., Milw., 1983, fellow Kenyon Coll. Summer Inst., 1983. Mem. Phi Kappa Phi (chpt. officer 1989). Personal E-mail: pritchardkj@aol.com.

PRITCHARD, KEVIN, professional sports team executive; b. Bloomington, Ind., July 17, 1967; Grad., U. Kans., 1990. Player Golden State Warriors, 1990—91, Boston Celtics, 1991—92, Phila. 76ers, 1994, Miami Heat, 1995, Washington Bullets, 1995—96; scout San Antonio Spurs; coach, gen. mgr., dir. player pers. Am. Basketball Assn. Kans. City Knights; dir. player pers. Portland Trail Blazers, 2004—05, interim head coach, 2005, asst. gen. mgr., 2006—07, gen. mgr., 2007—. Office: Portland Trail Blazers Rose Garden One Center Ct Portland OR 97227 *

PRITCHARD, LLEWELYN GEORGE, lawyer; b. NYC, Aug. 13, 1937; s. Llewelyn and Anne Mary (Streib) P.; m. Joan Ashby, June 20, 1959; children: David Ashby, Jennifer Pritchard Vick, Andrew Harrison, William Llewellyn. AB with honors, Drew U., 1958; LLB, Duke U., 1961. Ptnr. Helsell & Fetterman, Seattle. Trustee Allied Arts Found., pres. 2005-07; pres., trustee, corp. counsel Allied Arts Seattle, 1973-76; dir. Fifth Ave. Theatre, 2005-; trustee Meth. Ednl. Found., 1970-85, pres., 1991-92; life trustee PONCHO Patrons of Pacific N.W. Civil, Cultural and Charitable Orgns., pres., 1972-73; bd. dirs. Planned Parenthood of Seattle/King County, 1972-78; trustee Seattle Symphony Orch., 1979-83, chmn. bd., 1980-82, life trustee; trustee U. Puget Sound., 1972-99, exec. com., 1973-96, chmn. bd. visitors to Law Sch., 1984-88; trustee Mus. of Glass, 2000-07;mem. Betty Bowen com. Seattle Art Mus., 2007; chancellor Pacific N.W. Ann. conf. United Meth. Ch., 1969—. Fellow Am. Bar Found. (life, state chmn. 1988-98); mem. ABA (state del. 1982-86, bd. govs. 1986-89, chmn. program com. 1988-89, exec. com. 1988-89, Ho. of Dels. 1979—, nat. dir. young lawyers divsn. 1971, chmn. sect. of individual rights and responsibilities 1975-76, exec. coun. family law sect. 2002-05, chair standing com. on legal aid and indigent defendants 1973-75, chair legal needs study 1995-98, chair adv. com. to pro bono immigration project 1991-01, dir. Ctr. for Human Rights 2001-), Commn. Rule of Law Initiatives, Wash. State Bar Assn. (bd. govs. King County 1972-75), King County Bar Assn. (chair young lawyers sect. 1970). Avocations: reading, art collector. Home: 5229 140th Ave NE Bellevue WA 98005-1024 Office: Helsell & Fetterman 1001 Fourth Ave Ste 4200 Seattle WA 98154 Office Phone: 206-292-1144.

PRITCHARD, SARAH MARGARET, library director; b. Boston, Feb. 8, 1955; d. Wilbur Louis and Kathleen Hunton (Moss) P.; m. Timothy John Brennan, Aug. 20, 1977 (div. 1993); m. Neal Edward Blair, July 15, 2005. BA, U. Md., 1975; MA in French, U. Wis., 1976, MLS, 1977. Intern Libr. Congress, Washington, 1977-78, reference specialist in women's studies, 1978-88, head microform reading rm., 1988-90; sr. program officer Assn. Rsch. Librs., Washington, 1990-91, assoc. exec. dir., 1991-92; acad. libr. mgmt. intern Coun on Libr. Resources Princeton U., NJ, 1988-89; dir. librs. Smith Coll., Northampton, Mass., 1992-99; univ. libr. U. Calif., Santa Barbara, 1999—2006, Northwestern U., Evanston, Ill., 2006—. Editl. advisor Women's Rsch. and Edn. Inst., Washington, 1987-92; bd. dirs. Western Mass. Regional Libr. Sys., 1997-98; bd. dirs. U. Calif. So. Regional Libr. Facility, Gold Coast Libr. Network, Libr. Calif.; mem. steering com. Scholarly Pub. and Academic Resources Coalition, 2006—; Charles Deering McCormick disting. chair rsch. libr. U. Wis., 2006. Editor: The Women's Annual, 1984; compiler ARL Stats., 1990-92; contbr. articles to profl. jours.; mem. editl. bd. Jour. Acad. Librarianship, 1993-99, Portal: Librs. and the Acad., 2000—; contbg. editor Libr. Issues, 1994-99. Trustee Leroy C. Merritt Humanitarian Fund, 1991-94. Named Wis. Alumni Rsch. Found. fellow, 1975-77, Outstanding Alumna U. Wis. Sch. of Libr. and Info. Studies, 1997. Mem. ALA (chair machine assisted reference sect. 1986-87, chair women's studies sect. 1989-90, coun. 1990-98, 2000-04, chair stds. com. 1998-2002, chair ethics com. 2002-06, Equality award 1997), Nat. Women's Studies Assn., Cosmos Club, Phi Beta Kappa. Democrat. Office: Northwestern Univ Libr Evanston IL 60208

PRITCHARD, THERESE D., lawyer; AB, Bryn Mawr Coll., 1975; JD, Boston Coll., 1978. Bar: Mass. 1978. Asst. dir. Enforcement SEC, 1986—91; dep. chief counsel for enforcement Office of Thrift Supervision, 1991—94; ptnr., group leader Securities Enforcement, Compliance and Litig. Bryan Cave LLP, Washington, DC. Office: Bryan Cave LLP 700 Thirteenth Street NW Washington DC 20005 Office Phone: 202-508-6252. E-mail: tdpritchard@bryancave.com.

PRITCHARD, WILLIAM H., literature educator, writer; AB, Amherst Coll., 1953; MA, Harvard Univ., 1956, PhD, 1960. Henry Clay Folger prof. of English Amherst Coll. Author: (books) Wyndham Lewis, 1968, W.B. Yeats, 1972, Seeing Through Everything: English Writers 1918-1940, 1977, Frost: A Literary Life Reconsidered, 1984, Randall Jarrell: A Literary Life, 1990, Playing It By Ear: Literary Essays & Reviews, 1994, English Papers: A Teaching Life, 1995, Under Criticism: Essays for William H. Pritchard, 1998, Talking Back to Emily Dickinson & Other Essays, 1998, Lives of the Modern Poets, 1980, 1997, Updike: America's Man of Letters, 2000, 2005, Shelf Life: Literary Essays and Reviews, 2003. Fellow: Am. Acad. Arts & Sci. Office: Dept English Amherst College Amherst MA 01002-5000 Office Phone: 413-542-2079. Business E-Mail: whpritchard@amherst.edu.

PRITCHARD, WILLIAM ROY, former university systems administrator; b. Portage, Wis., Nov. 15, 1924; s. William Roy and Lillian Edith (Roberts) P.; m. Deanna Elaine Pritchard; children: Rosan June, William Roy, Caryl Jean, Alyn Evan, Cynthia Bedeau. Student, U. Wis., 1942-43; DVM, Kans. State U., 1946; PhD, U. Minn., 1953; JD, Ind. U., 1957; DSc (hon.), Kans. State U., 1970, Tufts U., 1988, Purdue U., 1977, U. Guelph, 1998. Asst. prof. U. Wis., 1946-49; assoc. prof. U. Minn., 1949-53; prof. Purdue U., 1953-57; prof., head vet. sci. U. Fla., 1957-61; assoc. dir. Vet. Med. Rsch. Inst., Ia. State U., 1961-62; prof. U. Calif., Davis, 1962—, dean Sch. Vet Medicine, 1962-82; assoc. dir. Agrl. Expt. Sta., 1962-72; coord. internat. agrl. programs U. Calif. system, 1977-81. Vis. fellow Woodrow Wilson Sch. Pub and Internat. Affairs, Princeton, 1968-69; John Thomson lectr. U. Queensland, 1966; co-dir. nat. vet. edn. program Duke U., 1987-92; spl. research hemmorrhagic diseases animals. Cons. Dept. Agr., Def. Dept., USPHS, VA, Calif. Dept. Health, FDA, 1962-97; bd. cons. agr. Rockefeller Found., 1962-66; nat. med. cons. surgeon gen. USAF, 1962-64; mem. FAO/WHO Expert Panel Vet. Edn., Pres.'s Sci. Adv. Com. Panel World Food Supply, 1966-67, President's Sci. Adv. Com. Panel Biology and Med. Sci., 1969-70, Joint Rsch. Com. Bd. Internat. Food and Agr. AID, 1977-81; Recognition lectr. Assn. Am. Vet. Med. Colls., 2005. With U.S. Army, 1942-44. Recipient Gov. Fla. award, 1961, Disting. Svc. award Kans. State U., 1963, Outstanding Achievement award U. Minn., 1976, Disting. Pub. Svc. award U. Calif., Davis, 1991, Gold Headed Cane award Am. Soc. Vet. Epidemiology, 1992. Mem. AAAS, APHA, Am. Vet. Med. Assn. (Internat. Vet. Congress award 1988), Nat. Acad. of Practice in Vet. Medicine (elected 1986), Am. Soc. Vet. Epidemiologists, Conf. of Pub. Health Vets. (hon. life), U.S. Animal Health Assn., Nat. Assn. State Univs. and Land-Grant Colls. (internat. affairs com. 1965-70), Order of Coif, Sigma Xi, Phi Zeta, Gamma Alpha. Home: 2409 Madrid Ct Davis CA 95616-0141

PRITCHETT, AMY R., aerospace engineer, educator; m. Eric N. Johnson; 2 children. BSc in Aeronautics and Astronautics Avionics Option, MIT, 1992, MSc in Aeronautics and Astronautics, 1994, DSc in Aeronautics and Astronautics, 1996. Joint asst. prof. aerospace engring. Ga. Inst. Tech., Atlanta, 1997—2003, asst. prof. indsl. & systems engring., 1997—2003, joint assoc. prof. aerospace engring., 2003—04, assoc. prof. indsl. & systems engring., 2003—04, joint assoc. prof. sch. indsl. and systems engring., 2005—, assoc. prof. aerospace engring., 2005, David S. Lewis Jr. assoc. prof. cognitive engring. Daniel Guggenheim sch. aerospace engring., 2005—. Sr. tech. fellow aerospace engring. Delft U. Tech., Netherlands, 2002; mem. aeronautics and space engring. bd. NRC, 2004—. Contbr. articles to sci. jours.; assoc. editor: AIAA Jour. Aerospace Computation, Info. and Communication, 2003—, mem. editl. adv. bd.: Jour. Cognitive Engring. and Decision Making, 2004—. Recipient Wings Club of Am. Merit award, 1992. Mem.: Am. Soc. Engring. Educators, Soc. Computer Simulation, Human Factors and Ergonomics Soc., AIAA (Lawrence Sperry award 2007), Sigma Gamma Tau (MIT chpt. pres. 1991—92, MIT chpt. treas. 1990—91), Tau Beta Pi. Office: Daniel Guggenheim Sch Aerospace Engring Ga Inst Tech 270 Ferst Dr Atlanta GA 30332-0150 E-mail: amy.pritchett@ae.gatech.edu.

PRITCHETT, DANIEL R., music educator; b. Indpls., Feb. 22, 1954; s. Jewell and Ruth Pritchett; children: Katie, Josh. BS, Ball State U., 1975; MA in Liberal Studies, Valparaiso U., 1978. Lic. tchr. Ind. Math tchr. Valparaiso (Ind.) H.S., 1975—86, assoc. dir. bands, 1975—95, dir. bands, chmn. music dept., 1995—; pvt. saxophone instr. Valparaiso, 1975—; profl. musician Ind. Named Oustanding H.S. Music Tchr., Ind. Music Educators Assn., 2004; named one of Fifty Directors Who Make A Difference, Sch. Band and Orch. Mag., 2001, 2005; recipient Music Alumni award, Ball State U., 1992, Greater Chicagoland H.S. Band Dir. ward, Quinalan & Fabish Music Co., 2005. Mem.: Internat. Assn. Jazz Educators, Coll. Band Dirs. Assn., Ind. State Sch. Music Assn. (pres. 1995), Ind. Bandmasters Assn. (pres. 1991—92, 1997—98), Pi Kappa Lambda, Phi Beta Mu, Phi Mu Alpha Sinfonia. Avocations: travel, music, fitness. Office: Valparaiso HS 2727 Campbell St Valparaiso IN 46385 Home Phone: 219-477-6873; Office Phone: 219-531-3070.

PRITCHETT, MERI KATHERINE, filmmaker; b. Richmond, Va., Aug. 28, 1973; d. Samuel Travis and Bertha Yates Pritchett. BA, Bard Coll., Annadale-on-Hudson, NY, 1997; MFA, U. So. Calif., LA, 2000. Rschr. A&E TV "Biography", LA, 2000—01; writer, prodr. Travel Channel "Worlds Best", LA, 2002; field prodr. Animal Planet "That's My Baby", LA, 2003; field dir., story prodr. Discovery Channel "Monster Nation", LA, 2004; sr. field dir. A&E TV "Intervention", LA, 2005—. Juror awards and fact film series Internat. Documentary Assn., LA, 2003—04; planning com. mem. Internat. Docuemntary Assn., Acad. Motion Picture Arts and Scis., 2001; prodr., dir. Charles Phoenix's Video Projects, LA, 2002—. Dir.: (films) Desertiopia, 2000 (Coll. Emmy, 2000); writer, prodr., dir., editor (Bunny Woman films), 1997, wirter, prodr., dir. (films) For Th e Love Of Cline, 1996. Hist., cultural monument nominatin writer LA Consservancy Modern Com., 2002—05, outreach chair, 2004—06. Scholar, Harold C. Lloyd Found., 1999, Women in Film. Avocations: hiking, knitting, travel.

PRITCHETT, SAMUEL TRAVIS, finance and insurance educator, researcher, consultant; b. Emporia, Va., Dec. 18, 1938; s. Harvey Eugene and Mary (Brown) P.; m. Bertha Yates, Feb. 20, 1960; children: John Travis, Meri Katherine. BSBA, Va. Poly. Inst. and State U., 1960, MSBA, 1967; DBA, Ind. U., 1969. CLU, ChFC, CPCU. Claim rep. Equitable Life Assurance Soc., Richmond, Va., 1960-64, asst. div. claim mgr., 1964-65; asst. prof. bus. adminstrn. U. Richmond, 1969-70; asst. prof. ins. Va. Commonwealth U., Richmond, 1970-72, assoc. prof. ins., 1972-73; assoc. prof. fin. and ins. U. S.C., Columbia, 1973-76, prof. fin. and ins., 1976-99, J.H. Fellers prof., 1981-83, W.F. Hipp prof. ins., 1983-2000, program dir., chair banking, fin., ins. and real estate, 1977-83, 99-00, acad. dir. MBA program, 1993-95, disting. prof. finance and ins., 1999-2000, disting. prof. emeritus, 2000—. Vis. prof. ins. Ind. U., Bloomington, 1995-96; chmn. Risk Theory Soc., Columbus, Ohio, 1987-88; acad. dir. internat. exec. devel. program Bamerindus Seguros, Curtiba, Brazil, 1995; mem., investment commr. S.C. Retirement Sys., 2005—. Author: Risk Management and Insurance, 7th edit., 1996, Stock Life Insurance Company Profitability, 1986, Individual Annuities as a Source of Retirement Income, 2d edit., 1982, An Economic Analysis of Workers' Compensation in South Carolina, 1994; assoc. editor Jour. Risk and Ins., 1982-86, editor, 1987-91; assoc. editor Fin. Svcs. Rev., 1989-95, 97-99; asst. editor Jour. Am. Soc. CLU and ChFC, 1993-98; mem. acad. rev. bd. Jour. Fin. Planning, 1990-91; mem. editl. bd. Jour. Bus. Rsch., 1976-83, Am. Jour. Small Bus., 1975-79; contbr. articles to profl. jours. Active S.C. Joint Ins. Study Com., 1981-86, 89-95; commr. S.C. Retirement Systems Investment Commn., 2005—. Mem. Am. Risk and Ins. Assn. (pres. 1980-81), Acad. Fin. Svcs. (pres. 1987-88), So. Risk and Ins. Assn. (pres. 1977-78), Fin. Mgmt. Assn., Profl. Ins. Agts. Found. (named Ins. Educator of Yr. 1989), Beta Gamma Sigma (pres. chpt. 1980-81), Gamma Iota Sigma (nat. trustee 1976-92), State Retirees Assn., (bd. mem., 2004—). Office: U SC Moore Sch Bus Columbia SC 29208-0001 Office Phone: 843-762-2645. Personal E-mail: tpritch@comcast.net. *Apply to others religious values such as honesty, humility, respect, and service. Cultivate a strong work ethic and select admirable mentors.*

PRITIKIN, DAVID T., lawyer; b. Freeport, Ill., May 2, 1949; BA summa cum laude, Cornell U., 1971; JD magna cum laude, Harvard U., 1974. Bar: Ill. 1974, US Ct. Appeals (9th cir.) 1975, US Ct. Appeals (7th cir.) 1976, U.S. Supreme Ct. 1977, US Ct. Appeals (fed. cir.) 1993. Ptnr. Sidley Austin LLP, Chgo., chair, nat. intellectual property practice. Fellow: Am. Coll. of Trial Lawyers. Office: Sidley Austin LLP 1 S Dearborn St Chicago IL 60603 Office Phone: 312-853-7359. Office Fax: 312-853-7036. Business E-Mail: dpritikin@sidley.com.

PRITIKIN, JAMES B., lawyer; b. Chgo., Feb. 18, 1939; s. Stan and Anne (Schwartz) P.; m. Barbara Cheryl Demovsky, Apr. 20, 1968 (dec. 1988); children: Gregory, David, Randi; m. Mary Szatkowski, July 7, 1990; 1 child, Peyton. BS, U. Ill., 1961; JD, DePaul U., 1965. Bar: Ill. 1965, U.S. Dist. Ct. (no. dist.) Ill. 1965, U.S. Supreme Ct. 1985; cert. matrimonial arbitrator. Pvt. practice, Chgo., 1965-68, 1984—; ptnr. Sudak, Grubman, Pritikin, Rosenthal & Feldman, Chgo., 1969-80, Pritikin & Sohn, Chgo., 1980-84, Nadler, Pritikin & Mirabelli, Chgo., 1997—. Hearing officer State of Ill. Atty. Registration and Disciplinary Commn. Named one of Best 100 Lawyers in Ill., Law and Politics, 2005. Fellow Internat. Acad. Matrimonial Lawyers, Am. Acad. Matrimonial Lawyers (past pres.); mem. ABA, Am. Acad. Matrimonial Lawyers (past pres. Ill. chpt.), Ill. Bar Assn., Chgo. Bar Assn. (cir. ct. Cook County liaison com.). Office: 1 Prudential Plz 130 E Randolph Dr Chicago IL 60601-6207 Office Phone: 312-861-4600.

PRITZKER, JEAN, film producer; Formerly with BBC; co-owner Dee Gee Entertainment. Prodr.: (films) The Phantom of the Opera, 1989, Simple Justice, 1990, Hostile Intent, 1997, Ricochet River, 1998, Wedding Planner, 2001, The Wedding Planner, 2001, Mean Creek, 2004, Hooligans, 2005, The Living Hell, 2006. Office: Dee Gee Entertainment Coronet Theater 366 N La Cienega Blvd Los Angeles CA 90048

PRITZKER, JOHN A., leisure services executive; s. Robert Pritzker; m. Lisa S. Pritzker; 3 children. Grad., Menlo Coll., U. Denver Coll. Hotel and Restaurant Mgmt. Various positions to divisional v.p. Calif. Hyatt; pres. Hyatt Ventures, Inc.; founder, pres. Red Sail Sports, Inc., 1988—. Exec. v.p. bus. devel. Key3Media Events, Inc., 2000; bd. dirs. Zoomedia Inc. Trustee San Francisco Mus. Modern Art; dir. Pritzker Found., Pritzker Cousins Found., Children Now; bd. dirs. U. Calif. San Francisco Found. Named one of Forbes Richest Americans, 2006, Top 200 Collectors, ARTnews mag., 2005—06. Office: Red Sail Sports 1 Ferry Bldg Ste 255 San Francisco CA 94111

PRITZKER, NICHOLAS J., diversified financial services company executive; BA, Lake Forest Coll.; JD, Univ. Chgo. Bar: Ill. 1975. Joined Hyatt Corp., 1978, formerly exec. v.p. devel. Chgo.; pres. Hyatt Devel. Corp., Chgo., 1981—99, chmn., 1999—; and vice chmn. Hyatt Internat. and Hyatt Corp., Chgo.; also ptnr. Pritzker & Pritzker law, Chgo. Chmn. bd. Eos Biotechnology, San Francisco, 2000—. Named one of Forbes' Richest Americans, 2006. Office: Hyatt Devel Corp 200 W Madison St Chicago IL 60606-3414

PRITZKER, PENNY, investor; b. Chgo., May 2, 1959; d. Donald N. and Sue Ann (Sandel) Pritzker; m. Bryan Traubert, Sept. 10, 1988; children: Donald Pritzker Traubert, Rose Pritzker Traubert. B in Econs., Harvard U., 1981; JD, MBA, Stanford U., 1985. Bar: Ill. 1985. Mgr. Hyatt Devel. Corp., Chgo., 1985-87; pres. Classic Residence by Hyatt, Chgo., 1987—; ptnr. Pritzker & Pritzker, Chgo., 1987—; pres. Pritzker Realty Grp. (formerly Penguin Group, L.P.), Chgo., 1990—; chmn. TransUnion Corp., 2005—. Chmn. exec. com. Encore Sr. Living, Portland, Oreg.; corp. adv.

bd. mem. Mayor Daley's Exec. Fellows Prog., Chgo.; mem. Mayor Daley's fin. com.; bd. dirs. William Wrigley, Jr. Co., Chgo., Coast-to-Coast Fin. Corp., NYC, Nat. Investment Conf., Washington.; Nat. Fin. chmn., Obama for Pres. Chair Mus. Contemporary Art, Chgo.; adv. bd. dirs. Chgo. Cares; mem. dean's coun. Harvard U.; mem. Women's Issues Network, Chgo., 1991—, The Chgo. Network, 1992—, Internat. Women's Forum, Chgo., Coun. Fgn. Rels., NY. Named a Woman to Watch, Crain's Chgo. Bus., 2007; named one of 50 Women to Watch, Wall St. Jour., 2005, 100 Most Powerful Women in World, Forbes mag., 2005, 400 Richest Ams., 2006; recipient Brick & Mortar award, Chgo. Equity Fund, 1991, Disting. Svc. award, REIA Kellogg, 1995. Mem. Nat. Assn. Sr. Living Industry Execs. (bd. dirs. 1989-91), Urban Land Inst., Young Pres.'s Orgn. Office: Classic Residence By Hyatt 71 S Wacker Dr Ste 900 Chicago IL 60606-4637 *

PRITZKER, THOMAS JAY, hotel executive; b. Chgo., June 6, 1950; s. Jay Arthur and Marian (Friend) P.; m. Margot Lyn Barrow-Sicree, Sept. 4, 1977; 3 children. BA, Claremont Men's Coll., Calif., 1971; MBA, U. Chgo., 1976, JD, 1976. Assoc. Katten, Muchin, Zavis, Pearl and Galler, Chgo., 1976-77; exec. v.p. Hyatt Corp., Chgo., 1977-80, pres., 1980—2002, chmn., CEO, 1999—2004; chmn. Hyatt Hotels Corp., 1980—2002, Hyatt Internat. Corp., 1999—2004; ptnr. Pritzker & Pritzker, Chgo., 1980—; CEO Global Hyatt Corp., Chgo., 2005—06, chmn., 2005—. Chmn. bd. dirs. The Pritzker Orgn., 1998—; bd. dirs. Royal Caribbean Cruises Ltd. Bd. trustees, chmn. Art Inst. Chgo., 1988—; bd. trustees U. Chgo. Named one of Forbes' Richest Americans, 2006. Mem. ABA, Ill. Bar Assn., Chgo. Bar Assn., Standard Club, Lake Shore Country Club. Office: Hyatt Ctr 71 S Wacker Dr Ste 4700 Chicago IL 60606 Office Phone: 312-873-4901.

PRIVES, CAROL, biologist, educator; PhD, McGill U. Prof. biology Columbia U., NYC, chmn. Dept. Biol. Scis. Mem. Damon Runyon Fellowship Com.; mem. sci. adv. bd. NIH Virology Study Section, N.J. Cancer Commn., Howard Hughes Med. Inst., GeminX. Mem. editl. bd.: Cell, Genes & Devel., Jour. Biology, Chemistry and Cancer Rsch.; editor: Jour. Virology, 1991—99. Fellow: Am. Acad. Arts and Scis.; mem.: Inst. Medicine. Office: Dept Biological Scis Columbia Univ 816 Fairchild Center MC422 1212 Amsterdam Ave New York NY 10027

PRIVETT, STEPHEN A., academic administrator, priest; b. San Francisco; BA in Philosophy and Classics, Gonzaga U., 1966; MDiv, U. Calif., Berkeley, 1972; postgrad., U. Calif., Santa Barbara, 1973—74; MA in Catechetics/Religious Edn., Cath. U. Am., 1982, PhD in Catechetics, 1985. Entered Soc. of Jesus, 1960. Instr. Latin, western civilization and religion Jesuit H.S., Sacramento, 1966—69; dir. Project 50 Santa Clara U., 1970—71; asst. dir. novices Coll. Queen of Peace, Santa Barbara, 1972—73; instr. modern European history, Latin and English Bellarmine Coll. Preparatory, San Jose, Calif., 1974—80, prin., 1975—80; asst. prof. religious studies dept. Santa Clara U., 1985—90, assoc. prof. religious studies dept., 1990—2000, co-dir. The Eastside Project, 1985—91, dir. Voice of the Voiceless: Inst. on Human Rights and Social Justice, 1989—91, v.p. acad. affairs, 1991—97, provost, v.p. acad. affairs, 1997—2000; pres. U. San Francisco, 2000—. Mem. U.S. Cath. Conf. on Certification and Accreditation, 1990—99; mem. Strategic Planning Commn. Calif. Province of the Soc. of Jesus, 1996—2002; mem. Nat. Seminar on Jesuit Higher Edn. U. Scranton, 1999—. Contbr. articles to profl. jours.; author: The U.S. Catholic Church and Its Hispanic Members: The Pastoral Vision of Robert E. Lucey, 1988. Vol. pastoral worker Jesuit Refugee Svc., El Salvador, 1988; bd. dirs. Jesuit Vol. Corps S.W., 1987—95, chair, 1988—91; bd. dirs. Christians for Peace in El Salvador, 1997—2000, Fromm Inst. for Lifelong Learning, U. San Francisco, 2000—; trustee Brophy Coll. Preparatory, Phoenix, 1996—, Seattle U., 2000—, U. Iberoamericana, Mexico City, 2001—; hon. mem. San Francisco Host Com., 2000—. Mem.: Assn. Grad. Programs in Ministry, Assn. Profs. and Rschrs. in Religious Edn. (mem. Cath. Assembly), Religious Edn. Assn., Assn. Cath. Colls. and Univs. (bd. dirs. 2002—), Assn. Jesuit Colls. and Univs. (bd. dirs. 2000—), Commonwealth Club Calif. (bd. govs.). Office: Univ San Francisco Office of the Pres 2130 Fulton St San Francisco CA 94117 Office Phone: 415-422-6762. *

PRIVETTE, JANET BROWN, elementary school educator; b. Raleigh, NC, Mar. 5, 1958; d. Dwight Dale and Peggy Hurt Brown; m. Randy Lee Privette, Dec. 21, 1980; children: Andrew Scott, Todd McLean. BS in Elem. Edn., East Carolina U., Greenville, NC, 1980; MEd in Elem. Edn., N.C. Ctrl. U., Durham, NC, 2000. Cert. tchr. Nat. Bd. Edn., 2000. Tchr. kindergarten Franklin County Schs., Louisburg, NC; reading specialist Wake County Pub. Schs., Zebulon, NC. Mem.: Internat. Reading Assn., Internat. Soc. Women Educators, Delta Kappa Gamma. Baptist. Home: 8409 Halifax Rd Youngsville NC 27596 Office: Zebulon Elem Sch 700 Proctor St Zebulon NC 27597

PRIZZI, JACK ANTHONY, investment banking executive; b. Rochester, NY, July 5, 1935; s. Samuel Anthony and Mary Ann (Emanuele) P.; m. Geraldine A. Bias, Feb. 16, 1957 (div. 1971); children: Lynne Marie, Michael Vincent, Karen Annette; m. Serafina M. Iacono, Sept. 30, 1995. BS in Chemistry, Va. Mil. Inst., 1956; MS in Phys. Chemistry, U. Va., 1961, MBA, 1963. Chem. engr. E.I. duPont DeNemours & Co., Inc., Niagara Falls, NY, 1956-57; engr. Project Mercury, NASA, 1959; mgr. planning and devel. PPG Industries, Pitts., 1963-68; gen. mgr. Process Components Inc., Norfolk, Va., 1968-70; ptrn. Alan Patricof Assocs., NYC, 1970-74, Beacon Ptnrs., NYC, 1974-76, 77-79, Stuart Bros., NYC, 1976-77; v.p. Walter E. Heller & Co.; exec. v.p. Heller Capital Svcs. Inc., NYC, 1979-84; sr. v.p. DG Am. Banking Corp., NYC, 1984-86; mng. dir. DnC Capital Corp., 1986-89; pres., CEO Jack A. Prizzi & Co., 1989-98. Founder, mng. prin. CoE Assocs., L.L.C., NYC, 1998—; spl. ltd. ptnr. Harvest Ptnrs., 1993-97; instr. advanced grades NY Power Squadron; bd. dirs. Meridian Resource Corp., 1993-2004. Capt. US Army, 1958-59. Capt. US Army, 1958—59. Grantee Office Naval Rsch., 1960, Calif. Rsch. Corp., 1960-61. Mem. Assn. for Corp. Growth, Natl. Assn. of Corp. Dir., Am. Chem. Soc., Raven Soc. Office: CoE Assocs LLC 156 W 56th St Ste 1400 New York NY 10019-3800 Office Phone: 212-265-7474 ext. 209. Business E-Mail: info@coeassociatesllc.com.

PRO, PHILIP MARTIN, judge; b. Richmond, Calif., Dec. 12, 1946; s. Leo Martin and Mildred Louise (Beck) P.; m. Dori Sue Hallas, Nov. 13, 1982; 1 child, Brenda Kay. BA, San Francisco State U., 1968; JD, Golden Gate U., 1972. Bar: Calif. 1972, Nev. 1973, U.S. Ct. Appeals (9th cir.) 1973, U.S. Dist. Ct. Nev. 1973, U.S. Supreme Ct. 1976. Pub. defender, Las Vegas, 1973-75; asst. U.S. atty. Dist. Nev., Las Vegas, 1975-78; dep. atty. gen. State of Nev., Carson City, 1979-80; magistrate US Dist. Ct. Nev., Las Vegas, 1980-87, judge, 1987—, chief judge, 2002—. Instr. Atty. Gen.'s Advocacy Inst., Nat. Inst. Trial Advocacy, 1992; chmn. com. adminstrn. of magistrate judge system Jud. Conf. U.S., 1993—; bd. dirs. Fed. Jud. Cts. Program com. and issues in justice com. NCCJ, Las Vegas, 1982—. Mem. ABA, Fed. Judges Assn. (bd. dirs. 1992—, v.p. 1997-2001), Nev. State Bar Assn., Calif. State Bar Assn., Nev. Judges Assn. (instr.), Assn. Trial Lawyers Am., Nev. Am. Inn Ct. (pres. 1989-91), Ninth Cir. Jury (instructions com.), Nat. Conf. U.S. Magistrates (sec.). Republican. Office: US Dist Ct 7015 Fed Bldg 333 Las Vegas Blvd S Ste 7015 Las Vegas NV 89101-5883 Office Phone: 702-464-5510. Business E-Mail: philip_pro@nvd.uscourts.gov.

PROBASCO, PEGGY LEE, lawyer; b. Ogden, Utah, Aug. 13, 1952; d. Robert Vere and Dorleen Elfrieda (Oppliger) P.; m. John Matthias Verburg, Dec. 18, 1972 (div.). Student, Weber State Coll., 1971-72, Utah State U., 1972-74, U. Utah, 1977-79; BA in Philosophy, U. Mont., 1980, JD, 1983. Bar: Mont. 1983. Unit mgr. Univ. Med. Ctr., Salt Lake City, 1975-81; inventory controller U. Mont., Missoula, 1981-82, research asst. Sch. Law, 1981-82; legal intern Petersen & Berndt, Missoula, 1982, Robinson, Doyle & Bell, Hamilton, Mont., 1982-83; assoc. Law Office of Gerald D. Schultz, Hamilton, 1983-86; staff atty. Dist. XI Human Resource Council, Inc., Missoula, 1985; dep. county atty. Ravalli County, 1986-87; city judge, Stevensville, 1985-86; rep. Women's Law Caucus, Missoula, 1980-83; researcher Rocky Mountain Natural Resource Clinic, Missoula, 1981-83, atty. specialist, Child Support Enforcement Divsn. Mont. Dept. Pub. Health and Human Services, 1991-. Del. Utah Dem. Conv., Salt Lake City, 1972; candidate Mont. Ho. of Reps., 1984. Mem. ABA, Mont. Bar Assn. (pres. 2006-07), Assn. Trial Lawyers Am., Am. Judicature Soc., Mont. Magistrates Assn. (dist. chmn.), LWV, Phi Delta Phi. Lodge: Soroptimists (1st v.p.). Office: Child Support Enforcement Divsn PO Box 202943 Helena MT 59620-2943

PROBST, LAWRENCE F., III, interactive software/gaming executive; b. 1950; BS, U. Del., 1972. Dist. sales mgr. Johnson & Johnson, 1972-80; nat. accounts mgr. The Clorox Co., 1980-82, Mediagenic (formerly Activision Inc.), 1982-84; v.p. sales Electronic Arts, Inc., 1984—86, sr. v.p., distbn., 1987—91, pres., 1991—98, CEO Redwood City, Calif., 1991—2007, exec. chmn., 1994—. Bd. dirs. Electronic Arts, Inc., 1991—, MP3.com, Inc., 1999—. Office: Electronic Arts Inc 209 Redwood Shores Pkwy Redwood City CA 94065 *

PROBSTEIN, RONALD FILMORE, mechanical engineering educator; b. NYC, Mar. 11, 1928; s. Sidney and Sally (Rosenstein) P.; m. Irene Weindling, July 30, 1950; 1 child, Sidney. BME, NYU, 1948; MSE, Princeton U., NJ, 1950, AM, 1951, PhD, 1952; ScD (hon.), Brown U., 1997. Rsch. asst. physics NYU, 1946-48, instr. engring. mechanics, 1947-48; rsch. asst. dept. aero. engring. Princeton U., 1948-52, rsch. assoc., 1952-53, asst. prof., 1953-54; asst. prof. divs. engring., applied math. Brown U., 1954-55, assoc. prof., 1955-59, prof., 1959-62; prof. mech. engring. MIT, Cambridge, 1962—89, Ford prof. engring., 1989-96, prof. mech. engring., 1996—2001, Ford prof. engring. emeritus, 1996—; Disting. prof. engring. U. Utah, 1973; sr. ptnr. Water Purification Assoc., Cambridge, 1974-82; chmn. bd. Water Gen. Corp., Cambridge, 1982-83; sr. corp. tech. advisor Foster-Miller, Inc., 1983-91. Commr. commn. on engring. and tech. systems NRC, 1980-83, mem. space studies bd., 2004-07; sci. advisor to bd. Corrpro Cos., 1993-2001. Author: Hypersonic Flow Theory, 1959, Hypersonic Flow, Inviscid Flows, 1966, 03, Water in Synthetic Fuel Production, 1978, Synthetic Fuels, 1982, 2006, Physicochemical Hydrodynamics, 1989, 03; editor: Introduction to Hypersonic Flow, 1961, Physics of Shock Waves, 1966, 02, Jour. PhysicoChem. Hydrodynamics, 1987-89; contbr. articles to profl. jours.; patentee in field. Guggenheim fellow, 1960-61; R.F. Probstein Lecture Series in Engring. Sci., MIT, established 1999. Fellow AAAS, AIAA, Am. Acad. Arts and Sci. (councilor 1975-79), Am. Phys. Soc., ASME (Freeman award 1971); mem. AIChE, NAS (chmn. engring. sci. sect. 2005—), NAE (com. membership 2001-05, chmn. 2005), Internat. Acad. Astronautics. Home: 5 Seaver St Brookline MA 02445-5714 Office: 77 Massachusetts Ave Cambridge MA 02139-4301 Office Phone: 617-253-2240. Business E-Mail: rfprobst@mit.edu.

PROCHASKA, ALICE, historian, librarian; m. Franklyn Kimmel Prochaska, June 25, 1971; children: Elizabeth, William. BA in Modern History, Somerville Coll., U. Oxford, 1968; MA in History, U. Oxford, 1973, DPhil in Modern History, 1975. Asst. keeper Pub. Record Office, England, 1975—84; sec. & libr. Inst. Hist. Rsch. U. London, 1984—92; dir. spl. collections Brit. Libr., 1992—2001; univ. libr. Yale U., New Haven, 2001—. Mem. dept. edn. sci. history working group, Nat. Curriculum, 1989-90; trusteeSir Winston Churchill Archive Trust, 1995-2001; chair Nat. Coun. Archives, UK, 1992-95; gov. London Guildhall U. (now London Metro. U.), 1995-2001; commr. Royal Commn. Hist. Manuscripts, 1998-2001; mem. Rare Books and Manuscripts Standing com. Internat. Fed. Libr. Assn., 1997-, chair 1999-2003; chair collection and access issues com., Assn. Rsch. Libr., 2003-05, spl. collections working group, 2007-; mem. adv. com. for global resources network Assn. Am. Univs.2003-; bd. mem. Ctr. Rsch. Libr., 2003-, vice chair 2005-07, chair 2007-; bd. mem. Yale U. Press 2004. Author: History of the General Federation of Trade Unions, 1982, Irish History from 1700: A Guide to Sources in the Public Record Office, 1986; co-editor (with Frank Prochaska): Margaretta Acworth's Georgian Cookery Book, 1987; contbr. numerous articles in scholarly and profl. jours. Named an Hon. Fellow, Royal Holloway U. of London, 2002, Inst. Hist. Rsch. U. London, 2001; recipient JJ Astor prize in Libr. Sci., Checkpoint Charlie Found., Berlin, 2006. Fellow: Royal Hist. Soc. (v.p. 1995—99). Avocations: history, theater, collecting watercolors, gardening. Office: Libr Adminstrv Services Sterling Meml Libr Yale U 130 Wall St PO Box 208240 New Haven CT 06520-8240 Home Phone: 203-624-3683; Office Phone: 203-432-1818. Business E-Mail: alice.prochaska@yale.edu.

PROCHNOW, DOUGLAS LEE, lawyer; b. Omaha, Jan. 9, 1952; s. Albert Delmer and Betty Jean (Wood) Prochnow. BA with high distinction, U. Nebr., 1974; JD, Northwestern U., 1977. Bar: Ill. 1977, U.S. Dist. Ct. (no. dist.) Ill. 1977, U.S. Ct. Appeals (7th cir.) 1989, U.S. Supreme Ct. 2000. Assoc. Wildman, Harrold, Allen & Dixon, Chgo., 1977-84, ptnr., 1985—. Spl. asst. corp. counsel City of Chgo., 1986—87; adj. prof. law Northwestern U. Sch. Law, 2005—. Pres. Chgo. bd. Prevent Child Abuse Am. Mem. ABA, ATLA (assoc.), Ill. Bar Assn., Chgo. Bar Assn., Soc. Trial Lawyers, Def. Rsch. Inst., Am. Health Lawyers Assn., Phi Beta Kappa, Phi Eta Sigma. Office: Wildman Harrold Allen & Dixon 225 W Wacker Dr Ste 2700 Chicago IL 60606-1224 Home: 159 E Walton St Unit 12B Chicago IL 60611 Home Phone: 312-951-8975; Office Phone: 312-201-2526. Business E-Mail: prochnow@wildman.com.

PROCKOP, DARWIN JOHNSON, biochemist, medical educator; b. Palmerton, Pa., Aug. 31, 1929; s. John and Sophie (Gurski) Prockop; m. Elinor Sacks, Apr. 15, 1961; children: Susan Elizabeth, David John. AB, Haverford Coll., 1951; MA, Oxford U., 1953; MD, U. Pa., 1956; PhD, George Washington U., 1962; DSc (hon.) (hon.), U. Oulu, Finland, 1983, U. So. Fla., 1993. Investigator NIH, 1957—61; assoc., asst. prof., asso. prof., prof. medicine and biochemistry U. Pa., Phila., 1961—72; prof., chmn. dept. biochemistry U. Medicine and Dentistry of N.J. (Rutgers Med. Sch.), Piscataway, NJ, 1972—86; prof., chmn. dept. biochemistry and molecular biology Jefferson Med. Coll., Phila., 1986—96, dir. Jefferson Inst. Molecular Medicine, 1986—96; prof., dir. Ctr. for Gene Therapy, MCP/Hahnemann Med. Coll., Phila., 1996—2000; prof., dir. Ctr. Gene Therapy Tulane U. Med. Ctr., New Orleans, 2000—. Contbr. Served with USPHS, 1958—61. Named hon. companion, U. Manchester, 1999; recipient Disting. Alumnus award, George Washington U., 1991, U. Pa., 1994, Hopkins Meml. medal., Brit. Biochem. Soc, 1998; fellow Fulbright Found., 1951—53; grantee, NIH, 1961—. Mem.: NAS, Am. Assn. Physicians, Am. Soc. Clin. Investigation, Am. Soc. Biol. Chemists, Acad. Finland, Inst. Medicine, Alpha Omega Alpha, Phi Beta Kappa. Achievements include research in on collagen and gene therapy. Home: 291 Locust St Philadelphia PA 19106-3913 Office: Ctr Gene Therapy Tulane U Med Ctr 1430 Tulane Ave New Orleans LA 70112-2699 E-mail: dprocko@tulane.edu.

PROCOPE, ERNESTA GERTRUDE, insurance company executive; b. Bklyn. d. Clarence and Elvira Forster; m. Albin Bowman (dec. 1952); m. John L. Procope, July 3, 1954. Student, Bklyn. Coll., Coll. Ins., Pohs Inst. Ins.; LLD (hon.), Adelphi U., Marymount Manhattan Coll., 1987, Howard U., 1989; HHD (hon.), Morgan State U., 1978. Founder, pres., CEO E.G. Bowman Co. Inc., NYC, 1953—. Panelist corp. governance and advancement of women US Dept. Labor, 1981; former bd. dir. Avon Products, Inc., Chubb Corp., Columbia Gas Sys. Amb. 10th anniversary independence celebration Republic of Gambia, 1975; trustee NY Zool. Soc., Cornell U., Adelphi U. Named Disting. Black Woman in Corp. Role, Nat. Coun. Negro Women, Inc., 1981, Bus. Person of Yr., Urban Bankers Coalition, 1990; named to African Am. Bus. Hall of Fame & Mus., 2003, Minority Bus. Hall of Fame and Mus., 2006; recipient Achievement award, Thelma T. Johnson Meml. Scholarship Fund, 1972, Interracial Coun. for Bus. Opportunity, 1973, Women of the Yr. award, presented at White House by First Lady Patricia Nixon, 1972, Cmty. Svc. award, F & M Schaefer Brewing Co., 1974, Sojourner Truth award, Negro Bus. and Profl. Women's Club, Inc., 1974, Bus. Achievement award, Nat. Bus. League, 1976, Catalyst award, Women Dirs. of Corps., 1977, Torch of Liberty award, Anti-Defammation League, 1990, Disting. Svc. award, NAACP, 1991, Entrepreneurial Excellence award, Dow Jones/Wall Street Jour., 1992, Whitney M. Young, Jr. award, 1992, Trumpet award, Turner Broadcasting Sys., 2002, Essence Power award, 2004, Women of Power Legacy award, Black Enterprise Mag., 2006. Mem.: Nat. Assn. Ins. Women, Nat. Assn. Ins. Brokers, Cosmopolitan Club, Women's Forum, Alpha Kappa Alpha (hon.). Presbyterian. Office: EG Bowman Co Inc 97 Wall St New York NY 10005-4302 Office Phone: 212-425-8150. Business E-Mail: procope@egbowman.com.

PROCTOR, CONRAD ARNOLD, physician; b. Ann Arbor, Mich., July 14, 1934; s. Bruce and Luena Marie (Crawford) P.; m. Phyllis Darlene Anderson, June 23, 1956; children: Sharon Heimbach Pins, Barbara Jan Brown, David Conrad, Todd Bruce. MD, U. Mich., 1959, MS, 1964. Cert. Am. Bd. Otolaryngology. Intern St. Joseph Mercy Hosp., Ann Arbor, 1959-60; jr. clin. instr. Univ. Hosp., Ann Arbor, 1961-63, sr. clin. instr., 1963-65; chief dept. otolaryngology Munson Army Hosp., Ft. Leavenworth, Kans., 1965-67; mem. attending staff William Beaumont Hosp., Royal Oak, Mich., 1967—. Instr. Am. Acad. Otolaryngology, Washington, 1968-82, guest examiner, Chgo., 1978-79. Author: Current Therapy in Otolaryngology, 1984-85; (booklet) Dietary Treatment of Meniere's Syndrome, 1983, Hyperinsulinemia and Tinnitus, 1988; (manual) Hereditary Sensorineural Hearing Loss, 1978, Etiology, Treatment of Fluid Retention in Meniere's Syndrome, 1992; (med. jour.) Abnormal Insulin Levels and Vertigo, 1981. Mem. US 5th Army Basketball, Tennis teams, 1965-67; dir. Christian edn. Bloomfield Hills (Mich.) Bapt. Ch., 1969-72, fin. chmn., 1975-78, Sunday sch. tchr., 1967—. Served to capt. U.S. Army, 1965-67. Recipient 1st pl. award med. rsch. Students Am. Med. Assn., 1959, Commdg. Gen.'s Acheivement award Ft. Leavenworth, Kans., 1967, Merit award Am. Acad. Otolaryngology, 1978; holder 8 world records Internat. Game Fish Assn., 6 world records Nat. Fresh Water Fishing Hall Fame. Mem. AMA, Mich. State Med. Assn., Oakland County Med. Assn., Am. Bd. Otolaryngology, ACS, Triological Soc., Otosclerosis Study Group, Internat. Game Fish Assn. (Nat. Fresh Water Fishing Hall of Fame), Am. Legion, U.S. Tennis Assn., Victors and Presidents Club (Ann Arbor), Phi Eta Sigma, Phi Kappa Phi, Phi Beta Kappa. Republican. Avocation: Arctic exploration. Office: 3535 W 13 Mile Rd Ste 307 Royal Oak MI 48073-6710 Office Phone: 248-288-2137.

PROCTOR, DAVID RAY, lawyer; b. Nashville, Apr. 18, 1956; s. Raymond Douglas and Margaret Florence (Coffey) Proctor; m. Robbin Lynn Fuqua, May 12, 1984 (div.); children: Rachael Lynne, Benjamin David; m. Shana T. Murdoch, Mar. 30, 2002; stepchildren: Sarah-Rachael Murdoch, Rebecca Caroline Murdoch. AA in Polit. Sci., Cumberland Jr. Coll., 1976; BA in Polit. Sci., Vanderbilt U., 1978; JD, Cumberland Sch. Law, 1981; LLM in Taxation, U. Fla., 1983. Bar: Ala. 1981, Tenn. 1983, US Tax Ct. 1983. Law clk. to presiding justice Ala. Supreme Ct., Montgomery, 1981-82; assoc. Thrailkill & Goodman, Nashville, 1983-84; v.p. taxes Alfa Mut. Ins. Co., Montgomery, 1984—. Conbtg. editor: Cumberland Law Rev., 1980—81; contbr. articles to profl. jours. Tchr. Rsch. Bd., Birmingham, Ala., 1980; active Montgomery Area United Way, 1985—; mem. adv. bd. Montgomery Therapeutic Recreation Ctr., 2000—, pres., 2001; treas. Taylor Rd. Bapt. Ch., 1994—95, 1997—98, 2007—, asst. treas., 1996, 1999—2006. Mem.: ABA, Am. Coun. Life Insurers (mem. tax com. 2007—), Am. Coun. Life Ins. Tax Com., Montgomery Bar Assn., Tenn. Bar Assn., Ala. Bar Assn., Nat. Assn. Mut. Ins. Cos. (mem. tax com. 1988—, chmn. 1997—99, mem. exec. tax com. 2000—), Property Casualty Insurers Assn. Am. (mem. exec. tax com. 2000—03), Sunrise Exch. Club Montgomery (treas. 1989—91), Pi Sigma Alpha, Phi Alpha Delta. Avocations: running, music, sports, charities. Home: 9224 Sturbridge Pl Montgomery AL 36116 Office: Alfa Mut Ins Co 2108 E South Blvd Montgomery AL 36116-2015 Office Phone: 334-613-4498. Business E-Mail: dproctor@alfains.com.

PROCTOR, GEORGANNE C., investment company executive; b. 1956; m. Robert Proctor. BS in Bus. Mgmt., U. S.D.; MBA in Fin., Calif. State U., Hayward. From fin. analyst Bechtel Financing Svcs. (now part of Bechtel Enterprises), 1982-89; mgr. Bechtel Info. Tech. Group., 1989-91, mgr. project cost controls for Disney MGM Studio project Paris, 1991; dir. fin. & acctg. Buena Vista Home Video Internat., 1991-93; dir. project & divsn. fin. Walt Disney Imagineering, 1993-94; CFO Bechtel Enterprises, 1994-97; sr. v.p., CFO Bechtel Group, Inc., San Francisco, 1997—2002; exec. v.p., CFO Golden West Fin. Corp., 2002—06, Teachers Ins. & Annuity Found. Coll. Retirement Equities Fund (TIAA-CREF), NYC, 2006—. Bd. dirs. The Bechtel Group, 1994—2002. Amb. Calif. State. U., Hayward. Office: TIAA-CREF 730 3rd Ave New York NY 10017 *

PROCTOR, KENNETH DONALD, lawyer; b. Balt., Apr. 28, 1944; s. Kenneth Chauncey and Sarah Elizabeth (Kent) P.; m. Judith Danner Harris, Aug. 2, 1969; children: Kenneth Scott, Kent Harris, Janet Cameron BS, Lehigh U., 1966; JD, U. Md., 1969. Bar: Md. 1969, U.S. Dist. Ct. Md. 1970, U.S. Supreme Ct. 1974, U.S. Ct. Appeals (4th cir.) 1980. Law clk. to judge Md. Ct. Appeals, 1969-70; assoc. Miles & Stockbridge, Balt., 1970-73, 74-76, ptnr., 1976-81, Towson, Md., 1981-96; asst. atty. gen. State of Md., Balt., 1973-74. Trustee Gilman Sch., Balt., 1982-85. Mem. ABA, Md. Bar Assn., Baltimore County Bar Assn. Democrat. Episcopalian. Office: Proctor & McKee PA 102 W Pennsylvania Ave Ste 505 Towson MD 21204-4542 Office Phone: 410-823-2258. E-mail: kdproctor@proctorlaw.com.

PROCTOR, RICHARD JAMES, geologist, consultant; b. LA, Aug. 2, 1931; s. George Arthur and Margaret Y. (Goodman) P.; m. Ena McLaren, Feb. 12, 1955; children: Mitchell, Jill, Randall. BA, Calif. State U., LA, 1954; MA, UCLA, 1958. Engring. geologist, Calif.; cert. profl. geologist Am. Inst. Profl. Geologists. Chief geologist Met. Water Dist., LA, 1958-80; pres., cons. geologist Richard J. Proctor, Inc., Arcadia, Calif., 1980-95. Vis. assoc. prof. Calif. Inst. Tech., Pasadena, 1975-78. Author: History of AIPG, 2003; co-author: Citizens Guide to Geologic Hazards, 1993; editor: Professional Practice Guidelines, 1985, Engineering Geology Practice in Southern California, 1992, (screenplays) My Friend Tom Horn, 2005, Stopping by Woods, 2006. Pres., dir. Arcadia Hist. Soc., 1993-96. Fellow Geol. Soc. Am. (Burwell Meml. award 1972); mem. Assn. Engring. Geologists (hon., pres. 1979), Am. Inst. Profl. Geologists (hon., pres. 1989, Van Couvering Meml. award 1990, Parker Meml. medal 2003), Am. Geol. Inst. (sec.-treas. 1979-83), Conf. Calif. Hist. Socs. (pres. 2004-06).

PROCTOR, RICHARD JEROME, JR., business educator, expert witness, accountant; b. NYC, Oct. 6, 1941; s. Richard Jerome and Edith (Decker) P.; m. Elfriede N. Neundorfer, Aug. 19, 1967; children: Courtney, John, David. BS, Columbia U., 1963, MBA, 1970. CPA, N.Y., Conn.; cert. valuation analyst, cert. govt. fin. mgr.; cert. forensic acct. Am. Bd. Forensic Acctg. Sr. acct. Arthur Andersen, NYC, 1970-72; dir. acctg. N.Y. Stock Exchange, NYC, 1972-75; chief fin. officer Executrans, Greenwich, Conn., 1975-77; dir. planning Irvin Industries, Stamford, Conn., 1977-79; asst. prof. acctg. and taxation U. Hartford (Conn.), 1979-82; prof., dir. Ctr. for Fin. Forensics Western Conn. State U., Danbury, 1983—. Pvt. practice,

1979—; cons., expert witness in field. Author (textbook): Proli Footwear-A Team Based Audit Simulation, 2002. Mem. AICPA, Conn. Soc. CPAs (Disting. Authors award 1983, 92), Nat. Assn. Cert. Valuation Analysts, Inst. Bus. Appraisers, Am. Acctg. Assn., Inst. Mgmt. Accts., Am. Bd. Forensic Acctg. (diplomate). Home: 31 Cooper Hill Rd Ridgefield CT 06877-5903 Office: Western Conn State U 181 White St Danbury CT 06810-6826 Home Phone: 203-438-7742; Office Phone: 203-438-7742.

PROCTOR, ROBERT NEEL, history educator; b. Corpus Christi, Tex., June 25, 1954; s. Norman Neel Proctor and Eugenia K. (Milton) P.; children: Jonathan N. Proctor, Geoffrey R. Schiebinger. BS in Biology, Ind. U., 1976; MA in History of Sci., Harvard U., 1977, PhD in History of Sci., 1984. Instr. and teaching fellow biology, history of sci. Harvard U., Cambridge, Mass., 1976-84; Andrew Mellon postdoctoral fellow history of sci. program Stanford (Calif.) U., 1984-86; faculty mem./organizer program in sci., tech. and power Eugene Lang Coll., New Sch. for Social Rsch., NYC, 1986-90; assoc. prof. dept. history Pa. State U., University Park, 1990-93, prof. history, 1993-2000, disting. prof. history, 2000—. Vis. asst. prof. history Va. Poly. Inst. and State U., Blacksburg, summer 1984; vis. lectr. dept. history U. Calif.-Berkeley, Fall 1985. Author: Racial Hygiene: Medicine Under the Nazis, 1988, Value-Free Science? Purity and Power in Modern Knowledge, 1991, Cancer Wars: How Politics Shapes What We Know and Don't Know About Cancer, 1995, The Nazi War on Cancer, 1999. Recipient Disting. Alumni Svc. award Ind. U., 1975, Viseltear prize, 1999; Fulbright grad. scholar, Free U., Berlin, 1980-81; NSF grad. fellow, 1976-79, Charlotte W. Newcombe doctoral dissertation fellow, 1982-83, Andrew Mellon postdoctoral fellow, Stanford U., 1984-86, Ctr. for Advanced Study in the Behavioral Scis. summer fellow, 1986, George A. and Eliza Gardner Howard Found. fellow, 1989-90, Max Planck Inst. for History of Sci. fellow 1999-2000; NEH summer stipend, 1989; grantee ACLS, 1989, Nat. Ctr. Human Genome Rsch, 1992-93; sr. scholar in residence U.S. Holocaust Meml. Mus., 1994. Mem. Am. Acad. Arts and Scis., Phi Beta Kappa.

PROCTOR, WILLIAM GILBERT, JR., writer, editor; b. Atlanta, Oct. 11, 1941; s. William Gilbert and Maud (Moore) P.; A.B. magna cum laude in History, Harvard U., 1963, J.D., 1966; m. Priscilla Adrian Moore, June 17, 1967. Admitted to Tex. bar, 1966; reporter NY Daily News, 1969-73; editor-in-chief Ch. Bus. Report, NYC, 1976-82; pres. Inkslingers, Inc.; free-lance writer, NYC and Fla., 1973-; writer, lectr.-in-residence Teen Writers Workshop, Vero Beach, Fla., 2000-; works include Survival on the Campus, 1972, Help Wanted: Faith Required, 1974, The Commune Kidnapping, 1975, Women in the Pulpit, 1976, PDA-Personal Death Awareness, 1976, On the Trail of God, 1977, The Born-Again Christian Catalog, 1979, Return of the Star of Bethlehem, 1980, Too Mean to Die, 1982, The Preconception Gender Diet, 1982, Adventures in Immortality, 1982, How to Go From Rags to Riches in Real Estate, 1982, The Templeton Touch, 1983, The Ethical Executive, 1984, Beyond the Relaxation Response, 1984, Forecast 2000, 1984, Beyond Reason, 1984, The Great American Success Story, 1985, Tough Marriage, 1986, The G-Index Diet, 1993, The Terrible Speller, 1993, Work a 4-Hour Day, 1994, Patient Power, 1996, The Resurrection Report, 1998, The Last Star, 2000, The Gospel According to the New York Times, 2000, Moongate, 2002, The Breakout Principle, 2003; writer, collaborator, Kenneth H. Cooper's Controlling Cholesterol, 1989, Charles Schwab's How to Be Your Own Stockbroker, 1991, Art Linkletter's Yes You Can!, 1982, Warren Avis's Take a Chance to Be First, 1987; editor The Light Speed Study Bible, 2005; co-author: Kenneth and Tyler Cooper's Start Strong, Finish Strong, 2007. Served with USMC, 1966-69. Mem. Authors Guild, Tex. Bar, NYC Bar Assn. Address: PO Box 643511 Vero Beach FL 32964

PROCTOR, WILLIAM LEE, college chancellor; b. Atlanta, Jan. 27, 1933; s. Samuel Cook and Rose Elizabeth (Nottingham) P.; m. Pamela Evans Duke; children: Samuel Matthews (dec.), Priscilla Nottingham. BS, Fla. State U., 1956, MS, 1964, PhD, 1968; DHL (hon.), Nova Southeastern U., 2003; LLD (hon.), Flagler Coll., 2004. Tchr. Seminole County Pub. Schs., Longwood, Fla., 1956-57, 58-62, Orange County Fla. Pub. Schs., Orlando, 1957-58; athletic coach Fla. State U., Tallahassee, 1962-65, asst. dean men, 1965-67, grad. fellow, 1967-68; supt. of schs. Rock Hill (S.C.) Sch. Dist. #3, 1968-69; dean of men U. Ctrl. Fla., Orlando, 1969-71; pres. Flagler Coll., St. Augustine, Fla., 1971-2001, chancellor, 2001—; mem. representing Dist. 20, Fla. Ho. of Reps., 2004. Cons. on higher edn. policy Heritage Found., Washington, 1983—, Fla. Bd. Edn., 2001-03, State Bd. Edn., 2003-2004; mem. Commn. on Colls., So. Assn. Colls. and Schs., 1995-2000; dir. Tchr. Edn. Accreditation Coun. Vice-chmn. Fla. Edn. Stds. Commn., 1995-2001; bd. dirs. Penney Retirement Cmty., chmn., 1991-2004; bd. dirs. Vicar's Landing Retirement Cmty., chmn., 1992-95, bd., 1990-96; trustee, chmn. Fla. Sch. for Deaf and Blind, St. Augustine, 1984-2001; adv. coun. Salvation Army, St. Johns County; devel. coun. First Coast Work Force, 1998-2001; mem. Bus./Higher Edn. Partnership, 2000-01; chmn. Cmtys. in Schs., St. Johns County, Fla., 2002—; elected mem. Fla. Ho. Reps. Dist. 20, 2004. Recipient Disting. Educator award Fla. State U. Coll. Edn., 1989, Phil Carroll award Soc. for Advancement Mgmt., 1990, Disting. Svc. award Fla. Sch. for Deaf and Blind, 1990, Patrick Henry Medallion patriotic achievement Mil. Order of World Wars, 1991, Stetson S Club Achievement award, 1993, Order of the South So. Acad. Letters, Arts, and Scis., Excellence in Mgmt. award Soc. for Advancement of Mgmt., 2000, Lifetime Edn. Achievement award, 2001, Disting. Svc. award Fla. Assn. Colls. and Univs., 2002, Sec. Jim Horne's Life Edn. Leadership award; named to Fla. State U. Athletic Hall of Fame, 1988, Order of La Florida, 2001. Mem. Am. Assn. Pres. of Ind. Colls., State Hist. Assn., Ind. Colls. and Univs. of Fla. (legis. chmn. 1974-77, vice chmn. 1976-77, chmn. 1978-79, Liberty Bell award 2003), Rotary (pres. 1978-79, bd. govs. dist. 697 1988-89). Republican. Presbyterian. Avocations: history, jogging, Karate. Office: Flagler Coll Office of the Chancellor PO Box 1027 Saint Augustine FL 32085-1027 Office Phone: 904-829-6481 ext. 210. Business E-Mail: proctorw@flagler.edu.

PROEBSTING, EDWARD LOUIS, JR., retired horticulturist; b. Woodland, Calif., Mar. 2, 1926; s. Edward Louis and Dorothy (Critzer) P.; m. Patricia Jean Connolly, June 28, 1947; children: William Martin, Patricia Louise, Thomas Alan (dec.). BS, U. Calif., Davis, 1948; PhD, Mich. State U., 1951. Asst. horticulturist Wash. State U., Prosser, 1951-57, assoc. horticulturist, 1957-63, horticulturist, 1963-93, supt. Irrigated Agrl. Rsch. and Ext. Ctr., 1990-93; ret., 1993. Vis. prof. Cornell U., Ithaca, N.Y., 1966; vis. scientist Hokkaido U., Sapporo, Japan, 1978, Victoria Dept. Agr., Tatura, Australia, 1986—. Contbr. numerous articles to profl. jours. Scoutmaster Boy Scouts Am., Prosser, 1963-76, dist. chmn., 1976-78. Served to lt. USNR, 1943-46, 52-54. Recipient Silver Beaver award Boy Scouts Am.; fellow Japan Soc. Promotion Sci., Sapporo, 1978, Res. Bank. Australia, 1986. Fellow AAAS, Am. Soc. Hort. Sci. (pres. 1983-84, sci. editor jour. 1993-98). Methodist. Avocations: backpacking, native plants. Home: 1929 Miller Ave Prosser WA 99350-1532

PROEFROCK, CARL KENNETH, academic medical administrator; b. Curtis, Ill., Mar. 30, 1928; s. Carl Robert and Anna Lorraine (Hagel) Proefrock; m. Margaret Muntz (dec. Apr. 1984); 4 children; m. Janelle Dillon, Sept. 8, 1988 (dec. Sept. 2001). BA, Carthage Coll., Kenosha, Wis., 1949; MDiv, Chgo. Luth. Theol. Sem., 1953. Pastor Evang. Luth. Ch. Am., 1953—66; sr. com. orgn. specialist N.Y.C. Housing and Devel. Adminstrn., 1966-68; exec. dir. Model Cities Program, Manchester, NH, 1968-70, Health Assn. Rochester and Monroe (N.Y.), 1970-73, Mahoning Shenango Area Health Edn. Network, Youngstown, Ohio, 1973-78; spl. asst. to dean Northeastern Ohio Univs. Coll. Medicine, Rootstown, 1978-79; v.p. Med. Coll. Ohio, Toledo, 1979-88, sr. v.p. govtl. affairs, 1988-93; pres. KPA Assocs., Inc., 1993—. V.p. Found. for Applied Rsch., Washington, 1976; chmn. adv. bd. Ohio AHEC, Columbus, 1976; program adminstr. Ohio Statewide Area Health Edn. Ctr., Toledo, 1988-93. Chmn. Toledo Area Coun. Tech., 1986; spl. asst. to clergy All Saints Parish, Pawleys Island, S.C., 1998-2000. Mem. Nat. Area Health Edn. Ctrs. Assn. (bd. dir. 1988-95), Nat. Assn. Univ. Rsch. Adminstrs., Soc. Rsch. Adminstrs., Internat. Assn. Univ. Rsch. Parks, Soc. Univ. Patent Adminstrs., Nat. Assn. Health Manpower Edn. Systems, Northeastern Ohio Med. Educators Assn. (bd. dir.), Rotary. Anglican. Home: 46 Pawleys Pl Dr Pawleys Island SC 29585-7254 Office: KPA Assocs PO Box 194 Pawleys Island SC 29585-0194 E-mail: kenkpa@sccoast.net.

PROENZA, BILL (XAVIER WILLIAM PROENZA), meteorologist, former federal agency administrator; b. Oct. 30, 1944; Grad. in Meteorology, Fla. State U. With NOAA/Nat. Weather Svc., Miami, Fla., 1963—, Huntsville, Ala., 1968, Columbus, Ga., 1969—, NOAA Nat. Weather Svc., Atlanta, 1970; asst. and acting nat. prog. leader Pub. Weather Br. Air Pollution and Fire NOAA/Nat. Weather Svc., Silver Spring, Md., 1970—72, mgr. regional pub., marine, forestry, agrl. and air pollution progs. Ctrl. Region Kansas City, Mo., 1973—75, forecaster regional warning coordination ctr. Ctrl. Region, 1974, exec. officer so. region Ft. Worth, 1976, acting dep. dir. so. region, 1986—87, dep. dir. so. region, 1987—97, acting dir. so. region, 1990, 1998—99, dir. so. region, 1999—2007, dir. Nat. Hurricane Ctr., 2007. Fellow: Am. Meteorol. Soc. (Francis W. Reichelderfer award 2001); mem.: Nat. Weather Assn. *

PROFETA, SALVATORE, JR., chemist, educator; m. Catherine Mary Cherry, Sept. 20, 1980; children: Luisa, Theresa. BA in Pharm. Chemistry, Temple U., Phila., 1973; PhD in Phys. Organic Chemistry, U. Ga., Athens, 1978. Fellow chemistry dept. Fla. State U., Tallahassee, 1979-80; fellow pharm. chemistry dept. U. Calif., San Francisco, 1980-81, teaching fellow, 1981-82; instr. chemistry dept. La. State U., Baton Rouge, 1982-84; sr. scientist Allergan Pharms., Inc., Irvine, Calif., 1984-87; project mgr. computational chemistry Glaxo Rsch. Inst., Research Triangle Park, N.C., 1987-90, head chemistry systems, 1990-93; dir. N.C. Supercomputing Ctr. Rsch. Inst. at MCNC, Research Triangle Park, N.C., 1993-95; prin. computational chemist Monsanto, St. Louis, 1996-2000; dir. computational chemistry and structural biology Millennium Pharm., Cambridge, Mass., 2000—02; assoc. prof. dept. pharm. chemistry U. S.C., Columbia, SC, 2003—06, rsch. prof. dept. chemistry/biochemistry, 2006—. Cons. CADD-CAMM Smith, Kline & French, Phila., 1980-82, Squibb Rsch. Inst., Princeton, N.J., 1982-84; allocation com. N.C. Supercomputing Ctr., 1989-94. Mem. editl. bd. Jour. Molecular Graphics, 1989-2000; contbg. editor Chem. Design Automation News, 1991-2000; contbr. articles to Jour. Am. Chem. Soc. NSF fellow, 1976-78; Petroleum Rsch. Found. grantee, 1984-88. Mem. Am. Chem. Soc., Am. Crystal. Assn. Achievements include patents in anticancer drug design; co-author MM1, MM2, MM3 and AMBER molecular mechanical force fields. Office Phone: 803-808-2701. Business E-Mail: profeta.s@mail.chem.sc.edu.

PROFFIT, WILLIAM ROBERT, orthodontics educator; b. Harnett County, NC, Apr. 19, 1936; s. Glenn Theodore and Edna Marie (Queener) P.; m. Sara Thomas, Sept. 20, 1953; children: Lola Ann, Edward Thomas, Glenn Theodore. BS, U. N.C., 1956, DDS, 1959; student, Campbell Coll., Buies Creek, NC, 1952-53; PhD, Med. Coll. Va., 1962; MS, U. Wash., 1963; FDS, Royal Coll. Surgeons, 1990. Cert. Am. Bd. Orthodontics. Investigator Nat. Inst. Dental Research, Bethesda, Md., 1963-65; asst. prof. orthodontics U. Ky., Lexington, 1965-68, assoc. prof., 1968-71; prof. U.Ky., Lexington, 1971-73; prof. orthodontics U. Fla., Gainesville, 1973-75; prof., chmn. dept. orthodontics U. NC, Chapel Hill, 1975—, Kenan prof., 1992. Cons. NIH, Bethesda, 1974, 76— Author: Contemporary Orthodontics, 1986, 4th edit., 2006; co-author: Surgical Correction of Dentofacial Deformity, 1980, Surgical-Orthodontic Treatment, 1990, Contemporary Treatment of Dentofacial Deformity, 2003; contbr. articles to sci. jours. Served to lt. comdr. USPHS, 1963-65. Fulbright research scholar U. Adelaide, Australia, 1972 Mem. ADA, Am. Assn. Orthodontists (coun. on rsch. 1970-76), Internat. Assn. Dental Rsch., Phi Beta Kappa. Democrat. Presbyterian. Home: 620 Rock Creek Rd Chapel Hill NC 27514-6716 Office: UNC Sch Dentistry Dept Orthodontics Chapel Hill NC 27599-7450 Office Phone: 919-966-4428. E-mail: william_proffit@dentistry.unc.edu.

PROFFITT, JOHN RICHARD, information technology executive, educator, public official; b. Grand Junction, Colo., Sept. 12, 1930; s. Hillus D. and Joy Elaine (Lindsay) P.; m. Claire Boyer Miller, May 8, 1965 (div. 1992); children: Cameron Lindsay Taylor, William Boyer. BA in Edn., U. Ky., 1953, MA in Polit. Sci., 1961; postgrad., U. Mich., 1959-65. Asst. dean of men, instr. polit. sci. dept. U. Ky., Lexington, 1957-59; teaching fellow U. Mich., Ann Arbor, 1961-63, 63-65; asst. dir. Nat. Commn. on Accrediting, Washington, 1966-68; dir. accreditation and eligibility staff U.S. Dept. HEW, Washington, 1968-75; dir. divsn. eligibility and agy. evaluation U.S. Dept. Edn., Washington, 1975-80, dir. divsn. instnl. and state incentive programs, 1980-82; pres. The Clairion Corp., Bethesda, Md., 1982-84, Nat. Asbestos Removal, Inc., Beltsville, Md., 1985-90, Commonwealth Environ. Svcs., Inc., Alexandria, Va., 1987-91, also chmn. bd. dirs.; chmn. Internat. Environ. Engrs., Inc., Alexandria, Va., 1991-92; pres. Canterbury Internat., Vienna, Va., 1992-95; cons., 1995-99; v.p. E-Pass Techs., Inc., McLean, Va., 1999—. Cons. Conn. State Commn. Higher Edn., Hartford, 1967, Am. Coun. Edn., Washington, 1970; cons. U.S. Dept. Hew, Washington, 1967, 68; mem. study steering com. Am. Vocat. Assn., Washington, 1968; exec. sec. Nat. Adv. Com. on Accreditation and Instnl. Eligibility, Washington, 1968-80; mem. gen. com. Nat. Study Sch. evaluation, Alexandria, 1970-78; mem. task force Edn. Commn. of the States, Denver, 1972; subcom. chmn. Fed. Interagy. Com. on Edn., Washington, 1974-76; lectr., presenter profl. confs.; chmn. Commn. Accrediting. Co-author: Accreditation and Certification in Relation to Allied Health Manpower, 1971; contbg. author: Health Manpower: Adapting in the Seventies, 1971, Accreditation in Teacher Education, 1975, Transferring Experiential Credit, 1979; contbr. articles to profl. and govtl. agy. publs., 1968-79. Bd. dirs. and chmn. accrediting commn. Nat. Accreditation Coun. for Agys. Serving the Blind, N.Y.C., 1983-89, v.p. and bd. dirs., 1985-89; pres., chmn. bd. dirs. Found. for Advancement of Quality Svcs. for the Blind, Alexandria, 1988. 1st lt. USAF, 1953-55, Japan and Korea. 1st lt. USAF, 1953—55, Japan, Korea, capt. USAFR. Higher edn. fellow Univ. Mich., 1959; decorated Korean War UN and Nat. Defense Svc. medals. Mem. Optimist Club (Lexington, Ky.), Club Internat. (Chgo.), Island Club (Hobe Sound, Fla.), Thoroughbred Club Am. (Lexington), Tower Club (Vienna, Va.), Sigma Nu, Omicron Delta Kappa. Democrat. Episcopalian. Avocations: travel, antiques, art, animal welfare, conservation. Home: 515 Beall Ave Rockville MD 20850-2106 Office Phone: 703-575-8486. E-mail: johnproff@aol.com.

PROFFITT, KEVIN, archivist; b. Hamilton, Ohio, Dec. 24, 1956; s. Henry C. and Marjorie O. (Elam) P.; m. Joan Moriarity, May 17, 1986. BA, Miami U., Oxford, Ohio, 1979; MA, Wright State U., 1980; MLS, U. Ky., 1998. Archivist Am. Jewish Archives, Cin., 1981—. Contbr. articles to profl. jours. Mem. Soc. Am. Archivists, Acad. Cert. Archivists (cert.), Midwest Archives Conf., Soc. Ohio Archivists (pres. 1987-89). Office: Am Jewish Archives 3101 Clifton Ave Cincinnati OH 45220-2404

PROFFITT, WALDO, JR., newspaper editor; b. Plainview, Tex., Oct. 8, 1924; s. Waldo and Susan Ann (Smith) P.; m. Marjorie Baltzegar, Sept. 14, 1946 (div. 1963); children: Ann Herbert, Deborah, Geoffrey Harrison, Laurence Scott; m. Anne Collier Greene, Feb. 6, 1966; 1 child, Robert Waldo. BA cum laude, Harvard U., 1948. Reporter Bangor (Maine) Commercial, 1948-50; assoc. dir. Harvard News Office, Cambridge, Mass., 1952-54; city editor Charlotte (N.C.) News, 1954-58; mng. editor Journal, Lorain, Ohio, 1958-61; editorial dir. Sarasota (Fla.) Herald-Tribune, 1961-84; editor, 1984-98; columnist Sarasota-Herald Tribune, 1998—. Lt. U.S. Army, 1943-46, ETO, lt. USAF, 1950-52. Recipient Global Media Lifetime Achievement award, Population Inst., 2003. Mem. Am. Soc. Newspaper Editors, Fla. Soc. Newspaper Editors (pres. 1978). Democrat. Unitarian Universalist. Home: 1581 Hillview Dr Sarasota FL 34239-2047 Office: Sarasota Herald-Tribune PO Box 1719 Sarasota FL 34230-1719 Personal E-mail: wproffitt@comcast.net.

PROFUSEK, ROBERT ALAN, lawyer; b. Cleve., Jan. 14, 1950; s. George John and Geraldine (Hobl) P.; m. Linda Gail Schmidt, May 7, 1972; children: Robert Charles, Kathryn Anne. BA, Cornell U., 1972; JD, NYU, 1975. Bar: Ohio 1975, Tex. 1981, NY 1994. Assoc. Jones Day, Cleve., 1975-81, Dallas, 1981-82, ptnr., 1982—, NY, 1993. bd. dirs., CTS Corporcitum and Valero, LP; Contbr. articles to profl. jours.; spkr. in field. Mem. ABA, NY Bar Assn., Assn. Bar City of NY, Tex. Bar Assn., Greenwich Country Club. Republican. Episcopalian. Home: 541 North St Greenwich CT 06830-3424 Office: Jones Day 222 E 41st St 15th Fl New York NY 10017 Office Phone: 212-326-3800. Office Fax: 212-755-7306. E-mail: raprofusek@jonesday.com.

PROGER, PHILLIP A., lawyer; b. NYC, Apr. 8, 1948; BA, Univ. Maryland, 1969, JD with honors, 1973. Bar: Ohio 1973, D.C. 1978, U.S. Supreme Ct. 1978. Head Antitrust Divsn. Jones Day, Washington. Adj. prof. Georgetown Univ. Law Ctr., 1983-84; adv. bds. BNA (antitrust & trade regulation report), M&A Lawyer. Mem. editl. bd. Law Rev. Moot Ct., 1973; contbr. articles to profl. jours. Fellow Am. Bar Found.; mem. ABA (chmn. Antitrust Law sect. 1998-99, bd. gov. 2003-2006), Am. Law Inst., Ohio State Bar Assn., D.C. Bar Assn., Am. Acad. Hosp. Attys. (pres. 1994-95). Office: Jones Day 5th Fl 51 Louisiana Ave Washington DC 20001-2113 Office Phone: 202-879-4668. Office Fax: 202-626-1700. Business E-Mail: paproger@jonesday.com.

PROHOFSKY, DENNIS E., lawyer, insurance company executive; BA, U. Minn., 1965; JD, William Mitchell Coll. Law, 1972. Bar: Minn. 1972. Sr. underwriter Minn. Life Ins. Co., St. Paul, 1962—72, second v.p., 1982—94, sr. v.p., gen. counsel, sec., 1994—2002, exec. v.p., gen. counsel, sec., 2002—. Office: Minn Life Ins Co 400 Robert St N Saint Paul MN 55101 Office Phone: 651-665-3500. Business E-Mail: dennis.prohofsky@minnesotamutual.com.

PROKASY, WILLIAM FREDERICK, academic administrator; b. Cleve., Nov. 27, 1930; s. William Frederick and Margaret Lovinia (Chapman) P.; m. Pamela Pearson; children: Kathi Lynn, Cheryl Anne; stepchildren: Lisa Wier Cauthen, Kevin Wier. BA, Baldwin-Wallace Coll., 1952; MA, Kent State U., 1954; PhD, U. Wis., 1957. Grad. asst. Kent State U., 1953-54; W.A.R.F. fellow U. Wis., 1954-55, teaching asst., 1955-57; asst. prof., then asso. prof. Pa. State U., 1957-66; prof. psychology, chmn. dept. U. Utah, 1966-69, Disting. rsch. prof., 1971-72, dean social and behavioral sci., 1968-70; dean U. Utah (Coll. Social and Behavioral Sci.), 1970-79; acting dean U. Utah (Grad. Sch. Social Work), 1979-80; prof. psychology dean Coll. Liberal Arts and Scis., U. Ill., Champaign-Urbana, 1980-88; prof., v.p. for acad. affairs U. Ga., 1988-98. Cons. in field. Editor: Classical Conditioning, 1965, (with A.H. Black) Classical Conditioning II, 1971, (with D. Raskin) Electrodermal Responding in Psychological Research, 1973, Psychophysiology, 1974-77; editor (with I. Gormezano and R. Thompson) Classical Conditioning III, 1986; assoc. editor Learning and Motivation, 1969-76; cons. editor Jour. Exptl. Psychology, 1968-80. Trustee Utah Planned Parenthood Assn., 1977—80; Utah bd. dirs. ACLU, 1978—80; v.p., bd. dirs. Champaign-Urbana Symphony, 1986—88; mem. bd. advisors Ga. Mus. Art, 1989—, U. Ga. Performing Arts Ctr., 1998—2003; mem. bd. visitors U. Ga. Librs., 1998—2007; mem. Athens-Clarke County Libr. Bd., 1999—2007; treas. Athens Opera Co. Guild, 2001—06; pres. Friends Ga. Mus. Art, 2002—03, Athens-Clarke County Libr. Bd., 2003—04, Friends of Dance, 2003—04; v.p. Athens-Clarke County Libr. Endowment Bd., 2003—; mem. Classic Ctr. Cultural Found., 2003—, treas., 2006—; mem. adv. bd. Franklin Coll. Arts and Scis., 2003—06; chmn. Athens chapt., Am. Wine Soc., 2007—; del. Utah Dem. Conv., 1968—70, 1972—74; mem. Athens Regional Libr., 2002—, chmn., 2006—. Recipient Alumni Merit award Baldwin Wallace Coll., 1992, Disting. Alumni award Piedmont Coll., 1998, U. Ga. Alumni award of excellence, 1998; NSF sr. postdoctoral fellow, 1963-64. Fellow AAAS, Am. Psychol. Assn. (chmn. bd. sci. affairs 1977-78, coun. of reps. 1980-86, bd. dirs. 1983-86, bd. ednl. affairs 1993-96); mem. Fedn. Behavioral, Pyschol. and Cognitive Scis. (v.p. 1984-85, pres. 1985-87), coun. of Sci. Soc. Pres.'s (exec. bd. 1987-91, chmn. 1990), Psychonomic Soc., Coun. Rsch. Librs. (bd. dirs. 1990-96), NASULGC (exec. com. coun. on acad. affairs 1995-96), Am. Assn. Higher Edn., Soc. Psychophysiol. Rsch. (bd. dirs. 1978-84, pres. 1982-83), Utah Psychol. Assn. (exec. bd. 1968-70, pres. 1971-72), Assn. Advancement Psychology (bd. dirs. 1982-83), Sigma Xi (pres. U. Utah chpt. 1972-73), Phi Kappa Phi. Avocations: genealogy, wine tasting, reading. Personal E-mail: wfp@charter.net.

PROKOP, KEVIN, investment company executive; b. 1968; BBA, Georgetown U., 1990; MBA, U. Chgo. Investment profl. First Chgo.-NBD Capital Markets; assoc. Kleinwort Benson, Ltd.; assoc., engagement mgr. McKinsey & Co., 1994—97; dir. Questor Mgmt. Co., Southfield, Mich., 1998—. Former bd. mem. GeoLogistics Corp.; bd. mem. Internet Ops. Ctr., U. Cancer Found., New Detroit. Named one of 40 Under 40, Crain's Detroit Bus., 2006; recipient Turnaround of Yr. award, Buyouts mag., 2006. Office: Questor Management Co 2000 Town Ctr Ste 2450 Southfield MI 48075 Office Phone: 248-213-2200. Office Fax: 248-213-2215.

PROKOPANKO, JAMES T., agricultural products executive; b. 1953; BS, U. Manitoba; MBA, U. We. Ontario. With Cargill Inc., 1978—2006, v.p. N.Am. crop inputs bus., corp. v.p. procurement, 2002—06; exec. v.p., CEO The Mosaic Co., Plymouth, Minn., 2006—07, pres., CEO, 2007—. Office: The Mosaic Co Atria Corp Ctr 3033 Campus Dr Ste E490 Plymouth MN 55441 Office Phone: 800-918-8270. Office Fax: 763-559-2960. *

PROKOSCH, MARK DAVID, research scientist; b. Albuquerque, Jan. 25, 1980; s. Barbara and Donald Prokosch. BS, U. N.Mex., Albuquerque, 2002; postgrad., U. Calif., Davis, 2003—. Instr. U. Calif., Davis, 2007—. Contbr. articles to profl. jours. Grantee Rsch. Grant, U. Calif., 2003—06; Gardner Zemke scholar, 1998—2007. Mem.: Internat. Soc. Intelligence Rsch. Soc., Human Behavior and Evolution Soc., Psi Chi, Phi Kappa Phi, Golden Key, Phi Eta Sigma, Sigma Xi (assoc.). Home: 1175 Lake Blvd #150 Davis CA 95616 Office: Univ Calif One Sheilds Ave Davis CA 95616 Home Phone: 530-220-3009; Office Phone: 530-754-8291. Personal E-mail: markpro10@msn.com. Business E-Mail: mdprokosch@ucdavis.edu.

PROMISLO, DANIEL, lawyer, small business owner; b. Bryn Mawr, Pa., Nov. 15, 1932; s. Charles and Pearl (Backman) Promislo; m. Estelle Carasso, June 10, 1961 (dec. Apr. 2006); children: Mark, Jacqueline, Steven. BSBA, Drexel U., 1955; JD magna cum laude, U. Pa., 1966. Bar: Pa. 1966. Pres., owner Hist. Souvenir Co., Phila., 1957—; assoc. Wolf, Block, Schorr & Solis-Cohen, Phila., 1966-70, ptnr., 1977-94, exec. com., 1987-89, mng. dir., 1997-2001, of counsel, 1994—; founder, pres. dir. Inst. Paralegal Tng., Phila., 1970-75, cons., 1975-77; pres., owner Hist. Documents Co., 1992—. Editor: Corporate Law, 1970, Real Estate Law, 1971, Estates and Trusts, 1971, Civil Litigation, 1972, Employee Benefit Plans, 1973, Criminal Law, 1974; contbr. articles to profl. jours. Bd. dirs. Phila. Drama Guild, 1977—95, chmn., 1982—86; bd. dirs. Phila. Israel Econ. Devel. Program, 1983—88, Inst. Arts in Edn., 1990—93, WHYY, Inc., 1994—2003, vice-chmn., 1995—96, chmn., 1996—97; bd. dirs. U.S.

Physicians, Inc., 1995—98; chmn. Phila. Jewish Sports Hall Fame, 2006—; trustee RAIT Fin. Trust, 1997—; bd. advisors Drexel U. Coll. Arts and Scis., 2001—; bd. dirs. Jewish Cmty. Ctrs. Greater Phila., 2006—. Mem.: Drexel U. 100, Blue Key, Order of Coif, Phi Kappa Phi. Democrat. Jewish. Avocations: movies, basketball, tennis, golf. Office: Wolf Block Schorr & Solis-Cohen 1650 Arch St Fl 22 Philadelphia PA 19103-2097 E-mail: dpromislo@comcast.net.

PRONGER, CHRIS, professional hockey player; b. Dryden, Ont., Can., Oct. 10, 1974; m. Lauren Pronger, 2001. Defenseman Hartford Whalers, 1993—95, St. Louis Blues, 1995—2005, Edmonton Oilers, 2005—06, Anaheim Ducks, 2006—; mem. Can. Nat. Hockey Team, 1992—93, 1996—97, 1997—98, 2001—02. Member NHL All-Rookie Team, 1994; player NHL All-star game, 1999, 2000, 02, 04. Finalist Lester B. Pearson award, 2000; named to Second All-Star Team, NHL, 2007; recipient Gold medal, Can. Under 18 Team, Phoenix Cup, 1991, World Jr. Hockey Championship, 1993, World Championship, 1997, Bud Ice Plus-Minus award, 1997—98, Norris Trophy, 2000, Hart Trophy, 2000. Achievements include being a member of gold medal Canadian Hockey team, Salt Lake City Olympic Games, 2002; being a member of Stanley Cup Champion Anaheim Ducks, 2007. Office: Anaheim Ducks 2695 E Katella Ave Anaheim CA 92806 *

PRONOVOST, AMY LYNNE, dancer, educator; b. Royal Oak, Mich., Aug. 5, 1976; d. Gerald and MaryAnn Pronovost. BA in Dance and English, Western Mich. U., Kalamazoo, 1998. Cert. Stott Pilates, Gyrotonic and pilates for golf. Ballet dir., tchr. Dance Dynamics, Walled Lake, Mich., 2000—. Pilates and gyrotonic instr. Equilibrium, Bloomfield Hills, Mich., 2000—, stott pilates instr. trainer. Home: 7073 Magnolia Ln Waterford MI 48327-4419 Personal E-mail: amypronovost@sbcglobal.net.

PRONZINI, BILL JOHN (WILLIAM PRONZINI), writer; b. Petaluma, Calif., Apr. 13, 1943; s. Joseph and Helene (Guder) P.; m. Marcia Muller. Author: 67 novels (including under pseudonyms), 4 books of non-fiction, 19 collections of short stories, 1971—; first novel, The Stalker, 1971; editor 80 anthologies; contbr. numerous short stories to publs. Recipient 6 scroll awards Mystery Writers Am.; recipient Life Achievement award Pvt. Eye Writers Am., 1987, 2 Shamus awards. Office: PO Box 2536 Petaluma CA 94953-2536 E-mail: pronhack@comcast.net.

PROPERZIO, PAUL J., classicist, educator; b. Keene, NH, May 20, 1947; s. Joseph M. and Virginia T. Properzio; m. Deborah E. Jewett, Jan. 31, 1970; 1 child, Lucy A. BA in Latin and Greek, U. NH, 1969; PhD in Classical Studies, Loyola U., Chgo., 1982. Lic. educator Mass. Chair, assoc. prof. classics Drew U., Madison, NJ, 1975—87; tchr. Latin Hanover HS, NH, 1987—88; tchr. Latin, history, mythology Reading Meml. HS, Mass., 1988—93; assoc. prof. classics and humanities St. Anselm Coll., Manchester, NH, 1993—97; tchr. Latin and Greek Boston Latin Acad., 1997—. V.p. Archaeol. Inst. of Am. (Boston Soc.), Boston, 2002—. Editor: (jour.) Am. Classical League Newsletter, 2003—; contbr. presentation,; author: (book chpt.) Heroic Epithets in Early Greek and Han Chinese Literature, New Light on the Cults of Apollo and Artemis in Marseilles, Heroic Honor and Responsibility: The Iliad as a Reflection of Global Conflict, Social Values, and Human Interaction in the Modern World; contbr. presentations, presentation, articles to profl. jours. Lector St. Joseph's Ch., Andover, Mass., 1988—. Capt. M.I. US Army, 1971—79. Recipient Rome and China Participant grant, NEH, 2000—02, Elaine G. Batting Meml. scholarship, Mass. Fgn. Lang. Assn., 2003, Arthur P. McKinley scholarship, Am. Classical League, 2002, FIPSE (Fund for Improvement of Post Secondary Edn.) fellowship, Woodrow Wilson Found., Princeton U., 1985; Fulbright scholar, Italy, 1969. Mem.: Classical Assn. of the Atlantic States (pres. 1984—85), Classical Assn. of New Eng. (pres. 1993—94), Am. Philol Assn. (minority students scholarship com. 2002—05), Prof. John C. Rouman Classical Lecture Series, U. of N.H. (adv. bd. 1997—). Independent. Roman Catholic. Avocations: travel, cooking, tennis, theater, walking. Home: 15 Ballardvale Rd Andover MA 01810 Office: Boston Latin Acad 205 Townsend St Boston MA 02121 Home Phone: 978-474-0195; Office Phone: 617-635-9957. Office Fax: 617-635-6696; Home Fax: 603-864-2496. Personal E-mail: pjpropertius@comcast.net.

PROPP, STEVEN H., personnel director; b. Berkeley, Calif., Oct. 2, 1955; s. Harry and Dorothy S. Propp; m. Nancy L. Jones Slaughter, Mar. 3, 2005. BA, Calif. State U., Sacramento, 1978. Membership mgr. Pub. Employees' Retirement Sys., Sacramento, 1979—. Author: Work, Death and Taxes, 2000, Tattered Pilgrims, 2001, Inquiries: Philosophical, 2002, Beyond Heaven and Earth, 2003, Utopia On the 6th Floor, 2004, A Multicultural Christmas, 2005, Josué, Prisoner At Shalem, 2005, Family Lessons, 2006, Saved By Philosophy, 2007, Three Brothers, 2007. Avocations: music, reading. Personal E-mail: stevenhpropp@hotmail.com.

PROPST, ANTHONY MARK, obstetrician, gynecologist; b. Tampa, Fla., July 26, 1966; s. Clyde Lewis and Audrey Elizabeth Propst; m. Wendy Wilson, June 12, 2004; children: Isabela, Elena, Pierce Wilson, Preston Clyde. BS, USAF Acad., Colorado Springs, Colo., 1988; MD, U. NC, Chapel Hill, 1992. Diplomate Am. Bd. Ob/Gyn., 2001. With USAF, 1984, advanced through grades to lt. col., 2004; intern David Grant USAF Med. Ctr., 1992—93, resident, 1992—96; fellow reproductive endocrinology and infertility Harvard Med. Sch., 1997—2000; dir. in vitro fertilization Wilford Hall Med. Ctr., San Antonio, 2001—04, chief, reproductive endocrinology and infertility, 2004—. Elder U. Presbyn. Ch., San Antonio, 2005—. Fellow: ACOG (assoc.; air force sect. chair 2005—, com. residency edn. ob-gyn. 2006—). Presbyterian. Achievements include research in randomized contolled trials of infertility treatment. Office Phone: 210-292-6125.

PROPST, CATHERINE LAMB, biotechnology and pharmaceutical company executive; b. Charlotte, NC, Mar. 10, 1946; d. James Pinckney and Eliza M. Propst. BA magna cum laude, Vanderbilt U., 1967; M of Philosophy, Yale U., 1970, PhD, 1973. Head microbiology div. GTE Labs., Waltham, Mass., 1974-77; various sr. mgmt. positions Abbott Labs., North Chicago, Ill., 1977-80; v.p. rsch. and devel. Ayerst (Wyeth) Labs., Plainview, NY, 1980-83; v.p. rsch. and devel. worldwide Flow Gen. Inc., McLean, Va., 1983-85; pres., CEO Affiliated Sci. Inc., Ingleside, Ill., 1985-97; pres., chmn., CEO Tex. Biotech. Found., Hempstead, Tex., 1997—. Vis. prof. genetics U. Ill., Chgo., 1989—90; founder, exec. dir. Ctr. for Biotech., Northwestern U., 1990—95; pres. Ill. Biotech. Ctr., 1995—97; bd. dirs. several cos.; bd. dirs., mem. sci. adv. bd. Keystone Symposia on Molecular and Cellular Biology, 1997—2002. Author, editor Computer-Aided Drug Design, 1989, Nucleic Acid Targeted Drug Design, 1992; contbr. articles to profl. jours. Named to Outstanding Working Women in the U.S., 1982; recipient many sci. and bus. awards. Fellow: Soc. Indsl. Microbiology (bd. dirs. 1990—93), Nat. Coun. Biotech Ctrs. (bd. dirs. 1995—97); mem.: AAAS, Nat. Wildlife Fedn., Consortium for Plant Biotech. Rsch. (bd. dirs. 1994—99), Phi Beta Kappa, Sigma Xi. Episcopalian. Avocations: horseback riding, skiing, raising Black Angus and Black Brangus cattle. Office: Texas Biotech Found PO Box 17 Hempstead TX 77445-0017 Office Phone: 979-826-3075. Office Fax: 979-826-9710.

PROPST, HAROLD DEAN, retired academic administrator; b. Newton, NC, Feb. 7, 1934; s. Charles Clayton and Sarah Isabel (Hilderbrand) P. BA, Wake Forest Coll., 1956; MA, Peabody Coll., 1959, PhD, 1964; LLD, Mercer U., 1985; LittD, Armstrong Atlantic State U., 2003. Tchr. Vandalia Pub. Schs., Ohio, 1959-60; instr. Wake Forest Coll., Winston-Salem, N.C., 1960-61; asst. prof. English, Radford Coll., Va., 1962-64, assoc. prof. Va., 1964-65, prof. Va., 1965-69, chmn. dept. English Va., 1965-66, 68-69; dean Armstrong State Coll., Savannah, Ga., 1969-76, v.p. for acad. affairs, 1976-79; vice chancellor for acad. devel. Univ. System Ga., Atlanta, 1979-81, exec. vice chancellor, 1981-85, chancellor, 1985-94. Editor: (novel) John Brent, 1970; contbr. articles to profl. jours., monographs, books Bd. visitors Radford Coll., 1970-74; former pres. bd. Family Counseling Ctr., Savannah; former pres. bd. Family Counseling Ctr., Savannah; former bd. dirs. Savannah Symphony, Savannah Heart Assn., Alliance Theatre, Atlanta; mem. So. Region Edn. Bd., 1985-94; mem. adv. bd. Peabody Coll. Vanderbilt U., 1994-98; mem. adv. bd. Mars Hill Coll., 1996-2002. With USN, 1956-58. Fellow Carnegie Found., 1958, Ford Found. fellow, 1960; recipient Disting. Alumnus award Wake Forest U., 1986, Disting. Svc. award Mens Hill Coll., 1997, Disting. Alumnus award Peabody Coll. Vanderbilt U., 2003. Mem. Am. Assn. State Colls and Univs. (com. on accreditation 1982-86), Acad. for Ednl. Devel. (study com. on campus govt. 1976-77) Baptist.

PROPST, M. TERESA CARSON, historian; b. Balt., Jan. 7, 1976; d. John Rian and Maria Patricia (Romagnoli) Carson; m. Anthony Michael Propst, Nov. 10, 2001. BA, Towson U., 1999. Patient svcs. rep. Advanced Radiology, Towson, 1999—. Adult youth ministry vol. St. William of York Cath. Ch., Balt., 2000—04. Mem.: Order of Omega, Golden Key Nat. Honor Soc., Phi Alpha Theta, Alpha Xi Delta (chpt. life advisor Towson U. 2003—04, programs adv. 2005—). Democrat. Roman Catholic. Avocations: entertaining, travel, camping. Home: 439 Old Home Rd Baltimore MD 21206 Office: Advanced Radiology 124 Sister Pierre Dr Towson MD 21204

PROSPER, PIERRE-RICHARD, former federal agency administrator; b. Denver, 1963; BA, Boston Coll., 1985; JD, Pepperdine U., 1989. Bar: Calif. Dep. dist. atty. L.A. County, 1989—94; asst. U.S. atty. (ctrl. dist.) Calif. US Dept. Justice, 1994—96; war crimes prosecutor U.N. Internat. Criminal Tribunal for Rwanda, 1996—98; spl. asst. to asst. atty. gen. for criminal divsn. US Dept. State, Washington, spl. counsel & policy adv. to amb. at large for war crimes issues, 1999—2001, amb. at large for war crimes issues, 2001—05. Recipient Alumni award of Excellence, Boston Coll., 1999, Dist. Alumnus award, Pepperdine U. Sch. Law Alumni, 2000; fellow Wasserstein fellow, Harvard U., 2000—01. Mem.: Calif. Bar Assn. *

PROSSER, DAVID THOMAS, JR., state supreme court justice and former legislator; b. Chgo., Dec. 24, 1942; s. David Thomas, Sr. and Elizabeth Averell (Patterson) Prosser. BA, DePauw U., 1965; JD, U. Wis., 1968. Bar: Wis. 1968. Lectr. Ind. U., Indpls., 1968-69; advisor U.S. Dept. Justice, Washington, 1969-72; adminstrv. asst. to U.S. Rep. Harold V. Froehlich, Washington, 1973-74; pvt. practice Washington, 1975, Appleton, Wis., 1976; dist. atty. Outagamie County Wis., Appleton, 1977-78; state rep. State of Wis., Madison, 1979-96; commr. Tax Appeals Commn., 1997-98; justice Supreme Ct. Wis., 1998—, Jud. Coun., 2002—06. Commr. Nat. Conf. Commrs. Uniform State Laws, 1982—96, 2005—07; mem. Wis. Sesquicentennial Commn., Madison, 1993—99; minority leader Wis. Assembly, 1989—94, spkr., 1995—96. Mem.: Outagamie Bar Assn., Milw. Bar Assn., Dane Bar Assn., Wis. Bar Assn. Presbyterian. Avocation: art collector of American prints. Office: Supreme Ct Wis PO Box 1688 Madison WI 53701-1688 Office Phone: 608-266-1882.

PROSSER, FRANKLIN PIERCE, computer scientist; b. Atlanta, July 4, 1935; s. Edward Theron and Eunice (McDaniel) P.; m. Brenda Mary Lau, June 16, 1960; children: Edward, Andrea. BS, Ga. Inst. Tech., 1956, MS, 1958; PhD, Pa. State U., 1961. Prof. computer sci. Ind. U., Bloomington, 1969-99; asso. dir. Wrubel Computing Center, 1969-81, chmn. dept. computer sci., 1971-77, 87-93, spl. asst. for acad. computing, 1979-81; v.p. Logic Design, Inc., 1982-92. Cons. Lockheed Theoretical Physics Lab., Palo Alto, Calif., 1967 Home: 1200 S Longwood Dr Bloomington IN 47401-6072 Office: Ind U Dept Computer Sci Bloomington IN 47405

PROSSER, JOHN MARTIN, architecture educator; b. Wichita, Kans., Dec. 28, 1932; s. Francis Ware and Harriet Corinne (Osborne) P.; m. Judith Adams, Aug. 28, 1954 (dec. 1982); children: Thomas, Anne, Edward; m. Karen Ann Cleary, Dec. 30, 1983; 1 child, Jennifer. BSc in Architecture, U. Kans., 1955; MArch, Carnegie Mellon U., 1961. Registered architect, Kans., Colo. Architect Robinson and Hissem, Wichita, 1954-56, Guirey, Srnka, and Arnold, Phoenix, 1961-62, James Sudler Assocs., Denver, 1962-68; ptnr., architect Nuzum, Prosser and Vetter, Boulder, 1969-73; from asst. prof. to prof. U. Colo., Boulder and Denver, 1968—, acting dean, 1980-84, dean, 1984, dir. environ. design Boulder, 1969-72, dir. urban design Denver, 1972-85. Cons. John M. Prosser Assocs., Boulder and Denver, 1974—; vis. prof. urban design Oxford Brooks, England, 1979; vis. critic Carnegie Mellon U., U. N.Mex., Colo. Coll.; pres. Denver chpt. AIA, 1983; prin. investigator Fitsimmons-U. Colo. Health Scis. City Rsch. Study, 1997—99; vis. urban design scholar Nat. U. Ireland, 2003—07; vis. fellow Urban Inst. Ireland, 2003—04. Author, narrator: (PBS TV documentary) Cities Are For Kids, Too, 1984; prin. works include (with others) hist. redesign Mus. Western Art, Denver, Villa Italia, Lakewood, Colo., Denver, Auraria Higher Edn. Ctr., Pueblo C.C. campus plan and new acad. facilities, comprehensive campus plan Denver U., Ft. Lewis Coll., Westminster Golf Course Cmty., Denver Botanic Gardens 20-Yr. Concept Plan, Colo. Coll. Historic Preservation Plan, Buffalo Hills Ranch Golf Course Cmty., Fountain Valley Sch., Urban Design, Ctrl. Colo. Springs 2001—; urban design cons. McDonough & Ptnrs., New China City, 2005—. Bd. dirs. Denver Parks and Recreation Bd., 1987-93, 96-2003; chmn. design rev. bd. univs. Colo., Boulder, Denver, Aurora, and Colorado Springs, 1981-2006, mem., 2006-07; archtl. control com. Denver Tech. Ctr., 1984—, Meridian Internat. Bus. Ctr., 1984—, DTC West, 1991—, Denver Internat. Bus. Ctr., 1993—, Nat. Renewable Energy Lab., 1996—, Greenwood Village Ctr., 2007—; planning cons. Denver Internat. Airport Environs., 1984—; Nucleus co-founder U. Colo. Real Estate Ctr., 1989-2000. Capt. USAF, 1956—59. Co-recipient 2d pl. award Am. Soc. Interior Designers, 1984; recipient Honor award Colo. Soc. Architects, 1984. Mem. Urban Land Inst. (panel adv. svcs. 1990, 2001, 02, 04, 06), Denver Country Club (bd. dirs. 1984-88, pres. 1986-87), Beta Theta Pi Democrat. Avocations: skiing, golf, hiking, bicycling. Office: 390 Emerson St Denver CO 80218 Home Phone: 303-333-1857; Office Phone: 303-880-3813. Personal E-mail: jmpros@aol.com.

PROSSER, MICHAEL HUBERT, communications educator; b. Indpls., Mar. 29, 1936; arrived in China, 2001; s. Marshall Herbert and Clydia Catharine (O'Dea) P.; m. Carol Mary Hogle, Nov. 27, 1958 (div. 1983); children: Michelle Ann, Leo Michael, Louis Mark; m. Joan Ann Kirkeby, Dec. 6, 1986 (div. 2001). BA, Ball State U., 1958, MA, 1959; PhD, U. Ill., 1964. Tchr. Latin Urbana Jr. HS, Ill., 1960-63; asst. prof. speech SUNY, Buffalo, 1963-69; assoc. prof. speech Ind. U., Bloomington, 1969-72; prof. rhetoric and comm. U. Va., Charlottesville, 1972-2001, chair, 1972-77, prof. emeritus, 2001—; William A. Kern prof. in comm. Rochester Inst. Tech., 1994—98; chair internat. adv. bd. Coll. English Shanghai Internat. Studies U. Intercultural Inst., 1998—2001, disting. prof., 2006—. Vis. lectr. comm. CUNY Queens Coll., 1966—67; vis. assoc. prof. speech Calif. State U., Hayward, 1971; vis. prof. curriculum Meml. U., Newfoundland, St. John's U., 1972, St. Paul U., 1975, U. Ottawa, Canada, 1975; cons. U.S. Info. Agy., Washington, 1977; disting. vis. prof. speech Kent State U., Ohio, 1978; Fullbright prof. English U. Swaziland, Kwalusene, 1990—91; disting. vis. prof. comm. Rochester Inst. Tech., 1998—2001; adj prof. SUNY, Brockport, 1998—99; prof. English Yangzhou U., 2001—02; disting. prof. English Beijing Lang. and Culture U., China, 2002—05, Shanghai Internat. Studies U., China, 2005—; keynote spkr. various Chinese comm. confs., India, Russia. Author: The Cultural Dialogue, 1978 (translated into Japanese 1982); co-author: Diplomatic Discourse: International Conflict at the United Nations: Addresses and Analysis, 1997; editor: An Ethic for Survival: Adlai Stevenson Speaks on International Affairs, 1936-65, 1969, Sow the Wind, Reap the Whirlwind: Heads of State Address the United Nations (2 vols.), 1970, Intercommunication Among Nations and Peoples, 1973; co-editor: Readings in Classical Rhetoric, 1969, Readings in Medieval Rhetoric, 1973, Civic Discourse: Multiculturalism, Cultural Diversity, and Global Communication, 1998, Civic Discourse: Intercultural, International and Global Media, 1999, Sino-American Compositions of Shared Topics, 2003, Intercultural Perspectives on Chinese Communication, 2007; series editor Civic Discourse for the Third Millennium, 1998-2004, Ablex Pub. Co., Praeger, Greenwood Pub. Co., 2005; featured in China Talent Semimonthly, Chinese edit. Chair AFS Global Awareness Day, U. Va., 1983-90, RIT Global Awareness Day, 1995-98; bd. dirs., v.p. Assn. Rochester UN, 1996-97, pres., 1997-98; pres. Rochester Area Fulbright chpt., 1995-97; mem. Nat. Comm. Assn. Recipient Disting. Alumnus award Ball State U., 1978, Excellence award Prosser-Sitaram, 2000. Mem. Internat. Soc. for Intercultural Edn., Tng. and Rsch. (pres. 1984-86, Citizen of World 1986, Outstanding Sr. Interculturalist 1990), Internat. Comm. Assn. (v.p., Disting. Svc. award 1978), UN Assn. U.S.A., Fulbright Assn., Nat. Comm. Assn., UN Assn. of Rochester (bd. dirs., v.p., pres.), Am. Field Svc. (pres. intercultural programs 1982-86, Charlottesville). Democrat. Roman Catholic. Avocation: travel. Office: Shanghai Internat Studies U Intercultural Inst Coll Journalism and Comm 121 Guanglingyilu Shanghai 200083 China Home Phone: 086 21 6542 3070; Office Phone: 086 21 6542 3070 ext. 1303. Office Fax: 86 21 6544 8852. Personal E-mail: michaelhprosser@yahoo.com.

PROST, SHARON, federal judge; b. Newburyport, Mass., May 24, 1951; m. Kenneth F. Greene, June 24, 1984; 1 child, Matthew Prost-Greene. BS, Cornell U., 1973; MBA, George Washington U., 1975, LLM in Taxation, 1984; JD, Am. U., 1979. Bar: D.C. Labor rels. specialist Office of Personnel Mgmt., 1973-76; with Gen. Acctg. Office, 1976-79; trial atty. Fed. Labor Rels. Authority, 1980-83; atty. chief counsel's office Dept. of Treasury, 1983-84; assoc. solicitor Nat. Labor Rels. Bd., 1984-89; chief minority labor counsel Senate Com. on Labor and Human Resources, 1989-93; minority chief counsel Senate Com. on the Judiciary, 1993—2001; judge US Ct. Appeals, (Fed. cir.), 2001—. Office: US Court Appeals Fed Cir 717 Madison Pl NW Washington DC 20439 *

PROTAS, ELIZABETH J., physical therapist, academic administrator; m. Eugene D. Protas, Mar. 6, 1950; 1 child, Mark Jason. PhD, SUNY, Buffalo, 1974—80. Cert. phys. therapist Tex., 1980. Assoc. dean, sch. phys. therapy Tex. Woman's U., Houston, 1980—2002; chair, dept. phys. therapy U. Tex. Med. Br., Galveston, 2002—. Bd. trustees Am. Coll. Sports Medicine, Indpls., 2002—04. Recipient Joseph Valley Gerontologica Profl. of Yr. award, U. Tex. Health Sci. Ctr., 2000; fellow Founding Fellow, Am. Assn. Cardiovasc. and Pulmonary Rehab.; grantee Support Rsch. and Tng. Grad. Students, Dept. of Veterans. Mem.: Am. Phys. Therapy Assn. Achievements include research in Rehabilitation outcomes for persons with chronic disabilities. Office: U Tex Med Branch 301 U Blvd Galveston TX 77555-1144

PROTAS, JOSH, non-profit organization director; b. 1975; Grad., Wesleyan U.; M in Pub. Hist., Ariz. State U. Exec. dir. Stone Ave. Temple; dir., Jewish Cmty. Rels. Coun. Jewish Fedn. Southern Ariz. Mem. Pima Coun. on Aging and Jewish Family & Children's Svc. Involved with Salvation Army, Cmty. Food Bank, Southern Ariz. Cmty. Diaper Bank, YWCA, Tucson Save Darfur Coalition; men's shelter meal team Primavera Svc. Named one of 40 Under 40, Tucson Bus. Edge, 2006. Office: Jewish Cmty Relations Council 3822 E River Rd Tucson AZ 85718 Office Phone: 520-577-9393. Office Fax: 520-577-0734.

PROTHRO, JERRY ROBERT, lawyer; b. Midland, Tex., Dec. 22, 1946; s. Jack William Prothro and Nita Marie (Stovall) Milligan; m. Leslie Joan Lepar, Aug. 15, 1970 (div. 1994); ptnr. David Majeau; children: Laura Kay, Evan Jackson. BA, Southwestern U., 1969; JD, U. Tex. Sch. Law, 1972. Lawyer, capt. U.S. Army, JAGC, 1972-76; ptnr. Turpin, Smith & Dyer, Midland, 1975-85, Boyd, Sanders, Wade, Cropper & Prothro, Midland, 1985-91; pvt. practice Dallas and Midland, Tex., 1991—95. Mem. admissions com. M/O div. U.S. Dist. Ct. for Western Dist. Tex., 1987-2000; staff atty. Dallas Legal Hospice, 2000-06; spkr. in field, real estate appraisals. Treas., v.p. Southwestern U. Alumni Bd., Georgetown, Tex., 1980-90, pres.-elect, 1991, pres., 1992-94; trustee, Southwestern U., 1992-94; adminstrv. bd. First United Meth. Ch., Midland, 1989-96; vice chmn. Permian Basin AIDS Coalition Bd., 1994; active Midland County Hist. Commn., 1980-85. Named Univ. scholar Southwestern U., 1969; recipient Disting. Svc. medal U.S. Army, 1974. Mem. Midland County Young Lawyers (pres. 1979-80), Midland County Bar Assn., 5th Cir. Bar Assn., Pi Kappa Alpha Social Frat., Blue Key Leadership Frat., Pi Gamma Mu Social Sci. Frat. Methodist. Avocations: antiques, camping. Home: Ste 211 4021 Cole Ave Dallas TX 75204 Office: 9 Rue Lavel No 1 Quebec City PQ Canada Personal E-mail: prothro@swbell.net.

PROUD, ROBERT DONALD (ROBERT PAYTON), broadcast executive; b. Cleve., Nov. 1, 1949; s. Lloyd Donald and Eleanore Matilda (Cihon) Proud; m. K. Diane Siler, Feb. 17, 1979; 1 child, James S. Owen. Grad., Cleve. Inst. Broadcasting, 1969; student, U. N.Mex., Albuquerque, 1982, Instituto Bilingue Cultural, 1989-90. Program dir. Sta. WGCL-FM, Cleve., 1972-74; ops. mgr. Sta. WRBR-FM, South Bend, Ind., 1974-75, Sta. XEROK, Juarez, Mexico, 1975-77; program dir. Sta. WZZP-FM, Cleve., 1977-78; gen. mgr. Sta. KELP, El Paso, Tex., 1978-82; sales mgr. Sta. KAMZ-FM, El Paso, 1982-86; gen. mgr. Sts. KAMA/KAMZ-FM, El Paso, 1982-86; dir. nat. sales Thrash Broadcasting, El Paso, Lubbock, Tex., 1987-88; gen. mgr. Sta. KVIV, El Paso, 1987-89; v.p., gen. mgr. Sta. KEZB, El Paso, Tex., 1989-91; gen. mgr. Sta. KFRR, Denver, 1991-92; gen. sta. mgr. Sta. KQQK, Houston, 1992-95; v.p., gen. mgr. Entravision Comm., Dallas, 1995—2003; v.p. sales OM Media Networks, Sacramento, 2003—04; v.p. ops. Border Media Ptnrs., Tex., 2004—. Office: 8828 North Stemmons Dallas TX 75247 Personal E-mail: krvabob@aol.com. Business E-Mail: bproud@bmpradio.com.

PROULX, (EDNA) ANNIE, writer; b. Norwich, Conn., Aug. 22, 1935; d. George Napolean and Lois Nellie (Gill) Proulx; m. James Hamilton Lang, June 22, 1969 (div. 1990); children: Sylvia Marion Bullock Clarkson, Jonathan Edward Lang, Gillis Crowell Lang, Morgan Hamilton Lang. BA cum laude, U. Vt., 1969; MA, Sir George Williams U., Montreal, Can., 1973; DHL (hon.), U. Maine, 1994; LLD, Concordia U., Montreal, 2002; DLitt (hon.), U. Toronto, 2000. Author: Heart Songs and Other Stories, 1988, Postcards, 1991 (PEN/Faulkner award 1993), The Shipping News, 1993 (Chgo. Tribune Heartland award 1993, Irish Times Internat. Fiction award 1993, Nat. Book award for fiction 1994, Pulitzer Prize for fiction 1994), Accordion Crimes, 1996 (Dos Passos prize for lit. 1996), Brokeback Mountain, 1998 (Nat. Mag. award 1998), Brokeback Mountain, 1998 (later adapted into film), Close Range: Wyoming Stories, 1999, That Old Ace in the Hole, 2002, Bad Dirt: Wyoming Stories 2, 2004; contbr. more than 50 articles to mags. and jours.; editor: Best American Short Stories of 1997. Recipient Dos Passos prize for Lit., Longwood Coll., 1997, Ambassador Book award English Speaking Union, 2000, Best Fiction 1999 Book award The New Yorker, 2000, Willa award, 2000, Evil Companions Lit. award, 2001; Kress fellow Harvard U., 1974, fellow Vt. Coun. Arts, 1989, NEA, 1991, Guggenheim Found., 1992; rsch. grantee Inter.-U. Ctr., 1975; resident Ucross Found., 1990, 92. Mem. PEN Am. Ctr., Phi Beta Kappa, Phi Alpha Theta. Avocations: canoeing, reading, fishing.

PROUNIS, OTHON A., lawyer; b. NYC, July 23, 1961; AB, Columbia Univ., 1983, JD, 1986. Bar: N.Y. 1987. Ptnr. Reboul MacMurray Hewitt & Maynard; ptnr. corp. dept. & co-head private equity practice group Ropes & Gray, NYC, 2003—. Mem.: ABA. Office: Ropes & Gray 45 Rockefeller Plz New York NY 10111-0087 Office Phone: 212-841-5785. Office Fax: 212-841-5725. Business E-Mail: othon.prounis@ropesgray.com.

PROUST, JOYCELYN ANN, retired librarian; d. Merry Aylor and Alice Wilhelmina (Morgan); m. George Edward Proust (dec.); children: Gabrielle Cynara, Bertrand Gerard. BA, U. Denver, 1950, MA, 1955; cert., U. Paris Sorbonne, 1953. Lifetime French tchg. credential Calif. C.C., lifetime libr. credential C.C. Libr. Colo. Sch. Mines, Golden, 1955—62; prof. libr. sci. Long Beach (Calif.) City Coll., 1962—92, prof. emerita, 1992—. Chair Calif. C.C. Libr. Cooperative, 1968—75; exec. dir., pres. Libr./Learning Resources Assn., Calif., 1985—86. Bd. mem. Long Beach Mozart Festival, 1975—95, chair; active 1976 Bicentennial Com., LA, 1976. Mem.: Alpha Gamma Delta, Phi Sigma Iota, Alpha Lambda Delta. Unitarian. Home: 5249 Village Rd Long Beach CA 90808

PROUT, CURTIS, internist, educator; b. Swampscott, Mass., Oct. 13, 1915; s. Henry Byrd and Eloise (Willett) P.; m. Daphne Brooks, June 27, 1939 (div. 1985); children: Diana P. Cherot, Daphne P. Cook, Rosamond P. Warren, Phyllis P.; m. Diane Neal Emmons, Dec. 7, 1985. AB, Harvard U., 1937, MD, 1941. Diplomate Am. Bd. Internal Medicine. Intern Peter Bent Brigham Hosp., Boston, 1942; resident in internal medicine Johns Hopkins Hosp., Balt., 1943; research fellow Mass. Gen. Hosp., Boston, 1944—45; practice medicine specializing in internal medicine, 1945—; asst. dir. Univ. Health Services Harvard U., Cambridge, Mass., 1961-72; dir. prison health project Office of Econ. Opportunity, 1972-74; asst. dean Harvard Med. Sch., Boston, 1980-94, asst. clin. prof. medicine, 1975-82. Trustee Humane Soc. Mass., Boston, 1975-2005, pres., 2004; bd. dirs. Nat. Commn. on Correctional Health Care, 1980-98, chmn., 1990; dir., treas. The Med. Found., Boston, 1980-98. Chmn. Bd. Health, Dover, Mass., 1960-75. Fellow ACP, Mass. Med. Soc.; mem. AMA, Am. Clin. and Climatol. Assn., Tavern Club of Boston (pres. 1980-82). Avocations: sailing, writing. Home and Office: 115 School St Manchester MA 01944-1232 Personal E-mail: dr.curtisprout@adelphia.net.

PROUT, GEORGE RUSSELL, JR., medical educator, urologist; b. Boston, July 23, 1924; s. George Russell and Marion (Snow) P.; m. Loa Katherine Wheatley, Oct. 17, 1950; children: George Russell III, Elizabeth Louise. Student, Union Coll., 1943, DSc (hon.), 1990; MD, Albany Med. Coll., 1947, DSc (hon.), 1988; MA (hon.), Harvard U., 1969. Intern Grasslands Hosp., Valhalla, NY, 1947-48; asst. resident in surgery, 1948-50; surg. resident Grasslands Hosp., Valhalla, NY, 1948-50; resident N.Y. Hosp., NYC, 1952-56; fellow in surgery Meml. Ctr. Cancer & Allied Diseases, 1954—55; asst. attending physician Meml. Ctr. for Cancer and Allied Disease, NYC, 1956-57; asst. clinician in surgery James Ewing Hosp., NYC, 1956-57; assoc. prof., chmn. div. urology U. Miami, 1957-60; prof., chmn. div. urology Med. Coll. Va., 1960-69; chief urol. svc. Mass. Gen. Hosp., Boston, 1969-89; prof. surgery Harvard Med. Sch., 1969-89, emeritus prof. surgery Boston, 1989—; hon. urologist Mass. Gen. Hosp., Boston, 1989—. Chmn. Adjuvants in Surg. Treatment of Bladder Cancer; mem. adv. task force Nat. Cancer Inst., 1968—, cons., 1990—; expert cons. divsn. surveillance, 1991—; Finland coop. ATBC study, 1991—; chmn. Nat. Bladder Cancer Group, 1973—86. Editor-in-chief: Urologic Oncology, 1994—2000. With USNR, 1950-52. Fellow ACS, Acad. Medicine Toronto (corr.); mem. AMA, AAUP, Am. Urol. Assn., Can. Urol. Assn., Japanese Urol. Soc. (hon.), Am. Cancer Soc., Soc. Surg. Oncology, Soc. Univ. Urologists, Dallas So. Clin. Soc. (hon.), Am. Assn. Genitourinary Surgeons, Soc. Pediat. Urology, Soc. Urol. Oncology, Soc. Internat. Urologists, Soc. Basic Urol. Rsch., Alpha Omega Alpha. Home (Winter): 224 Corsair Rd Duck Key FL 33050 Home and Office: 1800 River Watch Ave Annapolis MD 21401 Personal E-mail: drurocsal@aol.com.

PROUT, ROBERT STEPHEN, higher education consultant, law enforcement consultant; b. June 24, 1944; Degree in law, LaSalle Ext. U., Chgo., 1967; BA, Muskingum Coll., New Concord, Ohio, 1969; MEd, Ohio U., Athens, 1970; PhD, Ohio State U., Columbus, 1972. State trooper Ohio Hwy. Patrol, Akron, Ohio, 1965-68; coord. Zane State Coll., Zanesville, Ohio, 1969—72; dept. chair criminal justice St. Cloud State U., Minn., 1972—96, 2002—, dir. grad. program criminal justice, 1988—. Adj. faculty St. John's U., Coll. St. Thomas, U. Louisville; chmn. Govs. Com. on Crime Prevention-Region D, Minn., 1976-77. Author: Meeting Ohio's Law Enforcement Needs, 1973; contbr. articles to profl. jours. Recipient Tchr. of Yr. award, 1988. Office: St Cloud State U 241 Stewart Hall Saint Cloud MN 56301 Business E-Mail: prout@stcloudstate.edu.

PROUT, WILLIAM H., JR., lawyer; b. New Haven, 1945; BA, Yale U., 1967; JD cum laude, Boston U., 1973. Bar: Conn. 1973, US Dist. Ct. (Dist. Conn.), US Ct. Appeals (2d Cir.), US Supreme Ct. Ptnr. Wiggin & Dana, New Haven. Mem. Fed. Grievance Com. Counsel. Mem.: Fed. Bar Coun., New Haven Inn of Ct., New England Bar Assn., New Haven County Bar Assn. (past pres.), ABA (litig. sect., antitrust sect.), Conn. Bar Assn. (pres.-elect 2006). Office: Wiggin & Dana One Century Tower 265 Church St PO Box 1832 New Haven CT 06508 Office Phone: 203-498-4320. Office Fax: 203-782-2889. E-mail: wprout@wiggin.com.

PROVENCHER, CATHERINE A., state official; b. Merrimack, NH; married; 2 children. BS in Acctg., Bentley Coll.; MBA, So. NH Univ. CPA. With NH Office of Legislative Budget, 1985—2006, dir. audits, 1997—2006; state treas. State of NH, 2007—. Chair New England Govtl. Forum. Grantee Caroline Gross Fellowship, 2006. Mem.: NH Soc. CPA, AICPA. Office: State Treas Rm 121 25 Capitol St Concord NH 03301 Office Phone: 603-271-2621. Office Fax: 603-271-3922. Business E-Mail: treasury@treasury.state.nh.us. *

PROVENCIO, LINDA KAY, music educator; b. Ft. Benning, Ga., Feb. 24, 1955; d. Dean D. and Marilyn A. (Johnson) Johnson; m. Roberto E. Provencio, Aug. 18, 1984; children: Robert Phillip, Charles Raymond, Elizabeth Anne, Victoria Lynn. BMus, U. Ariz., Tucson, 1980; MA in Curriculum and Instrn., Calif. State U., Bakersfield, 2005; postgrad., U. Tex., El Paso, 1983-84, SW Tex. State U., San Marcos, 1985-86, U. Colo., Boulder, 1987—88. Music tchr. El Paso Ind. Sch. Dist., Tex., 1980-84; choir dir., music tchr. Lockhart Ind. Sch. Dist., Tex., 1984-86; music tchr. Nativity of Our Lord Sch., Broomfield, Colo., 1987-88; music specialist Panama Buena Vista Sch. Dist., Bakersfield, Calif., 1989-90, Fruitvale Sch. Dist., Bakersfield, 1995—. Curriculum author Lockhart Ind. Sch. Dist., 1985-86; adminstrv. asst. Hill Country Choral Camp, S.W. Tex. State U., summer 1985; part-time instr. Calif. State U., Bakersfield, 2005-. Singer: CSUB Chamber Singers, 2004—. Mem. Music Educators Nat. Conf., Calif. Music Educators, Soc. Gen. Music, Kern County Music Educators Assn., Kern Cmty. Tennis Assn. (sec. jr. com., 2001-2006), U.S. Tennis Assn. Republican. Roman Catholic. Avocations: reading, singing, travel, gardening.

PROVENCIO, ROBERTO ENRIQUE, music educator, music minister; b. El Paso, Tex., July 14, 1957; s. Jesus Roberto and Velia Rivero Provencio; m. Linda Kay Johnson, Aug. 18, 1984; children: Robert Phillip, Charles Raymond, Elizabeth Anne, Victoria Lynn. MusB, U. Ariz., 1980; MusM, Tex. State U., 1986; D Musical Arts, U. Colo., 1993. Prof. music Calif. State U., Bakersfield, 1988—; min. music First Presbyn. Ch., Bakersfield, 1995—. Pvt. practice cons., Bakersfield, 1980—. Mem. editl. bd. The Choral Jour.; translator: History of the Choral Movement of Venezuela; author: Releasing the Artist Within: Mnemonics for Achieving Artistic Choral Performance. Mem. Adult Rehab. Ctr. Salvation Army, Bakersfield, 1999; bd. dirs. The Beethoven Festival, Bakersfield, 1992—95. Named Outstanding Hispanic Alumnus, Tex. State U., 1994, Outstanding Music Educator, Calif. Music Educators Assn., 1994, Outstanding Prof., 2001;, Calif. State U. fellow, 1988—92, Choral Rsch. fellow, U. of Colo., Boulder, 1986—88. Mem.: Nat. Assn. Ch. Musicians (bd. govs. 1998—, chair publs. com. jour.), Internat. Fedn. Choral Music, Am. Choral Directors Assn. (life; chair multicultural perspectives western divsn. 1992—96, mem. editl. bd. 1995—), Rotary (dir., scholarship chair 1994, Bakersfield East), Pi Kappa Lambda (life). Conservative. Avocations: motorcycle touring, fly fishing, tennis, photography, tobacciana. Home: 101 Camino del Oeste Bakersfield CA 93309 Office: Calif State U 9001 Stockdale Hwy Bakersfield CA 93311 Office Phone: 661-654-3073. Business E-Mail: rprovencio@csub.edu.

PROVENSEN, ALICE, artist, writer; b. Chgo. d. Jay Horace and Kathryn (Zelanis) Twitchell; m. Martin Provensen, Apr. 17, 1944 (dec.); 1 child, Karen Anna. Student, Art Inst. of Chgo., 1930-31, U. Calif., LA, 1939, Art Student League, NYC, 1940-41; D.H.L. (hon.), Marist Coll., 1986. With Walter Lanz Studios, Los Angeles, 1942-43; OSS, 1944-45. Author, illustrator Karen's Opposites, 1963, Karen's Curiosity, 1963, What is a Color?, 1967, author, illustrator (with Martin Provensen) Who's in the Egg?, 1970, author, illustrator The Provensen Book of Fairy Tales, 1971, Play on Words, 1972, My Little Hen, 1973, Roses are Red, 1973, Our Animal Friends, 1974, The Year at Maple Hill Farm, 1978, A Horse and a Hound, A Goat and a Gander, 1979, The Owl and Three Pussycats, 1981, Town and Country, 1984, Shaker Lane, 1987, The Buck Stops Here, 1990, Punch in New York, 1991 (Best Books N.Y. Times, 1991), My Fellow Americans, 1995, Count on Me, 1998 (Book of Yr. Parenting Mag., 1998), The Master Swordsman, 2001, The Magic Doorway, 2001, A Day in the Life of Murphy, 2003 (named One of the Three Best Childrens Books, 2003), Klondike Gold, 2005 (Spur award Western Writers Am., 2006), illustrator (with Martin Provensen) Mother Goose Book, 1976, illustrator Old Mother Hubbard, 1977, A Peaceable Kingdom, 1978, The Golden Serpent, 1980, A Visit to William Blake's Inn, 1981 (Caldecott honor book, 1981), Birds, Beasts and the Third Thing, 1982, The Glorious Flight, 1984 (Caldecott medal, 1984), The Voyage of Ludgate Hill, 1987, also textbooks; exhibitions include with Martin Provensen Balt. Mus., 1954, exhibitions include Am. Inst. Graphic Arts, NYC, 1959, Botolph Group, Boston, 1964, Eric Carle Mus., Amherst, Mass., 2005—06, one-woman shows include Henry Feiwel Gallery, NYC, 1991, Children's Mus., Washington, 1991, Moscarelle Mus. Art, Williamsburg, Va., 1991, Eric Carle Mus. Picture Book Art, Amherst, Mass., 2005—06; books represented Fifty Book of Yr. selections Am. Inst. Graphic Arts, 1947, 1948, 1952 (The Charge of the Light Brigade named Best Illustrated Children's Book of Yr. N.Y. Times, 1964, co-recipient medal Soc. Illustrators, 1960). Named to Soc. Illustrators Hall of Fame, 2000; recipient Empire State award, Youth Svcs. sect. NY Libr. Assn., 2004.

PROVINE, JOHN CALHOUN, retired lawyer; b. Asheville, NC, May 15, 1938; s. Robert Calhoun and Harriet Josephine (Thoms) P.; m. Martha Ann Monson, Aug. 26, 1966 (div. Jan. 1975); m. Nancy Frances Lunsford, Apr. 17, 1976 (div. Mar. 1996); children: Robert, Frances, Harriet. AB, Harvard U., 1960; JD, U. Mich., 1966; MBA, NYU, 1972, LLM in Taxation, 1975. Bar: NY, Tenn., US Dist. Ct. (so. and ea. dists.) NY, US Ct. Appeals (2nd and 6th cirs.), US Dist. Ct. (mid. dist.) Tenn., US Supreme Ct. From assoc. to ptnr. White & Case, NYC, 1966—74, ptnr., 1974—82, 1992—94, Jakarta and Ankara, 1982—91; counsel Dearborn & Ewing, Nashville, 1981—82; ret., 1994. Lt. USN, 1960-63. Mem. ABA, NY Bar Assn., Tenn. Bar Assn., Assn. of Bar of City of NY Avocations: bluegrass music, rural activities. Home and Office: 6630 Manley Ln Brentwood TN 37027-3401 Personal E-mail: jprovine@bellsouth.net.

PROVINE, LORRAINE, retired mathematics educator; b. Altus, Okla., Oct. 6, 1944; d. Claud Edward and Emmie Lorraine (Gasper) Allmon; m. Joe A. Provine, Aug. 14, 1966; children: Sharon Kay, John David. BS, U. Okla., 1966; MS, Okla. State U., 1988. Tchr. math. US Grant HS, Oklahoma City Schs., 1966-69; tchr. Ponca City East Jr. HS, Okla., 1969-70, 1978-79, 81-96; lectr. dept. math. Okla. State U., Stillwater, 1996-99. Mem.: Cleve. County Ret. Educators Assn., Cleve. McClain County Ret. Educators Assn., Ponca City Assn. Classroom Tchrs. (treas. 1983—86, 1991—96), Assn. Women in Math, Okla. Coun. Tchrs. Math, Okla. Edn. Assn., Sch. Sci. and Math Assn., Nat. Coun. Tchrs. Math, Math. Assn. Am., Internat. Soc. Tech. in Edn., Coun. Exceptional Children, Nat. Ret. Educators Assn. (life), Okla. Ret. Educators Assn. (life), Okla. State U. Alumni Assn. (life), U. Okla. Alumni Assn. (life), Okla. Assn. Mothers Club (life; state bd. dirs. 1977—87, pres. 1984—85), Delta Kappa Gamma Soc. Internat. (Delta chpt. treas. 1996—98, Eta chpt. treas. 2000—04, Eta chpt. pres. 2004—, chair Gamma state essay com. 2005—07, Okla./Cleve county area dir. 2007—, S.W. regional com. chmn. 2007). Republican. Baptist. Avocations: reading, knitting, sewing, genealogy, quilting. Home: 1019 Greenway Cir Norman OK 73072-6125 Personal E-mail: lorraineprovine@cox.net.

PROVINE, WILLIAM B., biology professor; BS, U. Chgo., 1962, MA in Hist. of Sci., 1965, PhD, 1970. Asst. prof. hist. Cornell U., Ithaca, NY, 1969, mem. faculty divsn. biol. scis., 1974, mem. faculty sect. ecology and systematics, 1986, Charles A. Alexander prof. biol. scis. dept. ecology and evolutionary biology. Contbr. articles to profl. jours., chapters to books; author: The Origins of Theoretical Population Genetics, 1971, Sewall Wright and Evolutionary Biology, 1986; co-editor: The Evolutionary Synthesis, 1980; editor: Evolution: Selected Papers by Sewall Wright, 1986. Grantee Guggenheim fellowship, 1984. Fellow: AAAS, Am. Acad. Arts & Scis. Office: Dept Ecology and Evolutionary Biology Cornell U E139 Corson Hall Ithaca NY 14853 E-mail: wbp2@cornell.edu.

PROVITT, LINDA K., forensic specialist, mental health services professional, consultant; b. Cleve., Ohio, Nov. 26, 1965; d. Raymond Emery and Barbara Calhoun Provitt. BA, Oberlin Coll., Ohio, 1987; MD, U. Toledo, Ohio, 1993; MEd, Kent State U., Ohio, 2004. Psychiatrist U. Hosps. Cleve., 1993—2000; grad. rsch. asst. Kent State U., 2003—06, instr., 2004; forensic caseworker Cleve. Ho. Corrections, 2006—. Mental health screening cons. Cleve. Ho. Corrections, 2006—. Mem. St. James AME Choir, 1997—2007. Mem.: So. Poverty Law Ctr., Alpha Kappa Mu. Avocations: movies, music, collage, writing, poetry.

PROVORNY, FREDERICK ALAN, lawyer, educator; b. Bklyn., Sept. 7, 1946; s. Daniel and Anna (Wurm) P.; m. Nancy Ileene Wilkins, Nov. 21, 1971; children: Michelle C., Cheryl A., Lisa T., Robert D. BS summa cum laude, NYU, 1966; JD magna cum laude, Columbia U., 1969. Bar: NY 1970, US Supreme Ct. 1973, DC 1975, Mo. 1977, Md. 1987, Calif. 1989; CPA, Md., Mo. Law clk. to Judge Harold R. Medina U.S. Ct. Appeals (2d cir.), NYC, 1969-70; asst. prof. law Syracuse (NY) U., 1970-72; assoc. Debevoise, Plimpton, Lyons & Gates, NYC, 1972-75, Cole & Groner PC, Washington, 1975-76; with Monsanto Co., St. Louis, 1976-86, asst. co. counsel, 1978-86; pvt. practice Washington, 1986-89; ptnr. Provorny & Jacoby, Washington, 1989-91; counsel Shaw, Pittman, Potts & Trowbridge, Washington, 1991-93; ptnr. Tydings & Rosenberg, Balt., 1993-94; pvt. practice Balt., 1994—98; Harold R. Tyler prof. law and tech. Sci. and Tech. Law Ctr., Albany (NY) Law Sch., 1998—2004, dir., 1998—2003; pres. Empire State Venture Group, Inc., 2001—03; dir. Md. Intellectual Property Legal Resource Ctr., Rockville, 2004—. Vis. prof. U. Md. Sch. Law, 2004-; lectr. Bklyn Law Sch., 1973-74; adj. prof. U. Balt. Sch. of Law, 1996-98, Rensselaer Poly Inst., 2004; pres. Sci. and Tech. Assocs., Inc., 1986-91. Contbr. articles to profl. jours. Trustee Christian Woman's Benevolent Assn. Youth Home, 1979-83, Jewish Family Svcs. of N.E. NY, 1999—2004. Mem. ABA, Am. Law Inst., Am. Arbitration Assn. (panel comml. abitrators), Am. Intellectual Property Lawyers Assn., Licensing Execs. Soc. (U.S., Can.), Assn. Univ. Tech. Mgrs., Philo-Mt. Sinai Lodge 968, Masons, Beta Gamma Sigma. Jewish. Home: 11803 Kemp Mill Rd Silver Spring MD 20902-1511 Office: U Md Sch Law 500 W Baltimore St Baltimore MD 21201 also: Md Intellectual Property Legal Resource Ctr 9700 Great Seneca Hwy Rockville MD 20850 Home Phone: 301-593-9115; Office Phone: 410-706-1190, 240-453-6246. E-mail: fprovorny@law.umaryland.edu.

PROVOST, THOMAS TAYLOR, dermatology educator, researcher; b. Pitts., Mar. 21, 1938; s. Charles Thomas and Marcelle K. (Taylor) P.; m. Carol Sara Christie, July 2, 1960; children: Charles T., Christie Lynn, Thomas Wright. AB, U. Pitts., 1958, MD, 1962. Intern Mary Hitchcock Meml. Hosp., Hanover, N.H., 1962-63; resident in dermatology Dartmouth Med. Ctr., Hanover, N.H., 1966-67, U. Oreg. Med. Ctr., Portland, 1967-68; fellow in immunology SUNY, Buffalo, 1969-72, asst. prof. dermatology, 1972-75, assoc. prof., 1975-78, Johns Hopkins U. Med. Sch., Balt., 1978-82, prof. dermatology, 1982—, chmn. dept. dermatology, 1997—. Lt. commdr. USPHS, 1962-64. Mem. Soc. Investigative Dermatology, Soc. Clin. Investigation. Avocation: boating. Home: PO Box 230 Milton DE 19968-0230

PROVUS, BARBARA LEE, retired executive search consultant; b. Washington, Nov. 20, 1949; d. Severn and Birdell (Eck) P.; m. Frederick W. Wackerle, Mar. 29, 1985. Student, NYU, 1969-70; BA in Sociology, Russell Sage Coll., 1971; MS in Indsl. Rels., Loyola U., Chgo., 1978; postgrad., Smith Coll., 1971. Sec. Booz, Allen & Hamilton, Chgo., 1973-74, mgr. tng., 1974-77, dir. rsch., 1977-79, cons. search, 1979-80; mgr. mgmt. devel. Federated Dept. Stores, Cin., 1980-82; v.p. Lamalie Assocs., Chgo., 1982-86; prin., founder Sweeney, Shepherd, Bueschel, Provus, Harbert & Mummert, Inc., Chgo., 1986-91; founder Shepherd Bueschel & Provus Inc., Chgo., 1992—2005; ret., 2005. Bd. dirs. Anti-Cruelty Soc., Chgo., 1990—, pres., 1996-97; trustee Sage Colls., Troy, N.Y., 1999-2000. Mem. Assn. Exec. Search Cons. (dir. 1989-92), The Chgo. Network (bd. dirs. 1993—, chair 2002-03), Econ. Club Chgo. Avocations: collecting rubber bands, modern art, baseball. Home: 3750 N Lake Shore Dr Chicago IL 60613-4238 Home Phone: 773-935-0141.

PROWN, JULES DAVID, art historian, educator; b. Freehold, NJ, Mar. 14, 1930; s. Max and Matilda (Cassileth) P.; m. Shirley Ann Martin, June 23, 1956; children: Elizabeth Anderson, David Martin, Jonathan, Peter Cassileth, Sarah Peiter. AB, Lafayette Coll., 1951, DFA (hon.), 1979; AM, U. Del., 1956, Harvard U., 1953, PhD, 1961. Dir. Hist. Soc. Old Newbury, Newburyport, Mass., 1957-58, Old Gaol Mus., York, Maine, 1958-59; asst. to dir. Harvard U., Fogg Art Mus., Cambridge, Mass., 1959-61; instr. to Paul Mellon prof. history of art Yale U., New Haven, 1961-99, Paul Mellon prof. emeritus history of art, 1999—; curator Am. art Yale U. Art Gallery, New Haven, 1963-68; vis. lectr. Smith Coll., Northampton, Mass., 1966-67; dir. Yale Ctr. for Brit. Art, New Haven, 1968-76, sr. rsch. fellow, 1999—; assoc. dir. Nat. Humanities Inst., New Haven, 1977. Trustee Whitney Mus., N.Y.C., 1975-94; mem. editorial adv. bd. Am. Art-Smithsonian, Washington, 1986-2001, On Common Ground, 1993—; mem. vis. com. Harvard U. Art Museums, 1993-98. Author: John Singleton Copley, 2 Vols., 1966, American Painting from Its Beginnings to the Armory Show, 1969, The Architecture of the Yale Center for British Art, 1977; Art as Evidence: Writings on Art and Material Culture, 2002, (catalogue) American Art from Alumni Collections, 1968; editor (with Kenneth Haltman) American Artifacts: Essays in Material Culture, 2000. Recipient George Washington Kidd award Lafayette Coll., 1986, recipient Iris Found. award outstanding contbns. to the decorative arts, 2001, Lawrence A. Fleischman award Scholarly Excellence Am. Art History, 2001, William Clyde DeVane award Scholarship and Tchg. Phi Beta Kappa, Yale U., 2005. Fellow The Athenaeum of Phila. (hon.); mem. Am. Antiquarian Soc., Coll. Art Assn. (Disting. Tchg. of Art History award 1996), Am. Studies Assn., Conn. Acad. Arts & Scis., Walpole Soc., Royal Soc. Arts. Office: Yale Ctr for Brit Art PO Box 208280 New Haven CT 06520-8280 Business E-Mail: jules.prown@yale.edu.

PROZES, ANDREW, publishing executive; b. Jan. 21, 1946; BA in Math, U. Waterloo, Ont., Can.; MBA, York U., Toronto. Former group pres. Southam Inc., Don Mills, Ont., Can.; exec. v.p., COO Westlaw, The West Group (subs. Thomson Corp.), Eagan, Minn., 1997-99; CEO global legal pub. & info. divsn. Reed Elsevier, NYC, 2000—. Mem. bd. dirs. Reed Elsevier Group plc and Reed Elsevier PLC, 2000—. Office: Reed Elsevier 125 Park Ave 23rd fl New York NY 10017

PRUCHA, JOHN JAMES, geologist, educator; b. River Falls, Wis., Sept. 22, 1924; s. Edward Joseph and Katharine (Schladweiler) P.; m. Mary Elizabeth Helfrich, June 12, 1948; children: David, Stephen, Katharine, Carol, Mark, Barbara, Margaret, Christopher, Anne, Andrew. Student, Wis. State U., River Falls, 1941—43; PhB, U. Wis., 1945, PhM, 1946; MA, Princeton U., 1948, PhD, 1950. Asst. prof. geology Rutgers U., 1948-51; sr. geologist NY State Geol. Survey, 1951-56; rsch. geologist Shell Devel. Co., 1956-63; prof. geology Syracuse (NY) U., 1963-90, prof. emeritus, 1990—, chmn. dept., 1963-70, 88-89, dean Coll. Arts and Scis., 1970-72, vice chancellor acad. affairs, 1972-85; pres. Syracuse U. Press, 1973-85, bd. dirs., 1985-90. Author: Basement Tectonics of Rocky Mountains, 1965, Structural Behavior of Salt, 1967, Stratigraphy and Structure of Southeastern New York, 1959, Fracture Patterns, 1979, Zones of Structural Weakness, 1992; (with Norman A. Foss) Kinnickinnic Years, 1993. Trustee Le Moyne Coll., 1971-78; bd. dirs. Cultural Resources Coun., Syracuse, 1974—, pres., 1978-80; bd. dirs. Everson Mus. Art, Syracuse, 1977-83, v.p., 1980-81; regents vis. com. NY State Mus., 1993-96. Recipient John Mason Clarke medal NY State Geol. Survey, 1990. Fellow AAAS, Geol. Soc. Am.; mem. Am. Assn. Petroleum Geologists, Am. Geophys. Union, NY State Coun. Profl. Geologists. Home: 112 Ardsley Dr Syracuse NY 13214-2110 Office: Syracuse Univ 204 Heroy Geology Lab Syracuse NY 13244-0001

PRUCINO, DIANE L., lawyer; b. Wilmington, Del., July 15, 1957; d. Lawrence Joseph and Marjorie (Lowe) P. AB summa cum laude, Duke U., 1978; JD, U. Va., 1982. Bar: Ga. 1982, US Dist. Ct. (no. dist.) Ga. 1982, US Ct. Appeals (9th cir.) 1984, US Ct. Appeals (6th cir.) 1985, US Ct. Appeals (DC cir.). Assoc. Kilpatrick & Cody, Atlanta, 1982—97; ptnr., dept. head Labor and Employment and Employee Benefits Practice Grp. Kilpatrick Stockton LLP, Atlanta, 1997—2006, mem. exec. com., co-mng. ptnr., 2007—. Contbr. articles to profl. jours.; mem. editl. bd. Va. Law Rev., 1980-82. Bd. dirs. Homes for Children Internat., Inc., Atlanta, 1986—; vol. atty. Atlanta Legal Aid, 1983-84. Mem. ABA, Atlanta Bar Assn. Democrat. Presbyterian. Avocation: travel. Office: Kilpatrick Stockton LLP Ste 2800 1100 Peachtree St NE Atlanta GA 30309-4530 Office Fax: 404-541-3350. E-mail: DPrucino@KilpatrickStockton.com. *

PRUDEN, ANN LORETTE, chemical engineer, researcher, management consultant; b. Norfolk, Va., Sept. 3, 1948; d. James Otis and Elora Maie Pruden; m. Alan Todd Royer, Aug. 13, 1983; children: James Sebastian Royer, Annabelle Grace Royer. BS in Chemistry, Maryville Coll., Tenn., 1970; MA in Chem. Engrng., Princeton U., NJ, 1978; PhD, 1981. Rsch. and develop. chemist and chem. engr. Mobil Corp., Princeton, 1970—92; supr. Mobil Chem. Co., Edison, N.J., 1992-97, lab. mgr., 1997-2000, tech. mgmt. team, 1997-2000; prin. Inventive Strategies, 2000—. Mem. Process Effectiveness Network, Indsl. Rsch. Inst., Washington, 1992-98. Contbg. author: Photocatalytic Purification and Treatment of Water and Air, 1993; contbr. articles to profl. jours. Fellow Mobil R&D Corp., Princeton, N.J., 1976-79. Mem.: AIChE, Nat. Spkrs. Assn., Inst. Mgmt. Cons., Am. Chem.

Soc. Achievements include organizational effectiveness, platform speaking and catalysis research. Office Phone: 908-359-4787. Business E-Mail: pruden@inv-strat.com.

PRUDHOMME, PAUL, chef, restaurant owner; Owner, chef K-Paul's Louisiana Kitchen, New Orleans, 1979—. Creator Chef Paul Prudhomme's Magic Seasoning Blends. Author: (cookbooks) Fork in the Road, Fiery Foods That I Love, Kitchen Expedition, Louisiana Kitchen, Louisiana Tastes, Pure Magic, Still Cooking!, 2007. Vol. Meals on Wheels, Easter Seals, March of Dimes, Big Brothers/Big Sisters, Chef and the Child. Named Culinarian of Yr., Culinary Diplomat, Am. Culinary Fedn., 1994; recipient Restaurateur of Yr., La. State Restaurant Assn., 1983. Office: K-Paul's Louisiana Kitchen 416 Chartres New Orleans LA 70130 *

PRUEHSNER, WILLIAM ROBERT, biomedical engineer; b. June 12, 1957; s. Robert Edward and Lois Gay Pruehsner; m. Mary Ann Millsback, 1991. AS, Norwalk Tech. Coll., 1978—80; BS, U. of New Haven, 1980—85; MSc, U. of Conn., 1996—2002. Mech. engr. Frigitronics, Shelton, 1980—85; chief engr. Wallach Surg. Devices, Milford, Conn., 1985—89; mfg. engr. Anton Bauer, Shelton, 1989—91; project mgr./engr. Corometrics Med. Systems, Wallingford, Conn., 1991—96; grad. student U. of Conn., 1996—2002, doctoral candidate, 2002—. Biomedical engring. cons. Euro-Tech Mfg., Kernnersville, NC, 2000—. Editor: (hiking guide) Harriman Trails, 1990, New York Walk Book, 1992. Mem. Freemasons, Meriden, Conn., 1995—. Recipient Pro Deo Et Patria, Boy Scouts of Am., 1971, Eagle Scout, 1973, Bronze Palm, 1974, NY Long Path thru Kike to End award, Conn. 400 Club, 1993. Mem.: Rocky Mountain Biomedical Symposium (bd. mem. 2001—, exec. bd. mem. 2005—, student paper com. 2003—). Achievements include 5 patents pending for Fetal Pulse Oximeter in 1995. Avocations: hiking, letterboxing, long-distance backpacking, volksmarching, state high point hiking. Home Phone: 203-237-1026. Business E-Mail: pruehsnr@engr.uconn.edu.

PRUESSNER, DAVID MORGAN, lawyer; b. Corpus Christi, Tex., May 13, 1955; s. Harold Trebus and Alma (Morgan) Pruessner; m. Becky McKinney, May 21, 1977; children: Jennifer, Daniel, Heather. BA cum laude, Baylor U., 1977, JD cum laude, 1980; LLM, So. Meth. U., 2006. Bar: Tex. 1980, U.S. Dist. Ct. (no. dist.) Tex. 1980, U.S. Ct. Appeals (5th cir.) 1986, U.S. Supreme Ct. 1989. Atty. Coke & Coke, Dallas, 1980-83, Shank, Irwin & Conant, Dallas, 1983-90, Pettit & Martin, Dallas, 1990-92, Fletcher & Springer, Dallas, 1992-99; pvt. practice Dallas, 1999—. Mem. editl. bd. Baylor Law Rev., 1980. Avocations: world religions, history, chess. Office: Law Office David M Pruessner Three Galleria Tower 13155 Noel Rd Ste 1025 Dallas TX 75240 Office Phone: 972-991-6700. Business E-Mail: david@prulaw.com.

PRUETT, JAMES WORRELL, librarian, educator, musicologist; b. Mt. Airy, NC, Dec. 23, 1932; s. Samuel Richard and Gladys Dorne (Worrell) P.; m. Lilian Maria-Irene Pibernik, July 20, 1957; children— Mark, Ellen. BA, U. N.C., Chapel Hill, 1955, MA, 1957, PhD, 1962. Mem. faculty U. N.C., Chapel Hill., 1961-87, prof. music, 1974-87, music librarian, 1961-76, chmn. dept. music, 1976-86; chief music div. Library of Congress, Washington, 1987-95. Vis. prof. U. Toronto, 1976; cons. in music, 1995—. Editor: Studies in the History, Style and Bibliography of Music in Memory of Glen Haydon, 1969; author: Research Guide to Musicology, 1985. Contbr. profl. jours., encys. Newberry Libr. fellow, 1966. Mem. Internat. Musicol. Soc., Am. Musicol. Soc. (chpt. chmn. 1964-66, mem. coun. 1974-77), Music Libr. Assn. (pres. 1973-75, editor jour. 1974-77), Cosmos Club (Washington). Home: 343 Wesley Dr Chapel Hill NC 27516-1520

PRUETZ, ADRIAN MARY, lawyer; b. Nov. 13, 1948; Student, U. Wis., 1966—69; BA, Loyola U., Chgo., 1972, postgrad., 1972—73; JD magna cum laude, Marquette U., 1982. Bar: Wis. 1982, Calif. 1985. Assoc. Whyte and Hirschboeck, SC, 1982—84, Morrison and Foerster, 1984—88, ptnr., 1988—94, Quinn Emanuel Urquhart Oliver & Hedges, LLP, LA, 1994—2007, co-chair intellectual property litigation group; with Pruetz Law Group LLP, Manhattan Beach, Calif., 2007—. Spkr., lectr. Price Waterhouse Intellectual Property Forum, Licensing Execs. Soc., Am. Soc. Indsl. Security. Named one of Calif. Top 50 Litigators, LA Daily Jour., 2001—07, Most Influential Trial Lawyers in Calif., 2002—07, State's Top 25 Intellectual Property Lawyers, 2003—05, Calif.'s Most Successful Lawyers, Calif. Law Bus. Mem.: ABA (past chair com. U.S. lit. affecting internat. patent problems, past chair com. impact 1991 amendments), Los Angeles County Bar, State Bar Calif., Fed. Bar Assn. (spkr., lectr.). Office: Pruetz Law Group LLP 1600 Rosecrans Ave 4th Fl Manhattan Beach CA 90266 Office Phone: 310-321-7640. Business E-Mail: ampruetz@pruetzlaw.com.

PRUGH, WILLIAM BYRON, lawyer; b. Kansas City, Mo., Jan. 3, 1945; s. Byron E. and Helen Prugh; m. Linda Stuart, Aug. 12, 1968; 1 child, K. Niccole. BA, U. Mo., Kansas City, 1966, JD, 1969, LLM in Taxation, 1971. Bar: Mo. 1969, U.S. Tax Ct. 1975, U.S. Supreme Ct. 1975, Kans. 1982. Mem. Shughart Thomson & Kilroy, P.C., Kansas City, 1969—. Author, editor: Missouri Corporation Law and Practice, 1985, Missouri Taxation Law and Practice, 1987, 3d edit., 1996. Mem.: ABA, Kansas City Met. Bar Assn. (chmn. tax com. 1989—90, chmn. computer law com. 1989—91, Pres. award 1988), Mo. Bar Assn. (chmn. taxation com. 1988—90, chmn. computer tech. com. 1989—90). Republican. Methodist. Office: Shughart Thomson & Kilroy 12 Wyandotte Plz 120 W 12th St Fl 18 Kansas City MO 64105-1902 Office Phone: 816-421-3355 ext 3570. Business E-Mail: wprugh@stklaw.com.

PRUIS, JOHN J., manufacturing executive; b. Borculo, Mich., Dec. 13, 1923; s. Ties J. and Trientje (Koop) P.; m. Angeline Rosemary Zull, Sept. 14, 1944; children: David Lofton, Daniel J., Dirk Thomas. BS, Western Mich. U., 1947; MA, Northwestern U., 1949, PhD, 1951; Litt.D. (hon.), Yeungnam U., Taegu, Korea, Ind. State U.; LL.D. (hon.), Ball State U., U. So. Ind.; DHL (hon.), Keuka Coll. Tchr. pub. schs., Mich., 1942-43; supervising tchr. Campus Sch., Western Mich. U., 1947-48; instr. speech U. No Ia., 1951-52; from asst. prof. to assoc. prof. speech So. Ill. U., 1952-55; mem. faculty Western Mich. U., 1955-68, sec. bd. trustees, 1964-68, v.p. adminstrn., 1966-68; pres. Ball State U., 1968-78; v.p. corp. rels. Ball Corp., 1978-88. Cons., examiner North Central Assn., 1959-78; also bd. dirs. N. Central Assn. V.p. Country dr. chmn. Kalamazoo Cmty. Chest, 1964; bd. dirs. Kalamazoo chpt. Am. Cancer Soc., 1963-68, Del. County United Way, Muncie Symphony Assn., Ball Meml. Hosp., Big Bros./Big Sisters, Ind. Legal Found.; trustee U. So. Ind., 1985-90; exec. v.p. George and Frances Ball Found. With USNR, 1943-46; capt. Res., ret. Mem. Am. Assn. Higher Edn., Speech Communication Assn., Muncie C. of C., Blue Key, Rotary, Phi Delta Kappa, Omicron Delta Kappa, Beta Gamma Sigma Presbyterian. Personal E-mail: jjpruis@iquest.net.

PRUITT, ALICE FAY, mathematician, engineer; b. Montgomery, Ala., Dec. 17, 1943; d. Virgil Edwin and Ocie Victoria (Mobley) Maye; m. Mickey Don Pruitt, Nov. 5, 1967; children: Derrell Gene, Christine Marie. BS in Math., U. Ala., Huntsville, 1977; postgrad., Calif. State U., Northridge, 1978—79. Instr. math. Antelope Valley Coll., Quartz Hill, Calif., 1977—78; space shuttle engr. Rockwell Internat., Palmdale, Calif., 1979—81; programmer-analyst Sci. Support Svcs., Inc., Paso Robles, Calif., 1982—85; sr. engring. specialist Loral Vought Sys. Corp., Dallas, 1985—92; dir. concepts and analysis, advanced sys. engring. Nichols Rsch. Corp., Huntsville, Ala., 1992-99; sr. prin. engr. Computer Sci. Corp., Huntsville, 1999—. Mem. DeSoto (Tex.) Coun. Cultural Arts, 1987-89; bd. dirs. Churchill Condominium ASsn., Inc., 2005—. Mem. AAUW (sch. bd. rep. 1982, legal advocacy fund chairperson 1989-91), Toastmasters, Phi Kappa Phi. Republican. Methodist. Avocations: dance, gourmet cooking. Office: PO Box 400002 4090 S Memorial Pky Ste A Huntsville AL 35815-1502 Business E-Mail: apruitt@csc.com.

PRUITT, ANNE LORING, academic administrator, education educator; b. Bainbridge, Ga., Sept. 19, 1929; d. Loring Alphonzo and Anne Lee (Ward) Smith; m. Harold G. Logan; 1 child, Leslie; stepchildren: Dianne, Pamela, Sharon, Ralph Pruitt, Jr., Harold, Minda, Andrew Logan. BS, Howard U., Washington, 1949; MA, Columbia U., NYC, 1950, EdD, 1964; HumD hon., Ctrl. State U., Wilberforce, Ohio, 1982. Counsel for women Howard U., 1950-52; tchr., dir. guidance Hutto H.S., Bainbridge, 1952-55; dean students Albany State Coll., Ga., 1955-59, Fisk U., Nashville, 1959-61; prof. edn. Case Western Res. U., Cleve., 1963-79; prof. ednl. policy and leadership Ohio State U., Columbus, 1979-95, prof. emeritus, 1995—; assoc. dean Ohio State U. Grad. Sch., Columbus, 1979-84; assoc. provost Ohio State U., Columbus, 1984-86, dir. Ctr. for Tchg. Excellence, 1986-94; dean in residence Coun. Grad. Schs., Washington, 1994-96, scholar in residence, 1996—2002. Cons. So. Regional Edn. Bd., Atlanta, 1967-78, So. Edn. Found., Atlanta, 1978-87; co-dir. Preparing Future Faculty program, 1994-2002. Author: New Students and Coordinated Counseling, 1973, Black Employees in Traditionally White Institutions in the Adams States 1975-77, 1981, In Pursuit of Equality in Higher Education, 1987; co-author: (with Paul Isaac) Student Services for the Changing Graduate Student Population, 1995, (with Jerry Gaff and Richard Weibl) Building the Faculty We Need: Colleges and Universities Working Together, 2000, (with Jerry Gaff and Joyce Jentoft) Preparing Future Faculty in the Sciences and Mathematics, 2002, (with Jerry Gaff, Leslie Sims and Daniel Denecke) Preparing Future Faculty in the Humanities and Social Sciences: A Guide for Change, 2003. Trustee Urban League, Cleve., 1965-71, Ctrl. State U., 1973-82, Case Western Res. U., 1987-02, Columbus Area Leadership Program, 1988-91; bd. dirs. ARC, Cleve., 1978-79, Am. West Airlines Found., 1992-95; mem. adv. com. USCG Acad., New London, Conn., 1980-83; Ohio State U. rep. to AAUW, 1989-94; univ. co-chairperson United Way, 1990-91; trustee Marburn Acad., 1991-95; mem. Columbus 1992 Edn. Com., 1988-92; mem. edn. subcom. Columbus Found., 1991-94; mem. exec. com. Renaissance League, 1992-94; mem. vis. panel on rsch., Ednl. Testing Svc., 1996-02; mem. Commn. on Future Clemson U., 1997-98; bd. dirs. Black Women's Agenda, Inc., 1997-, pres. 1998-2002; deacon Peoples Congregational United Ch. of Christ, 1998—; mem. B.E.S.T. Expert Panel, 2002-04; evaluation external expert NSF Grad. Tchg. Fellows in K-12 Edn. Program, 2002-04. Named sr. scholar, Am. Coll. Pers. Assn., 1989, Godmother of Minority Grad. Edn., Black Issues in Higher Edn., 1995, inducted, Ohio State U. Coll. Edn. Hall of Fame, 2004; named one of Am.'s Top 100 Black Bus. and Profl. Women, Dollars & Sense Mag., 1986; recipient Outstanding Alumnus award, Howard U. Alumni Assn., 1975, Disting. Affirmative Action award, Ohio State U., 1988, Disting. Svc. award, 2005, Woman of Achievement award, YMCA, 1993; fellow Am. Coun. on Edn., 1977. Mem. NSF (mem. com. on equal opportunities in sci. and engring. 1989-95), Am. Coll. Pers. Assn. (pres. 1976-77), Coun. Grad. Schs. in U.S. (chairperson com. on minority grad. edn. 1980-84), Am. Ednl. Rsch. Assn., Ohio Assn. Counselor Edn. (pres. 1966-67), Links Inc., Cosmos Club, Alpha Kappa Alpha.

PRUITT, BASIL ARTHUR, JR., surgeon, retired military officer; b. Nyack, NY, Aug. 21, 1930; s. Basil Arthur and Myrtle Flo (Knowles) P.; m. Mary Sessions Gibson, Sept. 4, 1954; children: Scott Knowles, Laura Sessions, Jeffrey Hamilton. AB, Harvard U., 1952, postgrad., 1952—53; MD, Tufts U., 1957. Diplomate Am. Bd. Surgery. Intern Boston City Hosp., 1957—58, resident surgery, 1958—59, 1961—62; commd. capt., M.C. U.S. Army, 1959, advanced through grades to col., 1972; resident Brooke Gen. Hosp., Ft. Sam Houston, Tex., 1962—64; chief clin. divsn. Inst. Surg. Rsch., Ft. Sam Houston, 1965—67; chief profl. svcs. 12th Evacuation Hosp., Vietnam, 1967—68; comdr., dir. U.S. Army Inst. Surg. Rsch., Brooke Army Med. Ctr., Ft. Sam Houston, 1968—95, ret., 1995; clin. prof. gen. surgery U. Tex. Health Sci. Ctr., San Antonio, 1975—; prof. surgery Uniformed Svcs. U. Health Scis., Bethesda, Md., 1978—. Mem. surgery, anaesthesiology and trauma study sect. NIH, 1978—82; mem. Shriners Burns Adv. Bd., 1985—92, Shriners Med. Adv. Bd., 1992—95, Shriners Rsch. Adv. Bd., 1996—2006, Shriners Clin. Outcomes Studies Adv. Bd., 1999—; merit rev. bd. for surgery VA, 1990—93; bd. dirs. Am. Bd. Surgery, 1982—88, sr. mem., 1989—. Author med. books; contbr. chpts. to textbooks, articles to profl. jours.; mem. editl. bd. Jour. Trauma, 1975-94, editor, 1995—; mem. edit. bd.: Archives Surgery, 1981-93, Consultations in Surgery, Correspondence Society of Surgeons, Collected Letters, 1978-2000, Circulatory Shock, 1985-93, Jour. Burn Care and Rehab., 1984-87, Jour. Investigative Surgery, 1987-97, Shock, 1993—, Current Opinion in Surg. Infections, 1993-2001, Sepsis, 1996-2002, Injury, 1998-2003, Turkish Jour. Trauma, 2002—, English edit. Chinese Jour. Traumatology, 1998—, Med. Jour. Chinese People's Liberation Army, 2005—. Decorated Bronze Star, Legion of Merit, DSM; recipient ISS/SIC Danis prize, 1995, G. Whitaker Internat. Burns prize, 2000, Tanner-Vandeput-Boswick Burn prize, 2006, Roswell Park medal, 2007. Fellow: ACS (pre and postoperative care com. 1969—79, vice chmn. 1973—75, gov. 1973—79, com. on trauma 1974—84, internat. rels. com. 1983—93, chmn. 1987—89), Am. Coll. Critical Care Medicine (Disting. Investigator award 2000); mem.: We. Trauma Assn., Ea. Assn. Surgery Trauma, N.Am. Burn Soc. (pres. 1993—94), Shock Soc. (clin. counselor 1995—98, pres.-elect 2006—07, pres. 2007—, chmn. 2005 program com.), Internat. Surg. Group, Surg. Infection Soc. (recorder 1980—84, pres. 1985—86), Assn. Acad. Surgery, Internat. Soc. Surgery, Surg. Biol. Club III, Am. Assn. Surgery Trauma (recorder 1976—80, pres. 1982—83), Halsted Soc. (pres. 1985—86), So. Surg. Assn. (pres. 2004—05), We. Surg. Assn. (dist. rep. 1984—88, pres. 1993—94), Tex. Surg. Assn., Am. Surg. Assn. (2d v.p. 1980—81, pres. 1999—2000, Medallion 1998), Soc. Univ. Surgeons (Lifetime Achievement award 2007), Am. Trauma Soc. (pres. Tex. divsn. 1974—75, dir. 1974—, sec. 1986—88, v.p. 1988—90, pres.-elect 1990—92, pres. 1992—94), Smoke Burn and Fire Assn. (adv. coun.), Internat. Soc. Burn Injuries (nat. rep. 1974—82, co-chmn. disaster planning com. 1982—86, pres.-elect 1990—94, pres. 1994—98), Am. Burn Assn. (pres. 1975—76), Mediterranean Club Burns and Fire Disasters (regional rep. Ams.), Surgeons' Travel Club (pres. 2002—03). Home: 402 Tidecrest Dr San Antonio TX 78239-2517 Office: U Tex Health Sci Ctr Dept Surgery 7703 Floyd Curl Dr San Antonio TX 78229-3900 also: Editl Office Jour Trauma 7330 San Pedro Ste 654 San Antonio TX 78216-6236 Home Phone: 210-655-4769; Office Phone: 210-342-7903. Business E-Mail: pruitt@uthscsa.edu.

PRUITT, DEAN GARNER, psychologist, educator; b. Phila., Dec. 26, 1930; s. Dudley McConnell and Grace (Garner) P.; m. France Juliard, Dec. 27, 1959; children: Andre Juliard, Paul Dudley, Charles Alexandre. AB, Oberlin Coll., 1952; MS, Yale U., 1954, PhD, 1957. Postdoctoral fellow U. Mich., 1957-59; rsch. assoc. Northwestern U., 1959-61; asst. prof., then assoc. prof. U. Del., 1961-66; assoc. prof. to prof. SUNY, Buffalo, 1966—96, disting. prof., 1996—2001, disting. prof. emeritus, 2001—, dir. grad. program in social psychology, 1969—73, 1976—77, 1985—88, 1998—2001; disting. scholar in residence George Mason U., 2001—. Author: Negotiation Behavior, 1981, (with J. Z. Rubin and S.H. Kim) Social Conflict, 1986, 94, 2004, (with P.J. Carnevale) Negotiation in Social Conflict, 1993; editor; (with R.C. Snyder) Theory and Research on the Causes of War, 1969, (with K. Kressel) Mediation Research, 1989. Grantee Office Naval Rsch., 1965, NIMH, 1969, NSF, 1969, 74, 76, 80, 83, 86, 88, 93, Guggenheim Found., 1978-79. Fellow APA, Am. Psychol. Soc., Soc. for Psychol. Study Social Issues; mem. Internat. Assn. for Conflict Mgmt. (pres. 1990-92, Lifetime Achievement award 1997), Internat. Soc. Polit. Psychology (v.p. 1984-85, Harold D. Lasswell award 1992), Phi Beta Kappa, Sigma Xi. Home: 9006 Friars Rd Bethesda MD 20817-3320 Office: George Mason U Inst Conflict Analysis and Resolution Fairfax VA 22030-4444 E-mail: dean@pruittfamily.com.

PRUITT, GARY B., publishing company executive; b. 1957; m. Abby Pruitt; children: Katherine, Allison. BA summa cum laude, U. Fla., 1978; MA in Pub. Policy, U. Calif. Berkeley, 1981, JD, 1982. Counsel The McClatchy Co., 1984—87, gen. counsel, corp. sec., 1987—91, v.p. ops. & tech., 1994-95, pres., 1995—, COO, 1995—96, CEO, 1996—, chmn., 2001—; pub. The Fresno Bee, 1991-94. Bd. dirs. The McClatchy Co., 1995—. Mem. chancellors com. U. Calif., Berkeley, mem. bd. advisors Goldman Sch. Pub. Policy. Mem.: James Irvine Found. (bd. dirs. 1999—, vice chmn. 2003—05, chmn. 2006—), Newspaper Assn. Am, Phi Beta Kappa. Office: The McClatchy Co 2100 Q St Sacramento CA 95816-6816 *

PRUITT, GEORGE ALBERT, college president; b. Canton, Miss., July 9, 1946; s. Joseph Henry and Lillie Irene (Carmichael) P.; m. Pamela Young; 1 child, Shayla Nicole. BS, Ill. State U., 1968, MS, 1970, DHL (hon.), 1994; PhD, Union Grad. Sch., Cin., 1974; D Pub. Svc. (hon.), Bridgewater State Coll., 1990, MA (hon.), 1990; LLD (hon.), Ill. State U., 1994; DHL (hon.), SUNY Empire State Coll., 1996. Asst. to v.p. for acad. affairs Ill. State U., Normal, 1968-70, dir. high potential students program, 1968-70; dean students Towson State U., 1970-72; v.p., exec. asst. to pres., assoc. prof. urban affairs Morgan State U., 1972-75; v.p., prof. Tenn. State U., 1975-81; exec. v.p. Council for Advancement Experiential Learning, Columbia, Md., 1981-82; pres. Thomas A. Edison State Coll., Trenton, 1982—. Commn. on ednl. credit and credentials, labor/higher edn. coun. Am. Coun. on Edn.; advisor group XII, Nat. Fellowship program W.K. Kellogg Found., 1990-94, advisor group XV, 1995-99; bd. dirs. SEEDCO, Sun Nat. Bank, Vineland, N.J.; nat. adv. com. on instnl. quality and integrity U.S. Dept. Edn., 1994—; chmn. N.J. Pres. Coun., 2004-2006; chair N.J. Capital Region Conv. and Vis. Bur., 2004-2006. Past chair Mercer County Chamber of Commerce; mem. Govs. Edn. Cabinet, 2002—05, N.J. State Planning Commn., 2002—; trustee Union Inst., Cin., 1988—, Rider U., Lawrenceville, NJ, 2001—, Econ. Devel. Corp., Trenton, 2001—06; bd. dirs. N.J. Assn. Colls. and Univs. Recipient Resolution of Commendation Bd., Trustees Morgan State U., 1975, Outstanding Svc. to Edn. award Tenn. State U., 1981, Gubernatorial citation Gov. of Tenn., 1981, Good Guy award George Washington coun. Boy Scouts Am., 1991, Humanitarian award NCCJ, 1992, Educator of Yr. award Black N.J. Mag., 1993, Disting. Alumni award Ill. State U., 1996; apptd. hon. mem. Gen. Assembly Tenn., 1981, hon. mem. U.S. Congress from 5th Tenn. dist., 1981; named ofcr. of the Most Effective Coll. Pres. in U.S., Exxon Edn. Found. Study, 1986; named to Coll. of Edn. Hall of Fame, Ill. State U., 1995; named Mercer Co. N.J. Citizen of Yr., Mercer Co. C. of C., 1997. Mem. Coun. for Advancement Exptl. Learning, Am. Assn. State Colls.and Univs., Coun. for Advancement and Support of Edn., Am. Coun. Edn., Mid. States Assn. Colls. and Schs. (accreditation evaluator commn. on higher edn.). Office: Thomas Edison Coll 101 W State St Trenton NJ 08608-1176 Office Phone: 609-984-1105. E-mail: gpruitt@tesc.edu.

PRUITT, ROBERT A., artist; b. Houston, 1975; BFA, Tex. So. U.; MFA, U. Tex., Austin. Mem. Otabenga Jones & Assocs., Houston, 2002—; arts coord. Project Row Houses, Houston. Prin. works include This Do in Remembrance of Me, 2005, exhibited in group shows at Splat Boom Pow!: The Influence of Cartoons in Contemporary Art, Contemporary Art Mus., Come Forward: Emerging Art in Tex., Dallas Mus. Art, Whitney Biennial: Day for Night, Whitney Mus. Am. Art, 2006, exhibitions include I Call My Brother Sun Because He Shines Like One, Clementine Gallery, NYC. Recipient Artadia award, 2004. Mailing: Project Row Houses 2500 Holman PO Box 1011 Houston TX 77251-1011

PRUITT, ROSALYN JOLENA, science educator; b. Denville, NJ, Sept. 7, 1977; d. John Henry Jr. and Arlena Cobb Pruitt. BS, U. Memphis, 2001. Lab. technician GTW Analytical Svcs., Memphis, 2000—03; sci. educator Memphis City Schs., 2003. Head softball coach Kirby HS, Memphis, 2005. Profl. Devel. grantee, Exxon/Mobil, 2005. Office: Kirby HS 4080 Kirby Pkwy Memphis TN 38115 Office Phone: 901-416-1960.

PRUITT, STEPHEN WALLACE, finance educator; b. Indpls., Feb. 3, 1957; s. Harry Wallace and Dorothy (Thorp) P.; m. Mary Melinda Settle, Dec. 19, 1981; children: Rebecca Elizabeth, Victoria Barrick. BS in Mgmt., Purdue U., 1979; MBA in Fin., Ohio State U., 1980; PhD in Fin., Fla. State U., 1987. Internat. cash mgr. Marathon Oil Co., Findlay, Ohio, 1980-81; fin. analyst Nat. Svc. Industries, Crawfordsville, Ind., 1981-83; asst. prof. fin. U. Miss., Oxford, 1986-88, Ind. U., Bloomington, 1988-93; assoc. prof. fin. U. Memphis, 1993-96, prof. fin., 1996-2000; Arvin Gottlieb/Mo. chmn. in bus. econs. and fin. U. Mo., Kansas City, 2005—. Cons. in field. Contbr. articles to profl. jours. Bd. dirs. Art Mus. U. Memphis, 1995-2000; founder, pres. Memphis Print Club, 1995-2000. Mem. So. Fin. Assn., Fin. Mgmt. Assn. Avocations: collecting art and antiques, recording original music, making original films. Office: U Mo Henry W Bloch Sch Bus & Pub 5100 Rockhill Rd Kansas City MO 64110-2481 Home: 5316 W 140th St Overland Park KS 66224 Office Phone: 816-235-2334. E-mail: pruittst@umkc.edu.

PRUITT LEMLEY, CYNTHIA KAYE, computer educator; b. Linden, Tex., Apr. 8, 1955; m. Terry M. Lemley, Oct. 20, 2001; 1 child from previous marriage, Carlin Dominic Conan Morris. Student, L.A. City Coll., 1978-79, Pasadena City Coll., 1981-82. Tchrs. aide Ola's Ednl. Lab. & Day Care Ctr., LA, 1973-74; file clk. divsn. property Loan Guaranty, LA, 1984; armed security Mahoney's Silver Nugget and Sahara Hotel & Casino, Las Vegas, Nev., 1993—93, Desert Passage, 2000—01; recreation aid, ceramics instr. Nellis Air Force Skills Devel., 1996—97; armed security Wet' N Wild Water Park, 2000—. Dictation clk. Dept. Welfare, Las Vegas, 1989-90. New member chair The Walker African-Am. Mus. & Rsch. Ctr., 1995—; office clk. Rose Garden Townhouses, Las Vegas, 1995-97; explorer adv. Boy Scouts Am., Las Vegas, 1995-97, instr. high adventure team, 1995—, asst. scoutmaster, 1994-98, scoutmaster, 1998-2004; vol. mcpl. ct. traffic sch. City of Las Vegas, 1994-95. Sgt. US Army, 1975-78, 90-91, Desert Storm, USAR (active) 1978-1990, 91-96ret. Mem. Order Ea. Star, Golden Cir., Daus. Isis. Democrat. Baptist. Avocations: hiking, sewing, beading, ceramics, church.

PRUNES, FERNANDO, plastic surgeon, educator; b. Chihuahua, Mex. m. Linda R. Underwood; children: Alexander, Ariadne, Anthony. MD, U. Chihuahua, Mex., 1968. Surg. intern Booth Meml. Med. Ctr., Flushing, NY, 1971-72; resident in gen. surgery Tucson Hosps. Med. Edn. Program, 1972-76; resident in plastic surgery Mayo Grad. Sch. Medicine, 1979-81; chief divsn. plastic surgery Kern Med. Ctr., Bakersfield, Calif., 1983—. Asst. clin. prof. surgery U. Calif., San Diego, 1983-98. Mem. Am. Soc. Plastic Surgeons, Mayo Alumni Assn. Avocations: golf, computers. Office: Kern Med Ctr 1830 Flower St Bakersfield CA 93305-4186 Office Phone: 661-326-2274.

PRUSAK, MAXIMILIAN MICHAEL, lawyer; b. Granite City, Ill., Mar. 22, 1943; s. Max Emil and Catherine Theresa (Jakich) P.; m. Carolyn Irene Pinkel, July 2, 1966; children: Scott Michael, Stephanie K. BS in Math., U. Ill., 1965, JD, 1968. Bar: Ill. 1968, U.S. Dist. Ct. (so. dist.) Ill. 1973. Staff atty. Atty.'s Title Guaranty Fund, Champaign, Ill., 1968-69; ptnr. Goldsworthy, Fifield & Prusak, Peoria, Ill., 1973-80, Nicol, Newell, Prusak & Winne, Peoria, 1980-83, Prusak & Winne, Peoria, Ill., 1983-88, Prusak, Winne & Wombacher, Peoria, 1988-93, Prusak & Winne, Ltd., Peoria,

1993—. Contbr. articles to profl. publs. Bd. dirs. Human Svc. Ctr., Peoria, 1970's, Friendship House, Peoria, 1980, Southside Mission, Peoria, 1988-89; pres. adminstrv. bd. 1st United Meth. Ch., Peoria, 1990—. Capt. USAF, 1969-73. Mem. Ill. State Bar Assn. (chmn. law office cons. sect. coun. 1997-98), Internat. Assn. Def. Counsel, Ill. Assn. Def. Trial Counsel, Peoria County Bar Assn. (bd. dirs. 1982, 94, 98-99, v.p. 1999, pres. 2000), Union League Club Chgo., Ill. Valley Yacht Club. Avocations: computers, sailing, reading. Home: 5821 N Mar Vista Dr Peoria IL 61614-3850 Office Phone: 309-674-4222. Personal E-mail: mprusak2@mtco.com.

PRUSINER, STANLEY BEN, neurologist, biochemist, virologist, educator; b. Des Moines, May 28, 1942; s. Lawrence Albert and Miriam (Spigel) Prusiner; children: Helen Chloe, Leah Anne. AB cum laude, U. Pa., Phila., 1964, MD, 1968, DS (hon.), 1998; PhD (hon.), Hebrew U., Jerusalem, 1995, René Descartes U., Paris, 1996; DS (hon.), Dartmouth Coll., Hanover, NH, 1999, U. Liege, 2000; MD (hon.), U. Bologna, Italy, 2000; DSc (hon.), Pa. State U., 2001; DVM (hon.), U. Cardenal Herrera, 2005; PhD (hon.), Claremont Grad. U., Calif., 2007. Diplomate Am. Bd. Neurology. Intern in medicine U. Calif., San Francisco, 1968—69, resident in neurology, 1972—74, asst. prof. neurology, 1974—80, assoc. prof., 1980—84, prof., 1984—, prof. biochemistry, 1988—, acad. senate faculty rsch. lectr., 1989—90, prof. virology Berkeley, 1984—, dir. Inst. for Neurodegenerative Diseases, 1999—; founder, chmn. bd. dirs. InPro Biotech. Inc., South San Francisco, Calif., 2001—. Mem. neurology rev. com. Nat. Inst. for Neurodegenerative Diseases, NIH, Bethesda, Md., 1982—86, Bethesda, 1990—92; mem. Coun. Nat. Inst. Aging, NIH, Bethesda, Md., 2001—04; mem. sci. adv. bd. French Found., LA, 1985—, chmn. sci. adv. bd., 1996—; mem. sci. rev. com. Alzheimer's Disease Diagnosic Ctr. & Rsch Grant Program, State of Calif., 1985—89; chmn. sci. adv. bd. Am. Health Assistance Found., Rockville, Md., 1986—2000, hon. mem. bd. dirs., 2001—; mem. spongiform encephalopathy adv. com. FDA, 1997—2001; mem. adv. bd.Family Survival Project for Adults with Chronic Brain Disorders, San Francisco, 1982—90; mem. adv. bd. San Francisco chpt. Alzheimer's Disease and Related Disorders Found., 1985—91; mem. bd. dirs. Fromm Inst. for Lifelong Learning, San Francisco, 2002—; cons. Inst. of Medicine Com. on Advancing Prion Sci., Washington, 2002—03; mem. bd. govs. Found. for Biomed. Rsch., Washington, 2002—; bd. dirs. Internat. Longevity Ctr., NYC, 2003—. Editor: The Enzymes of Glutamine Metabolism, 1973, Slow Transmissible Diseases of the Nervous System, 2 vols., 1979, Prions--Novel Infectious Pathogens Causing Scrapie and CJD, 1987, Prion Diseases of Humans and Animals, 1992, Molecular and Genetic Basis of Neurologic Disease, 3d edit., 2003, Prions Prions Prions, 1996, Prion Biology and Diseases, 2d edit., 2004; contbr. more than 350 articles to profl. jours. Trustee U. Pa., 2000—05, Congregation Sherith Israel, San Francisco, 1999—2002. Lt. comdr. USPHS, 1969—72. Recipient Leadership and Excellence for Alzheimer's Disease award, NIH, 1990—97, Potamkin prize for Alzheimer's Disease Rsch., 1991, Disting. Med. Grad. award, U. Pa. Sch. Medicine, 1991, Med. Rsch. award, Met. Life Found., 1992, Christopher Columbus Discovery award, NIH and Med. Soc. Genoa, Italy, 1992, Charles A. Dana award, 1992, Dickson prize, U. Pitts., 1992, Max Planck Rsch. award, Alexander von Humboldt Found. and Max Planck Soc., 1992, Gairdner Found. Internat. award, 1993, Disting. Achievement in Neurosci. Rsch. award, Bristol-Myers Squibb, 1994, Albert Lasker award for Basic Med. Rsch., 1994, Caledonian Rsch. Found. prize, Royal Soc. Edinburgh, 1995, Paul Ehrlich and Ludwig Darmstaedter award, Germany, 1995, Paul Hoch award, Am. Psychopathol. Assn., 1995, Wolf prize in medicine, 1996, ICN Virology prize, 1996, Victor and Clara Soriano award, World Fedn. Neurology, 1996, Pasarow Found. prize, 1996, Charles Leopole Mayer prize, French Acad. Scis., 1996, Keio Internat. prize, 1996, Baxter award, Am. Assn. Med. Colls., 1996, Louisa Gross Horwitz prize, Columbia U., 1997, Nobel Prize for Medicine, 1997, K.J. Zulch prize, Gertrude Reemtsma Found., 1997, Benjamin Franklin medal, Franklin Inst., 1998, Jubilee medal, Swedish Med. Soc., 1998, Prize Lecture medal, U. Coll. London, 1999, Sir Hans Krebs medal, Fedn. European Biochem. Socs., 1999, Ellen Browning Scripps medal, 2000, Disting. Alumni award, Coll. Arts and Scis., U. of Pa., 2003, Commonwealth award, 2004, William Beaumont medal, 2005, T.S. Srinivasan Gold Medal, Srinivasan Trust, Chennai, India, 2007; fellow Alfred P. Sloan Rsch. fellow, U. Calif., 1976—78; grantee Med. Investigator grantee, Howard Hughes Med. Inst., 1976—81, grantee for excellence in neurosci., Senator Jacob Javits Ctr., NIH, 1985—90. Fellow: AAAS, Royal Coll. Physicians, Am. Acad. Arts & Scis., Am. Soc. Microbiology; mem.: NAS (mem. coun. 2007—, Inst. Medicine, Richard Lounsbery award for extraordinary achievements in biology and medicine 1993), World Jewish Acad. Scis., Serbian Acad. Scis., Protein Soc. (Amgen award 1997), Royal Soc. London, Am. Philos. Soc., Am. Soc. Molecular Biol. Biochemistry, Am. Soc. Cellular Biology, Am. Soc. Cell Biology, Genetics Soc. Am., Am. Soc. Human Genetics, Soc. Neurosci., Am. Chem. Soc., Am. Soc. Biochemistry and Molecular Biology, Am. Soc. Clin. Investigation, Am. Neurol. Assn., Am. Soc. Virology, Am. Soc. Neurochemistry, Am. Soc. Neurochemistry, Am. Assn. Physicians, Am. Acad. Neurology (George Cotzias award for outstanding rsch. 1987, Presdl. award 1993, Disting. Achievement award 1998), Bohemian Club, Concordia Argonaut Club (bd. dirs. 1997—2005).

PRUSSIN, JEFFREY A., management consultant; b. Bklyn., Aug. 11, 1943; s. Samuel and Shirley (Solomon) P.; m. Judith H. May; children: Aaron Justin, Leya Monique. AB, UCLA, 1965; MA, Johns Hopkins U., 1967. Dir. edn. and tng. Group Health Assn. Am., Washington, 1971-72; mgr. prog. devel. Health System div. Westinghouse, Columbia, Md., 1972-73; prin. Health Care Orgn., Delivery & Fin. System, Kensington, Md., 1973-80; exec. asst. for policy Bur. Health Facilities, HHS, Washington, 1980-81; exec. v.p. Comprehensive Am. Care, Miami, Fla., 1981-84; sr. v.p. Internat. Med. Ctrs., Miami, 1984-86; pres. Health Sys. Devel. Corp., South Miami, Fla., 1986-99, J&JP Funding Corp., Jacksonville, Fla., 1999—. Cons. in field; lectr. in field; adj. prof. U. Miami, Fla., 1982-99; vis. asst. prof. Oreg. State U., Eugene, 1970; adj. asst. prof. Linfield Coll., Oreg., 1969-70, Portland State U., 1969-70. Contbr. numerous articles to profl. jours.; author: Health Maintenance Organization Legislation in 1973-74, 1974, Employee Health Benefits: HMOs and Mandatory Dual Choide, 1976, Results of a State-of-the-Art Review of Health Assurance for the Elderly, 1979, (with Judith M. Prussin), Health Services and the Elderly: A Comprehensive, Annotated Bibliography, 1982, (with Jack C. Wood), Topics in Health Care Financing: Private Third Party Reimbursement, 1975. Mem. Fla. Assn. Health, Maint. Orgns. (pres. 1985-86), Group Health Assn. Am. Office: J & JP Funding Corp PO Box 600580 Jacksonville FL 32260-0580

PRUSSING, LAUREL LUNT, mayor, economist; b. NYC, Feb. 21, 1941; d. Richard Valentine and Maria (Rinaldi) Lunt; m. John Edward Prussing, May 29, 1965; children: Heidi Elizabeth, Erica Stephanie, Victoria Nicole Johanna. AB, Wellesley Coll., 1962; MA, Boston U., 1964; postgrad., U. Calif., San Diego, 1968-69, U. Ill., 1970-76. Economist Arthur D. Little, Cambridge, Mass., 1963-67, U. Ill., Urbana, 1971-72; mem. county bd. Champaign County, Urbana, 1972-76, county auditor, 1976-92; legis. dir. ERA Ill., 2002—03; founder ERA Yes!, 2003. Mem. local audit adv. bd. Office Ill. Compt., Chgo., 1984-92. Contbr. to Illinois Local Government: A Handbook, 1990. Founding mem. Citizens Forum on Gambling and Campaign Fin. Reform, 1999; downstate program dir. Citizen Action/Ill., 1999; legis. dir. AAUW, Ill., Inc., 2001, lobbyist, 2004; active Champaign-Urbana Mass Transit Dist. Bd., 2004—05; state rep. 103d dist. Ill. Gen. Assembly, 1993—95; Dem. nominee Ill. 15th dist. U.S. Congress, 1996—98; mayor Urbana, 2005—. Named Best Freshman Legislator Ind. Voters Ill., 1994; recipient Friend of Agriculture award Ill. Farm Bur., 1994; named to Legis. Honor Roll Ill. Environ. Coun., 1994. Mem. AAUW, NAACP, LWV, Govt. Fin. Officers Assn., U.S. and Can. (com. on acctg., auditing and fin. reporting 1980-88, Fin. Reporting award 1981-91, Disting. Budget award 1986), Nat. Assn. Local Govt. Auditors (charter), Ill. Assn. County Auditors (pres. 1984-85). Democrat. Home: 2106 Grange Dr Urbana IL 61801-6609 Office Phone: 217-328-2071.

PRUTER, MARGARET FRANSON, editor; b. Oak Park, Ill., Jan. 16; d. Frederick G. and Margaret K. (Svoboda) Franson; m. Robert D. Pruter, July 22, 1972; 1 child, Robin. AB, Dominican U., River Forest, Ill., 1961; MA, Northwestern U., Evanston, Ill., 1965. Asst. editor Am. People's Ency., Chgo., 1961-62; rsch. assoc. AMA, Chgo., 1962-63; asst. editor New Standard Ency., Chgo., 1964-66, assoc. editor, 1966-75, sr. editor, 1975-96; editl. dir. Elmhurst Editl. Svcs., Ill., 1996—2005; editor McDougal Littell, Evanston, Ill., 1997—2004; sr. editor The Book Edit Group, 2005—. Exec. dir. Militaria Archives, Elmhurst, Ill., 1972—. Co-author: DuPage Roots, 1985 (Ill. State Hist. Publ. award 1986); contbr. Encyclopedia of Chgo., 2004. Mem. Elmhurst Hist. Commn., 1981—, v.p., 1995—2000, pres., 2000—01; mem. Friends of Elmhurst Pub. Libr., Elmhurst Art Mus. Found.; exec. bd. North Ctrl. Coll. Parents Assn., 1995—98; bd. dirs. DuPage County Hist. Soc., Wheaton, Ill., 1982—, 1st v.p., 2004—; bd. dirs. DuPage County Sesquicentennial Com., Wheaton, Ill., 1988—89. Mem.: AAUW (bd. dirs. Elmhurst br. 1995—99), Ocean Conservancy, Nature Conservancy, Arch. Conservancy, Am. Studies Assn., Nat. Women's History Mus., Nat. Trust Historic Preservation, Orgn. Am. Historians, Am. Philat. Soc., Ill. Hist. Soc., Elmhurst Hist. Soc., Chgo. Hist. Soc., Chgo. Architecture Found., Nat. Parks and Conservation Assn., World Wildlife Fedn., Chgo. Women in Pub., Byrd's Nest Chapel Questers (pres. 1992—94, 2003—07), Sisters in Crime, Nat. Wildlife Fedn., Sierra Club. Office: The Book Edit Group PO Box 245 Elmhurst IL 60126-0768 Business E-Mail: bookedit1@yahoo.com.

PRUTER, ROBERT DOUGLAS, librarian; b. Phila., July 1, 1944; s. Hugo Rehling and Nancy Lee (Taylor) P.; m. Margaret Franson; 1 child, Robin Franson. BA, Roosevelt U., 1967, MA, 1976; MLS, Dominican U., 2000. Asst. editor New Std. Ency., Chgo., 1969-74, assoc. editor, 1974-79, sr. editor, 1979-96; sr. rsch. assoc. Planning Comms., 1996-97; asst. editor Charles D. Spencer & Assocs., Chgo., 1997-98, assoc. editor, 1999-2001; govt. documents lib. Lewis U., Romeoville, Ill., 2001—. Author: Chicago Soul, 1991, Doowop: The Chicago Scene, 1996; editor: Blackwell Guide to Soul Recordings, 1993; adv. editor Popular Music and Society, 1995—; rhythm and blues editor Goldmine Mag., 1984-2007. Mem. adv. com. Chgo. Blues Festival, 1992—. Served U.S. Army, 1967-69, Vietnam. Mem.: NARAS, Soc. Midland Authors, Chgo. Hist. Soc., N.Am. Soc. for Sport History. Democrat. Avocations: collecting records, sports history rsch. Office Phone: 815-836-5664. Personal E-mail: pruterro@lewisu.edu.

PRUZAN, IRENE, musician, educator, public relations executive, art association administrator; b. Watertown, NY, Jan. 3, 1949; d. John Edward and Esther (Coahn) P.; m. Charles G. Ullery, Jan. 30, 1972 (div. 1978); m. Charles Robert Freeman, May 20, 1988 (dec. Sept. 2005). Student, U. Ariz., Tucson, 1966-68; MusB, U. So. Calif., 1971; postgrad., San Francisco State U., Calif., 1972-74, U. Minn., 1976-80. Tchr. flute, coach chamber music MacPhail Ctr. for Arts, U. Minn., Mpls., 1976-85, coordinator instrumental music, 1978-81, program dir. instrumental music, 1982-85, div. head of programs, 1985-86; regional dir. Music On The Move, Inc., Valley Cottage, NY, 1986-87; pres. Music On the Move Minn., Inc., St. Paul, 1987—2002; dir. pub. rels. Nat. Flute Assn., 2004—. Founding mem. Crocus Hill Trio, 1976-2004; pub. rels. cons. Sch. of Music, U. Minn., 1991; faculty Nat. Music Camp, Interlochen, Mich., 1983, 84; cons. edn. and festival Ordway Music Theatre, St. Paul, 1985-87; mgr. Sartory String Quartet, Mpls., 1986-93; cons., program dir. Young Audiences, Mpls., 1986-1988; developer numerous master classes; cons. in field. Writer teaching materials for flute. Bd. directors Twin Cities Friends of Chamber Music, 1982—89; mem. Ariz. Chamber Orch., Tucson, 1967, San Gabriel (Calif.) Symphony, 1968—71, San Francisco Symphony, 1972—75; extra player St. Paul Chamber Orch., 1977—91; organizer German jazz residency USIA, Minn. and Wis., 1986; edn. com. Orlando Philharm., 2001—04. Mem.: AAUW (Orlando br. pub. rels. and web master 2003—), Orlando Musicians Union, Twin Cities Musicians Union, Nat. Flute Assn. (dir. mktg. 1987—90).

PRUZANSKY, JOSHUA MURDOCK, lawyer; b. NYC, Mar. 16, 1940; s. Louis and Rose (Murdock) P.; m. Susan R. Bernstein, Aug. 31, 1980; 1 child, Dina Gabrielle. BA, Columbia Coll., 1960, JD, 1965. Bar: NY, 1965, US Dist. Ct. (ea. and so. dists.) NY, 1968, US Supreme Ct., 1980. Ptnr. Scheinberg, DePetris & Pruzansky, Riverhead, NY, 1965-85, Greshin, Ziegler & Pruzansky, Smithtown, NY, 1985-2000, Pruzansky & Besunder, LLP, Islandia, NY, 2001—06; spl. counsel Bracken & Margolin, LLP, 2006—. Pres. NY State Bar Assn., house of dels. 1982-, exec. com. 1992-99, spl. com. women and law 1986-91, chmn. spl. com., fiduciary appts., 2003—, trusts and estates sect., gen. practice, elder law sects., 1997-98, chmn. spl. com. solo and small firm practices, 2006-; exec. coun. NY State Conf. Bar Leaders, 1984—, chmn., 1988-89; grievance com. Appellate Divsn. 10th Judicial Dist., 1992-96; LI adv. bd. HSBC Bank, 1995-2007. Mem. bd. visitors Columbia Law Sch., 1998—; chair bd. visitors Touro Law Sch., 1998-2004; dir., sec. L.I. Mus., 1998-2004. Fellow ABA Found., NY State Bar Found. (bd. dir. 1994-03); mem. ABA (house of dels. 1997-03, standing com. on solo and small firm practitioners 1998-00, NY state del. Caucus State Bar Assns.), Suffolk County Bar Assn. (bd. dir. 1979-89, pres. 1985-86), Nassau County Bar Assn. Office: Bracken & Margolin LLP Ste 300 One Suffolk Sq Islandia NY 11749 Office Phone: 631-234-8585. Business E-Mail: jmp@pruzlaw.com.

PRYCE, DEBORAH DENINE, congresswoman; b. Warren, Ohio, July 29, 1951; m. Randy Walker (div.); 1 child. BA cum laude, Ohio State U., 1973; JD with honors, Capital U. Law Sch., 1976. Bar: Ohio 1976. Adminstrv. law judge Ohio State Dept. Ins., 1976—78; first asst. city prosecutor, sr. asst. city atty., asst. city mgr. Columbus City Atty.'s Office, Ohio, 1978—85; judge Franklin County Mcpl. Ct., Columbus, 1989, 1990, 1992; mem. US Congress from 15th Ohio dist., 1993—, chair Ho. Rep. Conf., 2003—, mem. fin. svcs. com., ranking mem. subcommittee on capital markets, ins. and govt. sponsored enterprises, 2007—, dep. whip, co-chair cancer caucus. Republican. Presbyterian. Avocation: skiing. Office: 500 S Front St Ste 1130 Columbus OH 43215 Office Phone: 202-225-2015, 614-469-5614. *

PRYCE, JONATHAN, actor; b. North Wales, June 1, 1947; Appearences include (stage) Liverpool Everyman, 1972, Nottingham Playhouse, Comedians, 1977 (Tony award, Theatre World award), 1980, Hamlet (Olivier award), 1986, Macbeth, The Caretaker, 1981, Accidental Death of an Anarchist, 1984, The Seagull, 1986, Uncle Vanya, 1989, Miss Saigon, 1991 (Tony award, Olivier award), Oliver, 1995, My Fair Lady, 2001-02, A Reckoning, 2003, The Goat or Who Is Sylvia, 2004, Dirty Rotten Scoundrels, N.Y.C., 2006; (films) Voyage of the Damned, 1976, Breaking Glass, 1980, Loophole, 1981, Praying Mantis, 1982, The Plowman's Lunch, 1983, Something Wicked This Way Comes, 1983, Brazil, 1985, The Doctor and the Devils, 1985, Haunted Honeymoon, 1986, Jumpin Jack Flash, 1986, Hotel London, 1987, Man On Fire, 1987, The Adventures of Baron Munchausen, 1988, Consuming Passions, 1988, The Rachel Papers, 1989, Glengarry Glen Ross, 1992, The Age of Innocence, 1993, Shopping, 1994, A Business Affair, 1994, Carrington, 1996 (Best Actor award Cannes Film Festival 1995), Evita, 1996, Tomorrow Never Dies, 1997, Regeneration, 1997, Ronin, 1998, Stigmata, 1999, Very Annie Mary, 2001, Unconditional Love, 2001, Bride of the Wind, 2002, The Affair of the Necklace, 2002, What a Girl Wants, 2003, Pirates of the Caribbean, 2003, De Lovely, 2004, The Brothers Grimm, 2004, The New World, 2005, Pirates of the Caribbean 2: Dead Man's Chest, 2006, The Moon and The Stars, 2007, Pirates of the Carribean 3: At World's End, 2007, Leatherheads, 2007; (TV movie) Barbarians at the Gate, HBO, 1993 (Emmy nomination, Supporting Actor - Miniseries or Special, 1993), David, 1997, Confessions of an Ugly Stepsister, 2002, The Baker Street Irregulars, 2007. Recipient BAFTA Cymru spl. award, 2002. Address: UTA 9560 Wilshire Blvd Beverly Hills CA 90212 Mailing: Julian Belfrage Assocs ADAM House 16 New Burlington St London W1S 3BQ England

PRYOR, CAROL GRAHAM, obstetrician, gynecologist; b. Savannah, Ga. m. Louis O.J. Manganiello, June 11, 1950; children: Carol Helen, Victoria Manganiello Mudano. AB, Ga. Coll., 1943; MD, Med. Coll. Ga., 1947. Rotating intern City Hosps., Balt., 1947-48; asst. resident pathology Baroness Erlanger Hosp., Chattanooga, 1948; intern. obstetrics City Colls., Balt., 1949; coll. physician Ga. State Coll. for Women, Milledgeville, Ga., 1949-50; resident obstetrics City Hosps., Balt., 1950-51; asst. resident gynecology Univ. Hosp., Balt., 1951-52, sr. resident ob-gyn. Augusta, Ga., 1952; pvt. practice ob-gyn. Augusta, 1952—; chmn. ob-gyn. St. Joseph Hosp., Augusta, 1997—. Chair ob-gyn. dept. St. Joseph Hosp., Augusta. Mem., former pres. Iris Garden Club, Augusta; mem. coun. on maternal and infant health State of Ga., Atlanta, 1981-90; mem. edn. found. AAUW, 1961-63, state v.p., state pres., 1963-65. Recipient Cert. of Achievement-Community Leadersip, Ga. div. AAUW, 1982; named Med. Woman of Yr., Ga. br. 51 Am. Med. Women's Assn., 1961; Heritage award Ga. Coll. and State U., 2001, Achievement award, Ga. Coll. U., 1982. Fellow ACS (1st woman mem. Ga. chpt. 1956), ACOG; mem. AMA, Richmond County Med. Soc., So. Med. Assn., So. Surg. Congress, Delta Kappa Gamma. Democrat. Methodist. Office: 2316 Wrightsboro Rd Augusta GA 30904-6220 Office Phone: 706-738-2503. Personal E-mail: cpryor@bellsouth.net.

PRYOR, DAVID BRAM, health science association administrator; b. Charleston, SC, Oct. 18, 1951; s. Sydney and Grace Prystowsky; m. Christin Marie Kennedy; children: Rebecca Whitaker, Rachel Celia, Grace Eileen. Attended, U. Mich., Ann Arbor, 1969—72; MD, U. Mich. Med. Sch., 1972—76. Cert. Am. Bd. Internal Medicine, 1979, bd. cert. cardiovascular diseases 1983, lic. Pa., 1976, NC, 1979, Mass., 1994, Minn., 1996, Mo., 2004. Intern in medicine Pa. Hosp., Phila., 1976—77, resident in medicine, 1977—79; fellow in cardiology Duke U. Med. Ctr., Durham, NC, 1979—81, asst. prof. medicine, 1983—89, assoc. prof. medicine, 1989—94; sr. staff mem. cardiovascular divsn. Duke U., Durham, NC, 1981—94, dir. section clinical epidemiology and biostatistics, 1984—89, dir. clinical program devel., 1993—94; pres. New England Med. Ctr. Hosp., Boston, 1994—95; prof. medicine Tufts U. Sch. Medicine, 1994—97; sr. v.p./chief info. officer Allina Health Sys., Mpls., 1995—2001; sr. v.p. clinical excellence Ascension Health, St. Louis, 2001—. Program com. and biometry track chair 11th Symposium on Computer Applications in Med. Care, 1987; bd. dir. Clinical Rsch. Internat., Inc., 1989—90, PatientKeeper (Virtmed) Inc., 2001—06; chmn. task force reducing med. uncertainty Joint Commn. Accreditation Healthcare Orgn., 1989—91, adv. coun. performance measurement, 1995—, chmn. adv. coun. performance measurement, 1998—2003, mem. performance measurement coord. com., 1998—2000; chmn. epidemiology and prevention track Am. Coll. Cardiology Sci. Session Com., 1991—92, chmn. health svc. delivery track, 1991—92; mem. exec. com. and steering com. Health Care Financing Adminstrn., Coop. Cardiovascular Project, 1992—94; chmn. ops. com. Acad. Med. Ctr. Consortium, 1992—94; mem. sci. session program com. Am. Heart Assn., 1994—96; chmn. bd. dir. Strategicare, Inc., 1996—99; bd. gov. Bioengineering Inst., U. Minn., Mpls., 1996—2002; mem. 2000 Spring Congress Sci. Program com. Am. Med. Informatics Assn. (AMIA), 1999—2000; mem. IT expert adv. panel Nat. Quality Forum (NQF) Nat. Forum for Health Care Quality Measurement and Reporting, 2001—02; mem. adv. bd. Ctr. Info. Tech. Leadership (CITL), 2001—; cons. prof. Cardiovascular Inst., Favaloro Found., Buenos Aires, 1994—97; cons. assoc. prof. medicine Duke U. Med. Ctr., 1994—; adj. prof. epidemiology U. Minn. Sch. Pub. Health, Mpls., 1996—2002; pres. New England Med. Ctr., Boston, 1994—95; adj. prof. St. Louis U. Sch. Pub. Health; numerous positions with Allina Health Sys., Mpls., 1995—2001; reviewer numerous jour. and rsch. grants; presenter in field; mem. numerous nat. and internat. com.; cons. in field. Contbr. articles to jour., chapters to books. Named Laureate, Computerworld Smithsonian award, Allina Health Sys., 1999, Lifetime Scholar, Barton Haynes Soc., Duke U., 2005; named one of 100 Most Powerful People in Healthcare, Modern Healthcare, 2002, 2005, 50 Most Powerful Physician Execs., Modern Physician, 2005, Modern Healthcare, 2006; recipient Innovations in IT awards, 2nd place, HIMMS and Deloitte and Touche (Allina Health Sys.), 1998, Tng. for Future, 3rd place, Allina Health Sys., 1998, Quest for Best award, 2000, Silver award, 2001, CareScience Exec. Leadership award, 2006; fellow, Am. Coll. Med. Informatics, 1986, Am. Soc. Clinical Investigation, 1992. Fellow: Am. Coll. Med. Informatics, Am. Coll. Physicians, Am. Coll. Cardiology; mem.: Am. Med. Informatics Assn., Am. Heart Assn. (fellow coun. on clinical cardiology), Am. Soc. Clinical Investigation, Am. Fedn. Clinical Rsch. Office: Ascension Health 4600 Edmundson Rd Saint Louis MO 63134 Office Phone: 314-733-8192, 314-733-8196. Business E-Mail: dpryor@ascensionhealth.org.

PRYOR, DAVID HAMPTON, former senator; b. Camden, Ark., Aug. 29, 1934; s. Edgar and Susan (Newton) P.; m. Barbara Lunsford, Nov. 27, 1957; children— David, Mark, Scott. BA in Polit. Sci, U. Ark., Fayetteville, 1957; LL.B., U. Ark., 1961. Bar: Ark. 1964. Lawyer, Camden; mem. firm Pryor and Barnes; founder, pub. Ouachita Citizen newspaper, Camden, 1957-60; mem. Ark. Ho. of Reps., 1961-65, 89th-92d Congresses from 4th Ark. dist.; gov. of Ark., 1974-79; senator from Ark., 1979-96; Fulbright Disting. Fellow Law and Pub. Affairs U. Ark., 1997; fellow Inst. Politics, John F. Kennedy Sch. Govt., Harvard U., 1999—2000, dir., 2000, 2001; founding dean, Clinton Sch. Pub. Svc. Clinton Presdl. Libr., Little Rock, 2004—06, prof., Clinton Sch. Pub. Svc., 2004—. Ranking min. mem. Select Com. On Aging, Nutrition and Forestry Subcom. on Prodn. and Price Competitiveness, Fin. Subcom. on Long Term Growth, Debt. and Deficit Reduction; mem. Govt. Affairs, Sen. Dem. Conf. Com., Sen. Dem. Steering and Coord. Com., Dem. Senatorial Campign Com. Bd. trustees William Jefferson Clinton Presdl. Libr. Found. Office: 2701 Kavanaugh Blvd Ste 300 Little Rock AR 72205-3800 *

PRYOR, HAROLD S., retired college president; b. Overton County, Tenn., Oct. 3, 1920; s. Hubert S. and Ethel (Stockton) P.; m. LaRue Vaughn, June 26, 1946. BS, Austin Peay State U., 1946; MA, George Peabody Coll., 1947; Ed.D., U. Tenn., 1951. Instr. George Peabody Coll., Vanderbilt U., 1946-47, E. Tenn. State U., 1947-49, U. Tenn., Knoxville, 1949-51; head dept. edn. Austin Peay State U., 1952, dir. tchr. edn., 1954-68; pres. Columbia (Tenn.) State Community Coll., 1968-84, now pres. emeritus, 1984—. Dir. First Farmers and Merchants Nat. Bank, Columbia, 1970—, First Farmers and Mchts. Corp., 1982—; Columbia State Found., 1971—. Contbr. articles to profl. jours. With U.S. Army, 1943-46. Grantee Dept. Labor; Grantee HEW. Mem. NEA, Tenn. Coll. Assn. (past pres.), Tenn. Edn. Assn., Am. Assn. Higher Edn., Comparative Edn. Soc., Graymere Country Club, Kiwanis, Kappa Delta Pi, Phi Delta Kappa. Democrat. Presbyterian.

PRYOR, HUBERT, editor, writer, consultant; b. Buenos Aires, Mar. 18, 1916; (parents Am. citizens); s. John W. and Hilda A. (Cowes) P.; m. Ellen M. Ach, 1940 (div. 1959); children: Alan, Gerald, David. Grad., St. George's Coll., Argentina, 1932; student, U. London, Eng., 1934-36. Corr. in S.Am. for United Press, 1937-39; pub. relations rep. Pan Am. Airways in Buenos Aires, 1939-40; reporter N.Y. Herald Tribune, 1940-41; writer, dir. short-wave newsroom CBS, 1941-46; asst. mng. editor Knickerbocker Weekly, 1946-47; sr. editor Look mag., 1947-62; creative supr. Wilson, Haight & Welch, 1962-63; editor Science Digest, 1963-67; mng. editor

Med. World News, 1967; editor NRTA Jour. Modern Maturity, 1967-82; editl. dir. Dynamic Years, 1977-82; publs. coord. Modern Maturity, Dynamic Years, 1982-84; editl. cons., writer, 1985—. Author: Soul Talk, 1995, Eleanor of Palm Beach, 2002. Lt. USNR, 1943-46. Mem. Am. Soc. Mag. Editors, Author's Guild, Overseas Press Club. Home: 3560 S Ocean Blvd Palm Beach FL 33480-5772

PRYOR, MARK LUNSFORD, senator; b. Fayetteville, Ark., Jan. 10, 1963; s. David H. Pryor; m. Jill Pryor; children: Adams, Porter. BA in History, U. Ark., 1985, JD, 1988. Pvt. practice Wright, Lindsey & Jennings, Little Rock, 1988—97; mem. Ark. Ho. of Reps., 1990—98, chmn. Freshman Caucus, mem. judiciary com., com. on aging and legis. affairs; atty. gen. State of Ark., 1999—2002; US Senator from Ark., 2003—. Mem. com. commerce, sci. and transp. US Senate, com. homeland security and govt. affairs, com. small bus. and entrepreneurship, spl. com. ethics, armed svcs. com., com. rules and adminstrn. Chmn. Alliance to Save Energy; mem. cardiovascular cabinet Ark. Heart Assn.; mem. Friends of Carousel. Recipient Spirit of Enterprise award, US C. of C., 2005. Democrat. Presbyterian. Office: US Senate 257 Dirksen Senate Office Bldg Washington DC 20510 also: The River Market Ste 401 500 President Clinton Ave Little Rock AR 72201-1745 Office Phone: 202-224-2353, 501-324-6336. Office Fax: 202-228-0908, 501-324-5320.

PRYOR, RICHARD WALTER, telecommunications executive, retired air force officer; b. Poplar Bluff, Mo., Nov. 6, 1932; s. Walter V. and Mary (Clifford) P.; m. Barbara LeCompte, Feb. 19, 1955; children: Richard, Susan Davis, Robert, William. B in Gen. Studies, U. Nebr., Omaha, 1972; MA, Webster Coll., St. Louis, 1975. Commd. 2d lt. USAF, 1953, advanced through grades to maj. gen., 1982, ret., 1982; instr. U.S. Air Force Acad.; DVMT engr. space and missile systems USAF, chief of staff Comm. Svcs.; dir. worldwide def. comm. sys. Def. Comm. Agy., 1980-81; pres. ITT World Comm., NYC, 1982-84, ITT Indsl. Transmission Co., NYC; sr. v.p. engring. ops. ITT Comm. Svcs. GP; pres., gen. mgr. ITT Christian Rovsing-Copenhagen DK, 1984-86; chmn. Christian-Rovsing Inc., Tulsa; exec. v.p. Electronic Data Sys. (EDS) Comm. Corp., Dallas, 1986-89; pres., COO IMM Corp.-Interdigital AMEX, Phila., 1989-92; chmn., CEO. officer Ultranav Corp, Dallas, 1992—; chmn. Prism Video, Dallas, 1994—; pres. Trans-Tech Holdings Corp., Dallas, 1996—; pres., CEO Unison Corp., Dallas, 1998—, Video Net, Addison, Tex.; chmn., CEO Mega Link Tech., LA, 2003—, MIUSA, LA, 2003—; ptnr. BOR Assoc., 2005—. Dir. RPost, LA, 2000—. Contbr. articles to tech. publs. Assoc. dir. Boy Soucts Am., N.Y.C., 1983. Recipient Cert. of Appreciation Okla. Mental Health Assn., 1979, Kansas City Lions Club, 1974. Mem. Armed Forces Communications and Electronics Assn. (pres. N.Y.C. 1983, nat. dir.), Air Force Assn., Oklahoma City Soc. Profl. Engrs., Canoe Brook Country Club, Army-Navy Club, Phi Alpha Theta. Republican. Roman Catholic. E-mail: dick1955@tx.rr.com.

PRYOR, STEFAN I., city manager, real estate developer; b. NYC, Jan. 14, 1972; JD, Yale U., 1998. Policy adv. to mayor City of New Haven; v.p. Partnership for NYC, exec. dir. sch. reform program; sr. v.p. policy and programs Lower Manhattan Devel. Corp., NYC, 2001—05, pres., 2005—06; dep. mayor for econ. devel. City of Newark, NJ, 2006—. Founder ReStart Ctrl., NYC, Achievement First; co-founder Amistad Acad., New Haven. Grantee John V. Lindsay Pub. Svc. Fellowship, Yale U., 2000. Office: City Hall 920 Broad St Ste 200 Newark NJ 07102

PRYOR, WILLIAM C., judge; b. Washington, May 29, 1932; BA, Dartmouth Coll., 1954; LLB with honors, Georgetown U., 1959. Bar: D.C. 1959, Ohio 1964, U.S. Supreme Ct. 1965. With U.S. Dept. Justice, Washington, 1959-68; judge D.C. Dist. Ct., Washington, 1968—; former chief judge; now sr. judge DC Ct. of Appeals, Washington, 1993—. Instr. Georgetown U., Washington, 1969, 71, Potomac Law Sch., 1976—; now disting. prof. of law, resident scholar, D.C. U. David A. Clarke Sch. of Law. Bd. dirs. YMCA, St. Albans Sch., Opportunities Industrialization Ctr., Am. Cancer Soc. Lt. USAS, 1955-56. Mem. ABA, Washington Bar Assn., D.C. Bar, Washington Athletic Club. Office: Dist of Columbia Ct of Appeals 500 Indiana Ave NW Washington DC 20001-2131 also: David Clarke Sch of Law DC U 4200 Conn Ave NW Washington DC 20008

PRYOR, WILLIAM DANIEL LEE, humanities educator; b. Lakeland, Fla., Oct. 29, 1926; s. Dahl and Lottie Mae (Merchant) P. AB, Fla. So. Coll., 1949; MA, Fla. State U., Tallahassee, 1950, PhD, 1959; postgrad., U. NC, Chapel Hill, 1952—53; pvt. art studies with Florence Wilde; pvt. voice studies with Colin O'More, Anna Kaskas; pvt. piano studies with Waldemar Hille and audited piano master classes of Ernst von Dohnányi. Asst. prof. English, dir. drama Bridgewater Coll., Va., 1950-52; grad. tchg. fellow humanities Fla. State U., Tallahassee, 1953-55, 57-58; instr. English U. Houston, University Park, Houston, 1955-59, asst. prof. University Park, 1959-62, assoc. prof., 1962-71, prof., 1971-97, prof. emeritus, 1997. Vis. instr. English, Fla. So. Coll., Lakeland, MacDill Army Air Base, Tampa, Fla., summer 1951, Tex. So. U., 1961-63, humanities, govt. U. Tex. Dental Br., Houston, 1962-63; lectr. The Women's Inst., Houston, 1967-72, humanities series Jewish Cmty. Ctr., Houston, 1972-73; originator, moderator TV and radio program The Arts in Houston Stas. KUHT-TV and KUHF-FM, 1956-57, 58-63. Author: An Examination of the Southern Milieu in Representative Plays by Southern Dramatists, 1963; contbg. author: National Poetry Anthology, 1952, Panorama das Literaturas das Americas, vol. 2, 1958-60, Perspectives on Ernst von Dohnányi, 2005, Dohnányi Evkönyu 2005, 2006; assoc. editor Forum, 1967, editor, 1967-82; contbr. articles to profl. jours.; dir. Murder in the Cathedral (T.S. Elliot), U. Houston, 1965; performed in opera as Sir Edgar in Der Junge Lord (Henze), Houston Grand Opera Assn., 1967; played the title role in Aella (Chatterton), Am. premiere, U. Houston, 1970. Bd. dir., founding mem. Contemporary Music Soc., Houston, 1958-63, Houston Shakespeare Soc., 1964-67; bd. dirs., founding mem., program annotator Houston Chamber Orch. Soc., 1964-76; narrator Houston Symphony Orch., Houston Summer Symphony Orch., Houston Chamber Orch. (with Charles Rosekrans), U. Houston Symphony Orch., St. Stephen's Music Festival Symphony Orch., New Harmony, Ind.; narrator world premier of the Bells (Jerry McCathern), 1969, U. Houston Symphony Orch., 1969, Am. premier Symphony No. Seven, Antartica (Vaughn-Williams), Houston Symphony Orch. (with Andre Previn), 1967, L'Histoire du Soldat (Stravinski), U. Houston Symphony Orch., 1957, Am. premier Babar the Elephant (Poulenc-Francais), Houston Chamber Orch. (with Charles Rosekrans), 1967, Le Roi David (Honegger), 1979, Voice of God in opera Noye's Fludde (Britten), St. Stephen's Music Festival, 1981; bd. dir., program annotator Music Guild, Houston, 1960-67, v.p., 1963-67, adv. bd., 1967-70; mem.-at-large, bd. dir. Houston Grand Opera Guild, 1966-67; repertory com. Houston Grand Opera Assn., 1967-70; bd. dir. Houston Grand Opera, 1970-75, adv. bd. 1978-79; cultural adv. com. Jewish Cmty. Ctr., 1960-66; bd. dir. Houston Friends Pub. Libr., 1962-67, 73-75, 1st v.p., 1963-67; adv. mem. cultural affairs com. Houston C. of C., 1972-75; adv. bd. dir. The Wilhelm Schole, 1980-98, Buffalo Bayou Support Com., 1985-87, bd. dir. Moores Sch. Music Soc., 1998—, trustee, 2002-04, advisory bd. dir., 2004—; bd. dir. U. Houston Retiree Assn., 1999-2001, v.p., 2000-2001; founding bd. dir. Internat. Dohnányi Rsch. Ctr., Inc., 2002-. Recipient Master Tchg. award Coll. Humanities and Fine Arts U., Houston, 1980, Favorite Prof. award Bapt. Student Union, U. Houston, 1991. Mem. MLA, AAUP, Coll. English Assn., L'Alliance Francaise, English-Speaking Union, Alumni Assn. Fla. So. Coll., Fla. State U., South Ctrl. MLA, Conf. Editors Learned Jours., Coll. Conf. Tchrs. English, Nat. Coun. Tchrs. English, Am. Studies Assn., Shepard Soc. Rice U., Nature Conservancy, Nat. Trust for Hist. Preservation, Inst. Internat. Edn., Century Club, Fla. So. Coll., President's Club, James D. Westcott Legacy Soc., Fla. State U., Tex. Ret. Tchrs. Assn., Phi Beta (patron), Phi Mu Alpha Sinfonia, Alpha Psi Omega, Pi Kappa Alpha, Sigma Tau Delta (Outstanding Prof. English U. Houston chpt. 1990), 1927 Soc. U. Houston, Houston Philos. Soc., Caledonian Club (London), Tau Kappa Alpha, Phi Kappa Phi. Episcopalian. Avocations: tennis, racquetball, swimming, travel. Home: 2625 Arbuckle St West University Place TX 77005-3929 Office: U Houston Dept English Univ Park 3801 Cullen Blvd Houston TX 77004-2602 Office Phone: 713-665-2401. *My commitment is to the humanities. I believe that the most important thing that a teacher can do is to help a student to stand on his/her own intellectual hind legs; to help him/her to learn how to aquire facts; to help him/her to learn how to organize and utilize these facts in intelligent, responsible ways.*

PRYOR, WILLIAM HOLCOMBE, JR., federal judge, former state attorney general, educator; b. Mobile, Ala., Apr. 26, 1962; s. William Holcombe Sr. and Laura Louise (Bowles) Pryor; m. Kristan Camille Wilson, Aug. 15, 1987; children: Caroline Elizabeth, Victoria Camille. BA in Legal Studies with honors, N.E. La. U., 1984; JD with honors, Tulane U., 1987. Law clk. US Ct. Appeals (5th cir.), Judge John Minor Wisdom, New Orleans, 1987—88; assoc. Cabaniss, Johnston, Gardner, Dumas & O'Neil, Birmingham, Ala., 1988—91, Walston, Stabler, Wells, Anderson & Bains, Birmingham, 1991—95; dep. atty. gen. State of Ala., Montgomery, 1995—97, atty. gen., 1997—2004; judge US Ct. Appeals (11th cir.), 2004—. Adj. prof. Samford U. Cumberland Sch. Law, Birmingham, 1989—94, U. Ala. Sch. Law, 2006—. Bd. student editors: Tulane Law Rev., 1985—86, editor-in-chief:, 1986—87, bd. adv. editors:, 1995—. La. nat. com. Young Rep. Nat. Fedn., 1984—86; mem. Ala. Rep. Exec. Com., 1994—95. Mem.: Federalist Soc. (assoc.), Amer. Law Inst. (assoc.), Order of Coif, Omicron Delta Kappa, Phi Kappa Phi. Republican. Roman Catholic. Office: US Court of Appeals 900 Federal Courthouse 1729 5th Ave N Birmingham AL 35203 *

PRYPCHAN, LIDA D., psychiatrist; b. Caracas, DF, Venezuela, July 8, 1960; d. Roman Orestes Prypchan and Edel Sayagues. MD, U. Carabobo, Venezuela, 1986; psychiatrist, U. Ctrl., Venezuela, 1999; postgrad., Mt. Sinai Sch. Medicine, NYC, 2005. Intern, med. asst. Clinica Residencia Carabobo, Valencia, Venezuela, 1986—89; rsch. assoc. We. Psychiatric Inst. and Clinic U. Pitts. Med. Ctr., 1989—90, sr. rsch. assoc. World Psychiatric Assn., 1990—94; psychiatric resident Hosp. U. Caracas, 1996—99, Elmhurst Hosp. Ctr., NY, 2001—05; fellow Child and Adolescent Psychiatry Elmhurst Hosp. Ctr./Mt. Sinai Sch. Medicine, 2005—. Sr. rsch. assoc. Elmhurst Hosp. Ctr./World Psychiatric Assn., 2003—05. Contbr. articles to profl. jours. Recipient Nat. Sci. Journalism award, Venezuela, 1987, 1988, 1989. Mem.: Acad. Child and Adolescent Psychiatry, Am. Psychiatric Assn. Avocations: movies, theater, travel, walking. Home: 4005 Hampton St #415 Elmhurst NY 11373 Office: Elmhurst Hosp Ctr Dept Psychiatry 7901 Broadway Ave Elmhurst NY 11373 Office Phone: 718-372-6339. Personal E-mail: lidaprypchan@hotmail.com.

PRYSTAUK, ELISSA, artist; b. 1953; BFA, Rutgers U., Newark; postgrad., Urbino U., Newark Sch. Find and Ind. Advisor NJ Pastel Soc., 2005—. Work included in book, Best of Oil Painting, 1996, The Art of Pastel, 2005, North American Pastel Artists, 2007. Recipient Best of Show award, Avila Arts, NJ, 2003, Excellence award, Internat. Pastel Exhgn., Giverny, France, 2006. Fellow: Am. Artists Profl. League (medal of honor 2005); mem.: Hudson Valley Art Assn., Millburn Short Hills Art (treas. 2002—04), Pastel Soc. Am. (treas. 2004—). Home: 20 Knox Hill Rd Morristown NJ 07960-3502

PRZEMIENIECKI, JANUSZ STANISLAW, engineering executive, former government senior executive and college dean; b. Lipno, Poland, Jan. 30, 1927; came to U.S., 1961, naturalized, 1967; s. Leon and Maria (Sarnacka) P.; m. Stefania (Fiona) Rudnicka, July 17, 1954; children: Anita, Christopher. BS, U. London, 1949, PhD, 1958; diploma in Aeros., Imperial Coll. Sci. and Tech., 1953; DSc in Engring., U. London, 1988; doctorate (hon.), Warsaw U. Tech., 1999. Registered profl. engr., Ohio. Head structural R & D sect. Bristol Aircraft Ltd., Eng., 1954-61; from assoc. prof. to prof. mechanics Sch. Engring., Air Force Inst. Tech., Wright-Patterson AFB, Ohio, 1961-66, from asst. dean, assoc. dean rsch. to dean, 1966-89, sr. dean, 1970-95; pres. Astra Technologies, Inc., Fla., 1996—. Cons. in field. Author: Theory of Matrix Structural Analysis, 1968, Mathematical Methods in Defense Analyses, 3d edit., 2000, Defense Analyses Software, 1991; assoc. editor: Jour. Aircraft, 1970-71; editl. bd.: Internat. Jour. Numerical Methods in Engring., 1969-75; editor: Mechanics of Structural Systems (textbook series) 1973-89; editor: Critical Technologies for Nat. Defense, 1991, Acquisition of Defense Systems, 1993; contbr. articles to profl. jours. Chmn. bd. trustees The Air Force Inst. Tech. Found., Ohio, 1987-88, trustee, 1993-95; trustee Engring. and Sci. Found. of Dayton, 1984-95. Decorated Polish Underground Army Cross, Warsaw Uprising Cross, Armed Forces medal; recipient USAF superior performance award, 1965, exceptional civilian svc. decoration, 1978, Presdl. rank of Meritorious Exec., 1981, Disting. Exec., 1982, Outstanding Engr. award Dayton Engring. and Sci. Found., 1986, Outstanding Civilian Svc. medal, 1995, Comdrs. Cross of the Polonia Restituta Order by Pres. of Poland, 1995, Disting. Svc. award, Am. Inst. of Polish Culture, 1997. Fellow Royal Aeros. Soc. (Usborne Meml. prize 1959), AIAA (editor-in-chief ednl. series 1981—, Pendray medal 1992), City and Guilds of London Inst.; mem. Am. Soc. Engring. Edn., Ohio Acad. Sci., Polish Inst. Arts and Scis., Tau Beta Pi. Home: 510 Pennyroyal Pl Venice FL 34293-7233

PRZYPYSZNY, JOHN R., lawyer; b. Chgo., 1965; AB, Georgetown Univ., 1987, JD, 1990. Bar: Ill. 1990, DC 1991. Negotiator US Dept. Edn.; ptnr., head, edn. law practice group Drinker Biddle & Reath LLP, Washington, 2001—. Frequent lectr. in field. Office: Drinker Biddle & Reath LLP Ste 1100 1500 K St NW Washington DC 20005-1209 Office Phone: 202-842-8858. Office Fax: 202-842-8465. Business E-Mail: john.przypyszny@dbr.com.

PSARRAS, MARY AUTEN, language educator, tax specialist; b. Bridgeport, Conn., Dec. 26, 1945; d. James Ernest and Mary Dillon Auten; m. Georgios Psarras, Dec. 21, 1974 (dec.); children: Demetrios, Patrick. BA in Modern Spanish and Am. Lit., Brown U., Providence, RI, 1967; MS in Elem. Edn., U. Bridgeport, Conn., 1973. Cert. tchr. pre-K-8, Spanish grades 7-12, ESL pre-K-12 Conn. Cmty. vol. Peace Corps, Itapuranga, Goias, Brazil, 1967—69; tchr. ESL Bridgeport Bd. Edn., Conn., 1970—78, 1984—97, tchr., English lang. learner assessment and data specialist, 1997—. Pres., v.p. and treas. Bridgeport Assn. for Childhood Edn.; pres. and v.p. Conn. Assn. Childhood Edn., 1972—79; mem. steering com. Stratford Tchrs. Applying Whole Lang., 1992—97; mem. election com. Bridgeport Edn. Assn.; del. rep. assy. Conn. Edn. Assn. Grantee, Bridgeport Pub. Edn. Fund, Am. Brands. Mem.: Bridgeport Edn. Assn. (bldg. del. 1997—), Alpha Delta Kappa. Home: 106 Bridgeview Pl Stratford CT 06614 Office: Bridgeport Bd Edn Bilingual Dept 948 Main St Bridgeport CT 06606 Personal E-mail: mpsarras@optonline.net.

PSOMIADES, HARRY JOHN, political science professor; b. Boston, Sept. 8, 1928; s. John and Koula (Yalmanides) P.; m. Dorothy Smith, Aug. 18, 1962 (dec. Aug. 27, 1984); children— Kathy Alexis, Christine Anne. BA, Boston U., 1953; M.Internat. Affairs, Columbia U., 1955; cert., Middle East Inst., 1956, PhD (Ford Found. fellow), 1962; Litt.D. (hon.), Holy Cross/Hellenic Coll., 1985. Lectr. govt. Columbia U., 1959-65, asst. dean Grad. Sch. Internat. Affairs, 1959-65, dir. Carnegie Endowment Fellowships in Diplomacy, 1959-71; assoc. prof. polit. sci. Queens Coll., City U. N.Y., 1965-69, prof., 1970—2003, chmn. dept. polit. sci., 1967-71, dep. exec. officer Ph.D. program in polit. sci., 1975-76, program dir. seminar on the modern Greek state, 1976—2004; dir. Ctr. Byzantine and Modern Greek Studies, 1976—2004. Cons. faculty U.S. Army Command and Gen. Staff Coll., 1968-86; U.S. Dept. State Fgn. Service Inst., 1968-71; mem. screening com. Fgn. Area Fellowships Program for Asia and Middle East Joint Com., Social Sci. Research Council and Am. Council Learned Socs., 1967-69 Author: Greece and Turkey: Mutual Economic Interests, 1964, (with Thomas Spelios) A Pictorial History of the Greeks, 1967, The Eastern Question: The Last Phase, 1968, 2d edition, 2000, Greek edit., 2004, (with T.A. Couloumbis) Foreign Interference in Greek Polics: An Historical Perspective, 1976, (with A. Scourby) The Greek American Community in Transition, 1982, (with R.S. Orfanos) Education and Greek Americans: Proccess and Prospects, 1987, (with S. Thomadakes) Greece, The New Europe and the Changing International Order, 1993, (with Van Coufoudakis) Greece and the New Balkans: Challenges and Opportunities, 1999, (with Sam Tsemberis) Greek American Famiilies: Traditions and Transformations, 1999; editor: Jour. Modern Hellenism, 1984—; contbr, articles to profl. jours. Served with U.S. Army, 1946-50; to col. AUS, 1950-83. Hon. fellow Soc. Macedonian Studies, Thessaloniki, Greece, 1970—; named Comdr. Order of Honor The Republic of Greece, 1996. Fellow Middle East Studies Assn. N.Am.; mem. Am. Polit. Sci. Assn., Middle East Inst., Modern Greek Studies Assn. (mem. exec. com. 1972-76), Phi Beta Kappa. Greek Orthodox. Home: 440 Riverside Dr New York NY 10027-6828

PSUTY, NORBERT PHILLIP, marine sciences educator; b. Hamtramck, Mich., June 13, 1937; s. Phillip and Jessie (Proszkowski) P.; m. Sylvia Helen Zurinsky, June 13, 1959; children: Eric Anthony, Scott Patrick, Ross Phillip. BS, Wayne State U., 1959; MS, Miami U., Oxford, Ohio, 1960; PhD, La. State U., 1966. Rsch. assoc. Coastal Studies Inst., La. State U., Baton Rouge, 1962-64; instr. dept. geography and dept. geology U. Miami, Coral Gables, Fla., 1964-65; asst. prof. geography U. Wis., Madison, 1965-69; assoc. prof. geography and geol. scis. Rutgers U., New Brunswick, NJ, 1969-73, prof., 1973—2002, chmn. dept. marine and coastal scis., 1991-99, prof. marine and coastal scis., geog., geol. scis., 1989—2002, dir. Marine Scis. Ctr., 1972-76, dir. Ctr. for Coastal and Environ. Studies, 1976-90; assoc. dir. Inst. Marine and Coastal Scis., New Brunswick, 1990—2002; prof. emeritus Rutgers U., 2002—; dir. Sandy Hook Coop. Programs, 2002—. Mem. sci. com. Thalassas, Vigo, Spain, 1985—; mem. geog. scis. com. US NRC, 2007—. Co-author: Living with the New Jersey Shore, 1986, Coastal Dunes, 1990, Coastal Hazard Management, 2002, Coastal Dune Ecology, 2004; mem. editl. bd. Coastal Mgmt., 1981—, Jour. Coastal Rsch., 1987—, Jour. of Coastal Conservation, 1996—; contbr. numerous articles to scholarly jours., chapters to books, monographs. Mem. Water Policy Bd., East Brunswick, NJ, 1981—83, N.J. Shoreline Adv. Bd., Trenton, 1984—86; chmn. N.J. Gov.'s Sea Level Rise Com., Trenton, 1987—90; mem. N.J. State Beach Erosion Commn., 1994—99. Recipient Disting. Pub. Svc. award Pres. Rutgers U. 1988, Mel Marcus Disting. Career award, 2003, Natural Resources Rsch. award North Atlantic Region, US Nat. Park Svc., 2006; named Natural Resources Scientist of Yr., US Nat. Pk. Svc., 2006; grantee NSF, Nat. Park Svc., EPA, Office Naval Rsch., Nat. Sea Grant Program, NOAA, 1961—, others. Mem.: AAAS, N.J. Acad. Sci. (pres. 1982), Internat. Geog. Union (editor newsletter 1984—96, vice chair commn. on coastal environment 1988—92, chmn. commn. on coastal systems 1992—96, editor newsletter 2002—), Coastal Soc. (pres. 1980—82), Assn. Am. Geographers (Honors award 1993), Profl. Assn. Volleyball Ofcls. (chair N.J. bd. 2000—). Avocations: gardening, reading. Office: Rutgers U Inst Marine & Coastal Scis 74 Magruder Rd Highlands NJ 07732 Office Phone: 732-708-1462.

PTACEK, WILLIAM H., library director; BA in English and Psychology, U. Ill., 1972; MLS, SUNY, Geneseo, 1974; cert. of advanced study, U. Ill., Chgo., 1979. Reference libr. South Br. Chgo. Pub. Libr., 1974-75, head libr. Mt. Greenwood br., 1975-76, head system-wide circulation, 1976-77, asst. dir. pers., 1977-78, chief NE dist., 1978-79; dir. Idaho Falls Pub. Libr., 1979-83, Louisville Free Pub. Libr., 1984-89, King County Libr. Sys., Wash., 1989—. Co-author: (with Peggy Sullivan) Public Libraries: Smart Practices in Personnel, 1982; contbr. articles to profl. jours. Mem.: Pub. Libr. Assn., Bellevue Rotary Club (pres. 2002—03). Office: King County Libr Sys 960 Newport Way NW Issaquah WA 98027-2702 Office Phone: 425-369-3232. E-mail: billp@kcls.org. *

PTAK, FRANK STANLEY, manufacturing executive; b. Chgo., Apr. 23, 1943; s. Frank J. and Stella R. (Los) P.; m. Karen M. Novoselsky, May 2, 1971; children: Jeffrey B., Jacquelyn F., Russell E. BSc, De Paul U., 1965. CPA, Ill. Sr. auditor Arthur Young & Co., Chgo., 1965-69; sr. rsch. cons. Kemper Fin. Svcs., Chgo., 1969-71; asst. sec., mgr. acquisitions Sara Lee Corp., Chgo., 1971-73, asst. treas., 1973-74, asst. to chmn., 1974, v.p. planning, 1974-75; bus. devel. mgr. ITW Conex, Des Plaines, Ill., 1975-77; mktg. mgr. ITW Shakeproof, Elgin, Ill., 1977-78, group pres., 1977-78, ITW Metal Components Cos., Glenview, Ill., 1978-91; exec. v.p. Global Automotive Components ITW Corp., Glenview, 1991-95, vice-chmn., 1996—2005; pres., CEO, The Marmon Group, Inc., Chgo., 2006—. Bd. dir. The Marmon Group, Morningstar Inc.; adv. coun. DePaul U. Coll. Commerce, Chgo., 1998. Patentee in field. Mem. AICPA, Assn. Corp. Growth, ITW Patent Soc., Econ. Club Chgo., Comml. Club Chgo., Executives CLub Chgo. Jewish. Home: 1415 Waverly Rd Highland Park IL 60035-3714 Office: The Marmon Group 181 W Madison Chicago IL 60602 Business E-Mail: fptak@itw.com. *

PTASHNE, MARK STEVEN, molecular biology professor; b. Chgo., June 5, 1940; s. Fred and Mildred P.; m. Lucy Gordon, 1994. BA, Reed Coll., 1961; PhD, Harvard U., 1968. Lectr. biochemistry Harvard U., Cambridge, Mass., 1968-71, prof., 1971—73, chmn. dept. biochemistry and molecular biology, 1980-83, Herchel Smith prof. of molecular biology, 1993-97; Ludwig prof. molecular biology Sloan Kettering Cancer Rsch. Ctr., NYC, 1997—. Feodor Lynen lectr. U. Miami, Fla., 1988. Author: A Genetic Switch, 1986; contbr. numerous articles to sci. jours. Recipient Eli Lilly award, 1975, prix. Charles-Leopold Mayer Acad. des Scis., Inst. de France, 1977, Louisa Gross Horwitz prize Bd. Trustees Columbia U., 1985, Gairdner Found. Internat. award, 1985, Albert Lasker award for Basic Med. Rsch., Lasker Found., 1997; co-recipient Ledle award Harvard U., 1986, GM Sloan prize, 1990. Fellow N.Y. Acad. Sci., Am. Acad. Sci.; mem. NAS, Fedn. Am. Scis. (bd. sponsors 1981). Avocations: opera, classical music, violin. Office: Sloan Kettering Cancer Rsch Ctr 1275 York Ave # New York NY 10021-6094

PTASYNSKI, HARRY, geologist, oil industry executive; b. Milw., May 26, 1926; s. Stanley S. and Frances V. (Stawicki) Ptasynski; m. Nola G. Whitestine, Sept. 15, 1951; children: Rosa F., Lisa Joy. BS, Stanford U., 1950. Cert. profl. geologist, petroleum geologist. Dist. geologist Pure Oil Co., Amarillo, Tex., 1951-55, Casper, Wyo., 1955-58; ind. geologist, oil prodr. Casper, 1958—. With USN, 1943—46, PTO. Mem.: Soc. Petroleum Engrs., Rocky Mountain Oil and Gas Assn. (bd. dirs., mem. exec. com. 1980—96), Ind. Petroleum Assn. Mountain States (v.p., bd. dirs. 1976—80), Ind. Petroleum Assn. Am. (v.p., bd. dirs. 1976—85), Am. Inst. Profl. Geologists, Am. Assn. Petroleum Geologists. Republican. Episcopalian. Avocations: tennis, trout and salmon fishing, western history, golf. Home: 1515 Brookview Dr Casper WY 82604-4895 Office: 123 W 1st St Ste 560 Casper WY 82601-2483 Office Phone: 307-234-8392. Business E-Mail: hptasyn@tribcsp.com.

PU, CALTON, computer scientist; BS in Physics, U. Sao Paulo, Brazil, 1978, BS in Computer Sci., 1979; MS, U. Wash., 1983, PhD, 1986. From asst. to assoc. prof. dept. computer sci. Columbia U., 1986-92; assoc. prof. dept. computer sci. and engring. Oreg. Grad. Inst. Sci. and Tech., Portland, 1993-96, prof. dept. computer sci. and engring., 1996-99; prof., John P. Imlay Jr. chair in software Ga. Inst. Tech., Atlanta, 1999—. Vis. rsch. scientist IBM T.J. Watson Rsch. Ctr., summer 1990-91; co-gen. chair

Internat. Conf. on Data Engring., 1997, co-PC chair, 1999; vice-chair Heterogeneous Sys. Interoperability, 1995, program com. 1993-95; program. com. Internat. Conf. on Partial Evaluation and Program Manipulation, 1997, Internat. Conf. on Distributed Computing Sys., 1989, 91, 93, 97; co-chair program com. Am. and Pacific Rim Internat. Symposium on Reliable Distributed Sys., 1995, 2003; presenter in field. Mem. editl. bd. Internat. Jour. Digital Libr., 1995—, Jour. Brazilian Computer Soc.; patentee apparatus and method for certifying the delivery of information. Grantee NSF, 1991—, DARPA, 1994—. Mem. ACM; sr. mem. IEEE; fellow AAAS. Office: Ga Inst Tech Coll of Computing 801 Atlantic Dr Atlanta GA 30332-0280 Office Phone: 404-385-1106. Business E-Mail: calton.pu@cc.gatech.edu.

PUCCINELLI, ANDREW JAMES, lawyer; b. Elko, Nev., July 21, 1953; BA cum laude, U. of the Pacific, 1975, JD, 1978. Bar: Nev. 1978. Ptnr. Puccinelli & Puccinelli, Elko, Nev., 1978—2002; dist. judge 4th Judicial Dist. Ct., 2002—. Bus. law adj. prof. No. Nev. C.C., 1982-93; legal advisor Nev. Home Health Svcs., 1980-88. Bd. dirs. Nev. Legal Svcs., 1986-93. Mem. ATLA, Nev. Trial Lawyers Assn., Nev. State Bar Assn. (bd. govs. 1993-2000, v.p. 1996-97, pres.-elect 1997-98, pres. 1998-99, No. Nev. disciplinary bd. 1988-93, CLE com. 1981-85), Elko County Bar Assn. (pres. 1985-86), Phi Delta Phi. Office: 4th Jud Dist Ct Elko County Cthse 571 Idaho St Elko NV 89801 Office Phone: 775-753-4602.

PUCCIO, THOMAS PHILLIP, lawyer; b. Bklyn., Sept. 12, 1944; s. Matthew and Jeanette Puccio; m. Carol L. Ziegler (div.); m. Kathy Puccio. BA, Fordham U., 1966, JD, 1969. Bar: N.Y. 1969, U.S. Ct. Appeals (2d cir.) 1970, D.C. 1982, U.S. Supreme Ct. 1982, U.S. Ct. Appeals (4th and 9th cirs.) 1993. Lawyer Office U.S. Atty. Ea. Dist. N.Y., 1969—76, chief criminal divsn., 1973—75; exec. asst. U.S. atty., 1975—76; chief U.S. Dept. Justice Organized Crime Strike Force (ea. dist.) NY, 1976—82; atty. Booth, Lipton & Lipton, NYC, 1982—83; ptnr. Fisher, Puccio & Wilker, 1983—85, Stroock & Stroock & Lavan, 1985—87, Milbank, Tweed, Hadley & McCloy, 1987—92; mem. Law Offices of Thomas P. Puccio, NYC, 1992—. Co-author (with Dan Collins): In the Name of the Law: Confessions of a Trial Lawyer, 1995. Mem.: Assn. Bar City N.Y., D.C. Bar, Fed. Bar Coun. Office: Law Offices of Thomas P Puccio 230 Park Ave Ste 301 New York NY 10169 E-mail: tpuccio@lotpp.com. *

PUCEL, ROBERT ALBIN, electronics engineer, researcher; b. Ely, Minn., Dec. 27, 1926; s. Joseph and Theresa (Francel) P.; m. Catherine Ann Silva, June 30, 1952; children: Robert W., James J., Valerie A., Marc R., David J. BS, MS, MIT, 1951, DSc, 1955. With rsch. div. Research div. Raytheon Co., Lexington, Mass., 1955-93, staff mem. microwave tube group, 1951-55, solid state physics group, 1955-65, project mgr. microwave semicondr. group, 1965-70, cons. to microwave semicondr. group, 1970-74, cons. scientist semicondr. group, 1974-93; pres. RCP Cons., Jewett City, Conn., 1994—. Editor: Monolithic Microwave Integrated Circuits, 1985; contbg. author: Advances in Electronics and Electron Physics, vol. 38, 1975, Gallium Arsenide Technology, 1985. Served with USNR, 1945-46. Recipient Excellence in Technology award, Raytheon, 1988. Fellow IEEE (life; Third Millenium medal, 2000); mem. Microwave Theory and Techniques Soc. (editl. rev. bd., nat. lectr. 1980-81, Microwave prize 1976, Microwave Career award, 1990, Microwave Pioneer award, 2005), Nat. Acad. Engring., Electron Devices Soc. Inventor low-distortion FET; co-inventor Spacistor, Overlay FET. Home and Office: RCP Cons 45 Vandy Dr Jewett City CT 06351 Office Phone: 860-376-1339. Personal E-mail: bobpucel@yahoo.com.

PUCHALSKI, CHRISTINA M., physician, medical educator; d. Anthony R. and Krystyna J. Puchalski. BS, UCLA, 1976, MA, 1977; MD, George Washington U., 1994. Rsch. chemist NIH, Bethesda, Md., 1977—84, adj. scientist, 1984—90; intern George Wash. U. Med. Ctr., 1994—95, resident in internal medicine/primary care, 1997—98, fellowship in primary care, 1997—98; dir. edn. NIHR (Nat. Inst. Healthcare Rsch.), Bethesda, Md., 1997—2001; dir., founder George Washington Inst. for Spirituality and Health, 2001—. Asst. prof. medicine George Washington U. Sch. Medicine, Washington, 1998—2003, assoc. prof. medicine and healthcare scis., clin. leadership and mgmt., 2003—. V.p. bd. dirs. Virginia Square Condo, Arlington, Va., 1999—2002, pres. bd. dirs., 2002—. Recipient Humanitarian in Medicine award, Pfizer-AAMC, 1999, John Templeton award, John Templeton Found., 2001—, Humanitarian award, N.J. Healthcare Found., 2002; grantee, NIH, 2002. Fellow: ACP. Roman Catholic. Avocations: piano, hiking. Office: George Washington Univ 2150 Pennsylvania Ave NW Washington DC 20037

PUCK, WOLFGANG, chef; b. St. Veit, Austria, July 8, 1949; m. Marie France, 1976 (div. 1979); m. Barbara Lazaroff, 1984 (div. Nov. 27, 2002); children: Cameron, Bryon; life ptnr. Gelila Assefa; 1 child, Oliver Wolfgang. Doctor of Culinary Arts (hon.), Johnson & Wales U., Providence, RI, 1998. Former chef Hotel de Paris, Monaco, Maxim's, Paris, L'Oustau de Baumanière, Provence; chef, part owner Ma Maison, LA, 1975—; exec. chef, ptnr. Spago, 1982—, Chinois on Main, Santa Monica, 1983—, Postrio, San Francisco, 1989—, Trattoria del Lupo, Las Vegas, 1989—, Granita, Malibu, Calif., 1991—, Spago Las Vegas, 1992—, Chinois Las Vegas, 1998—, Postrio Las Vegas, 1998—, Wolfgang Puck Bar & Grill, Las Vegas, 2004—, 20 21, Mpls., 2005—, Vert, Hollywood, Calif., CUT, Beverly Hills, Calif., 2006—; owner Wolfgang Puck Express, Wolfgang Puck Cafes, 1993—; owner, chef Wolfgang Puck Catering, 1998—; ptnr. Wolfgang Puck Worldwide, Inc., 2000—. Fund raising Meals on Wheels, A. Cancer Soc. LA; exec. chef Governor's Ball, The Oscars, 1995-, ptnr. with Humane Soc. US, factory farming animal welfare prog., 2007- Author: (cookbooks) Modern French Cooking for the American Kitchen, 1982, The Wolfgang Puck Cookbook: Recipes from Spago and Chinois, 1986, Adventures in the Kitchen with Wolfgang Puck, 1991, Pizza, Pasta and More!, 2000, Live, Love, Eat! The Best of Wolfgang Puck, 2002, Wolfgang Puck Makes It Easy, 2004, (newspaper columns) Wolfgang Puck's Kitchen, 2003-; producer (instructional cooking video) Spago Cooking with Wolfgang Puck; appeared in TV series Wolfgang Puck, 2001 (Daytime Emmy for Outstanding Service Show, 2004), Wolfgang Puck's Cooking Class, 2003-; actor: (guest appearances) (films) The Weather Man, 2005, (TV series) Who's the Boss?, 1987, Blossom, 1991, Tales from the Crypt, 1992, Ellen, 1996, Frasier, 2000, 2002, Good Morning Am., Late Night with David Letterman, Tonight Show with Jay Leno, Entertainment Tonight, Hollywood Squares, Wheel of Fortune, ABC News, CBS News, Politically Incorrect with Bill Maher, Las Vegas, 2006, (voice) The Simpsons, 2002. Founder Puck-Lazaroff Charitable Found., 1982—. Named Outstanding Chef of the Yr., James Beard Found., 1991; recipient Humanitarian of Yr. award, 1994, Bus. Statesman of Yr. award, Harvard Bus. Sch. of So. Calif., 2001, Smithfield Foods Outstanding Service award, James Beard Found., 2005. *

PUCKETT, CHARLES LINWOOD, plastic surgeon, educator; b. Burlington, NC, Oct. 19, 1940; s. Harry W. and Lula C. Puckett; m. Florence Elizabeth Loy, June 18, 1961 (div. 1976); children: Loy C., Lisa A., Leslie A.; m. Patricia Louise Wells, June 17, 1984 (div. 1994); 1 child, Harry James; m. Teresa G. Teel, Nov. 24, 1995. Student, Elon Coll., 1959—62; MD, Wake Forest Coll., 1966. Diplomate in plastic surgery and surgery of the hand Am. Bd. Plastic Surgery, Am. Bd. Surgery. Intern Duke U., Durham, NC, 1966—67, jr. asst. resident gen. and thoracic surgery, 1967—68, sr. asst. resident gen. surgery, 1968—70, chief resident, instr. surgery, 1970—71, fellow gen. and thoracic surgery, 1971—72, asst. resident plastic surgery, 1973—75, instr., chief resident plastic surgery, 1975—76; fellow hand surgery U. Louisville Hosps., 1974; assoc. prof. plastic surgery U. Mo. Health Scis. Ctr., 1976—80, prof. plastic surgery, 1980—, vice chmn. dept. surgery, 1986—. Instr. surgery Duke Hosp., 1970—72, assoc. surgery, 1972—73. Contbr. articles to profl. jours. Maj. US Army, 1971—76. Fellow: ACS (gov. 1991—97, Mo. chpt.); mem.: AMA, So. Med. Assn., Plastic Surgery Rsch. Coun., Plastic Surgery Ednl. Found., Lipolysis Soc. N.Am. Inc., Internat. Microsurgical Soc., Assn. Acad. Chmn. Plastic Surgery (bd. dirs. 1985—87, pres.-elect 1986—87, pres. 1987—88), Am. Trauma Soc., Am. Soc. Plastic Surgeons, Inc. (bd. dirs. member-at-large 1985—88, asst. sec. 1988—89, trustee 1989—92, 2003—, chmn. bd. trustees 1991—92, parliamentarian 1992—93, historian 1994—95, sec. 1995—97, v.p. 1997—98, pres.-elect 1998—99, pres. 1999—2000, Spl. Hon. Citation 2002), Am. Soc. Surgery of the Hand, Am. Soc. for Aesthetic Plastic Surgery, Inc. (bd. dirs. 1989—2000, traveling prof. 2002), Am. Cleft Palate Assn., Am. Bd. Plastic Surgery (dir. 1988—94, chmn. 1993—94), Am. Assn. Plastic Surgeons (trustee 1995—98), Am. Assn. Hand Surgery (bd. dirs. 1982—84, 1990, 1991, v.p. 1986—87, pres.-elect 1987—88, pres. 1988—89, parliamentarian 1992), Alpha Omega Alpha, Sigma Xi. Republican. Avocation: cattle and horse farming. Office: Univ Mo Divsn Plastic Surgery One Hospital Dr Columbia MO 65212

PUCKETT, ELIZABETH ANN, law librarian, educator; b. Evansville, Ind., Nov. 10, 1943; d. Buell Charles and Lula Ruth (Gray) P.; m. Joel E. Hendricks, June 1, 1964 (div. June 1973); 1 child, Andrew Charles; m. Thomas A. Wilson, July 19, 1985. BS in Edn., Eastern Ill. U., 1964; JD, U. Ill., 1977, MS in L.S., 1977. Bar: Kans. 1978, Ill. 1979. Acquisitions/reader services librarian U. Kans. Law Library, Lawrence, 1978-79; asst. reader services librarian So. Ill. U. Law Library, Carbondale, 1979-81, reader services librarian, 1981-83; assoc. dir. Northwestern U. Law Library, Chgo., 1983-86, co-acting dir., 1986-87; dir./assoc. prof. South Tex. Coll. Law Library, Houston, 1987-89; dir./prof. South Tex. Coll. Law Libr., Houston, 1990-94, U. Ga. Law Libr., Athens, 1994—. Co-author: Evaluation of System-Provided Library Services to State Correctional Centers in Illinois, 1983; co-editor Uniform Commercial Code: Confidential Drafts, 1993. Mem. ABA, Am. Assn. Law Librs. (mem. exec. bd. 1993-96). Avocations: reading, antiques. Office: U Georgia Law Libr Athens GA 30602-6018 Office Phone: 706-542-5078. E-mail: apuckett@uga.edu.

PUCKETT, MARY ALICE, primary school educator, consultant; d. Bernard Louis and Alida Josepha Stork; m. Gary Michael Puckett, Dec. 27, 1981; 1 child, Sean. BS in Edn., North Tex. State U., 1976; MA in Edn., Tex. Wesleyan U., 1989. Cert. tchr. Tex. State Bd. Edn. 1st grade tchr.-Hill Arlington (Tex.) Ind. Sch. Dist., 1977—2000, 1st grade tchr.-Amos, 2000—01, 1st grade tchr.-Goodman, 2001—03, 1st grade tchr.-Pope, 2003—. Author: (video) It Takes Two Mainstreaming, 1989 (Ptnrs. in Mainstreaming award, 1990), (booklet) The Happy Teacher Campaign, 2000. Vol. Riding Unlimited, Keller, Tex., 1991; ednl. cons. Met. Adventist Cmty. Svc., Grand Prairie, Tex., 2000. Mem.: Courage to Teach. Avocations: reading, travel, writing. Home: 1901 Montana Trail Grand Prairie TX 75052 Personal E-mail: thtc@sbcglobal.net.

PUCKETT, RICHARD EDWARD, artist, consultant, former recreation executive; b. Klamath Falls, Oreg., Sept. 9, 1932; s. Vernon Elijah P., Leona Belle (Clevenger) P.; m. Velma Faye Hamrick, Apr. 14, 1957 (dec. 1985); children: Katherine Michelle Briggs, Deborah Alison Bolinger, Susan Lin Rowland, Gregory Richard. Student, So. Oreg. Coll. Edn., 1951—56, Lake Forest Coll., 1957—58, Hartnell Jr. Coll., 1960—70; BA, U. San Francisco, 1978. Acting arts and crafts dir., Ft. Leonard Wood, Mo., 1956-57; arts and crafts dir., asst. spl. svcs. officer, mus. dir. Ft. Sheridan, Ill., 1957-59; arts and crafts dir. Ft. Irwin, Calif., 1959-60, Ft. Ord, Calif., 1960-86; dir. arts and crafts br. Art Gallery, Arts and Crafts Ctr. Materials Sales Store, 1960; opening dir. Presidio Monterey Army Mus., 1968; dir. Model Army Arts and Crafts Program. One-man shows include Seaside City Hall, 1967—86, 2002, Ft. Ord Arts and Crafts Ctr. Gallery, 1967, 1973, 1979, 1981, 1984, 1986, Presidio of Monterey Art Gallery, Del Messa Gallery, Carmel, Calif., 1998, So. Oreg. Art Gallery, Medford, 2000, Country Rose Gallery, Hollister, Calif., 2001—03, Walter Avery Gallery Seaside City Hall, 2002, Sasoontsi Gallery, Salinas, Calif., 2004, also pvt. collections, designed and opened first Ft. Sheridan Army Mus., Presidio of Monterey Mus., exhibited in group shows at Salinas Valley Art Gallery, Glass on Holiday, Gatlinburg, Tenn., 1981—82, Internat. Congress on Arts and Comm., 1997, Del Messa Gallery, 2001—06. Donated over 4000 photographs, slides, paintings, arts and crafts to U. Monterey Bay; donated photo collection, art slides and books to Hartnell Jr. Coll. Recipient 1st pl. Dept. Army and US Army Forces Command awards for programming and publicity, 1979-81, 83-85 (exhibited in Smithsonian), 1st and 3d pl. sculpture awards Monterey County Fair Fine Arts Exhibit, 1979, Comdrs. medal civilian svcs., 1986, Golden Acad. award, Internat. Man of Yr. award, 1991-92, Champion of Arts-Friend of Arts Spl. Tribute award Art Coun. Monterey County, 2007, Spl. Congl. Recognition cert. Salimos City Coun., 2007, others. Mem.: Internat. Soc. Acrylic Painters, Ft. Ord Alumni Assn., Salinas Valley Art Assn. (pres. 2000—), Monterey Peninsula Art Mus. Assn. Home: 210 San Miguel Ave Salinas CA 93901-3021

PUCKETT, RUBY PARKER, nutritionist, food service executive, writer; b. Dora, Ala., Nov. 26, 1932; d. John Franklin Parker and Ethel V. (Short) Tuggle; m. Larry Willard Puckett, July 2, 1955; children: Laurel Lynn Puckett Brown, Hollie Kristina Puckett Walker. BS in Food and Nutrition, Auburn U., Ala., 1954; postgrad. in vocat. edn., U. Fla., 1970-80; MA in Health Sci. Edn., Cen. Mich. U., 1976. Registered dietitian, foodservice adminstr., food svc. exec., military traveller. Dietetic intern Henry Ford Hosp., Detroit, 1955; staff dietitian VA Hosp., Houston, 1955-56; dietitian Matty Hersee Hosp., Meridian, Miss., 1957-58; asst. dir. U. Miss. Med. Ctr., Jackson, 1960-61; dir. dietetics Ft. Sanders Presbyn. Hosp., Knoxville, Tenn., 1961-63, Waterman Meml. Hosp., Eustis, Fla., 1963-68; dir. food and nutrition U. Fla. Shands Hosp., Gainesville, 1968-95; pres. Square One Cons. Service, Gainesville, 1979-85; pres., owner Food Svc. Mgmt. Cons., 1995—. Adv. com. on jr. coll. dietetic programs Fla. Dept. Edn., 1967-69; nominating com. Southeastern Hosp. Conf. for Dietitians, 1969, sec., 1974-75; pres. Field Agy. Nutrition, 1970; instr. U. Fla., 1972-73, 82-85, clin. and cmty. coordinated undergrad. dietetic program adv. bd., 1974-89; instr. Santa Fe Jr. Coll., Gainesville, 1977-81; adv. com. Marquis Libr. Soc., Inc., 1974; health project rev. com. North Ctrl. Fla. Planning Coun., 1974-76; named to White House Conf. on Food and Nutrition, 1976, Senate Select Com. on Food and Nutrition, 1976; com. on animal products NRC Adv. Bd. on Mil. Pers. Supplies, 1978-81; site evaluator dietetic programs in colls and univs., 1998-; mem. Commn. on Accrediation Dietetic Edn., 1997-, program reviewer for dietary mgr. tng., 2003-06; reviewer abstracts, articles Jour. Am. Dietetic Assn.; spkr. in field. Author: Food Service Manual for Health Care Institutions, 1988 (Jim Rose Pub.award, 2005), 3d edit., 2004, Basic Nutrition and Diet Modification Shands Hospital, 1992, revised edit., 2002, Managing Foodservice Operations, 1992, HACCP The Future Challenge, 4th edit., Nutrition Diet Modification Meal Patterns, 4th edit., Disaster and Emergency Preparedness for Food Service Operations, 2003, Dietary Managers Course by Correspondence, 12th edit., Nutrition for the Elderly, Safety, Sanitation and Security for Food Service Operation, Topics in Practice: Productivity Measures for Food Service Operations, 2005; mem. editl. adv. com.: Stokes Report, 1980—84, editl. advisor: Food Management, 1986—, Topics in Clinical Nutrition, 1988—, Aspen's Focus, 1984—91, Aspen's Hosp. Nutrition and Foodservice Forms; editl. advisor Marketlink, 2006; contbr. articles to profl. jours.; developer nutrition and older adult distance edn.course. V.p. Campus USA Credit Union, 1980—81, pres.-elect, 1981—82; chmn. Shands Hosp. chpt. United Way, 1978, mem. speakers bur., 1985—86; profl. adv. bd. Shands Home Care; vol. Mothers Supporting Daus. with Breast Cancer, 2000—; mem. Sexual Phys. Abuse Bd.; courtesy faculty appt. Divsn Youth, Family and Ext.; election clk., inspector Alachua County (Fla.) Elections, 2000—06; bd. dir. Campus USA Credit Union, 1978—, chmn. bd., 1998—2000; mem. budget and allocations com. United Way, 1983—2005; mem. adv. bd. Harvest Gainesville, 1991—93, Children's Miracle Telethon, 1992—95; adv. bd. Sta. WRUF Pub. Radio, 1992; bd. dir. Fla. 4-H Found., 2000—04, North Fla. Regional Vocat. Sch. Named Alumni of Yr., Auburn U. Sch. Home Econs., 1985, Disting. Woman, Alachua County, Fla., 1992; named to Woodlawn H.S. Hall of Fame, 1982, Fla. Women's Hall of Fame, 1986; recipient Community Leader award, Sta. WRUF-FM, 1972, Ivy award, Restauranteurs of Distinction, 1980, Disting. Pace Setter award, Roundtable for Women in Foodservice, 1984, Award of Distinction, Sch. Human Svc., Auburn U., 1991. Mem.: Food Svc. Consultants Internat. Soc. (N.Am. divsn. bd. trustees 2006—, program planning com. 2007, Silver Plate award 1978), Fla. Coun. on Aging (sec. nutrition sect. 1974—76, chmn. 1974—76, adv. bd. 1974—76), Nat. U. Continuing Edn. Assn. (disting. ind. study course 1986, 1989), Nutrition Edn. Soc. (liaison with industry com. 1974, legis. com. 1974, charter), Dietary Mgr. Assn. Found. Fla. (steering com., Disting. Svc. award 2005, 2006), Am. Soc. Hosp. Food Service Adminstrs. (edn. com. 1968—71, nomination com. 1978, chmn. publ. com. 1981—82, chmn. legis. com. 1984, adv. bd. Trends 2006, task force HACCP cert., Jim Rose Pub. award 2005), Gainesville Dietetic Assn. (v.p. 1969, pres. 1970, 1976), Fla. Dietetic Assn. (sec. 1968—70, pres. 1973—74, del. 1980—87, chmn. by-laws com. 1985, numerous other offices), Am. Dietetic Assn. (house of delegates 1981—85, pres. practice group 41 1982—84, area III coord. 1985—88, chair DPG41 Area III Found. 1988—91, chair practice group mgmt. in food and nutrition svc. 2001, hons. award com. 2005, emergency task force 2006—07, chmn. stds. of profl. practice, Excellence in Mgmt. Practice award 1994, Medallion for Profl. Cmty. and Career Achievement 1996, Marjorie Hulsizer Copher award 2003), The Athenaeum Soc., Internat. Gold and Silver Plate Soc. (sec. bd. trustees 1983—85), Ivy Soc., Altrusa, Pi Lambda Beta, Kappa Sigma Phi. Democrat. Mem. Lds Ch. Avocations: whitewater rafting, hiking, gardening. Office: 5200 NW 43d St Ste 102-302 Gainesville FL 32606 Office Phone: 352-371-6160. Personal E-mail: puckerp@juno.com.

PUDDY, WILLIAM (BILL) CURTISS, retired military officer, not-for-profit developer; s. Harry Curtiss and Lee Puddy; m. Laryn Gail Puddy, Oct. 7, 1972; children: Karel Marie Decker, Steffany Lyn, Alan Curtiss. BS, US Mil. Acad., West Point, NY, 1972; MS in Systems Mgmt., U. So. Calif., LA, 1982; Resident Grad. Diploma, US Army War Coll., Carlisle Barracks, Pa., 1994. Lic. Life, Health, Annuities, Property and Casualty, Long Term Care ins. Va. Bur. Ins., 2005; cert. investment advisor Series 65 Nat. Securities Administrators Assn., 2004. Commd. 2d lt. US Army, 1972, advanced through grades to col., 1995, comdr. Co. B 9th Tng. Bn. Ft. Lewis, Wash., 1976, comdr. Co. A 1st Bn. 7th Inf. Aschaffenburg, Germany, 1977—79, com. chief and comdr. light weapons com. Co. C infantry tng. group Ft. Benning, Ga., 1984—85, comdr. 5th Bn. 10th Inf. Regiment Ft. Leonard Wood, Mo., 1990—92, comdt. Inst. for Profl. Devel., Tng. Support Ctr. Ft. Eustis, Va., 1996—2000, chief of staff mil. dist. Washington Washington, 2000—02, ret., 2002; registered rep. and agt. First Command Fin. Planning, Woodbridge, 2002—05; exec. dir., sec., treas. Emmanuel Farms Outreach, Inc., Lonaconing, Md., 2005—. Sound ministry Cornerstone Bapt. Ch., Cumberland, Md., 2007; youth soccer and baseball coach Army Dependent Youth Activities, Forts Benning, Detrick, Leonard Wood, 1986—92. Decorated Nat. Defense medal with two stars Dept. Defense, Ga. Commendation medal Ga. Dept. of Def., Legion of Merit Hdqs., Tng. and Doctrine Command, US Army Mil. Dist. Wash.; recipient Primicerius level, Order of St. Maurice medal, Nat. Inf. Assn., 1972—2002, Army Commendation medal, 9th Infantry divsn., 1976, Meritorious Svc. medal, US Army Europe, 3rd Infantry divsn., 1980, Combined Arms Ctr., 1983, Infantry Sch. Ft. Benning, 1986, Army Staff, DCS Ops., 1988, Engr. Sch., Ft. Leonard Wood, 1992, 24th Infantry divsn., 1993, Army Tng. Support Ctr., 2000, Army Achievement medal, 29th Infantry Regiment, 1985, Bronze level, Order of de Fleury medal, US Army Engr. Rgt., 1990—92, Defense Meritorious Svc. medal, Joint Staff, 1990, Distance Learning XXI Contract award, Joint Svc. Commendation medal, HQ NATO Stabilization Force, Bosnia, 1999, Svc. medal, Dept. Army, 1980, Armed Forces Expeditionary medal, 1999, Global War on Terrorism Svc. medal, 2001, Overseas Ribbon, 1980, NATO medal, 1999, Army Superior Unit medal, 2000, Expert Infantry badge, Joint Staff Badge, Army Staff badge, Cold War cert., Dept. Defense, 2000, Ga. Commendation medal, State Ga., Dept. Defense, Mil. divsn., HQ 48th Brigade, Ga. Nat. Guard, 1993, Joint Meritorious medal, Joint Staff, Pentagon, 1990. Mem.: Nat. Soccer Coaches Assn. Am., U. So. Calif. Trojan Family Assn., Nat. Inf. Assn., Non-Commd. Officers Assn. Am. (hon.), Assn. Grads. US Mil. Acad. (life), Army War Coll. Alumni Assn. (life), Mil. Officers' Assn. Am. (life). Independent. Achievements include development of National Training Center Instrumentation System. Avocations: soccer, leadership and management science, music, martial arts, history. Office: Emmanuel Farms Outreach Inc 1054 Pea Ridge Rd Lonaconing MD 21539

PUDLIN, HELEN POMERANTZ, lawyer; d. George and Claire Pomerantz; m. David B. Pudlin, Dec. 23, 1973; children: Alexander R., Julia H. BA cum laude, U. Pa., 1970, MS, 1971, JD, 1974. Bar: Pa. 1974. Lectr. U. Pa. Law Sch., 1983-87; asssoc. Ballard, Spahr, Andreas & Ingersoll, Phila., 1974-81, ptnr., 1981-89; gen. counsel Provident Nat. Bank, Phila., 1989-93; sr. v.p., dep. gen. counsel PNC Fin. Corp., Pitts., 1992-93; sr. v.p., mng. gen. counsel PNC Bank Corp., Pitts., 1993; sr. v.p., gen. counsel The PNC Fin. Svc. Group, Pitts., 1993—. Speaker in field. Author: (with others) Review of Antitrust Laws and Procedures, 1983, Criminal Antitrust Litigation Manual, 1983, Pennsylvania Medical Society Handbook, 1989; co-author: Joint Ventures in Healthcare. Former mem. Bd. of Ethics City of Phila.; former mem. bd. dirs. Phila. Facilities Mgmt. Corp.; bd. advisors Pub. Interest Law Ctr. Phila.; former mem. bd. overseers U. Pa.; bd. trustees Wistar Inst. Mem. ABA (antitrust sect., litigation sect., bus. law sect.), Pa. Bar Assn. (former mem. ho. of dels., judiciary com.), Phila. Bar Assn. (bd. govs. 1989-91, fed. cts. com., bus. law sect.), Acad. Natural Scis. (former bd. dirs., trustee), Duquesne Club. Office: The PNC Fin Svc Group 249 5th Ave Pittsburgh PA 15222-2709

PUDLO, STEVEN EDWARD, computer technician; s. Chester Joseph and Mary Ann Pudlo; life ptnr. Linda Sue Jacobsen; 1 child, Julia Briggs. AS in Data Processing, Thames Valley State Tech. Coll., Norwich, Conn., 1982; BS in Computer Sci., Ea. Conn. State U., Willimantic, Conn., 1985—86; AS in Indsl. Mgmt., Three Rivers CC, Norwich, 1986—87; MBA, Rensselaer Polytech, Hartford, Conn., 1992—95. Asst dir. IT Three Rivers CC, 1985—. Contbr. book. Sec. Ancient Accepted Scottich Rite, Preston, Conn., 1998—2006; mem. Norwich Rep. Town Com., 1990—94; master Somerset-St. James Lodge #34, Preston, 2000—03. Mem.: Masonic Motorcycle Assn. Australia, Patriot Guard Riders, Masonic Motorcycle Club, Internat. R-Consevative. Avocations: motorcycling, travel. Home: 59 Saint Regis Ave Norwich CT 06360 Office: Three Rivers CC 574 New London Turnpike Norwich CT 06360 Home Phone: 860-908-0512. Office Fax: 860-886-4960. Business E-Mail: spudlo@trcc.commnet.edu.

PUENTE, AUDREY, meteorologist; b. NYC; d. Tito Puente. BA, Syracuse U.; attended, Hunter Coll.; M in Meteorology, Mississippi State U. Prodn. asst. WNYW, 1993—94; weekday weather anchor WJCL-TV, Savannah, Ga.; weekend weather anchor WXVT-TV, Greenville, Miss., 1998—99; weekend meteorologist WAPT-TV, Jackson, Miss., WNBC Channel 4, 1999—2003; meteorologist WCBS Channel 2, 2003—07; chief weather anchor WWOR My9, 2007—. Hon. mem. jr. advisory bd. Com. Hispanic Children and Families. Mem.: Nat. Weather Assn., Am. Meteorological Soc., Nat. Assn. Hispanic Journalists. Office: My9 WWOR-TV 9 Broadcast Plz Secaucus NJ 07096

PUEPPKE, GLENN HOWARD, farmer, agricultural products executive; b. Amenia, ND, Apr. 12, 1927; s. Howard Monroe and Malinda Wilmelmina (Judisch) Pueppke; m. Ruth Bernice Kleinjasser, Sept. 19, 1965; children: Howard, Clinton; m. Letha Pauline Mitchell (dec.); children: Steven, David, Eric. Student, Concordia Coll., Moorhead, Minn., 1945—46, U. Okla., Oklahoma City, 1947, NY U., NYC, 1974—77. Owner, mgr. Pueppke Farms, Erie, ND, 1950—2007. Salesman G&G Transport Co., 1947—78; co-founder, pres. Arkota Industries Inc., 1978—84; pres. PAI Internat. Inc., 1980—82, Pan African Contractors, Inc., 1980—82; cons. agr. tech., 1975—2007; chmn., CEO Pan Asia Corp., 1990—; pres., CEO Pent-Asia Internat. Inc., 1997—98; bd. dirs. Met. Energy Sys. Inc., 1998—; v.p. project planning Frontier Fuels, Cin., 2005—. Mem. ND Rep. Party; founder, assoc. mem. Dollars for Scholars. Recipient Rerd Lantern award, Minnkota Power Coop, 1993. Mem.: NRA (life), Internat. Trade Assn. (past pres., past bd. dirs.), Fraternal Order of Eagles, N.Am. Hunting Club (life). Republican. Methodist. Avocations: coin collecting/numismatics, archaeology. Home: 2490 147th Ave SE Erie ND 58029

PUESCHEL, SIEGFRIED M., pediatrician, educator; b. Waldenburg, Germany, July 28, 1931; came to U.S., 1961; naturalized, 1971; widowed. Student, Braunschweig Coll., Germany, 1953-55, Leibniz Coll., Tubingen, Germany, 1955-56, U. Tubingen, Germany, 1955-57, Free U., Berlin, 1957-58, U. Freiburg, Germany, 1958; MD summa cum laude, Med. Acad., Dusseldorf, Germany, 1960; MPH, Harvard U., 1967; PhD, U. R.I., 1985; JD, So. New Eng. Sch. Law, 1996. Diplomate Am. Bd. Pediatrics, Am. Bd. Med. Genetics. Intern Mercer Hosp., Trenton, NJ, 1961-62; jr. resident in pediatrics Children's Hosp., Honolulu, 1962-63; asst. resident in pediatrics Children's Hosp. Med. Ctr., Boston, 1963-64, asst. in mental retardation, 1967-68, assoc. in mental retardation, 1968-75, dir. Down Syndrome Program, 1970-75, dir. PKU Clinic, 1972-75; sr. resident in pediatrics Montreal Children's Hosp., 1964-65, fellow in biochemical genetics/metabolism, 1965-66; assoc. physician R.I. Hosp., Providence, 1975-79, dir. child devel. ctr., 1975-94, dir. PKU and Amino Acid Program, 1975—, dir. Down Syndrome Program, 1978—, physician, 1979—. Instr. pediatrics Harvard U., Cambridge, Mass., 1968-74, asst. prof. in pediatrics, 1974-75, lectr. in pediatrics, 1975—; asst. prof. in pediatrics Brown U., Providence, 1975-77, assoc. prof. in pediatrics, 1977-85, prof. in pediatrics, 1985—; consulting pediatrician Waltham (Mass.) Hosp., 1968-75; cons. in genetics Lying in Hosp., Boston, 1969-75, Women and Infants Hosp., Providence, 1975—; cons. Devel. Evaluation Clinic Children's Hosp. Med. Ctr., Boston, 1975—; mem. prevention of mental retardation com. Internat. League of Socs. for Persons with Mental Handicaps; mem. rsch., prevention and program svc. com. Assn. for Retarded Citizens U.S.; mem. nat. conf. on rsch. perspectives in down syndrome Nat. Inst. Child Health and Rehab. Svcs.; mem. state-of-the-art conf. on down syndrome Office Spl. Edn. and Rehab. Svcs. U.S. Dept. Edn.; mem. nat. adv. child health and human devel. coun. NIH, Washington; mem. sub-com. on tng., edn. and quality assurance-tech. assistance Devel. Disabilities Coun., R.I.; mem. med. adv. com. Spl. Olympics. Author chpts. to books; mem. editl. bd. Down Syndrome Papers and Abstracts for Profls., Exceptional Parents, Down's Syndrome: Rsch. and Practice; reviewer numerous jours.; contbr. articles to profl. jours. Grantee Mass. Dept. Health, 1968, Vigneron Meml. Fund, 1984-85, Charlotte Taylor Fund, 1985-86, Dept. Health and Human Svcs., 1982-86, March of Dimes Nat. Found., 1987-89, Sigma-Tau Pharm., Inc., 1990-93; recipient Reconngnition award March of Dimes, 1976, Recognition award Blackstone Valley chpt. R.I. Assn. for Retarded Citizens, 1979, Fogarty Founders award, 1988, Edn. award Muscular Dystrophy Assn., 1985, 86, Muscular Dystrophy Tchg. award, 1988, Recognition award Devel. Ctr. for Handicapped Personsn-Utah State U., 1986, Down Syndrome Assn. of Greater Cin. award, 1986, Colegion John Langdown Down award Mexico City, 1987, Disting. Rsch. award Assn. for Retarded Citizens of U.S., 1990, Conn. Down Syndrome Assn. award, 1991, Sindrome de Down award Asociación Down de Monterrey (Mexico), 1994. Fellow Am. Acad. Pediatrics, Am. Coll. Med. Genetics (founder); mem. AAAS, Am. Assn. Mental Retardation (Profl. Contbn. award 1991), Am. Acad. Cerebral Palsy and Devel. Medicine, Am. Pediatric Soc., Am. Soc. Human Genetics, Nat. Down Syndrome Congress (past pres., Recognition for Disting. Svc. award 1980, Mid-Hudson Valley award 1983, Achievement in Rsch. award 1988, Outstanding Physician award 1991), N.Y. Acad. Sci., R.I. Med. Soc., New Eng. Regional Genetics Group, Soc. Inherited Metabolic Disorders, Down Syndrome Soc. R.I. (award 1985), Assn. for Children with Down Syndrome (bd. dirs.). Office: RI Hosp Child Devel Ctr 593 Eddy St Providence RI 02903-4923 Office Phone: 401-444-8477.

PUFFER, JAMES C., sports medicine physician, educator, medical association administrator; married. BS, UCLA, MD, 1976. Prof., chief, divsn. family medicine UCLA; prof., family medicine Univ. Ky., Lexington; exec. dir., sec. Am. Bd. Family Medicine, Lexington, Ky., 2003—05, pres., CEO, 2005—. Physician US Winter Olympic Team, Sarajevo, 1984; head team physician US Summer Olympic Team, Seoul, 1988; mem., sports medicine, sports sci. coun. US Olympic Com., 1985—92; com. mem. NCAA Com. on Competitive Safeguards and Med. Aspects of Sports, 1983—90; cons. Pres. Coun. on Physical Fitness and Sports, 1988—90. Assoc. editor Medicine and Science in Sports and Exercise, 1989—98, editor-in-chief Sports Medicine Digest, 1992—, editl. bd. mem., peer reviewer numerous profl. jours. Recipient Duke Paoa Kahanamoku award, USA Water Polo, 2004. Fellow: Am. Coll. Sports Medicine; mem.: US Olympic Sports Medicine Soc. (bd. dir. 1993—96), Am. Med. Soc. for Sports Medicine (pres. 1996—97, founding mem.), Am. Bd. Family Medicine (bd. dir. 1989—94, exec. com. mem.-at-large 1993—94, v.p. bd. dir. 1993—94). Avocation: water polo. Office: ABFM 2228 Young Dr Lexington KY 40505-4294 Office Phone: 859-269-5626. Business E-Mail: jpuffer@theabfm.org.

PUFFER, RICHARD JUDSON, retired college chancellor; b. Chgo., Aug. 20, 1931; s. Noble Judson and Lillian Katherine (Olson) P.; m. Alison Foster Cope, June 28, 1952; children— Lynn, Mark, Andrew. Ph.B., Ill. Wesleyan U., 1953; MS in Edn, Ill. State U., 1962; PhD (Roy Clark Meml. scholar), Northwestern U., 1967. Asst. plant supt. J.A. Olson Co., Winona, Miss., 1957-59; tchr. Leroy Community Unit Dist. (Ill.), 1959-60; tchr., prin. Community Unit, Dist. 7, Lexington, Ill., 1960-62; asst. county supt. schs. Cook County, Ill., 1962-65; dean arts and scis. Kirkwood Community Coll., Cedar Rapids, Iowa, 1967-69; v.p. Black Hawk Coll., Moline, Ill., 1969-77, pres., 1977-82, chancellor, 1982-87; pres. The Ark Computer Ctr., 1989-92. Dir. W. Ctrl. Ill. Ednl. TV Corp., Springfield, Ill., 1977-87; cons. examiner North Central Assn., 1978-87. Editor: Cook County Ednl. Digest, 1962-65. Bd. dirs. Cedar Rapids Symphony, 1967-69, United Way of Rock Island and Scott Counties, Ill., 1978-80, Unitarian Universalist Dist. of Mich., 1995-98; bd. dirs., sec. West Shore Unitarian Universalist Congregation, 1996-99; sec., treas. Ill. Ednl. Retirement Cts., 1987-91; vice-chmn. Illini Hosp. Bd., 1988-93, chmn., 1993-95; bd. dirs. Illowa coun. Boy Scouts Am., 1979-83, v.p., 1981-83. With USNR, 1953-57. Mem. Rotary (pres. 1975-76, East Moline, Ill.), Green Medallion, Blue Key, Phi Delta Kappa, Pi Gamma Mu. Home and Office: 6191 Grace Ave Ludington MI 49431-8629

PUGH, ARTHUR JAMES (JAY PUGH), retired retail executive; b. Glen Morrison, W.Va., Sept. 24, 1937; s. Arthur James and Mary Pugh; m. Sharon Hubacher, Sept. 26, 1961; children: James Gregory, Mary Elizabeth. BSBA, W.Va. U., 1959; Master of Retailing, U. Pitts., 1960. Mgmt. trainee, buyer Woodward & Lothrop, Washington, 1960-71, v.p., 1971-77, sr. v.p., 1977-80, exec. v.p., 1980-87, Coun. of Better Bus. Bur., Arlington, Va., 1987-90, bd. dir.; cons., bd. dir. Fairfax, Va., 1990—. Trustee, chmn. audit com. Calvert Mut. Funds, Washington, 1983—; bd. dirs. Acacia Capital Corp., Washington; bd. dirs., exec. com. compensation com., chmn. investment com. Acacia Fed. Savs. Bank, Falls Church, Va. Chmn. bd. dirs Better Bus. Bur. Met. Washington, 1987. Mem. Rotary Found. of Washington (pres. 1990-91), Nat. Retail Mchts. Assn. (bd. dirs. 1986), W.Va. U. Alumni Assn. (bd. dirs. 1993-98), Fairfax Country Club (bd. dirs. 1990-92), Rotary Club of Washington (Rotarian of Yr. 1982, pres. 1984). Republican. Presbyterian. Avocations: golf, skiing, swimming. Home and Office: 4823 Prestwick Dr Fairfax VA 22030-4533 Home Phone: 763-385-8879; Office Phone: 703-385-1312. Personal E-mail: jaypugh@prodigy.net.

PUGH, CARLA M., surgeon, educator; b. Oakland, Calif., Feb. 3, 1966; d. Tillman and Helen (Abram) Pugh; m. Joseph D. Towles, Aug. 16. BA, U. Calif., Berkeley, 1988; MD, Howard U., Washington, 1992; PhD, Stanford U., Calif., 2001. Surg. intern Howard U. Hosp., 1992—93, resident in surgery, 1993—97; staff surgeon Kaiser Med. Group, Redwood City, Calif., 1998—2003; rsch. assoc. Stanford U. Sch. Med., 2002—03; assoc. dir., asst. prof. edn. and surgery Northwestern U., Chgo., 2003—; staff surgeon Chgo. VA Westside, 2004—. Office: Galter 10-105 201 E Huron St Chicago IL 60611-3197 Office Phone: 312-695-0641.

PUGH, DAVID L., manufacturing executive; b. Lynchburg, Va. m. Barbara Pugh; 2 children. BSEE, Duke U. Former chief mktg. officer, v.p. and gen. mgr. power equipment bus. unit Square D Co.; former plant mgr., v.p. constrn. sales Westinghouse Electric Corp.; sr. v.p. indsl control group Rockwell Automation, 1994-99; pres., COO Applied Indsl. Technologies, Cleve., 1999-2000, chmn., CEO, 2000—. Bd. dir. J.L.G. Industries, R.W. Beckett Corp. Office: Applied Indsl Technologies 1 Applied Plz 3301 Euclid Ave Cleveland OH 44115 *

PUGH, DOROTHY GUNTHER, performing company executive; b. Memphis, May 8, 1951; Grad. magna cum laude, Vanderbilt U., 1973; studied with Raymond Clay, studied with Donna Carver, studied with David Howard; student, Royal Acad. Dancing, London. Founder Ballet Memphis, 1985, also artistic dir., 1985—. Named one of city's influential citizens, Memphis Mag.; recipient Woman of Achievement award for Initiative, 1987, Gordon Holl Artistic Adminstr. of Yr. award, State of Tenn., 1999. Office: Ballet Memphis PO Box 3675 Cordova TN 38088-3675 E-mail: info@balletmemphis.com. *

PUGH, EMERSON WILLIAM, electrical engineer; b. Pasadena, Calif., May 1, 1929; s. Emerson Martindale and Ruth Hazel (Edgin) P.; m. Elizabeth Burnam Russell; children: William Russell, Sarah Elizabeth, David Emerson. BS in Physics, Carnegie Mellon U., 1951, PhD in Physics, 1956. Asst. prof. physics Carnegie Mellon U., Pitts., 1956-57; with IBM, 1957-93, rsch. staff mem. rsch. div., Poughkeepsie, N.Y., 1957-61, engring. mgr. components div., 1962-65, group dir. data processing group, Harrison, N.Y., 1965-66, dir. tech. planning rsch. div., Yorktown Heights, N.Y., 1966-68, asst. to v.p. IBM Corp., Armonk, N.Y., 1968-71, rsch. mgr. rsch. div., Yorktown Heights, 1971-85, mgr. tech. history, 1985-93. Vis. scientist IBM Lab., Zurich, Switzerland, 1961-62; mem. United Engring. Trustees Bd., N.Y.C., 1986-92; mem. Engring. Soc. Libr. Bd., N.Y.C., 1986-89; trustee Charles Babbage Found., 1990—, Samuel Morse Hist. Site, 1998-99. Author: Principles of Electricity and Magnetism, 1960, Memories That Shaped an Industry, 1984, IBM's Early Computers, 1986, IBM's 360 and Early 370 Systems, 1991, Building IBM, 1995; also articles; 10 patents. Fellow IEEE (v.p. 1986-87, pres. 1989, chmn. friends com. Ctr. for History Elec. Engring. 1991-94, chmn. history com. 1995-98, dir. found. 1996-2005, pres. found. 2000-04 treas. trustees History Ctr., 2006—), AAAS, Am. Phys. Soc. Home: 3 Rock St Cold Spring NY 10516-2911

PUGH, GEORGE WILLARD, law educator; b. Napoleonville, La., Aug. 17, 1925; s. William Whitmell and Evelyn (Foley) P.; m. Jean Earle Hemphill, Sept. 6, 1952; children: William Whitmell III, George Willard Jr., David Nicholls, James Hemphill. BA, La. State U., Baton Rouge, 1947, JD, 1950; J.S.D., Yale U., New Haven, Conn., 1952; Dr. h.c., U. Aix-Marseille III, France, 1984. Bar: La. 1950. Instr. La. State U. Law Sch., 1950, mem. faculty, 1952-94, prof. law, 1959-94, Julius B. Nachman prof. law, 1984-94; prof. law emeritus, 1994—. Faculty U. Thessaloniki Greece 1974, Aix-en-Provence, France, 1985, 91; faculty U. San Diego, Paris, 1977; rsch. cons. La. State Law Inst., 1953-54; 1st jud. adminstr. Jud. Coun. Supreme Ct. La., 1954-56; vis. prof. U. Tex., 1961; vis. Doherty prof. law U. Va., 1966-67; faculty orientation program in Am. law Assn. Am. Law Schs., 1968, law teaching clinic, 1969; vis. prof. U. Aix-Marseille III, France, 1983, 1987, U. Catholique de Louvain, Belgium, 1987; cons. La. State U.S. Vietnam Legal Adminstrn. Project, 1969; coord., reporter Code of Evidence for La., 1981-95. Author: Louisiana Evidence Law, 1974, supplement, 1978; co-author: Cases and Materials on the Adminstration of Criminal Justice, 2d edit., 1969, Handbook on Louisiana Evidence Law, 1989, 20th edit., 2007. Bd. dirs. Legal Aid Soc. Baton Rouge, 1965-89, chmn., 1963-64; adv. bd. St. Alban's Episcopal Student Ctr., La. State U., 1965-68, 70-72. Served with AUS, World War II. Named George W. and Jean H. Pugh Inst. for Justice in his honor, La. State U. Law Ctr., 1997; fellow, Comparative Study Adminstrn. Justice, 1962—65. Mem. Am., La., Baton Rouge bar assns., Order of Coif, Omicron Delta Kappa, Lambda Chi Alpha. Democrat. Episcopalian. Home: 167 Sunset Blvd Baton Rouge LA 70808-5073

PUGH, JOHN ROBERT, academic administrator, educator, retired state official; b. New Orleans, Dec. 20, 1945; s. Edward Nicholls and Yvonne Marie (Duplantier) P.; m. Margaret Louise McMullen, Aug. 26, 1975; children— Margaret Elizabeth, John Robert. BA in Philosophy, Baylor U., 1967; M. in Social Work, U. Tex.-Austin, 1970. Program dir. McLaughlin Youth Ctr., Anchorage, Alaska, 1973-78; dep. dir. Alaska Div. Social Services, Juneau, 1978-80; dir. Alaska Family and Youth Services, Juneau, 1980-83; dep. commr. Alaska Dept. Health and Social Services, Juneau, 1983, commr., 1983-86; dean, Sch. of Education Univ. Alaska Southeast, Juneau, 1986-95, chancellor, 1995—. Cons., lectr. in field Mem., Blue Ribbon Commn. for Revision of Children's Code, 1975-77; supt. Sunday Sch., No. Light United Ch., Juneau, 1979—; mem. Gov.'s Council for Handicapped and Gifted, 1980-84; mem. precinct com. Greater Juneau Democratic Com., 1983—; bd. dirs. Alaska State Fin. Corp., 1985—; coach Juneau Little League, 1984—. Served to capt. USAF, 1969-73 Mem. Nat. Assn. Social Workers (pres. 1975-76), Am. Pub. Welfare Assn., Am. Correctional Assn., Alaska Pub. Employees Assn. (pres. 1977-79), Acad. Cert. Social Workers (cert.) Methodist. Avocations: fishing, sports. Office: U Alaska Southeast 11120 Glacier Hwy Juneau AK 99801 *

PUGH, RICHARD CRAWFORD, lawyer, educator; b. Phila., Apr. 28, 1929; s. William and Myrtle P.; m. Nanette Bannen, Feb. 27, 1954; children: Richard Crawford, Andrew Lembert, Catherine Elizabeth. AB summa cum laude, Dartmouth Coll., 1951; BA in Jurisprudence, Oxford U., Eng., 1953; LLB, Columbia U., 1958. Bar: N.Y. 1958. Assoc. firm Cleary, Gottlieb, Steen & Hamilton, NYC, 1958—61, ptnr., 1969—89; disting. prof. law U. San Diego, 1989—, univ. prof., 1998—99. Mem. faculty Law Sch. Columbia U., 1961-89, prof., 1964-69, adj. prof., 1969-89; lectr. Columbia-Amsterdam-Leyden (Netherlands) summer program Am. law, 1963, 79; dep. asst. atty. gen. tax div. U.S. Dept. Justice, 1966-68; Cons. fiscal and fin. br. UN Secretariat, 1962, 64. Editor: Columbia Law Rev., 1957—58; co-editor: Legal Aspects of Foreign Investment, 1959; co-author: International Law, 2001, Taxation of Business Enterprises, 2002, Taxation of International Transactions, 2006. With USNR, 1954—56. Rhodes scholar, 1951-53. Mem. ABA, Am. Law Inst., Am. Coll. Tax Counsel, Internat. Fiscal Assn. (pres. U.S. br. 1978-79). Home: 7335 Encelia Dr La Jolla CA 92037-5729 Office: U San Diego Sch Law Alcala Park San Diego CA 92110-2429 Office Phone: 619-260-2322. Business E-Mail: rpugh@sandiego.edu.

PUGH, THOMAS WILFRED, lawyer; b. St. Paul, Aug. 3, 1949; s. Thomas Leslie and Joann Marie (Tauer) P.; m. Susan Elizabeth Beattie, Sept. 12, 1971; children: Aimee Elizabeth, Douglas Thomas. AB cum laude, Dartmouth Coll., 1971; JD cum laude, U. Minn., 1976. Assoc. Thuet & Lynch, South St. Paul, 1976-79; ptnr. Thuet, Lynch & Pugh, South St. Paul, 1980-85; atty., pres. Thuet, Pugh, Rogosheske & Atkins, Ltd., South St. Paul, 1986—; mem. Minn. Ho. of Reps., St. Paul, 1989—2004, Dem. leader, 1999—2002; commr. Minn. Pub. Utilities Commn., 2004—. Mem. Supreme Ct. Task Force Conciliation Ct., St. Paul, 1992, Dakota County Tech. Coll. Adv. Bd., 1991-96. Bd. dirs. Wakota Arena, South St. Paul, 1984-87; pres. Luther Meml. Ch., South St. Paul, 1983-84. Daniel Webster scholar Dartmouth Coll., 1970, Rufus Choate scholar, 1971. Mem. Minn. State Bar Assn., 1st Dist. Bar Assn., Ducks Unltd., Pheasants Forever, South St. Paul C. of C. (local issues chair 1982, Dedicated Svc. award 1983), South St. Paul Jaycees (pres. 1978-79, Key award 1979), Lions. Lutheran. Avocations: tennis, golf, hunting, fishing, reading. Office: Thuet Pugh & Rogosheske 222 Grand Ave South Saint Paul MN 55075-2237

PUGH, WILLIAM WHITMELL HILL, III, lawyer; b. Baton Rouge, June 25, 1954; s. George Willard and Jean (Hemphill) P.; m. Beth Smith, Mar. 12, 1983; children: Brendan Kelly, Bryan Clayton, Katharine Elaine. BA, U. Va., 1976; JD, La. State U., 1979. Bar: La. 1979, Tex. 2005, U.S. Supreme Ct. 1986, U.S. Ct. Appeals (5th and 11th cirs.) 1983. Law clk. to presiding justice U.S. Ct. Appeals (5th cir.), New Orleans, 1979-80. Editor-in-chief La. Law Rev., 1978-79. Mem. Maritime Law Assn., La. Assn. Def. Counsel, La. State Bar Assn., Coun. of La. State Law Inst. (young lawyers rep. 1988-91, mem. 1992—). Office: Liskow & Lewis Three Allen Ctr 333 Clay St Ste 3485 Houston TX 77002 Home Phone: 713-861-2457; Office Phone: 713-651-2949. Business E-Mail: wwpugh@liskow.com.

PUGLIESE, STANISLAO, history educator, researcher; b. NYC, Mar. 24, 1965; s. Angelo and Lena Pugliese; m. Maria Jennifer Romanello, June 27, 1992; children: Alessandro, Giulia. BA, Hofstra U., 1987; MA, CUNY, 1990, PhD, 1995. Adj. lectr. CUNY, 1989-93; asst. prof. history Hofstra U., Hempstead, N.Y., 1994-2000, assoc. prof., 2000—. Author: Carlo Rosselli: Socialist Heretic and Antifascist Exile, 1999, Italian Fascism/Antifascism, 2001. Business E-Mail: stanislao.pugliese@hofstra.edu.

PUGSLEY, ROBERT ADRIAN, law educator; b. Mineola, NY, Dec. 27, 1946; s. Irvin Harold and Mary Catherine P. BA, SUNY-Stony Brook, 1968; JD, NYU, 1975, LLM in Criminal Justice, 1977. Instr. sociology New Sch. Social Rsch., NYC, 1969-71; coord. Peace Edn. programs The Christophers, NYC, 1971-78; assoc. prof. law Southwestern U., LA, 1978-81, prof., 1981—, Paul E. Treusch prof. law, 2000-01. Adj. asst. prof. criminology and criminal justice Southampton Coll.-Long Island U., 1975-76; acting dep. dir. Criminal Law Edn. and Rsch. Ctr., NYU, 1983-86; bd. advisors Ctr. Legal Edn. CCNY-CUNY, 1978, Sta. KPFK-FM, 1985-86; founder, coord. The Wednesday Evening Soc., L.A., 1979-86; vis. prof. Jacob D. Fuchsberg Law Ctr. Touro Coll., L.I., N.Y., summers, 1988, 89; lectr. in criminal law and procedure Legal Edn. Conf. Ctr., L.A., 1982-96; prof., dir. Comparative Criminal Law and Procedure Program U. B.C., Vancouver, summers, 1994, 98-2003; chair pub. interest law com. Southwestern U., 1990-2001; lectr. legal profl. responsibility West Bar Rev. Faculty, Calif., 1996-98; legal analyst/commentator for print and electronic media, 1992—. Creative advisor (syndicated TV program) Christopher Closeup, 1975-83; host (cable TV) Earth Alert, 1983-87; prodr., moderator (TV program) Inside L.A., Sta. KPFK-FM, 1979-86, Open Jour. program, Sta. KPFK-FM, 1991-94; contbr. articles to profl. jours. Founding mem. Southwestern U. Pub. Interest Law com., 1992—; mem. L.A. County Bar Assn. Adv. Com. on Alcohol & Drug Abuse, 1991-95, co-chair, 1993-95; mem. exec. com. non-govtl. orgns. UN Office Pub. Info., 1977; mem. issues task force L.A. Conservancy, 1980-81, seminar for law tchrs. NEH UCLA, 1979; co-convenor So. Calif. Coalition Against Death Penalty, 1981-83, convener, 1983-84; mem. death penalty com. Lawyer's Support Group, Amnesty Internat., U.S.A.; founding mem. Ch.-State Coun., L.A., 1984-88; bd. dirs. Equal Rights Sentencing Found., 1983-85, Earth Alert, Inc., 1984-87; mem. adv. bd. First Amendment Info. Resources Ctr., Grad. Sch. Libr. and Info. Scis., UCLA, 1990—; mem. coun. Friends UCLA Libr., 1993—, pres., 1996-2002; mem. adv. bd. Project Prevention, 1998-. Robert Marshall fellow Criminal Law Edn. and Rsch. Ctr., NYU Sch. Law, 1976-78. Mem. ABA (sect. criminal justice 1978-, Ctr. Profl. Responsibility 1995-), Am. Legal Studies Assn., Am. Soc. Polit. and Legal Philosophy, Assn. Am. Law Schs., Inst. Soc. Ethics and Life Scis., Soc. Am. Law Tchrs., Internat. Platform Assn., Internat. Soc. Reform of Criminal Law, The Scribes. Democrat. Roman Catholic. Office: Southwestern U Sch Law 675 S Westmoreland Ave Los Angeles CA 90005-3905 Office Phone: 213-738-6757. Business E-Mail: rpugsley@swlaw.edu.

PUJOL, ERNESTO, artist; b. Havana, Cuba, 1957; BA in Visual Arts magna cum laude, U. Puerto Rico, 1979; postgrad., Pratt Inst., 1987, Hunter Coll. Artist The Marketplace Program, Bronx Mus. Arts, NY, 1991. One-man shows include Taller D'Jevarez, San Juan, 1984, Cavin-Morris, N.Y.C., 1993, INTAR, 1994, Galeria Ramis Barquet, Monterrey, Mex., 1995, Casa de las Americas, Havana, 1995, Frederic Snitzer Gallery, Miami, Fla., 1995, Iturralde Gallery, L.A., 1996, exhibited in group shows at Galeria Interamericana, P.R., 1984, Nat. Arts Club, N.Y.C., 1990, Hudson Guild Gallery, 1991, Cavin Morris Gallery, 1992, The Space, Boston, 1992, Paine Weber Gallery, N.Y., 1992, Reed Coll. Art Gallery, Portland, Oreg., 1994, Seton Hill Coll., Pa., 1995, Iturralde Gallery, L.A., 1995, Spectrum Gallery, Rochester, N.Y., 1996, PS 122, N.Y.C., 1996, numerous others, Represented in permanent collections Casa de las Americas, Havana, El Museo del Barrio, N.Y., Assn. Artistas Plasticas de Cuba, Havana, Mus. Art, Ft. Laderdale, Fla., Cintas Found. Fellows Collection, Art Mus., Fla., Internat. U. Miami, Bronx Coun. Arts, Longwood, N.Y. Recipient Breakthrough award for creativity, Acad. Ednl. Devel., Washington, 1990, Cert. of Appreciation, Dept. Cultural Affairs, L.A., 1995; fellow Cintas Found. fellow, Arts Internat., Inst. Internat. Edn., 1991, Visual Arts fellow, Pollock-Krasner Found., 1993, Regional fellow in painting, Mid-Atlantic Arts Found./Nat. Endowment Arts, 1994; scholar Studio scholar, Bronx Coun. Arts, 1991. Office: Galeria Ramis Barquet 41 E 57th St New York NY 10022-1908

PUJOLS, ALBERT (JOSE ALBERTO PUJOLS), professional baseball player; b. Santo Domingo, Dominican Republic, Jan. 16, 1980; m. Deidre Pujols, Jan. 1, 2000; 3 children. Draft pick St. Louis Cardinals, 1999, first baseman, 2001—. First baseman Dominican Republic Team World Baseball Classic, 2006. Founder Pujols Family Found. Named Nat. League Rookie of Yr., 2001, Maj. League Player of Yr., 2003, Nat. League Championship Series MVP, 2004, Nat. League MVP, 2005, Best Maj. League Baseball Player, ESPY awards, 2005, 2006, Best Internat. Player, 2006, Man of Yr., Players Choice awards, 2006; named to Nat. League All-Star Team, Maj. League Baseball, 2001, 2003—07; recipient Silver Slugger award, 2001, 2003—04, Hank Aaron award, 2003, Gold Glove award, 2006. Achievements include winning the National League batting title (.359 average), 2003; leading the National League in runs (137), 2003; being fourth player in MLB history to start career with 4 straight 100 RBI season's, 2004; being first player in MLB history to hit 30 HR and 100 RBI's in first 5 seasons, 2005; tying consecutive record for at-bats resulting in a HR, 2006. Office: St Louis Cardinals Busch Stadium 250 Stadium Plaza Saint Louis MO 63102 *

PUKEL, CLIFFORD STUART, physician; b. Bronx, NY, Nov. 15, 1955; s. Bayas William and Pearl (Buchholtz) P.; m. Victoria Perry; children: Zachariah, Jacob. BA in Biology, Queens Coll. CUNY, 1979; MD, U. Miami, 1991. Rsch. technician Sloan-Kettering Inst. for Cancer Rsch., NYC, 1980-83, rsch. asst., 1983-85; rsch. assoc. dept. medicine U. Miami, Fla., 1985-87; resident dept. internal medicine U. W.Va., Charleston, 1991-94; fellow hematology, oncology, instr. medicine Dartmouth-Hitchcock Med. Ctr., Lebanon, NH, 1994-97; pvt. practice Wichita, 1998—2000, Eau Claire, Wis., 2000—02, Vince Lombardi Cancer Clinic, Green Bay, Wis., 2002—07, Aurora Bay Care Med. Ctr., Green Bay, 2002—07; asst. prof. clin. medicine U. Kans. Sch. Medicine, Wichita, 1998-99, U. Wis. Sch. Medicine, Madison, 2000—; pres., CEO Global Cancer Inst., Green Bay, 2007—. Vis. scientist Escola Paulista de Medicina, Sao Paulo, Brazil, 1984. Contbr. articles to profl. jours. Free Sons of Israel scholar, 1974, N.Y. State Regents scholar, 1974, U. Miami Med. Sch. scholar, 1990. Jewish. Achievements include patent for Method for Detecting the Presence of GD3 Ganglioside; notable findings on role of gangliosides in human cancer, on role of cytokines in diabetes mellitus. Office: Global Cancer Inst 1562 Manderly Way # 1 Green Bay WI 54311 Office Phone: 920-360-5692. E-mail: cspmdmd@aol.com.

PULANCO, TONYA BETH, special education educator; b. Portland, Oreg., Apr. 17, 1933; d. Anthony Lorenzo and Adelfa Elizabeth (Dewey) P. BA, San Jose State U., 1955; MA, Columbia U., 1966. Occupl. therapist Langley Porter Hosp., San Francisco, 1958-60; writer ednl. sub-contracts Columbia U., NYC, 1961-64; from tchr. to dir. edn. Gateway Sch. N.Y., NYC, 1965—. Mem. Assn. for Children with Learning Disabilities, Am. Occupl. Therapy Assn., Japanese Am. Citizens League. Avocations: tap dancing, walkathons, silversmithing, jazz, opera. Office: Gateway Sch NY 236 2d Ave New York NY 10003 E-mail: tobytap@aol.com.

PULEO, FRANK CHARLES, lawyer; b. Montclair, NJ, Nov. 25, 1945; s. Frank and Kathren (Despenzerie) P.; m. Alice Kathren Leek, June 1, 1968; children— Frank C., Richard James. BSE cum laude, Princeton U., 1967; JD, NYU, 1970. Bar: NY, 1971. Assoc., Milbank, Tweed, Hadley & McCloy, NYC, 1970—76, ptnr. 1976-, mem. exec. com. 1982-91, 1996-2002, co-chmn. Global Fin. group. Mem. ABA (mem. com. on fed. regulation securities), NY State Bar Assn. Office: Milbank Tweed Hadley & McCloy 1 Chase Manhattan Plz Fl 49 New York NY 10005-1413 Office Phone: 212-530-5134. Office Fax: 212-530-5219. Business E-Mail: fpuleo@milbank.com.

PULGRAM, WILLIAM LEOPOLD, architect, space designer; b. Vienna, Jan. 1, 1921; came to U.S., 1940; s. Sigmund and Gisela (Bauer) P.; married, Jan. 12, 1952; children: Deirdre, Laurence, Anthony, Christopher. BS, Ga. Inst. Tech., 1949, BArch, 1950; postgrad., Ecole des Beaux Arts, Fontainebleau, France, 1951. Archtl. designer various firms, Atlanta, 1951-58; assoc., chief interior design FABR&P, Atlanta, 1958-63; exec. v.p., gen. mgr. Associated Space Design Inc., Atlanta, 1963-70, pres., CEO, 1971-85, chmn., CEO, 1985-86, chmn. emeritus, 1986-88; arch., cons. Atlanta, 1988—. Cons. UN, 1986; com. mem. NAS, 1980-84; lectr. at colls., univs., U.S. and abroad. Author: Designing the Automated Office, 1984, Japanese transl., 1985; contbr. articles to jours. in field. Mem., lectr. High Mus. Art, Atlanta, 1970—. With U.S. Army, 1943-46. Named to Hall of Fame Interior Design mag., 1986. Fellow AIA (chmn. interiors 1978-84, archtl. res. coun. AIA Found. 1983-85); mem. Archs., Designers and Planners for Social Responsibility (nat. bd. dirs. 1989-93), Am. Soc. Interior Designers, Atlanta C. of C., Atlanta City Club, Lake Lanier Sailing Club. Mem. Unitarian Universalist Ch. Home and Office: W L Pulgram FAIA Cons 4317 E Conway Dr NW Atlanta GA 30327-3528 E-mail: pulgramga@mindspring.com.

PULHAMUS, MARLENE LOUISE, retired elementary school educator; b. Paterson, NJ, Sept. 11, 1937; d. David Weeder and Elfrieda (Ehler) Wemmell; m. Aaron R. Pulhamus, Aug. 20, 1960; children: Steven, Thomas, Nancy. Student, Trenton State U., 1957; BS, William Paterson U., 1959; postgrad., Rutgers U., 1992. Cert. elem. tchr., NJ. Kindergarten tchr. Wayne Bd. Edn., NJ, 1959-63, Paterson Bd. Edn., 1974-75, 2d grade tchr., 1975-81; basic skills instr. Paterson Pub. Schs., 1981—, tchr. accelerated program 1st grade, 1992—; cons. lang. arts, literacy Kendall Hunt Pegasus, Wayne; ret., 1997. Trainer for insvc. groups of learning ctrs. and math. with manipulatives for local pub. schs., trainer for local pub. schs. Contbr. Lessons 4Mat in Action, 3d edit., 4Mat: A Quest for Wholeness, 1977—. Pres. Friends of Eisenhower Libr., Totowa, NJ, 1975-77; coord. ch. sch. Preakness Reformed Ch., Wayne, 1990-93, elder, chair outreach commn.; exec. bd. United Meth. Women Altar GUild, Asbury United Meth. Ch.; sec. VTTC Homeowners Assn., Salisbury, Md. Recipient Gov.'s award for tchg. excellence State of NJ Commn. Edn., 1991, 4Mation program award, 1994. Mem. ASCD, NEA, AAUW, Nat. Coun. Tchrs. Math., Nat. Assn. for Edn. Young Children, NJ Edn. Assn., Passaic County Edn. Assn., Paterson Edn. Assn. (mem. exec. bd., 1985-89, legis. chmn. 1986-89). Personal E-mail: mylilycat@verizon.net.

PULIAFITO, CARMEN ANTHONY, ophthalmologist, healthcare executive; b. Buffalo, Jan. 5, 1951; s. Dominic F. and Marie A. (Nigro) P.; m. Janet H. Pine, May 19, 1979 AB cum laude, Harvard Coll., 1973, MD magna cum laude, 1978; MBA, U. Pa., 1997. Diplomate Am. Bd. Ophthalmology. Intern Faulkner Hosp., Tufts U. Sch. Medicine, 1978-79; resident Mass. Eye and Ear Infirmary, Boston, 1979-82, retina fellow, 1982-83; instr. Harvard Med. Sch., Boston, 1983-85, asst. prof., 1985-89, assoc. prof., 1989-91, dir. divsn. continuing edn. dept. ophthalmology, 1989-91; dir. Bascon Palmer Eye Inst., Miami, 2001—. Vis. scientist MIT Regional Laser Ctr., Cambridge, 1982—, asst. prof. health scis. and tech. program, 1987-89, assoc. prof., 1989-91; mem. staff Mass. Eye and Ear Infirmary, Boston, 1983; dir. Morse Laser Ctr., Mass. Eye and Ear Infirmary, 1986-91, dir. New Eng. Eye Ctr., 1991-2001; prof., chmn. dept. ophthalmology Tufts U. Sch. Medicine, 1991-2001, prof. ophthalmology and health mgmt., 1997-2001; adj. prof. biomed. engring. Tufts U., 1991—; chmn. med. bd. New Eng. Med. Ctr. Hosps., 1994-95, ophthalmologist in chief, 1991-2001; assoc. examiner Am. Bd. Ophthalmology, 1990—; sr. v.p. for network devel. Lifespan, 1997-2001; prof., chmn. dept. ophthalmology U. Miami Sch. Medicine, 2001—; med. dir. Anne Bates Leach Eye Hosp., 2001—. Author: (with D. Albert) Foundations of Ophthalmic Pathology, 1979, (with R. Steinert) Principles and Practice of Ophthalmic YAG Laser Surgery, 1984, Lasers in Surgery and Medicine: Principles and Practice, 1996, (with M.R. Hee, J.S. Schuman and J.G. Fujimoto) Optical Coherence Tomography of Ocular Diseases, 1996, (with E. Reichel) Atlas of Indocyanine Green Angiography, 1996; editor-in-chief Lasers in Surgery and Medicine, 1987-95, Ophthalmic Surgery and Lasers, 1995—; contbr. about 120 articles to profl. jours. Pres. Am. Soc. for Laser Medicine and Surgery, 1994-95; v.p. Mass. Soc. Eye Physicians and Surgeons, 1994-96; assoc. examiner Am. Bd. Ophthalmology, 1990—; retina trustee Assn. Rsch. in Vision and Ophthalmology, 1995-99, pres., 2000-01. Recipient Richard and Hinda Rosenthal award in visual scis., 1994, Man of Vision award Boston Aid to the Blind, 1993, Leon Goldman award Biomed. Optics Soc., 1993, I Migliori award Pirandello Lyceum of Mass., 1994. Fellow Am. Acad. Ophthalmology, Am. Soc. for Laser Medicine and Surgery (pres. 1994-95); mem. Assn. Rsch. in Vision and Ophthalmology (pres.-elect 1998-99, pres. 1999-2000, immediate past pres. 2000-2001), Mass. Soc. Eye Physicians and Surgeons (v.p. 1994-96). Roman Catholic. Home: 9321 SW 63rd Ct Miami FL 33156-1814 Office: Bascom Palmer Eye Inst 900 NW 17th St Miami FL 33136 Office Phone: 305-326-6303. Business E-Mail: cpuliafito@miami.edu.

PULIDO, JOSE S., physician; b. Apr. 29, 1956; BA with hons., U. Chgo., 1976, MS, 1977; MD, Tulane U., New Orleans, 1981; MBA, U. Iowa, 1993; MPH, U. Ill., 2005. Diplomate Am. Bd. Ophthalmology. Intern Tulane Affil. Hosps.-Charity Hosp., New Orleans, 1981-82; resident in ophthalmology U. Ill., Chgo., 1982-85, chief resident in ophthalmology, 1985-86; fellow vitreoretinal surgery Bascome Palmer Eye Inst./U. Miami Sch. Medicine, 1986-87, fellow retina rsch., 1987; fellow ocular oncology Wills Eye Hosp./Thomas Jefferson U. Sch. Medicine, Phila., 1998; head and prof. dept. ophthalmology and visual scis. U. Ill., Chgo., 1998—. Instr. organic chemistry U. Chgo., 1976-77; asst. prof. ophthalmology Coll. of Medicine, U. Iowa, Iowa City, 1987-92, assoc. prof., 1992-97, prof. 1997-98; prof. and chmn. U. Ill., 1998-2004; prof. Mayo Clinic, 2005. Reviewer numerous jours., including: Archives of Ophthalmology, 1985—, Ophthalmology, 1987—, Am. Jour. of Ophthalmology, 1992—, others; abstract editor: Diabetes 2000 Newsletter, 1992—, Ophthalmology World News, 1994-96, others; editor: Evidence-Based Eye Care, 1998—; contbr. articles to profl. jours. Mem. Am. Diabetes Assn. (del.), Am. Acad. Ophthalmology, Pan-Am. Acad. Ophthalmology, Retina Soc., Vitreous Soc., Fluorescein Reading and Macular Evaluation, Assn. for Rsch. in Vision and Ophthalmology, Am. Coll. Surgeons, Schepens Internat. Soc., Am. Ophthal. Soc., Macula Soc. Office: Mayo Clinic 200 First St SW Rochester MN 55905

PULITZER, EMILY RAUH (MRS. JOSEPH PULITZER JR.), art historian, consultant; b. Cin., July 23, 1933; d. Frederick and Harriet (Frank) Rauh; m. Joseph Pulitzer Jr., 1973 (dec. 1993). AB, Bryn Mawr Coll., Pa., 1955; student, Ecole du Louvre, Paris, 1955-56; MA, Harvard U., Cambridge, Mass., 1963; LHD honoris causa (hon.), U. Mo., 1989; DFA honoris causa (hon.), Aquinas Inst., St. Louis, 2002, St. Louis U., 2003; HHD honoris causa (hon.), Washington U., St. Louis, 2005. Mem. staff Cin. Art Mus., 1956-57; asst. curator drawings Harvard U. Fogg Art Mus., 1957-64, asst. to dir., 1962-63; curator City Art Mus., St. Louis, 1964-73; mem. painting and sculpture com. Mus. Modern Art, 1985—, trustee, 1994—, vice chair paintings and sculpture com., 1996—, mem. drawings com., 2003—; chmn. visual arts com. Mo. Arts Coun., 1976-81; bd. mem. Inst. Mus. Svcs., 1979-84; commr. St. Louis Art Mus., 1981-88, vice chmn., 1988; bd. dir. Pulitzer, Inc., 1993—2005; founder, chmn. Pulitzer Found. for the Arts, 2001—. Bd. dirs. Contemporary Art Mus., St. Louis, 1980-2003, 2004-, pres., 1990-95; bd. dirs. Mark Rothko Found., 1980-89, Grand Ctr., 1993-95,, 99—, arts strategy com. chair, 2003—; bd. trustees St. Louis Symphony Orch., 1994-2004, bd. overseers, 2005—; bd. dirs. arts in transit com. Bi-State Devel. Agy., vice-chmn. and co-founder, 1987-98; mem. Leadership St. Louis, 1990-91; trustee Mus. Modern Art, 1994—; mem. overseer's com. to visit the art mus. Harvard U., 1990—, chair, 2004—, mem. collections com., 1992—, chair, 1992-2004, mem. Fogg Fellows, 1978—, co-chair, 1978-94, bd. overseers, 2006—, pres.'s adv. com. on Allston Initiative, 2005—; chair collections com. St. Louis Art Mus., 2007-. Named one of Top 200 Collectors, ARTnews Mag., 2003—06; recipient St. Louis award, Contbn. to Arts Cmty., 2003. Mem. Am. Fedn. Arts (dir. 1976-89), St. Louis Mercantile Libr. Assn. (bd. dirs. 1987-93), Mo. Women's Forum.

PULITZER, ROSLYN KITTY, social worker, psychotherapist; b. Bronx, NY, Apr. 25, 1930; d. George and Laura Eleanor (Holtz) P. BS in Human Devel. and Life Cycle, SUNY, NYC, 1983; MSW, Fordham U., 1987; postgrad., Masterson Inst., NYC, 1991. cert. in psychoanalytic psychotherapy of the personality disorders, Masterson Inst., N.Y.C.; lic. clin. social worker, N.Y. Clinic dir. Resources Counseling and Psychotherapy Ctr., NYC, 1985-89; social worker, clin. supr. methadone maintenance treatment program Beth Israel Med. Ctr., NYC, 1989-97; psychotherapist pvt. practice, 1989—. Cons. therapist, clin. supr. Identity House, N.Y.C., 1980-97, exec. dir., 1985, clin. dir., 1993-94. Mem. regional adv. coun. N.Y. State Div. Human Rights, N.Y.C., 1975-76; mem. Community Bd. 6, N.Y.C., 1978-81; founder, legis. chmn. N.Y. State Women's Polit. Caucus, 1978-80. Mem. NASW, Acad. Cert. Social Workers, Soc. Masterson Inst., N.Y. Milton Erickson Soc. for Psychotherapy and Hypnosis (cert.). Avocations: photography, snorkeling. Home: 2742 La Silla Dorada Santa Fe NM 87505-6703 Office Phone: 505-473-9694. Fax: 505-438-2884. E-mail: rkp-imagestudio@comcast.net.

PULLEN, BRUCE REED, retired pastor; b. Princeton, NJ, Sept. 2, 1936; s. Leroy Cox and Dorothea Reed Pullen; m. Judith Ann Gunnemann, Aug. 15, 1959; children: Bonnie Jean, Beth Ann. D of Chiropractic, Nat. Coll., Lombard, Ill., 1960; BA, Rutgers U., New Brunswick, NJ, 1967; BD, Colgate Rochester Divinity Sch., NY, 1970; ThM, Princeton Theol. Sch., NJ, 1974; D of Ministry, Ea. Bapt. Theol. Seminary, Phila., 1979. Lic. chiropractor NJ, Maine, 1961. Chiropractor pvt. practice, Farmington, Maine, 1961—65; pastor Am. Baptist Ch., Hopewell, NJ, 1970—77, First Baptist Ch., Burlington, Iowa, 1977—84, Alton, Ill., 1984—90, Ctrl. Bapt. Ch., Westfield, Mass., 1990—2002, First Bapt. Ch., Williamstown, Mass., 2002—03; ret. Gen. bd. mem. Am. Bapt. Chs. USA, Valley Forge, Pa., 1981—84, 1994—2000; bd. mgr. Mins. and Missionaries Benefit Bd., NYC, 1986—94; bd. mem. Noble Hosp. Hospice, Westfield, Mass., 1991—99. Author: (books) Discovering Celtic Christianity, 1999, Profiles in Faith Discovering Baptist Beginnings, 2006. Chair, bd. mem. To Go Walk Camp, Westfield, Mass., 1992—2000. Mem.: Rotary Internat. (Svc. award 2006). Baptist. Avocations: travel, photography.

PULLEN, DAVID JOHN, physicist, researcher; b. Merton, Surrey, Eng., June 28, 1936; came to U.S. 1963; s. Arthur Lester and Alexandra Q. (Griffiths) P.; m. Heather Morgan, Aug. 6, 1960; children: Katrina, Adrian, Lester, Andrew. BSc with first class honors, London U., 1958; DPhil, Oxford U., Eng., 1963. "1851" rsch. fellow Oxford U., 1961-63; instr. MIT, 1963-65; asst. prof. physics U. Pa., Phila., 1965-70; assoc. prof. Lowell (Mass.) Tech. Inst., 1970-73; prof. physics U. Mass. Lowell, 1973—2002, prof. emeritus, 2002—. Ptnr. CPS Nuc., 1990—; cons. Internat. Atomic Energy Agy., Vienna, 1991—99. Author: Physics Laboratory Experiments, 1975, 6th edit., 2006; contbr. over 70 articles to profl. jours. Royal Commn. for Exhbn. of 1851 rsch. fellowship, 1961-63. Mem. Am. Phys. Soc., Am. Assn. Physics Tchrs., Sigma Xi. Home: 2 Reeves Rd Bedford MA 01730-1335 Office: U Mass Lowell 1 University Ave Lowell MA 01854-5009 Office Phone: 978-934-3765. Business E-Mail: david_pullen@uml.edu.

PULLEN, PENNY LYNNE, non-profit organization administrator, retired state legislator; b. Buffalo, Mar. 2, 1947; d. John William and Alice Nettie (McConkey) P. BA in Speech, U. Ill., 1969. Tv technician Office Instnl. Resources, U. Ill., 1966-68; cmty. newspaper reporter Des Plaines (Ill.) Pub. Co., 1967-72; legis. asst. to Ill. legislators, 1968-77; mem. Ill. Ho. of Reps., 1977-93, chmn. ho. exec. com., 1981-82, minority whip, 1983-87, asst. minority leader, 1987-93; pres., founder Life Advocacy Resource Project, Arlington Heights, Ill., 1992—. Exec. dir. Ill. Family Inst., 1993-94; dir. Legal Svcs. Corp., 1989-93; mem. Pres.'s Commn. on AIDS Epidemic, 1987-88; mem. Ill. Goodwill Del. to Republic of China, 1987. Summit conf. observer as mem. adhoc Women for SDI, Geneva, 1985; active Nat. Coun. Ednl. Rsch., 1983—88; dir. Eagle Forum of Ill., 1999—2003, pres., 2003—; del. Rep. Nat. Conv., 1984; mem. Rep. Nat. Com., 1984—88; del. Atlantic Alliance Young Polit. Leaders, Brussels, 1977; pres. Maine Twp. Rep. Women's Club, 1997—99, Rep. Women of Park Ridge, Ill., 2001—03, Rep. Women of Wheeling Twp., Ill., 2004—. Recipient George Washington Honor medal Freedoms Found., 1978, Dwight Eisenhower Freedom medal Chgo. Captive Nations Com., 1977, Outstanding Legislator awards Ill. Press Assn., Ill. Podiatry Soc., Ill. Coroners Assn., Ill. County Clks. Assn., Ill. Hosp. Assn., Ill. Health Care Assn.; named Ill. Young Republican, 1968, Outstanding Young Person, Park Ridge Jaycees, 1981, One of 10 Outstanding Young Persons, Ill. Jaycees, 1981. Mem. DAR, Am. Legis. Exch. Coun. (dir. 1977-91, exec. com. 1978-83, 2d vice chmn. 1980-83), Com. on the Status of Women (sec. 1997—).

PULLEN, TIMOTHY L., corporate financial executive; BS, Rochester Inst. Tech.; MBA, Seattle Univ. Positions through v.p. fin. Hillhaven Corp., 1983—95; v.p., controller Tenet Healthcare Corp., Dallas, 1995—99, sr. v.p., controller, 1999—2003, exec. v.p., chief acctg. officer, 2003—, interim CFO, 2005. Office: Tenet Healthcare Corp Ste 100 13737 Noel Rd Dallas TX 75240

PULLEY, BRETT A., communications executive; b. 1967; m. Stacey Pulley; children: Zoe, Blake. B, Hampton U.; M in Journalism, Northwestern U. Journalist Wall St. Jour., Chgo., NYC; nat. corr. NY Times; sr. editor Forbes Mag., 1999—2007; CEO NewYork.com, 2007—. Appearances on CNN, CNBC, E! Entertainment, MSNBC, Entertainment Tonight, Showbiz Tonight, Inside Edit., Access Hollywood, 48 Hours; author: The Billion Dollar BET, 2004; featured in Ebony Mag., 2007. Recipient Nat. Assn. Black Journalists' award, 1994, 2002.

PULLEY, LEWIS C., lawyer; b. Oklahoma City, Aug. 19, 1954; Student, Oxford U., England, 1974; BA with high honors, U. Okla., 1976; JD, Am. U., 1979. Bar: Pa. 1981, DC 1987, US Ct. Mil. Appeals 1982, US Ct. Appeals (DC cir.) 1985, US Supreme Ct. 1985. Asst. chief policy divsn. media bur. FCC, 2002—. Avocations: travel, political paraphernalia. Office: FCC Media Bur Policy Divsn 445 12th St SW Washington DC 20554

PULLEY, (J.) WAVERLY. (III), lawyer; b. Franklin, Va., May 19, 1946; BA in English, Univ. Richmond, 1968, JD, 1972. Bar: Va. 1972. Ptnr., capital fin., real estate Hunton & Williams LLP, Richmond, Va. Editor-in-chief Univ. Richmond Law Rev., 1971—72. Fellow: Am. Bar Found.; mem.: ABA, Va. State Bar Assn., McNeill Law Soc., Phi Delta Phi, Omicron Delta Kappa. Office: Hunton & Williams LLP Riverfront Plz East Tower 951 E Byrd St Richmond VA 23219-4074 Office Phone: 804-788-8783. Office Fax: 804-788-8218. Business E-Mail: wpulley@hunton.com.

PULLIAM, FREDERICK CAMERON, educational administrator; b. Mesa, Ariz., Jan. 5, 1936; s. Frederick Posy and Nathana Laura (Cameron) P.; m. Deborah Jean Botts, June 1, 1979; 1 child, Sarah Elizabeth; children by previous marraige: Cameron Dale, Joy Renee. AA, Hannibal LaGrange Coll., 1955; AB, Grand Canyon Coll., 1958; MEd, U. Mo., 1966, EdS, 1976, EdD, 1981. Ordained to ministry So. Bapt. Conv., 1955. Tchr. Centerview (Mo.) Pub. Scsh., 1958-59; min. Bethel Bapt. Ch., Kansas City, Mo., 1959-61; adminstr. Fiti'uta Manu'a Sch., Am. Somoa, 1966-68; cons. in fin. Mo. State Tchrs. Assn., Columbia, 1969-79; supt. schs. Midway Heights C-VII, Columbia, 1979-83; dir. elem. edn. Brentwood (Mo.) Pub. Schs., 1983-90; pres. Life Long Learning Sys. St. Louis, Mt. Vernon, Mo., 1989—; dir. clin. and field experiences in tchr. edn. Mo. So. State Coll., 1994—99. Pastor Patten Chapel and Miller United Meth. Chs., Mo., 1997-2001; assoc. pastor First United Meth. Ch., Mt. Vernon, Mo., 2002-03, St. Paul's United Meth. Ch., Joplin, Mo., 2003-05, pastor emeritus, 2005—; sr. pastor Kendricktown United Meth. Ch., Mo., 2007—; founder, coord. Mo. Computer-Using Educators Conf., 1982-84; contbg. writer St. Louis Computing News, 1984-95; adj. asst. profl. ednl. studies U. Mo., St. Louis, 1986-90; adj. assoc. prof. grad. studies S.W. Bapt. U., 1991-98; cons. in field. Contbr. articles to profl. jours. Active Columbia Am. Revolution Bicentennial Commn.; edn. adv. com. Mo. Gov.'s Transition Team, 1992-93. Inst. Devel. Ednl. Activity fellow, 1969, 1978—84. Mem.: ACLU, ASCD (bd. dirs. 1984—90), Am. Assn. Ret. Persons, Mo. Ret. Tchrs. Assn., Nat. Middle Sch. Assn., Nat. Assn. Gifted Children, Assn. Childhood Edn. Internat., Rotary Internat., Phi Delta Kappa. Democrat. Home: 102 Rocky Cir Carl Junction MO 64834 Office Phone: 417-437-3924. Personal E-mail: cpulliam@mchsi.com.

PULLIAM, YVONNE ANTOINETTE, gifted education educator; b. Chgo. d. Virgil D. Sr. and Velma (Hunter) P. BA in Edn., Lane Coll., Jackson, Tenn., 1966; MA in Ednl. Adminstrn. and Supervision, Roosevelt U., Chgo., 1988. Cert. intermediate tchr. Tchr. Howalton Day Sch., Chgo., 1968—69; actress NYC, 1970—75; tchr. gifted Chgo. Bd. Edn., 1975—78, 1981—; tutor Broadway play Raisin, NYC, 1977—78, Annie, NYC, 1980—82. Coordinator Adopt-a-Sch. program, Chgo., 1984-85; tchr. rep. PTA O'Keefe Sch., Chgo., 1984-85. Cartoonist 1st Nat. Bank Chgo. newsletter 1969; stand-in for Diana Ross In Mahogany, 1976; appeared on All My Children, The Hosp. and indsl. films and voiceovers; assoc. dir.: (TV comedy) From Chicago. Recipient cert. of merit Glamour mag., 1965, award for innovative teaching Bus.Week, 1990; named featured designer V2 Fashions, Chgo., 1967, Essence mag., 1971. Mem. AFTRA, Chgo. Tchrs. Union, Am. Film. Inst., Phi Delta Kappa. Democrat. Home: 2d FL 7134 S Cornell Ave Chicago IL 60649

PULLMAN, BILL, actor; b. Hornell, NY, Dec. 17, 1953; m. Tamara Hurwitz, 1987; children: Maesa, Jack, Louis. BFA, SUNY, Oneonta; MFA, U. Mass., Amherst. Theatre instr. Mont. State U., Bozeman. Actor: (theatre) The Rover, 1981, Ah, Wilderness!, 1983, The Old Flag, 1983, Dramathon '84, 1984, Curse of the Starving Class, 1985, All My Sons, 1986, Barabbas, 1986, Nanawatai, 1986, Demon Wine, 1988, Control Freaks, 1993, The Subject Was Roses, 2006; (films) Ruthless People, 1986, Spaceballs, 1987, The Serpent and the Rainbow, 1988, Rocket Gibraltar, 1988, The Accidental Tourist, 1989, Cold Feet, 1989, Brain Dead, 1989, Sibling Rivalry, 1990, Going Under, 1991, Bright Angel, 1991, Newsies, 1992, A League of Their Own, 1992, Singles, 1992, Sommersby, 1993, Sleepless in Seattle, 1993, Malice, 1993, Mr. Jones, 1993, The Favor, 1994, Wyatt Earp, 1994, While You Were Sleeping, 1995, Casper, 1995, Mr. Wrong, 1996, Independence Day, 1996, Lost Highway, 1997, The End of Violence, 1997, The Thin Red Line, 1998, Brokedown Palace, 1998, Zero Effect, 1998, A Man is Mostly Water, 1999, History Is Made at Night, 1999, The Guilt, 1999, Brokedown Palace, 1999, Lake Placid, 1999, (voice) Coming to Light: Edward S. Curtis and the North American Indians, 2000, (voice) Titan A.E., 2000, Numbers, 2000, Ignition, 2001, Igby Goes Down, 2002, 29 Palms, 2002, Rick, 2003, The Grudge, 2004, The Orphan King, 2005, Dear Wendy, 2005, Scary Movie 4, 2006; (TV movies) Home Fires Burning, 1989, Crazy in Love, 1992, The Last Seduction, 1994, Mistrial, 1996, Merry Christmas George Bailey, 1997, The Virginian, 2000, Tiger Cruise, 2004; (TV series) Revelations, 2005-. Office: UTA care JJ Harris 9560 Wilshire Blvd Ste 500 Beverly Hills CA 90212-2427 also: Big Town Prodns Ste 80 6201 Sunset Blvd Los Angeles CA 90028-8704

PULLMAN, JENNIFER KING, art educator, artist; d. John Lindsay King, Jr. and Leila Luening King; 1 child, Ian Thomas. BA, Stockton Coll. N.J., 1978; MA in Tchg., Marygrove Coll., 1999; PhD, Walden U., 2007. Cert. elem. educator N.J., art edn. N.J. Artist, interior designer, Pomona, NJ, 1978—, Egg Harbor, 1978—, McKee City, 1978—; tchr. kindergarten Our Lady of Sea Sch., Atlantic City, 1985—89; tchr. 3d grade Atlantic City Pub. Schs., 1989—93, educator art, 1993—. Leader curriculum task force Atlantic City Pub. Schs., 2001—02, new tchr. mentor, 1992—, advisor art club, 1993—. Contbg. editor: Jour. of Educational Practice and Social Change, 2006—. Recipient Govs. Recognition award, N.J. Edn. Dept., 1998, Recognition award, Atlantic City Edn. Found., 2006. Mem.: Am. Edn. Rsch. Assn., NJ Art Educators Assn., Nat. Art Educators Assn., Noyes Mus. Art, Atlantic City Art Ctr., Phi Delta Kappa (v.p. programs 2004—). Avocations: interior decorating, singing, guitar, gardening, exercise. Office Phone: 609-343-7300. Personal E-mail: cyberhen@verizon.net.

PULLMAN, MAYNARD EDWARD, biochemist; b. Chgo., Oct. 26, 1927; s. Harry and Gertrude (Atlas) P.; m. E. Phyllis Light, Sept. 12, 1948; children: H. Cydney, B. Valerie, Jacky Leigh. BS, U. Ill., 1948, MS, 1950; PhD (NIH fellow), Johns Hopkins U., 1953. Fellow in pediatrics Johns Hopkins Hosp., 1953-54; asst. Pub. Health Rsch. Inst., NYC, 1954-56, assoc., 1956-61, assoc. mem., 1961-65, mem., 1965-89, chief, 1973-87, assoc. dir., 1983-89; sr. rsch. scientist Coll. Physicians and Surgeons Columbia U., 1989-92. Vis. prof. biochemistry U. São Paulo (Brazil) Sch. Medicine, 1963-64; research assoc. prof. biochemistry Sch. Medicine NYU, 1966-76, research prof., 1976-90; biochemistry study section mem. NIH, 1969-73. Editorial bd.: Jour. Biol. Chemistry, 1967-71, 78-80. NIH grantee, 1956-85; Shubert Found. grantee, 1972-74. Fellow N.Y. Acad. Scis.; mem. AAAS, Am. Soc. Biol. Chemistry and Molecular Biology, Brit. Biochem. Soc., Am. Chem. Soc. Home and Office: 338 Archer St Freeport NY 11520-4233 Home Phone: 516-378-7442. E-mail: mep2658@aol.com.

PULLMAN, PHILIP NICHOLAS, writer, educator; b. Norwich, Norfolk, Eng., Oct. 19, 1946; s. Alfred Outram and Audrey Evelyn (Merrifield) Pullman; m. Judith Speller, Aug. 15, 1970; children: James, Thomas. BA, Oxford U., 1968. Tchr. Oxfordshire Edn. Authority, Oxford, Eng., 1972-88; lectr. Westminster Coll., Oxford, 1988-96. Author: Count Karlstein, 1982, The Ruby in the Smoke, 1987 (Best Book award Internat. Reading Assn., 1988), Shadow in the North, 1988, The Tiger in the Well, 1991, Spring-Heeled Jack, 1991, The Broken Bridge, 1992, The White Mercedes, 1993, The Subtle Knife, 1997, Clockwork or All Wound Up, 1998, I Was a Rat!, 1999, The Amber Spyglass, 2000 (Whitbread Book of Yr., 2001), The Golden Compass, 2001 (Guardian Children's Fiction award, 1996, Carnegie medal, 1996), Lyra's Oxford, 2003, The Scarecrow and his Servant, 2005. Recipient Astrid Lindgren Meml. award lit., Govt. Sweden, 2005. Avocations: music, drawing.

PULOS, VIRGINIA KATE, actress, consultant; b. Dayton, Ohio, Oct. 12, 1947; d. James C. and Mary M. Pulos; m. Georgios S. Georgiou; 1 child, Kate Elizabeth Chiemingo. BFA in Music summa cum laude, U. Cin., 1970. Singer, actor Broadway, Off Broadway, Stock, Film, Regional Theatre, more, 1970-89; founder, pres. Ginny Pulos Comms., Inc., 1989—. Speech, media and tng. cons.; asst. prof comm. NYU Sch. Continuing and Profl. Studies; speaker confs. in field. Actress: Portrait of Jenny (Eugene O'Neil award, Richard Rodgers award), regular appearances on TV shows: All My Children, As the World Turns, The Doctors, 1982-88; numerous major opera and musical theatre roles, including: (Broadway) A Little Night Music, (Regional) My Fair Lady, others, 1970—; numerous radio and TV commls., 1970-80; guest soloist: Bklyn. Kingsboro Symphony in the Parks, 1984, 85, others. Program chair The Matrix Awards, 1993, 95, 96, others. Named Corbett Found. Internat. Opera fellow, Hamburg, Germany, 1969, N.Y.C., 1970-77. Mem. SAG, Actors Equity Assn., Am. Fedn. TV and Radio Actors, Pub. Rels. Soc. Am. (pres.-elect internat. sect 2005), N.Y. Women in Comm. (bd. dirs. 1992-99). Office: Ginny Pulos Comms Inc 4th Fl 1120 Ave of the Americas New York NY 10036-6700 Office Phone: 212-626-6597. Business E-Mail: info@ginnypulos.com.

PULOS, WILLIAM WHITAKER, lawyer; b. Hornell, NY, Aug. 29, 1955; s. William Leroy and Juanita (Whitaker) P. BA in Econs. magna cum laude, Alfred U., 1977; JD, Union U., 1980. Bar: N.Y. 1982, U.S. Supreme Ct. 1987. Pvt. practice, Alfred, NY, 1982—92, Hornell, NY, 1992—. Adj. prof. law Alfred U., 1981-90; prof. bus. adminstrn. SUNY-Alfred, 1982-84; tutor Empire State Coll., 1982-85; atty. Town of Alfred, 1982-99, Village of Almond (N.Y.), 1983-97, Town of West Almond (N.Y.), 1987-97, Town of Jasper, N.Y., 1988-91, Town of Almond, 1990-97, Town of West Union (N.Y.), 1992-98, Town of Birdsall (N.Y.), 1993-97; mem. Allegany County and Steuben County Assigned Counsel Program for Indigent Defendants, 1982-85; asst. counsel N.Y. State Assembly, 1980; hearing officer NY State Small Claims Assessment Rev., 1983-87, NY State Bd. Equalization and Assessment, 1988-91; tax atty. NY State Dept. Tax and Fin., 1983-91; pres. Alfred Dombec, Ltd., 1985-99, Maple City Way, Inc., 1990-97, Saxon Properties, Ltd., 1984-92. Active Alfred Sta. Vol. Fireman's Assn., Inc., 1985-98, 2d chief, 1988-92, pres. 1994-96, life mem; pres. Alfred Lions Club Inc., 1988-89. Recipient Outstanding Young Man Am. award U.S. Jaycees, 1982, 86, Internat. Humanitarian award Lions Club Internat., 1991. Mem. ABA, ATLA, N.Y. State Bar Assn. (lawyer referral program 1983-90, 98—), Steuben County Bar Assn., NYS Acad. Trial Lawyers, Phi Kappa Phi, Pi GAmma Mu, Delta Mu Delta, Alpha Iota Delta. Office: PO Box 337 70 Main St Hornell NY 14843-0337 Home Phone: 607-587-8403; Office Phone: 607-324-7333. Business E-Mail: wpulos@stny.rr.com.

PULSIFER, EDGAR DARLING, retired leasing and sales company executive; b. Natick, Mass., Jan. 11, 1934; s. Howard George and Elvie Marion (Morris) P.; m. Alice Minarik, Feb. 16, 1957 (div. Oct. 1979); children: Mark Edgar, Audrey Carol, Lee Howard; m. Barbara Ann Chuhak, Apr. 19, 1980. BSEE, MIT, 1955. With sales and service dept. Beckman Instruments, Fullerton, Calif., 1956-59; regional sales mgr. Hewlett Packard, Palo Alto, Calif., 1959-72, Gen. Automation, Anaheim, Calif., 1973-74; exec. v.p. Systems Mktg., Elk Grove Vlg., Ill., 1975-79; pres. Consol. Funding, Mt. Prospect, Ill., 1979—. Served as 1st lt. U.S. Army, 1956. Mem. MENSA, Coast Guard Auxiliary. Republican. Episcopalian. Avocations: coins, stamps, curling, scuba diving, golf. Home and Office: Consol Funding Corp 3914 Dundee Rd Northbrook IL 60062 Personal E-mail: edpulsifer@comcast.net. Business E-Mail: consfunding@comcast.net.

PULTE, WILLIAM J., construction executive; married; 14 children. Founder, pres. William J. Pulte, Inc., 1950—69; pres. Pulte Homes Corp. (formerly William J. Pulte, Inc.), 1969—, chmn. of exec. com. of bd., 1972—90, chmn., 1991—99, 2001—. Named one of Forbes' Richest Ams., 2005—06. Avocations: golf, art. Office: Pulte Homes 100 Bloomfield Hills Pky Ste 300 Bloomfield Hills MI 48304 *

PULWERS, JACK EDWARD, news executive, writer, historian, journalism educator, lecturer, broadcaster; b. NYC, July 2, 1924; s. Leon and Frances Pulwers; m. Florence Jeanette Prisaznick, Apr. 29, 1989; children: George Conlon, Christina Carter, Marilyn Smith, John Pulwers, Mary Komm, Peter Conlon, Paul Conlon, Jack E. Pulwers Jr., Therese Conlon, Clare Conlon, David Pulwers, Patrick Conlon, Gerard Conlon, Abbe Pulwers, Anne Johnson. Student, Centenary Coll., Shreveport, La., La. State U., Baton Rouge, BA, 1948; Masters in Polit. Sci. and History, La. State U., 1955; graduate, USAF Air War Coll., 1972; Doctorate in History with distinction, Catholic U. Am., 1983. News and pub. affairs dir. leading stations in US and on major networks; news and pub. affairs chief WABC NY; head Armed Forces Radio and Television; broadcast and news chief US Armed Forces Radio and Television, 1966—82; PA action officer Sec. Weinberger's Defense Pub. Affairs News Br., Washington, 1982—89; head depts. history and journalism Inst. Arts and Design, Bklyn., Washington Hall Coll., Penn Media Ctr., Washington; assoc. prof., co-founder journalism dept. Bowie State U. Among the first disc jockeys in Am.; vis. prof. various institutions; expert in WWII history and military journalism; advisor to several TV networks on special documentaries; writer, rschr., lectr., narrator. Author: The Press of Battle: The GI Reporter and the American People, My Sons Wore Gray, Mr. Smith Comes to Washington, Jefferson's Newsman, The Biggest Bang: The U.S. Army's Information Explosion of World War II, A History of the U.S. Army Public Affairs, 1783-1983; contbr. numerous manuscripts, tapes, narrative documentaries, interviews, special events broadcasts, and essays to archives, libraries, and universities. Pvt. US Army, 1943—45. Recipient Mayor's award, Detroit, 1957, Mich. Constitution award, former Gov. George Romney, 1958, Citizen's Budget Com. award, NYC, 1962, Documentary award, Ohio State U., 1963, Equitable Savings award, NYC, 1964, Governor's award, NJ Gov. Richard Hughes, 1964, Mayor's award, Mayor Robert Wagner, NYC, 1964, DuPont Journalism award, 1965, Dept. Defense Quality awards, 1978, 1980, 1982, 1984, Medal award for WWII rsch. and writings, Stars and Stripes Newspaper, 2005, Hall of Fame, Byrd HS, Shreveport La., 2005, Alumni Achievement award, Catholic U. Am., 2006. Mem.: KC (Fourth Degree as Sir Knight), Diplomatic and Consular Orgn. Retired, Aviation and Space Writers Soc. (founding mem.), Nat. Hist. Soc. (founding mem.), Orgn. Am. Historians, Am. Hist. Assn., Nat. Radio-TV News Dir. Assn., Soc. Profl. Journalists, European and Pacific Stars and Stripes Assn., Internat. Combat Camera Assn., Assn. US Army, USAF Assn., Nat. Fed. Retired and Active Govt. Employees, USAF Pub. Affairs Assn., US Marine Combat Correspondents Assn., Am. Legion, Uniformed Firemen's Assn. of NY (life), Catholic U. Am. Alumni Assn., NYU Alumni Assn., La. State U. Alumni Assn., Loyal Order of the Moose (Legionaire mem.), Overseas Press Club. Am., Nat. Press Club (mem. oral history com.), Phi Alpha Theta (Theta Omricon br., life), Sigma Delta Chi. Achievements include among the first radio documentarians; produced 365 documentaries and social commentaries for both individual radio stations and networks, 1945-1982; introduced the world to the first around-the-clock 24-hours a day worldwide news broadcasting service on cable and shortware; organized and supervised the broadcast; first to record, produce and narrate a documentary on vinyl records, on the first trip to America by a Pope of the Catholic Church (Pope Paul VI); interviewed notable individuals such as the Beatles (exclusive interview on their first trip to America, 1964), Malcolm X, Elvis Presley, Eleanor Roosevelt, Harry Truman, Bob Hope, and others; first in America to offer 24-hour news coverage from a news street patrol; a founding member of one of the first post-WWII American Legion and Amvets Posts, Shreveport, Louisiana. Avocations: travel, history. Personal E-mail: jpnews@cox.net.

PUMA, VINCENT DOUGLAS, literature and language professor; b. Buffalo, Feb. 1, 1949; s. Lena and Thomas Massaro (Stepfather); m. Dorothy Paillou, Jan. 4, 1982; children: Jeremy Vincent, Alexander Jonathan. PhD, Ind. U. Pa., 1987. Instr. Wilberforce U., Ohio, 1971—73; prof. English Flagler Coll., St. Augustine, Fla., 1973—. Adv. UOAA, 2002. Office: Flagler Coll 74 King St Saint Augustine FL 32085 Office Phone: 904-819-6278.

PUMARIEGA, ANDRES JULIO, medical administrator, educator, researcher; b. Matanzas, Cuba, Jan. 25, 1953; came to U.S., 1962; s. Andrès Augustin and America Maria (Mechoso) P.; m. JoAnne Buttacavoli, Dec. 26, 1975; children: Christina Marie, Nicole Marie. BS, U. Miami, Coral Gables, Fla., 1973; MD, U. Miami, Fla., 1976. Resident in psychiatry Duke U., Durham, N.C., 1976-78, fellow in child psychiatry, 1978-80; dir. child psychiatry consultation/liaison svc. Vanderbilt U., Nashville, 1980-83; dir. pediat. psychiatry consultation/liaison svc. Tex. Children's Hosp. Baylor Coll. Medicine, Houston, 1983-86; dir. divsn. child adolescent psychiatry U. Tex. Med. Bd., Galveston, 1986-91, dir. residency program, 1987-92; prof. neuropsychiatry and behavioral scis. U. S.C., Columbia, 1992-96, dir. divsn. child and adolescent psychiatry, 1992-96, vice-chmn. dept. neuropsychiatry and behavior sci., 1994-96; assoc. dir. William S. Hall Psychiat. Inst., Columbia, 1992-96; prof. psychiatry and behavioral scis. East Tenn. State U., Johnson City, 1996—2006, chmn. dept. psychiatry and behavioral scis., 1996-2001, dir. divsn. child and adolescent psychiatry, 1996—2006, dir. Ctr. of Excellence Children in Custody, 2002—06; chmn. dept. psychiatry Reading Hosp. and Med. Ctr., Pa., 2006—; prof. psychiatry Temple U., Phila., 2006—; clin. prof. psychiatry U. Medicine and Dentistry NJ, Camden, 2006—. Examiner in child psychiatry and gen. psychiatry Am. Bd. Psychiatry and Neurology, Chgo., 1983—; co-investigator, mem. exec. com. Ctr. Cross-Cultural Rsch., Galveston, 1989-91; chmn. rsch. com. and exec. bd. S.C. Pub. Acad. Mental Health Consortium, 1994-96; chair Nat. Latin Behavioral Work Group, 1995—2000; chair Hispanic panel managed care initiative Ctr. for Mental Health Svcs. Abuse and MH Adminstrn., 1996—2000; cons. Ctr. for Substance Abuse Treatment USPHS, 1995-96; mem. nat. adv. coun. Ctr. Mental Health Svcs., Substance Abuse and Mental Health Adminstrn. U.S. Dept. HHS, 1997-2001. Editor: (with H. Vance) Clinical Assessment of Child and Adolescent Behavior, 2001; (with N. Winters) Handbook of Child and Adolescent Systems of Care: The New Community Psychiatry, 2003; editor Psychline Jour. Hispanic Am. Psychiatry, 2005-06; assoc. editor Jour. Child and Family Studies, 1996-2002, Am. Jour. Orthopsychiatry, 2005-; contbr. over 150 articles, chpts., monographs, and over 150 abstracts to profl. jours. Bd. dirs. Tex. Network for Children, Austin, 1986-88; mem. adv. coun. Ptnrs. Advocacy Network, 1990-92. Named to Alumni Hall of Fame, U. Miami Sch. Medicine, 1999; recipient Exemplary Psychiatrist award, Nat. Alliance for Mentally Ill, 1993, 1997, cert. of merit for beneficiary svc., Health Care Fin. Adminstrn., U.S. Dept. HHS, 1996; grantee, Ctr. for Cross-Cultural Rsch., NIMH, Bethesda, Md., 1988—92, Fullerton Found., 1993—95; Minority Child Psychiatrist Tng. grant, NIMH, 1988—92, site coord., grantee, Nat. Assn. State Mental Health Dir. Rsch. Fellowship, 1993—, Forest Pharm., 2000. Fellow: Coll. Physicians Phila., Tenn. Coun. Child and Adolescent Psychiatry (pres. 2001—06), Acad. Psychosomatic Medicine, Am. Psychiat. Assn. (disting.) (chair Hispanic com. 2006—, Simon Bolivar award 2004, Silver award outstanding svcs. 2004), Am. Acad. Child Psychiatry (chmn. work group on sys. of care 1994—2001, chmn. cmty. psych. com. 2001—07, chmn. diversity and culture com. 2007—, Outstanding Mentor award 1994, Catchers in the Rye award 2001, Jeanne Spurlock Diversity and Culture award and lectr. 2007), Am. Acad. Pediat.; mem.: Am. Orthopsychiat. Assn. (bd. dir. 2004—), S.C. Soc. Child and Adolescent Psychiatry (founding pres. 1996—97), Tex. Mental Health Assn. (mem. children's adv. com. 1991—92), Tenn. Soc. Child Psychiatry (sec. 1982—83, pres. 2001—06), Bay Area Pediat. Soc. (pres. 1990—91), Soc. Profs. of Child Psychiatry, Am. Assn. Cmty. Psychiatrists (bd. dir. 1996—2006, Ethics in Pub. Managed Care award 2000), Am. Coll. Psychiatrists, Nat. Mental Health Assn. (bd. dir. 1999). Roman Catholic. Avocations: swimming, political history, public affairs. Home: 27 Linree Ave Reading PA 19606-9075 Office: Reading Hosp & Med Ctr Dept Psychiatry Sixth Ave and Spruce St Reading PA 19611 Office Phone: 610-988-9318. Personal E-mail: pumarieg@verizon.net. Business E-Mail: pumariegaa@readinghospital.org.

PUMARIEGA, JOANNE BUTTACAVOLI, mathematics educator; b. Coral Gables, Fla., May 27, 1952; d. Ciro Charles and Rosaria Frances (Calabrese) Buttacavoli; m. Andres Julio Pumariega, Dec. 26, 1975; children: Christina Marie, Nicole Marie. BA in Math. and Edn. magna cum laude, U. Miami, 1973, MA in Math., 1974; postgrad., U. Houston, 1991-92. Cert. secondary math. tchr., Tex., Fla., Tenn., N.C. Grad. tchg. asst. U. Miami, Coral Gables, 1973-74; substitute tchr. Dade County Pub. Schs., Miami, 1975; math. instr. Miami Dade C.C., 1975-76; math. and G.E.D. instr. Durham (N.C.) Tech. Inst., 1976-77; math. instr. Durham H.S., 1977-78, Durham Acad., 1978-80, Univ. Sch. of Nashville, 1980-83; pvt. practice math. instr. Houston, 1984-86; tutor Clear Lake Tutoring Svc., Houston, 1987-90; pvt. practice, S.A.T, lang. instr. League City, Tex., 1990-92; pvt. practice math. and S.A.T. instr. Johnson City, Tenn., 1996—; lang. instr. Nelson Elem. Sch., Columbia, 1993-96. Instr. fgn. langs. and math. Lonnie B. Nelson Elem. Sch., Columbia, SC; faculty math. East Tenn. State U., 1999-2006, Pa. State-Berks., 2006—. Author (with F. Rodriguez and A. Pumariega): HIV/AIDS in Children and Adolescents, 1999; co-author (with A. Pumariega): Risk Factors of Mental Illness and Addiction Amongst Hispanic Immigrant Youth, 2002; contbr. articles to profl. jours. Chair bd. edn. St. Mary Parish, League City, 1988-90, lector, 1992, v.p. coun. Cath. Women, Johnson City, 1997-99; C.C.E. tchr. St. John Neumann Cath. Ch., Columbia, SC, Johnson City, Tenn., 1993-95, lector, 1992-96; lector St. Mary's Ch., Johnson City, 1996-2006, St. Catharine of Siena Ch., Reading, Pa., 2006—; treas. St. Thomas More Women's Club, Houston, 1985-86; v.p., then pres. housestaff med. wives Duke U., Durham, NC, 1978-80; mem. Wash./Unicoi/Johnson County Med. Alliance, 1999-2004, chair pub. rels. com., 1999-2002, asst. treas., 2002-03, membership chair, 2003-04, co-chair caring com., 2004-05, corr. sec., 2005-06; co-chair Am. Med. Assn., 2004-05. Recipient Above and Beyond award, East Tenn. State U., 2002. Mem. Berks County Med. Alliance, Newcomers of Greater Columbia (chmn. pub. rels. chpt. 1993,95), Newcomers of Greater Colo. (com. chair coord. 1994-95), Welcome Neighbors of Bay Area (v.p., program chmn. 1991-92), Tex. Med. Aux., Bay Area Med. Wives, East Tenn. State U. Women's Club (v.p. 1997-98, pres. 1998-99, parliamentarian 1999-2000), U. S.C. Faculty Women's Club (v.p. 1993-94, pres. 1994-95, parliamentarian, advisor 1995-96), Phi Kappa Phi, Kappa Delta Pi, Delta Kappa Gamma (corr. sec. Gamma chpt. 2004-06), Alpha Lamba Delta (Woman of Yr. 1972). Roman Catholic. Avocations: reading, travel. Home: 27 Linree Ave Reading PA 19606-9075 Office Phone: 610-396-6007. Personal E-mail: pumarieg@verizon.net.

PUMPHREY, GERALD ROBERT, lawyer; b. Flushing, NY, May 31, 1947; s. Fred Paul and Anne (Afferman) Pumphrey; m. Joann DeLillo, Oct. 6, 1968; children: Gerald, Christopher, Elena. BBA, St. John's U., 1969, MBA, 1974; JD, Nova U., 1978. Bar: Fla. 1978. Assoc. Walden & Walden, Dania, Fla., 1978; v.p. legal svcs. Golden Bear, Inc., North Palm Beach, Fla., Jack Nicklaus & Assocs., Air Bear, Inc., also bd. dirs.; v.p., sec. Triple P., Inc., 1978-83; pvt. practice, 1983—. Bd. advisor Benjamin Sch. Found. Athletics Assn., 1980—83; coord. Benjamin Sch. Found., Inc.; mem. golf com. St. Clare's Sch.; pres. St. Clare's Home and Sch. Assn., 1983—84; bd. dirs. Deaf Svc. Ctr. Palm Beach County, Inc., 1988—89. Mem.: North Palm Beach County Bar Assn. (pres. 1991—92), Palm Beach County Bar Assn., North Palm Beaches C. of C. (counsel 1987—2003), Palm Beach Gardens C. of C., Rotary (bd. dirs. North Palm Beach 1998—2003, pres. 2001—02), Kiwanis (charter mem., bd. dirs. Palm Beach Gardens 1983—87), Phi Alpha Delta. Office: 4495 Military Trail Ste 201 Jupiter FL 33458 Office Phone: 561-622-5446. Office Fax: 561-626-4824. Business E-Mail: pumphreypa@aol.com.

PUNDMANN, ED JOHN, JR., automotive company executive; b. St. Charles, Mo., Feb. 24, 1939; s. Ed J. Sr. and Ruth O. (Brehme) P.; m. Dolores Anne Lienau, June 15, 1963 (dec.); children: Mary Ann, Steven A., Susan K. BA, Westminster Coll., 1961. Jr. accountant Peat, Marwick & Mitchell, St. Louis, 1961-62; salesman Pundmann Ford, St. Charles, 1962-82, gen. mgr., 1982-92, pres., 1992—. Bd. dirs., chmn. First State Bank; mem. St. Charles City Tax Incremental Financing Commn., 1990-99; mem. Ford Motor Dispute Settlement Bd., 1993-94, St. Charles County Work Force Devel. Bd., 2002-05, Ford Motor Co. Nat. Dealer Coun., 2001-03. Treas. St. Charles City Charter Commn., 1981; mem. St. Charles City Park Bd., 1981-82; chmn. St. Charles City Econ. Devel. Commn.; mem. St. Charles City Park Found. Bd., 1985—, also past pres.; St. Louis Regional Commerce and Growth Assn.; adv. bd. St. Charles County; mem. Handicapped Facilities Bd. St. Charles County, 1986-94, also past pres.; active St. Charles County Road Bd., 1996-2005; past pres. St. John United Ch. of Christ; bd. dirs. Emmaus Homes, 1981-91, Parkside Meadows Retirement Facility, 1982-2001; chmn. St. Charles City Charter Rev. Commn., 1991; bd. dirs. St. Charles Jaycee Village Retirement Home, 1980-90, Boone Ctr. Workshop, 1982-92, Parkside Found., 2001-, St. Charles City Schs. Found., 1995-2006, St. Charles Crime Stoppers, 1999—; dist. chmn. Boy Scouts Am., 1979-82. Recipient Gov. of Mo. award, 1989, Mo. Time Quality Dealer award, 1995, United Ch. of Christ award, 1993, Jefferson award TV Sta. KSDK, St. Louis, 1996, Profl. Excellence Achievement award St. Charles C.C., 2002. Mem. Mo. Auto Dealers Assn. (bd. dirs. 1983—, treas. 1997-98, 2d v.p. 1998-99, 1st v.p. 1999-2000, pres. 2000-2001), Greater St. Louis Ford Dealers Assn. (past pres.), St. Charles C. of C. (past bd. dirs., pres., Citizen of Yr. award 1986, Small Bus. Person of Yr. 2002), Rotary (past pres.). Lodges: Rotary. Home: 3304 Lennox Dr Saint Charles MO 63301-0632 Office: Pundmann Ford 2727 W Clay St Saint Charles MO 63301-2566 Business E-Mail: edp@pundmannford.com.

PUNDT, RICHARD ARTHUR, lawyer; b. Apr. 18, 1944; s. Arthur Herman and Johanna Celeste (Pasterik) Pundt; m. Joyce Kay Schoenfelder, Dec. 1, 1968; children: Vincent Arthur, Jennifer Johanna, Heather Ann. BA, State U. Iowa, 1966; JD, Drake U., 1969. Temporary claims dep. Iowa Employment Security Commn., 1968—69; admitted to Iowa bar, 1969; staff atty. Polk County Legal Aid Office Econ. Opportunity, 1969; spl. agt. FBI, 1969—71; prin. Richard A. Pundt. Law Office; pres. and CEO enlighten techs., Inc (IP video network); pres. Lawchek Ltd. Dir. Cedar Rapids Profl. Football Corp., 1972—73, pres., 1972—73. Exec. dir. Iowans for Rockefeller, 1968, Polk County Republican Com., 1968—69; mem. Linn County Rep. Ctrl. Com., 1972—78; chmn. Linn County Rep. party, 1977—78; asst. prosecuting atty. Linn County, 1972—76. Mem.: Linn County Bar Assn., Iowa Bar Assn., Am. Iowa Bar Assn., Metro Athletic Assn. (dir. 1976—), Sertoma. Roman Catholic. Home: 3851 Hickory Ridge Ln SE Cedar Rapids IA 52403-3765 Office: 330 1st St SE Cedar Rapids IA 52401-1702 Office Phone: 319-363-8800. Business E-Mail: rpundt@lawchek.net.

PUNWANEY, JUANITA, dermatologist; d. Bhagwan Sitaldas and Lavina B. Punwaney. BA summa cum laude, Columbia U., NYC, 1987; MD in Parasitology, Nutrition and Biostats. with honors, Columbia Coll., NYC, 1991. Diplomate Am. Bd. Dermatology, Nat. Bd. Med. Examiners. Intern Columbia Presbyn. Med. Ctr., NYC, 1991—92; resident in dermatology Wayne State U./Detroit Med. Ctr., 1992—95; dermatologist Allied Dermatology Svcs., PC, Detroit, 1995—96, Midwest Health Ctr., PC, Dearborn, Mich., 1997—98, Advanced Dermatology, PC, Fresh Meadows, NY, 1998—99, DOCS Physicians Affiliated with Beth Israel Med. Ctr., Valhalla, NY, 2001—03, ProHEALTH Care Assocs., LLP, Lake Success, NY, 2004—06, North Shore-Long Islane Jewish Health Sys., Lake Success, 2006—. Cons. in field. Fellow: Am. Acad. Dermatology; mem.: Met. Mus. ARt, Young Patrons Soc. Lincoln Ctr., Delta Beta Beta Kappa. Avocations: walking, jogging, swimming, travel. Office: North Shore-LI Jewish Health Sys Faculty Practice 2800 Marcus Ave Ste # 200 New Hyde Park NY 11042

PUNYANUNT-CARTER, NARISSRA, communications educator; BA, Tex. Tech. U., 1995, MA, 1996; PhD, Kent State U., Ohio, 2000. Asst. prof. Tex. Tech. U., Lubbock, 2002—. Recipient Tchr. of Yr. award nominee, Nat. Spkrs. Assn., 2005, Grad. Student Senate Dissertation award, Kent State U., Grad. Sch., 2003, Dissertation award, Kent State U., Sch. Comm., 2003, Rsch. award, 2002, Kent State U., Grad. Student Senate, 2002, Kent State U., Sch. of Comm. Studies, 2001, Summer Dissertation Fellow sScholarship, Kent State U., 2001, Leadership Excellence award, 2001, Outstanding Tchg. Asst. award, Internat. Comm. Assn., 2000. Mem.: Nat. Comm. Assn. Office: Texas Tech U Dept Comms PO Box 43083 Lubbock TX 79409-3083 Home Phone: 806-742-3273. E-mail: n.punyanunt@ttu.edu.

PUOTINEN, ARTHUR EDWIN, college president, minister; b. Crystal Falls, Mich., Sept. 7, 1941; s. Kaleva Weikko and Ines Pauline (Maki) P.; m. Judith Cathleen Kapoun, Aug. 8, 1964; children: Anne, Marjetta, Sara. AA, Suomi Coll., 1961; BA, Augustana Coll., Rock Island, Ill., 1963; MDiv, Luth. Sch. Theology, Chgo., 1967; MA, U. Chgo., 1969, PhD, 1973; MBA, Wake Forest U., 1984. Pastor Trinity Luth. Ch., Chgo., 1968-70; asst. prof. religion Cen. Mich. U., Mt. Pleasant, 1971-74; dean faculty Suomi Coll., Hancock, Mich., 1974-78; v.p. acad. affairs Lenoir-Rhyne Coll., Hickory, N.C., 1978-83; assoc. dean acad. affairs Roanoke Coll., Salem, Va., 1983-84; exec. dir. Luth. Ednl. Conf. of N.Am., Washington, 1984-88; pres. Grand View Coll., Des Moines, 1988-96; v.p., provost Finlandia U., Hancock, Mich., 1996—2002; pastor Bethlehem Luth. Ch.,

Elgin, Ill., 2004—. Pastor ELCA Met. Chgo. Synod, Evang.-Luth. Ch. Am. Author: Finnish Radicals..., 1979; contbr. articles to books and jours. Grantee NEH, U.S. Dept. Edn. Democrat. Avocations: jogging, reading, travel. Home: 2885 Weld Rd Elgin IL 60124 Office Phone: 847-741-8434. E-mail: artpuotinen@sbcglobal.net.

PUPKIN, BARRY A., lawyer; b. Chgo., 1950; AB summa cum laude, Calif. State U. - San Diego, 1972; JD, Stanford U., 1975. Bar: Calif. 1976, DC 1976. Trial atty. Fed. Trade Commn., 1975—76; ptnr. Squire, Sanders & Dempsey LLP, Washington, chmn., Econ. Regulation Practice Group. Bd. adv. The Antitrust Counselor. Office: Squire Sanders & Dempsey LLP 1201 Pennsylvania Ave NW PO Box 407 Washington DC 20044-0407 Office Phone: 202-626-6662. Office Fax: 202-626-6780. Business E-Mail: bpupkin@ssd.com.

PURCELL, AARON D., archivist, historian; b. Lexington, Ky., May 30, 1972; s. R.D. and Betty A. Purcell; m. Laura Stevralia Purcell, June 30, 2000; 1 child, Samuel Sullivan. BS in Edn., Cumberland Coll., 1994; MA in History, U. Louisville, 1996; MLS in Archives, U. Md., 1999; PhD in History, U. Tenn., 2006. Univ. archivist U. Tenn., Knoxville, 2000—. Grantee nat. leadership grantee, Inst. Mus. and Libr. Svcs., 2005—. Mem.: Soc. Am. Archivists. Office: Spl Collections Libr 1401 Cumberland Ave Knoxville TN 37996 Office Phone: 865-974-3674. Office Fax: 865-974-0560. E-mail: apurcel2@utk.edu.

PURCELL, ALEXANDER HOLMES, entomologist, educator; b. Summit, Miss., Oct. 12, 1942; s. Alexander H. and Dorothy (Adams) P.; m. Rita Hall, Oct. 14, 1946. BS, USAF Acad., 1964; PhD, U. Calif., Davis, 1974. Commd. capt. USAF, 1964, officer, pilot, 1964-70, resigned, 1970; grad. rsch. asst. U. Calif., Davis, 1971-74, prof. entomology Berkeley, 1974—, dept. chair, 1993, head div. entomology and plant and soil microbiology, 1994, head divsn. environ. biology dept. environ. sci., policy and mgmt. Cons. FAO (UN), 1981. Contbr. articles to profl. jours. Fellow Calif. Acad. Sci.; mem. AAAS, Am. Soc. for Microbiology, Entomological Soc. Am., Am. Phytopath. Soc. Avocations: flying, fishing. Office: U Calif Dept Environ Sci and Policy and Mgmt 137 Mulford Hall MC 3114 Berkeley CA 94720-3114

PURCELL, ANN RUSHING, state legislator, human services manager; b. Reidsville, Ga., May 12, 1945; d. William Robert and Katie (Dasher) Rushing; m. Dent Wiley Purcell, May 26, 1966; children: Edwin Wiley, Mieke Ann, Mikki Marie. BS in Edn., Ga. So. Coll., 1966; degree (hon.), Ga. Future Farmers Am., 1999. Cert. secondary tchr. Tchr. math. Evans H.S., Ga., 1966-68; tchr. math., earth and sci. Beaumont Jr. H.S., Lexington, Ky., 1969-70; substitute tchr. Tallahassee, 1970's; agt. Noblin Realty, Tallahassee, 1970's; office mgr. Radiation Therapy Assocs., PC, Savannah, Ga., 1979—; state legislator Ho. of Reps. Ga. Gen. Assembly, Atlanta, 1991—2005. Author: Purcells of South Georgia and Other Related Families, 1976. Bd. dirs. Med. Assn. Ga. Polit. Action Com., Atlanta, 1988-89, Girl Scout Coun. Savannah, 1991-93, Effingham YMCA, 1999-, New Ebenezer Retreat Ctr., 2006—; Effingham County fin. chmn. State YMCA, 1991-05, vice chmn. steering com., 1999, bd. dirs., 1999; trustee Ga. So. U. Found., 1992—, Armstrong Atlantic U. Found., 2004-05, 06, 07, sec., 2005, 06, 07; mem. adv. com. Effingham County Extension Svc., 1992—; chmn. steering com. Effingham YMCA Bd., 2004, 05, 06, 07, chmn. fin. devel., 2005-; mem. adv. com. Treutlin Home, 1999-04; bd. adv. Claxton Youth Detention Ctr. Hon. comdr. 165th Ga. Air Guard Airlift, 1997-04; hon. mem. Civil Air Patrol, 2001-05, Ga. State Patrol, 2001; state bd. mem. Ga. Dept. Tech. and Adult Edn., 2005-; co-chmn. Ga. Edn. Joint Edn. Com., 2006, 07; mem. adv. bd. Ga. Pacific, 2006—; bd. dirs. New Ebenezer Retreat Ctr., 2006. Decorated WA-PO-HE award Ga. Nat. Air Guard, Minuteman award, Dept. Def. Commendatino medal; named Ga.'s Legislator of Yr., Ga. Sch. Counselors Assn., 1996, Ga. Legislator of Yr., Coastal Conservation Assn. Ga., 1998, Vol. of Yr., Effingham YMCA, 2006; named to Hon. Ga. State Patrol, 2001; recipient Friend of Medicine award, Med. Assn. Ga., 1991, 1993, 1994, 1996, Ga. Vet. award, 2003, Guardian of Small Bus. award, Nat. Fedn. Ind. Bus., 1992, 1994, 1996, Commendation cert., Ga. Emergency Mgmt. Agy., 1995, Vol. of Yr. award, Effingham 4-H, 1998, Nat. Am. hon. degree, Future Farmers Am., 1999, Friend of State 4-H award, 1999, Svc. award, Effingham Recreation Dept., 2000, Cmty. Svc. award, Guyton Masonic Lodge, 2000, Hon. Family Consumer Cmty. Leaders of Ga. award, 2001, Ga. Pub. Health award, 2003, Effingham Jr. Adv. Family Connection award, 2003, 2004, Environ. Leadership award, Ga. Conservation Voters, 2003, 2004, Pub. Rels. award, Ga. Ext. Assn. of Family and Consumer Scis., 2003, Leadership award, Ga. Water Coalition, 2003, 2004, Charles Dick award, U.S. Nat. Guard, 2003, Air Nat. Guardsmen award, Savannah Assn. Flying, 2003, City of Pembroke award, 2004, Bryan County Svc. award, 2004, Friend of Effingham 4-H award, 2005, Friends award, Ga. Med. Soc., 2005, Vol. Yr., Coastal Ga. YMCA, 2007. Mem. Aux. to the Med. Assn. Ga. (pres. 1985), Aux. to the Ga. Med. Soc. (pres. 1981-82), Ga. Salzburger Soc. (bd. dirs. 2005, v.p. 2005, 06, 07, pres., 2007—), Effingham County Pub. Ofcls. Assn., Rotary Internat. (Effingham bd. dirs., 2007—, Paul Harris fellow 2003), Ga. Peace Officers Assn. (hon.), Rincon Noon Lions Club, Exch. Club. Republican. Methodist. Avocations: painting, genealogy, fishing. Home: 410 Willowpeg Way Rincon GA 31326-9157

PURCELL, BILL, mayor; b. Phila., Oct. 25, 1953; s. William Paxson, Jr. and Mary (Hamilton) Purcell; m. Deborah Lee Miller, Aug. 9, 1986; 1 child, Jesse Miller. AB, Hamilton Coll., 1976; JD, Vanderbilt U., 1979. Bar: Tenn. 1979, U.S. Ct. Appeals (6th cir.) 1985, U.S. Supreme Ct. 1988. Staff atty. W. Tenn. Legal Svcs., Jackson, 1979—81; asst. pub. defender Metro Pub. Defender, Nashville, 1981—84, sr. asst. pub. defender, 1984—85; assoc. Lionel R. Barrett, P.C., Nashville, 1985—86; ptnr. Farmer, Berry & Purcell, Nashville, 1986—90; mem. Tenn. Ho. of Reps., Nashville, 1986—96, also majority leader, 1990—96; dir. child and family policy ctr. Inst. Pub. Policy Studies, Vanderbilt U., Nashville, 1996—99; mayor Met. Govt. of Nashville and Davidson County, 1999—. Chmn. select com. on children and youth Tenn. Gen. Assembly, 1989—96; exec. dir. Vanderbilt Legal Aid Soc., 1978—79; chmn. NCSL Assembly State Issues, 1995; chmn. policy makers' program adv. bd. Danforth Found., 1993—2002; mem. adv. bd. U.S. Conf. Mayors, 2001—02, trustee, 2002—, chmn. task force hunger and homelessness, 2001—05. Vice chmn. Nat. League Cities, 2000—02, chmn. coun. youth, edn. and families, 2003; chmn. human svcs. com. Nat. Conf. State Legislatures, Washington, 1993; mem. exec. com. Dem. Nat. Com., 1994—97; exec. com. 6th Dist. Dems., Nashville, 1986—88; mem. Tenn. State Gen. Assembly, Nashville, 1986—96, majority leader, 1990—96; chmn. Dem. Legis. Campaign Com., 1994—96. Named Legislator of Yr., Dist. Atty.'s Gen. Conf., 1989, Tenn. Conservation League, 1991; recipient Disting. Alumnus award, Vanderbilt Law Sch., 2004, Pub. Ofcl. of Yr., Governing mag., 2006; Toll fellow, Coun. State Govts., 1988. Mem.: ABA, Nashville Bar Assn., Tenn. Bar Assn. Methodist. Office Phone: 615-862-6000. Office Fax: 615-862-6040. Business E-Mail: mayor@nashville.gov. *

PURCELL, BRADFORD MOORE, publishing company executive; b. Garden City, NY, Oct. 1, 1929; s. William Lawrence and Margaret (Moore) P.; m. Louise Rauth, July 10, 1954; children: Margaret, Philip, Mark, Louisa, Christopher. BA, Williams Coll., 1951; MBA, Columbia U., 1957. Sr. v.p. devel. McGraw Hill Inc., 1976-79, sr. v.p., 1979-81, group v.p. tng. systems, 1981-83, sr. v.p. mktg., 1983-85; pres. W.H. Smith Pubs Inc., NYC, 1985-91; v.p. admin. and fin. Rsch. Books Inc., 1992. Served to 1st lt. USAF, 1951-53. Home: 106 Tantumorantum Rd Lyme CT 06371-3137 Office: Rsch Books Inc PO Box 555 Old Saybrook CT 06475 E-mail: bradfordpurcell@yahoo.com.

PURCELL, GEORGE RICHARD, artist; b. Clayton, NY, May 4, 1921; s. George Thomas and Katherine Eileen (Eagan) P.; m. Mary Sutter, Apr. 3, 1961. BS, Niagara U., 1947; postgrad., Syracuse U., 1952-53, 55-56. With Eagan Real Estate, Syracuse, 1948-49; claims interviewer NY State Divsn. Unemployment Ins., 1949-50, 52; with US Postal Svc., Syracuse, 1957—, cert. classifier of mails, 1975-77, with registry dept., 1977—. Tutor in philosophy, 1971—; mem. world peace and diplomacy forum Internat. Biog. Ctr., Cambridge, Eng., rsch. coun. Exhibited in Ctrl. NY Art Open, 1981, Drake Gallery, Fayetteville, NY, 1982, Assoc. Artists Gallery, Syracuse, 1983, 91, Fayetteville Art Festival, 1984, Recreation Generation Art Exhibit, 1982—, DeWitt Libr., NY, 1986-94, NY State Fair, 1990, 99, Art Telauc WCNY-TV, Syracuse, 1990-01, Cazenovia Coll. Art Auction, 1994, Old Forge Art Show, NY, 2005. Founder, pres. Syracuse chpt. Cath. Med. Mission Bd., 1973-76, rep., 1976—; del. Presdl. Trust, 1992; active Cath. Near-East Welfare Assn., Book Mission Program, New Mems. Art Show Manlius Libr., 1991, Rep. Nat. Com., Heritage Found., Washington; dep. dir. gen. Internat. Biog. Assn., Cambridge, Eng. Served with U.S. Army, 1943-46. Decorated capt. Legion of the Eagle of the Sea, Order of Holy Cross of Jerusalem, knight Order of Lofsensian Ursinius, baron Royal Order of Bohemian Crown, knight Holy Cross of Jerusalem-Grand Priory of US; named to Hall of Fame, Am. Biog. Inst., Raleigh, NC; NY State War Svc. scholar, 1955. Fellow: Australian Inst. Coordinated Rsch. (life); mem.: French Nat. Acad., Confedn. Chivalry (chevalier), Italian Acad. Arts and Scis., Order of Templar (knight), Sovereign and Mil. Order of the Holy Sepulcher (knight), Order Holy Grail (knight), Acad. of Ho. of Internat. Intellectuals, Cross of Gold, Albert Sweitzer Austrian Soc., Alliance Universal for Peace (hon. prof.), Inst. High Studies, Am. Biog. Inst. (life assoc., rsch. bd. advisors nat. divsn., apptd. dep. dir., editl. adv. bd., nat. bd. advisors). Roman Catholic.

PURCELL, HENRY, III, real estate developer; b. Watertown, NY, Dec. 21, 1929; s. John Cecil and Elizabeth (Hathway) P.; m. L. Betty Collier; children: Robert William, Emmy Purcell Reynolds, Jenny Purcell Hawley. BS in Mil. Engring., U.S. Mil. Acad., 1953; MBA in Econs. and Fin., U. Utah, 1975; postgrad., Princeton, 1960-61; PhD in Bus., Kennedy Western U., 2001. Cert. Middle East specialist, Turkish linguist. Commd. 1st lt. U.S. Army, Augsburg, Republic of Germany, 1953, advanced through grades to lt. col., 1967, commdr. Co. K. 1st regiment, 5th infantry div. Augsburg, Fed. Republic of Germany, 1955-56, chief translation, U.S. Mil. Mission to Turkey Ankara, Turkey, 1957-59, batallion commdr., tng. div. Ft. Ord, Calif., 1965, sr. regimental adv. 7th ARVN regiment, 5th ARVN div. South Vietnam, 1966, adv. G3 plans, III Corps ARVN, 1966-67, with Middle East Plans div., U.S. Strike Commd. Tampa, Fla., 1968-70, asst. chief staff, G5 101st Airborne/Ambl div. I Corps, South Vietnam, 1970, with G3Plans, Iv Corps ARVN South Vietnam, 1970, sr. regimental adv. 32d regiment, 1971, with war plans div., deputy chief of staff, ops., The Pentagon, 1971, Middle East Specialist U.S. Readiness command Tampa, Fla., 1972-74, retired, 1974; Middle East specialist U.S. Attache's Office, Ankara, Istanbul, 1961-63; with Spacos, G3 Plans and nuclear weapons employment div. NATO, Izmir, Turkey, 1963-65; pres. Henry Purcell, Inc., Tampa, 1976—, Warn-a-Prowler Inc., Tampa, 1994—. Personal interpreter/Turkish translator for Lyndon B. Johnson. Author: Valuation of Publicly Traded Companies: Indicating Investment Targets, 2001. Pres. Nat. Sojourners, Tampa, 1969, 70, 72, Wilson Jr. High Sch. PTA, Tampa, 1977; commdr. Heroes of '76, Tampa, Fla., 1969, 70. Decorated DFC, Bronze Star for Valor with two oak leaf clusters, Cross of Gallantry, Gold Star, Silver Star (Vietnam), 10 Air medals, Army Commendation medal for valor with one oak leaf cluster with "V" device. Mem. Unified Constrn. Trades Bd., Nat. Assn. Realtors, Fla. West Coast Roofing Assn., Nat. Builders Assn., Greater Tampa C. of C. (com. of 100 1980—). Office: 825 W Platt St Tampa FL 33606-2251 Office Phone: 813-251-1698. E-mail: purcellh@aol.com.

PURCELL, JAMES NELSON, JR., cultural organization administrator; b. Nashville, July 16, 1938; s. James Nelson and Mary Helen P.; m. Walda Jean Primm, July 16, 1961; children: Deirdre Ann, Carole Elizabeth. BA in Polit. Sci., Furman U., 1961; M.P.A. (Maxwell Grad. Sch. fellow), Syracuse U., 1962. Mgmt. intern U.S. AEC, NYC, Washington, Oak Ridge, 1962, budget analyst Oak Ridge, Washington, 1962-66; mgmt. analyst AID, State Dept., Washington, 1966-68; budget preparation specialist Office Mgmt. and Budget/Exec. Office of the Pres., 1968-69, dept. chief budget preparation, 1969-72, sr. budget examiner Internat. Ednl. Exch. program, 1972-74, chief Justice-Treasury br., 1974-76; chief resources programming and mgmt. div. Bur. Ednl. and Cultural Affairs, Dept. State, Washington, 1976-77; exec. dir. Bur. Adminstrn., Dept. State, Washington, 1978-79; dep. asst. sec. Bur. Refugee Programs, Dept. State, Washington, 1979-82, dir., 1982-87; dir. gen. Internat. Orgn. for Migration, Geneva, 1988-98; internat. cons., 1998—; CEO Opine Pub., Columbia, Md., 2002—. Bd. dirs. Coun. for Cmty. of Democracies; sr. adv. Inst. for Study of Internat. Migration, Georgetown U. Mem. Am. Soc. Pub. Adminstrn. Home: 5113 W Running Brook Rd Columbia MD 21044 Home Phone: 410-730-1353; Office Phone: 443-745-2380. Personal E-mail: jpurcellatcol@comcast.net.

PURCELL, JOHN F., lawyer; b. Bellingham, Wash., Apr. 25, 1954; AB with honors, Stanford U., 1976; JD, Lewis and Clark Coll., 1980. Bar: Oreg. 1980. Ptnr. Miller Nash LLP, Portland, 1987—. Mem. Oreg. State Bar. Office: Miller Nash LLP 111 SW 5th Ave Ste 3500 Portland OR 97204-3638 Office Phone: 503-224-5858.

PURCELL, LEE (LEE JEUNE WILLIAMS), actress, film producer; b. Cherry Point, NC, June 15, 1957; 1 child, Dylan D. Purcell. Studies with Margot Lister, London; studies with Milton Katselas, Jeff Corey, U.S. Pres., owner Silver Strand Entertainment, LA, 1995—. Appeared in (films) Adam at 6 A.M., 1970, The Toy Factory, 1971, Dirty Little Billy, 1972, Kid Blue, 1973, Mr. Majestyk, 1974, Almost Summer, Big Wednesday, 1978, Stir Crazy, 1980, Valley Girl, Eddie Macon's Run, 1983, Laura's Dream, 1986, Airplane II, 1989, Trackers, 1990, Money & Murder, 1993, The Joke, 1994, Malaika, 1997, Dizzyland, 1998, The Unknown, 2004, (TV) Hijack, 1973, Stranger in Our House, 1978, Howard, The Amazing Mr. Hughes, 1979, Kenny Rogers as the Gambler, 1980, Killing At Hell's Gate, 1981, My Wicked Wicked Ways: The Legend of Errol Flynn, 1986, Betrayed by Innocence, 1989, Long Road Home (Emmy nominee Lead Actress-Special), 1991, To Heal a Nation, 1992, Dazzle, 1994, Secret Sins of the Father (Emmy nominee Supporting Actress-Special), 1994, Due South (recurring role), 1995-96, Promised Land, 1999, (stage) One Flew Over the Cuckoo's Nest, Richard III, A Streetcar Named Desire, The Taming of the Shrew, A Midsummer's Night Dream. Recipient Bronze Star Halo Career Achievement award So. Calif. Motion Picture Council, 1985, Golden Star Halo award, 1986, Silver Medal award N.Y. Film and TV Festival, 1987. Mem. AFTRA, SAG, Actors' Equity Assn., Acad. Motion Picture Arts and Scis., Acad. TV Arts And Scis. Avocations: writing, collecting antiques and art. Office: PO Box 12581 La Crescenta CA 91224-5581

PURCELL, MARY HAMILTON, speech educator; b. Ft. Worth; d. Josseph Hants and Letha (Gibson) Hamilton; m. William Paxson Purcell, Jr., Dec. 28, 1950; children: William Paxson III, David Hamilton. BA, Mary Hardin-Baylor Coll., 1947, HHD (hon.), 1986; MA, La. State U., 1948; HHD (hon.), U. New Eng., 2000. Instr. dept speech and dramatic arts Temple U., Phila., 1948-53, 60-61; part-time instr. speech Cushing Jr. Coll., Bryn Mawr, Pa., 1966-78. Pres. Pa. Program for Women and Girl Offend, 1968—73, Nether Providence Parent Tchr. Orgn., 1975—76; treas. Virginia Gildersleeve Internat. Fund U. Women, 1975—81, bd. dirs., 1987—93; US del. UN Commn. on Status of Women, 1996; co-chmn. NGO Com. for UNICEF, 1994—2000, mem. global forum, 2001—; bd. dirs. Wallingford-Swarthmore Sch. Dist., 1977—83, Ministers and Missionaries Fund Am. Bapt. Conv., 1985—94, pres., 1995—2003, Internat. Devel. Conf., 1986—; bd. dirs. Nat. Peace Inst. Found., 1983—86; active Big Bros./Big Sisters of Am., 1985—90; bd. dirs. Citizens Crime Commn. of Phila., 1976—, Pa. Women's Campaign Fund, 1985—88, 1993—. Named Outstanding Alumna, Mary Hardin-Baylor Coll., 1972, Disting. Dau. Pa., 1982, v.p., 1994—95, pres., 1995—97, Woman of Yr., DECO Women's Conf., 1998; recipient Eleanor Schnurr award, UNA/USA, 2000. Mem. AAUW (Pa. state pres. 1968-70, v.p. mid. Atlantic region, 1973-77, program v.p. 1979-81, pres. 1981-85, rep. to UN 1985-89), Internat. Fedn. Univ. Women (1st v.p. 1986-89, pres. 1989-92, rep. to UN 1992-2005; pres. UN Dept. Pub. Info. Non Govt. Orgn. ann. conf. 1993), Speech Assn. Am. (Zeta Phi Eta award for excellence in comm. 1983), Pi Kappa Delta, Pi Gamma Mu, Delta Sigma Rho, Alpha Psi Omega, Alpha Chi. Democrat. Baptist. Home: 10 Willowbrook Ave Lansdowne PA 19050

PURCELL, MARY LOUISE GERLINGER, retired adult education educator; b. Thief River Falls, Minn., July 17, 1923; d. Charles and Lajla (Dale) Gerlinger; m. Walter A. Kuyawski, June 9, 1950 (dec. July 1954); children: Amelia Allerton, Jon Allerton; m. Dale Purcell, Aug. 26, 1962 (dec. Nov. 2005). Student, Yankton Coll., 1941-45, Yale Div. Sch., 1949-50, NYU, 1949; MA, Columbia U., 1959, EdD, 1963. Teenage program dir. YWCA, New Haven, 1945-52; dir. program in family rels. Earlham Coll., Richmond, Ind., 1959-62, asst. prof. sociology and psychology, 1959-62, conf. coord. undergrad. edn. for women, 1962; chmn. divsn. home and cmty. Stephens Coll., Columbia, Mo., 1962-73, chmn. family and cmty. studies, 1962-78; dir. continuing edn. women Learning Unltd., 1974-78; prof. Auburn (Ala.) U., 1978-88, head dept. family and child devel., 1978-84, chmn. search com. for v.p. acad. affairs, 1984, spl. asst. to v.p. acad. affairs, 1985-86, prof. emerita, 1988—. Developer course, cons. Contemporary Am. Woman, 1962; vis. prof. Ind. U. Summer Sch., 1970; cons. student pers. svcs. Trenton (N.J.) State Coll., 1958—59, 1961. Contbr. articles to coll. bulls., jours. V.p. Falls Villate-Canaan Hist. Soc., 1998—2001, pres., 2002—. Recipient Alumni Achievement award, Yankton Coll., 1975; Alumni fellow, Tchrs. Coll. Columbia U., 1959. Mem.: AAUW, Nat. Coun. Family Rels., Groves Conf. Family (nat. program chmn. 1977, dir., chmn.-elect affiliated couns. 1981—82, chmn. 1982—84, chmn. film awards com., chmn. spl. emphases sect., bd. dirs.), Am. Home Econs. Assn. (bd. dirs. 1967—69, chair 1st subject matter unit 1969, family rels. and child devel. sect. 1986—89), Falls Village Can. Hist. Soc. (v.p. 1998—2001, pres. 2002—07), Litchfield County Univ. Club (mem. scholarship com. 2001—, bd. dirs. 2001—06), Housatonic Camera Club (co-pres. 1996—2000), Delta Kappa Gamma. Congregationalist. Home: 120 Belden St Falls Village CT 06031-1124 E-mail: mlgp@sbcglobal.net.

PURCELL, PATRICK JOSEPH, newspaper publisher; b. NYC, Nov. 9, 1947; s. Patrick Joseph and Sarah (Muller) P.; m. Maureen T. Shuart, Aug. 8, 1970; children: Kathleen, Erin, Patrick, Kerry. BBA, St. John's U., 1969; MBA, Hofstra U., 1977. Various supr. positions N.Y. Daily News, NYC, 1969-80; assoc. pub. Village Voice, NYC, 1980-82; v.p. advt. N.Y. Post, NYC, 1982-83; v.p. sales and mktg. Skyband Inc., NYC, 1983; pres., pub. Boston Herald, 1984—, owner, 1994—; pub. The N.Y. Post, 1986-88; exec. v.p. News Am./Newspapers, 1986-90, pres., 1990-93, CEO, 1993-94; East Coast pres. Am. Ireland Fund, 1996—. Bd. dirs. Bay Bank, MetroWest Sub. Regional Bd., The Genesis Fund. Bd. dirs. NCCJ, Boston, 1984-86, Boy Scouts Am., Boston, 1984-85, Cath. Charitable Bur., Boston, 1984-86, John F. Kennedy Found.; mem. Greater Boston Assn. Retarded Citizens, 1984-86; chmn. Boston Against Drugs, 1988—; mem. White House Conf. for a Drug Free Am., 1987. Mem. Boston Better Bus. Bur., Am. Newspaper Pub. Assn., New Eng. Newspaper Assn., Boston C. of C. (bd. dirs. 1984-86), Downtown Crossing Assn. (bd. dirs.) Clubs: Publicity, Ad (Boston). Roman Catholic. Avocations: jogging, skiing. Office: Boston Herald PO Box 55843 Boston MA 02205-5843

PURCELL, PHILIP JAMES, retired diversified financial services company executive; b. Salt Lake City, Sept. 5, 1943; m. Anne Marie Mc Namara, Apr. 2, 1964; 7 children. BBA, U. Notre Dame, 1964; M.Sc. in Econs., London Sch. Econs. and Polit. Sci., U. London, 1966; MBA, U. Chgo., 1967. Mng. dir., cons. McKinsey & Co., Inc., Chgo., 1967-78; sr. v.p. corp. planning and adminstrn. Sears, Roebuck and Co., Chgo., 1978-82; from pres., CEO, to chmn., CEO Dean Witter Discover & Co., NYC, 1982-97; chmn., CEO Morgan Stanley (name changed from Morgan Stanley, Dean Witter & Co. 2002), NYC, 1997—2005. Dir. N.Y. Stock Exch., 1995-96, AMR Corp., 2000-; mem. coun. U. Chgo. Grad. Sch. Bus. Trustee U. Notre Dame. With USNR. Mem. Econ. Club Chgo., Chgo. Club, Links. Roman Catholic.

PURCELL, ROBERT HARRY, virologist, researcher; b. Keokuk, Iowa, Dec. 19, 1935; s. Edward Harold and Elsie Thelma (Melzl) P.; children: David Edward, John Leslie. BA in Chemistry, Okla. State U., 1957; MS Biochemistry, Baylor U., 1960; MD, Duke U., 1962. Intern in pediatrics Duke U. Hosp., Durham, NC, 1962-63; officer USPHS, 1963; with Epidemic Intelligence Svc., Communicable Disease Ctr. Atlanta; assigned to vaccine br. Nat. Inst. Allergy and Infectious Diseases, Bethesda, Md., 1963-65; sr. surgeon Lab. Infectious Diseases, NIH, Bethesda, Md., 1965-69, med. officer, 1969-72, med. dir., 1972-74, head hepatitis viruses sect., 1974-2001, co-chief, 2001—. Organizer, invited participant, speaker numerous nat. and internat. symposia, confs., workshops, meetings; temporary advisor WHO, 1967—; expert cons. in hepatitis U.S.—China, U.S.—Taiwan, U.S.—Japan, U.S.—Russia, U.S.—India, U.S.—Pakistan Bilateral Sci. Agreements; lectr. various virology classes. Reviewer numerous sci. jours.; contbr. 700 articles to profl. jours., chpts. to books; 40 patents in field. Recipient Superior Svc. award USPHS, 1972, Meritorious Svc. medal USPHS, 1974, Gorgas medal, 1977, Disting. Svc. medal USPHS, 1978, Disting. Alumni award Duke U. Sch. Medicine, 1978, Eppinger prize 5th Internat. FALK Symposium on Virus and Liver, Switzerland, 1979, Medal of City of Turin, Italy, 1983, Gold medal Can. Liver Found., 1984, King Faisal Internat. prize for Medicine, 1998, Rsch. Sci. award Hepatitis Found. Internats., 1999; named to Alumni Hall of Fame East Okla. State Coll., 1996. Fellow AAAS, Washington Acad. Scis., Am. Acad. Microbiology, Molecular Medicine Soc.; mem. Am. Epidemiology Soc., Am. Soc. Microbiology, Am. Soc. Virology, Soc. Epidemiol. Rsch., Infectious Diseases Soc. Am. (Squibb award 1980), N.Y. Acad. Scis., Am. Soc. Clin. Investigation, Assn. Am. Physicians, Am. Coll. Epidemiology, Am. Assn. Study of Liver Diseases (Disting. Achievement award 2000), Internat. Assn. Study and Prevention Virus Associated Cancers, Internat. Assn. Biol. Standardization, Internat. Assn. Study Liver, Soc. Exptl. Biology and Medicine (Disting. Scientist award 1986), Nat. Acad. Scis. (Washington chpt.). Office: NIH Lab Infectious Diseases 50 S Dr MSC 8009 Rm 6523 Bethesda MD 20892-8009 Office Phone: 301-496-5090. Business E-Mail: rpurcell@niaid.nih.gov.

PURCELL, STEVEN RICHARD, international management consultant, engineer, economist; B in Mech. and Indsl. Engring., NYU Coll. Engring., 1950; MS in Indsl. Engring., Columbia U., 1951; EdM, Harvard U., 1968. Registered profl. engr., Can. Lectr. engring. NYU Coll. Engring., NYC, 1948-50; gen. mgr. Dapol Plastics Co., Inc., Boston, 1956-58; gen. div. mgr. Am. Cyanamid Co., Sanford, Maine, 1958-61; sr. prin., mgmt. cons. investment banking Purcell & Assocs., NYC, 1961-66; prof., chmn. Bristol Coll., Fall River, Mass., 1966-68; assoc. dean grad. faculty adminstrv. studies York U., Toronto, Ont., Can., 1969-71; chief economist Dept. Manpower and Immigration, Ottawa, Ont., Can., 1970-71; cons. Treasury Bd., Ottawa, 1971-72; dir. urban and internat. environ. policy Ministry of State for Urban Affairs Internat. Activities, Ottawa, 1973-74; mem. com. on challenges of modern soc. NATO, Ottawa, 1973-74; mem. sci., econ. policy com. OECD UN, Ottawa, 1973-74; prof. Grad. Sch. Bus. Adminstrn. and Econs. Algonquin Coll., Ottawa, 1974-76; advisor, cons. House of Commons, 1976-77; sr. prin. Purcell & Assocs., Internat. Mgmt. Cons.,

Washington, 1977-80, chmn., CEO, 1981—, Phoenix Internat. Capital Associates, Washington, 1981—; exec. dir. nat. coastal zone mgmt. adv. com. NOAA U.S. Dept. Commerce, Washington, 1980-81. Profl. lectr. Northeastern U. Grad. Sch. Bus. Adminstrn., Boston, 1953-56, U. Toronto, 1968-69, George Washington U. Grad. Sch. Bus. Adminstrn., Washington, 1979; vis. prof. Rensselaer Poly. Inst. Advanced Mgmt. Program, 1967, U. Ottawa Grad. Sch. Bus. Adminstrn., 1971-74; lectr. Council for Internat. Progress in Mgmt., N.Y.C., 1960, Royal Bank Can. Mgmt. Assn., Toronto, Ont., 1970; corp. appointment cons. Harvard U., Cambridge, Mass., 1967-68; cons. Govt. Venezuela, 1967-68, Can. Inst. Bankers, Toronto, 1969-70; internat. sr. adviser NASA, 1985-86, mem. nat. adv. bd. Ctr. for Nat. Policy; dir. Rental Resource Corp., 1986-89. Contbr. articles on indsl. orgn., sci. policy and fin. to profl. jours. Lt. AC, USNR, 1943-46. Mem. UN Assn., Soc. for Advancement of Mgmt. (pres. 1949-50, leadership award 1950), Tau Beta Pi, Alpha Pi Mu (v.p. 1949-50), Columbia Univ. Club (Washington, trustee 1982-84, chmn., sr. trustee 1984-85), Harvard Univ. Club. Office: PO Box 2928 Petaluma CA 94953-2928

PURCHASE-OWENS, FRANCENA, marketing professional, consultant, educator; b. Milw., Nov. 14, 1960; d. Johnny Purchase Sr. and Arlene (Roberts) Pleas Brown. Cert., Mich. Profl. Sch. Modeling, 1980; AA cum laude, Bryant Stratton Coll., 1982; BS in Applied Liberal Studies, Western Mich. U., 1997, M in Ednl. Leadership cum laude, 2004; MBA, U. Phoenix, Grand Rapids, Mich., 2006—; student, Capella U., Grand Rapids, 2006—. Various office/clerical positions, 1972—84; sec. internat. mktg. dept. Am. Seating, Grand Rapids, 1980—81; adminstrv. asst. to Elizabeth Kubler-Ross Ga. State U., 1980; investment mgmt. sec. M&I Bank, Milw., 1984-85; cons. United Devel. Corp., Milw., 1986-88; sales Weathermakers Industries, Milw., 1989; paraprofessional Grand Rapids Pub. Schs., Mich., 1990-92; temp. helper Dayton Hudson, Grand Rapids, 1990; customer svc. rep. Kent County Conv. and Visitors Bur., Grand Rapids, 1995; customer svc. rep. children's dept. Meijers, Inc., 1995; mktg. rschr. Wirthlin Worldwide, Grand Rapids, 1996-98; pres. Creative Works, Grand Rapids, 1988—, Francena Purchase Internat. Honor Soc., Grand Rapids, 1999—, Francena Purchase Internat. Applied Studies, 1999—, Francena Purchase Internat. Applied Profl. Studies Soc., 2000—, Purchase Bus. Inst., Grand Rapids, 1999—; mktg. rschr. Directions in Rsch., Grand Rapids, 2004—05, Francena Purchase Cons. Svcs., Grand Rapids, 2006—. Bookkeeper Helen Smith Mart, Milw., 1972; sec. Mich. Nat. Bank, Grand Rapids, 1980-81, Volt. Tech. Svcs., Milw, 1980; asst. exec. sec. Manpower Internat. Inc., Milw., 1982-84; cons. NASW; sec., cons. United Devel. Corp, Access, Milw., 1988; human resource asst., computer programmer, sec., Patricia Stevens Coll., Milw., 1985-86; asst. to pres. Alissia Cosmetics, Miss Black Pageant, 1980; legal sec. to atty. David Clowers, Milw., 1980; student asst. gerontology dept., Ga. State U., Atlanta, 1980; student asst. main office, Ottawa Hills H.S., Grand Rapids, 1976-77, asst. Madison Mid. Sch. (formerly Iroquois Mid. Sch.), 1975; mem. contract divsn. Fed. Govt., Grand Rapids, 1977-78; grad. student adv. bd. Western Mich. U., Kalamazoo, 2000; mem. Nat. Honor Soc. Iroquois Mid. Sch., 1974-75, Grand Rapids, Ottawa Hills Montessori H.S., 1976-79; cons. in field. Co-editor: Smoke Signal, 1975; contbr. articles to profl. jours. Vol. United Way, Grand Rapids, 1990, co-chair, 2006-, vol. TV (GVSU-TV) fundraiser, basic needs investment com., 2006-; vol. Grand Valley State U.; vol. Cmty. Media Ctr. (GRTV), Cmty. Media Ctr. Scholarships; reading condr. S.E. Neighborhood Assn., Grand Rapids, 1990, Cmty. Media Ctr., GRTV; mem. literacy coun. Kent County Literacy Coun., Grand Rapids, 1991—, task force Dwelling Pl., Grand Rapids, 1999, First Call Help United Way, Grand Rapids, 1992; model Miss J. Fashion bd. Jacobson's Dept. store, East Grand Rapids Mich., 1979, mem. pub. com., refreshment com., Miss. jr. fashion bd., 1979; finalist Miss Black Wis. pageant, Milw., 1981; bd. dirs. Program and Quality Com., Pers. Com., Fin. Com., Consumer Adv. bd., Touchstone innovaré mental health, Grand Rapids, 2000—, mem. nominating com, Touchstone Innovare Mental Health, 2000-01, Kent County Cmty. Mental Health, 1999—; mem. Task Force Herkimer Apartment Projects, Weston Apartments Dwelling place of Grand Rapids, 1999; reading program asst. S.E. End Neigborhood Assn., Grand Rapids, 1993, mem. exec. bd. dirs, 2006; rehab. asst. Kent Cmty. Hosp. Complex, Grand Rapids, 1991; intake asst. Baxter Cmty. Ctr., Grand Rapids, 1989; tutor Kent County Literacy Coun., Grand Rapids, 1988; facilitator trainer Employers Coalition for Healing Racism, Grand Rapids, 1997, Citizens Cirs. Resource Ctr., Grand Rapids, 1998, Ptnrs. in Pub. Edn., Grand Rapids, 1999, United Way Champions of Diversity, Grand Rapids, 1999; project help tutor Iroquois Mid. Sch., Grand Rapids, 1975; student tutor Washington Elem., Kalamazoo, 1974; fundraiser Spl. Olympics Office Edn. Assn. Ottawa Hills HS, 1978; asst. sec. First Missionary Bapt. Ch., Grand Rapids, 2005—, fin. asst., 2005-, program com., 2006-, exec. bd. dirs., 2006-07; chair cmty. investment coun. United Way, 2006—; pastors asst. First Missionary Bapt. Ch., Grand Rapids, 2005—, adult usher bd., kitchen com., 2007—; program com. First vol. Cancer Soc.; mem. Grand Rapids TV, Cmty. Media Ctr. Recipient Creative Writing award, 1975, Secretarial award Grand Rapids Pub. Schs., 1978, Shorthand award Ottawa Hills HS, 1979, Shorthand awards Milw. Stratton Coll., 1981-82, Century award, 1982, Machine Transcription award Milw. Area Tech. Coll., 1981, Appreciation cert. Southeast End Neighborhood Assn., Grand Rapids, 1993, Recognition cert. United Way, Grand Rapids, 1999, Appreciation cert. Touchstone Ins., 1999, Recognition cert. Mark Kistler's Summer Art Camp, Grand Rapids, 2006; Phillip Morris scholar Alverno Coll., 1981, Personal Svc. and Sales Accomplishment cert. Manpower, Inc., 1982; Nontraditional Student grantee Western Mich. U., 1994, 2000, Thurgood Marshall Tuition grant, Western Mich. U. 2000; Thurgood Marshall Assistantship scholar Western Mich. U.1989, 1998; 1st place spkr., 3rd place typist and secretarial job application Office Edn. Assn. Extemporaneous Speaking; 1st Pl. with Letter of Recognition from Senator Berger of Wis. Milw. Area Tech. Coll., 1981; Internat. Faces finalist, Milw., 1985, Internat. finalist theatre arts, Milw., 1986, Young Alumni Student Spotlight recognition Western Mich. U., Grand Rapids, Alumni Spotlight recognition, Bryant and Stratton Coll., 2007, Milw., other honors and awards. Mem.: Cmty. Media Ctr., Soc. Human Resource Mgmt., Am. Mgmt. Assn., Am. Soc. Tng. and Devel., Parkinson's Assn., Alzheimer's Assn., Rotary Internat., Internat. Jaycees, Praprofessional Assn., Western Mich. U. Alumni, Phi Lambda Theta. Avocations: modern dancing, reading, tennis, writing. Address: PO Box 7421 Grand Rapids MI 49510-7421

PURCIFULL, DAN ELWOOD, retired plant virologist, retired educator; b. Woodland, Calif., July 1, 1935; s. Ernest Lee and Virginia (Margaroli) P.; m. Marcia Ann Weatherby, Sept. 7, 1966; children: Scott, Douglas. BS, U. Calif., Davis, 1957, MS, 1959, PhD, 1964. Asst. prof. plant pathology U. Fla., Gainesville, 1964-69, assoc. prof., 1969-75, prof., 1975-99, prof. emeritus, 2000—; ret., 2000. Plant virus subcom. Internat. Com. for Taxonomy of Viruses, 1973-75, mem. potyvirus study group, 1987-93; mem. plant virology adv. com. Am. Type Culture Collection, 1993-99; mem. Internat. Legume Virus Working Group, 1999. Assoc. editor Phytopathology, 1971-73, Plant Disease, 1987-89; contbr. articles to profl. jours. Mem. Morningside Nature Center Commn., City of Gainesville, 1978-81, treas., 1981. With US Army, 1957. Fellow AAAS, Am. Phytopathol Soc. (Lee Hutchins award 1981, Ruth Allen award 1992); mem. Fla. State Hort. Soc., N.Y. Acad. Sci., Am. Soc. Virology, Phytopathol. Soc. Japan, Brazilian Phytopathol. Soc., Australasian Plant Pathology Soc., U.S. Golf Assn., Nat. Wildlife Fedn. (assoc.), The Nature Conservancy, Nat. Geographic Soc., Smithsonian Instn. (assoc.), Sigma Xi, Gamma Sigma Delta. Home: 3106 NW 1st Ave Gainesville FL 32607-2504 Home Phone: 352-376-9926. Personal E-mail: depurc@aol.com.

PURDES, ALICE MARIE, retired adult education educator; b. St. Louis, Jan. 8, 1931; d. Joseph Louis and Angeline Cecilia (Mozier) P. AA, Belleville Area Coll., 1951; BS, Ill. State U., Normal, 1953, MS, 1954; cert., Sorbonne U., Paris, 1964; PhD, Fla. State U., Tallahassee, 1976. Cert. in music edn., elem. edn., secondary edn., adult edn. Tchg. and grad. asst. Ill. State U., 1953-54; music supr. Princeton Pub. Schs., Ill., 1954-55; music dir. Venice Pub. Schs., Ill., 1955-72, secondary vocal music dir. Ill., 1955-72; coord. literacy program Venice-Lincoln Tech. Ctr., 1983-86, chmn. lang. arts dept., 1983-96; ret., 1996. Tchr. in space candidate, 1985. Mem. St. Louis chpt. World Affairs Coun., UN Assn., Nat. Mus. of Women in the Arts, Humane Soc. of Am.; charter mem. St. Louis Sci. Ctr., Harry S. Truman Inst.; contbr. Old Six Mile Mus., 1981, Midland Repertory Players, Alton, Ill., 1991; chair Cystic Fibrosis Spring Bike-A-Thon, Madison, Ill., 1981, Granite City, Ill., 1985. Named to Ill. Sr. Hall of Fame, 2001, Gov's Sr. Hall of Fame, 2001; recipient Gold medal, Nat. Senior Olympics, 1989, 600 others, Sr. World Games, Generations of Success Alumni award, Belleville Area Coll., 1998, several scholarships. Mem.: AAUW, Am. Fedn. Tchrs. (pres. 1957—58), Ill. Adult and Continuing Educators Assn., Am. Choral Dirs. Assn., Ill. Music Educators Assn. (Svc. award 2002), Music Educators Nat. Conf., Ill. State U. Alumni Assn., Slavic and East European Friends (life), Fla. State Alumni Assn., Lovejoy Libr. Friends, Nat. Space Soc., Western Cath. Union, Croation Fraternal Union, St. Louis Numis. Assn., Friends St. Louis Art Mus., Archaeol. Inst. Am., Travelers Abroad (pres. 1966—68, 1989—), Madison Rotary Club (internat. amb., Humanitarian award 1975). Roman Catholic. Avocations: bowling, travel. Home: 1610 4th St Madison IL 62060

PURDOM, PAUL WALTON, JR., computer scientist; b. Atlanta, Apr. 5, 1940; s. Paul Walton and Bettie (Miller) P.; m. Donna Armstrong; children: Barbara, Linda, Paul BS, Calif. Inst. Tech., 1961, MS, 1962, PhD, 1966. Asst. prof. computer sci. U. Wis.-Madison, 1965-70, asst. prof., 1970-71; mem. tech. staff Bell Telephone Labs., Naperville, Ill., 1970-71; assoc. prof., chmn. computer sci. dept. Ind. U., Bloomington, 1977-82, prof. computer sci., 1982—. Grant researcher FAW, Ulm, Germany. Author: (with Cynthia Brown) The Analysis of Algorithms; assoc. editor: Computer Surveys; contbr. articles to profl. jours. NSF grantee, 1979, 81, 83, 92, 94. Mem. AAAS, Soc. for Indsl. and Applied Math., Assn. Computing Machinery, Sigma Xi. Democrat. Methodist. Home: 2212 S Belhaven Ct Bloomington IN 47401-6803 Office: Ind U Dept Computer Science 215 Lindley Hall Bloomington IN 47405-4101 Office Phone: 812-855-1501. Business E-Mail: pwp@cs.indiana.edu.

PURDOM, THOMAS JAMES, lawyer; b. Seymour, Tex., Apr. 7, 1937; s. Thomas Exer and Juanita Florida (Kuykendall) P.; m. Betty Marie Shoemaker, May 31, 1969; 1 son, James Robert. Student, U. Syracuse, 1956—57, U. Md., 1958—59; BA, Tex. Tech. Coll., 1962; JD, Georgetown U., 1966. Bar: Tex. 1966, U.S. Supreme Ct. 1978, U.S. Ct. Appeals (5th cir.) 1983. Ptnr. Griffith & Purdom, Lubbock, Tex., 1966-67; asst. dist. atty. 72d Jud. Dist., Lubbock, 1967-68; county atty. Lubbock County, Tex., 1968-72; pres. Purdom Law Offices, P.C., Lubbock, 1972—. Mem. com. for Vol. 5 pattern jury charges, 1988-97. Author: West's Texas Forms Vols. 16, 17, 18, 1984-96, Family Law, Texas Practice and Procedure, 1981. Served with USAF, 1956-60. Recipient Sam Emison award Tex. Acad. Family Law Specialists, 2000. Fellow Tex. Bar Found.; mem ABA, Lubbock County Bar Assn. (bd. dirs. 1970, Disting. Sr. Lawyer award 2000), State Bar Assn. Tex. (sec. family law sect. 1974-75, chmn. family law sect. 1975-76, mem. examining commn. for family law specialization), Am. Acad. Matrimonial Lawyers (cert. family law, Tex. bd. legal specialization), Delta Theta Phi. Democrat. Baptist. Home: 3619 55th St Lubbock TX 79413-4713 Office: Purdom Law Offices PC 3619 55th St Lubbock TX 79413-5713 E-mail: purdom6@aol.com.

PURDY, ALAN HARRIS, biomedical engineer; b. Mt. Clemens, Mich., Dec. 13, 1923; s. Harry Martin and Elinor (Harris) P.; m. Anna Elizabeth Sohn, Aug. 16, 1968 (dec.); children: Catherine, Charles, Susan, Harry; m. Margaret Josephine Kelley, Mar. 5, 1997. BSME, U. Miami, 1954; MS in Physiology, UCLA, 1967; PhD in Engring., U. Mo., 1970. Cert. clin. engr., Washington. Project engr. in acoustics Arvin Industries, Columbus, Ind., 1954-56, AC Spark Plug Co., Flint, Mich., 1956-60; asst. prof. engring. Calif. Poly. U., Pomona, 1960-62; assoc. dir. biomed. engring. U. Mo., Columbia, 1967-71; dep. assoc. dir., assoc. dir. Nat. Inst. for Occupational Safety and Health, Rockville, Md., 1971-81, scientist, biomed. engr. Cin., 1983-86; asst. dir. Fla. Inst. Oceanography, St. Petersburg, 1981-83; pres. Alpha Beta R & D Corp., San Marcos, Calif., 1986—. Cons. Smithy Muffler Corp., L.A., 1961-62, Statham Instruments, L.A., 1966; cons. faculty, Tex. Tech. U., Lubbock, 1972-73; lectr. U. Cin., 1980. Patentee in diving, acoustical and occupational safety fields. Pilot CG Aux., 1989-98. With USAF, 1942-43. Nat. Heart Inst. spl. fellow, 1963-67; Fulbright scholar, Yugoslavia, 1984. Mem. Acoustical Soc. Am., Biomed. Engring. Soc., Am. Inst. Physics, Exptl. Aircraft Assn., Aircraft Owners and Pilots Assn., DAV. Democrat. Home and Office: 941 Cycad Dr San Marcos CA 92078-5013 E-mail: ahpurdy@nethere.com.

PURDY, DAVID LAWRENCE, medical products executive; b. NYC, Sept. 18, 1928; s. Earl and Mabel (Roberts) Purdy; m. Margaret Helen Rye, July 7, 1951; children: Susan Lee, John F.(dec.), Ross David(dec.), Thomas Griffith. BME, Cornell U., 1951; degree in advanced & creative engring., GE, 1955, degree in profl. bus. mgmt., 1956. Devel. engr. GE, Valley Forge, Pa., 1953—64; mgr. energy conversion divsn. Nuc. Materials and Equipment Corp. (acquired by ARCO), Apollo, Pa., 1964—69, Atlantic Richfield Corp., Apollo, 1969—72; founder, pres., chmn. Biocontrol Tech., Inc., Indiana, Pa., 1972—2000; chmn., treas. Diasense, Inc. Biomedical Engring., Indiana, 1989—2000; pres., founder Purdy Tech., Inc., Marion Center, Pa., 2000—. Contbr. articles to profl. jours. 1st lt. USAF, 1961—63. Fellow: ASME (life); mem.: AAAS. Achievements include 32 patents in field; patents for generator of electrical energy by radioisotope thermoelectric conversion; radioisotope powered cardiac pacemaker; radioisotope powered artificial heart; thermoelectric apparatus for high thermoelectric efficiency by cascading materials; method of metals joining and articles produced by such method including brazing copper to tungsten; rate responsive pacemaker; artificial pancreas; noninvasive glucose sensor; multi-leaflet heart valve. Office: Purdy Tech Inc 1482 Ambrose Rd Marion Center PA 15759 Personal E-mail: penllwyn@yourinter.net.

PURDY, G. MICHAEL, observatory director; Student, London U.; PhD in Marine Geophysics, Cambridge U., Eng., 1974. Postdoctoral scholar Woods Hole Oceanographic Instn., Mass., 1974, chmn. dept. geology and geophysics Mass., 1991-95; dir. divsn. ocean scis. Geoscis. Directorate NSF, 1995-2000; dir. Lamont-Doherty Earth Obs. Columbia U., Palisades, NY, 2000—. Participated in several rsch. cruises. Contbr. rsch. articles in peer reviewed jours.:, author (of several conf. abstracts). Recipient Maurice Ewing medal, Am. Geophysical Union, 2006. Office: Lamont-Doherty Earth Obs PO Box 1000 61 Rt 9W Palisades NY 10964-1000 *

PURDY, JAMES AARON, medical physics professor; b. Tyler, Tex., July 16, 1941; s. Walter Bethel and Florence (Hardy) P.; m. Marilyn Janette Coers, Jan. 29, 1965; children: Katherine, Laura. BS, Lamar U., 1967; MA, U. Tex., 1968, PhD, 1971. Asst. rsch. scientist U. Tex., Austin, 1969-71; rsch. asst. M.D. Anderson Hosp. and Tumor Inst., Houston, 1968-69, fellow in med. physics, 1972-73; from instr. physics to prof. Sch. of Medicine, Washington U., St. Louis, 1973—83, chief physics sect., 1976—2004, prof., 1983—2004, assoc. dir. Radiation Oncology Ctr., 1987—2004; prof., vice chmn. Med. Ctr. Dept. Radiology Oncology U. Calif., Davis, 2004—. Mem. NIH Radiaton Study sect. Divsn. Rsch. Grantes, 1991-95; Landauer lectr., Oakland, Calif., 1991. Editor: Three Dimensional Treatment Planning, 1991, Advances in Radiation Oncology, 1992, 3D Radiation Treatment Planning and Conformal Therapy, 1995, A Practical Guide to 3D Planning and Conformal Radiation Therapy, 1999, 3-D Conformal and Intensity Modulated Radiation Therapy: Physics and Clinical Applications, 2001; sr. physics editor: Internat. Jour. Radiation Oncology, Biology, and Physics, 1996—2003. With USMC, 1961-64. Fellow Am. Assn. Physicists in Medicine (pres. 1985, William D. Coolidge award 1997), Am. Coll. Radiology (ACR Gold Medal 2002), Am. Coll. Med. Physics (chmn. bd. chancellors 1990, Marvin M.D. Williams award 1996); mem. Am. Inst. Physics, Am. Bd. Med. Physics (vice chmn. 1988-92), Am. Bd. Radiology, Am. Soc. Therapeutic Radiology and Oncology (ASTRO Gold medal 2000). Methodist. Avocation: travel. Home: 918 Eucalyptus St Davis CA 95616 Office: Univ Calif Davis Med Ctr Dept Rad Oncology 4501 X St Ste G126 Sacramento CA 95817 Home Phone: 530-758-9149; Office Phone: 916-734-3932. Business E-Mail: james.purdy@ucdmc.ucdavis.edu.

PURDY, JAN RAE, music educator; b. Detroit, July 11, 1937; d. Fred B. and Irma B. Purdy; m. Norman R. Rapp (div.); children: Lisa Ann Rapp, Lynda Rae Rapp. BA in music, Madonna U., Livonia, Mich., 1992. Tchr. voice and piano Mich. Conservatory, Detroit, Birmingham Conservatory, Mich., Plymouth Music Acad., Mich.; tchr. voice Marion HS, Birmingham, Immaculata HS, Detroit, Ant Ctr. Music Sch., Detroit, Orchard Lake Sch. Music, West Bloomfield, Mich., 2007—. Performed with Mt. Clemens Symphony, Dearborn Symphony, Pontiac Symphony, Clarion Symphony Orch., Sarnia, Ont., Cambodia, 2001, Mich. Opera Co., Mich. Opera Theatre Outreach Program, Detroit Lyric Opera, Dearborn Opera Group, Boris Goldovsky Opera Workshop and Performance Co., Verdi Opera Theatre, Oakway Symphony, Warren Symphony, Little Detroit Symphony. Soloist: Mich. Rep. Coun., Pres. Gerald Ford, Sen. Griffin, Detroit Mayor J. Cavanagh, astronaut James A. McDivitt, Detroit Symphony, 1955, 1969, Ctrl. Meth. Ch., Detroit, various area chs. Former mem. Birmingham Musicale; mem. Tuesday Musicale, 2005—. Recipient Belle Isle award, Detroit Symphony, 1955. Mem.: Sigma Alpha IOta. Republican. Avocations: movies, theater, concerts. Home and Office: 23235 Canfield Farmington Hills MI 48336 Office Phone: 248-471-1604.

PURDY, JESSE E., psychology professor; b. Denver, Colo., Sept. 7, 1952; s. Howard E. and Mary F. Purdy; m. Karen L. Culp; children: Kristopher L., Matthew A. BS, Colo. State U., Ft. Collins, 1974, MS, 1976, PhD, 1978. Prof. psychology Southwestern U., Georgetown, Tex., 1978—. Assoc. nat. resource coun. Nat. Marine Fisheries Svc., Seattle, 1984—85. Author: (book) Learning and Memory; contbr. chapters to books, articles to profl. jours. Fellow, Nat. Resource Coun., 1984; grantee, NSF, 1981, 2002. Mem.: Southwestern Psychol. Assn. (pres. 1998—99), Internat. Soc. Behavioral Ecology, Animal Behavior Soc., Psi Chi (pres. 2000—01). Democrat. Home: 301 S Pine St Georgetown TX 78626 Office: Southwestern Univ 1001 E Univ and Maple Sts Georgetown TX 78626 Home Phone: 512-863-4205; Office Phone: 512-863-1985. Office Fax: 512-863-1846. Business E-Mail: purdy@southwestern.edu.

PURDY, KEVIN MOORE, estate planner; b. Escondido, Calif., Jan. 26, 1952; s. Kenneth C. and Helen M. (Moore) P.; m. Janice M. Cook, May 12, 1982. BA in Philosophy, Psychology, U. Redlands, 1974. Pres. Timeline Pub., San Diego, Calif., 1980-90; estate planner Sagemark Cons., San Diego, Calif., 1990—. Pub. spkr.; digital artist. Author: A Brief History of the Earth and Mankind, 1986, A Brief History of Mankind, 1987. Avocations: photography, music, travel, investment analysis. Personal E-mail: kpurdy@home.com.

PURE, PAMELA J., health products executive; B in Health Adminstrn., U. NC. Various mgmt., product devel. and mktg. positions Shared Med. Sys. (now divsn. Siemens); COO Channel Health Subs. IDX Systems, 1999—2001; grp. pres. product devel. and support McKesson Corp., San Francisco, 2001—02, COO McKesson Info. Solutions, 2002—04, exec. v.p., pres. McKesson Provider Technologies, 2004—. Named Woman of Yr. Tech. (enterprise bus.), (WIT) Women in Tech., 2005. Office: McKesson Corpn 1 Post St San Francisco CA 94104 Office Phone: 415-983-8300. Office Fax: 415-983-9400. *

PURI, MADAN LAL, mathematics professor; b. Sialkot, Feb. 20, 1929; came to U.S., 1957, naturalized, 1973; s. Ganesh Das and S. W. P.; m. Uma Kapur, Aug. 24, 1962; 3 children. BA, Punjab U., India, 1948, MA, 1950, DSc, 1975; PhD, U. Calif., Berkeley, 1962. Head dept. math. D.A.V. Coll., Punjab U., 1955-57; instr. U. Colo., 1957-58; tchg. asst., rsch. asst., jr. rsch. statistician U. Calif. at Berkeley, 1958-62; asst. prof., assoc. prof. math. Courant Inst., NYU, 1962-68; prof. math. Ind. U., Bloomington, 1968—, Coll. Arts and Scis. Disting. Rsch. scholar, 2004—. Vis. assoc. prof. U. NC., 1966-67; guest prof. stats. U. Gottingen, West Germany, 1972, Alexander von Humboldt guest prof., 1974-75; guest prof. U. Dortmund, West Germany, 1972, Technische Hochschule Aachen, West Germany, 1973, U. Goteborg, Chalmers U. Tech., both Sweden, 1974; vis. prof. U. Auckland, N.Z., 1977, U. Calif., Irvine, 1978, U. Wash., Seattle, 1978-79, U. Bern, Switzerland, 1982, Va. Poly. Inst., 1988; disting. vis. London Sch. Econs. and Polit. Sci., 1991; vis. prof. U. Göttingen, Germany, 1991-92; rsch. fellow Katholieke U., Nijmegen, The Netherlands, 1992; vis. prof. U. Des Scis. et Tech. de Lille, France, 1994, U. Basel, Switzerland, 1995—, U. NSW, Australia, 1996; vis. fellow Australian Nat. U., Canberra, Australia, 1999; guest prof. U. Konstanz, Germany, 2000, U. Gottingen, 2001. Co-author: Non Parametric Methods in Multivariate Analysis, 1971, Non Parametric Methods in General Linear Models, 1985. Editor Stochastic Process and Related Topics, 1975, Statistical Inference and Related Topics, 1975, Non Parametric Techniques in Statistical Inference, 1970; co-editor: Nonparametric Statistical Inference, Vols. I and II, 1982, New Perspectives in Theoretical and Applied Statistics, 1987, Mathematical Statistics and Probability Theory, Vol. A, 1987, Statistical Sciences and Data Analysis, 1993, Recent Advances in Statistics and Probability, 1994, Asymptotics in Statistics and Probability, 2000, Probability, Statistics and their Applications, 2003. Recipient Sr. U.S. Scientist award, Humboldt Preis, 1974-75, 83, Rsch. award Humboldt Found., U. Göttingen, 2001; disting. vis. scholar Inst. for Advanced Study, Ind. U., 2007. Fellow Royal Statis. Soc. (adv. editor statistics book series Taylor and Francis Book Group Inc., 2005), Inst. Math. Statistics, Am. Statis. Assn., Internat. Indian Statis. Assn. (hon.); mem. Internat. Statis. Inst. Office: Ind U Dept Math Rawles Hall Bloomington IN 47405 Office Phone: 812-855-9537. Business E-Mail: puri@indiana.edu.

PURI, RAJENDRA KUMAR, business and tax specialist, consultant; b. Hoshiarpur, Punjab, India, Dec. 22, 1932; came to the U.S., 1965, naturalized, 1969; s. Harbans Lal and Satya Vati (Jerath) P.; children: Neena, Veena, Ram. BS, Agra U., 1952; diploma in Russian lang. and lit., U. Dehli, 1958; BA, U. Wash., 1968, MBA, 1969; MS in Taxation, Golden Gate U., 1982. Customs officer Govt. of India, New Delhi, 1955-60; asst. treas. Merc. Bank Ltd., New Delhi, 1960-65; mem. staff Peat, Marwick, Mitchell & Co., CPAs, Seattle, 1969-70; state examiner State of Wash., Seattle, 1970-72, asst. supervising state examiner, 1972-74, supervising state examiner, 1974-77; sr. internal auditor Lockheed Corp., Sunnyvale, Calif., 1977-79; sci. programming analyst Lockheed Missile and Space Co., Sunnyvale, 1979-80, data processing specialist, 1980-84, sci. programming specialist, 1984-88; chief acct. Tex. Dept. Health, Austin, 1989-90; dir. internal audit, internal auditor Tex. Workers' Compensation Commn., Austin, 1990-95; bus. and tax cons., 1996—2003. Del. Wash. State Rep. Conv., 1976, Snohomish County Rep. Conv., 1976; Rep. nominee for state auditor, Wash., 1976; spl. advisor U.S. Congl. Adv. Bd., 1982-83. Mem. AICPA. Home: 2608 Hunlac Cove Round Rock TX 78681-7107 E-mail: rkpi_2000@yahoo.com.

PURIS, MARTIN FORD, media company executive; b. Chgo., Feb. 22, 1939; s. Martin and Virginia Lee (Farmer) Puris; m. Mary M. Herrmann; children: Kimberly Mayo, Jason Patterson, Mary Elizabeth. Student,

DePauw U., 1961. With Campbell-Ewald Co., Detroit, 1962—64, Young & Rubicam, Inc., NYC, 1964-66; v.p. Carl Ally, Inc., NYC, 1966-74; pres., CEO Ammirati & Puris, Inc., NYC, 1974-94; chmn., CEO, chief creative officer Ammirati, Puris, Lintas, NYC, 1995—99; chmn., CEO Not Traditional Media, NYC, 2004—. Media advisor Pres. George Bush; dir. IPG Group, 1995—99; vice chmn. Sheltering Arms; mng. dir. New Things Investment Group; treasurer Hampton Classic; exec. com The Quills. Author: Comeback: How Seven Straight-Shooting CEO's Turned Around Troubled Companies, 1999. Recipient awards Art Dir. Club, Copy Club, N.Y.C., Cannes Film Festival. Mem.: Devon Yacht Club, Union Club, Am. Yacht Club, Nantucket Yacht Club, N.Y. Yacht Club. Republican. Roman Catholic. Avocations: sailing, tennis, horseback riding, hunting. Office: NTM Inc 32 E 57th St 10th Fl New York NY 10022 Office Phone: 212-371-0088. Office Fax: 212-371-8884.

PURKERSON, MABEL LOUISE, physician, educator, physiologist; b. Goldville, SC, Apr. 3, 1931; d. James Clifton and Louise (Smith) P. AB, Erskine Coll., 1951; MD, U. SC, Charleston, 1956. Diplomate Am. Bd. Pediat. Instr. pediat. Washington U. Sch. Medicine, St. Louis, 1961-67, instr. medicine, 1966-67, asst. prof. pediat., 1967-98, asst. prof. medicine, 1967-76, assoc. prof. medicine, 1976-89, prof., 1989-98, prof. emerita, 1998—, assoc. dean curriculum, 1976-94, assoc. dean acad. projects, 1994-98. Cons. in field. Editl. bd. Am. Jour. Kidney Diseases, 1981-87; contbr. articles to profl. jours. Mem. bd. counselors Erskine Coll., 1971—87, trustee, 2000—06, The Maisel Dorn Reeder Found.; historian St. Louis Symphony Orch., trustee. USPHS spl. fellow, 1971-72. Mem. Am. Heart Assn. Coun. on the Kidney (exec. com. 1973-81), Am. Physiol. Soc., Am. Soc. Nephrology, Internat. Soc. Nephrology, Ctrl. Soc. Clin. Rsch., Am. Soc. Renal Biochemistry and Metabolism, Internat. Assn. History Nephrology, Am. Osler Soc., Explorer's Club (chair St. Louis chpt., 2005-), Sigma Xi (chpt. sec. 1974-76), Alpha Omega Alpha. Home: 20 Haven View Dr Saint Louis MO 63141-7902 Office: Bernard Becker Med Libr Renal Div Dept PO Box 8132 Saint Louis MO 63110-1093 Home Phone: 314-994-1649; Office Phone: 314-362-4234. Business E-Mail: purkerm@msnotes.wustl.edu.

PURL, O. THOMAS, retired electronics company executive; b. East St. Louis, Ill., June 5, 1924; s. Ruthford Keith and Muriel Agnes (Thompson) P.; m. Martha Elaine Smalley, Feb. 21, 1948; children— Thomas Keith, Jeanne Marie Purl Elder. BS, U. Ill., 1948, BS, 1951, MS, 1952, PhD, 1955. Head high-power traveling wave tube sect., mem. tech. staff Hughes Research Lab., Culver City, Calif., 1955-58; sect. head, dept. mgr., group v.p., v.p. shareholder relations and planning coordination Watkins-Johnson Co., Palo Alto, Calif., 1958-86. Contbr. articles to profl. jours.; patentee in field. Chmn. career guidance com. Santa Clara Valley Joint Engring. Council, 1971-73; bd. dirs. Jr. Achievement of Santa Clara County, 1975-79. Served to 1st lt. USAAF, 1943-46. Fellow IEEE (chmn. Santa Clara Valley subsect. 1972); mem. Sigma Xi, Eta Kappa Nu, Phi Kappa Phi, Sigma Tau. Clubs: Commonwealth of Calif. Home: 300 Hot Springs Rd K220 Montecito CA 93108

PURNELL, MAURICE EUGENE, JR., lawyer; b. Dallas, Feb. 17, 1940; s. Maurice Eugene Sr. and Marjorie (Maillot) P.; m. Diane Blake, Aug. 19, 1966; children: Maurice Eugene III, Blake Maillot. BA, Washington and Lee U., 1961; MBA, U. Pa., 1963; LLB, So. Meth. U., 1966. Bar: Tex. 1966. Ptnr. Locke, Purnell, Boren, Laney & Neely, Dallas, 1966-87; shareholder Locke Purnell Rain Harrell PC, Dallas, 1987-99; ptnr. Locke Liddell & Sapp LLP, Dallas, 1999—2002, of counsel, 2002—. Bd. dirs. Leggett & Platt, Inc. Bd. dirs. Dallas Summer Musicals. Mem. ABA, Tex. Bar Assn., Tex. Bar Found., Dallas Bar Assn. Am. Judicature Soc., Dallas C. of C, Brook Hollow Golf Club. Home: 4409 S Versailles Ave Dallas TX 75205-3044 Office: Locke Liddell & Sapp LLP 2200 Ross Ave Ste 2200 Dallas TX 75201-6776 Office Phone: 214-740-8444.

PURNELL, OLIVER GORDON, JR., men's college basketball coach; b. Berlin, Md., May 19, 1953; m. Vicky Purnell; children: Olivia, Lindsay. BS in Health and Phys. Edn., Old Dominion U., 1975, MA in Phys. Edn. and Adminstrn., 1978. Draft pick Milw. Bucks, 1975; grad. asst. Old Dominion U., 1975—77, asst. coach, 1978—85, head coach, 1991—94; asst. coach U. Md., 1985—88; head coach Radford U., 1988—91, U. Dayton, Ohio, 1994—2003, Clemson U., SC, 2003—. Head coach US Olympic Festival, 1994; asst. coach World U. Games, 1995, head coach, 99; mem. USA Basketball Men's Collegiate Com., 2000; asst. coach Goodwill Games, 2001, Olympic Qualifying, 2003, US Olympic Team, Athens, Greece, 2004. Named Big South Conf. Coach of Yr., 1991, Colonial Athletic Assn. Coach of Yr., 1993, Coach of Yr. in State of Va., 1993, Atlantic 10 Coach of Yr., 1998; named to Old Dominion Athletic Hall of Fame, 1988, All-Time Old Dominion U. Basketball Squard, 2006; recipient Devel. Coach of Yr. award, USA Basketball, 1999. Mem.: Nat. Assn. Basketball Coaches (pres. 2006—, bd. dirs. 1998, Dist. Coach of Yr. 1998, Dist. IV Coach of Yr. 1993). Avocations: jogging, cooking. Office: Clemson U Mens Basketball Jervey Athletic Ctr 100 Perimeter Rd Clemson SC 29633 Office Phone: 864-656-1954. E-mail: opurnel@clemson.edu. *

PURNELL, OLIVER JAMES, III, judge; b. Richmond, Va., Jan. 18, 1949; s. Oliver James Jr. and Margaret Helen (Hodges) P.; m. Cheryl Naomi Williams, June 30, 1973; children: Oliver James IV, Amy Susan. AA, U. Hartford, 1969; AB, Middlebury Coll., 1972; MSLS, Case Western Res. U., 1976; JD, Western New England Sch. Law, 1982. Bar: Conn. 1982, U.S. Dist. Ct. Conn. 1982. Dir., pharmacy libr. U. Conn. Sch. Pharmacy, Storrs, Conn., 1977-81; assoc. Lavitt, Hutchinson & Kaplan, Vernon, Conn., 1981-84, DuBeau & Ryan, Vernon, Conn., 1984-87, Howard, Kohn Sprague & Fitzgerald, Hartford, Conn., 1987-89; pvt. practice Vernon, 1989—; reference libr. U. Conn. Sch. Law, Hartford, 1992-98; regional info. mgr. Lexis-Nexis, Vernon, 1998—99; judge Ellington Dist. Probate Ct., Vernon, 1999—. Adj. prof. U. Hartford. Contbr. articles to profl. jours. Scoutmaster Boy Scouts Am., Rockville, Conn., 1990—; trustee Rockville (Conn.) Pub. Libr.; corporator Ea. Conn. Health Network; mem. U. Hartford Alumni Coun.; mem. Hillyer Coll. Bd. Vis. Mem. Am. Assn. Law Libraries, So. New England Law Libr. Assn. (pres. 1998-99), Conn. Bar Assn. (coun. of bar pres. 1995-96), Tolland County Bar Assn. (pres. 1995-96), Nat. Coll. Probate Judges, Masonic Lodge, A.F. & A.M. (master Fayette Lodge 1970) Avocations: skiing, camping, hiking, church organist. Office: 1257 Hartford Tpke Vernon Rockville CT 06066 Office Phone: 860-870-1000. Personal E-mail: jpurnell3@att.net.

PUROHIT, RAJEEV, advocate, writer; LLB, Sussex U., 1995; LLM in Internat. Legal Studies, Am. U. Washington Coll. Law, 1997. Dir. legal svcs. Ctr. Conscience and War; legis. dir. NACDL, Human Rights First; sr. fellow internat. law & justice prog. Citizens for Global Solutions, Washington, 2005—. Adj. faculty mem. Am. U. Washington Coll. Law, 2006. Contbr. articles to profl. publs. Office: Citizens for Global Solutions 418 7th St SE Washington DC 20003-2769 Office Phone: 202-546-3950 ext. 108. E-mail: rpurohit@globalsolutions.org. *

PUROL, R.M. SCOTT, psychiatric nurse; b. Phila., Sept. 16, 1946; d. Sylvester Steven and Josephine Veronica (Czarnecka) P.; m. Stephen Chas Hershey, Dec. 27, 1986. Diploma in nursing, St. Joseph's Hosp., 1968; BA, Lone Mtn. Coll., 1974; BSN, U. San Francisco, 1976; M in Nursing, Emory U., 1990. Staff nurse Meth. Hosp., Phila., 1968—. Clin. nurse specialist Interdisciplinary Practice, Columbus, 1991-95; found. Health Mentors, Columbus, 1995—. Served in U.S. Army Nurse Corps, 1967-87. Grantee NIH, 1976. Mem. ANA, Am. Psychiat. Nurses Assn., Am. Holistic Nurses Assn., Ga. Nurses Assn. (Dist. Honoree 1996), Internat. Soc. Consultative Liaison Nurses, Assn. Child and Adolescent Psychiat. Nurses, Nat. Registry of Cert. Group Psychotherapists, Am. Group Psychotherapy Assn. (clin.), Am. Coll. Nurse Practitioners, Sigma Theta Tau. Avocations: singing, piano, music therapy research. Home and Office: Health Mentors PO Box 7937 Columbus GA 31908-7937

PURPURA, DOMINICK P., dean emeritus, neuroscientist; b. NYC, Apr. 2, 1927; m. Florence Williams, 1948; children: Craig, Kent, Keith, Allyson. AB, Columbia U., 1949; MD, Harvard U., 1953. Intern Presbyn Hosp., NYC, 1953—54; asst. resident in neurology Neurol. Inst., NYC, 1954—55; prof., chmn. dept. anatomy Albert Einstein Coll. Medicine, Yeshiva U., NYC, 1967—74, sci. dir. Kennedy Ctr., 1969—72, dir. Kennedy Ctr., 1972—82, prof., chmn. dept. neurosci., 1974—82, dean, 1984—2006, dean emeritus, 2006—; dean Stanford U., 1982—84. Editor-in-chief Brain Rsch. Revs., 1975—2000, Developmental Brain Rsch., 1981—2000, Molecular Brain Rsch., 1985—2000, Cognitive Brain Rsch., 1991—2000, Brain Rsch., 1975—2000, mem. editl. bd., 1965—2000. Served with USAAF, 1945-47. Fellow N.Y. Acad. Scis.; mem. NAS, Inst. Medicine of NAS, Am. Acad. Neurology, Am. Assn. Anatomists, Am. Assn. Neurol. Surgeons, Am. Epilepsy Soc., Am. Physiol. Soc., Assn. Rsch. in Nervous and Mental Disease, Soc. Neurosci., Sigma Xi. Office: Albert Einstein Coll Medicine Dept Neurosci 1300 Morris Park Ave Kennedy 912D Bronx NY 10461-1926 Office Phone: 718-430-2801. Office Fax: 718-430-8821. Business E-Mail: dpurpura@aecomyu.edu.

PURSCELL, KEITH WILLIAM, minister; b. Council Bluffs, Iowa, Feb. 12, 1931; s. Benjamin William and Marie Esther (Lowe) Purscell; m. Mary Louise Elliott, May 16, 1952 (dec. Jan. 22, 1993); children: Kenneth, Sally, David, Glenda; m. Helen Margaret Duncan, June 17, 1994. Student, Johnson Bible Coll., Knoxville, Tenn., 1949—51; BA in Religion, Nebr. Christian Coll., Norfolk, 1953; postgrad. studies, Lincoln Christian Coll. Sem., Ill., 1953—54; MDiv. in Ministrey, with hon., Phillips Grad. Sem., Enid, Okla., 1970. Ordained Clergy The Christian Ch., 1951. Pastor Ch. Christ, Red Cloud, Nebr., 1954—58, Clay Ctr. Christian Ch., Nebr., 1958—60, First Christian Ch., Florence, Kans., 1962—67, Spencer, Iowa, 1970—79, Douglass, Kans., 1967—70, Broadway Christian Ch., Wichita, Kans., 1979—82, 1st Christian Ch., Independence, Kans., 1982—86, La Junta, Colo., 1986—90, Mankato, Minn., 1990—96; interim pastor Congl. UCC Ch., Webster City, Iowa, 1998—99, Fairmont, Minn., 2005, St. Lukes, Fairbault, Minn., 1999—2000; retired; interim pastor United Ch. Mapleton, Minn., 2005—06. Chaplain NW Iowa Alcoholism & Drug Treatment Unit, Spencer, Iowa, 1971—78; vice moderator Christian Ch. in the Upper-Midwest Region, 1976—79; chmn. com. on scholarships for ministry Disciples of Christ, Kans., 1979—86; chmn. com. on ministry Disciples of Christ Colo., and Wyoming, 1989—90; organising pres., v.p. Living at Home Block Nurse Program, Mankato, Minn., 1991—2005; pres. Minn. State U. for Srs. Orgn., Mankato, 2005—06. Co-author: (devotional prayer) Secret Place, 1982; contbr. articles to Christian mags., 1955—95. Mem. adv. com. hospice Wesley Hosp., Wichita, Kans., 1981—82; creator sr. ctr. and county transportation for Clay County Iowa, 1976—79; pres. consumer adv. coun. Kans. Gas and Electric Co., 1984—86. Named Disting. alumus, Phillips U. Alumni, 2001. Disciples Of Christ. Achievements include design of regional policy on sexual abuse by clergy or staff for Christian Church in the Central Rockies Region. Avocation: photography. Home and Office: PO Box 3639 Mankato MN 56002 Office Phone: 507-625-3309.

PURSE, CHARLES ROE, investment banker; b. Redhill, Surrey, Eng., May 19, 1960; arrived in U.S., 1960; s. James Nathanial II and Rolande Marie-Louise (Redon) Purse; m. Carole Lynn Sadler, July 5, 1986; children: Hayley Elizabeth, Cameron James, Andrew Lang. BA, Dartmouth Coll., 1982; MBA, Northwestern U., 1985. Account officer No. Trust Bank, Chgo., 1982—85; asst. v.p. Citicorp Real Estate, Inc., Chgo., 1985—88; v.p. Citibank, Ltd., Sydney, 1988—91, Citibank Realty Investment Advisors, NYC, 1991—94; sr. v.p. Yarmouth Group, NYC, 1994—96; mng. dir. DRA Advisors, Inc., NYC, 1996—2000; mng. dir. real estate pvt. fund group Credit Suisse First Boston, NYC, 2000—05; mng. prin. Park Hill Real Estate Group, LLC, NYC, 2005—. Mem.: Pension Real Estate Assn., Bald Peak Colony Club, Belle Haven Club, Hillsboro Club (Hillsboro Beach, Fla.), Cromer Golf Club (Sydney), Country Club (Cleve.). Republican. Avocations: golf, photography, skiing, tennis. Office: Park Hill Real Estate Group LLC 345 Park Ave 15th Fl New York NY 10154

PURSEY, DEREK LINDSAY, retired physics professor; b. Glasgow, Scotland, Oct. 22, 1927; came to U.S., 1964; s. Henry Edwin and Margaret Martin (Lindsay) P.; m. Barbara Ann Parker, Aug. 4, 1962; 1 child, John BS, U. Glasgow, 1948, PhD, 1952. Asst. lectr. theoretical physics King's Coll., London, 1951-54; lectr. math. physics U. Edinburgh, Scotland, 1954-59; vis. lectr. UCLA, 1959-60; mem. sch. math. Inst. for Advanced Studies, Princeton, 1960-61; lectr. in theoretical physics U. Glasgow, Scotland, 1961-64; vis. prof. Iowa State U., Ames, 1964-65, prof. physics, 1965-93, emeritus prof. physics, 1993—. Vis. prof. UCLA, 1979-80. Contbr. articles to profl. jours. Fellow Royal Soc. Edinburgh, Am. Phys. Soc.; mem. AAAS, Presbyn. Assn. on Sci., Tech. and Christian Faith (sec.-treas. 1998-2002, pres. 2002—), Sigma Xi. Democrat. Presbyterian. Avocations: church-related activities, photography, music, reading, wilderness camping. Personal E-mail: dlpursey@mwci.net.

PURSLEY, FRANK JAMES, retired personal development specialist; b. Durham, NC, May 5, 1927; s. James Alton and Vesta Andwers Pursley; m. Dymple Edwards (dec.); children: Cynthia, Susan, Frank Jr.; m. Barbara Jean Pursley; children: Charles, Keith, Vanessa. AA, Ctrl. Va. C.C., Lynchburg, 1978. Sales mgr. WLVA-T Inc., Lynchburg, 1953—75; pers. devel. Va. Dept. Transp., Lynchburg, 1976—98; ret., 1998. Mem. adv. bd. Va. C.C., Lynchburg, adj. instr., 1998—2002; chmn. Svc. Corps. Ret. Exec. (SCORE) 529, 2003—. Mem. adv. bd. Local Red Cross, Lynchburg; active Rep. Nat. Com.; chair adminstrv. bd. Ct. St. Meth. Ch., Lynchburg, 1978—80. 1st. lt. US Army, 1956, col. US Army, 1980. Mem.: Mil. Order World Wars, Oakwood Country Club (golf com. 2000—). Avocations: golf, music, fishing, hunting. Home: 517 Midvale St Lynchburg VA 24502 Office: Score 529 Fed bldg Ste A42 1101 Court St Lynchburg VA 24504 Office Phone: 434-846-3235. Personal E-mail: fpurs17868@aol.com.

PURSLEY, MICHAEL BADER, engineering educator, communications systems researcher, consultant; b. Winchester, Ind., Aug. 10, 1945; s. Bader E. and Evelyn L. (Bennett) P.; m. Lou Ann Hinchman, July 6, 1968; 1 child, Jessica Ann. BS, Purdue U., 1967, MS, 1968; PhD, U. So. Calif., 1974. Mem. tech. staff Hughes Aircraft Co., Los Angeles, 1967; engr. Northrop Co., Hawthorne, Calif., 1968; staff engr. Hughes Aircraft Co., Los Angeles, 1968-74; acting asst. prof. UCLA, 1974; asst. prof., then assoc. prof. elec. engring. U. Ill., Urbana, 1974-80, prof., 1980-93; Holcombe prof. elec. and computer engring. Clemson (S.C.) U., 1992—; assoc. Ctr. Advanced Study, 1980-81; vis. prof. UCLA, 1985; cons. U.S. Army, Huntsville, Ala., 1977, Ft. Monmouth, NJ, 1983-86, 91, ITT, Ft. Wayne, Ind., 1979—; pres. SIGCOM, Inc., 1986-90; prin. scientist Techno-Scis. Inc., 1990—96. Author: Random Processes in Linear Systems, 2002, Introduction to Digital Communications, 2005; contbr. chapters to books. Recipient Fred W. Ellersick award Comms. Soc., 1996, Tech. Achievement award Mil. Comm. Conf., 1999, Edwin Howard Armstrong Achievement award, 2002. Fellow IEEE (pres. info. theory group 1983, Centennial medal 1984, Millennium medal 2000); mem. Inst. Math. Stats. Office: Clemson U 303 Fluor Daniel Bldg Dept ECE Clemson SC 29634

PURTELL, LAWRENCE ROBERT, lawyer; b. Quincy, Mass., May 2, 1947; s. Lawrence Joseph and Louise Maria (Loria) P.; m. Cheryl Lynn Tymon, Aug. 3, 1968; children: Lisa Ann, Susan Elizabeth. AB, Villanova U., 1969; JD, Columbia U., 1972. Bar: N.Y. 1973, N.J. 1978, Conn. 1988. Assoc. White & Case, NYC, 1972-73; judge advocate USMC, Washington, 1973-76; assoc. White & Case, NYC, 1977-79; corp. counsel Great Atlantic & Pacific Tea Co., Montvale, N.J., 1979-81; asst. gen. counsel United Techs. Corp., Hartford, Conn., 1981-84, assoc. gen. counsel, 1984-92, sec., gen. counsel, 1989-92; v.p., gen. counsel and sec. Carrier Corp., 1992-93; sr. v.p., gen. counsel and corp. sec. Mc Dermott Internat., New Orleans, 1993-96; sr. v.p., gen. counsel Koch Industries, Wichita, Kans., 1996-97; exec. v.p., gen. counsel Alcoa, Pitts., 1997—. Capt. USMC, 1973-76. Roman Catholic. Avocation: running. Home: 637 Shoreline Dr Naples FL 34119 Office: Alcoa 390 Park Ave New York NY 10022 Office Phone: 212-836-2650. *

PURTLE, JOHN INGRAM, lawyer, former state supreme court justice; b. Enola, Ark., Sept. 7, 1923; s. John Wesley and Edna Gertrude (Ingram) P.; m. Marian Ruth White, Dec. 31, 1951 (dec. 1995); children: Jeffrey, Lisa K.; m. Phyllis Kelly Purtle. Student, U. Ctrl. Ark., 1946—47; LLB, U. Ark., 1950. Bar: Ark. 1950, U.S. Dist. Ct. (ea. dist.) Ark. 1950. Pvt. practice, Conway, Ark., 1950-53, Little Rock, 1953—78, 1990—; mem. Ark. State Legislature, 1951-52, 69-70; assoc. justice Ark. Supreme Ct., 1979-90. Tchr., deacon Baptist Ch. Served with U.S. Army, 1940-45. Mem. ABA, Ark. Bar Assn., Am. Judicature Soc., Ark. Jud. Coun. Democrat.

PURVES, DENNIS PATRICK, library director; b. Elizabeth, NJ, Dec. 25, 1970; s. Dennis Patrick and Mary Theresa Purves. BA, Seton Hall U., 1993; MLS, Rutgers U., 1994. Libr. page Linden (N.J.) Pub. Libr., 1987—95, libr., 1996—2004, sr. libr., 2004—; libr. Alexander Libr. Rutgers U., New Brunswick, NJ, 1995; freelance subject cataloger Bowker-Reed Reference, New Providence, NJ, 1996—97. Mem.: ALA, Librs. of Union County Consortium (v.p. 2005, pres. 2006), N.J. Libr. Assn. Roman Catholic. Home: 38 E Elm Street Apt 3A Linden NJ 07036 Office: Linden Pub Libr 31 E Henry St Linden NJ 07036 Office Phone: 908-298-3830 11. Business E-Mail: dpurves@lindenpl.org.

PURVES, WILLIAM KIRKWOOD, biologist, educator; b. Sacramento, Oct. 28, 1934; s. William Kirkwood and Dorothy (Brandenburger) P.; m. Jean McCauley, June 9, 1959; 1 son, David William. BS, Calif. Inst. Tech., 1956; MS, Yale U., 1957, PhD, 1959. NSF postdoctoral fellow U. Tubingen, Germany, 1959-60; Nat. Cancer Inst. postdoctoral fellow UCLA, 1960-61; asst. prof. botany U. Calif., Santa Barbara, 1961-65, assoc. prof. biochemistry, 1965-70, prof. biology, 1970-73, chmn. dept. biol. scis., 1972-73; prof. biology, head biol. sci. group U. Conn., Storrs, 1973-77; Stuart Mudd prof. biology Harvey Mudd Coll., Claremont, Calif., 1977-95, prof. emeritus, 1996—, chmn. dept. biol., 1985-95, chmn. dept. computer sci., 1985-90; adj. prof. plant physiology U. Calif., Riverside, 1979-85. V.p., sci. dir. The Mona Group LLC, 1996-2004. Author: Life, the Science of Biology, 1983, 8th edit., 2007. NSF sr. postdoctoral fellow U. London, 1967, Harvard U., 1968; vis. fellow computer sci. Yale U., 1983-84; vis. scholar Northwestern U., 1991; NSF rsch. grantee, 1962-83, 97-2001. Fellow AAAS; mem. Sigma Xi. E-mail: Bill_Purves@hmc.edu.

PURVEZ, AKHTAR, interventional pain management specialist, writer, speaker, advocate; b. Srinagar, India, Apr. 1, 1958; s. Muzaffar Aazim and Padshah (Jan) Mir; m. Mudhasir Bashir; children: Ana Mir, Sama Mir. MB, BS, Govt. Med. Coll., Srinagar, India, 1981, M of Surgery with honors, 1986. Diplomate and cert. in pain medicine Am. Bd. Anesthesiology, Am. Bd. Pain Medicine, Am. Bd. Disability Analysts. Intern medicine Govt. Med. Coll. Associated Hosps., Srinagar, India, 1981—82, resident house surgeon, 1982—83, asst. surgeon, 1983—84, postgrad. scholar, 1984—86, registrar, asst. surgeon, 1986—87; registrar Govt. Med. Coll., 1987—89, resident anesthesiology, 1998—2001, fellow in pain mgmt., 2002; med. dir. Ctr. for Pain Mgmt., Charlottesville, Va., 2002—. Avocations: literature, mountain climbing, riding, charities, metaphysics, metacommunication. E-mail: apurvez@hotmail.com.

PURVIN, JACK MITCHELL, physician; b. Bklyn., May 27, 1953; s. Saul and Sylvia (Masey) P. BA in Psychology, U. Denver, 1975; postgrad., U. Autonoma de Guadalajara, Mex., 1978-81; MD, Dominica Sch. of Medicine, 1983. Pres. P.E.C. Inc., Del. Developer diabetic food products, pmlis sys. Patentee in field. Owner Jack M. Purvin Found. Mem. Am. Diabetes Assn., Montana Hist. Soc. Avocations: chess, coin collecting/numismatics, philatelic collections, rare documents, sports. Home: 1901 84th St Apt 4A Brooklyn NY 11214-3032 Office: PEC Inc PO Box 140028 Brooklyn NY 11214-0028 Home Phone: 718-759-7335; Office Phone: 718-333-9198. Personal E-mail: jackpurvin@aol.com.

PURVIS, JOHN ANDERSON, lawyer, educator; b. Aug. 31, 1942; s. Virgil J. and Emma Lou (Anderson) P.; m. Charlotte Johnson, Apr. 3, 1976; 1 child, Whitney; children by previous marriage: Jennifer, Matt. BA cum laude, Harvard U., 1965; JD, U. Colo., 1968. Bar: Colo. 1968, U.S. Dist. Ct. Colo. 1968, U.S. Ct. Appeals (10th cir.) 1978. Dep. dist. atty., Boulder, Colo., 1968-69; asst. dir., dir. legal aid U. Colo. Sch. Law, 1969; assoc. Williams, Taussig & Trine, Boulder, 1969; head Boulder office Colo. Pub. Defender Sys., 1970-72; assoc., ptnr. Hutchinson, Black, Hill, Buchanan & Cook, Boulder, 1972-85; ptnr. Purvis, Gray, Schuetze and Gordon, 1985-98, Purvis, Gray & Gordon, LLP, 1999—2001, Purvis Gray LLP, 2001—03, Purvis Gray & Murphy, 2003—. Acting Colo. State Pub. Defender, 1978; adj. prof. law U. Colo., 1981, 84-88, 94, others; lectr. in field; chmn. Colo. Pub. Defender Commn., 1979-89; mem. nominating commn. Colo. Supreme Ct., 1984-90; mem. com. on conduct U.S. Dist. Ct., 1991-97, chmn., 1996-97; chmn. Boulder County Criminal Justice Com., 1975-81. Recipient Recipient Ames award, Harvard U., 1964, Outstanding Young Lawyer award, Colo. Bar Assn., 1978, Dist. Achievement award, U. Colo. Law Sch. Alumni Assn., 1997. Mem.: ATLA, Am. Bar Found., Colo. Bar Found., Trial Lawyers for Pub. Justice, Colo. Trial Lawyers Assn., Boulder County Bar Assn., Colo. Bar Assn. (chair litigation sect. 1994—95), Am. Coll. Trial Lawyers (state chmn. 1998—2000), Am. Bd. Trial Advs., Internat. Acad. Trial Lawyers (state chmn. 2002—), Internat. Soc. Barristers, Faculty of Fed. Advs. (bd. dirs. 1999—2001), Supreme Ct. Hist. Soc. (state chmn. 1998—2002). Democrat. Address: 1050 Walnut St Ste 501 Boulder CO 80302-5144 Home Phone: 303-444-0744; Office Phone: 303-442-3366. Personal E-mail: jpurvis@purvisgray.net.

PURVIS, RANDALL W. B., lawyer; b. Summit, NJ, Mar. 2, 1957; s. Merton B. and Marjory L. (Baker) P.; m. Robin Head Intemann Purvis; children: Zachary, Timothy, Andrew. BS, Ohio State U., 1979; JD, Georgetown U., 1982. Bar: Colo. 1983, U.S. Dist. Ct. Colo. 1983, U.S. Ct. Appeals (10th cir.) 1983. Pvt. practice, Colorado Springs, Colo., 1983—. Adj. prof. Colo. Coll., 2001—. Steering com. Nat. League of Cities, Washington; trustee Meml. Hosp. Colorado Springs, 1991—99; councilman Colorado Springs City Coun., 1987—; elder 1st Presbyn. Ch., Colorado Springs, 1987—91. Mem. Colo. Bar Assn., El Paso County Bar Assn. (com. chmn. 1986), Colorado Springs C. of C. (com. chmn. 1986), Colorado Springs Bridge Club, Phi Beta Kappa. Republican. Avocations: bridge, woodworking. Office: 128 S Tejon Ste 402 Colorado Springs CO 80903-1520 Office Phone: 719-578-9800. E-mail: rwbpurvis@hotmail.com.

PURYEAR, JAMES BURTON, college administrator; b. Jackson, Miss., Sept. 2, 1938; s. Harry Henton and Doris (Smith) P.; m. Joan Copeland, June 13, 1965; children: John James, Jeffrey Burton, Joel Harry. BS, Miss. State U., Miss. State, 1960, MEd, 1961; PhD, Fla. State U., Tallahassee, 1969. Lic. profl. counselor, Ga. Assoc. dir. YMCA Miss. State U., Starkville, 1962-64; dir. YMCA, Starkville, Miss., 1964-65; dir. fin. aid Fla. State U., Tallahassee, 1967-69; asst. dir. student affairs Med. Coll. of Ga., Augusta, 1969-70, dir. student affairs, 1970-86, v.p. student affairs,

1986-2000, v.p. emeritus, student affairs, 2000—. Mem. adv. bd. Ga. Fed. Bank, Augusta, 1978-85; deacon, 1971-, chmn. bd. First Bapt. Ch., Augusta, 1978-80; pres. Learning Disabilities Assn., Augusta, 1987, PTA, 1994, Band Assn.,1996; bd. dirs. Augusta Tng. Shop for Handicapped, 1994-98; mem. exec. bd., v.p. Boy Scouts Am., 1996-02; mem. bd. Consumer Credit Counseling Svc., 2004-06. Yearbook Dedication MCG Student Yearbook, 1975; scholar Med. Coll. Ga., 1988; recipient Svc. to Mankind award Sertoma, 1988, Silver Beaver award Boy Scouts Am. Mem. Nat. Assn. Student Pers. (S.E. regional bd. 1985), Am. Coll. Pers. Assn., So. Assn. Coll. Student Affairs, Rotary (pres. 1978, dist. lt. gov. 1997-99, dist. gov. 2001-02, Paul Harris fellow 1985, Will Watt fellow). Baptist. Avocations: golf, photography, scouting.

PURYEAR, JOAN COPELAND, academic administrator; b. Columbus, Miss., May 10, 1944; d. John Thomas and Mamie (Cunningham) Copeland.; m. James Burton Puryear, June 13, 1965; children: John James, Jeffrey Burton, Joel Harry. BA summa cum laude, Miss. State U., Starkville, 1965; MA, Fla. State U., 1969; EdD, U. Ga., 1987. Instr. English, Fla. State U., Tallahassee, 1965-69, Augusta (Ga.) State U., 1987-88; head English dept. Augusta Tech. Coll., 1989-93, chairperson gen. edn. and devel. studies, 1993-96, mem. dean's coun., mgmt. team, 1994—, dean gen. edn. and devel. studies, 1997—, dean allied health scis., 1997—2004. Chmn. State Exec. Bd. English, Ga., 1990-92, East Ctrl. Consortium English, Ga., 1990-92; facilitator Total Quality Mgmt. Tech. Tng.; mem. exec. steering com. Continous Improvement Coun., 1996-02; mem. and co-chmn. Continous Improvement Coun., 1996-97. Mem. Cmtys. in Schs., 1996-06; trustee Augusta Tech. Inst. Found. Bd., 1996-07; mem. founding bd. Junior Achievement, 2001-02; co-pres. Davidson Fine Arts Sch. PTA, 1995, co-pres. bd. assn., 1996; pres. Med. Coll. Spouse's Club, Augusta, 1972; dir. Women's Mission Orgn., First Bapt. Ch., Augusta, 1982, dir. youth Sunday Sch., 1992-98, chmn. 175th Anniversary, 1992, deacon, 1996—, vice moderator, 1998-99, mem. ministerial adv. com., 1992-01, chair, 2003, vice chmn. scholarship and edn. com., 2002, chmn. nominating com., 2004, Sunday Sch. tchr.; mem. found. bd. Walton Rehab. Ctr. Mem.: Rotary (chmn. dist. membership 2003—04, asst. dist. gov. 2006—, literacy chair 2005), Augusta South Rotary Club (pres. 2002—03), Phi Theta Kappa (advisor 1992—, Horizon regional award for outstanding advisor 1997). Baptist. Avocations: flower arranging, home decorating, reading, travel. Office: Augusta Tech Coll 3200 Augusta Tech Dr Augusta GA 30906-3375

PURYEAR, MARTIN, artist, educator; b. Washington, May 23, 1941; s. Reginald Thomas and Martina Alice (Morse) P. BA, Cath. U., 1963; postgrad., Swedish Royal Acad., Stockholm, 1966-68; M.F.A., Yale U., 1971, Doctorate (hon.), 1994. Mem. Peace Corps, Sierra Leone, 1964—66; asst. prof. Fisk U., Nashville, 1971-73, U. Md., College Park, 1974-77; assoc. prof. art U. Ill., Chgo., 1978-86, prof., 1986-88; staff Calder Atelier, Saché, France, 1992—93; resident Am. Acad., Rome, 1997; represented by Donald Young Gallery, Chgo. Exhibited in group shows at Whitney Biennial Exhbn., 1979, 81, 89, Whitney Mus. Am. Art, N.Y., Guggenheim Mus., N.Y.C., 1978, 85, 87, Mus. Modern Art, N.Y.C., 1984, St. Louis Art Mus., 1988, Donald Young Gallery, Chgo., 2002, 03, McKee Gallery, N.Y.C., 2002, Irish Mus. Modern Art, Dublin, 2004, others; one-man shows include Corcoran Gallery Art, 1977, Joslyn Art Mus., 1980, Univ. Art Mus., 1985, Bklyn. Mus., 1988; commd. sculptures include Bodard Art, Nathan Manila Sculpture Pk., Govs. State U., University Park, Ill., Chevy Chase Garden Pla., Md.; traveling retrospective Art Inst. Chgo., Hirshorn Museum, Washington, D.C., Museum of Contemporary Art, Los Angeles, 1991-92; Documenta IX, Kassel, Germany, 1992. Recipient Purchase prize Balt. Mus. Art, 1962, award Francis J. Greenburger Found., 1988, Best Artist prize Sao Paulo Bienal, 1989, Creative Arts award for sculpture Brandeis U., 1989, medal for sculpture Skowhegan Sch. Painting & Sculpture, 1990, award Coll. Art Assn.; Louis Comfort Tiffany Found. grantee, 1981; Guggenheim fellow, 1982 Mem.: Am. Acad. and Inst. Arts and Letters.

PUSATERI, DAVID P., lawyer; b. Pitts., 1959; BA, U. Notre Dame, 1981, JD, 1984. Bar: Pa. 1984, US Dist. Ct. We. Dist. Pa. 1986. Law clk. to Hon. Gustave Diamond US Dist. Ct. We. Dist. Pa., 1984—86; v.p., assoc. gen. counsel, asst. sec. Robertson-Ceco Corp., San Ramon, Calif.; shareholder Sable, Makoroff & Gusky PC; mng. ptnr. Sable Pusateri Rosen Gordon & Adams LLC (merged with McGuireWoods LLP), Pitts.; ptnr., real estate & environ. dept. McGuireWoods LLP, Pitts., 2001—, co-mng. ptnr. Pitts. office, 2001—02, mng. ptnr., 2002—. Recipient Internat. Acad. Trial Lawyers Award. Fellow: Allegheny County Bar Found.; mem.: ABA (environment, energy & resources sect., bus. law sect.), Pa. Bar Assn. (environ. mineral & natural resource law sect.), Allegheny County Bar Assn. (bus. law sect., environ. law sect.). Office: McGuireWoods LLP Dominion Tower 23rd Fl 625 Liberty Ave Pittsburgh PA 15222-3142 Office Phone: 412-667-7924. Office Fax: 412-667-7963. Business E-Mail: DPusateri@mcguirewoods.com.

PUSCHEL, PHILIP P., textiles executive; m. Roberta J. Green. AB, Hamilton Coll., 1960; MBA, Stanford U., 1962. V.p. F Schumacher & Co., NYC, 1971, pres., CEO, 1981, chmn. bd., 1981—, CEO officer, 1989—99. With USN, 1962-65. Office: F Schumacher & Co 79 Madison Ave Fl 15 New York NY 10016-7802

PUSEY, WILLIAM ANDERSON, lawyer; b. Richmond, Va., Mar. 17, 1936; s. Paul H. and Vernelle (Barnes) P.; m. Patricia Powell, Sept. 3, 1960; children: Patricia Brent, William A. Jr., Margaret Glen. AB, Princeton U., 1958; JD, U. Va., 1962. Bar: Va. 1964. Assoc. McCutchen, Brown, et al, San Francisco, 1962-63; dep. dist. atty. Alameda County, Oakland, Calif., 1963-64; assoc., ptnr., sr. counsel Hunton & Williams, Washington, Fairfax and Richmond, Va., 1964—. Trustee Ea. Mineral Law Found., pres., 1987-88. Chmn. bd. dirs. Presbyn. Sch. Christian Edn., Richmond, 1984-85. Mem. Am. Hort. Soc. (bd. dirs. and sec. 1995-2002, gen. counsel 2002—06), Order of Coif, Phi Beta Kappa, Omicron Delta Kappa. Office: Hunton & Williams 1900 K St NW Washington DC 20006-1110 Home: 57 E Square Ln Richmond VA 23238

PUSKAR, MILAN, pharmaceuticals executive; b. 1935; Grad., Youngstown State U., 1961. V.p. Mylan Pharm. Inc., 1961-72; divsn. v.p. ICN Pharms., Inc., 1972-75; pres., CEO, chmn. Mylan Lab. Inc., 1976-2000, chmn., CEO, 2000—. Vice chmn. bd. dirs. Mylan Lab. Inc., 1980-93, chmn. bd., CEO, 1993—. Office: STE 400 1500 Corporate DR Canonsburg PA 15317-8580

PUST, RONALD E., physician, educator; b. Sidney, Mont., May 5, 1941; s. Erich W. Pust and Marie Leis; m. Karen J. Blomquist, June 12, 1966; children: Joel E., Sara M. Meza, Rachel K. Durazo, Brian P. BA, Wheaton Coll., Ill., 1962; MD, U. Wash., Seattle, 1962—66. Cert. Am. Bd. Preventive Medicine, 1973, Amercan Bd. Family Medicine, 1978, qualification Am. Soc. Tropical Medicine & Hygiene, 2000. TB control physician Indian Health Svc., Window Rock, Ariz., 1969—71; med. epidemiologist CDC, USPHS, Enugu, Nigeria, 1971—73; med. officer, dir. Immanuel Luth. Hosp., Wapenamanda, Papua New Guinea, 1973—79; prof. family medicine and pub. health U. Ariz., Tucson, 1979—. Pres. Global Health Edn. Consortium, NYC, 1992—93; prof. and head family health Moi U., Eldoret, Kenya, 2004—05. Med. missionary to Papua New Guinea Luth. Ch., St Louis, 1973—79. Recipient Smallpox Target Zero, WHO, 1980, Smilkstein Internat. Family Medicine award, STFM, 2007. Democrat. Presyterian. Avocations: travel, photography. Office Phone: 520-626-7822. Business E-Mail: rpust@email.arizona.edu.

PUSTILNIK, DAVID DANIEL, lawyer; b. NYC, Mar. 10, 1931; s. Philip and Belle (Gerberholtz) P.; m. Helen Jean Todd, Aug. 15, 1959; children: Palma Elyse, Leslie Royce, Bradley Todd. BS, NYU, 1952, JD, 1958, LLM, 1959; postgrad., Air War Coll., 1976. Bar: N.Y. 1959, U.S. Supreme Ct. 1962, Conn. 1964. Legis. tax atty. legis. and regulations div. Office Chief Counsel, IRS, Washington, 1959-63; atty. Travelers Ins. Co., Hartford, Conn., 1963-68, assoc. counsel, 1968-73, counsel, 1973-75, assoc. gen. counsel, 1975-87, dep. gen. counsel, 1987-93. Mem. adv. coun. Hartford Inst. on Ins. Taxation, 1978-93, vice chmn., 1991-92, chmn., 1992-93. Grad. editor NYU Tax Law Rev., 1958-59. Trustee Hartford Coll. for Women, 1985-91; life sponsor Am. Tax Policy Inst.; dir. Congregation Beth Yam, 1996-99. Served to col. USAFR. Kenneson fellow NYU, 1958-59. Fellow Am. Coll. Tax Counsel; mem. ABA (chmn. ins. cos. com. 1976-78), Am. Coun. Life Ins. (chmn. co. tax com. 1982-84), Am. Ins. Assn. (chmn. tax com. 1979-81), Assn. Life Ins. Counsel (chmn. tax sect. 1991-93), Mil. Officers Assn. Am. (dir. Hilton Head area chpt.), Twentieth Century Club, Sea Pines Country Club (co-chair social com. 1997-99).

PUTH, DAVID W., diversified financial services company executive; 3 children. With Bank New Eng., 1980; v.p. fgn. exch. Citigroup; mng. dir., global head FX Connect; global head currencies J.P. Morgan Chase & Co., global head fgn. exch. and commodities, mng. dir., head North Am. rates, mng. dir., head North Am. FX trading. Chmn. fgn. exch. com. Fed. Res. Bank, 2000—. Office: JP Morgan Chase & Co 270 Park Ave New York NY 10017-2070

PUTH, JOHN WELLS, manufacturing executive, consultant; b. Orange, NJ, Mar. 14, 1929; s. Leonard G. and Elizabeth R. (Wells) P.; m. Betsey Leeds Tait, Mar.1, 1952; children: David Wells, Jonathan Craig, Alison Leeds. BS cum laude, Lehigh U., 1952. Dir. mktg. Purolator Products, Rahway, NJ, 1955-61; pres., chief exec. officer Bridgeport (Conn.) Hardware Mfg. Co. subs. Purolator, 1962-65; group v.p. H.K. Porter Co., Pitts., 1965-72; pres., CEO Disston Inc., Pitts., 1972-75, Vapor Corp., Niles, Ill., 1975-83; chmn., pres., CEO Clevite Industries Inc., Glenview, Ill., 1983-89; pres. JW Puth Assocs., Skokie, Ill., 1989—. Bd. dir. Adam Street Ptnrs., L.B. Foster, Pitts., A.M. Castle & Co., Franklin Park, Ill., V.J. Growers Inc., Apopka, Fla., George W. Schmidt Inc., Niles, Ill.; advisor GTCR Funds. Chmn. bd. trustees Hadley Sch. for Blind, Winnetka, Ill., 1982-84; former trustee Lehigh U., Kenilworth Union Ch.; bd. dirs. Iaccoca Inst. With US Army, 1946—47. Mem.: Loblolly Pines Club, Old Elm Club, Indian Hill Country Club, Comml. Club, Chgo. Club. Republican. Presbyterian. Home: 180 De Windt Rd Winnetka IL 60093-3744 Office Phone: 847-967-4390.

PUTHENPURAKAL, JOSEPH MATHEW, information technology executive; b. Changanacherry, India, Feb. 12, 1949; arrived in U.S., 1978; s. Mathew Joseph and Teresa Mathew P.; m. Mary Jose Shirly, Aug. 21, 1977; children: Mathew Joseph, Thomas Joseph, Sherin Jose. BS, Kerala U., India, 1976; MS, Kerala U., 1978; AA, Dupage Coll., Glen Ellyn, Ill., 1982; BA, North Cen. Coll., Naperville, Ill., 1984; MBA, Thornewood U., Amsterdam, Netherlands, 1998, PhD, 2001. Software engr. AT&T Tech., Lisle, Ill., 1983-84; mem. tech. staff AT&T Bell Labs., Naperville, Ill., 1984-87; info. systems cons. Indecon, Inc., Chicago, 1987-89; pres. Chicagoland Star Telephone Co., 1988, Global Resources Co., Chgo., 1988—; mgr. Jewel Info. Systems Group, Melrose Park, Ill., 1989—91; pres. Optimum Techs. Inc., Lisle, Ill., 1992—2005; owner Optimum Real Estate, 2003—; pres. Alert IT Solutions, Inc., Woodridge, Ill., 2006—. Trustee Rep. Presdl. Task Force, Washington, 1986. Mem. Data Processing Mgmt. Assn., Am. Entrepreneurs Assn., Internat. Traders. Avocations: reading, travel, swimming, investing. Home and Office: Alert IT Solutions Inc PO Box 5433 1230 Golfview Dr Woodridge IL 60517 Office Phone: 630-854-3762. Personal E-mail: jputhen1@gmail.com. Business E-Mail: jputhen@alertitsolutions.com.

PUTHOFF, MARK ALLEN, lawyer; b. Ft. Loramie, Ohio, Dec. 13, 1972; s. Robert Lee and Teresa Francis Puthoff; m. Jennifer Ellen Ondera, Nov. 17, 2001; children: Jordyn Taylor, Milan Isabelle, Hunter Ty. B, Hawaii Pacific U., Honolulu, 1996; JD, Thomas M. Cooley Law Sch., Lansing, Mich., 2003. Bar: Ohio 2005. Intern asst. prosecutor Montgomery County Prosecutor's Office, Dayton, Ohio, 2002—03; adminstr. contracts and real estate Pacific LightNet, Inc., Honolulu, 2003—04; atty. Dungan & LeFevre Co., L.P.A., Troy, Ohio, 2004—07, Puthoff & Assocs. LLC, Troy, Ohio, 2007—. Amb. Troy Area C. of C., Ohio, 2006; chmn. Taste of Troy, 2006; participant Leadership Troy, 2006—06; asst. Strawberry Festival, Troy, 2005; basketball ofcl. Ohio H.S. Athletic Assn., Miami Valley, 2005; mem. Mayor's Roundtable, 2007—; v.p. Troy Main St., 2006; legal advisor Troy Sr. Citizens Ctr., 2006. Scholar, Thomas M. Cooley Law Sch., 2001—03. Mem.: KC (assoc.), Miami County Bar Assn., Ohio Bar Assn., Home Builders Assn. (assoc.), Kiwanis (assoc.). Home: 514 S Plum St Troy OH 45373 Office: Puthoff & Assocs LLC 16 S Cherry St Troy OH 45373 Personal E-mail: puthoffmark@hotmail.com. Business E-Mail: mark@puthoff.us.

PUTKA, ANDREW CHARLES, lawyer; b. Cleve., Nov. 14, 1926; s. Andrew George and Lillian M. (Koryta) Putka. Student, John Carroll U., 1944, U.S. Naval Acad., 1945-46; AB, Adelbert Coll., Western Res. U., 1949, JD, 1952. Bar: Ohio 1952. Practice law, Cleve.; instr. govt. Notre Dame Coll.; v.p. Koryta Bros. Coal Co., Cleve., 1952-56; supt. divsn. bldg. and loan assns. Ohio Dept. Commerce, 1959-63; pres., chmn. bd., CEO Am. Nat. Bank, Parma, Ohio, 1963-69; dir. fin. City of Cleve., 1971-74; dir. port control, 1974-78; dir. Cleve. Hopkins Internat. Airport, 1974-78. Mem. Ohio Ho. of Reps., 1953-56, Ohio Senate, 1957-58; dep. auditor, acting sec. Cuyahoga County Bd. Revision, 1970-71; mem. exec. com. Cuyahoga County Democratic Com., 1973-81, Assn. Ind. Colls. and Univs. Ohio, 1983-89; bd. govs. Sch. Law, Western Res. U., 1953-56; mem. exec. com. World Service Student Fund, 1950-52; U.S. rep. Internat. Pax Romana Congress, Amsterdam, 1950, Toronto, 1952; mem. lay adv. bd. Notre Dame Coll., 1968-90, trustee, 1990-93, hon. trustee, 1993—, life mem., 1993—; mem. adv. bd. St. Andrew's Abbey, 1976-88; trustee Case-Western Res. U., Newman Found. No. Ohio, 1980-93, hon. trustee, life mem., 1993—; 1st v.p. First Cath. Slovak Union of U.S., 1977-80; pres. USO Council of Cuyahoga County, 1980-83. Voted an outstanding legislator Ohio Press Corrs., 1953; named to All-Star Legislative team Ohio Newspaper Corrs., 1955; named one of Fabulous Clevelanders Cleve. Plain Dealer, John Henry Newman honor Soc. Mem. DAV (life), KC (4th degree), NCCJ, Cuyahoga County, Cleve. Bar Assn., Nat. Assn. State Savs. and Loan Suprs. (past. nat. pres.), US Savs. and Loan League (mem. legis com, 1960-63), Am. Legion, Ohio Mcpl. League (bd. trustees 1973), Parma C. of C. (bd. dir., treas. 1965-67), Newman Fedn. (past nat. pres.), Cath. Lawyers Guild (treas.), Am. Ohio Bankers Assn., Am. Inst. Banking, Adelbert Alumni Assn. (exec. com.), Cathedral Latin Alumni Assn. (trustee 1952—), Internat. Order Alhambra (internat. parliamentarian 1971—, past grand comdr., supreme advocate 1973), Amvets, Pi Kappa Alpha, Delta Theta Phi (past. pres. Cleve. alumni senate, master inspector 1975). Office: 28 Pond Dr Cleveland OH 44116-1062

PUTMAN, CAROL JEAN, photographer, artist; b. San Francisco, Jan. 1, 1943; d. Joe Alfred and Jessie Jane (Harris) P. BA, Calif. State U., Hayward, 1968. Photographer, artist, Clayton, Calif., 1975—; exec. sec. Bank of Am., San Francisco, 1980; group sec. physics dept. Lawrence Berkeley Lab. U. Calif., Berkeley, 1974-75, sec. civil engring. dept., 1981-84, faculty sec. journalism dept., 1984-85, adminstrv. asst., sec. Dept. Math., 1985-86, 87-88. Exhibitions include Walnut Creek Civic Arts, Calif., 1982, Bedford Gallery, Walnut Creek, Calif., 2005, 2007, Ironstone Vineyards, Murphys, Calif., 2006, 2007, Sanchez Art Ctr., Pacifica, Calif., 2006, Sola, Silicon Valley Arts, Palo Alto, Calif., 2006, Plaza Art Ctr., Healdsburg, Calif., 2006, Bay Area Arts, San Jose, Calif., 2007, Los Gatos Art Assn., Calif., 2007, Santa Cruz Art League, 2007. Mem.: Creekside Artists Guild. Avocations: sailing, bicycling.

PUTMAN, DALE CORNELIUS, management consultant, lawyer; b. Ponca, Nebr., Apr. 29, 1927; s. Merle H. and Catherine V. (Sheahan) P.; m. Alice Anselmi, Sept. 8, 1951; children: Mark, Lee, Neil, Bruce, Kirk, Nancy, Wendy. BS, U. Nebr., 1949, LL.D., 1951. Bar: Nebr. 1951, Iowa 1951, Mo. 1977. Mgr. Interstate Assn. Credit Mgmt., Sioux City, Iowa, 1951-52; sec., legal counsel Metz Baking Co., Sioux City, 1953-66, v.p., 1966-69, exec. v.p., 1969-72, pres., 1972-76; chief operating officer Interstate Brands Corp., Kansas City, Mo., 1976-77, pres., dir., 1977-80, pres., chief exec. officer, 1980-84; chmn., chief exec. officer, pres., dir. Interstate Bakeries (formerly DPF, Inc.), 1980-84; pvt. practice mgmt. cons., 1984—. Served with U.S. Army, 1945-46. Knight, Order of the Holy Sepulchre of Jerusalem, knight Order of Malta. Mem. KC (4th degree), Serra Internat., Mensa. Republican. Roman Catholic. Home: 8405 Reinhardt Ln Shawnee Mission KS 66206-1316 Personal E-mail: putman9752@aol.com.

PUTMAN, (JAMES) MICHAEL, lawyer; b. San Antonio, May 12, 1948; s. Harold David and Elizabeth Finley (Henderson) P.; m. Kris J. Bird. BBA, S.W. Tex. State U., 1969; JD, St. Mary's U., 1972. Bar: Tex. 1972, US Dist. Ct. (we. dist.) Tex. 1980, US Ct. Appeals (5th and 11th cirs.) 1981, US Supreme Ct. 2003; cert. in personal injury trial law Tex. Bd. Legal Specialization. Ptnr. Putman & Putman (Inc. 1981), San Antonio, 1972-81, officer, dir., 1981—. Mem. ATLA, State Bar Tex., Nat. Employment Lawyers Assn., Tex. Trial Lawyers Assn. (assoc. dir. 1995, dir. 1996-99, dir. emeritus 1999), Tex. Employment Lawyers Assn. (founding mem. 1998—), San Antonio Trial Lawyers Assn. (dir., officer 1975—, Am. Bd. Trial Advocates. Office: 310 S Saint Marys St 28th Fl San Antonio TX 78205-3104 Office Phone: 210-226-0221.

PUTNAM, ADAM HUGHES, congressman, farmer, rancher; b. Bartow, Fla., July 31, 1974; s. William Dudley and Sara Elizabeth (Hughes) P.; m. Melissa Putnam; children: Abbie Anna, Elizabeth Langford, Emma Katherine. BS in Food and Resource Econs., U. Fla., 1995. Co-owner Dudley Putnam, Inc., Bartow, Fla., 1988—; mem. Fla. Ho. of Reps., Tallahassee, 1996—2000, U.S. Congress from 12th Fla. dist., Washington, 2001—06, mem. budget com., rules com., 2004—06, chmn. Rep. policy com., 2006; chmn. rep. conf., 2007—. V.p. Fla. 4-H Found., 1997—. Mem. Fla. Cattlemen's Assn., Fla. Farm Bur., Bartow Kiwanis Club. Republican. Episcopalian. Avocations: hunting, fishing, reading. Office: US Ho of Reps 1725 Longworth HOB Washington DC 20515-0912

PUTNAM, ALFRED W., JR., lawyer; b. Phila., 1951; married; 1 child. AB summa cum laude, Harvard U., 1973; BA, U. Oxford, Eng., 1975; JD, U. Pa., 1978. Bar: Pa. 1978. Assoc. Drinker Biddle & Reath LLP, Phila., 1979—85, ptnr., civil litig., 1985—, chmn. bd., 2005—. Sec., gen. counsel People for John Heinz; southeastern fin. chmn. Rick Santorum polit. campaign. Trustee, chmn. Lankenau Hosp., Main Line Health Sys., Jefferson Health Sys., 2004—. Mem.: Univ. Pa. Law Sch. Am. Inn of Ct. (pres.). Republican. Office: Drinker Biddle & Reath LLP One Logan Sq 18th & Cherry Sts Philadelphia PA 19103-6996 Office Phone: 215-988-2907. Office Fax: 215-988-2757. E-mail: alfred.putnam@dbr.com.

PUTNAM, GEORGE W., JR., retired army officer; b. Ft. Fairfield, Maine, May 5, 1920; s. George W. and Rae B. (Merrithew) P.; m. Elaine Anderson (dec. 1973); m. Claudine Mahin (div. 1995); m. Helen Guerin, 1995; children: James M., J. Glenn; stepchildren: Philip Mahin, Leslie Mahin. Enlisted man U.S. Army, 1941-42, commd. 2d lt., 1942, advanced through grades to maj. gen., 1970; comdg. gen. 1st Aviation Brigade, Vietnam, 1970, 1st Cav, Divsn., Vietnam, 1970-71; dir. Mil. Personnel Mgmt., Hdqrs. Dept. Army, Washington, 1971-75; comdg. gen. U.S. Army So. European Task Force, Vicenza, Italy, 1975-77, U.S. Army Phys. Disability Agy., Washington, 1977-81; ret. U.S. Army, 1981. Dir. Army Coun. Rev. Bds., 1977-81; pres. Nat. Capital Retiree Coun., 1982-85. Internat. judge 5th and 6th World Helicopter Championships, 1986, 89, 94, chief judge 7th World Championship, 1992; U.S. mem. Internat. Helicopter com. Fedn. Aeronautique Internationale, 1988-91, 93-95; bd. dirs. Army Aviation Mus. Found., 1987—, pres., 1993-96; chmn. bd. trustees Army Aviation Hall of Fame, 1996-2001. Recipient Elder Statesman of Aviation award, 1998; inducted Army Aviation Hall of Fame, 1980. Mem. Nat. Aero. Assn. (sr. v.p. 1991-98, Fedn. Aero. Internat. (v.p. 1995-98), Army Aviation Assn. Am. (sr. v.p., pres. 1983-87, pres. scholarship found. 1991-93), Helicopter Club Am. (pres. 1988-90). Home: 4106 N Richmond St Arlington VA 22207-4816 Personal E-mail: gputj@aol.com.

PUTNAM, JERRY (GERALD D. PUTNAM), stock exchange executive; b. May 21, 1958; BS, U. Pa., 1981. With Walsh Greenwood, 1983—87, Jefferies & Co., PaineWebber, Prudential, Geldermann Securities, Inc.; founder, pres. Terra Nova, 1994—99; founder, CEO Archipelago Holdings, Inc., Chgo., 1999—2006; pres., co-COO NYSE Group, Inc., NYC, 2006—07; vice chmn. NYSE Euronext, NYC, 2007, sr. advisor, 2007—. Named one of Outstanding Innovators, Time mag., 2000; named to Entrepreneurship Hall of Fame, U. Ill., 2000. Avocation: hunting. Office: NYSE Euronext 11 Wall St New York NY 10005 *

PUTNAM, JONATHAN, lawyer; b. 1966; BA, Harvard U., 1988, JD, 1992. Bar: NY 1994. Clerk US Ct. of Appeals, DC Cir., 1992—93; ptnr. Kirkland & Ellis LLP, NYC. Named one of Litigation's Rising Stars, The Am. Lawyer, 2007. Office: Kirland & Ellis LLP Citigroup Ctr 153 E 53rd St New York NY 10022-4675 Office Phone: 212-446-4914. Office Fax: 212-446-4900. Business E-Mail: jputnam@kirkland.com. *

PUTNAM, KERI, film company executive; married; 2 children. Grad., Harvard U. Asst. HBO; with literary dept. Arena Stage, Washington; dir. develop. Devillier Donegan Enterprises, Washington; dir. devel. HBO, 1992—95; v.p. NYC Productions HBO Films, 1995—99, sr. v.p. LA, 1999—2004, exec. v.p., 2004—06; pres. prodn. Miramax Film Unit Walt Disney Co., 2006—. Named one of 100 Most Powerful Women in Entertainment, Hollywood Reporter, 2006; recipient Excellence in Media award, Women in Film, 2005. Office: Miramax 375 Greenwich St New York NY 10013 *

PUTNAM, MICHAEL COURTNEY JENKINS, classics educator; b. Springfield, Mass., Sept. 20, 1933; s. Roger Lowell and Caroline (Jenkins) P. AB, Harvard U., Cambridge, Mass., 1954, AM, 1956, PhD, 1959; LLD (hon.), Lawrence U., Appleton, Wis., 1985. Instr. classics Smith Coll., Northampton, Mass., 1959-60; faculty classics Brown U., Providence, 1960—, prof., 1967—, chmn., 2000-2001, prof. comparative lit., 1980—, MacMillan prof. of classics, 1985—; acting dir. Ctr. for Hellenic Studies, Harvard U., 1961-62, sr. fellow, 1971-86; Townsend prof. classics Cornell U., 1985; Mellon prof.-in-charge Am. Acad. in Rome, 1989-91; Martin classical lectr. Oberlin Coll., 2004. Scholar in residence Am. Acad. in Rome, 1969-70, classical jury, 1982-83, trustee, 1991—; assoc. univ. seminar on classical civilization Columbia U., N.Y.C., 1972—; mem. cath. Commn. on Intellectual and Cultural Affairs, 1969—; adv. coun. dept. classics Princeton U., 1981-87, chmn., 1983-87; cons. Am. Coun. Learned Socs., 1987-89; mem. Inst. for Advanced Study, 1987-88; vis. scholar Phi Beta Kappa, 1994-95; councillor Assn. of Lit. Scholars and Critics, 1996-99. Author: The Poetry of the Aeneid, 1965, Virgil's Pastoral Art, 1970, Tibullus: A Commentary, 1973, Virgil's Poem of the Earth, 1979, Essays on Latin Lyric, Elegy and Epic, 1982, Artifices of Eternity: Horace's Fourth Book of Odes, 1986, Virgil's Aeneid: Interpretation and

Influence, 1995, Virgil's Epic Designs, 1998, Horace's Carmen Saeculare, 2000, Maffeo Vegio: Short Epics, 2004, Poetic Interplay: Catullus and Horace, 2006; contbr. articles to profl. jours. Trustee Lowell Obs., Flagstaff, Ariz., 1967-87, bd. advisors, 1987—; trustee Bay Chamber Concerts, Camden, Maine, 1972-88, incorporator, 1988-94; mem. bd. cons. Portsmouth Abbey Sch., 1985-89; hon. sec. Keats-Shelley Meml. Assn., Rome, 1989-91. Rome Prize fellow Am. Acad. in Rome, 1963-64; Guggenheim Meml. fellow, 1966-67; sr. fellow NEH, 1973-74, cons. 1974-78, 87-90; Am. Council Learned Soc. fellow, 1983-84. Fellow Am. Acad. Arts and Sci. 1996—; mem. Am. Philol. Assn. (bd. dir. 1972-75, mem. com. on award of merit 1975-78, chmn. 1977-78, 1st v.p. 1981, pres. 1982, del. Am. Coun. Learned Soc. 1984-87, Charles J. Goodwin award of merit 1971, fin. trustee 1997-2004), mem. Am. Philosophical Soc., 1998—; Archaeol. Inst. Am., Classical Assn. New Eng., Medieval Acad. Am., Vergilian Soc. Am. (trustee 1969-73, v.p. 1974-76), Accademia Nazionale Virgiliana, Art Club. Office: Brown U Dept Classics Providence RI 02912-1856 E-mail: michael_putnam@brown.edu.

PUTNAM, PAUL ADIN, federal agency administrator; b. Springfield, Vt., July 12, 1930; s. Horace Adin and Beatrice Nellie (Baldwin) P.; m. Elsie Mae (Ramseyer) June 12, 1956; children: Pamela Ann, Penelope Jayne, Adin Tyler II, Paula Anna. BS, U. Vt., 1952; MS, Wash. State U., 1954; PhD, Cornell U., 1957. Research animal scientist Agrl. Rsch. Svc., USDA, Beltsville, Md., 1957-66, investigation leader beef cattle nutrition, 1966-68, chief beef cattle research br., 1968-72; asst. dir. Beltsville Agrl. Rsch. Ctr., 1972-80, dir., 1980-84; dir. cen. plains area Ames, Iowa, 1984-87; assoc. dir. mid. south area Stoneville, Miss., 1987-88; dir. mid south area, 1988-94; ret., 1994; selectman Town of Springfield, Vt., 1996—2002, 2004—06. Contbr. articles to profl. jours. Recipient Kidder medal U. Vt.; Outstanding Performance awards USDA, also cert. merit; Danforth fellow; Borden fellow; Purina Research fellow. Fellow AAAS (rep. sect. O), Am. Soc. Animal Sci. (pres., North Atlantic sect., chmn. various coms., N.E. sect. Disting. Service award); mem. Am. Dairy Sci. Assn., Orgn. Profl. Employees USDA (pres. Beltsville chpt.), Council for Agrl. Sci. and Tech. Home: 36 Putnam Rd Springfield VT 05156-9115 E-mail: pputnam8@vermontel.net.

PUTNAM, ROBERT D., education educator; m. Rosemary Werner; children: Jonathan, Lara. BA, Swarthmore Coll., Pa., 1963, LLD (hon.), 1990; Fellowship, Oxford U., Eng., 1964; MA, Yale U., New Haven, 1965, PhD with distinction, 1970; PhD (hon.), Stockholm U., 1993, Ohio State U., 2000, U. Antwerp, 2000, U. Edinburgh, 2003, John Cabot U., Rome, 2006. From lectr. to prof. polit. sci. U. Mich., Ann Arbor, 1968—79; prof. govt. Harvard U., Cambridge, Mass., 1979—, chmn. dept. govt., 1984—88, assoc. dean faculty arts and scis., 1986—88, 1992—94, stanfield prof. internat. peace, 1996—2000, Peter and Isabel Malkin prof. pub. policy, 2000—; dir. Ctr. for Int'l Affairs, Harvard U., Cambridge, Mass., 1993—96; dir., saguaro seminar civic engagement in Am. Harvard U., JFK Sch. Govt., Cambridge, Mass., 1995—, dean, 1989—91. Mem. Coun. on Fgn. Rels., 1981—, Internat. Inst. Strategic Studies, 1986—, Trilateral Commn., 1990—98; exec. com. Brit. Politics Group, 1974—79, Coun. on European Studies, 1983—86; pres. Conf. Group on Italian Politics, 1981—83; adv. coun. on environmentally sustainable devel. World Bank, 1992—96; adv. bd. Swedish Collegium for Advanced Study in the Social Sciences, 1987—89, Westchester Children's Mus., NY, Thomas C. Wales Found., Seattle; Leverhulme vis. prof. faculty history St. Johns Coll., Cambridge U., 2002—03; vis. prof. of polit. sci. U. Catania, Italy, 1977, Stockholm U., 1974; cons. in field. Author: Better Together: Restoring the American Community; mem. editl. bd.: Am. Polit. Sci. Rev., 1971—76, Brit. Jour. Polit. Sci., 1975—79, Comparative Polit. Studies, 1982—2005, Legislative Studies Quar., 1983—89, Internat. Orgn., 1989, Nonprofit and Voluntary Sector Qrly., 2000—04, Am. Sociol. Rev., 2004—, Critical Rev., 2004—. Staff US NSC, Washington, 1978; active President's Coun. on Svc. & Civic Participation, Washington, 2003; pres.-elect. Am. Polit. Sci. Assn., 2000—01, pres., 2001—02, v.p., 1997—98; adv. bd. Anne E. Borghesani Cmty. Found., Lexington, Mass. Recipient Louis Brownlow Book award, Nat. Acad. Pub. Adminstrn., 1993, Gregory Luebbert award, Am. Polit. Sci. Assn., 1994, Ithiel de Sola Pool award, 1995, Charles H. Levin award, Internat. Polit. Sci. Assn., 1994, Wilbur Lucius Cross medal, Yale U. Grad. Sch. Arts & Science, 2003, Commendatore in the Order of the Star of Italian Solidarity, Pres., Italian Republic, 2004, Johan Skytte prize in Polit. Sci., Statsvetenskapliga Inst., Uppsala U., 2006; fellow, SSRC-ACLS, 1966—68, Ford Found., 1970, Ctr. for Advanced Study in the Behavioral Sciences, 1974—75, 1988—89, Woodrow Wilson Internat. Ctr. for Scholars, 1977, 1979, Coun. on Fgn. Rels., 1977—78, German Marshall Fund, 1979, SSRC-Fulbright, 1982, SSRC-Foreign Policy Studies, 1988—89, Guggenheim fellow, 1988—89; Fulbright fellow, 1964—65, 1977, Marshall Lectr. fellow, U. Cambridge, 1999. Fellow: Nat. Acad. Pub. Adminstrn., Am. Acad. Arts & Sciences, Brit. Acad. (corr.); mem.: Coun. on Fgn. Rels., Am. Acad. of Polit. & Social Sci., NAS (assembly of behavioral & social sciences 1978—81), Phi Beta Kappa, Am. Philos. Soc. Office: Harvard Univ JFK Sch Govt 79 JFK St T370 Cambridge MA 02139 Office Phone: 617-495-1148.

PUTNAM, ROBERT ERVIN, chemist, consultant; b. Northampton, Mass., Oct. 18, 1927; s. Ervin Earl and Mary Gertrude (Connelly) P.; m. Caroline Wright, Aug. 23, 1952; children: David Earl, Mary Caroline, Robert Edward, Andrew Wright. BS in Chemistry, U. Mass., 1950; PhD in Organic Chemistry, U. Ill., 1953. Rsch. chemist E.I. du Pont de Nemours, Wilmington, Del., 1953-59, rsch. supr., 1959-65, sr. rsch. supr., 1965-67, Parkersburg, W.Va., 1967-78, rsch. lab. supt., 1978-82, rsch. mgr., 1982-85; adj. faculty Washington State C.C., Marietta, Ohio, 1985-95; pvt. practice Marietta, 1985-95. Alumni adv. coun. dept. chemistry U. Mass., Amherst, 1975-78; instr. chemistry Marietta Coll., 1982-89, adv. coun., 1989-95, dir. Inst. for Learning in Retirement, 1995-98. Editor Bull. Am. Friends of Puttenham, 1984-2000; contbr. 20 articles to profl. jours. With USNR, 1945-46. NSF fellow, U. Ill., 1952-53. Fellow AAAS; mem. Am. Chem. Soc. (chmn. Ohio Valley sect. 1976-78), Rsch. Soc. Am., Valley Renaissance Consort, Mid-Ohio Valley Aviation Assn., Sigma Xi, Gamma Alpha, Phi Lambda Upsilon. Democrat. Mem. Unitarian Ch. Achievements include patents on fluorine containing polymers and monomers, ion exchange resins; research on industrial processes for nylon, polyacetals, acrylics, rubber toughened plastics, fluorinated plastics. Address: 100 Alden Ave Marietta OH 45750-1138 Home Phone: 740-373-4510; Office Phone: 740-373-4510. E-mail: putnamr@suddenlink.net.

PUTNAM, THOMAS J., library director; b. 1962; m. Phyliis Wentworth; 2 children. Grad., Bowdoin Coll., 1984; MPA, Princeton U., 1987. Dir. ednl. programs John Fitzgerald Kennedy Libr., Boston, 1999—2003, dep. dir., 2003—06, acting. libr. dir., 2006—07, dir., 2007—. Office: John Fitzgerald Kennedy Libr Columbia Point Boston MA 02125-3398 Office Phone: 617-514-1651. Office Fax: 617-514-1652. E-mail: thomas.putnam@nara.gov. *

PUTNEY, MARK WILLIAM, lawyer, utilities executive; b. Marshalltown, Iowa, Jan. 25, 1929; s. Lawrence Charles and Geneva (Eldridge) P.; m. Ray Ann Bartnek, May 25, 1962 (dec. Feb. 2000); children: Andi Bartnek, William Bradford, Blake Reinhart; m. Linda Phelps, July 21, 2003. BA, U. Iowa, 1951, JD, 1957. Bar: Iowa 1957, U.S. Supreme Ct. 1960. Ptnr. Bradshaw, Fowler, Proctor & Fairgrave, Des Moines, 1961-72, of counsel, 1992-94; chmn., CEO. Bradford & Blake Ltd., Dakota Dunes, SD, 1992—; pres., chmn., chief exec. officer Iowa Resources, Inc., 1984-90; chmn., chief exec. officer Iowa Power & Light Co., 1984-90, Iowa Gas Co., 1984-85, Midwest Resources Inc., 1990-92. Civilian aide to Sec. Army Iowa, 1975-77; bd. dirs. Greater Des Moines YMCA, 1976-86, Boys' Home Iowa, 1982-86, Hoover Presdl. Libr. Assn., 1983—, U. Iowa Found., 1984—, Edison Electric Inst., 1986-89, Greater Des Moines Com., 1984—, pres. 1988; bd. dirs. Assoc. Edison Illuminating Cos., 1988-93, pres., 1991-92; chmn. Iowa Com. Employer Support of Guard and Res., 1979-86; bd. dirs. Des Moines Devel. Corp., 1984-92, chmn., 1989-90; bd. dirs. Iowa Law Sch. Found., 2006-. With USAF, 1951-53. Recipient Disting. Alumnus award U. Iowa, 1995. Mem. Iowa Utility Assn. (chmn. 1989, dir.), Des Moines Club (pres. 1977), Desert Forest Golf Club (Carefree, Ariz.), Masons, Shriners, Delta Chi, Phi Delta Phi. Republican. Episcopalian. Home: PO Box 1126 Carefree AZ 85377 Office Phone: 602-549-7731. Personal E-mail: markwputney@aol.com.

PUTTER, DAVID SETH, lawyer; b. NYC, Mar. 11, 1944; s. Norton Seth and Ruth Crystal P. Student, U. Granada, Spain, 1964; BA in Biology, Beloit Coll., 1965; JD, Syracuse U., 1968. Bar: Vt. 1970, N.Y. 1971, U.S. Dist. Ct. Vt. 1970, U.S. Ct. Appeals (2d cir.) 1975, U.S. Ct. Claims 1998. Atty. Putter & Carrington, Arlington, Vt., 1970-73; Bennington County pub. defender State of Vt., Bennington, 1973-76, law clk. to Superior Ct. judges Burlington, 1976-78, asst. atty. gen. Montpelier, 1979-81; with Putter & Unger, Montpelier, 1981-88, Saxer, Anderson, Wolinsky & Sunshine, Montpelier, 1988-2000; ptnr. Putter and Edson, LLP, Montpelier, 2001—02; pvt. practice Law Offices of David Putter, 2002—. Contbr. articles to profl. jours. Acting Superior Ct. judge, 1997-2001; chair legal panel ACLU Vt., 1988—; sponsored advisor on assembly, free press, free speech USIA, Lusaka, Zambia, Kampala, Uganda, 1996. Recipient Jonathan Chase award, ACLU Vt., 1991, 1997. Avocations: hiking, camping, theater, travel, music (folk and rock). Home: 6 Towne St Montpelier VT 05602-4231 Office: 15 E State St Montpelier VT 05602-3010 Home Phone: 802-223-6618.

PUTTER, IRVING, retired French language educator; b. NYC, Dec. 3, 1917; s. Joseph and Anna (Schrank) P.; children— Paul Stephen, Candace Anne Putter. BA, CCNY, 1938; MA, State U. Iowa, 1941; PhD, Yale U., 1949. Mem. faculty U. Calif. at Berkeley, 1947-88, prof. French, 1961-88, chmn. dept., 1968-71, humanities research fellow, 1971-72, 78-79, 84-85; ret., 1988. Author: Leconte de Lisle and His Contemporaries, 1951, The Pessimism of Leconte de Lisle: Sources and Evolution, 1954, The Pessimism of Leconte de Lisle: The Work and The Time, 1961, La Dernière Illusion de Leconte de Lisle: Lettres Inédites a Emilie Leforestier, 1968; also numerous articles.; editor, translator: Chateaubriand: Atala, René, 1952. Guggenheim fellow, 1955-56; Fulbright fellow, 1955-56 Home: 115 Saint James Dr Piedmont CA 94611-3603

PUTTERMAN, LOUIS G., economics professor; b. NYC, Apr. 27, 1952; s. Milton and Eileen L. (Goldstein) P.; (div.); 1 child, Laura Lee; m. Vivian Tseng, Apr. 5, 1981; children: Serena Rose, Mark Isaac. BA summa cum laude, Columbia U., 1976; MA in Internat. Relations, Yale U., 1978, PhD in Econs., 1980; MA (hon.), Brown U., 1983. From asst. prof. to prof. econs. Brown U., R.I., 1980—; rsch. assoc., Ctr. for East Asian Rsch. Harvard U., Cambridge, Mass., 1987-93. Dir. devel. studies program Brown U., Providence. Author: Peasants, Collectives and Choice, 1986, Division of Labor and Welfare, 1990, Continuity and Change in China's Rural Development: Collective and Reform Eras in Perspective, 1993, Dollars and Change: Economics in Context, 2001; co-author: Economics of Cooperation and the Labor-Managed Economy, 1987; editor: The Economic Nature of the Firm, 1986, (with Randall Kroszner) 2d edit., 1996, (with Dietrich Rueschemeyer) State and Market in Development: Synergy or Rivalry, (with Avner Ben-Ner) Economics, Values and Organization, 1998; mem. editl. bd. Modern China, 1990—, Comparative Economic Studies, 1991-93, Annals of Public and Cooperative Economics, 1992—, Jour. Comparative Econs., 1989-91, 97-99, China Econ. Rev., 2001—; assoc. editor Pacific Econ. Rev., 1996-2004. Recipient Sloan Rsch. fellow, Alfred P. Sloan Found., 1983, Fellow in Chinese Studies, Wang Inst., 1986, Am. Coun. Learned Socs., 1997. Mem. Am. Economic Assn., Assn. for Comparative Economic Studies, Econ. Sci. Assn., Phi Beta Kappa. Office: Brown U Dept Econs 64 Waterman St Providence RI 02912-9029 Home Phone: 978-287-4491. Business E-Mail: Louis_Putterman@brown.edu.

PUTTLER, BENJAMIN, entomologist; b. Bronx, Dec. 21, 1930; s. Isodor Puttler and Ida Lehrer; m. Virginia Witten Puttler, Oct. 6, 1961; children: Donna, Shari. BS in Agrl., U. Calif., 1955. Rsch. entomologist U.S. Dept. Agrl., Albany, Calif., 1955—57, Riverside, Calif., 1957—59, Moorestown, NJ, 1959—64, Columbia, Mo., 1964—89; extension entomologist U. Mo., Columbia, Mo., 1989—95, emeritus asst. prof., 1995. Contbr. articles over 60 scientific jours. Recipient Superior Svc. award, U.S. Dept. Agrl., 1987, Cert. Appreciation, U. Mo., Dept. Entomology, 1988, Faculty Staff award, 1999, 2000, 2002. Mem.: C.V. Riley Entomological Soc., Internat. Organ. Biological Control, Entomological Soc. Am. Independent. Jewish. Achievements include patents for virus to kill insects 1990; discovery of explorations for beneficial insects resulting in discovery of new species. Avocations: golf, stamp collecting/philately, coin collecting/numismatics. Home: 505 Bourn Ave Columbia MO 65203 Office: U Mo Divsn Plant Scis 1 31 Agrl Bldg Columbia MO 65211 Office Phone: 573-882-1457. Business E-Mail: puttlerbe@missouri.edu.

PUTTLITZ, DONALD HERBERT, microbiologist; b. Kingston, NY, Apr. 21, 1938; s. Adalbert Siegfried and Elizabeth Ann (Barthel) P.; m. Barbara Ann Dingman, July 19, 1969; children: Michelle, Brian, Laura. BS with distinction, SUNY, New Paltz, 1959; MS, SUNY, Albany, 1961; PhD, Cornell U., 1965. Diplomate emeritus Am. Bd. Med. Microbiology. Assoc. microbiologist Beth Israel Med. Ctr., NYC, 1967-85; supr. microbiology Jamaica (N.Y.) Hosp., 1985-92; instr. physician asst. program Touro Coll., NYC, 1986-88; supr. microbiology Sound Shore Med. Ctr. of Westchester, New Rochelle, NY, 1993-97. Mem. faculty Mt. Sinai Coll. Medicine, 1972-85. Mem. N.Y.C. Bd. Edn., 1997—. Predoctoral traineeship fellow NIH, 1964-65, postdoctoral traineeship fellow USPHS, 1965-67. Mem. Am. Soc. Microbiology, N.Y.C. Soc. Microbiology. Roman Catholic. Home: 116 Horace Harding Blvd Great Neck NY 11020-1107

PUTZ, J.J. (JOSEPH JASON PUTZ), professional baseball player; b. Trenton, Mich., Feb. 22, 1977; m. Kelsey Putz; children: Lauren, Kaelyn. Student, U. Mich., Ann Arbor. Draft pick Seattle Mariners, 1999, pitcher, 2003—. Named to Am. League All-Star Team, 2007. Mailing: Seattle Mariners PO Box 4100 Seattle WA 98194-0100 *

PUTZEL, CONSTANCE KELLNER, lawyer; b. Balt., Sept. 5, 1922; d. William Stummer and Corinne (Strauss) Kellner; m. William L. Putzel, Aug. 28, 1945; 1 son, Arthur William. AB, Goucher Coll., 1942; LLB, U. Md., 1945, JD, 1969. Bar: Md. 1945. Social worker Balt. Dept. Pub. Welfare, 1945-46; atty. New Amsterdam Casualty Co., Balt., 1947; staff atty. Legal Aid Bur., Balt., 1947-49; mem. Putzel & Putzel, P.A., Balt., 1950-89; pvt. practice Balt., 1989—; instr. U. Balt. Sch. Law, 1975-77, Goucher Coll., 1976-77. Chair character com. Ct. Appeals for 3d Cir., 1976-97. Author: A Practice Guide to Divorce, 1999, Representing the Older Client in Divorce, 1992. Commr. Md. Com. on Status of Women, 1972-76, Com. to Implement ERA, 1973-76; Pres. U. Md. Law Alumni Assn., 1978; bd. dirs. Legal Aid Bur., 1951-52, 71-73. Fellow Am. Acad. Matrimonial Lawyers (chair elder issues com. 1996); mem. ABA (co-chair elder issues com., mem. coun. sr. lawyers divsn. 1996-2000, editl. bd. 1996-99, family law sect.), Md. Bar Assn. (bd. govs. 1972-73, chmn. family law sect. 1978-79, chair sr. lawyers divsn. 2001-03). Home: 7121 Park Heights Ave Unit 401 Baltimore MD 21215-1610 Office: 3835 Naylor s Ln Pikesville MD 21208 Home Phone: 410-358-4099. Personal E-mail: lawtowson@aol.com.

PUTZEL, MICHAEL, journalist, editor; b. Washington, Sept. 16, 1942; s. Max and Nell (Converse) P.; m. Ann Blackman, Feb. 23, 1974; children: Leila Elizabeth, Christof Blackman. BA, UNC in Polit. Sci., 1967. Reporter Charleston (W.Va.) Gazette, 1963-66; newsman AP, Raleigh, NC, 1967-68, NYC, 1968-69, war corr. Vietnam, 1969-72, reporter Washington, 1972-79; asst. metro editor Washington Post, Washington, 1979; White House corr. AP, Washington, 1979-84, chief White House corr., 1984-87, chief of bur. Moscow, 1987—90, diplomatic corr. Washington, 1990-91; Washington bureau chief Boston Globe, 1991-92, White House corr. Washington, 1993-94; columnist "Plugged In", 1994-95; founder, CEO Trysail, Inc., Washington, 1996—; founder, pres. Milestones Inc., Washington, 1999—2000; v.p. Continental Computer Corp., Washington, 2000; freelance writer, book doctor Washington, 2003—. Lectr. Georgetown U., Washington, 1999—. With USAR, 1964-65. Recipient AP Mgn. Editors citation, 1975, 81, Merriman Smith Meml. award White House Corr. Assn., 1986. Home: 4938 Quebec St NW Washington DC 20016-3231 Office Phone: 202-362-3133. Personal E-mail: mputzel@trysail.com.

PUYAU, FRANCIS ALBERT, retired radiology educator, physician; b. New Orleans, Dec. 1, 1928; s. Frank Albert and Rose Sue (Jones) P.; m. Geraldine Sally diBenedetto, June 6, 1951; children: Michael, Stephen, Jeanne Marie, Julie, Melissa. BS, Notre Dame U., 1948; MD, La. State U., 1952. Diplomate Am. Bd. Pediat., Am. Bd. Pediat. Cardiology, Am. Bd. Radiology. Intern Charity Hosp., New Orleans, 1952-53, resident in pediat., 1955-57; from instr. pediat. to prof. radiology and pediat. La. State U. Sch. Medicine, New Orleans, 1957-74, acting head dept. radiology, 1971-72, head dept., 1972-74; asst. prof. pediat. Vanderbilt U., 1961-68; fellow dept. diagnostic radiology Charity Hosp., New Orleans, 1968-70; prof. radiology and pediat. Tulane U. Sch. Medicine, New Orleans, 1974-97, prof. medicine, 1974-95, acting chmn. dept. pediat., 1976-78; cons. St. Tammany Hosps., Covington, La., 1968-81; dir. cardiac catherization lab. dept. cardiology Charity Hosp., New Orleans, 1970-85; staff radiologist Our Lady of the Lake Regional Med. Ctr., Baton Rouge, 1986-93, ret., 1997. Mem. staff Hotel Dieu, New Orleans, 1973-80; head x-ray dept. Children's Hosp. of New Orleans, 1976-82. Contbr. articles to profl. jours. With USPHS, 1953-55. Fellow Am. Coll. Cardiology, Am. Coll. Radiology; mem. East Baton Rouge Med. Soc., So. Soc. Pediatric Research, Am. Coll. Radiology, La. Radiology Soc., New Orleans Radiology Soc. (pres. 1985), New Orleans Pediatric Soc., Soc. Chmn. Acad. Radiology Depts., Radiol. Soc. N.Am., Am. Roentgen Ray Soc., Assn. Univ. Radiologists, Southern Yacht Club (New Orleans), Alpha Omega Alpha. Roman Catholic. Home: 458 Shady Lake Pkwy Baton Rouge LA 70810-4322

PUZDER, ANDREW F., food service executive, lawyer; b. Cleve., July 11, 1950; s. Andrew F. and Winifried M. Puzder; m. Deanna L. Descher, Sept. 26, 1987. BA, Cleve. State U., 1975; JD, Washington U., 1978. Atty. Offices of Morris A. Shenker, 1978—84, Stolar Partnership, 1984—91; ptnr. Lewis, D'Amato, Brisbois, & Bisgaard, 1991—94, Yocca, Carlson & Rauth, 1994—95; exec. v.p., gen. counsel Fidelity Nat. Fin., Inc., 1995—97; CEO Santa Barbara Restaurant Group, 1997—2000; gen. counsel, exec. v.p. CKE Restaurants, Inc., Carpinteria, Calif., 1997-99; CEO Hardee's Food Systems, Inc., 2000—; pres., CEO CKE Restaurants, Inc., Carpinteria, Calif., 2000—. Editor Washington U. Law Quarterly, 1977-78. Mem. State Bar Nev., The Mo. Bar, State Bar Calif., Phi Alpha Theta. Office: CKE Restaurants Inc Ste A 6307 Carpinteria Ave Carpinteria CA 93013 *

PYATT, EVERETT ARNO, federal official; b. Kansas City, Mo., July 22, 1939; s. Arno Doyne and Myrl Elizabeth (Osborn) P.; m. Susan Evelyn Kristal, Sept. 28, 1968; children: Jennifer, Laura, Jeffrey. B.E., BS, Yale U., 1962; MBA, U. Pa., 1977. Staff engr. office dir. def. research and devel. Office Sec. Def., Dept. Def., Washington, 1962-72; dir. acquisition planning Office Asst. Sec. Def. for Program Analysis and Evaluation, 1972-75; dir. logistics resources Office Asst. Sec. Def. for Installations and Logistics, 1975-77; prin. dep. asst. sec. for logistics Dept. Navy, Washington, 1977-79, prin. dep. asst. sec. for shipbldg. and logistics, 1981-84, asst. sec. for shipbldg. and logistics, 1984-89; exec. advisor Coopers & Lybrand, 1989—; pres. EV Ventures; dep. chief fin. officer Dept. Energy, 1979-81; dir. Dept. Energy (Office of Alcohol Fuels), 1980. Recipient Disting. Civilian Svc. medal USN, 1980-81, 87, Superior Civilian Svc. medal, 1981, Outstanding Svc. medal Dept. Energy, 1981, Pres.'s award of meritorious excellence, 1983, Disting. Civilian Pub. Svc. award Dept. Def., 1989; Office of Sec. Def. fellow, 1975-77. Mem.: IEEE, Yale Club. Home: 4560 25th Rd N Arlington VA 22207-4147 Home Phone: 703-528-5828; Office Phone: 703-841-8318. Personal E-mail: epyatt1@comcast.net.

PYATT, KEDAR DAVIS, JR., research and development company executive; b. Wadesboro, NC, May 20, 1933; s. Kedar D. and Frances (Hales) P.; m. Mary Mackenzie, June 2, 1956; children: Geoffrey, Kira, David, Rebecca. BS in Physics, Duke U., 1955; PhD in Physics, Yale U., 1960. With Gen. Atomic, San Diego, 1959-67; sr. v.p. Fed. sys. divsn. Maxwell Techs., San Diego, 1967—2001, sr. v.p. just Sys. Divsn.; chief scientist Scientific Applications Internat. Co., San Diego, 2001—. Recipient Exceptional Pub. Svc. medal Dept. Def., 1985, Lifetime Achievement medal DSWA, 1997. Office Phone: 858-826-1629. Personal E-mail: budmary@att.net. Business E-Mail: kedar.d.pyatt@saic.com. E-mail: bud@maxwell.com.

PYATT, LEO ANTHONY, retired real estate broker; b. Key Port, NJ, Oct. 20, 1925; s. Ralph James and Anna Regina (Kussmaul) Pyatt; m. Geraldine Genevive Gibb, May 31, 1947; children: Steven Lee, Rebecca Lynn. Student, Franklin U., 1947-49. Salesperson Standard Oil Co., Columbus, Ohio, 1947-49, Borden Dairy Co., Columbus, 1950-57, Frito-Lay, Inc., Columbus, 1958-74; sec., treas. Snack Time, Inc., Columbus, 1974-75; agt. N. NE Realty Co., Columbus, 1976-86; owner-broker Pyatt's Rose Realty Co., Columbus, 1986—2003; ret., 2003. Mem. Citizens for An Alternative Tax Sys. With U.S. Naval Air Force, 1943—46, PTO. Decorated DFC, Air medal with silver star, Philippine Liberation award; inducted into Combat Aircrew Hall of Fame. Roman Catholic. Avocations: writing, travel, reading. Home: 4400 Wanda Lane Rd Columbus OH 43224-1026

PYCH, RICK, professional sports team executive; b. Hartford, Conn. m. Marilou Pych; 1 child, Zach. Grad. in Acctg., Fairfield U. CPA. CFO Spurs Sports & Entertainment (parent co. of NBA Spurs, Am. Hockey League Rampage and WNBA Silver Stars), San Antonio, 1993—2000, chief devel. officer AT&T Ctr., 1999—, exec. v.p. fin. and corp. devel., 2000—. San Antonio Rampage repr. Am. Hockey League Bd. Govs. Bd. trustees Via Met. Transit; bd. dirs. San Antonio Sports Found., 1989—, Boys and Girls Clubs San Antonio; bd. mem. San Antonio Tax Increment Reinvestment Zone. Office: San Antonio Spurs One AT&T Ctr San Antonio TX 78219 *

PYE, GORDON BRUCE, economist; b. Oak Park, Ill., Oct. 30, 1933; s. Harold Charles and Florence Martha P BS in Chem. Engring, M.I.T., 1955, PhD in Econs, 1963. Asst. prof. bus. adminstrn. U. Calif., Berkeley, 1963-66, assoc. prof., 1966-69, prof., 1969-72; econ. cons. Standard Oil Co. Calif. (name changed to Chevron Corp.), San Francisco, 1972-74; v.p., sr. economist Irving Trust Co., NYC, 1974-78, sr. v.p., mgr. econ. research and planning div., 1978-89; prin. Gordon B. Pye Assocs., NYC, 1990—. Assoc. editor: Fin. Analysts Jour, 1972-89 Mem. Forecasters Club N.Y. (pres. 1980-81) Home: 230 E 50th St New York NY 10022-7702 Personal E-mail: GBPye@aol.com.

PYE, LENWOOD DAVID, materials science educator, researcher, consultant; b. Little Falls, NY, May 16, 1937; s. Lenwood George and Elizabeth Marie Pye; m. Constance Lee Lanphere, Sept. 6, 1958; children: DeAnn, Lorie, Lisa, Brien. BS, Alfred U., 1959, PhD, 1968. Rsch. engr. PPG Industries, Pitts., 1959-60; rsch. scientist Bausch & Lomb, Rochester, NY, 1960-61, 62-64; prof. glass sci. N.Y. State Coll. Ceramics Alfred U., 1968—2003, dir. Inst. Glass Sci. and Engring., 1984-96, dir. Industry-Univ. Ctr. Glass Rsch., 1986-96, dean N.Y. State Coll. Ceramics, 1996—2002, dean and prof. emeritus, 2003—. Pres. Internat. Commn. on Glass, 1997-00; vis. scientist Johns Hopkins U., 2005-. 1st lt. US Army, 1960—62. Recipient Dominick Labino lectr. 1995, Phoenix award as Glassman of Yr., 1996, Excellence in Tchg. award Am. Soc. Engring. Edn., 1980, Presdl. Order of Merit, Alfred U., 2002, Chancellors award for scholarship and creativity SUNY, 2002, S.R. Scholes award lectr., NYSCC, 2005, Glass Art Soc. award. Fellow Am. Ceramics Soc. (trustee 1992-95), U.K. Soc. Glass Tech. (hon.); mem. Worldwide Acad. Ceramics, German Soc. Glass Tech. (hon.), Am. Ceramics Soc. (pres.-elect, 2000). Office: NY State Coll Ceramics Alfred Univ 2 Pine St Alfred NY 14802-1214 E-mail: pye@alfred.edu.

PYE, LUCIAN WILMOT, political science professor; b. Shansi, China, Oct. 21, 1921; s. Watts Orson and Gertrude (Chaney) P.; m. Mary Toombs Waddill, Dec. 24, 1944; children: Evelyn, L. Christopher, Virginia. BA, Carleton Coll., 1943, LLD, 1982; MA, Yale U., 1949, PhD, 1951. From instr. to asst. prof. polit. sci. Washington U., St. Louis, 1949-52; rsch. assoc. Yale U., 1951-52, Princeton, 1952-56; vis. lectr. Columbia U., 1956; faculty Mass. Inst. Tech., 1956-92, prof. polit. sci., 1960-92, Ford prof., 1972-92, chmn. sect., 1961-63; sr. staff mem. Mass. Inst. Tech. (Center Internat. Studies), 1956—. Vis. assoc. prof. Yale U., 1959-61; vis. prof. George Washington U., 1993, Balliol Coll., Oxford U., 1994, Fletcher Sch., Tufts U., 1994; chmn. com. comparative politics Social Sci. Rsch. Coun., 1963-73; assoc. Fairbank Ctr., Harvard U., 1995—; mem. adv. com. adminstr. AID, 1961-68; cons. Dept. State, 1962-68, NSC, 1968-72; trustee Asia Found., 1963-2002; gov. East-West Ctr., Honolulu, 1976-80; bd. dirs., v.p. Nat. Com. U.S.-China Rels. Author: Guerrilla Communism in Malaya, 1956, Politics, Personality and Nation Building, 1961, Aspects of Political Developments, 1966, Southeast Asia's Political Systems, 1967, The Spirit of Chinese Politics, 1968, Warlord Politics, 1971, China: An Introduction, 1972, Mao Tse-tung: The Man in The Leader, 1976, Dynamics of Chinese Politics, 1982, Asian Power and Politics, 1985; co-author: The Politics of the Developing Areas, 1960, The Emerging Nations, 1961; Editor: Communications and Political Development, 1963, Political Culture and Political Development, 1965, Political Science and Area Studies, 1975. 1st lt. USMCR, 1945-46. Fellow Center Advanced Study Behavioral Scis., 1963 Fellow Am. Acad. Arts and Scis., Am. Philos. Soc.; mem. Assn. Asian Studies (dir.), Am. Polit. Sci. Assn. (dir., pres. 1989), Council Fgn. Relations (dir.), Asia Soc. (dir.), Pilgrim Soc., Phi Beta Kappa. Clubs: Cosmos. Unitarian Universalist. Office: Mass Inst Tech Dept Polit Sci Cambridge MA 02139 Home: Apt H 587 1010 Waltham St Lexington MA 02421 Office Phone: 617-253-3379. Business E-Mail: pye@mit.edu.

PYERITZ, REED EDWIN, geneticist, educator, medical researcher; b. Pitts., Nov. 2, 1947; s. Paul L. and Ida Mae (Meier) P.; m. Jane Ellen Tumpson, May 28, 1972; 2 children. SB in Chemistry, U. Del., 1968; AM, Harvard U., 1971, PhD in Biochemistry, 1972, MD, 1975. Diplomate Am. Bd. Internal Medicine, Am. Bd. Med. Genetics. Intern Peter Bent Brigham Hosp., Boston, 1975-76; resident Peter Bent Bingham Hosp., Boston, 1976-77, Johns Hopkins Hosp., Balt., 1977-78; from instr. to prof. medicine and pediatrics Sch. Medicine, John Hopkins Hosp., Balt., 1977-93, chair dept. human genetics, 1994-00, prof. human genetics, medicine and pediatrics, 1994-01, MCP Hahnemann Sch. Medicine, 1993-00; prof. medicine and genetics U. Pa. Sch. Medicine, Phila., 2001—, chief divsn. med. genetics, 2001—, chair com. on appointments and promotions, 2004—, mem. faculty senate, 2006—. Dir. Inst. Genetics, Allegheny U. Health Sci., 1993-99; dir. Ctr. for Med. Genetics, Allegheny Gen. Hosp., 1995-00; chief physician Md. Athletic Commn., Balt., 1978-93; med. adv. bd. Nat. Marfan Found., N.Y.C., 1982—, chmn. 1982-93, clin. care adv. bd., Nat. Neurofibromatosis Found., 1985—; med. adviser Alliance of Genetic Support Groups, 1994-01; mem. rsch. adv. bd. Nat. Orgn. Rare Disorders, 1989-00; mem. rsch. adv. com. Am. Heart Assn., 1996-98; mem. genetic adv. bd. Nat. Cancer Inst., 1996-99; mem. med. adv. bd. Can. Marfan Assn., 1999-, chmn., 2003-; mem. sci. adv. bd. Hereditary Hemorrhagic Telangiectasia Found., 2003—, chair med. adv. bd., Canadian Marfan Assn., 2003-, Can. Inst. Health Rsch., 2005-. Co-editor Principles and Practice of Medical Genetics, 1992-; mem. editl. bd. New Eng. Jour. Medicine, 1993-96, JAMA, 1997-2001, Circulation, 2004—; contbr. over 300 articles to profl. publs. Lt. col. USAR Med. Corp., 1981—91. NIH grantee. Fellow: ACP, Am. Coll. Med. Genetics (dir. 1992—94, pres.-elect 1995—96, pres. 1997—98, past pres. 1999—2000); mem.: AAAS, AMA, Coll. Physicians Phila., Am. Med. Accred. Program (spl. adv. com. 1998—2000), Assn. Profs. Human Med. Genetics (pres. elect 1998—99, pres. 2000—02), Assn. Am. Physicians, Am. Soc. Clin. Investigation, Am. Fedn. Med. Rsch., Physician Consortium for Performance Improvement, Am. Heart Assn., Am. Soc. Human Genetics (chmn. program com. 1994—95, bd. dirs. 2005—). Office: Divsn Med Genetics Maloney 538 U Pa Sch Medicine 3400 Spruce St Philadelphia PA 19104-4283 Office Phone: 215-662-4740. Business E-Mail: reed.pyeritz@uphs.upenn.edu.

PYFER, JOHN FREDERICK, JR., lawyer, director; b. Lancaster, Pa., July 25, 1946; s. John Frederick and Myrtle Ann (Greiner) P.; m. Carol Trice, Nov. 25, 1970; children: John Frederick III, Carol Lee. Grad. cum laude, Peddie Sch., 1965; BA in Polit. Sci. and Econs., Haverford Coll., 1969; JD, Vanderbilt U., 1972. Bar: Pa. 1972, U.S. Dist. Ct. (ea. dist.) Pa. 1973, U.S. Tax Ct. 1975, U.S. Supreme Ct. 1975, U.S. Dist. Ct. (mid. dist.) Pa. 1984, U.S. Ct. Appeals (3d cir.) 1986. Law clk. to presiding justice Ct. Common Pleas, Lancaster, Pa., 1972-74; assoc. Xakellis, Perezous & Mongiovi, Lancaster, 1972-76; founding ptnr. Allison & Pyfer, Lancaster, 1976-85; pres. Pyfer & Assocs., Lancaster, 1986-88, Pyfer & Reese, Lancaster, 1988—2006, Pyfer Ptnrs., Lancaster, 2006—. Prof. para-legal tng. Pa. State Ext. Svc., 1989-93; fed. ct. mediator, 1992-2001. Contbr. articles to law revs., law treatises. Pres. Lancaster-Lebanon Coun., Boy Scouts Am., 1989—93, coun. commr., 1987—89, mem. nat. com., 1996—, exec. bd. N.E. region, 1998—, area pres., 2000—03, v.p., 2004—; bd. dirs. World of Scouting Mus.; achieved Eagle Scout, 1962; elder, pres. United Ch. of Christ, 1989, 1995, 2004. Named one of Pa. Super Lawyers, 2004, 2005; recipient Silver Beaver, Boy Scouts Am., 1988, Silver Antelope, 1998, Disting. Eagle Scout, 2001, Internat. Scouter's award, 2003; Baden Powel fellow, 2000. Fellow Am. Bd. Criminal Lawyers, Lancaster Heritage Ctr. (chair 2006-); mem. ABA (First prize Howard C. Schwab Nat. Essay Contest in Writing 1972), SAR, Am. Arbitration Assn., Lancaster Bar Assn., Inns Ct. (founder, pres. W. Hensel Brown 1993-94), Christian Lawyers Soc., Train Collector Assn. (divsn. pres. 1984), Am. Orchid Soc. (affiliate pres. 1998), Lions Club (pres. 1980-82, 00-01) (Willow Street, Pa.), Masons (Lancaster). Republican. Home: 1100 Little Brook Rd Lancaster PA 17603-6116 Office: Pyfer & Reese 128 N Lime St Lancaster PA 17602-2951 Home Phone: 717-872-6322; Office Phone: 717-299-7342. Personal E-mail: jfpyfer@comcast.net. Business E-Mail: jpyfer@pyferpartners.com.

PYKE, THOMAS NICHOLAS, JR., science administrator; b. Washington, July 16, 1942; s. Thomas Nicholas and Pauline Marie (Pingitore) Pyke; m. Carol June Renville, June 22, 1968 (dec. Oct. 2002); children: Christopher Renville, Alexander Nicholas. BS, Carnegie Inst. Tech., 1964; MS in Engring., U. Pa., 1965. Electronic engr. Nat. Bur. Standards, Gaithersburg, Md., 1964-69, chief computer networking sect., 1969-75, chief computer systems engring. div., 1975-79, dir. ctr. for computer systems engring., 1979-81, dir. ctr. programming sci. and tech., 1981-86; asst. adminstr. for satellite and info. services NOAA, Washington, 1986-92, dir. high performance computing and com., 1992-00, dir. The Globe Program, 1994—2002, chief info. officer, dir. high performance computing and comm., 2000—01; chief info. officer US Dept. Commerce, 2001—05, US Dept. Energy, 2005—. Organizer profl. computer confs., 1970-86; mem. Presdl. Adv. Com. on Networking Structure and Function, 1980, Interagy. com. on Info. Resources Mgmt., 1983-84, bd. dirs., 1984-87, vice chmn. 1986-87 (Exec. Excellence award 1991), chmn. Interagy. Working Group on Data Mgmt. for Global Change, 1987-93; speaker in field. Mem. editl. bd. Computer Networks Jour., 1976-86; contbr. articles to profl. jours. Mem. Task Force on Computers in Schs., Arlington, 1982—85; co-pres. Jamestown Elem. Sch. PTA, Arlington, 1984—85; bd. dirs. Glebe Commons Assn., Arlington, Va., 1976—79, v.p., 1977—79. Recipient silver medal Dept. Commerce, 1973, gold medal, 1995; award for exemplary achievement in pub. adminstrn. William A. Jump Found., 1975, 76, Presdl. Rank award of Meritorious Exec., 1988, 99; Westinghouse scholar Carnegie Inst. Tech., 1960-64; Ford Found. fellow U. Pa., 1964-66. Fellow Washington Acad. Scis. (Engring. Sci. award 1974); mem. IEEE (sr. mem.), Computer Soc. of IEEE (bd. govs. 1971-73, 75-77, vice chmn. tech. com. on personal computing 1982-86, chmn. 1986-87), AAAS, Assn. Computing Machinery, Sigma Xi, Eta Kappa Nu, Omicron Delta Kappa, Pi Kappa Alpha (chpt. v.p. 1963-64) Episcopalian. Office: US Dept Energy 1000 Independence Ave SW Washington DC 20585 Business E-Mail: tom.pyke@hq.doe.gov.

PYLE, ARTIMUS (THOMAS DELMAR PYLE), musician; b. Louisville, July 15, 1948; s. Clarence and Mildred Pyle. Drummer Volunteer Jam, Marshall Tucker Band, Lynyrd Skynyrd, 1975—77, 1987—92; founder Artimus Pyle Band, 1981—. Musician: (albums) A.P.B., 1982, Nightcaller, 1983, Live from Planet Earth, 2000, (with Lynyrd Skynyrd) Nuthin' Fancy, 1975, Gimme Back My Bullets, 1976, One More from the Road, 1976, Street Survivors, 1977, Southern by the Grace of God, 1988, Lynyrd Skynyrd 1991, Freebird: The Movie, 1996. USMC, 1968. Named to Rock and Roll Hall of Fame, 2006. Office: Lustig Talent Enterprises Inc PO Box 770850 Orlando FL 32877 Office Phone: 407-816-8960. Office Fax: 407-816-8959. E-mail: artimus@artimuspyle.com.

PYLE, GERALD FREDRIC, geographer, educator; b. Akron, Ohio, Dec. 22, 1937; s. Russell Roy and Ruth (Martin) P.; m. Carole Wood, Aug. 29, 1959; children: Eric, Frances. BA, Kent State U., 1963; MA, U. Chgo., 1968, PhD, 1970. Cartographer Rand McNally, Chgo., 1962-64; rsch. geographer Ency. Brit., Chgo., 1964-65; cartographer U. Chgo., 1965-70; from asst. prof. to prof. U. Akron, 1970-80; prof. geography and earth sci. U. N.C., Charlotte, 1980-98, prof. health promotion, 1995—2002, prof. health behavior and adminstrn., 2002—04, emeritus prof., 2004—. Vis. fellow Macquarie U., Sydney, 1988; rsch. dir. Ctr. for Urban Studies, Akron, Ohio, 1973—80; tech. dir. Akron Area Census File, 1974—80; vis. scholar U. SC, 1977; interim dir. health adminstrn. program U. NC, Charlotte, 2001—02. Author: Heart Disease, Cancer and Stroke in Chicago, 1971, Spatial Dynamics of Crime, 1974, Applied Medical Geography, 1979, Diffusion of Influenza: Patterns and Paradigms, 1986, (with Shannon and Bashshur) The Geography of AIDS, 1990, (with shannon) Medical Atlas of the Twentieth Century, 1993; sr. editor Med. Geography, Social Sci. and Medicine, 1977-84; book rev. editor Social Sci. and Medicine, 1990-2005. Recipient Scholars medal First Citizens Bank, 1992; grantee Ill. Regional Med., 1969, Law Enforcement Adminstrn. Agy., 1972, 74, NSF, 1979, 82, Nat. Geog. Soc., 1988, NRC, 1995, Smart Start 1999-2001. Fellow Ohio Acad. Sci.; mem. APHA, Am. Coll. Epidemiology, Assn. Am. Geographers (Rsch. Honors S.E. divsn. 1994), Phi Kappa Phi. Democrat. Anglican. Achievements include research in spatial diffusion of infectious diseases and the location of health care delivery facilities. Home: PO Box 641 Matthews NC 28106 Office: U NC Dept Health Behavior and Adminstrn 9201 University City Blvd Charlotte NC 28223-0002 Personal E-mail: gfpyle@msn.com.

PYLE, HOWARD, lawyer, consultant; b. Richmond, Va., Feb. 1, 1940; s. Wilfrid and Anne Woolston (Roller) P.; m. Victoria M. Sheffield; children: Elizabeth Roller Ross, Howard. AB, Princeton U., 1962; JD, U. Va., 1967. Bar: Va. 1967, D.C. 1969. Career trainee CIA, Washington, 1967-69; adminstrv. asst. to Congressman Odin Langen, U.S. Ho. of Reps., Washington, 1969-70, to Congressman Hastings Keith, 1971; asst. to sec. Dept. Interior, Washington, 1971-73; Washington rep. Std. Oil Co. Ind., 1973-77; mgr. fed. pub. affairs R.J. Reynolds Industries, Inc., Winston-Salem, NC, 1977-80; dir. fed. rels. Houston Industries, Washington, 1980-99; pres. HPYLE Cons., Alexandria, Va., 1999—. Mem.: SAR, NRA, Va. Bar, DC Bar, Washington Assembly, Naval Res. Assn., Alexandria Assn., Res. Officers Assn., Delta Theta Phi. Republican. Episcopalian. Home: 125 N Lee St Alexandria VA 22314-3260 also: PO Box 19645 Alexandria VA 22320-0645 Office: HPYLE Cons Po Box 19645 Alexandria VA 22320-0645 Office Phone: 703-608-4742. Personal E-mail: howard@hpyle.net.

PYLE, ROBERT MILNER, JR., financial consultant; b. Orange, NJ, Oct. 24, 1938; s. Robert M. and Dorothy (Collings) Pyle; m. C. Page Neville, May 31, 1969; children: Cynthia Neville, Laura Collings. BA, Williams Coll., 1960; JD, U. Va., 1963. Bar: N.Y. 1964. Assoc. Mudge Rose Guthrie & Alexander, NYC, 1963—68; with Studebaker-Worthington, Inc., NYC, 1968—77, sec., 1972—76, assoc. gen. counsel, 1974—77; with Singer Co., NYC, 1977—79; v.p., counsel Am. Soc. Corp. Secs., Inc., NYC, 1979—89, v.p., sec., counsel, 1989—91; v.p., sr. asst. sec. Am. Express Co., NYC, 1991—96, cons., 1997—. Career counseling rep. Williams Coll., 1977—. Trustee Pingry Sch., Martinsville, NJ, 1972—74, Arts Coun. Suburban Essex Inc., 1979—84, chmn. bd., 1981—84; trustee Suburban Cmty. Music Ctr., 1985—87; mem. Millburn-Short Hills Rep. Mcpl. Com. Essex County, 1998—2003; bd. govs. Colonial Dances, Ltd., NYC, 1970—74; bd. dirs. Millburn-Short Hills Hist. Soc., 1985—90, v.p., 1985—87. Mem.: ABA, Assn. Bar City N.Y., Am. Soc. Corp. Secs. (hon.), Pilgrims U.S., Pingry Sch. Alumni Assn. (bd. dirs. 1966—78, pres. 1972—74, cert. of merit 1968, Nelson Carr Svc. award 2006), Hillsboro Club (Fla.), Short Hills Club, Bay Head Yacht Club (N.J.), No. N.J. Squash Racquets Assn. (past sec., trustee, Disting. Svc. award 2005), Met. Squash Racquets Assn. (past treas.), Racquet and Tennis Club, Pi Delta Epsilon, Delta Theta Phi, Sigma Phi. Episcopalian. E-mail: rmpylejr@aol.com.

PYLE, ROBERT NOBLE, public relations executive; b. Wilmington, Del., Oct. 23, 1926; s. Joseph Lybr and LaVerne Ruth (Noble) Pyle; m. Patricia Carlile Pyle, Jan. 21, 2006; children: Robert Noble Jr., Mark C., Nicholas A., Louis P. Crosier, Sarah P. Moore. BA, Dickinson Coll., 1948; postgrad., Wharton Sch., U. Pa., 1949, U. Minn. Pres. Robert N. Pyle, Inc., Wilmington, 1949-52; adminstrv. asst. to US Congress, Washington, 1952-63; bus. and polit. cons. Robert N. Pyle & Assoc., Washington, 1970—2007, chmn. Sec./treas. Bulgarian Am. Bus. Ctr.; cons. in field. Contbr. numerous articles to profl. jours.; reporter covering Nurnburg Trials, Paris Peace Conf. for, Stars & Stripes, Europe, 1946. Dir. World Affairs Coun.; pres. La Quinta Sr. Ctr.; moderator Great Decisions; dir. English Speaking Union; field man Rep. Nat. Congl. Com., 1959—74. With US Army, 1945—46, ETO. Mem.: Newport Beach Tennis Club, Palm Valley Golf Club, Kenwood Country Club, City Tavern Club, La Quinta Resort and Club, Lincoln Club. Presbyterian. Home: 50255 Via Simpatico La Quinta CA 92253 Office: 1223 Potomac St NW Washington DC 20007-3212 Office Phone: 202-333-8190. Personal E-mail: carlile8@verizon.net.

PYLES, LEE ALLAN, cardiologist, biomedical researcher; m. Marie Elizabeth Steiner, July 15, 1989; children: Richard, Cynthia. BS in Chemistry, W.Va. U., Morgantown, 1979, MD, 1983. Diplomate Am. Bd. Pediat., Am. Bd. Pediat. Cardiology. Intern pediat. U. Minn. Sch. Medicine, Mpls., 1983—84, resident pediat., 1984—86; fellow pediat. cardiology U. Minn., Mpls., 1986—89, asst. prof. pediat., 1998—; asst. prof. pediat. sect. pediat. cardiology and pediat. critical care W.Va. U., 1990—90, assoc. prof. pediat. sect. pediat. cardiology and pediat. critical care, 1995—96; assoc. prof. pediat. with tenure W.Va. U. Sch. Medicine, Morgantown, 1996—98; assoc. prof. pediat. and emergency medicine U. Minn., 2007. Privacy and security officer U. Minn. Physicians, Mpls., 2002—07; pediatrician mem. Minn. Emergency Med. Svcs. Regulatory Bd., 2007. Dir.(grant principal investigator): Minnesota Emergency Medical Services for Children Information System. Named one of Best Doctors in Am., Best Doctors, Inc, 1998—2006, Twin Cities Top Docs, Twin Cities Mag., 2004—07; recipient Samuel L. Channel award for Excellence in EMS, W.Va. EMS Tech. Support Network, 2000. Fellow: Am. Coll. Cardiology, Am. Acad. Pediat. (disting. svc. citation 1996—2002). Avocations: swimming, camping. Office: U Minn Mayo Mail Code # 94 420 Delaware St Minneapolis MN 55455 Office Phone: 612-626-2755. Business E-Mail: pyles001@umn.edu.

PYLES, RODNEY ALLEN, archivist, county official; b. Morgantown, W.Va., June 21, 1945; s. Melford John and Luci L. (Scarcella) P.; m. Carol Louise Wrobleski, May 20, 1972; 1 child, Janessa Louise. BA, MA (Benedum scholar 1966-67, grad. research asst. 1967-68, grad. teaching fellow 1968-69), W.Va. U., 1967-69. Instr. polit. sci. Alderson-Broaddus Coll., Philippi, W.Va., 1969-71; asst. curator W.Va. U. Library, 1971-77; dir. archives and history div. W.Va. Dept. Culture and History, 1977-85; dep. chief Assessor's Office Monongalia County, 1985-88; assessor Monongalia County, 1989—. Mng. editor: W.Va. History quar, 1977-85 Mem. Morgantown (W.Va.) Dem. exec. com., 1966-69, Monongalia County (W.Va.) Dem. exec. com., 1972-76; mem. Morgantown Libr. Bd., 1988-91, Morgantown Hist. Landmarks Commn., 1986—; trustee W.Va. Pub. Theatre, 1999—, treas., 2004. Mem. Soc. Am. Archivists, W.Va. Hist. Soc. (exec. sec. 1977-90, bd. dirs. 1990—), Am. Assn. State and Local History (state awards chmn. 1980-85, state membership com. 1981-87), Monongalia Hist. Soc. (pres. 1986-88, bd. dirs. 1988—), W.Va. Polit. Sci. Assn. (treas. 1991—), W.Va. Assessors' Assn. (pres. 1992-93, bd. dirs. 2005—), KC (pres. bowling league 1995-96, 4th deg., faithful capt. 1996—, chancellor 1998-2000, dep. Grand Knight 2000-02, Grand Knight, 2002-2007), Sons of Italy (treas. 1995—). Roman Catholic. Home: 536 Harvard Ave Morgantown WV 26505-2157 Office: County Court House Rm 215 Morgantown WV 26505 Office Phone: 304-291-7222. Business E-Mail: rpyles@assessor.org.

PYLES, STEPHEN, chef; b. Tex. Chef, owner Routh St. Cafe, 1983—93, Baby Routh, 1983—93, Goodfellow's, 1987—93, Tejas, Mpls., 1987—93, Star Canyon, AquaKnox, 1997—98, Stephan Pyles Restaurant, 2005—. Founder Taste of the Nation event, Dallas, 1988; co-founder The Hunger Link; founding bd. mem. Share Our Strength; bd. mem. North Tex. Food Bank; adv. bd. mem. Nat. Culinary of The Art Institutes; cons. Ama Lur, Gaylord Texan Resort & Convention Ctr., Grapevine, Tex. Author: The New Texas Cuisine (Top Ten Chef's Cookbooks of the Decade, Bon Appetit), Southwestern Vegetarian, 2001; co-author: Tamales, New Tastes from Texas; host (TV series) New Tastes from Texas (Emmy award), guest appearances on Food Morning America, The Today Show. Recipient Best Chef: Southwest award, James Beard Found., 1991, AAA Five Diamond award, Fine Dining Hall of Fame award, Nation's Restaurant News, Ivy award, Restaurants and Institutions, Am. Acad. Achievement award, Outstanding Restaurateur of Yr. award, Minn. Restaurant Assn., Tex. Restaurant Assn., Humanitarian of Yr. award, Share Our Strength, 1998. Office: 1807 Ross Ave Ste 200 Dallas TX 75201 Office Phone: 214-580-7000. *

PYLIPOW, STANLEY ROSS, retired manufacturing company executive; b. Coudersport, Pa., Apr. 4, 1936; s. Stanley Edward and Helen L. (Haskins) P.; m. Phyllis Beverly Moore, Dec. 1, 1956; children— David, James, Vicky, Kenneth, Sandra BBA in Acctg. cum laude, St. Bonaventure U., 1957. Various fin. positions Chicopee Mfg., New Brunswick, NJ, 1957-65; various positions to v.p., gen. mgr. Domestic Coatings div. Mobil Chem. Co., NYC, 1965-73; asst. corp. controller Monsanto Co., St. Louis, 1974-76; controller, dir. planning Monsanto Comml. Products, St. Louis, 1976-79; sr. v.p., bd. dirs., chief fin. officer Fisher Controls Internat., Inc., St. Louis, 1979-92; ret., 1992; bd. dirs. RBA Group. Treas. Ulster Project, St. Louis, 1998—2002. Treas., City of Town and Country, Mo., 1980-84; bd. dirs. Ecumenical Housing Prodn. Corp., St. Louis, 1980-90; mem. Acctg. Edn. Change Commn., 1992-96. Served to 1st lt., U.S. Army, 1958. Named Exec. of Yr., Profl. Secs. Internat., 1982 Mem. Inst. Mgmt. Accts. (pres. 1990-91, chmn. 1991-92), Fin. Execs. Inst., Winghaven Country Club, Silverthorn Country Club. Republican. Avocations: golf, exercise, spectator sports. Office Phone: 352-796-6903. Personal E-mail: stanpylipow@centurytel.net.

PYNCHON, THOMAS RUGGLES, JR., author; b. Glen Cove, NY, May 8, 1937; s. Thomas R. Pynchon. BA, Cornell U., 1958. Former editorial writer Boeing Aircraft Co., Seattle. Author: V, 1963 (William Faulkner novel award 1963), The Crying of Lot 49, 1966 (Rosenthal Found. award Nat. Inst. Arts and Letters 1967), Gravity's Rainbow, 1973 (Nat. Book award 1974), Slow Learner, 1984, Vineland, 1989, Deadly Sins, 1994, Mason and Dixon, 1997, Against the Day, 2006; contbr. short stories to publs. including N.Y. Times Mag., N.Y. Times Book Rev., Cornell Writer, Saturday Evening Post, Kenyon Rev. Served with USNR. Recipient Howells medal Nat. Inst. and Am. Acad. Arts and Letters, 1975. *

PYOTT, DAVID EDMUND IAN, pharmaceutical executive; b. London, Eng., Oct. 13, 1953; married; 4 children. MA, U. Edinburgh, 1975; diploma in German and European Law, U. Amsterdam, 1976; MBA, London Bus. Sch., 1980. Numerous positions Sandoz Nutrition, Barcelona, 1980-90, gen. mgr., 1990-92; pres., CEO Sandoz Nutrition Corp., Mpls., 1992-95; head divsn. nutrition Sandoz Internat. AG, 1995—97; mem., exec. com. Novartis AG (merger Sandoz and Ciba), 1995—97; pres. Allergan, Inc., Irvine, Calif., 1998—2006, CEO, 1998—, chmn., 2001—. Bd. dirs. PhRMA, Avery Dennison Corp., Edwards Lifescis. Corp., Advanced Med. Optics, Inc.; chmn. Calif. Healthcare Inst.; mem. bd. dirs. U. Calif. (Irvine) Grad. Sch. Mgmt.; mem.LA Bus. Advisors; vice-chair Chief Exec. Roundtable for UCI Bd. dirs. Internat. Coun. of Ophthalmology Found., Eyecare Am.; pres. Pan-Am. Ophthalmological Found. Mem. Pharm. Rsch. and Mfrs. Am. (bd. dirs., Allergan rep.), Pan Am. Assn. Ophthalmology (bd. dirs.), L.A. Bus. Advisors. Achievements include transforming Botox, an obsure treatment for rare muscular diseases, into a cultural and medical phenomenon. Office: Allergan Inc 2525 Dupont Dr Irvine CA 92612-1531 Address: Allergan Inc PO Box 19534 Irvine CA 92623 *

PYSH, JOSEPH JOHN, neurologist; b. Olyphant, Pa., Nov. 14, 1935; s. John Andrew and Anna Mary (Marusin) P.; m. Deborah Ann Prass, Dec. 15, 1991. BA in Biology, Wayne State U., 1958; DO, Chgo. Coll. Osteo. Medicine, 1962; PhD in Neuroanatomy, Northwestern U., Chgo., 1967. From instr. to assoc. prof. anatomy Northwestern U., Chgo., 1966-86, acting chmn. cell biology and anatomy, 1978-81, resident physician in neurology, 1983-86; assoc. prof. neurology Mich. State U., East Lansing, 1986-95, prof. neurology, 1995—, dir. neurology residency program, 2001—03. Grant referee NSF, Washington, 1974—; frequent CME neurology speaker in field. Contbr. numerous articles to profl. jours; manuscript reviewer various orgns., Washington and N.Y.C. Recipient Tchg. award Northwestern U.; NIH grantee, 1969-82. Fellow Am. Coll. Neuropsychiatrists; mem. AAAS (life), NIH (mem. rsch. grant neurology study sect. 1976-77), Am. Acad. Neurology, Am. Soc. Cell Biology, Am. Assn. Anatomists, Soc. Neurosci., Sigma Xi. Republican. Achievements include research in synaptic transmission and brain development. Avocations: rare book collecting, sailing. Office: Mich State U Coll Osteo Medicine Dept Neurology 138 Service Rd A217 Clin East Lansing MI 48824 Office Phone: 517-353-8122. Business E-Mail: pysh@msu.edu.

PYSHER, THEODORE JAMES, pathologist, medical educator; b. Youngstown, Ohio, July 3, 1947; s. Ernest Raymond and Ruth Regina Pysher; m. Yanett Hall, Oct. 20, 1974; children: Nathaniel Hall, Jason Hall, Alexander Hall. BS, Youngstown State U., Ohio, 1969; MD, U. Chgo., 1973. Diplomate Am. Bd. Pediat., 1978, anatomic and clin. pathology Am. Bd. Pathology, 1978, pediat. pathology Am. Bd. Pathology, 1990. Pediat. intern Cleve. Met. Gen. Hosp., 1973—74, pathology resident, 1974—76; pediat. resident Rainbow Babies and Childrens Hosp., Cleve., 1976—77; chief resident, fellow pediat. pathology Children Hosp. LA, 1977—79; asst. prof. pathology and pediat. U. Okla., Oklahoma City, 1979—84, assoc. prof. pathology and pediat., 1984—85; adj. assoc. prof. pathology U. Utah, Salt Lake City, 1985—94, clin. prof. pathology, adj. prof. pediat., 1994—. Med. dir. labs. Primary Children's Med. Ctr., Salt Lake City, 1988—. Fellow: Am. Soc. Clin. Pathology, Coll. Am. Pathologists (lab. insp. 1980—2007); mem.: Children's Oncology Group (vice chmn. pathology 2001—07), Soc. Pediatric Pathology (pres. 2007—, Spl. Distinction 1996, 2000). Office: Primary Children's Med Ctr 100 North Medical Dr Salt Lake City UT 84113

PYSHKIN, SERGEI L., physics professor, researcher; b. St. Petersburg, Russia, July 5, 1941; s. Lev Nikolaevich Pyshkina and Lidia Yakovlevna Pyshkin; m. Tatiana V. Krasnojon, Jan. 27, 1973; children: Kirill S., Marina S. Samarina, Tatiana S. Pyshkina; m. Tatiana N. Moiseiuk, Aug. 19, 1961 (div. Nov. 25, 1972). Student, St. Petersburg State Tech. U., 1958—64; postgrad., State U. Moldova, Kishinev, 1967; DSc in Physics, Moscow State U., 1978. Rschr. Inst. Applied Physics, 1967—86, head laser rsch. lab, 1986—2001, prin. investigator, 2001—; prof. Free Internat. U., Kishinev, 1998—2005; adj. prof. Clemson U., 2005—, sr. fellow Ctr. Optical Materials Sci. and Engring. Techs. Anderson, SC, 2006—. Contbr. articles to profl. jours. Grantee, USAF, 1995, 1997, 1998, 1999, US Civilian R&D Found., 2003, 2005, 2007, UNESCO, Italy, 2007; Fulbright fellow, US Dept. State, 2005—06, Rsch. grant, Soros Found., 1991, 2001. Achievements include research in light emissive structures for optoelectronics. Home: 55/3 Shosse Hinceshti Apt 51 Kishinev MD2028 Moldova Office: Inst Applied Physics 5 Academy St Kishinev MD2028 Moldova also: Ctr for Optical Materials Sci and Engring Techs Clemson Rsch Park Technology Dr 91 Anderson SC Office Phone: (37322) 738406. Office Fax: (37322) 738149. Business E-Mail: spyshkin@clemson.edu, spyshkin@phys.asm.md.

PYTELL, ROBERT HENRY, retired lawyer, former judge; b. Detroit, Sept. 27, 1926; s. Henry Carl and Helen (Zielinski) P.; m. Laurie Mazur, June 2, 1956; children: Mary Beth, Mark Henry, Robert Michael. JD, U. Detroit, 1951. Bar: Mich. 1952. Of counsel Pytell & Varchetti, P.C., Detroit, 1952-2001; asst. U.S. atty. Ea. Dist. Mich., 1962-65; judge Mcpl. Ct., Grosse Pointe Farms, Mich., 1967-85. With USNR, 1945-46. Mem. Am. Coll. Trust and Estate Counsel, State Bar Mich. (mem. probate coun. probate sect. 1998-2000), Crescent Sail Yacht Club (Grosse Pointe), Delta Theta Phi. Roman Catholic.

PYTKA, STEPHEN MILTON, office equipment executive; b. Ludlow, Mass., Apr. 29, 1947; s. Milton Ignatius and Jean Marie (Kmiecik) P.; m. Linda Rachel Madsen, May 25, 1969; children: Jonathan Stephen, Justin Stephen, Brendan Stephen. BSEE, Worcester Poly. Inst., 1968; MBA, Dartmouth Coll., 1977. Design engr. AT&T, Whippany, N.J., 1968-69, Kwajalein, Marshall Islands, 1970-71, Greensboro, N.C., 1969-70, Langdon, N.D., 1971-73; sys. engr. GE, Pittsfield, Mass., 1973-75; planning mgr. Xerox Corp., Rochester, N.Y., 1977-81; mktg. mgr. Wang Labs., Inc., 1982-83; exec. v.p. Cap. Internat., Marshfield, Mass., 1983—; mng. ptnr. Consilium Ptnrs. LLC, Boston, 2004—. Co-founder P&R Microtech, 1982-83; exec. v.p. BIS Cap Internat., 1983-89; pres., chief ops. officer BISCOM, Inc., 1990-96; v.p. The Onstott Group, 1997-98; chmn., CEO Streamware, Inc., 1998-2000; pres., CEO eChinaLink, 2000-01; CEO Talksender, Inc., 2000-01, Hellotech, 2001-02, Gazelle Systems, Inc., 2002-03; mng dir., Consilium Ptnrs., 2004; mem. exec. bd. WPI Venture Forum; mem Touch Applications, HUB Angels, Common Angels; panelist MIT Enterprise Forum; trustee Andover YMCA; spkr. in field. Mem. Am. Mgmt. Assn, HubAngels, CommonAngels. Republican. Roman Catholic. Home: 9 Langley Ln Andover MA 01810-4259 Office: Consilium Ptnrs 399 Boylston St Boston MA 02116

PYTLEWSKI, LAURA JEAN, chemistry professor; b. Freeport, Ill., Aug. 26, 1959; d. James Franklin and Darlene Ann Donahue; m. James Andrew Pytlewski, Oct. 8, 1983; children: Michael Steven, Matthew John. BS in Biology, St. Xavier U., 1981; MS in Analytical Chemistry, Govs. State U., 1992. Cert. med. technologist Am. Soc. Clin. Pathologists, 1983. Adj. prof. chemistry Moraine Valley C.C., Palos Hills, Ill., 1993—2003; prof. chemistry Triton Coll., River Grove, Ill., 2002—06; adj. prof. chemistry Lewis U., Romeoville, Ill., 2006—; lab. supr. natural sci. dept. U. St. Francis, Joliet, Ill., 2006—07; mem. faculty Lewis U., Romeoville, 2007—. Mem. focus group Benjamin Cummings Publishers, San Francisco, 2004; adj. prof. Govs. State U., Univ. Pk., Ill., 2006—. Author: Biology for Life, 2001; reviewer: Chemistry: A World of Choices, 1998. Mem. com. devel. of new lab. St. Joseph's Sch., Lockport, Ill., 2005—06. Scholar, St. Xavier U., 1980—81. Democrat. Roman Catholic. Achievements include development of a visual factoring method for algebra II. Avocations: painting, reading, rollerblading, swimming, travel. Home Phone: 708-301-0211. E-mail: pytlewla@lewisu.edu.

PYTLINSKI, JERZY TEODOR, physicist, educator, research scientist; b. Warsaw, Apr. 1, 1938; s. Stanislaw and Natalia (Matuszewska) P.; m. Bonnie Laurie Bennett, Dec. 30, 1969; 1 child, Christine Barbara. MS, Tech. U. Warsaw, 1962; PhD Plasma Physics with distinction, U. Paris, 1967. Program mgr., acting divsn. head N.Mex. State U., Las Cruces, 1977—80; sr. scientist, divsn. head U. PR, Mayaguez, 1981—83, program dir., sr. scientist San Juan, 1983—86, sr. scientist, founding dir. Univ.-Industry Rsch. Ctr. Tampa, Fla., 1986—89; pres. Univ.-Industry Rsch. Ctr., Tampa, Fla., 1989—, prof., 1989—. Mem.adv. bd. on solar energy UNESCO, 1979-85; referee Am. Jour. Physics, 1980—, Solar Energy Jour., 1983-87, 38th Internat. Sci. and Engring. Fair, 1987; mem. U.S. tech. adv. group of ISO TC-180, 1981— Mem. editl. bd. Internat. Jour. Energy, Environ. Econs., 1990—; co-editor Procs. Internat. Conf. Energy for Ams., 1987; contbr. more than 85 articles to profl. jours. and procs. Grantee state and fed. agys., various edn. and rsch. founds.; Postdoctoral fellow U. Liverpool, Eng., 1968-69; recipient commendation State of Kans., 1977. Mem. Am. Phys. Soc., Nat. Coun. Univ. Rsch. Adminstrs., Soc. Rsch. Adminstrs., Internat. Solar Energy Soc., Internat. Energy Soc. (sci. coun. 1985—), Sigma Phi Sigma. Republican. Roman Catholic. Achievements include pioneering research in plasma physics, alternative energy sources. Avocations: reading, tennis, travel.

PYTTE, AGNAR, physicist, retired academic administrator; b. Kongsberg, Norway, Dec. 23, 1932; arrived in U.S., 1949, naturalized, 1965; s. Ole and Edith (Christiansen) Pytte; m. Anah Currie Loeb, June 18, 1955; children: Anders H., Anthony M., Alyson C. AB, Princeton U., 1953; AM, Harvard U., 1954, PhD, 1958. Faculty Dartmouth Coll., 1958—87, prof. physics, 1967—87, chmn. dept. physics and astronomy, 1971—75, assoc. dean faculty, 1975—78, dean grad. studies, 1975—78, provost, 1982—87; pres. Case Western Res. U., Cleve., 1987—99; adj. prof. physics Dartmouth Coll., 1999—. Rschr. in plasma physics; mem. Project Matterhorn Princeton U., 1959—60, 1978—79, U. Brussels, 1966—67. Bd. dirs. Goodyear Tire and Rubber Co., 1988—2004, Accreditation Coun. for Grad. Med. Edn., 2000—04, A.O. Smith Corp., 1991—2003, Sherman Fairchild Found., Inc., 1987—2006. Mem.: Am. Phys. Soc., Sigma Xi, Phi Beta Kappa. Personal E-mail: agnar.x.pytte@dartmouth.edu.

QAHWASH, MURAD, engineer, educator; b. West Bank, Palestine, Feb. 26, 1974; s. Mohammad Qahwash and Huda Latifa; MS, U. Ctrl. Fla., Orlando, 1999; PhD, U. Ctrl. Fla., 2002, MBA, 2006. Grad. rsch. asst. NASA, Cape Canaveral, Fla., 1998—99, wireless comm. rsch. grp., U. Ctrl. Fla., 1998—2000; programmer Joseph Comm. Rsch., Orlando, 1999—2000; digital signal processing engr. Global2Way, Melbourne, Fla., 2000—03; sr. dsp engr. LocusUSA, Melbourne, 2004—. Assoc. prof. Devry U., Orlando, 2003—; cons. Apecor, Orlando, 2004—05, Electrodynamics Assocs., Orlando, 2005—06. Mem.: IEEE. Achievements include patents pending for a demodulator for GFSK burst messages with time of arrival information. Office: Devry Univ 4000 Millenia Blvd Orlando FL 32839 Office Fax: 407-355-4790; Home Fax: 407-355-4790. Business E-Mail: mqahwash@orl.devry.edu.

QASIM, IMAD ISA, lawyer; b. Tripoli, Libya, Sept. 14, 1957; came to US, 1973; s. Isa and Nawal Q.; m. Nancy Meloy Qasim, May 19, 1990. AB with honors, Hamilton Coll., 1979; JD, Georgetown U., 1982. Bar: NY 1983, Ill. 1987, DC 1989. Assoc. Sidley & Austin, Chgo., 1983, 85-88, Muscat, Oman, 1983-85, Washington, 1988-91, ptnr., 1991—2001, Sidley, Austin, Brown & Wood, Chgo., 2001—. Mem. ABA (mem. securities law sect.), DC Bar Assn. Office: Sidley Austin Brown & Wood 1 S Dearborn Chicago IL 60603 Office Phone: 312-853-7000, 312-853-7094. Office Fax: 312-853-7036. *

QAZI, ASHRAF JEHANGIR, ambassador; b. Pakistan, 1942; married; 2 children. With Fgn. Svc. of Pakistan, 1965—; ambassador of Pakistan to Syria, 1986—88, East Germany, 1990—91, Russia, 1991—94, China, 1994—97, India, 1997—2002, U.S.A, 2002—04, Iraq, 2004—. Various diplomatic assignments Copenhagen, Tokyo, Cairo, Tripoli, London. Office: c/o UN Headquarters First Avenue at 46th Street New York NY 10017 Office Phone: 212-963-1234. Office Fax: 212-963-4879.

QI, HUAQING, special education educator; d. Zhenhua Qi and Qingduo Sun; m. Matthew Schlecht; 1 child, Isaac Schlecht; 1 child, Peter Li. MEd, Belmont U., Nashville, 1992, Vanderbilt U., 1998, PhD, 2001. Cert. early childhood spl. edn. Nashville. Asst. prof. West Chester U., Pa., 2001—04, U. of N.Mex, Albuquerque, 2004—. Grant reviewer, jour. reviewer profl. agys. Editor: Editing for a Professional Newsletter; contbr. articles to profl. jours. (Frederick Douglass scholarship, 2000). Mem.: CEC, Autism Soc. of Am., Am. Assn. of Mental Retardation, Soc. of Rsch. and Children Devel., Am. Speech, Lang., and Hearing Assn. (travel fellowship 2002, 2003). Office: Univ NMex Dept Ednl Specialties Hokona Hall 248 Albuquerque NM 87131 Home Phone: 505-850-6800; Office Phone: 505-277-4452. Business E-Mail: hqi@unm.edu.

QI, XIAOJUN, engineering educator; BS, Donghau U., Shanghai, 1993; Master's, Shenyang Inst. Automation, 1996; PhD, La. State U., Baton Rouge, 2001. Vis. asst. prof. U. Miss., University, 2002; asst. prof. Utah State U., Logan, 2002—. Mem. program coms. various orgns. Reviewer in field:. Grantee Simulation Projects, Air Force Rsch. Lab., 2004—06, Image Compression, Utah State U. New Faculty Rsch. Grant, 2003—04, Eye-Tracking, Cmty. U. Rsch. Initiatives, 2006—07, Computer Vision Assisted Nav., 2005—06. Mem.: IEEE. Office: Utah State U 4205 Old Main Hill Logan UT 84322 Office Phone: 435-797-8155.

QI, XIAONING, electrical engineer, electronics engineer, researcher; PhD, Stanford U., Calif., 2001. Sr. engr. R&D Sun Microsystems, Inc., Sunnyvale, Calif., 2001—05; staff engr. R&D Synopsys, Inc., Mountain View, Calif., 2005—06; sr. staff engr. R&D Synopsys Inc., 2006—07; sr. mem. tech. staff R&D Rambus, Inc., 2007—. Mem.: IEEE (sr.), Toastmaster Internat. (v.p. edn.). Avocation: tai chi.

QI, ZHIGANG, materials scientist, chemist; s. Pengling Qi and Fengzhi Jing; children: Lydia Cong Zhang, Albert Jie, Brian Lin. BSc in Chemistry, U. Sci. and Tech., Beijing, 1985; PhD, McGill U., 1996. Post-doctoral fellow Meml. U. of Newfoundland, St. John's, Newfoundland, Canada, 1996—97; sr. staff scientist H Power Corp., Belleville, NJ, 1997—2003; fellow Plug Power Inc., Latham, NY, 2003—. Contbr. articles to profl. jours.; mem. editl. bd.: Jour. Power Sources. Mem.: Am. Chem. Soc., The Electrochem. Soc. Achievements include first to ground breaking research in PEM fuel cells and conductive polymers; patents in field. Home Phone: 518-207-5273; Office Phone: 518-738-0229. Business E-Mail: zhigang_qi@plugpower.com.

QIAN, JIN, law librarian; b. Shanghai; came to the U.S., 1987; s. Bingchun and Shiyi Qian. BA, Shanghai Tchrs. U.,;, 1981; MA, Fordham U., 1988; MLS, St. John's U., 1990. Libr. trainee N.Y. Pub. Libr., NYC, 1988; reference asst. N.Y. Hist. Soc., NYC, 1989-90; asst. libr. Wilson, Elser, NYC, 1990—92, head libr., 1992—2004, dir. info. and rsch. svc., 2004—. Presdl. scholar Fordham U., 1987. Mem. ALA, Law Libr. Assn. Greater N.Y., Am. Assn. Law Librs., Spl. Librs. Assn., Assn. Legal Adminstrs. Home: PO Box 811 New York NY 10163-0811 Office: Wilson Elser 150 E 42nd St New York NY 10017-5612 E-mail: jin.qian@wilsonelser.com.

QIAN, LI, engineering educator; b. Lixian, China, Oct. 14, 1972; PhD (hon.), Kans. State U., 2002. Asst. prof. SD State U., Brookings, 2004—. Achievements include research in cost estimation and supply chain management. Office: SD State U Solberg Hall 115B Brookings SD 57006 Office Phone: 6056886419.

QIAN, ZIFEN, artist, editor-in-chief; b. Shanghai, Dec. 30, 1957; came to U.S., 1987; s. Mingkong and Xuan Wu (Chen) Q.; m. Li Dai, Mar. 27, 1992; 1 child, Kristin. BA, Shanghai Normal U., 1983; MFA, Portland State U., 1989. Sr. artist Carol Wilson Fine Arts, Portland, 1992—; art instr. Pacific Northwest Coll. Art, Portland, 1989-95, Portland State U., 1987-89; art dir. Classic Clay Concept Inc., 1990-92; art editor Youth and Health mag. WHO, Shanghai, 1983-87; pres. Northwest Chinese Artists Assn., Portland, 1993-95; editor-in-chief World Arts Pub. Co., Portland, 1997—. Fine artist: (paintings, art philosophy) The Oregonian newspaper, 1987, Stepping Out Arts mag., 1988, (paintings in a book) Entertaining with Betsy Bloomingdale, 1994, (paintings prints) Carol Wilson Fine Arts, 1992—, (art experience) The Dictionary of World Chinese Artists Achievements, 1994. One-man exhbns. Denise Amato Galleries, 1989-98, Indigo Gallery, 1992, Portland State U. Gallery, 1989 (fine artist award), U.S. Nat. Bank Tower, 1987, Broderick Gallery, 2000, Internat. Artexpo, NYC, 2002, Dragon Gallery, NYC, 2002, 03, Kavanaugh Art Gallery, West Des Moines, Iowa, 2002; group exhbns. include Shanghai Fine Arts Acad. Shows, 1982, 84, Across East China Nat. Art Show, 1986, San Francisco World Exposition, 1987, Pacific N.W. Coll. Art, 1992, Denise Amato Galleries, 1991, 93, 94, 96, 97, Emerly Fine Arts Gallery, 1997, Portland Art Mus., 1999, Malovat Art Gallery, Chgo., 2003, Broderick Gallery, 2004, Artexpo NY, 2006; featured in The Washington Post, 1995, The Houston Chronicle, 1995, The Oregonian newspaper, 1987, (book) Always Bright (Paintings From 1970-1999), 1999; painting on cover of book Traditions and Encounters-A Global Perspective on The Past (From 1500 To The Present), 2000; oil painting Classical Meditation pub. on The Asian Reporter; represented in permanent collections at State Senate of Oreg., State House of Oreg., City Hall of Portland, Portland Christian Ctr., Portland Art Mus.; watercolors printed in art products shown in over 40,000 art galleries and gift stores, U.K., France, Finland, Italy, Germany, Denmark, Australia, N.Z., Japan, Can., U.S. Pres. Chinese Friendship Assn. Portland, 2004—05. Recipient Outstanding Painting award Lucil S. Welch Meml. Found., 1988. Avocations: creating poetry, singing, tennis. E-mail: lzwap@aol.com.

QIAO, FENGXIANG, transportation engineer, educator; b. Taizhou, Jiangsu Province, China, Sept. 26, 1963; s. Deheng Qiao and Sufang Shen; m. Jinghong Ma, Sept. 28, 1988; 1 child, Yijun. Bachelor of Engring. in Automatic Control, Nanjing Inst. Tech., China, 1985; Master of Engring. in Mech. Engring., SE U., China, 1988; PhD in Civil Engring., Hong Kong U. Sci. and Tech., 2000. Asst. prof., dir. transp. lab SE U., Nanjing, 1988—97; rsch. and tchg. asst. Hong Kong U. Sci. and Tech., Hong Kong, 1997—2000; post doctoral rsch. assoc. and rsch. asst. prof. Tex. So. U., Houston, 2000—05, asst. prof., 2005—. Dir. Ctr. for Modeling and Simulation Tex. So. U., dir. Ctr. for Intelligent Transp. Sys. Recipient 2d Pl. award for transp. planning, Henan Province, China, 1992, 2d Pl. award for sci. and tech. progress, Chinese Edn. Com., 1992; Tex. So. U. Seed grantee, Tex. So. U., 2006. Master: Houston Area Nat. Summer Transp. Inst. (mentor 2002—06), United Assns. Chinese Alumni in Greater Houston Area (life; pres. 2005—07); mem.: N.Am. China Overseas Transp. Assn., Transp. Rsch. Bd., Air & Waste Mgmt. Assn., Am. Assn. Civil Engring. (assoc.), Tex. Dept. Transp. (mem. tech. adv. panel, Award for rsch. on symbols and warrants for major traffic generator guide signing), SW. Region U. Transp. Ctr. (prin. investigator 2004—07, Award for rsch. on intelligent transp. sys. data compression 2004, Award for rsch. on using GPS and ITS data to calibrate micro simulation model VISSIM 2005, Award for rsch. on computer simulation based algorithm for optimizing evacuation plans 2006). Achievements include first to develop Wavelet Transformation based approach for Intelligent Transportation System data aggregation and compression; research on collecting and evaluating on-road vehicle emission for mobile source air quality control; research in computer simulation based optimization strategy for evacuation under unexpected events in large urban areas; improving framework and systematic calibration for intersection left-turn yellow intervals including red clearance time; intelligent intersection delay estimation methogology by using Fuzzy logic theory; synthesizing warrants for major traffic generator guide signing; intelligent classification of traffic flow states using Neural Network Pattern Recognition technique; intelligent simulation and prediction of taffic flow dispersion; an equity-based model to control massive transit rail passenger flow; updating crash record data property based on new crash for improving regional air quality. Home: 5606 Bissonet St # 12 Houston TX 77081 Office: Texas Southern University Transp D 3100 Cleburne Ave Houston TX 77004 Office Phone: 713-313-1915. Office Fax: 713-313-1856. Personal E-mail: ceqfx@yahoo.com. Business E-Mail: qiao_fg@tsu.edu.

QIAO, JIAN-HUA, pathologist, researcher; b. Shanghai, Sept. 17, 1960; m. Mei-Qian Guan, Sept. 27, 1985; children: Mona G., George S. Qiao-Guan. MD, Shanghai Med. U., 1984. Diplomate Am. Bd. Pathology, 2003. Resident diagnostic radiology Children's Hosp., Shanghai Med. U., 1984—90, chief resident diagnostic radiology, 1988—90; rsch. fellow cardiology Cedars-Sinai Med. Ctr., LA, 1990—91, resident pathology, 1997—2002; asst. rschr. cardiology UCLA Med. Ctr., 1991—97, fellow cardiac and pulmonary pathology, 2002—03, clin. instr., 2003—04; staff attending pathologist Mercy Hosp., Bakersfield, Calif., 2004—06, Cath. Healthcare West, 2004—, Calif. Hosp. Med. Ctr., 2006—. Contbr. articles to profl. jours. Recipient Physician Recognition award, AMA, 2001—07, Nathan B. Friedman, M.D. prize for rsch., Cedars-Sinai Med. Ctr., 2002. Fellow: Coll. Am. Pathologists; mem.: L.A. Soc. Pathologists, US and Can. Acad. Pathology. Achievements include research in size of atherosclerotic plaque in coronary arteries in patients who died from acute myocardial infarction; rejection in cardiac transplantation; mouse models for athersclerosis; discovery of define genetic determination of arterial calcification heart diesease and HIV infection; describe cartilage cells in artery wall in human calcified diabetic peripheral vascular disease; research in imaging studies of pulmonary hypertension in Chinese children with congenital heart disease; gated MRI in diagnosis of congenital heart disease in children in Shanghai. Avocations: swimming, bicycling, stamp collecting/philately, photography. Office: Calif Hosp Med Ctr Dept Pathology 1401 S Grand Ave Los Angeles CA 90015 Office Phone: 213-742-5791. Personal E-mail: jianhuaqiao@yahoo.com. Business E-Mail: jian-hua.qiao@chw.edu.

QIN, YUFEN, immunologist, researcher; m. Yiping Zhang. MD (hon.), Harbin Med. U., China, 1977, MD in Immunology, 1982; PhD summa cum laude (hon.), U. Würzburg, Germany, 1990. Resident First Tchg. Hosp., Harbin Med. U., 1982—85; rsch. fellow Dept. Neurology U. Calif., Irvine, 1990—93; rsch. scientist Inst. Pathology, U. Würzburg, 1993—95, Dept. Virology, U. Quebec Inst. Armand-Frappier, Laval, 1995—96, Montreal Nuerol. Inst. Hosp., McGill U., 1996—99; asst. rschr. Dept. Neurology, U. Calif., Irvine, 1999—2003, asst. prof., 2003—. Contbr. articles to profl. jours. Recipient Rsch. award, Max-Planck Soc., 1986—90, Deutsche Forschungsgemeinschaft, 1993—95, van den Noort award, U. Calif., Dept. Neurology, 2005; fellow, U. Calif., 1990—93; grantee, Nat. Multiple Sclerosis Soc., 2000—03, NIH, 2001—06. Mem.: AAAS (assoc.), NY Acad. Sci. (assoc.), Am. Acad. Neurology (assoc.; multiple sclerosis sect.). Peace Party. Achievements include discovery of multiple sclerosis being considered as a neural and axonal autoimmune disease; glycolytic enzymes glyceraldehyde-3-phosphate dehydrogenase (GAPDH) and triosephosphate isomerase (TPI) being identified as target antigens in MS; antobodies in MS brains attack glycolytic enzymes in neuron and axon of a majoriey of MS patients; patents for B cell-mediated immune response in MS, in particular the patents at early stages of clinically isolated syndromes for the early diagnosis and treatment; patents pending for development of diagnosis kits for early detect glycolytic enzyme autoimmunoty in patients with MS and patients with other diseases. Avocations: philosophy, writing, travel, logical argumentation, photography. Office: U Calif 100 Irvine Hall Irvine CA 92697-4275 Office Phone: 949-824-1641. Business E-Mail: qiny@uci.edu.

QINGWEN, XU, law educator, social worker, educator; b. Beijing; LLM, Peking U., Beijing, 1997, NY U., NYC, 2000; PhD, U. Denver, 2002—02. Bar: NY 2000. Prof. San Francisco State U., 2002—04; asst. prof. Boston Coll., 2004—. Office: Boston Coll 140 Commonwealth Ave Chestnut Hill MA 02467 Office Phone: 617-552-1634. Business E-Mail: xuq@bc.edu.

QIU, WULIN, chemist, materials scientist, materials engineer; s. Shiqing Qiu and Chengcui Xu; m. Suya Wang, June 18, 1997; 1 child, Zhiyuan. BS, East China Inst. Tech., 1989, MS, 1992; PhD, Nanjing U. Sci. and Tech., China, 1995. Guest rschr. Nat. Inst. of Advanced Indsl. Sci. and Tech., Takamatsu, Kagawa, Japan, 1999—2004; postdoctoral rsch. assoc. U. of Tenn., Knoxville, Tenn., 2004—. Contbr. more than 60 sci. papers to peer reviewed jours. Recipient Excellent Grad. award, Nanjing U. of Sci. and Tech., 1996, Sci. and Tech. Devel. award, Sci. and Tech. Com. Jiangsu Province, China, 1997, Excellent U. Student award, Jiangsu Province, 1995; grantee Sci. Funds for the Postdoctoral fellows of China, Ednl. Com., 1996, Sci. Funds for the Postdoctoral fellow, Guangdong Province, 1996. Achievements include patents for novel thermal-resistance polymers; research in reversibility between glass and melting transition of polymers; observed glass transition within the polymer crystals; proved interfacial esterification between cellulose and maleated polyolefins in solid state; nanocomposites of polymer/inorganic hybrid; prepared inorganic nanoparticles with a new method; developed a novel macromolecular coupling agents, studied its effect on properties of polymer composites; synthesized novel metal-containing diamines; synthesized novel polymers (thermal-resistance, metal-containing, non-linear optical, liquid crystalline); synthesized dendrimers and hyperbranched polymer hybrids. Avocations: reading, travel, photography, badminton. Office: U Tenn Chem Dept 1420 Circle Dr Knoxville TN 37996-1600 Home Phone: 865-964-4123. Personal E-mail: qiuwulin@yahoo.com.

QIU, XIANGJUN, mining engineer; s. Anren Zhao and Peijin Qiu; m. Hong Lin, Jan. 17, 1961; children: Joanna Lin, Grace. BS, Nanjing U. Aeronautics and Astronautics, China, 1982, MS, 1984; PhD, U. Wis., Madison, 1990. Mgr. applied mechanics Conveyor Dynamics, Inc., Bellingham, Wash., 1990—2002; chief scientist high fidelity simulation Metso Minerals Industries, Inc., Colorado Springs, Colo., 2002—. Contbr. articles to profl. jours. Achievements include first to precisely solve equations for belt conveyor rolling resistance; development of numerical approach to madel mill linear wear. Home Phone: 719-266-1136.

QUAAL, WARD LOUIS, broadcast executive; b. Ishpeming, Mich., Apr. 7, 1919; s. Sigfred Emil and Alma Charlotte (Larson) Q.; m. Dorothy J. Graham, Mar. 9, 1944; children: Graham Ward, Jennifer Anne. AB, U. Mich., 1941; LL.D. (hon.), Mundelein Coll., 1962, No. Mich. U., 1967; D.Pub.Svc., Elmhurst Coll., 1967; D.H.L. (hon.), Lincoln Coll., 1968, DePaul U., 1974. Announcer-writer Sta. WBEO (now sta. WDMJ), Marquette, Mich., 1936—37; announcer, writer, producer Sta. WJR, Detroit, 1937—41; spl. events announcer-producer WGN, Chgo., 1941—42, asst. to gen. mgr., 1945—49; exec. dir. Clear Channel Broadcasting Service, Washington, 1949—52, pres., chief exec. officer, 1964—74; v.p., asst. gen. mgr. Crosley Broadcasting Corp., Cin., 1952—56; v.p., gen. mgr., mem. bd. WGN Inc., Chgo., 1956; exec. v.p., then pres. WGN Continental Broadcasting Co. (now Tribune Broadcasting Co.), 1960—75; pres. Ward L. Quaal Co, 1975—; dir. Tribune Co., 1961—75; dir., mem. exec. com. U.S. Satellite Broadcasting Co., 1982—2000. Bd. dirs. Christine Valmy Inc.; chmn. exec. com., dir. WLW Radio Inc., Cin., 1975-81; co-founder, dir. Universal Resources Inc., 1961-86; mem. FCC Adv. Com. on Advanced TV Sys., 1988-96. Author: (with others) Broadcast Management, 1968, rev. edit., 1979, new edit. 1997; co-prodr. (Broadway play) Teddy and Alice, 1988. Mem., Hoover Commn. Exec. Br. Task Force, 1949-59; mem. U.S.-Japan Cultural Exchange Commn., 1960-70; mem. Pres.'s Council Phys. Fitness and Sports, 1983-93; bd. dirs. Farm Found., 1963-73; bd. trustees Hollywood (Calif.) Mus., 1964-78, MacCormac Jr. Coll., Chgo., 1974-80; chmn. exec. com. Council for TV Devel., 1969-72; mem. bus. adv. coun. Chgo. Urban League, 1964-74; bd. dirs. Broadcasters Found., Internat. Radio and TV Found., Sears Roebuck Found., 1970-73; trustee Mundelein Coll., 1962-72, Hillsdale Coll., 1966-72. Served as lt. USNR, 1942-45. Named Radio Man of Yr., Am. Coll. Radio, Arts, Crafts & Scis., 1961, Laureate in Order of Lincoln, Lincoln Acad. Ill., 1965, Communicator of Yr., Jewish United Fund, 1969, Advt. Club Man of Yr., 1973; named one of Top 100 Mems., Delta Tau Delta, 1999, 1st 100 5th Estaters, Broadcasting 20th Century, 1999, First 50 Giants of Broadcasting, Libr. Am. Broadcasting, 2003; named to Delta Tau Delta Disting. Svc. Chpt., 1970, Broadcasting Mag. Hall of Fame, 1991, Mgmt. Hall of Fame, NATAS/TV Bur. Advt., 2003; recipient Disting. Bd. Gov.'s award, NATAS, 1966, 1987, Inaugural Inductee Mgmt. Hall of Fame, 2003, Freedoms Found. award, Valley Forge, 1966, 1968, 1970, Disting. Alumnus award, U. Mich., 1967, Loyola U. Key, 1970, Advt. Man of Yr. Gold medallion, Chgo. Advt. Club, 1968, Disting. Svc. award, Nat. Assn. Broadcasters, 1973, Ill. Broadcaster of Yr. award, 1973, Press Vet. of Yr. award, 1973, Comm. award of distinction, Brandeis U., 1973, Founder & Leadership award, Broadcast Pioneers Libr., 1991, 1st recipient Sterling medal, Barren Found., 1985, Lifetime Achievement award in broadcasting, Ill. Broadcasters Assn., 1989, Lifetime Achievement award, WGN TV, 1998, 1st person named to Better Bus. Bur. Hall of Fame, Coun. on Better Bus. Burs., Inc., 1975. Mem. NATAS (bd. govs. 1966-76, Silver Circle award 1993), Nat. Press Found. (bd. dirs. 1991-99), Nat. Assn. Broadcasters (bd. dirs. 1952-56), Fed. Comm. Bar Assn., Broadcast Music Inc. (bd. dirs. 1953-70), Assn. Maximum Svc. Telecasters Inc. (bd. dirs. 1952-72), Broadcast Pioneers (pres., bd. dirs. 1962-73), Broadcast Pioneers Libr. (pres. 1981-84), Broadcast Pioneers Ednl. Fund Inc., Broadcasters Found. (chmn. bd. 1996-99). Office: Ward L Quaal Co PO Box 336 Winnetka IL 60093

QUACKENBUSH, JUSTIN LOWE, federal judge; b. Spokane, Wash., Oct. 3, 1929; s. Carl Clifford and Marian Huldah (Lowe) Q.; m. Marie McAtee; children: Karl Justin, Kathleen Marie, Robert Craig. Student, U. Ill., 1947-49; BA, U. Idaho, 1951; LLB, Gonzaga U., Spokane, 1957. Bar: Wash. 1957. Dep. pros. atty., Spokane County, 1957-59; ptnr. Quackenbush, Dean, Bailey & Henderson, Spokane, 1959-80; dist. judge U.S. Dist. Ct. (ea. dist.) Wash., Spokane, 1980—, now sr. judge. Part-time instr. Gonzaga U. Law Sch., 1960-67 Chmn. Spokane County Planning Commn., 1969-73. Served with USN, 1951-54. Mem. Wash. Bar Assn., Spokane County Bar Assn. (trustee 1976-78), Internat. Footprint Assn. (nat. pres. 1967), Shriners. Episcopalian. Office: US Dist Ct PO Box 1432 Spokane WA 99210-1432 Office Phone: 509-458-5280.

QUACKENBUSH, MARGERY CLOUSER, psychoanalyst, researcher; b. Reading, Pa., Apr. 30, 1938; d. Carl Brumbach and Katherine Elvina (Althouse) Clouser; m. Robert Mead Quackenbush, July 3, 1971; 1 child, Piet Robert. BFA, Pratt Inst., 1960; MA, Calif. Grad. Inst., 1982; PhD in Psychoanalysis, Internat. U. Grad. Studies, NYC, 2001. Cert. in psychoanalysis Ctr. for Modern Psychoanalytic Studies, 1992. Instr. Pratt Inst., Bklyn., 1978-79, Fashion Inst. of Tech., NYC, 1980-81; counselor Wiltwyck, Bronx Ctr., 1981-82; exec. dir. Nat. Assn. for Advancement of Psychoanalysis, NYC, 1982—; pvt. practice in psychoanalysis NYC, 1980—. Adj. prof. Union Inst., 2007. Mem. Lenox Hill Dem. Club, N.Y.C., 1993-95; spkr. various cmty. groups, 1991—. Recipient Maison Blanche award, 1959, Miriam Berkman Spotnitz award, 1992, Am. Bd. Accreditation Profl. Svc. award, 2000-04. Mem. Nat. Assn. for Advancement of Psychoanalysis, Nat. Soc. DAR, Alumni Assn. of the Ctr. for Modern Psych. Studies (sec. 1992-94, Alumni Assn. program dir., v.p. 1995-98), Soc. Modern Psychoanalysts. Democrat. Avocations: reading, writing, golf, horseback riding. Home: 460 E 79th St Apt 14E New York NY 10021-1447 Office: Nat Assn Advancement Psychoanalysis 80 8th Ave # 1501 New York NY 10011-5126 Personal E-mail: margeryquackenbush@yahoo.com. Business E-Mail: mq@naap.org.

QUACKENBUSH, ROBERT MEAD, artist, writer, psychoanalyst; b. Hollywood, Calif., July 23, 1929; s. Roy Maynard and Virginia (Arbogast) Q.; m. Margery Clouser, July 3, 1971; 1 child: Piet Robert. B of Profl. Arts, Art Ctr. Coll. of Design, Pasadena, Calif., 1956; grad., Ctr. Modern Psychoanalytic Studies, NYC, 1991; MSW, Fordham U., NYC, 1994; PhD, Internat. U. Grad. Studies, NYC, 1999. Art dir. Scandinavian Airlines Sys., NYC and Stockholm, 1956-61; pvt. practice NYC, 1961—; psychoanalyst/psychtherapist New Hope Guild Ctrs. for Emotionally Disturbed Children, Bklyn., 1994-2000. Educator Robert Quackenbush Studios, NYC; lectr. US, Europe, Middle East and South Am.; TV performer Ednl. TV; mem. faculty NJ Ctr. for Modern Psychoanalysis. Author/artist: over 180 books including; author: (novels) Robert Quackenbush's Treasury of Humor, 1990, Benjamin Franklin and His Friends, 1991, Evil Under the Sea, 1992, James Madison & Dolly Madison and Their Times, 1993, Arthur Ashe and His Match with History, 1994, Clara Barton and Her Victory Over Fear, 1995, Batbaby, 1997 (Gradiva award, 1998), (under pen name Richard Gobbletree) Treasure Hunt, 1997, Two Miss Mallard Mysteries: Surfboard to Peril and Stage Door to Terror, 1998, Daughter of Liberty, 1999, Flamenco to Mischief: A Miss Mallard Mystery, 2000, Miss Mallard's Case Book, 2000, Batbaby Finds a Home, 2001, Mishap in Kaiserslautern: A Miss Mallard Mystery, 2001, Henry's Awful Mistake, 2005, The Return of Pete Pack Rat, 2005; prodr.: (TV series) Dear Mr. Quackenbush and The Great American Storybook, 1988; Represented in permanent collections Whitney Mus., The Smithsonian Inst., numerous pvt. collections; prodr.: (TV series) The Miss Mallard Mysteries, 1999; (TV series, DVD) Miss Mallard Rides to the Rescue, 2005, Miss Mallard Meets Masters of Mischief, 2005. With US Army, 1951—53. Recipient 2 Citations for outstanding Troop Info. & Edn. instrn. from commdg. gen. 31st Inf. Divsn. 1953, Am. Flag Inst. award, 1976, 77, 81, 99, Edgar Allen Poe Spl. award, 1982, Gradiva award, 1998, Holland Soc. Gold medal for distinction in art and lit., 2000, Nat. Assn. for Advancement of Psychoanalysis Vison award, 2004 Mem. Mystery Writers of Am., Authors' Guild, Authors' League of Am., Holland Soc. of NY, Nat. Assn. for Advancement of Psychoanalysis (trustee, v.p. pub. info., founder, chair Gradiva awards), Soc. Modern Psychoanalysts, Soc. of Illustrators. Avocations: travel, antique restoration. Home: 460 E 79th St Apt 14E New York NY 10021-1447 Office: Robert Quackenbush Studios 223 E 78th St New York NY 10021-1222 Office Phone: 212-744-3822. Personal E-mail: rqstudios@aol.com. *Humor became a key to survival in my family when I was growing up during the depression and World War II. Thus humor became the keynote of all the books I write and illustrate - I want young readers to know that as long as we keep our sense of humor, our spirits cannot be crushed. In my analytic practice I encourage children to verbalize their emotional conflicts through art and writing projects.*

QUACKENBUSH, ROGER E., retired secondary school educator; b. Cooperstown, NY, Jan. 22, 1940; s. Eugene W. and Marion I. (Clark) Q.; m. Cathy E. Quackenbush, Mar. 31, 1973; children: Michele, Stacey, Thomas. BS, SUNY, Albany, 1961, MS, 1966; PhD, Columbia Pacific U., San Rafael, Calif., 1984; postgrad., numerous univs. Cert. permanent biology and gen. sci. tchr., N.Y. Tchr. gen. sci. and math Troy (N.Y.) Pub. Sch. System, 1961-64; tchr. earth sci. and biology Schuylerville (N.Y.) Cen. H.S., 1964-66; tchr. biology Bethlehem Cen. H.S., Delmar, NY, 1966-95; cons. advanced placement biology Niskayuna (N.Y.) H.S., 1995-96; instr. anatomy and physiology lab. Russell Sage Coll., Troy, NY, 1996-97. Mentor student tchrs., 1968-90; instr. Tchr. Expectation Student Achievement program, 1985-91; lectr. on marine mammals SUNY, Albany, 1986; instr. DNA Sci. and Tech. for h.s. students SUNY, Albany, 1996; lectr. on whales; workshop leader on use microcomputers in classroom; former mem. Mid States Commn. on Evaluation Local H.S.'s; past mem. adv. bd. Upstate N.Y. Jr. Sci. and Humanities Symposium; test writer Regents biology exams. N.Y. State Dept. Edn.; presenter/cons. N.Y. State Edn. Dept. alt. assessment writer's workshop, 1994; leader, naturalist for whale watch trips and Kenya safaris; presenter for DNA-molecular biology lab. techniques; presenter on use of Tex. Instruments calculator and the Calculator Based Lab. sys. in the sci. classroom; mem Select Seminar on Evaluating Tchrs., 1985; mem. Wells Conf. Regents Biology Syllabus Revision, 1991; faculty cons. AP Biology reading Coll. Bd. Advanced Placement Program, 1997-98; cons. DNA molecular biology technology Greater Capital Region Tchr. Ctr., 1988-2001; instnl. animal care and use com. N.Y. State Health Dept., 1999-2001. Author: Once Upon a Yesterday, 2000, Adrift Upon the Air, 2001, Sketches of the Mind, 2002; editor/writer of alternative assessments for N.Y. State Edn. Dept., 1993-94; contbr. articles to profl. jours.; author: Swahili Phrasebook, 1993. Hon. admissions liaison officer USAF Acad., 1988. Named Hon. Grad. Marshal, 1991, 1994, hon. NY State Biology Mentor, 1995, Fla. Master Naturalist, 2006; recipient Eagle award, Boy Scouts Am., 1956, Excellence in Tchg. award, 1989, letter of commendation, U. Chgo., 1978, MIT, 1985, US Army, 1989, Tufts U., 1990, 1994, 1997, Tchr. of Yr. award, 1985, Golub Tchr.-Scholar award, SUNY, 1991, 1996, hon. mention, Tandy Tech. Scholar award, 1994, Tandy Tech. Scholar prize for excellence in sci. tchg., 1995, Outstanding Tchr. award, U. Chgo., 1995; grantee NSF, 1965, 1967, 1968, 1972, 1987, 1990, Future Directions, 1990, Greenwall Found., 1993; Chpt. II grantee, NY State Dept. Edn., 1987. Mem.: SAR, BALSA, NEA, NEA of NY, Sci. Tchrs. Assn. NY State (past sect. dir., past state bd. dirs.), Cetacean Soc. Internat., Am. Cetacean Soc., Soc. Marine Mammalogy, Nat. Assn. Biology Tchrs., Sons of Union Vets. of the Civil War, Phi Delta Kappa. Home: 2930 Banyan Hill Ln Land O Lakes FL 34639-6785 Personal E-mail: rogquacken@yahoo.com.

QUACKENBUSH, SCHUYLER, engineer, consultant; b. Plainfield, NJ, June 9, 1953; s. Arthur David and Nancy Chivvis Quackenbush; m. Lisa Lieberman; children: Christopher, Shanna, Adric. BS, Princeton U., NJ, 1975; MSEE, Ga. Inst. Tech., Atlanta, 1980; PhD, Ga. Inst. Tech., 1985. Mem. tech. staff AT&T Bell Labs., Murry Hill, NJ, 1986—97, AT&T Labs., Florham Park, NJ, 1997—2002; pres. Audio Rsch. Labs., Scotch Plains, NJ, 2002—. Chair, mpeg audio subgrp. Internat. Standards Orgn., Geneva, 2000—. Fellow: Audio Engring. Soc.; mem.: IEEE. Office: Audio RschLabs 336 Park Ave Ste 200 Scotch Plains NJ 07090

QUADAY-GRAY, AILENE DIANN, retired speech pathology/audiology services professional; b. Blue Earth, Minn., Aug. 26, 1937; d. Carl Frederick Quaday and Arlene Alice Pringle; m. Maurice Clayton Maine, Aug. 18, 1956 (div. May 1975); children: Keith Mauricé, Kevin Richard; m. Francis Moulton Gray Jr., May 7, 1989 (dec. Dec. 1994). BA, St. Cloud State U., Minn., 1971; postgrad., San Diego State U., 1979—81, various colls., 1971—85, West Hills and Fresno Pacific, 1987—94. Lic. speech pathologist Calif., cert. presch. tchr. Calif. Speech pathologist Comprehensive Health Ctrs., Inc., San Diego, 1981—82; speech pathologist pilot project Kings Rehab. Ctr., Inc., Hanford, Calif., 1983; tchr., dir. First Luth Ch. Presch., Hanford, 1983—85; speech specialist Fresno County Office Edn., Calif., 1985—87, Kings County Office of Edn., Hanford, 1987—91, Reef-Sunset Unified Sch. Dist., Avenal, Kettleman City, Calif., 1991—94, Kingsburg Joint Union Charter Elem. Schs., Calif., 1994—2001; part-time presch. speech therapist Sanger Unified Sch. Dist., Calif., 2001—02. Cons. Headstart: Tech. Assistance Mgmt., 1971-72; speech therapist Selma Unified Sch. Dist., Calif., 2001-04. Vice chmn. bd. edn. St. James Luth., San Diego, 1979-80; del. Consortium on County Health Needs, Wright County, Minn., 1972-75; advisor Wright County Minn. Commrs. on Handicapped, 1973-75; vol. children's waiting rm. Navy Hosp., Bremerton, Wash., 1976-77; tchr. Sunday sch., evangelism chair Calvary United Meth. Ch., Arnold's Park, Iowa. Democrat. Methodist. Avocations: playing flute, teaching language, reading, poetry. Home: 2408-25th St # 47 Spirit Lake IA 51360

QUADE, VICKI, editor, writer, playwright, theater producer; b. Chgo., Aug. 15, 1953; d. Victor and Virginia (Uryasz) Q.; m. Charles J. White III, Feb. 15, 1986 (div. Aug. 1996); children: Michael, David, Catherine. BS in Journalism, No. Ill. U., 1974. Staff reporter news divsn. The News-Tribune, LaSalle, Ill., 1975-77; staff writer news divsn. The News-Sun, Waukegan, Ill., 1977-81; staff writer ABA Jour., Chgo., 1981-85; mng. editor ABA Press, Chgo., 1985-90, editor, 1990-2000, sr. editor, 1994-2000. Author: (poetry) Rain and Other Poems, 1976, Laughing Eyes, 1979, Two Under the Covers, 1981, (biography) I Remember Bob Collins, 2000; playwright Late Nite Catechism, 1993, Room for Advancement, 1994, Mr. Nanny, 1997, (musical) Lost in Wonderland, 1998, (musical) Here Come the Famous Brothers, 2001, Put the Nuns in Charge!, 2005, Sunday School Cinema, 2007; prodr. Late Nite Catechism, Mr. Nanny, Here Come the Famous Brothers, Christopher Carter Messes With Your Mind, Forever Plaid, Cast on a Hot Tin Roof, Verbatim Verboten, Put the Nuns in Charge; U.S. premiere of Drapes, 2005; contbr. to numerous anthologies and publs.; contbd. to: 20th Century Chicago: 100 Years, 100 Voices (contbd. the year 1953), owner/operator Crossroads Theater, Naperville, Ill Recipient numerous awards from Soc. Nat. Assn. Publs., AP, UPI, Spirit of Benedict award Benedictine Sisters Chgo., 2003, Partners in Mission award Sisters of the Living Word, 2005 Mem. Am. Soc. Bus. Press Editors (award), Chgo. Newspaper Guild (award), Am. Soc. Assn. Execs. (Gold Circle award 1989, 90). Avocations: travel, photography.

QUADRI, FAZLE RAB, lawyer, government official; b. Dacca, Pakistan, Aug. 5, 1948; came to U.S., 1967; s. Gholam Moula and Jehan (Ara) Q.; children: Ryan F., Tania M. AA, Western Wyo. Coll., 1969; BA, Calif. State U., 1972; JD, Western State U., 1978; postgrad. cert. in criminal advocacy, U. Calif., San Francisco, 1988. Cert. program of learning for lawyers, Harvard Law Sch., 2002, 03, 04. Sr. adminstrv. analyst San Bernardino County, Calif., 1978-82, acting legis. adv. Calif., 1982, sr. legis. analyst Calif., 1982-90, county legis. analyst Calif., 1990-93, acting pub. defender Calif., 1984; dist. counsel Mojave Desert Air Quality Mgmt. Dist., Victorville, Calif., 1993—; dist. cousnel Antelope Valley Air Pollution Control Dist., 1997—. Local gov. rep. State Hazardous Waste Mgmt. Coun., Sacramento, 1982-84; county rep. South Coast Air Quality Mgmt. Dist., El Monte, Calif., 1983-87. Trustee Law Libr., 1984-85, 93-95. Mem. ABA, Calif. Bar Assn. (mem. exec. com. pub. law sect. 2000—05, chair 2003-04.), Calif. State U. Alumni Assn. (bd. dirs. 1985-86), Masons, Shriners. Republican. Islamic. Avocations: reading, music, travel, Karate, water sports. Office: Mojave Desert AQMD 14306 Park Ave Victorville CA 92392-2310 Office Phone: 760-245-1661. Business E-Mail: quadri@mdaqmd.ca.gov.

QUADROS, ORPHA MAY, retired social worker, educator; b. Park City, Mont., Dec. 25, 1915; d. John Howard and Helen Elinor (Donielson) Dasch; m. Milton Francis Quadros; 1 child, Kevin Karl. BS, U. Oreg., Eugene, 1938; attended Columbia U., NYC, 1945—46; MSW, U. Calif., Berkeley, 1952. LCSW Calif., diplomate. Caseworker Oreg. State Pub. Welfare Commn., Astoria, 1941—45; caseworker, office mgr. ARC, Salem, Oreg., 1943—45, Hayward, Calif., 1946—48; caseworker, supr. Santa Clara County Welfare Office, 1949—51; juvenile probation officer Santa Clara County, San Jose, Calif., 1951—52; psychiat. social worker Adult and Child Guidance Clinic, San Jose, 1952—56, San Jose State U., 1956—83, counselor, 1957—77, prof. social work, 1977—81, acting dean, 1981—83; ret., 1983. Kindergarten vol. Pomeroy Sch., San Jose, Calif., 1999—2004; sec. Santa Clara Dem. Party at The Villages, San Jose, Calif., 1949—73, bd. mem., 1949—73; bd. chairwoman CLE, 1940—93. Named Vol. of Yr., Pomeroy Sch., 2003. Mem.: NASW (local chairperson 1960—64). Democrat. Home: 8662 American Oak Dr San Jose CA 95135-2149

QUAID, DENNIS, actor; b. Houston, Apr. 9, 1954; s. William Rudy and Juanita B.; m. P.J. Soles, Nov. 25, 1978 (div. Jan. 23, 1983); m. Meg Ryan, Feb. 14, 1991 (div. July 16, 2001); 1 child, Jack Henry; m. Kimberly Buffington, July 4, 2004. Student, U. Houston, 1972-75. Actor (films) Crazy Mama, 1975, I Never Promised You A Rosegarden, 1977, Sept. 30, 1955, 1977, Our Winning Season, 1978, The Seniors, 1978, Breaking Away, 1979, G.O.R.P., 1980, The Long Riders, 1980, Caveman, 1981, All Night Long, 1981, The Night the Lights Went Out in Georgia, 1981, Tough Enough, 1983, Jaws 3-D, 1983, The Right Stuff, 1983, Dreamscape, 1984, Enemy Mine, 1985, Innerspace, 1987, The Big Easy, 1987, Suspect, 1987, D.O.A., 1988, Everybody's All-American, 1988, Great Balls of Fire, 1989, Postcards from the Edge, 1990, Come See the Paradise, 1990, Undercover Blues, 1993, Wilder Napalm, 1993, Flesh and Bone, 1993, Wyatt Earp, 1994, Something to Talk About, 1995, Dragonheart, 1996, Criminal Element, 1997, Going West, 1997, Gang Related, 1997, Savior, 1997, Switchback, 1997, The Parent Trap, 1998, On Any Given Sunday, 1999, Frequency, 2000, Traffic, 2000, The Rookie, 2002, Far From Heaven, 2002, Cold Creek Manor, 2003, The Alamo, 2004, The Day After Tomorrow, 2004, Flight of the Phoenix, 2004, In Good Company, 2004, Yours, Mine and Ours, 2005, Am. Dreamz, 2006; (theatre) The Last of the Knucklemen, 1983, True West, 1984; (TV movies) Are You In the House Alone?, 1978, Amateur Night at the Dixie Bar and Grill, 1979, Bill, 1981, Johnny Belinda, 1982, Bill: On His Own, 1983, Everything That Rises (also dir, prod.), 1998, Dinner with Friends, 2001; (TV appearances) Baretta, 1977. Named Hollywood Walk of Fame, 2005. Office: The William Morris Agy One William Morris Pl Beverly Hills CA 90212 *An artist must take chances in performing his craft. If he is to succeed he must be willing to fall flat on his face.*

QUAIL, PETER HUGH, biologist, educator; b. Australia, Feb. 4, 1944; BSc, U. Sydney, 1964, PhD, 1968. Rsch. assoc. Mich. State U./AEC Plant Rsch. Lab., East Lansing, 1968—71, U. Freiburg, Biologisches Inst., Germany, 1971—73; rsch. fellow, group leader photobiology lab. Australian Nat. U., Sch. Biol. Scis., Canberra, Australia, 1973—77; sr. fellow dept. biology Stanford (Calif.) U., Carnegie Instn., 1977—79; assoc. prof. botany U. Wis., Madison, 1979—84, prof. botany and genetics, 1984—87; rsch. dir., prof. molecular plant biology U. Calif.-Berkeley, Plant Gene Expression Ctr., 1987—89, rsch. dir., prof. dept. plant biology, 1989—. Cons. Resources Devel. Found., 1988, Rockefeller Found. Internat. Rice Rsch. Program, 1988—89; vis. scientist plant genetics Weizmann Inst. Sci., Rehovot, Israel, 1977; mem. NSF Oversight Panel, 1982; mem. rev. com. dept. energy U. Ga., Complex Carbohydrate Ctr., 1986; mem. NSF Grant Rev. Panel, 1988; mem. biochem. genetics program NSF, 1993; ad hoc mem. Biochem. Genetics/Mechanisms of Gene Expression Program, NSF Panel, 1996—2000; mem. sci. adv. com. Rockefeller Found. Biotech., Breeding and Seed Sys. for African Crops Program, 2001—. Reviewer: Dept. Energy, Plant Molecular Biology, Genes and Devel., others, mem. editl. bd.: Planta, 1980—87, Plant Physiology, 1980—87, Plant Molecular Biology, 1980—87. Recipient Commonwealth scholarship, 1961—64, Sibella MacArthur Onslow Meml. prize, 1964, Commonwealth Rsch. studentship, 1965—68, Fulbright-Hays travel grantee, 1968, Alexander von Humboldt stipend, 1971—73, Romnes Faculty fellow, U. Wis., 1984, Am. Soc. Photobiologists Rsch. award, 1988, award for disting. contbns. to photochemistry/photobiology, LI-COR Inc., 1995, Anton Lang Meml. award, Australian Soc. Plant Physiologists, 2000. Mem.: NAS, Internat. Soc. Plant Molecular Biology (bd. dirs. 1992—96), Am. Soc. Plant Physiologists (chmn. phytochrome session 1977). Office: Plant Gene Expression Ctr 800 Buchanan St Berkeley CA 94710 E-mail: quail@nature.berkeley.edu.

QUAINI, DUANE C., lawyer; b. Napa, Calif., Mar. 30, 1945; BA summa cum laude, Claremont Men's Coll., 1967; JD, Stanford U., 1970. Bar: Ill. 1970. Assoc. Sonnenschein Nath & Rosenthal LLP, Chgo., 1970—76, ptnr., 1976—, chmn., 1997—2007. Note editor Stanford Law Rev., 1969-70. Mem. exec. com. bd. visitors Stanford Law Sch., 1995—, chmn.; vice chmn. bd. Jane Addams Juvenile Ct. Found.; dir. emeritus Les Turner ALS Found. Office: Sonnenschein Nath & Rosenthal LLP 8000 Sears Tower 233 S Wacker Dr Chicago IL 60606 Office Phone: 312-876-8051. Office Fax: 312-876-7934. Business E-Mail: dquaini@sonnenschein.com. *

QUAINTON, ANTHONY CECIL EDEN, diplomat; b. Seattle, Apr. 4, 1934; s. Cecil Eden and Marjorie Josephine (Oates) Q.; m. Susan Long, Aug. 7, 1958; children: Katherine, Eden, Elizabeth. BA, Princeton U., 1955; BLitt, Oxford U., Eng., 1958; LHD (hon.), LaRoche Coll., Pitts., 2006. Rsch. fellow St. Antony's Coll., Oxford, 1958-59; with Fgn. Svc., State Dept., 1959-97; vice consul Sydney, Australia, 1960-62; Urdu lang. trainee, 1962-63; 2d sec., econ. officer Am. embassy, Karachi, Pakistan, 1963-64, Rawalpindi, Pakistan, 1964-66, 2d sec., polit. officer New Delhi, 1966-69; sr. polit. officer for India Dept. State, Washington, 1969-72; 1st sec. Am. embassy, Paris, 1972-73, counselor, dep. chief mission Kathmandu, Nepal, 1973-76; amb. to Ctrl. African Empire, Bangui, 1976-78, Managua, Nicaragua, 1982—84, Kuwait, 1984—87; dir. Office for Combating Terrorism, Dept. State, Washington, 1978-81; dep. insp. gen. Dept.

State, 1987-89; amb. Lima, Peru, 1989-92; asst. sec. of state for diplomatic security Dept. State, Washington, 1992-95, dir. gen. fgn. svc., 1995-97. Exec. dir. Una Chapman Cox Found., 1998—99; vis. lectr. Princeton U., 1998—99; pres., CEO Nat. Policy Assn., 1999—2003; diplomat in residence Am. U., 2003—; cons. internat. policy com. U.S. Conf. Cath. Bishops, 1999—2005; chmn. bd. dirs. Washington Theol. Consortium; bd. dirs. Interfaith Conf. of Washington; project dir. Am. Acad. Diplomacy, 2004—05. V.p. Washington Lions Found., Pub. Diplomacy Coun.; bd. trustees LaRoche Coll., Pitts. English Speaking Union fellow, 1951-52; Marshall scholar, 1955-58; recipient Rivkin award, 1972, Herter award, 1984, Disting. Honor award Dept. State, 1997. Fellow Fgn. Policy Assn.; mem. Coun. on Fgn. Rels., Am. Fgn. Svc. Assn., Washington Inst. Fgn. Affairs, Lions Internat., Met. Club, Phi Beta Kappa. Home: 3424 Porter St NW Washington DC 20016-3126 Office Phone: 303-885-1669. Personal E-mail: aquainton@aol.com.

QUAKE, STEPHEN R., physics professor, researcher; BS in Physics, Stanford U., 1991, MS in Math., 1991; PhD in Physics, U. Oxford, 1994. Asst. prof. applied physics Calif. Inst. Tech., 1996—99, assoc. prof., 1999—2002, assoc. prof. applied physics and physics, 2002—03, prof., 2003—04, Thomas E. and Doris Everhard prof., 2004; prof. dept. bioengineering Stanford U. Mem. Quake Group, Calif. Inst. Tech., Pasadena, CSULA-Calif. Inst. Tech. Partnerships for Rsch. and Edn. in Materials (PREM) Collaborative, 2004—; co-founder Fluidigm Corp. Contbr. articles to profl. jours. Named one of Brilliant 10, Popular Sci. mag., 2003; named to TR100 "Young Innovators that will create the Future", MIT Tech. Rev., 2002; recipient Career award, 1997, R29 "First" award, NIH, 1997, Pioneer award, 2004; Packard fellow, 1999. Achievements include research in fundamental and applied topics in biophysics, specifically single molecule science. Office: Stanford U Dept Bioengineering James H Clark Ctr Rm E300 318 Campus Dr Stanford CA 94305 Office Phone: 650-736-7890. E-mail: quake@stanford.edu.

QUALE, ANDREW CHRISTOPHER, JR., lawyer; b. Boston, July 7, 1942; s. Andrew Christopher and Luella (Meland) Q.; m. Sally Sterling Ellis, Oct. 15, 1977; children: Andrew, Addison. BA magna cum laude, Harvard U., 1963, LLB cum laude, 1966; postgrad., Cambridge U., Eng., 1966-67. Bar: Mass. 1967, N.Y. 1971. Fellow Internat. Legal Ctr., Bogota, Colombia, 1967-68; cons. Republic of Colombia, Bogota, 1968-69; assoc. Cleary, Gottlieb, Steen and Hamilton, NYC, 1969-75; ptnr. Coudert Brothers, NYC, 1975-82, Sidley Austin, LLP, NYC, 1982—. Adj. prof. Sch. of Law U. Va., Charlottesville, 1976—88; cons. privatizations and internat. financings World Bank, Inter-Am. Devel. Bank, UN, Harvard Inst. Internat. Devel., 1982—; bd. dirs. Battell Stoeckel Assocs., Norfolk. Contbr. articles to profl. jours. Pres. Bronxville (NY) Sch. Bd., 1991-93; founder, bd. dirs. Bronxville Sch. Found., 1991-95, 96-2002; bd. dirs. Coun. of the Ams., Youth Orch. Am., Doolittle Lake Co. Knox fellow, 1966—67. Mem.: ABA, The Little Forum (co-chair Bronxville 2000—03), Colombian-Am. Assn. (v.p., bd. dirs.), NY State Bar Assn., Assn. Bar City NY (chmn. Inter-Am. affairs com. 1982—85), Anglers' Club, Norfolk (Conn.) Country Club, Bronxville Field Club. Office: Sidley Austin LLP 787 7th Ave New York NY 10019 Office Phone: 212-839-7360.

QUALE, JOHN CARTER, lawyer; b. Boston, Aug. 16, 1946; s. Andrew C. and Luella (Meland) Q.; m. Diane Zipursky, Jan. 19, 1992; children: Virginia Ann, Jane Harris, John Andrew; stepchildren: Rachel Goldman, Alisa Goldman. AB cum laude, Harvard U., 1968, JD cum laude, 1971. Bar: Mass. 1971, D.C. 1972. Assoc. Kirkland & Ellis, Washington, 1971-78, ptnr., 1978-83, Wiley, Rein & Fielding, Washington, 1983-96, Skadden, Arps, Slate, Meagher & Flom L.L.P., Washington, 1996—. Spkr. mass media trade groups. Contbr. articles to profl. jours. Trustee Fed. Comm. Bar Assn. Found., 1992-93. Mem. ABA, Fed. Comm. Bar Assn. (treas. 1982-83, 98-99, mem. exec. com. 1993-98), Barristers, Met. Club. Office: Skadden Arps Slate Meagher & Flom LLP 1440 New York Ave NW Washington DC 20005-2111 Office Phone: 202-371-7200. Business E-Mail: jquale@skadden.com.

QUALLEY, CHARLES ALBERT, art educator; b. Creston, Iowa, Mar. 19, 1930; s. Albert Olaf and Cleora (Dietrick) Q.; m. Betty Jean Griffith, Nov. 26, 1954; children: Janet Lynn, John Stuart. BFA, Drake U., 1952; MA, U. Iowa, 1956, MFA, 1958; EdD, Ill. State U., 1967. Art tchr. Des Moines Pub. Schs., 1952, 1954—55; critic art tchr. U. Iowa, 1955-57; prof. fine arts U. Colo., Boulder, 1958-90, prof. emeritus, 1990—, chmn. dept. fine arts, 1968-71, assoc. chmn., 1981-82. Vis. prof. Inst. for Shipboard Edn., semester at sea, 1979, vis. disting. prof. Ill. State U., 1985. Author: Safety in the Art Room, 1986, rev. edit., 2005; contbg. editor Sch. Arts, 1978-85, mem. editl. adv. bd., 1985-87; author column Safetypoint, 1981-85. Served with AUS, 1952-54, Korea. Fellow Nat. Art Edn. Assn. (v.p. 1980-82, pres. 1987-89, dir. conv. svcs. 1990-99, Art Educator of Yr. 1993); mem. Nat. Art Edn. Found. (trustee 1987—, chair bd. trustees 1996-2004), Colo. Art Edn. Assn. (editor 1965-67, 75, pres. 1976- 78), Delta Phi Delta, Omicron Delta Kappa, Pi Kappa Delta. Home: 9025 Natalie Ave NE Albuquerque NM 87111-3131

QUALLS, BARRY V., literature professor; b. Ky. BA, Fla. State U., Tallahassee; MA, PhD, Northwestern U. Asst. prof. English to prof. Rutgers U., New Brunswick, NJ, 1971—, interim v.p. undergraduate edn., 2006—. Chair English dept. Rutgers U., 1989—97. Contbr. articles to profl. publs.; author: The Secular Pilgrims of Victorian Fiction: The Novel as Book of Life, 1982. Recipient US Prof. of Yr. award, Carnegie Found. for Advancement of Tchg. and Coun. for Advancement and Support of Edn., 2006. Mem.: Phi Beta Kappa (sec. Alpha chpt. NJ). Office: Rutgers U Undergraduate Edn Old Queens Bldg Rm 302 83 Somerset St New Brunswick NJ 08901 Office Phone: 732-932-4001. Office Fax: 732-932-1956. E-mail: qualls@oldqueens.rutgers.edu. *

QUALLS, ROBERT L., manufacturing and bank executive, educator, retired state official; b. Burnsville, Miss., Nov. 6, 1933; s. Wes E. and Letha (Parker) Q.; m. Carolyn Morgan, Feb. 10, 1979 (dec. July 1996); 1 child, Stephanie Elizabeth; m. Nancy Martin, Sept. 11, 1999. BS, Miss. State U., 1954, MS, 1958; PhD, La. State U., 1962; LLD, Whitworth Coll., 1974; DBA (hon.), U. of the Ozarks, 1984. Prof., chmn. div. econs. and bus. Belhaven Coll., Jackson, Miss., 1962-66, asst. to pres., 1965-66; asst. prof. finance Miss. State U., State College, 1967-69, adj. prof., 1969-73; sr. v.p., chmn. venture com. Bancorp South, Tupelo, Miss., 1969-73; v.p. Wesleyan Coll., Macon, Ga., 1974; pres. U. of the Ozarks, Clarksville, Ark., 1974-79; mem. cabinet Bill Clinton Gov. of Ark., 1979-80; exec. v.p. Bank of America, Little Rock, 1980-85, chmn., CEO, dir. Harrison, Ark., 1985-86; pres., dir. First Bank Fin. Services, Inc., 1980-85, Advt. Assocs., Inc., 1980-85; pres., chief oper. officer Baldor Electric Co., Ft. Smith, Ark., 1986-91, CEO, 1992-97, vice chmn., 1998—2000, dir., mem. exec. com., 1987—, chmn. corp. governance com., presiding non-mgmt. dir., 2004—. Mktg. cons. Ill. Central Industries, Chgo., 1964; mem. faculty, thesis examiner Stonier Grad. Sch. Banking, Rutgers U., 1973-86; mem. faculty Miss. Sch. Banking, U. Miss., 1973-78; course coord. Sch. Banking of the South, La. State U., 1978-88, Banking Sch., Duke U., 1977; lectr. Southwestern Sch. Banking, So. Meth. U., 1983; adj. prof. bus. adminstrn. U. Central Ark., 1985-86; bd. dirs. Bank of Ozarks, 1997—, mem. audit com., chmn. corp. governance com., presiding ind. dir., 2003—. Author: Entrepreneurial Wit and Wisdom, 1986; co-author: Strategic Planning for Colleges and Universities: A Systems Approach to Planning and Resource Allocation, 1979; mem. editorial adv. bd.: Bank Mktg. Mag., 1984-86. Chmn. cmty. svc. and continuing edn. com. Tupelo Cmty. Devel. Found., 1972-73; mem. Miss. 4-H adv. coun., 1969; active Boys Scouts Am.; mem. Lee County Dem. Exec. Com., 1973-74; trustee Walton Family Found., 1975-79, Oklahoma City U., 1990-95; trustee, mem. exec. com. U. Ozarks, 1982-88, chmn. bd., 2000-03; mem. Pres.'s Roundtable U. Ctrl. Ark., 1982-87; mem. exec. com. Coll. Bus. Adv. Bd., U. Ark., Little Rock, 1980-85; bd. dirs. U. Ark. Med. Sch. Found., 1991-97, Ark. Inst., 1991-94; chmn. bd. Petit Jean Youth Found., 2001-03; mem. Clarksville Light and Water Commn., 2000-01; elder Clarksville Presbyn. Ch., 1997-2000; bd. dirs. Vera Lloyd Presbyn. Home and Family Svcs., 2004-05. Lt. AUS, 1954-56. Found. for Econ. Edn. fellow, 1964; Ford Found. faculty research fellow Vanderbilt U., 1963-64; recipient Pillar of Progress award Johnson County, 1977 Mem. Am. Bankers Assn. (mktg. planning and rsch. com. 1972-73), Ark. Coun. Ind. Colls. and Univs. (chmn. 1978-79), Johnson County C. of C. (pres. 1977), Fort Smith C. of C. (dir. 1995-98), Blue Key, Omicron Delta Kappa, Delta Sigma Pi, Sigma Phi Epsilon (citation 1977), Beta Gamma Sigma, Masons (32 deg.), Clarksville Rotary (pres. 1979). Presbyterian. Personal E-mail: nancy_qualls@msn.com.

QUALLS, ROXANNE, mayor; D (hon.), Cin. State Tech. and C.C., 1996. Former exec. dir. Women Helping Women; former dir. No. Ky. Rape Crisis Ctr.; former dir. Cin. office Ohio Citizen Action; councilwoman City of Cin., 1991-93, mayor, 1993-98, founder youth summer jobs program Artworks, Cin. Homeownership Partnership. Former chairperson Cin. City Council's Intergovtl. Affairs and Environment Com.; former vice chairperson Community Devel., Housing and Zoning Com.; mem. Gov.'s Commn. on Storage and Use of Toxic and Hazardous Materials, Solid Waste Adv. Com. of State of Ohio, Gov.'s Waste Minimization Task Force; former chair bd. commrs. Cin. Met. Housing Authority; bd. dirs. Shuttlesworth Housing Found. Hon. chair Friends of Women's Studies; mem. Jr. League Adv. Coun.; bd. dirs. Nat. Underground Railroad Freedom Ctr., Ctr. Voting and Democracy; past bd. didrs. No. Ky. Cath. Commn. Soc. Jusitice. Recipient Woman of Distinction award Girl Scouts U.S., 1992, Woman of Distinction award Soroptimists, 1993, Outstanding Achievement award Cin. Woman's Polit. Caucus, 1993, Women of Achievement award YWCA, 1994, Outstanding Svc. award Ohio Pub. Employees Lawyers Assn., 1996, Pub. Offcl. of Yr. award State of Cinn., 1996, Nat. Assn. Soc. Workers, 1996, Nat. Homebuilders Assn., 1997. Mem. Nat. Assn. Regional Couns. (former pres., 1st v.p., 2d v.p.), Ohio Ky. Ind. Regional Coun. Govts. (1st v.p., 2d v.p.). Fax: 513-352-5201.

QUALSET, CALVIN O., agronomist, educator; b. Newman Grove, Nebr., Apr. 24, 1937; s. Herman Qualset and Adeline (Hanson) Vakoc; m. Kathleen Boehler; children: Douglas, Cheryl, Gary. BS, U. Nebr., 1958; MS, U. Calif., Davis, 1960, PhD, 1964. Asst. prof. U. Tenn., Knoxville, 1964-67; from asst. prof. to assoc. prof. U. Calif., Davis, 1967, prof., 1973-94, prof. emeritus, 1994—, chmn. dept. agronomy and range sci., 1975-81, 91-94, assoc. dean Coll. Agrl. and Environ. Sci., 1981-86, dir. Genetic Resources Conservation Program, 1985—2002, dir. Agrl. Sustainability Inst., 2005—06. Sci. liaison officer U.S. AID, Washington, 1985-93, rsch. adv. com., 1989-92; nat. plant genetic resources bd. USDA, Washington, 1982-88; trustee Am. Type Culture Collection, 1993-99, Internat. Rice Rsch. Inst., 1999-2004, Agronomic Sci. Found., 1999—, chmn., 2006—. Contbr. over 300 articles to profl. jours. and tech. publs. Bd. dirs. Auksuciai Found., 1999—; contbr. to wheat improvement in Mex. citation, 1988. Fulbright fellow, Australia, 1976, Yugoslavia, 1984; recipient Pub. Plant Breeding award U.S. Coun. Comml. Plant Breeders, 1996, Master Alumni award U. Nebr., 1997, Charles Black award Coun. Agrl. Sci. and Tech., 2002, William L. Brown award Mo. Bot. Garden, 2002, Citation for Excellence, U. Calif., Calif. Aggie Alumni Assn., 2003, Citation for contbns. to Calif. agr. State Calif. Senate, 2003, award of excellence Coll. Agrl. and Environ. Sci., U. Calif., Davis, 2003, Citation for contbns. to agr. in Lithuania, 2004, 06. Fellow AAAS (chmn. agr. sect. 1992), Am. Soc. Agronomy (pres. 1994, agronomy honoree Calif. sect. 2001), Crop Sci. Soc. Am. (pres. 1989, editor-in-chief 1980-84, Frank N. Meyer medal for plant genetic resources 2006); mem. Soc. Conservation Biology, Soc. Econ. Botany, Genetic Soc. Am., Internat. Union Biol. Scis. (mem. U.S. nat. com. 2000-06), Am. Genetic Assn., U. Nebr. Alumni Assn. Achievements include development of more than 18 cultivars of wheat, oat, triticale. Office: U Calif Genetic Res Conserv Prog One Shields Ave Davis CA 95616

QUAM, LOIS, insurance company executive; b. June 12, 1961; m. Matt Entenza; children: Ben, Steve. BA magna cum laude, Macalaster Coll., Minn.; MA in Philos., Politics, Econs., U. Oxford, 1985. Dir. rsch. and eval. UnitedHealth Group, 1989-93, v.p. pub. sector svcs., 1993; sr. adv. White House Task Force Nat. Health Care Reform, 1993-96; CEO AARP/United divsn. UnitedHealth Group, Mpls., 1996-98, exec. v.p., CEO Ovations, 2002—06, exec. v.p., pres. public & sr. markets group, 2006—. Bd. dirs. George C. Marshall Found., Coun. Fgn. Rels.; adv. com. Am. Democracy Inst. Mem. editl. bd.: British Med. Jour.; contbr. articles to profl. jours. Bd. trustees Macalester Coll. Named one of Next 20 Female CEOs, Pink Mag. & Forté Found., 2006, 50 Most Powerful Women in Bus., Fortune mag., 2006; recipient America-Norway Heritage Fund award, Nordmann-Forbundett Norway-Am. Assn. Mailing: UnitedHealth Group PO Box 1459 Minneapolis MN 55440-1459 *

QUAN, GANG, engineering educator; m. Yanjun Tian, 1998; children: Joy Tianlin, Cathy Tianlu. PhD, U. Notre Dame, Ind., 2001. Asst. prof. U. SC Columbia, 2002—. Recipient Faculty Early Career award, NSF, 2006—. Mem.: IEEE (corr. Best Paper award design automation conf. 2001). Office Phone: 803-777-5872.

QUAN, STUART FUN, internist, educator; b. San Francisco, May 16, 1949; s. Stuart Fun and Mabel (Wing) Q.; m. Diana Lee, Dec. 18, 1971; children: Jason Stuart, Jeremy Ryan-Stuart. AB, U. Calif., Berkeley, 1970; MD, U. Calif., San Francisco, 1974. Diplomate Am. Bd. Internal Medicine, Am. Bd. Pulmonary Diseases, Am. Bd. Critical Care Medicine, Am. Bd. Sleep Medicine. Intern in internal medicine U. Wis., Madison, 1974-75, resident, 1975-77; fellow in critical care and emergency medicine U. Calif., San Francisco, 1977-79; fellow in pulmonary medicine U. Ariz., Tucson, 1979-80, from instr. to assoc. prof. medicine, 1980-86, assoc. prof. medicine, 1986-1992, prof. medicine & anesthesiology, 1992—2006, prof. emeritus, 2006—, med. dir. respiratory care, 1980—; med. dir. ICU Univ. Med. Ctr., Tucson, 1980-87; med. dir. Kindred Hosp., Tucson, 1994—; dir. Sleep Disorders Ctr. U. Ariz., Tucson, 1984—, chief pulmonary and crit. care medicine sect., 1987—, assoc. head dept. medicine, 1995—2006, prof. pub. health, 2002—06. Chmn. and cons. adv. panel on anesthesia and respiratory devices FDA, 1987-89; vis. prof. medicine Harvard Med. Sch., 1987-; mem. Am. Bd. Sleep Medicine, 1991-96; mem. adv. bd. Nat. Ctr. Sleep Disorder Rsch., 2002—; mem. rev. com. internal medicine Accreditation Council on Graduate Med. Edn., 2005—; co-chmn. test writing com. sleep medicine Am. Bd. Internal Medicine. Co-author: Respiratory Diseases--A Pathophysiological Approach, 1984; editor-in-chief Jour. Clinical Sleep Medicine, 2005-; contbd. chpts. to various books; contbr. numerous articles to med. jours. Pres. Gymnastics Support Orgn., Tucson, 1985-87. Recipient Helmut S. Schmidt award, Am. Bd. Sleep Medicine, 1995, Nathaniel Kletman award Disting. Svc., Am. Acad. Sleep Medicine, 2005. Fellow Am. Coll. Chest Physicians, Am. Acad. Sleep Medicine (chmn. accreditation com. 1995-96, pres. 1999-2000, bd. dirs. 1996-2005); mem. Am. Thoracic Soc., Am. Fedn. Clin. Rsch., Nat. Assn. Med. Dirs. Respiratory Care, Soc. for Critical Care Medicine, Phi Beta Kappa, Alpha Omega Alpha. Avocations: skiing, hiking, swimming. Office: U Ariz Div Respiratory Scis 1501 N Campbell Ave Tucson AZ 85724-0001 Business E-Mail: squan@arc.arizona.edu.

QUANDT, JOSEPH EDWARD, lawyer, educator; b. Port Huron, Mich., May 21, 1963; s. Herbert Raymond and Mary Katherine (West) Q.; m. Christine Ann Reilly, Aug. 21, 1993. BA, Oakland U., 1990; JD, Thomas M. Cooley Law Sch., Lansing, Mich., 1993. Bar: Mich. 1994, U.S. Dist. Ct. (ea. and we. dists.) Mich. 1994. Exec. dir. Lord & Taylor, Sterling Heights, Mich., 1985-90; compliance and enforcement specialist Mich. Dept. Environ. Quality, Lansing, 1990-93, adv. bd., 1997—; assoc. Stowe, Draling & Boyd, Traverse City, Mich., 1993-94, Smith & Johnson, 1994-98; ptnr. Zimmerman, Kuhn, Darling, Boyd, Quandt & Phelps, PLC, 1998—. Lectr., commentator Inst. CLE, Ann Arbor, Mich., 1994—; adj. prof. Thomas M. Cooley Law Sch., 1997—; co-chair environ. law sect., mem. Environ. Law Coun. State Bar Mich., chair, natural resources sect. Contbr. articles to profl. jours. Bd. dirs. Involved Citizens Enterprises, Traverse City, 1995—. Mem. Nat. Honor Soc. for Polit. Scientists, Ancient Order Hibernians, Pi Sigma Alpha. Republican. Roman Catholic. Avocations: ice hockey, golf, fly fishing. Office: Zimmerman Kuhn Darling Boyd Quandt & Phelps PLC 412 S Union St Traverse City MI 49684-2404 Office Phone: 231-947-7900. Business E-Mail: jequandt@zimmerman-kuhn.com.

QUANDT, RICHARD EMERIC, economics professor; b. Budapest, Hungary, June 1, 1930; arrived in US, 1949, naturalized, 1954; s. Richard F. and Elisabeth Q. Quandt; m. Jean H. Briggs, Aug. 6, 1955; 1 child, Stephen. BA, Princeton U., NJ, 1952; MA, Harvard U., 1955, PhD, 1957; Dr. Econs. (hon.), Budapest U. Econs. Scis., 1991, Kossuth Lajos U., Hungary, 1994, Gödöllö Agrl. U., 1995, Comenius U., Slovakia, 1996; DrLaws (hon.), Queens U., Can., 1996. Mem. faculty Princeton U., 1956-95, prof. econs., 1964-95, prof. emeritus, sr. rsch. economist, 1995—, Hughes-Rogers prof. econs., 1976-95, chmn. dept., 1968-71, 85-88; dir. Fin. Rsch. Ctr., 1982-95; rsch. prof. Ford Found., 1967-68. Cons. Anderson Assocs., 1959—61, Internat. Air Transport Assn., 1974—75, NY Stock Exch., 1976—77, NY State Dept. Edn., 1978; sr. cons. Mathematica, Inc., 1961—67; editl. adviser Holt, Rinehart & Winston, 1968—72; adviser Am-Hungarian Found., 1977—78; vis. prof. Birkbeck Coll., 1981, U. Leicester, 1989—92; mem. Census Adv. Com., 1983—86; fin. adviser Inst. Rsch. History, 1986; sr. advisor Andrew W. Mellon Found., 1989—; mem. adv. coun. Budapest U. Econ. Scis., 1992—93; mem. adv. com. Coll. Fin. and Acctg., Budapest, 1993—94; bd. dirs. Ctr. Econ. Rsch. and Grad. Edn.-Econ. Inst. Found., Prague, 2002—05. Author (with J. M. Henderson): Microeconomic Theory: A Mathematical Approach, 1958, 3d edit., 1980; author: (with W. L. Thorp) The New Inflation, 1959; author: (with B. G. Malkiel) Strategies and Rational Decisions in the Securities Option Market, 1969; editor: The Demand for Travel: Theory and Measurement, 1970; author: The Econometrics of Disequilibrium, 1988, The Changing Landscape in Eastern Europe: A Personal Perspective on Philanthropy and Technology Transfer, 2002; author: (with P. Asch) Ractrack Betting: The Professor's Guide to Strategies, 1986; author: (with H. S. Rosen) The Conflict Between Equilibrium and Disequilibrium Theories, 1988; editor (with S.H. Goldfeld): Studies in Nonlinear Estimation, 1976; editor: (with S. M. Goldfeld) Nonlinear Methods in Econometrics, 1972; editor: (with M. Peston) Prices, Competition and Equilibrium, 1986; editor: (with R. Ekman) Technology and Scholarly Communication, 1999; editor: (with A. Lass) Library Automation Transitional Societies, 2000, Union Catalogs at the Crossroads, 2004; assoc. editor: Econometrica, 1976—80, Jour. Am. Statis. Assn., 1974—80, Bell Jour. Econs., Jour. Comparative Econs., 1988—91, Empirica, 1988—93; mem. editl. bd. Applied Econs., Econs. Planning Rev. Econ. and Stats., 1980—91; exec. editor: Oxford U. Press, 2001—; translator: If Dogs Could Talk (V. Csányi), 2005; contbr. articles to profl. jours. Trustee Corvina Found., 1992—. Recipient Merit citation, Jagiellonian U., Poland, 1991, medal Merentibus, 1998, Gold medal, Eötvös Lóránd U., 1991, Order of Merit, Govt. of Hungary, 1997, Karel Englis medal, Czech Acad. Sci., 2002; Guggenheim fellow, 1958—59, McCosh fellow, 1964, NSF Sr. Postdoctoral fellow, 1971—72. Fellow: Am. Acad. Arts and Scis., Econometric Soc. (mem. coun. 1985—88), Am. Statis. Assn.; mem.: Am. Philos. Soc., Am. Econ. Assn., Hungarian Librs. Assn. (hon.). Home: 162 Springdale Rd Princeton NJ 08540-4948 Office: Princeton U Dept Econs Princeton NJ 08544-1021

QUANDT, WILLIAM BAUER, political scientist; b. LA, Nov. 23, 1941; s. William Carl and Dorothy Elaine (Bauer) Q.; m. Anna Spitzer, June 21, 1964 (div. 1980); m. Helena Cobban, Apr. 21, 1984; 1 child, Lorna. BA, Stanford U., 1963; PhD, MIT, 1968. Researcher Rand Corp., Santa Monica, Calif., 1968-72; staff mem. Nat. Security Council, Washington, 1972-74, sr. staff mem., 1977-79; assoc. prof. U. Pa., Phila., 1974-76; sr. fellow Brookings Instn., Washington, 1979-94; prof. govt. and fgn. affairs U. Va., Charlottesville, 1994—, and vice provost internat. affairs, 2000—03. Sr. assoc., Cambridge Energy Research Assocs., Mass., 1983-90. Author: Revolution and Political Leadership: Algeria, 1954-68, The Politics of Palestinian Nationalism, 1973, Decade of Decisions, 1977, Saudi Arabia in the 1980's, 1981, Camp David: Peacemaking and Politics, 1986, The United States and Egypt, 1990, Peace Process, 1993, revised edit., 2001, 3rd. edit., 2005, Between Ballots and Bullets, 1998. Social Scis. Research Council fellow, 1966; Council Fgn. Relations fellow, 1972; NDEA fellow, 1963 Fellow: Am. Acad. Arts & Sci. Mem. Council Fgn. Relations, Middle East Inst., Middle East Studies Assn. (pres. 1987-88). Avocations: tennis, travel, photography. Office: U Va Dept Politics Cabell Hall 255 Charlottesville VA 22901 Home Phone: 434-924-7896. Business E-Mail: wbq8f@virginia.edu.

QUANT, HAROLD EDWARD, retired financial services company executive, rancher; b. Aug. 21, 1948; s. Harold Atwell and Dorothy Ann Quant; m. Michelle Bumpers, June 27, 1982; children: Andrew, Angela, Emily. BSBA, San Jose State U., 1976. Account exec. Dun & Bradstreet, San Jose, Calif., 1970-81; pres. Telecredit Collection Svcs., Inc., LA, 1981-85; v.p. FCA, Arlington, Tex., 1986-90; pres., CEO Creditwatch, Inc., Arlington, 1990-2000, chmn. bd. dirs.; ret., 2000. Sgt. USMC, 1965—70, Vietnam. Mem.: City Club. Republican. Mem. United Ch. Of God. Avocation: horses.

QUARANTA, PHILIP, lawyer; b. 1960; BA, Fordham U., 1981; JD with honors, Pace U., 1985. Bar: NY 1985, US Dist. Ct. No. Dist. NY, US Dist. Ct. So. Dist. NY, US Dist. Ct. Ea. Dist. NY, registered: Japan (Gaikokuho Jimu Bengoshi). Ptnr. Wilson, Elser, Moskowitz, Edelman & Dicker LLP, White Plains, NYC, past mng. ptnr. Tokyo office. Mem.: ABA, Inter-Pacific Bar Assn., Def. Rsch. Inst., Soc. for Advancement Automotive Medicine, Soc. Automotive Engineers, NY State Bar Assn. Office: Wilson Elser Moskowitz Edelman & Dicker LLP 3 Gannett Dr White Plains NY 10604 Office Phone: 914-323-7000 ext. 4238. Office Fax: 914-323-7001. Business E-Mail: quarantap@wemed.com.

QUARLES, BRANDON, law librarian; m. Debbie Quarles; children: Ashtyn, Corban. BA, Southwestern U., 1990; JD, U. Miss., 1993; MLS, U. North Tex., 1995. Atty. Passman & Jones, Dallas, 1993—94; reference/rsch. svc. libr. U. Richmond Sch. Law, Va., 1996—98; reference libr. Baylor U. Law Sch., Waco, Tex., 1998—2000, dir. Law Libr., 2000—. Contbr. articles to profl. jours. Avocations: running, skiing, bicycling. Office: Baylor Law Libr 1114 S University Parks Dr One Bear Place, Box 97128 Waco TX 76798-7128 Office Phone: 254-710-4916. Office Fax: 254-710-2294. E-mail: brandon_quarles@baylor.edu. *

QUARLES, CARROLL ADAIR, JR., physicist, researcher; b. Abilene, Tex., Nov. 24, 1938; s. Carroll Adair and Marguerite Marie (Vollmers) Q.; m. Sonja Gale Bandy, May 14, 1971; children: Jennifer Anne, John Patrick. BA, Tex. Christian U., 1960; PhD, Princeton U., 1964. Rsch. physicist Brookhaven Nat. Lab., Upton, NY, 1964-67; mem. faculty Tex. Christian U., Ft.Worth, 1967—, assoc. prof. physics Ft. Worth, 1970-76, prof. Ft.Worth, 1976—, W.A. Moncrief Jr. prof. physics, 1986—, chmn. dept. physics Ft. Worth, 1978-84, 96-99, assoc. dean Coll. Arts and Scis. Ft.Worth, 1976-78. Contbr. articles to profl. jours. Mem. AAAS, Am. Phys. Soc. (sec.-treas. Tex. sect. 1993-99, chair Tex. sect. 2003, mem. exec. com. Forum on Physics and Soc., 1999-2002), Am. Assn. Physics Tchrs. (pres.

Tex. sect. 1984), Sigma Xi, Phi Beta Kappa (pres. Delta of Tex. chpt. 1982-84). Roman Catholic. Office: Tex Christian U Dept Physics Fort Worth TX 76129-0001 Home Phone: 817-926-7584. Business E-Mail: c.quarles@tcu.edu.

QUARLES, JAMES LINWOOD, III, lawyer; b. Huntington, W.Va., Oct. 12, 1946; s. James Linwood Jr. and Beatrice (Hardwick) Q.; m. Sharon Taft, Dec. 20, 1969; children: Jessica, Matthew. BS cum laude, Denison U., 1968; JD cum laude, Harvard U., 1972. Bar: Mass. 1974, U.S. Dist. Ct. Mass. 1975, U.S. Ct. Appeals (D.C. cir.) 1975, U.S. Ct. Appeals (6th cir.) 1979, U.S. Supreme Ct. 1980, D.C. 1981, U.S. Ct. Appeals (2d cir.) 1981, U.S. Ct. Appeals (1st and 4th cirs.) 1983, Md. 1985, Va. 2000. Law clk. Judge Frank A. Kaufman, U.S. Dist. Ct. Md., Balt., 1972-73; asst. spl. prosecutor Watergate Spl. Pros. Force, Washington, 1973-75; from assoc. to sr. ptnr. Wilmer Cutler Pickering Hale & Dorr, Washington, 1975—, co-chmn. Appellate & Supreme Ct. Litigation group, mem. exec. com. Mem. Am. Law Inst., ABA, DC Bar Assn., Mass. Bar Assn., Boston Bar Assn., Phi Beta Kappa. Democrat. Home Phone: 301-229-9449; Office Phone: 202-663-6236. Business E-Mail: james.quarles@wilmerhale.com.

QUARLES, RANDAL KEITH, former federal agency administrator, lawyer; b. San Francisco, Sept. 5, 1957; s. Ralph Ray and Beverly Kay (Hulse) Q.; m. C. Hope Eccles, Sept. 13, 1997; children: Randal, Spencer, Hope. AB, Columbia U., 1981; JD, Yale U., 1984. Assoc. Davis Polk & Wardwell, NYC, 1984-91, ptnr., 1993—2001; spl. asst. to sec. US Dept. Treasury, Washington, 1991-92, deputy asst. sec., fin. insts. policy, 1992-93, asst. sec. internat. affairs, 2002—05, under sec. for domestic fin., 2005—06. U.S. exec. dir. IMF, 2001—02, European Bank Reconstrn. and Devel., 2002; mem. bd. dirs. Overseas Pvt. Investment Corp., 2004—05. Mem. fin. adv. com. Dole Presdl. Campaign, Washington, 1996. Mem. Yale Club, Salt Lake Country Club. Mem. Lds Ch. Avocations: aviation, skiing.

QUARLES, STEVEN PRINCETON, lawyer; b. Kansas City, Mo., May 9, 1942; s. Samuel Princeton and Marianna (Platt) Q.; m. Suzanne Margaret-Mary Cleary, June 2, 1970. AB, Princeton U., 1964; JD, Yale U., 1968. Bar: NY 1980, DC 1981. Counsel Senate Com. Energy and Natural Resources, Washington, 1971-78; dir. office coal leasing U.S. Dept. Interior, Washington, 1978-79, dep. under sec., 1979-81; ptnr. Nossaman, Guthner, Knox & Elliott, Washington, 1981-83, Crowell & Moring, Washington, 1983—. Mem. energy and mineral resources bd. Nat. Acad. Scis., 1985-88, abandoned mine lands com., 1985-86, oil and gas leasing com., 1988-89. Chmn. Sugarloaf Citizens Assn., Dickerson, Md., 1977-81, Md. Hazardous Waste Facilities Siting Bd., Annapolis, 1985-87; mem. Md. Sewage Sludge Mgmt. Commn., Annapolis, 1984, Bi-National Softwood Lumber Coun., 2007-; chmn. Montgomery County Solid Waste Adv. Com., Rockville, Md., 1980-85; pres. Frederick County Civic Fedn., 1989-94. Fulbright scholar India, 1964-65. Mem. ABA (enviroment, energy and resources sect.), N.Y. State Bar Assn., D.C. Bar Assn. Independent. Episcopalian. Avocation: horse breeding. Home: Some Day Soon Farm 13549 Glissans Mill Rd Mount Airy MD 21771-8509 Office: Crowell & Moring LLP 1001 Pennsylvania Ave NW Fl 10 Washington DC 20004-2595 Office Phone: 202-624-2665. Business E-Mail: squarles@crowell.com.

QUARTARARO, PHILIP, JR., mathematics professor; s. Philip Quartararo and Laura Nicoll, Joseph Nicoll (Stepfather), Angeline S. Quartararo (Stepmother); m. Dorothy Marie Morvant; children: Philip III, Sharon Campbell, Deborah Michael, Beth Davis. B in Math., La. State U., New Orleans, 1964; M in Math., La. State U., Baton Rouge, 1966, PhD in Math., 1972. Instr, asst. prof., assoc. prof. So. U., Baton Rouge, 1967—76, prof. math., 1976—2002, asst. to vice chancellor acad. affairs, 1989—91; ret., 2002. Developer ednl. material. Co-author: (textbooks) College Algebra: The UNCPAL Approach, Elementary Applied Mathematics; contbr. rsch. pubs. in Commutative Ring Theory. Bd. dirs. Lamar YMCA, 1971—85, bd. chair, 1974—79. Recipient grants in field. Mem.: Math. Edn. Reform, Nat. Coun. Tchrs. Math., Am. Math. Soc., Math. Assn. Am. (chmn. LA-MS sect. 1995—96), Kiwanis Internat. (life; bd. dirs., lt. gov., pres., cert. leadership trainer, dist. chmn. Hugh O'Brian Youth Leadership com.), Phi Delta Kappa. Presbyterian. Achievements include research in commutative ring theory; developing educational material. Avocations: swimming, home repair projects, small goat farm, golf, church choir singing. Office: So U PO Box 9261 Baton Rouge LA 70813 Home Phone: 225-933-6057; Office Phone: 225-933-6057. Personal E-mail: pquartjr@yahoo.com.

QUATAERT, DONALD, historian, educator; b. Rochester, NY, Sept. 10, 1941; s. William Leonard and Norine Louise (Katzenberger) Q.; m. 1963 (div.); 1 child, Laurie; m. Jean H. Grebler, Jan. 24, 1970; 1 child, Eliot. AB, Boston U., 1966; MA, Harvard U., 1968; PhD, UCLA, 1974. Asst. prof. U. Houston, 1974-79, assoc. prof., 1979-87, Binghamton (N.Y.) U., 1988-94, prof., 1994—. Vis. assoc. prof. Binghamton U., 1987-88. Author: Social Disintegration, 1983, Manufacturing and Technology, 1992, Ottoman Manufacturing, 1993; co-editor: An Economic and Social History of the Ottoman Empire, 1300-1914, 1994, The Ottoman Empire 1700-1922, 2000, 2d edit., 2005, Coal Miners and the State in the Ottoman Empire, 2006. NEH Sr. fellow, 1985-86, 1999-2000, Social Sci. Rsch. fellow, 1985-86, 1998, Fgn. Area fellow, 1980-81, Guggenheim fellow, 2004—05. Mem. Am. Hist. Assn., Mid. East Studies Assn., Turkish Studies Assn. Avocations: tennis, golf, stamp collecting/philately, birdwatching. Home: 4600 Deerfield Pl Vestal NY 13850-3757 Business E-Mail: dquataer@binghamton.edu.

QUATE, CALVIN FORREST, engineering educator; b. Baker, Nev., Dec. 7, 1923; s. Graham Shepard and Margie (Lake) Quate; m. Dorothy Marshall, June 28, 1945 (div. 1985); children: Robin, Claudia, Holly, Rhodalee; m. Arnice Streit, Jan. 1987; children: Christine, Carol, Richard. BS in Elec. Engring, U. Utah, 1944; PhD, Stanford U., 1950. Mem. tech. staff Bell Telephone Labs., Murray Hill, NJ, 1949-58; dir. research Sandia Corp., Albuquerque, 1959-60, v.p. research, 1960-61; prof. dept. applied physics and elec. engring. Stanford (Calif.) U., 1961-95, chmn. applied physics, 1969-72, 78-81, Leland T. Edwards prof. engring., 1986—, assoc. dean Sch. Humanities and Scis., 1972-74, 82-83, rsch. prof. dept. elec. engring., 1995—. Sr. rsch. fellow Xerox Rsch. Ctr., Palo Alto, Calif., 1984—94. Served as lt. (j.g.) USNR, 1944—46. Recipient Rank prize for Opto-electronics, 1982, Pres.'s Nat. medal of Sci., 1992. Fellow: Acoustical Soc., Am. Acad. Arts and Scis., IEEE (Morris N. Liebmann award 1981, IEEE medal of honor 1988, Third Millennium award 2000, Ultrasonics Rayleigh award 2002); mem.: Royal Soc., Royal Microscop. Soc., Am. Phys. Soc. (Keithly award), NAS, NAE, Tau Beta Pi, Sigma Xi. Office: Stanford U E L Ginzton Lab Palo Alto CA 94305-4085 Office Phone: 650-723-0213.

QUAY, THOMAS EMERY, lawyer; b. Cleve., Apr. 3, 1934; s. Harold Emery and Esther Ann (Thomas) Q.; divorced; children: Martha Wyndham, Glynis Cobb, Eliza Emery; m. Winnifred B. Cutler, May 13, 1989. AB in Humanities magna cum laude (Univ. scholar), Princeton U., 1956; LLB (Univ. scholar), U. Pa., 1963. Bar: Pa. 1964. Assoc. Pepper, Hamilton & Scheetz, Phila., 1963-65; with William H. Rorer, Inc., Ft. Washington, Pa., 1965—, sec., counsel, 1974-79, v.p., gen. counsel, sec., 1979-88; v.p. legal planning and adminstrn. Rorer Group, 1988-90; counsel Reed Smith Shaw and McClay, Phila., 1991-93; v.p., gen. counsel Athena Inst., Chester Springs, Pa., 1993—. Bd. dirs. Main Line YMCA, Ardmore, Pa., 1971-73, chmn. bd., 1972-73; editor 10th Reunion Book Princeton Class of 1956, 1966, 25th Reunion Book, 1981—, class sec., 1966-71, class v.p., 1971-81, pres., 1981-86. Lt. (j.g.) USNR, 1957-60. Recipient Commendation award, Main Line YMCA, 1984. Mem. ABA, Pa. Bar Assn., Phila. Bar Assn., Pharm. Mfrs. Assn. (chmn. law sect. 1983), Pa. Biotech. Assn. (chmn. legis. com., mem. exec. com. 1991-93), Phila. Drug Exch. (chmn. legis. com. 1975-78), Cannon Club of Princeton U., Sharswood Law Club of U. Pa., Princeton Club of Phila. Democrat. Presbyterian.

QUAYLE, DAN (JAMES DANFORTH QUAYLE), former Vice President of the United States; b. Indpls., Feb. 4, 1947; s. James C. and Corinne (Pulliam) Q.; m. Marilyn Tucker, Nov. 18, 1972; children: Tucker Danforth, Benjamin Eugene, Mary Corinne Berger. BS in Polit. Sci., DePauw U., Greencastle, Ind., 1969; JD, Ind. U., 1974. Bar: Ind. 1974. Ct. reporter, pressman Huntington (Ind.) Herald-Press, 1965-69, assoc. pub., gen. mgr., 1974-76; with consumer protection divn. Office Atty. Gen., State of Ind., 1970-71; adminstrv. asst. to gov. State of Ind., 1971-73; dir. Ind. Inheritance Tax Div., 1973-74; tchr. bus. law Huntington Coll., 1975; mem. US Congress from 4th Ind. dist., Washington, 1977—81; US Senator from Ind. Washington, 1981-89; v.p. US, Washington, 1989-93; founder BTC, 1994; chmn. global investments Cerebrus Capital Mgmt., 2000—. Disting. vis. prof. Am. Grad. Sch. Internat. Mgmt., 1997-99; cons. in field. Author: Standing Firm: A Vice-Presidential Memoir, 1994, Worth Fighting For, 1999; co-author (with Diane Medved) The American Family: Discovering the Values that Make Us Strong, 1996 Chmn. Campaign Am., 1995-99; hon. trustee emeriti Hudson Inst. With Ind. Army N.G., 1970-76. Office: Cerberus Investments 7001 N Scottsdale Rd Ste 2010 Scottsdale AZ 85253-3644

QUAYLE, DWIGHT W., lawyer; b. Apr. 21, 1951; BA magna cum laude, Williams Coll., 1973; JD cum laude, George Washington Univ., 1978; MTS, Harvard Divinity Sch. Bar: Mass. 1978. Assoc. Ropes & Gray, Boston, 1978—87, ptnr., 1987—, chmn. corp. dept. Lectr. Boston Coll. Law Sch. Mem. bd. deacons & minister search com. First Parish in Lincoln, Mass. Mem.: Phi Beta Kappa. Office: Ropes & Gray 1 International Pl Boston MA 02110-2624 Office Phone: 617-951-7406. Office Fax: 617-951-7050. Business E-Mail: dwight.quayle@ropesgray.com.

QUAYLE, MARILYN TUCKER, wife of former United States Vice President, lawyer; b. 1949; d. Warren S. and Mary Alice (Craig) Tucker; m. J. Danforth Quayle, Nov. 18, 1972; children: Tucker Danforth, Benjamin Eugene, Mary Corinne. BA in Polit. Sci., Purdue U., 1971; JD, Ind. U., 1974. Pvt. practice atty., Huntington, Ind., 1974—77; ptnr. Krieg, DeVault, Alexander & Capehart, Indpls., 1993—2001; pres. BTC Inc., Phoenix, 2001—. Author (with Nancy T. Northcott): Embrace the Serpent, 1992; author: The Campaign, 1996. Office: Quayle and Associates Ste 2010 7001 N Scottsdale Rd Scottsdale AZ 85253-3644 *

QUEEN, JOYCE, elementary school educator; b. Cleve., Mar. 17, 1945; d. Wilbur and Mae Closterhouse; m. Robert Graham Queen, Mar. 17, 1973. BA in Biology, Macalester Coll., 1966; MS in Conservation and Natural Resource Mgmt., U. Mich., 1968. Cert. tchr. biol. and earth scis., Ohio. Exhibitor, docent, coord. Grand Rapids (Mich.) Pub. Mus., 1967-68; tchr., naturalist Rose Tree-Media (Pa.) Outdoor Edn., 1967, Willoughby-Eastlake (Ohio) Schs., 1969-70, Independence (Ohio) Schs., 1970-78; sci. tchr. Hathaway Brown Sch., Cleve., 1970—, chmn. dept. primary sci., 1998—. Designer Courtland Woods nature trail, 1986, designer sci. greenhouse, 1990-92; designer sci. classroom Van Dyke Architects/Hathaway Brown Sch., 1990-92; designer, coord. Dampeer Primary sci. courtyard, 1993, Oliva Herb Garden, 1998, Colini Landscape Design/Hathaway Brown Sch., Shaker Hts., Ohio; ednl. adv. com. William G. Mather Vessel Mus., Cleve., 1992, Holden Arboretum, Kirtland, Ohio, 1992-97, Shaker Lakes Nature Ctr., 2005-06, Squire Valleyvue Farm, 2006; youth divsn. judge Cleve. Botanic Garden Show, 1999, 2000, 02, 05, 07, NOAA Live From Antarctica, 2003; presenter in field. Contbr. articles to profl. jours. Active Belize (Ctrl. Am.) Tchrs. Workshop, 1994; Sagamore Adirondack Great Camps Workshop, 2003; vol. PARI Radio Telescope, 2005; task force, agrl. edn. commn. HB Engring., 2005-06. Catalyst grant Hathaway Brown Sch. Gt. Lks. Curriculum, 1991; recipient Ohio Alliance for Environment, 1986, Presdl. Excellence in Elem. Sci. Tchg. award NSF, 1992, Sheldon Exemplary Equipment and Facilities award, 1992, Garden Club Am. Hull award, 2005; Great Lakes Lighthouse Keepers Assn. scholar, Marine Ecology scholar Marine Resources, Inc., 1989, Internat. Space Sta. Conf. scholar, 2000, Maine Salt Marsh Ecology Curriculum scholar, 2001, Calif. Coastal Wetlands and Desert Study scholar, 2002, NASA Mars Mission Scholar, 2006, Hong Kong-Sci./Tech. China scholar, 2006. Mem. NSTA, Cleve. Regional Coun. Sci. Tchrs., Cleve. Natural Hist. Mus., Cleve. Zool. Park, Ind. Sch. Assn. Ctrl. Sts., Internat. Pen Pal Exch. Progam, Great Lakes Sci. Ctr. Holden Arboretum (mem. profl. women's adv. bd. 2007). Presbyterian. Avocations: orchardist, naturalist, horticulturist. Office: Hathaway Brown Sch 19600 N Park Blvd Cleveland OH 44122-1899

QUEENEY, DEBORAH ANN, special education educator; b. Allentown, Pa., Feb. 4, 1949; d. William and Jane Swartz; m. Stephen Francis Queeney, Aug. 5, 1978; children: Nicole Ellen, Jessica Elaine. BSc, Kutztown State Coll., 1972; MEd, U. Pitts., 1975. Tchr. blind, multi-handicapped Lincoln Intermediate Unit 12, York, Pa., 1973—74; tchr. Monmouth Assn. Retarded Children, Shrewsbury, NJ, 1975—78; instrnl. assoc., tutor Amherst Sch. Dist. Regional Svcs. and Edn. Ctr., NH, 1988—91; spl. needs tchr. Milford Sch. Dist., NH, 1991—. Named NH Tchr. of Yr., Assn. Retarded Citizens NH, 1994; recipient Monmouth County Tchr. of Yr., Monmouth Assn. Retarded Citizens, 1977, Excellence in Edn. award, Nat. Ctr. Low Incidence Disabilities, Denver, 2004. Mem.: NH Connections. Avocations: seashell collecting, sketching. Home: 7 Roberts Rd Amherst NH 03031 Office: Milford Mid Sch 33 Osgood Rd Milford NH 03055

QUEEN LATIFAH, (DANA ELAINE OWENS), actress, musician; b. Newark, Mar. 18, 1970; d. Lance and Rita Owens Student, Borough of Manhattan C.C. Co-founder, CEO Flavor Unit Entertainment, 1993—; spokeswoman Revlon. Model, spokesperson Covergirl. Actress: (films) House Party 2, 1991, Jungle Fever, 1991, Juice, 1992, Who's the Man, 1993, My Life, 1993, Set It Off, 1996, Hoodlum, 1997, The Wizard of Oz, 1998, Living Out Loud, 1998, Sphere, 1998, The Bone Collector, 1999, (voice only) Bringing Out the Dead, 1999, The Country Bears, 2002, Brown Sugar, 2002, (voice only) Pinocchio, 2002, Chicago, 2002 (Acad. Award Nomination for Best Supporting. Actress, 2003), Scary Movie 3, Barbershop 2: Back in Business, 2004, Taxi, 2004, Last Holiday, 2006, (voice only) Ice Age: The Meltdown, 2006, Stranger Than Fiction, 2006, Hairspray, 2007; actor, exec. prodr.: (films) Bringing Down the House, 2003; actor, prodr.: (films) The Cookout, 2004, Beauty Shop, 2005; actor: (TV movies) Sister in the Name of Rap, 1992, Mama Flora's Family, 1998, Living with the Dead, 2002, (voice only) Crash Nebula, 2004, The Muppets' Wonderful Wizard of Oz, 2005; (TV appearances) In Living Color, 1991, Fresh Prince of Bel Air, 1991, Living Single, 1993, Mad TV, 1997, Living Single, 1996, 1997, Spin City, 2001, Kung Faux, 2003, The Fairly OdParents, 2004, Eve, 2004; host, exec. prodr.: The Queen Latifah Show, 1999-2001; composer (films) New Jack City, 1991, White Man Can't Jump, 1992, Girls Town, 1996; singer (albums) All Hail the Queen, 1990, The Nature of Sista, 1991, X-tra Naked, 1992, Black Reign, 1994, Order In The Court, 1998, She's the Queen: A Collection of Hits, 2002, The Dana Owens Album, 2004; Author: Ladies First: Revelations of a Strong Woman, 1999, Queen of the Scene, 2006 Recipient Grammy award nomination, 1990, Soul Train Music award, 1995, Sammy Davis Jr. award, 1995, Entertainer of Yr. award, 1995, Grammy award for best rap solo performance, 1995, Arist of the Yr. award, Harvard Found., 2003; named Best New Artist, New Music Seminar, 1990, Best Female Rapper, Rolling Stone Readers' Poll, 1990, Woman of the Yr. Glamour mag., 2006; named one of 50 Most Influential African-Americans, Ebony Magazine 2004, named to Hollywood Walk of Fame, 2005. Achievements include becoming first hip-hop artist honored with star on the Hollywood Walk of Fame. Office: Flavor Unit Entertainment 155 Morgan St Jersey City NJ 07302-2932 *

QUELER, EVE, conductor; b. NYC; Student, Mannes Coll. Music, CCNY. Music staff N.Y.C. Opera, 1958-70; assoc. condr. Ft. Wayne (Ind.) Philharm., 1970-71; founder, music dir. Opera Orch., N.Y., 1968; condr. Lake George Opera Festival, Glen Falls, N.Y., 1971-72, Oberlin (Ohio) Music Festival, 1972, Romantic Festival, Indpls., 1972, Mostly Mozart Festival, Lincoln Center, 1972, New Philharmonia, London, 1974, Teatro Liceu, Barcelona, 1974, 77, San Antonio Symphony, 1975; guest condr. Paris Radio Orch., 1972, P.R. Symphony Orch., 1975, 77, Mich. Chamber Orch., 1975, Phila. Orch., 1976, Montreal Symphony, 1977, Cleve. Orch., 1977 (Recipient Martha Baird Rockefeller Fund for Music award 1968, named Musician of Month Mus. Am. Mag. 1972), N.Y.C. Opera, 1978, Opera Las Palmas, 1978, Opera de Nice, 1979, Nat. Theatre of Prague, 1980, Opera Caracas, Venezuela, 1981, San Diego Opera, 1984, Australian Opera, Sydney, 1985, Kirov Opera, St. Petersburg, Russia, 1993, Hamburg Opera, Germany, 1994, Pretoria, South Africa, 1995, Hamilton, Ont., 1995, Hawaii Philharmonic, 1997, Hong Kong Sinfonietta, 1998, Hong Kong Philharmonic, 1999, Orch. dello State de Mexico, 1999-2002, Macau Festival, 2000, Festival Euro Mediteranneo, Italy, 2002; Opei Bonn, 1994-96; recording CBS Masterworks, 1974, 76, Hungaroton Records, 1982-85. Decorated Chevalier de l'ordre des Arts et des Lettres; named Woman in Music, N.Y.C., 2002; recipient Butterfly award, Licia Albanese-Puccini Foundation, 1995. Office: Opera Orch 239 W 72nd St Ste 2R New York NY 10023-2734

QUELLO, JAMES HENRY, government official; b. Laurium, Mich., Apr. 21, 1914; s. Bartholomew and Mary Katherine (Cochis) Q.; m. Mary Elizabeth Butler, Sept. 14, 1937 (dec. 1999); children: James Michael, Richard Butler. BA, Mich. State U., 1935, D of Humanities (hon.), 1977; D of Pub. Svc. (hon.), No. Mich. U., 1975. V.p., sta. mgr. Goodwill Stas., Inc., Detroit, 1947-72; v.p. Capital Cities Comm. Corp., 1968; commr. FCC, Washington, 1974—98. Comm. cons., Detroit, 1972-74; commr. Detroit Housing and Urban Renewal Commn., 1951-72 Contbr. articles to mags., newspapers. Bd. dirs. Greater Detroit Hosp. Assn.; trustee Mich. Vet. Trust Fund; mem. Gov.'s Spl. Commn. on Urban Problems, Mich., Gov.'s Spl. Study Com. on Legis. Compensation, Mayor's Com. on Human Relations; bd. dirs. Am. Negro Emancipation Centennial; mem. exec. bd. Boy Scouts Am.; TV-radio chmn. United Found. Lt. col. AUS, 1940-45. Decorated Bronze Star with oak leaf cluster, Croix de Guerre (France); recipient Internat. Pres.'s award Nat. Assn. TV Program Execs., 1985, Silver Satellite award Am. Women in Radio and TV, 1988, 93, Sol Taishoff award Washington Area Broadcasters Assn., 1989, 93, Pub. Svc. award Fed. Comm. Bar Assn., 1993, Disting. Svc. award Media Inst., 1993, Golden Eagle Amb. award Pa. Assn. Broadcasters, 1993, Disting. Alumni award Mich. State U., Club Dir. award Detroit Adcraft Club, 1993, L.I. Coalition for Fair Broadcasting award, 1993, Nat. Disting. Svc. award Nat. Assn. Pub. TV, 1993, Obie award Ohio Ednl. TV Stas., 1993, Gold Eagle Leadership award Wireless Cable Assn. Internat., 1993, Pres. award Alaska Broadcasting Assn., 1994, Chmn. award Nat. Religious Broadcasters, 1994, Ga. Broadcasters award Broadcasters of Am., 1994, 1st Amendment award Radio & TV News Dirs. Found., 1994. Mem. Nat. Assn. Broadcaster (gov. liaison com. 1964-72, Keystone award 1990, Disting. Svc. award 1994, Honor award for protecting the technical integrity of radio and TV 1994, Broadcasting Cable Hall of Fame, 1995, Nat. Radio Hall of Fame 1996), Mich. Assn. Broadcasters (pres. 1958, legis. chmn. 1959-72, dir., Outstanding Mich. Citizen 1989, Pioneer award 1994, Ellis Island honor award 1997), Greater Detroit Bd. Commerce, Sigma Alpha Epsilon. Clubs: Adcraft (Detroit); Detroit Athletic, Army and Navy Country; Nat. Press (Washington). Office: FCC Wiley Rein and Fielding 1776 K St NW Washington DC 20006-2304 Office Phone: 202-719-7052. Personal E-mail: jquello@wrf.com.

QUENCER, ROBERT MOORE, neuroradiologist, researcher; b. Jersey City, Nov. 14, 1937; s. Arthur Bauer and Isabell (Moore) Quencer; m. Christine F. Thomas, Sept. 16, 1972; children: Kevin, Keith. BS, Cornell U., 1959, MS, 1963; MD, SUNY, Syracuse, 1967. Diplomate Am. Bd. Radiology, Nat. Bd. Med. Examiners; cert. of added qualifications in neuroradiology. Intern Jackson Meml. Hosp., Miami, Fla., 1967-68; resident in radiology Columbia U., NYC, 1968-71, fellow in neuroradiology, 1971-72; asst. prof. Downstate Med. Ctr., Bklyn., 1972-76; assoc. prof. U. Miami, 1976-79, prof., 1979-92, chmn., prof., 1992—, chief sect. neuroradiology, 1976-86, dir. divsn. magnetic resonance imaging, 1986-92, Robert Shapiro MD prof. radiology. Vis. prof. U. Tenn. Coll. Medicine, Memphis, 1982, Downstate Med. Ctr. Coll. Medicine, Bklyn., 1992, U. Vt. Coll. Medicine, Burlington, 1983, NY Med. Coll., Valhalla, 1984, U. Va. Sch. Medicine, Charlottesville, 1984, U. Ky. Sch. Medicine, Lexington, 1985, Yale U. Sch. Medicine, New Haven, 1986, 2000, Columbia U. Sch. Medicine, NYC, 1986, The Mayo Clinic & Found., Rochester, Minn., 1987, Med. Coll. Va., Richmond, 1988, U. Pa. Sch. Medicine, Phila., 1988, Harvard U. Sch. Medicine/Mass. Gen. Hosp., Boston, 1989, U. Conn., Farmington, 1990, Kumamoto, Japan, 1993, U. Man., Can., 1992, Mich. State U., 1996, Mt. Sinai Med. Ctr., 1997, Cornell U. Sch. Medicine, 1998, U. Minn., 2001, U. Ky., 2002; UTMB Galveston, 2003; Dartmouth Hitchcock Med. Sch., 2003, Duke Univ. Sch. of Med., 2003, U. Calif., San Francisco, 2005, U. Mass., 2006; guest lectr. Asian Oceanic Soc. Neuroradiology, 2001, Internat. Med. Soc. Paraplegic, Lucerne, Switzerland, 2001; Phaler lectr. Phila. Roentgen Soc., 1995; dir. programs in dept. radiology U. Miami Sch. Medicine, 1984, 86, Med. Coll. Wis., 1990, 92, Kauai, Hawaii, 1991, Whistler, B.C., 1990; guest lectr. at ASEAN Congress of Radiology, Malaysia, 1992, Royal Australia Radiology Soc., Brisbane, 1993, Brazilian Congress Neurology, 1996, NY Roentgen Soc., 1997, Somerset MR course, Torquay, UK, 1998, Republic of China, 1999, Yale U., 2000, U. Minn., 2001, U. Tex., 2003, Duke U., 2003, U. Calif., San Francisco, 2005; adv. cons. NIH, 1987, 90; sci. merit reviewer V.A., 1987; presenter, lectr. in field. Author: Neurosonography, 1988; dep. editor Am. Jour. Neuroradiology, 1984-96, editor-in-chief, 1998—; assoc. editor for neuroimaging Yearbook of Neurology and Neurosurgery, 1991—; manuscript reviewer Am. Jour. Neuroradiology, 1984—, Paraplegia, 1989—, Radiographics, 1991—, Pediatrics, 1993—, Radiology, 1994—; mem. editl. bd. Jour. Clin. Neuro-Ophthalmology, 1980-90; contbr. articles to profl. jours. Pres. Am. Soc. Neuroradiology, 1994-95; prin. investigator NIH Grant on imaging/pathology of spinal cord injury; chmn. Commn. Neuroradiological Socs. World Fedn. Neuroradiology Soc., 2003-, Neuroradiology Sci. Program Com. Radiological Soc. North Am., Scientific RSNA Program, dir. for neuroradiology, 2004-; Lt. (j.g.) USN, 1959-61. Fellow Am. Coll. Radiology, Am. Soc. Neuroradiology (pres. 1994-95, program com. 1985-89, 92, editl. com. 1984—, publs. com. 1984—, Gold medal 2007); mem. AMA, Radiol. Soc. N.Am. (program subcom. on neuroradiology 1990-94, chmn. neuroradiology program 2004—), Southeastern Neuroradiol. Soc. (founder, pres. 1980-81, examiner for bd. certification in radiology and neuroradiology), Fla. Radiol. Soc. (magnetic resonance com. 1991-92), Alpha Omega Alpha. Avocations: golf, travel. Business E-Mail: rquencer@med.miami.edu.

QUENEAU, PAUL ETIENNE, retired metallurgical engineering educator; b. Phila., Mar. 20, 1911; s. Augustin L. and Jean (Blaisdell) Q.; m. Joan Osgood Hodges, May 20, 1939; children: Paul Blaisdell, Josephine Downs. BA, Columbia U., 1931, BSc, 1932, M of Engring., 1933; postgrad., Cambridge U., Eng., 1934; DSc, Delft U. Tech., Netherlands, 1971. With INCO, 1934-69; rsch. supt. Internat. Nickel Co., 1940-41, 46-48, v.p., 1958-69, chief tech. officer, tech. asst. to pres., 1960-66, asst. to chmn., 1967-69; vis. scientist Delft U. Tech., 1970-71; prof. engring. Dartmouth

Coll., 1971-87, prof. emeritus, 1987. Cons. engr., 1972—; vis. prof. U. Minn., 1974-75, U. Utah, 1987-91; geographer Perry River Arctic Expdn., 1949; chmn. arctic rsch. adv. com. USN, 1957; gov. Arctic Inst. N.Am., 1957-62; mem. engring. coun. Columbia U., 1965-70; mem. vis. com. MIT, Cambridge, 1967-70; mem. extractive metallurgy and mineral processing panels NAS; pres. Q-S Oxygen Processes Inc., 1974-79, also bd. dir. Author: (with Hanson) Geography, Birds and Mammals of the Perry River Region, 1956; Cobalt and the Nickeliferous Limonites, 1971; editor: Extractive Metallurgy of Copper, Nickel and Cobalt, 1961; (with Anderson) Pyrometallurgical Processes in Nonferrous Metallurgy, 1965; The Winning of Nickel, 1967; contbr. articles to profl. jours.; patentee 500 internat. patents, 36 U.S. patents including processes and apparatus employed in the pyrometallurgy, hydrometallurgy and vapometallurgy of nickel, copper, cobalt, lead, zinc, iron and steel, extractive metallurgy oxygen tech. including INCO oxygen flash smelting, oxygen top-blown rotary converter, lateritic ore matte smelting, nickel high pressure carbonyl and iron ore recovery processes; co-inventor Lurgi QSL direct lead-making, QSOP direct coppermaking and nickelmaking reactors, Lurgi direct steelmaking reactors, and Dravo oxygen sprinkle smelting copper furnaces. Bd. dir. Engring. Found., 1966-76, chmn. bd. dir., 1973-75. With C.E. US Army, 1937—45, ETO, to col. US Army, 1945—71. Decorated Bronze Star, ETO medal with 5 Battlestars, Army Commendation medal; recipient Appreciation Cert. US Army, Egleston medal Columbia U., 1965, Fletcher award Dartmouth Coll., 1991, Chem. Engring Personal Achievement McGraw Hill, 1996; Evans fellow Cambridge U., 1933-34. Fellow Metall. Soc. of AIME (dir. 1964, 68-71, pres. 1969, Extractive Metallurgy Lecture award 1977, Paul E. Queneau TMS Internat. Symposium on Extractive Metallurgy of Copper, Nickel and Cobalt 1993); mem. AIME (Douglas Gold medal 1968, v.p. 1970, dir. 1968-71, Henry Krumb lectr. 1984, keynote lectr. ann. meeting 1990, McGraw Hill award personal achievement in chem. engring.), NAE, NSPE, Can. Inst. Mining and Metallurgy, Inst. Mining and Metallurgy U.K. (overseas mem. council 1970-80, Gold medal 1980), Sigma Xi, Tau Beta Pi. Achievements include 36 U.S. patents and 500 foreign patents. Office: Dartmouth Coll Thayer Sch Engring Hanover NH 03755

QUENELLE, SUSANNAH SHERMAN, music educator; b. Albion, NY, Apr. 4, 1955; d. Moses H. and Margaret (McKirdy) Sherman; m. Anthony M. Quenelle, July 23, 1983; children: Kayla N., Taylor R. Mus B in Edn., SUNY, Potsdam, 1977; Mus M in Edn., SUNY, 1983. Tchr. K-6 music Gen. Brown Sch. Dist., Brownville, NY, 1978—83; tchr. 9-12 music St. Anne Inst., Albany, 1983—87; tchr. 6-8 music, vocal theater East Greenbush Sch. Dist., 1987—2006; tchr. 9-12 vocal music, theatre Columbia H.S., 2006—. Music dir. East Greenbush Youth Theatre, 2003—04; bd. dirs. Spotlight Players. Mem. soloist First United Meth. Ch., 1992—; conducted Rensselaer County Elem. Choir, 1998. Recipient Tchr. Recognition award, Albany Civic Theater, 2004. Mem.: Music Educators Nat. Conf., Am. Choral Dir. Assn. Methodist. Avocations: reading, exercise. Office: Columbia HS 962 Luther Rd East Greenbush NY 12061

QUENNELL, NICHOLAS, landscape architect, educator; b. London, Sept. 30, 1935; s. Cecil William and Beatrice Irene Quennell; m. Grace Tankersley, Apr. 30, 1983. AA, Archtl. Assn., London, 1957; MLA, Harvard U., 1969. Registered architect, N.Y., Pa., N.J., Conn., U.K.; registered landscape architect, N.Y., N.J., Conn., Mass., N.C. Architect London County Coun., 1959-61, Jose Luis Sert, Cambridge, Mass., 1961-62, Lawrence Halprin & Assocs., San Francisco, 1962-65, Vollmer Assocs., NYC, 1965-68; prin. Nicholas Quennell Assocs., NYC, 1968-79, Quennell Rothschild Assocs., NYC, 1979-97, Quennell, Rothschild & Ptnrs., NYC, 1998—. V.p. The Mcpl. Art Soc. (dir. 1978-85), N.Y.C., 1985-92, dir. The Archtl. League, N.Y.C., 1984-89. Bd. dirs. Nat. Assn. for Olmsted Pks., Washington, 1988-90, chmn., 1990-93; mem. Art Commn. of City of N.Y., 1992-97, pres., 1993-97. Fellow Am. Soc. of Landscape Architects; mem. Century Assn. Office: Quennell Rothschild & Ptnrs 118 W 22nd St New York NY 10011-2416 E-mail: quennell@qrpartners.com.

QUENNEVILLE, JOEL, professional hockey coach; b. Windsor, Ont., Can., Sept. 15, 1958; m. Elizabeth Quenneville; children: Dylan, Lily, Anna. Hockey player, player coach St. John's Maple Leafs, 79-92; head coach Springfield Indians, Am. Hockey League, 1993-94; asst. coach Colorado Avalanche, 1995-96; head coach St. Louis Blues, 1997—2004, Colo. Avalanche, 2004—. Named Most Valuable Defensemen, 1985, 86, Coach of Yr., NHL, 1999-2000. Office: c/o Colorado Avalanche Pepsi Center 1000 Chopper Circle Denver CO 80204

QUENTEL, ALBERT DREW, lawyer; b. Miami, Fla., Nov. 27, 1934; s. Charles Edward Jr. and Alberta Amelia (Drew) Q.; m. Paula Staelin Hagar, Feb. 9, 1957 (dec. Mar. 1998); children: Albert D. Jr., Stephen C., Marshall Lee, Paul G., Peter E., Michael J. BA, U. Fla., 1956, JD with honors, 1959. Bar: Fla. 1959. Assoc. Mershon, Sawyer, Johnston, Dunwody & Cole, Miami, 1959-64, ptnr., 1965-71; prin., shareholder Greenberg Traurig P.A., Miami, 1971—. Editor-in-chief U. Fla. Law Rev., 1959; contbg. author: Florida Real Property Practice, 1965, Real Estate Partnerships Selected Problems and Solutions, 1991, Commercial Real Estate Finance, 1993. Mem. Gov.'s Growth Mgmt. Adv. Com., Tallahassee, 1985-87; bd. dirs. Nat. Parkinson Found., Miami, 1980-98, v.p., 1985-97. Mem. NRA (life 1989—), Am. Coll. Real Estate Lawyers, Fla. Bar Assn. (chmn. pub. rels. com. 1970-72, chmn. editorial com. jour. 1972-73), Lions (pres. Key Biscayne, Fla. club 1973), Miami Club (pres. 1991-92), Bath Club, Blue Key, Beta Theta Pi (pres. local chpt. 1954-55), Phi Eta Sigma, Phi Kappa Phi. Republican. Congregationalist. Avocations: reading, shooting, photography. Home: 825 Algeria Ave Coral Gables FL 33134-2401 Office: Greenberg Traurig 1221 Brickell Ave Miami FL 33131-3224 Home Phone: 305-442-8788; Office Phone: 305-579-0505. Business E-Mail: QuentelA@gtlaw.com.

QUERESHI, MOHAMMED YOUNUS, retired psychology professor; b. Haripur Hazara, Pakistan, Dec. 12, 1929; arrived in U.S., 1953; s. Mohammed Noor and Meryam Khatoon Qureshi; m. Nora Jane Knapp, May 27, 1958 (div. Nov. 1979); children: Ahmed, Amna, Shukria, Shawn; m. Farzana Kaukab, May 17, 1980; children: Ajmel, Sabeeha, Azem. PhD, U. Ill., 1958. Lic. psychologist Wis., diplomate Am. Bd. Psychol. Specialties. Asst. prof. psychology U. Minn., Duluth, 1960-62, U. N.D., Grand Forks, 1962-64; assoc. prof. psychology Marquette U., Milw., 1964-70, prof., 1970—2003, prof. emeritus psychology, 2003—, chmn. dept. psychology, 1971-77. Cons. psychologist. Author: Statistics and Behavior: An Introduction, 1980, 2d edit., 1991; contbr. articles to sci. and profl. jours. Pres. 81st St. Sch. PTA, 1968—70; merit badge counselor Milwaukee County coun. Boy Scouts Am., 1973—88; pres. Islamic Assn. Greater Milw., 1978—83; chmn. bd. trustees Islamic Soc. Milw., 2004—. Grantee, NIH, 1962—69, TOPS Club, 1969—76, Office of Edn., 1970—71. Mem.: Psychometric Soc., Am. Psychol. Assn., Sigma Xi. Home: 15660 Monet Ct Brookfield WI 53005-5125 Office: Marquette U Schroeder Health Complex PO Box 1881 Milwaukee WI 53201-1881 Office Phone: 414-288-7468.

QUERY, LANCE D., dean, university librarian; EdB in History, Spanish, U. Mo., 1969; MA in Latin Am. History, Ind. U., PhD; MLS, U. Chgo. Acting univ. libr. Northwestern Univ., Chgo.; asst. univ. libr., planning and adminstrn. We. Mich. U., and faculty, history dept., to dean, univ. libraries; dean libraries and academic info. resources Tulane U., New Orleans, 2000—; interim dir. Law Libr. Tulane U. Law Sch., 2005—. Office: Dean Libr Academic Info Resources Tulane Univ 6823 St Charles Ave New Orleans LA 70118-5698 Office Phone: 504-865-5131. Office Fax: 504-865-6773. Business E-Mail: lquery@tulane.edu. *

QUERY, LOIS A., elementary school educator; b. Ft. Scott, Kans., Sept. 8, 1940; d. Lawrence B. and Ida M. Query. BS in Elem. Edn., Pitts. State U., Kans., 1962, MS in Elem. Edn., 1968. Cert. tchr. Kans. Dept. Edn., 2006. Elem. tchr. Sch. Dist. #1, Hickman Mills, Mo., 1963—65, Ft. Scott Christian Heights, Kans., 1966—73; reading specialist Sch. Dist. R-4, Cabool, Mo., 1974—75; tchr., prin. Tutu Ch. of God Elem. Sch., St. Thomas, Virgin Islands, 1976—81; early childhood tchr. Barton-Dade-Jaspe County Spl. Edn. Coop., Lockwood, Mo., 1989—91; reading specialist U.S.D. #246, Arma, Kans., 1992—2006; ret., 2006. Master of ceremonies Title I Parent Meeting, Arma, 2002—06; coord. Young Author's Conf., Arma, 2004, Arma, 06. Treas. Harmony Hill Youth Camp, Fulton, Mo., 1960—68; activities dir. Harmony Hill Girls Camp, Fulton, 1968—75; twp. chmn. Am. Cancer Soc., Ft. Scott, 1974. Nominee Kans. Tchr. of Yr., U.S.D. #246, 2006; Jr. scholar, Pitts. State U., Kans., 1961, Sr. scholar, 1962. Mem.: Phi Kappa Phi, Kappa Delta Pi. Republican. Ch. Of God. Avocations: music, gardening, reading, sewing. E-mail: laqfarm@terraworld.net.

QUESENBERRY, KENNETH HAYS, agronomy educator; b. Springfield, Tenn., Feb. 28, 1947; s. James William and Cora Geneva (Moore) Quesenberry; m. Joyce Ann Kaze; children: James Kenneth, Kendra Joyce. BS, Western Ky. U., 1969; PhD, U. Ky., 1975. D.F. Jones predoctoral fellow U. Ky., Lexington, 1972—75; asst. prof. U. Fla., Gainesville, 1975—80, assoc. prof. agronomy, 1980—86, prof. agronomy, 1986—. Contbr. articles to profl. jours. With US Army, 1969—71, Vietnam. Fellow: Crop Sci. Soc. Am. (chair divsn. C-8 1993—94, bd. reps. 2005—07), Am. Soc. Agronomy. Achievements include research in germplasm enhancement of forages with release of four cultivars of tropical grasses and three clovers and genetic transformation of clovers; specialist Trifolium species germplasm and forage breeding and genetics. Avocations: sports, antique furniture refinishing. Office: U Fla PO Box 110500 Gainesville FL 32611-0500 Office Phone: 351-392-1811 ext. 213. Business E-Mail: clover@ifas.ufl.edu.

QUESENBERY, ERIKA LYNN, media specialist, curator; b. Balt., Apr. 29, 1969; d. Lonnie Ray Quesenbery Jr. and Ruth Ann Pierce. Student, Harford CC, 1987—89; grad., Cecil Leadership Acad., 2006. News dir. Delmarva Broadcasting, Sta. WXCY, Havre de Grace, Md., 1989—91; editor The Rising Sun Herald and Herald County edit. Octoraro Pub. Co., Rising Sun, Md., 1995—2000; grant writer, media rels. specialist Boys & Girls Club of Cecil County, North East, Md., 2000—05; mktg. assoc. Stewart Assoc., Perryville, Md., 2005—. Curator Paw Paw Mus., Port Deposit Heritage Corp., Port Deposit, Md., 1998—. Author (researcher): (non-fiction) A Snowball's Chance: Captain Alonzo Snow's 1st Maryland Light Artillery, Battery B, 1861-1865; author: Images of America: United States Naval Training Center Bainbridge, 2007; contbr. chapters to books. Co-founder Torne Sch. clean-up vols. Naval Tng. Ctr. Bainbridge, Port Deposit, 1997—2000; vol., tour guide, first civilian mem. US Naval Tng. Ctr. Bainbridge Hist. Assn., Port Deposit, 1999—2006; chmn. event com. Capt. John Smith 400th Anniversary Am. in Port Deposit, 2007; bd. dirs., former tour com. chair, vol. Port Deposit Heritage Corp., Port Deposit, 1996—98. Recipient Non-Metro Radio Editl. Writing award, AP, Balt., 1989, Non-Metro Radio Enterprise in Reporting award, 1990, Sch. Bell award for media coverage of edn., Md. State Tchrs.' Assn., 1997, U.S. Navy Civilian Citizen Recognition for Bainbridge/NAPS and Tome Sch. Clean-Up Volunteers, USN, 2000. Mem.: Port Deposit C. of C. (v.p. 2006—07). Democrat. Presbyterian. Avocations: historic preservation, local and regional history, genealogy, Irish heritage, travel. Home: 704 Main St Delta PA 17314 Office: Stewart Assoc 1723 Principio Furnace Rd Perryville MD 21903 Home Phone: 717-456-2957; Office Phone: 410-642-3074. Personal E-mail: historacle@verizon.net. E-mail: erikaq@stewartrealestatedev.com.

QUESTER, GEORGE HERMAN, political science professor; b. Bklyn., July 14, 1936; s. Jacob George and Elizabeth (Mattern) Q.; m. Aline Marie Olson, June 20, 1964; children: Theodore, Amanda. AB, Columbia U., 1958; MA, Harvard U., 1964, PhD, 1965. Instr., then asst. prof. govt. Harvard U., 1965-70; assoc. prof. govt. Cornell U., 1970-73, prof., 1973-82; prof. polit. sci. U. Md., College Park, 1982—. Vis. prof. U.S. Naval Acad., Annapolis, Md., 1991-93. Author: Deterrence Before Hiroshima, 1966, Nuclear Diplomacy, 1970, The Politics of Nuclear Proliferation, 1973, The Continuing Problem of International Relations, 1974, Offense and Defense in the International System, 1977, American Foreign Policy: The Lost Consensus, 1982, The Future of Nuclear Deterrence, 1986, The International Politics of Television, 1990, Nuclear Monopoly, 2000, Before And After The Cold War, 2002, Nuclear First Strike, 2006. Served with USAF, 1958-61. Fellow Center Advanced Study Behavioral Scis., 1974-75 Mem. Council Fgn. Relations, Inst. Strategic Studies, Am. Polit. Sci. Assn. Home: 5124 37th St N Arlington VA 22207-1862 Office: Univ Md 3140 Tydings College Park MD 20742-0001 Office Phone: 301-405-4146. Business E-Mail: gqueste@gvpt.umd.edu.

QUEVEDO, HECTOR ADOLF, operations research specialist, environmental scientist; b. Juarez, Mexico, June 25, 1940; arrived in U.S.A., 1973. s. Robert and Margaret (Urias) Quevedo Endlich; m. Gloria (Guijarro), June 2, 1971; children: Gloria, Hector. BA, U. Tex., El Paso, 1966; MS in Environ. Sci., U. Okla., 1972, PhD in Environ. Sci., 1977. Part time instr. math. U. Tex., El Paso, 1977—80; environ. engr. El Paso Natural Gas Co., El Paso, 1978—79; systems analyst U.S. Army, White Sands Missile Range, N.Mex., 1980—84, Ft. Bliss, Tex., 1985—98; ret., 1998. Instr. environ. engring. and stats., rschr. Univ. Autonoma de Juarez, Juarez, Mexico, 1998. Author: Una Nueva Filosofía Médica Racionalist, 1998. Democrat. Avocations: classical music, reading, outdoor recreation, writing. Home: 11148 Voyager Cove St El Paso TX 79936-3007 Office Phone: 915-240-1310. Personal E-mail: hqnatura@aol.com.

QUIALA, MARIBEL, psychotherapist, consultant; d. Guillermo H. Quiala and Neris Aroche; m. Jesus A. Rios, Apr. 24, 1993; children: Natalie, Jesus. BA in Psychology and Music, Seton Hall U., 1985; MSW, Barry U., 1995. LCSW, bd. cert. Fla. Pvt. pracitce, Miami, Fla., 2000—. S.E. regional coord. Nat. Latina Health Network, Washington, 2000—; field instr. Barry U., Miami, Fla., 2000—, Fla. Internat. U., Miami, 2000—, Nova Southeastern U., Ft. Lauderdale, Fla., 2000—, Carlos Albizu U., Miami, 2000—; internship dir. Psychiat. Solutions Inc., Ft. Lauderdale, 2000—, Hispanic Devel., Leeza Gibbons Memory Found.; mem. Minority Tobacco Control Task Force, Dept. Health, Fla., 1999—2002; spokesperson HIV/AIDS Awareness Campaign, State Fla., Breast/Cervical Cancer Campaign, State Fla., Hispanic Heart Healthy Day Campaign, S.E. Region. Named Most Dynamic Woman, Am. Cancer Soc., 2005. Mem.: NASW (MSW Gosnell Meml. Scholarship Panel 2003—06, Nat. Com. on Women's Issues 2005—), Am. Coll. Musicians, Nat. Guild Piano Tchrs. Roman Catholic. Avocations: dance, piano, meditation. Office Phone: 305-571-9996. Personal E-mail: mquiala@bellsouth.net.

QUIAT, GERALD M., lawyer; b. Denver, Jan. 9, 1924; s. Ira L. and Esther (Greenblatt) Q.; m. Roberta M. Nicholson, Sept. 26, 1962; children: James M., Audrey R., Melinda A., Daniel P., Ilana L., Leonard E. AA, U. Calif., Berkeley, 1942; AB, LLB, U. Denver, 1948, changed to JD, 1970. Bar: Colo. 1948, Fed. Ct. 1948, U.S. Dist. Ct. Colo. 1948, U.S. Ct. Appeals (10th cir.) 1948, U.S. Surpeme Ct. 1970. Dep. dist. atty. City and Co. of Denver, Colo., 1949-52; partner firm Quiat, Seeman & Quiat, Denver, 1952-67, Quiat & Quiat (later changed to Quiat, Bucholtz & Bull, P.C.), 1968; pres. Quiat, Bucholtz & Bull & Laff, P.C. (and predecessors), Denver, 1968-85; pvt. practice Denver, 1985—. Bd. dirs., past chmn. audit com. Guaranty Bank & Trust Co., Denver. Past trustee Holding Co.; pres., chmn. bd. dirs. Rose Med. Ctr., Denver, 1976—79; mem. Colo. Civil Rights Com., 1963—71, chmn., 1966—67, 1969—70, hearing officer, 1963—71; bd. dirs. AMC Cancer Rsch. Ctr., Denver, 1971—2004, chmn. bd., 1991—93, sec. treas., 2000—04; chmn. bd. Am. Med. Ctr., 1993—95; hon. mem. nat. civil rights com. Anti-Defamation League, hon. mem. nat. exec. com., hon. nat. commr.; chmn. Mountain State region, 1980—82; mem. exec. com., bd. mem. Mountain States region Anti-Defamation League. With inf. US Army, 1942—45. Decorated Combat Infantry Badge, Bronze Star. Mem. ABA, Colo. Bar Assn., Am. Legion (comdr. Leyden-Chiles-Wickersham post 1 1955-56, past judge adv. Colo. dept.). Home: 5361 Nassau Cir E Englewood CO 80110-5100 Office: 1873 S Bellaire St Ste 900 Denver CO 80222-4304 Home Phone: 303-300-0722; Office Phone: 303-759-1000 ext. 102. E-mail: gqph@aol.com.

QUICK, ADAM D., neurologist; b. Sturgis, Mich., July 29, 1975; s. William and Janice Quick; m. Allison Quick, Aug. 26, 2003. BA, Wabash Coll., Crawfordsville, 1998; MD, Ind. U., Indpls., 2002. Neurologist U. Vt., Burlington, 2002—, neuromuscular fellow, 2006—. Rsch. U. Vt., Billington, 2006—07. Contbr. chapters to books. Mem.: Am. Acad. Neurology. Avocations: snowboarding, running, travel.

QUICK, DANNY RICHARD, computer systems engineer; b. Millen, Ga., Aug. 7, 1948; s. John Francis and Olene (Crane) Q.; m. Donna Kay Nobles, Oct. 13, 1973; children: Dexter Brian, Debby Kim. Cert. data processing, Strayer Coll., 1989. Enlisted USAF, 1967, advanced through grades to sr. master sgt., 1984; chief Message Processing Br. Orgn. Joints Chiefs of Staff, Pentagon, Washington, 1984—88, ret., 1988; sys. analyst Potomac Sys. Engring., Annandale, Va., 1988—89; sr. sys. cons. Wang Labs., Inc., Bethesda, Md., 1989—93; prin. sys. engr. Computer Scis. Corp., Falls Church, Va., 1993—2002; computer specialist Dept. of State, Washington, 2002—. Methods & procedures panel U.S. Mil. Comm.-Electronics Bd., Washington, 1984-88, call signs panel, 1984-88. Recipient Def. Meritorious Svc. medal Sec. Def., Washington, 1987, Meritorious Svc. medal Sec. Air Force, Washington, 1980; named one of 50 Outstanding Airmen of Yr., Airforce Mil. Pers. Ctr., Randolph AFB, Tex., 1983-84. Mem.: Am. Legion (editor Post-O-Gram 1983—84, exec. com. 1984—86). Republican. Methodist. Achievements include merge of the principal officers e-mail system and the foreign affairs information systems networks; led the Dept. of State test and deploy team in testing and deploying a Lotus Notes locally developed database program, which is installed on a Microsoft Windows NT/2000/2003 LAN, for distributing inbound and transmitting outbound diplomatic telegrams, throughout the Department of State and at American embassies and consulates; provide Tier 4 IT support for domestic and overseas operations. Home: 4 Caledon Ct Stafford VA 22556-1608 Office: Dept of State IRM/OPS/MSO/MSP/TD 7374 Boston Blvd Springfield VA 22153-2804 Personal E-mail: catpaws777@aol.com.

QUICK, EDWARD RAYMOND, museum director, educator, curator; b. LA, Mar. 22, 1943; s. Donald Russell Quick and Gertrude Ruth (Albin) Thornbrough; m. Ruth Ann Lessig; children: Jeannette Lee, Russell Raymond. BA, U. Calif., Santa Barbara, 1970, MA, 1977. Adminstr. supr. Civil Service, Santa Ana, Calif., 1971-75; sr. computer operator Santa Barbara Rsch. Ctr., 1975-77; asst. collections curator Santa Barbara Mus. Art, 1977-78; collections mgr. Montgomery (Ala.) Mus. Fine Arts, 1978-80; asst. dir. Joslyn Art Mus., Omaha, 1980-85; dir. Sheldon Swope Art Mus., Terre Haute, Ind., 1985-95, Berman Mus., Anniston, Ala., 1995-97; mus. curator National Archives, Washington, 1998-2000, William Clinton Presdl. Libr. and Mus., 2000—04; staff curator mus. mgmt. Nat. Archives Office Presdl. Librs., Washington, 2004—. Adv. Ind. Arts Commn., Indpls., 1986-91; mem. Arts in Pub. Places Commn., Terre Haute, Ind., 1986-93; pres. Friends Vigo County Pub. Libr., 1988-95, treas., 1990-93. Author: Code of Practice for Couriering Museum Objects, 1985, Gilbert Brown Wilson and Herman Melville's Moby Dick, 1993, The American West in the Berman Collections, 1997, Cattle Drive, 1997 others; co-author: Registrars in Record, 1987; contbg. author: Dante Marioni: Blown Glass, 2000. Bd. dirs. Vol. Action Ctr., Terre Haute, 1987-90, Terre Haute Cmty. Relief Effort for Environ. and Civic Spirit, 1989. With USAF, 1961-65, Air N.G., 1979-96. Mem. Am. Assn. Mus. (adv. 1994—, mgmt. and long-range planning com. 1994—), Assn. Ind. Mus., Am. Assn. State and Local History, Internat. Coun. Mus., Washington Print Club, Rotary Internat., Kiwanis Internat., English Conv. Club (leader 2007—), Alpha Gamma Sigma. Office: Nat Archives Presdl Librs 8601 Adelphi Rd Rm 1320 College Park MD 20740-6001 Office Phone: 301-837-0611. Business E-Mail: edward.quick@nara.gov.

QUICK, ELIZABETH L., lawyer; b. Izmir, Turkey, May 22, 1948; BA, Duke U., 1970; JD with honors, U. NC, 1974. Bar: NC 1974. Mem., trusts & estates Womble Carlyle Sandridge & Rice, Winston-Salem, NC, mem. mgmt. com. Vis. lectr. U. NC Sch. Law, 1977. Mem. U. NC Law Review, 1973—74, co-author, editor NC Estate Adminstrn. Manual, 1984; contbr. articles to profl. jours. Bd. dir. Cannon Found., Concord, NC, Reynolda House, inc., Winston-Salem, NC; bd. trustee Salem Coll. & Acad., Winston-Salem, NC; mem. Winston-Salem Found. Com. Fellow Am. Coll. Trust and Estate Counsel (past chmn.); mem. ABA, NC Bar Assn. (pres. 1997-98), Forsyth County Bar Assn. (treas.), Order of Coif. Mailing: Womble Carlyle Sandridge & Rice PLLC PO Box 84 Winston Salem NC 27102 Office: Womble Carlyle Sandridge & Rice PLLC One West 4th St Winston Salem NC 27101 Office Phone: 336-721-3638. Office Fax: 336-733-8359. Business E-Mail: equick@wcsr.com.

QUICK, FRANCES KING, lawyer; b. Florence, Ala., Apr. 6, 1957; d. Percy Madding Jr. and Ruby Jones King; m. James Keith Quick, Oct. 9, 1999. BA, U. Ala., Tuscaloosa, 1979, JD, 1991. With Aetna Casualty and Surety, Birmingham, Ala., 1981—88; law clk. to chief judge Sam C. Pointer Jr. US Dist. Ct. (no. dist.) Ala., Birmingham, 1991—92; assoc. Adama and Reese, LLP, Birmingham, 1992—. Trustee U. Ala. Sch. Law Found., Tuscaloosa, 2006—; bd. dirs. Am. Heart Assn., Birmingham, 2003—, Women's Network, Birmingham, 2005—. Mem.: ABA, Birmingham Bar Assn. (chmn. exec. com. women's lawyer sect. 2006, mem. exec. com. 2005—, Disting. Svc. award women lawyers sect. 2001, Shining Star award 1999). Methodist. Avocations: bridge, growing dahlias. Office: Adams and Reese LLP 2100 3d Ave N Birmingham AL 35203

QUICK, JONATHAN DICKINSON, health organization executive; b. Albany, NY, June 5, 1951; s. James F. and Olva F. (Faust) Q.; m. Tina L. Burdick, May 1, 1982; children: Janneke C., Katrina F., Kimberly C. AB magna cum laude, Harvard U., 1974; MPH, MD, U. Rochester, 1979. Diplomate Am. Bd. Family Practice, Am. Bd. Preventive Medicine. Resident/chief resident family medicine Duke U., Durham, NC, 1982; chief of staff USPHS Hosp., Talihina, Okla., 1982-84; dir. drug mgmt. program Mgmt. Scis. for Health, Boston, 1984-89, health svcs. advisor Peshawar, Pakistan, 1989-91; health planner Min. of Health, Nairobi, Kenya, 1991-94; med. officer WHO, Geneva, 1995-96, dir. essential drugs, 1996-98, dir. essential drugs and medicines policy, 1999—2004; pres., CEO Mgmt Scis. For Health, Boston, 2004—. Adj. assoc. prof. Boston U. Sch. Pub. Health, 1990—; cons. Aga Khan Health Scis., Tanzania, 1982-83. Editor: Managing Drug Supply, 1997; co-editor: Preventive Stress Management in Organizations, 1997; co-author: Stress and Challenge at the Top, 1990, Rhinos in the Rough: A Golfer's Guide to Kenya, 1993, Financial Times Guide to executive Health, 2002; editl. bd. Jour. Occupl. Health Psychology, 1995—. Mem. worship team Hope Christian Ch., Ferney-Voltaine, France, 1996—. Lt. USPHS, 1982-84. Fellow Royal Soc. Medicine, Am. Coll. Preventive Medicine; mem. Am. Acad. Family Physicians, Rotary Interant. (com. mem. 1992-94). Avocations: jazz and rock 'n roll drumming, jogging, skiing, writing. Office: Mgmt Scis Health 165 Allandale Rd Boston MA 02130 Office Phone: 617-250-9396.

QUICK, PETER, stock exchange executive; married. BS in Engring., U. Va.; postgrad., Stanford U. With U.S. Clearing Corp., 1983-94, pres., 1990-94, Quick & Reilly Group, Inc., 1994-96, Quick & Reilly, Inc., NYC, 1996—2000, Am. Stock Exch., NYC, 2000—, also bd. govs. Bd. dirs. Securities Industry Automation Corp., Reckson Associates Realty Corp. Bd. dirs. St. Francis Hospital, Good Shepherd Hospice; trustee Securities Industry Inst., Wharton Sch. U. Penn.; mem. nat. selection com. Jefferson scholar program U. Va.; trustee Museum of Am. Financial History. Recipient Ellis Island Medal of Honor award, 2001. Office: The Am Stock Exch 86 Trinity Pl New York NY 10006

QUICKSILVER, WILLIAM TODD, lawyer; b. St. Louis, July 26, 1952; AB magna cum laude, Princeton U., NJ, 1974; JD, U. Chgo., 1978. Bar: Calif. 1978. COO, dep. mng. ptnr. Manatt, Phelps & Phillips, LLP, LA, 2003—06, chief exec., mng. ptnr., bd. dirs., co-chair bus. and transactions divsn., 2007—. Dir. Pub. Counsel Law Ctr.; spkr. in field. Assoc. editor: U. Chgo. Law Rev. Mem.: ABA, Century City Bar Assn. Office: Manatt Phelps & Phillips LLP 11355 W Olympic Blvd Los Angeles CA 90064-1614 Office Phone: 310-312-4210. Office Fax: 310-312-4224. E-mail: wquicksilver@manatt.com. *

QUIE, PAUL GERHARDT, pediatrician, educator; b. Dennison, Minn., Feb. 3, 1925; s. Albert Knute and Nettie Marie (Jacobson) Quie; m. Elizabeth Holmes, Aug. 10, 1951; children: Katie, Bill, Paul, David. BA, St. Olaf Coll., 1949; MD, Yale U., 1953; PhD (hon.), U. Lund, 1993. Diplomate Am. Bd. Pediat., Nat. Bd. Med. Examiners (mem.). Intern Hennepin County Hosp., 1953—54; pediatric resident U. Minn. Hosps., 1957—59; mem. faculty U. Minn. Med. Sch., 1959—, prof. pediatrics, 1968—99, prof. microbiology, 1974—99, assoc. dean of students, 1992—, Am. Legion meml. heart research prof., 1974—91, Regents prof., 1991; Regent's prof. emeritus, 1999—; interim dir. Ctr. for Biomed. Ethics U. Minn. Med. Sch., 1985—86; attending physician Hennepin County Hosp., 1959—91. Cons. U. Minn. Nursery Sch., 1959—91; chief of staff U. Minn. Hosp., 1979—84; vis. physician Radcliffe Infirmary, Oxford, England, 1971—72; mem. Adv. Allergy and Infectious Disease Coun., 1976—80; mem. pediat. com. NRC, 1978; mem. bd. sci. counselors Gamble Inst., 1985—90; vis. prof. U. Bergen, 1991; hon. prof. U. Hong Kong Med. Sch., 1995; vis. prof. pediat. Chubu Hosp., Nagasaki, Japan, 1996; co-dir. internat. med. edn. and rsch. program U. Minn. Med. Sch., 1998—. Editl. bd. Pediat., 1970—76, Rev. Infectious Diseases, 1989—92. Pres. Fairview Found., 1998—2007; bd. dirs. Ctr. for Victims of Torture, Elizabeth Glaser Pediat. AIDS Found., 1998—2005. Med. officer USNR, 1954—57. Recipient E. Mead-Johnson award, Am. Acad. Pediat., 1971, Shotwell award, Hennipen Med. Soc., 2001, Gold Headed Cane award in Pediatrics, 2005; fellow Guggenheim, 1971—72, Alexander von Humboldt, 1986; scholar John and Mary R. Markle, 1960—65. Mem.: Minn. Acad. Medicine (pres. 1993—94), Assn. Am. Physicians, Am. Acad. Pediat., Minn. Acad. Pediat., Am. Soc. Clin. Investigation, Am. Pediatric Soc. (coun. 1976—83, pres. 1987—88), Soc. Pediatric Rsch., Infectious Diseases Soc. Am. (coun. 1977—82, pres. 1985, Bristol award 1994), Am. Soc. Microbiology, Am. Fedn. Clin. Rsch., Minn. Med. Found. (pres. 1986—88), N.W. Pediat. Soc., Inst. Medicine of NAS. Achievements include research in function of human leukocytes and international medical education and research. Home: 2154 Commonwealth Ave Saint Paul MN 55108 Office: PO Box 293 Minneapolis MN 55455-0374 Office Phone: 612-626-2558. Business E-Mail: quiex001@umn.edu.

QUIGGINS, LARRY DALE, theater educator; b. St. Louis, Jan. 6, 1962; s. Walter Louis Quiggins and Mildred Hoskinson; m. Elizabeth Marie McEvoy, May 30, 1986; children: Benjamin T'omas, James Tiberious. A in Comm., Florissant Valley C.C., St. Louis, 1983; BA, Lindenwood U., St. Charles, Mo., 1998, MFA, 2000. Owner Bug's Comics & Games, Inc., St. Louis, 1991—; prof. Lindenwood U., 2001—. Tour dir. Florissant Valley C.C., St. Louis, 1984—91, Off the Cuff Prodns., 2000—01. Author: (theatrical play: adaptation) Scrooge: A Christmas Carol, (children's play) The Adventures of Cookie-Man; actor: (improvisation troupe) NIghtshift Improv Troupe; dir.: The Nick of Time Players. Avocations: theater, comic book collecting, creative writing, music. Home: 3218 Catesby Ln Saint Charles MO 63301 Office: Lindenwood U 209 S Kings Hwy Saint Charles MO 63301 Home Phone: 636-949-3912; Office Phone: 636-949-4850. Personal E-mail: nevellah@msn.com. E-mail: lquiggins@lindenwood.edu.

QUIGLEY, JAMES B., diversified financial services company executive; BS in Internat. Econs., George Washington U. Elliott Sch. Internat. Affairs. With NY Syndicate Grp. Merrill Lynch, 1983, exec. dir. London Syndicate Grp., head US High Grade Syndicate Grp., head Debt Transactions Grp., head global issuer client grp. for global debt markets, sr. v.p., head client strategies for global debt markets, vice chmn. exec. client coverage grp., 2002—, vice-chmn., head Latin Am. global markets and investment banking, 2006—, pres. Merrill Lynch Internat., Inc. Office: Merrill Lynch 4 World Fin Ctr 250 Vesey St New York NY 10080

QUIGLEY, JAMES H., accounting firm executive; b. Utah, 1953; m. Bonnie Quigley; 3 children. BS, Utah State U., 1974; PhD in comml. sci. (hon.), Bentley Coll., Waltham, Mass., 2005. With Deloitte & Touche USA LLP, 1974—, asst. to chmn., sec. to bd. dirs., chief staff to office of chmn., nat. industry leader mfg. practice, vice chmn., regional mng. ptnr. N.E. practice, 1999—2003, CEO, 2003—, also bd. dirs.; bd. dirs. Deloitte Touche Tohmatsu. Bd. dirs. US C. of C., Catalyst; bd. trustees Fin. Acctg. Found. Bd. dirs. Partnership for NYC; bd. trustees Ctrl. Park Conservancy; nat. adv. coun. Brigham Young U. Marriott Sch. Mgmt.; mem leadership com. Lincoln Ctr. Corp. Fund. Mem.: Union League Club, Econ. Club NY. Office: Deloitte & Touche USA LLP 1633 Broadway New York NY 10019-6754 Office Phone: 212-489-1600. Office Fax: 212-489-1687. *

QUIGLEY, JOHN BERNARD, law educator; b. St. Louis, Oct. 1, 1940; s. John Bernard and Ruth Rosina (Schieber) Q. BA, Harvard U., 1962, MA, LLB, 1966. Bar: Ohio 1973, Mass. 1967, U.S. Dist. Ct. (so. dist.) Ohio 1976, U.S. Ct. Appeals (6th cir.) 1986, U.S. Supreme Ct. 1989. Research assoc. Harvard U. Law Sch., Cambridge, Mass., 1967-69; prof. law Ohio State U., Columbus, 1969—. Author: Basic Laws on the Structure of the Soviet State, 1969, The Soviet Foreign Trade Monopoly, 1974, Palestine and Israel: A Challenge to Justice, 1990, The Ruses for War: American Interventionism since World War II, 1992, 2nd edit., 2007, Flight into the Maelstrom: Soviet Immigration to Israel and Middle East Peace, 1997, Genocide in Cambodia, 2000, The Case for Palestine: An International Law Perspective, 2005, The Genocide Convention: An International Law Analysis, 2006, Soviet Legal Innovation and the Law of the Western World, 2007. Mem. Nat. Lawyers Guild (v.p. 1977-79), Am. Soc. Internat. Law, AAUP. Avocations: tennis, speed skating, violin. Office: Ohio State U Coll of Law Coll of Law 55 W 12th Ave Columbus OH 43210-1338

QUIGLEY, JOHN MICHAEL, economist, educator; b. NYC, Feb. 12, 1942; BS with distinction, U.S. Air Force Acad., 1964; MSc with honors, U. Stockholm, Sweden, 1965; AM, Harvard U., 1971, PhD, 1972. Commd. 2d lt. USAF, 1964, advanced through grades to capt., 1968; asst. prof. econs. Yale U., 1972-74, assoc. prof., 1974-81; prof. pub. policy U. Calif., Berkeley, 1979—, prof. econs., 1981—, Chancellor's prof., 1997—, prof. bus., 1999—, I. Donald Terner disting. prof., 1999—, chmn. dept. econs., 1992-95; vis. prof. econs. and stats. U. Gothenberg, 1978. Cons. numerous govt. agys. and pvt. firms; econometrician Hdqrs. U.S. Air Force, Pentagon, 1965-68; research assoc. Nat. Bur. Econ. Research, N.Y.C., 1968-78; mem. com. on nat. urban policy NAS, 1985-93. Author, editor, contbr. articles to profl. jours.; editor in chief Reg. Sci. and Urban Econs., 1987-2003; mem. editl. bd. many sci. and scholarly jours. Fulbright scholar, 1964-65; fellow NSF, 1968-69, Woodrow Wilson, 1968-71, Harvard IBM, 1969-71, NDEA, 1969-71, Thord-Gray Am. Scandinavian Found. 1971-72, Social Sci. Research Council, 1971-72. Mem. Am. Econ. Assn., Econometric Soc., Regional Sci. Assn. (bd. dirs. 1986—), Nat. Tax Assn., Assn. for Pub. Policy and Mgmt. (bd. dirs. 1986-89, v.p. 1987-89), Am. Real Estate and Urban Econs. Assn. (bd. dirs. 1987-2001, pres. 1995-97), Royal Swedish Acad. Engring. Scis. (fgn.). Home: 875 Hilldale Ave Berkeley CA 94708-1319 Office: U Calif 2607 Hearst Ave Berkeley CA 94720-7305 Business E-Mail: quigley@econ.berkeley.edu.

QUIGLEY, MARTIN SCHOFIELD, writer, educator; b. Chgo., Nov. 24, 1917; s. Martin Joseph and Gertrude Margaret (Schofield) Q.; m. Katherine J. Dunphy, July 2, 1946; children: Martin, Elin, William, Kevin, Karen, Patricia, John, Mary Katherine, Peter. AB magna cum laude, Georgetown U., 1939; MA, Columbia U., 1973, EdD, 1975. Reporter Motion Picture Herald, NYC and Hollywood, Calif., 1939-41; with overseas br. OWI, 1942; secret war work U.S. Govt., 1943-45; various editl. and mgmt. posts Quigley Pub. Co., Inc., NYC, 1946—2001, pres., 1964-2001, chmn., 2001—; staff, dept. higher and adult edn. Tchrs. Coll., 1974-75; prof. higher edn. grad. courses Baruch Coll. CUNY, 1977-89; prof. higher edn. grad. courses Tchrs. Coll. Columbia U., 1979-80, 90; prof. higher edn. grad. courses Seton Hall U., 1981-82. Pres. QWS, Inc., 1975-80; ednl. cons.; cons. supt. schs. N.Y. Archdiocese, 1962-70 Author: Great Gaels, 1944, 2d edit. 1997, Roman Notes, 1946, Magic Shadows--the story of the origin of motion pictures, 1948, Government Relations of Five Universities in Washington, 1975, Peace Without Hiroshima-Secret Action at the Vatican in Spring of 1945, 1991, First Century of Film, 1995, A U.S. Spy in Ireland, 1999, Community College Movement in Perspective, 2003, Martin J. Quigley and the Glory Days of American Film-1915-65, 2006; co-author: Catholic Action in Practice, 1962, Films in America, 1969; editor: New Screen Techniques, 1953. Pres. NY Christian Family Movement, 1960-62, nat. exec. com., 1960-65; founder, chmn. NY Ind. Schs. Opportunity Project, 1965-77; pres. Found. Internat. Coop., 1960-65; bd. dirs. Will Rogers Inst., Motion Picture Pioneers; treas. Religious Edn. Assn. US and Can., 1975-81, chmn., 1981-84; trustee Village of Larchmont, NY, 1977-79, mayor, 1980-84; trustee Am. Bible Soc., 1984-2007; bd. dirs. William J. Donovan Meml. Found., 1994-2001. Mem.: Larchmont Yacht. Roman Catholic. Personal E-mail: greatgaels@aol.com.

QUIGLEY, MATTHEW RICHARD, neurosurgeon; b. Bklyn., Nov. 7, 1955; s. Daniel Nolan and Helen Marie Quigley; m. Heidi Margarite Martin, Sept. 5, 1987; children: Matthew, Madeline. BS, Trinity Coll., Hartford, Conn., 1977; MD, Northwestern U., Chgo., 1987. Cert. Am. Bd. Neurol. Surgeons. Staff neurosurgeon Allegheny Gen. Hosp., Pitts., 1989—, chmn. IRB, 2000—, program dir. neurosurgery residency, 2005—; assoc. prof. neurosurgery Drexel U., Phila., 1996—. Contbr. articles to profl. jours. Mem.: Congress Neurol. Surgeons, Am. Assn. Neurol. Surgeons. Achievements include design of balloon-in-balloon chemotherapy device. Avocations: squash, wine collecting. Office: Allegheny Gen Hosp 420 E North Ave Pittsburgh PA 15212

QUIGLEY, MICHAEL, lawyer; b. Flushing, NY; AB, Univ. Calif., Berkeley, 1980; JD cum laude, Pepperdine Univ., 1980. Bar: Calif. 1983, US Ct. of Fed. Claims 1987, US Tax Ct. 1988, DC 1989, US Supreme Ct. 1991, US Ct. of Appeals (fed. cir.) 1991. Trial atty., tax divsn. US Dept. Justice; ptnr., internat. taxation and mem. mgmt. com. Akin Gump Strauss Hauer & Feld LLP, Washington; ptnr., head tax controversy practice White & Case LLP, Washington, 2006—. Mem.: ABA, DC Bar Assn., State Bar of Calif., Fed. Bar Assn. (chmn. sect. taxation 1993—94, 1995—96). Office: White & Case LLP 701 Thirteenth St NW Washington DC 20005 E-mail: michaelquigley@whitecase.com.

QUIGLEY, ROB WELLINGTON, architect; b. Calif., 1945; B, Univ. Utah, 1969. Registered Architect, Calif., 1976. Architect Peace Corps, Chile; prin. Quigley Architects, San Diego, Palo Alto, 1974—. Adj. prof. arch. Univ. Calif., San Diego; vis. design prof. Harvard Univ. Grad. Sch. Design, 1991, Univ. Tex., Austin, 1994, Univ. Calif., Berkeley, 1997, 98; spkr. in field; invited juror and advisor. Prin. works include San Diego New Main Libr. (Honor award, AIA San Diego, 1998), Sherman Heights Cmty. Ctr. (Citation, AIA San Diego, 1990, Orchid, San Diego Chpt. AIA, 1992, Merit award, AIA San Diego, 1996), Golden Hill Community Ctr., Baltic Inn, San Diego (Honor award, AIA San Diego, 1987, Panda award, City of San Diego, 1988), 202 Island Inn (One of "Ten Best Designs of 1992," Time Mag., 1993, Nat. AIA Honor award, 1993, Merit award, AIA San Diego, 1993, Honor award with Distinction, AIA Calif. Coun., 1994), Solana Beach Transit Sta. (Orchid, San Diego Chpt., AIA, 1996, Honor award, AIA Calif. Coun., 1998), Escondido Transit Sta. (Citation, AIA San Diego, 1990, Orchid,AIA San Diego, 1991, Beautification award, City of Escondido, 1990), San Diego Children's Mus., Calif., Student Academic Services Facility, U. Calif. San Diego, San Diego Historic Harbor Front, West Valley Branch Libr. (Divine Detail, AIA San Diego, 2003, Merit award, AIA Santa Clara, 2004), Leslie Shao-ming Sun Field Station, Stanford U. (Merit award, AIA San Diego, 2003, Honor award, AIA Santa Clara, 2004, COTE Top Ten Green Buildings, Nat. AIA, 2005), Opportunity Ctr. for the Midpeninsula (Advocacy Planning award, Northern Sect. Am. Planning Assn., 2003), Shaw Lopez Park, Casa Feliz, and several others, solo exhibitions, Retrospective, So. Calif. Inst. of Architecture, Santa Monica, 1982, Exhibit of Recent Work, UCLA, 1984, Recent Work, Portland State U., 1991, exhibitions include Visual Communication Towards Architecture, Installation Gallery, San Diego, 1982, Don Clos Pegase Competition, San Francisco Mus. Contemporary Art, 1985, The Emerging Generation in the USA, Global Architecture Gallery, Tokyo, Japan, 1987, Five Choose Five, Nat. AIA Conf., St. Louis, 1989, Fabrications, San Francisco Mus. Modern Art, 1998, Books, Bytes and Mortar, Mus. Contemporary Art, San Diego, 2001, Modern Trains and Splendid Stations, Art Inst. Chgo., 2002, and several others; co-author: (monograph) Buildings & Projects, 1996. Named Headliner of Yr. in Architecture, San Diego Press Club, 1995; named one of 100 Foremost Architects of the World, AD 100, Architectural Digest, 1991, 88 San Diegans to Watch in '88', San Diego Mag., 1988, The San Diego 50 People to Watch in 1997, 1997; recipient Presdl. Commendation for Exemplary Cmty. Svc., 1988, Firm award, AIA Calif. Coun., 1995, Maybeck award, 2005, The Irving Gill award, AIA San Diego, 1997, several mag. and cmty. program awards, several awards for design excellence from the Nat. AIA, AIA Santa Clara, AIA San Diego, and AIA Calif. Coun.; fellow Inst. for Urban Design, 1996. Fellow: AIA; mem.: NAD. Office: Quigley Architects 434 W Cedar St San Diego CA 92101 also: 210 High St Palo Alto CA 94301 Office Phone: 619-232-0888, 650-328-8030. E-mail: office@robquigley.com.

QUIGLEY, ROBERT CHARLES, insurance industry consultant; b. Phila., 1949; s. James and Kathrine Regina (Kinckiner) Q.; m. Barbara Jeanne Browne, 1971; children: Robert J., Michael J., Brian A., Jason T. BS in Acctg., Pa. State U., 1970. CPA, Pa., NJ. Sr. acct. Touche Ross & Co., Phila., 1970—72; dir. acctg. policy and rsch. Ins. Co. of N.Am., Phila., 1972—81; asst. treas. Reliance Ins. Co., Phila., 1981—85; v.p., treas. Mut. Fire Marine and Inland Ins. Co., Phila., 1985—86; owner Quigley & Assocs., Hatboro, Pa., 1987—. Team leader accreditation Nat. Assn. of Ins. Commrs., Kansas City, 1992—. Author: (with others) Property and Liability Insurance Accounting, 5th edit., 1991. With USMCR, 1967. Mem.: AICPAs, Internat. Assn. Ins. Receivers, AIDA Reinsurance and Ins. Arbitration Soc. U.S. (cert. arbitrator), Soc. of Ins. Fin. Mgmt. Republican. Presbyterian. Avocations: reading, writing. Office: PO Box 147 Hatboro PA 19040-0147 Home Phone: 215-443-0591. Business E-Mail: RCQCPA@aol.com.

QUIGLEY, STEPHEN HOWARD, executive editor; b. Boston, May 29, 1951; s. John Joseph Sr. and Anne Margaret (O'Brien) Quigley; m. Suzanne Elizabeth Daley, July 21, 1980; children: Benjamin Parker, Theodore Hunter, Margaret Hunter. BA in French and Internat. Rels., Dartmouth Coll., 1973. Sales rep. Addison-Wesley Pub. Co., Inc., Reading, Mass., 1973—75, math. editor, 1975—81, regional sales mgr., 1981—85; sr. math. editor Scott, Foresman and Co., Chgo., 1985—88, PWS-KENT Pub. Co., Boston, 1988—95; exec. editor math. and stats. sci., tech. and med. pub. divsn. John Wiley and Sons, Inc., Marblehead, Mass., 1995—. Mem. Independence Day Celebration Commn., 1987—88; mem. Eveleth Sch. liaison Sch. PTA, Marblehead, Mass., 1989—90, vice chair sch. com., 1991—92, chair sch. comm., 1992—93; water safety chmn., bd. dirs. Greater Lynn chpt. ARC, 1978—81; leader Boy Scouts Am., Explorers Group, Marblehead, 1976—79; swim ofcl. Ill. High Sch. Ofcls. Assn., 1984—88; lector Star of Sea Ch., Marblehead, 1988—; dir. Goldthwait Reservation, Marblehead; vol. Marblehead Little Theatre, 2001—, Marblehead/Swampsott YMCA Nostalgia Weekend Swim Off, 2005. Recipient Club of Yr. award, Darmouth Coll., 1988, Disting. Book award, Assn. Am. Publ., 2001, 2002, 2007, 2d Place award, Bay State Swimming Masters, 2006. Mem.: ASCD, Nat. Coun. Tchrs. Math., Nat. Fedn. Interscholastic Ofcls. Assn., Am. Math. Assn. Two-Yr. Colls., Am. Statis. Assn., Math. Assn. Am., Am. Math. Soc., Geol. Soc. Am., Glenview C. of C. (mem. accreditation team 1988), Friends of the Performing Arts, North Shore Friends in Pub. (founding group), Chgo. Dartmouth Club (pres. 1988—89), North Shore (Mass.) Dartmouth Club, Corinthian Yacht Club (rec. chair, operating com. 1997—2000), Rotary (bd. dirs. Boston 1990—95, Svc. award 1988). Republican. Roman Catholic. Avocations: swimming, sailing, tennis, singing, computers. Home: 10 Leicester Rd Marblehead MA 01945-1817 Office: Wiley Pub 2 Hooper St Marblehead MA 01945-3431 Office Phone: 781-631-0062. Business E-Mail: squigley@wiley.com.

QUIGNEY, THERESA ANN, special education educator; b. East Cleveland, Ohio, June 19, 1952; d. James and Lenora Mary (McDonald) Q.; m. Joseph Carl Lang, July 23, 1983. BA, Notre Dame Coll., 1974; MEd, Cleve. State U., 1980; PhD, Kent State U., 1992. Cert. tchr. handicapped K-12; cert. ednl. adminstrv. specialist edn. of exceptional pupils; cert. ednl. supr.; cert. elem. prin.; cert. h.s. prin. cert. tchr. French K-12, Ohio. Spl. edn. tchr. Newbury (Ohio) Local Schs., 1974—80; county supr., specific learning disabilities and behavior handicaps Geauga County Bd. Edn., Chardon, Ohio, 1980—86, 1987—88; asst. prof. spl. edn. West Chester (Pa.) U., 1992—93; asst. prof. edn. Heidelberg Coll., Tiffin, Ohio, 1993—94; assoc. prof. spl. edn. Cleve. State U., 1994—, coord. spl. edn. program Coll. Edn., 2000—02. Ednl. rschr.; presenter in field. Contbr. articles to profl. jours., chapters to books. Vol. cons. Tchrs. for Action Rsch. South Euclid/Lyndhurst (Ohio) Sch. Dist., 1996—; past participant issues task force Ohio Coun. for Exceptional Children; presenter, participant Oxford Round Table, Oxford U., England; past bd. mem. Camp Sue Osborne, Lake County, Ohio; mem. steering com. State Improvement Grant (Edn.), 2000—02. Grantee Ohio State Supt.'s Task Force on Spl. Edn., 1997, Cleve. State U. Coll. Edn., 1997, Am. Sch. Counselor's Assn.; recipient achievement recognition Assn. for Children and Adults with Learning Disabilities, Ohio, 1980. Mem. CEC, ASCD, Am. Ednl. Rsch. Assn., Learning Disabilities Assn., Mid-We. Ednl. Rsch. Assn., Coun. for Learning Disabilities, Kappa Delta Pi, Phi Delta Kappa, Pi Lambda Theta. Avocations: travel, writing, reading, sketching. Office: Cleveland State Univ Euclid Ave at E 24th St Cleveland OH 44115 Business E-Mail: t.quigney@csuohio.edu.

QUILLEN, CECIL DYER, JR., lawyer, consultant; b. Kingsport, Tenn., Jan. 21, 1937; s. Cecil and Mary Louise (Carter) Q.; m. Vicey Ann Childress, Apr. 1, 1961; children: Cecil III, Ann C. Macaulay. BS, Va. Poly. Inst., Blacksburg, 1958; LLB, U. Va., Charlottesville, 1962. Bar: Va. 1962, NY 1963, Tenn. 1974; cert. in exec. devel., U. Tenn., Knoxville, 1976. Atty. patent dept. Eastman Kodak Co., Rochester, NY, 1962—65; atty. patent sect. Tenn. Eastman Co. (divsn. Eastman Kodak), Kingsport, 1965—69, mgr. patent sect., 1969—72, mgr. licensing, 1972—74, sec. and asst. chief counsel, 1974—76, v.p., chief counsel, 1983—85; dir. patent litigation Eastman Kodak, 1976—82, dir. antitrust litigation, 1978—82, v.p., assoc. gen. counsel, 1986, sr. v.p., gen. counsel, dir., 1986—92; sr. advisor Putnam, Hayes, Bartlett and PHB Hagler Bailly, Washington, 1992—2000, Cornerstone Rsch., Washington, 2000—. Contbr. articles to profl. jours. Bd. dirs. Pub. Patent Found., 2006—; former mem. law alumni adv. coun. U. Va Law Sch. Mem. ABA, Va. State Bar, Am. Intellectual Property Law Assn., Va. Poly. Inst. Com. of 100, Assn. Gen. Counsel, Phi Kappa Phi, Omicron Delta Kappa, Tau Beta Pi, Phi Lambda Upsilon. Office Phone: 202-912-8930. Personal E-mail: cecilquillen@comcast.net. Business E-Mail: cquillen@cornerstone.com.

QUILLEN, CECIL DYER, III, lawyer; b. Rochester, NY, Aug. 15, 1963; s. Cecil Dyer, Jr. and Vicey Ann (Childress) Q.; m. Mary Stuart Humes, Oct. 20, 1990; children: Caroline, James C.D., George, Elizabeth. AB magna cum laude, Harvard U., 1985; JD, U. Va., 1988. Bar: N.Y. 1989, D.C. 1991, U.S. Ct. Appeals (4th cir.) 1989. Law clk., Sr. Cir. Judge U.S. Ct. Appeals (4th cir.), Richmond, Va., 1988-89; assoc. Sullivan & Cromwell, NYC, 1989-95, Linklaters, NYC, 1995-96, ptnr., 1996—, ptnr. London office, 2000—. Bd. dirs. European High Yield Assn.; spkr. various profl. confs. Notes editor Va. Law Rev., 1987-88. Mem. ABA, N.Y. State Bar Assn., Assn. Bar City of N.Y., Raven Soc., Order of Coif, Phi Beta Kappa. Office: Linklaters One Silk St London EC2Y 8HQ England

QUILLEN, LLOYD DOUGLAS, oil and gas executive; b. Red House, Ky., Sept. 9, 1943; s. Carter Livingston and Irene (Bolson) Q.; m. Leslie J. Johnsen (div. Jan. 1980); children: Tracey, David; m. Debra Gale Wagner, Aug. 7, 1982; children: Justin, Meghan, Bradley. BA, U. Ky., 1965, JD, 1969; student, Emory U., 1966-67. Bar: Ky., 1970, Tex., 1986. Atty. Phillips Petroleum Co., Denver, 1970-76; mgr. real estate and claims Phillips Petroleum Co. Euro. Afr., London, 1976-79; dir. govt. and comml. affairs Phillips Petroleum Co. & Subs., Lagos, Nigeria, 1979-82; mgr. internat. gas devel. Phillips Petroleum Co., Bartlesville, Okla., 1982-84; dir. laws and regulations Phillips 66 Natural Gas Co., Bartlesville, Okla., 1984-88; mgr. bus. devel. and mktg. HUFFCO/VICO Indonesia Co., Jakarta, Indonesia, 1988-93; v.p. Lng Texaco Natural Gas Internat., 1997; sr. v.p. Texaco Global Gas and Power, 1997—2001; sr. LNG comml. advisor Chevron, 2002—. Cons. Govt. of Nigeria, Lagos, 1977-82; gas cons. LNG/Internat. Gas, Houston, 1993-97. Charter mem. Statue of Liberty Ellis Island Found., N.Y.C., 1983; pro bono counsel Landmark Preservation Coun., Bartlesville, 1986-87, Washington County Sr. Citizens, Inc., Bartlesville, 1987—, Pro Bono Coll., Tex. Bar Assn., 1997-2004; cubmaster Boy Scouts Am.; pres. Pine Brook Cmty. Assn., NASA Little League coach.; pres. Clear Lake Blvd. Assn. Recipient Speak Out award Am. Petroleum Inst., 1972; named to hon. order Ky. Cols., 1969. Mem.: Houston Vols. Lawyers Assn., Tex. Bar Assn. Republican. Avocations: woodworking, gardening, sailing, scuba diving, travel. Office Phone: 281-480-7874. Personal E-mail: quillld@att.net.

QUILLEN, MICHAEL J., energy executive; Grad., Va. Tech. U. Chmn., CEO Addington Inc.; v.p. ops. NERCO Coal Corp.; v.p. AMVEST Corp.; pres. Pittston Coal Sales Corp.; v.p. ops. Pittston Coal Co.; exec. v.p. ops. Am. Metals & Coal Internat., 1998—2002; pres. Alpha Natural Resources LLC, Abingdon, Va., 2002—, CEO, 2003—; pres. ANR Holdings Inc., Abingdon, Va., 2002—, CEO, 2003—; pres., CEO Alpha Natural Resources Inc., Abingdon, Va., 2004—06, chmn., CEO, 2006—. Office: Alpha Natural Resources 1 Alpha Pl PO Box 2345 Abingdon VA 24212 Office Phone: 276-719-4410.

QUILLEN, WILLIAM TATEM, retired judge, lawyer, educator; b. Camden, NJ, Jan. 15, 1935; s. Robert James and Gladys Collings (Tatem) Quillen; m. Marcia Everhart Stirling, June 27, 1959; children: Carol Everhart, Tracey Tatem. BA, Williams Coll., 1956; LLB, Harvard U., 1959; LLM, U. Va., 1982; LLD (hon.), Widener U. Sch. Law, 2002. Bar: Del. 1959. Assoc. Richards, Layton & Finger, Wilmington, Del., 1963—64; adminstrv. asst. to Gov. of Del., 1965; assoc. judge Superior Ct. of Del., 1966—73; chancellor State of Del., 1973—76; sr. v.p. Wilmington Trust Co., 1976—78; justice Supreme Ct. of Del., 1978—83; ptnr. Potter Anderson & Corroon, Wilmington, 1983—86; gen. counsel, v.p. Howard Hughes Med. Inst., 1986—91; sec. of state State of Del., Dover, 1993—94; assoc. judge Superior Ct. Del., Wilmington, 1994—2000; of counsel Drinker Biddle & Reath, Wilmington, 2003—. Mem. adj. faculty Widener U. Sch. Law, Wilmington, 1976—83, 1985—86, 1995—2000, 2002—, disting. vis. prof. law, 1992—94, 2001—02. Trustee Widener U., 1979—91; Dem. candidate for gov. Del., 1984. With JAGC USAF, 1959—62. Mem.: ABA, Del. State Bar Assn., Wilmington Club, Phi Beta Kappa. Democrat. Presbyterian. Office Phone: 302-467-4219. Business E-Mail: william.quillen@dbr.com.

QUILLIAN, J. KIRK, lawyer; b. Akron, Ohio, Mar. 1, 1946; BA, Emory U., 1968; JD, U. Va., 1973. Bar: Ga. 1973. Assoc. Troutman Sanders LLP, Atlanta, 1973—77, ptnr., 1978—, practice group leader, complex litig. Named a Super Lawyer, Atlanta Mag., 2004, Legal Elite in business litig., Ga. Trend Mag., 2004. Mem. ABA, State Bar Ga. (mem. bar-media conf. 1990—), Atlanta Bar Assn. (chmn. continuing legal edn. com. 1987-88), fellow, Am. Bar Found., Am. Inn of Ct. Master, Lamar Inn of Ct. Founding Master, Lawyers Club Atlanta. Office: Troutman Sanders LLP 600 Peachtree St NE Ste 5200 Atlanta GA 30308-2216 Office Phone: 404-885-3204. Office Fax: 404-962-6660. Business E-Mail: kirk.quillian@troutmansanders.com.

QUILLIAN, WARREN WILSON, II, pediatrician, educator; b. Miami, Fla., Jan. 21, 1936; s. Warren Wilson and Rosabel (Brown) Q.; m. Sallie Ruth Creel, July 26, 1958; children: Rutledge, Ruth, Warren C., Frances. MD, Emory U., 1961. Diplomate Am. Bd. Pediat. (examiner 1966—, bd. dirs. 1974-80, 1992-98, treas. 1978, v.p. 1979, pres. 1980). Intern in pediat. Vandertilt U., Nashville, 1961-62; resident Children's Hosp. Med. Ctr., Harvard U., Boston, 1962-63; chief resident Grady Meml. Hosp., Emory U., Atlanta, 1963-64; pvt. practice Coral Gables, Fla., 1966. Instr., asst. clin. prof., assoc. clin. prof., now clin. prof. pediat. U. Miami Med. Sch., 1966—; emeritus staff, bd. dirs. Miami Children's Hosp.; emeritus staff Jackson Meml. Hosp.; past chief pediat. Doctors' Hosp.; mem. hon. staff Mercy Hosp., Bapt. Hosp., South Miami Hosp.; chmn. health adv. com. Dade County Schs.; bd. dirs., v.p. Am. Bd. Pediat. Found., 1991-98; mem. adv. bd. McGlannon Sch.; cons. Fla. Divsn. Med. Svcs.; bd. dirs. Bank Coral Gables. Contbr. articles to med. jours. Hon. bd. dirs. Soc. Abused Children of Children's Home Soc., Miami, 1980-84; mem. Coral Gables Code Enforcement Bd., 1986-88; team-sch. physician Coral Gables Sr. H.G., 1980-88; bd. dirs. Dade County March of Dimes, Miami, 1968-72; bd. advisors Dade County Assn. Retarded Children, 1968-76; trustee Emory U., 1991-97; mem. coun. ministries, youth coord., mem. fin. com., Sunday Sch. tchr. United Meth. Ch. Coral Gables, 1966—; chair staff parish rels. com.; mem. bd. advisors The Growing Place; mem. Citizens Bd. U. Miami, 1997—; v.p. bd. Good Hope Equestrian Tng. Ctr. for Retarded, 1999—. Capt. M.C., U.S. Army, 1964-66. Recipient citation of merit Emory U., 1980, Alumni Commendation, Miami Children's Hosp., 1983, Tchg. award U. Miami Sch. Medicine, 1995, 2002, 06, Winston Churchhill medal, 1999, Commendation Key to City, City of Coral Gables, 2007, Lifetime Achievement award Miami Children's Hosp., 2007; named to CGHS Athletic Hall of Fame, 1996, Wisdom Hall of Fame, 1998. Fellow Am. Acad. Pediat.; mem. AMA, Fla. Med. Assn. (sch. health com.), Fla. Pediat. Soc. (past chmn. sch. health com.), So. Med. Assn., Dade County Med. Assn. (sch. health com., continuing edn. com.), Empirical Soc. (past pres.), Soc. for Pediat. Rsch., So. Perinatal Soc., Greater Miami Pediat. Soc. (past pres., chmn. legis. and sch. health com., Hall of Fame), Miami Med. Forum (past pres., Haverfield Cup 1985, Mansfield Trophy 1983, 88, 98), Sr. Soc. Emory U., Biscayne Bay Yacht Club (commodore, bd. govs.), DVS Sr. Honor Soc., Alpha Omega Alpha, Omicron Delta Kappa, Alpha Epsilon Upsilon, Phi Delta Theta. Democrat. Avocations: fishing, golf, boating. Office: 305 Granello Ave Coral Gables FL 33146-1806

QUILLIGAN, EDWARD JAMES, retired obstetrician, gynecologist, educator; b. Cleve., June 18, 1925; s. James Joseph and Maude Elvira (Ryan) Q.; m. Betty Jane Cleaton, Dec. 14, 1946; children: Bruce, Jay, Carol, Christopher, Linda, Ted. BA, MD, Ohio State U., 1951; MA (hon.), Yale, 1967. Intern Ohio State U. Hosp., 1951-52, resident, 1952-54, Western Res. U. Hosps., 1954-56; asst. prof. obstetrics and gynecology Western Res. U., 1957-63, prof., 1963-65; prof. obstetrics and gynecology UCLA, 1965-66; prof., chmn. dept. Ob-Gyn Yale U., 1966-69, U. So. Calif., 1969-78, asso. v.p. med. affairs, 1978-79; prof. Ob-Gyn. U. Calif., Irvine, 1980-83, vice chancellor health affairs, dean Sch. Medicine, 1987-89; prof., chmn. ob.-gyn. dept. U. Wis., 1983-85; prof., chmn. Ob-Gyn Davis Med. Ctr. U. Calif., Sacramento, 1985-87, vice chancellor Health Scis., dean Coll. Med. Irvine, 1987-89, prof. ob-gyn, 1987-94, prof. emeritus ob-gyn., 1994; exec. dir. med. edn. Long Beach (Calif.) Meml. Health Svcs., 1995—2005; ret., 2005. Contbr. articles to med. jours.; editor-in-chief emeritus: Am. Jour. Obstetrics and Gynecology. Served to 2d lt. AUS, 1944—46. Recipient Centennial award Ohio State U., 1970 Mem. Soc. Gynecologic Investigation, Am. Gynecol. Soc., Am. Coll. Ob-Gyn., Sigma Xi. Home: 1 Goldenglow Irvine CA 92612-4077 E-mail: equilligan@cox.net.

QUIMBY, FRED WILLIAM, pathology educator, veterinarian; b. Providence, Sept. 19, 1945; s. Edward Harold and Isabel (Barber) Q.; m. Cynthia Claire Connelly, Aug. 21, 1965; children: Kelly Ann, Cynthia Jane. VMD, U. Pa., 1970, PhD, 1974. Diplomate Am. Coll. Lab. Animal Medicine. Hematology fellow New Eng. Med. Ctr., Boston, 1974-75, instr. pathology, 1975-76, asst. prof., 1976-79; assoc. prof. pathology Cornell Med. Coll., NYC, 1979—92, prof. pathology, 1993—2000; assoc. v.p., sr. dir. Lab. Animal Rsch. Ctr. Rockefeller U., 2001—. Dir. lab. animal medicine Tufts-New Eng. Med. Ctr., Boston, 1975—79; dir. Ctr. Rsch. Animal Resources Cornell U., Ithaca, 1979—2001. Editor Animal Welfare, 1992, Lab. Animal Sci., 1992-93, consulting editor, 1993-95; editor: Clinical Chemistry of Laboratory Animals, 2d edit., 1999, Laboratory Animal Medicine, 2d edit., 2002, The Mouse in Biomedical Research, 2d edit., 2006; guest editor Applied Animal Behavior Sci., 1997; chmn. editl. bd. ILAr News, 1988-91; contbr. articles to profl. jours. Recipient Focused Giving award, Johnson and Johnson, 1987—90; Greenfield Trust scholar, 1966—70, N.H. Rural Rehab. Corp. scholar, 1966—70, U. Pa. scholar, 1969—70. Mem. Am. Vet. Med. Assn. (Charles River prize 1995), Am. Assn. Lab. Animal Sci. (pres. N.E. br. 1978-79, bd. trustees Metro NY br. 2003-05, N.E. br. Trum award 1979, Metro br. Veterinarian of Yr. award (now Fred W. Quimby award), 2007), Am. Soc. Lab. Animal Practitioners (Rsch. award 2004), World Vet. Assn. (sec. exec. com. animal welfare 1990-96). Roman Catholic. Home: Apt 24P 504 E 63d St New York NY 10021-7919 also: 46 South Shore Rd New Durham NH 03855 Office Phone: 212-327-8535. Business E-Mail: quimby@rockefeller.edu.

QUIN, JOSEPH MARVIN, manufacturing executive; b. Vicksburg, Miss., Aug. 18, 1947; m. Terry Gage, June 12, 1973; children: William C., Elizabeth G. BA in Finance, U. Miss., 1969; MBA, U. Va., 1972. Fin. analyst Ashland Chem. Co., Dublin, Ohio, 1972—74, mgr. project analysis, 1974—79, mgr. planning & analysis & dir. planning and devel., 1979—81, adminstrv. v.p., 1981-83; treas. Ashland Inc., 1983-87, adminstrv. v.p. fin., treas., 1987-92, sr. v.p., CFO, 1992—. Bd. mem. Marathon Ashland Petroleum, Kentucky Electric Steel; trustee Cin. Symphony Orch. Episcopalian. Office: Ashland Inc 50 E River Ctr Blvd Covington KY 41012-0391 *

QUIN, LOUIS DUBOSE, chemist, educator; b. Charleston, SC, Mar. 5, 1928; s. Louis DuBose and Olga vonOven (Jatho) Q.; children: Gordon, Howard, Carol. BS, The Citadel, 1947; MA, U. N.C., 1949, PhD, 1952. Research chemist Am. Cyanamid Co., Stamford, Conn., 1949-50; research project leader FMC Corp., South Charleston, W.Va., 1952-54, 56; mem. faculty dept. chemistry Duke U., Durham, NC, 1956-86, prof., 1967-81, James B. Duke prof. chemistry, 1981-86, prof. emeritus, 1986, chmn. dept., 1970-76; prof. chemistry U. Mass., Amherst, 1986-96, prof. emeritus, 1996—, head dept., 1986-94; adj. prof., disting. vis. prof. chemistry U. N.C., Wilmington, 1996—. Mem. Durham Human Relations Commn., 1978-81 Author: Heterocyclic Chemistry of Phosphorus, 1981, (with J.G. Verkade) Phosphorus-31 NMR Spectroscopy in Stereochemical Analysis, 1987, Phosphorus-31 NMR Spectral Properties in Compound Characterization and Structural Analysis, 1994, A Guide to Organophosphorus Chemistry, 2000, Practical Interpretation of P-31 NMR Spectra and Computer Assisted Structure Verification, 2004. Served to 1st lt. U.S. Army, 1954-56. Recipient Arbusovs award in phosphorus chemistry, 1997. Fellow AAAS; mem. Am. Chem. Soc. Office: 15 Aldersgate Ct Durham NC 27705 Office Phone: 919-384-2412.

QUINA, MARION ALBERT, JR., lawyer; b. Mobile, Ala., Apr. 18, 1949; s. Marion Albert Sr. and Tallulah (Dunlap) Q.; children: Marion Albert III, Elliott Richardson; m. Jamie Mayhall Curtis, May 2, 1998. BS, U. Ala., 1971; JD, Samford U., 1974. Bar: Ala. 1974, U.S. Dist. Ct. (so. dist.) Ala. 1975, U.S. Ct. Appeals (5th cir.) 1977, U.S. Ct. Appeals (11th cir.) 1981. Assoc. Lyons, Pipes & Cook, Mobile, 1974-77, ptnr., 1978-87; shareholder Lyons, Pipes & Cook, P.C., Mobile, 1988—. Past mem., bd. dirs. Mobile Touchdown Club, Presch. for the Sensory Impaired; mem. United Way, 1989—; past chmn. adv. bd. Cumberland Sch. of Law, Birmingham, 2003-05; sec., treas., vice chmn., chmn. Southeastern Admiralty Law Inst., Athens, Ga., 1996-99. 1st lt. U.S. Army. Mem. ABA, Ala. Bar Assn., Mobile Bar Assn. (past chmn. admiralty and maritime law com.), Maritime Law Assn. U.S. (assoc.), Ala. Wildlife Fedn. (past dir.), Mobile Area C. of C. (past vice chmn., gen. counsel), Kiwanis (past dir.), Mobile County Wildlife Assn., Mobile Propeller Club, Mobile Area C. of C. Diplomat Club, among others. Avocations: hunting, fishing. Office: Lyons Pipes & Cook PC 2 N Royal St Mobile AL 36602-3896 Office Phone: 334-441-8227. Business E-Mail: maq@lpclaw.com.

QUINAN, DEBORAH PECHET, lawyer; b. 1960; BA, Hamilton Coll., Clinton, NY, 1982; JD cum laude, Suffolk U., Boston, 1985; LLM in Taxation, Boston U., 1992. Bar: Mass. 1985. Atty. estate planning and probate dept. Mirick, O'Connell, DeMallie & Lougee, Worcester, Mass.; New Eng. area dir. estate and bus. succession planning Ernst & Young; assoc. dir. Ernst & Young Ctr. Family Wealth Planning; nat. dir. estate and fin. planning svcs. State St. Global Advs. Pvt. Asset Mgmt. Divsn. State St. Corp., 1997; dir. Rackemann, Sawyer & Brewster, Boston. Mem. curriculum adv. com. trusts & estates Mass. Continuing Legal Edn.; bd. advs. Bentley Coll. Fin. Planning and Taxation prog. Named one of Top 100 Attys., Worth mag., 2006. Mem.: Boston Probate and Estate Planning Forum, Boston Estate Planning Coun., Boston Bar Assn., Mass. Bar Assn., ABA. Office: Rackemann Sawyer & Brewster 1 Financial Ctr Boston MA 02111 Office Phone: 617-951-1109. E-mail: dquinan@rackemann.com. *

QUINBY, WILLIAM ALBERT, lawyer, arbitrator, mediator; b. Oakland, Calif., May 28, 1941; s. George W. and Marge (Diaz) Q.; m. Marion Bach, Nov. 27, 1964; 1 child, Michelle Kathleen. BA, Harvard U., 1963; JD, U. Calif., San Francisco, 1967. Bar: Calif. 1967. V.p., dir., shareholder Crosby, Heafey, Roach & May, Oakland, 1967-96; mediator, arbitrator Am. Arbitration Assn. and AAA Ctr. for Mediation, San Francisco, 1996—; ptnr. Wulff, Quinby & Sochynsky, 2001—. Bd. dirs. Haws Drinking Faucet Co., Berkeley, Calif.; mem. faculty Hastings Coll. Advocacy, San Francisco, 1980, instr. Boalt Hall Sch. Law, 1997; co-moderator Counsel Connect's Calif. ADR Discussion Group; lectr. currents devels. in banking arbitration and mediation; mem. fellowship rev. com. HEW; mem. mediation panel Nat. Assn. Securities Dealers; trustee Nat. Pre-Suit Mediation Program; adj. prof. Hastings Coll. of the Law, U. Calif., 1998, 99. Author: Six Reasons--Besides Time and Money--to Mediate Rather Than Litigate, Why Health Care Parties Should Mediate Rather Than Litigate, Starting an ADR Practice Group in a Law Firm, Mediation Process Can Amicably Solve Business Disputes and Not a Gold Rush (But Silver, Maybe), ADR Practice in a Large Law Firm Produces No Overnight Bonanzas, Making The Most of Mediation (Effective Mediation Advocacy). Bd. dirs. Big Bros. East Bay, Oakland, 1983-87, Easter Seals Soc. East Bay, 1973; past bd. dirs. Oakland East Bay Symphony, Oakland Pub. Libr. Found.; chmn. bd. dirs. Bay Area Tumor Inst. Scholar Harvard U., 1962-63. Fellow Coll. Comml. Arbitrators; mem. ABA (sect. on dispute resolution, chair programs, mediation coms.), Calif. Bar Assn., Alameda County Bar Assn., San Francisco Bar Assn., Contra Costa County Bar Assn., Calif. Bus. Trial Lawyers Assn., Am. Arbitration Assn. (large, complex case panel, internat., employment, constrn., and comml. mediation and arbitration panels), Oakland C. of C. (past bd. dirs., exec. com.), Alameda County Barristers Club (bd. dirs., pres. 1972), Harvard Club, San Francisco Calimari Club. Republican. Avocations: running, skiing, tennis, travel, gardening. Office: Wulff Quinby & Sochynsky Dispute Resolution 1901 Harrison St Ste 1420 Oakland CA 94612-3582 Office Phone: 510-663-5220. Personal E-mail: wquinby@aol.com.

QUINCE, PEGGY A., state supreme court justice; b. Norfolk, Va., Jan. 3, 1948; m. Fred L. Buckine; children: Peggy LaVerne, Laura LaVerne. BS in Zoology, Howard U., 1970; JD, Cath. U. of Am., 1975; LLD (hon.), Stetson U., 1999, St. Thomas U., 2004. Hearing officer Rental Accomodations Office, Washington; gen. practice Norfolk, 1977-78, Bradenton, Fla., 1978-80; asst. atty. gen. criminal divsn. Atty. Gen.'s Office, 1980; apptd. 2d Dist. Ct. of Appeals, 1994-98; justice Fla. Supreme Ct., 1998—. Lectr. in field. Former asst. Sunday sch. tchr., former mem. #3 usher bd. New Hope Missionary Bapt. Ch.; active Jack and Jill of Am., Inc., Urban League, NAACP, Tampa Orgn. for Black Affairs. Recipient award Cath.'s Neighborhood Legal Svcs. Clinic. Mem. Nat. Bar Assn., Fla. Bar, Va. State Bar, George Edgecomb Bar Assn., Fla. Assn. Women Lawyers, Tallahassee Women Lawyers, William H. Stafford Inn. Ct., Alpha Kappa Alpha. Office: Fla Supreme Ct 500 S Duval St Tallahassee FL 32399-1925 Office Phone: 850-922-5624. Business E-Mail: Larryg@flcourts.org.

QUINDLEN, ANNA, journalist, writer; b. Phila., July 8, 1952; d. Robert V. and Prudence Quindlen; m. Gerald Krovatin; children: Quindlen Krovatin, Christopher Krovatin, Maria Krovatin. BA, Barnard Coll., 1974. Reporter New York Post, NYC, 1974-77; gen. assignment, city hall reporter New York Times, NYC, 1977-81, columnist About New York, 1981-83, dep. met. editor, 1983-85, columnist Life in the 30's syndicated, 1986-89, columnist Public and Private, 1990-94; full-time novelist, 1995—; columnist, "Last Word" Newsweek mag. Author: (novels) Object Lessons, 1991, One True Thing, 1994, Black and Blue, 1998, Blessings, 2000, Rise and Shine, 2006, (non-fiction) A Short Guide to a Happy Life, 2000, Being Perfect, 2005 (Publishers Weekly Bestseller non-fiction list, 2005), (children's books) The Tree That Came to Stay, 1992, Happily Ever After, 1997, (compilation) Living Out Loud, 1988, Thinking Out Loud, 1993, Loud and Clear, 2004; wrote text for: coffee table pictorial Naked Babies, 1996, Siblings, 1998. Bd. mem. Nightingale-Bamford Sch., NYC, NARAL Found. Named Woman of Yr., Glamour Mag., 1991; recipient Mike Berger award for disting. reporting, 1983, Pulitzer Prize for commentary, 1992. Mem.: Planned Parenthood Fedn. of Am. (bd. adv.), Author's Guild (coun. mem.), Bd Trustees, Barnard Coll. (chmn. 2003—). Achievements include being first writer to ever appear on fiction, nonfiction & self-help NewYork Times Best Seller lists. Office: c/o ICM 40 W 57th St New York NY 10019-4001

QUIN-HARKIN, JANET ELIZABETH (RHYS BOWEN), writer; b. Bath, Somerset, Eng., Sept. 24, 1941; d. Frank Newcombe Lee, Margery Lee; m. John Quin-Harkin; children: Clare Broyles, Anne, Jane Hansen, Dominic. BA with honors, U. London, 1963. Author: (children's picture book) Peter Penny's Dance, 1976 (NY Times Best Book of Yr., ALA Book of Internat. Note, 1977), Heartbreak Cafe series novels, Sweet Dreams series, Wanted Date for Saturday Night, 1985 (Reader's Choice award, 1986), Madam Sarah, 1990, Fool's Gold, 1991, Amazing Grace, 1992; author: (as Rhys Bowen) (novels) Evans Above, 1997, Evan Help Us, 1998 (nominated--Barry award, best mystery novel, 1999), Evanly Choirs, 1999, Evan and Elle, 2000, Evan Can Wait, 2001, Murphy's Law, 2001 (Agatha award, 2002, Herodohis award, Reviewer's Choice award, 2002), Death of Riley, 2002 (nominated for Agatha award, nominated for Reviewer's Choice award), For the Love of Mike, 2003 (Anthony award, Bruce Alexander award), Evans Gate, 2004 (Edgar award nominee for best novel, 2005), In Like Flynn: A Molly Murphy Mystery, 2005, Evan Blessed: A Constable Evans Mystery, 2005, Oh Danny Boy, 2006, Evanly Bodies, 2006, In Dublin's Fair City, 2007, Her Royal Spyness, 2007. Treas. Daughters of the Brit. Empire, San Rafael, 1998—2000. Recipient award for best screenplay, Marin Arts Coun., 1995. Mem.: Soc. Children's Bookwriters, Sisters in Crime, Mystery Writers Am. (regional pres. No. Calif. chpt. 2001). Roman Catholic. Avocations: travel, hiking, singing, tennis. Office: c/o Meg Ruley Jane Rotrosen Agy 318 E 51st St New York NY 10022 Office Phone: 212-593-4330. Personal E-mail: rhysbowen@comcast.net.

QUINLAN, CATHERINE, university librarian; MusB, Queens U.; MLS, Dalhousie U.; MBA, Meml. U. Newfoundland. Dir. librs., chief libr. U. Western Ontario; univ. libr. U. BC, 1997—2007, dir. Irving K. Barber Learning Ctr., 2004—07; dean librs. U. So. Calif., 2007—. Mem.: Harry Hawthorne Found., Canadian Libr. Assn., Canadian Assn. Rsch. Libraries, Assn. Rsch. Libraries, Golden Key Soc., Coalition for Networked Info. Avocations: playing chamber music, opera, queuing theory, running. Office: U So Calif Dean Libr Los Angeles CA 90089 *

QUINLAN, GUY CHRISTIAN, lawyer; b. Cambridge, Mass., Oct. 28, 1939; m. Mary-Ella Holst, Apr. 18, 1987. AB, Harvard Coll., Cambridge, Mass., 1960; JD, Harvard U., Cambridge, 1963. Bar: NY 1964, US Dist. Ct. (so. and ea. dists.) NY 1965, US Ct. Appeals (2d cir.) 1967, US Supreme Ct. 1969, US Ct. Appeals (8th cir.) 1973, (10th cir.) 1977, (4th cir.) 1993, (11th cir.) 1995, US Tax Ct. 1977. Assoc. Clifford Chance, NYC, 1963-70, ptnr., 1970—90, of counsel, 1991—. Past pres. Unitarian Universalist Svc. Com., Yorkville Common Pantry; Unitarian Universalist Dist. of Met. N.Y.; mem. adv. council on ministerial studies Harvard U. Div. Sch.; chair nuclear disarmament task force All Souls Unitarian Ch. Mem.: ABA, Lawyers Com. on Nuclear Policy, Amnesty Internat. Legal Network, Arm Control Assn., Harvard Club. Democrat. Office: Clifford Chance US LLP 31 W 52d St New York NY 10019-6131 Office Phone: 212-878-8219. Business E-Mail: guy.quinlan@cliffordchance.com.

QUINLAN, J(OSEPH) MICHAEL, lawyer; b. Rockville Centre, NY, Nov. 2, 1941; s. Joseph Charles Quinlan and Harriet Veronica (Gorman) Greene; m. Agnes Mary Quinlan, May 5, 1973; children: Kara Quinlan Davis, Kristen Quinlan Calder. BS in Social Sci., Fairfield U., Conn., 1963; JD, Fordham U., Bronx, NY, 1966; LLM, George Washington U., Washington, DC, 1970. Bar: NY 1966, DC 1967, Va. 1993, US Ct. Mil. Appeals 1967, US Supreme Ct. 1970. Exec. asst. to warden US Penitentiary, Leavenworth, Kans., 1973-74; of counsel N.E. region US Bur. Prisons, Phila., 1974-75, exec. asst. to dir. Washington, 1975-78, from dep. asst. dir. to dir., 1985-92; supt. Fed. Prison Camp, Eglin AFB, Fla., 1978-80; warden Fed. Correctional Inst., Otisville, NY, 1980-85; dir. strategic planning Corrections Corp. Am., 1993-97; dir., bd. dirs. UK Detention Svcs., London, 1993-97; vice-chmn., bd. trustees Prison Realty Trust, 1997-99. 1st vice-chmn. bd. dirs. Horton Meml. Hosp., Middletown, NY, 1982-85; CEO Prison Realty Trust, 1997-99; pres. Corrections Corp of Am., 1999-2000, exec. v.p., COO, 2000-02, sr. v.p., 2002—. Bd. advisors BI Inc., 2001-05. Lt. col. USAFR, 1966-93. Recipient SES Presdl. Disting. Rank award, 1988, SES Presdl. Meritorious Rank award, 1991, Exceptional Leadership award US Atty. Gen., 1991, Nat. Pub. Svc. award Nat. Acad. Pub. Adminstrn./Am. Soc. Pub. Adminstrn., 1992, John Marshall award Dept. Justice, 1993, E.R. Cass award ACA, 2003. Fellow Nat. Acad. Pub. Adminstrn. (chair prisons com.); mem. ABA (corrections and sentencing com. 1985—), Am. Correctional Assn., Nat. Com. Comm. Corrections, NY Bar Assn., DC Bar Assn., Va. Bar Assn. Roman Catholic. Avocation: reading. Home: 420 Elmington Ave # 507 Nashville TN 37205 E-mail: mike.quinlan@correctionscorp.com.

QUINLAN, KATHLEEN, actress; b. Pasadena, Calif., Nov. 19, 1954; d. Robert and Josephine Quinlan; m. Bruce Abbott, Apr. 12, 1994; 2 children. Actress: (theatre) Taken in Marriage, 1979 (Theatre World award 1979), Accent on Youth, 1983, Les Liaisons Dangereuses, 1988, (feature films) One is a Lonely Number, 1972, American Graffiti, 1973, Lifeguard, 1976, Airport '77, 1977, I Never Promised You a Rose Garden, 1977, The Promise, 1979, The Runner Stumbles, 1979, Sunday Lovers, 1981, Hanky Panky, 1982, Independence Day, 1982, Twilight Zone: The Movie, 1983, The Last Winter, 1983, Warning Sign, 1985, Wild Thing, 1987, Sunset, 1988, Clara's Heart, 1988, The Doors, 1991, Trial by Jury, 1994, Apollo 13, 1995 (Acad. award nominee for best actress 1996), Zeus and Roxanne, 1997, Event Horizon, 1997, Lawn Dogs, 1997, A Civil Action, 1998, My Giant, 1998, The Battle of Shaker Heights, 2003, The Hills Have Eyes, 2006, American Fork, 2007, Breach, 2007; (TV movies) Can Ellen Be Saved?, 1974, Lucas Tanner, 1974, Where Have All the People Gone?, 1974, The Missing Are Deadly, 1975, The Turning Point of Jim Malloy, 1975, The Abduction of Saint Anne, 1975, Little Ladies of the Night, 1977, She's in the Army Now, 1981, When She Says No, 1984, Blackout, 1985, Children of the Night, 1985, Dreams Lost, Dreams Found, 1987, Trapped, 1989, The Operation, 1990, Strays, 1991, An American Story, 1992, Stolen Babies, 1993, Last Light, 1993, Perfect Alibi, 1994, Breakdown, 1996, In the Lake of the Woods, 1996, The Doris Duke Story, 1998, Blessings, 2003, The Riverman, 2004, The Dead Will Tell, 2004; (TV series) Family Law, 1999-2002. Mem. Actors' Equity Assn., Screen Actors Guild. *

QUINLAN, KENNETH J., JR., military officer; BSCE, U. RI; MS in Military Art and Sci., US Army Command & Gen. Staff Coll.; grad., Sch. Advanced Mil. Studies, Army War Coll. Advanced through ranks to maj. gen. U.S. Army; platoon comdr., ops. officer Delta Troop, 1st Cav., Alaska; ops. officer D Troop, 1st Squadron, 26th Cav. Regiment; chief force integration 101st Airborne Div., Fort Campbell; 101st Aviation Brigade S-3 Op. Desert Shield/Desert Storm; chief strategic plans div., strategic planning, policy dir. U.S. Pacific Command; commandant Joint Forces Staff Coll., 2003. Decorated Defense Superior Service Medal U.S. Army, Legion of Merit, Bronze Star, Army Commendation Medal, Expert Infantryman's Badge U.S. Army, Ranger Tab, Sr. Parachutist Badge, Air Assault Badge; recipient Meritorious Svc. Medal. Office: Joint Forces Staff Coll 7800 Hampton Blvd Norfolk VA 23511-1701

QUINLAN, MARY LOU, former advertising executive, consultant; b. 1953; BA, St. Joseph's U., 1975; MBA, Fordham U., 1982; doctorate (hon.), Alvernia Coll., 1996. Dir. comm. St. Joseph's U., 1975-78; dir. advtg. Avon Products, 1978-89; sr. v.p. Ally & Gargan, 1989-91; exec. v.p., mng. ptnr. DDB Needham N.Y., 1991-94; pres N.W. Ayer & Ptnrs., NYC, 1994-99, CEO, 1995—99; vice chairperson The MacManus Group, NYC, 1999; founder, CEO Just Ask a Woman, NYC, 1999—. Bd. dirs. 1800flowers.com, 2002—; trustee, lectr. St. Joseph's U., 2004—. Author: Just Ask a Woman: Cracking the Code of What Woman Want and How They Buy, 2003, Time Off for Good Behavior: Hardworking Women Can Take a Break and Change Their Lives, 2005. Bd. dirs. St. Joseph's U., Phila. Named Advt. Woman of Yr., Advt. Women of N.Y., 1995. Mem.: N.Y. Women in Comm. (Matrix Award for Advt. 1997). Office: Just Ask a Woman 670 Broadway Ste 301 New York NY 10012

QUINLAN, ROBERT CONRAD, real estate developer; married. Grad., Yale Univ., 1954. Ptnr. Quinlan & Field Real Estate, NYC. Bd. trustees Whitney Mus. Am. Art, NYC, Preservation League of NY State; bd. dir. NY Landmarks Conservancy, Hist. House Trust, Friends of Upper East Side Hist. Dist.; chmn. Columbus Ave. Bus. Improvement Dist. Office: Quinlan & Field 2N 101 W 70th St New York NY 10023

QUINLAN, THOMAS J., III, printing company executive; b. Feb. 3, 1963; m. Diane Quinlan; 4 children. BS, Pace U. Sr. v.p., treas. World Color Press Inc.; exec. v.p., treas. Walter Industries, Inc., 2000, Moore Wallace Inc., 2000—02, exec. v.p., bus. integration, 2003—04; exec. v.p. ops. R.R. Donnelley & Sons Co., Chgo., 2004—06, group pres. glob. services, CFO, 2006—07, pres., CEO, 2007. Office: RR Donnelley & Sons Co 111 S Wacker Dr Chicago IL 60606-4301 *

QUINLAN, WILLIAM J., lawyer; b. 1976; s. William R. and Jane Quinlan. Grad., U. Ill., Georgetown U. Law Sch. Atty. Gardner Carton & Douglas, Chgo., Quinlan & Carroll, Ltd., Chgo.; gen. counsel Ill. Gov.'s Office, Springfield, 2004—. Mem.: Ill. Bar Assn. Office: Office of the Gov 207 State House Springfield IL 62706 Office Phone: 312-814-8974. Office Fax: 217-782-1853.

QUINN, ANDREW PETER, JR., lawyer, retired insurance company executive; b. Providence, Oct. 22, 1923; s. Andrew Peter and Margaret (Canning) Q.; m. Sara G. Bullard, May 30, 1952 (dec. Feb. 2004); 1 child, Emily H. AB, Brown U., 1945; LLB, Yale U., 1950. Bar: R.I. 1949, Mass. 1960, U.S. Tax Ct. 1960, U.S. Supreme Ct. 1986. Pvt. practice, Providence, 1950-59; ptnr. Letts & Quinn, 1950-59; with Mass. Mut. Life Ins. Co., Springfield, 1959—88, exec. v.p., gen. counsel, 1971-88; of counsel Day, Berry & Howard, Hartford, Conn. and Boston, 1988-99; retired, 1999. Pres., trustee MML Series Investment Fund, 1971-88; pres. Sargasso Mut. Ins. Co., Ltd., 1986-89, chmn. bd. dirs., 1989-93. Trustee, MacDuffie Sch., 1974-87, chmn. bd., 1978-85; trustee Baystate Med., Springfield, 1977-80. Lt. (j.g.) USNR, 1944-46. Mem. ABA (co-chmn. nat. conf. lawyers and life ins. cos. 1973), Assn. Life Ins. Counsel (pres. 1983-84, Anderson Disting. Svc. award 1998), Am. Coun. Life Ins. (chmn. legal sect. 1971), Life Ins. Assn. Mass. (chmn. exec. com. 1975-77), Brown U. Alumni Assn. (bd. dirs. 1969-72), NY Yacht Club, Dunes Club, Hillsboro Club. Home (Winter): 1205 Meadow Ridge Redding CT 06896

QUINN, ART JAY, retired veterinarian, educator; b. Bennington, Kans., Aug. 2, 1936; s. Arthur Jess and Edith Mae (Reigle) Q. BS, Kans. State U., 1959, DVM, 1961. Diplomate Am. Coll. Vet. Ophthalmologists. Pvt. practice, Albuquerque, 1961-75; field rep. Am. Animal Hosp. Assn., Denver, 1968-69; prof. Coll. Vet. Medicine, Okla. State U., Stillwater, 1975-95, prof. emeritus, 1995—. Contbr. articles to profl. jours. Capt. U.S. Army, 1962-64. Recipient Small Animal Proficiency award, Kans. Vet. Med. Assn., 1961, Upjohn award, 1961, Western Region Practitioner award, AAHA, 1993, Meritorious Svc. award, Western Vet. Conf., 2002; grantee, Sarkey Found. grantee, 1981. Mem.: AVMA, Am. Coll. Vet. Ophthalmologists, Am. Animal Hosp. Assn. Democrat. Home: 210 Cedar Ln Diamond Head Sand Springs OK 74063-5309 Office Phone: 918-865-3419.

QUINN, BRADY (BRADY TYLER QUINN), professional football player; b. Dublin, Ohio, Oct. 27, 1984; s. Ty and Robin Quinn. BBA in Fin. Admin., U. Notre Dame, South Bend, Ind., 2006, BA in Polit. Sci., 2007. Quarterback Cleve. Browns, 2007—. Named Cingular All-Am. Player of Yr., 2006; named to All-American Team, Lindy's, Street and Smith, 2006; recipient Sammy Baugh trophy, 2005, College Football Player of Yr. award (Maxwell award), Maxwell Football Club, 2006, Johnny Unitas Golden Arm award, 2006. Achievements include holding 30 U. Notre Dame passing records for career yardage, single season yardage, single game yardage & touchdown passes. Office: Cleveland Browns 76 Lou Groza Blvd Berea OH 44017 *

QUINN, BRIAN GRANT, sculptor, art educator; b. Wahoo, Nebr., Oct. 21, 1950; s. Grant Scott and Goldie Maxine Quinn; m. Jennifer Ann Jackels. BA, Nebr. Wesleyan U., 1973; MFA, Ariz. State U., 1975. Preparator Phoenix Art Mus., Phoenix, 1975; artist-in-residence NEA, Mesa, Ariz., 1975—76; vis. instr. sculture Glendale C.C., Glendale, Ariz., 1976—90; lectr. sculpture Ariz. State U., Tempe, Ariz., 1980—81; prof. sculture and jewelry Glendale C. C., 1990—94, curator art collection, 1990—94; vis. instr. art hist. Scottsdale C. C., Scottsdale, Ariz., 1996—; instr. visual arts Scottsdale Pub. Sch., 1996—2006. Represented in numerous permanent collections. Fulbright Meml. Fund Scholarship, Fulbright Inst., Japan, 2001, scholarship, Tchr. Inst. Contemporary Art, 2005, Chgo. Art Inst., 2005, NEA, 2005. Mem.: Japanese Sword Soc. of U.S. (bd. dir. 1994—2004, pres. 2004—). Avocations: sculpting, painting, antiques, visual arts. Home: 6132 E Lincoln Dr Paradise Valley AZ 85253 E-mail: swords@cox.net.

QUINN, CHARLES NICHOLAS, journalist; b. Utica, NY, July 28, 1930; s. Charles Dunaway and Elsa (Zarth) Q.; children— Diana David, Ben, Jane. BA, Cornell U., 1951; MS, Columbia U. Sch. Journalism, 1954. Reporter Providence Jour., 1954-56, N.Y. Herald Tribune, 1956-62; corr. NBC News, NYC, 1962-66, Washington, 1966-71, Rome, 1971-74; mng. editor, chief corr. NBC Radio News, Washington, 1978-80; corr. Ind. Network News, Washington, 1980-81; electronic media rep. Am. Petroleum Inst., Washington, 1981-91. Reported on hunger in U.S. on: Huntley-Brinkley Report, (co-recipient Emmy 1969). Served with arty. U.S. Army, 1951-53. Mem. Nat. Press Club (bd. govs. 1990-91).

QUINN, CHRISTINE CALLAGHAN, councilwoman; b. Glen Cove, NY, July 25, 1966; d. Mary and Lawrence Quinn; life ptnr. Kim Catullo. BA in Urban Studies and Edn., Trinity Coll., Hartford, Conn., 1988. With Assn. Neighborhood and Housing Develop., 1989—91; chief staff Councilman Thomas K. Duane, 1992—96; exec. dir. NYC Gay and Lesbian Anti-Violence Project, 1996—98; city councilwoman Dist. 3 NYC, 1999—, council speaker, 2006—. Mem. NYC Police/Community Relations Task Force; del. DNC, 2000, mem. platform com., 04. Named one of Fifty Most Powerful Women in NYC, NY Post, Forty Under Forty, Gotham Mag. Avocation: reading. Office: Dist Office Christine Quinn 224 W 30th St Ste 1206 New York NY 10001 *

QUINN, CLARK NIVES, psychologist, consultant; b. LA, Nov. 7, 1956; s. J. Nives and Esther Elizabeth (Schwarz) Q.; m. Le Ann Woolsey Keane, Oct. 10, 1989. BA computer based edn., U. Calif., San Diego, 1980, PhD in Psychology, 1989. Programmer, analyst Design Ware, Inc., San Francisco, 1981-83; rsch. assoc. CRMSE San Diego (Calif.) State U., 1988-89; post doctoral fellow Learning Rsch. & Devel. Ctr. U. Pitts., 1989-91. Cons. The Consulting Group, Inc., San Diego, 1983, Cubic Corp., San Diego, 1985; instr. San Diego Community Colls., 1985, U. Pitts., 1990. Programmer: (software) Word Skills, 1981, Micro Discovery, 1981, Facemaker, 1982, Spellicopter, 1983; project mgr. Creative Creator, 1983; creator: Voodoo Adventure, 1990. Mem. Am. Psychol. Soc., Cognitive Sci. Soc., Am. Ednl. Rsch. Assn. Democrat. Avocations: surfing, skiing, snowboarding, travel, reading. Office: Univ Pitts Learning Rsch Devel Ctr Pittsburgh PA 15260

QUINN, D. MICHAEL, history professor; b. Pasadena, Calif., Mar. 26, 1944; s. Daniel Donald Pena-Quinn and Joyce Coila Workman; m. Janice L. Darley, June 20, 1967 (div. Jan. 1986); children: Mary, Lisa, Adam, Moshe. BA in English, Philosophy, Brigham Young U., 1968; MA in Hist., U. Utah, 1973; MPhil in Hist., Yale U., 1975, PhD in Hist., 1976; cert. of completion, Inst. Quantative Hist., Newberry Libr., 1982. Tchg. fellow III Yale U., Hist. Dept., New Haven, 1974—75; asst. prof. to assoc. prof. Brigham Young U., Hist. Dept., Provo, Utah, 1976—84, prof., 1984—88, dir. grad. program, 1986—88; vis. scholar Claremont (Calif.) Grad. U., 2000; affiliated scholar U. Southern Calif., Ctr. for Feminist Rsch., Los Angeles, 2000—02; Beinecke fellow, assoc. History Dept. Yale U., New Haven, 2002—03; external mem., doctoral com. Tex. A&M U., Hist. Dept., Coll. Sta., 2004—. Adv. coun. Redd Ctr. Western Studies, Provo, 1980—86; assoc. dir. Study Abroad Program, Vienna, 1983; TV documentary cons., 1990—2007. Author: Early Mormonism and the Magic World View, 1987; editor: The New Mormon History: Revisionist Essays on the Past, 1992; contbr. articles various profl. jours.; author: The Mormon Hierarchy: Origins of Power, 1994, Same-Sex Dynamics Among Nineteenth-Century Americans: A Mormon Example, 1996, The Mormon Hierarchy: Extensions of Power, 1997, Elder Statesman: A Biography of J. Reuben Clark, 2002. Spkr. various cmty. activities, Salt Lake City, 1981; bd. trustees Leonard J. Arrington Found., Salt Lake City, 1982—83; vol. One Inst. and Archives, LA, 2000—02. With M.I. US Army, 1968—71. Named Outstanding Tchr., Brigham Young U., 1986, Dist. Historian, Organ. Am. Historians, 2004; recipient Samuel F. Bemis prize, Yale U., 1974, George W. Egleston prize, 1976, Frederick W. Beinecke prize, 1976, Svc. award, One Inst., 2001; fellow, Mrs. Giles Whiting Found., 1975—76; grantee Glenn W. Irwin fellowship, Ind. U., Purdue U., 1990—91; Summer fellow, NEH, 1977, Giles Mead Dist. fellowship, Henry E. Huntington Libr., 1988, Dorothy Collins Brown fellowship, 1992—93, fellowship, NEH, 1993—94, Sr. fellowship, Yale U., 2002—03. Mem.: Am. Hist. Assn., Am. Civil Liberties Union, Organ. Am. Historians, John Whitmer Hist. Assn., Mormon Hist. Assn., Utah State Hist. Soc., Affirmation: Gay and Lesbian Mormons (awards com. 2000—05), Western Hist. Assn. (program com. 1981—82), Am. Acad. Religion, Move-On Organ., Southern Poverty Ctr., Human Rights Campaign, Ctr. Lesbian and Gay Studies, Amnesty Internat., Greenpeace. Democrat. Lds Ch. Avocation: photography. Home: 8348A Gabriel Dr Rancho Cucamonga CA 91730 Personal E-mail: mike.quinn@finefriends.net.

QUINN, EUGENE FREDERICK, diplomat, minister; b. Oil City, Pa., Sept. 16, 1935; s. Eugene Frederick and Wilma (Scott) Q.; m. Charlotte Alison Smith, Aug. 25, 1965 (dec. June 2000); children: Christopher Edward Vermilye, Alison Moore; m. Carolyn Tanner Irish, June 14, 2001. AB, Allegheny Coll., 1957; MA in African studies, UCLA, 1966, MA in History, 1969, PhD in History, 1970; diploma in theol. studies, Va. Theol. Sem., 1974. Ordained to ministry Episcopal Ch., 1975. Info. officer Am. Embassy, Rabat, Morocco, 1958-59, cultural affairs officer Port-au-Prince, Haiti, 1959-61; country pub. affairs officer Ouagadougou, Upper Volta, 1961-63; field rep. Joint U.S. Affairs Office, Saigon, Vietnam, 1964-66; country pub. affairs officer Am. embassy, Yaounde, Cameroon, 1966-68, counselor embassy for press and cultural affairs Prague, Czechoslovakia, 1975-78; apptd. career mem. Sr. Fgn. Service with class of counselor, 1981, minister-counselor, 1986; dir. fgn. service personnel Voice of Am., Washington, 1981-83; dep. asst. sec. pub. affairs Dept. Transp., 1983-85; dir. Office Pub. Affairs Voice of Am., 1985-86; internat. coord. for Bicentennial U.S. Constn., dir.'s office U.S. Info. Agy., 1986-91; cons. internat. affairs, 1992—. Dir. rule of law programs, conf. on security and cooperation in Europe, Office of Dem. Instns. and Human Rights, Warsaw, 1993-95. Author: Federalist Papers' Reader, 1992, To Heal the Earth, 1994, Democracy at Dawn, Notes from Poland and Points East, 1998, Human Rights and You, 1998, French Overseas Empire, 2000, To Be A Pilgrim, The Anglican Ethos in History, 2001, African Saints, Martyrs and Holy People, 2002, Courthouse at Indian Creek, 2002; co-author: Pride, Faith and Fear: Islam in Africa, 2003, Building the Goodly Fellowship of Faith, and History of the Episcopal Church in Utah 1867-1996, 2004, In Search of Salt, a History of the Beti People 1970-1960, 2006, The Sum of All Heresies, The Image of Islam in Western Thought, 2007; editor: Diplomacy for the Seventies, 1969; mem. editl. bd. Fgn. Svc. Jour., 1972—75, Dept. State Open Forum Jour., 1982—83; contbr. articles to profl. jours., chapters to books. Trustee N.J. Ednl. Consortium, 1970-72; coord. USIA Yorktown Bicentennial Activities, 1981; assisting clergyman St. Columba's Ch., Washington, 1973-75, 78-81, Nat. Cathedral, Washington, 1981-82, 95-2001, Grace Ch., Silver Spring, Md., 1981-82, Epiphany Ch., Washington, 1983, 86-92; chaplain Anglo-Am. Diplomatic Cmty., Prague, 1975-78, Warsaw, 1993-95; vicar St. James Ch., Bowie, Md., 1983-84; rector Christ Ch., Accokeek, Md., 1985, St. John's Ch., Pomonkey, Md.; assisting clergyman All Saints Ch., Chevy Chase, Md., 1981-82, 86-90; interim pastor Ch. of Holy Communion, Washington, 1992-93, St. Andrew's Leonardtown, Md., 1998-99; chair environ. com. Episcopal Diocese of Washington Peace Commn., 1991-92; mem. Environ. Stewardship Team, Episcopal Ch., 1992-95. Recipient Meritorious Honor award USIA, 1964, 66, 85; Merit medal Republic of Vietnam, 1965, medal of honor 2d class, 1966

QUINN, FRANCIS A., bishop; b. LA, Sept. 11, 1921; Student, St. Joseph's Coll., Mountain View, Calif., St. Patrick's Sem., Menlo Park, Calif., Cath. U., Washington, U. Calif., Berkeley. Ordained priest Roman Cath. Ch., 1946, ordained titular bishop of Numana and aux. bishop of San Francisco Roman Cath. Ch., 1978. Bishop Diocese of Sacramento, 1979—94, bishop emeritus, 1994—. Roman Catholic. Office: 2110 Broadway Sacramento CA 95818-2518 Office Phone: 916-733-0200.

QUINN, FRANCIS FLAHERTY, lawyer; b. Phila., Jan. 22, 1946; AB with honors, St. Joseph's U., 1967; JD, U. Pa., 1971. Bar: Pa. 1972, N.J. 1993, N.Y. 1995, U.S. Supreme Ct. 1985. Law clk. to Hon. Daniel H. Huyett III U.S. Dist. Ct. (ea. dist.) Pa., 1971-73; ptnr. Lavin, O'Neill, Ricci, Cedrone & DiSipio, NYC, 1973—. Lectr. in field. Mem. Phila. Bar Assn., Def. Rsch. and Trial Lawyers Assn., NY Assn. Def. Counsel, Bar Assn. City of NY, NY State Bar Assn., Alpha Sigma Nu. Office: Lavin O'Neil Ricci Cedrone & DiSipio 420 Lexington Ave Ste 2900 New York NY 10170 Office Phone: 212-415-8201. Business E-Mail: fquinn@lavin-law.com.

QUINN, FRANCIS XAVIER, arbitrator, mediator, writer, law educator; b. Dunmore, Pa., June 9, 1932; s. Frank T. and Alice B. (Maher) Q.; m. Marlene Stoker Quinn; children: Kimberly, Catherine, Cameron, Lindsay, Megan, Savannah, Jackson Blair. BA, Fordham U., NYC, 1956, MA, 1958; STB, Woodstock Coll., Md., 1964; MS in Indsl. Rels., Loyola U., Chgo., 1966; PhD in Indsl. Rels., Calif. Western U., LA, 1976. Assoc. dir. Inst. Indsl. Rels. St. Joseph's Coll., Phila., 1966-68; Manpower fellow Temple U., Phila., 1969-74, asst. to dean Sch. Bus. Adminstrn., 1972-78. Arbitrator Fed. Mediation and Conciliation Svc., Nat. Mediation Bd., Am. Arbitration Assn., Nat. Assn. Railroad Referees, Dem. Nat. Steering Com.; apptd. to Presdl. Emergency Bd., 1975, to Fgn. Svc. Grievance Bd., 1976, 78, 80. Author: The Ethical Aftermath of Automation, 1963, Ethics and Advertising, 1965, Population Ethics, 1968, The Evolving Role of Women in the World of Work, 1969, Developing Community Responsibility, 1970; editor: The Ethical Aftermath Series; contbr. articles to profl. jours. Chmn. Tulsa City-County Mayor's Task Force to Combat Homelessness, 1991-92; mem. exec. bd. Tulsa Met. Ministries, 1990-92, Labor-Religion Coun. Okla., 1990-98; pres. pastoral coun. Ft. Worth Holy Family Roman Cath. Ch., 2000-03, formation adv. bd., 2002-05. Named Tchr. of Yr. Freedom Found., 1959; recipient Human Rels. award City of Phila., 1970; inducted into Hall of Fame, Internat. Police Assn., 2000. Fellow Coll. of Labor and Employment Lawyers; mem. Nat. Acad. Arbitrators (v.p. 1999-2001), Indsl. Rels. Rsch. Assn., Assn. for Social Econs., Soc. for Dispute Resolution, Am. Arbitration Assn. (arbitrator), Nat. Assn. Railroad Refs. (pres. 2000-04), Internat. Soc. Labor Law and Social Security. Democrat. Home: 4213 Blackhaw Ave Fort Worth TX 76109-1618 Office Phone: 817-924-7372. Personal E-mail: Quinnfrank@msn.com.

QUINN, HELEN RHODA ARNOLD, physicist; b. Melbourne, Victoria, Australia, May 19, 1943; came to U.S. 1961; d. Ted Adamson and Helen Ruth (Down) Arnold; m. Daniel James Quinn, Oct. 8, 1966; children: Elizabeth Helen, James Arnold. BS in Physics, Stanford U., 1963, MS in Physics, 1964, PhD in Physics, 1967; DSc (hon.), Notre Dame U., 2002, U. Melbourne, 2005. Rsch. assoc. Stanford Linear Accelerator Ctr., 1967—68, 1978—79, mem. permanent sci. staff, 1979—2003, edn. coord., 1988—93, asst. to dir. edn. and pub. outreach, 1998—2003, prof. physics, 2003—; hon. rsch. fellow Harvard U., 1971, rsch. fellow, 1971—72, asst. prof. physics, 1972—76, assoc. prof. physics, 1976—77. Guest scientist (non German postdoctoral rschr.) Deutsches Elektronen Sychrotron, Hamburg, 1968—70; vis. assoc. prof. Stanford U., 1976—78; vis. scientist Stanford Linear Accelerator Ctr., 1977—78. Contbr. articles to profl. jours. Pres. Contemporary Physics Edn. Project, Portola Valley, Calif., 1989-95; vol., chair Town of Portola Valley Trails Com., 1988-98; pres. Am. Phys. Soc., 2004. Decorated Hon. officer Order of Australia, 2005; recipient DIRAC medal Internat. Ctr. Theoretical Physics, Trieste, Italy, 2000; fellow Alfred Sloan Found., 1975-79. Fellow AAAS, Am. Phys. Soc. (pres. 2004); mem. Nat. Acad. Sci. Avocations: hiking, native plants. Business E-Mail: quinn@slac.stanford.edu.

QUINN, IAIN, musician; arrived in US, 1994; s. Brian and Linda Quinn; m. Maxine Thévenot, June 19, 2005. MusB, U. Hartford, West Hartford, Conn., 2002; MusM, Yale U., New Haven, 2004. Organist St. Michael's Theol. Coll., Cardiff, Wales, 1987—89; faculty Blachheath Conservatoire, London, 1992—94; dir. music, organist Ch. of the Intercession, NYC, 1994—97, Ch. of the Holy Name, NYC, 1997—98; organist Temple Beth-El, Jersey City, 1997—98; dir. music, organist Trinity Episcopal Ch., Hartford, Conn., 1998—2005; dir. cathedral music, organist Cathedral Ch. St. John, Albuquerque, 2005—. Composer choral and organ works, musician commercial recs.; concert organist: St. Paul's Cathedral, Westminster Abbey, Washington Nat. Cathedral, Alice Tully Hall, Hong Kong Cultural Ctr., Melba Hall, Kaiser-Wilhelm Gedachtnis-Kirche, Internat. Organ Festivals; concert organist Tours for the Brit. Coun. Fellow, Winston Churchill Meml. Trust, 1994. Fellow: Royal Schs. Music; mem.: Friends Cathedral Music, Royal Coll. Organists, Ryal Sch. Ch. Music (examiner), Assn. Anglican Musicians, Am. Guild Organists. Anglican. Office: Cathedral Ch St John PO Box 1246 Albuquerque NM Personal E-mail: iain.quinn@musician.org.

QUINN, IAN, music educator; b. Warner-Robins, Ga., Mar. 19, 1972; s. John J. Quinn and Quinn C. McDonald. BA in Music, Columbia U., NYC, 1993; PhD in Music Theory, Eastman Sch. Music, Rochester, NY, 2004. Asst. prof. music & cognitive sci. Yale U., New Haven, 2004. Editor: Jour. Music Theory, 2004—; contbr. articles to profl. jours. Grantee fellowship, Mannes Inst. Advanced Study Music Theory, 2005—06; Postdoctoral fellowship, U. Chgo., 2002—03, fellowship, Mannes Inst. Advanced Study Music Theory, 2003, Morse Faculty fellowship, Yale U., 2006. Mem.: Am. Musicological Soc., New Eng. Conf. Music Theorists, Soc. Math. and Computation Music, Soc. Music Theory (Emerging Scholar award 2004). Office: Yale Univ Music Dept 143 Elm St New Haven CT 06520-8310 Business E-Mail: ian.quinn@yale.edu.

QUINN, JACK (JOHN FRANCIS QUINN), former congressman, English language educator; b. South Buffalo, NY, Apr. 13, 1951; s. Jack Sr. and Norma Ide Q.; m. Mary Beth McAndrews, 1974; children: Jack III, Kara. BA, Siena Coll.; MA in Edn., SUNY, Buffalo. English language tchr. Orchard Park (N.Y.) Schs., 1973—83; town councilman Town of Hamburg, 1982—84, also town supv.; mem. U.S. Congress from 30th N.Y. Dist., 1993—2002, U.S. Congress from 27th N.Y. Dist., 2003—05; mem. transp. and infrastructure com., chmn. subcom. on railroads, mem. vet. affairs com.; pres. Cassidy & Associates, Washington, 2005—. Recipient Humanitarian award Erie County for the Disabled, Pub. Svc. award Niagara Frontier Parks and Recreation Soc., Disting. Grad. award Nat. Cath. Elem. Schs. Assn., Bronze Good Citizen medal SAR, New Horizons award Drug Edn. of Internat. Assn. of Lions Club, Red, White and Blue award Am. Legion of N.Y., Honor medal Hilbert Coll., Fin. Reporting award Govt. Fin. Officer's Assn., Disting. Career Svc. award Siena Coll., 1995. Mem. Hamburg C. of C., Greater Buffalo C. of C., Buffalo KC, Hamburg Kiwanis Club. Republican. Roman Catholic. Office: Cassidy & Associates 700 13th St NW Washington DC 20005

QUINN, JAMES W., lawyer; b. Bronxville, NY, Oct. 1, 1945; s. James Joseph Quinn and Marie Joan (Blossy) Tisi; m. Kathleen Manning, Kellianne, Christopher, Tierney, Kerrin. AB cum laude, U. Notre Dame, 1967; LLB, Fordham U. Sch. Law, 1971. Bar: NY 1972, US Dist. Ct. (so. and ea. dists. NY) 1973, US Ct. Appeals (2nd cir.) 1974, US Supreme Ct. 1984, US Ct. Appeals (3rd cir.) 1984, US Ct. Appeals (7th cir.) 1985, US Ct. Appeals (9th cir.) 1986, US Ct. Appeals (8th cir.) 1991, US Ct. Appeals (fed. cir.) 2000, US Ct. Appeals (11th cir.) 2004. Assoc. Weil, Gotshal & Manges LLP, NYC, 1971-77, 78-79, ptnr. to sr. ptnr. global chair litig./regulatory dept., 1979—, mem. mgmt. com.; ptnr. Fleisher & Quinn, NYC, 1977-78. Adj. assoc. prof. law Fordham U., NYC, 1985-87; spkr. and lectr. in field. Co-author: ABA's Corporate Litigator, 1989, Corporate Counsellor's Deskbook, 1990, Litigating Complex Careers, 1997, ABA's Business and Commercial Litigation in Fed. Courts, 1998; editor: Fordham U. Law Rev., 1969—71; contbr. articles to profl. jours. Bd. dir. Am. Diabetes Assn., Landmark Found., The Respect for Law Alliance. Named one of Top 10 Trial Lawyers in Am., Nat. Law Jour., 1993, 2004. Fellow Internat. Acad. Trial Lawyers, Am. Coll. Trial Lawyers, NY Bar Found.; mem. ABA (forum com. on the entertainment and sports industries 1982-85, co-chmn. subcommittee alt. dispute resolution, com. corp. counsel 1983-90, litig. sect., prog. chmn. and chmn. of sports and entertainment subcommittee of the trial practice com. 1985-92), Assn. of Bar of City of NY (com. of state jurisdiction 1979-81, com. on entertainment & sports 1984-87, com. on anti-trust regulation 1987-89, chmn. com. sports law 1993-96); mem. adv. bd. Nat. Jud. Coll., Panel of Disting. Neutrals of the Ctr. Pub. Resources, Fed. Bar Coun. Avocations: golf, running, reading. Office: Weil Gotshal & Manges LLP 767 5th Ave New York NY 10153 Office Phone: 212-310-8385. Office Fax: 212-310-8007. E-mail: james.quinn@weil.com. *

QUINN, JANE BRYANT, journalist, writer; b. Niagara Falls, NY, Feb. 5, 1939; d. Frank Leonard and Ada (Laurie) Bryant; m. David Conrad Quinn, June 10, 1967; children: Matthew Alexander, Justin Bryant. BA magna cum laude, Middlebury Coll., 1960. Assoc. editor Insiders Newsletter, NYC, 1962-65, co-editor, 1966-67; sr. editor Cowles Book Co., NYC, 1968; editor-in-chief Bus. Week Letter, NYC, 1969-73, gen. mgr., 1973-74; syndicated fin. columnist Wash. Post Writers Group, 1974—2001; contbr. fin. column to Woman's Day mag., 1974-95, Good Housekeeping, 1995—; contbr. NBC News and Info. Service, 1976-77; contbg. editor Newsweek mag., 1978—; bus. corr. WCBS-TV, NYC, 1979, CBS-TV News, 1980-87, ABC-TV Home Show, 1991-93. Host PBS personal fin. series Take Charge!, 1988; dir. bd. dirs. Bloomberg LP. Author: Everyone's Money

Book, 1979, 2d edit., 1980, Making the Most of Your Money, 1991, 2d edit., 1997, A Hole in the Market, 1994, Smart and Simple Financial Strategies for Busy People, 2006; contbr. (software program) Quicken Financial Planner, 1995. Dean's coun. Harvard Sch. Pub. Health; mem. bd. advisors Jerome Levy Econs. Inst. Bard Coll. Named one of 25 Most Influential Women in US, World Almanac; recipient Emmy award for outstanding coverage fin. on TV, Gerald Loeb award for lifetime achievement and disting. bus. and fin. journalism, John Hancock award for excellence in bus. and fin. journalism, Janus award for excellence in TV and bus. reporting, Journalism award for excellence in personal fin. reporting, ICI-Am. U., three-time winner Nat. Press Club award for consumer journalism, two-time winner Nat. Headliner award, honored for outstanding consumer media svc., Consumer Fedn. Am. Mem. Phi Beta Kappa. Office: Newsweek Inc 251 W 57th St New York NY 10019-1802 Office Phone: 212-445-4000.

QUINN, JARUS WILLIAM, physicist, former association executive; b. West Grove, Pa., Aug. 25, 1930; s. William G. and Ellen C. (DuRoss) Q.; m. Margaret M. McNerney, June 27, 1953; children: J. Kevin, Megan, Jennifer, Colin, Kristin. BS, St. Joseph's Coll., 1952; postgrad., Johns Hopkins U., 1952-55; PhD, Cath. U. Am., 1964. Rsch. assoc. physics Johns Hopkins U., 1954-55; staff scientist Rsch. Inst. Advanced Study, 1956-57; rsch. assoc. physics Cath. U. Am., 1958-60, instr., 1961-64, asst. prof., 1965-69; exec. dir. Optical Soc. Am., Washington, 1969-93; governing bd. Am. Inst. Physics, 1973-94; pres. Stellar Focus, Sunnyvale, Calif., 1994-95. Bd. govs. Am. Assn. Engring. Socs., 1990-93. Fellow Optical Soc. Am. (Distinguished Service Award, 1993), mem. Am. Phys. Soc., Coun. Engring. and Sci. Soc. Execs. Home: 15 Forsythia Ct Durham NC 27705 E-mail: optics2010@yahoo.com.

QUINN, JEFFRY N., chemicals executive, lawyer; BS, Univ. Ky., 1981, JD, 1984. Sr. v.p. sec., gen. counsel Arch Coal Inc.; exec. v.p., chief adminstrv. officer, sec., gen. counsel Premcor Inc.; sr. v.p., gen. counsel, chief restructuring officer Solutia Inc., St. Louis, 2004—04, pres., CEO, 2004—06, chmn., pres., CEO, 2006—. Office: Solutia Inc 575 Maryville Centre Dr Saint Louis MO 63166 Business E-Mail: jnquin@solutia.com.

QUINN, JENNIFER J., mathematics professor; b. Princeton, NJ; m. Mark Martin, Dec. 19, 1998; children: Anson Robert Quinn Martin, Zachary Vincent Quinn Martin. BA in Math. and Biology magna cum laude, Williams Coll.; MS in Pure Math., U. Ill., Chgo., 1993; PhD in Combinators, U. Wis., Madison. With Occidental Coll., 1993—2005, full prof., dept. chair amth. Vis. mem. Math. Sciences Rsch. Inst., Inst. for Math. and its Applications; vis. rsch. scholar, math. and computer sci. U. Puget Sound, 2006—; vis. lectr. Pacific Lutheran U.; invited spkr. in field. Co-editor: Math Horizons; contbr. articles to profl. jours.; co-author (with Arthur Benjamin): Proofs That Really Count: The Art of Combinatorial Proof, 2003 (Beckenbach Book prize, 2006); assoc. editor Math. Magazine, past editl. bd. mem. Spectrum book series of Math. Assn. Am. Fellow: Inst. Combinatories and its Applications; mem.: Math. Assn. Am. (program chair and newsletter editor, Disting. Tchr. award, So. Calif. Sect. 2001, Deborah and Franklin Tepper Haimo award for Disting. Coll. or Univ. Tchg. Math. 2007), Assn. for Women Math. (exec. dir.), Phi Beta Kappa (pres. of the delta, Calif. Chpt.), Phi Beta Kappa Alpha Alumni Assn. Calif. (councilor, chair internat. scholarship com., v.p. bd.). Office: Math and Computer Sci U Puget Sound 1500 N Warner #1043 Tacoma WA 98416-1043 Office Phone: 253-879-3630. Office Fax: 253-572-5490. Business E-Mail: jjquinn@ups.edu. *

QUINN, JOHN ALBERT, chemical engineering professor; b. Springfield, Ill., Sept. 3, 1932; s. Edward Joseph and Marie (Von De Bur) Q.; m. Frances Wilkie Daly, June 22, 1957; children: Sarah D., Rebecca V., John E. BSChemE, U. Ill., 1954; PhDChemE, Princeton U., 1959. Mem. faculty chem. engring. U. Ill., Urbana, 1958-70; prof. U. Pa., Phila., 1971—, Robert D. Bent prof., 1978—, chmn. dept. chem. engring., 1980-85. Vis. prof. Imperial Coll. U. London, 1965-66; vis. scientist MIT, 1980; vis. prof. U. Rome/La Sapienza, 1992; mem. sci. adv. bds. Sepracor, Inc., Marlborough, Mass., 1984—, Whitaker Found., Mechanicsburg, Pa., 1987—; Mason lectr. Stanford U., 1981; Katz lectr. U. Mich., 1985; Reilly lectr. U. Notre Dame, 1987; Michael's lectr. MIT, 2001. Contbr. articles to profl. publs.; editl. advisor Jour. Membrane Sci., 1975—, Indsl. and Chem. Engring. Rsch., 1987-88, Revs. in Chem. Engring., 1980—; pioneer rschr. on mass transfer and interfacial phenomena. Sr. postdoctoral fellow NSF, 1965-66; Sherman Fairchild scholar Calif. Inst. Tech., 1985. Fellow AAAS, Am. Inst. Med. and Biol. Engring.; mem. NAE, AIChE (Allan P. Colburn award 1966, Alpha Chi Sigma award 1978), Am. Acad. Arts and Scis., Am. Chem. Soc., Internat. Soc. Oxygen Transport to Tissue, Sigma X, Phi Lambda Upsilon, Tau Beta Pi. Home: 275 E Wynnewood Rd Merion Station PA 19066-1627 Office: Univ Pa Towne Bldg 220 S 33rd St Philadelphia PA 19104-6393 Office Phone: 215-898-8503.

QUINN, JOHN B., lawyer; b. Ft. Belvoir, Va., June 20, 1951; BA magna cum laude, Claremont Men's Coll., 1973; JD cum laude, Harvard U., 1976. Bar: NY 1978, Calif. 1979. Assoc. Cravath, Swaine & Moore, 1976—79; founding ptnr. Quinn Emanual Urquhart Oliver & Hedges, LLP, 1979—. Gen. counsel Acad. Motion Picture Arts and Scis., 1987—; instr. Brigham Young U. Sch. Law, 1977; lectr. fed. practice Calif. Continuing Ed. of Bar; mem. Fed. Courts and Practice Com., Com. on Fed. Courts, Million Dollar Advocates Forum; dir. Rose Bowl Operating Co. Fellow: Internat. Acad. Trial Lawyers; mem.: ABA, Calif. Bar Assn., NY Bar Assn., Union Internationale Des Avocats, LA County Bar Assn. Office: Quinn Emanuel Urquhart Oliver & Hedges LLP 865 South Figueroa St 10th Fl Los Angeles CA 90017 Office Phone: 213-443-3000. Office Fax: 213-443-3100. E-mail: johnquinn@quinnemanuel.com.

QUINN, JOHN COLLINS, publishing executive, editor; b. Providence, Oct. 24, 1925; s. John A. and Kathryn H. (Collins) Q.; m. Lois R. Richardson, June 20, 1953; children: John Collins, Lo-anne, Richard B., Christopher A. AB, Providence Coll., 1945; MS, Columbia U. Sch. Journalism, 1946. Successively copy boy, reporter, asst. city editor, Washington corr., asst. mng. editor, day mng. editor Providence Jour.-Bull., 1943-66; with Gannett Co. Inc., Rochester, NY, 1966-90; exec. editor Rochester Democrat & Chronicle, Times-Union, 1966-71; gen. mgr. Gannett News Service, 1967-80, pres., 1980-88, v.p. parent co., 1971-75, sr. v.p. news and info., 1975-80, sr. v.p., chief news exec. parent co., editor USA TODAY, 1983-89; exec. v.p. Gannett Co., Arlington, Va., 1983-90; trustee Gannett Found., Arlington, 1988-91; dep. chmn. Freedom Forum, Arlington, 1991-97, trustee, 1991—. Named to R.I. Hall of Fame, 1975, Editor of Yr. Nat. Press Found., 1986; recipient William Allen White citation, 1987, Women in Communications Headliner award, 1986; Paul Miller/Okla. State U. medallion, 1988. Mem. AP Mng. Editors (past dir., nat. pres. 1973-74), Am. Soc. Newspaper Editors (dir., chmn. editorial bd., chmn. conv. program, nat. pres. 1982-83) Roman Catholic. Home: 365 S Atlantic Ave Cocoa Beach FL 32931-2719 Office: Freedom Forum 1101 Wilson Blvd Ste 2300 Arlington VA 22209-2265 Office Phone: 703-284-2871.

QUINN, JOHN J., lawyer; b. Sept. 19, 1932; BA, Univ. So. Calif., 1954, JD, 1959. Bar: Calif. 1959, US Supreme Ct. 1965. Ptnr., LA Office Mgmt. Arnold & Porter, LA. Past chmn. US Senator Barbara Boxer Fed. Judicial Selection Com.; chmn., Disciplinary Com. US Dist. Ct., Ctrl. Calif., 1995—2001. Recipient Learned Hand award, Am. Jewish Com., Disting. Svc. award, U.S. Ct. Appeals, Ninth Cir. Fellow: Am. Col. Trial Lawyers; mem.: ABA (mem. Ho. of Dels. 1977—82), L.A. County Bar Assn. (pres. 1976—77, Shattuck-Price award), Am. Bd. Trial Advocates, Order of the Coif. Office: Arnold & Porter 777 S Figueroa St Los Angeles CA 90017-2513 Office Phone: 213-243-4080. Office Fax: 213-243-4199. Business E-Mail: john.j.quinn@aporter.com.

QUINN, JOHN MICHAEL, physicist, geophysicist; b. Denver, May 8, 1946; s. Leonard Simon and Winifred Ruth (Doolan) Q.; m. Pamela Dagmar Shield, May 28, 1983. BS in Physics, U. Va., 1968; MS in Physics, U. Colo., 1982. Physicist U.S. Naval Rsch. Lab., Washington, 1967—73; prin. engr. Singer Simulation Products, Silver Spring, Md., 1973—74; rsch. physicist U.S. Naval Rsch. Lab, Washington, 1979—80; geophysicist U.S. Naval Oceanog. Office, Stennis Space Ctr., Miss., 1974—79, 1982—85, geophysicist, mathematician, 1985—95; rsch. geophysicist U.S. Geol. Survey, Denver, 1995—2002; ret., 2002. Investigator Polar Orbiting Geomagnetic Survey Experiment, 1990-94; prin. investigator Nat. Polar Orbiting Environ. Satellite Sys., 1989-2002; chmn. com. on earth and planetary geomagnetic survey satellites Internat. Assn. Geomagnetism and Aeronomy, 1991-99, mem. internat. geomagnetic ref. field com., 1989-2002; U.S. del. UN Internat. Stds. Orgn., 2000-2002; project coord. USN Project MAGNET; vis. scientist NOAA, 2003—; cons. in field. Author: Epoch World Geomagnetic Model, 1985, 90, 95, 2000. With US Army, 1968—71. Mem. Am. Geophys. Union, Am. Math. Soc., European Geophys. Soc., Math. Assn. Am. Achievements include devel. of official Dept. of Def. world magnetic models which are used by military and civilian agencies for navigational purposes and basic rsch. of earth's magnetic field, specialized remote geomagnetic sensing/modeling techniques to detect, in the lithosphere, magnetization due to meteorite impact shocks and hotspot basalt flows; engaged in geodynamo research, yielding high-resolution fluid-flow models at the core-mantle-boundary. Determined global lithspheric 3-D structure of the Earth to 200 kilometers depth by inverse modeling of CHAMP satellite magnetic field data; global change research. Home: 2732 S Braun Way Lakewood CO 80228-4954 Personal E-mail: p-j_quinn@comcast.net.

QUINN, KATHERINE SARAH, psychologist; d. George and Esther Blank; m. Ed Quinn (div. 1994); children: Adam(dec.), Molly Quinn Panepinto. BA in Psychology, U. Nev., 1982, MA in Psychology, 1987; PhD in Psychology (hon.), Calif. Sch. Profl. Psychology, 1999. Intern Children's Behavioral Svcs., Las Vegas, 1980—83, child devel. specialist, 1984—85; rsch. devel. coord. San Diego County Mental Health, 1988—97; intern Southwood Hosp., San Diego, 1991—92; therapist Child Sexual Abuse Treatment Ctr., San Diego, 1992—93; post-doctoral intern Neuropsychological Assessment and Psychotherapy, Solana Beach, Calif., 1999—2002; pvt. practice Solana Beach, 2002—04, Del Mar, Calif., 2004—. Mem.: APA, San Diego Psychol. Assn. Roman Catholic. Avocations: reading, music, opera, theater, hiking. Home: 721 Genter St La Jolla CA 92037 Office: 240 9th St Del Mar CA 92014 Office Phone: 858-720-0682. Business E-Mail: quinnphd@san.rr.com.

QUINN, KEVIN ANTHOMY, investment banker; b. 1964; m. Jane Katherine Zoidis, Aug. 28, 1993; 3 children. BS, Columbia Coll., NYC; MBA, Columbia U., NYC. Mng. dir., mergers and acquisitions Goldman Sachs & Co., Menlo Park, Calif. Named a Top Dealmaker, Dealmaker mag., 2006. Office: Goldman Sachs 2765 Sand Hill Rd Menlo Park CA 94025 Office Phone: 650-234-3300. *

QUINN, KEVIN J., utilities executive; BCE, U. Dayton, Ohio; MBA, Columbia U., NYC. Engr. Exxon Rsch. and Engring. Co.; mgmt. cons. McKinsey and Co., Inc.; dir. enterprise strategy PSEG, bus. strategy mgr. corp. planning, 1991, v.p. corp. planning; pres. PSEG Energy Resources & Trade, 2006—. Mem. parish fin. com. St. Patrick's Sch., Chatham, NJ. Office: PSEG Energy Resources & Trade PO Box 570 Newark NJ 07101 Office Phone: 973-430-7000. *

QUINN, MATTHEW J., educational association administrator; BA in Classics, Fordham U.; PhL with honors in Philosophy, Woodstock Coll.; MA in English, Fordham U.; PhD with highest distinction in Mgmt. of Higher Edn., Boston Coll.; JD, Fordham U.; LHD (hon.), Carroll Coll. Bar: Pa. Asst. to exec. v.p., asst. to dir. admissions and fin. aid Boston Coll.; dir. state colls. office NJ Dept. Higher Edn., Trenton; dean grad. sch. arts and scis. Iona Coll., New Rochelle, NY; v.p. acad. affairs St. Joseph's U., Phila.; pres. Carroll Coll. Helena, Mont., 1989—2000; founding exec. dir. Jack Kent Cooke Found., Lansdowne, Va., 2000—. Adv. Kellogg Nat. Leadership Prog. W.K. Kellogg Found.; bd. mem. Am. Assn. Univ. Adminstrs., Commn. Women in Higher Edn., Am. Coun. Edn.; chmn. bd. dirs. Fed. Res. Bank. Mpls., Helena Br.; mem. exec. com., bd. dirs. Assn. Cath. Colls. and Univs.; mem. adv. com. for exec. progs. and working group on stewardship principles for ind. founds. Coun. Founds.; bd. dirs. Coun. Ind. Colls., Washington Grantmakers; mem. Mission and Identity Task Force. Founding editor: Crossroads, The Holy Cross Quarterly. Office: Jack Kent Cooke Found 44325 Woodridge Pky Lansdowne VA 20176 *

QUINN, MICHAEL, economics professor; s. Tom and Grace Quinn. BA, Fairfield U., Conn., 1996; PhD in Econs., U. N.C., Chapel Hill, 2002. Asst. prof. of econs. Bentley Coll., Waltham, Mass., 2002—. Contbr. articles to profl. jours. Recipient Taner award for Excellence in Tchg., U. N.C.-Chapel Hill, 2000, Econ. Dept. award for Excellence in Tchg., 1999, Hohmann award in Econs., Fairfield U., 1996, Gregory Zec award in Econs., So. Conn. Bus. Economists, 1996; grantee Tech. Enhancement grantee, IBM and U. N.C., 2000; scholar Malcolm Baldridge scholar in Internat. Trade, Conn. Bus. and Industry Assn., 1994. Mem.: So. Econ. Assn., Am. Econ. Assn. Office: Bentley College 175 Forest St Waltham MA 02452 Office Phone: 781-891-2938. Office Fax: 781-891-2896. E-mail: mquinn@bentley.edu.

QUINN, NIGEL WILLIAM TREVELYAN, research scientist; b. Belfast, Northern Ireland, Dec. 28, 1955; arrived in U.S., 1978; s. Stanley Quinn and Elaine Elizabeth Hayes. BSc with honors, Cranfield U., 1977; MS, Iowa State U., 1981; PhD, Cornell U., 1987. Registered profl. engr., Calif. GE fellow Cornell U., 1984—86, sr. rsch. assoc., 1987—90; lead groundwater modeler San Joaquin Valley Drainage Program, 1987—90; geol. scientist, group leader Hydro Ecol. Engring. Advanced Decision Support Berkeley (Calif.) Nat. Lab., 1990—. Convener Calif. Water and Environ. Modeling Forum, Sacramento, 2002—; bd. dirs. Internat. Symposium on Environ. Software Sys., Germany; adj. prof. Calif. Water Inst.; assoc. rsch. prof. Calif. State U., Fresno; rsch. engr. U. Calif., Merced. Contbr. chapters to books, articles to profl. jours. Dir. UN Assn., Ames, 1978—81. Recipient Hunting Challenge Cup, Cranfield U., 1977. Mem.: ASCE, Calif. Water Inst., Water Environment Fedn., Am. Water Resources Assn., Am. Geophysical Union, Berkeley Yacht Club, Yolo Polo Club. Unitarian. Avocations: sailing, travel, polo. Home: 1123 Lochbrae Rd Sacramento CA 95815 Office: Berkeley Nat Lab 70A-3317H 1 Cyclotron Rd Berkeley CA 95815 Office Phone: 510-486-7056. Business E-Mail: nwquinn@lbl.gov.

QUINN, PATRICIA K., literary agent; b. Chico, Calif. d. Donald Joseph and Kathleen (Alexander) Q. BA, Bennington Coll.; MFA in Drama, Yale U. Prodr., devel. exec. various Off-Broadway and regional theatres, 1976-84; devel. cons. Sundance Film Inst., Utah, 1983—85; theatrical agt. I.C.M., LA, 1985-90; v.p. comedy devel. Warner Bros. TV, Burbank, Calif., 1990-92; lit. and packaging agt. various agys. LA, 1995—2006; cons. Quinn Media, 2006—. Instr. UCLA Ext., 1995—; spkr., lectr. Nat. Assn. of TV Programming Execs., Fla. Bar, NATAS, Media Xchange (Internat.); mem. TV com. Brit. Acad. Film and TV Arts, 2002-; prof. reps. peer group com. NATAS, 2002-04. Founding mem. N.Y. Theatre Workshop, NYC, 1980—86. Mem.: Women in Film (v.p. 1995—2001, bd. dirs. 2005—). Office: 330 S Spalding Dr #403 Beverly Hills CA 90212 Home Phone: 310-788-3810; Office Phone: 310-656-5141. E-mail: p_quinn@sbcglobal.net.

QUINN, PATRICK, lieutenant governor; b. Chgo., Sept. 22, 1948; 2 children. BS, Georgetown U., 1971; JD Northwestern U. Sch. of Law. Commr. Cook County Bd. of Tax Appeal, 1982; treas. State of Ill., 1990—94, lt. gov., 2003—. Chmn. Ill. River Coordinating Counc., Ill. Rural Affairs Counc., Ill. Rural Bond Bank. Democrat. Catholic. Office: Office Lt Governor James R Thompson Ctr 100 W Randolph Ste 15-200 Chicago IL 60601 also: Office Lt Governor State Capitol 214 State House Springfield IL 62706 Office Phone: 312-814-5220, 217-782-7884. Office Fax: 312-814-4862, 217-524-6262.

QUINN, PATRICK, transportation executive; BA, U. Nebr., 1968, JD, 1971. From assoc. to ptnr. Nelson & Harding, Lincoln, Nebr., 1971-77; gen. counsel S.W. Motor Freight, Chattanooga, 1977-85; pres., co-chmn. U.S Xpress Enterprises, Inc., Chattanooga, Tenn., 1985—. Office: US Xpress Enterprises Inc 4080 Jenkins Rd Chattanooga TN 37421-1174 Office Phone: 423-510-3000.

QUINN, PEGGY ARMSTRONG, elementary school educator, writer; b. Gorman, Tex., Nov. 12, 1943; d. Lowell Rogers and Alice Humphrey Armstrong; m. Robert Michael Quinn, Aug. 12, 1979; 2 children. BS, Tex. Woman's U., 1965; MEd, San Diego State U., 1976. Cert. elem. tchr. Calif. Dept. Educator, 1975, reading specialist Calif. Dept. Educator, 1975, kindergarten tchr. Calif. Dept. Educator, 1975, elem. tchr. Tex. Dept. Educator, 1981, kindergarten tchr. Tex. Dept. Educator, 1981, ESL tchr. Tex. Dept. Educator, 2001, Learning Resource Specialist Tex. Dept. Educator, 2001. Kindergarten tchr. North Hanover Schs., Wrightstown, N.J., 1966—69; elem. tchr., reading specialist San Diego City Schs., 1970—80; elem. tchr. Garland ISD, Tex., 1986—. Mem. AFT/CIO Educators Group, Dallas, 1987—. Author: (articles) Writer's Digest, 1984 (contest winner), Antique Weekly, 1985. Mem., supporter Weaver PTA, Garland, 1982—; vol. pianist Western Hills Nursing Home, Denton, Tex., 1980—, Comanche, Tex., 2004—05; supporter Dem. Party, Dallas, 2005. Democrat. Baptist. Avocations: music, writing. Office: Weaver Elem Sch 805 Pleasant Valley Rd Garland TX 75040 Office Phone: 972-494-8311. E-mail: pegqn@yahoo.com.

QUINN, SUSAN NICODEMUS, theater educator, director; d. Eugene Johnson Nicodemus, Jr. and Marsha Grottola Nicodemus; m. Thomas P. Quinn, Aug. 8, 1998; children: Nathaniel Nicodemus, Samantha Rose. BFA with honors, U. of Arts, Phila., 1991. Acct. exec., coord. art in edn. Am. Family Theatre, Phila., 1996—99; acct. exec., arts ed specialist Baylin Artist Mgmt., Doylestown, Pa., 1999; dir. edn. Walnut St. Theatre, Phila., 1999—. Mem. peer rev. panel Phila. Cultural Fund. Dir.: (plays) Walnut St. Theatre Mainstage; prodr.: Walnut St.Theater for Kids Series (Best of Philly 2000 Phila. Mag., 2000). Recipient Acting award, Charlotte Cushman Club, 1990, Beyond the Ramp Accesibility award, Creative Access, 2005. Mem.: ASSITEJ, Am. Alliance Theatre and Edn., Actors Equity Assn. Office: Walnut St Theatre 825 Walnut St Philadelphia PA 19107 Home Phone: 215-574-3500 566; Office Phone: 215-574-3550 566. Business E-Mail: education@wstonline.org.

QUINN, THOMAS CHARLES, medical researcher, educator; BS, U. Notre Dame, 1969, MS, 1970; MD, Northwestern U., 1974. Diplomate Am. Bd. Internal Med, 1977, Am. Bd. Infectious Disease, 1981. Intern, resident in internal medicine Albany (NY) Med. Ctr., 1974—77; prof. medicine, internat. health, epidemiology, molecular microbiology, immunology and pathology Johns Hopkins U., Balt., 1981—; dir. Johns Hopkins Ctr. Global Health, Balt.; sr. investigator, dir. internat. STD/HIV lab. Nat. Inst. Allergy & Infectious Diseases, Balt., 1982—. Med. cons. Academic Alliance, Washington, 2001—03. Capt. USPHS, 1977—. Decorated Disting. Svc. award USPHS. Fellow: Infectious Diseases Soc. Am. (bd. dirs. 2002—03); mem.: Inst. Medicine. Office: Johns Hopkins Univ Ross 1159 720 Rutland Ave Baltimore MD 21205 E-mail: tquinn@jhmi.edu.

QUINN, THOMAS H., lawyer; b. Pawtucket, RI, 1937; AB, Providence Coll., 1959; LLB, Georgetown Univ., 1963. Bar: RI 1963, DC 1964. Atty., legis. counsel, Office Comptroller Currency US Treasury Dept., 1963—66; ptnr. legis. and regulatory practice O'Connor & Hannan, Washington; ptnr., legis. affairs group Venable LLP, Washington, 2001—. Apptd. mem. US Govt. Bd Internat. Broadcasting, 1974—82; alt. US observer Internat. Fund for Ireland, 1993; trustee Dem. Senatorial Campaign Com., House Dem. Congl. Campaign Com. Mem.: ABA, RI Bar Assn., DC Bar Assn. Democrat. Office: Venable LLP 575 Seventh St NW Washington DC 20004 Office Phone: 202-344-4701. Office Fax: 202-344-8300. Business E-Mail: thquinn@venable.com.

QUINN, YVONNE SUSAN, lawyer; b. Spring Valley, Ill., May 13, 1951; d. Robert Leslie and Shirley Eilene (Morse) Quinn. BA, U. Ill., 1973; JD, U. Mich., 1976, MA in Econs., 1977. Bar: NY 1978, US Dist. Ct. (ea. and so. dists.) NY 1978,US Ct. Appeals (3d, 5th, 9th, 10th and DC cirs.) 1982, US Ct. Appeals (2d cir.) 1992, US Ct. Appeals (4th cir.) 1994, US Supreme Ct. 1982. Assoc. Cravath, Swaine & Moore, NYC, 1977-80, Sullivan & Cromwell, NYC, 1980-84, ptnr. litig., 1984—, and coord. antitrust practice area. Mem. ABA, Assn. of Bar of City of NY Office: Sullivan & Cromwell 125 Broad St New York NY 10004-2489 Home Phone: 212-628-0932; Office Phone: 212-558-3736. Office Fax: 212-558-3588. Business E-Mail: quinny@sullcrom.com.

QUINNAN, GERALD VINCENT, JR., medical educator; b. Boston, Sept. 7, 1947; s. Gerald Vincent and Mary (Lally) Q.; children: Kevin, Kylie, Kathleen, John, Gerald; m. Leigh A. Sawyer. AB in Chemistry, Coll. Holy Cross, 1969; MD cum laude, St. Louis U., 1973. Diplomate Am. Bd. Internal Medicine. Intern, resident, fellow Boston U. Med. Ctr., 1973-77; med. officer Bur. Biologics, USPHS, Bethesda, Md., 1977; advanced through grades to asst. surgeon gen. USPHS, 1992; dir. herpes virus br., dep. dir. div. virology Bur. Biologics, Bethesda, 1980-81; dir. div. virology Ctr. for Drugs and Biologics, Bethesda, 1981-88; dep. dir. Ctr. Biologics Evaluation and Rsch., Bethesda, 1988-93, acting dir., 1990-92; prof. Uniformed Svcs. U. Health Scis., Bethesda, 1993—, chair preventive medicine, 2002—. Contbr. chpts. to books, numerous articles to profl. jours.; editl. bd./reviewer several jours. Fellow Infectious Diseases Soc. Am.; mem. AAAS, Am. Soc. for Microbiology, Am. Soc. for Clin. Investigation, Sigma Xi, Alpha Omega Alpha. Roman Catholic. Office: Uniformed Svcs U Hlth Scis Dept Preventive Medicine & Biometrics 4301 Jones Bridge Rd Bethesda MD 20814-4712 Home Phone: 301-460-6625; Office Phone: 301-295-3173. Business E-Mail: gquinnan@usuhs.mil.

QUINN TRANK, CHRISTINE, education educator; b. Waterloo, Iowa, Feb. 27, 1953; d. Richard Peter and Irene Christine Quinn; m. Douglas Monty Trank, Jan. 15, 2001. BA, U. Iowa, Iowa City, 1975, PhD, 2001. Program asst., adminstrv. asst., coord. acad. adminstrn. U. Iowa, 1981; asst. prof. Tex. Tech U., Lubbock, 2004—. Mem. editl. bd. Acadm. Mgmt. Jour., 2004—, Acad. Mgmt. Learning and Edn., 2004—. Contbr. articles to profl. jours. Mem.: Acad. Mgmt., Am. Sociol. Assn.

QUINONES, MARISSA ESCOBAR, pharmacist; d. Roberto Escobar Sr. and Olivia Escobar; m. Eddy Anthony Quinones, Sept. 17, 2005. BS, Tex. State U., San Marcos, 2000; PharmD, Tex. Tech., Amarillo, 2004. Discharge pharmacist Vet. Affairs North Tex., Dallas, 2004—05; pharmacy practice resident, asst. instr. Veterans Affairs/Tex. Tech Health Scis. Ctr.

Sch. Pharmacy, Dallas, 2004—05; inpatient pharmacist Vet. Affairs, Dallas, 2005—06; primary care splty. resident/asst. instr. Tex. Tech Health Scis. Ctr. Sch. of Pharmacy/Vet. Affairs North Tex., Dallas, 2005—06; clin. pharmacist Ctrl. Dallas Ministries Cmty. Health Svcs., 2006—. Asst. prof. pharmacy practice Tex. Tech., Health Scis. Ctr. Sch. Pharmacy, Dallas, 2006—; presenter in field. Contbr. scientific papers. Vol. diabetes edn. Veterans Affairs Health Fair, Dallas, 2004; vol. Tarrant County Woman and Children Item Dr., Ft. Worth, 2004, Habitat for Humanity Project, Cleburne, Tex., 2004, Am. Diabetes Assn. Expo, Dallas, 2005, Camp Broncho-Asthma Camp, Tex., 2005, Tex. Lions Diabetes Camp, Kerville, 2005, Camp New Horizons Diabetes Camp, Dallas, 2006. Recipient Chief Resident award, Tex. Tech., Health Scis. Ctr. Sch. Pharmacy, 2004—05, Excellence in Pub. Health Pharmacy Practice award, USPHS, 2004, Controversial Topic award, Am. Coll. Clin. Pharmacy, Dallas-Ft. Worth Chpt., 2005; scholar, Amarillo Edn., 2000, Walgreens, 2001—02. Mem.: Tex. Soc. Hosp. Pharmacists, Am. Coll. Clin. Pharmacy (sec. 2006—07), Phi Delta Chi. Achievements include research in evaluation of first line therapy for the treatment of hypertension using thiazide diuretics in a VA population; utilization of glucose test strips improve glycemic control in patients treated with oral hypoglycemics. Office: Tex Tech Health Scis Ctr Sch Pharmacy 4500 S Lancaster Rd Bldg 7-R #119A Dallas TX 75216 Home Phone: 806-433-2288; Office Phone: 214-372-5300 ext. 236. Office Fax: 214-375-9366. Business E-Mail: marissa.escobar@ttuhsc.edu.

QUINONES-BURGOS, DAYNA, pharmacist, educator; d. Jose Quinones and Tita Burgos. PharmD, Midwestern U., Ill., 2003. Cert. SCUBA instr. Resident in pharmacy practice San Juan VA Med. Ctr., 2004; clin. pharmacist Ashford Presbyn. Cmty. Hosp., San Juan, 2004—05; asst. prof. U. Puerto Rico, San Juan, 2005—. Vol. Puerto Rico Alzheimer's Fedn., San Juan, 2005—07. Recipient 2d Pl. award for residency rsch. Mem.: Puerto Rico Commn. Health Sys. Pharmacists (pres.), Puerto Rico Pharmacists Assn., Am. Coll. Clin. Pharmacy, Am. Soc. Health-Sys. Pharmacists, Rho Chi. Avocation: scuba diving. Home: 506 Asuncion St San Juan PR 00920 Office: Univ Puerto Rico PO Box 365067 San Juan PR 00936 Home Phone: 787-406-9049; Office Phone: 787-758-2525. Business E-Mail: dquinones@rcm.upr.edu.

QUIÑONES KEBER, ELOISE, art historian, educator; b. LA; d. Rudy Jr. and Margaret Q. BA, Immaculate Heart Coll., 1966; MA, UCLA, 1967, Columbia U., 1979, PhD, 1984. Lectr. Columbia U., NYC, 1984-86; prof. art history Baruch Coll., The Grad. Ctr., CUNY, 1986—. Author: Codex Telleriano Remensis: Ritual, Divination, and History in a Pictorial Aztec Manuscript, 1995 (Getty Grant Program Publ. Subvention award, 1992); co-author: Art of Aztec Mexico: Treasures of Tenochtitlan, 1983; editor: Chipping Away on Earth: Studies in Prehispanic and Colonial Mexico in Honor of Arthur J.O. Anderson and Charles E. Dibble, 1995, In Chalchihuitl in Quetzalli: Mesoamerican Studies in Honor of Doris Heyden, 2000, Representing Aztec Ritual: Performance, Text, and Image in the Work of Sahaqún, 2002; co-editor: The Work of Bernardino de Sahagun: Pioneed Ethnographer of 16th-Century Aztec Mexico, 1988, Mixteca-Puebla: Discoveries and Research in Mesoamerican Archaeology and Art, 1994; contbr. articles to profl. jours. Mellon postdoctoral fellow Columbia U., 1984-86, fellow Ford Found./NRC, 1986-87, Am. Coun. of Learned Socs. fellow, 1987-88, 93-94, grantee, 1985, 95, NEH fellow, 1993-94, grantee, 1986, 91; grantee Am. Philos. Soc., 1986; fellow Guggenheim Found., 1998; recipient Ralph Waldo Emerson award Phi Beta Kappa Soc., 1996. Mem. Coll. Art Assn., Assn. Latin Am. Art, Am. Soc. for Ethnohistory. Office: CUNY Grad Ctr Art History Program 365 Fifth Ave New York NY 10016 also: CUNY Baruch Coll Dept Fine and Performing Arts 1 Bernard Baruch Way New York NY 10010-1703 Office Phone: 646-312-4052. Business E-Mail: EQuinones-Keber@gc.cuny.edu. E-mail: Eloise_Quinones-Keber@baruch.cuny.edu.

QUINONEZ, TASHA MARIE, elementary school educator; b. Mt. View, Calif., Oct. 30, 1972; m. Steven John Quinonez, Oct. 19, 1996; children: Emerson, Madison, Blake. BA, Hayward State U., Calif., 1995; M in Adminstrn., San Jose State U., Calif., 2002. Multiple subject clear credential with CLAD Calif., 1996. Tchr. Moreland Sch. Dist., San Jose, 1996—. Named Tchr. of Yr., Moreland Sch. Dist., 2005. Mem.: Calif. Tchrs. Assn. Home Phone: 408-378-4001; Office Phone: 408 874 3125. Personal E-mail: tquinonez@moreland.k12.ca.us.

QUINSON, BRUNO ANDRE, painter, retired publishing executive; b. Norwich, Conn., Jan. 1, 1938; s. Louis Jean and Suzanne Marie (Richard) Q.; m. Mary Ann Goodman, May 3, 1980; children by previous marriage: Timothy Bruno, Marc Albert (dec.), Christopher Louis; stepchildren: J. Geoffrey Taylor, Luke J. Taylor (dec.), Adam J. Taylor, Joshua P. Taylor. BA, Williams Coll., 1958; postgrad., NYU, 1960-61. Product mgr. Simon & Schuster, NYC, 1960-65; pub., gen. mgr. Golden Press (div. Western Pub. Co., Inc.), 1965-70; pres. Larousse & Co., Inc., NYC, 1970-82, also bd. dirs.; pres. trade and reference div. Macmillan Pub. Co., NYC, 1982-88; pres., chief exec. officer Henry Holt & Co. Inc., NYC, 1988-96, ret., 1996—. Bd. dirs. Nat. Book Found., chmn., 1993-96; treas. Columbia U. Press, 1994-03, vice chmn., 1997-03; exec. bd. Macmillan Ltd., 1995-96; nat. coun. Graywolf Press, 2005— Exhibitions include Nat. Acad. Art, Century Assn., NYC, Meeting House, Southfield, Mass., IS 183, Interlaken, Mass., Norfolk Libr.Conn., Frost Pl., Franconia, N.H. Bd. dirs. Rye (NY) Art Ctr., treas., 1973-74; bd. dirs. Northside Ctr. for Child Devel., 1981-89, chmn., 1987-89, adv. bd., 1990—; bd. dirs. 1115 Fifth Ave. Corp., 1983-94, 96-04, pres., 1998-03; bd. dirs. Mus. of the City of NY, 1999—, Lycee Francais NY, 1994-96, Vol. Cons. Group, 1997, Each Child a Reader Found., 1996; founding mem. Barrington Stage Co.; founding mem., bd. dirs. Interlaken Sch. Art, 1998-01; nat. adv. bd. Eudora Welty Found., 2002—; trustee Leopold Schepp Found., 2001—, PEN Am. Ctr., 2003-07; bd. dirs. Manhattan Theater Club, 1991-97, emeritus 1997— Decorated chevalier Des Arts et Lettres (France). Mem. Am. Assn. Pubs. (bd. dirs. 1991-95), Pubs.' Lunch Club (pres. 1990-93), Century Assn., Norfolk Country Club, The River Club. Office: 2 E 93rd St New York NY 10128-0610

QUINT, ARNOLD HARRIS, lawyer; b. Boston, Jan. 3, 1942; s. Milton and Esther Quint; m. Susan Arenson, July 23, 1967; children: Edward, Michael. AB, Haverford Coll., Pa., 1963; LLB, Yale U., 1966. Bar: D.C. 1967. Supervisory atty. Power Commn., Washington, 1967-70; assoc. Hunton & Williams, Washington, 1970-74, ptnr., 1974—2007, sr. counsel, 2007—. Mem. ABA, Energy Bar Assn. (com. chmn. 1979-83, bd. dirs. 1989-92). Office: Hunton & Williams 1900 K St NW Washington DC 20006-1110 Office Phone: 202-955-1542. E-mail: aquint@hunton.com.

QUINT, DAVID PAUL, investment banking executive; b. Independence, Iowa, July 24, 1950; s. Paul Theodore and Mary Ann (Connolly) Q.; m. Kathleen Mary Stern, May 25, 1973; children: Jennifer, Angela, David, Geoffrey. BA in Modern Langs., U. Notre Dame, 1972, JD, 1975. Assoc. Arter & Hadden, Cleve., 1975-82; mng. dir. Belden & Blake, London, 1983-92; pres., CEO RP&C Internat., London, 1992—. Mem. Notre Dame Law Rev., 1974. Rotary Internat. fellow, 1978. Mem. Ohio State Bar Assn. Republican. Roman Catholic. Avocation: travel. Home: Avallon East Rd KT1 30LF Weybridge Surrey England Office: RP&C Internat 31A St James Square SW1Y 4JR London England Office Phone: 011 44 207 766 7000. E-mail: dquint@rpcint.co.uk.

QUINT, IRA, retail executive; b. NYC, May 29, 1930; s. Theodore Isaac and Rebecca (Ginandes) Q.; m. Carol Ann Goldsmith (div. Feb. 1984); children: Susan Amy, Stephanie Ann. BS, NYU, 1951; MBA, Harvard U., 1954. Group nat. mdse. mgr. Sears Roebuck & Co., Chgo., 1954-78; pres. Colonial Corp. Am., NYC, 1978-79; pres., CEO Venture Stores, St. Louis, 1979-81; exec. v.p. Montgomery Ward, Chgo., 1981-85; pres. Lane Bryant Stores, NYC, 1985-90; pres., chief exec. officer Conston Corp., Phila., 1990-92; pres. Quint Consultancy, NYC. Mem.: Harvard (N.Y.C.). Home and Office: 130 E 67th St New York NY 10021-6136

QUINTANA-ALLENSON, ANA M., government agency executive; b. Chgo., Oct. 16, 1967; d. Sergio Antonio (Tony) Quintana and Ana Ilia Gonzalez; m. James M. Allenson, May 5, 2006. BA in Comm. cum laude, Loyola U. Chgo., 1989. Cert. Media Rels. Cmty. Media Workshop, 2001, U. of S.C., 2001. Claims rep. Social Security Adminstrn., Chgo., 1993—99, mgmt. support specialist, 2000—01, pub. affairs specialist, 2001—02, acting asst. dist. mgr., 2003, exec. staff asst., 2003—. President-Hispanic task force Gift of Hope Organ and Tissue Donation Network, Elmhurst, Ill., 2002—03. Mem.: Nat. Assn. Hispanic Journalists (mem. Chgo. region Hispanic action com. 1995—, Ill. vice chair 2003—04). D-Liberal. Avocations: photography, reading, drawing, art shows. Office Phone: 312-575-4109. E-mail: ana.quintana-allenson@ssa.gov.

QUINTANILLA, ANTONIO PAULET, retired physician, educator; b. Feb. 8, 1927; came to U.S., 1963, naturalized, 1974; s. Leandro Marino and Edel Paulet Quintanilla; m. Mary Parker Rodriguez, May 2, 1958; children: Antonio Paulet, Angela, Francis, Cecilia, John. PhD, San Marcos U., 1948, MD, 1957. Assoc. prof. physiology U. Arequipa, Peru, 1960-63; assoc. in physiology Cornell U., N.Y., 1963-64; prof. physiology U. Arequipa, 1964-68; assoc. prof. medicine Northwestern U., 1969-80, prof., 1980-2000; ret., 2000. Chief renal sect. VA Lakeside Hosp., 1976-90; cons. nephrologist Northwestern Meml. Hosp., Evanston Hosp., 1990-98, sr. attending emeritus; lectr. nat. Ctr. Advanced Med. Edn., Chgo.; mem. adv. bd. Am. Fedn. Clin. Rsch. Contbr. articles on renal disease to med. jours.; author books in English and Spanish, poetry, short stories. Fellow ACP; mem. Ctrl. Soc. Clin. Rsch., Internat. Soc. Nephrology, Am. Soc. Nephrology, Am. Physiol. Soc. Home: 650 S River Rd Unit 411 Des Plaines IL 60016-8428

QUINTERO, ELIAS MATTHEW, biomedical researcher; s. Elias and Delia Quintero; m. Cheryl Ann Byham, July 11, 1992. BS in Biology, Midwestern State U., Wichita Falls, Tex., 1988; MS in Anatomy, Baylor U., Dallas, 1994; PhD, Tex. A&M Health Sci. Ctr., Dallas, 2000; MS in Clin. Rsch., Med. U. SC., Charleston, 2005. Rsch. technician Baylor Coll. Dentistry, Dallas, 1988—91; asst. prof. Parker Coll. of Chiropractic, Dallas, 1992—99; rsch. assoc. U. Tex. Southwestern Med. Ctr., Dallas, 1993—94; instr. El Centro Coll., Dallas, 1995—97; postdoctoral fellow Med. U. SC., Charleston, 2000—06; scholar Inst. Rsch. Minority Mental Health and Aging, Charleston, 2003—06. Vol. KidSport Inc., Dallas, 1995—96; pub. spkr. Soc. Neurosci, Brain Awareness Week, Charleston, 2002—05; vol. venue head Spl. Olympics, Charleston, 2002—06. Recipient Paul McFarland Resident Rsch. award, U. Tex., Houston Health Sci. Ctr., 1999, Travel award, Internat. Stereology Workshop, 2002, Internat. Conf. on Neural Transplantation and Repair, 2003; fellow, Nat. Inst. on Aging, NIH, 2003—06; grantee, SC. Coop. Healthy Aging in Minority Populations, 2005—06. Mem.: Soc. Neuroscience (assoc.), Am. Soc. Neural Transplantation and Repair (assoc.), Am. Assn. Geriatric Psychiatry (assoc.). Achievements include research in characterized the therapeutic potential of tetracylines in Parkinson's Disease Pathology. Home Phone: 214-573-6673; Office Phone: 214-456-6146. Office Fax: 214-456-6199. Personal E-mail: tb4@att.net.

QUINTERO, RONALD GARY, management consultant; b. Detroit, Jan. 5, 1954; s. John Urdiales and Jean Lorraine (Morton) Q.; children: Jean Marie, Alexandra Lisa; m. Ellen Robin Leventhal, Sept. 2, 2004; stepchildren: Adam Leventhal, Daniel Leventhal. AB, Lafayette Coll., 1975; MS, NYU, 1976, APC, 1978. CPA, CFA, CFP, cert. mgmt. acct., cert. fraud examiner, cert. insolvency, cert. turnaround profl., cert. in distressed bus. valuation; accreditation in bus. valuation. Sr. mgr. Peat, Marwick, Mitchell & Co., NYC, 1975-85; workout cons. Zolfo, Cooper & Co., NYC, 1985-87; assoc. Bear, Stearns & Co., Inc., NYC, 1987-88; prin. R. G. Quintero & Co., NYC, 1988—. Mng. dir. Chartered Capital Advisers, Inc., N.Y.C., 1988—; adj. prof. New Sch. for Social Rsch., N.Y.C., 1983-85; internat. lectr.; adj. prof. N.Y. Inst. Fin., N.Y.C., 1988—; instr. Ctr. for Profl. Edn., Berwyn, Pa., 1991—; leading provider CFA Sems. Author: (book and cassette) Mergers and Acquisitions, 1990, CFA Review Notes, 2001, Q-Notes, 2002; contbr. articles to profl. jours.; chpts. to books; creator: Quintero Index of Bankrupt Stocks. Mem. AICPAs, Am. Bankruptcy Inst., N.Y. Soc. CPAs (chmn. com. 1990-91, Max Block Disting. Article award 1990, Outstanding Discussion Leader 1991), Turnaround Mgmt. Assn. (bd. dirs., exec. com.). Avocations: squash, softball, running, computers, reading. Office: R G Quintero & Co 145 4th Ave New York NY 10003-4906 Office Phone: 212-505-9743. Business E-Mail: q@rgquintero.com.

QUIRANTES, ALBERT M., lawyer; b. Cuba, Jan. 25, 1963; came to U.S., 1966; s. Alberto and Haydee (Mendez) Quirantes. B in Bus., U. Miami, Fla., 1984; JD, U. Fla., 1987. Bar: Fla. 1988, U.S. Dist. Ct. (so. dist.) Fla. 1990, U.S. Dist. Ct. (mid. dist.) Fla. 1990, U.S. Ct. Appeals (11th cir.) 1990, U.S. Supreme Ct. 1991, U.S. Dist. Ct. Ariz. 1991. Pub. defender Ct. 8th cir., Gainsville, Fla., 1988-89; pvt. practice Miami, Fla., 1989—; sr. ptnr. Ticket Law Ctr., P.A., Miami, Fla., 1990—. Mem. Fla. Traffic Ct. Rules Com., Tallahassee, 1991—. Mem. Fla. Assn. Criminal Def. Attys., Dade Bar (cts. com. 1992—, criminal cts. com. 1992—), Latin C. of C., Jaycees. Home and Office: 1815 NW 7th St Miami FL 33125-3504 Office Phone: 305-644-1800. E-mail: lawyer@ticketlawyer.com.

QUIRK, FRANK JOSEPH, management consulting company executive; b. NYC, Feb. 27, 1941; s. Frank J. and Madeline B. Quirk; m. Betty Josephine Mauldin, Jan. 7, 1967; children: Laura Josephine, Katherine Elizabeth. BA, Cornell U., 1962, MBA, 1964. Assoc. Booz, Allen & Hamilton, Inc., Chgo. and Washington, 1967-72; exec. v.p. Macro Internat., Inc., Calverton, Md., 1972-79, pres., CEO, 1980-98, CEO, 1998—2006, chmn., 1998—2006, ret., 2006; exec. v.p. Opinion Rsch. Corp., Princeton, NJ, 1999—2003, pres., 2003—05, ret., 2006; chmn. Alexandria Buick Pontiac GMC, 2005—. Bd. dirs. Smithsonian Inst. Libr. Capt. US Army, 1964—66. Mem.: Belle Haven Country Club. Home: 2110 Foresthill Rd Alexandria VA 22307-1128 Office: Macro Internat Inc 11785 Beltsville Dr Beltsville MD 20705-3121

QUIRK, JOHN JAMES, investment company executive; b. NYC, July 10, 1943; s. Francis J. and Madeline A. (Meizinger) Q.; m. Kathryn Anne O'Brien, Mar. 21, 1963; children: John James, Ashlin Carter, Merritt Andrew. BA, Georgetown U., 1965; MBA, U. Va., 1967. Asst. treas., mgr. corp. fin. dept. W.R. Grace & Co., NYC, 1967-74; asst. v.p., asst. treas. City Investing Co., NYC, 1974-77, v.p., treas., 1978-81, sr. v.p., treas., 1982-85; chmn. bd. Quirk Carson Peppet Inc., 1985-98; prin. Churchill Capital, Inc., 1999—2001; mng. dir. Morgan, Joseph & Co. Inc., 2001—. Bd. dirs. Environ. Opportunities Fund., Ltd., City Investing Co. Liquidating Trust. Mem.: Racquet and Tennis; Wee Burn (Conn.). Home: 445 Hollow Tree Ridge Rd Darien CT 06820-3030 Office: 600 5th Ave Fl 19 New York NY 10020-2302 Office Phone: 212-218-3726. Business E-Mail: jquirk@morganjoseph.com.

QUIRK, KENNETH PAUL, accountant; b. Lake Charles, La., Aug. 29, 1953; s. Charles Patrick and Helen (Lejeune) Q.; m. Teresa Ann Tucker, Mar. 26, 1982 (div. Mar. 1988); 1 child, Heather Marie; m. Ava Marie Angelle, July 13, 2002. BS in Acctg., McNeese State U., 1978; MBA, U. Phoenix, 1998. CPA, La.; cert. Microsoft product specialist in Windows NT 4.0., cert. info. tech. profl., AICPA, 2000; cert. Quickbooks ProAdvisor; Microsoft Profl. Accts. Network cons. Staff acct. Quirk, Cargile, Hicks & Reddin, Lake Charles, 1979-80, Browning-Ferris Industries, Lake Charles, 1980-81, La. Savs. Assn., Lake Charles, 1981-90, Calcasieu Marine Nat. Bank, Lake Charles, 1990-96, Hibernia Nat. Bank, Lake Charles, 1996-97; pres. Acctg. Tech. Strategies, 1997—2003; ptnr. Quirk and Assoc., LLC, 2005—. Instr. U. Phoenix-Online, 1999—. Author: fin. acctg. software sys. Mem. Young Men's Bus. Club, Lake Charles, 1986-90, Girl Scouts U.S., Lake Charles, 1989-90; bd. dirs. Ednl. and Treatment Coun., Inc., 2001—. Recipient Innovative User of Tech. award, La. CPA Soc., AICPA, 1999. Mem.: AICPA (cert. 1994), Inf. Systems Audit and Control Assn., Computer Soc. IEEE, Assn. Computing Machinery, Soc. La. CPAs (task force com. 2000—01), Assn. Cert. Fraud Examiners (assoc.). Republican. Episcopalian. Avocations: jazz drumming, genealogy, hunting.

QUIRK, MARY, writer, consultant; d. William and Mary Loretta Quirk; m. Steven Durben, May 6, 1989; 1 child, Emma Quirk-Durben. BS, U. Wis., Madison, 1991. Asst. scientist U. Minn., Mpls., 1985—97; editor, jour. news ican, Inc., Eden Prairie, Minn., 2000—01; cons. Immunization Action Coalition, St. Paul, 2001—. Contbr. articles to profl. jours. including The Lancet, Analytical Chemistry. Mem.: Nat. Assn. Sci. Writers.

QUIRK, RAYMOND R. (RANDY QUIRK), insurance company executive; b. 1946; m. Linda J. Quirk; 3 children. Pres. Fidelity Nat. Fin., Inc., Jacksonville, Fla., 2002—05, CEO Fidelity Nat. Title Group, Inc., 2005—, co-pres., 2007—. Mem. bd. dirs. Fidelity Nat. Title, Alamo Title, Chgo. Title, Home Warranty subsidiaries of Fidelity Nat. Fin. Avocation: golf. Office: Fidelity Nat Fin Inc 601 Riverside Ave Jacksonville FL 32204 Office Phone: 888-934-3354. *

QUIRMBACH, HERMAN CHARLES, economics professor; b. St. Paul, Oct. 6, 1950; s. William Herman and Elizabeth Lou (Ziegler) Q. AB in Govt. cum laude, Harvard U., 1972; AM in Econs., Princeton U., 1980, PhD in Econs., 1983. Assoc. economist, cons. Rand Corp., Santa Monica, Calif., 1981—; assoc. prof. econs. Iowa State U., Ames, 1990—. Vis. asst. prof. econs. U. Wis., Madison, 1983—84; mem. numerous coms. Iowa State Senate. Contbr. articles to profl. jours. Treas. Story County Dem. Party, Ames, 1992-94; councilman 4th ward Ames City Coun., 1995-03; pres. Iowa Civil Liberties Union, 2001-02, bd. dirs., 1996-02; bd. dirs. Ames Mcpl. Utility Retirement Sys., 1996-03, Ames Conv. and Visitors Bur., 1997-99; Ames mayor pro tem, 2002; mem. Iowa Coll. Student Aid Commn., 2003—, Iowa Property Tax Implementation Com., 2003-04, Gov's Task Force on Local Governance, 2005, Iowa Tobacco Use Prevention and Control Commn., 2005—; state senator Iowa Dist. 23, 2003—, chair, senate local govt. com., 2005—; co-chair Ames Vets. Meml. Com., 2001—. Recipient Don Biggs award for polit. leadership, 1998-99, Stick Your Neck Out award Nat. Assn. for Mentally Ill Ctrl. Iowa, 2005, Outstanding Contbns. to Tobacco Control Appreciation cert. Clean Air for Everyone of Iowa, 2006. Mem. AAUP, ACLU, Ames LWV, Am. Econ. Assn., Econometric Soc., Ames C. of C., Appalachian Mountain Club, White Mountain Four Thousand Footer Club, Ames Kiwanis Club, Ames Patriotic Coun. Office: Iowa State Senate The Statehouse Des Moines IA 50319

QUIROS-TEJEIRA, RUBEN ELOY, pediatrician, educator, researcher; b. Panama, July 5, 1962; s. Felix A. Quiros and Olimpia Tejeira de Quiros; m. Nubia Noemi Navarrete, Nov. 12, 1994; children: Ruben Eloy Quiros Jr., Jonathan Elias Quiros, Jacob Eli Quiros. MD, Nat. U. Panama, 1986. Cert. Am. Bd. Pediat., 1995, diplomate Am. Bd. Hosp. Physicians, 2005, Am. Coll. Ethical Physicians, 2005. Resident Children's Hosp. Panama, 1988—91; sci. rschr. duPont Hosp. Children, Thomas Jefferson U., Wilmington, Del., 1992; resident Thomas Jefferson U., Phila., 1993—95; asst. prof. pediat. U. Rochester, NY, 2000—01, dir. pediatric hepatology, 2000—01; asst. prof. pediat. and surgery Baylor Coll. Medicine, Houston, 2001—04, med. dir. pediatric liver transplantation, 2001—04; assoc. prof. pediat. and surgery U. Tex., 2004—, med. dir. pediatric liver, intestinal transplantation, 2004—, dir. pediatric hepatology, 2004—; assoc. prof. pediat. U.T. M.D. Anderson Cancer Ctr., Houston, 2005—. Chmn. med. adv. com. Am. Liver Found., South Tex. Chpt., Houston, 2004—, bd. dirs.; reviewer peer rev. jour. Am. Jour. Transplantation, Edmonton, Canada, 2004—, Jour. Pediatric Gastroent. and Nutrition, Denver, 2004—, Archives Med. Rsch., Mexico D.F., 2003—, Bone Marrow Transplantation Jour., London, 2002—; Jour. Pediat., Cin., 2004—; med. adv. bd. mem. Life Gift Organ Donation Ctr., Houston, 2002—, Alagille Syndrome Alliance, Tualatin, Oreg., 2004—, Hepatitis Mag., Houston, 2005—; internat. com. mem. N.Am. Soc. Pediatric Gastroent., Hepatology and Nutrition, Flourtown, Pa., 2004—. Contbr. articles to profl. jours. Mem. focus group Tex. Gulf Digestive Disease Ctr., 2004—. Recipient Herman Roseblum award, Thomas jefferson U., 1994—95; fellow, UCLA, 1995—98, 1998—2000; grantee, NIH. Fellow: AMA (assoc.), Am. Acad. Pediatric (assoc.); mem.: AAAS (assoc.), Assn. Med. Students U. Panama (hon.), Nat. Med. Assn. Panama (hon.), Panamanian Pediatric Soc. (hon.), Harris County Med. Soc. (assoc.), Internat. Liver Transplantation Soc. (assoc.), Am. Gastroent. Assn. (assoc.), Tex. Med. Assn. (assoc.), Am. Assn. Study Liver Disease (assoc.), Am. Soc. Transplantation (assoc.; mem. diversity and minority affairs com. 2006—), N.Am. Soc. Pediatric Gastroent., Hepatology and Nutrition (assoc.), Internat. Pediatric Transplant Assn. (assoc.), Am. Liver Found. (assoc.), Jefferson Med. Coll. Alumni Assn. (hon.). Roman Catholic. Office: U Tex 6431 Fannin St MSB 3140A Houston TX 77030 Home Phone: 713-436-2240; Office Phone: 713-500-6142. Office Fax: 713-500-5750.

QUISGARD, LIZ WHITNEY, artist, sculptor; b. Phila., Oct. 23, 1929; d. Kenneth E. and Elizabeth (Warwick) Whitney; children: Kristin, Berit. Grad. night sch., Md. Inst. Coll. Art, 1947, grad. day sch., 1949; student, Johns Hopkins U., 1952—58; pupil of, Morris Louis, 1958-60; BFA in Painting, Md. Inst., 1966, MFA in Sculpture, 1966. Pvt. tchr. painting, Balt., 1955-65. Tchr. Balt. Hebrew Congregation, 1962-80; mem. faculty Md. Inst. Coll. Art, 1965-76, Goucher Coll., 1966-68, Balt. Jewish Community Ctr., 1974-78, Villa Julie Coll., Stevenson, Md., 1978-80; art critic Balt. Sun, 1969-71, Craft Horizons, 1969-72, The Paper, 1971-72; designer prodns. Center Stage, Goucher Coll., Johns Hopkins U.; lectr. in Md., Va., W.Va., Pa., Ark., Ohio, NY, NJ One-woman exhbns. include Jefferson Place Gallery, Washington, 1960, Emmerich Gallery, NYC, 1962, Goucher Coll., Balt., 1966, U. Md., 1969, Gallery, 707, Los Angeles, 1974, Arts and Sci. Center, Nashua, NH, 1975, Mechanic Gallery, Balt., 1978, Marymount Manhatten Coll., NYC, 1983, Tiffany's windows, NYC, 1984, Starkman Gallery, NYC, 1984, Fordham U., NYC, 1985, Henri Gallery, Washington, 1987, Artemisia Gallery, Chgo., 1987, Savannah Coll. Art and Design, Ga., 1987, Life of Maryland Gallery, Balt., 1988, Franz Bader Gallery, Washington, 1989, Fairleigh Dickinson U., NJ, 1990, Herr-Chambliss Gallery, Hot Springs, Ark., 1990, Huntington Coll., Ind., 1991, Bergdorf Goodman Windows, 1991, Coll. of New Rochelle, NY, 1992, Broadway windows, NYC, 1992, Nexus Found., Phila., 1993, Carnegie Arts Ctr., Leavenworth, Kans., 1994, Asheville Mus., NC, 1995; group exhbns. include, Balt. Mus., 1951-53, 58, Corcoran Gallery Area Show, 1956, 64, Corcoran Biennial Show, 1963, Peale Mus., Balt., 1947, 56, Butler Inst. Am. Art, Youngstown, Ohio, 1957, Provincetown Art Assn., Mass., 1955, Pa. Acad. Am. Art ann., 1964, Chgo. Art Inst., 1965, Gallery 707, 1973, S. Houston St. Gallery, NYC, 1974, Balt. Mus. travelling show, 1978, Mus. of Hudson Highlands, Cornwall, NY, 1983; represented in permanent collections U. Ariz., U. Md., U. Balt., Johns Hopkins U., Lever House, NYC, Center Club, Balt., Libyan Mission to UN, Englewood, NJ, Datalogix Corp., Valhalla, NY, Gt. Northern Nekoosa Corp., Norwalk, Conn., Quality Inns, Newark, Can. Imperial Bank of Commerce, NYC, Rosenberg Diamond Co., NYC, Marsh, Inc., Indpls., Kirkpatrick and Lockhart, Pitts., Fordham U., NYC, Atlantic Realty, Atlanta, Miss. Mus.

Art, Jackson, St. Joseph Health Ctr., Hot Springs, Ark., Dermatology Assocs., Pitts., Scudder, Stevens & Clark, Boston, also pvt. collections; executed mural William Fell Elem. Sch., Balt., 1980, Urban Wall, Atlanta, 1990, floor painting Vet.'s Stadium, Phila., 1992, mural Med. Coll. Va., Richmond, 1994. Recipient Best in Show award Loyola Coll. Invitational, Balt., 1966, Florsheim Purchase Grant, 1991; scholar Md. Inst., 1947-49; Rinehart fellow in sculpture, 1964-66. Address: 113 Elizabeth St #B New York NY 10013 Office Phone: 212-571-4283.

QUIST, GORDON JAY, federal judge; b. Grand Rapids, Mich., Nov. 12, 1937; s. George J. and Ida F. (Hoekstra) Q.; m. Martha Jane Capito, Mar. 10, 1962; children: Scot D., George J., Susan E., Martha J., Peter K. BA, Mich. State U., 1959; JD with honors, George Washington U., 1962. Bar: DC 1962, Ill. 1964, US Dist. Ct. (no. dist.) Ill. 1964, US Supreme Ct. 1965, Mich. 1967, US Dist. Ct. (we. dist.) Mich. 1967, US Ct. Appeals (6th cir.) 1967. Assoc. Hollabaugh & Jacobs, Washington, 1962-64, Sonnenschein, Levinson, Carlin, Nath & Rosenthal, Chgo., 1964-66, Miller, Johnson, Snell & Cummiskey, Grand Rapids, 1967-72, ptnr., 1972-92, mng. ptnr., 1986-92; judge US Dist. Ct. (we. dist.) Mich., Grand Rapids, 1992—2006, sr. judge, 2006—. Mem. Code of Conduct com. U.S. Cts., 2000—, chmn., 2004—. Bd. dirs. Wedgewood Acres-Ch. Youth Home, 1968-74, Mary Free Bed Hosp., 1979-88, Christian Ref. Publs., 1968-78, 82-88, Opera Grand Rapids, 1986-92, Mary Free Bed Brace Shop, 1988-92, Better Bus. Bur., 1972-80, Calvin Theol. Sem., 1992-93; bd. dirs. Indian Trails Camp, 1970-78, 82-88, pres., 1978, 88. Recipient Disting. Alumnus award George Washington U. Law Sch. 1998 Mem. Fed. Bar Assn., Am. Judicature Soc., Mich. State Bar Found., Univ. Club Grand Rapids, Order of Coif. Avocations: reading, travel. Office: 482 Ford Fed Courthouse 110 Michigan St NW Grand Rapids MI 49503-2313 Business E-Mail: Gordon_J_Quist@miwd.uscourts.gov.

QUIST, ROXANNE GENEVIEVE, middle school teacher; BS in Indsl., Labor Rels., Cornell Univ., 2005; MPhil student in Comparative Social Politics, Oxford Univ., 2007—. Tchr. Charles Drew Middle Sch., LA, 2005—07. Rhodes Scholar. Achievements include tutors students; organized art enrichment program; served as a chaperone in a dist. program for girls considered at-risk. *

QUITTMEYER, PETER CHARLES, lawyer; b. Charlottesville, Va., Oct. 9, 1957; s. Charles L. and Maureen (Rankin) Q.; children: Charles Lake, Laura Slater. BA with high distinction, U. Va., Charlottesville, 1979, JD, 1982. Bar: Ga. 1985. Assoc. King & Spalding, Atlanta, 1982-87; shareholder Trotter, Smith & Jacobs, Atlanta, 1987-91; ptnr. Nelson Mullins Riley & Scarborough, Atlanta, 1991—2001, Sutherland Asbill & Brennan, Atlanta, 2001—. Adj. prof. computer law Emory U. Sch. Law, Atlanta, 1996, 98, 2000; spl. asst. atty. gen. State Ga., 2002; vice chmn. Ga. chpt. Arthritis Found. Author: Computer Software Agreements, 1985—; mem. editl. bd. Va. Law Rev., 1981-82; contbr. articles to profl. jours. Recipient Vol. award, Ga. chpt. Arthritis Found., 2005; Nat. Merit scholar semifinalist, Westinghouse Sci. Talent Contest. Mem. ABA, Ga. Bar Assn., Raven Soc., Order of Coif, Phi Beta Kappa. Office: Sutherland Asbill & Brennan 999 Peachtree St NE Ste 2300 Atlanta GA 30309 Office Phone: 404-853-8186. Business E-Mail: peter.quittmeyer@sablaw.com.

QUITTNER, JOSH, editor; m. Michelle Slatalla; 3 children. Grad., Grinnell Coll., Columbia U. With Bergen Record, NJ, Albuquerque Jour., Newsday; joined TIME, 1995, mng. editor time.com, mng. editor ON Mag., tech. editor; editor in chief Bus. 2.0, NYC, 2002—. Co-author (with M. Slatalla): Flame Wars: A Cyberthriller, 1995, Masters of Deception: The Gang That Ruled Cyberspace, 1997, Speeding the Net: The Inside Story of Netscape and How It Challenged Microsoft, 1998. Office: Business 2-0 One California St, 29th Fl San Francisco CA 94111 Office Phone: 415-293-4800.

QUIVERS, ROBIN, radio personality; b. Balt., Aug. 8, 1952; d. Charles and Louise Quivers. Student, U. Md., 1974. Morning anchor W100, Carlisle, Pa., 1980; co-host Howard Stern Show, 1981—; with WWDC, Wash., DC, 1981, WNBC, NYC, 1982—85, WXRK-FM, NYC, 1985—2005, Sirius Satellite Radio, NYC, 2006—. Co-author: Quivers: A Life, 1995; actor: (films) Private Parts, 1997; (TV films) Deadly Web, 1996; co-host (TV series) The Howard Stern Show (WOR-TV), 1990—92, The Howard Stern Show (E!), 1994—2005, Howard Stern On Demand, 2005—; guest appearance: (TV series) The Fresh Prince of Bel-Air, 1993; The Larry Sanders Show, 1993; The Magic Hour, 1998. RN, advanced through ranks to capt. USAF. Office: Sirius Satellite Radio 1221 Ave of the Americas New York NY 10020

QUON, MICHAEL JAMES, medical researcher, internist; b. Oakland, Calif, Apr. 26, 1960; s. Jimmie Earl and Helen (Tang) Quon; m. Huison Kim, June 22, 1985; children: Hana, James. BS in Biomed. Engring., Northwestern U., 1982, PhD in Biomed. Engring., 1987, MD, 1988. Diplomate Nat. Bd. Med. Examiners, Am. Bd. Internal Medicine. Resident in internal medicine U. Chgo., 1988—90; fellow in endocrinology NIH, Bethesda, Md., 1990—93, sr. clin. investigator, 1993—95, sr. investigator Nat. Heart, Lung and Blood Inst., 1995—2002, chief diabetes unit NCCAM, 2002—. Contbr. articles to profl. jours. Capt. USPHS, 1990—. Mem.: ACP, Juvenile Diabetes Found. Internat., Coun. for High Blood Pressure, Am. Heart Assn., Am. Diabetes Assn. (Rsch. award grant 1994—). Avocations: piano, violin. Office: NIH NCCAM Bldg 10 rm 6C 205 Bethesda MD 20892-0001

QURAISHI, MOHAMMED SAYEED, retired health facility administrator, research scientist; b. Jodhpur, India, June 23, 1924; arrived in US, 1946, naturalized, 1973; s. Mohammed Latif and Akhtar Jahan Q.; m. Akhtar Imtiaz, Nov. 12, 1953; children: Rana, Naveed, Sabah (dec.). B.Sc., St. John's Coll., 1942; M.Sc., Aligarh Muslim U., 1944; PhD, U. Mass., 1948. Sr. mem. UN, WHO Team to Bangladesh, 1949-51; entomologist Malaria Inst. Pakistan, 1951-55; sr. rsch. officer Pakistan Council Sci. and Indsl. Rsch., 1955-60; sr. sci. officer Pakistan AEC, 1960-64; assoc. prof. entomology U. Man., 1964-66, N.D. State U., Fargo, 1966-70, prof., 1970-74; chief scientist biology N.Y. State Sci. Svc., Albany, 1974-75; entomologist, toxicologist, chief pest control and consultation sect. NIH, Bethesda, Md., 1976-84; health scientist adminstr., exec. sec. microbiology and infectious disease rsch. com. Nat. Inst. Allergy and Infectious Diseases, Bethesda, Md., 1984-88, sci. rev. adminstr. spl. revs., 1988-96, sci. rev. adminstr. AIDS clin. epidemiol. rsch. rev. br., 1996-2000; ret., 2000; sr. scientist Inst. Nuclear Sci., CENTO, Tehran, Iran, 1960-64; program mgr. interdepartmental contract Project THEMIS, Dept. Def., 1968-74. Cons. breast cancer rsch. program UIS Dept. Def., 2001; vis. scientist Harvard Sch. Pub. Health, 1995. Author: Biochemical Insect Control: Its Impact on Economy, Environment and Natural Selection, 1977; mem. editorial bd. Jour. Environ. Toxicology and Chemistry, 1981-84; author numerous sci. papers. Chmn. NIH Asian-Am. Cultural Assn., 1980—81; mem. Montgomery County Bd. Social Svcs., 2002. Recipient Sustained High Quality Performance award, 1980, Merit Pay Performance awards, 1984, 86, 87, Recognition and Appreciation of Spl. Achievement award NIH, 1988, Spl. Recognition award for Svcs. to NIH, Asian Am. Cultural Com., 1989, Appreciation in Recognition of Outstanding Support for Combined Fed. Campaign, 1991. Mem. Am. Chem. Soc., Soc. Environ. Toxicology and Chemistry (mem. publs. com. in charge spl. publs. 1982-84), Sigma Xi, Phi Kappa Phi. Home: 19813 Cochrane Way Gaithersburg MD 20879-1637 Personal E-mail: sayeedquraishi@aol.com.

QURAISHI, SADEQ ALI, anesthesiologist, educator; s. Ali Akhtar and Rowshan Ara Quraishi; m. Ayesha Naz Khalid, Sept. 5, 1997; children: Sarah Ayesha, Mishael Amber. BSc in PT, McGill U., Montreal, Can., 1997; MD, Pa. State U., Hershey, 2004; MHA, Pa. State U., Middletown, 2004. Cert. ACLS Am. Heart Assn., 2004, ATLS ACS, 2004, BDLS Nat. Disaster Life Support Found., 2003. Resident dept. anesthesiology Pa. State Coll. Medicine, Hershey, 2004—; instr. world campus grad. sch. Pa. State U., University Park, 2006—. Author: (textbook) Elsevier's Integrated Pharmacology. Master: Brownstone Lodge; mem.: AMA (coun. on med. svc. 2002—07), Accreditation for Grad. Med. Edn. (bd. dirs. 2006—), Soc. for Critical Care Medicine, Am. Soc. Anesthesiologists. Republican. Achievements include research in faster reconstitution of life-saving dantrolene for patients with malignant hyperthermia; adverse effects of propofol use in pediatric patients; benefits and methods of encouraging perioperative tobacco cessation. Avocations: music, swimming, running. Office: Penn State College of Medicine 500 University Drive H 187 Hershey PA 17033 Office Phone: 717-531-8521. Business E-Mail: squraishi@psu.edu.

QUREISHI, A. SALAM, computer company executive; b. Aligarh, India, July 1, 1936; s. M.A. Jabbar and Saira (Sattar) Q.; m. Naheed Fatima; children: Lubna, Leila. BS in Physics and Math., Aligarth U., India, 1954; MS in Stats., Patna U., India, 1957. Mgr. applications IBM Corp., Palo Alto, Calif., 1961-67; founder, pres., chmn. bd. Optimum Sys., Inc., Palo Alto, Calif., 1967-71; CEO Sysorex Internat., Inc., Mountain View, Calif., 1972—. Republican. Home: 925 Mountain Home Rd Woodside CA 94062-2519 Office: A Salam Qureishi 506 Clyde Ave Mountain View CA 94043-2212

QURESHI, FAIQA, pediatric emergency physician; 1 child, Saamia. MBBS, King Edward Med. Coll., Lahore, Pakistan, 1973. Specialist in pediat. emergency medicine. Med. dir. emergency dept. Children's Hosp. of the King's Daus., Norfolk, Va., 1993—. Office: Children's Hosp of the King's Daus 601 Children's Ln Norfolk VA 23507 Home Phone: 757-233-8678; Office Phone: 757-668-9220. Office Fax: 757-668-7568. Business E-Mail: faiqa.qureshi@chkd.org.

QUTUB, AMINA ANN, biomedical researcher, entrepreneur; d. Shehryar and Nancy Qutub. BS, Rice U., Houston, Tex., 1999; PhD, U. Calif., Berkeley and San Francisco, 2004. Grad. rschr. U. Calif., San Francisco, 2000—04; founder, CEO B3io, Berkeley, Calif., 2002—03; postdoctoral fellow Sch. Medicine Johns Hopkins U., Balt., 2004—. Contbr. articles to profl. jours. Vol. dir. corp. partnerships Found. Internat. Med. Relief Children, 2005, v.p. adminstrn., 2004—05. Finalist Haas Bus. Plan Competition, U. Calif., Berkeley, 2002, Innovator's Challenge Competition, Berkeley and Stanford U., 2003; recipient Poster award, Gordon Rsch. Conf., 2004; fellow, Whitaker Found., 1999—2004; scholar Chem. Engring. Thomas Moore scholarship, Rice U., 1999; Ruth L. Kirschstein Nat. Svc. Rsch. grant, NIH, 2006—. Mem.: Am. Assn. Cancer Rsch. Achievements include first to agent-based blood-brain barrier model; research in intracellular oxygen-sensing computational model. Home Phone: 510-541-3497. Personal E-mail: aminaq@gmail.com.

QUTUB, MUSA YACUB, hydrogeologist, educator, consultant; b. Jerusalem, June 2, 1940; came to U.S., 1960; s. Yacub and Sarah Qutub; married; children: Hanhia, Jennan, Sarmad, Muntaser, Aya, Saif, Tasneem. BA in Geology, Simpson Coll., Indianola, Iowa, 1964; MS in Hydrogeology, Colo. State U., 1966; PhD in Water Resources, Iowa State U. Sci. and Tech., 1969. Instr. earth sci. Iowa State U., Ames, 1966-69; from asst. prof. to prof. Northeastern Ill., Chgo., 1969-80, prof. geography and environ. studies, 1980—. Cons. hydrogeology, Des Plaines, Ill., 1970—; sr. adviser Saudi Arabian Ministry Planning, Riyadh, 1977-78; leader U.S. environ. sci. del. to People's Republic of China, 1984; pres., founder Islamic Info. Ctr. Am. Author: Secondarty Environmental Science Methods, 1973; contbr. numerous articles to profl. jours.; editor Environ. Resource, Directory Environ. Educators and Cons. World. NSF grantee, 1970-71, 71-72, 72-73, 75, 76, Hew grantee, 1974, grantee Ill. Dept. Edn., 1970. Mem. AAAS, NSF (cons.), Am. Waterworks Assn., Am. Men and Women Sci., Nat. Assn. Geology Tchrs. (pres. central sect. 1974), Environ. Sci. Inst. (edn. com.), Internat. Assn. Advancement of Earth and Environ Sci. (pres. 1975—, founder), Ill. Earth Sci. Edn. (pres. 1971-73, founder), Phi Delta Kappa. Muslim. Avocations: tennis, track, cross country, soccer.

RA, HYUNGSHIM YOO, biologist, researcher; b. Kimje, Cheonrabook-Do, Republic of Korea, Jan. 12, 1964; d. Okdol Ra and Bokdong Seo; m. Sunhee Yoo, June 10, 1989; children: Suran Yoo, Aran Yoo, Daeyeon Yoo. B, Paichai U., Republic of Korea, 1986; M, Sungshin Women's U., Republic of Korea, 1991; PhD, U. Ill., 2002. Cert. Achieve. U. Ill., in bus. mgmt. U. Ill., grad. tchr. U. Ill. Rschr. U. Ill., Urbana-Champaign, 2002—. Contbr. articles to profl. jours. Tchr. Korean Lang. Sch., Champaign, 2005—06; group leader summer Christian youth conf. Mountain Top, 2003—04; group leader New Year Christian Youth Conf., 2003—05, Camp Grow, 2004; organizer Ch. Blending Week, 2004; treas. Ch. Champaign, Ill., 2004—05; bridge builder Korean Presbyn. Ch., 2006, pres. women's club, 2007; vol. Empty Tomb, 2007; pres. women's club Korean Presbyn. Ch., Champaign, 2007—; bd. dirs. Nat. Women's Hist. Mus., DC, 2005; rsch. bd. adv. Am. Biog. Inst., Inc., Raleigh, NC, 2005. Recipient Internat. Peace prize, United Cultural Conv., 2005, Lifetime Achievement award, World Congress Arts, Scis. & Comms., 2006. Mem.: AAUW (assoc.), Am. Bryological and Lichenological Soc. (assoc.), Habitat for Humanity (assoc.), Nat. Com. to Preserve Social Security and Medicare (assoc.), The Nature Conservancy (assoc.), Sierra Club (assoc.). Consumer. Office: U Illinois 265 Morrill Hall 505 S Goodwin Ave Urbana IL 61801 Home: 3906 Turnberry Dr Champaign IL 61822 Home Phone: 217-355-2501. Business E-Mail: hs-yoo@life.uiuc.edu.

RAAB, DIANE, special education educator; BA, Lewis and Clark Coll., 1987; MA, U. Ariz., 2005. Cert. tchr. Alaska, Ariz. Reporter Anchorage Times, 1990—92, Juneau Empire, Alaska, 1993—94; tchr. Annette Island Sch. Dist., Metlakatla, Alaska, 1994—96; city govt. reporter Sedona Red Rock News, Ariz., 1996—98; devel. dir. KRBD, Ketchikan, Alaska, 1999—2000; news reporter KAZM 780 AM, Sedona, Ariz., 2001; campaign mgr. Ketchikan, Alaska, 2000; tchr. Ariz. Sch. for Blind, Tucson, 2001—. Counselor Am. Cancer Soc., Ariz., 2002, Ariz., 2003; deacon St. Mark's Presbyn. Ch., Tucson, 2006. Avocations: caving, hiking. Office: Ariz Sch for Deaf and Blind 1200 W Speedway Blvd Tucson AZ 85745 Personal E-mail: diane_raab@hotmail.com.

RAAB, HARRY FREDERICK, JR., retired physicist; b. Johnstown, Pa., May 9, 1926; s. Harry Frederick and Marjorie Eleanor (Stiff) R.; m. Phebe Ann Duerr, June 16, 1951; children: Constance Diane, Harry Frederick, Cynthia Ann Raab Morgenthaler. Student, Navy Electronics Tech. Sch., 1944-45; SB and SM E.E., MIT, 1951; postgrad., Oak Ridge Sch. Reactor Tech., 1954-55. Reactor control engr. Bettis Atomic Power Lab Westinghouse Electric Corp., West Mifflin, Pa., 1951-54, mgr. surface ship physics, 1956—62, mgr. light water breeder reactor physics, 1962-72; chief physicist Navy Nuc. Propulson Directorate, Washington, 1972-95, ret., 1995. Patentee light water breeder reactor. Active Laymen's Missionary League, Episc. Diocese of Pitts., 1957-72; lay eucharistic min., lay intercessor and lector Episc. Ch. of Good Shepherd, Burke, Va., 1972-, Sunday sch. tchr. St. Paul's Episcopal Ch., Mt Lebanon, Pa., 1957-72, dir. liturgy, 1987-97, stewardship chmn., 1979-82, 84, 92-93, chmn. presch. bd., 1994-97, healing ministry, 1989—, sr. warden, 1983, 85, 97, Stephen Ministry leader, 1998—; trustee, 2006—; mem. stewardship com. Diocese of Va., 1983—, chmn. stewardship, 1995-2002; chaplain for mentally retarded No. Va. Tng. Ctr., 1983—, treas. religious adv bd., 1998—; bd. dirs. Phoenix Cmty. Svcs., 1995-99; lay pediat. chaplain Fairfax Hosp., 1995—. With USNR, 1944-46 Fellow Am. Nuc. Soc.; mem. Masons, Sigma Xi, Tau Beta Pi, Eta Kappa Nu. Republican. Home: 8202 Ector Ct Annandale VA 22003-1342 E-mail: hraabjr@aol.com. *Always treat others with respect. Strive for excellence. Always act with honesty and integrity. Remember Henry Ford's observation: "If you say that you can, or if you say you cannot, you are right.".*

RAAB, IRA JERRY, lawyer, judge; b. NYC, June 20, 1935; s. Benjamin and Fannie (Kirschner) R.; m. Regina Schneider, June 4, 1957 (div. 1978); children: Michael, Shelley; m. Katie Rachel McKeever, June 30, 1979 (div. 1991); children: Julie, Jennifer, Joseph; m. Gloria Silverman, Nov. 7, 1996; children: Jill, Todd, John. BBA, CCNY, 1955; JD, Bklyn. Law Sch., 1957; MPA, NYU, 1959, postgrad.; MS in Pub. Adminstrn., LI U., 1961; MBA, Adelphi U., Garden City, NY, 1990. Bar: NY 1958, US Dist. Ct. (so. and ea. dists.) N.Y. 1960, US Supreme Ct. 1967, US Tax Ct. 1976, US Ct. Appeals (2d cir.) 1977; notary public, Fla., 2006. Pvt. practice, Woodmere, NY, 1958-96, 2003—05, West Palm Beach, Fla., 2005—; agt. Westchester County Soc. Prevention of Cruelty to Children, White Plains, 1958; counsel Dept. Correction City of NY, 1959, trial commr. Dept. Correction, 1976, asst. corp. counsel Tort divsn. N.Y.C. Law Dept., 1963-70; staff counsel SBA, NYC, 1961-63; counsel Investigation Com. on Willowbrook State Sch., Boro Hall, SI, NY, 1970; gen. counsel Richmond County Soc. Prevention of Cruelty to Children, Boro Hall, SI, NY, 1970-81; pro bono counsel NYC Patrolmen's Benevolent Assn., 1974-81; rep. to UN Internat. Criminal Ct., 1977-78; arbitrator Small Claims Ct. Day Cts., NYC, 1970-96; arbitrator LI Better Bus. Bur., 1976-93, Nassau County Dist. Ct., 1978-93, 2003—, arbitrator Small Claims Ct., 1978-96; spl. master NY County Supreme Ct., 1977-96; judge Parking Violations Bur., NYC, 1991-93; arbitrator, 2003—; hearing ofcl. Nassau County Supreme Ct., 1982—96, 2003—. Small claims arbitrator NYC Civil Ct., 1970-96; arbitrator US Dist. Ct. (ea. dist.) NY, 1986-96, 2003—; lectr. cmty. and ednl. orgns.; instr. paralegal course Lawrence Sch. Dist., NY, 1982-84; law prof. Briarcliff Coll., Bethpage, NY, 1997; arbitrator Nat. Arbitration and Mediation, Inc., 2003-, NASD, 2003-06. Chmn. Businessmen's Luncheon Club, Wall St. Synagogue, 1968-79; exec. sec. Cmty. Mediation Ctr., Suffolk County, 1978-80, exec. v.p., 1980-81; vice chmn. Woodmere Inc., Com., 1980-81; mem. adv. bd. Nassau Expressway Com., 1979-80; bd. dirs. Woodmere Mchts. Assn., 1979-80, v.p., 1979-83, chmn., 1984-93; sec. Congregation Aish Kodesh, Woodmere, 1992-2002; candidate for dist. ct. judge Nassau County, 1987, 88, 89, 91, 93, 94, 96; candidate for supreme ct. justice Nassau and Suffolk Counties, 1995, 98; elected judge Nassau County Dist. Ct., 1997-99; candidate for county ct., Nassau County, 1997; elected presiding judge dist. ct., 1999-2000; elected justice Nassau County Supreme Ct., 2000-03; arbitrator Nat. Arbitration and Mediation Inc., 2003—; bd. dirs. Estates at Baywinds Neighborhood Assn., West Palm Beach, 2003—; mem. criminal justice adv. bd. City West Palm Beach, 2007—. Recipient Consumer Protection award FTC, 1974, 76, 79, Recognition award Pres. Ronald Reagan, 1986, Man of Yr. award LI Coun. of Chambers, 1987, NY State Ct. Reporters Assn., 1999. Mem. ABA (chmn. cts. and comty. com. 1988-93, exec. com. jud. adminstrn. divsn. lawyers conf. 1989-95), Am. Judges Assn. (rep. to UN 2000-03, bd. govs. 1973-78, 82-88, 89-96, 97-2003, nat. treas. 1978-82, chmn. civil ct. ops. com. 1975-76, chmn. ednl. film com. 1974-77, editl. bd. Ct. Rev. mag. 1975-79, 82-86, chmn. spkrs. bur. com. 1976-77, chmn. legis. com. 1983-95, chmn. resolutions com. 1995-98, 2000-2002, chmn. jud. concerns com. 1997-99, historian 1988-2006, William H. Burnett award 1983), Am. Judges Found. (pres. 1977-79, chmn. bd. trustees 1979-83, treas. 1974-75, 76-77, trustee 1983-97, 2000-06), Assn. Arbitrators of Civil Ct. City of NY (past pres.), NY State Bar Assn. (sec. dist., city, town and village cts. com.), Nassau County Bar Assn. (criminal cts. com., matrimonial and family ct. com., ct. com., ethics com., Supreme Ct. com.), Profl. Group Legal Svc. Assn. (past pres.), Internat. Assn. Jewish Lawyers and Jurists (com. to draft Internat. Bill of Rights to Privacy 1982, coun. 1981-95, bd. govs. 1984-95), adv. bd. comty. dispute ctr. 1979-81), K.P. (past chancellor comdr.). Democrat. Address: 9452 Lantern Bay Cir West Palm Beach FL 33411 Office Phone: 561-514-1047. Personal E-mail: irajraab@yahoo.com.

RAAB, JENNIFER J., city commissioner; AB with distinction, Cornell U., 1977; MPA, Princeton U., 1979; JD cum laude, Harvard U., 1985. Spl. projects mgr. S. Bronx Devel. Org., 1979-81; dir. pub. affairs Planning commn. City of N.Y., 1981-82, chmn. Landmarks Preservation commn., 1994—2001; litigation assoc. Cravath, Swaine & Moore, NYC, 1985-90; campaign dir. Rose State Senate Campaign, 1988; issues dir. Giuliani Mayorial Campaign, 1989; litigation assoc. Paul, Weiss, Rifkind, Wharton & Garrison, NYC, 1990-94; pres. Hunter Coll., 2001—. Bd. dirs. Argus Cmty., Inc., Bronx, N.Y., 1987-94, City Vol. Corps, 1994; active Manhattan Cmty. Bd. 5, 1990-94; pres. E. 154-155th St. Housing Corp., Bronx, 1992-94; vol. arbitrator Small Claims divsn. Bronx Civil Ct., 1993-94; mem. citizen's adv. coun., Mid-Town Cmty. Ct., 1994. Mem. Phi Beta Kappa. Office: Hunter College Room E1700 695 Park Ave New York NY 10021

RAAB, SHELDON, lawyer; b. Bklyn., Nov. 30, 1937; s. Morris and Eva (Shereshevsky) Raab; m. Judith Deutsch, Dec. 15, 1963; children: Michael Kenneth, Elisabeth Louise, Andrew John. AB, Columbia U., 1958; LLB cum laude, Harvard U., 1961. Bar: N.Y. 1961, U.S. Ct. Appeals (2d cir.) 1963, U.S. Dist. Ct. (so. and ea. dists.) 1967. Dep. asst. atty. gen. State of N.Y., 1961—63, asst. atty. gen., 1963—64; assoc. Frank, Harris, Shriver & Jacobson LLP (and predecessor firm), NYC, 1964—69, ptnr., 1970—81, inc. ptnr., 1981—2003, gen. counsel, of counsel, 2003—. Bd. dirs. lawyers com. Civil Rights Under Law, 1998—. Mem. exec. com. lawyers' divsn. United Jewish Appeal, 1982—93. Mem.: ABA, Assn. of Bar of City of N.Y. (adminstrv. law com. 1968—71, spl. com. electric power and environment 1971—73, chmn. energy com. 1974—79, fed. cts. com. 1981—84, state superior cts. juris. com. 1985—88), N.Y. State Bar Assn. (trial lawyers sect. 1968—), Am. Law Inst. Democrat. Office: Fried Frank Harris Shriver & Jacobson LLP 1 New York Plz New York NY 10004-1980 Office Phone: 212-859-8090. Business E-Mail: raabsh@ffhsj.com.

RAABE, GERHARD KARL, epidemiologist; b. Flushing, NY, Feb. 24, 1948; s. Oscar Albert and Eugenie (Loehr) R.; m. Barbara Irene Douglas, Nov. 27, 1969; children: Andrew John, Emily Jean. BA in Biology, Hofstra U., 1969; MS in Computer Sci., Pratt Inst., 1971; DrPH, Columbia U., 1987. Sr. rsch. scientist N.Y. State Dept. Mental Hygiene, NYC, 1970-77; med. systems analyst Mobil Oil Corp., NYC, 1977-79, indsl. med. advisor, 1979-81, mgr. epidemiology and med. info. svcs., 1982-89, dir. epidemiology and med. info. svcs. Princeton, N.J., 1990-97; dir. med. info. and health risk assessment Global Med. Svcs., Mobil Bus. Resources Corp., 1997-99; pres., prin. scientist occupl. and environ. health Health Risk Scis., Inc., New Hope, Pa., 1999—. Cons. spl. studies Cornell U. Med. Ctr., NYC, 1973-77; cons. NYC Health Systems Agy., 1976; chmn. occupational health com. Fla. Phosphate Coun., Lakeland, 1979-85; reviewer profl. jours.; expert panelist WHO, IARC, U.S. EPA. Contbr. articles to profl. jours., chpts. to books. Fellow Am. Coll. Epidemiology; mem. AAAS, Soc. for Epidemiologic Rsch., Internat. Soc. for Environ. Epidemiology, Am. Petroleum Inst. (chmn. epidemiology 1985-88, chmn. health and product stewardship 1996-2000), NY Acad. Scis., Soc. for Risk Analysis, Indsl. Epidemiology Forum (chmn. 1991), Internat. Commn. on Occupl. Health. Republican. Lutheran. Avocations: science fiction, tennis. Home: 2215 Aquetong Rd New Hope PA 18938-1149 Office: Health Risk Scis Inc PO Box 189 New Hope PA 18938-0189 Home Phone: 215-862-9747; Office Phone: 215-862-5718. Personal E-mail: gkraabe@cs.com.

RAABE, WILLIAM ALAN, tax writer, business educator; b. Milw., Dec. 14, 1953; s. William Arthur and Shirley R.; m. Nancy Elizabeth Miller, Mar. 1989; children: Margaret Elisabeth, Martin William. BS, Carroll Coll., 1975; MAS, U. Ill., Urbana, 1976, PhD, 1979. Wis. Disting. prof. U. Wis., Milw., 1979-96; tax edn. cons. Price Waterhouse Coopers, NYC, 1985—; prof., dir. acctg. programs Samford U., Birmingham, Ala., 1997-2001; founding dean Sch. Mgmt., disting. prof. Capital U., Columbus, Ohio, 2001—02; mem. tax faculty Fisher Coll. Bus. Ohio State U., Columbus, 2002—. Vis. assoc. prof. Ariz. State U., Tempe, 1985; vis. faculty Ernst & Young, NYC, 1990—, Deloitte & Touche, NYC, 1998—, Calif. CPA Found., 1986, AICPA, 1984-94, Wis. Bar Assn., 1992, Capital U. Law Sch., 2002—; developer Estate Tax Planner, McGraw Hill Software, NYC, 1980-88; expert witness, 1985—; cons. corp. income tax State Ala., 1997-01, State of Wis., 1995, 99; dir. Fisher/Ohio State U. Tax Clinic, 2003—. Author West's Federal Taxation, 1985—, Federal Tax Research, 1986—, Income Shifting After Tax Reform, 1987, Multistate Corporate Tax Guide, 1985-96, California Income Taxation, 1999-2006, Schedule M-3, 2006; editor CCH, 2005, Price Waterhouse Coopers Tax Case Studies, 2005-; contbr. articles to profl. jours. Bd. dirs., Luth. High Sch. Assn. Milw., 1991-96, pres., 1993-96, Bethesda Luth. Home, Watertown, Wis., 1989-91, Luth. Counseling and Family Svcs., 1982-88, Concord Chamber Orch., Milw., 1983-88; mem. Econ. Devel. Com., Wauwatosa, Wis., 1986-89; faculty athletic rep. to NCAA from U. Wis. Milw., 1990-96; mem. Milw. Symphony Chorus, Master Singers of Milw., Samford Master Singers; vice chair faculty senate Samford U., 2000-01. Named to Alumni Hall Fame, Milw. Luth. H.S., 1995, Carroll Coll., 2005; fellow, U. Ill., 1978, Nat. Ctr. Tax Edn. and Rsch., 1981. Fellow Am. Acctg. Assn., Wis. Inst. CPAs (Educator of Yr. 1987), Ala. Acctg. Educators Assn. (pres. 1999-2000). Office: Fisher Coll Bus 2100 Neil Ave Columbus OH 43210-1144 Office Phone: 614-292-4023. Business E-Mail: raabe.12@osu.edu.

RAAD, VIRGINIA, pianist, educator; b. Salem, W.Va., Aug. 13, 1925; d. Joseph M. and Martha (Joseph) R. BA in Art History, Wellesley Coll., 1947; spl. student, New Eng. Conservatory Music, 1947-48; student, Berthe Bert, 1949—55, Jeanne Blancard, 1949—55, student, 1968—70, Alfred Cortot, 1950—51, Jacques Chailley, 1953—55; PhD with honors, U. Paris, 1955; diplôme, Ecole Normale de Musique, Paris, 1950. Artist in residence Salem Coll., W.Va., 1957-70; ind. concert pianist, 1960—; musician in residence at cmty. colls. NC Arts Coun., 1971—. Adjudicator Nat. Guild Piano Tchrs., Nat. Fedn. Music Clubs; panelist, grant reviewer NEH, 1978-84, 92—; mem. com. Nat. Endowment Arts, 1978; Am. rep. Debussy Centennial Colloque, Paris, 1962. Perfomances, concerts, lectrs. master classes at West Ga. Coll., Carrollton, La Grange Coll., Ga., Columbus Coll., Ga., Young Harris Coll., Ga., U. Fla., Gainesville, Norton Gallery, Palm Beach, Fla., Alliance Française de Rollins Coll., Winter Park, Fla., Dixon Gallery and Gardens, Memphis, St. Jude Children's Rsch. Hosp., Memphis, Cleveland State CC, Tenn., Sampson Tech. Inst., Clinton, NC, Wayne CC, Goldsboro, NC, Brevard Coll., NC, Ctrl. Wesleyan Coll., SC, Ky. Wesleyan Coll., Owensboro, Berea Ky., Coll., Alice Lloyd Coll., Pippa Passes, Ky., Coll. of William and Mary, Williamsburg, Va., Eastern Mennonite Coll., Harrisonburg, Va., The Phillips Gallery, Washington, Trinity Coll., Washington, Manhattanville Coll., Purchase, NY, Elmira Coll., NY, Fordham U., NYC, The Piano Tchrs. Congress of NY, Middlebury Coll., Vt., St. Anselm's Coll., Manchester, N.H., Mount St. Mary's Coll., Hooksett, NH, Wellesley Coll., Mass., Curry Coll., Milton, Mass., So. Conn. State U., New Haven, Slippery Rock U., Pa., Seton Hill Coll., Greensboro, Pa., Alliance Française de Pitts. and U. Pitts., Channel 13 WQED (PBS) Pitts., Lincoln U., Oxford, Pa., The Grier Sch., Tyrone, Pa., Mount de Chantal Acad., Wheeling W.Va., Wheeling Jesuit U., among other colls. and univs.; contbg. author: Debussy et l'Evolution de la Musique au XX Siècle, 1965; author: The Piano Sonority of Claude Debussy, 1994; recording artist: EDUCO, 1995—; contbr. articles to profl. jours. Active Amnesty Internat. Urgent Action Network; alumna regional rep. Wellesley Coll.; mem bd. visitors New Eng. Conservatory of Music, 2004—. Named Outstanding W.Va. Woman Educator Delta Kappa Gamma, 1965; presented biography to Schlesinger Library on History of Women in Am. Radcliffe Coll., 1967; grantee Govt. France, Am. Coun. Learned Socs. Mem. Soc. Française de Musicologie, Am. Musicol. Soc. (regional officer 1960-65), Am. Coll. Musicians, Internat. Musicol. Soc., Music Tchrs. Nat. Assn. (adjudicator, musicology program chair 1983-87), W.Va. Music Tchrs. Assn., Audubon Activist, Alpha Delta Kappa (hon.). Republican. Roman Catholic. Avocations: hiking, gardening, birding. Home and Office: 60 Terrace Ave Salem WV 26426-1116 Office Phone: 304-782-2274. Personal E-mail: virginiaraad@aol.com.

RAAF, JOHN HART, surgeon, educator, health facility administrator; b. Portland, Oreg., Aug. 10, 1941; s. John E. and Lorene (Rardin) R.; m. Heather Neilson, June 15, 1965; children— Jennifer, John, Sabrina AB magna cum laude, Harvard U., 1963, MD cum laude, 1970; D.Phil., Oxford U., 1966. Diplomate Am. Bd. Surgery. Intern Mass. Gen. Hosp., Boston, 1970-71, resident in surgery, 1971-73, 75-77; research fellow Sloan-Kettering Inst., NYC, 1973-75; fellow in immunology Meml. Hosp., NYC, 1973-74; faculty assoc. in surgery M.D. Anderson Hosp. and Tumor Inst., Houston, 1977-78, asst. prof. surgery, 1978-79, Cornell U. Med. Coll., NYC, 1979-81; assoc. prof. surgery Meml. Sloan-Kettering Cancer Ctr., NYC, 1981-85; dir. Cleve. Clinic Cancer Ctr., 1985-90; chmn. dept. surgery Meridia Huron Hosp., Cleve., 1991-94; chief surg. svc. VA Med. Ctr. Cleve., 1994-2001; prof. surgery Case Western Res. U., 1994—, vice chmn. dept. surgery, 1994-2001. Mem. selection coms. for Rhodes scholarships, Vt., 1969-71, New Eng., 1969-71, La., 1977, Tex., 1978, Ohio, 1989-94; mem. soft tissue sarcoma discussion group Nat. Cancer Inst., 1980; mem. clin. trials com. Nat. Cancer Inst., NIH, 1984-88 Co-author Meml. Sloan-Kettering Cancer Ctr. publs., 1980; also numerous articles, chpts., abstracts, letters, short papers, movies, med. photographs; editor: Diagnosis and Treatment of Soft Tissue Sarcomas, 1993; editor-in-chief Primary Care and Cancer, 1981-92; mem. editorial bd. Meml. Sloan-Kettering Cancer Ctr. Clin. Bull., 1979-82; assoc. editor Oncology mag., 1987-92; mem. editorial com. Cleve Clinic Jour. Medicine, 1987-90. Rhodes scholar Oxford U., Eng., 1963; nat. scholar Harvard U. Med. Sch., 1966-70; Am. Cancer Soc. postdoctoral scholar Harvard U. Med. Sch., 1969-70; ACS scholar Mass. Gen. Hosp., Boston, 1975-77; Am. Cancer Soc. jr. faculty clin. fellow, 1980-83. Fellow ACS; mem. Am. Assn. Cancer Research, Am. Assn. Endocrine Surgeons, Am. Soc. Clin. Oncology, Assn. Acad. Surgery, Assn. Am. Rhodes Scholars, Cen. Surg. Assn., Soc. Surg. Oncology (publs. com. 1981-84, working group on edn. 1982, membership com. 2000), Meml. Hosp. Alumni Soc. (chmn. program com. 1982), Cleve. Skating Club, Charaka Club (N.Y.C.). Home: 12501 Fairhill Rd Cleveland OH 44120-1017

RAAFLAUB, KURT ARNOLD, classics educator; b. Buea, Cameroon, Feb. 15, 1941; s. Fritz and Heidi (Ninck) R.; m. Deborah Dickmann Boedeker, July 14, 1978. MA, U. Basel, Switzerland, 1967, PhD, 1970. Asst. prof. ancient history Free U. Berlin, 1972-78, Brown U., Providence, 1978-80, assoc. prof. classics and history, 1980-83, prof., 1983—, John Rowe Workman Disting. prof. classics and humanistic tradition, 1989-92, David Herlihy Univ. prof., 2001—, Royce Family prof. excellence in tchg., 2005—, chmn. dept. classics, 1984-89; co-dir. Ctr. for Hellenic Studies, Washington, 1992-2000, chmn. program in ancient studies, 2000—. Author: Dignitatis Contentio, 1974, Die Entdeckung der Freiheit, 1985, The Discovery of Freedom in Ancient Greece, 2004; co-author: Studien zum Attischen Seebund, 1984, Aspects of Athenian Democracy, 1990, Ancient History: Recent Work and New Directions, 1997, Origins of Democracy in Ancient Greece, 2007; editor or co-editor: Social Struggles in Archaic Rome, 1986, 2d edit., 2005, Between Republic and Empire: Interpretations of Augustus and His Principate, 1990, Athens and Rome, Florence and Venice: City-States in Classical Antiquity and Medieval Italy, 1991, Anfänge politischen Denkens in der Antike: Die nahöstlichen Kulturen und die Griechen, 1993, Studies in the Ancient Greek Polis, 1995, More Studies in the Ancient Greek Polis, 1996, Democracy 2500: Questions and Challenges, 1998, Democracy, Empire and the Arts in Fifth-Century Athens, 1998, War and Society in the Ancient and Medieval Worlds, 1999, War and Peace in the Ancient World, 2007; contbr. articles to profl. jours. Mem. Historisches Kolleg Munich, 1989-90. Am. Coun. Learned Socs. fellow, 1983-84, Ctr. for Hellenic Studies fellow, 1976-77, NEH fellow, 1989; faculty fellow U. New England, Armidale, Australia, 1996. Mem. Philol. Assn., Assn. Ancient Historians, Am. Inst. Archaeology, German Archaeol. Inst. (corr.). Avocation: music. Home: 495 Lloyd Ave Providence RI 02906-4547 Office: Brown U Dept Classics Providence RI 02912-1856 Office Phone: 401-863-2123. Business E-Mail: kurt_raaflaub@brown.edu.

RA'ANAN, URI (HEINZ FELIX FRISCHWASSER), international politics educator; b. June 10, 1926; m. Estelle Khan, 1949; children: Gavriel, Michael. BA, MA, MLitt, Oxford U. Polit. journalist, 1950-57; positions in internat. diplomacy, 1958-64; sr. fellow Rsch. Inst. on Communist Afairs, Columbia U., NYC, 1964-66, lectr. in govt., 1965-66; assoc. Ctr. for Internat. Studies MIT, Boston, 1966-76, vis. prof. polit. sci., 1966-68; prof. internat. politics, dir. Internat. Security Studies Fletcher Sch. Law and Diplomacy, Tufts U., Boston, 1967-87; univ. prof. Boston U., 1988—, dir. Inst. for Study of Conflict, Ideology and Policy, 1988—. Assoc. Davis Ctr. for Russian Studies, Harvard U.; cons. Nat. Inst. Justice and Temple U. Rsch. Program on Organized Crime, 1981-83, Battelle Columbus Labs./U.S. Army Ballistic Missile Def. Program, 1976-77, U.S. Senate Subcom. on Nat. Security, 1972; mem. Ronald Reagan's Fgn. Affairs and Def. Adv. Team, 1980. Author, editor 25 books; mem. adv. bd. Polit. Warfare; contbr. chpts. to numerous books, articles to profl. jours.; numerous appearances on TV and radio Mem. Am. Assn. Advancement of Slavic Studies, Internat. Inst. of Strategic Studies Office: Inst for Study of Conflict Ideology and Policy 141 Bay State Rd Boston MA 02215-1708 Office Phone: 617-353-5815. Business E-Mail: raanan@bu.edu.

RAAS, DANIEL ALAN, lawyer; b. Portland, Oreg., July 6, 1947; s. Alan Charles and Mitzi (Cooper) R.; m. Deborah Ann Becker, Aug. 5, 1973; children: Amanda Beth, Adam Louis. BA, Reed Coll., 1969; JD, NYU, 1972. Bar: Wash. 1973, Calif. 1973, U.S. Dist. Ct. (we. dist.) Wash. 1973, U.S. Ct. Appeals (9th cir.) 1975, U.S. Supreme Ct. 1977, U.S. Tax Ct. 1983, U.S. Ct. Claims 1984. Atty. Seattle Legal Svcs, VISTA, 1972-73; reservation atty. Quinault Indian Nation, Taholah, Wash., 1973-76, Lummi Indian Nation, Bellingham, Wash., 1976-97, spl. counsel, 1997—; mem. Raas, Johnsen & Stuen, P.S., Bellingham, 1982—; judge Tulalip Indian Tribe Ct. Appeals, 2004—; appellate justice N.W. Intertribal Ct. Sys., 2005—. Cons. Falmouth Inst., Fairfax, Va., 1992-2000, Nat. Am. Ind. Ct. Judges Assn., McLean, Va., 1976-80. Rules chmn. Whatcom County Dem. Conv., Bellingham, 1988, 92, 94, 96, 2004; bd. dirs. Congregation Beth Israel, Bellingham, 1985-2000, pres., 1990-92; adv. com. legal asst. program Bellingham Vocat. Tech. Inst., 1985-91; trustee Whatcom County Law Libr., 1978-2002; pres. Vol. Lawyer Program, 1990-93, bd. dirs., 1988-94; Samish Camp Fire Coun., 1988-94, pres. 1991-94, v.p., 1989-91, regional v.p. Union Am. Hebrew Congregations, 1986-93, nat. trustee, 1995—, exec. com., 1995-99, sec. Pacific N.W. region, 1993-95, pres., 1995-99. John Ben Snow scholar, NYU, 1969-70, Root-Tilden scholar, NYU, 1970-72. Mem. Wash. State Bar Assn. (trustee Ind. law sect. 1989-95, Pro Bono award 1991), Whatcom County Bar Assn. (v.p. 1981, pres. 1982, Pro Bono award 1991), Grays Harbor Bar Assn. (v.p. 1976). Home: 1929 Lake Crest Dr Bellingham WA 98229-4510 Office: Raas Johnsen & Stuen PS 1503 E St Bellingham WA 98225-3007 Office Phone: 360-647-0234.

RAB, GEORGE T., pediatric orthopedic surgeon; b. Cleve., Nov. 11, 1946; s. Thomas P. and Patricia S. Rab; m. Wendy Andereson Rab, Aug. 31, 1968; children: Geoffrey W., Nicholas A. BS, Northwestern U., Chgo., 1968; MD, Northwestern U., 1970; MS, U. Minn., Mpls., 1975. Lic. physician Calif., diplomate Am. Bd. Orthop. Surgery, Nat. Bd. Med. Examiners. Intern in surgery Chgo. Wesley Meml. Hosp., 1970—71; resident in orthop surgery Mayo Clinic, Rochester, Minn., 1971—75; resident in pediat. orthop. surgery Gillette Children's Hosp., St. Paul, 1974; asst. prof. dept. orthop. surgery Sch. Medicine, U. Calif., Davis, 1977—82, assoc. prof. dept. orthop. surgery, 1982—88, prof. dept. orthop., 1988—, Ben Ali chair in pediat. orthop., 1998—, chair dept. orthop. surgery, 2000—06. Guest lectr. Shriners Hosp. for Crippled Children and Sch. Medicine Oreg. Health Scis. U., Portland, 1985, Duncan Seminar Children's Orthop. Hosp. and Med. Ctr., Seattle, 1987; vis. prof., guest lectr. dept. orthop. Children's Hosp. Med. Ctr., Cin., 1986; vis. prof., guest lectr. Carrie Tingley Hosp. Annual Meeting, Albuquerque, 1992; vis. prof., guest lectr., Robert Samilson lectr., San Francisco, 96; vis. prof. U. Calif., Irvine, 1998, U. Colo., 1999, New Eng. Med. Ctr., 1999, Children's Hosp. Med. Ctr. of Akron, Ohio, 2001; Arthur A. Thibodeau vis. prof. Tufts U. Sch. Medicine, 1999; John M. Roberts vis. prof. Children's Hosp. of New Orleans, 2000; vis. prof., Leslie Meyers lectr. Shriners Hosp., Greenville, SC, 2001; Charles LeRoy Lowman vis. prof. Orthop. Hosp., LA, 2002; orthop. surgeon, med. dir. motion analysis lab. Shriners Hosp. for Children, 1995—; pediat. orthop. specialist Sutter Cmty. Hosps., Sacramento, 1987—; vis. assoc. prof. dept. orthop. Harvard Med. Sch., Boston, 1983—84; rsch. fellow gait lab. Children's Hosp., Boston, 1983—84; editl. cons. Am. Jour. Diseases of Children, 1990—93; cons., rev. com. Orthop. Rsch. and Edn. Found., 1994—99; civilian cons. med. specialist in pediat. orthop. surgery Oakland Naval Hosp., Calif., 1990—95; pediat. orthop. cons. Kaiser Permanente Hosp., Sacramento, 1977—98. Mem. editl. bd. Gait and Posture, 1992—97, bd. editors Jour. Pediat. Orthopedics, 1992—, Jour. Children's Orthopedics, 2006—. Bd. dirs. Sacramento Make-A-Wish Found., Inc., 1988—92. Maj. US Army, 1975—77. Named Outstanding Clin. Instr., U. Calif. Davis Sch. Medicine, 1980, Outstanding Tchr. of Yr. in Orthop. Surgery, 1991, 1996; named one of Best Drs. in Am., 2005—06; recipient Goldsmith Intern Humanitarian award, Chgo. Wesley Meml. Hosp., 1971, Frank Stitchfield award, Hip Soc., 1976, annual award for excellence in tchg. clin. scis., Kaiser Found. Hosp., 1978, Best Poster award, Gait and Clin. Analysis Soc. Meeting, 2000; Berg-Sloat Traveling fellow, 1977. Fellow: Am. Acad. Pediat., Am. Acad. Orthop. Surgeons (com. on biomed. engring. 1980—82, com. on psychomotor skills 1980—87, com. ednl. content 1981—82, sec. com. on biomed. engring. 1982—85, subcom. on pediat. of com. on exams. and evaluations 1985—91, chmn. com. on biomed. engring. 1986—87); mem.: Sierra Sacramento Valley Med. Soc., Sacramento Pediat. Soc., Paul R. Lipscomb Soc., West Coast Gait Lab. Group, Western Orthop. Assn., Calif. Med. Assn., Am. Orthop. Assn., Pediat. Orthop. Soc. N.Am. (com. on computer applications in pediat. orthop. 1985—90), Orthop. Rsch. Soc., Internat. Soc. Electrophysiol. Kinesiology, Internat. Pediat. Orthop. Think Tank (site selection com. 1998—2000), Gait and Clin. Movement Analysis Soc. (awards com. 2001—02), Am. Soc. Biomechanics (arrangements com. annual meeting 1987, pres.-elect 1989—90, exec. com. 1989—93, pres. 1990—91), Am. Bd. Orthop. Surgery (certifying examiner 1984—92), Am. Acad. Cerebral Palsy and Devel. Medicine (nominating com. 1990—94). Avocations: bicycling, sailing, hiking, cooking. Office: Dept Orthop Surgery U Calif-Davis 4860 Y St # 3800 Sacramento CA 95817 Office Phone: 916-734-5770. Office Fax: 916-734-7904. E-mail: george.rab@ucdmc.ucdavis.edu.

RABAK, DAVID WILLIAM, retired family practice physician, educator, consultant; b. Washington, Sept. 3, 1919; s. William Rabak and Jessie Garnet Hastings; m. Barbara Jean Rabak, Mar. 25, 1943 (dec. Mar. 6, 2005); children: Martha Jean Tatum, Thomas William, Judith Ann Wagoner. Degree, Edison Vocat. Coll., Seattle, 1938; BS, U. Wash., Seattle, 1942; MD, U. Calif., San Francisco, 1949. Diplomate Am. Bd. Family Practice, 1971, lic. physician Calif., 1949, Wash., 1950. Platoon leader, instr. US Army 10th Mountain Divsn., Ft. Lewis, Wash. and Denver, 1942—49; intern San Joaquin County Hosp., French Camp, Calif., 1949—50; resident The Dr.'s Hosp., Seattle, 1950—51; pvt. practice gen. and family medicine Seattle, 1951—73; pvt. practice FAA-United Airlines, Seattle and Washington, 1951—84; clin. asst. prof. U. Wash., Seattle, 1972—74, clin. assoc. prof., 1974—77; family physician, chief primary care and clinic svcs. USAF Clinic Ramstein, Germany, 1975—76, dir. base med. svcs., 1976, chief clinic svcs., 1976—78; assoc. prof. Uniformed Svcs. Med. Sch., Bethesda, Md., 1978—84; chief primary care clinic Malcolm Grow USAF Med. Ctr., Andrews AFB, Md., 1978—79, chmn. dept. primary care, 1979—80, chmn. dept. family practice, 1980—84. Cons. United Airlines, Seattle, 1955—73; aviation med. examiner FAA, 1960—75; med. dir., physician Alaska Airlines, Seattle, 1966; staff physician Sound Health Assocs., Tacoma, 1973—74; family practice cons. Surgeon Gen. USAF, 1980—84; program dir. family practice residency Malcolm Grow USAF Med. Ctr., 1980—84; preceptor dept. familly medicine Swedish Hosp., Seattle, 1984—85; tutor U. Wash. Sch. Medicine, Seattle, 1992. Contbr. articles to profl. jours. Col. USAF, 1942—84. Recipient Meritorious Svc. medal, US Govt., Washington, 1978—84. Fellow: Am. Acad. Family Physicians (pres. Seattle 1954—92, del. to state 1969—71, pres. King County chpt. 1970); mem.: AMA (pres. Wash. state 1972—73), Wash. Acad. Family Physicians (v.p. 1971—72, pres. 1973—74, chmn. liaison com. 1967—73, former del.), Soc. Tchrs. Family Medicine, King County Med. Soc. (past del. to state, formerly univ. com., program com.), Wash. State Med. Assn. (past mental health and liaison com.), Mountain Rescue Coun. Presbyterian. Avocations: skiing, mountaineering, golf, hiking. Home: 720 Seneca St # 909 Seattle WA 98101-2766 Personal E-mail: drabak@sprynet.com.

RABASSA, GREGORY, language educator, translator, poet; b. Yonkers, NY, Mar. 9, 1922; m. Clementine Christos, 1966; children: Kate, Clara. AB, Dartmouth Coll., 1945, Litt.D. hon., 1982; MA, Columbia U., 1947, PhD in Portuguese, 1954; Litt.D. (hon.), U. Hartford, 2005. Instr. Spanish Columbia U., 1947-52, assoc., 1952-58, asst. prof., 1958-63, assoc. prof. Spanish and Portuguese, 1963-68; prof. Romance langs. Queens Coll., CUNY Grad. Sch., Flushing, NY, 1968-86, Disting. prof., 1986—. Assoc. editor Odyssey Rev., 1961-64 Contbr. articles to profl. jours.; author If This Be Treason: Translation and Its Dyscontents, 2005, A Cloudy Day in Gray Minor, Early Poems, 1945-1948, 1992. Staff sgt. OSS, 1942-45. Decorated Croce al Merito di Guerra Italy, Order of San Carlos Colombia; recipient Nat. Book award for transl., 1967, Transl. prize, PEN Am. Ctr., 1977, Transl. medal, 1982, Gregory Kolovakos award, 2001, Martha Albrand award Art of Memoir, 2006, Transl. prize, Wheatland Found., 1988, Gode award, Am. Transl. Assn., 1980, Arts award, N.Y. Gov., 1985, Lit. award, Am. Acad. and Inst. Arts and Letters, 1989, Presdl. medal, Dartmouth Coll., 1991, Ivan Sandrof award, The Nat. Book Critics Cir., 1993, Lit. Lion award, N.Y. Pub. Libr., 1993, Mellon Humanities award, Loyola U., Chgo., 1995, Gabriela Mistral prize, Chile, 1996, John Steinbeck Writers award, Southampton Coll., 2002, Machado de Assis medal, Union Brazilian Writers, NY, 2005, Aurora Borealis award, Internat. Fedn. Translators, 2005, Nat. Medal of Arts, Nat. Endowment Arts, 2006; fellow Fulbright-Hays fellow, 1965—66, NEH fellow, 1979—80, Guggenheim fellow, 1988—89. Mem. Renaissance Soc. Am., MLA, Am. Assn. Tchrs. Spanish and Portuguese, Latin Am. Studies Assn., Am. Lit. Translators Assn., Hispanic Soc. Am., Century Assoc., PEN Club, Phi Beta Kappa. Office: Dept Hispanic Langs & Lits CUNY Queens Coll Flushing NY 11367 Office Phone: 212-439-6636.

RABAUT, THOMAS W., defense industry executive; b. Detroit, 1948; m. Sheila Rabaut; 3 children. BS, U.S. Mil. Acad., 1970; MBA, Harvard U., 1977. Trainee mfg. dept. dr. divsn., various mfg./mgmt. positions FMC, 1977-81, planning mgr. fluid control divsn., 1982, mfg. mgr., ops. mgr. fluid control divsn., mgr. steel products divsn., 1986-88, dir. ops. ground sys. divsn., 1989; gen. mgr. def. sys. group FMC Corp., 1993, v.p., 1994; pres., CEO United Defense Industries, Inc., Arlington, Va., 1994—. With U.S. Army, 1970-75. Mem. Am. Def. Preparedness Assn., Assn. of U.S. Army, Navy League, Surface Navy Assn. Office: United Defense Industries Inc 1525 Wilson Blvd Arlington VA 22209

RABB, BRUCE, lawyer; b. Cambridge, Mass., Oct. 4, 1941; s. Maxwell M. and Ruth (Criedenberg) R.; m. Harriet Rachel Schaffer, Jan. 4, 1970; children: Alexander Charles, Katherine Anne. AB, Harvard U., 1962; Cert. d'Etudes Politiques, Institut d'Etudes Politiques, Paris, 1963; LLB, Columbia U., 1966. Bar: NY 1966. Law clk. to judge U.S. Ct. Appeals (5th cir.), 1966-67; assoc. Stroock & Stroock & Lavan, NYC, 1967-68, 71-75, ptnr., 1976-91, Kramer Levin Naftalis & Frankel LLP, NYC, 1991—2003, counsel, 2003—; sr. v.p., gen counsel North Am. Bioenergy Resources, LLC, 2003—. Staff asst. to Pres. U.S., 1969-70; supr. bd. dir. Agora-Gazeta, sp.zo.o., 1993-98, Agora-Druk, sp.zo.o., 1995-98, Agora, SA, 2006—; pub. mem. Adminstrv. Conf. U.S., 1982-86, 89-92, spl. counsel, 1986-88; bd. dir. Helicor, Inc. 2005-. Mem. Human Rights First (formerly Lawyers Com. Human Rights, 1977-95), nat. coun., 1996—; sec. Lehrman Inst., 1978-88; bd. dirs. Citizens Union of NY, 1981-87, 88-94, 95-01, 02—, treas., 2002-05; bd. dirs. Human Rights Watch Ams., 1982-, Human Rights Watch Helsinki, 1985-97, Fund for Free Expression, 1987-97, Am. Friends Alliance Israelite Universelle, 1987-01; bd. dirs. Human Rights Watch Middle East No. Africa, 1989-, vice chmn., 1990-, Nat. Ctr. Law and Econ. Justice (formerly Welfare Law Ctr.), 1997-, Sabre Found., 2003—, Human Rights Watch Asia, 2003—, Nat. Com. Am. Fgn. Policy, 2004-05, Human Rights Watch, 2004—, Human Rights Watch, LGBT, 2005—, co-chair, 2006-, Cinereach, 2007-; mem. internat. adv. com. Internat. Parliamentary Group Human Rights in the Soviet Union, 1984-88; dir. Human Rights Watch Internat. Bd., 1988-03, dir. emeritus, 2003—,sec., 2003—; prin. Coun. Excellence in Govt., 1990—; mem. adv. coun. Drs. of World USA, 1996-, FilmAid Internat., 2000-03, dir., sec., 2003-; dir. Nat. Econ. and Social Rights Initiative, 2007-, Sustainable South Bronx, 2007-. With USCGR, 1967—72. Mem. ABA (adv. panel Internat. Human Rights Trial Observer project), Am. Law Inst., Assn. of Bar of City of N.Y. (fed. legis., internat. law chair 1992-95, internat. human rights, civil rights, legal edn. and admission to bar, internat. trade coms., coun. fgn. affairs, energy), Coun. Fgn. Rels., Harvard Club N.Y.C., Met. Club of Washington. Office: 1177 Ave Americas New York NY 10036-2714 Office Phone: 212-715-9484. Business E-Mail: brabb@kramerlevin.com.

RABB, GEORGE BERNARD, zoologist, conservationist; b. Charleston, SC, Jan. 2, 1930; s. Joseph and Teresa C. (Redmond) R.; m. Mary Sughrue, June 10, 1953. BS, Coll. Charleston, 1951, LHD (hon.), 1995; MA, U. Mich., 1952, PhD, 1957. Teaching fellow zoology U. Mich., 1954-56; curator, coord. rsch. Chgo. Zool. Park, Brookfield., Ill., 1956-64, assoc. dir. rsch. and edn., 1964-75, dep. dir., 1969-75, dir., 1976—2003, dir. emeritus, 2003—. Rsch. assoc. Field Mus., 1965—; lectr. dept. biology U. Chgo., 1965-89; mem. Com. on Evolutionary Biology, 1969—; pres. Chgo. Zool. Soc., 1976-2003, pres. emeritus, 2004—; mem. steering com. Species Survival Commn., Internat. Union Conservation of Nature/World Conservation Union, 1983—, vice-chmn. N.Am., 1986-88, dep. chmn., 1987-89, chmn., 1989-96, vice-chmn. comms., 1997—; chmn. policy adv. group Internat. Species Info. System, 1974-89, chmn. bd., 1989-92; pres. bd. dirs. Chgo. Wilderness Mag., 1999—; v.p. Fauna and Flora Internat., 1998—; chmn. bd. Ill. State Mus., 1999—; bd. dirs. Ctr. Humans and Nature. Bd. dirs. Defenders of Wildlife, 2002—. Fellow AAAS; mem. Am. Soc. Ichthyologists and Herpetologists (pres. 1978), Herpetologists League, Soc. Systematic Zoology, Soc. Mammalogists, Soc. Study Evolution, Ecol. Soc. Am., Soc. Conservation Biology (council mem. 1986), Soc. for Integrative and Comparative Zoology, Soc. Study Animal Behavior, Am.

Assn. Museums (named to Centennial Honor Roll, 2006), Am. Soc. Naturalists, Am. Assn. Zool. Parks and Aquariums (dir. 1979-80), World Assn. Zoos and Aquariums, World Conservation Union (hon. mem.), Sigma Xi. Office: 9236 Broadway Brookfield IL 60513 Personal E-mail: georgerabb@sbcglobal.net. *

RABB, HAMID, nephrologist, educator; b. Dhaka, Bangladesh, June 22, 1962; s. Abdur Rabb and Aishah Farhat; m. Nausheen Rabb, Apr. 10, 1987; children: Adam, Samy, Neil. MD, McGill U., 1985. Resident in medicine UCLA, 1985-88; fellow in nephrology Harvard U., Boston, 1988-91; scientist McGill U., Montreal, Que., Can., 1991-92; chief renal lab. U. South Fla., Tampa, 1992-98; assoc. prof. U. Minn., Mpls., 1998—; dir. Minn. Med. Rsch. Found. kidney lab. Hennepin County Med. Ctr., Mpls., 1998; assoc. prof. Johns Hopkins Univ. Med. Sch., Balt. Reviewer FDA, Rockville, Md., 1994. Contbr. chpts. to books, over 60 articles to profl. jours. Recipient Physician Leadership award AMA, 1990, Clin. Scientist award Nat. Kidney Found., NYC, 1999. Fellow ACP; mem. Am. Soc. Nephrology, Am. Soc. Advancement of Sci., Am. Soc. Transplantation (sci. adv. com. 1999—; Roche Clin. Sci. Investigator award (assoc. prof. level), 2007). Office: Nephrology Dept Johns Hopkins Sch Med 34 North Charles Baltimore MD 21218 *

RABB, HARRIET SCHAFFER, academic administrator, lawyer; b. Houston, Sept. 12, 1941; d. Samuel S. and Helen G. Schaffer; m. Bruce Rabb, Jan. 4, 1970; children: Alexander, Katherine. BA in Govt., Barnard Coll., 1963; JD, Columbia U., 1966. Bar: N.Y. 1966, U.S. Supreme Ct. 1969, D.C. 1970. Instr. seminar on constl. litig. Rutgers Law Sch., 1966-67; staff atty. Ctr. for Constl. Rights, 1966-69; spl. counsel to commr. consumer affairs NYC Dept. Consumer Affairs, 1969-70; sr. staff atty. Stern Cmty. Law Firm, Washington, 1970-71; asst. dean urban affairs Law Sch., Columbia U., NYC, 1971-84, prof. law, dir. clin. edn., 1984-99, George M. Jaffen prof. law and social responsibility, 1991-99, vice dean, 1992-93; gen. counsel Dept. Health and Human Svcs., Washington, 1993—2001; v.p., gen. counsel Rockefeller U., NYC, 2001—. Mem. faculty employment and tng. policy Harvard Summer Inst., Cambridge, Mass., 1975-79. Author: (with Agid, Cooper and Rubin) Fair Employment Litigation Manual, 1975, (with Cooper and Rubin) Fair Employment Litigation, 1975. Bd. dirs. Ford Found., 1977-89, NY Civil Liberties Union, 1972-83, Lawyers Com. for Civil Rights Under Law, 1978-86, Legal Def. Fund NAACP, 1978-93, Mex. Am. Legal Def. and Edn. Fund, 1986-90, Legal Aid Soc., 1990-93, The Hastings Ctr., 2004-; mem. exec. com. Human Rights Watch, 1991-93; trustee Trinity Episcopal Sch. Corp., 1991-93; mem. external adv. bd. Columbia U. Ctr. Bioethics, 2002-; mem. adv. bd. Howard Hughes Med. Inst. Bioethics, 2007—. Mem.: NAS (com. on sci., tech. and law 2007—). Office: Rockefeller U 1230 York Ave New York NY 10021 Office Phone: 212-327-8070. Business E-Mail: hrabb@rockefeller.edu.

RABB, THEODORE K., historian; b. Teplice-Sanov, Czechoslovakia, Mar. 5, 1937; came to U.S., 1956, naturalized, 1978; s. Oskar Kwasnik and Rose (Oliner) Rabinowicz; m. Tamar Miriam Janowsky, June 7, 1959; children: Susannah Rabb Bailin, Jonathan Richard, Jeremy David. BA, Queen's Coll. Oxford U., Eng., 1958; MA, Queen's Coll. Oxford U., 1962, Princeton U., 1960, PhD, 1961. Instr. Stanford U., Calif., 1961—62; instr. Northwestern U., Evanston, Ill., 1962—63; asst. prof. Harvard U., Cambridge, 1963—67; mem. faculty Princeton U., New Brunswick, 1967—2007, prof. history, 1976—2007; prof. emeritus, 2007. Vis. assoc. prof. Johns Hopkins U., 1969, SUNY-Binghamton, 1973-74; visitor Inst. Advanced Studies, Princeton, 1973, 82; mem. nat. bd. cons. NEH, Nat. Coun. History Edn. (chair); N.J. Com. for Humanities (chair); chief historian Renaissance Television Series; bd. dirs. Humanities West, Save Venice, Inc.; juror Rome Prize; cons. in field. Author: The Thirty Years War, 2d edit, 1972, Enterprise and Empire, 1967, The Struggle for Stability in Early Modern Europe, 1975, The Origins of Modern Nations, 1981, Renaissance Lives: Portraits of an Age, 1993, rev. edit., 2000, Origins of the Modern West, 1993, Jacobean Gentleman, 1998; co-author: The Western Experience, 8th edit., 2003, Peoples and Nations, 1982; editor: Jour. Interdisciplinary History, 1970—; co-editor: Action and Conviction in Early Modern Europe, 1969, The Family in History, 1973, Marriage and Fertility, 1981, Industrialization and Urbanization, 1981, Climate and History, 1981, The New History, 1982, Hunger and History, 1985, Population and Economy, 1986, Art and History, 1988, La Fame nella storia, 1991, Origin and Prevention of Major Wars, 1988, The Making and Unmaking of Democracy, 2003, The Last Days of the Renaissance, 2006. Bd. govs. Hebrew U. Fellow and/or grantee Folger Shakespeare Library, Am. Philos. Soc., Social Sci. Research Council, Am. Council Learned Socs., Guggenheim Found., NEH. Mem. Am. Hist. Assn. (chmn. com. quantitative rsch. history, chmn. nominating com.), Social Sci. History Assn. (exec. com., treas.), Am. Assn. Advancement Humanities (dir., sec.-treas.), Nat. Coun. History Stds., C.C. Humanities Assn. (steering com.), Royal Hist. Soc., Internat. Commn. History Parliamentary and Rep. Instns., Renaissance Soc. Am., Hakluyt Soc., Nat. Coun. History Edn. (chair), Historians Early Modern Europe, Conf. Brit. Studies. Office: Princeton University History Dept Princeton NJ 08544-1017 Business E-Mail: tkr@princeton.edu.

RABBAT, GUY, electronics executive, consultant; b. Cairo, Jan. 30, 1943; arrived in U.S., 1972; s. Victor and Alice R.; m. Elfriede Freitag, Aug. 3, 1968; children: Ralph, Shirley; m. Nadia Kobinger, Feb. 8, 1992; children: Richard, Jacques, Laurent. Baccalaureate, France; BS, Queens U., Eng., 1967; MS, Queens U., 1969, PhD Elec. Engring. honors, 1971. Design supr. Siemens AG, Germany, 1964—68; asst. lectr. Queens U., England, 1968—72; dir. ops. IBM, 1972—84; v.p. Austin ops., CAE sys. divsn. Tektronix, 1984—86; head elec. engring. GM Corp., Mich., 1986—87; pres., CEO Modular Computer Sys., Inc., Ft. Lauderdale, Fla., 1987—92; mng. dir., exec. bd. dirs. Rank Xerox, Ltd., Welwyn Garden City, Herts, England, 1992—96; corp. v.p. GE, Milw., 1996—98; chief tech. officer, chief info. officer Gen. Elec. Med. Sys., Milw., 1996—98; sr. v.p. Solectron Corp., 1998—2004; chmn., gen. ptnr. Corcica Tech. Ventures, 2001—05; pres., CEO HTC Corp., Sunnyvale, Calif., 2004—05; CEO Nest Group Cos., Foster City, Calif., 2005—. Chmn. Internat. IEEE Conf. on Circuits and Computers, 1980, Internat. IEEE Conf. on Computer Design, 1983; bd. dirs. indsl. affiliates Mich. State U., 1986-88; pres. Am. Automation Assn., 1984-86; chmn., founder High Tech. Consortium Yr. 2000 and Beyond, 1998-02 Author: Hardware and Software Concepts in VLSI, 1983, Advanced Semiconductor Technology and Computer Systems, 1988; contbr. numerous scis. tech. papers; patentee in field Fellow: IEEE (Eng. chpt., editor-in-chief, chmn. editl. bd. Circuits and Devices Mag. 1984—86, invention and outstanding contbn. awards), Royal Engring. Coun. (London). Avocations: history, archaeology, poetry, jogging. Home: 360 Saint Andrews Ln Half Moon Bay CA 94019 Office: Nest Group Cos 373E Vintage Park Dr Foster City CA 94404 Office Phone: 408-218-4393. Business E-Mail: guy.rabbat@nestgroup.net.

RABBAT, NASSER O., architecture educator; PhD, MIT, Cambridge, 1990. Prof. MIT, Cambridge, 1991—. Dir. aga khan program for islamic architecture MIT, Cambridge, 1999—. Pres. Ctr. for Arabic Culture, Boston, 2006—07. Independent. Office: Mit Room 10-390 77 Mass Ave Cambridge MA 02139 Office Phone: 617-253-1417. Business E-Mail: nasser@mit.edu.

RABBE, DAVID ELLSWORTH, oil industry executive; b. Alexandria, Va., Dec. 17, 1955; s. Raymond Leed and Judith Ann (Ayers) R.; m. Maryann Degroot, Sept. 25, 1982; children: Lisa Ann, Chelsea Nicole, Jamison David. BCE, U. Md., 1979. From terminal trainee to mgr. Amerada Hess Corp., Balt., 1980—87, mgr. gas station maintenance Woodbridge, NJ, 1987—91; from project mgr. to pres. Tierra Solutions, Inc., East Brunswick, NJ, 1991—. Mem. editl. bd., editor: Soil and Sediment Contamination, 2002—. Mem.: Md. Soc. Surveyors, World Affairs Coun. Republican. Episcopalian. Avocations: woodworking, sailing. Home: 33 Sorrel Run Mount Laurel NJ 08054-4819 Personal E-mail: Davermxs@aol.com.

RABBITT, DANIEL THOMAS, JR., lawyer; b. St. Louis, Sept. 19, 1940; s. Daniel Thomas and Charlotte Ann (Carpenter) R.; m. Susan Lee Scherger, July 26, 1969. BA in Commerce, St. Louis U., 1962, JD cum laude, 1964. Bar: Mo. 1964, U.S. Supreme Ct. 1970. Assoc. Moser, Marsalek, Carpenter, Cleary, Jaeckel, Keaney & Brown and predecessor, St. Louis, 1964-68; ptnr. Moser, Marsalek, Carpenter, Cleary, Jaeckel, Keaney & Brown, St. Louis, 1969-81, Brown, James & Rabbitt, P.C., St. Louis, 1981-91, Rabbitt, Pitzer & Snodgrass, P.C., St. Louis, 1991—. Recipient Lon Hocker Meml. Trial Atty. award Mo. Bar Found., 1975, award of Honor, Lawyer's Assn. St. Louis, 2007. Fellow: Am. Coll. Trial Lawyers; mem.: ABA (chmn. young lawyers sect. 1973—74), Mem. prod. Liability Adv. Coun., Bar Assn. Met. St. Louis, Internat. Assn. Def. Counsel (product liability com.), Mo. Bar Assn., Mo. Athletic Club (gov. 1978—81, v.p. 1980—81). Office: 100 S 4th St Ste 400 Saint Louis MO 63102 Home Phone: 314-991-0401. Business E-Mail: rabbitt@rabbitt.law.com.

RABCHENUK, PAUL THOMAS, lawyer; b. Salem, Mass. s. Nicholas and Apolonia Pauline (Napierski) R. BA, Suffolk U., 1962; MPA, U. Pitts., 1964; JD, New Eng. Law Sch., 1981; postgrad., Tufts U. Bar: Mass. 1981, U.S. Dist. Ct. 1982, U.S. Ct. Appeals 1982, U.S. Supreme Ct. 1986, U.S. Ct. Internat. Trade, 1999. Clk. Essex Superior Ct, Salem, Mass., 1958-61; negotiator Commonwealth of Mass., Boston, 1962-63; realty specialist D.C. Redevel. Agy., Washington, 1964-65; rsch. assoc. Boston Mcpl. Rsch. Bur., 1966-67; urban renewal dir. City of Nashua, N.H., 1967-68, City of Haverhill, Mass., 1969-73; town adminstr. North Reading, Mass., 1973-78; town mgr. Town of Saugus, Mass., 1982-87; pvt. practice law Salem, Mass., 1981—. Cons. numerous pub. entities, 1966-85; vis. prof. civil rights Salem (Mass.) State Coll., 2001—. Chmn. Topsfield (Mass.) Housing Authority, 1978-83, Mass. Bay Tranportation Authority, Boston, 1973-86. Mem. ATLA, Mass. Bar Assn. Avocation: Eastern European history. Home: 37 Glendale Rd Marblehead MA 01945-1804 Office: Rabchenuk Law Offices 81 Washington St Ste 311 Salem MA 01970-3514 Office Phone: 978-741-1163. Business E-Mail: rablaw@verizon.net.

RABECS, ROBERT NICHOLAS, lawyer; b. Scranton, Pa., Mar. 19, 1964; s. Nicholas and Anne Marie (Stull) R.; m. Kimberly Ann Rabecs. BA summa cum laude, U. Scranton, 1986; JD cum laude, Georgetown U., 1990. Bar: Pa. 1990, D.C. 1992. Assoc. Reed Smith Shaw & McClay, Washington, 1990-94; ptnr. Hogan & Hartson, Washington, 1994—. Adj. prof. law George Washington U. Law Sch., Washington, 2002—. Columnist Managed Healthcare News, Belle Meade, N.J., 1994-98. Fulbright scholar, 1986-87; NEH undergrad. fellow, 1985. Mem. ABA, Am. Health Lawyers Assn., Pa. Bar Assn. (health law com.), D.C. Bar Assn. (health law sect.), Alpha Sigma Nu. Roman Catholic. Home: 6809 Rannoch Rd Bethesda MD 20817- Office: Hogan & Hartson 555 13th St NW Washington DC 20004-1161 Home Phone: 301-320-4505; Office Phone: 202-637-5842. E-mail: rnrabecs@hhlaw.com.

RABEKOFF, ELISE JANE, lawyer; b. NYC, June 26, 1959; d. Sidney and Natalie (Kaufman) R.; m. Christopher Gladstone, June 7, 1986; children: Katherine, Nicholas. AB, Princeton U., 1980; JD, Yale U., 1986. Bar: Pa. 1986, D.C. 1988, U.S. Dist. Ct. (fed. dist.) D.C. 1988. Legis. asst. Sen. D.P. Moynihan, Washington, 1980-83; law clk. judge Charle Robert Richey U.S. Dist. Ct. D.C., Washington, 1986—88; assoc. Shea & Gardner, Washington, 1988-93; v.p., gen. counsel Quadrangle Devel. Corp., Washington, 1993—. Bd. dirs. Chelsea Sch., Silver Spring, Md., 1990-95. Fellow: Am. Bar Found. Office: Quadrangle Devel Corp 1001 G St NW Washington DC 20001-4545 E-mail: eliserabekoff@quad1.com.

RABENSTEIN, DALLAS LEROY, chemistry professor; b. Portland, Oreg., June 13, 1942; 8. Melvin Leroy and Rose Marie (Nelson) R.; m. Gloria Carolyn Duncan, Aug. 30, 1964; children: Mark, Lisa. BS, U. Wash., 1964; PhD, U. Wis., 1968. Lectr. U. Wis., Madison, 1967-68; research chemist Chevron Research Co., Richmond, Calif., 1968-69; from asst. prof. to prof. chemistry U. Alta., Edmonton, Can., 1969-85; prof. U. Calif., Riverside, 1985-97, chmn. dept. chemistry, 1989—92, 1998—2000, 2002—03, dean Coll. Natural and Agrl. Scis., 1993-94, disting. prof. chemistry, 1997—; dean grad. div., 2003—. Vis. prof. U. Oxford, 1976-77, U. Western Ont., 1982; McElvain lectr. U. Wis., 1981; Dow lectr. U. B.C., 1988; Eli Lilly lectr., Ind. U., 1993; faculty rsch. lectr. U. Calif., Riverside, 2000; cons. in field. Contbr. articles to profl. jours. NIH and NSF grantee. Fellow AAAS, Chem. Inst. Can. (Fisher Sci. Lecture award 1984); mem. Am. Chem. Soc., Internat. Soc. Magnetic Resource. Avocations: reading, gardening, music. Home: 5162 Palisade Cir Riverside CA 92506-1521 Office: U Calif Dept Chemistry Riverside CA 92521-0001 Office Phone: 951-827-4302. Business E-Mail: dallas.rabenstein@ucr.edu.

RABIDEAU, MARILYN ANN, elementary school educator; b. Green Bay, Wis., Sept. 23, 1939; d. Henry John and Irma Tornow Fink; m. Kenneth Francis Rabideau, June 9, 1962; children: Neil Kenneth Rabideau, Laurie Ann Rabideau Kleisinger. BS in Edn., U. Wis., 1961; MEd, Nat. Louis U., 1996. Life license elem. sch. tchr. grades 1-8 Wis. Dept. Pub. Instrn. Elem. educator Janesville (Wis.) Pub. Schs., 1961-2001, retired, 2001. Pres. Rock County (Wis.) Ext. Homemakers, 1968-70; pres., coun. mem. Faith Luth. Ch., Janesville, 1983-88; officer, bd. dirs. Faith Lutheran Endowment Found., 1996-2002. Recipient Cert. of Excellence, Wis. Ctr. for Academically Talented Youth, Inc., Madison, 1995. Mem. Phi Beta Kappa, Delta Kappa Gamma (chpt. pres. 1998-2000, 02). Avocations: writing, music, drawing, sports, handicrafts.

RABIDEAU, PETER WAYNE, dean, chemistry professor, educator; b. Johnstown, Pa., Mar. 4, 1940; s. Peter Nelson and Monica (Smalley) R.; m. Therese Charlene Newquist, Sept. 1, 1962 (div.); children: Steven, Michael, Christine, Susan; m. Jennifer Lee Mooney, Nov. 15, 1986; children: Mark, Leah. BS, Loyola U., Chgo., 1964; MS, Case Inst. Tech., Cleve., 1967; PhD, Case Western Res. U., Cleve., 1968. Postdoctoral asst. U. Chgo., 1968-69, instr., 1969-70; asst. prof. Ind. U.-Purdue U., Indpls., 1970-73, assoc. prof., 1973-76, prof., 1976-90, chmn. dept. chemistry, 1985-90; dean Coll. Basic Scis. La. State U., Baton Rouge, 1990-99; dean Coll. Liberal Arts and Scis. Iowa State U., Ames, 1999—2003; provost, v.p. acad. affairs Miss. State U., 2003—. Program officer NSF, 1988-89. Contbr. numerous articles to profl. jours. Recipient rsch. award Purdue Sch. Sci. at Indpls., 1982, Outstanding Alumnus award chemistry dept. Case Western U., 2001. Fellow AAAS; mem. Am. Chem. Soc. (chmn. Ind. sect. 1974, councilor 1981-90). Home: 105 Derbyshire Rd Starkville MS 39759 Office: Miss State U PO Box BQ Mississippi State MS 39762 Home Phone: 662-324-7778. E-mail: prabideau@provost.msstate.edu.

RABII, PATRICIA BERG, retired church administrator; b. Lynn, Mass., Nov. 7, 1942; d. Clarence Oscar and Naomi Ruth (MacHugh) B.; m. S. Rabii, Oct. 26, 1966 (div. 1988); children: Susan M., Elizabeth L. AA, Green Mtn. Coll., Poultney, Vt., 1962; BA cum laude, U. Pa., 1978. Cons. City of Phila., 1981; fin. svcs. officer U. Pa., Phila., 1981-90; asst. to exec. dir. Psi Upsilon Found., Paoli, Pa., 1990-92; parish adminstr. St. David's Radnor Episcopal Ch., Wayne, Pa., 1992—98; clergy, parish sec. St. David's Ch., Wayne, Pa., 1998—2006; ret., 2006. Co-dir. career planning/pub. rels. Resources Women, Phila., 1978-81. Counselor direct patient and care ARC, St. Louis, 1967-69; bd. dirs. Upper Merion PTA, 1976-78, Dental Clinic, King of Prussia, 1976-78; leader Girl Scouts U.S.A., King of Prussia, 1976-77, 80-81. Recipient ACT 101 Svc. award, Penn Cap, 1989. Mem. AAUW, U. Pa. Women's Club (bd. dir. 1975-80, v.p. 1979-80). Avocations: golf, bridge, travel. Home: 5 Drummers Ln Wayne PA 19087-1503 Personal E-mail: patrabii@comcast.net.

RABIL, ALBERT, JR., humanities educator; b. Rocky Mount, NC, May 8, 1934; s. Albert and Sophie Mae (Safy) R.; m. Janet Spain, Aug. 29, 1956; children: Albert III, J. Alison. BA, Duke U., 1957; MDiv, Union Theol. Sem., 1960; PhD, Columbia U., 1964. Instr. religion Trinity Coll., Hartford, Conn., 1964-65, asst. prof., 1965-68; assoc. prof. hist. theology Chgo. Theol. Sem., 1969-71; assoc. prof. SUNY-Old Westbury, 1971-74, prof., 1974-77, disting. tchg. prof. humanities, 1977-98, emeritus prof., 1998. Program dir. NEH Summer Inst., 1992, 94, 95, 96, 98, 2000, 01, 03, 04, 05. Author: Merleau-Ponty, 1967 (Ansley award 1964), Erasmus and the New Testament, 1972, Laura Cereta, 1981, (with others) Her Immaculate Hand, 1983, Erasmus' Paraphrases of Romans and Galatians, 1983, Erasmus' Annotations on Romans, 1994, Teaching Other Voices: Women and Religion in Early Modern Europe, 2006; editor: Renaissance Humanism (3 vols.), 1988; editor, translator: Knowledge, Goodness, and Power, 1991, Henricus Cornelius Agrippa Declamation on the Nobility and Preeminence of the Female Sex, 1996; co-editor Renaissance Quarterly, 1992-97; series co-editor The Other Voice in Early Modern Europe, 1993—; mem. editl. bd. Soundings: An Interdisciplinary Jour., 1992-94. Travelling fellow Union Theol. Sem., 1960, Soc. for Values in Higher Edn., 1961; grantee Fulbright Found., 1961, NEH, 1974, 81, 94, 2002, 03, 04. Mem. Erasmus Rotterdam Soc. (mem. editl. bd. 1980—), Soc. for Values in Higher Edn. (bd. dirs. 1981-90), Renaissance Soc. Am. (bd. dirs. 1991-97). Democrat. Home and Office: 2305 Honeysuckle Rd Chapel Hill NC 27514-1716 Office Phone: 919-967-0231. Personal E-mail: arabil@nc.rr.com.

RABIL, MITCHELL JOSEPH, lawyer; b. Smithfield, NC, Sept. 19, 1931; s. Albert G. and Eva (Nassif) R.; m. Antoinette M. Olivry, Nov. 25, 1956 (div. Oct. 1986); children: Elizabeth, Nathalie, Marcus, Gregory; m. Dolores E. Bleam, Jan. 21, 1989; children: Susan Starr Vermes, Scott Starr. BS, Wake Forest Coll., 1953; LLB, Georgetown U., 1961. Bar: N.C. 1961, N.J. 1967, D.C. 1980, Pa. 1981, U.S. Tax Ct. 1962, U.S. Supreme Ct. 1979; CPA, N.J., N.C. Supervisory acct. GAO, Washington, 1956—60; fin. analyst, staff acct. SEC, Washington, 1960—62; tax atty. Office of Chief Counsel, IRS, Phila. and NYC, 1962—66; assoc. Archer, Greiner, Hunter & Read, Camden, NJ, 1966—71; ptnr. Myers, Matteo, Rabil, Norcross & Landgraf, Cherry Hill, NJ, 1971—89, Montgomery, McCracken, Walker and Rhoads, Cherry Hill, 1989—95; sole stockholder, pres. Mitchell J. Rabil & Assocs., P.A., Cherry Hill, 1995—2000; mem. Rabil & Harris LLC, Cherry Hill, 1998—2000, Rabil & Ropka, LLC, Cherry Hill, 2000—02, Rabil, Ropka, Kingett & Hatzell LLC, Cherry Hill, 2002—04, Rabil, Ropka, Kingett & Stewart LLC, 2005—. Mcpl. chmn. Riverton (N.J.) Rep. Com., 1976-83; chmn. area 2 Burlington County Rep. Com., 1976-82; bd. dirs. West Jersey Chamber Music Soc., 1990-91, Zurbrugg Meml. Hosp., 1991-93; mem. N.J. New Capital Sources Bd., 1996-2000. With AUS, 1953-55 Mem. AICPA, N.J. Bar Assn., N.J. Soc. CPA, Phila. Bar Assn., Am. Assoc. Atty. CPA (bd. dirs., past pres.) Cherry Hill C. of C. (bd. dirs. 1990-94), World Affairs Coun. Phila., Union League (Phila.), Riverton Country Club, Rotary (pres. Cherry Hill chpt. 1980-81, past dir.). Roman Catholic. Home: 107 Wayside Ct Delran NJ 08075-2000 Office: 215 Fries Mill Rd Turnersville NJ 08012

RABIN, ALAN A., economics professor; b. NYC, June 16, 1947; s. Sidney and Claire Rabin. BA, Hamilton Coll., 1969; PhD, U. Va., 1977. NSF trainee U. Va., 1970—71, 1971—72; intern Coun. Econ. Advisors, 1971; instr. Calif. State U., Northridge, 1973-74, Georgetown U., Washington, 1975; asst. prof. econs. U. Tenn., Chattanooga, 1977-81, assoc. prof., 1981-86, prof., 1986—. Author: Monetary Theory, 2004; contbr. articles to profl. jours. NDEA fellow, 1969-70; U. Tenn.-Chattanooga faculty rsch. grantee, 1982. Mem. Am. Econs. Assn., So. Econs. Assn., Atlantic Econs. Soc., We. Econs. Assn., U. Tenn. Chattanooga Coun. Scholars, Omicron Delta Epsilon. Avocations: sports, stamp collecting/philately, theater. Home: 1175 Pineville Rd Apt 161 Chattanooga TN 37405-2653 Office: U Tenn-Chattanooga Dept Economics Chattanooga TN 37403 Office Phone: 423-425-4360. Business E-Mail: alan-rabin@utc.edu.

RABIN, HERBERT, physicist, educator, dean; b. Milw., Nov. 14, 1928; 2 children. BS, U. Wis., 1950; MS, U. Ill., 1951; PhD in Physics, U. Md., 1959. Physicist elec. divsn. U.S. Naval Rsch. Lab., 1952-54, physicist solid state physics divsn., 1954-62, head radiation effects sect. optical materials br., 1962-67, head quantum optics sect., applied optics br., 1967-68, head quantum optics br., 1968-71, assoc. dir. rsch. for space sci. and tech., 1971-77, assoc. dir. rsch. for space and comm. sci. and tech., 1977-79; dep. asst. sec. for rsch., applied and space tech. Office of Navy Secretariat, Washington, 1979-83; dir. engring. rsch. ctr., prof. elec. engring., assoc. dean Coll. Engring., U. Md., College Park, 1983—, interim dean coll. engring., 1999-2000, 2007—. Dir. GRC Internat., 1988—98, Washington Aluminum Co., 1992—95, Yurie Sys. Inc., 1995—98, VT Linx Multimedia Sys., Inc., 2000—02; vis. scientist Technisch Hochschule, Stuttgart, Germany, 1960—61; mem. staff physics dept. George Washington U., 1955—73; cons. Sch. Engring. Sao Carlos U., Sao Paulo, Brazil, 1964, Sao Paulo, 70; trustee Nat. Technol. U., 1984—2000, life trustee, 2000—03; vis. fellow SEEDA, England, 2003. Contbr. articles to tech. jours. Recipient Meritorious Civilian Svc. award, USN, 1969, Disting. Civilian Svc. award, 1976, 1993, Dept. Def., 1979, Cert. of Commendation, NASA, 1986, Centennial medal, U. Md. Coll. Engring., 1994. Fellow: AIAA, AAAS, Optical Soc. Am., Am. Phys. Soc.; mem.: IEEE (sr.), Brazilian Acad. Scis. (corr.). Achievements include patents in field. Home: 7109 Radnor Rd Bethesda MD 20817-6332 Office: U Md Engring Rsch Ctr College Park MD 20742-0001 Office Phone: 301-405-3906.

RABIN, JACK, lawyer; b. Aug. 19, 1930; s. Leo and Bertha Rabin; m. Roberta Edith Libson, Oct. 25, 1953; children: Keith Warren, Michael Jay, Adam Douglas. Student, Bklyn. Coll., 1948-50; LLB, Bklyn. Law Sch., 1953. Bar: N.Y. 1953, U.S. Tax Ct. 1960, U.S. Ct. Claims 1964, U.S. Supreme Ct. 1964, U.S. Ct. Appeals (2d cir.) 1968. Ptnr. Hoffberg, Rabin & Engler and predecessor firms, NYC, 1968-82, Javits, Hinckley, Rabin & Engler, NYC, 1982-84, Phillips, Nizer, Benjamin, Krim & Ballon, NYC, 1984-94, counsel, 1994—. Arbitrator gen. comml. and constrn. panel Am. Arbitration Assn., 1968—; instr. Real Estate Inst., NYU, 1976-78; ct. apptd. mediator U.S. Dist. Ct. (so. dist.), N.Y., 1994—, N.Y. Supreme Ct., N.Y. County, 1999. Assoc. editor Bklyn. Law Rev., 1952, editor-in-chief, 1953, also author law rev. note. 1st lt. JAGC, U.S. Army, 1954-57, col. res., ret., 1983. Mem. N.Y. State Bar Assn., Res. Officers Assn. U.S. (pres. Rockland County chpt. 1967-68), B'nai B'rith (pres. New City, N.Y. 1965-66). Jewish. Office: 10 W 66th St Ste 8G New York NY 10023 Office Phone: 212-724-1050. E-mail: sutleg@earthlink.net.

RABIN, JOSEPH HARRY, marketing research company executive; b. Chgo., Dec. 12, 1927; s. Morris and Libby (Broder) Rabinovitz; m. Barbara E. Leader, Oct. 31, 1954; children: Marc Jay, Michelle Ann, Deborah Susan. BSc, Roosevelt U., 1950; MBA, DePaul U., 1951. Account exec. Gould, Gleiss & Benn, 1951-56; asst. dir. mktg. rsch. Paper Mate Co., Chgo., 1956-63; pres. Rabin Rsch. Co., Chgo., 1963—. Pres. Mather HS Coun., 1972-74; mem. adv. coun. U. Toledo, 1976-77, Kellstadt Ctr. DePaul U., 1986-93; mem. adv. com. Bur. of the Census, 1978-83; bd. dirs. Market Rsch. Inst., 1973-75, Ner Tamid Synagogue, 1976-2007, Jewish Vocat. Svc., 1977-80. With AUS, 1946-47. Mem. Am. Mktg. Assn. (pres. Chgo. chpt. 1961-62, nat. dir. 1973-75, nat. v.p. mktg. rsch. 1978-79, nat. pres. 1981-82), Assn. Consumer Rsch., Am. Statis. Assn. (pres. Chgo. chpt.

1962-63), Am. Assn. Pub. Opinion Rsch. Home: 7061 N Kedzie Ave Chicago IL 60645-2846 Office: Rabin Rsch Co 150 E Huron St Chicago IL 60611-2999 Home Phone: 773-465-6661; Office Phone: 312-482-8500. Business E-Mail: jrabin@rabin-research.com.

RABIN, MICHAEL OSER, computer scientist, educator; b. Breslau, Germany, Sept. 1, 1931; s. Israel A. and Else (Hess) R.; m. Ruth Scherzer, May 31, 1954; children: Tal, Sharon. MSc in Math., Hebrew U., Jerusalem, 1953; PhD in Math., Princeton U., NJ, 1957. H.B. Fine instr. Princeton U., 1956—58; mem. Inst. Advanced Study, Princeton, 1958; sr. lectr. to assoc. prof. Hebrew U., Jerusalem, 1958—65, chmn. Inst. Math., 1964—66, prof., 1965—, chmn. computer sci. dept., 1970—71, rector (acad. head), 1972—75, pro-rector, 1976—80, Albert Einstein chair, 1980—99; vis. prof. U. Calif., Berkeley, 1962, U. Paris, 1965, Yale U., 1967, NYU, 1970, MIT, 1972-78; Gordon McKay prof. computer sci. Harvard U., Cambridge, Mass., 1981—83, Thomas J. Watson sr. prof. computer sci., 1983—; cons. computer industry. Inventor oblivious transfer algorithm. Recipient Rothschild prize in math., 1974, Turing award in computer sci., 1976, Harvey prize in sci. and tech., 1980, The Israel Prize in Exact Scis./Computer Sci., 1995, IEEE Charles Babbage award in Computer Sci., 2000, ACM Kanellakis Theory and Practice award, 2004, EMET Prize in Exact Scis./Computer Sci., 2004. Mem. Israel Acad. Scis. and Humanities, NAS (fgn. assoc. mem.), Am. Acad. Arts and Scis. (fgn. hon. mem.), Am. Philos. Soc. (fgn.), French Acad. Scis. (fgn.), Royal Soc. UK (fgn.). Office: Sch Engring and Applied Scis Harvard U 29 Oxford St Cambridge MA 02138 *

RABIN, MONROE STEPHEN ZANE, physicist; b. Bklyn., Dec. 19, 1939; s. Louis and Helen (Haspel) R.; m. Joan Greenblatt, Feb. 27, 1965; children: Elaine Judith, Carolyn Sandra. AB, Columbia Coll., 1961; PhD, Rutgers U., 1967. Physicist Lawrence Berkeley (Calif.) Lab., 1967-72; assoc. prof. physics U. Mass., Amherst, 1972-81, prof. physics, 1981—; vis. physicist Stanford Linear Accelerator Ctr., Palo Alto, Calif., 1979-80; vis. scholar Physics Dept. Harvard U., Cambridge, Mass., 1986-87; Soriano scholar in radiol. physics, radiation therapy dept. Mass. Gen. Hosp., Boston, 1986-87. Mem. oversight panel Proton Therapy Med. Facility, Mass. Gen. Hosp., Boston, 1991-96. Contbr. articles to Physical Rev., Physical Rev. Letters, Physics Letters, Nuclear Instruments and Methods. Mem. Am. Phys. Soc., Sigma Xi. Achievements include research in experimental particle physics, medical physics, cancer therapy using accelerated protons, ductal carcinoma in situ and heavy-ion physics. Home: 21 Atwater Cir Amherst MA 01002-3205 Office: U Mass Dept Physics Amherst MA 01003 Office Phone: 413-545-0424. Business E-Mail: rabin@physics.umass.edu.

RABIN, ROBERT L., law educator; b. 1939; BS, Northwestern U., 1960, JD, 1963, PhD in Polit. Sci., 1967. Bar: Ill. 1963. Asst. prof. law U. Wis., Madison, 1966-69, assoc. prof., 1969-70; vis. assoc. prof. Stanford Law Sch., Calif., 1970-71, assoc. prof. Calif., 1971-73, prof. Calif., 1973-84, A. Calder Mackay prof. Calif., 1984—. Sr. environ. fellow EPA, 1979—80; vis. fellow Centre Sociolegal Studies Wolfson Coll., Oxford U., 1982; vis. prof. Harvard Law Sch., 1987—88, NYU Law Sch., 1999—2000; Jack N. Pritzker disting. vis. prof. Northwestern Sch. Law., 1994. Author: Perspectives on the Administrative Process, 1979, Perspective on Tort Law, 1995; co-author: Smoking Policy: Law, Politics and Culture, 1993, Cases and Materials on Tort Law and Alternatives, 2001, Regulating Tobacco, 2001, Torts Stories, 2006. Fellow, Ctr. Advanced Study Behavioral Scis., 1982—83. Office: Stanford Law Sch Crown Quadrangle 559 Nathan Abbott Way Stanford CA 94305-8610 Office Phone: 650-723-3073. Business E-Mail: rrabin@stanford.edu.

RABIN, STANLEY ARTHUR, metal products manufacturer; b. NYC, 1938; BA, BS in Metall. Engring., Columbia U., 1958; MBA, U. Santa Clara, 1969. With Comml. Metals Co., Inc., Irving, 1970—, pres., 1978—2006, CEO, 1979—2006, chmn., 1999—. Mailing: Commercial Metals Co PO Box 1046 Dallas TX 75221-1046 Office: Commercial Metals Co Ste 800 6565 N MacArthur Blvd Irving TX 75039 *

RABINOVICH, EGLA CONSUELO, pediatrician, rheumatologist; d. Sergio and Nelly Rabinovich; m. Kenneth Wayne Jordan, May 3, 1986; children: Danielle Jordan, Nicholas Jordan, Kyle Jordan. BS, U. Ill., Champaign-Urbana, 1981; MD, So. Ill. U., 1985; MPH, U. NC, Chapel Hill, 1991. Cert. in pediat. rheumatology Am. Bd. Pediats., 2006. Assoc. pediat. Duke U., Durham, NC, 1991—93, asst. prof., 2002—, U. Chgo., 1993—2001. Mem.: Am. Coll. Rheumatology (pediatric exec. com. 1992—2006, Amgen/REF Vis. Professorship 2006). Office: Duke U Med Ctr Box 3212 Durham NC 27710 Office Phone: 919-684-6475. Office Fax: 919-684-6616.

RABINOVITCH, BENTON SEYMOUR, chemist, educator emeritus; b. Montreal, Que., Can., Feb. 19, 1919; came to U.S., 1946; s. Samuel and Rachel (Schachter) R.; m. Marilyn Werby, Sept. 18, 1949; children: Peter Samuel, Ruth Anne, Judith Nancy, Frank Benjamin; m. Flora Reitman, 1980. BSc, McGill U., 1939, PhD, 1942; DSc (hon.), Technion Inst., Haifa, 1991. Postdoctoral fellow Harvard, 1946-48; mem. faculty U. Wash., Seattle, 1948—, prof. chemistry, 1957—, prof. chemistry emeritus, 1985—. Cons. and/or mem. sci. adv. panels, coms. NSF, Nat. Acad. Scis.-NRC; adv. com. phys. chemistry Nat. Bur. Standards. Author Antique Silver Servers, 1991, Contemporary Silver, 2000, Contemporary Silver Part II, 2005; co-author: Physical Chemistry, 1964; former editor: Ann. Rev. Phys. Chemistry; mem. editorial bd.: Internat. Jour. Chem. Kinetics, Rev. of Chem. Intermediates, Jour. Phys. Chemistry Served to capt. Canadian Army, 1942-46, ETO. Nat. Research Council Can. fellow, 1940-42; Royal Soc. Can. Research fellow, 1946-47; Milton Research fellow Harvard, 1948; Guggenheim fellow, 1961; vis. fellow Trinity Coll., Oxford, 1971; recipient Sigma Xi award for original research, Debye award in phys. chemistry, 1984, Polanyi medal Royal Soc. Chemistry; named hon. liveryman Worshipful Co. of Goldsmiths, London, 2000. Fellow Am. Phys. Soc., Am. Acad. Arts and Scis., Royal Soc. London; mem. Am. Chem. Soc. (past chmn. Puget Sound sect., past chmn. phys. chemistry divsn., assoc. editor jour.), Faraday Soc. Achievements include rsch. in Unimolecular gas phase reaction and history and design of silver implements. Home: 12530 42nd Ave NE Seattle WA 98125-4621 Office: Univ Washington Chemistry Box 351700 Seattle WA 98195 Office Fax: 206-285-8665.

RABINOVITZ, BRUCE H., lawyer; b. Spokane, Wash., Dec. 15, 1945; BA, Washington U., 1967; JD with honors, George Washington U., 1971. Bar: Va. 1971, D.C. 1977, Calif. 1982. Atty.-advisor procurement divsn. Gen. Svcs. Adminstrn., Washington, 1971-72; rates and agreements divsn. Office Gen. Counsel Civil Aeronautics Bd., Washington, 1972-76; atty. Ginsburg, Feldman and Bress, Washington; ptnr., chmn. Aviation dept. Wilmer Cutler Pickering Hale & Dorr, Washington. Mem. D.C. Bar, State Bar Calif., Fed. Bar Assn., Va. State Bar, Order of the Coif. Office: Wilmer Cutler Pickering Hale & Dorr 1899 Pennsylvania Ave NW Washington DC 20006 Mailing: Wilmer Cutler Pickering Hale & Dorr 2445 M St NW Washington DC 20037 Office Phone: 202-663-6960. Office Fax: 202-663-6363. Business E-Mail: bruce.rabinovitz@wilmerhale.com.

RABINOVITZ, JOEL, lawyer, educator; b. 1939; AB, Cornell U., 1960; LLB, Harvard U., 1963. Bar: N.Y. 1963, Calif. 1981. Asst. prof. U. Fla., Gainesville, Fla., 1966—68; vis. assoc. prof. UCLA, 1968—69, acting prof., 1969—72, prof., 1972—79; vis. prof. NYU, 1976; dep. Internat. Tax Counsel, Dept. Treasury, 1980—81; ptnr. with Irell & Manella LLP, LA, 1981—. Office: Irell & Manella LLP 1800 Avenue Of The Stars Los Angeles CA 90067-4212

RABINOWITZ, JACK GRANT, radiologist, educator; b. Monticello, NY, July 9, 1927; s. Abraham and Bessie (Sussman) R.; m. Rica Gedalia Arnon, Oct. 19, 1972; children— Antoine, Anne, Pierre, Yaron, Tal. BA, UCLA, 1949; MD, U. Berne, Switzerland, 1955. Diplomate: Am. Bd. Radiology. Intern Kings County Hosp., Bklyn., 1955-56, resident, 1956-59; instr. radiology Downstate Med. Center, Bklyn., 1960-61, asst. prof. radiology, 1967-70, prof. radiology, 1970-73; asst. radiologist Mt. Sinai Sch. Medicine, NYC, 1962-65, asst. prof. radiology, 1965-66, asso. prof. radiology, 1966-67, prof., chmn. dept. radiology, 1978-95, prof., 1995—. Asso. attending radiologist Mt. Sinai Hosp., N.Y.C., 1965-67, dir. radiology, 1978—; radiologist-in-chief Bklyn.-Cumberland Med. Center, Bklyn., 1967-70; dir. diagnostic radiology Kings County Hosp. Center, Bklyn., 1970-73; prof., chmn. dept. diagnostic radiology U. Tenn., Memphis, 1973-78; cons. in radiology VA Hosp., Bronx, N.Y. Author: Pediatric Radiology, 1978, Radiology for the Primary and Emergency Care of Physicians, 1981. Fellow Am. Coll. Radiology; mem. Radiol. Soc. N. Am., Am. Roentgen Ray Soc., Assn. Univ. Radiologists, AMA, Soc. Chmn. Acad. Radiology Depts. Office: Mt Sinai Hosp 1 Gustave L Levy Pl New York NY 10029-6500 Home Phone: 201-501-8190; Office Phone: 212-241-7427. Business E-Mail: jack-rabinowitz@msnyu.health.org.

RABINOWITZ, MARK I., lawyer; b. Phila., Feb. 7, 1959; BS, Pa. State U., 1981; JD summa cum laude, Temple U., 1988. Bar: Pa. 1988, NJ 1988, Fla. 1990. Law clerk Blank Rome LLP, Phila., 1987, ptnr., practice group leader, fin. svcs. group, 1988—. Co-author: Golden Books Case Creates New Golden Rule for Lessors, 2002, The Case of the Continuing Guaranty, 2000, How Effective Is An Acceptance Certificate Under Article 2A?, 1999, Georgia Upholds the Integrity of Hell or High Water, 1998. Mem.: Equipment Leasing Assn. (former bd. mem. legal com., former bd. mem. ea. regional com.), Ea. Assn. of Equipment Lessors, Pa. Bar Assn. (former vice-chmn. Article 2A Task Force, mem. bus. section), Fla. Bar Assn., NJ Bar Assn., Phila. Bar Assn. Office: Blank Rome LLP One Logan Sq Philadelphia PA 19103-6998 Office Phone: 215-569-5629. Office Fax: 215-832-5629. E-mail: mrabinowitz@BlankRome.com.

RABINOWITZ, STEPHEN L., lawyer; b. Bklyn., June 8, 1962; AB, Brandeis Univ., 1983; JD, Am. Univ., Washington, 1986. Bar: NY 1987. Law clk. to Chief Judge, James C. Turk US Dist. Ct. (we. dist.) Va., 1986; shareholder, real estate dept., bd. dir. Greenberg Traurig LLP, NYC. Adj. prof. NY Law Sch. Office: Greenberg Traurig MetLife Bldg 200 Park Ave New York NY 10166-1400 Office Phone: 212-801-9295. Office Fax: 212-801-6400. Business E-Mail: rabinowitzs@gtlaw.com.

RABINOWITZ, YARON GIL, psychologist, military officer; b. Memphis, Dec. 21, 1973; s. Jack Grant and Rica Rabinowitz; m. Stephanie Lynn Maislen, Sept. 1, 2001 (div. Dec. 1, 2005); 1 child, Mia Jaden. AB in Govt., Harvard U., Cambridge, Mass., 1996; MA in History, Stanford U., Calif., 2000; PhD in Clin. Psychology, Pacific Grad. Sch. Psychology, Palo Alto, Calif., 2005. History tchr. Blair Acad., Blairstown, NJ, 1996—98; clin. rschr. Stanford U. Sch. Medicine, 2000—04; commd. 2d lt. US Army, 2004, advanced through grades to capt., 2004; clin. psychology resident Walter Reed Army Med. Ctr., Washington, 2004—05; dep. command psychologist JFK Spl. Warfare Ctr. and Sch., Fort Bragg, NC, 2005—06; command psychologist Spl. Forces Assessment and Selection Program, JFK Spl. Warfare Ctr. and Sch., Fort Bragg, NC, 2006—. Contbr. articles to profl. publs. Decorated Nat. Svc. ribbon, Army Parachutist badge, Army Commendation medal, Global War on Terrorism ribbon; recipient Student Award for Excellence in Alzheimer's Rsch., California-Nevada Alzheimer's Assn., 2004, STAR award for achievement, Palo Alto VA Health Care Sys., 2004; Health Profession scholar, US Army Med. Dept., 2002—04, Jared and Mae Tincklenberg fellow, Pacific Grad. Sch. Psychology, 2002—03, Rabbi Stephen S. Pearce fellow, 2003—04. Mem.: APA (chmn. grad. students 2004—05, chmn. advocacy coord. team 2003—04), Divsn. Mil. Psychology. Avocations: triathlons, wrestling, music, travel, accordion. Home Phone: 650-814-5355.

RABIU, BADRU I.O., federal official; b. Lagos, Nigeria, Aug. 18, 1935; came to U.S., 1972; divorced; six children. Polit., labor specialist Am. Embassy, Lagos, 1951-72; dir. Liberty Immigration and Citizenship Svc., NY, 1984—. Adminstrv. asst. Arlington (Va.) County, 1981-83; labor writer U.S. Dept. Labor, Washington, 1979-80. Contbr. articles to profl. jours. Mem. Rep. Nat. Com. (life), Rep. Senatorial Inner Circle, Nigeria Muslim Orgn., UN Assn. of U.S. Muslim. Home: 2840 Ocean Pkwy Apt 9E Brooklyn NY 11235-7956 Office: 72 Maiden Ln Ste 312 New York NY 10038

RABKIN, MITCHELL THORNTON, physician, educator, hospital administrator; b. Boston, Nov. 27, 1930; s. Morris Aaron and Esther (Quint) Rabkin; m. Adrienne M. Najarian, June 24, 1956; children: Julia Margaret, David Gregory. AB magna cum laude, Harvard U., 1951, MD cum laude, 1955; DSc (hon.), Brandeis U., 1983; DPharm (hon.), Mass. Coll. Pharmacy, 1983; DSc (hon.), Curry Coll., 1989, Northeastern U., 1994; DHumLet (hon.), Salem State Coll., Mass., 1995. Intern Mass. Gen. Hosp., Boston, 1955—56, resident in internal medicine, 1956—57, 1959—60, chief resident, 1962, mem. staff, 1963—72, bd. consultation, 1972—80, hon. physician, 1981—; clin. fellow NIH, Bethesda, Md., 1957—59; gen. dir. Beth Israel Hosp., Boston, 1966—80, pres., 1980—96; CEO CareGroup, Boston, 1996—98; now disting. inst. scholar Carl J. Shapiro Inst. for Edn. and Rsch. Harvard Med. Sch. and Beth Israel Deaconess Med. Ctr., Boston, 1996—; dir. Washington Adv. Group LECG, 1999—. Asst. prof. medicine Harvard U., 1969—70, assoc. prof., 1971—83, prof., 1983—, pres. med. alumni coun., 2002—03; v.p. NYU Sch. Medicine Found. Bd.; chmn. Albert Schweitzer Fellowship, 2005—, bd. dirs. With USPHS, 1957—59. Fellow: AAAS, ACP, Am. Acad. Arts and Scis.; mem.: Inst. Medicine of NAS, Assn. Am. Med. Colls. (chmn. 1996—97), Soc. Med. Adminstrs., Mass. Med. Soc., Tavern Club Boston, Harvard Club of Boston. Jewish. Office: Beth Israel Deaconess Med Ctr/Harvard U Shapiro Inst Edn and Rsch 330 Brookline Ave Boston MA 02215-5400 Office Phone: 617-549-0176. Personal E-mail: mtrabkin@mindspring.com. Business E-Mail: mrabkin@theadvisorygroup.com.

RABNER, STUART JEFF, state supreme court justice, former state attorney general; b. Passaic, NJ, June 30, 1960; s. George and Stella (Litwok) Rabner; m. Deborah Wiener, July 2, 1989; children: Erica, Carly, Jacob. AB, Princeton U., 1982; JD, Harvard U., 1985. Bar: NJ 1986, NY 1986, US Dist. Ct. NJ 1986, US Ct. Appeals (3rd cir.) 1986. Law clk. to Hon. Dickinson R. Debevoise US Dist. Ct. NJ, 1985-86; asst. U.S. atty. US Dept. Justice, Newark, dep. chief criminal divsn., 1991—2005, dep. chief spl. prosecutions divsn., exec. asst. U.S. atty., chief criminal divsn.; chief counsel to gov. State of NJ, Trenton, 2006, atty. gen., 2006—07; chief justice NJ Supreme Ct., Trenton, NJ, 2007—. Chmn. Holocaust Resource Ctr., Clifton, NJ, 1986—. Named one of 2007 People to Watch, Sunday Star Ledger. Office: NJ Supreme Ct PO Box 23 Trenton NJ 08625 *

RABÓ, JULE ANTHONY, research scientist, consultant; b. Budapest, Hungary; came to U.S., 1957; m. Sheelagh Ennis; children: Benedict, Sebastian. BSChemE, Poly. U., Budapest, 1946, DSc in Chemistry, 1949, D honoris causa, 1986, U. Veszprem, Hungary, 2002. From asst. prof. to assoc. prof. Poly. U., Budapest, 1946—54; assoc. dir. Hydrocarbon Rsch. Inst., Budapest, 1951—56; rsch. assoc. Union Carbide Corp., Buffalo, 1957-60, rsch. mgr. Tarrytown, NY, 1960-72, corp. fellow, 1969-82, sr. corp. rsch. fellow, 1982—, UOP, Tarrytown, 1988—. Cons. in chemistry and catalysis, Armonk, N.Y.; former mem. adv. bd. Ctr. for Advanced Materials, Lawrence-Berkeley Lab.; mem. adv. bd. dept. chemistry Lehigh U. Author: Zeolite Chemisty and Catalysts; former mem. editorial bd. Jour. Catalysis, Applied Catalysis; contbr. articles to profl. jours.; patentee in field. Recipient Kossuth award Govt. of Hungary, 1953, Excellence in Catalysis award N.Y. Catalysis Soc., 1982, Humboldt award, Fed. Republic of Germany, 1990. Mem. Am. Chem. Soc. (E.V. Murphree award 1988), Am. Catalysis Soc. (Eugene J. Houdry award 1989), Hungarian Acad. Sci. (Varga medal 1991), Am. Inst. Chemists (Chem. Pioneer award 1993).

RABON, ANTHONY PEREZ, protective services official; s. Francisco R. Rabon and Engracia B. Perez. BS, Almeda U., Boise, 2006. Cert. emergency med. technician Office Emergency Med. Svcs., Guam, 1990. Fire insp., capt. Guam Fire Dept., Hagatna, 1990—96, asst. fire chief, 1996—. Acting fire chief Guam Fire Dept., 2000. Internat. v.p. Isla Latte Jaycees, Hagatna, 1995—96; sec. Fraternal Order of Eagles, Hagatna, 1986—87, Asia Pacific Lions Club, Hagatna, 1987—88; mem. mcpl. planning coun. Office of Mayor of Barrigada, Barrigada, 1987—2007; dir. bd. dirs. Young Men's League Guam, Hagatna, 1995—96. Recipient Fire Chief's Citation of Honor, Guam Fire Dept., 1997, cert., Congl. Fire Svcs. Inst., 2007. Mem.: Nat. Fire Protection Assn. (assoc.), KC (life; fin. sec. 2000—01, Knight of Fourth Degree 1987). Office Phone: 671-472-3337.

RABON, WILLIAM JAMES, JR., architect; b. Marion, SC, Feb. 7, 1931; s. Williams James and Beatrice (Baker) R.; m. Martha Ann Hibbitts, Mar. 6, 1987. BS in Arch., Clemson Coll., 1951; BArch, N.C. State Coll., 1955; MArch, MIT, 1956; postgrad., Inst. Urbanistico, Rome, 1957-58. Registered architect, Calif., N.C., Ohio, Pa., Ga. Designer archtl. firms, NYC & Birmingham, Mich., 1958-61; designer, assoc. John Carl Warnecke & Assocs., San Francisco, 1961-63, 64-66; designer, assoc. Keyes, Lethbridge & Condon, Washington, 1966-68; prin. archtl. ptnr. A.M. Kinney Assocs. & William J. Rabon, Cin., 1968-85; v.p., dir. archtl. design A.M. Kinney, Inc., Cin., 1977-85; v.p., dir. programming svcs. Design Art Corp., 1977-85; sr. architect John Portman & Assocs., Atlanta, 1985-88; dir. archtl. design Robert & Co., Atlanta, 1988-89; design prin. Carlson Assocs., Atlanta, 1990-93; prin., dir. rsch. & med. facilities programming & design Rosser Internat., 1993-97, William J. Rabon, Arch., 1995—. Lectr. U. Calif., Berkeley, 1963-65; asst. prof. archtl. design Cath. U. Am., 1967-68; planning cons. Nat. Bur. Stds. Lab., China, 1982. Prin. works include Kaiser Tech. Ctr., Pleasanton, Calif., 1970 (Rsch. Devel. Lab. of Yr. award), Clermont Nat. Bank, Milford, Ohio, 1971, Pavilion Bldg. Children's Hosp. Med. Ctr., Cin., 1973 (Cin. AIA design award), EG&G, Hydrospace, Inc., Rockville, Md., 1970 (Potomac Valley AIA design award), Mead Johnson Pk., Evansville, Inc., 1973 (Rsch. Devel. lab. of Yr. merit award), Hamilton County Vocat. Sch., Cin., 1972, Hdqrs. Lab. EPA, 1975, Arapahoe Chem. Co. Rsch. Ctr., Boulder, Colo., 1976 (Rsch. Devel. lab. of Yr. award, 1976, Concrete Reinforced Steel Inst. Nat. Design award, Regional AIA design award), Corp. Hdqrs. Ohio River Co., Cin., 1977, Children's Hosp. Therapy Ctr., 1981 (Cin. AIA design award, 1978, award of merit Am. Wood Coun., 1981), Va. Hosp. addition (Cin. ASHRAE Design award, 1980), NALCO Chem. Co. Rsch. Ctr., Naperville, Ill., 1980 (Ohio and Cin. AIA design awards, 1980, 1981), NALCO Chem. Co. Co. Hdqs., 1987, Proctor and Gamble-Winton Hill Tunnel, Cin., 1978 (Ohio AIA design award), Toyota Regional Ctr., Blue Ash, Ohio (Ohio AIA and Ohio Masonry Coun. combined design award, 1981), U. Cin. Med. Ctr. Lab., Cin., 1981, Children's Hosp. Ambulatory Svc. Ctr., 1984, East and West fleethdqrs. and Data Ctr. Librs. of Royal Saudi Arabian Navy, 1985, corp. hdqrs. The Drackett Co., Cin., 1983, corp. hdqrs. Brown & Williamson, Louisville, 1984, Children's Hosp. Med. Ctr. Ambulatory Svcs. Ctr., Cin., 1984, Olin Corp. Rsch. Ctr., Cheshire, Conn., 1985, Inst. Paper Sci. & Tech., Atlanta, 1989, Citicorp. Data Ctr., Napa, Calif., 1992, Sci. Complex, Athens, Ga., 1996, Biocontainment Rsch. Ctr., 1998. 1st lt., co. comdr., Battalion S-2 and Platoon leader AUS, 1951—53, Korean War. Company awarded Presdl. Unit Citation; recipient Silver Star, Bronze Star for Valor, Bronze Star for Meritorious Svc., Purple Heart with bronze cluster; MIT Grad. scholar, 1956; Fulbright scholar, Italy, 1957-58. Mem. AIA, Nat. Coun. Archtl. Registration Bds.

RABOSKY, JOSEPH GEORGE, engineering consulting company executive; b. Sewickley, Pa., May 20, 1944; m. Suzanne Lazzelle, Aug. 23, 1969. BS, Pa. State U., 1966; MS in Engring., W.Va. U., 1969; MSCE, U. Pitts., 1973, PhD, 1984. Registered profl. engr., Pa., Ohio. Project engr. Chester Engrs., Coraopolis, Pa., 1969-70, mgr., 1989-92; project mgr. Calgon Corp., Pitts., 1970-73, sect. leader, 1979-85, mktg. mgr., 1985-86; sr. environ. specialist Mobay Chem. Corp., Pitts., 1975-79; project engr. Morris Knowles, Inc., Pitts., 1973-74; project mgr. Penn Environ. Cons., 1974-75; engring. mgr. Baker/TSA, Inc., Pitts., 1986-89; pres. AquaTerra, Inc., Moon Twp., Pa., 1992-95, Rabosky & Assocs., Moon Twp., Pa., 1995—. Adj. prof. U. Pitts., 1985-88, Pa. State U.-Beaver, McKeesport and New Kensington campuses, 1985-2007, Youngstown State U., 2003. Mem. Western Pa. Water Pollution Control Assn. (officer 1984-94, pres. 1992-93), Internat. Water Conf. (mem. exec. bd. 1989-94, gen. chmn. 1992-93), Pa. Water Environ. Assn. (pres. 1996-97). Home and Office: 104 Wynview Dr Moon Township PA 15108-1033 Personal E-mail: joera1co@aol.com.

RABSON, ALAN SAUL, federal agency administrator, pathologist, educator; b. NYC, July 1, 1926; s. Abraham and Florence (Shulman) Rabson; m. Ruth L. Kirschstein, June 11, 1950; 1 child, Arnold. BA, U. Rochester, 1948; MD, SUNY, Bklyn., 1950. Intern Mass. Meml. Hosp., Boston, 1951—52; resident in pathology NYU Hosp., 1952—54, USPHS Hosp., New Orleans, 1954—55; pathologist Nat. Cancer Inst., Bethesda, Md., 1955—; prof. pathology Georgetown U. Med. Sch., 1974—, Uniformed Services U. Health Scis., 1978—, George Washington U., 1978—; dep. dir. Nat. Cancer Inst., Bethesda, 1995—, acting dir., 2001—02. Contbr. articles to med. jours. Mem.: Am. Assn. Pathologists, Alpha Omega Alpha, Sigma Xi, Phi Beta Kappa. Address: NIH-Nat Cancer Inst 9000 Rockville Pike Bldg 31 Bethesda MD 20892-0001

RABSTEJNEK, GEORGE JOHN, healthcare executive; b. Queens, NY, June 14, 1932; s. George John and Rose Anna (Krasa) R.; m. Patsy Kidd, July 17, 1964; 1 child, Marley Ann. B in Indsl. Engring., Ga. Inst. Tech., 1954; postgrad., U. Conn. Sch. Law, 1960, NYU Sch. Bus., 1965-69; advanced mgmt. program, Harvard U., 1975. Dir. material mgmt. svcs. divsn. Harbridge House, Inc., Boston, 1965-69, v.p., group head, 1969-75, exec. v.p., 1975-76, pres., 1976-83, CEO, 1983-92, chmn., 1983-93, ret., 1993. Chmn. bd. dirs. R.P.W., Inc., Bluelight, Inc.; chmn. bd. dirs. C.T.C., Inc. (Ctr. for Tech. Commercialization), 2002; founder, mem. exec. com. Keck Neural Prothesis Rsch. Ctr.; chmn. emeritus Mass. Eye and Ear Infirmary. Contbr. articles to profl. jours. Vice chmn. World Affairs Coun. Boston, 1988, pres., 1984-87; trustee Internat. Coord. Coun., Boston, 1984-2003; trustee, chmn. bd. dirs. Mass. Eye and Ear Infirmary, Boston, 1984—, vice chmn. bd. dirs., chmn. emeritus, 2006—; bd. emeritus Draper Labs. Corp., 1994, chmn. bd. dirs., 2002; mem. adv. bd. Town of Cohasset, Mass., 1975; chmn. nat. adv. bd. Ga. Inst. Tech., 1991-92; mem. exec. adv. bd. Ivan Allen Coll.; mem. bd. visitors Northeastern U. Comdr. USNR, 1954-75, ret. Recipient Disting. Alumni award Sch. Indsl. and Sys. Engring., Ga. Inst. Tech., named to Acad. Disting. Engring. Alumni. Mem. Am. Inst. Indsl. Engrs., Nat. Security Indsl. Assn. (v.p. 1987—), Nat. Def. Transp. Assn. (Def. Transp. award 1980), Assn. Naval Aviators, Navy League, Reynolds Soc. (chmn.), Nat. Security Industry Assn. (trustee 1990-93), Harvard Club, Algonquin Club (Boston), Cohasset Golf Club

(Mass.), Cohasset Yacht Club, Cohasset Tennis and Squash Club, Mill Reef Club, Antigua, B.W.I., Comml. Club, F St. Club (Washington), Phi Kappa Sigma. Republican. Unitarian Universalist. Home: 181 Border St Cohasset MA 02025-2043

RABUN, DANIEL W., oil and gas industry executive; BBA in Acctg., U. Houston; JD, So. Meth. U., Dallas. CPA 1976. Positions up to ptnr. Baker & McKenzie, 1986—2001, ptnr., 2001—06; v.p., gen. counsel, sec. Chorum Techs. Inc., 2000—01; pres., bd. dirs. ENSCO Internat. Inc., 2006—, CEO, 2007—, chmn., 2007—. Office: ENSCO Internat Inc 500 N Akard St Ste 4300 Dallas TX 75201-3331 Office Phone: 214-397-3000. *

RABUN, JOHN BREWTON, JR., criminal justice agency administrator; b. Augusta, Ga., Aug. 16, 1946; s. John Brewton and Alsie Imor (Bateman) R.; m. Anna Betsy Park, Dec. 27, 1967; children: Kerry Kristin, John Candler. BA, Mercer U., 1967; postgrad., So. Bapt. Theol. Sem., 1967—70; MSW, U. Louisville, 1971. Cert. social worker Ky., DC. Exec. dir. Ky. Civil Liberties Union, Louisville, 1971—72; dir. Cmty. Residential Treatment Svcs., Louisville, 1973—78; program mgr. Field Svcs., Louisville, 1978—80, Exploited and Missing Child Unit, Louisville, 1980—84; exec. v.p., COO Nat. Ctr. for Missing and Exploited Children, Washington, 1984—2006, COO, 1984—, exec. v.p., 2006—. Mem. Alderman's Task Force on Social Svcs., Louisville, 1982, Mayor's City Youth Commn., Louisville, 1983-84; trainer and/or cons. to numerous agys. in U.S., U.K., Can., Mex., Belgium, Germany, Austria, Netherlands. Contbr. articles to profl. jours., chapters to books. Recipient Key to City of Louisville, 1983, Disting. Alumnus award U. Louisville, 1985, 2003, Russell L. Colling Lit. award Internat. Assn. for Healthcare Security and Safety, 1991; named hon. chief of police City of Louisville, 1982; Alumni fellow U. Louisville, 1999. Mem. ACLU, NASW, Nat. Sheriff's Assn., Nat. Coun. Juvenile and Family Ct. Judges, Internat. Juvenile Officers Assn., Acad. Cert. Social Workers, Internat. Assn. Healthcare Safety and Security, Am. Soc. Indsl. Security, Internat. Assn. Chiefs of Police. Baptist (deacon). Avocations: photography, hunting, fishing, internet. Home: 13519 Oak Ivy Ln Fairfax VA 22033-1230 Office: Nat Ctr for Missing and Exploited Children 699 Prince St Alexandria VA 22314-3117 Office Phone: 703-837-6216. Business E-Mail: jrabun@ncmec.org.

RABURN, VERN L., air transportation executive, former internet company executive; b. Okla., 1950; m. Dottie Raburn. Student in Aeronautical Engring., Calif. Polytechnical Inst., San Luis Obispo; BS in Indsl. Tech., Long Beach State Univ., 1976. With 3M Corp.; pres., consumer products divsn., to corp. v.p. Microsoft Corp., 1979—82; exec. v.p., gen. mgr. Lotus Devel. Corp.; chmn., CEO Symantec Corp., Slate Corp.; pres. Paul Allen Group; founder Eclipse Aviation, Albuquerque, 1998—. Bd. dir. Experimental Aircraft Assn.; exec. coun., Rsch., Engring, Devel. Adv. Com. FAA; presdl. adv. bd. Embry-Riddle Aeronautical Univ. Named a Time 100 Innovator, 2001; named one of 50 Who Matter Now, Business 2.0, 2007; recipient Michael A. Chowdry Aviation Entrepreneur of Yr. award, Airport Jour., 2005. Office: Eclipse Aviation 2503 Clark Carr Loop SE Albuquerque NM 87106 Office Phone: 505-245-7555. *

RABUS, DOMINIK GERHARD, electrical engineer, researcher; b. Stuttgart, Germany, July 21, 1973; arrived in U.S., 2005; s. Gerhard Eugen and Rosemarie Irmgard Rabus; m. Regina Maria Elisabeth Fischer-Fels, July 20, 2002; children: Anouk Marjorie, Tizian Dominik. Dipl.-Ing., U. Stuttgart, Germany, 1999; Dr.-Ing., Tech. U. Berlin, 2002. Rsch. assoc. Fraunhofer Inst. for Telecom., Heinrich-Hertz-Inst., Berlin, 1999—2002, postdoctoral rsch. fellow, 2002—03; sr. rsch. scientist Forschungszentrum Karlsruhe GmbH, Germany, 2003—05; Feodor Lynen fellow U. Calif., Santa Cruz, 2006—07. Reviewer European Commn., Directorate Gen. Info. Soc., Natural Sciences and Engring. Rsch. Coun. Can. Author: (textbook) Integrated Ring Resonators, 2007. With Germany Navy, 1993—94. Recipient Exceptional reward "power engring.", 28. Landeswettbewerb of "Jugend forscht", 1993, Environ. award, City of Stuttgart, 1992, Umweltwettbewerb der Terratec, 1993. Mem.: IEEE Laser and Electro-optics Soc., Conv. of Socs. of Elec. Engrs. of Europe, Assn. for Elec., Electronic and Info. Techs./Info. Tech. Soc. Achievements include patents in field; patents pending in field. Avocations: sailing, motor biking, windsurfing. Office: U Calif Santa Cruz 1156 High St Santa Cruz CA 95064 Home Phone: 18314201892. Office Fax: 18314594829. Business E-Mail: rabus@soe.ucsc.edu.

RABUZZI, DANIEL D., medical association administrator; b. Pitts., June 19, 1935; s. Daniel Ralph and Victoria (Bruni) R.; m. Kathryn Allen, June 11, 1958; children: Daniel, Matthew, Douglas. AB, Harvard Coll., 1957; MD, U. Pa., 1961. Diplomate Am. Bd. Otolaryngology. Instr. otolaryngology U. Md., Balt., 1967-68; asst. prof. SUNY, Syracuse, 1968-71, assoc. prof., 1971-77, prof., 1977-81, clin. prof. otolaryngology, 1984-97, emeritus prof., 1997—; prof., chmn. N.Y. Med. Coll. and N.Y. Eye & Ear Infirmary, NYC, 1981-84. Pres. St. Joseph's Hops. Med. Staff, Syracuse, 1990-92; med. dir. Harrison Surgery Ctr., 1996—. Contbr. 55 articles to profl. jours., chpts. to books. Capt. U.S. Army, 1966-68. Fellow ACS; mem. Am. Soc. Head and Neck Surgery, Am. Acad. Otoloaryngology, Am. Cancer Soc. (pres. County unit 1978-80), Onondaga County Med. Soc. (pres. 1987-88). Avocations: roman archeology, european travel, golf, historical readings. Office: Harrison Outpatient Surgery Ctr 550 Harrison St Ste 230 Syracuse NY 13202-3064 Home Phone: 315-446-5225; Office Phone: 315-472-4424. Personal E-mail: buzdoc@verizon.net.

RABY, AREND CHRISTOPHER, sales executive; s. Mark and Linda Raby; m. Jennifer L. Raby, June 8, 2001; children: Rilee E., Kennedy G. Student (hon.), Sweetwater U., Fort Wayne, Ind., 2002—04. Cert. computer specialist Apple, Inc, Cupertino, Calif., 2002, Digidesign ProTools 100 level Digidesign, Palo Alto, Calif., 2003; lic. real estate agt. Ind., 2007. Sales team leader Sweetwater Sound, Inc, Fort Wayne, 2002—; CEO, cons., educator ABM Holdings, DBA, Fort Wayne, Ind., 2003—. Author: (manual) A?V Electronics: How A/D Converters Work; editor: (catalog) Sweetwater Gear Encyclopedia, 2002—05; tech. cons. (DVDdocumentary) Type O Negative: Symphony for the Devil, 2006, (album) Type O Negative: Dead Again, 2007. Worship leader Christian Family Ctr., Adrian, Mich., 1994—96. Mem.: Mensa (Top 2 award). Office: Sweetwater Sound Inc 5501 US Hwy 30 W Fort Wayne IN 46818 Home Phone: 260-484-3407; Office Phone: 800-222-4700 1276.

RABY, JULIAN, art gallery director; b. London, Eng., 1950; m. Lorna Raby. PhD in Oriental Stdues, Univ. Oxford, 1981. Lectr. in Islamic Art & Architecture Univ. Oxford, England, 1979—2002; chmn. of curators Oriental Inst., 1991—93, 1995—2000, chmn. of bd, faculty of Oriental Studies, 1993—95; dir. Freer Gallery of Art and Arthur M. Sackler Gallery, Smithsonian Instn., Washington, 2002—. Founder, former co-owner Azimuth Editors publisher. Series founder and editor Oxford Studies in Islamic Art; author: Venice, Durer, and the Oriental Mode, 1982, IZNIK: The Pottery of Ottoman Turkey, 1989, Turkish Bookbinding in the 15th Century, The foundation of a Court Style, 1993, Qajar Portraits, 1999. Fellow: Soc. of Antiquaries; mem.: Coun. of Britis Inst. of Archaeology and History, Amman, Jordan. Office: Freer Gallery of Art Smithsonian Instn MCR707 PO Box 37012 Washington DC 20013-7012 Office Phone: 202-633-4880. Office Fax: 202-357-4911.

RABY, KENNETH ALAN, lawyer, retired military officer; b. Dec. 29, 1935; s. Carl George and Helen Josette (Milne) R.; m. Shirley Rae Nelson, June 2, 1957; children: Randolph Carlton, Shelly Ann. BA, U. S.D., 1957, JD, 1960; grad. with honors, Command and Gen. Staff Coll., 1975, U.S. Army War Coll., 1981. Bar: US Ct. Mil. Appeals 1961, Supreme Ct. SD 1960, US Supreme Ct. 1968, US Ct. Mil. Review 1983, DC Ct. Appeals 1983, Ga. 1988, Ga. Ct. Appeals 1988. Commd. 2d lt. U.S. Army, 1957, chief mil. def. counsel U.S. vs. Calley (My Lai Massacre), 1969—71, chief legal team Inf. Sch. Ft. Benning, Ga., 1969-71, advanced through grades to col. JAGC, 1979, staff judge adv. Armor Ctr. Ft. Knox, Ky., 1979—80, ret., 1987; dep. staff judge adv. Am. Divsn., Chu Lai, Vietnam, 1968-69; team chief, acting divsn. chief adminstrv. law divsn. Dept. Army Dept. Army, TJAG, 1971-74, chief criminal law divsn., 1981-84; staff judge adv. Hdqs. 24th Inf. Divsn., Ft. Stewart, Ga., 1974-79; sr. judge Army Ct. Mil. Rev., Falls Church, Va., 1984-87; staff atty. Ga. Ct. Appeals, 1987—2005; ret., 2006. Former chmn., mem. Joint Svc. Com. on Mil. Justice, 1981-84; mem. Mil. Justice Act of 1983 Adv. Commn., 1984-87; army liaison to criminal law sect. ABA, 1981-84. Eagle Scout Boy Scouts Am., 1952—53. Decorated Legion of Merit, Bronze Star with oak leaf cluster, Meritorious Svc. medal with 2 oak leaf clusters, Joint Svc. Commendation medal, Air medal, Army Commendation medal with oak leaf cluster, Army Achievement medal. Mem.: FBA (chmn. law enforcement liaison com. 1986—87), SD Bar Assn., Ga. Bar Assn., Assn. U.S. Army, Masons (32d degree, KCCH), Order Ea. Star (grand chpt. Ga. 1999—2000, worthy grand patron 1999—2000, gen. grand chpt. parliamentarian 2003—06, 2006—), Scottish Rite, Royal Order Scotland (hon.), Arturo Reghine Lodge (Italy) (hon.), Theta Xi, Delta Theta Phi. Home: 575 Spender Trace Atlanta GA 30350-5017 Personal E-mail: alanraby@bellsouth.net.

RABY, WILLIAM LOUIS, writer, consultant; b. Chgo., July 16, 1927; s. Gustave E. and Helen (Burgess) R.; m. Norma Claire Schreiner, Sept. 8, 1956 (dec. Feb. 2006); children: Burgess, Marianne, Marlene. BSBA, Northwestern U., 1949; MBA, U. Ariz., 1961, PhD, 1971. Ptnr. VAR CPA Firms, 1950-76, Touche Ross & Co., NYC, 1977-87; ret. ptnr. Deloitte & Touche, NYC. Pres. Ariz. State Bd. Accountancy, 1993-94; mem. Ariz. State Bd. Tax Appeals, 1994-2006, chmn., 1997-99, 2003-05; prof. acctg. emeritus Ariz. State U.; columnist Tax Notes mag., Arlington, Va., 1990—; cons. on video and audio tax edn. tapes Bisk Pub. Co., 1992—. Author: The Income Tax and Business Decisions, 1964, Building and Maintaining a Successful Tax Practice, 1964, The Reluctant Taxpayer, 1970, Tax Practice Management, 1974, Introduction to Federal Taxation, annually, 1980-91, Tax Practice Management: Client Servicing, 1986; editor: Raby Report on Tax Practice, 1986-96, PPC Guide To Successful Tax Practice, 1991; mem. editorial adv. bd. Practical Tax Strategies; contbr. articles to profl. jours. Mem. AICPA (chmn. fed. tax divsn. 1980-83, v.p. 1983-84, coun. 1983-90), Tax Ct. Bar. Presbyterian (elder, United Presbyn. Ch. chmn. adv. coun. on ch. and soc. 1979-81). Office: PO Box 26846 Tempe AZ 85285-6846 Home Phone: 480-756-4333; Office Phone: 480-967-1501. Personal E-mail: rabyw@aol.com.

RACCAH, DOMINIQUE MARCELLE, publisher; b. Paris, Aug. 24, 1956; arrived in U.S., 1964; d. Paul and Colette Raccah; m. Raymond W. Bennett, Aug. 20, 1980; 3 children. BA, U. Ill., Chgo., 1978; MS, U. Ill., Champaign-Urbana, 1981. Rsch. analyst Leo Burnett Advt., Chgo., 1980-81, rsch. supr., 1981-84, assoc. rsch. dir., 1984-87; pres., pub., owner Sourcebooks, Inc., Naperville, Ill., 1987—; co-CEO Login Pubs. Consortium, Chgo., 1990-99. Author: Financial Sourcebooks' Sources, 1987; editor: Poetry Speaks, 2001, Poetry Speaks to Children, 2005, The Sourcebooks Shakespeare, 2005. Bd. dirs. Com. of 200, Book Industry Study Group. Recipient Blue Chip Enterprise award, 2000, Ernst & Young Entrepreneur of Yr. Ill. and N.W. Ind., 2000; named to Inc. 500 list; inducted into Univ. Ill. Entrepreneurship Hall of Fame, 2001. Mem. Pubs. Mktg. Assn., Am. Booksellers Assn., Am. Assn. Pubs. Office: Sourcebooks Inc 1935 Brookdale Rd # 139 Naperville IL 60563-9245 Office Phone: 630-961-3900. Business E-Mail: dominique.raccah@sourcebooks.com.

RACE, GEORGE JUSTICE, pathology educator; b. Everman, Tex., Mar. 2, 1926; s. Claude Ernest and Lila Eunice (Bunch) R.; m. Annette Isabelle Rinker, Dec. 21, 1946; children: George William Daryl, Jonathan Clark, Mark Christopher, Jennifer Anne (dec.), Elizabeth Margaret Rinker. MD, U. Tex., Southwestern Med. Sch., 1947; MS in Pub. Health, U. N.C., 1953; PhD in Ultrastructural Anatomy and Microbiology, Baylor U., 1969. Intern Duke Hosp., 1947-48, asst. resident pathology, 1951-53; intern Boston City Hosp., 1948-49; asst. pathologist Peter Bent Brigham Hosp., Boston, 1953-54; pathologist St. Anthony's Hosp., St. Petersburg, Fla., 1954-55; staff pathologist Children's Med. Center, Dallas, 1955-59; dir. labs. Baylor U. Med. Center, Dallas, 1959-86, chief dept. pathology, 1959-86, vice chmn. exec. com. med. bd., 1970-72; cons. pathologist VA Hosp., Dallas, 1955-71; adj. prof. anthropology and biology So. Meth. U., Dallas, 1969; instr. pathology Duke, 1951-53, Harvard Med. Sch., 1953-54; asst. prof. pathology U. Tex. Southwestern Med. Sch., 1955-58, clin. assoc. prof., 1958-64, clin. prof., 1964-72, prof., 1973-94, prof. emeritus, 1994—, dir. Cancer Center, 1973-76, assoc. dean for continuing edn., 1973-94, emeritus assoc. dean, 1994—. Pathologist-in-chief Baylor U. Med. Ctr., 1959-86, prof. biomed. studies Baylor Grad. sch., 1989-94; chmn. Baylor Rsch. Found., 1986-89; prof. microbiology Baylor Coll. Dentistry, 1962-68, prof. pathology, 1964-68, prof., chmn. dept. pathology 1969-73, dean A. Webb Roberts Continuing Edn., 1973-94; spl. advisor on human and animal diseases to gov. State of Tex., 1979-83. Editor: Laboratory Medicine (4 vols.), 1973, 10th edit., 1983; Contbr. articles to profl. jours., chpts. to textbooks. Pres., Tex. div. Am. Cancer Soc., 1970; chmn. Gov.'s Task Force on Higher Edn., 1981. Served with AUS, 1944-46; flight surgeon USAF, 1948-51, Korea. Decorated Air medal. Fellow AAAS, Coll. Am. Pathologists, Am. Soc. Clin. Pathologists; mem. AMA (chmn. multiple discipline research forum 1969), Am. Assn. Pathologists, Internat. Acad. Pathology, Am. Assn. Med. Colls., Explorers Club (dir., v.p. 1993-2000), Sigma Xi, Alpha Omega Alpha. Fax: 214-526-8607. E-mail: georgejrace@yahoo.com.

RACE, TIM, editor; BA, Miami Univ., 1978; MA, Bowling Green State Univ., 1980; MS in journalism, Am. Univ., 1983. Editor CMP Publications; exec. editor Comm. Week; editor, Bus. World sect. New York Times, 1989—91, info. tech. & media editor, 1991—97, founding editor, Circuits sect., 1997—98, editor, Monday Bus. sect., 1998—2004, tech. & health care editor, 2004—. Mem.: Assn. Healthcare Journalists. Office: New York Times 620 8th Ave New York NY 10018 Office Phone: 212-556-1526. Office Fax: 212-556-1448. Business E-Mail: timrace@nytimes.com.

RACER, WILLIAM EUGENE, retired music educator; b. Kansas City, Mo., Sept. 20, 1942; s. Hershcel F. and Alice Taylor Racer; m. Janice Mullinix, Jan. 3, 2007; children: James Mullinix, Jonathan Mullinix, Tim, Brent, Holly Rector, William Akin. B Music Edn., Okla. Bapt. U., Shawnee, 1963; M Music Edn., Wichita State U., Kans., 1968; MS in Edn., Ctrl. Mo. State U., Warrensburg, 1975; EdD, U. Kans., Lawrence, 1985. Tchr. Attica schs., Kans., 1963—65, Wichita Unified Sch. Dist., 1965—66, Augusta Unified Sch. Dist., Kans., 1966—67, Rose Hill schs., Kans., 1967—70, Belton schs., Mo., 1971—80, Henderson CC, Ky., 1981—82; reading supr. English Augusta Pub. Sch., 1982—2001; tchr. Butler CC, 1996—. Adj. instr. Wichita State U., 1995, Newman Coll., Wichita, 1997; organist Bethany Luth. Ch., Kansas City, Mo., 1970—82, Gloria Dei Luth. Ch., Wichita, 1982—2003; concert organist, 1965—2005. Pres. Kiwanis, Augusta, 1987. Grantee, NDEA, Burlington, Vt., 1969. Mem.: Assn. Disciples Musicians (lectr. 1995), Am. Guild Organists (pres. Kansas City chpt. 1964, cert., bd. dirs.). Democrat. Mem. Christian Ch. (Disciples Of Christ). Home: 805 Glenmoor Wichita KS 67206

RACHANOW, GERALD MARVIN, lawyer, pharmacist; b. Balt., Aug. 7, 1942; s. Louis and Lillyan (Binstock) R.; m. Sally Davis, July 26, 1964; children: Mindy, Shelly, Gary. BS in Pharmacy, U. Md., 1965; JD, U. Balt., 1972. Bar: Md. 1973, U.S. Dist. Ct. Md. 1977, U.S. Supreme Ct. 1977. Consumer safety officer FDA, Rockville, Md., 1973-96, dep. dir. divsn. OTC drug evaluation, 1978-96, regulatory counsel divsn. OTC drug products, 1996—2005, regulatory counsel office nonprescription products, 2005—; ptnr. Rachanow & Wolfson, Owings Mills, Eldersburg, Md., 1975—. Contbr. fed. drug law exam. Nat. Assn. Bds. Pharmacy, 1985. Contbr. articles to profl. jours. Fellow Am. Soc. Pharmacy Law; mem. ABA, Soc. FDA Pharmacists, Heuisler Honor Soc. Avocations: chess, stamp and coin collecting, sports. Home: 6700 Sweet Clover Ct Eldersburg MD 21784-6385 Office: US FDA 10903 New Hampshire Ave Bldg 22 Rm 5496 Silver Spring MD 20903-0002 Home Phone: 410-549-7713; Office Phone: 301-796-0977. Business E-Mail: gerald.rachanow@fda.hhs.gov.

RACHEL, DAVID P., lawyer; JD, John Marshall Law Sch., Atlanta, 2003. Atty. The Rachel Law Group, P.C., Atlanta, 2004—. Mem.: ABA (assoc.). Office: The Rachel Law Group PC 2625 Cumberland Pky SE Ste 110 Atlanta GA 30339 Office Phone: 770-805-0087. Office Fax: 770-805-0089. Business E-Mail: drachel@rachellaw.com.

RACHELEFSKY, GARY STUART, medical educator; b. NYC, 1942; BS, Columbia Coll., 1963. Intern Bellevue Hosp. Ctr., NYC, 1967-68; resident in pediatrics Johns Hopkins Hosp., 1968-70, Ctr. Disease Control, 1970-72; fellow UCLA Med. Ctr., 1972-74; prof. allergy and immunology, dir. exec. care UCLA, Ctr. Asthma, Allergy and Immunology. Fellow Am. Acad. Allergy, Asthma and Immunology (bd. dirs., past pres.). Mailing: 14933 Alva Dr Pacific Palisades CA 90272 Office Phone: 310-754-6884. Personal E-mail: rachruss@ix.netcom.com.

RACHLIN, HARVEY BRANT, writer; b. Phila., June 23, 1951; s. Philip and Mazie (Drucker) R.; m. Marla Sivak Goldwert, June 28, 1987; 1 child, Glenn. BA in Biology, Hofstra U., Hempstead, NY, 1973. With music pub. cos., 1973—; owner Western Hemisphere Music Co., Ellipsis Music Mgmt. Co., Manhasset Hills, NY, 1975—, pres., 1982-92; mem. faculty Five Towns Coll., Seaford, NY, 1978-84, Manhattanville Coll., Purchase, NY, 1995—. Author: The Songwriter's Handbook, 1977 (NY Pub. Libr. Book for Teen Age 1979-82); The Encyclopedia of the Music Business, 1981 (Outstanding Music Reference Source ALA 1981, ASCAP-Deems Taylor award 1982, Writer's Digest Book Club Spl. Selection, included in Selected Bibliography for Musicians Libr. of Congress); Love Grams, 1983; The Money Encyclopedia, 1984 (Outstanding Fin. Reference Book, Libr. Jour., 1984, Ency. Britannica Home Libr. selection); The Kennedys: A Chronological History 1823--, 1986; The Songwriter's and Musician's Guide to Making Great Demos, 1988 (NY Pub. Libr. Book for Teen Age 1989); The Making of a Cop, 1991 (NY Pub. Libr. Book for Teen Age, 1992), The Songwriter's Workshop, 1991, The TV and Movie Business: An Encyclopedia of Careers, Technologies, and Practices, 1991 (Fireside Theatre Book Club main selection), The Making of a Detective, 1995 (featured on Good Morning America, NYPD Retired Detectives Assn. award), Lucy's Bones, Sacred Stones, and Einstein's Brain, 1996 (History Book Club selection, named one of best books in print The Reader's Catalog 1997, Best Books Young Adult Readers Grades 7-12, 1997, Pub. Libr Catalog, 1999, Sr. HS Libr. Catalog, 1997-02); co-writer, cons. adapted as three-part TV mini-series History's Lost and Found (daily series on The History Channel, CineGold Eagle award 2000), Jumbo's Hide, Elvis's Ride, and the Tooth of Buddha, 2000 (Book-of-the-Month Club's Quality Paperback Book Club selection), Scandals, Vandals, and Da Vincis: A Gallery of Remarkable Art Tales, 2007; free-lance music journalist; contbr. Songwriter Mag., 1978—, Law and Order Mag., 1992—, Songwriter's Market, 1979-80, 87, 92, The Writer, 2005, Wal St. Jour., 2007; guest on The Joe Franklin Show, 1977, 81, The Dinah Shore Show, 1978, Nine Broadcast Plaza, 1991, The Sally Jessy Raphael Show, 1993, The Late Late Show with Tom Snyder, 1996; compositions performed L.I. Mandolin and Guitar Orch., 1988; featured in NY Times, 1982, 96, Pro-Music, 1982, Something About the Author, 1987, Valley Stream Herald, 1995-96, 98, Writer's Market, 1994, Newsday, 1996, 99, 07, Sarasota Herald-Tribune, 1996, Coral Springs Forum, 1997, L.I. Lifestyles, 2000, City Line News, 2001, Recess for Tchrs., 2005, Northwest Herald, 2007, The Windsor Star, 2007. Recipient Outstanding Reference Book of Yr. award, ALA, 1981, award, Libr. Jour., 1984. Mem.: Am. Soc. Journalists and Authors. Home: 878 Warner Rd Valley Stream NY 11580-1526 Home Phone: 516-568-1795; Office Phone: 516-568-1795. Personal E-mail: hbrachlin@msn.com.

RACHLIN, LAUREN DAVID, lawyer; b. Buffalo, Feb. 6, 1929; s. Harry A. and Thelma (Goldberg) R.; m. Jean K. Rachlin, June 27, 1954; children: Laura Gail, Ellen Joan, James N. BS, U. Buffalo, 1948; JD, Harvard U., 1951. Bar: NY 1952, U.S. Dist. Ct. (no. and we. dists.) NY 1952, U.S. Tax Ct. 1952, U.S. Supreme Ct. 1958, U.S. Ct. Appeals (2d cir.) 1967, U.S. Ct. Internat. Trade 1978. Ptnr. Rachlin & Rachlin, Buffalo, 1952—81; sr. ptnr. Kavinoky & Cook, Buffalo, 1981—2003; ptnr. Hodgson Russ, LLP, Buffalo and Toronto, 2003—. U.S. appointee to Bi-nat. Dispute Settlement Panel created under U.S.-Can. Free Trade Agreement, 1989-93; U.S. appointee N.Am. Free Trade Agreement Bi-Nat. Dispute Settlement Panel, 1994-96, 2004-; arbitrator Internat. C. of C., Am. Arbitration Assn.; founder and dir. Can./U.S. Border Alliance regionalizing the bi-national trade corridor linking Toronto, Hamilton, Buffalo, Syracuse and Rochester, 1996—; founder, past pres., dir. World Trade Ctr.-Buffalo Niagara, 1986—; lectr. in field. U.S. del. to UN Human Rights Commn., 1970; cons. to temporary commn. NY State Constl. Conv.; mem. Erie County Charter Rev. Commn.; mem.-at-large U.S. Nat. Commn. for UNESCO, 1972-76, chmn. human rights task force; mem. industry functional adv. com. Customs for Trade Policy Matters of U.S. Dept. Commerce, Office U.S. Trade Rep., 1987—. Mem. ABA (fgn. investment in U.S. real estate com., internat. bus. law com., subcom. on trade import), NY State Bar Assn. (founding chmn. internat. sect. 1987-89, chmn. internat. divsn. 1989-94, chair legal edn. and admission to bar com. 1999-2002, ADR com. 2005—, award for distinction in internat. law and affairs Internat. Law and Practice sect. 2005), World Arbitration Inst. (adv. bd., bd. dirs.), Am. Assn. Exporters & Importers (trade policy com.), Interpacific Bar Assn., Interam. Bar Assn., Customs and Internat. Trade Bar Assn., Erie County Bar Assn, Industry Trade Adv. Commn. on Customs and Trade Facilitation, US Dept. Commerce. Office: Hodgson Russ LLP Ste 2000 1 M & T Plz Buffalo NY 14203-2391 Address: Ste 2309 150 King St W Toronto ON M5H 1J9 Canada Office Phone: 716-848-1460.

RACHOFSKY, DAVID J., lawyer; b. Oceanside, NY, Nov. 17, 1936; s. Lester M. and Marjorie A.; m. Faith Allen; children: Robert, Patricia, Edward. BSEE, MIT, 1958; JD, Temple U., 1968. Bar: Pa., U.S. Dist. Ct. (ea. dist.) Pa., U.S. Tax. Ct., U.S. Ct. Fed. Claims, Pa. Supreme Ct. 1968. Of counsel Dechert LLP, Phila., 1968—. Lectr. law Temple U. Law Sch., 1976-95. Contbr. articles to profl. jours. With USAF, 1969-72. Mem. Phila. Bar Assn., Internat. Fiscal Assn. (chmn. mid-Atlantic region 1985-87, mem. coun. 1986—, mem. exec. com. 1992—, v.p., sec. 1992-96, exec. v.p. 1996-98, pres. 1998-2000). Office: Dechert LLP 2929 Arch St Philadelphia PA 19104-2808

RACHOFSKY, HOWARD, retired investor, art collector, patron; m. Cindy Rachofsky, 2000; children: Meghan, Matthew. Former bd. chmn. Regal Securities Investment, L.P. Bd. dirs. Dallas Symphony Assn., Dallas Mus. Art, NYC Dia Ctr. for the Arts, East Dallas Cmty. Sch., Tate Lecture Series, So. Methodist U.; adv. dir. Booker T. Washington Magnet HS for the Performing and Visual Arts, Dallas Theater Ctr., Dallas Archtl. Found., U. Tex. Sch. Architecture; founder, bd. dirs. Dallas Ctr. for the Performing Arts Found., chair, site design com.; mem. adv. bd. Wharton Club, Dallas/Ft. Worth, Dallas Bus. Com. for the Arts; founder Howard Earl

Rachofsky Found.; mem. investment com. St. Phillips Acad. Named one of Top 200 Collectors, ARTnews mag., 2003—06. Avocation: Collector of Contemporary Art. Address: Dallas Ctr for the Performing Arts Found 2106 Boll St Dallas TX 75204

RACHOR, JEFFREY C., automotive supplies company executive; Region v.p. mid-south Sonic Automotive, Inc., Charlotte, NC, 1997—98, v.p. retail ops., 1998—99, exec. v.p. retail ops., 1999—2002, exec. v.p., COO, 2002—04, pres., COO, 2004—07; pres., CEO The Pep Boys-Manny, Moe & Jack, Phila., 2007—. Office: The Pep Boys-Manny Moe & Jack 3111 West Allegheny Ave Philadelphia PA 19132 *

RACHOW, LOUIS A(UGUST), librarian; b. Shickley, Nebr., Jan. 21, 1927; s. John Louis and Mable (Dondlinger) R. BS, York Coll., 1948; MS in L.S., Columbia U., 1959. Librarian York Coll., Nebr., 1949-54; instr. library asst. Queens Coll., NYC, 1956-57; serials acquisition asst. Columbia U. Law Library, NYC, 1957-58; asst. librarian Univ. Club, NYC, 1958-62; librarian Hampden-Booth Theatre Library at the Players, NYC, 1962-86, curator, 1986-88; library dir. Internat. Theatre Inst. U.S., NYC, 1989—2002. Cons. theatre sect. U. Calif., San Diego, new campuses program, 1964, Music Ctr. Operating Archives, Los Angeles, 1985; mem. library adv. bd. Eugene O'Neill Meml. Theatre Center, 1966— Editor, compiler: Guide to Performing Arts, 1968; assoc. editor Am. Notes and Queries, 1971-74, asst. editor, 1967-71; mem. editorial adv. bd. Nat. Dir. for Performing Arts and Civic Ctrs.; editor Performing Arts series Gale Info. Guide, 1976-83, Theatre and Performing Arts Collections, 1981; contbr. articles and revs. to profl. jours. Mem. adv. bd. Am. Theatre Co., OKC Theatre Prodns. Served with AUS, 1954-56 Mem. Theatre Libr. Assn. (rec. sec. 1966-67, pres. 1967-72, 81-83, v.p. 1976-80, editor Broadside 1973-81), ALA, Spl. Librs. Assn. (sec.-treas. mus. group N.Y.C. chpt. 1964-66), N.Y. Libr. Club (pres. 1979-80), Am. Theatre Assn., New Drama Forum Assn. (pres. 1983-86), Am. Soc. Theatre Rsch., N.Y. Tech. Svcs. Librs., Archons of Colophon (convener 1982-83), Episcopal Actors Guild Am. (bd. dirs. 1976-2002, v.p. 2002—), Drama Desk, Broadway Theatre Inst. Outer Critics Circle (treas. 1998—), Players Club, The Lambs Club. Home: 528 W 114th St New York NY 10025-7841

RACHOW, SHARON DIANNE, realtor; b. St. Joseph, Mo., Apr. 12, 1939; d. Norman DeLos Zancker and Sylvia Lavina (Hawkins) Trouel; m. Thomas Eugene Rachow, Oct. 22, 1968; children: Todd A., Tiffany K. Student, So. Ill. U., 1969-72. Sec. Westab, Inc. (now Mead), St. Joseph, 1957-60, Seitz Packing Co. (now Sara Lee), St. Joseph, 1960-66; exec. asst. to v.p., gen. mgr. Kansas City (Mo.) Chiefs, 1972; co-owner, mgr. Pool 'N Patio Plus, St. Joseph, 1973-84; realtor Coldwell Banker Gen. Realtors, St. Joseph, 1984-93, RE/MAX, 1993—2004, Evans Realty, 2004—. Trustee Nat. Multiple Sclerosis Soc., Mid Am. chpt., Midland M.S. Express Br., 1993-98. Mem.: Real Estate Buyers Agt. Coun. (accredited buyers rep. 1996—), St. Joseph Regional Bd. Realtors (residential specialist 1987—, Multi-List com. 1993—2002, bd. dirs. 1994, forms com. 1994—2002, Top Residential Sales award 1986—, Top 10), Multi Million Dollar Club (quality svc. cert. 2001, quality svc. cert. 2003). Republican. Lutheran. Home: 4211 Country Ln Saint Joseph MO 64506-2454 Office: Evans Realty 606 S Woodbine Rd Saint Joseph MO 64507 Office Phone: 816-390-8000. Business E-Mail: sharonr@stjoelive.com.

RACINE, KARL A., lawyer; b. Port au Prince, Haiti, Dec. 14, 1962; Student French, French civilization, Sorbonne, Paris; BA in Economics, U. Pa., 1985; JD, U. Va., 1989. Bar: Md. 1989, DC 1992. Litig. assoc. Venable LLP, Washington, 1989—92, ptnr., corp. and civil litig. groups, 2002—, dep. mng. ptnr., 2005—06, mng. ptnr., 2006—; staff atty. Pub. Defender Svc., Washington, 1992—94; ptnr. Cacheris & Treanor, Washington, 1994—97; assoc. counsel The White House, Washington, 1997—2000. Achievements include co-producing the first Haitian/Creole/English legal dictionary, 1994. Office: Venable LLP 575 Seventh St NW Washington DC 20004 Office Phone: 202-344-8322. Office Fax: 202-344-8300. E-mail: karacine@venable.com.

RACINE, RICHARD B., lawyer; b. Cleve., Mar. 20, 1956; BS in Chem., Georgetown U., 1978; JD, Case Western Reserve U., 1981. Bar: Ohio 1981, DC 1984, registered: US Patent & Trademark Office. Ptnr. Finnegan, Henderson, Farabow, Garrett & Dunner LLP, Washington, mng. ptnr., leader, chem. practice group, mem. mgmt. com., mem. compensation com. Mem.: ABA (subcom. chmn. atty. opinions com. 1993—94), Intellectual Property Owners Assn. (lectr. 2006), Southwestern Legal Found. (lectr. 1993—94, lectr. patent resources group 2005—), Fed. Cir. Bar Assn., Am. Chem. Soc. (program chmn. 1991—93, divsn. chmn. elect 1993, divsn. chmn. 1994), Am. Intellectual Property Law Assn., Bar Assn. DC, DC Bar. Office: Finnegan Henderson Farabow Garrett Dunner LLP 901 New York Ave NW Washington DC 20001-3315 Office Phone: 202-408-4038. Office Fax: 202-408-4400. Business E-Mail: rich.racine@finnegan.com.

RACINE, SCOTT H., lawyer; b. Chgo. BA, Bradley U., 1972; JD cum laude, Pepperdine U., 1978; LLM in Tax., NYU, 1979. Bar: Calif. 1978, US Dist. Ct. (ctrl., so. districts) Calif., US Ct. of Appeals (9th cir.), US Tax Ct., US Ct. of Claims. Law clk. Judge William M. Drennen US Tax Ct., 1979—80; shareholder tax specialty firm, LA; ptnr., chair, tax practice group LA Akin Gump Strauss Hauer & Feld LLP, LA. Adj. prof. law Pepperdine Univ., 1980—, Univ. San Diego, 1983—87, Loyola Univ., 2000—. Student writings editor Pepperdine Law Rev., 1976—78; author: numerous articles for profl. publs. Bd. visitors Pepperdine Univ. Sch. Law; bd. adv. Loyola Univ. Sch. Law; planning com. Univ. So. Calif. Tax Inst. Mem.: ABA (sect. on tax.), Calif. Bar Assn. (sect. on tax.), LA County Bar Assn. (sect. on tax.). Office: Akin Gump Strauss Hauer & Feld LLP Ste 2400 2029 Century Pk E Los Angeles CA 90067-3012 Office Phone: 310-229-1059. Office Fax: 310-229-1001. Business E-Mail: sracine@akingump.com.

RACITI, CHERIE, artist; b. Chgo., June 17, 1942; d. Russell J. and Jacque (Crimmins) R. Student, Memphis Coll. Art, 1963-65; BA in Art, San Francisco State U., 1968; M.F.A., Mills Coll., 1979. Assoc. prof. art San Francisco State U., 1984—89, prof., 1989—2007, prof. emeritus, 2007—. Lectr. Calif. State U., Hayward, 1974, San Francisco Art Inst., 1978; mem. artist com. San Francisco Art Inst., 1974-85, sec., 1980-81. One woman shows include U. Calif., Berkeley, 1972, Nicholas Wilder Gallery, L.A., 1975, San Francisco Art Inst., 1977, Marianne Deson Gallery, Chgo., 1980, Site 375, San Francisco, 1989, Reese Bullen Gallery, Humboldt State U., Arcata, Calif., 1990, Mills Coll. Art Mus., Oakland, Calif., 1998; group shows include Whitney Mus. Art, 1975, San Francisco Sci. Fiction, The Clocktower, N.Y.C., Otis-Parsons Gallery, Los Angeles, 1984-85, San Francisco Art Inst., 1985, Artists Space, N.Y.C., 1988, Angles Gallery, Santa Monica, 1987, Terrain Gallery, San Francisco, 1992, Ctr. for the Arts, San Francisco, 1993, Santa Monica Coll., 1998, 25/25 25th Anniversary Exhbn., So. Exposure Gallery, San Francisco, 1999, Santa Cruz Mus., 2003, Thacher Gallery U. San Francisco, 2004. Bd. dirs. New Langton Arts, 1988-92. Eureka fellow Fleishhacker Found., San Francisco, Va.Ctr. for Creative Arts fellow, Amherst, Va., 2005; recipient Adaline Kent award San Francisco Art Inst., 1976, Djerassi resident, 1994, Tyrone Guthrie Ctr. resident, Ireland, 1995, Millay Colony for Arts resident 1999, Juror's award Artadia San Francisco.

RACKLIN, BARBARA COHEN, fundraising consultant; b. NYC, Dec. 3, 1950; d. Harry Cohen and Shari Lillian (Greene) Cohen; m. Arthur Michael Racklin, Aug. 19, 1979 (div.); 1 child, Nicholas Michael. BA in Math., U. Tex., 1972; postgrad., U. LaVerne, 1981-82. Cert. histocompatability technologist, Am. Bd. Histocompatability and Immunogenetics; cert. fundraising exec. Asst. dir. transplant lab. Med. br. U. Tex., Galveston, 1974-76; transplant immunology specialist Montefiore Hosp., Bronx, N.Y., 1976-77; dir. pediat. immunology lab. Cedar Sinai Hosp., LA, 1977-79; supr. pathology lab. City of Hope Nat. Med. Ctr., Duarte, Calif., 1979-82, rsch. specialist transplant lab., 1982-85; staff coord. vol. devel. City of Hope Deve. Ctr., LA, 1986-88; coord. fin. devel. events ARC, Pasadena, Calif., 1995-99; co-owner benefit specialists Fundraising Cons., La Cañada, Calif., 1995-99; chief devel. officer San Gabriel chpt. ARC, 1999—2002; devel. dir. PSW region Anti-Defamation League, 2002—05; assoc. v.p. advancement Music Ctr. L.A. County, 2005—. Tour chmn. City of Hope Ann. Conv., Duarte, 1987, 89, 91. Contbr. or co-contbr. articles to profl. publs. Bd. dirs. City of Hope Med. Ctr., 1986-89, mem. bd. govs., 1991-93; mem. steering com. local parcel tax election, La Cañada, 1992, local sch. bd. election, 1995; mem. sch. bd. La Cañada Unified Sch. Dist., 1997-2001, clk. governing bd., 1999-2000, pres. gov. bd. 2000-01; pres. La Cañada Coun. PTA, 1995-97, City of Hope Aux., 1988-90; bd. dirs. LCF Ednl. Found., past pres., v.p., 1991-97; sec. Children's Hosp. Aux., 1994-97; auditor 1st Dist. PTA, 1997; chairperson youth com. Pasadena Temple, 1996-97; v.p. governing bd. La Canada Unified Sch. Dist., 1998-99; bd. dirs. southwest reg. B'nai B'rith Youth Orgn.; participant Leadership Pasadena, 1999-2000. Recipient Hon. Svc. award La Cañada Coun. PTA, 1996, Svc. award LCF Ednl. Found., 1995, Golden Apple award La Canada Unified Sch. Dist., 1996, Golden Bear award for Fundraising Excellence Am. Red Cross, 2001 Mem.: L.A. World Affairs Coun., Nat. Coun. Planned Giving, Calif. Advancement Rschrs. Assn., Assn. Fundraising Profls. Avocations: skiing, bowling, reading. Office: Music Ctr LA County 135 N Grand Ave Los Angeles CA 90012 Business E-Mail: bracklin@musiccenter.org.

RACKOW, ERIC C., hospital administrator; Grad., Franklin and Marshall Coll.; MD, SUNY, Downstate Med. Ctr., Brooklyn, 1971. Bd. cert. internal medicine, cardiovasc. diseases, critical care medicine, internal medicine, 1975, cardiology, 1977, critical care, 1987. Residency Kings County Hosp. Ctr., 1970—72, chief residency, 1972—73, clin. fellow, 1973—75; dir. clin. trials NYU Hosp. Ctr.; prof. heath care mgmt. NYU Med. Ctr., Sch. Medicine; sr. v.p., chief med. officer NYU Hosp. Ctr., NYC, 2000—04, pres., 2004—. Adj. prof. medicine NY Med. Coll.; chmn. emeritus St. Vincent's Hosp. & Med. Ctr. of NY, Dept. Medicine; hon. role, Physician-in-Chief Inst. Critical Care Medicine; past pres. Soc. Critical Care Medicine; past chair Am. Bd. Internal Medicine, Critical Care Medicine Subspecialty Bd. Contbr. articles to profl. jours. Office: NYU Hosps Ctr Sch Med HCC15 550 First Ave New York NY 10016 Office Phone: 212-263-2606. Business E-Mail: eric.rackow@nyumc.org.

RACKOW, JULIAN PAUL, lawyer; b. Phila., Dec. 16, 1941; s. Lawrence Lionel and Blanche (Wachman) R.; m. Paulette Schorr, June 23, 1963; children: Jeffrey A., Andrea B. AB, Cornell U., 1963; JD, Harvard U., 1966. Bar: Pa. 1966, US Dist. Ct. (ea. dist.) Pa. 1966. Assoc. atty. Goodis, Greenfield, Narin & Mann, Phila., 1966-69; ptnr., co-chmn. dept. real estate Blank, Rome LLP, Phila., 1970—. Exec. com., bd. dirs. Ctrl. Phila. Devel. Corp., 1990—, pres. 1996-2000, chmn., 2000—; bd. dirs. Ave of the Arts, Inc., 2000—, Parkway Coun. Found., 2004—. Mem. Phila. Bar Assn., Harvard Law Sch. Assn. Phila, Am. Coll. Real Estate Lawyers, Ave. of the Arts, Inc. Avocations: tennis, travel, piano. Office: Blank Rome LLP One Logan Sq Philadelphia PA 19103-6998 Office Phone: 215-569-5671. Business E-Mail: rackow@blankrome.com.

RACLIN, GRIER C., lawyer; BA, JD, Northwestern U. Vice chmn., mng. ptnr. Gardner, Carton & Douglas; exec. v.p., chief adminstrv. office, gen. counsel, corp. sec. Global TeleSystems, Inc.; chief legal officer, corp. sec. SAVVIS, Inc., St. Louis; exec. v.p., gen. counsel, corp. sec. Charter Comms., St. Louis, 2005—. Office: Charter Comms 12405 Powerscourt Dr Saint Louis MO 63131 Office Fax: 314-965-0555. *

RACTLIFFE, ROBERT EDWARD GEORGE, management executive; b. Hertfordshire, Eng., July 25, 1943; came to U.S., 1965; s. Augustus David John and Veronica Phyllis (Jones) R.; m. Nancy Jane Brumbaugh, June 29, 1968; children: Richard Alban, Tiffany Elizabeth, Courtney Veronica. BS with honors, U. London, 1965; MSEE, U. Pitts., 1969, MBA with honors, 1972; PMD, Harvard U., 1975. Engr. Westinghouse Electric Corp., Pitts., 1965-69, sales mgr. LRA Div., 1969-73, mfg. engr. mgr. LRA Div., 1974-76, dept. mgr. Hydrogenerator Dept., 1976-78, mgr. product mktg. Steam Turbine Generator Div. Phila., 1979-81, mgr. strategic planning Power Generation Bus. Unit, 1981-84, gen. mgr. Power Generation Comml. Div. Orlando, Fla., 1984-86; pres., North Am. Ops. United Tech. Carrier Corp., Syracuse, N.Y., 1986-88; pres., chief exec. officer NORDYNE Inc., St. Louis, 1989—. Patentee in field; contbr. articles to profl. jours. Mem. AAIM (bd. dirs.), Gas Appliance Mfrs. Assn. (co. rep.), Manufactured Housing Inst. (co. rep.), Air Conditioning and Refrigeration Inst. (bd. dirs., v.p. exec. com., com. chmn., co. rep.). Republican. Episcopalian. Avocations: golf, tennis, skiing. Office: NORDYNE Inc PO Box 8809 O Fallon MO 63366-8809

RACZKA, TONY MICHAEL, artist; b. Pottsville, Pa., Jan. 16, 1957; s. Albert Joseph and Rosemary Bernadette Raczka; m. Virginia Boone, 1974 (div. 1984); 1 child, Mesika; m. Patricia Martinez, June 20, 1986; 1 stepchild, Cynthia. BFA, No. Ariz. U., 1978; MFA, No. Ill. U., 1980; postgrad., U. Calif., San Diego, 1991-92. Instr. art Southwestern Coll., Chula Vista, Calif., 1981-84, No. Ariz. U., Flagstaff, Ariz., 1983; registrar Mingei Internat. Mus. World Folk Art, San Diego, 1985-86; instr. art San Diego State U., 1987; asst. dir. Quint Gallery, San Diego, 1987; sr. mus. preparator U. Art Gallery, U. Calif., San Diego, 1989—95. Presenter in field. One-man shows include Quint Gallery, 1982, 1983, Paris Green Gallery, La Jolla, Calif., 1987, Queens Coll. Art Ctr., CUNY, Flushing, 1999—, 2-person shows include, Printworks, Chgo., 1982, 1984, exhibited in group shows at Butler Inst. Arm. Art, Youngstown, Ohio, 1983, 1997, Drawing Ctr., 1994, Meridian Gallery, San Francisco, 1995 (Best of Show 2d pl.), Coll. and William and Mary, 1996, Trenton (NJ) State Coll., 1996, Laguna (Calif.) Art Mus., 1997, Carnegie Mus. Art, 1997, U. Richmond, Va., 1996, 1998, San Jacinto Coll., Houston, 1998 (Merit award), Palm Springs Mus., 1999, Weber State U., Ogden, Utah, 2000, Bradley U., Peoria, Ill., 2001, Anne Arundel CC, Arnold, Md., 2002, Hofstra U. Mus., Hempstead, NY, 2002; author: poetry. Recipient Pollock-Krasner Found. award, 2001. Mem.: San Diego Mus. Art, Internat. Soc. Phenomenology and Scis. Life. Home: 4430 42d St # 2 San Diego CA 92116 Personal E-mail: raczkatony@aol.com.

RADA, DAVID CHARLES, dermatologist; b. Chgo., Apr. 8, 1954; s. Irwin C. and Mary A. Rada; m. Christina Lynne Fogle, Mar. 27, 1981; children: Matthew D., Megan E., Rebecca C. BS in Microbiology, U. Nebr., Omaha, 1976, MD, 1980. Diplomate Am. Bd. Dermatology. Resident in dermatology U. Kans. Med. Ctr., 1982—85; pvt. practice Kansas City, Mo., 1985—; pres. CryoHist, Inc., Kansas City, 1995—. Inventor (in field). Fellow: Am. Soc. Dermatologic Surgery, Am. Acad. Dermatology; mem.: Kansas City Dermatologic Soc., Mo. Dermatologic Soc. Achievements include invention of technology to get the surface cut by the surgeon's knife onto glass slides for histologic margins, a technique applicable for cancer resection margins using frozen sections. Office: 4320 Wornall Rd Ste 728 Kansas City MO 64111 Office Phone: 816-561-3641. Personal E-mail: cryohist@aol.com. Business E-Mail: camargin@cryohist.com.

RADAKOVICH, DANIEL L., communications executive, consultant; b. Easton, Pa., Sept. 27, 1958; s. Daniel L. and Nancy A. Radakovich; life ptnr. Matthew W. Fluck. BA in History, Pa. State U., University Park, 1979. Overseas mktg. mgr. Investment and Income-Producing Properties Internat., Inc., Denver, 1983—84, exec. v.p. LA, 1984—85; substitute tchr. Philipsburg Sch. Dist., NJ, 1985—87; asst. warehouse mgr. Steelcrete, North Royalton, Ohio, 1991—93; v.p. Swing-Sling Inc., Strongsville, Ohio, 1994—96; rschr. DesertSun Films LLC, Garfield, NJ, 2003—04; sr. exec. v.p. prodn. DesertSun Films, LLC, Garfield, NJ, 2004—, chief rsch. officer, 2005—. Cons. Strategicon, Inc., Fullerton, Calif., 1981—85, Diverse Talents Inc., LA, 1985, New Universe Project SF Convs., Fullerton, 1986—88, GuardTower Games, Brunswick, Ohio, 1999—2005; spl. cons. HollyDanWorks, Belgrade, 2003—04, Ontario, 2003—04, lead specialist cons., 2005—06; staff mem. Alpha Young Writer's Workshop, Greensburg, Pa., 2003—06. Actor: (films) Darkest Days (NY Ind. Film Festival Best thriller award, 2005); contbr. articles to profl. jours. Mem. Cleve. Ams. Mid. Ea. Origin, 1997—2001, Polish-Ams., Inc., Cleve., 1997—2001; exec. com. mem. Cuyahoga County Dems., Cleve., 1994—2000; mem. Cosmopolitan Dem. League, Cleve., 1997—2001, Ward 15 Dem. Club, Cleve., 1998—2001; Dem. candidate 2000 US senate primary, Ohio. Mem.: PARSEC, KC. Democrat. Roman Catholic. Avocations: reading, writing, strategic gaming, acting, politics. Office: DesertSun Films LLC TDS Studios 31 4th Ave Westwood NJ 07675 Home Phone: 412-264-9777; Office Phone: 862-703-3090. Business E-Mail: info@teamdesertsun.com, hollydanworks@gmail.com.

RADANOVICH, GEORGE P., congressman; b. Mariposa, Calif., June 20, 1955; s. Joan and George F.; m. Ethie Weaver; 1 child, George King. BS in Agr. Bus. Mgmt., Calif. State Polytechnic U., 1978. County supr. County Planning Comm., 1988-92; mem. U.S. Congress from 19th Calif. dist., Washington, 1995—; mem. energy and com. com., resources com., chmn. natural parks subcom. Chmn. Water and Power Sub Com.; co-chair Congl. Wine Caucus. Mem. Calif. Agrl. Leadership Program Class XXI, Rotary (Paul Harris Fellowship). Republican. Roman Catholic. Office: US Ho Reps 438 Cannon Ho Office Bldg Washington DC 20515-0519 *

RADCLIFF, JOYCE B., librarian; d. Robert and Rosanna Bullard; m. Doc Radcliff, June 24, 1968; children: Nicole Lynn, Rasheda Asia. BA, U. South Ala., Mobile, 1973, MLS, 1996. Tech. asst. U. S. Ala., Mobile, 1974—99; cataloging libr. U. So. Miss., Hattisburg, 1999—2001; serials libr. Tenn. State U., Nashville, 2001—; cons. Libr. of Congress, Washington, 1996; mem. exec. bd. Reading Is Fundamental, Nashville, 2004—06. Exec. bd. Libr. Sch. Assn. U. Ala., 1997—2002. Contbr. articles to profl. jours. Advisor ABeneefuo KUO Honor Soc., 1989—99; greeter Frist Mus., Nashville, 2002—; advisor Girl Scouts Am., Mobile, 1982—86. Named Staff of Yr., U. S. Ala., 1999; recipient Award of Appreciation, Libr. Congress, Washington, 1996, Congress award, Congressman Sonny Callahan, 2000. Mem.: ALA, Tenn. Libr. Assn., Delta Sigma Theta. Avocations: walking, reading, travel, computers. Office: Tenn State Univ 330 10th Ave N Nashville TN 37203 Office Phone: 615-963-7383. Personal E-mail: joydoc987@aol.com.

RADCLIFFE, DANIEL, actor; b. London, July 23, 1989; Actor: (films) Tailor of Panama, 2001, Harry Potter and the Sorcerer's Stone, 2001, Harry Potter and the Chamber of Secret's, 2002, Harry Potter and the Prisoner of Azkaban, 2004, Harry Potter and the Goblet of Fire, 2005, Harry Potter and the Order of the Phoenix, 2007; appearances (TV) The Today Show, 2001, The Oprah Winfrey Show, 2001, Late Night with Conan O'Brien, 2004, (TV special) David Copperfield, 1999; actor: (plays) Equus, 2007. *

RADCLIFFE, MARK FLOHN, lawyer; b. Dayton, Ohio, Mar. 11, 1952; Cert. of completion, Sorbonne, Paris, 1972; BS in Chem. magna cum laude, U. Mich., 1974; JD, Harvard U., 1981. Bar: Calif. 1982. Law clk. to chief judge U.S. Dist. Ct. (so. dist.) Calif., San Diego, 1981-82; assoc. Brobeck, Phleger & Harrison, San Francisco, 1982-86; assoc. to ptnr. Gray Cary Ware & Freidenrich, Palo Alto, Calif., 1986—2004; ptnr. DLA Piper, 2004—, co-chmn. Technology and Sourcing Group Ea. Palo Alto, Calif., 2005—. Gen. counsel The Open Source Initiative; chair com. C for reviewing GPLv3. Mem. editorial bd.: Computer Lawyer, 1988—, Cyberspace Lawyer; mem. adv. bd. BNA Electronic Commerce & Law Report, Global Intellectual Property Asset Mgmt. Report; country corr. European Intellectual Property Rev.; editor-in-chief Jour. Internet Law; co-author Multimedia Law, Internet Law and Business; contbr. articles to profl. law jours. Lt. (j.g.) USNR, 1974-77. Named one of Am. 100 Most Influential Lawyers, Nat. Law Jour., 1997, World's Leading Trademark Lawyers, Expert Guide, 2003, No. Calif Super Lawyer & one of Top 100 No. Calif. IP Lawyers, San Francisco mag., 2004, Best Lawyers in Am., 2005—06, Am. Leading Lawyers for Bus., Chanbers USA, 2006; recipient Disting. Alumni award, Harvard Univ., 1998. Mem. ABA (chmn. subcom. 1985-88), Am. Intellectual Property Law Assn., Internat. Trademark Assn., San Francisco Bar Assn. (chmn. computer law sect. 1985-86), Computer Law Assn. (dir.), Licensing Exec. Soc., South Bay Trademark Lawyers Assn. (founder), Harvard Club. Office: DLA Piper 2000 University Ave Palo Alto CA 94303 Office Phone: 650-833-2266. Office Fax: 650-833-2001. Business E-Mail: mark.radcliffe@dlapiper.com.

RADCLIFFE, REDONIA (DONNIE RADCLIFFE), journalist, writer; m. Robert C. Radcliffe; 1 child, M. Donnel Nunes. BA, San Jose State U., Calif., 1951. Reporter, women's editor, county editor The Salinas Californian, 1951-59; free-lance writer Europe, 1959—66; reporter Washington Star, 1967-72; White Ho. reporter, columnist Washington Post, 1972-95. Author: Simply Barbara Bush: A Portrait of America's Candid First Lady, 1989, Hillary Rodham Clinton: A First Lady for Our Time, 1993, reissued as Hillary Rodham Clinton: The Evolution of a First Lady, 1999; contbr.: The Fall of a President, 1974, Guide to Washington, 1989. Trustee Calvert County (Md.) Libr.; bd. dirs. Nat. 1st Ladies' Libr. Home Phone: 410-326-1577. E-mail: redrad@erols.com.

RADDATZ, MARTHA, news correspondent; b. Idaho Falls, 1953; m. Tom Gjelten; children: Greta Bradlee, Jake. Chief corr. WCVB-TV, Boston; Pentagon corr. Nat. Pub. Radio, 1993—98; State Dept. corr. ABC News, 1999—2003, nat. security corr., 2003—05, chief White House corr., 2005—. Contbr. The New Republic, Washington Week, PBS. Author: The Long Road Home: A Story of War & Family, 2007. Recipient Overseas Press Club award, 1996, Nat. Headliner award, 1998, 3 Emmy awards, 1999—2001, Merriman Smith Meml. award, White House Corrs. Assn., 2007. Achievements include being first corr. to report on the death of Abu Musab al-Zarqawi. Office: ABC News 1717 DeSales St Washington DC 20036

RADDE, BRUCE, retired architecture educator; b. Milw., Mar. 2, 1935; s. Elwin F. Radde and Jeanette Helane Behrend; m. Sally Ernstrom Parker, Oct. 20, 1972. BA, U. Wis., Madison, 1957; MA, U. Calif., Berkeley, 1967, PhD, 1975. Prof. San Jose State U., Calif., 1968—2000; ret. Vis. prof. U. Calif., Berkeley, 1975—76, Conn. Coll., New London, 1989, U. Hartford, Conn., 1990. Contbr. articles to profl. jours. Bd. dirs. San Jose Mus. Art, San Jose, 1976—78; commr. Hist. Landmarks, San Jose, 1978—85. Fellow, McCloud Lewis Found., 1958. Mem.: Soc. Arch. Historians. Democrat. Avocations: cooking, reading.

RADDING, ANDREW, lawyer; b. NYC, Nov. 30, 1944; m. Bonnie A. Levinson, Oct. 7, 1972; children: Judith Lynne, Joshua David. BBA, CCNY-Baruch Sch., 1965; JD, Boston U., 1969. Bar: N.Y. 1968, Md. 1977, D.C. 1977, U.S. Supreme Ct. Grad. fellow Northwestern U. Sch. Law, 1968-69; asst. counsel U.S. Ho. of Reps. Select Com. on Crime, 1969-72; asst. U.S. atty. for Dist. Md., 1972-77; ptnr. Francomano, Radding & Mannes, Balt., 1977-80, Burke, Gerber, Wilen, Francomano & Radding, Balt., 1980-85, Blades & Rosenfeld P.A., Balt., 1985-97, Adelberg, Rudow, Dorf and Hendler LLC, Balt., 1997—. Mem. adj. faculty clin. practice skills, criminal law, fed. criminal practice U. Balt. Sch. Law, 1980—; mem. trial experience com. U.S. Dist. ct., 1986-88; apptd. by gov. State Adminstrv. Bd. of Election Laws, 1995-96; instr. professionalism course Md. State Bar Assn., 1999—; mem. inquiry panel and peer rev. panel Atty. Grievance Commn., 1991—. Bd. dirs. Copper Hill Condominium, 1979-82, pres., 1981-82; vice chair Lawyers for Erlich for Gov. Com., 2002; mem. subcom. Md. Republican Conv., 1981; sen. C.M. Mathias Jud. Selection com., 1986; chmn. U.S. Dist. Ct. Bicentennial Program, 1989-90; mem. Mayor's Domestic Violence Coord. com., 2001—. Mem.: ABA, Nat. Arbitration Forum (arbitrator), U.S. Arbitration and Mediation, Md. Inst. Continuing Profl. Edn. for Lawyers (bd. govs. 1987—92), U.S. Atty. Alumni Assn. Md. (pres. 1978—), Fed. Bar Assn. (Balt. chpt. pres. 1986—87), Balt. City Bar Assn. (jud. selection com. 1990—92, chmn. 1996—97, co-chmn. membership com. 1999—2000, exec. coun. 2000—, chmn. fee arbitration com. 2001—02, jud. selection com. 2004—), Md. Bar Assn. (CLE com. 2002—, chair program com. 2005—, bd. govs. 2005—). Jewish. Office: Adelberg Rudow et al LLC 7 St Paul St Ste 600 Baltimore MD 21202 Home Phone: 410-486-1229; Office Phone: 410-986-0824. Business E-Mail: aradding@adelbergrudow.com.

RADEBOLDT-DALY, KAREN ELAINE, retired medical/surgical nurse; b. Bklyn., Mar. 3, 1944; d. Harry Phillip and Lillian Florence (Renton) McAnaney; m. Richard William Radeboldt, Aug. 19, 1968 (dec. Aug. 1985); children: Karyn, Kellianne, Kimberly, Kristi-Jo, Richard; m. William J. Daly, Sr., Jan. 22, 1995. Lic. practical nurse, Wyckoff Heights Sch. Nursing, Bklyn., 1968; RN, Orange County C.C., Middletown, NY, 1990. LPN, N.Y., RN, N.Y.; cert. med.-surg. nurse, N.Y. Nurses aide, lic. practical nurse Wyckoff Heights Hosp., Bklyn., 1967-90; staff nurse, med.-surg. nurse Westchester Med. Ctr., Valhalla, NY, 1990—96, staff nurse, trauma unit, 1996—98, staff nurse, critical care-trauma ICU, 1988—2004; ret., 2004. Mem. Am. Jour. Nursing. Adventist. Avocations: reading, sewing, bowling, walking, motorcycling. Home: 101 Daly Rd Middletown NY 10940-7356

RADECKI, JEFFREY, sports medicine physician; s. Jan and Irene Radecki. BA, NYU, NY, 2000; MD, U. MDNJ, Piscataway, NJ, 2004. Lic. physician NY, 2006. Resident phys. medicine and rehab. NY Presbyn. Hosp., NY, 2005—. Mem.: Am. Coll. Sports Medicine (corr.). Office: NY Presbyn Hosp 180 Ft Washington Ste 199 New York NY 10032

RADEL, EVA, pediatrician, hematologist; b. Vienna, Apr. 10, 1934; came to U.S., 1939; d. Ernest O. and Marian (Feiks) Grossman; m. Stanley Robert Radel, May 31, 1954; children: Carol, Laura. AB, N.Y. U., 1954, MD, 1958. Pediatric intern, resident Bronx Mcpl. Hosp. Ctr., 1958-61; pediatric hematology rsch. fellow Albert Einstein Coll. Medicine, Bronx, 1961-63; pediatrician, head pediatric hematology Morrisania city Hosp., Bronx, 1963-76; assoc. dir. pediatrics North Cen. Bronx Hosp., 1978-82; attending physician pediatric hemetology out patients Montefiore Med. Ctr., Bronx, 1965-79, svc. head pediatric hematology-oncology, 1979—2004; head pediatric hematology North Cen. Bronx Hosp., 1976-97. Responsible investigator Children's Cancer Study Group, 1980-2001; dir. pediatric hematology-oncology Albert Einstein Coll. Medicine, Bronx, 1980-2004; prin. investigator Children's Oncology Group, 2001-05 Fellow Am. Acad Pediatrics; mem. Am. Soc. Hematology, Am. Soc. Pediatric Hematology-Oncology, Soc. for the Study of Blood. Office: Childrens Hosp at Montefiore Sect Pediat Hematology-Oncology 3415 Bainbridge Ave Bronx NY 10467-2401 Office Phone: 718-741-2342. Business E-Mail: eradel@montefiore.org.

RADEMACHER, DANA ELLIS, urologist; b. Denver, Sept. 25, 1964; s. James Dennis and Barbara Jane Rademacher; m. Jonella Gross, Sept. 5, 1987; children: Ryan John, Erin Janelle, Connor Jacob. MD, U. Colo., Denver, 1992. Diplomate Wis., Minn., 1998, cert. bd. cert. urologist 2003. Intern in gen. surgery U. Calif. Davis Med. Ctr., Sacramento, 1992—94, resident in urology, 1994—98; urologist FranciscanSkemp Mayo Healthcare, LaCrosse, Wis., 1998—. Chmn. fin. com. FranciscanSkemp Mayo Healthcare, 2001—07. Recipient Am. Outstanding Dr. award, 2006. Mem.: N.Ctrl. Cancer Treatment Grp. (assoc.), N.Ctrl. Urol. Assn. (assoc.), Am. Urol. Assn. (assoc.). Office: FranciscanSkemp Mayo Healthcare 800 West Ave S La Crosse WI 54601

RADEMAKER, STEPHEN GEOFFREY, legislative staff member, former federal agency administrator; b. Balt., July 18, 1959; s. Thomas Joseph and Ruth Virginia (Wentz) R.; m. Danielle Pletka; children: Andrew, Olivia, Sophia, Nicola. BA with highest distinction, U. Va., 1981, JD, 1984, MA in Fgn. Affairs, 1985. Bar: Va. 1984, D.C. 1985. Assoc. Covington & Burling LLP, Washington, 1984-86; law clk. to Hon. James L. Buckley US Ct. Appeals (D.C. Cir.), Washington, 1986; counsel to vice chmn. US Internat. Trade Commn., Washington, 1986-87; spl. asst. to asst. sec. for Inter-Am. affairs US Dept. State, Washington, 1987-89; assoc. counsel to Pres. of U.S. and dep. legal advisor to NSC, Washington, 1989-92; gen. counsel Peace Corps, Washington, 1992-93; Rep. chief counsel Com. Fgn. Affairs US Ho. of Reps., Washington, 1993-95, chief counsel Com. Internat. Rels., 1995—2001, dep. staff dir., chief counsel Com. Internat. Rels., 2001—02, chief counsel Select Com. on Homeland Security, 2002; asst. sec. for arms control US Dept. State, Washington, 2002—05, acting asst. sec. for internat. security & nonproliferation, 2005—06; dir. nat. security for Senator Bill Frist US Senate, Washington, 2006—. Mem. UN Sec. Gen.'s Adv. Bd. on Disarmament Matters, 2003—. Recipient Raven award U. Va., 1984; S. Philip Heiner scholar U. Va., 1983. Mem. Va. Bar Assn., D.C. Bar Assn., Phi Beta Kappa, Omicron Delta Kappa. Republican. Lutheran. Avocations: skiing, bicycling, scuba diving. Office: 509 Hart Senate Office Bldg Washington DC 20510

RADER, DOTSON CARLYLE, writer, journalist; b. Minn., July 25, 1941; s. Paul Carlyle and Lois (Schacht) R. Student, Columbia, 1962-68. Editor Defiance: A Radical Rev. (Warner Communications, Inc.), 1969-71; contbg. editor Evergreen Rev., 1969-73, Esquire, NYC, 1973-77, N.Y. mag., 1977-80; cons. Nat. Com. for Lit. Arts at Lincoln Center, NYC, 1980—. Mem. sponsoring bd. New Politics, 1972—; host Free Time Show, WNET-TV, N.Y.C., 1972-73 Author: I Ain't Marchin' Anymore!, 1969, Government Inspected Meat and Other Fun Summer Things, 1971, Blood Dues, 1973, Tennessee: Cry of the Heart: An Intimate Memoir of Tennessee Williams, 1985; screenplay The Bronze Lily, 1974, The Dream's on Me: A Love Story, 1976, Miracle, 1978; novel Beau Monde, 1981; play (with Mike Miller) Shattered Glass, 1990; contbg. editor Parade Mag., 1984—. Mem. Student Peace Union, 1961-63, Students for a Democratic Soc., 1964-69, War Resisters League, 1970—; pres. Humanitas, Columbia, 1963-67; vice chmn. Peoples Coalition for Peace and Justice, 1972. Named hon. ambassador State of W. Va., 1982; recipient award for nat. journalism Odyssey Inst., 1982, Spl. Olympics award for nat. journalism Joseph P. Kennedy Found., 1985 Mem. PEN, Overseas Press Club, The Dramatists Guild.

RADER, NANCY LOUISE DE VILLIERS, psychology professor, consultant; b. Danbury, Conn., May 21, 1948; d. Martin Anthony and Elsie Concetta (Lauricella) R.; m. David Strutt de Villiers, Sept. 6, 1975; 1 child, Alyssa Jane. AB magna cum laude, Smith Coll., 1970; PhD, Cornell U., 1976. Asst. prof. psychology UCLA, 1974-82, dir. Infant and Child Lab., 1979-82, scholar Found. for Child Devel., 1982-83, postdoctoral fellow, rsch. psychologist Neuropsychiat. Inst., 1983-84; vis. scholar Cornell U., Ithaca, N.Y., 1979, rsch. assoc., 1984-85; asst. prof. Ithaca Coll., 1985-90, assoc. prof., 1990—2004, prof., 2004—, chair psychology dept., 2000—03. Contbr. articles to profl. jours., chpts. to books. Bd. dirs. Coddington Community Ctr., Ithaca, 1991-94, Family and Children Svcs., 1999-2002. Fellow NDEA, 1968, 71-74, Ford Found., 1970-74; grantee NIMH, 1982, NSF, 2001—. Mem. APA, Am. Psychol. Soc., Soc. for Rsch. in Child Devel., Internat. Soc. for Study Behavioral Devel., Internat. Soc. for Ecol. Psychology, Ea. Psychol. Assn., Sigma Xi (pres. Ithaca Coll. chpt. 1988-89), Phi Kappa Phi. Avocations: gardening, mystery. Home: 201 Eastman Hill Rd Willseyville NY 13864-1229 Office: Ithaca Coll Psychology Dept Ithaca NY 14850 Office Phone: 607-274-3510. E-mail: rader@ithaca.edu.

RADER, RALPH TERRANCE, lawyer; b. Clarksburg, W.Va., Dec. 5, 1947; s. Ralph Coolidge and Jeanne (Cover) R.; m. Rebecca Jo Vorderman, Mar. 22, 1969; children: Melissa Michelle, Allison Suzanne. BSME, Va. Poly. Inst., 1970; JD, Am. U., 1974. Bar: Va. 1975, U.S. Ct. Customs and Patent Appeals, 1977, U.S. Dist. Ct. (ea. dist.) Mich. 1978, Mich. 1979, U.S. Ct. Appeals (6th cir.) 1979, U.S. Dist. Ct. (we. dist.) Mich. 1981, U.S. Ct. Appeals (fed. cir.) 1983. Supervisory patent examiner U.S. Patent Office, Washington, 1970-77; patent atty., ptnr. Cullen, Sloman, Cantor, Grauer, Scott & Rutherford, Detroit, 1977-88; ptnr. Dykema, Gossett, Detroit, 1989-96; founder, ptnr. Rader, Fishman & Grauer, Bloomfield Hills, Mich., 1996—. Contbr. articles to profl. jours. Mem. adminstrv. bd. 1st United Meth. Ch., Birmingham, Mich., 1980—. With U.S. Army, 1970-76. Mem. ABA, Am. Patent Law Assn., Mich. Patent Law Assn., Mich. Bar (governing coun. patent, trademark and copyright law sect. 1981-84), Engring. Soc. Detroit, Masons, Tau Beta Pi, Pi Tau Sigma, Phi Kappa Phi. Methodist. Home: 4713 Riverchase Dr Troy MI 48098-4186 Office: Rader Fishman & Grauer 39533 Woodward Ave Ste 140 Bloomfield Hills MI 48304-5098 Office Phone: 248-594-0620. Business E-Mail: rtr@raderfishman.com.

RADER, RANDALL RAY, federal judge; b. Hastings, Nebr., Apr. 21, 1949; BA magna cum laude, BYU, 1974; JD with honors, George Washington U., 1978. Bar: DC, US Ct. Appeals (fed. cir.) 1990, US Claims Ct., US Supreme Ct. Legis. asst. to Congresswoman Virginia Smith US Ho. of Reps., 1975—78, mem. staff Ways and Means Com., 1978—81; chief counsel subcom. on Constn. US Senate Judiciary Com., 1981—86, chief counsel, staff dir. subcom. on patents, copyrights and trademarks, 1987—88; counsel to Senator Orrin Hatch, 1981—88; judge US Ct. Claims, Washington, 1988—90, US Ct. Appeals (Fed. cir.), Washington, 1990—. Lectr. patent law U. Va. Sch. Law, 1993—99; lectr. trial advocacy, lectr. George Washington U. Nat. Law Ctr., Washington, 1993—97; lectr. comparative patent law Georgetown U. Law Ctr., Washington, 1998—99. Co-author: Patent Law, 1997; co-editor: Criminal Justice Reform, 1983; contbr. articles to profl. jours. Mem.: FBA. Office: US Ct Appeals Fed Cir 717 Madison Pl NW Ste 913 Washington DC 20439-0002 *

RADER, STEVEN PALMER, lawyer; b. Charlotte, NC, Dec. 30, 1952; s. Alvin Marion Jr. and Shirley Ninabelle (Palmer) Rader; m. Victoria Rolinsky, 2001; 1 child, Tudor R. AB, Duke U., 1975; postgrad., Stetson U., 1975-76; JD, Wake Forest U., 1978. Bar: N.C. 1978, U.S. Dist. Ct. (ea. dist.) N.C. 1979. Assoc. Wilkinson and Vosburgh, Washington, N.C., 1978-81; pvt. practice Washington, 1981-88; spl. asst. to sec. N.C. Dept. Human Resources, Raleigh, 1988-89, asst. dir. office legal affairs, 1989-91, gen. counsel, 1991-93; ptnr. Wilkinson & Rader, P.A., Washington, 1993—. Commr. Nat. Conf. Commrs. on Uniform State Laws, 1985-93; gen. counsel N.C. Rep. Party, 1992-97; commr. N.C. Rules Rev. Commn., 1997-99. Mem., sec. City of Washington Human Rels. Coun., 1981-83; chmn. Beaufort County Rep. party, Washington, 1983-87, 1st Congl. Dist. Rep. party, N.C., 1985-92; v.p. East Main St. Area Neighborhood Assn., 1983-85, 1st v.p., Ocean Villas Homeowners Assn., 1999-2003, pres. 2003—; del. Rep. Nat. Conv., 1984, 88, 92; Presdl. elector from N.C., U.S. Electoral Coll., 2000. Mem. N.C. State Bar, 2d Jud. Dist. Bar, Beaufort County Hist. Soc. (v.p. 1981-85, pres. 1985-86). Lutheran. Avocations: boating, classic automobiles, travel. Home: PO Box 1901 Washington NC 27889-1901 Office: Wilkinson & Rader PA PO Box 732 Washington NC 27889-0732 Office Phone: 252-946-7167.

RADFORD, JAMES H., retired military officer, political science professor; b. Portland, Oreg., Mar. 18, 1947; s. Edwin Smith and Miriam Elizabeth Bentley Radford; m. Carole L. Seyfrit, Apr. 7, 1991. BS in Occupl. Edn., So. Ill. U., Carbondale, 1976; MPA, Shippensburg U., Pa., 1995; PhD in Internat. Studies, Old Dominion U., Norfolk, Va., 2005. Instr. Christopher Newport U., Newport News, Va., 1998—2001, Radford U., Va., 2003—. Lt. col. Signal Corps US Army, 1968—98, US, Vietnam, Germany. Independent. Avocations: bookbinding, clockmaking. Home: 412 Vista Ridge Radford VA 24141 Office: Radford Univ Dept Polit Sci Box 6945 Radford VA 24142 Personal E-mail: radfordj1@earthlink.net. Business E-Mail: jradford2@radford.edu.

RADFORD, MARIE LOUISE, library science educator; b. Lakewood, NJ, Aug. 1, 1951; d. Charles and Marion Esther (Nuccio) Hein; m. Gary Paul Radford, June 17, 1989; 1 child, Meg Kathleen. BA, Coll. of N.J., 1973; MSLS, Syracuse U., 1975; PhD, Rutgers U., 1993. Libr. Franklin Twp. Elem. Sch., Quakertown, N.J., 1976-80, Belvidere (N.J.) H.S., 1980-84; head of curriculum materials William Paterson U. Libr., Wayne, N.J., 1984-96; assoc. prof. Pratt Inst., Bklyn., 1996—2004, acting dean, 2002—04; assoc. prof. Sch. Communication, Info. & Library Studies Rutgers U., 2004—. Founder Radford Consulting. Author: The Reference Encounter: Interpersonal Communication in the Academic Library, 1999; mem. editl. bd. N.J. Jour. of Comm., 1992—, assoc. editor 1994—. Mem. ALA, Assn. Coll. and Rsch. Librs., N.J. Comm. Assn. (sec. 1996—, editl. bd. sec. 1997—), Nat. Comms. Assn., Ea. Comm. Assn. (interest groupchair 1994—, chair nonverbal comm. interest group 1996-97), Beta Phi Mu (dir. at large). Office: Rutgers U 4 Huntington St Room 329 New Brunswick NJ 08901-1071 Office Phone: 732-932-7500 Ext. 8233. Office Fax: 732-932-2644. Business E-Mail: mradford@scils.rutgers.edu. *

RADFORD, R. S., lawyer, law educator; b. Independence, Kans., July 30, 1945; s. Lloyd Raymond and Arlene (Bacon) R.; m. Sharon L. Browne, Nov. 24, 1992; children: Jessica Siegel, Jacob Siegel. BS in Bus. Adminstrn., Rockhurst Coll., 1974; MA in Econs., U. So. Calif., 1976; JD, 1988. Bar: Calif. 1988, Supreme Ct. 1992. Prin. atty. Pacific Legal Found., Sacramento, Calif., 1988—; dir. progrm for jud. awareness, 1999—. Adj. prof. law U. Pacific McGeorge Sch. Law, Sacramento, 2001—. Contbr. numerous articles to profl. jours. Named Laywer of Yr. Calif. Lawyer, 1997 Office Phone: 916-419-7111. Fax: (916) 362-2932. E-mail: radford@cal.com, rsr@pacificlegal.org.

RADHAKRISHNAN, MALATHI, biologist, educator; d. Sundarrajan Chakravarthy and Shanbagam Sundarrajan; m. Radhakrishnan Palaniswamy, Nov. 11, 1983; children: Deepa, Veena. Prof. biology Balt. City C.C., 2002—. Contbr. articles to profl. jours. Mem.: Paleobotanical Soc. (life). Achievements include research in medicinal plants. Avocations: drawing, painting, doll making, music. Office: Balt City Cmty Coll 2901 Liberty Heights Ave Baltimore MD 21215 Home Phone: 410-484-6632; Office Phone: 410-462-8428.

RADHAKRISHNAN, RAVI, science educator; b. Chennai, Tamilnadu, India, Sept. 1, 1974; s. Thimmakudy Sambasiva and Ganga Radhakrishnan; m. Deboleena Dutta, Apr. 28, 2004; 1 child, Radhakrishnan Anshul Ved. B of Technology, Indian Inst. Tech., Madras, 1995; PhD, Cornell U., Ithaca, NY, 2000, DPhil, 2001. Rsch. assoc. MIT, Cambridge, 2000—02, NYU, Howard Hughes Med. Inst., NYC, 2002—04; asst. prof. U. Pa., Phila., 2004—. Cons. U. Pa. Med. Sch., Phila., 2004—07. Fellow, Coun. Sci. and Indsl. India, 1995, Cornell U., 1995. Mem.: Biomed. Engring. Soc., AIChE, Biophysical Soc., Am. Chem. Soc. Office Phone: 215-898-0487.

RADICE, ANNE-IMELDA MARINO, museum director, former federal agency administrator; b. Buffalo, Feb. 29, 1948; d. Lawrence and Anne (Marino) R. AB, Wheaton Coll., 1969; MA, Villa SchiFanoia, Florence, Italy, 1971; PhD, U. N.C., 1976; MBA, Am. U., 1984. Asst. curator, staff lectr. Nat. Gallery of Art, Washington, 1972-76; archtl. historian U.S. Capitol, Washington, 1976—81, curator Office of Architect, 1981—85; dir. Nat. Mus. Women in the Arts, 1985-89; chief divsn. of creative arts USIA, 1989-91; sr. dep. chmn. Nat. Endowment for Arts, Washington, 1991-92, acting chmn., 1992-93; exec. v.p. Gray & Co. II, Miami, Fla., 1993; prodr. World Affairs TV Prodn., 1994; assoc. producer Think Tank, 1994; chief spl. projects, confidential adviser Courtney Sale Ross, 1994-96; v.p., COO ICL Internat., 1996; exec. dir. Friends of Dresden Inc., 1998—2001; exec. dir. appeal Conscience Found., NYC, 2001—03; chief staff to sec. US Dept. Edn., Washington, 2003—05; acting asst. chmn. for programs Nat. Endowment Humanities, Washington, 2005—06; dir. The Inst. Mus. & Library Services, Washington, 2006—. Cons. in pub. rels. and TV, 1994—. Contbr. articles to profl. jours. Office: The Inst Mus & Library Services 1800 M St NW 9th Fl Washington DC 20036

RADICE, FRANK J., communications executive; b. Washington, Dec. 13, 1949; m. Vida S. Radice, July 4, 1995. Student, U. Md., 1968-72. Film editor WRC/NBC-TV, Washington, 1971-72, ABC News, Washington, 1972, assignment editor, 1976, assoc. prodr. Good Morning Am., 1978, ops. prodr. World News Tonight, 1979-80; prodr. Nightline NYC, 1980-83; program prodr. The Last Word ABC News, NYC, 1983; field dir. Entertainment Tonight Paramount Motion Pictures, NYC, 1984; prodr., developer Live At 5:00 WRC/NBC-TV, Washington, 1985; exec. prodr. Entertainment News, Cable News Network, NYC, 1987-89; InterActive sr. producer/prodr. devel., producer advt. and promotion ABC News, NYC, 1989-91; advt. mgr. WCBS-TV, NYC, 1991; v.p. advt. and promotion NBC Entertainment, NYC, 1996; sr. v.p. The NBC Agy., NYC, 2000—07, exec. v.p., 2007—. Exec. prodr. NBC on Ted, 2004—05, NBC Inflight on United Airlines, 1984—2005; v.p. Vida F.R. Co., 1999; chmn. mktg. Nat. Acad. TV Arts and Scis., 2005—. Author: (with Vida Radice) Sam Katz On The Loose, 2005; prodr. A Line in the Sand, War of Peace, War in the Gulf; writer, prodr., 1992; co-exec. prodr. (CD): The Best of The Today Show Summer Concerts, Vols. 1 and 2, 2000. Bd. govs. N.Y. Festivals, 2003—. Recipient award Coll. Emergency Physicians, 1983, Emmy award NATAS, 1984, 1990, 7 NY Festival awards, 2000-03; Alfred I Dupont grantee Columbia U., NYC, 1984, 91, Mobius award, 1998, 2005, Cine Golden Eagle award 2002-04; Brand Builder award, B & C, 2003; inductee Promax Hall of Fame, 2004; Emmy nomination for Outstanding Original Song, 2006. Mem. Broadcast Music Inc. (writer affiliate), AFTRA, Nat. Assn. Broadcast Employees and Technicians, Internat. Alliance Theatrical and Stage Employees, Writers Guild Am., Dirs. Guild Am., Congressional Country Club, Friars (N.Y.C.). Democrat. Roman Catholic. Office: NBC Ste 1891E 30 Rockefeller Plz New York NY 10112-0002 Office Phone: 212-664-3555. Business E-Mail: frank.radice@nbc.com.

RADIGAN, FRANK XAVIER, retired pharmaceutical executive; b. Paterson, NJ, Apr. 13, 1933; s. John Joseph and Susan Clair (Brett) R.; m. Julia Lou Smith, Aug. 27, 1960 (div. Nov. 1988); children: Francis Gregory, Patricia Louise, Brett Frasier; m. Carol E. Berkley, June 26, 1992; children: Dana, Traci. AB in Sociology, Seton Hall U., 1955; MBA Mktg., U. Hartford, 1968. Asst. mgr. Beneficial Fin. Co., Newark, 1955-57; hosp. rep. Becton-Dickinson Co., Rutherford, N.J., 1957-58; dist. mgr. Merck Human Health Divsn., West Point, Pa., 1958-98; ret., 1998. Horse breeder, 1976—86. Active Greater Balt. SCORE; mem. Passaic County Dem. Com., 1955—56; chmn. St. John the Baptist Social Justice, New Freedom, Pa., 1981—85. Capt. USAR. Mem.: Md. Mental Health Assn. (legis. com. 1969—73), Balt. Pharm. Assn. (hon. pres. 1989), W.Va. Pharm. Soc., Md. Pharmacists Assn. (hon. pres. 1999—2000, past chmn. indsl. rels. com.), Am. Mgmt. Assn., Am. Pharm. Assn., Hopewell Fish and Game Assn., Pleasant Valley Golf Club, Bon Air Country Club, Lions (pres. Glen Rock, Pa. chpt. 1975—76, 1986—88), Elks. Roman Catholic. Home: 2440 Bradenbaugh Rd White Hall MD 21161-9661 Personal E-mail: fxr333@msn.com.

RADIN, ALEX, former association executive, consultant; b. Chattanooga, June 14, 1921; s. Joseph and Mollie (Pernat) R.; m. Sara Leah Gordon, Sept. 6, 1943 (dec. Nov. 20, 1964); children— Jay Jacob, William Gordon m. Carol Nita Schuman, Sept. 21, 1979 BA, U. Chattanooga, 1947. Reporter Chattanooga Times, Chattanooga, 1938-42; adminstrv. asst. Office of Price Adminstrn., Washington, 1942-43; adminstrv. analyst Dept. of State, Washington, 1945-48; asst. to gen. mgr. Am. Pub. Power Assn., Washington, 1948-51, exec. dir., 1951-86; pres. Radin & Assocs. Inc., 1986—. Cons. U.S. Senate Com. on Interior and Insular Affairs, Washington, 1959; mem. exec. com. Am. Nuclear Energy Coun., Washington, 1973-88; v.p. Consumer Fedn. Am., Washington, 1978-86; mem. So. States Energy Bd.'s Adv. Com. on TVA, 1986-87; chmn. Monitored Retrievable Storage Rev. Commn., 1988-89; rep., sec. U.S. Dept. Energy, Independent Mgmt. and Fin. Rev. of Yucca Mt. (Nev.) Project, 1994-95; mem. adv. bd. Ford Found. Energy Policy Project, 1973-74; bd. dirs. Consumer Energy Coun. Am., 1999—2006. Columnist, Pub. Power Mag.; contbr. articles to newspapers and mags.; author Public Power, Private Life, 2003. Mem. adv. bd. Dance Theatre of Harlem, N.Y.C., 1985—. Recipient Leland Olds award Western States Water and Power Consumers Conf., 1970, Philip Hart Disting. Consumer Svc. award Consumer Fedn. Am., 1985, Alex Radin Disting. Svc. award Am. Pub. Power Assn., 1986, named Disting. Alumnus of 2001 U. Tenn. Chattanooga, 2001, Lifetime Achievement award Energy Daily, 2003. Mem. Alpha Soc. Clubs: Nat. Press. Democrat. Jewish. Avocations: photography, music, art, hiking. Home: 2510 Virginia Ave NW Apt 610N Washington DC 20037-1904 Office: Radin & Assocs Inc Ste 609 2510 Virginia Ave NW Washington DC 20037-1904 Home Phone: 202-338-0607; Office Phone: 202-338-0607.

RADIN, AMY JANINE, financial services company executive; b. Mar. 30, 1958; d. Harold I. and Selma M. Friedman; m. Mitchell E. Radin, Nov. 1984; 3 children. BA magna cum laude, Coll. Letters and Spanish, Wesleyan U.; MBA, Wharton Sch., U. Pa. Mktg. develop. mgr. KMG Main Hurdman, NY; various positions in mgmt., customer loyalty, new product develop. and channel mgmt. American Express; exec. v.p., chief mktg. officer Dime Savings Bank of NY; exec. v.p., citi cards e-business Citigroup, Inc., 2000, exec. v.p., customer engagement, 2005, chief innovation officer, global consumer group, 2005—, mem. mgmt. com., mem. global consumer group planning com. Spkr. in field. Trustee The Healthcare Chaplaincy, 2006—; founder, pres. The Small Acts of Kindness Found., Inc. Named one of 25 Masters of Innovation, BusinessWeek. Office: Citigroup Inc 399 Park Ave New York NY 10043

RADIN, SAM, lawyer; b. NYC, Aug. 1, 1951; s. Clarence and Marjorie (Rembar) R.; m. Pamela Anderson, Sept. 13, 1981; children: Clarence Andrew, Elizabeth Rebecca. BA, Columbia U., 1973; JD, Boston U., 1976. Bar: N.J. 1976, U.S. Dist. Ct. N.J. 1976, N.Y. 1978, U.S. Dist. Ct. (so. dist.) N.Y. 1978, U.S. Ct. Appeals (D.C. cir.) 1978, U.S. Supreme Ct. 1980. Assoc. Burns, Van Kirk, NYC, 1976-79, Lovejoy Wasson successor to Burns, Van Kirk, NYC, 1979-80; pvt. practice, NYC, 1980-84; v.p., gen. counsel Nat. Madison Group, Inc., NYC, 1984-99, pres., 1999—. Mem. adv. coun. Harry Ranson Humanities Rsch. Ctr., U. Tex., 2005—. Contbg. author: Executive Compensation Answer Book, 1998; contbg. author, editor: Estate and Retirement Planning Answer Book, 1999; also articles. Bd. dirs. Student Athletes Inc., N.Y.C., 1992-98, Westchester Conservatory Music, White Plains, N.Y., 1995-97; trustee Payomet Performing Arts Charitable Trust, 1999—, Nat. Lighthouse Ctr. and Mus., 2000—, pres., 2001—; mem. adv. coun. Harry Ransom Humanities Rsch. Ctr., U. Tex., Austin. Recipient Nathan Burkan Meml. prize ASCAP, 1975. Mem. ABA (subcom. on life ins. tax sect. 1996—), N.Y. State Bar Assn., Assn. Bar City N.Y., Assn. Advanced Life Underwriting, Comm. on Estate Taxation. Avocations: salt water fly fishing, collecting books, skiing, running. Home: 71 Greenacres Ave Scarsdale NY 10583-1442 Office: Nat Madison Group Inc 200 Pk Ave 21st Flr New York NY 10166-2401 E-mail: sradin@nationalmadison.com.

RADKE, KIRK A., lawyer; b. Mar. 21, 1958; m. Erin M. Radke. BA, Stanford U., 1980; JD, MBA, U. Va., 1984. Bar: Ill. 1985, NY 1991. Ptnr., mem. NY ops. Kirkland & Ellis LLP. Adj. prof. VCPE, HBS, Inc. Office: Kirkland & Ellis LLP Citigroup Ctr 153 E 53rd St New York NY 10022-4675 Home Phone: 212-874-0455; Office Phone: 212-446-4940. Office Fax: 212-446-4900. Business E-Mail: kradke@kirkland.com.

RADKOWSKY, KAREN, advertising research specialist; b. Washington, Nov. 8, 1957; d. Lawrence and Florence (Kramer) Radkowsky. BA, Columbia U., 1979. Rsch. analyst Cosmair, Inc., NYC, 1979-82, sr. rsch. analyst, 1982-84; asst. rsch. mgr. Am. Express Co., NYC, 1984-85; account rsch. mgr. BBDO, Inc., NYC, 1985-88, v.p., assoc. rsch. dir., 1988-94, sr. v.p., assoc. rsch. dir., 1994-95; sr. v.p., rsch. dir. BBDO N.Y., NYC, 1995-99; sr. ptnr., dir. mktg. intelligence Ogilvy & Mather, NYC, 2000—. Bd. dirs. Advt. Rsch. Found., 2001—. E-mail: karen.radkowsky@ogilvy.com.

RADLAUER, STEVE, freelance writer, journalist, producer; b. NYC, Nov. 2, 1948; s. Marvin and Gladys (Steltzer) R.; m. Kerry K. Willis, June 7, 1985; 1 child, Kate. Student, Union Coll., Schenectady, NY; BS, U. State of NY. Dir. A-Space, Toronto, Ontario, Canada, 1971-73; co-owner The Ritz Cafe, Toronto, Ontario, Canada, 1973-77; program dir. Dry Salvages Film Group, NYC, 1978-85. Co-author: The Hist. Shops and Restaurants of NY, 2002; editor-in-chief (online news comedy site) Today's Other News on American Online, 1996; co-author: Dan Quayle: Airhead Apparent, 1992, Special Moments, 1984; freelance writer articles for various pubs. incl. N.Y. Mag., Spy, Esquire, N.Y. Times, L.A. Times. Mem. Authors Guild. E-mail: steve@radz.org.

RADLO, EDWARD JOHN, lawyer, mathematician; b. Pawtucket, RI, Mar. 7, 1946; s. Edward Zygmund and Sue Mary (Borek) Radlo; m. Patricia Jackson, Feb. 22, 1989; children: Heather Sue, Graeme Michael, Connor Andrew. BS, MIT, 1967; JD, Harvard U., 1972. Bar: Calif. 1972, U.S. Dist. Ct. (no. dist.) Calif. 1972, R.I. 1973, U.S. Patent Office 1973, Can. Patent Office 1974. Staff. dir. Atty. Gen.'s Adv. Commn. on Juvenile Code Revision, Boston, 1970—72; law clk. R.I. Supreme Ct., 1972—73; patent atty. Honeywell Info. Systems, Waltham, Mass., 1973—74, Varian Assoc., Palo Alto, Calif., 1974—78, Ford Aerospace Corp., 1978—83, patent counsel, 1983—90; ptnr. Fenwick & West LLP, Mountain View, Calif., 1991—2004, Sonnenschein Nath & Rosenthal LLP, San Francisco, 2004—. Lectr. U. Calif., San Jose State U., U. Santa Clara, 1975—78. Organizer So. Peninsula Emergency Comm. Sys., 1970; mem. Los Altos Hills (Calif.) Emergency Comm. Com, Lawyers' Alliance for Nuclear Arms Control, 1982—83, Environ. Def. Fund, 1979—; bd. dir. Tomahawks Lacrosse Club, Menlo Park, Calif., 2002—05; bd. dirs. No. Calif. Jr. Lacrosse Assn., Corte Madera, Calif., 2004—05. Lt. (jg.) USPHS, 1967—69. Mem.: ABA, Calif. Bar (intellectual property sect.), Silicon Valley Intellectual Property Law Assn., Assn. Radio Amateurs of So. New England Inc. (sec. 1962—63), No. Calif. Contest Club (pres. 1984—85), Sigma Xi. Home: 28040 Elena Rd Los Altos Hills CA 94022-2454 Office: Sonnenschein Nath & Rosenthal LLP 525 Market St San Francisco CA 94105

RADLOFF, ROBERT ALBERT, real estate company executive; b. Chgo., Mar. 30, 1947; s. Henry O. and Virginia G. (Grothus) R.; m. Ann Macy Beha, June 21, 1975; children: Macy, Allison. BS in Fin., Boston U., 1969. V.p. Kuras & Co., Inc., Boston, 1971-76; sr. v.p. Boston Co. Real Estate Counsel, Inc., 1976-81, pres., 1981-89, chmn., 1989-91; real estate investments counselor Boston, 1991—. Bd. dirs. Mass. Cultural Coun., 1992, Friends of Vieilles Maison Francais, 1992, The Augustus Saint-Gaudens Meml.; trustee Isabella Stewart Gardner Mus., 1995; chmn., bd. overseers WGBH Ednl. Found. Mem. Am. Soc. Real Estate Counselors (cert.), Somerset Club. Avocations: art, tennis, travel. Office: 33 Kingston St Boston MA 02111-2208

RADMER, MICHAEL JOHN, lawyer, educator; b. Wisconsin Rapids, Apr. 28, 1945; s. Donald Richard and Thelma Loretta (Donahue) R.; children from previous marriage: Christina Nicole, Ryan Michael; m. Laurie J. Anshus, Dec. 22, 1983; 1 child, Michael John BS, Northwestern U., 1967; JD, Harvard U., 1970. Bar: Minn. 1970. Assoc. Dorsey & Whitney, Mpls., 1970-75, ptnr., corp. practice group, 1976—, chmn., funds practice. Lectr. law Hamline U. Law Sch., St. Paul, 1981-84; gen. counsel, rep., sec. 63 federally registered investment cos., Mpls. and St. Paul, 1977—. Contbr. articles to legal jours. Active legal work Hennepin County Legal Advice Clinic, Mpls., 1971—. Mem. ABA, Minn. Bar Assn., Hennepin County Bar Assn., Mpls. Athletic Club. Office: Dorsey & Whitney 50 South 6th St Ste 1500 Minneapolis MN 55402 Home Phone: 612-824-6919; Office Phone: 612-340-2724. Office Fax: 612-340-8738. Business E-Mail: radmer.michael@dorsey.com. *A key to a successful and happy life is achieving a balance. Intellectual, academic and vocational goals are important, but their pursuit should be balanced with ample time spent with family and friends, travel and enjoying reading, music, art and sports. Don't be afraid to try something new; realize that education should be a lifelong pursuit. Much frustration can be avoided by realizing that life is full of trade-offs. You can't experience the joy of raising children and have the complete freedom of the child-free. Finally, while you should strive for perfection, be content with less. We are only human, and live in an imperfect, yet wonderful, world.*

RADMILOVIC, VELIMIR, materials scientist, researcher; arrived in US, 1986; s. Radivoje and Jelena Radmilovic; m. Vesna Mihailovic, Nov. 18, 1978; 1 child, Vuk. BS in Metallurgy, U. Belgrade, Yugoslavia, MS in Phys. Metallurgy, PhD, 1985. Prof. U. Belgrade, Belgrade, Serbia, 1985—2002; prin. investigator Nat. Ctr. for Electron Microscopy, Lawrence Berkeley Nat. Lab., U. Calif., Berkeley, 2002—. V.p. Yugoslav Materials Rsch. Soc., Belgrade, 1996—, Yugoslav Microscopical Soc., Belgrade. Contbr. over 200 articles to profl. jours. and confs. Fulbright scholar, 1986. Mem.: ASM Internat., TMS, Microscopical Soc. Am., Materials Rsch. Soc. Home Phone: 510-238-8990; Office Phone: 510-486-5663. Business E-Mail: vrradmilovic@lbl.gov.

RADNER, ROY, economist, educator, researcher; b. Chgo., June 29, 1927; s. Samuel and Ella (Kulansky) R.; m. Virginia L. Honoski, July 26, 1949 (dec. Apr. 1976); children: Hilary A., Erica H. (dec.), Amy E., Ephraim L.; m. Charlotte Virginia Kuh, Jan. 22, 1978. PhB with honors, U. Chgo, 1945, BS in Math., 1950, MS in Math., 1951, PhD in Math. Stats., 1956. Rsch. asst. Cowles Commn. for Rsch. in Econs. U. Chgo., 1951, rsch. assoc., 1951-54, asst. prof., 1954-55; mem. Cowles Found. for Rsch. in Econs. Yale U., New Haven, 1955-57, asst. prof. econs., 1955-57; assoc. prof. econs. and stats. U. Calif., Berkeley, 1957-61, prof. econs. and stats., 1961-79, chmn. dept. econs., 1966-69; Taussig prof. econs. Harvard U., Cambridge, Mass., 1977-78, vis. prof. Kennedy Sch. Govt., 1978-79; mem. tech. staff AT&T Bell Labs, Murray Hill, NJ, 1979-84, disting. mem. tech. staff, 1985-95; rsch. prof. econs. NYU, NYC, 1983—95, prof. econs. and info. sys., 1995, L.N. Stern Sch. prof. bus., 1996—, prof. environ. studies, 2006—. Mem. tech. adv. com. Carnegie Commn. on Future of Higher Edn., 1967-73; com. on fundamental rsch. relevant to edn. NRC-NAS, 1976-77, commn. on human resources, 1976-79; assembly of behavioral and social scis. NRC, 1979-82, com. on risk and decision making, 1980-81, working group on basic rsch. in behavioral and social scis., 1985-86, com. on info. tech. workforce, 1999-2000, com. on geophys. and environ. data, 2001-05; panel on contingent valuation methology NOAA, U.S. Dept. Commerce, 1992-93; steering com. Enjeux et Procedures de Decentralization Commissariat du Plan, Paris, 1992-95; mem. Com. on Prevention of Nuc. War. Author: Notes on Theory of Econ. Planning, 1963; co-author (with D. Jorgensen and J.J. McCall): Optimal Replacement Policy, 1967; co-author: (with J. Marshack) Econ. Theory of Teams, 1972; co-author: (with L.S. Miller) Demand and Supply in U.S. Higher Edn., 1975; co-author: (with C.V.Kuh) Mathematicians in Academia, 1980; co-editor: Decision and Orgn., 1972, Edn. as an Industry, 1976, Info., Incentives and Econ. Mechanisms, 1987, Perspectives on Deterrence, 1989, Bargaining with Incomplete Info., 1992; mem. editl. bd.: Mgmt. Sci., 1959—70, Econometricia, 1961—68, Jour. Econ. Theory, 1968—2005, Am. Econ. Review, 1979—82, Games and Econ. Behavior, 1989—2005, Econ. Theory, 1991—2003, Econ. Design, 1993—, Info. Sys. Frontiers, 2000—, Theoretical Econ., 2005—; contbr. articles to profl. jours. 2d lt. U.S. Army, 1945-48, PTO. William Cook scholar U. Chgo., 1944-45; fellow Ctr. Advanced Study in Behavioral Scis., Stanford, Calif., 1955-56, Guggenheim Found. fellow, 1961-62, 65-66, overseas fellow Churchill Coll., Cambridge U., Eng., 1969-70, 89. Fellow AAAS (disting. fellow), Econometric Soc. (v.p. 1970-72, pres. 1972-73), Am. Acad. Arts and Scis., Am. Econ. Assn. (disting. fellow); mem. NAS (chair econ. sect. 1994-97, sec. class 5 2004—07, chair class 5 2007-), Inst. Math. Stats. Avocations: music, hiking, cross country skiing. Home: 3203 Davenport St NW Washington DC 20008-2211 Business E-Mail: rradner@stern.nyu.edu.

RADNER, SIDNEY HOLLIS, retired retail executive; b. Holyoke, Mass., Dec. 8, 1919; s. William I. Radner; m. Helen Jane Cohen, Dec. 12, 1946; children: William Marc, Richard Scott. Student, Yale U., 1941. Ret. pres. Am. Rug Co., Holyoke. Lectr., cons., investigator on crooked gambling U.S. Armed Forces, Govt. of Can., state and mcpl. police squads; dir. Houdini Magical Hall of Fame, Niagara Falls, Ont., Canada; dir., organizer Ann. Ofcl. Houdini Seance. Author: Radner on Poker, Radner on Dice, Radner on Roulette and Casino Games, How to Detect Card Sharks; contbr. articles to profl. jours.; appeared in (TV series) Turn of a Card, 1953, Tonight Show, 1956, BBC Omnibus: Houdini, 1971, CNN, 1993—94, Today Show, Merv Griffin Show, CNBC, PBS, CBC, In Search Of..., Can. Discovery on magic, 1998, History Channel on Houdini, 2000, Ripley's Believe It or Not, History Channel, 2000, (TV series) Today Show, 2004, BBC History of Magic, 2004, cons. (TV films) Houdini, 1998, cons., participant (TV Spl.) A&E Houdini, 1996, appeared in (TV spl.) E Network Houdini documentary, 1998; cons., participant: (TV spl.) History Channel show on the world's largest Houdini collection, 2005; cons., participant (TV films) Discovery Channel documentary, 1997. Past pres. Holyoke C. of C.; co-founder Volleyball Hall of Fame; past bd. dirs. Greater Springfield (Mass.) Better Bus. Bur.; hon. curator, dir. Houdini Hist. Ctr., Appleton, Wis. With criminal investigation divsn. US Army, 1942—46. Named to Volleyball Hall of Fame, 1999. Mem.: Acad. Magical Arts, Nat. Assn. Bunco Investigators, Magicians Guild (charter), Magic Cir. London (mem. Inner Magic Cir.), Internat. Brotherhood Magicians, Soc. Am. Magicians (mem. occult investigation com.), Profs. Against Confidence Crime, China-Burma-India Vets. Assn. (life), Magic Collector's Assn. (charter, Honor award 1992), Houdini Club Wis. (hon.), Shriners, Masons, Rotary, Soc. Osaris (hon.). Jewish. Home (Summer): 1050 Northampton St Holyoke MA 01040-1321 Home (Winter): 3200 S Ocean Blvd Apt C203 Palm Beach FL 33480-6670

RADNOR, ALAN T., lawyer; b. Cleve., Mar. 10, 1946; s. Robert Clark and Rose (Chester) R.; m. Carol Sue Hirsch, June 22, 1969; children: Melanie, Joshua, Joanna. BA, Kenyon Coll., 1967; MS in Anatomy, Ohio State U., 1969, JD, 1972. Bar: Ohio 1972. Ptnr. Vorys, Sater, Seymour & Pease, Columbus, Ohio, 1972—. Adj. prof. law Ohio State U., Columbus, 1979-99. Author: Cross-Examining Doctors: A Practical Guide, 1999; contbr. articles to profl. jours. Bd. dirs., trustee Congregation Tifereth Israel, Columbus, 1975—, pres., 1985-87; trustee Columbus Mus. Art, 1995-98; pres. The Thurber House., 2004. Named Boss or Yr., Columbus Assn. Legal Secs., 1983. Fellow Am. Coll. Trial Lawyers; mem. ABA, Ohio State Bar Assn., Columbus Bar Assn., Def. Rsch. Inst., Internat. Assn. Def. Counsel. Avocations: reading, sculpture. Home: 400 S Columbia Ave Columbus OH 43209-1629 Office: Vorys Sater Seymour & Pease 52 E Gay St PO Box 1008 Columbus OH 43216-1008

RADO, PETER THOMAS, lawyer; b. Berlin, Nov. 12, 1928; came to U.S., 1931; naturalized, 1937; s. Sandor and Emmy (Chrisler) R.; m. Jacqueline Danenberg, Sept. 11, 1977. AB, HArvard U., 1949, LLB, 1952, LLM, 1953. Bar: N.Y. 1952. Assoc. Ide, Haigney & Rado, NYC, 1956-61, ptnr., 1961—. With U.S. Army, 1953-55. Mem. ABA, N.Y. State Bar Assn., Assn. of Bar of City of N.Y., Harvard Club (N.Y.C.). Home: 176 E 71st St New York NY 10021-5159 Office: Ide Haigney & Rado 176 E 71st St New York NY 10021-5159 E-mail: radopandj@aol.com.

RADOFF, LEONARD IRVING, librarian, consultant; b. Houston, Jan. 9, 1927; s. Morris Aaron and Jenny (Goldberg) R.; m. Lisel Ruth Ephraim, July 25, 1953; 1 child, Lesley Radoff Rappaport BA, Rice U., Houston, 1949; M.L.S., U. Tex., Austin, 1965. Cert. secondary sch. tchr., Tex. Tchr. math Aldine Ind. Sch. Dist., Houston, 1959-61, sch. librarian, 1961-63; head pub. services Abilene Pub. Library, Tex., 1964-65; library dir. Pasadena Pub. Library, Tex., 1966-70; chief br. services Houston Pub. Library, 1971-92, ret., 1992; library bldg. cons. Houston, 1975—. Treas. Literacy Vol. Am., Houston, 1984-85; mem. Northside Interests, Houston, 1982-85. Served with USN, 1945-46 Hoenthal scholar, 1948 Mem. Tex. Library Assn., ALA, Freedom to Read Found., Houston Great Books Council (leader trainer 1953-59, pres. 1967-69) Avocations: tutoring, music, stamp collecting/philately. Home: 4013 Gano St Houston TX 77009-4119

RADOMSKI, ROBYN L., marketing executive; b. Pitts., 1956; d. Robert G. and Helen L. Moses; m. A. David Radomski; children: Lauren E., Kristen L. BA in Journalism, Pa. State U., 1975; MBA in Mktg., DePaul U., 1989. Dir. Sedgwick-James, Inc., Chgo., 1977-81; v.p. Edelman Worldwide, Chgo., 1981-84, Playboy Enterprises, Inc., Chgo., 1984-91; sr. v.p. Bozell Worldwide, Chgo., 1991-92; v.p. mktg. Fluid Mgmt., L.P., Wheeling, Ill., 1992-96; v.p. mktg., CMO Wace, The Imaging Network, Chgo., 1996—98; v.p. mktg., pub. rels. and physician svcs. Northwestern Meml. Hosp., 1998—99; chief mktg. officer Sonnenschein Nath & Rosenthal, Chgo., 1999—; chmn. worldwide mktg. N.Am. Lex Mundi, 2003—. Bd. dirs. Playboy Found., Chgo. Mem.: Internat. Assn. Bus. Communicators (bd. dirs.), Pub. Rels. Clinic, Pub. Rels. Soc. Am., Nat. Investor Rels. Assn., Am. Mktg. Assn., Sigma Delta Chi. Avocation: yacht sailing. Office: Sonnenschein Nath & Rosenthal 8000 Sears Tower Chicago IL 60606

RADON, JENIK RICHARD, lawyer; b. Berlin, Jan. 14, 1946; arrived in U.S., 1951, naturalized, 1956; s. Louis and Irmgard (Hinz) R.; m. Heidi B. Duerbeck, June 10, 1971 (dec. Sept. 1999); 1 child, Kaara H.D. BA, Columbia Coll., 1967; MCP, U. Calif., Berkeley, 1971; JD, Stanford U., 1971. Bar: Calif. 1972, NY 1975, US Ct. Appeals (2d cir.) 1975, US Dist. Ct. (so. dist.) NY 1975. Atty. Radon & Ishizumi, NYC, 1981—. Bd. dirs. Gland Pharma Ltd., India; pub. Baltic Rev., 1993-04, City Paper (Baltic), 1993-03; trustee, executor Vetter Pharma, Germany, 1999—; adj. faculty Sch. Law Stanford U., 2000-02, Bus. Sch., 2000-01, Sch. Internat. Pub. Affairs Columbia U., 2002-, Indira Gandhi Inst. Devel. Rsch., Bombay, 2004—; lectr. in field. Editor-in-chief Stanford Jour. Internat. Studies, 1970-71; contbr. The Internat. Acquisitions Handbook, 1987, Negotiating and Financing Joint Ventures Abroad, 1989, How to Form and Manage Successful Strategic Alliances, 1990, Risks Mgmt. in Internat. Bus. 1991, Investing in Reform, 1991, Comrade Goes Pvt., 1992, Covering Energy and Development. A Reporter's Handbook, 2005; contbr. articles to profl. jours. Active Am. Coun. on Germany, NYC, 1978—; vice-chmn. US.-Polish Econ. Coun., 1989-93; mem. exec. com. Afghanistan Relief Com., NYC, 1980-95; bd. dirs. Columbia Coll. Alumni Assn., 1988-92, nat. coun., 1996-98, Freedom Medicine, 1987-94, chmn., 1989-94; trustee Direct Relief Internat., Santa Barbara, Calif., 1987-89; founder, dir. Eesti and Eurasian Fellowship of Columbia U., 1990—; profl. advisor Estonian Ministry Economy, Reform and Justice, 1991-95, Harriman Inst., 1993-2004; advisor to Parliament Republic of Georgia, 1996-98, to Pres. of Georgia, 1999-03; advisor Min. of Fin. of Georgia, 1998-00, Georgian Internat. Oil Corp., 1998-04; chmn. Estonian-Am. C. of C., 1990-93, Deutsche Stiftung for internat. rechtliche Zusammenarbeit, Estonia Commn., Beirat, 1992-94, Ctr. for Global Change and Governance Rutgers U., 2004-. Recipient Order of Honor award Republic of Georgia, 2000. Mem. ABA, German-Am. Law Assn. Roman Catholic. Office: Radon & Ishizumi 269 W 71st St New York NY 10023-3701

RADOUSKY, HARRY BRIAN, physicist; b. Chgo., May 14, 1955; s. Rudy and Esther R.; m. Judith, March 19, 1978; children: Ari, Elan, Oren, Yonah. BA in Physics, U. Ill., 1976, PhD in Physics, 1982. Postdoctoral rschr. Argonne Nat. Lab., Ill., 1982; exptl. physicist Lawrence Livermore at. Lab., Calif., 1982—, dep. dir. univ. rels. program, 1996—2007, acting dir. univ. rels. program, 2000-2001, divsn. leader for strategic recruiting program, 2007—; founding dir. Materials Rsch. Inst., 1997-2000; dir. lab. collaborations U. Calif. Office Pres., 2000—02; sci. editor Sci. and Tech. Rev., 2006—07; asst. assoc. dir. Nat. Ignition Facility, 2007—08. Adj. prof. physics U. Calif., Davis, 1991—. Editor: Magnetic Properties of Heavy Fermion Systems, 2000; contbr. over 100 articles to profl. jours. Fellow: Am. Phys. Soc. Achievements include the discovery of shock induced cooling in nitrogen; the development of a model to explain the destruction of superconductivity in $YBa_2Cu_3O_7$ when Pr replaces Y; breakthrough experiments and theory for understanding laser damage in optical materials. Office: Lawrence Livermore National Lab PO Box 808 Livermore CA 94551-0808 Business E-Mail: radouskyl@llnl.gov.

RADOVIC, MILADIN, engineering educator, researcher; s. Nedeljko and Milica Radovic. BSME, U. Belgrade, Serbia, 1992, MSME, 1997; PhD in Materials Engring., Drexel U., Phila., 2001. Tchg. asst., rsch. assoc. U. Belgrade, 1992—98; rsch. asst., assoc. dept. materials engring. Drexel U., Phila., 1998—2001; postdoctoral fellow Oak Ridge Nat. Lab., Tenn., 2001—06; asst. prof. dept. mech. engring. Tex. A&M U., College Station, 2006—. Guest scientist Nat. Inst. Stds. and Tech., Gaithersburg, Md., 1991—2001. Recipient A.W. Grosvenor award Acad. Performance, Drexel U., 2001; scholar, Ministry Sci. and Tech. Republic of Serbia, 1993, Gordon Rsch. Conf., Solid State Studies Ceramics, 2001. Mem.: ASM, European Structural Integrity Soc., Am. Ceramic Soc. Achievements include research in processing and characterization of nano-laminated MAX phases; reliability and durability of materials and components for solid oxide fuel cells; processing and characterization of the high-temperature. Office: Texas A&M Univ 3123 Tamu College Station TX 77843-3123 Home: 301 Holleman Dr E Apt 717 College Station TX 77840-7047 Home Phone: 865-560-9148; Office Phone: 979-845-5114. Office Fax: 979-845-3081. Business E-Mail: mradovic@tamu.edu.

RADOVICH, DONALD, painter, illustrator, retired art educator; b. Nazareth, Pa., Jan. 3, 1932; s. Zivan and Angeline (Trumich) R.; m. Sheryl Ann Nash; children: Steven Michael, Nicholas Daniel. BFA, U. N.Mex., 1956, MA in Painting, 1960; postgrad., San Miguél Allende, Gto, Mex., 1970. Instr. of art to prof. of art Western State Coll., Gunnison, Colo., 1964-88, prof. emeritus, 1988—; owner Canyon Creek Gallery, Ouray, Colo. Illustrator U. N.Mex. Press, 1963, Western State Press, 1980, Reader's Digest Corp., 1990, Phil. Acad. of Sci., 1990, Denver Colo. Sci., 1990, Nat. Wildlife Fedn., 1990, Birds of West Indies, 1998, Birds of Western Colorado, 2004, many others; invitational exhibit Wave Hill Mus., 1982; one person exhibit Nat. Wildlife Fedn., 1988, two person, Tohono Chul Pk. Gallery, Tucson, 2003. With US Army, 1956-58. Avocation: gardening. Home: 17232 Woodgate Rd Montrose CO 81401-7722

RADOWICH, JEFFREY J., lawyer; b. Balt., 1945; BA in humanities, Villanova U., 1967; MA in philos., Yale U., 1971, JD in taxation, 1971. Bar: Md. 1972. Atty. Ober, Kaler, Grimes & Shriver, Balt.; ptnr. Venable LLP, Balt. Trustee Bar Assns. Insurance Trust, 1993—. Recipient Best Lawyers in Am., Woodward White, Inc., 1993—2007. Fellow Am. Coll. Trust and Probate Counsel; mem. ABA, Md. State Bar Assn. (mem. sect. coun., sect. estate and trust law 1987-89, sec. 1989-90, chair-elect 1990-91, chmn. 1991-92), Bar Assn. Balt. City. Office: Venable LLP 2 Hopkins Plaza 1800 Mercantile Bank & Trust Bldg Baltimore MD 21201 Office Phone: 410-244-7516. Office Fax: 410-244-7742. Business E-Mail: jjradowich@venable.com.

RADTKE, DUANE C., energy executive; B in Mining Engring., U. Wis., 1971. With Tex. Pacific Oil Co., 1971, Coquina Oil & Gas, Midland, Tex., Fluor Oil & Gas, Denver, Primary Fuels, Houston and Denver, Santa Fe Snyder Corp., Houston; pres. internat. divsn. Devon Energy Corp., Oklahoma City; exec. v.p., pres. and CEO Dominion Exploration & Prodn. Dominion, Richmond, Va., 2001—. Bd. dirs. Offshore Energy Ctr., Nat. Ocean Industries Assn. Mem.: Soc. Petroleum Engrs., Tex. Ind. Prodrs. and Royalty Owners Assn., Ind. Petroleum Assn. Am. Office: Dominion PO Box 26532 Richmond VA 23261-6532 *

RADU, BOGDAN, aerospace engineer; b. Bucharest, Romania, Jan. 29, 1957; arrived in USA, 1991; s. Ionel and Maria Radu; m. Doina Radu, Jan. 17, 1981; 1 child, Ana. MS in Aerospace Engring., Poly. Inst., Bucharest, 1981. Cert. airframe and powerplant engr., Romanian Aero. Civil Authority, 1982, profl. engr., ASME, 1993, AIAA, 1993, airframe and powerplant engr., Airframe and Powerplant Fed. Aviation Adminstrn., 1993, profl. engring. maintenance engr., Profl. Airframe Maintainence Assn., 1994, aerospace engr., Seattle Profl. Engring. Assn., 1994, profl. engr., Seattle Profl. Engring. Assn., 1995. Mgr. engring. Tarom, Bucharest, 1981—91; sr. lead engr. Tower Air, NYC, 1991—94; sr. engr. design devel. Boeing, Seattle, 1994—96; sr. lead engr. design devel., project engr. Pratt & Whitney Can., Toronto, Ont., 1996—99; sr. lead engr. R&D Ketkert, Detroit, 1999—2001; mgr. project door sys. Lear Corp., 2001—04; CEO Advanced Sys. Tech., 2004—05; gen. mgr. country MGI Coutier Romania, Timisoara, 2005—06; sr. lead engr. ops. project design fabrication Sikorsky Helicopters, Stratford, Conn., 2006—. Achievements include 24 patents in field; 49 patents pending. Home: 5 7th Ave Garden City Park NY 11040 Personal E-mail: bogdanradu@yahoo.com.

RADWIN, JEROME J., public health service officer; BA in Polit. sci., Idaho State U., 1965. Fundraiser March of Dimes Birth Defects Found., NY, 1967, dir., gen. solicitation NYC, dir., devel. Chgo., 1971—74, exec. dir., 1974, exec. dir., nat. field svcs. dir., 1974—78, exec. dir., nat. field svcs. dir., asst. v.p., chpt. programs for nat. office, 1978, dir., chpt. NYC, v.p., corp. comms. and v.p., planning and mktg., 1984—88; founder J. Radwin Cons. Svc., 1989—; exec. dir. Nat. Victim Ctr., 1990—93; v.p., opers. Am. Found. for AIDS Rsch., NYC, 1993, sr. v.p., 1993—95, sr. v.p., COO, 1995—97, exec. v.p., CEO, 1997—2000, CEO, 2000—. Office: Am Found for AIDS Rsch 120 Wall St 13th fl New York NY 10005-3902 E-mail: jerry.radwin@amfar.org.

RADY, ERNEST S., thrift and loan association executive; b. Winnipeg, Canada, Aug. 28, 1937; s. Max and Rose Rady; m. Evelyn Rady; 3 children. B in Commerce (U. Gold Medal), U. Manitoba, JD. Founder, chmn. Am. Assets Inc., San Diego, 1967—; chmn. Ins. Co. West (ICW Group), 1972—; chmn. bd., CEO, founder Westcorp as the holding company for Western Thrift & Loan Assn. (sold to Wachovia in 2005 for $3.42 billion), Irvine, Calif., 1974—2005; acquired Amfac Thrift & Loan Assn. Westcorp, 1977, acquired Evergreen Savings and Loan Assn. (name changed to Western Financial Savings Bank), 1982; bd. dirs. Wachovia, 2006—, chmn. consumer fin. divsn. and Calif. bank, 2006—. Principal shareholder Coast Distributing, a distributor of Anheuser-Busch products in San Diego, PAR Broadcasting; purchased with Leon Parma KIOZ/FM 105.3, KOGO/AM 600, KLNV/FM 106.5 (then known as Q106), and KCBQ/AM 1170 (Sold to Clear Channel for $75 million in 1998); past part owner San Diego Sockers, San Diego Padres, 1990—94. Chmn. bd. trustees Children's Hosp. and Health Ctr. San Diego, 1990—93; chmn. Dean's Advisory Bd. Univ. Calif. San Diego Rady Sch. Mgmt.; trustee Salk Inst. Biological Sciences, Scripps Health; founder Rady Family Found.; pres. United Jewish Fedn., 1980—81; past chmn. Nat. Conf. Christians and Jews; involved Congregation Beth Israel Synagogue, San Diego. Named one of Forbes' Richest Americans, 2004—06; recipient Thomas F. Carter Leadership award, Children's Hosp. and Health Ctr. San Diego, 2003. Mem.: World Presidents Orgn., The Exec. Com. Achievements include $30 million contribution to UC San Diego's new School of Management in 2004 - renamed Rady School of Management; $60 million contribution to Children's Hosp. and Health Ctr. San Diego in 2006 - renamed Rady Children's Hosp. and Health Ctr. Office: Insurance Co West 11455 El Camino Real San Diego CA 92130 *

RADZELY, HOWARD M., federal agency administrator, lawyer; b. 1970; m. Lisa Radzely; 2 children. BS summa cum laude, U. Pa. Wharton Sch. Bus., 1992; JD magna cum laude, Harvard Law Sch. Law clk. to Hon. J. Michael Luttig US Ct. Appeals (4th Cir.); law clk. to Justice Antonin Scalia US Supreme Ct.; pvt. practice, law and employment law Washington; dep. solicitor labor US Dept. Labor, Washington, 2001, dep. solicitor, acting solicitor, 2001—02, acting solicitor, 2003, solicitor, 2003—07, acting dep. sec., 2007—. Office: US Dept Labor Frances Perkins Bldg Rm S2002 200 Constitution Ave NW Washington DC 20210-0001 Office Phone: 202-693-5260. Office Fax: 202-693-5278. Business E-Mail: radzely.howard@dol.gov.

RADZIK, ALBIN F., federal analyst, military consultant; b. Berwyn, Ill., Oct. 21, 1947; s. Albin F. and Evelyn Clara Radzik; children: Melanie Rose, Amy Marie. BS, Northwestern U.; MBA, Georgetown U., 1994; HHD (hon.), Kalinin U., St. Petersburg, 1995. Analyst U.S. Govt., Washington, 1976—, mil. cons., 1978—2001. Author: (poetry) Love and Distance, 1967 (Hole Creative Writing award, 1967). Mem. and vol. Cambodian Land Mine Relief Org.; vol. Chechnya Refugee Org.; open space com. City of Redlands, Calif., 1985—86. Served to capt. US Army, 1966—82. Decorated Bronze Star for Valor, Purple Heart, Disting. Svc. Cross, Army Commendation medal for valor, Air medal for valor, Combat Inf. badge, Parachutist badge, hon. capt. Russian Army; recipient Cold War Recognition cert., U.S. Sec. Def., 2003, cert. Special Merit, City Police Dept., Redwood City, Calif. Mem.: MENSA, VFW, Royal Order of the Purple Heart. Roman Catholic. Office Phone: 909-478-0659. Personal E-mail: aradzik@netzero.net.

RADZINOWICZ, MARY ANN, language educator; b. Champaign, Ill., Apr. 18, 1925; d. Arthur Seymour and Ann (Stacy) Nevins; m. Leon Radzinowicz, June 16, 1958 (div. 1978); children: Ann Stacy Radzinowicz Prior, William Francis Henry. BA, Radcliffe Coll., 1945; MA, Columbia U., 1947, PhD, 1953; MA (hon.), U. Cambridge, Eng., 1960. Prof. Vassar Coll., Poughkeepsie, NY, 1947-50, 52-59, Girton Coll., Cambridge, England, 1960-80, U. Cambridge, 1973-80, Cornell U., Ithaca, NY, 1980-90, Jacob Gould Schurman prof. English emeritus, 1990—. Mem. adv. bd. 2d, 3d, 4th Internat. Milton Symposia, 1985—. Author: Toward Samson Agonistes, 1978 (Hanford prize 1979), Milton's Epics and Psalms, 1989, Milton and the Tragic Women of Genesis, 1995 (Hanford prize); editor American Colonial Prose, 1984, Paradise Lost, Book VIII, 1974; mem. editl. bd. Milton Quar., 1981-2005, Christianity and Lit., 1989—. Mem. MLA, Renaissance Soc. Am., Milton Soc. Am. (honored scholar 1987), John Donne Soc. Home: Ballyconry House Ballyvaughan County Clare Ireland Office: Cornell U Dept English Lit Ithaca NY 14850 Home Phone: 353-65-7077085; Office Phone: 353-65-7077-085. E-mail: manr@eircom.net.

RAE, BARBARA JOYCE, employee placement company executive; b. Prince George, BC, Can., May 17, 1930; d. Alfred and Lottie Kathleen (Davis) Holmwood; m. George Suart, Feb. 14, 1984; children: James, Glenn, John. MBA, Simon Fraser U., Burnaby, B.C., 1975, LLD (hon.), 1998. Chmn., CEO Adia Can., Ltd., Vancouver, 1953-95; CEO Dekora Staging Inc., Vancouver, B.C., 2003—. Bd. dirs. emeritus Can. Imperial Bank Commerce, Grosvenor Internat. Ltd., Noranda, Inc., Telus, Xerox Can.; dir. VLINX.Com., Can. Inst. Adv. Rsch., 1995-2001, KTCS Pub. Broadcasting; bd. govs. Multiple Sclerosis Soc., 1995—; mem. Fed. Task Force on Future of Can. Fin. Svcs. Sector, 1997-98; past chmn. B.C. Women's Hosp. Found., 1994-97. Chancellor Simon Fraser U., 1987—93; mem. Jud. Appts. Com., B.C., 1988—90; commr. Triennial Commn. Judges Salaries and Benefits; mem. Premier's Econ. Adv. Coun., B.C., 1987—91, Prime Minister's Com. on Sci. and Tech., 1989—94; gen. chmn. United Way Lower Mainland, 1987; chair Salvation Army Red Shield Vancouver Campaign, 1986; bd. dirs. Vancouver Bd. Trade, 1972—76; dir. Royal B.C. Mus.; patron Can. Coun. Christians and Jews; mem. adv. bd. Salvation Army, 1985—2004. Decorated Order of Can., Order of B.C.; recipient Outstanding Alumnae award Simon Fraser U., 1985, Disting. Alumni Svc. award, 1995, Bus. Women of Yr. award Vancouver YWCA, 1986, West Vancouver Achievers award, 1987, B.C. Entrepreneur of Yr. award, 1987, Nat. Vol. award, 1990, Can. Woman Entrepreneur B.C. award, 1992, Queen's Jubilee medal, 2003, Clan Leader award Simon Fraser U., 2004. Home: 3355 Osprey Box 508 Whistler Canada V0N 1B3 Personal E-mail: brae@dekora.com.

RAE, JENEANNE, new product development and innovation consultant, educator; married; 2 children. BS in Commerce, U. Va.; MBA, Harvard Bus. Sch. Prin., sr. mgmt. team mem. IDEO, Palo Alto, Calif.; co-founder Peer Insight, LLC, Alexandria, Va. Adj. prof. mktg. Georgetown U. McDonough Sch. Bus. Contbr. articles to profl. jours. Named one of Magnificent Seven Gurus of Innovation, BusinessWeek, 2005. Office: Peer Insight LLC 901 King St Ste 400 Alexandria VA 22314 Office Phone: 703-778-5543. Office Fax: 703-535-8176. Business E-Mail: jrae@peerinsight.com.

RAE, MATTHEW SANDERSON, JR., lawyer; b. Pitts., Sept. 12, 1922; s. Matthew Sanderson and Olive (Waite) R.; m. Janet Hettman, May 2, 1953; children: Mary-Anna, Margaret Rae Mallory, Janet S. Rae Dupree. AB, Duke, 1946, LLB, 1947; postgrad., Stanford U., 1951. Bar: Md. 1948, Calif. 1951. Asst. to dean Duke Sch. Law, Durham, NC, 1947-48; assoc. Karl F. Steinmann, Balt., 1948-49, Guthrie, Darling & Shattuck, LA, 1953-54; nat. field rep. Phi Alpha Delta Law Frat., LA, 1949-51; research atty. Calif. Supreme Ct., San Francisco, 1951-52; ptnr. Darling, Hall & Rae (and predecessor firms), LA, 1955—. Mem. Calif. Commn. Uniform State Laws, 1985—, chmn., 1993-94; chmn. drafting com. for revision Uniform Prin. and Income Act of Nat. Conf., 1991-97, Probate and Mental Health Task Force, Jud. Coun. Calif., 1996-2000. Vice pres. L.A. County Rep. Assembly, 1959-64; mem. L.A. County Rep. Ctrl. Com., 1960-64, 77-90, 2000—, exec. com., 1977-90; vice chmn. 17th Congl. Dist., 1960-62, 28th Congl. Dist., 1962-64; chmn. 46th Assy. Dist., 1962-64, 27th Senatorial Dist., 1977-85, 29th Senatorial Dist., 1985-90, sec. 53d Assembly Dist., 2000-; mem. Calif. Rep. State Ctrl. Com., 1966—, exec. com., 1966-67; pres. Calif. Rep. League, 1966-67; trustee Rep. Assocs., 1979-94, pres., 1983-85, chmn. bd. dirs., 1985-87. 2d lt. USAAF, WWII. Fellow Am. Coll. Trust and Estate Counsel; academician Internat. Acad. Estate and Trust Law (exec. coun. 1974-78); mem. ABA, L.A. County Bar Assn. (chmn. probate and trust law com. 1964-66, chmn. legis. com. 1980-86, chmn. program com. 1981-82, chmn. membership retention com. 1982-83, trustee 1983-85, dir. Bar Found., 1987-93, Arthur K. Marshall award probate and trust law sect. 1984, Shattuck-Price Meml. award 1990), South Bay Bar Assn., State Bar of Calif. (chmn. state bar jour. com. 1970-71, probate com. 1974-75; exec. com. estate planning trust and probate law sect. 1977-83, chmn. legis. com. 1977-89; co-chmn. 1991-92; probate law cons. group Calif. Bd. Legal Specialization 1977-88; chmn. conf. dels. resolutions com. 1987, exec. com. conf. dels. 1987-90), Lawyers Club L.A. (bd. govs. 1981-87, 1st v.p. 1982-83), Am. Legion (comdr. Allied post 1969-70), Legion Lex (bd. dirs. 1964-99, pres. 1969-71), Air Force Assn., Aircraft Owners and Pilots Assn., Town Hall (gov. 1970-78, pres. 1975), World Affairs Coun., Internat. Platform Assn., Breakfast Club (law, pres. 1989-90), Commonwealth Club, Chancery Club (pres. 1996-97), Rotary, Phi Beta Kappa (councilor Alpha Assn. 1983—, pres. 1996), Omicron Delta Kappa, Phi Alpha Delta (supreme justice 1972-74, elected to Disting. Svc. chpt. 1978), Sigma Nu. Presbyterian. Home: 600 John St Manhattan Beach CA 90266-5837

RAE, NANCY A., human resources specialist, automotive executive; 1 child. Diploma in Bus. Adminstrn., Ea. Mich. U., M in Indsl. Rels. Interviewer Chrysler Corp., Warren, Mich., 1978; various positions DaimlerChrysler Corp., Auburn Hills, Mich., 1978—92, group personnel exec., procurement and supply and product strategy and regulatory affairs, 1992—94, mgr. workforce diversity and econ. equality, 1994, group personnel mgr., Chrysler Tech. Ctr., 1994—96, group human resources mgr. tech. ops., 1996—98, mgr. health ins. and disability, 1998, v.p. compensation and benefits, 1998—2000, sr. v.p. human resources, 2000—. Office: DaimlerChrysler Corp 1000 Chrysler Dr Auburn Hills MI 48326-2766 Office Phone: 248-576-5741. Office Fax: 248-576-4742.

RAEBER, JOHN ARTHUR, architect, construction consultant; b. St. Louis, Nov. 24, 1947; s. Arthur William and Marie (Laux) R. AA, Jefferson Coll., 1968; AB, Washington U., 1970, MArch, 1973. Registered architect, Calif., Mo.; cert. constrn. specifier; cert. Nat. Coun. Arch. Specification writer Hellmuth, Obata & Kassabaum, St. Louis, 1973-78, constrn. administr., 1978-79; mgr. of specifications Gensler & Assocs., San Francisco, 1979-82; ind. constrn. specifier San Francisco, 1982—. Adj. prof. architecture Calif. Coll. Arts and Crafts, San Francisco, 1986—; access code advisor Constrn. Industry & Owners, 1982—; spkr., instr. seminars orgns., univs., 1982—; mem. Calif. State Bldg. Standards Commn. Accessibility Adv. Panel, Sacramento, 1981, Calif. Subcom. Rights of Disabled Adv. Panel, Sacramento, 1993; cons. Nat. Inst. Bldg. Scis., 1996—. Author: CAL/ABL: Interpretative Manual to California's Access Barriers Laws, 1982; co-author: (with Peter S. Hopf) Access for the Handicapped, 1984; columnist Constrn. Specifier Mag., 1988-95. Vol. Calif. Office Emergency Svcs. Safety Assessment, Sacramento, 1991—. Fellow AIA (San Francisco chpt. codes com., Calif. coun. codes and standards com., nat. masterspec rev. com. 1982-84, nat. codes com. corr.), Contrns. Specifications Inst. (cert., columnist newsletter San Francisco chpt. 1984-95, Ben John Small award for Outstanding Stature as practicing specifications writer 1994, pres. St. Louis chpt. 1978-79, pres. San Francisco chpt. 1993-94, tech. com., edn. com., publs. com., Specifications Proficiency award San Francisco chpt. 1989, Tech. Commendation award 1987); mem. Specifications Cons. in Ind. Practice (nat. pres. 1990-92, nat. sec./treas. 1988-90), Internat. Conf. Bldg. Officials, Phi Theta Kappa. Avocations: history, anthropology, science fiction. Home and Office: 3962 26th St San Francisco CA 94131-2002

RAEBURN, ANDREW HARVEY, performing arts consultant, recording industry executive; b. London, July 22, 1933; arrived in U.S., 1964, Can., 1993; s. Walter Augustus Leopold and Dora Adelaide Harvey (Williams) R. BA in History, King's Coll., Cambridge U., 1958, MA, 1962; diploma in music performance (hon.), Mt. Royal Coll., 1998; LLD (hon.), U. Calgary, 2005. Mus. dir. Argo Record Co., London, 1959—64; asst. to music dir., program editor Boston Symphony Orch., 1964—73; dir. artists and repertory New World Records, NYC, 1975—79; artistic adminstr. Detroit Symphony Orch., 1979—82; exec. dir. Van Cliburn Found. Inc., Ft. Worth, 1982—85; performing arts cons., 1985—93; exec. v.p. The Peter Pan Children's Fund, 1990—91; exec. dir. Esther Honens Internat. Piano Competition Found., 1993—95, pres., 1995—99, vice chmn., artistic dir., 1999—2001, pres., artistic dir., 2001—04; freelance cons. Calgary, Canada, 2004—. Cons. music; radio and TV commentator; mem. faculty Boston U., 1966-67; condr. New World String Orch., 1978; v.p. World Fedn. Internat. Music Competitions, 2003-06. Author record liner notes, Argo, RCA, Time-Life records, 1960-79, program notes, Boston Symphony Orch., 1968-73. Served with Royal Arty. Brit. Army, 1952-55; founding dean Prague Mozart Acad. 1992-93. Recipient Lifetime Achievement award, World Fedn. Internat. Music Competitions, 2006. Home and Office: 702 235 15th Ave SW Calgary AB Canada T2R 0P6 Office Phone: 403-263-9939. Personal E-mail: araeburn@telus.net, ar@andrewraeburn.com.

RAEBURN, JOHN HAY, language educator; b. Indpls., July 18, 1941; s. Gordon Maurice and Katherine (Calwell) R.; m. Gillian Kimble, Aug. 18, 1963 (div. July 1979); children— Daniel Kennedy, Nicholas Kimble; m. Kathleen Kamerick, July 5, 1986. AB with honors, Ind. U., 1963; A.M., U. Pa., 1964, PhD, 1969. Asst. prof. U. Mich., Ann Arbor, 1967-74; vis. lectr. U. Iowa, Iowa City, 1974-75, assoc. prof., 1976-83, prof. English, 1983—; chmn. Am. Studies dept., 1983-85, 94-2000; chmn. English dept. U. Iowa, Iowa City, 1985-91; assoc. prof. U. Louisville, 1975-76. Author: Fame Became of Him: Hemingway as Public Writer, 1984, A Staggering Revolution: A Cultural History of Thirties Photography, 2006; editor: (with others) Frank Capra: The Man and His Films, 1975. Mem.: Am. Studies Assn., Orgn. Am. Historians. Democrat. Home: 321 Hutchinson Ave Iowa City IA 52246-2407 Office: U Iowa Dept Am Studies 210 Jefferson Bldg Iowa City IA 52242-1418 Home Phone: 319-338-5590; Office Phone: 319-335-0320. Business E-Mail: john-raeburn@iowa.edu.

RAEDER, MYRNA SHARON, lawyer, educator; b. NYC, Feb. 4, 1947; d. Samuel and Estelle (Auslander) R.; m. Terry Oliver Kelly, July 13, 1975; children: Thomas Oliver, Michael Lawrence. BA, Hunter Coll., 1968; JD, NYU, 1971; LLM, Georgetown U., 1975. Bar: N.Y. 1972, D.C. 1972, Calif. 1972. Spl. asst. U.S. atty. U.S. Atty's Office, Washington, 1972-73; asst. prof. U. San Fransisco Sch. Law, 1973-75; assoc. O'Melveny & Myers, LA, 1975-79; assoc. prof. Southwestern U. Sch. Law., LA, 1979-82, prof., 1983—, Irwin R. Buchalter prof. law, 1990, Paul E. Treusch prof. law, 2002; mem. faculty Nat. Judicial Coll., 1993—. Prettyman fellow Georgetown Law Ctr., Washington, 1971—73. Author: Federal Pretrial Practice, 3d edit., 2000; co-author: Evidence, State and Federal Rules in a Nutshell, 4th edit., 2003, Evidence, Cases, Materials and Problems, 3d edit., 2006; co-editor: Acheiveing Justice: Freeing the Innocent, Convicting the Guilty, 2006. Named to Alumni Hall of Fame, Hunter Coll., 2005. Mem.: ABA (trial evidence com. 1980—, criminal justice sect. 1994—97, adv. to nat. conf. commrs. uniform state laws drafting com. 1996—99, vice-chair planning 1997—98, chair elect 1997—98, chair 1998—99, mem. mag. bd. 2000—, co-chair ad hoc innocence com. 2002—, mem. youth at risk commn. 2006—07, mem. litig. sect. 1980—, Margaret Brent Women Lawyers of Achievement award 2002), Am. Law Inst., Assn. Am. Law Schs. (chair women in legal edn. sect. 1982, com. on sects. 1984—87, chair elect evidence sect. 1996, chair 1997), Nat. Assn. Women Lawyers (bd. dirs. 1991—98, pres.-elect 1993, pres. 1994—96), Women Lawyers Assn. LA (coord. mothers support group 1987—96, bd. dirs., Ernestine Stallhutt award 2003), Am. Bar Found. (life), Order of Coif, Phi Beta Kappa. Office: Southwestern U Sch Law 675 S Westmoreland Ave Los Angeles CA 90005-3905 Business E-Mail: mraeder@swlaw.edu.

RAEL, HENRY SYLVESTER, SR., retired health administrator, financial and management consultant; b. Pueblo, Colo., Oct. 2, 1928; s. Daniel and Grace (Abeyta) R.; m. Helen Warner Loring Brace, June 30, 1956 (dec. Aug. 1980); children: Henry Sylvester Jr., Loring Victoria, Thomas Warner Bush. AB, U. So. Colo., 1955; BA in Bus. Adminstrn., U. Denver, 1957, MBA, 1958. Sr. boys counselor Denver Juvenile Hall, 1955-58; adminstrv. asst. to pres. Stanley Aviation Corp., Denver, 1958-61; Titan III budget and fin. control supr. Martin Marietta Corp., Denver, 1961-65; mgmt. adv. services officer U. Colo. Med. Center, Denver, 1965-72; v.p. fin., treas. Loretto Heights Coll., Denver, 1972-73; dir. fin. and adminstrn. Colo. Found. for Med. Care, 1973-86, Tri-County Health Dept., 1987—96; ret., 1996. Instr. fin. mgmt., mem. fin. com. am. Assn. Profl. Standards Rev. orgn., 1980-85; speaker systems devel., design assns., univs., 1967-71. Mem. budget lay adv. com. Park Hill Elem. Sch., Denver, 1967-68, chmn., 1968-69; vol. worker Boy and Girl Scouts, 1967-73; bd. dirs. Community Arts Symphony, 1981-83, 85-87; controller St. John's Episcopal Cathedral, 1982-83; charter mem. Pueblo (Colo.) Coll. Young Democrats, 1954-55; block worker Republican Party, Denver, 1965-68, precinct committeeman, 1978-84; trustee Van Nattan Scholarship Fund, 1974-96; bd. dirs. Vis. Nurse Assn., 1977-84, treas., 1982-84; cons. to dir. Clayton Found., 1996; cons. Colo. Dept. Health Contr., 1997. Served with USAF, 1947-53, res., 1954-61. Recipient Disting. Service award Denver Astron. Soc., 1968, Citation Chamberlin Obs., 1985; Stanley Aviation masters scholar, 1957; Ballard scholar, 1956. Mem.: Nat. Astronomers Assn. (exec. bd. 1965—97), Am. Assn. Founds. for Med. Care (fin. com. 1981—82), Denver Astron. Soc. (pres. 1965—66, bd. dirs. 1982—94), Colo. Pub. Employees Retirement Assn. (bd. dirs. 1993), Budget Execs. Inst. (sec. 1963—64, v.p. chpt. 1964—65), Hosp. Systems Mgmt. Soc., Assn. Systems. Mgmt. (pres. 1971—72), Whispering Pines of Denver Homeowners Assn. (pres. bd. dirs. 1998, dir.-at-large 2001), Brandy Chase Homeowners Assn. (bd. dirs. 1997), Delta Psi Omega, Epsilon Xi. Home: 7755 E Quincy Ave Apt 57 Denver CO 80237-2312

RAESE, DAVID SENNA, aerospace and mass properties engineer, consultant; b. Morgantown, W.Va. s. John Thomas and Joan Marie (Keeney) Raese. BSCE, Washington State U., Pullman, 1981, BS in Gen. Sci., 1981; attended, U. Bonn, Germany, 1978—79. Cert. profl. engr., Wash., 1995. Engr. Boeing Comml. Airplanes, Everett, Wash., 1981—85, Renton, 1981—85, Boeing Space and Comm., Huntsville, Ala., 1985—87; engrng. team leader Boeing Missile Sys. Divsn., Kent, Wash., 1987—91, Boeing Comml. Space Co., Tukwila, 1997—99; engr., auditor, cons. Boeing Helicopters Divsn., Ridley Park, Pa., 1991—93; engrng. team leader, cons. Boeing Def. and Space Divsn., Kent, Wash., 1993—97, Boeing Integrated Def. Sys., Kent, 1999—. Mass properties engrng. mentor Boeing Ed Wells Mentoring Program NW Region, 2005—; tech. focal cons., Boeing assoc. tech. fellow N.W. Region, 2006. Contbr. chapters to books. Mem.: SAR, Soc. Automotive Engrs., Soc. Allied Weight Engrs., Inc., Am. Inst. Aeronautics and Astronautics (sr.), Descendants of Knights of Garter, Friends of St. George's, Nat. Hugenot Soc. Wash., Nat. Soc. Magna Charta Dames and Barons. Independent. Presbyterian. Avocations: travel, hiking, art, history. Office: The Boeing Co PO Box 3999 Seattle WA 98124-2499 Office Phone: 253-657-6731. Business E-Mail: david.s.raese@boeing.com.

RAETZ, CHRISTIAN R. H., biochemistry professor; b. Berlin, Nov. 17, 1946; BS in Chemistry, Yale U., 1967; MD, Harvard U., 1973, PhD. House officer Peter Bent Brigham Hosp., Boston, 1973-74; research assoc. Nat. Inst. Gen. Med. Scis., USPHS, Bethesda, Md., 1974-76; asst. prof. biochemistry U. Wis.-Madison, 1976-79, assoc. prof., 1979-82, prof., dir. Ctr. for Membrane Biosynthesis Research, 1982—87; exec. dir biochemistry Merck Rsch. Lab., Rahway, NJ, 1987—91, v.p. basic rsch., biochemistry and mircobiology, 1992—93; George Barth Geller prof., chmn. of biochemistry Duke Univ. Med. Ctr., Durham, NC, 1993—. Mem. biochemistry study sect. NIH Contbr. numerous articles to profl. jours. Mem. editorial bd. Jour. Biol. Chemistry Recipient James Tolbert Shipley Research prize Harvard U. Med. Sch., 1973, Harry and Evelyn Steenbock Career Advancement award, 1976, Research Career Devel. award NIH, 1978-83, Dreyfus Tchr.-Scholar award, 1979; H. I. Romnes Faculty fellow U. Wis., 1984; NIH grantee Mem. Am. Soc. Biol. Chemists, Japanese Soc. Promotion Sci., Phi Beta Kappa, Alpha Omega Alpha, NAS. Office: Duke U Dept Biochemistry 255 Nanaline H Duke PO Box 3711 DUMC Durham NC 27710-0001 Home: 7411 Bill Poole Rd Rougemont NC 27572

RAEUCHLE, JOHN STEVEN, application developer; b. Washington, Sept. 21, 1955; s. Richard Frank and Ruth Darlene (Fulton) R. BS, Tex. Christian U., 1978. Programmer Tex. Christian U., Ft. Worth, 1976-78, Warrex Computer Sys., Ft. Worth, 1978-79; sys. programmer Tandy Data Processing, Ft. Worth, 1979-84; sr. programmer, analyst Commodity News Svcs., Leawood, Kans., 1984-86, Logica Data Archs., St. Louis, 1986-89; computer analyst Credit Sys., Inc., St. Louis, 1989-95; sr. software engr. Master Card Internat., St. Louis, 1995—. Mem. St. Louis Ambassadors, 1989—98; active Boy Scouts Am., 1964—95. Recipient awrd of merit Boy Scouts Am., Commrs. Key, 1982. Mem. St. Louis Jaycees Found. (treas. 1990-94, 2001—, sec. 1994-96, 99-2001, pres. 1996-99), U.S. Jr. C. of C. Senate Found., Mo. Jr. C. of C. Internat. Senate (treas. 1997-98, v.p. 1998-99, pres. 1999-2000, chmn. bd. 2000-01, comm. dir. 2004—), Mo. Jaycees (state officer 1989-94), Kansas City Jaycees (bd. dirs. 1985-87), Kansas City Jaycees Found., St. Louis Jr. C. of C. (pres. 1988-89). Democrat. Methodist. Avocations: camping, bowling, hiking. Office: Master Card Internat 2200 Master Card Blvd O Fallon MO 63366 Home: 8682 Garfield Ave Huntington Beach CA 92646-2150 Office Phone: 636-722-2342. Personal E-mail: jraeuchle@aol.com.

RAFALSKI, BRIAN, professional hockey player; b. Dearborn, Mich., Sept. 28, 1973; m. Felicity Rafalski; children: Danny, Evan James, Matthew. Grad., U. Wis., 1995. Defenseman NJ Devils, 1999—2007, Detroit Red Wings, 2007—. Player NHL All-Star Game, 2002, 04; mem. USA Olympic Hockey Team, Salt Lake City, 2002, Torino, Italy, 06. Named to All-Rookie Team, NHL, 2000. Achievements include being a member of Stanley Cup Champion NJ Devils, 2000, 2003; being a member of silver medal winning USA Hockey Team, Salt Lake City Olympics, 2002. Office: Detroit Red Wings Joe Louis Arena 600 Civic Center Dr Detroit MI 48226 *

RAFEEDIE, EDWARD, federal judge; b. Orange, NJ, Jan. 6, 1929; s. Fred and Nabeeha (Hishmeh) R.; m. Ruth Alice Horton, Oct. 8, 1961; children: Fredrick Alexander, Jennifer Ann. BS in Law, U. So. Calif., 1957, JD, 1959; LLD (hon.), Pepperdine U., 1978. Bar: Calif. 1960. Pvt. practice, Santa Monica, Calif., 1960-69; mcpl. ct. judge Santa Monica Jud. Dist., 1969-71; judge Superior Ct. State of Calif., LA, 1971-82; dist. judge U.S. Dist. Court (cen. dist.) Calif., LA, 1982-96, sr. judge, 1996—. With U.S. Army, 1950-52, Korea. Office: US Dist Ct 312 N Spring St Ste 244P Los Angeles CA 90012-4704 Office Phone: 213-894-6927.

RAFEYAN, ROUEEN, psychiatrist, educator; b. Tehran, Iran, Oct. 1, 1961; came to U.S., 1979; s. Majid Rafeyan and Nezhat Babanoury; m. Helena Linda Hernandez, Feb. 15, 1991; 1 child, Ryan Michael. BA, Knox Coll., 1981; MD, U. Istanbul, Turkey, 1989. Cert. Am. Bd. Psychiatry &

Neurology, 2001; Am. Bd. Psychiatry and Neurology. Resident U. Ill. Chgo., 1996; dir. outpatient clin. svcs., dir. med. student edn. Michael Reese Hosp., Chgo., 1996-99; med. dir. Rush Presbyn., Chgo., 1997—; asst. clin. prof. psychiatry U. Ill., Chgo., 1996—; asst. prof psychiatry Rush U., 2005—. Cons. Threshold Cmty. Mental Health Ctr., Chgo., 1996—. Mem. AMA, Am. Psychiatric Assn., Ill. Psychiatric Soc., Chgo. Med. Soc. Avocations: tennis, music, world history. Office: Michael Reese Hosp 2959 S Cottage Grove Ave Chicago IL 60616 Office Phone: 312-791-3930. Personal E-mail: roueen@msn.com.

RAFFAY, STEPHEN JOSEPH, manufacturing executive, director; b. McAdoo, Pa., Oct. 25, 1927; s. Stephen John and Stephanie (Severa) R.; m. Audree Eugenia Kuehne, Sept. 12, 1953; children: Andrea, Stephen, Leslie. BA, Columbia U., NYC, 1950, MS, 1951. C.P.A., N.Y. Sr. accountant Arthur Andersen & Co., NYC, 1951-56; asst. controller Emhart Corp., Farmington, Conn., 1956-61, asst. treas., 1961-63, treas., 1963-67, v.p. internat., 1967-72, v.p., group pres., 1972-79, exec. v.p., 1979-84, vice chmn., chief adminstrv. officer, 1984-87, dir., 1980-87; sr. v.p. Dexter Corp., Windsor Locks, Conn., 1987-90. Bd. dirs. United Plumbing Tech., Inc., EDAC Techs. Inc. Bd. dirs. Hartford Symphony Soc. With AUS, 1946-47. Mem. AICPA, Conn. Soc. CPAs. Home: 93 Westmont St West Hartford CT 06117-2929

RAFFEGEAU, JEAN MICHEL, audit and consulting company executive; b. St. Germain en Laye, Yvelines, France, Sept. 24, 1930; s. Louis and Irene (Pithon) R.; m. Nicole Laporte, Jan. 19, 1962; children: Catherine, Brigitte. Diploma in law, Sorbonne U., Paris, 1954; diploma in bus. adminstrn., H.E.C., Paris, 1954. Chartered acct. Commissaire aux Comptes, 1966. Asst. mgr. Banque de Paris et des Pays-Bas, Paris, 1955-57; adminstrv. and fin. mgr. Société Industrielle de Transmissions, 1958-66; chmn., mng. dir. Befec, Paris, 1966-89, Befec-Price Waterhouse, 1989-94; regional mng. pntr. French-speaking Europe and Africa Price Waterhouse, Paris, 1994-96, hon. pres., 1995—. Legal expert Court Appeal, Paris, 1979, adminstv. court, Paris, 1982. Co-author: L'Audit Opérationnel, 1993; co-author, editor: Les Comptes Consolidés, 1989, Guide du Financement des Entreprises, 1993, Le Mémento Comptable, 1997, Evaluation of Enterprise, 4th edit., 2003. Recipient silver medal Order of Experts Comptables, Paris, 1979, Chevalier de la Légion d'Honneur, Govt. France, Paris, 1995, Mem. Chartered Accountancy Exams. Jury, Rotary (Paris) (treas. 1987-88), Cercle Union Interalliée. Avocations: reading, cinema, photography. Office Phone: 33-1-47-47-80-45. E-mail: j.raffegeau@free.fr.

RAFFEL, BURTON NATHAN, literature educator, poet, translator; b. NYC, 1928; married, six children. BA cum laude, Bklyn. Coll., 1948; MA, Ohio State U., 1949; JD, Yale U., 1958. Lawyer Milbank, Tweed, Hadley & McCloy, NYC, 1958-60; editor Foundation News, 1960-63; instr. English SUNY, Stony Brook, 1964-65, asst. prof. of English, 1965-66, assoc. prof. English Buffalo, 1966-68; prof. English and Classics U. Tex., Austin, 1969-71; sr. tutor, dean Ont. Coll. Art, Toronto, Can., 1971-72; prof. English U. Denver, 1975-87; dir. Adirondack Mountain Found., 1987-89; Disting. prof. arts and humanitites, prof. English U. La., Lafayette, 1989—2003; assoc. prof. English U. Haifa, 1968—69. Lectr. English dept. Bklyn. Coll., 1950-51; instr. Ford Found. English Lang. Tchr. Tng. program in Indonesia, resident in Makassar, 1953-55; vis. prof. Humanities York U., Toronto, 1972-75, vis. prof. English Emory U., 1974; sr. editor, cons. McDonnell Douglas Computer-Based Systems Tng. Group, Denver, 1985-87; lectr. in law U. Denver, 1986-87. Author: The Development of Modern Indonesian Poetry, 1967, Mia Poems, 1968, The Forked Tongue: A Study of the Translation Process, 1971, Why Re-Create?, 1973, Four Humours, 1979, (film) The Legend of Alfred Packer, 1979, Robert Lowell, 1981, T.S. Eliot, 1982, Changing the Angle of the Sun-Dial, 1984, Grice, 1985, Evenly Distributed Rubble, 1985, Ezra Pound: The Prime Minister of Poetry, 1985, The Art of Translating Poetry, 1988, American Victorians: Exploration in Emotional History, 1984, Possum and Ole Ez in the Public Eye, 1985, After Such Ignorance, 1986, Man as a Social Animal, 1986, Artists All, 1986, Politicians, Poets, and Con Men, 1986, Founder's Fury, 1988, The Art of Translating Poetry, 1988, Founder's Fortune, 1989, From Stress to Stress: An Autobiography of English Prosody, 1992, The Art of Translating Prose, 1994, The Annotated Milton, 1999, Beethoven in Denver and Other Poems, 1999, The Annotated Hamlet, 2003, The Annotated Romeo and Juliet, 2004, Macbeth, 2005, Midsummer Night's Dream, 2005, Othello, 2005, Taming of the Shrew, 2005, The Tempest, 2006, Henry IV, Part One, 2006, The Merchant of Venice, 2006, Julius Ceasar, 2006, Twelfth Night, 2007, King Lear, 2007, Richard III, 2007, Antony and Cleopatra, 2007; mem. editl. bd. Oral Tradition, 1983—, Literature East and West, 1967-70; adv. editor The Lit. Rev., 1987-03; reviewer/writer Asian Wall St. Jour., 1978-85; contbr. articles to profl. jours. Mem. Bar of the State of N.Y., The Nat. Faculty. Home: 203 S Mannering Ave Lafayette LA 70508-4829 E-mail: bnraffel@cox.net.

RAFFEL, LEROY B., real estate developer; b. Zanesville, Ohio, Mar. 13, 1927; s. Jacob E. and Anne M. (Oliker) R.; m. Shirley Balbot, Sept. 11, 1949; children: Kenneth, Janet, James, Nancy. BS, U. Pa., 1949. Pres. Raffel Bros., Inc., Youngstown, Ohio, 1949-78, York Mahoning Co., Youngstown, 1950-64, Arby's, Inc., Youngstown, 1964-70, chmn. bd., 1971-79; pres. Brom Equity Devel., Inc., Miami, Fla., 1979—. Served with USNR, 1945-46. Home: 2141 NE 190th Ter North Miami Beach FL 33179-4352 Office: Brom Equity Devel Inc Ste 207 1380 NE Miami Gardens Dr Miami FL 33179-4709 Home Phone: 305-935-2187; Office Phone: 305-949-6445.

RAFFERTY, EMILY KERNAN, museum administrator; b. NYC, Mar. 13, 1949; m. John Rafferty; children: Nicholas, Sara. BA cum laude, Boston U., 1971. Arts and philanthropy asst. to David Rockefeller, Jr., Boston, 1971; deputy dir. edn. Inst. Contemporary Art, Boston, 1973—75; adminstr. corp., found. and individual fundraising Met. Mus. of Art, NYC, 1976—81, mgr. devel., 1981—84, v.p. devel. and membership, 1984—96, sr. v.p. devel. and membership, 1996—99, sr. v.p. external affairs, 1999—2005, pres., 2005—. Mem. blue ribbon com Am. Cancer Soc. Found., 1999—2000; lifetime honorary trustee Convent of the Sacred Heart; v.p. bd. Independent Sch. Chmn. Assn.; pres. Blue Hill Troupe, 1998—99. Recipient ArtTable award for disting. svc. to visual arts, 2007. Mem.: Independent Sector (Met. Mus. rep.), Am. Assn. Museums (devel. com. 1984—94), Women in Financial Devel., Assn. Fundraising Professionals, ArtTable (bd. dirs. 1991—94). Office: Met Museum of Art 1000 Fifth Ave New York NY 10028-1098

RAFFERTY, GENEVIEVE KENNEDY, social service agency administrator; b. Davenport, Iowa, Jan. 21, 1922; d. Thomas Cyril and Mabel Veronica (Finefield) Kennedy; B.A., St. Ambrose Coll., 1942; postgrad. U. Iowa, 1972; m. Daniel J. Rafferty, Aug. 22, 1942 (dec. 1984); children—Daniel D., Michele M., Genevieve, Thomas K., Eileen M., Margaret M., Sheila M. Real estate saleswoman Manhard Realty, Moline, Ill., 1950-59; substitute tchr., Rock Island, Ill., 1963-67; head start tchr. Rock Island-Scott County Dept. Social Services, 1966; public welfare worker Scott County Dept. Social Services, Davenport, Iowa, 1967-72; exec. dir. Info. and Referral of the Quad-Cities, Rock Island, 1972—92, ret.; mem. Travelers Aid Internat.; chair Rock Island Housing Authority; mem. Quad-City Council on Crime and Delinquency, 1977-80; mem. Rock Island County Council on Alcoholism, 1976-82; chairperson CETA Adv. Bd., 1982-84, bi state regional commn. 1986—; steering com., Quad-City Vision for the Future, 1987; bd. dirs. Quint-City Drug Abuse; chair Just Kids Day Care, 1991—; with United Way Bay Area, 1992-94; Peace Corps vol., Uzbekistan, 1994-96. Named Social Worker of Yr. Quad-City, Nat Assn. Social Workers, 1973, Jefferson award for Cmty. Svc., 2003; Mem. Nat. Assn. Social Workers, Iowa Council Info. and Referral Providers, Nat. Conf. Social Welfare, Ill. Welfare Assn., NOW, Ill. Alliance Info. and Referral Services (dir.). Democrat. Roman Catholic. Office: 1818 3rd Ave Ste 202 Rock Island IL 61201-8030 Office Phone: 309-737-6931.

RAFFERTY, JAMES PAUL, telecommunications executive; b. Hartford, Conn., Oct. 26, 1952; s. James Paul and Kathleen Marie (LeHane) Rafferty; m. Lucinda Anne Link, Sept. 16, 1989. BS in Mgmt. Engring., Rensselaer Poly. Inst., Troy, NY, 1974, M in Mgmt. Engring., 1975. MIS analyst Burroughs, Danbury, Conn., 1977—80, MIS project leader, 1981—83, mgr. resource planning, 1984, mgr. materials, 1985—86; mgr. product program Fujitsu, Danbury, 1987—88, mgr. R&D, 1989—92; pres. Human Comm., 1992—99, dir, product mgr., 2007—; sr. mgr. product Cantata Tech., Needham, Mass., 2000—05, 2006—. Pub. industry newsletter Human Comm. Digest, 1992—99, Human Commn. Stds. Update, 1996—99; US del. Internat. Telecom. Union Study Group 8, 1993—2000, Study Group 16, 2000—; chair Internet Engring. Task Force, 1997—2000; del., editor Third Generation Partnership Project, 2006—; lectr. in field. Editor: Enterprise Telephony Forum, 1995—2000; contbr. articles to profl. jours. Pres. Deer Ridge Condo Assn., Danbury, 1987—90; merit badge counselor Boy Scouts Am., 2003—, chair endowed commn., 2007—; active Caucus Conn. Dems., 1986; mem. endowment com. Fed. Ch. Norfolk, 2003—; bd. dirs. Internat. Bus. Communicators Assn., 1999—2000. Recipient Computer Facsimile Industry award, 1996. Mem.: Telecom. Industry Assn., Electronic Messaging Assn. (Disting. Svc. award 1998), Internat. Packet Comm. Consortium, Alliance Francaise, Danbury Golf League (team capt. 1984—85), Epsilon Delta Sigma (mem. Fed. Ch. Norfolk endowment com. 2993—). Avocations: golf, cooking, hiking, music, skiing. Office: Cantata Tech 15 Crawford St Needham MA 02494-2618 Office Phone: 781-449-4100. Personal E-mail: jrafferty@humancomm.com. Business E-Mail: jraff@cantata.com.

RAFFERTY, THOMAS G., lawyer; b. Rockaway Beach, NY, Mar. 23, 1955; BA, SUNY, Old Westbury, 1985; JD, Harvard Univ., 1988. Bar: NY 1989. Assoc. Cravath Swaine & Moore LLP, NYC, 1988—94, ptnr., litig., 1994—. Office: Cravath Swaine & Moore LLP Worldwide Plz 825 Eighth Ave New York NY 10019-7475 Office Phone: 212-474-1837. Office Fax: 212-474-3700. Business E-Mail: trafferty@cravath.com.

RAFFIN, THOMAS A., physician; b. San Francisco, Jan. 25, 1947; s. Bennett L. and Carolyn M. Raffin; m. Michele Raffin, June 19, 1987; children: Elizabeth S., Ross Daniel, Jason Bennett, Nicholas Ethan. AB in Biol. Sci., Stanford Med. Sch., 1968, MD, 1973. Diplomate Am. Bd. Pulmonary Medicine, Am. Bd. Internal Medicine, Am. Bd. Critical Care Medicine. Intern Peter Bent Brigham Hosp., 1973-75; fellow in respiratory medicine sch. medicine Stanford U., Stanford, Calif., 1975-78, med. fiberoptic bronchoscopy service dir. med. ctr., 1978—, acting asst. prof. sch. medicine, 1978-80, assoc. dir. med. ctr. intensive care units, med. dir. dept. respiratory therapy hosp., 1978—, assoc. prof. medicine sch. medicine, 1986-95, acting chief div. respiratory medicine, 1988—2004, chief divsn. pulmonary and critical care, 1990—2004, prof. medicine sch. of medicine, 1995—, Colleen and Robert Haas emeritus prof. medicine/biomed. ethics, 1999—; dir. emeritus Stanford U. Ctr. for Biomed. Ethics, 1989—; co-founder Rigel Pharms., Inc. Gen. ptnr. Telegraph Hill Ptnrs., 2002; bd. dirs. New Link Genetics, AngioScore, Pneum Rx. Author: Intensive Care: Facing the Critical Choices, 1988; contbr. articles to profl. jours. V.p. lung cancer com. No. Calif. Oncology Group, 1983—85; com. mem. NIH Workshop, 1984. Recipient award, Henry J. Kaiser Found., 1981, 1984, 1988, 1997, Arthur L. Bloomfield award, 1981. Fellow: ACP (rep. coun. subspecialty socs. 1986), Am. Coll. Chest Physicians (program com. mem. 1985—86); mem.: AAAS, Calif. Thoracic Soc., Soc. Critical Care Medicine, Calif. Med. Assn. (chmn. sect. chest diseases 1984—85), Santa Clara County Med. Soc., Santa Clara County Lung Assn., Am. Thoracic Soc., Am. Fedn. Clin. Rsch. Jewish. Avocations: painting, gardening, raising miniature donkeys. Home: 13468 Three Forks Ln Los Altos CA 94022-2432 Office: Stanford Ctr For Biomedical 701 Welch Rd Ste A1105 Palo Alto CA 94304-1709 Office Phone: 415-765-6980. Business E-Mail: tar@stanford.edu.

RAFI, MOSTAFA, ophthalmologist; b. Oujda, Morocco, May 20, 1947; s. Miloud Rafi and Fatna (Hemri) R.; m. Amina Samir Rafi, Aug. 5, 1973; children: Fedoua, Nada. PhD in Medicine, U. Rabat, 1974; diploma in Ophthalmology, U. Paris, 1976. Cert. ophthalmologist Paris. Asst. prof., Sale, 1976; prof. Auicenne's Hosp., Rabat, 1980-86, Specialty Hosp., Rabat, 1986-97; head dept., 1990—; pvt. practice Clinique d'Ophthalmologie, Rabat. Dir. Sale's Hosp., 1983-85; head of OTO-Neuro-Ophthalmology Dept., 1990—; pres. 1982-85, v.p., 1986-89, Moroccan Ophthalmological Soc., pres. Qualification's Commn. in Ophthalmology, 1987-93. Mem. Direction of the Social Assn. Anjoad, 1983—; pres. Assn. Against Blindness, 1993—. Recipient Gov.'s award, Oujda, 1989, Settat, 1995, Honor award Moroccan Soc. of Ophthalmology, 2004. Avocations: golf, hunting, tennis. Home: 252 rue Beni Garfat Rabat Morocco Office: Specialty Hosp Afdal Rabat Morocco Home Phone: 21237751805; Office Phone: 212 37660389/90.

RAFIQ, MUHAMMAD AMIR, nephrologist; b. Lahore, Pakistan, Aug. 19, 1974; s. Muhammad Rafiq and Parveen Akhter; m. Hina Chaudhry, Apr. 12, 2002; children: Ridha Fatima, Amir Abdullah. MBBS, King Edward Med. Coll., Lahore, 1998. Physician critical care unit Drs. Hosp. and Med. Ctr., Lahore, 1999—2002; resident LI Coll. Hosp., Bklyn., 2002—05, nephrology fellow, 2005—. Named Best Ho. Officer, Mayo Hosp., 1998, Intern of Yr., LI Coll. Hosp., 2003, Resident of Yr., 2005; recipient 2d pl. in 1st profl. MBBS exam., King Edward Med. Coll., 1994, Silver medal, 1995; Kidney and Pancreas Transplant fellow, Mt. Sinai Sch. Medicine, 2007—. Mem.: Renal Physician Assn. (assoc.), Nat. Kidney Found. (assoc.), Am. Soc. Nephrology (assoc.). Achievements include research in malnutrition and inflammation as predictors of mortality in peritoneal dialysis patients; relationship of peritoneal transport rate and dialysis adequacy with inflammation in peritoneal dialysis patients; association of serum fructosamine, an alternative marker for glycemic control, but not glycated hemoglobin, with morbidity and mortality in non-diabetic hemodialysis patients; the changing face of diabetic nephropathy; clinical correlates of C-reactive (CRP) in peritoneal dialysis (PD) patients; bioimpidence analysis (BIA) to measure body cell mass (BCM) in peritoneal dialysis patients; pulmonary hypertension in peritoneal dialysis patients. Avocations: travel, cricket. Office: LI Coll Hosp 339 Hicks St Brooklyn NY 11201 Office Phone: 718-780-1247.

RAFUSE, NANCY E., lawyer, director; b. Columbia, SC, Dec. 14, 1966; m. Mark Rafuse; 2 children. BBA cum laude, U. Ga., 1988, JD magna cum laude, 1991. Ptnr., chair dept. employment law Paul, Hastings, Janofsky & Walker, Atlanta, 1991—2003; co-founder, mng. ptnr. Ashe, Rafuse & Hill, Atlanta, 2003—. Spkr. in field; mem. bar coun. and disciplinary com. No. Dist. Ga., 2002—05. Contbr. articles to profl. jours. Bd. dirs. Atlanta Urban League, Zoo Atlanta; mem. Atlanta United Way Women's Leadership Coun. Named one of Georgia's Legal Elite, Georgia Trend mag., 2003—04, Top 40 Lawyers Under 40, Nat. Law Jour., 2005. Mem.: ABA (mem. labor and employment law sect.), Atlanta Bar Assn. (mem. labor and employment law sect.), State Bar Ga. (mem. labor and employment law sect.). Office: Ashe Rafuse & Hill LLP 1355 Peachtree St Ste 500 Atlanta GA 30309 Office Phone: 404-253-6002. Office Fax: 404-253-6060. E-mail: nancyrafuse@asherafuse.com.

RAGAN, AMANDA, state senator; b. Mason City, Sept. 1954; m. James Ragan; children: Edith, Charles. AA, N. Iowa Area CC; BA in Human Svcs., cum laude, Buena Vista U. Legis. asst. to Rep. Ed Parker; co-chair Ho. Majority Leader John Groninga, 1987—89; dist. rep. Iowa Dem. State Ctrl. Com., 1992—2002; legis. page Iowa State Senate, 1973, mem. DesMoines, 2002—, asst. leader, co-chair human resources com., mem. agr. com., mem. econ. growth com., mem. rules and adminstrn. com., mem. appropriations com., mem. health & human svcs. com., mem. budget com.; co-chair Senate Human Resources Com. Active Mason City Sesquicentennial Com., Sesquicentennial Com.; mem. Birth Defects Adv. Bd., HAWK-I Bd.; exec. dir. Meals on Wheels, Mason City, Cmty. Kitchen North Iowa, Inc., Mason City; mem. N. Iowa Band Festival Planning Com., Buena Vista Alumni Found., Coun. Social Agencies, Maternal Health Adv. Coun.; active Iowa Dem. Party State Ctrl. Com.; asst. leader Dem. Caucus; mem. Cerro Gordo County Dem. Ctrl. Com.; past chair. Cerro Gordo Re-Elect Clinton-Gore Com.; bd. dirs. Charles City C. of C., Osage C. of C., Francis Lauer Youth Svc. Mem.: N Iowa Fund-Raising Profls. Assn., Mason City C. of C., Mason City Sunrise Rotary (bd. dirs.). Office: State Capitol Bldg East 12th and Grand Des Moines IA 50319 Home: 20 Granite Ct Mason City IA 50401

RAGAN, ANN TALMADGE, media and production consultant, actor; b. Raleigh, NC, July 6, 1951; d. Samuel Talmadge and Marjorie Lois (Usher) R.; m. L. Worth Keeter III, Aug. 22, 1992. Student, U. N.C., 1969-71, Finch Coll., 1972-73, New Sch. Social Rsch., 1973-74, Western Wash. U., 1978. Acct. estimator Benton & Bowles Inc., NYC, 1971-72, media buyer, 1974-77; speechwriter, press aide Senator Robert Morgan, Washington, 1978-79; asst. prodr., casting dir. John F. Murray Inc., NYC, 1979—80; prod., sales dir. Grand St. Films, NYC, 1980-84; ind. prod. for various clients NYC, 1984-86; asst. pub. The Pilot, Inc., Southern Pines, NC, 1986-96, bd. dirs. Prodn. mgr. Anglo Am. Media Workshops, London, 1988—90; dir. SAG Conservatory Am. Film Inst., LA, 2003—, coach Film Camp, 2005—, cons.; mgr., exec. prodr. films, commercials, audio books Blue Kiss, LLC, 2000—; prodn. mgr., coach Directing Workshop for Women; workshop leader in field; ind. feature project West Find, 2007—. Contbr. articles to newspapers and jours. Life mem. Roanoke Island Hist. Assn.; mem. Moore County Arts Coun., 1986-89; mem. adv. bd. Art & Soul. Mem.: SAG (conservatory com., rec. sec. 1997—2006, cons., vice-chair 2003—), AFTRA, Women in Film, Women in Theatre (adminstrv. dir. 1995—97, treas. 1997—99, bd. dirs. 1997—99, pres. 2004—), Actors Equity Assn., Kings and Clowns Ednl. Shakespeare Alliance (treas. bd. dirs. 1999—2002, adv. bd. 2003—), Pi Beta Phi. Democrat. Methodist. Home and Office: 10542 Bloomfield St Toluca Lake CA 91602-2813 Home Phone: 818-762-1926; Office Phone: 818-762-6339. E-mail: bluekissllc@aol.com.

RAGAN, CHARLES RANSOM, lawyer; b. NYC, Aug. 13, 1947; s. Charles Alexander Jr. and Josephine Forbes (Parker) R.; m. Barbara Thiel McMahon, Aug. 30, 1969; children: Alexandra Watson, Madeline McCue. AB, Princeton U., 1969; JD, Fordham U., 1974. Bar: N.Y. 1975, U.S. Ct. Appeals (3d cir.) 1975, Calif. 1976, U.S. Ct. Appeals (9th cir.) 1976, U.S. Dist. Ct. (no. dist.) Calif. 1976, U.S. Supreme Ct. 1981, U.S. Dist. Ct. (so. dist.) N.Y. 1982, U.S. Ct. Appeals (2d cir.) 1984. Law clk. to Hon. R.J. Aldisert U.S. Ct. Appeals (3rd cir.), 1974-76; assoc. Pillsbury, Madison & Sutro, San Francisco, 1976-81, ptnr., 1982-97, Palo Alto, 1997-2000, Pillsbury Winthrop, Palo Alto, San Francisco, 2001—05; founder, ptnr. Redgrave Daley Ragan & Wagner, 2005—. Mem. exec. com. 9th Cir. Judicial Conf., 1987-91. Avocations: bicycling, swimming, sports. Office: Redgrave Daley Ragan & Wagner LLP 1750 Montgomery St San Francisco CA 94111 Office Phone: 612-455-4403. Business E-Mail: cragan@rdrw.com.

RAGAN, DAVID, publishing company executive; b. Jackson, Tenn., Aug. 26, 1925; s. Amos and Esther Lee (Tacker) R.; m. Violet Claire Sills, Dec. 27, 1948; children— David Nathaniel, Sarah Sills, Jennifer Leigh. BA in English, Union U., Jackson, 1947; M. Theatre Arts, Calif. Sch. Theatre, 1950. Radio writer Grand Central Sta., 1950; syndicated columnist Hollywood South Side, 1951; mng. editor Tele-Views mag., 1952; free-lance writer, 1952-57, 74-77, 82—; editor TV and Movie Screen Sterling Group, Inc., NYC, 1957-61; mng. editor Motion Picture mag. Fawcett Pub. Co., NYC, 1961-64; editor TV Radio Mirror, Macfadden-Bartell Pub. Co., NYC, 1964-71; pub., editorial dir. Movie Digest, Words and Music, Planet mags. Nat. Periodical Publs. (Warner Communications), NYC, 1971-74; editorial dir. Photoplay, Motion Picture, TV Mirror mags.; Macfadden Women's Group, NYC, 1977-79; entertainment editor Globe Nat. Weekly, NYC, 1979-82. Author: Who's Who in Hollywood 1900-1976, 1977, Movie Stars of the '30s, 1985, Movie Stars of the '40s, 1985, Mel Gibson: An Intimate Biography, 1985, Who's Who in Hollywood: The Largest Cast of Film Personalities Ever Assembled, rev., 1992; co-author: Richard Pryor: This Cat's Got Nine Lives, 1982; contbr. articles to profl. jours. Served with U.S. Army, 1952-54. Mem. Screen Actors Guild, TV Acad., Alpha Tau Omega, Tau Kappa Alpha. Republican. Presbyterian. Home: Landmark Apts Apt 2-M 232 Main St Port Washington NY 11050

RAGAN, JAMES THOMAS, communications executive; b. San Diego, Mar. 15, 1929; m. Susan Held, Nov. 9, 1957; children: James, Maria, Carey, Andrew. BA, Oxford U., Eng., 1951, MA, 1955; elect. engring. vocat. cert., U. State of N.Y., 1954. With Gen. Electric Co., 1954-69; pres., chief operating officer Athena Communications Corp. subs. Gulf & Western Industries, Inc., NYC, 1969-74; v.p. broadcast services Western Union Telegraph Co., 1974-76, v.p. satellite services, 1976-82, pres. Western Union personal communications corp., v.p. communication systems group, 1982-85; pres. Associated Info. Services Corp., 1985-86, Bunting, Inc., 1985-88; ptnr. Pierce Kennedy Hearth, 1988-91; CEO Nat. Lang. Assocs. Lanarea Pub., Guilford, Conn., 1990—. Patentee recreational sports equipment; author: The Ultimate Diet, The First Alaskans, A Guide to the Geography of the Native Languages, Cultures, Their Communities, and Populations, 1996. Pres. Wilton Pop Warner Football League, Wilton, Conn., 1972—73. Maj. USMCR, 1952—54, Korea. Home: PO Box 1112 Green Valley AZ 85622 Office: Nat Lang Assocs PO Box 1112 Green Valley AZ 85622 Office Phone: 520-399-2294. Personal E-mail: jtrnla@aol.com.

RAGAN, ROBERT ALLISON, private investment executive, financial consultant; b. Gastonia, NC, Aug. 21, 1938; s. Caldwell and Jocelyn (Sikes) R. BS in Bus. Adminstrn., U. NC, 1961; postgrad., Rutgers U., 1968. V.p. N.C. Nat. Bank (now Bank of Am.), Charlotte, 1961-81; pres., treas. R.A. Ragan & Co., Inc., Charlotte, 1981—. Dir. Carolina Mills, Inc., Maiden, N.C., 1977—. Author, pub.: The Ragans of Gastonia (1790-1995), 1995, The Textile Heritage of Gaston County, N.C. (1848-2000), 2000. Founder, pres. bd. govs. The Gaston Soc. of Mecklenburg County, Charlotte, NC, 1999—; trustee, bd. visitors Darlington Sch., Rome, Ga., 1981—; mem. bd. visitors Daniel Stowe Bot. Gardens, Belmont, NC, 2001—; pres. bd. trustees Gaston County Mus. Art and History, Dallas, NC, 1978—81, 1997—99. Mem. Charlotte City Club, DeBordieu Colony Country Club (Georgetown, S.C.), Linville (N.C.) Ridge Country Club. Republican. Presbyn. Avocations: preservation and recording of local and North Carolina history, travel. Home: 227 Fenton Pl Charlotte NC 28207-1913 Office: R A Ragan & Co PO Drawer 6158 Charlotte NC 28207-0001 also: 407 DeBordieu Blvd Georgetown SC 29440 Personal E-mail: rragan@carolina.rr.com.

RAGANS, ROSALIND DOROTHY, writer, artist, retired educator; b. Bklyn., Feb. 28, 1933; d. Sidney Guy Gordon and Beatrice (Zuckerman) Safier; m. John Franklin Ragans, July 31, 1965; 1 child, John Lee. BFA, CUNY-Hunter Coll., 1955; MEd, Ga. So. Coll., 1967; EdD, U. Ga., 1971. Cert. tchr. art, Ga. Tchr. art Union City (N.J.) Bd. Edn., 1956-62; tchr. 1st grade Chatham Bd. Edn., Savannah, Ga., 1962-64; instr. art Ga. So. U., Statesboro, 1964-69, asst. prof., 1969-76, assoc. prof., 1976-89, prof.

emeritus, 1989—. Keynote speaker art edn. confs.; presenter in field. Author: (textbooks) ArtTalk, 1988, 4th edit., 2005, Introducing Art, 1997, 2d edit., 2005, Exploring Art, 1990, 3d edit., 2005, Understanding Art, 1990, 3d edit., 2005; sr. author Art Connections K-5, 1997, 2d edit., 2000, K-6. 3d edit., 2005 Mem. Nat. Assn. Educators (life), Ga. Assn. Educators (life), Nat. Art Edn. Assn. (Southeastern Art Educator of Yr. 1991, Nat. Art Educator of Yr. 1992), Ga. Art Edn. Assn. (Ga. Art Educator of Yr. 1990), Pilot Club Internat. (Ga. dist., Ga. Profl. Handicapped Woman of Yr. 1988). Jewish. Avocation: painting. Personal E-mail: rozragans@comcast.net.

RAGATZ, THOMAS GEORGE, lawyer; b. Madison, Wis., Feb. 18, 1934; s. Wilmer Leroy and Rosanna (Kindschi) Ragatz; m. Karen Christensen, Dec. 19, 1965; children: Thomas Rolf, William Leslie, Erik Douglas. BBA, U. Wis., 1957, LLB, 1961. CPA Wis.; bar: Wis. 1961, U.S. Dist. Ct. (ea. and we. dists.) Wis. 1961, U.S. Tax Ct. 1963, U.S. Ct. Appeals (7th cir.) 1965, U.S. Supreme Ct. 1968. Staff acct. Peat, Marwick, Mitchell & Co., Mpls., 1958; instr. Sch. Bus., U. Wis., Madison, 1958-60; formerly lectr. in acctg. and law Law Sch. U. Wis.; law clk. Wis. Supreme Ct., 1961-62; assoc. Boardman Suhr Curry & Field, Madison, 1962-64, ptnr., 1965-78, Foley & Lardner, Madison, 1978—2002, mng. ptnr., 1984-93, chmn. budget com., 1994-99. Bd. dirs. Wolf Appliance Co., LLC, Sub-Zero Freezer Co., Inc., Norman Bassett Found., Wis. Sports Found., United Way Found.; pres. Courtier Found.; bd. dirs., pres. Wis. Sports Devel. Corp.; lectr. seminars on tax subjects. Editor-in-chief Wis. Law Rev., 1960—61, chmn. Nat. Conf. Law Revs., 1960—61; author: The Ragatz History, 1989; contbr. articles to profl. jours. Formerly dir. United Way, Meth. Hosp. Found; mem. U. Wis. Found.; chmn. site selection com. U. Wis. Hosp. Com.; past pres., past moderator 1st Congl. Ch.; bd. dirs. Found. for Madison Pub. Schs.; pres. Bus. and Edn. Partnership, 1983—89, bd. dirs.; past pres., vice pres. HospiceCare Found.; bd. regents U. Wis., panel provision of legal svcs.; bd. dirs. Met. YMCA, Madison, 1983—90. Fellow: Am. Bar Found.; mem.: ABA, Dane County Bar Assn. (pres. 1978—79, chmn. jud. qualification com., sec.), Wis. Inst. CPA, State Bar Wis. (sec. 1969—70, bd. govs. 1971—75, chmn. fin. com. 1975—80, chmn. tax sect., chmn. spl. com. on econs., chmn. svcs. for lawyers com.), Wis. Bar Found., Seventh Cir. Bar Assn., Am. Judicature Soc., Order of Constantine, Bascom Hill Soc., Order of Coif, Madison Club (pres. 1980—81), Madison Club House Corp. (pres. 1999—, bd. dirs.), Sigma Chi, Beta Gamma Sigma. Republican. Home: 3334 Lake Mendota Dr Madison WI 53705-1469 Office: Foley & Lardner LLP PO Box 1497 Madison WI 53701-1497 also: Foley & Lardner LLP 1st Wisconsin Ctr 777 E Wisconsin Ave Ste 3800 Milwaukee WI 53202-5302 E-mail: tgragatz@yahoo.com.

RAGAUSS, PETER A., oil industry executive; B. in mech. engring., Mich. State U., 1980; MBA, Harvard U., 1987. V.p. corp. devel. Tenneco Energy Inc.; v.p. fin. El Paso Energy Internat. Corp.; v.p. fin. & portfolio mgmt. Amoco Energy Internat.; asst to grp. chief exec. BP plc, 1998; CEO Air BP; segment contr. refining & mktg. BP plc, London, 2003—06; sr. v.p. & CFO Baker Hughes Inc., Houston, 2006—. Office: Baker Hughes Inc 3900 Essex Ln Houston TX 77027-5177 Office Phone: 713-439-8600. Office Fax: 713-439-8699.

RAGAVAN, ANPALAKI JEYABALASINKHAM, software developer, researcher; arrived in U.S., 1992; d. George Nagularajah and Thangaranee Veluppillai Jeyabalasingham; m. Ragavan Vinasithamby, July 1, 1993; 1 child, Muhundhan. BS (hon.), U. Sri Lanka, 1985, MPhil (hon.) in Hydrology, 1989; MS in Hydrogeology (hon.), U. Nev., 1996, MS in Civil Engring., 2003, MS in Math., 2004—, MS in Hydrology, 2005, postgrad, 2006—. Cert. BASIC computer programmer, geographic info. sys., Visual Basic programmer, GIS and web design, well drilling with LS 100. Asst. prof. U. Sri Lanka, Kilinochchi, Jaffna, 1989—92; rsch. asst. Ind. State U., Tere Haute, 1992—93; rsch./tchg. asst. U. of Nev., Reno, 1993—96; software developer Bur. Labor Stats., Washington, 1996—99; rsch. asst. U. of Nev., Reno, 1999—. Grad. fellow U. Nev., Reno, 1993—96; presenter in field. Contbr. articles to profl. jours. (Excellence in Abstract Submission award Am. Jour. Pub. Health, 2001); author: Introductory Statistics, Lab-Guide - SAS, 1st edition., 1993. Named Woman of Achievement, Am. Biog. Inst., 2006, Woman of Yr., 2006; recipient Cert. of Appreciation, Nev. State Mental Health and Devel. Services, 2000, Excellence in Abstract Submission award, APHA, HIV/AIDS Sect., 2001, Poster award, SAS Inst., Inc., 2007, 2007; grantee, State of Nev., 2002; scholar, Asian Inst. Of Tech. in Thailand, 1991, Ind. State U., 1992—93, U. of Nev., Reno, 1993—, Soroptimist Internat. of Reno, Sierra Nev. Region, 2000, Water Resources Assn., 2005, Grad. Student Assn., 2005—06; Overseas Devel. Adminstrn. scholar, Govt. of UK, 1986—89, Conf. scholar, Western Users SAS, 2007. Mem.: AAAS (Travel award 2007), Nature Pub. Group, Am. Geophys. Union, Nat. Ground Water Assn., Nev. Water Resources Assn., Am. Math. Soc., Am. Statis. Assn., Geol. Soc. Am., Great Woman of the 21st Century (profl. women's adv. bd.), Alumni Assn. U. Nev. (mem. profl. women's adv. bd.). Mem. Lds Ch. Avocations: dance, music, guitar, swimming, sports. Office: U Nev Dept Internal Med Reno NV 89512 Home: 3952 Clear Acre Ln #276 Reno NV 89512-1202 Office Phone: 775-784-4433. Business E-Mail: ragavan@unr.edu.

RAGENT, BORIS, physicist; b. Cleve., Mar. 2, 1924; s. Samuel and Bertha (Lev) R.; m. Dorothy Kohn, Sept. 11, 1949; children: David Stefan, Lawrence Stanton, Jesse Ron. Student, Ohio State U., 1941—44; BSEE, Marquette U., 1944; PhD in Physics, U. Calif., Berkeley, 1953. Registered profl. engr., Calif. Engr. Victoreen Instrument Co., Cleve., 1946-48; engr., physicist Radiation Lab., U. Calif., Berkeley, 1948-53; physicist Livermore, Calif., 1953-56, Broadview Rsch. Corp., Burlingame, Calif., 1956-59, Vidya divsn. Itek Corp., Palo Alto, Calif., 1959-66, Ames Rsch. Ctr., NASA, Moffett Field, Calif., 1966-87, San Jose (Calif.) State U. Found., 1987-98. Lectr. Stanford U., U. Calif. Ext. Served in USNR, 1944-46. Mem. AAAS, Am. Phys. Soc., Optical Soc. Am., Am. Geophys. Union, Sigma Xi.

RAGER, RUDOLPH RUSSELL, retired lawyer; b. Miles City, Mont., Jan. 15, 1932; s. Harry E. and Esther (Anderson) R.; m. Sharon E. Keeling, Dec. 30, 1959; children: Sean, Kurt, Quita, Elani, Valari, Jordan. BBA, U. ND, Grand Forks, 1956; JD, U. N.Mex., Albuquerque, 1958. Bar: N.Mex. 1958, US Dist. Ct. N.Mex. 1959. Sole practice, Albuquerque, 1958—60, 1970—2003; ptnr. Grantham, Spann, Sanchez & Rager, 1961—69. Atty. Village of Corrales, 1971-81; bd. dirs. Anderson Devel. Corp., Albuquerque, Anderson Western Corp., Albuquerque. Pres., bd. dirs. Albuquerque Tutoring Assn., 1967; co-founder, bd. dirs., sec. Security Escrow Corp., 1974-80, Intermountain Conservation Trust, 1996-2005; bd. dirs. Luth. Coordinating Coun., Albuquerque, 1975, Corrales Hist. Soc., 1988-94; bd. dirs., sec. Anderson Charitable Found., 1994-, Anderson Abruzzo, Internat. Balloon Mus., Albuquerque, 1984-2006; adv. bd. dirs. Albuquerque City Balloon Mus., 1991-2006; bd. dirs., treas. San Pedro Creek Homeowners Assn., 1996-2000. Gold Seal scholar, 1949. Mem. N.Mex. Bar Assn., Albuquerque Bar Assn. Lodges: Kiwanis (pres. Albuquerque chpt. 1966). Republican. Lutheran. Home: 20 Canada Vista Dr Sandia Park NM 87047-9645 Personal E-mail: rrager@msn.com.

RAGGI, REENA, federal judge; b. Jersey City, May 11, 1951; BA, Wellesley Coll., 1973; JD cum laude, Harvard U., 1976. Bar: NY 1977, US Dist. Ct. (ea. dist.) NY 1987, US Ct. Appeals (2d cir.) 2002. Law clerk US Ct. of Appeals, 7th Circuit, 1976—77; assoc. Cahill, Gordon & Reindel, NY, 1977—79; asst. U.S. atty. Dept. Justice, Bklyn., 1979—86; ptnr. Windels, Marx, Davies & Ives, NYC, 1986—87; judge US Dist. Ct. (Ea. dist.) NY, 1987—2002, US Ct. Appeals (2nd cir.), NYC, 2002—. Office: US Courthouse 225 Cadman Plz E Brooklyn NY 11201 *

RAGGIO, THOMAS LOUIS, lawyer; b. Dallas, Sept. 11, 1946; s. Grier H. and Louise (Ballerstadt) R.; m. Janice B. Savage, May 23, 1970; children: Stephen, Kristen. BA, U. Tex., 1968; JD, So. Meth. U., 1971. Bar: US Dist. Ct. (no. dist. Tex.) 1971; cert. family law specialist. Atty. Raggio & Raggio, PLLC, Dallas, 1971—, mng. ptnr., 1985—. Author, spkr. in field of family law. Named one of Best Lawyers in Dallas, D Mag., 2001, 2003, 2005, 2007, Tex. Super Lawyers, Tex. Top 100 Super Lawyers, 2005, Best Lawyers in Am., 2007. Mem. Am. Acad. Matrimonial Lawyers, Tex. Bar Found. Office: Raggio and Raggio PLLC 3316 Oak Grove Ave Ste 100 Dallas TX 75204-2338 Office Phone: 214-880-7500. E-mail: tom@raggiolaw.com.

RAGGIO, WILLIAM JOHN, state legislator; b. Reno, Oct. 30, 1926; s. William John and Clara M. (Cardelli) R.; m. Dorothy Brigman, August 15, 1948 (dec. Apr. 1998); children: Leslie Ann, Tracy Lynn, Mark William; m. Dale Checket, Apr. 27, 2003. Student, La. Poly. Inst., 1944-45, U. Okla., 1945-46; BA, U. Nev., 1948; JD, U. Calif. at Hastings, 1951. Bar: Nev. 1951, U.S. Supreme Ct. 1959. Atty., Reno and Las Vegas; asst. dist. atty. Washoe County, Nev., 1952-58; dist. atty., 1958-71; ptnr. firm Wiener, Goldwater, Galatz & Raggio, Ltd., 1971-72, Raggio, Walker & Wooster, Reno and Las Vegas, 1974-78, Raggio, Wooster & Lindell, 1978-92; sr. ptnr. Vargas & Bartlett, 1992-98; then Jones-Vargas (formerly Vargas & Bartlett), 1998—; mem. Nev. Senate, Washoe Dist. 3, Carson City, 1973—. Mem. Nev. Senate, 1973—, minority floor leader, 1977-81, 82-87, 91, majority fl. leader, 1987-2007; mem. legis. commn., vice chmn. criminal law and adminstrn. com. council State Govts., 1972-75; v.p., dir. Archon Corp. Mem. Nev. Am. Revolutionary Bicentennial Commn., 1975-81; mem. Republican State Cen. Com.; past nat. chmn., current dir. Am. Legislative Exchange Council, dir. Sierra Health Svcs.; republican candidate for U.S. Senate, 1970. Served with USNR, 1944-46; to 2d lt. USMCR, 1946-47. Named Young Man of Yr., Reno-Sparks Jr. C. of C., 1959, Alumnus of Yr. U. Nev. Reno, 2000, Civic Leader of Yr Greater Reno C. of C., Disting. Eagle Scout, 1989; named to Jr. Achievement of Nev. Hall of Fame, 1999, Reg. Trans. Commn. Hall of Fame; recipient Disting. Nevadan award, 1968, Fellows award The Salvation Army, Torch of Liberty award The Anti-Defamation League, SIR award Assoc. Gen. Contractors, 1995, Outstanding Svc. award Airport Authority of Washor County, Pres.'s medal UNLV, 2000. Fellow Am. Bd. Criminal Lawyers; mem. ABA (state chmn. jr. bar conf. 1957-60, ho. dels.) Am. Judicature Soc., Am. Coll. Trail Lawyers, Am. Bd. Trial Advocates, Am. Inns of Ct., Navy League, Air Force Assn., Nat. (nat. pres. 1967-68; named Outstanding Prosecutor 1965), Nev. State (sec. 1959, pres. 1960-63) Dist. Attys. Assn., NCJ (Brotherhood award 1965), Nev. Peace Officers Assn., Internat. Assn. Chiefs Police, Am. Leg. Exch. Coun. (nat. chmn. 1991-92, The William J. Raggio Excellence in Leadership Outstanding award 2007), Coll. of Edn. U. Nev. (life), Am. Legion, Elks, Lion Club, Prospectors Club, Alpha Tau Omega, Phi Alpha Delta. Republican. Roman Catholic. Home: PO Box 281 Reno NV 89504-0281

RAGHAVAN, DEREK, oncologist, medical researcher, educator; b. Aug. 11, 1949; came to U.S., 1991; divorced; 2 children. MB, BS with honors, Sydney U., 1974; PhD, London U., 1984. Cert. Royal Australian Coll. Physicians, Fgn. Lic. Exam Coun., Ednl. Coun. Fgn. Med. Grads., Gen. Med. Coun. (U.K.), NSW Med. Bd. (Australia). Resident, registrar Royal Prince Alfred Hosp., Sydney, 1974-77; lectr., sr. registrar Royal Marsden Hosp., London, 1978-80; rsch. fellow Ludwig Inst. Cancer Rsch., London, 1978-80; med. rsch. specialist U. Minn., Mpls., 1980-81; sr. specialist med. oncology Royal Prince Alfred Hosp., Sydney, 1981-91; prof., chief solid tumor oncology and investigational therapeutics Roswell Park Cancer Inst. and SUNY, Buffalo, 1991-97; prof. medicine and urology U. So. Calif., LA, 1997—2003, chief divsn. med. oncology, 1997—2003, assoc. dir. Norris Cancer Ctr., 1997—2004; prof., dir. Cleve. Clinic Taussig Cancer Ctr., 2004—. Pres. med. staff Roswell Park Cancer Inst., Buffalo, 1995—96; mem. oncology drug adv. com. FDA, 1996—2000; mem. cancer ctrs. support rev. com. Nat. Cancer Inst., 2000—; prof. medicine SUNY, Buffalo, 1991—97, prof. urology, 1996—97; assoc. dir. U. So. Calif.-Norris Cancer Ctr. U. So. Calif., 1997—2003; mem. sci. adv. bd. Southwest Oncology Group, 1998—2005, bd. govs., 1998—2004, vice chair genitournairy com., 1998—2006; vice chair genitouring cancer com. Radiation Therapy Oncology Group, 1995—97; mem. sci. adv. com. European Orgn. for Rsch. and Treatment of Cancer, 2000—, mem. external sci. audit com., 2001—; mem. external adv. bd. Comprehensive Cancer Ctr. U. Ala., Birmingham, 2002—04; mem. external adv. bd. Ohio State U. James Comprehensive Cancer Ctr., 2002—; mem. clin. trials and awards adv. com. Cancer Rsch. UK, 2002—06; mem. NCI Clin. Oncology Study Sect., 2007—; mem. clin. oncology study sect. Nat. Cancer Inst., 2007—. Editor: The Management of Bladder Cancer, 1988, Textbook of Uncommon Cancer, 1988, 3d edit. 2006, Principles and Practice of Genitourinary Oncology, 1997, ACS Atlas of Clinical Oncology-Germ Cell Tumors, 2002, Fast Facts: Bladder Cancer, 2006; assoc. editor Urologic Oncology, 1995—, Clin. Cancer Rsch., 1996—; mem. editl. bd. Jour. Clin. Oncology, 1990-94, 2006—, European Jour. Cancer, The Prostate, The Breast, Prostate Cancer, Advances in Oncology, Abstracts in Hematology and Oncology, 1998-2000, Oncology, Brit. Jour. Urology; bd. cons. Jour. Urology, 1996-2006; contbr. articles to profl. jours. Rsch. grantee Nat. Health amd Med. Rsch. Coun., Australia, 1983-90; traveling fellow NSW Cancer Coun., Sydney, 1978; named Hospice Physician of Yr., Hospice of Buffalo, 1994. Fellow: ACP (MKSAP XI com. 1997—98, sci. program com. 2000), Royal Australian Coll. Physicians (chair specialist adv. com. in med. oncology 1988—90); mem.: Sydney U. Med. Soc. (pres. 1974), Med. Oncology Group Australia (chmn. 1988—90), Soc. Urologic Oncology, Am. Assn. Cancer Rsch., Am. Soc. Clin. Oncology (liaison Am. joint com. on cancer 1995—2000, AJCC liaison 1995—2000, chair cancer comms. com. 1998—2000, 1998—2000, program com. 1999—2000, mem. pub. issues com. 2000—02, chair Diversity Working Party 2006—, assoc. editor People Living With Cancer Website). Avocations: tennis, squash. Office: Cleve Clinic Taussig Cancer Ctr Euclid Ave Cleveland OH 44195 Office Phone: 216-445-6888.

RAGHAVAN, RAJAGOPAL S., retired petroleum engineer; BS, Birla Inst. Tech., India, U. Birmingham; PhD in Petroleum Engring., Stanford U., 1970. Rschr., lectr. Tex. A&M U., Stanford U., U. Tulsa; sr. staff assoc. Phillips Petroleum Co., Tulsa; ret. Contbr. articles to profl. jours. Mem.: NAE, Am. Geophysical Union, NY Acad. Scis., Soc. Petroleum Engrs. (former chmn. Edn. and Accreditation Com. & Symbols Accreditation Com.).

RAGHAVAN, SIVAKUMAR, food scientist; s. Raghavan; m. Mahalakshmi Vasan. BS in Food and Fermentation, U. Dept. Chem. Tech., Mumbai, India, 2000; BS in Chemistry, U. Madras, India, 1997; D, U. Mass., Amherst, 2004. Cert. hazard analysis and critical control pt. Rsch. assoc. U. Wis., Madison, 2004—05, U. Fla., Gainesville, 2005—. Contbr. articles to profl. jours. Mem.: Sigma Xi, Inst. Food Tech., Am. Oil Chemists Soc. (member-at-large 2005—). Achievements include research in lipid and protein chemistry. Office: University of Florida 359 FSHN Building Newell Drive Gainesville FL 32611 Office Phone: 352-392-1991 ext. 501. Personal E-mail: siva.kr@gmail.com. Business E-Mail: siva2000@ufl.edu.

RAGHAVAN, SUDHEER, hotel executive; b. Singapore; MS, Cranfield Inst. Tech. Various postions including jr. exec., and sr. v.p. cargo co. Singapore Airlines, 1981—2005, corp. v.p. worldwide revenue mgmt., v.p. Singapore, v.p. ea. U.S. and S.Am. region; pres. Millennium Hotels and Resorts, 2005—. Avocation: reading. Office: Millennium Hotels and Resorts 145 W 44th St New York NY 10036

RAGHEB, SAMIA, immunologist, educator; d. Shafik and Carmen Ragheb. BA, U. Pa., Phila., 1980; PhD, Wayne State U., Detroit, 1988. Post-doctoral fellow Wayne State U., Detroit, 1988—92, asst. prof. neurology, 1992—, assoc. immunology and microbiology, 1993—. Contbr. articles to profl. jours. Interviewer U. Pa. alumni secondary sch. com. network U. Pa., Phila., 2004—06. Osserman Rsch. fellow, Myasthenia Gravis Found., 1992. Mem.: Am. Assn. Immunologists. Avocations: travel, cooking, gardening.

RAGHU, GANESH, physician, educator; s. Adgula and Jayamma Ganesh; m. Tina Lowenstein, May 2, 2002; children: Shanthi P., Preethi P., Raghavendra Amit, Anand Sathyanarayan. MD, U. Mysore, India, 1972. Cert. in Internal Medicine Am. Bd. Internal Medicine, 1981, in Pulmonary Diseases Am. Bd. Internal Medicine, 1991, in Critical Care Medicine Am. Bd. Internal Medicine, 1992. Prof. medicine U. Wash., Seattle, 2000—. Med. dir. lung transplant program U. Wash., Seattle; cons. in field. Contbr. articles to profl. jours. Recipient rsch. awards, NIH. Fellow: Am. Coll. Chest Physicians (life); mem.: European Respiratory Soc. (mem. editl. bd.), Am. Thoracic Soc. (mem. editl. bd.). Office: U Wash 1959 Pacific Ave Seattle WA 98195

RAGINSKY, NINA, artist; d. Bernard Boris and Helen Theresa R.; 1 child, Sofya Katrina. BA, Rutgers U., 1962; studied painting with, Roy Lichtenstein; studied sculpture with, George Segal; studied Art History with Allan Kaprow, Rutgers U. Freelance photographer Nat. Film Bd., Ottawa, Ont., Canada, 1963-81; instr. metaphysics Emily Car Coll. Art, Vancouver, B.C., Canada, 1973-81; painter Salt Spring Island, B.C., 1989—. Sr. artist, jury Can. Coun.; selected Can. rep. in Sweden for Sweden Now Mag., 1979; tchr., lectr. in field, 1973—. One woman shows include Vancouver Art Gallery, Victoria Art Gallery, Edmonton Art Gallery, Art Gallery Ont., San Francisco Mus. Art, Acadia U., Nancy Hoffman Gallery, N.Y.C., Meml. U. Newfoundland Art Gallery; exhibited in group shows at Rutgers U., 1962, Montreal Mus. Fine Arts, 1963, Nat. Film Bd., Ottawa, 1964, 65, 67, 70, 71, 76, 77, Internat. Salon Photography, Bordeaux, France, 1968, Nat. Gallery Ottawa, 1968, Eastman House, Rochester, N.Y., 1969, Vancouver Art Gallery, 1973, 80, Mural for Conf. Ctr. Ottawa, 1973, Field Mus., Chgo., 1976, Edmonton Art Gallery, 1978, 79, Walter Philips Gallery, 1979, Glenbow Mus. Gallery, 1979, Harbour Front Community Gallery, 1980, Hamilton Art Gallery, 1980, Musée Maisil de St. Lambert, 1981, Mendel Art Gallery, 1981, Dunlop Art Gallery, Regina, Can., 1981, Vancouver Art Gallery, 2001; represented in permanent collections Nat. Film Bd. Stills divsn., Ottawa, Ont., Banff (Alta.) Sch. Fine Arts, Nat Gallery Ottawa, Can., George Eastman House, Rochester, NY, Wadsworth Atheneum, Conn., Edmonton Art Gallery, U. Victoria, B.C., various pvt. collections. Bd. dirs. Island Watch, Salt Spring Island, B.C., 1993; founder, coord. Salt Spring Island Ecosys. Stewardship Project, 1993; founder, coord. Salt Spring Island Waterbird Watch Collective, 1994—. Decorated officer Order of Can., 1984; recipient Kees Vermeer award for edn. and conservation Simon Fraser U., 1997, Burns Bog award for environ. excellence, Vancouver, 2005. Mem.: Soc. for Advancement of Slow, Royal Can. Acad. Arts. Avocations: gardening, birding, subject of numerous publs. Home and Office: 272 Beddis Rd Salt Spring Island BC Canada V8K 2J1

RAGLAND, GEORGE A., lawyer; b. Charleston, W.Va., May 14, 1943; BS, U. Va., 1965; LLB cum laude, Washington & Lee U., 1968. Bar: NC 1978. With Wachovia Bank & Trust Co., Winston-Salem, NC, 1968—78; mem. Womble Carlyle Sandridge & Rice PLLC, Winston-Salem, trust & estates practice group leader. Fellow Am. Coll. Trust and Estate Counsel; mem. ABA, NC Bar Assn. (chair estate planning and fiduciary law sect., 1990-91), Forsyth County Bar Assn., Phi Delta Phi. Office: Womble Carlyle Sandridge & Rice PLLC PO Box 84 Winston Salem NC 27102 Office Phone: 336-721-3646. Office Fax: 336-733-8401. Business E-Mail: gragland@wcsr.com.

RAGLAND, JACK WHITNEY, artist; b. El Monte, Calif., Feb. 25, 1938; s. Jack Rider and Dorsey (Whitney) R.; m. Marilee J. Weaver, July 31, 1969; children— Roxanne, Natasha. BA, Ariz. State U., Tempe, 1960, MA, 1964; postgrad., UCLA, 1961-64. Grad. asst. tchr. Ariz. State U., 1960-61; grad. teaching asst. UCLA, 1961-64; head art dept. Simpson Coll., Indianola, Iowa, 1964-76. Demonstrator Nat. Art Materials Trade Assn., Denver, 1993, Pasadena Conv. Ctr., 1994 One-man shows include Kleine Gallery, Vienna, Austria, Simpson Coll., Internat. Art Svc., Pan Pacific Hotel, San Diego, Lakes Art Ctr., Okaboji, Iowa, Hilltop Ctr., Fallbrook, 1996-98, Desert Art Source Gallery, 1999-2007; exhibited in group shows, Lyn Kottler Gallery, NYC, Phoenix Art Mus., Tucson Festival Art, Talisman Gallery, Bartlesville, Okla., Exhibiting Artists Fedn., Poultney, Vt., Des Moines Art Center, Joslyn Mus. Art, Omaha, Lagerquist Gallery, Atlanta, Desert Art Source Gallery, Palm Desert, Calif., Desert Pleine Air Show, La Quinta, Calif., San Diego, NAMTA Art Show, San Francisco, 1995, Christian Art Show Jubilee 2000, 04, Fall Brook, Calif., Pleine Air San Diego/Calif. Art Club, La Quinta Festival, 2000, Eagle Gallery, La Jolla, Calif., Encouragment Gallery, Fallbrook, Calif., Show Case Houses, Pasadena, Rancho Santa Fe, Calif., 1995, 96, Palm Springs Paradise, 2000, San Diego, 97, 98, 99, French Gallery, Fallbrook, 2005; represented in permanent collections, Albertina Museum, Vienna, Kunstmus., Basel, Switzerland, Bibliothèque National, Paris, Los Angeles County Mus., Simpson Coll., Phoenix Art Mus., Ariz. State collection, Graphische Bundes Versuchsanstalt, Vienna, Austria, Equitable ns. Co., Des Moines, also pvt. collections, works include stained glass windows, Meth. Ch., Perry, Iowa.; works reproduced Applause mag, 1971, New Woman mag, 1974, Artists of Cen. and No. Calif., Vol. II, San Diego Better Homes and Gardens Lifestyles mag., 1995, San Diego Decorating mag., 1995, 98, Pasadena Showcase House Design Mag., 1995, San Diego Decor and Style, 1996, 97, 98, Sci. of Mind Mag., 1997, Desert Art Scene Mag., 1999-; poster artist Vintage Car Show, Fallbrook, 2003-; signature artist Malabar Homes, 2007; commd. J.D. Properties, Stockton, Calif., 2007. Selected for Calif. State Fair, Sacramento, 2005, recipient grand purchase prize Ariz. Ann. Art Show, 1961, 1st prize in prints Iowa State Fair, 1974, 1st prize So. Calif. Expn., Del Mar, 1984, 1st prize Fall Brook Art Assn., 2000, Best of Show, 2003, 1st prize San Diego County Fair, 2005, 3rd prize, Best of Show, 1st, 3d, hon. mention, 2006, 3d prize Kirkland's Next Great Am. Artist, 2nd prize and two 3d prize mentions, 2007, others; featured in Am. Artist mag. Oct. 1993, San Diego Decor and Style mag. June 2005. Mem. Calif. Art Club, Oil Painters Am. Home and Office: 5555 8th St Fallbrook CA 92028-9619 Personal E-mail: jackragland@sbcglobal.net.

RAGLAND, KATHRYN MARIE, dancer, educator; b. Lakewood, Ohio, Nov. 22, 1948; d. Earl Albert and Alice Maxine (Outzs) R.; m. Donald Glen Rubright, Sept. 1, 1973 (div. 1977); m. Jack Victor Rutberg, Mar. 9, 1980 (div. 1988); 1 child, Jessica Erin; m. Johnny Anthony Vergona, Oct. 9, 1988; 1 child, David Sean; stepchildren: Danielle Evelyn Vergona, Jonathan Chaunch Vergona. AA, L.A. Valley Coll., 1971; BFA cum laude, U. Utah, 1973, MFA in Dance, 1975; MA in Marriage, Family and Child Counseling/Clin. Child Devel., Pacific Oaks Coll., 1993; EdD in Ednl. Leadership and Change, Fielding Grad. U., 2005. Lic. marriage and family therapist; cert. ednl. specialist, Calif. With Momentum Dance Co., LA, 1975-77; dance spl. pub. sch. LA, 1975-76; instr. Scripps Coll., Claremont, Calif., 1976-77; dir. dance Cypress Coll., Calif., 1978-85, instr. dance Calif., 1978—85, Calif., 1986—2002; owner, operator Gymboree, 1985-88. Adj. faculty Antioch U., 1998—, Pacific Oaks Coll., 2006—; faculty facilitator MA-CEL program Fielding Grad. U.; dance instr. Hollywood (Calif.) Little Red Sch. Ho., Hollywood, 1985—89, sch. coun., 1997—, asst. head of sch., 2000—02, Hollywood Schoolhouse prin., 2002—04; inclusion specialist Milagro Charter Sch., 2004—; spl. products coord.

Learning Ctr., 2004—05; dance instr. McGroarty Arts Ctr., 1992—97, bd. dirs., 1991—92, 1997—2002; mem. arts assistance team L.A. Supt. Schs.; curriculum coun. L.A. H.S. Performing Arts, adv. bd., 1986—88, Dance Resource Ctr., 1991—92; intern Julie Ann Singer Ctr. Therapeutic Sch., 1991—92; coord. infant devel. program Santa Clara Valley Child and Family Devel. Ctr., 1992—93; therapist Julia Ann Singer Ctr. Family Stress Program, 1994—95, Verdugo Mental Health Ctr., 1994—; crisis counselor Verdugo Disaster Recovery Program, 1994—95; trainer Project COPE, 1995—96; co-dir. Verdugo Creative Arts Group, 1995—2002; program coord. Atwater Park Ctr., 1996—97; coach L.A. Odyssey of the Mind, 1998—, L.A. regional dir., 2002, bd. dirs., 2002—, bd. dirs. L.A. Basin, 2002—. Author/choreographer Kitty Kats, 1986; choreographer: Man of La Mancha, 1976-80, Pippin, 1981, Fiddler on the Roof, 1982, Music Man, 1983, Spanish Suite, 1983, A Funny Thing Happened on the Way to the Forum, 1984, Skaters Edge, 1984, Cartoon, 1984, Urban Primitive, 1985, Cabaret, 1985, Healings, 1987, Cloud Reveries, 1988, Guys and Dolls, 1988, The Lottery, 1988, Cabaret, 1989, Atmos, 1990, Damn Yankees, 1990, Conflict of Interest, 1990; author, dir., choreographer We Saved the Day, 1987, The Visit, 1988, Where the Wild Things Are, 1991, Evening's After Image, 1992, Hair, 1992, South Pacific, 1993, Hello Dolly, 1993, In Search of Quieter Times and Places, 1993, Fiddler on the Roof, 1994, Pajama Game, 1994, Nine, 1994, Testosteroni Baloney, 1994, Guys and Dolls, 1995, Into the Woods, 1995, Alice in Wonderland, 1996, Pirates of Penzance, 1997, Rags, 1997; dir. Courage of the Heart, 1998; dir./choreographer Bye Bye Birdie, 1998; choreographer Mikado, 1998, Sweeney Todd, 1999, Funny Thing Happened on the Way to the Forum, 1999, Jesus Christ Superstar, 1999, Oklahoma, 2000, Rocky Horror Show, 2000, Man of La Mancha, 2001, Joseph and the Amazing Technicolor Dreamcoat, 2001, Cabaret, 2002, Fiddler on the Roof, 2005, Nightmare Before Christmas, 2005. Mem. So. Calif. steering com. Legis. Action Coalition Arts Edn.; den leader Cub Scouts, 1996-2000. Mem. AAHPERD, ASCD, AARP, AERA, ASCD, Dance Resource Ctr., Calif. Dance Educators Assn. (v.p. 1980-82, legis. rep. 1982-86), Calif. Music Educators (legis. com. 1982-86), L.A. Area Dance Alliance, Faculty Assn. C.C., Calif. Assn. Health, Phys. Edn., Recreation and Dance, Calif. Assn. Marriage and Family Therapists, So. Calif. Assn. Edn. Young Children (bd. dirs. South Bay chpt.), Calif. Confedn. Arts, Calif. Learning Disabilities Assn., Calif. Elem. Edn. Assn., Josephson Inst. Ethics (mem. shared leadership coun. Millikin Middle Sch. 1994-96, mem. learn coun. Apperson Sch. 1994-95), Assn. Ednl. Therapists, Learning Disabilities Assn. L.A., Calif. Elem. Edn. Assn. Democrat. Personal E-mail: kragland@juno.com, kmragland@verizon.net. Business E-Mail: kmragland@pubschools.org.

RAGLAND, ROBERT ALLEN, lawyer; b. Bartlesville, Okla., Apr. 18, 1954; s. Thomas Martin and Joan Ethel (Murphy) R. BA, U. Md., 1976; JD, George Mason Sch. of Law, 1980. Dir. regulatory reform and govt. orgn. Nat. Assn. Mfrs., Washington, 1979-82, asst. v.p. taxation, 1983-86; mgr. congl. rels. The Clorox Co., Oakland, Calif., 1982-83; dir. tax rsch. U.S. C. of C., Washington, 1988-93; v.p., officer Wachovia Bank, 1995—2004; v.p. SunTrust Bank, Orlando, Fla., 2004—05, Fifth Third Bank, Cin., 2006; ptnr. The Ragland Law Firm, Orlando, Fla., 2006—. Chief tax counsel, mng. dir. Nat. Chamber Found., Washington, 1989-93. Author: Transportation Reform, 1980, Employee Stock Ownership Plans, 1989, Taxation of Foreign Source Income, Distributional Impact of Excise Taxes, 1990; editor Taxation of Intercorporate Profits, 1990, Jour. Regulation and Social Costs, 1992-93, Jour. Regulation, 1992-93. Active Boy Scouts Am., Washington, 1967—, bd. dirs. nat. capital area coun.; dep. dir. duPont for Pres., 1987-88; v.p. Nat. Chamber Found. U.S. C. of C., 1989-93, dir., Liz Lerman Dance Exchange, 1993-2001, dir. Our House, Inc., 1988-2000. Republican. Roman Catholic. Home: The Waverly 803 322 E Central Blvd Orlando FL 32801

RAGLAND, WILLIAM MCKENZIE, JR., lawyer, real estate developer; b. Raleigh, NC, Feb. 12, 1960; s. William McKenzie and Elizabeth White (Johnson) R. AB, U. N.C., 1982; JD, U. Va., 1986. Bar: Ga. 1986, D.C. 1987, U.S. Dist. Ct. (no. dist.) Ga. 1987, U.S. Dist. Ct. Calif. (no. dist.) 1987, U.S. Ct. Appeals (11th cir.) 1987, U.S. Ct. Appeals (D.C. and Fed. cirs.) 1990, U.S. Supreme Ct. 1990. Staff asst. Com. on Commerce, Sci. and Transp., U.S. Senate, Washington, 1982-83; legis. asst. U.S. Rep. Jim Cooper, Washington, 1983; assoc. Powell, Goldstein, Frazer & Murphy, Atlanta, 1986—. Faculty Atlanta Coll. of Trial Advocacy, 1994—. Sr. editor Jour. of Law and Politics, 1984-86; contbr. articles to profl. publs. Mem. ABA, State Bar Ga. (co-founder products liability sect.), Fed. Cir. Bar Assn., Atlanta Bar Assn. (vice-chmn./chmn.-elect 1997-98, sec/treas. 1996, dir.—, litigation sect., bd. dirs. 1997—, trustee 1997—), D.C. Bar Assn., Am. Inns. Ct. Episcopalian. Home: 2 Albemarle Dr NW Atlanta GA 30327-1856

RAGLIN, JONNY, Bar Chef; With Pearls Oyster Bar; bartender Bodega Bay, Calif., Stars Bar and Dining, San Francisco, 2001, Incanto, San Francisco; bar chef Absinthe, San Francisco, 2004—. Named one of San Francisco's Rising Stars, StarChefs.com, 2007; recipient Plymouth Gin competition award, 2006. Mem.: US Bartender's Guild. Office: Absinthe 398 Hayes St San Francisco CA 94110 Office Phone: 415-551-5127. *

RAGO, DOROTHY ASHTON, retired elementary school educator; b. NYC, Oct. 10, 1925; d. Thomas Percy and Isabel (Seddon) Ashton; divorced, 1958; 1 child, Thomas Ashton. BA, Wellesley Coll., 1946; MA, Columbia U., 1964. Cert. early childhood edn. tchr., N.Y. Editor Alford Baby Group mags., NYC, 1948-52; kindergarten tchr. N.Y.C. Bd. Edn., 1964-86, ret., 1986. Mem. vestry Chapel of St. John, Saunderstown, R.I., 1988-91; mem. Human Rights Com., North Kingstown, R.I., 1988-94; treas. Pettaquamscutt Hist. Soc., 1991-98; mem. exec. bd. Friends of Oceanography/GSO-URI, 1997-2001. Mem. South County Mus., Gilbert Stuart Mus., South County Women's Club, Saunderstown Yacht Club, R.I. Wellesley Club. Episcopalian. Avocations: local history, hand bell ringing.

RAGO, JOHN THOMAS, law educator; b. Pitts., May 11, 1955; s. Joseph Thomas and Louise Rose (Libetti) Rago; m. Anna Marie D'Amico, Aug. 31, 1984; 3 children. BA, Duquesne U., 1979, JD, 1987. Bar: Pa. 1987. Atty. Superior Ct. Pa., Pitts., 1987-88; atty. criminal div. Ct. Common Pleas, Pitts, 1988-90; law clk. US Dist. Ct. for Western Dist., Pa., 1990; asst. prof. law Duquesne U., Pitts., founding exec. dir. Cyril H. Wecht Inst. Forensic Sci. and Law, founding dir. Post-Conviction DNA Project, asst. dean law sch., 1993—96, assoc. dean adminstrn., 1996—2003. Mem. Innocence Project's Northeast Pub. Policy Com., Cordoza Law Sch.; adj. faculty mem. Justice Studies Dept. Calif. U. of Pa. Editor: Juris, 1986—87; contbr. articles to profl. jours. Mem.: ABA, Pa. Bar Assn., Serra Club Pitts. Democrat. Roman Catholic. Avocations: beatles afficianado, music, travel, reading. Office: Duquesne U 600 Forbes Ave Pittsburgh PA 15282 Office Phone: 412-396-1039. Office Fax: 412-396-4014. E-mail: ragoj@duq.edu. *

RAGON, ROBERT RONALD, clergyman; b. Flintstone, Ga., Sept. 10, 1939; s. Robert Emmett and Frances Cora (Stoner) R.; m. Judith Ann Ward, Apr. 27, 1962; children: Ronald Russell, Regina Renee. BS, U. Chattanooga, 1962; BDiv, MDiv, Columbia Theol. Sem., Decatur, Ga., 1967. Ordained to ministry Presbyn. Ch., 1967. Pastor Trion (Ga.) Presbyn. Ch., 1967-72; dir., pastor Chattooga County Presbyn. Ministries, Trion, 1971-72; pastor Brainerd Presbyn. Ch., Chattanooga, 1972—2007. Moderator Knoxville Presbytery, 1979-80; founder An Order of Slaves of Christ, Chattanooga, 1970; stated clk. Presbytery of S.E., 1990-93, moderator, 1995-96. Author: Covenant Agreement: O.S.C., 1970, The Journey, 1990. Trustee King Coll., Bristol, Tenn., 1983-86. Mem. Masons (Ga. chaplain 1980), KT (sec. 1991), Shriners. Republican. Presbyterian. Avocation: investments. Home: 4229 Happy Valley Rd Flintstone GA 30725-2222

RAGONE, DAVID VINCENT, former university president; b. NYC, May 16, 1930; s. Armando Frederick and Mary (Napier) R.; m. Katherine H. Spaulding, Dec. 18, 1954; children: Christine M., Peter V. BS, MIT, 1951, MS, 1952, DSc, 1953. Asst. prof. chem. and metall. engring. U. Mich., Ann Arbor, 1953-57, assoc. prof., 1957-61, prof., 1961-62; asst. dir. John J. Hopkins Lab. for Pure and Applied Sci., also chmn. metallurgy dept. Gen. Atomic divsn. Gen. Dynamics, La Jolla, 1962-67; Alcoa prof. metallurgy Carnegie-Mellon U., Pitts., 1967-69, assoc. dean Sch. Urban and Pub. Affairs, 1969-70; dean Thayer Sch. Engring. Dartmouth Coll., 1970-72; dean Coll. Engring. U. Mich., 1972-80; pres. Case Western Res. U., Cleve., 1980-87; vis. prof., dept. materials sci. and engring. MIT, Cambridge, 1987-88, sr. lectr. dept. materials sci. and engring., 1988-98; gen. ptnr. Ampersand Ventures, 1988-92, ptnr., 1992—2005. Mem. Nat. Sci. Bd., 1978-84; mem. tech adv. bd. US Dept. Commerce, 1967-75; chmn. adv. com. advanced auto power systems Coun. on Environ. Quality, 1971-75; trustee Henry Luce Found. Named Outstanding Young Engr., Engring. Soc. Detroit, 1957. Mem. Univ. Club (NYC), Longwood Cricket Club (Boston), Sigma Xi, Tau Beta Pi. Home Phone: 781-237-9676. Business E-Mail: ragone@mit.edu.

RAGONE, TARA ADAMS, lawyer; b. Paterson, NJ, Apr. 24, 1974; d. John Joseph and Maryellen Adams; m. Alexander B. Ragone, July 6, 1996; children: Elisabeth Alexandra, Evan Philip, Claire May. BA, Coll. William and Mary, Williamsburg, Va., 1996; JD, NYU, NYC, 2001. Bar: NJ 2001, NY 2002. Rsch. asst. Brookings Instn., Washington, 1996—98; law clerk US Dist. Ct. (ea. dist. NY), Bklyn., 2001—02, US Ct. Appeals (2d cir.), NYC, 2002—03; dep. atty. gen. State N.J., 2003—. Contbr. articles in field. Office Phone: 973-648-7093.

RAGSDALE, FRANK WAYNE, voice educator, singer; b. Dallas, Dec. 10, 1965; s. Dorothy Joyce Goodall and Dannie Murle Ragsdale, Ronald Goodall (Stepfather) and Lynda Ragsdale (Stepmother). MusB, Atlantic Union Coll., South Lancaster, Mass., 1990; MusM, Longy Sch. of Music, Cambridge, Mass., 1994; D in Mus. Arts, U. Miami, Fla., 2004. Asst. prof. of voice Columbia Union Coll., Takoma Park, Md., 1994—98; assoc. prof. of voice Oklahoma City U., 2004—; tchg. asst. U. Miami, Coral Gables, Fla., 2001—04. Young artist studio mgr. Fla. Grand Opera, Coral Gables, 1999—2001; dramatic interpretation coach U. of Miami in Salzburg, Salzburg, Austria, 2003—; performer in venues including Carnegie Hall, N.Y., Avery Fischer Hall, N.Y., Cairo Opera House, Notre Dame, Paris and Martin-in-the-Fields, London. Singer (rodolfo): (opera) La Boheme; singer: (alfredo) La Traviata; singer: (don ottavio) Don Giovanni; singer: (garrison) Walker; singer: (tony) (musical) West Side Story. Mem.: Coll. Music Soc., Nat. Assn. of Teachers of Singing, Pi Kappa Lambda (hon.). D-Liberal. Achievements include research in belting and nonclassical styles of singing. Avocations: cooking, reading, exercise. Home: 249 NW Eubanks St Oklahoma City OK 73118 Home Phone: 405-604-6807. Fax: 405-208-5971. Personal E-mail: frankragsdale@cox.net.

RAGSDALE, SANDRA RUSSELL, special education educator; b. Billings, Mont., Mar. 15, 1957; d. Alexander Emmett and Cleora Jean (Saunders) Russell; children: Naomi Jo, Andrea Renee, James Russell. BS, Mont. State U., 1979, MS in Spl. Edn., 2005, MEd in Reading, 2006. cert. childbirth educator. Spl. edn. and reading tchr. Anchorage Sch. Dist., 2005—06, Matanuska-Susitna Sch. Dist., 2006—. U.S. western dir. Inter Childbirth Edn. Assn., Mpls., 1990-92, pres. elect 1992-94, pres. 1994-95. Contbr. articles to profl. jours. Avocations: skiing, reading, writing, quilting, white-water rafting. Personal E-mail: sandyragsdale1@yahoo.com.

RAGUCKAS, SARAH, pharmacist, educator; b. Lansing, Mich., Apr. 14, 1979; d. Robert and Susan Christiansen; m. James Raguckas, Sept. 17, 2005. D of Pharmacy, Ferris State U., Big Rapids, Mich., 2004. Resident KCMS/MSU/IBA Health Plans/Pfizer/Blue Care Network, Kalamazoo, 2004—05; asst. prof. pharmacy practice Ferris State U., Grand Rapids, Mich., 2005—. Office Phone: 616-235-7272 3195.

RAHAIM, STEPHEN, lawyer; BA in Geology, U. Del., 1983, MS in Organic Geochemistry, 1986; JD, Rutgers U. Sch. Law, 1992. Bar: US Ct. Appeals (10th cir.), US Ct. Appeals (11th cir.), US Dist. Ct. (ea. dist.) Pa., US Dist. Ct. (no. dist.) Ga., US Dist. Ct. (dist. Del.), Pa. 1993, Ga. 1994. Sr. project mgr. nat. environ. consulting firm; environ. scientist NJ Dep. Environ. Protection; ptnr. Duane Morris, Baker & Hostetler, Washington, 2006—. Mem.: Ga. Bar Assn., Del. Bar Assn., Pa. Bar Assn. Office: Baker Hostetler Washington Sq Ste 1100 1050 Conn Ave Washington DC 20036-5304 Office Phone: 202-861-1573. Office Fax: 202-861-1783. *

RAHAL, IMAD, computer science educator; b. Nomeire, Lebanon, Aug. 2, 1978; BS (hon.), Lebanese Am. U., Beirut, 2001; MS in Computer Sci., ND State U., Fargo, 2003, PhD, 2005. Web developer ABEO, Beirut, 1999—2001; rsch., tchg. asst. ND State U., Fargo, 2001—05; asst. prof. Coll. St. Benedict, St. John's U., St. Cloud, Minn., 2005—. Recipient Cert. Achievement award, ACM-ICPC, 2006, Cert. Appreciation award, ISCA, 2006; Grant, NSF, 2003—05, Coll. of St. Benedict, St. Johns U., 2006—. Mem.: ACM (assoc.). Independent.

RAHALL, NICK JOE, II, (NICK RAHALL), congressman; b. Beckley, W.Va., May 20, 1949; s. N. Joe and Alice Rahall; m. Melinda Ross; children: Rebecca Ashley, Nick Joe III, Suzanne Nicole. BA, Duke U., 1971. Asst. Staff of US Senator Robert C. Byrd, 1971-74; sales rep. Sta. WWNR, Beckley, 1974; pres. Mountaineer Travel Co., Beckley, 1975-77, W.Va. Broadcasting, 1980; mem. US Congress from 3rd W.Va. dist., 1977—, ranking mem. resources com., mem. transp. and infrastructure com. Bd. dirs. Rahall Comm. Corpn.; served on US Constn. Bicentennial Commn. of Mo. Del. Dem. Nat. Conv., 1972, 74, 78, 80, 84, 88, 92, 96; W.Va. chmn. March of Dimes, 1979; mem. profl. adv. bd. Alsac-St. Jude Children's Rsch. Hosp. Named Young Man of Yr. Beckley Jaycees, 1972; Outstanding Young Man in W.Va. W.Va. Jaycees, 1977; recipient Achievement award Logan Cripple Children Soc., 1978; Citizenship award KC, 1978, Disting. Svc. award Am. Fedn. Govt. Employees W.Va., 1984, Young Dem. of Yr. Dem. Nat. Conv., 1980, Outfitter of Yr. Profl. Outfitters, 1987, Seneca award Sierra Club, 1988, River Conservation award Am. River, 1988; named Coal Man of Yr. Coal Industry News, 1979, W.Va. Son of Yr., W.Va. Soc. of Washington, 1996. Mem. NAACP, NRA (life), Elks, Moose, Masons (33rd degree) Shriners. Democrat. Presbyterian. Office: US Ho Reps 2307 Rayburn Ho Office Bldg Washington DC 20515-4803 Office Phone: 202-225-3452. *

RAHARINAIVO, ANDRÉ LÉON, research scientist, educator; b. Tananarive, Madagascar, Sept. 1, 1940; arrived in France, 1954; s. Ignace Léon and Marthe (Rasoazanamalala) R.; m. Christiane Martine Laurent, May 7, 1966 (div. June 1994); 1 child, Jacques Yves. Engr. mining and metallurgy, Ecole des Mines, Nancy, France, 1964; degree superior scientific studies, U. Nancy, France, 1964; PhD, U. Compiegne, France, 1982. Cert. engr. Head sect. Lab. Ctrl. Ponts et Chaussées, Paris, 1971-80, dep. head dept., 1980-83, sec. sci. coun., 1983-91, rsch. mgr., 1991—2005; cons. Cefracor, 2005—. Author: Fracture Mechanics and Mechanisms, 1990; patentee in field. Capt. Equipment, 1967-69, France. Mem. Ctr. Français Anticorrosion, Nat. Assn. Corrosion Engrs. Avocation: singing gospel music. Home: 378 rue de Vaugirard F-75015 Paris France Personal E-mail: andraha@aol.com.

RAHE, MARIBETH SEMBACH, investment management executive; b. Evanston, Ill., Oct. 3, 1948; d. Daniel F. and Boysie (Beebe) Sembach; m. Martin E. Rahe, May 31, 1975. BA, Bowling Green State U., 1970; postgrad., Ohio State U., 1970—72; MBA, Thunderbird Garvin Grad. Sch. Internat. Mgmt., 1974. Internat. banking officer Harris Bank, Chgo., 1974-77, asst. v.p. London, 1977-80; v.p. Morgan Guaranty Trust Co., London, 1980-83, NYC, 1983-84; sr. rep. Sparebanken Oslo Akershus, NYC, 1984-85; v.p. Morgan Guaranty Trust Co., NYC, 1985-87, J.P. Morgan Investment Mgmt., NYC, 1987-88; sr. v.p. Harris Bank, Chgo., 1988-91, dept. exec., 1991-94, sr. exec. v.p., 1994-95, vice chmn. bd., 1995-97; vice chmn. U.S. Trust Co. N.Y., 1997—2001, pres., 2001—02; pres., CEO Fort Washington Investment Advisors, Cin., 2003—. Bd. dirs. N.Y. Landmark Conservancy, Rush Presbyn. Hosp., Nat. Trust, Thunderbird Garwin Grad. Sch. Internat. Mgmt.; com. 200 Found. Bd.; mem. investment oversight com. United Way; mem. Fin. Svcs. Roundtable, The Chgo. Network, Women's Forum, Inc. Recipient Outstanding Alumni award, Thunderbird Garvin Am. Grad. Sch., 1991. Mem.: Chgo. Women's Network, Econ. Club N.Y., Econ. Club Chgo., Am. Bankers Assn., Univ. Club, Queen City Club, Chgo. Club. Republican. Lutheran. Office Phone: 513-361-7619. Business E-Mail: maribeth.rahe@fortwashington.com.

RAHER, PATRICK MICHAEL, lawyer; b. Kalamazoo, June 15, 1947; BBA, U. Notre Dame, 1969; JD, Georgetown U., 1972. Bar: Va. 1972, D.C. 1973. Prof. legal rsch. and creditors rights Internat. Sch. Law, Washington, 1972-75; law clk. to Hon. Roger Robb U.S. Ct. Appeals, Washington, 1972-73; ptnr. Hogan & Hartson LLP, Washington, environ. practice group dir. Vice chair DC Jud. Disabilities and Tenure Commn., 1986-92; mem. EPA Clean Air Act Adv. Com., 1994—. Mem. ABA, DC Bar. Office: Hogan & Hartson LLP Columbia Sq 555 13th St NW 13E-300 Washington DC 20004-1161 Office Phone: 202-637-5682. Office Fax: 202-637-5910. Business E-Mail: pmraher@hhlaw.com.

RAHIMI, HESSAM, dentist; b. Strasburg, France, Aug. 11, 1979; s. Mohammad Farhad Rahimi and Malekbanou Asgari; m. Niloofar Khalesseh, Aug. 10, 2004. DDS, Mashhad Sch. Dental Medicine, Iran, 2003. Pvt. practice, Tehran, Iran, 2003—06; rsch. asst. Harvard Sch. Dental Medicine, Boston, 2007—. Author: (book) Textbook of Canal Preparation, Fundamentals, Instruments and Techniques (Yr. book award, 2007); contbr. articles to profl. jours. Mem.: Internat. Assn. Dental Rsch. (exec. dir. Iranian sect. 2003—04). Achievements include patents for osteoconductive material based on calcium sulfate. Home Phone: 310-666-5730.

RAHJA, VIRGINIA H., retired art educator, artist; b. Aurora, Minn., Apr. 21, 1921; d. Emil Rahja and Mae Amanda Nevala. BA, Hamline U., St. Paul, 1944. Art instr. Hamline U., St. Paul, 1944—48, dir. galleries, 1944—48; asst. supt. art Art Gallery, Minn. State Fair, St. Paul, 1945—50; co-founder Coll. Visual Arts, St. Paul, 1948, art instr., 1948—60, dean, 1960—72, pres., 1972—86; ret., 1986. Mem.: AAUW. Presbyterian. Avocations: reading, volunteering, gardening, walking, travel. Home: 2940 E 94th Pl #1014 Tulsa OK 74137

RAHM, SUSAN BERKMAN, lawyer; b. Pitts., June 25, 1943; d. Allen Hugh and Selma (Wiener) Berkman; m. David Alan Rahm, Nov. 23, 1972; children: Katherine, William. BA with honors, Wellesley Coll., 1965; postgrad., Harvard U., 1966-68; JD, NYU, 1973. Bar: N.Y. 1974, D.C. 1988. Assoc. Marshall, Bratter, Greene, Allison & Tucker, NYC, 1973-81, ptnr., 1981-82, Kaye Scholer LLP, NYC, 1982—2005, ptnr, chair real estate dept., 1993—98, chair internat. practice group, 1999—2005. N.Y. adv. bd., Chgo. Title Ins. Co., 1995. Editor: New York Real Property Service, 1987. Bd. dirs. Girls Inc., 1989-93; mem. aux. bd. Mt. Sinai Hosp., N.Y.C., 1976-78. Recipient cert. of outstanding svc. D.C. Redevel. Land Agy., 1969, She Knows Where She's Going award Girls' Clubs of Am., 1987, Woman of Yr. award CREW.NY, 1999 Mem. ABA, Assn. Bar City N.Y., N.Y. Bar Assn. (real property law com., co-chmn. real-estate devel. 1987-91), Am. Coll. Real Estate Lawyers, WX formerly known as Comml. Real Estate Women N.Y. (bd. dirs. 1988-94, v.p. 1988-91, pres. 1991-93), Assn. Fgn. Investors in Real Estate, Assn. Real Estate Women (Outstanding Achievement award 2003). Office: Kaye Scholer LLP 425 Park Ave New York NY 10022-3506

RAHMAN, ABU TAYEB RAFIQUR, former United Nations official; b. Ashrafpur, Feni, Bangladesh, July 1, 1936; came to U.S., 1958; s. Abidur Rahman and Fatima Begum; m. Saleha Choudhury, Sept. 1, 1963; children: Farhana, Tamanna, Nashra. M Polit. Sci., Dacca U., 1956; MPA, Karachi U., 1958; PhD, Duke U., 1969. Expert in pub. adminstrn. Rural Devel. Acad., Comilla, Bangladesh; assoc. prof. polit. sci. Dacca U., Bangladesh, 1969-71; assoc. dir. Internat. Devel. Rsch. Ctr., Ottawa, Ont., Can., 1971-80, sr. cons., 1971-72; with devel. adminstrn. divsn. UN, NYC, 1981—94, chief divsn., 1981—94, now consultant, div. of governance, public. admin. & fin.; pres. Vols. Assn. for Bangladesh, 1998—. Now adjunct prof. Baruch Coll., John Jay Coll. of Criminal Justice; guest lecturer Harvard Inst. of Internat. Develop. Pres. Bangladesh-Can. Soc., Ottawa, 1976, Deshantari Cmty. Group, Ottawa, 1977; bd. dirs. United Way of Westchester-Putnam County, NY, 1999-2006. Mem. Bangladesh Polit. Sci. Assn., Bangladesh Devel. Forum, East Pakistan Polit. Sci. Assn. (sec. 1970), Rivertowns Lions Club (pres. 2004-06).

RAHMAN, MUHAMMAD ABDUR, mechanical engineer; b. Sylhet, Assam, India, Mar. 1, 1930; came to U.S., 1950; s. Haji Sajjad Ali Khan and Momotaj Khanom. BSME, U. Toledo, 1953, MSME, 1968; PhD in Engring., Calif. Coast U., 1985. Registered profl. engr., Calif. Mech. design engr. various cons. firms, LA, 1955-61; aerospace engr. Douglas Aircraft Co., Santa Monica, Calif., 1962-63, N.Am. Aviation, Inc., LA, 1963-64, NASA Manned Spacecraft Ctr. Gemini & Apollo Program Office, Houston, 1964-70; safety engr. U.S. Dept. Labor, OSHA, Washington, 1975-86; invention researcher Arlington, Va., 1987—. Contbr. articles to profl. jours. Mem. N.Y. Acad. Scis. Democrat. Muslim. Achievements include patent for solar energy collector, supersonic MHD generator system; copyrights for hypothesis on unified field theory and creation of the universe, on the gravitoenergy in the creation of cosmic matters in the space, on the mechanism of superconductivity, a note of caution for superconductivity in reference to permeability and permitivity, concentration on suggesting methods to build superconductors and biomedical engineering instrumentation for cancer in particular, others. Home and Office: 1805 Crystal Dr Apt 1013 Arlington VA 22202-4407

RAHMAN, RAFIQ UR, oncologist, educator; b. Mirali, Pakistan, Mar. 3, 1957; came to U.S., 1985; s. Rakhman and Bibi (Sana) Gul; m. Shamim Ara Bangash; children: Maryam, Hassan, Haider. BS, MB, U. Peshawar, Pakistan, 1980. Bd. cert. internal medicine, med. oncology, hematology; lic. physician Pa., Ala., Ky. House officer in internal medicine Khyber Tchg. Hosp.-U. Peshawar, 1980-81, house officer in gen. surgery, 1981, jr. registrar med. ICU, 1983-84; jr. registrar internal medicine Khyber Tchg. Hosp., 1981-82; sr. registrar internal medicine Khyber Tchg. Hosp.-Lady Reading Hosp. & Postgrad. Inst., Peshawar, 1984-85; Audrey Meyer Mars fellow in med. oncology Roswell Park Cancer Inst., Buffalo, 1985-86; resident in internal medicine SUNY-Buffalo Gen. Hosp.-Erie County Med. Ctr.-VA Med. Ctr., 1986-88; chief resident in internal medicine SUNY-Buffalo-Erie County Med. Ctr., 1988; fellow in hematology and med. oncology SUNY-Buffalo-Roswell Park Cancer Inst., 1989-90; hematologist, med. oncologist Daniel Boone Clinic and Harlan A.R.H., 1991-92; clin. asst. prof. medicine U. Ky., 1991—; attending physician, hematology, med. oncologist Hardin Meml. Hosp., Elizabethtown, Ky., 1993—, chief medicine, 1996, pres.-elect med. staff, 2001—02, pres. med. staff, 2002—03. Tchr. med. students Med. Sch., SUNY; participant CALGB protocol studies Roswell Park Cancer Inst., investigator. Editor English sect. Cenna mag.; contbr. articles to profl. jours. Founder Cmty. Uplift Program, Pakistan; founding dir. Pakistan Human Devel. Fund, Pakistan Am. Leadership Ctr., Washington. Mem.: Assn. Pakistan Physicians Ky.

and Ind. (pres. 2002—03), Ky. Med. Assn. Avocations: travel, aeromodeling, swimming, studying political science and history. Home: 400 Briarwood Cir Elizabethtown KY 42701-6915 Office: 1107 Woodland Dr Ste 105 Elizabethtown KY 42701-2789 Home Phone: 270-769-2003; Office Phone: 270-769-6665. Personal E-mail: rahmanrafiq@hotmail.com.

RAHMAN, SALEH MAHMUDUR, medical educator; s. Afaz Uddin Sarkar and Feroza Begum; m. Selina Rahman, Dec. 10, 1992; children: Tishian Mahmud, Renoa Mahmud. MBBS, Sir Salimullah Med. Coll., Dhaka, Bangladesh, 1992; MPH, Harvard U., Boston, 1997; PhD, U. Ala., Birmingham, 2001. Lic. Joslin Health Behavior Diabetes Ctr., Harvard Med. Sch., 1995. Cons. ACIPCO, Birmingham, Ala., 1999—2000; asst. prof. NW Ohio Consortium Pub. Health, Bowling Green, Ohio, 2000—04; adj. asst. prof. Med. U. Ohio, Toledo, 2000—04, cons., co-investigator, 2001—02; asst. prof. Fla. A&M U., Tallahassee, 2004—. Author: (books) Social Marketing and Community Based Participatory Research, 2002; reviewer Jour. Behavioral Services & Research, 2003—, Ethnicity and Diseases, 2003—, Cancer Causes and Control, 2004—, Jour. Health Disparities Research & Practice, 2006; contbr. articles to profl. jours. Recipient Nat. Acad. Children award, Nat. Acad. for Children, Bangladesh, 1989, Our Pride award, Bangladesh Am. Found. Inc., 2005, Outstanding Achievement award, Alabama Power Found., B award, ENHR; grantee Rsch. grant, Bowling Green State U., 2003, NIH-NCMHD, 2004—, 2005—. Mem.: APHA (pub. health edn. & health promotion workgrp. 2006, Early Career award 2006), Bangladesh Med. Assn. N.Am., Am. Assn. Diabetes Educators, European Assn. Study Diabetes, Internat. Diabetes Fedn., South Asian HIV Network (steering com. 2000—05). Office: Fla A&M Univ COPPS IPH 209-A FSH Sci Rsch Ctr Tallahassee FL 32307 Office Phone: 850-599-8840. Office Fax: 850-599-8830; Home Fax: 850-599-8830. Business E-Mail: saleh_rahman_97@post.harvard.edu, saleh.rahman@famu.edu.

RAHMAN, SHAFIQUR, neuropharmacologist, scientist, educator; b. Faridgonj, Chandpur, Bangladesh, Jan. 1, 1963; d. Mohammad Ali and Momotaj Begum; m. Moursheda Rahman, May 24, 1993; 2 children, Zarin and Kashfia. BSc with honors, Dhaka U., Bangladesh, 1985, MSc, 1987; PhD, Meml. U., Newfoundland, Can., 1995. Lectr. Jahangirnagar U., Dhaka, 1988-93, asst. prof., 1993-97, assoc. prof., 1997—; rsch. assoc. Ind. U. Sch. Medicine, Indpls., 1998—2001; scientist Ctr. Addiction Mental Health, 2001—04; asst. prof. dept. psychiatry and neurosci. U. Toronto, Canada, 2002—04; sr. rsch. sci. Ctr. Drug Abuse Rsch. Translation, U. Ky., 2005—. Cons. Inst. Psychiat. Rsch., Indpls., 1998—; rschr., investigator in field. Contbr. articles to profl. jours.; investigator, rschr. for profl. jour. articles. Active Lions Club Dhaka Topekhana, 1984-88, ADHUNIK, Dhaka, 1989-98. Recipient Chancellor and Pres. Bangladesh, Dhaka, 1987, rsch. grant, Ctr. Drug Addiction and Mental Health, Toronto, Can., 2001, U. Toronto, Can., 2001, Nat. Inst. on Drug Abuse, US, 2002, Canadian Inst. Health Rsch., 2003; vis. scientist rsch. grantee Ind. U. Sch. Medicine, 1998; Meml. Rsch. fellow Meml. U., Newfoundland, 1990, Clark Found. Postdoctoral fellow Clarke Inst. Psychiatry, U. Toronto, Can., 1995. Mem. Internat. Brain Rsch. Orgn., Soc. for Neurosci., Bangladesh Physiol. and Pharmacol. Soc., Bangladesh Assn. Advancement Sci., Am. Soc. Pharmacology Expert Therpeutics, Soc. Rsch. Nicotine and Tobacco, Canadian Ctr. of Substance Abuse. Avocations: writing, reading, travel. Office: U Ky Ctr Drug Abuse Rsch Translation 206 Brekenridge Hall Lexington KY 40506 Home: 336 Greenbriar Rd Lexington KY 40503 Office Fax: 859-323-0232. Business E-Mail: s.rahman@uky.edu.

RAHMAN, YUEH-ERH, biologist; b. Kwangtung, China, June 10, 1928; came to U.S., 1960; d. Khon and Kwei-Phan (Chan) Li; m. Aneesur Rahman, Nov. 3, 1956; 1 dau., Aneesa. BS, U. Paris, 1950; MD magna cum laude, U. Louvain, Belgium, 1956. Clin. and postdoctoral research fellow Louvain U., 1956-60; mem. staff Argonne (Ill.) Nat. Lab., 1960-72, biologist, 1972-81, sr. biologist, 1981-85; prof. pharmaceutics Coll. Pharmacy, U. Minn., Mpls., 1985—2002, prof. emeritus, 2002—, dir. grad. studies, pharmaceutics, 1989-92, head dept. pharmaceutics, 1991-96, 97-98. Vis. scientist State U. Utrecht, Netherlands, 1968-69; adj. prof. No. Ill. U., DeKalb, 1971-85; cons. NIH.; Mem. com. of rev. group, div. research grants NIH, 1979-83 Author; patentee in field. Recipient IR-100 award, 1976; grantee Nat. Cancer Inst., Nat. Inst. Arthritis, Metabolic and Digestive Diseases. Fellow Am. Assn. Pharm. Scientists; mem. AAAS, Am. Soc. Cell Biology, N.Y. Acad. Scis., Radiation Rsch. Soc., Assn. for Women in Sci. (1st pres. Chgo. area chpt. 1978-79). Unitarian Universalist. Home: 939 Coast Blvd Unit 6G La Jolla CA 92037-4115

RAHMANI, CAROL HIPP, retired school system administrator, psychologist; b. Loris, SC, May 4, 1950; d. James Chester and Edith Bedenbaugh Hipp; m. Abdul Manan Rahmani, May 18, 1985. BA, NC State U., 1972, MS, 1976, PhD, 1981. Lic. psychologist NC, sch. psychologist NC, cert. health svcs. provider-psychologist NC. Sch. psychologist Wake County Pub. Sch. Sys., Raleigh, NC, 1978—80, coord. psychol. svcs., 1980—90, sr. dir. related svcs., 1990—2003, sr. dir. counseling and student svcs., 2003—07; ret., 2007. Mem.: Nat. Assn. Sch. Psychologists, NC Sch. Psychology Assn. (Practitioner of Yr. 1998). Democrat. Methodist. Avocations: beach-combing, tennis, reading, sports, walking. Home: 6802 Phillips Ct Raleigh NC 27607 Personal E-mail: acrahmani@bellsouth.net.

RAHMANI, RAMIN KHOSRAVI, mechanical engineer, researcher; s. Rasoul Khosravi Rahmani and Nayereh Lajevardi Qamsari; m. Anahita Ayasoufi, May 5, 1997; 1 child, Cyrus Khosravi. BS in Mech. Engring., Sharif U. Tech., 1994, MS in Mech. Engring., 1997; PhD in Mech. Engring., U. Toledo, 2004. Project mgr. and rschr. Niroo Rsch. Inst., Tehran, 1997—99; computational fluid dynamics engr. Ill. Tool Works, Maumee, Ohio, 2001—04; postdoctoral rschr. U. Ala., Birmingham, 2005—06; applied rsch. engr. A.O. Smith, 2006—. Mem.: AIAA, ASME. Achievements include research in new grid generation algorithm; new algorithm to solve heat conduction. Home: 1825 W Lakeview Dr Apt L96 Johnson City TN 37601 Office: 1100 E Fairview Johnson City TN 37601 Home Phone: 205-822-5303. Personal E-mail: rrahmani@uab.edu.

RAHMANI, REZA MOSSAVER, writer, retired Iranian Air Force officer, banker, tour operator; b. Tehran, Iran, Jan. 17, 1912; came to U.S., 1963; s. Aliasghar M. and Khadijeh M. R.; m. Behjatmolook Lazgui, 1939 (div. 1947); children: Farhad, Sohrab; m. Poorandokht Amir Fazli, 1949; children: Ali M., Jasmin M. Rahmani Dugan. BS, Mil. Cadet Acad., Tehran, 1934; MS, Air Obs. Acad., Tehran, 1935, Higher Acad. Air Navigation, Cazaux, France, 1949; PhD equivalent, Staff and War Coll., Tehran, 1942; LLB, U. Tehran, 1945; MBA, Columbia U., NYC, 1967. Commd. officer Iranian Air Force, 1948, advanced through grades to col., 1949; tchr., operator 1st Wing Iranian Air Force, Tehran, 1942-45; prof. Mil. Cadet Acad., 1945-46, Staff and War Coll., Tehran, Iran, 1946-48; reorganizer ednl. sys. Iranian Air Force, 1948-52; ret., 1952; air, mil. and naval attache Iranian Embassy, Baghdad, Iraq, 1952-54; mgr. Bank Saderat, Ekbatan, Iran, 1954-55, head internat. dept. Tehran, 1955-60, gen. mgr. Hamburg, Germany, 1961-63, Paris, 1962-63, London, 1962-63; founder head Persepolis Travel, Ltd., NYC, 1967-91; ret., 1991. Ofcl.guest ednl. orgns., U.S., Gt. Britain, France, also aircraft factories in all three countries. Author: The Old Soldier, Vol. 1, 1985, Vol. 2, 1992, Vol. 3, 1993. Active Freedom Party, 1952. Decorated Sci. medal 3, Sci. medal 2 (Iran). Mem. Columbia U. Alumni Assn., Rancho Bernardo Swim and Tennis Club. Democrat. Home: 17199 Prado Pl San Diego CA 92128-2163

RAHMING, ETTA LORRAINE, social worker, consultant, psychotherapist, school psychologist; b. Bronx, Mar. 6, 1957; d. Henry Lewis and Irene (Linen) R. BA in Sociology, CCNY, 1979; MSW, Howard U., 1981; EdS, U. VI, 2006. Lic. social worker, N.Y.; lic. counselor, N.Y., alchohol and substance abuse counselor. Investigative probation officer N.Y.C. Dept. Probation, 1981-85; social worker E.N.T.E.R. Alcoholism O.P.D., 1985-86; psychiat. social worker Bronx Lebanon Alcoholism O.P.D., 1986-88; clin. supr. residential treatment program E.N.T.E.R. Inc., 1988-89; supr. Comprehensive Employment Opportunity Support Ctr. Fedn. Employment Guidance Ctr., 1989-92; therapist Our Lady of Mercy Mental Health Clinic, Bronx, 1994—96; sch. psychologist intern Dept. of Svcs. Virgin Islands Dist., 1997—. Dist. mgr. Dept. Human Svc., 1997—. Mem. APA, NASW, Nat. Assn. Black Social Workers, Inc., N.Y. Fedn. Alcoholism Counselors. Home Phone: 803-842-1017. Personal E-mail: ettarahming@yahoo.com.

RAHMING, JOHN CHRISTOPHER, investment company executive, consultant; b. Mt. Vernon, Ohio, Oct. 25, 1937; s. Norris Walton and Mary Catherine (Arndt) Rahming; m. Ann Gail Smith, June 12, 1959 (div. Aug. 1974); children: Charles, Jennifer; m. Penelope Watson Bevan, Dec. 17, 1988; 1 child, Jason Bevan. BA, Harvard U., Cambridge, Mass., 1959; MBA, Harvard U., Boston, 1965. Mgr Citibank, NYC and Buenos Aires, 1966-70; v.p. Security Pacific Bank, London and L.A., 1970-76, Alexander Proudfoot, L.A., Paris, London, 1976-81; mng. dir. London Interstate Bank, 1981-88; ops. mgr. Inter-Am. Investment Corp., Washington, 1989-93, gen. mgr., 1993-99, cons., 2000—07. Chmn. bd. dirs. Environ. Enterprise Assistance Fund, 2001—06; chmn. Ctrl. Am. Small Enterprise Investment Fund, 2001—. Lt. USN, 1959-63. Mem. Met. Club, Harvard Club (N.Y.C.), Harvard Bus. Sch. Club, Roehampton Club (London). Avocations: sailing, golf, music, theater. Home: 400 Madison St Apt 1202 Alexandria VA 22314-1721 Home Phone: 703-549-1833.

RAHNEMA, FARZAD, engineering educator, department chairman; m. Mahnaz Rahnema; children: Tina, Nina, Sara. BSME, Ill. Inst. Tech., 1975; PhD, UCLA, 1981. Prin. engr. GE Nuc. Energy, San Jose, Calif., 1981—92; prof., chair nuc. engring. Ga. Inst. Tech., Atlanta, 1992—. Cons. Can. Nuc. Safety Commn., Atlanta, 1998—2006. Contbr. articles to profl. jours. Fellow: Am. Nuc. Soc.; mem.: Am. Assn. Physicists in Medicine. Office: Ga Inst Tech Atlanta GA 30332-0405 Home Phone: 404-451-4686; Office Phone: 404-894-3731. Personal E-mail: farzad@nazconsulting.com. Business E-Mail: farzad@gatech.edu.

RAHNFELD, VINCENT D., counseling administrator; b. Chgo. m. Amy L. Rahnfeld; children: Michelle, Kim. BMus, U. Cin. Coll. Conservatory of Music, 1980; MEd, Xavier U., Cin., 1991. Tchr. music Milford Village Schs., Ohio, 1980—82, New Richmond Village Schs., Ohio, 1982—89, Sycamore Cmty. Sch., Cin., 1989—97, sch. counselor, 1997—. Musician, Cin., 1982—; adj. instr. Xavier U., Cin., 2004—; counselor adv. bd. Miami U., Oxford, Ohio, 2004—07; out-of-state counselor adv. bd. U. Buffalo/SUNY, 2005—. Mem.: NACAC, ASCD, Greater Cin. Counseling Assn., Ohio Counseling Assn., Ohio Assn. Coll. Admissions Counselors, Am. Sch. Counselor Assn., Music Educators Nat. Conf. Avocations: running, cycling. Office: Sycamore High School 7400 Cornell Rd Cincinnati OH 45242

RAHR, STEWART, health medical products executive; b. Feb. 19, 1948; m. Carol Rahr. BA, N.Y. Univ., 1968. Owner Kinray Inc., Whitestone, NY, 1975—, pres., 1978—, also CEO, 1984—. Named one of Top 200 Collectors, ARTnews Mag., 2004, 400 Richest Americans, Forbes, 2006. Avocation: Collector of Impressionist and Modern Art. Office: Kinray Inc 152-35 10th Ave Whitestone NY 11357-1233

RAHRIG, CAROL ANN, literature and language educator; b. Bridgeport, Conn., Sept. 16, 1954; d. Albert George and Elsie Gross Rahrig. BA in Spanish cum laude, Sacred Heart U., Bridgeport, Conn., 1976; MA in Edn., Fairfield U., Conn., 1980. Tchr. grades 3 & 4 Assumption Sch., Fairfield, Conn., 1976—86; tchr. h.s. Stamford Pub. Schs., Conn., 1986—. Tchr. summer sch. Assumption Sch.; tutor fgn. lang. Ruppowam Mid. Sch., Stamford, 2006, translator, interpretor, 2000—. Mem.: Am. Coun. Tchrs. Fgn. Langs., Stamford Edn. Assn., Conn. Edn. Assn., Delta Epsilon Sigma. Roman Catholic. Avocation: ballroom dancing. Home: 462 GLendale Ave #14 Bridgeport CT 06606

RAI, AISHWARYA, actress; b. Mangalore, Karnataka, India, Nov. 1, 1973; m. Abhishek Bachchan, Apr. 20, 2007. Jury mem. Cannes Internat. Film Festival. Actor: (films) Mamagaru, 1991, Iruvar, 1997, ...Aur Pyaar Ho Gaya, 1997, Jeans, 1998, Let's Go Back, 1999, Straight from the Heart, 1999, Taal, 1999, I Have Found it, 2000, Josh, 2000, You Have My Heart, 2000, Dhaai Akshar Prem Ke, 2000, Love Stories, 2000, Albela, 2001, Devdas, 2002, Hum Kisi Se Kum Nahin, 2002, Shakti: The Power, 2002, Heart of Gold, 2003, Choker Bali: A Passion Play, 2003, Don't Say a Word, 2003, The Uniform, 2004, Raincoat, 2004, Kyun...! Ho Gaya Na, 2004, Bride and Prejudice, 2004, Shabd, 2004, (TV commls.) Loreal. Achievements include being crowned Miss World 1994 (also named Miss Photogenic); being first actress and performer from India to appear on cover of Time Mag.(as one of 100 most influential people in world), 2004; being fluent in English, Hindi, Kannada, Tamil and Urdu. Mailing: c/o Wm Morris Agy 1 Wm Morris Pl Beverly Hills CA 90212

RAI, VARUN, physical chemist; b. Ghazipur, India, June 1, 1981; arrived in US, 2002; s. Vidya Shanker and Shanti Rai. B in Tech., IIT Kharagpar, India, 2002; MS, PhD, Stanford U., Calif., 2004—. Rsch. asst. Stanford U., 2003—. Guest rschr. MIT, Cambridge, Mass., 2006. Fundraiser Pratham, Santa Clara, Calif., 2005; vol. AIDS Relief, Stanford, Calif., 2006—07. Recipient Indian Nat. Math. Olympiad award, Nat. Bd. Higher Math., Dept. Atomic Energy, Govt. India, 1995, Outstanding Contbns. award, Grad. Student Programming Bd., Stanford U., 2003; scholar, Found. Excellence, 2001, 2002. Achievements include research in the field of electrochemistry for fuel cells. Home: 126 Blackwelder Ct Apt 402 Stanford CA 94305 Home Phone: 650-450-1236.

RAIBLEY, PARVIN RUDOLPH, dentist; b. Boonville, Ind., Nov. 19, 1926; s. Otto Sr. and Hallie Marie (Hedges) R.; m. Mary Helen Holder, Aug. 31, 1946; children: Bruce D., Brian L., Brent A. Student, Purdue U., 1945, U. Evansville, 1946—50; BS in Dentistry, Ind. U., 1951, DDS, 1954. Practice gen. dentistry, Evansville, Ind., 1954—. Counselor Boy Scouts Am. With U.S. Army, 1944-45. Named Dentist of Yr. Ind. Acad. Gen. Dentistry, 1992. Fellow Acad. Gen. Dentistry, Internat. Coll. Dentists; mem. ADA, First Dist. Dental Soc., Ind. Dental Assn., Ind. Acad. Gen. Dentistry, S.W. Ind. Oral Health Found. (disbursement com.), Masons. Republican. Methodist. Avocations: farming, forestry, fishing, poetry, gardening. Home: 7100 Olive St Evansville IN 47715-3625 Office: 207 S Green River Rd Evansville IN 47715-7334 Personal E-mail: praibley@aol.com.

RAICHLE, MARCUS EDWARD, radiology, neurology educator; b. Hoquiam, Wash., Mar. 15, 1937; m. Mary Elizabeth Rupert, 1964; children: Marcus Edward, Timothy Stephen, Sarah Elizabeth, Katherine Ann. BS, U. Wash., 1960, MD, 1964. Diplomate Am. Bd. Psychiatry and Neurology. Intern Balt. City Hosps., 1964—65, resident, 1965—66; asst. neurologist N.Y. Hosp. Cornell Med. Ctr., NYC, 1966—68, neurologist, chief resident, 1968—69; clin. instr. dept. medicine divsn. neurosci. U. Tex. Med. Sch., San Antonio, 1969—70; rsch. instr. Washington U. Sch. Med., St. Louis, 1971—72, from asst. prof. neurology to assoc. prof. neurology, 1972—78, from asst. prof. radiology (radiation scis.) to assoc. prof. radiology Edward Mallinckrodt Inst. Radiology, 1972—79, from asst. prof. to assoc. prof. biomedical engring., 1974-79, prof. neurology, 1978—, prof. radiology Edward Mallinckrodt Inst. Radiology, 1979—, prof. biomedical engring., 1979—; and prof. psychology Washington Univ., St. Louis, 2000—. Instr. dept. neurology Cornell U. Med. Coll., NYC, 1968—69; asst. neurologist Barnes Hosp., St. Louis, 1971—75, assoc. neurologist, 1975—78, neurologist, 1978—; cons. neurologist St. Louis Children's Hosp., 1975—; neurologist Jewish Hosp., St. Louis, 1984—, St. Louis Regional Hosp., St. Louis, 1984—; mem. neurology study sect. A NIH, 1975—79; mem. com. cerebrovascular diseases Nat. Inst. Neurol. Diseases and Stroke, long range planning effort, 1978, basic sci. task force, 78; mem ad hoc adv. panel Nat. Inst. Neurol. Diseases and Stroke, 1983, chmn. PET grants spl. rev. com., 83, chmn. brain imaging ctrs. spl. rev. com., 85; mem. adv. bd. McDonnell-Pew Program cognitive neuroscience, 1989; other coms. Mem. editl. bd.: Stroke, 1982, Neurology, 1976—82, Annals of Neurology, 1979—86, Brain, 1985—90, Journal Cerebral Blood Flow and Metabolism, 1983—86, dep. chief editor:, 1981—83, mem. editl. bd.: Human Neurobiology, 1985—87, Brain Rsch., 1985—90, Synapse, 1987—90, Jour. Neurosci., 1989—95, Jour. Cognitive Neurosci., 1989—, Cerebral Cortex, 1990—, Jour. Nuclear Medicine, 1990—96. Maj. USAF, 1969—71. Recipient umerous awards, lectrs., fellows including Charles A. Dana award for pioneering achievements in health and edn., Dana Found., 1996. Fellow: Am. Assn. Advancement of Sci.; mem.: NAS, Inst. Medicine of NAS.

RAIFFA, HOWARD, economics educator; Faculty mem. Harvard U., 1957—, Frank Plumpton Ramsay prof. managerial econs., Frank P. Ramsey prof. managerial econs. Kennedy Sch. Govt., prof. emeritus. Co-author: Games and Decisions: Introduction and Critical Survey, 1989, Decisions with Multiple Objectives: Preferences and Value Trade-offs, 1993, Introduction to Statistical Decision Theory, 1995, Negotiation Analysis: The Science and Art of Collaborative Decision Making, 2003. Mem.: NAE. Mailing: 175 Somerset St Belmont MA 02478 Office Phone: 617-495-6289. E-mail: hraiffa@hbs.edu.

RAIJMAN, ISAAC, gastroenterologist, educator; b. Empalme, Sonora, Mex., July 6, 1959; arrived in US, 1985, naturalized, 2000; s. Jose and Amalia (Langsam) R. MD, Nat. Autonomous U., Mexico City, 1985; postgrad., U. Wis., Milw., 1985—89, U. Tex., Houston, 1989—92. Diplomate Am. Bd. Internal Medicine, Am. Bd. Gastroenterology. Resident in medicine Mt. Sinai Hosp., Milw., 1986-88, chief resident, 1989; fellow in therapeutic endoscopy Wellesley Hosp., U. Toronto, 1992—93; rsch. fellow in gastroenterology U. Tex., Houston, 1989-90, clin. fellow, 1990-92, asst. prof. medicine, 1993-97, dir. therapeutic endoscopy, 1993-97, asst. prof. M.D. Anderson Cancer Ctr., 1993—2000, dir. ann. therapeutic endoscopy course, 1995-97, assoc. prof., 2002—, dir. therapeutic endoscopy, 2002—; assoc. prof. Baylor Coll., Houston, U. Houston. Chair Ann. Therapeutic Endoscopy Meeting; chair gastroenterology and endoscopy sub. com., GI subcom. on endoscopic credentialing and quality assurance Hermann Hosp., Houston. Author: Pancreas, 1993, Bockus Textbook of Gastroenterology, 1993; also numerous articles; reviewer jours. in field. Fellow Am. Gastroenterology Assn.; mem. Am. Coll. Gastroenterology, Internat. Assn. Pancreatology, Am. Soc. Gastrointestinal Endoscopy, Am. Soc. Internal Medicine. Jewish. Avocation: painting. Office: 6620 Main Ste 1510 Houston TX 77030 Office Phone: 713-795-4444. E-mail: iraijman@dahpa.com.

RAIKES, CHARLES FITZGERALD, retired lawyer; b. Mpls., Oct. 6, 1930; s. Arthur FitzGerald and Margaret (Hawthorne) R.; m. Antonia Raikes, Dec. 20, 1969; children: Jennifer Catherine, Victoria Samantha. BA, Washington U., 1952; MA, Harvard U., 1955, LL.B., 1958. Bar: N.Y. State 1959. Assoc. White & Case, NYC, 1958-69; assoc. gen. counsel Dun & Bradstreet, Inc., NYC, 1969-72, v.p., gen. counsel, 1972-73, The Dun & Bradstreet Corp., NYC, 1973-76, sr. v.p., gen. counsel, 1976-94, of counsel, 1994-95; ret., 1995. Cons. Bd. Govs. Fed. Reserve System, 1958-95. Served with U.S. Army, 1952-54. Woodrow Wilson fellow, 1952 Mem. Assn. Bar City of N.Y., Harvard Club, Phi Beta Kappa. Home: 26 Crooked Trl Norwalk CT 06853-1106

RAIKES, JEFF, information technology executive; B of Engring. and Econ. Systems, Stanford U. Software devel. mgr. Apple Computer Inc.; product mgr. Microsoft Corp., Redmond, Wash., 1981—84, dir., applications mktg., 1984, chief strategist, v.p. office sys., sr. v.p., Microsoft N.Am., 1993, group v.p. worldwide sales and support group Redmond, Wash., group v.p., information worker bus., pres., bus. divsn., 2005—. Ptnr. Seattle Mariners Baseball Club, 1992—; mem. Sr. Leadership Team, Bus. Leadership Team, Microsoft Corp.; bd. dirs. XO Comm. Inc., Washington Technology Ctr. Mem. U. Nebr. Found., trustee; leader Online Wash. State U. Initiative; trustee Wash. State U. Found. Named to Computer Industry Hall of Fame, Computer Reseller News Mag., 2003. Mem.: Software Publishers Assn. (bd. dir. 1987—93, chmn. bd. (twice)). Office: Microsoft One Microsoft Way Redmond WA 98052-6399 *

RAILSBACK, SHERRIE LEE, management consultant, educator; b. Phila., Mar. 12, 1942; children: Ricky, Cindy. BBA, U. Ky., 1981. Sales mgr. Marjo Cosmetics, Ft. Wayne, Ind.; asst. dir. patient fin. svcs. Riverside Meth. Hosp., Columbus, Ohio; cons. Railsback and Assocs., Long Beach, Calif.; adoption search/reunion cons., educator Spirited Comm., L.A. Mem.: ASTD, NAFE, Book Publicists So. Calif., Nat. Spkrs. Assn. Office Phone: 714-468-9686. Personal E-mail: sherrierailsback@yahoo.com.

RAILTON, PETER ALBERT, philosophy educator; b. Elgin, Ill., May 23, 1950; s. Arthur Roy and Marjorie Elizabeth Marks Railton; m. Rebecca Jarvis Scott, Apr. 21, 1978; children: John Scott-Railton, Thomas Scott-Railton. AB magna cum laude, Harvard U., 1971; PhD, Princeton U., 1980. From asst. prof. philosophy to assoc. prof. U. Mich., Ann Arbor, 1979—90, prof. philosophy, 1990—, Nelson prof., 1999—2001, Perrin Collegiate prof., 2001—, dept. chair, 2002—05. Vis. prof. U. Calif., Berkeley, 1984-85, Princeton (N.J.) U., 1990; mem. Coun. for Philos. Studies, N.Y.C., 1992-94; rsch. assoc. Ecole Poly., Paris, 1995—, CSMN, U. Oslo. Co-editor, author: Moral Discourse and Practice, 1997; author: Facts, Values and Norms, 2003; mem. editl. bd.: Ethics, Utilitas; contbr. articles to profl. jours. Am. Coun. Learned Socs. fellow, 1988-89, 2000, NEH fellow, 1999, Guggenheim fellow, 2001-2002, Am. Acad. Arts and Scis. fellow, 2004—. Mem. Am. Philos. Assn. (various coms. 1978—), Am. Soc. for Polit. and Legal Philosophy, Philosophy of Scis. Assn. (com. mem. 1978—), Soc. for Philosophy and Psychology, Mich. Soc. Fellows (jr. fellow 1979-82, sr. fellow 2005-). Office: U Mich Dept Philosophy 2215 Angell Hall Ann Arbor MI 48109 Office Phone: 734-764-6285.

RAILTON, W(ILLIAM) SCOTT, retired commissioner; b. Newark, July 30, 1935; s. William Scott and Carolyn Elizabeth (Guiberson) R.; m. Karen Elizabeth Walsh, Mar. 31, 1979; 1 son, William August; children by previous marriage: William Scott, Anne Greenwood. BSEE, U. Wash., 1962; JD with honors, George Washington U., 1965. Bar: D.C. 1966, Md. 1966, Va. 1993, U.S. Patent Office 1966. Assoc., then ptnr. Kemon, Palmer & Estabrook, Washington, 1966-70; sr. trial atty. Dept. Labor, Washington, 1970-71, asst. counsel for trial litigation, 1971-72; chief counsel U.S. Occupational Safety and Health Rev. Commn., Washington, 1972-77, acting gen. counsel, 1975-77; ptnr. Reed Smith LLP, Pitts., 1977—2002, ret., 2002; commr., chmn. U.S. Occupl. Safety and Health Rev. Commn., 2002—07, ret., 2007. Lectr. George Washington U. Law Sch., 1977-79, seminar chmn. Occupational Safety and Health Act, Govt. Inst., 1979-96; lectr. Practicing Law Inst., 1976-79. Author: (legal handbooks) The Examination System and the Backlog, 1965, The OSHA General Duty Clause, 1977, The OSHA Health Standards, 1977; OSHA Compliance Handbook, 1992; contbg. author: Occupational Safety and Health Law, 1988, 93. Regional chmn. Montgomery County (Md.) Republican party, 1968-70; pres. Montgomery Sq. Citizens Assn., 1970-71; bd. dirs., pres.

Foxvale Farms Homeowners Assn., 1979-82; pres. Orchards on the Potomac Homeowners Assn., 1990-92; dir. Great Falls Hist. Soc., 1991-94; scoutmaster Troop 55 Boy Scouts Am., 1993-98. With USMC, 1953-58. Recipient Meritorious Achievement medal Dept. Labor, 1972, Outstanding Service award OSHA Rev. Commn., 1977, elected fell. Coll. Labor and Employment Lawyers, 1998. Fellow Coll. Labor and Employment Lawyers; mem. ABA (mgmt. co-chmn. occupational safety and health law com. 1995-98), Md. Bar Assn., Va. Bar Assn., Bar Assn. D.C. (vice chmn. young lawyers sect. 1971), Order of Coif, Sigma Phi Epsilon, Phi Delta Phi. Home: 10102 Walker Lake Dr Great Falls VA 22066-3502 Office: US Occupational Safety and Health Rev Commn 1120 20th Street NW Washington DC 20036 Business E-Mail: fysh4it@aol.com. *Lawsuits are won by pre-trial preparation. A litigator should be candid with his clients and honest in his dealings with associates, opponents and the courts; an attorney should also volunteer his service to the community of which he is a part.*

RAIM, DAVID MATTHEW, lawyer; b. NYC, Mar. 11, 1953; s. Murray S. and Joan D. (Feldman) Raim; m. Leslie K. Sheldon, June 12, 1983. BA cum laude, Yale U., 1975; JD cum laude, U. Pa., 1978. Bar: NY 1979, US Dist. Ct. (So. & Ea. Dist.) NY 1979, US Ct. Appeals (2nd Cir.) 1981, US Supreme Ct. 1982, DC 1985, US Dist. Ct. (Dist. DC) 1985, US Ct. Appeals (3rd Cir.) 1988. Asst. dir. nat. law dept. Anti-Defamation League of B'nai B'rith, NYC, 1981-82, chmn. civil rights com.; assoc. Leboeuf, Lamb, Leiby & McRae, NYC and Washington, 1978-81, 83-86, Hughes Hubbard & Reed PC, Washington, 1986—88; ptnr. Chadbourne & Parke LLP, Washington, chmn., Reinsurance & Ins. Practice Group, 1989—. Contbr. articles to profl. jour.; lectr. in field. Mem.: DC Bar (chmn. members benefit com. 1988—94). Office: Chadbourne & Parke LLP 1200 New Hampshire Ave NW Washington DC 20036 Office Phone: 202-974-5625. Office Fax: 202-974-5602. Business E-Mail: draim@chadbourne.com.

RAIMAN, ROSEMARY A., advocate; d. Claude and Emma Butch; m. John L. Davidson (div.); children: Jennifer Lynne Davidson, Jacqueline Rose Davidson; m. Irwin Raiman, Aug. 29, 1981. Cert. nat. victims acad. Am. U., 1998, victim assistance specialist Greenville, SC, 2000, trauma svcs. specialist Irmo, SC, 2001, domestic violence counselor Am. Coll. Cert. Forensic Counselors, 2001, advanced care advocate Nat. Advocate Credential, Washington, 2004, roper victim asst. U. Balt., 2004. Program coord. Del. Opportunities Inc., Delhi, NY, 1977—81; dir. Title IIIC Nutrition/Supportive Svcs. for Elderly, Delhi, 1981—85; office coord. Psychol. Svcs. Inc., Annapolis, Md., 1986—91; office mgr. Reliance Comm., Inc., Latham, Md., 1991—94; agy. receptionist Sanders Ins. Agy., LaPiata, Md., 1994—96; cert. victim advocate/admin. dep. Ctr. for Abused Persons, Waldorf, Md., 1996—. Chairperson Charles County Dept. Social Svcs., 1996—2005, bd. mem., 1996—2005; mem. Md. Divsn. Parole and Probation Victim's Adv. Bd., 1998—2001; bd. mem. Md. Assn. Social Svc., 1999—2003; founder Silent Witness Program for Charles County, 1999—, co-coord., 1999—; bd. mem. Md. Network Against Domestic Violence, Bowie, Md., 2000—; crisis respondent Charles County Sheriff's Victim Svc. Unit, LaPlata, 2001—06; bd. chair Md. Assn. Social Svc., 2002—03; mem. Family Violence Coord. Coun. Charles County, 2003—, mem. pro bono legal svcs. com., 2003—; co-chairperson Legal Advocates Task Force, Bowie, Md., 2004—; chair Charles County Commn. for Women, 2004—05. Nominee Spirit of Cmty. award, Med. Ctr., Svc. award, Charles County Comm. for Women, 2007; recipient Silver Tray of Appointment, Del. Opportunities Inc., Outstanding Svc. award, Psychol. Svcs. Inc., Cert. Appreciation, Ctr. for Abused Persons, Charles County Commn. Women, 1999—2007, Md. Most Beautiful Nominee and 1st Runner-Up, Charles County Commissioners, Silent Witness Plaque award, Charles County Co-Coord., Cmty. Svc. award, Commn. for Women, Gov. Victim Assistance award, Crime Control and Prevention Bd. Victims Svc., Bd. Mem. of Yr., Dept. Social Svc., Cmty. Svc. award, Dept. Social Svcs., Appreciation Plaque, Md. State Bd. Mem., Svc. award, Ctr. for Abused Persons, Plaque of Appreciation, Charles County Sheriff's Dept., Achievement award, Md. Coalition Against Sexal Assault, 2006. Mem.: Assn. Traumatic Stress Specialist. Republican. Methodist. Office: Ctr for Abused Persons 2670 Crain Hwy Ste 303 Waldorf MD 20601

RAIMI, BURTON LOUIS, lawyer; b. Detroit, May 5, 1938; s. Irving and Rae (Abel) R.; m. Judith Morse, Mar. 31, 1963 (div. Mar. 1985); children: Diane L., and Matthew. BA, Brandeis U., 1960; JD with honors, U. Mich., 1963; LLM, George Washington U., 1964. Bar: Mich. 1963, D.C. 1964, Fla. 1991, U.S. Ct. Appeals (4th, 7th, 8th, 9th, 10th, 11th and DC cirs.), U.S. Ct. of Fed. Claims, U.S. Supreme Ct. Atty. appelate ct. sect. NLRB, Washington, 1964-69; assoc. Morgan, Lewis & Bockius, Washington, 1969-71; dep. gen. counsel FDIC, Washington, 1971-78; ptnr. Rosenman and Colin, Washington, 1978-86, Dechert Price & Rhoads, Washington, 1986-93; shareholder McCaffrey & Raimi, P.A., Naples and Sarasota, Fla., 1994—2002, Law Offices of Burton L. Raimi PA, Sarasota, Fla., 2003—05, 2007—; gen. counsel Washington Mgmt. Corp., 2005—07. Spkr. various insts. Mem. ABA (past chmn. bank receiverships subcom. of banking com.), D.C. Bar Assn. (past chmn. banking law com., com. on interest on lawyers trust accounts), Fla. Bar (bus. law com.), Am. Arbitration Assn. (panel of arbitrators), Nat. Arbitration Forum (arbitrator). Avocations: travel, golf, fishing. Office: 8499 S Tamiami Trail No 266 Sarasota FL 34238 Office Phone: 941-927-1603. Office Fax: 941-927-1703. Business E-Mail: burt@moneylaw.com.

RAIMI, SAMUEL M., film director; b. Royal Oak, Mich., Oct. 23, 1959; s. Leonard Ronald and Celia Barbara (Abrams) R.; m. Gillian Greene, 1993; 5 children. Student in humanities study, Mich. State U., East Lansing, 1977-79. V.p. Renaissance Pictures, Ferndale, Mich., 1979—. Writer, dir. (films) Crimewave, 1985 (Best Dir. award 1986), Evil Dead II, 1986, Darkman, 1990, Army of Darkness: Evil Dead 3, 1993; co-writer: (screenplay) The Hudsucker Proxy, 1994; prodr. Hard Target, 1993, Timecop, 1994, Boogeyman, 2005; dir. (films) The Quick and the Dead, 1995, A Simple Plan, 1998, For Love of the Game, 1999, The Gift, 2000, Spider-Man, 2002, Spider-Man 2, 2004, Boogeyman, 2005, The Messengers, 2007, Spider-Man 3, 2007; appeared in films Spies Like Us, 1985, Thou Shall Not Kill...Except, 1987, Maniac Cop, 1988, Miller's Crossing, 1990, Innocent Blood, 1992, Intruder, 1994, Terminal Force, 1995, others; exec. prodr., writer, dir.: (films) The Evil Dead, 1981; exec. prodr., writer (films) Easy Wheels, 1989, (TV films) M.A.N.T.I.S., 1994; exec. prodr. (films) Lunatics: A love Story, 1991, Hard Target, 1993, The Grudge, 2004, The Grudge 2, 2006, (TV series) Hercules: The Legendary Journeys, 1995-99, Xena: Warrior Princess, 1995-2001, American Gothic, 1995-96, Spy Game, 1997, Young Hercules, 1998, Jack of All Trades, 2000, Cleopatra 2525, 2000-2001. Recipient Best Horror Film, Knokke'heist Film Festival Belgium, 1982, Best Horror Film and Best Spl. Effects, Sitges Film Festival, Spain, 1982, 1st Prize of the Critics, 1st Prize of the Pub., Paris Festival Sci. Fiction, Fantasy and Horror, 1983, Best Horror Film of Yr., Fangoria Mag., 1983; named one of 50 Most Powerful People in Hollywood Premiere mag., 2004-06. Mem. Mich. State U. Soc. for Creative Film Making (founder, pres. 1978, 79), Calif. Rare Fruit Growers. *

RAIMO, BERNARD (BERNIE), lawyer; b. Kansas City, Mo., May 29, 1944; m. Sharon Marie Brady, Aug. 23, 1974; children: Sarah Elizabeth, Peter Bernard. BA, U. Notre Dame, 1965; MA, U. Md., 1967; JD with honors, George Washington U., 1972. Bar: D.C. Staff asst. to Sen. Stuart Symington, Mo., 1968-72; asst. corp. counsel D.C., Washington, 1972-76; legis. analyst Am. Petroleum Inst., 1976-78; counsel Permanent Select Com. Intelligence US Ho. Reps., Washington, 1978—91, chief counsel Ho. Com. Standards of Official Conduct, 1991—95, counsel to Dem. leader, 1997—2006, counsel to the spkr., 2007—; minority counsel Ho. Com. Stds. of Official Conduct, 1995—97. Office: Office of the Spkr H-333 The Capitol Washington DC 20515-0001 E-mail: bernard.raimo@mail.house.gov.

RAIMONDI, RUGGERO, opera singer; b. Bologna, Italy, Oct. 3, 1941; m. Isabel Maier, 1987. Studies with, Teresa Pediconi, Armando Piervenanzi. Debut in La Boheme, Spoleto, Italy, 1964; singer in major houses, Europe and US; Met. debut in Ernani, NYC, 1970; favorite roles include Don Giovanni, Philip II, Boris and Don Quichotte; recorded Verdi Requiem, Vespri Siciliani, La Boheme, Aida, Attila, Don Carlos, Macbeth, Simon Boccanegra, Don Giovanni, Boris Godunov, Tosca, Turandot, Barbiere di Siviglia, Mosè, Nozze di Figaro, Italiana in Algieri, Cenerentola, Il Viaggio a Reims, and others; appeared in films Don Giovanni (Joseph Losey), 1979, Six Characters in Search of a Singer (Maurice Bejart), 1983, Carmen (Francesco Rosi), 1986, Tosca (B. Jaquot), 2001, others; opera prodn. since, 1986—. Decorated Comdr. Arts et Lettres, Officier de la Légion d'Honneur (France), chevalier Ordre de Malte, Grand Ufficiale della Repubblica Italiana, comdr. Mérite Culturel (Monaco), others; named Citizen of Honor, City of Athens, Greece. Office: 140 bis rue Lecourbe F-75015 Paris France

RAIN, See JEONG, JI-HOON

RAINAL, ATTILIO JOSEPH, retired electronics engineer; b. Marion Heights, Pa., Feb. 14, 1930; m. Violet Dorothy Robel, June 29, 1957; children: Valery, Eric. BS in Engring. Sci., Pa. State U., University Park, 1956; MSEE, Drexel U., Phila., 1959; D of Elec. Engring., Johns Hopkins U., Balt., 1963. Engr. Applied Physics Lab. Johns Hopkins U., Silver Spring, Md., 1955; engr. Martin Co., Balt., 1956-59; mem. rsch. staff Carlyle Barton Lab. Johns Hopkins U., Balt., 1959-64; mem. tech. staff R & D AT&T Bell Labs., Whippany, Murray Hill, NJ, 1964-83, mem. disting. tech. staff R & D, 1983—2003; ret., 2003. Contbr. articles to profl. jours. With USAF, 1948—52. Mem.: IEEE (life), Info. Theory, Component, Hybrids and Mfg. Tech. Achievements include research in noise theory; signal detection and estimation; radiometry; radar; FM; first passage times of random processes; crosstalk; voltage breakdown; current carrying capacity of printed wires; performance limits of electrical interconnections; patents for balanced interconnections; laser intensity modulation; patents in field. Home: 28 Woodruff Rd Morristown NJ 07960-4620

RAINE, STANLEY M., lawyer; b. Seattle, Dec. 23, 1949; BA summa cum laude, U. Pa., 1975; JD cum laude, Harvard U., 1978. Bar: Colo. 1978. Atty. Sherman & Howard LLC, Denver, 1978—84, mem., 1984—. Named Best Lawyers Am. Mem. ABA, Denver Bar Assn., Colo. Bar Assn., Nat. Assn. Bond Lawyers, Phi Beta Kappa. Office: Sherman & Howard 633 17th St Ste 3000 Denver CO 80202 Office Phone: 303-299-8254. Office Fax: 303-298-0940.

RAINER, REX KELLY, civil engineer, educator; b. Montgomery, Ala., July 17, 1924; s. Kelly Kenyon and Pearl (Jones) R.; m. Betty Ann Page, Aug. 28, 1945; children: Rex Kelly, John Kenyon. BS, Auburn U., Ala., 1944, MS, 1946; PhD, Okla. State U., 1967. Asst. engr. L. & N. R.R. Co., Cin., 1944-45; design engr. Polglaze & Basenberg, Birmingham, Ala., 1945-51; pres., chmn. Rainer Co., Inc., Orlando, Fla., 1951-62; prof. civil engring. Auburn U., 1962-67, head civil engring. dept., 1967; exec. v.p., 1980; hwy. dir. State of Ala., 1979-80, fin. dir., 1981-82; spl. asst. to gov. of Ala., 1981-82; dir. Office for Advancement Devel. Industry U. Ala., Birmingham, 1982-86; pres., cons. engr. Rex K. Rainer, Inc., 1982-98, ret., 1998. Cons. to ins. cos., constrn. engring. firms; mem. Ala. Bd. Registration Profl. Engrs. and Land Surveyors, 1977-89. Contbr. articles to profl. jours Mem. Municipal Planning Bd., 1963-65, Indsl. Park Devel. Bd., 1969-71, So. Regional Edn. Bd., 1982-86. Served with AUS, 1943. Fellow ASCE (sec., treas. 1970, pres. Ala. chpt. 1976-77, chmn. Constrn. Rsch. Coun., chmn. hwy. div. publs. com.; Civil Govt. award 1981); mem. Assn. Gen. Contractors Am. (bd. dirs. 1955), Am. Soc. for Engring. Edn. (chmn. constrn. engring. com.), Am. Pub. Works Assn., Phi Kappa Phi, Tau Beta Pi, Chi Epsilon. Personal E-mail: rkrainer@charter.net.

RAINER, THOMAS SPRATLING, pastor; b. Union Springs, Ala., July 16, 1955; s. Samuel Solomon Sr. and Amelia Nan (Keller) R.; m. Nellie Jo King, Dec. 17, 1977; children: Samuel III, Arthur, Jess. BS summa cum laude, U. Ala., Tuscaloosa, 1977; MDiv, So. Bapt. Theol. Sem., 1985, PhD, 1988. Ordained to ministry So. Bapt. Conv., 1984. Pastor Hopewell Bapt. Ch., Madison, Ind., 1984-86, Louisville, 1986-88; sr. pastor Azalea Bapt. Ch., St. Petersburg, Fla., 1988-90, Green Valley Bapt. Ch., Birmingham, Ala., 1990-94; dean Billy Graham Sch. Missions, Evangelism and Ch. Growth The So. Bapt. Theol. Sem., Louisville, 1994—. Trustee Bay Area Pregnancy Ctr., Clearwater, Fla., 1988-90; mem. bd. overseers Criswell Coll., Dallas, 1991—; adj. prof. Beeson Div. Sch., Samford U., Birmingham, 1991-94. Author/editor: Evangelism in the 21st Century, 1989, The Book of Church Growth, 1993, Eating the Elephant, 1994, Breakout Churches: Discover How to Make the Leap, 2005; contbr. revs. and articles to profl. jours. Garrett fellow So. Bapt. Theol. Sem., 1986-88. Mem. Acad. for Evangelism in Theol. Edn., Beta Gamma Sigma, Omicron Delta Epsilon. Home: 13505 Rock Bay Ct Louisville KY 40245-2097 Office: The Southern Bapt Theol Sem 2825 Lexington Rd Louisville KY 40207 *Life is a series of never-ending choices which compete for our limited resource of time. I have found that my life takes on its fullest meaning when my priorities for time are my God, my family, and my church.*

RAINER, WILLIAM GERALD, cardiac surgeon; b. Gordo, Ala., Nov. 13, 1927; s. Jamie Flournoy and Lula (Davis) R.; m. Lois Sayre, Oct. 7, 1950; children: Vickie, Bill, Julia, Leslie. Student, Emory U., Atlanta, Ga., 1943-44, U. Ala., 1944-45; MD, U. Tenn., Memphis, 1948; MS in Surgery, U. Colo., Denver, 1958. Diplomate Am. Bd. Surgery, Am. Bd. Thoracic Surgery. Intern Wesley Hosp., Chgo., 1949; gen. practice medicine Blue Island, Ill., 1950-52; resident Denver VA Hosp., 1954-59; practice medicine specializing in cardiac surgery Denver, 1960—. Bd. dirs. St. Joseph Hosp. Found., Denver; disting. clin. prof. surgery U. Colo. Health Sci. Ctr. Contbr. articles to profl. jours. Active Colo. Symphony Assn.; dir. emeritus St. Joseph Hosp. Found. Bd. Lt. U.S. Army, 1952-54. Decorated Bronze Star; recipient Disting. Alumnus award U. Tenn. Health Sci. Ctr., 1992, Florence Sabin award U. Colo. Health Sci. Ctr., 1998, Disting. Svc. award U. Colo., 2004, Outstanding Clin. Vol., U. Colo. Health Sci. Ctr., 2006, Disting. Svc. award We. Thoracic Surg. Assn., 2007. Mem. Soc. Thoracic Surgeons (sec. 1980-85, pres. 1989, historian 1992—, Disting. Svc. award 1998), Colo. Med. Soc. (pres. 1984-85), Denver Med. Soc. (pres. 1984), Denver Clin. and Pathology Soc. (pres. 1997), Am. Coll. Chest Physicians (pres. 1984), Am. Bd. Thoracic Surgeons (bd. dirs. 1982-88), Am. Surg. Assn., Am. Assn. Thoracic Surgery, Societé Internationale de Chirugie, Cactus Club. Avocations: photography, travel. Office: 2552 E Alameda 48 Denver CO 80209 Office Phone: 303-601-0532. Personal E-mail: wrainer@qwest.net.

RAINER, YVONNE, choreographer, filmmaker; b. San Francisco, Nov. 24, 1934; Choreographer US, Scandinavia, London, Germany, and Italy, 1964—72; co-founder Judson Dance Theater, 1962; disting. prof., Claire Trevor Sch. of Arts Univ. Calif., Irvine. Dir.: (films) Film About a Woman, 1974, Christina Taking Pictures, 1976, (also actor, editor) Journeys from Berlin, 1980, (also editor, screenwriter) The Man Who Envied Women, 1985,: Privilege, 1990 (Filmmaker's Trophy Sundance Film Fest., 1990), (also editor, prodr., screenwriter): (films) Murder and Murder, 1996 (Teddy award Berlin Film Fest., 1996, Spl. Jury award Miami Lesbian and Gay Film Fest., 1999), Many a Summer Dies the Swan, 2002; actor: Underground and Emigrants, 1976, Rainer Variations, 2002. Grantee MacArthur Fellow, 1995. Fellow: NY Found. Arts, Am. Acad. Arts & Scis. Office: NY Found for Arts 155 Ave Americas New York NY 10013-1507 also: Arts-Studio Art 2231 ACT Univ Calif Irvine CA 92697-2775 Office Phone: 949-824-0350. Office Fax: 949-834-5297. Business E-Mail: yrainer@uci.edu. *

RAINES, EDGAR FRANK, JR., historian; b. Murphysboro, Ill., Aug. 17, 1944; s. Edgar Frank and Mary Bernice (Mohlenbrock) R.; m. Gretchen Rose Beuscher, Aug. 9, 1975 (div. Dec. 1982); 1 child, Edgar Jacob; m. Rebecca Celia Robbins, June 20, 1987. BA, So. Ill. U., 1966, MA, 1968; PhD, U. Wis., 1976. Asst. acad. dean Silver Lake Coll., Manitowoc, Wis., 1976-79; historian Office of Air Force History, Washington, 1979-80, U.S. Army Ctr. of Mil. History, Washington, 1980—. Chmn. book selection com. Mil. Classics Seminar, Washington, 1984-86, 89-92; ad hoc com. on Dept. of Def. Reform, Dept. of Army, 1985, historian Directorate of Roles and Missions, Office of Dep. Chief of Staff for Ops. and Plans, 1994-95, historian sec. Army Realignment Task Force, 2001-02; pres. Mil. Classics Seminar, Washington, 2001-02. Co-author: The Army and the Joint Chiefs of Staff, 1986; author: Eyes of Artillery, 2000. Sec. of the Army fellow Dept. of the Army, 1987. Mem. Am. Hist. Assn., Orgn. Am. Historians, Soc. Mil. History, Soc. History in the Fed. Govt., Wis. Hist. Soc., Soc. Historians Am. Fgn. Rels. Office: US Army Ctr of Mil History 103 3d Ave Fort McNair DC 20319-5058 Office Phone: 202-685-2094. E-mail: edgar.raines@hqda.army.mil.

RAINES, FRANKLIN DELANO, former finance company executive; b. Seattle, Jan. 14, 1949; s. Delno Thomas and Ida Mae Raines; m. Wendy Farrow. BA magna cum laude, Harvard U., 1971, JD cum laude, 1976; postgrad., Oxford U., 1971-73. Assoc. dir. Seattle Model Cities Program, 1972-73; assoc. Preston, Thorgrimson, Ellis, Holman & Fletcher, Seattle, 1976-77; asst. dir. White House Domestic Policy Staff, Washington, 1977-78; assoc. dir. Office Mgmt. & Budget Exec. Office of the Pres., Washington, 1978-79; v.p. Lazard, Freres & Co., NYC, 1979-82, sr. v.p., 1983-84, ptnr., 1985—91; dir. Office Mgmt. & Budget Exec. Office of the Pres., Washington, 1996-98; vice-chmn. Fannie Mae, Washington, 1991-96, chmn., CEO, 1999—2004. Vice chmn. bd. dirs. Revolution Health Group LLC. Former pres. bd. overseers Harvard U.; former chmn. Fannie Mae Found.; former co-chmn. Bus. Roundtable; vice-chmn. bus. council Nat. Urban League; Enterprise Found.; Black Student Fund. Rhodes scholar, 1971. Mem. AAAS, Coun. Fgn. Rels., Nat. Acad. Social Ins., Washington State Bar Assn., D.C. Bar Assn. Avocations: running, golf.

RAINES, HOWELL HIRAM, former newspaper editor, journalist; b. Birmingham, Ala., Feb. 5, 1943; s. W.S. and Bertha Estelle (Walker) R.; m. Laure Susan Woodley, Mar. 22, 1969 (div.); children: Ben Hayes, Jeffrey Howell; m. Krystyna Anna Stachowiak, March 8, 2003 BA, Birmingham So. Coll., 1964; MA, U. Ala., 1973. Reporter Birmingham Post-Herald, 1964-65, Sta. WBRC-TV, Birmingham, 1965-67, Tuscaloosa News, Ala., 1968-69, Birmingham News, 1970-71; polit. editor Atlanta Constitution, 1971-74, St. Petersburg (Fla.) Times, 1976-78; Atlanta bur. chief NY Times, 1978-80, White Ho. corr., 1980-82, nat. polit. corr., 1982-84, dep. Washington editor, 1985-86, London bur. chief, 1987-88, Washington editor, 1988-92, editl. page editor NYC, 1993—2001, exec. editor, 2001—03; polit. commentator The Guardian. Author: Whiskey Man, 1977, My Soul is Rested: Movement Days in the Deep South Remembered, 1977, Fly Fishing Through the Midlife Crisis, 1993, The One That Got Away: A Memoir, 2006. Recipient Pulitzer Prize for feature writing, 1992.

RAINES, JEFF, biomedical scientist, medical research director; b. NYC, Sept. 5, 1943; s. Otis J. and Mildred C. (Wetzler) Raines; children: Gretchen Christena, Victoria Jean. BSME, Clemson U., 1965; MME, U. Fla., 1967; PhD in Biomed. Engring., MIT, 1972. Mem. staff MIT, Cambridge, 1968—70; biophysicist dept. surgery Mass. Gen. Hosp., Boston, 1972—77, dir. Vascular Lab., 1972—77; instr. surgery Harvard Med. Sch., Boston, 1973—77; preceptor Harvard/MIT Sch. Health Scis., 1976—77; rsch. dir., dir. Vascular Lab. Miami (Fla.) Heart Inst., Miami Beach, 1977—88; adj. prof. bioengring. U. Miami, Coral Gables, 1977—; prof. surgery U. Miami (Fla.) Sch. Medicine, 1977—; with Miami Vein Ctr., 2004—. Prin. investigator series NIH programs and pharm. firms, 1977—; Harvard Travelling fellow lectr. in Europe, 1975. Contbr. numerous articles on biomechanics, cardiovasc. diagnosis, dynamics and instrumentation to sci. jours. Recipient Apollo Achievement award, NASA, 1969; fellow, NIH, 1972. Fellow: Am. Assn. Physicists in Medicine, Am. Coll. Radiology, Am. Coll. Cardiology; mem.: AAAS, Cardiovasc. Sys. Dynamics Soc. (founding mem., editor 1976—, pres. 1980—82), Internat. Cardiovasc. Soc., Instrument Soc. Am., Biomed. Engring. Soc., New Eng. Cardiovasc. Soc., Am. Heart Assn., MIT Club, Harvard Club, Coral Gables Club, Kiwanis, Sigma Xi, Tau Beta Pi. Republican. Presbyterian. Achievements include patents for medical devices; development of mathematical models of arterial hemodynamics and clinical use of autotransfusion. Home Phone: 305-246-0333; Office Phone: 305-854-1555, 305-585-5284. E-mail: drjraines@yahoo.com.

RAINES, JIM NEAL, lawyer; b. Memphis, Sept. 11, 1943; s. J.E. and Amelia C. Raines; m. Julia Walters, Sept. 1, 1979; 1 dau., Lee Pierceson. BBA, Memphis State U., 1965, JD, 1968. Bar: Tenn. 1968, U.S. Dist. Ct. (we. dist.) Tenn. 1968, U.S. Ct. Appeals (6th cir.) 1970, U.S. Ct. Appeals (5th cir.) 1975, U.S. Supreme Ct. 1974. Trial atty. antitrust divsn. U.S. Dept. Justice, Washington, 1968-70; asst. U.S. atty. We. Dist. Tenn., Memphis, 1970-74; ptnr. Burch, Porter & Johnson, Memphis, 1975-76, Glankler, Brown, Gilliland, Chase, Robinson, Raines, Memphis, 1976—2001; v.p., sec., gen. counsel Thomas & Betts Corp., Memphis, 2001—. Served with USMC, 1960-64. Mem. ABA, Memphis Bar Assn., Shelby County Bar Assn., Univ. Club. Office: Thomas & Betts Corp 8155 T&B Blvd Memphis TN 38125 Business E-Mail: jim_raines@tnb.com.

RAINES, SHIRLEY CAROL, academic administrator; b. Jackson, Tenn., Apr. 15, 1945; m. Robert J. Canady; 1 stepchild, Brian Scott Smith. BS, U. Tenn., Martin; MS, EdD, U. Tenn., Knoxville; grad. mgmt. program, Harvard Grad. Sch. of Edn. Dept. head Northeastern State U, 1983—87; assoc. prof. edn. George Mason U., Fairfax, Va., 1987—92; prof. and chmn. dept. of childhood/ lang. arts/ reading U. South Fla., 1992—95; prof. U. Ky. Coll. of Edn., 1995—2001, vice chancellor acad. svcs. and dean of coll., 1998—2001; pres. U. Memphis, 2001—. Author books; contbr. articles to profl. jours. Recipient Dist. Svc. to Edn., Phi Delta Kappa, Dist. Paper awards, Ednl. Rsch. Assn. Office: U Memphis 341 Adminstrn Bldg Memphis TN 38152 Office Phone: 901-678-2234. E-mail: sraines@memphis.edu.

RAINESS, ALAN EDWARD, psychiatrist, neurologist, educator; b. NYC, Sept. 24, 1935; s. George W. and Ida Rainess; m. Alice Maree Haber, June 5, 1968 (dec May 24, 2007); children: Alice Jeanne Rainess Jordan, James Alan (dec.). AB, Columbia Coll., 1957; MD, U. Paris, 1965. Diplomate Am. Bd. Psychiatry and Neurology. Intern Meadowbrook Hosp., East Meadow, L.I., 1965-66; resident in psychiatry NY VA Hosp., NYC, 1966-67; teaching fellow in psychiatry Harvard Med. Sch., Boston, 1967; chief resident in psychiatry Boston City Hosp., 1967; psychiatrist U.S. Army Hosp., Heidelberg, Germany, 1968—70; resident in psychiatry Walter Reed Med. Ctr., Washington, 1970-72; clin. dir. Noyes Divsn. St. Elizabeths Hosp., Washington, 1973-76; asst. chief psychiatry Andrews AFB Hosp., Camp Springs, Md., 1976-80, chief neurology, 1989-91; resident in neurology Wilford Hall USAF Med. Ctr., San Antonio, 1980-83; chief medicine and neuropsychiatry Air Univ. Hosp., Maxwell AFB, Ala., 1983-89, chief neurology, 1991-94; psychiatrist Manhattan Psychiat. Ctr., NYC, 1994—97, 1999—2002, clin. dir., 1997-99; psychiatrist Prison

Health Svcs., Riker's Island, NYC, 2002—. Asst. clin. prof. psychiatry Georgetown U. Med. Sch., Washington, 1974-79, NYU Sch. Medicine, 1997-2002; assoc. prof. neurology and asst. prof. psychiatry Uniformed Svcs. U. Health Scis., Bethesda, Md., 1989-94. Maj. U.S. Army, 1968-73, col. USAF, 1976-94, ret. Fellow: Am. Psychiat. Assn. (disting. life); mem.: AMA, Am. Soc. Psychoanalytic Physicians (past pres. 1995—96), Uniformed Svcs. Soc. Neurologists (past pres. 1985—86), Med. Soc. State of NY, Harvard Club (N.Y.C.). Office: OBCC Riker's Island New York NY Office Phone: 718-546-6580. Personal E-mail: alan.rainess@verizon.net.

RAINEY, BARBARA WHITE, insurance company executive; d. Harry Jennings and Grace Frances White; m. James Pugh Gillmore (div.); children: James C., Cheryl, Katherine, Barbara C.; m. Frank Cobb Rainey, July 11, 1974. BA in TV and Speech, U. Ala., Tuscaloosa, 1953; postgrad., U. Nev., Reno, 1965. Cert. life, accident, health, property and casualty ins. agt. Calif., Colo.; tchr. Nev., Calif., Colo. Spokesperson WDSU TV, New Orleans, 1954—59; fashion model, model Motion Picture Adv., New Orleans, 1954—59; ski instr. Vail Resort Assn., Colo., 1965—70, coord. ctrl. reservations and info., 1967—68; tchr. grades K-4 Vail Country Day Sch., 1966—67; tchr. grade 5 Minturn Grade Sch., Colo., 1968—69; counselor Best Agy., San Francisco, 1970—71; ins. agt. Met. Life, San Francisco, 1971—72; ins. agt., asst. Strong & Co., Barry O'Neill & Diercks, San Francisco, 1972—75; v.p., pres., owner Vail Ins. Agy., 1977—82; real estate agt. Mich. Homes, Priscilla Murphy, Ft. Myers, Fla., 1983—93; v.p., sec., co-owner Rainey Ins. Cons., Inc., Ft. Myers and Bonita Springs, Fla., 1994—. Mem.: Mensa, Alpha Chi Omega. Avocations: skiing, dance, art collecting, swimming, exercise. Home and Office: Rainey Ins Cons Inc 9650 Village Vw Blvd #201 Bonita Springs FL 34135

RAINEY, DEANA LEE PARKS, language educator; b. Casper, Wyo., Sept. 26, 1972; d. Bryan Dean and Estella Marie Parks; m. Brian Krieg Rainey, Apr. 6, 2002; 1 child, Tristan. BA, Midland Luth. Coll., Fremont, Nebr., 1995. Cert. tchr. Nebr. 4th grade tchr. Trinity Sch., Omaha, 1995—96; paralegal Ronald J. Palagi Law Offices, Omaha, 1996—99; lang. arts tchr. Omaha Pub. Schs., 1999—2001, tchr., gifted edn. facilitator, 2001—. Cons. Coll. Bd., 2005—. Mem.: NEA. Democrat. Mem. Christian Ch. (Disciples Of Christ). Avocations: running, reading. Office: Monroe Mic Sch 5105 Bedford Dr Omaha NE 68104

RAINEY, GORDON FRYER, JR., lawyer; b. Oklahoma City, Apr. 26, 1940; s. Gordon F. and Esther (Bliss) R.; m. Selina Norman, Aug. 3, 1968; children: Kate, Melissa, Gordon III. BA in English, U. Va., 1962, LLB, 1967. Bar: Okla. 1967, Va. 1968. Assoc. Rainey, Flynn, Wallace, Ross & Cooper, Oklahoma City, 1967-68, Hunton & Williams LLP, Richmond, Va., 1968-75, ptnr., 1975—, chmn. exec. com., 1994—2006, chmn. emeritus, 2006—. Chmn. emeritus Hunton & Williams; bd. dirs. Bon Secours Richmond Health Sys., Inc., Colonial Williamsburg Co.; bd. visitors, past rector U. Va. Past pres. U. Va. Alumni Assn.; trustee Colonial Williamsburg Found., Va. Found. Ind. Colls.; mem. Gov.'s Blue Ribbon Commn. on Higher Edn.; campaign chmn. United Way of Greater Richmond, 1982, trustee, 1981-84; bd. dirs., past pres. Sheltering Arms Hosp., 1984; trustee Sheltering Arms Found.; chmn. Gov.'s Econ. Devel. Adv. Coun. Dist. 12; mem. Gov.'s Adv. Com. for Va. Strategy on Econ. Devel.; mem. Bd. Housing and Cmty. Devel.; past mem. bd. govs. St. Catherine's Sch.; past chmn. bd. dirs. Leadership Met. Richmond.; past pres., bd. dirs. Met. Bus. Found. 1st lt. U.S. Army, 1962-64, Korea. Recipient Disting. Grad. award Casady Sch., Comm. and Leadership award toastmasters Internat., 1983, Humanitarian award Nat. Conf. Cmty. and Justice, 2003, Disting. Alumni award U. Va. Coll. Found., 2005, Ukrop Cmty. Vision award, 2006. Mem. ABA (sect. on bus. law, banking law com., com. on devel. in investment svcs.), Richmond Metro C. of C. (bd. dirs., past chmn.), Commonwealth Club, Country Club of Va., The Brook (NYC), Forum Club (Richmond). Republican. Episcopalian. Office: Hunton & Williams Riverfront Plz East Tower PO Box 1535 Richmond VA 23219-4074 Home Phone: 804-353-3004; Office Phone: 804-788-8275. Office Fax: 804-788-8218. Business E-Mail: grainey@hunton.com.

RAINEY, JEAN OSGOOD, public relations executive; b. Lansing, Mich., Apr. 5, 1925; d. Earle Victor and Blanche Mae (Eberly) Osgood; m. John Larimer Rainey, Nov. 29, 1957 (dec. Oct. 1991); children: Cynthia, John Larimer, Ruth. Grad., Lansing Bus. U., 1942. Pub. rels. dir. Nat. Assn. Food Chains, Washington, 1954-59; v.p. pub. rels. Manchester Orgns., Washington, 1959-61; ptnr. Rainey, McEnroe & Manning, Washington, 1962-73; v.p. Manning, Selvage & Lee, Washington, 1973-79, pres. Washington divsn., 1979-84, sr. counsellor, 1985; owner Jean Rainey Assocs., Washington, 1986-87; sr. v.p. Daniel J. Edelman Inc., 1987-96; owner Jean Rainey Assocs., Washington, 1996—. Chmn. bd. Windward Mortgage, 1997—2001. Author: How to Shop for Food, 1972. Pres. Hyde Home and Sch. Assn., Washington, 1969-71; co-chmn. Nat. Adv. Com. for Reelection of the Pres., 1972; chmn. bd. trustees St. John's Presch., 1996-99, vice chair, 2003-04; pres. Sherwood Forest Endowment Fund, 1995-97; adminstr. A Few Good Women-Advancing the Cause of Women in Govt., 1969-74, 97-; bd. dirs. Westchester Corp., 2001-04. Mem. Internat. Women's Forum, Pub. Rels. Soc. Am. (accredited, Hall of Fame 1999), Am. Women in Radio and TV (pres. Washington chpt. 1962-63, mem. nat. bd. 1963-65), Am. News Women's Club (pres. 1973-75), City Tavern Club. Republican. Episcopalian. Home: 4000 Cathedral Ave NW Apt 250B Washington DC 20016-5279 Office: PO Box 251 Main Lobby W 4000 Cathedral Ave NW Washington DC 20016-5249 E-mail: jorainey@aol.com.

RAINEY, JO ANNE, psychologist, educator; b. Oak Ridge, Tenn., Sept. 17; d. Robert H. Rainey, Sr. and Margaret Elizabeth Walker Rainey; children: Regina Elizabeth, Robert Joseph, Gavin Walker. BA, Emory U., Atlanta, 1973; MEd, Ga. State U., Atlanta, 1978; PhD, U. Tex., Austin, 1998. Lic. psychologist Ky., 2000, sch. psychologist Nat. Bd. Sch. Psychologists, 2004, Ky., 1999, cert. early care and edn. trainer 2007. Dir. Phoenix Sch., Atlanta, 1980—83; tchr. spl. edn. Ga. Mental Health Inst., Atlanta, 1980—92; sch. psychologist Lafourche Parish Schs., Thibodaux, La., 1997—99; asst. prof. Ky. State U., Frankfort, 1999—2005, assoc. prof., 2005—. Cons. in field. Contbr. chapters to books, articles to profl. jours. Fellow, Hogg Found. Mental Health, 1995—96; scholar, Joseph L. and Katherine D. Henderson Found., 1992—93, 1993—94, 1994—95, 1995—96. Mem.: NASP, APA, Coun. for Exceptional Children, Ky. Psychol. Assn. Quaker. Avocations: travel, hiking. Office: Ky State Univ 400 East Main St Frankfort KY 40601 Office Phone: 502-597-5574.

RAINEY, SUSAN J., school system administrator; m. Jack Rainey; 1 child, Jordan. BA, MA, U. Redlands; PhD, U. So. Calif. Tchr. Moore Jr. H.S., Redlands Unified Sch. Dist.; tchr. Palo Alto, Calif., Yucaipa H.S., 1972—76, dir. activities, 1976—78; asst. prin. Monrovia H.S.; h.s. prin. Brea-Olinda High, Brea, Calif.; asst. supt. for adminstrv. svcs. Helmet Unified Sch. Dist., asst. supt. for personnel svcs., assoc. supt.; supt. Charter Oak Unified Sch. Dist., Covina, Calif., 1991—98; sutp. Riverside Unified Sch. Dist., 1998—. Avocations: travel, reading detective novels, golf. Office: Riverside Unified Sch Dist 3380 14th St Riverside CA 92501 Office Phone: 951-788-7134. Business E-Mail: srainey@rusd.k12.ca.us.

RAINEY, TIMOTHY J., air transportation executive; married. Grad. in Bus. Adminstrn., U. Minn. With NW Airlines Corp., Minn., 1977—, various mgmt. positions in systems ops. control and ground ops., mng. dir. ops. control, with sys. ops. control ctr., v.p. sys. ops. control, 1999, sr. v.p. flight ops. and sys. ops. control, 2001—. Office: NW Airlines Corp 2700 Lone Oak Pky Eagan MN 55121 Office Phone: 612-726-2111. *

RAINEY, WILLIAM JOEL, lawyer; b. Flint, Mich., Oct. 11, 1946; s. Ralph Jefferson and Elsie Matilda (Erickson) R.; m. Cynthia Hetsko, June 15, 1968; children: Joel Michael, Allison Elizabeth. AB, Harvard U., 1968; JD, U. Mich., 1971. Bar: NY 1973, Wash. 1977, Ariz. 1987, Mass. 1992, Oreg. 2007, US Dist. Ct. (so. and ea. dists.) NY 1973, US Ct. Appeals (2nd cir.) NY 1973, US Dist. Ct. (we. dist.) Wash. 1977, US Supreme Ct. 1976, US Ct. Appeals (9th cir.) Wash. 1978, US Dist. Ct. Ariz. 1987, US Dist. Ct. Mass. 1992; registered in-house counsel, Calif., 2005. Assoc. atty. Curtis, Mallet-Prevost, Colt & Mosle, NYC, 1971-76; atty., asst. corp. sec. Weyerhaeuser Co., Tacoma, 1976-85; v.p., corp. sec., gen. counsel Southwest Forest Industries Inc., Phoenix, 1985-87; sr. v.p., corp. sec., gen. counsel Valley Nat. Corp. and Valley Nat. Bank, Phoenix, 1987-91; v.p., gen. counsel Cabot Corp., Boston, 1991-93; exec. v.p., gen. counsel, corp. sec. Fourth Fin. Corp., Wichita, Kans., 1994-96; sr. v.p., gen. counsel, corp. sec. Payless ShoeSource, Inc., Topeka, 1996—2003, Longs Drug Stores Corp., Walnut Creek, Calif., 2003—. Editor U. Mich. Jour. Law Reform, 1970-71. Bd. dirs. Big Bros./Big Sisters, 1994—96. Maj. USAR, 1970—91. Mem. ABA (chmn. task force 1984-91, com. of corp. gen. counsel, 1993—), Wash. State Bar Assn., State Bar of Ariz., Assn. Bank Holding Cos. (steering com. 1989-91, chmn. lawyers com. 1990-91), Assn. Corp. Coun., Soc. Corp. Secs. and Governance Profls., Harvard Club of Phoenix (bd. dirs. 1989-91). Avocations: hiking, running, bicycling. Home: 1208 Bridlewood Ct Clayton CA 94517 Office: Longs Drug Stores Corp 141 N Civic Dr Walnut Creek CA 94596 Office Phone: 925-210-6720. Business E-Mail: brainey@longs.com.

RAINIER, ROBERT PAUL, publisher, consultant; b. Adrian, Mich., Oct. 19, 1940; s. Paul Leslie and Mildred Sofia (Magdefrau) R.; m. Dorothy Krauss, May 28, 1966; children: Michele Carole, Kenneth Charles. BA, Northwestern U., 1962, MA, 1964. From mem. staff to editor-in-chief McGraw Hill Book Co., NYC, 1964—74, editor-in-chief humanities, 1974—79; edit. exec. CBS Coll. Pub., NYC, 1979—86, v.p., editor in chief, 1984-86; dir. publs. AICPA, NYC, 1986-97, dir. prof. devel., 1997-99, sr. cons. strategic devel., 1999—2003; pres. Rainier Assocs., 2003—. Vestryman St. Johns Episcopal Ch., Larchmont, NY, 1987-90, 2006-, treas., 2007-. Staff sgt. NY Nat. Guard, 1964-70. Mem. The Dessoff Choirs (pres. 2000-04), Soc. Nat. Assn. Publs. (pres. 1992-93). Democrat. Episcopalian. Avocations: music, sports. Home: 21 Summit Ave Larchmont NY 10538-2913 Office Phone: 914-643-0994. Personal E-mail: rainier.inc@verizon.net.

RAINIS, EUGENE CHARLES, bank executive; b. NYC, Sept. 24, 1940; s. Charles William and Louise Theresa (Nold) Rainis; m. Jane Margaret Micucci, Nov. 28, 1964; children: Ellen, David, Mark. BS, Fordham U., 1962; MBA, U. Pa., 1964. Security analyst trainee Merrill, Lynch Pierce Fenner & Smith, NYC, 1963-65; ptnr. Brown Bros. Harriman & Co., NYC, 1965—. Bd. dirs. Bio-Brite, Inc.; hon. consul Govt. Lithuania. Trustee Robert Brunner Found., Gregorian U. Found., St. Vincents Cath. Med. Ctrs., Cristo Rey NY HS, NYC; trustee fellow Fordham U. Mem.: Inst. Chartered Fin. Analysts, Knights of Malta, Down Town Assn. (N.Y.C.), Harbour Ridge Golf Club (Palm City, Fla.). Republican. Roman Catholic. Avocations: fishing, golf. Office: Brown Bros Harriman & Co 140 Broadway New York NY 10005 Office Phone: 212-493-7830.

RAINONE, MICHAEL CARMINE, lawyer; b. Phila., Mar. 4, 1918; m. Ledena Tonioni, Apr. 10, 1944; children: Sebastian, Francine. LLB, U. Pa., 1941. Bar: Pa. 1944, U.S. Dist. Ct. Pa. 1944, U.S. Supreme Ct. 1956. Apptd. arbitrator U.S. Dist. Ct. (ea. dist.) Pa., 2003—. Del. 3d cir. Jud. Conf., 1984—85; mem. Fed. Cts. Com., 2004—. Past pres. Nationalities Svc. Ctr., hon. bd. dirs.; commr. Fellowship Commn., 1973—82; internat. pres. Orphans of Italy, Inc., 1975—83; bd. dirs., mem. govt. rels. com. Mental Health Assn. Southeastern Pa., 1979—91; pres. Columbus Civic Assn. Pa., Inc., 1984—91; regional v.p. Nat. Italian-Am. Found.; pres. Seaview Harbor Civic Assn., 1990—95, pres. emeritus, 1996—; apptd. judge Final Law Sch. Trial Advocacy Program N.E., 1996—; mem. nominating com. NIABA, 1996, bd. dirs., 1996; counsel, v.p. Piccola Opera Com., Phila., 1997—; task force chmn. Mazzei Nat. Constn. Ctr., 2001; trustee Chapel of the Four Chaplains, 2005; bd. dirs. State of Pa., Phila., 1970—85; chmn. lawyers' biog. com. Hist. Soc., U.S. Dist. Ct.; trustee Balch Inst. Ethnic Studies, 1989—92; pres. Grad. Club, bd. dirs., 2000. Recipient Man of the Yr. award, Columbus Civic Assn., 1969, Disting. Svc. award, Nationalities Svc. Ctr., 1975, Legion of Honor, Chapel of Four Chaplains, 1979, Bronze Medallion award, 1982, commendation, Pa. Senate, 1982, Appreciation award, Villanova Law Sch., 1993, Achievement award, Syracuse U., 1994, Hon. Lifetime award, KC, 1997, Resolution of Praise, Pres. City Coun. Phila., 1999, Svc. to Legal Profession and Cmty. award, City Coun. of Phila., 2003. Mem.: ATLA (supr. judge law sch. trial advocacy competition 2000, Phila. chpt. emeritus chmn. Justice Michael A. Musmanno award 2000, Supervising Judge Advocacy award Phila. region 2000), ABA (chmn. U.S. Supreme Ct. admissions com. 2001), Am. Arbitration Assn. (arbitrator 1950—), Nat. Itlaian-Am. Bar Assn. (bd. govs. 1986—2003, historian 1987—90, pres. 1991—93, bd. chmn. 1993—95, chmn. Supreme Ct. admissions com. 2000), Phila. Trial Lawyers Assn. (pres. 1982—83, Disting. Svc. award 2000), Lawyers Club Phila. (pres. 1982—84, chmn. nominating com. 2000—, chmn. Centennial Celebration 2001, Achievement and Svc. award 2003), Phila. Bar Assn. (bd. dirs. 1980—83, asst. sec. 1983, 1984, chmn. emeritus Beccaria award 1993—, Cesare Beccaria award 2006), Pa. Trial Lawyers Assn. (bd. govs. 1982—84), Pa. Bar Assn. (Dist. Svc. award 2006), Justinian Soc. (bd. govs. 1980—83, Sr. Lawyer award 2000, Chancellor's Becuma award 1997), Internat. Acad. Law and Sci., N.Y. Trial Lawyers Assn. (assoc.), Sons of Italy (Man of the Yr. award 1995). Home: 2401 Pennsylvania Ave Philadelphia PA 19130-3010 Office: 1617 John F Kennedy Blvd Ste 1500 Philadelphia PA 19103 Office Phone: 215-557-7066. Office Fax: 215-557-3750. Personal E-mail: mcrainone@cs.com. E-mail: mcrainone@cypress.com.

RAINS, BAXTER SMITH, sculptor, consultant; b. Atlanta, July 2, 1938; s. Baxter, Jr. and Elinor (Nelson) Rains; m. Barbara Osmundsen, Sept. 20, 1986; children: Anne Douglass, David Sinclair, Elinor Houston, Holly Christine Delaney. Studied, Ga. Inst. Tech., Atlanta, 1964—65, Atlanta Coll. Art, 1966—68; B of Visual Arts, Ga. State U., Atlanta, 1968; MFA, U. Guanajuato, San Miguel de Allende, Mex., 1975. Tchr. The Westminster Schs., Atlanta, 1969—71; instr. Atlanta Coll. Art, 1969—71, U. Guanajuato, San Miguel de Allende, Mexico, 1972—75, Brevard Art Ctr. and Mus., Melbourne, Fla., 1992; prof. Ctr. for the Arts, Vero Beach, Fla., 2000—02; adj. prof. Indian River CC, Fort Pierce, Fla., 2000—02; adj. prof. art Brovard CC, Melbourne, Fla., 2006—. Dir., evening sch. Atlanta Coll. Art, 1970; founder, exec. dir. Sculptural Arts Mus., Atlanta, 1980—82; cons. U.S. Pres.'s Coun. on Handicapped, 1981—82, Brevard Cultural Alliance, Viera, Fla., 2003, Brevard Mus. Art and Sci., Melbourne, Fla., 2003—04; bd. dirs. Arts Festival of Atlanta, 1982—85; artist-in-charge Hope Dragon Found., Merritt Island, Fla., 1996. One-man shows include Ga. State U., Atlanta, 1967—68, The Westminster Schs., 1969, 1971, Galeria Roma, San Miguel de Allende, Mex., 1973—74, Pine Valley Ranch, Pine, Colo., 1977, El Rancho, Colo., 1977, Gallery Danielli, Toronto, 1979, Washington World Galleries, 1979, Southside Studio Sculpture Show, Richmond, Va., 1990—91, Fifth Ave. Art Gallery, Melbourne, Fla., 1992, Brevard Mus. Art & Sci., 2003, Indian River Sculpture Gallery, Vero Beach, Fla., 2004, Vero Beach (Fla.) Mus. Art, 2005, exhibitions include High Mus. Art, Atlanta, 1969, Mint Mus. Art, Charlotte, N.C., 1970, Galeria Del Conde, San Miguel de Allende, 1972—73, Fiesta de Santa Fe, 1977, Mus. of Touch, Atlanta, 1980, Christian-Brydon Gallery, Richmond, Va., 1989—91, Brigantine Gallery, Cocoa Beach, Fla., 1993, Raleigh Gallery, Design Ctr. of Ams., Dania, Fla., 1992—95, Gaier Contemp. Gallery, Orlando, Fla., 1994—96, Raleigh Gallery, Boca Raton, Fla., 1995—97, Vero Beach Mus. Art, 2000—03, Represented in permanent collections Brevard Mus. Art & Sci., Melbourne, Fla., Radford U. Sculpture Garden, Va., The Westminster Schs., Atlanta, Piedmont Hosp., Ga. State U. Mus., The Trane Corp., Our Lady of Perpetual Help Hosp., Bklyn., City of Atlanta, Office of the Mayor, First Presbyn. Ch., Atlanta, St. Francis Gardens, Albuquerque, Holy Name of Jesus Cath. Ch., Melbourne, Fla., commissioned, Parkway Indsl. Pk., Balt., 1987, Freedom 7 Cmty. Ctr., Cocoa Beach, Fla., 1992, Child Care Assn. of Brevard, Cocoa, Fla., 2004. Mem. Internat. Sculpture Ctr., Washington, 1988—94; bd. govs. Vector Arts Endowment, Indian Harbour Beach, Fla., 1997—. Avocations: archery, gardening. Home and Studio: Osmundsen-Rains Studios PO Box 372628 Satellite Beach FL 32937 Personal E-mail: baxterrains@yahoo.com.

RAINS, CAMERON JAY, lawyer; BA cum laude, Coll. Holy Cross, 1978; JD summa cum laude, Notre Dame Univ., 1981. Bar: Calif. 1981, US Dist. Ct. (so. dist. Calif.) 1981. Ptnr., co-chmn. Corp. & Securities practice group DLA Piper US LLP, San Diego. Editor (assoc.): Notre Dame Lawyer. Mem.: State Bar Calif., San Diego County Bar Assn., U.S. Golf Assn. (mem. exec. com., chmn. 2008 U.S. Open Com.), Century Club San Diego (past pres., gen. chmn. 2000 Buick Invitational), Phi Alpha Delta. Office: DLA Piper US LLP 4365 Executive Dr Ste 1100 San Diego CA 92121 Office Phone: 858-677-1476. Office Fax: 858-677-1401. Business E-Mail: jay.rains@dlapiper.com.

RAINS, M. NEAL, lawyer; b. Burlington, Iowa, July 26, 1943; s. Merritt and Lucille Rains; children: Robert Baldwin, Kathleen Kellogg. BA in Polit. Sci. with honors, U. Iowa, 1965; JD, Northwestern U., 1968. Bar: Ohio 1968. Assoc. Arter & Hadden, Cleve., 1968-76, ptnr., 1976—2001, mem. exec. com., 1981-90, Cleve. mng. ptnr., 1990-92; ptnr. Frantz Ward LLP, Cleve., 2001—. Lectr. on profl. topics, including alternative dispute resolution, distbn. law, litigation practice and procedure, and antitrust. Contbr. articles to profl. jours. With U.S. Army, 1968-70 Fellow: Am. Bar Found.; mem.: ABA, William K. Thomas Am. Inn Ct. (pres. 1999—2000), Cleve. Bar Found. (pres. 2005—07, v.p. 2007—), Cleve. Bar Assn., Ohio Bar Assn., Rowfant Club, Union Club, City Club, Print Club, Phi Delta Phi, Omicron Delta Kappa, Phi Beta Kappa. Home: 18400 Shelburne Rd Shaker Heights OH 44118 Office: Frantz Ward LLP 2500 Key Ctr 127 Public Sq Cleveland OH 44114 Office Phone: 216-515-1660. Business E-Mail: nrains@frantzward.com.

RAINS, MARY JO, banker; b. Konawa, Okla., Oct. 27, 1935; d. Albert Wood and Mary Leona (Winfield) Starns; m. Billy Z. Rains, June 17, 1956; one child, Nicky Z. Student, Okla. Sch. Banking, 1969, Seminole Jr. Coll., 1970—72, East Ctrl. State U., 1978—79; diploma, Am. Inst. Banking, 1981—83; student, Okla. State U., 1987, Adult Vocat. Tech. Ctr., Pontotoc County, 1987. With acctg. divsn. Universal C.I.T., Okla. City, 1953—56; cashier Okla. State Bank (now Bancfirst), Konawa, 1957—89, sr. v.p., 1989—95; sr. v.p., br. mgr. Bancfirst, Konawa, 1995—2002; bd. sec. Seminole County Election Bd., Okla., 2003—. Mem. consulting bd. dirs. Bancfist, Konawa, 2006—. Sec. First Bapt. Ch., Konawa, Okla. 1969-79, budgeting com., 1982-92, 2006-, chmn. fin. com., 1994-2004, 06-, lectureship adminstr.; fin. bd. Kennedy Libr., 1997—; bd. dir. Sacred Heart Mission Hist. Soc.; mem. exec. bd. Ctrl. Okla. Family Med. Ctr., 2004-, fin. com., 2004-. Mem. Okla. Bankers Assn. (dir. women's divsn. 1974-76), Konawa C. of C., Am. Legion, Wewoka C. of C. Home: RR 2 Box 28 Konawa OK 74849 Office: Courthouse Ste 101 Wewoka OK 74884 Office Phone: 405-257-2786.

RAINSBERRY, PATRICK RYAN, engineer; BS, U. Calif., Berkeley, 2001; MS, U. Calif., LA, 2004. Home: 6074 La Costa Fontana CA 92336

RAINVILLE, ALLISON M., language educator; d. Robert F., Jr. and Nancy Rainville. BA, Syracuse U., NY, 1996; MA, Monterey Inst. Internat. Studies, Calif., 2000. Peace corps vol. US Peace Corps, Bourgas, Bulgaria, 1998—2000; adj. instr. Monterey Inst. Internat. Studies, Calif., 2000—01; tchr. ESL Cushing Acad., Ashburnham, Mass., 2002—; ESL tchr., coord. ESL program Phillips Acad. Andover Summer Session, Mass., 2002—. Mem. Monadnock Chorus, Peterborough, NH, 2004—. Mem.: TESOL (chair awards com. 2004—07), Mensa. Avocations: singing, languages. Office Phone: 978-827-7097.

RAINVILLE, CHRISTINA, lawyer; b. NYC, Feb. 7, 1962; d. Dewey and Nancy Rainville; m. Peter S. Greenberg, May 1994. BS, Northwestern U., 1984, JD, 1988. Atty. Schnader Harrison Segal & Lewis, Phila., 1988—. Mem. ABA (pro bono publico award 1999), Nat. Assn. Criminal Def. Lawyers. Presbyterian.

RAINWATER, ERIC, composer, music educator; b. Long Beach, Calif., July 23, 1955; s. Paul Eugene Rainwater and Billye Ree Wallace; m. Candy Marie Layne, Mar. 29, 1980; children: Autumn, Crescent, Shiloh. BA in Music Composition, Azusa Pacific U., Calif., 1988. Dir. 5 home sch. choirs, Sacramento, 1992—; owner Rainwater Music Co., Sacramento, 1995—; dir. 3 home sch. bands Sacramento, 1997—. Music dir. River Ridge Neighborhood Ch., Elk Grove, Calif., 2004—; children's dir., seminar spkr. various music conventions, 1993—. Author, songwriter, arranger: children's musical The Not-So-Silent Night!, 1998 (Top Best Selling Musical award), Samson, The Day God Brought Down the House, 1997 (Top Best Selling Musical award), composer 25 adult, teen and children's musicals; author, songwriter, arranger: children's musical Check Out That Star!, 1995 (Top Best Selling Musical award), arranger: I've Been Working on the Railroad, Sacramento Light Rail Assn. Recipient Hall of Fame award, Azusa Pacific U., 2000, 1st Pl. Novelty Song award, Christian Artists Sem. in Rockies, Estes Park, Colo., 1989. Mem.: Yellowstone Assn. Socialist. Avocations: hiking, swimming. Home and Office: 932 Shellwood Way Sacramento CA 95831 Office Phone: 866-428-2056. Personal E-mail: rainh2omusic@sbcglobal.net.

RAINWATER, GARY L., electric power industry executive; BSEE, U. Mo., Columbia; M of Systems Mgmt., U. So. Calif. Engr. electric transmission and distbn. Union Electric Co. (now Ameren Corp.), v.p. corp. planning, 1993—97; exec. v.p. Ameren CIPS, 1997, pres., CEO, 1997—2001, Ameren CILCO, 2000—01; pres., COO Ameren Corp., St. Louis, 2001—04, chmn., pres., CEO, 2004—. Mem. dean's adv. coun. U. Mo. Sch. Engring.; mem. adv. coun. engring. mgmt. and engring. tech. Washington U.; bd. dirs. AmerenUE, Ameren CILCO, Ameren CIPS and other Ameren subs., Mo. Hist. Soc., St. Louis USO, Ill. Energy Assn., Urban League Met. St. Louis, US Bank. Recipient Mo. Honor award for disting. svc. in engring., U. Mo.-Columbia Coll. Engring., 2000. Mem.: Engrs.' Club (Knight of St. Patrick 2000). Office: Ameren 1901 Chouteau Saint Louis MO 63166-6149 *

RAINWATER, R. STEVEN, systems engineer; b. Tyler, Tex., Dec. 13, 1962; s. Clois Miles and Nancy Jane Rainwater; m. Susan C. Chance, May 11, 1991. AA, Northlake Coll., Irving, Tex., 1981-83; student, U. Tex., 1983-88. Programmer Profl. Info. Libr., Dallas, Tex., 1984-89; systems engr. Kimball Computer Video Tech., Irving, Tex., 1989-91; pres. Network Cybernetics Corp., Irving, 1992—. Sys. operator The Interocitor BBS, Irving, 1990-94; editor new site, 2001-. Author computer software. Mem. Soc. Motion Picture and TV Engrs., Dallas Personal Robotics Group. Avocation: artificial intelligence rsch. Home: 2821 Vassar Dr Irving TX 75062-4575 Office: Network Cybernetics Corp 3720 Canton St Ste 202 Dallas TX 75226

RAINWATER, RICHARD EDWARD, financial consultant, investor; b. Ft. Worth, June 15, 1944; m. Darla D. Moore; 3 children. BA in Math., U. Tex., 1966; MBA in Fin. and Mktg., Stanford U., 1968. With Goldman, Sachs & Co., NYC, Dallas; chief fin. arch. Bass Orgn., Ft. Worth, 1970-86; ind. investor Ft. Worth, 1986-94; founder ENSCO Internat. Inc., 1986; co-founder Columbia Hosp. Corp. (now Columbia/HCA Healthcare Corp.), 1988, Mid Ocean Ltd.; founder, chmn. bd. Crescent Real Estate Equities, Inc., Ft. Worth, 1994—; chief investor Mesa Inc., 1994—. Spkr. Harvard Bus. Sch., Stanford U., U. Tex. Bus. Sch. Appeared on cover of Bus. Week mag., Oct. 1986; recipient Man of Yr. award, 1989, Kupfer Disting. Exec. award Tex. A&M U., 1991, Golden Plate award Am. Acad. Achievement, 1992; named one of Forbes' Richest Americans, 2006. Office: Crescent Real Estate Equities Co 777 Main St Ste 2100 Fort Worth TX 76102-5325

RAINWATER, TERRY I., counseling administrator; b. Ft. Morgan, Colo., Mar. 28, 1953; d. Agnes Marian Rainwater; children: Tylor S. Willis, Chase P. Willis. PhD in Philosophy and Counseling, U. N.Mex, Albuquerque, 2006. Cert. Nat. Bd. Counselor Cert., 1998. Dist. sch. counselor Evergreen Sch. Dist. #50, Kalispell, Mont., 1981—2001; project asst., coder U. N.Mex Ctr. on Alcoholism, Substance Abuse, and Addictions, Albuquerque, 2001—04. Traverse cons. U. N.Mex, Albuquerque, 2001—04. Bd. dirs. Flathead C.A.R.E., Kalispell, Mont., 1988—95. Grantee, Educators for Dialogue and Inquiry, 2004. Mem.: U. Wis. AODA Coalition (mem. 2006—07). Achievements include research in principal-counselor relationships impact counselors' perceived self-efficacy and autonomy in elementary schools. Home: 2085 White Swan Dr Oshkosh WI 54901 Office: Univ Wis Oshkosh 800 Algoma Blvd Oshkosh WI 54901 Office Phone: 920-424-1475. Business E-Mail: rainwatt@uwosh.edu.

RAIRDIN, CRAIG ALLEN, software company executive, software developer; b. Cedar Rapids, Iowa, Oct. 23, 1959; s. Ernie W. and Sherryl E. (Asklund) R.; m. Johnna L. Miller, Jan. 9, 1982. BS in Computer Sci. with distinction, U. Iowa, 1981. Software engr. Rockwell Internat., Cedar Rapids, 1982-88; divsn. dir. Parsons Tech., Cedar Rapids, 1988-90, v.p., 1990-98; ind. software developer, 1999—; pres. Laridian, Cedar Rapids, 1999—. Cons. Creative Computer Systems, Cedar Rapids, 1987-90. Author: (software) Juliet, 1987, QuickVerse, 1988, Bible Illustrator, 1990, Standard Template for Electronic Publishing (STEP), 1995, PalmBible, 1998, PocketBible, 2000. Chmn. Area Liaison Com., Campus Bible Fellowship, Iowa City, 1983-90; precinct chmn. Linn. County Rep. Party, Cedar Rapids, 1986-90; founder Bible Software Industry Standards Group, 1995; vol. pilot Angel Flight Ctrl., 2001—. Republican. Christian. Avocations: church, amateur radio, flying.

RAIRDON, JAMES LEE, paralegal, educator; b. Marion, Ohio, Oct. 25, 1947; s. James Russell and Eleanor Jane (Gandert) Rairdon; m. Ellen Kathryn Findley, Feb. 6, 1977; children: Devin Michael, Patrick Alex. BA in Internat. Studies, Ohio State U., Columbus, 1976; MA in Mgmt., Webster U., Denver, 1993; D in Mgmt., Colo. Tech. U., Colorado Springs, 2006. Regional mgr. group sales Hartford Ins. Group, Denver, 1979—89; paralegal Dept. Justice, Denver, 1989—90; sr. paralegal Great West Life and Annuity Ins. Co., Greenwood Village, Colo., 1990—. Adj. faculty Nat Am. U, Denver, 1993—. 1st. lt. US Army, 1976—79, Ft. Carson, Colo. Fellow: Life Mgmt. Inst.; mem.: Front Range Fly Fishing, Acad. Mgmt. Avocations: fly fishing, hiking. Office: Great West Life adn Annuity Ins Co 8525 E Orchard Rd Greenwood Village CO 80111

RAISBECK, GORDON, systems engineer, consultant; b. NYC, May 4, 1925; s. Milton Joseph and Marcelle (Ellinger) R.; m. Barbara Wiener, Dec. 22, 1948; children: Michael Norbert, Lucy Margaret, Alison Jane, Timothy Gordon, James Gregory. Rhodes scholar, Oxford U., Eng., 1947-48; BA, Stanford U., 1944; PhD, MIT, 1949. Registered profl. engr., Mass., Maine. Instr. M.I.T., Cambridge, 1948-49; mem. tech. staff Bell Telephone Labs., Inc., Murray Hill, NJ, 1949-61; dir. transmission line research Bell Telephone Labs., Inc. (now Lucent), 1954-61; mem. profl. staff research and devel. Advanced Research Projects Agy., Washington, 1959-60; mem. profl. staff Arthur D. Little, Inc., Cambridge, 1961-86, dir. systems engring., 1966-70, dir. phys. systems research, 1970-75, v.p. systems engring., 1973-86, part-time 1982-86; cons. mgmt. of technol. innovation, 1982-94; ret., 2004. Instr. Drew U., Stanford U., MIT. Contbr. articles to profl. jours.; author: Information Theory: An Introduction for Engineers and Scientists, 1964; patentee in field (22). Served to lt. (j.g.) USNR, 1944-46, ATO, PTO. Rhodes scholar, 1947 Fellow IEEE, Acoustical Soc. Am.; mem. Math. Assn. Am., Oceanic Engring. Soc. IEEE (sec. 1988-92), New Coll. Soc., Oxford Soc., Assn. Am. Rhodes Scholars, Amateur Chamber Music Players, Chamber Music Am., Sigma Xi. Democrat. Episcopalian. Home: 15 Piper Rd Apt J202 Scarborough ME 04074-7545 Personal E-mail: raisbeck7@netscape.net.

RAISH, DAVID LANGDON, lawyer; b. Cleve., Mar. 12, 1947; s. John E. Raish and Roslyn V. (Skeels) Pettibone; m. Roslyn Anne Dinnick, Sept. 12, 1969; children: David Jr., Anne, Julia. BA, Yale U., 1969; JD, Harvard U., 1973. Bar: Mass. 1975, DC 1981. Law clk. to hon. James R. Browning U.S. Ct. Appeals-9th Cir., San Francisco, 1973-74; assoc. Ropes & Gray, Boston, 1974-82, ptnr., 1982—. Mem. ABA Tax sect. 1991—, mem. Employee Benefits Com., 1993—, mem. coun., 1999-2004, vice chair, 2002-04. Author: Cafeteria Plans, 2000, Cash or Deferred Arrangements, 1997, Compensation and Benefits for Key Employees of Tax-Exempt Organizations, 1995; bd. advisors Jour. Taxation of Employee Benefits, 1990-2000. Tenor Tanglewood Festival Chorus; mem. bd. visitors New Eng. Conservatory. Office: Ropes & Gray One International Pl Boston MA 02110 Business E-Mail: draish@ropesgray.com.

RAISIAN, JOHN, academic administrator, economist; b. Conneaut, Ohio, July 30, 1949; s. Ernest James and Ruby Lee (Owens) Raisian; m. Joyce Ann Klak, Aug. 17, 1984; children: Alison Kathleen, Sarah Elizabeth. BA, Ohio U., 1971; PhD, UCLA, 1978; LLD (hon.), Albertson Coll. Idaho, 1995. Rsch. assoc. Human Resources Rsch. Ctr., U. So. Calif., LA, 1972—73; cons. Rand Corp., Santa Monica, Calif., 1974—75; vis. asst. prof. econs. U. Wash., Seattle, 1975—76; asst. prof. econs. U. Houston, 1976—80; sr. economist Office Rsch. and Evaluation, U.S. Bur. Labor Stats., Washington, 1980—81; spl. asst. for econ. policy Office Asst. Sc. for Policy, U.S. Dept. Labor, Washington, 1981—83, dir. rsch. and tech. support, 1981—84; pres. Unicon Rsch. Corp., LA, 1984-86; sr. fellow Hoover Instn., Stanford, Calif., 1986—, assoc. dir., dep. dir., 1986—90, dir., 1990—. Advisor Nat. Coun. on Handicapped, Washington, 1985—86, Nat. Commn. on Employment Policy, Washington, 1987—88; chmn. minimum wage bd. Calif. Indsl. Welfare Commn., 1987; mem. nat. adv. com. Student Fin. Assistance, Washington, 1987—89; corp. mem. Blue Shield Calif., 1994—96; bd. dirs. Sentinel Groups Fund, Inc., 1997—; mem. Pacific Coun. Internat. Policy; nat. adv. bd. City Innovation. Editor (editl. bd.): (jour.) Jour. Labor Rsch., 1983—; contbr. articles to profl. jours. Exec. dir. Presdl. Task Force on Food Assistance, Washington, 1983—84. Recipient Best Publ. of Yr. award, Econ. Inquiry, Western Econ. Assn., 1979, Disting. Tchg. award, U. Houston Coll. Social Scis., 1980, Disting. Svc. award, U.S. Dept. Labor, 1983; fellow predoctoral fellow, Rand Corp., 1976. Mem.: Nat. Assn. Scholars, Coun. on Fgn. Rels., Mont Pelerin Soc., World Affairs Coun., Commonwealth Club of Calif., We. Econs. Assn., Am. Econs. Assn., Phi Beta Kappa. Republican. Avocation: wine collecting, sports enthusiast. Office: Hoover Instn Stanford Univ 434 Galvez Mall Stanford CA 94305-6010 *

RAISIG, PAUL JONES, JR., lawyer; b. Jamestown, NY, June 21, 1932; s. Paul Jones and Marian Elizabeth (Christian) R.; m. Carolyn Virginia Sides, June 12, 1955; children: Dawn Virginia, Paul Christian, Anne Sibley. B.G.E., U. Nebr., 1961; MBA, U. Ala., 1965; JD, Campbell U., 1989. Bar: NC, 1989, US Supreme Ct. 1992. Commd. 2d lt. U.S. Army, 1953, advanced through grades to col., 1973, ret., 1977, served in Vietnam, 1963, btn. comdr., Vietnam, 1968; dep. dir. U.S. Army Reorganization, 1973; v.p. Armed Forces Relief and Benefit Assn., Washington, 1977-79; sr. cons. Dept. Def., Washington, 1979-80; exec. dir. Am. Fedn. Info. Processing Socs., Arlington, Va., 1980-84; v.p., dir. Designs, Ltd., Alexandria, Va., 1985-86; ptnr. Barrington, Herndon & Raisig, P.A., Fayetteville, NC, 1989-92. Adj. prof. bus. law and bus. mgmt. Campbell U., 1992-2004; cons. in field; mediator for Superior Ct. and arbitrator for Dist. Ct. Decorated Legion of Merit (3), Bronze Star medal (2), Air medal (5), Purple Heart (2), Meritorious Service medal, Army Commendation medal with V Device (3), Combat Inf. badge. Mem. U.S. Coun. for World Comms., Beta Gamma Sigma. Home and Office: Buffalo Lake 325 Mallard Rd Sanford NC 27332-1142 *As we go about climbing the mountains in our lives, we must always remember to take the high road - for that is the only way to truly reach the top.*

RAISLER, KENNETH MARK, lawyer; b. New Rochelle, NY, May 15, 1951; s. Herbert A. and Norma (Glaubach) R.; children: Caroline Elisabeth, Katharine Kelsey, David Mark. BSBA, Yale Coll., 1973; JD, NYU, 1976. Bar: NY 1977, DC 1977, US Dist. Ct. (so. dist.) NY 1977, US Dist. Ct. DC 1977, US Ct. Appeals (2d cir.) 1977, US Ct. Appeals (DC cir.) 1977, US Ct. Appeals (7th cir.) 1982, US Ct. Appeals (10th cir.) 1983, US Supreme Ct. 1985. Law clk. US Dist. Ct. (so. dist.) NY, NYC, 1976-77; asst. US atty., Washington, 1977-82; dep. gen. counsel Commodity Futures Trading Commn., Washington, 1982-83, gen. counsel, 1983-87; ptnr. Rogers & Wells, NYC, 1987-92; ptnr., coord. commodities, futures and derivatives practice area Sullivan & Cromwell, NYC, 1992—. Mem. Assn. of Bar of City of NY (chair futures regulation com. 1988-91). Office: Sullivan & Cromwell 125 Broad St 33d Fl New York NY 10004-2498 Office Phone: 212-558-4675. Office Fax: 212-558-3588. Business E-Mail: raislerk@sullcrom.com.

RAITT, BONNIE LYNN, singer, musician; b. Burbank, Calif., Nov. 8, 1949; Student, Radcliffe Coll. Performer: blues clubs, East Coast, concert tours in Britain, 1976, 1977; albums include Bonnie Raitt, 1971, Give It Up, 1972, Takin' My Time, 1973, Streetlights, 1974, Home Plate, 1975, Sweet Forgiveness, 1977, The Glow, 1979, Green Light, 1982, Nine Lives, 1986, Nick of Time, 1989 (Grammys 1990, Rock-Best Vocal Performance, Female, Pop-Best Vocal Performance, Female, Album of Yr., 1990), I'm in the Mood (with John Lee Hooker) (Grammy 1990, Blues-Best Traditional Record, 1990), The Bonnie Raitt Collection, 1990, Luck of the Draw, 1991 (Grammy, Rock-Best Vocal Performance, Female, Grammy for Best Duet with Delbert McClinton, 1992), Longing In Their Hearts, 1994 (Grammy award Best Pop Album, 1994), Road Tested, 1996, Fundamental, I Can't Make You Love Me, 1998, Silver Lining, 2002, songs include Something to Talk About (Grammy, Best Pop Vocal Performance, Female, 1992), Good Man, Good Woman (with Delbert McClinton) (Grammy, Rock-Best Vocal by a Duo or Group, 1992). Founding mem. Musicians United for Safe Energy, Rhythm and Blues Found.

RAIZEN, SENTA AMON, educational association administrator, researcher; b. Vienna, Oct. 28, 1924; came to U.S., 1940; d. John and Helen (Krys) Amon; m. Abraham A. Raizen, Apr. 18, 1948; children: Helen S., Michael B., Daniel J. BS, Guilford Coll., 1944; MA, Bryn Mawr, 1945; Tchr. Cert., U. Va., 1960. Rsch. chemist Sun Oil Co., Norwood, Pa., 1945-48; rsch. asst. NAS, Washington, 1960-62; assoc. program dir. NSF, Washington, 1962-69, spl. asst., 1969-72; sr. researcher The Rand Corp., Washington, 1972-74; assoc. dir. Nat. Inst. Edn., Washington, 1974-78; ind. cons. Washington, 1978-80; study dir. NAS, Washington, 1980-88; dir. Nat. Ctr. for Improving Sci. Edn., Washington, 1988—. Cons. Nat. Ctr. for Edn. Stats., Washington, 1987—, Ednl. Testing Svc., Princeton, N.J., 1988—, Nat. Goals Panel, Washington, 1990-2000, Third Internat. Math. and Sci. Study, Internat. Assn. Evaluation Ednl. Achievement, The Netherlands, 1990—, SRI Internat., 1998—, Orgns. for Econ. Cooperation and Devel., Paris, 1998—. Contbr. articles to profl. jours., encys., books, reports in field. Pres. Cooperative Nursery Sch., Arlington, Va., 1953-57; leader Brownies, Girl Scouts, U.S. and Cub Scouts, Boy Scouts, Am., Arlington, 1958-64. Recipient Disting. Lifetime award WestEd, 2000; grantee NSF, U.S. Dept. Edn., U.S Dept. Energy, pvt. founds., 1988-2000, fellowship for grad. study NSF, 1944-45, Meritorious Svc. award, 1968, The Network Pres.' award, 1991. Fellow AAAS; mem. Am. Chem. Soc., Am. Ednl. Rsch. Assn. Avocations: dance, swimming, reading, knitting, stitchery. Home: 5513 31st St N Arlington VA 22207-1532 Office: Nat Ctr Improving Sci Edn 1940 Wilson Blvd Ste 400 Arlington VA 22201 Home Phone: 703-241-1973; Office Phone: 703-875-0496.

RAIZER, VICTOR, physicist, researcher; b. Leningrad, Russia, July 30, 1951; arrived in US, 1996; MS, Inst. Physics and Tech., Moscow, 1974. Engr., scientist, sr. scientist Space Rsch. Inst. Acad. Scis., Moscow, 1974—96; sr. scientist Sci. and Tech. Corp., Fairfax, Va., 1997—2001, Zel Technologies, LLC, Fairfax, Va., 2001—. Presenter in field. Co-author (with I. Cherny): Passive Microwave Remote Sensing of Oceans, 1998; contbr. articles to profl. jours. Mem.: IEEE, NY Acad. Scis. Office: Zel Technologies LLC Fairfax VA Home Phone: 703-764-2308. Personal E-mail: vraizer@aol.com.

RAJ, SATISH RAMNARAYAN, cardiologist, researcher; s. Kidambi and Sugantha Raj; m. Vidya Sundararajan, Jan. 23, 2003; 1 child, Priya L. BS, Rensellaer Poly. Inst., Troy, NY, 1991; MD, Queen's U., Kingston, Ont., Can., 1993; MSCI, Vanderbilt U., Nashville, 2004. Diplomate Am. Bd. Internal Medicine, 1996, Am. Bd. Cardiology, 1999, Am. Bd. Clin. Cardiac Electrophysiology, 2001. Fellow in cardiac electrophysiology U. Calgary, Alta., Canada, 1999—2002; fellow in clin. pharmacology Vanderbilt U., Nashville, 2002—03, asst. prof. medicine & pharmacology, 2004—. Contbr. articles to profl. jours. Mentored Clin. Rsch. grantee, NIH, 2005—. Fellow: Am. Coll. Cardiology; mem.: Assn. Patient-Oriented Rsch., Am. Soc. Pharmacology & Exptl. Therapeutics, Am. Heart Assn. (assoc.), Am. Autonomic Soc. Achievements include research in Postural Tachycardia Syndrome. Office: Vanderbilt U AA3228 MCN 1161 21st Ave S Nashville TN 37232-2195 Office Phone: 615-343-6499. Office Fax: 615-343-8649. Business E-Mail: satish.raj@vanderbilt.edu.

RAJA, RAJENDRAN, physicist; b. Guruvayur, Kerala, India, July 14, 1948; arrived in US, 1974; s. P.K. Sreeveerarayan and Chandramathi Raja; m. Selitha Barbara Freundorfer, 1976; 1 child, Anjali. BA with honors, Cambridge U., Eng., 1970, MA with honors, 1974, PhD, 1974. Rsch. assoc. Fermilab, Batavia, Ill., 1975—78, assoc. scientist, 1978—83, scientist I, 1983—88, scientist II, 1988—. Monte Carlo convenor DO Expt., 1986—97, top quark physics convenor, 1990—94; head DO Software Support Group, 1986—93, DO Electron ID Group, 1989—94; head emittance exch./ring coolers group Muon Collider/Neutrino Factory Collaboration, 2001—03; spokesman Mipp Expt. Fermilab, Batavia, 2001—; fellow Trinity Coll. Cambridge U., 1973. Contbr. over 300 articles to profl. jours. Pres. Cambridge U. India Soc., 1969—70. Mem.: AAAS, Planetary Soc., Am. Phys. Soc. Achievements include discovery of top quark. Home: 1304 Margate Ct Naperville IL 60540 Office: Fermi Nat Accelerator Lab PO Box 500 Batavia IL 60510 Office Phone: 630-840-4092. Business E-Mail: raja@fnal.gov.

RAJAGOPAL, USHA, plastic surgeon; married; 2 children. MD, Southwestern Med. Sch., Dallas. Cert. Am. Bd. Plastic & Reconstructive Surgery, Am. Bd. Gen. Surgery. Surg. resident Parkland Hosp., Dallas; fellow in plastic surgery U. Calif., San Francisco; pvt. practice San Francisco. Mem.: Am. Soc. Laser Medicine & Surgery, Calif. Soc. Plastic Surgeons, Am. Soc. Plastic Surgeons, Alpha Omega Alpha. Office: 490 Post St #430 San Francisco CA 94102 Office Phone: 415-392-3333. Office Fax: 415-392-5327. E-mail: info@sfcosmeticsurgery.com. *

RAJANI, PREM RAJARAM, transportation company financial executive; b. Bombay, Nov. 9, 1949; came to U.S., 1973; s. Rajaram N. and Devibai Rajani; m. Rekha Rohera, Apr. 21, 1977; children: Anand, Harshada. B Tech., Indian Inst. Tech., Bombay, 1973; MBA in Acctg. and Fin., Columbia U., 1975. Sr. ops. auditor Pfizer, Inc., NYC, 1975-78; sr. projects fin. analyst Sea-Land Industries subs. RJR, Edison, NJ, 1978-80, fin. mgr. joint ventures, 1980-81, mgr. corp. planning and analysis, 1981-84; mgr. corp. fin. Sea-Land Corp., Edison, 1984-87; asst. treas.-internat. Sea-Land Svc. Inc. subs. CSX Corp., Edison, 1987-88, asst. treas.-domestic, 1988, staff v.p., treas., 1988-94, staff v.p. fin. and planning Americas, 1994-97, staff v.p. fin. projects, 1998—2001, fin. cons., 2001—. Personal E-mail: prajani@carolina.rr.com.

RAJARAM, SRI-SUJANTHY, internist, medical educator; arrived in US, 1993, permanent resident, 1998; d. Vel and Sribalasaras Veluppillai; m. K. Rajaram, June 4, 1989; children: Sanjev, Sankavi, Sweda. MBBS, U. Jaffna, Srilanka, 1989. Diplomate Am. Bd. of Internal Medicine 1996, Critical Care 1998, Am. Acad. Sleep Medicine 2003. Asst. prof. medicine Albert Einstein Sch. Medicine, Bronx, NY, 1998—2003; med. dir. Cardio Sleep Ctr., Oldbridge, NJ, 2003—04; intensivist Robertwood Johnson U. Hosp., New Brunswick, NJ, 2003—05; asst. prof. medicine Robertwood Johnson Med. Sch. UMDNJ, NJ, 2003—05; asst. prof. medicine Cooper U. Hosp., NJ, 2005—, intensivist, 2005—. Intern, pediats. ob-gyn. U. Colombo, Sri Lanka, 1991—92, sr. house officer, anesthesiology, 1992; residency, internal medicine LI Coll. Hosp., NY, 1993—96; fellowship, critical care medicine Mt. Siani Sch. Medicine, 1996—98; sleep medicine NJ Neuro-Sleep Inst., JFK Med. Ctr., Edison, NJ, 2001—02. Contbr. chapters to books, articles to profl. jours., abstracts to profl. jours. Cmty. svc. project, primary health care svcs. to Sri Lanka, 2004, 2005; bd. dir. Internat. Med. Health Orgn. USA, 2003—; dir., continuous med. edn. Internat. Med. Health Orgn., 2004—; NJ coordinator Internat. Med. Health Orgn. USA, 2003—. Fellow: Am. Acad. Sleep Medicine, American Coll. Chest Physicians (Gov.'s Cmty. Svc. award 2004); mem.: Soc. Critical Care Medicine. Hindu. Home: 5 Rushton Ct West Windsor NJ 08550 Office: Cooper U Hosp One Cooper Plaza Camden NJ 08103 Home Phone: 609-452-1344. Business E-Mail: rajaram-sri-sujanthy@cooperhealth.edu.

RAJASEKAR, ARCOT, computer scientist; s. Kuppuswamy and Sakunthala Arcot; m. Malini Govindaraj Purasawalkam, Aug. 21, 1989; 1 child, Bhairavi. B with honors in engring., Coll. of Engring., U. of Madras, India, 1979; MS, Indian Inst. of Tech., India, 1982; PhD, U. Md., 1984. Post doctoral rsch. assoc. U. Md. Inst. for Advanced Computer Studies, Coll. Pk., Md., 1989—90; asst. prof. U. Ky., Lexington, 1990—96; scientist to principle scientist San Diego Supercomputer Ctr., La Jolla, Calif., 1996—2001, dir., data grid technologies group, 2001—. Vice thrust area liaison Nat. Partnership for Advanced Computational Infrastructure, La Jolla, Calif., 1997—2003; reviewer NSF, Washington, 2000—02. Author: (research monograph) Foundations of Disjunctive Logic Programming; guest editor Annals of Mathematics and Artificial Intelligence; contbr. articles various profl. jours., chapters to books various profl. text. Founder, dir. South India Heritage Found. Various scientific grants, NSF, 1991—, Storage Resource Broker Performance Optimization grant, Dept. of Def., 2000—01, Biomedical Imaging Rsch. Network Coordinating Ctr. grant, NIH, 2001—, Nat. Archives and Records Agency, Persistent Archive Testbed, 2001—, Libr. of Congress Digital Archives Project, 2005—07, Portal Web Services: Support of DOE SciDAC Collaborations grant, Dept. of Energy, 2002-2005, Rsch. in String-oriented Databases grant, Dept. of Def., 1996. Mem.: Global Grid Forum. Hindu. Achievements include development of storage resource broker; patents for collection-based persistent digital archive; development of MCAT - a metadata catalog, iRODS - integrated Rule Oriented Data System; research in data grid technology; logic programming. Avocations: reading, fish-breeding, web-surfing, camping, hiking. Office: San Diego Supercomputer Ctr UCSD 9500 Gilman Dr La Jolla CA 92014-0505 Office Phone: 858-534-8378. Business E-Mail: sekar@sdsc.edu.

RAJASEKARAN, SANGUTHEVAR, computer science educator; b. Andipatty, India, June 7, 1957; came to U.S., 1983; s. Subbiah and Ponnuthayammal (Sonai Servai) Sanguthevar; m. Krishnavadhana Ramaswami, Feb. 4, 1988; 1 child, Keeran. BSc in Spl. Physics, Madurai Kamaraj U., 1977; BE in Elec. Tech., Indian Inst. Sci., 1981, ME in Automation, 1983; PhD in Computer Sci., Harvard U., 1988. Teaching asst. Aiken Computing Lab., Harvard U., Cambridge, Mass., 1983-86; assoc. in rsch. dept. computer sci. Duke U., Durham, N.C., 1986-88; asst. prof. computer and info. sci. U. Pa., Phila., 1988-94; assoc. prof. computer and info. sci. U. Fla., Gainesville, 1994-99, prof., 1999—2000; chief scientist Arcef Sys., 2000—02; UTC chmn., prof. CSE U. Conn., Storrs, 2002—. Vis. scientist U. Saarlandes, Saarbrücken, Germany, 1991; vis. scholar U. Md. Inst. for Advanced Computer Studies, 1993; mem. program com. Internat. Parallel Processing Symposium, 1996-97; chmn. workshop on randomized parallel computing, 1996, 97; lectr., presenter numerous seminars; referee numerous profl. jours., including Jour. Computer and Systems Sci., IEEE Trans. on Computers, Parallel Processing Letters, Soc. Indsl. and Applied Math. Jour. on Computing. Contbg. author: Advances in Parallel Algorithms, 1992, Synthesis of Parallel Algorithms, 1993, Parallel Algorithm Derivation and Program Transformation, 1993, Computer Algorithms/C++, 1997; contbr. numerous articles to profl. jours. Rsch. grantee NSF, 1989—, Army Rsch. Office, 1989-93, NSF, 1992. Mem. IEEE Computer Soc. (sr.), Assn. for Computing Machinery. Office: Univ Conn 257 ITE Bldg CSE Storrs Mansfield CT 06269-2155 Business E-Mail: rajasek@engr.uconn.edu.

RAJE, SACHIN, information technology manager; m. Sana Garud, Feb. 23, 1987; 1 child, Jay Karan. MS in Computer Sci. and Info. Sys., Marist Coll., Poughkeepsie, NY, 1997. Cert. Project Mgmt. Profl. Project Mgmt. Inst., 2000. Head EAI and PMO practices Avesta Computer Svcs., Jersey City, 2003—04; SVP and global head PMO Ness IBS, Scotch Plains, NJ, 2004—. Pres. Multi Tasks CAD Svcs., Pune, India, 1988—96. Author: (tech. book) Thinking in AutoCAD. Mem.: Rotary Internat. (life). Home Phone: 908-281-9837. Personal E-mail: sachin.raje@gmail.com.

RAJENDRAN, KADIAMPATTI NATARAJAN, marketing educator; b. Begunia, West Bengal, India, Oct. 18, 1949; s. Kadiampatti Subramania Iyer and Meenakshi Natarajan; m. Mythili Sundaram, Nov. 10, 1976; children: Hari, Aditi. BSc in Engring., Banaras Hindu U., Varanasi, India, 1971, M in Bus. Mgmt., 1973; PhD in Bus. Mgmt., Mktg., U. Iowa, Iowa City, 1990. Cert. Indian Inst. Bankers, 1982. Probationary officer State Bank India, India, 1974—76, officer, consultancy cell Chennai, Tamil Nadu, India, 1976—81, dep. mgr., sib divsn. Tirupur, Tamil Nadu, India, mgr., pb divsn. Avanashi, Tamil Nadu, India, 1982—83; asst. prof., mktg. U. No. Iowa, Cedar Falls, 1988—96, assoc. prof., mktg., 1996—. Faculty tng. programs for bankers World Bank, 1979—82. Contbr. articles to profl. jours., chapters to books. Fellow: Acad. of Mktg. Sci.; mem.: Mktg. Mgmt. Assn., Inst. Ops. Rsch. Mgmt. Sci., Am. Mktg. Assn. Home: 2510 Neola Street Cedar Falls IA 50613 Office: Univ No Iowa 342 Curris Business Bldg Cedar Falls IA 50614 Home Phone: 319-266-3623; Office Phone: 319-273-6011. Office Fax: 319-273-2922. Personal E-mail: raj@cfu.net. Business E-Mail: raj.rajendran@uni.edu.

RAJKOWSKI, E. MARK, corporate financial executive; BS, Lehigh Univ. CPA NY, NJ, Pa. Positions through mng. ptnr. Pricewaterhouse Coopers LLP, 1981—98; corp. contr. Eastman Kodak Co., 1998—2001, v.p. fin., 2001—03, COO consumer digital bus., 2003, v.p., gen. mgr.

worldwide ops imaging systems, 2004; sr. v.p., CFO MeadWestvaco Corp., Glen Allen, Va., 2004—. Bd. dir. Performance Technologies Inc. Mem.: Fin. Executives Inst., Am. Inst. CPAs. Office: MeadWestvaco Corp 11013 W Broad St Glen Allen VA 23060 *

RAJPURKAR, ATUL DATTATRAYA, urologist; b. Mumbai, India, Apr. 1, 1963; s. Dattatraya and Sudha Rajpurkar; m. Madhvi Atul Jadhav; children: Asavari, Athary. MS, Seth G.S. Med. Coll., Mumbai, 1986, MS in Gen. Surgery, 1990; FRCS, Royal Coll. Surgeons, Glasgow, 1995. Med. officer King-Edward Meml. Hosp., Mumbai, India, 1991—92; surgery resident Royal Oldham Tameside Hosp., England, 1993—96; surgery in house staff Episc. Hosp., Phila., 1996—97; rsch. assoc. Wayne State U., Detroit, 1997—99; surgical cons. R.K. Hosp., Mumbai, 2000—02; rsch. fellow assoc. Wayne State U., 2002—04, in house staff urology, 2004—. Rsch. assoc. Wayne State U., 1997—99, 2002—04. Contbr. articles various profl. jours. Fellow: Royal Coll. Surgeons and Physicians Glasgow; mem.: Sexual Medicine Soc. North Am., Am. Urological Assn. Office: 4160 John Rd Ste 1017 Detroit MI 48201 Personal E-mail: arajpurkar@hotmail.com.

RAJU, MINNIE M., application analyst, critical care nurse; arrived in U.S., 1974; d. Pazhavilla I. and Mary Raju. BS in Biology, Albany State U., 1994; ADN, Rockland CC, Suffern, NY, 1997; BSN, U. Md., 2003, MS in Nursing Informatics, 2005. RN N.Y., Md., DC. Clin. nurse Nyack Hosp., NY, 1997—99, Washington Hosp. Ctr., 1999—, clin. mgr., 2004—05, applications devel. mgr., 2005—. Mem.: Am. Assn. Critical Care Nurses, Health Info. Mgmt. Sys. Soc., Am. Med. Informatics Assn., Greater Washington Area Chamber Am. Assn. Critical Care Nurses, Sigma Theta Tau. Seventh Day Adventist.

RAJUPALEPU, RAHI K., technologist, consultant; s. Seshagiri Rao Venkata and Padmavathi Rajupalepu; m. Vidya Vidyakumar, Oct. 18, 2001; children: Pranav, Mayukha Anasuya. B of Engring., Osmania U., 1995; MBA, Am. Intercontinental U. Programmer Beechwood Computing/Deloitte, Norwalk, Calif., 1996—97; sr. tech. cons. Exec Search Inc, Milw., 1998—2000; sr. tech., data arch. Commerceone, Arlington/Columbia, Va., 2000—02; sr. tech. cons., arch. Plateau Systems Ltd, Arlington, 2002—05; pres., CEO Prometheus Technologies LLC, Ashburn, 2003—. Pres. Prometheus Technologies LLC, Ashburn, 2003—. Contbr. Rajdhani Mandir, Chantilly, Va. Achievements include various patents pending for technological ideas. Home Phone: 571-333-2662; Office Phone: 703-975-7244. Personal E-mail: rrajupalepu@yahoo.com. E-mail: contact@prometheusllc.com.

RAK, LORRAINE KAREN, lawyer; b. Trenton, NJ, Jan. 8, 1959; d. Charles Walter and Lottie Mary (Debiec) R. BA in Polit. Sci., Seton Hall U., South Orange, NJ, 1981; JD, Cornell U., Ithaca, NY, 1984. Bar: NJ 1986, NY 1986, US Dist. Ct. NJ 1986, US Dist. Ct. (so. and ea. dists.) NY 1988, US Dist. Ct. (no. dist.) NY 1991, US Ct. Appeals (4th cir.) 1989, US Ct. Appeals (2d cir.) 1990, US Ct. Appeals (3d cir.) 1991. Assoc. Shearman & Sterling, NYC, 1984-91, Robinson, St. John & Wayne, NYC, 1992-93; dep. atty. gen. State of NJ, Newark, 1993—2003, dep. atty. gen., sect. chief consumer fraud prosecution, 2003—. Mem. Lawyers' Com. for Human Rights, NYC. Mem. ABA, ACLU, LWV, NJ State Bar Assn., Cornell Law Assn., Amnesty Internat., Polish Arts Club Trenton. Democrat. Roman Catholic. Office: 124 Halsey St Fl 5 Newark NJ 07102-3017 Office Phone: 973-648-4429. Business E-Mail: lorraine.rak@dol.lps.state.nj.us.

RAKEL, DAVID PAUL, sports medicine physician, director; b. Newport Beach, Calif., Nov. 30, 1964; s. Robert Edwin and Margaret Ann Rakel; m. Denise Ann Oliveto, Aug. 13, 1988; children: Justin Paul, Sarah Ann, Lucas Alexander. MD, Baylor Coll. Medicine, Houston, Tex., 1991. Cert. family medicine Am. Acad. Family Physicians, 1994, sports medicine Am. Acad. Family Physicians, 1998, interactive guided imagery Acad. Guided Imagery, 2001, diplomate Am. Bd. Holistic Medicine, 2001. Dir. integrative medicine sch. medicine and pub. health U. Wis., Madison, 2001—. Editor: Integrative Medicine. Named Resident Tchr. of Yr., North Colo. Family Medicine Residency Program, 1994, Faculty Educator of Yr., U. Wis. Dept. Family Medicine Residents, 2005; recipient Mark Hanson Faculty Lectr. award, U. Wis. Dept. Family Medicine, 2003, Faculty Excellence in Edn. award, 2004. Office: Univ Wis Med Sch 777 S Mills St Madison WI 53715 Home Phone: 608-277-9107; Office Phone: 608-265-8421.

RAKEL, ROBERT EDWIN, physician, educator; b. Cin., July 13, 1932; s. Edwin J. and Elsie (Machino) R.; m. Peggy Klare; children: Barbara, Cindy, Linda, David. BS in Zoology, U. Cin., 1954, MD, 1958. Diplomate Am. Bd. Family Practice. Intern St. Mary's Hosp., Cin., 1958-59; resident in internal medicine USPHS Hosp., Seattle, 1959-61; resident in gen. practice Monterey County Hosp., Salinas, Calif., 1961-62; practice medicine Newport Beach, Calif., 1962-69; chmn. family practice program U. Calif., Irvine, 1969-71; prof., head dept. family practice U. Iowa, 1971-85; assoc. dean acad. and clin. affairs, Richard M. Kleberg, Sr. prof., chmn. dept. family medicine Baylor Coll. Medicine, Houston, 1985-97, prof. dept. family and cmty. medicine, 1997—. Dir. family practice residency program Hoag Meml. Hosp., Newport Beach, 1969-71; med. staff Mercy Hosp., Iowa City, 1971-85; chief family practice svc. St. Luke's Episc. Hosp., The Meth. Hosp., Houston, 1985-97; trustee The Hospice of Tex. Med. Ctr., 1986-97, Inst. of Religion Tex. Author (forward): Neurology for the Everyday Practice of Medicine, R.G. Feldman, 1984; author: selected References in Family Medicine, 1973; editor (with H.F. Conn & T.W. Johnson): Family Practice, 1973; editor: (with H.F. Conn) Textbook of Family Practice, 1978; editor: Principles of Family Medicine, 1977, Conn's Current Therapy, 1984—, Yearbook of Family Practice, 1977—90, (series) Procedures for Your Practice Patient Care, Vol. 18, Essentials of Family Practice, 1992, 2d edit., 1998, Saunders Manual Med. Practice, 1996, 2d edit., 2000, Essential Family Medicine, 3rd edit., 2006, Textbook of Family Medicine, 2007; mem. 13 editorial bds. med. jours.; contbr. articles to profl. jours., chapters to books. Served with USPHS, 1959-61. Recipient Mead-Johnson Scholar award in Gen. Practice, 1971, Max Cheplove award, NY Acad. Family Physicians, 2001, Lifetime Achievement award, Am. Med. Student Assn., 2002, McGovern award, Am. Med. Writers Assn., 2004. Fellow Am. Acad. Family Physicians (pres. Orange County chpt. Calif. 1969, commn. on edn. 1970-76, Thomas W. Johnson award 1973); mem. AMA (sect. on med. schs. 1985-97, gov. coun. of sect. 1986-88), Tex. Med. Assn., Am. Bd. Family Practice (bd. dirs. 1973-79, v.p. 1977-79, chmn. exam. com. 1974-79, recert. com. 1973-79, others), Am. Bd. Med. Spltys. (com. splty. evaluation 1978-81), Nat. Bd. Med. Examiners (bd. dirs. 1975-79), Soc. Tchrs. Family Medicine (dir. 1971-79, sec. 1971-73, F. Marian Bishop Leadership award, 1992), Coun. Acad. Socs., Assn. Am. Med. Colls., History of Medicine Soc. (founder, chmn. U. Iowa 1978-85, founder, chmn. Baylor Coll. Medicine 1986—), Am. Osler Soc. (bd. dirs. 1989-96, pres. 1994). Roman Catholic. Home: 2420 Underwood St Houston TX 77030-3506 Office: Baylor College Medicine Dept Family and Cmty Medicine 3701 Kirby Dr Ste 600 Houston TX 77098 Business E-Mail: rrakel@bcm.edu.

RAKER, IRMA S., judge; b. Bklyn. m. Samuel K. Raker. BA, Syracuse U., 1959; cert. of attendance (hon.), Hague (The Netherlands) Acad. Internat. Law, 1959; JD, Am. U., 1972. Bar: Md. 1973, D.C. 1974, U.S. Dist. Ct. Md. 1977, U.S. Ct. Appeals (4th cir.) 1977. Asst. state's atty. State's Atty.'s Office Montgomery County, Md., 1973-79; ptnr. Sachs, Greenebaum & Tayler, Washington, 1979-80; judge Dist. Ct. Md., Rockville, 1980-82, Cir. Ct. for Montgomery County, Md., 1982-94, Md. Ct. of Appeals, 1994—. Adj. prof. Washington Coll. Law, Am. U., 1980—; mem. faculty Md. Jud. Inst., Nat. Criminal Def. Inst., 1980, 81, 82; mem. legis. com. Md. Jud. Conf., mem. exec. com., 1985-89, mem. commn. to study bail bond and surety industry in Md.; mem. spl. com. to revise article 27 on crimes and punishment State of Md., 1991—; mem. inquiry com. atty. Grievance Commn. Md., 1978-81; chair jud. compensation com. Md. Jud. Conf., 1997—. Treas., v.p. West Bradley Citizens Assn., 1964-68; mem. adv. com. to county exec. on child abuse Montgomery County, 1976-77, mem. adv. com. to county exec. on battered spouses, 1977-78, mem. adv. com. on environ. protection, 1980; mem. citizens adv. bd. Montgomery County Crisis Ctr., 1980. Recipient Robert C. Heeney award Md. State Bar Assn., 1993, Dorothy Beatty Meml. award Women's Law Ctr., 1994, Rita Davidson award Women's Bar Md., 1995, Margaret Brent Trailblazers award ABA Commn. on Women in the Profession/Women's Bar Assn. Md., 1995, Elizabeth Dole Woman of Achievement award ARC, 1998, Leadership in Law award The Daily Record, 2001, Nat. Assn. Social Workers' Pub. Citizen of Yr. award, 2001, others; named of Md.'s Top 100 Women Warfield's Bus. Record, 1997, 99, 2001. Fellow Md. Bar Found.; mem. ABA (chair criminal justice stds. com. 1995-96, mem. coun. criminal law sect. 1997—, del. nat. conf. state trial judges, active various coms.), Am. Law Rev., Md. State Bar Assn. (chair coun. criminal law and practice sect., mem. bd. govs. 1981, 82, 85, 86, 90, mem. coun. litigation sect., active coms., chair com. to draft pattern jury instrns. in civil and criminal cases 1980—), Nat. Assn. Women Judges, Internat. Acad. Trial Judges, Am. Law Inst., Montgomery County Bar Assn. (chair criminal law sect. 1978-79, mem. exec. com. 1979-80, active other coms., Outstanding Jurist award 2000), Montgomery County Bar Leaders, Women's Bar Assn. Md., Women's Bar Assn. D.C., Hadassah Women's Orgn. (life), Pioneer Women Na'amat (Celebration of Women award 1985), Pi Sigma Alpha. Office: Ct of Appeals of Md 50 Maryland Ave Rockville MD 20850-2320 *

RAKES, GANAS KAYE, retired finance and banking educator; b. Floyd, Va., May 2, 1938; s. Samuel D. and Ocie J. (Peters) R.; m. Mary Ann Simmons, Oct. 1, 1961; 1 child, Sabrina Darrow. BS, Va. Tech., 1960, MS, 1964; D of Bus. Adminstrn., Washington U., St. Louis, 1971. Assoc. prof. commerce U. Va., Charlottesville, 1968-80; O'Bleness prof. fin. and banking Ohio U., Athens, 1980—2003, chmn. fin. dept. Coll. of Bus. Adminstrn., 1983—2003, O'Bleness prof. emeritus fin., 2003—. Contbr. articles to profl. jours. Served to 1st lt. U.S. Army, 1961-63. Mem. Fin. Mgmt. Assn., Eastern Fin. Assn., Two Rivers Country Club. Republican. Episcopalian. Avocations: golf, sailing. E-mail: rakes1@verizon.net.

RAKHNO, IGOR, physicist; s. Leonid and Elena Rakhno; m. Olga Kopeliovich, Nov. 24, 1984; 1 child, Eugenia. MS in Physics, Belarusian State U., Minsk, Belarus, 1981; postgrad. in nuc. engring., Nuc. Power Engring. Inst., Minsk, 1988. PhD Diploma Supreme Exam. Bd., Moscow, 1991. Jr. scientist Nuc. Power Engring. Inst., Minsk, 1981—91; scientist Radiation Physics and Chemistry Problems Inst., Minsk, 1991—93, sr. scientist, 1993—2000; rsch. assoc. Fermi Nat. Accelerator Lab., Batavia, Ill., 2000—03, guest scientist, 2004—; rsch. assoc. U. Ill., Urbana-Champaign, 2003—04. Fellow, Matsumae Internat. Found., Tokyo, 1994. Achievements include research in theoretical and experimental research on nuclear waste transmutation with low-energy neutrons and high-energy hadrons; theoretical research on radiation environment in high-luminosity regions in the Large Hadron Collider to be built at CERN (Geneva, Switzerland) to study proton-proton collisions at 14 TeV. Office: Fermi National Accelerator Lab MS 220 PO Box 500 Batavia IL 60510-0500 Home Phone: 630-978-1281; Office Phone: 630-840-6763. Office Fax: 630-840-6039. Business E-Mail: rakhno@fnal.gov.

RAKITA, LOUIS, retired cardiologist; b. Montreal, Que., Can., July 2, 1922; came to U.S., 1951, naturalized, 1962; s. S. and Rose (Weinman) R.; m. G. Blanche Michlin, Dec. 4, 1945; 1 son, Robert M. BA, Sir George Williams Coll., Montreal, 1942; MD, C.M., McGill U., 1949. Diplomate: Am. Bd. Internal Medicine. Intern Montreal Gen. Hosp., 1949-50; resident in medicine Jewish Gen. Hosp., Montreal, 1950-51; fellow in medicine Alton Ochsner Med. Found., New Orleans, 1951-52; chief resident in medicine Cleve. City Hosp., 1952-53, Am. Heart Assn. fellow, 1954-55, Inst. for Med. Research, Cedars of Lebanon Hosp., Los Angeles, 1953-54; practice medicine specializing in internal medicine and cardiology Cleve., 1954—2005; instr. medicine Western Res. U., Cleve., 1954-55, sr. instr., 1955-57, asst. prof., 1957-61, asso. prof., 1961-71; asst. vis. physician Cleve. City Hosp., 1954-57, vis. physician, 1957—; advanced fellow Cleve. Met. Gen. Hosp., 1959-61, dir. cardiology, 1966-87, immediate past dir., div. cardiology, 1987—2005; assoc. div. of research in med. edn. Case Western Res. U., Cleve., 1969-75, prof. medicine, 1971-93, prof. emeritus medicine, 1993; ret., 2005. Chmn. Phase IIA Cardiovascular com. Case Western Res. U., 1965-70, Faculty Senate Subcom. for Devel. and Evaluation of Ednl. Methods, 1969, chmn. Univ. Com. on Ednl. Planning, 1971-73, Faculty Coun. Sch. Medicine, 1979-80, Faculty Coun., chmn. Steering Com. Sch. Medicine, 1979-80, mem. bd. trustees Com. on Univ. Plans, 1971-73, Faculty Senate, Exec. Coun.; cons. in cardiology Luth. Med. Ctr., Cleve., 1970—, Crile VA Hosp., Cleve., 1969—; vis. cardiologist Sunny Acres Hosp., Cleve., 1973—; cardiologist rep. of del. to USSR, 1973. Author: (with M. Broder) Cardiac Arrhythmias, 1970, (with M. Kaplan) Immunological Diseases, 1972; Contbr. (with M. Kaplan) articles on cardiovascular diseases to profl. publs. Served with RCAF, 1942-45. Recipient Research Career Devel. award USPHS, 1962-69, Saltzman award Mt. Sinai Med. Health Found., 1997. Fellow ACP (Laureate award Ohio chpt. 1992), Am. Coll. Cardiology, Royal Coll. Physicians and Surgeons Can. (cert.), Am. Heart Assn. (mem. exec. com. N.E. Ohio chpt. 1972—, trustee 1969—, pres. N.E. Ohio chpt. 1972-74, coun. on clin. cardiology 1972—, chmn. various coms., v.p. North Ctrl. Region 1985-86, bd. dirs. 1985-86, hon. life trustee Northeast Ohio affiliate, vice chmn. task force on product licensing feasibility 1987—, Award of Merit 1987, Gold Heart award 1989); mem. AAUP, Am. Fedn. Clin. Rsch., Ctrl. Soc. Clin. Rsch., Soc. Exptl. Biology and Medicine, Cleve. Med. Libr. Assn. (trustee 1972—), Nat. Bd. Med. Examiners, The Press of Case Western Res. U. (adv. com. 1970), Nat. Heart and Lung Inst., Nat. Insts. Health (left ventricular assist device clin. trial program divsn. extramural affairs, data rev. bd. 1981—, adv. com. med. devices applications program 1971-75), Sigma Xi. Home: 24151 S Woodland Rd Cleveland OH 44122-3315 Personal E-mail: lrakita@earthlink.net.

RAKO, SUSAN, psychiatrist, writer; b. Springfield, Mass., Sept. 4, 1939; d. Robert and Ann (Melnikoff) Mandell; 1 child, Jennifer Sarah. Student, Wellesley Coll., 1957-60; BS, U. Cin., 1961; MS in Film, Boston U., 1988; MD, Albert Einstein Coll. Medicine, 1966. Med. rsch. asst. neuroendocrinology Worcester Found. Exptl. Biology, Shrewsbury, Mass., 1959; med. rsch. asst. May Inst., Cin., 1961-62; intern in medicine, surgery Mt. Auburn Hosp., Cambridge, Mass., 1966-67; resident in adult psychiatry Mass. Mental Health Ctr., Boston, 1967-69; tchg. fellow in psychiatry Harvard Med. Sch., Boston, 1967-69, clin. fellow in psychiatry, 1969-70; pvt. practice Newton, Mass., 1970—; clin. instr. psychiatry Harvard Med. Sch., Boston, 1970-75; resident in child and adult psychiatry Beth Israel Hosp., Boston, 1969-70; psychiatrist Mass. Mental Health Ctr., Boston, 1970-77, Newton-Wellesley Hosp., 1982. Cons. Cutler Counseling Ctr., Norwood, Mass., 1983, VA Hosp., San Juan, 1990—94; founder, pres. Women's Health on Alert, Inc., 2003—; spkr. in field. Author: No More Periods? The Risks of Menstrual Suppression, 2003, The Hormone of Desire: The Truth About Testosterone, Sexuality, and Menopause, 1996, 2d edit., 1999, That's How the Light Gets In: Memoir of a Psychiatrist, 2005, The Blessings of the Curse, 2006; co-editor: Semrad: The Heart of a Therapist, 1980, (paperback) 2004; film maker Susan and Jenni, 1987; exec. prodr. play Hysterics, 2005. Business E-Mail: susanrako@aol.com.

RAKOFF, JED SAUL, federal judge, author; b. Phila., Aug. 1, 1943; s. Abraham Edward and Doris Tobiah (Michell) R.; m. Ann Rosenberg, Aug. 4, 1974; children: Jena Lynn, Elana Beth, Keira Jan. BA, Swarthmore Coll., 1964, LLD (hon.), 2003; MPhil, Balliol Coll., Oxford U., Eng., 1966; JD, Harvard U., 1969; LLD (hon.), St. Francis U., 2005. Bar: N.Y. 1971, D.C. 1983, U.S. Supreme Ct. 1986. Law clk. U.S. Ct. Appeals (3rd cir.), Phila., 1969-70; assoc. Debevoise, Plimpton, Lyons & Gates, NYC, 1970-73; asst. U.S. atty. So. Dist. N.Y., NYC, 1973-80, chief bus. and securities fraud prosecutions U.S. Atty.'s Office, 1978-80; ptnr. Mudge Rose Guthrie Alexander & Ferdon, NYC, 1980-90, Fried Frank Harris Shriver & Jacobson, NYC, 1990-96; judge U.S. Dist. Ct. (So. Dist.), 1996—. Lectr. in law Columbia Law Sch., 1988-; mem. bd. mgrs. Swarthmore Coll., 2003—; mem. governing bd. project law and neuroscience MacArthur Found., 2007—. Author: (with S. Arkin et al) Business Crime, 6 vols., 1982, Criminal Defense Techniques, 6 vols., 1982, (with H. Goldstein) RICO: Civil and Criminal Law and Strategy, 1989, (with L. Blumkin and R. Sauber) Corporate Sentencing Guidelines,: Compliance and Mitigation, 1993; editor-in-chief Bus. Crimes Bull., 1994-95; columnist N.Y. Law Jour., 1985-95; contbr. numerous articles to law revs. Mem. exec. bd. N.Y. chpt. Am. Jewish Com., 1971-95. Fellow Am. Coll. Trial Lawyers (chmn. N.Y. State 1993-94), Am. Bd. Criminal Lawyers; mem. ABA, N.Y. State Bar Assn., Assn. of Bar of City of N.Y. (chmn. criminal law com. 1986-89), Fed. Bar Coun., N.Y. Coun. Def. Lawyers (dir. 1990-94). Democrat. Jewish. Office: US Courthouse 500 Pearl St Rm 1340 New York NY 10007-1316 Office Phone: 212-805-0401. Business E-Mail: Jed_S_Rakoff@nysd.uscourts.gov.

RAKOS, BALÁZS, physicist, researcher; b. Budapest, Hungary, Oct. 21, 1975; s. Miklós Rakos and Zsuzsanna Szendro. MS in Physics, U. Debrecen, Hungary, 2001; PhD, U. Notre Dame, 2006. Rsch. asst. U. Notre Dame, Ind., 2001—06; rschr. Inst. Isotopes, Hungarian Acad. Sci., Budapest, 2006—. Home: 76/A Szeher ut Budapest 1021 Hungary Personal E-mail: rakos@iki.kfki.hu.

RAKOTOARISOA, JEAN AIMÉ, director museum; b. Toamasina, Madagascar, Aug. 23, 1946; s. Rakotobe Joseph Zackarie and Raveloarisoa (Geneviée) R.; m. Rajaonah Victoire, Feb. 13, 1971; children: Hanta, Zefa, Jao. License es lettres, U. Madagascar, 1970, maitrise, 1971; doctorat de Géographie, U. Antananarivo, 1980; doctorat ed lettres, INALCO, Paris, 1994. Tchr. Secondary Sch., Antananarivo, 1971-72; dir. U. Museum, Antananarivo, Madagascar, 1973—. Cons. UNESCO, World Bank, UNDP, and others; assoc. prof. Mich. Univ. Editor: Taloha; co-organizer Madagascar, Island of Ancesters. Pers. adviser Malagasy Minister of Edn. Recipient Chevalier de l'ordre National Malagasy Govt., mem. Malagasy Acad. Social Scis. Mem. Nat. Com. Museums (pres.), Malagasy Assn. Archaelogy (sec. gen.), Indian Ocean Assn. Museums (adv.), NAS (fgn. assoc.). Roman Catholic. Avocations: tennis, classical jazz music, malagasy traditional folk songs, cartoons. Office: Univ Museum Antananarivo 101 Madagascar

RAKOW, JAY, lawyer, film company executive; AB, NYU, 1974; JD, Cornell U., 1977. Bar: Calif. 1980, DC 1980. Assoc. Dewey, Ballantine, 1977—80, Wyman, Bautzer, Christensen, Kuchel & Silbert; ptnr. Christensen, Miller, Fink, Jacobs, Glaser, Weil & Shapiro, LLP, 1988—93, 1996—2000; sr. v.p., gen. counsel Paramount Pictures Corp., 1993—96; sr. exec. v.p., gen. counsel Metro-Goldwyn-Mayer Inc., LA, 2000—05, mediator, arbitrator, 2005—. Office: 1925 Century Park East Ste 1975 Los Angeles CA 90067 Office Phone: 310-277-3669.

RAKSIN, ALEX, reporter, writer; b. Nov. 9, 1960; m. Victoria Hendrick; children: Tobias, Leonid. BA in Journalism, U. So. Calif., 1984. Columnist LA Times, 1985—93, dep. book editor, 1993—96, editl. writer, 1996—2005, sci. corr., 2005—. Freelance writer, 1984—93; instr. UCLA Ext., 1986—89; dir. Lit. awards PEN USA West, 1998—2000. Recipient Outstanding Media award for Editl. Writing, Nat. Alliance for Mentally Ill, 2001, Nat. Headliner award for Editl. Writing, Calif. Alliance for Mentally Ill, 2001, 1999, Aaron Price Child Health and Welfare Scholarship and Journalism award, 1999, Sigma Delta Chi award for editl. writing, 2002, Pulitzer prize for editl. writing, 2002, L.A. Times prize for best editl. series, 2004. Mem.: Nat. Conf. Editl. Writers, Nat. Com. Concerned Journalists, Nat. Book Critics Cir. Office: LA Times 202 W 1st St Los Angeles CA 90012

RALEIGH, CECIL BARING, geophysicist; b. Little Rock, Aug. 11, 1934; s. Cecil Baring and Lucile Nell (Stewart) R.; m. Diane Lauster, July 17, 1982; children: Alison, Marianne, Lawrence, David. BA, Pomona Coll., Calif., 1956; MA, Claremont Grad. Sch., Calif., 1958; PhD, UCLA, 1963. Fellow Research Sch. Phys. Sci., Australian Nat. U., Canberra, 1963-66; geophysicist U.S. Geol. Survey, Menlo Park, Calif., 1966-80, program mgr. for earthquake prediction research program, 1980-81; dir. Lamont-Doherty Geol. Obs. and prof. geol. scis. Columbia U., Palisades, NY, 1981-89; dean Sch. Ocean and Earth Sci. and Tech. U. Hawaii, Honolulu, 1989—2003; rschr. Hawaii Nat. Energy Inst. U. Hawaii, 2003—. CEO Ctr. for a Sustainable Future, Inc., 1996-2005, HR Biopetroleum, 2004—; mem. Gov.'s Task Force on Sci. Tech., 1996-98; mem. NAS/NRC Ocean Studies Bd.; chmn. NAS/NRC Yucca Mountain Panel. Author papers control earthquakes, rheology of the mantle, mechanics of faulting, crystal plasticity. Trustee Bishop Mus., 1997—2003. Recipient Interdisciplinary award U.S. Nat. Com. Rock Mechanics, 1969, 74; Meritorious Service award Dept. Interior, 1974; Barrows Centennial Dist. Alumnus award Pomona Coll. Fellow Am. Geophys. Union, Geol. Soc. Am. Democrat. Inventor formation fracturing method. Office: U Hawaii Sch Ocean Earth Sci & Tech Honolulu HI 96822

RALES, MITCHELL P., automotive parts company executive; b. 1956; married; 2 children. B, DePauw U.; grad., Miami U., Ohio, 1978. Ptnr. Equity Grp. Holdings, Washington, 1979—; pres. Danaher Corp., Washington, 1984—, bd. dirs., chmn. exec. com., 1990—; founder, dir. Colfax Corp., 1995—. Chmn. Capital Campaign for Hosp. Sick Children; treas., trustee, chmn. Capital Campaign of Norwood Sch.; mem. adv. coun. Miami U., Ohio; bd. trustees Hirshorn Mus. and Sculpture Garden; mem. trustees coun. Nat. Gallery Art. Named one of Top 200 Collectors, ARTnews mag., 2003—06, Forbes' Richest Americans, 2006. Avocation: Collector of Modern and Contemporary Art. Office: Danaher Corpn 2099 Pennsylvania Ave NW 12th Fl Washington DC 20006-6800 *

RALES, STEVEN M., automotive parts company executive; b. Pitts., Mar. 31, 1951; m. Christine Plank Rales (div. 2002). BA, DePauw U., 1973; JD, America U., 1978. Ptnr. Equity Grp. Holdings, Washington, 1979—; chmn., CEO Danaher Corp., Washington, 1984—2001, chmn., 2001—. Named one of Top 200 Collectors, ARTnews mag., 2003—06, Forbes' Richest Americans, 2006. Avocation: Collector of Impressionism, Modern and Contemporary Art. Office: Danaher Corpn 2099 Pennsylvania Ave NW 12th Fl Washington DC 20006 *

RALEY, BENNETT WILLIAM, former federal agency administrator; b. 1956; BS in Agrl. Bus., Colo. State U., 1979, JD, 1983. Assoc. Davis, Graham & Stubbs, Denver, 1983, ptnr., 1990; shareholder Trout & Raley, P.C. (formerly known as Hobbs, Trout & Raley, P.C.), 1992—2001; gen. counsel No. Colo. Water Conservancy Dist.; spl. asst. atty. gen. State of N.Mex., 1998—2001; asst. sec. water and sci. US Dept. Interior, Washington, 2001—04. Staff counsel US Senator Hank Brown (Rep.-Colo.), 1991—92; chief counsel US Senate Judiciary Subcom. on Constn., Federalism and Property Rights, 1995; co-chair Fed. Water Rights Task Force.

RALEY, JOHN WESLEY, JR., lawyer; b. May 23, 1932; s. John Wesley and Helen Thames; children: John Wesley III, Robert Thames. AB, Okla. Baptist U., 1954; JD, U. Okla., 1959. Bar: Okla. 1959, U.S. Supreme Ct. 1973, U.S. Ct. Appeals (10th cir.), 1962, U.S. Dist. Ct. (we. dist.) Okla. 1961, U.S. Dist. Ct. (no. dist.) Okla. 1988, U.S. Dist. Ct. (ea. dist.) Okla. 1989. Asst. U.S. atty. We. Dist. Okla. U.S. Dept. Justice, 1961-69; ptnr. Northcutt, Raley, Clark and Gardner, Ponca City, Okla., 1969-90; U.S. atty. Ea. Dist. Okla. U.S. Dept. Justice, 1990-97; of counsel Northcutt, Clark, Gardner & Hron, Ponca City, 1997—; mcpl. ct. judge Ponca City, 2001—05. Mayor of Ponca City, Okla., 1980-83; mem. Okla. Ethics Commn., 2002—, chmn., 2005-06. Capt. USNR, 1950-84, ret. Recipient George Washington Honor medal Freedoms Found. at Valley Forge, 1971, Spl. Initiative award U.S. Dept. Justice, 1994, Outstanding Alumni Achievement award Okla. Bapt. U., 1981, Outstanding Citizen award Ponca City, 1984. Fellow Am. Coll. Trial Lawyers; mem. ABA, Am. Bd. Trial Advs. (pres. Okla. chpt. 2005), Okla. Bar Assn. (bd. govs. 1988-90), Kay County Bar Assn. (pres. 1980), Am. Legion, Masons, Res. Officers Assn., Naval Res. Assn., VFW. Republican. Southern Baptist. Office: 400 E Central Ave Ste 401 Ponca City OK 74601-5428 Address: PO Box 1412 Ponca City OK 74602-1412 Office Phone: 580-762-1655.

RALEY, JOHN WESLEY, III, lawyer; b. Oklahoma City, Oct. 19, 1959; s. John Wesley Raley Jr. and Mary Lane Mallett; m. Kelly Elaine Williams, Sept. 22, 1984; children: Katherine Elise, William Thomas, James Wesley. BA summa cum laude, U. Okla., 1981, JD, 1984; LLM, U. Aberdeen, Scotland, 1988. Bar: Tex. 1985, U.S. Dist. Ct. (so. dist.) Tex. 1985, U.S. Ct. Appeals (5th cir.) 1985; bd. cert. personal injury trial law Tex. Bd. Legal Specialization. With Fulbright & Jaworski, LLP, Houston, 1985-96, ptnr., 1996-2000; shareholder, mng. ptnr. Cooper & Scully, P.C., Houston, 2001—. Lectr. civil litigation U. Houston CLE, 1995—; bd. dirs. Houston Pub. TV, on-air spokesman, 1996—. Vol. Habitat for Humanity, Houston, 1998. Fellow Tex. Bar Found. (life); mem. ABA, State Bar Tex., Houston Bar Assn. (interdisciplinary ednl. alliance, spkrs. bur.), U. Okla. Varsity O Club, Phi Beta Kappa. Avocations: basketball, golf, tennis, local amateur drama performances. Home: 1 Stayton Cir Houston TX 77024 Office: 700 Louisiana St Ste 3850 Houston TX 77002 Office Phone: 713-236-6800. E-mail: john.raley@coopersally.com.

RALEY, KELLI B., forensic specialist; d. Ronald and Barbara Langley; m. Stewart Raley; 1 child, Elizabeth. BS in Biomedical Sci., Western Mich. U., Kalamazoo, 1993; MS in Forensic Sci., U. Ala., Birmingham, 1997. Criminalist IV Office Chief Med. Examiner, NYC, 1997—2003; forensic scientist III North La. Criminalistics Lab, Shreveport, 2003—. Mem.: Am. Acad. Forensic Scis. Achievements include research in use of laser microdissection as a means to expedite forensic sexual assault casework. Office: N La Criminalistics Lab 1115 Brooks St Shreveport LA 71101 Home Phone: 318-865-3082; Office Phone: 318-227-2889. Office Fax: 318-227-9013. Business E-Mail: kraley@nlcl.org.

RALL, PRISCILLA, artist, educator; b. NYC, Nov. 15, 1950; d. Joseph Edward Rall and Caroline Ruth Domm; m. Donald Lee Smith (div.); children: Caroline E. Smith, Amanda M. Smith; m. Richard Harvey Stambaugh, July 7, 2002. AA, Cornell U., Ithaca, NY, 1970; BA, Hood Coll., Frederick, Md., 1994; MLA, McDaniels Coll., Westminster, Md., 2003. Bot. illustrator Smithsonian Inst., Washington, 1968; cabinetmaker MRK Woodworking, Newark, 1971—73; cabinetmaker, designer Ridgeville, Ohio, 1973—76, Credgerstown, Md., 1977—94; art tchr. Hagerstown, Md., 1994—2003; pvt. art tchr. Rocky Ridge, Md., 2003—. Presenter P. Buckley Mass. Found., 1999—2002. Vol. PTA Thurmont Schs., Md., 1984—2001; vol. Catoctin Sports Assn., 1985—98; pres. PTA Catoctin HS, Thurmont, 1995—97; vol., chmn. Vets. History Project, Frederick, Md., 2004—. Democrat. Avocation: genealogy. Home: 9901 Longs Mill Rd Rocky Ridge MD 21778

RALLI, CONSTANTINE PANDIA, lawyer; b. Bronxville, NY, Apr. 6, 1948; s. Pandia C. and Mary (Motter) R.; m. Alison Rhoads, Aug. 11, 1973; children: Pandia C., Christopher A. BA, Middlebury Coll., 1970; JD, Fordham U., 1973; LLM in Taxation, NYU, 1986. Bar: NY 1974, US Ct. Appeals (2nd cir.) 1974, US Dist. Ct. (so. and ea. dists.) NY 1975, US Tax Ct. 1977, Fla. 1985, Conn. 1985, US Dist. Ct. Conn. 1987. Assoc. Davis Polk & Wardwell, NYC, 1973-81; ptnr. Hall, McNicol, Hamilton & Clark, NYC, 1981-88, LeBoeuf, Lamb, Greene & MacRae LLP, NYC, 1988—, chmn. trust & estates dept. Sec., bd. dirs. Fairfield-Maxwell Ltd., Campo Tankers SA, NYC, 1987—95. Bd. dirs. Samaritan Counseling Ctr., Rye, NY, 1987-90, Rye Free Reading Room, 1990-93, Rye Presbyn. Ch., 1986-89. Mem. Union Club, Am. Yacht Club, Ekwanok Country Club (Manchester, Vt.). Republican. Presbyterian. Office: LeBoeuf Lamb Greene & MacRae 125 W 55th St New York NY 10019-5369 Office Phone: 212-424-8394. Office Fax: 212-424-8500. Business E-Mail: cralli@llgm.com.

RALLO, DOUGLAS, lawyer; b. Orange, NJ, Nov. 22, 1953; s. Vito and Mary (Spiduro) Rallo. BA, Montclair State U., NJ, 1975; cert., Inst. Internat. and Comparative Law, 1977; JD, John Marshall Law Sch., 1978. Bar: Ill 1979, US Dist Ct (no dist) Ill 1979, US Ct Appeals (7th cir) 1979, US Dist Ct (ea dist) Wis 1995, Wis 1998, US Dist Ct (we dist) Wis 2001. Corp. lawyer Bendix Corp., NYC, 1979-81; assoc. David T. Rallo & Assocs., Ltd., Chgo., 1981-83, Horwitz & Assocs., Ltd., Chgo., 1983-84, Semmelman & Bertucci Ltd., Lake Forest, Ill., 1984-98; pvt. practice Law Offices of Douglas Rallo, P.C., Libertyville, Ill., 1998—. Research asst A Functional Analysis of the Criminal Code Reform Act of 1978 for US Congress; panel atty Ill State Appellate Defender's Office, 1980; profiled in Newsweek mag, 1989, Chicago Tribune, 1989; tchr adult legal educ programs Libertyville High Sch, Ill., 1988—90, Mundelein High Sch, Ill., 1989; Notable cases include: Sherrod vs. Berry, 629F. Supp. 159 (1985) and 59F Supp. 433 (1984). Contbr. articles to profl jours. V.p. Lake County chpt. MADD, 1989—91; mem. Libertyville Youth Commn., 1990—94; bd. dirs. Civic Ctr. Found., Libertyville. Mem.: Vernon Hills, Mundelein and Libertyville C. of C., Lake County Bar Assn., State Bar Wis., Ill. Trial Lawyers Assn., Ill. State Bar Assn. (lectr hedonic damages, civil practice procedure, sem expert witnesses 1989), Pi Sigma Alpha. Avocations: water sports, swimming, softball. Office: Law Offices Douglas Rallo P C 611 S Milwaukee Ave Libertyville IL 60048-3256

RALLO, HARRY, architectural firm executive; b. NYC, Sept. 28, 1951; s. Angelo and Rose Rallo; m. Bridgette Louise Bruno, May 5, 1979; 1 child, Matthew Henry. Student, CUNY, 1968-69; BS in Architecture, CCNY, 1973, BArch, 1977; student, Palm Beach Armory Art Ctr., 1994-97; studied under Douglas Ferrin, West Palm Beach, Fla., 1997-98. Registered arch., N.Y., Conn., Fla. Project engr. Turner Constrn. Co., NYC, 1973-87; prin. Harry Rallo, Arch., Deerfield Beach, Fla., 1987—2003. Editl. cartoonist Observer, North Broward, weekly newspaper, Deerfield Beach, 1993—2000. One-man shows include Cultural Arts Com., Lighthouse Point, Fla., 1995, Cultural Com., Deerfield Beach, 1995, Meml. Hosp., Hallandale, Fla., 1997, Norfolk Artisan's Guild, Conn, 2002, Falls Village Hunt Libr., Conn., 2005; group show at Cooley Gallery, Old Lyme, Conn., 2006; commns. include Wellington Forum, Fla., 1995, Ft. Lauderdale St. Patrick's Day Com., 1995, Roman Cath. Archdiocese, Miami, Fla., 1996, Fla. Urban Forestry Coun., 1995; exhbns. include (mural) Historic Stranahan House, Ft. Lauderdale, 2001; featured in Art Bus. News, 2006; contbr. articles to various publs. Recipient 4th pl., Palm Beach Soc. Four Arts. E-mail: BLRallo@aol.com.

RALLO, JAMES GILBERT, management company executive; b. Balt., Mar. 1, 1942; s. James Vincent and Thelma Mary (Hannahs) R.; m. Frances Elaine Petro, June 13, 1965; children: James Michael, Robert Francis. BS, U. Md., 1965; postgrad., George Washington U., 1967—. Mktg. trainee Chessie Sys., Balt., 1965—66; market analyst Bendix Corp., Balt., 1966—68, contract adminstr. NYC, 1968—70; account exec. Peterson, Howell & Heather, Inc. (name changed to PHH Arval) PHH Vehicle Mgmt. Svcs., Hunt Valley, Md., 1970—75; regional mgr. Peterson, Howell & Heather, Inc., Hunt Valley, 1975—80, v.p. sales, 1980—83, v.p. sales and client rels., 1983—87, sr. v.p. sales and client rels., 1987—91, sr. v.p. client and industry rels., 1991—94, v.p. industry rels., 1994—2003, v.p. strategic partnership, 2003—. Bd. dirs., mem. fin. com. Towson YMCA, Md., 1981-93, mem. fundraising com., mem. budget com.; coach Cockeysville-Springlake Recreation Coun., 1973-82; advisor Jr. Achievement, 1975-76; fund solicitor United Way, 1983-84; v.p. NAFA Found., 1995—. Mem.: Balt. County C. of C. (legis. com. mem.), Am. Automotive Leasing Assn. (sponsor Industry Standards project), Automotive Fleet and Leasing Assn. (dir. lessors 1993—95, conf. com. 1993—2001, v.p. 1999—2000, exec. v.p. 2000—01, pres. 2001—02, bd. dirs., ednl. com.), Nat. Assn. Fleet Adminstrs. (affiliate chmn. intercounty chpt. 1978—80, nat. affiliate com. 1990—2000, editl. com. 1992—96, mem. conf./program com. 1993—98, bd. govs. 1993—, chmn. affiliates com. 1995—97, co-chair edn. com. 1999—2001, affiliate trustee 2000—03, bd. trustees 2001—03, Hon. award for disting. svc. 1997), Optimists Club (v.p. Springdale-Cockeysville 1982—84, chmn. fundraising com.). Avocations: skiing, sports, classic cars, reading, golf. Office: PHH Arval 940 Ridgebrook Rd Sparks MD 21152 Office Phone: 410-771-2371. Business E-Mail: jim.rallo@phh.com.

RALPH, DAMANI, professional soccer player; b. Kingston, Jamaica, Nov. 6, 1980; Attended, Merdian Cmty. Coll., Miss., 1999—2001, U. Conn., 2001—03. Forward, men's soccer Meridian Cmty. Coll., 1999—2001, U, Conn., 2001—03; forward DC United Major League Soccer, Washington, 2004—. Named MVP, Nat. Junior Coll. Athletic Assn. Tournament, 2000, Offensive Player of Yr., Big East, 2002; named to First Team, Big East, 2002; recipient Finalist, Hermann Trophy, MO Athletic Commn., 2002. Achievements include team leader in goals scored (10) and points (26) for men's soccer at the U. Conn. in 2001. Office: Soldier Stadium 425 E McFetridge Dr Chicago IL 60605

RALPH, DAVID CLINTON, communications educator; b. Muskogee, Okla., Jan. 12, 1922; s. Earl Clinton and Rea Jane (Potter) R.; m. Kathryn Juanita Wicklund, Nov. 29, 1947; children: David Randall, Steven Wicklund. AA, Muskogee Jr. Coll., 1941; BS in Theatre, Northwestern U., 1947, MA in Theatre, 1948, PhD in Speech, 1953. Lectr. Ind. U., Hammond, 1947-48; instr. speech U. Mo., Columbia, 1948-53; tchr. debate-forensics summer program for high sch. students Northwestern U., Evanston, Ill., 1949-51; asst. prof. speech Mich. State U., East Lansing, 1953-57, assoc. prof., 1957-64, prof. speech and theatre, 1964-68, prof. communication, 1968-94, prof. emeritus, 1994—, dir. comm. undergrad. program, 1968-88. Cons. in field. Co-author: Group Discussion, 1954, 2d edit., 1956, Principles of Speaking, 1962, 3d edit., 1975; contbr. articles to profl. jours., chpts. to books. Coach Jr. League Boys' Baseball, Lansing, Mich., 1958-74; mem. civilian aux. to Lansing Fire Dept., 1987—. Lt. USNR, 1942-46, PTO, ETO. Named Hon. State Farmer, Future Farmers Am., 1965; recipient Community Svc. award Mich. State U. Sr. Class Coun., 1979, Outstanding Faculty award, 1987, 91; Teaching Excellence award State of Mich., 1990. Mem. AAUP, Nat. Communication Assn., Cen. States Communication Assn., Golden Key (hon., faculty advisor), Omicron Delta Kappa. Democrat. Methodist. Avocation: model trains and fire engines. Office: Mich State U Dept Communication East Lansing MI 48824

RALPH, NANCYJO, retired music educator; d. Alfred M. and Phyllis L. Niles; m. Dwight G. Ralph, Mar. 28, 1970; children: Victoria L. Fortna, Erik C. MusB in Edn., Grove City Coll., Pa., 1969; M in Elem. Edn., Edinboro U. Pa., 1974; postgrad. in Music Edn., Kent State U., Ohio, 1989. Registered music educator. Elem. music tchr. Lakeview Sch. Dist., Sandy Lake, Pa., 1969; h.s. music tchr. Cambridge Springs H.S., Penncrest Sch. Dist., Pa., 1970—2000, elem. music tchr., 2000—05; pvt. piano tchr. Vol. music tchr. Cornerstone Day Care and Penncrest Day Care Ctrs., Penncrest Day Care; with Tool City Bell Ringers, 2005—. Choir mem., pianist, various com. Saegertown (Pa.) United Meth. Ch., 1970—; dir. Justified By Faith, Saegertown, 2002—. Named to Nat. Honor Roll for Am. Outstanding Tchrs., 2005—06. Mem.: Pa. Music Educators Assn. (curriculum and instrn. chair dist. 2 1993—2003), Pa. State Edn. Assn. (alt. profl. rights and responsibilities commn. 2001—05), Penncrest Area Edn. Assn. (assoc.; v.p. 1982—84, negotiator 1982—86, pres. 1984—86, negotiator 2000—01, v.p. 2001—02, pres. 2001—03), Tool City Ringers. Methodist. Avocations: music, reading, painting. Home: 17768 Grange Center Rd Saegertown PA 16433-4506 Personal E-mail: schoolmarm@zoominternet.net.

RALPH, ROBERT ALAN, ophthalmologist, educator; b. New Haven, Jan. 29, 1941; s. Joseph S. and Elsie S. Ralph; m. Jan Eden; children: Alison, Stephanie. AB, Harvard U., Cambridge, Mass., 1961; MD, Tufts U., Boston, 1965. Diplomate Am. Bd. Ophthalmology. Intern, then resident in surgery Yale Med. Ctr., New Haven, 1965—67; clin. assoc. Nat. Cancer Inst., Bethesda, Md., 1967—69; resident in ophthalmology Georgetown U., Washington, 1969—72, clin. prof. ophthalmology, 1995—; fellow in cornea rsch. Mass. Eye and Ear Infirmary, Boston, 1972—74; pvt. practice ophthalmology Washington and Rockville, Md., 1974—; asst. prof. ophthalmology Wilmer Eye Inst., Johns Hopkins U., Balt., 1995—. With USPHS, 1967—69. Fellow: ACS, Am. Acad. Ophthalmology; mem.: Photographic Soc. Am., Cosmos Club. Avocations: photography, art, creative writing. Home: 11400 Grundy Ct Potomac MD 20854 Office: 6212 Montrose Rd Rockville MD 20852

RALSTON, ANTHONY, computer scientist, mathematician, educator; b. NYC, Dec. 24, 1930; s. Alfred Joseph and Ruth (Bien) R.; m. Jayne Madeleine Rosenthal, Feb. 14, 1958; children: Jonathan, Geoffrey, Steven, Elizabeth. BS, MIT, 1952, PhD, 1956. Mem. tech. staff Bell Tel. Labs., 1956-59; lectr. U. Leeds, 1959-60; mgr. tech. computing Am. Cyanamid Co., 1960-61; assoc. prof. math. Stevens Inst. Tech., 1961-64, prof., 1964-65; dir. computer svcs. SUNY, Buffalo, 1965-70, prof., 1965-95, chmn. dept. computer sci., 1967-80, prof. emeritus, 1995—. Bd. examiners Grad. Record Exam in Computer Sci., 1976-82; mem. computer sci. and tech. bd. NRC, 1976-79, math. sci. edn. bd., 1985-89; acad. visitor Imperial Coll., London, 1995-2003. Author: A First Course in Numerical Analysis, 1965, 2d edit., 1978, Introduction to Programming and Computer Science, 1971, Discrete Algorithmic Mathematics, 1991, 3d edit., 2004, Algorithms, 1997; editor: Ency. of Computer Science, 1976, 2d edit., 1982, 3d edit., 1992, 4th edit., 2000, concise edit., 2004, ABACUS, 1983-88; co-editor: Mathematical Methods for Digital Computers, Vol. 1, 1960, Vol. 2, 1967, Vol. 3, 1977, The Influence of Computers and Informatics in Mathematics and Its Teaching, 1993. 2d lt. U.S. Army, 1957. Fellow AAAS, Royal Soc. of Arts, Assn. Computing Machinery (pres. 1972-74, mem. coun. 1968-76, Disting. Svc. award 1982); mem. Math. Assn. Am. (bd. govs. 1984-87), Am. Fedn. Info. Processing Soc. (pres. 1975-76), Com. Concerned Scientists (bd. dirs.). Home: Flat 4 58 Prince Consort Rd London SW7 2BA England Home Phone: 44-20-75892195; Office Phone: 44-20-75892195. E-mail: ar9@doc.ic.ac.uk.

RALSTON, BARBARA JO, bank executive; b. Youngstown, Ohio, Apr. 11, 1940; d. Fred Kenneth and Juanita Ruth (Welch) Roof; m. Donald Gene Ralston, Jan. 9, 1960; children: Mark David, Lori Sue. Cert., Pacific Coast Banking Sch. U. Wash., Seattle, 1981; AA in fin., Maricopa County CC. Sec. Bank of Scottsdale, Ariz., 1962-66; adminstrv. asst. Talley Industries, Mesa, Ariz., 1966-73; asst. mgr. Continental Bank, Phoenix, 1973-77; exec. v.p. Continental Bank Service Corp., Phoenix, 1977-85, pres., dir., 1985—86; chmn., pres. to sr. v.p. electronic and convenience banking to exec. v.p. personal banking group Chase Bank of Ariz., exec. v.p., COO; exec. v.p., mgr. northeast Ariz. retail area First Interstate Bank, 1994—95, Phoenix area pres., 1995—96; sr. v.p., mgr. in-store banking Wells Fargo Bank, Ariz., 1996—97; founder, pres., CEO Camelback Cmty. Bank, Phoenix, 1998—. Pres. Ariz. Bus. Leadership. Bd. dirs. Valley Big Bros.-Big Sisters, Phoenix, 1986; mem. Ariz. Acad., Phoenix, 1984; treas. Phoenix Together Town Hall, 1986; chair Am. West Airlines Edn. Found.; immediate past chair, Fresh State Women's Found.; past chair Ariz. Town Hall; past internat. pres. Financial Women Internat. Recipient You Too Can Make A Difference award Valley Christian Ctrs., Phoenix, 1985. Mem. Nat. Assn. Bank Women (state pres. 1981-82), Am. Inst. Banking (state edn. chmn. Ariz. chpt. 1984), Tumbleweed (pres. 1983); Am. Bankers Assn. (state membership chair for Ariz., chair ABA Edn. Found, 2003-), Ariz Bankers Assn. (bd. dirs., 2001-03, pres., 2001-02. Lodges: Soroptimists (pres. 1982, Women Helping Women award 1984). Republican. Methodist. Avocations: reading, travel, sewing. Office: Camelback Cmty Bank 2777 E Camelback Rd Ste 100 Phoenix AZ 85016

RALSTON, JOANNE SMOOT, public relations executive; b. Phoenix, May 13, 1939; d. A. Glen and Viriginia (Lee) Smoot; m. W. Hamilton Weigelt, Aug. 15, 1991 (dec.). BA in Journalism, Ariz. State U., 1960. Reporter The Ariz. Rep., Phoenix, 1960-62; co-owner, pub. rels. dir. The Patton Agy., Phoenix, 1962-71; founder, pres., owner Joanne Ralston & Assocs., Inc., Phoenix, 1971-87, 92—. Pres. Nelson Ralston Robb Comm., Phoenix, 1987—91, Joanne Ralston & Assocs., Inc., Scottsdale, 1991—, Kapaau, Hawaii, 2000—. Contbr. articles to profl. jours. Bd. dirs. Ariz. Parklands Found., 1984-86, Gov.'s Coun. on Health, Phys. Fitness and Sports, 1984-86; mem. task force Water and Natural Resources Coun., Phoenix, 1984-86; mem. Hawaii Gov.'s Adv. Bd., 2003-05, Hawaii Gov.'s Coun. Advisors, 2005—, others. Recipient Lulu awards (36) L.A. Advt. Women, 1964—, Gold Quill (2) Internat. Assn. Bus. Communicators, Excellence awards Fin. World mag., 1982-93, others; named to Walter Cronkite Sch. Journalism Hall of Fame, Coll. Pub. Programs Ariz. State U., 1987; named one of 25 Most Influential Arizonians, Phoenix Mag., 1991. Mem. Pub. Rels. Soc. Am. (counselor sect.), Internat. Assn. Bus. Communicators, Phoenix Press Club (pres. bd.), Investor Rels. Inst., Phoenix Met. C. of C. (bd. dirs. 1977-84, 85-91), Rotary Internat. Republican. Avocations: horses, dog training. Address: PO Box 808 Kapaau HI 96755-0808 Office Phone: 808-889-6433. Personal E-mail: joanne-ralston@juno.com.

RALSTON, JOSEPH W., retired military officer; b. Hopkinsville, Ky., Nov. 4, 1943; m. Diane Dougherty; children: Christopher, Paige, David, Sarah. BA in Chemistry, Miami U., Ohio, 1965; MA in Pers. Mgmt., Ctrl. Mich. U., 1976; student, Army Command and Gen. Staff Coll., Ft. Leavenworth, Kans., 1975—76, Nat. War Coll., Ft. McNair, Wash. DC, 1983—84, Harvard U., 1989. Commd. 2d lt. res. officer tng. corps. program USAF, 1965, advanced through grades to gen., 1995, ret., 2003, student pilot training Laughlin AFB, Tex., 1965—66, student, F-105 combat crew training sch. Nellis AFB, Nev., 1966—67, F-105 combat crew mem. 67th Tactical Fighter Squadron later 12th Tactical Fighter Squadron Kadena AFB, Japan, 1967—69, student, F-105 combat crew training sch. Nellis AFB, Nev., 1969, F-105 Wild Weasel instr. pilot 66th Fighter Weapons Squadron, 1970—71, F-105 Wild Weasel pilot, 354th Tactical Fighter Takhli Royal Thai AFB, Thailand, 1970, fighter requirements officer & project officer for F-15 & lightweight fighter programs, Office of the Dep. Chief of Staff for requirements Langley AFB, 1971—73, asst. ops. officer, 335th Tactical Fighter Squadron, the chief Standardization & Evaluation, 4th Tactical Fighter Wing Seymour Johnson AFB, NC, 1973—75, tactical fighter requirements officer, Office of the Dep. Chief of Staff for Rsch. & Devel. Washington, 1976—79, ops. officer later comdr. 68th Tactical fighter Squadron Moody AFB, Ga., 1979—80, spl. asst. later exec. officer to the comdr. Hdqs. Tactical Air Command Langley AFB, 1980—83, spl. asst. for low observables tech., Office of Dep. Chief of Staff for Rsch., Devel., & Acquisition Washington, 1984—86, comdr., 56th tactical training wing MacDill AFB, Fla., 1986—87, asst. dep. chief of staff for ops., later dep. chief of staff for requirements, Hdqs. Tactical Air Command Langley AFB, Va., 1987—90, dir. tactical programs Office of the Asst. Sec. for acquisition Washington, 1990—91, dir. operational requirements, Office of the Dep. Chief of Staff for plans & ops., 1991—92, comdr. Alaskan Command, Alaskan N. Am. Aerospace Def. Command Region, 11th Air Force & Joint Task Force Elmendorff AFB, Alaska, 1992—94, dep. chief of staff plans & ops., 1994—95, comdr., Hdqs. Air Combat Command Langley AFB, Va., 1995—96; vice chmn. Joint Chiefs of Staff The Pentagon, Washington, 1996—2000; comdr. US European Command (USEUCOM), Mons, Belgium, 2000—03; supreme allied comdr. NATO, Europe (SACEUR), Brussels, 2000—03; vice chmn. The Cohen Group, Washington, 2003—; spl. envoy for Countering the Kurdistan Worker's Party (PKK) US Dept. State, 2006—. Bd. dirs. Lockheed Martin Corp., 2003—, The Timken Co., 2003—, URS Corp., 2003—. Recipient Def. Disting. Svc. medal with oak leaf cluster, Disting. Svc. medal, Legion of Merit with two oak leaf cluster, Disting. Flying Cross with three oak leaf cluster, Meritorious Svc. medal with two oak leaf cluster, Air medal with 19 oak leaf cluster, Air Force Commendation medal with four oak leaf cluster Office: The Cohen Group 1200 19th St NW Ste 400 Washington DC 20036 E-mail: jralston@cohengroup.net. *

RALSTON, RONALD LEE, retired manufacturing tradesman; b. Vincennes, Ind., May 22, 1942; s. Joe Franklin and Anna Lee Ralston. Student, Purdue U., 1963—66; degree in indsl. mgmt., Ivy Tech., Indpls., 1980. Machinist Allison Aircraft & Transmission, Indpls., 1962—78; skilled tradesman Allison Transmission Plants, Indpls., 1978—2005; ret., 2005. Sgt./tank comdr. US Army, 1966—68. Mem.: Shriners, Scottish Rite, Masons. Republican. Methodist. Avocation: woodworking. Home: 1814 Inisheer Ct Indianapolis IN 46217 Personal E-mail: mrronralston@aol.com.

RALSTON, STEVEN PHILIP, portfolio manager, financial analyst; b. Trenton, NJ, Mar. 29, 1954; s. George and Edith Martha Ralston; m. Miriam Mercedes Font, July 14, 1979. BS, MIT, 1975. CFA. Account exec. Merrill, Lynch, Pierce, Fenner & Smith, Balt., 1979—80; security analyst Fidelity and Deposit Co. of Md., Balt., 1980—83; security analyst, v.p. First Nat. Bank of Md., Balt., 1983—95; dir. rsch. 1st Nat. Bank of Md., Balt., 1990—95; portfolio mgr., analyst, v.p. Gen. Accident, Phila., 1995—98; equity investment mgr., v.p. BlackRock, Phila., 1998—2003; pres. Ralston Fin. Mgmt., Glenside, Pa., 2003—. Instr. Johns Hopkins U., Balt., 1985—87. Mem. Howard County Hist. Soc., Ellicott City, Md., 1969-92; mem. Lake Falls Improvement Assn., 1984-95, treas., 1987, pres., 1988; mem. Northwoods Assn., 1995—, bd. dir. 1996-2006, pres. 2007—; mem. Springfield Twp. Hist. Soc., 1997—. Mem. CFA Inst., Balt. Security Analysts Soc. (bd. dir., v.p. 1984-89), Fin. Analysts Phila., Consumer Analysts Group N.Y. Avocation: auctions. Home: 515 Edann Rd Glenside PA 19038-1404 Office Phone: 215-887-2965. E-mail: sralston@ralstonfinancial.com.

RALSTON, SUSAN BONZON, former federal official; b. Pa., Oct. 15, 1967; d. Teotimo D. and Lagman Bonzon; m. Troy Alan Ralston. BA in English and Lit., Loyola U., Chgo.; MBA, Keller Grad. Sch. Mgmt. Office adminstr. M&J Wilkow, Ltd., Chgo.; exec. asst. to Jack Abramoff Preston Gates & Ellis, Washington; asst. dir. govtl. affairs Greenberg Traurig LLP; White House liaison to Bush-Cheney campaign; spl. asst. to Pres. George W. Bush The White House, 2001—06, exec. asst. to sr. presdl. adv. Karl Rove, 2001—06; pres. SBR Enterprises, LLC, 2006—. Mem. adv. coun. Filipino-American Rep. of Va., Inc., 2006—07. *

RAM, CHITTA VENKATA, physician; b. Machilipatnam, India, Oct. 24, 1948; s. Chitta M. Row and Chitta (Cheruvu) Sarojini; m. Ashalata Ram, Feb. 17, 1979; children: Gita, Radha. B.Sci, Marathwada U., Aurangabad,

India, 1966; MD, Osmania U., Hyderabad, India, 1972. Diplomate Am. Bd. Internal Medicine. Resident in internal medicine Brown U., R.I. Hosp., Providence, 1974-76; fellow in hypertension Hosp. U. Pa., Phila., 1976-77; faculty assoc. U. Tex. Southwestern Med. Ctr., Dallas, 1977-78, asst. prof., 1978-83, assoc. prof., 1983-89, prof. internal medicine, 1989—. Dir. Tex. Blood Pressure Inst., Dallas; dir. rsch. and edn. Dallas Nephrology Assocs.; dir. hypertension clinic Parkland Meml. Hosp., Dallas, hypertension unit St. Paul Med. Ctr., Dallas, dir. continuing med. edn. dept., 1996-98, chmn. instnl. rev. com., 1996-98, pres. med. staff, 1997-98; dir. Tex. Blood Pressure Inst., Dallas. Contbr. numerous articles to profl. jours. and chpts. to textbooks; editl. cons., reviewer numerous nat. and internat. jours. and pubs. Pres. Tex. IndoAm. Physician Soc., Dallas, 1988; trustee Dallas/Ft. Worth Hindu Temple Soc., Dallas, 1988. Named Outstanding Tchr. St. Paul Med. Ctr., 1982; recipient Mother of India award, 1992. Master ACP; fellow Am. Coll. Cardiology, Am. Coll. Chest Physicians (regent), Am. Coll. Clin. Pharmacology; mem. Am. Assn. Physicians from India (pres.-elect 1994-95, pres. 1995-96), Tex. Indo-Am. Physicians Soc. Office Phone: 214-358-2300. E-mail: ramv@dneph.com.

RAMACHANDRA, GOUTHAM K., software architect, software developer; s. K. T. and Venkatasamy Vijayalakshmi Ramachandra. M in Engring., Indian Inst. Sci., Bangalore, 1993. V.p. Goldman Sachs Japan Ltd., Tokyo, 1998—2002, Goldman Sachs and Co., NYC, 2002—. Recipient Merit cert. Outstanding Achievements, Govt. of India. Mem.: IEEE (assoc.; assoc. mem. 1993). Achievements include development of financial software. Office: Goldman Sachs and Co 85 Broad St New York NY 10004 Home Phone: 201-626-6188; Office Phone: 917-699-6384.

RAMACHANDRAN, VASAN SRINI, medical educator; b. Madras, India, Jan. 8, 1959; arrived in U.S., 1992; m. Sudha Seshadri; 1 child, Aditi. MBBS, All India Inst. Med. Sci., New Delhi, 1983; MD, All India Inst. Med. Sci., 1986, DM, 1990. Lic. physician India. Resident in internal medicine All India Inst. Med. Sci., New Delhi, 1983—86, fellow in cardiology, 1986—88; fellow in echocardiography Washington Hosp. Ctr., Washington, 1992—93; rsch. fellow in cardiology Framingham Heart Study, 1993—96; asst. prof. cardiology All India Inst. Med. Sci., 1991—92; assoc. prof. medicine Sri Chitra Tinnal Inst. Med. Sci., Trivandrum, 1996—98; clin. assoc. prof. medicine Boston U., 1998—2006, prof. medicine, 2006—. Staff cardiologist Sitaram Bhartia Inst. Med. Sci., New Delhi, 1996, All India Inst. Med. Sci., 1990—92; co-dir. echocardiography lab. Framingham Heart Study, 1998—, co-dir. fellowship program in cardiovascular epidemiology, 2001—; dir., MPH course coord. Achutha Menon Ctr. for Health Sci. Studies, Trivandrum, 1996—98; mem. K-23-K34 rev. panel study sect. NIH, NHLBI, Washington, 2000—; ad hoc reviewer Health Rsch. Bd. Iceland, 2004—, Med. Rsch. Coun. U.K., 2004—; guest editor Current Sci., 1998, Biomarkers of Congestive Heart Failure, 2005; assoc. editor Circulation, 2004; jour. reviewer Annals of Internal Medicine, 1995—, Lancet, 1995—, Jour. Hypertension, 1995—, Nat. Med. Jour. India, 1995—, Circulation, 1998—, Am. Jour. Medicine, 1998—, Am. Jour. Hypertension, 1998—, Hypertension, 1999—, New Eng. Jour. Medicine, 2002—, European Jour. Medicine, 2004—; lectr. in field. Contbr. nover 150 articles to profl. jours., chapters to books; author: Textbook of Internal Medicine, 1998, Medicine at a Glance - a companion to Textbook of Internal Medicine, 1998; contbr. abstracts. Recipient Dorabjee Tata award for excellence in biochemistry, All India Inst. Med. Sci., 1979, Inst. prize for excellence in gen. surgery, 1982, Jagdish Lal Kapila Gold Medal for excellence in cardiology, 1989, Searle award, Cardiology Soc. India, 1989. Fellow: Am. Heart Assn./Coun. on Epidemiology and Prevention, Am. Coll. Cardiology. Home: 2000 Commonwealth Ave #1705 Brighton MA 02135 Office: The Framingham Heart Study 73 Mount Wayte Ave Framingham MA 01702 E-mail: vasan@bu.edu. *

RAMACHANDRAN, VENKATANARAYANA DEEKSHIT, electrical engineering educator; b. Mysore, India, May 3, 1934; s. K.C. Venkatanarayana Deekshit and Subbamma Deekshit R.; m. Kamala Visweswaraiya, June 12, 1960; 1 child, Ravi P. BS, U. Mysore, 1953; B in Engring., Indian Inst. Sci., Bangalore, 1956, M in Electronics, 1958, PhD, 1965. Registered profl. engr. Sr. research asst. Indian Inst. Sci., 1958-59, lectr., 1959-66; asst. prof. N.S. Tech. Coll., Halifax, Can., 1966-69; prof. elec. engring. Concordia U. (formerly Sir George Williams Univ.), Halifax, Can., 1971—; acting chmn. dept. elec. and computer engring. Montreal, various times; grad. program dir. dept., 1969-84. Adj. prof. U. Windsor, Ont., Can., 1983—, Ecole Tech. Superieure U. Quebec, Montreal, 1989—; mem. program com. Internat. Symposium on Operator Theory of Networks and Systems, 1975; vice chmn. Internat. Symposium on Circuits and Systems IEEE, Montreal, 1984, mem. tech. program com., 1987; internat. coordinator Internat. Conf. on Computers, Systems and Signal Processing, Indian Inst. Sci., 1984. Author papers in profl. jours., over 125 papers presented to confs., others. Named to Order of Engrs. of Que.; recipient Merit award Concordia Council on Student Life, 1981-82, Outstanding Contbn. award Engring. and Computer Sci. Assn., Concordia U., 1996. Fellow Inst. Electronics and Telecomms. India (edit. bd. jour. 1986), Inst. Engrs. India, Inst. Elec. Engrs. Eng., Engring. Inst. Can. (sec. Montreal chpt. 1979-80, centennial bd. 1983-84), IEEE (Outstanding Engring. Educator award IEEE Can. 2003); mem. Circuits and Systems chpt. IEEE (chmn. Montreal sect. 1978-84), Can. Soc. Elec. Engrs. (editor jour. 1983-85, editor bull. 1981-83), Am. Soc. Engring. Edn. (chmn. awards com. St. Lawrence chpt. 1987-88, Western Elec. Fund award 1983, Myril B. Reed Best Rsch. Paper award 1984, Outstanding Svc. 1993) Office: Concordia U Faculty of Engring 1455 de Maisonneuve Blvd W Montreal PQ Canada H3G 1M8 Office Phone: 514-848-2424 ext. 3078. Business E-Mail: kamala@ece.concordia.ca.

RAMAGE, JAMES ALFRED, history professor; b. Paducah, Ky., May 6, 1940; s. Willis Newman and Lora Helen Ramage; m. Judith Ann Winstead, June 6, 1964; 1 child, Andrea Susanne Watkins. BS, Murray State U., Ky., 1965, MA, 1968; PhD, U. Ky., Lexington, 1972. Tchr. history Mehlville H.S., St. Louis, 1965—67; prof. history No. Ky. U., Highland Heights, Ky., 1972—. Author: John Wesley Hunt, 1974, Rebel Raider, 1986 (Freeman award, 1986), Gray Ghost, 1999 (History Book Club selection). Chair Recreation Commn. City of Highland Heights, Ky., 1975—81. With USAF, 1958—62. Named Outstanding Prof., No. Ky. U., 1988; recipient Ky. Gov.s Vol. Activist award, 1978, Regents Prof. award, No. Ky. U., 1994, Acorn award, Ky. Advocates Higher Edn., 2003. Mem.: Ky. Hist. Soc., So. Hist. Assn., Phi Alpha Theta (faculty advisor (No. Ky. U. chpt.) 1985—2004, nat. coun. mem. 2002—03, nat. v.p. 2006—). Baptist. Achievements include preservation work on Civil War Battery Hooper honored in James A Ramage Civil War Museum. Avocation: reading. Office: History Dept No Ky Univ One Nunn Dr Highland Heights KY 41099

RAMAGE, MARTIS DONALD, JR., banker; b. Tupelo, Miss., Oct. 6, 1957; s. Martis Donald and Helen Frances (Estes) Ramage. AA, Itawamba Jr. Coll., Fulton, Miss., 1978; BBA in Banking and Fin., U. Miss., 1980; grad., Mid South Sch. of Banking, 1989. Mgmt. trainee Renasant Bank (formerly Peoples Bank & Trust Co.), Tupelo, 1981-82, asst. cashier, 1983-89, asst. v.p., 1989-90, v.p., 1990-93, 1st v.p., 1993-2000, sr. v.p., 2000—02, divsn. v.p., 2002—. Sec. Renasant Corp., 1993—96, v.p., 1996—. Author: Our Ramage Family, 1986, Mississippi Society SAR 1909-1993, Tupelo, Mississippi, Tornado 1936, 1997; co-editor: The Peoles Bank & Trust Co-In Partnership with the Community, 1989; editor: N.E. Miss. Hist. Geneal. Soc. Quar., 1991—2000. Sec. United Way Greater Lee County, Tupelo, 1991—2000, Leadership Lee, 1987; pres. Friends of Lee County Libr., 1995—97; bd. dirs. Brice's Battlefield Commn., Inc., 1995—, Tupelo Cmty. concert, 1998—, Regional Rehab. Ctr., 2003—; trustee Miss. Dept. Archives and History, 1996—, Lee/Itawamba County Libr., 1998—, chmn., 2004—, Christmas Festival Com., Tupelo, 1990—91; mem. Miss. rev. bd. Nat. Register Hist. Places, 1999—2002. Mem.: Miss. Hist. Soc. (bd. dirs. 1995—97), Tupelo Artist Guild (bd. dirs. 1993—98, 1993—98, sec. 1996—98), Bank Adminstrn. Inst. (v.p. N. Miss. chpt. 1990—94, pres. 1994—95), Am. Inst. Banking (pres. Tupelo chpt. 1986—87), Itawamba CC Alumni Assn. (bd. dirs. 2002—), Regional Rehab. Ctr. (bd. dirs. 2003—), Itawamba Jr. Coll. Alumni Assn. (pres. 1982—83), Ole Miss. Alumni Assn., Civitan Club, Masons, Mil. Order Stars and Bars, SCV, SAR (pres. Miss. 1991—92, trustee 1992—94, Silver Good Citizenship medal 1990). Home: 4218 Ridgemont Dr Belden MS 38826-9785 Office: Renasant Bank 209 Troy St Tupelo MS 38804-4827 Home Phone: 662-840-0508; Office Phone: 662-680-1306. Personal E-mail: martyr@tsixroads.com. Business E-Mail: martyr@renasant.com.

RAMAKRISHNAN, DIVAKAR, pharmaceutical executive; s. Thirumanilayur Venkataramanan and Sivakamasundari Ramakrishnan; m. Abira Pyne, Nov. 2003; 1 child, Arjun Venkat. B in Tech. in Chem. Engring., Anna U., Madras, India, 1991; PhD in Chem. Engring., Pa. State U., University Park, 1997; MBA, Harvard U., Boston, 2005. Sr. chem. engr. Mobil Oil Corp., Dallas, 1997—98; sr. scientist Eli Lilly and Co., Indpls., 1998—2002, rsch. scientist, 2002, head bioprocess r&d, 2002—03; dir. biotech mfg. strategy, 2005—05, dir. strategic facilities planning, 2005—. Mgmt. cons. Cook Pharmica, LLC, Bloomington, Ind., 2004—05. Contbr. chapters to books, articles to profl. jours. Office: Eli Lilly and Company Lilly Corporate Center Indianapolis IN 46285 Home Phone: 317-848-1675; Office Phone: 317-277-5856.

RAMAKRISHNAN, KANNAN, mechanical engineer; arrived in US, 1996; s. Sivarama Subramanium and Sarasa Ramakrishnan. B in Mech. Engring., Walchand Inst. Tech., Solapur, Maharashtra, India, 1994; MME, Lamar U., 1998, DEng, 2001. Prodn., purchase engr. Walchandnagar Industries Ltd., Pune, Maharashtra, India, 1994—96; rsch. asst. Lamar U., Beaumont, Tex., 1996—98, tchg. fellow, 1998—2001; design engr. GEMCO Port Lavaca, Inc., 2001—. Contbr. scientific papers. Mem.: ASME, ASM Internat. Metallographic Soc., ASM Thermal Spray Soc., Soc. Plastics Engrs., ASM Internat. Material Info. Soc. Avocations: travel, sports, music, winemaking. Home Phone: 361-574-8780; Office Phone: 361-552-5122. Personal E-mail: kanna_ramakrishnan@hotmail.com.

RAMAKRISHNAN, VENKATASWAMY, civil engineer, educator; b. Coimbatore, India, Feb. 27, 1929; came to U.S., 1969, naturalized, 1981; s. Venkataswamy and Kondammal (Krishnaswamy) R.; m. Vijayalakshmi Unnava, Nov. 7, 1962; children: Aravind, Anand. BEng, U. Madras, India, 1952, DSS, 1953; Diploma in Hydropower and Concrete Tech, Imperial Coll., London, 1957; PhD, Univ. Coll., London, 1960. From lectr. to prof. civil engring., head dept. P.S.G. Coll. Tech., U. Madras, 1952-69; vis. prof. S.D. Sch. Mines and Tech., Rapid City, 1969-70, prof. civil engring., 1970—, dir. concrete tech. research, 1970-71, head grad. div. structural mechanic and concrete tech., 1971—, program coordinator materials engring. and sci. Ph.D. program, 1985-86, disting. prof., 1996—. Emeritus mem. TRB. Author: Ultimate Strength Design for Structural Concrete, 1969; contbr. over 350 articles to profl. jours. Recipient Outstanding Prof. award, S.D. Sch. Mines and Tech., 1980, 1st Rsch. award, 1994; Colombo Plan fellow, 1955—60. Mem. ASCE (vice chmn. constrn. divsn. publs. com. 1974), NSPE, Internat. Assn. Bridge and Structural Engring., Am. Concrete Inst. (chmn. subcom. gen. considerations for founds., chmn. com. 214 on evaluation of strength test results, sec.-treas. Dakota chpt. 1974-79, v.p. 1980, pres. 1981, Robert Philio Rsch. Excellence award), Instn. Hwy. Engrs., Transp. Rsch. Bd. (chmn. com. on admixtures and curing, chmn. com. on mech. properties concrete), Am. Soc. Engring. Edn., Internat. Coun. Gap-Graded Concrete Rsch. and Application, Sigma Xi. Address: 5260 Autumn Place Rapid City SD 57702 Office Phone: 605-394-2403. Personal E-mail: vramakrishnan@rushmore.com. *To me, success is a coin with hard work on one side and perseverance with devotion on the other. No matter what—head or tails—the message is the same: keep on working. Goals in my life were pursuit of truth and beauty. The structures I have created, and my writings based on research have given me greater satisfaction than any wealth, position, or power.*

RAMAKRISHNAN, VENKATRAMAN (VENKI RAMAKRISHNAN), scientist; BSc in physics, Baroda U.; PhD in physics, Ohio U., 1976. Staff Brookhaven Nat. Lab.; prof., dept. of biochemistry U. UT., 1995; sr. sci. and group leader, structural studies divsn. MCR Lab. of Molecular Bio., 2000—. Contbr. articles to profl. jours. Mem.: Royal Soc., NAS. Office: MRC Laboratory of Molecular Biology Hills Rd Cambridge CB2 2QH England Business E-Mail: dramak@mrc-lmb.cam.ac.uk.

RAMANAN, SUNDARAM V., internist, hematologist, oncologist; s. Tarakad Appadoraier Subndaram. MD, MS, Vellore Christian Med. Coll., India, 1959. Prof. medicine U. Conn., Farmington, 1976—; emeritus attending physician St. Francis Hosp., Hartford, Conn., 1993—; assoc. prof. medicine West Va. U. Fellow: ACP (corr.), Royal Soc. Medicine (London), Royal Coll. Physicians (Edinburgh). Office: St Francis Hosp 1000 Asylum Ave Ste # 1004 Hartford CT 06105 Office Phone: 860-714-4152.

RAMANATHAN, CHITRA, artist, art educator; BFA, U. Madras, India, 1979; BFA in Painting with hons., U. Ill., Urbana-Champaign, 1993, MBA in Art Mus. Adminstrn., 1997. Adminstrv. asst. New Mus. Contemporary Art, NYC, 1996; devel. intern Krannert Art Mus., Champaign, Ill., 1996—97; profl. artist Chitra Ramanathan Art Studio, Indpls., 2003—; faculty painting Indpls. Art Ctr., 2004—. Vis. art lectr. in field. Exhibitions include Agora Gallery, SoHo, NY, 1995, Montserrat Gallery, 1995, 1997, 1998, Indpls. Artsgarden Circle Ctr., 2006, Chase Towers Arts Coun. Ind., Indpls., 2006—07, one-woman shows include ARC Gallery, Edn. Found., Chgo., 1994, Represented in permanent collections Hotel Bellagio, LV. Recipient Corp. Commn. for Painting award, MGM Mirage, 2004. Mem.: Indpls. Mus. Art (vol. Lilly house and Oldfield gardens), Coll. Art Assn. Am. (assoc.; mem. svcs. to artists com. 2003—06, mem. com. cultural diversity 2007—). Avocations: travel, gardening, golf, swimming, bicycling. Office: 10445 Stonegate Dr Fortville IN 46040 Home Phone: 317-336-9877; Office Phone: 317-223-1823.

RAMANATHAN, RANGASAMY, pediatrician; arrived in US, 1982; s. Rangaswamy Naidu and Gunavathi Rangaswamy; m. Prema Naidu, July 12, 1978; children: Anusha, Vinitha. MBBS, Stanley Med. Coll., Chennai, India, 1975; D, Madras Med. Coll., Chennai, India, 1978, MD in Pediat., 1981, NY Med. Coll., NY, 1984. Diplomate Am. Bd. Pediat., 1987, neonatal-perinatal medicine Am. Bd. Pediat., 1987. Intern Lincoln Med. Ctr., NY, 1982—83, resident, 1983—84; clin. instr. pediat. U. So. Calif., LA, 1984—86; rsch. fellow Harbor U. Calif. Med. Ctr., LA, 1987—88; asst. prof. pediat. sch. medicine Olive View med. ctr. U. Calif., Sylmar, Calif., 1988; asst. prof. of pediat. Keck sch. medicine U. So. Calif., LA, 1988—98, assoc. prof. of pediat. Keck sch. medicine, 1998—2002, prof. pediat. Keck sch. medicine, 2003—, assoc. divsn. chief divsn. neonatology Keck sch. medicine, 2003—. Program dir, neonatal-perinatal medicine fellowship Keck sch. medicine U. So. Calif., 2002—; med. dir. newborn icu Women's and Chlidren's Hosp., LA, 1988—; sect. head divsn. neonatology Women's and Children's Hosp., 2001—, med. dir. respiratory therapy dept., 1991—; assoc. med. dir. Good Smaritan Hosp., LA, 1989—; dir. high risk infant follow-up program Good Samaritan Hosp., 1990—, chief neonatolgy sect., 2003—; lectr. in field. Contbr. articles to profl. jours. Named Physician of Yr., Good Samaritan Hosp., LA, 2004; named one of Best Doctors in Am., Best Doctors, Inc., Boston, 2005; recipient Outstanding Tchr. award, Dept. Pediat., U. So. Calif., 2004, Richard H. Paul Disting. Tchg. award, U. So. Calif., 2005. Mem.: Am. Acad. Pediat. (regional trainer 1991—). Achievements include research in molecular basis of lung injury and oxgen radical mediated disorders in newborn infants. Avocation: travel. Office: Women's & Children's Hosp LAC+USC 1240 North Mission Rd Room L-919 Los Angeles CA 90033 Office Phone: 323-226-3406. Business E-Mail: ramanath@usc.edu.

RAMANI, GIRISH, marketing educator, researcher; s. Venkateswaran and Jayalakshmi Ramani; m. Jayanthi Rajan, Aug. 9, 1990; 1 child, Neharika Girish. BSc in Mech. Engring., Regional Engring. Coll., Kurukshetra, India, 1984; MBA, Indian Inst. Mgmt., Ahmedabad, 1988; PhD in Mktg., U. Conn., Storrs, 2006. V.p. Lowe Lintas & Ptnrs., Bangalore, India, 1989—2001; rsch. asst., instr. U. Conn., 2002—06; asst. prof. mktg. Drexel U., Phila., 2006—. Contbr. chapter to book, articles to profl. jours. Recipient Best Paper award, Interactive Mktg., 2006; grantee Rsch. grant, Mktg. Sci. Inst., 2006. Mem.: Beta Gamma Sigma (life). Avocation: kayaking. Office: Drexel Univ Mktg Dept Matheson 502A 3141 Chestnut St Philadelphia PA 19104-2875 Business E-Mail: girish.ramani@drexel.edu.

RAMANI, RAJA VENKAT, engineering educator; b. Madras, India, Aug. 4, 1938; came to U.S., 1966; s. Natesa and Meenakshi (Srinivasan) Rajaraman; m. Geetha V. Chalam, July 9, 1972; children: Deepak, Gautam. BSc with honors, Indian Sch. Mines, Dhanbad, Bihar, 1962, DSc (hon.), 1997; MS, Pa. State U., 1968, PhD, 1970. Registered profl. engr., Pa., 1971; lic. first class mine mgr., 1965. Mining engr., mgr. Andrew Yule & Co., Asansol, West Bengal, India, 1962-66; grad. asst. Pa. State U., University Park, 1966-70, asst. prof., 1970-74, assoc. prof., 1974-78, prof. mining engring., 1978—, chmn. mineral engring. mgmt. sect., 1974—, head dept. mineral engring., 1987-98, George and Anne Deike chair in mining engring., 1997—2001, prof. emeritus, 2001—, Deike chair emeritus, 2001—. Chmn. com. post-disaster survival/rescue NAS, Washington, 1979-81; mem. health rsch. panel NAS Com. on the Rsch. Programs of the U.S. Bur. of Mines, 1994; mem. NAS Com. on Techs. for the Mineral Industries, 2000-01; mem. NAS Com. on Coal Waste Impoundments, 2001-02; mem. NAS Com. on NIOSH programs, 2005—; chmn. Gov.'s Commn. on Mine Voids and Mine Safety, Pa., 2002; cons. UN, UN Devel. Program, Dept. Econ. and Social Devel., N.Y.C., 1983-97, World Bank, 1998-99, Nat. Safety Coun., 2003-; cons., expert panels U.S. Dept. Labor, 1979, 92, 96, HHS, 1977, 92, U.S. Dept. State, 1986, 87, U.S. Dept. Interior, 1995, Dept. Environ. Resources, Commonwealth of Pa., 1990, 92; co-dir. Generic Mineral Tech. Ctr. on Respirable Dust, U.S. Bur. Mines, 1983—, Nat. Mines/Land Reclamation Ctr., 1988—, Std. Oil Ctr. of Excellence on Longwall Tech., 1983-89; presenter in field. Sect. editor, author: Computer Methods for the Eighties, 1979, SME Mining Engineering Handbook, 1992; editor State-of-the-Art in Longwall-Shortwall Mining, 1981, Longwall Thick Seam Mining, 1988, Computers in Mineral Industry, 1994, Internat. Mine Ventilation Congress, 1997. Recipient Disting. Alumni award Indian Sch. Mines, Dhanbad, 1978, Ednl. Excellence award Pitts. Coal Mining Inst., 1986, Environ. Conservation award AIME, N.Y.C., 1990, Howard N. Eavenson award SME/AIME, N.Y.C., 1991, Robert Stefanko Best Paper award, 1993, Coal Divsn. Disting. Svc. award, 1993, Howard L. Hartman award, 1997, Percy H. Nicholls award AIME/ASME Joint Soc., 1994, Mineral Industry Edn. award Am. Inst. Mining Engrs., 1999, The Thornton medal Instn. Mining and Metallurgy, 2000, Erskine Ramsay medal AIME, 2005; Fulbright scholar to Soviet Union Coun. Internat. Exch. of Scholars, Washington,, 1989-90; Henry Krumb lectr. AIME, 1994. Mem. NAE, Internat. Coun. for Application of Computers in the Mineral Industry (chmn. 1984-87, Disting. Achievement award 1989), Soc. Mining, Metallurgy & Exploration, Inc. Found. (pres. 2001-04), Soc. Mining, Metall. and Exploration (Disting. Mem. 1989, pres. 1995), Mine Ventillation Soc. South Africa, Inst. for Ops. Rsch. and Mgmt. Scis. Achievements include research in health, safety, environmental and productivity aspects in underground and surface mining engineering. Home: 285 Oakley Dr State College PA 16803-1349 Office: Dept Mineral Engring Pa State U University Park PA 16802 Home Phone: 814-237-6062; Office Phone: 814-863-1617. Business E-Mail: RVR@PSU.edu.

RAMAPRASAD, KACKADASAM RAGHAVACHAR, physical chemist; b. Dec. 8, 1938; came to U.S., 1965, permanent resident, 1971; s. Kackadasam Raghavachar and Saroja (Narasimhachar) R.; m. Rukmani Raghavachari, July 14, 1968; children: Saroja, Venkat. BS in Chemistry (hon.), U. Mysore, Bangalore, 1958; MS in Phys. Chemistry, NYU, 1971; PhD, 1972. Trainee Bhabha Atomic Rsch. Ctr. Tng. Sch., Bombay, India, 1958-59; rsch. asst., jr. sci. officer chemistry divsn., 1959-65; teaching fellow N.Y.C., 1965-71; duPont teaching asst., 1967-68; maitre-asst. dept. de chimie physique U. Geneva, 1972-73; chemist Ecole Poly-Technique Federale de lausanne, Switzerland, 1974; rsch. assoc. dept. chemistry Princeton (N.J.) U., 1974-77; rsch. assoc., mem. profl. rsch. staff dept. chem. engring., 1977-79; sr. scientist Chronar Corp., Princeton, 1979-89, Electron Transfer Techs., Inc., Princeton, 1990-93; staff scientist TRI-Princeton, 1993-96, sr. scientist, 1996-2001, sr. scientist, group leader, 2001—. Contbr. articles to profl. publs. Recipient Founder's Day award, NYU, 1972. Mem. Am. Chem. Soc., Sigma Xi. Office: TRI/Princeton PO Box 625 Princeton NJ 08542-0625

RAMBERG, WALTER DODD, architect; b. Charlotte, NC, Feb. 17, 1932; s. Walter Gustav Charles and Julia Elisabeth (Lineberger) R.; m. Lucinda Jenifer Ballard, Nov. 25, 1961 (dec. 1989); children: Lucinda E.G., Jenny S.F., Julia E.L.; m. Seska Peck Dunne, Sept. 14, 1996. BA, Yale U., 1953, M.Arch., 1956. Fulbright fellow Kyoto (Japan) U., 1956-58; apprentice architect Paul Rudolph, New Haven, 1958-61; project designer Meyer & Ayers, Balt., 1961-63; partner Howe & Ramberg, Washington, 1963-65; prin. Walter Dodd Ramberg (Architect), Washington, 1965—. Prof. architecture Cath. U. Am., 1977-2006, prof. emeritus, 2006—; mem. design adv. panel Balt. Dept. Housing and Cmty., 1973—; mem. bd. architecture rev. Baltimore County, 1986-89. Designer: N.W. Balt. High Sch, 1963 (P.A. Excellence in Design award); architect: Bridge for Washington Cathedral, 1965 (Excellence in Design award Washington Bd. Trade, AIA), Kidder Guest House, 1965 (1st Honor award Balt. AIA), Azrael House, 1969 (Honor award Balt. AIA), Cutts House, 1973 (Honor award Balt. AIA), Woody House, 1975 (Merit award Balt. AIA), Lineberger Meml. Library, 1976 (Merit award Nat. AIA, ALA); contbr. articles to profl. publs. Served to lt. USCGR, 1958-59. Mem. AIA (corp.), AAUP, Soc. Archtl. Historians. Clubs: Met. (Washington). Episcopalian. Home: 1651 Belfast Rd Sparks MD 21152-9788 Office: 1830 T St NW Washington DC 20009-7138

RAMBO, KELLY CLIFFORD, lawyer; b. Easton, Pa., Apr. 26, 1961; d. Brian D. and Roslyn Clifford; m. William K. Rambo, Apr. 11, 1987; children: William Clifford, Grace Caroline, Luke Evan. BS cum laude, Pa. State U., University Park, 1983; JD with high distinction, Temple U. Sch. Law, Phila., 1986. Bar: Pa. 1986. Assoc. atty. White & Williams, Phila., 1986—87, Cohen & Feeley, Easton, 1987—91; prin. atty. Kelly Clifford Rambo, Atty. at Law, Easton, 1991—95; atty./mng. atty. worker's compensation dept. Post & Schell, Allentown, Pa., 1995—97; ptnr. Cohen & Feeley, Bethlehem, Pa., 1997—. Author: (article) The Legal Field and the Health Care Professional: Weathering Involvement. Fellow Rotary Club, Easton, 2005; mem. Third St. Alliance for Women and Children, Easton, 1994. Mem.: Pa. Trial Lawyers Assn. (assoc.), Pa. Bar Assn. (assoc.), Northampton County Bar Assn. (assoc.). Avocations: travel, reading. Office: Cohen & Feeley 2851 Baglyos Cir Ste 200 Bethlehem PA 18020 Home Phone: 610-559-0403; Office Phone: 610-332-2718. Office Fax: 610-332-2722. Business E-Mail: krambo@cohenfeeley.com.

RAMBO, SYLVIA H., federal judge; b. Royersford, Pa., Apr. 17, 1936; d. Granville A. and Hilda E. (Leonhardt) R.; m. George F. Douglas, Jr., Aug. 1, 1970. BA, Dickinson Coll., 1958; JD, Dickinson Sch Law, 1962; LLD (hon.), Wilson Coll., 1980, Dickinson Sch. Law, 1993, Dickinson Coll., 1994, Shippensburg U., 1996, Widener U., 1999. Bar: Pa. 1962. Atty. trust dept. Bank of Del., Wilmington, 1962-63; pvt. practice Carlisle, 1963-76; from public defender to chief public defender Cumberland County, Pa., 1974-76; judge Ct. Common Pleas, Cumberland County, 1976-78, U.S. Dist. Ct. (mid. dist.) Pa., Harrisburg, 1979—, chief judge, 1992-99; federal judge U.S. Dist. Ct., Harrisburg, 2000—. Asst. prof., adj. prof. Dickinson Sch. Law, 1974—76; mem. Jud. Conf. Com. on Adminstrn. of Magistrate Judges Sys., 1996—2002. Bd. dirs. Dickinson Sch. Law., Pa. State U., bd. govs., 2000—05, mem. bd. counselors, 2005—. Mem. Pa. Bar Assn. (mem. task force legal svcs. to needy 2000-03, mem. third cir. com. devel. model criminal jury instrns. 2004—), Phi Alpha Delta. Democrat. Presbyterian. Office: US Dist Ct Federal Bldg PO Box 868 Harrisburg PA 17108-0868 Office Phone: 717-221-3960.

RAMCHARAN, BERTRAND, former international organization official; LLD, London Sch. Econ. and polit. Sci.; diploma in Internat. Law, Hague Acad. of Internat. Law. Adviser peace negotiators in the Yugoslavia conflict, UN; dir. peace keeping oper. UN in Yugoslavia; chief speech writer Sec.-Gen.; spl. asst. Ctr. for Human Rights; dir. studies Hague Acad. Internat. Law; adj. prof. of internat. human rights Columbia U.; mem. Permanent Ct. Arbitration; commr. Internat. Commn. Jurists; dep. high commr. for human rights UN, 1998—2003, acting high commr. for human rights, 2003—04; chancellor U. Guyana; vis. prof., Internat. Law Lund U., Sweden. Carr Fellow, JFK Sch. Govt Harvard U., Cambridge, Mass., 2004—; sr. fellow Ralph Bunche Inst. Internat. Studies. Author of over 15 books. Office: Carr Ctr for Human Rights Policy JFK Sch Govt 79 JFK St Cambridge MA 02138

RAMDAS, JAGADEESH, physician; arrived in U.S., 1995; s. Ramdas and Sharada Shenoy; children: Ganesh, Maya. MBBS, Calicut Med. Coll., 1989, MD, 1994. Bd. Cert. Pediats. and Oncology Am. Bd. Pediats. Fellow pediat. hematology/oncology LSU Med. Ctr., New Orleans, 1997, pediat. resident, 1998; pediat. hematology/oncology fellowship LSU, Tulane U., New Orleans, 1999—2002; pediat. hematologist/oncologist Geisinger Med. Ctr., Danville, Pa., 2002—; pediat. oncologist Jefferson Med. Coll., Phila., 2003—. Mem.: Am. Soc. Pediat. Hematolgy/Oncology (investigator 2002—), Am. Soc. Hematology (investigator 2002—), Children's Oncology Group (investigator 2002—). Office: Divsn Pediat Hematology/Oncology 100 N Academy Ave Danville PA 17821 Office Phone: 570-271-6848. E-mail: jramdas@geisinger.edu.

RAMER, BRUCE M., lawyer; b. Teaneck, NJ, Aug. 2, 1933; s. Sidney and Anne S. (Strassman) R.; children: Gregg B., Marc K., Neal I. BA, Princeton U., 1955; LLB, Harvard U., 1958. Bar: Calif. 1963, NJ 1958. Assoc., Morrison, Lloyd & Griggs, Hackensack, NJ, 1959-60; ptnr. Gang, Tyre, Ramer & Brown, Inc., LA, 1963—. Exec. dir. Entertainment Law Inst., Law Ctr. U. So. Calif., bd. councilors; chmn., nat. bd. govs. Am. Jewish Com., 1995-98, nat. v.p., 1982-88, pres., 1998—, LA chpt., 1980-83, chair Western region, 1984-86, Cmty. Svc. award, 1987, nat. pres., 1998—, adv. bd. Skirball Inst. on Am. Values, 1998—; chmn. Asia Pacific Rim Inst., 1989-98; trustee Loyola Marymount U., LA Children's Mus., 1986-89; vice chair United Way, 1991-93, corp. bd. dirs., 1981-93, chair coun. pres. 1989-90, mem. cmty. issues coun., 1989-90, chair discretionary fund distbn. com., 1987-89; bd. dirs., chair Geffen Playhouse, 1995-98, founding chair, 1998—; bd. dirs. LA Urban League, 1987-93, 96—, Jewish Fedn. Coun. of Greater LA (mem. Cmty. Rels. com., bd. dirs., exec. com.), Jewish TV Network, Sta. KCET-TV; mem., bd. dirs. Rebuild LA, 1992-96; mem. bd. govs. Calif. Cmty. Found., 1988-98; recipient Ann. Brotherhood award NCCJs, 1990; mem. Fellows of Am. Bar Found.; mem. econ. strategy panel State Calif., 1997—; bd. dirs. Shoah Visual History Found., Righteous Persons Found., LA 2012 Bid Com. for So. Calif. Olympic Games; bd. dirs. Jewish Fedn. Coun. Greater LA, mem. exec. com., cmty. rels. com. Pvt. US Army, 1958-59, 2d lt., 1961-62. Mem. ABA (mem. spl. com. jud. ind.), LA County Bar Assn., Calif. Bar Assn., Beverly Hills Bar Assn. (Exec. Dirs. award 1988, Entertainment Lawyer of Yr. award 1996), LA Copyright Soc. (pres. 1974-75), Calif. Copyright Conf. (pres. 1973-74), Princeton Club (pres. 1975-78). Office: Gang Tyre Ramer & Brown Inc 132 S Rodeo Dr Beverly Hills CA 90212-2415

RAMER, HAL REED, retired academic administrator; b. Kenton, Tenn., June 8, 1923; s. Claude Orion and Dixie Clayton (Carroll) R. BS, George Peabody Coll., 1947; MSW, U. Tenn., 1952; PhD, Ohio State U., 1963. Asst. dean men Ohio State U., Columbus, 1953-58, dir. internat. house, 1958-60, staff asst. to pres., 1960-62; asst. commr. State Dept. Edn., Nashville, 1963-70; founding pres. Vol. State C.C., Gallatin, Tenn., 1970—2003, pres. emeritus, 2003—; ret. Bd. dirs. Sumner Regional Health Sys., Inc. Com. mem. March of Dimes, Gallatin; trustee Nashville United Way, 1970, Hiwassee Coll., 2001; bd. advisors Aquinas Coll., Nashville, 1967—; former chmn. Tenn. Fulbright-Hays Sch. Commn.; bd. visitors U. Tenn. Sch. Social Work; YMCA. With U.S. Army Air Corps, 1943—45. Recipient Distinctive Svc. award Devel. Coun. Peabody Coll., Nashville, 1960s, Disting. Svc. award Tenn. Dept. Edn., 1970, Outstanding Leader award Vanderbilt U. chpt. Phi Delta Kappa, 1987, Gov.'s Svc. award State of Tenn., 1993, Sertoma Club Svc. to Mankind award, 1995-96, Disting. Alumnus award Peabody Coll., 1996, Disting. Svc. award Tenn. Bd. Regents, 1997, Svc. award Am. Assn. Cmty. Col., 1999, Otis Floyd Jr. award for excellence Tenn. Coll. Pub. Rels. Assn., 1999, Lifetime Achievement award Peabody Coll. of Vanderbilt U., 2003; named Rotarian of the Yr., 1979; Paul Harris fellow Rotary Internat., 1981. Mem. Am. Legion, Coun. Pres. C.Cs. (chmn. state Tenn. 1988-89), Tenn. Coll. Assn. (pres. 1985-86), Nat. Alumni Assn. Peabody Coll. (pres. 1970-71, trustee), Tenn. Acad. Sci., Tenn. and Sumner County Hist. Socs. (bd. dirs.), English Speaking Union Internat. (Nashville chpt.), So. Assn. Colls. and Schs., Univ. Club Nashville, Gallatin and Hendersonville C. of C., St. Thomas Aquinas Soc., Torch Club, Alpha Tau Omega, Kappa Phi Kappa, Alpha Phi Omega, Phi Delta Kappa. Methodist. Avocations: antiques, antique cars, photography. Home: 120 Abbottsford Nashville TN 37215-2440

RAMER, JAMES LEROY, civil engineer; b. Marshalltown, Iowa, Dec. 7, 1935; s. LeRoy Frederick and Irene (Wengert) Ramer; m. Jacqueline L. Orr, Dec. 15, 1957; children: Sarah T., Robert H., Eric A., Susan L. Student, U. Iowa, Iowa City, 1953-57; MCE, Washington U., St. Louis, 1976, MA in Polit. Sci., 1978; postgrad., U. Mo., Columbia, 1984—. Registered profl. engr., land surveyor. Civil and constrn. engr. US Army C.E., Tulsa, 1960-63; civil and relocations engr. US State Dept., Del Rio, Tex., 1964; project engr. H.B. Zachary Co., San Antonio, 1965-66; civil and constrn. engr. US Army C.E., St. Louis, 1967-76, tech. advisor for planning and nat. hydropower coord., 1976-78; project mgr. for EPA constrn. grants Milw., 1978-80; chief arch. and engring. HUD, Indpls., 1980-81; civil design and pavements engr. Whiteman AFB, Mo., 1982-86; project mgr. maintenance, 1993—; soil and pavements engr. Hdqrs. Mil. Airlift Command, Scott AFB, Ill., 1986-88. Project mgr. AF-1 maintenance hangar; cattle and grain farmer, 1982—; pvt. practice civil-mech. engr., constrn. mgmt., estimating, cost analysis, cash flow, project scheduling, expert witness, profl. land surveying, Fortuna, Mo., 1988—2001; chief constrn. inspector divsn. design and constrn. State of Mo., 1992—93; project engr. Mil. Housing, 2001—; adj. faculty civil engring. Washington U., 1968—78, U. Wis., Milw., 1978—80, Ga. Mil. Coll., Whiteman AFB, Longview Coll., Kansas City; adj. rsch. engr. U. Mo., Columbia, 1985—86; project engr., quality control officer Korte Constrn. Co. Mem.: AAUP, NSPE, ASCE, Soc. Am. Mil. Engrs., Optimists Internat. Lutheran. Achievements include patents for in diverse art, 9 copyrights; development of solar waterstill, deep shaft hydropower concept. Office Phone: 660-882-9444. Business E-Mail: jlramer@iland.net.

RAMER, LAWRENCE JEROME, corporation executive; b. Bayonne, NJ, July 29, 1928; s. Sidney and Anne (Strassman) R.; m. Ina Lee Brown, June 30, 1957; children: Stephanie Beryl, Susan Meredith, Douglas Strassman. BA in Econs, Lafayette Coll., 1950; MBA, Harvard U., 1957; LLD (hon.), Lafayette Coll., 1992. Sales rep., then v.p. United Sheet Metal Co., Bayonne, 1953-55; with Am. Cement Corp., 1957-64; v.p. mktg. div. Riverside Cement Co., 1960-62, v.p. mktg. parent co., 1962-64; vice chmn. bd., chief exec. officer Clavier Corp., NYC, 1965-66; exec. v.p., vice chmn. bd. Pacific Western Industries, LA, 1966-70; pres., chief exec. officer Nat. Portland Cement Co. Fla., 1975-89; chmn. bd. Sutro Partners, Inc., LA, 1977-89, Somerset Mgmt. Group, 1975-92, Luminall Paints Inc., LA, 1972-95; chmn. bd., CEO Bruning Paint Co., Balt., 1979—2000; chmn. bd., chief exec. officer Pacific Coast Cement Co., LA, 1979-90; pres., CEO Ramer Equities, Inc., 1990—2000, chmn., 2000—; chmn. bd. Scott Paint Co., Sarasota, Fla., 2000—. Chmn. Lee and Lawrence J. Ramer Family Found., 1986—; bd. dirs. The Music Ctr., LA, Canyon Ranch, Tucson; bd. dirs. Ctr. Theatre Group-Mark Taper Ahmanson Theatres, LA, pres. and chmn., 1987-97. Mem. Coun. on Fgn. Rels., NYC; chmn. bd. trustees Lafayette Coll., Easton, Pa., 1992—2001, bd. trustees, 1976—2001, Helen Keller Internat., NYC, Calif. Inst. Arts, Valencia, 2000—, chmn. bd. trustees, 1995—2006; nat. bd. govs. Am. Jewish Com., NY, treas. NY; bd. dirs. LA World Affairs Coun., Pacific Coun. Internat. Policy; bd. govs. Hebrew Union Coll.; trustee Leo Baeck Inst., NY; bd. dirs. RAND Corp. Ctr. on Mid. East Policy. Office: Ramer Equities Inc 10900 Wilshire Blvd Ste 550 Los Angeles CA 90024-6501 Office Phone: 310-209-0442.

RAMESH, SRIKRISHNAPERUMAL THANGA, engineering educator; b. Nagercoil, India, July 5, 1976; s. Neelathangam Srikrishnaperumal and Muthiah Kalaichelvi; m. Gandhimathi Rajan, Dec. 9, 2005. BS in Engring., GCT, 1998, MS in Engring., 2000; PhD, Indian Inst. Tech., Chennai, Madras, 2006. Project officer Indian Inst. Tech., 2002—04; lectr. Nat. Inst. Tech., Tiruchirappalli, India, 2006—. Recipient Best Project award, TSCST, 1998. Mem.: ISTE (assoc.). Home: Nat Inst Tech Campus No 8 12 St Tiruchirappalli 620 015 India Office: Nat Inst Tech Civil Engring Tiruchirappalli 620015 India Office Fax: 0431 2500133; Home Fax: 0431 2500133. Business E-Mail: stramesh@nitt.edu.

RAMETTE, RICHARD WALES, chemistry professor; b. Stafford, Conn., Oct. 9, 1927; s. Joel Edward and Grace Margaret (Wales) R.; m. Lenora Kathryn Kelleher, Aug., 21, 1949; children: Cheryl Lee, James Edward, John Richard, David Joel, William Michael. BA, Wesleyan U., Middletown, Conn., 1950; PhD, U. Minn., 1954. Prof. chemistry Carleton Coll., Northfield, Minn., 1954-90, Laurence M. Gould prof. chemistry, 1971-90, prof. emeritus, 1990—. Sci. advisor FDA, Mpls., 1969-80. Author: Chemical Equilibrium and Analysis, 1981. Asst. scoutmaster Boy Scouts Am., Northfield, 1968-73; calligraphy instr. Northfield Arts Guild, 1974-80; sec. Unitarian Universalist Congregation Green Valley, 1998-2001, pres., 2001-2002. Recipient Chemistry Teaching award Mfg. Chemists, 1966, Analytical Chemistry Teaching award Am. Chem. Soc., 1991, Disting. Alumnus award Wesleyan U., 1995. Mem.: Am. Chem. Soc. (Analytical Chemistry Tchg. award, 50 yr. mem. award 2002). Home: 765 W Fountain Creek Dr Green Valley AZ 85614-3272 Personal E-mail: rramette@carleton.edu.

RAMEY, CARL ROBERT, lawyer; b. Binghamton, NY, Feb. 15, 1941; s. Clinton W. and Hester May (Wisdom) R.; m. Maryan Sitzenkopf, Aug. 11, 1962 (div. Sept. 1987); children: Mark Alan, Christian David; m. Karen Reichard, Nov. 28, 1987. AB, Marietta Coll., 1962; MA, Mich. State U., 1964; JD, George Washington U., 1967. Bar: D.C. 1968, U.S. Dist. Ct. D.C. 1968, U.S. Ct. Appeals (D.C., 2d, 3d, 4th, 5th, 7th and 9th cirs.), U.S. Supreme Ct. 1972, Md. 1999. Assoc. McKenna, Wilkinson & Kittner, Washington, 1967-71, ptnr., 1971-86, Wiley, Rein & Fielding, Washington, 1986—. Contbr. articles to profl. jours., chpt. to Copyright Law Symposium, 1969; editorial staff George Washington Law Rev., 1965-67. Recipient First Prize award Nat. Nathan Burkan Meml. Writing Competition, ASCAP, 1969. Mem. ABA, Fed. Communications Bar Assn. (treas. 1977-78, co-chair editl. adv. bd. Fed. Comms. Law Jour. 1993-96), D.C. Bar Assn., Md. Bar Assn. Republican. Episcopalian. Avocations: skiing, tennis, boating, biking. Office: Wiley Rein & Fielding 1776 K St NW Washington DC 20006-2304 Home: 409 Rehoboth Ave Apt 23 Rehoboth Beach DE 19971-3142

RAMEY, DENNY L., bar association executive director; b. Portsmouth, Ohio, Feb. 22, 1947; s. Howard Leroy and Norma Wylodine (Richards) R.; m. Jeannine Gayle Dunmyer, Sept. 24, 1971 (div. Nov. 1991); children: Elizabeth Michelle, Brian Michael. BBA, Ohio U., 1970; MBA, Capital U., 1976. Cert. assn. exec. Adminstrv. mgr. Transit Warehouse div. Elston Richards Storage Co., Columbus, Ohio, 1970-73; mgr. continuing profl. edn. Ohio Soc. CPA's, Columbus, 1973-79; exec. dir. Engrs. Found. of Ohio, Columbus, 1979-80; asst. exec. Ohio State Bar Assn., Columbus, 1980-86, exec. dir., sec., treas., 1986—. Treas., exec. com., bd. dirs. Ohio Bar Liability Ins. Co., Columbus, 1986—; treas. Ohio State Bar Found., 1986—; treas. Ohio Legal Ctr. Ins., Columbus, 1988-91; sec. Ohio Printing Co., Ltd., 1991; v.p. Osbanet, Inc., 1993—; chmn. Lawriter LLC, 2000—; bd. dirs. OSBA.com, LLC. Mem.: Ohio Soc. Assn. Execs., Am. Soc. Assn. Execs., Nat. Assn. Bar Execs., Scioto Country Club. Methodist. Avocations: golf, sports, music, art. Office: Ohio State Bar Assn 1700 Lake Shore Dr PO Box 16562 Columbus OH 43216-6562 Office Phone: 614-487-4405. Business E-Mail: dramey@ohiobar.org.

RAMEY, EUDORA MALOIS, minister; b. Maywood, Ill., Oct. 26, 1923; d. Cleonus and Ora Helen Garner; m. Edward F Ramey, July 27, 1947; children: Jonathan, RoseMary, Paul. Student, Herzl Jr. Coll., Chgo., Peter's Bus. Coll., Master's Sewing Coll., Vennard Bible Coll., Moody Bible Inst. Ordained minister African Episcopal Ch., 1951. Mem. Dist. 9 Bd. Edn., McKinley Sch., Chgo., 1966—75; counselor aide Bd. Edn./Whitney Young Magnet Sch., Chgo., 1975—80; implementor Job Club/Pres.'s Office/Employment Tng., Chgo., 1980—92. Advisor Garfield Pk. Conservatory, Chgo., 1991—, bd. dirs., 1996—. Mem. Chgo. Urban League, 1943—68, PUSH (People United to Serve Humanity), Chgo., 1970—91; ordained local elder/min. St. Stephen AME Ch., Chgo., 1951—; mem. NAACP, Chgo., 1943—68. Named Sr. of Yr., Christian Edn. Commn., 2005; recipient Chgo. Sr. Citizen's Hall of Fame, 1997, Svc. award, North Dist. Sunday Schs. Chgo. Conf., 1990, Garfield Pk. Conservatory Alliance, Chgo., 1998, Unsung Heroes award, Christian Edn. Commn., 1998, Cert. of Honor, Internat. Way of Life /City of Chgo., 1999, Trailblazer for Women in Ministry award, 4th Dist. of the AME Ch., 2001. Avocations: Scrabble, Bingo, reading, checkers, crossword puzzles. Personal E-mail: rev.eudora1026@sbc.global.net.

RAMIREZ, AINISSA, materials scientist; BSc, Brown U.; MS, PhD, Stanford U. Rschr., scientist Hewlett Packard Lab., Bell Lab., Lucent Tech., sci. curriculum developer pub. sch.; current asst. prof. mech. engring. Yale U. Named one of 100 Top Young Innovators, MIT's Tech. Review, 2003. Office: Yale Univ Mech Engring Dept PO Box 208284 New Haven CT 06520

RAMIREZ, CIRO, mechanical engineer, consultant; s. Ciro Benito Ramirez and Nancy Maiden Hockett; m. Denise Etter, Aug. 2, 1975; children: Rachel Marie Titsworth, Monica Ann. BS in Mech. Engring., Rice U., Houston, 1973, MME, 1974; PhD in Mech. Engring., U. Tex., Austin, 1991. Lic. profl. engr., Tex., registered Miss.; accredited accident reconstructionist Accreditation Commn. Traffic Accident Reconstructionists, cert. safety and health ofcl. OSHA and Tex. Engring. Ext. Svc. Sr. engr. IBM Corp., Austin, 1974—99; forensic mech. engr. Thornhill, Ramirez & Associates, Leander, Tex., 1996—. Music min. St. Helen Cath. Ch., Georgetown, Tex., 1997—2007. Recipient Outstanding Innovation award, IBM Corp., 1979, 1984, First Invention Achievement award, 1980, Corp. Achievement award, 1984. Mem.: ASME, Tex. Assn. Accident Reconstructionists, Soc. Automotive Engrs., Phi Kappa Phi, Tau Beta Pi. Achievements include patents in field. Office: Thornhill Ramirez & Associates 550 Oak Grove Rd Leander TX 78641 Home Phone: 512-869-8353; Office Phone: 512-259-1120. Office Fax: 512-259-4667. Personal E-mail: ciro.ramirez@gmail.com. Business E-Mail: cramirez@trengineer.com.

RAMIREZ, ENEIDA SARAHI, biology professor; b. Rio Piedras, PR, May 15, 1968; d. Nelson Sotelo (Stepfather); m. Noel Soto, May 1, 1993 (div. Mar. 8, 2005); children: Alejandro Soto-Ramirez, Gustavo Soto-Ramirez. BS, U. PR, Mayaguez, 1991, MS, 1995; postgrad., Marywood U., Scranton, Pa, 2001—. Biology instr. HACC Ctrl. Pa. CC, Harrisburg, Pa., 2001—. Office: HACC One Hacc Dr Harrisburg PA 17110 Office Phone: 717-780-2396. E-mail: esramire@hacc.edu.

RAMIREZ, EVANGELINE ROSE, elementary school educator; d. Alfredo and Rose Ramirez. BS in Criminal Justice, U. Tex., El Paso, 1980, MPA, 1987. Tchr. Desert View Mid. Sch., El Paso, 2001—05. Named Tchr. of Yr., Desert View Mid. Sch., 1999, 2004, Outstanding Tchr., Tex. Mis. Sch. Assn., 2004; named to Cheerleader Hall Fame, City El Paso, 2003. Mem.: Coun. Social Studies, Tex. Classroom Tchrs. Assn. Office Phone: 915-434-5300. E-mail: eramirez11@yisd.net.

RAMIREZ, HANLEY, professional baseball player; b. Samana, Dominican Republic, Dec. 23, 1983; s. Toribio and Isabel Ramirez. Shortstop Fla. Marlins, 2005—. Named Nat. League Rookie Yr., MLB Baseball Writers Assn., 2006; named to Eastern League All-Star Game, 2005, All-Stars Future Game, 2005. Achievements include hitting 7 leadoff home runs in 2006, a franchise first; being the first Marlin ever to post double digits in triples (11), home runs (17) and stolen bases (51) in 2006. Office: Dolphin Stadium 2267 Dan Marino Blvd Miami FL 33056 Office Phone: 305-626-7400. *

RAMIREZ, JUAN, mechanical engineer, researcher; b. Maracay, Aragua, Venezuela, Dec. 18, 1974; permanent resident, US; s. Jose Antonio Ramirez and Albea Julia Darias; m. Susana Bustamante; 1 child, Sara Valentina. PhD, U. Iowa, Iowa City, 2004. Post-doctoral rsch. assoc. Los Alamos Nat. Lab., N.Mex., 2004—. Office: Los Alamos Nat Lab Mailstop G755 Los Alamos NM Business E-Mail: jcramirez@lanl.gov.

RAMIREZ, LEO ARMANDO, SR., mathematics educator; Math. tchr. McAllen HS, Tex., 1985—; founder, owner Ram Materials, Inc., McAllen, Tex. Named Hero in Edn., Reader's Digest, 1992, Tex. State Math. Tchr. of Yr., 1993, Disney's Am. Teacher award finalist, 1994, Teacher award Honorable Mention, USA Today, 1999, HEB Excellence award finalist, 2004; recipient Denius Univ. Interscholastic League Sponsors Excellence award, 1991, Tandy Corp. Scholar award, 1995. Mem.: Tex. Math and Sci. Coaches Assn. (Numerous Coach of Yr. award), Univ. Interscholastic League. Achievements include has written more Number Sense, Calculator, and Mathematics tests for invitational tournaments and more workbooks/practice tests than any person in the history of University Interscholastic League. Office: Ram Inc Materials 2908 Flamingo Mcallen TX 78504 Office Phone: 956-682-5185. Office Fax: 956-682-7281. Business E-Mail: toywiz127@aol.com.

RAMIREZ, LINDA MANNING, counselor; b. San Antonio, July 13, 1951; d. Elmer Eugene Manning and Celeste E. (Campbell) Siner; m. Javier Ramirez, Oct. 22, 1977; children: Andrea, Xavier, Eric. BSN, U. Tex. Health Sci. Ctr., Houston, 1974; MEd in counseling, U. Tex. Pan-Am., Edinburg, 1993. RN Tex.; lic. profl. counselor supr. Bd. Profl. Counseling, registered play therapist supr. Assn. for Play Therapists. Vol. tchr. Our Lady of Sorrows Sch., McAllen, Tex., 1988-98, counseling intern, 1992—95; pvt. practice counseling children McAllen, 1996—. Presenter profl. continuing edn. workshops, parenting tng.; co-author children's books in English and Spanish. Bd. dirs. Diocese of Brownsville Sch. Coun., 1997-2000. Mem.: Assn. Play Therapists, Tex. Assn. Play Therapy (bd. dir. 1997—99, treas 2002—), Rio Grande Valley Assn. Play Therapy (pres. 1997—99, 2000—01), Border Equestrian Sports Assn. (sec. 1992), Phi Kappa Phi. Republican. Roman Catholic. Avocations: weightlifting, equestrian sports, reading. Home: 12 Villas Jardin Mcallen TX 78503-3138

RAMIREZ, MANNY (MANUEL ARISTIDES RAMIREZ), professional baseball player; b. Santo Domingo, Dominican Republic, May 30, 1972; m. Juliana Ramirez. Draft pick Cleve. Indians, 1991, outfielder, 1993—2000, Boston Red Sox, 2000—. Named World Series MVP, 2004; named to The Sporting News Am. League Silver Slugger Team, 1995, 1999—2006, Am. League All-Star Team, 1995, 1998—2007; recipient Players Choice award for Am. League Outstanding Player, 1999, Hank Aaron award, 1999, 2004, Am. League Batting Title, 2002. Achievements include led the American League in RBIs (165), 1999, home runs (43), 2004; being a member of World Series Champion Boston Red Sox, 2004. Office: Boston Red Sox Fenway Park 4 Yawkey Way Boston MA 02215 *

RAMIREZ, MARI CARMEN, curator; b. San Juan, 1955; m. Hector Olea. M in art history, PhD in art history, U. Chgo. Dir. Mus. Anthropology, History, and Art U. PR, Rio Piedras; curator L.Am. art Jack S. Blanton Mus. Art, U. Tex., Austin, 1989—2001; Worthman Curator L.Am. Art Mus. Fine Arts, Houston, 2001—, dir. Internat. Ctr. for the Arts of the Americas, 2001—. Adj. lectr. art dept. U. Tex., Austin. Editor: (books) El Taller Torres-Garcia: The School of the South and Its Legacy, 1992, Collecting L.Am. Art for the 21st Century, 2002, Questioning the Line: Gego in Context, 2003; co-author (with Hector Olea): Inverted Utopias: Avant-Garde Art in L.Am., 2004; co-curator Re-Aligning Vision: Alternative Currents in South American Drawing, 1997, co-curator (with Hector Olea) (exhibitions) Inverted Utopias: Avant-Garde Art in L.Am., 2004, co-curator (with Beverly Adams) Encounters/Displacements: Alfredo Jaar, Luis Camnitzer, Cildo Meireles, curator Cantos Paralelos: Visual Parody in Contemporary Argentinean Art, Global Conceptualism: Points of Origin (L.Am. sect.). Named one of 25 Most Influential Hispanics, Time Mag., 2005; recipient Peter Norton Family Found. Award for Curatorial Excellence, Ann. award for curatorial excellence, Ctr. for Curatorial Studies, Bard Coll., 2005; Getty Curatorial Residence Fellowship. Office: Mus Fine Arts PO Box 6826 Houston TX 77265-6826

RAMIREZ, MARIA FIORINI, financial consultant; b. Naples, Italy, Jan. 1, 1948; came to U.S., 1961; d. Fernando and Clelia Ambrosio Fiorini; m. George M. Ramirez, 1973. BBA, Pace U., 1972, postgrad., 1974-76. Analyst Meinhard-CIT Comml. Fin., NYC, 1967-68; credit analyst Am. Express Internat. Bank, NYC, 1968-72; credit mgr. Banca Nazionale del Lavoro, NYC, 1972-73; credit mgr., asst. v.p. Merrill Lynch G.S.I., 1973-74, economist, 1974—81, v.p., sr. money market economist Merrill Lynch Econs. Inc., 1981-84; sr. v.p., sr. money market economist Becker Paribas Inc., NYC, 1984; corp. first v.p., money market economist Drexel Burnham Lambert Inc., NYC, 1984-86, mng. dir., chief money market economist, 1986—90; pres. Maria Ramirez Capital Cons. Inc. (subs. Hancock Freedom), NYC, 1990—92; pres., CEO Maria Fiorini Ramirez, Inc., 1992—. Bd. dirs. Statewide Savings Bank, 1989—2000, Arlington

Capital, 1991—2000, Security Benefit Life, 1996—98, Independence Community Bank, 2000—06, Schroder Hedge Funds, 2004—, AMF funds, 2005—, Sovereign Bancorp, Inc., 2006—, Security Mutual Ins., Binghamton, NY, 2006, Monavie, Salt Lake City, 2007; mem. investment policy com. & product review com. Edward Jones & Co., 1996—. Mem. advisory bd. Pace U. Lunblin Sch. Bus., 1997—2007; trustee Notre Dame H.S., 2001, Pace U., 2002—; founding mem. 100 Woman in Hedge Fund, 2004. Named Woman of the Yr., Women Bouse Club NY, 1986; recipient Lubin Alumni Achievement award, Pace U., 2001, Metro Internat. Fulbright award for Contributing to Internat. Understanding, 2004, Ellis I. Medal of Honor, 2004. Mem.: The Econ. Club NY. Roman Catholic. Office: 675 3rd Ave New York NY 10017

RAMIREZ, MARIO EFRAIN, physician; b. Roma, Tex., Apr. 3, 1926; s. Efren M. and Carmen (Hinojosa) R.; m. Sarah B. Aycock, Nov. 25, 1949; children: Mario, Patricia Ann, Norman Michael, Jaime Eduardo, Roberto Luis. Student, U. Tex., 1942—45; MD, U. Tenn., 1948. Diplomate Am. Bd. Family Physicians. Intern Shreveport Charity Hosp., La., 1949, resident, practice medicine specializing in family practice; pvt. family practice Roma, 1950—75, Rio Grande City, Tex., 1975—93; owner, adminstr. Ramirez Meml. Hosp., Roma, 1958—75. Assoc. med. dir. South Tex. Blue Cross Blue Shield Tex., McAllen, 1993-95 County judge Starr County, Rio Grande City, 1969-78; chmn. South Tex. Devel. Coun., 1975-76, Tri-County Cmty. Action Coun., 1971-78; mem. coordinated bd. Tex. Colls. and Univs., 1979-85; mem. devel. bd. U. Tex., 1986—; presdl. appointee bd. regents Uniformed Svcs. U. Tex. Health Scis., 1985-92; mem. bd. regents U. Tex. Sys., 1989-95, vice chmn. bd., 1991-92 Recipient Spl. citation Surgeon Gen., 1967, Disting. Alumnus award U. Tex., 1975, 78, Achievement award Lab World, 1978, Presdl. citation U. Tex., 1979, Outstanding Alumnus award U. Tenn., 1991, Mirabeau B. Lamar medal Assn. Tex. Colls. and Univs., 1997; named Family Dr. of Yr., Good Housekeeping mag. and Am. Acad. Family Physicians, 1978, Border Texan of the Yr., 1995; honoree Founder's Day for contbns. to higher edn. U. Tex. Pan Am., 1989; honored by elem. sch. named Dr. Mario E. Ramirez elem. sch., Rio Grande City, Tex., 2006. Fellow Am. Acad. Family Physicians; mem. AMA (vice chmn. com. health care of poor 1971-75, Benjamin Rush Bicentennial award 1976, Coun. Med. Svcs. 1985-94), Tex. Med. Assn. (chmn. com. health care of poor 1971, Disting. Svc. award 1972, pres. 1979-80), Tex. Acad. Family Physicians (v.p. 1973, pres. 1975, Disting. Svc. award 1967, Outstanding Leadership award 1975-76, v.p. Valley chpt. 1960-61, pres. 1961-62), Hidalgo-Starr Counties Med. Soc. (pres. 1964), Lions, K.C, Rotary, Alhambra Club Address: 212 W Pine Ridge Ln Mcallen TX 78503-3129 Personal E-mail: mramirezmd@aol.com.

RAMIREZ, MARTIN RUBEN, engineering educator; BS, Northwestern U., 1984, MS, 1986, PhD, 1991. Asst. to v.p. engring. Perkins & Will, Chgo., 1980-84; cons. engr. Alfred Benesch & Co., Chgo., 1985-86, Teng & Assocs., Chgo.; prof. engring. Johns Hopkins U., Balt., 1990-94; pres. I.D.E.A.S., Chgo., 1994—99; pres., chief product officer 5Ps, Chgo., 1999—. Cons. Wiss-Jenney Elstner, Northbrook, Ill., 1985—86, Mitsubishi Heavy Industries, Hunt Valley, Md.; cons. to forune 500 corps., govts., dists. and instns.; founder, dir. program on engring. Johns Hopkins U., Balt., 1993. Reviewer for several jours.; editor Needs Database. Recipient Fazlur Khan Meml. prize, 1986, Young Investigator award NSF, 1993; Lilly fellow, 1992; NSF grad. fellow, 1985. Mem.: ASME, ASCD, ASCE (assoc.), Am. Acad. Mechanics, IEEE Computer Soc., U.S. Assn. for Computational Mechanics, Am. Soc. Engring. Edn. (chair Frontiers in Edn. Conf. 1993), Am. Edn. Rsch. Assn., Tau Beta Pi. Achievements include major innovations e-business usability, business strategy, learning, integration; orbitz.com, Sprint PCS vision designer. Avocations: bicycling, cars, travel, music. Office Phone: 312-446-9487. Personal E-mail: martin.ramirez@yahoo.com.

RAMIREZ, MONICA E., education educator, consultant; b. New York, NY, Nov. 27, 1952; d. Luis Ramirez de Arellano and Margarete Brendel; m. Neil Allen, Aug. 17, 2002; children: Luis Preiss, Suellen Melzer-Drinnen. BA, MS, U. Munich, 1979; EdS, Novasout Eastern, 1989; PhD, Columbia Pacific U., 1992. Assoc. prof. Fla. Atlantic U., Boca Raton, 1994—97; prof. geology Aims Coll., Greeley, Colo., 1997—2004; assoc. prof. Colo. State U. at Pueblo, 2004—. Stormwater adv. bd. City of Greeley, 2003—; tchr. edn. bd. Colo. State U., 2004—05; geology state chmn. Aims Coll., 2001—04. Contbr. articles to jours.; lang. editor Ctrl. European Sci. Jour., 2002—. Nominee Fla. Governor's award, Fla. Dept. Environ. Edn., 1993; recipient grant, NSF, 2000—04;, Math and Sci. Initiative, Colo. Commn., 2004—05. Avocations: rock climbing, mountain climbing. Office: Colo State U 2200 Bonforte Blvd Pueblo CO 81001 Business E-Mail: monica.ramirez@colostate-pueblo.edu.

RAMIREZ, NOLA MARIE, librarian; b. Painesville, Ohio, July 25, 1953; d. Ruth Alice Young; m. Robert Cisneros Ramirez, Dec. 20, 1983; 1 child, Geoffrey Michael Ross. Attended, West Valley Jr. Coll., San Jose, Calif. Vol. Merced County Libr., Gustine, Calif., 1988—90, libr. asst., 1990—92, branch mgr., 1992—. Co-leader Girl Scouts Am., 1998—. Avocation: reading. Home: 263 Laurel Ave Gustine CA 95322 Office: Merced County Libr Gustine Branch 205 Sixth St Gustine CA 95322 Office Phone: 209-854-3013. Personal E-mail: nolar55@hotmail.com.

RAMIREZ, RALPH HENRY, nurse, corporate executive; b. Oakland, Calif., Sept. 25, 1949; s. Hector Ramirez and Genevieve (Figueroa) Ingraham. BS in Nursing, San Jose State U., 1974; M in Health Svcs. Adminstrn., St. Joseph's Coll., 1995. RN; cert. critical care nurse. DON nursing Chgo. Ctr. Hosp., 1980-84; adminstr. Med. Profls. Supplemental Staffing, Chgo., 1984-85; pres. Progressive Svcs., Chgo., 1985-92; v.p. Seville Internat. Tours, Inc., 1990—; pres. Progressive Health Svcs. Ctrs., Inc., 1992-94, Merchants Nat. Fin. and Mgmt., Houston, 1994-95; ops. mgr. Ravenswood Home Care, Chgo., 1995-98; adminstr. United Home Health Svcs., Homewood, Ill., 1998—2003; br. mgr. Patient Care, Inc., Chgo., 2003—04; v.p. nursing Gentle Home Care, Inc., Deerfield, Ill., 2004—. Contbr. articles to profl. jours. Sponsor nursing symposium, Chgo., 1991—; bd. dirs. AIDS Found. of Chgo., 1991-95, chmn. Gala com., 1993, 94, Chase House, Chgo., 1998-2000; co-chair Bonaventure House Benefit, 1993. Mem. Am. Biog. Inst. (Disting. Leadership award for Outstanding Svc. to Nursing Profession, Golden Acad. award), Chgo. Nurses Assn., Ill. Nurses Assn., Sigma Theta Tau. Democrat. Episcopalian. Avocations: swimming, weightlifting. Office: Gentle Home Care Inc 570 Lake Cook Rd Deerfield IL 60015 Office Phone: 847-444-1222. E-mail: r5218us@yahoo.com.

RAMIREZ, RONALDO VICTOR, science educator; s. Rolando C. and Amor Ramirez; m. Tina Louise Coffman, June 17, 1995; children: Ronaldo Christopher, Gavin Lee. MPH, W.Va. U., Morgantown, 2005. Microbiologist WVDHHR BPH Office Lab. Svcs., South Charleston, W.Va., 1994—2006; lab. instr. U. Charleston Sch. Pharmacy, W.Va., 2006—. Democrat. Roman Catholic. Home Phone: 304-548-7917; Office Phone: 304-357-4394.

RAMIREZ, SANDRA IVELISSE, case manager; d. Anania and Paula Ramirez; m. Rafael Corona, 1983 (div. 1992); children: Omar Corona, Max Corona, Alexander Corona, Cassandra Corona. BS, Springfield Coll., Boston, 1993. Family support worker Roca, Inc., Chelsea, Mass., 1993—2001; social worker Cath. Charities, Inc., Waterbury, Conn., 2001—06; recovery case mgr. Advanced Behavioral Health, Inc., Middletown, Conn., 2006—. Observer Nat. Electoral Coun., DC, 2006; mem. Nat. Assn. Latinos Elected Ofcl., 2003—07; alderwoman City of Waterbury, 2003—07; mem. Conn. Hispanic Dem. Caucus, 2004—07; leader Aspira, Inc., Waterbury. Named Role Model and Mentor on ensuring the optimal health of the child, prevent child abuse and neglect, Dept. Social Svcs., 1997—2000, Human Services Worker of Yr., Chelsea Human Svcs. Collaborative, Inc., 1999—2001; recipient Cmty. Svc. award, Hispanic Profl. Providers, 2006, Accomplishment award, City of Boston, 2006, Hispanic Voter Edn., Cmty. Empowerment award, Commonwealth of PR, 2004. Mem.: Black Dem. Club (assoc.; treas. 2006—07). Democrat. Home: 33 Norton St Waterbury CT 06708 Home Phone: 203-597-1870.

RAMIREZ, SARA, actress; b. Mazatlan, Mexico, Aug. 31, 1976; Actress (Broadway plays) The Capeman, 1998, The Gershwins' Fascinating Rhythm, 1999, A Class Act, 2001, Dreamgirls, 2001, Monty Python's Spamalot, 2005 (Tony award, best performance by featured actress in a musical, 2005, Outer Critics Circle award, outstanding featured actress in a musical, 2005), (off-Broadway plays) The Vagina Monologues, (films) You've Got Mail, 1998, actress (voice) UnJammer Lammy, 1999, actress PaRappa the Rapper 2, 2001, Spider-Man, 2002, Washington Heights, 2002, Chicago, 2002, (TV series) Baseball Wives, 2002, (guest appearance) Law & Order SVU, As the World Turns, 2002, NYPD Blue, 2004, Grey's Anatomy, 2006— (Outstanding Performance by an Ensemble in a Drama Series, SAG, 2007). Office: Cornerstone Talent Agency 37 W 20th St Ste 1108 New York NY 10011-3713 *

RAMIREZ, STEVAN G., consumer products company executive; BS in Bus. Mgmt., Univ. Redlands, Calif.; MBA, Univ. Rochester. Various positions to customer svc. v.p. Xerox Corp., 1972—2000; v.p., worldwide quality, supply chain, consumer imaging Eastman Kodak Co., 2000—01, chief quality officer, v.p., 2001; gen. mgr. customer care Health Group, 2006—. Mgmt. sponsor Kodak Hispanic Orgn. for Leadership, Advancement (HOLA); steering com. chair United Way Latino Leadership Devel. Program. Named one of 50 Most Important Hispanics in Tech. and Bus., Hispanic Engineer Info. Tech. mag., 2003, 2004, 2005. Office: Chief Quality Officer Eastman Kodak 343 State St Rochester NY 14650

RAMIREZ, TED L., lawyer; b. San Antonio, Aug. 16, 1952; BA cum laude, Southwestern Adventist Coll., 1974; JD, Ohio State Univ., 1976. Bar: Ohio 1977, US Tax Ct. 1978. Ptnr. Arter & Hadden, LLP; ptnr., co-chair health care practice Venable LLP, Washington, 2003—. Adj. faculty Columbia Union Coll., Moritz Coll. Law, Ohio State Univ. Contbr. articles profl. journals. Legal affairs com. Loma Linda Univ. and Medical Ctr.; Gen. Conf., exec.com. Seventh-Day Adventists. Mem.: Am. Health Lawyers Assn., Ohio State Bar Assn., Dayton (Ohio) Bar Assn., Columbus (Ohio) Bar Assn. Office: Venable LLP 575 Seventh St NW Washington DC 20004 Office Phone: 202-344-4622. Office Fax: 202-344-8300. Business E-Mail: tramirez@venable.com.

RAMIREZ, TINA, performing company executive; b. Caracas, Venezuela; d. Gloria Maria Cestero and Jose Ramirez Gaonita. Studied dance with Lola Bravo, Alexandra Danilova, Anna Sokolow. Toured with Federico Rey Dance Co.; founder, artistic dir. Ballet Hispanico, NYC, 1970—. Panelist NEA N.Y. Sate Coun. on Arts; mem. advisory panel N.Y.C. Dept. Cultural Affairs; bd. dirs Dance Theater Workshop. Appearances (Broadway plays) Kismet, Lute Song, (TV series) Man of La Mancha. Bd. mem. The New 42nd Street, Inc. Named one of ten people of yr., AARP Mag., 2004; recipient Arts and Culture Honor award, Mayor of NYC, 1983, Ethnic New Yorker award, NYC, 1986, Gov.'s Arts award, NY State Gov. Mario Cuomo, 1987, honoree Nat. Puerto Rican Forum, Hispanic Inst. for Performing Arts., Hispanic Heritage Award, 1999, Dance Magazine Award, 2002, Nat. Medal of Arts, Nat. Endowment for the Arts, 2005. Office: Ballet Hispanico 167 W 89th St New York NY 10024-1901 *

RAMIREZ GARZA, ELIZABETH ANN, biology professor, researcher; d. Joe E. Ramirez Sr. and Diamantina Ramirez; m. Simon Garza, Jr., Sept. 18, 1982; children: Jonathan David Garza, Aaron Zachary Garza, Joshua Joseph Garza, Caleb Daniel Garza. BS in Biology, U. Tex., San Antonio, 1981, MS in Biology, 1986. Cert. radiology Tex. State Bd. Dental Examiners, 1989, dental practice mgmt. asst. Tex., 1990. Rsch. asst. U. Tex. Health Sci. Ctr., San Antonio, 1981—82, 1985—86; student intern genetics lab U. Tex., San Antonio, 1984—85; biology tutor St. Edward's U., Austin, Tex., 1991; lectr. Incarnate Word Coll., San Antonio, 1991—92; adj. faculty biology Austin C.C., 1993—2004, asst. prof. biology, 2004—06; adj. faculty biology Concordia U., Austin, 2002—03. Coll. assistance migrant program mentor St. Edward's U., Austin, 1991—92; biology faculty mentor Dept. Biology, Austin, 1999, biology 1408 com. chmn., 2005. Mem. campus adv. coun. Lyndon Baines Johnson H.S., Austin, 2002—04; active City Charter Commn., Yoakum, Tex., 1987; pres. Bailey Mid. Sch. PTA, Austin, 1999—2000. Nat. Hispanic scholar, Nat. Hispanic Scholarship Com., 1984. Mem.: Tex. C.C. Tchr. Assn. (assoc.). Avocations: hiking, camping, swimming, bicycling. Office: Austin Community College 1212 Rio Grande Austin TX 78701 Home Phone: 512-288-6232; Office Phone: 512-293-1799 23714. Personal E-mail: lramlgarz@msn.com. Business E-Mail: lramirez@austincc.edu.

RAMIREZ-MIRELES, FERNANDO, electrical engineer; s. Fernando Ramirez Matuk and Maria Elia Mireles Tabares; m. Gina Miroslava Guerrero Barja; children: Tania Fernanda Ramirez Guerrero, Thalia Miroslava Ramirez Guerrero. BSc in Electronics Comm., Met. Autonomous U., Mexico City; MScEE, Ctr. for Rsch. and Advanced Studies of Nat. Politechnic Inst., Mexico City; PhDEE, U. So. Calif. Intern Mex. Tel. Co., Mexico City, Distrito Federal, 1987—88; rschr. Ctr. for Rsch. and Advanced Studies Nat. Politechnic Inst., Mexico City, 1988—92; rsch. asst. U. So. Calif., LA, 1996—98; summer intern Torrey Sci. Corp., San Diego, 1997; mem. tech. staff Glenayre/Wireless Access, Santa Clara, Calif., 1998—99; comm. sys. engr. Aware, Inc., Lafayette, Calif., 1999—2001; sr. comm. sys. engr. Ikanos Comms., Fremont, Calif., 2001—03; prof. Inst. Tech Autonomo, Mexico, 2003—. Cons. Nat. Bank Mex., Mexico City, 1991; invited spkr. at tech. confs. Referee: profl. jours.; contbr. articles to profl. jours. and confs. Named Candidate to Nat. Rschr., Nat. Sys. Rschrs., Mex., 1993—94; named one of Best Students of Mex., Best Students of Mex. Orgn., 1989; recipient Fulbright Scholarship, Fulbright-Garcia Robles Comm., 1992—97, Universitarian Merit medal, Met. Autonomous Univ., Mex., 1987, Honorific Mention, IV Ericsson's Nat. Prize of Sci. and Tech., Mex., 1990. Mem.: IEEE (sr.), Soc. Hispanic Profl. Engrs., Tau Beta Pi. Achievements include patents in field of DSL communications. Avocation: travel. Office: Inst Tech Autonomo Rio Hondo 1 Caolniatizapan Mexico Office Phone: +525 55 628 4000 ext. 3620. Personal E-mail: fernandomireles@yahoo.com. Business E-Mail: ramirezm@ieee.org.

RAMIREZ NAFARRATE, ADRIAN, industrial engineer; b. Hermosillo, Sonora, Mexico, Jan. 13, 1979; s. David Ramirez Zayas and Maria de los Angeles Nafarrate Alvarez. Degree in Indsl. and Sys. Engring., U. Sonora, Hermosillo. Mexico, 2000; MS in Mfg. Sys., Monterrey Tech. Inst., Mexico, 2002; postgrad., Ariz. State U. Rsch. asst. Monterrey Tech. Inst., prof. engring. dept. Hermosillo, 2003—05; jr. engr. Motorola Broadband Comm. Sector, Nogales, Mexico, 2000; prof. dept. indsl. engring. U. Sonora, Hermosillo, 2002—06. Exhibitor workshops and confs. in field. Editl. adviser Newspaper El Imparcial, Hermosillo, 2006. Recipient 2d pl. award, U. Sonora, 2006, 3d pl. award, 2005; fellow, TELMEX Found., 1997—2002; scholar, Monterrey Tech and Sci. and Tech. Nat. Coun., 2001—02, Sci. and Tech. Nat. Coun., Mex., 2006—. Mem.: INFORMS. Roman Catholic. Achievements include research in algorithms for the reduction of processing time for printed circuit boards; analysis of the traffic in Hermosillo. Avocations: baseball, languages, movies, soccer, Karate, acting. Home Phone: 480-343-3964. Personal E-mail: adrian.ramirez@asu.edu.

RAMIREZ-RIVERA, JOSE, physician; b. Mayaguez, PR, June 26, 1929; s. Jesus Ramirez and Nieves Rivera; m. Leila Suner, May 14, 1971; children: Frederico, Steven, Sally, Juliette, Natasha, Leila. BA, Johns Hopkins U., 1949; MD, Yale U., 1953. Diplomate Am Bd Internal Med, re-certified 1974. Intern U. Md. Hosp., 1953-54; resident in medicine Univ. Hosp., Balt., 1954-55, fellow in hematology, 1958-59, resident, 1959; staff physician VA Hosp., Balt., 1960-67, assoc. chief of staff, 1962-68; asst. in medicine Johns Hopkins U., 1960-67, instr. in medicine, 1967-68; asst. prof. medicine U. Md., 1961-68; assoc. prof. Duke U., Durham, NC, 1968-70; dir. med. edn. and clin. investigation Western Region P.R., 1970-80; chief medicine Mayaguez (P.R.) Med. Ctr., 1971-82. Prof med Univ PR, San Juan, 1974—, dir univ med servs Med Sci Campus, 1982—86; prof med Univ Cent del Caribe, 1998—; dir Rincon Rural Health Project, 1975—82; assoc chief staff educ VA Med Ctr, San Juan, 1990—92; dir clin investigation La Concepcion Hosp, San German, 1996—. Contbr. articles to med. jours.;, author books of Puerto Rican Legends. Bd dirs Soc Educ Suroeste. With USPHS, 1955—57. Decorated Comendador Imperial Orden Hispanica de Carlos V; named Man of Yr., PR Med. Soc. Western Sect., 1975, 1981. Master: ACP (pres. PR chpt. 1986—88, Blaine Brower Traveling Scholar 1967, Laureate award 2005); fellow: Coll. Chest Physicians, Royal Soc. Med (London); mem.: Imperial Orden Hispanica de Carlos V, Puerto Rican Fedn. Bioethics (bd. dirs. 1999—2002, pres. 2002—), Soc. Autores Puertorriguenos, PR Lung Assn. (bd. dirs. 1975—80), Casa Espanã (bd. dirs. 1998—), Alliance Francaise PR (v.p. 1995—96, pres. 1996—2000, bd. dirs. 2006—), PEN Club. Roman Catholic. Achievements include creating a technique of lung lavage for alveolar proteinosis. Avocations: classical music, literature. Office Phone: 787-793-6576. Personal E-mail: ramirj@hotmail.com.

RAMKRISHNA, DORAISWAMI, chemical engineering educator, researcher; b. Trichur, Kerala, India, Oct. 29, 1938; came to U.S., 1974; s. M.R. and Ponnu (Raman) Doraiswami; married, 1966; children: Sriram, Arvind. B in Chem. Engring., Bombay U., 1960; PhD in Chem. Engring., U. Minn., 1965, DSc (hon.), 2004. From asst. to assoc. prof. chem. engring. Indian Inst. Tech., Kanpur, 1967-75, prof., 1975-76; prof. chem. engring. Purdue U., West Lafayette, Ind., 1976—, Harry Creighton Peffer disting. prof., 1994—. Vis. assoc. prof. U. Wis., Madison, 1974-75; vis. prof. U. Minn., Mpls., 1975-76, George T. Piercy disting. vis. prof., 1988; Kane vis. prof. dept. chem. tech. Bombay U., 1983; Melchor vis. prof. U. Notre Dame, Ind., 1994. Co-author: (with Neal R. Amundson) Linear Operator Methods in Chemical Engineering, 1985, Population Balances, 2000; contbr. over 190 papers to profl. jours. Named Disting. Engring. alumnus Bombay U., 1994. Fellow Am. Inst. Med. and Biol. Engring.; mem. AIChE (Alpha Chi Sigma award 1987, RH Wilhelm award in Chem. Reaction Engring., 1998, Thomas Baron award, 2004), von Humboldt Found. (Sr. Humboldt award 2001). Democrat. Hindu. Achievements include application of operator theory, population balances and stochastic methods to numerous chemical engineering problems. Home: 3517 Woodwind Pl West Lafayette IN 47906-8861 Office: Purdue U Sch Chem Engring Northwestern Ave West Lafayette IN 47907 Home Phone: 765-463-5637; Office Phone: 765-494-4066. Business E-Mail: ramkrish@ecn.purdue.edu.

RAMLER, SIEGFRIED, foundation administrator, researcher; b. Vienna, Oct. 30, 1924; s. Lazar and Eugenia Ramler; m. Piilani A. Ahuna, Dec. 1948 (dec. July 2003); children: David K., Dita L., Laurence K., Malia R.; m. Kiyoko Koizumi, Dec. 1, 2003. Diplôme supérieur, U. Paris, 1958; MA, U. Hawaii, 1961. Interpreter Internat. Mil. Tribunal, Nuremberg, Germany, 1945—46, chief interpreting br., 1946—49; chair fgn. lang. dept. Punahou Sch., Honolulu, 1951-71, dir. instnl. svcs., 1971-91, dir. Wo Internat. Ctr., 1990-95; exec. dir. Found. Study in Hawaii and Abroad, Honolulu, 1969-90. Sr. adj. fellow East-West Ctr., 1995—; pres. adv. bd. Pacific Basin Consortium, Hawaii, 1997-02. Contbr. articles to profl. publs. Vice chair, sec., bd. dir. Crown Prince Akihito Scholarship Found., 1989—; trustee St. Francis Sch., Honolulu, 1996— Decorated Order of the Palmes Académiques, Ordre National du Mérite (France); Order of the Sacred Treasure (Japan); recipient medal Freedom Found., 1958. Mem. ASCD, Internat./Global Edn. Com. (chair nat. adv. com. 1987-93), Japan-Am. Soc. Hawaii (pres. 1986-87, program chmn. 1975-94, Alliance Française Hawaii (pres. and founder 1961, bd. dir. 1992-2001, regent 2001-), World Assn. Internat. Studies (bd. dir. 2000—). Avocations: running, travel, swimming. Home: 921 Maunawili Cir Kailua HI 96734-4620 Office: East West Ctr 1777 E West Rd Honolulu HI 96848 Personal E-mail: ramlers001@hawaii.rr.com.

RAMM, DOUGLAS ROBERT, psychologist; b. New Haven, Dec. 11, 1949; s. Robert Frederick and Gladys (Torgrimson) R.; m. Barbara Stephens, Aug. 10, 1974; children: Jennifer, Jessica. BA, Ithaca Coll., 1972; MA, Duquesne U., 1974, PhD, 1979. Diplomate Am. Bd. Profl. Psychology; bd. cert. clin. psychologist Am. Bd. Profl. Psychology. Staff psychologist Westmoreland Hosp., Greensburg, Pa., 1976-79, chief clin. psychologist, dir. child & adolescent psychiat., 1979-82; pvt. practice Greensburg, Pa., 1980—. Pres. Ethics, Inc., Ctr. for Sci. Study of Values and Morality, 1995-98; cons. U. Pitts., Pa. Bur. Vocat. Rehab., Westmoreland County Ct. of Common Pleas; past pres. Mental Health Assn. Westmoreland County. Author: Clinically Formulated Principles of Morality, 1996, Consider the Scientific Study of Morality, 1998, The Formula for Happiness, 2004, Principles for Achieving Emotional Well-Being, 2005. Mem. APA, ASCD, Am. Philos. Assn., Pa. Psychol. Assn., Acad. Clin. Psychology, Soc. Personality Assessment, Nat. Acad. Neuropsychologists, Nat. Register Health Svc. Providers in Psychology, Am. Coll. Forensic Examiners (diplomate), Soc. Bus. Ethics, Rotary Club. Methodist. Office: 225 Humphrey Rd Ste 4 Greensburg PA 15601-4571 Office Phone: 724-832-9096. Personal E-mail: rammpsychsvcs@aol.com.

RAMMES, LISA M., lawyer; b. Dayton, Ohio, Mar. 4, 1969; BA, Miami U., 1991; JD, U. Cin., 1996. Bar: Ohio 1996, US Dist. Ct. Southern Dist. Ohio 1997. Atty. Wood & Lamping LLP, Cin., 1996—. Mem., Bd. Dirs. CancerFree Kids Pediatric Cancer Rsch. Alliance, mem., Bd. Advisors. Named one of Ohio's Rising Stars, Super Lawyers, 2006. Mem.: Ohio State Bar Assn., Cin. Bar Assn. Office: Wood & Lamping LLP 600 Vine St Ste 2500 Cincinnati OH 45202-2491 Office Phone: 513-852-6000. Office Fax: 513-852-6087.

RAMMING, MICHAEL ALEXANDER, retired school system administrator; b. St. Louis, Feb. 4, 1940; s. William Alexander and Emily Louise (Reingruber) Ramming; m. Susan Ray Oliver, July 9, 1962; children: Michael Murray, Todd Alexander. BS, Centenary Coll., 1963; MA, Washington U., St. Louis, 1968. Cert. adminstr. secondary schs. Mo. Tchr., coach Ladue Sch. Dist., St. Louis, 1963-88, adminstr., 1988—2002; ret., 2002. Adj. prof. Lindenwood U., 2002—; cons. Ladue Sch. Dist., St. Louis, 2002—. Vol. Sr. Olympics, St. Louis, 1992, 1993. Mem.: Mo. Interscholastic Athletic Adminstrs. Assn. (25 Yr. Svc. award), Nat. Interscholastic Athletic Adminstrs., Mo. Assn. Secondary Sch. Prins., Nat. Assn. Secondary Sch. Prins. Avocations: tennis, walking, travel. Home: 18128 Dawns Trail Wildwood MO 63005 Office: Ladue Horton Watkins High Sch 1201 S Warson Rd Saint Louis MO 63124-1266 Personal E-mail: mikeramming@earthlink.net. *As I look back I feel that participation in sports as a player, coach, and fan provided me with a wealth of leadership, community building, daring, sharing, and the ability to accept success and failure.*

RAMO, SIMON, retired engineering executive; b. Salt Lake City, May 7, 1913; s. Benjamin and Clara (Trestman) Ramo; m. Virgina Smith, July 25, 1937; children: James Brian, Alan Martin. BS, U. Utah, 1933, DSc (hon.), 1961; PhD, Calif. Inst. Tech., 1936; DEng (hon.), Case Western Res. U., 1960, U. Mich., 1966, Poly. Inst. NY, 1971; DSc (hon.), Union Coll., 1963,

Worcester Polytechnic Inst., 1968, U. Akron, 1969, Cleve. State U., 1976; LLD (hon.), Carnegie-Mellon U., 1970, U. So. Calif., 1972, Gonzaga U., 1983, Occidental Coll., 1984, Claremont U., 1985. With Gen. Electric Co., 1936—46; v.p. ops. Hughes Aircraft Co., 1946—53; with Ramo-Woolridge Corp., 1953—58; dir. U.S. Intercontinental Ballistic Missile Program, 1954—58, TRW Inc., 1954—85, exec. v.p., 1958—61, vice chmn. bd., 1961—78, chmn. exec. com., 1969—78, cons., 1978—; pres. The Bunker-Ramo Corp., 1964—66; chmn. bd. TRW-Fujitsu Co., 1980—83. Vis. prof. mgmt. sci. Calif. Inst. Tech., 1978—; Regents lectr. UCLA, 1981—82, U. Calif. at Santa Cruz, 1978—79; chmn. Ctr. for Study Am. Experience, U. So. Calif., 1978—80; Faculty fellow John F. Kennedy Sch. Govt., Harvard U., 1980—84; mem. White House Energy Rsch. and Devel. Adv. Coun., 1973—75; chmn. Pres.'s Com. on Sci. and Tech., 1976—77; bd. advisors for sci. and tech. Repu. of China, 1981—84; chmn. bd. Aetna, Jacobs & Ramo Venture Capital, 1987—90, Allenwood Ventures, Inc., 1987—. Author: The Business of Science, 1988, other sci., engring. and mgmt. books, (non-fiction) Meetings, Meetings and More Meetings, 2005. Life trustee Calif. Inst. Tech., Nat. Symphony Orch. Assn., 1973—83; trustee emeritus Calif. State U.; bd. govs., pres. Performing Arts Coun. Mus. Ctr. LA, 1976—77; co-chair bd. overseers Keck Sch. Medicine, U. So. Calif., 1999—; bd. dirs. W. M. Keck Found., 1983—, LA World Affairs Coun., 1973—85, Mus. Ctr. Found., LA, LA Philharm. Assn., 1981—84. Named to Bus. Hall of Fame, 1984; recipient IAS, 1956, award, Am. Inst. Elec. Engrs., 1959, Am. Iron and Steel Inst., 1968, Medal of Achievement, AEA, 1970, DSM, Armed Forces Comm. and Electronics Assn., 1970, medal of achievement, WEMA, 1970, Kayan medal, Columbia U., 1972, award, Am. Cons. Engrs. Coun., 1974, Nat. Medal of Sci., Pres. of US, 1976, 1979, medal, Franklin Inst., 1978, awards, U. So. Calif., 1979, Pres. medal Sci., 1981, UCLA medal, 1982, Presdl. Medal of Freedom, Pres. of US, 1983, Aesculapian award, UCLA, 1984, Durand medal, AAIA, 1984, John Fritz medal, 1986, Henry Townley Heald award, Ill. Inst. Tech., 1988, Nat. Engring. award, Am. Assn. Engring. Socs., 1988, Franklin-Jefferson medal, 1988, Howard Hughes meml. award, 1989, Air Force Space and Missile Pioneers award, 1989, Pioneer award, Internat. Coun. on Sys. Engring., 1997, Disting. pub. Svc. medal, NASA, 1999, Lifetime Achievement trophy, Smithsonian Inst., 1999, John F. Kennedy Astronautics award, Am. Astronautical Soc., 2000, John R. Alison award for indsl. leadership, Air Force Assn., 2000, Presdl. Medallion, U. So. Calif., 2002, Founders award, USC Thornton Sch. of Music, 2003, Lifetime Space Achievement award, Space Found., 2007. Fellow: IEEE (Electronic Achievement award 1953, Golden Omega award 1975, Founders medal 1980, Centennial medal 1984), Am. Acad. Polit. Sci., Am. Acad. Arts and Scis.; mem.: NAS, Nat. Acad. Engring. (founder, coun. mem. Bueche award), Internat. Acad. Astronautics, Pacific Coun. Internat. Policy, Coun. Fgn. Rels., Inst. advancement Engring., Am. Philos. Soc., Am. Phys. Soc., NY Acad. Scis., Theta Tau (Hall of Fame laureate), Eta Kappa Nu (eminent mem. award 1966). Office: 9200 W Sunset Blvd Ste 801 Los Angeles CA 90069-3603

RAMO, VIRGINIA M. SMITH, civic worker; b. Yonkers, NY; d. Abraham Harold and Freda (Kasnetz) Smith; m. Simon Ramo; children: James Brian, Alan Martin. BS in Edn., U. So. Calif., DHL (hon.), 1978. Nat. co-chmn., ann. giving U. So. Calif., 1968-70, vice chmn., trustee, 1971—, co-chmn. bd. councilors Sch. Performing Arts, 1975-76, co-chmn. bd. councillors Schs. Med. and Engring. Vice-chmn. bd. overseers Hebrew Union Coll., 1972-75; bd. dirs. The Muses of Calif. Mus. Sci. and Industry, UCLA Affiliates, Estelle Doheny Eye Found., U. So. Calif. Sch. Medicine; mem. adv. coun. L.A. County Heart Assn., chmn. com. to endow Chair in cardiology at U. So. Calif.; vice chmn., bd. dirs. Friends of Libr. U. So. Calif.; bd. dirs., nat. pres. Achievement Rewards for Coll. Scientists Found., 1975-77; bd. dirs. Les Dames L.A., Cmty. TV So. Calif.; bd. dirs., v.p. Founders L.A. Music Ctr.; v.p. L.A. Music Ctr. Opera Assn.; v.p. corp. bd. United Way; v.p. Blue Ribbon-400 Performing Arts Coun.; chmn. com. to endow chair in gerontology U. So. Calif.; vice chmn. campaign Doheny Eye Inst,. 1986; co-chair, bd. overseers Keck Sch. Medicine U. So. Calif., 1999—. Recipient Svc. award Friends of Librs., 1974, Nat. Cmty. Svc. award Alpha Epsilon Phi, 1975, Disting. Svc. award Am. Heart Assn., 1978, Svc. award U. So. Calif., Spl. award U. So. Calif. Music Alumni Assn., 1979, Life Achievement award Mannequins of L.A. Assistance League, 1979, Woman of Yr. award Pan Hellenic Assn., 1981, Disting. Svc. award U. So. Calif. Sch. Medicine, 1981, U. So. Calif. Town and Gown Recognition award, 1986, Asa V. Call Achievement award U. So. Calif., 1986, Phi Kappa Phi scholarship award U. So. Calif., 1986, Vision award Luminaires of Doheny Eye Inst., 1994, Presdl. medallion U. So. Calif., 2002, USC Thornton Sch. of Music Founder's award, 2003. Mem. UCLA Med. Aux., U. So. Calif. Pres.'s Cir., Commerce Assocs. U. So. Calif., Cedars of Lebanon Hosp. Women's Guild (dir. 1967-68), Blue Key, Skull and Dagger.

RAMOS, ALBERT A., electrical engineer; b. L.A., Feb. 28, 1927; s. Jesus D. and Carmen F. (Fontes) R.; B.S. in Elec. Engring., U. So. Calif., 1950, M.S. in Systems Mgmt., 1972; Ph.D., U.S. Internat. U., 1975; m. Joan C. Pailing, Sept. 23, 1950; children— Albert A., Richard R., James J., Katherine. With guided missile test group Hughes Aircraft Co., 1950-60; with TRW DSG, 1960-91, sr. staff engr. Norton AFB, San Bernardino, Calif., 1969-91, ret., 1991. Served with USNR, 1945-46. Registered profl. engr., Calif. Mem. IEEE, NSPE, Air Force Assn., Mexican-Am. Engring. Soc., Mexican-Am. Profl. Mgmt. Assn. (mem. administering commn. dept. community svcs.), Sigma Phi Delta, Eta Kappa Nu, Tau Beta Pi. Home: 8937 Napoli Dr Las Vegas NV 89117-1182

RAMOS, DENISE L., corporate financial executive; MBA, Univ. Chgo., 1979. Fin. mgmt. positions through asst. treas. Atlantic Richfield Co., LA; sr. v.p., treas., CFO KFC Yum! Brands, 2000—05; CFO Furniture Brands Internat., 2005—07; sr. v.p., CFO ITT Corp., White Plains, NY, 2007—. Office: ITT Corp 4 W Red Oak Ln White Plains NY 10604 *

RAMOS, JAMIE, information scientist; s. David and Sue Ramos; m. Crystal Ramos, July 10, 1999; children: Alyssa, Andrew. Micro tech. Ind. U., Kokomo, 1998—2000; instrnl. systems coord. Kokomo-Ctr. Schs., 2000—. Office: Kokomo-Center Schools 2501 S Berkley Kokomo IN 46902 Office Phone: 765-455-8095. Office Fax: 765-455-8098. Business E-Mail: jdramos@kokomoschools.com.

RAMOS, JORGE, newscaster; b. Mex. City, Mar. 16, 1958; arrived in U.S., 1983; 2 children. Grad. in Comm., Ibero-Am. U., Mex. City; M in Internat. Studies, U. Miami. News reporter Univision, LA, 1984—86; host Mundo Latino, Univision TV prog., 1986; anchorman Noticiero Univision, 1986—. Founder Wake Up Reading book club, 2002—. Author: (autobiography) No Borders: a Journalist's Search for Home, Behind the Mask, The Other Face of America, What I Saw, Hunting the Lion, The Latino Wave, Dying to Cross; contbr. weekly column, NY Times Syndicate. Named one of Ten Most Admired Latinos, Latino Leaders mag., 2004, 25 Most Influential Hispanics, Time Mag., 2005; recipient Maria Moors Cabot award, Columbia Univ., 2001, Ruben Salazar award, Nat. Council La Raza, 2002, Ron Brown award, Nat. Child Labor Com., 2002, David Brinkley award for Journalistic Excellence, Barry Univ., 2003, 8 Emmy awards, Nat. Acad. Television Arts & Sci. Office: Univision Communications Ste 3050 1999 Ave of the Stars Los Angeles CA 90067 Studio: WNJU-TV Noticiero 47 6th Fl 2200 Fletcher Ave Fort Lee NJ 07024 Office Phone: 201-969-4247. Office Fax: 201-969-4120. E-mail: jramos@univision.net, jorge.ramos@nbcuni.com.

RAMOS-CANO, HAZEL BALATERO, caterer, chef, innkeeper, restaurateur, entrepreneur; b. Davao City, Mindanao, Philippines, Sept. 2, 1936; came to U. S., 1960. d. Mauricio C. and Felicidad (Balatero) Ramos; m. William Harold Snyder, Feb. 17, 1964 (div. 1981); children: John Byron, Snyder, Jennifer Ruth; m. Nelson Allen Blue, May 30, 1986 (div. 1990); m. A. Richard Cano, June 25, 1994. BA in Social Work, U. Philippines, Quezon City, 1958; MA in Sociology, Pa. State U., 1963, postgrad., 1966—67. Cert. exec. chef, Am. Culinary Fedn. Faculty, tng. staff Peace Corps Philippine Project, University Park, Pa., 1961-63; sociology instr. Albright Coll., Reading, Pa., 1963-64; rsch. asst. Meth. Ch. U.S.A., State College, Pa., 1965-66; rsch. asst. dept. child devel. & family rels. Pa. State U., University Park, 1966-67; exec. dir. Presbyn. Urban Coun. Raleigh Halifax Ct. Child Care and Family Svc. Ctr., 1973-79; early childhood educator Learning Together, Inc., Raleigh, NC, 1982-83; loan mortgage specialist Raleigh Savs. & Loan, 1983-84; restaurant owner, mgr. Hazel's on Hargett, Raleigh, 1985-86; admissions coord., social worker Brian Corp. Nursing Home, Raleigh, 1986-88, food svc. dir., 1989-90; regional dir. La Petite Acad., Raleigh, 1989-90; asst. food svc. mgr. Granville Towers, Chapel Hill, NC, 1990-92; mgr. trainee Child Nutrition Svcs. Wake County Pub. Sch. Sys., Raleigh, 1993-94; food svc. dir. S.W. Va. 4-H Ednl. Conf. Ctr., Abingdon, 1994-95; caterer, owner The Eclectic Chef's Catering, 1995—; innkeeper, owner Love House Bed and Breakfast, 1996—; pres. Ramos-Cano Inc., 1996—, Ramos-Cano Mgmt. Svcs., LLC, 2002—; owner Withers Hardware Restaurant, Abingdon, 2002—, The Frame Shop, Abingdon, 2004—, The Victoria and Albert Inn, 2000—. Cooking instr. Wake Cmty. Tech. Coll., Raleigh, 1986-92; freelance caterer, 1964-95; chair Internat. Cooking Demonstrations Raleigh Internat. Festival, 1990-93. Pres. Wake County Day Care United Coun., 1974-75, NC Assn. Edn. Young Children (Raleigh chpt.), 1975-76; bd. dirs. Project Enlightenment Wake County Pub. Schs., 1976-77; active Pines of Carolina coun. Girl Scout USA, 1976-85; chmn. Philippine Health and Medical Aid Com., Phil-Am Assn. Raleigh 1985-88 (publicity chmn.); elder Trinity Presbyn. Ch., Raleigh, 1979-81, bd. deacons, 1993-94; elder, session mem. Sinking Spring Presbyn. Ch., 1997—; treas. Abingdon Newcomers Club, 1997—, Presbyn. Women, Sinking Spring Presbyn. Ch., Abingdon, 1999—; master gardener Va. Tech. Master Gardeners Program, 1998—. Rockefeller grant Rockefeller Found., 1958-59; recipient Ramon Magsaysay Presdl. award Philippine Leadership Youth Movement, 1957; Gov.'s Cert. Appreciation State NC, 1990, Raleigh Mayor's award Quality Childcare Svcs., 1990, award for keeping hist. Abington beautiful Abington Kiwanis Club, 1997 Mem. Am. Culinary Fedn., Presby. Women, Raleigh, (historian 1975-76), Penn State Dames (pres. 1968-69). Democrat. Office: Victoria & Albert Inn 224 Oak Hill St Abingdon VA 24210 also: The Love House Bed and Breakfast 210 E Valley St Abingdon VA 24210 also: Withers Hardware Restaurant 260 W Main St Abingdon VA 24210 also: The Frame Shop 115 Charwood Dr Abingdon VA 24210 also: Somethyme Bistro 115 Charwood Dr Abingdon VA 24210 Home Phone: 276-623-1281; Office Phone: 276-628-1111. E-mail: v&ainn@naxs.com, rcano@naxs.com.

RAMOS-CARO, FRANCISCO A., dermatologist, educator; MD, U. PR, San Juan, 1977. Diplomate Am. Bd. Dermatology. Assoc. prof. medicine U. Fla., Gainesville. Fellow: Am. Acad. Dermatology; mem.: Alpha Omega Alpha. Office: U Fla Divsn Dermatology PO Box 100277 Gainesville FL 32610

RAMPACHER, HERMANN HANS, writer, consultant; b. Ulm, Germany, Dec. 29, 1934; s. Hermann Alexander and Pauline Katharine (Milch) R.; m. Ursel Hanna Brand; 1 child, Carsten. BS, Coll. Stuttgart, 1954, MSc in Physics, 1962; Dr.rer.nat., U. Munich, 1968. Charter IT profl. Brit. Computer Soc. Rsch. asst. Max Planck Gesellschaft, Munich, 1965-68; asst. prof. U. Tuebingen, 1968-70; systems engr. IBM Deutschland, Stuttgart, 1970-79; rschr. GMD German Nat. Rsch. Ctr. for Info. Tech., Bonn, 1979-81; chief exec. German Informatics Soc., Bonn, 1982-99; mng. dir. German Info. Acad. GmbH (DIA), 1997-2000; ptnr. DLGI Ltd. Bd. dirs. Internat. Conf. and Rsch. Ctr. for Computer Sci., Castle Dagstuhl, 1995-99; founder Coun. European Profl. Informatics Socs Fellow Brit. Computer Soc. (chartered info. tech. profl.); mem. Max-Planck Gesellschaft, German Soc. Philosophy, Gesellschaft Deutscher Naturforscher und Aerzte. Avocations: normative theories, history, classical music. Office: DLGI Wissenschaftszentrum Ahrstr D-53175 Bonn Germany Fax: 49 0 228 302-161. E-mail: hrampacher@dlgi.de.

RAMPE, DAVID, editor; Asst. fgn. editor, weekend New York Times. Office: New York Times 229 W 43d St New York NY 10036 Office Phone: 212-556-7415. Office Fax: 212-556-7278.

RAMPE, KEVIN M., real estate developer; b. 1966; m. Christine Rampe; children: William, Mathhew. BA cum laude, Union Coll.; JD magna cum laude, Albany U.; grad. in Sr. Exec. Program, Harvard U.; LLD (hon.), Union Coll., 2004. Litig. assoc. Shearman & Stearling, 1992—96; first asst. counsel Gov. Pataki's Office, 1996—99; from dep. supt. and gen. counsel to first dep. supt. Ins. Dept. N.Y. State Ins. Dept., 1999—2004, first dep. supt., COO, 2004—05; exec. v.p., gen. counsel Lower Manhattan Devel. Corp, NYC, 2002—03; pres. Lower Manhattan Devel. Corp., NYC, 2003—05, chmn., 2006—. Named one of 40 Under 40, Crain's NY Bus., 2005. Office: Lower Manhattan Development Corp One Liberty Plaza 20th Fl New York NY 10006

RAMPERSAD, PEGGY A. SNELLINGS, sociologist, consultant; b. Fredericksburg, Va., Jan. 12, 1933; d. George Daniel and Virginia Riley (Bowler) Snellings; m. Oliver Ronald Rampersad, Mar. 19, 1955; 1 child, Gita. BA, Mary Washington Coll., Fredericksburg, 1953; student, Sch. Art Inst. Chgo., 1953—55; MA, U. Chgo., 1965, PhD, 1978. Grad. admissions counselor U. Chgo., 1954—57, adviser fgn. students, 1958, dir. admissions Grad. Sch. Bus., 1958—63, rsch. project specialist, 1970—78, pers. mgr., 1979—80, mgr. orgnl. devel., 1980—82, adminstr. dept. econs., 1983—95; cons. PSR Consulting, Chgo., 1995—. Cons. North Ctrl. Assn. Colls. and Secondary Schs., Chgo., 1964—70, Orchestral Assn. Chgo. Symphony Orch., 1982, Chgo. Ctr. Decision Rsch., 1982, Harvard U., 1993—97. Exhibitions include Va. Mus. Fine Arts, Art Inst. Chgo., others; editor: North Ctrl. Assn. Quar., 1972; contbr. articles to profl. jours. Grad. fellow, U. Chgo., 1963—67. Mem.: AAUW, Am. Acad. Polit. and Social Sci., Am. Econ. Assn., Art Inst. Chgo. (assoc.), Pi Lambda Theta (past pres.). Episcopalian. Avocations: painting, drawing, opera, reading, walking. Home and Office: 28 Seneca Ter Fredericksburg VA 22401-1115

RAMPERSAUD LUNDY, SHERYLL, special education educator; b. Portsmouth, Va., Dec. 30, 1947; d. Rebecca Greene and Freddie Lee Drake; children: Vincent Earle Rampersaud, Sean Derrik Rampersaud, Sharon Antoinette Rampersaud. BS in Acctg., Norfolk State U., 1971—74, Advanced Studies Tchr. Certification, 2000—01. Spl. Educator Emotional Disturbance and Specific Learning Disabilities Va. Bd. Edn., 2002. Fire rates clk. Geico, Friendship Heights, Md., 1968—70; staff acct. Peat, Marwick, Mitchell CPAs, Washington, 1974—76; asst. internal auditor Howard U., Washington, 1976—80; pension acct./ cons. Qualified Pension Consultants/ Compdesign Inc., Bethesda, Md., 1983—98, Thomas F. Barrett, Inc., Bethesda, 1998—99; spl. edn. tchr. The Pines Residential Treatment Ctr., Portsmouth, Va., 2000—. Dir. Sankofa Cultural and Learning Ctr., Inc., Portsmouth, 1999—. Chief officer John F. Kennedy Poling Sta., Portsmouth, 1999—2001. Mem. Christian Ch. Home: 3204 Gwin St Portsmouth VA 23704 Office: The Pines Residential Treatment Center 825 Crawford Pky Portsmouth VA 23070 Home Phone: 757-397-1951; Office Phone: 757-391-6588. Personal E-mail: srampersaud@cox.net. E-mail: sheryl.rampersaud@absfirst.com.

RAMPHAL, JULIE FRANCES, retired secondary school educator; b. Sioux Falls, SD, Jan. 31, 1944; d. Shelton Russell and Frances Pauline (Hospers) Tilgner; m. Cecil Edward Ramphal, Aug. 29, 1976 (dec. Apr. 2000); stepchildren: Richard Andre, Rani. BA in English, Macalester Coll., 1966; MS in Ednl. Computing, Pepperdine U., 1985. Secondary tchr. Glendora Unified Sch. Dist., Calif., 1966—69, Tustin Unified Sch. Dist., Calif., 1969—2000. Coll. instr. Nat. U., Irvine, Calif., 1987; mentor tchr. Tustin Unified Sch. Dist., Calif., 1995—97; workshop leader Orange County Dept. of Edn., Costa Mesa, Calif., 1998. Workshop presenter Computer Using Educators (CUE) State Confs., Palm Springs, Calif., 1988—95. Recipient Exemplary Achievement in the field of Ednl. Tech., Ednl. Computing Alumni of Pepperdine U., 1992, grant, Women's Action Alliance of NYC, 1991—93, Mentor Tchr. in Tech., Tustin Unified Sch. Dist., 1995—97; grant, Calif. Academic Partnership Program, 1992. Mem.: Am. Assn. of U. Women (v.p. membership 2004—06, legal advocacy fund chair 2006—). Avocations: swimming, singing, gardening, piano, travel. Home: 20141 Crown Reef Lane Huntington Beach CA 92646 Home Phone: 714-964-5682. Personal E-mail: julieps23@aol.com.

RAMSAUR, ALLAN FIELDS, legal association administrator, lobbyist; b. Rocky Mount, NC, Dec. 30, 1951; s. Carl Hamilton and Celestine (Fields) R.; m. Jimmie Lynn Brewer, Sept. 2, 1972; children: Katherine Celeste, Benjamin Allan. BA in Polit. Sci., Lambuth U., 1974; JD, U. Tenn., 1977. Bar: Tenn. 1977. Staff atty. Tenn. Dept. Mental Health, Nashville, 1977—80; dir. Tenn. Assn. Legal Svcs., Nashville, 1980—86; campaign dir. Steve Cobb, Nashville, 1986; exec. dir. Nashville Bar Assn., 1986—98, Tenn. Bar Assn., 1999—. Pres. Woodland-in-Waverly Neighborhood Assn., Nashville, 1985; bd. dirs. SAGA, Nashville, 1984-86, Bethlehem Ctr., Nashville, 1990-96 (sec. 1992, v.p. 1994-95). Recipient Leadership Nashville award, 1988. Mem. ABA (liaison to standing com. on legal aid and indigent defendants 1984-86, spl. com. on prepaid legal svcs. 1988-89, standing com. on lawyer referral and info. svc. 1990-92), Nat. Assn. Bar Execs. (chair edn. com.), Tenn. Bar Assn. (pres. young lawyers divsn. 1985-86), Nat. Legal Aid and Defender Assn. (chmn. legis com. 1984-86), Tenn. Soc. Assn. Execs. (pres. 2000, named Assn. Exec. of Yr. 2007). Democrat. Methodist. Home: 1417 Beddington Park Nashville TN 37215-5815 Office Phone: 615-383-7421. Business E-Mail: aramsaur@tnbar.org.

RAMSAY, DAVID LESLIE, physician, dermatologist, educator; b. Rochester, NY, Apr. 25, 1943; s. Joseph Walter and Jean (Eastwood) R. AB in English with honors, Ind. U., 1965, MD, 1969; MEd, U. Ill., 1973. Diplomate Am. Bd. Dermatology. Assoc. faculty mem. Ind. U., Indpls., 1965-69; intern in medicine George Washington U. Med. Ctr., 1969-70; resident in dermatology NYU Med. Ctr., 1970-73; dir. dermatology residency tng. Nat. Naval Med. Ctr., Bethesda, Md., 1973-75; asst. prof. medicine Georgetown U., Washington, 1974-75; asst. prof. dermatology NYU, 1974-78, assoc. prof. dermatology, 1978-95, prof. dermatology, 1995—2003, clin. prof. dermatology, 2003—, senator, 1986-94, pres. faculty coun., 1988-90, dir. ednl. affairs dermatology, 1975—2002, dir. cutaneous lymphoma sect., 1975—. Author: Simulations in Dermatology, 1974; contbg. author: Adolescent Dermatology, Basic Mechanisms of Physiologic and Aberrant Lymphoproliferation in the Skin, Hematology and Oncology Clinics in North America; sr. editor: Jour. of Drugs in Dermatology, 2003-; contbr. more than 25 articles to profl. jours. Pres., bd. dirs. One Fifth Ave. Apt. Corp., N.Y.C., 1978-80; trustee Bklyn. Acad. Music, 1989—, chmn. visual arts com., chmn. edn. com; bd. dirs. Cutaneous Lymphoma Found., 2003—. Lt. comdr. USN, 1973-75. NIH fellow U. Ill., 1972-73. Fellow ACP, Internat. Soc. Cutaneous Lymphomas, Am. Acad. Dermatology; mem. Am. Dermatologic Assn. Roman Catholic. Avocations: collecting visual art, swimming, reading. Home: One Fifth Ave New York NY 10003 Office: NYU Med Ctr 530 5th Ave New York NY 10036-5101 E-mail: DRamsay1@nuc.rr.com.

RAMSAY, DONALD ALLAN, physical chemist; b. London, July 11, 1922; s. Norman and Thirza Elizabeth (Beckley) Ramsay; m. Nancy Brayshaw, June 8, 1946 (dec. July 25, 1998); children: Shirley Margaret, Wendy Kathleen, Catharine Jean, Linda Mary; m. Marjorie Craven Findlay, Apr. 13, 2000. BA, Cambridge U., Eng., 1943, MA, PhD, Cambridge U., Eng., 1947, ScD, 1976; D honoris causa, U. Reims, France, 1969; Filosofie hedersdoktor, U. Stockholm, Sweden, 1982. With divsn. chemistry Nat. Rsch. Coun. Can., Ottawa, 1947-49, with divsn. physics, 1949-75; with Herzberg Inst. Astrophysics, 1975-87, sr. research officer, 1961-68, prin. research officer, 1968-87, guest worker, 1987—2001, Steacie Inst. Molecular Scis., rschr. emeritus, 2002—. Vis. prof. U. Minn., 1964, U. Orsay, 1966, U. Stockholm, 1967, 71, 74, U. Calif., Irvine, 1970, U. Sao Paulo, 1972, 78, U. Bologna (Italy), 1973, U. We. Australia, 1976, Australian Nat. U., 1976, East China Normal U., Shanghai, 1987, Tex. Christian U., 1988, U. Wuppertal, Germany, 1988, U. Canterbury, Christchurch, New Zealand, 1991, 96, U. Ulm, Germany, 1992, Germany, 96, Germany, 97. Editor: (with J. Hinze) Selected Works of Robert S. Mulliken, 1975; contbr. articles to profl. jours. Recipient commemorative medal for 125th anniversary Confederation Can., 1992, Alexander von Humboldt Rsch. award, 1993-95; decorated Queen Elizabeth Silver Jubilee medal. Fellow: Chem. Inst. Can. (Chem. Inst. Can. medal 1992), Am. Phys. Soc., Royal Soc. London, Royal Soc. Can. (life; treas. 1976—79, 1988—91, Centennial medal 1982); mem.: Order of Can. Mem. United Ch. of Canada (organist 1954-97). Club: Leander (Henley-on-Thames, Eng.). Achievements include research in molecular spectra and molecular structure. Home: 400 Laurier Ave E Apt 11 Ottawa ON Canada K1N 8Y2 Office: Nat Rsch Coun 100 Sussex Dr Ottawa ON Canada K1A 0R6 E-mail: donald.ramsay@nrc.ca.

RAMSAY, J. RUSSELL, psychologist; s. J. Roger and Mary Ann Ramsay; m. Amy D. Bozzuto; children: Abigail G., Brynn A. BA in Psychology, U. Miami, 1988; MS in Clin. Psychology, Pacific Grad. Sch. Psychology, 1994, PhD in Clin. Psychology, 1995. Instr. U. Pa. Sch. Medicine, Phila., 1997—2000, asst. prof. psychology in psychiatry, 2001—. Editl. cons. Oxford U. Press, 2003. Mem. editl. bd. Jour. Attention Disorders, 2005—, Jour. Psychotherapy Integration, 2005—; author: Cognitive Behavioral Therapy for Adult ADHD, 2007; contbr. articles to profl. jours., chapters to books. Fellow, Ctr. Cognitive Therapy, Phila., 1995—96; Henry King Stanford scholar, U. Miami, 1984—88. Fellow: Pa. Psychol. Assn.; mem.: APA, Internat. Assn. Cognitive Psychotherapy, Psi Chi, Golden Key Honor Soc. Avocations: soccer, exercise, reading.

RAMSAY, KARIN KINSEY, publisher, educator; b. Brownwood, Tex., Aug. 10, 1930; d. Kirby Luther and Ina Rebecca (Wood) Kinsey; m. Jack Cummins Ramsay Jr., Aug. 31, 1951; children: Annetta Jean, Robin Andrew. BA, Trinity U., 1951. Cert. assoc. ch. edn., 1980. Youth coord. Covenant Presbyn. Ch., Carrollton, Tex., 1961-76; dir. ch. edn. Northminster Presbyn. Ch., Dallas, 1976-80, Univ. Presbyn. Ch., Chapel Hill, N.C., 1987-90, Oak Grove Presbyn. Ch., Bloomington, Minn., 1990-93; coord. ecum. ministry Flood Relief for Iowa, Des Moines, 1993; program coord. 1st Presbyn. Ch., Green Bay, Wis., 1994—98; owner, sole proprietor Hist. Resources Press, Corinth and Denton, Tex., 1994—. Dir. Godspell tour Covenant Presbyn. Ch., 1972-75; mem. Presbytery Candidates Com., Dallas, 1977-82, Presbytery Exams. Com. Dallas, 1979-81; clk. coun. New Hope Presbytery, Rocky Mount, NC, 1989-90; creator, dir. Thee Holy Fools mime/musical group and This Is Me retreats. Author: Ramsay's Resources, 1983—; co-author: I Can Feel the Sunshine, 2006; pub., editor: Patton's Ill-Fated Raid, 2002, Angel Kisses and My Beating Heart, 2004; contbr. articles to profl. jours. Design cons. Brookhaven Hosp. Chapel, Dallas, 1977-78; elder Presbyn. Ch. U.S.A., 1982—; coord. Lifeline Emergency Response, Dallas, 1982-84. Mem. Internat. Platform Assn., Small Publisher's Assn. of N. Am.,Pub. Marketing Assoc., Writer's League of Tex. Home Phone: 940-321-1066; Office Phone: 940-321-1066. *Yesterday taught me the lessons which made today possible. Today is the challenging link between yesterday and tomorrow. Tomorrow is an opportunity built on the foundation of today. Today is special.*

RAMSAY, MICHAEL, communications company executive; BSEE, U. Edinburgh, Scotland. Sr. v.p., gen. mgr., visual systems group Silicon Graphics, Inc., 1991—94, pres. Silicon Studio, Inc, 1994—96, sr. v.p. Silicon Desktop Group, 1996—97; CEO TiVo Inc., 1997—2005, chmn., 1997—. Bd. dir. Netflix. Office: TiVo Inc 2160 Gold St Alviso CA 95002-2160

RAMSAY, RICHARD L., lawyer; b. Pine Bluff, Ark., Apr. 30, 1952; BA, U. Ark., 1974, JD, 1977. Bar: Ark. 1977, US Dist. Ct. (Ea. Dist. Ark.) 1977, US Dist. Ct. (We. Dist. Ark.) 1977, US Ct. Appeals (8th Cir.) 1980. Ptnr. Eichenbaum, Liles & Hester PA, Little Rock. Mem.: Debtor-Creditor Bar Ctrl. Ark., ABA (exec. coun. mem. 1987), Ark. Bar Assn. (pres. young lawyers divsn. 1986, pres.-elect 2006—07, pres. 2007—08). Office: Eichenbaum Liles & Hester PA Ste 1400 124 W Capitol Ave Little Rock AR 72201-3736 Office Phone: 501-376-4531. Office Fax: 501-376-8433.

RAMSAY, VIOLETA, language educator, consultant; b. Chihuahua, Mexico, Sept. 29, 1949; d. Manuel Martinez and Bertha Blanco Munoz; m. Keith A. Ramsay; 1 child, Odysseus E. PhD magna cum laude, U. Oreg., Eugene, 1990. Assoc. prof. Spanish Linfield Coll., McMinnville, Oreg., 1998—, chair dept. modern langs., 2006—. Mem. Rainbow Family Svcs., McMinnville, 2000—05. Mem.: ADFL, Pacific NW Coun. for Langs., Confederation in Oreg. for Lang. Tchg., Am. Coun. for the Tchg. of Fgn. Langs., Phi Beta Kappa. American Independent. Avocations: yoga, travel. Office: Linfield Coll 900 SE Baker St Mcminnville OR 97128 Home Phone: 503-434-6488; Office Phone: 503-883-2544. Business E-Mail: vramsay@linfield.edu.

RAMSAY, WILLIAM CHARLES, writer, composer; b. NYC, Nov. 6, 1930; s. Claude Barnett and Myrtle Marie (Scott) Ramsay; m. Jane Coutant Evans, July 7, 1997; children from previous marriage: Alice, John, Carol Ramsay Scott, David. BA in English Lit., U. Colo., 1952; MA in Physics, UCLA, 1957, PhD in Physics, 1962. NFS postdoctoral fellow U. Calif., San Diego, 1962-64, asst. prof. Santa Barbara, 1964-67; tech. mgr. Sys. Assocs., Inc., Long Beach, Calif., 1967-72; sr. environ. economist U.S. AEC, Bethesda, Md., 1972-75; tech. adviser U.S. Nuc. Regulatory Agy., Washington, 1975-76; sr. fellow Resources for the Future, Washington, 1976-83, Ctr. Strategic and Internat. Studies, Washington, 1983-85; sr. staff officer NAS, Washington, 1985-86; freelance writer, editor, publ. Washington, Santa Barbara, 1986—. Cons. Vols. Tech. Assistance, Arlington, Va., 1987—90, Arlington, 1998—, Internat. Resources Group, Washington, 1991. Author: (book) Unpaid Costs of Electrical Energy, 1979, Bioenergy and Economic Development, 1985, (plays) Agamemnon, 2000; co-author: (book) Managing the Environment, 1972, Energy in America's Future, 1979; composer: Glory Road, The Hawk, Genesis, Spring Dawn. Bd. dirs. Opera Santa Barbara. Buenos Aires Conv. fellow, 1952, NSF fellow, 1962, NATO scholar, 1960, 1962. Mem.: Internat. Assn. Energy Economists, Am. Astron. Soc., Am. Phys. Soc. Avocation: piano. Home and Office: 115 Summit Ln Santa Barbara CA 93108-2323 E-mail: ram556@cox.net.

RAMSBY, MARK DELIVAN, lighting designer, consultant; b. Portland, Oreg., Nov. 20, 1947; s. Marshall Delivan and Verna Pansy (Culver) R.; married; children: Aaron Delivan, Venessa Mercedes. Student, Portland State U., Oreg., 1966-67. With C.E.D., Portland, 1970-75; minority ptnr. The Light Source, Portland, 1975-78, pres., 1978-87; prin. Illume Lighting Design, Portland, 1987-90; ptnr. Ramsby, Dupuy & Seats, Inc., Portland, 1990-91; dir. lighting design PAE Cons. Engrs., Inc., Portland, 1991—2001; dir. design LUMA, Portland, 2001—. Pvt. practice cons. Portland, 1979—. Recipient Top 100 Outstanding Achievement award Metalux Lighting, 1981-85, 100% award, 1985, Edwin F. Guth award of merit, 1990, 95, 96, 99, 2001, 03, Edison award of excellence, 1990, Edwin F. Guth award of excellence, 1993, 94, Paul Waterbury award of Merit, 1995. Mem. Illuminating Engring. Soc. Am. (sec.-treas. Oreg. sect. 1978-79, Oreg. sect. pres. 2002-03, Oreg. Section and Regional and Internat. awards 1989, 90, 93, 94, Lighting Design awards), Internat. Assn. Lighting Designers. Lutheran. Avocations: lighting design, historical restoration, fly fishing, downhill skiing. Office: LUMA 808 SW 3d Ave Ste 450 Portland OR 97204-2426 Office Phone: 503-226-3905.

RAMSDEN, MARY CATHERINE, substance abuse specialist; Diploma, St. Joseph Mercy Hosp., 1966; postgrad., Mason City Jr. Coll., Kirkwood Community Coll. Cert. alcohol and drug counselor; RN Iowa, cert. chem. dependency nurse. Nursing supr. children's unit State Mental Health Inst., Cherokee, Iowa, 1966-69, Iowa Security Med. Facility, Oakdale, 1969; staff nurse psychiatry St. Luke's Meth. Hosp., Cedar Rapids, Iowa, 1969-74, asst. psychiat. nursing instr., 1970-74; mem. staff Sedlacek Treatment Ctr. Mercy Hosp., Cedar Rapids, 1974-85; cons. drug and alcohol CareUnit, Jacksonville Beach, Fla., 1985-86; nursing mgr. adolescent chem. dependency unit Broadlawns Med. Ctr., Des Moines, 1987-88; tng. mgr. Div. Substance Abuse and Heath Promotion Iowa Dept. Pub. Health, 1988-91; clin. program dir. Forest City (Iowa) Treatment Ctr., 1991-92; facilitator Employee & Family Resources Enhancement Women Pr Iowa Correctional Instn. for Women, Mitchellville, 1992-97; cast mgmt. tng. coord. Employee & Family Resources, Des Moines, 1998-99; substance abuse cons., trainer Des Moines, 1999—; sr. counselor Powell Chem. Dependency Ctr. Iowa Luth Hosp., Des Moines, 1999—2003; case mgr., substance abuse counselor drug ct. 5th Jud. Dist., Employee & Family Resources, 2003—. Mem. licensing rev. com. Iowa Bd. of Nursing. Author: (with others) Nurses Quick Reference, 1989. Vol. Project Enduring Families, 2004—. Lt. comdr. Nurse Corps USNR. Named Nurse Expert Coll. Nursing U. Iowa., 1985. Mem.: Iowa Assn. Addiction Profls. (v.p.), Iowa Corrections Assn., Consortium Behavioral Health Nurses and Assoc., Nat. Assn. Alcoholism and Drug Abuse Counselors, Res. Officers Assn. Home: 1519 Idaho St Des Moines IA 50316-2425 Office: 65 Gruber Des Moines IA 50315 Office Phone: 515-242-6982. Personal E-mail: mrrncd@yahoo.com.

RAMSER, WANDA TENE, librarian, educator; b. Atlanta, Ga., June 4, 1951; d. Galen Eugene Ramser and Christine Elizabeth Owen; children: Catherine Nicole Hannabach, David Richmond Hannabach. BA in History, U. Calif., Santa Barbara, 1973; MLS in Libr. and Info. Sci., UCLA, 1976, MLS in L.Am. Studies, 1977. With UCLA L.Am. Ctr., 1973—78; literacy coord. County of L.A. Libr., 1978—83; assoc. faculty South Orange County C.C. Dist., Mission Viejo, 1986, 2002—03, 2005—; with City of Oceanside (Calif.) Libr., 2001—. Chancellors assoc. UCLA, 1993—. Mem.: NOW, ALA (affiliate to Latinos and Spanish spkg., pres. San Diego chpt.), AAUW, Calif. Libr. Assn. (pres. svcs. to Latinos roundtable), UCLA Women Philanthropy, Habitat for Humanity, Mex. Am. Nat. Assn., Palomar Libr. Assn. (pres.). Business E-Mail: wanda.ramser@uclalumni.net.

RAMSEY, CHARLES, retired government agency administrator; b. Pineapple, Ala., Aug. 2, 1937; s. James Augustus and Ophelia Ramsey; m. Maratha Ann Reed, Aug. 31, 1968; children: Charles Jr., Kevin. Master degree, U. Pitts., 1974. Cert. draftsman, Cleve. Engring. Soc., 1970. Commr. divsn. of rehab. and conservation City of Cleve., 1980—88; dep. dir. Ohio Dept. of Transp. State of Ohio, Columbus, 1990—92. Organizer and campaign dir. 21 Congl. Dist. Caucus, Cleve. With USAF, 1955—63. Mem.: Paralyzed Vets. of Am. (assoc.; bd. dirs. 2000—06). Independent. Home: 25801 Lakeshore Blvd Condo # 61 Euclid OH 44132 Home Phone: 216-261-7788. Personal E-mail: cramsey37@yahoo.com.

RAMSEY, CHARLES ESTEL, retired physician, retired surgeon; b. Ridgway, Ill., Mar. 2, 1927; s. Jesse Charles Ramsey and Ethel Pearl Rister; m. Marjorie Jean Wegmet, Dec. 22, 1951; children: Laurel, Charles, Kenneth, Joyce, Martha, Joseph. BS, U. Ill., Chgo., 1949, MD, 1950. Intern Cook County Hosp., Chgo., 1950—51, surg. resident, 1951; resident US Naval Hosp., 1953—54; mini resident in radiology Trudeau Sanitarium, 1953; pvt. practice Ridgway, Ill., 1952, Charleston, Ill., 1954—93; staff physician Ea. Ill. U., Charleston, 1993—2005; ret., 2005. Chief of staff Charleston Hosp., 1973—77; pre-med. adv. bd. Ea. Ill. U., Charleston, 1960—68; mem. sheriffs merit commn. Coles County, Charleston, 1993—2005, mem. pub. health bd., 2006—; bd. dirs. The Bank, Charleston. Docent Lincoln Douglas Debate Mus., Charleston, 2002—07; vol. Charleston Pub. Libr., 2005—07; big brother Big Bros. Big Sisters, Coles County, 2006—07; substitute tchr. Charleston A&B&C Sch., 2006—. Ot. USN, 1952—54. Mem.: AMA (pres. Coles County 1957—59). Avocations: dog training, volunteering. Home: 2108 Edgewood Dr Charleston IL 61920-3700

RAMSEY, CHARLES EUGENE, sociologist, educator; b. Paragon, Ind., Apr. 24, 1923; s. Sarcefield Dodson and Stella (Goss) R.; m. Alberta Mae Jordan, July 19, 1943; children— James D., Charles W., Jane E., Suzanne. BS, Ind. State Tchrs. Coll., 1947; MS, U. Wis., 1950, PhD, 1952. Faculty U. Wis., 1951-52, U. Minn., 1952-54, Cornell U., 1954-62, Colo. State U., 1962-65; prof. sociology U. Minn., Mpls., 1965-77; chmn. dept. sociology U. Tex., Arlington, 1977-83. Vis. prof. Inter-Am. Instn. Agrl. Sci., Costa Rica, 1961, Exptl. Sta., U. P.R., 1961-62; research cons. to various univs., agys. Author: (with Lowry Nelson and Cooley Verner) Community Structure and Change, 1960, (with David Gottlieb) The American Adolescent, 1965, Understanding the Deprived Child, S.R.A, 1967, Problems of Youth, 1967, (with D.J. McCarty) The School Managers: Power and Conflict in American Public Education, 1971, (with William A. Stacey) Social Statistics, 1992; also articles. Achievements include developing and testing theory of variations in community power structure, types of sch. bds., and roles of sch. supt., developed method of comparative measurement of level of living for different countries. Home: 1102 De Pauw Dr Arlington TX 76012-5339 Office: U Tex Dept Sociology Arlington TX 76004

RAMSEY, CHARLES H., former police chief; b. Chgo., 1950; BA in Criminal Justice, Lewis U., 1990, MS in Criminal Justice, 1991; grad., FBI Nat. Acad., 1986. Cadet Chgo. Police Dept., 1968—71, police officer, 1971—77, sergeant, 1977—84, lt., 1984—88, captain, 1988—92, comdr. narcotics units, 1989—92, dep. chief, patrol divsn., 1992—94, dep. supt., 1994—98; chief of police Met. Police Dept., Washington, 1998—2006. Spkr. in field; adj. faculty mem. Northwestern U. Traffic Inst. Sch. Police and Command, Lewis U. Recipient Gary P. Hayes award, Police Exec. Rsch. Forum, 1994, Robert Lamb Humanitarian award, Nat. Orgn. Black Law Enforcement Exec., 2001, Civil Rights award, Internat. Assn. Chiefs of Police, 2001. *

RAMSEY, DAVID SELMER, retired health facility administrator; b. Mpls., Feb. 19, 1931; s. Selmer A. and Esther D. (Dahl) R.; m. Betty Seiler, May 15, 1953; children— Scott, Stewart, Thomas BS, U. Mich., 1953, MS in Microbiology, 1954, M.H.A., 1962. Research asst. Detroit Inst. Cancer Research, 1954-60; asst. adminstr. Harper Hosp., Detroit, 1962-68, assoc. adminstr., 1968-72; exec. v.p. Iowa Meth. Med. Ctr., Des Moines, 1972-83, pres., 1983-93, Iowa Health Sys., 1993-95, Fine Wood Designs, 1996—. Avocations: golf, tennis, photography. Home: 18710 Poco Rio Dr Rio Verde AZ 85263-7108

RAMSEY, FORREST GLADSTONE, JR., retired engineering company executive; b. Wichita, Kans., Oct. 25, 1930; s. Forrest Gladstone and Anastasia Ruth (Linot) R.; m. Gwendolyn Moreton, June 22, 1953 (div. Jan. 1982); children: Deborah Jenkins, Rebecca Johnson, Susan Klopp, Diane Hayes, Forrest G. III, Mark, Kenneth; m. Carmen Bergen, Apr. 30, 1988. BS in Engring., U.S. Naval Acad., 1952; postgrad., Wichita State U., 1957-58, U. Colo., 1958-64. Commd. ensign USN, 1952, res., 1957; planner, engr. Boeing Corp., Wichita, Kans., 1957-58; engr., logistician Martin-Marietta, Denver, 1959-65; div. dir. Computer Scis., Washington, 1965-73; program dir. Systems Cons., Washington, 1973-76; CEO Am. Sys. Corp., Washington, 1976-92, chmn., bd. dirs., 1992-97; ret., 1997. Mem. Profl. Svcs. Coun. (vice chmn. 1990), Naval Submarine League (bd. dirs. 1982-90). Roman Catholic. Home: 1700 Stony Brook Rd Bedford VA 24523 Personal E-mail: forrest.ramsey@1952.usna.com.

RAMSEY, FRANK ALLEN, veterinarian, retired army officer; b. Rocksprings, Tex., May 1, 1929; s. Reynolds Allen and June (Burdette) R.; m. Lucette C. Reboul, Jan. 1958; children: Randal R., Ramsay A.; m. 2d, Mary Lou Cain, June 1991. D.V.M., Tex. A & M U., 1954; grad., U.S. Army Command and Gen. Staff Coll., 1965, U.S. Army War Coll., 1972. Commd. 1st. lt. U.S. Army Vet. Corps, 1955, advanced through grades to brig. gen., 1980; chief vet. service Ft. Leonard Wood, Mo., 1958-61; acad. vet. U.S. Mil. Acad., West Point, NY, 1962-64; vet. staff officer U.S. Army Combat Devel. Command Med. Service, Ft. Sam Houston, Tex., 1965-67; asst. chief profl. programming and planning br. Office Surgeon Gen., Washington, 1967-68, chief profl. programming and planning br., 1968-71, chief food inspection policy office, 1972-73, sr. vet. staff officer, 1973-77; asst. chief of staff Vet. Service, 7th Med. Command, Army Europe and 7th Army, Heidelberg, W. Ger., 1977-80; asst. for vet. services to surgeon gen. and chief U.S. Army Vet. Corps, Hdqrs. Dept. Army, Washington, 1980-85; ret., 1985. Decorated Army Commendation medal, Legion of Merit with oak leaf cluster, D.S.M. Mem. AVMA, Assn. Fed. Veterinarians, Assn. Mil. Surgeons U.S., Assn. Equine Practitioners, Am. Assn. Food Hygiene Veterinarians, Conf. Pub. Health Veterinarians, Tex. Vet. Med. Assn. Lodges: Masons (32 degree). Presbyterian. Home: 8 El Norte Cir Uvalde TX 78801-4021

RAMSEY, INEZ LINN, librarian, educator; b. Martins Ferry, Ohio, Mar. 25, 1938; d. George and Leona (Smith) Linn; m. Jackson Eugene Ramsey, Apr. 22, 1961; children: John Earl, James Leonard. BA in History, SUNY, Buffalo, 1971, MLS, 1972; EdD in Audiovisual Edn., U. Va., 1980. Libr. Iroquois Ctrl. H.S., Elma, N.Y., 1971-73, Lucy Simms Elem. Sch., Harrisonburg, Va., 1973-75; instr. James Madison U., Harrisonburg, 1975-80, asst. prof., 1980-85, assoc. prof., 1985-91, prof., 1991-98; ret., 1998. Mem. Va. State Library Bd., Richmond, 1975-80; cons. in field. Author: (with Jackson E. Ramsey) Budgeting Basics, Library Planning and Budgeti;g; contbr. to Ency., articles to profl. jours.; project developer Internet Sch. Libr. Media Ctr.; project dir. Oral (tape) History Black Community in Harrisonburg, 1977-78; storyteller, puppeteer. Recipient Pierian Press's Libr. Hi Tech (periodical) award, 1998; rsch. grantee James Madison U., Harrisonburg, 1981, Commonwealth Ctr. State Va., 1989. Mem. ALA, Am. Assn. Sch. Librs., Assn. Edn. Comm. Tech. (exec. bd. DSMS 1989-98, DSMT Meritorious Svc. award 1998), Va. Ednl. Media Assn. (sec. 1981-83, citation 1983, pres. 1985-86, Educator of Yr. award 1984-85, Meritorious Svc. award 1987-88), Phi Beta Kappa (pres. Shenandoah chpt. 1980-81), Beta Phi Mu, Phi Delta Kappa. Home: 3215 S Torrey Pines Dr Las Vegas NV 89146-6529 Personal E-mail: inezramsey@cox.net.

RAMSEY, IRA CLAYTON, retired petroleum industry executive; b. Quitman, Ga., May 13, 1931; s. James Redding and Ruth Frances (Treadaway) R.; m. Marianne Vinzant, Dec. 23, 1962; children: Clayton Hamilton, Robin Leigh. BBA, U. Ga., Atlanta, 1954; LLB, Atlanta Law Sch., 1950; postgrad., U. Tex., 1968, U. Pitts., 1973. With Plantation Pipe Line Co., Atlanta, 1948-96, asst. sec., 1967-70, treas., contr., 1970-90, v.p. fin., 1990-96. Life trustee Ga. Found. for Ind. Colls.; trustee emeritus KingsBridge Retirement Ctr., Inc. Baptist. Home: 780 Wesley Oak Rd NW Atlanta GA 30328-4738

RAMSEY, JACKSON EUGENE, management educator; b. Cin., Dec. 20, 1938; s. Leonard Pershing and Edna Willa (Blakeman) R.; m. Inez Mae Linn, Apr. 22, 1961; children: John Earl, James Leonard. BS in Metallurgical Engring., U. Cin., 1961; MBA, SUNY, Buffalo, 1969, PhD, 1975. Registered profl. engr., Ohio. Welding engr. Gen. Electric Co., Cin., 1961-62, Westinghouse-Bettis Lab., Pitts., 1962-66; mgr. prodn. ctrl. Columbus-McKinnon Corp., Buffalo, 1966-71; asst. prof. mgmt. SUNY, Buffalo, 1971-73; prof. mgmt. James Madison U., Harrisonburg, Va., 1973—. Cons. in field. Author: R D Strategic Decision Criteria, 1986, Handbook for Professional Managers, 1985, Budgeting Basics, 1985, Library Planning and Budgeting, 1986; contbr. articles to profl. jours. Vice chmn. Harrisonburg Reps., 1974-78, chmn., 1978-86; vice chmn. 6th dist. Rep. com., 1984-94. Served with USMCR, 1956-62. Named Outstanding Young Scholar, Xerox Corp., 1976. Mem. Acad. Mgmt., Am. Inst. Decision Scis., Inst. Mgmt. Sci., Am. Soc. Metals, Nat. Soc. Profl. Engrs. Baptist. Home: 3215 S Torrey Pines Dr Las Vegas NV 89146-6529 Office: James Madison U Coll Intergrated Sci & Tech Harrisonburg VA 22807-0001 Office Phone: 702-251-0589. E-mail: jackramsey@cox.net.

RAMSEY, JAMES R., academic administrator; m. Jane Ramsey; children: Jenny, Jacque. BA, We. Ky. U.; MA, PhD, U. Ky. Vice chancellor fin. and adminstrn. U. NC, Chapel Hill, We. Ky. U.; assoc. dean, asst. dean, dir. pub. adminstrn. Coll. Bus. Adminstrn., Loyola U.; rsch. assoc. Ctr. Pub. Affairs, U. Ky.; interim commr. Office of New Economy; spl. advisor to chmn. Ky. Coun. on Postsecondary Edn.; sr. policy advisor, state budget dir. Commonwealth Ky.; sr. prof. econs. U. Louisville, pres., 2002—. Named Ky.'s Disting. Economist of Yr., 1999; recipient Outstanding Pub. Svc. Award, National Gov.'s Assn., 2001. Office: Office of Pres Grawemeyer Hall U Louisville Louisville KY 40292 Office Phone: 502-852-5417. Office Fax: 502-852-7226. *

RAMSEY, JAMIE M., lawyer; b. Ft. Thomas, Ky., Mar. 14, 1974; BS, Northern Ky. U., 1996; JD, Salmon P. Chase Coll. Law, Northern Ky. U., 1999. Bar: Ohio 1999, US Dist. Ct. Southern Dist. Ohio 1999, Ky. 2000, US Dist. Ct. Eastern Dist. Ky. 2000, US Ct. of Appeals Sixth Cir. 2001, US Dist. Ct. Western Dist. Ky. 2003, US Tax Ct. 2004, US Supreme Ct. 2005. Ptnr. Keating Muething & Klekamp PLL, Cin. Former sec., treasurer Kenton County Dem. Party; mem., bd. dirs. Children's Law Ctr. Named one of Ohio's Rising Stars, Super Lawyers, 2005, 2006. Mem.: Northern Ky. U. Alumni Assn. (bd. mem., former pres.), Northern Ky. Bar Assn., Ohio State Bar Assn., Ky. Bar Assn., Cin. Bar Assn., ABA. Office: Keating Muething & Klekamp PLL One E Fourth St Ste 1400 Cincinnati OH 45202 Office Phone: 513-639-3928. Office Fax: 513-579-6457.

RAMSEY, JAROLD WILLIAM, literature and language professor, writer; b. Bend, Oreg., Sept. 1, 1937; s. Augustus S. and Wilma E. Ramsey; m. Dorothy Ann Quinn, Aug. 16, 1959; children: Kate, Sophia, John. BA with honors, U. Oreg., 1959; Ph. D., U. Wash., 1966. Acting instr. U. Wash., Seattle, 1963-65; asst. prof. English U. Rochester, NY, 1965-70, assoc. prof. NY, 1970-81, prof. NY, 1981-97; prof. emeritus, 1997—; dir. undergrad. rsch. U. Rochester, NY, 1990-96. Vis. prof. English U. Victoria, B.C., Can., 1974, 75-76; dir. NEH summer seminars on Indian lit., 1985, 88. Author: The Space Between Us, 1970, Love in an Earthquake, 1973 (Lillian Fairchild award 1973), Dermographia, 1982, Reading the Fire, 1983, rev. edit., 1999, Hand-shadows, 1989, (play) Coyote Goes Upriver, premier 1985, (cantata) (with Samuel Adler) The Lodge of Shadows, premiere 1988; editor: Coyote Was Going There, 1977, Nehalem Tillamook Tales, 1990, The Stories We Tell: Oregon Folk Literature (with Suzi Jones), 1994, New Era: Reflections on the Human and Natural History of Central Oregon, 2003, (with Dorothy Ramsey) The Piper of Cloone: Father Keegan and the Early Gaelic Revival, 2005. Recipient Don Walker award Western Am. Lit., 1979, Borestone Mount Found. Best Poems award, 1972, 75, 76; Helen Bullis prize, 1984, Poetry prize Quar. Rev., 1989; Alumni Achievement award U. Oreg. Alumni Assn, 1990; Nat. Endowment Arts writing grantee, 1974, 76; Ingram Merrill Found. writing grantee, 1976 Mem.: MLA (chair com. on lits. and langs. of Am. 1991—92), Assn. Study Am. Indian Lit. (pres. 1981), Phi Beta Kappa. Democrat. Home: 5884 NW Highway 26 Madras OR 97741-9543 E-mail: jwr1937@madras.net.

RAMSEY, JOHN ARTHUR, lawyer; b. Apr. 1, 1942; s. Wilbert Lewis and Lillian (Anderson) R.; m. Nikki Ann Ramsey, Feb. 9, 1943; children: John William, Bret Anderson, Heather Nichole. AB, San Diego State U., 1965; JD, Calif. Western Sch. Law, 1969. Bar: Colo. 1969, Tex. 1978. Assoc. Henry, Cockrell, Quinn & Creighton, 1969-72; atty. Texaco Inc., 1972-80; asst. to pres. Texaco U.S.A., 1980-81, asst. to divsn. v.p. Houston, 1981-82, divsn. atty. Denver, 1982-88; ptnr. Holland & Hart, 1989—. Editor-in-chief: Calif. Western Law Rev., 1969. Bd. dirs. Selective Svc., Englewood, Colo., 1972-76; chmn. coun. Bethany Luth. Ch., Englewood, 1976; mem. exec. bd. Denver Area coun. Boy Scouts Am., 1999—. Mem. ABA (vice-chmn. oil, natural gas exploration and prodn. com. sect. natural resource law 1983-88, chmn. 1989, coun. sect. natural resources, energy and environ. law 1990-93). Republican. Office: Holland & Hart 8390 E Crescent Pkwy Ste 400 Greenwood Village CO 80111-2822 Office Phone: 303-290-1600.

RAMSEY, JOHN MICHAEL, chemistry professor, researcher; b. Mansfield, Ohio, May 9, 1952; BS, Bowling Green State U., Ohio, 1974; PhD, Ind. U., 1979. Rsch. assoc. Ind. U., Bloomington, Ind., 1974—79, assoc. instr., 1974—79; Eugene P. Wigner Fellow Oak Ridge Nat. Lab., Tenn., 1979—81, rsch. assoc. III Tenn., 1981—82, rsch. staff I Tenn., 1982—85, R&D group leader II Tenn., 1985—86, group leader, rsch. staff II Tenn., 1986—89, group leader, sr. rsch. staff I Tenn., 1989—92, group leader, sr. staff scientist II Tenn., 1992—96, group leader, corp. rsch. fellow Tenn., 1997—2004; co-founder, scientific adv. bd. mem. Caliper Technologies, Inc., Mountain View, Calif., 1995—2003; Minnie N. Goldby Disting. prof. chemistry U. NC, Chapel Hill, 2004—. Invited lectr. in field; vis. scientist Lawrence Livermore Lab., Calif., 1977—78; mem. permanent scientific com., High Performance Capillary Electrophoresis, 1996—; mem. steering com. μTAS, 1998—. Contbr. articles to peer-reviewed jours.; assoc. editor Journal of Microcolumn Separations, 2001, mem. editl. adv. bd. Journal of Proteome Research, 2001—, mem. editl. bd. Biomedical Microdevices, 1997—, Chromotographia, 1999—, Assay and Drug Development Technologies, 2002—, Combinatorial Chemistry & High Throughput Screening, 2004—. Recipient Merck Index award, 1971, Am. Inst. Chemists award, 1974, Martin Marietta Energy Systems, Publications award, 1985, 1994, Martin Marietta Energy Systems, Significant Achievement award, 1987, 1992, Lockheed Martin Energy Systems, Publication award, R&D Accomplishments award & Scientist of Yr. award, 1996, Lockheed Martin NOVA award, 1996, Lockheed Martin Energy Systems, Publication award, 1998, Discover Mag. Annual Tech. award, 1996, R&D 100 award Lab-on-a-Clip Technology, 1996, Alexander von Humboldt award for Sr. Scientist, 1999, Frederick Conf. Capillary Electrophoresis award, 2000, R&D 100 Top 40, Lab-on-a-Chip Technology, 2001, Energy@23 award, 2001, A.J.P. Martin Gold medal for Separation Sci., 2001, Jacob Heskel Gabbay award in Biotechnology and Medicine, 2001, Battelle Disting. Inventor award, 2003, Marcel J.E. Golay award in Capillary Chromatography, 2003, R&D 100 award μTrapMS, 2003, Southeast Region Fed. Lab. Consortium Tech. Transfer award, 2003, Fed. Lab. Consortium Excellence in Tech. Transfer award, 2004; Lockheed Martin Corp. Rsch. Fellow, 1997. Fellow: Optical Soc. Am.; mem.: Sigma Xi, Delta Phi Alpha, AAAS, Analytical Divsn. Am. Chem. Soc. (mem. program adv. com. 1986—88, chmn. program adv. com. 1989—91, mem. award selection com. 1991—94, mem. program adv. com. 1992, chair 1999, undergraduate award in analytical chemistry 1974, award in chem. instrumentation 2003, summer fellowship 1977), Am. Chem. Soc. (mem. award selection com.

1994—96, Toledo sect. graduating sr. award 1974, award in chromatography 2007), Sigma Pi Sigma, Kappa Mu Epsilon. Achievements include patents in field; patents pending in field. Office: Univ NC UNC-CH Dept Chemistry CB# 3290 Chapel Hill NC 27599-3290 Office Phone: 919-962-7492. Office Fax: 919-962-4952. Business E-Mail: jmramsey@unc.edu. *

RAMSEY, MARGIE, librarian; b. Bay City, Tex., Aug. 29, 1921; d. Cyrus Otis Lansford and Myra Lenore Ferrell; m. Joe Bryan Ramsey, July 29, 1945 (dec. 2003); children: Ronald Lansford, Kevin Bryan. BA in Libr. Sci., Tex. State U., 1942. Cert. tchr., Tex. Libr. Talco (Tex.) Ind. Sch. Dist., 1942-44; sec. Consolidated Aircraft, San Diego, summer 1943; bookkeeper Lockheed Aircraft, Dallas, 1944; libr. Dallas Pub. Libr., 1944-45; sec. Steck Co., Austin, Tex., 1946-48; libr. U. Tex., Austin, 1948-51. Author, poet:. Vol. libr. Hyde Park United Meth., Austin, 1963-2002, Leander (Tex.) Ind. Sch. Dist., 1982-92, Aspen Ridge Lodge, Los Alamos, N.Mex.; mem. The Internat. Libr. of Poetry. Named Outstanding Vol., Nat. Assn. Ptnrs. in Edn., Kraft-Disney, 1989. Fellow AAUW. Democrat. Avocations: teaching, camping, computers, reading, collecting rare books. Home: 1010 Sombrillo Ct 313 Los Alamos NM 87544 Personal E-mail: laraishere8321@aol.com.

RAMSEY, MARY CATHERINE, mechanical engineer, consultant; b. Dumas, Tex., Sept. 16, 1955; d. E. Edward and Mary V. Roberts; m. Jimmy Paul Ramsey, Aug. 18, 1984. BSME, Tex. Tech U., 1979. Registered profl. engr., Tex. Fatigue and fracture engr. Gen. Dynamics, 1979—80; design engr. Barnard & Burke, Baton Rouge, 1980—81; project engr. Ruston Gas Turbines, Houston, 1981—88, Hawker Siddeley, Houston, 1988—90; project mgr. No. Engring., Houston, 1990—95; project devel. mgr. Air Liquide Am., Houston, 1995—97; cons. Power Project Solutions, Cat Spring, Tex., 1997—. NSF rsch. scholar, 1974; Welch Rsch. Found. grantee, 1974; named Nat. Merit finalist, 1974. Avocations: llama raising, wildlife rehabitation, needlecrafts, cooking, piano. Office: 17425 Tranquil Ln Cat Spring TX 78933 Home Phone: 979-992-3120. Business E-Mail: cramsey@industryinet.com.

RAMSEY, MICHAEL W., lawyer; b. Galveston, Tex., Feb. 18, 1940; s. V.V. Ramsey; married; 2 children. BA, So. Meth. U., 1962, JD, 1965. Bar: 1965. With Richard Haynes & Assoc., 1965—72; ptnr. Ramsey & Tyson, 1972—85; pvt. practice, 1985—. Named Criminal Def. Lawyer of the Year, Tex. State Bar Assn., 1999. Office: Law Office of Michael Ramsey 2120 Welch St Houston TX 77019 *

RAMSEY, NATALIE D., lawyer; b. Greeneville, Tenn., Dec. 6, 1959; d. William Trent and Nancy Elizabeth (Maupin) Ramsey. BS, U. Del., 1981; JD, Villanova U., 1984. Bar: Pa. 1984, US Dist. Ct. (ea. dist.) Pa., US Ct. Appeals (3d and 11th cirs.), US Supreme Ct. 2004. Assoc. Montgomery, McCracken, Walker & Rhoads, LLP, Phila., 1985-93; ptnr. Montgomery, McCracken, Walker & Rhoads, Phila., 1993—, chair bankruptcy and reorgn. group, 1997—. Dir. Consumer Bankruptcy Advocacy Project, 1998—; chair Ea. Dist. Pa. Bankruptcy Conf., 2005—06. Contbr. articles to profl. jours. Pres. bd. dirs. Delaware County Habitat for Humanity, 1997—2002. Mem.: Turnaround Mgmt. Assn., Comml. Law League. Presbyterian. Avocations: travel, reading. Office: Montgomery McCracken Walker & Rhoads LLP 123 S Broad St Ste 2538 Philadelphia PA 19109-1099

RAMSEY, NORMAN F., physicist, researcher; b. Washington, Aug. 27, 1915; s. Norman F. and Minna (Bauer) Ramsey; m. Elinor Jameson, June 3, 1940 (dec. Dec. 1983); children: Margaret, Patricia, Janet, Winifred; m. Ellie Welch, May 11, 1985. AB, Columbia U., NYC, 1935, PhD, 1940; BA, Cambridge U., Eng., 1937, MA, 1941, DSc, 1954; DSc (hon.), Harvard U., Cambridge, Mass., 2006, MA (hon.), 1947; DSc (hon.), Case Western Res. U., Cleve., 1968, Middlebury Coll., Vt., 1969, Oxford U., Eng., 1973, DCL (hon.), 1990; DSc (hon.), Rockefeller U., 1986, U. Chgo., 1989, U. Sussex, 1990, U. Houston, 1991, Carleton Coll., Northfield, Minn., 1991, Lake Forest Coll., Ill., 1992, U. Mich., 1993, Phila. Coll. Pharmacy & Sci., 1995, Colby Coll., Waterville, Maine, 1998. Kellett fellow Columbia U., 1935—37, Tyndall fellow, 1938—39; Carnegie fellow Carnegie Inst. Washington, 1939—40; assoc. U. Ill., 1940—42; asst. prof. Columbia U., 1942—46; assoc. MIT Radiation Lab., 1940—43; cons. Nat. Def. Rsch. Com., 1940—45; expert cons. sec. of war, 1942—45; group leader, asso. div. head Los Alamos Lab., 1943—45; assoc. prof. Columbia U., 1945—47; head physics dept. Brookhaven Nat. Lab. of AEC, 1946—47; assoc. prof. physics Harvard U., 1947—50, prof. physics, 1950—66, Higgins prof. physics, 1966—86, Higgins prof. emeritus, 1986—. Sr. fellow Harvard Soc. Fellows, 1970—; Eastman prof. Oxford U., 1973—74; Luce prof. cosmology Mt. Holyoke Coll., 1982—83; prof. U. Va., 1983—84; dir. Harvard Nuc. Lab., 1948—50, 1952—53, Varlan Assocs., 1963—66; mem. Air Forces Sci. Adv. Com., 1947—54; sci. advisor NATO, 1958—59; mem. Dept. Def. Panel Atomic Energy; exec. com. Cambridge Electron Accelerator; gen. adv. com. AEC. Author: Nuclear Moments and Statistics, 1953, Nuclear Two Body Problems, 1953, Molecular Beams, 1956, 2d edit., 1985, Quick Calculus, 1965, Spectroscopy with Coherent Radiation, 1998; contbr. articles to profl. jours. Trustee Assoc. Univs., Inc., Brookhaven Nat. Lab., Carnegie Endowment Internat. Peace, 1962—85, Rockefeller U., 1977—90; pres. Univs. Rsch. Assocs., Inc., 1966—72, 1973—81, pres. emeritus, 1981—. Recipient Presdl. Order of Merit for radar devel. work, 1947, award, E.O. Lawrence and AEC, 1960, Columbia award for excellence in sci., 1980, medal of honor, IEEE, 1983, Rabi prize, 1985, Monte Ferst award, 1985, Compton medal, 1985, Rumford premium, 1985, Oersted medal, 1988, Nat. medal of Sci., 1988, Nobel prize for Physics, 1989, Pupin medal, Columbia Engring. Sch. Alumni Assn., 1992, Sci. for Peace prize, 1992, Einstein medal, 1993, Vannevar Bush award, 1995, Svc. award, PTTL, 2005; fellow Guggenheim, Oxford U., 1954—55. Fellow: Am. Phys. Soc. (coun. 1956—60, pres. 1978—79, Davisson-Germer prize 1974), Am. Acad. Sci.; mem.: AAAS (chmn. physics sect. 1977), NAS, Am. Inst. Physics (chmn. bd. govs. 1980—87), Am. Philos. Assn., French Acad. Sci., Sigma Xi, Phi Beta Kappa (senator 1979—88, v.p. 1982—85). Achievements include research in nuc. physics, molecular beam experiments, radar, nuc. magnetic moments, radiofrequency spectroscopy, masers, nucleon scattering. Home: 24 Monmouth Ct Brookline MA 02446-5634 Office: Harvard U Lyman Physics Lab Cambridge MA 02138 Office Phone: 617-495-2864.

RAMSEY, PAUL GLENN, dean, internist; b. Pitts., 1949; MD, Harvard U., 1975. Diplomate Am. Bd. Internal Medicine. Intern Cambridge Hosp., 1975-76; resident in medicine Mass. Gen. Hosp., Boston, 1976-78, U. Wash., Seattle, 1980-81, fellow infectious diseases, 1978-80, prof., 1991—, chmn. dept. medicine, 1992-97; physician-in-chief U. Wash. Med. Ctr., 1992-97; v.p. for med. affairs, dean Sch. Medicine U. Wash., Seattle, 1997—. Mem.: Inst. Medicine, AAAS, Assn. Am. Physicians, Am. Fedn. Clin. Rsch., ACP. Office: U Wash Sch Medicine PO Box 356350 Seattle WA 98195-6350

RAMSEY, RONALD L., lieutenant governor, state senator, realtor; b. Johnson City, Tenn., Nov. 20, 1955; married; three children. BS in Indsl. Tech., East Tenn. State U., 1978. Real estate broker/auctioneer; mem. Tenn. Ho. Reps., 1993—97, Tenn. State Senate, 1997—, spkr., 2007—; lt. gov. State of Tenn., Nashville, 2007—. Mem. Elizabeth Chapel United Meth. Ch.; mem. adv. bd. Farm Credit Assn. Mem. Bristol Tenn.-Va. Assn. Realtors (past pres.), Blountville Ruritan, Blountville Bus. Assn. (past pres.). Republican. Office: Office Lt Gov One Legislative Plz Nashville TN 37243 also: Tenn State Senate 2132 Feathers Chapel Rd Blountville TN 37617 E-mail: sen.ron.ramsey@legislature.state.tn.us. *

RAMSEY, SALLY JUDITH WEINE, chemist, research and development company executive; married; 2 children. B in Chemistry, Hiram Coll.; attended grad. study in chemistry, Iowa State U. Founder, v.p. new product devel. Ecology Coatings, Inc., Akron, Ohio, 1990—. Named Best Inventions 2005: Thin Skins, Time Mag.; recipient Silver winner and Materials and other Base Technologies winner, Wall Street Jour. Technology Innovation award, 2005. Achievements include patents pending for; patents in field. Office: Ecology Coating 1238 Brittain Rd Akron OH 44310 Office Phone: 330-633-3500. Office Fax: 330-633-3464. Business E-Mail: sally@ecologycoatings.com.

RAMSEY, STEPHANIE DENISE, medical transcriptionist; b. Chattanooga, Tenn., Aug. 28, 1975; m. Ronald Foster Ramsey, Aug. 31, 1996; children: Garrett F., Carson L., Jackson G. AS, Chattanooga State Tech. CC, 1996. Cert. med. transcription Chattanooga State Tech. CC, 2002. Med. transcriptionist Am. Transcription, Rome, Ga., 2002—04, Chattanooga Allergy Clinic, 2004—. Children's ch. instr. Meadowview Bapt. Ch., Georgetown, Tenn., 2006—07. Mem.: Am. Assn. Med. Transcription (assoc.; co-pres. 2006—07, cert., treas. Chattanooga chpt. 2004—05). Home: 7854 Grasshopper Road Georgetown TN 37336 Office: Chattanooga Allergy Clinic 6624 Lee Hwy Chattanooga TN 37421 Home Phone: 423-961-0555; Office Phone: 423-899-0431. Personal E-mail: ramsfam@peoplepc.com.

RAMSEYER, J. MARK, law educator; b. 1954; BA, Goshen Coll., 1976; AM, Mich. U., 1978; JD, Harvard U., 1982. Bar: Ill. 1983. Law clk. to Hon. S. Breyer U.S. Ct. Appeals (1st cir.), Boston, 1982-83; assoc. Sidley & Austin, Chgo., 1983-85; acting prof. UCLA, 1986-89, prof., 1989-92, U. Chgo. Law Sch., 1992-98; Mitsubishi prof. of Japanese Legal Studies Harvard U., Cambridge, Mass., 1998—. Office: Harvard U Sch of Law Cambridge MA 02138

RAMSEY-GOLDMAN, ROSALIND, physician; b. NYC, Mar. 22, 1954; d. Abraham L. and Miriam (Colen) Goldman; m. Glenn Ramsey, June 29,1 975; children: Ethan Ramsey, Caitlin Ramsey. BA, Case We. Res. U., 1975, MD, 1978; MPH, U. Pitts., 1988, DPH, 1992. Med. resident U. Rochester, NY, 1978—81; chief resident Rochester Gen. Hosp., 1981—82; staff physician U. Health Svc., Rochester, 1982—83; rheumatology fellow U. Pitts., 1983—86, instr. medicine, 1986—87, asst. prof., 1987—91, co-dir. Lupus Treatment and Diagnostic Ctr., 1987—91; asst. prof. medicine Northwestern U., Chgo., 1991—96, assoc. prof. medicine, 1996—2001, prof. medicine, 2001—. Dir. Chgo. Lupus Registry, Northwestern U., Chgo., 1991—, chairperson Systemic Lupus Internat. Collaborating Clinics Group, 2003—; program dir. Gen. Clin. Rsch. Ctr. at NCRR/NIH, 2005—. Contbr. rsch. articles to profl. jours. Recipient Finkelstein award Hershey (Pa.) Med. Ctr., 1986. Fellow ACP, Am. Coll. Rheumatology; mem. Soc. for Epidemiologic Rsch., Ctrl. Soc. Clin. Rsch. Office: Northwestern U Feinberg Sch Medicine McGaw Pavilion 240 E Huron Ste M-300 Chicago IL 60611 Office Phone: 312-503-8003. Business E-Mail: rgramsey@northwestern.edu.

RAMSTAD, JAMES, congressman, lawyer; b. Jamestown, ND, May 6, 1946; s. Marvin Joseph and Della Mae (Fode) Ramstad. BA, U. Minn., 1968; JD with honors, George Washington U., 1973. Bar: ND 1973, DC 1973, Minn. 1979, admitted to practice: US Supreme Ct. 1976. Adminstrv. asst. to LL Duxbury Minn. Ho. Reps., 1969, spl. asst. to Congressman Tom Kleppe, 1970; pvt. practice law Jamestown, 1973, Washington, 1974—78, Mpls., 1978—90; asst. campaign mgr. for Congressman William E. Frenzel US Ho. Reps., 1978; mem. Minn. Senate, 1981—90, asst. minority leader, 1983—87; mem. US Congress from 3rd Minn. dist., 1991—. Adj. prof. Am. U., Washington, 1975—78. Bd. dir. D.A.R.E., Minn., Children's Heart Fund, Lake Country Food Bank; mem. C. of C., Twin West, Wayzata, North Metro. 1st lt. USAR, 1968—74. Named Representative of Yr., Nat. Assn. of Police Organizations, 1997, 2000, Legislator of Yr., Nat. Assn. of Alcoholism and Drug Addiction Counselors, 1998, Nat. Mental Health Assn., 1999; recipient Fulbright Disting. Pub. Service award. Mem.: Hennepin County Bar Assn., ND Bar Assn., DC Bar Assn., Minn. Bar Assn., Minn. Prayer Breakfast Com., Plymouth Lions Club, U. Minn. Alumni Assn., Am. Legion, Phi Delta Theta, Phi Beta Kappa. Republican. Office: US Ho Reps 103 Cannon Ho Office Bldg Washington DC 20515-2303 *

RAMUNDO, KIMBERLY E., lawyer; b. Covington, Ky., Dec. 23, 1971; BA, Miami U., 1993; JD, U. Cin., 1996. Bar: Ohio 1996, US Dist. Ct. Southern Dist. Ohio 1998, US Ct. of Appeals Sixth Cir. 2001, Ky. 2002, US Dist. Ct. Eastern Dist. Ky. 2002; cert. Constrn. Industry Technician. Ptnr. Thompson Hine LLP, Cin. Mem., Bd. Dirs., sec. Tallstacks Music Arts & Heritage Festival. Named Rising Star, YWCA, 2003; named one of Ohio's Rising Stars, Super Lawyers, 2006. Mem.: Ky. Bar Assn., Ohio Bar Assn., Cin. Bar Assn., ABA, Nat. Assn. Women in Constrn., Cin. Acad. Leadership for Lawyers. Office: Thompson Hine LLP 312 Walnut St 14th Fl Cincinnati OH 45202-4089 Office Phone: 513-352-6656. Office Fax: 513-241-4771.

RANA, HARMINDERPAL SINGH, lawyer; b. Bombay, July 4, 1968; came to U.S., 1970; s. Baljit Singh and Devinder (Kaur) R.; m. Aasjot Kaur Sidhu, Mar. 8, 1998. BS in Fgn. Svc., cert. in Asian studies, Georgetown U., 1990; JD cert. in internat. law, Rutgers U., 1994; cert. info. sys. analysis, Columbia U., 2002. Bar: N.J. 1994, U.S. Dist. Ct. N.J. 1994, N.Y. 1995, U.S. Dist. Ct. (so. and ea. dists.) N.Y. 1995. Pvt. practice, Warren, NJ, 1994—. Assoc. staff analyst N.Y.C. Dept. Mental Health, Bklyn., 1995-97, region coord., Bklyn. and S.I., 1997-2004; asst. gen. coun. N.Y.C. Dept. Health, 2004—. Mem. traffic safety com. Warren Twp. Coun., 1997-2000. NYU Trustees scholar, 1986, N.Y. State Regents scholar, 1986. Mem. ABA, Assn. Bar City N.Y. (health law com. 1997-2000). Sikh. Avocations: literature, philosophy, world affairs, cross training, writing. Office: 3 Krausche Rd Warren NJ 07059 Personal E-mail: hsresq@msn.com.

RANCK, EDNA RUNNELS, academic administrator, researcher; b. Waterville, Maine, Aug. 24, 1935; d. Everett Elias and Edna May (King) Runnels; m. James Gilmour Ranck, June 30, 1971 (dec. May 1979); children: Matthew, Christopher, Joshua Duggan; m. Martin Fleischer, Apr. 19, 1982; stepchildren: Christina, Laura. BA cum laude, Fla. State U., Tallahassee, 1957; MDiv magna cum laude, Drew U. Theol. Sch., Madison, NJ, 1971, MEd in Edn. Adminstrn., 1978; EdD in Curriculum and Tchg., Columbia U., NYC, 1986. Dir. Collinsville Child Care Ctr., Morristown, NJ, 1971-78; exec. dir. Children's Svcs. Morris County, Morristown, 1980-84; co-mgr. NJ Child Care Clearinghouse, Trenton, NJ; coord. NJ Child Care Adv. Coun., Trenton, 1987-92; dir. NJ Office Child Care Devel., Trenton, 1992; child care coord. NJ Dept. Human Svcs., Trenton, 1992-98, Nat. Assn. Child Care Resource & Referral Agys., Washington, 1998—2002, Westover Consultants, Inc., Bethesda, Md., 2002—. Adj. faculty Kean U. NJ, Union, 1983; dir. Sprout House Presch., Chatham, NJ, 1984-87; mem. Morris County Human Svcs. Adv. Coun., Morristown, NJ, 1986-87, spkr. in field. Author: Dodge Foundation Project, 1984, Young Children, 1997, Our History, Our Vision: A History of the National Association of Child Care Rsource and Referral Agencies, 1997, NAFCC@25: 1982-2007, 2007, Early Childhood Education: An International Encyclopedia, 2007; writer monthly Policy Perspectives column, 2000-02; contbr. chapters to books, articles to profl. jours. Exec. bd. Drew U. Alumni Assn. Theol. Sch., 1986-92; active Drew U. Alumni Study Commn., 1993, Non-Govt. Orgn. rep. to UN Internat. Fedn. Educative Cmtys., 1992-99; mem. history/archives panel Nat. Assn. for Edn. of Young Children, 1999-2001. Recipient Volpe Commitment in Child Care award, NJ Child Care Assn., 1991, Essex C.C. Early Childhood award, 1997, Aletha Wright award for Excellence in Early Edn., 1998. Mem. Internat. Assn. Presch. Edn. N.Am. (bd. dirs.), Child Care Action Campaign Panel, Acad. Child and Youth Care Workers, Nat. Assn. Regulatory Adminstrn. (bd. dirs. 2000-05), World Orgn. Presch. Edn. USA (bd. dirs. 2000—, pres. 2006—), Nat. Assn. Edn. Young Children (moderator history seminar 2002—, contbr. Exch. Everyday 2004—), Tchrs. Coll. Columbia U. Washington Alumni Assn. (co-chmn.), Fla. State U. Emeritus Alumni Soc., GCH Found. (sec./treas. bd. dirs. 2004—), Phi Beta Kappa, Pi Sigma Alpha, Sigma Delta Pi. Republican. United Methodist. Avocations: writing, travel, clothing design, art collecting, walking. Home: 4447 MacArthur Blvd NW Washington DC 20007-2564 Personal E-mail: edna.ranck@verizon.net.

RAND, CALVIN GORDON, art educator, educational consultant; b. Buffalo, May 15, 1929; s. George Franklin and Isabel (Williams) R.; m. Patricia Clemens Andrew, Aug. 18, 1951; children: Robin, Melissa, Jennifer, Lucinda, Elizabeth BA, Princeton U., 1951; MA, Columbia U., 1954; LHD (hon.), York U., Can., 1984. Head history dept. Riverdale Sch., NYC, 1955-60; lectr. philosophy SUNY-Buffalo, 1961-68, acting dir. cultural affairs, 1968-71; founder, pres. The Niagara Inst., Niagara-on-the-Lake, Canada, 1971-79; pres. Am. Acad. in Rome, NYC, 1980-84; ind. producer, theatre and film cons., NYC, 1985-90. Founding chmn., dir. Shaw Festival Theatre, Niagara-on-the-Lake, 1964-78,. bd. govs., 1979—; trustee Playwrights Horizons Theatre, N.Y.C., 1982-92; bd. dirs. Arts in Edn. Inst.; mem. N.Y. State Coun. on Arts, 1978-82, Arts Coun. Western N.Y., 1987-93; chmn. World Ency. Contemporary Theater; chmn. arts coun. SUNY, Buffalo, 1987-94, adj. prof. theater, 1988—. Contbr. articles to profl. jours. Bd. dirs. Burchfield-Penney Art Ctr., Buffalo, 1991—, vice-chair, 1999—; bd. dirs. Irish Classical Theater, 1993—, pres., 1998-2004; trustee Albright-Knox Gallery, Buffalo, 1976-80, 84-88, 90-94. Recipient spl. citation Ont. Arts Coun., 1976, Fellowship Fund award Niagara Inst., 1980, Centennial Arts award Nichols Sch., 1992, Red Jacket award, Erie County Hist. Soc., 2000, Arts award Nat. Conf. Cmty. and Justice, 2007; named Man of Yr., Coun. World Affairs, 1976, Buffalo Courier Express, 1976, Arts Patron of Yr., Western N.Y. Arts Coun. and C. of C., 1989, Disting Non-Alumni, SUNY, Buffalo, Man of Yr., 1997, YMCA of Western NY, 1999; Vanier Coll. fellow York U. Mem. Princeton Club, Saturn Club. Home Phone: 716-883-7238; Office Phone: 716-883-2942.

RAND, DUNCAN DAWSON, retired librarian; b. Biggar, Sask., Can., Oct. 28, 1940; s. Dawson Ellis and Elizabeth Edna (Gabie) R.; m. Nancy Jean Daugherty, Sept. 7, 1963; children: Jacqueline Nancy, Duncan Dawson, Thomas Nelson, John David, Jennifer Nancy. BA, U. Sask., 1963; B.L.S., McGill U., 1964. Young adult librarian Regina Pub. Library, Sask., 1964-65; coordinator library services Regina Separate Sch. Bd., 1965-68; asst. chief librarian Regina Pub. Library, 1968-71; dep. dir. London Pub. Library and Art Mus., 1971-73, acting dir., 1973-74; chief librarian Lethbridge Pub. Library, Alta., 1974-2000, ret. Alta., 2001. Dir. So. Alta. Art Gallery, Alberta Libr., 1996—. Editor: Sask. Geneal. Soc. Bull, 1968-71. Vice pres. Alta. council Boy Scouts. Mem. Libr. Assn. Alta (dir., pres. 1986-87), Can. Libr. Assn. (dir.), Can. Assn. Pub. Librs. (chair 1976-77), Sask. Geneal. Soc. (pres.), Assn. Profl. Librs. of Lethbridge (chmn. 1982-84), So. Alta. Regional Info. Network (chmn. 1996-2000), Samaritans (pres. 1998-2001), Allied Arts Coun. (bd. dirs. 1993-98), Southern Alberta Regional Info. Network (chmn.), Rotary, Ipalosh (archivist, sec. 1980-94). Office: 810 5th Ave S Lethbridge AB Canada T1J 4C4

RAND, JOELLA MAE, retired nursing educator, counselor; b. Akron, Ohio, July 9, 1932; d. Harry S. and Elizabeth May (Miller) Halberg; m. Martin Rand (dec.); children: Craig, Debbi Stark. BSN, U. Akron, 1961, MEd in Guidance, 1968; PhD in Higher Edn. Adminstrn., Syracuse U., 1981. Lic. mental health counselor 2006. Staff nurse Akron Gen. Hosp., 1953-54; staff-head nurse-instr. Summit County Receiving, Cuyahoga Falls, Ohio, 1954-56; head nurse psychiat. unit Akron Gen. Hosp., 1956-57; instr. psychiatric nursing Summit County Receiving, Cuyahoga Falls, 1957-61; head nurse, in-service instr. Willard (N.Y.) State Hosp., 1961-62; asst. prof. Alfred (N.Y.) U., 1962-76, assoc. prof., assoc. dean, 1976-78, acting dean, 1978-79, dean, 1979-90, dean coll. profl. studies, 1990-91, prof. counseling, 1991-2000; ret., 2000. Cons. N.Y. State Regents Program for Non-Collegiate Sponsored Instrn., 1984; cons. collegiate programs N.Y. State Dept. Edn., 1985, Elmira Coll., 1991, U. Rochester, 1992-93; accreditation visitor Nat. League for Nursing, 1984-92; ednl. cons. Willard Psychiat. Hosp., 1992-93; mem. profl. practice exam. subcom. Regents Coll., 1990-95. Vol. Williard Drug Treatment Ctr., 1997—, bd. dirs., Romulus Zoning Bd., 2002—; vol. Red Cross, 2003—, co-capt. disaster team, 2004—05; bd. dirs. Five Point Correctional Facility, Willard Drug Treatment Ctr. Recipient Tchg. Excellence award Alfred U., 1977, Mary E. Gladwin Outstanding Alumni award Akron U. Coll. Nursing, 1983, Alfred Alumni Friends award, 1989, Grand Marshall commencement Alfred U., 1993, Vol. of Yr. award Willard Drug Treatment Ctr., 1999, Cert. Appreciation, Seneca County Cmty. Svcs. Bd., 2005. Mem.: ACA (NAR rep. 2000—04, co-capt. disaster team Red Cross-Finger Lakes chpt. 2003—05, pres. NYCA 2005, Seneca County Med. Reserve Corps. 2005—), Genesee Valley Edn. Com. (chair 1984—86), Western N.Y. League Nursing (bd. dirs. 1991—93), Genesee Regional Consortium (v.p.), N.Y. State Coun. of Deans (treas. 1984—88), N.Y. State Counseling Assn. (v.p.-elect profl. svcs. 1995—96, v.p. profl. svcs. 1996—98, 1999—2000, pres. 2005—06), Sigma Theta Tau (treas. Alfred chpt. 1984—85). Avocations: boating, fishing, public speaking in areas of family and child abuse. Personal E-mail: drand@rochester.rr.com.

RAND, KATHY SUE, public relations executive, consultant; b. Miami Beach, Fla., Feb. 24, 1945; d. William R. and Rose (Lasser) R.; m. Peter C. Ritsos, Feb. 19, 1982. BA, Mich. State U., 1965; MBA, Northwestern U., 1980. Asst. editor Lyons & Carnahan, Chgo., 1967-68; mng. editor Cahners Pub. Co., Chgo., 1968-71; pub. rels. writer Super Market Inst., Chgo., 1972-73; account supr. Pub. Communications Inc., Chgo., 1973-77; divisional mgr. pub. rels. Quaker Oats Co., Chgo., 1977-82; exec. v.p., dep. gen. mgr. Golin/Harris Communications, Chgo., 1982-90; exec. v.p. Lesnik Pub. Rels., Northbrook, Ill., 1990-91; mng. dir. Manning, Selvage & Lee, Chgo., 1991—2002; public rels. cons., 2002—. Dir. midwest region NOW, 1972-74; mem. Kellogg Alumni Adv. Bd.; bd. dirs. Jr. Achievement of Chgo. Mem. Pub. Rels. Soc. Am. (Silver Anvil award 1986, 87), Pub. Club Chgo. (Golden Trumpet awards 1982-87, 90, 94, 95, 97, 98, 99, 00), Vet. Feminists of Am. (bd. dirs., v.p. pub. rels.), Northwestern Club Chgo., Kellogg Alumni Club, Beta Gamma Sigma. Home: 400 Riverwoods Rd Lake Forest IL 60045-2547 Personal E-mail: ksrand@aol.com.

RAND, LAWRENCE ANTHONY, investor, finance company executive; b. Bklyn., Nov. 19, 1942; s. Gerald M. and Elaine Shirley Rand; m. Madelon L., July 4, 1942; children: Allan, Joshua, Emily. AB with honors, Brown U., 1964; MA, NYU, 1965, PhD, 1998. Lectr. NYU, 1967, CUNY, 1968; analyst CIA, Langley, Va., 1967-68; account supr. Ruder & Finn Inc., NYC, 1968-71; co-founder, sr. v.p. Kekst & Co., NYC, 1971—, also bd. dirs. Chmn., bd. dirs. ALS Assn., L.A., 1987-92. Chmn. ethics com. Village Rye Brook, NY, 1993—2000, village trustee, 2000—02, mayor, 2004—; bd. dirs. U.S. Tennis Assn. Tennis and Edn. Found. Mem. Brown U. Club, Bailiwick Club (Greenwich, Conn.). Office: Kekst & Co 437 Madison Ave 19th Fl New York NY 10022-7195 Home Phone: 914-939-4762; Office Phone: 212-521-4800. Personal E-mail: lar@kekst.com.

RAND, LEON, academic administrator; b. Boston, Oct. 8, 1930; s. Max B. and Ricka (Muscanto) Rakisky; m. Marian L. Newton, Aug. 29, 1959; children: Debra Ruth, Paul Martin, Marta Leah. BS, Northeastern U., 1953; MA, U. Tex., 1956, PhD, 1958. Postdoctoral fellow Purdue U., 1958-59;

asst. prof. to prof. U. Detroit, 1959-68; prof., chmn. dept. chemistry Youngstown (Ohio) State U., 1968-74, dean grad. studies and research, 1974-81, acting acad. v.p., 1980; vice chancellor acad. affairs U. N.C., Pembroke, 1981—85; chancellor Ind. U.-S.E., New Albany, 1986-96; chancellor emeritus Ind. U., 1996—, prof. emeritus, 1999—; spl. asst. to chancellor IUPUI, 1996-98. Bd. dirs. Floyd Meml. Hosp., New Albany, 1987—90, Jewish Hosp., Louisville, 1991—96. Bd. dirs., mem. exec. com. Louisville (Ind.) area chpt. ARC; docent Indpls. Mus. Art, 1998—. Mem.: Metroversity (bd. dirs.), Am. Inst. Chemists, Am. Chem. Soc., Sigma Xi, Phi Kappa Phi. Home: 1785 Arrowwood Dr Carmel IN 46033-9019 E-mail: LRand7658@sbcglobal.net.

RAND, PETER, writer, editor, educator; b. San Francisco, Feb. 23, 1942; s. Christopher T.E. Rand and Margaret Aldrich Demott; m. Bliss I. Rand, Dec. 19, 1976; 1 child, James. Student, U. Calif., Berkeley; MA, Johns Hopkins U., 1975. Adv. fiction editor Antaeus, NYC, 1970-73; editor Washington Monthly, 1974-75; instr. Columbia U., NYC, 1976-91; preceptor Harvard U., Cambridge, Mass., 1997-98, Boston U., 1999—. Freelance editor, Belmont, Mass., 1994—. Author: Firestorm, 1969, The Time of the Emergency, 1977, The Private Rich, 1984, Gold from Heaven, 1988, China Hands, 1995; editor: Deng Xiaoping, Chronicle of an Empire (by Ruan Ming), 1994, Scarlet Memorial, Tales of Cannibalism in Modern China (by Zheng Yi), 1996, Tiananmen Follies (by Dai Qing), 2004, Zou Enlai, The Perfect Revolutionary (by Gao Wenqian), 2007. Trustee Belmont Citizens Forum, 1999—2002. Grantee Creative Artists Performing Svc., NYC, 1977. Mem. PEN, J.K. Fairbank Ctr. for East Asian Rsch. (affiliate), Tavern Club (sec.). Avocation: tennis. Home: 35 Falmouth St Belmont MA 02478 Business E-Mail: prand@bu.edu. E-mail: inuirand@aol.com.

RAND, RICHARD P., plastic surgeon; AB, Stanford U.; MD, U. Mich. Cert. Am. Bd. Plastic Surgery, Am. Bd. Surgery, Nat. Bd. Med. Examiners. Gen. surgery trainee Tufts-New Eng. Med. Ctr., Boston; plastic surgery trainee Emory U.; craniofacial surgery fellow U. Miami; chief of plastic surgery U. Wash. Med. Ctr.; owner & dir. Northwest Ctr. Aesthetic Plastic Surgery, Bellevue, Wash. Examiner Am. Bd. Plastic Surgery. Named one of Top 250 Golf Doctors in Am., Golf Digest, 2006; recipient Sr. Resident Chmn.'s award in Gen. Surgery, Tufts-New Eng. Med. Ctr. Fellow: Am. Coll. Surgeons; mem.: Wash. State Med. Assn., Ralph A. Deterling Surg. Soc., Maurice J. Jurkiewicz Soc., King County Med. Soc., Royal & Ancient Assn. Plastic Surgeons, Seattle Surg. Soc., Wash. Soc. Plastic Surgeons (Golden Hands/Golden Scalpel award), Northwest Soc. Plastic Surgeons, Am. Soc. Maxillofacial Surgeons, Am. Soc. Plastic Surgeons, Am. Soc. Aesthetic Plastic Surgery, Am. Soc. Plastic Surgeons, Phi Beta Kappa. Office: Northwest Ctr for Aesthetic Plastic Surgery Ste 630 1135 116th Ave NE Bellevue WA 98004 Office Phone: 866-616-6183. Office Fax: 425-455-0921. *

RAND, ROBERT WHEELER, neurosurgeon, educator; b. LA, Jan. 28, 1923; s. Carl W. and Catherine (Humphrey) R.; m. Helen L. Pierce, Dec. 17, 1949; children: Carl W., Richard P. Student, Harvard U., 1940-42, UCLA, 1942-44; MD, U. So. Calif., 1947; MS, U. Mich., 1951, PhD in Anatomy, 1952; JD, U. West L.A., 1974. Intern, resident in neurosurgery U. Mich., Ann Arbor, 1947-52; from instr. to prof. neurol. surgery UCLA, 1953-89; assoc. med. dir. John Wayne Cancer Inst., Santa Monica, Calif., 1989—. Expert witness malpractice cases Superior Ct. Author: Spinal Cord Tumors in Childhood, 1960, Microneurosurgery, 3d edit., 1985; contbr. articles to profl. jours.; inventor neuropledgets, thermomagnetic surgery coil system, microballoon for aneurysm occlusion, Malcolm-Rand graphite cranial frame, cobalt scalpel. Lt. comdr. USNR, 1943-46, 54-56. Recipient Profl. award UCLA, 1973. Fellow ACS; mem. AMA, Calif. Med. Assn., L.A. County Med. Assn., Am. Surg. Assn., Internat. Coll. Surgeons, Am. Assn. Neurol. Surgeons, Assn. Neurol. Surgeons, Soc. Neurol. Surgeons, Western Neurosurg. Soc., L.A. Country Club. Office: John Wayne Cancer Inst St John's Hosp 2200 Santa Monica Blvd Santa Monica CA 90404-2302 Office Phone: 310-472-0155. Personal E-mail: rwrand@verizon.net.

RAND, WILLIAM, lawyer, retired judge; b. NYC, Oct. 11, 1926; s. William and Barbara (Burr) R.; married; children: Alicia, Carley Coudert, William Coudert, Paula Burr. AB, Harvard U., 1948; LLB, Columbia U., 1951. Bar: N.Y. 1951, U.S. Dist. Ct. N.Y. 1951, U.S. Supreme Ct., 1958, U.S. Ct. Appeals (2d cir.) 1961, U.S. Ct. Appeals (4th cir.) 1985, U.S. Ct. Appeals (3rd cir.) 2004. Asst. dist. atty. New York County, 1954-59; asst. counsel to gov. of State of N.Y., 1959-60; assoc. Coudert Bros., NYC, 1961-62, ptnr., 1963-98; justice N.Y. State Supreme Ct., 1962. Justice Village of Cove Neck, Oyster Bay, N.Y., 1974-98. Mem. exec. com. New York County Reps., 1968-72. Served with USN, 1944-46, PTO. Mem.: Racquet and Tennis Club (N.Y.C.), Piping Rock Club (Locust Valley, N.Y.). Home: 73 Cove Neck Rd Oyster Bay NY 11771-1821 Office: Coudert Bros Fl 43 1114 Avenue of the Americas New York NY 10036-7710 Home Phone: 212-369-8841; Office Phone: 212-626-4433. E-mail: randw@coudert.com.

RANDA, JAMES PAUL, physicist, electrical engineer; b. Chgo., Jan. 26, 1947; s. John Joseph and Catherine Anne (Baier) R.; m. Susan Bulmann, June 12, 1980; 1 child, David. BS, Ill. Benedictine Coll., 1969; MS, U. Ill., 1970, PhD, 1974. Vis. asst. prof. Tex. A&M U., College Station, 1974-75; postdoctoral fellow U. Manchester, Eng., 1975-78; asst. prof. U. Colo., Boulder, 1978-83; physicist, sr. project leader Nat. Inst. of Stds. and Tech., Boulder, 1983—. Lectr. physics dept. U. Colo., Boulder, 1985-89; lectr., cons. Productivity and Stds. Bd., Singapore, 2000; U.S. rep. to working group on radiofrequency quantities Internat. Com. of Weights and Measures, Sevres, France, 1999—, chmn., 2002—. Editor: Quantum Flavordynamics, Quantum Chromodynamics, and Unified Field Theories, 1980; contbr. articles to profl. jours. Recipient Bronze medal, U.S. Dept. Commerce, 1992, 1999, award for best paper, IEEE Transactions on Electromagnetic Compatibility, 1992. Mem. IEEE, MTT Soc., EMC Soc. (tech. com., chair 1990-94), Am. Phys. Soc., Automated RF Techniques Group, Geoscience and Remote Sensing Soc. of IEEE. Avocations: reading, hiking, gardening, writing. Office: NIST 818-01 325 Broadway Boulder CO 80305-3328 Business E-Mail: randa@boulder.nist.gov.

RANDALL, CLAIRE, retired religious organization administrator; b. Dallas, Oct. 15, 1919; d. Arthur Godfrey and Annie Laua (Fulton) Randall. AA, Schreiner Coll., 1948; BA, Scarritt Coll., 1950; DD (hon.), Berkley Div. Sch., New Haven, Conn., 1974; LHD (hon.), Austin Coll., 1982; LLD (hon.), Notre Dame U., 1984. Assoc. missionary edn. Bd. World Missions Presbyn. Ch., U.S., Nashville, 1949-57, dir. art Gen. Coun. Atlanta, 1957-61; dir. Christian World Mission, program dir., assoc. dir. Ch. Women United, NYC, 1962-73; gen. sec. Nat. Coun. Ch. of Christ U.S.A., NYC, 1974-84; nat. pres. Ch. Women United, NYC, 1988-92; ret., 1992. Mem. Nat. Commn. Internat. Women's Yr., 1975—77, Martin Luther King Jr. Fed. Holiday Commn., 1985. Recipient Woman of Yr. in Religion award, Heritage Soc., 1977, Empire State woman of Yr. in Religion award, State of NY, 1984, medal Order of St. Vladimir, Russian Orthodox Ch., 1984. Democrat. Episcopalian. Avocations: golf, swimming, painting, reading, music. Mailing: PO Box 2338 Sun City AZ 85372-2338

RANDALL, CLIFFORD WENDELL, civil engineer, educator; b. Somerset, Ky., May 1, 1936; s. William Lesbert and Geneva (James) R.; m. Phyllis Amis, Aug. 15, 1959; children: Andrew Amis, William Otis. BSCE, U. Ky., 1959, MS in Sanitary Engring., 1963; PhD in Environ. Health Engring., U. Tex., 1966. Asst. prof. civil engring. U. Tex., Arlington, 1965-68; mem. faculty Va. Poly. Inst. and State U., 1968—2001, prof. civil engring., 1972-81, Charles Lunsford prof., 1981—2001; vis. prof. U. Cape Town, South Africa, 1983; chmn. environ. engring. and scis. program Va. Poly. Inst. and State U., 1979-97, Charles Lunsford prof. emeritus, 2001—. Lectr. Shanghai Archtl. and Mcpl. Engring. Inst., Wuhan Tech. U., 1987; dir. Occoquan Watershed Monitoring Program, 1971-2001; mem. Occoquan watershed monitoring subcom. Va. State Water Control Bd., 1971—, chair, 1971-85, 2001-, vice chair, 1986-2001; US nat. com. Internat. Water Quality, 1976-88, chair 1986-88, mem. 1992 IAWQ Biennial Conf. Com., chair conf. arrangements, Washington; tng. grant cons. EPA, 1970-71; cons. to industry, 1969—; WHO cons. to Nat. Environ. Engring. Rsch. Inst. India, 1983-84; Va. gov. appointee sci. and tech. adv. com. Chesapeake Bay Program; sci. and tech. adv. com. Chesapeake Bay Program, 1984-2006, chmn. 1993-97; nitrogen tech. adv. com. NYC Dept. Environ. Protection, 1994-2006; blue ribbon panel wastewater treatment City of Atlanta, 1997-2001. Author tech. papers in field; co-author: Biological Process Design for Wastewater Treatment, 1980, Stormwater Management in Urbanizing Areas, 1983, Design and Retrofit of Wastewater Treatment Plants for Biological Nutrient Removal, 1992. Troop com. chmn. Boy Scouts Am., 1978-82, chmn. dist. Camporee com., 1977; camp pres. Gideons Internat., 1976-78, 80, 95-97, state cabinet mem., 1985-88, v.p., 2005—; vice moderator Highlands Bapt. Assn., 1980-81, moderator, 1982-83; bd. deacons Blacksburg Bapt. Ch., 1971-74, 79-82, chmn., 1974. Lt. U.S. Coast and Godetic Survey, 1959-62. Ford Found. fellow, 1964-65; recipient citation Engring. News-Record, 1988, Disting. Svc. award US nat. com. Internat. Assn. Water Quality, 1989, Salute to Excellence Gov. of Md., 1994, Alumni Pub. Svc. award Va. Tech., 1996, Mathias medal for sci. excellence Chesapeake Rsch. Consortium and the Sea Grant Offices of Md. and Va., 1996, Dean's award Excellence Pub. Svc., Va. Tech. Engring., 1997, Disting. Svc. award Assn. Environ. Engrs. and Scientists Profs., 1997, Gordon Maskew Fair medal Achievement in Engring. Edn. Water Environ. Fedn., 1998; Lifetime Achievement award Va. Water Resources Ctr., 2006, Leadership award Va. Water Rsch. Ctr., 2006; named Conservationist of Yr. Chesapeake Bay Found., 1986; AEC trainee U. Tex., 1963-65. Mem. ASCE (hon.; chmn. water resources mgmt. com. 1977, environ. engring. rsch. coun. 1989-90, svc. award 1978, 80, meritorious tech. paper award 1969), Am. Water Works Assn. (cert. recognition for acad. excellence 1980, 89), Water Environ. Fedn. (bd. dirs. 1981-84, Morgan cert. of merit for full scale rsch. 1982, Bedell award 1983, svc. award 1984, Gordon M. Fair medal for excellence in engring. edn. 1998), Internat. Water Assn. (nat. com., 1978-88, chair, 1986-88, governing bd. 1986-88, USA rep. on sci. and tech. com. 1994-98, mem. nutrient removal specialist group mgmt. com. 1990-2002, chmn. 1994-98), Va. Water Environment Assn. (v.p. 1974-75, pres. 1975-76), Assn. Environ. Engring. Profs. (sec.-treas. 1979-80, bd. dirs. 1978-80, 93-97, v.p. 1994-95, pres. 1995-96, past pres. 1996-97, Lifetime Achievement award 2005). Home: 1302 Crestview Dr Blacksburg VA 24060-5609 Office: Va Tech Dept Civil and Environ Engring 418 Durham Hall Blacksburg VA 24061-0246 Office Phone: 540-231-6018. Business E-Mail: cliff@vt.edu.

RANDALL, DOUGLAS D., biochemist, educator; b. Cheyenne, Wyo. BS, SD State U., 1965; PhD, Mich. State U., 1970. With U. Mo.-Columbia, 1971—, prof. emeritus biochemistry, dir. interdisciplinary program on plant biochemistry-physiology. Past officer, chair bd. trustees Am. Soc. Plant Biologists; bd. dirs. Nat. Sci. Bd., 2002—; mem. Great Barrier Reef Photorespiration Expdn. Nat. Sci. Found., 1973. Mem. editl. bd. Plant Physiology, Annual Reviews Plant Physiology and Plant Molecular Biology, Protein Expression and Purification, Biochemical Archives, Current Topics in Plant Biochemistry and Physiology; contbr. articles to profl. jours. Mem.: Am. Chemical Soc., Am. Soc. Biol. Chemistry. Achievements include research in plant metabolism, signal transduction, regulation of plant enzymes and understanding the metabolic interations between photosynthesis, photorespiration and respiration. Office: U Mo Columbia Biochemistry Dept 117 Schweitzer Hall Office 213 Columbia MO 65211 Office Phone: 573-882-4847. Office Fax: 573-882-5635. Business E-Mail: randalld@missouri.edu.

RANDALL, FRANCES, technical writer; b. Frederick, Md., Oct. 6, 1924; d. George Birely and Ruth Carty Delaplaine; m. Myron William Randall, Apr. 10, 1949; children: George Elliott, Myron William Jr., Ruth Ann Randall, Eleanor Jane Randall Luttrell. BA, Hood Coll., 1945; MS, Johns Hopkins U., 1947; DHL (hon.), Hood Coll., 2006. Chemist U.S. Army Lab., Frederick, Md., 1947—49; writer-historian Frederick News-Post, 1965—. Chmn. bd. dirs. The Randall Family LLC, 2001—. Author: Mirror on Frederick, 1998, More Reflections on the History of Frederick, 2005 Bd. dir. Cmty. Found. Frederick County, 1988-96, Braddock Hts. Cmty. Assn.; past bd. dirs. Penn Laurel coun. Girl Scouts US. Recipient Cmty. Svc. award Ch. Transfiguration, Braddock Heights, Md., 1999, Thanks Badge, Penn Laurel Girl Scout Coun., 1988, Alumnae Achievement award Hood Coll., 1998, Woman of Distinction award Penn Laurel coun. Girl Scouts US, 2000, Families Plus! Cmty. Svc. award, 2004. Mem. DAR (Woman of Yr. in History, 2005), Hood Coll. Alumnae Assn. (pres., sec.), Frederick Woman's Civic Club (publicity chair, pres.), bd. trustees,Hood Coll, 1988-2000, Hist Soc. Frederick County (bd. dir. 2005-) Avocations: swimming, photography, travel, music. Home: 6301 Jefferson Blvd Frederick MD 21703-5809

RANDALL, FRANCIS BALLARD, retired historian, educator, writer; b. NYC, Dec. 17, 1931; s. John Herman, Jr. and Mercedes (Moritz) R.; m. Laura Regina Rosenbaum, June 11, 1957; children: David R., Ariane R. BA, Amherst Coll., 1952; MA, Columbia, 1954, PhD, 1960. Instr. history Amherst Coll., 1956-59; from instr. to asst. prof. history Columbia, 1959-61, vis. prof., 1967-68; humanities faculty Sarah Lawrence Coll., Bronxville, NY, 1961—2002, chmn., 1985—89, 1998—2001, trustee, 1971-76. Author: (with others) Essays in Russian and Soviet History, 1963, Stalin's Russia, an Historical Reconsideration, 1965, N.G. Chernyshevskii, 1967, Vissarion Belinskii, 1987, History Papers: A Teaching Life, 2000. Freedom rider civil disobedience to racism, 1961, war draft resistance arrests, 1967, 70. Fulbright fellow for study in India, 1965, Wye fellow, 1986. Mem.: AAUP (chpt. chmn. 1966—69), Am. Assn. for Advancement Slavic Studies, Am. Hist. Assn., Sigma Xi, Phi Beta Kappa. Home: 425 Riverside Dr Apt 10I New York NY 10025-7730

RANDALL, JEFFREY G., lawyer; BS in Fin., U. Oreg.; JD, U. Calif. Ptnr. Skadden, Arps, Slate, Meagher & Flom LLP, Palo Alto, Calif. Named one of California's Top 30 IP Attorneys, Daily Jour., Litigation's Rising Stars, The Am. Lawyer, 2007. Office: Skadden Arps Slate Meagher & Flom LLP 525 University Ave Ste 1100 Palo Alto CA 94301 Office Phone: 650-470-4500. Office Fax: 650-470-4570.

RANDALL, JESSIE, apparel executive; m. Brian Murphy, 2003. Grad., U. Va., Fashion Inst. Tech., Parsons New Sch.of Design. Assistantship Katayone Adeli, NYC, 2001; with Gap Inc.; pres., creative dir. Loeffler Randall Inc., NYC, 2004—. Recipient Swarovski award for Emerging Talent Accessory Design, Coun. Fashion Designers Am., 2007. Office: Loeffler Randall Inc 525 Broadway Ste 200 New York NY 10012 Office Phone: 212-226-8787. Office Fax: 212-226-7959. *

RANDALL, JESSY, curator, writer; b. Hornell, NY, Dec. 25, 1969; d. Katherine Cronk Randall; m. Ross Gresham, May 27, 2000; children: William Randall Gresham, Celia Randall Gresham. AB, Columbia U., NYC, 1992; MLS, U. NC, Chapel Hill, 1994. Rare book cataloger Glenn Horowitz, Bookseller, Inc., NYC, 1994—96; reference libr. and curator women's studies collection Libr. Co. Phila., 1996—2000; curator spl. collections Colo. Coll., Colo. Springs, 2001—. Author: Slumber Party at the Aquarium, 2004, Because Mona is in the Psychiatric Hospital, 2005, Broken Heart Diet, 2007, A Day in Boyland, 2007; occasional guest editor: online poetry jour. Snakeskin, 2001—07; contbr. Verbatim: The Language Quar., 1999—2007. Office: Special Collections Colorado Coll 1021 North Cascade Ave Colorado Springs CO 80903 Office Phone: 719-389-6668. Business E-Mail: jrandall@coloradocollege.edu.

RANDALL, KARL W., air transportation executive, lawyer; b. Mount Pleasant, Mich., Feb. 12, 1951; s. Herbert J. and Wilma E. (Worstell) R.; m. Natalie Kilmer Randall, Dec. 17, 1971; children: Adam B., Kara J. AA, Mich. Christian Coll., Rochester, 1971; BA, Oakland U., Rochester, 1977; JD, Wayne State U. Law Sch., Detroit, 1981. Bar: Mich., 1981, U.S. Dist. Ct., 1981, U.S. Ct. Appeals, 1983; cert. airport mgr., Mich., 1993. Quality contr. Staley SNO BOL Corp., Pontiac, Mich., 1971-72; engring. tech. Oakland Co. Drain Comm., Pontiac, 1972-83; sr. asst. corp. counsel Oakland County Corp. Counsel, Pontiac, 1983-93; mgr. aviation Oakland County Internat. Airport, Waterford, Mich., 1993—. Dir. Integrity Jour., Mt. Pleasant, 1980-98, Oakland County Coord. Child Care Coun., Waterford, 1992-97. Author, editor: (religious jour.) Integrity, 1982, 94-95. Mem. Rep. Com. Oakland County, 1988—, Exec. Club Oakland County, 1993—. Mem. Mich. Assn. Airport Execs. (exec., pres., 2005—), Langsford Men's Chorus. Republican. Mem. Ch. of Christ. Avocations: physical fitness, motorcycling, jogging, golf, piano. Office: Oakland County Internat Airport 6500 Highland Rd Waterford MI 48327-1607 Office Phone: 248-666-3900. E-mail: randallk@co.oakland.mi.us.

RANDALL, KAY TEMPLE, accountant, retired real estate agent; b. Chattanooga, Sept. 23, 1952; d. James H. Temple and Hortense N. (Dailey) Goodner; m. Gary F. Goodner, Feb. 9, 1968 (div. July 1972); 1 child, Jeffrey F. Goodner; m. Rodney B. Randall, Oct. 3, 1987. Student, Chattanooga State Coll., 1970-77, 82-83, Am. Inst. Banking, 1977-79. Lic. real estate agt., Tenn., ret.; notary public, Tenn. Ins. rep. Colonial Life Accident and Health, Columbia, SC, 1980-82; real estate appraiser, agt. Chattanooga, 1983-88; acct. Mr. Transmission of Chattanooga, Inc., 1987—; real estate agt. Chattanooga, 1989—. Adminstrv. asst. to legal profession, Chattanooga, 1972-75. Adv. bd. United Meth. Ch., Chattanooga, 1979-82, tchr., 1979-83; fellow cen. br. YMCA, Chattanooga, 1977-97. Fellow Walden's Club. Republican. Episcopalian. Avocation: collecting art. Home: 1858 Rivergate Ter Soddy Daisy TN 37379-5947 Office: Mr Transmission of Chattanooga Inc PO Box 1395 Soddy Daisy TN 37384-1395 E-mail: rodkayj@aol.com.

RANDALL, KENNETH C., dean, law educator; JD, Hofstra U., 1981; MA, Yale U., 1982, Columbia U., 1985, PhD, 1988. Practice law Simpson Thacher & Bartlett, NYC, 1982-84; with faculty U. Ala. Sch. Law, Tuscaloosa, 1985—, vice dean, 1989-93, dean, 1993—. Author book on international law; contbr. articles to law jours. and revs. W. Bayard Cutting Jr. fellow of internat. law Columbia U. Sch. Law, 1984-85. Office: U Ala Law Sch PO Box 870382 Tuscaloosa AL 35487-0001 Office Phone: 205-348-5117. E-mail: krandal@law.ua.edu. *

RANDALL, LILIAN MARIA CHARLOTTE, museum curator; b. Berlin, Feb. 1, 1931; came to U.S., 1938; d. Frederick Henry and Elizabeth Agnes (Ziegler) Cramer; m. Richard Harding Randall, Apr. 11, 1953; children: Christopher, Julia, Katharine. BA cum laude, Mount Holyoke Coll., 1950; MA, Radcliffe Coll., 1951, PhD, 1955; LHD (hon.), Towson State U., 1993; D of Arts (hon.), Mt. Holyoke Coll., 1998. Asst. dir. Md. State Arts Coun., 1972-73; curator manuscripts and rare books Walters Art Gallery, Balt., 1974-85, rsch. curator manuscripts, 1985-95; rsch. cons., 1995-97. Vis. lectr. dept. art history Johns Hopkins U., 1964-68; hon. vis. lectr. U. Mich., Ann Arbor; lectr. in field; bd. dirs. Digital Scriptorium: Electronic Access to Medieval Manuscripts; advisor Union Manuscript Computer Catalogue, 1996—. Author: Images in the Margins of Gothic Manuscripts, 1966; co-editor: Gatherings in Honor of Dorothy Miner, 1974, The Diary of George A. Lucas: An American Art Agent in Paris, 1909-1957, 1979, Illuminated Manuscripts: Masterpieces in Miniature, 1984, Medieval and Renaissance Manuscripts in the Walters Art Gallery, Vol. I, France, 875-1420, 1989, Vol. II, France, 1420-1540, 1992, Vol. III, Belgium, 1250-1530, 1997; contbr. articles to profl. jours. Mem. Williston Libr. com., 1988-89; reviewer, panelist NEH, 1980. Grantee AAUW, 1953-54, ACLS, 1960, 65, Bunting Inst., 1961-63, Ford Found., 1967-69, Am. Philos. Soc., 1971, NEA, 1975, Samuel H. Kress Found., 1979, 81-84, NEH, 1977-84, 89-95; grantee publ. subsidy Md. State Arts Coun., 1972, Mcpl. Art Soc. Balt., 1972, Andrew W. Mellon Found., 1988, Getty Grant program, 1990-92, NEA Mus. program, 1992-93; recipient Festschrift, Walters Art Gallery, ed. Elizabeth Burin, 1996, Sesquicentennial award Mount Holyoke Coll., 1987. Fellow Medieval Acad. Am. (libr. preservation com., various coms. 1985-87, 90-93, 2004—); mem. Internat. Ctr. Medieval Art (bd. dir. 1978-82, 96-99, mem. com. 2004—), Coll. Art Assn. (Arthur Kingsley Porter prize 1957), Balt. Bibliophiles (bd. dir. 1966-80, pres. 1980-83), Pyramid Atlantic (bd. dir. 1985-88), Mus. Fine Arts Boston (vis. com. Art of Europe dept. 2002-2007, adv. bd. Manuscripta 2004—), Grolier Club, Phi Beta Kappa. Home: 370 Adams St Milton MA 02186-4233 Personal E-mail: lmcrand@ix.netcom.com.

RANDALL, LINDA LEA, biochemist, educator; b. Montclair, NJ, Aug. 7, 1946; d. Lowell Neal and Helen (Watts) Randall; m. Gerald Lee Hazelbauer, Aug. 29, 1970. BS, Colo. State U., 1968; PhD, U. Wis., 1971. Postdoctoral fellow Inst. Pasteur, Paris, 1971—73; asst. prof. Uppsala (Sweden) U., 1975—81; assoc. prof. Wash. State U., Pullman, 1981—83, prof. biochemistry, 1983—2000; Wurdock prof. biochemistry U. Mo., Columbia, 2000—. Guest scientist Wallenberg Lab. Uppsala U., 1973—75; mem. study sect. NIH, 1984—88. Contbr. articles to profl. jours.; co-editor: (book) Virus Receptors Part I, 1980; mem. editl. bd.: Jour. Bacteriology, 1982—96. Recipient Eli Lilly award in Microbiology and Immunology, 1984, Faculty Excellence Award in Rsch., Wash. State U., 1988, Parke-Davis award, 1995. Fellow: AAAS, Am. Acad. Arts and Scis., Am. Acad. Microbiology; mem.: NAS, Protein Soc., Am. Soc. Biol. Chemists, Am. Microbiological Soc. Avocation: dance. Office: Univ Mo Dept Biochemistry 117 Schweitzer Hall Columbia MO 65211 Home Phone: 573-449-2042; Office Phone: 573-884-4160.

RANDALL, LISA, physics professor; b. June 18, 1962; BA in Physics, Harvard U., 1983, PhD in Particle Physics, 1987. Pres.'s fellow U. Calif., Berkeley, 1987—89; postdoctoral fellow Lawrence Berkeley Lab., 1989—90; jr. fellow Harvard Soc. Fellows, 1990—91; asst. prof. physics MIT, 1991—95, assoc. prof., 1995—98, prof., 1998—2001, Princeton U., 1998—2000, Harvard U., 2001—; fellow Radcliffe Inst., 2002; chair Radcliffe Inst. Cosmology & Theoretical Astrophysics Cluster, 2003. Contbr. articles to sci. jours. and popular publs., chapters to books; editor: Jour. High Energy Physics, 1997—98, 2000—06, Ann. Rev. Nuc. and Particle Sci., 1997—2000; assoc. editor: Nuc. Physics B, 1999—; author: Warped Passages: Unraveling the Mysteries of the Universe's Hidden Dimensions, 2005; featured in Vogue Mag., 2007. Named a 2005 Year in Sci. Icon, Seed Magazine, 2005; named one of the World's Most Influential People, TIME Mag., 2007; named to Who's Next in 2006, Newsweek, 2006; recipient Young Investigator award, NSF, 1992, Outstanding Jr. Investigator award, Dept. Energy, 1992, Premio Caterina Tomassoni e Felice Pietro Chisesi award, U. Rome, 2003, Klopsteg award, Am. Assn. Physics Tchrs., 2006, Elizabeth A. Wood award, Am. Crystallographic Assn., 2007; grantee Alfred P. Sloan Found. Rsch. fellowship, 1992. Fellow: Am. Phys. Soc. (Julius Edgar Lilienfeld prize 2007), Am. Acad. Arts & Sciences. Office: Dept Physics Harvard U 17 Oxford St Cambridge MA 02138 Office Phone: 617-496-8188. E-mail: randall@physics.harvard.edu. *

RANDALL, LYNN ELLEN, librarian; b. Chgo., Oct. 10, 1951; d. Ward W. and Hazel A. R. BA, King's Coll., 1970; MA, Seton Hall U., 1973; MLS, Rutgers U., 1978. Libr. asst. Newark Coll. Engring, Newark,

1970-75; libr. dir. N.E. Bible Coll., Essex Fells, N.J., 1975-81; reference libr. Seton Hall U., South Orange, N.J., 1983-85; dir. libr. svc. Berkeley Coll., NJ, 1985-89; with Caldwell Coll., NJ, 1989—2006, exec. dir. libr. svcs.; dir. human resources Am.'s Keswick, Whiting, NJ, 2006—. Reference libr., instr. Morris (N.J.) County Coll., 1981-83; panelist/facilitator Middle States Self-Study Inst., 1996, 97, 2004. 05; Evaluator, Middle States, 1994-. Mem. N.J. Libr. Assn. (pres. 1996-97), Am. Libr. Assn. Office: America's Keswick 601 Route 530 Whiting NJ 08759 Office Phone: 732-350-1187 18. Business E-Mail: lrandall@americaskeswick.org.

RANDALL, MARILYN MAE, writer; d. Dice A. and Margaret L. Hartman; m. Charles D. Randall, Aug. 24, 1991; children: Philip E. Marechal, Cheryl L. Pittman. BA magna cum laude, Trinity Coll., Washington, 1988. Registrar Va. Theol. Sem., 1974—87; bus. mgr. St. Margaret's Episcopal Ch., 1987—89; bus. owner, 1989—95. Vis. author/lectr. various elem. and mid. schs., Tenn., 2002—; featured lectr./workshop presenter Christian Writers' Conf., Memphis, 2002, 06, Ea. Tenn. State U. Celebration Books and Authors, 2004; featured local author Fall for the Book George Mason U., 2004; workshop presenter; contest judge Life Press, 2006. Author: (children's books) Southern Christmas, 2001, Wishes for Christmas, 2002, Wellington's Windows, 2003, The Three Wives of Hero the Second, 2004, The Meanie, 2006, A Marine Salute (endorsed by USMC and Young Marine Orgn.); editor: The Forty Days of Lent; composer, lyricist: Angel with an Attitude, 2004. Pres. Good Samaritan chpt. Daus. of the King, Knoxville, 1998—2004. Mem.: Alpha Sigma Lambda, Phi Beta Kappa. Episcopalian. Avocations: composing, poetry. Home: 1550 Scenic View Dr Loudon TN 37774 Personal E-mail: mmrandall@hughesnet.com.

RANDALL, NEIL WARREN, gastroenterologist; b. White Plains, NY, Mar. 24, 1957; s. Leroy Bruce and Libby Cynthia (Brandt) R.; m. Linda Ilene Zell, Oct. 31, 1992. BA, U. Va., 1978; MD, U. Md., 1983. Diplomate Am. Bd. Internal Medicine with subspecialty in gastroenterology, geriat. Resident in internal medicine Ochsner Clinic, New Orleans, 1983-86; fellow in gastroenterology Tufts U., Boston, 1986-88; staff gastroenterologist Cleve. Clinic Fla., Fort Lauderdale, 1988-92, Geisinger Clinic, Danville, Pa., 1992-97, Pa. State Geisinger Health Sys., Danville, 1997-98; med. dir. gastrointestinal endoscopy Geisinger Health Sys., 1999-2000; gastroenterologist Gastroenterology Group of Naples, 2001—. Fellow ACP, Am. Coll. Gastroenterology; mem. Am. Soc for Gastroent. Endoscopy. Avocations: theater, travel, wine. Office: Gasterenterology Group of Naples 1064 Goodlette-Frank Rd Naples FL 34102-5449 Office Phone: 239-649-1186.

RANDALL, PETER, retired plastic surgeon; b. Phila., Mar. 29, 1923; s. Alexander and Edith Tilghman (Kneedler) R.; m. Rose Gordon Johnson, May 1, 1948; children: Deborah K., Peter G., Julia B., Susanna T. BA, Princeton U., 1944; MD, Johns Hopkins U., 1946; MS (hon.), U. Pa., 1969. Diplomate Am. Bd. Plastic Surgery. Intern Union Meml. Hosp., Balt., 1946—47; asst. resident in surgery Hosp. of U. of Pa., Phila., 1949—50; fellow in plastic surgery Barnes Hosp.-St. Louis Childrens Hosp., 1950—52, resident in plastic surgery, 1952—53; asst. instr. plastic surgery Washington U., St. Louis, 1950—53; from asst. prof. to assoc. prof. plastic surgery U. Pa. Hosp., Phila., 1953—69, prof. plastic surgery, 1969—92, emeritus prof. plastic surgery, 1992—; chief div. plastic surgery sch. medicine U. Pa., Phila., 1979—87; ret., 1994. Sr. surgeon Children's Hosp. Phila., 1965—. Contbr. articles to profl. jours. Pres. Plastic Surgery Edn. Found., 1972-73. Lt. (j.g.) USNR, 1947-49. Fellow: ACS (bd. govs., chmn. 1982—84, 1st v.p. 1985—86), Am. Assn. Plastic Surgeons (hon. Clinician of Yr. award 1987, disting. fellow 1994); mem.: AMA, Am. Cleft Palate Assn. (pres. 1965—66, Honors award 1986), Plastic Surgery Rsch. Coun. (founder, chmn. 1964—65), Phila. Acad. Surgery, Phila. County Med. Soc., Northea. Soc. Plastic Surgery (founder), Am. Surg. Assn., Coll. Physicians of Phila., Am. Soc. Plastic Surgeons (pres. 1978—79, Spl. Achievement award 1987), Am. Bd. Plastic Surgery (vice-chmn. 1976—77), Am. Cleft Palate Ednl. Found. (founder, pres. 1972—73), Robert H. Ivy Soc. (founder, pres. 1966—67), Halsted Soc., Sigma Xi.

RANDALL, RICHARD J., academic administrator; BA, U. Maine, 1966, MA, 1967, LLD, 2004. Instr. sociology U. Maine at Augusta, 1967, asst. prof., assoc. prof., prof., dir. student affairs, 1968—71, dean student affairs and ednl. svcs., 1971—78, acting dean, 1984—85, dean, 1985—87, provost, 1989—93, provost, v.p. academic affairs, 1993—2001, interim assoc. provost, 2005, interim pres., 2005—06, pres., 2006—. Office: U Maine at Augusta Off of Pres 46 University Dr Augusta ME 04330-9410 Office Phone: 207-621-3403. Office Fax: 207-621-3496. E-mail: rrandall@maine.edu.

RANDALL, RICHARD RAINIER, geographer; b. Toledo, July 21, 1925; s. Robert Henry and Maree (Gard) R.; m. Patricia Lee Spencer, June 9, 1962; children: Allison Maree, Susan Rebecca, Richard Rainier Jr. BA, George Washington U., 1949, MA, 1950; PhD, Clark U., 1955. Fulbright scholar Graz U., Austria, 1953—54; Geog. analyst CIA, Washington, 1955-61; Washington rep. Rand McNally & Co., Washington, 1961-72; owner Randall Assocs., Washington, 1972-73; exec. sec. U.S. Bd. Geog. Names, Washington, 1973-93; geographer Def. Mapping Agy., Washington, 1973-93; ret., 1993; cons. on geog. names, 1993—. Convenor UN Working Group on Undersea and Maritime Feature Names, 1975-84; mem., prin. U.S. tech. advisor U.S. and U.K. Conf. on Geog. Names, 1976, 79, 81, 84, 86, 88, 92; dep. head U.S. del. UN Conf. on Geog. Names, 1977, head, 1982, 87, 92; 1st v.p. of 6th UN Conf. 92; prin. U.S. expert UN Group Experts on Geog. Names, 1975, 77, 79, 82, 84, 86, 87, 89, 92; pres. com. on geog. terminology Pan Am. Inst. Geography and History, 1973-77, pres. working group on geog. names and gazetters, 1981-94. Author: Place Names: How they Define the World—And More, 2001; contbr. articles to profl. jours.; inventor flexible fishhook. V.p. North Cleveland Park Citizens Assn., Washington, 1968. With U.S. Army, 1943-46, ETO. Decorated ETO ribbon with 4 battle stars, Bronze Star, Combat Infantryman's badge; recipient Pioneer Achievement award United Black Christians Region III United Ch. Christ, 1994. Mem. Am. Congress on Surveying and Mapping (dir. cartography divsn. 1973-75, dir. press rels. 1961-72, program dir. cartography divsn. ann. meeting 1967), Am. Geog. Soc., Assn. Am. Geographers (chmn. Mid-Atlantic divsn. 1978, dir. press rels. ann. conf. 1968), Am. Names Soc., Am. Austrian Soc. (v.p. 1955-57), Explorers Club (Washington group steering com.), Cosmos Club. Republican.

RANDALL, ROBERT L(EE), ecological economist; b. Aberdeen, SD, Dec. 28, 1936; s. Harry Eugene and Juanita Alice (Barstow) Randall. MS in Phys. Chemistry, U. Chgo., 1960, MBA, 1963. Market devel. chemist E.I. du Pont de Nemours & Co., Inc., Wilmington, Del., 1963-65; chem. economist Battelle Meml. Inst., Columbus, Ohio, 1965-68; mgr. market and econ. rsch. Kennecott Copper Corp., NYC, 1968-74, economist, 1974-79, dir. new bus. venture devel., 1979-81; pres., mng. dir. R.L. Randall Assocs., Inc., 1981—; economist U.S. Internat. Trade Commn., Washington, 1983—. Founder, pres., exec. dir. RainForest ReGeneration Inst., 1986—, ind. internat. press corr., 1997—, indsl. panel policy rev. of effect of regulation on innovation and U.S.-internat. competition U.S. Dept. Commerce, 1980-81; participant preparatory com. UN Conf. on Environ. and Devel., Rio de Janeiro, 1991; del. observer internat. negotiating com. UN Framework Conv. on Climate Change, 1991—. Contbg. author: Computer Methods for the 80's; sect. lead author, editor: World Energy Assessment, 2000; pub. reviewer intergovtl. panel on climate change Third Assessment Report; addresser 4th Internat. Greenhouse Gas Tech. conf., Interlaken, Switzerland, 1998; contbr. articles to profl. jours. Mem. Gay Activists Alliance, N.Y.C., 1971-75, chmn. state and fed. legislation com., 1975. Mem. AAAS (organizer ann. meeting, Tropical Forest Regeneration Symposium), AIME (econ. coun., mineral econ. subsect.), Internat. Soc. Ecol. Health, Internat. Soc. Ecol. Economists, Am. Econ. Assn., Am. Statis. Assn., Am. Chem. Soc., Soc. Mining Engrs., Chemists Club of N.Y.C., Metall. Soc., N.Y. Acad. Scis., Nat. Econs. Club Washington (sec., reporter), Assn. Environ. and Resource Economists, Marine Biol. Assn. (Plymouth, Eng.), Wanderbirds Hiking Club (hike leader, treas.), Capital Hiking Club (hike leader, Washington). Home: 1727 Massachusetts Ave NW Washington DC 20036-2153 Office: US Internat Trade Com 500 E St SW Washington DC 20436-0003 E-mail: randall@usitc.gov. *Like thousands of organizations around the world, The RainForest ReGeneration Institute is trying to find a practical and effective way forward, through United Nations-sponsored treaty negotiations, appropriate national actions, and imaginative project work, on the ground, in local communities. Tropical rainforests must have recognizable community value if they are to be viable. Global value is not enough for the conservation of the tropical rainforests. Ultimate wisdom does not reside in any individual or organization. All must work together through every available forum and mechanism, and to create new modalities where those presently in existence are inadequate or ineffective.*

RANDALL, ROGER DAVID, publishing executive; b. St. Charles, Minn., Dec. 24, 1953; s. Curtis Clark and Virginia Mae (Tollefson) Randall; m. Mary Barnard, Aug. 25, 1979; children: Sara Louise, Clark Robinson. BA, Morningside Coll., 1976. Advt. dir. Nutra-Flo Chem. Co., Kay Dee Feed Co., Sioux City, Iowa, 1976-78; agrl. account svc. Lewis & Gilman, Phila., 1978-80, Creswell, Munsell, Fultz & Zirbel, Cedar Rapids, Iowa, 1980-81, Richardson, Myers & Donofrio, Inc., Balt., 1981-84; mktg. mgr. Farm Jour., Inc., Phila., 1984-85, v.p., 1986-89, v.p., pub., 1989-95, pres., 1995-99, CEO, 1999-2000, also bd. dirs.; pres., CEO AgWeb.com, 1999-2001; exec. v.p. Miller Meester, Inc., 2001—03. Mem. bus. adv. com. Nat. Assn. Conser. Dist. Bd. dirs. Planned Parenthood Sioux City, 1977-78, Iowa Planned Parenthood Fedn., 1978, Sioux City Pub. Mus., 1977-78; trustee Old 1st Reformed Ch., 1994-95. Recipient Disting. Alumni award, Morningside Coll., 1997. Mem. Nat. Agri-Mktg. Assn. (pres. Chesapeake chpt. 1984, nat. awards agri. excellence 1988, exec. com. 1990-92, sec.-treas. 1992-93), Queen Village Neighbors Assn. (dir., treas. 1987-90, pres. 1994-95), Preservation Alliance of Minn. (dir., vice chair, commn. com. co-chair, chair 2005) Mem. United Ch. Of Christ. Home: 4270 Norwood Ln N Minneapolis MN 55442 E-mail: rrandall112953@msn.com.

RANDAZZO, GARY WAYNE, newspaper executive; b. Georgetown, Tex., Sept. 23, 1947; s. Frank Birchmans and Edna Earle (Forbis) R.; m. Joyce Sue McNorton, Oct. 7, 1966; children: Gary Wayne Jr., Vanessa Rene, Michael Jason, Daniel Paul. BBA, U. Tex., 1974; MBA, Tex. A&I U., 1976. Instr. Del Mar Coll., Corpus Christi, 1974—76; bus. mgr. Corpus Christi Caller-Times, 1976—81; pres., pub. Huntsville Item, Tex., 1981—83; pres. Am. Property Data, Houston, 1984—87; gen. mgr. Health Care News, Houston, 1987—89; sr. v.p. sales and mktg. Houston Chronicle, 1989—2002; exec. v.p., gen. mgr. San Francisco Chronicle, 2002—05; pres. G.W. News Corp., 2005—. Chmn., bd. dirs. Leadership Houston; bd. dirs. Downtown Houston Assn., treas.; bd. dirs. Better Bus. Bur., Alley Theatre, Houston; chmn. Big Bros./Big Sisters; mem. adv. coun. San Francisco Unified Sch. Dist. Mem. Kiwanis (bd. dirs.). Home: 8306 Glenn Elm Dr Spring TX 77379 Home Phone: 832-717-4272; Office Phone: 832-717-0604. Business E-Mail: garyrandazzo@sbcglobal.net.

RANDAZZO, MARISA R., psychologist; d. Hilary Phillip and Susan Hilborn Reddy; m. Robert Salvatore Randazzo, May 15, 2004. BA in Psychology and Religion, Williams Coll., 1989; MA in Psychology, PhD in Psychology, Princeton U., 1995. Chief rsch. psychologist US Secret Svc., Washington, 1996—2004; sr. expert Bus. Intelligence Advisors, Boston, 2004—06; pres. Threat Assessment Resources Internat., Reno, 2006—. Editl. bd. Jour. Threat Assessment, 2001—. Recipient Bicentennial Medal Recipient, Williams Coll., 2005; fellow, Soc. Psychol. Study Social Issues, Washington, 1995—96. Mem.: APA, Am. Psychology-Law Soc. (program chair 1998—2000). Achievements include research in American school shooters; preventing violence in schools. Office Phone: 775-424-6685. Business E-Mail: mrr@threatresources.com.

RANDEL, DON MICHAEL, foundation administrator, former academic administrator, musicologist; m. Carol Randel; children: Amy Elizabeth Keating, Julia, Emily Catherine Pershing, Sally Randel Eggert. AB magna cum laude, Princeton U., 1962, MFA in Music, 1964, PhD in Music, 1967. Asst. prof., dept. fine arts Syracuse U., 1966—68; asst. prof. music Cornell U., Ithaca, NY, 1968—71, assoc. prof. music, 1971—75, chair dept. music, 1971—76, prof. music, 1975—2000, vice provost, 1978—79, assoc. dean Coll. Arts and Scis., 1989—91, Given Found. prof. musicology, 1990—2000, Harold Tanner dean Coll. Arts and Scis., 1991—95, provost, 1995—2000; pres. U. Chgo., 2000—06, Andrew W. Mellon Found., NYC, 2006—. V.p. Am. Musicological Soc., 1977—78; mem. adv. com. dept. music Princeton U., 1987—99; mem. Penn Nat. Commn. Soc., Culture and Cmty., 1996—99; bd. govenors Argonne Nat. Lab., 2000—; bd. trustees Chgo. Symphony Orch. Assn., 2001—06; bd. dirs. Chgo. Coun. Fgn. Relations, 2001, CNA Fin. Corp., 2002—; bd. mem. Lyric Opera Chgo., 2004—06. Editor: New Harvard Dictionary of Music, 1986, Harvard Biographical Dictionary of Music, 1996, Harvard Concise Dictionary of Music and Musicians, 1999, The Harvard Dictionary of Music, 2003; mem. editl. bd. advisors Ency. Britannica, editor-in-chief Jour. Am. Musicological Soc., 1972—74. Bd. mem. Internet2, 2004—. Recipient Fulbright award; Hon. Woodrow Wilson fellow, Danforth Grad. fellow, 1962—66. Fellow: Am. Acad. Arts and Scis.; mem.: Am. Assn. Advancement Sci., Modern Language Assn., Am. Musicological Soc., Am. Philos. Soc. Office: Andrew W Mellon Found 140 E 62nd St New York NY 10021

RANDELL, CORTES W., news service executive; b. Washington, 1935; m. Joan. V. (Wirz) 1968; children: Cortes John, Christina Alexis. BSME, U. Va., 1959; student, Darden Sch., U. Va., 1962. Engr. Gen. Electric, N.Y., 1959-61, Internat. Telephone & Telegraph, Chgo., 1962-64; pres. Nat. Student Mktg., N.Y., 1964-71; cons. and trustee Washington Trust, 1972-84; pres. Federal News Svc., Washington, 1985—2002; mcht. banker, 2002—. Author: Taking the Stand, Testimony of Oliver North, 1987, The National Press Club's Best Contemporary Speakers, 1995. Mem. Nat. Press Club, Yale Club. Avocations: ballooning, boating. Office: 9017 Swift Creek Rd Fairfax Station VA 22039-2815 Office Phone: 703-685-4828. E-mail: cort.randell@cox.net.

RANDELL, LINDA L., utilities executive, lawyer; b. Chgo., 1950; AB magna cum laude with high distinction in econ., U. Mich., 1970; JD, Yale U., 1973. Bar: N.Y. 1974, Ill. 1974, Conn. 1976. Assoc. Wiggin & Dana, 1976—80, ptnr., 1980—2007; sr. v.p., gen. counsel UIL Holdings Corpn., New Haven, 2007—. Recipient Best Lawyers in Am., 1995. Mem. Conn. Bar Assn. (chmn. antitrust sect.) 1988-1991, NY Bar Assn., Ill. Bar Assn., Phi Beta Kappa, ABA (coun, sec. pub. utility comm. and transp. law, vice chair, fuel and energy com.), vice chair (antitrust com., elec. com.), Statewide Grievance Com. 1991-1994, James W. Cooper Fellow Conn. Bar Found., Yale Law Jour. Alumni Adv. Bd. Office: UIL Holdings Corpn 157 Church St PO Box 1564 New Haven CT 06506

RANDELS, DAVID GEORGE, retired secondary school educator; b. Bryan, Ohio, Feb. 6, 1943; s. George D. and Doris L. Randels; 1 child, Kellie R. BS in Edn., Bowling Green State U., 1965, MusM, 1971. Instr., counselor Culver (Ind.) Mil. Acad., 1962-67; instr. music Port Clinton (Ohio) City Schs., 1965—2004; ret., 2004. Tchr., drummer various jazz bands, 1960—; drummer Jamie Wight New Orleans Joymakers, 1980—. Musician (drummer): (albums) 6 recordings. Named Outstanding Bandsman, Bowling Green State U., 1965; recipient John Phillips Sousa Band award, Bryan HS, 1961, Dist. Svc. award, Ottawa County, Ohio, 2004, Mayor's Svc. award, Port Clinton, Ohio, 2004. Mem.: Music Educators Nat. Conf., Port Clinton Fedn. Tchrs. (Lifetime Achievement award 1984), U.S. Capital Hist. Soc., Nat. Sch. Orch. Assn. (Disting. Svc. award 1994), Port Clinton Model R.R. Club (pres. 1965), Elks, Phi Kappa Psi, Phi Delta Kappa, Kappa Kappa Psi. Democrat. Avocations: model railroading, music, antique cars, camping, fishing. Home: PO Box 182 Port Clinton OH 43452-1901 Office: 8060 W Mud Creek Rd Oak Harbor OH 43449-9642 Home Phone: 419-898-1896; Office Phone: 419-898-2442. Business E-Mail: davidrandels@cnos.net.

RANDELS, ED L., lawyer; b. Albuquerque, Nov. 17, 1953; s. James L. and Betty J. (Ridgeway) R.; m. Kathryn J. Eddleman, July 11, 1975; children: Nancy L, Joshua L. BA, Mid-Am. Nazarene Coll., Olathe, Kans., 1975; JD, U. Kans., 1982. Bar: Kans. 1982, U.S. Dist. Ct. Kans. 1982, U.S. Ct. Appeals (10th cir.) 1994. Asst. county atty. Montgomery County, Independence, Kans., 1982—85, Miami County, Paola, Kans., 1985—86; asst. city atty. City of Wichita, Kans., 1986—92; asst. county counselor Sedgwick County, Wichita, Kans., 1992—. Law day dir. Miami County Bar Assn., Paola, Kans., 1985-86. Contbr. articles to profl. jours. Mem. ABA, Kans. Bar Assn., Wichita Bar Assn. (chair law in edn. com. 1999-2000, mem. mcpl. practice com.), Christian Legal Soc. (pres. Wichita chpt. 1998-99, 2000-01), County Counselor Assn. Kans. (pres. 2005-2006). Republican. Nazarene. Office: Sedgwick County Counselor 525 N Main St Ste 359 Wichita KS 67203-3731 Home Phone: 316-773-6047; Office Phone: 316-660-9340. Business E-Mail: erandels@sedgwick.gov.

RANDERSON, JAMES T., geophysicist, educator; s. Tremper and Laurie Randerson. BS in Chemistry, Stanford U., Calif., 1992, PhD in Biol. Scis., 1998. Postdoctoral scholar U. Calif. Berkeley and U. Alaska, 1998—2000; asst. prof. biogeochemistry and environ. sci. and engring. Calif. Inst. Tech., Pasadena, 2000—03; assoc. prof. dept. earth sys. sci. U. Calif., Irvine, 2003—. Contbr. articles to sci. jours. Fellow: Am. Geophys. Union (James B. Macelwane medal 2005); mem.: AAAS, Ecol. Soc. Am., Sigma Xi. Office: Dept Earth Sys Sci U Calif Irvine 3212 Croul Hall Irvine CA 92697 Office Phone: 949-824-9030. Office Fax: 949-824-3874. E-mail: jranders@uci.edu. *

RANDHAWA, BIKKAR SINGH, retired psychologist, retired educator; b. Jullundur, India, June 14, 1933; came to Can., 1961, naturalized, 1966; s. Pritam S. and Sawaran K. (Basakhi) R.; m. Leona Emily Bujnowski, Oct. 8, 1966; children: Jason, Lisa. BA in Math., Panjab U., India, 1954, BT in Edn., 1955, MA in History, 1959; BEd, U. Alta., Can., 1963; MEd in Measurement and Evaluation, U. Toronto, 1967, PhD, 1969. Tchr. secondary sch. math., Panjab, 1955-61; asst. headmaster, then headmaster, 1955-61; tchr. h.s. math. and sci. Camrose County, Canada, 1961—64, Beaver County, 1964—65, Edmonton (Alta.) Pub. Schs., 1965-67; tutor in math. for social sci. Ont. Inst. Studies in Edn., Toronto, 1968-69; mem. faculty U. Sask., Saskatoon, Canada, 1969—76, 1977—, prof. ednl. psychology, 1977-2000, prof. emeritus, 2000—, asst. dean rsch. and field svcs., 1982-87. Prof., coord. Visual Scholars' Program, U. Iowa, 1976-77; adj. prof. edu. psychology, U. Alta., 2002-; cons. in field. Contbr. articles to profl. jours. Treas. St. Albert Crime Stoppers, 2002—05. Fellow APA, Am. Psychol. Soc. (charter), Can. Psychol. Assn.; mem. Can. Ednl. Rsch. Assn. (pres. 1997-99), Can. Soc. Study Edn., St. Albert Rotary Club (treas. 2003-05), Phi Delta Kappa (pres. Saskatoon chpt. 1971, 85). Home: 14 Harwood Dr Saint Albert AB Canada T8N 5V5 Home Phone: 780-419-2547; Office Phone: 780-419-2549. Personal E-mail: randy.randhawa@shaw.ca.

RANDI, JAMES (RANDALL JAMES HAMILTON ZWINGE), magician, educator; b. Toronto, Aug. 7, 1928; naturalized U.S. citizen, 1987; s. George Randall and Marie Alice (Paradis) Zwinge. Student, Oakwood Collegiate Inst., Toronto, 1940-45; LittD (hon.), U. Indpls., 1995. Internationally known conjuror, lectr., author, investigator. Regent's lectr. UCLA, 1984; skeptical lectr. on paranormal subjects. Author: The Magic of Uri Geller, 1975 (with Bert Sugar) Houdini, His Life and Art, 1978, Flim-Flam, 1982, Test Your ESP Potential, 1983, The Faith Healers, 1987, The Magic World of the Amazing Randi, 1989, The Mask of Nostradamus, 1990, James Randi: Psychic Investigator, 1991, Conjuring, 1992, An Encyclopedia of Claims, Frauds, and Hoaxes of the Occult and Supernatural, 1995 (English, Chinese, French, Italian, German, Japanese, Korean, Norwegian, Punjabi, Polish and Spanish edits.); host TV spls. Recipient Blackstone award Internat. Platform Assn., 1983, 87, Forum award Am. Phys. Soc., 1988, Nat. Consumer Svc. award Nat. Coun. Against Health Fraud, 1988, Gold medal U. Ghent, Belgium, 1989, Humanist Disting. Svc. award Am. Humanist Assn., 1990, medal with golden wreath Hungarian Soc. for Dissemination of Scientific Knowledge, 1992; MacArthur Found. fellow, 1986, Spl. fellow Acad. Magical Arts and Scis., 1987; inducted into Soc. Am. Magicians Hall of Fame, 1988. Founding fellow Com. for Scientific Investigation of Claims of the Paranormal (exec. bd. dirs. 1973-91). Achievements include performing at White House, 1974. Home: 12000 NW 8th St Fort Lauderdale FL 33325-1406 Office: James Randi Ednl Found 201 SE 12th St Fort Lauderdale FL 33316-1815 Office Phone: 954-467-1112. Personal E-mail: randi@randi.org. *We are well into the third millennium with quack medicine, "Creation Science," faith "healing" and other pseudo-scientific matters heedlessly and increasingly embraced by the public, and major TV programs feature performers who claim to "speak to the dead." These con artists, feeding on the grief and vulnerability of their victims, are ignored, even tolerated, by our state and federal agencies. TV "magazine" shows promote belief in superstition by failing to properly research their subjects, and thereby serve their audiences poorly. Medieval notions and an anti-science movement threaten our very survival. We must reach out to our youth and develop in them a respect and understanding for real science. Acceptance of "politically correct" and "faith-based" standards, and of unquestioning belief in obviously crackpot theories, have brought us to a crisis in education. We need to adopt higher standards for our young people in respect to critical thinking, and encourage them to question the claims of the quacks and scam artists. The one-million dollar prize offered by my Foundation for proof of any paranormal power is still unclaimed. Why?.*

RANDICH, STEVEN J., financial services company executive; BS in computer sci., No. Ill. U.; MBA, U. Chgo. Mgr. KPMG Peat Marwick; joined IBM, 1989; mng. prin. IBM Global Services; exec. v.p., chief info. officer Chgo. Stock Exch.; exec. v.p., chief tech. officer NASDAQ Stock Market Inc., 2000—01, exec. v.p. ops. and tech., chief info. officer, 2001—05; chief info. officer, Citi markets and banking Citigroup, 2005—. Named one of Premier 100 IT Leaders, Computerworld, 2005. Office: Citigroup Inc 388 Greenwich St New York NY 10013

RANDINELLI, TRACEY ANNE, magazine editor; b. Morristown, NJ, Apr. 6, 1963; d. Andrew R. and Patricia Ann (Brenner) Randinelli. BA in Comm., U. Del., 1985. Copywriter Macy's N.J., Newark, 1985-86; editl. asst. Globe Comms. Corp., NYC, 1986-87; from asst. editor to assoc. editor Scholastic Math and DynaMath Mags. Scholastic, Inc., NYC, 1987-89, editor Scholastic Math Mag., 1989-95; mng. editor Zig Zag Mag. Games Pub. Group, NYC, 1995; sr. editor Contact Kids Mag./ Sesame Workshop, NYC, 1996-2001; freelance writer, 2001—02; sr. editor Pearson Learning Group, 2002—04, supervising editor, 2004—. Mem. Soc. Children's Book Writers, Ednl. Press Assn. Am. (Disting. Achievement award feature articles divsn. 1991, 95, coverdesign 1996, how-to feature divsn. 1998, 99). Personal E-mail: pen4kidz@aol.com.

RANDLE, BERNADETTE, musician, composer, graphics designer; b. St. Louis, Jan. 8, 1947; d. William George Randle and Louise Robinmae Randle-Ware. BA summa cum laude, Concordia U. Wis., 1993; MA, Lindenwood U., 1994. Dir. employment programs YMCA of Greater St. Louis, 1980—83; freelance studio musician Platinum Chess Record, Englewood, NJ, 1983—86; office clk. Def. Contract Audit Agy. & HUD, St. Louis, 1986—87; mktg. specialist Tailored Software Corp., Maryland Heights, Mo., 1987—89; graphic illustrator The Bionetics Corp., St. Louis, 1989—97; concept developer/tech. writer Bus. Blueprints, St. Louis, 1997—2000; composer, arranger ReMembered/The Gozz Ensemble; creative dir. Prosit Media Group; min. music Third United Presbyn. Ch., St. Louis. Mktg. cons. The Enterprise Found., St. Louis, 2002—03. Author: (short story) Chicken Soup for the Surviving Soul; pianist, arranger, composer numerous recs., 1974—. Vol. counselor CanSurmount, St. Louis, 1991—96; vol. visitor Am. Heartland Hospice, St. Louis, 1994. Grantee, Mo. Arts Coun., 1991. Mem.: Broadcast Music Inc., Mensa, Sigma Phi Omega. Avocations: reading religious histories, surfing the web, collecting baseball caps and kaleidoscopes. Office: Prosit Media Group 11621 Olive Street Rd Creve Coeur MO 63141 Personal E-mail: bernadettrandle@sbcglobal.net.

RANDLE, CAMMON C., filmmaker; b. Provo, Utah, 1981; m. Lorri Randle. Student in Multi-media, Utah Valley State Coll.; B in Comm., Brigham Young U., Provo, Utah. Founder, dir. photography CopperRain Prodns., Provo, Utah, 2004—. Attendee Provo Labs, Utah. Lighting technician intern: The Work and the Glory: Pillar of Light, 2005. Named one of Best Entrepreneurs Under 25, BusinessWeek mag., 2006. Office: CopperRain Prodns 2419 W 180 South Provo UT 84601-3678 Office Phone: 801-836-0182. E-mail: cammon@copperrain.com. *

RANDLE, ELLEN EUGENIA FOSTER, opera and classical singer, educator; b. New Haven, Oct. 2, 1948; d. Richard A.G. and Thelma Lousie (Brooks) Foster; m. Ira James William, 1967 (div. 1972); m. John Willis Randle, Dec. 24, 1983. Student, Calif. State Coll., Sonoma, 1970; studied with Boris Goldovsky, 1970; student, Grad. Sch. Fine Arts, Florence, Italy, 1974; studied with Tito Gobbi, Florence, 1974; student, U. Calif., Berkeley, 1977; BA in World History, Lone Mountain Coll., 1976, MA in Performing Arts, 1978; studied with Madam Eleanor Steber, Graz, Austria, 1979; studied with Patricia Goehl, Munich, Germany, 1979; MA in Counseling and Psychology, U. San Francisco, 1990, MA in Marriage and Family Therapy, 1994, EdD in Internat. Multicultural Edn., 1998. Asst. artistic dir. Opera Piccola, Oakland, Calif., 1990—92; instr. African Am. culture and humanities Mission C.C., Santa Clara, Calif., 1997—; instr. Peralta C.C. Dist., Oakland, 1998—; psychotherapy intern, sr. peer counseling program City of Fremont, Calif., 1999—2000; psychotherapist, marriage family therapist intern Portia Bell Human Behavioral Health and Tng. Ctr., Concord, Calif., 2000—01; family facilitator EMQ Family and Children Svcs., Sacramento, 2002; family cons. Positive Options Family Svcs., Sacramento, 2002—; pvt. practice (with Dr. Harmesh Kumar), dir. residential svcs. Therapeutic Residential Svc., Inc., Concord, 2004—. Instr. East Bay Performing Art Ctr., Richmond, 1986, Chapman Coll., 1986, Las Positas C.C., Livermore, Calif., 1999—; adj. prof. U. Pheonix, 1999-2000, adj. prof. U. Pheonix, Northern Calif., 2001-. Singer opera prodns. Porgy & Bess, Oakland, Calif., 1980-81, LaTraviata, Oakland, Calif., 1981-82, Aida, Oakland, 1981-82, Madame Butterfly, Oakland, 1982-83, The Magic Flute, Oakland, 1984, numerous others; performances include TV specials, religous concerts, musicals; music dir. Natural Man, Berkeley, 1986; asst. artistic dir. Opera Piccola, Oakland, Calif., 1990—. Art commr. City of Richmond, Calif. Recipient Black Am. Achievement award. Mem. Music Tchrs. Assn., Internat. Black Writers and Artists Inc. (life, local #5), Nat. Coun. Negro Women, Nat. Assn. Negro Musicians, Calif. Arts Fedn., Calif. Assn. for Counseling and Devel. (black caucus), Nat. Black Child Devel. Inst., The Calif.-Nebraskan Orgn., Inc., Calif. Marital & Family Therapist Assn. (San Francisco chpt.), Black Psychotherpist of San Francisco and East Bay Area, San Francisco Commonwealth Club, Gamma Phi Delta. Democrat. Mem. A.M.E. Zion Ch. Avocations: cooking, entertaining. Home: 5314 Boyd Ave Oakland CA 94618 Office: Therapeutic Residential Svc Inc 2063 Pacheco St Concord CA 94520 Office Phone: 925-356-0122. E-mail: ellenefoster@comcast.net.

RANDLE, RODGER A., human relations professor, political science professor; b. Oct. 26, 1943; BA, U. Okla., 1967; LLB, U. Tulsa, 1978. Bar: Okla. 1978. Mem. Okla. Ho. of Reps., 1971-72, Okla. Senate, 1973-88; mayor City of Tulsa, 1988-92; pres. U. Ctr., Tulsa, 1992-96, Rogers U., 1996-98; prof. human rels. U. Okla., Tulsa, 1999—. Hon. Brit. consul State of Okla. Chmn. bd. dirs. Sister Cities Internat., 1998-00. Home: 1395 E 26th St Tulsa OK 74114-2733 Office: U Okla 4502 E 41st St Tulsa OK 74135 Home Phone: 918-744-8017; Office Phone: 918-660-3495. Personal E-mail: rarandle@gmail.com.

RANDLETT, MARY WILLIS, photographer; b. Seattle, May 5, 1924; d. Cecil Durand and Elizabeth (Bayley) Willis; m. Herbert B. Randlett, Oct. 19, 1950 (div.); children: Robert, Mary Ann, Peter, Susan. BA, Whitman Coll., Walla Walla, Wash., 1947. Freelance photographer, 1949—. One-woman shows include Seattle Sci. Ctr., 1971, Western Wash. State U., 1971, Seattle Art Mus., 1971, Art Gallery Greater Victoria, 1972, Alaska State Mus., 1972, State Capitol Mus., 1983, Whatcom Mus. History and Art, Bellingham, Wash., 1986, Janet Huston Gallery, LaConner, Wash., 1990, Gov.'s Gallery, Office of Gov., Olympia, Wash., 1991, Stonington Gallery, Seattle, 1992, Valley Mus. Art, LaConner, 1992, Grad. Sch. Design Dept. Landscape Arch. Harvard U., Cambridge, Mass., 1996, Mus. N.W. Art, LaConner, 1998, Mary Randlett Portraits in the Arts Cmty., Wright Exhbn. Space, Seattle, 2002—03, Safco Plaza, Seattle and Richmond, Wash., 2003, Seattle's One Percent for Art, 2004, Walla Walla CC, 2004, Wash. State Libr., Olympia, 2005, Thomas Art Mus., 2007—, others, exhibited in group shows at Am. Soc. Mag. Photographers, 1970, Whatcom Mus., Bellingham, Henry Gallery, Seattle, 1971, 1974, Royal Photg. Soc., 1979, Heard Mus., Phoenix, 1979, State Capital Mus., Olympia, Wash., 1983, 1984, 1988, 1989, 1993, Santa Fe Ctr. for Photography, 1987, Tacoma Art Mus., 1989, Helen Day Art Ctr., Stowe, Vt., 1989, Valley Mus. N.W. Art, LaConner, 1991, 1994, 1996—98, Allen Libr. U. Wash., Seattle, 1991, Wing Luke Asian Mus., 1991, Cheney Cowles Mus., Spokane, 1991, 1998, Security Pacific Gallery, Seattle, 1992, Benham Gallery, 1993, Stonington Gallery, 1993, 1998, Rainier Club, Seattle, 1994, Port Angeles (Wash.) Fine Arts Ctr., 1994, Mus. History and Industry, Seattle, 1994, Whatcom Mus., Bellingham, 1994, Pacific N.W. Annual Bellevue Art Mus., Wash., 1995, Skagit Valley Hist. Mus., LaConner, 1995, Seattle Art Mus., 1996—98, Kirkland (Wash.) Arts Ctr., 1997, Bainbridge Arts and Crafts, Bainbridge Island, Wash., 1997, Lucia Douglas Gallery, Bellingham, 1997, Anchorage Mus. History & Art, 1997, Burke Mus. Natural History and Culture, Seattle, 1998, Henderson House, Turnwater, Wash., 1998, Whatcom Arco Exhibit Gallery, Bellingham, 1998, Sea First Gallery, Seattle, 1998, 1999, Citizens Cultural Ctr., Fujinomita, Japan, 1999, Mus. Am. Indian, N.Y.C., 1999, Cheney Cowels Mus., Spokane, 1999, J. Paul Horiuchi Seattle Asian Art Mus., 2000, Mus. NW Art, 2000, Seattle Art Mus., 2002, Whitney Mus. Am. Art, N.Y.C., 2002, High Mus., Atlanta, 2002, Mus. NW Art, 2003, Seattle Art Mus., 2003, Tacoma Art Mus., 2003, Whatcom Mus., 2003, MONA, La Conner, Wash., 2004, Lucia Douglas Gallery, Bellingham, Wash., 2005, U. Wash. Press, Seattle, 2005, U. Portland, Oreg., 2006, Whatcom Mus., Bellingham, 2006—07, Stonington Gallery, Seattle, 2007, Grays Harbor Coll., 2007, and numerous others. Represented in permanent collections Met. Mus., Nat. Collection of Fine Arts, Nat. Portrait Gallery, Washington State Libr., Manuscript divsn. U. Wash., Pacific Northwest Bell, Seattle, Swedish Med. Ctr., Whatcom Mus., Bellingham, Henry Gallery, Seattle, Wash. State Capitol Mus., Olympia, Phillips Collection, Wash.; works appeared in books The Master and His Fish (Roderick Haig-Brown), 1982, Theodore Roethke: The Journey to I and Otherwide (Neal Bowers), 1982, Mountain in the Clouds (Bruce Brown), 1982, Masonry in Architecture (Louis Redstone), 1982, Writings and Reflections from the World of Roderick Haig-Brown, 1982, Pike Place Market (Alice Shorett and Murray Morgan), 1982, The Dancing Blanket, (Cheryl Samuel), 1982, Collected Poems of Theodore Roethke, 1982, Spires of Form (Victor Scheffer), 1983, Assault on Mount Helicon (Mary Barnard), 1983, New as a Wave (Eve Triem), 1983, Sketchbook: A Memoir of the '30's and the Northwest School (William Cumming), 1983, Good Intentions (Jane Adams), 1985, Blackbirds of the Americas (Gordon Orians and Tony Angell), 1985, Historic Preservation in Seattle (Larry Kreisman), 1985, Down Town Seattle Walking Tours (Mary Randlett and Carol Tobin), 1986, Seattle, the Seattle Book, 1986, When Orchids Were Flowers (Kate Knap Johnson), 1986, Jacob Lawrence, American Painter, (Ellen Wheat), 1986, Manic Power: Robert Lowell and His Circle (Jeffrey Meyers), 1987, The Isamu Noguchi Garden Museum (Isamu Noguchi), 1987, Washington's Audacious State Capitol an its Builders (Norman Johnston), 1988, The Bloedel Reserve: Gardens in the Forest (Lawrence Kreisman), 1988, Washingtonians: A Biographical Portrait of the State on the Occasion of its Centennial, 1988, Directory of Literary Biography: Canadian Writers 1920-59, 2d series, 1989, Crafts of America, 1989, The Lone Tree Tragedy (Bruce Brown), 1989, Northwest Coast Handbook of North American Indians, 1990, Dancing on the Rim of the World, 1990, Openings, Original Essays by Contemporary Soviet and American Writers (eds. Robert Atwan, Valeri Vinokurov), 1990, George Tsutakawa (Martha Kingsbury), 1990, Contemporary American Poetry (ed. Al Polin Jr.), 1991, Natural History of Puget Sound Country (Arthur Kruckberg), 1991, Bones (Joyce Thompson), 1991, Cebu (Peter Basho), 1991, Catalogue of Historic Preservation Publications, 1992, Art in Seattle's Public Places (James Rupp), 1992, The Olympic Rainforest (Ruth Kirk with Jerry Franklin), 1992, Steelhead Fly Fishing (Trey Combs), 1992, Illustrated Guidelines for Rehabilitation Historic Buildings, 1993, A History of African American Artists (Bearden and Henderson), 1994, Childrens Literature Review Vol. 1, 1994, Invisible Gardens: The Search for Modernism the American Landscape (Walker and Simo), 1994, Seeing Seattle (Roger Sale), 1994, Reaching Home (Jay and Matson), 1994, Redesigning the American Lawn: A Search for Environmental Harmony (Gordone Geballe, Diana Balmari and F. Herbert Bormann), 1995, Reaching Home: Pacific Salmon, Pacific People (Foves, Jay and Matson), 1995, Carl F. Gould: A Life in Architecture and the Arts (T. William Booth and William H. Wuksib), 1995, Destination Zero (Sam Hamill), 1996, Market Sketchbook, 25th Anniversary Edition, 1996, Spririts of the Ordinary, 1997, Instrument of Change: Jim Schoppert 1947-1992, 1997, Looking for Eulabee Dix (JoAnn Ridley), 1997, Jack Lenor Larsen: A Memoir, 1998, Museo Nacional Centro de Arte Reina (Mark Tobey), 1998, Fountains Splash, and Spectacle: Water and Design from the Renaissance to Present (ed. Marilyn Symmes), 1998, Ghost Dancing (Anna Linzer), 1998, The Flower in the Skull (Kathleen Alcala), 1998, This Great Unknowing: Last Poems (Denise Levertov), 1999, Building Washington (Paul Dorpat, Genevier McCoy), 1999, The Wright Collection, Seattle Art Museum, 1999, Made to Last: Historic Preservation in Seattle and King County (Larry Kreisman), 1999, Isamu Noguchi: A Study of Space (Ana Maria Torres), 2000, The Tiger Iris (Joan Swift), 2000, The Eighth Lively Art (Wesley Wehr), 2000, All Powers Necessary and Convenient (Mark F. Jenkins), 2000, Ice Breakers: Alaska's Most Innovative Artists (Julie Decker), 2000, Over the Line: The Life and Art of Jacob Lawrence (Peter Nesbett and Michelle Dubois), 2000, Iridescent Light: The Emergence of Northwest Art (Delores Tarzan Ament), 2001, Messages from Frank's Landing, 2000, Leo Kenney: A Retrospective, 2000, Building for Learning: Seattle Public Schools History 1860-2000, 2001, Geology and Plant Life, 2001, and numerous others; works also appeared in newspapers and mags., book, Maritime Seattle, 2002, Picture Bainbridge Island: A Pictorial History, Distant Corner, 2003, Child of the Oemulgee, Passing the Three Gates, 2003, Northwest Mythologies, The Interactions of Mark Tobey, Morris Graves, Kenneth Callahan and Guy Anderson, 2003, The Accidental Collector, Art, Fossils, Friendships, 2004, Isamu Noguchi and Sky Viewing Sculpture, 2004, A San Juan Island's Journal, 2004, Poems From Ish River Country, 2004, American Knees, 2005, Groundswell: Constructing the Contemporary Landscape, 2005, Vanishing Seattle, Archaeology in Washington, 2007, Mary Randlett: Landscapes, 2007. Recipient Wash. State Gov.'s award for spl. commendation for contbns. in field of photography, 1983, Individual Artist award, King County Arts Commn., 1989, Lifetime Achievement award, Artist Trust, 2001, Matrix Table, Seattle Women of Achievement, 1999, Nancy Blankenship Pryor award, 2001, Alumnus of Merit award, Whitman Coll, 2003, History Maker's award, Mus. History and Industry, 2003; grantee, Nat. Endowment for Arts, 1976, Allied Arts Found., 2000. Mem. AIA (hon.), Am. Soc. Mag. Photographers. Home: PO Box 11238 Olympia WA 98508-1238 Office Phone: 360-352-1716.

RANDMAN, BARRY I., real estate developer; b. Cin., Apr. 1, 1958; s. David I. and Marilyn June (Garfinkel) F. BBA in Fin., U. Denver, 1980. With acctg. dept. Rookwood Pottery & Celestial Restaurants, Cin., 1976-80; asst. to pres., head mktg. and real estate branching Great Am. Banks Inc., Miami, 1980-83; pres. Tower Mgmt. Inc., Cin., 1983-85, bd. dirs.; pres. Ohio Jet Svcs. Inc., Cin., 1983-85; v.p. Home State Fin. Svcs. Inc., Cin., 1984-85; pres. East Hill Devel. Corp., Cin., 1985—, B.I.R. Properties Inc., Cin., 1985—. Pres. Golden Devel. Corp., 1988-91, SRB Food Corp., 1988-92, Scarborough Devel. Corp., 1989, Redmont Devel Corp., 1990—, Eastridge, Inc., 1993-99, 613 Race LLC, Hale Justis, LLC, 1999—, Middleton-Ludlow LLC, 2004, Butterfield Pl. Devel., LLC, 2002—, Bulluck Terr. Devel. LLC, Gilbert Ave. Devel. LLC. Mem. Jewish Welfare Fund, Cin., 1980. Avocations: skiing, tennis, gardening. Home: 9 Hill and Hollow Ln Cincinnati OH 45208-3357 Office: 2321 Kemper Ln Cincinnati OH 45206-2610 Office Phone: 513-751-9700. E-mail: brand1111@aol.com.

RANDO, JOHN, theater director; MA, UCLA. Asst. dir. Old Globe Theater, San Diego, Acting Co., NY. Dir.: (plays) The Dinner Party, 2000, A Thousand Clowns, 2001, Urinetown, 2001 (Tony award, best direction of a musical, 2002), Dance of the Vampires, 2002, My Beautiful Goddamn City, 2005, Miami, 2005, The Wedding Singer, 2006, The Underpants, 2006, Of Thee I Sing, 2006, Pig Farm, 2006. Mailing: c/o Geffen Playhouse 10886 Le Conte Ave Los Angeles CA 90024

RANDOLPH, A(RTHUR) RAYMOND, federal judge; b. Riverside, NJ, Nov. 1, 1943; m. Eileen J. O'Connor, May 18, 1984; children: John Trevor, Cynthia Lee. BS, Drexel U., 1966; JD summa cum laude, U. Pa., 1969. Bar: Calif. 1970, DC 1973, US Supreme Ct. 1973. Law clk. to Hon. Henry J. Friendly US Ct. Appeals (2d cir.), NYC, 1969—70; asst. to solicitor gen. US Dept. Justice, Washington, 1970—73, dep. solicitor gen., 1975—77; ptnr. Sharp, Randolph & Green, Washington, 1977—83, Randolph & Truitt, Washington, 1983—87, Pepper, Hamilton & Scheetz, Washington, 1987—90; judge US Ct. Appeals (DC cir.), Washington, 1990—. Spl. asst. atty. gen. State of Mont., 1983—90, State of N.Mex., 1985—90, State of Utah, 1986—90; adv. panel Fed. Cts. Study Com., 1989—90; spl. counsel Com. on Stds. Ofcl. Conduct, US Ho. of Reps., 1979—80; adj. prof. Georgetown U. Law Ctr., 1974—78; exec. sec. Atty. Gen.'s Com. on Reform of Fed. Jud. Sys., 1975—77; com. on fed. rules evidence US Justice Dept., 1972; chmn. Com. on Govtl. Structures, McLean, Va., 1973—74; adj. prof. law sch. George Mason U., 1992, disting. prof., 1998—; com. codes conduct Jud. Conf. US, 1992—95, chmn., 1995—98. Recipient Spl. Achievement award, U.S. Dept. Justice, 1971, James Wilson Disting. Alumnus award, U. Pa. Law Sch., 2004, Drexel 100 award, Drexel U., 2005. Mem.: DC Bar Assn., Calif. Bar Assn., Am. Law Inst., Order of Coif. Office: US Court of Appeals 333 Constitution Ave NW Washington DC 20001-2866 *

RANDOLPH, CARL LOWELL, chemicals executive; b. Pasadena, Calif., May 30, 1922; s. Carl L. and Lulu (McBride) R.; m. Jane Taber, June 25, 1943; children: Margaret, Stephen. BA, Whittier Coll., 1943; MS, U. So. Calif., 1947, PhD, 1949; LLD, Whittier Coll., 1982; D in Pub. Svc. (hon.), U. Alaska, 1983. Prin. chemist Aerojet-Gen. Corp., 1949-57; v.p. U.S. Borax Rsch. Corp., Anaheim, Calif., 1957-63; asst. to pres. U.S. Borax & Chem. Corp., LA, 1963-66, v.p., 1966-68, exec. v.p., 1968-69, pres., 1969-86, vice chmn., 1983-87. Trustee, chmn. bd. Whittier Coll., emeritus, 1969—; bd. dirs., chmn. Ind. Colls. So. Calif., 1982—. Lt. (j.g.) USNR, 1944-46. Mem.: Phi Beta Kappa, Sigma Xi. Home: 1300 O Ave Anacortes WA 98221

RANDOLPH, CHRISTOPHER CRAVEN, lawyer; b. Washington, May 26, 1956; s. William Barksdale and Elizabeth Page (Craven) R.; m. Linda Bubernak Dressler, June 6, 1982; children: Alexander Dressler, Brian Donovan. BA summa cum laude, U. Va., 1978; JD cum laude, Harvard U., 1982. Bar: D.C. 1983, NY 1983. Assoc. Debevoise & Plimpton, NYC, 1982-86, Washington, 1987-92; atty. advisor Agy. for Internat. Devel., Washington, 1992-95; investor, entrepreneur Vienna, Va., 1995—2002, Oakton, Va., 2004—; assoc. gen. counsel Peace Corps, 2002—04. Editor Harvard Law Rev., 1980-82; contbr. articles to profl. jours. Mem. ABA, D.C. Bar Assn., Phi Beta Kappa. Republican. Episcopalian. Avocations: travel, reading, sports. Home and Office: 2784 Marshall Lake Dr Oakton VA 22124-1148

RANDOLPH, DAVID, conductor; b. NYC, Dec. 21, 1914; s. Morris and Elsie (Goodman) R.; m. Mildred Greenberg, July 18, 1948. BS, CCNY, 1936; MA, Tchrs. Coll., Columbia U., 1942; LHD (hon.), Saint Peter's Coll., Jersey City, 2006; DFA (hon.), CUNY, 2006. Music specialist OWI, NYC, 1943-47. Adj. prof. music NYU, 1948-85, Mostly Mozart course, 1976-85; lectr. Town Hall, N.Y.C., 1955-60, Columbia U., 1957, Cosmopolitan Club, N.Y.C., 1962-63; pre-concert lectr. N.Y. Philharm., Avery Fisher Hall, 1964-86,Cleve. Orch., 1981, Vienna Symphony Orch., 1988; tchr. conducting Dalcroze Sch., 1948-49; music commentator Little Orch. Soc. Concerts and Broadcasts, 1950-62, Met. Opera Intermission Broadcasts, 1951, 52; intermission commentator Lewisohn Stadium Concert Broadcasts, 1952-58; vis. prof. music SUNY, New Paltz, 1970-72, Fordham U., 1972-73; lectr. New Sch. for Social Rsch., 1973-90, IBM, N.Y.C., 1978-86, Beethoven Soc., 1977, 83; prof. music Montclair State Coll., Upper Montclair, N.J., 1973-87; guest condr. Rockland County (N.Y.) Ann. Choral Festival, 1972, 73; adviser film Music to Live By, mem. N.J. Arts Coun., 1967-70; mem. music com. Gov. N.J.'s Commn. to Study Arts, 1965; honored guest Handel Festival, Halle, Germany, 1991. Condr. Randolph Singers, 1944-62 (appeared on NBC Today, and Tonight Shows), concerts Town Hall, NYC, Carnegie Recital Hall, recs. for Columbia, Concert Hall Soc., Esoteric Records, Vanguard, Westminster Records, The Triumphs of Oriana, 1953, Monteverdi's Lagrime d'amante, Beethoven's Elegischer Gesang, Satie's Mass for the Poor, CRI, 13 Modern American Madrigals composed for the Randolph Singers, condr. United Choral Soc., LI, NY, 1961-86, NJ Ballet Orch., 1977, 83, Masterwork Chamber Orch., 1982-83, Philharmonia Orch. in Brahms' Requiem, Barbican Ctr., London, 1988, Barge Concert, NYC, 1987, 89; guest condr., Conn. Symphony Orch., 1961; condr. concert tour Spain with Am. choruses and Radio TV Orch. of Moscow, 1992; music annotator, CBS, NYC, 1947-48; choral seminar leader Mohonk Mountain House, 1986-95; music dir., condr. Masterwork Chorus and Orch., 1955-93, St. Cecilia Chorus and Orch., NYC, 1965—; performances at Carnegie Hall, Avery Fisher Hall, Lincoln Ctr., Kennedy Ctr. including Brahms' Requiem, Schicksalslied, Nänie, Gesang der Parzen, Mozart's Requiem, C Minor Mass, Vesperae de Confessore, Beethoven's Missa Solemnis, Symphony No. 3 (Eroica), Symphony No. 9, Mass in C Major, Choral Fantasy, Bach's Mass in B Minor, St. John Passion, St. Matthew Passion, Christmas Oratorio, Magnificat, C.P.E. Bach's Magnificat, Haydn's St. Cecilia Mass, Theresienmesse, Paukenmesse, Lord Nelson Mass, The Creation, Heiligmesse, Schöpfungsmesse, Michael Haydn's Requiem, Bruckner's Mass in E Minor, Requiem, Vaughan Williams' A Sea Symphony, Dona Nobis Pacem, Mass in G Minor, Hodie, Verdi's Requiem, Four Sacred Pieces, Honegger's King David, Elgar's The Music Makers, Corigliano's Fern Hill, Salieri's Mass in D, Purcell's The Fairy Queen, Mendelssohn's Elijah, Die erste Walpurgisnacht, Lobgesang, Lauda Sion, Poulenc's Gloria, Rutter's Gloria, Dvorak's Requiem, Te Deum, Kodaly's Te Deum, Berlioz' Requiem, Messe solennelle, Cherubini's Requiem, Schubert's Masses 5 and 6, Stabat Mater, Vivaldi's Gloria, Dixit Dominus, Zelenka's Missa Dei Patris, Gounod's St. Cecilia Mass, Handel's Solomon, Israel in Egypt, Judas Maccabaeus, Dixit Dominus and 172 complete performances of Handel's Messiah, Orff's Carmina Burana, Saint-Saëns' Requiem, Puccini's Messa di Gloria, Zimmermann's Psalmkonzert, Finzi's For St. Cecilia, In Terra Pax, Rachmaninoff's The Bells, others; broadcaster: David Randolph Concerts, WNYC and radio stas. of Nat. Assn. Ednl. Broadcasters, 1946-79, Young Audience telecasts, CBS-TV, 1958-59, series of candid rehearsals of Bach's Mass in B minor, PBS, 1967; host: weekly broadcasts Lincoln Ctr. Spotlight, Sta. WQXR, NYC, 1966-67; regular guest critic First Hearing program Sta. WQXR, NYC, and 68 other stas., 1986-95; author: This Is Music, 1964, 98, numerous album jacket notes; A New Music Made with a Machine, Horizon Magazine, 1959; editor: David Randolph Choral Series; writer, narrator: Instruments of the Orchestra, 1958, compact disc 1995, Stereo Review's Guide to Understanding Music, 1973; music critic, High Fidelity Mag., 1952-57; composer: A Song for Humanity, 1968, Andante for Strings, 1937, Edward, 1937; contbg. author: NY Times Guide to Listening Pleasure, 1968; analyzed Mendelssohn's Symphony No. 3 on records for Book of Month Club. Recipient 1st award for edn. by radio Ohio State Inst., 1948, 50, 51, Sylvania TV award, 1959, Disting. Alumni award Columbia U., 1982, cert. of appreciation Mayor of City of N.Y. at Carnegie Hall, 1991, Townsend Harris medal CCNY, 1996, Lifetime Achievement award Carnegie Hall, MidAmerica Prodns., 2000; St. Cecilia Chorus endowed David Randolph Disting. Artist-in-Residence Program at New Sch. in N.Y., 1996. Home: 420 E 86th St Apt 4-c New York NY 10028-6456 Home Phone: 212-744-1444; Office Phone: 212-744-1444.

RANDOLPH, JENNINGS, JR., (JAY RANDOLPH), sportscaster; b. Cumberland, Md., Sept. 19, 1934; s. Jennings and Mary Katherine (Babb) R.; m. Sue Henderson, May 28, 1966; children: Jennings, Brian Robert, Rebecca Sue. Student, George Washington U., 1952—54, student, 1957—58; BA, Salem Coll., W.Va., 1963. Sports and promotion dir. Sta. WHAR, Clarksburg, W.Va., 1958-61; sportscaster Sta. KLIF, Dallas, 1963-66; Sta. KMOX, St. Louis, 1966-68; with Sta. KSDK-TV, St. Louis, 1968—, sports dir., 1968-88, spl. sports corr., 1988—, also on nationally televised broadcasts for various sports events including Sr. PGA tour; TV announcer Fla. Marlins Baseball Club, Ft. Lauderdale, 1993—2002; announcer PGA Tour Classic on Golf Channel, 2002—06; staff KFNS Radio, St. Louis, 2002—06; St. Louis Cardinals announcer Sta. KSDK-TV, 2007—. Interviewer analyst Champions Tour on Golf Channel and CNBC; broadcaster coll. basketball ESPN regional TV; TV announcer St. Louis Cardinals, 1970-87, Cin. Reds., 1988; mem. NBC's broadcast staff for 1988 Olympics, Seoul, Korea and 1992 Summer Games, Barcelona, Spain; host The Golf Show. Trustee Salem Coll., 1976-89. With U.S. Army, 1954-56. Named to Boys and Girls Clubs of Am. Hall of Fame, 1990, Tex. Radio Hall Fame, 2005, Mo. Sports Hall of Fame, 2007; named Champion, So. Conf. Golf, 1958 Mem. Nat. Assn. Sportscasters, Delta Tau Delta (Disting. Alumni award 2006) Achievements include being an amateur golf champion. Home: 12021 Charter Oakpky Saint Louis MO 63146

RANDOLPH, JESSE See CASTILE, RAND

RANDOLPH, JUDSON GRAVES, pediatric surgeon; b. Macon, Ga., July 19, 1927; s. Milton Fitz and Abigail Theresa (Graves) R.; m. Susan Comfort Adams, June 14, 1952 (dec.); children: Somers, Garrett, Judson, Adam, Comfort, m. Joyce Dunn, Oct. 11, 2003. BA, Vanderbilt U., 1950, MD, 1953. Intern in surgery U. Rochester, NY, 1953-54; asst. resident in pathology Vanderbilt U., 1954-55; asst. resident, then sr. resident in surgery Mass. Gen. Hosp., Boston, 1956-58; asst. resident in surgery Children's Hosp., Boston, 1955-56, sr. resident, then chief resident, 1958-61, asst. surgeon, 1961-63; teaching fellow to instr. surgery Med. Sch. Harvard U., 1960-63; jr. assoc. in surgery Peter Bent Brigham Hosp., Boston, 1961-63; surgeon-in-chief Children's Hosp., Washington, 1964-91; mem. faculty Med. Sch. George Washington U., 1964-91, prof. surgery and child health, 1968-91; prof. surgery Meharry Med. Coll., 1992-96. Cons. Nat. Naval Med. Ctr., NIH, Walter Reed Army Med. Ctr.; trustee Vanderbilt U., 1980—. Editor: Pediatric Surgery, 3d edit., 2 vols., 1979, 4th edit., 2 vols., 1985, The Injured Child, 1980; mem. editl. bd. Surgery, 1978-92; contbr. articles to profl. jours. With USNR, 1945-46, PTO. Mem. ACS (gov. 1969-75), AMA, Am. Acad. Pediats. (chmn. exec. com. surg. sect. 1974-75), Am. Assn. Thoracic Surgery, Am. Pediat. Surg. Assn. (gov. 1980—, pres. 1984), Washington Acad. Surgery (pres. 1989), Soc. U. Surgeons, Am. Surg. Assn., So. Surg. Assn., Am. Bd. Surgery (bd. dirs. 1973-79, diplomate), Alpha Omega Alpha (faculty), Cosmos Club (Washington), Belle Meade Club. Methodist. Home Phone: 615-383-3757. Personal E-mail: jrpedsurg@aol.com.

RANDOLPH, LEONARD MCELROY, JR., career officer; b. Washington, Sept. 22, 1943; s. Leonard McElRoy and Jessie Marshall (Stockton) R.; m. Linda Fleming Raney, Aug. 1, 1987; children: Nathaniel Randolph, Brion Randolph, Holly Tocknell, Chad Muterspaw, Judd Muterspaw. BS in Biology, Marietta Coll., Ohio, 1965; MS in Microbiology, Howard U., Washington, 1967; MD, Meharry Med. Coll., Nashville, 1972; DHL (hon.), Meharry Med. Coll., 2001. Diplomate Am. Bd. Surgery, Am. Bd. Med. Mgmt., Am. Coll. Physician Execs.; cert. physician exec. Grad. tchg. asst. Howard U., Washington, 1966-67; rsch. microbiologist Georgetown U., Washington, 1966-67; chemistry tchr. Ballou H.S., Washington, 1967-68; commd. 2d lt. USAF, 1968, advanced through grades to maj. gen., 1998, intern Keesler AFB, Miss., 1972-73, resident, 1973-77, gen. surgeon Bergstrom AFB, Tex., 1977-78, chief gen. surgery, 1978-80, chief surg. svcs., 1980-83, attending surgeon Wright-Patterson AFB, Ohio, 1983-84, dir. med. edn., 1984-85, chief med. officer Minot AFB, ND, 1985-86, hosp. cmdr. George AFB, Calif., 1988-90, dep. command surgeon HQ Tactical Air Command Langley AFB, Va., 1990-91, forward command surgeon Desert Storm Riyahd, Saudi Arabia, 1990-91, med. ctr. comdr. Travis AFB, Calif., 1994-97; asst. prof. surgery Wright State U. Sch. Medicine, Dayton, Ohio, 1983-88; command surgeon U.S. Ctrl. Command, MacDill AFB, Fla., 1991-94, U.S. Transp. Command and Air Mobility Command, Scott AFB, Ill., 1997-99. Lead agt. DOD Health Svc. Region 10, 1994-97; spec. asst. to USAF Surg. Gen., 1999, dep. surgeon gen., 1999-2001; dep. exec. dir. Tricare Mgmt. Activity, Office of Under Sec. Def., Washington, 2001-03; assoc. prof. surgery U. Calif. Davis Sch. Medicine, 1995-97; assoc. prof. mil. medicine and emergency medicine Uniformed Svcs. U. of Health Scis., 1995—; acting dep. asst. sec. def. Health Plan Adminstrn., TRICARE Mgmt. Activity, 2003—04, COO, 2003-04; v.p. med. ops. Cath. Healthcare West, 2003-05; sr. v.p. and chief med. officer, Mercy Health Ptnrs., 2005-. Contbr. articles to profl. jours. Bd. trustees Marietta Coll., 2001—. Decorated Def. Superior Svc. medal for Operation Restore Hope, Legion of Merit Operation Desert Storm, Disting. Svc. medal USAF; selected for Boys State (Georgetown U.); recipient Excellence award Fed. Healthcare Execs., 1997, Disting. Alumni of Yr. award Nat. Assn. for Equal Opportunity in Higher Edn., 1999, Disting. Alumnus award Marietta Coll. Alumni Assn., 2000, Exceptional Svc. award Uniformed Svcs. U. of the Health Scis., 2003; named to Hall of Excellence, Ohio Found. Ind. Colls., 2003. Fellow ACS (bd. govs. 1996—2002), Am. Coll. Physician Execs. (disting. pres. 2000-2001), Am. Acad. Med. Adminstrs. (hon.); mem. Soc. Air Force Clin. Surgeons (bd. govs. 1996-2002), Soc. Med. Adminstrs., Soc. Med. Cons to Armed Forces, Assn. Mil. Surgeons of the U.S., Air Force Assn. (life), Christian Med. Assn., Aerospace Med. Assn., Alpha Omega Alpha, Beta Kappa Chi, Beta Beta Beta. Avocations: reading, sports, writing. Office: Mercy Health Partners 4600 McAuley Pl 6th Fl Cincinnati OH 45242-4745 Office Phone: 513-981-6347. Office Fax: 513-981-6133. Business E-Mail: lmrandolph@health-partners.org. E-mail: caprand@aol.com.

RANDOLPH, MICHAEL K., state supreme court justice; b. 1946; m. Kathy Webb; 3 children. BA in Bus. Administration, Rollins Coll., Winter Park, Fla., 1972; JD, U. Miss. Sch. of Law, 1974. Atty. Ross, King and Randolph, Biloxi, 1975—76, Bryan, Nelson, Allen, Schroder and Randolph, Hattiesburg, 1976—2004; justice Miss. Supreme Ct., 2004—. Former mem. Nat. Coal Council. Mem. adv. bd. Hattiesburg Salvation Army; former pres. Hattiesburg Civic Assn.; mem. Hattiesburg Area Development Partnership; mem. bd. dirs. William Carey Coll., Boys and Girls Club of Hattiesburg, Hattiesburg Girls Shelter. Air traffic controller US Army, atty., Judge Advocate General Corps USN. Mem.: ABA, Fifth Federal Circuit Bar Assn., Miss. Bar Assn. (Com. on Continuing Legal Ed. 1975—76), S. Central Miss. Bar Assn. (pres. 1986). Office: Miss Supreme Ct PO Box 117 Jackson MS 39205

RANDOLPH, ROBERT DEWITT, lawyer; b. Sligo, Pa., Mar. 6, 1929; s. DeWitt Lyman and Hazel Irene (McCall) R.; m. Betty Ann McElhattan, May 8, 1953 (dec. Aug. 1979); children: Douglas, Andrew; m. Susan Denise Hopkins, Oct. 15, 1988 BA, Westminster Coll., 1951; LLB, Harvard U., 1957. Bar: Ohio 1958, Pa. 1960, U.S. Supreme Ct. 1981. Assoc. Buckingham, Doolittle & Burroughs, Akron, Ohio, 1957-59, Rose, Houston, Cooper & Schmidt, Pitts., 1959-60, 61-65; fgn. svc. officer U.S. Dept. State, Washington, 1960-61; ptnr. Houston, Cooper, Spear & German, Pitts., 1965-70, Randolph & O'Connor, Pitts., 1970-74, Buchanan Ingersoll P.C., Pitts., 1974-93. Pres. Assn. Retarded Citizens Allegheny, Pitts., 1990-92; mem. Allegheny County Mental Health/Mental Retardation Bd., 2002-. With US Army, 1951—54. Mem. St. Clair Country Club. Democrat. Presbyterian. Avocations: golf, skiing. Home: 750 Washington Rd Pittsburgh PA 15228-2051

RANDOLPH, VIRGELLA, retired federal official; d. Russell and Catherine (Smith) Snowden; m. Alphonso L. Randolph, 1960; children: Victor, Pebble, Deborah. At, D.C. C.C., 1976, Georgetown U. Clk. typist census bur. U.S. Dept. Commerce, Suitland, Md., 1955—56; clk. typist to dep. chief fed. acquisition and assistance divsn. Nat. Bur. Stds. (now Nat. Inst. Sci. Tech.) U.S. Dept. Commerce, Gaithersburg, 1956—87; ret. Vol. Providence Hosp., 1987; past mem., pres. We Chick, Inc.; past mem. The Musical Choraleers; past mem., v.p. The Stereophonic Chorale; deaconess Greater First Baptist Ch., Washington, 2004—; mem. Gospel Chorus, Pres., v.p., fin. sec.; mem. Fellowship Choir; co-chair Elevator Ministry. Recipient Bronze medal, U.S. Dept. Commerce, 1974. Mem.: Choir Dirs. and Organists Guils, Hampton U. Annual Minister's Conf. Democrat. Baptist. Achievements include development of in-house procurement training program for Nat. Bur. Stds; subject of Black History Week at Nat. Bur. Stds. for accomplishments. Avocations: flower arranging, singing, writing. Personal E-mail: virgella7@aol.com.

RANDOLPH, WILLIE (WILLIE LARRY RANDOLPH JR.), professional baseball team manager, retired professional baseball player; b. Holy Hill, SC, July 6, 1954; m. Gretchen Foster; children: Taniesha, Chantre, Ciara, Andre. DHL (hon.), Fordham U., 2007. Second baseman Pitts. Pirates, 1975—76, NY Yankees, 1976—88, LA Dodgers, 1989—90, Oakland A's, 1990, Milw. Brewers, 1991, NY Mets, 1992; asst. gen. mgr. NY Yankees, 1993, third base coach, 1993—2003, bench coach, 2004; mgr. NY Mets, 2004—. Named Dodgers' MVP Anaheim/L.A. chpt. BBWAA, 1989; named to Am. League All-Star Team 1976-77, 1980-81, 1987, Nat. League All-Star Team, 1989; recipient James P. Dawson award, 1976 Office: c/o NY Mets 123 01 Roosevelt Ave Flushing NY 11368 *

RANDT, CLARK THORP, JR., ambassador, lawyer; b. Cleve., Nov. 24, 1945; s. Clark Thorp and Mary-Louise (Mitchell) R.; m. Sarah Talcott, Nov. 3, 1979; children: Clark Thorp III, Paull Mitchell, Clare Talcott. BA, Yale U., 1968; JD, U. Mich., 1975; People's Republic China law diploma, U. East Asia, 1988. Bar: NY 1976, Hong Kong 1992. Assoc. Milbank, Tweed, Hadley & McCloy, NYC, Hong Kong and Tokyo, 1975-82; lst sec., comml. attache Am. Embassy, Beijing, 1982-84; ptnr. Heller, Ehrman, White & McAuliffe, San Francisco and Hong Kong, 1985-87, Gibson, Dunn and Crutcher, Hong Kong, 1987—91, Shearman & Sterling, Hong Kong, 1991—2001; US amb. to China US Dept. State, 2001—. Legal adv. Nat. Coun. US-China Trade, 1974. Contbr. articles to profl. jours. and books. Mem. nat. steering com. George Bush for Pres., 1988; vice chmn. Reps. Abroad Com., Hong Kong, 1988-93; chmn. George Bush for Pres., Hong Kong, 1998-00. With USAF, 1968-72. Recipient Disting. Svc. medal US Dept. Commerce, 1984. Mem. ABA, NY Bar Assn., Hong Kong Bar Assn., Am. Soc. Internat. Law, Am. C. of C. in Hong Kong (v.p., gov.), Yale Club (pres. 1987-95), Am. Club in Hong Kong, Ladies Recreation Club. Office: DOS Amb 7300 Beijing Pl Washington DC 20521-7300 also: US Embassy 3 Xiu Shui Bei Jie Beijing 100600 China Office Phone: 86 10 6532 3831. *

RANEY, MIRIAM DAY, actress; b. Florence, SC, Sept. 30, 1922; d. Lewis Griffith and Iola Lewis (Edwards) Day; m. Robert William Raney, Mar. 31, 1946 (div. Sept. 1976); children: Robert William Jr., Miriam, Kevin Paige, Megan. BSM in Voice, Music Edn., U. NC, Greensboro, 1943; student, Julliard Sch. Music, 1942—43; BA in Music History and Lit., U. Ark., Little Rock, 1981; cert., Adam Roarke Film Actors Lab., Irving, Tex., 1989. Singing chorus NYC Ctr. Opera Co., 1943-44; understudy, singing chorus Oklahoma, Theater Guild, NYC, 1944-45; ingenue lead Connecticut Yankee, Geosan Subway Cir., NYC, 1945; understudy, singing chorus Up In Central Park, Michael Todd, NYC, 1945-46. Beauty cons. Mary Kay Cosmetics, Inc., Dallas, 1993—98. Author: Ark Women in Music, 1982; composer, lyricist: songs The Bend and the Wiillow, 1982, Ballad of Petit Jean, 1983; actor: (plays) Hedda Gabler, 1990, Time of Your Life, 1991, Our Town, 1991, Evening with Women II, 1991; (TV series) Unsolved Mysteries, 1988; (films) Killing Time with Aunt Olene, 1988, commls. and tng. films, 1987—99; reviewer: Ency of Ark. History, 2005—07; print model, Little Rock, Memphis, Ft. Worth, 1988—98. Sec. sr. adult coun. Pulaski Heights United Meth. Ch., 2004—07. Named Illustrious Alumna, U. NC, Greensboro, 1945; recipient Thanks Badge, Girl Scouts USA, Oachita Coun., Little Rock, 1962. Mem.: AAUW (mem. Little Rock br. legis. com., mem. program com. 1973—79, cultural interest rep. 1975—77, 1996—98, state rep. cultural interests 1976—78), Ctrl. Ark. Guild Organists (pres. student chpt. 1977—80). Democrat. Avocations: birdwatching, gardening, reading, movies. Home and Office: 25 Valley Forge Dr Little Rock AR 72212-2613 Personal E-mail: mimraney@comcast.net.

RANGANATHAN, PARTHASARATHY, computer scientist; BTech, Indian Inst. Tech., 1994; MS in Elec. and Computer Engring., Rice U., 1997; PhD in Elec. and Computer Engring., Rice U., Houston, 2000. Sr. rsch. scientist Compaq/Hewlett Packard Labs., Palo Alto, Calif., 2000—05; prin. rsch. scientist Hewlett Packard Labs., Palo Alto, 2005—. Dir. IIT Madras Alumni Assn. N.Am., Houston, 1996—2007. Achievements include patents pending in field. Office: Hewlett Packard Labs 1501 Page Mill Rd MS 1177 Palo Alto CA 94304 Business E-Mail: partha.ranganathan@hp.com.

RANGARI, VIJAYA KUMAR, chemistry professor, researcher; s. Ranganath Rao and Chendramani Rangari; m. Vatsalya Rao, Dec. 19, 1995; children: Shivani, Shashank Kumar. BSc, Osmania U., India, PhD, 1996. Rschr. Indian Inst. Sci., Bangalore, 1996—98, Barilan U., Ramatgan, Israel, 1999—2001; rsch. asst. prof. Tuskegee U., Ala., 2001—. Fellow, Coun. Sci. Rsch. India, 1996. Mem.: Soc. for the Advancement of Material and Process Engring. (assoc.). Achievements include research in nanomaterials for structural applications. Office: Tuskegee Univ 101 James Ctr T-Cam Tuskegee AL 36088 Home Phone: 334-826-5410; Office Phone: 334-724-4875. Office Fax: 334-727-2286. Business E-Mail: rangariv@tuskegee.edu.

RANGEL, CHARLIE (CHARLES BERNARD RANGEL), congressman; b. NYC, June 11, 1930; s. Ralph and Blanche (Wharton) Rangel; m. Alma Carter, July 26, 1964; children: Steven, Alicia. BS, NYU, 1957; JD, St. John's U. Sch. Law, 1960; LLD (hon.), Wagner Coll., 1982, Atlanta U., 1983, St. John's U., 1988, Mt. Sinai Sch. Medicine, 1988, NYU, 1988, Howard. U., 1988, Hofstra U., 1989. Bar: NY 1960. Counsel NYC Housing and Redevelopment Bd.; asst. US atty. (So. dist.) NY US Dept. Justice, 1961-62; mem. NY State Assembly, 1966-70, US Congress from 15th NY dist., 1971—, mem. ways and means com., 1975—, ranking minority mem. ways and means com., 1996—2007, chmn. ways and means com., 2007—, chmn. bd. Dem. Congl. Campaign Com., dean NY State Congl. Del. Chmn. Congl. Narcotics Abuse and Control Caucus US Congress, mem. Congl. Black Caucus; co-chair African Trade and Investment Caucus, Congressional Glaucoma Caucus; mem. Congressional Human Rights Caucus. Co-author (with Leon Wynter): And I Haven't Had a Bad Day Since: From the Streets of Harlem to the Halls of Congress, 2007. Served in US Army, 1948—52, Korea. Decorated Bronze Star, Purple Heart; named one of Most Influential Black Americans, Ebony Mag., 2006; recipient Korean Presdl. citations, Henry F. Scheig Nat. Pub. Svc. award, Aid Assn. Luths., 1987, Excellence in Pub. Svc. award, Am. Acad. Pediat., 1988, Marcus Garvey Lifetime Achievement award, Inst. Caribbean Studies, 1995, Edmund S. Muskie Disting. Pub. Svc. award, Ctr. Nat. Policy, 2002. Mem.: NY State Bar Assn., Nat. Assn. State Legislators, 369th Vets. Assn., NAACP. Democrat. Roman Catholic. Office: US House Reps 2354 Rayburn House Office Bldg Washington DC 20515-0001 Office Phone: 202-225-4365. Office Fax: 202-225-0816. *

RANIS, GUSTAV, economist, educator; b. Darmstadt, Germany, Oct. 24, 1929; s. Max and Bettina (Goldschmidt) R.; m. Ray Lee Finkelstein, June 15, 1958; children: Michael Bruce, Alan Jonathan, Bettina Suzanne. BA summa cum laude, Brandeis U., 1952, hon. degree, 1982; MA, Yale U., 1953, PhD, 1956. Asst. adminstr. program and policy AID/Dept. of State, 1965-67; dir. Econ. Growth Ctr. Yale U., New Haven, 1967-75, prof. econs., 1964—81, Frank Altschul prof. internat. econs., 1981—2005, Frank Altschul prof. emeritus internat. econs., 2005—, dir. Ctr. Internat. and Area Studies, 1996—2004. Ford Found. vis. prof. U. De Los Andes, Bogota, Colombia, 1976-77; Ford Found. vis. prof. Colegio de Mex., 1971-72; fellow Inst. for Advanced Study, Berlin, 1993-94; cons. World Bank, AID, Ford Found., ILO, FAO, Inter-Am. Devel. Bank. Author: (with John Fei) Development of the Labor Surplus Economy: Theory and Policy, 1964,; (with Fei and Shirley Kuo) Growth with Equity: The Taiwan Case, 1979; (with Keijiro Otsuka and Gary Saxonhouse) Comparative Technology Choice in Development, 1988; (with F. Stewart and E. Angeles-Reyes) Linkages in Developing Economies: A Philippine Study, 1990; (with S.A. Mahmood) Political Economy of Development Policy Change, 1992; (with John C. H. Fei) Growth and Development from an Evolutionary Perspective, 1997, Globalization and the Nation State, 2006; editor: Taiwan: From Developing to Mature Economy, 1992, En Route to Modern Economic Growth: Latin America in the 1990s, 1994, Japan and the U.S. in the Developing World, 1997,; co-editor: The State of Development Economics, 1988, Science and Technology: Lessons for Development Policy, 1990; mem. editl. bd. Jour. Internat. Devel., 1995—, Oxford Devel. Studies, 1996—, Internat. Econ. Jour., 2005-. Trustee Brandeis U., 1967-93, chmn. acad. affairs com., 1986-93. Social Sci. Rsch. Coun. fellow, Japan, 1955-56, Carnegie scholar, 2004-06. Mem. Am. Econ. Assn., Coun. Fgn. Rels., Overseas Develop. Coun. (mem. adv. com.). Home: 7 Mulberry Rd Woodbridge CT 06525-1716 Office: Econ Growth Ctr Yale 27 Hillhouse Ave New Haven CT 06520 Office Phone: 203-432-3632. Business E-Mail: gustav.ranis@yale.edu.

RANJAN, RAHUL, engineer, researcher; b. Ranchi, Jharakhand, India, June 28, 1980; arrived in US, 2004; s. Rajendra Prasad and Asha Chaudhary. BTech, Indian Inst. Tech., Kharagpur, 2002; MS, Wayne State U., Detroit, 2006. Rsch. engr. CDOT, New Delhi, 2002—04; high speed circuit design engr. Altera Corp., San Jose, Calif., 2006—. Author (and co-author): jour. articles and conf. papers. Recipient GRA award, Wayne State U., 2004, Outstanding Grad./Profl. Leadership award, 2005; Thomas C. Rumble Fellow, 2005. Mem.: SPIE, IEEE, Asha, Sillicon Valley, Calif. Achievements include development of Video Image Fusion using Fuzzy and Neuro Fuzzy Logic; research in Image Fusion using Subtractive Clustering Approach; Fuzzy Applications. Avocations: reading, travel. Home Phone: 313-623-2771; Office Phone: 408-544-8190. Personal E-mail: rahulr@wayne.edu. Business E-Mail: rranjan@altera.com.

RANKAITIS, SUSAN, artist; b. Cambridge, Mass., Sept. 10, 1949; d. Alfred Edward and Isabel (Shimkus) Rankaitis; m. Robbert Flick, June 5, 1976. BFA in Painting, U. Ill., 1971; MFA in Visual Arts, U. So. Calif., 1977. Rsch. asst., art dir. Plato Lab., U. Ill., Urbana, 1971-75; art instr. Orange Coast Coll., Costa Mesa, Calif., 1977-83; chair dept. art Chapman Coll., Orange, Calif., 1983-90; Fletcher Jones chair art Scripps Coll., Claremont, Calif., 1990—. Represented by Robert Mann Gallery, NYC; overview panelist visual arts Nat. Endowment for Arts, 1983, 84; selector Bingham Ednl. Trust, 1997—2002; scholar-in-residence Borchard Found., Missillac, France, 2004; artist-in-residence Europos Parkus, 2005. One-woman shows include LA County Mus. Art, 1983, Internat. Mus. Photography, George Eastman House, 1983, Gallery Min. Tokyo, 1988, Ruth Bloom Gallery, Santa Monica, 1989, 90, 92, Schneider Mus., Portland, Ore., 1990; Ctr. Creative Photography, 1991, Robert Mann Gallery, NYC, 1994, 97, 2007, Mus. Contemporary Photography, Chgo., 1994, Mus. Photog. Arts, 2000, Europos Parkas, Vilnius, 2005; represented in permanent collections MOCA, LA, U. N.Mex Art, Ctr. Creative Photography, Mus. Contemporary Photography, Chgo., Santa Barbara Mus. Art, LA County Mus. Art, Mpls. Inst. Arts, St. Louis Art Mus., San Francisco Mus. Modern Art, Art Inst. Chgo., Mus. Modern Art, Lodz, Poland, Princeton U. Art Mus., Stanford U. Art Mus., Contemporary Art Mus., Honolulu, Mus. Contemporary Photography, Art Inst. Chgo., St. Louis Art Mus., others. Active art auction Venice Family Clinic, 1980-2005. Recipient Graves award in Humanities, 1985; fellow NEA, 1980, 88, US, France, 1989, Agnes Bourne fellow Djerassi Found., 1989, Award in the Visual Arts, Flintridge Found., 2004; Durfee Chinese/Am. grantee, 2000-2001, Cultural Affairs grantee City L.A., 2001, grantee Mellon Found., 2005, 06; Borchard Found. scholar-in-residence, France, 2004. Mem. CMDPA, oll. Art Assn., LA County Mus. Art, Mus. Contemporary Art. Home: 3117 N Lansbury Ave Claremont CA 91711-4146 Office Phone: 909-607-4439, 909-920-5969. Business E-Mail: srankait@scrippscollege.edu.

RANKIN, ALEX C., management executive; B in Commerce, BA in Psychology, MBA. With Agra Industries, Ltd., 1976-94; pres., CEO NexCycle, Inc., Irving, Tex., 1994—. Office: Nexcycle 26021 Business Center Dr Redlands CA 92374-4553 E-mail: arankin@nexcycle.com.

RANKIN, ALFRED MARSHALL, JR., manufacturing executive; b. Cleve., Oct. 8, 1941; s. Alfred Marshall and Clara Louise (Taplin) R.; m. Victoire Conley Griffin, June 3, 1967; children: Helen P., Clara T. BA in Econs. magna cum laude, Yale U., 1963, JD, 1966. Mgmt. cons. McKinsey & Co., Inc., Cleve., 1970-73; with Eaton Corp., Cleve., 1974-81, pres. materials handling group, 1981-83, pres. indsl. group, 1984-86, exec. v.p., 1986, vice chmn., chief oper. officer, 1986-89; pres., COO NACCO Industries, Inc., Cleve., 1989-91, pres., CEO, 1991-94, also bd. dirs., chmn., pres., CEO, 1994—. Bd. dir. Goodrich Corp., Vanguard Group. Former pres., trustee Hathaway Brown Sch.; trustee U. Hosps. Health Sys., Cleve., Mus. Arts Assn., Univ. Circle, Inc., Cleve. Mus. Art, John Huntington Art Trust, Greater Cleve. Partnership; dir., exec. com. mem. Nat. Assn. Manufacturers; past chairperson The Cleve. Found. Mem. Ohio Bar Assn. Clubs: Chagrin Valley Hunt, Union, Tavern, Pepper Pike, Kirtland Country (Cleve.); Rolling Rock (Ligonier, Pa.); Met. (Washington). Republican. Office: NACCO Industries Inc 5875 Landerbrook Dr Ste 300 Mayfield Heights OH 44124 *

RANKIN, CLYDE EVAN, III, lawyer; b. Phila., July 3, 1950; s. Clyde Evan, Jr. and Mary E. (Peluso) R.; m. Camille Cozzone, Aug. 24, 1997; AB, Princeton U., 1972; JD, Columbia U., 1975; postgrad. Hague Acad. Internat. Law, 1975. Bar: NY 1976, NJ 1976, DC 1978, U.S. Supreme Ct. 1980. Law clk. to Judge Dudley B. Bonsal US Dist. Ct. So. Dist. NY, 1975-77; assoc. Debevoise, Plimpton, Lyons & Gates, NYC, 1977-79; assoc. Coudert Bros., NYC, 1979-83, ptnr., Corp. & Fin. Practice, 1984-2005, chmn., 2005; ptnr. Baker & McKenzie LLP, NYC, 2005—. Trustee Rensselaerville (NY) Inst., 1989-, chmn. 2001-; mem. Coun. on Fgn. Rels., 1996—, bd. vis. Columbia U. Law Sch., 1991-; chmn. alumni coun. Princeton U., 2003-05. Stone scholar, 1974. Mem. ABA, Assn. Bar City NY, NY State Bar Assn., DC Bar Assn., NJ Bar Assn. Roman Catholic. Amateur Comedy Club (NYC). Contbr. articles to profl. jours. Office: Baker & McKenzie LLP 1114 Ave of Americas New York NY 10036-7703 Office Phone: 212-626-4740. Office Fax: 212-310-1639. Business E-Mail: clyde.e.rankin@bakernet.com.

RANKIN, EDWARD ANTHONY, orthopedist, surgeon; b. Holly Springs, Miss., July 6, 1940; s. Edgar Everett and Robbie Lee Rankin; m. Frances Espy, June 8, 1965; children: Tony(dec.), Marc Espy. BS, Lincoln U., 1961; MD, Meharry Med. Coll., 1965. Cert. Am. Bd. Orthop. Surgery. Pvt. practice Epps Gladden Rankin, Washington, 1973—87; prof. surgery Howard U., Washington, 1988—; ptnr. Rankin Orthopaedic Ctr., Washington, 1988—. Editor-in-chief: Am. Acad. Orthop. Surgery Bulletin, 2001—. Bd. dirs. Blue Cross Blue Shield, 1985—88, Meharry Med. Coll., Nashville, 1990—2000. Maj. US Army, 1965—73. Named to Hall of Fame, Lincoln U., Jefferson City, Mo.; recipient Disting. Svc. award, 33 deg. Masons, 2002, Cmty. Svc. award, DC Med. Soc., 2004. Mem.: ACS (gov.-at-large), Ea. Orthop. Soc. (pres. 2002—03), Am. Acad. Orthop. Surgeons (bd. dirs. 1996—98, sec. 2001—04, bd. dirs. 2001—04, 2d v.p. 2006—07, 1st v.p. 2007—), Daus. of Charity, Sigma Phi Phi. Catholic. Avocations: travel, golf, reading, music. Office: 1160 Varnum St NE Washington DC 20017 Office Phone: 202-526-7031.

RANKIN, GENE RAYMOND, lawyer; b. Madison, Wis., Sept. 29, 1940; s. Eugene Carleton and Mildred Florence (Blomster) R.; m. Katherine E. Hundt, Aug. 25, 1979; 1 child, Abigail Hundt. BS, U. Wis., 1966, MS in Planning, 1973, JD, 1980. Bar: Wis. 1980, U.S. Dist. Ct. (we. dist.) Wis. 1980, U.S. Ct. Appeals (7th cir.) 1992. Systems analyst U. Wis. Primate Rsch. Ctr., Madison, 1967-72; planner Dane County Regional Planning Commn., Madison, 1973-79; pres. Mendota Rsch., 1978—; with Risser and Risser, Madison, 1980-89; dir. land regulation and records dept. Dane County, Madison, 1984-89; pvt. practice Madison, 1989—; dir. bd. examiners Wis. Supreme Ct., Madison, 1994—2006. Planning cons., Madison, 1973-77; guest lectr. land use, ethics and admiralty law Law Sch. U. Wis., 1982, 86, 93-96, 2003-05, guest lectr. land econs. Planning Sch., 1973-81; guest lectr. U. Wis. Ext., 1988-90; guest lectr. ethics Marquette U. Law Sch., 2005; paralegal task force State Bar Wis., 1998-2004; unauthorized practice of law com. State Bar Wis., 2005—. Author: Historic Preservation Law in Wisconsin, 1982; The First Bite at the Apple: State Supreme Court Takings Jurisprudence Antedating First English, 1990; (with others) Boundary Law in Wisconsin, 1991; contbr. articles to profl. jours. Bd. dirs. Madison Trust for Hist. Preservation, 1984-87, Madison Zoning Bd. Appeals, 1986-94, Dane County Humane Soc., 1988-90, Dane County Housing Devel. Corp., 1975-79, Music Makers Inc., 2006-, vice chair, 2006-; spl. counsel City Fitchburg, 1983-84, Nat. Trust for Hist. Preservation, 1989-90, City Shullsburg, 1990-98; gen. counsel Cat Fanciers' Assn. Midwestern Region, 1990-95, Hist. Madison, Inc., 1981-2005, Wis. Lead Region Hist. Trust, Inc., 1992-2000; mem. legis. coun. Spl. Com. Condominium Issues, Madison, 1984-85; commr. and vice-chmn. Dane County Housing Authority, 1979-84; chmn. Wis. Chamber Orch. Bd., 1979-81; state chmn. McCarthy 1976 campaign, Madison, 1974-76. With USCGR, 1958-60. Fellow Nat. Endowment for the Arts and Humanities, 1972; Olympic finalist for Internat. 470 yachting competition, 1976. Mem.: Coun. Bar Admission Adminstrs., Dane County Bar Assn., State Bar Wis. (bd. dirs., treas., founder environ. law sect., unauthorized practice of law com.), Urban and Regional Info. Sys. Assn., Urban Land Inst., Am. Planning Assn., US Yacht Racing Union, Ixion, Downtown Madison Rotary, Meml. Union Club, U. Wis. Hoofers Sailing Club (vice commodore 1972). Avocations: sailing, racquet sports, music, skating, motorcycling. Home and Office: 2818 Ridge Rd Madison WI 53705 Office Phone: 608-658-4431, 608-658-4431. Business E-Mail: rankinlaw@gmail.com.

RANKIN, JAMES, finance company executive; b. Morris Plains, NJ, Jan. 25, 1957; s. Bernard James and Carol Joyce (Cooper) R.; m. Rebecca R. Samuel, May 11, 1989. BS, U. Calif., Davis, 1980; postgrad., U. Calif., Berkeley, 1981-83; MBA, Harvard U., 1986. Asst. v.p. Wells Fargo Bank, San Francisco, 1979-88; v.p. T. Rowe Price, LA, 1988-93; v.p., chmn. oper. com. Founders Asset Mgmt., Denver, 1993-98; v.p. customer support FOLIOfn Investments, LLC, Vienna, Va., 1999-2000; sr. mng. dir. product mgmt. EquiServe, Jersey City, 2000—03; assoc. dir. Pacific Alternative Asset Mgmt. Co., Irvine, Calif., 2004—. Mem. Harvard Bus. Sch. Club of So. Calif. Avocations: skiing, bicycling, travel. Office: Pacific Alternative Asset Mgmt Co 1920 Main St Irvine CA 92614 Home: 120 Sidney Bay Dr Newport Coast CA 92657-2112 Office Phone: 949-261-4937. E-mail: rankinjp@yahoo.com.

RANKIN, JAMES WINTON, lawyer; b. Norfolk, Va., Sept. 9, 1943; s. Winton Blair and Edith (Griffin) R.; m. Donna Lee Carpenter, June 25, 1966 (dec.); children— Thomas James, William Joseph, Elizabeth Jeanne; m. JoAnne Katherine Murray, Feb. 11, 1978. AB magna cum laude, Oberlin Coll., 1965; JD cum laude, U. Chgo., 1968. Bar: Ill. 1968, U.S. Dist. Ct. (no. dist.) Ill. 1969, U.S. Ct. Appeals (7th cir.) 1971, U.S. Ct. Appeals (5th cir.) 1979, U.S. Supreme Ct. 1975, Calif. 1986. Law clk. U.S. Dist. Ct. (no. dist.) Ill., 1968-69; assoc. Kirkland & Ellis, Chgo., 1969-73, ptnr., 1973—. Fellow Am. Bar Found.; mem. ABA, Order of Coif, Mid-Am. Club, Univ. Club, Mich. Shores Club, Kenilworth Club, Ephriam Yacht Club. Presbyterian. Home: 633 Kenilworth Ave Kenilworth IL 60043-1070 Office: Kirkland & Ellis 200 E Randolph St Fl 54 Chicago IL 60601-6636

RANKIN, MARGARET MCISAAC, elementary school educator; b. Selma, Ala., Apr. 1, 1977; d. William Dickason and Lucile Coleman Rankin. Attended, U. South, Sewanee, Tenn., 1995—97; BEd, Auburn U., Ala., 1997—99; MEd in Elem. Edn., U. Ala., Tuscaloosa, 2003. Cert. elem. edn. tchr. Ala., 1999, Commonwealth Va., 2001. 5th grade tchr. Loudoun County Schs., Sterling, Va., 2000—02; 6th grade math & English tchr. Tuscaloosa County Schs., 2002—. Math & engring. club sponsor Hillcrest Mid. Sch., Tuscaloosa, 2003, adopt-a-school rep./student recognition, 03; K-12 tchr. NSF, Tuscaloosa, 2005. Mem.: NEA (licentiate), Nat. Coun. Tchrs. Math. (licentiate), Kappa Delta Pi (life). Home: 1115 Tuscaloosa St Greensboro AL 36744 Office: Hillcrest Mid Sch 401 Hillcrest School Rd Tuscaloosa AL 35405 Home Phone: 334-624-4718. Business E-Mail: meg.rankin.hcms@tcss.net.

RANKIN, PRESSLEY ROBINSON, JR., physician; b. Mt. Gilead, NC, Dec. 7, 1920; s. Pressley R. and Katie (McAuley) Rankin; m. Paula S. Story, Apr. 30, 1992; children: Pressley III, Susan, Rebecca. BS, Davidson Coll, NC, 1942; MD, Bowman Gray Sch. Medicine, 1947; grad., USAF Sch. Aviation Medicine, San Antonio, 1951. Rotating intern Watts Hosp., Durham, NC, 1948; family practice physician Mt. Gilead, NC, 1949; pvt. practice Ellerbe, NC, 1957—. Mem. Montgomery Meml. Hosp., 1957—87, Richmond Meml. Hosp., 1957—87, Moore Regional Hosp., 1957—87; med. examiner Richmond County Med. Examiner, NC, 1970—2000. Bd. mem. Richmond County Health Dept., 1973—95, 2005—; appointed to Govs. Waste Mgmt. Bd., 1990; dir. Town Creek Indian Mound, 1980—2000, Land Trust Ctrl. NC, 1995—99, United Mills, Mt. Gilead, 1949—56, Mt. Gilead Bldg. and Loan, NC, 1949—56, Mt. Gilead Brick Co., 1949—56; bd. dirs. Mt. Gilead Untied Carolina Bank, Southern Nat. Bank, Mt. Gilead, 1952—94; bd. mem. Richmond County Health Dept., 1973—95. With US Army, 1942—46, flight surgeon USAF, 1951—54, Europe and North Africa, capt. USAAF, 1954—72. Recipient Honor award, Smithsonian Mus. Am. Indians, 2006, Citizen of Yr. award, Richmond County, 1987. Mem.: Rankin Mus. Am. Heritage (founding mem. 1985), Richmond County Scottish Heritage Soc., Richmond County Hist. Soc. (pres. 1984—86), NC Med. Soc., Am. Acad. Family Physicians (charter mem.), Mason (Thirty Third Degree), NC Forestry Assn. (Recognition award 1983). Office: PO Box 40 Ellerbe NC 28338

RANKIN, ROBERT ARTHUR, journalist; b. Richmond, Va., May 31, 1949; s. Arthur Norton and Martha Louise (Rountree) Rankin; m. Janis Johnson, May 11, 1979 (div. May 2001); 1 child, Benjamin John; m. Judy A. Stromberg, Apr. 9, 2005. BA in Polit. Sci., Randolph Macon Coll., 1971; MA in Govt., U. Va., 1974; Walter Bagehot fellowship, Columbia U., 1978-79. Reporter Richmond News Leader, Va., 1972-75; reporter Congl. Quar., Washington, 1975-78; editorial writer Miami Herald, Fla., 1980-85, Phila. Inquirer, 1985-87; nat. corr. Washington bur. Knight Ridder Newspapers, Washington, 1987—99, govt. and politics editor, 2000—06, McClatchy Newspapers, Washington, 2006—. V.p. Civic Assn. Hollin Hills, Alexandria, Va., 1991—92. Co-recipient Pulitzer prize for editl. writing, 1983; recipient Olive Br. award, NYU Ctr. War, Peace and News Media, 1990, 1st prize, Va. Press Assn., 1974, Best Editl. award, Phila. chpt. Sigma Delta Chi, 1987. Mem.: Nat. Press Club, White House Corr. Assn. (bd. govs. 1996—98). Office: McClatchy Newspapers 700 12th St NW Ste 1000 Washington DC 20005-3994 Office Phone: 202-383-6017. Business E-Mail: rrankin@mcclatchydc.com.

RANKIN, SCOTT DAVID, artist, educator; b. Newark, Mar. 21, 1954; s. Clymont J. and Jean L. (Lane) R.; m. Linda K. Piemonte, Sept. 3, 1989 (div. Apr. 2000); m. Stephanie Volz, Apr. 23, 2005. BFA, Tyler Sch. of Art, Phila., 1976; MFA, UCLA, 1980. Asst. prof. U. Iowa, Iowa City, 1985-86, U. Chgo., 1986-94; assoc. prof. Ill. State U., Normal, 1994—2005, prof., 2005—. Video cons. Math. Edn. Rsch. Project, LA, 1991—93, 3d internat. math. and sci. study UCLA dept. psychology, 1994—95, 1998—99. Prodr., dir.: (videotapes) Fugue, 1985, This and that (version 1), 1987, (version 2), 1990, The Pure, 1993, Wire, 1998, Flow, 2000, Central, 2001, Path, 2003, Piccadilly, 2004. Regional media arts fellow, Nat. Endowment for Arts, 1984, visual artists fellow, Ill. Arts Coun., 1989, 1990, Nat. Endowment for Arts, 1990, 1993. Office Phone: 309-438-8090. Business E-Mail: sdranki@ilstu.edu.

RANKIN, WILLIAM PARKMAN, communications educator, academic administrator; b. Boston, Feb. 6, 1917; s. George William and Bertha W. (Clowe) Rankin; m. Ruth E. Gerard, Sept. 12, 1942; children: Douglas W., Joan W. BS, Syracuse U., 1941; MBA, NYU, 1949, PhD, 1979. Sales exec. Redbook mag., NYC, 1945-49, This Week mag., NYC, 1949-55, adminstrv. exec., 1955-60, v.p., 1957-60, v.p., dir. advt. sales, sales devel. dir., 1960-63, exec. v.p., 1963-69; gen. exec. newspaper divsn. Time Inc., NYC, 1969-70; gen. mgr. feature svc. Newsweek Inc., NYC, 1970-74, fin. and ins. advt. mgr., 1974-81; prof., asst. to dir. Walter Cronkite Sch. Journalism & Telecom., Ariz. State U., Tempe, 1981-98, prof. emeritus, 1998—, also bd. dirs. Lectr. Syracuse U., NYU, NYC, Berkeley Sch. Author: Selling Retail Advertising, 1944, The Technique of Selling Magazine Advertising, 1949, Business Management of Consumer Magazines, 1980, 2d edit., 1984, The Practice of Newspaper Management, 1986. Mem.: Dutch Treat Club (N.Y.C.). Home: 2625 E Southern Ave Cottage 18 Tempe AZ 85282-7615 Office: Ariz State U Walter Cronkite Sch Journalism and Mass Communication Tempe AZ 85287-1305

RANKINS, DARREN BARNARD, poet; b. Murfreesboro, Tenn., Sept. 24, 1966; s. James William and Barbara Elizabeth Rankins; children: Joshua, Michael, Ashley, Amy. Student, Mid. Tenn. State U., Munfreesboro, 1998. Author: Pure Thoughts, 2003, vol. 2, 2003, vol. 3, 2004; contbr. articles to profl. jours. Avocations: tennis, poetry. Home: 117 Winsford Ct Murfreesboro TN 37130

RANNEBERGER, MICHAEL E., ambassador; BA, Towson State U.; MA, U. Va., 1973. Angola desk officer Bur. African affairs US Dept. State, spl asst. to under sec., 1984—85, dep. chief of mission Office US amb. to Mozambique, 1986—89, dep. chief of mission Office US amb. to Paraguay, 1989—92, dep. dir. Office Ctrl. Am. and Panamanian Affairs, Bur. We. Hemisphere Affairs, 1992—94, dep. chief of mission Office US amb. to Somalia, 1994, coord. Cuban affairs, 1995—99, US amb. to Mali, 1999—2002, spl adv. Office Sudan Programs Group, 2002—04, prin. dep. asst. sec. Bur. African Affairs, 2004—05, US amb. to Kenya Nairobi, 2006—. Office: 8900 Nairobi Pl Washington DC 20521

RANNER, SHANNA, music educator; d. Gare and Shirley Kraemer; m. Christopher Ranner, May 31, 1997; 1 child, Jayson. BA with Instrumental Emphasis, Truman State U., Kirkville, Mo., 1997; MusB in Percussion Performance, Truman State U., Kirksville, Mo, 1997; MusM in Edn., U. Mo.-St. Louis, 2003. Cert. instrumental music edn. K-12 Mo., 2003, vocal music edn. K-12 Mo., 2006. Tchr. music Lincoln County R-III Sch. Dist., Troy, Mo., 2000—04, U. City Sch. Dist., University City, Mo., 2004—. Musician: (mallet keyboard competition) Percussive Arts Soc. Internat. Mallet Keyboard Competition, Music Tchrs. Nat. Assn. Competition-Percussion. Named to Nat. Dean's List, Truman State U., 1995. Mem.: Sigma Alpha Iota, Mo. Music Educators Assn., Music Educators Nat. Conf., Phi Kappa Phi. Lutheran. Avocations: water aerobics, crafts. Home: 12 Fairfield Court Saint Peters MO 63376 Home Phone: 636-441-0668.

RANNEY, BROOKS, gynecologist, educator; b. Daytona Beach, Fla., Jan. 31, 1915; s. Milo Miles and Ruth Farrell (Schertz) R.; m. Ruth Vail Snow, Oct. 14, 1939 (dec. 1979); children: Robert Lawrence, David Francis, Carol Elizabeth; m. Viona Inez Thum, Aug. 29, 1981. BA, Oberlin Coll., 1936; MD, Northwestern U., 1940, MS, 1947. Diplomate: Am. Bd. Ob-Gyn. Resident ob-gyn Wesley Meml. Hosp., Chgo., 1945-48; chmn. dept. ob-gyn Yankton (S.D.) Clinic, 1948—, Sacred Heart Hosp., 1948—, Human Services Ctr., 1948—; prof., chmn. dept. ob-gyn U. S.D. Sch. Medicine, Vermillion, 1950-76. Contbr. articles to profl. jours. Mem. Yankton City Commn., 1958-64; mayor City of Yankton, 1963-64; trustee Yankton Coll., 1970—, First Congregational Ch., Yankton, 1955-58. Served to maj. AUS, 1941-53, ETO. Recipient Faculty Recognition award U. S.D. Sch. Medicine, 1980 Fellow Am. Coll. Ob-Gyn (pres. 1982-83, chmn. dist. VI 1965-68, v.p. 1978), Central Assn. Ob-Gyn (pres. 1975) Clubs: Elks. Republican. Home: 705 W 10th St Yankton SD 57078-3411

RANNEY, CARLETON DAVID, retired plant pathologist; b. Jackson, Minn., Jan. 23, 1928; s. Carleton Oran and Ada Elizabeth (Harriman) R.; m. Mary Kathryn Ransleben, July 16, 1949; children: David Clayton, Mary Elizabeth. AA, Chaffey Jr. Coll., Ontario, Calif., 1952; BS, Tex. A&M U., 1954, MS, 1955, PhD, 1959. Plant pathologist Crops Rsch. Divsn. Agrl. Rsch. Svc. USDA, College Station, Tex., 1955-58, Stoneville, Miss., 1958-70, investigations leader Beltsville, Md., 1970-72; area dir. Ala. No. Miss. area Agrl. Rsch. Svc. USDA, Starkville, Miss., 1973-78, area dir. Delta States area Stoneville, Miss., 1978-84, area dir. Mid-South area, 1984-87; asst. dir. Miss. Agrl. and Forestry Exptl. Stas., Stoneville, 1987-94, head Delta Rsch. and Ext. Ctr., 1987-94, emeritus plant pathologist, 1994—. Adj. prof. agronomy Miss. State U., 1972—94; sr. exec. svc. USDA, Stoneville, 1984—87; adv. bd. belt wide meetings Nat. Cotton Coun., Memphis, 1987—96. Contbr. articles to profl. jours. Sect. advisor SE2 Order of Arrow, Boy Scouts Am., Miss. and West Tenn., 1973-83; pres. Delta Area coun. Boy Scouts Am., Clarksdale, Miss., 1990-91, Eagle Scout; v.p. Leland Habitat for Humanity, 1995-2000, bd. dirs. 2000-06. Served with USAAC, 1946-49. Recipient Silver Beaver Boy Scouts Am., 1981, Disting. Svc. Order of Arrow Boy Scouts Am., 1983, Superior Svc. award USDA, 1981, Cert. of Merit USDA, 1983. Mem. Agron. Soc. Am., Nat. Cotton Disease Coun. (sec. 1959-60, chmn. 1961-62), Lions (pres. Leland club 1995-96), Sigma Xi, Alpha Zeta, Phi Kappa Phi. Methodist. Achievements include development of fungicide control seedling diseases; definition of relationship of microclimate to boll rot of cotton; development of non-mercurial seed treatments. Office: Delta Rsch & Ext Ctr PO Box 226 Stoneville MS 38776-0226 Office Phone: 662-686-9311. E-mail: rs2dk49@tecinfo.net.

RANNEY, GEORGE A., JR., lawyer; b. Chgo., Apr. 11, 1940; BA magna cum laude, Harvard U., 1962; JD, U. Chgo., 1966. Bar: Ill. 1966. Law clk. to Hon. Carl McGowan U.S. Ct. Appeals, Washington, 1966-67; dep. dir. Bur. Budget, State of Ill., 1969-73; counsel, v.p. Inland Steel Co., 1973-86; now sr. counsel Mayer, Brown & Platt, Chgo.; and pres., CEO Chigo. Metropolis 2020; also chmn., CEO Prairie Holdings Corp., Grayslake, Ill. Mem. Commn. Uniform State Laws, Campaign for RTA 1969-73; chmn. State Task Force on Future Ill., 1978-80; lectr. U. Chgo., 1975-79. Editor-in-chief U. Chgo. Law Rev., 1966-67. Fellow Am. Acad. Arts & Scis.; mem. ABA, Chgo. Bar Assn. Office: Mayer Brown & Platt 190 S La Salle St Ste 3900 Chicago IL 60603-3410 Office Phone: 312-701-7360. Office Fax: 312-706-8191. *

RANNEY, HELEN MARGARET, retired internist, hematologist, educator; b. Summer Hill, NY, Apr. 12, 1920; d. Arthur C. and Alesia (Toolan) Ranney. AB, Barnard Coll., 1941; MD, Columbia U., 1947; ScD, U. S.C., 1979, SUNY, Buffalo, 1996. Diplomate Am. Bd. Internal Medicine. Intern Presbyn. Hosp., NYC, 1947—48, resident, 1948—50, asst. physician, 1954—60; practice medicine specializing in internal medicine, hematology NYC, 1954—70; instr. Coll. Phys. and Surg. Columbia, NYC, 1954—60; from assoc. prof. to prof. medicine Albert Einstein Coll. Medicine, NYC, 1960—70; prof. medicine SUNY, Buffalo, 1970—73, U. Calif., San Diego, 1973—90, chmn. dept. medicine, 1973—86, Disting. physician vet. adminstr., 1986—91; cons. Alliance Pharm. Corp., San Diego, 1991—2004; ret., 2004. Master: ACP; fellow: AAAS; mem.: NAS, Am. Acad. Arts and Scis., Am. Assn. Physicians, Harvey Soc., Am. Soc. Hematology, Am. Soc. for Clin. Investigation, Inst. Medicine, Alpha Omega Alpha, Sigma Xi, Phi Beta Kappa. Personal E-mail: hranney@ucsd.edu.

RANNEY, JOSEPH AUSTIN, lawyer; b. Urbana, Ill., May 19, 1952; s. Joseph Austin and Elizabeth (Mackay) R.; m. Rebecca S. Rice, Sept. 5, 1982; 1 child, Emily M. BA, U. Chgo., 1972; JD, Yale U., 1978. Bar: Wis. 1978, U.S. Dist. Ct. (ea. dist. 1978, we. dist. 1988) Wis., U.S. Ct. Appeals (7th cir.) 1995, U.S. Ct. Appeals (Fed. cir.) 2000. Assoc. Gibbs, Roper, Loots & Williams, Milw., 1978-81, Trowbridge, Planert & Schaefer, Green Bay, Wis., 1981-88, Ross & Stevens, S.C., Madison, Wis., 1988-90, ptnr., 1990-94, DeWitt Ross & Stevens S.C., Madison, Wis., 1995—. Dir., pres. Legal Svcs. of Northeastern Wis., Green Bay, 1982-88; adj. prof. Marquette Law Sch., Milw., Wis., 2000—. Author: Trusting Nothing to Providence: A History of Wisconsin's Legal System, 1999, In the Wake of Slavery: Civil War, Civil Rights and the Reconstruction of Southern Law, 2006; contbr. articles to profl. law refs. Chmn. Brown County Dem. Party, Green Bay, 1984-86, Wis. 8th Congl. Dist., Dem. Party, 1986-88. With U.S. Army, 1972-75. Recipient Charles Dunn Author award Wis. State Bar, 1993. Office: DeWitt Ross & Stevens SC Two E Mifflin St Madison WI 53703 Home: 595 Fargo Tr Middleton WI 53562 Home Phone: 608-827-3057; Office Phone: 608-255-8891. Business E-Mail: jar@dewittross.net.

RANNEY, RICHARD RAYMOND, periodontist educator, researcher, dean; b. Atlanta, July 11, 1939; s. Russell Ballou and Maureen Joan (Bannon) R.; m. Beverly Anne Toton, June 10, 1961 (div.); children: Christine Marie, Kathleen Anne; m. Patricia Marie DeNoto, Feb. 22, 1969; children: Maureen Frances, Russell Christopher. DDS, U. Iowa, 1963; MS, U. Rochester, 1969; D (hon.), U. Buenos Aires, 1995. Asst. prof. periodontology U. Oreg., 1969-72; assoc. prof. periodontics Va. Commonwealth U., Richmond, Va., 1972-78, prof., 1978-86, dir. grad. periodontics, 1972-76, chmn. dept. periodontics, 1974-77, asst. dean rsch. and grad. affairs, 1977-84, asst. dean rsch., 1984-86; dir. Clin. Rsch. Ctr. Periodontal Diseases, Richmond, 1978-86; prof. Sch. Dentistry U. Ala., Birmingham, 1986-91, dean, 1986-89; prof. U. Md., Balt., 1991—2005, prof. emeritus, 2005, dean, 1991—2002; Sr. Policy fellow Am. Dental Edn. Assn., 2003—04, Gies Edn. fellow, 2004—05; dir. Eastman Dental Ctr. Found., Inc., 2005—. Contbr. chpts. to books, articles to profl. jours. With USPHS, 1963-66. Nat. Inst. Dental Rsch. grantee, 1970-86. Fellow: AAAS, Am. Coll. Dentists, Internat. Coll. Dentists; mem.: ADA, Am. Dental Edn. Assn. (sr. policy fellow 2003—04, Presdl. citation 2005), Am. Assn. Dental Rsch. (pres. 1990—91), Internat. Assn. Dental Rsch. (pres. 1995—96, basic rsch. periodontology award 1985), Am. Acad. Periodontology, Omicron Kappa Upsilon, Sigma Xi. Home Phone: 410-923-1049. Personal E-mail: pranney3@comcast.net.

RANONE, JOHN LOUIS, school board executive; b. NYC, July 7, 1940; s. Michael Nicholas and Josephine Clara (Iannone) R.; m. Carolyn Margaret Smith, June 13, 1964; children: Michelle Mary, Margaret Anne. AA in data processing, Fairleigh Dickinson, 1960; BA in Elem. Edn., Jersey City State Coll., 1964; AA/Classroom Renaissance, Montclair State Coll., 1969; MA in Adminstrn., Monmouth Coll., 1974. Cert. elem. tchr., adminstr., sex edn., classroom renaissance. Teaching prin. Hollie M. Davis Sch., River Edge, N.J., 1972-77; prin. Lincoln Sch., Ridgefield Park (N.J.) Bd. Edn., 1977-89; dir. curriculum and instruction Ridgefield Park Bd. Edn., 1989—. Cons., lectr., N.J. State Dept. Edn., Trenton, 1974—; chmn. N.J. State Adv. Council, Trenton, 1976—; lectr. Jersey City State Coll., 1979—; rep. U.S. Council for Individually Guided Edn., Atlanta, 1979-87; bd. trustees for teacher edn. Felician Coll. Trustee River Edge Pub. Libr., 1978-85. Recipient Outstanding Svc. award, Cath. Youth Orgn., Newark. 1965, Bergen County Outstanding Tchr. award, PTA, 1971, Child Assault Prevention award, N.J. State Dept. Edn., 1988, Halls Motor Co. scholarship, Jersey City, N.J., 1958-59; named to Edn. at the Met., Met. Opera Co., N.Y.C., Workshop Series I, 1988. Mem. Assn. Supervision and Curriculum Devel., Prins. and Suprs. Assn., River Edge Edn. Assn. (pres. 1974-76, v.p. 1972-74), Ridgefield Park Adminstr. Assn. (treas. 1981-98), River Edge Dem. Club, Friends of the Libr. Roman Catholic. Avocations: travel, reading, ceramic, collector. Home: 5 Oakmont Ln Jackson NJ 08527-3988 Office Phone: 201-819-8649.

RANSEL, DAVID LORIMER, history professor; b. Gary, Ind., Feb. 20, 1939; s. Joseph A. and Patricia (Lorimer) R.; m. Therese Holma; children: Shairstin, Annaliisa. BA, Coe Coll., 1961; MA, Northwestern U., 1962; PhD, Yale U., 1969. Instr. Tollare Folkhogskola, Boo, Sweden, 1959-60; asst. instr. Yale U., New Haven, 1966-67; instr. U. Ill., Urbana, 1967-69, asst. prof., 1969-73, assoc. prof., 1973-81, prof., 1981-85, Ind. U., Bloomington, 1985—, Robert F. Byrnes prof. history, 2001—, dir. Russian and East European Inst., 1995—; co-dir. European Union Ctr., 2005—. Author: The Politics of Catherinian Russia, 1975, Mothers of Misery, 1988, Village Mothers: Three Generations of Change in Russia and Tataria, 2000; editor: The Family in Imperial Russia, 1978, Imperial Russia: New Histories for the Empire, 1998, Polish Encounters, Russian Identity, 2005; editor/translator: Village Life in Late Tsarist Russia, 1993; editor Slavic Rev., Urbana, 1980-85, Am. Hist. Rev., Bloomington, 1985-95; bd. editors The History of the Family: An International Quarterly, Historisk Tidskrift, Forum for Anthropology and Culture, Kritika: Explorations in Russian and Eurasian History, Jour. Modern History, 2005—. Fellow Guggenheim Found., 1989-90, Wilson Nat. Fellowship Found., 1989-90, NEH, 1998-99, Bogliasco Found., 2007; Fulbright-Hays grantee, 1979, 90, Irex grantee, 1990, 93. Mem. Am. Hist. Assn. (gov. coun. 1985-95, fin. com. 1989-95), Am. Assn. for Advancement of Slavic Studies (bd. dirs. 1979-85, mem. fin. com. 1980-85, chmn. com. on status of women 1991-93, v.p., pres.-elect 2003, pres. 2004-05, immediate past pres. 2005), Irex (program com. 1995-99). Avocations: classical guitar, sailing, swimming. Office: Ind Univ Russian/East European Inst 565 Ballantine Hall Bloomington IN 47401-5017 Office Phone: 812-855-7309. Business E-Mail: ransel@indiana.edu.

RANSOHOFF, RICHARD MILTON, neurologist, researcher; b. Cin., Aug. 18, 1946; s. Jerry Nathan and Sue (Westheimer) R.; m. Margaret Seidler, Mar. 26, 1988; children: Amy Julia, Lena Jane. BA, Bard Coll., 1968; MD, Case Western Reserve U., 1978. Diplomate Am. Bd. Psychiatry and Neurology, Am. Bd. Internal Medicine. Resident in internal medicine Mt. Sinai Hosp., Cleve., 1978-81; resident in neurology The Cleve. Clinic Found., 1981-83, chief resident in neurology, 1983-84, mem. assoc. staff in neurology, 1984-93, mem. asst. staff in molecular biology Rsch. Inst., 1989-94, mem. staff neurology dept., 1993—; mem. staff in molecular biology Lerner Rsch. Inst., 1994—97, mem. staff in neuroscis. Lerner Rsch. Inst., 1994—; prof. dept. med. virology, immunology and molecular genetics Ohio State U. Health Sci. Ctr., Cleve. Clinic Found., 1997—2001; postdoctoral fellow in molecular biology Case Western Reserve U., Cleve., 1984-89; adj. prof. Case Med. Sch., Dept. Pathology, 2004—; dir. Neuroinflammation Rsch. Ctr., Cleve. Clinic Found., 2005—. Mem. neurology C study sect., Washington, 1995—98; cons. Rsch. Ctr. for AIDS Dementia, Johns Hopkins U., 1998—2002; mem. clin. adv. bd. LeukoSite, Inc., Cambridge, Mass., 1998—2000; mem. sci. adv. bd. ChemoCentryx, Santa Clara, Calif., 2001—; cons. Ctr. Neurobiology & Neurodegeneration U. Nebr. Med. Ctr.; external adv. European Union Project on Brain Inflammation, 2004—06. Co-author: Transcriptional Regulation in the Interferon System, 1997; co-editor: Cytokines in the CNS, 1996, 2d edit., 2005; editor: Chemokines in the CNS, 2002; assoc. editor: Neurology, 2006, sect. editor: Jour. Immunology, 2002—05, editl. bd.: Jour. of Neuroimmunology, 1998—, Ency. Neurol. Scis., 2003, mem. editl. adv. bd.: Trends in Immunology; mem. editl. adv. bd. Nature Review Immunology, 2005—; contbr. more than 215 articles to profl. jours. Chair profl. adv. com. Nat. Multiple Sclerosis Soc., N.E. Ohio, 1985-95, trustee, 1985-97, mem. med. adv. bd. Nat. Multiple Sclerosis Soc., N.Y.C. 1996—, chmn. peer rev. com. B, 2003—; mem. corp. Hathaway Brown Sch., Shaker Heights, Ohio; ad hoc reviewer Charles Dana Fund, N.Y.C., Wellcome Trust, U.K. Grantee NIH, Washington, 1988—, Harry Weaver Neurosci. scholar Nat. Multiple Sclerosis Soc., N.Y.C., 1987-92; recipient Physicians Rsch. Tng. award Am. Cancer Soc., N.Y.C., 1984-86, Clin. Investigator Devel. award Nat. Inst. Neurol. and Communicative Diseases and Stroke, Washington, 1988-93, John and Samuel Bard award for Sci. and Medicine, 2002, Excellence in Sci. award Lerner Rsch. Inst., 2006.

Mem.: Nat. Inst. Neurol. and Stroke (mem. steering com. 2003—), Assn. Am. Physicians, Am. Assn. Immunologists, Am. Assn. Neurology, Am. Neurol. Assn. (mem. sci. program com. 1996—98). Office: Lerner Rsch Inst NC-30 Cleve Clinic Found 9500 Euclid Ave Cleveland OH 44195-0001 Office Phone: 216-444-8939. E-mail: ransohr@ccf.org.

RANSOM, MARGARET PALMQUIST, public relations executive; b. Davenport, Iowa, Aug. 13, 1935; d. Herman Philip and Margaret (Burchell) Palmquist; m. David Duane Ransom, July 16, 1960; 1 child, David Burke. BA in Speech and English, Augustana Coll., 1957. Tchr. speech and English Beloit (Wis.) High Sch., 1957-59; tchr. English Lake Forest (Ill.) High Sch., 1959-60, Warren High Sch., Gurnee, Ill., 1960-62, 64-66; asst. to dean Grad. Sch. Bowling Green (Ohio) State U., 1963; freelance writer Coll. Bd. Examinations, 1966; market rsch. analyst Kitchens of Sara Lee, Deerfield, Ill., 1972-74; pub. affairs mgr. Sara Lee Bakery, Deerfield, 1975-89; sr. cons. Ransom Pub. Svc. Cons., Libertyville, Ill., 1990-94; cons. Olsten Staffing Svcs., Chgo., 1994-96, Kelly Svcs. Chgo. Region, 1996—. Judge nat. competitions Pub. Rels. Soc. Am., 1986-89; spkr. on motivation and orgn.; chmn. employer coun. Ill. Dept. Employment Security, 1995-96; cons. Kelly Svcs., 1996-98. Bd. dirs. Early Childhood Adv. Coun., Northeastern Ill. State U., 1989-91; mem. Main St. Libertyville com., 1990-92; creator Job Market Place '96, Lake County; ct.-appts. spl. advocate, 2003; adult Christian edn. vol. coord. Hope EPC, 2004-06; literacy vol., 2007-. Recipient Ill. Citizens Svc. medal, 1993. Mem.: AAUW, Bus. and Profl. Women Lake County, Mid-Lake County Garden Club, Mortar Bd. Avocations: computers, reading, art. *This is the day the Lord has made. Let us rejoice and be glad.*

RANSOM, RANDY, marketing executive; BA, U. Calif., Berkeley; MBA, UCLA. Dir. internat. bus. devel. FEMSA Corp.; chief mktg. officer FEMSA Cerveza; sr. v.p. portfolio strategy Coca-Cola N.Am.; pres. ConvergencePoint Group; exec. v.p., chief mktg. officer Miller Brewing Co., Milw., 2006—. Office: Miller Brewing Co 3939 W Highland Blvd Milwaukee WI 53208 *

RANSOM, TASHA ELANA, news production assistant, producer; d. Vincent Allen and Mary Geraldine Ransom. BS, Drake U., Des Moines, 1995; postgrad., Valparaiso U., Ind., 1996—97; MA, Columbia Coll., Chgo., 2002. Law clk. Vickie Pasley & Assocs., Chgo., 1992, 1994; product mgr. Zachs Investment & Rsch., Chgo., 1996; law clk. Hoeppner Wagner & Evans, Valparaiso, Ind., 1997—98; intern Lawyers for the Creative Arts, Chgo., 1999—2000; asst. Linda S. Mensch P.C., Chgo., 1999—2001; intern, prodn. cmty. affairs Fox News Chgo., 2000—01, asst. to news dir., 2001—05, asst. to news dir., prodr., 2005—. Bd. mem. Metro. and Family Svc., 2005—. Recipient Alumni of the Yr., Outstanding Contbn. in the African Am. Cmty., Youth Action Ministry, 2003; Chuck Suber scholarship, Columbia Coll., 2001—02. Mem.: Nat. Assn. Black Journalists, Phi Alpha Delta, Delta Sigma Pi.

RANTS, CAROLYN JEAN, academic administrator, educator; b. Hastings, Nebr., Oct. 3, 1936; d. John Leon and Christine (Helzer) Halloran; m. Marvin L. Rants, June 1, 1957 (div. July 1984); children: Christopher Charles, Douglas John. Student, Hastings Coll., 1954—56; BS, U. Omaha, 1960; EdM, U. Nebr., 1968; EdD, U. S.D., 1982. Elem. sch. tchr. Ogallala (Nebr.) Cmty. Sch., 1956-58, Omaha Pub. Schs., 1958-60, Hastings Pub. Schs., 1960-64, Grosse Pointe (Mich.) Cmty. Schs., 1964-67; asst. prof., instr. Morningside Coll., Sioux City, Iowa, 1974-82, dean for student devel., 1982-84, v.p. for student affairs, 1984-94, interim v.p. for acad. affairs, 1992-94, v.p. enrollment and student svcs., 1994-96, v.p. adminstrn., 1996-99; exec. dir. enrollment svcs. Western Iowa Tech C.C., 1999—, dean of students, 2000—06, interim v.p. instrn. and student svcs. Iowa, 2006—. Pres. New Perspectives, Inc., 1999—2000. New agy. com., chmn. fund distbn. and resource deployment com. United Way, Sioux City, 1987-94, co-chair, United Way Day of Caring, 1996; active Iowa Civil Rights Commn., 1989-97; bd. dirs. Leadership Sioux City, 1988-93, pres., 1992-93; bd. dirs. Siouxland Y, Sioux City, 1985-90, pres., 1988; bd. dirs. Girls, Inc., 1995-2000, Sioux City Symphony, 2001—, Red Cross, 2002—; mem. Vision 2020 Cmty. Planning Task Force, 1990-92; pres. bd. dirs. Siouxland Youth Chorus, 2001—, treas., 2002—; mem. Vision Iowa Bd., 2005—. Mem. Iowa Women in Ednl. Leadership (pres. Sioux City chpt. 1986), Nat. Assn. Student Pers. Adminstrs.(region IV-E adv. bd.), Nat. Assn. for Women Deans, Adminstrs. and Counselors, Iowa Student Pers. Adminstr. (chmn. profl. devel. Iowa chpt. 1988-89, pres. 1991-92, Outstanding Svc. award 1992, Disting. Svc. award 1994), AAUW (corp. rep., coll./univ. rep. 1994-96), P.E.O. (pres. Sioux City chpt., Tri-State Women's Bus. Conf. (treas., planning com. Sioux City chpt. 1987-89), Quota Club (com. chmn. Sioux City 1987-89, v.p. 1992-94, pres. 1994-95, Siouxland Woman of Yr. award 1988), Sertoma (officer, bd. govs., regional dir.), Omicron Delta Kappa (faculty dir. province X 1996-99), Delta Kappa Gamma (state 1st v.p. 1993-95, state pres. 1995-97, internat. com. 1998-2000, 2002-04, N.W. regional dir. 2004-06, 1st v.p. 2006—), Phi Delta Kappa (pres. 1988-89, Excellence in Leadership award 1998, Spl. Commendation Bessie Gabbard award 2001). Republican. Methodist. Avocations: handbells, cross-stitching. Home: 2904 S Cedar St # 4 Sioux City IA 51106-4246 Office: Western Iowa Tech Comm Coll PO Box 5199 4647 Stone Ave Sioux City IA 51102-5199 E-mail: rantsc@witcc.com, cjrants@willinet.net.

RANU, HARCHARAN SINGH, biomedical scientist, administrator, orthopaedic biomechanics educator; b. Lyallpur, India; came to U.S., 1976; s. Jodh Singh and Harnam Kaur R. BSc, De Montfort U., Eng., 1963; MSc, U. Surrey, Guilford, Eng., 1967, Cambridge U., Eng., 1972; PhD, Middlesex Hosp. Med. Sch. and U. Westminster, London, 1975; diploma, MIT, 1984. Chartered engr., scientist, Eng. Med. scientist Nat. Inst. Med. Rsch. of the Med. Rsch. Coun., London, 1967-70; rsch. fellow Middlesex Hosp. Med. Sch. and Poly. of Cen. London, 1971-76; rsch. scientist Plastics Rsch. Assn. of Great Britain, Shawbury, Eng., 1977; asst. prof. Wayne State U., Detroit, 1977-81; prof. biomed. engring./orthopaedic biomechanics biomaterials La. Tech. U., Ruston, 1982—; prof., chmn. dept. biomechanics N.Y. Coll. Osteo. Medicine, Old Westbury, 1989-93; dir. tng. Rehab. R&D Ctr., 1983-85; mem. La. Tech. U. Libr. Com., 1983-85; chmn. design competition Assn. Biomed. Engrs.; mem. steering com. So. Biomed. Engring. Confs., 1983—; chmn. tech. in health care conf. U. Cambridge, 1985; chmn. Internat. Symposium on Bioengring., Calcutta, India, 1985; dir. orthopaedic biomechanics rsch. labs., staff Nassau County Med. Ctr., Long Island, 1989—; prof., exec. asst. to pres., and dir. doctoral program Life U., Marietta, Ga., 1993—; pres. Am. Orthop. Biomechanics Rsch. Inst., Atlanta, 1997—. Biomed. engring. faculty com. La. Tech. U., faculty com., rsch. awards com., grad. studies com., grad. faculty, acad. bd. dirs; vis. scientist Dryburn Hosp., Durham, Eng., 1985-87, cons., 1988—; vis. prof. U. Istanbul, 1982, Lab. de Recherch Orthopediques, Paris, 1985—, Kings Coll. Med. Sch. U. London, 1989—, Indian Inst. Tech., New Delhi, Postgrad Inst. Med. Edn. and Rsch., Chandigarh, India, 1989—, Polytech. Ctrl. London, 1991—, U. Buenos Aires, Pontific Cath. U. Chile, Fed. U. Rio de Janeiro; adj. prof. Coll. Physicians and Surgeons Columbia U., NYC, 1988—, Inst. Biol. Physics USSR Acad. Sci., Moscow, 1990, NY Coll. Podiatric Medicine, 1991—, CUNY, 1992—; cons. Lincoln Gen. Hosp., Ruston, La., 1982-85, La. State U. Med. Ctr., Shreveport, 1982—, St. Luke's and Roosevelt Hosp. Ctr., NY, 1988—, Foot Clinics N., 1991—, Vets. Affairs Med. Ctr., NY, 1992—, others; media resource svc. Inst. Pub. Info., NY, 1989—; med. scientist, cons. NATO, 1982—; presenter, lectr. in field; external examiner for doctoral candidates All India Inst. Med. Scis., New Delhi, Indian Inst. Tech., New Delhi, Banaras Hindu U., Varanasi, India, 1994— Author: Rheological Behavior of Articular Cartiliage Under Tensile Loads, 1967, Effects of Ionizing Radiation on the Mechanical Properties of Skin, 1975, Effects of Fractionated Doses of X-irradiation on the Mechanical Properties of Skin--A Long Term Study, 1980, Effects of Ionizing Radiation on the Structure & Physical Properties of the Skin, 1983, 3-D Model of Vertebra for Spinal Surgery, 1985, Application of Carbon Fibers in Orthopaedic Surgery, 1985, Relation Between Metal Corrision & Electrical Polarization, 1989, The Distribution of Stresses in the Human Lumbar Spine, 1989, Medical Devices & Orthopaedic Implants in the United States, 1989, Spinal Surgery by Modeling, 1989, Multipoint Determination of Pressure-Volume Curves in Human Intervertebral Discs, 1993, Evaluation of Volume-Pressure Relationship in Lumbar Discs Using Model and Experimental Studies, 1994, A Mechanism of Laser Nuclectomy, 1994, Microminiaturization in Laser Surgery in Vivo Intradiscal Pressure Measurements in Lumbar Intervertebral Discs, 1994, An Experimental and Mathematical Simulation of Fracture of Human Bone Due to Jumping, 1994; editor The Lower Extremity, 1993—; guest editor IEEE Engring. in Medicine & Biology, 1991; mem. editl. bd. Med. Instrumentation, 1988—, Jour. Biomed. Instrumentation & Tech., 1988—, Jour. Med. Engring. & Tech., 1989—, Jour. Med. Design & Material, 1990—, Jour. Long-Term Effects Med. Implants, 1991—, Biomed. Sci. & Tech., 1991—; reviewer Jour. Biomechanics, 1981—, Clin. Biomechanics, 1984—, Jour. Biomed. Engring., 1981, Phys. Therapy, 1990—, IEEE Biomed. Transactions, 1991—, Jour. Engring. in Medicine, 1989—; contbr. articles to profl. jours. Faculty advisor India Students Assn. Wayne State U., 1980. Recipient Edwin Tate award U. Surrey, 1968, Third Internat. Olympic Com. World Congress On Sprots Scis. award, Atlanta, 1995; numerous rsch. grants. Fellow ASME (bioengring. com. 1990—, award L.I. chpt. 1991), Biol. Engring. Soc. (London, President's prize 1984), Instn. Mech. Engrs. (chmn. revv. bd. for corp. memberships, James Clayton awards 1974-76), Inst. Physics and Engring. in Medicine; mem. AAAS, Am. Soc. Biomechanics (edn. com. 1990—), Orthopaedic Rsch. Soc., Am. Coll. Sports Medicine, Biomed. Engring. Soc., India Assn., India Assn. North La., Sci. Coun. Eng. (chartered scientist). Sikh. Achievements include research in microfracture simulation of human vertebrae under compressive loading, laserectomy of the human nucleus pulposus and its effect on the intradiscal pressure, pressure-volume relation in human intervertebral discs, in vitro and in vivo intradiscal pressure measurements before and after laserectomy of the human nucleus pulposus, gait analysis of a diabetic foot, bioengineering in the millennium, bioengineering-building the future of biology and medicine, bioengineering the cutting edge of biology and medicine in the millennium, in vivo micro-fracture simulation in Indian Olympic field hockey players, relief from low-back pain in sports by infusion of saline into the human nucleus pulposus and establishing the pressure-volume relationship, clinical applications of bioinstrumentation for better health, fifth IOC World Congress on sports sciences, microfracture simulation in tennis players, human gait analysis normal and pathological, simulation of micro-fracture injury in female gymnasts-an in vivo study, pattern recognition in human gait, identification of ethnicity from human gait; micro-fracture injury simulation in pole-vaulting and female gymnasts; 3-D simulation of drop in intradiscal pressure in spinal discs due to laserectomy; Ranu's principle and laserectomy to relieve low back pain; Ranu's cumulative gait effect phenomenon, invivo microfracture simulation in skiers; 3-D foot pressure measurements in normal and diabetic persons; normal and abnormal gait of successive steps with miniature triaxial load cells; gait analysis of amputees initally and one month later for successive steps; stress-fracture simulationi n ski jumpers. Office: Life Univ Sch Grad Studies Marietta GA 30060 Personal E-mail: profranu@yahoo.com.

RANUM, OREST ALLEN, historian, educator; b. Lyle, Minn., Feb. 18, 1933; s. Luther George and Nada (Chaffee) R.; m. Patricia McGroder, July 4, 1955; children— Kristin, Marcus BA, Macalester Coll., St. Paul, 1955; MA, U. Minn., 1957, PhD, 1961. Asst. prof. U. So. Calif., 1960-61; asst. prof. Columbia U., NYC, 1961-63, assoc. prof., 1963-69; prof. history Johns Hopkins U., Balt., 1969-99; ret., 1999. Mem., chmn. GRE Ednl. Testing Service, Princeton, 1973-78 Author: Richelieu and Councilors, 1963, Paris, Age of Absolutism, 1968, revised and expanded edit., 2002, Artisans of Glory, 1981, The Fronde, 1993, Paris in the Age of Absolutism, 2002. Recipient Bronze medal City of Tours, France, 1980. Mem. Am. Hist. Assn., Soc. French Hist. Studies, Inst. de France (corr.), Académie des Sciences Morales et Politiques (Paris; corr. 1989), Société de l'Histoire de France, Collège de France (internat. chair 1994-95). Home: 208 Ridgewood Rd Baltimore MD 21210-2539 Office: History Dept Johns Hopkins U Baltimore MD 21218 Office Phone: 410-516-7575. E-mail: orestranum@cs.com.

RANZ, JULES M., psychiatrist, director; s. Sidney and Evelyn Hoffman Ranz; m. Bonnie T. Horen, June 28, 1990; children: David Jeremy, Joshua Hillel. BA, Harvard Coll., Cambridge, Mass., 1962; MD, NYU Sch. Medicine, NYC, 1966. Lic. psychiatrist Am. Bd. Psychiatry and Neurology, 1973. Dir., pub. psychiatry fellow Columbia U., NYS Psychiat. Inst., NYC, 1992—. Bd. dir. Project Renewal, Inc., NYC, 1994—. Office: Columbia Univ NYS Psychiatr Inst 1051 Riverside Dr Box 111 New York NY 10032 Home Phone: 914-693-9484; Office Phone: 212-543-5655. Business E-Mail: jmr1@columbia.edu.

RANZAN, DAVID ALDRICH, archivist; b. East Stroudsburg, Pa., Feb. 21, 1973; s. William Theodore Ranzan and Audrey Dorothy (Meier) Ranzan; m. Kelly Gene Smith, May 31, 2002; 1 child, Eric Walter. BA in History, East Stroudsburg U., 2000, MA in History, 2002; MLIS, Rutgers U., 2006. Grad. asst. Papers of War Dept., 1784-1800, East Stroudsburg, Pa., 1999—2000, asst. editor, 2004—05; documentary editor Thomas A. Edison Papers, Piscataway, NJ, 2000—; cons. The Hist. Speedwell, Morristown, 2004—; archivist Rutgers U. Archives, New Brunswick, 2005—07; reference libr. Wayne Pub. Lib., NJ, 2006—. Adj. asst. archivist Coll. SI, 2007—. Co-editor: Thomas A. Edison Papers, A Selective Microfilm Edition: Part V (1911-1919), Sussex County (N.J.) Marriage and Obituary Dates (1814-1903), Passaic County (N.J.) Military Service Records from World War I and Other Wars. Fellow, NHPRC, 2001. Mem.: ALA, Assn. Documentary Editing, NJ. Libr. Assn., Phi Alpha Theta. Home: PO Box 334 Saylorsburg PA 18353 Office: Thomas A Edison Papers 44 Rd 3 Piscataway NJ 08854-8049 Home Phone: 570-992-8856; Office Phone: 732-445-8511 ext. 18. Office Fax: 732-445-8512.

RAO, ANJANA, immunologist, educator; MS in Physics, Osmania U., Hyderabad, India; PhD in Biophysics, Harvard U. Postdoctoral rschr. Harvard Med. Sch. and Dana-Farber Cancer Inst.; prof. pathology Dana Farber Cancer Inst., Harvard Med. Sch.; sr. investigator CBR Inst. Biomedical Rsch. Contbr. articles to profl. jours. Recipient Am. Assn. Immunologists-Huang Found. Meritorious Career award, 2000. Office: Harvard Med Sch Dept Pathology CBR Inst Biomedical Rsch 200 Longwood Ave Rm 152 Boston MA 02115 E-mail: arao@cbr.med.harvard.edu.

RAO, BALAKRISHNA, plant pathologist, mycologist, botanist; b. Yelluru, South Kanara, India, July 23, 1944; came to U.S., 1969; d. Y. Venkatramanayya and B. Padmavathiamma; m. Sudaxina B. Rao, Mar. 1, 1981; children: Anita B., Vinod B. BS, U. Mysore, India, 1964; MS, U. Bombay, 1966, U. N.C., 1971; PhD, Ohio State U., 1976. Postdoctoral fellow O.A.R.D.C., Wooster, Ohio, 1976-77; plant pathologist Davey Tree Expert Co., Kent, Ohio, 1977-84, dir. lawncare tech. resources, 1984-87, mgr. diagnostic lab., 1977—, mgr. tech. resources, 1987—. Lectr. in field. Contbg. editor: Landscape Mgmt. 1982—; contbr. papers to sci. jours. U. Bombay Merrit scholar, 1965, U. Madras Grant Commn. scholar, 1967. Mem. Am. Phytopathological Soc., Am. Mycological Soc., Mich. Turfgrass Found., N.Y. State Turfgrass Assn., Inc., Ont. Turfgrass Rsch. Found., So. Turfgrass Found. Avocations: gardening, indoor plantscape, travel, photography, stamp collecting/philately. Home: 4445 Bunker Ln Stow OH 44224-5129

RAO, DABEERU C. (D.C. RAO), epidemiologist, educator; b. Apr. 6, 1946; came to U.S., 1972; naturalized. s. Ramarao Patnaik and Venkataratnam (Raghupatruni) R.; m. Sarada Patnaik, 1974; children: Ravi, Lakshmi. BS in Stats., Indian Statis. Inst., Calcutta, 1967, MS, 1968, PhD, 1971. Rsch. fellow U. Sheffield, England, 1971-72; asst. geneticist U. Hawaii, Honolulu, 1972-78, assoc. geneticist, 1978-80; dir. divsn. biostats. Washington U. Med. Sch., 1980—, assoc. prof. St. Louis, 1980-82, prof. depts. biostats., psychiatry and genetics, 1982—. Adj. prof. math., 1982—. Author: A Source Book for Linkage in Man, 1979, Methods in Genetic Epidemiology, 1983, Genetic Epidemiology of Coronary Heart Disease, 1984; editor-in-chief Genetic Epidemiology jour., 1984-91; contbr. over 400 articles to profl. jours. Grantee NIH, 1978—; Telugu Assn. N.Am. Mem. Am. Statis. Assn., Am. Soc. Human Genetics, Internat. Genetic Epidemiology Soc. (pres. 1996), Behavior Genetics Assn., Soc. Epidemiol. Rsch., Biomed. soc. Office: Washington U Sch Medicine Divsn Biostats Box 8067 660 S Euclid Ave Saint Louis MO 63110-1010 E-mail: rao@wubios.wustl.edu.

RAO, K.V.R. MOHAN See KOTTAMASU, MOHAN

RAO, NANNAPANENI NARAYANA, electrical engineer; b. Kakumanu, Andhra Pradesh, India; m. Sarojini Jonnalagadda, June 10, 1955; children: Vanaja, Durgaprasad, Hariprasad. BSc in Physics, U. Madras, India, 1952; DMIT in Electronics, Madras Inst. Tech., 1955; MSEE, U. Wash., Seattle, 1960, PhD in Elec. Engring, 1965. Acting instr. elec. engring. U. Wash., 1960-64, acting asst. prof., 1964-65; asst. prof. elec. engring. U. Ill., Urbana, 1965-69, asso. prof., 1969-75, prof., 1975—2007, Edward C. Jordan prof., 2003—07, Edward C. Jordan prof. emeritus, 2007—, assoc. head elec. and computer engring., 1987—2007; disting. prof. Amrita U., India, 2006—. Cons. Fakultas Teknik, Univ. Indonesia, Jakarta, 1985-86, 87. Author: Basic Electromagnetics with Applications, 1972, Elements of Engineering Electromagnetics, 6th edit., 2004; contbr. numerous articles to profl. jours. Recipient Engring. award Telugu Assn. N.Am., 1983, Excellence in Edn. award, 1999, Fakultas Teknik award Universitas Indonesia, 1986. Fellow IEEE (Undergrad. Teaching award 1994); mem. Am. Soc. Engring. Edn. (AT&T Found. award for excellence in instrn. engring. students 1991), Internat. Union Radio Sci. (US Commn. G). Achievements include contributions to engineering education in the United States and abroad. Home: 2509 S Lynn St Urbana IL 61801-6841 E-mail: rao@ece.uiuc.edu.

RAO, NARSING A., ophthalmologist, pathologist, educator; arrived in U.S., 1968; MD, Osmania U., Hyderabad, India, 1967. Cert. Am. Bd. Ophthalmology, Am. Bd. Pathology. Prof. ophthalmology and pathology U. So. Calif., LA, 1983—; dir. uveitis and ophthalmic pathology Doheny Eye Inst., LA, 1983—. Contbr. articles to profl. jours. Pres. Internat. Uveitis Soc., Bethesda, Md., 2000—05. Recipient Zimmerman Gold medal, Am. Acad. Ophthalmology, 2003; grantee, NIH, 1985—2007. Mem.: Am. Ophthal. Soc. Achievements include research in free radical biology. Office: Doheny Eye Inst 1450 San Pablo St Los Angeles CA 90033 Office Phone: 323-442-6645. Office Fax: 323-442-6634. Business E-Mail: nrao@usc.edu.

RAO, NATTI SREERAMA, small business owner, consultant; b. Pulivendla, Andhra Pradesh, India, Oct. 28, 1935; arrived in US, 2002, permanent resident; s. Natti Sreeramulu and Bhadipetla Satyanarayanamma; m. Rosemarie Ruth Dorrer, July 1, 1966; children: Steffen Schneider, Sylvia Van Ledden. B in Mech. Engring. with honors, Indian Inst. Tech. Madras, India, M in Chem. Engring.; PhD in Chem. Engring., U. Karlsruhe, Germany, 1960—64. Lic. chem. engr., U. Karlsruhe, 1964. Sr. rsch. engr. Basf Ag, Ludwigshafen/Rh, Germany, 1964—81; propr. Plastics Solutions Internat. Cons., Ghent, NY, 1987—. Vis. prof. Indian Inst. Tech. Madras, Chennai, India, 1983—84. Author: (book) Formulas for Plastics Engineers. Fellow: Soc. Plastics Engrs. USA; mem.: Tech. Assn. Paper and Pulp Industry. Achievements include research in computer aided design of plasticating screws; design of machines and dies for polymer processing with computer programs. Home and Office: Plastics Solutions Internat Cons 327 County Rte 21 C Ghent NY 12075 Home Phone: 518-672-4281; Office Phone: 518-672-4281. Office Fax: 518-672-4281; Home Fax: 518-672-7608. Business E-Mail: raonatti@aol.com.

RAO, PANDURANGA S., nephrologist, educator; b. Madras, Tamilnadu, India, Dec. 1, 1961; s. Sadashiua and Shalini Rao; m. Deepa Mukundaw Rao, Nov. 9, 1988; 1 child, Harsha. MBBS, Stanley Med. Coll., Madras, India, 1979—86; MD, Kilpauk Med. Coll., Madras, 1986—89; DNB, Apollo Hosp., Madras, 1990—93; MS, U. Mich., Ann Arbor, 2003—05. Asst. prof. Medical Coll. Ohio, Toledo, 2000—03, U. Mich., 2003—. Recipient Faculty Tchg. award, Medical Coll. Ohio, 2003. Mem.: Am. Soc. Nephrology. Achievements include research in outcome studies in transplantation. Office: Univ Mich 102 Observatory Ann Arbor MI 48109

RAO, POTARAZU KRISHNA, environmental consultant; b. Andhra Pradesh, India, Mar. 26, 1930; s. Satyanarayana and Annapooma (Mullapudi) Rao; m. Rukmani Krutivinti, Aug. 5, 1954; children: Ramanarayan, Sreedhar. BS, Andhra U., 1950, MS, 1952, Fla. State U., 1957; PhD, NYU, 1968. Meteorologist Can. Meteorol. Svc., Montreal, Canada, 1960-61; rsch. phys. scientist Nat. Oceanic and Atmospheric Adminstrn./Nat. Environ. Satellite Data and Info. Svc., Washington, 1961-74, chief atmospheric energetics br., acting dir., 1976-80, chief satellite applications lab., 1980-86, dir. office of rsch. and applications, 1986-96; chief scientist for satellite and info. svcs. Nat. Oceanic and Atmospheric Adminstrn., Washington, 1996—2002; program dir., weather modification NSF, Washington, 1971-72; advisor on satellite programs World Meteorological Orgn., Geneva, 1974-76; cons. TRW, ITT. Bd. dirs. Climate and Global Change Program Nat. Oceanic and Atmospheric Adminstrn., Washington; mem. adv. bd. Coop. Inst. for Rsch. in Atmospheres, Ft. Collins, 1986—. Editor: Weather Satellites, 1990; contbr. articles to profl. jours. Founder, trustee Sri Siva Vishnu Temple, Lanham, Md. Fellow: N.Y. Acad. Scis., Royal Meteorol. Soc. U.K., Am. Meteorol. Soc. Hindu. Avocations: tennis, photography. Home: 15824 Buena Vista Dr Rockville MD 20855-2658 E-mail: potarazukrao@netscape.net.

RAO, RAMA KRISHNA R., pharmaceutical company executive; b. Tanuku, Andhra Province, India, Nov. 20, 1955; came to U.S., 1998; s. R.R. and Satyavani R. (Gudipati) R.; m. Kavitha Advikolanu, May 19, 1996. B in Tech., Indian Inst. Tech., Delhi, 1977; postgrad. diploma in mgmt., Indian Inst. Mgmt., Calcutta, 1981; MBA, INSEAD, Fontainebleu, France, 1989. Asst. mgr. Metal Box India, Calcutta, 1977-84; exec. asst. to gen. mgr. Bank of Bahrain & Kuwait, Bahrain, 1985-88; fin. assoc. Eli Lilly, Geneva, credit and customer svc. mgr., 1993-94, fin. mgr. Africa, 1994-95; mgr. (global treasury) Gems Eli Lilly, Brussels, 1995-97; fin. advisor corp. fin. and investment banking Lilly Corp. Ctr., Indpls., 1998-99; CFO, fin. mgr. PC/NS Lilly USA, Indpls., 1999—2001; fin. dir. intercontinental region Novartis Oncology Bus. Unit, East Hanover, NJ, 2001—04; CFO, v.p. fin. Novartis Can., Dorval, Canada, 2004—06; exec. dir., head fin., global devel. and oncology unit Novartis, 2006—. Alumni mem. panel for INSEAD interviews, Belgium, U.S., 1995-99. Contbr. journalist Students' Newsletter, IIT, Delhi, co-editor Students' Newsletter, I.I.M., Calcutta, INSEAD, Fontainebleu, France. Vol. Samaritans/Befrienders, Bahrain, 1987, 88; donor of blood Red

Cross/Crescent, India, Belgium, US, Bahrain, 1974-97. Recipient First prize Nat. Young Mgrs. Competition, All India Mgmt. Assn., 1983. Mem. AMA, Assn. Investment Mgmt. and Rsch., Inst. Mgmt. Accts. Hindu. Avocations: travel, military history, foreign policy. Office Phone: 862-778-5459. Business E-Mail: rama.rao@novartis.com.

RAO, SETHURAMIAH LAKSHMINARAYANA, demographer, United Nations official; b. Mysore, Karnataka, India, Apr. 28, 1942; came to U.S., 1967; s. Ramakrishniah Sethuramiah and Bhageerathi; m. Sudha Bagur Viswanath, Aug. 1, 1971; children: Rekha, Kumar. MSc, U. Mysore, 1963; MPH, U. N.C., 1968; cert., U. Mich., 1969; PhD, U. Pa., 1971. Cert. Demographic Tng. and Rsch. Ctr., Bombay. Asst. prof. Brown U., Providence, 1971-73; UN adviser Govt. of Sri Lanka, Colombo, 1974-77; chief population and devel. UN Population Fund, NYC, 1978-82, chief policy br., 1982-90, country dir. Addis Ababa, Ethiopia, 1991-92, dep. dir. info. & extern rels. NYC, 1992-95, dir. tech. and evaluation divsn., 1995-97, dir. divsn. adminstrn. fin. and mgmt., 1998-2000, dir. strategic planning & coord. divsn., 2001—03, sr. advisor, 2004—05, Ptnrs. in Population and Devel., NYC, 2006—. Sec. UN Population Fund segment of UN Devel. Program/UN Population Fund exec. bd.; leader UN tech. missions to several countries. Author: Socio-Religious Factors in Fertility, 1973; co-author: Population Problems of Sri Lanka, 1977, Population Program Experience, 1991; contbr. articles to profl. jours. V.p. Mysore Self Reliance Assn., Mangalore, 1963-65, Indo-Am. Forum for Polit. Edn., N.Y., 1989-90; founder, pres. New Eng. Kannada Koota, Providence, 1972-73. Recipient several acad. honors and gold medals, U. Pa., 1971, U. Mysore, 1961, 63. Mem. Delta Omega, Internat. Union for the Scientific Study of Population. Avocations: travel, debate, bridge playing. Home: 143 Nelson Rd Scarsdale NY 10583-5811 Office: UN Population Fund 220 E 42nd St New York NY 10017-5806 E-mail: rao2108@yahoo.com.

RAO, SHAOQI, medical educator; BS in Animal Sci., Xing Jiang Agrl. U., China, 1983; MS in Biostatistics, Case We. Res. U., Cleve., 2001; PhD in Genetics, Va. Tech, Blacksburg, 1997. Scientist Cleve. Clinic Found., 2001—; prof. Harbin Med. U., China, 2004—. Longjiang scholar Heilongjiang Province Govt., Harbin, 2006—; guest prof. China People Liberation Army Gen. Hosp., Beijing, 2006—; prof. Beijing Mcpl. Govt., 2007—. Editor: (book) Analysis of Medical Data: An Introduction to Bioinformatics, 2001; translator: Hereditary Hearing Loss and Its Syndromes, 2006; contbr. chapters to books. Mem.: Internat. Genetic Epidemiology Soc., Am. Soc. Human Genetics. Achievements include research in genome-wide linkage to early heart attacks; an angiogenic factor that when mutated causes susceptibility to Klippel-Trenaunay syndrome; genomewide linkage scan that identifies a novel susceptibility locus for restless legs syndrome; discovery of gene mining approach to hunting for disease genes using microarray expression profiling. Office: Lerner Rsch Inst NE40 Cleveland Clinic Found 9500 Euclid Ave Cleveland OH 44195 Office Phone: 216-444-0056. Personal E-mail: shaoqir@yahoo.com. Business E-Mail: raos@ccf.org.

RAO, SREERAMOJU GAUTAMI, oncologist; b. India, May 27, 1960; MD, Coimbatore Med. Coll., India, 1983. Cert. Internal Medicine, Hematology, Med. Oncology. Intern Kingsbrook Jewish Med. Ctr., Bklyn., 1998; fellow, hematology & oncology Brookdale U. Hosp., Bklyn., 1991—93; fellow, hematology Thomas Jefferson U., The Cardeza Found., 1993; attending physician Southern NH Med, Ctr., 1993; mem., Norris Cotton Cancer Ctr. Dartmouth-Hitchcock Med. Ctr., Lebanon, NH, 2003—. Named one of Top Doctor, NH Mag., 2007. Office: Norris Cotton Cancer Ctr Dartmouth-Hitchcock Med Ctr 1 Medical Center Dr Lebanon NH 03756 also: Dartmouth-Hitchcock Manchester 100 Hitchcock Way Manchester NH 03104 Address: Dartmouth-Hitchcock Nashua 21 E Hollis St Nashua NH 03060 Office Phone: 603-629-1828, 603-577-3460. Office Fax: 603-695-2855, 603-577-3459. *

RAO, SUDHAKAR, aerospace engineer, researcher; b. Tenali, Andhra Pradesh, India, July 15, 1951; arrived in US, 1996, naturalized, 2004; s. Baparao and Hymavathi Krothapalli; m. Rajani Krothapalli, Apr. 30, 1978; 1 child, Neha. BE, JNT U., Warangal, India, 1974; ME, Indian Inst. Tech., Kharaghpur, 1976; PhD, Indian Inst. Tech., Madras, 1980. Tech. officer Electronic Corp. India Ltd., Hyderabad, Andhra Pradesh, India, 1976—77; sr. sci. officer Electronic and Radar Devel. Establishment, Bangalore, Karnataka, India, 1980—81; postdoctoral rsch. fellow U. Trondheim, Norway, 1981—82; rsch. assoc. U. Man., Winnipeg, Canada, 1982—83; staff scientist Spar Aerospace Ltd., Ste-Anne-de-Bellevue, Que., Canada, 1983—96; chief scientist Boeing Satellite Sys., El Segundo, Calif., 1996—2003; divsn. fellow Lockheed Martin Comml. Space Sys., Newtown, Pa., 2003—. Mem. intellectual property rev. bd. Lockheed Martin. Contbr. more than 100 articles to profl. jours. Sponsored eye camps Rotary Club India, Vijayawada, Andhra Pradesh, 2005—06. Recipient Boeing's Spl. Invention award, 2002, Lockheed Martin's Key Inventor award, 2005, 2007, Lockheed Martin Corp. Sr. Fellow award, 2006; NTNF Postdoctoral fellow, Norwegian Coun. Sci. and Indsl. Rsch., 1981, 1982. Fellow: IEEE (Benjamin Franklin Key award 2006). Republican. Hindu. Achievements include 30 US patents for advanced payloads for satellite communications; development of radiation templates for interference analysis of various satellite systems. Avocations: tennis, basketball. Home: 125 Livery Dr Churchville PA 18966 Office: Lockheed Martin Comml Space Sys 100 Campus Dr Newtown PA 18940 Office Phone: 215-497-2265. Personal E-mail: skraoks@yahoo.com.

RAO, VITTAL SRIRANGAM, electrical engineering educator; b. Inumpamula, India, June 8, 1944; came to U.S., 1981; s. Rangaiah Srirangam and Lakshmamma (Immadi) R.; m. Vijaya Morishetti, Feb. 28, 1965; children: Asha, Ajay. M of Tech., Indian Inst. Tech., 1972, PhD, 1975. Asst. prof. Indian Inst. of Tech., New Delhi, India, 1975-79; vis. prof. T.U., Halifax, N.S., Can., 1980-81; assoc. prof. U. Mo., Rolla, 1981-88, prof., 1988—; dir. Intelligent Systems Ctr., Rolla, 1991—. Cons. Delco Remy, Anderson, Ind., 1985-87, Allison Gas Turbines, Indpls., 1986-87, U.S. Army Picatinny Arsenal, N.J., 1988-91. Contbr. articles to profl. jours. including Suboptimal/Near Optimal Control, Reduced Order Modeling Techniques, Robust Control, Large Space Structures, Smart Structures. Fellow AIAA (assoc.); mem. IEEE (sr., subsect. 1981-88, Centennial medal 1984). Achievements include devel. of reduced order modeling techniques for large space structures, interdisciplinary approach for control of smart structures and structural health monitoring. Home: 501 Oak Knoll Rd Rolla MO 65401-4727 Office: U Mo Intelligent Systems Ctr Rolla MO 65401

RAO, YALLAPRAGADA S., oncologist; b. Repalle, India, Aug. 14, 1949; arrived in US, 1974; s. Y. Narasimha and Bhagyalaxmi Rao; m. Shailaja Rambhatla, Aug. 27, 1977; children: Vikas, Vivek, Svetha. MBBS, Guntur Med. Coll., India, 1972. Diplomate Am. Bd. Radiology. Intern Elyria Meml. Hosp., Ohio, 1975; resident Michael Reese Med. Ctr., Chgo., 1975—78; radiation oncologist U. Calif., Irvine Med. Ctr., Orange, 1978—83; dir. radiation oncology Pomona Valley Hosp. Med. Ctr., Calif., 1984—, med. dir. Cancer Care Ctr., 2004—. Assoc. clin. prof. U. Calif., Irvine, 1982—. Fellow: Am. Coll. Radiation Oncology; mem.: Am. Soc. Clin. Oncology, Am. Coll. Radiology, Am. Soc. Therapeutic Radiology Oncology. Office: Cancer Care Ctr 1910 Royalty Dr Pomona CA 91767

RAOUFI, AZADEH, music educator; arrived in U.S., 1998; d. Mohammad Sadogh Raoufi and Fatemeh (Mali) Fakoor-Sevvom. B in Piano and Computer Sci., U. Iowa, 2004, postgrad., 2005—. Tchr. English Shokoh, Mashad, 1995—98; with Info. Tech. Ctr., Iowa City, 2001—02; with internal med. rsch. lab. U. Iowa, Iowa City, 2001—02; piano tchr. West Music, Iowa City, 2002—. Mem.: Iowa City Ind. Piano Tchrs. (v.p.), Iowa Music Tchr. Assn. (pub. rels. person 2004—), Music Tchr. Nat. Assn., Phi Theta Kappa. E-mail: azadeh-raoufi@uiowa.edu.

RAPADAS, LEONARDO M., prosecutor, lawyer; b. 1960; BS, Pacific Univ.; JD, Williamette Univ. Coll of Law. Pros. Guam Atty. Gen. office, 1989—97, chief pros., 1997—99; US Atty. dist. Guam & Mariana Islands US Dept. Justice, Saipan, 2003—. Office: US Attys Office Sirena Plz Ste 500 108 Hernan Cortez PO Box 500377 Saipan MP 96950-0377 *

RAPELYE, JANET LAVIN, dean; m. Peter Rapelye. Grad. with honors, Williams Coll.; MEd, Stanford U. Tchr. English, Wells River, Vt.; asst. dir. admissions Williams Coll., 1982; counselor admissions office Stanford U.; assoc. dir. admissions Bowdoin Coll., 1986; dean admissions Wellesley Coll., 1991—2003, Princeton U., 2003—. Office: Princeton U Dean of Admissions 201 West College, Rm 110 Princeton NJ 08544 Office Phone: 609-258-6150. Office Fax: 609-258-6743. Business E-Mail: jrapelye@princeton.edu. *

RAPER, CHARLES ALBERT, retired management consultant; b. Charleston, W.Va., Aug. 18, 1926; s. Kenneth B. and Louise (Williams) R.; m. Margaret Ann Weers, Dec. 26, 1947; children: Kathleen, Josephine, Charles. Student, Okla. State U., 1945; BS, U. Ill., 1949. Sales mgr. Meyer Furnace Co., Peoria, Ill., 1949-54; v.p. mktg. Master Consol., Inc., Dayton, Ohio, 1954-61; mgmt. cons. McKinsey & Co., Inc., Chgo., 1961-67; v.p. mktg. Gen. Portland Inc., Dallas, 1967-69, pres., also dir., 1969-75; v.p., gen. mgr. Scholl Inc., Chgo., 1975-81; pres. Oxford Group of Sara Lee, 1981-84; mgmt. cons. McKinsey & Co., 1984—. Vice-chmn. devel. bd. U. Tex., Dallas; exec. bd. Circle 10 coun. Boy Scouts Am.; Svc. Corp. of Ret. Execs. counselor. With USN, 1944-46. Mem. Dallas C. of C. (chmn. bd. dirs. 1974—), Sales Execs. Club, Cherokee Country Club, Chattooga Club, Atlanta Mallet Club (pres.), Phi Gamma Delta. Methodist. Home: 3750 Peachtree Rd Apt 482 Atlanta GA 30319

RAPER, WILLIAM BURKETTE, retired college president; b. nr. Wilson, NC, Sept. 10, 1927; s. William Cecil and Beulah Maybelle (Davis) R.; m. Rose Mallard, Aug. 19, 1951; children: Olivia, Kristie, Burkette, Elizabeth, Stephen (dec.), Laura. AB, Duke U., 1947, MDiv, 1951; MS (Kellogg fellow), Fla. State U., 1962; LLD, Atlantic Christian Coll. (now Barton Coll.), 1960. Ordained to ministry Free Will Baptist Ch., 1946; pastor Hull Rd. Free Will Bapt. Ch., Snow Hill, NC, 1951-55; pres. Mt. Olive (N.C.) Coll., 1954-95, ret. pres. emeritus, 1995. Dir. Wachovia Bank and Trust Co., 1979-97; promotional dir. Free Will Bapt. State Conv. N.C., 1953-54; pres. council Ch.-Related Colls. N.C., 1966-67; mem. N.C. Edn. Assistance Authority, 1972-76; sec. Ind. Coll. Fund of N.C., 1976-78; Mem. N.C. Gov.'s Com. on Hwy. Traffic Safety, 1968; regional coordinator U.S. Office Edn. Program with Developing Instns., 1968-70; dir. Edn. Professions Devel. Act Grant for Strengthening Devel. in Pvt. Two-Year Colls., 1970-72; trustee N.C. Coll. Found., 1977-94; adv. com. Ind. Coll. Presidents, U. N.C. Pres. N.C. Found. Christian Ministries, 2005. Recipient Disting. Service award Mt. Olive Jr. C. of C., 1961; named N.C. Young Man of Year, 1961 Mem. Am. Assn. Community and Jr. Colls. (commn. on legislation 1963-66, cons. 1968-71, chmn. commn. on student personnel 1970-71), N.C. Assn. Ind. Colls. and Univs. (exec. com. 1967-70, 76-77, 83-85), N.C. Assn. Colls. and Univs. (pres. 1969-70), Masons. Democrat. Office: Mt Olive Coll Office of Pres Emeritus Mount Olive NC 28365 Home Phone: 919-658-3855; Office Phone: 919-658-5250. E-mail: wraper@moc.edu.

RAPHAEL, ALBERT ASH, JR., retired lawyer; b. NYC, June 4, 1925; s. Albert Ash and Clare (Schindler) R.; m. Dorothy Buck, Oct. 7, 1960; 1 child, Bruce William. AB, Yale U., 1947; LL.D., Harvard U., 1950. Bar: N.Y. 1950, Vt. 1972. Mem. firm Gallert, Hilborn & Raphael, NYC, 1950-60, Alter, Lefevre, Raphael, Lowry, and Gould, NYC, 1960-78; pvt.practice Waitsfield, Vt., 1972—86; pvt. practice, 1995—2002; ptnr. Raphael and Ware, Waitsfield, 1986-95; ret., 2002. Dir. various real estate cos. Mem. bd. zoning appeals, Waitsfield, 1974-83, selectman, 1976-82, chmn. bd. selectmen, 1981-82 Mem. Waitsfield Planning Commn., 1996-2003. Served with F.A., AUS, 1943-46. Mem. Vt. Bar Assn., Assn. of Bar of City of N.Y. Home: PO Box 113 Warren VT 05674-0113

RAPHAEL, CAROL, health care administrator; b. NYC, Apr. 21, 1942; BA, CUNY, 1962; MEd, Boston U., 1965; MPA, Harvard U., 1979. Dir. EDP planning and contract mgmt. Human Resources Adminstrn., NYC, 1979-82, asst. dep. adminstr. office home care svcs., 1982-84, dep. commr. med. assistance program, 1984-88, exec. dep. commr. income and med. assistance adminstrn., 1988-89; dir. ops. mgmt. Mount Sinai Med. Ctr. N.Y., 1989; pres., chief exec. officer Vis. Nurse Svc. N.Y., 1989—. Office Phone: 212-609-1510.

RAPHAEL, LOUISE ARAKELIAN, mathematician, educator; b. NYC, Oct. 24, 1937; d. Aristakes and Antionette (Sudbeaz) Arakelian; m. Robert Barnett Raphael, June 12, 1966 (div. 1985); children: Therese Denise, Marc Philippe. BS in Math., St. John's U., 1959; MS in Math., Cath. U., Washington, 1962; PhD in Math, Cath. U., 1967. Asst. prof. math. Howard U., Washington, 1966-70, vis. prof., 1981-82, assoc. prof., 1982-86, prof., 1986—; assoc. prof. Clark Coll., Atlanta, 1971-79, prof., 1979-82. Vis. assoc. prof. MIT, Cambridge, 1977-78, vis. prof., 1989-90; vis. mem. Courant Inst. Math. Scis., NYU, 1996-97; vis. scholar Cornell U., 2004. Contbr. over 40 rsch. articles to profl. jours. Program dir. NSF, Washington, 1986—88; acting adminstrv. officer Conf. Bd. Math. Scis., 1985—86. Grantee NSF, 1975-76, 79-81, 89-91, Army Rsch. Office, 1981-89, Air Force Sci. Rsch., 1981-82, 91-95, Nat. Security Agy., 1994-96. Mem.: Soc. Indsl. and Applied Math., Math. Assn. Am. (1st v.p. 1996—98, chmn. minorities in math. task force 1988), Am. Math. Soc. (coun. 2001—04, com. mem.), Sigma Xi. Democrat. Roman Catholic. Office: Howard U Dept Math Washington DC 20059-0001 Office Phone: 202-806-6836.

RAPHAEL, MOLLY (MARY E. RAPHAEL), library director; b. Columbus, Ohio; d. Paul and Dorothy Osborn Horst; m. Ted Raphael. B in Psychology, Oberlin Coll., Ohio, 1967; MLS, Simmons Coll., Boston, 1969. Various positions starting with asst. children's libr. DC Pub. Libr., 1970—98, dir., 1998—2003; dir. librs. Multnomah County Libr., Portland, Oreg., 2003—. Mem. Freedom to Read Found., Friends of Librs. USA. Recipient Alumni Achievement award, Simmons Coll. Grad. Sch. Libr. and Info. Sci., 2007. Mem.: ALA (mem. governing bd.), Urban Librs. Coun. Office: Multnomah County Libr 801 SW 10th Ave Portland OR 97205 Office Phone: 503-988-5403. E-mail: mollyr@multcolib.org.

RAPHAELSON, JOEL, retired advertising agency executive; b. NYC, Sept. 27, 1928; s. Samson and Dorothy (Wegman) R.; m. Mary Kathryn Hartigan, Aug. 20, 1960; children: Matthew, Katherine, Paul. BA, Harvard U., 1949. Copywriter Macy's, NYC, 1950-51, BBDO, NYC, 1953-58; with Ogilvy & Mather, Inc., NYC, 1958-94, sr. v.p., dir., 1966-75, mem. exec. com., 1970-75, exec. creative dir. Chgo., 1976—82; sr. v.p. internat. creative svcs. Ogilvy & Mather Worldwide, 1982-92, spl. assignments as editor, writer, speechwriter, cons., 1993-94, ret., 1995. Lectr. Am. Assn. Advt. Agys., others; cons. Art Inst. Chgo., 2007—. Author: (with Kenneth Roman) How To Write Better, 1978, Writing That Works, 1981, rev. expanded edit., 1992, 00; editor: The Unpublished David Ogilvy, 1986, Viewpoint (co. jour.), 1983-94; contbr. Harvard Bus. Rev., Advertising Age, other bus. publs. Cons. Lyric Opera Chgo., 1983-2005, Exec. Svc. Corps, Chgo.; dir. Santa for the Very Poor, 1988— Home: 20 E Cedar St Apt 8A Chicago IL 60611-5115 Home Phone: 312-751-0987. Personal E-mail: joelr28@aol.com.

RAPINI, RONALD PETER, dermatology educator; b. Akron, Ohio, Feb. 15, 1954; s. Vincent Thomas and Joann Irene (Tufexis) R.; m. Mary Jo Beigel, June 16, 1979; children: Brianna Marie, Sarina Elizabeth. BS in Biology, U. Akron, 1975; MD, Ohio State U., 1978. Diplomate Am. Bd. Dermatology (bd. dirs. 1996-2004, pres. 2004), Am. Bd. Dermatopathology. Assoc. prof. U. Tex. Med. Sch., Houston, 1983-93; prof. and chair dermatology dept. Tex. Tech. U., Lubbock, 1994—2002; prof., chair dept. dermatology U. Tex. Med. Sch., Houston, 2002—, MD Anderson Cancer Ctr., Houston, 2002—. Author (with K.G. Gross and H.K. Steinman): Mohs Surgery, 1999; author: (with J. Bolognia and J. Jorizzo) Dermatology, 2003; author: Practical Dermatopathology, 2005, of over 150 other publications. Fellow Am. Acad. Dermatology, Am. Soc. Dermatol. Surgery (bd. dir. 1995-98), Soc. Investigative Dermatology; mem. AMA, Am. Soc. Dermatopathology (pres. 1998-99), Am. Soc. Mohs Surgery (pres. 2003), Internat. Soc. Dermatopathology, Tex. Dermatol. Soc. (pres. 2006—). Avocations: tennis, entomology, piano. Office: U TEx Med Sch 6655 Travis St 980 Houston TX 77030-0001 Office Phone: 713-745-1113.

RAPINO, MICHAEL, music company executive; b. Can. Grad. in Bus., Lakehead U., Thunder Bay, Ont. Dir. entertainment and sports Labatt's Breweries Can., head mktg. brands; ptnr. Core Audience Entertainment (acquired by SFX in 1999), Canada; head Internat. Music divsn. Clear Channel Entertainment (formerly SFX), London; CEO, pres. Global Music Clear Channel Music Group; CEO Live Nation, 2005—. Office: Live Nation 9348 Civic Center Dr Beverly Hills CA 90210 Office Phone: 310-867-7000. *

RAPOPORT, BERNARD ROBERT, lawyer; b. NYC, Jan. 18, 1919; s. Max and Rose (Gerard) R.; m. Robyrta Wechter, May 31, 1959; 1 son: Michael. AB, Cornell U., 1939, JD, 1941. Bar: NY 1941, Fed. Ct. (so. dist.) 1946. Assoc. firm Proskauer, Rose, Goetz, Mendelsohn, NYC, 1941-50; gen. counsel M. Lowenstein Corp., NYC, 1950-86; dir., treas., sec. Leon Lowenstein Found. Capt. Signal Corps, U.S. Army, 1942-45. Mem. ABA, Assn. of Bar of City of N.Y. Address: 910 5th Ave New York NY 10021-4155

RAPOPORT, JUDITH, psychiatrist; b. NYC, July 12, 1933; d. Louis and Minna (Enteen) Livant; m. Stanley Rapoport, June 25, 1961; children: Stuart, Erik. BA, Swarthmore Coll., 1955; MD, Harvard U., 1959. Lic. psychiatrist. Cons., child psychiatrist NIMH/St. Elizabeth's Hosp., Washington, 1969—72; clin. asst. prof Georgetown U. Med. Sch., Washington, 1972—82, clin. assoc. prof., 1982—85, clin. prof. psychiat., 1985—; med. officer biol. psychiatry br. NIMH, Bethesda, Md., 1979—82, chief, child psychiatry lab. of clin. scis., 1982—84, chief, child psychiatry div. intramural rsch. programs, 1984—; prof. psychiatry George Washington U. Sch. Med., Washington, 1979—; prof. pediat. Georgetown U., Washington, 1985—. Cons. in field. Author: (non-fiction) The Boy Who Couldn't Stop Washing, 1989 (best seller literary guild selection, 1989), Childhood Obsessive Compulsive Disorder, 1989. Recipient Scolnick award, MIT, 2005. Fellow: Am. Acad. Arts & Sci., Am. Acad. Child Psychiatry, Am. Psychiat. Assn.; mem.: Inst. Medicine, D.C. Psychiat. Assn. Home: 3010 44th Pl NW Washington DC 20016-3557 Office: NIMH Rm 3N202 10 Center Dr Bldg 10 Bethesda MD 20892-0001 Office Phone: 301-496-6081. Business E-Mail: rapoport@helix.nih.gov.

RAPOPORT, MILES S., former state official; m. Sandra Luciano; children: Jeff, Ross. BA in Polit. sci., N.Y. U., 1971. Exec. dir. Conn. Citizen Action Group, 1979-84; mem. Conn. Ho. of Reps., asst. majority leader, 1987-92, house chmn. govt. adminstrn. and elections com., mem. fin., revenue and bonding com.; sec. of state State of Conn., 1994-98; exec. dir. Democracy Works, Hartford, Conn., 1999—2001. Office: President Demos 5th Fl 220 Fifth Ave New York NY 10001

RAPOPORT, NANCY B., law educator; m. Jeffrey D. Van Niel, Oct. 13, 1996. BA in Legal Studies, Psychology with hon., summa cum laude, Rice U., 1982; JD, Stanford Law Sch., 1985. Bar: Calif. 1987, Ohio 1993, Nebr. 1999, Calif. Supreme Ct. 1987, Ohio Supreme Ct. 1993, Nebr. Supreme Ct. 1999, US Dist. Ct. Hawaii 1988, US Dist. Ct. (no., ea., ctrl., and so. dists.) Calif. 1987, US Dist. Ct. (no. dist.) Tex. 2003, US Ct. Appeals (9th cir.) 1987, US Supreme Ct. 2000. Jud. clk. Hon. Joseph T. Sneed, U.S. Ct. Appeals (9th cir.), San Francisco, 1985—86; assoc. bus.dept. of bankruptcy and workouts group Morrison & Foerster, San Francisco, 1986—91; asst. prof. Ohio State U. Coll. Law, Columbus, 1991—95, tenured assoc. prof., 1995—98, assoc. dean student affairs, 1996—98, prof., 1998; dean, prof. law U. Nebr. Coll. Law, Lincoln, 1998—2000; dean U. Houston Law Ctr., 2000—06, prof. law, 2000—06; with Gordon & Silver Ltd., 2006—07; prof. law. William S. Boyd Sch. Law, U. Nev., Las Vegas, 2007—. Invited spkr., panelist, and presenter in field. Co-editor (with Bala G. Dharan): Enron: Corporate Fiascos and Their Implications, 2004. Bd. trustees Law Sch. Admissions Coun., 2001—04; bd. dir. ADL Southwest Regional Bd., 2001—, Houston Area Women's Ctr., 2003—; bd. mem. Mayor's Adv. Bd. of World Energy Cities Partnership, 2001—04, Houston Disaster Relief Adv. Bd., 2001—04, Houston Chpt. Tex. Gen. Counsel Forum, 2001—05, Anti-Defamation League Southwest Regional Bd., 2001—06, Advisory Coun., WWW United Inc., 2002—06, Tex. Environ. Health Inst., 2002—04, Houston Hillel, 2002—07, Vinson & Elkins Women's Initiative Adv. Bd., 2003—, Houston Area Women's Ctr., 2003—06, Tex. Ctr. for Legal Ethics, 2004—06, Tex. Supreme Ct. Hist. Soc. Adv. Bd., 2004—06, Houston World Affairs Coun., 2002—05, NALP Found. for Law Career Rsch. and Edn., 2005—, Assn. Rice Alumni Bd., 2006—, Am. Bd. Cert., 2007—. Named Outstanding Prof. of Yr., Ohio State U. Coll. Law., 1997, fellow, Am. Bankruptcy Law Jour., 1998; recipient Rice U. Dist. Alumna award. Fellow: Am. Coll. Bankruptcy, Am. Bar Found., Houston Bar Found. (selection com. 2000—, Best Article award); mem.: ABA (task force atty. discipline 2005—, commn. legal debt and forgiveness), Assn. Am. Law Sch.'s Profl. Develop. Com., Ohio State Bar Assn. (legal edn. com. 1997—98), Am. Bankruptcy Inst. (law sch. com. 1994—), Bar Assn. San Francisco, Nat. Assn. Coll. and U. Attys., Nebr. State Bar Assn. (Named Legal Pioneer for Women in Law 1999), Houston Bar Assn., Am. Law Inst. Democrat. Jewish. Avocations: dance, photography, music, movies, history. Office: Univ Nev Las Vegas William Boyd Sch Law Box 451003 4505 S Maryland Pkwy Las Vegas NV 89154-1003 Business E-Mail: nrapoport@money-law.org.

RAPOPORT, RONALD JON, journalist; b. Detroit, Aug. 14, 1940; s. Daniel B. and Shirley G.; m. Joan Zucker, Sept. 2, 1968; children—Rebecca, Julie. BA, Stanford U., 1962; MS, Columbia U., 1963. Reporter Mpls. Star, 1963-65; assoc. editor Sport mag., 1965-66; sports reporter AP, NYC, San Francisco, 1966-70, Los Angeles Times, 1970-77; sports columnist Chgo. Sun-Times, 1977-88, Los Angeles Daily News, 1988-95; sports commentator Weekend Edit. Nat. Pub. Radio, 1986—; dep. sports editor Chgo. Sun-Times, 1996-98, sports columnist, 1998—2006. Author: (with Chip Oliver) High for the Game, 1971; (with Stan Love) Love in the NBA, 1975, (with Jim McGregor) Called for Travelling, 1979; editor: A Kind of Grace: A Treasury of Sportswriting by Women, 1994; (with Betty Garrett) Betty Garrett and Other Songs, 1998, See How She Runs: Marion Jones and the Making of a Champion, 2000, The Immortal Bobby: Bobby Jones and the Golden Age of Golf, 2005, (with Eddie Einhorn) How March Became Madness: How the NCAA Tournament Became the Greatest Sporting Event in America, 2006. Served with U.S. Army Res., 1963. Personal E-mail: rjrapoport@ameritech.net.

RAPOPORT, TOM ABRAHAM, cell biology professor; b. Cin., June 17, 1947; s. Samuel M. and Ingeborg A. R.; m. Iris Hirsch; children: Daniel, Tobias, Esther. PhD, Humboldt Univ., 1972; habilitation, Humboldt Univ., Berlin, 1977; MA, Harvard Univ., 1995. Rsch. assoc. Acad. Sci., Berlin,

1972-85, prof., 1985-90, Max-Delbrueck Ctr., Berlin, 1991-94, Harvard Medical Sch., Boston, 1995—; investigator Howard Hughes Med. Inst., 1997—. Editorial bd. Jour. of Cell Biology, The New Biologist, Jour. Molecular Recognition, European Jour. Biochemistry, FEBS Letters. Recipient Johannes-Mueller award Soc. Exptl. Medicine, 1972, Rudolf-Virchow award, 1978. Fellow Am. Acad. Arts and Sciences; mem. German Biochemical Soc., Acad. Scis., Academea European, EMBO, NAS. Office: Harvard Medical Sch Dept Cell Biology 240 Longwood Ave Boston MA 02115-5701

RAPP, ADAM, writer, playwright; b. Chgo. Grad., Clarke Coll., Dubuque, Iowa. Artist-in-residence Vassar Coll., Dartmouth Coll.; playwright-in-residence The Juilliard Sch.; resident playwright Edge Theater Co., NYC. Author: (plays) Gompers, Ghosts in the Cottonwoods, 1996, Dreams of the Salthorse, Trueblinka, 1997, Faster, Finer Noble Gases, 2001, Stone Cold Dead Serious, Blackbird, Animals and Plants, 2001, Nocturne, 2001, Red Light Winter, 2005 (OBIE award spl. citation, Village Voice, 2006), Cagelove, 2006, Essential Self-Defense, 2007, (young adult novels) Missing the Piano, 1994, The Buffalo Tree, The Copper Elephant, 1999, Little Chicago, 2002, 33 Snowfish, 2003, Under the Wolf, Under the Dog, 2004, (adult novels) The Year of Endless Sorrows, 2005; writer & dir. (films) Winter Passing, 2005. Recipient Princess Grace award for playwrighting, 1999, Roger L. Stevens award, Kennedy Ctr. Fund for New Am. Plays, 2000, Helen Merrill award for emerging playwrights, 2001, Elliot Norton award, Le Compte de Nuoy awards, Lincoln Ctr.; Herbert & Patricia Brodkin Scholarship, 1997, Camargo Found. fellowship, Cassis, France. Office: Resident Playwright Edge Theater Co 880 Third Ave 16th Floor New York NY 10022 Office Phone: 212-350-7223. Office Fax: 212-350-7295. *

RAPP, GEORGE ROBERT (RIP RAPP), geology and archeology educator; b. Toledo, Sept. 19, 1930; s. George Robert and Gladys Mae (Warner) R.; m. Jeannette Messner, June 15, 1956; children: Kathryn, Karen. BA, U. Minn., 1952; PhD, Pa. State U., 1960. Asst. then assoc. prof. S.D. Sch. Mines, Rapid City, 1957-65; assoc. prof. U. Minn., Mpls., 1965-75, prof. geology and archeology Duluth, 1975-95, dean Coll. Letters and Sci., 1975-84, dean Coll. Sci. and Engring., 1984-89, dir. Archeometry Lab., 1975—2004, Regents' prof. geoarchaeology, 1995—2003, emeritus, 2003—. Prof. Ctr. for Ancient Studies, U. Minn., Mpls., 1970-93, prof. interdisciplinary archaeol. studies, 1993—; cons. USIA, Westinghouse Corp., Exxon Corp., Ford Found. Author, editor: Excavations at Nichoria, 1978, Troy: Archeological Geology, 1982, Archeological Geology, 1985, Excavations at Tel Michal, 1989, Encyclopedia of Minerals, 1989, Phytolith Systematics, 1992, Geoarchaeology, 1998, Artifact Copper Sources, 2000, Archaeomineralogy, 2002; mem. editl. bd. Jour. Field Archeology, 1976-85, Jour. Archeol. Sci., 1977-79, Geoarcheology Jour., 1984-92, Am. Jour. Archeology, 1985-92. NSF postdoctoral fellow, 1963-64, Fulbright-Hayes sr. rsch. fellow, 1972-73. Fellow AAAS (chmn. sect. E, 1987-88, nat. coun. 1992-95), Geol. Soc. Am. (Archeol. Geology award 1983), Mineral. Soc. Am.; mem. Nat. Assn. Geology Tchrs. (pres. 1986-89), Soc. for Archeol. Sci. (pres. 1983-84), Assn. Field Archeology (pres. 1979-81), Archaeol. Inst. Am. (Pomerance medal 1988), Sigma Xi (bd. dirs. 1990-98). Avocations: classical music, exercise, nutrition. Office: U Minn-Duluth Dept Geol Scis Duluth MN 55812 Business E-Mail: grapp@d.umn.edu.

RAPP, ROBERT ANTHONY, metallurgical engineering educator; s. Frank J. and Goldie M. (Royer) R.; m. Heidi B. Sartorius, June 3, 1960; children: Kathleen Rapp Raynaud, Thomas, Stephen, Stephanie Rapp Surface. BSMetE, Purdue U., 1956; MSMetE, Carnegie Inst. Tech., 1959, PhDMetE, 1960; D (hon.), Inst. Polytech., Toulouse, France, 1995. Asst. prof. metall. engring. Ohio State U., Columbus, 1963—66, 1966—69, prof., 1969—, M.G. Fontana prof., 1988—95, prof., 1989—95, disting. univ. prof. emeritus, 1995—. Vis. prof. Ecole Nat. Superior d'Electrochimie, Grenoble, France, 1972-73, U. Paris-Sud, Orsay, 1985-86, Ecole Nat. Superior de Chimie, Toulouse, France, 1985-86, U. New South Wales, Australia, 1987; Acta/Scripta Metallurgica lectr., 1991; rsch. metallurgist WPAFB, Ohio, 1960-63. Editor: Techniques of Metals Research, vol. IV, 1982, High Temperature Corrosion, 1984; translator Metallic Corrosion (Kaesche), 1986; bd. rev. jour. Oxid. Metals; contbr. 265 publs. and numerous articles to profl. jours. First lt. USAF, 1960—63, Wright-Patterson AFB. Decorated chevalier des Palmes Academiques; recipient Disting. Engring. Alumnus award Purdue U., 1988, B.F. Goodrich Collegiate Inventor's award, 1991, 92, Ulrick Evans award Brit. Inst. Corrosion, 1992; Guggenheim fellow, 1972; Fulbright scholar Max Planck Inst. Phys. Chemistry, 1959-60, Linford award for Disting. Tchg.,The Electrochem. Soc., 1998. Fellow: Nat. Assn. Corrosion Engrs. (W.R. Whitney award 1986), Electrochem. Soc. (HTM Divsn. Outstanding Achievement award 1992, Linford Tchr. award 1998, Olin Palladium award 2005), Mining Metals and Materials Soc. (R.F. Mehl medal 2000, Educator award 2003), Am. Soc. Metals Internat. (Zay Jeffries lectr. 2006, B. Stoughton award 1968, Howe gold medal 1974, Gold medal 2000); mem.: Nat. Acad. Engring., French Soc. Metals and Materials (hon.). Lutheran. Achievements include about twenty patents. Avocations: gardening, golf, travel. Home: 1379 Southport Dr Columbus OH 43235-7649 Office Phone: 614-292-6178. E-mail: rrapp001@columbus.rr.com, rapp.4@osu.edu.

RAPP, ROBERT DAVID, lawyer; b. NYC, Mar. 19, 1950; s. Melville Benjamin and Rachel (Marx) R. BA in Econs., U. Tenn., 1973; JD, Antioch U., 1982. Bar: Tex. 1982, US Dist. Ct. (so. dist.) Tex. 1983, US Ct. Appeals (5th cir.) 1983, US Supreme Ct. 1985. Law clk. to presiding judge US Dist. Ct. (so. dist.) Tex., Houston, 1982-83; ptnr., dir., shareholder Mandell & Wright, P.C., Houston, 1983—97; pvt. practice Houston, 1997—. Instr. CLE Bates Coll. Law, U. Houston, 1986-87. Contbr. articles to law revs., profl. jours. and treatises. Mem. Fed. Bar Assn. (bd. dirs. Houston chpt. 1986-87, lectr. 1987), Houston Bar Assn. Home: 5110 San Felipe St Unit 152 W Houston TX 77056-3610 Office: 3 Riverway Ste 150 Houston TX 77056-1982 Office Phone: 713-520-8250. Personal E-mail: robertrapp@sbcglobal.net.

RAPP, ROBERT NEIL, lawyer; b. Erie, Pa., Sept. 10, 1947; m. Sally K. Meder; 1 child: Jeffrey David. BA, Case Western Res. U., 1969, JD, 1972; MBA, Cleve. State U., 1989. Bar: Ohio 1972, U.S. dist. Ct. (no. dist.) Ohio 1973, U.S. Ct. Appeals (6th crct.) 1981, U.S. Supreme Ct. 1980. Assoc. Metzenbaum, Gaines & Stern, Co., L.P.A., Cleve., 1972-75; ptnr. Calfee, Halter & Griswold, Cleve., 1975—. Adj. prof. law Case Western Res. U., 1975—78, 1994—98, Cleve. Marshall Coll. Law, Cleve. State U., 1976—82; practitioner-in-residence Cornell U. Law Sch., 1993; mem. legal adv. bd. Nat. Assn. Securities Dealers, 1992—96; mem. market ops. rev. com. Nasdaq Stock Market, 1996—; arbitrator, practitioner mediator Nat. Futures Assn. Author: Blue Sky Regulation, 2d edit., 2003; contbr. numerous articles to law jours. Mem. ABA (sect. bus. law: mem. com. fed. regulation of securities, subcom. broker-dealer regulation, sect. litigation: mem. com. securities litigation), Am. Arbitration Assn. (securities arbitrator, mem. comml. adv. coun. Cleve. region), Ohio State Bar Assn. (elected mem. coun. dels. 1976-82, corp. law com. 1980—), Cleve. Bar Assn. (chmn. young lawyers sect. 1976-77), assoc. mem. cert. grievance com., sect. securities law: exec. coun. 1980-85, chmn. govt. liaison com. 1980-81). Office: Calfee Halter & Griswold LLP 1400 McDonald Investment Ct Cleveland OH 44114-2688

RAPP, STEPHEN JOHN, international prosecutor; b. Waterloo, Iowa, Jan. 26, 1949; s. Spurgeon John and Beverly (Leckington) R.; m. Donna J.E. Maier, 1981; children: Alexander, Stephanie. AB cum laude, Harvard U., 1971; JD with honors, Drake U., 1973. Bar: Iowa 1974, US Dist. Ct. (no. and so. dists.) Iowa 1978, US Ct. Appeals (8th cir.) 1979, US Supreme Ct. 1979. Rsch. asst. Office of US Senator Birch Bayh, Ind., 1970; community program asst. HUD, Chgo., 1971; mem. Iowa Ho. Reps., 1972-74, 79-83, Coun. to Majority Caucus, Iowa Ho. Reps., 1975; staff dir., counsel subcom. on juvenile delinquency US Senate, Washington, 1977-78; ptnr. Rapp & Gilliam, Waterloo, 1979-83; pvt. practice Waterloo, 1983-93; U.S. atty. US Dist. Ct. (no. dist.) Iowa, 1993—2001; sr. prosecuting atty. UN Internat. Crime Tribunal Rwanda, 2001—05, chief prosecutions, 2005—07; prosecutor Spl. Ct. for Sierra Leone, 2007—. Del., mem. com. Dem. Nat. Conv., 1976, 80, 84, 88, 92; mem. Dem. Nat. Adv. Com. on Econ., 1982-84, chmn. Black Hawk Dem. Com., 1986-91; mem. Iowa Dem. Com., 1990-93, chair 2d C.D. Dem. Com., 1991-93. Mem. ABA, Iowa Bar Assn., Order of Coif. Methodist. Home: 219 Highland Blvd Waterloo IA 50703-4229 Office: SC52 Jomo Kenyatta Rd Freetown Sierra Leone Office Phone: 212-963-9915 ext. 1787380. E-mail: rapp@un.org.

RAPP, STEVEN M., lawyer, consumer products company executive; BA in English, SUNY, Buffalo, 1975; JD, St. John's U. Sch. Law. Atty. Willkie, Farr & Gallagher; corp. lawyer PepsiCo. Inc., 1986, divsn. counsel, 1994; v.p., dep. gen. counsel, asst. sec. Pepsi Bottling Group, Inc., Somers, NY, 1999—2004, sr. v.p., gen. counsel, sec., 2005—. Office: Pepsi Bottling Grp Inc 1 Pepsi Way Somers NY 10589-2201 Office Phone: 914-767-6000. *

RAPPAPORT, CHARLES OWEN, lawyer; b. NYC, May 15, 1950; s. Edward and Edith (Novick) R.; m. Valerie B. Ackerman, Oct. 11, 1987; children: Emily Randle, Sarah Elisabeth. BA, Columbia U., 1970; JD, NYU, 1975. Bar: N.Y. 1976. Assoc. Simpson, Thacher & Bartlett LLP, NYC, 1975—82, ptnr., 1982. Home: 26 N Moore St Apt 4W New York NY 10013-2436 Office: Simpson Thacher & Bartlett LLP 425 Lexington Ave 14th Fl New York NY 10017-3954 E-mail: corappaport@stblaw.com.

RAPPAPORT, IRVING S., entrepreneur, lawyer, consultant; s. Melvin Rappaport and Minette Grober; m. Lesley Radoff; children: Steven, Matthew, Diana Robinson, David. BSEE, Wash. U., St. Louis, 1962; JD (hons.), George Wash. U. Law Sch., Washington, DC, 1966; MBA, Boston Univ. Grad. Sch. Mgmt., 1969. Bar: Mo. State Bar 1966, Ct. Appeals (fed. cir.) 1966, US Supreme Ct. 2005, registered: US Patent & Trademark Office (patent atty.) 1966, Can. Intellectual Property Office (patent agent) 1980. Patent examiner US Patent & Trademark Office, Washington, 1962—63; 1st lt. US Army, Ft. Meade, Md., 1963—65; patent agt. RCA, Washington, 1965—66, Philpitt, Steininger & Priddy, Washington, 1965; patent and trademark atty. Raytheon Co., Lexington, Mass., 1966—70, Schiller & Pandiscio, Waltham, Mass., 1970—71; asst. gen. counsel for patents, asst. sec. Medtronic, Inc., Mpls., 1971—77; corp. sec., gen. counsel Renal Sys., Inc., Mpls., 1977—78; chief patent counsel Data Gen. Corp., Westboro, Mass., 1978—82; assoc. gen. counsel for intellectual property and licensing Bally Mfg., Chgo., 1982—84, Apple Computer, Inc., Cupertino, Calif., 1984—90; intellectual property cons. Intel Corp., Santa Clara, Calif., 1990—91; v.p., assoc. gen. counsel for intellectual property and licensing Nat. Semiconductor Corp., Santa Clara, 1991—93; founder, dir. and v.p. intellectual property Aurigin Sys., Inc., Cupertino, 1993—2002; v.p. intellectual property licensing bus. Symyx Technologies, Inc., Sunnyvale, Calif., 2002—03; intellectual property lawyer and cons. Irving S. Rappaport, Palo Alto, Calif., 2003—; co-founder, mng. dir. IP Checkups, LLC, Berkeley, Calif., 2004—. Sec. Minn. Patent & Trademark Law Assoc., Mpls., 1977—78; mem. bd. dirs. Aurigin Sys., Inc., Cupertino, Calif., 1993—2002; bd. of advisors Intellectual Property Innovations, Charlotte, NC, 2004—, Altitude Capital Ptnrs., NYC, 2006—; mng. dir. Telemaze LLC, Los Altos, Calif., 2005—; strategic advisors bd. Patent-Cafe.com, Inc., Yuba City, Calif., 2006—. Author over 60 articles and presentations on intellectual property matters. First lt. Army Sec. Agy. US Army, 1963—65. Recipient Svc. to U.S. Gov't. on Trade Related IP Matters, 3 U.S. Secretaries of Commerce & 3 U.S. Trade Rep., 1987—94. Mem.: Ill. State Bar, Minn. State Bar, Mass. State Bar, Minn. Patent & Trademark Law Assn. (sec. 1977—78), Boston Patent Law Assn., Am. Intellectual Property Law Assn., Licensing Execs. Soc., ABA. Achievements include having 18 US patents. Avocations: jogging, bicycling, tennis, squash. Home Phone: 650-321-7024; Office Phone: 650-321-7024 publish. Business E-Mail: isport1@yahoo.com.

RAPPAPORT, JAMES WYANT, lawyer, real estate developer; b. Boston, May 9, 1956; s. Jerome Lyle and Nancy (Vahey) R.; m. Cecelia Catherine Ewald; children: James, Jessica, Joshua. BS in Econs., Wharton, U. Pa., 1977; JD, Boston U., 1980. Assoc. Law Offices of Alan Jacobs, Boston, 1980-81; atty. Rappaport and Rakov, Boston, 1981-93; ptnr. Rappaport, Aserkoff & Rappaport, Boston, 1994-2000, New Boston Fund Inc, 2000—. Gen. ptnr. Charles River Park, Boston, 1982-2001; prin. New Boston Funds, 1992—; pres. Charles River Properties, Ltd., 1986-93, Charles River Hawaii Devel. Corp., 1987-90; chmn. Park Transit Displays, 1992-2000, Silent Sys., Inc., 1994-98; dir. Jillians Holding Co., 1998—. Class chmn. Roxbury Latin Sch., 1978-95; vice chmn. Rep. 3d ward, Boston, 1978-83, chmn., 1988-89; mem. Young Eagle sect. Rep. Nat. Com., Boston, 1985-88, Rep. state fin. com., Boston, 1985—, Concord (Mass.) Rep. Town Com., 1985-87, 1989—; bd. dirs. Mass. Taxpayers Com., Needham, Mass., 1984-91, chmn., 1988-91; gen. ptnr. Charles River Hawaii L.P., Kauai, 1986-89; Rep. candidate U.S. Senate, 1990; chmn. Mass. Rep. Party, 1992-97; mem. Rep. Nat. Com., 1992-97; bd. dirs. Jewish Vocat. Svcs., Jewish Community Rels. Coun., Dana Farber Cancer Inst., 1998—, Children's Hosp., 2000—; mem. fin. com. Rep. Nat. Com., 1992-2000. Mem. ABA, Mass. Bar Assn., Vt. Bar Assn., Boston Bar Assn., Greater Boston Real Estate Bd., King David Soc. (chmn. 1999—). Jewish. Avocations: hiking, golf. E-mail: jwrappinc@aol.com.

RAPPAPORT, LAWRENCE, plant physiology and horticulture educator; b. NYC, May 28, 1928; s. Aaron and Elsie R.; m. Norma, Nov. 21, 1953; children: Meryl, Debra Kramer, Craig. BS in Horticulture, U. Idaho, 1950; MS in Horticulture, Mich. State Coll., 1951; PhD in Horticulture, Mich. State U., 1956. Lectr. U. Calif., Davis, 1956-67, jr. olericulturist, dept. vegetable crops, 1956-58, asst. olericulturist, 1958-63, assoc. olericulturist, 1963-67, prof., 1968—, prof. emeritus, 1991—, dir. plant growth lab., 1975-78, chairperson dept. vegetable crops, 1978-84. Vis. scientist Calif. Inst. Tech., 1958; co-dir. Horticulture Subproject, Calif./Egypt project, 1978-82. Contbr. articles to profl. jours. 1st pres. Davis Human Rels. Coun., 1964-66; v.p. Jewish Fedn. Sacramento, 1969; pres. Jewish Fellowship, Davis, 1985-89; founder, 1st dir. Hillel Counselership at Davis, 1965-76. Decorated Bronze star; Guggenheim Found. fellow, 1963, Fulbright fellow, 1964, USPHS Spl. fellow, 1970, Am. Soc. Horticulture Sci. fellow, 1987, Sir Frederick McMaster fellow, 1991. Achievements include discovery of evidence for gibberellin-binding protein in plants; evidence for the signal hypothesis operating in plants, positive evidence for phytochrome-mediated gibberellin metabolism and stem growth; isolation of somaclonal variants of celery bearing stable resistance to Fusarium oxysporum f. sp. apii. Home: 637 Elmwood Dr Davis CA 95616-3514 Office: Dept Plant Environ Sci One Shields Ave Davis CA 95616 Business E-Mail: lrappaport@ucdavis.edu.

RAPPAPORT, LINDA ELLEN, lawyer; b. Freeport, NY, Jan. 12, 1952; d. William Jay and Marcia Ann (Wiland) Rappaport; m. Leonard Chazen, June 1, 1980; 1 child, Matthew Ross Chazen. BA, Wesleyan U., Middletown, Conn., 1974; JD, NYU, 1977. Bar: N.Y. 1977. Law clk. Chief Judge James S. Holden U.S. Dist. Ct. Vt., Rutland, 1978; assoc. Shearman & Sterling, NYC, 1979—85, ptnr., 1986—, elected mem. policy com., 1995—2005, mem. exec. group, 2005—. Adv.bd. dirs. NYC Ballet, 2006—; bd. dirs. NY Women's Found., NYC, 1995—2001, AIESEC Internat., NYC, 1994—2000; bd. govs. Mannes Coll. Music, 2004—; bd. dirs. Legal Aid Soc. N.Y., 2005—, exec. com., 2005—. Fellow: Am. Coll. Employee Benefits Coun.; mem.: Bar Assn. City of N.Y. (employee benefits com. 1986—, employment law com. 1986—). Office: Shearman & Sterling 599 Lexington Ave Fl 13 New York NY 10022-6069 E-mail: lrappaport@shearman.com.

RAPPAPORT, MARGARET MARY WILLIAMS EWING, psychologist, physician, writer, pilot, consultant; b. Nov. 16, 1947; d. Leo J. and Marie L. (Rischle) Williams; m. Herbert Rappaport (div.); children: Amanda, Alexander. BA, U. Buffalo; MA, SUNY; PhD, MD, U. Colo. Zone Perfect cert. instr. Prof., rschr. U. Dar es Salaam, Tanzania; with Rappaport Assocs., Phila., 1974-94; exec. dir. Inst. for Parent/Child Svcs., Phila., 1978-94; pres., CEO Diabetes Edn. Ctr. Cape Cod, 2002—03. Mem. adj. faculty Temple U., Phila., 1974—94; aviation safety counselor FAA; cons., spkr. in field.; pres. Reach New Heights, Inc., 1994—2005; founder Fit to Fly. Mem. AAUP, Nat. Profl. Spkrs. Assn., Cosmopolitan Club, Orleans Yacht Club. Home: PO Box 1845 Orleans MA 02653-1845 Office Phone: 508-255-9570. Personal E-mail: rappaportmm@yahoo.com.

RAPPAPORT, MARTIN PAUL, internist, nephrologist, educator; b. Bronx, NY, Apr. 25, 1935; s. Joseph and Anne (Kramer) R.; m. Bethany Ann Mitchell; children: Karen, Steven; stepchildren: Aaron Cole, Kevin Cole. BS, Tulane U., 1957, MD, 1960. Diplomate Am. Bd. Internal Medicine, Nat. Bd. Med. Examiners. Intern Charity Hosp. of La., New Orleans, 1960-61, resident in internal medicine, 1961-64; pvt. practice internal medicine and nephrology, Seabrook, Tex., 1968-72, Webster, Tex., 1972-98; internist Univ. Med. Group, Houston, 1998; mem. courtesy staff Mainland Ctr. Hosp. (formerly Galveston County Meml. Hosp.), Texas City, 1968-96, Bapt. Meml. System, 1969-72, 88-98; mem. staff Clear Lake Regional Med. Ctr., 1972-98; cons. staff St. Mary's Hosp., 1973-79; cons. nephrology St. John's Hosp., Nassau Bay, Tex.; fellow in nephrology Northwestern U. Med. Sch., Chgo., 1967—68; clin. asst. prof. in medicine and nephrology U. Tex., Galveston, 1969—2006; part-time physician dept. family medicine outpatient clinics U. Tex. Med. Br., Galveston, 2000; locum tenens, 2000—06; ret., 2006. Lectr. emergency med. technician cours e, 1974-76; adviser on respiratory therapy program Alvin (Tex.) Jr. Coll., 1976-82; cons. nephrology USPHS, 1979-80. Served to capt. M.C. U.S. Army, 1961-67. Fellow ACP, Am. Coll. Chest Physicians; mem. Internat., Am. Socs. Nephrology, So. Med. Assn., Tex. Med. Assn., Tex. Soc. Internal Medicine (bd. govs. 1994-96), Am. Soc. Artificial Internal Organs, Tex. Acad. Internal Medicine, Harris County Med. Soc., Am. Geriatrics Soc., Bay Area Heart Assn. (bd. govs. 1969-75), Clear Lake C. of C., Conroe Rotary Club, Rotary, Phi Delta Epsilon, Alpha Epsilon Pi, Tulane Alumni Assn. Home: 15913 Malibu W Willis TX 77318-6784 Office Phone: 936-890-0673. Personal E-mail: mrappapo@msn.com.

RAPPAPORT, NORMAN HARVEY, plastic surgeon; b. Phila., Apr. 23, 1947; s. Herbert and Ruth Rappaport; m. Deborah Ann Finn, Oct. 2, 1982; children: Jonathan David, Betsy, William. BA, LaSalle Coll., 1969; DDS, Temple U., 1972; MD, Hahnemann Med. Coll., 1975. Diplomate Am. Bd. Plastic Surgery. Resident in gen. surgery Abington (Pa.) Meml. Hosp., 1975-78; fellow in hand surgery U. Pa., Phila., 1978; resident in plastic surgery Baylor Coll. Medicine, Houston, 1978-80; clin. assoc. prof. surgery Baylor Coll. Surgery, Houston, 1994—. Contbr. articles to profl. jours. Fellow: ACS; mem.: AMA, Houston Surg. Soc. (pres. 2001), Tex. Soc. Plastic Surgeons, Tex. Med. Assn., N.Am. Burn Soc., Houston Soc. Plastic Surgeons (pres. 2002), Harris County Med. Soc., Am. Assn. Hand Surgeons, Am. Assn. Plastic Surgeons, Am. Soc. for Aesthetic Plastic Surgery, Am. Soc. Plastic Surgeons (bd. dirs. 1998—2000), Plastic Surgery Ednl. Found. (bd. dirs. 1994—2000), Am. Soc. Maxillofacial Surgeons (pres. 2000), Omicron Kappa Upsilon. Office: 6560 Fannin St Ste 1812 Houston TX 77030-2775 Office Phone: 713-790-4500. E-mail: nhr@hcps.cc.

RAPPAPORT, RICHARD J., lawyer; b. Chgo., Aug. 13, 1943; m. Roberta Rappaport; children: Michael, Barbara. BS, Loyola U., 1965, JD cum laude, 1967. Bar: Ill. 1967, Fla. 1993, US Dist. Ct. No. Dist. Ill. 1967, US Ct. Appeals 7th Cir. 1978, 10th Cir. 1978, 6th Cir. 1986, 4th Cir. 1988, 11th Cir. 1997, 8th Cir. 2000, 2d Cir. 2006, US Tax Ct. 1988, US Supreme Ct. 1979. Trial atty. antitrust divsn. US Dept. Justice, Washington, 1967-69; ptnr. Ross & Hardies (merged with McGuireWoods LLP in 2003), Chgo., McGuireWoods LLP, Chgo., 2003—, co-mng. ptnr. Chgo. office, 2003—04. Bd. dirs. Am. Assn. for Klinefelter Syndrome Info. & Support; bd. mem. Loyola U. Sch. Law Inst. Consumer Antitrust Studies. Fellow: Am. Bar Found.; mem.: ABA, Lawyers Club of City of Chgo., Chgo. Bar Assn. Office: McGuireWoods LLP Ste 4100 77 W Wacker Dr Chicago IL 60601-1818 Office Phone: 312-750-8618. Office Fax: 312-920-3696. Business E-Mail: rrappaport@mcguirewoods.com.

RAPPAPORT, STUART RAMON, lawyer; b. Detroit, Apr. 13, 1935; s. Reuben and Zella (Golechen) R.; m. Anne M. Plotnick; children: Douglas, Erica Rappaport Witt. BA in History, U. Mich., 1956; JD, Harvard U., 1959. Bar: Calif. 1962. Trial lawyer, chief trials, bur. chief, chief. asst. pub. defender L.A. County Pub. Defender's Office, LA, 1962-87; pub. defender Santa Clara County, San Jose, Calif., 1987-95; pvt. practice, 1995—. Mem. standing adv. com. on criminal law Jud. Coun. Calif., San Francisco, 1993—; mem. discipline evaluation com. State Bar of Calif. Contbr. articles to profl. jours. Recipient Lifetime Achievement award Calif. Attys. for Criminal Justice. Mem. Calif. Pub. Defenders Asn. (pres. 1982-83, Lifetime Achievement award), L.A. County Pub. Defenders Assn. (pres.). Democrat. Jewish. Home: 4500 Bloomfield Rd Sebastopol CA 95472 Business E-Mail: sturap@mcn.org.

RAPPEPORT, IRA J., lawyer; b. Phila., Jan. 13, 1954; BA with honors, Washington U., 1975; JD with honors, Villanova U., 1978. Bar: Calif. 1978. Assoc. Pillstory Madison & Sutro, 1978-83, Memel, Jacobs, Pietro & Gersh, 1983-85, ptnr., 1985-87, McDermott, Will & Emery, LA, 1987—. Mng. editor Villanova Law Rev., 1977-78. Recipient Scribes award Villanova Sch. Law, 1978. Mem. Am. Acad. Hosp. Attys., L.A. County Bar Assn. (mem. healthcare law sect.), Beverly Hills Bar Assn. (mem. healthcare law sect.), Century City Bar Assn. (mem. healthcare law sect.), Nat. Health Lawyers Assn., Calif. Soc. Healthcare Attys. Office: McDermott Will & Emery 2049 Century Park E Fl 34 Los Angeles CA 90067-3101

RAPPUOLI, RINO, immunologist; BS in Biological Sciences, PhD in Biological Sciences, U. Siena. Vis. scientist Rockefeller U., NY, Harvard Med. Sch.; head rsch. and devel. Sclavo SpA, Italy; head European vaccines rsch. Chiron Corp., Italy, 1992, v.p. vaccines rsch., acting chief scientific officer, chief scientific officer, 2004—. Mem. rsch. dirs. group European Commn. Recipient Paul Ehrlich and Ludwig Darmstaedter prize. Mem.: Am. Soc. Microbiology, European Molecular Biology Orgn., NAS. Office: Chiron Via Fiorentina 1 53100 Siena Italy

RAPSON, RICHARD (RIP RAPSON), foundation administrator; b. Bonn, Fed. Republic Germany, Mar. 16, 1952; came to U.S., 1954. s. Ralph E. and Mary Christine (Dolan) R.; m. Gail M. Johnson, Aug. 19, 1989. BA, Pomona Coll., 1974; JD, Columbia U., 1981. Legis. asst. to U.S. Rep. Donald M. Fraser US Congress, Washington, 1974-78; assoc. Leonard, Street & Deinard, Mpls., 1981-86, ptnr., 1987-89; dep. mayor City of Mpls., 1989—93; sr. fellow Design Ctr. for Am. Urban Landscape U. Minn.; pres. McKnight Found., Mpls., 1999—2005, The Kresge Found, Troy, Mich., 2005—. Counsel Harriet Tubman Women's Shelter, Mpls., 1982-89, Coffee House Press., Mpls., 1986-89. Trustee, Mpls. Pub. Library, 1983, pres. bd.; bd. dirs. Mpls. Bd. Estimate and Taxation,

1985-88, Mpls. Youth Coordinating Bd., Mpls., 1986-89. Recipient Sigurd Olsen award for outstanding vol. svc. to environment, Sierra Club Northstar Chpt. Mem. ABA, Minn. Bar Assn., Hennepin County Bar Assn. Democrat. Avocations: art collecting, running, tennis, literature. Office: The Kresge Found 3215 W Big Beaver Rd Troy MI 48084 Business E-Mail: rrapson@kresge.org.

RARICK, PHILIP JOSEPH, lawyer, retired state supreme court justice; b. Troy, Ill., Nov. 10, 1940; s. Philip J. and Mary (Buckman) R.; m. Janet N. Arnovitz, Feb. 1, 1963; 1 child, Philip J. IV. BA, So. Ill. U., 1962; JD, St. Louis U., 1966. Bar: Ill. 1966, U.S. Dist. Ct. Ill. 1966. Twp. atty. Collinsville & Jarvis, Collinsville, Ill., 1966-75; asst. state's atty. Madison County, Edwardsville, Ill., 1966-75; city atty. City of Collinsville, 1967-75; cir. judge Third Jud. Cir., Edwardsville, 1975-88; presiding judge Criminal Div. in Madison County, Ill., 1982—85; chief cir. judge Third Jud. Cir., Edwardsville, 1985-87; presiding judge Criminal Div. in Madison County, Ill., 1987—88; elected judge Appellate Ct., Fifth Dist., Ill., 1988; judge indsl. commn. divsn. Ill. Appellate Ct., 1988—2002; elected judge, retained Appellate Ct., Fifth Dist., Ill., 1998; justice Ill. Supreme Ct., 2002—04; with Callis, Papa, Hale, Szewczyk, Rongey & Danzinger, PC, Granite City, Ill., 2004—. Mem. exec. com. Ill. Jud. Conf., Springfield, 1985—2000, chmn. complex litigation com., 1988—2000, mem. Industrial Comm. Div. of the Appellate Ct., 1992-2002, Ill. Cts. Commn. State of Ill., Springfield, 1992—99. Chmn. (manual) Illinois Manual for Complex Litigation. Mem. Ill. State Bar Assn., Ill. Judges Assn. (dir. 1977—82), Madison County Bar Assn., Tri-City Bar Assn. Office: Callis Papa Hale Szewczyk Rongey & Danzinger PC 1326 Niedringhaus Ave Granite City IL 62040 Office Phone: 618-452-1323.

RARIDON, RICHARD JAY, retired computer scientist; b. Newton, Iowa, Oct. 25, 1931; s. Jack Allison and Letha Helen (Woods) R.; m. Mona Marie Herndon, May 28, 1956; children— Susan Gayle, Ann Chaney. BA, Grinnell Coll., 1953; MA, Vanderbilt U., 1955, PhD, 1959. Assoc. prof. phys. sci. Memphis State U., 1958-62; rsch. scientist Oak Ridge Nat. Lab., 1962-92; cons. ORNL, 1992—2004. Environ. specialist Coop. Sci. Edn. Center, Oak Ridge, 1971-72 Contbr. articles to profl. jours. Radiol. Physics fellow AEC, 1953-55 Fellow AAAS, Tenn. Acad. Sci. (pres. 1971); mem. Assn. Acads. Sci. (sec.-treas. 1972-76, pres. 1977), Sigma Xi. Home: 111 Columbia Dr Oak Ridge TN 37830-7720 Personal E-mail: raridon@hotmail.com.

RASCHE, ROBERT HAROLD, banker, retired economics educator; b. New Haven, June 29, 1941; s. Harold A. and Elsa (Bloomquist) R.; m. Dorothy Anita Bensen, Dec. 28, 1963; children: Jeanette Dorothy, Karl Robert. BA, Yale U., 1963; A.M., U. Mich., 1965, PhD, 1966. Asst. prof. U. Pa., Phila., 1966-72; assoc. prof. econs. Mich. State U., East Lansing, 1972-75, prof., 1975-98, prof. emeritus, 1999—; sr. v.p., dir. rsch. St. Louis Fed. Res. Bank, 1999—. Vis. scholar St. Louis Fed. Res., 1971-72, 76-77, 94-98, San Francisco Fed. Rsch. Bank, 1985, Bank of Japan, Tokyo, 1990; disting. vis. prof. econs. Ariz. State U., Tempe, 1986; rsch. assoc. Nat. Bur. Econ. Rsch., Cambridge, Mass., 1982-91; mem. Mich. Gov. Coun. Econ. Advisers, 1992-96; mem. Shadow Open Market Com., 1973-98. Mem. Am. Econs. Assn. Lutheran. Home: 14531 Radcliffeborough Ct Chesterfield MO 63017-5626 Office: Fed Res Bank St Louis Rsch Divsn PO Box 442 Saint Louis MO 63166-0442 Home Phone: 636-728-1918. Business E-Mail: rasche@msu.edu.

RASCOE, PAUL STEPHEN, librarian, researcher; b. Corpus Christi, Tex., July 7, 1954; s. Stephen Thomas and Barbara Jean (Butler) R. BA, U. Tex., Arlington, 1975, U. Tex., Austin, 1976, M Libr. Info. Sci., 1983; MA, U. London, 1977. Govt. documents and electronic info. svcs. libr. U. Tex., Austin, 1985-96, libr., 1978-85, libr. govt. documents maps and electronic info. svcs., 1996—. Dir. rsch. Weissmann Travel Reports, Austin, 1990-96. Avocation: travel. Office: U Tex Austin Documents Collection Gen Librs PCL 2-400 Austin TX 78713-7330 Home Phone: 512-472-7429; Office Phone: 512-495-4262.

RASCON, ALFRED V., former federal agency administrator; b. Chihuahua, Mexico, 1945; s. Alfredo and Andrea Rascon; m. Carol Lee Richardson; 2 children. Grad. US Army's Infantry Officers Candidate Sch., 1970. Commd. 2d lt. U.S. Army, ret., 1976; with Immigration & Naturalization Svc. US Dept. Justice, with Drug Enforcement Adminstrn., with internat. criminal police orgn.; insp. gen. Selective Svc. System, Arlington, Va., 1996—2001, dir., 2001—03. Served US Army, 1963—66, South Vietnam. Decorated Congl. Medal of Honor.

RASGON, JASON LAURENCE, entomologist, microbiologist, educator; AA in Liberal Arts, LA Pierce Coll., 1995; BS cum laude in Zoology, San Jose State U., 1998; PhD in Entomology, U. Calif., Davis, 2003. Academic cons. terrorism tech. support office, tech. support working grp. Maxim Systems and US Dept. Def., 2003; postdoctoral rsch. assoc. dept. entomology U. Calif., Davis, 2003, NC State U., 2003; asst. prof. dept. molecular microbiol. and immunology Johns Hopkins U. Bloomberg Sch. Pub. Health, Balt. Contbr. articles to sci. jours. Achievements include leading the development of a malaria-resistant mosquito in the laboratory. Office: Dept Molecular Microbiol and Immunology Johns Hopkins U Bloomberg Sch Pub Health 615 N Wolfe St E4626 Baltimore MD 21205 Office Phone: 410-502-2584. E-mail: jrasgon@jhsph.edu. *

RASH, DAVID C., lawyer; b. Colorado Springs, Aug. 18, 1962; m. Vicki Rash; children: Rebecca, Charlie. BA, Fla. State U., 1986; JD, Loyola U. of New Orleans, 1990. Bar: La., Fla., US Dist. Ct. (ea., we. and mid. dists.), US Dist. Ct. (so. and mid. dists. of Fla.), US Ct. Appeals (11th cir.). Atty., New Orleans, with Stanley Rosenblatt, Miami; ptnr. Alters, Boldt, Brown, Rash & Culmo, PA. Mem.: Fla. Admiralty Trial Lawyers Assn., Southeastern Admiralty Law Inst., Broward County Trial Lawyers Assn., Miami-Dade County Trial Lawyers Assn., Fla. Justice Assn. (Eagle mem.), Am. Assn. Justice (admiralty law sect.), Fla. Bar, La. Bar Assn. Achievements include practice in admiralty and maritime law, catastrophic personal injury and death claims involving crew members and passengers; crew member wage claims; medical malpractice resulting in catastrophic injury or death; automobile and trucking accidents involving catastrophic injury or death; defective products resulting in catastrophic injury or death; reported and argued landmark cases including Herzfeld v. Herzfeld, 732 So.2d 1102 (Fla. 3d 1999), Herzfeld v. Herzfeld, 781 So.2d 1070 (Fla. 2001).

RASHAD, AHMAD, sports broadcaster, former professional football player; b. Portland, Oreg., Nov. 19, 1949; m. Phylicia Ayers-Allen, 1985 (div. 2001); children: Keva, Maiysha, Ahmad Jr., Codola Phylea. BA, U. Oreg., 1972. With St. Louis Cardinals, 1972-73, Buffalo Bills, 1974-76, Seattle Seahawks, 1976, Minn. Vikings, 1976-82; sports broadcaster NBC Sports, NYC, 1982—; exec. prodr., mng. editor NBA Inside Stuff NBC Sports/NBA Entertainment, Secaucus, N.J., 1989—. Author: Vikes, Mikes and Something on the Backside, 1988. Recipient, Emmy Award in Sports Broadcast; named to Nat. Football Conf. All-Star Team Sporting News, 1978, 79, NFC Pro-Bowl, NFL, 1979, Nat. Coll. Football Hall of Fame, 2007. Office: NBC Sports 30 Rockefeller Plz Fl 2 New York NY 10112-0036 also: NBA Entertainment 450 Harmon Meadow Blvd Ste 200 Secaucus NJ 07094-3618 *

RASHAD, PHYLICIA, actress, singer, dancer; b. Houston; m. Ahmad Rashad; children: William Bowles, Condola Phylea. Grad. magna cum laude, Howard U., NYC. Mem. Negro Ensemble Co.; founder Phylicia Rashad and Co., 1990. Actor: (plays) The Cherry Orchard, 1973, Zora, 1981, A Raisin in the Sun, 1984, Gem of the Ocean, 2005, (Off-Broadway) The Duplex, 1972, Zooman and the Sign, 1980—81, Weep Not for Me, 1981, In an Upstate Motel, 1981, Puppetplay, 1983, Sons and Fathers of Sons, 1983; (Broadway plays) Ain't Supposed to Die a Natural Death, 1971, The Wiz, 1975, Dreamgirls, 1981, Into the Woods, 1988, Jelly's Last Jam, 1992—93, A Raisin in the Sun, 2004 (Tony award best actress in a play, 2004, Drama Desk award best actress in a play, 2004), Bernarda Alba, 2006; (films) The Broad Coalition, 1972, The Wiz, 1978, Once Upon a Time When We Were Colored, 1995, Free of Eden, 1999, Loving Jezebel, 1999, The Visit, 2000; (TV films) We're Fighting Back, 1981, Uncle Tom's Cabin, 1987 (Cable ACE award nom. best sup. actress, 1987), False Witness, 1989, Polly, 1989, Polly: Comin Home, 1990, Jailbirds, 1991, Hallelujah, 1993, David's Mother, 1994, The Possession of Michael D., 1995, The Babysitters Seduction, 1996, Free of Eden, 1999, The Old Settler, 2001, Murder, She Wrote: The Last Free Man, 2001; (TV series) One Life to Live, 1983—84, The Cosby Show, 1984—92 (NAACP Image award best actress, 1987, Emmy award nom. best actress, 1985, 1986), Santa Barbara, 1985, Cosby, 1996—2000, (voice) Little Bill, 1999—,: (TV guest appearances) The Love Boat, 1985, A Different World, 1988—90, Blossom, 1991, Touched by an Angel, 1994, 2002, The Cosby Mysteries, 1994, In the House, 1995, Bull, 2001; host Theatre Hall of Fame Ceremony, Am. Theatre Critics Assn., 2007. Recipient Theatre Artist award, Nat. Corp. Theatre Fund, 2006. *

RASHEED, ADAM, aerospace engineer, researcher; b. Edmundston, New Brunswick, Canada, Nov. 16, 1973; s. Mahmood and Safia Rasheed; m. Taslim Shaikh, Aug. 14, 2005. B Engring. in Aerospace Engring., Carleton U., Ottawa, Canada, 1995; MS in Aeronautics, Calif. Inst. Tech., Pasadena, 1998, PhD in Aeronautics, 2001. Registered profl. engr., Ont., 1996. Sys. analyst GasTOPS Ltd., Gloucester, Ont., 1995—96; aerospace rsch. engr. GE Global Rsch., Niskayuna, NY, 2001—. Mem. in tng. Registered Engrs. Disaster Relief, Ottawa, 2004. Named one of TR35 World's Top 35 Innovators, 05MIT Tech. Rev. Mag., 2005; recipient Global Indus Technovator award, MIT Sloan, Indian Bus. Club, 2006; ISU Summer Session Program fellow, Can. Found. Internat. Space U., 2007. Mem.: AIAA (sr.; mem. airbreathing propulsion tech. com. 2005). Achievements include research in experimental hypervelocity aerothermodynamics; turbine-based hybrid pulsed detonation engines. Office: GE Global Rsch One Research Cir Niskayuna NY 12309

RASHEED, JEROME NAJEE See NAJEE

RASHLEIGH, BRENDA, ecologist; d. John Lyle and Louise Rashleigh. BS in Biol. Sci., U. Vt., Burlington, 1988; MS in Environ. Sci., Ind. U., Bloomington, 1992; PhD in Ecology & Evolutionary Biology, U. Tenn., Knoxville, 1998. Pk. ranger Acadia Nat. Pk., 1991; environ. edn. tchr. Nature's Classroom, 1991—92; instr. Village Camps, Lecyn, Switzerland, 1992; marine sci. educator instr., sci. ctr. coord. U. Ga. Marine Ext. Svc., Tybee Island, 1992; prin. instr. Ind. U., 1992; rsch. assoc. Oak Ridge Nat. Lab., Tenn., 1992—94; natural heritage program rschr. TVA, Norris, Tenn., 1994—95; biologist, ecologist U.S. Geol. Survey, Knoxville, 1995—98; rsch. ecologist US EPA, Athens, Ga., 1998—. Bd. pres. Ga. River Network, Athens, 2004—; v.p. Upper Oconee Watershed Network, Athens, 2005; regional coord. Ga. Adopt-A-Stream Program, Atlanta, 2006. Editor: (book) Assessment of the Fate and Effects of Toxic Agents on Water Resources, 2007; contbr. articles to profl. jours. Recipient Bronze Medal Team award, US EPA, 2005, Cmty. Svc. award, 2006. Mem.: Sigma Xi, Toastmasters Internat. (sec. 2006—07). Achievements include research in multi-scale analysis of unionid freshwater mussel community structure in the upper Tennessee River basin; development of watershed health assessment tools investigating fisheries. Avocation: kayaking. Office: US Environ Protection Agy 960 College Station Rd Athens GA 30605

RASI, HUMBERTO MARIO, editor, educator; b. Buenos Aires, Mar. 23, 1935; arrived in USA, 1962, naturalized, 1968; s. Mario and Gertrudis Frida (Heyde) R.; m. Julia Cuchma, Feb. 28, 1957; children: Leroy Mario, Sylvia Beatrice. BA, Instituto Superior del Profesorado, Buenos Aires, 1960; MA, San Jose State U., 1966; PhD, Stanford U., 1971; D honoris causa, U. Peruana Union, Peru, 1999, U. Adventista del Plata, Argentina, 2001, U. Montemorelos, Mex., 2003. Ordained to ministry Seventh-day Adventist Ch., 1980. Mem. faculty Instituto Florida, Buenos Aires, 1957-61; asst. editor Pacific Press Publ. Assn., Mountain View, Calif., 1962-66; asst. prof., assoc. prof. modern langs. Andrews U., 1969-76, prof., dean Sch. Grad. Studies, 1976-78; chief editor internat. publs. Pacific Press Publ. Assn., 1978-83, v.p. editorial devel., 1984-86; assoc. world dir. edn. Gen. Conf. Seventh-day Adventists, Silver Spring, Md., 1987-90, world dir. edn., 1990—2002; ret., 2002. Exec. dir. Inst. for Christian Teaching, 1987—. Author: The Life of Jesus, 3 vols., 1984—85; contbg. editor: Handbook of L.Am. Studies, Libr. of Congress, 1972—82; editor: Comentario Biblico Adventista, 7 vols., 1978—90; co-editor: Meeting the Secular Mind, 1985; founder, editor-in-chief: Coll. and Univ. Dialogue, 1989—, compiler: Christ in the Classroom, 35 vols., 1991—; contbr. articles on modern Hispanic lit., cultural issues, and religious trends. Exec. sec. Found. Adventist Edn., 2005-. NEH postdoctoral fellow Johns Hopkins U., 1975-76. Personal E-mail: h.rasi@adelphia.net.

RASIMAS, JOSEPH JAMES, psychiatrist; b. Wilkes-Barre, Pa., Sept. 11, 1974; s. Joseph Anthony Rasimas and Judith Ann Gardner. BA in Philosophy summa cum laude, U. Scranton, Pa., 1996, BS in Biochemistry and Math., 2006; PhD, Pa. State. Coll. Medicine, Hershey, 2003. Life scis. consortium fellow Pa. State U., State College, 1996—2003; chief resident, mayo clinic psychiaty Mayo Clinic, Rochester, Minn., 2006—07; clin. rsch. fellow NIMH, Bethesda, Md., 2007—. Resident coord. free good samaritan med. clinic Salvation Army, Rochester, 2004—. Recipient Outstanding Resident award, Nat. Inst. Mental Health, 2005; Laughlin fellow, Am. Coll. Psychiatrists, 2007—. Mem.: AMA, Acad. Psychosomatic Medicine, Assn. Advancement Philosophy and Psychiatry, Pi Mu Epsilon, Phi Lambda Upsilon, Phi Sigma Tau, Alpha Sigma Nu. Office: Mayo Clinic 200 First St SW Rochester MN 55905 Home Phone: 507-288-2570; Office Phone: 507-284-0557. Office Fax: 507-284-3933. Personal E-mail: sophrosyne_@msn.com.

RASIN, RUDOLPH STEPHEN, corporate financial executive; b. Newark, July 5, 1930; m. Joy Kennedy Peterkin, Apr. 11, 1959; children: Rudolph Stephen, James Stenning, Jennifer Shaw Denniston. BA, Rutgers U., 1953; postgrad., Columbia U., 1958-59. Mgr. Miles Labs., Inc., 1959-61; devel. mgr. Gen. Foods Corp., White Plains, NY, 1961-62; asst. to pres., chmn. Morton Internat. Inc., Chgo., 1962-72; pres. Rasin Corp., Chgo., 1971—, Alliance Brands, LLC. Bd. dirs. Facets Media. Bd. dirs. Geneva Lakes Conservancy, Gatherings Water Land Trust, Poetry Found. With USAF, 1954—56. Mem. Hinsdale Golf Club, Mid Am. Club (Chgo.), Lake Geneva Country Club, Williams Coll. Club (N.Y.C.), Casino Club (Chgo.), Chgo. Club. Mem. United Ch. of Christ. Office: Alliance Brands LLC 30 W Monroe St Chicago IL 60603 Office Phone: 312-236-8453.

RASKA, KAREL FRANTISEK JULIAN, JR., pathologist, virologist, educator; b. Prague, Czech Republic, May 26, 1939; arrived in U.S., 1965; s. Karel Raska and Helena (Heller) Raskova; m. Jana Dostalova, Feb. 18, 1960; children: Karel III, Francis. MD, Charles U., Prague, 1962; PhD in Biochemistry, Czechoslovak Acad. Scis., Prague, 1965. Diplomate Am. Bd. Pathology (anatomic and clin., immunopathology). Fellow Yale U. Sch. Medicine, New Haven, 1965—66; assoc. Waksman Inst. Microbiology, New Brunswick, NJ, 1966—67; scientist Czech Acad. Sci., Prague, 1967—68; prof. microbiology and pathology Rutgers Med. Sch., Piscataway, NJ, 1968—82; profl. pathology, lab. medicine, microbiology U. Medicine and Dentistry-Robert Wood Johnson Med. Sch., New Brunswick, 1982—; prof., chmn. dept. lab medicine and pathology U. Medicine and Dentistry NJ Med. Sch., Newark, 1989—92; chmn. dept. lab medicine and pathology St. Peter's U. Hosp., New Brunswick, 1992—. Cons. Newark Beth Israel Med. Ctr., Newark, 1991—2001, E. Orange (NJ) VA Med. Ctr., 1991—; vis. prof. Charles U. Med. Sch., Prague, 1993—94; prof. path. and lab. medicine Drexel U., Coll. Medicine, Phila., 2005—. Contbr. articles to profl. jours., chapters to books. Trustee N.J. Organ Sharing Network, Springfield, 1991—2000; pres. Czechoslovak Soc. for Arts and Scis. in Am., 2006—. Lt. Czechoslovak Air Force, 1962—63. Grantee, NIH, 1975—93, Damon Runyon-Walter Winchell Cancer Rsch. Fund, 1975, NJ Commn. Cancer Rsch., 1985—86, 1994—95. Mem.: Learned Soc. of the Czech. Republic, Am. Soc. Cell Biologists, Am. Soc. Virology, NJ Soc. Pathology, Assn. Univ. Pathologists, Internat. Acad. Pathology, Am. Assn. Cancer Rsch., Am. Soc. Clin. Immunology, Am. Assn. Immunology, Am. Soc. Investigative Pathology. Avocations: skiing, boating. Office: St Peters Univ Hosp Dept Lab Medicine & Pathology 254 Easton Ave New Brunswick NJ 08901 Office Phone: 732-745-8504. Personal E-mail: jkraskamd@aol.com.

RASKIN, FRED CHARLES, retired transportation and utility holding company executive, educator; b. NYC, Sept. 11, 1948; s. Harry and Isabel Raskin; m. Lorraine Mary Sabourin, Apr. 25, 1974; children: Elizabeth Harris, Alexander Eastwood. BS, Syracuse U., 1970; JD, NYU, 1973. Bar: R.I. 1973, Mass. 1974; CPA, Ohio. Assoc. counsel Fleet Nat. Bank, Providence, 1973-75, Bank of Boston, 1975-78; asst. gen. counsel Eastern Enterprises, Boston, 1978-79, treas., 1979-81, v.p., treas., 1981-84; sr. v.p. fin. Eastern Assoc. Coal Co., Pitts., 1984-87; exec. v.p. Midland Enterprises, Inc., Cin., 1987-90, pres., 1991-98; pres., COO Eastern Enterprises, Weston, Mass., 1998-2000; CEO Woods Hole, Martha's Vineyard and Nantucket Steamship Authority, 2002—04; ret., 2004. Lectr. Boston U., 2001—; adj. prof. Merrimack Coll., 2005-. Trustee Boston Heart Found. Personal E-mail: derfniksar@comcast.net.

RASKIN, MICHAEL A., retail executive, director; b. N.J., Feb. 26, 1925; s. Harry and Elizabeth Rose (Furstenberg) R.; m. Mary Bonetta Whalen, June 12, 1948; children: Robin Raskin Crowell, Hillary Raskin Maass, Mary Allison Sullivan. AB, Pa. State Coll., 1947; MBA, Columbia U., 1948. With Abraham & Straus, 1949-65; successively mdse. v.p., dir. stores, sr. v.p. Abercrombie & Fitch, NYC, 1966-68; exec. v.p. Dayton's div. Dayton Hudson Corp.; pres. Jos. Magnin Co., San Francisco, 1978—, Chmn., CEO, bd. dirs. Imnar Corp., San Francisco, Info. Please; chmn. More Investments; chmn. exec. com. Acajoe Internat.; bd. dirs. Fortune Almac, Canterbury Cuisine, Cultural Devel. Assocs., HELP Inc., Express Yourself Through Art, Inc., Munsingwear, Inc., B&B Acceptance Corp. Bd. dirs. Amyotrophic Lateral Sclerosis Assn.

RASKIN, RICHARD D., lawyer; b. St. Louis, Aug. 7, 1957; s. Lawrence M and Miriam S Raskin; m. Alba Alexander, July 16, 2000; children: Samuel David, Abby Rachel, Molly Rose. AB, Brown U., 1979; JD, U. Cin., 1985. Bar: Ill. 1985. Jud. clk. Hon. Hubert L. Will, Chgo., 1985—87. Bd. mem. Cmty. Counseling Centers, Chgo., 1994—98, Ill. Assn. Healthcare Attorneys, Chgo., 1995—98; feature editor Antitrust Health Care Chronicle, 1997—2001; adv. bd. mem. Health Law Reporter, Washington, 2000—. Contbr. articles to profl. jours. Mem. Cmty. Counseling Centers of Chgo., Chgo., 1994—98, Oak Park. Temple B'Nai Abraham Zion, Ill., 1993—97. Recipient William Worthington award, U. Cin. Coll. Law, 1984, Paxton & Seasongood prize, 1985; Fellow, Urban Morgan Inst. for Human Rights, 1982—84. Mem.: ABA (vice chair antitrust sect. 2002—), Order of the Coif, Am. Lawyers Assn. Jewish. Avocations: music, travel, literature. Office: Sidley Austin LLP One South Dearborn St Chicago IL 60603 Home Phone: 312-853-2170; Office Phone: 312-853-2170. Office Fax: 312-853-7036; Home Fax: 312-853-7036. Business E-Mail: rraskin@sidley.com.

RASKIND, LEO JOSEPH, law educator; b. Newark, Nov. 2, 1919; s. Isaac and Fannie (Michelson) R.; m. Mollie Gordon, June 14, 1948; children— Carol Inge, John Richard. AB, UCLA, 1942; MA, U. Wash., 1949; PhD, London Sch. Econs., 1952; LLB, Yale U., 1955. Faculty Stanford Law Sch., 1955-56; lectr., research asso. Yale Law Sch., 1956-58; faculty Vanderbilt Law Sch., 1958-64, Ohio State U. Coll. of Law, 1964-70, U. Minn., 1970-90, emeritus, 1991—. Counsel Am. Econ. Assn., 1979—88; vis. tchr. NYU, 1964, 83, U. Tex., 1964, U. Utah, 1967, So. Meth. U., 1973, U. N.C., 1978, Lyon III, 1984, Kiel U., 1988; vis. prof. Coll. Law, U. Tenn., Knoxville, 1994, Law Sch., U. Calif., Davis, 1995, U. Minn., 1998, Bklyn. Law Sch., 1998—2004. Co-author: Casebook Corporate Taxation, 1978, Casebook Antitrust Law, 2001; mem. adv. bd. BNA jour. Served to capt. AUS, 1942-46. Fulbright fellow, London Sch. Econs., 1952. Mem. Am. Law Inst. Office: U Minn Law Ctr 229 19th Ave S Minneapolis MN 55455 Personal E-mail: ljraskind@aol.com.

RASKIND, PETER E., bank executive; B in Econs., Dartmouth Coll., Hanover, NH, 1978, MBA in Fin., 1979. Various positions in corp. fin. and cash mgmt. svcs. Harris Bank, Chgo.; vice chmn. US Bancorp, Mpls., 1999—2000; exec. v.p. consumer fin. Nat. City Corp., Cleve., 2000—04, vice chmn., 2004—06, pres., 2006—07, pres., CEO, 2007—. Bd. dirs. Visa USA, Visa Internat., Inovant, LLC. Bd. trustees Cleve. Orch. Office: Nat City Corp Nat City Ctr 1900 E Ninth St Cleveland OH 44114-3484 Office Phone: 216-222-2000. *

RASKY, HARRY, producer, director, writer; b. Toronto, Ont., Can., May 9, 1928; emigrated to U.S., 1955; s. Louis Leib and Pearl (Krazner) R.; m. Ruth Arlene Werkhoven, Mar. 21, 1965; children: Holly Laura, Adam Louis. BA, U. Toronto, 1949, LLD, 1984. Reporter No. Daily News, Kirkland Lake, Ont., 1949; news editor-producer Sta. CHUM, Toronto, 1950, Sta. CKEY, 1951-52; co-founder new documentary dept. CBC, 1952-55; assoc. editor Saturday Night Mag., 1955; producer-dir-writer Columbia Broadcasting Corp., 1955-60, NBC-TV, NYC, 1960-61, ABC-TV, NYC, 1963-69, CBC-TV, Toronto, 1971-78; pres. Harry Rasky Prodns., NYC and Toronto, 1971—, Maragall Prodns., Toronto, 1978—. Guest lectr. film and TV at various univs., colls.; lectr. U. Toronto, York U. Creator (films) Raskymentary (Emmy 1978, 86, San Francisco Film Festival 1978, Grand prize N.Y. TV-Film Festival 1978, Jerusalem medal 1975), Travels Through Life with Leacock, 1976, Arthur Miller on Home Ground, 1979, (TV films) Hall of Kings (Emmy, 1965), prodr., dir., writer (films) Next Year in Jerusalem, 1973, The Wit and World of G. Bernard Shaw, 1974, Tennessee Williams South, 1975, (films) Homage to Chagall-The Colours of Love, 1977 (200 internat. prizes including Oscar nomination Emmy, 1986), Stratasphere, The Mystery of Henry Moore, Karsh: The Searching Eye, (plays) Tiger Tale, 1978, Christopher Plummer: King of Players, 1988, The War Against the Indians, 1992 (Humanities prize, Great Plains Film Festival, Lincoln, Nebr., Golden Hugo award Chgo. Film Festival), Prophecy, 1994 (Golden Angel, honored by Smithsonian, Jerusalem Found.), William Hutt: A Fortunate Man, 1997; author: (memoirs) Nobody Swings on Sunday-The Many Lives of Harry Rasky, 1980, Tennessee Williams a Portrait in Laughter and Lamentation, 1986, Karsh: The Searching Eye, 1986, To Mend the World, 1987, Stratas: An Affectionate Tribute, 1988, Book 2001: The Song of Leonard Cohen, The Great Teacher, 1989, Robertson-Davies-The Magic Season, 1989; author (19 hour retrospective of films including documentaries) Rasky's Gallery: Poets, Painters, Singers and Saints, CBC, 1988, The War Against the Indians, 1993 (12 Internat. awards, adopted Huron Nation title Keeper of the Flame, The Three Harrys, 1999), Modigliani Body & Soul, 2005. Mem. YMCA; mem. adv. coun. Univ. Coll./U. Toronto. Decorated Order of Can.; recipient honors City of Venice, Italy, 1970, Golden Eagle, Grand prize N.Y. Intenat. TV and Film Festival of N.Y., 1977, Cert. of Merit, Acad. Motion Picture Arts and Scis., 1984, Red Ribbon, Am. Assn. Film and Video, N.Y.C., 1988, Blue Ribbon, Am. Film Festival, Emmy award, 1990, Moscow award for cultural contbn. to 20th Century USSR, 1991, Retrospective of Films, 1990, Golden Hugo award Chgo. Film Festival, 1993; named Best Non-Fiction Dir., Dirs. Guild Am., N.Y.C. and L.A., 1988, hon. Mayor N.Y.C., 1977, City of Toronto, 1979; Harry Rasky Day named in his honor, City of Toronto, 1988; Moscow Film Festival honoree, 1991; adopted by Huron Indians, named Keeper of the Spirit, adopted by Ojibway Tribe, named Mountain Eagle; presented to Her Royal Majesty Queen Elizabeth, 2002. Mem. Writers Guild Am. (best non-fiction dir. 1986), Dirs. Guild Am., Writers Union Can., Am., Acad. TV Arts and Scis., Assn. Can. TV and Radio Artists, Producers Assn. Can., Acad. Motion Picture Arts and Scis., Overseas Press Club, Acad. of Can. TV and Film Can. (lifetime achievement award 1992), PEN (Toronto), Nat. Arts Club. Jewish. Avocations: swimming, lecturing. Home: 15 Gregory Ave Toronto ON Canada M4W 2X7 Office: care CBC Box 500 Terminal A Toronto ON Canada M5W 1E6 E-mail: harryrasky@cbc.ca. *I have tried to find the positive forces in life and out of them create works of art of a lasting nature with the idea of improving the lives of others. This, plus the adventure of passing on the tradition of my father and his, is my life.*

RASMUS, JOHN CHARLES, trade association administrator, lawyer; b. Rochester, NY, Dec. 27, 1941; s. Harold Charles and Myrtle Leota (Dybevik) R.; m. Elaine Green Reeves, Mar. 19, 1982; children: Kristin, Stuart, Karin. AB, Cornell U., 1963; JD, U. Va., 1966. Bar: Va. 1970, U.S. Supreme Ct. 1974. Spl. agt. Def. Dept., Washington, 1966-70; v.p., adminstrv. officer, legis. rsch. counsel U.S. League Savs. Instns., Washington, 1970-83; asst. to exec. v.p. Nat. Assn. Fed. Credit Unions, 1983-84; sr. fed. adminstrv. counsel, mgr. regulatory & trust affairs Am. Bankers Assn., 1985—. Bd. trustees The Appraisal Found. Mem. ABA, FBA (disting. svc. award 1980, 82, past chmn. long range planning com., past chmn. coun. fin. instns. and economy), Univ. Club, Exchequer Club, Masons. Office: Am Bankers Assn 1120 Connecticut Ave NW Washington DC 20036 Home: 3302 Alabama Ave Alexandria VA 22305-1734 Home Phone: 703-683-3891; Office Phone: 202-663-5333. Business E-Mail: jrasmus@aba.com.

RASMUSON, BRENT J., photographer, small business owner; b. Logan, Utah, Nov. 28, 1950; s. Eleroy West and Fae (Jacobsen) Rasmuson; m. Tess Bullen, Sept. 30, 1981 (div. Jan. 2003); children: John, Mark, Lisa. Grad. auto repair and painting sch., Utah State U. Pre-press supr., ptnr. Herald Printing Co., Logan, 1969—80; profl. drummer, 1971-75; owner, builder auto racing engines Valley Automotive Specialties, 1971-76; exec. sec. Herald Printing Co., 1980—89; owner Brent Rasmuson Photography, Logan, 1986—, Temple Picture Classics, Logan, 1996—. Author photo prints of LDS temples: Logan, 1987, 95, 98, 2000, 04, Manti, 1989, 2000, Jordan River, 1989, 96, 98, 2000, Provo, 1990, 2001, Mesa, Ariz., 1990, 96, Boise, Idaho, 1990, 96, 2000, Salt Lake Temple, 1990, 96, 2001, 04, Idaho Falls, 1991, 94, 2000, St. George, 1991, 93, 2000, Portland, Oreg., 1991, 96, 97, 2000, LA, 1991, 96, 97, 2000, Las Vegas, Nev., 1991, Seattle, 1992, Oakland, Calif., 1993, 94, Ogden, 1992, 2001, Bountiful, 2002, Mt. Timpanogos, 2002; author photo print: Statue of Angel Moroni, 1994; author photos used to make neckties and watch dials of LDS temples: Salt Lake, Manti, Logan, LA, Oakland, Seattle, Las Vegas, Mesa, Portland, St. George, Jordan River, scenic tie Mammoth Hot Springs in Yellowstone Park, 1995; landscape scenic photographs featured in Best of Photography Ann., 1987-89, also in calendars and book covers; author photo print of Harris Rsch., Inc. Internat. Hdqrs. (recipient 1st prize nat. archtl. photo competition); designer several bus. logos. Mem.: Internat. Freelance Photographers Orgn., Assoc. Photographers, Internat. Platform Assn., Nat. Air and Space Soc., Nat. Trust Hist. Preservation. Republican. Mem. Lds Ch. Avocations: automobile collecting, travel, reading, coin collecting/numismatics, stamp collecting/philately. Home and Office: 66 W 100 N Logan UT 84321-4506 Office Phone: 435-755-0668. Personal E-mail: bjr021@msn.com.

RASMUSON, EDWARD BERNARD, banker; b. Aug. 27, 1940; s. Elmer Edwin and Lile Vivian Rasmuson; m. Cathryn Elaine Robertson, Sept. 11, 1969; children: Natasha Ann, Laura Lile, David Edward. BA, Harvard U., 1962. Mgmt. trainee Brown Brothers Harriman, 1963, Chem. NY, 1964; asst. cashier Nat. Bank Alaska, Anchorage, 1964—66, asst. v.p., 1966—68, v.p., 1968—73, pres., 1973—85, chmn. bd. dirs., 1986—2001; chmn. adv. bd. Wells Fargo Bank, Anchorage, 2001—02. Bd. regents U. Alaska, 1975—89; mem. Rasmuson Found., 1973—; past trustee Sheldon Jackson Coll.; past pres. Anchorage United Way; Hon. Consul of Sweden State of Alaska. Mem.: World Bus. Coun., Young Pres.'s Orgn., Harvard Club (N.Y.C.), Rainier Club, Seattle Yacht Club, Wash. Athletic Club, Metropolitan Club, Pioneers Club Am., Explorers Club, Elks, Rotary. Office: Wells Fargo K3212-051 PO Box 196127 Anchorage AK 99519 Home Phone: 907-243-1155; Office Phone: 907-265-2927. Personal E-mail: erasmuson@gei.net.

RASMUSSEN, DOUGLAS JOHN, lawyer; b. Mt. Clemens, Mich., Jan. 18, 1941; s. Kenneth Edward and Laura Jean (Fletcher) R.; m. Andrea Marie Smart, Aug. 22, 1964; children: Mark Douglas, Michael Andrew. BBA, U. Mich., 1962, MBA, JD, 1965. Bar: Mich. 1965, US Dist. Ct. (ea. dist.) Mich. 1965, US Tax Ct. 1973, US Ct. Appeals (6th cir.) 1973. Assoc. Clark Hill PLC, Detroit, 1965—73, mem., 1973—2007, CEO, 1994—2000, of counsel, 2007—. Trustee Cmty. Found. for S.E. Mich., 1988-2004, Holley Found., bd. dirs. S.E. chpt. ARC, Detroit, 1987—, chmn., 1994-96; bd. dirs. YMCA of Metro Detroit, chmn., 1992-93; unit chmn. United Way, Detroit, 1987-92; bd. dirs. Detroit Symphony Orch., 1999-06, Friends of Detroit Pub. Libr., 2000—, pres., 2001-03, Grand Rapids Symphony, 2007-, Holland Symphony Orch., 2007-. Recipient Outstanding Vol. award Mich. Chpt. Nat. Assn. Fund Raising Execs., 1988, Fundraiser of Yr. award Nat. ARC, 1997, Outstanding Vol. award Mich. ARC, 2002, John McBean award YMCA, 2006. Fellow Am. Coll. Trust and Estate Counsel (regent 1987-93); mem. ABA, State Bar Mich., Internat. Acad. Estate and Trust Law, Fin. and Estate Planning Coun. Met. Detroit (pres. 1986-87), Detroit Athletic Club (bd. dirs. 1992, pres. 1997), Detroit Econ. Club Detroit (bd. dirs. 1999-06), Rotary (Paul Harris fellow, Stanley S. Kresge award). Republican. Reformed Ch. Am. Avocations: music, photography, nordic skiing, golf. Home: 2003 W Lakewood Blvd Holland MI 49424 Office: Clark Hill PLC 200 Ottawa Ave NW Ste 500 Grand Rapids MI 49503 Office Phone: 313-965-8234. Business E-Mail: drasmussen@clarkhill.com.

RASMUSSEN, HARRY PAUL, horticulture and landscape educator; b. Tremonton, Utah, July 18, 1939; s. Peter Y. and Lorna (Nielsen) R.; m. Mary Jane Dalley, Sept. 4, 1959; children: Randy Paul, Lorianne, Trent Dalley, Rachelle. AS, Coll. of So. Utah, 1959; BS, Utah State U., 1961; MS, Mich. State U., 1962, PhD, 1965. Rsch. scientist Conn. Agr. Expt. Sta., New Haven, 1965-66; rschr., instr. Mich. State U., East Lansing, 1966-81; chmn. dept. horticulture and landscape architecture Wash. State U., Pullman, 1981-88; dir. Utah Agrl. Expt. Sta. Utah State U., 1988—, assoc. v.p., 1992—99, 2002—06. Contbr. articles to profl. jours., chpts. to books. Mem. bd. control YMCA, Lansing, Mich., 1976; mem. coun. Boy Scouts Am., Lansing, 1980; stake pres. Ch. of Jesus Christ of Latter Day Saints, Lansing, 1973-81. NDEA fellow, 1961-65. Fellow Am. Soc. Horticulture Sci.; mem. AAAS, Scanning Electron Microscopy (chmn. plant sect. 1976-83, chmn. exptl. sta. com. on orgn. and policy 1996-97). Home: 1949 N 950 E Logan UT 84341-1813 Office: Utah State U 225 Agr Sci Bldg Logan UT 84322-0001

RASMUSSEN, JOHN OSCAR, nuclear research scientist; b. St. Petersburg, Fla., Aug. 8, 1926; s. John Oscar and Hazel R.; m. Louise Brooks, Aug. 27, 1950; children: Nancy, Jane, David, Stephen. BS, Calif. Inst. Tech., 1948; PhD, U. Calif., Berkeley, 1952; MA (hon.), Yale U., 1969. Mem. faculty dept. chemistry U. Calif., Berkeley, 1952-68, 73-91, prof. chemistry, 1971-91, ret., 1991, mem. research staff, 1952-68; sr. rsch. assoc. Lawrence Berkeley Nat. Lab., 1972—91, participating retiree, 1991—; cons., mem. panel nuclear isomer energy project U.S. Dept. Energy, 2004—06. Prof. chemistry Yale U. 1969-73; assoc. dir. Yale Heavy Ion Accelerator Lab., 1970-73; vis. research prof. Nobel Inst. Physics, Stockholm, 1953; vis. prof. Inst. Nuclear Sci. U. Tokyo, 1974, Fudan U., Shanghai, 1979, hon. prof., 1984. Contbr. articles to profl. jours. Served with USN, 1944-46. Recipient E.O. Lawrence Meml. award AEC, 1967; NSF sr. postdoctoral fellow Niels Bohr Inst., Copenhagen, 1961-62, NORDITA fellow, 1979, Guggenheim Meml. fellow, 1973, Alexander von Humboldt sr. rsch. fellow Tech. U. Munich, 1991. Fellow Am. Phys. Soc., AAAS; mem. Am. Chem. Soc. (Nuclear Applications in Chemistry award 1976), Fedn. Am. Scientists (chmn. 1969). Office: Lawrence Berkeley Nat Lab MS 70 319 Berkeley CA 94720-0001

RASMUSSEN, KERRIE L., theater educator; b. Brigham City, Utah, Mar. 21, 1962; d. Eugene McLaws and Sharon B. Rasmussen. BFA, Idaho State U., Pocatello, 1985; MA, U. N.Mex., Albuquerque, 1988; postgrad., U. N.Mex., 1998. Drama tchr. Albuquerque Acad., 1998—99, West Mesa HS, Albuquerque, 1999—. Mem.: Ednl. Theater Assn., Order Ea. Star. Avocations: karate (3d deg. black belt), poetry, stage managing, short stories. Office: West Mesa HS 6701 Fortuna Rd NW Albuquerque NM 87121

RASMUSSEN, RICHARD ROBERT, lawyer; b. Chgo., July 5, 1946; s. Robert Kersten Rasmussen and Marisa Bruna Batistoni; children: Kathryn, William. BS, U. Oreg., 1970, JD, 1973. Bar: Oreg. 1973. Atty. U.S. Bancorp, Portland, Oreg., 1973-83, 95-00, v.p. law divsn., 1983-87, mgr. law divsn., 1983-95, sr. v.p., 1987-95, mgr. corp. sec. divsn., 1990—95; exec. v.p., gen. counsel, sec. West Coast Bancorp, Lake Oswego, Oreg., 2000—. Mem. editl. bd. Oreg. Bus. Law Digest, 1979-81, Oreg. Debtor/Creditor newsletter, 1980-84; contbr. articles to profl. jours. Chmn. mgmt. com. YMCA of Columbia-Willamette, Portland, 1978-79; bd. dirs. Camp Fire, 1988-89, v.p., 1990-91; bd. dirs. Portland Repertory Theatre, 1994-96. Mem.: ABA, Am. Bankers Assn. (bank counsel com. 1996—99), Multnomah County Bar Assn., Oreg. State Bar Assn. (chmn. corp. counsel com. 1979—81, debtor/creditor sect. 1982—83, sec. com. on sects. 1982—83, award of merit, debtor/creditor sect. 2003), Beta Gamma Sigma. Avocations: mountain climbing, white-water rafting, tennis, basketball. Office: West Coast Bancorp 5335 Meadows Rd Ste 201 Lake Oswego OR 97035

RASMUSSEN, ROBERT DEE, retired real estate appraiser; b. Lincoln, Kans., Dec. 24, 1936; s. Sam and Kristena (Andersen) R.; m. Beverly Bert Rowden, Mar. 22, 1959; children: Robert Denis, Kay Lynn. B Gen. Edn., U. Nebr., 1965; MA, Ariz. State U., 1970. Cert. gen. real estate appraiser, Fla. Commd. USAF, 1957, advanced through grades to col., 1978, fighter pilot various locations, 1956-75, comdr. 59th Tactical Fighter Squadron Eglin AFB, Fla., 1975-77, chief Europe/Nato Plans Washington, 1978-80, vice-comdr. 474th Tactical Fighter Wing Nellis AFB, Nev., 1980-81; chief of plans U.S. European Command Joint Chiefs of Staff, Stuttgart, Germany, 1981-84; dir. joint matters Hdqrs. Tactical Air Command USAF, Langley AFB, Va., 1984-86, ret., 1986; appraiser, cons. Appraisal House Inc., Ft. Walton Beach, Fla., 1987-94; gen. appraiser Niceville, Fla., 1994-2000; ret., 2000. Dir. U.S. Power Squadrons, Ft. Walton Beach, 1988-90. Decorated Defense Superior Svc. Medal, Legion of Merit, D.F.C. Mem. Ret. Officers Assn., Am. Assn. Ind. Investors, Porsche Club Am. (v.p. Germany region 1983-84, pres. North Fla. region 1989, 97, dir. 1988-94), Mid-Bay Rotary Club (charter, dir. 1995-96). Avocations: boating, fishing, sports cars. Home: 2421 Duncan Dr Niceville FL 32578-2915

RASMUSSEN, ROBERT KENNETH, dean, law educator; b. Brunswick, Ga., Mar. 13, 1960; s. Robert Edward and Marlene Joan (Kus) Rasmussen; m. Rebecca Brown. BA magna cum laude, Loyola U., Chgo., 1982; JD cum laude, U. Chgo., 1985. Bar: Calif. 1987, US Ct. Appeals (1st, 2nd, 5th, 9th cirs.) 1987, US Ct. Appeals (DC, 4th cirs.) 1988. Law clk. for Hon. John C. Godbold US Ct. Appeals (11th cir.), Montgomery, Ala., 1985-86; atty. US Dept. Justice, Washington, 1986-89; asst. prof. law Vanderbilt U. Law Sch., Nashville, 1989—92, assoc. prof., 1992—94, prof., 1994—, dir. law and econs. program, 1998—2006, assoc. dean academic affairs, 2002—04, Fed Ex rsch. prof., 2004—05, Milton Underwood prof. law, 2004—07, dir. Ctr. Law and Human Behavior, 2006—07; dean Gould Sch. Law, U. So. Calif., LA, 2007—. Vis. prof. law U. Mich. Law Sch., 1994, U. Chgo. Law Sch., 2004. Contbr. articles to law jours. Mem.: ABA, Order of the Coif. Democrat. Roman Catholic. Avocations: softball, astronomy, cooking. Office: Gould Sch Law U So Calif Los Angeles CA 90089-0071 *

RASMUSSEN, STEPHEN S., insurance company executive; BS in Bus. Adminstrn., U. Iowa. Underwriting & mktg. Allied, 1974—82, regional v.p., pacific coast regional office, 1982—86, v.p., underwriting, 1986—98, exec. v.p., product mgmt., 1998—2001; pres., COO CalFarm Ins., 2001—03; pres., COO, property casualty ins. ops. Nationwide Mutual Ins. Co., Columbus, Ohio, 2003—. Trustee Grand View Coll.; 2002 Walk corp. chair, ctrl. Iowa chpt. Juvenile Diabetes Rsch. Found. Office: Nationwide One Nationwide Pl Columbus OH 43215-2220 *

RASMUSSEN, TERESA J., lawyer, insurance company executive; b. Fergus Falls, Minn., Oct. 9, 1956; BS magna cum laude, Moorhead State U., 1981; JD, U. ND, 1984. CPA 1981; bar: Colo. 1984, Minn. 1986. Trial atty. tax divsn. US Dept. Justice, Washington, 1984—86; assoc. Oppenheimer, Wolff & Donnelly, Mpls., 1986—89; exec. v.p., gen. counsel N.E. Securities Corp., Mpls., 1989—90; legal positions up to v.p., gen. counsel, IDS Life Ins. subs. Am. Express Fin. Corp., 1990—2005; sr. v.p., gen. counsel, sec. Thrivent Fin. for Luths., Mpls., 2005—. Mem.: ABA, Minn. State Bar Assn., Hennepin County Bar Assn. Office: Thrivent Financial for Lutherans 625 4th Ave S Minneapolis MN 55415-1624 *

RASMUSSEN, THEODORE PETER, biology professor; s. Theodore Peter and Greta Jean Rasmussen. BS, U. Wash., Seattle, 1992; PhD, U. Wis., Madison, 1997. Postdoctoral fellow Whitehead inst. biomed. rsch. MIT, Cambridge, Mass., 1997—2002; asst. prof. ctr. regenerative biology U. Conn., Storrs, 2002—. Spkr. in field. Author: (films) Stem Cells, Therapy, and Medical Research, 2005; contbr. articles to profl. jours. Expert testimony pub. health legislators State of Conn., Hartord, 2004—06. Fellow, NIH, 1998—2001, Merck, 2001—02; grantee, R.L. and C.G. Patterson Trusts for Biomedical Rsch., 2004—05, NIH, 2005—, Conn. State Stem Cell Rsch. Program, 2007—; scholar, Merck, 2001—02. Mem.: AAAS, Internat. Soc. Stem Cell Rsch., Orgn. Study of Sex Differences, Soc. Women's Health Rsch. Achievements include research in molecular genetics and stem cells. Office: Univ Connecticut 1392 Storrs Rd U-4243 Storrs Mansfield CT 06269 Office Phone: 860-486-8339.

RASMUSSEN, THOMAS VAL, JR., lawyer, small business owner; b. Salt Lake City, Aug. 11, 1954; s. Thomas Val and Georgia (Smedley) R.; m. Donita Gubler, Aug. 15, 1978; children: James, Katherine, Kristin. BA magna cum laude, U. Utah, 1978, JD, 1981. Bar: Utah 1981, U.S. Dist. Ct. Utah 1981, U.S. Supreme Ct. 1985, U.S. Ct. Appeals (10th cir.) 1999. Atty. Salt Lake Legal Defender Assn., Salt Lake City, 1981-83, Utah Power and Light Co., Salt Lake City, 1983-89; of counsel Hatch, Morton & Skeen, Salt Lake City, 1989-90; ptnr. Morton, Skeen & Rasmussen, Salt Lake City, 1991-94, Skeen & Rasmussen, Salt Lake City, 1994-97; pvt. practice, Salt Lake City, 1997—. Co-owner, developer Handi Self-Storage, Kaysville, Utah, 1984-93; instr. bus. law Brigham Young U., Salt Lake City, 1988-90. Adminstrv. editor Jour. Contemporary Law, 1980-81, Jour. Energy Law and Policy, 1980-81. Missionary Ch. of Jesus Christ of Latter-Day Sts., Brazil, 1973-75. Mem. Utah, Salt Lake County Bar Assn., Intermountain Miniature Horse Club (pres. 1989, 2d v.p. 1990), Phi Eta Sigma, Phi Kappa Phi, Beta Gamma Sigma. Avocations: tennis, scuba diving, breeding and showing horses, travel, collecting art. Home: 3094 Whitewater Dr Salt Lake City UT 84121-1561 Office: 4659 Highland Dr Salt Lake City UT 84117-5137 Office Phone: 801-484-3000.

RASMUSSEN, WILLIAM MEADE STITH, curator, historian; b. Richmond, Va., Feb. 23, 1946; s. John Curtis and Dena Lee Rasmussen; m. Maria Payne Rasmussen, Aug. 8, 2003; children: Drury Alexander Stith, Marc Emerson Townes, Elizabeth Maria Joynes, Alexandra Mercedes Joynes. BA in History, Wash. & Lee U., Lexington, Va., 1964—68; MA in Art History, U. Del., Newark, 1972—75, PhD in Art History, 1975—80. Tchr. Va. Mus. Fine Arts, Richmond, 1977—81; prof. Wash. & Lee U., 1981—82; curator Va. Hist. Soc., Richmond, 1991—. Curator Va. Hist. Soc., Richmond, Va., 1991—. Author: (books) The Making of Virginia Architecture, 1992 (Exhbn. Catalog award, Soc. Archtl. Historians, 1992), Pocahontas: Her Life and Legend, 1994, Pocahontas: Her Life and Legend, 2d edit., 2007, George Washington: The Man Behind the Myths, 1999 (Merit award, Am. Assn. State & Local History, 2000), The Virginia Landscape: A Cultural History, 2000, Lost Virginia: Vanished Architecture of the Old Dominion, 2001 (Gabriella Page Hist. Preservation award, Assn. Preservation Va. Antiquities, 2002), Old Virginia: The Pursuit of a Pastoral Ideal, 2003, Lee and Grant, 2007; contbr. articles to profl. jours. Recipient Excellence award, Soc. Archtl. Historians, 1993; grantee, Nat. Endowment Humanities, 2006. Home: 5408 Bewdley Rd Richmond VA 23226 Office: Va Historical Soc 428 North Blvd Richmond VA 23221 Home Phone: 804-288-2210.

RASMUSSON, THOMAS, lawyer; b. Lansing, Mich., Dec. 5, 1941; s. William and Mary Jane Rasmusson; m. Alice Wolo, Oct. 1, 1989; children: David, Jane. BA, Mich. State U., 1963; JD, U. Mich., 1966; MA, Tufts/Harvard Fletcher Sch., 1988. Bar: Mich. 1967, U.S. Ct. Appeals (6th cir.) 1982, U.S. Supreme Ct. 1982. Law clk. to presiding justice Mich. Supreme Ct., Lansing, 1966-68; asst. prosecutor Ingham Prosecutor's Office, Lansing, 1968-72, criminal divsn. chief, 1972-75; spl. prosecutor Ingham County, Lansing, 1975-76; pvt. practice Lansing, 1975—. Trustee and audit chair Lansing Cmty. Coll., 1998-; cons. U.S. AID, Monrovia, Liberia, 1989-90; contractor U.S. Dept. of State, Monrovia, 1987-90; adj. prof. Cooley Law Sch., Lansing, 1991—; rsch. assoc. program on negotiation Harvard U., Cambridge, 1987-88; mem. Ct. Rule Com., Lansing, 1979-81; dir. Educated Solutions, LLC, 2000-03. Editor: Jurisprudence and System Science, 1986, Interactive Systems, 1988, (series) Liberian Law Reports, 1988-90; contbr. articles to profl. jours. Chair fin. Ingham Rep. Party, Lansing, 1994-98, mem. exec. com., 1994—; mem. 8th Congl. Com., Lansing, 1997—; trustee and audit com. Lansing C.C., 1998—; bus. edn. coun. conf. bd., N.Y., 2004—. Recipient Outstanding Svc. award US Edn. Found., 1987; grantee Fulbright, 1986 US Edn. Found., 1987. Mem. AAAS, State Bar Mich. Republican. Methodist. Avocations: physics, history of science. Office: Rasmusson and Assoc 712 Abbott E East Lansing MI 48823 Home: 1713 Willow Creek Dr Lansing MI 48917-7815

RASOCHOVA, LADA, research scientist; d. Vlastimil Rasocha and Marie Rasochova. BS, MS, Czech Agrl. U., Prague, 1986, Iowa State U., Ames, 1993, PhD, 1996. Cert. clin. trials mgmt. Calif., 2006. Scientist Biol. Rsch. Ctr., Szeged, Hungary, 1989—91; postdoctoral rsch. assoc. Iowa State U., Ames, 1996—97; scientist Inst. Genetic Engring. and Cell Biology, Kiev, Ukraine, 1988, Rsch. Inst. for Crop Prodn., Prague, Czech Republic, 1986—88; postdoctoral rsch. assoc. U. Wis., Madison, 1997—98; scientist Mycogen, San Diego, 1998—99, Dow Chem. Co., San Diego, 1999—2003, r&d group leader, 2003—06; mgr., vaccine product devel. Dowpharma, Dow Chem. Co., San Diego, 2007—. Recipient Rsch. Excellence award, Czech Acad. Scis., 1989, Spl. Recognition award, TDCC, 2001, 2005, 2006; fellow, Internat. Union Microbiol. Socs., Virology Divsn., 1996, UN, UNESCO, 1988, 1989—91; Mary J. Brinton Grad. scholar, Iowa State U., 1991—93, Profl. Travel grant, 1993, 1995, 1996. Mem.: Am. Soc. Microbiology, Americal Chem. Soc., Am. Soc. Virology (Travel Grant from the Am. Soc. for Virology 1993, 1995, 1998), Gamma Sigma Delta, Sigma Xi. Achievements include research in virology; vaccines; 15 patents pending. Office: Dowpharma Dow Chem Co 5501 Oberlin Dr San Diego CA 92121 Home Phone: 858-352-4457; Office Phone: 858-352-4457. Business E-Mail: lrasochova@dow.com.

RASOR, DINA LYNN, journalist, private investigator; b. Downey, Calif., Mar. 21, 1956; d. Ned Shaurer and Genevieve Mercia (Eads) R.; m. Thomas Taylor Lawson, Oct. 4, 1980. BA in Polit. Sci., U. Calif., Berkeley, 1978. Editorial asst. ABC News, Washington, 1978-79; researcher Pres.'s Commn. on Coal, Washington, 1979; legis. asst. Nat. Taxpayers Union, Washington, 1979-81; founder, dir. Project on Mil. Procurement, Washington, 1981-89; investigative reporter Lawson-Rasor Assocs., El Cerrito, Calif., 1990-92; pres., CEO, investigator Bauman & Rasor Group, El Cerrito, Calif., 1993—; chief investigator Follow the Money Project, 2005—. Author: The Pentagon Underground, 1985, Betraying Our Troops, 2007; editor: More Bucks, Less Bang, 1983; contbr. articles to profl. jours. Recipient Sigma Delta Chi Outstanding Leadership award Soc. Profl. Journalists, 1986; named to register Esquire Mag., 1986, Nat. Jour., 1986. Mem. United Ch. Christ. Office Phone: 510-235-5021.

RASPBERRY, WILLIAM JAMES, journalist; b. Okolona, Miss., Oct. 12, 1935; s. James Lee and Willie Mae (Tucker) R.; m. Sondra Patricia Dodson, Nov. 12, 1966; children— Patricia D., Angela D., Mark J. BS in History, Ind. Central Coll., 1958, LHD, 1973. Reporter-editor Indpls. Recorder, 1956-60; reporter-editor Washington Post, 1962-65, urban affairs columnist, 1966—2005; instr. journalism Howard U., 1971-73; prof. pub. policy Duke U., Durham, NC, 1995—. Lectr. on race relations and pub. edn. Mem. Pulitzer Prize Bd., 1979-86 TV commentator, Sta. WTTG, Washington, 1973-75, TV discussion panelist, Sta. WRC-TV, Washington, 1974-75; Contbr. articles on race relations and pub. edn. to popular mags; author, Looking Backward at US, 1991. Bd. visitors U. Md. Sch. Journalism, 1985—; bd. advisors Poynter Inst. for Media Studies, 1984-94. With US Army, 1960-62. Recipient Pulitzer Prize for commentary, 1994; Elijah Parish Lovejoy Fellowship, 1999; Lifetime Achievement Award, Nat Assn Black Journalists, 1994. Mem. Nat. Press Club, Capital Press Club, Kappa Alpha Psi. Clubs: Gridiron. Home: 1301 Iris St NW Washington DC 20012-1434 Home Phone: 202-722-1558; Office Phone: 919-613-7388. E-mail: wr3@duke.edu.

RASPINO, LOUIS A., energy executive; b. 1953; Various positions to sr. v.p. fin., adminstrn., CFO La. Land & Exploration Co. (merged with Burlington), 1978—97; sr. v.p. Burlington Resources, 1997—98; v.p., fin. Halliburton Co., 1999—2000; exec. v.p., CFO, COO JRL Enterprises Inc., 2000—01; sr. v.p., fin., CFO Grant Prideco. Inc., Houston, 2001—03; exec. v.p., CFO Pride Internat. Inc., Houston, 2003—05, pres., CEO, dir., 2005—. Office: Pride Internat Inc 5847 San Felipe Houston TX 77057 Office Phone: 713-789-1400. *

RASSBACH, HERBERT DAVID, marketing executive; b. Glen Ridge, NJ, Mar. 23, 1944; s. Merrill Augustus and Ruth Bruce (Sims) Rassbach. BS, Del. State Coll., 1971; MBA, Drexel U., 1979. Prodn. planning mgr. Standard Brands Chem. Industries, Edison, NJ, 1971-74; order fulfillment mgr. P Q Corp., Valley Forge, Pa., 1974-77, mkt. devel. project mgr., 1977-82; market mgr. Willson Safety Products, Reading, Pa., 1983-85; pres. HDR Group, mktg. and mgmt. cons., Wayne, Pa., 1986—. Guest speaker Wharton Sch. U. Pa., 1988, Temple U., Phila., 1989, Wharton Club, 1995. Media comms. bd. Upper Merion Twp., 1989, vice-chmn., 1990, 1992—2004, chmn., 1991, 2005—, ex-officio mem. Citizens Police

Adv. Bd., 2005—, committeeman, 1977. With USAF, 1962—66, hon. discharged, 1968. Mem. Drexel U. Alumni Assn. (v.p. Montgomery County chpt. 1988-91), Alpha Kappa Mu, Delta Mu Delta. Avocations: golf, tennis, running, travel, american history. Home: 635 Mallard Rd Wayne PA 19087-2346 Office: HDR Group PO Box 2164 Southeastern PA 19399-2164 Office Phone: 610-964-8555. Business E-Mail: hdrassbach@hdrgroup.com.

RASSEL, RICHARD EDWARD, lawyer; b. Toledo, Jan. 10, 1942; s. Richard Edward and Madonna Mary (Tuohy) R.; m. Elizabeth Ann Frederick, Dec. 5, 1967 (dec. June 1977); children: Richard III, Elizabeth; m. Dawn Ann Lynch, Sept. 17, 1983; children: Lauren, Brian. BA, U. Notre Dame, 1964; JD, U. Mich., 1966; cert. judge advocate, USN Judge Advocate Sch., 1967. Law clk. Mich. Ct. Appeals, Detroit, 1966-70; shareholder, v.p. Butzel Long, Detroit, 1970-94, chmn., CEO, 1994—2006, dir. global client rels., 2006—. Bd. dirs. Robertson-Jamieson Corp., Birmingham, Mich., WTVS-Channel 56. Pres. Birmingham Cmty. House; bd. advisors U. Detroit Mercy Grad. Sch. Bus.; bd. dirs. Detroit Legal News, Detroit Police Athletic League, Internat. Visitors Coun., William Beaumont Hosp.; chair meta. affairs coalition Oakland U. Coll. Arts and Scis.; past pres., past bd. dirs. Rosa Parks Scholarship Found.; trustee Seed Found. Lt. USNR, 1967-69. Mem. ABA (vice chmn. media and law com.), State Bar of Mich. (chmn. multidisciplinary practice law com.), Am. Coll. Trial Lawyers, Birmingham Athletic Club, Detroit Athletic Club, Otsego Ski Club, Village Club. Office: Butzel Long 150 W Jefferson Ave Ste 900 Detroit MI 48226-4416 E-mail: rassel@butzel.com.

RASSMANN, JOEL H. H., corporate financial executive; b. NYC, May 16, 1945; Grad., Bernard Baruch Coll., 1967. CPA, N.Y. Acct. S.D. Leidesdorf & Co., 1967—72; ptnr. Kenneth Leventhal & Co., 1972—84; sr. v.p., treas., CFO Toll Brothers Inc., Horsham, Pa., 1984—2002, exec. v.p., treas., CFO, 2002—. Mem. AICPA, N.Y. State Soc. CPA's. Achievements include appearing frequently as commentator on CNBC, CNN, Fox, Bloomberg TV & Radio. Office: Toll Brothers Inc 250 Gibraltar Rd Horsham PA 19044 *

RASTETTER, WILLIAM H., biotechnology company executive; BS in Chemistry, MIT; MA, Harvard U., PhD in Chemistry. Faculty MIT, Cambridge, Mass., 1975—82; scientist/rschr. biocatalysis and chem. scis. groups Genentech, 1982—84, dir. corp. ventures, 1984—86; pres. & CEO IDEC Pharms. Corp., San Diego, 1986—2002, CFO, 1988—93; dir. IDEC Pharms. Corp. (now Biogen IDEC), 1986—; chmn. bd. dirs. IDEC Pharms. Corp., 1996—2002; CEO Biogen IDEC, 2002—03, exec. chmn., 2003—. Bd. dir. Argonaut Technologies, Inc., Illumina, Inc., 1998—, non-exec. chmn., 2005—; mem. Calif. Healthcare Inst.; R.B. Woodward vis. scholar, dept. chem. and chem. biology Harvard U. Office: Biogen IDEC 5200 Research Pl San Diego CA 92122 also: Biogen IDEC 14 Cambridge Ctr Cambridge MA 02142

RASTOGI, ANIL KUMAR, health products executive; b. India, July 13, 1942; came to U.S., 1969, naturalized, 1978; s. R.S. and K.V. Rastogi; m. Anjali Capur, Mar. 18, 1970; children: Priya, Sonya. BS with honors, Lucknow U., 1963, MS, 1964; PhD in Polymer Sci., McGill U., 1969. From staff to dir. corp. diversification portfolio Owens-Corning Tech. Ctr., Granville, Ohio, 1969—87; v.p. Mead Imaging, Miamisburg, Ohio, 1987-89; pres. Mead Cycolor Divsn., Dayton, Ohio, 1989-92; v.p., gen. mgr.infusion systems div. Pharmacia Deltec, Inc., St. Paul, 1992-93, exec. v.p., 1993-94; COO SIMS Deltec, Inc., St. Paul, 1994-95; pres., COO Sabratek Corp., Niles, Ill., 1995—98; pres., CEO NOMOS Corp., Sewickley, Pa., 1998—2002; v.p. entrepreneurship and tech. commercialization Drexel U., Phila., 2002—05; pvt. investor Reston, Va., 2005—. Mem. adv. bd. Central Ohio Tech. Coll.; lectr., cons. in field. Author of 15 bus. and tech. publs.; patentee in field. Bd. dirs. Licking County Family Services Assn.; bd. dirs. Tech. Alliance of Central Ohio; v.p. local United Way; bd. dirs. and treas. Columbus Bus. Tech. Ctr.; mem. Overview Adv. Com. Strategic Hwy. Research Program. Fellow NRC Can., 1966-69 Mem. AAAS, Am. Mgmt. Assn., Am. Chem. Soc., Soc. Plastics Engrs., Comml. Devel. Assn., Med. Alley (bd. dirs.), Health Ind. Mfrs. Assn., Nat. Infusion Therapy Alliance (bd. dirs.), Toastmasters (past pres.), Rotary, Sigma Xi. Home and Office: 1584 Regatta Lane Reston VA 20194

RASTOGI, SHIPRA, cell biologist; d. Satya Prakash and R. Rastogi. Postdoctoral fellow H. Lee Moffitt Cancer Ctr., Tampa, Fla., 2002—. Mem.: AAAS (assoc.).

RASULO, JAMES A., theme park executive; Grad. in Econs., Columbia U., 1978; MA in Econs., U. Chgo., 1982, MBA, 1984. Exch. rate/interest rate forecaster Chase Manhattan Bank; mgr. corp. planning Marriott Corp.; from dir. to sr. v.p. corp. strategic planning Walt Disney Co., Lake Buena Vista, Fla., 1986—93, sr. v.p. corp. alliances, 1993—95; exec. v.p. Euro Disney S.C.A., Paris, 1998—2000, also pres., COO, 1999—2000, chmn., CEO, 2000—02; pres. Walt Disney Pks. and Resorts Worldwide Walt Disney Co., Lake Buena Vista, Fla., 2002—. Mem.: Am. C. of C. (France), Columbia U. Club France. Office: Walt Disney Co 1375 N Buena Vista Dr Lake Buena Vista FL 32830-8402

RATCHEV, BORIS A, management consultant; b. Sofia, Bulgaria, July 16, 1969; s. Anton Slavov and Blaga Borisova Ratchev; m. Leticia G. Ratchev, Mar. 22, 1996. BSc, U. of Wis., 1990—93, MSc, 1993—95, Stanford U., 2000—05. Summer intern-analyst Siemens Power Sys. Control Divsn., Mpls., 1995; sr. reliability engr. Altera Corp., San Jose, Calif., 1996—2000, sr. software engineer-arch., 2000—05; mgmt. cons. Pittiglio Rabin Todd and McGrath, Mountain View, 2005—. Grad. fellowship, U. of Wisconsin-Madison, 1993. Mem.: IEEE (life). Achievements include patents for technology mapping technique for fracturable logic; novel method of using randomly generated; techniques for automated sweeping of parameters in computer aided design to achieve optimum performance and resource usage. Avocations: skiing, soccer, reading, travel. Home: 992 Belmont Terrace #9 Sunnyvale CA 94086

RATCHFORD MERCHANT, BETTY JO, retired elementary school educator; b. Huntsville, Ala., Feb. 9, 1937; d. Howard Clyde and Margaret (Kyle) Wikle; m. McClellan Ratchford, 1960 (div.); children: McClellan III, Margaret Lee, Rosalyn Hampton; m. Curtis Merchant, 1992. BS, Auburn U.; MEd, Ala. A&M U., 1998. Cert. tchr. elem. Tchr. elem. Gilbert Sch., Atlanta, Madison County Sch. Sys., Huntsville, Ala., Riverton Elem. Sch., Mt. Carmel Elem. Sch., 2003. Named Tchr. of Yr. for Madison County, 1992. Mem. NEA, AAUW, Ala. Edn. Assn., Environ. Edn. Assn. Ala., Madison County Edn. Assn. Episcopalian. Avocations: poetry, singing, reading, painting, rock climbing. Home: 11033 Everest Cr Huntsville AL 35803

RATCHYE, BOYD HAVENS, lawyer; b. Helena, Mont., June 10, 1938; s. John Frederick and Leanora (Boyd) R.; m. Jean P. Cunningham, Sept. 1, 1962 (div. Oct. 1985); children: Ellen C., Stephen B.; m. Susan Light, May 21, 1994. BA cum laude, Harvard U., 1960, JD, 1963. Bar: Minn. 1964, U.S. Dist. Ct. (Minn. 1964, ND 1993), U.S. Ct. Appeals (8th cir.) 1967, U.S. Supreme Ct. 1972, U.S. Ct. Appeals (fed. cir.) 1983. Law clk. to justice J.C. Otis Supreme Ct. Minn., St. Paul, 1963-64; assoc. Erickson, Popham, Haik & Schnobrich, Mpls., 1964-65; assoc. to ptnr. Doherty, Rumble & Butler, P.A., St. Paul, 1966—99; shareholder, civil litig. Bassford Remele, Mpls., 1999—. Adj. prof. William Mitchell Coll. of Law, 1975-94. Chmn., bd. dir. Yellowstone Assn. Named a Minn. Super Lawyer, Mpls.-St. Paul Mag. and Minn. Law and Politics mag., 2000—07; named one of Best Lawyers in Am., 1986—2007. Mem. ABA, Am. Bd. Trial Advocates (pres. Minn. chpt. 1990-91), Minn. State Bar Assn., Minn. Def. Lawyers Assn., Hennepin County Bar Assn., Harvard Radcliffe Club Minn., Inns of Ct. (Warren Burger chpt., pres. 1999-2000, counselor 2000-01). Episcopalian. Avocations: rowing, running, cross country skiing, scuba diving, snorkeling. Office: Bassford Remele Ste 3800 33 S 6th St Minneapolis MN 55402 Office Phone: 612-376-1604. Office Fax: 612-333-8829. Business E-Mail: boydr@bassford.com.

RATCLIFF, CARTER GOODRICH, writer, critic, poet; b. Seattle, Aug. 20, 1941; s. Francis Kenneth and Marian Elizabeth (Carter) R.; m. Phyllis Derfner, Jan. 28, 1976. BA, U. Chgo., 1963. Dir. poetry workshop St. Mark's Poetry Project, NYC, 1969-70; editorial assoc. Artnews, NYC, 1969-72; advisory editor Art Internat., Lugano, Switzerland, 1970-75; instr. modern and contemporary art and art theory The Sch. of Visual Arts, NYC, 1972-83; instr. modern and contemporary art Phila. Coll. of Art, 1973; instr. art history NYU Sch. of Continuing Edn., 1973-75; contbg. editor Saturday Review, NYC, 1980-82, Art in America, NYC, 1976—; mem. editorial adv. com. Sculpture, Washington, 1992—. Vis. prof. post-war Am. art SUNY, Purchase, 1983-84, Pratt Inst., Bkyn., 1984-85, Hunter Coll., CUNY, 1985-89, 95-99, 2002; lectr. in field. Author: (books, poetry), Fever Coast, 1973, Give Me Tomorrow, 1983, Arrievederci, Modernismo, 2007; (books) John Singer Sargent, 1982, Andy Warhol, 1983, Robert Longo, 1985, Komar and Melamid, 1989, Gilbert and George: The Singing Sculpture, 1993, The Fate of a Gesture: Jackson Pollock and Post War American Art, 1996, paperback edit., 1998, Out of the Box: The Reinvention of Art, 1965-1975, 2001; (essays) Joseph Cornell, 1980, Willem de Kooning: The North Atlantic Light, 1983, Roy Lichtenstein, 1989, Barnett Newman, 1991, Gilbert & George, 1993, Ellsworth Kelly, 1996, Francis Bacon, 1998, William Blake, 2001, Barnett Newman, 2002, Georgia O' Keeffe, 2003, Alex Katz, 2005, What "Evidence" Tells Us About Art, 2006, Andy Warhol: Portraits, 2007; contbg. editor Art in America, 1976—, Art on Paper, 2001—, Sculpture Mag., 2001—; mem. editl. bd. Sculpture Mag., 1992—; contbr. over 500 articles on art to mags. and catalogs. Recipient of the Frank Jewett Mather award for art criticism Coll. Art Assn., 1987; Poets Found. grantee, 1969, NEA Arts Critics grantee, 1972, 76; Guggenheim fellow, 1976. Home and Office: PO Box 448 Tivoli NY 12583 Office Phone: 917-821-2681. E-mail: carterratcliff@gmail.com.

RATCLIFFE, DAVID M., utilities executive; b. Tifton, Ga. BS in Biology, Valdosta State U., Ga., 1970; JD, Woodrow Wilson Coll. Law, 1975. Bar: Ga. Biologist Ga. Power, 1971; v.p. fuel svcs. Southern Co., 1986—89, exec. v.p., 1989—91, pres., CEO Miss. Power, 1991—95, sr. v.p. external affairs, 1995—98, exec. v.p., treas., CFO Ga. Power, 1998—99, CEO Ga. Power, 1999—2003, chmn., pres., CEO, 2004—. Bd. dirs. Edison Electric Inst., CSX Transp., Ga. Rsch. Alliance, Ctrl. Atlanta Progress, Ga. Partnership for Excellence in Edn., chair, 2001—04; bd. dirs. Fed. Res. Bank Atlanta, chair, 2004. Trustee Woodruff Arts Ctr.; mem. adv. bd. Salvation Army. Mem.: Metro Atlanta C. of C. (chair econ. devel.), Ga. Bar Assn. Office: Southern Co 30 Ivan Allen Jr Blvd NW Atlanta GA 30308 Office Phone: 404-506-5000. *

RATH, ALAN T., sculptor; b. Cin., Nov. 25, 1959; s. George and Carolyn R. BSEE, MIT, 1982. One-man exhbns. include San Jose (Calif.) Art Mus., 1990, Dorothy Goldeen Gallery, Santa Monica, Calif., 1990, 92, Walker Art Ctr., Mpls., 1991, Mus. Contemporary Art, Chgo., 1991, Carl Solway Gallery, Cin., 1991, Inst. Contemporary Mus., Honolulu, 1992, Ctr. Fine Art, Miami, Fla., 1992, Galerie Hans Mayer, Dusseldorf, Germany, 1992, Hiroshima (Japan) City Mus. Contemporary Art, 1994, Worcester (Mass.) Art Mus., 1994, John Weber Gallery, N.Y.C., 1994, Haines Gallery, San Francisco, 1995, 96, 98, Contemporary Art Mus., Houston, 1995, Aspen Art Mus., Colo., 1996, Dorfman Projects, N.Y.C., 1998, Yerba Buena Ctr. for the Arts, San Francisco, 1998, Site Santa Fe (N.Mex.), 1998, Mus. of Art, Austin, Tex., 1999, Scottsdale Mus. of Contemporary Art, 1999; group exhbns. include Visiona, Zurich, 1989, Ars Electronica, Linz, Austria, 1989, L.A. Contemporary Exhbns., 1989, Mus. Folkwang, Essen, Germany, 1989, Cite des Arts et des Nouvelles Technologies, Montreal, 1990, Stadtmuseum Siegburg, Siegburg, Germany, 1990, San Francisco Mus. Modern Art, 1990, 95, 98, Denver ArtMus., 1991, Whitney Am. Art, N.Y.C., 1991, Alvar Alto Mus., Jyvaskyla, Finland, 1992, Internat. Ctr. Photography, N.Y.C., 1992, Padiglione d'Arte Contemporanea, Ferrara, Italy, 1992, John Weber Gallery, N.Y.C., 1993, Spiral Art Ctr., Tokyo, 1994, Aldrich Mus. of Contemporary Art, Ridgefield, Conn., 1995, Otso Gallery, Espo Finland, 1996, LaLonja, Palma de Malloren, Spain, 1996, Kunsthalle, Vienna, 1998, L.A. Mus. Contemporary Art, 1999, Taipei ICA, Taiwan, 2001, Bienal de Valencia, Spain, 2001. Grantee NEA, 1988; Guggenheim fellow, 1994. Office: IKON 830 E 15th St Oakland CA 94606-3631

RATH, ERIC CLEMENCE, history professor; PhD, U. Mich., Ann Arbor, 1998. Postdoctoral fellow Reischauer inst. Harvard U., Cambridge, Mass., 1998—99; assoc. prof. U. Kans., Lawrence, 1999—. Author: (book) The Ethos of Noh. Office: Univ Kansas 1445 Jayhawk Blvd Lawrence KS 66045 Office Phone: 785-864-9470.

RATH, HOWARD GRANT, JR., lawyer; b. LA, Sept. 2, 1931; s. Howard Grant and Helen (Cowell) R.; m. Peyton McComb, Sept. 13, 1958 (dec. Apr. 1984); children: Parthenia Peyton, Francis Cowell; m. Dorothy Moser, Aug. 29, 1986. BS, U. Calif., 1953; JD, U. So. Calif., 1958. Bar: Calif. 1959, US Dist. Ct. (cen. dist.) Calif., 1959, US Ct. Claims 1974, US Tax Ct. 1960. Assoc. O'Melveny & Myers, LA, 1959-66; tax counsel, dir. tax adminstrn., asst. treas. Northrop Corp. LA, 1966-74; sr. tax ptnr. Macdonald, Halsted & Laybourne, LA, 1974-86, Hill & Weiss, LA, 1986-90; ptnr. Lewis Brisbois Bisgaard & Smith, LA, 1990—; dir. Rath Packing Co., Waterloo, Iowa, 1966-81. 1st lt. US Army, 1953-55. Mem. State Bar Calif., LA County Bar Assn., LA Yacht Club, The Athenaeum, Order of Coif, Phi Beta Kappa. Republican. Episcopalian. Office: Lewis Brisbois Bisgaard & Smith 221 N Figueroa St Ste 1200 Los Angeles CA 90012-2646 Business E-Mail: rath@lbbslaw.com.

RATH, MANIK K., lawyer; b. Pitts., 1969; m. Wendy Rath. BA, U. Va., 1991, JD, 1994. Admitted: State Bar of Tex., Va. State Bar, DC Bar Assn., US Dist. Ct., US Ct. of Appeals. Atty. Baker & McKenzie LLP, Dallas, McGuire Woods LLP, Richmond, Va., 1997—99, McKenna Long & Aldridge LLP, 1999; v.p., dep. gen. counsel, asst. sec. Alion Sciences and Tech. Corp., 2002—05; gen. counsel, corp. sec., v.p. adminstrn. LMI, McLean, Va., 2005—. Bd. dirs. Alion Sci. and Tech. Corp. Office: LMI Hdqs 200 Corporate Ridge Mc Lean VA 22102-7805 Office Phone: 800-213-4817. Office Fax: 703-917-9800.

RATH, THOMAS DAVID, lawyer, retired prosecutor; b. East Orange, NJ, June 1, 1945; s. Harvey and Helen R.; m. Christine Casey, Dec. 18, 1971; children— Erin, Timothy. AB, Dartmouth Coll., 1967; JD, Georgetown U., 1971. Bar: N.J. 1971, N.H. 1972, U.S. Supreme Ct. 1978. Law clk. Judge Clarkson Fisher, U.S. Dist. Ct. N.J., 1971-72; atty. criminal div. Office of Atty. Gen., NH, 1972-73, asst. atty. gen., 1973-76, dep. atty. gen., 1976-78, atty. gen., 1978-80; ptnr. Orr & Reno, P.A., Concord, NH, 1980-87, Rath & Young, P.A., Concord, 1987-91; founding ptnr. Rath, Young, Pignatelli & Oyer, P.A., Concord, 1991—. Polit. analyst WHDH-TV, Boston, WGBH Pub. TV, Boston, WENH, N.H. Pub. TV, WBUR-Boston Radio; chief strategist Alexander for Pres.; vice chmn. of bd. Primary Bank, 1995-97; pres. Play Ball, N.H., 1994—; commentator, polit. analyst WMUR-TV and Yankee Network; bd. dirs. Assoc. Grocers New England, Chubb Am. Fund. Host State of the State, Yankee Cable Network; co-host Close-Up, WMUR-TV. Chmn. campaign Warren B. Rudman for U.S. Senate, 1980, 86; bd. overseers Aquinas House, Dartmouth Coll., com. on trustees Rockefeller Ctr. Bd. Visitors; bd. oversers Dartmouth Med. Sch.; nat. dir. Baker Exploratory Com., 1986-87; sec. bd. trustees Concord Hosp.; treas. N.H. Rep. party, 1981-93; trustee DWC, 1981-87, chmn., 1982-86; mem. Baker Exploratory Com., 1986-87; trustee Concord Hosp., 1980-86; sr. nat. cons. Dole for Pres.; del. Rep. Nat. Conv., 1984, 88, 92, rules com., 1988, 92, N.H. committeeman, 1996—; Rep. nat. committeeman State of N.H., 1996; bd. dirs. New Eng. Coun., 1997. Mem. Nat. Assn. Attys. Gen. (vice-chmn. Eastern region, vice chmn. standing com. on energy), N.H. Bar Assn. (Spl. Pres. award 1992). Clubs: Dartmouth Coll. (v.p. Merrimack County). Roman Catholic. Office: Rath Young and Pignatelli One Capital Plaza PO Box 1500 Concord NH 03302-1500 Business E-Mail: tdr@rathlaw.com.

RATHBONE, PETER B., art appraiser; BA in Art History, Boston U. Dir., Am. paintings, drawings and sculpture dept. Sotheby's, NYC, 1972—. Office: Sotheby's 1334 York Ave New York NY 10021 Office Phone: 212-606-7280. Office Fax: 212-606-7039. Business E-Mail: peter.rathbone@sothebys.com.

RATHBUN, ANDREW J., music educator; MA, New Eng. Conservatory, Boston, 1994. Adj. prof. Kingsborough C.C., Bklyn., 2002—. Composer (musician): (albums) Shadow Forms, Renderings, Sculptures, True Stories, Jade. Fellow, MacDowell Found.; grantee, Am. Music Ctr., Can. Coun. for Arts. Home: 315 St Johns Pl 1B Brooklyn NY 11238 Home Phone: 718 636-7414. Personal E-mail: andrewrathbun@optonline.net.

RATHBURN, KENT, chef; Chef Mr. B's, New Orleans, Am. Restaurant, Kans. City, Milano, Kans. City, The Mansion on Turtle Creek, Dallas, Landmark Restaurant, Dallas, Dusit Hotel Co., Bangkok; proprietor, exec. chef Abacus, Dallas, 1999—, Jasper's, Dallas, 2003—, The Woodlands, 2005—. Featured chef Pres. Bush 2001 Inaugural Ball; guest chef Taste of the NFL. Featured on (TV series) Chef du Jour, Cooking Live with Sara Moulton, Ready Set Cook, CBS Early Show, Rosie O'Donnell Show, Today Show, NBC, featured in Better Homes and Gardens, Rosie Mag., Bon Appetit, Southern Living Mag., Nation's Restaurant News, Elle, Veranda Mag., USA Today, Wall St. Jour., Esquire Mag., NY Times, Dallas Morning News. Nominee Best Chef: Southwest, James Beard Found., 2000, 2002, 2003, 2004; named Best Chef, D Mag. Office: Abacus 4511 Mckinney Ave Dallas TX 75205-4213 *

RATHER, DAN, news correspondent, former network news anchor; b. Wharton, Tex., Oct. 31, 1931; m. Jean Goebel, 1957; children: Dawn Robin, Daniel Martin. BA in Journalism, Sam Houston State Tchrs. Coll., Huntsville, Tex., 1953; student, U. Houston, South Tex. Sch. Law. Instr. journalism Sam Houston State Coll.; reporter AP, Huntsville, Tex., 1950, UPI, 1950—52, Houston Chronicle, 1954—55; news writer, reporter, news dir. KTRH Radio, Houston, 1956; dir. news and pub. affairs KHOU (CBS TV affiliate), Houston, 1959—61; chief southwestern bur. CBS, Dallas, 1961—64, White House corr., 1963, 1966—74, chief London bureau, 1965—66, war corr. Vietnam, 1966; anchor, corr. CBS Reports, 1974—75; corr., co-editor 60 Minutes, 1975—81; anchor Dan Rather Reporting, CBS Radio Network, 1977—2005; anchor, mng. editor CBS Evening News with Dan Rather, 1981—2005; anchor 48 Hours, 1988—2002; corr. 60 Minutes II, 1998—2006; prodr., host, Dan Rather Reports HDNet, 2006—. Co-editor show Who's Who, CBS-TV, 1977; anchored numerous CBS News spl. programs. Author: (with Gary Gates) The Palace Guard, 1974, (with Mickey Herskowitz) The Camera Never Blinks, 1977, (with Peter Wyden) Memoirs, I Remember, 1991, The Camera Never Blinks Twice: The Further Adventures of a Television Journalist, 1994, The American Dream, 2001; editor Our Times, 1994. Recipient ten Emmy awards, George Foster Peabody award, 2005; honors include dedication of Dan Rather Comm. Bldg., classroom facility Sam Houston State U., Huntsville, Tex. Office: HDNet 320 S Walton St Dallas TX 75226

RATHER, LUCIA PORCHER JOHNSON, library administrator; b. Durham, NC, Sept. 12, 1934; d. Cecil Slayton and Lucia Lockwood (Porcher) Johnson; m. John Carson Rather, July 11, 1964; children: Susan Wright, Bruce Carson. Student, Westhampton Coll., 1951-53; AB in History, U. N.C., 1955, MS in Library Sci., 1957; PhD in History, George Washington U., 1994. Cataloger Library of Congress, Washington, 1957-64, bibliographer, 1964-66, systems analyst, 1966-70; group head MARC Devel. Office, 1970-73, asst. chief, 1973-76, acting chief, 1976-77, dir. for cataloging, 1976-91. Chmn. standing com. on cataloguing Internat. Fedn. Library Assns., 1976-81; sec. Working Group on Content Designators, 1972-77; chmn. Working Group on Corp. Headings, 1978-79, Internat. ISBD Rev. Com., 1981-87. Co-author: the MARC II Format, 1968. Recipient Libr. Congress Disting. Svc. award, 1991, Disting. Alumnus award U. N.C. Sch. Libr. and Info. Sci., 1992. Mem. ALA (Margaret Mann award 1985, Melvil Dewey award 1991), Phi Beta Kappa. Democrat. Presbyterian. Home: 438 Heron Point Chestertown MD 21620-1680

RATHJE, JAMES LEE, broker; b. Davenport, Iowa, Nov. 23, 1947; s. Gilbert L. and Wanda L. (Henning) R.; m. Karen L. Mangels, May 15, 1980. BBA with high distinction, U. Iowa, 1970, MBA, 1972. Plant acct. Container Corp. Am., Wilmington, Del., 1972-73; portfolio mgr. Davenport Bank and Trust, 1973-76; investment broker Loewi and Co., Davenport, 1976-78; fin. cons. A.G. Edwards and Sons, Inc., Davenport, 1978—. With USAR, 1970-76. Republican. Lutheran. Avocations: basketball, baseball, golf, bicycling. Home: 3861 Parkdale Dr Bettendorf IA 52722-1974

RATHKE, SHEILA WELLS, strategic planning and marketing executive; b. Columbia, SC, Aug. 9, 1943; d. Walter John and Betty Marie (McLaughlin) Wells; m. David Bray Rathke, Sept. 1966 (dec. 1997); 1 child, Erinn Michele. BA summa cum laude, U. Pitts., 1976, postgrad., 1976-77. Loan coord. Equibank, Pitts., 1961-65; office mgr. U.S. Steel Corp., Pitts., 1966-70; various account and mgmt. positions Burson-Marsteller, Pitts., 1977-87, exec. v.p., gen. mgr., 1987-94, CEO Can. ops. Toronto, Montreal, Ottawa, Vancouver, 1994-95; sr. v.p., dir. corp. devel. Young and Rubicam, Inc., NYC, 1995-99, COO, 1999-2000; asst. provost strategic and program devel. U. Pitts., 2001—. Instr. Slippery Rock Coll., Pitts., 1984-85; adviser Exec. Report Mag., Pitts., 1986-88, A Better Chance, N.Y.C., 1996-2000, N.Y. Philharm., 1997-99. Trustee U. Pitts., 1976-80, mem. alumni bd. dirs., 1990-94; trustee Robert Morris Coll., 1992-95; bd. dirs. Vocat. Rehab. Ctr., 1987-93, Freewheelers, 1989-92, Pitts. Hist. Soc., River City Brass Band, Quantam Theatre, 2003-07. Named Disting. Alumnus, U. Pitts., 1992, Legacy Laureate, 2000. Mem. AAUW, Female Execs. Am., Am. Assn. Advt. Agys. (chair ea. region 1994-95), Pitts. Advt. Club (bd. dirs. 1988-91, pres. 1990), Alpha Sigma Lambda (charter). Avocations: skiing, reading, gardening, travel, photography. Home: 1819 Sarah St Apt 2 Pittsburgh PA 15203 Office: U Pitts Cathedral of Learning Pittsburgh PA 15260- E-mail: sheilarathke@msn.com.

RATHKOPF, DAREN ANTHONY, lawyer; b. Lynbrook, NY, May 12, 1933; s. Arden Herman and Florence Marie (Gortikov) R.; m. Mira Torgersen, Mar. 30, 1963; children: Ann, Erika. BA, Columbia U., 1955, LLB, 1958. Bar: N.Y. 1958, U.S. Dist. Ct. (ea., so. dists.) N.Y. 1962. Assoc. Mendes & Mount, NYC, 1961-62, Rathkopf & Rathkopf, NYC, 1962-66, ptnr. Glen Cove, N.Y., 1966-81, Payne, Wood & Littlejohn, Glen Cove and Melville, N.Y., 1982-98, of counsel Melville, Bridgehampton, Locust Valley, NY, 1999-2001, Farrell Fritz, P.C., Uniondale, Melville, Bridghampton, Locust Valley, NY, 2001—02; ptnr. Chase, Rathkopf & Chase, LLP, Glen Cove, NY, 2002—. Author: (with others) The Law of Zoning and Planning, 4th edit., 1977. Mem.: Nassau County Bar Assn., NY State Bar Assn. Home: 149 Turkey Ln Cold Spring Harbor NY 11724-1712 Office: Chase Rathkopf & Chase LLP 48 Forest Ave Glen Cove NY 11542 Office Phone: 516-671-5880. E-mail: chaserathkopf@aol.com.

RATHMAN, WILLIAM ERNEST, retired lawyer, minister; b. Middletown, Ohio, Jan. 10, 1927; s. Ernest Daniel and Marguerite (Sebald) R.; m. Constance Schedler, Nov. 28, 1958; children: Marchie, William E. Jr. Grad., Phillips Exeter Acad., 1944; BA, Kenyon Coll., 1948; postgrad., Harvard U., 1950, Ohio State U. Coll. of Law, 1951, United Theol. Seminary, Dayton, Ohio, 1975. Bar: Ohio 1952; ordained to ministry Episc. Ch., 1975. Pvt. practice law, Middletown, Ohio, 1952-78; sr. ptnr. Rathman, Elliott & Boyd, Middletown, 1979-84, Rathman, Combs, Schaefer, Valen & Kaup, Middletown, 1985-88, Rathman, Combs, Schaefer & Kaup, Middletown, 1989-95, ret., 1995—. Spl. counsel to County of Butler, 1956-64, City of Middletown, 1965-66, Ohio Atty. Gen., 1967-69; acting judge Middletown Mcpl. Ct., 1969-74. Pres. Middletown Community Found., 1972-76, Middletown Chamber Found., 1977-80, Butler County Park Commn., 1986-90; trustee-at-large Ohio Found. of Ind. Colls., Columbus, 1972-90; trustee, mem. exec. com. Middletown United Way, 1963-90; trustee Middleton Req. Hosp. Found., 1986-90; adv. bd. Middletown campus Miami U., 1984-90. With USN, 1944-46, capt. USAF, 1959, comdr. Am. Legion, 1965. Named Exec. Yr., Middletown chpt. Nat. Secs. Assn., 1969; recipient Outstanding Community Svc. award Middletown post Am. Legion, 1975, Outstanding Svc. award Parstoral Counselling Svc., 1983, Vol. of Yr. award Middletown Area United Way, 1986. Fellow Am. Coll. Trust and Estate Counsel; mem. ABA (estate tax com. 1966-69), Ohio Bar Assn. (coun. del. 1980-93), Butler County Bar Assn. (pres. 1980), Middletown Bar Assn. (pres. 1967), Fed. Bar Assn. (pres. Cin. chpt. 1975), Ohio State Bar Found. (trustee 1992-96, Ohio Supreme Ct. bd. commrs. on grievances and discipline 1996-99), Masons (master 1959-60, 33d deg.), Scottish Rite Valley of Cin. (treas. 1986, chmn. bd. 1990), Sea Pines Country Club. Episcopalian. Home (Summer): 501 Thorn Hill Ln Middletown OH 45042-3750 Home: 1924 S Beach Club Hilton Head Island SC 29928-3750 Personal E-mail: crathman@aol.com.

RATHMANN, GEORGE BLATZ, genetic engineering company executive; b. Milw., Dec. 25, 1927; s. Louis and Edna Lorle (Blatz) R.; m. Frances Joy Anderson, June 24, 1950; children: James, Margaret, Laura, Sally, Richard. BS in Phys. Chemistry, Northwestern U., 1948; MS, Princeton U., 1950, PhD in Phys. Chemistry, 1952. With 3M Co., St. Paul, 1951-72, various positions including rsch. chemist, rsch. dir., group tech. dir., mgr. X-ray products; with Litton Med. Systems, Des Plaines, Ill., 1972-75; v.p. R & D diagnostics div. Abbott Labs., North Chicago, Ill., 1975-80; pres., chief exec. officer Amgen Inc., Thousand Oaks, Calif., 1980-88, chmn. Newbury Park, Calif., 1980—90, chmn. emeritus; founder, chmn. ICOS Corp., 1990-2000; pres & CEO Hyseq, Inc., Sunnyvale, Calif., 2000—01, chmn., 2000—; chmn. bd. dir. ZymoGenetics Inc., Seattle, 2000—05. Bd. dirs. ZymoGenetics Inc., Seattle. Mem. NAE, AAAS, Am. Chem. Soc., Indsl. Biotech. Assn. (bd. dirs.), Nat. Sci. and Tech. Medals Found. (bd. dir., pres.), Phi Beta Kappa, Sigma Xi. Office: Hyseq Inc 201 Industrial Rd # 310 San Carlos CA 94070-6211

RATHMANN, PEGGY, writer, illustrator; b. St. Paul; BA in Psychology, U. Minn.; student, Am. Acad. Chgo., Atelier Lack, Mpls., Otis Parsons Sch. Design, LA. Author: Ruby the Copycat (Most Promising New Author Cuffie award Pubs. Weekly 1991), Good Night, Gorilla (ALA Notable Children's Book 1994), Officer Buckle and Gloria (Caldecott medal 1996), Ten Minutes Till Bedtime, 1998 (ALA Notable Children's Book 1998), The Day The Babies Crawled Away, 2003; illustrator: Bootsie Barker Bites, 1992. Office: Penguin Putnam Inc 345 Hudson St Fl 15 New York NY 10014-4502

RATHMELL, ROBERT D., physicist; b. Springfield, Mo., Apr. 24, 1942; s. William and Mardell Rathmell; m. Bonnie Blue Thompson, June 15, 1963; children: Mark A., Keith E. PhD, U. Wis., Madison, 1971. Sr. v.p. Nat. Electrostatics Corp., Middleton, Wis., 1970—94; staff scientist Axcelis Techs., Inc., Beverly, Mass., 1994—. Recipient Disting. Technologist award, Axcelis Techs., Inc, 2001. Achievements include 10 patens on various implantation related inventions. Home: 401 Love Bird Ln Murphy TX 75094 Home Phone: 972-881-3831; Office Phone: 972-690-8914 78607. Personal E-mail: rober.rathmell@verizon.net.

RATHNAU, HEATHER HEARN, music educator, writer; b. San Antonio, Tex., Mar. 8, 1958; d. Claude Adam Hearn, Jr. and Mildred Ruby Damron; m. Ronald Alan Rathnau, Aug. 1, 1981; children: Alison Renee, Mallory Dawn. MusB magna cum laude, Baylor U., 1980, MusM, 1982. Pvt. music and voice tchr., Houston, 1984—; prin., owner Theory Time, Mo. City, Tex., 1996—. Guest instr. Schmitt Music Expo, 1999, Mpls., 2005; lectr. in field. Author: Theory Time, 1996, 2002. Mem.: Music Tchrs. Nat. Assn., Tex. Music Tchrs. Assn., Forum Music Tchrs. Assn. (pres. 1992—94), Nat. Piano Tchrs. Guild (adjudicator 1990—2007), Houston (Tex.) Music Tchrs. Assn. (v.p. 1989—90), Music Tchrs. Nat. Conf., Houston (Tex.) Fedn. Music Clubs, Mu Phi Epsilon. Republican. Baptist. Avocations: travel, reading, gardening. Home: 6639 Sutters Creek Trail Missouri City TX 77459

RATHOD, MULCHAND, mechanical engineering educator; b. Pathri, India, Mar. 3, 1945; came to U.S., 1970, naturalized, 1981; s. Shamjibhai Laljibhai and Ramaben Rathod; m. Damayanti Thakor, Aug. 15, 1970; children: Prerana, Falgun, Sejal. BS in Mech. Engring., Sardar Patel U., India, 1970; MS, Miss. State U., 1972, PhD, 1975. Rsch. grad. asst. Miss. State U., 1970-75; cons. engr. Bowron & Butler, Jackson, Miss., 1975-76; asst. prof. Tuskegee Inst., Ala., 1976-78; assoc. prof., coord. MET program SUNY, Binghamton, 1979-87; prof. Wayne State U., Detroit, 1987—, dir. engring. tech. divsn., 1987—2003. Cons. Interpine, Hattiesburg, Miss., 1977-79, Jet Propulsion Lab., 1980-83, IBM Corp., 1982-85; pres. Shiv-Parvati, Inc. 1982—. Contbr. articles to profl. jours.; patentee in field. Den leader Susquahanna coun. Boy Scouts Am., Vestal, N.Y., 1983-84. Recipient award NASA, 1981; grantee SUNY Found., 1984, Dept. Energy, 1978, GM, 1988-92, UAW Chrysler, 1990-91, Hudson-Webber Found., 1991-92, Ford, 1992-93, Kellogg Found., 1993-94, SME Found., 1994, Mich. Dept. Edn., 1994, NSF, 1995-2001. Fellow: ASME (cert. of appreciation 1982—89, 1991—2005, Dedicated Svc. award 1995, Ben C. Sparks medal 1998, BMW award 2001); mem.: ASHRAE, Profl. Order Engring. Tech., N.Y. State Engring. Tech. Assn., Am. Soc. Engring. Edn. (reviewer), India Assn. Miss. State U. (pres. 1972—73), Tau Beta Pi, Tau Alpha Phi (founder, faculty advisor 1989—), Pi Tau Sigma. Home: 1042 Woods Ln Grosse Pointe Woods MI 48236-1157 Office: Wayne State U Div Engring Tech Detroit MI 48202

RATHORE, AKSHAY KUMAR, electrical engineer, researcher; b. Bhawani Mandi, Rajasthan, India, Dec. 8, 1979; s. Ramesh Chandra Rathore and Saroj Rani Pancholi. B in Engring., Coll. Tech. and Engring., Udaipur, India, 2001; M in Tech., Banaras Hindu U., Varanasi, India, 2003; postgrad., U. Victoria, B.C., Can. Lectr. elec. engring. Mody Inst. Tech. and Sci., Lakshmangarh, India, 2003—04, Coll. Tech. and Engring., Udaipur, 2003; rsch. asst., lab instr. dept. elec. and computer engring. U. Victoria, 2004—. Reviewer numerous internat. confs. Contbr. articles to profl. jours. Recipient gold medal, Banaras Hindu U., India, 2003; fellow, U. Victoria, 2004—05; scholar, U. Grant Commn., 2001—03; Thouvenelle Grad. scholar, 2006—07. Mem.: IEEE (travel grantee 2003, 2004). Achievements include research in soft-switching techniques for high frequency link power converters; utility interactive inverters for renewable energy sources; linear induction motor. Home: 1590 Mortimer St British Columbia Victoria BC Canada V8P 3A6 Office: Univ Victoria ELW B 308 Dept ECE Victoria BC Canada V8P 5C2 Home Phone: +1-250-477-3037; Office Phone: +1-250-472-4233. Office Fax: +1-250-721-6052; Home Fax: +1-250-721-6052. Personal E-mail: akshay@uvic.ca. E-mail: akshay@engr.uvic.ca.

RATI, ROBERT DEAN, retired data processing executive; b. Pittsburg, Kans., Jan. 8, 1939; s. Steve Julius Rati and Dorothy Bill (Rodebush) McWilliams; m. Margaret Fort Henry, June 7, 1969; children: Susan Margaret, Robert Henry. BA, U. Kans., Lawrence, 1961; MA, Northeastern U., Boston, 1970; MBA, Columbia U., NYC, 1973. Systems engr. IBM Corp., Boston, 1965-72; mgr. mgmt. services Arthur Young and Co., NYC, 1973-75; mgr. client systems Touche Ross and Co., NYC, 1975-76; mgr. systems and programs Walker Mfg. div. Tenneco, Racine, Wis., 1976-78; mgr. data processing Schwitzer div. Household Internat., Indpls., 1979-87; mgr. mgmt. info. systems Nat. Machinery Co., Tiffin, Ohio, 1988-90; pres. Dunhill Profl. Search of Carmel (Ind.), 1990-97; mgr. Muncie MIS Power Transformer div. Asea Brown Boveri, Muncie, Ind., 1991-94; dir. info. svcs. State Lottery Commn. Ind., Indpls., 1995-97; mgmt. cons. Aerotek-Maxim Group, Indpls., 1998-2000; project mgr. corp. info. tech. AT&T (formerly SBC Comms.), Indpls., 2000—05; ret., 2005. Contbr. articles to publs. of fraternal orgns. Mem. Rep. Com., Ramsey, NJ, 1972-74; treas. Rep. Club Ramsey, 1972-75; vice chmn. Swimming Pool Commn., Ramsey, 1972-74; bd. dirs., exec. com. Near Eastside Multi-Svc. Ctr., Indpls., 1984-87; fin. com. Carmel (Ind.) United Meth. Ch., 1984-87, adminstrv. bd., 1987-90. Lt. (j.g.) USN, 1961-64. Recipient Regional Mgrs. award, IBM Corp., 1967. Mem. SAR (pres. 1979), Soc. Ind. Pioneers (pres. 1996-98), Huguenot Soc. Ind. (pres. 1985-89), S.R. in State of Ill. (pres. 1980-82), Ind. Soc. Colonial Wars (gov. 1995-98), Gen. Soc. Sons of the Revolution (chmn. awards com. 1983-91, Gen. Pres. Commendation award 1985, 91), Sons of the Revolution State of Ind. (sec. 2006—, pres. 2007—), Pi Mu Epsilon. Republican. Avocations: genealogy, home computer. Home: 4919 Regency Pl Carmel IN 46033-5959

RATLIFF, BEN, music critic; Contbr. Coda mag., Option, Village Voice; popular music critic NY Times, NYC. Author: The New York Times Essential Library: Jazz: A Critic's Guide to the 100 Most Important Recordings, 2002. Office: NY Times Culture Desk 229 W 43rd St New York NY 10036 Office Phone: 212-556-4922. Office Fax: 212-556-1516.

RATLIFF, LOUIS JACKSON, JR., mathematics professor; b. Cedar Rapids, Iowa, Sept. 1, 1931; s. Louis Jackson and Ruth Sara (Sidlinger) R.; m. Georgia Lee Smith, May 9, 1996. BA, State U. Iowa, 1953, MA, 1958, PhD, 1961. Lectr. Ind. U., Bloomington, 1961-63, U. Calif., Riverside, 1963-64, asst. prof. math., 1964-67, assoc. prof., 1967-69, prof., 1969—. Author: Chain Conjectures in Ring Theory, 1978; assoc. editor Procs. of AMS, 1987-92, Comm. in Algebra, 1990-95; contbr. articles to profl. jours. 1st lt. USAF, 1953-57. NSF fellow, 1960-62, grantee, 1965-69, 71-88; recipient Disting. Teaching award, U. Calif.-Riverside, 1983. Mem. Am. Math. Soc., Phi Beta Kappa. Democrat. Seventh Day Adventist. Home: 26660 Ridgemoor Rd Sun City CA 92587 Office: U Calif Dept Math Riverside CA 92521-0001 Office Phone: 951-827-5024. Business E-Mail: ratliff@math.ucr.edu.

RATLIFF, THOMAS ASBURY, JR., retired engineer; b. Phila., May 5, 1919; s. Thomas Asbury and Edna Dorothy (Overman) R.; m. Lucy Lila Graydon, Aug. 15, 1942; children: Deborah Ratliff Miller, Anne Ratliff Naberhaus. Test technician GE, Cin., 1951; quality engr. Am. Standard Corp., Cin., 1951-54, asst. dir. rsch., 1956-58; chief inspector Gruen Watch Co., Cin., 1954-58; cons. Hyde Engring. Co., Cin., 1958-60, Badgett & Smith, Inc., Cin., 1963-67; sales mgr. Lehmann Corp., Cin., 1960-63; purchasing mgr. Access Corp., Cin., 1967-70; pres. Ratliff & Assoc., Inc., Cin., 1970-96; ret., 1996. Adj. prof. engring. U. Cin., 1998-2000. Author: Basic Statistics for Lab Workers, 1992, The Laboratory Quality Assurance System, 1993, 3d. edit., 2003. Col. U.S. Army, 1940-72. Fellow Am. Soc. for Quality (various coms.). Republican. Mem. Soc. Of Friends. Avocation: collecting model cannons. Home: 755 Greenville Ave Cincinnati OH 45246-4608 Personal E-mail: tarqc19@aol.com.

RATLIFF, WILLIAM, former state senator, lieutenant governor, civil engineer; b. Aug. 16, 1936; BS in Civil Engring., U. Tex., 1960. City mgr., Copperas Cove, Tex.; pvt. practice civil engr. Mt. Pleasant, Tex.; mem. Tex. Senate Dist. 1, 1989—2003, chair fin. com., mem. edn. com., mem. adminstrn. com.; mem. internat. rels., trade and tech. com.; lt. gov. Tex., 2000—; dist. 1 state senator Tex., 2003—04. Pres. Mt. Pleasant Indsl. Found.; mem. exec. com. N.E. Tex. Econ. Devel. Dist., Inc.; Sunday sch. tchr.; lay reader; chair fin. com.; bd. trustees Tennison Meml. United Meth. Ch.; Sgt. USAR. Recipient Outstanding State Leader award, 2001, John F. Kennedy Profile in Courage award John F. Kennedy Libr. Found., 2005. Mem. Am. Consulting Engr. Coun. (past pres.). Republican.

RATNER, BRUCE C., professional sports team owner, real estate developer; b. Cleve., Jan. 23, 1945; children: Rebecca, Elizabeth. BA cum laude, Harvard U., 1967; JD, Columbia U., 1970. Dir. Model Cities Prog., head Consumer Protection Divsn. NYC, 1970—73, commr. consumer affairs, 1978—82; prof. law NYU, 1974—78; pres., CEO Forest City Ratner Cos., NYC, 1982—; owner NJ Nets, 2004—. Trustee Bklyn. Acad. Music, 1989, chmn., 1992—2001; bd. dirs. Mus. Jewish Heritage, Met. Mus. Art, City Pks. Found., Internat. Rescue Com., Bklyn. C. of C., NYC Partnership. Named The Top NYC Exec., Crain's NY Bus., 1992; named one of NY's Most Influential Bus. Leaders, 2002; recipient NY State Gov.'s Arts award, 1994. Office: Forest City Ratner Cos 1 Metrotech Ctr N Brooklyn NY 11201 *

RATNER, BUDDY DENNIS, biomedical engineer, educator; b. Bklyn., Jan. 19, 1947; s. Philip and Ruth Ratner; m. Cheryl Cromer; 1 child, Daniel Martin. BS in Chemistry, Bklyn. Coll., 1967; PhD in Polymer Chemistry, Bklyn. Poly. U., 1972. From fellow to prof. U. Wash., Seattle, 1972—86, prof., 1986—, Darland prof. bioengring., 2005—. Dir. U. Wash. Engineered Biomaterials Engring. Ctr.; founder Asemblon, Inc., Healionics, Inc. Editor: Surface Characterization of Biomaterials, 1989, Plasmas and Polymers, 1994-99, Biomaterials Science: An Introduction to Materials in Medicine, 2d edit., 2004, Characterization of Polymeric Biomaterials, 1997; mem. editl. bds. 9 jours. and book series; editor Jour. Undergrad. Rsch. in Bioengring., 1998—; contbr. over 300 articles to profl. jours. Recipient Faculty Achievement/Outstanding Rsch. award, Burlington Resources Found., 1990, Perkin Elmer Phys. Electronics award for excellence in surface sci. Fellow AAAS, Internat. Acad. Med. and Biol. Engring., Am. Inst. Med. Biol. Engring. (founder, pres. 2002-03), AVS Sci. Technol. Soc. (Medard Welsh medal 2002); mem. AIChE (C.M.A. Stine award 1998), Nat. Acad. Engring., Am. Chem. Soc., Internat. Soc. Contact Lens Rsch., Materials Rsch. Soc., Soc. for Biomaterials (pres. 1991-92, Clemson award 1989, fellow 1994, Founders award 2004, C.W. Hall award 2006), Biomed. Engring. Soc. Achievements include patents in field. Home Phone: 206-286-0969; Office Phone: 206-685-1005. E-mail: ratner@uweb.engr.washington.edu.

RATNER, CARL JOSEPH, opera stage director, baritone; b. Memphis, Sept. 17, 1957; MusB, Oberlin Conservatory of Music, 1980; MA, Northeastern Ill. U., 1999; DM, Northwestern U., 2005. Intern Juilliard Sch., NYC, 1980-81, N.Y.C. Opera, 1981-82; asst. dir. Lyric Opera Chgo., 1982-84; prodn. asst. San Francisco Opera, 1985-86; asst. dir. Metropolitan Opera, NYC, 1989-90; artistic dir. Chamber Opera Chgo., 1985-93, Chgo. Opera Theater, 1994-99; opera dir. Western Mich. U., 2001—. Cons. in field. Home: 3440 N Lake Shore Dr Apt 9D Chicago IL 60657-2848 Office: Western Michigan Univ Sch Music Dalton Ctr 1903 W Michigan Ave Kalamazoo MI 49008-5434 Office Phone: 269-387-4706, 773-454-4919. Personal E-mail: carlratner@aol.com.

RATNER, DAVID LOUIS, retired law educator; b. London, Sept. 2, 1931; AB magna cum laude, Harvard U., 1952, LLB magna cum laude, 1955. Bar: N.Y. 1955. Assoc. Sullivan & Cromwell, NYC, 1955-64; assoc. prof. Cornell Law Sch., Ithaca, NY, 1964-68, prof., 1968-82; prof. law U. San Francisco Law Sch., 1982-99, dean, 1982-89, prof. emeritus, 1999—. Exec. asst. to chmn. SEC, Washington, 1966-68; chief counsel Securities Industry Study, Senate Banking Com., Washington, 1971-73; vis. prof. Stanford (Calif.) U., 1974, Ariz. State U., Tempe, 1974, U. San Francisco, 1980, Georgetown U., Washington, 1989-90, U. Calif., Hastings, San Francisco, 1992, U. Ariz., 2004; mem. Larkspur (Calif.) Planning Commn., 1992-2004. Author: Institutional Investors: Teaching Materials, 1978, Securities Regulation: Cases and Materials, 6th edit., 2002, Securities Regulation in a Nutshell, 9th edit., 2006. Fulbright scholar Monash U., Australia, 1981. Mem. Cosmos Club (Washington), Harvard Club of San Francisco (pres. 1999-2000), Phi Beta Kappa. Home and Office: 84 Polhemus Way Larkspur CA 94939-1928 E-mail: dlratner@aol.com.

RATNER, ELLEN FAITH, news analyst and correspondent, writer; b. Cleve., Aug. 28, 1951; d. Harry Ratner and Anne Spott. BA, Goddard Coll., 1974; EdM, Harvard U., 1978. Coord. women's svcs. Homophile Comty. Health Svc., Boston, 1971-73; co-dir., co-founder Boundaries Therapy Ctr., Acton, Mass., 1973-86; dir. psychiat. day treatment program South Shore Mental Health Ctr., Quincy, Mass., 1974-81; v.p. rsch., devel. and svc., dir. ARC Rsch. Found. Addiction Recovery Corp., Rockville, Mass., 1986-90; health care cons., dir. Found. for Addiction Rsch., 1990-94; White House reporter, bur. chief Talk Radio News Svc., Washington, 1991—, chief polit. corr., news analyst; polit. analyst FOX News Channel, 1997—; Washington bur. chief, polit. editor Talkers Mag., 1996—; CEO Coll. Media News Co. Tchr. Curry Coll., Milton, Mass., 1979-80; cons. program devel. Addiction Recovery Corp., 1984-86; developer, planner The Art's in Mileau Treatment of Phychiatric Outpatients, Quincy, 1980, New Eng.'s first conf. on Chem. Dependency and AIDS, 1988. Author: The Other Side of the Family: A Book for Recovery from Abuse, Incest and Neglect, 1990, 101 Ways to Get Your Progressive Issues on Talk Radio, 1997; mem. adv. bd. The Counselor Mag., 1987-90; appeared on nat. TV and radio shows including C-SPAN, The Oprah Winfrey Show, CNN, Nat. Empowerment TV, others; co-host (radio) Washington Reality Check, Good Day USA, New World Chronicle; polit. corr, Talk Radio Countdown Show; prodr. Talk Daily. Bd. trustees, mem. exec. com., vis. com. presdl. search com. Goddard Col., Plainfield, Vt. 1977-81; bd. trustees Samaritan Coll., L.A., 1988-90; bd. dirs. Nat. Lesbian and Gay Health Found., Washington, 1985-92, pres., exec. com., program com., program chair; v.p. Harry Ratner Human Svcs. Fund, Cleve., 1991—; mem. adv. bd. Women of Washington, Inc., 1992—; bd. dirs. Theater Chamber Players, Kennedy Ctr., Washington, 1988-91, An Uncommon Legacy Found., N.Y.C., 1993—, The Ctr. for Spiritual Enlightment, Falls Church, Va., 1994—. Recipient Comty. Svc. award Lesbian and Gay Counseling Svc., Boston, 1985, The Addams-Brown award Nat. Lesbian and Gay Health Found., 1993. Mem. Nat. Assn. Radio Talk Show Hosts, Mass. Assn. Day treatment Adminstrs. (chair regulations and standards com. 1979-81), Lily Dale Assembly. Democrat. Jewish. Avocation: writing works on spiritualism. Office: Talk Radio News Svc 2514 Mill Rd NW Washington DC 20007-2950 Address: FOX News Channel 1211 Avenue of the Americas New York NY 10036

RATNER, GAYLE, special education educator; b. Bronx, NY; BS, SUNY, Plattsburgh, 1991, MS in Edn., 1993. Cert. spl. edn. grades K-12 and elem. edn. grades N-6. Spl. edn. tchr. Chazy (N.Y.) Ctrl. Rural Sch., 1991—. Asst. chief reader N.Y. State Tchr. Cert. Examinations, mem. students with disabilities content adv. com.; instr. N.Y. State United Tchrs. Effective Tchg. Program, 1999—, mentor coord.; mem. policy bd. North Country Tchr. Resource Ctr.; new tchr. mentor coord. Chazy Ctrl. Rural Sch. Mem.: N.Y. State United Tchrs., Chazy Tchrs. Assn. (pres. 1995—2005, newsletter editor 2003—), Nat. Bd. Profl. Tchg. Stds. (spl. edn. and elem. edn. com. 2000—, bd. dirs.). Office: Chazy Ctrl Rural Sch 609 Route 191 Chazy NY 12921

RATNER, GERALD, lawyer; b. Chgo., Dec. 17, 1913; s. Peter I. and Sarah (Soreson) R.; m. Eunice Payton, June 18, 1948. PhB, U. Chgo., 1935, JD cum laude, 1937. Bar: Ill. 1937. Since practiced in, Chgo.; sr. ptnr. Gould & Ratner and predecessor firm, 1949—. Officer Henry Crown & Co., CC Industries, Inc., Material Svc. Corp., Freeman United Coal Mining Co., Mineral and Land Resources Corp.; lectr., writer on real estate law. Capt. US Army, 1942—46. Gerald Ratner Athletics Ctr. named in his honor, U. Chgo.; recipient Disting. Svc. medal U. Chgo., 2005 Mem. ABA, Ill. Bar Assn., Chgo. Bar Assn., Order of Coif, Phi Beta Kappa. Home: 180 E Pearson St Apt 6205 Chicago IL 60611-2191 Office: 222 N La Salle St Ste 800 Chicago IL 60601-1086 Office Phone: 312-236-3003. Business E-Mail: gratner@gouldratner.com.

RATNER, MICHAEL D., lawyer; b. June 13, 1943; s. Harry and Anne (Spott) Ratner. BA, Brandeis U., 1966; JD magna cum laude, Columbia U., 1971. Bar: N.Y. 1971, U.S. Supreme Ct. 1983. Law clk. U.S. Dist. Ct. (so. dist.), NYC, 1971-72; prof. NYU Law Sch., NYC, 1973-74; atty. Ctr. for Constl. Rights, NYC, 1978-85, legal dir., 1985-90, pres. Adj. prof. Yale Law Sch., New Haven, 1990—95, lectr., 2000; spl. counsel for human rights Govt. of Haiti, 1996; lectr. Columbia Law Sch., NYC, 1999—. Author: International Human Rights Litigtion in U.S. Courts, 1997, Che Guevara and the FBI, 1997, The Pinochet Papers: The Case of Augusto Pinochet Ugarte in Spain and Britain, 2000; co-author (with Barbara Olshansky & Jennie Green): Against War with Iraq, 2003; co-author: (with Ellen Ray) Guantanamo: What the World Should Know, 2004; contbr. articles to profl. jours.; co-author: Disappeared in America, 2005. Named Trial Lawyer of Yr., Trial Lawyers for the Pub. Interest; named one of 100 Most Influential Lawyers, Nat. Law Jour.; recipient medal of excellence, Columbia Law Sch., 2004, John Minor Wisdom pro bono award, ABA, 2006, Brandeis Alumni award, 2006, Hans Litten prize, 2006; Lennon Ono Peace grantee, 2006, Skelly Wright fellow, Yale Law Sch., 2000, Hon fellow, U. Pa. Law Sch., 2005. Mem. Nat. Lawyers Guild (pres. 1982-83). Office Phone: 212-614-6429. E-mail: mratner@igc.org.

RATTERREE, JOHN ERIC, academic administrator; b. Spartanburg, SC, Feb. 20, 1962; s. Hugh Bryson and Jane Goins Ratterree; m. Allison Albee, Mar. 4, 1995. BS, Clemson U., SC, 1985; MEd, Converse Coll., Spartanburg, 1988. Curriculum facilitator James F. Byrnes HS, Duncan, SC, 1999—; dist. energy mgr. Sch. Dist. 5 of Spartanburg County, Duncan, 2001—. Adj. prof. Converse Coll., Spartanburg, 1998—. Mem. SC Acad. Learning Environment, Duncan, 2000—. Named Spartanburg Conservation Tchr. of the Yr., Spartanburg Soil and Water Conservation Dist., 1995, Lockhart HS Tchr. of the Yr., Union County Schs., 1990. Mem.: ASCD (assoc.), Am. Ednl. Rsch. Assn., Nat. Sci. Tchrs. Assn., Assn. Energy Engrs. (cert. energy mgr.), SC Acad. Sci., Sierra Club. Avocations: woodworking, natural science, cooking. Personal E-mail: cu85tiger@yahoo.com.

RATTI, CARLO FILIPPO, architect, researcher, educator; b. Turin, Italy, Jan. 7, 1971; s. Giuseppe Enrico Ratti and Anna Chiara Frisa. MSc Civil Engring., Poly. Inst. Turin, 1995; MSc, Ecole Nationale des Ponts et Chaussées, Paris, 1995; PhD, U. Cambridge, Eng., 2002, MPhil, 1996. Registered arch., U.K.; engr., Italy, France. Dir. archtl. firm Carlo Ratti Associati, Turin, 2002—; prof., dir. MIT SENSEable City Lab., Cambridge, Mass., 2002—. Co-designer SandScape (Ars Electronica Exhbn., Lintz, Austria, 2002); contbr. articles to profl. publs., newspapers. Founder Coll. Milan, 2000—; pres. Comitato Valdo Fusi, Turin, 2005; mem. Associazione Effetto-T, Turin. Aspen for the New Leadership fellow,

Aspen Inst. Italy, 2000—, Fulbright scholar, Fulbright Commn., 2001—02. Achievements include patents in field. Office: Mit 77 Massachusetts Ave Cambridge MA 02139 Office Fax: 617-258-8081; Home Fax: 0039-011-8393218.

RATTIE, KEITH O., gas industry executive; Sr. v.p. The Coastal Corp., 1996—2001; pres. Questar Corp., 2001—02, pres., CEO, 2002—03, chmn., pres., CEO, 2003—. Dir. Zions First Nat. Bank, Interstate Natural Gas Assoc. of Am., Gas Technology Institute, Gas Inst. of Salt Lake, U. Wyo. Energy Resources Coun. Mem.: Salt Lake C. of C. (chmn.). Office: c/o Questar 180 E 100 S Salt Lake City UT 84145 *

RATTMAN, WILLIAM JOHN, electronics and electro-optic engineer; b. Springfield, Mass., Nov. 16, 1933; s. Frank William and Sylvia Mary (Berry) R.; m. Jayne Winona Crockett, Aug. 19, 1954; children: Joy Diane, Beth Jayne, Amy Cathryn. BSEE, U. Mass, 1955; MSEE, Northeastern U., 1961. Sr. engr. Raytheon Co., Bedford, Mass., 1955-63; prin. engr., 1967-72; engrng. specialist Sylvania Applied Rsch. Lab., Waltham, Mass., 1963-67; mgr. R&D Electro Signal Lab., Inc., Rockland, Mass., 1972-86. Cons. electronics, electro-optics to mfg. firms. Patentee optical depth finder, contrast detector, low drive power wideband optical modulator, laser ablative printing system, photoelectric smoke detector, self diagnostic smoke detector. Co-chmn. Town of Needham United Way Campaign, 1973. Mem. Soc. Photo-Optical Instrumentation Egnrs., S. Yarmouth Hist. soc. (pres. 1974-75). Home and Office: 303 Bellingrath Terr Deland FL 32724 Office Phone: 386-736-3232. E-mail: wrattman@cfl.rr.com.

RATTNER, DAVID W., surgeon; MD, Johns Hopkins U. Sch. Medicine, 1978. Diplomate Am. Bd. of Surgery, 1986. Intern, surgery Mass. Gen. Hosp., Boston, 1978—79, resident, surgery, 1979—85, chief gen. and gastrointestinal surgery divsn., 1999—; prof. surgery Harvard Med. Sch., Boston. Contbr. articles to profl. jours. Mem.: ACS, Am. Surgical Assn., Soc. for Surgery Alimentary Tract, Soc. Surgical Oncology, Soc. Am. Gastrointestinal and Endoscopic Surgeons (pres. 2004—05). Office: Mass Gen Hosp Divsn Gen Surgery 15 Parkmans St WANG (WACC) 460 Boston MA 02114 Office Phone: 617-726-1893. Office Fax: 617-724-0355. Business E-Mail: drattner@partners.org.

RATTNER, STEVEN LAWRENCE, investment banker; b. NYC, July 5, 1952; s. George Seymour and Selma Ann (Silberman) R.; m. P. Maureen White, June 22, 1986; children: Rebecca White, Daniel Irvin, David William, James Brennan. AB in Econs. with honors, Brown U., 1974. Asst. to James Reston, corr. NY Times, Washington, NYC, London, 1974-82; assoc., v.p. Lehman Bros. Kuhn Loeb, NYC, 1982-84; assoc., v.p., prin., mng. dir., head communications group Morgan Stanley & Co., NYC, 1984-89; mng. dir., head comms. group Lazard Fréres & Co., LLC, NYC, 1989-97, dep. chief exec., dep. chmn., 1998—2000; mng. prin. Quadrangle Group LLC, NYC, 2000—. Dir. Falcon Cable Holding Group, 1993—. Contbr. articles to various publs. including NY Times, Wall St. Jour., LA Times, Fin. Times. Trustee Brookings Instn., 1998—, Met. Mus. Art, 1996—; trustee Ednl. Broadcasting Corp., 1990—, vice chmn., 1994-98, chmn., 1998-2006; fellow & chmn. budget & fin. com. Brown Univ.; adv. coun. NYC Outward Bound Ctr., 1990—; past trustee Mus. TV & Radio. Harvey Baker fellow Brown U. 1974, Poynter fellow Yale, 1979. Mem. Coun. Fgn. Rels., Royal Inst. for Internat. Affairs (assoc.). Office: Quadrangle Group LLC 375 Park Ave New York NY 10152 *

RATUM, CECILIA BANGLOY, retired psychologist; b. Jones, Isabela, Philippines, Feb. 1, 1935; arrived in U.S., 1968, naturalized, 1974; d. Federico Reyes and Vivina Pastor Bangloy; m. Pablo Agpaoa Ratum, Apr. 21, 1958; children: Nympha, Locelia. Psychology program, U. San Francisco, 1980—81; MA in Elem. Counseling, San Francisco State U., 1975; grad. program, Philippine Normal U., 1963, BS in Elem. Edn., 1955. Cert. tchr. Ilocos Norte Normal Sch., Philippines, 1953, nat. cert. sch. psychologist 1989. Instr. Philippine Wesleyan Coll., Cabanatuan, Philippines, 1955—56; critic tchr. Philippine Women's U., Manila, 1956—57; head tchr., classroom tchr. Philippine Pub. Schs., Jones, 1957—60, dist. guidance coord., 1960—68; filing clk. Pacific Telephone, San Francisco, 1968—69; substitute tchr. San Francisco Unified Sch. Dist., 1969—70, counselor, 1970—78, tchr., 1978—79, counselor, 1979—81, psychologist, 1981—98; ret., 1998—2002; psychologist San Francisco Unified Sch. Dist., 2002—04; ret., 2004. Team leader for sch. pschologist San Francisco Unified Sch. Dist., 1984—86, supr. sch. psychology intern, 1993—96, cadre leader for sch. psychologists, 1997—98. Mem. JCC, San Francisco. Mem.: Calif. Ret. Tchrs. Assn. (San Francisco Divsn.), Sixty Plus San Francisco U. Beta Chpt., Internat. Dyslexia Assn., Calif. Assn. Sch. Psychologists, Nat. Assn. Sch. Psychologists, San Francisco State U. Alumni Assn. (life), San Francisco State U. Osher Learning Inst. (life). Avocations: reading, writing, music, writing. Home: 168 Lowell St San Francisco CA 94112-4307 Personal E-mail: ratum5f@sbcglobal.net.

RATZ, JOHN LOUIS, dermatologist; b. Aurora, Ill., May 18, 1947; s. Augustin and Veronica Ratz; m. Shirley Mary Fayfar, June 7, 1969; children: Kristen Noel, Timothy John (T.J.) Michael, Stacie Michelle. BS, Aurora Coll., 1970; MD, Case Western Res. U., Cleve., 1975; MBA, Auburn U., Ala., 2001. Diplomate Am. Bd. Dermatology, 1979. Assoc. prof., dir. dermatol. surgery U. Cin., 1980—84; co-dir. dermatol. surgery Cleve. Clinic Found., 1984—89; clin. assoc. prof., dir. dermagol. surgery Ochsner Clinic, New Orleans, 1992—96; prof., dir. dermatologic surgery Med. Coll. Ga., Augusta, 1998—2004; dir. dermatology Cosmetic and Surg. Assocs. at Veranda, Albany, Ga., 2006—. Editor: (textbook) Lasers in Medicine and Surgery, Textbook of Dermatologic Surgery;, co-editor: Roenigk's Dermatologic Surgery: Current Techniques in Procedural Dermatology; contbr. more than 100 articles to sci. jours., chpts. to books. Fellow: ACP, Am. Soc. Dermatologic Surgery, Am. Soc. Laser Medicine and Surgery, Am. Coll. Mohs Micrographic Surgery and Cutaneous Oncology, Am. Acad. Dermatology. Independent. Byzantine Catholic. Avocations: art, collecting guns, collecting timepieces, photography, boating. Office: Cosmetic and Surgical Dermatology Associ 2701 Meredyth Dr Albany GA 31707 Home Phone: 864-993-8855; Office Phone: 229-883-7010. Business E-Mail: jlratz@theveranda.org.

RATZENBERGER, JOHN DESZO, actor, writer, film director; b. Bridgeport, Conn., Apr. 6, 1947; s. Dezso Alexander and Bertha (Grohowski) R.; m. Elizabeth Georgia Stiny, Sept. 9, 1984 (div. May 27, 2004); children: James John, Nina Katherine. Grad. high sch., Bridgeport, Conn.; PhD, Sacred Heart U., 1992, LHD (hon.), 2002. Actor, writer, dir. own theater troupe Sal's Meat Market, 1971-76; touring actor, 1971-81. Owner, pres., founder Eco-Pack Industries, Kent, Wash. Performed various one-man shows and directed, Stowe Playhouse, Vermont; appeared in plays Curse of the Starving Class, The Connection; films include The Ritz, 1974, Twilight's Last Gleaming, 1977, A Bridge Too Far, 1977, Valentino, 1977, Warlords of Atlantis, 1978, Superman, 1978, The Bitch, 1979, Arabian Adventure, 1979, Yanks, 1979, Star Wars: Episode V-The Empire Strikes Back, 1980, Motel Hell, 1980, Superman II, 1980, Outland, 1981, Ragtime, 1981, Warlords of the 21st Century, 1982, Firefox, 1982, Gandhi, 1982, House II: The Second Story, 1987, Going to the Chapel, 1988, Toy Story (voice), 1995, That Darn Cat, 1997, One Night Stand, 1997, Bad Day on the Block, 1997, A Fare to Remember, 1998, A Bug's Life (voice), 1998, Toy Story 2 (voice), 1999, Tic Tock, 2000, Determination of Death, 2001, Monsters, Inc., 2002, Finding Nemo (voice), 2003, The Incredibles (voice), 2004, All In, 2005, Something New, 2006, (voice) Cars, 2006, Superman II (voice), 2006, Ratatouille (voice), 2007; (TV films) The Good Soldier, 1981, Goliath Awaits, 1981, Combat High, 1986, Timestalkers, 1987, Friends in Space, 1990 (also writer), Camp Cucamonga, 1990, Dog's Best Friend, 1997, The Pennsylvania Miners' Story, 2002, Mystery Woman: Redemption, 2006; video (voice) Toy Racer, 2001, Extreme Skate Adventure, 2003, The Incredibles: Rise of the Underminer, 2005; TV performances include Songs of a Sourdough, Secret Amy, 1979, (series) Cheers, 1982-1993 (also dir. several episodes 1988-93); guest appearences include Hill Street Blues, 1982, Wizards and Warriors, 1983, Magnum P.I., 1984, St. Elsewhere, 1985, The Love Boat, 1985, The Tortellis, 1987, Mickey's 60th Birthday, 1988, Disneyland, 1990, Wings, 1990, Captain Planet and the Planeteers, 1990, Nurses, 1992, Bill Nye, the Science Guy, 1993, Moon Over Miami, 1993, (voice) The Simpsons, 1994, Murphy Brown, 1995, Caroline in the City, 1996, Sabrina, The Teenage Witch, 1997, The Detectives, 1997, Remember WENN, 1998, Touched by an Angel, 2000, (voice) Pigs Next Door, 2000, That '70's Show, 2001, Fraiser, 2002, 8 Simple Rules for Dating My Teenage Daughter, 2003; (TV mini series) Small World, 1988; dir. (TV series) Sister, Sister, 1994, (1 episode) Evening Shade, 1994, Pearl, 1996; prodr., screenwriter BBC, Paravision, Royal Court Theater, Hampstead Theater Club, Royal Acad. Dramatic Arts, and Granada TV; co-author TV plays: Friends in Space, 1978, Scalped, 1979; exec. prodr., creator, (TV) Locals, 1994; host Pixar's 20th Anniversary Special, 2006; performer Dancing with the Stars, 2007; co-author with Joel Engel We've Got It Made In America: A Common Man's Salute to an Uncommon Country, 2006. Chmn., largest internet venture connecting diabetes info. & rsch. www.childrenwithdiabetes.com; nat. walk chmn. Juvenile Diabetes Found.; actively involved with other various diabetes organizations; founder, actively involved Nuts, Bolts and Thingamajigs Found.; road trip (Travel Channel) Made in America. Recipient cash award Arts Council of Great Britain, Father of Yr. award, Father's Day Coun. Am., 1996, Outstanding Role Model award, Am. Diabetes Assn., for writing, directing and producing, awarded Cleo and 3 Aegis awards. Mem. AFTRA, SAG, Writers Guild Am., Dirs. Guild, Am. Farmland Trust, Brit. Actors Equity Assn., Greenpeace, Wilderness Soc., Nat. Resources Def. Coun., Sierra Club (San Francisco). Achievements include development of packaging alternatives in 1989 made from biodegradable and non-toxic recycled paper; rowed a boat non-stop for more than 36 miles around Vashon Island, Wash. State to raise money for Special Olympics, 1993. Holds record as only person to make this 16 hour trip non-stop; drove Harley Davidson cross-country from NY to Las Vegas to raise awareness for Juvenile Diabetes, 1998. Avocations: sailing, reading, woodworking. Mailing: c/o Schachter Entertainment 1157 S Beverly Dr Los Angeles CA 90035 *

RATZLAFF, RUBEN MENNO, theology studies educator, minister; b. Burrton, Kans., Jan. 8, 1917; s. Henry and Julia (Foth) R.; m. Frances Irene King, Sept. 7, 1941; children: Keith Lowell, Paul Dennis, Mark Henry, Loren Lee; m. Doris Carr Arneson, Aug. 1, 1992; m. Marian McCuistion, June 10, 2006. BA, Johnson Bible Coll., 1940; BD, Butler U., 1955, MA, 1959. Ordained to ministry Chs. of Christ, 1938. Min. Pleasant Hill Christian Ch., Hall, Ind., 1948-50, Christian Ch., Clermont, Ind., 1950-55, Kennard, Ind., 1955-59; prof. San Jose (Calif.) Christian Coll., 1959-98, prof. emeritus, 1998—. Ann. vis. lectr. Springdale Coll., Selly Oak Colls., Birmingham, Eng., 1985-97; vis. lectr. Zimbabwe Christian Coll., Harare, 1995, Philippine Coll. Ministry, Baguio City, 1998. Author: Ezra Nehemiah, 1982; contbr. articles to profl. jours. Recipient Hebrew award Hebrew Synagogue, 1950. Mem. Theta Phi. Home: 5345 Boise St SE Turner OR 97392 Personal E-mail: rubenotprof@juno.com. *What amazes me most is that God the Almighty sends His Son to knock at our door, and wait with His hat in His hand while we decide whether to follow Him.*

RAU, LEE ARTHUR, lawyer; b. Mpls., July 22, 1940; s. Arthur W. and Selma A. (Lund) R.; m. Janice R. Childress, June 27, 1964; children: Brendan D., Patrick C., Brian T. BSB, U. Minn., 1962; JD, UCLA, 1965. Bar: Calif. 1966, DC 1972, Va. 1986, US Dist. Ct. DC 1973, US Dist. Ct. (ea. dist.) Va. 1988, US Ct. Mil. Appeals 1966, US Ct. Appeals (DC cir.) 1972, US Ct. Appeals (3d cir.) 1975, US Ct. Appeals (6th cir.) 1980, US Ct. Appeals (4th cir.) 1988, US Supreme Ct. 1971. Trial atty. evaluation sect. antitrust div. US Dept. Justice, Washington, 1965-66, appellate sect., 1970-72; assoc. Reed Smith Shaw & McClay, Washington, 1972-74, ptnr., 1975—2002; commr. Fairfax County Redevel. and Housing Authority, 2002—. Former mem. constl. and adminstrv. law adv. com. Nat. Chamber Litigation Ctr. Inc.; sec., bd. dirs. Old Dominion Land Co., Inc. Contbr. articles to profl. jours. Mem. Washington Dulles Task Force, 1982—91; mem. exec. com., ops. com. Fairfax-Falls Church United Way, mem. regional coun., 1988—92; chair Fair Fairfax Cts., High Rise Panel, 2006—; sec. bd. dirs. Reston Found., 1982—93; bd. dirs. Reston Interfaith Inc., 1973—89, pres., 1984—88; bd. dirs. Greater Reston Arts Ctr., 1988—96, pres., 1989—91, sec., 1991—95. Capt. JAGC US Army, 1966—70. Named Restonian of Yr., 1990; decorated Commendation with oak leaf cluster; recipient Best of Reston award, Merit citation Washington Post and Fairfax County Fedn. Civic Assns., 2006. Mem.: D.C. Bar Assn. (past chmn. energy study group). Democrat. Lutheran. Home: 11654 Mediterranean Ct Reston VA 20190-3401 Personal E-mail: leerau@verizon.net.

RAU, MAGDA, ophthalmologist; b. Zlin, Czechoslovakia, Aug. 31, 1952; arrived in Germany, 1982; d. Jaromir Broul and Vera Broulova; m. Hans-Konrad Pfeiffer, Dec. 26, 2001; m. Čestmir Mičán, Dec. 20, 1975 (div. 1992); 1 child, Čestmir Mičán; m. Björn Rau, Dec. 23, 1996 (div. 1998). Degree, Coll., Frydlant, Czechoslovakia, 1970; med. diploma, Palacky U., Olomouc, 1976; ophthalmologist diploma, Prag, Czechoslovakia, 1980, Munich, 1984. Intern Residency Hosp., Frydek-Mistek, Czech Republic, 1976—82; ophthalmologist Prof. Dr. Dausch Eye Dept., Amberg, Germany, 1983—85; practice owner Furth Im Wald, 1985—; day clinic owner Tageskliník, Cham, 1995—; chief ophthalmologist Hosp., 1995—; pvt. clinic owner Privatklinik Rau, 2000—. Contbr. articles to profl. jours. including multifokal IO Lenses, LASEK, LASEK-Viscodissection; author: (interactive CD-ROM) ICRS (Intrastromal Corneal Ring Segments), 1999, 2001. Mem. Albert Schweizer Stiftung Lambarene, 1996. Mem.: European Soc. Cataract and Refractice Surgery, Internat. Soc. Refractive Surgery, Internat. Soc. Cataract and Refractice Surgery. Roman Catholic. Avocations: tennis, horseback riding, skiing, skating. Home: Aepflet 24 93437 Furth Germany Office: Ophtalmologist Practice Von Mueller Str 12 93437 Furth Germany

RAU, RAGHAVENDRA, economist, educator; MBA, Indian Inst. Mgmt., Bangalore, 1989; MSc in Mgmt., INSEAD, France, 1993, PhD, 1997. Asst. prof. Purdue U., West Lafayette, Ind., 1997—2003, assoc. prof., 2003—. Exec. edn. cons. Univentures, Phoenix, 2005—. Recipient Best of the Best award, FMA, 1997. Office: Purdue University 403 W State St West Lafayette IN 47907

RAU, RALPH RONALD, retired physicist; b. Tacoma, Sept. 1, 1920; s. Ralph Campbell and Ida (Montgall) R.; m. Maryjane Uhrlaub, June 2, 1944; children: Whitney Leslie, Littie Elise. BS in Physics, Coll. Puget Sound, 1941; MS in Physics, Calif. Inst. Tech., 1943, PhD in Physics, 1948; LHD (hon.), U. Puget Sound, 2002. Asst. prof. physics Princeton U., 1947-56; Fulbright research prof. physics Ecole Polytechnique, Paris, 1954-55; physicist Brookhaven Nat. Lab., Upton, NY, 1956-66, chmn. dept. physics, 1966-70, assoc. dir. for high energy physics, 1970-81. Adj. prof. U. Wyo.; vis. prof. MIT, 1984-88; staff scientist Desy Lab., Hamburg, Fed. Republic Germany, 1984-85. Trustee U. Puget Sound, 1978-84 Named Alumnus Cum Laude U. Puget Sound, 1968; recipient Alexander von Humboldt U.S. Sr. Scientist award 1988. Mem. Am. Phys. Soc. Office: Brookhaven Nat Lab Upton NY 11973

RAUCH, ALLAN N., lawyer; BA, U. Pa., 1980, JD, 1983. Bar: NY 1983. Mgr., dir. law dept. Bed Bath & Beyond, Union, NJ, gen. counsel, 1997—. Contbr. articles to law jours. Office: Bed Bath & Beyond 650 Liberty Ave Union NJ 07083 Office Phone: 902-688-0888. Office Fax: 908-688-8385. E-mail: allan.rauch@bedbath.com.

RAUCH, ARTHUR IRVING, management consultant; b. NYC, Sept. 18, 1933; s. David and Miriam (Frankel) R.; m. Roxane M. Spiller, Aug. 19, 1962 (div. 1977); children: David S., Janine B.; m. Lynn R. Saidenberg, Oct. 11, 1987. BA magna cum laude, Dartmouth Coll., 1954, MS, 1955. Chartered fin. analyst. Security analyst Lionel D. Edie & Co., NYC, 1959-64; group dir. rsch. Eastman Dillon, Union Securities & Co., NYC, 1964-68; v.p., sr. analyst Laird, Inc., NYC, 1968-69, dir. rsch., 1969-71, sr. v.p., 1970-73; ptnr. Oppenheimer & Co., NYC, 1973-77; v.p. corp. devel. Rorer Group, Inc., Ft. Washington, Pa., 1977-84; v.p. corp. fin. Arnhold & S. Bleichroeder, Inc., NYC, 1984-88; cons. corp. devel. ICN Pharms., Inc., NYC, 1988-89. Mem. investment com. Becker Fund, 1969-73. Exec. com. Dartmouth Class of 1954, 1968-79, 94-2004. Lt. (j.g.) USNR, 1956-59. Rufus Choate scholar Dartmouth Coll., 1951. Mem. NY Soc. Security Analysts, Assn. Corp. Growth, Fin. Analysts Fedn. (corp. fin. com.), Phi Beta Kappa. Home and Office: 115 Central Park W Apt 9D New York NY 10023-4153 Personal E-mail: arauch@rcn.com.

RAUCH, GEORGE WASHINGTON, lawyer, director; b. Marion, Ind., July 18, 1919; s. George W. and Emma Asenath (Nolen) R.; m. Audrey M. Cranfield, Feb. 28, 1943 (div.); children: George Washington III, Nancy Lynn, Jane Nolen; m. Dorothy D. Farlow, June 26, 1970. BS, Ind. U., 1941; LL.B., U. Va., 1947. Bar: Ind. 1948, Ill. 1957, Mass. and Fla. 1972. Practice law Batton, Harker and Rauch (and predecessor firms), Marion, Ind., 1948-57; v.p., gen. counsel The Greyhound Corp., Chgo., 1957-61; mem. firm Hubachek & Kelly Ltd. and predecessor firms, Chgo., 1961-82; pres. Hubachek & Kelly Ltd., 1972-80; of counsel firm Chapman and Cutler, Chgo., 1982-95; gen. counsel Household Internat., 1967-78, dir., 1967-92, mem. fin. com., 1969-92, exec. com., 1972-92; dir. Edwards Engring. Corp., Constrn. Materials Co., Indsl. Air & Hydraulics Co., 1976-90, Burch Co., 1972-97, pres., 1975-97; dir. 1242 Lake Shore Dr. Corp., 1971-83, pres., 1973-74. Mem. Nat. Conf. Commrs. on Uniform Laws, 1955-57. Served as aviator USNR, 1941-45; lt. comdr. Mem. Raven Soc., Sankaty Head Golf Club (Nantucket, Mass.), Casino Club (Nantucket), Masons, Shriners, Phi Delta Phi, Delta Tau Delta. Home: 83 Baxter Rd PO Box 149 Siasconset MA 02564

RAUCH, IRMENGARD, linguist, educator; b. Dayton, Ohio, Apr. 17, 1933; d. Konrad and Elsa (Knott) R.; m. Gerald F. Carr, June 12, 1965; children: Christopher, Gregory. Student, Nat. U. Mex., summer 1954; BS with honors, U. Dayton, 1955; MA, Ohio State U., 1957; postgrad. (Fulbright fellow), U. Munich, Fed. Republic Germany, 1957-58; PhD, U. Mich., 1962. Instr., German and linguistics U. Wis., Madison, 1962-63, asst. prof., 1963-66; assoc. prof. German U. Pitts., 1966-68; assoc. prof. German and linguistics U. Ill., Urbana, 1968-72, prof., 1972-79, U. Calif., Berkeley, 1979—. Author: The Old High German Diphthongization: A Description of a Phonemic Change, 1967, The Old Saxon Language: Grammar, Epic Narrative, Linguistic Interference, 1992, Semiotic Insights: The Data Do the Talking, 1998, The Gothic Language: Genetic Provenance and Typology, Readings, 2002; editor (with others): Approaches in Linguistic Methodology, 1967; editor: Spanish edit., 1974, Der Heliand, 1974, Linguistic Method: Essays in Honor of Herbert Penzl, 1979, The Signifying Animal: The Grammar of Language and Experience, 1980, Language Change, 1983, The Semiotic Bridge: Trends from California, 1989, On Germanic Linguistics: Issues and Methods, 1992, Insights in Germanic Linguistics I: Methodology in Transition, 1995, Across the Oceans: Studies from East to West in Honor of Richard K. Seymour, 1995, Insights in Germanic Linguistics II: Classic and Contemporary, 1996, Synthesis in Diversity: Semiotics Around the World, 1997, New Insights in Germanic Linguistics I, 1999, II, 2001, III, 2002; editor of three series: Berkeley Insights in Linguistics and Semiotics, Berkeley Models of Grammars, Studies in Old Germanic Languages and Literatures; founder, co-editor Interdisciplinary Jour. for Germanic Linguistics and Semiotic Analysis; contbr. articles to profl. jours. Named outstanding woman on campus U. Ill. Sta. WILL, 1975; recipient Disting. Alumnus award U. Dayton, 1985; research grantee U. Wis., summer 1966, U. Ill., 1975-79, Eastern Ill. U., 1976, Nat. Endowment Humanities, 1978, U. Calif., Berkeley, 1979—; travel grantee NSF, Linguistics Soc. Am., 1972; Guggenheim fellow, 1982-83; IBM Distributed Acad. Computing Environment, 1986; NEH grantee, 1988; Festschrift: Interdigitations: Essays for Irmengard Rauch, 1999. Mem. Linguistics Soc. Am., MLA, Am. Assn. Tchrs. German (hon.), Society for Germanic Philogy, Philogical Assn. of the West Coast, Phonetics Assn., Semiotic Soc. Am. (pres. 1982-83), Semiotic Circle of Calif. (founder), Internat. Assn. for Semiotic Studies (pres., dir. 5th congress 1994), Alpha Sigma Tau, Delta Phi Alpha. Home: 862 Camden Ct Benicia CA 94510-3633 Office: U Calif Dept German Berkeley CA 94720-0001

RAUCH, JAMES E., economics professor; b. Trenton, NJ, Jan. 18, 1959; s. Harry E. and Helen F. Rauch; m. Doris E. Bittar, June 16, 1984; children: Joseph Benjamin Bittar, Gabriel James Bittar. BA, Princeton U., 1980; PhD, Yale U., New Haven, Conn., 1985. Rsch. assoc. Nat. Bur. Econ. Rsch., Cambridge, Mass., 1993—; asst. prof. econs. U. Calif., La Jolla, 1986—92, assoc. prof. econs., 1992—98, prof. econs., 1998—. Prin. investigator NSF, 1990—2002. Author: Networks and Markets, 2001, Leading Issues in Economic Development, 8th edit., 2005, The Missing Links: Formation and Decay of Economic Networks, 2007; co-editor: Jour. Internat. Econs., 2001—. Vis. Ind. scholar, Russell Sage Found., 1995—96. Mem.: Am. Econ. Assn. Home: 3026 Granada Ave San Diego CA 92104 Office: Dept Econs U Calif San Diego La Jolla CA 92093-0508 Office Phone: 858-534-2405. Office Fax: 858-534-7040. E-mail: jrauch@ucsd.edu.

RAUCH, JOHN KEISER, JR., architect; b. Phila., Oct. 23, 1930; s. John Keiser and Marjorie (Gretz) R.; m. Carol Pfaff, Mar. 11, 1953 (div. June 1978); children: John David, Charles Daniel, Kathryn Mari, Peter, Carol Anne; m. Carol A. McConochie, Jan. 10, 1981. Student, Wesleyan U., Middletown, Conn., 1948-51; BArch., U. Pa., 1957; grad. cert. program, Pa. Acad. Fine Arts, 2001. Draftsman Cope & Lippincott, Phila., 1957-60; architect Venturi and Short, Phila., 1960-64; partner Venturi and Rauch (Architects and Planners), Phila., 1964-79, Venturi, Rauch and Scott Brown, 1980-82, v.p., mng. prin., 1982-87, mgmt. cons., mediator, arbitrator, 1988-96; instr. U. Pa. Grad. Sch. Fine Arts, 1969-70, 89. Lectr. dept. architecture Princeton (N.J.) U., 1990-94. Trustee Found. for Architecture, 1977-84, mem. adv. com., 1994-2002; treas. Phila. Rehab., Inc., 1984-94; pres. Reading Terminal Market Pres. Fund, 1988-93, bd. dirs., 1994-2001; bd. dirs. United Cerebral Palsy Assn., 1988-91. Recipient Good Neighbor award Mellon/PSFS Bank, 1992. Fellow AIA (emeritus; Firm award 1983, John Harbeson Disting Svc. Phila. Chpt. award 1992); mem. Pa. Soc. Architects. Democrat. Home: 620 Gate House Ln Philadelphia PA 19118-4303

RAUCHER, HERMAN, screenwriter, novelist; b. Bklyn., Apr. 13, 1928; s. Benjamin Brooks and Sophie (Weinshank) R.; m. Mary Kathryn Martinet, Apr. 20, 1960; children: Jacqueline Leigh, Jennifer Brooke. BS, NYU, 1949. Asst. trade ad mgr. 20th Century Fox Films, NYC and Los Angeles, 1950-54; copy dir. Walt Disney Studios, NYC, 1954-55; copy supr. Calkins & Holden Advt., NYC, 1955-57; copy dir., v.p., dir. Reach McClinton Advt., NYC, 1957-63; v.p., creative dir. Maxon Advt., NYC, 1963-64; creative supr. Gardner Advt., NYC, 1964-65; v.p. advt., cons. Benton & Bowles Advt., NYC, 1965-67; freelance novelist, screenwriter,

1967—; pres. Bearfilm Prodns., 1971-96. Author: (novels and screenplays) Watermelon Man, 1970, Summer of '42 (nominated Acad. award for best original screenplay 1971, Writers Guild award nomination, Photoplay award), Ode to Billy Joe, 1975, A Glimpse of Tiger, 1972, (novel) Maynard's House, 1979, (screenplays) Sweet November, 1968, The Other Side of Midnight, 1977, Class of 44, 1972, Hieronymus Merkin (Best Original Screenplay award Writers Guild of Great Britain 1969), There Should Have Been Castles, 1978, Ginger, 1995, ARA/Froom, 2001 also various dramas appearing on TV in Alcoa Hour, Studio One, Matinee Theatre, Goodyear Playhouse, (TV mini-series under pseudonym) Master of the Game, 1984, (TV pilot) Remember When, 1974; playwright: Harold, 1962, Two Weeks Somewhere Else, 1967, Red Lights and Dragons, 1996, Kitty Hawk (musical), 2000; contbg. editor: Greenwich Time; contbr. to book revs. to N.Y. Times. Served with U.S. Army, 1950-52. Mem. Writers Guild Am., Authors League Am., Am. Film Inst., Dramatists Guild, Acad. of Motion Picture Arts and Scis.

RAUE, JORG EMIL, electrical engineer; b. Stettin, Germany, June 13, 1936; came to U.S., 1952; s. Ludwig and Liselotte (Barth) R.; m. Anke Volkmann, June 29, 1957; children: Monika Kay, Jennifer Faye. BSEE, Milw. Sch. Engring., 1961; MSEE, Marquette U., 1965, PhDEE, 1968. Mem. faculty Milw. Sch. Engring., 1961-68, chmn. dept., 1968-69; research engr. TRW Systems, Redondo Beach, Calif., 1969-76, mgr. dept., 1976-79; sr. research scientist TRW Electronic Systems, Rendondo Beach, advanced systems mgr., 1980-93; tech. cons. Calif., 1993—; chmn. dept. elec. engring. Calif. Poly. State U., San Luis Opispo, 1979-80. Mem. faculty Marquette U., Milw., 1968-69, Loyola U., L.A., 1970-72, U. So. Calif., L.A., 1983—. Contbr. articles to profl. jours. Served with U.S. Army, 1955-58. Recipient Disting. Tchr. award Milw. Sch. Engring., 1968; named Outstanding Alumnus Milw. Sch. Engring., 1985. Fellow IEEE; mem. Microwave Soc. of IEEE (sec. adminstrn. com. 1985—), Sigma Xi. Avocations: tennis, bicycling, flying, bridge. Home and Office: 28813 Rothrock Dr Palos Verdes Estates CA 90275-3060

RAUH, CARL STEPHEN, lawyer; b. Washington, Dec. 14, 1940; s. Joseph L. and Olie (Westheimer) R. AB, Columbia U., 1962; LL.B., U. Pa., 1965; LL.M., Georgetown U., 1968. Bar: D.C. 1966, U.S. Supreme Ct. 1969. Asst. U.S. atty. for D.C., 1966-69; atty. Dep. Atty Gen.'s Office Dept. Justice, Washington, 1969-71; 1st asst. atty. gen. U.S. V.I., 1971-73; prin. asst. U.S. atty. for D.C., 1974-79; U.S. atty. for D.C., 1979; ptnr. Dunnells, Duvall, Bennett & Porter, Washington, 1980-90, Skadden, Arps, Slate, Meagher & Flom, Washington, 1990—. Mem. D.C. Jud. Nomination Commn., 1985-90. Recipient Dir.'s award Dept. Justice, 1976; Atty. Gen.'s Disting. Service award, 1980 Fellow Am. Coll. Trial Lawyers; mem. ABA, D.C. Bar Assn., Nat. Assn. Former U.S. Attys., Asst. U.S. Attys. Assn. (Harold J. Sullivan award 1980). Office: 1440 New York Ave NW Washington DC 20005-2111 Office Phone: 202-371-7000.

RAUH, JOSHUA D., finance educator; b. Waltham, Mass., July 24, 1974; s. Robert David and Roberta Gottlieb Rauh; m. Carolyn Carlson, Aug. 16, 2003; 1 child, Samantha. BA, Yale U., New Haven, 1996; PhD in Econs., MIT, Cambridge, Mass., 2004. Asst. prof. finance U. Chgo., 2004—. Office Phone: 773-834-1710.

RAUH, LINDA ANN, rehabilitation services professional, counselor; d. John Matthew and Edna Ruth Rauh. MA in Counseling Edn., Kean U., 1997. Cert. counselor Nat. Bd. for Cert. Counselors, clin. hypnotherapist Md., psychosocial rehab. practitioner Md., marriage and family therapist N.J., lic. profl. counselor. Sr. counselor Bridgeway Rehab. Svcs., Inc., Elizabeth, NJ, 1999—2001, dir. staff devel. and quality improvement, 2001—. Clinician SERV Behavioral Healthcare, Elizabeth, 1997—99. Counselor Ctr. for Hope Hospice, Linden, NJ, 1996—97. Mem.: Am. Mental Health Counselors Assn., N.J. Counseling Assn. (Grad. Student of Yr. award 1997). Avocations: guitar, reading, swimming. Office: Bridgeway Rehab Svcs Inc 615 N Broad St Elizabeth NJ 07208 Home Phone: 732-541-1618; Office Phone: 908-355-7886. Office Fax: 908-355-6668. Personal E-mail: msrauh@comcast.net. E-mail: linda.rauh@bridgewayinc.com.

RAUL, ALAN CHARLES, lawyer; b. Bronx, NY, Sept. 9, 1954; s. Eugene and Eduarda (Müller-Mañas) R.; m. Mary Tinsley, Jan. 30, 1988; children: Caroline Tinsley, William Eduardo Tinsley, Alexander Tinsley. AB magna cum laude, Harvard U., 1975, MPA, 1977; JD, Yale U., 1980. Bar: N.Y. 1982, D.C. 1982, U.S. Ct. Appeals (D.C. cir.) 1982, U.S. Supreme Ct. 1988. Law clk. to judge U.S. Ct. Appeals (D.C. cir.), Washington, 1980-81; assoc. Debevoise & Plimpton LLP, NYC, 1981-86; assoc. counsel to Pres. The White House, Washington, 1986-88; gen. counsel Office Mgmt. & Budget, Exec. Office of the Pres., Washington, 1988-89, USDA, Washington, 1989-93; prin. Beveridge & Diamond P.C., Washington, 1993-97; ptnr. Sidley Austin LLP, Washington, 1997—. Vice chmn., Pres. Oversight Bd. on Privacy and Civil Liberties, 2006- Author: (book) Privacy and the Digital State, 2001. Co-chair, co-founder Lawyers Have Heart; chmn. bd. USDA Grad. Sch., 1991-93; bd. dirs. Nation's Capital affiliate Am. Heart Assn., 1993-97, Greater Washington region, 2002-; bd. dir. Wash. Tennis and Edn. Found., 2007-; treas., dir. Citizens Assn. Georgetown, 1993-97; mem. adv. coun. Atlantic Legal Found., 2001—. Recipient Disting. Achievement award Am. Heart Assn., 1991, Vol. of Yr. award, 1993, Lifetime Achievement award, 1999, Outstanding Support award 2006. Mem. ABA (chmn. com. on nat. security and internat. law 1990-92, coun. sect. internat. law and practice 1992-98, standing com. on election law 1995-99, sect. internat. law and practice govt. affairs officer 1996-98, coun. sect. adminstrv. law and regulatory practice 2004-05), Assn. of Bar of City of N.Y. (chmn. subcom. on Cen. Am. issues 1985, mem. com. on inter-Am. affairs 1983), Federalist Soc. (mem. nat. practitioners adv. coun., chair environ. and property rights practice group 1996-99), Coun. on Fgn. Rels. Office: Sidley Austin LLP 1501 K St NW Washington DC 20005 Office Phone: 202-736-8477. Business E-Mail: araul@sidley.com.

RAULINAITIS, PRANAS ALGIS, electronics executive, consultant; b. Kaunas, Lithuania, May 13, 1927; came to U.S., 1954, naturalized, 1960; s. Pranas Viktoras and Paulina (Gervaite) R.; m. Angele Staugaityte, Oct. 4, 1952; 1 son, Pranas Darius. With Commonwealth Rys. of Australia, Melbourne, 1949-53; asst. to fin. acct. Kitchen & Sons, Pty. Ltd., Melbourne, 1953-54; v.p. photo divsn. Interphoto Corp., LA, 1954-71; sr. v.p. fin., sec. Craig Corp., LA, 1971-87; pres. PAR Enterprises, Burbank, Calif., 1987—. Adviser Ministry Fgn. Affairs Republic of Lithuania, 1992; asst. sec. M & F Corp. Enterprises, Ltd., Chgo., 2004-. Former pres. Lithuanian Am. Coun., Inc. of Calif.; bd. dirs. Lithuanian-Am. Assns.; founder, former dir., v.p. Baltic Am. Freedom League; former mem. Am. Soc. Internat. Law. Home and Office: PAR Enterprises 1501 W Riverside Dr Burbank CA 91506-3027 Personal E-mail: raulalgis@juno.com.

RAULLERSON, CALVIN HENRY, retired political scientist, consultant; b. Utica, NY, Dec. 18, 1920; s. Calvin Thomas and Cora (White) R.; m. Olive Lewis, Dec. 1, 1956; children: Kevin Greer, Cheryl Harp, Earl Henry. AB, Lincoln U., Pa., 1943; MPA, NYU, 1949; postgrad., Harvard, 1947, Harvard Bus. Sch., 1979. Instr. polit. sci. Lincoln U., 1946, 49; editor, dir. research Christian E. Burckell Assocs., Yonkers, NY, 1950-52; asst. to exec. dir. United Negro Coll. Fund, 1952-57, dir. ednl. services, 1957-61; dir. African programs Am. Soc. African Culture, Lagos, Nigeria, 1961-64, exec. dir. NYC, 1964-66; chief Peace Corps, East and So. Africa, 1966-69; dir. Kenya, 1969-71; Africa regional dir., 1971-73; exec. asst. to dean Sch. Medicine, spl. asst. to pres. for internat. programs, spl. cons. research and devel., exec. dir. Internat. Ctr. for Arid and Semi-Arid Lands, Tex. Tech U., 1973-78; asst. prof. health orgn. mgmt., Health Scis. Ctr. Tex. Tech U., 1973-78; asst. adminstr. Bur. Pvt. Devel. Cooperation, AID, 1978-81; v.p. African Am. Inst., 1981-84; assoc. Keene, Monk Assocs., Middleburg, Va., 1985-86; dir. internat. programs One Am., Inc., 1987-88; pres. internat. group LABAT Anderson, 1988-94; v.p. internat. group Gardner Kamya Inc., Washington, 1994-95; sr. project mgr. Labat-Anderson Inc., McLean, Va., 1995—, ret., 2003—. Mgmt. cons. Mgmt. Devel. Consortium, Phelps Stokes Fund, 1973-75; Mem. information resources com. group on bus. affairs Assn. Am. Med. Colls.; mem. adv. com. on desertification AAAS, 1976-78; mem. Career Ministers Selection Bd., Dept. State, 1980; US del. UN Conf. Desertification Nairobi, 1977; chmn. US del. Com. on Food Aid and Policy, World Food Program, Rome, 1980; rsch. analyst Pres.'s Com. on Fair Employment Practices, 1944; treas. US planning com. 1st World Festival Negro Art, Dakar, 1965-66; del. Internat. Conf. on African History, U. Ibadan (Nigeria), 1962, Internat. Conf. on African Affairs, U. Ghana, 1963. Assoc. editor: Who's Who in the United Nations, 1952; Contbr. to: Negro Yearbook, 1952. Mem. nat. adv. com. Peace Corps, 1986-89; trustee African Wildlife Found., 1992—, chmn. strategic planning com., 1993-95. Rockefeller travel grantee East and Central Africa, 1960; Woodrow Wilson scholar, 1978-79 Mem. Harvard Club (Washington), Nat. Press Club. Home: 5823 Bradley Blvd Bethesda MD 20814-1104 E-mail: olrchr@msn.com.

RAUM, MARY BETH, performing arts educator; b. Takoma Park, Md., Oct. 14, 1957; d. Lawrence Arthur and Catherine Tompkins Raum. BS cum laude, U. Md., 1979; M in Adminstrv. Sci. magna cum laude, Johns Hopkins U., 1979; PhD summa cum laude, U. Wash., 1992. Adminstr. Johns Hopkins U./APL, Laurel, Md., 1976—82; adj. faculty/tech. mgmt U. Md. Open Univ., College Park, 1980—84; cons. Lawrence A. Raum & Assocs., Inc., Tacoma, 1982—92; doctoral rsch. assoc. George Washington U., Washington, 1983; asst. prof. orgnl. leadership Chapman U., Bangor, Wash., 1984—2005; adj. grad. faculty City U., Silverdale, Wash., 1986—88; corps de ballet/instr. Pacific Regional Ballet, Bremerton, Wash., 1996—2004; doctoral rsch. assoc. U. Wash., Seattle; ballet instr. MK Ballet Studio, Bremerton, Wash.; adj. faculty Pacific U., Dept. Econs., 2005; nat. security decision making prof. Naval War Coll., 2006—. Ballet mistress Pacific Regional Ballet, Bremerton, Wash., 2002—. Classical dance pointe, Raymonda (High Second Pl. Regional Dance Competition, 2002), character dance, Untitled (Internat. Dance Competition Sterling Silver Champion, 2001), classical ballet pointe, Raymonda (Dance Magic Regional High Score 2nd Pl., 2002), Spanish character dance, Voz de la Referencia (Regional lst Pl. & Championship High Score Adult Trophy, 2002)., NSF grantee, 1985. Mem.: Soc. Judgement and Decision Making, European Assn. Decision Making, Women in Internat. Security, Women in Aviation Internat., Phi Kappa Phi. Methodist. Avocation: free lance writer. Office: Naval War Coll 686 Cushing Rd Newport RI 02840 Home: 97 Narragansett Ave Unit C-4 Newport RI 02840-6903 Personal E-mail: maryraumphd@aol.com. Business E-Mail: mary.raum@nwc.navy.mil.

RAUP, DAVID MALCOLM, paleontology educator; b. Boston, Apr. 24, 1933; s. Hugh Miller and Lucy (Gibson) R.; m. Susan Creer Shepard, Aug. 25, 1956; 1 son, Mitchell D.; m. Judith T. Yamamoto, May 30, 1987. BS, U. Chgo., 1953; MA, Harvard U., 1955, PhD, 1957. Instr. Calif. Inst. Tech., 1956-57; mem. faculty Johns Hopkins U., 1957-65, assoc. prof., 1963-65; mem. faculty U. Rochester, 1965-78, prof. geology, 1966-78, chmn. dept. geol. scis., 1968-71, dir. Center for Evolution and Paleobiology, 1977-78; curator geology, chmn. dept. geology Field Mus. Natural History, Chgo., 1978-80, dean of sci., 1980-82; prof. geophys. sci. U. Chgo., 1980-95, chmn. dept., 1982-85, Sewell L. Avery disting. service prof., 1984-95; prof. emeritus, Sewell L. Avery disting. svc. prof. emeritus, 1995—. Geologist U.S. Geol. Survey, part-time, 1959-77; vis. prof. U. Tubingen, Germany, 1965, 72 Author: (with S. Stanley) Principles of Paleontology, 1971, 78, The Nemesis Affair, 1986, 2d edit., 1999, Extinction: Bad Genes of Bad Luck?, 1991; editor: (with B. Kummel) Handbook of Paleontological Techniques, 1965; contbr. articles to profl. jours. Recipient Best Paper award Jour. Paleontology, 1966; Schuchert award Paleontol. Soc., 1973; grantee Calif. Rsch. Corp., 1955-56, Am. Assn. Petroleum Geologists, 1957, Am. Philos. Soc., 1957, NSF, 1960-66, 75-81, Chem. Soc., 1965-71, NASA, 1983-95. Mem. AAAS, Am. Acad. Arts and Scis., Nat. Acad. Sci., Paleontol. Soc. (pres. 1976-77, medal 1997), Am. Soc. Naturalists (v.p. 1983), Am. Philos. Soc. Home: 423 Johnson Dr Washington Island WI 54246-9753 Home Phone: 920-847-2714. Personal E-mail: draup@itol.com.

RAUSCH, PAUL MATTHEW, financial executive; b. Lafayette, Ind., Dec. 14, 1953; s. Richard Leo and Vernice Ruth R. Student, Purdue U., 1976. County supr. Farmers Home Adminstrn., Richmond and Falmouth, Ky., 1979-87; loan officer spl. accounts team Farm Credit Svcs., LaPorte, Ind., 1987; br. mgr. Nat. Mortgage Corp., Merrillville, Ind., 1987-89; collection mgr. Greentree Acceptance, Lexington, Ky., 1989; county supr. Farmers Home Adminstrn., Springfield and Alamosa, Colo., 1990-96; v.p. Hershey State Bank, Nebr., 1996-98; fin. svcs. mgr. Coop. Fin. Assn. for Elsie, Chappell and Stapleton, Nebr., 1998-2000; econ. devel. fin. specialist West Ctrl. Nebr. Devel. Dist., Ogallala, 2001—05; exec. dir. Nat. Children's Found., 2003—; v.p. comml. and agrl. lending Sunflower Bank, Monte Vista, Colo., 2005—. Pres. rural devel. Madison County, Richmond, 1980-85; bd. dirs. Mosca-Hooper Soil Conservation Dist., 1993-94, San Luis Valley Rural Devel. Coun., Alamosa, 1993-94, Nat. Children's Found., Hooper, Colo., 1993-2003; mem. Monte Vista Econ. Devel. Recipient Dedication to Cmty. award Madison County, Richmond, 1983; named Ky. Col., Richmond, 1985. Mem. Nat. Parks and Conservation Assn., Am. Soc. Farm Mgrs. and Rural Appraisers, Nature Conservancy, Wilderness Soc., Sierra Club (agr. com. 1987-94), Kiwanis (bd. dirs. 1980-85). Avocations: music collecting, antiques and art collecting, studebaker vehicle restoration, hunting, farming. Home: 9531 Lane 9N Mosca CO 81146 Office: 104 Adams St Monte Vista CO 81144

RAUSCHENBERG, BRADFORD LEE, museum program director; b. Atlanta, Sept. 11, 1940; BS in Archaeology and Biology, Ga. State Coll., 1963; MA in History, Wake Forest U., 1995; PhD (hon.), Kendal Coll. Arts and Design, 2006. Archaeologist Ga. Hist. Commn., 1963-64; site supr., asst. Stanley South, State Archaeologist of N.C., 1964-66; antiquarian, asst. Dir. Restoration Old Salem, Inc., Winston-Salem, NC, 1966-73; asst. to dir. Mus. Early So. Decorative Arts, Winston-Salem, 1973-76, rsch. fellow, 1976-87, dir. rsch., 1987-93, Mus. Early So. Decorative Arts and Old Salem, Inc., Winston-Salem, 1993—, sr. fellow emeritus. Cons., lectr. in field. Author: British Regional Carving (1600-1640), and Furniture (1600-1800), 1984, Wachovia Historical Society: 1895-1995, 1995, Charleston Furniture, 1680-1820, 3 vols., 2003. With USCG, 1964-72. Recipient Halifax Resolves award, 1986; grantee NEH, 1972-81, Kaufman Americana Found., 1981-82. Mem. Am. Ceramic Circle (grantee), Orgn. Am. Historians, No. Ceramic Soc., So. Hist. Assn., Friends of Swiss Ceramic Circle, Regional Furniture Soc., Furniture History Soc., Soc. Hist. Archaeology, Soc. Post-Medieval Archaeology, Soc. Historians Early Am. Republic. Address: 221 Harmon Ct Winston Salem NC 27106-4613 Office: Mus Early So Decorative Arts PO Box 10310 Winston Salem NC 27108-0310 E-mail: k4blr@triad.rr.com.

RAUSCHENBERG, ROBERT, artist; b. Port Arthur, Tex., Oct. 22, 1925; m. Susan Weil, 1950 (div. 1952); 1 child, Christopher. Student, U. Tex., Kansas City Art Inst., Academie Julian, Paris, Black Mountain Coll., NC, Art Students League, NYC; LHD (hon.), Grinnell Coll., 1967; DFA (hon.), U. So. Fla., 1976. Neuropsychiat. tech. Calif. Naval Hosps. Founder Overseas Culture Interchange traveling exhbn., 1985—. One-man shows include Parsons Gallery, N.Y.C., 1951, Stable Gallery, 1953, White Chapel Art Gallery, London, 1964, Galerie Ileana Sonnabend, Paris, 1971, 1972, 1973, Leo Castelli Gallery, N.Y.C., 1972, 1973, Ace Gallery, L.A., 1973, Nat. Collection Fine Arts, Smithsonian Inst., Washington, 1976, Mus. Modern Art, N.Y.C., 1977, Albright Knox Gallery, 1977, Art Inst. Chgo., 1977, San Francisco Mus. Modern Art, 1977, Vancouver Art Gallery, 1978, Staatliche Kunsthalle, Berlin, 1980, Kunstalle, Düsseldorf, 1980, Louisiana Mus., Copenhagen, 1980, Stadelsches Kunstinst., Frankfurt, 1981, Tate Galery, London, 1981, Städtische Galerie im Lembacchaus, Munich, 1981, Phoenix Art Mus., 1982, G.H. Dalsheimer Gallery, Balt., 1983, Castelli Graphics, 1984, Galerie Bayeler, Basle, 1984, Juan March, Madrid, 1985, L.A. County Mus. Art, 1987, Inst. Contemporary Art, London, 1987, Galerie Alfred Kren, Cologne, 1988—89, Tretyakov Gallery, Moscow, 1989, Nat. Art Gallery, Kuala Lumpur, Malaysia, 1990, Mus. Contemporary Art, L.A., 1995—97, Pace Wilder Stein Gallery, N.Y.C., 1996, L.A., 1996—97, Guggenheim Mus., 1998, others, exhibited in group shows at Sao Paulo Biennial, 1959, Exposition Internat. Surrealisme, Paris, 1959—60, Mus. Modern Art, 1959, Guggenheim Mus., 1961, 1992, Mus. South Tex., Corpus Christi, 1974, N.Y. Collection in Stockholm, 1972, Whitney Mus. Am. Art, N.Y.C., 1972, 1973, Garage Show, Rome, 1973, Automme Festival d'Artes, Paris, 1973, N.Y. Cultural Ctr., 1973, Represented in permanent collections Albright-Knox Art Gallery, Whitney Mus. am. Art, Wadsworth Atheneum, Tate Gallery, Mus. Modern Art, Neue Galerie Aachen, Germany, Hirshhorn Mus., Moderna Museet, Stockholm, others, prin. works include electronic sculpture Soundings, prin. works include painting Tut-Scape; set and costume designer, lighting expert, stage mgr. Merce Cunningham Dance Co., 1964; choreographer others. With USMC, 1947—48. Recipient 1st Prize, Internat. Exhbn. Prints Gallery Modern Art, Ljubljana, Yugoslavia, 1963, Venice Biennale, 1964, Corcoran Biennal Contemporary Am. Painters, 1965, Skowhegan Sch. Painting and Sculpture medal, 1982, Grammy award, 1984. Mem.: NAD (assoc.), Am. Acad. and Inst. Arts and Letters. Gallery: Pace Wildenstein Gallery 32 E 57th St New York NY 10022-2513

RAUSCHENBUSCH, STEPHANIE, artist, educator, poet; b. Washington, July 27, 1942; d. Stephen and Josephine Burns Raushenbush; m. Joseph Marchant Hayman, Dec. 29, 1984; m. Louis R. Rowan, June 20, 1964 (div. June 20, 1979); 1 child, Quentin Rowan. BA magna cum laude, Radcliffe Coll., Cambridge, Mass., 1964; MA summa cum laude, Columbia U., NYC, 1966. Treas. Noho Gallery, NYC, 1999—; docent Bklyn. Mus. Art. One-woman shows include Noho Gallery, NYC, 1983, 1987, 1989, 1991, 1993, 1995, 1997, 1999, 2002, 2005, 2007—, exhibited in group shows at Woodstock (NY) Guild, 1986, Art and the Law traveling exhibit, 1988—1889, Biennale d'Arte Contemporanea, Florence, 2001, in pvt. collections; author: (book of poetry) The Heart's Ice Thaws, 1999; contbr. poetry to lit. jours.; exhibitions include, 1986—. Trustee Friends Sem., NYC, 1998—2001. Fellow, Woodrow Wilson Found., 1964—65; grantee Kent fellowship grad. studies, Danforth Found., 1966—70. Mem.: N.Y. Soc. Women Artists (pres. 2006—), Women's Caucus for Art, Catherine Lorillard Wolfe Art Club. Democrat. Mem. Soc. Of Friends. Avocation: gardening. Home: 46 Sherman St Brooklyn NY 11215

RAUSCHER, GREGORY EDWIN, plastic surgeon; b. Englewood, NJ, Sept. 18, 1946; s. Edwin and Catherine (Smullen) R.; m. Irene Boucher, Aug. 22, 1970; children: Greg, Jr., Geoffrey, Eric, Daniel. BS in Biology, Fairfield U., 1968; MD, SUNY Downstate, 1972. Diplomate Am. Bd. Surgery, Am. Bd. Plastic Surgery. Intern, gen. surgery Kings County-SUNY Med. Ctr., Bklyn., 1971—72, resident, plastic surgery, 1972—76, resident, 1976—78; fellow Kings County-Downstate Med. Ctr., Bklyn., 1974—75; chmn., dir. plastic surgery U. Dentistry and Medicine N.J., Newark, 1984-96, prof. plastic surgery; prof. U. Dentistry and Medicine N.J. Univ. Hosp., Newark; dir. plastic surgery Hackensack U. Med. Ctr., NJ, 1990-99, sect. chief, cosmetic surgery NJ, dir. cosmetic surgery dept. plastic surgery NJ, 1999—; private practice Hackensack, NJ, 1980—. Exec. coun. N.Y. Regional Plastic Soc., N.Y.C., 1995-96. Contbg. author: Aesthetic Male Surgery, 1996. Named one of America's Cosmetic Doctors and Dentists, 2003, 2005, Top Doctors NY Metro Area, 2001, 2003, 2004, 2005, 2006, Top Doctors for Women, NJ Life Mag., 2004, Top 10 Doctors, NY Mag., 2005, 2006, Premiere Plastic Surgeons correcting cosmetic deformities of the breast, Fox Channel 5. Mem. N.J. Plastic Surgery Soc. (pres. 1995-96), N.Y. Regional Plastic Surgery Soc. (exec. bd. 1996, v.p.), Am. Burn Assn., Am. Soc. Hand Surgery, Am. Assn. for Surgery of the Hand, Am. Soc. for Aesthetic Plastic Surgery, Internat. Coll. Surgeons in Plastic Surgery, Am. Soc. Plastic and Reconstructive Surgery, N.Y. Acad. Medicine. Avocation: tennis. Office: 20 Prospect Ave Ste 600 Hackensack NJ 07601 Office Phone: 201-488-1036. Office Fax: 201-488-2264. *

RAUSCHER, RICHARD CONRAD, psychotherapist, writer; b. Rochester, NY, Oct. 3, 1940; s. Orville Conrad and Mabel Emily Rauscher; m. Linda Howland (div.); children: Thomas, Kristina, Rebecca, Michael; m. Melinda S. Stanfield, Dec. 31, 1990. BEE, Clarkson U., Potsdam, NY, 1962; ThM, Colgate Rochester Div., 1986. Lic. mental health counselor NY. Engr. GM, Rochester, 1960—63, Xerox, Webster, NY, 1963—65; founder, pres. Woric Corp., Shortville, NY, 1965—69; engr., mgr. Singer Bus. Machines, Rochester, 1969—73; owner Silversmith-Kiva Jewelry, Naples, NY, 1973—80; pvt. practice psychotherapist Naples, 1981—2006. Editor, author: Stonyhill Newsletter; contbr. articles to profl. jours. Bd. ordained ministry United Meth. Ch., 1992—2006. Lt. USN, 1968—71. Fellow: Am. Assn. Pastoral Counselors. Avocations: writing, Blue Grass mandelin. Home: 167 Rainbow Dr # 6729 Livingston TX 77399

RAUSEN, AARON REUBEN, pediatric hematologist, oncologist; b. Jersey City, June 30, 1930; s. David and Ruth (Schwartz) R.; m. Emalou Watkins, Apr. 7, 1968; children: David, Susan, Elisabeth. Degree, Dartmouth Coll., 1950; MD, SUNY, Bklyn., 1954. Intern, then resident in pediat. Bellevue Hosp. Ctr., NYC, 1954-56; chief resident in pediats. Mt. Sinai Hosp., NYC, 1958-59, asst. assoc. and attending pediatrician, 1961-81; fellow in hematology Children's Hosp. and Harvard Med. Sch., Boston, 1959-61; chief of pediat. City Hosp. Ctr., Elmhurst, NY, 1964-72; dir. pediat. Beth Israel Med. Ctr., NYC, 1972-81; dir. pediatric oncology NYU Med. Ctr., NYC, 1981-97; prof. pediat. NYU Sch. Medicine, NYC, 1981—. Prof. pediat. Mt. Sinai Sch. Medicine, NYC, 1971—81, professorial lectr., 1981—; dir. Stephen D. Hassenfeld Children's Ctr. for Cancer and Blood Disorders, NYC, 1990—97, founding dir., 1997—; cons. Lenox Hill Hosp., NYC, 1981—; vis. prof. Dartmouth Med. Sch., Hanover, NH, 1984—86; prin. investigator Children's Oncology Group, 1999—2005; vis. staff pediat. Greenwich (Conn.) Hosp., 2005—; attending pediat. Stamford (Conn.) Hosp., 2005—. Contbr. articles to profl. jours. Bd. dirs. N.Y.C. chpt. Am. Cancer Soc., 1984-1996, Nat. Childhood Cancer Found., 1992—, Children's Oncology Soc. N.Y., 1993—, Ovarian Cancer Rsch. Fund, 1994-99. Capt. Med. Corps, U.S. Army, 1956-58. Fellow Am. Acad. Pediatrics; mem. Am. Pediatric Soc., Am. Soc. Hematology, Am. Soc. Clin. Oncology, Am. Assn. Cancer Rsch., Am. Soc. Pediatric Hematology-Oncology, N.Y. Pediatric Soc. (pres. 1974), Yale Club N.Y.C., Phi Beta Kappa, Alpha Omega Alpha. Office: 160 E 32d St Fl2 New York NY 10016 Office Phone: 212-263-7144. Personal E-mail: aaron.rausen@nyumc.org.

RAUSHENBUSH, WALTER BRANDEIS, retired law educator; b. Madison, Wis., June 13, 1928; s. Paul A. and Elizabeth (Brandeis) R.; m. Marylu de Watteville, May 3, 1956; children: Lorraine Elizabeth, Richard Walter, Carla de Watteville, Paul Brandeis. AB magna cum laude in Govt., Harvard U., 1950; JD with high honors, U. Wis., 1953. Bar: Wis. 1953. Ptnr. LaFollette, Sinykin & Doyle, Madison, 1956-58; mem. faculty U. Wis., Madison, 1958—, prof. law, 1966-95, prof. emeritus, 1995—; vis. prof. law U. San Diego, 1992—94, 1996—; project dir. real estate transfer study Am. Bar Found., 1967-72. Trustee nat. Law Sch. Admission Coun., 1968-70, 72-95, chmn. pre-law com., 1970-74, chmn. svcs. com., 1976-78, pres., 1980-82; legal advisor Madison Citizens Fair Housing, 1961-63, Wis. Citizens Family Planning, 1965-73; real property drafting com.

Multistate Bar Exam., 1986-2002. Author: Wisconsin Construction Lien Law, 1974, (with others) Wisconsin Real Estate Law, 1984, 4th edit., 1994, Brown on Personal Property, 3d edit., 1975, Real Estate Transactions Cases and Materials, 1997. With USAF, 1953-56, col. Res. ret. Mem. ABA, State Bar Wis., Order of Coif, Stage Harbor Yacht Club (Chatham, Mass.), Cape Cod Nat. Golf Club (Harwich, Mass.), Phi Beta Kappa, Phi Delta Phi (province pres. 1963-75). Presbyterian (Elder). Home: Unit 908 1730 Avenida Del Mundo Coronado CA 92118-3026

RAUSHER, DAVID BENJAMIN, internist, gastroenterologist; b. Bklyn., Sept. 15, 1952; s. Herbert and Shirley Ruth R.; m. Judy A. Steinlauf, Aug. 8, 1976; children: Scott, Michael, Steven. BA, Hamilton Coll., 1973; MD, SUNY, Bklyn., 1977. Diplomate Am. Bd. Internal Medicine, Am. Bd. Gastroenterology. Resident Emory U. Hosps., Atlanta, 1977-80, fellow in gastroenterology, 1980-82; pres. Atlanta Ctr. for Gastroenterology, Decatur, Ga., 1982—; med. dir. Atlanta Endoscopy Ctr., Decatur, 1994—. Chmn. diagnostic treatment ctr. DeKalb Med. Ctr., Decatur, Ga., 1985—, co-chief gastroenterology, 1995-97, chief sect. gastroenterology, 1998—. Fellow: Am. Gastroenterology Assn., Am. Coll. Gastroenterology. Office Phone: 404-296-1986.

RAUSSER, GORDON C(LYDE), agricultural and resource economics educator; b. Lodi, Calif., July 21, 1943; s. Elmer A. and Doyve Ester (Meyers) R.; children: Sloan, Stephanie, Paige. BS summa cum laude, Calif. State U., 1965; MS with highest honors, U. Calif., Davis, 1968, PhD with highest honors, 1971. Prof. econs. and agrl. econs. U. Calif., Davis, 1969-74; vis. prof. U. Chgo., 1972-74; prof. econs. and stats. Iowa State U., 1974-75; prof. bus. adminstrn. Harvard U., 1975-78; prof., chmn. dept. agrl. and resource econs. U. Calif., Berkeley, 1979-85, 93-94, Robert Gordon Sproul disting. prof., 1985—, dean nat. resources, 1994-2000; dir. Giannini Found., Berkeley, 1984-86. Vis. prof. Hebrew U. and Ben-Gurion U., Israel, 1978; Ford Found. vis. prof., Argentina, 72; spl. cons. and sr. economist Coun. Econ. Advisors, 1986—87; chief economist AID, 1988—90; advisor econ. rsch. svc. USDA, 1978—80, 1986—88, Agr. Can., 1977—79, Bur. Agrl. Econs., Australia, 1987, U.S. Office Mgmt. and Budget, 1986; mem., chmn. planning com. Sch. Bus. Adminstrn. U. Calif., Berkeley, 1986—87, mem. adv. com. Agrl. Issues Ctr., 1984—85, mem. planning com. Agrl. and Natural Resources Program, 1986, mem. econs. programs evaluation com., 1987—88; mem. Citrus Planning Commn., Brazil, 1984; pres. Inst. for Policy Reform, Washington, 1989—94; prin., founder Law & Econ. Cons. Group, Berkeley, Washington, Chgo., NYC, 1990—2000; sr. cons. CRA Internat., 2000—06. Author: Macroeconomic Environment for U.S. Agricultural Policy, Alternative Agricultural and Food Policies and the 1985 Farm Bill, The Emergence of Market Economies in Eastern Europe, New Directions in Econometric Modeling and Forecasting, Dynamics of Agricultural Systems: Economic Prediction and Control, Quantitative Methods in Agricultural Economics, GATT Negotiations and the Political Economy of Policy Reform; co-editor: Handbook of Agricultural Economics, Vol. 2A, 2002, Vol. 2B, 2002, Vol. 1A, 2001, Vol. 1B, 2001; editor Decision-Making in Business and Economics, 1977-79, Am. Jour. Agrl. Econs., 1983-86, Ann. Rev. Resource Econs., 2006. Mem. western nutrition ctr. coordinating com. USDA, 1980-83; mem. Arab-Am. Coun. for Cultural and Econ. Exch., 1979-81; bd. dirs. Giannini Found. Agrl. Econs., 1979-84, mem. exec. com., 1979-84; mem. planning com. Berkeley Food Coop., 1980-83, planning com. for food policy Resources for the Future, 1984-85; mem. adv. com. Calif. State Dept. Agr., 1982-84; bd. dirs. Am. Agrl. Econs. Awards. Grantee USDA, NSF, World Bank, Chgo. Merc. Exch., U.S. Bur. Mines; Fulbright scholar, Australia, 1987; Sr. fellow Resources for Future, 1984-85. Fellow: AAAS, Am. Agrl. Econs. Assn. (oustanding enduring rsch. contbn. com. 1982—84, outstanding PhD dissertation com. 1974—76, chmn. outstanding article com. 1983—86, rsch. awards of merit 1976, 1978, 1980, 1982, 1986, 1989, 1992, Pub. Enduring quality award 1993, rsch. awards of merit 1993, Disting. Policy Contbn. award 1993, rsch. awards of merit 1994, 2000, 2001), Am. Statis. Assn.; mem.: Coll. Natural Resources Citation, Western Agrl. Econ. Assn. (Best Pub. Rsch. award 1978, Outstanding Pub. Rsch. award 1994), Ops. Rsch. Soc., Math. Assn. Am., Econometric Soc., Am. Acad. Polit. and Social Sci., Am. Econ. Assn., Commonwealth Club (dir. agr. study group 1983—84), Alpha Zeta, Alpha Gamma Rho. Home: 661 San Luis Rd Berkeley CA 94707-1725 Office: U Calif Berkeley ARE 230 Giannini Hall Berkeley CA 94720-3310 Business E-Mail: rausser@are.berkeley.edu.

RAUTENSTRAUCH, GARY M., marketing executive; BBA, Miami U., 1975; MBA, NYU. Exec. v.p. technology Baker & Taylor, Inc., exec. v.p. distribution, COO, pres., CEO, 2001—03; CEO Blackwell's Book Svcs., 2005—06; pres., CEO Advanced Mktg. Svcs., Inc., 2006—. Office: Advanced Mktg Svcs Inc 5880 Oberlin Dr Ste 400 San Diego CA 92121 Office Phone: 858-457-2500, 858-452-2237.

RAUTIOLA, NORMAN A., manufacturing executive; b. Hancock, Mich., Aug. 6, 1932; s. Arnold and Irene Rautiola; m. Sarah-Binah Rautiola, Dec. 5, 1997; children: Jeffrey, Jordan, Leijona, Niikolas, Ari. BS in Metal Engring., Mich. Tech. U., 1954; MBA, George Washington U., 1960. Engring. officer U.S. Air Force, Hamilton AFB, Calif., 1954—56; sr. patent examiner U.S. Patent Office, Washington, 1957—60; patent devel. mgr. Tex. Instruments, Dallas, 1960—65; asst. to president Bunker Ramo Corp., Canoga Park, Calif., 1965—66; dir., corp. devel. Sparton Corp., Jackson, Mich., 1966—68; pres. Nartron Corp., Reed City, Mich., 1968—; founder, chmn. Smart Power Sys. Inc., Sylvan Lake, Mich., 1986—. Dir. Smart Power Sys. Inc., Sylvan Lake, Mich., 1985—, Nartron Corp., Reed City, Mich., 1968—; chmn. Nonometal LLC, Birmingham, Mich., 2004—. Bd. of control Mich. Tech. U., Houghton, Mich., 2002—. Cpt. USAF, 1954—68. Mem.: IEEE (sr.). Achievements include patents in field. Office: Nartron Corp 5000 N US 131 Reed City MI 49677 Office Phone: 231-832-5525. Business E-Mail: hhuber@nartron.com.

RAUWERDINK, WILLIAM JAY, accountant; b. Sheboygan, Wis., Mar. 3, 1950; s. Harvard M. and Dorothy M. (Duenk) R.; m. Ann Catherine Geske, July 14, 1979; 1 child, Margaret Allene. BBA, U. Wis., 1972; MBA, Harvard U., 1974. CPA, N.Y., Mich., Mass. Ptnr. Deloitte & Touche, Detroit, 1978—93; exec. v.p., CFO, treas., sec. The MEDSTAT Group, Inc., Ann Arbor, Mich., 1994—96, Lason, Inc., Troy, Mich., 1996—2000; exec. v.p., CFO, treas. Hotwire.com, San Francisco, 2001; interim pres., CFO, Gyricon, LLC, Ann Arbor, 2002—04; mng. dir. BAM Investments, LLC, West Bloomfield, Mich., 2005—. Bd. dirs. Trinity Health Svcs., Novi, Mich. Mem. Wis. Bus. Alumni Assn. (bd. dirs. 1980-89, 92—, pres. 1984-85), Harvard Club (Boston). Mailing: 5382 Pembrooke Crossing Ct West Bloomfield MI 48322

RAVAGO, MIGUEL, chef, Restaurant Owner; Co-founder San Angel Inn, Houston, Fonda San Miguel, Austin, 1975—. Co-author: Cocina de la Familia, 1997 (Julia Child cookbook award, 1998), Fonda San Miguel: Thirty Years of Food and Art, 2006 (Cookbook award for Design, Internat. Assn. Culinary Professionals, 2006). Mem.: Internat. Assn. Culinary Professionals. Office: Fonda San Miguel Restaurant 2330 W N Loop Blvd Austin TX 78758 Office Phone: 512-459-4121. *

RAVECHÉ, HAROLD JOSEPH, academic administrator; b. NYC, Mar. 18, 1943; s. Harold Edward Raveche and Helen Patricia (DeVincent) Gravino; m. Elizabeth Marie Scott, Jan. 26, 1974; children: John Vincent, Justin Blaise, Bernice Helen, Elizabeth Ann. BA in Chemistry, Hofstra U., 1963; PhD in Phys. Chemistry, U. Calif., San Diego, 1968. NRC postdoctoral assoc. Nat. Bur. Stds., Gaithersburg, Md., 1968—70, rsch. chemist, 1970—78, chief thermophysics divsn., 1978—85; dean Sch. of Sci., prof. chemistry Rensselaer Poly. Inst., Troy, NY, 1985—88; pres. Stevens Inst. Tech., Hoboken, NJ, 1988—. Bd. dirs. Nat. West NJ and Bancorp, Atlantic Energy Inc.; commr. sci. and tech., NJ. Editor: Perspectives in Statistical Physics, 1980; contbr. articles to profl. jours. Pres. Potomac Highlands Citizens Assn., Md., 1978-80 Recipient Disting. Young Scientist of Yr. award Md. Acad. Scis., 1975, US Sr. Exec. Svc. award Nat. Bur. Stds., 1983, Equal Employment Opportunity award, 1984. Mem. AAAS (commn. sci. edn. 1972-75), Am. Phys. Soc. (adv. coun. 1975-78), Soc. Indsl. and Applied Math. (adv. bd. conf. on large-scale computational problems 1984-88), Am. Chem. Soc., Sigma Xi. Roman Catholic. Avocations: hiking, swimming, skiing, music, theater. Office: Stevens Inst Tech Office of Pres Castle Point On Hudson Hoboken NJ 07030 Office Phone: 201-216-5213. E-mail: hraveche@stevens.edu. *

RAVEN, ABBE, broadcast executive; b. NY, 1953; 1 child. BA in Theater, U. Buffalo, 1974; MA in Cinema and Theater, Hunter Coll. Prodn. mgr., stage mgr. Manhattan Theater Club, Bklyn. Acad. Music, NYC; mgr. prodn. Hearst/ABC Video Svcs.; dir. prodn. svcs. A&E TV Networks, 1984-88, sr. v.p. prodn., 1988—95; sr. v.p. programming and prodn. The History Channel and HTV Prodns., 1995-97; sr. v.p. programming The History Channel, 1997—2000, gen. mgr., exec. v.p., 2000—02, A&E Network-USA, pres., 2004—05; pres., CEO A&E Television Networks, 2005—. Instr. various ednl. instns. Active Competition Com. CableACE Awards, chair 12 Ann. Ceremonies; active coms. focusing on violence in TV. Named one of 100 Most Powerful Women in Entertainment, Hollywood Reporter, 2006; named to Hunter Coll. Hall of Fame; recipient U. Buffalo Alumni award, National History Day Org. Corp. Leadership Award, 2000. Mem. NATAS, Women in Cable, Am. Women in Radio and TV, PROMAX, Nat. Acad. Cable Programming. Office: A&E TV Networks The Hearst Corp 235 E 45th St 9th Fl New York NY 10017-3305 *

RAVEN, BERTRAM H(ERBERT), psychology professor; b. Youngstown, Ohio, Sept. 26, 1926; s. Morris and Lillian R.; m. Celia Cutler, Jan. 21, 1961; children: Michelle G., Jonathan H. BA in psychology summa cum laude with great distinction, Ohio State U., 1949, MA in psychology, 1950; PhD in social psychology, U. Mich., 1953. Rsch. assoc. Rsch. Ctr. for Group Dynamics, Ann Arbor, Mich., 1952-54; lectr. psychology U. Mich., Ann Arbor, 1953-54; vis. prof. U. Nijmegen, U. Utrecht, Netherlands, 1954-55; psychologist RAND Corp., Santa Monica, Calif., 1955-56; prof. UCLA, 1956—, chair dept. psychology, 1983-88, prof. emeritus, 1991—. Vis. prof. Hebrew U., Jerusalem, 1962-63, U. Wash., Seattle, 1965, U. Hawaii, Honolulu, 1968, London Sch. Econs. and Polit. Sci., 1969-70; external examiner U. of the W.I., Trinidad and Jamaica, 1980—, rsch. assoc. Psychol. Rsch. Ctr., 1993—; participant Internat. Expert Conf. on Health Psychology, Tilburg, Netherlands, 1986; cons., expert witness in field, 1979—; mem. internat. adv. bd. Acad. Freedom, Bar-Ilan U., 2005—; mem. sci. bd. Kurt Lewin Ctr. Psychol. Rsch. Kazimierza Wielkiego U., Poland; affiliate prof. U. Haifa, 2006—. Author: (with others) People in Groups, 1976, Discovering Psychology, 1977, Social Psychology, 1983, Social Psychology: People in Groups (Chinese edit.), 1994; editor: (with others) Contemporary Health Services, 1982, Policy Studies Rev. Ann., 1980; editor: (with others) Lewinian Psychology, 2006; editor: Jour. Social Issues, 1969-74; mem. editl. bd. Jour. of Criminology and Social Psychology, 2001-, Revista de Psicologia de la Salud, 1995-; mem. adv. bd. Jour. Entrepreneurship, 2004-; contbr. articles to profl. jours. Co-dir. Tng. Program in Health Psychology, UCLA, 1979-88; cons. WHO, Manila, 1985-86; cons., expert witness various Calif. cts., 1978—. Guggenheim fellow, Israel, 1962-63; Fulbright scholar Netherlands, 1954-55, Israel, 1962-63, Britain, 1969-70; recipient Citation from L.A. City Coun., 1966, 2006, Rsch. on Soc. power by Calif. Sch. of profl. psychology, L.A., 1991; NATO sr. fellow, Italy, 1989. Fellow APA (chair bd. social and ethical responsibility 1978-82, ethics com. 2003-06), Am. Psychol. Soc., Soc. for Psychol. Study of Social Issues (pres. 1973-74, coun. 1995-97, Kurt Lewin award 1998), Soc. for Personality and Social Psychology; mem. AAAS, Am. Sociol. Assn., Internat. Assn. Applied Psychology, Soc. Exptl. Social Psychology, Assn. Advancement of Psychology (founding, bd. dirs. 1974-81), Internat. Soc. Polit. Psychology (governing coun. 1996-98), Interam. Psychol. Soc., Am. Psychology-Law Soc., Scholars for Peace in the Middle East. Democrat. Jewish. Avocations: guitar, travel, international studies. Home: 2212 Camden Ave Los Angeles CA 90064-1906 Office: UCLA Dept Psychology Los Angeles CA 90095-1563 Home Phone: 310-479-1607; Office Phone: 310-825-2296.

RAVEN, FRANCIS HARVEY, mechanical engineer, educator; b. Erie, Pa., July 29, 1928; s. Frederick James and Eleanor Elizabeth (Sopp) R.; m. Therese Mary Strobel, June 21, 1952; children: Betty, Ann Raven McCarthy, Paul, John, Mary Raven Mansmann, Cathy, Linda. BS in Math., Gannon U., Erie, Pa., 1948; BSME, Pa. State U., University Park, 1950, MSME, 1951; PhD, Cornell U., Ithaca, NY, 1958. Design engr. Hamilton Standard div. United Techs., Hartford, Conn., 1951-54; instr. Cornell U., Ithaca, N.Y., 1954-58; asst. prof. mech. engring. U. Notre Dame, 1958-62, assoc. prof., 1962-66, prof., 1966—. Cons. microprocessor and computer control of robots and mech. systems; devel. Vector Loop Method (first analytical method for the design of mechanisms and cam systems.). Author: Automatic Control Engineering, 1961, 5th edit., 1995, Mathematics of Engineering Systems, 1966, Engineering Mechanics, 1973; pub. McGraw-Hill Book Co. Mem. ASME, Am. Soc. for Engring. Edn. (AT&T Teaching award 1968-69), Sigma Xi. Roman Catholic. Office Phone: 574-631-7381. Business E-Mail: fraven@nd.edu.

RAVEN, LUISA ANTONIA, psychotherapist, nurse; b. NYC, Sept. 25, 1939; d. Joseph A. and Mary Louise (Swann) R. BSN, St. Louis U., 1976; BA in Edn., Caldwell Coll., NJ, 1970; MSN, Columbia U., 1982. RN, N.J. Joined Order Sisters of St. Joseph of Peace, Roman Cath. Ch., 1962. Pvt. practice nurse psychotherapist, Englewood Cliffs, N.J.; instr. nursing Felician Coll., Lodi, N.J.; clin. specialist psychiat. nursing Greystone Park (N.J.) Psychiat. Hosp.; staff nurse med./surg. psychiat. unit St. Mary's Hosp., Passaic, NJ. Adj. faculty Bergen C.C., Paramus, N.J. Mem. N.J. Nurses Assn. (Psychiat. Nurse of Yr. award 1984), Sigma Theta Tau, Alpha Sigma Nu. Home: 5 Oakdale Manor Apt B18 Suffern NY 10901-5700 Office Phone: 201-871-2266.

RAVEN, PATRICIA ELAINE (PENNY RAVEN), real estate broker, developer, columnist; b. Oakland, Calif., Apr. 27, 1943; d. Allen James and Patricia Elaine (McClure) Nichelini; m. Larry Joseph Raven, June 15, 1963; children: Laurence Tagge Allen, Corbyn Lance. Student, U. So. Calif., 1961—62, U. Calif., Fresno, 1962—63, Fresno City Coll., 1973. Model, Fresno, Calif., 1960—; owner, operator Del Mar Motel and apts., Fresno, 1963—64; owner R Pantry Markets, 1965—72, v.p., 1968—72; owner Holy Cow Meat Markets, Fresno, 1965—72; real estate salesman, developer, 1973; real estate broker, owner The Raven Co., Fresno, 1974—; owner Raven Alcohol Distillery, 1979—89; pres. Am. Gasohol, Inc., 1980—; spl. events cons. Royal Cruise Line, 1986. Co-author: National Handbook on Toll Roads, 1977; columnist: Party Line, Fresno Bee, 1978—87, Central Valley Homes & Lifestyles, 2003—; contbg. editor: Fresno Weekly, 2001—02, Fresno Mag., 2003—, Fresno Mag. Lunch Ladies, 2006—07; actress: (TV miniseries) Fresno, 1986; (films) Pretty Woman, 1989; Princess Diaries 2, 2004. Pres. Fresno Cancer League, 1972—73, Jackson Sch. PTA, 1980—82; hon mem. Fresno Zool. Soc.; commr. Fresno County Hist. Landmarks and Records Commn., 2005—; Democratic candidate for lt. gov. Calif., 1978; Fresno County Dem. ctrl. com. alt., 1977; bd. dirs. Women's Symphony League, 1973—74; pres. Huntington Blvd. Homeowners Hist. Assn., 1987—97, officer, 1997—. Named Betty Crocker Homemaker of Tomorrow, 1961; named one of 50 Most Influential People in Fresno, 2007; recipient Mayor's award, 1976, Hon. Svc. award, Jackson Sch. PTA, 1982, Appreciation award, United Cerebral Palsy Assn., 1982—86, Fresno Zool. Soc., 1982, Calif. State Senate, 1983, San Joaquin chpt. Assn. Gen. Contractors, 1983, Holland Sch., 1984, Huntington Blvd. Neighbors, 1985, proclamation in her honor, City of Fresno, 1985, others, San Joaquin Valley's Most Fashionable award, 1984, Appreciation award, Huntington Blvd. Neighbors, 1986, hon. mayor, City of Fresno, 1986. Roman Catholic. Office Phone: 559-486-7710.

RAVEN, PETER HAMILTON, botanical garden director, botany educator; b. Shanghai, June 13, 1936; s. Walter Francis and Isabelle Marion (Breen) R.; children— Alice Catherine, Elizabeth Marie, Francis Clark, Kathryn Amelia. AB with highest honors, U. Calif.-Berkeley, 1957; PhD, UCLA, 1960; DSc (hon.), St. Louis U., 1982, Knox Coll., 1983, So. Ill. U., 1983, Miami U., 1986, U. Goteborg, 1987, Rutgers U., 1988, U. Mass., 1988, Leiden U., The Netherlands, 1990; HHD (hon.), Webster U., 1989; D.Sc. (hon.), Universidad Nacional de La Plata, Argentina, 1991, Westminster Coll., 1992, U. Mo., 1992, Washington U., 1993, U. Conn., 1993; DSc (hon.), U. Cordoba, Argentina, 1993. Taxonomist, curator Rancho Santa Ana Botanic Garden, Claremont, Calif., 1961-62; asst. prof., then assoc. prof. biol. scis. Stanford U., Calif., 1962-71; dir. Mo. Bot. Garden, St. Louis, 1971—; adj. prof. biology St. Louis U., 1973—; Engelmann prof. botany Washington U., St. Louis, 1971—; adj. prof. biology U. Mo., St. Louis, 1976—. Sr. rsch. fellow New Zealand Dept. Sci. and Indsl. Rsch., 1969-70; v.p. XIII Internat. Bot. Congress, Sydney, 1981; Home Sec. Nat. Acad. Scis., 1987—; chmn. report rev. com. NRC, 1989—; mem. pres. com. Adv. on Sci. and Tech., 1994—; hon. vice-chair 27th Internat. Geographical Cong., 1992; hon. v.p. XV Internt. Bot. Cong., Tokyo, 1993; mem. Nat. Sci. Bd., 1990-94; mem. jury Internat. St. Francis Prize for Environment, 1990-93; mem. exec. com. Joint Appeal by Religion and Sci. for Environment, 1991—; mem. external adv. bd. Com. on Peabody Mus., Yale U., 1992-94; mem. coun. World Resources Inst., 1992—; mem. adv. com. Africa Ctr. for Resources and Environment, 1992—, Third World Found. N.Am., 1993; mem. adv. com. to biodiversity com. Chinese Acad. Scis., 1993—; mem. Exec. Com. Round Table, St. Louis, 1993—; mem. hon. fgn. adv. bd. Botanical Garden Orgn. Thailand, 1993—. Author: Native Shrubs of Southern California, 1966, (with P.R. Ehrlich, R.W. Holm) Papers on Evolution, 1969, (with H. Curtis) Biology of Plants, 1971, 4th edit., 1986, (with R.F. Evert and S.E. Eichhorn) 5th edit., 1992, (with B. Berlin and D. Breedlove) Principles of Tzeltal Plant Classification, 1974, (with G.B. Johnson) Biology, 1986, 3d edit., 1992, Understanding Biology, 1988, 3d edit., 1995; editor: (with L.E. Gilbert) Coevolution of Animals and Plants, 1981, (with F.J. Radovsky & S.H. Sohmer) Biogeography of the Tropical Pacific, 1984, (with others) Topics in Plant Population Biology, 1979, (with K. Iwatsuki and W.J. Bock) Modern Aspects of Species, 1986; editor-in-chief Brittonia, 1963-66; mme. editorial bd. Flora Neotropica, 1965-84; editor (with D.E. Osterbrock) Origins and Extinctions, 1988, paperback, 1992, (with R.M. Polhill) Advances in Legume Systematics, 1981 (with L. Berg and G.B. Johnson) Environment, 1995; mem. editorial bd. Evolution, 1963-65, 76-79, Memoirs of N.Y. Botanical Garden, 1966-84, N.Am. Flora, 1966-84, Am. Naturalist, 1967-70, Annual Rev. Ecology and Systematics, 1971-75, Flora of Ecuador, 1974—, Evolutionary Theory, 1975—, Adansonia, 1976—, Jour. Biogeography, 1978—, Science, 1979-82, Proceedings of U.S. Nat. Acad. Scis., 1980-87, World Book, Inc., 1982-86, Diversity, 1985-90, Bothalia, 1985—, Serie Botánica of the Anales del Instituto de Biología UNAM, 1989, Ecol. Applications, 1989-92, others; mem. adv. bd. Applied Botany Abstracts, 1981—, Tropical Plant Sci. Research, 1982—, Darwiniana, 1985—; mem. internat. editl. com. Acta Botánica Mexicana, 1987—; mem. internat. editl. adv. bd. Candollea, 1995—; mem. editl. bd. Botanical Bulletin Academia Sinica, 1988—, Botanical Mag., 1988-92, Chinese Jour. of Botany, 1991—, Edinburgh Jour. of Botany, 1994—; co-chmn. editl. com. Flora of China, 1988—; advisor Plants Today, 1988-89; contbr. over 400 articles to profl. jours. Bd. curators U. Mo., 1985-90; commr. Tower Grove Park, St. Louis, 1971—; mem. Arnold Arboretum Vis. Com., 1974-81, chmn. 1976-81; bd. overseers Morris Arboretum, 1977-81; mem. sci. adv. bd. Nat. Tropical Botanical Garden, 1975—; mem. Smithsonian Council, 1985-90; chmn. St. Louis Area Mus. Collaborative, 1985-91, Commn. for Flora Neotropica, 1985—; mem. Comm. on Mus. for New Century, 1981-84; mem. sci. and engring. panel Com. on Scholarly Communication with People's Republic China, 1981-85; chmn. com. to visit dept. organismic and evolutionary biology Harvard U., 1982-84, mem. 84-85; ednl. adv. bd. John Simon Guggenheim Meml. Found., 1986—; research assoc. botany Bernice P. Bishop Mus., 1985—; hon. trustee Acad. Sci. of St. Louis, 1986—; chmn. Internat. Union for the Conservation of Nature, World Wildlife Fund, 1984-87, hon. chmn. 1987-90; mem. adv. and tech. bd. Fundación de Parques Nacionales and Fundación Neotrópica, Costa Rica, 1988—; mem. Nat. Coun. World Wildlife Fund and Conservation Foun., 1989—, U.S. bd. dirs. 1983-88, bd. dirs. Conservation Found., 1985-88, sci. adv. com. Conservation Internat., 1988—, chmn's. coun., 1989, World Wildlife Fund, 1987-90, Conservation Found., 1989—, Found. Flora Malesianna, 1992—, Sci. Svc., 1993—; hon. scientific adv. com. XVII Pacific Sci. Congress, 1990-91; adv. bd. The Winslow Found., 1993—, The Internat. Sci. Camp The Earth We Share, 1993—; exec. bd. Internat. Sci. Found. for the Former Soviet Union, 1992—; internat. adv. bd. Fifth ICSEB Congress, Hungary, 1994—. Commn. mem. U.S. MAB, 1994-95. Recipient A.P. DeCandolle prize, Geneva, 1970; Disting. Service award Japan Am. Soc. So. Calif., 1977; award of Merit, Bot. Soc. Am., 1977; Achievement medal Garden Club Am., 1978; Willdenow medal Berlin Bot. Garden, 1979; Disting. Service award Am. Inst. Biol. Scis., 1981; Joseph Priestly medal, Dickinson Coll., 1982; Gold Seal medal Nat. Council of State Garden Clubs, 1982; Internat. Environ. Leadership medal UN Environ. Program, 1982; Spl. citiation Doña Doris Yankelewitz de Monge, 1985, Internat. Prize for Biology, Govt. Japan, 1986, Hutchinson medal Chgo. Hort. Soc., 1986, Archie F. Carr medal, 1987, Global 500 Honor Roll UN Environ. Program, 1987, Am. Fuchsia Soc. Achievement Medal, 1987, George Robert White Medal of Honor Mass. Horticultural Soc., 1987, Robert Allerton Medal Nat. Tropical Bot. Garden, 1988, Nat. Conservation Achievement award Nat. Wildlife Fedn., 1989, Delmer S. Fahrney medal Franklin Inst., Phila., 1989, (with E.O. Wilson) Environ. prize Institut de la Vie (Paris), 1990, Order of Golden Ark (officer), The Netherlands, 1990, award for Support of Sci. Coun. Sci. Soc. Pres., 1990, (with Norman Myers) Volvo Environ. prize, 1992, Pres.'s Conservation Achievement Awd., 1993, Nature Conservancyvement award TNC, 1993, Internat. award Internat. Inst. of St. Louis, 1994, Founder's Coun. Centennial Merit award The Field Mus. of Natural History, 1994, Sword of St. Ignatius Loyola award St. Louis U., 1994, Tyler Environ. Achievement prize, 1994, and numerous other botanical awards and honors; Guggenheim fellow, 1969-70; John D. and Catherine T. MacArthur Found. fellow, 1985-90, NSF postdoctoral fellow, Brit. Mus. London, 1960-61. Fellow Am. Acad. Arts and Scis. (com. on membership 1980-82), Linnean Soc. London (fgn. mem.), Calif. Acad. Scis. (CAS Fellow, Fellows' medal 1988), AAAS, Indian Nat. Sci. Acad., Third World Acad. Scis., World Acad. Art & Sci.; mem. NSF (systematic biology panel 1973-76, chmn. adv. com. for biol. behavioral and social scis. 1984-90), NAS (com. on human rights 1984-87, home sec. 1987—), Royal Danish Acad. Scis. and Letters (fgn. hon.), Royal Swedish Acad. Scis. (fgn.), Royal Soc. New Zealand (hon.), NRC (gov. bd. 1983-86, 87-88, chmn. com. on research priorities in tropical biology 1977-79, assembly life scis. 1979-81, com. on selected research problems in humid tropics 1980-82, commn. internat. relations 1981-82), Calif. Bot. Soc. (v.p. 1968-69), Am. Soc. Plant Taxonomists (pres. 1972), Assn. Systematics Collections (pres. 1980-82, Fed. Council Arts and Humanities, Nat. Geographic Soc. (com. on research and exploration 1982—), Internat. Orgn. Plant Biosystematists (v.p. 1989-92, pres. 92-95), Internat. Assn. for Plant Taxonomy (council 1981—), Orgn. Tropical Studies (treas. 1981-84, v.p. elect. 1984-85, pres. 1985-88, past pres. 1988-90, bd. dirs. 1981-91), Am. Soc. Naturalists (pres. 1983), Miller Inst. Basic Research in Sci. (adv. bd. 1983-89), Am. Inst. Biol. Scis. (pres. 1983-84), Mo. Acad. Scis., Geol. Soc. Am., Bot. Soc. Am. (pres. 1975, chmn. com. on sci. exchange with People's Republic China 1978-84), Assn. Tropical Biology (bd. dirs. 1981-85), Am. Assn. Mus. (exec. com. 1980-83, named to Centennial Honor Roll, 2006), Assn. Sci. Mus. Dirs., Assn. Pacific Systematists, Sociedad Argentina de Botanica (socio honorario), Fundación Miguel Lillo (hon.), Soc. Systematic Zool., Sociedad Botánica de México (life), Assn. pour l'Etude Taxonomique de la Flore d'Afrique Tropicale, Orgn. for Phyto-Taxonomic Investigation of Mediterranean Area (council 1975-89), All-Union Botanical Soc. USSR (hon. fgn. mem.), Accademia Nazionale delle Scienze detta dei XL (fgn.), Am. Philosophical Soc, Russian Acad. Scis. (fgn. mem.), Nat. Acad. Scis. India (fgn. fellow 1990—), Academia de Ciencias Exactas, Físicas y Naturales, Austrian Acad. Scis., Academia Chilena de Ciencias, Academia Nacional de Ciencias, Academy Scis. Ukraine, Chinese Acad. Scis., Nature Conservancy (Pres. Conservation Achievement Awd., 1993), Phi Beta Kappa, Sigma Xi Office: Missouri Botanical Garden PO Box 299 Saint Louis MO 63166-0299 Office Phone: 314-577-5111. Office Fax: 314-577-9595. E-mail: peter.raven@mobot.org. *

RAVENAL, EARL CEDRIC, international relations educator, writer; b. NYC, Mar. 29, 1931; s. Alan M. and Mildred S. (Sherman) R.; m. Carol Bird Myers, May 26, 1956; children: Cornelia Jane, John Brodhead, Rebecca Eliza. BA, Harvard U., 1952; postgrad., U. Cambridge, Eng., 1952-53; M.M.P. diploma, Harvard Bus. Sch., 1958; MA, Johns Hopkins U., 1971, PhD, 1975. Treas. Elbe File & Binder Co., Inc., Fall River, Mass., 1955-64, pres., 1965-67; dir. Asian div. systems analysis Office Sec. Def., Washington, 1967-69; prof. internat. relations Johns Hopkins U. Sch. Advanced Internat. Studies, Washington, 1973-78, Georgetown U. Sch. Fgn. Service, Washington, 1976—. Bd. advisors Ctr. for Def. Info., Washington, 1971-97, Ctr. for Study Conflict, 1983—; bd. dirs. Critical Rev. Author: (with others) Peace with China?, 1971, (with others) Atlantis Lost, 1976, Never Again, 1979, Toward World Security, 1978, Strategic Disengagement and World Peace, 1979, NATO's Unremarked Demise, 1979, Defining Def., 1984, NATO: The Tides of Discontent, 1985, Large-Scale Foreign Policy Change, 1989, Designing Defense, 1991, Defending America in an Uncontrollable World, 2002; contbg. editor Inquiry Mag., 1976-85, Critical Rev., 1987—; contbr. articles to profl. jours. Advisor Democratic Presdl. Campaign, 1972; advisor Jerry Brown Presdl. Campaign, 1976, Libertarian Presdl. Campaigns, 1980, 84. Served with JAGC U.S. Army, 1953-55. Henry fellow U. Cambridge, 1952-53; mem. faculty Salzburg Seminar in Am. Studies, 1977; fellow Bellagio Ctr. Rockefeller Found., 1975, Woodrow Wilson Internat. Ctr. for Scholars, 1973, Washington Ctr. of Fgn. Policy Research, 1974; sr. fellow Cato Inst., 1985-91, 97—. Mem. Council Fgn. Relations, Am. Polit. Sci. Assn., Internat. Inst. Strategic Studies, Fed. Am. Scientists, Internat. Studies Assn. Clubs: Cosmos (Washington); Fed. City (Washington); Harvard (N.Y.C.); Signet (Cambridge, Mass.); Tred Avon Yacht (Oxford, Md.). Libertarian. Home and Office: 4439 Cathedral Ave NW Washington DC 20016-3562

RAVENAL, JOHN B., curator; BA in Art History, Wesleyan U., 1982; MA in Art History, Columbia U., 1987, MPhil in Art History, 1990. Rschr. in contemporary art Wadsworth Atheneum, Hartford, Conn., 1982—85; asst. curator 20th-century art Phila. Mus. Art, 1991—97, assoc. curator 20th-century art, 1997—98; curator of modern and contemporary art Va. Mus. Fine Arts, Richmond, 1998—. Curator (exhibitions) robert lazzarini, Va. Mus. Fine Arts, 2003—04 (Award for Best Exhbn. of Digital Art, Assn. Independent Art Critics/USA, 2005). Office: Va Mus Fine Arts 200 N Blvd Richmond VA 23220-4007 Office Phone: 804-340-1606.

RAVENEL, SHANNON, book publishing professional; b. Charlotte, NC, Aug. 13, 1938; d. Elias Prioleau and Harriett Shannon (Steedman) R.; m. Dale Purves, May 25, 1968; children: Sara Blake, Harriett. BA, Hollins Coll., 1960. Mktg. asst., sch. dept. Holt, Rinehart & Winston, Inc., NYC, 1960-61; editl. asst. Houghton Mifflin Co., Boston, 1961-64, editor, 1964—70; editl. cons. pvt. practice, St. Louis, 1973-90; sr. editor, co-founder Algonquin Books of Chapel Hill, NC, 1982-91, editl. dir., 1992-2000; dir. Algonquin imprint Shannon Ravenel Books, 2001—. Series editor: Best American Short Stories, 1978-90; editor: Best American Short Stories of the Eighties, 1990, New Stories From the South, 1986-2005 Recipient Disting. Achievement award Coun. Lit. Mags. & Presses, NYC, 1990, R. Hunt Parker Meml. award for contbns. to the lit. of N.C., 2004. Mem. PEN Am. Ctr. Democrat. Office: Algonquin Books of Chapel Hill PO Box 2225 Chapel Hill NC 27515-2225 Business E-Mail: shannonr@algonquin.com.

RAVENELL, KENNETH W., lawyer; b. Cross, SC, May 9, 1959; BA cum laude, SC State Coll., 1981; JD, U. Md., 1985. Bar: Md. 1985, US Dist. Ct. (dist. Md.) 1990, US Dist. Ct. (DC dist.). Asst. editor U. Md. Law Forum, 1983—84; asst. states atty. Balt., 1985—88; ptnr. Schulman, Treem, Kaminkov, Gilden & Ravenell, P.A., Balt. Mem. jud. nominating. com. Trial Courts; instr. bar exam tutorial prog. U. Md., 1987—90. Named one of Balt.'s Top Lawyers, Balt. Mag., 2003, Top Criminal Lawyers in Balt., 2004. Mem.: Fed. Bar Assn., Bar Assn. Balt. City, Md. Criminal Def. Attys. Assn., Monumental Bar Assn., Md. State Bar Assn. Office: Schulman Treem Kaminkow Gilden & Ravenell PA 1800 World Trade Ctr 401 E Pratt St Baltimore MD 21202-3004 Office Phone: 410-659-0111. Office Fax: 410-332-0866. *

RAVENHOLT, REIMERT THOROLF, epidemiologist, researcher; b. Milltown, Wis., Mar. 9, 1925; s. Ansgar Benedikt and Kristine Henriette (Petersen) R.; divorced; children: Janna, Mark, Lisa, Dane; m. Betty Butler Howell, Sept. 26, 1981. BS, U. Minn., 1948, MB, 1951, MD, 1952; MPH, U. Calif., Berkeley, 1956. Bd. cert. preventive medicine. Intern USPHS Hosp., San Francisco, 1951-52; epidemic intelligence service officer USPHS Communicable Disease Ctr., Atlanta, 1952-54; dir. epidemiology and communicable disease div. Seattle-King County Health Dept., 1954-61; epidemiology cons. European area USPHS, Paris, 1961-63; assoc. prof. preventive medicine U. Wash. Med. Sch., Seattle, 1963-66; dir. Office of Population, AID, Washington, 1966-79, World Health Surveys, Ctrs. for Disease Control, 1980-82; asst. dir. epidemiology and research Nat. Inst. Drug Abuse, Rockville, Md., 1982-84; chief epidemiology br. FDA, Rockville, Md., 1984-87; dir. World Health Surveys, Inc., Seattle, 1987-93; pres. Population Health Imperatives, Seattle, 1993—. Author/designer website Adventures in Epidemiology. Served with USPHS, 1951-54, 61-63. Recipient Disting Honor award AID, 1973, Hugh Moore Meml. award IPPF and Population Crisis Com., 1974. Fellow Am. Coll. Epidemiology, APHA (Carl Schultz award 1978), mem. Am. Coun. on Sci. and Health (bd. dirs.); mem. Cosmos Club (Washington). Independent. Achievements include discovery of cause of Meriwether Lewis' death of progressive neurosyphilis. Home: 3156 E Laurelhurst Dr NE Seattle WA 98105-5333 E-mail: ravenrt@oz.net.

RAVENSTAHL, LUKE R., mayor; b. Pitts., Pa., Feb. 6, 1980; s. Robert P. and Cindy Ravenstahl; m. Erin Lynn Feith, July 2004. Attended, Mercyhurst Coll., U. Pitts.; BBA with honors, Washington and Jefferson Coll., 2002. Account mgr. for courier svc.; mem., Coun. Dist. 1 Pitts. City Coun., 2004—05, pres., 2005—06; mayor City of Pitts., 2006—. Bd. mem. City of Pitts. Mcpl. Pension Fund. Bd. pres. Neighborhood Enterprises; mem. Allegheny County Democratic Com., 1998—2004; bd. mem. Fireman's Relief and Pension Fund, Comprehensive Mcpl. Pension Trust Fund., Pitts. Cultural Trust, Sports and Exhbn. Authroity, Carnegie Libr.; bd. trustee Carnegie Mellon U.; mem. adv. bd. North Catholic HS; mem. Northside Cmty. Develop. Fund, City-County Summit Com. of Pub. Works, Parks, and Facilities. Office: Rm 512 City County Bldg 414 Grant St Pittsburgh PA 15219 Office Phone: 412-255-2626. Office Fax: 412-255-2687. Business E-Mail: mayorcompl@city.pittsburgh.pa.us. *

RAVETCH, IRVING, screenwriter; b. Newark, Nov. 14, 1920; s. I. Shalom and Sylvia (Shapiro) R.; m. Harriet Frank Jr., Nov. 24, 1946. BA, UCLA, 1941. Screenwriter: (films) (with La Cava) Living in a Big Way, 1947, The Outriders, 1950, Vengeance Valley, 1951; (with Harriet Frank, Jr.) The Long, Hot Summer, 1958, The Sound and the Fury, 1959, Home from the Hill, 1959, The Dark at the Top of the Stairs, 1960, House of Cards, 1969, The Cowboys, 1972, Conrack, 1974, The Spikes Gang, 1974, Norma Rae, 1979 (Academy award nomination best adapted screenplay 1979), Murphy's Romance, 1985, Stanley and Iris, 1990; writer, prodr.: (with Frank) Hud, 1963 (Academy award nomination best adapted screenplay 1963, N.Y. Film Critics Circle award best screenplay 1963), Hombre, 1967, The Reivers, 1969; story: (with Frank) Ten Wanted Men, 1955. Recipient N.Y. Film Critics award, 1963, Writers' Guild Am. award, 1988; Oscar nomination for Hud, Acad. Motion Picture Arts and Scis., 1963, Norma Rae, 1979.

RAVETCH, JEFFREY VICTOR, molecular biologist, immunologist, educator; s. Sylvia and Paul H. Ravetch; m. Wendy Evans Joseph, Oct. 27, 2001. Grad., Yale U., New Haven; PhD in Genetics, Rockefeller U.; MD, Cornell U. Postdoctoral rschr. NIH; mem. faculty Meml. Sloan-Kettering Cancer Ctr. and Cornell Med. Coll., 1982; Theresa and Eugene M. Lang prof. Rockefeller U., NYC. Mem. sci. adv. bd. Cancer Rsch. Inst., Irvington Inst. Med. Rsch., Damon Runyon Found.; co-founder, dir. MacroGenics, Rockville, Md., 2000—. Contbr. articles to profl. jours. Named a Pew Scholar, 1985. Fellow: NAS. Office: Leonard Wagner Lab Molecular Genetics and Immunology Rockefeller U 1230 York Ave New York NY 10021 E-mail: ravetch@rockefeller.edu.

RAVINSKY, ANTHONY, music educator; s. Tony and Anna Ravinsky. MusB, Crane Sch. Music, 2003. Carpenter N.Y. Stage and Film, Poughkeepsie, 2002—04; choral dir. Cornwall (N.Y.) Ctrl. H.S., 2003—. Mem.: N.Y. State Theater Educators Assn., Music Educators Nat. Conf., Am. Choral Dir. Assn.

RAVISH, I. R., urologist, surgeon; b. Feb. 7, 1971; MBBS, Mysore U, 1996; MS in Gen. Surgery, Mysore U., 2002; MCh in Urology, J.N.M. Coll., Bangalore, 2007. Registrar, dept. gen. surgery, 1997—98; resident dept. urology, 2002—04. Spkr. and presenter in field. Contbr. articles to profl. jours. Achievements include research in effect of pygeum africanum on symptomatic BPH; comparative study between dutasteride finesteride in symptmatic BPH; RIRS for renal stones; flexible uretroscopy for post ESWL fragments; results of surgical repair of delayed presentations of penile fractures as against the conservative management; phase III trial for overacitve bladder. Avocation: football. Office: Nehru Nagar Karnataka 590010 India

RAVISHANKARA, AKKIHEBAL R., chemist; PhD, U. Fla., 1975. Chief atmospheric chem. kinetics group NOAA, Boulder, Colo. Adj. prof. dept. chemistry U. Colo., Boulder; postdoctoral rsch. assoc. U. Md., 1976. Named Robertson Meml. lectr., NAS, 1999. Office: DSRC Rm 1A123 325 Broadway Boulder CO 80305-3328

RAVITCH, DIANE SILVERS, historian, educator, writer, government official; b. Houston, July 1, 1938; d. Walter Cracker and Ann Celia (Katz) Silvers; m. Richard Ravitch, June 26, 1960 (div. 1986); children: Joseph, Steven (dec.), Michael. BA, Wellesley Coll., 1960; PhD, Columbia U., 1975; LHD (hon.), Williams Coll., 1984, Reed Coll., 1985, Amherst Coll., 1986, SUNY, 1988, Ramapo Coll., 1990, St. Joseph's Coll., NYC, 1991, Middlebury Coll., 1997, Union Coll., 1998. Adj. asst. prof. Tchrs. Coll., Columbia U., NYC, 1975-78, assoc. prof., 1978-83, adj. prof., 1983-91; asst. sec. office ednl. rsch. and improvement U.S. Dept. Edn., Washington, 1991-93, counselor to the sec. edn., 1991-93. Vis. fellow Brookings Instn., Washington, 1993-94, non-resident sr. fellow, 1994-, editor papers on edn. policy, 1997-05, Brown chair in edn. policy, 1997-05; rsch. prof. NYU, 1994-; mem. Nat. Assessment Governing Bd., 1997-04; com. on edn. policy Nat. Acad. Scis., 2003-05; mem. Koret task force Hoover Instn., 1999-, sr. fellow, 2005-. Author: The Great School Wars, 1974, The Revisionists Revised, 1977, The Troubled Crusade, 1983, The Schools We Deserve, 1985, National Standards in American Education, A Citizens Guide, 1995, Left Back, 2000, The Language Police, 2003; author: (with others) Educating an Urban People, 1981; author: The School and the City, 1983, Against Mediocrity, 1984, Challenges to the Humanities, 1985, What Do Our 17 Year Olds Know?, 1987, Edspeak, 2007; editor: The American Reader, 1990; co-editor: The Democracy Reader, 1992, New Schools for a New Century, 1997, City Schools, 2000, Making Good Citizens, 2001, Kid Stuff, 2003, Forgotten Heroes of American Education, 2006, The English Reader, 2006; editor: Learning from the Past, 1995, Debating the Future of American Education, 1995. Chair Ednl. Excellence Network, 1988—91, 1994—96; trustee Nat. Humanities Ctr., 1999—2000, NY Pub. Libr., 1981—87, hon. life trustee, 1988—; trustee NY Coun. on Humanities, 1996—2004; mem. Landmarks Preservation Commn., Southold, NY, 2000—02; bd. dirs. Woodrow Wilson Nat. Fellowship Found., 1987—91, Coun. Basic Edn., 1989—91, Thomas B. Fordham Found., 1998—, New Am. Found., 2000—06, Albert Shanker Inst., 2002—, Core Knowledge Found., 2003—, Hunt Inst. Ednl. Policy and Leadership, 2002—, Nat. History Ctr., 2007—, John Dewey Ednl. Found., 2007—. Recipient Disting. Svc. award NY Acad. Pub. Edn., 1994, Alumnae Achievement award Wellesley Coll., 1989, Uncommon Book award Hoover Instn., 2004, John Dewey award United Fedn. Tchrs., 2005, Gaudium award Breukelein Inst., 2005, Pub. Svc. award Am. Jewish Hist. Soc., 2006; Guggenheim fellow, 1977-78; Phi Beta Kappa vis. scholar. Mem. Nat. Acad. Edn., Am. Acad. Arts and Scis., Soc. Am. Historians, N.Y. Hist. Soc. (trustee 1995-98), PEN Internat. Office: NYU 82 Wash Sq E New York NY 10003-6644

RAVIV, TAL, ophthalmologist; b. Aug. 20, 1970; s. Michael and Nava Raviv. BS, Brown U., Providence, RI, 1992, MD, 1995—95. Diplomate Am. Bd. Ophthalmology, 2001. Founding ptnr. NY Laser Eye, LLP, NYC, 2001—. Mem.: Am. Soc. Cataract and Refractive Surgeons, Am. Acad. Ophthalmology. Office: New York Laser Eye LLP 30 E 40th St Ste 203 New York NY 10016 Home Phone: 212-481-0001; Office Phone: 212-448-1005. Business E-Mail: tal.raviv@nylasereye.com.

RAWITCH, ALLEN BARRY, medical educator, academic administrator; b. Chgo., Dec. 29, 1940; s. Sam and Jean Rawitch; m. Patricia Nan Karlan, July 21, 1962; children: Bruce, David. BS in Chemistry, UCLA, 1963, PhD in Biol. Chemistry, 1967. Rsch. fellow U. Ill., Urbana, 1967-69; asst. prof. Kent (Ohio) State U., 1969-73, assoc. prof., 1973-75, U. Kans. Med. Ctr., Kansas City, 1975-80, prof., 1980—, asst. dean student affairs, 1999-2000, vice chancellor acad. affairs, dean grad. studies, 2000—, chmn. biochemistry and molecular biology, 2002—03. Vice chair biochemistry U. Kans. Med. Ctr., 1977-95, chair edn. coun., 1995-99 Editor Med. Biochemistry Question Bank, 1985-94; contbr. articles to profl. jours. Res. police officer capt. Overland Park Police Dept., 1979—. Rsch. grant NIH, 1971-2000, NSF, 1970, Am. Heart Assn., 1998-2002. Mem. Am. Soc. for Biochemistry and Molecular Biology, The Protein Soc., Am. Thyroid Assn., Sigma Xi. Avocations: amateur radio, woodworking, target shooting. Office: Office Acad Affairs U Kans Med Ctr 3901 Rainbow Blvd Mail Stop 1040 Kansas City KS 66160-0001 Office Phone: 913-588-1258. Business E-Mail: arawitch@kumc.edu.

RAWITCH, ROBERT JOE, journalist, educator; b. LA, Oct. 11, 1945; s. Sam and Jean (Reifman) R.; m. Cynthia Z. Knee, Oct. 27, 1968; children: Dana Leigh, Jeremy Aaron, Joshua Eric. BA in Journalism, Calif. State U., Northridge, 1967; MS in Journalism, Northwestern U., 1968. Reporter L.A. Times, 1968-80, asst. met. editor, 1980-82, editor Valley sect., 1982-83, suburban editor, 1983-89, exec. editor Valley and Ventura County edits., 1989-93; dir. editl. ops. Valley and Ventura County edits., 1993-95; sr. v.p. Winner and Assocs., 1996—. Lectr. Calif. State U., Northridge, 1971-83, 95-96, 03-. Co-author: Adat Ari El, The First Fifty Years, 1988. Chmn. Calif. Freedom of Info. Com., 1978-79; pres. Calif. First Amendment coalition, 1991-93; bd. dirs. Temple Adat Ari El, 1987-92, Calif. State U. Northridge Found., 1999-, Univ. Corp., 2000-. Recipient Greater L.A. Press Club award, 1973, 75, 79, L.A. Jewish Youth of Yr. award United Jewish Fund, 1963, Clarence Darrow Found. award, 1979, Heitz award outstanding vol. Calif. State U. Northridge, 2003. Mem. Soc. Profl. Journalists (nat. bd. dirs. 1979-82), Calif. Soc. Newspaper Editors (pres. 1995-96), Medill Alumni Assn. (bd. dirs. 1994-2000), CSUN Journalism Alumni Assn. (bd. dirs. 2002—). Office: Winner & Assocs 16501 Ventura Blvd Encino CA 91436-2007 Office Phone: 818-385-1900. Business E-Mail: brawitch@winnr.com.

RAWL, ARTHUR JULIAN (LORD OF CURSONS), corporate director, retail executive, consultant, accountant, writer; b. Boston, July 6, 1942; s. Philip and Evelyn (Rosoff) R.; m. Karen Lee Werby, June 4, 1967; 1 child, Kristen Alexandra. BBA, Boston U., 1967, postgrad, 1974; DBA in Business (hon.), St. George's U., London, 1995. CPA, Mass., N.Y., La. Audit mgr. Touche Ross & Co., Boston, 1967-77, NYC, 1977-79, ptnr., 1979, Newark, 1980-88, NYC, 1988-89, Deloite & Touche, NYC, 1989-90; exec. v.p., CFO Hanlin Group, Inc., Linden, NJ, 1990-94, United Auto Group, Inc., NYC, 1994-97; pres., CEO, bd. dirs. Brazil Internat. Motors, Brazil Am. Auto Group, São Paulo, Brazil, 1999—2003; chmn., CEO Auto Alliance, Englewood, NJ, 2003—, Rawl & Assocs., Miami, Fla., 2003—. Bd. dirs. BiakalInterPlast (USSR), Kuperwood Enterprises, Hanlin Group, Inc., Quipp, Inc., XL Generation, Inc., Zug Switzerland; chmn. Tiger Ethanol, Inc., Montreal, Canada; mem. adj. faculty Boston U., 1971-75, Lectr. Practicing Law Institute, NY 2007, KPMG Audit Committee Institue 2006-. Contbr. articles to profl. journals, mags. and trade publs. Mem. Newton Upper Falls (Mass.) Hist. Commn., 1977; bd. dirs. Sherburne Scholarship Fund Boston U., 1977-80; mem. Englewood (N.J.) Planning Bd., 1981-83; trustee Englewood Bd. Edn., 1983-85, 89-93, pres., 1991-92; trustee, treas. exec. com. Englewood Econ. Devel. Corp., 1986-89; fin. and compensation com. Dwight Englewood Sch., 1985-90; mem. parent devel. com. Mt. Holyoke Coll., 1991-94; chmn. Brit. Meml. Garden Trust, NY, 2003—; chmn. British Meml. Garden Trust, London, 2007-. Served to 2d class Petty Officer, Aviation Electronics and Combat Air Crewman (hon. discharge 1967) USN, 1960—63. Decorated Naval Expeditionary medal, Armed Forces Expeditionary Medal, Good Conduct Medal, National Defense medal; named member, Her Majesty's Most Excellent Order of the British Empire. Fellow AICPA, Mass. Soc. CPAs, NY Soc. CPAs; mem. VFW, Am. Legion, Navy League U.S., N.J. Hist. Soc. (bd. govs., exec. com., nominating com., treas. 1987-99), St. George's Soc. NY (treas. exec. com. 1998-2005), H.M. Sovereign Order of St. John, Coll. Arms Found. (v.p. 2001—), Brit. Am. Inst., Fin. Execs. Internat. Officer of Most Venerable Order of Hosp. of St. John of Jerusalem, Univ. Club (NY), Essex Club, Sloane Club (London). Conservative. Home: 1581 Brickell Ave Ste 1003 Miami FL 33129 Business E-Mail: a.rawl@att.net.

RAWLES, EDWARD HUGH, lawyer; b. Chgo., May 7, 1945; s. Fred Wilson and Nancy (Hughes) Rawles; m. Margaret Mary O'Donoghue, Oct. 20, 1979; children: Lee Kathryn, Jacklyn Ann. BA, U. Ill., 1967; JD summa cum laude, Ill. Inst. Tech., Chgo., 1970. Bar: Ill. 1970, Colo. 1984, US Dist. Ct.(ctrl. dist.) Ill. 1970, US Ct. Appeals (7th cir.), US Supreme Ct. 1973, diplomate: Nat. Bd. Trial Advocacy. Assoc. Reno, O'Byrne & Kepley, Champaign, Ill., 1970—73, ptnr., 1973—84, Rawles, O'Byrne, Stanko & Kepley P.C., 1984—98, pres., 1990—97. Student legal svc. adv. bd. U. Ill., Urbana, Ill., 1982—; hearing officer Ill. Fair Employment Practice Commn., Springfield, Ill., 1972—74; mem. rules com. U.S. Dist. Ct. (ctrl. dist.) Ill., 1994—2006; mem. com. fitness Ill. Supreme Ct., 2005—. Named one of, Ill. Super Lawyers, 2007. Fellow: Ill. State Bar Found.; mem.: Colo. Trial Lawyers Assn., Ill. Trial Lawyers Assn., Assn. Trial Lawyers Am., Bar Assn. 7th Fed. Cir., Ill. Bar Assn., Kent Soc. Honor Men, Phi Delta Theta. Roman Catholic. Home: 6 Alice Dr White Heath IL 61884-9747 Office: Rawles O'Byrne Stanko Kepley & Jefferson PC 501 W Church St Champaign IL 61820-3412 Office Phone: 217-352-7661. Business E-Mail: ehrkwles@rosklaw.com.

RAWLINGS, BOYNTON MOTT, lawyer; b. El Paso, Tex., Dec. 6, 1935; s. Junius Mott and Laura Bassett (Boynton) R.; m. Nancy Mary Peay, Aug. 24, 1962 (div. 1973); children: Laura Bassett, James Mott; m. Judith Reed, Dec. 10, 1977; 1 child, William Reed. AB, Princeton U., 1958; LLB, Stanford U., 1961; diploma, U. Strasbourg, France, 1963. Bar: Calif. 1962, D.C. 1980, Conseil Juridique Paris, 1973, Avocat Paris, 1992. Assoc. Broad, Busterud & Khourie, San Francisco, 1963-65, Homer G. Angelo, Brussels, 1966; assoc., ptnr. S.G. Archibald, Paris, 1967-74; ptnr. Boynton M. Rawlings, Paris, L.A., 1974-84, Kevorkian & Rawlings, Paris, 1984-90, Oppenheimer, Wolff and Donnelly, Paris, 1990-99, Rawlings & Giles LLP., Paris, 2000—. Contbr. articles to profl. jours. Mem. L.A. Bar Assn. (bd. dirs. sect. internat. law 1975-82), French Am. C. of C. L.A. (bd. dirs. 1985—). Republican. Episcopalian. Avocations: music, tennis, skiing, hiking. Office: Rawlings & Giles 53 Ave Montaigne 75008 Paris France also: The Farragut Bldg 500 17th St NW Ste 700 Washington DC 20006-4804 Home: 38 Elliott St Charleston SC 29401-2529

RAWLINGS, GREGORY OWEN, science educator, consultant; b. Roswell, N.Mex., Jan. 29, 1951; s. Vernon Keith and Mildred Mary Rawlings; m. Virginia Lee Murphy, Oct. 25, 1985; 1 adopted child, Gwyndolyn Nicole 1 child, Stephanie Janiece. BS, U. of Kans., 1973. Cert. edn. Kans. State Dept. of Edn. Intermediate sci. tchr. Unified Sch. Dist. #497, Lawrence, Kans., 1973—78, Unified Sch. Dist. #305, Salina, Kans., 1978—82; asst. mgr., cashier supr. Wal-Mart #558, Salina, 1983—84; account rep. Burroughs Computer Corp., Rochester, NY, 1984—85; tchr. 8th grade earth sci. and algebra Unified Sch. Dist. 469, Lansing, Kans., 1986—2005; assoc. prof. algebra, bus. ethics, and profl. devel. Brown Mackie Coll., Kansas City, Kans., 2006—. Resource person Harvard-Smithsonian Ctr. for Astrophysics - Project ESTEEM. Mem. Dist. Site Coun., Lansing, 1995—2002, Dist. Steering Com., Lansing, 1986—94; mem. blue ribbon adv. bd. ShareNet Pan Ednl. Inst., Independence, Mo., 1989—93. Mem.: NEA, Kans. Nat. Edn. Assn. (adminstrv. bd. dirs. 2003—04), Nat. Sci. Tchrs. Assn. Home: 210 Jayhawk Ct Lansing KS 66043-1811 Office: Brown Mackie Coll 9705 Lenexa Dr Lenexa KS 66215 Personal E-mail: g.rawlings.bmckc@gmail.com.

RAWLINGS, HUNTER RIPLEY, III, classicist, former academic administrator; b. Norfolk, Va., Dec. 14, 1944; m. Elizabeth Trapnell Rawlings; 4 children. BA, Haverford Coll., 1966; PhD Classics, Princeton U., 1970. Asst. prof. U. Colo., Boulder, 1970—75, assoc. prof., 1975—80, prof. classics, 1980—88, v.p. acad. affairs, rsch., dean System Grad. Sch., 1984—88; pres. U. Iowa, 1988—95, Cornell U., Ithaca, NY, 1995—2003, prof. greek classics, 1995—, pres. emeritus, 2003—, interim pres., 2005—06. Chair Iowa Commn. Fgn. Lang. Studies and Internat. Edn., 1988—91; bd. dirs. Tokpkins County Trust Co.; bd. dirs. Brookhaven Sci. Assocs. Author: The Structure of Thucydides' History, 1981; editor-in-chief: Classical Jour., 1977—83; contbr. articles to profl. jours. Bd. dirs. Norwest Bank Iowa N.A., 1988—95. Fellow, Ctr. Hellenic Studies, 1975—76. Fellow: Am. Acad. Arts and Scis.; mem.: Nat. Fgn. Lang. Ctr. (mem. nat. adv. bd. 1995—), Am. Coun. Edn. (bd. dirs. 1994—97), Assn. Am. Univs. (exec. com. 1990—92). Home: 54 Woodard RD Newfield NY 14867-9267 Office: Cornell U Dept Classics 120 Goldwin Smith Hall Ithaca NY 14853-3201

RAWLINGS, PAUL C., retired government official; b. Cave City, Ark., June 21, 1928; s. Otha A. and Leona (King) R.; m. Catherine Terral, 1951 (div. 1970); children: William A., Rebecca, Neal; m. Erma Martin, June 20, 1971 (div. Jan. 1997). Grad., Little Rock Jr. Coll.; LL.B., Ark. Law Sch., 1950. Bar: Ark. 1950. Practiced in, Little Rock, 1950, 52-73; adminstrv. law judge Office Hearings and Appeals, Social Security Adminstrn., HEW, Hattiesburg, Miss., 1973-92; ret.; ptnr. firm Terral, Rawlings, Matthews & Purtle, until 1973. Asst. atty. gen., Ark., 1955-56 Bd. dirs. Ark. Enterprises for Blind, 1964-67; del. White House Conf. on Aging, 1995. Served with AUS, 1950-52 Mem. Ark. Bar Assn., Law Sci. Acad. Methodist (past chmn. bd. adminstrn., trustee). Club: Lion (past pres.). Home: 100 # 14 Swinging Bridge Dr Heber Springs AR 72543-8717

RAWLINS, DONALD RAY, lawyer; b. Dyersburg, Tenn., Apr. 28, 1965; s. Dal M. and Rebecca S. Rawlins. BBA, U. Memphis, 1987; JD, Am. U., 1990. Bar: Tenn., 1990. V.p., asst. gen. counsel, asst. sec. AutoZone, Inc., Memphis, 1990—2004; asst. gen. counsel Thomas & Betts Corp., Memphis, 2004—05, asst. sec., 2004—05, chief compliance officer, 2004—05; counsel Alston and Bird LLP, Charlotte, NC, 2007—. Vice chmn. Memphis Landmarks Commn., 2004—05. Recipient Best Brief award ATLA, 1990. Republican. Methodist. Office: Alston and Bird 101 S Tryan St #4000 Charlotte NC 28280

RAWLINS, V. LANE, economics professor, retired academic administrator; b. Rigby, Idaho, Nov. 30, 1937; m. Mary Jo Rawlins, three children. BA in Economics, Brigham Young U., 1963; PhD in Economics, U of Calif., Berkeley, 1969. Faculty Wash. State U., Pullman, 1968-86, chair. economics, 1977-82, vice provost, 1982—86; vice chancellor, academic affairs U. of Alabama, 1986-91; pres. Memphis St. U., Memphis, 1991-00, Wash. State U., Pullman, 2000—07, prof. econs.; mem. William D. Ruckelshaus Ctr. Office: Washington State U Hulbert 121C Pullman WA 99164-1048 Office Phone: 509-335-6666. E-mail: rawlins@wsu.edu. *

RAWLINS, W. SCOTT, art educator; b. New Brunswick, NJ, Oct. 28, 1954; s. Stokes Smith and Hazel Mae Rawlins. BA in Biology, Earlham Coll., Richmond, Ind., 1976; MA in Tchr. in Museum Edn., George Washington U., Washington, 1981; MFA in Med. Illustration, U. Mich., Ann Arbor, 1989. Cert. EMT. Asst. curator natural sci. Children's Mus., Indpls., 1978—79; ednl. cons., exhibit designer Trailside Mus. and Sci. Ctr., Mountainside, NJ, 1981—82; dir. edn. Calvert Marine Mus., Solomons, Md., 1982—86; curator natural sci. Pub. Mus. Grand Rapids, Mich., 1990—94; from asst. prof. to assoc. prof., chair fine arts dept. Arcadia U., Glenside, Pa., 1994—. Adj. prof. Kendall Coll. Art and Design, Grand Rapids, 1990—94; contractor Nat. Mus. Natural History, Washington, 1981—82. Contbg. author: The Guild Handbook of Scientific Illustration, 2003. Canvasser Move On, Pa., 2004. Mem.: Am. Assn. Museums, Guild Natural Sci. Illustrators (bd. dirs., dir. edn., Members' Choice award 2002), Am. Soc. Bot. Artists (bd. dirs., pres.), Phi Beta Delta, Phi Kappa Phi. Office: Arcadia U Dept Fine Arts 450 S Easton Rd Glenside PA 19038

RAWLINSON, HELEN ANN, librarian; b. Columbia, SC, Mar. 30, 1948; d. Alfred Harris and Mary Taylor (Moon) R. BA, U. S.C., 1970; MLS, Emory U., 1972. Asst. children's librarian Greenville (S.C.) County Library, 1972-74, br. supr., 1974-76, asst. head extension div., 1976-78; children's room librarian Richland County Pub. Library, Columbia, 1978-81, sr. adult services librarian, 1981-82, chief adult services, 1982-85, dep. dir., 1985—. Mem. adv. com. S.C. Pre-White House Conf. on Libr. and Info. Svcs., chmn. program com. Recipient Outstanding S.C. Librarian award by S.C. Library Assn., 1998. Mem. ALA, S.E. Libr. Assn., S.C. Libr. Assn. (2d v.p. 1987-89, editl. com. 1993, chmn. pub. libr. sect. 1995), U. S.C. Thomas Cooper Soc. (bd. dirs., v.p., pres.-elect, pres.). Baptist. Home: 1316 Guignard Ave West Columbia SC 29169-6137 Office: Richland County Pub Libr 1431 Assembly St Columbia SC 29201-3101 Office Phone: 803-799-9084. E-mail: harawlin@richland.lib.sc.us.

RAWLINSON, JOHNNIE BLAKENEY, federal judge; b. Concord, NC, Dec. 16, 1952; BS in Psychology summa cum laude, NC A&T State U., 1974; JD, U. of Pacific, 1979. Private practice, Las Vegas, 1979—80; staff atty. Nevada Legal Services, 1980; from dep. dist. atty. to asst. dist. atty. Clark County Dist. Atty.'s Office, 1980—98; judge US Dist. Ct. Nev., 1998—2000, US Ct. Appeals (9th cir.), 2000—. Office: 333 Las Vegas Blvd S Rm 7072 Las Vegas NV 89101 *

RAWLINSON, JOSEPH ELI, foundation administrator, lawyer; b. Delta, Utah, May 9, 1915; s. Eli Wilford and Dora Pearl (Day) Rawlinson; m. Elaine Millicent Andersen, June 2, 1947; children: James, Jolene, Nancy, Rex, Anina, Cheryl, Mark, Lisa, David. BS, U. Utah, 1936; JD, Loyola U., 1958. CPA Calif.; bar: Calif. 1959. Agt. IRS, Wichita, Kans., 1938—52; acct. Serene Koster, Barbour, Calif., 1952—62; pvt. practice Calif., 1959; pres., CEO Fritz B. Burns Found., Burbank, Calif., 1980—. Recipient Silver medal, Am. Inst. Accts., 1942. Office: Fritz B Burns Found 4001 W Alameda Ave Ste 203 Burbank CA 91505-4338 Home Phone: 818-886-3142. Personal E-mail: josepheli@sbcglobal.net.

RAWLS, FRANK MACKLIN, lawyer; b. Suffolk, Va., Aug. 24, 1952; s. John Lewis and Mary Helen (Macklin) R.; m. Sally Hallum Blanchard, June 26, 1976; children: Matthew Christopher, John Stephen, Michael Andrew. BA in History cum laude, Hampden Sydney Coll., 1974; JD, U. Va., 1977. Bar: Va. 1977, U.S. Dist. Ct. (ea. dist.) Va. 1977, U.S. Ct. Appeals (4th cir.) 1977. Assoc. Rawls, Habel & Rawls, Suffolk, 1977-78, ptnr., 1978-91, Ferguson & Rawls, Suffolk, 1991-96, Ferguson, Rawls, MacDonald, Overton & Grissom PC, Suffolk, 1996-98, Ferguson, Rawls, MacDonald & Overton PC, Suffolk, 1999—2002, Ferguson, Rawls & Raines, P.C., 2002—. Sec., Suffolk Title Ltd., 1986-95; bd. dirs. Secure Title, Inc. Deacon Westminster Reformed Presbyn. Ch., Suffolk, 1979-83, elder, clk. of session, 1984-91, 94-99, elder, 2004—, co-chmn. forward by faith capital campaign, 2001—; chmn. bd. dirs. Suffolk Crime Line, 1982-90, Suffolk Cheer Fund, 1982—, Covenant Christian Schs., Suffolk, 1982-84; bd. dirs. Norfolk Christian Schs., 1990-2004, v.p., 1998-99, pres., 1999-2004; pres. Parent Tchr. Fellowship, 1995-97, vice-chmn. steering com. for capital campaign, 1996-98, v.p., 1997-98; adv. bd. dirs. Salvation Army, Suffolk, 1977-95, chmn., 1989-90; chmn. Suffolk Com. on Affordable Housing, 1989-90; bd. dirs. Suffolk YMCA, 1988-90, Suffolk Youth Athletic Assn., 1999-2000. Mem. ATLA, Suffolk Bar Assn. (past pres.), Va. State Bar, Va. Bar Assn., Christian Legal Soc., Va. Trial Lawyers Assn., Suffolk Bar Assn. Office Phone: 757-539-2400. Business E-Mail: frawls@frrlaw.com.

RAWLS, JAMES C., lawyer; b. Jackson, Miss., June 20, 1948; BA with highest distinction, Miss. State U., 1970; JD, Yale U., 1973. Bar: Ga. 1973, US Dist. Ct.(no. dist.) Ga. 1973, Georgia State Cts 1973, US Ct. Appeals (11th cir.) 1981, US Supreme Ct. 1985. Mem. Powell, Goldstein, Frazer & Murphy, Atlanta; ptnr. Powell Goldstein LLP, Atlanta. Mem. ABA (litig. sect.), State Bar Ga. (gen. practice sect., trial sect.), Atlanta Bar Assn. (bd. dirs. 1987-88, chmn.-elect litigation sect. 1988-89, chmn. 1989-90), Atlanta Coll. Trial Advocacy (chmn. 1986), Lawyers Club Atlanta, Lamar Inn of Ct (pres. 1998-2000, master 1995-, exec. com. 1996-, Phi Eta Sigma, Phi Kappa Phi, Omnicron Delta Kappa. Office: Powell Goldstein LLP 1201 W Peachtree St NW 14th Fl 1 Atlantic Center Atlanta GA 30309 Office Phone: 404-572-6870. Business E-Mail: jrawls@pogolaw.com.

RAWN, WILLIAM LEETE, III, architect; b. Berkeley, Calif. s. William Leete Jr. and Betsy (Blanckenburg) R. BA, Yale U., 1965; JD, Harvard U., 1969; MArch, MIT, 1979. Bar: D.C., 1969. Assoc. Arent, Fox, Kintner, Plotkin & Kahn, Washington, 1969-71; asst. to pres. U. Mass., Boston, 1971-73, asst. chancellor phys. planning, 1973-75; architect Davis Brody & Assocs., NYC, 1979-83, William Rawn Assocs., Boston, 1983—. Vis. prof. urban design Harvard U. Grad. Sch. Design, 1993, 94. Designer serigraphs, 1971-79; contbr. articles to profl. jours., newspapers. Mem. Boston Civic Design Com., 1990; Inst. Contemporary Art, Boston, 1994. Fellow AIA (hon., Excellence award, 1993, 7 Honor awards in Arch. 1994, 95, 96, 00 (2 awards), 04, 05, Louis Sullivan award 1995); mem. Boston Soc. Architects (over 80 regional and local design awards 1985—, Harleston Parker medal 2005), DC Bar Assn., Yale Club of NYC, Harvard Club (Boston). Office: William Rawn Assocs Archs Inc 10 Post Office Sq Ste 1010 Boston MA 02109

RAWNSLEY, HOWARD MELODY, pathologist, educator; b. Long Branch, NJ, Nov. 20, 1925; s. Walter A. and Elizabeth (Melody) R.; m. B. Eileen Fiddes, Sept. 5, 1967; children: Virgilia Ingram, Elizabeth Sue. AB, Haverford Coll., Pa., 1949; MD, U. Pa., Phila., 1952. Diplomate Am. Bd. Pathology (trustee 1988-96). Intern Hosp. U. Pa., 1952-53, resident, 1953-57; practice medicine, specializing in pathology Phila., 1957-75; mem. Wm. Pepper Lab., U. Pa., 1957-75, asst. dir., 1960-68, dir., 1968-75; assoc. dir. Clin. Research Ctr., 1962-67, acting dir., 1969— 70, asst. prof. pathology and medicine, 1960-65, assoc. prof., 1965-69; prof. Clin. Rsch. Ctr., 1969-75; prof. pathology Dartmouth Hitchcock Med. Ctr., Hanover, NH, 1975-95, chmn. dept., 1980-87, sr. v.p. med. affairs, 1987-94. Cons. VA Hosp.; mem. exec. com. Am. Bd. Med. Spltys., 1998-2001. Chmn. bd. dirs. New Eng. Blood Svcs. ARC, 1996—2000, 2002—05. With US Army, 1944—46. Woodward fellow in chemistry, 1953-55 Mem. AMA, ARC (biomed. svcs. com. 1990-92), Pathology Soc. Phila. (pres.), Coll. Am. Pathologists (bd. govs. 1985-93), Coll. Am. Pathologists Found. (bd. dirs. 2003-), Am. Soc. Clin. Pathology (Disting. Svc. award 1995).

RAWSKI, EVELYN SAKAKIDA, history professor; b. Honolulu, Feb. 2, 1939; d. Evan T. and Teruko (Watase) Sakakida; m. Thomas G. Rawski, Dec. 16, 1967. BA, Cornell U., 1961; MA, Radcliffe Coll., 1962; PhD, Harvard U., 1968. Asst. prof. history U. Pitts., 1967-72, assoc. prof., 1973-79, prof. history, 1980—; univ. prof., 1996—. Mem. Sch. Hist. Studies, Inst. for Advanced Study, Princeton, NJ, 2007. Author: Agricultural Change and the Peasant Economy of South China, 1972, Education and Popular Literacy in Ch'ing China, 1979, The Last Emperors: A Social History of Qing Imperial Institutions, 1998; co-author: Chinese Society in the Eighteenth Century, 1987, Worshiping the Ancestors: Chinese Commemorative Portraits, 2001; co-editor: Popular Culture in Late Imperial and Modern China, 1985, Death Ritual in Late Imperial and Modern China, 1988, Harmony and Counterpoint: Chinese Music in Ritual Context, 1996, China: The Three Emperors, 1662-1795. Mem. Inst. for Advanced Study, 2007. Grantee Am. Coun. Learned Socs., 1973-74; NEH fellow, 1979-80, Chinese Studies fellow Am. Coun. Learned Socs./Social Sci. Rsch. Coun., 1989, Guggenheim fellow, 1990, Woodrow Wilson Internat. Ctr. fellow 1992-93, NEH fellow, 2006-07. Mem.: Assn. Asian Studies (China-Inner Asia coun., bd. dirs. 1976—79, v.p. 1994—95, pres. 1995—96). Home: 5317 Westminster Pl Pittsburgh PA 15232-2120 Office: U Pitts Dept History Pittsburgh PA 15260 Office Phone: 412-648-7458. Business E-Mail: esrx@pitt.edu.

RAWSKI, FREDERICK, lawyer; BA in Psychology, Coll. William and Mary, 1992; MA in Anthropology, SUNY, 1995; JD, NYU, 2002. Bar: NY State Bar Assn. 2003. Lectr., rschr. SUNY, Buffalo, 1993—98; field coord. Carter Ctr., Dili, 1999; human rights officer UN Transitional Adminstrn. East Timor, Dili, 2000—01; student asst. dist. atty. NY County Dist. Attorney's Office, NYC, 2001—02; litig. assoc. Stroock & Stroock & Lavan LLP, NYC, 2002—; law clk. UN Internat. Criminal Tribunal for Rwanda, Arusha, Tanzania, 2002. Election monitor/deployment advance staff Nat. Dem. Inst. Internat. Affairs, Jakarta, Indonesia, 1999; cons. East Timor Commn. for Reception, Truth and Reconciliation, Dili, 2004; rsch. intern Human Rights Watch Asia, NYC. Contbr. articles to jour., chapters to books. Bd. advisors Am. Coll. Program, U. Fribourg, Switzerland, 2004. Fellow Marion White Grad. Fellowship, SUNY, 1993-1997; grantee Global Law Sch. Clerkship Grant, NYU Sch. Law, 2002. Mem.: Assn. Polit. and Legal Anthropology, Am. Anthropology Assn., Am. Soc. Internat. Law. Office: Stroock & Stroock & Lavan LLP 180 Maiden Ln New York NY 10038-4982 Home Phone: 718-302-5859; Office Phone: 212-806-6236. Office Fax: 212-806-9236. E-mail: frawski@stroock.com.

RAWSON, CLAUDE JULIEN, literature and language professor; b. Shanghai, Feb. 8, 1935; came to U.S., 1985; m. Judith Ann Hammond, July 14, 1959; children: Hugh, Tim, Mark, Harriet, Annabel. BA, Oxford U., Eng., 1955, MA, BLitt, 1959; DLitt (hon.), U. Keele, Eng., 2007. English lectr. U. Newcastle, Eng., 1957-65; from lectr. to prof., chmn. dept. U. Warwick, Coventry, Eng., 1965-85, hon. prof., 1986—; George Sherburn prof. English U. Ill., Urbana, 1985-86; George M. Bodman prof. English Yale U., New Haven, Conn., 1986-96, Maynard Mack prof. English, 1996—. Vis. prof. U. Pa., Phila., 1973, U. Calif., Berkeley, 1980; chmn. Yale Boswell Papers, 1990—2001; del. for lang. and lit. Oxford U. Press, NY, 2001—05; mem. ednl. adv. bd. John Simon Guggenheim Meml. Found., 2005—. Author: Henry Fielding and the Augustan Ideal, 1972, 2d edit., 1991, Gulliver and the Gentle Reader, 1973, 2d edit., 1991, The Character of Swift's Satire, 1983, Order from Confusion Sprung, 1985, 2d edit., 1992, (with F.P. Lock) Collected Poems of Thomas Parnell, 1989, Satire and Sentiment 1660-1830, 1994, 2d edit., 2000, (with H. B. Nisbet) Cambridge History of Literary Criticism, vol. 4: The Eighteenth Century, 1997, God, Gulliver, and Genocide, 2001, 2d edit. 2002, Basic Writings of Jonathan Swift, 2002, Cambridge Companion to Henry Fielding, 2007, Henry Fielding: Playwright, Novelist, Journalist, Magistrae, 1707-1754, 2007; editor: Modern Lang. Rev. and Yearbook of English Studies, London, 1974-88; gen. editor: Cambridge (Eng.) History of Literary Criticism, 1983—, Unwin Critical Libr., London, 1974—, Blackwell Critical Biographies, 1985—, Cambridge Edition of the Works of Jonathan Swift, 2001—, Essential Writings of Jonathan Swift, 2007. Recipient Cert. of Merit for Disting. Svc. Conf. of Editors of Learned Jours., 1988; Andrew Mellon fellow Clark and Huntington Libr., 1980, 90, Guggenheim fellow, 1991-92, Sr. Faculty fellow Yale U., 1991-92; NEH grantee, 1991. Fellow Am. Acad. Arts and Scis.; mem. Modern Humanities Rsch. Assn. (life mem., com. mem. 1974-88), Internat. Soc. 18th Century Studies, Am. Soc. for 18th Century Studies, Brit. Soc. for 18th Century Studies (pres. 1973-74). Office: Yale U Dept English PO Box 208302 New Haven CT 06520-8302

RAWSON, JIM CHARLES, finance company executive; b. Houston, Apr. 20, 1947; s. Charles Manly and Georgie (Kearse) R.; m. Linda Eidman, Arp. 12, 1968; children: John Erich, Susan Margaret. BBA, Tex. Christian U., 1969. CPA, Tex. Acctg. clk. Tenneco, Inc., Houston, 1969—71, Projects Am. Corp., Houston, 1971—74, office mgr., 1974—77, v.p., gen. mgr., 1977—82, pres., 1982—. Recipient Gold award, Am. Land Devel. Assn., 1983, Silver award, 1983, Bronze award, 1985. Mem. Sports Car Club Am. Methodist. Avocations: sports car racing, salt water fishing. Office: Projects Am Corp 6124 Beverlyhill St Houston TX 77057-6610

RAWSON, JOHN ELTON, neonatologist, medical educator; b. Okolona, Miss., Jan. 31, 1938; s. Elton Phlemuel and Marjorie Morgan Jones Rawson; m. Mary Crouch Rawson, June 23, 1962; children: Katherine Asbury Rawson Kronzer, Edwin Lauderdale. BS in Chemisty, Millsaps Coll., 1960; MD, U. Miss., 1965. Diplomate Am. Bd. Pediat., Am. Bd. Neonatology and Perinatal Medicine; lic. physician, Miss. Clin. assoc. prof. pediat. U. Miss. Sch. Medicine, Jackson, 1972—; attending neonatologist, chief newborn medicine Ctrl. Miss. Med. Ctr., Jackson, 1978—; attending neonatologist Miss. Bapt. Med. Ctr., Jackson, 1982—. Chmn. bd. dirs. Health Choice of Miss., Jackson, 1991-98, Integrity Health Plan, Inc., Jackson, 1995-98, State Watch, Inc., Jackson, 1988-96; chief of staff Meth. Healthcare, Inc., Jackson, 1994-95. Editor: Newborn Ventilation, 1976. State chmn. March of Dimes, Jackson, 1972-82; mem. vestry St. James Episcopal Ch., Jackson, 1975-78; trustee St. Andrew's Day Sch., Madison, Miss., 1978-89, Meth. Lebouner Found., Memphis, 1991-2000. Capt. USAF, 1968-70. Mem. Rotary (Paul Harris fellow 1984). Office: Ctrl Miss Med Ctr 1850 Chadwick Dr Jackson MS 39204 Home: 632 Lake Cavalier Rd Madison MS 39110-7155 Office Phone: 601-376-1370. Personal E-mail: jackrawson@hotmail.com.

RAWSON, RACHEL L., lawyer; BA magna cum laude, Kenyon Coll., 1987; JD, Columbia U., 1990. Bar: N.Y. 1991, Ohio 1995. With Jones Day, Cleve., 1992—, ptnr., 2003—. Mem.: ABA (bus. law sect.), Cleve. Bar Assn. (banking and bus. law sect.). Office: Jones Day North Point 901 Lakeside Ave Cleveland OH 44114-1190

RAWSON, RICHARD J., telecommunications industry executive, lawyer; b. Florham Park, NJ, Nov. 22, 1952; BS, Notre Dame U.; JD, Rutgers U. Formerly with Sullivan & Cromwell, NYC and Washington; various positions with Law Divsn. AT&T, 1984—96, sr. v.p., gen. counsel, 1995, Lucent Technologies, Murray Hill, NJ, 1996—. Mem. ABA, Am. Corp. Counsel Assn.

RAWSON, ROBERT H., JR., lawyer; b. Washington, Oct. 18, 1944; AB, Princeton U., 1966; MA, Oxford U., Eng., 1968; JD, Harvard U., 1971. Bar: Ohio 1971, D.C. 1972. Ptnr. Jones, Day, Cleve.; ptnr.-in-charge Jones Day, Cleve. Rhodes scholar. Mem.: ABA, Bar Assn. of DC, Cleve. Bar Assn., Ohio State Bar Assn., Phi Beta Kappa. Office: Jones Day North Point 901 Lakeside Ave E Cleveland OH 44114-1190 Office Phone: 216-586-3939. Office Fax: 216-579-0212. Business E-Mail: rrawson@jonesday.com.

RAY, ALBERT, physician, educator; b. NYC, Aug. 8, 1948; s. Herman and Stella (Meritz) R.; m. Cheryl Antecol, Oct. 8, 1977; children: Heather, Erin, Samantha. BA, Bklyn. Coll., 1969; MD, Cath. U. Louvain, Belgium, 1976. Diplomate Am. Bd. Family Practice, Can. Coll. Family Physicians. Intern Meml. U. of Nfld., St. John's, Can., 1976; resident McGill U., Montreal, 1978; family physician SCPMG, San Diego, 1978—. Clin. prof. U. Calif., San Diego, 1978—; cmty. faculty UCLA, USD, U. Calif., Davis, USC; clerkship cmty. adv. bd. U. Calif., San Diego, 1995—; pres. profl. staff Kaiser Found. Hosp.; bd. dirs. So. Calif. Permanente Med Group; asst. chief family medicine Kaiser Permanente, San Diego; physician coord. health promotion and preventive care Kaiser Permanente. Author: Lecons d'Histologie, 1973; contbr. to profl. jours. Program chair adult edn. Congregation Beth Israel, 1995; bd. dirs. Temple Emanuel, San Diego, 1990, Agy. for Jewish Edn.; expert reviewer Med. Bd. Calif., 1995; spl. med. cons. Calif. Dept. of Corps., 1996; hon. chmn. physician's adv. bd. Nat. Rep. Congl. Com. Named Family Physician of Yr., Calif. Acad. Family Physicians, 2002. Fellow: Am. Acad. Family Physicians; mem.: Calif. Acad. Family Physicians, San Diego Acad. Family Physicians, San Diego County Med. Soc. (councilor 2002—03, treas. 2004—06, pres.-elect 2006—07, pres. 2007—08), Calif. Med. Assn. (ho. of dels.), AMA (alt. del.). Avocations: golf, tennis, travel, antiques, gardening. Office: Kaiser Permanente 4405 Vandever Ave San Diego CA 92120-3315 Office Phone: 619-516-7400.

RAY, AMY, vocalist, guitarist; b. Decatur, Ga., Apr. 12, 1964; BA, Emory U., 1986. Vocalist, guitarist Saliers & Ray, 1980-83, Indigo Girls, 1983—; signed to Epic Records, 1988—2006, Hollywood Records, 2006—. Founder, pres. Daemon Records, Decatur, Ga., 1990—. Musician: (albums) Stag, 2001, Prom, 2005; musician: (with Emily Saliers) Early 45, 1985, Strange Fire, 1987, Indigo Girls, 1989 (Grammy Award for Best Contemporary Folk Album, 1990), Nomads Indians Saints, 1990, Back On the Bus, Y'All, 1991, Rites of Passage, 1992, Swamp Ophelia, 1994, 1200 Curfews, 1995, Shaming of the Sun, 1997, Come On Now Social, 1999, Retrospective, 2000, Become You, 2002, All That We Let In, 2004, Rarities, 2005, Despite Our Differences, 2006, (songs) Closer to Fine, 1989, Hammer and Nail, 1990, Galileo, 1992, Least Complicated, 1994, Shame on You, 1997; appears in (films) Boys on the Side, 1995, Join the Resistance: Fall in Love, 2003, (documentaries) Trudell, 2005, Wordplay, 2006. Nominee Best New Artist, Grammy Awards, 1990; named one of Greatest Women of Rock'n'Roll, VH1. Office: c/o Russell Carter Artist Mgmt Ste 75 315 W Ponce de Leon Ave Decatur GA 30030 Office Phone: 404-377-9900. E-mail: igfan@rcam.com.

RAY, ASOK KUMAR, physicist, researcher; s. Chittaranjan and Anita Roy; m. Swati Ray. BS in Physics, Calcutta U., 1967, B of Tech. in Radio-Physics and Elecs., 1969; MS in Physics, Okla. State U., Stillwater, 1973; MS in Math., Tex. Tech. U., 1975, PhD in Physics, 1977. Postdoctoral rsch. fellow U. Fla., 1979—81; asst. prof. physics Mich. Tech. U., 1981—82; vis. asst. prof. physics U. Tex, Arlington, 1982—84; asst. prof. physics U. Tex., Arlington, 1984—88, assoc. prof. physics, 1988—92, prof. physics, 1992—. Grantee, U. S. Dept. Energy, Welch Found., 2003—. Mem.: Materials Rsch. Soc., Am. Phys. Soc. Achievements include research in Over 130 Publications in Peer-Reviewed Journals; computational condensed matt. Office: Physics Univ of Texas 502 Yates St Arlington TX 76019 Home Phone: 817-274-5981; Office Phone: 817-272-2503. Office Fax: 817-272-3637. Business E-Mail: akr@uta.edu.

RAY, BETTY JEAN G., retired lawyer; b. New Orleans, June 7, 1943; d. William E. George and Iris U. (Berthold) Grizzell; m. Gerald L. Ray, June 9, 1962; children: Gerald L. Ray, Jr., Brian P. BS Psychology, La. State U., 1976, JD, 1980. Bar: La., 1980; U.S. Dist. Ct. (ea., mid. and we. dists.) La. 1981; U.S. Ct. Appeal (5th cir.) 1981. Jud. law clk. 19th Jud. Dist. Ct., Baton Rouge, 1980-81; atty. Jean G. Ray, Baton Rouge, 1981-83; counsel Gulf Stream, Inc., Baton Rouge, 1982-83; staff atty. La. Dept. Justice, Baton Rouge, 1983-84, asst. atty. gen., 1984-87; staff atty. FDIC, Shreveport, La., 1987-88, mng. atty., 1988-94; spl. dep. receiver Receivership Office, La. Dept. Ins., Baton Rouge, 1994-95; spl. counsel Brook, Pizza & van Loon, L.L.P., Baton Rouge, 1995-2000. Mem. La. Bar Assn., Order of Coif, Phi Beta Kappa, Phi Delta Phi (scholar 1980). Episcopalian. Home: 12154 County Rd 99 Lillian AL 36549-5120 E-mail: jeangray@gulftel.com.

RAY, BRADLEY STEPHEN, petroleum geologist; b. Ada, Okla., Feb. 15, 1957; s. Walter Lloyd and Betty Louise (McCurley) R. BS in Geology, Baylor U., 1980; MS in Geology, U. Tex., 1985. Cert. geologist. Asst. geologist Hunt Oil Co., Dallas, 1978, geologist, 1979-81; ind. oil and gas producer Dallas, 1981—. Chmn. adv. bd. Geol. Info. Libr. Dallas, 1988—; bd. dirs. Global Mapping Internat. Trustee Dallas Bapt. U., 1988-94, Criswell Coll., 1990-92; chmn. The Habitats Project, 1993—; mem. Peoples Info. Network. Mem. Am. Assn. Petroleum Geologists, Ind. Petroleum Assn. Am., Soc. Ind. Profl. Earth Scientists, Dallas Geol. Soc., Tex. Ind. Producers and Royalty Owners, Okla. Ind. Petroleum Assn., Geol. Soc. Am., Computer Oriented Geol. Soc., Nat. Stripper Well Assn., Energy Club, Oklahoma City Geol. Soc., Colbert-Tracht Club. Republican. Baptist. Home: 4925 Greenville Ave Ste 1348 Dallas TX 75206-4021 Office: 1348 One Energy Sq Dallas TX 75206

RAY, BRITTANY E., literature and language educator; m. Ronald Smith; 3 children. BA, Colby Coll., Maine, 1990; student Grad. Edn. Program, Univ. Maine. English tchr. Narraguagus H.S., Harrington, Maine, 1995—. Named Maine Tchr. of Yr., 2007. Office: Narraguagus High Sch RR 1 Box 489 Harrington ME 04643 Business E-Mail: bray@sad37.com. *

RAY, CARLOS See NORRIS, CHUCK

RAY, CAROL RENEÉ, researcher; b. Petersburg, Va. d. Frederick Chester Ray and Brenda Ray-Moore. BSc, Spelman Coll., 1987; MSc, N.C. Agrl. and Tech. State U., 1995; PhD, U. Nebr.-Lincoln, 2003. Tutor coord. U. Nebr., Lincoln, 2000, prin. investigator, 1998—2003; instr. chemistry Fayetteville Tech. C.C., 2002; TV tutor comcast, coord. allied health project U. Md. Eastern Shore, 2004, coord. sr. rsch. program, 2005; rschr. Johns Hopkins Sch. Medicine, Balt., 2006—. Adj. faculty Sojouriner Douglass Coll., Salisbury, Md., 2004—; cons. Nebr. Divsn. on Aging., 1998. Contbr. articles to profl. jours. Nominee Avon scholarship, 1984; Chemistry Scholarship, Spelman Coll., 1984. Mem.: Phi Upsilon Omicron Nat. Honor Soc. Avocations: flute, reading, tennis, writing. Home: 3409 Greenway Apt 3A Baltimore MD 21218

RAY, CHARLES AARON, ambassador; b. Center, Tex., July 5, 1945; m. Myung Wook Soe, Nov. 3, 1973; children: David Edward, Denise Ellen, Gayle Denene, Jason Andre. BSBA, Benedictine Coll., 1972; MS in Sys. Mgmt., U. So. Calif., 1981; MS in Nat. Security Strategy, Nat. War Coll., 1997. Commd. 2nd lt. US Army, 1965, advanced through grades to maj., ret., 1982; consular officer US Consulate Gen., Guangzhou, China, 1983-84, chief consular sect. Shenyang, China, 1985-87, chief adminstrv. sect. Chiangmai, Thailand, 1988-91; spl. asst. to dir. Office Def. Trade Controls, Washington, 1991-93; dep. chief of mission Am. Embassy, Freetown, Sierra Leone, 1993-96; detailed to Nat. War Coll., Washington, 1996-97, Nat. Fgn. Affairs Tng. Ctr., Arlington, Va., 1997-98; consul gen. US Consulate Gen., Ho Chi Minh City, Vietnam, 1998-2001; sr. seminar Nat. Fgn. Affairs Tng. Ctr., 2001—02; US amb. to Cambodia US Dept. State, Phnom Penh, Cambodia, 2002—05; dep. asst. sec. def. POW/missing pers. affairs Dept Def., 2006—. Editl. cartoonist Spring Lake News, 1975-79; contbr. articles to Asia Mag., 1974-79; editor mag. Psyop Digest, 1976-78; exec. editor Def. Trade News, 1992-93. Avocations: golf, taekwondo, softball, tennis, painting, poetry. Office: DPMO 2400 Defense Pentagon Washington DC 20301-2400 Home Phone: (855) 23 218 932; Office Phone: 703-699-1101. Business E-Mail: charles.ray@osd.mil. E-mail: rayc@state.gov.

RAY, CHARLES DEAN, neurosurgeon, spine surgeon, bioengineer, inventor; b. Americus, Ga., Aug. 1, 1927; s. Oliver Tinsley and Katherine (Broadfield) Ray; children: Bruce, Marlene. AB, Emory U., Atlanta, 1950; MS, U. Miami, Coral Gables, 1952; MD, Med. Coll. Ga., 1956. Diplomate Am. Bd. Neurol. Surgery, Am. Bd. Spine Surgery. Intern Bapt. Meml. Hosp., Memphis, 1956-57; resident, rsch. assoc. neurosurgery U. Tenn. Hosp., Memphis, 1957-62; fellow, rsch. asst. Mayo Clinic and Found., Rochester, Minn., 1962-64; asst. prof. neurosurgery, lectr. bioengring. Johns Hopkins U. Med. Sch., Balt., 1964-68; chief dept. engring. F. Hoffmann-LaRoche, Basel, Switzerland, 1968-73; clin. assoc. prof. medicine U. Minn., Mpls., 1973; practice medicine specializing in neurosurgery Norfolk, Williamsburg, Va., 1996—2000. Lectr. U. Basel, Switzerland, 1968—73; dir. emeritus Inst. Low Back and Neck Care; med. dir. The Spine Program Ea. Va. Med. Sch., Norfolk, Va.; pres. Am. Coll. Spine Surgery; mem. staff Sentara Hosps., Norfolk; chmn. bd. pres. Cedar Devel. Corp., Cedar Surg., Inc., 1985—; v.p. med. rsch. Medtronic, Inc., Mpls., 1972—79; bd. dirs. Herman Miller, Inc.; chmn. emeritus, med. dir. Raymedia, Inc., Mpls.; cons. in field; adj. prof. orthopedics Ain Shams U., Cairo, 2002—, U. Colo., Denver, 2002—. Author: Principles of Engineering Applied to Medicine, 1964, Medical Engineering, 1974, Lumbar Spine Surgery, 1988; contbr. over 360 articles to profl. publs. Chmn. com. materials and devices World Fedn. Neurosurg. Socs., 1977—, Cosmos Club, 1976—; vestry St. Martin's Episcopal Ch., Wayzata, Minn., 1976-79. With USN, 1945-49. Named Disting. Alumnus, Med. Coll. Ga., 1999; recipient Gold award for Best Med. Device Design of Yr. R&D 100, 2000. Fellow: ACS, Royal Soc. Health, Am. Coll. Spine Surgery (pres.); mem.: ASTM, AMA (sr.), IEEE (sr.), Internat. Spine Arthroplasty Soc. (pres.), N.Am. Spine Soc. (past pres., chmn., Wiltse award 1999), Internat. Orgn. Standardization, Pan-Am. Med. Assn. (life), Am. Assn. Neurol. Surgeons (sr.), Internat. Soc. Stereotaxic and Functional Neurosurgery, Internat. Fedn. Med. Biol. Engring., West Germany Armed Forces Med. Soc., Congress Neurol. Surgeons, Mpls. Club, Sigma Xi. Achievements include over 53 US patents and over 100 foreign patents. Home and Office: 4320 Via Presada Santa Barbara CA 93110 Office Phone: 805-964-7026. Personal E-mail: inveray@aol.com.

RAY, CHARLES KENDALL, retired dean; b. Boise City, Okla., Mar. 15, 1928; s. Volney Holt and Mamie (Burton) R.; m. Doris Derby, Aug. 26, 1951. BA, U. Colo., 1951; MA, Columbia, 1955, Ed.D., 1959. Teaching prin. Bur. Indian Affairs, Savoonga, Alaska, 1951-54; mem. faculty U. Alaska, 1957-93, prof. edn., 1960-93, dean Sch. Behavioral Scis. and Edn., 1961-80, dir. summer sessions, 1980-93. Author: A Program of Education for Alaska Natives, 1959, Alaskan Native Secondary School Dropouts, 1961. Mem. N.E.A., Phi Delta Kappa. Home: 2000 1st Ave Apt 2204 Seattle WA 98121-2171

RAY, CREAD L., JR., retired judge; b. Waskom, Tex., Mar. 10, 1931; s. Cread L. and Antonia (Hardesty) Ray; m. Janet Watson Keller, Aug. 12, 1977; children: Sue Ann(dec.), Robert E., Glenn L., David B., Marcie Lynn, Anne Marie. BBA, Tex. A&M U., 1952; JD, U. Tex., 1957; LHD (hon.), Wiley Coll., Marshall, Tex., 1980. Bar: Tex. 1957. Pvt. practice law, Marshall, 1957-59; judge Harrison County, 1959-61; justice 6th dist. Ct. Civil Appeals, Texarkana, 1970-80, Supreme Ct. Tex., Austin, 1980-90; ret., 1990; prin. C.L Ray, Austin, 1991—. Prin. C. L. Ray, Austin, 1991—; pres., CEO White Oil, Inc. Past pres. Marshall Jaycees, Marshall C. of C.; active Boy Scouts Am.; mem. Tex. Ho. of Reps., 1966—70; trustee Wiley Coll. Lt. col. USAF, 1952—54, Korea. Recipient awards, Boy Scouts Am. Mem.: N.E. Tex. Bar Assn. (past pres.), State Bar Tex., Tex. Aggies, Rotary. Democrat. Methodist. Home and Office: 604 Beardsley Ln Austin TX 78746-4929 Home Phone: 512-327-6137; Office Phone: 512-328-9238. Personal E-mail: clray4523@hotmail.com. E-mail: judgeclray@aol.com, judgeclray@msn.com.

RAY, DOUGLAS KENT, newspaper executive; Pres., CEO Daily Herald/Sunday Herald, Arlington Heights, Ill., 1970—. Named Pubisher of Yr., Editor & Publisher, 2006. Office: Daily Herald/Sunday Herald Paddock Publs PO Box 280 Arlington Heights IL 60006-0280

RAY, EDWARD JOHN, economics professor, academic administrator; b. Jackson Heights, NY, Sept. 10, 1944; s. Thomas Paul and Cecelia Francis (Hiney) R.; m. Virginia Beth Phelps, June 14, 1969; children: Stephanie Elizabeth, Katherine Rebecca, Michael Edward. BA, CUNY, 1966; MA, Stanford U., 1969, PhD, 1971. Asst. prof. econs. Ohio State U., Columbus, 1970-74, assoc. prof., 1974-77, prof., 1977—2003, chmn. dept. econs., 1976-92, assoc. provost acad. affairs Office Acad. Affairs, 1992-93, sr. vice provost, chief info. officer Ohio Office Acad. Affairs, 1993-98, acting sr. v.p. and provost, 1997-98, exec. v.p., provost, 1998—2003; pres. Oreg. State U., 2003—, prof., 2003—. Mem. bd. dirs. Com. Instl. Cooperation Net, 1994—97, Midwest Universities Consortium for Internat. Activities, 1994—95, Columbus Coun. World Affairs, 1994—, Ohio State U. Rsch. Found., 1998—, John Glenn Inst. Pub. Svc. and Pub. Policy, 1998—; provost Consortium Instl. Cooperation, 1998—, Ohio Inter-U. Coun., 1999—; bd. chair Ohio Principals Leadership Acad., 2000—; mem. Ohio Tchr. Edn. and Certification Adv. Commn., 2000—03, Ohio Higher Edn. Funding Commn., 2002—. Contbr. articles to profl. jours. Active Upper Arlington Civic Assn., Columbus, 1983—, Wexner Ctr. Found. Bd., 1998-. Recipient Chairperson's Recognition award, Ohio State U., 1989, Disting. Svc. award, 2006. Mem. Am. Econs. Assn., Western Econ. Assn., Econ. Hist. Assn., Internat. Trade and Fin. Assn., Phi Beta Kappa Home: 3700 SW Brooklane Dr Corvallis OR 97333 Office: Office of Pres Oreg State U Corvallis OR 97331-2128 *

RAY, FRANK ALLEN, lawyer; b. Lafayette, Ind., Jan. 30, 1949; s. Dale Allen and Merry Ann (Fleming) R.; m. Carol Ann Olmutz, Oct. 1, 1982; children: Erica Fleming, Robert Allen. BA, Ohio State U., 1970, JD, 1973. Bar: Ohio 1973, U.S. Dist. Ct. (so. dist.) Ohio 1975, U.S. Supreme Ct. 1976, U.S. Tax Ct. 1977, U.S. Ct. Appeals (6th cir.) 1977, U.S. Dist. Ct. (no. dist.) Ohio 1980, U.S. Dist. Ct. (ea. dist.) Mich. 1983, U.S. Ct. Appeals (1st cir.) 1986; cert. civil trial adv. Nat. Bd. Trial Advocacy. Asst. pros. atty. Franklin County, Ohio, 1973-75, chief civil counsel, 1976-78; dir. econ. crime project Nat. Dist. Attys. Assn., Washington, 1975-76; assoc. Brownfield, Kosydar, Bowen, Bally & Sturtz, Columbus, Ohio, 1978, Michael F. Colley Co., L.P.A., Columbus, 1979-83; pres. Frank A. Ray Co., L.P.A., Columbus, 1983—93, 2000—05, Ray & Todaro Co., LPA, Columbus, 1993-94, Ray, Todaro & Alton Co., L.P.A., Columbus, 1994-96, Ray, Todaro, Alton & Kirstein Co., L.P.A., Columbus, 1996, Ray, Alton & Kirstein Co., L.P.A., Columbus, 1996—98; sr. ptnr. Ray & Alton, L.L.P., Columbus, 1998—2000; ptnr. Chester, Willcox & Saxbe, LLP, 2006—; adj. prof. Moritz Coll. of Law, Ohio State U., 2003—. Mem. seminar faculty Nat. Coll. Dist. Attys., Houston, 1975-77; mem. nat. conf. faculty Fed. Jud. Ctr., Washington, 1976-77; bd. editors Man. for Complex Litigation, Fed. Jud. Ctr., 1999—2004; bd. mem. bar examiners Ohio Supreme Ct., 1992-95, mem. rules adv. com., 1995-99. Editor: Economic Crime Digest, 1975-76; co-author: Personal Injury Litigation Practice in Ohio, 1988, 91. Fin. com. Franklin County Rep. Orgn., Columbus, 1979-84, 2005—; trustee Ohio State U. Coll. Humanities Alumni Soc., 1991-93, Nat. Coun. Ohio State U., Moritz Coll. Law Alumni Soc., 1998—; capital campaign fund cabinet Legal Aid Soc. of Columbus, 1998. Capt. inf. U.S. Army, 1976. Named to Ten Outstanding Young Citizens of Columbus, Columbus Jaycees, 1976; recipient Nat. award of Distinctive Svc., Nat. Dist. Attys. Assn., 1977, Worthy Adversary award Ohio Assn. Civil Trial Attys., 2005, Disting. Alumnus award Ohio State U. Moritz Coll. Law, 2006. Fellow: Ohio Acad. Trial Lawyers (pres. 1989—90, Pres.'s award 1986), Ohio State Bar Found., Roscoe Pound Found., Am. Coll. Trial Lawyers, Internat. Soc. Barristers, Columbus Bar Found. (trustee 2003—); mem.: ATLA (state del. 1990—92), Franklin County Trial Lawyers Assn. (pres. 1987—88, Pres.'s award 1990), Ohio State Bar Assn. (com. negligence law 1990—97, mem. com. jury instrns. 2002—06, Friend of Legal Edn. award 2005), Million Dollar Advs. Forum, Columbus Bar Assn. (pres. 2001—02, Profl. award 1987), Am. Bd. Trial Advs. (pres., Ohio Chpt. 2004), Inns of Ct. (pres. Judge Robert M. Duncan chpt. 1993—94). Presbyterian. Home: 2030 Tremont Rd Columbus OH 43221-4330 Office: 65 E State St Ste 1000 Columbus OH 43215-4216 Office Phone: 614-221-4000. Business E-Mail: fray@cwslaw.com.

RAY, GENE WELLS, industrial executive; b. Murray, Ky., Apr. 23, 1938; s. Terry Lee and Loreen (Lovett) R.; m. Becky Huie, Mar. 5, 1956 (dec. 1976); m. Taffin Ray; children: Don Dickerson, Kathy Pratt, Nancy Solomon. BS in Math., Physics and Chemistry, Murray State U., 1956; MS in Physics, U. Tenn., 1962, PhD in Theoretical Physics, 1965. With tech. staff Aerospace Corp., San Bernardino, Calif., 1965-68; mgr. strategic div. USAF (OA), Washington, 1968-70; scientist, sr. v.p., systems group mgr. Sci. Applications Inc., La Jolla, Calif., 1970-81, also bd. dirs.; pres., chief exec. officer Titan Systems Inc., San Diego, 1981-85, CEO, 1985—, CEO, pres., chmn.; assoc. prof. Carson Newman Coll., Tenn., 1964-65. Inventor mass flow meter. 1st lt. USAR, 1963-68. Republican. Avocations: tennis, wine collecting. Home: PO Box 2464 Rancho Santa Fe CA 92067-2464 Office: Titan Corp 3033 Science Park Rd San Diego CA 92121-1199

RAY, GILBERT T., lawyer; b. Mansfield, Ohio, Sept. 18, 1944; s. Robert Lee Ray and Renatha (Goldie) Washington; m. Valerie J. Reynolds, June 14, 1969; children: Tanika, Tarlin. BA, Ashland Coll., 1966; MBA, U. Toledo, 1968; JD, Howard U., 1972. Assoc. O'Melveny & Myers, LA, 1972-79, ptnr., 1980-2000, ret. ptnr., 2000—. Bd. dirs. Sierra Monolithics, Inc., IHOP Corp., Watson, Wyatt & Co., Advance Auto Parts, Automobile Club of So. Calif., Haynes Found., DiamondRock Hospitality, Inc., Seasons Series Fund, SunAmerica Series Trust. Mem. The Calif. Club, L.A. Country Club. Democrat. Office: 400 S Hope St Ste 1900 Los Angeles CA 90071-2899

RAY, HILLOL KUMAR, environmental engineer, poet; arrived in US, 1975, permanent resident, 1986; s. Nibaran Chandra and Angur Lata Ray; m. Seema Ray; children: Brian Kumar, Ryan Kumar Ray. BS in Civil Engring., U. Calcutta, India, 1973; MS in Environ. Engring., ND State U., Fargo, 1977. Environ. engr. Brown & Root Inc., Houston, 1978—80; civil/structural engr. PLACON Ltd., Calcutta, India, 1973—75; rsch. asst. N. Dakota State U., Fargo, 1975—77; sr. environ. engr. Ecology and Environment Inc., Dallas, 1980—92; program mgr., environ. engr. US EPA, Dallas, 1992—. Author poetry. Chmn., editor North Tex. Bengali Assn., Dallas, 1992—99. Recipient Bronze medal, US EPA, 2001, Excellence in Customer Svc. award, 2002, Nat. Liberal & Fine Arts award, Nat. Fedn. Indian Am. Assn., 2006. Hindu. Avocations: creative writing, poetry, watch repair, antique cars, stamp collecting/philately. Home: Milestone 2723 Riviera Ct Garland TX 75040 Office: US EPA 1445 Ross Ave Dallas TX 75202-2733 Office Phone: 214-665-7502. Personal E-mail: mukhosh@verizon.net. Business E-Mail: ray.hillol@epa.gov.

RAY, HUGH MASSEY, JR., lawyer; b. Vicksburg, Miss., Feb. 1, 1943; s. Hugh Massey and Lollie Landon (Powell) R.; m. Carroll Robertson, Sept. 7, 2002; children: Hugh, Hallie. BA, Vanderbilt U., 1965, JD, 1967. Bar: Tex. 1967, U.S. Dist. Ct. (so. dist.) Tex. 1967, U.S. Dist.Ct. (we. dist.) La. 1979, U.S. Dist. Ct. (we. dist.) Tex. 1979, U.S. Dist. Ct. (no. dist.) Tex. 1980, U.S. Ct. Appeals 1st, 5th, 9th, 11th cirs.) 1982, U.S. Dist. Ct. (no. dist.) Calif. 1989, N.Y. 1992; cert. Tex. Bd. Legal Specialization. Asst. U.S. atty. So. Dist. Tex., 1967-68; assoc. Andrews & Kurth, Houston, 1968-77, ptnr., Bankruptcy Dept., 1977—. Lectr. Ctrl. and Ea. European Law Initiative, Vilnius, Lithuania, 1996. Co-author: Bankruptcy Investing, 1992, Creditor's Rights in Texas, vol. 1 & 2, 1998, Last Rights--Liquidating a company, 2007; contbr. articles to profl. jours. Mem.: ABA (chmn. real property practice com. 1975—77, chmn. cont. legal edn. com. young lawyers divsn. 1976—78, vice-chmn. 1979, chmn. oil and gas subcom. bus. bankruptcy com. 1985—89, chmn. executory contracts subcom. 1989—93, chmn. bus. bankruptcy com. 1993—96, chmn. com. on trust indentures and indenture trustees 1995—97, mem. standing com. on jud. selection, tenure and compensation 1996—97, chmn. ad hoc com. on bankruptcy ct. structure 1996—2001, mem. bus. law sect. 1997—2001, chair energy com. 2001—06), South Tex. Coll. Law (trustee 2003—), Houston Symphony Orch. (governing trustee 2004—06), Am. Coll. Bankruptcy., Am. Law Inst., Tex. Bar Assn. (chmn. bankruptcy com. 1985—88), Houston Bar Assn., River Oaks Country Club, Houston Country Club. Episcopalian. Office: Andrews & Kurth 600 Travis St Ste 4200 Houston TX 77002-2910 Office Fax: 713-238-7225. Business E-Mail: hray@andrewskurth.com.

RAY, HUGH MASSEY, III, lawyer; b. Houston, June 25, 1970; s. Hugh Massey and Florence Hargrove Ray; m. Katheryn Elaine Shaffer, June 19, 1993; children: James Henry, Mary Carol, John William. BA, Vanderbilt U., Nashville, 1992; MDiv, JD, Vanderbilt U., 1996. Cert.: Tex. Bd. Legal Specialization (bus. bankruptcy law) 2005, bar: Tex. 1998, US Ct. Appeals (5th cir.) 2001, US Ct. Appeals (11th cir.) 2001, US Supreme Ct. 2001. Shareholder Weycer, Kaplan, Pulaski & Zuber, P.C., Houston, 2001—. Barrister of Davis-Foltz Inn of Ct. Am. Inns of Ct., Houston, 2004—, barrister of Garland Walker, 2006—. Patron Houston Symphony, 2004, Houston Mus. Natural Sci., 2004—; mem. St. Martin's Episc. Ch., Houston, 1993—. Mem.: ABA (editl. bd. young lawyers mag. 2004—05, young lawyer divsn. profl. devel. team 2005—06), State Bar Tex. (mem. disciplinary rules com. 2000—), Am. Law Inst., Houston Bar Assn. (disting. spkr. 2004—, disting. faculty 2005—, CLE com. 2006—, mem. bankruptcy sect.), Coll. of State Bar Tex., Houston Livestock Show and Rodeo (life), Ritz Club (London), Houston Club, Briar Club, Phi Alpha Delta, Lambda Chi Alpha. Episcopalian. Avocations: running, hunting, triathlon. Office: Weycer Kaplan Pulaski & Zuber PC 11 Greenway Plz Ste 1400 Houston TX 77046 Office Phone: 713-341-1158. Office Fax: 713-961-5341.

RAY, JAMES LEE, military officer; b. Roanoke, Va., Mar. 28, 1971; s. Dale Eugene and Judy Ann Ray; m. Cheri Elizabeth Gabel, July 17, 2004; m. Janice Blomeyer, May 4, 1994 (div. Mar. 1996); children: Ariel Alexis Johnson, Ryan Pierce, Jordyn Gabrielle Johnson. BBA, Roanoke Coll., Salem, Va., 1994; postgrad., Ctrl. Mich. U. Commd. officer USAF, 1995, advanced through grades to capt., wing weather officer 7th Operational Support Squadron Dyess AFB, Tex., 2000—01, officer-in-charge, combat weather team 3d Air Support Operation Squadron Ft. Wainwright, Alaska, 2001—03, chief resources and tech. health 28th Operational Weather Squadron Shaw AFB, SC, 2003—05, flight comdr. 28th Operational Weather Squadron, 2005—06; civilian inst. program mgr. Air Force Inst. Tech., Wright-Patterson AFB, Ohio, 2007—. Decorated US Achievement medal Air Combat Command, Pacific Air Forces, Joint Svc. Achievement medal US So. Command, Air Force Commendation medal US Ctrl. Command, 28th Operational Weather Squadron. Mem.: VFW (life), Mil. Officers Assn. Am., Am. Legion, Alpha Kappa Psi (life; v.p. efficiency 2001—03). Avocation: travel. Home: 5503 Cottonrose Dr Dayton OH 45431 Office: AFIT/ENEL Bldg 16 Room 120 D St Wright Patterson Afb OH 45433 Home Phone: 937-422-5050; Office Phone: 937-255-2259 3026.

RAY, JANE ZIMRUDE, retired machine shop executive; b. Strawn, Tex., May 9, 1937; d. M.A. and Susie Matilda (Kitchens) Wooton; m. Earl Vernon Ray, Oct. 19, 1956; children: Marcus Vernon, Martha Ruth Ray O'Grady, Douglas Wayne, Patricia Ann Grad., Stephenville (Tex.) High Sch., 1955. Bookkeeper Ray's Texaco Svc. Ctr., Ft. Worth, Tex., 1967-74, Ray's Repair & Mfg., Ft. Worth, Tex., 1974-79, pres., 1979-80, Cisco, Tex., 1980-92. Sunday sch. tchr., Cisco, Tex., 1983-92, sub. tchr., 1992—; mem. Civic League of Cisco, 1990—; instr. Community Svc. course Cisco Jr. Coll., 1991.

RAY, JOHN WALKER, otolaryngologist, educator, broadcast commentator; b. Columbus, Ohio, Jan. 12, 1936; s. Kenneth Clark and Hope (Walker) R.; m. Susanne Gettings, July 15, 1961; children: Nancy Ann, Susan Christy. AB magna cum laude, Marietta Coll., Ohio, 1956; MD cum laude, Ohio State U., 1960; postgrad., Temple U., Phila., 1964, Mt. Sinai Hosp., Columbia U., NYC, 1964-66, Northwestern U., Evanston, Ill., 1967-71, U. Ill., 1968, U. Ind., 1969, Tulane U., New Orleans, 1969. Diplomate Am. Bd. Otolaryngology. Intern Ohio State U. Hosps., Columbus, 1960-61, clin. rsch. trainee NIH, 1963-65, resident dept. otolaryngology, 1963-65, 66-67, resident dept. surgery, 1965-66, instr. dept. otolaryngology, 1966-67, 70-75, clin. asst. prof., 1975-82, clin. assoc. prof., 1982-92, clin. prof., 1992-2000, clin. prof. emeritus, 2000—; hon. staff, past chief of staff Good Samaritan Hosp., Zanesville, Ohio, 1967—, Bethesda Hosp., Zanesville, 1967—. Hon. active staff Meml. Hosp., Marietta, Ohio, 1992—; radio-TV health commentator, 1982—2006. Contbr. articles to profl. jours.; collaborator with surg. motion picture: Laryngectomy and Neck Dissection, 1964. Past pres. Muskingum chpt. Am. Cancer Soc. Capt. USAF, 1961-63. Recipient Barraquer Meml. award, 1965; named to Order of Ky. Col., 1966, Muskingum County Country Music Hall of Fame. Fellow ACS, Am. Soc. Otolaryn. Allergy, Am. Acad. Otolaryngology-Head and Neck Surgery (past gov.), Am. Acad. Facial Plastic and Reconstructive Surgery; mem. AMA, Nat. Assn. Physician Broadcasters, Muskingum County Acad. Medicine (past pres.), Ohio Med. Assn., Columbus Ophthalmol. and Otolaryn. Soc. (past pres.), Ohio Soc. Otolaryngology (past pres.), Am. Soc. Contemporary Medicine and Surgery, Acad. Radio and TV Health Commentators, Fraternal Order of Police Assocs., Internat. Bluegrass Music Assn., Phi Beta Kappa, Alpha Omega Alpha, Beta Beta Beta, Alpha Tau Omega, Alpha Kappa Kappa. Presbyterian. Home: 1245 East Dr Zanesville OH 43701-1445 Personal E-mail: jray42@columbus.rr.com.

RAY, JOYCE MARIE, archivist, historian; b. Mobile, Ala., Dec. 29, 1948; d. Jack W. and Juliet (Craddock) Butler; m. Dennis A. Ray, Apr. 1, 1972 (div. 1980); 1 child, Nathan C.; m. F. G. Gosling, Aug. 13, 1982. BA, U. Houston, 1970; MLS, U. Tex., 1974, PhD, 1992. Tech. svcs. libr., archivist Tusculum Coll., Greeneville, Tenn., 1974-76; head hist. collections U. Tex. Health Sci. Ctr., San Antonio, 1977-87; archivist Office Nat. Archives Nat. Archives and Records Adminstrn., Washington, 1988, appraisal archivist Office Records Adminstrn., 1989, archives specialist Office Mgmt. and Adminstrn., 1989-93, spl. asst. to the Archivist, 1993-95; asst. program dir. for techl. evaluation Nat. Hist. Publs. and Records Commn., Washington, 1995; assoc. deputy dir. library services Inst. Mus. and Library Services, 1997—. Tchr. Georgetown U., 1992, 93; presenter in field. Contbr. articles to profl. jours. Rsch. fellow Med. Coll. Pa., 1989. Mem. Soc. Am. Archivists (mem. acquisitions and appraisal sec., sect. chair 1987-88, chair nominating com. 1989, cons. SAA basic archival conservation program 1989), Soc. S.W. Archives (exec. bd. 1986-87, chair profl. devel. com. 1984-85, local arrangements com. 1984-85), Mid-Atlantic Regional Archives Conf., Orgn. Am. Historians. Democrat. Office: Inst Mus and Library Services 1800 M Street NW 9th Fl Washington DC 20036-5802 *

RAY, MARILYN ANNE, nursing educator, researcher; b. Hamilton, Ont., Can., Jan. 24, 1938; d. Arthur William Anthony and Elvera Caroline (Montag) Ray; m. James L. Droesbeke, Aug. 18, 1979 (dec. Nov. 2001). Diploma, St. Joseph's Hosp. Sch. Nursing, Hamilton, 1958; BSN, U. Colo. Denver, 1968, MSN, 1969; MA in Anthropology, McMaster U, 1978; PhD of Nursing, U. Utah, 1981; HD (hon.), Nev. State Coll., 2005. RN Fla., cert. transcultural nurse, CTN. Instr. sch. nursing U. San Francisco, 1970—72; asst. prof. sch. nursing McMaster U., 1973—76; asst. prof. U. Colo., 1984—89; Christine E. Lynn eminent scholar Coll. Nursing Fla. Atlantic U., Boca Raton, 1989—94, prof. Coll. Nursing, 1995—2004, adj. prof., 2004—05, prof. emeritus, 2006—. Vis. prof. U. Colo., 1989—2004; Yingling vis. scholar Va. Commonwealth U., Richmond, 1994—95; vis. prof. Alta. Heritage Found. U., 2005—. Contbr. articles to profl. jours. Col. USAF, 1967—99. Recipient Leininger award, 1989, Disting. Alumni award, U. Utah Coll. Nursing, 2007; Transcultural Nursing scholar, 2005. Mem.: ANA, Space Nursing Soc. (charter), Aerospace Human Factors Assn. (charter), Coll. Nurses Ont., Transcultural Nursing Soc. (cert., mem. editl. bd. jour.), Am. Anthrop. Assn., Sigma Theta Tau. Business E-Mail: mray@fau.edu.

RAY, MARJORIE, retired financial planner; b. Hemingway, SC, Mar. 6, 1927; d. James Earl Ray and Maybelle Jordan; divorced; 2 children, Debra Boyd and Roberta Jill Sharp. AB in English and History, U. Calif., Berkeley, 1962, MLS, 1965; teaching degree, U. Ill., 1966. Lic. real estate agt., Conn. Dir. libr. program Sch. Dist. 57, Westmont, Ill., 1965—67; instr. English coll. edn. Evanston, Ill., 1966—67; coord. children's and adult svcs. Tampa Pub. Libr., Fla., 1967; dir. profl. svcs. Weston (Conn.) Woods Film Studios, 1968-69; asst. dir. Danbury (Conn.) Pub. Libr., 1970-73, Westport (Conn.) Pub. Libr., 1973-74; cons. Conn. State Libr., Hartford, 1974-76, assoc. state libr., 1977-79; broker rep. P&I Equities, White Plains, N.Y., 1980-82, MHA Fin. Corp., Braintree, Mass., 1983-84, Townsley Assocs., Corning, N.Y., 1984-89, v.p. corp. devel., 1985-89; v.p. Planned

Mgmt. Co. Savs. Bank Rockville, Conn., 1989-90; sr. v.p. Specialized Investments, 1991-92; investment officer FSC Securities Corp., 1993—97, Conn. regional sales mgr., 1995—; investment officer and asst. treas. Rockville (Conn.) Bank, 1998—2002, ret., 2002. Cons., propr. Colmar, Glastonbury, Conn., 1985—; instr. grad. English West Conn. Star Coll., 1971. Mem. Internat. Assn. Fin. Planning (bd. dirs. Hartford 1983-84, Disting. Svc. award 1984), Glastonbury Bus. and Profl. Women. Republican. Congregationalist. Avocations: travel, theater, literature, tennis, golf, ballroom dancing.

RAY, MARY LOUISE RYAN, lawyer; b. Houston, Dec. 8, 1954; d. Cornelius O'Brien and Mary Anne (Kelley) R.; m. Marshall Ransome Ray, Jan. 30, 1982; children: Siobhan Elisabeth Kelley, Johanna Frances Morris, Jonathan Jordan Willson. BA with honors, U. Tex., 1976; JD, St. Mary's Univ., San Antonio, 1980. Bar: Tex. 1980, U.S. Dist. Ct. (so. dist.) Tex. 1981, U.S. Ct. Appeals (5th cir.) 1993, U.S. Supreme Ct. 1994. Assoc. Kelley & Ryan, Houston, 1980-82, R.W. Armstrong, Brownsville, Tex., 1982-83; ptnr. Armstrong & Ray, Brownsville, 1983-87; shareholder Ransome and Ray, P.C., Brownsville, 1987—. Bd. dirs. Brownsville Soc. for Crippled Children, 1984-95, pres., 1992-93; bd. dirs. Valley Zool. Soc., 1990—, pres., 2005-06; bd. dirs. United Way of Southern Cameron County, 1989-95, pres., 1994; bd. dirs. Crippled Children's Found., Brownsville, 1989—; bd. dirs. Episcopal Day Sch. Found., 1995-2002, 04—, pres., 1995-2002; bd. dirs. Brownsville Econ. Devel. Coun., 2006—. Fellow Tex. Bar Found. (life); mem. Tex. Bar Assn., Cameron County Bar Assn. (bd. dirs. 1990-99, pres. 1998), Brownsville C. of C. (bd. dirs. 1998-99). Episcopalian. Office: Ransome & Ray PC 550 E Levee St Brownsville TX 78520-5343 Business E-Mail: marylou@ransomeray.com.

RAY, NELDA HOWTON, financial consultant; Grad., U. Montevallo, Ala., 1962. Fin. cons. Merrill Lynch, Tuscaloosa, Ala. Mem.: Rotary Internat. (local and dist. officer). Home: 4704 Oneida Ave Northport AL 35473-1431 Office: Merrill Lynch 302 Merchants Walk Ste 100 Tuscaloosa AL 35406-2214

RAY, PAUL SUKHAMAY, engineering educator, researcher; b. Bengal, India, Feb. 1, 1933; arrived in U.S., 1974; s. Suresh Chandra and Radha Rani Ray; m. Sudha Karmakar, Apr. 29, 1961; children: Steve S., Sumit S. B in Mech. Engring. with first class honors, Jadavpur U., Calcutta, India, 1956; M in Mech. Engring., Indian Inst. Tech., Kharagpur, India, 1961; MBA in Mgmt., Golden Gate U., 1978; PhD in Indsl. Engring., U. Okla., 1988. Registered profl. engr., Tex., chartered engr., Engring. Coun., London; cert. safety profl. Bd. Cert. Safety Profls. Sr. indsl. engr. Hindustan Motors Ltd., India, 1960—63; sr. asst. Union Carbide (I) Ltd., India, 1963—72; mgr. mgmt. svcs. Hindustan Copper Ltd., India, 1972—74; project plan-scheduling engr. Bechtel Corp., San Francisco, 1974—87; asst. prof. U. Ala., Tuscaloosa, 1989—95, assoc. prof., 1995—2005, prof., 2005—. Presenter in field. Mem. editl. bd. Internat. Jour. Indsl. Engring., Theory, Applications and Practice; contbr. chapters to books, articles to profl. jours. Recipient Outstanding advisor Departmental Hon. award Ala. chpt. Alpha Pi Mu, Coordinating Coun. Student Orgns. U. Ala., 2004—05; Gordon fellow, U. Okla., 1985, recipient numerous rsch. grants. Mem.: Campus Safety Assn., Nat. Safety Coun., Sys. Safety Soc. (Educator of the Yr.), Human Factors and Ergonomics Soc. (newsletter editor indsl. ergonomics tech. group 1990—91), Internat. Soc. Occupl. Ergonomics & Safety (pres. elect 2002—03, pres. 2003—04), Am. Soc. Safety Engrs. (Safety Rsch. award 1999), Inst. Indsl. Engrs. (sr.; v.p. publ. Okla. chpt. 1988—89, 2d v.p. Birmingham chpt. 1992—93, sec. 1994—95, bd. dirs. 1995—96, v.p. Region 3 2006—), Alpha Pi Mu. Achievements include patents pending for. Avocations: travel, TV, reading. Home: 3 Highland Manor Dr Tuscaloosa AL 35406 Office: Univ Ala Tuscaloosa Dept Indsl Engring PO Box 870288 Tuscaloosa AL 35487 Office Phone: 205-348-1603. Personal E-mail: rpl9825@aol.com. Business E-Mail: pray@eng.ua.edu.

RAY, RACHAEL DOMENICA, chef, television personality; b. Cape Cod, Mass., Aug. 25, 1968; m. John Cusimano, Sept. 24, 2005. Student, Pace Univ. Mgr. fresh foods dept. Macy's Marketplace, NY; store mgr., buyer Agata & Valentina, NY; mgr., pub and rest. Sagamore Resort, Lake George, NY; food buyer Cowan & Lobel, Albany; editor-in-chief Everyday with Rachael Ray mag., 2005—. Spokesperson Dunkin Donuts, 2007—. Author: 30-Minute Meals, 1999, Veggie Meals, 2001, Comfort Foods, 2001, 30-Minute Meals 2, 2003, Get Togethers: Rachael Ray 30 Minute Meals, 2003, Cooking 'Round the Clock: Rachael Ray's 30-Minute Meals, 2004, Cooking Rocks!: Rachael Ray's 30-Minute Meals for Kids, 2004, 30-Minute Get Real Meals: Eat Healthy Without Going to Extremes, 2005 (Quills award cookbook The Quills Literacy Found., 2005), Comfort Food: Rachael Ray's Top 30 30-Minute Meals, 2005, Rachael Ray 365: No Repeats, 2005 (Quills award cookbook The Quills Literacy Found., 2006), Express Lane Meals, 2006, 2, 4, 6, 8: Great Meals for Couples or Crowds, 2006; host 30 Minute Meals, Food Network, 2002— (Emmy award for outstanding svc. show, 2006), $40 A Day, 2004—, Inside Dish, 2004—, Rachael Ray's Tasty Travels, 2005—, (syndicated talk show) The Rachel Ray Show, 2006—, guest appearances Pyramid, 2003, The Tony Danza Show, 2004, 2005, Live With Regis and Kelly, 2004, 2005, Sidewalks Entertainment, 2004, Good Day Live, 2004, The View, 2005, Isaac Mizrahi, 2005, Tonight Show with Jay Leno, 2005, Late Show with David Letterman, 2005, Oprah Winfrey Show, 2005, 2006. Named one of 100 Sexiest Women, FHM-US Mag., 2004, 100 Most Influential People, Time Mag., 2006. Office: c/o Everyday with Rachael Ray Fifth Floor 260 Madison Ave New York NY 10016-2402 *

RAY, RAYMOND B., federal judge; b. 1943; BA, U. South Fla., 1965; JD, U. Fla., 1971. Bar: Fla. Asst. U.S. atty. Dept. Justice, So. Dist. Fla., Miami, 1971-74; bankruptcy judge U.S. Bankruptcy Ct. (so. dist.) Fla., Ft. Lauderdale, 1993—. Comdr. USNR, 1961—85, ret. Office: US Courthouse Rm 306 299 E Broward Blvd Fort Lauderdale FL 33301-1944 Business E-Mail: raymond_ray@flsb.uscourts.gov.

RAY, ROMITA, art historian, educator; b. Calcutta, Mar. 28, 1970; arrived in US, 1988; d. Jyoti P. and Arundhati Ray. BA, Smith Coll., Northampton, Mass., 1992; MA, Yale U., New Haven, 1994, MPhil, 1995, PhD, 1999. Vis. asst. prof. art Colby Coll., Waterville, Maine, 1998—99; Franklin postdoctoral fellow U. Ga., Athens, 1999—2000, curator prints and drawings, 2000—06, adj. asst. prof. art history, 2000—06; asst. prof. art history Syracuse U., NY, 2006—. Author mus. catalogs. Panelist women artists panel Lyndon Ho. Arts Ctr., Athens, 2001; founding mem. Ga. Mus. Art, Athens, organizer symposium, 2004; founding mem. Pierre Daura Ctr. Grantee, Ga. Humanities Coun., Atlanta, 2006; Andrew W. Mellon dissertation writing fellow, Yale U., 1997—98. Mem.: Coll. Art Assn. (mem. com. diversity practices 2007—). Office: Syracuse U Dept Fine Arts 308 Bowne Hall Syracuse NY 13244

RAY, RONALD DUDLEY, lawyer; b. Hazard, Ky., Oct. 30, 1942; BA in Psychology and English, Centre Coll., 1964; JD magna cum laude, U. Louisville, 1971. Assoc. Greenebaum, Doll & McDonald, 1971-75, ptnr., 1975-84, 85-86, Ray & Morris, Louisville, 1986-89; mng. ptnr. Ronald Ray Attys., Louisville, 1990—; dep. asst. sec. def. Pentagon, Washington, 1984-85. Adj. prof. law U. Louisville Sch. Law, 1972-80; comm. Presdl. Commn. on Assignment Women in Mil., 1992. Author: Military Necessity & Homosexuality, 1993; sr. legal editor: Personnel Policy Manual, Bank Supervisory Policies, The Bank Employee Handbook, 1985-86; mil. historian. State fin. chmn. Nat. Fin. Com. for George Bush for Pres.; chmn. Vietnam Vets. Leadership Program in Ky., 1982-85, Ky. Vietnam Vets. Meml. Fund, 1985-91; trustee Marine Corps Command and Staff Found., 1985-92; mem. exec. com. State Cen. Com., Ky. Rep. Party, 1986-90; mem. Am. Battle Monuments Commn., 1990-94; chmn. Vets. for Bush in Ky., 2000; mem. Nat. Com. Vets. for Bush, 2000; spokesman Coalition of Am. Vets., 1998—, chmn., 1999—; spl. coun. Naval Aviation Found., 1994—. With USMC, 1964-69; col. USMCR (ret.). Decorated Silver Star medal with gold star, Bronze Star medal, Purple Heart, Vietnamese Cross of Gallantry, Vietnamese Honor Medal; recipient Nat. Eagle award Nat. Guard Assn., 1985. Mem. Naval Inst. (life), Marine Corps Res. Officers' Assn. Home: Halls Hill Farm 3317 Halls Hill Rd Crestwood KY 40014-9523 Office Phone: 502-241-5552. Personal E-mail: colray@aye.net.

RAY, ROSABELL HARRIET See BATTIN, R.

RAY, RUTH ALICE YANCEY, retired rancher, real estate developer; b. Birmingham, Ala., July 26, 1931; d. John Grayson and Ruth Ethel (Lutman) Yancey; (div. July 1986); children: Virginia Ruth, John Edward, William Arthur. Student, Fla. State U., 1949-50; BS, Appalachian State U., 1954; postgrad., Stetson U., 1966-67, Appalachian State U., 1962-63, Stetson U., 1964-67. Tchr. pub. schs., Nenana, Alaska, 1955-56; tchr. 1st Christian Ch., Clermont, Fla., 1965-67, Lake County Sch. Bd., Clermont, 1969-70; rancher Rays' Ranch, Clermont, 1963-97; pvt. real estate developer Clermont, 1990—; substitute tchr. Buncombe County Asheville City Sch. Sys., 1999—; tchr. Marion County Sch. Bd., 2006—. Chmn. Clermont Planning and Zoning Commn., 1973-81; mem. Heart of Fla. Girl Scout Coun., 1988—, life mem. Ctr. Fla. Gir. Scout Coun.; life mem. Friends of Cooper Mem. Libr., South Lake Art League; assoc. Sisters of St. Mary. Named Conservation Farmer of Yr., State of Fla., 1982. Mem. Lake County Farm Bur. (bd. dirs. 1977-81), Lake County Cattlemen's Assn. (v.p. 1979-81), Lake County Farmer's Home Adminstrn. (bd. dirs. 1984-88, 1990—, chmn. 1985, 88, 90-91), Nat. Cutting Horse Assn. (life), Am. Quarter Horse Assn., Am. Paint Horse Assn., E.S.A. Internat., Daus. of King (pres., sec.), St. Bridcats Guild, Order St. Luke, Sigma Kappa. Republican. Episcopalian (sr. warden, eucharistic min.). Avocations: needlepoint, fishing, hiking, reading. Home: 3001 SE Lake Weir Ave Apt 1101 Ocala FL 34471-6778

RAY, SIBA PRASAD, materials scientist, ceramics scientist; b. Dinhata, India, Jan. 4, 1944; came to U.S., 1969; s. Nilmony P. and Bina Pani Ray; m. Liplka Ray, May 28, 1977; children: Sourav, Leena. B in Engring., Calcutta U., India, 1964; MS, Columbia U., NYC, 1970, D in Engring. Sci., 1974. Sci. officer Bhabha Atomic Rsch. Ctr., Bombay, 1964-68; rsch. assoc. Pa. State U., University Park, 1974-76; scientist Alcoa Labs., Alcoa Ctr., Pa., 1977-78, sr. scientist, 1978-82, sci. assoc. Alcoa Center, Pa., 1982-91, sr. sci. assoc., 1991-98; program mgr. materials devel. NGAP, Alcoa, Alcoa Center, 1999—. Cons. Alcoa Separations Tech., Warrendale, Pa., 1991, Electro Metallurgy and Electrochemistry Cons., New Kensington, Pa., 1992. Contbr. articles to Jour. Solid State Chemistry, J. Am. Ceramic Soc., Light Metals, Bull. Am. Ceramic Soc. Pres. Bengali Assn. Pitts., 1988. Mem. The Metall. Soc., Am. Ceramic Soc., Sigma Xi. Achievements include 52 patents in the area of inert elctrodes, ceramic composites and reaction sintering. Home: 6007 Pilgrim Ct Murrysville PA 15668-8533 Office: Alcoa Labs Alcoa Tech Ctr New Kensington PA 15069 Office Phone: 724-337-2803. Business E-Mail: siba.ray@alcoa.com.

RAY, STEPHEN ALAN, academic administrator, lawyer; b. Oklahoma City, Aug. 26, 1956; s. Stephen Harold Ray and Dorothea Hodges. BA summa cum laude, St. Thomas Sem., 1978; PhD, Harvard U., Cambridge, Mass., 1986; JD, U. Calif., Hastings, 1990. Bar: Calif. 1990, Mass. 1994. Assoc. Richards, Watson & Gershon, LA, 1990—93; pvt. practice, 1994—95; staff counsel Houghton Mifflin Co., 1995—96; dir. acad. affairs Harvard Law Sch., 1996—98, asst. dean acad. affairs, 1998—2001, assoc. dean acad. affairs, 2001—04, lectr. law, 2004; vice provost acad. affairs U. New Hampshire, Durham, 2004—06, sr. vice provost, 2006—, affiliate assoc. prof. of polit. sci., philosophy and justice studies, 2004—. Vis. lectr. religion Harvard Divinity Sch., 1995; adv. bd. Harvard Native Am. Program, 1999—2004. Author: The Modern Soul, 1987, Native American Identity and the Challenge of Kennewick Man, 2006. Vol. AIDS action com., Boston, 1994-96; atty. vol. AIDS Project L.A., 1991-93; Native Am. Adv. Com. on Repatriation, Peabody Mus., 1999-2002. Mem. Cherokee Nation Okla., Phi Beta Kappa (hon.). Office: U New Hampshire Thompson Hall 207 Durham NH 03824 Business E-Mail: alan.ray@unh.edu.

RAY, SUSAN ELAINE, principal; b. Huntington, W.Va. d. Emory Joseph and Frances Fulkerson Ray. BS, Fla. State U., Tallahassee, 1974, MS in Edn., 1976; MS in Edn. Adminstrn., Coll. New Rochelle, NYC, 2003; post grad., St. Johns U. Cert. tchr. N.Y., Fla., admistr. N.Y., Fla. Tchr. Longwood Ctrl. Schs., Middle Island, NY, 1979—85; instr. Elon Coll., NC, 1986—87; tchr. Riverside H.S., Durham, 1988—2000; instr. edn. Kamuzu Coll., Lilogwe, Malawi, 2000; asst. prin. Lake Grove (N.Y.) Sch., 2001—02, Copiague Mid. Sch., 2003—04; prin. The Broach Sch., St. Petersburg, Fla., 2005—. Staff developer Tchg. Children of Poverty and Tng. New Tchrs., Copiague, NY, 2003—04; dir. The Broach Sch., St. Petersburg, Fla., 2005—. Youth coach U.S. Volleyball Assn., Durham, NC, 1988—99; site dir. Internat. Spl. Olympics, 1999; active Tchrs. Africa Fellowship, 2000—01. Named Durham County Tchr. of Yr., 1998, State Volleyball Coach of Yr., N.C. H.S. Athletic Assn., 1998; recipient Outstanding Achievement in Edn award, Duke U., 1998. Mem.: ASCD, Phi Delta Kappa.

RAY, WILLIAM JACKSON, psychologist; b. Birmingham, Ala., Sept. 3, 1945; s. Norman M. and Mary K. Agnew; m. Judith Mebane, Aug. 22, 1987; children from previous marriage: Adam, Lauren. BA, Eckerd Coll., 1967; MA, Vanderbilt U., 1969, PhD, 1971; Fellow in med. psychology, Langley Porter Neuropsychiat. Inst., U. Calif. Med. Center, San Francisco, 1971-72. Prof., dir. clin. psychology tng. program Pa. State U., 1972—, dir. clin. trng., 1991-97. Author: (with R.M. Stern) Biofeedback, 1977, (with others) Evaluation of Clinical Biofeedback, 1979, (with R.M. Stern and C.M. Davis) Psychophysiological Recording, 1980, 2d edit. (with R.M. Stern and K. Quigley), 2000, Methods Toward a Science of Behavior and Experience, 1981, 8th edit., 2006, (with E. Susman & L. Feajous) Emotion, Cognition, Health and Development in Children and Adolescents, 1992, (with L. Michelson) Handbook of Dissociation, 1996 (Cornelia Wilbur award ISSD); series editor: Plenum Series in Behavioral Psychophysiology and Medicine. Recipient Nat. Media award Am. Psychol. Found., 1976, 78, Rsch. award Best Empirical Paper, Soc. Clin. Experimental Hypnosis. Mem. AAAS, APA, APS, Soc. Psychophysiol. Rsch. Office: Dept Psychology Pa State U University Park PA 16802 Home Phone: 814-234-3402; Office Phone: 814-863-1726. Business E-Mail: wjr@psu.edu.

RAYALA, SURESH KUMAR, medical educator; b. Khammam, Andhra Pradesh, India, July 25, 1976; arrived in US, 2003; s. Venkatappaiah and Krishnaveni Rayala. BSc in Biol. Scis., Kakatiya U., India, 1996; MS in Animal Physiology, S.V. U., Tirupati, India, 1998; PhD in Biochemistry, U. Madras, India, 2002. Scientist Shanta Biotechnics, Hyderabad, India, 2002—03; postdoctoral fellow MD Anderson Cancer Ctr., Houston, 2003—07, asst. prof., 2007—. Contbr. articles to profl. jours. Recipient Young Scientist award, Indian Soc. Oncology, 2002. Mem.: Sci. Adv. Bd. (life). Achievements include research in cancer. Home: 7900 Cambridge Apt # 10-1B Houston TX 77054 Office: U Texas MD Anderson Cancer Ctr 1515 Holcombe Blvd Houston TX 77030 Home Phone: 713-796-2634; Office Phone: 713-745-3559. Business E-Mail: srayala@mdanderson.org.

RAYBURN, CAROLE ANN (MARY AIDA), psychologist, researcher, writer, consultant; b. Washington, Feb. 14, 1938; d. Carl Frederick and Mary Helen (Milkie) Miller; m. Ronald Allen Rayburn (dec. Apr. 1970). BA in Psychology, Am. U., 1961; MA in Clin. Psychology, George Washington U., 1965; PhD in Ednl. Psychology, Cath. U. Am., 1969; MDiv in Ministry, Andrews U., 1980. Lic. psychologist, Md. Psychometrician Columbian Prep. Sch., Washington, 1963; clin. psychologist Spring Grove State Hosp., Catonsville, Md., 1966—68; pvt. practice, 1969, 1971—; staff clin. psychologist Instl. Care Svcs. Divsn. D.C. Children's Ctr., Laurel, Md., 1970—78; psychologist Md. Dept. Vocat. Rehab., 1973—74; psychometrician Montgomery County Pub. Schs., 1981—85. Lectr. Strayer Coll., Washington, 1969-70; forensic psychology expert witness, 1973—; guest lectr. Andrews U., Berrien Springs, Mich., 1979, Hood Coll, Frederick, Md., 1986-88; instr. Johns Hopkins U., 1986, 88-89; adj. faculty Profl. Sch. Psychology Studies, San Diego, 1987; adj. asst. prof. Loyola Coll., Columbia, Md., 1987; cons. Julia Brown Montessori Schs., 1972, 78, 82—, VA Ctr., 1978, 91-93. Editor: (with M.J. Meadow) A Time to Weep and a Time to Sing, 1985, (with Violet Franks) Focus on Women Co-ed, 2005; contbg. author: Montessori: Her Method and the Movement (What You Need to Know), 1973, Drugs, Alcohol and Women: A National Forum Source Book, 1975, The Other Side of the Couch: Faith of the Psychotherapist, 1981, Clinical Handbook of Pastoral Counseling, 1985, An Encyclopedic Dictionary of Pastoral Care and Counseling, 1990, Religion Personality and Mental Health, 1993; co-editor (with Violet Franks) Springer Focus on Women series; author copyrighted inventories Religious Occupational and Stress Questionnaire, 1986, Organizational Relationships Survey, 1987, Attitudes Toward Children Inventory, 1987, State-Trait Morality Inventory, 1987, Body Awareness and Sexual Intimacy Comfort Scale (BASICS), 1993, Inventory in Religiousness, 1996, Inventory on Spirituality, 1996, Sports, Exercise, Leadership and Friendship Questionnaire, 1997, Peacefulness Inventory, Life Choices Inventory, 1998, Inventory on the Supreme and Work, 1999, Children's and Adolescents' Peace Inventory, 2002, Inventory on Well-Being, 2004, TEACH: Traumatic Experiences and Children's and Adolescents' Health, 2005, Creative Personality Inventory, 2005, Intuition Inventory, 2005, Health and Traumatic Experiences in Adults, 2005, Inventory on Religiousness, Children's Version, 2005; cons. editor Profl. Psychology, 1980-83; assoc. editor Jour. Pastoral Counseling, 1985-90, guest editor, 1988; co-proposer (with Lee Richmond) The Theory and Field of Theobiology: interfacing of theology and the sciences, 1998; mem. editl. bd. Internat. Jour. Ethics (Nova Sci.), 2004—; contbr. numerous articles to profl. jours. Bd. dirs. Psychologists Ethical Treatment of Animals, 1998-2000; spkrs. TF Mont County NOW, 2002-07, treas., 2005-07, chair TF women's spirituality pres., 2007-. Recipient Svc. award Coun. for Advancement Psychol. Professions and Scis., 1975, cert. D.C. Dept. Human Resources, 1975, 76, cert. recognition D.C. Psychol. Assn., 1976, 1985; AAUW rsch. grantee, 1983. Fellow: APA (editl. bd. Jour. Child Clin. Psychology 1978—82, divsn. psychology women chair task force on women and religion 1980—81, chair equal opportunity affirmative action divsn. clin. psychology 1980—82, clin. psychology women's sect. 1984—86, divsn. psychology issues in grad. edn. and clin. tng. 1988—, program chair 1991—94, pres. divsn. psychology of religion 1995—96, gen. psych. divsn. liaison to commn. internat. rels. 2004—, fellow, divsn. on internat. psychology, divsn. psychology of religion, psychology of women, clin. psychology, cons. psychology, gen. psychology, psychotherapy, state assn. affairs, divsn. media psychology, divsn. family psychology, Mentoring award divsn. clin. psychology, sect. of clin. psychology of women 1997, divsn. psychology of religion 1997, William C. Bier rsch. award divsn. psychology of religion 2000), Md. Psychol. Assn. (editor newsletter 1975—76, chair ins. com. 1981—83, pres. 1984—85, exec. adv. com. 1985—, chpt. recognition 1978), Am. Assn. Applied & Preventive Psychology (sec. 1992—93, chair fellows com. 1992—93), Am. Orthopsychiat. Assn.; mem.: NOW (pres. Montgomery County, Md. chpt. 2004—), Md. Assn. Counseling and Devel., Md. Asn. Measurement and Evaluation (pres. 2005—), Balt. Assn. Cons. Psychologists (pres. 1991—92), Assn. Practicing Psychologists Montgomery-Prince George's Counties (pres. 1986—88, editor newsletter 1990—, treas. 1996—98), Internat. Soc. Polit. Psychology, Psi Chi (hon.). Achievements include research in stress in religious professionals, women and stress, women and religion, pastoral counseling, state-trait morality inventory, leadership, mentoring, clergy stress, psychotherapy, children, body image; intimacy, peacefulness, spirituality, life choices, religiousness, well-being, work, traumatic experiences and health, creative personality, intuition. Address: 1200 Morningside Dr Silver Spring MD 20904-3149 Personal E-mail: valentinecarole@copper.net.

RAYBURN, DAVID B., manufacturing executive; b. Gallipolis, Ohio, May 24, 1948; BS, Pa. State Univ., 1970; MBA, Xavier Univ., 1979. Mgmt. positions through dir. mfg. Rockwell Internat., 1970—91; v.p., gen. mgr. heavy duty & indsl. div. Modine Mfg. Co., Racine, Wis., 1991—93, v.p., gen. mgr. automotive div., 1993—94, group v.p. highway products, 1994—98, exec. v.p., 1998—2002, pres., COO, 2002—03, pres., CEO, 2003—, bd. dir., 2003—. Bd. dir. Marshall & Ilsley Bank, Twin Disc, Jason Holdings Inc., RAMAC. Mem.: Soc. Automotive Engineers. Office: Modine Mfg Co 1500 DeKoven Ave Racine WI 53403 *

RAYBURN, WENDELL GILBERT, SR., educational consultant; b. Detroit, May 20, 1929; s. Charles Jefferson and Grace Victoria (Winston) R.; m. Gloria Ann Myers, Aug. 19; children: Rhonda Renee, Wendell Gilbert; 1 stepson, Mark K. Williams. BA, Eastern Mich. U., 1951; MA, U. Mich., 1952; Ed.D., Wayne State U., Detroit, 1972. Tchr., adminstr. Detroit public schs., 1954-68; from asst. dir. to dir. spl. projects U. Detroit, 1968-72, asso. dean acad. support programs, 1972-74; dean Univ. Coll., U. Louisville, 1974-80; pres. Savannah (Ga.) State Coll., 1980-88, Lincoln U., Jefferson City, Mo., 1988-97; v.p. fin. Am. Assn. State Colls. and Univs., Washington, 1997—2001; v.p., sec., treas., sr. assoc. Penson Associates, Chevy Chase, Md. Chmn. adv. com. Office for Advancement of Pub. Black Colls., 1989-97. Trustee Candler Gen. Hosp., 1982-85, Telfair Acad. Arts, 1980-87; bd. dirs. Candler Health Svcs., 1985-88, YMCA Blue Ridge Assembly, 1986-88, Internat. Food and Agrl. Devel. and Econ. Cooperation, 1988-94, Meml. Cmty. Hosp., Jefferson City, 1988-94, United Way Mo., 1989-97, Mo. Capital Punishment Resource Ctr., 1990-95, Stephens Coll., Columbia, Mo., 1993-97, Capital Regional Med. Ctr., 1994-97; campaign chmn. Jefferson City Area United Way, 1994-95. With AUS, 1952-59. Decorated Commendation medal with pendant; recipient Disting. Alumni award Wayne State U., 1993, Whitney M. Young Jr. award Lincoln Found., 1980, Disting. Citizens award City of Louisville, 1980. Mem. Mo. Bar Assn. (foresight com.), Am. Assn. Higher Edn., Am. Assn. State Colls. and Univs. (bd. dirs. 1988—, chmn. 1992-93), Nat. Assn. State Univs. and Land Grant Colls., Nat. Assn. for Equal Opportunity in Higher Edn., Coun. on Pub. Higher Edn. for Mo. (chmn. 1991-93), Coun. of 1890 Colls. and Univs., Jefferson City C. of C. (bd. dirs. 1988-97), Rotary (bd. dirs. Jefferson City 1989-96, pres. 1994-95), Kappa Alpha Psi, Sigma Pi Phi. Episcopalian. Mailing: Penson Associates Apt 1735 4701 Willard Ave Chevy Chase MD 20815-4632

RAYFIELD, ELLIOT JAMES, medical educator; b. Phila., May 6, 1942; s. Joseph and Rachel Evelyn (Aisenstein) Rayfield. AB, U. Pa., 1963; MD, Jefferson Med. Coll., 1967. Asst. prof. medicine Mt. Sinai Sch. Medicine, NYC, 1974—77, assoc. prof. medicine, 1977—82, prof. medicine, 1982—88, clin. prof. medicine, 1988—. Mem. med. adv. bd. Mirro Islet, San Diego, 2001—05. Author (with C. Soelmani): (book) Diabetes - Beating the Cure, 1992. Maj. US Army, 1971—73. Recipient Recognition award, Endocrine Soc. Devel. Com., 2004, 1st Profl. Edn. Sci. award, N.Y. Downstate Affiliate, Rsch. Career R&D award, NIH, 1975—80, Disting. Rsch. award, Dept. Medicine, Mt. Sinai Sch. Medicine, 1985. Fellow: ACP, Am. Assn. Clin. Endocrinology (charter); mem.: Mt. Sinai Alumni Assn. (v.p. 2005—07), Am. Diabetes Assn. (1st Profl. Edn. Sci. award N.Y. downstate affiliate 1989), Am. Soc. for Clin. Investigation (pres. N.Y.

downstate affiliate 1993—94), Mt. Sinai Alumni Assn. (pres. 2007—), Alpha Omega Alpha. Avocation: running. Office: 1150 Park Ave New York NY 10028 Office Phone: 212-427-9191. Personal E-mail: ejrayfield@aol.com.

RAYLE, HEATHER LYNNETTE, chemist; b. Greensboro, NC, June 10, 1968; d. Donald Lee and Sharon Sue R. BS in Chemistry with high distinction, Pa. State U., 1989; PhD in Chemistry, UCLA, 1994; MBA, Lehigh U., 2001. Sr. scientist Rohm & Haas Co., Spring House, Pa., 1994-98, rsch. sect. mgr., 1998-99, mgr. tech. planning, 1999-2000, bus. devel. mgr., 2001—03, mktg. dir., 2003—05, dir. slurry technology, 2006—. Bd. dirs. Rohm & Haas Tech. Comty. Orgn., Spring House, Pa., 1997-2000, chair 1999; alumni bd. Pa. State U. Coll. Sci., 2001—, treas., 2005—, v.p., 2007—; vice chair exec. com. SEMI Chems. and Gas Mfrs. Group, 2007—. Braddock scholarship, Pa. State U. Coll. of Sci., 1985-89; fellow NSF, 1989-92, fellow UCLA, 1989-94; recipient Otto Haas award for Scientific Achievement, 1998. Mem. Am. Chem. Soc., Phi Beta Kappa. Achievements include development of commerical processes to manufacture agricultural chemicals and their intermediates; commercial marketing and technology management of consumables for semiconductor processing. Office: Rohm and Haas Electronic Materials 451 Bellevue Rd Newark DE 19713 Business E-Mail: hrayle@rohmhaas.com.

RAYLE, STEPHEN LANE, criminal justice educator; b. Orlando, Fla., Aug. 6, 1958; s. Charles Wesley and June Elizabeth Rayle; m. Suk Cha Yang; children: James, Angel, Tara. BS, Nova Southeastern U., Ft. Lauderdale, Fla., 2001, MS, postgrad., Nova Southeastern U., Ft. Lauderdale, Fla., 2003—. Cert. correctional officer Fla., 2002. Correctional officer sgt. Fla. Dept. Corrections, Orlando, 2002—; prof. criminal justice Keiser Coll., Orlando, 2005—05, Valencia C.C., Orlando, 2005—; online criminal justice instr. ECPI Coll. Tech., Virginia Beach, Va., 2006—. Sgt. USMC, 1976—80. Mem.: Am. Mensa (assoc.; testing proctor 2004—). Avocations: self-education, reading. Home: 6016 Bent Pine Dr Apt 2619 Orlando FL 32822-6809 Home Phone: 407-928-2641.

RAYLESBERG, ALAN IRA, lawyer; b. NYC, Dec. 6, 1950; s. Daniel David and Sally Doris (Mantell) Raylesberg; m. Caren Thea Coven, Nov. 20, 1983; children: Lisa Maris, Jason Todd. BA in Polit. Sci., NYU, 1972; JD cum laude, Boston U., 1975. Bar: NY 1976, US Dist. Ct. (so. dist.) NY 1976, US Dist. Ct. (ea. dist.) NY 1978, US Tax Ct. 1981, US Ct. Appeals (2d and 5th cirs.) 1982, US Ct. Appeals (1st cir.) 1986, US Ct. Appeals (9th cir.) 1996, US Ct. Appeals (fed. cir.) 2004. Assoc. Orans, Elsen & Polstein, NYC, 1975-77; from assoc. to ptnr. Guggenheimer & Untermyer, NYC, 1977—85; ptnr. Rosenman & Colin, NYC, 1985—2002, co-chmn. litig. dept., 1998—99, chmn. litig. dept., 1999—2002; ptnr., sect. head litig. group Vinson & Elkins, NYC, 2002—04; ptnr. Chadbourne & Parke, NYC, 2004—, co-head comml. litig. group, 2006—. Adj. instr. NY Law Sch., 1980—83; instr. Nat. Inst. Trial Advocacy; mem. adv. group comml. divsn., mem. mediation panel NY State Supreme Ct.; mem. arbitration panel US Dist. Ct. (ea. dist.) NY; mem. CPR Inst. Dispute Resolution Panel Disting. Neutrals, NYC; judge Nat. Moot Ct. Competition, 1980—. Author: Case Evaluation, Commercial Litigation in New York State Courts, 2005; editor: Boston U. Law Rev., 1974—75. Bd. dirs. Fund Modern Cts., 1994—. Recipient Humanitarian award, Award of Courage Found., 2006. Fellow: NY Bar Found.; mem.: ABA, NY Coun. Def. Lawyers, Securities Industry Assn. Legal and Compliance Divsn. (legal and compliance divsn.), NY State Bar Assn. (house of dels. 1996—2000), NY County Lawyers Assn. Found. (bd. dirs. 1998—2003), NY County Lawyers Assn. (mem. fed. ct. com. 1988—, mem. appellate ct. com. 1990—, co-chmn. appellate ct. com. 1992—93, chair appellate ct. com. 1993—96, bd. dirs. 1995—98, 1999—2002), Assn. Bar City NY, Fed. Bar Coun., Town Club New Castle (mem. exec. com. 1987—91). Democrat. Jewish. Office: Chadbourne & Parke LLP 30 Rockefeller Plz New York NY 10112 Office Phone: 212-408-5198. Business E-Mail: araylesberg@chadbourne.com.

RAYMAN, RUSSELL BARRY, physician; b. Toledo, Ohio, Jan. 13, 1936; m. Ludy Rayman; children: Joseph, David, Ariel. MD, U. Mich., 1961. Diplomate Am. Bd. Family Practice, Am. Bd. Aerospace Medicine. Intern Jackson Meml. Hosp., Miami, Fla., 1961-62; commd. 2d lt. USAF, 1962, advanced through grades to col., 1989; resident in aerospace medicine Brooks AFB, Tex., 1969-72; mgr. operational medicine Lockheed, Washington, 1989-92; exec. dir. Aerospace Med. Assn., Alexandria, Va., 1992—. Author: Clinical Aviation Medicine, 1982, 4th edit., 2006. Decorated numerous mil. awards. Office: Aerospace Med Assn 320 S Henry St Alexandria VA 22314-3524

RAYMER, DANIEL P., aeronautical engineering company executive, aeronautical engineer; BS in Astronautics and Aeronautics, MS in Astronautics and Aeronautics, Purdue U.; MBA in Entrepreneurship and Venture Mgmt., U. So. Calif.; DEng, Swedish Royal Inst. Tech. (KTH). Project mgr. engring. Rockwell North Am. Aviation, 1976—86; dir. future missions Aerojet Propulsion Rsch. Inst., 1986—87; dir. advanced design Lockheed Aero. Systems, 1987—90; prof. Calif. State U., Northridge, 1990—93; pres. Conceptual Rsch. Corp., Calif., 1990—; rsch. engr., aerospace design cons. RAND Corp., 1993—2004. Contbr. articles to sci. jours.; author: Aircraft Design: A Conceptual Approach, Dan Raymer's Simplified Aircraft Design for Homebuilders; mem. editl. bd.: AIAA Jour. Aircraft, Aircraft Design: An Internat. Jour. Recipient Award of Excellence, Aviation/Space Writers Assn., 1991, Engring. Merit award, San Fernando Valley Engrs. Coun., 1991. Fellow: Inst. for Advancement of Engring., AIAA (disting. lectr. 1990—92); mem.: Exptl. Aircraft Assn., Soc. Allied Weights Engrs., Soc. Automotive Engrs. Achievements include patents in field. Avocations: flying, music, travel, gardening, cooking. Office: Conceptual Rsch Corp PO Box 5429 Playa Del Rey CA 90296 Office Phone: 310-577-3773. Office Fax: 818-743-7483. *

RAYMER, JOHN DAVID, literature and language professor; b. Elkhart, Ind., July 9, 1948; m. Kathleen Russell, June 24, 2006; children: Thomas, Carolyn Mary McEachran, Janet Theresa, Thomas Joseph, Mariah Trench. BA, Wittenberg U., Springfield, Ohio, 1970; MA, Nat. U. Ireland, Dublin, 1971; PhD, Ohio U., Athens, 1975; postdoctoral, Purdue U., West Lafayette, Ind. Asst. prof. English Purdue U., Hammond, Ind., 1976—80; ins. agt. C.M. Alliance Group Inc., South Bend, Ind., 1980—90; adj. asst. prof. Ind. U., South Bend, 1989—94; assoc. prof. English Holy Cross Coll., Notre Dame, Ind., 1990—. Chair faculty forum Holy Cross Coll., Notre Dame, 1991—93, homework tutoring campus coord., 1994—2006, co-founder, dir. homework tutoring program, 1995—, acad. affairs faculty rep., 1997—98, chair promotions and retention com., 2005—; mem. Ind. Middle Grades Reading Network, 1993—, Nat. Scholastic Hon.; adv. editor Collegiate Press, 1995—2004; mentee Midwest Tech. Tchg. Acad., Chgo., 2000—01. Contbg. editor: The Hole in Me Since the Day You Died, 2005. Leader student groups South Bend Walk for Hospice; sr. warden St. Michael and All Angels Episcopal Ch., South Bend, Ind., 2004—; founding mem. English Connection; former bd. mem., pres. Big Brothers/Big Sisters, South Bend; bd. mem. Dismas House, South Bend, Ind., 2007. Named Outstanding Mentoree of U. Notre Dame bound students, 2005; recipient Outstanding Cmty.-Coll. Collaboration award, Coll. Compact, Miami Beach, Fla., 1998, Attendance award, Kiwanis Internat., 2003, 2004, George Hixson award, 2004, Outstanding Young Men of Am. award. Mem.: Internat. Reading Assn., Knute Rockne Kiwanis Club, Phi Kappa Phi. Democrat. Episcopalian. Avocations: travel, swimming, canoeing, hiking, reading. Home: 1613 E Madison St South Bend IN 46617 Office: Holy Cross Coll 54515 State Rd 933 Notre Dame IN 46556-0308 Home Phone: 574-386-1239; Office Phone: 574-239-8385.

RAYMOND, BRUCE ALLEN, retired surgeon, medical association administrator; b. Aberdeen, SD, Dec. 8, 1924; s. Samuel A. and Pearl (Blackstone) R.; m. Virginia Stratton, Apr. 2, 1948 (div. 1969); children: Judith Ann, Jaqueline Marie, Bruce Allen Jr., Brian Andrew; m. Jane Molnar, Nov. 15, 1969; children: Douglas A., Andrew D., Colin K. BS, Leland Stanford U., U. S.D., 1945; MD, Washington U., St. Louis, 1949. Diplomate Am. Bd. Surgery, Am. Bd. Thoracic Surgery. Intern U. Ored. Med. Sch. Hosps., Portland, 1949-50; resident Walter Reed Gen. Hosp., Washington, 1953—60, asst. chief thoracic surgery, 1959-60; chief thoracic and cardiovascular surgery Letterman Gen. Hosp., San Francisco, 1960-64, Fitzsimmons Gen. Hosp., Denver, 1967-69, chief dept. surgery, 1969-71; pvt. practice surgery Warwick, RI, 1975-86; sr. med. dir. various insurance co.; med. dir. The Health Plan of the Upper Ohio Valley, 1996—2003. Asst. clin. prof. U. Colo., 1967-71; assoc. clin. prof. surgery Northwestern U., Chgo., 1973-80; mem. staff Kent County Med. Mem. Hosp., Warwick, 1975-86, Miriam hosp., Providence, 1975-86; cons. in field. Contbr. articles to profl. jours. Col. MC US Army, 1949—72. Decorated Legion of Merit. Fellow ACS, Am. Coll. Cardiology, Am. Coll. Chest Physicians; mem. Soc. Thoracic Surgeons. Avocation: downhill skiing. Home: 218 Salem Dr Upper Saint Clair PA 15241-2226 Personal E-mail: braymond66@adelphia.net.

RAYMOND, DAVID WALKER, lawyer; b. Chelsea, Mass., Aug. 23, 1945; s. John Walker and Jane (Beck) R.; m. Sandra Sue Broadwater, Aug. 12, 1967 (div.); m. Margaret Byrd Payne, May 25, 1974; children: Pamela Payne, Russell Wyatt. BA, Gettysburg Coll., 1967; JD, Temple U., 1970. Bar: Pa. 1970, D.C. 1971, Ill. 1975, U.S. Dist. Ct. (no. dist.) Ill. 1981, U.S. Supreme Ct. 1974. Govtl. affairs atty. Sears, Roebuck and Co., Washington, 1970-74, atty. Sears Hdqrs. law dept. Chgo., 1974-80, asst. gen. counsel advt., trademarks and customs, 1981-84, asst. gen. counsel adminstrn., 1984-86, mgr. planning and analysis corp. planning dept., 1986-89, sr. corp. counsel pub. policy corp. law dept., 1989-90; assoc. gen. counsel litigation and adminstrn. law dept. Sears Mdse. Group, 1990-92, dep. gen. counsel, 1992-93, v.p., gen. counsel, 1993-95; v.p. law Sears Roebuck and Co., 1996; of counsel Winston & Strawn, Washington, 1996-2001; v.p., gen. counsel C-NAV Systems, Inc., Gettysburg, Pa., 2001—03. Mem. staff Temple Law Quar., 1968—69; editor: Temple Law Quar., 1969—70. Trustee No. Ill. U., 1996—98; bd. vis. Christopher Newport U., 1999—2003; bd. fellows Gettysburg Coll., 1999—2003; bd. dirs. ATO House Corp., 1997—, pres., 2004—. Mem.: ABA, Phi Alpha Delta. Presbyterian. Personal E-mail: dwraymond74@cox.net.

RAYMOND, DOROTHY SARNOFF, communications consultant, former actress, former singer; b. NYC; d. Jacob and Belle (Roossin) S.; m. Milton Harold Raymond, Mar. 15, 1957. BA, Cornell U., 1935. Cons. 5 adminstrns., over 12 years; cons. 5 adminstrns. U.S. Dept. State; founder, chmn. Dorothy Sarnoff Speech Dynamics and Communications Svcs. Inc. subs. Oglivy & Mather, NYC, 1975—2000. Lectr., cons. nat. and internat. orgns., 1975—. Appeared in Broadway plays: Rosalinda, 1942, Magdalena, 1948, The King and I, 1951, My Darling Aida, 1953; debut in opera as Marquerite in Faust, Phila. Opera, 1942; leading roles with N.Y.C., Phila., L.A. and San Francisco Civic Light, New Orleans, St. Louis Mcpl., Salt Lake City operas include La Boheme, Tosca, Tales of Hoffmann, Carmen, Merry Widow, Fleidermaus, Pagliacci, New Moon, Chocolate Soldier, Great Waltz, Vagabond King; soprano soloist with various symphony orchs., soloist and guest on numerous TV programs incl. Ed Sullivan Shows, 1951—; author: Speech Can Change Your Life, 1970, Make the Most of Your Best, 1981, Never Be Nervous Again, 1988, contbr. articles to profl. jours. and mags. Mem. spl. med. adv. bd. N.Y. Cornell Hosp. Recipient Gold Medal of Honor award for disting. svc. to humanity Nat. Inst. Social Scis.; named Woman of Achievement Albert Einstein Med. Coll. Mem. Women's Forum, Women in Communication, Mortar Bd., Tower Club (Cornell U. chpt.), Lotos Club, N.Y. Hosp. Med. Adv. Bd. Home: 150 E 69th St New York NY 10021-5704

RAYMOND, GEORGE MARC, city planner, educator; b. Odessa, Russia, Jan. 1, 1919; came to U.S., 1937, naturalized, 1942; s. Mark J. and Rachelle (Schneiderman) R.; m. Kathleen E. Waid, Oct. 3, 1942 (div. Mar. 1978); 1 dau., Valerie M.; m. Lois Jean Gainsboro, Mar. 26, 1979. BArch, Columbia, 1946. Planning dir. Harrison, Ballard & Allen, Inc., NYC, 1952-54; founder, pres. Raymond, Parish, Pine & Weiner, Inc., 1954-83; pres. George M. Raymond Assocs., 1983—2006; prof. planning, chmn. dept. city and regional planning Pratt Inst., Bklyn., 1959-75; founder, dir. Pratt Ctr. for Community Improvement, Bklyn., 1963-70. Lectr. planning Columbia U., 1955-58; lectr. planning and urban renewal New Sch. Social Rsch., 1967-72; pres. Assn. Collegiate Sch. Planning, 1968-69; chmn. Westchester County Housing Implementation Commn., 1992-93. Editor: Pratt Planning Papers, 1963-73, (with Astrid Monson) Pratt Guide to Housing, Planning and Urban Renewal for New Yorkers, 1965. V.p. Citizens Housing and Planning Coun. N.Y.C., 1967-86, N.Y. Assn. Environ. Profls., 1977-79; pres. Westchester Citizens Housing Coun., 1964-66, Met. Com. on Planning, 1950-51; founder, pres. Friends of Music Concerts, 1954-57, Spoken Arts Soc., 1966-67; past 1st v.p. Federated Conservationists Westchester County; past dir. Nat. Housing Conf., Phipps Houses, Wave Hill, Settlement Housing Fund; chmn. Westchester County Housing Opportunity Commn., 1994—; land use adv. com. N.Y. State Legis. Commn. on Rural Resources, 1992-98. Fellow: Am. Inst. Cert. Planners; mem.: Am. Planning Assn. (pres. NY met. chpt. 1983—85), Am. Soc. Cons. Planners (pres. 1968—70). Home: 192 Locust Ln Irvington NY 10533-2315 Office: 101 Executive Blvd Elmsford NY 10523-1316

RAYMOND, KAY E(NGELMANN), Spanish language educator, consultant; b. Cin., Feb. 1, 1939; d. Gerson Silas and Pauline Coleman (Early) Engelmann; m. Ralph Raymond II, Feb. 1, 1964 (div. Nov. 1977); 1 child, Jenifer Kay Raymond-Judy. AB magna cum laude, Radcliffe Coll., 1961; MA, Brown U., Providence, 1964; PhD, Ind. U., 1983. Lectr. Boston U., 1965—68, Assumption Coll., Worcester, 1965—67; instr. Regis Coll., Weston, 1967—71; assoc. instr. Ind. U., Bloomington, 1972—83; lectr. Emporia State U., Kans., 1983—84; asst. prof. U. Ala., Huntsville, 1984—89, Sam Houston State U., Huntsville, 1989—94, assoc. prof., 1995—, coord. fgn. langs., 1995—98. Adv. fgn. lang. program Sam Houston State U., Huntsville, Tex., 2004—. Advisor Internat. Hispanic Assn., Sam Houston State U., 1990—; vol. translator City of Huntsville, 1993-98. Named Top Prof Sam Houston State U. Bapt. Student Ministry, 1996, Outstanding Advisor Internat. Hispanic Assn., 1996-97, Sammy award Sam Houston State U. Student Activities, 2003. Mem.: Tex. Fgn. Lang. Assn., Tex. Assn. Coll. and Univ. Lang. Suprs., Harvard Univ. Club Houston (schs. and scholarship com. 1997—), Sigma Delta Pi, Pi Delta Phi, Phi Sigma Iota. Home: 3644 Youpon Ln Huntsville TX 77340-8920 Office: Sam Houston State U Dept Fgn Langs PO Box 2147 Huntsville TX 77341-2147 Office Phone: 936-294-1444. Business E-Mail: fol_ker@shsu.edu.

RAYMOND, KENNETH NORMAN, chemistry professor, researcher; b. Astoria, Oreg., Jan. 7, 1942; s. George Norman and Helen May (Dunn) R.; m. Jane Galbraith Shell, June 19, 1965 (div. 1976); children: Mary Katherine, Alan Norman; m. Barbara Gabriele Sternitzke, June 17, 1977; children: Gabriella Petra, Christopher Norman. BA, Reed Coll., 1964; PhD, Northwestern U., 1968. Asst. prof. chemistry U. Calif.-Berkeley, 1967-74, assoc. prof., 1974-78, prof., 1978—; vice chmn. dept. U. Calif. Berkeley, 1982-84, 1999—2000, chmn., 1993-96; faculty sr. scientist Lawrence Berkeley Lab., 1996—; dir. Seaborg Ctr., 2002—. Mem. study sect. NIH, 1983—86, 2006—; adv. com. NSF, 1985—87; co-chmn. bd. chem. scis. & tech. NRC, 2000—; co-founder Lumiphore, Inc., 2001; Chancellor's prof. U. Calif., Berkeley, 2007—. Editor: Bioinorganic Chemistry II, 1977; assoc. editor Biology of Metals, 1987-91; editl. bd. Inorganic Chemistry, 1976-86, Accounts Chem. Rsch., 1982-90, Inorganica Chemica Acta f-Block Elements, 1984-90, Jour. Coordination Chemistry, 1981-2003, Jour. Inorganic and Nuclear Chemistry, 1974-81, Jour. Am. Chem. Soc., 1983-95, Topics in Current Chemistry, 1981-97, Metals in Biology, 1993—, Jour. Supramolecular Chemistry, 1992—, Jour. Biol. Inorganic Chemistry, 1996-2004, Procs. NAS USA, 2002-04, Accts. Chem. Rsch., 1982-88, 2005—; US editl. advisor Springer-Verlag in Chemistry, 1972-91; contbr. articles to profl. jours.; author more than 400 papers. Alfred P. Sloan rsch. fellow, 1971-73; Miller rsch. prof., 1977-78, 96, 2004; Guggenheim fellow, 1980-81; recipient E.O. Lawrence award Dept. Energy, 1984, Humboldt Rsch. award for U.S. Scientists, 1992, 2000, Alfred R. Bader award Am. Chem. Soc., 1994, Vollum award Reed Coll., 2002, Izatt/Christensen award, 2005. Mem. NAS, Am. Acad. Arts and Scis., Am. Chem. Soc. (chair divsn. inorganic chemistry 1996), Am. Crystallographic Soc., Sigma Xi. Democrat. Achievements include 15 patents in field. Office: U Calif Berkeley Dept Chemistry Berkeley CA 94720-1460 E-mail: raymond@socrates.berkeley.edu.

RAYMOND, LEE R., retired oil company executive; b. Watertown, SD, Aug. 13, 1938; m. Charlene Raymond, 1960. BSChemE, U. Wis., 1960; PhD ChemE, U. Minn., 1963, LLD (hon.), 2001. Joined Exxon Corp., Tulsa, Okla., 1963; various positions Exxon Co. USA and Creole Petroleum Corp., Houston and Caracas, Venezuela, 1963—72; mgr. planning Exxon Internat. Co., NYC, 1972—75; v.p. Lago Oil, Aruba, 1975—76, pres., 1976—79, Exxon Nuclear Co., Inc., Bellevue, Wash., 1979—81; exec. v.p. Exxon Enterprises Inc., NYC, 1981—83; pres. Esso Inter-Am. Inc., Coral Gables, Fla., 1983—84; sr. v.p. Exxon Corp., NYC, 1984—86, pres., 1987—93, 1996—99, chmn., CEO, 1993—99, Exxon Mobil Corp., Irving, Tex., 1999—2006; chmn. Nat. Petroleum Coun., Washington, 2006—. Bd. dirs. Exxon Corp., 1984—99, ExxonMobil Corp., 1999—2005, J.P. Morgan & Co., Inc., NYC, 1987—2000; co-chmn. corp. governance and nominating com., mem. compensation and mgmt. develop. com. J.P. Morgan and Co., Inc., NYC; bd. dirs. Morgan Guaranty Trust Co. of N.Y., NYC; bd. dirs., mem. exec. and policy coms. Am. Petroleum Inst., 1987—; mem. Emergency Com. for Am. Trade, President's Export Coun.; vice chmn. bd. trustees Am. Enterprise Inst. Bd. dirs. United Negro Coll. Fund, 1991—; mem. adv. bd. Project Shelter Pro-Am, Sect. Energy; trustee Wis. Alumni Rsch. Found., 1987—; bd. dirs., hon. trustee bus. coun. Internat. Understanding, Inc.; mem. innovations in medicine leadership coun. U. Tex. Southwestern Med. Ctr.; ptnr. emeritus N.Y.C. Partnership; vice chmn., bd. trustee Am. Enterprise Inst., Washington; mem. Dallas Citizens Coun., U. Wis. Found., Am. Coun. on Germany, Dallas Com. Fgn. Rels., Coun. on Fgn. Rels., Emergency Com. for Am. Trade, Singapore-US Bus. Coun., Trilateral Commn. Mem.: Am. Inst. Chem. Engrs. (mem. exec. com. of the 21st Century Campaign), Trilateral Commn., Occupl. Physicians Scholarship Fund (chmn. fundraising campaign 1995), Am. Soc. Engring. Edn. (nat. adv. coun.), Singapore-U.S. Bus. Coun., Coun. Fgn. Rels., Nat. Petroleum Coun. (mem. nom. and natural gas coms.), Bus. Roundtable (mem. policy com., security task force, taxation task force, govt. rels. working group), Bus. Coun., NAE. Office: The Nat Petroleum Coun 1625 K St NW Ste 600 Washington DC 20006 *

RAYMOND, LISA, professional tennis player; b. Norristown, Pa., Aug. 10, 1973; d. Ted and Nancy Raymond. Student, U. Fla. Profl. tennis player WTA Tour, 1993—. Mem. US Fed Cup Team, 1997—98, 2000, 2002—03. Recipient 4 Career singles title, 65 Career Doubles Titles, WTA Tour, 1 career doubles title, ITF; winner US Open, 1996, 2002, Wimbledon, 1999, Australian Open Grand Slam doubles, 2000, Wimbledon, 2001, US Open Grand Slam doubles, 2001, WTA Doubles Championship, 2001, Mixed Doubles Roland Garros, 2003; named NCAA Singles Champion, 1992, 1993; named Doubles Team of Yr., WTA 2006 Player Awards. Avocations: shopping, hanging out with friends, watching television, football, volleyball.

RAYMOND, RICHARD GERARD, JR., lawyer; b. Detroit, Jan. 1, 1959; s. Richard G. Raymond Sr. and Mary Jo (Bradley) Raymond; m. Holly Lyn Russell, Aug. 4, 1984; 3 children. BS in chemistry, U. Mich., 1981; JD, U. Detroit, 1986. Bar: Mich. 1986, US Dist. Ct. Ea. Dist. Mich. 1986. Indsl. chemist Product-Sol Inc., Birmingham, Mich., 1982-83; assoc. Johnson & Valentine, Detroit, 1986—89; asst. gen. counsel Fruehauf Trailer Corp., 1989; assoc. gen. counsel, asst. sec. Gen. Automotive Corp.; corp. counsel Am. Axle & Mfg. Holdings Inc., 1995—2000, gen. counsel, 2000—. Mem. ABA, Mich. Bar Assn., Detroit Bar Assn., Am. Chem. Soc. Roman Catholic. Office: Am Axle & Mfg Holdings Inc 1840 Holbrook Ave Detroit MI 48212 *

RAYMOND, URAL WAYNE, retired retail executive; b. Missoula, Mont., May 20, 1944; s. Ural Daniel and Fayetta Arilla Raymond. Student, U. NC, 1969-70, U. Mont., 1962-66, 93-94. Enlisted man U.S. Army, 1966-69, 70-89; advanced through grades to master sgt. U.S. Army, 1985; ret., 1989; advt. mgr. Sears & Roebuck, Missoula, 1993-99; ret., 1999. Chmn. western dist. Am. Legion Baseball, Missoula, 1997—; pres. Friends of the Libr., Missoula, 1997-99. With U.S. Army, 1966-69. Decorated Bronze Star. Mem. Nev. Internat. Lic. Plate Soc. (treas. state br. 1998—). Democrat. Evangelical. Avocations: collecting license plates, collecting flags, baseball, collecting stamps, collecting coins.

RAYMOND, USHER, IV, (USHER), vocalist, actor; b. Chattanooga, Tenn., Oct. 14, 1978; s. Jonnetta Patton and Usher Raymond; m. Tameka Foster, Aug. 3, 2007. Co-owner Cleve. Cavaliers NBA team. Singer: (albums) Usher, 1994, My Way, 1997 (Soul Train award Best R&B/Soul Single for "You Make Me Wanna", 1998), Live, 1999, All About U, 2000, 8701, 2001 (Grammy award Best Male R&B Vocal Performance, 2001, 2002, Platinum 7 times), Confessions, 2004 (MTV Video Music award Best Dance Video for song "Yeah!", 2004, MTV Video Music award Best Male Video for the song "Yeah!", 2004, Am. Music Award Favorite Album Pop or Rock, 2004, Am. Music Award Favorite Album Soul/Rhythm & Blues Music, 2004, Billboard 200 Album of Yr., 2004, Hot 100 Single of the Yr.: "Yeah!", Billboard Music Awards, 2004, Hot 100 Airplay Single of Yr.: "Yeah!", Billboard Music Awards, 2004, Mainstream Top 40 Single of Yr.:"Yeah!", Billboard Music Awards, 2004, R&B/Hip Hop Album of Yr., Billboard Music Awards, 2004), In the Mix soundtrack, 2005; actor: (films) The Faculty, 1998, She's All That, 1999, Light It Up, 1999, Texas Rangers, 2001, In the Mix, 2005; (TV films) Gepetto, 2000; (TV series) Moesha, 1997—98, The Bold and the Beautiful, 1998, (TV guest appearances) The Famous Jett Jackson, 2000, Sabrina the Teenage Witch, 2002, The Twilight Zone, 2002, American Dreams, 2002, 7th Heaven, 2002, Soul Food, 2003; (Broadway plays) Chicago, 2006—. Named Artist of Yr., Billboard Music Awards, 1998, 2004, Mainstream Top 40 Artist of Yr., 2004, Hot 100 Artist of Yr., 2004, Billboard 200 Artist of Yr., 2004, Artist of Yr., Radio Music Awards, 2004; recipient Pop Music award, ASCAP, 2003, Favorite Male Artist award Pop or Rock, Am. Music Awards, 2004, Favorite Male Artist award Soul/Rhythm & Blues Music, 2004, R&B/Hip Hop Artist of Yr., Billboard Music Awards, 2004, R&B/Hip-Hop Albums Artist of Yr., 2004, Male Entertainer of Yr., World Music Awards, 2005. Achievements include First place on the Star Search TV talent series, 1992. Mailing: c/o JPat Mgmt 3996 Pleasantdale Rd # 104A Atlanta GA 30340 *

RAYMUND, STEVEN A., computer company executive; b. Van Nuys, Calif., Nov. 16, 1955; s. Edward C. and Annette Leah Raymund. BS in Economics, U. Oreg., 1978; MA in Internat. Polit., Georgetown U. Sch. Fgn. Svc., 1980. With Manufacturers Hanover Corp., NYC, 1980—81; ops. mgr. Tech Data Corp., 1981—84, COO, 1984—86, CEO, 1986—2006, chmn., 1991—2006, non-exec. chmn., 2006—. Bd. dir. Jabil Circuit. Named Entrepreneur of the Yr., Arthur Young Entrepreneurial

Services, 1988; named one of 25 Most Influential Executives in the PC Industry, Computer Reseller News, 1989—2004; named to Industry Hall of Fame, 1999. Office: Tech Data Corp 5350 Tech Data Dr Clearwater FL 33760-3122 *

RAYNAL, LAZAR POL, lawyer; b. 1963; BS, U. Wis., 1985; JD cum laude, U. Notre Dame, 1988. Bar: Ill. 1988, US Dist. Ct. (no. dist. Ill.), US Ct. Appeals (7th & 10th cirs.), US Supreme Ct. Ptnr. McDermott, Will & Emery, Chgo., co-chair Trust & Estate Controversy practice. Named one of Litig.'s Rising Stars, The Am. Lawyer, 2007. Mem.: Def. Rsch. Inst., Fed. Defender Prog. Panel No. Ill. Office: McDermott Will & Emery 227 W Monroe St Chicago IL 60606-5096 Office Phone: 312-984-3653. Office Fax: 312-984-7700. E-mail: lraynal@mwe.com. *

RAYNAULD, ANDRE, economist, educator; b. Quebec, Can., Oct. 20, 1927; s. Léopold and Blanche (Gauthier) R.; m. Michelle Nolin, Oct. 15, 1951; children: Francoy, Olivier, Dominique, Isabelle. BA cum laude, U. Montreal, 1948, MA in Indsl. Rels. magna cum laude, 1951; D. in Econs., U. Paris, 1954; D. in Econs. (hon.), U. Ottawa, 1976, U. Sherbrooke, 1976. Mem. faculty U. Montreal, 1954-71, founder, dir. Ctr. Econ. Research and Devel., 1970-72; vis. prof. U. Toronto, 1962-63; chmn. Economic Council Can., Ottawa, 1971-76; mem. Que. Nat. Assembly, Montreal, 1976-80; prof. U. Montreal, 1980-93, prof. emeritus, 1993—. Exec. com. Can. Social Sci. Rsch. Coun., 1961-63, 64-65; pres. Inst. Canadien Affaires Publiques, 1961-62; bd. govs. Can. Labour Coll., 1962-66; dir., exec. com. CBC, 1964-67; trustee CBC Pension Fund, 1967-70; pres. Soc. Canadienne de Sci. Economique, 1967-69; mem. Royal Commn. Bilingualism and Biculturalism, 1969-70, Can. Coun. Urban and Regional Rsch., 1971, Quebec Coun. Planning and Devel., 1971; chmn. com. inquiry French-lang. tchr.-tng. Western provinces Dept. Sec. State, 1971; interfutures study group OECD, Paris, 1976-78; bd. dirs. Inst. Rsch. Pub. Policy, 1980—; rsch. fellow Devel. Ctr. OECD, Paris, 1986—; invited prof. College de France, Paris, 1987. Author: Economic Growth in Quebec, 1961, The Canadian Economic System, 1967, La propriete des entreprises au Quebec, 1974, Institutions Economiques Canadiennes, 2d edition, 1977, Le financement des exportations, 1979, Government Assistance to Export Financing, 1984, The External Financing of Tunisia's Imports, OECD, 1988, Financing Exports to Developing Countries, OECD, 1992; co-editor: Economic Integration in Europe and North America, 1992, Labour Standards and International Competitiveness, 1998; co-author: L'Etat Providence des Entreprises, 1999; editor Can. Jour. Econs., 1965-70. Recipient ann. award des Diplomes de l'U. de Montreal, 1974; apptd. Officer of Order of Can., 1986; fellow Walter Levy Coun. on Fgn. Rels., Boston, 1977. Fellow Royal Soc. Can.; mem. Can. Econs. Assn. (pres. 1983-84), Am. Econs. Assn., Atlantic Econ. Soc. (distng. assoc.). Liberal. Roman Catholic. Home: 4820 Roslyn St Montreal PQ Canada H3W 2L2

RAYNER, ARNO ALFRED, investment company executive, consultant; b. San Francisco, Sept. 23, 1928; BS in Econs., U. Calif., Berkeley, 1949, MBA, 1954. Security analyst Bank of Calif., San Francisco, 1950—54; various positions to sr. v.p. Indsl. Indemnity, San Francisco, 1954—74; v.p. internat. svcs. Bechtel Group, San Francisco, 1975—76; pres. Rayner & Haynor, Mill Valley, Calif., 1977—99, chmn. bd., 1999—; pres. Raynor Found. Recipient Investment prof. of the yr., San Francisco Bond Club, 1999, Disting. Citizen of the Yr., Marin Coun. Boy Scouts of Am., 2000. Mem.: Security Analysts (San Francisco) (life). Home: 7 Venado Dr Belvedere Tiburon CA 94920-1625 E-mail: arnorayner@aol.com.

RAYNER, VICTORIA LEIGH, medical educator, consultant; b. Sacramento, Mar. 6, 1954; d. Harold Edward Rayner and Angela Jane Allitore; m. Vallucci Rayner, July 20, 1997. BA, Coll. of Marin, 1974; AA in Bus. Studies, Highline CC, Seattle, 1976. Lic. post-secondary instr. Calif., 1995, continuing edn. instr. Calif. Bd. of Registered Nursing, 1996. Founder and pres. Bay Area Skin Assn., San Francisco, 1981; founder and dir. Ctr. Appearance and Esteem, 1987; founder Camouflage Therapy Clinic, dept. dermatology San Francisco Gen. Hosp., 1987, clin. assoc. Camouflage Therapy Clinic, 1986—; clin. assoc. Alta Bates Hosp., Berkeley; founder Rayner Inst. Career Advancement, Washington; owner Creative Career Bldg. Inst. Contbg. mem. and presenter U. Calif. Arts and Lectrs., San Francisco, 1988—; adv. bd. Dermascope, Sunnyvale, Tex., 1990—, Les Nouvelle Esthetique, Coral Gables, Fla., 1990—; adv. com. rsch. divsn. Almay Cosmetics, Oxford, NC, 1992—93; cons. and rep. Nat. Assn. Women in Bus., mem. public rels. com., 1993—95; founder Women's Forum for Discussion Group, San Francisco, 1996; spokesperson Fibroid Ctr. Wash. Med. Ctr.; lectr. on med. esthetics; presenter in field. Author: Clin. Cosmetology; A Med. Approach to Aesthetic Procedures, 1993, A Survival Guide for Today's Career Woman, 1994; columnist Skin Inc. Mag.; contbr. articles to profl. jours., chapters to books. Hon. chmn. Bus. Adv. Coun., Washington, 2005; leader medical esthetics trng. and care Task Force Legis. Reform of Patients' Rights, Sacramento, 1993—95; bd. dirs. Alissa Ann Ruch Burn Found., San Francisco, 1991—93. Recipient For Those Who Care Vol. award, KRON-TV, 1989, Merit award, Commn. on Status of Women of City and County of San Francisco, 1993, Contribn. to Cosmetology, Internat. Congress of Esthetics, 2003. Mem.: NAFE, Am. Med. Women Assn. (author online distance edn. course 2006), Nat. Cosmetology Esthetic Assn., Am. Soc. Plastic Surgery Skin Care Specialists, Dermatology Nursing Assn. Independent. Roman Catholic. Achievements include development of long distance learning programs in esthetic procedures; women over forty, reentry career devel. programs; four outpatient cosmetic rehabilitation clinics for women and children. Avocations: interior design, cooking, reading, painting. Office: Rayner Inst for Career Advancement #300 1201 Penn Ave NW Washington DC 20004 Office Phone: 202-667-9596. Fax: 202-667-6297. Personal E-mail: victoriarayner@hotmail.com.

RAYNER, WILLIAM ALEXANDER, retired newspaper editor, author; b. Winnipeg, Man., Can., Nov. 7, 1929; s. William and Annie Mitchell (McDonald) R.; divorced; 1 child, Robert William. Student Can. schs. Sports editor Trail Times, B.C., 1954-55; sportswriter Victoria (B.C.) Times, 1955-57, Vancouver (B.C.) Herald, 1957; copy editor, reporter Montreal (Que.) Star, 1957-58; asst. sports editor Vancouver Sun, 1958-62, copy editor, then slotman, 1962-74, news editor, 1974-83, systems mgr., 1983-88, ret., 1988; copy editor Toronto Globe & Mail, 1962. Author: Vancouver Sun Style Guide, 1976, Images of History - Twentieth Century British Columbia Through the Front Pages, 1997, British Columbia's Premiers in Profile-The Good, The Bad and the Transient, 2000, Scandal! 130 Years of Damnable Deeds in Canada's Lotus Land, 2001, The Canadian Journey - Provocative Glimpses into Canada's Past, 2006. Dir. B.C. Newspaper Found. Mem. Writers Union Can. Personal E-mail: wrayner@telus.net.

RAYNOLDS, DAVID ROBERT, buffalo breeder, writer; b. NY, Feb. 15, 1928; s. Robert Frederick and Marguerite Evelyn (Gerdau) R.; m. May (Kean) Raynolds, May 12, 1951; children: Robert, Linda, Martha, Laura, David A.F. AB, Dartmouth Coll., 1949; MA, Wesleyan U., Middletown, Conn., 1955; predoctoral, Johns Hopkins Sch. Advanced Internat. Studies, Washington, 1956; grad., Nat. War Coll., Washington, 1973. Account exec. R.H. Morris Assoc., Newtown, Conn., 1949-50; fgn. svc. officer Dept. of State, Washington, 1956-76; pres. Ranch Rangers, Inc., Lander, Wyo., 1976—. Pres. Nat. Buffalo Assn., Ft. Pierre, S.D., 1987-88. Author: Rapid Development in Small Economies (Praeger); contbr. articles to profl. jours. Trustee, bd. dirs. Liberty Hall Found.; dir. Leader Corp.; mem. steering com. Wyo. Bus. Alliance; chmn. bd. govs. Mus. of the Am. West. With US Army, 1950—53. Recipient Meritorious Svc. Award, Dept. of State, Washington, 1966. Mem. The Explorers Club, Dacor Assn., Fremont County Farm Bur., Fgn. Svc. Assn., Am. Legion, Rotary, Elks. Republican. Episcopalian. Avocation: travel. Office: Table Mountain Group PO Box 1310 Lander WY 82520-1310

RAYNOLDS, ELAINE SPALDING, sales executive, photojournalist; b. Flushing, NY, June 26, 1940; d. John Arpad and Thelma Smith Rado; m. Arthur Reginald Raynolds, Nov. 21, 1992; m. Larry Lee Spalding (div.); children: Timothy A. Spalding, Linda Spalding Morrison. Student, Coll. Wooster, Ohio, 1959—60, NYU, NYC, 1961—62. Administrv. asst. Bus. Internat., NYC, 1960—64; pub. rels. staff Duke Med. Ctr., Durham, NC, 1967—70; sales exec. Seyforth Labs., Clearwater, 1975—95; adminstrv. aide Pinellas County, Clearwater, Fla., 1980—90; sales exec. Herbalife Internat., Lake Toxaway, NC, 1995—. Photojournalist Mountain Voice, Lake Toxaway, 2004—. Musician: Brevard (N.C.) Cmty. Band, 2003—04; co-author: Art on a Shoestring. Mem. Brevard C. of C., NC. Mem.: Nat. Mus. Women in the Arts, Friends Libr., Transylvania Arts Coun., Transylvania Choral Soc. (treas. 2003—). Avocations: travel, photography, music, nature, wildlife. Home: PO Box 334 Lake Toxaway NC 28747 Personal E-mail: eraynolds@citcom.net.

RAYNOR, BRUCE S., labor union administrator; m. Joan Raynor; children: Alvin Carter, Kudjo Sogadzi, Candice, Robin Sydney. Grad., Cornell U., 1972. Edn. dir. edn. dept. Textile Workers Union Am., 1973, edn. dir., 1974; so. regional dir., internat. v.p. Amalgamated Clothing and Textile Workers Union, 1981, exec. v.p., 1993, Union Needletrades, Indusl., and Textile Employees, 1995, sec.-treas., 1998; pres. Union Needletrades, Indusl., and Textile Employees (now UNITE HERE!), 2001—. Mem. bd. trustees N.Y. State Statutory Affairs Com. Cornell U., 1989; v.p. AFL-CIO, mem. exec. bd. Pres. The Sidney Hillman Found.; bd. trustees Cornell U., adv. bd., Sch. Indsl. and Labor Rels. Recipient Groat award for disting. alumni, Sch. Indsl. and Labor Rels., Cornell U., 1999. Mem.: Cornell Sch Indusl. and Labor Rels. (mem adv. com.). Office: 275 7th Ave Fl 11 New York NY 10001-6708 *

RAYNOR, EILEEN MARGOLIES, otolaryngologist, educator; b. NYC, Feb. 11, 1965; d. Allan Fred and Noemi (Schmerz) Margolies; m. Dewey Lee Raynor, Jr., Nov. 9, 1991; children: Stephanie Dianne, Logan Foster. AB in Chemistry, Duke U., 1987; MD, U. N.C., 1993. Cert. Am. Bd. Otolaryngology. Resident otolaryngology Med. Coll. Ga., Augusta, 1993—98; asst. prof. otolaryngology U. Fla., Jacksonville, 1998—2006, assoc. prof., 2006—. Cons. Medimetrics Corp., Jacksonville, Fla., 1999—; med. dir. Pediat. Hearing Program, Jacksonville, 2000—; mem. Cleft Palate Team Childrens Med. Svcs., Jacksonville, 2000—. Contbr. articles to profl. jours., chapters to books. Recipient Nat. Leadership award, Rep. Nat. Com., 2003; Deafness Rsch. Found. rsch. grantee, 1991. Fellow: Am. Acad. Otolaryngology (cmty., acad. rels. com. 2002—); mem.: AMA, Assn. for Rsch. in Otolaryngology, Triological Soc. (James Harrell award So. sect. 1997), Am. Acad. Facial Plastic Surgery, Duke Alumni Club (bd. dirs. 2000—). Avocations: cooking, skiing, photography, jewelry design. Home: 1031 River Oaks Rd Jacksonville FL 32207 Office: U Fla Jacksonville 653-2 W 8th St Jacksonville FL 32209 Office Phone: 904-244-3498. E-mail: eileen.raynor@jax.ufl.edu.

RAYNOR, RICHARD BENJAMIN, neurosurgeon, educator; b. NYC, Aug. 16, 1928; s. Murray and Mildred (Pitt) R.; m. Barbara Golob; children: Geoffrey, Michele. BSME, U. Mich., 1950; MD, U. Vt., 1955. Diplomate Am. Bd. Neurol. Surgery. Intern Mt. Sinai, NYC, 1955-56; residency Neurol. Inst. Presbyn. Hosp., NYC, 1956-57, Nat. Hosp., London, 1957; residency neurosurgery Neurol. Inst. Presbyn. Hosp., 1958-62; assoc. in neurosurgery Coll. Physicians and Surgeons Columbia U., NYC, 1965-77; clin. assoc. prof. NYU, NYC, 1977-2000, clin. prof., 1984—. Pvt. practice neurosurgery, N.Y.C., 1965—. Cons. editor Spine; contbr. over 50 articles to profl. jours., chpts. to books. Served as capt. U.S. Army, 1962-64. Fellow Am. Coll. Surgeons; mem. Cervical Spine Research Soc. (pres. 1986-87), Am. Assn. Neurol. Surgeons, Congress Neurol. Surgeons. Clubs: University (N.Y.C.). Avocations: skiing, squash. Office: 112 E 74th St New York NY 10021-3535 Office Phone: 212-535-1255.

RAYNOVICH, GEORGE, JR., retired lawyer; b. Pitts., Dec. 30, 1931; s. George Sr. and Zora (Mamula) R.; m. Mary Ann Senay, July 11, 1953; children: George III, Andrew. BS, U. Pitts., 1957; JD, Duquesne U., 1961. Bar: Pa. 1962, U.S. Dist. Ct. (we. dist.) Pa. 1962, U.S. Patent and Trademark Office 1962, U.S. Supreme Ct. 1966, U.S. Ct. Appeals (fed. cir.) 1986. Patent agt. Consolidation Coal Co., Library, Pa., 1959-62; ptnr. Stone & Raynovich, Pitts., 1962-75; atty. Wheeling-Pitts. Steel Corp., Pitts., 1975-77, gen. counsel, sec., 1978-85, v.p., 1980-85; sr. atty. Buchanan Ingersoll P.C., Pitts., 1986-88, 89-96; ptnr. Price & Raynovich, Pitts., 1988-89; of counsel Gorr Moser Dell and Loughney, Pitts., 1997-2000, Paul A. Beck and Assocs., Pitts., 2001—04; ret., 2004. Councilman Borough of Baldwin, Allegheny County, Pa., 1972-75, govt. study commr., 1973. 1st lt. USAF, 1952-56. Mem. Allegheny County Bar Assn., Pitts. Intellectual Property Law Assn., Acad. Trial Lawyers Allegheny County. Democrat. Mem. Serbian Orthodox Ch. Home: 335 Jean Dr Pittsburgh PA 15236-2511

RAYSON, GARY DONN, chemistry educator; s. Ralph LeRoy and Muriel Rayson; m. Jenny Ruth Moorer, June 18, 1988. BS, Baker U., 1979; PhD, U. Tex., Austin, 1983. Teaching asst. U. Tex., Austin, 1979-80, rsch. asst., 1980-83; rsch. assoc. Ind. U., Bloomington, 1983-86; asst. prof. N.Mex. State U., Las Cruces, 1986-93, assoc. prof., 1993—2005, prof., 2005—. Inventor in field. Mem. Am. Chem. Soc., Soc. Applied Spectroscopy, Optical Soc. Am. Republican. Methodist. Avocations: photography, camping, hiking,. Office: NM State U PO Box 30001 # 3C Las Cruces NM 88003-8001 Business E-Mail: garayson@nmsu.edu.

RAYSON, GLENDON ENNES, internist, preventive medicine specialist, writer; b. Oak Park, Ill., Dec. 2, 1915; s. Ennes Charles and Beatrice Margaret (Rowland) R.; m. Sarah Weida. AB, U. Rochester, NY, 1939; MD, U. Ill., Chgo., 1948; MPH, Johns Hopkins U., Balt., 1965; MA, Northwestern U., Evanston, Ill., 1965. Diplomate Am. Bd. Internal Medicine, Am. Bd. Preventive Medicine, Am. Bd. Forensic Medicine, Am. Bd. Forensic Examiners. Resident in internal medicine Presbyn.-St. Luke's Hosp., Chgo., 1953-56; physician-in-charge Contagious Disease Hosp., Chgo., 1956-58, asst. med. supt., 1958-64; rsch. assoc. Sch. Hygiene and Pub. Health Johns Hopkins U., Balt., 1966-71; internist Johns Hopkins Hosp., 1971-82, Columbia Free State Health Plan, Balt., 1984-91; pvt. practice Balt., 1984—; with Neurodiagnostics Assocs., 1990—2001. Attending internist emergency rm. South Balt. Gen. Hosp., 1982-84; asst. prof. health sci. U. Ill., Chgo., 1958-64; fellow in gastroenterology and endocrinology Presbyn.-St. Luke's Hosp., 1956-58. Contbr. articles to med. jours., chpt. to book. Vol. physician, Vietnam, 1968, 71, 72, 73; mem. Citizens Amb. Program Delegation to Vietnam, 1993. Capt. M.C., USAF, 1951-53. Fellow: Am. Acad. Cardiology, Am. Coll. Forensic Examiners Inst., Am. Col. Preventive Medicine, Am. Geriatrics Soc.; mem.: APHA, ACP-Am. Soc. Internal Medicine, AMA. Avocations: poetry, writing, composing songs. Office: 218 N Charles St Apt 1407 Baltimore MD 21201-4024 Office Phone: 410-547-8285.

RAYWARD, WARDEN BOYD, librarian, educator; b. Inverell, NSW, Australia, June 24, 1939; s. Warden and Ellie Rayward. BA, U. Sydney, 1960; diploma in libr., U. NSW, 1964; MS in L.S. U. Ill., 1965; PhD, U. Chgo., 1973. Asst. state library, NSW, 1961-64; research librarian planning and devel. NSW, 1970; lectr. Sch. Librarianship U. NSW, Sydney, 1971-72, head sch. Info., Libr. and Archive Studies, 1986-92, prof., 1986-00, dean Faculty Profl. Studies, 1993-96, prof. emeritus, 2000—; asst. prof. U. Western Ont., 1973-74, Grad. Library Sch. U. Chgo., 1975-77, assoc. prof., 1978-80, prof., 1980-86; dean U. Chgo. Grad. Library Sch., 1980-86; rsch. prof. U. Ill., Champaign, 2000—, prof., 2004—. Cons. NEH, 1976-79, U.S. Dept. Edn., 1981; bd. govs. Charles Stuart U., 1994-96; bd. dirs. Internat. House-U. NSW, 1992-97; George A. Miller vis. prof. U. Ill., 1997-98; Leverhulme Trust vis. prof. Leed Met. U., 2002; vis. prof. Leeds Met. U., 2004—. Author: The Universe of Information: The Work of Paul Otlet for Documentation and International Organization, 1975 (also transl. Russian and Spanish), Hasta la documentacion electronica, 2002; editor: The Variety of Librarianship: Essays in Honour of John Wallace Metcalfe, 1976, The Public Library: Circumstances and Prospects, 1978, Library Quar., 1975-79, Library History in Context, 1988, Libraries and Life in a Changing World: the Metcalfe Years 1920-1970, 1993; editor, translator: International Organization and the Dissemination of Knowledge: Selected Papers of Paul Otlet, 1990; editor Confronting the Future, University Libraries in the Next Decade, 1992, Developing a Profession in Librarianship in Australia: Travel Diaries and Other Papers of John Wallace Metcalfe, 1996, Aware and Responsible: Papers of The Nordic-International Colloquium (Scarlid), 2004; (with Christine Jenkins) Libraries in Time of War Revolution and Social Change; mem. editl. bd. World Book of Encyclopedia, 1990-97; co-editor: History and Heritage of Scientiful and Technological Information Systems, 2004; contbr. articles to profl. jours. Coun. on Library Resources fellow, 1978, vis. fellow U. Coll. London, 1986, 90, Mortenson fellow U. Ill., 1992-93, Garfield fellow in hist. sci. lit., 2000. Mem.: ALA, Union Internat. Assns., Am. Soc. Info. Sci. (Rsch. award 2004), Australian Libr. and Info. Assn. (hon.). Office: U Ill Grad Sch Libr and Info Scis 501 E Daniel St Champaign IL 61820-6211 Office Phone: 217-244-9741. Business E-Mail: wrayward@uiuc.edu.

RAZ, JOSEPH, philosophy and law educator; b. Haifa, Israel, Mar. 21, 1939; arrived in Great Britain, 1970; M in Juris summa cum laude, Hebrew U., Jerusalem, 1963; PhD, Oxford U., Eng., 1967; Doctorate (hon.), Cath. U., Brussels, 1993. Lectr. then sr. lectr. depts. law and philosophy Hebrew U., Jerusalem, 1967-72; fellow, tutor in law Balliol Coll., Oxford, 1972-85, fellow, 1985—2006; prof. philosophy of law Oxford U., 1985—2006, rsch. prof., 2006—. Author: (book) Practical Reason and Norms, 1975, The Authority of Law, 1979, The Concept of a Legal Sys., 1970—80, The Morality of Freedom, 1986, Practical Reason and Norms, 2d edit., 1990, Ethics in the Pub. Domain, 1995, Engaging Reason, 2000, Value, Respect and Attachment, 2001, The Practice of Value, 2003. Recipient The W.J.M. Mackenzie Book prize The Polit. Studies Assn. of the U.K., 1987, The Elaine and David Spitz Book prize The Conf. for the Study of Political Though, 1988, Internat. Hector Fix-Zamndio prize Legal Rsch. UNAM, Mexico City, 2005. Fellow Brit. Acad.; mem. Am. Acad. Arts and Scis. (fgn. hon.). Office: Balliol Coll Broad St Oxford OX1 3BJ England also: Columbia Law Sch 435 W 116th St New York NY 10027 Office Phone: 212-845-5191. E-mail: raz@law.columbia.edu.

RAZA, ASIM, psychiatrist; b. Rawalpindi, Pakistan, Apr. 27, 1958; s. Kamal and Sughra Raza. FSc, Sir Syed Sch. and Coll., Rawalpindi, 1975; BSc, B Medicine and Surgery, Rawalpindi Med. Coll., 1983. Diplomate Am. Bd. Psychiatry and Neurology. Intern dept. medicine Rawalpindi Gen. Hosp., 1983; med. officer dept. medicine Cantonment Gen. Hosp., Rawalpindi, 1984—91, med. officer outpatient dept., 1991—92; resident dept. psychiatry U. Mo. Sch. Medicine, Kansas City, 1993—97, chief resident dept. psychiatry, 1996—97; mem. staff Counseling Assocs., Inc., Conway, Ark., 1998—. Cons. in field; mem. spkrs. bur. Pfizer Inc., Wyeth Pharms., Sanofi-Aventis Pharms. Treas. Residents Assn. Western Mo., Kansas City, 1994—95, v.p., 1995—96, pres., 1996—97. Recipient Psychiatry Resident of Yr. award, Pfizer, 1997; fellow, Eli Lilly, 1994. Fellow: Am. Psychiat. Assn. (Wyeth Ayerst Resident Reporter 1996, mem.-in-tng. rep. Western Mo. br. 1996—97); mem.: Ark. Psychiat. Soc. Home: 1801 Champlin Dr 112 Little Rock AR 72223 Office Phone: 501-336-8300. Personal E-mail: selfless@sbcglobal.net.

RAZIQ, YAQUB, telecommunications engineer; b. Peshawar, Pakistan, Dec. 15, 1961; s. Yaqub Masih and Alice (Bibi) Yaqub; m. Kiran Raziq Gill, Nov. 9, 1989; children: Anita, Monica, Zimran BSc, U. Peshawar, Pakistan, 1981; BSc in engring. with honors, N.W. Frontier Province U. Engring. & Tech., Peshawar, 1985; MSc with honors, N.W. Frontier Province U. Engring & Tech., Peshawar, 1993; PhD, Keio U., Yokohama, Japan, 1998; MBA, Fairleigh Dickinson U., NJ, 2002—04. Aircraft engr. Pakistan Internat. Airlines, Karachi, 1986-87; shift engr. Pakistan Water & Power Devel. Authority, Peshawar, 1987-88; asst. divisional engr. Pakistan Telecom. Corp., Peshawar, 1988-98; rsch. engr. Nokia Rsch. Ctr., Tokyo, 1998-99; asst. mgr. DDI Corp., Japan, 1999-2001; rsch. dir. Toshiba Am. Rsch. Inc., Morristown, NJ, 2001—. Vis. rschr. Rikkyo U., Tokyo; tech. advisor Initiatives N.W.F.P. Pakistan for Hearing Impaired Children, Pehswar, 1991-93; participant, presenter IEEE Internat. Symposium on Info. Theory and its Applications, Victoria, Can., 1996, IEEE Internat. Conf. Comm., Montreal, 1997, Asia Pacific Symposium on Info. and Telecom. Tech., Vietnam, 1997, Internat. Conf. Telecom., Melbourne, Australia, 1997, IASTED Applied Informatics, Garmisch, Germany, 1998, Global Summit 3d Generation Mobile Comm., Japan, 1999, Internat. Symposium Computers and Comm., Red Sea, Egypt, 1999, Vehicular Comm. Techs., Houston, Amsterdam, 1999, IEEE Vehicular Tech. Conf., Amsterdam, 1999, Internat. Workshop on Distributed Computing and Comms., Pakistan, 2000-02; chmn., project mgr. working group 1 Mobile Wireless Internet Forum, chmn. Internat. Multi Conf. in Computer Sci. and Engring. panel discussion, 2004; also others. Contbr. rsch. papers to profl. jours. and conf. procs.; editor, writer English newspaper Keio U., Tokyo, 1994-95. English tchr. YMCA, Minami Jr. H.S. Tsurugashima, Saitama, Japan, 1995-98; mem. Anglican Ch. Peshawar, Pakistan. ScholarRikkyo U., Tokyo, 1993-95, Keio U., 1995-96, Ministry of Edn., Govt. of Japan, 1996-98. Mem. IEICE, Christian Student Fellowship Pakistan (sec. 1986-93). Anglican. Avocations: teaching, writing articles. Office: Toshiba Rsch Am Inc Ste 1B268B 445 South St Morristown NJ 07960-6454 Home: 15 Cook Ct Stewartsville NJ 08886

RAZNICK, CAROL, lawyer; b. Omaha, Nebr., Mar. 9, 1954; d. Byron and Tillie Chorney Raznick. BA, U. Colo., Boulder, Colo., 1976; JD, Emory U. Sch. Law, Atlanta, 1979. V.p. legal real estate MDC Holdings Inc., Denver, 1986—2000; shareholder Shugart Thomson & Kilroy P.C., Denver, 2000—04, Shughart Thomson & Kilroy, Denver, 2001—04; of counsel Solomon Pearl Heymann & Stich LLP, Denver, 2004—06; ptnr. Wolf Slatkin & Madison P.C., Denver, 2005—. Fused glass artist. Mem.: Colo. Bar Assn. Office: Wolf Slatkin & Madison PC 44 Cook St #1000 Denver CO 80209 Home Phone: 303-322-6540; Office Phone: 303-355-2999. Business E-Mail: craznick@wolfslatkin.com.

RAZZANO, FRANK CHARLES, lawyer; b. Bklyn., Feb. 25, 1948; s. Pasquale Anthony and Agnes Mary (Borgia) R.; m. Stephanie Anne Lucas, Jan. 10, 1970; children: Joseph, Francis, Catherine. BA, St. Louis U., 1969; JD, Georgetown U., 1972. Bar: NY 1973, US Dist. Ct. (so. and ea. dists.) NY 1973, NJ 1976, DC 1981, Va. 1984, US Dist. Ct. NJ 1976, US Dist. Ct. Md. 1977, US Dist. Ct. (no. dist.) Calif. 1981, US Dist. Ct. DC 1982, US Dist. Ct. (ea. dist.) Va. 1989, US Dist. Ct. (we. dist.) Va. 1990, US Ct. Appeals (2d cir.) 1973, US Ct. Appeals (3d cir.) 1975, US Ct. Appeals (DC and 5th cirs.) 1983, US Ct. Appeals (4th cir.) 1984, US Ct. Appeals (6th cir.) 1990, US Ct. Appeals (8th and 9th cirs.) 2000, US Supreme Ct. 1976. Assoc. Shea & Gould, NYC, 1972-75; asst. US atty. Dist. of NJ, Newark, 1975-78; asst. chief trial atty. SEC, Washington, 1978-82; ptnr. Shea & Gould, Washington, 1982-94, mng. ptnr., 1991-92; ptnr. Camhy Karlinsky Stein Razzano & Rubin, Washington, 1994-96, Dickstein, Shapiro LLP,

Washington, 1996—. Lectr. in field; adv. bd. Securities Litigation Reform Act Reporter, Securities Regulation Law Jour.; adj. prof. law U. Md. Sch. Law. Civil law editor Rico Law Reporter; hon. adv. com. Jour. Internat. Law and Practice, Detroit Coll. Law; contbr. articles to legal jours. Scoutmaster Vienna coun. Boy Scouts Am., 1984. Recipient spl. achievement award Justice Dept., 1977, spl. commendation, 1978, Outstanding Achievement award Detroit Coll. of Law, 1993. Mem. ABA (chmn. criminal law com., sect. bus. law 1996-98), Va. Bar, D.C. Bar (chmn. litigation sect. 1987-89, vice-chmn. coun. sects. 1988-89), Assn. Securities & Exch. Commn. Alumni (pres. 1993-95), Phi Beta Kappa, Eta Sigma Phi. Roman Catholic. Home: 2425 L St NW Apt 623 Washington DC 20037 Office Phone: 202-420-2291. Business E-Mail: razzanof@dicksteinshapiro.com.

RAZZANO, PASQUALE ANGELO, lawyer; b. Bklyn., Apr. 3, 1943; s. Pasquale Anthony and Agnes Mary (Borgia) R.; m. Maryann Walker, Jan. 29, 1966; children: Elizabeth, Pasquale, Susan, ChristyAnn. BSCE, Poly. Inst. Bklyn., 1964; student law, NYU, 1964-66; JD, Georgetown U., 1969. Bar: Va. 1969, N.Y. 1970, U.S. Ct. Appeals (2d, 3d, 7th, 9th and fed. cirs.), U.S. Supreme Ct., U.S. Dist. Ct. (so., ea. and western dists.) N.Y., U.S. Dist. Ct. (we. dist.) Tex., U.S. Dist. Ct. Hawaii, U.S. Dist. Ct. Conn. Examiner U.S. Patent Office, 1966-69; assoc. Curtis, Morris & Safford, P.C., 1969-71, ptnr., 1971-91, Fitzpatrick, Cella, Harper & Scinto, 1991—. Guest lectr. U.S. Trademark Assn., Am. Intellectual Property Law Assn., Practicing Law Inst., NYU Law Ctr., ABA, N.Y. Intellectual Property Law Assn. Mem. bd. editors Licensing Jour., 1986—; mem. bd. editors Trademark Reporter, 1987—, book rev. editor, 1989-91, pub. articles editor, 1991-94, domestic articles editor, 1992-93, 95, editor-in-chief 1996-98. Rep. committeeman Rockland County. Recipient Robert Ridgeway award, 1964. Mem.: FBA (chmn. patent law com. 1999—2002, bd. govs. 2002—), ABA (guest lectr.), Columban Laws Assn., Bar Assn. City N.Y., Italian Am. Bar Assn., Va. Bar Assn., N.Y. Coun. Bar Leaders (exec. coun. 1993—94), N.Y. Bar Assn., Am. Intellectual Property Law Assn., Internat. Trademark Assn. (bd. dirs. 1996—99), Licensing Exec. Soc. (chmn. N.Y. chpt. 1996—99), N.Y. Intellectual Property Law Assn. (bd. dirs. 1985—93, sec. 1988—91, pres. 1994—95), Shorehaven Golf Club (bd. dirs. 2005—), Minute Man Yacht Club, N.Y. Athletic Club. Republican. Roman Catholic. Address: 21 Covlee Dr Westport CT 06880-6407 also: 14 Deerwood Trl Lake Placid NY 12946-1834 Office Phone: 212-218-2253. Business E-Mail: prazzano@fchs.com.

RAZZOUK, BASSEM IBRAHIM, hematologist, oncologist; b. Afisdeek, Lebanon, Aug. 13, 1964; US, 1990; s. Ibrahim M. and Lamia C. Razzouk; m. Jacky F. Farah, Sept. 7, 1997; children: Lamya Celina, Ralph Bassem, Carla Janet, Nour Grace. BSc, Am. U. Beirut, Lebanon, 1983, MD, 1987. Diplomate in pediat. Am. Bd. Pediat., 1992, in hematology and oncology Am. Bd. of Pediat., 1996. Internship, residency Am. U. Beirut, 1987—90; resident to chief resident SUNY Health Sci. Ctr., Syracuse, 1990—92; fellowship in pediat. St. Jude Children's Rsch. Hosp., Memphis, 1992—95; attending pediatrician Boaz-Albertville Med. Ctr., Ala., 1995—98; asst. St. Jude Children's Rsch. Hosp., 1998—2004, assoc., 2004—. Med. dir., Mid. East and Telemedicine Programs St. Jude Children's Rsch. Hosp., 1998—, chmn. clin. protocol sci. rev. and monitoring com., 2004—. Contbr. articles to profl. jours. Fellow: Am. Acad. Pediat.; mem.: Am. Soc. Hematology. Achievements include research in new agents for relapsed leukemia, prognostic factors in pediatric leukemia. Home: 1948 Autumndale Cove Cordova TN 38016 Office: St Jude Children's Research Hospital 332 North Lauderdale Memphis TN 38105 Home Phone: 901-309-0336; Office Phone: 901-495-3940. Office Fax: 901-495-3122. Business E-Mail: bassem.razzouk@stjude.org.

RE, JOSEPH R., lawyer; BS in Civil Engring., Rutgers U. Coll. Engring., NJ, 1982; JD, St. John's U. Sch. Law, NYC, 1985. Bar: NY, Calif., U.S. Supreme Ct., U.S. Ct. of Appeals for the Federal, Fourth and Ninth Circuits, U.S. Ct. of Federal Claims, U.S. Ct. of Internat.Trade. Clk. Hon. Howard T. Markey, Chief Judge of the U.S. Ct. of Appeals for Federal Cir., 1985—87; assoc. Knobbe Martens Olson & Bear LLP, Irvine, Calif., 1987—90, ptnr., 1990—; adj. prof. Whittier Law Sch., Costa Mesa, Calif. Named one of 100 Leading Lawyers in Calif., Daily Jour., 2006, 100 Most Influential Lawyers, Nat. Law Jour., 2006; recipient 20th Annual Rossman Meml. Award, U.S. Patent and Trademark Office, 1993, Calif. Lawyer Atty. of Yr. for Intellectual Property, 2004. Mem.: U.S. Ct. of Appeals for Fed. Cir. (adv. coun. 2005—), Am. Intellectual Property Law Assn. (bd. dirs. 2003—06), Fed. Cir. Bar Assn. (bd. dirs. 2001—04, treas. 2004—06, vice-pres. 2006—), Amicus Comm. (chmn. 1997—99), Chi Epsilon. Office: Knobbe Martens Olson & Bear LLP 2040 Main St 14th Floor Irvine CA 92614-3641 Business E-Mail: jre@kmob.com.

REA, ANN W., librarian; b. Jefferson City, Mo., Aug. 3, 1944; d. William H. and Ruby (Fogleman) Webb; m. Glen N. Rea, Sept. 28, 1974; children: Sarah, Rebecca. BA, U. Mo., 1966; MLS, U. So. Calif., 1968. Libr. St. Charles (Mo.) County Libr., 1967-71; libr. adult svcs. Paterson (N.J.) Free Pub. Libr., 1971-74; libr. Beal Coll. Libr., Bangor, Maine, 1983—. Mem ALA, Maine Libr. Assn.(scholarship and loan com.). Office: Beal Coll Libr 99 Farm Rd Bangor ME 04401 Office Phone: 207-947-4591.

REA, ANNE E., lawyer; b. 1959; AB, Brown U., 1981; JD, U. Cgho., 1984. Bar: Ill. 1984. With Sidley Austin Brown & Wood, Chgo., 1984—, ptnr., 1992—. Selected as one of 15 Rising Stars You Won't Want to Oppose in Ct., Ill. Legal Times. Mem.: ABA, Leadership Greater Chgo., Chgo. Bar Assn., Ill. State Bar Assn.

READ, IAN C., pharmaceutical executive; BSChemE, London U. Imperial Coll., 1974. Cert. Chartered Acct., Inst. Chartered Accts. of Eng. and Wales, 1978. Operational auditor Pfizer, Inc., 1978, CFO Pfizer Mex. to country mgr. Brazil, pres. Internat. Pharms. Grp. L.Am./Can., 1996, exec. v.p. Europe/Can., 2000, v.p., 2001—, exec. v.p. Africa/Mid. East, 2004, exec. v.p. L.Am., 2006, pres. worldwide pharm. ops., 2006—. Pfizer rep. internat. sect. exec. com. Pharm. Rsch. and Mfrs. Am. Office: Pfizer Inc 235 E 42nd St New York NY 10017 *

READ, JOHN CONYERS, non-profit company executive; b. NYC, May 21, 1947; s. Edward Cameron Kirk and Louise (Geary) R.; m. Alexandra Gould, Mar. 30, 1968; children: Cameron Kirk, Trevor Conyers, Alexandra. AB, Harvard, 1969, MBA, 1971; LHD (hon.), Centenary Coll., 2004. Ops. rsch. analyst HEW, Washington, 1971-72; exec. asst. to dir. Cost of Living Council, Washington, 1973; chief econ. adviser to Gov. Mass., 1974; exec. asst., counselor to sec. labor Washington, 1975; asst. sec. labor for employment standards, 1976—77; dir. corp. employee rels., pers. Cummins Engine Co., Columbus, Ind., 1977-80, plant mgr., 1980-85; v.p. Midrange Engines, 1986-90; v.p., gen. mgr. engine group Donaldson Co., Inc., Mpls., 1990-92; exec. v.p., 1992-94; ptnr. Hidden Creek Industries, Mpls., 1996—2000; pres., CEO Heavy Duty Holdings, Mpls., 1997-2000; pres. Read Ptnrs. Inc., Mpls., 2001—02; pres., CEO Outward Bound USA, Garrison, NY, 2002—. Cons. nat. productivity and energy policies; chmn. NAM Task Force on Wage and Price Policies, 1978-80; bd. dirs. MAC Equipment Co., Active Leasing Co., Summer Search. Contbr. articles to newspapers and mags. Trustee Summer Search, Nat. Ctr. Occupl. Readjustment, 1984-87; trustee NC Outward Bound Sch., dir., 1995—, chmn., 1997-2000; chmn. Charleston Pvt. Industry Coun., 1985; plant closing task force US Dept. Labor, 1986, mfg. task force NRC, 1989, critical industries task force Def. Dept., 1989 Mem. Nat. Assn. Mfrs. (bd. dirs., chair employee rels. com. 1993-95). Home: 111 Marlborough Rd Briarcliff Manor NY 10510 E-mail: jread@outwardbound.org.

READ, MICHAEL OSCAR, editor, consultant; b. Amarillo, Tex., July 11, 1942; s. Harold Eugene and Madeline (Welch) R.; m. Jill Kay Vanderby, July 6, 1963 (div. Apr. 1967); 1 child, Rebecca Anne; m. Fawn Dale Barby, Apr. 10, 1977; 1 child, Nathan Michael. AA in Chemistry, Amarillo Coll., 1962; BA in Journalism, Tex. Tech. U., 1965. News editor Olton Enterprise, Tex., 1963—64; reporter, photographer Lubbock Avalanche-Jour., Tex., 1964—67, copy editor, 1967—70, city editor, 1970—72; copy editor Houston Post, 1972—74, sys. editor, 1974—89, dir. news tech., 1989—95; coord. electronic media content Houston Chronicle, 1995—2000, editor web ops. and devel., 2000—. Bd. dirs. Shell Employees Fed. Credit Union, Houston, vice chmn., 2002—, supervisory com., 1996-2001; tchr. Let's Compute!, Stafford, Tex., 1985—; cons. Newspaper Pub. Sys., Stafford, 1989—; mem. joint Newspaper Assn. Am.-Internat. Press. Telecomm. Coun. Com. Wire Svc. Stds.; mem. adv. bd. Found. for Am. Comms. FACSNET; mem. adv. com. Sch. of Mass Comm., Tex. Tech U., chmn., 2001-04 Author weekly newspaper column, 1977—. Vol. United Way, Houston, 1973—; bd. dirs. Meadows (Tex.) Cmty. Improvement Assn., 1985-95, Meadows Utility Dist., 1988-93, Meadows Econ. Devel. Corp., 1994-99. Named among Outstanding Alumni, Tex. Tech U. Sch. Mass Comms., 2001; Eldon Durrett scholar, 1961-65. Mem. Am. MENSA, Am. Philatelic Soc., Am. 1st Day Cov. Soc. (life), U.S. Chess Fedn. (life), Soc. Profl. Journalists (conv. com. 1989-90), Press Club of Houston. Avocations: stamp collecting/philately, photography, gardening. Office: Houston Chronicle 801 Texas St Houston TX 77002-2996 Home Phone: 213-277-7213; Office Phone: 713-362-2905. E-mail: mike.read@chron.com.

READ, PIERS PAUL, author; b. Beaconsfield, Eng., Mar. 7, 1941; s. Herbert Edward and Margaret (Ludwig) R.; m. Emily Albertine Boothby, July 29, 1967; children: Albert Nathaniel, Martha Marianna, William Edward, Beatrice Mary. BA, St. John's Coll., Cambridge U., 1962, MA, 1963. Sub-editor Times Lit. Supplement, 1963-64. Adj. prof. writing Columbia U., 1980; lit. panel mem. Arts Coun. Gt. Britain, 1974-76; gov. Cardinal Manning Boys Sch., 1985; chmn. Cath. Writers Guild, 1993-97. Author: (novels) Game in Heaven with Tussy Marx, 1966, The Junkers, 1968 (Sir Geoffrey Faber Meml. prize, 1969), Monk Dawson, 1970 (Somerset Maugham award, Hawthornden prize, 1970), The Professor's Daughter, 1971, The Upstart, 1973, Polonaise, 1976, A Married Man, 1980, The Villa Golitsyn, 1982, The Free Frenchman, 1986, A Season in the West, 1988 (James Tait Black Meml. prize), On the Third Day, 1990, The Patriot, 1995, Knights of the Cross, 1997, (non-fiction) Alive: The Story of the Andes Survivors, 1974 (Thomas More medal), The Train Robbers, 1978, Ablaze: The Heroes and Victims of Chernobyl, 1993, The Patriot, 1996, (songs) Knights of the Cross, 1997, The Templars, 1999, The Gospel of St. John: The Story of the Son of God, 1999, Alice in Exile, 2001, Alec Guiness: The Authorised Biography, 2003, Hell and Other Destinations, 2006, (TV plays) Coincidence, The Family Firm, The House of Highburgh Hill. Mem. Brit. bd. of Aid to Church in Need, 1988. Ford Found. fellow, 1963-64; Harkness fellow, 1967-68 Fellow Royal Soc. Lit.; mem. Soc. Authors (com. mgmt. 1972-74), Inst. Contemporary Arts (com. mgmt. 1972-74) Roman Catholic. Address: 50 Portland Rd W11 4LG London England E-mail: piersread@dial.pipex.com.

READ, RICHARD EATON, newspaper reporter; b. St. Andrews, Scotland, Sept. 3, 1957; s. Arthur H. and Katharine (Eaton) R.; m. Kim R. Kunkle, July 26, 1986; 1 child, Nehalem Kunkle-Read. BA in English, Amherst Coll., 1980; postgrad., Harvard U., 1996—97; LHD (hon.), Williamette U., 2003. Press sec. Mass. Commn. on State and County Bldgs., 1980; staff writer The Oregonian, 1981-86; fellow The Henry Luce Found./The Nation, Bangkok, 1986-87; freelance writer Tokyo, 1987-89; Asia bur. chief The Oregonian, Tokyo, 1989-94; sec., 1st dir., 1st v.p. Fgn. Corrs. Club of Japan, 1990-93; internat. bus. writer The Oregonian, Portland, 1994-99, sr. writer internat. affairs, 1999—. V.p., bd. dirs. The Internat. Sch., Portland, 2002—. Recipient Pulitzer prize for explanatory reporting, 1999, Overseas Press Club award for bus. reporting from abroad, 1999, Scripps Howard Found. award for bus. reporting, 1999, Blethen award for enterprise reporting Pacific Northwest Newspaper Assn., 1999, 2001, Pacific Northwest Soc. Prof. Journalists first place award for social issues, 2001, 05, bus. 1998, 2004, spot news 1997, edn. 1990, Oreg. Gov.'s award for achievement in internat. bus., 2000, Pulitzer prize for pub. svc., 2001, Unity award in media investigative reporting, Lincoln U., 2001, Blethen award, 2001, Bruce Baer award, 2001, Media Leadership award Am. Immigration Lawyers Assn., 2001; named Internat. Citizen of Yr. 1999 World Affairs Coun. Oreg., named Internat. Citizen of Yr. 2002 Oreg. Assn. Consuls Eisenhower Exch. fellow, Peru, 1997; Nieman fellow, 1996-97; U. Md. CASE fellow, 2002.

READ, SUSAN PHILLIPS, state appeals court judge; b. Gallipolis, Ohio, June 27, 1947; d. Gomer Wesley and Elizabeth Molineaux Phillips; m. Howard John Read. BA summa cum laude, Ohio Wesleyan U., 1969; JD Floyd R. Mechem Prize Scholar, U. Chgo., 1972. Bar: NY 1974. Legal intern US Atomic Energy Commn., 1972—73; asst. counsel SUNY, 1974—77; in-house counsel GE Co., 1977—88, chief environ. counsel, 1980—85; ptnr. Bond, Schoeneck & King, Albany, NY, 1988—94; dep. counsel to Gov. Pataki State of NY, Albany, 1995—97; judge (confirmed for an unexpired term in 1998 and full term in 1999) NY Ct. of Claims, 1998—2003, presiding judge, 1999; assoc. judge NY State Ct. Appeals, Schenectady, 2003—. Mem.: Phi Beta Kappa. Office: NY State Ct Appeals 20 Eagle St Albany NY 12207-1095 *

READ, TONY JOHN, information scientist, consultant; BSc, Loughborough U., Leicestershire, UK, 1981; MBA, Kingston U., London, 1989; MEd, Vanderbuilt U., Nashville, 1997; PhD, Nova Southeastern U., Miami, 2005. V.p. IT Nortel Networks, Maidenhead, 1992—2000, Nashville, 1992—2000, Miami, 1992—2000; CIO sr. v.p. IT CCI, Miami, 2000—01; sr. v.p. T & O, Toronto, Canada, 2001—02; mng. ptnr. Read Assoc., Toronto, Canada, 2003—. Contbr. articles, various publs. and confs. Recipient Upsilon Pi Epsilon, Hon. Soc. Computer Sci. Home Phone: 905 342 2713; Office Phone: 905 342 2713. Business E-Mail: tread@readassociates.net.

READ, VIRGINIA HALL, retired biochemistry professor; b. Louisville, Miss., Oct. 15, 1937; d. Angus R. and Hassie (Bowie) Hall; m. Dale Gilbert Read Sr., Mar. 5, 1960; children: Laura Read Sprabery, Dale Gilbert Jr., Eva Read Warden. BS, U. Miss., 1959; MS, U. Miss., Jackson, 1962, PhD, 1964. Instr. biochemistry U. Miss., Jackson, 1965-66, asst. prof. biochemistry, 1966-68, 70-74, assoc. prof. biochemistry, 1974-2000, assoc prof. pathology, 1979-2000; asst. prof. medicine U. Ala., Birmingham, 1968-70. Contbr. articles to Jour. Clin. Investigation, Jour. Clin. Endocrinology and Metabolism, Nature, Biochem. Pharmacology. Grantee U.S. Pub. Health Svc., 1960-62, fellow, 1968-70. Mem. Am. Assn. Clin. Chemistry, Acad. Clin. Biochemistry, Endocrine Soc., Sigma Xi. United Methodist. Personal E-mail: dread@ayrix.net.

READE, CLAIRE ELIZABETH, lawyer; b. Waltham, Mass., June 2, 1952; d. Kemp Brownell and Suzanne Helen (Dorntge) R.; m. Earl Phillip Steinberg, Nov. 22, 1980; children: Evan Samuel, Emma Miriam. BA, Conn. Wesleyan U., 1973; JD, Harvard U., 1979; MA in Law and Diplomacy, Tufts U., 1979. Bar: Mass. 1980, D.C. 1983. Sheldon fellow Harvard U., Cambridge, Mass. and, Republic of China, 1979-80; assoc. Ropes & Gray, Boston, 1980-82, Arnold & Porter, Washington, 1982-86, ptnr. internat. law, chmn. Hiring Com., 1987—2006; chief counsel China trade enforcement Office U.S. Trade Rep., Washington, 2006—. Exec. editor: International Trade Policy: The Lawyer's Perspective, 1985; contbr. articles to profl. jours. Mem. ABA (co-chair internat. trade com.), DC Bar Assn., Coun. on Foreign Rels. Office: US Trade Rep 600 17th St NW Washington DC 20508

READE, LEWIS P., diplomat, engineer, consultant; b. NYC, Nov. 1, 1932; s. Herman Ross and Dorothy Stella (Pollock) R.; m. Anne Carol Kulka, July 3, 1955 (div. Feb. 1968); children: Steven Gordon, Nicholas Edward; m. Margaret Ann Kilpatrick, Mar. 30, 1968; 1 child, Jonathan Collins. BS in Mech. Engrin., U. Miami, 1953; postgrad., Hofstra U., 1953-54, U. Balt., 1957-59, U. N.Mex., 1997—. Product engr. Sperry Gyroscope, Lake Success, N.Y., 1953-54; project engr. ARMA, Garden City, N.Y., 1954-55; field engr. Westinghouse Electric Corp., Balt. & Rome, 1957-66; v.p. Westinghouse Learning Corp., Washington & Pitts., 1966-70; v.p. corp. planning & devel. Tyco Labs., Waltham, Mass., 1970-71; chmn., chief exec. officer, treas. Kellett Corp., Willow Grove, Pa., 1971-72; exec. v.p., CEO Big Bros./Big Sisters of Am., Phila., 1973-80; mission dir. U.S. Agy. Internat. Devel., Kingston, Jamaica, 1982-85; sr. dep. asst. adminstr. Pvt. Enterprise Bur., Washington, 1985-86; mission dir. U.S. Agy. Internat. Devel., Amman, Jordan, 1986-90, Jakarta, Indonesia, 1990-92; dir. gen. U.S.-Asia Environ. Partnership, Washington, 1992-97; ret., 1997; pres., CEO Jordan-U.S. Bus. Partnership, Amman, 1998—2000; cons. UN Devel. Program, 2003. Sgt. USAR, 1955—57. Named to Hall Fame, Big Bros. Big Sisters, 2004. Mem. Am. Fgn. Svc. Assn. Home: 92 Vista Montana Loop Placitas NM 87043-9518

READER, GEORGE G., retired internal-public health medicine educator; b. Bklyn., 1919; m. Helen Brown, May 23, 1942; 4 children. BA in Animal Biology, Cornell U., Ithaca, NY, 1940; MD, Cornell U., NYC, 1943; ScD (hon.), Drew U., 1988. Intern in medicine N.Y. Hosp., NYC, 1944-45, resident and fellow in medicine, 1946—50, resident in hematology, 1950—51; instr. medicine Cornell U. Med. Ctr., 1951—52, from asst. prof. to prof., 1952—89, emeritus prof. medicine, 1989—, Livingston Farrand prof. pub. health, 1989—. Former advisor Social Security Adminstrn.; former chmn. human ecology study sect. NIH; former chmn. tech. com. on tng. White House Conf. on Aging; former cons. OEO, Office Sec. of HEW, Health Svcs. and Mental Health Adminstrn.; head transition task force health adv. coun. N.Y. State Dept. Health, 1974—84; former chmn. N.Y. State Task Force on Health of Sch. Age Child and Health Manpower; rep. Cornell U. Med. Ctr. in Health Planning for N.Y.C.; mem. master plan com. N.Y.C. Hosp. Coun. Mem. N.Y.C. Mayor's Organized Task Force for Health Planning; mem. local planning bd. representing N.Y. Hosp., Health Sys. Agy., NYC. Scholar Regents scholar, Cornell U., 1940. Mem.: AOA, Inst. of Medicine (sr.), Skulls.

READER, JOSEPH, physicist; b. Chgo., Dec. 1, 1934; BS, Purdue U., 1956, MS, 1957; PhD in Physics, U. Calif., 1962. Rsch. assoc. physics Argonne Nat. Lab., 1962-63; staff physicist Nat. Inst. Standards and Tech., Gaithersburg, Md., 1963-99, group leader atomic spectroscopy group, 1999—. Recipient Gold medal Dept. Commerce, 1989. Fellow Am. Phys. Soc., Optical Soc. Am. (William F. Meggers award 1992). Achievements include research in experimental atomic physics, optical spectroscopy, hyperfine structure, electronic structure of highly ionized atoms, wavelength standards, and ionization energies of atoms and ions. Office: Natl Inst Of Stds & Tech Gaithersburg MD 20899-8422

READEY, MARIJO, artist, educator; d. J. and A. Readey. PhD in Zoology, U. Toronto, Ontario, Canada, 1986. Postdoctoral rschr. Argonne Nat. Lab., Ill., 1986—90; adj. faculty Roosevelt U., Chgo., 1992—2007; adj. instr. Northeastern Ill. U., Chgo., 1998—; artist Prairie Ho. Gallery, Hansboro, ND, 2005—. Giclee print porfolios, Human Experience of Love/of Nature/of Spirituality; contbr. chapter to book, articles to profl. jours. Vol. Names Project, Chgo., 1988, DC, 1988; art donor Weiss Meml. Hosp. Art Against AIDS, Chgo., 1992—93, Oshawa Rape Crisis Ctr., Oshawa, Ontario, Canada, 2006; vol. educator, trainer Stop AIDS Chgo., 1994—96; vol. Mitchel Mus. Am. Indian, Evanston, Ill., 2006—07. Mem.: Art in Can., Artists Blue Book. Avocations: bicycling, paleontology.

READING, ANTHONY JOHN, retired psychiatrist, educator; b. Sydney, Sept. 10, 1933; s. Abe Stanley and Esma Daisy R.; m. Elisabeth Ann Hoffman, July 27, 1975; children— Wendy Virginia Elisabeth, Sarah Alexandra Jane. MBBS, U. Sydney, 1956; MPH, Johns Hopkins U., Balt., 1961, DSc, 1964. Intern Sydney Hosp., 1957-58; resident in psychiatry Johns Hopkins Hosp., Balt., 1965-68; asst. prof. psychiatry and medicine Johns Hopkins U. Sch. Medicine, Balt., 1968-73, assoc. prof. psychiatry, 1973-75, dir. psychiat. liaison service, 1974-75; dir. comprehensive alcoholism program Johns Hopkins Hosp., 1972-75; prof. U. South Fla. Coll. Medicine, 1975—2006, chmn. dept. psychiatry and behavioral medicine, 1975—2002, assoc. dean, 1993-96; med. dir. Bay Med. Behavioral Health Ctr., Panama City, Fla., 2004—05; ret., 2006. Mem.: AAAS. Home: 3202 Magnolia Islands Blvd Panama City Beach FL 32408-7176 Personal E-mail: tonytoo@comcast.net.

READING, JAMES EDWARD, transportation executive; b. Milw., June 26, 1924; s. James Edwards and Helen Marie (Boehm) R.; m. Ada Irene Kelly, May 24, 1944; children: Wendy Irene, James David, Christopher Kelly, Mary Katherine, Kevin Sinclair. Student, San Diego State U., 1942, Ga. Inst. Tech., 1944. With Union-Tribune Pub. Co., San Diego, 1942-59, dist. mgr., 1953-58, circulation promotion mgr., 1958-59; adminstrv. asst. to v.p. Copley Newspapers, La Jolla, Calif., 1959-60; dir. advt. and pub. rels. San Diego Transit System, 1960-67; dir. mktg. Calif. Motor Express, 1967-68; asst. to exec. v.p. Am. Transit Assn., Washington, 1968; v.p. Nat. City Mgmt. Co.; resident mgr. Regional Transit Service, Rochester, N.Y., 1968-74; asst. gen. mgr. ops. Regional Transit Dist., Denver, 1974-77; gen. mgr. Central Ohio Transit Authority, Columbus, 1977-85; dir. Santa Clara County Transp. Agy., San Jose, Calif., 1985-90; ind. cons. San Diego, 1990—. Lectr. in field. Treas. Contg. Edn. Ctr., Rancho Bernardo. With ETO US Army, 1943—46. Named Pub. Rels. Man of Yr. Pub. Rels. Club, San Diego, 1962; recipient Urban Mass Transp. Adminstrs. award for outstanding pub. service, 1980, 82; charter mem. Herbert Hoover H.S. Achievement Hall of Fame, San Diego, 1998; named to Rancho Bernardo Hall of Fame, 2000. Mem. Am. Pub. Transit Assn. (bd. dirs., past v.p., elected Hall of Fame 1995), Am. Legion, Rotary Club Rancho Bernardo (past pres.), Press Club No. San Diego County (past pres.), Rancho Bernardo Spirit of Fourth (past pres., treas.), Tau Kappa Epsilon. Republican. Roman Catholic. Home: 11728 Caminito Corriente San Diego CA 92128-4548

READY, ROBERT JAMES, finance company executive; b. Bridgeport, Conn., June 26, 1952; s. John Edward and Anne (Salata) R.; m. Margaret S. Neale, Aug. 23, 1975; children: Carolyn, Christopher and Steven (twins). AS, Housatonic Community Coll., 1972; BS, Babson Coll., 1974. CLU; chartered fin. cons.; registered fin. cons.; cert. ins. cons; cert. retirement cons.; cert. retirement adminstr. Agt. John Hancock Mut. Life Ins. Co., Hamden, Conn., 1975-77; broker Beardsley, Brown & Bassett Inc., Bridgeport, Conn., 1977-80; agt. Aetna Life and Casualty Ins. Co., Trumbull, Conn., 1980-83; v.p. Crestview Fin. Services Inc., Westport, Conn., 1983-2000, Crestview Securities Inc., Westport, Conn., 1983-2000, Crestview Investment Advisors Inc., Westport, Conn., 1983-2000; sr. v.p. ins. RDM Ins. Svcs. Inc., Westport, Conn., 2000—. Mem. Nat. Assn. Life Underwriters, Conn. Assn. Life Underwriters, Bridgeport Life Underwriters (bd. dirs. 1977), New Haven County CLU and Chartered Fin. Cons., Soc. of Fin. Svc. Profls. (Fairfield county chpt.). Roman Catholic. Avocations: golf, tennis, softball. Office: RDM Financial Group Inc 1555 Post Rd E Westport CT 06880-5602 Office Phone: 203-255-0222. E-mail: bready@rdmfinancial.com.

REAGAN, GARY DON, state legislator, lawyer; b. Amarillo, Tex., Aug. 23, 1941; s. Hester and Lois Irene (Marcum) R.; m. Nedra Ann Nash, Sept. 12, 1964; children: Marc Kristi, Kari, Brent. BA, Stanford U., 1963, JD, 1965. Bar: N.Mex. 1965, US Dist. Ct. N.Mex. 1965, US Supreme Ct. 1986.

Assoc. Smith & Ransom, Albuquerque, 1965—67; ptnr. Smith, Ransom, Deaton & Reagan, Albuquerque, 1967—68, Williams, Johnson, Houston, Reagan & Porter, Hobbs, N.Mex., 1968—77, Williams, Johnson, Reagan, Porter & Love, Hobbs, 1977—82; pvt. practice Hobbs, 1982—; city atty. City of Hobbs, 1978—80, 1997—2004, City of Eunice, N.Mex., 1980—2004; mem. N.Mex. State Senate, 1993—96. Instr. N.Mex. Jr. Coll. and Coll. of S.W., Hobbs, 1978-84; N.Mex. commr. Nat. Conf. Commrs. Uniform State Laws, 1993-96; adv. mem. N.Mex. Constl. Revision Commn., 1993-95. Mayor City of Hobbs, 1972-73, 76-77, city commr., 1970-78; pres., dir. Jr. Achievement of Hobbs, 1974-85; pres., trustee Landsun Homes, Inc., Carlsbad, N.Mex., 1972-84; trustee Lydia Patterson Inst., El Paso, Tex., 1972-84, N.Mex. Conf. United Meth. Ch., 1988—, Coll. SW Hobbs, 1989-2001 Mem. ABA, State Bar N.Mex. (coms. 1989-96, v.p. 1992-93, pres. 1994-95), Lea County Bar Assn. (pres. 1976-77), Hobbs C. of C. (pres. 1989-90), Rotary (pres. Hobbs 1985-86), Hobbs Tennis Club (pres. 1974-75). Home: 200 E Eagle Dr Hobbs NM 88240-5323 Office: 1819 N Turner Ste G Hobbs NM 88240-3834 Home Phone: 505-393-9072; Office Phone: 505-397-6551. Business E-Mail: lglregan@nm.net.

REAGAN, HARRY EDWIN, III, lawyer; b. Wichita, Kans., Sept. 9, 1940; s. Harry E. II and Mary Elizabeth (O'Steen) R.; m. Marvene R. Rogers, June 17, 1965; children: Kathleen, Leigh, Mairen. BS, U. Pa., 1962, JD, 1965. Bar: Pa. 1965, U.S. Dist. Ct. (ea. dist.) Pa. 1965, U.S. Ct. Appeals (3d cir.) 1965. From assoc. to ptnr. Morgan, Lewis & Bockius, Phila., 1965-98. Chmn. Northhampton Twp. Planning Commn., Bucks County, Pa., 1974-79; mem. Warwick Twp. Planning Commn., 1980-95, chmn., 1994; supr. Warwick Twp., 1996-98; mem. San Miguel County (Colo.) Open Space Commn., 1998—, chmn., 2001-05; mem. Town of Telluride Open Space Commn., 1999-2002, San Miguel County Planning Commn., 2002—. Mem. ABA (labor sect.), Pa. Bar Assn. (labor sect.), Phila. Bar Assn. (labor sect.), Indsl. Rels. Assn. (pres. Phila. chpt. 1990-91). Republican. Presbyterian. Avocations: rugby, skiing, raising horses, bicycling. Home and Office: Box 190 Norwood CO 81423

REAGAN, JOSEPH BERNARD, retired aerospace executive, management consultant; b. Somerville, Mass., Nov. 26, 1934; s. Joseph B. and Helen Lowry R.; m. Dorothy Hughes; children: Patrick, Michael, Kevin, Kathleen, Brian, John, Maureen. BS in Physics, Boston Coll., 1956, MS in Physics, 1959; PhD in Space Sci., Stanford U., 1975; postgrad. exec. mgmt., Pa. State U., State College, 1981. Staff scientist, rsch. scientist, sr. scientist, scientist Lockheed Rsch. & Devel. Div., Palo Alto, Calif., 1959-75, mgr., 1975-84, dir., 1984-86, dep. gen. mgr., 1986-88, v.p., asst. gen. mgr., 1988-90; v.p. gen. mgr. Lockheed Missle and Space Co., 1991-96. Contbr. articles to profl. jours. Bd. dirs. SM&A, Newport Beach, Calif. Capt. U.S. Army, 1956-64. Recipient Career Achievement in Sci. award Boston Coll. Alumni Assn., 1993. Fellow AIAA (outstanding engr. San Francisco chpt. 1988); mem. Am. Geophys. Union, Nat. Acad. of Engring., Nat. Rsch. Coun. Republican. Roman Catholic. Avocation: computer and woodworking hobbies. Home and Office: 13554 Mandarin Way Saratoga CA 95070-4847 Home Phone: 408-867-0557. Personal E-mail: jbr733@comcast.net.

REAGAN, LAWRENCE PAUL, JR., engineering executive, consultant; b. Honolulu, Nov. 5, 1957; s. Lawrence Paul Sr. and Laura Louise (Sears) R.; m. Ann Marie Decker, Apr. 15, 1989; children: Lawrence P. III, Andrew Scott, Kelly Rene, Ryan Joshua. BS in Mech. & Aerospace Engring., Ill. Inst. Tech., Chgo., 1979; MS in Acquisition & Contract Mgmt., West Coast U., Santa Barbara, Calif., 1986; advanced cert. in Chinese/Soviet/Middle East/North Africa Studies, Nat. Cryptological Sch., 1992. Cert. Air Force Acquisition Level 3. Product engr. R.G. Ray Corp., Schaumburg, Ill., 1978—80; launch integration mgr. USAF Hqrs. Space Divsn., L.A. AFB, 1980—84; chief Titan program mgmt. USAF Aerospace Test Group, Vandenberg AFB, Calif., 1984—89; chief joint comm. br. USAF Pentagon, Washington, 1989—91; sr. sys. engr. Dynamics Rsch. Corp., Arlington, Va., 1992—96, dir. Md. ops. California, Md., 1996—97; fed. programs mgr. Info. Builders, Inc., Arlington, 1997—98, dir. fed. programs, 1998—2003; v.p. PRICE Systems LLC, Arlington, 2003—. CEO Jacob's Well, Inc., Lexington Park, Md., 1993—. Contbr. papers to profl. publs. Officer USAF, 1979—92. Named Outstanding Young Engr., Air Force Assn. Mem. AIAA, Soc. Logistics Engring., Air Force Assn., Armed Forces Comms. Electronics Assn., Govt. Electronic Industry Assn. (bd. dirs.), Industry Adv. Coun. Ptnr. Program Avocations: boating, water sports, reading, photography. Home: PO Box 22 Lusby MD 20657-0022 Office: PRICE Systems LLC 1700 N Moore St Ste 1100 Arlington VA 22209 Office Phone: 703-740-0078. Business E-Mail: larry.reagan@pricesystems.com.

REAGAN, NANCY DAVIS (ANNE FRANCIS ROBBINS), former First Lady of the United States, volunteer; b. NYC, July 6, 1921; d. Kenneth and Edith (Luckett) Robbins, Loyal Davis (Stepfather); m. Ronald Reagan, Mar. 4, 1952 (dec. June 5, 2004); children: Patricia Ann, Ronald Prescott stepchildren: Maureen(dec.), Michael. BA in Theatre, Smith Coll., 1943; LLD (hon.), Pepperdine U., 1983; LHD (hon.), Georgetown U., 1987. Sales clk. Marshall Fields Dept. Store, Chgo.; First Lady of the US Washington, 1981—89. Contract actress, MGM, 1949-56; films include Portrait of Jennie, 1948, East Side, West Side, 1949, Doctor and the Girl, 1949, Shadow on the Wall, 1950, The Next Voice You Hear, 1950, Night into Morning, 1951, It's a Big Country, 1951, Shadow in the Sky, 1952, Talk About a Stranger, 1952, Donovan's Brain, 1953, Hellcats of the Navy, 1957, Crash Landing, 1958, You Can't Hurry Love, 1988, Lunar: Silver Star Story, 1992; TV credits include Schlitz Playhouse of Stars, 1951, Climax, 1954, General Electric Theater, 1953, Zane Grey Theater, 1956, The Tall Man, 1960, 87th Precint, 1961, Wagon Train, 1957, Different Strokes, 1978, Dynasty, 1981; Broadway: Lute Song, 1946; formerly author syndicated column on prisoner-of-war and missing-in-action soldiers and their families; author: Nancy, 1980; (with Jane Wilkie) To Love a Child, 1982, (with William Novak) My Turn: The Memoirs of Nancy Reagan, 1989. Civic worker, visited wounded Viet Nam vets., sr. citizens, hosps. and schs. for physically and emotionally handicapped children, active in furthering foster grandparents for handicapped children program; hon. nat. chmn. Aid to Adoption of Spl. Kids, 1977; spl. interest in fighting alcohol and drug abuse among youth: hosted first ladies from around the world for 2d Internat. Drug Conf., 1985; hon. chmn. Just Say No Found., Nat. Fedn. of Parents for Drug-Free Youth, Nat. Child Watch Campaign, President's Com. on the Arts and Humanities, Wolf Trap Found. bd. of trustees, Nat. Trust for Historic Preservation, Cystic Fibrosis Found., Nat. Republican Women's Club; hon. pres. Girl Scouts of Am. Named one of Ten Most Admired Am. Women, Good Housekeeping mag., ranking #1 in poll, 1984, 85, 86; Woman of Yr. Los Angeles Times, 1977; permanent mem. Hall of Fame of Ten Best Dressed Women in U.S.; recipient humanitarian awards from Am. Camping Assn., Nat. Council on Alcoholism, United Cerebral Palsy Assn., Internat. Ctr. for Disabled; Boys Town Father Flanagan award; 1986 Kiwanis World Service medal; Variety Clubs Internat. Lifeline award; numerous awards for her role in fight against drug abuse. Republican. Presbyterian. *

REALS ELLIG, JANICE, marketing professional, human resources specialist; b. NYC, May 14, 1946; d. Otto Peter and Anne (Briganti) Astolfi; m. Paul T. Reals, 1971 (div.); m. Bruce Robert Ellig, July 16, 1994; 1 child, Meredith Evans. BBA, U. Iowa, 1968; MA, Rider Coll., Princeton, NJ, 1978. Dir. Shareholders Mgmt., LA, 1968—71; v.p. human resources Cooper Med. Ctr., NJ, 1971—80; dir. human resources Pfizer, NYC, 1980—86; v.p. human resources Citibank, 1986—91; sr. v.p. mktg., human resources, adminstrn. Ambac Fin. Group, 1991—2000; prin. Heidrick & Struggles, 2000; pres., owner Gould, McCoy, Chadick, Ellig, NYC, 2000—06; owner, co-CEO Chadick, Ellig, NYC, 2007. Chmn. bd. Women's Econ. Roundtable, NYC, 1997—98. Author: What Every Successful Woman Knows, 2001, Driving the Career Highway, 2007. Bd. dirs. Fountain House, NYC, Nat. Exec. Svc. Corp., NYC, 2000-03, U. Iowa Found., 2003—, pres. club, 2000—, YMCA of Greater NY, 2004—, chair, 2007-; dir. adv. coun. Bus. Sch., U. Iowa, Iowa City, 1998-2004; bd. dirs. Women in the State and House, Washington, 1998-2006; bus. com. Met. Mus. Art, NYC, 1994—; bd. dirs. Women's Forum, NYC, 2004—; adv. coun. Children's Aid Soc., NYC, 1995-97; leadership cir. Women's Campaign Fund, NYC, 1990—2003. Named Woman of Yr., Rhinelander's Children Ctr./Children's Aid Soc., 1999; recipient Woman of Excellence award TV Channel 21, 2002, 21 Women in the 21st Century award, 2007. Mem. Fin. Women's Assn., Econ. Club N.Y.C. Republican. Avocations: writing, gourmet cooking, reading, travel, tennis. Home: Apt 12G 10 Gracie Sq New York NY 10028-7052 Office: Chadick Ellig 300 Park Ave New York NY 10022 Office Phone: 212-688-8671. Business E-Mail: ellig@chadickellig.com.

REAM, JAMES B. (JIM REAM), air transportation executive; married; 1 child. MBA, Northwestern Univ. Mng. dir. fin. planning Am. Airlines Inc.; v.p. fin. Continental Airlines, 1994—96; exec. v.p., COO Continental Micronesia Inc., Guam, 1996, pres., COO Guam, 1996—98; sr. v.p. Asia Continental Airlines, 1998—99; pres. ExpressJet Holdings, Houston, 1999—, CEO, 2002—. Office: ExpressJet Holdings Ste 200 700 N Sam Houston Pkwy W Houston TX 77067 Office Phone: 713-324-4722. Office Fax: 713-324-4716. *

REAMAN, GREGORY HAROLD, pediatric hematologist, oncologist; b. Akron, Ohio, Sept. 9, 1947; s. Harold J. and Margaret U. (D'Alfonso) R.; m. Susan J. Pristo, Sept. 7, 1974; children: Emily Margaret, Sarah Elizabeth. BS in Biology, U. Detroit, 1969; MD, Loyola U., Chgo., 1973. Diplomate Nat. Bd. Med. Examiners, Am. Bd. Pediats. with subspecialty in pediat. hematology and oncology. Pediatric intern Loyola U. Med. Ctr., 1973-74; resident in pediatrics Montreal Children's Hosp., McGill U., 1974-76; clin. assoc. pediatric oncology br. Nat. Cancer Inst., NIH, Bethesda, Md., 1976-78, investigator pediatric oncology br., 1978-79; assoc. dept. hematology/oncology, attending physician Children's Nat. Med. Ctr., Washington, 1979—, chmn. dept. hematology/oncology, 1985—2003, dir. med. spl. svcs., 1995—99, exec. dir. Ctr. for Cancer and Blood Disorders, 1999—2002; asst. prof. pediats. Sch. Medicine and Health Scis. George Washington U., 1979—82, assoc. prof. pediats., 1982—87, prof. pediats., 1987—. Assoc. chmn. Children's Cancer Group; strategic planning com. Children's Oncology Svcs. of Met. Washington; exec. v.p. for sci. and med. affairs Nat. Childhood Cancer Found./Children's Oncology Group, chmn., 2000-; mem. oncologic drugs adv. com., FDA, 2002-06; chmn. Pediat. sub-com., bd. dir. Am. Soc. Clin. Oncology. Mem. editl. bd. Cancer Data Query, Nat. Cancer Inst., Jour. Clin. Oncology, Am. Jour. Pediat. Hematology Oncology, Cancer, Pediatric Blood and Cancer, Leukemia and Lymphoma, The Oncologist; reviewer Blood, Jour. Clin. Oncology; assoc. editor: Cancer, 1990-2000; contbr. articles to profl. publs. Trustee Nat. Childhood Cancer Found., Arcadia, Calif.; bd. dirs. Am. Cancer Soc., Atlanta; trustee, chmn. patient care and profl. edn. coms. Leukemia Soc. Am. Lt. comdr. USPHS, 1976-79, Res., 1979—. With US Pub. Health Svc., 1976—80, with active reserves, 1980—99. Folger Summer scholar Am. Cancer Soc.; recipient Spl. Fellowship Rsch. award Leukemia Soc. Am., 1980-82, Tree of Life award, Leukemia and Lymphoma Soc.; grantee DHHS, Nat. Cancer Inst., 1987—. Mem. Soc. Pediat. Rsch., Am. Soc. Hematology, Am. Pediat. Soc., Am. Fedn. Clin. Rsch., Am. Soc. Clin. Oncology, Am. Assn. Cancer Rsch., Am. Soc. Pediat. Hematology/Oncology, Children's Oncology Group, Washington Blood Club, Alpha Omega Alpha. Democrat. Roman Catholic. Home: 7306 Brennon Ln Chevy Chase MD 20815-4064 Office: Children's Nat Med Ctr 111 Michigan Ave NW Washington DC 20010-2916 Office Phone: 240-235-2220. Business E-Mail: greaman@childrensoncologygroup.org.

REAMS, BERNARD DINSMORE, JR., law educator; b. Lynchburg, Va., Aug. 17, 1943; s. Bernard Dinsmore and Martha Eloise (Hickman) Reams; m. Rosemarie Bridget Boyle, Oct. 26, 1968 (dec. Oct. 1996); children: Andrew Dennet, Adriane Bevin; m. Lee Anne Oberhofer, Apr. 19, 2003. BA, Lynchburg Coll., 1965; MS, Drexel U., 1966; JD, U. Kans., 1972; PhD, St. Louis U., 1983. Bar: Kans. 1973, Mo. 1986, N.Y. 1996, Tex. 2002. Instr., asst. libr. Rutgers U., 1966—69; asst. prof. law, libr. U. Kans., Lawrence, 1969—74; mem. faculty law sch. Washington U., St. Louis, 1974—95, prof. law, 1976—95, prof. tech. mgmt., 1990—95, libr., 1974—76, acting dean univ. libraries, 1987—88; prof. law, assoc. dean, dir. Law Libr. St. John's U. Sch. Law, Jamaica, NY, 1995—97, assoc. dean acad. affairs, 1997—98; prof., dir. law libr. and info. tech. St. Mary's U., San Antonio, 2000—03, prof. law, 2000. Vis. fellow Max-Planck Inst., Hamburg, 1995, 97-98, 2001; vis. prof. law Seton Hall U., 1998-2000, Inst. World Legal Problems, Innsbruck, Austria, 2002, 05-07. Author: Law For The Businessman, 1974, Reader in Law Librarianship, 1976, Federal Price and Wage Control Programs 1917-1979: Legis. Histories and Laws, 1980, Education of the Handicapped: Laws, Legislative Histories, and Administrative Documents, 1983, Internal Revenue Acts of the United States: The Revenue Act of 1954 with Legislative Histories and Congressional Documents, 1983, Congress and the Courts: A Legislative History 1978-1984, 1984, University-Industry Research Partnerships: The Major Issues in Research and Development Agreements, 1986, Deficit Control and the Gramm-Rudman-Hollings Act, 1986, The Semiconductor Chip and the Law: A Legislative History of the Semiconductor Chip Protection Act of 1984, 1986, American International Law Cases, 2d series, 1986, Technology Transfer Law: The Export Administration Acts of the U.S., 1987, Insider Trading and the Law: A Legislative History of the Insider Trading Sanctions Act, 1989, Insider Trading and Securities Fraud, 1989, The Health Care Quality Improvement Act of 1989: A Legislative History of P.L. No. 99-660, 1990, The National Organ Transplant Act of 1984: A Legislative History of P.L. No. 98-507, 1990, A Legislative History of Individuals with Disabilities Education Act, 1994, Federal Legislative Histories: An Annotated Bibliography and Index to Officially Published Sources, 1994, Electronic Contracting Law, 1996, Health Care Reform, 1994, The American Experience: Clinton and Congress, 1997, The Omnibus Anti-Crime Act, 1997, The Law of E-SIGN: A Legislative History of the Electronic Signature in Global and National Commerce Act, 2001; co-author: Segregation and the Fourteenth Amendment in the States, 1975, Historic Preservation Law: An Annotated Bibliography, 1976, Congress and the Courts: A Legislative History 1787-1977, 1978, Federal Consumer Protection Laws, Rules and Regulations, 1979, A Guide and Analytical Index to the Internal Revenue Acts of the U.S., 1909-1950, 1979, The Numerical Lists and Schedule of Volumes of the U.S. Congressional Serial Set: 73d Congress through the 96th Congress, 1984, Human Experimentation: Federal Laws, Legislative Histories, Regulations and Related Documents, 1985, American Legal Literature: A Guide to Selected Legal Resources, 1985, U.S.A. Patriot Act: A Legislative History, 2002, Supplement, 2005, Intelligence Reform: A Legislative History of the Intelligence Reform and Terrorism Prevention Act, 2006. Trustees Quincy Found. for Med. Rsch. Charitable Trust, San Francisco; bd. dirs. San Antonio Lighthouse for Blind Fellow Am. Bar Found.; recipient Thornton award for excellence Lynchburg Coll., 1986, Joseph L. Andrews Bibliog. award, 1995; named to Hon. Order Ky. Cols., 1992; named Admiral Tex. Navy, 2005. Mem. ABA, ALA, Am. Law Inst., Am. Soc. Law and Medicine, Nat. Health Lawyers Assn., Am. Assn. Higher Edn., Spl. Librs. Assn., Internat. Assn. Law Libr. Coll. and Univ. Attys., Order of Coif, Phi Beta Kappa, Sigma Xi, Beta Phi Mu, Phi Delta Phi, Phi Delta Epsilon, Kappa Delta Pi, Pi Lambda Theta. Office: St Marys U Sch Law One Camino Santa Maria San Antonio TX 78228 Home Phone: 210-479-1316; Office Phone: 210-431-5030. E-mail: breams@stmarytx.edu.

REAMS, LEE ROY, actor; b. Covington, Ky., Aug. 23, 1942; s. Robert David and Flora (Moore) R. BA, U. Cin., 1964, MA, 1982. Appeared in several Broadway musicals including Sweet Charity, 1966, Applause, 1970, Lorelei, 1973, Hello Dolly, 1978, 42d Street, 1980, La Cage aux Folles, 1985, Beauty and the Beast, 1995, An Evening with Jerry Herman, 1998, The Producers, 2004 (Helen Hayes award, Outstanding Supporting Performer, Non-Resident Prodn., 2005); other stage appearances include The Producers (Las Vegas), 2007; acted in numerous TV shows including Jerry Herman at the Hollywood Bowl, 1994, Show Boat, 1989, In Performance at the White House, 1988, Night of 100 Stars II, 1985, Happy Birthday Hollywood, 1987; dir., stage mgr. Hello Dolly (Broadway), 1995. Office: 262 W 89th St New York NY 10024-1705 *

REAMS, PATRICIA LYNN, retired elementary school educator; b. Fresno, Calif., Dec. 10, 1938; d. Chris H. and Marjorie Lois (nee Maul) Pedersen; m. William Everett Harvey (dec.); m. George William Reams, Nov. 10, 1972; children: Holly, Richard, George, Susan, Kristin. AA, Colo. Women's Coll., 1958; BA with honors, San Jose State U., Calif., 1960. Cert. tchg. life diploma 1966. Tchr. Salinas Sch. Dist., Calif., 1960—61, Cupertino Sch. Dist., Calif., 1961—63, Spreckels Sch. Dist., Salinas, 1963—68, Alisal Sch. Dist., Salinas, 1971—74, Kingsburg Charter Sch., Calif., 1987—2002. BITSA trainer Fresno County Sch., Kingsburg, 1996—98. Pink lady, women's aux. local hosp., Salinas, Calif., 1972—83, Boulder City, Nev., 1984—87; adv. Rainbow Girls, Salinas, 1980—83; sec. PTA, Boulder City, 1984—86; brownie leader, 1985—86; Girl Scout leader, 1986—87; sec. Kingsburg HS Music Boosters, 1992—94; classroom vol. Lincoln Sch., Kingsburg, 2002—07. Recipient Grand Cross of Color award, Rainbow Girls, 1983. Mem.: PEO (pres. 2004—06, guard 2007), Ladies Oriental Shrine. Republican. Avocations: reading, gardening, travel. E-mail: plreams@sbcglobal.net.

REARDEN, CAROLE ANN, clinical pathologist, educator; b. Belleville, Ont., Can., June 11, 1946; d. Joseph Brady and Honora Patricia (O'Halloran) R. BSc, McGill U., 1969, MSc, MDCM, 1971. Diplomate Am. Bd. Pathology, Am. Bd. Immunohematology and Blood Banking, Am. Bd. HIstocompatibility and Immunogenetics. Resident and fellow Children's Meml. Hosp., Chgo., 1971-73; resident in pediatrics U. Calif., San Diego, 1974, resident then fellow, 1975-79, asst. prof. pathology, 1979-86, dir. histocompatability and immunogenetics lab., 1979-94, assoc. prof., 1986-92, prof., 1992—, head divsn. lab. medicine, 1989-94; dir. med. ctr. U. Calif. Thornton Hosp. Clin. Labs., San Diego, 1993—. Prin. investigator devel. monoclonal antibodies to erythroid antigens, recombinant autoantigens; dir. lab. exam. com. Am. Bd. Histocompatibility and Immunogenetics. Contbr. articles to profl. jours.; patentee autoantigen pinch. Mem. Mayor's Task Force on AIDS, San Diego, 1983. Recipient Young Investigator Rsch. award NIH, 1979; grantee U. Calif. Cancer Rsch. Coordinating Com., 1982, NIH, 1983; scholar Nat. Blood Found. Mem. Am. Soc. Investigative Pathology, Am. Soc. Hematology, Am. Assn. Blood Banks (com. organ transplantation and tissue typing 1982-87, tech. com. 13 and 14 edit. tech. manual 1996-2002). Office: U Calif San Diego Dept Pathology 0612 9500 Gilman Dr La Jolla CA 92093-0612 E-mail: arearden@ucsd.edu.

REARDON, FRANK EMOND, lawyer; b. Providence, May 22, 1953; s. J. Clarke and Dorothy (Emond) R.; m. Deborah Walsh, Sept. 30, 1978; children: Kathleen Elizabeth, Brendan Francis, William James, Sean Patrick. BA, Holy Cross Coll., Worcester, Mass., 1975; JD, Suffolk U., 1978; MS, Harvard U., 1981. Bar: Mass. 1978, R.I. 1978, U.S. Dist. Ct. Mass. 1980, U.S. Dist. Ct. R.I. 1980, U.S. Supreme Ct. 1986. Counsel Nat. Assn. Govtl. Employment and Internat. Brotherhood Police Officers, Cranston, R.I., 1978-81; asst. gen. counsel Brigham and Women's Hosp., Boston, 1981-84; litigation counsel Risk Mgmt. Found. Harvard Med. Instns., Cambridge, Mass., 1984-87; ptnr. Hassan and Reardon, Boston, 1987—. Chmn. bd. dirs. St. Monica's Nursing Home, 1984-89, Med. Area Fed. Credit Union, 1984-89; clk., trustee Deaconness Glover Hosp., Needham, Mass.; ethics com. Boston Children's Hosp., 1993-96. Contbr. articles to profl. jours. Chmn. fin. com. Town of Needham, Mass.; mem. pres.'s council Coll. Holy Cross, 1985—. Beuilacqua scholar, 1978. Mem. ABA, Mass. Bar Assn. (chmn. health law sect. 1987—), Assn. Trial Lawyers Am., Am. Soc. Law and Medicine (cmty. rep. children's hosp. ethics com.). Democrat. Roman Catholic. Avocations: tennis, sailing, golf, writing. Home: 44 Sargent St Needham MA 02492-3434 Office: Hassan & Reardon 535 Boylston St Boston MA 02116-3720

REARDON, GEORGE MARTIN, lawyer; b. Detroit, Aug. 7, 1947; BS in bus., Ind. U., 1972; JD, U. Fla., Gainesville, 1975. Bar: Fla. 1976, US Ct. Appeals 5th Cir. 1976, US Dist. Ct. Mid., No., So. Districts Fla. 1976, Tex. 1992, US Dist. Ct. So. Dist. Tex. 1992, Mich. 1999. V.p., gen. counsel Charles Stedman & Co. Inc., 1976—82; v.p., asst. gen. counsel Snelling & Snelling, Inc., 1983—90; v.p., gen. counsel, corp. sec. The Talent Tree Corp., 1990-94; atty. pvt. practice, Houston, 1994-98; sr. v.p., gen. counsel Kelly Services Inc., Troy, Mich., 1998—2004, Adecco Group N.Am., 2005—. Served Adj. Gen. Corps US Army, 1970—72, Vietnam. Office: Adecco 175 Broadhollow Rd Melville NY 11747 *

REARDON, JAMES F., adult education educator; s. Joseph Reardon. PhD, U. North Tex., Denton. Wells Fargo prof. U. North Colo., Greeley, 1997—. Office: U N Colo Campus Box 128 Greeley CO 80639 Office Phone: 970-351-1251.

REARDON, JOHN B., III, state agency administrator; b. Youngstown, Ohio, Nov. 25, 1957; s. John B. Jr. and Carole Ann (Shutrump) R. BBA in Econs., Kent State U., Ohio, 1979; MA in Econs., Youngstown State U., 1985. Mgr. contract adminstrn. Rep. Storage Systems Co., Canton, Ohio, 1980; treas. Mahoning County, Ohio, 1998—2007; supt. Ohio Divsn. Fin. Instns., 2006—07. Tchr. econs. Youngstown State U. Republican. Roman Catholic. Avocations: reading, music, sports, games, travel. Office: Divsn Fin Instns Ohio Dept Commerce 77 S High St 21st Fl Columbus OH 43215-6120 Office Phone: 614-728-8400. Office Fax: 614-752-9029. E-mail: john.reardon@com.state.oh.us.

REARDON, JOHN E., broadcast executive; b. Chgo., Jan. 26, 1954; BA in Bus. Adminstrn. and Fin., Loyola U., 1977. Account exec. WGN-TV, Chgo., 1985—86, regional sales mgr., 1986—87, local sales mgr., 1979—89, dir. sales, 1989—92; sta. mgr. KTLA-TV, LA, 1992—96, v.p. & gen. mgr., 1996—2004; group v.p. Tribune Broadcasting Co., 2004—05, pres. & CEO Chgo., 2005—. Bd. dirs. Lincoln Park Zoo, Chgo. Mem.: Nat. Assn. Broadcasters (TV bd. dirs.), TV Bur. Advt. (bd. dirs.). Office: Tribune Co 435 N Michigan Ave Chicago IL 60611 Office Phone: 312-222-9100. *

REARDON, MICHAEL J., finance company executive; Mng. dir. high yield leverage fin. Salomon Smith Barney, NYC, 1994—96; mng. dir. fin. planning and analysis Travelers Group, 1996—98; mng. dir. Strategy and Bus. Devel. Group Citigroup, 1999—2002, chief adminstrn. officer Consumer Fin. and Consumer Assets Div., 2000—02, CFO Consumer Assets Div., 2000—04; acting CFO Student Loan Corp., Stamford, Conn., 2004, CEO, 2004—, pres., 2005—, chmn., 2006—. Office: Student Loan Corp 750 Washington Blvd Stamford CT 06901

REARDON, NANCY ANNE, food products executive; b. Little Falls, NY, Sept. 19, 1952; d. Warren Joseph and Elizabeth Owen (Tiel) Reardon; m. Steven Jonathan Sayer, Aug. 28, 1976; children: Scott Jason, Kathryn Anne. BS in Psychology, Union Coll., 1974; MS in Social Psychology, Syracuse U., 1978. With GE Co., NYC, 1979-85, Avon Products Inc., NYC, 1985-89, Am. Express, NYC, 1989-91; sr. v.p. human resources

Duracell Internat., Inc., Bethel, Conn., 1991-97; sr. v.p. corp. affairs & human resources Borden Inc., Columbus, Ohio, 1997—2004; sr. v.p., chief human resources and comm. officer Campbell Soup Co., Camden, NJ, 2004—. Bd. dir. Warnaco Group Inc. 2006-; adv. bd. mem. Catalyst, 1995. Mem. Human Resource Planning Soc. (bd. dirs. 1991-94, treas. 1992-93), N.Y. Human Resource Planners (bd. dirs., pres. 1989-91), Sr. Pers. Execs. Forum, Nat. Fgn. Trade Coun. (bd. dirs. 1995), Soc. Human Resource Mgmt., Phila. Women's Forum. Avocation: skiing. Office: Campbell Soup Co 1 Campbell Pl Camden NJ 08103-1799

REARDON, ROBERT IGNATIUS, JR., lawyer; b. NYC, Nov. 28, 1945; s. Robert I. and Mildred (Lomax) R.; m. Lise Hofffman; children: Colleen Brooke, Kelly Elizabeth. BS in Econs., Boston Coll., 1967; JD, Fordham U., 1970. Bar: Conn. 1970, U.S. Dist. Ct. Conn. 1974, U.S. Ct. Mil. Appeals 1971, U.S. Ct. Appeals (2d cir.) 1974, U.S. Supreme Ct. 1974, U.S. Ct. Claims 1986. Ptnr. Shapiro & Reardon, P.C., New London, Conn., 1973-83; pres. Reardon Law Firm P.C., New London, 1983—. State trial referee Conn. Superior Ct., 1985—. Chmn. Bd. Fin. Town of Waterford, Conn., 1974-79; mem. Bd. Edn. Town of East Lyme, Conn., 1981-84; trustee Eugene O'Neill Meml. Theater, Inc., 1978-84; active Conn. Commn. Pub. Trust, 1998-2000. Served as capt. USMC, 1970-73. Recipient Disting. Alumnus award, Fordham Law Sch., 2004. Mem. ABA (award of achievement young lawyers sect. 1975), ATLA (bd. dirs. 1998—), Conn. Trial Lawyers Assn. (pres. 1997-98), Conn. Bar Assn. (bd. govs. 1979-81, ho. of dels. 1975-79), New London County Bar Assn. (mem. exec. com. 1975-79)Fordham Law Sch. (Dist. Alumnus award, 2004) Office: 160 Hempstead St New London CT 06320-5638 Office Phone: 860-442-0444. Personal E-mail: reardonlaw@aol.com.

REASON, J. PAUL, naval officer; b. Washington, Mar. 22, 1941; s. Joseph Henry and Bernice (Chism) R.; m. Dianne Lillian Fowler, June 12, 1965; children: Rebecca, Joseph. BS, U.S. Naval Acad., 1965; MS, USN Postgrad. Sch., 1970. Cert. nuclear propulsion engr. Commd. ens. USN, 1965, advanced through grades to adm., 1996; naval aide to pres. The White Ho., Washington, 1976-79; exec. officer USS Miss., 1979-81; comdg. officer USS Coontz, 1981-83, USS Bainbridge, 1983-86; comdr. Naval Base, Seattle, 1986-88, Cruiser-Destroyer Group 1, 1988-90, Naval Surface Force Atlantic, 1991-94; dep. chief naval ops. plans, policy and ops. Dept. Navy, Washington, 1994-96; comdr.-in-chief U.S. Atlantic Fleet, 1996-99; retired, 1999; v.p. Syntek, Inc., Arlington, Va., 1999-2000; pres. Metro Machine Corp., Norfolk, Va., 2000—. Bd. dirs. Wal-Mart Stores Inc., 2000—06, Amgen, 2001—, Norfolk Southern Corp., 2002—. Decorated DSM, Legion of Merit, other mil. awards. Achievements include the first African-American in naval history to achieve the rank of four-star admiral. Avocations: fishing, tennis. Address: 201 W Tazewell St Apt 319 Norfolk VA 23510-1319

REASONER, BARRETT HODGES, lawyer; b. Houston, Apr. 16, 1964; s. Harry Max and Macey (Hodges) Reasoner; m. Susan Hardig; children: Matthew Joseph, Caroline Macey, William Harry, Olivia Lucille, Eloise Susan. BA cum laude, Duke U., 1986; Grad. Dipl., London Sch. Econs., 1987; JD with honors, U. Tex., 1990. Bar: Tex. 1990, U.S. Dist. Ct. (ea., so., we., and no. dists.) Tex. 1993, U.S. Ct. Appeals (5th cir.) 1993, U.S. Supreme Ct. 1997. Asst. dist. atty. Harris County Dist. Atty.'s Office, Houston, 1990-92; ptnr. Gibbs & Bruns, L.L.P., Houston, 1992—. Fellow: Houston Bar Found., Tex. Bar Found.; mem.: Houston Vol. Lawyers Program (bd. dirs. 2001—, chmn. bd. dirs. 2005—06), Houston Young Lawyers Assn. (mem. pub. schs. and pub. edn. com. 1994—99, chmn. 1997—99, outstanding com. chair 1999), Houston Bar Assn. (bd. dirs. 2000—, outstanding com. chmn. 2003, treas. 2007—), State Bar Tex. (mem. jud. rels. com. 1999—2001), Am. Judicature Soc. (bd. dirs. 1994—99, mem. exec. com. 1997—99), Am. Law Inst., Order of Barristers. Episcopalian. Office: Gibbs & Bruns LLP 1100 Louisiana St Ste 5300 Houston TX 77002-5215 Office Phone: 713-650-8805. Business E-Mail: breasoner@gibbs-bruns.com.

REASONER, HARRY MAX, lawyer; b. San Marcos, Tex., July 15, 1939; s. Harry Edward and Joyce Majorie (Barrett) Reasoner; m. Elizabeth Macey Hodges, Apr. 15, 1963; children: Barrett Hodges, Elizabeth Macey Reasoner Stokes. BA summa cum laude in Philosophy, Rice U., 1960; JD with hons., U. Tex., 1962; postgrad., U. London, 1962—63. Bar: Tex., DC, NY. Law clk. U.S. Ct. Appeals (2d cir.), 1963—64; assoc. Vinson & Elkins, Houston, 1964—69, ptnr., 1970—, mng. ptnr., 1992—2001, ex-officio mem. Mgmt. Com. Vis. prof. U. Tex. Sch. Law, 1971, Rice U., 1976, U. Houston Sch. Law, 1977; chair adv. group U.S. Dist. Ct. (so. dist.) Tex.; mem. adv. com. Supreme Ct. Tex.; at-large rep. Supreme Ct. Tex. Access to Justice Commn., 2006—. Author (with Charles Alan Wright): Procedure: The Handmaid of Justice, 1965; mem. editl. bd.: Nat. Law Jour., 2004—. Trustee U. Tex. Law Sch. Found., Ctr. Am. and Internat. Law, Baylor Coll. Medicine; chair Tex. Higher Edn. Coordinating Bd., 1991; bd. dirs. Houston A+ Challenge, Houston, 1997—, Supreme Ct. of U.S. Bd. Hist. Soc, 2000—. Named Disting. Alumnus, U. Tex., 1997, U. Tex. Sch. Law, 1998, Rice U., 2003; recipient Professionalism award, US Court Appeals, Fifth Circuit, Am. Inns Court Found., 2004; fellow, Rotary Found., 1962—63. Fellow: Tex. Bar Found., ABA Found., Internat. Soc. Barristers, Am. Coll. Trial Lawyers, Internat. Acad. Trial Lawyers (bd. dirs. 2005—07); mem.: ABA (chmn. antitrust sect. 1989—90), Am. Bd. Trial Advocates, Philos. Soc. Tex., Houston Philos. Soc., Am. Law Inst., Assn. Bar City of NY, Houston Bar Assn., Century Assn. N.Y.C., U.S. Hist. Soc., Chancellors, Cosmos Club (DC), Phi Delta Phi, Phi Beta Kappa. Office: Vinson & Elkins LLP 1001 Fannin St Ste 2500 Houston TX 77002-6760 Office Phone: 713-758-2358.

REASONER, WILLIS IRL, III, lawyer; b. Hamilton, Ohio, Dec. 24, 1951; s. W. Irl Jr. and Nancy Jane (Mitchell) R.; m. Lana Jean Mayes, Apr. 19, 1975 (div. Sept. 1985); 1 child, Erick; m. Joan Marie Mogil, Dec. 30, 1985; children: Scott, Sally. BA in History, Ind. U., 1974; JD cum laude, U. S.C., 1978. Bar: Ohio 1978, U.S. Dist. Ct. (so. dist.) Ohio 1978, U.S. Dist. Ct. (no. dist.) Ohio 1979, U.S. Ct. Appeals (6th cir.) 1988, U.S. Ct. Appeals (1st cir.) 1991, U.S. Ct. Appeals (7th cir.) 1999. Assoc. Porter, Wright, Morris & Arthur, Columbus, Ohio, 1978-83; ptnr. Baker & Hostetler, Columbus, 1983-94, Habash, Reasoner & Frazier, 1994—. Mem. ABA, Ohio Bar Assn., Columbus Bar Assn. Home: 4005 Redford Ct New Albany OH 43054-9500 Office: Habash, Reasoner & Frazier 471 E Broad St Ste 800 Columbus OH 43215-3854 Office Phone: 614-221-9400. E-mail: jreasoner@hrf-law.com.

REATH, DAVID BROOKE, plastic surgeon; b. Phila., Mar. 18, 1953; married; 3 children. MD, U. Tex., Dallas, 1979. Cert. Am. Bd. Plastic Surgery, 1988. Gen. surgery intern Med. Coll. Va., Richmond, 1979—80, plastic surgery resident, 1980—84; resident Hosp. U. Pa., Phila., 1984—86; with U. Tenn. Med. Ctr., Knoxville, assoc. prof.; with Plastic Surgery Knoxville. Assoc. prof. plastic surgery U. Tenn. Guest (radio shows) The Phil Williams Show, 2005; featured: magazines Self, 2005, Plastic Surgery News, 2007. Named one of Knoxville's Top Docs, Cityview Mag., 2006. Fellow: Am. Coll. Surgeons; mem.: Ea. Assn. for Surgery of Trauma (pres. emeritus), Am. Soc. Aesthetic Plastic Surgery, Tenn. Soc. Plastic Surgeons (pres. emeritus), Am. Soc. Plastic Surgeons (bd. dirs. 2006). Avocations: rowing, sailing, football. Office: Northshore Dr Ste 101 Knoxville TN 37919 Office Phone: 865-450-9253. Office Fax: 865-450-9949.

REATH, GEORGE, JR., lawyer, mediator, arbitrator; b. Phila., Mar. 14, 1939; s. George and Isabel Duer (West) Reath; m. Ann B. Rowland, 1990; children from previous marriage: Eric(dec.), Amanda. BA, Williams Coll., 1961; LLB, Harvard U., 1964. Bar: Pa. 1965, US Dist. Ct. (ea. dist.) Pa. 1966, US Ct. Appeals (3d cir.) 1996. Assoc. Dechert Price & Rhoads, Phila., 1964-70, Brussels, 1971-74; atty. Pennwalt Corp., Phila., 1974-78, mgr. legal dept., asst. sec., 1978-87, sr. v.p. law, sec., 1987-89; sr. v.p., gen. counsel, sec. Elf Atochem N.Am., Inc. (formerly Pennwalt Corp.), Phila., 1990-92; sr. v.p., gen counsel, sec. Legal Triage Svcs., Inc., Phila., 1993-98; sr. v.p., gen. counsel, sec. Triage Mediation Svcs., Inc., Phila., 1999—. Trustee Children's Hosp., Phila., 1974—2003, sec., 1980—81, vice chmn., 1984—97, trustee emeritus, 2003; bd. mgrs. Phila. City Inst. Libr., 1974—, treas., 1981—88, pres., 1989—99; bd. dirs. Phila. Festival Theatre New Plays, 1983—94, Ctrl. Phila. Devel. Corp., 1987—93, Bach Festival Phila., 1990—98, v.p., 1992—93; bd. dirs. Citizens Crim Commn. Delaware Valley, 1st vice chmn., 1992—94, chmn., 1994—96, exec. com., 1996—; bd. trustees Episcopal Cmty. Svcs., 1999—, treas., 2000—06. Mem.: ABA, Assn. Conflict Resolution, Am. Corp. Counsel Assn., Phila. Bar Assn., Pa. Bar Assn., Penn Club, Winter Harbor Yacht Club, Penllyn Club, Phi Beta Kappa. Office Phone: 215-235-7711. Business E-Mail: gr@triagemediation.com. E-mail: greath@comcast.net.

REAVES, MELVIN JUNIOR, retired small business owner; b. Benson, NC, May 4, 1919; s. Edgar Washington and Bess Ann (Rowsey) Reaves; m. Cynthia Thomas, Nov. 18, 1937; children: Sherwood, Sharon, Dennis, Jackie. Owner Reaves Music Co., Odessa, Tex., San Angelo, Tex., House Beautiful, Odessa, Tex., Austin Piano Co., Austin P&O Inc., Seguin (Tex.) Piano Co., Mel Reaves Realty, Austin, Tex. Author: West Texas - 1947, 2006, What Color Blue, 2006, Romance in Prose and Poems, 2006, Writer's Aid, 2006. Mem. C. of C., Odessa, Tex. With USN, WWII. Mem.: DAV, VFW, Am. Legion, Lions Club. Presbyterian. Home: 512 Green Valley Dr Unit A Bastrop TX 78602-6873 Personal E-mail: melreaves@academicplanet.com.

REAVES, RAY DONALD, civil engineer; b. Jacksonville, Ala., Aug. 6, 1935; s. William Ozzie and Josephine (Jackson) R.; m. Annette Baird, Dec. 18, 1959; children: Tanya Ann Walker, Ronald Ray. BS in Civil Engring., Auburn U., Ala., 1960; MBA, U. Utah, 1976; postgrad., U. Mo., Kansas City. Registered profl. engr., Okla.; diplomate Am. Acad. Environ. Engrs. Commd. 2d lt. USAF, 1961, advanced through grades to col., 1981; comdt. Airlift Ops. Sch., Scott AFB, Ill., 1980-82; dep. base comdr. Little Rock AFB, 1982-83; base comdr. Kunsan Air Base, Korea, 1983-84, Tinker AFB, Oklahoma City, 1984-85; dir. environ. mgr. Oklahoma City Air Logistics Ctr., Tinker AFB, 1985-89; ret. USAF, 1989; mgr. environ. engring. Oklahoma County, Oklahoma City, 1989-95, Okla. county engr., 1995—2007. Bus. Tech. Delegation Citizen to Citizen ambassador to Russia and Ukraine, 1992. Mem. ASCE, NSPE, Okla. Soc. Profl. Engrs. (citizen ambassador to Russia and Ukraine 1992), Midwest City C. of C., Rotary, Masons, Shriners. Avocations: golf, boating, tinkering.

REAVIS, CHARLES BENTON, choir director, educator; b. Salisbury, NC, Nov. 20, 1946; s. James Clyde and Mildred Benton Reavis; m. Muriel Marjorie Roberts, July 4, 1949; children: Christopher Benton, Heather Reavis Fullerton. M of Secondary Edn., Salisbury U., 1978. Cert. advanced profl. Md., 1985. Tchr. Daniels Jr. HS, Raleigh, NC, 1969—71, Carneige Jr. HS, Raleigh, 1971—73, James M. Bennett HS, Salisbury, Md., 1973—; choir dir. St. Stephen's United Meth. Ch., Delmar, Del., 1973—, WorWic CC, Salisbury, 2006—. Mem. state curriculum task force Md. State Dept. Edn., Balti., 1986—88. Coun. mem. St. Stephen's United Meth. Ch., 1973. Mem.: NEA (life). Office Phone: 410-677-5141.

REAVIS, HUBERT GRAY, JR., retired metal products executive; b. Winston-Salem, NC, May 4, 1945; s. Hubert Gray and Marie R.; m. Brenda Todd, Oct. 19, 1969; children: Anna Caroline, Jennifer Rebecca. BS in Engring., N.C. State U., 1967. Metall. engr. Alumninum Co. Am., Alcoa, Tenn., 1967-73; divisional metall. engr. Aluminum Co. Am., Newburgh, Ind., 1973-79, product metall. engr. Pitts., 1979-86; quality assurance mgr. Alumninum Co. Am., Newburgh, Ind., 1986-88; tech. mgr. Aluminum Co. Am., Newburgh, Ind., 1988-96, mgr. materials devel. group, 1997—2002, sr. mgr. tech., 2002—04, ret., 2004; cons., 2005—. Patentee in field. Mem. Alumninum Co. Am. Polit. Action, Pitts., 1979-86, Newburgh, 1986—. Recipient 3 Arthur Vining Davis awards. Mem. Am. Soc. for Metals, N.C. State Alumni Loyalty Fund, Phi Kappa Phi, Theta Tau, Alpha Sigma Mu, Tau Beta Pi.

REAVLEY, THOMAS MORROW, federal judge; b. Quitman, Tex., June 21, 1921; s. Thomas Mark and Mattie (Morrow) Reavley; m. Florence Montgomery Wilson, July 24, 1943 (dec.); children: Thomas Wilson, Marian, Paul Stewart, Margaret; m. Carolyn Dineen King, Aug. 27, 2004. BA, U. Tex., 1942; JD, Harvard U., 1948; LLD, Austin Coll., 1974, Southwestern U., 1977, Tex. Wesleyan, 1982; LLM, U. Va., 1983; LLD, Pepperdine U., 1993. Bar: Tex. 1948. Asst. dist. atty., Dallas, 1948—49; mem. Bell & Reavley, Nacogdoches, Tex., 1949—51; county atty. Nacogdoches, Tex., 1951; with Collins, Garrison, Renfro & Zeleskey, 1951—52; mem. Fisher, Tonahill & Reavley, Jasper, Tex., 1952—55; sec. state Tex., 1955—57; mem. Powell, Rauhut, McGinnis & Reavley, Austin, Tex., 1957—64; dist. judge Austin, Tex., 1964—68; justice Tex. Supreme Ct., Tex., 1968—77; counsel Scott & Douglass, 1977—79; judge US Ct. Appeals (5th cir.), Austin, Tex., 1979—90, sr. judge, 1990—. Lectr. Baylor U. Law Sch., 1976—94; adj. prof. U. Tex. Law Sch., 1958—59, 1978—79, 1988—95, South Tex. Sch. Law, Pepperdine Law Sch., 1990, Tex. Tech. Law Sch., 1998; mem. Am. Bar Assn., Am Bar Found., Tex. Bar Assn, Am. Law Inst., Am. Judicature Soc. Chancellor S.W. Tex. conf. United Meth. Ch., 1972—93. Lt. USNR, 1943—45. Mem.: Masons (33 degree). Office: US Ct Appeals Rm 11009 515 Rusk St Houston TX 77002-2605 Home Phone: 713-960-9512; Office Phone: 713-250-5185. *

REAY, STEFANIE, application developer, educator; d. Rick and Ruth Lagerquist; m. Brent Reay, Feb. 14, 2004; children: Katelynn, Adrianna. BS in Math. and Stats., U. Conn., Storrs, 1999, MS in Stats., 2001. Lectr. U. Conn., Storrs, 1999—; analyst CentrPort, Westport, Conn., 2001; portfolio rev. analyst People's Bank Credit Card Divsn., Bridgeport, Conn., 2002—03, sr. quantitative analyst, 2003; analyst The Student Loan Corp., Pittsford, NY, 2004—06; bus. intelligence client svc. mgr., 2007. Adj. lectr. U. New Haven, 2002—. Mem.: Am. Statis. Assn. Avocation: volleyball. Home Phone: 860-584-1305. Personal E-mail: stefanie_reay@hotmail.com.

REAY-JONES, FRANCIS PETER FORTNUM, entomologist, researcher; b. Oxford, England, May 23, 1978; arrived in U.S., 2002; s. Nigel S. and Georgea Reay-Jones. BS in Organism Biology, U. Bordeaux 1, 1999; MS in Plant Tech., U. d'Angers, 2001; PhD in Entomology, La. State U., 2005. Grad. rsch. asst. C.I.R.A.D, St-Denis-de-la-Réunion, France, 2001, La. State U., Baton Rouge, 2002—05, post-doctoral rsch. assoc., 2005, Tex. A&M U., Beaumont, Tex., 2006; asst. prof. Clemson U., Forence, SC, 2006—. Contbr. articles to profl. jours. Co-chair movie com. Internat. Cultural Ctr. La. State U., 2002—03. Recipient L.D. Newsom Outstanding PhD Student award, La. State U., 2004;, Sigma Xi grantee, 2004. Mem.: Am. Soc. Sugar Cane Technologists (D.T. Loupe Best Paper Presentation award 2005), La. Plant Protection Assn., Entomol. Soc. Am. (Robert T. Gast Best Rsch. Presentation PhD Student award S.E. br. 2004). Avocations: movies, travel. Office: Clemson Univ Pee Dee Rsch and Edn Ctr 2200 Pocket Rd Florence SC 29506 Office Fax: 843-661-5676.

REBACK, GARY, lawyer; b. Knoxville, Tenn., 1949; married; 2 children. BA magna cum laude, Yale U., 1971; LD, Stanford Law Sch. Clk. Fifth Cir., Atlanta, 1974—75; atty. Covington & Burling LLP, Washington, 1975—81, Fenwick & West LLP, Palo Alto, Calif., 1981—91, Wilson Sonsini Goodrich & Rosati LLP, Palo Alto, Calif., 1991—2000, Carr & Ferrell LLP, Palo Alto, Calif., 2003—. Author: (Article) Why Microsoft Must Be Stopped, 1995; contbr. articles to Forbes Mag. Named one of 100 Most Influential Lawyers, Nat. Law Jour., 1997, 2006, Elite 100, Upside Mag., Top 100, Micro Times, Lawyers of the Yr., Calif. Lawyer Mag. Achievements include successfully opposing Microsoft's acquisition of Intuit. Office: Carr & Ferrell LLP 2200 Geng Rd Palo Alto CA 94303

REBACK, JOYCE ELLEN, lawyer; b. Phila., July 11, 1948; d. William and Sue (Goldstein) R.; m. Itzhak Brook, Aug. 2, 1981; children: Jonathan Zev, Sara Jennie. BA magna cum laude, Brown U., 1970; JD with honors, George Washington U., 1976. Bar: D.C. 1976, U.S. Dist. Ct. D.C. 1976, U.S. Ct. Appeals (D.C. cir.) 1976, U.S. Ct. Appeals (3d cir.) 1983, U.S. Ct. Appeals (Fed. cir.) 1985. Assoc. Fulbright & Jaworski, Washington, 1976—84, ptnr., 1984—87; legal svcs. cons. IMF, Washington, 1987—. Contbr. articles to profl. jours. Mem. ABA, D.C. Bar Assn., Phi Beta Kappa. Jewish. Office: Internat Monetary Fund 700 19th St NW Washington DC 20431-0001

REBAY, LUCIANO, language educator, literary critic; b. Milan, Apr. 23, 1928; came to U.S., 1955; s. Angelo and Pierina (Doniselli) R.; m. Martha Virginia Krauss, Aug. 2, 1952; children: Alexandra, Ilaria. Maturita classica Liceo Manzoni, Milan, 1946; Licence es lettres, U. Aix-en-Provence, France, 1951; PhD, Columbia U., 1960. Instr. Italian Columbia U., NYC, 1957-60, asst. prof., 1960-63, assoc. prof., 1963-65, prof., 1965-73, Giuseppe Ungaretti prof. Italian lit., 1973—, chmn. Italian Dept., 1970-73; dir. Ctr. Italian Studies, 1985-88. Cons. to scholarly jours.; mem. Nat. Bd. Translators, Columbia U. Transl. Ctr. Author: Le origini della poesia di Giuseppe Ungaretti, 1962, Invitation to Italian Poetry, 1969, Alberto Moravia, 1970, Giuseppe Ungaretti, Gli scritti egiziani, 1909-1912, 1980, Montale, Clizia e l'America, 1982, Montale per amico, 1994, Montale: del dire e del non dire, 1998; editor: Giuseppe Ungaretti, Saggi e interventi, 1974, Jean Paulhan-Giuseppe Ungaretti, Correspondance, 1921-68, 1989. Guggenheim fellow, 1966-67; Am. Council Learned Socs. fellow, 1970-71; NEH fellow, 1980-81; Am. Philos. Soc. research grantee, 1970, 75 Mem. MLA, Am. Assn. Tchrs. of Italian, Associazione Internazionale per gli Studi di Lingua e Letteratura Italiana

REBEI, ADNAN, physicist, researcher; PhD, U. Wis., Madison, 1998. Mem.: Am. Math. Soc., Am. Phys. Soc. Achievements include research in dissipation and noise in magnetic recording heads. Office: Seagate Research Center 1251 Waterfront Pl Pittsburgh PA 1522 Home Phone: 412-776-7207; Office Phone: 412-918-7231. Personal E-mail: arebei@mailaps.org. E-mail: adnan.rebei@seagate.com.

REBEIN, DAVID JAMES, lawyer; b. Dodge City, Kans., Mar. 13, 1955; AA, Dodge City Community Coll., 1975; BA summa cum laude, Washburn U., 1977; JD, Kans. U., 1980. Bar: Kans. 1980, US Dist. Ct. (Dist. Kans.) 1980. Trial atty. Mangan, Dalton, Trenkle, Rebein & Doll, Dodge City, Kans., 1982; ptnr. Rebein Bangerter, Dodge City, Kans. Bd. dirs. Kans. Assn. Commerce and Industry, 1977—2000; bd. gov. U. Kans. Coll. Law; bd. trustees Dodge City Cmty. Coll., endowment bd.; bd. dirs. Kans. Agrl. and Rural Leadership; mem. Leadership Kans., 1997; bd. dirs. Manna House; adv. bd. Manor of the Plains; pres. bd. dirs. New Chance; nominating commn. Kans. Supreme Ct., 2002—06; citizen adv. com. Kans. Sunflower Found., 2005—. Fellow: Kans. Bar Found. (pres. litig. sect. 1991—92), Am. Bar Found.; mem.: Southwest Kans. Bar Assn., Kans. Trial Lawyers Assn., Kans. Assn. Def. Counsel (bd. dirs. 1992, pres. 2001), Kans. Bar Assn. (pres. 2006), Ford-Gray County Bar Assn. (pres. 1985), Am. Trial Lawyers Assn., Internat. Assn. Def. Counsel, ABA. Office: Rebein Bangerter 810 Frontview PO Box 1147 Dodge City KS 67801 Office Phone: 620-227-8126. E-mail: drebein@rebeinbangerter.com.

REBEIZ, CONSTANTIN ANIS, plant biochemist, educator, lab administrator, foundation administrator; b. Beirut, July 11, 1936; arrived in U.S., 1959, naturalized, 1975; s. Anis C. and Valentine A. (Choueyri) Rebeiz; m. Conness Carole Louise, Aug. 18, 1962; children: Paul A., Natalie, Mark J. BS, Am. U., Beirut, 1959; MS, U. Calif., Davis, 1960, PhD, 1965. Dir. dept. biol. scis. Agrl. Rsch. Inst., Beirut, 1965—69; rsch. assoc. biology U. Calif., Davis, 1969—71; assoc. prof. biochem. plant physiology U. Ill., Urbana-Champaign, 1972—76, prof., 1976—2005, dir. Lab. Plant Biochemistry and Photobiology, 1973—2005, prof. emeritus, 2005—; pres. Rebeiz Found. for Basic Rsch., Champaign, 2005—. Adj. prof. U. Limerick, Ireland, 2003. Contbr. articles to profl. jours. Bd. dirs. Rebeiz Found. for Basic Rsch. Named one of 100 Outstanding Innovators, Sci. Digest, 1984—85; recipient Beckman Rsch. award, 1982, 1985, Funk award, 1985, Sr. Rsch. award, U. Ill., 1994, Presdl. Green Chemistry Challenge award, 1999, Outstanding Sci. Achievement award, Faculty of Agrl. and Food Sci., Am. U. Beirut, 2002; grantee John P. Trebellas Rsch. Endowment, 1986, C.A. and C.C. Rebeiz Endowment for basic rsch., 2000. Mem.: AAAS, Lebanese Assn. Advancement Scis. (exec. com. 1967—69). Achievements include research in pathway of chlorophyll biosynthesis; chloroplast development; bioengineering of photosynthetic reactors; first to biosynthesis of chlorophyll in vitro; duplication of greening process of plants in test tube; development of demonstration of operation of multi-branched chlorophyll biosynthetic pathway in nature; formulation of a blue-print chloroplast bioengineering in green plants aimed at improving plant productivity; formulation and design of laser herbicides, insecticides and cancer chemotherapeutic agents. Home: 2209 Edgewater Pl Champaign IL 61822 Office: Rebeiz Found Basic Rsch 2209 Edgewater Pl Champaign IL 61822 Office Phone: 217-377-9148. Business E-Mail: crebeiz@uiuc.edu. *Meaningful scientific discoveries are those that help humans achieve a better understanding of themselves, of their environment or of the universe at large, as well as those that contribute to the betterment of the human spiritual, psychological and physical condition.*

REBELL, ARTHUR LESLIE, diversified holding company executive; Prof. mergers & acquisitions NYU Stern Grad. Sch. Bus.; various positions Schroder Wertheim & Co., NYC; mng. dir. High View Capital Corp., Strategic Mgmt. Co., LLC, NYC, 1997—98; sr. v.p., chief investment officer Loews Corp., NYC, 1998—. Office: Loews Corp 667 Madison Ave New York NY 10021-8087 Office Phone: 212-521-2450. *

REBELLO, MARLENE MUNSON, speech pathologist, consultant; b. San Jose, Calif., Oct. 15, 1948; d. Alfred Vernon and Rose Zita (Pereira) Nunes; m. Steven Del Munson, Mar. 21, 1970 (div. 1982); m. William Wayne Rebello, Dec. 5, 1992. BA, San Jose State U., 1970, MA, 1971; MS in Counseling, U. LaVerne, 1990. Speech pathologist Newark Unified Sch. Dist., Calif., 1971—2005, Washington Hosp., Fremont, Calif., 1980-89; pvt. practice Fremont and Pleasanton, Calif., 1980—. Cons. in field. Recipient Bank of Am. award, 1966, Cabrillo scholarship, Nat. Merit scholarship, 1966, Maria Leonard award Outstanding Sr. Grade Point Average, 1970; fellow VA, 1970. Mem. Calif. Speech and Hearing Assn., Pleasanton Sister City Assn. (v.p. 1996-2002, pres. 2003, mem. pres. 2005-, fundraising chair 2005-), Newark Tchrs. Assn. (treas. 1971), Save Our Sunol Found., Calif. Tchrs. Assn., Arthur & Elena Court Conservation Soc., Pleasanton North Rotary (Paul Harris fellow). Avocations: antiques, decorating, gourmet cooking. Home and Office: 10579 Foothill Rd Sunol CA 94586-9464 Personal E-mail: marspot@aol.com.

REBENACK, JOHN HENRY, retired librarian; b. Wilkinsburg, Pa., Feb. 10, 1918; s. Charles Lewis and Carrie (Fielding) R.; m. Dorothy Merle Treat, Oct. 31, 1942 (dec. Apr. 1971); children: Charles Edwin, Christine (Mrs. Clair N. Hayes III); m. Frances Stribley Krieger, May 6, 1972. AB, U. Pitts., 1942; BS in L.S, Carnegie Library Sch., 1947. Reference asst. Carnegie Library, Pitts., 1947-50; librarian Salem (Ohio) Pub. Library,

1950-53, Elyria (Ohio) Library, 1953-57; asst. librarian Akron (Ohio) Public Library, 1957-65, asso. librarian, 1965-67, librarian-dir., 1967-80. Dir. U.S. Book Exchange, Inc., 1972 Mem. United Community Council, Citizens' Com. Pub. Welfare, 1965-66, chmn. group work and recreation div., 1963-66, v.p., 1967-68, pres. conf. of execs., 1975-76; mem. steering com., planning div. United Way; mem. Akron Mayor's Task Force on Human Relations, 1962; mem. library com. President's Com. on Employment of Handicapped, 1967-80, chmn., 1973-80, mem. sch. library manpower adv. com., 1967-73; mem. coll. adv. com. U. Akron, 1972-85; mem. adv. council on fed. programs State Library of Ohio, 1975-79; Bd. visitors Grad. Sch. Library and Info. Sci., U. Pitts., 1968-74; mem. exec. bd. Gt. Trail council Boy Scouts Am., 1977-80; bd. dirs. Summit County unit Am. Cancer Soc., 1976—, pres., 1979-81; bd. dirs. Ohio div., 1981-91, chmn. pub. info. com., 1989-90, exec. com. 1988-91. With AUS, 1942-45. Recipient Newton D. Baker citation, 1968 Mem. ALA (chmn. personnel adminstrv. sect. 1966-67, chmn. bldgs. and equipment sect. 1971-73, chmn. legislation assembly 1976-77), Ohio Library Assn. (exec. bd. 1957-60, chmn. adult edn. round table 1963, chmn. legis. com. 1965-66, 70-72, 76-80, pres. 1966-67, Librarian of Year 1979, named to Hall of Fame 1989), Ohio Library Found. (privileged mem. 1980, privileged dir. 1988—), Carnegie Library Sch. Assn. (pres. 1961-63), U. Pitts. Grad. Sch. Library and Info. Sci. Alumni Assn. (exec. com. 1978-79, Disting. Alumnus award 1980), Am. Assn. UN (v.p. Akron chpt. 1960), Kiwanis Internat. Found. (Tablet of Honor 1997, George F. Hixson fellow 1998), Torch Club (pres. 1968-69), Kiwanis (pres. Akron 1978-79, Man of Yr. 2004), Beta Phi Mu. Congregationalist. Home: 2095 Brookshire Rd Akron OH 44313-5323

REBER, DAVID JAMES, lawyer; b. Las Vegas, Mar. 1, 1944; s. James Rice and Helen Ruth (Cusick) R.; m. Jacqueline Yee, Aug. 31, 1968; children: Emily, Brad, Cecily. BA, Occidental Coll., LA, 1965; JD, Harvard U., 1968. Bar: Calif. 1969, Hawaii 1975, U.S. Dist. Ct. Hawaii, U.S. Ct. Appeals (9th cir.), U.S. Supreme Ct. Asst. prof. law U. Iowa, Iowa City, 1968-70; assoc. Sheppard Mullin Richter & Hampton, LA, 1970-75, Goodsill Anderson Quinn & Stifel, Honolulu, 1975-76, ptnr., 1976—. Bd. dirs. Enterprise Honolulu, pres. Legal Aid Soc. Hawaii. Mem. ABA (bus. and pub. utilities sects.), Hawaii Bar Assn. Avocations: golf, tennis, softball, travel. Office: Goodsill Anderson Et Al 1099 Alakea St Ste 1800 Honolulu HI 96813-4511 Office Phone: 808-547-5611. E-mail: dreber@goodsill.com.

REBER, RAYMOND ANDREW, chemical engineer; b. Bklyn., Apr. 16, 1942; s. Herbert and Dorothy Agnes (Schmidt) R.; m. Anita Jean Roe, June 22, 1963; children: Laura Jean Bucci, Paul Raymond, Jill Anita Atkinson. BChemE, NYU, 1963, MChemE, 1966. Engr. M.W. Kellogg, NYC, 1964-69; devel. engr. Union Carbide, 1970—81, licensing bus. mgr., 1982-84, tech. mgr., 1985-87; dir. tech. UOP, Tarrytown, 1988-93; exec. v.p., COO Balchem Corp., Slate Hill, NY, 1994-96, pres., CEO, 1997; cons., 1999—. Patentee in field. Commr. Montrose Improvement Dist., NY, 1970—; soccer referee, 1977—93; trustee No. Westchester Joint Water Works, 1995, 1998—2001, cons., 2001—, dir., 2003—07. Recipient Kirkpatrick award McGraw-Hill, 1967, 87. Mem.: NSPE, AIChE. Episcopalian. Avocations: soccer, table games, philately. Home: 10 Bonnie Hollow Ln Montrose NY 10548-1314

REBERT, JEPHREY LEE, urban planner, musician; b. Carlisle, Pa., June 10, 1959; s. John Alton and Mary Anna (Feeman) Rebert. BS, Pa. State U., 1982. Residential appraiser County of York, Pa., 1984-85; phys. and environ. planner York County Planning Commn., 1985-87, transp. planner, 1987-93, sr. transp. planner, 1993—. Musician, prodr.: audiotape Peace of Mind (Loose Cannons), 1995; musician: (albums) Colonial Pagoda (Namaste), 1997, Smoke Signals (Anderson's Tool Shed), 2004. Alumni mem. Pa. State Blue Band; treas., bd. dirs. Ctr. Ind. Living Opportunities; mem. Susquehanna Regional Transp. Partnership; ptnr. York Resuce Mission. Mem.: ASCE, Inst. Transp. Engrs., Am. Planning Assn., Phi Mu Alpha Sinphonia (Alpha Zeta chpt., alumnus). Avocations: anthropology, racquet sports, coin collecting/numismatics. Office: York County Planning Commn 28 E Market St Rm 301 York PA 17401-1580 Personal E-mail: zoombangi@netzero.net.

REBHUN, JOSEPH, allergist, immunologist, medical educator; b. Przemysl, Poland, Oct. 7, 1921; came to U.S., 1950; s. Baruch and Serel R.; m. Maria Birkenhejm, Aug. 10, 1945; children: Lillian Friedland, Richard B.R., Donald. MD, U. Innsbruck, Austria, 1950; MS in Medicine, Northwestern U., 1954. Diplomate Am. Bd. Allergy and Immunology. Intern Barnert Meml. Hosp., Patterson, NJ; resident in internal medicine Tompkins County Meml. Hosp. and Cornell U., NY, 1951-52; fellow in allergy Northwestern U. Med. Sch./Children's Meml. Hosp., Chgo., 1952-54; fellow instr. Northwestern U. Med. Sch., 1954; asst. clin. prof. medicine Loma Linda U., 1957-93; clin. prof. medicine U. So. Calif., LA, 1965-91, ret., 1998. Chief allergy Chgo. Eye, Ear, Nose and Throat Hosp., 1953-55; cons. Pacific State Hosp., Spadra Pomona Valley Cmty. Hosp., Pomona Casa Colina Hosp. Author: SOS, 1946, The Cry of Democracy for Help, God and Man in Two Worlds, 1985, The Embers of Michael, 1993, Crisis of Morality and Reaction to the Holocaust, 1998, Leap to Life: Triumph Over Nazi Evil, 2000, Why Me?, 2004; contbr. numerous articles to med. jours. Pres. Am. Congress Jews from Poland, 1969—70. Capt. U.S. Mil., San Francisco, capt. med. reserve corps., L.A. Recipient honors City and County of L.A., L.A. Office Dist. Atty., Senate of State of Calif., all 1985. Fellow Am. Acad. Allergy (rsch. coun. 1960-65), Am. Coll. Allergy, Assn. Clin. Allergy and Immunology; mem. West Coast Allergy Soc., Calif. Allergy Assn., L.A. Soc. Allergy, L.A. Med. Assn., Calif. Med. Assn. Personal E-mail: joerebhun@yahoo.com.

REBICH, LOIS J., elementary school educator; m. Eli Rebich; 3 children. BBA, MBA, Univ. Pitts. Cert. elem. edn. Chatham Coll. Buyer H.J. Heinz; fin. analyst Rockwell Internat.; tchr. Pitts. City Schs., 1989—91; instructional support tchr., head tchr. Ross Elem. Sch., Pitts., 1991—. Named Pa. Tchr. of Yr., 2007. Office: Ross Elem Sch 90 Houston Rd Pittsburgh PA 15237 Business E-Mail: rebichl@nhsd.k12.pa.us. *

REBOLLO LÓPEZ, FRANCISCO, judge; b. San Juan, Aug. 5, 1938; BA, U. PR, 1959, JD, 1963. Asst. dist atty. San Juan, PR, 1966; asst. prosecutor US Dist. Ct. of PR; judge PR Superior Ct., 1973—77; atty. priv. practice, 1977—82; justice PR Supreme Ct., San Juan, 1982—. Office: Supreme Court PO Box 2392 San Juan PR 00902-2392 *

REBOUL, JOHN W., lawyer; b. NYC, Nov. 12, 1937; AB, Harvard Univ., 1959, LLB, 1963; Doctorat de l'Universite, Faculte de Droit et Sciences Economiques, Univ. Paris, 1964. Bar: N.Y. 1965. Founding ptnr. Reboul Mac Murray Hewitt & Maynard, NYC, 1973—2003; ptnr. corp. dept. & co-head internat. practice group Ropes & Gray, NYC, 2003—. Mem.: ABA, Assn. Bar City of N.Y., Internat. Law Assn. (Am. branch), Union Internationale des Avocats. Office: Ropes & Gray 45 Rockefeller Plz New York NY 10111-0087 Office Phone: 212-841-5705. Office Fax: 212-841-5725. Business E-Mail: jreboul@ropesgray.com.

REBSTOCK, THEODORE LYNN, chemist, educator, retired research scientist; b. Elkhart, Ind., June 24, 1925; s. Adolph Rebstock and Redna Dunkelberger; m. Barbara Jean Lee, Nov. 30, 1957; children: David Lynn, Donald Lee. BA, North Ctrl. Coll., Naperville, Ill., 1949; MS, Mich. State U., 1951, PhD, 1956. Instr. rsch. Mich. State U., East Lansing, 1951—56, asst. prof. agrl. chemistry, 1956—59, vis. prof., 1965; assoc. prof. chemistry Westmar Coll., Le Mars, Iowa, 1959—66, prof. chemistry, 1966—83, chmn. chemistry dept., 1963—83; mgr. R&D Lab. Harkers, Inc., Le Mars, Iowa, 1984—90; ret., 1990. Dir. divsn. natural scis. Westmar Coll., Le Mars, Iowa, 1970. Contbr. articles to profl. jours. Fellow: AAAS; mem.: Am. Chem. Soc., Kiwanis Club (pres. 1993), Sigma Xi. Methodist. Avocations: golf, bowling, gardening, woodworking. Home: 1026 Sixth Ave SE Le Mars IA 51031

REBUELTA, AVELINO LUIS, public administration educator; b. June 22, 1944; MPA, Am. U., Washington, 1982; M in Ednl. Adminstrn., U. Tex., Edinburg, 1999. Prof. Universidad Nacional Autonoma De Mexico, Mexico City, 1962—, Instituto Politecnico Nacional, Mexico City, 1962—, Universidad Pedagogica Nacional, Mexico City, 1982—. Home: 701 Hibiscus Ave Apt 5 Mcallen TX 78501-1858 Home Phone: 956-630-6417; Office Phone: 956-630-6417. E-mail: al_rebuelta@hotmail.com.

RECCHI, MARK, professional hockey player; b. Kamloops, BC, Can., Feb. 1, 1968; Right wing Pitts. Penguins, 1988—92, 2004—06, 2006—, Phila. Flyers, 1992—95, 1999—2004, Montreal Canadiens, 1995—99, Carolina Hurricanes, 2006. Named Most Valuable Player, All-Star Game, 1997; named to NHL All-Star Game, 1991, 1993, 1994, 1997—2000. Achievements include being a member of Stanley Cup Champion Pitts. Penguins, 1991, Carolina Hurricanes, 2006. Office: c/o Pittsburgh Penguins 66 Mario Lemieux Pl Pittsburgh PA 15219

RECH, LINDSAY FAITH, writer; b. Phila., Mar. 30, 1978; d. Ivan Blaine and Hillary-Sue Resnick; m. Scott Rech, Oct. 21, 2000. BFA in Theater and English, Rider U., 2000. Writing tutor Rider U., Lawrenceville, NJ, 2000; columnist Pennington (NJ) Post, 2000—01; freelance reporter, theater critic Times Pub. Newspapers, Inc., Yardley, Pa., 2000, asst. editor, 2000—02; author Red Dress Ink, NYC, 2003—04; editl. quality control assoc. Law Sch. Admission Coun., Newtown, Pa., 2005—. Spkr. Northampton Writers Group, Richboro, Pa., 2003. Columnist: A Different Voice, 2000—01; author: Losing It, 2003, Joyride, 2004. Acad. achievement scholar, presdl. scholar, Rider U., 1996—2000, Clayton Family scholar, 1997—2000. Mem.: Authors Guild, Honor Key Soc., Sigma Tau Delta, Alpha Lambda Delta. Jewish. Avocations: vegetarianism, 80's pop culture. Personal E-mail: lindsay@lindsayfaithrech.com.

RECHARD, PAUL ALBERT, retired civil engineering company executive, consultant; b. Laramie, Wyo., June 4, 1927; s. Ottis H. and Mary R. (Bird) R.; m. Mary Lou Roper, June 26, 1949; children: Robert Paul, Karen Ann. BS, U. Wyo., 1948, MS, 1949, CE, 1955. Registered land surveyor, Wyo.; registered profl. engr., Wyo.; cert. profl. hydrologist Am. Inst. Hydrology. Hydraulic engr. U.S. Bur. Reclamation, Cody, Wyo. and Billings, Mont., 1949-54; dir. water resources Natural Resource Bd., Cheyenne, Wyo., 1954-58; prin. hydraulic engr. Upper Colorado River Commn., Salt Lake City, 1958-64; dir. Water Resources Rsch. Inst. U. Wyo., Laramie, 1964-81, mem. faculty dept. civil engring., 1964-82, prof., 1964-82; pres. Western Water Cons., Laramie, 1980-2001, Hydrology Assocs., Laramie, 1978-80; ret. Western Water Consults., Inc., 2001. Owner Paul A. Rechard, P.E., Laramie, 1964-1978, 2001-. Editor: Compacts, Treaties and Court Decrees Affecting Wyoming Water, 1956; contbr. articles to tech. publs. Pres., Thayer Sch. PTA, Laramie, 1965; mem. Laramie City Planning Commn., 1974-80. Served with USNR, 1945-46. Recipient Wyo. Eminent Engr. award Tau Beta Pi, 1993; named Disting. Alumnus U. Wyo., 1998; named Outstanding Engr. Wyo. Engring. Soc., 1999. Fellow ASCE (life mem., pres. Wyo. sect. 1968); mem. NSPE (life), Am. Geophys. Union, Wyo. Engring. Soc. (pres. 1976, hon.), U.S. Com. on Irrigation and Drainage, Lions (pres. Laramie 1968), Masons, Sigma Xi (pres. Wyo. chpt. 1973), Phi Kappa Phi (pres. Wyo. chpt. 1969), Gamma Sigma Delta, Sigma Tau (pres. Wyo. chpt. 1948, selected Wyo. Eminent Engr. 1993). Republican. Presbyterian. Home and Office: 316 Stuart St Laramie WY 82070-4866 Office Phone: 307-745-7477. Personal E-mail: prechard@msn.com.

RECHY, JOHN FRANCISCO, writer; b. El Paso, Tex. s. Roberto Sixto and Guadalupe (Flores) R. BA, U. Tex., El Paso; student, New Sch. Social Research. Instr. creative writing UCLA, Occidental Coll., U. So. Calif. Author: City of Night, 1963, Numbers, 1967, This Day's Death, 1969, The Vampires, 1971, The Fourth Angel, 1973, The Sexual Outlaw, 1977, Rushes, 1979, Bodies and Souls, 1983, Marilyn's Daughter, 1988, The Miraculous Day of Amalia Gõmez, 1991, Our Lady of Babylon, 1996, The Coming of the Night, 1999, The Life and Adventures of Lyle Clemens, 2003, Outlaw: The Life and Careers of John Rechy, 2004; (essays) Beneath the Skin, 2004; (plays) Momma As She Became-Not As She Was, 1968, Rushes, 1978, Tigers Wild, 1986; (CD-Rom) Mysteries and Desire: Exploring the Worlds of John Rechy, 2000; contbr.: short stories and articles to Tex. Observer, The Nation, Village Voice, London mag., Saturday Rev., N.Y. Times Book Rev., L.A. Times, San Francisco Chronicle Books, Washington Post Book World, Phila. Inquirer, Contemporary Fiction, Big Table, others; also anthologies Chicano Voices, Black Humor, Urban Reader, Evergreen Rev. Reader, New Am. Story, The Moderns, Rediscoveries, Men on Men, others; trans.: stories and articles for Tex. Quar., Evergreen Rev. Served with AUS. Recipient Lifetime Achievement award PEN-USA, 1997, Pub. Triangle's William Whitehead award for lifetime achievement in lit., 1999, Longview Found. award for short story The Fabulous Wedding of Miss Destiny, 1960, Golden Nugget Outstanding Alumni award U. Tex El Paso, 2002; Nat. Endowment for Arts grantee, 1976. Fellow L.A. Inst. Humanities; mem. Authors Guild, Tex. Inst. Letters, PEN, Nat. Writers Union.

RECK, ANDREW JOSEPH, philosopher; b. New Orleans, Oct. 29, 1927; s. Andrew Gervais and Katie (Mangiaracina) R.; m. Elizabeth Lassiter Torre, June 17, 1987. BA, Tulane U., 1947, MA, 1949; postgrad., U. St. Andrews, Scotland, 1952—53; PhD, Yale U., 1954; student, U. Paris, 1962, student, 1964. Instr. English U. Conn., 1949-50; instr. philosophy Yale U., 1951-52, 55-58; faculty Tulane U., 1958—2003, prof. philosophy, 1964—2003, chmn. dept., 1969-89, dir. Master Liberal Arts program, 1984—2003, emeritus prof. philosophy, 2003—. Thomasfest lectr. Xavier U., Cin., 1970; Suarez Lectr. Spring Hill Coll., 1971; Niebuhr lectr. Elmhurst Coll., Ill., 1976; vis. prof. Fordham U., 1979; vis. scholar Hastings Ctr., NY, 1981; Woodruff lectr. Emory U., 1982; Fairchild lectr. U. So. Miss., 1982, 87; Matchette Found. lectr. Cath. U. Am., 1991, 95; sr. scholar Inst. Humane Studies, Menlo Park, Calif., 1982; vis. scholar Poynter Ctr., Ind. U., Bloomington, 1983; faculty rep. to bd. adminstrs. Tulane Ednl. Fund., 1988-91; bd. dirs. Internat. Soc. for Study of Human Ideas of Ultimate Reality and Meaning, 1989-2005, La. Endowment for Humanities, 1990-96; mem. philosophy screening com. Coun. Internat. Rsch. Scholars, 1974-76; mem. am. studies adv. com. Am. Coun. Learned Socs., 1972-76. Author: Recent American Philosophy, 1964, Introduction to William James, 1967, New American Philosophers, 1968, Speculative Philosophy, 1972; co-author: Die Philosophie des 18. Jahrhunderts 1, 2004; editor: George Herbert Mead Selected Writings, 1964, 2d edit., 1981, Knowledge and Value, 1972, (with T. Horvath, T. Krittek and S. Grean) American Philosophers' Ideas of Ultimate Reality and Meaning, 1993; co-editor Ultimate Reality and Meaning, Interdisciplinary Studies in the Philosophy of Understanding, 1990-2005; former mem. adv. editl. bd. Internat. Jour. World Peace, Trans. Charles Peirce Soc., Santayana edit. So. Jour. Philosophy, Library of Living Philosophers; editor History of Philosophy Quar., 1993-98. Soldier US Army, 1953—55. Howard fellow, 1962-63, Liberty Fund grantee, 1982, Newcomb fellow, 1991-93; Fulbright scholar, 1952-53; Am. Coun. Learned Socs. grantee, 1961-62, Am. Philos. Soc. grantee, 1972, Huntington Libr. grantee, 1973, La. Ednl. Quality State Found. grantee, 1994-96, U.S. Info. Agy. grantee, Brazil, 1993. Mem.: Internat. Soc. for Study of Human Ideas of Ultimate Reality and Meaning (bd. dirs. 1989—2005, treas. 2001—03, sec., treas. 2003—05), Charles S. Peirce Soc. (sec., treas. 1985—86, v.p. 1986—87, pres. 1987—88), Soc. Advancement Am. Philosophy (exec. com. 1980—82, pres.-elect 1997—98, pres. 1998—2000, exec. com. 2001—03, chair nominating com. 2002—04), Metaphys. Soc. Am. (councillor 1971—75, pres. 1977—78, program com. 1989—90, chair program com. 1995—96), So. Soc. Philosophy and Psychology (treas. 1968—71, pres. 1976—77), Southwestern Philos. Soc. (exec. com. 1965—69, v.p. 1971—72, pres. 1972—73), Am. Philos. Assn. (program com. ea. divsn. 1969, nominating com. western divsn. 1975—76, 1981—82, adv. com. to program com. ea. divsn. 1994—97, chair ad hoc com. on history 1996—2004), Tulane U. Emeritus Club (Outstanding Grad. of Class of 1947 award 1997), Omicron Delta Kappa, Alpha Sigma Lambda (hon. Theta chpt. of La.), Phi Beta Kappa (pres. Alpha of La. 1966—67). Home: 6125 Patton St New Orleans LA 70118-5832 Home Phone: 504-895-5629. Personal E-mail: ereck@cox.net.

RECK, ELIZABETH TORRE, social worker, educator; b. Winston-Salem, NC, June 17, 1931; d. Vernon Clark and Mary (Pfohl) Lassiter; m. Mottram Peter Torre, Apr. 13, 1957 (dec.); m. Andrew Joseph Reck, June 17, 1987. Student, Wellesley Coll., Mass., 1948-49; BA, Duke U., 1952; MRE, Union Theol. Sem., 1957; MSW, Tulane U., 1966, PhD, 1972. Cert. social worker, La. Field dir. undergrad. admissions Duke U., Durham, NC, 1952—53; head tchr. primary dept. Riverside Ch., NYC, 1957—60; instr. Sch. Social Work Tulane U., New Orleans, 1966—72, assoc. prof., 1972—2000, coord. Indsl. Social Work Program, 1982—88, mem. faculty senate, 1972—88, prof. emeritus, 2000—. Non-govtl. orgn. rep. UNICEF, World Fedn. Mental Health, 1957—63; cons. to v.p. cmty. affairs WETA, Washington, 1979; cons. Office Spl. Symposia and Seminars, Smithsonian Instn., Washington, 1979-86; treas. N.Y. Jr. League, 1961-62, v.p., 1962-63; bd. dirs. Cmty. Vol. Svcs., New Orleans, 1965-68; mem. profl. adv. com. Project Pre-Kindergarten, Orleans Paris Sch. Bd., New Orleans, 1967-69; mem. adv. bd. DePaul Cmty. Mental Health Ctr., New Orleans, 1971-72; mem. citizens adv. com. Orleans Parish Juvenile Ct., New Orleans, 1970-73; mem. Coun. on Social Work Edn. Task Force on Prevention, 1981-87; mem. New Orleans Women's Coalition Task Force on Employers and Working Parents, 1985-90; mem. med. social svcs. subcom. Mayor's Adv. Com. on Domestic Violence, 1995-96; v.p. Torre Realty Bd., 1996-2006, mem. exec. bd., 2006-. Grantee NIMH, Summer Inst. grantee Nat. Endowment Humanities, 1982; Newcomb Coll. fellow, 1989-2002. Mem. AAUW (Tulane Corp. rep. 1990-2000), NASW (bd. dir. La. chpt. 1987-89), AAUP (treas. Tulane chpt. 1984-86, 88-91, exec. com. 1991-95, v.p. New Orleans chpt. 1996), World Fedn. Mental Health, Coun. Social Work Edn., Am. Orthopsychiat. Assn. (life), Tulane U. Women's Assn. (v.p. 1996-97, pres. 1997-98, bd. mem. 2006-07), Phi Beta Kappa (Tulane chpt. exec. com. 1990-2002, pres. Tulane chpt. 1991, regional sec. 1994—2002). Personal E-mail: ereck@cox.net.

RECKERS, PHILIP MERLE, accountant, educator; b. Quincy, Ill., May 1, 1946; s. Merle Joseph and Frances Adelaide (Friye) R.; m. Patricia Anne Polchinski, May 12, 1979; children: Brian, Colleen, Ashley. BS, Quincy Coll., Ill., 1968; MBA, Washington U., St. Louis, 1972; PhD, U. Ill., 1978. Asst. prof. U. Md., College Park, 1976—80; assoc. prof. Ariz. State U., Tempe, 1980—83, prof. acctg., 1983—; dir. Sch. Accountancy, 1993—2002; dir. rsch. Ctr. for Advancing Bus. through Info. Tech., 2002—05. Vis. prof. Notre Dame, 2004—07. Assoc. editor: Advances in Acctg., 1985—93, mem. editl. bd.: Auditing, 1987—2003, Behavioral Rsch. in Acctg., 1992—2002, Internat. Jour. Auditing, 1999—2007; editor: Advanes in Acctg., 1994—; contbr. articles to profl. jours. With US Army, 1970—72, Vietnam. Auditing rsch. grantee, Peat Marwick Found., 1976, 1985, 1989, 1990, 1991, tax rsch. grantee, Ernst and Young Found., 1991. Mem. Am. Acctg. Assn. (v.p. 2006—, Innovations in Acctg. Edn. award 2003, Edn. Rsch. grant 1982), Fedn. Schs. Accountancy (pres. 2002, Joseph Silvoso Lifetime Achievement award 2006), AICPA (pre-cert. edn. exec. com.), Acctg. Programs Leadership Group (v.p. 2005—) Roman Catholic. Home: 7461 S Rita Ln Tempe AZ 85283-4796 Office: Ariz State U Sch Accountancy Ba 301D Tempe AZ 85287 Office Phone: 480-965-2283. Business E-Mail: philip.reckers@asu.edu.

RECKFORD, JONATHAN THOMAS MORE, nonprofit organization administrator; b. Chapel Hill, NC, Aug. 31, 1962; s. Kenneth and Mary (Stevens) Reckford; m. Ashley Louise Richards, June 9, 1990; 3 children. BA in polit. sci., U. NC, Chapel Hill, 1984; MBA, Stanford U., 1989. Fin. analyst Goldman, Sachs & Co., 1984—86; mgr. svc. group strategy and bus. devel. Host Marriott Corp.; mgr. bus. planning The Walt Disney Co., 1991—92, mktg. mgr. Disney Vacation Club, 1993, dir. fin. and bus. planning Disney's Am., 1994, dir. bus. planning and devel. Disney Design and Devel., 1994—95; v.p. Circuit City Stores, Inc., 1995—97, sr. v.p. corp. planning and comm., 1997—99; pres. mall stores divsn. The Musicland Group, Inc., 1999—2000, pres. stores, 2000—02; exec. pastor Christ Presbyn. Ch. of Edina, Minn., 2003—05; CEO Habitat for Humanity Internat., Inc., Americus, Ga., 2005—. Henry Luce Found. Scholarship for Young Am. Leaders. Office: Habitat for Humanity Internat Inc 121 Habitat St Americus GA 31709-3498 Office Phone: 229-924-6935.

RECKLINE, SIGMUND JOSEPH, publishing executive, editor; b. Balt., Oct. 29, 1956; s. Sigmund Joseph Reckline and Regina Ann DeBarry; m. Marilyn Louise Windes, May 2000; children: Clarissa Irene, Sigmund Joseph III, William Joseph, Quinten Christopher. BA in Liberal Arts, W.Va. U., 2002; BS in Applied Sci., Siena Heights U., 2002; MBA, U. Notre Dame, 2002; PhD in Bus. Adminstrn., Madison U., 2003; postgrad., Capella U., 2006, U. Md. Ordained Ch. of Spiritual Humanism. I&C technician Va. Electric Power Co., 1981—82; tech. writer, technician Nuc. Support Svcs., 1982, 1986—88; field engr. Johnson Controls, 1983—84; tech. writer Butler Svc. Group, 1984—85; field engr. Westinghouse Instrument Svc. Co., 1985—86; ops. mgr. Chesapeake Internat., 1988—91; sys. engr. Peak Tech. Svcs., 1991—92; tech. editor GTS/Duratek, Rockhill, SC, 1992—97; engring. mgr. Duke Engring and Svcs., Bridgman, 1997—99, Estes Group, Bridgman, Mich., 1999—2000; aux. operator CMS Energy, Covert, Mich., 2000—02; online instr., instr. Siena Heights U., Adrian, Mich., 2002—05; with Global Transitions Pub., Baroda, Mich., 2005—. Founder Environ. Cancer Res. Inst., Baroda, Mich. Co-author: America Rewired. Mem. Berrien County Cancer Ctr., Bridgman, 2002; amb. Am. Cancer Soc., Kalamazoo, 2005; pres. South Potomac Forest Property Owners Assn., Springfield, W.Va., 1986—88; comdr. Antioch Commandery Knights Templar, 2000; hereditary chief Clan Recklein, 1990—. Sgt. USAF, 1981—87. Mem.: Am. Coll. Heraldry, Royal Order Scotland (life), St. Andrews Soc. Balt. (life), Phi Theta Kappa (disting. prof. 2004), Alpha Sigma Lambda. Republican. Presbyterian. Avocations: writing, genealogy, collecting swords, jewelry design. Office: Global Transitions Pub PO Box 41 Baroda MI 49101 Office Phone: 269-369-9897. E-mail: reckline@hotmail.com.

RECORD, M. THOMAS, JR., biochemist, educator; BA, Yale Univ.; PhD, Univ. Calif., San Diego. Steenbrook prof., chem. sci., John D. Ferry prof., chemistry, biochemistry Univ. Wis., Madison. Recipient Biophysical Soc. Founders award, 2001. Fellow: Am. Assn. Advancement Sci., Biophys. Soc., Am. Acad. Arts & Scis. Office: 4419 Biochemistry Addn 433 Babcock Dr Madison WI 53706 Office Phone: 608-262-5332. Business E-Mail: record@chem.wisc.edu.

RECORD, PHILLIP JULIUS, journalist; b. Ft. Worth, Jan. 12, 1929; s. Phillip Cross and Frances Virginia (McElwee) R.; m. Patricia Ann Edwards, Sept. 29, 1954; children: Christopher Phillip, Gregory Edwards, Timothy James. BA in Journalism, U. Notre Dame, Ind., 1950. Gen. reporter Lubbock Avalanche-Jour., Tex., 1950-54; copy editor, reporter Fort Worth Star-Telegram, 1954-67, asst. city editor, 1967-68, city editor evening edit., 1968-76, mng. editor, 1976-80, assoc. exec. editor, 1980-91, spl. asst. to pub., ombudsman, 1991-97, columnist, 1997—2001. Mem.

mass comms. com. Tex. Tech. U., 1971—2000, chmn., 1990—92, bd. dirs., 1992—; journalism profl. in residence Tex. Christian U., 1999—. Mem. Friends of Ft. Worth Pub. Libr.; bd. visitors Tex. Christian U.; conciliation/arbitration bd. Cath. Diocese of Ft. Worth, 1994—, chair, 1996—, publs. adv. com., 1982—; bd. dirs. Tarrant County Mental Health Assn., 1990—95; dir. Freedom Info. Found., Tex., 1987—93; bd. dirs. Depression Connection Team, 1999—, Cassata H.S., 2006—; founding mem. Ft. Worth Theatre. With US Army, 1950—52. Recipient Ethics award Tex. Christian U., 1991, others for reporting, photography and headline writing; named to Tex. Tech U. Mass Comms. Hall of Fame. Mem. ABA (nat. commn. on pub. understanding about law 1984-90, commn. on partnership programs 1990-93), Investigative Reporters and Editors Inc., Soc. Profl. Journalists (pres. 1983-84, bd. dirs. Found. 1980-2001, v.p. Found., 1991-94, bd. chair 1994-01, Wells Key 1991), Creative Thinking Assn., Orgn. News Ombudsmen (dir. 1994-98, v.p. 1995-96, pres. 1996-97). Avocation: tennis. Office: 6144 Walla Ave Fort Worth TX 76133 *As a journalist, I strive to be a servant of the truth and a servant of the people. As a follower of Jesus, I try to live my life as he would. But, being human, I fail frequently. But I try and I care. I think that makes me OK in God's eyes.*

RECORD, WILLIAM JOHN, librarian; b. NYC, June 21, 1931; s. William and Betty (Collins) R.; m. Betty Lowrey, Oct. 7, 1950; children: Linda, William John, Jr., Michael, John. BA, George Peabody Coll. for Tchrs, 1961; MLS, Pratt Inst., 1965. Cert. pub. librarian, N.Y. State. Cataloger N.Y. Pub. Library, NYC, 1963-66; cataloger Coll. Dentistry, NYU, 1966-67; achivist Sch. Medicine, NYU, 1967-68; librarian Milton Helpern Libr. Legal Medicine, NYC, 1969-70, Fordham Hosp., Bronx, N.Y., 1973-76, Misericordia Hosp., Bronx, 1976-81, Assn. Vol. Surg. Contraception, NYC, 1981-97, ret., 1997. Periodicals librarian Met. Hosp., N.Y.C., 1971-72. Editor Odyssey, pres. parents group phase III, Odyssey House, N.Y.C., 1970. With U.S. Army, 1947-58, Korea. Mem. Assn. for Population/Family Planning Libraries Internat. (pres. 1987-88), Med. Library Assn. Home: 437 E 80th St Apt 26 New York NY 10021-0611

RECTOR, DONNA LYNN, writer, photographer, vocalist; b. Warrenton, Va., July 8, 1959; d. Allen Leon and Elizabeth Ann (Godfrey) R. Freelance photographer, journalist, calligrapher, poet, Culpeper, Va., 1985—; corr. Culpeper Star Exponent, Culpeper News, Culpeper, Va., 1987-95. Pub. info. coord. Va. Dept. Transp., Culpeper, 1988-89; advisor CommonHealth, 1989; with Donna Lynn and the Bluesmen, 1996-98; cons. in field. Editor: Va. Dept. Transp. Newsletter, 1989; columnist, photographer: Va.'s Music Line, The Corridor; blues vocalist, 1996—; pub.: Stylus newsletter; columnist: Corridor Mag., Rock and Read Mag., SHAKE! Mag. Vol. Svcs. to Abused Families, Culpeper, 1987-92; vol. art instr. Culpeper County Sch. Vis. Artisan Program; vol. Culpeper Renaissance Downtown Assn.; canvasser United Way, 1987-88; coord. fundraisers & major charity events, pub. rels. coord. for charity and community orgns.; spl. events/fund raiser coord. Nat. Multiple Sclerosis Soc., Blue Ridge chpt., 1990-91; coord., publicist Culpeper Music Festival, 2004-05. Recipient First Place awd. for Poetry, Germanna Community Coll., 1988, 92, 98, Bus. and Profl. Women's Assn. Young Career Woman of Yr. award, Spl. Svc. award Va. Dept. Transp., 1989, Cert. Appreciation Blue Ridge chpt. Nat. Multiple Sclerosis Soc., 1991, Piedmont United Way Gold award, 1993, Cert. Appreciation, Vocat. Indsl. Clubs Am., 1993, Cert. Appreciation Culpeper Downtown Renaissance Inc., 1990, Cert. Recognition for exceptional contribution to Va. employee suggestion program Gov. George Allen, Va., 1994, Top Hat award Windmore Found. for Arts, 1999, Mem. Phi Theta Kappa, Alpha Beta Gamma. Avocations: writing, singing, photography, public relations, music.

RECTOR, JOHN MICHAEL, pharmaceutical association executive, lawyer; b. Seattle, Aug. 15, 1943; s. Michael Robert and Bernice Jane (Allison) R.; m. Carmen De Ortiz, 1994; children: Christian Phillip, Ciera Rose, Zachary Ryan BA, U. Calif., Berkeley, 1966; JD, U. Calif., Hastings, 1969; PharmD (hon.), Ark. State Bd. Pharmacy, 1991. Bar: Calif. 1970, U.S. Supreme Ct. 1974; registered corp. counsel Va. Bar, 2006. Trial atty. civil rights divsn. Dept. Justice, 1969-71; dep. chief counsel judiciary com. U.S. Senate, 1971-73, counsel to Sen. Birch Bayh, 1971-77, chief counsel, staff dir., 1973-77; confirmed by U.S. Senate as assoc. adminstr. to Law Enforcement Assistance Adminstrn. and adminstr. of Office Juvenile Justice Dept. Justice, 1977-79; spl. counsel to U.S. Atty. Gen., 1979-80; dir. govt. affairs Nat. Assn. Retail Druggists, Washington, 1980-85; sr. v.p. govt. affairs, gen. counsel Nat. Cmty. Pharmacists Assn., Alexandria, Va., 1986—2005, sr. v.p., gen. counsel, 2006—. Chmn. adv. bd. Nat. Juvenile Law Ctr., 1973-77; mem. HEW panel Drug Use and Criminal Behavior, 1974-77; cons. panel Nat. Commn. Protection Human Subjects Biomed. and Behavioral Rsch., 1975-76; chmn. US Interdepartmental Coun. Juvenile Justice, 1977-79; mem. bd. com. civil rights and liberties Am. Dem. Action, 1976-80, Pres.'s Com. Mental Health-Justice Group, 1978; mem. Pharm. Industry Adv. Com.; treas. polit. action com. Nat. Pharmacists Assn., 1981-2006; exec. dir. Retail Druggist Legal Legis. Def. Fund, 1985-2005, founder, chmn. Washington Pharmacy Industry Forum; owner Second Genesis. Mem. editl. bd. Managed Care Law; mem. Hastings Law Jour. 1967-9; contbr. articles to profl. jours. Mem. exec. com. small bus. and fin. couns. Dem. Nat. Com., 1988-92; dir. Dem. Leadership Coun.'s Network, 1989-92, bd. advisers, 1992-94, Clinton-Gore Washington Bus. adv. com.; bd. dirs. Small Bus. Legis. Coun., 1987—, sec., 1999, treas., 2000, chmn. elect, 2001, chmn., 2002; bd. dirs. Nat. Bus. Coalition for Fair Competition, 1984—; policy advisor Presdl. campaigns; active Reagan for Pres. Task Force on Criminal Justice. Perry E. Towne scholar, 1966-67; recipient Children's Express Birch Bayh Juvenile Justice award, 1981, John W. Dargavel medal Nat. Assn. Retail Drug Assts. 2003, J. Leon Lascoff Meml. award Am. Coll. Apothecares, 2004. Mem. ABA (mem. com. youth citizenship 1978-84), ATLA, Calif. Bar Assn., Nat. Health Lawyers Assn., Am. Soc. Assn. Execs. (mem. govt. affairs sect.), Washington Coun. Lawyers, Assn. Former Sr. Senate Aides, Vinifera Wine Growers Assn. Va. (life), Health R Us, Am. League Lobbyists, Theta Chi, Germanna Found. Libertarian. Avocations: antiques, books and documents. Office: Nat Cmty Pharmacists Assn 100 Daingerfield Rd Alexandria VA 22314-2885 Business E-Mail: john.rector@ncpanet.org.

RECTOR, SUSAN DARNELL, lawyer; b. Wilmington, Del., Feb. 14, 1959; d. W. Thomas and Barbara Joan (Shafer) Darnell; m. Neil Kenyon Rector, Aug. 7, 1982. BA in Econs., Wake Forest U., Winston-Salem, NC, 1981; JD, U. N.C., Chapel Hill, 1984. Bar: Ohio 1984. Lawyer Ohio Legislative Svc. Commn., Columbus, Ohio, 1984-87; assoc. Schottenstein, Zox & Dunn, Columbus, Ohio, 1987-93, ptnr., 1993—. Bd. trustees Firstlink, Inc., 1990-95, v.p., 1993, pres., 1994; apt. to Ohio Small Bus. and Entrepreneurship Coun., 1991-95; bd. dirs. The Wilds. Contbr. articles to profl. jours. Mem. allocation com. United Way, Columbus, 1990-96, campaign cabinet, 1991, 2006, co-chair planning, evaluation and allocation com., 1993-94, bd. trustees, 1996-05, chair health vision com., 1996-99; trustee Columbus Zool. Park Assn., 2001—, v.p., 2003-04, pres. 2005-06, chmn., 2007—; chmn. devel. com., 2001-03, 07—, chmn. zoo fund, 2000; bd. dir., sec., treas. Cmty. Rsch. Ptnrs., 2000-02. Harry S. Truman scholar, Truman Scholarship Found., 1979, named one of 10 Outstanding Young Citizens, Columbus Jaycees, 1993, 40 under 40, Bus. (Columbus); grad. Columbus Area Leadership Program; named one of Best Lawyers in Am., 2003-07. Fellow Am. Bar Found.; mem. Ohio Bar Assn., Columbus Bar Assn. (Cmty. Svc. award 1997), Columbus Bar Found. (trustee 1995—2004, pres. 2003), Women Lawyers of Franklin County, Jr. League of Columbus (bd. trustees, sec. 1989-90, 95-98, pres. 1997-98), Columbus Club, Columbus Met. Club, Columbus Women's Network (Cmty. Leader award), Mortar Bd., Phi Beta Kappa, Omicron Delta Kappa. Home: 67 E Deshler Ave Columbus OH 43206-2655 Office: Schottenstein Zox & Dunn 250 West Street Columbus OH 43215 Office Phone: 614-462-2219. Business E-Mail: srector@szd.com.

RECUPERO-FAIELLA, ANNA ANTONIETTA, poet; b. Boston, Nov. 22, 1966; d. Vittorio and Anna Maria Recupero; m. Mark Stephan James Faiella, May 30, 1998; 1 child, Dante Vincenzo Faiella. Cert. early edn., Wheelock Coll. Tchr. N. Bennet St. Sch., Boston, 1981-87; clk. Post Office, Boston, 1988—. Art coord. N. Bennett Sch., Boston, 1985-87; acting extra films and commls. Author: A View From the Edge, 1992, Dusting Off Dreams, 1994, Echoes From the Silence, 1995, Treasure the Moment, 1996, Whispers, 1996, Sensations, 1997; co-author: Distinguished Poets of Amercia, 1993, Outstanding Poets of 1994, 1994, Treasured Poems of America, 1995, Treasured Poems of America, 1996, Best Poems of the 90's, 1996, Best Poems of '97, 1997, Ten Years of Excellence, 1998. Co-chair Wall of Tolerance, 2003. Recipient Internat. Writer Yr. award, Internat. Biographical Ctr., 2003, Outstanding Writer award, Internat. Soc. Poetry, 2004, Outstanding Achievement in amateur photography award, Internat. Soc. Photographers, 2004; Mass. State Gen. scholar, 1985. Mem. Internat. Soc. Poets (disting. mem. adv. com. 1994), Nat. Mus. Women Arts, Point of Pines Assn. Democrat. Roman Catholic. Avocations: painting, writing poems, travel, nascar racing, comedy. Home: 40 Bickford Ave Revere MA 02151-1723

REDA, JAMES FRANCIS, business consultant; b. Bklyn., Aug. 27, 1953; s. Ralph Charles and Evelyn Susan (Buchan) R.; m. Susan Rosemary Hisnay, June 10, 1982 (div. Oct. 1993); 1 child, Jennifer Beryl; m. Deborah Linda Grannis, July 4, 1994; children: Jennifer Rose, James Francis Jr., Linda Victoria. BS in Indsl. Engring., Columbia U., 1981; MS in Mgmt., MIT, 1983. 1st class lic., FCC; lic. internat. fin. analyst. Indsl. engr. IBM Corp., Bklyn., 1980, East Fishkill, NY, 1981; process engr. Hewlett-Packard Co., Andover, Mass., 1982; bus. mgr. Wang Labs., Inc., Lowell, Mass., 1983-85; sr. product mgr. Honeywell Fed. Systems, Inc., McLean, Va., 1985-87; assoc. cons. Touche Ross & Co., NYC, 1987; v.p., cons. The Bachelder Group, NYC, 1987-96; cons. Buck Cons., NYC, 1996-97, Hewitt Assocs., Atlanta, 1997-99; sr. mgr. Arthur Andersen LLP, Atlanta, 1999-2000; prin., regional practice leader Buck Cons., Inc., Atlanta, 2000—03; founder, mng. dir. James F. Reda & Assocs., LLC, NYC, 2003—. Campaign advisor Friends of Vincent Gentile, Bklyn., 1994. With USN, 1971-77; lt. comdr. USCGR. Mem. Internat. Inst. Indsl. Engrs. (sr. mem., chpt. pres. 1979-81, Walter Rautenstrauch award 1981), Res. Officers Assn. (Top Grad. award 1983), N.Y. Soc. Security Analysts (mem. com. corp. governance), CFA Inst., Soc. Corporate Governance Profls., World at Work, U.S. Naval Inst., Armed Forces Comms. Assn., Ret. Officers Assn., Nat. Assn. Stock Plan Profls., Nat. Assn. Corp. Dirs., Naval War Coll. Found., Am. Legion, Tau Beta Pi, Alpha Pi Mu. Republican. Methodist. Avocations: spectator sports, exercise, travel, history, current events. Office: 1500 Broadway 9th Fl New York NY 10036-4055 Home: 5 Howard Dr Princeton Junction NJ 08550-2150 Office Phone: 646-367-4466. Personal E-mail: jfreda@jfreda.com.

REDBURN, TOM, newspaper editor; BA in Sociology, Pomona Coll., 1972. With OSHA, U.S. Dept. Labor, 1972—73; editor & reporter The Washington Monthly, 1974—75, Environ. Action, 1975—76; reporter & chief econ. correspondent LA Times, 1977—90; internat. econ. correspondent Internat. Herald Tribune, 1991—93; reporter NY Times, 1993—94, editor, Bus. Day sect., 1994—97, asst. bus. editor, 1997—2003, tech. editor, 2003—04, dep. bus. editor, 2004—. Named to Athletic Hall of Fame, Pomona Coll., 1992. Office: New York Times 229 W 43d St New York NY 10036 Office Phone: 212-556-1548. Business E-Mail: redburn@nytimes.com.

REDD, KENNETH ERIC, statistician, researcher; b. Boston, June 17, 1965; s. Phyllis and Charles William Redd. BA, Tufts U., Medford, Mass., 1983—87; MA, U. Minn., Mpls., 1987—89. Analyst in social legislation Congl. Rsch. Svc., Washington, 1989—91; rsch. assoc. Pa. Higher Edn. Assistance Agy., Harrisburg, 1991—94; rsch. and policy analyst Nat. Assn. of Indsl. Colls. and Univs., Washington, 1994—96; rsch. assoc. Am. Assn. State Colls. and Univs., Washington, 1997—98; sr. rsch. assoc. Sallie Mae, Inc., Washington, 1998—99; dir. of higher edn. rsch. USA Group Found., Indpls., 1999—2000; dir. of rsch. and policy analysis Nat. Assn. of Student Fin. Aid Administrs., Washington, 2000—. Bd. dirs. Sallie Mae Fund, Reston, Va., 2003—. Contbr. articles to profl. jours., chapters to books. Recipient Governor's Award for Outstanding Cmty. Svc., Office of Gov. Michael S. Dukakis, 1985, Commendation for Outstanding Svc., Social Security Adminstrn., 1985; fellow, Assn. for Pub. Policy Analysis and Mgmt., 1986, Nat. Ctr. for Pub. Policy and Higher Edn., 2001—02. Mem.: Toastmasters. Home: 7290 Mandan Rd Greenbelt MD 20770 Office: Nat Assn Student Fin Aid Adminstrs 1129 20th St NW Ste 400 Washington DC 20036 Home Phone: 301-486-4631; Office Phone: 202-785-0453. Office Fax: 202-785-1487. E-mail: reddk@nasfaa.org, kredd31@comcast.net.

REDD, L. HUGH, manufacturing executive; B in Acctg., Brigham Young U., Provo, Utah; M of Profl. Accountancy in Tax Acctg., U. Tex. With tax dept. Arthur Andersen, 1983—86; sr. fin. analyst Gen. Dynamics, 1986—89, sr. tax adminstr. Falls Church, Va., 1989—94, dir. treasury planning and analysis, 1994—98, staff v.p., asst. treas., 1998—2000, v.p., contr. Land Systems Sterling Heights, Mich., 2000—06, sr. v.p., CFO, 2006—. Office: Gen Dynamics 2941 Fairview Park Dr Ste 100 Falls Church VA 22042-4513 Office Phone: 703-876-3000. Office Fax: 703-876-3125. *

REDD, MICHAEL, professional basketball player; b. Aug. 24, 1979; Attended, Ohio State Univ. Basketball player Milw. Bucks, 2001—. Named to All-American Team Hon. Mention, 2000—01, NBA All-Star Team, 2004. Office: Milwaukee Bucks 1001 N Fourth St Milwaukee WI 53203

REDD, SCOTT (JOHN SCOTT REDD), federal official, retired military officer; b. Sidney, Iowa, Sept. 10, 1944; m. Donna Ford; children: Anne, Scott Jr., Adam. BSc in Math. and Physics, U.S. Naval Acad., 1966; postgrad. studies, Uruguay; MS in Ops. Analysis, Naval Post Grad. Sch.; postgrad. studies for Sr. Execs., MIT; grad., Armed Forces Staff Coll. Commd. ensign USN, 1966, advanced through grades to rear admiral, 1994, ret., 1998; mem. staff Sec. Defense, Washington; naval officer 5 operational commands USN destroyers and frigates; acting dep. chief naval ops. for plans, policy and ops. USN, Washington; comdr. US Naval Forces, US Ctrl. Command US Dept. Def., 1994—96; commdr. Fifth Fleet USN, 1995; dir. strategic plans and policy The Joint Staff, Washington, 1996—98; chmn., pres., CEO NetSchools Corp., Atlanta, 1999—2002; COO, dep. adminstr. Civilian Provisional Authority, Baghdad, Iraq, 2003—04; dir. Nat. Counterterrorism Ctr. Office Nat. Intelligence, Washington, 2005—. Pres. Naval Acad. Class, 1966; exec. dir. Commn. on the Intelligence Capabilities of the US Regarding Weapons of Mass Destruction, 2004-05 Decorated Order Bahrain 1st degree, Legion of Merit (2 awards), Disting. Svc. medal (2 awards), Meritorious Svc. medal (2 awards), Navy Commendation medal (2 awards). Mem. U.S. Naval Acad. Alumni Assn. (past bd. dirs.) Avocation: amateur radio.

REDDEL, CARL WALTER, academic administrator; b. Gurley, Nebr., May 31, 1937; s. Walter Julius and Friedora Regina (Sorge) R.; m. Colette Marie Antoinette Mansuy, Oct. 26, 1963; children: Eric, Damien. BSED, Drake U., 1959; MA in Russian Studies, Syracuse U., 1962; PhD in Russian History, Ind. U., 1973, cert. Russian Studies, 1973. Lectr. U. Md., Toul-Rosieres, France, 1963-66; instr. U.S.A.F. Acad., Colorado Springs, Colo., 1967-68, 71-72, from asst. prof. to assoc. prof., 1972—80; from assoc. prof. to prof., head dept. history, fellow U. Edinburgh, 1980—82; pres., CEO, Eisenhower World Affairs Inst., 1999—2000; pub. svc. fellow Gettysburg (Pa.) Coll., 2000-01; cons. coord. Dwight D. Eisenhower Meml. Commn., Washington, 2001—02, exec. dir., 2002—. Nat. coord., regional World History Assn., Phila., 1990-95; bd. editors, mem. Joun. Slavic Mil., London, 1988—; series editor Military Hist. Symposium Series, Colorado Springs, 1993-2001. Editor: Transformation in Russian and Soviet Military History, 1990; contbr. articles to profl. jours. Mem. Rotary Internat., 1994—. Served to brig. gen. U.S. Air Force, 1962-99. Recipient Young Faculty exch. Internat. Rsch. Exchs. Bd., Moscow State U., 1975; Woodrow Wilson fellow, 1959-60, Danforth Found. fellow, 1959-61. Mem.: World History Assn., Am. Assn. Advancement of Slavic Studies, Am. Hist. Assn., Phi Alpha Theta. Lutheran. Home: 420 7th St NW Apt 809 Washington DC 20004-2214 Office: 1629 K St NW Ste 801 Washington DC 20006-3837 Office Phone: 202-296-0005. Personal E-mail: soloviev@msn.com. Business E-Mail: creddel@eisenhowermemorial.org.

REDDEN, JAMES ANTHONY, federal judge; b. Springfield, Mass., Mar. 13, 1929; s. James A. and Alma (Cheek) R.; m. Joan Ida Johnson, July 13, 1950; children: James A., William F. Student, Boston U., 1951; LL.B., Boston Coll., 1954. Bar: Mass., 1954, Oreg., 1955. Pvt. practice, Mass., 1954-55; title examiner Title & Trust Ins. Co., Oreg., 1955; claims adjuster Allstate Ins. Co., 1956; mem. firm Collins, Redden, Ferris & Velure, Medford, Oreg., 1957-73; treas. Oreg., 1973-77; atty. gen., 1977-80; U.S. dist. judge, now sr. judge U.S. Dist. Ct. Oreg., Portland, 1980—. Chmn. Oreg. Pub. Employee Relations Bd.; mem. Oreg. Ho. of Reps., 1963-69, minority leader, 1967-69. With AUS, 1946-48. Mem. ABA, Mass. Bar Assn., Oreg. State Bar. Office: US Dist Ct 1527 US Courthouse 1000 SW 3d Ave Portland OR 97204-2902 Office Phone: 503-326-8370.

REDDEN, TAYLOR TILGHMAN, musician; b. Swarthmore, Pa., Mar. 2, 1946; s. O. Tilghman Redden and Virginia Dare (Martin) Martin-Redden. Artist diploma, Phila. Conservatory of Music, 1965; BA, Phila. Music Acad., 1967, BFA in Music, 1967. Artist, tchr. Phila. Settlement Music Schs., 1968—70; prof. piano Bryn Mawr Conservatory of Music, Bryn Mawr, Pa., 1971—. Mem.: Music Tchrs. N. Am., U. of Arts Alumni Assn. Home: 539 Cornell Ave Swarthmore PA 19081

REDDICK, BRYAN DEWITT, academic administrator; b. Austin, Tex., Feb. 4, 1942; s. DeWitt Carter and Marjorie Alice (Bryan) R.; m. Sheila Ann Farrell, Oct. 3, 1970; children: Bridget Louise, George William. BA, U. Iowa, 1964; MA, Syracuse U., 1966; PhD, U. Calif., Davis, 1969. Fulbright teaching fellow U. Lyon, France, 1969-70; Maitre de Confs. U. Grenoble, France, 1970-71; asst. prof. English Am. U., Washington, 1971-75; prof. Olivet (Mich.) Coll., 1980-86, assoc. dean, 1981-82, acad. v.p., 1982-86, Elmira Coll., NY, 1986—. Author: Student Journalist and Effective Writing Style, 1976; editor: Mass Media and the School, 1984. Contbr. articles to profl. jours. Chmn. Olivet Planning Commn., Mich., 1978; mem. Sch./Community Adv. Coun., 1986-89; mem. exec. com. Sullivan Coun. BSA, 1988-92; trustee Chemung Valley History Mus., 1992—. NDEA fellow, 1966-69. Mem. Phi Beta Kappa. Home: 85 Decker Pkwy W Elmira NY 14905-2303 Office: Elmira Coll 1 Park Pl Elmira NY 14901-2085 E-mail: breddick@elmira.edu.

REDDICK, CATHERINE ANNE (CAT REDDICK), Olympic athlete; b. Richmond, Va., Feb. 10, 1982; Majoring in comm., U. N.C., 2000—. Mem. Under-16 Nat. Team, 1998, Under-18 Nat. Team, 1998—99, capt., 2000; mem. Under-21 Nat. Team, 2003; soccer player, defender U.S. Women's Nat. Team, 2000—; mem. U.S. Olympic Soccer Team, Athens, 2004. Co-recipient U-18 Soccer Gold medal, Pan Am. Games, 1999, Nordic Cup, Denmark, 2000, 2001, 2002, 2003; named Defensive MVP, NCAA Final Four, 2000, Freshman All-Am. Team, NSCAA, 2000, Second Team All-Am., 2001, First Team All-Am., 2002; named to First Team All-ACC, 2002. Achievements include being a member of gold medal winning US Women's Soccer Team, Athens Olympic Games, 2004. Office: US Soccer Fedn 1801 S Prairie Ave Chicago IL 60616

REDDICK, C.N. (FRANK)LIN, III, lawyer; b. Quantico, Va. BA with high honors, Calif. State Univ., San Jose, 1977; JD, Univ. Calif., 1980. Bar: Calif. 1980. Mng. ptnr., chair, corp. practice group Troop Steuber Pasich Reddick & Tobey LLP, LA; ptnr., chair corp. and securities practice group and mem. mgmt. com. Akin Gump Strauss Hauer & Feld LLP, LA, 2001—. Bd. dir. VCA Antech Inc., LA, 2002—. Mem. Hastings Law Jour., 1978—79, note and comment editor, 1979—80. Mem.: ABA, Thurston Soc., Order of Coif. Office: Akin Gump Strauss Hauer & Feld LLP Ste 2400 2029 Century Pk E Los Angeles CA 90067-3012 Office Phone: 310-728-3204. Office Fax: 310-229-1001. Business E-Mail: freddick@akingump.com.

REDDIEN, CHARLES HENRY, II, lawyer, diversified financial services company executive, consultant; b. San Diego, Aug. 27, 1944; s. Charles Henry and Betty Jane (McCormick) R.; m. Paula Gayle, June 16, 1974; 1 child, Tyler Charles. BSEE, U. Colo., Boulder, 1966; MSEE, U. So. Calif., 1968; JD, Loyola U., LA, 1972. Bar: Calif. 1972, Colo. 1981, U.S. Dist. Ct. 1981. Mgr. Hughes Aircraft Co., 1966-81; pvt. practice, 1972—. Pres., broker R&D Realty Ltd., 1978-91; mem. spl. staff, co-dir. tax advantage group OTC Net Inc., 1981-82; pres., chmn. Heritage Group Inc., investment banking holding co., 1982-84, Plans and Assistance Inc., mgmt. cons., 1982-83, Orchard Group Ltd., investment banking holding co., 1982-84, J.W. Gant & Assocs., Inc., investment bankers, 1983-84; mng. ptnr., CEO J.W. Gant & Assocs., Ltd., 1984-85; chmn. bd. Kalamath Group Ltd., 1985-87, Heritage group Ltd. Investment Bankers, 1985-87; dir. Virtusonics Corp., 1985-92; v.p., dir. Heritage Fin. Planners Inc., 1982-83; pres., chmn. PDN Inc., 1987-89; pub., exec. v.p., dir. World News Digest Inc., 1987-90, LeisureNet Entertainment, Inc., 1989-90; chief exec. officer, Somerset Group Ltd., 1988-93, Inland Pacific Corp., 1989-91, World Info. Network, Inc., 1990-92, pres., CEO, chmn., Europa Cruises Corp., 1992-94; CEO, chmn. Casino World Inc., 1993-97, Miss. Gaming Corp., 1993-97; pres., chmn., CEO Chart Group LLC, 1997—, SkyData Corp., 2000-05; pres., Miss. Corrections, L.L.C. 2000-05; COO IAG Holding, Ltd., 2004—. Contbr. articles to profl. jours. Pres. Diamondhead Business and Profl. Assn.; commr. Diamondhead Fire Dist.; dir. Internat. Trade Club South Miss. Recipient tchg. internship award, 1964. Mem. AIAA, IEEE (chmn. U. Colo. chpt. 1965), Calif. Bar Assn., Nat. Assn. Securities Dealers, Phi Alpha Delta, Tau Beta Pi, Eta Kappa Nu. Office: PO Box 6133 Diamondhead MS 39525-6002 Personal E-mail: chartgroup@aol.com.

REDDING, BOBBIE NEWMAN, lawyer; b. Guilford County, NC, Mar. 30, 1935; d. John J. Newman and Flora Pearl (Kirkman) Brower; m. Marshall S. Redding, June 2, 1957 (div. 1982); children: Joan Lucile, Rebecca Marie Redding Greene. Student, U. N.C., Greensboro, 1952-54; BA in Edn., U. N.C., 1956, MSLS, 1957; JD, Campbell U., 1985. Bar: N.C. 1986. Staff atty. Lumbee River Legal Svcs., Fayetteville, NC, 1986-88, Cumberland County Dept. Social Svcs., Fayetteville, 1988—. Local adv. coun. Legal Aid N.C. Mem. ABA, N.C. Bar Assn., N.C. Assn. Social Svcs. Attys., N.C. State Bar Assn., N.C. Guardianship Assn. (bd. dirs.), Cumberland County Bar, Twelth Judicial Bar Home: Box F Unit 106 1100 Clarendon St Fayetteville NC 28305-4800 Office: Cumberland County DSS 1225 Ramsey St Fayetteville NC 28301 Office Phone: 910-677-2667. Business E-Mail: lg2@ccdssnc.com.

REDDING, MARKUS CARL, management consultant, educator; s. Robert E. and Betty J. Redding; m. Heidi Cornell Horsley; children: Alexander Aristotle Horsley-Redding, Samantha Horsley-Redding. BS in History, U. Utah, Salt Lake City, 1990, BS in Polit. Sci., 1990; JD, Loyola U., New Orleans, 1994; MSW, Columbia U. Social Work Sch., New York, 1996. Adj. prof. Columbia U., NYC, 2004—; chief mktg. officer Herrick, Feinstein LLP, NYC, 2005—06, Lovells Internat. Law Firm, 2003—05; state ct. atty. NYS Unified Ct. Sys., NYC, 2001—03; dir. mktg. Sedgwick, Detert, Moran & Arnold, San Francisco; founder Aristotle Consulting, NYC, 2006—, prin., 2006—. Recipient Outstanding Achievement award, NY Unified Ct. Sys., 1996. Fellow: So. Poverty Law Ctr. (leadership coun.); mem.: Phi Theta Kappa. Office: Columbia Univ 1255 Amsterdam Ave Rm 308 New York NY 10027 Office Phone: 646-267-2859. Personal E-mail: mcr24@columbia.edu.

REDDING, ROBERT ELLSWORTH, lawyer; b. South Bend, Ind., Mar. 23, 1919; s. Harry Ellsworth and Lorraine (Livengood) R.; m. Blanche Breisch, Apr. 14, 1941 (div.); children: Rosemary, Robert Ellsworth Jr., Douglas; m. A. Virginia Boender Korn, July 22, 1972 (dec. Aug. 2004). AB, Ohio State U., 1940; LLB, JD, Georgetown U., 1946. Bar: DC 1946, Md. 1949, US Supreme Ct. 1951. Legal asst. to judge U.S. Tax Ct., Wash., 1947—48; legal asst. to mem. CAB, Washington, 1949-51; mem. Bradshaw Shearin Redding & Thomas, Silver Spring, Md., 1951-59; v.p., gen. counsel Transp. Assn. Am., Washington, 1960-69; dir. Office Facilitation Dept. Transp., 1970-76; pvt. practice Washington, Md., 1976—2006. Sec. Cert. Claims Profl. Accreditation Council, Washington, 1981-85; chief judge Appeal Tax Ct., Rockville, Md., 1953-55; internat. cons. GE Co., 1977; cons. Ford Motor Co., 1978-79, UN Devel. Program, NYC, 1980-81, Montgomery County, Md. Office Inspector Gen., 1997-2004; dir. fed. affairs Shippers Nat. Freight Claim Coun., Washington, 1979-89; Washington counsel Japan Airlines; chmn. US dels. at various internat. transp. confs. Author: Community Planning for Air Transportation, 1960; Washington editor Handling and Shipping mag., 1976—81, dir. Olney Big Band, 2005—. Pres. Allied Civic Group (50 assns.), Silver Spring, 1956-58; chmn. rsch. com. Md. Rep. Com., 1965-70; chmn. fin. adv. com. to county coun., Rockville, 1965-70; exec. dir. Montgomery County Taxpayers League, 1994-97. 2d lt. US Army, 1943-46. Mem.: Assn. Intelligence Officers, Univ. Club (bd. govs., Washington), 33 Degree Scottish Rite Mason, Phi Beta Kappa, Phi Alpha Delta (supreme justice 1966—68, exec. v.p. Pub. Svc. Ctr. 1984—91, Disting. Svc. chpt.). Home: 9105 Falls Chapel Way Potomac MD 20854-2452 Personal E-mail: robredding@comcast.net.

REDDING, ROGERS WALKER, physics professor, academic administrator; b. Louisville, July 15, 1942; s. George Walker and Carolyn Lorraine (Rogers) R.; m. Jennie Ruth Fincher, Sept. 6, 1966 (div.); children: Jeffrey Walker, Jonathan Hull; m. Shirley Rubrecht, Aug. 24, 1991. BS, Georgia Tech., 1965; PhD, Vanderbilt U., 1969. Rsch. assoc. Nat. Bur. Standards, Washington, 1969-70; from asst. prof. to assoc. prof. North Tex. State U. (name now U. North Tex.), Denton, 1970-78, prof. physics, 1978-94, dept. chmn., 1980-87, dir. Tex. Acad. Math. and Sci., 1987-89, assoc. dean arts and scis., 1990-94; prof. physics, dean Coll. Arts and Scis. No. Ky. U., Highland Heights, 1994—, v.p. acad. affairs, provost. Disting. vis. prof. USAF Acad., 1989-90. Author: Exploring Physics, 1984; contbr. articles to profl. jours. Mem. Am. Phys. Soc., Am. Assn. Physics Tchrs., AAAS, Optical Soc. Am. Lodges: Kiwanis. Democrat. Avocations: handball, jogging, referee college football, little league coach. E-mail: redding@nku.edu.

REDDINGTON, MARY JANE, retired secondary school educator; b. New Rochelle, NY, July 21, 1923; d. Gordon William and Katharine Regina (Coleman) Kann; m. John Martin Reddington, Oct. 11, 1947; children: Terence, Martha, Robert. BA cum laude, Coll. New Rochelle, 1945; postgrad., Columbia U., 1947—49; MA, Hunter Coll., 1954; PhD (hon.), Iona Coll., 1996. Tchr. St. Gabriel's H.S., New Rochelle, NY, 1945—51, Albert Leonard Jr. H.S., New Rochelle, NY, 1960—81; dir. devel. The Ursuline Sch., New Rochelle, NY, 1981—88; ret., 1988. Active Bd. Edn., New Rochelle, 1983—, v.p., 1985—87, pres., 1987—89, Colburn Meml. Home; active New Rochelle Pub. Libr. Found. Bd., New Rochelle Cmty. Svcs. Bd.; vol. Sound Shore Med. Ctr.; bd. dirs. United Way New Rochelle, 1972—, pres., 1979—82, campaign chair, 1976—82; trustee Coll. New Rochelle, 1967—73; lector Holy Family Ch.; active Holy Family Ch. Ladies Guild. Named to Westchester County Hall of Fame, 2005; recipient Gold Key award, Columbia Scholastic Press Assn., 1976, Ursula Laurus citation, Coll. New Rochelle, 1962, St. Angela Merici medal, 1970, citation, United Way New Rochelle, 1970—82, Spl. Recognition award, 1986, 2001, St. Angela award, The Ursuline Sch., 1977, Nat. Cmty. Svc. award, AARP, 1994, Loyal Svc. and Dedication award, Colburn Home, 1992, Cmty. Salute honoree, New Rochelle Pub. Libr. Found., 1999, Cmty. Svc. award, New Rochelle YMCA, 2001, honoree, Sr. Pers. Placement Bur., 2002, Interreligious Coun. of New Rochelle, 2002, Meals-On-Wheels of New Rochelle, 2003, New Rochelle Fund for Ednl. Excellence, 2004, Marie Vitt award, Sound Share Med. Ctr., 2005. Mem.: Bus. and Profl. Women's Club New Rochelle (past pres., Woman of Yr. 1979), So. Westchester Ret. Tchrs. Assn. (co-pres.), Coll. New Rochelle Alumnae Assn. (past pres.), Ladies of Charity (past pres.), Cath. Women's Club Westchester (founder, past pres.), Woman's Club New Rochelle (pres.), LWV, Alpha Delta Kappa (past pres.). Roman Catholic. Avocations: travel, reading, antiques, writing, cross country skiing. Home: 56 Wykagyl Terr New Rochelle NY 10804

REDDY, DANIEL JOSEPH, vascular surgeon; b. Jackson, Mich., June 2, 1947; s. Martin Joseph and Phyllis Watson Reddy; m. Diane Marie D'Angelo; children: Caitlin Marie, Daniel Martin. BS, Georgetown U., 1969; MD, U. Mich., 1973. Diplomate in gen. surgery and vascular surgery Am. Bd. Surgery. Sr. staff vascular surgeon Henry Ford Hosp., Detroit, 1979—, chief of vascular surgery, 1997—, dir. vascular surgery fellowship tng. program, 1997—, d. emerick szilagyi chair in vascular surgery, 2002—. Mem. bd. govs. Henry Ford Med. Group, Detroit, 1995—2002. Author numerous papers, exhibits, movies, abstracts. Bd. mem. Christus Medicus, Metro Detroit, 1999—. Ignatius Academic scholar, Georgetown U., 1965—69, Traveling Pub. Health fellow to Yugoslavia, Am. Assn. Med. Colls., 1973. Fellow: ACS (Fredrick Coller award 1975); mem.: Ctrl. Surg. Assn., Western Surg. Assn., Soc. Vascular Surgery. Independent. Roman Catholic. Achievements include patents for Reddy Treadle Asssessing Arterial Systems. Avocation: ice hockey. Office: Henry Ford Hosp 2799 W Grand Blvd Detroit MI 48202 Business E-Mail: dreddy1@hfhs.org.

REDDY, GERARD ANTHONY, financial consultant; b. NYC, Sept. 25, 1958; s. Warren and Julia (O'Reilly) R.; m. Lorraine (Bush), Feb. 20, 1994; 1 child, Katelyn Grace. BA in English Writing and Comm. Media, Queens Coll., 1981. Rsch. analyst John Blair and Co., NYC, 1981—82, Katz Ind. TV Sales, NYC, 1982—83; sr. rsch. analyst Seltel, NYC, 1983—84; sales presentation writer Capital Cities ABC TV Sales, NYC, 1984—86; client svc. exec. A.C. Nielsen Co., NYC, 1986—87; rsch. mgr. off network programming MCA-TV, NYC, 1987—88; mgr. corp. tng. and instrn. Dale Carnegie Tng., NYC, 1989—96, major accounts bus. mgr., 1996—97; tng. supr. Americhoice Inc., Newark, 1998; sr. tng. specialist The Dreyfus Corp., Uniondale, NY, 1999—2000; fin. advisor Am. Express Fin. Advisors, Inc., Mitchel Field, NY, 2000—03, para planner, 2004—05; consumer banker J.P. Morgan Chase, Gt. Neck, NY, 2003—04; tng. specialist Wm. Fin. Svcs., Inc., Uniondale, NY, 2005—. Mgr. Little League Our Lady Miraculous Medal, Ridgewood, N.Y., 1993-94; campaigned for Rudolph Guliani for Mayor, N.Y.C., Ridgewood, 1994. Avocations: script writing, motorcycling, meditation, jogging. Home: 3 Smith St East Rockaway NY 11518-1716 Office: Wm Fin Svcs Inc Reckson Plz 11th Fl E Tower Uniondale NY 11556-0125 E-mail: gerard.reddy@wamu.net.

REDDY, J. N., mechanical engineering educator; b. Warangal, AP, India, Aug. 12, 1945; m. Aruna Reddy; children: Anita, Anil. BE in Mech. Engring., Osmania U., 1968; MS in Mech. Engring, Okla. State U., 1970; PhD in Engring. Mechanics, U. Ala., 1973. Rsch. scientist Lockheed Missiles & Space Co., 1974-75; asst. prof. U. Okla., 1975-78, assoc. prof., 1978-80; prof. mech. engring. Va. Poly. Inst. and State U., Blacksburg, Va., 1980-85, Clifton G. Garvin prof., 1986-92; Oscar S. Wyatt Jr. chair Tex. A&M U., College Station, 1992—, Univ. Disting. prof., 1998—. Author: Energy Principles and Variational Methods in Applied Mechanics, 1984, 2nd edit., 2002, Applied Functional Analysis and Variational Methods in Engineering, 1986, An Introduction to the Finite Element Method, 2d edit., 1993, Mechanics of Laminated Composite Plates and Shells: Theory and Analysis, 2d edit., 2004, Theory and Analysis of Elastic Plates, 1999, An Introduction to Nonlinear Finite Element Analysis, 2004, (with others) Variational Methods in Theoretical Mechanics, 1976, A Mathematical Theory of Finite Elements, 1976, Advanced Engineering Analysis, 1982, Finite Element Analysis of Composite Laminates, 1992, The Finite Element Method in Heat Transfer and Fluid Dynamics, 1994, 2d edit., 2001, Practical Analysis of Laminated Composite Structures, 1995; editor-in-chief Mechanics of Advanced Materials and Structures, Internat. Jour. Computational Methods Engring. Sci. Mechanics, Internat. Jour. Structural Stability and Dynamics; mem. editl. bd. Jour. Applied Mechanics, Internat. Jour. Numerical Methods in Engring., Internat. Jour. Numerical Methods in Fluids, others; contbr. over 300 papers to profl. jours. Recipient Ralph R. Teetor Edn. award Soc. Automotive Engrs., 1976, Technical Achievement award NAE, 1995, Archie Higdon Disting. Educator award Am. Soc. Engring. Edn., 1997. Fellow ASME (Worcester Reed Warner medal 1992, Charles Russ Richards Meml. award 1995), ASCE (Walter L. Huber Civil Engring Rsch. prize 1983, Nathan M. Newmark medal 1998), AIAA (assoc.), Am. Acad. Mechanics, Aeronautical Soc. India, U.S. Assn. Computational Mechanics (Computational Solid Mechanics award 2003), Internat. Assn. Computational Mechanics, Am. Soc. Composites (Excellence in the Field of Composite award 2000, Outstanding Rsch. award 2004). Office: Texas A&M Univ Dept Mech Engring College Station TX 77843-3123 Office Phone: 979-862-2417. Fax: 979-862-3989. Business E-Mail: jmreddy@tamu.edu.

REDDY, J. PATRICK, gas industry executive; Grad., UCLA; MBA, Univ. So. Calif. Mgmt. positions through v.p. planning & adv. services Pacific Enterprises, 1980—98; v.p. corp. develop Atmos Energy, Dallas, 1998, v.p., treas., 1998—2000, sr. v.p., CFO, 2000—. Mailing: Atmos Energy PO Box 650205 Dallas TX 75265-0205 *

REDDY, K. SRINATH, cardiologist; b. India; BS, Osmania Med. Coll., Hyperabad, India, 1973; MD, All India Inst. Med. Scis., New Delhi, 1977, DM in cardiology, 1980; MSc in clin. epidemiology, McMaster U., Hamilton, Can., 1988. Prof., chief dept. cardiology All India Inst. Med. Scis., New Delhi. Editor: Nat. Med. Jour. India; mem. editorial adv. bd. World Health Bulletin, Ethnicity & Health, Indian Heart Jour., Current Sci. Chair, scientific coun. on epidemiology & prevention WHO, mem. adv. panel on cardiovascular diseases, 1993—, mem. sci. adv. com. on tobacco product regulation, active. Recipient Dir.-Gen.'s award for Outstanding Contbn. to Global Tobacco Control, WHO, 2004, Padma Bhushan, India, 2005, Queen Elizabeth Medal, Royal Soc. for the Promotion of Health, UK, 2005. Fellow: Nat. Acad. Med. Scis. India; mem.: Inst. Medicine (fgn. assoc.), Nat. Acad. Med. Scis. India. Office: All India Inst Med Sciences Dept Cardiology Ansari Nagar New Delhi 110 029 India Office Phone: 91-11-2659-4681. Office Fax: 91-11-2658-8663. E-mail: ksreddy@aiims.ac.in.

REDDY, KAMBHAM RAJA, botanist, educator; b. Ambuvari Palli, India, July 1, 1953; s. Kambi Kambham and Ammannamma (Reddy) R.; m. Anasuya Reddy; 1 son, Sasank. BSc in Biology, S.V. U., Tirupati, India, 1975, MSc in Botany, 1977, PhD in Botany, 1984. Curator in botany S.V. U., 1977-88; prof. plant physiology Miss. State U., 1991—. Editor: Climate Change and Global Crop Productivity, 2000; contbg. author: Climate Change and Agriculture: Analysis of Potential International Impacts, 1995; contbr. articles to profl. jour., chpt. to books. Recipient Career Rsch. award, So. Br. Am. Soc. Agronomy and Assn. Agrl. Scientists Indian Origin, 2004. Fellow Agronomy Soc. Am., Crop Sci. Soc. Am.; mem. Biol. Sys. Simulation Work Group, Gamma Sigma Delta (Rsch. award of merit 1995). Achievements include development of new theories and concepts in plant growth regulation and incorporated into a cotton simulation model GOSSYM, used by cotton producers, consultants and rschr. across the cotton belt; extensive contributions to the field of climate change, environmental plant physiology, ethnobotany, remote sensing and crop simulation modeling. Home: 505 Banyan Rd Starkville MS 39759-4348 Office: Mississippi State U Box 9555 Mississippi State MS 39762-9555 Home Phone: 662-324-5323; Office Phone: 662-325-9463.

REDDY, KRISHNA NARAYANA, artist, educator; b. Chittoor, India, July 15, 1925; s. Narayana B. and Laksmamma Reddy; m. Judith Blum, June 30, 1967; 1 child, Aparna. Diploma in Fine Arts, Internat. U. Santiniketan, India, 1947; cert. in Fine Arts, Slade Sch. Fine Arts, U. London, 1952; student of Zadkine in sculpture, Academie Grande Chaumière, Paris, 1952—55; student of Marino Marini in sculpture, Academia di Belle Arti di Brera, Milan, 1956—57; specialist in Gravure, Internat. Ctr. for Graphics, Atelier 17, Paris, 1953—55; DLitt (hon.), S.V. Univ., India, 1984. Asst. dir. Internat. Ctr. for Graphics, Atelier 17, Paris, 1957—64, prof., co-dir., 1964—76; from prof. art to prof. emeritus NYU, NYC, 1977—2001, prof. emeritus art and art edn., 2001—. Dir. dept. art Coll. Fine Arts, Kalakshetra, Madras, India, 1947—49; lectr. art Arundale Montessori Tchrs. Tng. Ctr., 1948—49; vis. prof. Am. U., 1964; prof. U. Calif., Davis, 1970—71, U. Wis., Madison, 1973; guest prof. Yale U. Summer Sch. Music and Art, 1973; Andrew Mellon vis. prof. Cooper Union Sch. Art and Arch., 1977; vis. prof. Yale U. Summer Sch. Music and Art, 1978, Kala Inst. Graphics, Berkeley, Calif., 1979, U. Calif., Santa Cruz, 1979. Author: Intaglio Simultaneous Color Printmaking: Significance of Materials and Processes, 1989, New Ways of Colour Printmaking, 1997; exhibitions include Bronx Mus. Arts, 1981-82, Indian Coun. for Cultual Relations, Ministry Culture and India Nat. Acad. Fine Arts, 1984-85, Mus. del Palacio de Bellas Artes, Mexico City, 1988-89. Recipient Gagan-Abani Puraskar Nat. award Viswa-Bharati, 1983, Printmaker Emeritus award So. Graphics Coun. Am., 2000, Kala Ratna award Nat. Acad. Fine Arts, Govt. India, 2007, Lifetime Achievement award Soc. Am. Graphic Artists, 2005; named Featured Guest Artist-Printmaker at the Northwest Print Coun. Ann. Meeting, 1985; Title of Padma Shree awarded by Pres. of India, 1972. Home: 80 Wooster St New York NY 10012-4347 Office Phone: 212-998-5756. Personal E-mail: jreddy5@nyc.rr.com.

REDDY, LIKITH V., maxillofacial surgeon, director; s. Vootukuru Reddy; m. Deval Reddy, May 1, 2001. MD, DDS, U. Tex., Dallas, 2003. Lic. Medicine Ohio, 2003. Asst. prof. surgery U. Cin. Med. Ctr., 2003—06, resident dir. oral and maxillofacial surgery, 2005—. Fellow, ACS, 2003. Achievements include development of surgical specialty. Office: U Cin Med Ctr 231 Albert Sabin Way Cincinnati OH 45267-0558 Office Phone: 513-886-0600. Business E-Mail: likith.reddy@uc.edu.

REDDY, RAJ, science educator, academic administrator; married; 2 children. BE in Civil Engring., Guindy Engring. Coll. (Currently named Anna Univ.), Univ. Madras, India, 1958; MTech, Univ. New South Wales, 1960; PhD in Computer Sci., Stanford Univ., 1966; DSc (hon.), Sri Venkateswara Univ., India, Univ. Henri-Poincare, France, Univ. South Wales, Australia, Jawaharial Nehru Technological Univ., India, Univ. Mass. Applied sci. rep. IBM Corp., Australia, 1960—63; asst. prof. Stanford Univ., 1966—69; assoc. prof. computer sci. Carnegie Mellon U., Pitts., 1969—73, full prof. computer sci., 1973—84, univ. prof., 1984—92, dir., Robotics Inst., 1979—91, dean sch. computer sci., 1991-99, Herbert A. Simon prof. computer sci. and robotics, sch. computer sci., 1992—2005; Mozah Bint Nasser univ. prof. computer sci. and robotics, sch. computer sci. Carnegie Mellon U. (awarded by Qatar Found.), Pitts., 2005—. Co-chair President's Clinton and Bush Adv. Com. on Info. Tech., 1999—2001. Bd. gov. Peres Inst. for Peace in Israel. Recipient Legion Honor, President Mitterand of France, 1984, IBM Rsch. Ralph Gomory Fellow award, 1991, A.M. Turing award Assn. Computing Machinery, 1994, Padma Bhushan, President of India, 2001, Okawa prize, 2004, Honda prize. 2005, Vannevar Bush award, Nat. Sci. Bd., 2006. Fellow IEEE, Acoustical Soc. Am., Am. Assn. for Artificial Intelligence (pres. 1987-89); mem. NAE, Am. Acad. Arts and Sciences. Avocations: walking, reading. Office: Carnegie Mellon U Sch Computer Sci Wean Hall 5325 Pittsburgh PA 15213-3891 Office Phone: 412-268-2597. Office Fax: 412-683-5348. Business E-Mail: rr@cmu.edu. *

REDDY, RANGA VALLELA, anesthesiologist; b. India, Jan. 1, 1946; came to US, 1976; MS in Gen. Surgery, Kurool Med. Coll., 1970. Residency, gen. surgery Kurnool Gen. Hosp., Kurnool, India, 1971—74; med. superintendent St. Raphael's Hosp., Giddalur, India, 1975—76; physician St. John Hosp., Yonkers, NY, 1976-77; resident, anesthesiology dept. SUNY Health Sci. Ctr., Brooklyn, NY, 1977—79, asst. prof., 1979—82; attending anesthesiologist, asst. prof. St. Louis U. Med. Ctr., St. Louis, 1979—82; attending anesthesiologist Veteran Hosp. Med. Ctr., St. Louis, 1979—82; clinical assoc. prof. So. Ill. U. Sch. of Med., 1982—; attending anesthesiologist Meml. Med. Ctr., Springfield, Ill., 1982—, chmn. dept. anesthesiology, 1996—98. Pres. AAPI, 1997-98. Mem. AMA, Am. Surg. Assn., Internat. Anesthesia Rsch. Soc., Ill. Med. Assn., Ill. Surg. Assn., Am. Assn. Physicians of Indian Origin (pres. 1997-98). Office: Memorial Medical Center 701 N First St Springfield IL 62781 E-mail: rankris@aol.com.

REDDY, RAVINDER, medical educator, director; m. Vasantha Reddy; 1 child, Rishika. PhD in Chemistry, Indian Inst. Tech. Kanpur, Kanpur, India, 1989. Cert. German proficiency Indian Inst. Tech. Asst. prof. radiology U. Pa., Phila., 1994—2000, assoc. prof. radiology, 2000—06, prof. radiology, sch. medicine, 2006—. Dir. grad. level courses U. Pa., 1996—, sci. dir., Metabolic Magnetic Resonance Rsch. & Computing Ctr., 1996—, mem. bioengring. grad. grp., 1998—, dir., multinuclear magnetic resonance lab., 2000—, mem. biomed. grad. grp., 2000—. Contbr. articles to profl. jours. Grantee Rsch. grants, NIH, 1995—, Biomedical Rsch. grant, Whitaker Found., 1996—2000, Rsch. grant, Dana Found., 2004—. Mem.: Am. Chem. Soc., Osteoarthritis Rsch. Soc. Internat., NY Acad. Scis., Internat. Soc. Magnetic Resonance Medicine. Achievements include patents for diagnostic MRI technology.

REDDY, SHYAM K., lawyer; s. Mohan and Sujatha Reddy; m. Renee E. Dye, Nov. 23, 2002. BA in Polit. Sch., Emory U., Atlanta, 1996, MPH, 1997; JD, U. Ga., Athens, 2000. Assoc. Kilpatrick Stockton, Atlanta, Ga., 2000—. Founder. bd. dirs. Red Clay Democrats, Atlanta, 2002—05; bd. dirs. Common Cause Ga., Atlanta, 2006—; mentor Indus Entrepreneaurs, Atlanta, 2003. Named a Mover and Shaker, Multicultural Law, 2005; named L.E.A.D. Atlanta Class Mem., Leadership Atlanta, 2005; named one of Top 40 Under 40 Georgians, Ga. Trend Mag., 2005, Top 40 Under 40 Up and Comers, Atlanta Bus. Chronicle, 2005; recipient Ga. Rising Star award, Atlanta Mag. and Ga. Super Lawyers, 2005—06; Marshall fellow, German Marshall Fund of US, 2007. Mem.: Indus Bar. Home Phone: 404-949-5659; Office Phone: 404-815-6500.

REDDY, THIKKAVARAPU RAMACHANDRA, electrical engineer; b. Nellore, India, June 4, 1944; came to the U.S., 1979; s. Thikkavarapu Kota and Saraswathi T. (Sivareddy) R.; m. Padmavathi Reddy Kakuturu Thikkavarapu, Aug. 17, 1973; children: Lavanya T., Samatha T. BSEE, Osmania U., 1968, PhD in Bus. Adminstrn., 2005; diploma in Computer Sci., Coll. Engring., Madras, India, 1978. Cert. profl. engr., chartered engr. Supervising engr. APSE Bd., Hyderabad, India, 1969—79; engr. elec. design Sargent & Lundy, Chgo., 1979—80; engr. Bechtel Corp., San Francisco, 1980—82, supr. Athens, Ala., 1989—92; sr. project engr. EGS, Inc., Huntsville, Ala., 1983—84; sr. start-up engr. Gilbert Commonwealth Co., Reading, Pa., 1984—86; cons. Quantum Resources, Decatur, Ala., 1986—87; prin. engr. Ebasco Svcs. Inc., NYC, 1987—89; pres. LSP Internat. Inc., Huntsville, 1992—, LASA Internat., Huntsville, 1992—; project engr. Sargent & Lundy, Chgo., 1997—. Guest lectr. gen. interest and wide range of engring. issues. Author: Qualification of Electrical Distribution Components, 1984, Thermal Aging Techniques of Organic Materials, 1984, and others; contbr. articles to profl. jours.; guest lectr. on wide range of engring. issues. Mem. NSPE (Outstanding Profl. award 1991, Profl. Engr. of Yr. award 1996), IEEE (sr.; Meritorious Svc. award 1985), Commonwealth Engrs. Coun., Project Mgmt. Inst., Am. Telugu Assn. (life), Telugu Assn. N.Am. (life), Internat. Platform Assn., Soc. Fire Protection Egrs. (profl.), C. of C. Avocations: journalism, ping pong/table tennis, anthropology, archaeology, classic and modern art, literature. Home and Office: 100 Jersey Ln Rockville MD 20850 Personal E-mail: trr2020@yahoo.com.

REDDY, VADIYALA MOHAN, cardiothoracic surgeon; m. Anita Reddy. MD, Kakatiya Med. Coll., Warangal, India, 1983. Resident Delhi U., New Delhi, 1986, 1989; sr. resident, pediatric cardiac surgery Children's Hosp., Boston, 1991; fellow Miami Children's Hosp., Fla., 1992, U. Calif., San Francisco, 1992; dir., pediatric cardiac surgery U. Calif, San Francisco, 1992—2001, assoc. prof., 1992—2001; divsn. chief, pediatric cardiothoracic surgery Cardiothoracic Surgery Clinic, Lucile Packard Children's Hosp. at Stanford U. Med. Ctr., Palo Alto, Calif., 2001—; assoc. prof., cardiothoracic surgery Stanford U. Sch. Medicine, Stanford, Calif., 2001—. Contbr. articles to profl. publs. Mem.: Soc. Thoracic Surgeons, Am. Heart Assn., Am. Assn. for Thoracic Surgeons. Office: Cardiothoracic Surgery 300 Pasteur Dr CVRB MC 5407 Stanford CA 94305 Address: Lucile Packard Childrens Hosp 725 Welsh Rd Palo Alto CA 94304 Office Phone: 650-724-2925, 650-497-8000, 415-476-3501. Fax: 650-724-0707, 415-476-9678; Office Fax: 650-725-3846. Business E-Mail: vmreddy@stanford.edu.

REDDY, VARDHAN JONNALA, surgeon; b. Kollipara, India, Nov. 26, 1960; MBBS, Guntur Med. Coll., Andhra U., 1985. Diplomate Am. Bd. Surgery, Am. Bd. Thoracic Surgery. Internist Robert Packer Hosp., Sayre, Pa., 1990-91; res. L.I. Jewish Med. Ctr., New Hyde Park, NY, 1991-95; fellowship Tex. Heart Inst., Houston, 1995-96; staff surgeon Glades Gen. Hosp., Belle Glade, Fla., 1996-98, chief surgery, 1998—99; cardiothoracic surgeon U. Miss., Jackson, Miss., 1999—2001, Shadyside Hosp., Pitts., 2001—. V.p. Med. Staff Assocs. of Glades Inc., 1998, pres., CEO Heartcom Inc., 1999. Mem. AMA, Internat. Coll. Angiology, Royal Coll. Surgeons Edinburgh (diplomate), Am. Coll. Angiology. Home and Office: 504 Greenbrier Ct Steubenville OH 43953-3335 E-mail: vardhanreddy@usa.net.

REDDY, VENKAT NARSIMHA, ophthalmologist, researcher; b. Hyderabad, India, Nov. 4, 1922; came to U.S., 1947; s. Malla and Manik (Devi) R.; m. Alvira M. DeMello, Dec. 10, 1955; children: Vinay Neville, Marlita Alvira. BSc, U. Madras, 1945; MS, PhD, Fordham U., 1952. Rsch. assoc. Coll. of Physicians and Surgeons Columbia U., NYC, 1952-56, Banting and Best Inst., Toronto, Can., 1956; ass. and assoc. prof.

ophthalmology Kresge Eye Inst. Wayne State U., Detroit, 1957-68; prof., biomed. scis., asst. dir. Eye Rsch. Inst. Oakland U., Rochester, Mich., 1968-75, prof., dir., 1975-98, Disting. prof. biomed. scis., dir., 1996-98; prof. ophthalmology Kellogg Eye Ctr. U. Mich., Ann Arbor, 1998—. Mem. study sect. NIH, Bethesda, 1966-70, nat. adv. eye coun., 1982-87, mem. bd. sci. counselors Nat. Eye Inst., 1977-81 Mem. editl. bd. Investigative Ophthalmology and Visual Scis., 1969-72, 78-88, Ophthalmic Research, 1978-90, Experimental Eye Research, 1985-2000; contbr. articles to profl. jours. Recipient Friendenwald award Assn. Rsch. in Ophthalmology, 1979, Rsch. award Cataract Rsch. Found., 1987, Merit award Nat. Eye Inst., 1989; named Scientist of Yr. State of Mich., 1991, Disting. Faculty Mem. Mich. Assn. Governing Bds. State Univs., 1994. Mem. AAAS, Internat. Soc. Eye Rsch., The Biochem. Soc., Assn. Rsch. in Vision and Ophthalmology (pres. 1985), Am. Soc. for Biochemistry and Molecular Biology, Soc. Free Radicals, Oxygen Soc. Sigma Xi. Achievements include research on cataract etiology, intraocular fluids dynamics relating to glaucoma, cell biology of lens, ciliary body and retinal pigment epithelium, cell differentiation. Office: U Mich Kellogg Eye Ctr 1000 Wall St Ann Arbor MI 48105-1912 Home Phone: 248-334-9339; Office Phone: 734-763-7246. Business E-Mail: venreddy@med.umich.edu.

REDFEARN, PAUL L., III, lawyer; b. Camp Cook, Calif., Oct. 1, 1951; s. Paul Leslie Jr. and Alice Ruby Redfearn; children: Ashley, Lauren; m. Denise Jean Davis, July 24, 1993. BS, S.W. Mo. State U., 1973; JD, Oklahoma City U., 1976. Bar: Mo. 1977, U.S. Dist. Ct. (we. and ea. dists.) Mo., U.S. Dist. Ct. Kans., U.S. Dist. Ct. N.D., U.S. Dist. Ct. Mont., U.S. Ct. Appeal (8th ant 11th cirs.); bd. cert. civil trial advocate. Assoc. Sheridan, Sanders & Simpson, P.C., 1977-79, William H. Pickett, P.C., 1979-84; pvt. practice Kansas City, Mo., 1984—. Mem. bd. dirs. Lawyers Encouraging Acad. Performance (LEAP), treas.; lectr. and presenter in field. Contbr. chpts. to books. Bd. govs. S.W. Mo. State U., 1998-2003; instr. Ross T. Roberts Inn of Ct. Program, Kansas City. Mo. Named Best of the Bar, Business Jour., 2003, Mo. and Kans. Super Lawyers, 2005, 2006. Mem. ABA, Am. Assn. Justice, Mo. Bar Assn., Mo. Assn. Trial Attys. (bd. govs. 1986-94, exec. com. 1990—, pres. 1992), Am. Bd. Trial Advs. (charter, pres. chpt. 1996-97, adv.), Pub. Justice Found., Kansas City Met. Bar Assn., Millon Dollar Advs. Forum. Democrat. Avocation: tennis. Office: 1125 Grand Blvd Ste 1805 Kansas City MO 64106-2518 Office Phone: 816-421-5301. Business E-Mail: predfearn@redfearnlawfirm.com.

REDFIELD, CAROL ANN LUCKHARDT, computer scientist, educator; b. Greencastle, Ind., July 19, 1958; d. Robert Luckhardt and Helen Kinoshta; m. Josiah Beckley Redfield, Mar. 17, 1990; children: Neil, Crystal. BS Edn., U. Mich., 1980, MS Math, 1982, MS Computer & Controls, 1982, PhD Computer Sci. & Engring., 1989. Cert. secondary tchr. Tchg. asst. U. Mich., Ann Arbor, 1979—87; rsch. engr. Southwest Rsch. Inst., San Antonio, 1987—94; sr. scientist Mei Tech. Corp., San Antonio, 1995—98; asst. prof. St. Mary's U., San Antonio, 1998—2003, assoc. prof., 2003—, dir. Grad. Program, 2004—. Chair Internat. Space Devel. Conf., San Antonio, 1991, co-chair, ITS, 1998, AI in Edn., 2001. Author: AI and Game Playing, 1986; editor, author: Intelligent Tutoring Systems, 1991, 98; editor: 1991 ISDC Procs., 1991, AI in Education, 2001 Dir. Internet team Landmark Edn.; founder Radiance Acad. West Charter Sch. Named to San Antonio Women's Hall of Fame, 1993; recipient Ultimate Frisbee Nat. champion, 1993. Mem. AAAI, Nat. Space Soc., San Antonio Space Soc. (pres. 1988—) Mem. Soc. Of Friends. Avocations: science fiction, games, ultimate frisbee. Home: 609 Ridge View Dr San Antonio TX 78253-5348 Office: St Marys U 1 Camino Santa Maria St San Antonio TX 78228-8524 Office Phone: 210-436-3298. Business E-Mail: CRedfield@stmarytx.edu.

REDFIELD, PAMELA A., state legislator; b. Chgo., Aug. 11, 1948; m. Jerry Redfield; 6 children. BS in Edn., U. Nebr., 1969. Mem. Nebr. Legislature 12th dist., Lincoln, 1998—. Mem. Ralston Bd. Edn. 1992-1998. Coun. State Govt.; Nat. Conf. State Legislatures; Am. Legis. Exch. Conf.; Nat. Coun. Ins. Legislators Mem.: Am. Legis. Exch. conf., Nat. Conf. State Legis., Nat. Coun. Ins. State Legis.

REDFIELD, ROBERT HORACE, mathematician, educator; b. Schenectady, NY, Feb. 24, 1945; s. Robert Horace Redfield and Elizabeth (Carlson) Cherrett; m. Rosemary Jeanne Gagne, Dec. 13, 1970 (div. 1979); 1 child, Signe Anne; m. Mary Eleanor Javorski, Aug. 18, 1984; children: Lisbeth Ellen Sarah, Catherine Mairi Sophia. BA, Reed Coll., 1967; MA, U. Oreg., 1969; PhD, Simon Fraser U., Can., 1973. Rsch. fellow Monash U., Clayton, Victoria, Australia, 1974-77, vis. assoc. prof., 1989-90; vis. asst. prof. math. U. Kans., Lawrence, 1977-78; instr. Okanagan Coll., Kelowna, 1978-86; assoc. prof. math. Hamilton Coll., Clinton, N.Y., 1986-93, prof., 1993-96, Samuel F. Pratt prof.math., 1996—. Vis. lectr. McMaster U., Hamilton, Ont., Canada, 1980; vis. assoc. prof. Simon Fraser U., Burnaby, B.C., Canada, 1985, Monash U., Victoria, Australia, 1989—90. Reviewer: for math reviews, published: textbook on abstract algebra; contbr. rsch. papers to math. publs. Organizer, tchr., Kelowna Internat. Dancers, 1981-86, Clinton Internat. Folk Dancers, 1992-2003 Grantee, Australian Rsch. Grants Com., 1974-77. Mem. Am. Math. Soc., Can. Math. Soc., Can. Soc. History and Philosophy of Math., Math. Assn. Am., Kelowna Scottish Country Dance Group (treas. 1981-86), Sigma Xi. Office: Hamilton Coll Dept Math Clinton NY 13323

REDFIELD, ROBERT R., virologist, medical educator; b. Chgo., 1951; BS, Georgetown U., 1973; MD, Georgetown U. Sch. Med., 1977; degree (hon.), N.Y. Med. Coll. Intern Walter Reed Army Med. Ctr, 1977—78, resident in med., 1978—80, fellow infectious diseases, 1980—82, fellow tropical med., 1982; project dir. HIV immunotherapy Walter Reed Army Inst. Rsch., chief dept. retroviral rsch.; project dir. HIV vaccine devel. for treatment and prevention Military Med. Consortium for Applied Retroviral Rsch., Dept. Def.; co-founder, assoc. dir. Inst. Human Virology U. Md., Baltimore, dir. clin. care & rsch. div. Inst. Human Virology; prof. med., immunology, microbiology, dept. infectious disease U. Md. Sch. Med.; dir. adult HIV program U. Md. Med. Mem. adv. bd. Fogarty Internat. Ctr.; mem. AIDS rsch. adv. coun. NIH. Bd. dirs. The Pendulum Project. Recipient Lifetime Science award, Inst. Advanced Studies in Immunology and Aging, Highest Achievement in Clinical Virology award, Ortho Diagnostic Systems Inc., Physician Recognition award, Surgeon Gen., multiple medals in virology, U.S. Army. Achievements include being the first to demonstrate the heterosexual transmission of the HIV virus; development of the first clinical staging system, now used around the world; originated efforts to examine viral replication and viral load at all of stages of disease. Office: Inst Human Virology 725 W Lombard St Baltimore MD 21201

REDFORD, DONALD BRUCE, historian, archaeologist; b. Toronto, Ont., Can., Sept. 2, 1934; s. Cyril Fitzjames and Kathleen Beryl (Coe) R.; m. Susan Pirritano, Jan. 30, 1982; children: Alexander, Aksel; children by previous marriage: Christopher, Philip. BA, U. Toronto, 1957, MA, 1958; PhD, Brown U., 1965. Lectr. Brown U., 1960-61; lectr. U. Toronto, 1961-64, asst. prof. Egyptian history and language, 1965-67, asso. prof., 1967-69, prof., 1969-98; site supr. Brit. Sch. Archaeol. Excavations, Jerusalem, 1964-67; dir. Soc. Study Egyptian Antiquities Expdn. to, Karnak, Egypt, 1970-72, Akhenaten Temple Project, Luxor, Egypt, 1972—; research assoc. Univ. Museum, U. Pa., Royal Ont. Mus.; prof. classics Pa. State U., 1998—. Vis. prof. Ben Gurion U., Beersheva, Israel, 1986, U. Pa., 1995-96; dir. excavations Mendes and Ted Kedwa, Egypt, 1991—. Author: History and Chronology of the Egyptian 18th Dynasty, 1967, A Study of the Biblical Joseph Story, 1970, Papyrus and Tablet, 1973, The Akhenaten Temple Project, vol. I, 1977, Akhenaten, the Heretic King, 1984; Annals, King-Lists and Daybooks, 1986, The Akhenaten Temple Project, vol. II, 1988, Egypt, Canaan and Israel in Ancient Times, 1992, The Wars in Syria and Palestine of Thutmose III, 2003; From Slave to Pharaoh: The Black Experience of Ancient Egypt, 2003. Killam grantee, 1975-79; Smithsonian Fgn. Currency grantee, 1973-76, 1979, Social Scis. Humanities Research Council Can. grantee, 1980—. Fellow Royal Soc. Can. Achievements include discovering Temple of Akhenaten at Luxor, 1976. Office: CAMS Weaver Bldg State College PA 16803 also: Pa State U Dept Classics & Mediterranean Studies 108 Weaver Bldg University Park PA 16802-5500 Business E-Mail: dbr3@psu.edu.

REDFORD, ROBERT (CHARLES ROBERT REDFORD), actor, film director; b. Santa Monica, Calif., Aug. 18, 1937; s. Charles Robert and Martha Redford; m. Lola Van Wegenen, Sept. 12, 1958 (div. 1985); children: Shauna, Jamie, Amy. Student, U. Colo., Pratt Inst. Design, Am. Acad. Dramatic Arts; LHD (hon.), U. Colo., 1987; D (hon.), U. Mass., 1990. Owner ski resort Sundance, Provo, Utah. Stage appearances include: Tall Story, The Highest Tree, Sunday in New York, Barefoot in the Park; films include: (actor) War Hunt, 1961, Situation Hopeless But Not Serious, 1965, Inside Daisy Clover, 1965, The Chase, 1966, This Property Is Condemned, 1966, Barefoot in the Park, 1967, Butch Cassidy and the Sundance Kid, 1969, Tell Them Willie Boy is Here, 1969, Little Fauss and Big Halsey, 1970, The Hot Rock, 1972, Jeremiah Johnson, 1972, The Way We Were, 1973, The Sting, 1973 (Academy award nominee), The Great Gatsby, 1974, The Great Waldo Pepper, 1975, Three Days of the Condor, 1975, A Bridge Too Far, 1977, The Electric Horseman, 1979, Brubaker, 1980, The Natural, 1984, Out of Africa, 1985, Legal Eagles, 1986, Havana, 1990, Sneakers, 1992, Indecent Proposal, 1993, Up Close and Personal, 1996, Anthem, 1997, Enredando sombras, 1998, Forever Hollywood, 1999, Spy Game, 2001, The Last Castle, 2001, The Clearing, 2004, An Unfinished Life, 2005, (voice) Charlotte's Web, 2006; actor, exec. prodr. Downhill Racer, 1969, The Candidate, 1972, All The President's Men, 1976; exec. prodr. Promised Land, 1988, Some Girls, 1988, She's the One, 1996, The Dark Wind, 1991, Slums of Beverly Hills, 1998, How to Kill Your Neighbor's Dog, 2000; exec. prodr., narrator Yosemite: The Fate of Heaven, 1989, Incident at Oglala, 1992 (TV) Independent's Day, 1998, Visions of Grace: Robert Redford and 'The Horse Whisperer' 1998 (Audience award); dir. Ordinary People, 1980 (Academy and Golden Globe Awards, Best Director), Quiz Show, 1994; dir., prodr. The Milagro Beanfield War, 1988, A River Runs Through It, 1993 (narrator); prodr. A Civil Action, 1998, The Legend of Bagger Vance, 2000. Founder, pres. The Sundance Inst., 1981—. Named Officer of French Ordre des Arts et des Lettres; named one of 100 Sexiest Stars in film history, Esquire mag., 1994; recipient Audubon medal, 1989, Dartmouth Film Soc. award, 1990, Cecil B. Demille Golden Globe Award for Lifetime Achievement, 1994, Screen Actors Guild Award for Life Achievement, 1996, Hon. award, Acad. Awards, 2002, Kennedy Ctr. Honor, John F. Kennedy Ctr. for Performing Arts, 2005. Fellow: Am. Acad. Arts & Scis.; mem.: Land Trust of Napa County (mem. adv. com.). Office: 1223 Wilshire Blvd # 412 Santa Monica CA 90403-5400 also: Creative Artists Agy c/o David O'Conner 9830 Wilshire Blvd Beverly Hills CA 90212-1804 *

REDGRAVE, MARTYN ROBERT, retail executive; BA in Economics, Princeton U.; MBA in Finance, N.Y.U. CPA Minn. Various fin. and gen. mgmt. positions PepsiCo, 1980—90; exec. v.p. fin., CFO Kentucky Fried Chicken Corp., 1990—94; CFO, exec. v.p Carlson Cos. Inc., Mpls., 1994—2005; exec. v.p., chief admin. officer Limited Brands, Inc., Columbus, Ohio, 2005—; CFO Limited Brands., Inc., Columbus, Ohio, 2006—07. Vol. United Way. Office: Limited Brands Inc 3 Limited Pkwy Columbus OH 43216 *

REDGRAVE, VANESSA, actress; b. London, Jan. 30, 1937; d. Michael and Rachel (Kempson) Redgrave; m. Tony Richardson, Apr. 29, 1962 (div. 1967); children: Joely Kim, Natasha, Carlo. Student, Central Sch. Speech and Drama, London, 1955-57. First stage appearances include: Reluctant Debutante, Frincton Summer Theater, 1957, Come On Jeeves, Arts Theater, Cambridge, 1957, A Touch of the Sun, Saville Theater, London, 1958, Major Barbara, Royal Court, 1958, Mother Goose, Leatherhead, 1958; Prin. theatrical roles include Helena in Midsummer Night's Dream, 1959, Stella in Tiger and the Horse, 1960, Katerina in The Taming of the Shrew, 1961, Rosalind in As You Like It, 1962, Imogene in Cymbeline, 1962, Nina in The Seagull, 1969, Miss Brodie in The Prime of Miss Jean Brodie, 1966, Cato Street, 1971, Threepenny Opera, 1972, Twelfth Night, 1972, Antony and Cleopatra, 1973, Design for Living, 1973, Macbeth, 1975, Lady from the Sea, 1976, 78, 79, The Aspern Papers, 1984 (Laurence Olivier award for actress of yr. in a revival, 1985), The Seagull, 1969, 85, Chekhov's Women, 1985, The Taming of the Shrew, Ghosts, 1986, Touch of the Poet, 1988, Orpheus Descending, 1989, A Madhouse in Goa, 1989, Chekov's Women, 1989, Three Sisters, 1990, When She Danced, 1991, Heartbreak House, 1991, Maybe, 1993, Brecht in Hollywood, 1994, Vita and Virginia, 1994, Long Days Journey Into Night, 2003 (Tony award for best actress, 2003), The Year of Magical Thinking, 2007 (Drama Desk award outstanding solo performance, 2007); films include Behind The Mask, 1958, A Man For All Seasons, 1966, Morgan: A Suitable Case for Treatment, 1966 (Best Actress award, Cannes Film Festival, 1966), Blow-Up, 1966, Red And Blue, 1967, Camelot, 1967, The Sailor from Gibralter, 1967, Isadora, 1968 (Best Actress award, Cannes Film Festival, 1969), The Charge of the Light Brigade, 1968, The Seagull, 1968, A Quiet Place in the Country, 1969, Oh! What a Lovely War, 1969, Daniel Deronda, 1969, Dropout, 1969, The Trojan Women, 1970, The Devils, 1970, The Holiday, 1971, Mary, Queen of Scots, 1971, Murder on the Orient Express, 1974, Winter Rates, 1974, 7 per cent solution, 1975, Julia, 1977 (Academy award for best supporting actress, 1978, Golden Globe award for best supporting actress, 1978), Agatha, 1978, Yanks, 1978, Bear Island, 1979, Playing for Time, 1980, My Body My Child, 1981, Wagner, 1981, The Bostonians, 1983 (Best Actress Nat. Film Critics, Best Actress New Delhi Internat. Film Festival), Wetherby, 1985, Steaming, 1985, Prick Up Your Ears, 1987, Comrades, 1987, Consuming Passions, 1988, Diceria dell'Untore, 1989, The Ballad of the Sad Café, 1990, Young Catherine, 1990, Howard's End, 1992, Crime and Punishment, 1993, The House of the Spirits, 1994, Mother's Boys, 1994, A Month by the Lake, 1995, Little Odessa, 1995, Mission Impossible, 1996, For The Love Of Tyler, 1996, Smilla's Sense of Snow, 1996, Deep Impact, 1998, Celebrity, 1998, Lulu on the Bridge, 1998, Uninvited, 1999, Toscano, 1999, A Rumor of Angels, 1999, Mirka, 1999, An Interesting State, 1999, If These Walls Could Talk 2, 1999, The Cradle Will Rock, 1999, Girl, Interrupted, 1999, A Rumor of Angels, 2000, Crime and Punishment, 2000, The 3 Kings, 2000, The Pledge, 2001, Crime and Punishment, 2002, Good Boy!, 2003, The Fever, 2004, Short Order, 2005, The Keeper: The Legend of Omar Khayyam, 2005, The White Countess, 2005; TV movies and miniseries appearances include Playing for Time, 1980 (Emmy award for outstanding lead actress in a limited series or spl., 1981), Snow White and the Seven Dwarfs, 1985, Three Sovereigns for Sarah, 1985, Peter the Great, 1986, Second Serve, 1986 (Emmy award, Golden Globe award), A Man for All Seasons, 1988, Young Catherine, 1990, Whatever Happened to Baby Jane, 1990, The Three Sisters, 1990, When She Danced, 1991, Playing for Time (Emmy award, TV Times award), The Wall, 1992, Heartbreak House, 1992, Great Moments In Aviation, 1993, Down Came A Blackbird, 1994, The Young Indiana Jones Chronicles, 1992, If These Walls Could Talk 2, 2000 (Emmy award for outstanding supporting actress in a miniseries or movie, 2000, Golden Globe award for best supporting actress in a series, mini-series or motion picture made for TV, 2001, Screen Actors Guild award for best supporting actress in aTV movie or miniseries, 2001) The Gathering Storm, 2002, The Locket, 2002, Byron,2003; Author: Pussies and Tigers, 1964, (autobiography) Vanessa, 1991, Vanessa Redgrave: An Autobiography, 1994. Bd. govs. Central Sch. Speech and Drama, 1963—. Decorated comdr. Order Brit. Empire; recipient 4 times Drama award Evening Standard, 1961-91, Best Actress award, Variety Club, Gt. Brit., 1961, 66, Best Actress award, Brit. Guild TV Producers and Dirs., 1966, Variety Club of Great Britain award, 1992, Laurence Olivier award Actress of the Yr. in a Revival for A Touch of the Poet; fellow Brit. Film Inst., 1988. *

REDICK, J.J. (JONATHAN CLAY REDICK), college basketball player; b. Cookeville, Tenn., June 24, 1984; s. Ken and Jeanie. BA in History, Duke Univ., 2006. Coll. basketball player Duke Univ. Blue Devils, 2002—06. Recipient Sullivan award for Top Amateur Athlete, 2005, John Wooden award, 2006. Achievements include all-ACC Freshman Team honoree, 2002-2003; named Rupp Nat. Player Yr., 2004-2006, also unanimous First Team all-America coaches selection, First Team All-American AP, USBWA, NABC, ESPN.com, Sporting News, Baketball News, ACC Player Yr; eclipsed record for all-time ACC Leading Career Scorer, 2006; drafted 11th in NBA draft by Orlando Magic, 2006. Office: Orlando Magic 8701 Maitland Summit Blvd Orlando FL 32810

REDING, JOHN ANTHONY, JR., lawyer; b. Orange, Calif., May 26, 1944; AB, U. Calif., Berkeley, 1966, JD, 1969. Bar: Calif. 1970, U.S. Dist. Ct. (no., ctrl., ea. and so. dists.) Calif., U.S. Claims Ct., U.S. Supreme Ct. Formerly mem. Crosby, Heafey, Roach & May P.C., Oakland, Calif.; ptnr. Paul, Hastings, Janofsky & Walker, LLP, San Francisco, global chmn. litig. dept. Mem. ABA (sects. on litigation, intellectual property, and natural resources, energy and eviron. law, coms. on bus. torts, internat. law, trial practice and torts and insurance), Am. Intellectual Property Law Assn., State Bar Calif. (sect. on litigation), Bar Assn. San Francisco, Assn. Bus. Trial Lawyers. Office: Paul Hastings Janofsky & Walker LLP 55 Second St 24th Floor San Francisco CA 94105-3441 Office Phone: 415-856-7004. Office Fax: 415-856-7100. Business E-Mail: jackreding@paulhastings.com.

REDISH, EDWARD FREDERICK, physicist, researcher; b. NYC, Apr. 1, 1942; s. Jules and Sylvia Redish; m. Janice Copen, June 18, 1967; children: A. David, Deborah. AB, Princeton U., 1963; PhD, MIT, 1968. CTP fellow U. Md., College Park, 1968-70, from asst. prof. to assoc. prof., 1970-79, prof., 1979—, chmn. dept. phys. astronomy, 1982-85. Vis. scholar U. Calif., Berkeley, 1999-00; vis. prof. Ind. U., Bloomington, 1985-86, U. Wash., Seattle, 1992-93; vis. fgn. collaborator CEN, Saclay, France, 1973-74; co-dir. Md. U. Project in Physics and Ednl. Tech., 1983-93, Comprehensive Unified Physics Learning Environment, 1989-96; mem. Nuclear Sci. Adv. Com., Dept. of Energy/NSF, 1987-90; mem. program adv. com. Ind. U. Cyclotron Facility, 1985-89, chmn., 1986-89; mem. Internat. Commn. on Physics Edn., 1993-2002, sec., 1999-2002. Author: Teaching Physics with the Physics Suite, 2003, (textbook) Understanding Physics, 2003, (software) Orbits, 1989, The M.U.P.P.E.T. Utilities, 1994, The Comprehensive Unified Physics Learning Environment, 1994; editor: (conf. procs.) Computers in Physics Instrn., 1990, Internat. Conf. Undergrad. Physics Edn., 1997, Internat. Summ. Sch. Phys. Edn. Res., 2004, Jour. Physics Edn. Rsch. Supplement to Am. Jour. Physics., 1999—2004. Named Sr. Resident Rsch. Assoc., NAS-NRC, 1977—78; recipient Inst. medal, Ctrl. Rsch. Inst. Physics, 1979, Leo Schubert award, Wash. Acad. Sci., 1988, Educator award, Md. Assn. Higher Edn., 1989, Glover award, Dickinson Coll., 1991, Forman award, Vanderbilt U., 1996, Tchg. award, Univ. Sys. Md. Bd. Regents, 2007; Lilly fellow, U. Md., 2005, JILA fellow, U. Colo., 2007, NSF Disting. Tchg. scholar, 2005, U. Md. Dist. Scholar Tchr., 2006—07. Fellow AAAS, Am. Phys. Soc. (mem. com. edn. 2004-06, chair 2005), Wash. Acad. Sci.; mem. Am. Assn. Physics Tchrs. (Robert A. Millikan medal 1998). Office: U Md Dept Physics College Park MD 20742-4111 Home: 6820 Winterberry Ln Bethesda MD 20817

REDISH, MARTIN HARRIS, law educator; b. Lynbrook, NY, Aug. 16, 1945; m. Caren Beverly Redish; 1 child, Jessica. AB, U. Pa., 1967; JD magna cum laude, Harvard U., 1970. Bar: NY 1971, US Dist. Ct. (so. dist.) NY 1971, US Ct. Appeals (2d cir.) 1971, US Ct. Appeals (7th cir.) 1973. Law clk. Honorable J. Joseph Smith US Ct. Appeals (2d cir.), 1970—71; assoc. Proskauer, Rose, Goetz & Mendelsohn, NYC, 1971—73; asst. prof. Northwestern U. Sch. Law, Chgo., 1973—76, assoc. prof., 1976—78, prof., 1978—90, Louis and Harriet Ancel prof. law and pub. policy, 1990—. Vis. assoc. prof. law Cornell U., 1977, Stanford U., 1977; vis. prof. law U. Mich., 1987—88; mem. 7th Cir. Rules Adv. Com.; cons. U.S. Senate Jud. Com. Author: Federal Jurisdiction: Tensions in the Allocation of Judicial Power, 1980, Federal Courts: Cases, Comments and Questions, 1983, Freedom of Expression: A Critical Analysis, 1984, The Constitution as Political Structure, 1995, Money Talks: Speech, Economic Power and the Values of Democracy, 2001; co-author: Constitutional Law: Principles and Policy, 1987, Civil Procedure: A Modern Approach, 1989, Understanding Federal Court Jurisdiction, 1999; contbr. articles to profl. jours. Mem.: Am. Coll. Trial Lawyers, Am. Law Inst. Office: Northwestern U Sch Law 357 E Chicago Ave Chicago IL 60611-3059 Office Phone: 312-503-8545. E-mail: m-redish@law.northwestern.edu.

REDLENER, IRWIN ELLIOT, health facility administrator, educator; b. Bklyn., 1944; MD, U. Miami, 1969; DSc (hon.), Hunter Coll. Intern Columbia Presbyterian Med. Ctr, 1969—70; resident Colo. Med. Ctr., 1970—71, Jackson Meml. Hosp, 1973—74; dir. VISTA Health ctr., Ark., 1971—73; dir. grants, med. dir. USA for Africa, Hands Across Am., 1986—87; pres., founder Children's Health Fund, NYC, 1987—2003; pres. Children's Hosp. Montefiore Med. Ctr., dir. child health network and cmty. pediatrics; dir. Nat. Ctr. Disaster Preparedness Columbia U., 2003—, assoc. dean, prof. clin. pub. health and pediats. Mailman Sch. Pub. Health, 2006—. Former chmn. Nat. Adv. Coun. on Nat. Health Svc. Corps.; vice chmn. health profl. rev. group. The White House Task Force on Nat. Health Care Reform, 1993; spkr. in field. Office: Childrens Health Fund 215 W 125 th St New York NY 10027 Office Phone: 212-535-9400. Office Fax: 212-535-7488. E-mail: ir2110@columbia.edu.

REDLICH, MARC, lawyer; b. NYC, Nov. 25, 1946; s. Louis and Mollie R.; m. Janis Redlich, Jan. 16, 1982; children: Alison, Suzanne, Rachel. BA, Queens Coll., 1967; JD, Harvard U., 1971. Bar: Mass. 1971, U.S. Dist. Ct. 1971, U.S. Ct. Appeals (1st cir.) 1974, U.S. Ct. Appeals (5th cir.) 1984. Assoc. Rubin & Rudman, Boston, 1971-75; mem., sr. dir. Widett, Slater & Goldman, Boston, 1975-84; prin. Law Offices of Marc Redlich, Boston, 1984—. Seminar chmn. Mass. Continuing Legal Edn., Inc., "Resolving Complex Litigation" 1996, seminar panelist, dir., officer liability Suffolk U. Law Sch., 2003. Mem. Mass. Bar Assn. (governing coun. civil litigation sect., participant/panelist chpt. 93A in the bus. context seminar 1996), participant/panelist, Cambridge Bar Assn., Nat. Assn. Coll. and Univ. Attys., Harvard Sq. Bus. Assn. (bd. dirs. 1989-92, 93-94), Friends of Switzerland Inc. (bd. dirs. 1984—, assoc. pres. 1991-93, pres. 1993—), German Am. Bus. Club of Boston (exec. com. 1997-2001), Harvard Club Boston (co-chair music com. 1997-98, chair 1998—), Am. Council on Germany (Boston chpt. dir., 2001—), Phi Beta Kappa. Office: 155 Federal St 17th Fl Boston MA 02110-1727

REDLICH, NORMAN, lawyer, educator; b. NYC, Nov. 12, 1925; s. Milton and Pauline (Durst) R.; m. Evelyn Jane Grobow, June 3, 1951; children: Margaret Bonny-Claire, Carrie Ann, Edward Grobow. AB, Williams Coll., 1947, LLD (hon.), 1976; LLB, Yale U., 1950; LLM, NYU, 1955; LLD (hon.), John Marshall Law Sch., 1990. Bar: N.Y. 1951. Practiced in, NYC, 1951-59; assoc. prof. law NYU, 1960-62, prof. law, 1962-74, assoc. dean Sch. Law, 1974-75, dean Sch. Law, 1975-88, dean emeritus, 1992—, Judge Edward Weinfeld prof. law, 1982—; counsel Wachtell, Lipton, Rosen & Katz, NYC, 1988—. Editor-in-chief Tax Law Rev., 1960-66; mem. adv. com. Inst. Fed. Taxation, 1963-68; exec. asst. corp. counsel, N.Y.C., 1966-68, 1st asst. corp. counsel, 1970-72, corp. counsel, 1972-74; asst. counsel Pres. Commn. on Assassination Pres.

Kennedy, 1963-64; mem. com. on admissions and grievances U.S. 2d Circuit Ct. Appeals, 1978—, chmn., 1978-87. Author: Professional Responsibility: A Problem Approach, 1976, Constitutional Law, Cases and Materials, 1983, rev. edit., 1996, 2001, Understanding Constitutional Law, 1995, rev. edit., 1999; contbr. articles in field. Chmn. commn. on law and social action Am. Jewish Congress, 1978—, chmn. governing coun., 1996; mem. Borough Pres.'s Planning Bd. Number 2, 1959-70, counsel N.Y. Com. to Abolish Capital Punishment, 1958-77; mem. N.Y.C. Bd. Edn., 1969; mem. bd. overseers Jewish Theol. Sem., 1973—; trustee Law Ctr. Found. of NYU, 1975—, Freedom House, 1976-86, Vt. Law Sch., 1977-99, 2003—, Practicing Law Inst., 1980-99; trustee Lawyers Com. for Civil Rights Under Law, 1976—, co-chmn., 1979-81; bd. dirs. Legal Aid Soc., 1983-88, NAACP Legal Def. Fund, 1985—, Greenwich House, 1987—. Decorated Combat Infantryman's Badge. Mem. ABA (coun. legal edn. and admissions to bar 1981—, vice chmn. 1987-88, chmn. 1989-90, equal opportunities in legal profession 1986-92, ho. of dels. 1991—), Assn. of Bar of City of N.Y. (exec. com. 1975-79, professionalism com. 1988-92), com. on capital punishment 1998—). Office: 51 W 52nd St Fl 30 New York NY 10019-6119

REDMAN, BARBARA KLUG, nursing educator; b. Mitchell, SD; d. Harlan Lyle and Darlien Grace (Bock) Klug; m. Robert S. Redman, Sept. 14, 1958; 1 child, Melissa Darlien. BS, S.D. State U., 1958; MEd, U. Minn., 1959, PhD, 1964; LHD (hon.), Georgetown U., 1988; DSc (hon.), U. Colo., 1991; M in Bioethics, U. Pa., 2004, MBE, 2004. RN. Asst. prof. U. Wash., Seattle, 1964-69; assoc. dean U. Minn., Mpls., 1969-75; dean Sch. Nursing U. Colo., Denver, 1975-78; VA scholar VA Cen. Office, Washington, 1978-81; postdoctoral fellow Johns Hopkins U., Balt., 1982-83; exec. dir. Am. Assn. Colls. Nursing, Washington, 1983-89, ANA, Washington, 1989-93; prof. nursing Johns Hopkins U., Balt., 1993-95; dean, prof. Sch. Nursing U. Conn., Storrs, 1995-98; dean Coll. Nursing Wayne State U., Detroit. Vis. fellow Kennedy Inst. Ethics, Georgetown U., 1993-94; fellow in med. ethics Harvard Med. Sch., 1994-95. 2004—; vis. scholar U. Pa. Ctr. for Bioethics, 2004—. Author: Practice of Patient Education, 1968—; contbr. articles to profl. jours. Bd. dirs. Friends of Nat. Libr. of Medicine, Washington, 1987—. Recipient Disting. Alumnus award S.D. State U., 1975, Outstanding Achievement award U. Minn., 1989. Fellow Am. Acad. Nursing. Home: 12425 Bobbink Ct Potomac MD 20854-3005 Office: Wayne State U 5557 Cass Ave Detroit MI 48202-3615

REDMAN, CLARENCE OWEN, lawyer; b. Joliet, Ill., Nov. 23, 1942; s. Harold F. and Edith L. (Read) R.; m. Barbara Ann Pawlan, Jan. 26, 1964 (div.); children: Scott, Steven; m. 2d, Carla J. Rozycki, Sept. 24, 1983. BS, U. Ill., 1964, JD, 1966, MA, 1967. Bar: Ill. 1966, US Dist. Ct. (ea. dist.) Ill. 1967, US Ct. Appeals (7th cir.) 1973, US Ct. Appeals (4th cir.) 1982, US Supreme Ct. 1975. Assoc. Keck, Mahin & Cate, Chgo., 1969-73, ptnr., corp. ptnr., 1973—, CEO, 1986-97; of counsel Lord, Bissell & Brook, Chgo., 1997—2007. Spl. asst. atty. gen. Ill., 1975-8; bd. dirs. AMCOL Internat. Corp. Mem. bd. visitors U. Ill. Coll. of Law, 1991-95. Capt. U.S. Army, 1967-69. Decorated Bronze Star. Mem. Ill. State Bar Assn. (chmn. young lawyers sect. 1977-78, del. assembly 1978-81, 84-87), Seventh Cir. Bar Assn.

REDMAN, ERIC, lawyer; b. Seattle, June 3, 1948; s. M. Chandler and Marjorie Jane (Sachs) R.; children: Ian Michael, Graham James, Jing, Amanda; m. Heather Bell, 1996. AB, Harvard U., 1970, JD, 1975; BA, Oxford U., 1972, MA, 1980. Bar: Wash. 1975, U.S. Dist. Ct. (we. dist.) Wash. 1975, D.C. 1979, U.S. Ct. Appeals (9th cir.) 1981, U.S. Supreme Ct. 1983. Asst. U.S. senator W.G. Magnuson, Washington and Seattle, 1968-71, 74-75; assoc. Preston, Thorgrimson et al, Seattle, 1975-78, ptnr., 1979-82, Heller, Ehrman, White & McAuliffe, Seattle, 1983—. Author: Dance of Legislation, 1973; also book revs., articles. Office: Heller Ehrman LLP 701 5th Ave Ste 6100 Seattle WA 98104-7098 Home Phone: 206-935-5205; Office Phone: 206-389-6000. E-mail: eric.redman@hellerehrman.com.

REDMAN, GARY LON, II, lawyer; b. Denison, Tex., Sept. 19, 1976; Grad., U. North Tex., 1999; JD, Okla. City U. Sch. Law, 2002. Bar: Tex. 2002. Ptnr. Milner & Finn, Dallas, 2005—. Named a Rising Star, Tex. Super Lawyers mag., 2006. Mem.: Nat. Coll. DUI Def., Nat. Assn. Criminal Def. Lawyers, Tex. Criminal Def. Lawyers Assn., Dallas Assn. Young Lawyers, Dallas Criminal Def. Lawyers Assn., Dallas Bar Assn., Phi Delta Phi. Office: Milner & Finn 2828 N Harwood St Ste 1950 LB-9 Dallas TX 75201 Office Phone: 214-651-1121. E-mail: gary@milnerfinn.com. *

REDMAN, JANIS F., special education educator, department chairman; d. Thomas Edward and Margaret Fletcher (Rush) Fox; m. Timothy Duane Redman, Sept. 5, 1970; children: Megan, Molly, Ashley. BS in Elem. Edn., Ohio State U., Columbus, 1971; MA in Curriculum and Instrn., Ashland U., Ohio, 2002. Cert. spl. edn. Ohio State U., 1972. Tchr. spl. edn. Upper Arlington Schs., Ohio, 1971—74, pvt. tutor home and hosp., 1974—87; dir. edn. St. Patrick's Episcopal Ch., Dublin, 1987—92; tchr. spl. edn. Dublin City Schs., 1992—2003, tchr. spl. edn. intervention, dept. chmn., 2003—. Student coun. advisor Dublin City Schs., 1992—; tutor and cons. math, ACT, SAT tests, 1971—; presenter Sch. Study Coun. Ohio. Stencils, Mt. Carmel Hosp. Oncology Wing, 1977—, Worthington Inn, 1984—, Decorator's Showcase, —. Participant Columbus Marathon, Ohio. Named Wal-Mart Tchr. of Yr., Jennings scholar, Ohio State U.; recipient Golden Shamrock award, Excellence in Edn. award. Mem.: ASCD, Kappa Kappa Gamma. Avocations: reading, gardening, walking, scrapbooks. Office: Dublin Coffman HS 6780 Coffman Rd Dublin OH 43017-1027

REDMAN, JOHN FLETCHER, urologist, educator; b. Fort Smith, Ark., Nov. 14, 1940; s. John Walter and Berie Lee Redman; m. Anna Talley Redman, Apr. 23, 1994; children: Rachel Redman Brittain, Jacob Fletcher. MD, U. Ark., Little Rock, 1963. Diplomate Am. Bd. Urology, 1972. Prof. urology coll. medicine U. Ark., 1972—, chmn. dept. urology coll. medicine, 1972—98. Maj. USAF, 1968—70. Office Phone: 501-364-2632. Office Fax: 501-364-3960. Business E-Mail: redmanjohnf@uams.edu.

REDMAN, ROBERT SHELTON, pathologist, dentist; b. Fargo, ND, Aug. 1, 1935; s. Kenneth and Elizabeth Francis (McMillan) R.; m. Barbara Darlien Klug, Sept. 14, 1958; 1 child, Melissa Darlien Redman Johnson. Student, S.D. State U., 1953-55; BS, DDS, U. Minn., 1959, MSD, 1963; PhD, U. Wash., 1969. Cert. Am. Bd. Oral and Maxillofacial Pathology. Clin. asst. prof. sch. dentistry U. Minn., Mpls., 1963-64, assoc. prof., 1969-75; assoc. prof. sch. dentistry U. Colo., Denver, 1975-78; staff dentist, chief oral pathology rsch. lab. Dept. VA Med. Ctr., Denver, 1975-78, Washington, 1978—. Clin. assoc. prof. Balt. Coll. Dental Surgery U. Md., 1989—; cons. Children's Orthop. Hosp., Seattle, 1966-69; program specialist in oral biology Dept. VA, Washington, 1982-86; adj. scientist Nat. Inst. Dental and Craniofacial Rsch., NIH, 1997—. Contbr. 14 chpts. to books, over 100 articles to profl. jours.; mem. editl. bd. Jour. Dental Rsch., 1995-98, Biotech. and Histochemistry, 2000—; bd. reviewers Anatomical Record, 2004—. Mem. Biol. Stain Commn., 1999—, bd. trustees, 2002-2005. Capt. U.S. Army, 1959-61. Recipient Carl A. Schlack award Assn. Mil. Surgeons US, 1997. Fellow Am. Acad. Oral and Maxillofacial Pathology; mem. ADA, Am. Assn. Anatomists, Internat. Assn. Dental Rsch. (program chmn. salivary rsch. group 1982-86, sec.-treas. 1995-2001, Salivary Rschr. of the Yr., Salivary Rsch. Group 2001), Soc. for In Vitro Biology, Omicron Kappa Upsilon. Presbyterian. Achievements include discovery and naming of an unique minor salivary gland in the rat; documentation of the relationship between weaning and maturation of salivary glands, of mitotic division of well-differentiated salivary gland cells of all types, including acinar, ductal and myoepithelial cells, of constant cell cycle length and very low rate of apoptosis in salivary glands during development and into maturity; determination of mode of inheritance of benign migratory glossitis, co-developer method to maintain salivary gland acinar cells in culture and several cell lines of these cells, documentation of head and neck cancer in smad 4 deficient mice. Office: Dept VA Med Ctr (151-I) Oral Pathology Rsch Lab 50 Irving St NW Washington DC 20422-0001

REDMAN, TIMOTHY PAUL, language educator, writer; b. Elmhurst, Ill., June 26, 1950; s. William Charles and Eileen Marie (Keenan) Redman. BA, Loyola U., Chgo., 1973; MA, U. Chgo., 1974, PhD, 1987. Instr. Loyola U., Rome, 1977, Ill. Inst. Tech., Chgo., 1980-84; lectr. English dept. Loyola U., Chgo., 1982-84, DePaul U., 1982—84; lectr. U. Wis., Parkside, 1984-85; instr. Ohio State U., Lima, 1985-87, asst. prof., 1987-89, U. Tex., Dallas, 1989-91, assoc. prof., 1991-98, prof., 1998—, assoc. dean, coll. master, 1991-92. Author: Ezra Pound and Italian Fascism, 1991; editor: Official Rules of Chess, 3d edit., 1987. Whiting fellow, 1981—82, NEH fellow, 1992—93. Mem.: MLA, U.S. Chess Trust (v.p.), PEN U.S.A. (pres. Tex. chpt.), Nat. Coun. Tchrs. English, U.S. Chess Fedn. (past pres.), World Chess Fedn. (Chess schs. com.). Roman Catholic. Office: U Tex Dallas Sch Arts & Humanities JO31 PO Box 830688 Richardson TX 75083-0688: US Chess Fedn PO Box 3967 Crossville TN 38557 Office Phone: 972-883-2775. Business E-Mail: redman@utdallas.edu.

REDMAN, WILLIAM WALTER, JR., retired realtor; b. Statesville, NC, Oct. 15, 1933; s. William Walter and Mildred (Huie) R.; m. Elizabeth Ann Wilhelm, Dec. 28, 1956; children: Lisa Dawn, Kathryn Marlene, Adrienne Ann. Student, U. So. Calif., 1966; BS, Embry-Riddle Aeronat. U., 1972; postgrad., Jud. Coll., 1987. Enlisted U.S. Army, 1954, advanced trhough grades to lt. col., 1974, ret., 1974; dir. pub. rels. Northwestern State Bank, Statesville, 1974-76; pres. Redman Realty, Statesville, 1976-92; mem. N.C. Senate from 26th Dist., 1978-87, minority leader, 1986-87; commr. pub. utilities State of N.C., 1987-95; chmn. N.C. Utilities Commn., 1995—2001; ret., 2004. Exec. dir. N.C. Telecomm. Industry Assn.; exec. v.p. carolina Vas. Telephone Membership Assn.; mem. exec. com., vice chmn. com. on adminstrn., comm. com. Nat. Assn. Regulatory Utility Commrs.; chmn. bd. dirs. Nat. Regylatory Rsch. Inst., Ohio State U., 1993; mem. exec. com. Southeastern Assn. Regulatory Utilities Commrs.; past trustee Gardner-Webb Coll.; mem. bd. advisors Sch. Bus. Pub. Utility Regulatory Bd., N.Mex. State U.; dir. N.C. Solar Ctr.; past mem. N.C. Energy Policy Coun., N.C. Tax Rev. Bd.; bd. dirs. N.C. Child Advocay Inst., 1997, Assn. Excs. N.C. 1997—; adv. bd. ARC Carolina's chpt. Decorated DFC with oak leaf cluster, Bronze Star medal with two oak leaf clusters, Air medal with sixteen oak leaf clusters, Meritorious Svc. medal; recipient Valand award NC Mental Assns.; named to Inf. Officers Sch. Hall of Fame, Ft. Benning Ga., Disting. Mem. Regt., U.S. Transp. Corps, 1990; recipient 2 Long Leaf Pine award State of NC, 1987, 94. Mem. DAV (life), VFW (life), Ret. Officers Assn. (life), Nat. Assn. Adminstrv. Law Judges, Vietnam Helicopter Pilots Assn., Army Otter-Caribou Assn., Army Aviation Am. Assn., 1st Cavalry Divsn. Assn. (life), Am. Legion (life), Raleigh Exec. Club. Republican. Baptist. Home: 1320 Royalty Cir Statesville NC 28625-8230

REDMON, CYNTHIA ANN, poet, songwriter; b. Royal Oak, Mich., Feb. 10, 1951; d. Martin Lewis and Mary Elizabeth (Andrews) Hook; m. Robert Carl Nelson, Sept. 18, 1971 (div. Apr. 1983); children: Jennifer, Christina, David; m. Robert Marx Redmon, Mar. 23, 1985; 1 child, Karl. Grad., h.S., 1969. With Roses of Pearl, Miss. Contbr. poetry to 10 Best Poets of the 90s, Watermark Press, 10 Best Poets of the 90s, Nat. Library of Poetry, Poetic Voices of Am., 1998, The Best Poets, Nat. Library of Poets, 1991, others; pub. in numerous anthologies. Sgt. USAF, 1970-75. Recipient awards World of Poetry, 1991, 1997; named to Internat. Poetry Hall of Fame, 1997. Mem. Internat. Soc. Poets (life; bd. advisors), Humane Soc. U.S. Avocations: cooking, reading, gardening, spirituality. Home: 4169 Old Brandon Rd Jackson MS 39208-3010 Personal E-mail: cynthiaredmon@comcast.net.

REDMON, LARRY ALLEN, agronomist, educator; s. Billy Lee and Edith Bernice Redmon; m. Yvonne Louise Redmon; children: Rebecca Anne Flint, Monica Louise Randolph. BS in Agronomy, Stephen F. Austin State U., 1987, MS in Agr., 1989; PhD, Tex. A&M U., College Station, 1989—92. Cert. Grassland Profl. Am. Forage & Grassland Coun., U.S., 2006. Asst. prof. Okla. State U., Stillwater, 1994—99; prof. Tex. A&M U., 1999—. Recipient Outstanding State Ext. Specialist, Okla. Assn. Ext. Agr. Agents, 1996, Outstanding Tchr., Coll. Agrl. Scis. & Natural Resources, Okla. State U. Student Agrl. Coun., 1997—98, Early Career award for Tech. Transfer, Am. Soc. Agronomy, So. Br., 2002, award in Excellence, Vice Chancellor for Agr., Tex. A&M U., 2004. Mem.: Soc. Range Mgmt. (assoc. editor 2002—04), Am. Forage and Grassland Coun. (bd. dirs. 2000—03), Crop Sci. Soc. Am., Am. Soc. Agronomy (bd. dirs. 2002—05). Office Phone: 979-845-2425.

REDMOND, ANDREA, executive recruiter; b. Glen Ellyn, Ill., Feb. 21, 1956; m. Bill Ferguson; 1 child, Duke. BS, No. Ill. Univ.; MBA, George Williams Coll. Asst. v.p. First Nat. Bank of Chgo., 1981—86; with Russell Reynolds Assoc., Chgo., 1986—, mng. dir., co-head, CEO/bd. services practice, 1994—. Mutual fund bd. mem. Fischer, Francis, Trees & Watts. Co-author (with Charles A. Tribbett III): Business Evolves, Leadership Endures, 2004. Bd. dir. Y-Me Breast Cancer Orgn., Chgo. Children's Meml. Hosp. Named one of 100 Most Influential Women, Crain's Chgo. Bus., 2004. Mem.: Chgo. Econ. Forum, Chgo. Club, Executives Club. Office: Russell Reynolds Assoc Inc Ste 2900 200 S Wacker Dr Chicago IL 60606-5802 Office Phone: 312-993-0704. Office Fax: 312-876-1919. Business E-Mail: aredmond@russellreynolds.com.

REDMOND, DAVID DUDLEY, lawyer; b. Hartford, Conn., May 12, 1944; s. Robert LaVere and Dorothy Iva (Mylchreest) R.; m. Eugenia Blount Scott, Aug. 24, 1968; children: R. Scott, Sarah D. BA, Washington and Lee U., 1966, LLB, 1969. Bar: Va. 1970, U.S. Dist. Ct. (ea. dist.) Va. 1972, U.S. Ct. Appeals (4th cir.) 1972. Ptnr. Christisn & Barton LLP, Richmond, Va., 1972—. Mem. editl. bd. Washington and Lee U. Law Rev., 1968—69. Trustee St. Joseph's Villa, 1998—, chmn. bd. trustees, 2004—06. Capt. US Army, 1970—71. Decorated Bronze Star; named to Washington and Lee U. Athletic Hall of Fame. Mem.: George Washington Soc. (bd. dirs. 2002—06), Richmond Bar Assn. (exec. com. 1980), Va. Bar Assn., Va. State Bar, Washington and Lee Law Alumni Assn. (bd. dirs. 1993—2002, pres. 1995—96), Washington and Lee U. Alumni Assn. (pres. Richmond chpt. 1980—82, bd. dirs. 1997—99, 2003—07, exec. com. 2005—07), Omicron Delta Kappa. Office: Mutual Bldg Ste 1200 Richmond VA 23219 Office Phone: 804-697-4102. Business E-Mail: dredmond@cblaw.com.

REDMOND, DONALD EUGENE, JR., neuroscientist, educator; b. San Antonio, June 17, 1939; s. Donald Eugene and Viola (Kellum) R.; m. Patricia Welder (Robinson), Dec. 22, 1972; one child Andy J. BA, So. Meth. U., 1961; MD, Baylor U., 1968; MAH, Yale U., 1987. Diplomate Am. Bd. Psychiatry and Neurology. With Lab. of Clin. Sci., NIMH, Bethesda, Md., 1973-74; asst. prof. psychiatry Yale U., New Haven, 1974-77; assoc. chief clin. neurol. sci. unit Conn. Mental Health Ctr., New Haven, 1974-87; assoc. prof. psychiatry Yale U., New Haven, 1978-87; pres. St. Kitts Bio Med. Rsch. Found., St. Kitts, West Indies, 1983—, Axion Rsch. Found., Hamden, Conn., 1985—; prof. psychiatry, dir. neurol. behavior lab. Yale U., New Haven, 1987—, dir. neurol. transplant program for neurol. diseases, 1987—; prof. neurol. surgery, 1993—; with Yale Univ., New Haven, 1993. Contbr. articles to profl. jour.; patentee in field. With USPHS, 1972-74. Recipient Rsch. Scientist Award NIMH, 1980-2001; Found. Fund Prize, Am. Psychiatric Assoc., 1981; grantee NIMH, 1974-91; Nat. Inst. Neurol. Diseases and Stroke, 1986—; others. Mem.: Internat. Soc. Motor Disturbances, Am. Soc. Neural Transplantation and Repair (coun. mem. 1994—98, pres. 2002), Am. Coll. Neuropsychopharmacology (fellow 2002—03). Office: Neurobehavior Lab 300 George St Ste 8107 New Haven CT 06511-6624 Business E-Mail: eugene.redmond@yale.edu.

REDMOND, ELSA M., anthropologist; BA in Anthropology, Rice Univ., Houston, 1973; MPH, Yale Univ., 1976, PhD, 1981. Anthropology faculty Univ. Conn., Yale Univ., Hunter Coll., Columbia Univ.; rsch. assoc. Am. Mus. Natural History, NYC, 1991—. Fellow: Am. Acad. Arts & Scis. Office: Anthropology Divsn Am Mus Natural History Central Pk W at 79th St New York NY 10024 Office Phone: 212-769-5898. Office Fax: 212-769-5334. Business E-Mail: eredmond@amnh.org. *

REDMON-HOLLIDAY, ROSE MARIE, secondary school educator; b. Pasadena, Calif., Sept. 24, 1952; d. Earl Eugene and Rose Ellen (Jackson) R.; m. Dwight Holliday; 1 child, Matthew Eugene. AA, Midway Jr. Coll., 1972; BS, SUNY, Brockport, 1973; MS, Emporia State U., 1981. Cert. secondary edn. tchr., Minn., NY, Ky. Educator Kansas City (Kans.) Pub. Schs., 1974-81; instr. U. Minn., Morris, 1981-82; educator Spl. Sch. Dist. 1, Folwell Jr., Mpls., 1982-83; educator, mid. sch. coord. Webster Open Sch., Mpls., 1983-2000; mid. sch. coord. Jordan Park Sch. Extended Learning, Mpls., 2000—04; title I Math. tchr. Olson Middle Sch., Mpls., 2004—05; tchr. math. Christian County HS, Hopkinsville, Ky., 2005—. Bd. dirs. Grace Meth. Pre-sch., Mpls., 1988-96. Mem. NEA, ASCD, Am. Fedn. Tchrs., Mpls. Fedn. Tchrs., Nat. Coun. Tchrs. Math., Nat. Youth Leadership Coun., Secondary Edn. Task Force Mpls., Minn. Edl. Effectiveness Project, Mpls. Edn. Assn. Democrat. Mailing: PO Box 678 Murray KY 42071 Home: 906B Southwood Dr Murray KY 42071-3586 Office: Christian County HS 220 Glass Ave Hopkinsville KY 42240-2499 Home Phone: 270-767-1187. E-mail: mamaredmon@yahoo.com.

REDMONT, BERNARD SIDNEY, dean, communications educator; b. NYC, Nov. 8, 1918; s. Morris Abraham and Bessie (Kamerman) R.; m. Joan Rothenberg, Mar. 12, 1940; children: Dennis Foster, Jane Carol. BA, CCNY, 1938; M.J., Columbia U., 1939; D.H.L., Fla. Internat. U., 1980. Reporter, book reviewer Bklyn. Daily Eagle, 1936-38; free lance corr. Europe, 1939, Mexico City, 1939-40; telegraph editor, editorial writer Herkimer (N.Y.) Evening Telegram, 1941-42; newswriter U.S. Office of Inter-Am. Affairs (Washington shortwave radio newscasts to Latin Am.), 1942-43, dir. News div., 1944-46; staff corr., bur. chief U.S. News & World Report, Buenos Aires and Paris, 1946-51; columnist Continental Daily Mail, Paris, 1951-53; chief corr. English Lang. World News Service Agence France-Presse, Paris, 1953-65; European corr. Paris news bur. chief Westinghouse Broadcasting Co., Paris, 1961-76; corr., bur. chief CBS News, Moscow, 1976-79, corr. Paris, 1979-81; prof. journalism, dir. broadcast journalism program, dean Boston U. Coll. Communication, 1982-86, dean emeritus, prof. journalism, 1986—, mem. adv. bd. Latin Am. journalism program, 1989—. Cons. Exec. Svc. Corps. of New Eng., 1991—, Internat. Exec. Svc. Corps, 1992—. Author: Risks Worth Taking: The Odyssey of a Foreign Correspondent, Univ. Press of Am., 1992, Friendly Moderation, 1997. Served with USMCR, 1943-44. Decorated Purple Heart, chevalier Legion of Honor (France); recipient award for advancement of journalism Columbia U., 1986, Townsend Harris medal for life achievement, 1991, Yankee Quill award for disting. contbns. to betterment of journalism, 1995; Pulitzer travel fellow; named to Commns. Hall of Fame CCNY, 2002 Mem. Overseas Press Club (award best radio reporting from abroad 1968, 73), Soc. Profl. Journalists, Nat. Press Club, Anglo-American Press Assn. of Paris (pres. 1961, treas. 1970-73, sec. 1974-76) Unitarian Universalist. *Life has more meaning when it affirms, with grace, the Yang and the Yin, reconciling opposites--independence, yet cooperative effort and community caring; courage and hard work, yet moderation and generosity; hatred of injustice, yet kindness,fairness and compassion.*

REDNAM, KRISHNA RAO VENKATA, ophthalmologist; b. Visakhapatnam, India, Aug. 1, 1949; MD, Andhra Med. Coll., 1971. Diplomate Am. Bd. Ophthamology. Internist King George Hosp., Visakhapatnam, 1971-73, res. ophthamology, 1973-76; resident in surgery Jewish Hosp. and Med. Ctr., Bklyn., 1976-77; fellow in glaucoma Eye and Ear Infirmary, 1977-79; fellowship retina & citreous Ill. Eye and Ear Infirmary, Chgo., 1979-82; active staff St. Josephs Hosp., Kirkwood, Mo., 1983—; courtesy staff St. Lukes Hosp., Chesterfield, Mo., 1983—, Alexian Bros., St. Louis, Mo., 1984—; Lutheran Med. Ctr., St. Louis, Mo., 1985—; Courtesy staff St. Anthony Med. Ctr., St. Louis, 1985—; assoc. Depaul Med. Ctr., Bridgeton, Mo., 1985—; staff Out Patient Surg. Ctr., St. Louis, 1986—; assoc. St. Marys Eye Ctr., St. Louis, Mo., 1987—, 1988—; courtesy staff Christian Hosp., St. Louis, Mo., 1993—; provisional staff Mo. Bapt. Hosp., St. Louis, Mo., 1995—. Fellow ACS, Am. Acad. Ophthalmology, Internat. Coll. Surgeons; mem. AMA, Am. Assn. Opthamology. Office: St Louis Eye Clin 4530 Hampton Ave Saint Louis MO 63109-2238 also: St Louis Eye Clinic 135 W Adams Ave Kirkwood MO 63122-4043 Office Phone: 314-821-2002.

REDO, DAVID LUCIEN, investment company executive; b. Lakewood, Ohio, Sept. 1, 1937; s. Joseph L. and Florence M. (Morse) R.; m. Judy L. Ijams, Aug. 4, 1962; children: Jenny, Mark. BSEE, U. Calif., Berkeley, 1961; MBA, U. Santa Clara, Calif., 1967. Registered investment advisor. Asst. engring. mgr. AT&T, NYC, 1968-71; pension fund mgr. Pacific Telephone, San Francisco, 1971-77; mng. dir. Fremont Group (formerly Bechtel Investments Inc.), San Francisco, 1977—2002; chmn., CEO Fremont Investment Advisors, Inc., San Francisco, 1986—2000; prin., portfolio mgr. Wetherby Asset Mgmt., San Francisco, 2003—. Bd dirs. Sit/Kim Internat Investments; mem. adv. bd. Callan Assocs.; chmn. emeritus Fremont Mutual Funds, 2000—03, chmn., CEO, 1988—2000. Chmn. investment com. U. Calif. Found., 1988—2001; mem. bd. advisors Sentinel Pension Inst., 1978—2001; trustee U. Calif., Berkeley, 1988—2001, trustee emeritus, 2001—. Mem.: Internat. Assn. Fin. Planners. Avocations: golf, travel, reading, walking. Office: Wetherby Asset Mgmt 3rd Fl 417 Montgomery San Francisco CA 94104

REDO, S(AVERIO) FRANK, retired surgeon; b. Bklyn., Dec. 28, 1920; s. Frank and Maria (Guida) R.; m. Maria Lappano, June 27, 1948; children: Philip, Martha. BS, Queens Coll., 1942; MD, Cornell U., 1950. Diplomate Am. Bd. Thoracic Surgery, Am. Bd. Surgery (pediatric surgery). Intern in surgery NY Hosp., NYC, 1950-51, asst. resident surgeon, 1951-56, resident surgeon, 1956-57, asst. attending surgeon, 1958-60, assoc. attending surgeon, 1960-66, surgeon in charge pediatric surgery, 1960, attending surgeon, 1966—; practice medicine specializing in surgery; clin. asso. prof. surgery Cornell U. Med. Coll., 1963-72, prof., 1972—2006; ret. Author: Surgery in the Ambulatory Child, 1961, Principles of Surgery in the First Six Months of Life, 1976, Atlas of Surgery in the First Six Months of Life, 1977; contbr. articles to profl. jours.; patentee in field. Served to capt. USAAF, 1942-46. Fellow ACS, Am. Coll. Chest Physicians; mem. Harvey Soc., Pan Am. Med. Assn., Soc. Univ. Surgeons, Am. Acad. Pediatrics, Am. Fedn. for Clin. Research, Internat. Cardiovascular Soc., Am. Surg. Assn., Am. Assn. Thoracic Surgery, Soc. for Surgery Alimentary Tract, Am. Soc. Artificial Internat. Organs, Am. Acad. Pediatrics, Assn. Advancement Med. Instrumentation, Soc. Thoracic Surgeons, Internat. Soc. Surgery, NY Gastroent. Soc., NY Acad. Sci., NY Cardiovascular Soc., NY Acad. Medicine, NY Soc. Thoracic Surgery, NY Pediatric Soc., Med. Soc. County NY, Queens Coll. Alumni Assn. (pres. 1962—), Sigma Xi. Home: 435 E 70th St New York NY 10021-5342 Personal E-mail: sfredo1@aol.com. *My life is based on the principles of doing as much for others as possible and* *doing no harm; to offer advice only when asked; to apply myself unstintingly, but not selfishly, to my work; to learn from my mistakes; to strive for perfection; and to always have a project and a dream.*

REDPATH, JOHN SLONEKER, JR., lawyer, publishing executive; b. Temple, Tex., Mar. 14, 1944; BA, Princeton U., 1966; JD, U. Mich., 1973; LLM, NYU, 1978. Bar: U.S. Dist. Ct. (so. dist.) N.Y. 1975. Assoc. Dewey, Ballantine, Bushby, Palmer & Wood, NYC, 1974-78; assoc. counsel film programming Home Box Office, Inc., NYC, 1978-79, chief counsel programming, 1979-80, asst. gen. counsel, 1980-81, v.p., gen. counsel, 1981-83, sr. v.p., gen. counsel, 1983-94, exec. v.p., gen. counsel, 1994—2002; sr. v.p., gen. counsel Time Inc., NYC, 2003—. Lt. USNR, 1966-69. Mem. ABA, N.Y. State Bar Assn., Assn. Bar City N.Y. Office: Time Inc 1271 Ave of the Americas New York NY 10020 Business E-Mail: john_redpath@timeinc.com.

REDSHAW, JAMES DOUGLAS, neurologist; b. Montreal, Aug. 5, 1952; s. Robert Leslie Redshaw and Dorothy Ann Levine; m. Evelyn Lee Downs, Dec. 28, 1979; children: Jeffrey Devin, Timothy Douglas. BSc in Biology, Laurentian U., 1975; PhD in Med. Sci., McMaster U., 1980; MD, U. Calgary, 1986. Postdoctoral fellow Alta. Heritage Found. for Med. Rsch., Calgary, 1980-86; med. resident internal medicine U. Calgary Med. Sch., 1986-87; resident in neurology U. Western Ont., London, 1987-89; clin. fellow in neurology U. Alta., Edmonton, 1989-91; neurologist Boise (Idaho) Neurol. Cons., 1991—. Mem. med. staff St. Alphonsus Med. Ctr./St. Lukes Med. Ctr., Boise, 1991—, chmn. dept. neurology/neurosurgery, Boise, 1997-99. Contbr. articles to profl. jours. Mem. profl. adv. bd. Epilepsy Found. Idaho, Boise, 1991—. Mem. Am. Acad. neurology, Idaho Med. Assn., Idaho Neurol. Inst. (bd. dirs. 1994-2000), Nat. Stroke Assn. Avocations: photography, skiing, water-skiing. Home: 4155 W Quail Ridge Dr Boise ID 83703 Office: Boise Neurol Cons 999 N Curtis Rd Ste 506 Boise ID 83706

REDSTONE, SHARI ELLIN, amusement company executive; b. Washington, Apr. 14, 1954; d. Sumner and Phyllis Gloria (Raphael) Redstone; m. Yitzhak Aharon Korff (div.); 3 children. BS, Tufts U., 1975; JD, Boston U., 1978, M in Tax Law, 1980. Lawyer, Boston area, 1978-93; v.p. corp. planning & devel. Nat. Amusements, Dedham, 1993—94, exec. v.p., 1994—2000, pres., 2000—; non-exec. vice chmn. Viacom Inc., 2006—, CBS Corp., 2006—. Bd. dirs. Viacom Inc., 1994—, William Wrigley Jr. Co., 1994—2005, Midway Home Entertainment, 2004, Global Hyatt Corp., LaSalle Bank Corp.; bd. dir. The Marmon Group; chmn., CEO Rising Star Media, CineBridge Ventures, Inc.; co-chmn., co-CEO MovieTickets.com; mem. exec. com. Boston U. Sch. Law. Bd. dir. Jewish Philanthropies; bd. overseers Harvard U., 2002—, co-chair com. on Allston; bd. dir., exec. com. Nat. Assn. Theatre Owners; trustee, Dana Farber Cancer Inst. Tufts U.; mem. adv. com. Tufts Hillel. Named an 100 Most Powerful Women in Entertainment, Hollywood Reporter, 2006; named one of 50 Women to Watch, Wall St. Jour., 2005. *

REDSTONE, SUMNER MURRAY, broadcast executive, lawyer; b. Boston, May 27, 1923; s. Michael and Belle (Ostrovsky) R.; married; children: Brent Dale, Shari Ellin. BA, Harvard U., 1944, LLB, 1947; LLD (hon.), Boston U., 1994; LHD (hon.), NY Inst. Tech., 1996. Bar: Mass. 1947, US Ct. Appeals (1st cir.) 1948, US Ct. Appeals (8th cir.) 1950, US Ct. Appeals (9th cir.) 1948, DC 1951, US Supreme Ct. 1952. Law sec. US Ct. Appeals (9th cir.), San Francisco, 1947-48; instr. law and labor mgmt. U. San Francisco, 1947; spl. asst. to atty. gen. US Dept. Justice, Washington, 1948-51; ptnr. Ford, Bergson, Adams, Borkland & Redstone, Washington, 1951-54; CEO Nat. Amusements Inc., Dedham, Mass., 1967—, pres., 1967—99, chmn. bd., 1986—, Viacom, Inc., NYC, 1987—2006, CEO, 1996—2006, exec. chmn. bd., 2006—; chmn. bd. CBS Corp., 2006—. Prof. Boston U. Law Sch., 1982, 85-86; bd. dirs., adv. coun. TV Acad. Arts and Scis. Found.; vis. prof. Brandeis U., Waltham, Mass.; lectr. Harvard Law Sch., Cambridge, Mass.; Judge on Kennedy Libr. Found., (sel. comm. John F. Kennedy Profile in Courage award); bd. trustee Mus. TV and Radio; past pres. Theatre Owners Am. Chmn. met. divsn. NE Combined Jewish Philanthropies, Boston, 1963; mem. exec. bd. Combined Jewish Philanthropies of Greater Boston, chmn. met. divsn.; mem. corp. New Eng. Med. Ctr., 1967—, Mass. Gen. Hosp. Corp.; trustee Children's Cancer Rsch. Found.; founding trustee Am. Cancer Soc.; chmn. Am. Cancer Crusade, State of Mass., 1984-86; Art Lending Libr.; sponsor Boston Mus. Sci.; chmn. Jimmy Fund Found., 1960; v.p., mem. exec. com. Will Rogers Meml. Fund; hon. chmn. Will Rodgers Motion Picture Pioneers Found.; bd. dirs. Boston Arts Festival; bd. overseers Dana Farber Cancer Ctr., Boston Mus. Fine Arts; mem. presdl. adv. com. on arts John F. Kennedy Libr. Found., also judge ann. John F. Kennedy Profile in Courage Award com.; chmn. Corp. Commn. on Edn. Tech., 1996—, presdl. apptd. chmn., 1996. 1st lt. AUS, 1943-45. Decorated Army Commendation medal; named 1 of 10 Outstanding Young Men in New Eng., Boston Jr. C. of C., 1958; recipient William J. German Human Rels. award Am. Jewish Com. Entertainment/Comm. Divsn., 1977, Silver Shingle award Boston U. Law Sch., 1985, Variety New Eng. Humanitarian award, 1989, Golden Plate award Am. Acad. Achievement, 1993, 32d Ann. Salute to Excellence Program, 1993, Bus. Excellence award U. So. Calif. Sch. Bus. Adminstrn., 1994, The Stephen S. Wise award The Am. Jewish Congress, 1994, Man of Yr. award MIPCOM, the Internat. Film and Programme Market for TV, Video, Cable and Satellite, 1994, The Legends in Leadership award Emory U., 1995, Allan K. Jonas Lifetime Achievement award Am. Cancer Soc., 1995, Humanitarian award Variety Club Internat., 1995, Expeditioner's award NYC Outward Bound Ctr., 1996, Patron Arts award Songwriter's Hall Fame, 1996, Vision 21 award NY Inst. Tech., 1996, Trustees award NATAS, 1997, Ripple of Hope award Robert F. Kennedy Meml., 1998, Humanitarian award Nat. Conf. Christians and Jews, 1998; named Communicator of Yr., B'nai B'rith Comm./Cinema Lodge, 1980, Man of Yr., Entertainment Industries Divsn. of UJA Fedn., 1988, Pioneer of Yr., Motion Picture Pioneers, 1991, Grad. of Yr., Boston Latin Sch., 1989, Honoree 7th ann. fundraiser Montefiore Med. Ctr., 1995, Hall of Fame award Broadcasting and Cable mag., 1995; named one of World's Richest People, Forbes Mag., 1999-2007. Mem. ABA, Nat. Assn. Theatre Owners (chmn. bd. dirs. 1965-66, exec. comm. 1995—), Theatre Owners Am. (asst. pres. 1960-63, pres. 1964-65), Motion Picture Pioneers (bd. dirs.), Boston Bar Assn., Mass. Bar Assn., Harvard Law Sch. Assn., Am. Judicature Soc., Masons, Univ. Club, Harvard Club. Office: Viacom Inc 1515 Broadway New York NY 10036 also: Nat Amusements Inc PO Box 9126 Dedham MA 02027-9126 also: CBS Corp 51 W 52nd St New York NY 10019-6188 *

REDWINE, ROBERT PAGE, physicist, researcher; b. Raleigh, NC, Dec. 3, 1947; s. Robert Word and Hazel Virginia (Green) R.; m. Jacqueline Nina Hewitt, Nov. 22, 1986; children: Keith Hewitt, Jonathan Hewitt. AB, Cornell U., 1969; PhD, Northwestern U., 1973. Rsch. assoc. Los Alamos (N.Mex.) Nat. Lab, 1973-77, staff sci., 1977-79; rsch. assoc. U. Berne, Switzerland, 1974-75; asst. prof. physics MIT, Cambridge, Mass., 1979-82, assoc. prof., 1982-89, prof., 1989—, dir. lab. nuclear sci., 1992-2000, dean for undergrad. edn., 2000—05; dir. BATES Lab., 2006—. Contbr. articles to profl. jours. Fellow AAAS, Am. Phys. Soc. Office: MIT Bldg 26-453 Cambridge MA 02139

REECE, DAVID BRYSON, information systems administrator; b. Phoenix, Aug. 5, 1953; s. Frank Williams and Margaret Leonora (Bryson) W.; div.; children: Ashley Cambridge, Christopher David. ADN, Phoenix C.C., 1974; Baccalaureate Sci. Wholistic Nursing, Westbrook U., 1991, Master Sci. Wholistic Nursing, 1992, PhD, 1993. Lic. pvt. glide pilot. V.p. Young Nursing Svc., Kingman, Ariz., 1987-89; dean of nursing, co-founder Sch. Wholistic Nursing Westbrook U., Aztec, N.Mex., 1994-2000; co-founder Auditors Unlimited, Inc., Phoenix, 1997, bd. dirs., 1998-2000; CEO Ashfork (Ariz.) Inst., 2004—, Ashfork Rapid Prototyping R&D Ctr., 2006. Author: Minerals, Metals and Gemstones of the Holy Bible, 1998, Wholistic Nursing Theory, 1998, Homeopathy: Introduction to Healthcare Professional, Computer: Computer Based Training for Nursing, Database Administration Fraud & Abuse Analysis, Software Development, 1% Solution-Ergonomic Designs for the Exceptionally Tall and Big, 2000-04, Pre-Nursing, Preparing for Nursing School, 2004, others. Pres. Healingworks Inst. nursing rsch. ctr., Creative Wellness Inst. edn. ctr. Recipient Silver Badge, two gold and one diamond, Internat. Soaring awards. Mem. Ariz. Assn. Healthcare Agys. (bd. dirs. 1988-90), Soaring Soc. Am., Exptl. Aircraft Assn. Avocations: flying, treasure hunting, amateur radio.

REECE, GREGORY PAUL, plastic surgeon, educator; b. Lake Charles, La., Aug. 16, 1957; s. John Paul Reece and Mary Agnes Robicheaux; m. Kelley Baldwin; children: John, Kelley. BS, McNeese State U., 1978; MD, La. State U., 1982. Intern U. Hosp. Jacksonville, Fla., 1982—83, gen. surgery resident, 1983—87; plastic surgery resident Health Sci. Ctr., Houston, 1987—89; microsurgery fellow U. Tex. M.D. Anderson Cancer Ctr., Houston, 1989—90, asst. prof. plastic surgery, 1990—95, assoc. prof. plastic surgery, 1995—2002, prof., 2002—. Assoc. prof. plastic surgery U. Tex. Health Sci. Ctr., Houston; clin. prof. Baylor Coll. Medicine, Houston; assoc. mem. U. Tex. Ctr. Biomed. Engring., Houston. Contbr. web chpts. to profl. sites, articles to profl. jours. Grantee, Plastic Surgery Ednl. Found., 1999, NIH, 1999. Fellow: ACS; mem.: Tissue Engring. Soc., Am. Soc. Plastic Surgeons. Avocations: hiking, camping. Office: MD Anderson Cancer Ctr Dept Plastic Surgery Box 443 1515 Holcombe Blvd Houston TX 77030-4009 E-mail: greece@mdanderson.org.

REECE, JULIA RUTH, systems analyst, entrepreneur; b. Detroit, Oct. 25, 1958; d. William James and Julia Henrietta (Thomas) Coleman; m. Darnell Fuller, Nov. 10, 1984 (div. Dec. 1988); m. Terry Allen Reece, July 2, 2001. BA in Computer Sci., Wayne State U., 1980. Programmer analyst Mich. Bell Telephone Co., Detroit, 1980-82; tech. support analyst Unisys Corp. (formally Burroughs), Detroit, 1982-91; owner JR & Assocs. Computer Svcs., Detroit, 1991—; computer cons. Comprehensive Data Processing, Detroit, 1991-94; sr. programmer, analyst City of Detroit, 1994-00, prin. programmer/analyst, 2000—. Musician Met. Cmty. Tabernacle, Detroit, 1975—84, 1988—2000, Greater Faith New Covenant Assembly, Detroit, 1985—87. Independent. Avocations: reading, travel, music, cooking, computers. E-mail: fullerj@itsd.ci.detroit.mi.us, ladyjr@ameritech.net.

REECE, KARYN LYNN, business owner, consultant; d. George John and Eleanor Roberta (O'Donnell) R. BS in Bus., SUNY, Buffalo, 1998. Lic. stockbroker, series 7, insurance lic., fin. cons., NY. Lic. stockbroker, insurance Cook Fin. Group, Buffalo, 1990—; ind. fin. cons., 1992—; psychic cons. Author: Caught Between Two Worlds:" A Psychic Detectives Experience in Solving Crimes and Hidden Agendas, The Lighter Side of the Other Side. Mem. Women Everywhere. Independent. Avocations: drawing, aerobics, figure skating. Office Phone: 866-735-3715.

REECE, MAYNARD FRED, artist, writer; b. Arnolds Park, Iowa, Apr. 26, 1920; s. Waldo H. and Inez V. (Latson) R.; m. June Carman, Apr. 7, 1946; children: Mark A., Brad D. Privately educated. Artist Meredith Pub. Co., Des Moines, 1938-40; artist, asst., mus. dir. Iowa Dept. History and Archives, Des Moines, 1940-50. Artist: Fish and Fishing, 1963, Waterfowl of Iowa, 1943; watercolor Trout, Saturday Evening Post (award of Distinctive Merit 1962); watercolors 73 Fish, Life mag. (cert. of merit 1955); print of Water's Edge Canada Geese for Am. Artist Collection, Am. Artist Mag., 1985; author, artist: The Waterfowl Art of Maynard Reece, 1985, The Upland Bird Art of Maynard Reece, 1997. Chmn. Gov.'s Com. Conservation of Outdoor Resource, 1963-64; trustee Iowa Natural Heritage Found., Des Moines, 1979—; hon. trustee Ducks Unltd., Inc., 1983—; trustee J.N. "Ding" Darling Conservation Found., Inc., Des Moines, 1962—. Served with AUS, 1943-45. Recipient awards for duck stamps and others Dept. Interior, 1948, 51, 59, 69, 71; recipient award Govt. Bermuda, 1963, award Iowa Conservation Commn., 1972, 77, 80, 81, award Fish and Game Commn., Little Rock, 1982, 88, award Tex. Parks and Wild Life Dept., 1983, award Nat. Fish & Wildlife Found., 1988, award Wash. State Dept. Wildlife, 1989, award Idaho Dept. Fish & Game, 1998, 4 awards Ill. Dept. of Natural Resources, 1997-2000; named Artist of Yr. Ducks Unltd. Inc., 1973; chosen Master Artist 1989, Leigh Yawkey Woodson Art Mus., Wausau, Wis., 1989. Mem. Nat. Audubon Soc., Nat. Wildlife Fedn., Izaak Walton League Am. (hon. pres. 1974-75). Home and Office: 5315 Robertson Dr Des Moines IA 50312-2133 Office Phone: 515-277-3623.

REECE, RICHARD KENT, finance executive; b. Feb. 13, 1956; s. Robert Keith and Shirley (Fly) R.; m. Sonya Rebecca Branum, July 29, 1978; children: Emily, Eric, Ellen. BS in Acctg., Auburn U., 1978. CPA, Tex. Ptnr. Ernst & Young, Houston, 1978-93; v.p. fin., treas., CFO Belden Inc., St. Louis, 1993—2005; sr. v.p., CFO Acuity Brands, Inc., Atlanta, 2005—. Bd. dirs. Tex. Accts. & Lawyers for Arts, Houston, 1990-93, North Harriss County YMCA, Houston, 1991-93. Mem. AICPA, Nat. Investors Rels. Assn., Tex. Soc. CPAs. Office: Acuity Brands Inc 1170 Peachtree St NE Ste 2400 Atlanta GA 30309-7676 Office Phone: 404-853-1400.

REECE, TERRY ALLEN, travel company executive, Internet company executive; b. Texarkana, Ark., Jan. 2, 1958; s. Pendon and Mary Ella Reece; m. Julia Ruth Coleman, July 2, 2001; 5 children. Student, Cear Valley Coll.; cert. in bus. mgmt., Tex. Wesleyan U. Founder, chmn., pres., CEO Reece Enterprises, Detroit. Mem.: NAACP, Nat. Libr. Poetry, Tex. Writer's Assn., Internat. Poets Soc., Fellowship Christian Athletes (life). Address: 17175 Avon Ave Detroit MI 48219 Office Phone: 313-541-5255. E-mail: warrior_75210@yahoo.com.

REECE, THOMAS L., manufacturing executive; BA, Western Mich. Univ., 1964. Office mgr., Ronnigen-Petter Divsn. Dover Corp., 1965—71, pres., Ronnigen-Petter Divsn., 1971, corp. pres., COO, 1993—94, CEO, 1994—2005, chmn., 1999—. Recipient Disting. Alumni award, Western Mich. Univ. Alumni Assn., 1998. Mem.: Nat. Assn. Manufacturers (bd. dir. 2005—). Office: Dover Corp 280 Park Ave New York NY 10017-1216 *

REECE-PORTER, SHARON ANN, international human rights educator; b. Cin., Nov. 28, 1953; d. Edward and Claudia (Ownes) Reece; div., 1981; children: Erika Lynn, Melanie Joyce. BS in Textiles and Clothing, Edgecliff Coll., 1975; cert. clerical computer, So. Ohio Coll., 1984; MEd in Gen. Edn., SUNY, Buffalo, 1994; PhD in Internat. Human Rights Devel., Brentwick U., London, 2000; EdD in Global Edn. (hon.), Australian Inst. Coordinated Rsch., Victoria, 1995; postgrad. in photojournalism/profl. photography, NY Inst. Photography, 2002—. Cert. tchr. Ohio. Dept. supr., asst. buyer Mabley & Carew, Cin., 1975—76; claims adjuster Allstate Ins. Co., Cin., 1976—78; sales merchandiser Ekco Houseware, Cin., 1979—80; sales rep. Met. Life Inc., Cin., 1981—83; info. processing specialist GPA/Robert Half/Word Source, Cin., Dallas, 1985—87; tchr. adult edn. Princeton City Schs., Cin., 1984—90; with Rainbow Internat. Non-Profit Adult Ednl. Rsch. Ctr., Honolulu, 1990—98, Norfolk, Va., 1998—; specialist edn. rsch. found. SUNY, Buffalo, 1993; human rights investigator Citizens Commn. on Human Rights Internat., LA, 2005—. Prof. computer sci. So. Ohio Tech. and Bus. Coll., Cin., 1986-90; computer software tng. cons., 1987-89; part-time tchr. adult GED classes Adult Learning Ctr. Buffalo Bd. Edn., 1994-95; participant Am. Forum for Global Edn., Honolulu; lectr. photography N.Y. Inst. Photography, N.Y.C., N.Y., 2002—. Tutor U.S. divsn. Internat. Laubach Lit., Clermont County, Ohio, 1984; coordinate workshops Dianetics Found., Virginia Beach, Va.; human rights investigator Citizens Commission for Human Rights, Virgina Beach. Fellow Australian Inst. for Coordinated Rsch. (life); mem. NAFE, ASTD, Internat. DOS Users Group, Am. Ednl. Rsch. Assn., Nat. Assn. Women Bus. Owners, UN Assn., World Assn. Women Entrepreneurs, Boston Computer Soc., Cin. Orgn. Data Processing Educators and Trainers, Internat. Platform Assn., Cin. C. of C. (cert. minority supplier devel. coun.), Dianetics Found. (co-coord. workshops). Home: 2941 Chilton Pl Virginia Beach VA 23456 Office: Global Human Rights & Artistic Impressions PO Box 56544 Virginia Beach VA 23456 Personal E-mail: humanrtssharonann@msn.com.

REED, ADAM VICTOR, psychologist, engineer, information scientist; b. Torun, Poland, Jan. 11, 1946; arrived in US, 1959, naturalized, 1965; s. Henry Kenneth and Eva (Tenenbaum) Reed; m. Barbara Irene Birnbaum, 1982 (div. 2000); 1 child, Halina Brooke. BSEE, MIT, 1967, MS in Biology, MSEE, 1970; PhD, U. Oreg., 1974. Rsch. programmer Artificial Intelligence Lab. MIT, Cambridge, 1965; rsch. engr. Hewlett Packard Co., Palo Alto, Calif., 1966-67; mem. rsch. staff Riverside Rsch. Inst., NYC, 1970-71; postdoctoral fellow, adj. asst. prof. Rockefeller U., NYC, 1974-78; asst. prof., vis. lectr. psychology New Sch. Social Rsch., NYC, 1977-82; mem. tech. staff Bell Labs., 1981—99; from assoc. prof. to prof. Calif. State U., LA, 2000—06, prof. Info. Sys., 2006—. Peer rev. referee NSF, others. Contbr. articles to profl. jours. Sci. and tech. adv. LIbertarian v.p. candidate Tonie Nathan, 1972; mem. Marlboro Twp. Bd. Edn., N.J., 1994-97. NDEA Title IV fellow, 1967-70, NSF fellow, 1970-73, NIMH Rsch. Svc. fellow, 1974-77. Mem. IEEE, APA, AAAS, Soc. Engring. Psychologists, Assn. Computing Machinery, Am. Soc. Cybernetics, N.Y. Acad. Sci., Sigma Xi, Tau Beta Pi, Eta Kappa Nu. Achievements include patents in field; first implementation of steepest descent, first statistically adaptive user interface, first switch-based facsimile server, first commercially deployed autonomous expert system; research on experimental psychology-response signals method. Business E-Mail: areed2@calstatela.edu.

REED, ALFRED DOUGLAS, retired academic administrator; b. Bristol, Tenn., July 18, 1928; s. Roy Theodore and Elizabeth Brown (Tuft) R.; m. Emily Joyce Freeman, Mar. 18, 1950 (dec. March 2005); children: Roy Frederick, Robert Douglas, David Clark, Timothy Wayne, Joseph William AB, Erskine Coll., 1949. Reporter Citizen-Times, Asheville, NC, 1949—51, city editor, 1953—60, mng. editor, 1962—63, assoc. editor, 1963—66, capital corr., 1959—66; asst. editor Presbyn. Jour., Weaverville, NC, 1951—52; assoc. editor Shelby Daily Star, NC, 1961—62; dir. pub. info. We. Carolina U., Cullowhee, NC, 1966—96, asst. to chancellor, 1996—2002. Cons. Devel. Office, East Carolina U., Greenville, 1980; bd. dirs. Wachovia Bank, Sylva, N.C., 1969-2003. Author: Prologue, 1968, Decade of Development, 1984; exec. editor: Western, The Mag. of Western Carolina University, 1991-96. Mem. Asheville City Bd. Edn., 1958-62; vice chmn. bd. dirs. Sta. WCQS FM, We. N.C. Pub. Radio Inc., Asheville, 1978-88; bd. dirs., mem. exec. com. Cherokee Hist. Assn., 1985-2004, We. N.C. Assn. Cmtys., 1985-2001, Jackson County Fund of N.C. Cmty. Found., 1991-93; mem. Hunter Libr. Adv. Bd., 1991-98, Pack Pl. Adv. Coun., Asheville, 1991-95. Recipient Paul A. Reid Disting. Svc. award We. Carolina U., 1980, Disting. Svc. award, 1996. Mem. Pub. Rels. Assn. We. N.C. (bd. dirs. 1988-98, treas. 1966-86), Coll. News Assn. Carolinas (bd. dirs. 1968-71, 80-82), Smoky Mountain Host Assn. (bd. dirs., 1st v.p. 1994-96, pres. 1996-98), Great Smoky Mountains Assn. (bd. dirs. 1998-02, 05-06). Democrat. Presbyterian. Avocations: travel, stamps, gardening. Home: 931 University Heights Rd Cullowhee NC 28723-6953 Personal E-mail: douglasreed@earthlink.net.

REED, ANGELICA DENISE, sculptor, writer, illustrator; b. Murfreesboro, Tenn., Dec. 16, 1955; d. Keith Kenyon and Lester Faye (Todd) Reed; m. David Earl Myers, Apr. 19, 1975 (dec. Mar. 1978); m. John Gregory Bettis, May 11, 1979. Student, Mid. Tenn. State U., 1973-75, 77-78, UCLA, 1981-82, Venice Sculpture Studio, 1983-85, Brucchion Sch. of Art, Culver City, Calif., 1987-90. Artist-in-residence Reed Studio and Gallery, Venice, Calif., 1990-95, The Jerry Solomon Gallery, LA, 1997, Belle Art Galleries, Inc. at Bel Age Hotel, West Hollywood, Calif., 2000—. Cons. Sweet Harmony Music, Sunset Beach, Calif., 1978-83, Bettis Paradise Music, Sunset Beach, 1978-85, John Bettis Music, L.A., 1983—, John Bettis Property Mgmt., L.A., 1986—. Fundraiser Children's Hosp./Santa Monica Bay Aux., 1991, Nat. Acad. Songwriters, 1985, SEA Environ. Assn., Bonaventure Hotel, L.A., 1990, 91; mem. L.A. com. P.E.T.A. People for the Ethical Treatment of Animals, 1992; vol. St. John Hosp., 1998. Avocations: gymnastics, scuba diving, travel, ballet. Home and Office: 2251 Mid Tenn Blvd Murfreesboro TN 37130 E-mail: angelicadenise@comcast.net.

REED, ANNE F. THOMSON, management consultant; BA, Goucher Coll., 1973; MPA, Harvard U., 1981. Devel. rschr. Office of Alumni Devel. Vanderbilt U., Nashville, 1973—74; jr. cmty. planner Nashville City Planning Commn., 1974—76; staff asst. to asst. dean for adminstrn. Kennedy Sch. Harvard U., Cambridge, Mass., 1976—77, registrar, admissions officer John F. Kennedy Sch. Govt., 1977—80; presdl. mgmt. intern Dept. Navy, Washington, 1981—83, budget analyst for Naval Sea Sys. Command, 1983—86, numerous mgmt. positions Office Comptroller, 1986—93; dep. asst. sec. agr. for adminstrn. USDA, Washington, 1993—96, chief info. officer, 1997—2000; v.p. govt. global industry group EDS, 2000—02, pres. State and Local Govt., 2002—03; pres. Aquisition Solutions, Inc., 2003—. Office Phone: 703-253-6309.

REED, AUSTIN F., lawyer; b. Waterbury, Conn., Aug. 4, 1951; m. Mary Cincotta, Dec. 22, 1973; children: George, Patricia, Edward, John. AB in Econs. and Polit. Sci., Boston Coll., 1973; JD, U. Fla., 1975. Bar: Fla. 1976, Conn. 1982, Va. 1997. Atty. Fla. Pub. Employee Rels. Commn., 1976-77; sr. atty. Jack Eckerd Corp., 1977-81; assoc. Cummings & Lockwood, Stamford, Conn., 1981-87; asst. gen. counsel Pittston Co., Greenwich, Conn., 1987-89, v.p., gen. counsel Darien, Conn., 1989-93; v.p., gen. counsel, sec. The Brink's Co. (formerly Pittston Co.), Richmond, Va., 1994—. *

REED, BERENICE ANNE, cultural organization administrator, educator, artist; b. Memphis; d. Glenn Andrew and Berenice Marie (Kallaher) R. BFA, St. Mary-of-the-Woods Coll., Ind., 1955; MFA in Painting and Art History, Istituto Pio XII, Villa Schifanoia, Florence, Italy, 1964. Cert. art tchr. Tenn. Comml. artist Memphis Pub. Co., 1955—56; arts adminstr., educator pub. and pvt. instns., Washington, Memphis, 1957—70; arts adminstr. Nat. Park Svc., 1970—73; mem. staff U.S. Dept. Energy, Washington, 1973—81, U.S. Dept. Commerce, Washington, 1983—84, Exec. Office of Pres., Office of Mgmt. and Budget, Washington, 1985; with fin. mgmt. svc. U.S. Treasury Dept., Washington, 1985—2004. Ind. art history rschr. Nat. Gallery of Art, Ctr. Advanced Study in Visual Arts, Washington, 1998—; cons. on art and architecture in recreation AIA, 1972-73; artist-in-residence St. Mary-of-the-Woods Coll., Ind., 1965; guest lectr. instr. Nat. Sch. Fine Arts, Tegucigalpa, Honduras, 1968; exec. com. Parks, Arts and Leisure Project, Washington, 1972-73; rschr. art projects, Washington, 1981-83. Developer (video) In Your Interest, 1992; TV interviewer Am. Fin. Skylink satellite programs, 1996-98. Advisor Royal Oak Found.; bd. dirs. Am. Irish Bicentennial Com., 1974—76. Recipient various awards for painting; installed as Dama of Merit, Sacred Mil. Constantinian Order of St. George, Naples, 1997, awarded Star, 2001, installed as Dama, Order of St. Maurice and St. Lazarus, 2000; named one of 150 Women Who Made A Difference in 150 years of St. Agnes Acad., 2001. Mem. Soc. Woman Geographers, Nat. Soc. Arts and Letters, Ctr.

Advanced Study in Visual Arts, Art Barn Assn. (bd. dir. 1973-83), Patrons Arts in the Vatican Mus., Irish Georgian Soc. Roman Catholic. Avocations: photography, performing arts. Home: PO Box 34253 Bethesda MD 20827-0253

REED, BETTY JAMERSON, historian, educator; b. East Flat Rock, NC, July 27, 1937; d. Floyd Wesley and Ella Mae (Case) Jamerson; m. William Alonzo Reed, July 24, 1971; children: Floyd Allan, Sara-Ann Reed Sizemore, David Andrew. BA, Bryan Coll., Dayton, Tenn., 1959; MA in Edn., Western Carolina U., 1969, EdD, 2000. Tchr. NC Pub. Schs., 1960—99; adj. instr. Blue Ridge C.C., Brevard, NC, 1975—2005; instr. continuing edn. Brevard Coll., 2000—04, adj. supr. student tchrs., 2000—04. Trainer NC Tchr. Acad., 1993—2003; instr. Brevard Coll., 2004, Blue Ridge C.C., 2004—06. Author: The Brevard Rosenwald School, 2004 (cert. of commendation Am. Assn. State and Local History, 2005); contbg. author: Out of Our Hearts and Minds, 2006. Vol. interpreter, tutor El Centro Comunitario, Brevard, 2003—05; literacy instr. ESL Literacy Coun., Brevard, 2004—05; mem. Human Rels. Coun., Brevard, 2001—06, Abandoned Cemeteries Commn., Brevard, 2004—06. Named Outstanding Young Educator NC, NC Jaycees, 1971; recipient Gov.'s award Excellence in Tchg., Gov.'s NC, 1991, cert. of appreciation, Transylvania County Citizens Improvement Orgn., 2001. Mem.: NEA, Appalachian Studies Assn., Orgn. Am. Historians, NC Writers Network, Transylvania Writers Alliance, Buncombe Hist. Soc., Anderson County Hist. Soc., Transylvania County Hist. Soc., Nat. Trust Historic Preservation.

REED, CHARLES BASS, chief academic administrator; b. Harrisburg, Pa., Sept. 29, 1941; s. Samuel Ross and Elizabeth (Johnson) R.; m. Catherine A. Sayers, Aug. 22, 1964; children: Charles B. Jr., Susan Allison. BS, George Washington U., 1963, MS, 1964, EdD, 1970; postgrad. Summer Inst. for Chief State Sch. Officers, Harvard U. Grad Sch. Edn., 1977; D of Pub. Svc. (hon.), George Washington U., 1987; LLD (hon.), Stetson U., 1987; LHD (hon.), St. Thomas U., 1988; LittD (hon.), Waynesburg Coll., 1990; LHD, Fla. State Univ., 1997; d of the U. (hon.), British Open U., 2000. From asst. prof. to assoc. prof. George Washington U., Washington, 1963—70; asst. dir. Nat. Performance-Based Tchr. Edn. Project, Am. Assn. Colls. for Tchr. Edn., Washington, 1970—71; assoc. for planning and coordination Fla. Dept. Edn., Tallahassee, 1971—75, dir. Office Ednl. Planning, Budgeting, and Evaluation, 1975—79; edn. policy coord. Exec. Office of Gov., Tallahassee, 1979—80, dir. legis. affairs, 1980—81, dep. chief of staff, 1981—84, chief of staff, 1984—85; chancellor State Univ. System Fla., Tallahassee, 1985—98, Calif. State U. Sys., Long Beach, 1988—. Mem. Nat. Commn. on H.S. Sr. Yr., Pres. Leadership Group, Higher Edn. Ctr. for Alcohol and Other Drug Prevention, Coll. Edn. Nat. Bd., Policy Bd., EdVoice; mem. Rand Edn. Adv. Bd; bd. dirs. Nat. Ctr. for Ednl. Accountability, Mem. Coun. for Advancement and Support of Edn., Coun. on Fgn. Rels., Bus.-Higher Edn. Forum. Disting. fellow,Fullbright Commn. 50th Anniversary, Peru, 1996, Lamar R. Plunkett Award, So. Regional Edn. Bd., 2001. Mem. Am. Assn. State Colls. and Univs., Am. Assn. for Higher Edn., Am. Coun. on Edn., Assn. Governing Bds. of Univs. and Colls., Nat. Assn. State Univs. and Land-Grant Colls., Nat. Assn. Sys. Heads, Internat. Assn. Univ. Presidents, Hispanic Assn. Colls. and Univs. Democrat. Roman Catholic. Office: Calif State U Office Chancellor 401 Golden Shore St Fl 6 Long Beach CA 90802-4210 E-mail: creed@calstate.edu.

REED, CHARLES RUFUS (CHUCK REED), mayor, lawyer; b. Garden City, Kans., Aug. 15, 1948; s. Ambers Reed and Estelle (Robinson) Sinclair; m. Paula Marie Weeg; children: Kim Nicole, Alexander Ryan. BS, USAF Acad., 1970; M in Pub. Affairs, Princeton U., 1972; JD, Stanford U., 1978. Bar: Calif. 1978. Assoc. Campbell, Warburton et al, San Jose, Calif., 1978-80; ptnr. Glaspy, Elliott et al, San Jose, 1981-85; mng. ptnr. Reed, Elliott, Creech & Roth, San Jose, 1985-96; pres. Reed & Roth, San Jose, 1996—99; mem. San Jose City Council, San Jose, 2000—06; mayor City of San Jose, San Jose, 2006—. Mem. Berryessa Citizens Adv. Coun., 1984—, Friends of the Guadalupe River Park, 1986-88, Horizon 2000 Task Force, 1983-84, Sm. Bus. Assn., 1981-83, Enterprise Zone Design Com., 1983, fund raising com. Vinci Park Sch. Site Coun., 1981-82, Bay Area Lawyers for the Arts, 1981-82, Urban Svcs. and Constn. and Conveyance Tax Task Force, 1982, Citizens for Park Improvements, 1982, Mayor's Com. on Ballot Measures, 1982, Berryessa Union Sch. Dist. Human Rels. Task Force, 1980-81, chmn. community rels. subcom., 1981; mem. San Jose Planning Commn., 1982-90, vice chmn., 1985-86, chmn., 1986-87; mem. Mayor's Task Force on Homeless, 1987; mem. site coun. Piedmont Mid. Sch., 1986-88; bd. dirs. San Jose Repertory Co., 1981-83, bd. counsel, 1982-83; mem. adv. bd. San Jose Shelter Found., 1988—; chmn. Destination Downtown steering com., 1988; San Jose Symphony Chmn.'s Coun., 1989; mem. adv. bd. Community Leadership San Jose, 1989—; v.p. Friends of Edn. for Berryessa Students, 1991—; mem. Santa Clara County Planning Commn., 1994—, chair, 1995-96; chair Santa Clara County Charter Rev. Com., 1997—; co-chair San Jose Gen. Plan Task Force GP 2020, 1991-93; mem. Land Trust for Santa Clara County, 1997-98; mem. Walden West Outdoor Sch. Found., 1997—. Served to capt. USAF, 1970-75. Mem. ABA, NAACP, Calif. Bar Assn., Santa Clara County Bar Assn. (mem. exec. com. bus law com., pub. edn. com.), San Jose C. of C. (v.p., bd. dirs. 1985—, chmn. 1990, chmn. high tech. com. 1983-85, participant leadership San Jose program, chmn. cen. bus. dist. com. 1981-83, chmn. downtown roundtable 1987-88) San Jose Downtown Assn. (1987—, pres. 1989, downtown working rev. com 1989-90, urban design rev. bd. 1989-90, mayor's earthquake relief com. 1989-90), USAF Acad. Assn. of Grads. (founder No. Calif. chpt. 1987, pres. 1987-88). Democrat. Avocations: skiing, jogging, boating. Office: Office of Mayor 200 E Santa Clara St San Jose CA 95113 *

REED, DALE F., computer scientist, educator; PhD in Computer Sci., Northwestern U., Evanston, Ill., 1985—95. Assoc. prof. Loyola U., Chgo., 1990—95; lectr. U. Ill., Chgo., 1996—. Dir. music Grace Covenant Ch., Chgo., 1995—.

REED, DAVID GEORGE, entrepreneur; b. Alameda, Calif., July 19, 1945; s. David Francis and Anna Amelia Vangeline (Paulson) R.; m. Marianne Louise Watson, Apr. 7, 1971 (div. June 1975); m. Michele Ann Hock, June 28, 1989; 1 child, Casey Christine Michele. AA in Bus. Adminstrn., Diablo Valley Coll., Pleasant Hill, Calif., 1965; BA in Design and Industry, San Francisco State U., 1967, MBA in Mktg., 1969; cert. res. police officer, Los Medanos Coll., Pittsburg, Calif., 1977. Owner Western Furs, Ltd., Walnut Creek, Calif., 1963-72; mgmt. cons. Controlled Interval Scheduling, Rolling Hills Estates, Calif., 1972-73; owner Dave Reed's Texaco, Concord, Calif., 1973-76; mgmt. cons. Mgmt. Scheduling Systems, Houston, 1974-76, Thomas-Ross Assocs., Mercer Island, Wash., 1972-82; plant mgr. Bonner Packing, Morgan Hill, Calif., 1981; mfg. engr. Systron Donner, Concord, 1982-84, Beckman Instruments, San Ramon, Calif., 1984-90; owner Dave Reed & Co. Water Ski Sch., White Water Rafting, Chiloquin, Oreg., 1987—, Dave Reed & Co., design, market, mfg. Contender boats, Chiloquin, Oreg., 1976—. Lectr. wildlife mgmt. Dave Reed & Co., Chiloquin, 1965—, lectr. mgmt. seminars, 1982—; coach Japanese Water Ski Team, Bluff Water Ski Club, Tokyo, 1984; fin. mgr. Japanese investors Dave Reed & Co., Chiloquin, 1986—, design and supply solar electric power sys., 1994—. Res. dep. sheriff Contra Costa County Sheriff's Dept., Martinez, Calif., 1977-80. With U.S. Army, 1969-71, Vietnam. Recipient Gold medal internat. freestyle wrestling Sr. Olympics, Fullerton, Calif., 1983. Mem. Am. Water Ski Assn. (Calif. state water ski champion 1977, 86, western region water ski champion 1977, silver medal nat. water ski championships 1977), Bay Area Tournament Assn. (chmn. 1968—), Diablo Water Ski Club (bd. dirs. 1968—). Republican. Avocations: water-skiing, skiing, surfing, camping, fly fishing. Home: PO Box 336 Chiloquin OR 97624-0336

REED, DAVID PATRICK, information scientist; b. Portsmouth, Va., Jan. 30, 1952; s. Sherman Clark and Bernice Lois (Maul) R.; m. Lynn Susan Schwartz, June 10, 1973 (div. Mar. 1979); 1 child, Colin Alexander; m. Jessica Amy Kenn, Sept. 4, 1983; children: Katherine Anne, Carly Diana. BS, MIT, 1973, SM, 1975, Degree in Elec. Engring., 1976, PhD, 1978. Asst. prof. computer sci. and engring. MIT, Cambridge, 1978-84, lectr., 1984-86; chief scientist Software Arts, Wellesley, Mass., 1983-84, v.p. R&D, 1984-85; v.p. R&D, chief scientist Lotus Devel., Cambridge, 1985-92; sr. scientist Interval Rsch. Corp., 1992-96; pvt. practice, 1996—; mem. adv. bd. Vanguard, 1991—. Fellow Diamond Tech. Ptnrs. Exch. program, 1997—; vis. scientist MIT Media Lab., 2001-02; adj. prof. MIT Media Lab., 2003—; mem. tech. adv. coun., FCC, 2003-2004. Contbr. articles to profl. jours. Recipient Tchg. award MIT Elec. Engring. Dept., 1975, Tech. award World Tech. Network Comms., 2004, IP3 award Pub. Knowledge, 2005; fellow Hewlett-Packard Labs., 2003—. Mem. IEEE, Assn. Computing Machinery, Computer Soc., Sigma Xi. Democrat. Achievements include multiple US patents.

REED, DIANE MARIE, retired psychologist; b. Joplin, Mo., Jan. 11, 1934; d. William Marion and Olive Francis (Smith) Kinney; m. William J. Shotton; children: Wendy Robison, Douglas Funkhouser. Student, Art Ctr. Col., LA, 1951-54; BS, U. Oreg., 1976, MS, 1977, PhD, 1981. Lic. psychologist. Illustrator J.L. Hudson Co., Detroit, 1954-56; designer, stylist NYC, 1960-70; designer, owner Decor To You, Inc., Stamford, Conn., 1970-76; founder, exec. dir. Alcohol Counseling and Edn. Svcs., Inc., Eugene, Oreg., 1981-86, clin. supr., 1986, Christian Family Svcs., Eugene, 1986-87; pvt. practice Eugene, 1985—94; co-founder Reed Consulting, Bend, Oreg., 1995—2000; pvt. practice Bend, Oreg., 2000—04; ret., 2005. Evaluator Vocat. Rehab. Div., Eugene, 1982—; alcohol and drug evaluator and commitment examiner Oreg. Mental Health Div., 1981—86. Named Disting. Alumnus, Ctrl. Oreg. region U. Oreg. Coll. Edn., 2003. Mem.: AAUW, APA, Ctr. Ore. Psychological Assn. (pres. elect), Lane County Psychol. Assn. (pres. 1989—90), Oreg. Psychol. Assn., U. Oreg. Nat. Alumni, Ctrl. Oreg. Llama Assn. (pres. 1999—2000), Bend C. of C., Sunriver Area C. of. C. (bd. dirs. 1997—98), Sunriver Women's Club (comm. chair), Toastmasters Internat., Rotary (pres. 1997—98, Rotarian Yr. 1996—97, 1997—98). Avocations: photography, skiing, hiking, backpacking.

REED, DONNA MARIE, editor; b. Dayton, Ohio, Mar. 29, 1950; d. Andrew Levi and Golda Mabel (Branham) Tatman; m. Donald Ray Newsome, May 12, 1973 (div. Sept. 1985); 1 child, Amanda Marie; m. James A. Reed, Sept. 26, 1987. BA, Morehead State U., 1973, MA, 1974. Junior high sch. tchr. English, 1974; part-time corr. Tampa Tribune, Fla., 1974—75, reporter, bur. chief, asst. suburban editor, suburban editor, asst. metro editor, state editor, dep. mng. editor, mng. editor Fla.; dir. comm. Hillsborough County Schs., Tampa, 1990-96. Bd. dirs. Tampa Edn. Channel; com. mem. Hillsborough Edn. Found., Tampa, 1990—. Recipient Sunshine Medallion award Sunshine State Sch. PR Assn., 1991-96, Prin.'s award Armwood H.S., 1994-95. Mem. Fla. Press Assn., Fla. Soc. Newspaper Editors, Hillsborough Assn. Sch. Adminstrs. (Pub. Rels. award 1991, 95), Plant City Little League, Delta Gamma Alumni Assn. Baptist. Avocations: reading, needlecrafts, sports, bike riding. Office: Tampa Tribune 202 S Parker St Tampa FL 33606-2395

REED, EDWARD CORNELIUS, JR., federal judge; b. Mason, Nev., July 8, 1924; s. Edward Cornelius Sr. and Evelyn (Walker) R.; m. Sally Torrance, June 14, 1952; children: Edward T., William W., John A., Mary E. BA, U. Nev., 1949; JD, Harvard U., 1952. Bar: Nev. 1952, U.S. Dist Ct. Nev. 1957, U.S. Supreme Ct. 1974. Atty. Arthur Andersen & Co., 1952-53; spl. dep. atty. gen. State of Nev., 1967-79; judge U.S. Dist. Ct. Nev., Reno, 1979—, chief judge, now sr. judge. Former vol. atty. Girl Scouts Am., Sierra Nevada Council, U. Nev., Nev. Agrl. Found., Nev. State Sch. Adminstrs. Assn., Nev. Congress of Parents and Teachers; mem. Washoe County Sch. Bd., 1956-72, pres. 1959, 63, 69; chmn. Gov.'s Sch. Survey Com., 1958-61; mem. Washoe County Bd. Tax Equalization, 1957-58, Washoe County Annexation Commn., 1968-72, Washoe County Personnel Com., 1973-77, chmn. 1973; mem. citizens adv. com. Washoe County Sch. Bond Issue, 1977-78, Sun Valley, Nev., Swimming Pool Com., 1978, Washoe County Blue Ribbon Task Force Com. on Growth, Nev. PTA (life); chmn. profl. div. United Way, 1978; bd. dirs. Reno Siver Sox, 1962-65. Served as staff sgt. U.S. Army, 1943-46, ETO, PTO. Mem. ABA (jud. adminstrn. sect.), Nev. State Bar Assn. (adminstrv. com. dist. 5, 1967-79, lien law com. 1965-78, chmn. 1965-72, probate law com. 1963-66, tax law com. 1962-65), Am. Judicature Soc. Democrat. Baptist. Named in his honor Edward C. Reed H.S., Sparks, Nev., 1972. Office: US Dist Ct 400 S Virginia St Ste 606 Reno NV 89501-2182 Office Phone: 775-686-5919.

REED, FRANCES BOOGHER, writer, actress; b. Marion, Ky., May 29, 1938; d. Charles Boogher and Evelyn Shelby (Roberts) R.; m. José Joaquín Solís, June 1, 1957 (div. Sept. 1964); children: Julie, Michael Charles; m. Arnold Haslund, Jan. 30, 1965 (div. May 1967); 1 child, Elizabeth Evelyn Marie; 1 adopted child, Leni Ellis. BA in English and Spanish, U. Houston, 1960; MPH, U. P.R., 1970. Tchr. English as 2d lang. Author: A Dream With Storms, 1979, Thoughts, Feelings and Dreams, 1985, Black Mexican Necklace, 1990, TOEIC Test Guide, 1997, Miguel's Aztec Calendar, 1997, (with Koji Shimada) From Chocolate Bars to CEO, A MacArthur's Kid, 2000, (with Francisco Diaz Infante M.) Pockets and Jingles: Something for His Pockets, 2000, Love Blooms in Mazatlan, 2004; co-artist (with Francisco Diaz Infante M.) Art Works Gallery, Hilton Head, SC, Museo de Arte, Mazatlan, Mex.; ghostwriter: Life On the Run; actress (television shows) General Hospital, Rescue-911, others, also movies. Mem. Am. Pub. Health Assn., Screen Actors' Guild, Mensa, Phi Kappa Phi. Democrat. Methodist. Avocations: teaching, dance, reading. Home: 239 Beach City Rd Apt 2113 Hilton Head Island SC 29926-4713 Office Phone: 843-689-9258. Personal E-mail: ml888888@aol.com.

REED, FRANK METCALF, bank executive, director; b. Seattle, Dec. 22, 1912; s. Frank Ivan and Pauline B. (Hovey) R.; m. Maxine Vivian McGary, June 11, 1937; children: Pauline Reed, Frank Metcalf. Student, U. Alaska, 1931-32; BA, U. Wash., 1937. V.p. Anchorage Light and Power Co., 1937-42; pres. Alaska Electric & Equipment Co., Anchorage, 1946-50; sec., mgr. Turnagain, Inc., Anchorage, 1950-56; mgr. Gen. Credit Corp., Anchorage, 1957; br. mgr. Alaska SBA, Anchorage, 1958-60; sr. v.p. First Interstate Bank of Alaska, Anchorage, 1960-87, also dir., corp. sec. Dir. First Interstate Corp. of Alaska, First Nat. Bank of Fairbanks; pres., dir. Anchorage Broadcasters, Inc.; past pres., chmn. Microfast Software Corp.; dir., treas. RM.R., Inc.; dir. Anchorage Light and Power Co., Turnagain, Inc., Alaska Fish and Farm, Inc., Life Ins. Co. Alaska. Pres., Anchorage Federated Charities, Inc., 1953-54; mem. adv. bd. Salvation Army, 1948-58; mem. Alaska adv. bd. Hugh O'Brian Youth Found., 1987-91; trustee Anchor Age Endowment Fund, 1988-96, chmn., 1991; mem. City of Anchorage Planning Commn., 1956; mem. City of Anchorage Coun., 1956-57; police commr. Territory of Alaska, 1957-58; chmn. City Charter Commn., 1958; mem. exec. com. Greater Anchorage, Inc., 1955-65; mem. Sch. Bd., 1961-64; mem. Gov.'s Investment adv. com., 1970-72; mem. Alaska State Bd. Edn.; mem. citizens adv. com. Alaska Meth. U.; chmn. Anchorage Charter Commn., 1975; chmn. bldg. fund dr. Cmty. YMCA, 1976 dir., 1976-97, hon. dir. 1998—; sec.-treas. Breakthrough, 1976-78; bd. dirs. Alaska Treatment Ctr., 1980-87, pres. 1985-86; trustee Marston Found., Inc., 1978, exec. dir. 1988. Served as lt. USNR, 1942-46. Elected to Hall of Fame, Alaska Press Club, 1969; named Outstanding Alaskan of Yr. Alaska C. of C., 1976, Alaskan of Yr., 1990, Outstanding Vol. in Philanthropy Alaska chpt. Nat. Soc. Fundraising Execs., 1991; laureate Jr. Achievement's Alaska Bus. Hall of Fame, 2000. Mem.: Alaska Bankers Assns. (pres. 1970—71), Nat. Assn. State Bds. Edn. (sec.-treas. 1969—70), Am. Inst. Banking Am. (exec. coun. 1971—72), Navy League (pres. Anchorage coun. 1961—62), Pioneers of Alaska, Anchorage C. of C. (presl 1966—67, dir.), San Francisco Tennis Club, Tower Club (life), Elks (life), Lions (life; sec. Anchorage 1953—54, pres. 1962—63, dir. 1988, treas. 2002—04, Melvin Jones fellow 2000—05). Home: 1361 W 12th Ave Anchorage AK 99501-4235

REED, GALEN K., music educator; s. Harold Elias and Barbara Keener Reed. BS in music edn., Millersville U., 1976—81. Instructional II Penna. Dept of Edn., 1981. Tchr. Ephrata Area Sch. Dist., Ephrata, Pa., 1983—. Mem.: Am. String Teachers Assn. Christian. Avocations: nature, music. Office: Ephrata Area Sch Dist 803 Oak Blvd Ephrata PA 17522 Home Phone: 717-560-2252; Office Phone: 717-721-1130. E-mail: g_reed@easdpa.org.

REED, GLEN ALFRED, lawyer; b. Memphis, Sept. 24, 1951; s. Thomas Henry and Evelyn Merle (Roddy) Reed; m. Edith Jean Renick, June 17, 1972; children: Adam Christopher, Alec Benjamin. BA, U. Tenn., 1972; JD, Yale U., 1976. Bar: Ga. 1976. Project dir. Tenn. Rsch. Coordinating Unit, Knoxville, 1972-73; assoc. Alston Miller & Gaines, Atlanta, 1976-77, Bordurant Miller Hishon & Stephenson, Atlanta, 1978-81, ptnr., 1981-85, King & Spalding, Atlanta, 1985—. Author: (book) Practical Hospital Law, 1979. Mem. adv. bd. CARE Atlanta, 1992—, chmn., 1994—99; v.p. Ga. Network People with Devel. Disabilities, 1991—92; legal advisor Ga. Gov.'s Commn. on Healthcare, 1994; bd. dirs. Ga. Partnership for Caring, 1999—2002, Ga. Comm. Support and Solutions, 2000—, vice chmn., 2005—; bd. dirs. Healthcare Ethics Consortium Ga., 2002—04, MedShare Internat., 1999—, chmn., 2005—06; bd. dirs. Ctrl. Health Ctr., 1989—95, Vis. Nurse Health Sys., 1992—2006, chmn., 1996—99; mem. dean's coun. Sch. Pub. Health Emory U., Atlanta, 1998—. Mem.: ABA, Ga. Acad. Hosp. Attys. (pres. 1991—92), Am. Health Lawyers Assn. (bd. dirs. 1997—2000, pres. 1998—99), Am. Acad. Hosp. Attys. (bd. dirs. 1991—97, pres.-elect 1997), Ga. Bar Assn., Assn. Retarded Citizens (gen. counsel 1979—, bd. dirs. 1986—2006, pres. 1992—96), Phi Beta Kappa. Methodist. Office: King & Spalding 1180 Peachtree St NE Atlanta GA 30309-1740 Home Phone: 404-266-3461; Office Phone: 404-572-3393. Business E-Mail: gareed@kslaw.com.

REED, GLENN W., lawyer; b. Melrose Park, Ill., Jan. 18, 1953; AB summa cum laude, Dartmouth Coll., 1975; JD cum laude, Harvard U., 1978. Bar: Ill. 1978, U.S. Dist. Ct. Ill. (No. dist.). With Gardner, Carton & Douglas, Chgo., 1978—99, ptnr., 1985—99; exec. v.p., gen. counsel UICI, North Richland Hills, Tex., 1999—, dir., 2001—. Mem. exec. com. bd. dirs. UICI, mem. privacy com., mem. investment com.; dir., v.p. MEGA Life and Health Ins. Co., Mid-West Nat. Life Ins. Co., Tenn., Chesapeake Life Ins. Co., Fidelity First Ins. Co.; dir. Pepper Companies, Inc., Chgo., 1990—, Peoples Bankcorp, Inc., Arlington Heights, Ill., 1999—. Mem.: Ill. State Bar Assn. Office: UICI 9151 Grapevine Hwy North Richland Hills TX 76180 Office Phone: 817-255-5200. Office Fax: 817-255-5394. *

REED, H. OWEN, retired music educator; b. Odessa, Mo., 1910; m. Esther M. Reed (dec.); children: Sara Jo Ferrar, Carol Ann Wetters; m. Mary L. Arwood, 1982. Student, U. Mo., 1929—33; MusB in Music Composition, La. State U., 1934, MusM in Music Composition, 1936, BA in French, 1937; PhD in Music Composition, U. Rochester, 1939. Educator Mich. State U., 1939—76, chmn. theory and composition, 1939—67, acting head, Sch. Music, 1957—58, chmn. music composition, Sch. Music, 1967—76, prof. emeritus, 1976—; ret., 1976. Physics educator Army Spec. Tng. Program, 1943—44; guest prof. Mont. State U., 1950, Gettysburg Coll., Pa., 1969, U. Pacific, Stockton, Calif., 1983; founding mem. Geriatric Six Plus One Jazz Ensemble. Asst. conductor, arranger: The La. Kings Brass Ensemble, second trumpet: Lansing Symphony Orchestra, band leader: The Missourians Jazz Ensemble; composer: (orchestral works) Evangeline, 1938, Symphony No. 1, 1939, Overture, 1940, Symphonic Dance, 1942, Concerto for Cello and Orchestra, 1949, Overture for Strings, 1961, La Fiesta Mexicana, 1964, The Turning Mind, 1968, Ut Re Mi, 1979;: Christmas Eve, 2001, Song of Acapulco, 2001, (winds and percussion) Spiritual, 1947, Missouri Shindig, 1951, Theme and Variations, 1954, Renascence, 1958;: Che-Ba-Kun-Ah, 1959, The Touch of the Earth, 1971, For the Unfortunate, 1972, Ut Re Mi, 1980, The Awakening of the Ents, 1985, La Fiesta Mexicana, 1986, Of Loth Lorien, 1987, The Heart of the Morn, 1987, Frolicking Winds, 2006, The Song of Acapulco, 2001, (chamber work) Piano Sonata, 1934, String Quartet, 1937, The Passing of John Blackfeather, 1945, Scherzo for Clarinet & Piano, 1947, Three Nationalities, 1947, Dusk, 1947, Wondrous Love, 1948, Mountain Meditation, 1948, Nocturne, 1953, Symphonic Dance, 1954, Christmas Eve, 1954, The Song of Acapulco, 1954, El Muchacho, 1962, El Son De La Negra, 1975, Give the Fiddler a Dram, 1976, Fanfare for Remembrance, 1986, Make a Joyful Noise, 2005, (choral works) Two Tongue Twisters, 1950, Close Beside the Winding Cedar, 1957, Ripley Ferry, 1958, Proud Chieftains, 1958, A Tabernacle for the Sun, 1963, Lord God of Sea, 1963, Rejoice! Rejoice!, 1977, Make a Joyful Noise, 2004, (stage works) The Masque of Red Death, 1936, Michigan Dream, 1955, Earth Trapped, 1960; author: A Workbook in the Fundamentals of Music, 1947, Basic Music, 1954, Basic Music Workbook, 1954, Composition Analysis Chart, 2004; co-author (with Paul Harder): Basic Contrapuntal Technique, 1964; co-author: (with Greg Steinke) rev. edit., 2003; co-author: (with Joel T. Leach) Scoring for Percussion and the Instruments of the Percussion Section, 1969, rev. edit., 1979; co-author: (with Robert G. Sidnell) The Materials of Music Composition, 1978. Recipient Composers Press Symphonic award for Concerto for Cello and Orchestra, 1949, Disting. $1000 award, Mich. State U., 1962, Recognition and Honors for Scholarly Contbns. and Publ. of La Fiesta Mexicana, 1999, award for Psalm of Praise, Basic Contrapuntal Techniques, Belwin Mills Pub., 2004, Libr. Pub. award for sound recording of Awakening of the Ents, La Fiesta Mexicana, For the Unfortunate, and Missouri Shindig, 2005, Citation for Disting. Contbns. in Arts, George Romney and Greater Mich. Found., 1963, Neil A. Kjos Meml. award for For The Unfortunate, 1975, various ann. awards, ASCAP, 1978—, award of Merit, Youth Arts Festival, 1978, Hon. Mention for Rejoice! Rejoice!, Brown U. Choral Composition Competition, 1978, Nat. Arts Assoc. award, Sigma Alpha Iota, 1983, First Place award for Butterfly Girl and Mirage Boy, Bklyn. Coll. Chamber Opera Competition, 1985, Edwin Franco Goldman Meml. Citation for conspicuous svc. in interest of bands and band music in Am., Am. Bandmasters Assn., 1994; fellow for Creative Work in Musical Composition, Guggenheim, 1948—49; Resident Fellowship, Huntington Hartford Found., Pacific Palisades, Calif., 1960, Helene Wurlitzer Found., Taos, N.Mex, 1967. Mem.: Nat. Assn. Composers (mem. nat. coun.), Am. Music Ctr., ASCAP, Music Tchrs. Nat. Assn. (chmn. theory composition section), Mich. Sch. Band and Orchestra Assn. (hon.), Phi Mu Alpha Sinfonia (Orpheus award, Gamma Epsilon chpt. 1976). Office Phone: 520-648-1096. Personal E-mail: homlreed@cox.net.

REED, HELEN SKUGGEDAL, law librarian, musician; b. Halifax, NS, Can., June 19, 1948; came to U.S., 1971; d. Johan Martin Skuggedal and Anna Gurine (Ringdal) Burns; m. Robert Douglas Reed, Aug. 14, 1971 (div. 1996); 1 child, Eric Douglas Reed. BA with honors, Dalhousie U., Halifax, 1969; MM, U. Mich., 1971. Libr. Hochstein Sch. Music, Rochester, 1972-75; organist Neu Chapel U. Evansville, 1976-83; acting archivist U. So. Ind., Evansville, 1978-80; organist Washington Ave. Presbyn., Evansville, 1984-90; prin. harpsichordist Evansville Philharm., 1984—; law libr. William H. Miller Law Libr., Evansville, 1985—. Archival cons. Evansville Mus. of Arts and Scis., 1984-85; exec. bd. mem.

Four Rivers area Libr. Svcs. Authority, Evansville, 1988-91; bd. dirs., mem. adv. coun. Ind. Coop. Libr. Svcs. Authority, 1995-2000; adj. instr. U. Evansville, 2004—. Recitalist Royal Can. Coll. of Organists Conv., 1973; artist-fellow Bach Aria Festival and Inst., 1992. Founding mem. Evansville Chamber Orch., 1981—; organist Eastminster Presbyn. Ch., Evansville, 1991—. Grantee Nova Scotia Talent Trust, 1969-70. Mem. Am. Assn. Law Librs., Am. Guild Organists (Evansville chpt. exec. 1982-91, 94—), Evansville Area Librs. Consortium, Friends of UE Music (sec., treas. 1988-91), Ohio Regional Assn. Law Librs., Midwestern Hist. Keyboard Soc. (dir. at large 2004—), Evansville Philharmonic Youth Orch. (mem. adv. coun.). Home: 1435 Brookside Dr Evansville IN 47714-2043 Office: William H Miller Law Libr 825 Sycamore St Ste 207 Evansville IN 47708-1849 Home Phone: 812-476-0673; Office Phone: 812-435-5175. Personal E-mail: hsr@evansville.net.

REED, IRVING STOY, electrical engineer; BS in Math., Cal. Inst. Tech., 1944, PhD in Math., 1949. With Northrop Aircraft Co., 1949-50, Computer Rsch. Corp., 1950-51; with Lincoln Lab. MIT, 1951-60; with Rand Corp., 1960-63; prof. dept. elec. engring. and computer sci. U. So. Calif., LA, 1963—. Cons. Jet Propulsion Lab., Hughes Aircraft Co., Rand Corp., Mitre Corp.; Shannon lectr. Internat. Symposium Info. Theory, Les Arcs, France, 1982. Co-author: Theory and Design of Digital Machines, 1962, Error—Control Coding for Data Networks, 1994; contbr. articles to profl. jours. Recipient Roy Carlton award for Outstanding Paper 1985, Disting. Alumni award Calif. Inst. Tech., 1992. Fellow IEEE (life, Charles Babbage Outstanding Sci. award 1986, Richard W. Hamming medal 1989, Masaru Ibuka Consumer Electronics award 1995, Warren White Radar medal 2001); mem. NAE. Office: U So Calif Dept Elec Engring Sys Los Angeles CA 90089-2560 Office Phone: 213-740-7335.

REED, JAMES ELDIN, historian, consultant, educator; b. Walla Walla, Wash., Mar. 13, 1945; s. Eldin Wallace and Mary Ellen (White) R.; m. Deborah Jane Addis, Apr. 14, 1983. AB, Ripon Coll., 1967; AM, Harvard U., 1968, MTS, 1971, PhD, 1976. Cert. mgmt. cons., 1984-89. Tchg. fellow Harvard U., Cambridge, Mass., 1972-77; lectr. Boston Coll., 1973—74; dir. summer writing program Harvard U., 1977-78; founder, pres., chmn. Addis & Reed Cons., Inc., Boston, 1977—; pub. ARC Publs., Boston, 1995—99; sr. rsch. fellow Ctr. on Internat. Governance Innovation, 2004—05. Vis. scholar Harvard U., 1992-94, 96—; rsch. assoc. North Pacific program Fletcher Sch. Law and Diplomacy, Medford, Mass., 1994-96; v.p., pres. Assn. Mgmt. Cons., Boston, 1985-89; founder, bd. dirs. Nat. Coun. Pub. History, Washington, 1980-83; vis. prof., Fulbright Disting. chair U. Waterloo, 2004-05; participant internat. confs.; cons. in field. Author: The Missionary Mind and American East Asia Policy, 1983, China On Our Minds, 2006; contbg. author: Enhancing Global Governance, 2002; editor: American Canada Watch, 1995-99; contbr. numerous articles, papers, and revs. to profl. publs., Christian Sci. Monitor, Boston Globe, Toronto Globe and Mail, others. Cons. House Agr. Com. Washington, 1978, House Judiciary Com., 1999-2000, invited witness Senate Judiciary Com., 1990, Ontario Coun. on Grad. Studies, 1999-2000; legis. dir. Asbestos Victims Campaign, Boston, 1987-90. Woodrow Wilson fellow, 1967-68, Harvard Grad. Prize fellow, 1967-68, fellow Newberry Libr., Chgo., 1965, Ctr. for Internat. Affairs, Harvard U., 1993-94, James Luther Adams Soc., Harvard Div. Sch., 2001—; Fulbright disting. scholar, 2004-05; Fulbright sr. specialist, 2006—. Mem. Am. Hist. Assn., Am. Acad. Religion, Can. Inst. Internat. Affairs (pres. Boston br. 1998—), Fulbright Assn. (bd. dirs. Mass. chpt. 2006—), Soc. for Historians of Am. Fgn. Rels., Boston Athenaeum, Harvard Club Boston, Phi Beta Kappa. Home: 25 Holly Ln Brookline MA 02467-2156 Office: Addis & Reed Cons PO Box 85 Chestnut Hill MA 02467 Office Phone: 617-232-3378. Business E-Mail: jimreed@post.harvard.edu.

REED, JAMES MICHAEL, church musician; b. London, Aug. 22, 1980; s. Barry and Margaret Reed. Dir. music and fine arts Trinity Luth. Ch., Washington, 2004—05; v.p. Musica Sacra, Odessa, Tex., 2005—. Cons. sacred music Beta Records, London, 2000. Sec. Conservative Future, Peterborough, England, 2002—03. Fellow: Guild Musicians and Singers. Conservative. Avocations: travel, reading, tennis, fencing. Office: Musica Sacra LLC 1507 E 18th St Odessa TX 79761 Home Phone: 432-664-4335; Office Phone: 432-664-4335.

REED, JAMES TABOR, history educator, consultant; m. Kathy Ann Sanders, May 17, 1975; children: Katie Elizabeth, Judyth Kassidy. Student, Itawomba CC, Fultom, Miss., 1974—76; EdB, Miss. State U., Starksville, 1978, MEd, 1992. Nat. bd. cert. history. Tchr., coach Kennedy HS, Ala., 1979—82, Hamilton HS, Miss., 1983—93, Caledonia HS, Miss., 1993—; coach Caldwell HS, Columbus, Miss., 1983. Named Star Tchr., Hamilton HS, 1990, 1994, Caledonia HS, 1996, 2000, History Tchr. of the Yr., Miss. Coun. Social Studies, 2001. Mem.: Miss. Coun. Social Studies (bd. dirs. 2003—04, 2006—, pres. 2005), Miss. Profl. Educators. Home: 40149 Holloway Rd Hamilton MS 39746 Office: Caledonia HS 111 Confederate Dr Caledonia MS 39740-9405

REED, JAMES WALTER, JR., educational association administrator; b. Boussac, France, Sept. 6, 1962; arrived in US, 1963; s. James Walter and Helene Thornton Reed; m. Courtney Cosgroye Reed, Dec. 7, 1996; 1 child, Fiona Loveland. BS, U. Wis., LaCrosse, 1986; JD, Hamline U., St. Paul, 1990. Jud. clk. Mich. Supreme Ct., Detroit, 1990—91; assoc. Cassiday, Schade & Gloor, Chgo., 1991—93; sr. tax analyst No. Trust Co., Chgo., 1993—97; asst. comptroller Diversified Fin. Mgmt. Corp., Chgo., 1997; tax specialist KPMG Peat Marwick, Chgo., 1998; field coord. Stragetic Cons. Group, Rock Island, Ill., 1998, campaign mgr. Chgo., 1998—99; legis. assoc. Citizen Action/Ill., Chgo., 1999—2000; city dir. NAACP Nat. Voter Fund, Chgo., 2000; legis. dir. Citizen Action/Ill., 2001—03; dep. dir. legis. affairs Office Ill. Atty. Gen., 2003—; dir. govt. rels. Ill. Edn. Assn., Springfield, 2006—. Vice chair, bd. dirs. Meth. Youth Svcs., 2000—. Mem.: ABA (mem. coalition justice 2002—). Methodist. Avocations: golf, basketball, travel, hiking. Office: Ill Edn Assn 100 E Edwards Springfield IL 62704

REED, JAMES WESLEY, social historian, educator; b. New Orleans, Oct. 17, 1944; married. BA, U. New Orleans, 1967; AM, Harvard U., 1968, PhD, 1974. Research fellow in history Schlesinger Library, 1973-75; prof. history Rutgers U., New Brunswick, NJ, 1975—; dean Rutgers Coll., Rutgers U., New Brunswick, 1985-94. Author: From Private Vice to Public Virtue: The Birth Control Movement and American Society Since 1830, 1978. Office: Rutgers U Dept History Van Dyck Hall Rm 118 New Brunswick NJ 08901 E-mail: reed@history.rutgers.edu.

REED, JAMES WHITFIELD, internist, educator, endocrinologist; b. Pahokee, Fla., Nov. 1, 1935; s. Thomas Reed and Chineater (Grey) Whitfield; married; children: David M., Robert A., Mary I., Katherine E. BS summa cum laude, W.Va. State Coll., Institute, 1954; MD, Howard U., Washington, DC, 1963. Diplomate Am. Bd. Internal Medicine, Am. Bd. Endocrinology and Metabolism; cert. specialist Am. Soc. Hypertension. Commd. US Army, 1963, advanced through grades to col., 1981; postdoctoral rsch. fellow U. Calif. Med. Ctr., San Francisco, 1969—71; resident in internal medicine Madigan Army Med. Ctr., Tacoma, 1966—69, chief endocrinology and metabolism, 1971—76, chief dept. clin. rsch., 1976—78; chief dept. medicine Eisenhower Army Med. Ctr., Augusta, Ga., 1978-81; assoc. prof. internal medicine edn. for FP program U. Tex., Dallas, 1981—84; prof. medicine Morehouse Sch. Medicine, Atlanta, 1985—, chmn. dept., 1985—92, chmn. grad. med. edn., 1992—96, activity chmn., 1986—88, dir. internal medicine residency, 1992—98, dir. Clin. Rsch. Ctr., 1998—2000, assoc. chair and prof. medicine, 1992—, chief endocrinology, 1992—, chief of medicine svc. at Grady. Dir. endocrinology, fellowship Madigan Army Med. Ctr., 1976-78; dir., chief medicine and program dir. internal medicine residency program Eisenhower Army Med. Ctr., 1978-81, chmn. directorate of clin. investigation, 1978-81, dir. endocrinology fellowship program; med. cons. Tuskegee VA Hosp., Ala., 1985—; mem. nat. high blood pressure edn. com. NHLBI/NIH, Nat. Diabetes Mellitus Adv. Coun., Nat. Diabetes Adv. Bd., NHLBI working Com. on Hypertension and Diabetes; chmn. Sub Com. Special Population and Situations, chmn. subcom., exec. com. Joint Nat. Commn. Detection Evaluation and Treatment of High Blood Pressure; diabetes epidemic action coun. Am. Diabetes Assn. Author: Black Man's Guide to Good Health, 1994, rev. edit., 2000, High Blood Pressure: The Black Man and Woman's Guide to Living with Hypertension, 2002, Living with Diabetes: A Guide for Patients and Parents, 2005; contbr. articles to profl. jours. Med. advisor, chmn. March of Dimes, Pierce County, Tacoma, 1976-78; pres. Charles Drew Sickle Cell and Health Bd., Tacoma, 1976-78; task force on cardiovascular risk reduction Am. Heart Assn. Decorated Legion of Merit; recipient Disting. Alumni award Nat. Assn. for Equal Opportunity in Higher Edn., 1988, Nat. Alumnus of Yr. award W.Va. State Coll., 1987; named to ROTC Hall of Fame, W.Va. State Coll., 1987. Master ACP; fellow Am. Coll. Clin. Endocrinologists; mem. Assn. Profs. Medicine, Endocrine Soc., Internat. Soc. Hypertension in Blacks (v.p. 1986-92, pres. 1992—2001, Lifetime Achievement award), Assn. Program Dirs. in Internal Medicine, Am. Heart Assn. (task force on cardiovasc. risk), Alpha Phi Alpha. Democrat. Avocations: bowling, skiing. Home: 380 Mcgill Pl NE Atlanta GA 30312-1069 Office: Morehouse Sch Medicine 720 Westview Dr SW Atlanta GA 30310-1495 Office Phone: 404-756-5788. Business E-Mail: jreed@msm.edu. *One cannot control the circumstance of one's birth, but with keen alertness and honest hard work there are no limits to what one can achieve. So hitch your wagon to a star and never lose sight of it.*

REED, JAN STERN, lawyer; Asst. corp. sec., legal counsel Wheelabrator Technologies Inc., 1995—97; asst. corp. sec., asst. gen. counsel Baxter Internat., 1997—98, corp. sec.; assoc. gen. counsel, 1998—2004, chief governance officer, 2003—04; sr. v.p., gen. counsel, sec. Solo Cup Co., Highland Park, Ill., 2004—05, exec. v.p., gen. counsel, sec., 2005—. Office: Solo Cup Co 1700 Old Deerfield Rd Highland Park IL 60035 *

REED, JOAN-MARIE, special education educator; b. St. Paul, Sept. 8, 1960; d. William Martin Reed and Diana-Marie (Miller) Reed Moss. BA, U. Minn., 1982, BS, 1983; MEd, Tex. Woman's U., 1986. Cert. tchr., Tex. Tchr. emotionally disturbed Birdville Ind. Sch. Dist., Ft. Worth, 1984-86, Goose Creek Ind. Sch. Dist., Baytown, Tex., 1986-92, ctr. leader, 1992-93, dept. chairperson, 1987-91; tchr. emotionally disturbed Conroe (Tex.) Ind. Sch. Dist., 1993-94, Willis (Tex.) Ind. Sch. Dist., 1994-95, Jefferson County (Colo.) Pub. Schs., 1995—. Co-editor: New Teacher Handbook, 1986—87, Behavior Improvement Program Handbook, 1987—88, Student Teacher Supervisor, 1997, Intern Supervisor, 2005—, Middle School Team Leader, 2007. Mem.: NEA. Congregationalist. Avocations: reading, cooking, travel, running. Office: Sobesky Acad Adolescent Day Treatment Program 2001 Hoyt St Lakewood CO 80215 Business E-Mail: jmreed@jeffco.k12.co.us.

REED, JOANN A., corporate financial executive; BBA, St. Mary's Coll.; MBA, Fordham Univ. Fin. mgmt. positions Aetna/Am. Reinsurance, CBS, Standard & Poor's, Unisys/Timeplex; dir. fin. planning & analysis, then v.p. controller PAID subsidiary Medco Health Solutions, Franklin Lakes, NJ, 1988—92, sr. v.p. fin., 1992—, CFO, 2002—. Bd. dirs. Waters Corp., Am. Tower Corp., 2007—. Trustee St. Mary's Coll. Office: Medco Health Solutions 100 Parsons Pond Dr Franklin Lakes NJ 07417 *

REED, JOHN ALTON, lawyer; b. Washington, June 29, 1931; s. John Alton and Emma Powers (Ball) R.; m. Louisa Wardman, June 6, 1953; children: Donna, Joanne, Deborah. AB, Duke U., 1954, LLB, 1956. Bar: Fla. 1956. Assoc. Fowler-White, Tampa, Fla., 1956-57; ptnr. Rush, Reed & Marshall, Orlando, Fla., 1957-67; judge Fla. 4th Dist. Ct. Appeal, 1967-73, chief judge, 1971-73; judge U.S. Dist. Ct. for Middle Dist. Fla., Orlando, 1973-84; ptnr., chmn. dept. litigation Lowndes, Drosdick, Doster, Kantor & Reed, Orlando, 1985-99. Com. on standard civil jury instructions Fla. Supreme Ct., 1986-90. Bd. visitors Duke U. Law Sch., 1983—. Mem. ABA, Fla. Bar Assn., Orange County Bar Assn. Republican. Episcopalian. Office: PO Box 2809 215 N Eola Dr Orlando FL 32802 Home: 1600 US Hwy 64 W 203 Sapphire NC 28774-9513 Office Phone: 407-843-4600.

REED, JOHN C., physician, researcher; b. NYC, Oct. 11, 1958; s. Anthony J. and Patricia A. (Brown) R.; m. Martha Walker, June 7, 1986; children: Hunter Ashley, Tyler Austin. BA in Biochemistry, U. Va., 1980; MD, PhD, U. Pa., 1986. Resident, pathology and lab. medicine Hosp. U. of Pa., Phila., 1986-90; asst. dir. lab. molecular diagnosis U. Pa., Phila., 1990—; postdoctoral rsch. fellow, molecular biology Wistar Inst., Phila., 1986-88; asst. prof. U. Pa., Phila., 1990—92, dir., Lab. for Molecular Diagnosis; joined Burnham Inst., La Jolla, Calif., 1992—, scientific dir., 1995—2002, dep. dir., NCI-sponsored Cancer Ctr., 1994—2002, interim dir., NCI-sponsored Cancer Ctr., 2002, pres., CEO, 2002—, current bd. trustee. Mem. grant rev. com. Am. Cancer Soc., Atlanta, 1990—; cons. Genta, Inc., La Jolla, Calif., 1991—; adj. prof. U. Calif.-San Diego, San Diego State U.; advisor nat. Cancer Inst., Am. Cancer Soc., Am. Assn. for Cancer Rsch.; advisor and cons. to numerous biotechnology and pharm. cos.; sci. co-founder, scientific adv. bd., (current) bd. dir. IDUN Pharm., Inc.; sci. co-founder, sci. adv. bd. GMP/Diagnostics; current bd. dir. ISIS Pharm., Inc (also sci. adv. bd.), STRATAGENE, Inc. (also sci. adv. bd.), and BIOCOM; sci. adv. bds. Abbott Lab., Bristol-Myers-Squibb, Genta, Structural Bioinformatics, Genome Biosciences, Entropia, global Lifesciences Information Tech. initiative. Author 50 book chpts.; contbr. over 600 articles to profl. jours.; serves on editl. bds. of over 12 scientific jours. Leukemia Soc. Am. fellow, 1988-91, recipient scholar award, 1991—, Rsch. award Am. Cancer Soc., 1989—; grantee NIH, Nat. Cancer, Inst., Am. Cancer Soc., Leukemia Soc. Am., CaP-CURE, ABC2, and the Susan B. Komen Breast Cancer Found. Mem. AAAS, Am. Assn. Cancer Rsch., Am. Soc. Human Genetics, Am. Assn. Immunology. Republican. Episcopalian. Achievements include patent for DNA therapeutic strategy for treating cancer; research on cancer causing genes (oncogenes), on mechanism of action of immunomodulator Interleukin 2; his inventions have resulted in over 40 US Patents or Patent applications, and have spawn drug-discovery programs at several biopharmaceutical cos.; pioneer in delineating the fundamental mechanisms that regulate programmed cell death; has the distinction of having published more papers on programmed cell death (known as "apoptosis") during the past decade than any other scientist worldwide; recognized by the Institute for Scientific Information as the world's most cited scientist in all areas of research from 1997-99. Office: Burnham Inst 10901 N Torrey Pines Rd La Jolla CA 92037 Office Phone: 858-646-3132. Fax: 858-646-3199. Business E-Mail: president@burnham.org.

REED, JOHN FRANCIS (JACK), senator; b. Providence, Nov. 12, 1949; s. Joseph Anthony and Mary Louise (Monahan) R.; m. Julia Hart. BS in Engring., US Mil. Acad., 1971; MA in Pub. Policy, Harvard U., 1973, JD cum laude, 1982. Bar: DC 1982, RI 1983. Commd. 2d. lt. US Army, 1971, served with 82d Airborne Div., 1973-77; asst. prof. US Mil. Acad., West Point, NY, 1977-79; resigned US Army, 1979; assoc. Sutherland, Asbill & Brennan, Washington, 1982-83, Edwards & Angell, Providence, 1983-89; mem. RI Senate, 1984-90, 102nd-104th Congresses from 2d R.I. dist., 1991—97; US Senator from RI, 1997—. Mem. com. armed services US Senate, com. banking, housing, and urban affairs, com. health, edn., labor and pensions, joint econ. com. Author: (with others) American National Security, 1981. Served to Major US Army, 1967—79. Recipient Disting. Legis. award United Way Southeastern New Eng., 1988, Disting. Svc. award AARP, 1989, John Fogarty award, 1990, Crystal Apple award Am. Assn. Sch. Librarians, 1994, Excellence in Public Svc. award Am. Acad. Pediatrics, 1998, Excellence in Immunization award Nat. Partnership for Immunization, 2001, Congressional Leadership award Coalition to Stop Gun Violence and Edn. Fund to Stop Gun Violence, 2002, Nat. Excellence in Public Health award Assn. State and Territorial Health Officials, 2002, Joan Gallagher Legis. award Mass. Sch. Libr. Media Assn., 2003. Mem. ABA, RI Bar Assn., DC Bar Assn., Environ. and Energy Study Inst., Phi Kappa Phi. Democrat. Roman Catholic. Avocations: reading, hiking. Office: US Senate 728 Hart Senate Ofc Bldg Washington DC 20510-0001 also: District Office Ste 200 201 Hillside Rd Cranston RI 02920 Office Phone: 202-224-4642, 401-943-3100. Office Fax: 202-224-4680, 401-464-6837. *

REED, JOHN HATHAWAY, former ambassador; b. Ft. Fairfield, Maine, Jan. 5, 1921; s. Walter and Eva Ruth (Seeley) R.; m. Cora Mitchell Davison, Mar. 24, 1944; children— Cheryl, Ruth. BS, U. Maine, 1942, LL.D. (hon.), 1960, Ricker Coll.; grad., Harvard Naval Supply Sch., 1944. Officer Reed Farms, Inc., Fort Fairfield, Maine, 1948-98; pres. Aroostook Raceway, Inc., 1958-59; adv. com. Fort Fairfield br. No. Nat. Bank of Presque Isle; mem. Nat. Transp. Safety Bd., Washington, 1967-75, chmn., 1969-75; ambassador to Sri Lanka Colombo, 1975-77; dir. govt. rels. Assoc. Builders & Contractors, Inc., Washington, 1978-81; ambassador to Sri Lanka and Republic of Maldives, 1982-85; cons. Dept. State, 1985-90; pvt. practice cons. Washington, 1990—. Chmn. Nat. Govs. Conf. Rep., 1966; rep. Fort Fairfield to Maine Legislature, 1954-56; mem. Senate, 1957-59, pres., 1959-60; gov. State of Maine, 1960-67. Pres. bd. Community Gen. Hosp., Fort Fairfield, 1952-54, No. Maine Fair, 1953-59; trustee Ricker Coll., 1953-60, Oak Grove Sch., Vassalboro, Maine; bd. advisors Coll. of Democracy, 1986—, chmn., 1991-2000. Served to lt. (j.g.) USNR, 1942-46. Mem. Am. Fgn. Svc. Assn., Coun. Am. Abassadors, Soc. Sr. Aerospace Execs. Inc. (bd. dirs. 1987-99, pres. 1988-91), Nat. Inst. Former Govs. (bd. dirs. 1992—), Am. Legion, VFW, Grange, Maine Assn. Agrl. Fairs (pres. 1956), Mil. Order of Carabao, Capitol Hill Club, Driving Club (Ft. Fairfield) (pres. 1950-53), Aeroclub of Washington, Internat. Aviation Club, Rotary, Masons, KP, Anah Temple Shrine. Republican. Congregationalist. Office: 410 O St SW Washington DC 20024-2239

REED, JOHN SHEDD, former railway executive; b. Chgo., June 9, 1917; s. Kersey Coates and Helen May (Shedd) R.; m. Marjorie Lindsay, May 4, 1946; children: Ginevra, Keith, Helen, Peter, John Shedd Jr. Student, Chgo. Latin Sch., Hotchkiss Sch.; BS in Indsl. Adminstrn., Yale U., 1939; grad., Advanced Mgmt. Program, Harvard U., 1955. With A.T. & S.F. Ry., 1939-83; test dept. asst., successively spl. rep. to gen. supt. transp. Chgo.; transp. insp. Amarillo, Tex.; trainmaster Slaton, Tex., Pueblo, Colo.; supt. Mo. div., Marceline, Mo.; asst. to v.p. Chgo., 1957-59; exec. asst. to pres., 1957-59; v.p. finance, 1959-64; v.p. exec. dept., 1964-67; pres., 1967-78; chief exec. officer, 1968-82; chmn. bd., 1973-83. Pres. Santa Fe Industries, Inc., 1966-78, chmn. bd. dirs., CEO Santa Fe So. Pacific Corp., 1987, chmn., 1987-88. Dir. Nat. Merit Scholarship Corp., 1996, past chmn.; trustee Shedd Aquarium, Chgo., 1996, past pres.; vice chmn., dir. Alliance Francaise de Chicago. With USNR, 1940-45. Mem. Chgo. Club, Old Elm Club, Shoreacres Club, Onwentsia Club (Lake Forest).

REED, JOHN SHEPARD, former stock exchange executive; b. Chgo., Feb. 7, 1939; divorced; 4 children; m. Cindy McCarthy, 1994. BA, Washington and Jefferson Coll., 1961; BS, MIT, 1961; MS, Sloan Sch. MIT, 1965. With Citicorp/Citibank, 1965—2000, chmn., CEO, 1984-98; co-chmn. CitiGroup, Inc., NYC, 1998—2000; interim chmn. NY Stock Exch., NYC, 2003—05, interim CEO, 2003—04; Robert S. Hatfield Fellow, Econ. Edn. Cornell Univ., Ithaca, 1998; sr. visiting fellow Princeton Univ., Bendheim Ctr. for Finance, 2002. Bd. dirs. Citicorp/Citibank, 1975-2000, Altria Group (formerly Philip Morris Inc.), 1975-, Monsanto Co.; mem. Bus. Coun.; mem. policy com., Bus. Roundtable; chmn. Coalition of Svc. Inds., svcs. policy adv. com. to the U.S. Trade Rep. Mem. bd. MIT, Meml. Sloan-Kettering Cancer Ctr., Rand Corp., Spencer Found., Am. Mus. Nat. History. Served with C.E. U.S. Army, Korea, 1962-64.

REED, JOHN WESLEY, lawyer, educator; b. Independence, Mo., Dec. 11, 1918; s. Novus H. and Lilian (Houchens) R.; m. Imogene Fay Vonada, Oct. 5, 1946 (div. 1958); m. Dorothy Elaine Floyd, Mar. 5, 1961; children: Alison A., John M. (dec.), Mary V., Randolph F., Suzanne M. AB, William Jewell Coll., 1939, LLD, 1995; LLB, Cornell U., 1942; LLM, Columbia U., 1949, JSD, 1957. Bar: Mo. 1942, Mich. 1953. Assoc. Stinson, Mag, Thomson, McEvers & Fizzell, Kansas City, Mo., 1942-46; assoc. prof. law U. Okla., 1946-49; assoc. prof. U. Mich., 1949-53, prof., 1953-64, 68-85, Thomas M. Cooley prof., 1985-87, Thomas M. Cooley prof. emeritus, 1987—; dean, prof. U. Colo., 1964-68, Wayne State U., Detroit, 1987-92, prof. emeritus, 1992—. Vis. prof. NYU, 1949, U. Chgo., 1960, Yale U., 1963-64, Harvard U., 1982, U. San Diego, 1993; dir. Inst. Continuing Legal Edn., 1968-73; reporter Mich. Rules of Evidence Com., 1975-78, 83-84; mem. faculty Salzburg Sem., 1962, chmn., 1964. Author: (with W.W. Blume) Pleading and Joinder, 1952; (with others) Introduction to Law and Equity, 1953, Advocacy Course Handbook series, 1963-81; editor in chief Cornell Law Quar., 1941-42; contbr. articles to profl. jours. Pres. bd. mgrs. of mins. and missionaries benefit bd. Am. Bapt. Chs. U.S.A., 1967-74, 82-85, 88-94; mem. com. visitors JAG Sch., 1971-76; trustee Kalamazoo Coll., 1954-64, 68-70; bd. dirs., Ann Arbor Area Cmty. Found., 2004-. Recipient Harrison Tweed award Assn. Continuing Legal Edn. Adminstrs., 1983, Samuel E. Gates award Am. Coll. Trial Lawyers, 1985, Roberts P. Hudson award State Bar Mich., 1989. Fellow Internat. Soc. Barristers (editor jour. 1980—); mem. ABA (mem. coun. litigation sect.), Assn. Am. Law Schs. (mem. exec. com. 1965-67), Am. Acad. Jud. Edn. (v.p. 1978-80), Colo. Bar Assn. (mem. bd. govs. 1964-68), Mich. Supreme Ct. Hist. Soc. (bd. dirs. 1991—), Sci. Club Mich., Order of Coif. Office: U Mich Sch Law Ann Arbor MI 48109-1215 Office Phone: 734-763-0165. Business E-Mail: reedj@umich.edu.

REED, JOSEPH WAYNE, American studies educator, artist; b. St. Petersburg, Fla., May 31, 1932; s. Joseph Wayne and Gertrude (Cain) R.; m. Kit Craig, Dec. 10, 1955; children: Joseph McKean, John Craig, Katherine Hyde Maruyama. BA, Yale U., New Haven, Conn., 1954, MA, 1958, PhD, 1961. Rsch. asst. Yale Libr., 1956-57; instr. English Wesleyan U., Middletown, Conn., 1960-61, assoc. prof., 1967-71, prof., 1971—, chmn. dept., 1971-73, 75-76, 85-86, prof. English and Am. studies, 1987—2004; prof. emeritus, 2004—. Vis. lectr. Yale U., New Haven, 1974; lectr. US dept. State and USIS, Can., India, Nepal, 1974; coord. cultural exch., New Delhi, Bombay, 1992, Mo., 2007; coord. music and writing workshop U. Va., Georgetown U; participant exch. program, New Delhi, 2007; lectr. in field. Author: English Biography in the Early Nineteenth Century, 1801-38, 1966, Faulkner's Narrative, 1973, Three American Originals: John Ford, William Faulkner, Charles Ives, 1984, American Scenarios, 1989; editor: Barbara Bodichon's American Diary, 1972, (with W.S. Lewis) Horace Walpole's Family Correspondence, 1975, (with F.A. Pottle) Boswell, Laird of Auchinleck, 1977, 2d edit., 1994; one-man shows include Portal Gallery, London, 1971, USIS Libr., New Delhi, 1974, 92, Addison/Ripley Gallery, Washington, 1987, 92, 95, 98, Sterling Meml. Libr., Yale U., 2004; sculptor Johnson Medal of the Johnsonians, 1984, Elizabethan Medal, Yale Elizabethan Club, 1986, Daniel Patrick Moynihan Medal, Citizens Com. NY, 1999, Vincent Scully Medal, Nat. Bldg. Mus., Wash., Freeman Medal, Wesleyan U., 1999, Moynihan plaque, D.P. Moynihan Courthouse, NYC, 2000. Chmn. Wesleyan Sesquicentennial, 1982; chmn. bd. trustees Yale Libr. Assocs., 1984-2000, hon. trustee,

2000—. Lt. (j.g.) USNR, 1954-56. Mem. Elizabethan Club, The Johnsonians (chmn. 1988). Democrat. Episcopalian. Home: 45 Lawn Ave Middletown CT 06457-3135 Office: 51 Lawn Ave Middletown CT 06459 Office Phone: 860-685-3637.

REED, KATHLYN LOUISE, occupational therapist, educator; b. Detroit, June 2, 1940; d. Herbert C. and Jessie R. (Krehbiel) R. BS in Occupl. Therapy, U. Kans., 1964; MA, Western Mich. U., 1966; PhD, U. Wash., 1973; MLIS, U. Okla., 1987. Occupl. therapist in psychiatry Kans. U. Med. Ctr., Kansas City, 1964-65; instr. occupl. therapy U. Wash., Seattle, 1967-70; assoc. prof. dept. occupl. therapy U. Okla. Health Scis. Ctr., Oklahoma City, 1973-77, prof., 1978-85, chmn. dept. occupl. therapy, 1973-85; libr. edn. info. svcs. Houston Acad. Medicine Tex. Med. Ctr. Libr., 1988-97. Cons. Okla. State Dept. Health, 1976-77, Children's Convalescent Ctr., Oklahoma City, 1977-80, Oklahoma City Pub. Schs., 1980-81; vis. scholars program Tex. Woman's U., 1991-94, adj. prof. Sch. Occupl. Therapy, 1992-97, vis. prof., 1997-2006, assoc. prof., 2006—; prof. Houston Ctr. Author: (with Sharon Sanderson) Concepts of Occupational Therapy, 1980, 4th edit., 1999, Models of Practice in Occupational Therapy, 1983, Quick Reference to Occupational Therapy, 1991, 2d edit., 2000, (with Julie Pauls) Quick Reference to Physical Therapy, 1996, 2d edit., 2004; (with S. Cunningham) Internet Guide for Rehabilitation Professionals, 1997; (with Sally Pore) Quick Reference to Speech-Language Pathology, 1999. Vol. crisis counselor Open Door Clinic, Seattle, 1968-72; mem. exec. bd. Seattle Mental Health Inst., 1971-72; Mem. Citizen Participation Liaison Coun., Seattle, 1970-72. Recipient Award of Merit, Can. Assn. Occupl. Therapists, 1988. Fellow: Am. Occupl. Therapy Assn. (Merit award 1983, Slagle lectr. award 1985, Svc. award 1985, 2001); mem.: Soc. for the Study of Occupations, Tex. Occupl. Therapy Found. (pres. 1998—), Neuro-Devel. Treatment Assn., Assn. Advancement Rehab. Tech., Am. Occupl. Therapy Found., Med. Libr. Assn. (Rittenhouse award 1987, Acad. Health Info. Professions), Tex. Occupl. Therapy Assn. (Roster of Merit award 2002, Disting. Svc. award 2004), Okla. Occupl. Therapy Assn. (pres. 1974—76), Coun. Exceptional Children, World Fedn. Occupl. Therapists, N.Am. Riding for Handicapped Assn., Sigma Kappa (Colby award 1994), Pi Theta Epsilon. Democrat. Home: 6699 De Moss Dr Houston TX 77074-5003 Office Phone: 713-794-2166. Personal E-mail: klreed3@juno.com.

REED, LEON SAMUEL, secondary school educator, photographer; b. Warren, Ohio, July 6, 1949; s. Walter Charles and Lois Avalene (Botroff) R.; m. Margaret Smith, Dec. 27, 1975 (div.); m. Lois S. Lembo, Aug. 5, 1997; children: Samuel, Stephen, Catherine. BA in Econs. and Journalism, Antioch Coll., Yellow Springs, Ohio, 1971. Project dir. Coun. on Econ. Priorities, NYC and Washington, 1970-75; sr. mem. profl. staff Joint Com. on Def. Prodn., U.S. Congress, Washington, 1975-77; mem. profl. staff Com. on Banking, Housing and Urban Affairs, U.S. Senate, Washington, 1977-81; analyst TASC, 1981-82, mgr. contingency planning, 1982-85, mgr. instl. resources dept., 1985-91, dir. indsl. and mfg. scis. divsn., 1991-97; rsch. staff Inst. Def. Analyses, 1998—2003; freelance writer, photographer, 2000—; rsch. asst. George Mason U., 2004—; tchr. Woodbridge H.S., 2005—. Author: Military Maneuvers, 1975, Resource Management: A Historical Perspective, 1988; co-author: Guide to Corporations, 1973, Report of the National Critical Technologies Panel, 1991; contbr. Strategic Survey, 1981-82, The American Defense Mobilization Infrastructure, 1983; corr. Potomac Almanac; author numerous congressional and exec. br. reports, also mag. and jour. articles. Del. White House Conf. on Youth, 1971; writer, photographer Md. Soccer News, 1996—2005; pres. Randolph Civic Assn., 1978—80; v.p. North Bethesda Congress of Citizens Assns., 1983—84, pres., 1984—86; v.p. Md. State Youth Soccer Assn., 1998—2005; bd. dirs. Coun. on Econ. Priorities, 1971—73, Montgomery Soccer, Inc., 1994—, pres., 2001—06.

REED, LORIJEAN KINSEY, anesthesiologist; m. Sean Reed. MD, Tex. Tech U., Lubbock, 1998—2002. Lic. LoriJean Reen. Anesthesiologist S. County Hosp., Wakefield, RI, 2006—. Office: S County Hosp 100 Kenyon Ave Wakefield RI 02879 Home Phone: 401-865-0884.

REED, LOWELL A., JR., federal judge; b. Westchester, Pa., 1930; BBA, U. Wis., 1952; JD, Temple U., 1958. Bar: Pa. 1959, U.S. Dist. Ct. (ea. dist.) Pa. 1961, U.S. Ct. Appeals (3d cir.) 1962, U.S. Supreme Ct. 1970. Corp. trial counsel PMA Group, Phila., 1958-63; assoc. Rawle & Henderson, Phila., 1963-65, gen. ptnr., 1966-88; judge U.S. Dist Ct., Phila., 1988-99; sr. judge U.S. Dist. Ct., Phila., 1999—. Lectr. law Temple U., 1965-81, faculty Acad. Advocacy, 1988—, Pa. Bar Inst., 1972—. Contbr. articles to profl. jours. Elder Abington (Pa.) Presbyn. Ch.; past. mem. Pa. Senate Select Com. Med. Malpractice; past pres., bd. dirs. Rydal Meadowbrook Civic Assn.; bd. dirs. Abington Sch. Bd., 1971, World Affairs Coun. Phila., 1983-88; trustee Abington Health Care Corp., 1983-88, 90-93. Lt. Comdr. USNR, 1952-57. Recipient Alumni Achievement award Temple U. 1988, Cert. of Honor, 2001, A. Sherman Christensen award Am. Inns. of Ct. Found., 2003. Mem. ABA, Phila. Bar Assn. (chmn. medico legal com. 1975, constl. bicentennial com. 1986-87, commn. on jud. selection and retention 1983-87), Temple Am. Inn of Ct. (pres. 1990-93, master of bench 1990—), Am. Judicature Soc., Temple U. Law Alumni Assn. (exec. com. 1987-90, 99—), Hist. Soc. U.S. Supreme Ct., Hist. Soc. U.S. Dist. Ct. Ea. Dist. Pa. Republican. Office: US Dist Ct US Courthouse Independence Mall W Philadelphia PA 19106

REED, M. SCOTT, accounting company executive; CFO Grant Thornton LLP, Chgo., 1997-99, CEO, 1999-2000. Office: Grant Thornton LLP 175 W Jackson Blvd #20 Chicago IL 60604-3033

REED, MARC C., telecommunications industry executive, human resources specialist; B in Bus. Adminstrn., State U. NY. Mem. human resources staff GTE World Hqtrs., 1986—87; various human resources exec. positions including dir. human resources GTE Wireless, 1987—97, v.p. human resources, 1997—2004, Verizon Wireless, NYC, exec. v.p. human resources, 2004—. Office: Verizon Comm Inc 1095 Avenue of the Americas New York NY 10036 Office Phone: 212-395-2121. Office Fax: 212-869-3265. *

REED, MARK ARTHUR, research scientist, educator; b. Suffern, NY, Jan. 4, 1955; s. Arthur Julius and Rita Margaret Reed; m. Elizabeth J. Schaffer; 1 child, Victor. BS in Physics with honors, Syracuse U., 1977, MS in Physics, 1979, PhD in Solid State Physics, 1983; MA (hon.), Yale U., 1990. Mem. tech. staff Ctrl. Rsch. Labs., Tex. Instruments, Dallas, 1983—88, sr. mem. tech. staff, 1988—90; prof. elec. engring. and applied physics Yale U., New Haven, 1990—, chmn. elec. engring. dept., 1995—2001, Harold Hodgkinson prof. engring. and applied sci., 1999—; chief tech. officer, dir. Molecular Electronics Corp., 1999—2001; assoc. dir. Yale Inst. Nanosci. and Quantum Engring. Chmn., organizer numerous confs.; speaker in field. Editor: Nanostructure Physics and Fabrication, 1989, Nanostructures and Mesoscopic Systems, 1992, Nanostructured Systems, 1992, Compound Semiconductors, 1997, Nanostructured Systems, Molecular Electronics, 2001, Molecular Nanolectronics, 2003; contbr. chapters to books, articles 175 pub. to profl. jours. Recipient Kilby Young Innovator award, 1994, Disting. Alumni award Syracuse U., 2000, Fujitsu Internat. Symposium on Compound Semicondrs. Quantum Device award, 2001, Yale Sci. and Engring. Assn. award for advancement of basic and applied sci., 2002; named one of Fortune Mag.'s 12 most promising young Am. Scientists. Fellow: Am. Phys. Soc.; mem.: IEEE (sr. Nanotech. Pioneer award 2007), Sigma Xi. Achievements include pioneered investigation of "Quantum Dots" and Quantum devices; invention of resonant tunneling transistor; 25 patents for novel quantum effect and heterojunction devices; pioneered research on molecular electronic systems. Office: Yale U PO Box 208284 New Haven CT 06520-8284

REED, MARY CAROLYN CAMBLIN, retired music educator, retired county official; b. North Platte, Nebr., June 22, 1938; d. Brick and Evelyn Camblin; m. Paul E. Reed, Dec. 20, 1960. BA, U. No. Colo., 1960; MA, Calif. State U., 1964; PhD in Ednl. Adminstrn., U. So. Calif., 1976. Cert. administr. Calif., 1970. Music educator Rowland Unified Sch. Dist, Rowland Heights, Calif., 1960—67; tchr and writer instrnl. TV LA County Office Edn., asst. to supt. and chief dep. supt., 1976—79; adminstr. Regional Ednl. TV Adv. Coun., LA, 1979—82; ednl. tech. unit adminstr. Calif. State Dept. Edn., Sacramento, 1982—83; dir. media svcs. Sacramento County Office Edn., 1983—94, dir. ednl. media, 1983—94; mng. cons. Northern Calif. Media/Tech. Consortium, 1994—2004, Ctrl. Calif. Ednl. Tech. Consortium, 1994—2004. Cons. music series PBS Sta. WETA, Washington, 1974—76; bd. dirs. LA (Calif.) Music Ctr., AMAN Folk Dance group, LA, 1975—77, PBS Sta. KQED, San Francisco, 1989—95. Musician: Am. Flute Orch., 2001, 2002, Internat. Flute Orch., 2004—07, Sacramento Symphonic Band, 1995, 2003, Camellia City Flute Choir, 2000—. Recipient Outstanding Alumnus, U. of No. Colo., 1983. Mem.: Calif. Music Educators Assn. (pres. 1976—78), Cosumnes Cmty. Orch, West Sacramento Orch. (prin. flutist 1990—). Office Phone: 916-928-9332.

REED, MICHAEL HAYWOOD, lawyer; b. Phila., Jan. 17, 1949; s. Soloman Taylor and Vivian (Haywood) Reed; m. Yalta Gilmore, Aug. 12, 1978; children: Alexandra Haywood, Michael Haywood Jr. BA in Polit. Sci., Temple U., 1969; JD, Yale U., 1972. Bar: Pa. 1972, U.S. Dist. Ct. (ea. dist.) Pa. 1972, U.S. Dist. Ct. (ea. dist.) Mich. 1982, U.S. Supreme Ct. 1982, U.S. Ct. Appeals (3d cir.) 1985. Assoc. Pepper, Hamilton & Scheetz, Phila., 1972-80; ptnr., corp. restructuring, bankruptcy practice Pepper Hamilton LLP (formerly Pepper, Hamilton & Scheetz), Phila., 1980—. Co-adj. prof. law Rutgers U., Camden, NJ, 1983, 85; adj. prof. sch. law Temple U., Phila., 1989; mem. Pa. Judicial Inquiry and Rev. Bd., 1990-93; chair Ea. Dist. Pa. Bankruptcy Conf., 1997-98; mem. Presdl. Adv. Coun. on Diversity in the Profession, 2006—; spkr. in field. Contbr. articles to profl. jours. Advisor Post 913 Law Explorers, Phila., 1974-84; trustee Acad. Natural Scis., Phila., 1988—, Episcopal Hosp., Phila., 1986-98; mem. bd. advisors Pub. Interest Law Ctr., Phila., 1992—; mem. Com. Seventy, Phila., 1981—. Recipient cert. of honor Alumnus of Yr. Coll. of Arts and Scis. Temple U., 1995, Award of Excellence, Thurgood Marshall Scholarship Fund, Inc., 2003, J. Austin Norris award, Barristers Assn. Phila., 2005. Fellow Am. Coll. Bankruptcy; mem. ABA (chmn. subcom. labor and employment law, bus bankruptcy com. sect. bus. law 1991-97, chmn. subcom. on labor and employment law 1997-02, subcom. on avoiding powers 2002-05, subcom. bankruptcy coms. 2005-, ho. of dels. 2002-, bd. govs. 2005-06, mem. standing com. on bar activities and svcs. 2007—, mem. presdl. adv. coun. on diversity in the profession 2006—), Nat. Bar Assn., Am. Law Inst., Am. Bankruptcy Inst., Pa. Bar Assn. (mem. ho. of dels. 1999-01, chmn. minority bar com. 1988-90, mem. bd. govs. 1993-96, co-chair 1994, v.p. 2002-03, pres.-elect 2003, pres. 2004-05, ann. meeting, Spl. Achievement award 1989, Cert. of Honor award 1995), Barristers Assn. Phila. (1st v.p. 1974-76), Phila. Bar Assn. (chair profl. guidance com. 1986), Yale Club (Phila.), Alpha Phi Alpha, Sigma Pi Phi. Democrat. Baptist. Avocations: racquetball, films, theater, biking, piano. Office: Pepper Hamilton LLP 3000 Two Logan Sq 18th and Arch Streets Philadelphia PA 19103-2799 Office Phone: 215-981-4416. Office Fax: 215-981-4750. Business E-Mail: reedm@pepperlaw.com.

REED, MICHAEL JOHN, dentist, dean, oral biology educator; b. Wednesbury, Eng., Dec. 25, 1940; came to U.S., 1967, naturalized, 1972; s. Harry Ernest and Ida Veva (Heywood) R.; m. Pamela Twycross, July 4, 1965 (div. Feb. 1976); children: Justine Marianne, Helena Clare; m. Ingrid Liepins, Sept. 8, 1978; children: Kathryn Anne, Matthew Harrison. BS with honors, U. Durham, Eng., 1963; B in Dental Surgery, U. Newcastle-Upon-Tyne, Eng., 1967; PhD, SUNY, Buffalo, 1971. Lic. dentist U.K., N.Y., Miss. Instr. oral biology SUNY, Buffalo, 1971-72, asst. prof. oral biology, 1972-77, assoc. prof., 1977-79; asst. dean Sch. Dentistry, U. Miss., Jackson, 1980-85, assoc. dean, 1985; dean, prof. oral biology Sch. Dentistry, U. Mo., Kansas City, 1985—. Cons. Nat. Inst. Dental Rsch., Washington, 1975-85. Contbr. numerous articles to profl. jours. Recipient rsch. career devel. award NIH, 1975-80. Fellow Acad. Dentistry Internat., Internat. Coll. Dentists, Am. Coll. Dentists; mem. ADA (cons. 1982—, joint com. on nat. dental exam., 1988-93, chair 1992-93), Am. Assn. Dental Schs. (sect. chair 1985-86. chmn. schs. coun. of deans, 1992-93, pres. 1997-98), Am. Assn. Dental Rsch. (councillor 1974-76), Fedn. Dentaire Internat., Am. Assn. for Microbiology, Mid-Am. Masters Club, Omicron Kappa Upsilon. Episcopalian. Avocations: running, European current affairs. Office: U Mo-Kansas City Sch Dentistry 650 E 25th St Kansas City MO 64108-2716 Office Phone: 816-235-2010. Office Fax: 816-235-2157. Business E-Mail: reedm@umkc.edu.

REED, MICHAEL ROBERT, agricultural economist; b. Lawrence, Kans., July 11, 1953; s. Robert Stanley and Marian Lucille (Karr) R.; m. Patricia Gail Gurtler, Mar. 16, 1973; children: Laura Gail, Brian Michael. BS, Kans. State U., 1974; MS, Iowa State U., 1976, PhD, 1979. Asst. prof. U. Ky., Lexington, 1978-83, assoc. prof., 1983-89; prof., 1989—; exec. dir. Ctr. for Export Devel., 1988-95; dir. office of internat. affairs U. Ky., Lexington, 1994-98, dir. office of internat. programs for agr., 1998—. Cons. USDA, 1994-97, 02—, US AID, Washington, 1983-86, 99-01, 04-. Author: (textbook) International Trade in Agricultural Products, 2000; mem. editl. bd. So. Jour. of Agrl. Econs., 1983-86; contbr. articles to profl. jours. Grantee Farmer Coop. Svcs., 1982-84, 87-88, TVA, 1982-85, Fed. Crop Ins. Corp., 1985-87, USDA, 1986-2003, 2005—; recipient Outstanding Jour. Article award Soc. Farm Mgrs. and Rural Appraisers, 1986, Jour. Agrl. and Applied Econs., 2002 Mem. Am. Agrl. Econs. Assn., So. Agrl. Econs. Assn., Gamma Sigma Delta. Home: 2216 Bonhaven Rd Lexington KY 40515-1150 Office: U Ky Dept Agrl Econs 308 Barnhart Bldg Lexington KY 40546-0001 Office Phone: 859-257-7259. Business E-Mail: mrreed@uky.edu.

REED, MIRIAM BELL, legislative staff member; b. NYC, May 31, 1930; d. Samuel Dennis and Miriam Wilkes Bell; m. John Grady Reed, May 1, 1954; children: Roberta, Christine, Karen, Laura, Margaret, Abigail, Elisabeth. BA, Mount Holyoke Coll., 1952. Asst. to adminstrv. asst. Rep. Harlan Hagan, Washington, 1953-54; asst. to econ. prof. Littauer Sch. Pub. Adminstrn., Cambridge, Mass., 1954; producer, treas. Video Ed Prodns., Inc., Hyattsville, Md., 1974-90; Singapore testing coord. Malaysian Am. Commn. on Ednl. Exch., Singapore, 1991-92; legis. aide Del. Constance A. Morella, Annapolis, Md., 1978-86; legis. asst. Hon. Constance A. Morella, Washington, 1987-90, 92, 94-97; staff Friends of Connie Morella for Congress, 1999-2000. Cons. Acad. Arrangements Abroad, NYC, 1974-99. Rsch. and writing of ednl. hist. videotapes, 1974-90 (Pratt Libr. award 1986). V.p., pres. bd. LWV, Bronxville, NY, 1957-74; mem. Montgomery County Commn. on the Humanities, 1985-88; mem. Montgomery County Com. to Celebrate Md.'s 350th Birthday. Mem. Montgomery County Hist. Soc. (dir. 1998-2001), C&O Canal Assn. (info. officer 2000, 02, 2004-06). Avocations: swimming, hiking, backpacking. Home: 8221 Burning Tree Rd Bethesda MD 20817-2908 Personal E-mail: mreed8221@aol.com.

REED, PEGGY ANNE, education educator; b. Kittaning, Pa., Apr. 25, 1954; d. Clarence Wade and Shirley Anne Pence; m. William Raymond Reed, Aug. 9, 1975; children: Meredith Anne Knapp, Kevin William, Christopher Paul. BS, Evangel U., Springfield, Mo., 1976; MEd, Mo. State U., Springfield, 1982; EdD, Nova Southeastern U., Ft. Lauderdale, Fla., 1990. Cert. tchr. Mo. Dept. Elem. and Secondary Edn., 1976. Kindergarten tchr. Fair Play Sch., Mo., 1976—84; substitute tchr. Pleasant Hope Schs., Mo., 1985, Bolivar Schs., Mo., 1985; assoc. prof. Evangel U., Springfield, Mo., 1985—. Dir. Early Childhood Ctr. Evangel U., 1985—97; child care training cons. State of Mo. Child Care Licensing, Jefferson City, 1998. Reader Ozarks Literacy Coun., Springfield, Mo., 2005—07; fifth grade tchr. First Assembly of God Missionettes, Bolivar, Mo., 1990—2005. Mem.: Nat. Assn. for Edn. of Young Children. Avocations: crafts, reading. Home: 829 W Hughs St Bolivar MO 65613-2817 Office: Evangel Univ 1111 N Glenstone Springfield MO 65802 Home Phone: 417-326-6341; Office Phone: 417-865-2815 ext. 8556. Business E-Mail: reedp@evangel.edu.

REED, R. DOUGLAS, music educator; b. Cheboygan, Mich., Apr. 17, 1947; s. Robert G. and Marian L. Reed; 1 child, Eric Douglas. MusB in Organ Performance, U. Mich., 1969, MusM in Organ Performance, 1971; cert. in Performance, U. Rochester, 1974, MusD in Performance and Lit., 1975. Prof. music U. Evansville, Ind., 1975—. Organist The Luth. Ch. Our Redeemer, Evansville, 1975—78; organist, dir. music First Presbyn. Ch., Evansville, 1980—88; prin. organist Cathedral Immaculate Conception, Memphis, 2001—02; cons. in field. Musician: Organ Concerts in United States, Europe, and Japan, William Albright: The King of Instruments, (albums) William Albright: Music for Organ and Harpsichord, Eastman American Music Series, Vol. 3, Douglas Reed Plays the C.B. Fisk Organ, Op. 98, Douglas Reed Plays the Taylor & Boody Organ, In Memoriam William Albright Douglas Reed Plays the C.B. Fisk Organ, Op. 110; author: (chapter) North American Organ Music after 1800 for Cambridge Companion to the Organ; contbr. articles to profl. jours. Recipient The Sadelle and Sidney Berger award, U. Evansville, 1998; grantee, The Mesker Trust Fund Evansville, Ind., 1978, U. Evansville, 1985, Ind. Arts Commn. and NEA, 1987, Friends U. Evansville Music, 1991, 2000, 2005. Mem.: Westfield Ctr. Early Keyboard Studies, Organ Hist. Soc., Am. Guild Organists (dean 1998—2001), Phi Kappa Phi, Pi Kappa Lamda. Avocations: travel, reading, photography. Office: University of Evansville 1800 Lincoln Avenue Evansville IN 47722 Home Phone: 812-422-0958; Office Phone: 812-488-2877. Business E-Mail: dr5@evansville.edu.

REED, RALPH EUGENE, JR., political consultant, former political organization administrator; b. Portsmouth, Va., June 24, 1961; s. Ralph Sr. and Marcy R.; m. Jo Anne Young, 1987; children: Brittany, Ralph III, Christopher, Nicole. BA in History, U. Ga., 1985; Ph.D in Am. History, Emory U., 1991. Exec. dir. Christian Coalition, Chesapeake, Va., 1989-97; founder, pres. Century Strategies, Strategies Cons. Co., Duluth, Ga., 1997—; chmn. Ga. Republican Party, 2001—03; southeast regional campaign chmn. George Bush re-election campaign, 2003—04. Founder Students for Am., Raleigh, N.C., 1984; lobbyist; spkr. in field. Author: Politically Incorrect: The Emerging Faith Factor in American Politics, 1994, After the Revolution: How the Christian Coalition is Impacting America, 1995, Active Faith: How Christians Are Changing the Face of American Politics, 1996. Office: Century Strategies 3235 Satellite Blvd Ste 575 Duluth GA 30096-9017

REED, ROBERT ALAN, lawyer; b. Pitts., Dec. 1, 1942; s. Thomas Frank and Elizabeth Mary (Kelly) R.; m. Rosemary Alice Werner, Dec. 26, 1967; children: Brian, Kevin. BSE, Purdue U., 1964; LLB, U. Pitts., 1967. Bar: Pa. 1967. Atty. ALCOA, Pitts., 1968-93, gen. atty., 1982-93, asst. gen. counsel, 1982—, asst. sec., 1983-84, sec., 1984-93; v.p., sec. and assoc. gen. counsel Jefferson-Pilot Corp., Greensboro, NC, 1994—. Mem. ABA, Am. Corp. Counsel Assocs., Am. Soc. Corp. Secs. (chair corp. practices com. 1992—), Allegheny County Bar Assn., Duquesne Club. Home: Jefferson-Pilot Corp 100 N Greene Greensboro NC 27401 Office Phone: 336-691-3000. Office Fax: 336-691-3258. E-mail: bob.reed@jpfinancial.com.

REED, ROBERT N., JR., retired announcer; b. Giles, Tenn., Aug. 24, 1928; s. Robert N. Reed Sr. and Bessie Louise Jones; m. Shirley A. Black; 1 child, Dora A.L.; m. Nettie M. McCarn (dec.); children: Cassandra Gail Parker, Lamar Reed, Karl D. Grad., Furman U., Greenville, SC, 1953. Author: (books) Early Radio, 1990, Gospel Music Rings In Nursery of South Warren County, Tenn., 1992. Staff sgt. USAF, 1949—71, Korea, staff sgt. USAF, 1973—98, Korea. Mem.: Warren Lodge 124 (sr. steward 2006—).

REED, ROBERT PHILLIP, lawyer; b. Springfield, Ill., June 14, 1952; s. Robert Edward and Rita Ann (Kane) R.; m. Janice Leigh Kloppenburg, Oct. 8, 1976; children: Kevin Michael, Matthew Carl, Jennifer Leigh, Rebecca Ann. AB, St. Louis U., 1974; JD, U. Ill., 1977. Bar: Ill. 1977, U.S. Dist. Ct. (ctrl. dist.) Ill. 1979, U.S.Ct. Appeals (7th cir.) 1983, U.S. Dist. Ct. (so. dist.) Ill. 1992, Colo. 1993. Intern Ill. Legislature, Springfield, 1977-78; assoc. Traynor & Hendricks, Springfield, 1979-80; ptnr. Traynor, Hendricks & Reed, Springfield, 1981-88; pvt. practice Springfield, 1988—. Pub. defender Sangamon County, Ill., Springfield, 1979-81; hearing examiner Ill. State Bd. Elections, Springfield, 1981-88; spl. asst. atty. gen. State of Ill., Springfield, 1983—; instr. Lincoln Land Community Coll., Springfield, 1988. Trustee Springfield Pk. Dist., 1985-89. Mem.: NY Stock Exch. (arbitrator 2006—), Bar Assn. Met. St. Louis, Attys Title Guaranty Fund, Inc., Colo. Bar Assn., Ill. State Bar Assn., Nat. Assn. Securities Dealers, Inc. (arbitrator 1996—), Phi Beta Kappa. Roman Catholic. Office: 1129 S 7th St Springfield IL 62703-2418 Office Phone: 217-528-7333. Personal E-mail: reedlaw@sbcglobal.net.

REED, SALLY GARDNER, cultural organization administrator; m. Harold F. Reed, 1981; children: Gardner F., Charles A. BA in English, Colo. State U., 1979; MLS, No. Ill. U., 1981. Dir. North Hampton (H.H.) Pub. Libr., 1981-85, Ilsley Pub. Libr., Middlebury, Vt., 1985-93, Ames (Iowa) Pub. Libr., 1993-95; dir. librs. Norfolk (Va.) Pub. Libr., 1995—2001; exec. dir. Friends of Librs. USA, Phila., 2001—. Author: Small Libraries: A Handbook for Successful Management, 1991, 2d edit., 2002, Saving Your Library: A Guide to Getting, Using and Keeping the Power You Need, 1992, Library Volunteers: Worth the Effort!, 1994; editor: Creating the Future: Essays on the Future of Librarianship in an Age of Great Change, 1996, Speaking Out: Voices in Celebration of Intellectual Freedom, 1999, Making the Case for Your Library, 2001, 101+ Great Ideas for Libraries and Friends, 2004, Getting Grants in Your Community, 2005; contbr. articles to profl. jours. Bd. dirs. Sheldon Art History Mus., Middlebury, 1988-93, United Way Story County, Ames, 1994-95; mem. cabinet United Way Norfolk, 1996-97, chair city campaign, 1997. Recipient Recognition award Tidewater Area Minority Libr. Network, 1997, Am. Libr. Assoc. Herb & Virginia White award for Promoting Librarianship, 2000. Mem. ALA (chpt. coun. 1989-93, adv. com. office libr. outreach svcs. 1993-94, nat. libr. week com. 1993-95, presdl. com. pub. awareness 1994-96, councilor at large 1995-99, chair membership com. 1996, resolutions com. 1997, exec. bd. 1997-2001, chair pub. awareness com. 2004-06). Office: Friends Libraries USA 1420 Walnut Ste 450 Philadelphia PA 19102 Home Phone: 267-210-0882; Office Phone: 215-790-1674. Business E-Mail: sreed@folusa.org.

REED, SAM, state official; b. Portland, Oreg. m. Margie Reed, 1963; children: David, Kristen. BA, MA, Wash. State U. Cert. profl. elections officer. Exec. dir. Gov. Evans' Urban Affairs Coun.; asst. sec. state State of Wash., Olympia, 1969—75; dir. State Constl. Reform Commn., 1975—77; auditor Thurston County, 1978—2000; sec. state State of Wash., Olympia, 2001—. Exec. dir. Gov. 's Urban Affairs Coun., 1967—69; sec. Nat. Assn. Secretaries State (NASS), 2004; bd. mem. Fed. Election Commn. Voting System; internat. election observer, Uganda; mem. Americorps Adv. Coun., Wash. State Election Admin. & Cert. Bd. Recipient Gov.'s Disting. Vol.

award, Thurston County Citizen of the Year Disting. Svc. award. Mem.: Mainstream Reps. of Wash., Wash. State Assn. County Auditors, Olympia Kiwanis. Republican. Avocations: running, piano, arts, tennis. Office: Office Sec of State Legislative Bldg 2nd Floor PO Box 40220 Olympia WA 98504 Office Phone: 360-902-4151. Office Fax: 360-586-5629. E-mail: sreed@secstate.wa.gov. *

REED, SCOTT C., musician, educator, writer; s. Vernon C. Reed and Betty M. Ryan. MusB, U. of So. Calif., 1981. Adj. prof. Gov.'s State U., U. Pk., Ill., 1989—95, Prairie State Coll., Chgo. Heights, Ill., 1994—2005. Author: Getting Into Guitar Improvising: A Systematic Approach To Soloing, 2002, Getting Into Guitar Styles, 2005. Fellow, NEA, 1992—93. Mem.: Las Vegas Fedn. Musicians, Chgo. Fedn. Musicians. Office: Prarie State College 202 South Halsted Chicago Heights IL 60411

REED, SHERMAN KENNEDY, chemicals executive, consultant; b. Chgo., Apr. 11, 1919; s. Frank Hynes and Helen Louise (Kennedy) R.; m. Octavia Bailey, Oct. 11, 1943; children: Martin Bailey, Holly Anne Johnson, Julie Marie Reed. BS with honors, U. Ill., 1940; PhD, Cornell U., 1949. Asst. instr. chemistry Cornell U., 1940-43; asst. rsch. scientist Manhattan Project, NYC, 1942-46; asst. prof. Bucknell U., Lewisburg, Pa., 1946-50; with FMC Corp., 1950—, mgr., asst. dir. rsch., 1950-60, divisional dir. rsch. and devel., ctrl. rsch. dir., 1960-76, v.p., 1976-82, cons. Chgo., 1983—; dir. Avicon, Inc., 1970-82; pres., dir. FMC Gold Corp.; mng. dir. COGAS Devel. Co., 1975—; dir. Indsl. Rsch. Inst., NYC, Franklin Inst., Phila., 1976-83; chmn. bd. Franklin Rsch. Ctr., Phila., 1976-83. Fellow Am. Inst. Chemists; mem. AAAS, Am. Chem. Soc., Assn. Rsch. Dirs. (pres. 1973). Republican. Home and Office: 2300 Indian Creek Blvd W #C211 Vero Beach FL 32966-2400 Home Phone: 772-562-2003; Office Phone: 772-539-2369. Personal E-mail: shermankreed@bellsouth.net.

REED, STUART C., electronics executive; BA, Mich. State Univ.; MS, MIT. V.p. integrated supply chain IBM, 1999—2002, v.p. strategy, process & systems, 2002—03, v.p. systems & storage, worldwide mfg. ops., 2003—04, v.p. systems, storage & software products, 2004—05; sr. v.p., chief supply chain officer Motorola, Inc., Schaumburg, Ill., 2005—06, exec. v.p., integrated supply chain, 2006—. Sloan Fellow. Office: Motorola Inc 1303 E Algonquin Rd Schaumburg IL 60196 *

REED, SUELLEN KINDER, school system administrator; BA in History, Polit. Sci. and Secondary Edn., Hanover Coll., 1967; MA in Elem. Edn. and History, Ball State U., 1970, EdD in Adminstrn. and Supervision, LLD (hon.), 1997; EdD (hon.), Vincennes U., 1996; LittD (hon.), U. Indpls., 1997; LHD (hon.), St. Joseph Coll., 1999, Hanover Coll., 2003; postgrad., Fla. Atlantic U., U. Scranton, Purdue U., Earlham Coll., Ind. U., Ind. State U., U. So. Ind., Butler U., U. Alaska, Edinburgh U., Scotland, Oxford U., Eng. Lic. supt., life lic. in elem. edn., U.S. history, world history, govt., adminstrn. and supervision and endorsement in edn. for gifted and talented K-12, Ind.; lic. adminstr., U.S. history, world history, govt., middle sch. lang. arts, social studies, elem. edn., gifted edn., Fla. Tchr. 5th and 6th grades Rushville Consol. Sch. Corp., Ind., 1967-70; tchr., world history and coll. prep Latin Am. history Shelbyville HS, Ind., 1970-71; tchr. 6th, 7th and 8th grade social studies and civic, curriculum coord., dir. gifted programs, homebase guidance dir., & handwriting inservice coord. Broward County Sch. Corp., Fla., 1971-76; reading tchr. Rushville Jr. HS, Ind., 1976-77; asst. prin. Rushville Elem. Sch., Ind., 1977-79; prin. Frazee Elem. Sch., Connersville, Ind., 1979-87; asst. supt. Rushville Consolidated Schs., Ind., 1987—91, supt. Ind., 1991-93; supt. pub. instrn., chairperson bd. edn., CEO dept. edn. State of Indiana, Indpls., 1993—. Pres. N. Ctrl. Regional Edn. Lab., Oak Brook, Ill., 1993—97, Oak Brook, 2002; mem. The Ctr. on Congress Outstanding Tchr. Award Selection Com., Task Force on Strengthening Profl. Practice, Western Interstate Commn. for Higher Edn., State Scholar Initiative Adv. Coun., 2005; co-chair Ind. Commn. for Early Learning and School Readiness, Ind. Edn. Roundtable, 1998—; visited schools & addresses administrators, teachers, parents, and students; prepared units of study on Japan, China, Singapore, Taiwan, former Union Soviet Socialist Republics, UK, Germany, France, Australia, Italy, The Netherlands, Austria, Hong Kong, & Spain. Contbr. articles to profl. jours.; regular contbr. Ind. Reading Assn. Jour., Ind. Principal's Assn. Indianagram. Bd. trustees Hanover Coll., Commn. Drug-Free Ind., Ind. Commn. Cmty. Svc., Ind. Higher Edn. Telecom. Sys., Ctr. Agrl. Sci. Heritage; hon. bd. mem. Rush County Cmty. Found.; alumni bd. Ball State U. Tchrs. Coll., 1999-; bd. dirs. Nat. Children's Film Festival; trustee, mem. New Salem United Meth. Ch.; bd. dirs. Ind. Historic Landmarks Found., Agy. for Instrnl. Tech., Project Lead the Way, Virtual H.S., 2003-; bd. visitors Ind. U.; mem. Commn. for Drug-Free Ind., Ind. Commn. on Cmty. Svc., Ind. Higher Edn. Telecommunication System, Ind. Commn. on the Social Status of Black Males, Ind. State Mus. Performing Arts and Edn. Adv. Com., Ctr. for Agr. Sci. and Heritage, Indpls. Art Mus., Indpls. Zoo; mem. adv. coun., Ball State U. Sch. Continuing Studies and Pub. Svc.; hon. bd. mem. Indpls. Zool. Soc.; hon. chair, Young Audiences Ind. Fundraising Campaign, 1994-95. Named Outstanding Sch. Edn. Alumnus, Ball State U., 1994, Govt. Leader Yr., Ind. C. of C., 2001, Exemplary Friend, Butler U., Coll. Edn., 2005; recipient Certificate of Appreciation, Fayette-Rush County NAACP, 1993, Certificate of Appreciation in Helping to Reduce Crime and to Improve Communities, Nat. Crime Prevention Coun., Partnership with the Bur. Justice Assistance, Office of Justice Programs, US Dept. of Justice, 1994, Pres. award, Ind. Assn. Sch. Prins., 1996, Achievement award, Ind. Network Women Adminstrs., 1996, Alumni award, Hanover Coll., 1997, Legis. award, Ind. Assn. for the Edn. Young Children, 1998, Pres. award, Ind. Middle Level Edn. Assn., 2001, Elizabeth Heywood Wyman award for alumnae, Alpha Omicron Pi, 2001, Friend Youth award, Ind. Sch. Counselors, 2001, Hoosier Heritage Civic Leadership award, 2002, Turn Off the Violence award, Ind. Crime Prevention Coalition, 2002, Ind. Sch. Safety Leadership award, 2002, Citizen's award, Ind. Libr. Fedn., Counselor's award, Assn. for Ind. Media Educators, Spl. Contributions to Edn. award, Ind. U. Sch. Adminstr. Assn., 2004, Disting. Alumni award, Ind. 4-H Found.-Ind. 4-H Centennial, 2004, Friend Fgn. Languages award, Ind. Fgn. Language Teachers Assn., 2004, Sagamore of the Wabash award, 1997, 2005, Leadership award for Continuing Advocacy for Gifted Children, Ind. Assn. for the Gifted, 2005, Indian Trails Career Cooperative for Continued Support to Career and Tech. Edn., 2005, Citation for Courage, Ind. Assn. for Adult and Continuing Edn., 2005. Mem. ASCD (nat. and Ind. chpts.), Internat. Reading Assn., Internat. Edn. Com., Nat. Coun. for Accreditation Tchr. Edn. (mem. exec. bd.), Nat. Assn. Elem. and Mid. Sch. Prins. (assoc.), Nat. Assn. Gifted Children (nat. adv. bd.), Internat. Tech. Edn. Assn. (mem. adv. com.), Ind. Assn. Pub. Sch. Supts.(Outstanding Educator award, 2004), Ind. Assn. Elem. and Mid. Sch. Prins. (assoc.), Women's Coun. on Literacy for the Ind. Literacy Found., Indpls. Bd. Associates, Rose Hulman Inst. Tech., Network Woman Adminstrs., Indpls. Bd. Assocs., Bus. and Profl. Women of Rushville, Connersville Area Reading Coun., Smithsonian, Rushville Rotary Club, Monday Cir., K-12 Compact Learning and Citizenship (first nat. chairwoman), Edn. Commn. States (commr., mem. exec. com., steering com. 1994-98, 2002-, treas., chair policy and priorities com.), Coun. Chief State Sch. Officers (v.p. 1999-2000, pres.-elect., 2000-01, pres., 2001-02), ex-officio bd. dir., North Ctrl. Assn., Ind. Hist. Soc., Ind. State Mus., Conner Prairie Farm, Order of Ea. Star (Andersonville chpt.), Delta Kappa Gamma (past pres.), Phi Lambda Theta, Phi Delta Kappa (Conner Prairie), Kappa Delta Pi, Altrusa Club Connersville (chmn. internat. rels., 1979-87), The Gathering. Office: Superintendent Edn Dept Room 229 State House Indianapolis IN 46204-2798 Office Phone: 317-232-6665. Office Fax: 317-232-8004. Business E-Mail: sureed@doe.state.in.us. *

REED, SUSAN J., elementary school educator; d. Eldora L. and James E. Kraby; m. Terry R. Reed, Apr. 15, 1950; children: Jamie R., Daniel C. BS Phys. Edn., N.D. State U., Fargo, 1972; Elem. Edn. Endorsement, Mayville State U., ND, 1982. Cert. Tchr. Reading N.D. Dept. Pub. Instrn., Title I, 2003, Tchr. Math. N.D. Dept. Pub. Instrn., Title I, 2003. Tchr. h.s. phys. edn. Linton Pub. Sch., ND, 1972—73; office asst. Farmers Home Adminstrn. USDA, Hillsboro, ND, 1974—81; tchr. elem. sch. Hillsboro Pub. Sch., 1984—. Dir. and treas. Hillsboro Scholarship Found., 2002—. Named to Who's Who Among Am. Tchrs., 2006, 2007; recipient Tchr. of Yr., Hillsboro Edn. Assn., 2005. Mem.: Hilsboro Edn. Assn., N.D. Edn. Assn. Avocations: reading, golf. Home Phone: 701-436-4117.

REED, THOMAS JAMES, law educator; b. Joliet, Ill., Jan. 1, 1940; s. Thomas p. and Bernardine M. (Dorsey) R.; m. Emily A. Fabrycki, Dec. 29, 1962; children: Martin, Valerie. BA, Marquette U., 1962; JD, Notre Dame Law Sch., 1969. Bar: Ind. 1969, US Dist. Ct. (so. dist.) Ind. 1969, US Ct. Appeals (7th cir.) 1974, Mass. 1977, US Dist. Ct. Mass. 1979, Pa. 1982, US Ct. Appeals (3rd cir.) 1982. Assoc. Reller, Mendenhall, Kleinknecht & Milligan, Richmond, Ind., 1969-76; asst. prof. law We. New Eng. Coll. Sch. Law, Springfield, Mass., 1976-79, assoc. prof., 1979-81, Widener U. Del. Law Sch., Wilmington, Del., 1981-84, prof., 1984—; assoc. dean Widener U. Law Sch., Wilmington, Del., 1984-93, prof. law, 1993—; dir. Vets. Law Clinic, 2006—. Hist. preservation planner City Planning Assn., Mishawaka, Ind., 1969-71, Hist. Centerville Inc., Ind., 1970-76, Old Richmond, 1975-76. Contbr. articles to profl. jours. Reporter Del. Appellate Handbook, Wilmington, 1984—. Mem. ABA, Fed. Bar Assn., Ind. Bar Assn., Pa. Bar Assn. Roman Catholic. Avocations: civil war history, genealogy, historic preservation. Office: Widener U Law Sch 4601 Concord Pike PO Box 7474 Wilmington DE 19803-0474 Business E-Mail: tjreed@mail.widener.edu.

REED, TRAVIS DEAN, public relations executive; b. Trinity, Tex., Sept. 27, 1930; s. Travis and Alma (Rains) R.; m. Caroline M. McDonald, June 15, 1957; children: Anne Reed Adams, Lisa Reed Lettau. Student, Tex. A&M U., 1948-51, U. Houston, 1951-53. Reporter Houston Post, 1951-53; Washington Bur. corr. McGraw-Hill Pub. Co., 1955-61, Boston Herald-Traveler, 1961-62; with Newhouse News Svc., Washington, 1962-79, chief corr., 1964-67, editor, 1967-79; pub. rels. cons. Washington, 1979—. *The T. Dean Reed Company is a Washington, D.C. based strategic communications management and public affairs consulting company providing services to corporations, trade associations, law firms, foreign governments and others in national and international markets. The company services its clients with a staff of skilled practitioners, including writers, media relations specialists, and former Capitol Hill staff.* 1st lt. U.S. Army, 1953-55. Mem. Nat. Press Club, Gridiron Club, Army and Navy Club. Home: 37277 Branchriver Rd Purcellville VA 20132-1922 Office: T Dean Reed Co PO Box 65276 Washington DC 20035

REED, VASTINA KATHRYN (TINA REED), child and adolescent psychotherapist; b. Chgo., Mar. 5, 1960; d. Alvin Hillard and Ruth Gwendolyn (Thomas) R.; 1 child, Alvin J. BA in Human Svcs. magna cum laude, Nat.-Louis U., Chgo., 1988; MA, Ill. Sch. Profl. Psychology, Chgo., 1991; tng. cert., Appelbaum Inst. Child Devel.; cert. family devel. specialist, U. Iowa, 2002; fashion cons. of Evangelist Audey Donson, Good Shepherd Grace Min., 2002—. Notary pub. Ill., lic. profl. counselor Ill., child and adolescent psychotherapist, nat. cert. counselor NBCC. Tchr. early childhood edn. Kendall Coll. Lab. Sch., Evanston, Ill., 1983-85, Rogers Park Children's Learning Ctr., Chgo., 1983-85; child life therapist Mt. Sinai Hosp., Chgo., 1988; child psychotherapist Nicholas Barnes Therapeutic Day Sch., Chgo., 1989-90; presch. instr. YMCA, 1999-2000; crisis line counselor Washington Security Corp., 2000—02; family support specialist Maywood (Ill.) Head Start, 2000—03; health care rep. Care Entrée, 2002—03; mental health svc. coord. Head Start Chgo. Dept. Children & Youth Svcs., 2005—. Den leader Boy Scouts Am., Chgo., 1989-92, scoutmaster, 1992-2000, merit badge counselor, 1999—, troop advisor for Order of the Arrow; vision ptnr., co-labourers Christ Ministry; editor, mem. praise and worship team Christ Outreach Deliverance Ctr. Ministry, 2001—; mem. Ill. Notary Public. Recipient Cub Scouter award Boy Scouts Am., 1990, Scoutmaster award of merit, 1993, 94, Scouters Vet. award, 1994, Scouters Tng. award, 1995, Scoutmasters Key award, 1996, Okpik Cold Weather Camping cert., 1994-95, Outstanding Women of 20th Century medal, 2000, Boy Scout Woodbadge Tng. award, 2001. Mem. APA, Nat. Orgn. for Human Svc. Edn., Order of the Arrow, Charles F. Menninger Soc. (patron), Phi Theta Kappa, Kappa Delta Pi. Democrat. Pentecostal. Avocations: camping, films, singing, music. Home: 1872 S Millard Ave Chicago IL 60623-2542 Office Phone: 773-921-8674. Personal E-mail: treed2010@aol.com.

REED, W. ALLEN, automotive executive; b. Nashville, Apr. 4, 1947; B in Engring., Auburn U., 1970; M in Bus. Adminstrn., Ga. State U., 1975. Cert. Chartered Fin. Analyst. Asst. treas. Delta Airlines, 1981—84; staff v.p., pres. investment mgmt. co. Hughes Aircraft Co., Hughes Investment Mgmt. Co., 1984—91; v.p., treas. Hughes Aircraft, 1991, Hughes Elecronics, 1992; chmn. HIMCO, 1984—92; v.p. GM, 1994—; pres., CEO GM Asset Mgmt., 1994—. Mem. investment adv. com. N.Y. State Retirement Sys.; mem. editl. bd. Morgan Stanley Capital Internat.; bd. dirs. GMAC, GMAC Ins. Holdings, iShares, Inc., Temple-Inland Inds. Office: GM Asset Mgmt 767 Fifth Ave 15th Fl New York NY 10153

REED, W. FRANKLIN, lawyer; b. Louisville, Dec. 30, 1946; s. William Ferguson and Stella Elizabeth (Richardson) R.; m. Sharon Ann Coss, June 16, 1973; children: Jonathan Franklin, William Brian, Carrie Ann. BA, Williams Coll., 1968; JD, Columbia U., 1971. Bar: N.Y. 1972, U.S. Dist. Ct. (so. dist.) N.Y. 1975, U.S. Ct. Appeals (2d cir.) 1975, Pa. 1982, U.S. Dist. Ct. (we. dist.) 1983. Assoc. Milbank, Tweed, Hadley & McCloy, NYC, 1971-82, Reed Smith Shaw & McClay, Pitts., 1982-83; ptnr. Reed, Smith, Shaw & McClay, Pitts., 1984—. Mem. instnl. devel. com. The Pitts. Cultural Trust; bd. dirs. Steel Industry Heritage Corp. Mem. ABA, Pa. Bar Assn., Allegheny Bar Assn., Carnegie 100, Williams Coll. Alumni Soc. W. Pa. (sec. 1983—), Rivers Club (Pitts.), St. Clair Country Club (Upper St. Clair, Pa.), Duquesne Club (Pitts.), Phi Beta Kappa. Democrat. Presbyterian. Avocations: fishing, golf. Home: 525 Miranda Dr Pittsburgh PA 15241-2039 Office: Reed Smith LLP 435 6th Ave Pittsburgh PA 15219-1886 E-mail: wreed@reedsmith.com.

REED, WALLACE ALLISON, anesthesiologist; b. Covina, Calif., May 19, 1916; s. Wallace Allison and Mary Julia (Birdsall) Reed; m. Maria Eva Wiemers, Jan. 20, 1938; children: Ellen E., Barbara R., Wallace J., Michael E., Kathryn L., Vikki T. AB, UCLA, 1937; postgrad., U. Cologne, 1937-38, U. Freiburg, 1938-39; MD, U. So. Calif., 1944. Diplomate Am. Bd. Anesthesiology. Intern Santa Fe Coast Lines Hosp., Los Angeles, 1943—44; resident Precept Sanders-Valley Forge Hosp., 1944—46, Los Angeles County Gen. Hosp., 1946-47; asst. to head dept. anesthesiology Precept Dillon-Los Angeles County Gen. Hosp., 1946-47; clin. instr. surgery U. So. Calif. Sch. Medicine, 1946-47; practice medicine, specializing in anesthesiology Phoenix, 1948-89; ret., 1989. Hon. staff mem. Good Samaritan Hosp., St. Joseph Hosp., Maricopa County Gen. Hosp.; mem. hon. staff Children's Hosp.; co-founder John L. Ford, M.D., Surgicenter, 1970; vice pres. Maricopa Found. for Med. Care, 1970-74, pres., 1975-76; mem. House Ways and Means Adv. Com.; adv. coun. Nat. Health Inst., 1975-76; mem. accreditation coun. for ambulatory health care Joint Commn. on Accreditation of Hosps., 1975-79; vice-chmn. Accreditation Assn. for Ambulatory Health Care, 1979-81, pres., 1981-83; mem. panel for study Nat. Health Ins., Congl. GAO; chmn. bd. Alterna Care Corp., 1984-87, now chmn. bd. emeritus; mem. adv. bd. Kino Inst., 1994-95. Bd. dirs. South Phoenix Montessori Sch., pres. bd., 1971—75; bd. dirs. Alzheimer's Assn., Greater Phoenix chpt., 1998—2000, co-v.p., 2000; co-chmn. med. and sci. adv. com. Desert S.W. chpt. Alzheimer's Assn., 2004—05; bd. dirs. Ctrl. Ariz. Health Sys. Agy., 1975—78; exec. dir. Surgictr. of Phoenix, 1987—97. Capt. M.C. AUS, 1944—46. Recipient Pinal award Ariz. Psychiat. Soc., 1967-68, Gerard B. Lambert Merit award for innovative ideas that improve patient care; John L. Ford M.D., 1972; recipient spirit of philanthropy award Alzheimer's Assn., 1996, Samba Disting. Svc. award, 2000; Disting. Svc. award Ariz. Soc. Anesthesiology, 2003. Fellow: Am. Coll. Anesthesiologists; mem.: AMA, Alzheimer's Assn. (co-chmn. med. and sci. adv. com. Desert S.W. chpt. 2004—05, co-v.p. Greater Phoenix (Ariz.) chpt. 2000), Soc. for Advancement Geriatric Anesthesia (charter mem.), Guedel Assn. (pres. 1972), Am. Assn. Founds. for Med. Care (dir. 1970—74), Central Ariz. Physicians Svc. Assn. (pres. 1982—83), Maricopa County Med. Soc. (pres. 1964, dir., Salsbury medal 1967, 1971, Thomas Dooley medal 1970), Internat. Assn. Amb. Surgery (hon.), Soc. for Ambulatory Anesthesia (bd. dirs. 1985—87), Federated Amb. Surgery Assn. (pres. 1974—75, dir.), Acad. Anesthesiology (dir. 1966—72, pres. 1969), Ariz., Maricopa County Socs. Anesthesiologists, Am. Soc. Anesthesiologists, WarMer Rsch. Found., Seed Money for Growth Found. (pres. 1984—). Methodist. Home: 4716 N Dromedary Rd Phoenix AZ 85018-2939 Office: 1040 E Mcdowell Rd Phoenix AZ 85006-2622 Office Phone: 602-258-1521. Personal E-mail: somnus4@cox.net.

REED, WALTER GEORGE, JR., retired osteopath; b. Ardmore, Okla., Sept. 10, 1928; s. Walter George and Lillian Dorene (Gee) Reed; children: Jay Walter, David George, Kimberly Sue. BA, Phillips U., 1955; DO, Kansas City U. Medicine and Biosci., 1959. Intern Des Moines Gen. Hosp., 1959—60; pvt. practice Oklahoma City, 1960-63, Atoka, Okla., 1963-80; flight surgeon USAF, Omaha, 1980-84, Lubbock, Tex., 1984-86; chief med. officer Army Health Clinic, McAlester, Okla., 1986-96; ret. USAF, 1996. Mayor City of Atoka, 1967—72; v.p. Atoka Bd. Edn., 1974—79. Lt. col. USAF, 1980—96. Mem.: Assn. Mil. Surgeons U.S., Okla. Osteo. Assn. (life), Assn. Mil. Osteo. Physicians and Surgeons (life), Ret. Officers Assn. (life), Air Force Assn. (life), Masons (32d degree). Avocations: flying, hunting, computers, plate collecting. Home: 9921 N 110th East Ave Owasso OK 74055-4358 Address: PO Box 119 Owasso OK 74055-0119 Office: Slim Care Owasso OK 74055 also: Slim Care Tulsa OK 74135

REED, WENDY, management consultant company executive, information technology executive; BS in Computer-Based Mgmt., minor in comm., Clarkson U., 1984. Mem. info. tech. dept. Accenture; with MSA (now Dun & Bradstreet Software), Viasoft, Clarus, Hayes Microcomputer Products. Spkr. in field. Bd. dir. AEA, Revegy, Inc., Milton HS Athletic Assn. Named Woman of Yr. Tech. (small/medium bus.), (WIT) Women in Tech., 2006; named one of 40 Under 40 Georgia's Brightest Stars, Ga. Trend Mag., 2002, Top 50 Entrepreneurs, Catalyst Mag., 2004, 2005; recipient Entrepreneurial Success award, Clarkson U., 2001, Entrepreneur of Yr. award, Ernest & Young, 2006. Office: InfoMentis Inc Ste 160 1750 Founders Parkway Alpharetta GA 30004 Office Phone: 770-667-5352. Office Fax: 770-752-9143.

REED, WILLIAM R., JR., bank executive; Chmn. Nat. Bank of Commerce; vice chmn. Nat. Commerce Bancorporation; COO Nat. Commerce Fin. Corp., 2000—03, pres., CEO, 2003—04; vice chmn. SunTrust Banks Inc., Atlanta, 2004—. Mailing: SunTrust Banks Inc PO Box 4418 Atlanta GA 30308-4418 Office Phone: 404-588-7711. Office Fax: 404-827-6173. *

REED, WILLIS, professional sports team executive; b. Hico, La., June 25, 1942; s. Willis and Inell R.; m. Geraldine Oliver (div.); children: Carl, Veronica.; m. Gale Reed. Student, Grambling Coll., 1960—64. Center, forward NY Knicks, 1964—74, head coach, 1977—78, spl. basketball adv., 2003—04; head coach Creighton U., Omaha, 1981—85, NJ Nets, 1988—89, sr. v.p. basketball ops., 1989—92, exec. v.p., gen mgr., 1992—96, sr. v.p. basketball ops, 1996—97, sr. v.p., 1997—2003; asst. coach Atlanta Hawks, 1985—87, Sacramento Kings, 1987—88; v.p. basketball ops. New Orleans/Okla. City (formerly Charlotte) Hornets, 2004—. Author: (with Phil Pepe) The View from the Rim, 1971. Named to NBA All-Star Team, 1965-71, Naismith Meml. Hall of Fame, 1982; named NBA Rookie of Yr., 1965, NBA All-Star Game MVP, 1970, NBA MVP, 1970, NBA Playoffs MVP, 1970, 73. Achievements include winning NBA Championships as a member of the Knicks, 1970, 73. Office: New Orleans Okla City Hornets 210 Park Ave Ste 1850 Oklahoma City OK 73102 *

REEDE, JOAN YVONNE, academic administrator, medical educator, pediatrician; b. Boston, 1953; 1 child, Loretta Jackson. BS, Brown U., 1977; MD, Mt. Sinai Sch. Med., 1980; MPH, Harvard Sch. Pub. Health, 1990, MS in Health Policy and Mgmt, 1992. Intern Johns Hopkins Hosp., Baltimore, 1980—81, pediat. resident, 1981—83; child psychology fellow Children's Hosp., Boston, 1986—88; med. dir. Cmty. Health Ctr., Boston, Commonwealth of Mass. Dept. Youth Services; dean diversity and cmty. partnership Harvard Med. Sch., 2002—, dir. minority faculty devel. program, faculty dir. cmty. outreach programs, assoc. prof. med.; asst. prof. maternal and child health Harvard Sch. Pub. Health; asst. in health policy Mass. Gen. Hosp. Founder Biomedical Sci. Careers Program, 1991; mem. bd. govs. Warren Grant Magnuson Clin. Ctr.; mem. adv. com. on minority health US Dept. Health and Human Services, 2000—, mem. adv. com. on genetics, health and soc., 2002—; bd. dirs. Mass. Tech. Park. Corp. Named a Ctr. for Disease Control and Prevention/U. Calif. Public Health Leadership Inst. Scholor; recipient Boston NAACP Health award, 1986, Community Service award, Epilepsy Assn. Mass., 1993, Exemplary Models Adminstrv. Leadership award, Am. Assn. U. Adminstrs., 1996. Achievements include being included in the Changing the Face of Medicine exhibit honoring women physicians. Office: Harvard Med Sch 25 Shattuck St Rm 152 Boston MA 02115

REEDER, CHARLES BENTON, retired economic consultant; b. Columbus, Ohio, Oct. 31, 1922; s. Charles Wells and Lydia (Morrow) R.; m. Carol Lincoln, June 25, 1949 (div. June 1972); 1 son, Charles; m. Beverly Lawrence, Nov. 11, 1972; adopted children: Keith, Sue. BS, Ohio State U., 1945, PhD, 1951; MBA, Harvard U., 1947. Econ. analyst Cleve. Elec. Illuminating Co., 1947-48; instr. Ohio State U., Columbus, 1948-51; econ. analyst, asst. economist Armstrong Cork. Co., Lancaster, Pa., 1951-55; assoc. economist E. I. DuPont de Nemours & Co., Inc., Wilmington, Del., 1955-70; chief economist E.I. DuPont de Nemours & Co., Inc., Wilmington, Del., 1970-85; pres. Charles Reeder Assocs., 1986-99. Bd. dirs. DP Am. Growth Fund, Amsterdam, The Netherlands. Author: The Sobering Seventies, 1981. Bd. dirs. Greater Wilmington Devel. Coun., 1963-84; treas. Del. Coun. on Econ. Edn., 1958-85, Bank of Del., Wilmington, 1975-92. 1st lt. Q.M.C., AUS, 1943-46. Recipient Silbert award Sterling Nat. Bank of N.Y., 1982 Fellow Nat. Assn. Bus. Economists (pres. 1966-67); mem. Nat. Bur. Econ. Research (past bd. dirs.) Clubs: Wilmington, Greenville Country. Presbyterian. Home: 1001 Kensington Ln Greenville DE 19807-2539 E-mail: cbrecon@aol.com.

REEDER, F. ROBERT, lawyer; b. Brigham City, Utah, Jan. 23, 1943; s. Frank O. and Helen H. (Heninger) R.; m. Joannie Anderson, May 4, 1974; children: David, Kristina, Adam. JD, U. Utah, 1967. Bar: Utah 1967, U.S. Ct. Appeals (10th cir.) 1967, U.S. Ct. Appeals (D.C. and 5th cirs.) 1979, U.S. Ct. Mil. Appeals 1968, U.S. Supreme Ct. 1972. Shareholder Parsons, Behle & Latimer, Salt Lake City, 1968—, bd. dirs., 1974—92. Bd. dir. Holy Cross Found., 1981-90, chmn., 1987-90; bd. dir. Holy Cross Hosp., 1990-93, treas., 1986-87, vice chmn., 1987-93; bd. dirs. Holy Cross Health Svcs. Utah, 1993-94, treas., 1993-94; bd. dir. Salt Lake Regional Med. Ctr.,

1995—, vice chmn., 1995-2000, chmn., 2000-07; trustee Univ. Hosp. Found.; hon. col. Salt Lake City Police, Salt Lake County Sheriff; bd. dir. Utah Hosp. and Health Sys. Assn.; 2005—, This is the Place Found., 2006-, Utah Facility Com., 2006-. With USAR, 1967—73. Mem. ABA, Utah Hosp. Health Sys. Assn. (bd. dir. 2006—), Utah State Bar, Salt Lake County Bar (ethics adv. com. 1989-94), Cottonwood Country Club (bd. dir. 1978-82, 83-86, pres. 1981-82), The Country Club (Salt Lake), Rotary. Office: Parsons Behle & Latimer PO Box 45898 Salt Lake City UT 84145-0898 Office Phone: 801-536-6769. Business E-Mail: bobreeder@parsonsbehle.com.

REEDER, JAMES ARTHUR, lawyer; b. Baton Rouge, June 29, 1933; s. James Brown and Grace (Britt) R.; m. Mary Leone Guthrie, Dec. 30, 1958; children: Mary Virginia, James Jr., Elizabeth Colby. BA, Washington and Lee U., Lexington, Va., 1955; LLB, U. Tex., 1960; JD, La. State U., 1961. Ptnr. Booth, Lockard, Jack et al, Shreveport, La., 1961-72; pres. and mgng. ptnr. Shreveport Broadcasting Co., 1972-86; CEO, mng. gen. ptnr. Radio USA Limited, Houston, 1986-89; pres. SW subsidiaries Sun Group, Inc., Houston, 1990-92; atty. Patton & Boggs, LLP, Washington, 1991-94; ptnr. Patton, Boggs LLP, Washington, 1994—. Dir. ABC Radio Sta. Affiliates adv. bd., N.Y.C., 1978-84. Dir. Boys Country, Houston, 1986-90; pres. Holiday in Dixie, Shreveport, 1968; chmn. Ambassadors Club, Shreveport, 1979. 1st lt. U.S. Army, 1955-57. Named La. Outstanding Young Man, La. Jaycees, 1969. Mem. ABA (bd. dirs. young lawyers sect. 1967-68, Gavel awards com. 1980), La. Bar Assn. (pres. young lawyers sect. 1966, La. Outstanding Young Lawyer award 1968), D.C. Bar Assn., Tex. Bar Assn., Nat. Assn. Broadcasters, Houston Country Club, Allegro Club (Houston). Roman Catholic.

REEDER, JOE ROBERT, lawyer, former federal official; b. Tacoma, Nov. 28, 1947; s. William Thomas and Marilyn Ruth (Parker) R.; m. Katharine Randolph Boyce, Jan 1, 1983; children: Rachael Anne, Aubrilyn, Julia, Kelsey. BS, U.S. Mil. Acad., West Point, NY, 1970; JD, U. Tex., 1975; LLM, Georgetown U., 1981. Bar: Tex. 1975, D.C. 1979, U.S. Dist. Ct. (so. dist.) Tex 1975, U.S. Ct. Appeals (5th cir.) 1989, U.S. Ct. Claims 1979, U.S. Dist. Ct. D.C. 1982, U.S. Ct. Appeals (Fed. cir.) 1984, U.S. Supreme Ct. 1988, U.S. Ct. Appeals (4th cir.) 1988, Md. 1989, U.S. Dist. Ct. (Md. dist) 1989, U.S. Dist. Ct. (no. dist.) Tex. 1991, U.S. Dist. Ct. (so. dist.) Tex. 1991. Commd. 2d lt. U.S. Army, 1970, advanced through grades to maj., 1985; law clk. to presiding justice U.S. Dist. Ct. (so. dist.) Tex., 1976; trial atty. litigation div. U.S. Army, Pentagon, DC, 1976-78, trial atty. contract appeals div., 1978-79; assoc. Patton, Boggs & Blow, Washington, 1979-82, ptnr., 1983-93; under sec. of U.S. Army U.S. Dept. Def., Washington, 1993; chmn. bd. Panama Canal Commn., 1994; now shareholder-in-charge Mid-Atlantic Region, bd. dir. Greenberg Traurig LLP, Washington. Mem. ABA (assoc. editor pub. contract law jour. 1985-93), ATLA, Am. Law Inst., Fed. Bar Assn., D.C. Bar Assn., Tex. Bar Assn., Bar Assn. 5th Fed. Circuit, Bd. Contract Appeals Bar Assn., Rotary. Episcopalian. Office: Greenberg Traurig LLP Ste 500 800 Connecticut Ave NW Washington DC 20006-2709 Office Phone: 202-331-3125. Office Fax: 202-331-3101. Business E-Mail: reederj@gtlaw.com.

REEDER, ROBERT HARRY, retired lawyer; b. Topeka, Dec. 3, 1930; s. William Harry and Florence Mae (Cochran) R. AB Washburn U., 1952, JD, 1960. Bar: U.S. Dist. Ct. Kans. 1960, Kans. 1960, U.S. Supreme Ct. 1968. Rsch. asst. Kans. Legis. Council Rsch. Dept., Topeka, 1955-60; asst. counsel Traffic Inst., Northwestern U., Evanston, Ill., 1960-67, gen. counsel, 1967-92; exec. dir. Nat. Com. on Uniform Traffic Laws and Ordinances, Evanston, 1982-90; ret. Co-author: Vehicle Traffic Law, 1974; The Evidence Handbook, 1980. Author: Interpretation of Implied Consent by the Courts, 1972. Served with U.S. Army, 1952-54. Mem. Com. Alcohol and Other Drugs (chmn. 1973-75). Republican. Methodist.

REED-PENTTINEN, DAPHNE STEVENSON, artist; b. Hartford, Conn. d. Edward McMurtry and Adele (Vaughan) Stevenson; m: Bruce Penttinen, 2001; children: Bonnie, Laurie, Rory. BA, Am. U., Washington, DC; MFA, U. Mass., Amherst, 1969. Rschr., author, editor, publisher, artist, Amherst, Mass., 1965—; instr., theatre dir. Mt. Holyoke Coll., South Hadley, Mass., 1970-72; tchr., adminstr., theatre dir. Hampshire Coll. and Amherst Coll., 1972-77; staff asst. Five Colls., Inc., Amherst, 1977-83; adminstr. U. Mass., Amherst, 1977-85; freelance editor, writer, artist, English lang. cons. Amherst, 1986—; writer, pub. Owl Pub., 1993—2006. Broadcaster Radio Reading Svcs. Western New Eng., Springfield, Mass., 1982-88; cons. in field. One woman show Artwork, 1994; author/dir. (plays) I Woman, 1970, This Thing Called Freedom, 1972; author The Secret World of Angels, 1999; editor Owl Angels Jour., 2000—06. Organizer Pioneer Valley (Mass.) chpt. P-FLAG, 1985, leader, 1994—, editor Owl Angels Jour. newsletter, 2001-06; founding charter mem. Com. on Race Rels., Amherst, 1970-73. Arts Coun. grantee, Amherst, 1987. Mem. Internat. Women's Writing Guild, Ednl. Theatre Assn., Mothers Against War (organizer 2002). Democrat. Congregationalist. Avocations: theater, literature, writing, painting, metaphysical and political research. Home: 305 Middle St Amherst MA 01002-3016 Office Phone: 413-253-3354. Personal E-mail: owlangels@aol.com.

REEDY, HARRY LEE, financial services executive; b. Lebanon, Pa., Dec. 25, 1945; s. Harry Lee and Charlotte (Weedmark) R.; m. Linda Bartley, Nov. 7, 1970; children: Jennifer Beth, Sara Emily. BS in Indsl Engring., Pa. State U., 1967; MBA, U. Conn., 1977. Cert. Six Sigma Master Black Belt 2006. Mgmt. asst. Bell Telephone Pa., Phila., 1967-70; field engring. rep. Travelers Cos., Hartford, Conn., 1971-72, ops. analyst, 1972-76, supervising ops. analyst, 1976-79, sr. mgmt. cons., 1979-83, adminstr. consumer affairs, 1983-85, asst. dir. consumer affairs, 1985-90; dir. corp. customer svc. John Hancock Fin. Svcs., Boston, 1990-91, dir. Ctr. for Quality, 1991-96; asst. v.p. quality State St. Corp., Boston, 1997—98, v.p., dir. quality, 1998—. Mem. consumer affairs com. Ins. Info. Inst., N.Y.C., 1988-90. Contbr. articles to trade publs. Participant Leadership Greater Hartford, 1985; bd. dirs., treas. Woodland Manor Condominium Assn., Manchester, Conn., 1986-87; bd. mgrs. Auburn Ct. Condominimum Assn., 2001-04; bd. examiners Malcolm Baldridge Nat. Quality award, 1995-2000, sr. examiner, 1997-2000, panel of judges, 2002-05, chmn., 2003-05; sr. examiner Mass. State Quality award, 1995-99, judge, 1999; judge New Hampshire Quality Award, 2002. With U.S. Army, 1968-70 Fellow Ins. Consumer Affairs Exch. (treas. 1985-87, v.p. 1987-88, pres. 1988-90). Soc. Consumer Affairs Profls. (v.p. New Eng. chpt. 1991-92); mem. Am. Coun. Life Ins. (consumer affairs com. 1987), Am. Soc. Quality Control, Am. productivity & Quality Ctr., Internat. Benchmarking Clearing House, Strategic Planning Inst., Mass. Coun. Quality (bd. dirs. 1998—, treas. exec. com. 1999-2001), Benchmarking Coun., Assn. Quality and Participation, Beta Gamma Sigma. Democrat. Avocations: photography, racquetball, swimming, reading. Home: 3 Auburn Ct # 2 Brookline MA 02446-6302 Office Phone: 617-662-7030. Business E-Mail: hlreedy@statestreet.com.

REEHER, JAMES IRWIN, minister; b. Sharon, Pa., Dec. 6, 1948; s. James William and Lillian (Irwin) R.; m. Marian Powell, Oct. 25, 1969; children: Elizabeth Margret, James Michael. BA, U. Tampa, 1975; MDiv, Emory U., 1978; DD, Boston U., 1989. Ordained to ministry United Ch. Ch., 1978. Min. Christ United Meth. Ch., Tampa, Fla., 1972-75, Lamar United Meth. Ch., Barnesville, Ga., 1975-78, 1st United Meth. Ch., Seffner, Fla., 1986-90; asst. min. Grace United Meth. Ch., Venice, Fla., 1978-79; founding min. 1st United Meth. Ch., Sarasota, Fla., 1980-86; min. Forest Hills United Meth. Ch., Tampa, 1990—. Del. bd. ordained ministry Tampa Dist., 1987—; del. stewardship com. Fla. United Meth. Ch., Tampa, 1988—; bd. dirs. Jim Russo Prison Ministries, Bradenton, Fla., 1990—; chmn. anti-gambling campaign Fla. United Meth. Conf., 1986; v.p. Shade and Fresh Water, Inc. Founding chmn. East Hillsborough Orgn., Seffner, 1988; bd. dirs. Life Enrichment Sr. Ctr., Tampa, 1990—; founder Family Hall of Fame. Recipient Outstanding Religious Leader award Sarasota Jaycees, 1985. Mem. Assn. for Clin. Pastoral Edn., Alban Inst., North Tampa Ministerial Assn., West Orange Ministerial Assn. Democrat. Office: First United Meth Ch 125 Lakeview Dr Winter Garden FL 34787 Home: 10370 Frankie Lane Dr Saint James City FL 33956-3233

REEMA, JAIN, pharmacist, pharmaceutical executive; d. Ashok and Kusum Jain. BS, PharmD, Ernest Mario Sch. Pharmacy, New Brunswick, NJ, 2003. Cert. pharmacist NJ. Bd. Pharmacy, 2002. Pharmacist CVS Pharmacy, Plainfield, NJ, 1998—2006, Mandell's Pharmacy, New Brunswick, NJ, 2002—; assoc. dir. Johnson & Johnson PRD, Titusville, NJ, 2003—. Office: Johnson & Johnson PRD 1125 Trenton Harbourton Road Titusville NJ 08560 Office Phone: 609-730-7663. Business E-Mail: rjain@brmus.jnj.com.

REENSTJERNA, FREDERICK ROBERTS, librarian, writer; b. Lexington, SC, Sept. 30, 1948; s. Otto Frederick and Miriam Swann (Roberts) R.; m. Hope Shields, June 3, 1971; 1 child, Elisabeth Shields. BA in Am. History, Coll. of Charleston, 1969; MLS, U. Md., 1971; M Adminstrn. in Human Resources, Lynchburg Coll., 1981; EdD, W.Va. U., 1991. Reference specialist congl. rsch. svc. Libr. of Congress, Washington, 1972-75; dir. Franklin County Libr., Rocky Mount, Va., 1975-77; br. libr. Hollins Br. Libr. Roanoke County (Va.) Pub. Libr., 1977-82, head reference main libr., 1982-84; bus. mgr. autism tng. ctr. Marshall U., Huntington, W.Va., 1984-86, asst. mgr. housing, 1986-88, head pub. svcs. Morrow Libr., 1989, asst. prof. instrnl. tech. Coll. Edn., 1989-90; freelance writer, Roseburg, Oreg., 1990-91; rsch. libr. Douglas County Mus., Roseburg, 1991—. Author: Library Survival Skills: A Guide to the Resources of the James Morrow Library, 1990, (with Jena Mitchell) Life in Douglas County, Oregon: The Western Experience, 1993; contbr. articles to various publs. Mem. needs task force Douglas County United Way, 1994. Mem. Soc. Am. Archivists. Avocation: fly fishing. Office: Douglas County Mus 123 Museum Dr Roseburg OR 97470-5308 Home: 1760 NW 17th St Corvallis OR 97330-1919

REEP, EDWARD ARNOLD, artist; b. Bklyn., May 10, 1918; s. Joseph and Elsie (Abramson) R.; m. Karen Patricia Stevens, Dec. 9, 1942; children— Susan Kay, Cristine Elyse, Janine J., Mitchell Jules. Student, Art Center Coll. Design, 1936-41. Instr. painting and drawing Art Center Coll. Design, Los Angeles, 1946-50, Chouinard Art Inst., Los Angeles, 1950-69; prof. painting, chmn. dept., artist in residence E. Carolina U., 1970-85, prof. emeritus, 1985—. Cons. editor Van Nostrand Reinhold Pub. Co.; ofcl. war artist-corr. WWII, Africa and Italy. Author: The Content of Watercolor, 1968, A Combat Artist in World War II, 1987; shows include Whitney Mus. Am. Art Ann., N.Y.C., 1946-48, Los Angeles County Mus. Ann., 1946-60, Corcoran Gallery Art Biennial, Washington, 1949, Nat. Gallery Art, Washington, 1945, They Drew Fire, 2000, Mus. Modern Art, N.Y.C.; represented in permanent collections Los Angeles County Mus., U.S. War Dept., Grunwald Graphic Arts Collection, UCLA, Nat. Mus. Am. Art, Washington, Lytton Collection, Los Angeles, State of Calif. Collection, Sacramento. Guggenheim fellow, 1945-46; Nat. Endowment for Arts grantee, 1975 Mem. AAUP, Nat. Watercolor Soc. (past pres., Lifetime Achievement award 2002), Watercolor USA Honor Soc. (lifetime achievement gold medal 1997). Democrat. Home: 9021 Crowningshield Dr Bakersfield CA 93311-1901 *I once was consumed by the desire to become an artist. I feel no differently today. There is work ahead. If I had set goals for myself I no longer can recall what they may have been; I go along painting as well or as inventively as I can. Never have I sacrificed living life as I feel I must for my art. My work is a reflection of my life—experiences real and imagined.*

REES, CLIFFORD HARCOURT, JR., (TED REES), consulting company executive, retired trade association administrator, military officer; b. Newport News, Va., Dec. 11, 1936; s. Clifford Harcourt Sr. and Mary Evelyn (Brooks) R.; m. Joan Elizabeth Mittong, July 26, 1958; children—Clifford Harcourt III, Steven M., Daniel B., William B. BS in Fgn. Svc., Georgetown U., 1958; MS in Polit. Sci., Auburn U., 1969; grad., Air War Coll., Montgomery, Ala., 1978; grad. program for sr. exec. in nat. and internat. security, JFK Sch. Govt., Harvard U. Commd. 2d lt. U.S. Air Force, 1958; advanced through grades to lt. gen., 1988; comdr. 421st Tactical Fighter Squadron, Udorn Royal Thai AFB, 1974-75; chief, house liaison office U.S. Ho. Reps., Washington, 1978-80; asst. col. assignments Randolph AFB, 1980-82; vice-comdr. Air Force Manpower and Personnel Ctr., 1982; dep. dir. legis. liaison Office Sec. Air Force, 1982-84, dir. legis. liaison, 1984-86; comdr. USAF Air Defense Weapons Ctr., Tyndall AFB, Fla., 1986-88; vice comdr. in chief USAF in Europe, Ramstein AB, Federal Republic of Germany, 1988-92, ret., 1992; founder, pres. Rees Group Cons., 1992—; pres. Air Conditioning and Refrigeration Inst., Arlington, Va., 1992—2002. U.S. rep. to v.p. Internat. Coun. Mil. Sports, Brussels, 1982-94; dir. bd. dirs. Armed Forces Benefit Assn. Investment Mgmt. Co., 1996—. Decorated D.S.M. with one oak leaf cluster, DFC with one oak leaf cluster, Legion of Merit with one oak leaf cluster, Meritorious Svc. medal with one oak leaf cluster, Air medal with 11 oak leaf clusters, Das Grosse Verdienstkreuz Mit Stern, Fed. Republic Germany; named comdr. Order of Meritorious Svc. Internat. Mil. Sports Coun., 1993, Order of the Sword, US Air Forces in Europe, 1992. Mem. Delta Phi Epsilon (v.p. membership 1957-58, nat. pres. 1984-86) Methodist. Home: 20 Spring Valley Ct Pinehurst NC 28374 E-mail: ted@thereesgroup.com.

REES, ELAINE, chemistry educator; b. Springhill, La., Feb. 23, 1956; d. Jimmie Dale and Lillie Serena Jackson; m. Dwane Rees, Aug. 1, 1980; children: Kristin Lynne, Kameka Anne, Kameron Michael. BS, La. Tech., Ruston, 1978; MS, Ctrl. Mo. State U., Warrensburg, 1994. Gen. sci. tchr. Plaquemine Jr. HS, La., 1978—80; sci. tchr. Vandalia Van-Far HS, Mo., 1980—90; chemistry tchr. Ft. Osage HS, Independence, Mo., 1991—. Mem.: Mo. State Tchrs. Assn. Avocations: gardening, sewing, travel. Home: 316 SE 2d St Blue Springs MO 64014 Office: Ft Osage HS 2101 N Twyman Independence MO 64058 Business E-Mail: erees@fortosage.net.

REES, FRANK WILLIAM, JR., architect; b. Rochester, NY, June 5, 1943; s. Frank William and Elizabeth R. (Miller) R.; m. Joan Mary Keevers, Apr. 1, 1967; children: Michelle, Christopher. BS in Architecture, U. Okla., 1970; postgrad., Harvard U., Boston, 1979-90; OPM, Harvard U., 1990; DArch, U. Hawaii, 2001. Registered architect, 39 states & D.C.; cert. Nat. Coun. Archtl. Registration Bds.; registered interior designer. Sales mgr. Sta. KFOM, Oklahoma City, 1967-70; project architect Benham-Blair & Affiliates, Oklahoma City, 1970-75; pres., CEO, founder Rees Assocs., Inc., Oklahoma City, 1975—. Pres., chmn. bd. Weatherscan Radio Network, Oklahoma City, 1973-78; chmn. bd. Weatherscan Internat., Oklahoma City, 1972-78; pres. Frontier Communications, Oklahoma City, 1980-84; chmn. architecture bd. U. Okla., Norman, 1988-91; bd. dirs. Century, Inc., Oklahoma City. Past pres. Lake Hefner Trails, Oklahoma City, Hosp. Hospitality House, Oklahoma City, Oklahoma City Beautiful; mem. Leadership Oklahoma City. Mem. AIA, Am. Assn. Hosp. Architects, Am. Healthcare Assn., Tex. Hosp. Assn., World Pres. Orgn. (chmn. 1997-98), Assisted Living Fedn. of Am., Am. Assn. Homes and Svcs. for the Agig. Home: 1104 Stone Gate Dr Irving TX 75063-4676 also: 1801 N Lamar St Ste 600 Dallas TX 75202-1711

REES, GROVER JOSEPH, III, lawyer, government official, diplomat; b. New Orleans, Oct. 11, 1951; s. Grover Joseph and Patricia (Byrne) R.; m. Lan Dai Nguyen; 1 child, Grover Joseph. BA, Yale U., New Haven, 1975; JD, La. State U., Baton Rouge, 1978. Bar: La. 1978, U.S. Supreme Ct. 1982. Asst. prof. law U. Tex., Austin, 1979-86; spl. asst. to Atty. Gen. US Dept. Justice, Washington, 1985, spl. counsel jud. selection, 1985-86; chief justice High Ct. Am. Samoa, Pago Pago, 1986-88, assoc. justice, 1988-91; gen. counsel US Immigration and Naturalization Svc., Washington, 1991—93; dir., chief counsel subcommittee on internat. ops. & human rights Com. Internat. Rels., 1995—2001, counsel, 2001—02; US amb. to East Timor US Dept. State, 2002—06, spl. rep. social issues, 2006—. Editor in chief La. Law Rev., 1977-78. Justice of Peace, New Haven, 1973-75. Mem. Order of Coif. Republican. Roman Catholic. Office: US Dept State 2201 C St NW Washington DC 20520 E-mail: reesgj@aol.com.

REES, LANE CHARLES, industrial relations consultant; b. Longview, Tex., June 23, 1951; s. Holly Elias and Charlene Elizabeth (Quin) R.; m. Brenda Faye Anderson, July 1, 1978; children: Brian Andrew, Lauren Catherine. BBA in Mgmt. magna cum laude, Tex. A&M U., 1973, MEd in Ednl. Adminstrn., 1978. Pers. rep. Tex. A&M U., College Station, 1973—77; v.p. Brazos Gen. Svcs., Bryan, Tex., 1977—78; successively pers. office supr., wage and salary adminstr., employee rels. rep., sr. employee rels. rep. ARCO, various cities, Tex., 1979—83, from sr. employee rels. rep. to employee rels. dir. Anchorage and Kuparuk, Alaska, 1983—87, dir. employee rels. Prudhoe Bay, Alaska, 1987—90, dir. human resources dept. engring., 1990—94; sr. human rels. advisor Algeria and engring. exploration Arco Internat. Oil and Gas, Plano, Tex., 1994—99; pres. Human Resources Solutions, Inc., Dallas/Santa Rosa Beach, Tex., 1999—. Ptnr. Rees and Assocs., Anchorage, Tex., Fla., 1978—. Mem. editl. staff Conf. Leadership, 1978. Vice chmn. Rep. Party of Alaska, 1993-94, chair, 1994; vice-chmn. Walton Co. GOP exec. com., 1999-2005; mem. ctrl. com. State of Alaska, 1990-94; chmn. utility regulatory commn. municipality of Anchorage, 1989-91; mem. com. sec. United Meth. Com. Commn., Nashville, 1988-97; evangelism chmn., mem. adv. coun. St. John United Meth. Ch., Anchorage, 1986-91, chmn. adminstrv. bd., 1991-93; trustee Nat. Found. Evangelism, Lake Junaluska, NC, 1988—, exec. com., 1995—, chmn. 2002—; conf. lay leader Ala. Missionary Conf.-Meth. Ch., 1992-94; chmn. evangelism and mem. adminstrv. bd. 1st United Meth. Ch., Allen, Tex., 1995-97; mem. adminstrv. bd. Suncreek (Tex.) United Meth. Ch., 1997-99, adv. bd. Freeport United Meth. Ch., lay del. to ann. conf., 1995-2001; active Port Washington United Meth. Ch., 2001—, mem. ch. coun. 2003—, del. ann. conf., 2004—; mem. internat. bd. George Bush Ctr., Tex. A&M U., 1996—; bd. dirs. Walton County C. of C., 1999—2005, interim pres., CEO, 2005; bd. dirs. Fla. Assn. Counties, 2002-04, Fla. Assn. Counties Trust, 2001-04, vice chair, 2002-04; commr. Walton County, 2000-04; vice chair Walton Bd. County Commrs., 2000-01, chair, 2001-02; mem. adv. bd. Walton Tourist Devel. Coun., 2001-04; mem. adv. coun. U. West Fla. Coll. Bus., 2002—. Recipient Denman award Alaska Missionary Conf. United Meth. Ch., 1989, Legis. citation State of Alaska, 1989. Mem. Acad. Mgmt., Tex. A&M U. Assn. Former Students (nat. councilman 1987-91, bd. dirs. 1996—), Am. Numis. Assn., Alaska Soc. SAR (pres. 1989-90, trustee Nat. Soc. 1991-94, Silver Good Citizenship award 1989), Phi Eta Sigma, Phi Kappa Phi, Sigma Iota Epsilon (pres. 1972-73), Beta Gamma Sigma. Avocations: golf, racquetball, reading, travel, coin collecting/numismatics. Home: 323 Lakeview Dr Santa Rosa Beach FL 32459-6604 Office Phone: 850-231-0735. Business E-Mail: solutionhr@aol.com.

REES, MARTIN JOHN, astronomy educator; b. York, Eng., June 23, 1942; s. Reginald and Joan (Bett) R. MA, PhD, Cambridge U., Eng., 1967; DSc (hon.), Sussex U., Eng., 1990, Leicester U., 1993, Uppsala U., Sweden, 1995, Keele U., Eng., 1995, Newcastle U., 1995, Copenhagen U., 1995, Toronto U., Can., 1997, Durham U., Eng., 1999, Oxford U., 2000. Rsch. fellow Calif. Tech. Inst., 1968; vis. rsch. fellow Inst. for Advanced Study, Princeton, NJ, 1969, 82, 96, 97; vis. scientist Harvard U., Cambridge, Mass., 1972, 87-90; Regents fellow Smithsonian Instn., 1984-87; prof. Sussex U., 1972-73; Plumian prof. astronomy Cambridge U., 1973-91; dir. Inst. Astronomy, Cambridge, 1977-91; rsch. prof. Royal Soc. Cambridge U., England, 1992—2003, prof. cosmology and astrophysics, 2002—; master Trinity Coll., Cambridge, 2004—; astronomer royal, 1995—2005. Fellow King's Coll., Cambridge U., England, 1969—2003; hon. fellow Trinity Coll., 1995—, Jesus Coll., 1996—, Cardiff U., Wales, 1998, Darwin Coll., 2004—; vis. prof. Harvard U., Princeton U., Calif. Tech., Imperial Coll., London, Leicester U., hon. prof.; bd. trustees Brit. Mus., 1996—2002, Nat. Endowment for Sci., Tech, and Arts, 1998—2001, Inst. for Advanced Study, Princeton, 1998—, Kennedy Meml. Trust, England, 1999—2004, Inst. for Pub. Policy Rsch., 2001—, Nat. Mus. of Sci. and Tech., 2003—. Author: (with M.C. Begelman) Gravity's Fatal Attraction, 1995, Perspectives in Astrophysical Cosmology, 1995, Before the Beginning, 1997, Just Six Numbers, 1999, Our Cosmic Habitat, 2001, Our Final Century?, 2003. Decorated officer Order of Arts and Letters (France); recipient Heinemann prize, Am. Inst. Physics, 1984, Gold medal, Royal Astron. Soc., 1987, Balzan prize, 1989, Robinson prize, 1990, Bruce medal, 1993, Sci. Writing award, Am. Inst. Physics, 1996, Bower award, Franklin Inst., 1998, Rossi prize, AAS, 2000, Cosmology prize, Gruber Found., 2001, Einstein award, World Sci. Coun., 2003, Crafoord prize, Royal Swedish Acad., 2005, Niels Bohr prize, UNESCO, 2005; created knight bachelor, 1992, created life peer, 2005. Fellow AAAS, Royal Soc. London (pres. 2005—, Henry Norris Russell lectureship, 2004), Royal Netherlands Acad. Arts and Scis., Indian Acad. Scis. (hon.), Russian Acad. Scis. (hon.), Swedish Acad. Scis., Am. Philosophy Soc.; mem. NAS (fgn. assoc.), Pontifical Acad. Scis., Academia Europea, Inst. Physics (Eng.) (Guthrie prize 1990—), Royal Astron. Soc. (pres. 1992-94), Brit. Assn. Advancement Sci. (pres. 1994-95), Norwegian Acad. Sci., Acad. Lincei (Rome), Finnish Acad. Arts and Sci. Anglican. Office: Inst Astronomy Cambridge England CB3 0HA also: Trinity Coll Cambridge CB2 1TQ England

REES, NINA SHOKRAII, educational association administrator, former federal agency administrator; b. Iran; BS in Psychology, Va. Polytech and State U., 1989; MS in Internat. Transactions, George Mason U., 1991. Mem. staff Rep. Porter Goss, Washington, 1990—92; policy analyst Ams. for Tax Reform, Washington, 1992—93; dir. outreach programs Inst. for Justice, Washington, 1993—97; chief edn. analyst The Heritage Found., Washington, 1997—2000; with Bush/Cheney transition team, 2000—01; aide to v.p. U.S. Govt., Washington, 2001—02; asst. deputy sec. Innovation and Improvement US Dept. Edn., Washington, 2002—06; sr. v.p. strategic initiatives Knowledge Learning Corp. Sch. Partnerships, 2006—. Contbr. commentaries in newspapers, TV, radio on ednl. issues, 1995. Education adviser to Bush Campaign, Phila., 2000; contbr. to Rep. platform in edn. area Rep. Paty, 2000. Recipient Rita Ricardo Campbell award, Heritage Found., 1999. Office: Knowledge Learning Corp 650 NE Holladay St # 1400 Portland OR 97232 Office Phone: 202-205-4500. Business E-Mail: nina.rees@ed.gov. *

REES, NORMA S., academic administrator; b. NYC, Dec. 27, 1929; d. Benjamin and Lottie (Schwartz) D.; m. Raymond R. Rees, Mar. 19, 1960; children— Evan Lloyd, Raymond Arthur BA, Queens Coll., 1952; Ma, Bklyn. Coll., 1954; PhD, NYU, 1959; D of Arts and Letters honoris causa, John F. Kennedy U., 2001. Cert. speech-language pathology, audiology. Prof. communicative disorders Hunter Coll., NYC, 1967-72; exec. officer, speech and hearing scis. grad. sch. CUNY, NYC, 1972-74, assoc. dean for grad. studies, 1974-76, dean grad. studies, 1976-82; vice chancellor for acad. affairs U. Wis., Milw., 1982-85, from 1986, acting chancellor, 1985-86; vice chancellor for acad. policy and planning Mass. Bd. Regents for Higher Edn., Boston, 1987-90; pres. Calif. State U. East Bay, Hayward, 1990—. Chmn. Commn. Recognition of Postsecondary Accreditation, 1994-96; mem. adv. com. quality and integrity U.S. Dept. Edn., commn. on internat. edn. Coun. on Higher Edn. Accreditation, 2003—. Contbr. articles to profl. jours. Trustee Citizens Govtl. Rsch. Bur., Milw., 1985-87; active Task Force on Wis. World Trade Ctr., 1985-87; bd. dirs. Am. Assn. State

Colls. and Univs., 1995-97, Coun. of Postsecondary Accreditation, Washington, 1985-94, Greater Boston YWCA, 1987-90; mem. Calif. Sch. to Career Coun.; bd. dir. Econ. Devel. Alliance for Bus., Alameda County, 1995—; sec. edn. Nat. Adv. Com. Institutional Quality and Integrity, 1998-2002; bd. dirs. Bay Area World Trade Ctr., 2001—, Alameda County Health Care Found., 2002-. Fellow Am. Speech-Lang-Hearing Assn. (honors); mem. Am. Coun. Edn. (com. internat. edn. 1991-93), Am. Assn. Colls. and Univs. (chair task force on quality assessment 1991-92), Nat. Assn. State Univs. and Land Grant Colls. (exec. com. divsn. urban affairs 1985-87, com. accreditation 1987-90), Hayward C. of C. (bd. dirs. 1995-98), Oakland C. of C. (bd. dirs. 1997-2004). Office: Calif State Univ East Bay 25800 Carlos Bee Blvd Hayward CA 94542-3001 Home Phone: 510-889-8069; Office Phone: 510-885-3877. E-mail: norma.rees@csueastbay.edu.

REES, RAYMOND F., military officer; b. Pendleton, Oreg., Sept. 29, 1944; s. Raymond Emmett and Lorna Doone (Gemmell) R.; m. Karen Kristine Young, Nov. 1966 (div. Mar. 1974); children: Raymond Gordon, Christian Frederick; m. Mary Len Middleton, Dec. 30, 1977; 1 child, Carrie Evelyn. BS, U.S. Mil. Acad., 1966; JD, U. Oreg., 1976. Commd. 2d lt. U.S. Army, 1966, 2005—; platoon leader, troop exec. officer, co. comdr. 2d Armored Cavalry Regiment, Bamberg, Fed. Republic Germany; troop comdr. 2-17 Cavalry 101 Airborn divsn., Camp Eagle, Vietnam, 1969; troop exec. officer 1-17 Cavalry 82 Airborn divsn., Ft. Bragg, N.C., 1972; resigned U.S. Army, 1973; with Oreg. Army Nat. Guard, 1973—, advanced through grades to maj. gen., 1990; asst. ops. officer Infantry Brigade; co. comdr. 2d Battalion, 162d Infantry, Corvallis, Oreg.; with 116th Armored Calvary Regiment, 1976-87; comdr. 116th cavalry regiment, adjutant gen. Oreg. Army Nat. Guard, 1987-91; dir. Army N.G., 1991-92; vice chief N.G. Bur., Washington, 1992-94; adjutant gen. Oreg. N.G., 1994-99; vice chief N.G. Bur., Washington, 1999—2002, acting chief, 2002—03; chief of staff Hdqrs. NORAD and U.S. No. Command, 2003—05. Decorated Bronze Star, Legion of Merit, D.S.M., Def. Disting. Svc. medal. Mem. VFW, Adjutant Gen. Assn. U.S., Nat. Guart Assn. U.S., Assn. of U.S. Army, Oreg. Nat. Guard Assn., U.S. Armor Assn., Oreg. Bar Assn., Am. Legion, Mil. Order World Wars, West Point Soc. Oreg., 101st Airborne Div. Assn., 116th Armored Cavalry Assn., 41st Infantry Div. Assn., Elks. Office Phone: 503-584-3991.

REESE, C. RICHARD, data processing executive; BS, MS in Ceramic Engring., Clemson Univ.; MBA, Harvard Univ. Former cons.; former pres., dir. PRISM Internat. trade assn.; lectr. Harvard Bus. Sch.; pres., CEO Iron Mountain Inc., Boston, 1981—95, chmn., pres., CEO, 1995—2005, chmn., CEO, 2005—. Bd. dir. Bird Dog Solutions, Continental Fire & Safety LLC; mem. investment com. Schooner Capital LLC. Recipient New England Entrepreneur of Yr., Ernst & Young, 2003. Office: Iron Mountain 745 Atlantic Ave Boston MA 02111 Office Phone: 617-535-4766. *

REESE, CARL THOMAS, urologist; b. Scranton, Pa., Dec. 7, 1961; s. T. Carlyle and Ruth May Reese; m. Valerie Ward, Nov. 14, 1981; children: T. Carlyle, Jason B., Daniel Ward. BSc cum laude, King's Coll., Wilkes-Barre, Pa., 1989; MD, Pa. State U., Hershey, Pa., 1997, MS in Health Evaluation Sci., 2003. Diplomate Am. Bd. Urology, 2004. Resident in urology M.S. Hershey Med. Ctr., 1997—2002; attending urologist coll. medicine Pa. State U., Hershey, 2002—, asst. prof. surgery coll. medicine, 2002—. Pres. med. staff Hershey Outpatient Surgery Ctr., 2004—; mem. curriculum com. coll. medicine Pa. State U., 2006—, mem. com. cancer inst., 2006—. Mem. editl. bd., reviewer: Jour. Urology; contbr. articles to profl. jours. Lt. col. US Army, 1979—2006. Decorated Armed Forces Res. medal US Army, Armed Forces Res. Commendation medal, Army Commendation medal with oak leaf cluster, Nat. Def. medal, Army Achievement medal with oak leaf cluster, Expert Field Med. badge, Meritorious Svc. medal, NATO medal, Armed Forces Expeditionary medal, Global War on Terror Svc. medal, Global War on Terror Expeditionary medal; recipient Scholars of Surgery award, Bristol- Myers Squibb, 1997, Resident in Urology award, Pfizer, 2002, Faculty Professionalism/ Humanism in Surgery award, Dept. Surgery, Pa. State U. Coll. Medicine, 2004. Fellow: ACS; mem.: Dauphin County Med. Soc., Pa. Med. Soc., Urol. Assn. Pa. (mem. exec. bd. 2006—), N.G. Assn. US, Alpha Omega Alpha. Avocations: hiking, skiing, running. Office: Division of Urology H055 500 Univ Dr Hershey PA 17036 Office Phone: 717-531-8848.

REESE, CHARLES EDGAR, columnist; b. Washington, Ga., Jan. 29, 1937; s. Edgar Ernest and Neoma (Moody) R.; m. Gretchen Elise Krughoff, May 16, 1965 (div. July 1984); children: Benjamin, Alice, Theodore. PhD (hon.), Webber Coll., 1989. Caption writer Planet Newspictures Ltd., London, 1956-57; reporter Pensacola (Fla.) News-Jour., 1957-67; account exec. Dodson, Craddock & Born, Pensacola, 1967-69, Fry, Hammond & Born, Pensacola, 1971-72; chief bur. media svcs. State of Fla. Dept. of Commerce, Tallahassee, 1969-71; asst. metro editor Orlando Sentinel, 1972-75, asst. to pub., 1975-78, columnist, mem. editorial bd., 1978—. Author: Great Gods of the Potomac, Common Sense for the 80s. Active Hist. Commn., Pensacola, 1968; bd. dirs. Holocaust Meml., Orlando, 1985-90. With USAR, 1959-65. Named Best Columnist, Fla. Press Club, 1984, Fla. Soc. Newspaper Editors. Mem. SCV. Avocations: pistol shooting, hunting, sketching. Office: Orlando Sentinel 633 N Orange Ave Orlando FL 32801-1349 Address: King Features Syndicate 235 E 45th St New York NY 10017

REESE, CHARLES WOODROW, JR., lawyer, real estate developer; b. San Antonio, June 21, 1944; s. Charles Woodrow and Mary Ruth (Gott) R.; m. Jill Fritschi, Aug. 10, 1979; children: Clarissa, Alexandra. BA cum laude, Washington and Lee U., 1966; JD, U. Calif., Berkeley, 1969. Bar: Calif. 1970, US Sup. Ct. 1976. Assoc. McCutchen, Doyle, Brown & Enersen, San Francisco, 1969-75; staff atty. Kaiser Industries Corp., Oakland, Calif., 1975-78; asst. gen. csl. Kaiser Cement Corp., Oakland, 1978-86; mng. dir. Reese Interests, Houston, 1978—; mng. trustee Clotilde deMartini Trusts, San Francisco, 1977-; prin Lempres & Wulfsberg PC, Oakland, 1986-98; exec. v.p. Wulfsberg Reese & Sykes PC, 1998-2002; pres., CFO Wulfsberg Reese Colvig & Firstman PC, 2002—. Hon. trustee Orinda Found., 1976-79; bd. dirs. Planned Parenthood Alameda/San Francisco, 1981-83, Brown and Caldwell, Walnut Creek, 1987-, PLA Holdings, Inc., Port Costa, 1991-2000. Robert E. Lee Rsch. scholar, 1965-66. Mem. State Bar Calif., ABA, Bar Assn. San Francisco, Alameda County Bar Assn. (coms.), Omicron Delta Upsilon, Pacific Union Club (San Francisco), Orinda (Calif.) Country Club. Republican. Episcopalian. Home: 89 La Salle Piedmont CA 94611 Office: 300 Lakeside Dr 24th Fl Oakland CA 94612-3534 E-mail: creese@wulfslaw.com.

REESE, DELLA (DELOREESE PATRICIA EARLY), singer, actress; b. Detroit, July 6, 1931; d. Richard and Nellie Early; m. Vermont Adolphus Bon Taliaferro (div.); m. Leroy Basil Gray (div.); m. Franklin Thomas Lett, Jr. Student, Wayne U. Ordained to ministry Ch. Understanding Principles for Better Living Inc., April, 1987. Choir singer, 1938—, with Mahalia Jackson troupe, 1945-49, Erskine Hawkins, N.Y.C.; solo artist, 1957—; organized gospel group at Wayne U.; appearances include: (radio shows) with Robert Q. Lewis; (TV series) Della, 1969, The Voyage of the Yes, 1972, Twice in a Lifetime, 1974, Cop on the Beat, 1975, Chico and the Man, 1974, 76-78, Nightmare in Badham County, 1976 (Emmy nomination), Roots: The Next Generation, 1979, It Takes Two, 1982, Charlie & Co., 1985, 86, The Kid Who Loved Christmas, 1990, The Royal Family, 1991, You Must Remember This, 1992, Touched By an Angel, 1994-2003, A Match Made in Heaven, 1997, Miracle in the Woods, 1997, Emma's Wish, 1998, The Secret Path, 1999, Having Our Say: The Delany Sisters' First 100 Years, 1999; spl. appearances with Jackie Gleason, Ed Sullivan, McCloud, 1971, Sanford and Son, 1972, Welcome Back, Kotter, 1975, The A-Team, 1983, Night Court, 1984, MacGyver, 1985, Designing Women, 1986, L.A. Law, 1986, Married People, 1990, Dream On, 1990, Picket Fences, 1992, Promised Land, 1996, Anya's Bell, 1999, The Moving of Sophia Myles, 2000; guest host The Tonight Show; actress (films) Let's Rock, 1958, Psychic Killer, 1975, Harlem Nights, 1989, A Thin Line Between Love and Hate, 1996, (voice) Dinosaur, 2000, Beauty Shop, 2005, (plays) Same Time Next Year, Ain't Misbehavin, Blues in the Night, The Last Minstrel Show; recs. for Jubilee, RCA Victor Records, ABC Paramount Records, Jazz Ala Carte, AIR Co. (Grammy nomination 1987); author: Angels Along the Way, 1997, (voice) Dinosaur, 2000. Voted Most Promising Singer of Yr. 1957; recipient Image awards, 1996, 98-2000, Star on Walk of Fame, 1994. Office: William Morris Agy c/o Jeff Kolodny 151 S El Camino Dr Beverly Hills CA 90212-2775

REESE, FRANCIS EDWARD, retired chemical company executive, consultant; b. Monaca, Pa., Nov. 3, 1919; s. Francis Edward and Vivian Iris (Hancuff) R.; m. Katherine Mary McBrien, June 29, 1946; 1 son, Francis Edward III. BS in Chem. Engring, Purdue U., 1941. Registered profl. engr., Pa. From rsch. engr. Plastics Divsn. to sr. v.p. Monsanto Co., 1941—79, sr. v.p., 1979-84. Pres. FTR Assocs., Inc., 1993-2005; mem. engring. found. adv. coun. U. Tex. Fellow AAAS, Am. Inst. Chem. Engrs.; mem. Am. Chem. Soc., Nat. Soc. Profl. Engrs., Soc. Chem. Industry, Tau Beta Pi, Phi Lambda Upsilon. Home and Office: Rydal Pk 271W 1515 The Fairway Rydal PA 19046-1435 Office Phone: 215-885-2095. Personal E-mail: ftrassoc@aol.com.

REESE, HARRY EDWIN, JR., electronics executive; b. Balt., Oct. 27, 1928; s. Harry Edwin and Margery Lee (Stroud) R.; m. Elizabeth Syra Pfeiffer, Oct. 15, 1955; children: Clifford Owen, Susan Syra, Peter Eyre. BSEE, Tufts U., 1950; MS in Stats., Villanova U., 1960. Engr. Philco Corp., Phila., 1950-54; project engr. Burroughs Corp., Paoli, Pa., 1956-59, dept. mgr., 1959-65, GE Co., King of Prussia, Pa., 1965-69; group staff mgr. Burroughs Corp., Paoli, Pa., 1969-75, gen. mgr. Plainfield, NJ, 1975-82, corp. staff dir. Detroit, 1982-83; v.p. quality assurance Am. Electronic Labs., Inc., Lansdale, Pa., 1984—90, ret., 1990. Chmn. Charlestown Twp. Planning Commn., Pa., 1973-75. With U.S. Army, 1954-56. Fellow IEEE (life, pres. Reliability Soc. 1969-70, gen. chmn. Rams symposium 1968, chmn. bd. 1969, Centennial medal 1984); mem. Nat. Mgmt. Assn. (life, chmn. formation com. Am. Electronics Labs. chpt. 1985, Leadership award 1973, 86), Lake Hopatcong Yacht Club (commodore 2000-01), Masons, Rotary (Paul Harris fellow, treas.). Republican. Episcopalian. Avocations: carpentry, architecture, boating, antiques, travel. Home: 300 Willow Valley Lakes Dr Apt B408 Willow Street PA 17584

REESE, HAYNE WARING, psychologist, educator; b. Comanche, Tex., Jan. 14, 1931; s. Tom F. and Marion (Waring) R.; m. Patsy Atwood, Aug. 24, 1957 (div. Apr. 1967); children: Anne, William, Margaret; m. Nancy Mann, Dec. 16, 1967; 1 child, Bradley. Student, So. Meth. U., 1949-50; BA, U. Tex., 1953, MA, 1955; PhD, U. Iowa, 1958. Asst. prof. U. Buffalo, 1958-62; assoc. prof. SUNY-Buffalo, 1962-66, prof., 1966-67, U. Kans., Lawrence, 1967-70; Centennial prof. psychology W.Va. U., Morgantown, 1970-2000, dir. grad. tng. in life-span devel. psychology, 1973-2000, Centennial prof. emeritus, 2000—. Mem. initial rev. groups div. research grants NIH, Washington, 1969-71, 74-78, 79-84; vis. prof. SUNY, Buffalo, 1970, U. Iowa, 1972, U. Hawaii, 1975, S.W. China Normal U., 1997, 2000. Author: Perception of Stimulus Relations, 1968, Basic Learning Processes in Childhood, 1976; co-author: Experimental Child Psychology, 1970, Life-Span Developmental Psychology, 1977, 1988, Child Development, 1979; editor: Advances in Child Development and Behavior, 26 vols., 1969-2001; co-editor: Life-Span Developmental Psychology, 8 vols., 1973-97; assoc. editor: Jour. Exptl. Child Psychology, 1975-83, editor, 1983-97, mem. editl. bd. 1965-74, 98-2000. Served with U.S. Army, 1954. Fellow AAAS, Assn. for Psychol. Sci.; mem. Soc. for Rsch. in Child Devel., Psychonomic Soc., Assn. for Behavior Analysis, Internat. Soc. for Study Behavioral Devel. Home Phone: 817-346-2865. Personal E-mail: haynereese@aol.com.

REESE, JERRY, professional sports team executive; b. Tiptonville, Tenn., July 22, 1963; m. Gwen Moore; children: Jasmyne, Jerry II. BS in Health & Physical Edn., Tenn.-Martin U., 1987, MA in Edn. Adminstrn. & Supervision, 1988. Grad. asst. Tenn.-Martin U., 1986—88, secondary coach, 1988—93, receivers coach, asst. head coach, 1993—94; regional scout NY Giants, 1994—99, asst., pro pers. dept., 1999—2002, dir. player pers., 2002—06, gen. mgr., 2007—. Named to Tenn.-Martin U. Hall of Fame, 1995. Achievements include being third African-American named Gen. Mgr. of Nat. Football League team, 2007. Office: NY Giants Giants Stadium Way East Rutherford NJ 07073 *

REESE, JOHN ROBERT, lawyer; b. Salt Lake City, Nov. 3, 1939; s. Robert McCann and Glade (Stauffer) R.; m. Francesca Marroquin Gardner, Sept. 5, 1964 (div.); children: Jennifer Marie, Justine Francesca; m. Robin Ann Gunsul, June 18, 1988. AB cum laude, Harvard U., 1962; LLB, Stanford U., 1965. Bar: Calif. 1966, U.S. Dist. Ct. (no. dist.) Calif. 1966, U.S. Ct. Appeals (9th cir.) 1966, U.S. Dist. Ct. (ctrl. dist.) Calif. 1974, U.S. Supreme Ct. 1976, U.S. Dist. Ct. (ea. dist.) Calif. 1977, U.S. Ct. Appeals (6th cir.) 1982, U.S. Ct. Appeals (8th cir.) 1985, U.S. Ct. Appeals (10th cir.) 1992, U.S. Ct. Appeals (Fed. cir.) 1994. Assoc. McCutchen, Doyle, Brown & Enersen, San Francisco, 1965—74, ptnr., 1974—2002, Bingham McCutchen, San Francisco, 2002—06, of counsel, 2007—. Adj. asst. prof. law Hastings Coll. of Law, 1991; lectr. U. Calif., Berkeley, 1987, Berkeley, 92. Mem. editl. and adv. bds.: Antitrust Bull., Jour. Reprints for Antitrust Law and Econs., 1981—99. Bd. dirs. Friends of San Francisco Pub. Libr., 1981-87; bd. vis. Stanford U. Law Sch., 1983-86. Capt. U.S. Army, 1966-68. Decorated Bronze Star. Mem. ABA, Am. Acad. Appellate Lawyers, State Bar Calif., San Francisco Bar Assn., U.S. Supreme Ct. Hist. Soc., Ninth Jud. Cir. Hist. Soc., Calif. Acad. Appellate Lawyers, Order of Coif. Avocation: gardening. Home: 9 Morning Sun Dr Petaluma CA 94952-4780 Office: Bingham McCutchen 3 Embarcadero Ctr San Francisco CA 94111-4003 Home Phone: 707-765-1941; Office Phone: 415-393-2225. Business E-Mail: john.reese@bingham.com.

REESE, LYMON CLIFTON, civil engineering educator; b. Murfreesboro, Ark., Apr. 27, 1917; s. Samuel Wesley and Nancy Elizabeth (Daniels) R.; m. Eva Lee Jett, May 28, 1948; children: Sally Reese Melant, John, Nancy. BS, U. Tex., Austin, 1949, MS, 1950; PhD, U. Calif., Berkeley, 1955; D in Civil Engring. (hon.), Inst. Bucharest, Romania, 1994. Diplomate: Registered profl. engr., Tex. Internat. Boundary Commn., San Benito, Tex., 1939-41; surveyor U.S. Naval Constrn. Bns., U.S., Aleutian Islands, Okinawa, 1942-45; field engr. Assoc. Contractors & Engrs., Houston, 1945; draftsman Phillips Petroleum Co., Austin, 1946-48; research engr. U. Tex., Austin, 1948-50; asst. prof. civil engring. Miss. State Coll., 1950-51, 53-55; asst. prof. U. Tex., Austin, 1955-57, assoc. prof., 1957-64, prof., 1964—, chmn. dept., 1965-72, Taylor prof. engring., 1972-81, assoc. dean engring. for program planning, 1972-79, Nasser I. Al-Rashid Chair, 1981-84; prin. Ensoft, Inc., 1985—, Lymon C. Reese Assocs. Contbr. articles to profl. jours. Recipient Thomas Middlebrooks award ASCE, 1958; Joe J. King Profl. Engring. Achievement award, 1977, Offshore Tech. Conf. Disting. Achievement award for Individuals, 1985, Disting. grad. Coll. of Engring., U. Tex., Austin., 1985. Mem. ASCE (Karl Terzaghi lectr. 1976 Terzaghi award, 1983, Tex. sect. award of Hon. 1985, hon. mem. 1984—), Nat. Acad. Engring. Baptist (deacon). Office: U Tex Dept Civil Engring Austin TX 78712-1104 Home: 11503 April Dr Austin TX 78753-2903 Home Phone: 512-833-5190; Office Phone: 512-244-6464 ext. 113. Personal E-mail: lymonreese@aol.com.

REESE, POKEY, professional baseball player; b. Columbia, SC, June 10, 1973; Player Cin. Reds, 1997—2001, Pittsburgh Pirates, 2002—03, Boston Red Sox, 2004, Seattle Mariners, 2005—. Recipient Nat. League Golden Glove Award, 1999—2000. Achievements include being a member of World Series Champion Boston Red Sox, 2004. Office: c/o Seattle Mariners 1250 1st Ave South Seattle WA 98134

REESE, STUART HARRY, insurance company executive; b. Richmond, Va., May 3, 1955; s. Allison and Virginia (Saul) R.; m. Elizabeth Garr, Aug. 21, 1976; children: Katharine, Elizabeth, Jillian, Thomas. BA, Gettysburg Coll., Pa., 1977; MBA, Dartmouth Coll., 1979. Securities analyst investment pvt. placements Aetna, Hartford, Conn., 1979-81, sr. securities analyst dept. fin. guaranty, 1981-82, dir. treas. investment planning, 1982-83, sr. investment officer, 1983-84, asst. v.p., 1984-85, mng. dir., 1985-89, v.p., mng. dir. capital markets, 1989—93; various sr. mgmt. positions, including chmn. & CEO Babson Capital Mgmt. subsidiary, Mass. Mutual Fin. Group, Springfield, Mass., 1993—99, exec. v.p. & chief investment officer, 1999—2005, pres. & CEO, 2005—. Mem. investment com. Vis. Nurses Assn., Simsbury, Conn., 1991—. Mem. Hartford Soc. Fin. Analysts (v.p. bd. 1991—). Office: Mass Mutual Financial Group 1295 State St Springfield MA 01111 *

REESE, TRACY, fashion designer; b. Detroit; d. Claude Reese. Degree, Parsons Sch. Design, 1984. Design asst. to Martine Sitbon Arlequin Paris, 1984-87; designer with Marc Jacobs Perry Ellis Portfolio; design dir. Magaschoni, Inc., 1990—95; launched own label Tracy Reese, 1987—89, 1997—, Plenty by Tracy Reese, 1998—, Plenty by Tracy Reese Home. Featured in Ebony mag., 2007. Office: c/o Factory PR 580 Broadway Ste 602 New York NY 10012 *

REESE, WILLIAM LEWIS, philosophy educator; b. Jefferson City, Mo., Feb. 15, 1921; s. William Lewis and Lillian Amelia (Fisher) R.; m. Louise Weeks, June 11, 1945; children: Claudia, Patricia, William Lewis III. AB, Drury Coll., 1942; B.D., U. Chgo., 1945, PhD, 1947; postdoctoral, Yale U., 1955-56. Asst. prof. philosophy Drake U., 1947-49, asso. prof. philosophy, 1949-57, head dept., 1954-57; asso. prof. philosophy Grinnell Coll., 1957-60; vis. prof. philosophy Iowa State U., 1958; prof. philosophy, chmn. dept. U. Del., Newark, 1960-67, dir. seminar in philosophy of sci., 1960-66, H. Rodney Sharp prof. philosophy, 1965-67; prof. philosophy SUNY-Albany, 1967-99, chmn. dept., 1968-74, 84, prof. philosophy emeritus, rsch. prof. philosophy, 1999—, dir. emeritus ctr., 2006—, pres. emeritus ctr. bd., 2006—. Tully Cleon Knoles lectr. U. Pacific, 1962; del. U.S. Nat. Commn. for UNESCO, 1963; gen. mem. 4th East-West Philosophers Conf., 1964 Author, contbr.: Studies in C.S. Peirce, 1952, (with Charles Hartshorne) Philosophers Speak of God, 1953, 2d edit., 2000, The Ascent from Below, 1959, 2d edit., 2000, (with Eugene Freeman) Process and Divinity, 1964, Dictionary of Philosophy and Religion: Eastern and Western Thought, 1980, 3d edit., 1999, Freedom, 2000, Values, 2000; gen. editor: Philosophy of Science, The Delaware Seminar, vols. 1, 2, 1963, vol. 3, 1967; editor: Philosophy and World Religions: The Reader's Adviser, vol. 4, 1988, Fundamental Issues in Philosophy Series, 2 vols., 2000; editl. bd.: State of N.Y. Press, 1968-78; contbr. articles to profl. jours Recipient Ford Found. Study award Argentina, 1967; Fulbright lectr. Argentina, summer 1971; Inst. Humanistic Studies fellow, 1977— Mem.: AAUP, Metaphysical Soc. Am. (sec. 1962—65, treas. 1962—65), Am. Philos. Assn. Mem. Christian Ch. (Disciples Of Christ). Home: Font Grove Rd Slingerlands NY 12159 Office: SUNY Dept Philosophy Albany NY 12222-0001 Personal E-mail: reesewl@aol.com. *To have before one always the realistic sense that if one has been successful in one way one has failed in others, and that one's failures surely outnumber one's successes.*

REES-JONES, TREVOR D., oil industry executive; b. Dallas, Tex., 1950; married; 2 children. BA, Darmouth Coll.; JD, So. Methodist U. Sch. Law, 1978. Atty. Thompson & Knight, Dallas, 1978—84; oil & gas investor, 1984—93; founder Chief Oil & Gas LLC (sold to Devon Energy), 1994—2006; founder, pres. & CEO Chief Operating LLC, Dallas, 2006—. Named one of 400 Richest Americans, Forbes, 2006. Office: Chief Operating LLC Ste 600 8111 Preston Rd Dallas TX 75225 Office Phone: 214-265-9590. Office Fax: 214-265-9593.

REEVE, DEBORAH B., art association administrator, art educator; Art teacher; adj. prof. Lesley Coll., Cambridge, Mass.; with US Dept. Edn.; assoc. exec. dir. develop. and special projects Nat. Assn. Elementary Sch. Principals, dep. exec. dir., advocacy and prof. develop., 2001—07; exec. dir. Nat. Art Ed. Assn., Reston, Va., 2007—. Paintings exhibited Gallery West, Alexandria, Va., Cranbury Gallery, Princeton, NJ; mem. curriculum develop. advisory team 100 People: A World Portrait. Office: Nat Art Ed Assn 1916 Association Dr Reston VA 20191 *

REEVES, BARBARA ANN, lawyer; b. Buffalo, Mar. 29, 1949; d. Prentice W. and Doris Reeves; m. Richard C. Neal; children: Timothy R. Neal, Stephen S. Neal (dec.), Robert S. Neal, Richard R. Neal. Student, Wellesley Coll., Mass., 1967-68; BA (NSF fellow, Lehman fellow), New Coll., Sarasota, Fla., 1970; JD cum laude, Harvard U., 1973. Bar: Calif. 1973, D.C. 1977. Law clk. U.S. Ct. Appeals, 9th Circuit, Portland, Oreg., 1973—74; assoc. firm Munger, Tolles and Rickershauser, LA, 1977—78; trial atty. spl. trial sect. Dept. Justice (Antitrust div.), 1974—75; spl. asst. to asst. atty. gen. Antitrust div. Dept. Justice, Washington, 1976—77; chief antitrust div. L.A. field office, 1978—81; ptnr. Morrison & Foerster, LA, 1981—94, Fried, Frank, Harris, Shriver & Jacobson, LA, 1995—97, Paul, Hastings, Janofsky & Walker, LA, 1997—99; assoc. gen. counsel So. Calif. Edison, 1999—2004, v.p. shared svcs., 2004—06; mediator, arbitrator JAMS, 2006—. Mem. exec. com. state bar conf. of dels. L.A. Delegation, 1982-91; del. 9th Cir. Jud. Conf., 1984-88; mem. Fed. Ct. Magistrate Selection Com., 1989; bd. dirs. Pub. Counsel, 1988-92, Western Ctr. Law and Poverty, 1992-98; lectr. in field. Editor: Federal Criminal Litigation, 1994; contbg. author: World Antitrust Law, 1995; contbr. articles to profl. jours. Mem. ABA (litigation sect., antitrust sect.), Fed. Bar Assn. (officer 1998—), Assn. Bus. Trial Lawyers (officer 1997—), Am. Arbitration Assn. (arbitrator, mediator, mem. adv. panel large complex case program), L.A. County Bar Assn. (antitrust sect. officer 1980-81, litigation sect. officer 1988-93 trustee 1990-92, chair alternative dispute resolution sec. 1992-95, L.A. County Ct. ADR com.). Home: 1410 Hillcrest Ave Pasadena CA 91106-4503 Office: 46th Fl 707 Wilshire Blvd Los Angeles CA 90017 Home Phone: 626-449-5809; Office Phone: 213-620-1133. Business E-Mail: breeves@jamsadr.com.

REEVES, DANIEL EDWARD, former professional football coach; b. Rome, Ga., Jan. 19, 1944; m. Pam Reeves; children: Dana, Laura, Lee. Grad., U. S.C. Running back Dallas Cowboys, NFL, 1965-72, player-coach, 1970-71, asst. coach, 1972, 74-80; head coach Denver Broncos, NFL, 1981-92, also v.p.; head coach N.Y. Giants, 1993-96, Atlanta Falcons, 1997—2003. Recipient NFL Coach of the Year award, 1984, 1989, 1991, 1993, 1998; named to S.C. Hall Fame.

REEVES, DENISE MOSELEY, dancer, educator; d. Margaret Ann Freeman and Kenneth Stewart Moseley; m. Dennis Dean Reeves, May 15, 1982. BS, U. N.C., Greensboro, 1979; MEd, Frostburg State U., Md., 1984. Cert. tchr. Royal Acad. of Dance, 1988, level 3 master tchr. True Pilates-Romana's Pilates, 2002. Dancer N.C. Sch. of the Arts, Winston-Salem, 1973; tchr. movement edn. sch. King Intermediate Sch., NC, 1978—82; dancer, instr. Hagerstown and W.Va. Youth Ballet Co., Md., 1982—83; profl. dancer San Jose Dance Theatre, Calif., 1986—88; ballet dir. Pam East Dance, Cupertino, Calif., 1986—92; profl. dancer Santa

Clara Ballet, Calif., 1988—92; dance dir., instr. Pebblebrook H.S., Mableton, Ga., 1994—; sch. dir., dancer Ga. Ballet, Marietta, 1992—97; instr., dancer Atlanta Ballet, 1996—98; dance dir. Ga. Gov.'s Honors Program, Atlanta, 1997—97; dir. Pilates Studio of Atlanta, 1999—2002. Coord., instr. Cobb County Schs. Gov.'s Honor Program, Marietta, Ga., 1994—2006. Mem.: Nat. Dance Edn. Orgn., Nat. Dance Assn. (corr.), Ams. for the Arts (corr.), Corps De Ballet Internat. (corr.), Gamma Beta Phi. Achievements include dance ambassador with Santa Clara University to dance in Poland and Soviet Union. Avocations: travel, fitness, musical theatre, dance. Home: 489 Timberlea Lake Dr Marietta GA 30067 Office: Pebblebrook HS 991 Old Alabama Rd Mableton GA 30126 Home Phone: 678-521-6666; Office Phone: 770-819-2521. Office Fax: 770-819-2524. Personal E-mail: dansin1@hotmail.com. E-mail: denise.reeves@cobbk12.org.

REEVES, DIANNE, singer; b. Detroit, 1956; Student, U. Colo., 1970s. Performed with trumpeteer Clark Terry; recorded sessions with Lenny White, Stanley Turrentine, Alphonso Johnson, 1970s; performer with Night Flight, 1970s, Sergio Mendes tour, 1981, Harry Belafonte, 1983-86; toured as trio with Billy Childs, 1986; rec. artist: (albums) Welcome to My Love, 1982, For Every Heart, 1986, Dianne Reeves, 1987, Never Too Far, 1989, I Remember, 1990, Art and Survival, 1993, Quiet After the Storm, 1994, The Grand Encounter, 1996, That Day..., 1997, Bridges, 1999, In the Moment: Live in Concert, 2000, The Calling, 2001, A Little Moonlight, 2003, Christmas Time is Here, 2004, Good Night and Good Luck motion picture soundtrack, 2005; actress (films) Good Night and Good Luck, 2005. Recipient Best Jazz Vocal Album for The Calling, Grammy Awards, 2001, Best Jazz Vocal Album for A Little Moonlight, 2003, Best Jazz Vocal Album for Good Night and Good Luck, 2006. Office: Blue Note Records 150 5th Ave New York NY 10011 Office Phone: 212-786-8600.

REEVES, GRAFTON DULANY, pediatric endocrinologist; b. Philadelphia, Del., June 17, 1945; s. William Handy and Eleanor Fotterall Reeves; m. Diana Burke Reeves, July 6, 1968; children: Pamela Reeves Gilmartin, Dulany Reeves Dent. MD, Temple U., Phila., 1973. Chief divsn. pediatric endocrinology duPont Hosp. for Children, Wilmington, Del., 1996—. Fellow: Am. Bd. Pediat., Am. Acad. Pediat. (life). Office: duPont Hosp for Children 1600 Rockland Rd Wilmington DE 19803 Office Phone: 302-651-5965. Business E-Mail: greeves@nemours.org.

REEVES, HALLIE LAWSON, retired music educator, retired chaplain; d. Andrew William and Gracie Elizabeth (Owens) Lawson; m. William A. Reeves, June 21, 1961 (div.); 1 child, Rona Omega; 1 child, M.C. BA, NC Ctrl. U., 1958; MDiv, Duke U., 1978; PhD in Humane Letters, Nat. Theol. Sem., 1985. Cert. supr. ACPE, 1992. Music tchr. Roxboro Pub. Schs., NC, 1958—59, Oxford Pub. Schs., NC, 1959—60, Durham Pub. Schs., NC, 1960—75; chaplain intern St. Elizabeth's Hosp., DC, 1979—80, chaplain resident, 1980—81, staff chaplain, 1985—2003; dir. chaplain svcs. Provident Hosp., Balt., 1981—85. Owner piano studio, 1958—2003. Mem.: NADCD, Phi Delta Kappa.

REEVES, JAMES N., lawyer; b. Albert Lea, Minn., Oct. 14, 1945; AB, Dartmouth Coll., 1967; student, George Washington U.; JD, U. Minn., 1970. Bar: Minn. 1970, Alaska 1972, U.S. Ct. Appeals (9th cir.), U.S. Supreme Ct. Law clk. U.S. Dist. Ct. Minn., 1970-71; asst. atty. gen. State of Alaska, 1971-78; mem. Bogle & Gates (now Dorsey & Whitney), Anchorage; ptnr.-in-charge, Anchorage; mem. trial dept., environ. and natural resources practice groups Dorsey & Whitney LLP, Anchorage. Sr. fellow East-West Ctr., Honolulu, 1977. Mem. ABA, Alaska Bar Assn. Office: Dorsey & Whitney 1031 W 4th Ave Ste 600 Anchorage AK 99501-5907 Office Phone: 907-276-4557. Office Fax: 907-276-4152. Business E-Mail: reeves.jim@dorsey.com.

REEVES, JENNIFER TODD, filmmaker; b. Colombo, Sri Lanka, 1971; MFA, U. Calif., San Diego. Founder Sparky Pictures, Inc., NYC, 2000—. Vis. asst. prof. film and electronic arts Yale U., New Haven; part-time tchr. Bard Coll. Milton Avery Sch. Arts, Cooper Union, Millennium Film Workshop. Filmmaker (prin. works) The Girl's Nervy, 1995, Chronic, 1996, Darling Internat. (with MM Serra), 1999 (Cinematography award, Cinetexas Film Festival, 2000), Fear of Blushing, 2001, The Time We Killed, 2004 (FIPRESCI Critics prize, Berlin Film Festival, Outstanding Artistic Achievement, OUTFEST, Best NY, NY Narrative Feature, Tribeca Film Festival), Shadows Choose Their Horrors, We Are Going Home (Film Co-op award, Ann Arbor Film Festival, 1999, Juror's Citation, Black Maria Film Festival, 1999), (group shows) Toronto Film Festival, Kill Your Timid Notion: Dundee Contemporary Arts Festival, Whitney Biennial: Day for Night, Whitney Mus. Am. Art, 2006. Recipient Princess Grace award, 2000; grantee Jacob K. Javits fellowship, 1997—2001, Andrea Frank Found. grant, 1999. Office: Sparky Pictures Inc PO Box 136 Planetarium Sta New York NY 10024

REEVES, JOAN HUTCHINS, painter; b. Seattle, June 22, 1932; d. John Marvin and Bess Irene (Sowler) Hutchins; m. George Catherwood Reeves, Sept. 5, 1953; children: David Alan, John Michael. Exhibitions include Whatcom Mus. History and Art. Mem. Art Stall Gallery Coop. (chmn. 1986-89), Nat. Mus. Women in the Arts (charter), N.W. Watercolor Soc. (life mem., exhbn. chmn. 1986, Purchase award 1988), Women Painters of Wash. (membership chmn. 1986-88, Transparent Watecolor award 1985, 86, 90, Best of Show 1989, 2001, Purchase award, 2004), Mont. Watercolor Soc. (signature mem.), Watercolor West (signature mem.), San Diego Watercolor Soc. (signature mem.) Avocation: travel. Home: 3901 Fremont Ave N Seattle WA 98103-7756

REEVES, JOHN DRUMMOND, retired English language professional, writer; b. Troy, NY, Dec. 8, 1914; s. Robert Brockway and Emma Caroline (Mausert) R.; m. Mary Markwick Moore, Sept. 1, 1951. AB, Williams Coll., Williamstown, Mass., 1937; AM, Columbia U., 1941. Instr. in Eng. Irving Sch., Tarrytown, NY, 1937-40, Horace Mann Sch., NYC, 1940-41, 46-47; asst. prof. of classics and Eng. Whitman Coll., Walla Walla, Wash., 1956-62; assoc. prof. English Millikin U., Decatur, Ill., 1962-65; lectr. in Eng. Hofstra U., Hempstead, NY, 1965-73, ret., 1973. Author: Windows on Melville, 2001; contbr. articles to profl. jours. Lt. USNR, 1941-45, PTO. Mem. AAUP, Coll. Eng. Assn., Am. Coun. Learned Soc. (reg. assoc. 1957-59), Walla Walla Archaeol. Assn. (pres. 1959-62), SR (Conn. state chpt.), Masons. Home: 20 Devonwood Dr Apt 161 Farmington CT 06032-1422

REEVES, KATHLEEN WALKER, English language educator; b. Mt. Pleasant, Mich., Dec. 7, 1950; d. John J. and Gladys M. W.; m. Daniel H. Reeves, Mar. 10, 1972; children: Sheila, Michael. BA, Ctrl. Mich. U., 1973, MA, 1984. English tchr. Shepherd (Mich.) High Sch., 1973-76, Chippewa Hills High Sch., Remus, Mich., 1978-79, Onekama (Mich.) Pub. Sch., 1983-86, Seaholm High Sch., Birmingham, Mich., 1986—. Bd. dirs. Nat. Bd. Profl. Tchg. Stds.

REEVES, KEANU, actor; b. Beirut, Sept. 2, 1964; s. Samuel Nowlin Reeves and Patricia Taylor. Stage appearances: Wolf Boy (debut), For Adults Only, Romeo and Juliet; films: Flying, 1986, Youngblood, 1986, River's Edge, 1987, Permanent Record, 1988, The Night Before, 1988, The Prince of Pennsylvania, 1988, Dangerous Liaisons, 1988, Bill and Ted's Excellent Adventure, 1989, Parenthood, 1989, I Love You to Death, 1990, Tune in Tomorrow, 1990, Bill and Ted's Bogus Journey, 1991, Point Break, 1991, My Own Private Idaho, 1991, Bram Stoker's Dracula, 1992, Much Ado About Nothing, 1993, Little Buddha, 1994, Even Cowgirls Get the Blues, 1994, Speed, 1994, Johnny Mnemonic, 1995, A Walk in the Clouds, 1995, Feeling Minnesota, 1996, Chain Reaction, 1996, Devil's Advocate, 1997, The Last Time I Committed Suicide, 1997, The Matrix, 1999, The Replacements, 2000, The Watcher, 2000, The Gift, 2000, Hard Ball, 2001, Sweet November, 2001, The Matrix Reloaded, 2003, The Matrix Revolutions, 2003, Something's Gotta Give, 2003, Thumbsucker, 2005, Constantine, 2005, A Scanner Darkly, 2006, The Lake House, 2006 (with Sandra Bullock Movie-Choice Liplock, Teen Choice Awards, 2006); TV films: Letting Go, 1985, Act of Vengeance, 1986, Young Again, 1986, Babes in Toyland, 1986, Under the Influence, 1986, Brotherhood of Justice, 1986, Life Under Water, 1989, Children Remember the Holocaust, 1995, (narrator) The Great Warning, 2003. Named one of 50 Most Powerful People in Hollywood, Premiere mag., 2004—06. Office: Creative Artists Agy care Kevin Houvane 9830 Wilshire Blvd Beverly Hills CA 90212-1825

REEVES, LUCY MARY, retired elementary school educator; b. Pewamo, Mich., July 2, 1932; d. Lavaldin Edgar and Marian S. (Lee) Hull; m. Walter Emery Reeves, Jan. 21, 1922. BS, Western Mich. U., Kalamazoo, 1965; postgrad., Western Mich. U., 1965-75. Tchr. Country Sch. One Room, Matherton, Mich., 1956-57, Ionia, Mich., 1957-58, Belding, Mich., 1958-62, Saranac, Mich., Belding, 1965, Belding Area Schs., 1965—89; ret., 1989. Vol. Frederick Meijers Garden, Grand Rapids, Point Man Internat. Ministries, Shiloh Cmty. Ch., United Meml. Health Ctr., Shiloh Cmty. Ch.; vol. United Meml. Health Ctr., Greenville. Mem. NEA, Mich. Edn. Assn., Belding Area Edn., Profl. Businesswomen's Assn. Avocations: computers, reading, travel, sewing.

REEVES, MICHAEL SPENCER, investment company executive; b. Memphis, Mar. 13, 1967; s. Rodger Clifton and Betty Lou Reeves; m. Julie Mackle; children: Spencer J.M., Kathleen Kohl, Vivian Asbridge. BA, U. South, Sewanee, Tenn., 1985—89; MBA, Duke U., Durham, NC, 1993—95. Vp New South Capital Mgmt., Inc., Memphis, 1995—2004; sr. mng. dir. Third Ave. Mgmt., LLC, NYC, 2004—06; mng. dir. Lapides Asset Mgmt., LLC, Greenwich, Conn., 2006—. Mem.: AIMSE, Assn. Investment Mgmt. Sales Executives, CFA Inst. Home Phone: 203-966-2581.

REEVES, RALPH BERNARD, III, publishing executive; b. Raleigh, NC, Apr. 2, 1947; s. Ralph Bernard Reeves Jr. and Frances Rhoda (Campbell) M.; m. Caroline Holton Green, Apr. 24, 1971 (div. 1986); children: Ralph B. IV, Daniel MacQuarrie; m. Katherine Drewry Reid, June 20, 1998. AB in History, U. NC, 1970. Field coord. FMI Mgmt. Group, Raleigh, NC, 1972-76; gen. mgr., v.p. The Leader Newspaper, Rsch. Triangle Pk., NC, 1976-78; pres., pub., founder Spectator Pubs. Inc., Raleigh, 1978-98, Triad Bus., Greensboro, NC, 1986-88, Triangle Bus., Raleigh, 1985-91, Spectator Pub., NC Architect, 1981-84; pres. Reeves Media, 1998—; pub., editor Raleigh Metro Mag., 1999—. Editor: Mr. Spectator, 1978—98; author: (monthly column) My Usual Charming Self in Metro Mag. 1st v.p. Mordecai Square Hist. Soc., Raleigh, 1980—83; pres. Hilltop Home, 1982—84; coun. mem. NC Mus. Art; founder Raleigh Internat. Spy Conf.; chmn. Downtown Adv. Com., 1983—85; bus. adv. com. NC Sec. of State, Raleigh, 1992—; bd. dirs. NC State U. Friends of Libr., Carolina Ballet. Gov's. Bus. award in the Arts and Humanities, 1986, Benjamin Fine award, 1991, AABP award Triangle Bus., 1st place award Feature Writing, 1991. Mem. Assn. Former Intelligence Officers (assoc.), Pumpkin Papers Irregulars, Fifty Group, English Speaking Union (past pres. RTP br. 1988—), Carolina Co. Club, Sphinx Club. Episcopalian. Avocations: golf, history, travel. Home: 3066 Granville Dr Raleigh NC 27609 Office Phone: 919-831-0999. E-mail: reevesmedia@msn.com.

REEVES, RICHARD, writer, historian; b. NYC, Nov. 28, 1936; s. Furman W. and Dorothy (Forshay) R.; m. Carol A. Wiegand, June 1, 1959 (div. 1971); m. Catherine E. O'Neill, July 28, 1979; children: Cynthia Ann, Jeffrey Richard, Colin O'Neill, Conor O'Neill, Fiona O'Neill. ME, Stevens Inst. Tech., 1960. Engr. Ingersoll-Rand Co., Phillipsburg, NJ, 1960-61; editor Phillipsburg Free Press, 1961-63; reporter Newark News, 1963-65, NY Herald Tribune, 1965-66; chief polit. corr. NY Times, 1966-71; editor NY, 1971-77; lectr. Hunter Coll., 1969-70, Columbia U., 1971-72; nat. editor, columnist Esquire, 1977-79; chief corr. Frontline, PBS, 1981—84; syndicated columnist, 1979—. Regents prof. polit. sci. UCLA, 1992-93, vis. prof. Annenberg Sch. for Comm., 1998; host "Sunday" NBC-TV, 1972-75, "American Journey" PBS-TV, 1983. Author: A Ford, Not a Lincoln, 1975, Old Faces of 1976, 1976, Convention, 1977, Jet Lag: The Running Commentary of a Bi-coastal Reporter, 1981, American Journey: Travelling with Tocqueville in Search of Democracy in America, 1982 (Christopher Book award 1983), The Reagan Detour: Conservative Revolutionary, 1985, A Passage to Peshawar: Pakistan Between the Hindu Kush and the Arabian Sea, 1985, President Kennedy: Profile of Power, 1993 (PEN Non-Fiction Book of Year, Time mag., Book of the Year, Wash. Monthly 1993), Running in Place: How Bill Clinton Disappointed America, 1996, Do the Media Govern?: Politicians, Voters, and Reporters in America, 1997, Family Travels: Around the World in 30 (or So) Days, 1997, What the People Know: Freedom and the Press, 1998, Richard Nixon: Alone in the White House, 2002, President Reagan: The Triumph of Imagination, 2006. Recipient Emmy award, 1980, Columbia-Peabody award, 1984, Carey McWilliams award, Am. Polit. Science Assn., 1998. E-mail: rr@richardreeves.com.

REEVES, ROBERT K., lawyer, oil industry executive; BSBA, JD, La. State U., Baton Rouge. Ptnr. energy sect. Onebane Law Firm, Lafayette, La., 1983—93; sr. v.p., gen. counsel, sec. Flores & Rucks, Inc., 1993—97; exec. v.p., gen. counsel, sec. Ocean Energy, Inc., 1997—2003; sr. v.p. corp. affairs and law Anadarko Petroleum Corp., The Woodlands, Tex., 2004—07, chief governance officer, 2004—07, sr. v.p., gen. counsel, chief adminstrv. officer, 2007—. Trustee Episcopal HS; mem. vestry St. Martin's Episcopal Ch.; bd. dirs. Family Svcs. Greater Houston. Mem.: ABA, Am. Corp. Counsel Assn., La. Bar Assn., Tex. Bar Assn. Office: Anadarko Petroleum Corp 1201 Lake Robbins Dr The Woodlands TX 77380-1046 Office Phone: 832-636-1000. *

REEVES, TATE, state official; b. Rankin County, Miss. m. Elee Williams; 1 child. BS in Econs., Millsaps Coll. CFA. Investment officer Trustmark, 2000; asst. v.p. AmSouth (formerly Deposit Guaranty Nat. Bank); state treas. State of Miss., 2003—. Bd. dir. Public Employees' Retirement Sys., Miss.; chmn. bd. College Savings Plans of Miss. Mem.: Nat. Assn. State Treas. (pres. so. region, sr. v.p., pres. 2007—), CFA Inst., CFA Soc. of Miss. (Miss. Soc. Fin. Analysts award 1996). Republican. Meth. Office: State Treas PO Box 138 Jackson MS 39205 Office Phone: 601-359-3600. Office Fax: 601-359-2001. *

REEVY-MANNING, GRETCHEN MARIA, psychologist, educator; b. Cortland, NY, Oct. 17, 1964; d. William Robert and Carole May Reevy; m. Todd Royal Manning. AB in Psychology, U. N.C., 1986; PhD in Psychology, U. Calif., Berkeley, 1994. Lectr. psychology dept. Dominican Coll., San Rafael, Calif., 1993—98; lectr. U. Calif., Davis, 1994, Profl. Sch. Psychology, San Francisco, 1995; lectr. psychology dept. Calif. State U., East Bay, 1994—. Co-editor: The Praeger Handbook on Stress and Coping, 2007. Grantee, Rand Corp., 1993. Mem.: APA, Soc. for Psychological Study of Social Issues, Am. Psychol. Soc., Western Psychol. Assn., Phi Beta Kappa, Psi Chi. Avocations: swimming, reading, running. Office: Calif State Univ Psychology Dept Hayward CA 94542 Office Phone: 510-885-3421. Business E-Mail: gretchen.reevy@csueastbay.edu.

REFAAT, TAMER F., electrical engineer, researcher; s. Fawzi Ibrahim Refaat and Zeinab Helmi; m. Rehab Hafez; 1 child, Mostafa. BS, Alexandria U., 1991, MS, 1995; PhD, Old Dominion U., 2000. Tchg. asst. and lectr. dept. elec. engring. Faculty of Engring., Alexandria U., Egypt, 1991—95; rsch. asst. elec. and computer engring. Phys. Electronics Rsch. Lab., Old Dominion U., Norfolk, Va., 1996, Old Dominion U., 1996—99; on-site contr. NASA Langley Rsch. Ctr., Hampton, Va., 1996—99; sr. lidar and instrumentation engr., Sci. and Engring. Svcs. Inc., Burtonsville, Md., 2000—01; rsch. elec. engr. Sci. and Tech. Corp., Hampton, 2001—06; on-site contr. NASA Langley Rsch. Ctr., Hampton, 2001—; sr. rsch. scientist Applied Rsch. Ctr. Old Dominion U., Norfolk, 2006—. Contbr. articles to profl. jours. Mem.: IEEE (corr.), Internat. Soc. Optical Engring. (corr.). Muslim. Achievements include design of advanced atmospheric water vapor and carbon dioxide differential absorption lidar detection systems; research in characterization and modelling of optical detectors. Office: NASA Langley Research Center 5 North Dryden St MS468 Hampton VA 23681 Office Phone: 757-864-1540. Personal E-mail: tamer.refaat@hotmail.com. Business E-Mail: trefaat@jlab.org.

REFINETTI, ROBERTO, biopsychologist; b. Sao Paulo, Brazil, Nov. 19, 1957; came to U.S., 1988; s. Renato and Maria Stella (Barroso) R.; m. Kathleen Diane Zylan, Mar. 5, 1988 (div. Aug. 1991); 1 child, Lauren Lynne; m. Theresa Kaye Tolleson, Aug. 11, 2000. BA in Philosophy, Pontifical Cath. U., Sao Paulo, 1981; BS in Psychology, U. Sao Paulo, 1981, MA in Psychology, 1983; PhD in Psychology, U. Calif., Santa Barbara, 1987. Asst. prof. U. Sao Paulo, 1986-88; fellow U. Calif., Santa Barbara, 1988-89, U. Ill., Champaign, 1989-90, U. Va., Charlottesville, 1990-92; asst. prof. Coll. William and Mary, Williamsburg, Va., 1992-97; mgr. profl. publs. Montage Media Corp., Mahwah, NJ, 1997-98; pvt. practice Birmingham, Ala., 1998-99; asst. prof. U. S.C., Salkehatchie, 1999—2005, prof., 2005—. Author: Circadian Physiology, 1999, 2d edit., 2005; editor-in-chief Jour. Circadian Rhythms, 2003-; contbr. over 150 articles to profl. jours Area grantee NIH, 1996, 2002; recipient Nat. Rsch. Svc. Individual award NIMH, 1991, Career award NSF, 1995, 2004. Mem. Am. Physiol. Soc., Am. Psychol. Soc., Soc. Neuroscience, Soc. Rsch. on Biol. Rhythms. Office: Circadian Rhythm Lab Univ SC 807 Hampton St Walterboro SC 29488 Home Phone: 843-549-9497; Office Phone: 843-549-6314. E-mail: refinetti@sc.edu.

REFO, PATRICIA LEE, lawyer; b. Alexandria, Va., Dec. 31, 1958; m. Don Bivens; 1 child, Andrew stepchildren: Jody, Lisa. BA with high honors and high distinction, U. Mich., 1980, JD cum laude, 1983. Bar: Ill. 1983, US Dist. Ct. No. Dist. Ill. 1983, US Ct. Appeals 7th cir. 1988, US Ct. Appeals 11th cir. 1989, US Ct. Appeals 5th cir. 1993, Ariz. 1996, US Dist. Ct. Ariz. 1997, US Ct. Appeals 9th cir. 1998, US Tax Ct. Assoc. Jenner & Block, Chgo., 1983—90, ptnr., 1990—96, Snell & Wilmer LLP, Phoenix, 1996—. Mem. faculty Nat. Inst. Trial Advocacy, 1989—; adv. com. on fed. rules of evidence, US Jud. Conf. 2000-06; mem. bd. advisors Comml. Lending Liability News, 1989-, Nat. Law Jour., 2005—; lectr. ALI/ABA and Practicing Law Inst. Chancellor Episcopal Parish of St. Barnabas on the Desert, 1999—; bd. dirs. Ariz. Academic Decathlon Assn., 1997—2001, bd. advisors, 2001—; bd. dirs. Ariz. Found. for Women, 1999—2005; dir. Greater Phoenix C. of C., 2005—. Named one of The 50 Most Influential Women Lawyers in Am., Nat. Law Jour., 2007. Fellow: Ariz. Found. for Legal Services and Edn., Am. Bar Found.; mem.: ABA (sec. sect. litig. 1994—98, exec. com. sect. litig. 1994—, ho. delegates 1998—2001, standing com. on membership 2000—03, chmn. sect. litig. 2003—04, chair Am. Jury Project 2004—05, ho. delegates 2005—). Office: Snell & Wilmer LLP One Arizona Ctr Phoenix AZ 85004-2202

REGAL, RANDALL NATHANIEL, policy analyst; s. Arthur N. and Mildred Fins Regal. BA, NYU, NYC, 2003. V.p. comm. ESB-USA, Inc., Hewlett Bay Park, NY, 1985—88; ptnr. Regal Realty Holdings, L.P., Lawrence, NY, 1987—2000, Hahn Assocs., Bayville, NY, 2000—. Trustee The Regal Found., Bellmore, NY, 1987—2005; mem. Cedarhurst Bus. Improvement Dist., NY, 1995—2000. Founding mem. Cedarhurst Comml. Property Owners Assn., 1993—2000. Merit scholar, NY State Bd. Regents, 1983. Mem.: NYU Young Alumni Leadership Cir. (corr.), The Princeton Club (assoc.), Am. Mensa (life). Conservative. Home Phone: 561-641-8028; Office Phone: 561-596-9734.

REGALMUTO, NANCY MARIE, small business owner, consultant; b. Bay Shore, NY, Aug. 24, 1956; d. Antonio J. Jr. and Agnes C. (Dietz) R. Student, SUNY, Stony Brook. Sales mgr. Fire, Inc., Hempstead, NY, 1976-78; sports handicapper Red Hot Sport, J. Dime Sports, Diamond Sports, Hicksville, NY, 1978—; small bus. owner, pres. Synergy (vitamin/nutritional product mfr. and distributor), Bellport, NY, 1981—. Cons. on medicine, fin., past life, bus. readings, hypnosis, substance abuse, archeology, law enforcement investigations, family, counseling, interspecies comm., animal therapy, psychic surgery, healing, 1989—; lectr. in field, specializing in holistic remedies and therapies, 1989-91. Columnist Daily Racing Form, 1989-91; appeared on numerous TV programs, worldwide radio, mags., newspapers. Lectr., seminar leader, written about in numerous books. Min. Universal Life Ch., 1996, 97, Ch. of Inner Wisdom, 1996, 97. Mem. NAFE, Internat. Platform Assn., Horse Protection Assn., Therapuetic Riding for the Handicapped, World Wildlife Fedn. Office: 18 Woodland Park Rd Bellport NY 11713-2315

REGAN, DAVID, neuroscientist; b. Scarborough, Eng., May 5, 1935; arrived in Can., 1976; m. Marian Pauline Marsh, Aug. 15, 1959; children: Douglas Lawrence, Howard Michael BSc, London U., 1957, MSc, 1958, PhD, 1964, DSc, 1974. Lectr. physics London U., 1960-65; reader neurosci. Keele U., England, 1965-75; prof. psychology Dalhousie U., Canada, 1976-80, prof. physiology, 1980-84, assoc. prof. medicine, 1978-84, prof. medicine, 1984-87, prof. ophthalmology, 1980-87, prof. otolaryngology, 1980-84, Killam rsch. prof., 1978-82; prof. engring. Rutgers U., 1985-86; prof. psychology York U., 1987—2003, prof. biology; prof. ophthalmology U. Toronto, Ont., Canada, 1987—. Retained inventor Wilkinson-Graviner Group, Eng., 1970-75; cons. Westinghouse, Pitts., 1980-86; co-dir. human performance in space lab. Inst. for Space and Terrestrial Sci., York U., 1989-2002, disting. rsch. prof., 1991-93, emeritus, 1993—; indsl. rsch. chair aviation vision Natural Sci. and Engring. Rsch. Coun. Can./Can. Aviation Electronics, 1993-2003; Spinoza profl. U. Amsterdam, The Netherlands, 1999. Author: Human Evoked Potentials, 1972, Human Brain Electrophysiology, 1989, Human Perception of Objects, 2000; editor: Spatial Vision, 1989, Binocular Vision, 1989, Vision Research, 1992; contbr. over 250 articles to profl. jours.; holder 8 patents. Recipient Forman prize for med. rsch., 1983, Prentice medal, 1990, Sir J.W. Dawson Medal, Royal Soc. Can., 1997, award of excellence Nat. Sci. and Engring. Rsch. Coun. Can., 2000, Proctor medal, 2000, Queen Elizabeth II medal, 2002, Hebb medal, 2003; rsch. grantee NIH, NRC, Air Force Office Sci. Rsch., Nat. Scis. and Engring. Rsch. Coun. Can., Med. Rsch. Coun.; mem. Order of Can., 2001; Killam fellow, 1990. Fellow: Optical Soc. Am., Royal Soc. Can.; mem.: Netherlands Royal Acad. (fgn.), Am. Acad. Optometry, Royal Coll. Sci. (London) (assoc.), Assn. Rsch. in Vision and Ophthalmology, Soc. Clin. Electroretinography, Exptl. Psychology Soc. Avocations: cricket, walking, modern european history. Office: York U Dept Psychology 4700 Keele St North York ON Canada M3J 1P3 Business E-Mail: dregan@yorku.ca.

REGAN, ELLEN FRANCES (MRS. WALSTON SHEPARD BROWN), ophthalmologist, educator; b. Boston, Feb. 1, 1919; d. Edward Francis and Margaret (Moynihan) R.; m. Walston Shepard Brown, Aug. 13, 1955. AB, Wellesley Coll., Mass., 1940; MD, Yale U., New Haven, Conn., 1943. Intern Boston City Hosp., 1944; asst. resident, resident Inst. Ophthalmology, Presbyn. Hosp., NYC, 1944-47, asst. ophthalmologist, 1947-56, asst. attending ophthalmologist, 1956-84; instr. ophthalmology Columbia Coll. Physicians and Surgeons, 1947-55, assoc. ophthalmology,

1955-67, asst. clin. prof., 1967-84; ret., 1984. Mem. AMA, Am. Ophthal. Soc., Am. Acad. Ophthalmology, NY Acad. Medicine, NY State Med. Soc., Mass. Med. Soc., River Club, Tuxedo Club. Home: PO Box 632 Tuxedo Park NY 10987-0632

REGAN, FRANCIS VINCENT, lawyer; b. Toronto, Ont., Can., Dec. 13, 1922; s. James Dennis and Irene Philomena (Duggan) R.; m. Barbara Jane Callahan, Apr. 26, 1947; children: Rosemary, Paul, Michael, Deborah, John, Mary Anne. BCom., U. Toronto, 1945; LLB, York U., 1949. Apptd. Queen's Counsel, Ont., 1964. Pvt. practice, Toronto, 1949—. Co-founder radio sta. C.K.S.L.-A.M., London, Ont., 1955, C.I.Q.M.-F.M., London, 1986. Pres. Toronto Dist. Liberal Assn., 1956-58, Liberal Bus. Men's Club of Toronto, 1961-63, The Ont. Club, Toronto, 1970-72; bd. dirs. Our Lady of Mercy Hosp., 1961-74, chmn., 1971-74; bd. dirs. St. John's Sch., Uxbridge, 1966-75, chmn., 1970-75; bd. dirs. Can. Opera Co., 1969-80; bd. dirs. Met. Toronto adv. bd. Salvation Army, 1980—, chmn., 1983-86. Named Knight Equestrian Order of Holy Sepulchre of Jerusalem, 1973, Knight Comdr. with Star Equestrian Order of Holy Sepulchre of Jerusalem, 1979. Mem. Can. Assn. of Knights of Sovereign Mil. Order of Malta (knight of magistral grace 1983, pres. 1992—, knight grand cross of magistral grace 1995), Venerable Order St. John (hon. life mem., grand priory of Can.), Ont. Club (hon. life mem.). Home: 611 Lonsdale Rd Toronto ON Canada M5P 1R8 Office: 65 Queen St W Ste 1507 Toronto ON Canada M5H 2M5

REGAN, JUDITH TERRANCE, former publishing executive; b. Leominster, Mass., Aug. 17, 1953; d. Leo James and Rita Ann (Imprescia) Regan; children: Patrick, Lara. BA, Vassar Coll., 1975. Reporter Nat. Enquirer; sr. editor, v.p. Simon & Schuster, NYC, 1989—94; pres., pub. Regan Books imprint of HarperCollins, NYC, 1994—2006. TV prodr. Entertainment Tonight, NYC, Geraldo, NYC; prodr. 20th Century Fox Films, Fox TV; anchor Full Disclosure, Fox TV; host Judith Regan Tonight, Fox News Channel. Editor, pub. (books) The Way Things Ought to Be (Rush Limbaugh), 1992, Rogue Warrior (Richard Marcinko), 1992, She's Come Undone (Wally Lamb), 1992, Shampoo Planet and Life After God (Douglas Coupland), 1992, Private Parts, Miss America (Howard Stern), 1993, Judge Robert Bork, Slouching Towards Gomorrah, 1993, I Can't Believe I Said That (Kathie Lee Gifford), 1994, Microserfs, 1996, Shabby Chic (Rachel Ashwell), 1996, The Zone (Dr. Barry Sears), 1996, Brain Lock (Dr. Jeffrey Schwartz), 1997, Wicked, 1997, Confessions of an Ugly Stepsister (Gregory Maguire), 1997—2000, Girlfriend in A Coma, 1998, I Know This Much is True, 1998, Marilu Henner's Total health Makeover, 1998, Story (Robert McKee), 1998, Have a Nice Day, Mick Foley (Mankind), 1999, The Rock Says, 2000, The September 11 Photo Project, 2002, How to Make Love Like a Porn Star (Jenna Jameson), 2004, Juiced (Jose Canseco), 2005, Nanny 911, 2005, The Confession (James McGreevey), 2006, The Confession (James E. McGreevey), 2006, A Million Little Lies (James Pinocchio), 2006, The Zero (Jess Walter), 2006, If I Did It (O.J. Simpson), 2006, and others; exec. prodr.: (TV series) Growing Up Gotti, 2004.

REGAN, MICHAEL PATRICK, lawyer; b. Bklyn., Feb. 22, 1941; s. Cornelius Francis and Marguerite (Cann) Regan; m. Susan Ann Light, July 13, 1974; children: Michael Patrick Jr., Brian Christopher, Mark Dennis. BA in English, U. Notre Dame, 1963; LLB, Union U., Albany, 1967, JD, 1968. Bar: NY 1967, Va. 1975, US Dist. Ct. (we. dist.) Va., US Dist. Ct. (so. dist.) NY, US Ct. Appeals (4th cir.), US Bankruptcy Ct., US Supreme Ct. Assoc. Medwin & McMahon, Albany, NY, 1967—69; asst. dist. atty. Albany County, NY, 1969; corp. atty. Mohasco Corp., Amsterdam, NY, 1969—74; asst. gen. consel Dan River, Inc., Danville, Va., 1975, assoc. gen. counsel, 1981—88, acting gen. counsel, asst. sec., 1988, gen. counsel, asst. sec., 1989; assoc. gen. counsel, asst. sec. Dan River Svc. Corp. of Va., Danville, 1984—88; gen. counsel Wunda Weve Carpets, Inc., Greenville, SC, 1990—93; pvt. practice Danville, 1990—. Clarinetist, saxophonist Tightsqueeze Philharm. Band, 1981—; active Danville Symphony Orch., 1991—, prin., 1997—2005; leader The DanceNotes, 1986—; active Starmont Swing Band, 1999—; sec. DanPac Polit. Action Com., 1976—89. Fellow Paul Harris fellow, Rotary Internat. Mem.: ABA, ATLA, Va. Trial Lawyers Assn., Danville Bar Assn., Va. Bar Assn., N.Y. State Bar Assn., Danville Golf Club. Republican. Roman Catholic. Home: 236 Cambridge Cir Danville VA 24541-5233 Office: 703 Patton St Danville VA 24541-1905 Office Phone: 434-793-9670.

REGAN, PAUL JEROME, JR., manufacturing company executive, consultant; b. Ithaca, NY, Mar. 13, 1940; s. Paul Jerome and Mildred (Dempsey) R.; m. Barbara Ann Easton, Feb. 4, 1962 (dec. Nov. 1996); children: Paul J. III, Timothy Andrew, Allison Ann; m. Susan Margaret Mulcair, Sept. 7, 2002. BS, Cornell U., 1962, MBA, 1965. Pers. asst. Corning (N.Y.) Glass Works, 1963, pers. mgr. Corning and State College, 1964-68, dept. mgr. mfg. State College, 1968-70, personnel devel. cons. Corning, 1970-72, prodn. supt. Wilmington, N.C., 1972-74, devel. mgr. Corning, 1974-77, corp. dir., 1977-83, v.p. human resources, 1983-86; sr. v.p. Corning Inc., Corning, 1986-93; ret. Mem. adv. bd. Cornell U., Ithaca, N.Y., 1970-82, lectr., 1977—; founding mem. Human Resource Planning Soc., 1974-93; dir. Corning Can. Inc., Toronto, 1983-93. Contbr. articles to books and profl. jours. including Human Resource Planning Soc. jour.; expert comment on exec. compensation and succession including Wall St. Jour., N.Y. Times, Bus. Week, Forbes. Mem. exec. bd. Thousand Islands Assn., Gananoque, Ont., Can., 1988—, pres., 1999—2001; chmn. Blue Ribbon Fund, Corning Hosp., 1989-93; mem. Rep. Nat. Com., Washington, 1984—; dir. State College C. of C., 1967-73, Half Moon Bay Found., dir. Friends of the 1000 Islands Mus., Inc., 2000—; chair Museums of 1000 Islands, Inc., 2002—; chmn. Historic Thousand Islands Village Found., 1998—. Johnson Soc. fellow Cornell U., 1991; named Ky. Col., State of Ky., 1984, Adm. Thousand Islands Navy, 1999. Mem. Am. Compensation Assn. (regional chair 1978-81), Am. Acad. Polit. and Social Sci., Heron Soc. (life.), Cornell Club, Smithsonian Nat. Mus. Am. Indian (charter, membership com. 1991—), Antique Boat Mus., Canadian Antique Boat Trust(dir. 2004—, pres., 2005—), Save the River Com. (adv. 1982—), Menninger Found. (patron), Trust for Historic Preservation, Delta Phi (past pres.). Avocations: antique wooden boats, decoys, photographs, Inuit art, poetry.

REGAN, PETER FRANCIS, III, physician, medical educator; b. Bklyn., Nov. 11, 1924; s. Peter Francis Jr. and Veronica (Tierney) R.; m. Laurette Patricia O'Connor, June 18, 1949; children: Peter, Stephen, William, Elizabeth, John, Carol. MD, Cornell U., Ithaca, NY, 1949. Diplomate Am. Bd. Psychiatry and Neurology, Nat. Bd. Med. Examiners. Intern in medicine N.Y. Hosp., 1949-50; asst. resident psychiatry Payne Whitney Psychiat. Clinic, 1950, 53-54, resident, 1954-56; asst. prof. psychiatry Cornell U. Med. Coll., 1956-58; prof., head dept. psychiatry U. Fla. Coll. Medicine, chief psychiat. svc. Univ. Teaching Hosp., 1958-64; prof. psychiatry SUNY, Buffalo, 1964-84, v.p. health affairs, 1964-67, exec. v.p. univ., 1967-69, exec. v.p., acting pres. univ., 1969-70, vice chancellor acad. programs, 1970-71; assoc. chief staff for edn. Buffalo VA Med. Ctr., 1979-84; prof. psychiatry U. Tex. Health Sci. Ctr., San Antonio, 1984-87, assoc. dean Sch. Medicine, 1986-87; assoc. chief staff for edn. San Antonio VA Med. Ctr., 1984-86, chief staff, 1986-87; dep. assoc. chief med. dir. for acad. affairs VA Cen. Office, Washington, 1987-88, assoc. chief med. dir. for acad. affairs, 1988-92; prof. emeritus / sen. cons. dept. psychiatry SUNY, Buffalo, 1992—; interim chair dept. psychiatry Med. U. S.C., 2001—02. Project dir. Ctr. for Ednl. Rsch. and Innovation, OECD, 1972-74. Author: (with F. Flach) Chemotherapy in Emotional Disorders, 1960, (With E. Pattishall) Behavioral Science Contributions to Psychiatry; contbr. articles to profl. jours. Capt. M.C. AUS, 1951-52. Fellow Am. Psychiat. Assn., Am. Coll. Psychiatrists (bd. regents 1986-95, 2d v.p. 1988, 1st v.p. 1989, pres.-elect 1990, pres. 1991); mem. AMA, Alpha Omega Alpha.

REGAN, ROBERT CHARLES, English language educator; b. Indpls., Mar. 13, 1930; s. Francis Bernard and Alma Ophelia (McBride) R.; m. Katherine Jeanclos, Aug. 11, 1989; children by previous marriage: Christopher, Alison, Amelia. BA, Centenary Coll., 1951; MA, Harvard U., 1952; PhD, U. Calif., Berkeley, 1965. Instr. English, Centenary Coll., 1956-57; asst. prof. English, U. Va., 1963-67; Fulbright-Hays lectr. Am. civilization U. Montpellier, France, 1967-68; assoc. prof. English, U. Pa., Phila., 1968-82, prof., 1982-2000, undergrad. chmn. dept. English, 1978-80, 81-83, 89-90, dir. Penn-in-London program, prof. emeritus, 2000—. Lectr. Internat. Communications Agy., Morocco, Algeria, Jordan, 1980, Main Line Sch. Night, Radnor, Pa., 2001—; vis. prof. King's Coll., London, 1983-84 Author: Unpromising Heroes; Mark Twain and His Characters, 1966, Poe: A Collection of Critical Essays, 1967; mng. editor: Am. Quar., 1969-72; mem. editl. bd. Mark Twain Papers, U. Calif., Berkeley, 1997-2001; contbr. articles to lit. jours. Served with USNR, 1952-56, 61-62. Woodrow Wilson fellow, 1962-63; Am. Philos. Soc. research grantee, 1970 Mem. Univ. Mews Assn. (pres. 1999-2001), Faculty Club U. Pa. (bd. govs. 1997-2001). Democrat. Episcopalian. Office: U Pa Dept English Philadelphia PA 19104 E-mail: robertregan@earthlink.net.

REGAN, SUSAN WRIGHT, dance educator, small business owner, choreographer; b. Cambridge, Mass., Dec. 12, 1946; d. Stephen Ellis Wright and Angela Louise Domenichello; m. David Joseph Regan, June 29, 1968 (dec.); children: Michele, David, Derek. BS in Edn., Lesley Coll., Cambridge, 1968. Tchr. Chelmsford schs., Mass.; owner, dance tchr., choreographer Susan Wright Sch. Dance, Watertown, Mass., 1964—. Performer NY World's Fair, appearances on numerous TV programs, dance cos. Recipient 2d and 3d pl. medals, NY World's Fair, 1st pl. regionals, Miss Dance New Eng., 5th pl., Miss Dance Am., Charles Burke award outstanding dedication and svc.; Sch. rated Best of the Best, Watertown, 1999—2005. Mem.: Watertown-Belmont C. of C. (Charles Burke award 2005), Dance Masters Am., Dance Tchrs. Club Boston, Sons of Italy. Avocations: travel, gardening, decorating, ballroom dancing, cooking. Office Phone: 617-924-6255. Personal E-mail: swrdance@comcast.net.

REGAN, TIMOTHY JAMES, grain company executive; b. Atchison, Kans., July 31, 1956; s. Vincent James and Phyllis (Brull) R.; m. Veronica Sue Kasten, June 25, 1977; children: Katrina Sue, Brian James. BS, Kans. State U., 1978. Corp. acct. Lincoln Grain Co., Atchison, 1978-80; acctg. supr. Pillsbury Co., St. Joseph, Mo., 1980, br. account mgr., 1980-82, Omaha, 1982, internal auditor Mpls., 1983, regional account mgr. Huron, Ohio, 1983-84, Scoular Grain Co., Omaha, 1984-87, controller, 1987-91, v.p., mem. exec. com., 1990-99, CFO, 1991—2000; sr. v.p., CFO J.D. Heiskell & Co., Tulare, Calif., 2000—06, Elkhorn, Nebr., 2006—. Fin. advisor Grace Abbott Sch. PTO, Omaha, 1987, treas., 1990-91. Fin. adviser Grace Abbott Sch. PTO, Omaha, 1987, treas., 1990-91; bd. dirs. Cath. Charities, 1994-2000, treas., 1997-99; coach Little League Baseball and Soccer. Mem. KC, Elks. Republican. Roman Catholic. Avocations: jogging, basketball, coaching little league baseball and soccer. Office: JD Heiskell & Co PO Box 1379 Tulare CA 93275-1379 Business E-Mail: tregan@heiskell.com.

REGAN, WILLIAM JOSEPH, JR., energy company executive; b. Bronx, NY, Mar. 7, 1946; s. William Joseph and Eleanor F. (Malone) R.; m. Mary Lee Wynn; children— Katrina Lee, Thomas Wynn, James William BS, U.S. Air Force Acad., 1967; MBA, U. Wis.-Madison, 1969, PhD, 1972. Asst. prof. Wayne State U., Detroit, 1971-75; with Nat. Bank Detroit, 1975-77; sr. bus. planner Am. Natural Resources Co., Detroit, 1977-78, dir. fin. planning, 1978-82, v.p., treas., 1982-85; v.p. corp. fin. United Svcs. Automobile Assn., San Antonio, 1986-88, sr. v.p., treas., 1988-95; v.p., treas. Entergy Corp., New Orleans, 1995-99; CFO Calif. Ind. Sys. Operator Corp., Folsom, Calif., 1999—. Home: 15181 De La Pena Cir Rancho Murieta CA 95683-9798 Office: 151 Blue Ravine Rd Folsom CA 95630 E-mail: wregan37@earthlink.net.

REGAN GOSSAGE, MURIEL, librarian; b. NYC, July 15, 1930; d. William and Matilda (Riebel) Blome; m. Robert Regan, 1966 (div. 1976); 1 child, Jeanne Booth; m. Wayne Gossage, 2003 (dec. 2006). BA, Hunter Coll., NYC, 1950; MLS, Columbia U., 1952; MBA, Pace U., NYC, 1982. Post libr. US Army, Okinawa, 1952-53; researcher P.F. Collier, NYC, 1953-57; asst. libr. to libr. Rockefeller Found., NYC, 1957-67; dep. chief libr. Manhattan Community Coll., NYC, 1967-68; libr. Booz Allen & Hamilton, NYC, 1968-69, Rockefeller Found., NYC, 1969-82; prin. Gossage Regan Assocs., Inc., NYC, 1980-95; pub. svcs. libr. Carlsbad (N.Mex.) Pub. Libr., 1995-2000. Dir. N.Y. Met. Reference and Rsch. Libr. Agy., 1988-95, Coun. Nat. Libr. and Info. Assns., 1991-95; cons. Librs. Info. Ctrs., Gossage Sager Assocs., 2001-05. Elder First Presbyn. Ch. of Carlsbad, 1997-99, 2006—, Stephen min., 2000-05, deacon, 2002-03. Mem. Spl. Librs. Assn. (pres. 1989-90), Archons of Colophon. Avocations: cats, reading, playing piano, travel. Home: 702 Lakeside Dr Carlsbad NM 88220-5209 Personal E-mail: murielregan@zianet.com.

REGAN-STANTON, CHRISTA MARIA, artist; b. Stuttgart, Germany, Dec. 30, 1930; arrived in U.S., 1952; d. Friedrich Wilhelm and Anna Katharina (Schiller) Hohnhausen; m. James Allen Stanton (dec.); m. James Dale Regan, Apr. 27, 1955 (div. 1983); children: Jessica Ute, Jeffrey William. M Interpretive Dance, Tanzmeister Sch. Vock, Stuttgart, Germany, 1950. Tchr. Christa Studio Dance, Stuttgart, Germany, Athens, Ohio, 1952—54, Miami U., 1955—56; mgr. Treehouse Gallery, Oak Ridge, Tenn., 1983—95; studio potter Oak Ridge, Tenn. Bd. dirs. Upstairs Gallery, Oak Ridge, Tenn.; show dir. Foothills Craft Guild, Oak Ridge, Tenn., 1985. Recipient Honorable Mention award, Oak Ridge Mus. Fine Arts, 1982, First Place award, 1983, Second Place award, 1985. Mem.: Nat Mus. Women in Arts, Southern Highland Crafts Guild, Tenn. Arts and Crafts Assn., Am. Craft Coun., Foothills Craft Guild. Home: 119 Cooper Cir Oak Ridge TN 37830-7156

REGAZZI, JOHN JAMES, III, dean, publishing executive; b. Bklyn., June 8, 1948; s. John James Jr. and Theresa Cecil (Fiore) R.; m. Marie Louise Ford, May 30, 1971; children: John James IV, Thomas Paul, Michael Rees. BS, St. John's U., Queens, NY, 1970; MA, U. Iowa, 1972; MS, Columbia U., 1974; PhD, Rutgers U., 1983. Systems mgr. No. Ill. U., De Kalb, Ill., 1974-76; dir. pub. Found. Ctr., NYC, 1976-79; assoc. prof. Rutgers U., New Brunswick, NJ, 1979-81; v.p. The H.W. Wilson Co., NYC, 1981-88; pres., CEO Engring. Info., Inc., NYC, 1988-99; CEO, pres. Elsevier Inc., NYC, 1999—2005; dean LI U. Coll. Info. and Computer Sci., Brookville, 2005—. Chmn. Article Express Internat., 1992-94; bd. dirs. Bristish Stds. Inst. Group, Nat. Tech. Info. Svc., CAB Internat., Engring. Info. Found., Elsevier Found.; adj. prof. SUNY, Albany, Columbia U., Rutgers U. Author: Guide to Periodicals in Religion, 1974. Mem. AAAS, IEEE, ALA, Am. Assn. Pubs. (bd. dirs. NYC chpt. 1987-88), Nat. Info. Standards Orgn. (vice chmn. 1989-90), Nat. Fedn. of Abstracting and Info. Svcs. (bd. dirs. 1980-81, 88, 2004-), Assn. Computing Machinery, NY Acad. Sci. Avocation: cycling. Office: LI U Coll Info & Computer Sci 720 Northern Blvd Greenvale NY 11548 Office Phone: 516-299-4109. Business E-Mail: john.regazzi@liu.edu.

REGEL, TERESA DIAMOND, elementary school educator; d. Frank Wesley and Delphine Margaret Kaminski; children: Jonathan F., Kristal D. BA, U. Wis., Eau Claire, 1971; M in profl. ednl. devel., U. Wis., La Cross, 1991. Adminstrv. lic. Edgewood Coll., Wis., 2003. Retail mgmt. Fish Bldg. Supply, Baraboo, Wis., 1973—79; Country Market, Lake Delton, Wis., 1979—93; bus. owner Fishin' Hut, Lake Delton, Wis., 1978—84; elem. tchr. Wis. Dells. Sch. Dist., 1993—; second grade tchr. Lake Delton Elem., Wis., 1995—. Trustee Kilbourn Pub. Libr. Mem.: Wis. Reading Assn. Avocations: reading, cooking, quilting. Personal E-mail: tregel@verizon.net.

REGELBRUGGE, ROGER RAFAEL, steel company executive; b. Eeklo, Belgium, May 22, 1930; arrived in U.S., 1953, naturalized, 1961; s. Victor and Rachel (Roesbeke) Regelbrugge; m. Dorcas Merchant; children: Anita, Marc, Laurie, Jon, Craig, Kurt, Christiane, Lauren, Lauren, Roger Rafael Jr. BSME, State Tech. Coll., Ghent, 1951; BS in Indsl. Engring. Gen. Motors Inst., Flint, Mich., 1955; MSME, Mich. State U., 1964. Supr. product engring. dept. Gen. Motors Corp., Antwerp, 1955—58; chief devel. engr., then gen. mgr. Airmaster div. Hayes Industries Inc., Jackson, Mich., 1958—66; with Koehring Co., 1966—74, group v.p. internat. ops. Milw., 1969—74; exec. v.p. Korf Industries, Inc., Charlotte, NC, 1974—77, chmn.; chmn., pres., CEO Georgetown Industries, Inc. (formerly Korf Industries, Inc.), 1977—95; chmn., CEO GS Industries Inc. (formerly Georgetown Industries), 1995—97, chmn., 1997—2001. Mem. adv. coun. Coll. Engring. U. Notre Dame; trustee Belmont (N.C.) Abbey Coll. Mem.: Am. Soc. Automotive Engrs., ASME, Georgetown Club, Carmel Country Club. Roman Catholic.

REGENBOGEN, ADAM, judge; b. Steyer, Austria, June 12, 1947; s. William and Pauline (Feuerstein) R.; m. Paula Ruth Rothenberg, June 27, 1970 (div. Oct. 1992); children: Stacy, Candice; m. Helen Busuttil Drwal, Apr. 20, 1996; 1 stepchild, Jason A. Drwal. BA, Temple U., 1969; MSW, U. Pa., 1972; JD, Temple U., 1980. Bar: N.Y. 1983. Social worker VA, Coatesville, Pa., 1974—78, supr. Northport, NY, 1978—80, quality assurance dir., 1980—87; dir. quality assurance N.Y. State Office Mental Health, Willard, 1987—91; workers compensation law judge Binghamton, Oneonta, Norwich, Ithaca, 1998—; pvt. practice NY, 1983—98; conciliator, acting judge Workers Compensation Bd., NY, 1992—98, judge NY, 1998—; judge assigned to World Trade Ctr. 9/11 cases, 2002. Organizer/incorporator Ithaca (N.Y.) Reform Temple, 1992; organizer Parents Without Partners, Ithaca, 1992. Recipient Pro Bono Svc. award Suffolk County Bar Assn., 1986. Home: 42 Hawkins Rd Nineveh NY 13813 Office: Workers Compensation Bd 44 Hawley St Binghamton NY 13901-4434 Home Phone: 607-639-4265; Office Phone: 607-721-8331. Business E-Mail: adam.regenbogen@wcb.state.ny.us.

REGENSTEIN, JOE M., food scientist, educator; b. Bklyn., Sept. 22, 1943; s. Alfred B. and Fannie Regenstein; m. Carrie Ellen Forsheit, June 12, 1966; children: Elliot Michael, Scott Lewis. BA in Chemistry, Cornell U., Ithaca, NY, 1965, MS in Dairy Chemistry, 1966; PhD in Biophysics, Brandeis U., Waltham, Mass., 1973. Postdoctoral Children Biomed. Ctr., Boston, 1973—74; asst. prof. Cornell U., 1974—80, assoc. prof., 1980—87, prof., 1987—. Gen. ptnr. C&J Assoc., Ithaca, 1990—2006; mem. animal welfare com. Food Mktg. Inst./Nat. Coun. Chain Restaurants, Washington, 2001—06; advisor Jewish Vegetarians of North Am., Humane Farm Animal Care. Columnist: Kashrus Mag., 1986—2002; author: (book) Food Protein Chemistry, 1984, Introduction to Fish Technology, 1991, (internet article) The Kosher and Halal Food Laws, 2003. Congl. fellow US Senate, 1996—97, Sacred Foods, 2005—, Shared Journeys, 2006—. Recipient Elizabeth Stier Humanitarian award, Inst. Food Technologists, 2000, Multicultural Diversity award, Cornell Coll. Agr. and Life Scis., 2003; fellow, Inst. Food Technologists, 1995; guest fellow, New Zealand Inst. Food Sci. and Tech., 1983. Mem.: Am. Assn. Advanced Sci., Poultry Sci. Assn., Assn. Orthodox Jewish Sci., Am. Meat Sci. Assn., Atlantic Fisheries Tech. Conf., Inst. Food Technologists (mem. exec. com. 1993—96). Liberal. Jewish. Avocations: deltiology, jogging, birdwatching. Office: Cornell Univ Dept Food Sci Stocking Hall Ithaca NY 14853 Business E-Mail: jmr9@cornell.edu.

REGENSTREIF, HERBERT, lawyer; b. NYC, May 13, 1935; s. Max and Jeannette (Hacker) R.; m. Patricia Friedman, Dec. 20, 1967 (div. July 1968); m. Charlotte Lois Levy, Dec. 11, 1980 (div. Sept. 2002); 1 child, Cara Rachael. BA, Hobart Coll., 1957; JD, NY Law Sch., 1960; MS, Pratt Inst., 1985. Bar: NY 1961, Ky. 1985, US Dist. Ct. (ea. and so. dists.) NY 1962, US Dist. Ct. (ea. dist.) Ky. 1998, US Tax Ct. 1967, US Ct. Appeals (2d cir.) 1962, US Supreme Ct. 1967. Ptnr. Fried & Regenstreif, P.C., Mineola, NY, 1963—; reservist atty. Fed. Emergency Mgmt. Agy., 1998-99. Cons. in field; arbitrator Dist. Ct., Nassau County, NY, 1989—, NYC Civil Ct., 1984-86; sec.-treas. Sta. WAHY-FM, Inc., 1998-2000. Contbr. articles to profl. jours. County committeeman Dem. Com., Queens County, NY, 1978-79. Mem. Bar Assn. Nassau County, Ky. Bar Assn., Am. Judges Assn., Phi Delta Phi, Beta Phi Mu, Hobart Club of NY (gov. 1968-69). Office Phone: 516-294-6442.

REGENSTREIF, S(AMUEL) PETER, political scientist, educator; b. Montreal, Que., Can., Sept. 9, 1936; s. Albert Benjamin and Miriam Lillian (Issenman) R.; children: Anne Erica, Mitchell Chester, Jeffrey Gershon, Gail Aviva. BA, McGill U., 1957; PhD, Cornell U., 1963. Mem. faculty U. Rochester, 1961—, prof. polit. sci., 1971—; coordinator Can. studies program, 1967—. Editl. cons. Toronto Star, 1968-82, Chgo. Sun-Times, 1988-89; polit. cons. Bunting Warburg, Toronto, 1973-90, Coopers & Lybrand, Ltd., 1981-89, Loewen, Ondaatje, McCutcheon, 1991-94; prin. Policy Concepts Inc., Toronto; broadcaster CKO Radio Network, 1983-89; pvt. polit. cons. Author: The Diefenbaker Interlude: Parties and Voting in Canada, 1965; syndicated columnist: Toronto Star, 1963-82; contbr. articles to profl. jours. Served to lt. Canadian Army, 1957. Ford. Found. fellow, 1960; Can. Council fellow, 1960, 65; Canadian Royal Commn. on Bilingualism and Biculturalism grantee, 1964-66; recipient Edward Peck Curtis award U. Rochester, 1979 Mem. AAAS, Am. Polit. Sci. Assn., Can. Polit. Sci. Assn., Assn. Can. Studies in U.S., Phi Beta Kappa. Jewish. Home: 438C Browncroft Blvd Rochester NY 14609 Office: Univ Rochester Dept Polit Sci Rochester NY 14627 Office Phone: 585-275-5466. Business E-Mail: peter.regenstreif@rochester.edu.

REGER, LAWRENCE LEE, trade association administrator; b. Lincoln, Nebr., June 23, 1939; s. Lawrence John and Bertha (Hergenrader) R. Student, U. Nebr., 1961; LL.B., Vanderbilt U., 1964. Bar: Nebr 1964. Asso. firm Crosby, Guenzel & Binning, Lincoln, 1964-70; gen. counsel Nat. Endowment Arts, 1970-72, dir. program devel. and coordination, 1972-78; dir. Am. Assn. Mus., Washington, 1978-86; pres. Heritage Preservation, Washington, 1988—. Mem. visual arts vis. com. U. Del., 1995—; mem. cultural property adv. com. USIA, 1996—2000; mem. bd. trustees St. Petersburg Internat. Preservation Ctr., 1996—; bd. dirs. Peck Stacpoole Found. Chmn. Nat. Humanities Alliance, 1982-86, bd. dirs., 2007—; bd. dirs. Nat. Musical Arts, 1990—. Recipient Forbes medal Am. Inst. Conservation, 2000, Alumni Achievement award Hixon-Leid Coll. Fine and Performing Arts, U. Nebr., 2004. Home: 5010 Garfield St NW Washington DC 20016-3469 Office: Heritage Preservation 1012 14th St NW Ste 1200 Washington DC 20005 Office Phone: 202-233-0800.

REGER, ROBERT J., JR., lawyer; b. Buffalo, June 6, 1948; BA summa cum laude, Fordham U., 1970; JD, U. Va., 1973. Bar: NY 1974. Ptnr. Thelen Reid & Priest LLP, NYC, mem. exec. com. Mem.: ABA, Phi Beta Kappa. Office: Thelen Reid & Priest LLP 875 Third Ave New York NY 10022-2001 Office Phone: 212-603-2204. Office Fax: 212-603-2001. Business E-Mail: rreger@thelenreid.com.

REGES, MARIANNA ALICE, marketing executive; b. Budapest, Hungary, Mar. 23, 1947; arrived in U.S., 1956, naturalized, 1963; d. Otto H. and Alice M. Reges; children: Rebecca, Charles III. AAS with honors, Fashion Inst. Tech., NYC, 1967; BBA magna cum laude, Baruch Coll., 1971, MBA in Stats., 1978. Media rsch. analyst Doyle, Dane, Bernbach Advt., NYC, 1967—70; rsch. supr. Sta. WCBS-TV, NYC, 1970—71; rsch. mgr. Woman's Day mag., NYC, 1971—72; asst. media dir. Benton & Bowles Advt., NYC, 1972—75; mgr. rsch. and sales devel. NBC Radio, NYC, 1975—77; sr. rsch. mgr. Ziff-Davis Pub. Co., NYC, 1977—84; media mgr. Bristol-Myers Squibb Co., 1984—2001, Procter & Gamble Co., 2001—. Mem. Spanish Radio Adv. Coun., NYC, 1986—88, Pan-European TV Audience Rsch. Mgmt. Com., 1988—. Mem. advisor Baruch Coll. Advt. Soc., 1975—; active First Presbyn. Ch., NYC. Mem.: Advt. Rsch. Found., Radio and TV Rsch. Coun., Media Rsch. Dirs. Assn., Am. Advt. Fedn., Am. Mktg. Assn., Anthroposophical Soc., Nature Conservancy, Baruch Alumni Assn., Gilda's Club, Beta Gamma Sigma. Home: 626 E 20th St New York NY 10009-1509 Personal E-mail: marianna10009@hotmail.com.

REGGIO, VITO ANTHONY, retired management consultant; b. Rochester, NY, Dec. 17, 1929; s. Salvatore and Carrie Angela (LoRe) R.; m. Mary Ann Dolores Pippie, Sept. 28, 1957; children: Salvatore, Angela. BS, Purdue U., 1952; postgrad. sch. modern langs., Middlebury Coll., 1948; postgrad. fellowship, U. Ky., U. Tenn. and U. Ala., 1952-53. Jr. engr. Rochester (N.Y.) Gas and Electric Co., 1950; designer/drafter Globe Constrn. Co., Rochester, 1951; rsch. analyst Commonwealth of Ky., Frankfort, 1952; orgn. & methods analyst, then wage adminstrn. specialist USN Dept. Indsl. Rels., Indpls., 1955-56; cons. mgmt. engr. to project mgr. to account exec. Bus. Rsch. Corp., Chgo., 1956-60; sr. cons. econ. feasibilities Ebasco Svcs., Inc., Chgo., 1960-63, dir. pers. mgmt. cons. dept., 1970-77; regional mgr., orgn. and pers. mgmt. svcs. EBS Mgmt. Cons., Chgo., 1963-65, nat. dir. orgn. and pers. mgmt. svcs., 1965-70; pres., bd. dirs. Reggio and Assocs., Inc., Chgo., 1977—2005; mng. dir. Pay Data Svc., 1977—2005, ret., 2005. Bd. dirs. Pay Data Svcs., Chgo. Contbr. papers to profl. publs. With U.S. Army, 1953-55. Named Solco Cultural Soc. fellow, Rochester, N.Y., 1948. Mem. Am. Compensation Assn., Am. Mgmt. Assn., Chgo. Compensation Assn., Soc. Human Resources Profls., Soc. Human Resources Mgmt., Human Resources Mgmt. Assn. Chgo., Western Soc. Engrs.

REGIER, BRYAN L., music educator; b. Topeka, Kans., Sept. 20, 1970; s. Russell L. and Nancy A. Regier; m. Kelly L. Hitt, Dec. 20, 2003. BS, Tabor Coll., 1992; MS, U. Nebr., Kearney, 2000. Grade 5-12 instrumental music tchr. Rushville (Nebr.) H.S., 1994—96; K-12 music, vocal tchr. Arcadia (Nebr.) H.S., 1996—98; grades 5-12 instr. music Bridgeport (Nebr.) H.S., 1998—2000; grades 6-12 instr. music McCook (Nebr.) H.S., 2000—. Bd. dirs. S.W. Nebr. Cmty. Theatre Assn., McCook, 2000—, McCook Arts Coun. Mem.: Nebr. State Bandmasters Assn., Nebr. Music Educators Assn., Masons. Republican. Mennonite. Avocations: trap shooting, golf, music, gardening. Home: PO Box 97 Indianola NE 69034 Office: McCook HS 600 W 7th Mc Cook NE 69001

REGIER, DARCY JOHN, professional sports team executive; b. Swift Current, Sask., Can., Nov. 27, 1956; came to U.S., 1977; s. John Melvin and Helen (Neufeld) Regier; m. Katherine Opyr, June 30, 1979; children: Jonathan, Justin, Jarrett. Student, U. Lethbridge (Alta., Can.), 1980-85. Head coach Indpls. Checkers, 1984-85; dir. hockey adminstrn. NY Islanders, Uniondale, 1985-89, asst. coach, 1989-91, Hartford Whalers, 1991—92; gen. mgr., v.p. Buffalo Sabres, 1997—. Mem. all-star team Cen. Hockey League, 1983. Mem. Profl. Hockey Players Assn. (chmn. exec. com. 1980-83). Avocations: bicycling, video productions on sports. Office: Buffalo Sabres HSBC Arena One Seymour H Knox III Plz Buffalo NY 14203-3096

REGISTER, ANNETTE ROWAN, literature educator; b. Doctors Inlet, Fla., Apr. 5, 1931; d. Ernest Ambors and Frances Perlena (Monroe) R.; Henry Ira Register, Oc. 31, 1954; 1 child, Andrew Henry. RN, Greenville Gen. Hosp. Sch. of Nursing, Greenville, 1948-51; BS, Tex. Woman's U., Denton, 1954; MEd, U. Fla., Gainesville, 1959; SEd, Fla. State U., 1983; student, U. West Fla., Okaloosa Walton C.C. Instrn. dir. nursing edn. Alachua Gen. Hosp., Gainesville, Fla., 1955-57; pub. sch. tchr. Okaloosa County, Ft. Walton Beach, Fla., 1966-93. V.p., Internat. Tng. in Communication Ft. Walton Beach, Fla.; active Inst. Sr. Profls. Okaloosa Walton C.C. Pres. Okaloosa Reading Coun., 1976—80; mem. Okaloosa Walton C.C. Symphony Guild, 1998—; pres. United Meth. Women, Ft. Walton Beach, Fla., 1985—87; dist. v.p. Mem. Fla. C. of C. (amb. 1996—), Phi Delta Kappa (1st v.p.). Methodist. Avocations: crafts, painting, sketching, travel. Office: Okaloosa County Sch Bd 10 Lowery Pl SE Fort Walton Beach FL 32548 Office Phone: 850-243-2250. Personal E-mail: registerannette@yahoo.com.

REGNERY, ALFRED SCATTERGOOD, publishing executive; b. Chgo., Nov. 21, 1942; s. Henry and Eleanor (Scattergood) R.; m. Christina Sparrow, Nov. 29, 1969 (dec.); children: George M., Louise S., Alfred W., Charles H. BA, Beloit Coll., 1965; JD, U. Wis., 1971. Bar: Wis. 1971, D.C. 1987. Pvt. practice law, Madison, Wis., 1971-78; minority counsel Senate Judiciary Com., Washington, 1978-81; dep. asst. atty. gen. land and natural resources div. Dept. Justice, Washington, 1981-82; adminstr. Office of Juvenile Justice and Delinquency Prevention, 1982-86; pres., chief exec. officer Regnery Pub. Inc., Washington, 1986—2003; publisher The Am. Spectator, Arlington, Va., 2003—. Counsel Keller and Heckman, Washington; bd. dirs. Eagle Pub., Inc., Washington. Vice chmn. Intercollegiate Studies Inst., Wilmington, Del., Inst. World Politics, Washington; bd. dirs. Found. for Am. Studies, Washington, Am. Fgn. Policy Coun., Washington, Jamestown Found. Served with USCG, 1966—67. Office: The American Spectator 1611 N Kent St Arlington VA 22209 Office Phone: 703-807-2011.

REGNI, JOHN F., academic administrator, career military officer; BS in Biology, USAF Acad., 1973; MS in Systems Mgmt., St. Mary's U., 1981; attended, Air Command and Staff Coll., Maxwell AFB, 1984, Air War College, 1990, Nat. Defense U., Fort Lesley J. McNair, 1997. Commd. 2d lt. USAF, 1973, advanced through grades to lt. gen., 2004; pers. officer Ogden Air Logistics Ctr., Hill AFB, Utah, 1973-76; chief, pers. utilization 40th Tactical Group, Aviano AB, Italy, 1976-78; chief force anlysis and asst., col. assignments Air Force Manpower and Pers. Ctr., Randolph AFB, Tex., 1978-81; asst. exec., dep. chief of staff for manpower and pers. Hdqrs. USAF, The Pentagon, Washington, 1981-83; asst. chief of staff Hdqrs. Air Tng. Command, Randolph AFB, Tex., 1984-87; dep. base comdr. 3380th Air Base Group, Keesler AFB, Miss., 1987-89; base comdr. 8th Combat Support Group, Kunsan AB, Republic of Korea, 1990-91; dir. manpower, pers. and support Hdqrs. U.S. Pacific Command, Camp H.M. Smith, Hawaii, 1991-94; dir. pers. Hdqrs. Air Mobility Command, Scott AFB, Ill., 1994-96; dir., mil. pers. policy, dep. chief of staff for pers. Hdqrs. USAF, the Pentagon, Washington, 1996-98, dir. pers. resources, dep. chief of staff for pers., 1998—2000; dir. Air Force Pers. Ops. Agy., Washington, 1998-2000; comdr. 2nd Air Force, Keesler AFB, Miss., 2000—04, Air Univ., Maxwell AFB, Ala., 2004—05; supt. USAF Acad., Colorado Springs, 2005—. Decorated Legion of Merit, Air Force Commendation Medal, Meritorious Svc. Medal with silver oak leaf cluster, Defense Superior Svc. Medal, Disting. Svc. Medal with oak leaf cluster. Office: Supt 2304 Cadet Dr, Ste 342 U S A F Academy CO 80840-5001 *

REGO, CESAR, science educator, researcher; b. Porto, Portugal, Apr. 9, 1963; s. Julio and Amelia Rego; 1 child, Bruno. PhD, U. of Versailles, 1996. Assoc. prof. Universidade Portucalense, Porto, Portugal, 1991—99, U. of Miss., Oxford, 1999—; invited prof. Instituto Superior Tecnico (IST-UTL), Lisbon, Portugal, 1996—98; asst. prof. Faculdade de Ciencias (FCUL), Lisbon, Portugal, 1998—99. Recipient IFORS-Lisbon Best Internat. Paper, IFORS/APDIO, Best Master Thesis, Portuguese Ops. Rsch. Soc.; PhD Scholarship, JNICT, Portugal, Rsch. Grant, Office of Naval Rsch. Mem.: INFORMS (assoc.). Home: 405 Whitney Oxford MS 38655 Office: University of Mississippi Oxford MS 38677 E-mail: crego@bus.olemiss.edu.

REGO, SIMON ALEXANDER, psychologist; s. Joseph A.V. and Barbara D. Rego; m. Katherine Lynn Muller, May 15, 2003. BSc with honors, Queen's U., Kingston, Ont., Can., 1994; MA, CUNY, NYC, 1995; M of Psychology, Rutgers U., Piscataway, NJ, 1999, PsyD, 2001. Cert. cognitive therapist Acad. Cognitive Therapy, 2004. Open clinic coord. Ctr. for the Treatment and Study of Anxiety, U. Pa., Phila., 2001—03; clin. and rsch. coord. Anxiety and Depression Clinic Montefiore Med. Ctr., Bronx, NY, 2003—04, assoc. dir. psychology tng., 2004—; asst. prof. psychiatry and behavioral scis. Albert Einstein Coll. Medicine, Bronx, 2004—. Mem. instl. rev. bd. for the protection of human subjects Montefiore Med. Ctr., Bronx, 2004—; clin. supr. Ferkauf Grad. Sch. Psychology, Yeshiva U., Bronx, 2004—, Psychol. Clinic, Grad. Sch. Applied and Profl. Psychology, Rutgers U., Piscataway, 2004—; mem. instl. rev. bd. Biomedical Rsch. Alliance NY, Great Neck, NY, 2005—. Sect. editor: the clinical psychologist Internet Update. Recipient GSAPP Scholars award, Grad. Sch. Applied and Profl. Psychology, 1996, Robert S. Morrow prize for Excellence in the Grad. Forensic Psychology Program, John Jay Coll. Criminal Justice, 1996, Dean's award for Contbn. to Student Life, Grad. Sch. Applied and Profl. Psychology, 1998, 1999, 2000, Robert D. Weitz award, 2002. Mem.: APA, Assn. for Behavioral and Cognitive Therapies (chair profl. issues com. 2004—, spl. interest group insomnia and other sleep disorders, spl. interest group anxiety disorders), Can. Psychol. Assn. (sect. on clin. psychology), NY State Psychol. Assn., Obsessive-Compulsive Found., APA Soc. Clin. Psychology, APA Soc. for a Sci. Clin. Psychology, Internat. Assn. for Cognitive Psychotherapy. Office: Montefiore Medical Center 111 E 210th St Klau 1 Bronx NY 10467 Home Phone: 914-965-8368; Office Phone: 718-920-7667. Office Fax: 718-920-6538. Business E-Mail: srego@montefiore.org.

REGULA, RALPH STRAUS, congressman, lawyer; b. Beach City, Ohio, Dec. 3, 1924; s. O.F. and Orpha (Walter) Regula; m. Mary Rogusky, Aug. 5, 1950; children: Martha, David, Richard. BA, Mt. Union Coll., 1948, LLD, 1981; LLB, William McKinley Sch. Law, 1952; LLD, Malone Coll., 1976. Bar: Ohio 1952. Sch. adminstr. Stark County Bd. Edn., 1948-55; lawyer Navarre, 1952—; mem. Ohio State Ho. Reps., 1965-66, Ohio State Senate, 1967-72, US Congress from 16th Ohio dist., 1973—, mem. appropriations com.; ptnr. Regula Bros. Mem. Pres.'s Commn. Fin. Structures and Regulation, 1970-71. Mem. Ohio Bd. Edn., 1960-64; hon. mem. adv. bd. Walsh Coll., Canton, Ohio; trustee Mt. Union Coll., Alliance, Ohio, Stark County Hist. Soc., Stark County Wilderness Soc. With USNR, 1944—46. Named Outstanding Young Man of Yr. Canton Jr. C. of C., 1957, Legis. Conservationist of Yr. Ohio League Sportsmen, 1969; recipient Cmty. Svc. award Navarre Kiwanis Club, 1963, Meritorious Svc. in Conservation award Canton Audubon Soc., 1965, Ohio Conservation award Gov. James Rhodes, 1969, J. Sterling Morton award Nat. Arbor Day Found., 2000, Sheldon Colemon Great Outdoors award Am. Recreation Coaltion, 2000, Award for Legis. Excellence, Nat. Assn. Mfrs., 2001, Legislator of Yr., Assn. Home Appliances Mfrs., 2001, Pick and Gavel award, Assn. Am. State Geologists, 2001, Spirit of Enterprise award, US C.of C., 2001, Vanguard award North County Trail Assn., 2001, Thomas Jefferson award, Food Distributors Internat., 2002, Disting. Cmty. Health Champion award, Nat. Assn. Cmty. Health Ctrs., 2002, Nat. Ednl. Svc. award Am. Assn. CC, 2002, Policy Maker of Yr. award, Assn. Corp. Travel Execs., 2002-03, Pub. Svc. award Creutzfeldt-Jacob Disease Found., 2003, Benjamin Franklin Pub.Policy award Nat. Assn. Mutual Ins. Cos., 2003, Crystal Apple award Affiliate Assembly of the Am. Assn. Sch. Librarians, 2003, Disting. Legis. award, Nat. Devel. & Rsch. Insts., Inc. 2003, Congl. Am. Spirit Medallion, Nat. D-Day Mus., 2004 Republican. Episcopalian. Office: US House Reps 2306 Rayburn House Office Bldg Washington DC 20515-3516 Office Phone: 202-225-3876. Office Fax: 202-225-3059. *

REHA, ROSE KRIVISKY, retired finance educator; b. NYC, Dec. 17, 1920; d. Boris and Freda (Gerstein) Krivisky; m. Rudolph John Reha, Apr. 11, 1941; children; Irene Gale, Phyllis BS Bus. and Music Edn., Ind. State U., 1965; MA Bus. and Psychology, U. Minn., 1967, PhD Ednl. Psychology and Counseling, 1971. With U.S. and State Civil Svc., 1941—63; tchr. pub. schs., Minn., 1965—66; tchg. assoc., instr. U. Minn., Mpls., 1966—68, 1968—85; prof. coll. bus. St. Cloud State U., Minn., 1968—85, prof. emeritus, 1985—, chmn. bus. edn. & office adminstrn. dept., 1982—83. Advisor Small Bus. Inst., 1972-85, SBA, 1972-85; ct. advocate for women in distress St. Cloud Women's Shelter, 1986-89; adj. prof. profl. and bus. comm. Fla. Atlantic U., Boca Raton, 1989-90; substitute tchr. Broward County, 1990—; tutor (reading) Lauderdale, Fla., 1990-92; moderator, counselor Posnack Jewish Cmty. Ctr., Davie, Fla.; lectr. comm. Soref Jewish Cmty. Ctr. Continuing Edn. for sr. groups, Sunrise, Fla., 1994—; cons., lectr. in field; small bus. cons. Small Bus. Inst. Coll. Bus. St. Cloud State U. Minn.; reviewer bus. comm. and consumer edn. textbooks Contbr. articles to profl. jours Camp dir. Girl Scouts U.S., 1960-62; active various cmty. fund drives; sec., mem. relicensure rev. Com. Minn. Bd. Tchg. Continuing Edn., 1984-85 Recipient Achievement award St. Cloud State U., 1985, St. Cloud State U. Rsch. and Faculty Improvement grantee, 1973, 78, 83 Mem. NEA, ACA (cert.), Am. Vocat. Assn. (cert.), Am. Mental Health Counselors Assn. (cert.), Minn. Econ. Assn., Minn. Women of Higher Edn., Minn. Edn. Assn. (pres. women's caucus 1981-83, award 1983), St. Cloud U. Faculty Assembly (pres. 1975-76), St. Cloud State U. Grad. Coun. (chmn. 1983-85), Fifty-five-plus Sr. Group (moderator 1994-97), Pi Omega Pi, Phi Chi Theta, Delta Pi Epsilon, Delta Kappa Gamma Jewish. Home: 6501 Woodlake Dr Apt 1006 Minneapolis MN 55423-1393 Office Phone: 612-866-0544.

REHAK, JAMES RICHARD, orthodontist; b. Chgo., Jan. 2, 1938; s. James Joseph and Lydia Ann (Thomas) R.; m. Joann Marie Tabbert, Oct. 15, 1969; 1 child, Suzanne Therese. BS, U. Ill., 1960, DDS cum laude, 1962, MS, 1967, cert. in orthodontics, 1965. Pvt. practice dentistry, Chgo., 1962-63; pvt. practice orthodontics Chgo., Arlington Heights, Ill., Cape Coral, Naples, Fla. Asst. prof. U. Ill. Coll. Dentistry, 1966-68. Pres. bd. trustees St. Ann Sch. Foun.; chmn. bd. dirs. St. John Neumann H.S.; organizer, dir. 1st Nat. Bank, Naples; trustee Catholic Cultural Ctr., Washington. Served to capt. U.S. Army Res., 1962-69. Kellogg Found. fellow, 1958; recipient Blessed Edmund Rice medal, Christian Bros., 1996. Fellow Royal Soc. Health; mem. ADA, Ill. Dental Assn., Chgo. Dental Soc., Fla. Dental Assn., West Coast Dental Soc., Collier County Dental Assn., Am. Assn. Orthodontists, Am. Assn. Lingual Orthodontists, Fedn. Dentaire Internationale, Psi Omega, Omicron Kappa Upsilon.

REHBEIN, EDWARD ANDREW, minister, geologist, consultant; b. Aug. 13, 1947; s. Edward Louis and Marjorie Ann (Simshaw) R.; m. Phyllis Jean Boyer, June 23, 1973; children: Matthew Louis, Angela Mae. BS in Geology, Calif. Inst. Tech., 1969. Geologist U. S. Forest Svcs., Elkins, W.Va., 1972—74, U.S. Geol. Survey, Billings, Mont., 1974—76; coal geologist W.Va. Geologic Survey, Morgantown, 1977; cons. Morgantown, 1978; geologist Allied Corp., Beckley, W.Va., 1979; sr. exploration geologist Kerr-McGee Corp., Beckley, W.Va., 1980—82, regional mgr. exploration Reno, 1983—85, exploration geologist Oklahoma City, 1985—88; assoc. min. Ch. of Christ, Beckley, 1989—90, min., 1990—; pres. M&R Computer Sales and Svc., Inc., Beckley, 1989—90. Author: Rememberich God's Word, 1991, Overcome by the Cross, 2003; contbr. articles. Mem.: Am. Assn. Petroleum Geologists, Shotokan Karate Am. Office: N Beckley Ch of Christ PO Box 951 Beckley WV 25802-0951 Personal E-mail: rehbein321@hotmail.com. *So God created man in his own image. (Genesis 1:27). Search the Scriptures, find the full meaning of this, and your life will never be the same.*

REHBERG, DENNIS R., congressman; b. Billings, Mont., Oct. 5, 1955; m. Janice Rehberg; 3 children. Student, Mont. State U., 1974; BA in Pub. Adminstrn. and Polit. Sci., Wash. State U., Pullman, 1977. Tchr. gymnastics, Billings, Mont., 1973—74; with Green Giant Co., Dayton, Wash., 1975—76, Ramada Inn, Billings, 1977; ditch digger Lockrem Constrn., Billings, 1977; real estate salesman Billings, 1977—79; legis. aide Staffs of State Senator Bill Mathers and State Senator Sonny Lockrem, 1977; legis. asst. Staff of US Rep. Ron Marlenee, Mont., 1979—82; mgr. Rehberg Ranch, Billings, 1982—2000; mem. Mont. State Ho. Reps. from Dist. 88, 1985—89; state dir. Staff of US Senator Conrad Burns, Mont., 1989—91; lt. gov. Mont., 1991—97; mem. US Congress from Mont. at large, 2001—, mem. appropriations com. Named Champion of Small Bus., Small Bus. Survival Com., 2001, 2002, Hero of the Taxpayer, Americans for Tax Reform, 2002; recipient Guardian of Senior's Rights award, 60 Plus Assn., 2002, Presdl. award, Leadership, Nat. Farmers Union, 2003. Republican. Episcopalian. Office: US House Reps 516 Cannon House Office Bldg Washington DC 20515-2601 Office Phone: 202-225-3211. Office Fax: 202-225-5687. *

REHG, KENNETH LEE, linguistics educator; b. East St. Louis, Ill., Nov. 21, 1939; s. Theophil Albert and Kathryn Louise (George) R.; m. Kimi Miyagi; 1 child, Laura Le'olani. BA, U. Ill., 1962; MA, So. Ill. U., 1965; PhD, U. Hawaii, 1986. Tng. officer Internat. Ctr. for Lang. Studies, Washington, 1966-67; lang. officer U.S. Peace Corp, Saipan, Micronesia, 1967-70; asst. rschr. Social Sci. Rsch. Inst. U. Hawaii, Honolulu, 1974-83, assoc. prof., 1984—. Cons. Micronesian govt., 1973-76, 97, 2000, 2003, 2004, Samoa Dept. Edn., Pago Pago, 1978, U.S. Geol. Survey, Menlo Park, Calif., 1979-81, Japan Nat. Mus. Ethnology, Osaka, 1986; participant Fulbright-Hays Study Group, Ea. Indonesia, 1991. Author: Ponapean Reference Grammar, 1981; co-author: Kitail Lokaiahn Pohnpei, 1969, Ponapean-English Dictionary, 1979; co-editor: Issues in Austronesian Morphology; mng. editor.: jour. Oceanic Linguistics; contbr. papers to profl. publs.; editor: (jour.) Lang. Documentation and Conservation. Rsch. fellow U. Hawaii, 1981-82; recipient Excellence in Teaching award Hawaii Tchrs. ESL, 1984, Mortar Bd., 1990, Presdl. Citation for meritorious tchg., 1996. Mem. Linguistic Soc. Am., Linguistic Soc. Hawaii. Office: U Hawaii Dept Linguistics Moore Hall 569 1890 E West Rd Honolulu HI 96822-2318 Home Phone: 808-988-7607; Office Phone: 808-956-3277. E-mail: rehg@hawaii.edu.

REHL, BEATRICE CLAIRE, editor; d. William Richard and Alicia Stein Rehl. BA, Princeton U., NJ, 1976; MA, NYU, NYC, 1978, PhD, 1984. Editor George Braziller, Inc., NYC, 1983—89; mgr. ednl. material WNET-Channel 13, NYC, 1987—89; sr. editor Cambridge U. Press, NYC, 1989—. Mem.: Archaeol. Inst. Am., Coll. Art Assn. (bd. dirs. 1995—99). Avocations: ballet, theater, literature, travel, piano. Office: Cambridge Univ Press 32 Avenue of the Americas New York NY 10013

REHM, PATRICE KOCH, radiologist, educator; b. DeSoto, Mo., Nov. 23, 1954; d. James Clarence and Eleanor (Koch) R. BA in Chemistry, U. Mo., 1977; MD, Yale U., 1981. Diplomate Am. Bd. Radiology, Am. Bd. Nuc. Medicine. Intern in medicine Waterbury (Conn.) Hosp., 1981-82; resident in radiology Yale New Haven Hosp., 1982-83, 84-85, fellow in neuroradiology, 1985-86, fellow in nuclear medicine, 1986-87; resident in radiology SUNY Upstate Med. Ctr., Syracuse, 1983-84; clin. assoc. Cleve. Clinic, 1987-88, staff physician, 1988-89, Presbyn. Hosp., Charlotte, N.C., 1989-91, Georgetown U. Med. Ctr., Washington, 1992—2000; assoc. prof. radiology, dir. nuc. medicine U. Va. Health Sys., Charlottesville, Va., 2000—. Fellow Am. Coll. Radiology, Radiologic Soc. N.Am., Soc. Nuc. Medicine. Office: U Va Health Sys PO Box 800170 Charlottesville VA 22908

REHM, SUSAN J., social services professional; b. Yorktown, Va., May 17, 1945; d. Gilbert F. and Jeradean Dolly (Field) R. BA, U. Redlands, 1967; MSW, San Diego State U., 1969. Diplomate in clin. social work; lic. social worker, Calif.; cert. tchr., Calif. Dir. clin. social work home health care and child devel. depts. UCLA Med. Ctr.; dir. social work svcs. Mercy Hosp. and Med. Ctr., San Diego, Calif.; lectr. Sch. Social Work San Diego State U.; exec. dir. Family Svc. Agy., Santa Barbara, Calif. Named state scholar, Calif., 1963-67, U.S. Children's Bur. Fellow, 1968-69. Mem. NASW, Family Svc. Am. (exec. coun.), Santa Barbara Sunrise Rotary, Nat. Found. Infectious Diseases (pres.). Office: Family Svc Agy 123 W Gutierrez St Santa Barbara CA 93101-3424

REHMAN, QAISER, rheumatologist, researcher; b. Karachi, Pakistan, Mar. 4, 1970; arrived in U.S., 1995; s. Malik Nazir Ahmed and Shahnawaz Begum; m. Nadia Jawed, Feb. 7, 2003. MBBS, Aga Khan U., Karachi, 1993. Diplomate Am. Bd. Internal Medicine, Am. Bd. Rheumatology. Resident in internal medicine U. Tex., Houston, 1995—98; fellow in rheumatology U. Calif., San Francisco, 1998—2001; physician Pratt (Kans.) Regional Med. Ctr., 2001—. Co-author: Rheumatoid Arthritis, 2004; manuscript reviewer European Jour. Pediat., 2005—. Fellow: Am. Coll. Angiology; mem.: ACP, Kans. Med. Soc., Am. Coll. Rheumatology. Office: S Ctrl Kans Bone and Joint Ctr 203 Watson St Ste 300 Pratt KS 67124 Office Phone: 620-672-1002. E-mail: rhumatologist@yahoo.com.

REHMUS, CHARLES MARTIN, arbitrator; b. Ann Arbor, Mich., June 27, 1926; s. Paul A. and Amy D. (Martin) R.; m. Carolyn Brown, Dec. 21, 1948 (div. July 1982); children— Paul, James, Jon, David; m. Laura Carlson, Sept. 4, 1982 AB, Kenyon Coll., 1947; MA, Stanford U., 1951, PhD, 1955. Commr. Fed. Mediation and Conciliation Service, San Francisco, 1952-58; staff dir. Presdl. R.R. Commn., Washington, 1959-61; prof. polit. sci. U. Mich., Ann Arbor, 1962-80, dir. Inst. Labor and Indsl. Relations, 1962-76; chmn. Mich. Employment Relations Commn., Detroit, 1976-80; dean N.Y. State Sch. Indsl. and Labor Relations, Cornell U., Ithaca, 1980-86; prof. law U. San Diego, 1988-97. Author: Final-Offer Arbitration, 1975, The Railway Labor Act at Fifty, 1977, Labor and American Politics, 1967, rev. edit., 1978, The National Mediation Board, 1984, Emergency Strikes Revisited, 1990. Chmn. 4 Presdl. emergency bds. at various times. Served to lt. USNR, 1943-45; PTO Mem. Internat. Inst. Labor Studies (bd. govs. 1984-92), Indsl. Rels. Rsch. Assn. (exec. bd. 1984-88), Nat. Acad. Arbitrators (bd. govs. 1979-82, v.p. 1993-95). Home: 18755 W Bernardo Dr Apt 1027 San Diego CA 92127-3011

REHNKE, MARY ANN, academic administrator; b. Faribault, Minn., Jan. 23, 1945; d. Wesley Arthur and Sarah Frances (Smith) Rehnke; m. Charles Orin Willis, Apr. 18, 1924. BA in English, Cornell Coll., 1967; MA in English, U. Chgo., 1968, PhD in Lit., 1974; MS in Ednl Adminstrn., U. Wis., 1975; Cert. of Completion, Shalem Inst. Spiritual Formation, 2000. Head resident Elizabeth Waters Hall, U. Wis., Madison, 1970-73; asst. prof. English No. Ky. U., Highland Heights, 1973-82, acad. adminstr., 1976-77, dir. summer sessions, 1977-80; dir. conf. planning Am. Assn. Higher Edn., Washington, 1980-82; assoc. dean for faculty relations and acad. programs Coll. St. Catherine, St. Paul, 1982-83; assoc. dean of coll. Daemen Coll., Buffalo, 1983-85; v.p. programs Council of Ind. Colls., Washington, 1986—. Mem. planning com. nat. identification program Am. Council Edn., Washington, 1978-85; mem. program com. Nat. Conf. Women Student Leaders and Women of Distinction, Washington, 1985-88. Author: Women in Higher Education Administration: A Brief Guide for Conference

Planners, 1982, Guide to Spiritual Retreats in the Washington, D.C. Area, 1997; editor: Creating Career Programs in a Liberal Arts Context, 1987; editor newsletter N. Ctrl. Regional Women's Studies, 1978-80. Vestry mem Ch. of St. Clement, Alexandria, Va., 1982, vice chair search com., 1986-87. Named one of Outstanding Young Women Am., 1976. Mem.: Nat. Women's Studies Assn., Jane Austen Soc., Soc. Values in Higher Edn., N.Am. Assn. Summer Sessions (rsch. chair 1979—80), Am. Assn. Higher Edn. (coord. nat. conf. roundtable 1982—86), Phi Beta Kappa, Phi Delta Kappa. Democrat. Episcopalian. Office Phone: 202-466-7230. E-mail: mrehnke@cic.nche.edu.

REHNQUIST, JANET, lawyer, former federal agency administrator; b. Phoenix, May 4, 1957; d. William and Margery (Peck) Rehnquist. BA, U. Va., 1979; JD, U. Va. Law School, 1985. Assoc. counsel to the Pres. The White House, Washington, 1990—93; asst. U.S. atty. (ea. dist.) Va. US Dept. Justice, Washington; insp. gen. US Dept. HHS, Washington, 2001—03; ptnr. Venable LLP, Washington, 2003—, co-chair Wash. Health Care practice. Counsel U.S. Senate Permanent Subcom. on Investigations. Office: Venable LLP 575 7th St NW Washington DC 20004 Office Phone: 202-344-8241. Office Fax: 202-344-8300. E-mail: jrehnquist@venable.com.

REHORN, LOIS M(ARIE) (LOIS MARIE SMITH), nursing administrator; b. Larned, Kans., Apr. 15, 1919; d. Charles and Ethel L. (Canaday) Williamson; m. C. Howard Smith, Feb. 15, 1946 (dec. Aug. 1980); 1 child, Cynthia A. Huddleston; m. Harlan W. Rehorn, Aug. 25, 1981. RN, Bethany Hosp. Sch. Nursing, Kansas City, Kans., 1943; BS, Ft. Hays Kans. State U., Hays, 1968, MS, 1970. RN, N.Mex.; lic. pvt. pilot. Office nurse, surg. asst. Dr. John H. Luke, Kansas City, Kans., 1943-47; supr. nursing unit Larned (Kans.) State Hosp., 1949-68, dir. nursing edn., 1968-71, dir. nursing, 1972-81, ret., 1981. Recipient Order of the Blue Key, 1942-43; named Nurse of Yr. DNA-4, 1986. Mem. Am. Nurses Assn., Kans. Nurses Assn. (dist. treas.), N.Mex. Nurses Assn. (dist. pres. 1982-86, dist. bd. dirs. 1986-88). Avocation: flying (pilot). Home: 410 W 2nd St Larned KS 67550-3508 *Keep within you a place where dreams may grow. The fountain of understanding is the willingness to listen.*

REHR, DAVID K., broadcast association executive; BS, St. Johns U., 1981; MA, George Mason U., 1989, PhD. Exec. asst. to U.S. Rep Vin Weber U.S. Ho. of Reps., mem. staff com. small bus., dir. fed. govt. rels.; dir. Nat. Fedn. Independent Businesses; pres. govt. affairs Nat. Beer Wholesalers Assn., Inc., sr. v.p.; pres., CEO Nat. Assn. Broadcasters, 2005—. Office: Nat Assn Broadcasters 1771 N St NW Washington DC 20036-2891 Office Phone: 202-429-5300. Office Fax: 202-429-4199. E-mail: irc@nab.org.

REHTH, ANN, counselor; b. Pennyan, NY, May 28, 1942; d. J. Allen and Jean Eleanor (Stanhope) Henderson; children: Nikki, Douglas, Scott. BA, U. South Fla., 1983; MS, Nova U., 1994. Cert. tchr., ESL tchr. Tchr. Venice H.S., Fla., 1984—94; mental health counselor Meridian Behavioral, Gainsville, Fla., 1994—98, YMCA, Sarasota, Fla., 1998—2001; tchr. Gulf Coast Marine Inst., Venice, 2000—01; tchr. ESOL and reading North Port H.S., Fla., 2001—06; ret., 2006; part-time tchr. Sarasota County Tech. Inst., 2005—. Dir. intervention program for children and teens Meridian Behavioral, Gainsville, Fla., 1994—98; cons. to schs. for abuse and crisis intervention YMCA, Venice, Fla., 1999—2001. Mem.: Sarasota Literacy Coun. Avocations: reading, volunteer projects, walking, tricycle riding. Personal E-mail: annrehth@verizon.net.

REIBEL, KURT, physicist, researcher; b. Vienna, May 23, 1926; came to U.S., 1938; s. Michael and Regina (Pak) R.; m. Eleanor Elvira Mannino, June 10, 1954; children— Leah, Michael, David BA, Temple U., 1954; MS, U. Pa., 1956, PhD, 1959. Jr. research assoc. in physics Brookhaven Nat. Lab., 1957-59; research assoc, U. Pa., Phila., 1959-61; asst. prof. Ohio State U., Columbus, 1961-64, assoc. prof., 1964-70, prof. physics, 1970-92, prof. emeritus, 1992—. Vis. scientist CERN, Geneva, Switzerland, 1968-69, 75-76 Author research papers on nuclear and elementary particle physics NSF fellow, 1954-56 Mem. Am. Phys. Soc., AAUP, Fedn. Am. Scientists, Union Concerned Scientists, Sigma Xi Jewish. Office: Ohio State U Dept Physics 191 W Woodruff Ave Columbus OH 43210-1117

REIBER, PAUL L., state supreme court chief justice; b. Pitts., June 20, 1947; BA, Hampden-Sydney Coll., Va., 1970; JD, Suffolk Law Sch., 1974. Prtnr. Reiber, Kenlan, Schwiebert and Facey, 1984—2003; town moderator Chittenden, 1985—; justice Vt. Supreme Ct., 2003—04, chief justice, 2004—. Former mem. Vt. Jud. Nomination Bd. Mem.: ABA, Vt. Bar Assn. Avocations: bicycling, reading. Office: Vt Supreme Ct 109 State St Montpelier VT 05609-0701 *

REIBLE, DANNY DAVID, environmental chemical engineer, educator; b. Rantoul, Ill., Dec. 21, 1954; s. George Anthony and Mavis Otilla (Prause) R.; m. Susanne Cecilia Schulte, Mar. 17, 1979; children: Kristin Nicole, Monica Lynn. BS, Lamar U., 1977; MS, Calif. Inst. Tech., 1979, PhD, 1982. Registered profl. engr., La.; diplomate environ. engr., 2004. Asst. prof. La. State U., Baton Rouge, 1981-86, assoc. prof., 1986-92, prof. chem. engring., 1992—2004, Chevron prof. chem. engring., 1998—2004, dir. Hazardous Substance Rsch. Ctr., 1995—; Shell prof. environ. engring. U. Sydney, Australia, 1993-95; Bettie Margaret Smith chair environ. health engring. U. Tex., Austin, 2004—. Vis. rschr. U.S. Army Engr. Waterways Experiment Sta., Vicksburg, Miss., 1990; sr. visitor Cambridge U., Eng., 1992; cons. in field. Author: Fundamentals of Environmental Engineering, 1999, Diffusion Models of Environmental Transport, 2000; contbr. articles to profl. publs. Environ. Sci. and Engring. fellow AAAS, 1987. Fellow AIChE (exec. bd. 1990-95, LK Cecil award 1992); mem. NAE, Am. Chem. Soc., Am. Geophys. Union, Am. Soc. Engring. Edn. (New Engring. Educator Excellence award 1985), Ak. Soc, Civil Engring., Assn. Environ. Engring. Sci. Profs., Coms. Nat. Rsch. Coun., Sigma Xi. Achievements include identification and evaluation of new mechanisms for contaminant release in the environment; advances in sediment management techniques; development of widely used methods of managing contaminated sediments. Home: 10300 Indigo Broom Loop Austin TX 78733 Office: U Tex 1 University Station C1786 Austin TX 78712 Office Phone: 512-471-4642. E-mail: reible@mail.utexas.edu.

REIBOLD, DOROTHY ANN, accountant, researcher; b. Leigh, Nebr., Feb. 22, 1922; d. Herman Ludwig Marty and Frances Jane Harvey; m. Wayne Henry Reibold, Mar. 27, 1947; children: Lillie Frances, Marty John. BEd, Wayne State Tchrs., 1945. Tchr., prin. Nenzel Sch., Nebr., 1941-42; tchr. Cozad Sch., Nebr., 1942-43; sec. Burroughs Adding Machine, Omaha, 1943-44; tchr. Lyons Pub. Sch., Nebr., 1945-47; office mgr. Yoelin Bros. Wholesale, Denver, 1947-52; freelance bookkeeper Henderson, Colo., 1960-00; bookkeeper Hazeltine Heights Water, Henderson, 1964—2007; dir. sch. lunch program Zion Luth. Sch., Brighton, Colo., 1969—78; dir. budget Hazeltine Heights Water, 1982—2007. Author: Ecklin Family Story, 1988, Life of Matthias Harvye, 1998. Mem.: DAR. Republican. Lutheran. Avocations: genealogy, travel. Home and Office: 8181 E 104th Ave Henderson CO 80640-9049 Home Phone: 303-288-8635. Personal E-mail: dotareibold@earthlink.net.

REICH, ABRAHAM CHARLES, lawyer; b. Waterbury, Conn., Apr. 17, 1949; s. Samuel and Esther (Gurvitz) Reich; m. Sherri Engelman, Aug. 15, 1971; children: Spencer, Alexander. BA, U. Conn., 1971; JD, Temple U., 1974. Bar: Pa. 1974, U.S. Supreme Ct. 1979. Assoc. Fox Rothschild LLP, Phila., 1974-81, ptnr., 1981—, mng. ptnr., 2001—05, co-chair, 2005—. Chair lawyers adv. com. U.S. Ct. Appeals (3d cir.), 1998. Fellow: Am. Coll. Trial Lawyers; mem.: ABA (house dels. 1997—2002, 2004—), Phila. Bar Assn. (chair profl. responsibility com. 1983—84, chair bench-bar com. 1985, chair profl. guidance com. 1987—88, bd. govs. 1987—89, chair bd. govs. 1989, chancellor 1995, del. ABA 1996—2000). Home: 2224 Mount Vernon St Philadelphia PA 19130-3115 Office: Fox Rothschild LLP 2000 Market St Ste 10 Philadelphia PA 19103-3231 Office Phone: 215-299-2090. Business E-Mail: areich@foxrothschild.com.

REICH, ALLAN J., lawyer; b. Chgo., July 9, 1948; s. H. Robert and Sonya (Minsky) R.; m. Lynne Susan Roth, May 23, 1971; children: Allison, Marissa, Scott. BA, Cornell U., 1970; JD cum laude, U. Mich., 1973. Bar: Ill. 1973, U.S. Dist. Ct. (no. dist.) Ill. 1973. Ptnr. McDermott, Will & Emery, Chgo., 1973-93; vice chmn. D'Ancona & Pflaum LLC, Chgo., 1993—2003; ptnr., chair nat. corp. practice group Seyfarth Shaw LLP, Chgo., 2003—. Trustee Oakmark Family of Mutual Funds, 1994—. V.p., mem. exec. com. Coun. for Jewish Elderly, 1989—97; mem. men's coun. Mus. Contemporary Art, Chgo., 1988—89; mem. Chgo. exec. bd. Am. Jewish Com., 1989—, nat. bd. govs., pres., 2007; mem. met. Chgo. bd. Am. Heart Assn.; bd. dirs. Young Men's Jewish Coun., Chgo., 1974—84, Coun. for Jewish Elderly, 1986—97. Fellow: Am. Bar Found.; mem.: ABA, Chgo. Bar Assn., Econ. Club Chgo., Northmoor Country Club (Highland Park, Ill.), Standard Club (Chgo.). Home: 936 Skokie Ridge Dr Glencoe IL 60022-1434 Office: Seyfarth Shaw LLP 131 S Dearborn St Ste 2400 Chicago IL 60603 Home Phone: 847-835-3225; Office Phone: 312-460-5650. Business E-Mail: areich@seyfarth.com.

REICH, BERNARD, political science professor; b. Bklyn., Dec. 5, 1941; s. Moe and Rosalyn (Hartglass) R.; m. Madelyn Sue Ingber, June 16, 1963; children— Barry, Norman, Michael, Jennifer BA cum laude with spl. honors, CCNY, 1961; MA, U. Va., 1963, PhD, 1964. Asst. prof. polit. sci. and internat. affairs George Washington U., Washington, 1964-70, assoc. prof., 1970-76, prof., 1976—, chmn. dept. polit. sci., 1976-82, 88-91. Vis. prof. U. Va., 1969, 94, Sch. Advanced Internat. Studies Johns Hopkins U., 1978-80; vis. rsch. assoc. Tel Aviv U., 1971-72. Author: Quest for Peace: United States-Israel Relations and the Arab-Israeli Conflict, 1977, The U.S. and Israel: Influence in the Special Relationship, 1984, Israel: Land of Tradition and Conflict, 1985, 1993, Historical Dictionary of Israel, 1992, Securing the Covenant: United States-Israel Relations After the Cold War, 1995, A Brief History of Israel, 2005, A Brief History of Isreal, 2005; co-author, co-editor: Government and Politics of the Middle East and North Africa, 1980, 1986, 1995, 2002, Israel Faces the Future, 1986, The Powers in the Middle East, 1987, Israeli National Security Policy: Political Actors and Perspectives, 1988, Political Leaders of the Contemporary Middle East and North Africa: A Biographical Dictionary, 1990;; co-author: Israeli Politics in the 1990's: Key Domestic and Foreign Policy Factors, 1991; co-editor: Israeli Politics in the 1990's Key Domestic and Foreign Policy Factors, 1991, Arab-Israeli Conflict and Conciliation: A Documentary History, 1995, An Historical Encyclopedia of the Arab-Israeli Conflict, 1996; editor, co-author: Handbook of Political Science Research on the Middle East and North Africa, 1998; co-author, co-editor: Government and Politics of the Middle East and North Africa, 2002, Israel Faces the Future, 1986, The Powers in the Middle East, 1987, Israeli National Security Policy: Political Actors and Perspectives, 1988, Political Leaders of the Contemporary Middle East and North Africa: A Biographical Dictionary, 1990, co-author: United States Foreign Policy and the Middle East/North Africa: A Bibliography of Twentieth-Century Research, 1990, Asian States' Relations with the Middle East and North Africa: A Bibliography, 1950-93, 1994, U.S. Foreign Relations with the Middle East and North Africa: A Bibliography, 1998, 1999, Political Dictionary of Israel, 2000; mem. adv. bd. editors Middle East Jour., 1977—, Terrorism, 1987—93, Jour. Israel Affairs, 1994—, Fgn. Svc. Jour., 1987—90, contbr. articles to profl. jours. Bd. govs. Middle East Inst. Fulbright research scholar, UAR, 1965; NSF postdoctoral fellow, 1971-72 Mem.: Phi Beta Kappa. Home: 13800 Turnmore Rd Silver Spring MD 20906-2134 Office: George Washington U Dept Polit Sci Washington DC 20052-0001 Office Phone: 202-994-6716. Business E-Mail: breich@gwu.edu.

REICH, BERNARD, communications engineer; b. NYC, Jan. 7, 1926; s. Adolph and Rose (Gluck) R.; m. Sylvia Greenberg, June 15, 1947; children: Robin Reich Murphy, Richard. BS in Physics, CCNY, 1948; MSc, Rutgers U., 2002. Electronic engr., supervisory electronic engr. U.S. Army Electronics R & D Command, Ft. Monmouth, N.J., 1948-81; unit mgr. Semcor, Farmingdale, N.J., 1981-88; telecommunications engr. Telos Corp., Shrewsbury, N.J., 1988-99, retired, 1999. Chmn. spl. working group on semicondrs. and microelectronics NATO, Brussels, 1959-80, chmn. group experts on electronic parts, 1972-80; adv. editor Microelectronics and Reliability, 1970—. Contbr. over 100 articles to tech. jours.; patentee in field. Mem. Juvenile Conf. Com., Ocean Twp., N.J., 1964—; pres. Manor at Wayside Condominium Assn., Ocean Twp., 1990-91. Sgt. U.S. Army, 1945-46, ETO. Recipient decoration for meritorious civilian svc. U.S. Army Electronics R & D Command, 1981. Fellow IEEE (chartered,), IEE (Eng.). Avocation: walking. Home: 45 Gimbel Pl Ocean NJ 07712-2565

REICH, DAVID LEE, library director; b. Orlando, Fla., Nov. 25, 1930; s. P.F. and Opal Katherine (Wood) Reichelderfer; m. Kathleen Johanna Weichel, Aug. 2, 1954 (div. Sept. 1964); 1 son, Robert Weichel. PhB magna cum laude, U. Detroit, 1961; AM in LS, U. Mich., 1963. Tchr. English Jefferson Davis Jr. Sch., San Antonio, 1961-62; dir. engring. library Radiation Inc., Melbourne, Fla., 1963-64; asst. to dir. libraries Miami-Dade Jr. Coll., Miami, Fla., 1964-65; dir. learning resources Monroe County C.C., Monroe, Mich., 1965-68; dep. dir. Dallas Pub. Library, 1968-73; dep. chief librarian Chgo. Pub. Library, 1973-74, commr., 1975-78; dir. Bd. Libr. Commrs., Commonwealth of Mass., Boston, 1978-80; exec. sec. New Eng. Libr. Bd., Augusta, Maine, 1980-82, vice chmn., 1979-80; dir. Lakeland (Fla.) Pub. Libr., 1983-99, ret., 1999; exec. sec. Soc. Fla. Archivists, 1999—2001, ret., 2001. Libr. cons. Macomb County C.C., Warren, Mich., 1967; chmn. adv. com. to libr. tech. asst. program El Centro Coll., Dallas, 1969-71; mem. inter-task working group Goals for Dallas, 1968-70, mem. Dallas Area Libr. planning coun., 1970-73; mem. adv. coun. dept. libr. sci. No. Ill. U., 1975-78; v.p., pres.-elect Tampa Bay Libr. Consortium, 1985-86, pres., 1986-87. Co-author: The Public Library in Non-traditional Education, 1974; editor The Villas II News, 1999—; contbr. articles to library jours. Bd. dirs. The Villas II Homeowners Assn., 1994-96, 98-2001; mem. steering com. Friends of Tampa Bay Libr. Consortium, 2000—. Sgt. U.S. Army, 1952-55. Recipient Disting. Alumnus award U. Mich., 1978; William B. Calkins Found. scholar Orlando, 1963; Carnegie L.S. Endowment scholar, 1963. Mem. ALA (coun.-at-large 1968-72, 75-79), S.E. Libr. Assn., Fla. Libr. Assn. (sec.-treas. coll. and spl. librs. divsn. 1965, steering com. mcpl. librs. caucus 1983-84, chmn. 1984-85, exec. bd. 1984-87), Soc. Fla. Archivists (exec. bd. 1994-96, sec. 1996-97, exec. sec. 1999-2001, treas. 2000-01), Fla. Pub. Libr. Assn. (pres. 1987-88, exec. bd. 1988-89, 94-95, pres. emeritus 1996-98, editor newsletter 1992-93, 96-97, chmn. libr. adminstrn. divsn. 1992, friends and trustees divsn. 1993, 95), Soc. Automotive Historians, Alumni Assn. U. Mich. (pres. Libr. Sch. alumni 1973), Nat. Soc. SAR, Polk Sr. Games (bd. dirs., 2004—, sec. 2007—). Home: 4011 Heron Ave Lakeland FL 33813-1123 E-mail: dreich@tampabay.rr.com.

REICH, HERB, editor; b. NYC; s. Herman S. and Hattie (Davis) R.; m. Gerri Toog, Aug. 7, 1960; children: Amanda Suri, Elizabeth Jo. BA, Bklyn. Coll., 1950; MA, Bklyn. Coll. and Kings County Hosp., 1951; postgrad., Columbia U., 1951-54. Author sketches and lyrics Tamiment Revues (Pa.), 1951; staff writer NBC-TV, NYC and Los Angeles, 1955-57; research coordinator Inst. for Motivational Research, Croton-on-Hudson, NY, 1958-59; research dir. Scientist and Engr. Technol. Inst., NYC, 1960-64; mng. editor SETI Pubs. Inc., NYC, 1961-64; sr. editor Odyssey Press, NYC, 1964-65; editorial dir. Profl. and Tech. Programs Inc., NYC, 1966-72; dir. Behavioral Sci. Book Service, NYC, 1966-72; dir. behavioral scis. program Basic Books Inc., NYC, 1973-79; editor intersci. div. John Wiley & Sons. Inc., NYC, 1979-87, sr. editor profl. and trade divsn., 1987-95; pres. H&G Reich, Cons., Hastings Hdsn., NY, 1980—. Publ., rsch., advt. and polit. cons.; rschr., statistician, rsch. cons. Am. Found. for Blind, Pepsi Cola Co., Nowland and Co., Comms. and Media Rsch. Svcs. Mng. editor: Odyssey Science Library Ency. of Engring., Signs and Symbols, 1965, Dictionary of Physics and Mathematics Abbreviations, Signs and Symbols, 1965, Dictionary of Electronics Abbreviations, Signs and Symbols, 1965, Dictionary of Computers and Control Systems Abbreviations, Signs and Symbols, 1965; contbr. Random House Dictionary of the English Language, 1967, rev. edit., 1987, The Greatest Revue Sketches, 1982, Ency. of Psychology, 2d edit., 1994, Corsini Encyclopedia of Psychology and Behavioral Scienses, 2001; TV writer: Broadway Open House, 1951, Olsen and Johnson Show, 1951, Milton Berle Texaco Star Theatre, 1952, All-Star Revue, 1952, Mel Torme Show, 1952, Eddie Cantor Show, 1953, Red Buttons Show, 1954, Summer Colgate Show, 1954, Jerry Lester Show, 1954, Jan Murray Time, 1955, Howdy Doody Show, 1955-56, Tonight Show, 1956, NBC Comedy Hour, 1956, Wayne and Schuster Hour, 1957. Co-founder, vice chmn. Mt. Vernon United for Better Edn., N.Y., 1970-73; mem. Westchester County Democratic Com., 1972-76; exec. com. Mt. Vernon Dem. City Com., 1973-76; mem. supt.'s adv. com. Hastings Schs., Hastings-on-Hudson, N.Y., 1981-82. Recipient Gold award of excellence for radio advt. Advt. Club of Westchester, 1980; recipient Gold and Bronze awards of excellence for radio advt. Advt. Club of Westchester, 1981 Mem. AAAS, APA, Alpha Phi Omega. Office: 127 Mount Hope Blvd Hastings On Hudson NY 10706 Office Phone: 914-478-4042. Personal E-mail: hgreich@yahoo.com.

REICH, JILL, dean; B.A., Regis College; PhD in Psychology, Dartmouth Coll. Fmr. dept. chair, assoc. dean Grad. school Loyola; fmr. dean of faculty Trinity College; fmr. exec. dir. of education American Psychology Assoc.; prof., dept. of psychology Bates Coll., v.p. of academic affairs, dean of faculty Lewiston, Maine, 2000—. Office: Bates Coll Lane Hall Rm 120A 2 Andrews Rd Lewiston ME 04240 Office Phone: 207-786-6066. E-mail: jreich@bates.edu. *

REICH, JOHN M., federal agency administrator; BS, So. Ill. U., 1961; MBA, U. South Fla.; graduate, Sch. Banking of South, La. State U. Cmty. banker, Ill., Fla.; pres., CEO Nat. Bank Sarasota, Fla.; staff mem. for US Senator Connie Mack, 1988—2000, chief of staff, 1998—2000; bd. dirs. FDIC, 2001—, acting chmn., 2001, vice chmn., 2002—05; dir. Office of Thrift Supervision, Washington, 2005—. Chmn. bd. dir. Sarasota Family YMCA, Fla. Office: Office of Thrift Supervision 1700 G St NW Washington DC 20552 Office Phone: 202-898-3888.

REICH, LARRY SAM, lawyer; b. Bklyn., Sept. 24, 1946; s. Sidney and Regina (Brown) R.; children: Ilysa Jill, Shari Beth; m. Marcia S. Koltun, Mar. 17, 2002. BA, Hofstra U., 1969; JD, Bklyn. Law Sch., 1973. Bar: NY 1974, US Dist. Ct. (so. and ea. dists.) NY 1974, US Ct. Appeals (2d cir.) 1974, US Ct. Appeals (3d cir.) 2002, US Supreme Ct. 1980. Assoc. S. Edward Orenstein PC, NYC, 1973-78; ptnr. Herzfeld & Rubin PC, NYC, 1978-98, Blank Rome LLP, NYC, 1999—. Arbitrator US Dist. Ct. (ea. dist.) NY, Bklyn., 1986—; mem. guest faculty Hofstra U. Sch. Law, 1994—. Mem. ABA, N.Y. State Bar Assn. (chmn. com. on supreme cts. 1986-89, chmn. com. on jud. adminstrn. 1989-92, com. jud. adminstrn. 1989-94), N.Y. County Bar Assn., Nassau County Bar Assn., Assn. Trial Lawyers Am., N.Y. State Trial Lawyers Assn. Avocations: running, rowing, biking, reading. Office: Blank Rome LLP The Chrysler Bldg New York NY 10174 Office Phone: 212-885-5514. Business E-Mail: lreich@blankrome.com.

REICH, LAURENCE, lawyer; b. Jersey City, Jan. 22, 1931; s. Victor and Miriam (Gross) R.; m. Doris Rita Diamond, Oct. 21, 1965 (dec. Apr. 15, 2002). BA, U. Chgo., 1951, JD, 1953. Bar: NJ 1954, NY 1982, US Dist. Ct. NJ 1954, US ct. appeals (3rd cir.) 1958, US Supreme ct. 1963, US Tax Ct. 1971, US Dist. Ct. (so. dist.) NY 1982, US Ct. Appeals (2nd cir.) 1987. From mem. firm to sr. counsel McElroy, Deutsch, Mulvaney & Carpenter, LLP (formerly Carpenter, Bennett & Morrissey), Newark, 1957—2003. Mem. Bur. Nat. Affairs Tax Adv. bd., 1972—; lectr. in field. Author: NJ Corporation Law and Practice; contbr. articles to profl. jours. With US Army, 1955-57. Fellow Am. Coll. Tax Counsel, Am. Bar Found.; mem. ABA (com. chmn. sect. taxation 1972-74, 85-86, mem. coun. 1991-94), NJ Bar Assn. (chmn. taxation sect. 1975-76), Assn. Fed. Bar State NJ (v.p. 1982-94, bd. trustees 1994-99), Essex County Bar Assn. Office Phone: 973-565-2003. Business E-Mail: lreich@mdmc-law.com.

REICH, MICHAEL, economics professor; b. Poland, Oct. 18, 1945; came to U.S., 1949; s. Melvin and Betty (Mandelbaum) R.; children: Rachel, Gabriel. BA, Swarthmore Coll., 1966; PhD, Harvard U., 1974. Asst. prof. Boston U., 1971-74, U. Calif., Berkeley, 1974-81, acting assoc. prof., 1981-82, assoc. prof., 1982-89, prof., 1989—. Rsch. dir. Nat. Ctr. for the Workplace, 1993-96, Inst. Labor and Employment, 2001-04; dir. Inst. Indsl. Rels., 2004-. Author: Segmented Work, Divided Workers, 1982, Racial Inequality, 1981, The Capitalist System, 1986, Social Structures of Accumulation, 1994, Work and Pay in the U.S. and Japan, 1997; editor: Indsl. Rels. Jour., 1986-94; contbr. articles to profl. jours. Mem. Am. Econ. Assn., Indsl. Rels. Rsch. Assn., Phi Beta Kappa, Sigma Xi. Office: Dept of Econs U Calif 611 Evans Hl Berkeley CA 94720-0001

REICH, RICHARD ALLEN, bank executive; b. Rhinelander, Wis., Mar. 12, 1962; s. John E. and Alma Louise (Post) R. BBA, U. Wis., Madison, 1984; MBA, NYU, NYC, 1989. CPA, Okla. Staff acct., cons. Deloitte, Haskins and Sells, NYC, 1984-86; fin. analyst Salomon Bros., Inc., NYC, 1986-89; treasury mgr. Citibank-US Card Products Group, NYC, 1989-92; with Bankers Trust Corp., NYC, 1992-93; v.p., dir. risk mgmt. Nikko Securities Internat., Inc., NYC, 1993-95, CDC Capital, Inc., NYC, 1995-99; dir. risk mgmt. and control OGE Energy Corp., Oklahoma City, 1999—2005; sr. v.p. corp. fin. BancFirst Corp., Oklahoma City, 2005—. Investment mgr. Wis. Eastern Scholarship Fund, 1996-2001. Mem. AICPA, Okla. Soc. CPA, Okla. Soc. Security Analysts, CFA Inst., U. Wis. Alumni Assn. NY (sec. 1989-91, v.p. 1991-92, pres. 1992-95). Avocations: golf, skiing. Office: BancFirst Corp 101 N Broadway Ste 900 Oklahoma City OK 73102-8405 Home: 2219 Windmere Dr Edmond OK 73034-6600 Office Phone: 405-218-4126. Personal E-mail: richard_a_reich@yahoo.com.

REICH, ROBERT BERNARD, political economics educator, former secretary of labor; b. Scranton, Pa., June 24, 1946; s. Edwin Saul and Mildred Dorf (Freshman) R.; m. Clare Dalton, July 7, 1973. BA, Dartmouth Coll., 1968, MA (hon.), 1988; MA, Oxford U., Eng., 1970; JD, Yale U., 1973. Asst. solicitor gen. US Dept. Justice, Washington, 1974-76; dir. policy planning FTC, Washington, 1976-81; mem. faculty John F. Kennedy Sch. Govt. Harvard U., Cambridge, Mass., 1981-92; sec. US Dept. Labor, Washington, 1993-97; Maurice B. Hexter prof. econ. & social policy Brandeis U., Waltham, 1997—2006; prof. pub. policy Richard & Rhoda Goldman Sch. Pub. Policy, U. Calif, Berkely, 2006—. Chmn. biotech. sect. U.S. Office Tech. Assessment, Washington, 1990-91; vis. prof., Richard & Rhoda Goldman Sch. Pub. Policy, U. Calif, 2004, 2005 Author: The Next American Frontier, 1983, New Deals: The Chrysler Revival and the American System, 1986, Tales of a New America: The Anxious Liberals's Guide to the Future, 1987, The Resurgent Liberal: And Other Unfashionable Prophecies, 1989, The Work of Nations: Preparing Ourselves for 21st Century Capitalism, 1991, Locked in the Cabinet, 1997,

The Future of Success: Working and Living in the New Economy, 2001, I'll Be Short: Essentials for a Decent Working Society, 2002, Reason: Why Liberals Will Win the Battle for America, 2004, Supercapitalism: The Transformation of Business, Democracy, and Everyday Life, 2007; editor: The Power of Public Ideas, 1987; contbg. editor The New Republic, Washington, 1982-93; co-founder, nat. editor, chmn. editl. bd. The Am. Prospect, 1990—; playwright Public Exposure, 2005. Mem. governing bd. Common Cause, Washington, 1981-85; bd. dirs. Bus. Enterprise Trust, Palo Alto, Calif., 1989-93; trustee Dartmouth Coll., Hanover, N.H., 1989-93. Rhodes scholar, 1968; recipient Louis Brownlow award ASPA, 1983, Vaclev Havel Found. prize, 2003 Office: Richard & Rhoda Goldman School Pub Policy U Calif Berkeley 2607 Hearst Ave Berkeley CA 94720 E-mail: rreich@berkeley.edu. *

REICH, ROBERT SIGMUND, landscape architect; b. NYC, Mar. 22, 1913; s. Ulysses S. and Adele G. R.; m. Helen Elizabeth Adams, May, 1945; children: Barbara, Betsy, Bob, Bill. BS, Cornell U., 1934, PhD, 1941; postgrad., U. So. Calif., 1951. Instr. landscape design Cornell U., 1936-39, 40-41; instr. landscape design U. Conn., 1939-40; Inst. Land Design La. State U., 1941-46, asst. prof. landscape architecture, 1946-49, asso. prof., 1949-60, prof., 1960—, Alumni prof., 1967—, head dept. landscape architecture, 1964-79, dir. Sch. Landscape Architecture, 1979-83; prof. Landscape Architecture, 1992—. Instr. Shrivenham (Eng.) Am. U., 1946, Biarritz (France) Am. U., 1947; vis. lectr. Tulane U., 1958-67; judge, instr. Nat. Council Garden Clubs, 1956—; mem. task force on parks, recreation and tourism Goals for La. Program; mem. com. to establish Chicot State Park Arboretum, Ville Plate, La., 1964, mem. steering com., 1964-75; examiner La. Bd. Examination for Landscape Architects, 1957-77 Co-author: Landscape and You, 1953. Mem. com. to establish City/Parish Beautification Commn., 1961-82; mem. area and facilities com. Baton Rouge Recreation and Pk. Commn., 1957-83; bd. dirs. Hubbard Edn. Trust, Weston, Mass., 1967—; adv. com. Friends of Frederick Law Olmsted Papers, 1983-95. With U.S. Army, 1942-45; in charge alter arrangements U. United Meth. Ch., 1945—. Recipient Tchg. award of merit Gamma Sigma Delta, 1963, Baton Rouge Green Individual Honor award, 1996. Fellow Am. Soc. Landscape Architects (trustee 1968-71, 83-86, 3d v.p. 1971-73, Medal 1992); mem. AIA (hon.), S.W. Park and Recreation Tng. Inst. (dir. 1975-77, award of merit 1968), Phi Kappa Phi, Pi Alpha xi, Omicron Delta Kappa, Sigma Lambda Alpha. Home: 333 E Boyd Dr Baton Rouge LA 70808-4507 Office: La State U Sch Landscape Architecture Coll Art & Design Bldg Baton Rouge LA 70803-0001 E-mail: doc@reichassociates.net.

REICH, STANLEY BENJAMIN, radiologist, medical educator; b. NYC, Feb. 20, 1921; s. Harry Max Reich and Bessie Bangel; m. Adele Axelrod, Dec. 15, 1944; children: Linda, James, Judi. AB, Cornell U., 1941; MD, NYU, 1944. Diplomate Am. Bd. Radiology, Am. Bd. Nuclear Medicine. Intern Bellevue Hosp., NYC, 1944-45, resident in radiology, 1946-49; asst. prof. NYU/Bellevue Hosp., NYC, 1949-50; clin. prof. radiology U. Calif., San Francisco, 1952-72, 77—; prof. radiology U. Colo., Denver, 1972-77, U. Calif. Davis, Sacramento, 1977—; chief radiology No. Calif. VA Clinics, Martinez, 1979-98. Contbr. articles to profl. jours. Pres. Concordia-Argonaut Club, San Francisco, 1963-65; cons. Travis AFB, Fairfield, Calif., 1977—, Exec. Svc. Corps., San Francisco, 1997-2002. Lt. (sr.) USN, 1944-47, 50-52. Fellow Am. Coll. Radiology; mem. Am. Soc. Thoracic Radiology (sec. 1967), Am. Radium Soc. Avocations: travel, photography. Home: 2 Abbott Way Piedmont CA 94618-2610 Personal E-mail: asreich@att.net, asreia@att.net.

REICH, STEVE, composer; b. NYC, Oct. 3, 1936; m. Beryl Korot; children: Ezra, Michael. Studies in percussion with Roland Kohloff, 1950—53; BA in Philosophy with honors, Cornell U., 1957; studies in composition with Hall Overton, 1957—58; studies with Bergsma and Persichetti, Julliard Sch. Music, 1958—61; MA in Music, Mills Coll., 1963; studies in drumming, Inst. for African Studies, U. Ghana, 1970; student, Am. Soc. for Ea. Arts, Seattle and Berkeley, 1973—74, Cantillation of Hebrew Scriptures, NYC and Jerusalem, 1976—77; D (hon.), Calif. Inst. Arts, 2000. Organized ensemble Steve Reich and Musicians, 1966; performed throughout the world, 1971—; recs. with various cos. including Columbia Records, Deutsche Grammophon, Nonesuch, Disques Shandar, Hungaraton, Angel, ECM, Phillips, Virgin Classics, Argo. Regents lectr. U. Calif., Berkeley, 2000. Composer, performer: (albums) Come Out, 1967, It's Gonna Rain, 1969, Violin Phase, 1969, Four Organs, 1970, Phase Patterns, 1970, Drumming, 1971, Four Organs, 1973, Six Pianos, 1973, Music for Mallet Instruments, Voices, and Organ, 1973, Music for Eighteen Musicians, 1978 (Grammy award 1999), Octet, 1980, Music for a Large Ensemble, 1980,Tehillim, 1982, The Desert Music, 1984, Sextet, 1986, Six Marimbas, 1986, Electric Counterpoint, 1987, Different Trains, 1988 (Grammy award 1989), The Four Sections, 1987, The Cave, 1994, City Life, 1995, Proverb, 1996, Triple Quartet, 1999, Three Tales, 2002, Dance Patterns, 2002, Cello Counterpoint, 2003, You Are, 2004, others; recordings include (10 CD boxed set) Steve Reich Works: 1965-1995; composer: Vermont Counterpoint, Variations for Winds, Strings and Keyboards, Eight Lines for Chamber Orchestra, Piano Phase, Clapping Music, Pendulum Music, Music for Pieces of Wood, Nagoya Marimbas, other works performed by major orchs. and ensembles; commd. to compose for Holland Festival, 1978, Radio Frankfurt, 1979, San Francisco Symphony, 1980, Rothko Chapel, 1981, West German Radio, Cologne, 1984, Fromm Music Found., 1985, Richard Stoltzman, 1985, Bklyn. Acad. Music, 1987, Kronos Quartet, 1988, St. Louis Sympnony, 1987, (with Beryl Korot) The Cave video opera commd. by Vienna Festival, Holland Festival, Festival d'Automne à Paris, Theatre de la Monnaie, Brussels, Hebbel Theatre, Berlin, South Bank Centre/Serious Speakout, London and the Brooklyn Acad. Music, Next Wave Festival, 1993; 4-concert retrospective Lincoln Ctr. Festival, NYC, 1999, video opera (with Beryl Korot) Three Tales, commd. by Vienna Festival, Barbican Ctr., London, SPoleto Festival, Bklyn. Acad. Music, Music Strassbourg, Hebbel Theater, Berlin. Recipient Koussevitzky Found. award, 1981, 2002, Schuman prize Columbia U., 2000, Praemium Imperiale award (Music), Japan Art Assn., 2006, Polar Music prize, 2007; named Composer of Yr., Musical Am., 2000; Rockefeller Found. grantee 1975, 78, 81, 90, Nat. Endowment for the Arts grantee, 1974, 76, 91, NY State Coun. Arts grantee, 1974; Guggenheim fellow, 1978, Montgomery fellow Dartmouth Coll., 2000; elected to Am. Acad. Arts and Letters, 1994, Bayerische Akademie der Schönen Künst, 1995; named Commr. dans l'Ordre des Arts et des Lettres, 1999. Fellow Am. Acad. Arts & Scis. Office: Howard Stokar Mgmt 879 West End Ave New York NY 10025-4918 also: c/o Elizabeth Sobol-Gomez IMG Artists 152 W 57th St 5th Fl New York NY 10019 also: Boosey & Hawkes Inc 35 E 21st St New York NY 10010-6212 also: Nonesuch Records 75 Rockefeller Plaza New York NY 10019 *

REICH, VICTORIA J., consumer products company executive; b. Southborough, Mass., Sept. 24, 1957; BS in Applied Math. & Econs., Brown U. With GE Co., 1979—96; v.p., contr. Brunswick Corp., Lake Forest, Ill., 1996-2000, sr. v.p., CFO, 2000—03, pres. Brunswick European Group, 2003—06; sr. v.p., CFO United Stationers Inc., Deerfield, Ill., 2007—. Office: United Stationers Inc One Pkwy N Blvd Ste 100 Deerfield IL 60015

REICH, WALTER, psychiatrist, medical educator, political science professor, writer, museum director; arrived in USA, 1947, naturalized; s. Simon and Anna (Nussbaum) R.; m. Tova Rachel Weiss, June 10, 1965; children: Daniel S., David E., Rebecca Z. AB, Columbia U., 1965; MD, NYU, 1970; cert. in Psychiatry, Yale U., 1975. Diplomate Am. Bd. Med. Examiners, Am. Bd. Psychiatry and Neurology. Fellow, asst. instr. psychiatry Yale U., New Haven, 1971-73, lectr., 1973—. Lt. comdr., comdr., capt. US Pub. Health Svc., 1973—94; assoc. rsch. psychiatrist NIMH, Bethesda, Md., 1973-75, dir. advanced studies Rockville, Md., 1976-86, sr. rsch. psychiatrist, 1976-94; chmn. program in med. and biolog. scis. Washington Sch. Psychiatry, 1975-85;psychiatrist The Pres.'s Biomed. Rsch. Panel, Washington, 1975-76; sr. rsch. assoc., then sr. scholar Woodrow Wilson Internat. Ctr. Scholars, Washington, 1985—, dir. project on health, sci. and pub. policy, 1992-95; rsch. assoc. Forum on Psychiatry and the Humanities, 1986-88; rsch. prof. psychiatry Uniformed Svcs. U. Health Scis., Bethesda, 1986-88, prof. psychiatry, 1988—; dir. US Holocaust Meml. Mus., Washington, 1995—98; prof. psychiatry and behavioral scis. George Washington U., 1995—. Yitzhak Rabin Meml. Prof. of Internat. Affairs, Ethics and Human Behavior, 1998—. Author: A Stranger in My House: Jews and Arabs in the West Bank, 1984; co-author: How to Beat Jet Lag, 1993; editor: Origins of Terrorism: Psychologies, Ideologies, Theologies, World Views, 1990, 98, King's Crown Essays, 1964-65, Yavneh Rev., 1965-66; mem. editl. bd. Columbia Rev., 1964; adv. editor Psychiatry: Interpersonal and Biological Processes, 1976-; contbg. editor The Wilson Quarterly, 1983-; contbr. numerous articles to profl. jours. Mem. Therapy/Social Control Study Group Inst. Soc., Ethics and the Life Scis., Hastings-on-Hudson NY 1974-75, Group for Advancement of Psychiatry, 1979-83; mem. edn. com. Fortunoff Video Archive for Holocaust Testimonies, Yale U., 1982-85, com. on Scientific Freedom and Responsibility AAAS,1985-91; residential scholar and writer, Mishkenot Sha'ananim, Jerusalem Found., 1984, 85, 87, 2004, 05, 06; mem. acad. bd. Yale Inst. for Study of Global Anti-Semitism, 2007-; adv. coun. mem. Edn. for Pub. Inquiry and Internat. Citizenship, Experimental Coll., Tufts U., 1990; vice chair for Psychiatry, Com. Concerned Scientists, NYC, 1985-95; nat. co-chmn., NYC, 1995—; founding adv. bd. mem. Internat. Inst. for Mediation and Hist. Conciliation, 2001-; mem. Nat. Adv. Coun. Am. Jewish Com., 2002-03; founding mem. Coun. Global Terrorism, 2006. Kennan Inst. Advanced Russian Studies Woodrow Wilson Internat. Ctr. Scholars fellow, 1982-83; Lustman fellow Davenport Coll. Yale U., 1984, 91—; recipient Adminstr.'s award for meritorious achievement Alcohol, Drug Abuse, and Mental Health Adminstrn., 1978; David J. Fish meml. lectr. Brown U., 1984, Art Dir. Club Merit Award, 1985, Albert Kahn meml. lectr. Boston, U., Muriel Gardiner lectr. Yale U., 1994, Solomon A. Berson Medical Alumni Achievement award, 1994; decorated Order of Military Medical Merit U.S. Army, 1991, Outstanding Svc. medal, 1992, Special Presdl. Commendation Am. Psychiatric Assn., 1998, Holocaust Humanitarian award Holocaust Meml. Com., 1999, AAAS award for Sci. Freedom and Responsibility, 2003, Human Rights Award Am. Psychiatric Assn., 2004, Bradley lectr., Am. Enterprise Inst., 2005. Fellow Am. Psychiat. Assn. (disting. life fellow,chair, com. human rights, task force on terrorism, Spl. Presidential Commendation 1998, Human Rights award 2004); mem. AMA. Jewish. Office: Elliott Sch Internat Affairs Geo Wash Univ 1957 E Street NW Washington DC 20052 Office Phone: 202-994-5075. Home Fax: 301-656-0106. Business E-Mail: wreich@gwu.edu.

REICH, WILLIAM ZEEV, lawyer; b. Tel Aviv, Oct. 5, 1947; came to U.S., 1958; s. Louis and Helen (Skura) R.; children: Eric, Justin, Zabrina, Aviva. BA, Queens Coll., CUNY, 1969; JD, SUNY, Buffalo, 1974. Bar: N.Y. 1974, U.S. Supreme Ct. 1980. Assoc. Serotte, Reich & Harasym, Buffalo, 1974—76; ptnr. Serotte, Reich, & Wilson, Buffalo, 1976—. Mem. ABA, N.Y. State Bar Assn., Erie County Bar Assn., Am. Immigration Lawyers Assn. (treas. Upstate chpt. 1982—, overseas practice com. 1984—, nat. liaison com. 1997). Home: 467 N Forest Rd Buffalo NY 14221-5036 Office: Serotte Reich & Wilson 300 Delaware Ave Ste 4 Buffalo NY 14202-1807 Office Phone: 716-854-7525. E-mail: wreich@srwlawyers.com.

REICHARD, ROBERT ROSS, pathologist; b. Dec. 18, 1970; m. Kaari Reichard. MS, U. Louisville, 1995; MD, U. Louisville Sch. Medicine, 1998. Cert. Anatomic Pathology, Neuropathology. Resident, neuropathology U. Tex. Southwestern Health Sciences, Dallas, 1998—2002, intern, pathology, 1999; resident, anatomic pathology Stanford U., 2002—03; fellow, forensic pathology U. N.Mex., 2003—04, asst. prof. pathology, 2004—. Achievements include swimming the English Channel from England to France in 12 hours and 23 minutes on August 16, 2006. Office: Pathology Dept MSCOB 4640 1 University of New Mexico Albuquerque NM 87131

REICHBLUM, AUDREY ROSENTHAL, public relations and publishing executive; b. Pitts., June 28, 1935; d. Emanuel Nathan and Willa (Handmacher) Rosenthal; m. M. Charles Reichblum, Jan. 25, 1956; children: Robert Nathan, William Mark. Student, Bennington Coll., 1952-53; BS, Carnegie Mellon U., 1956. Founder, creator, chmn. Pitts. Children's Mus., 1970-73; mag. writer Pitts. Mag., 1978; dir. pub. rels. Pitts. Pub. Theater, 1978-79; pres. arPR audrey reichblum PUB. RELS. inc., Pitts., 1980—, arpr, inc., 1996—; pub. "Knowledge in a Nutshell" Series, 1996—99, "The Edible Game A Smart Cookie", 1996—, "Sweet Smarts The Candy With A Brain", 2004. Pub. rels. cons., bd. mem. Pitts. Planned Parenthood, 1980-84, United Jewish Fedn., Bus. and Profl. Women, Pitts., 1980-85, Pitts. City Theater, 1985-94, Pa. Coun. on Aging, 1996-99; chmn. Villa de Marillac Nursing, 1999, Vincencian Collaborative Svcs. Bd.; syndicator The Dr. Knowledge Show. Recipient Gold Cindy award Info. Film Producers Am., 1982, award of excellence Internat. Assn. Bus. Communicators, Pitts., 1986, Matrix award for Three Rivers Arts Festival, Lifetime Achievement award NAWBO-YWCA, Y-Tribute to Women in Comms. award, 1998. Mem. Pub. Rels. Soc. Am. (accredited; award of merit 1983, G. Victor Barkman award for excellence 1984, 1st place award Race For The Cure), Women in Comm. (Matrix-sales promotion award 1987), Nat. Assn. Women Bus. Owners (Life Time Achievement award 1995). Office: 1420 Centre Ave Ste 2213 Pittsburgh PA 15219-3536

REICHE, FRANK PERLEY, lawyer, former federal commissioner; b. Hartford, Conn., May 8, 1929; s. Karl Augustus and LaFetra (Perley) R.; m. Janet Taylor, Sept. 26, 1953; children: Cynthia Reiche Schumacker, Dean S. AB, Williams Coll., 1951; LLB, Columbia U., 1959; MA, George Washington U., 1959; LLM in Taxation, NYU, 1966. Bar: N.J. 1960, D.C. 1981. Assoc. Stryker, Tams & Dill, Newark, 1959-61, Smith, Stratton, Wise & Heher, Princeton, NJ, 1962-64, ptnr., 1964-79; commr. Fed. Election Commn., Washington, 1979-85, chmn., 1982; ptnr. Katzenbach, Gildea & Rudner, Lawrenceville, NJ, 1986-93; pvt. practice law Princeton, 1993-97; of counsel Schragger, Lavine & Nagy, West Trenton, NJ, 1997-2000, Archer & Greiner, Princeton, 2001—. Trustee Westminster Choir Coll., Princeton, 1974-86, Ctr. Theol. Inquiry, Princeton, 1991-97, Wells Coll., Aurora, N.Y., 1994-2003; mem. planned giving com. Williams Coll., Williamstown, Mass., 1973-87, nat. chmn. planned giving, 1983-87; dir., Ctr. Responsive Politics, Washington, 2002—. Lt. USN, 1952-56. Mem. ABA, D.C. Bar Assn., N.J. Bar Assn., Am. Coll. Trust and Estate Counsel (N.J. state chair 1995-2000, bd. regents 2001-07). Clubs: Washington Golf and Country, Capitol Hill. Republican. Presbyterian.

REICHEK, MORTON ARTHUR, retired magazine editor, writer; b. NYC, Nov. 2, 1924; s. Meyer and Katherine (Rabinowitz) R.; m. Sybil Green, June 13, 1953; children: Amy, Marjorie (dec.), James. BS, NYU, 1948; postgrad., Am. U., 1948-50. Press officer, editor U.S. Fish & Wildlife Svc., Washington, 1948-49, U.S. Br. Labor Statistics, Washington, 1949-51, U.S. Nat. Prodn. Authority, Washington, 1951-52; Washington corr. McGraw-Hill Publs., 1952-63, Newhouse Newspapers, 1963-65; assoc. editor Forbes, NYC, 1965-66, Bus. Week, NYC, 1966-76, sr. editor, writer, 1978—89; dir. editl. svcs. Gulf & Western. Industries, Inc., NYC, 1976-78. U.S. rep. NATO journalist program U.S. Dept. State, France, 1957; adj. lectr. Columbia U. Graduate Sch. Journalism, N.Y.C., 1981. Contbr. articles to N.Y. Times Mag., New Republic, others. Staff sgt. U.S. Army, 1943-46, China-Burma-India. Journalist fellow Carnegie-Mellon U. Grad. Sch. Indsl. Adminstrn., 1979; grantee NEH, 1980. Home: 1 Worchester Dr Concordia Monroe Township NJ 08831-4723 Home (Winter): The Cascades 6975 Lismore Ave Boynton Beach FL 33437-6441 Personal E-mail: iankev@att.net.

REICHEL, AARON ISRAEL, lawyer, editor, writer, rabbi; b. NYC, Jan. 30, 1950; s. Oscar Asher and Josephine Hannah (Goldstein) R. BA, Yeshiva U., 1971, MA, 1974; JD, Fordham U., 1976. Bar: NJ 1977, NY 1978; ordained rabbi 1975. Atty. editor Securities Regulation Prentice-Hall, Englewood Cliffs, NJ, 1977-78, editor, founder govt. disclosure svc. Paramus, NJ, 1978-82, atty. editor fed. taxation, 1982-89; tech. editor Warren, Gorham & Lamont, Practical Acct., NYC, 1989—90; assoc. Firm A. Edward Major, 1990—91, Firm Allen L. Rothenberg, 1991—93, Bloom & Mintz, P.C., 1993—2006; pvt. practice, 2006—. Adminstr. Harry & Jane Fischel Found., 2005—. Author: The Maverick Rabbi, 1984, 2d edit. 1986, Back to the Past for Inspiration for the Future—West Side Institutional Synagogue Jubilee 1937-87, 1987, Fahrenheit 9-12--Rebuttal to Fahrenheit 9-11, 2004, 2nd edit., 2005; co-author (manual) Style and Usage, 1984; contbr. The 1986 Jewish Directory and Almanac, 1986, The 1987-88 Jewish Almanac, 1988; contbg. editor Complete Guide to the Tax Reform Act of 1986, Prentice-Hall's Explanation of the Tax Reform Act of 1986, 1986, Prentice Hall's Complete Guide to the Tax Law of 1987, 1988, Prentice Hall's Explanation of the Technical & Miscellaneous Revenue Act of 1988, 1988, Guide to Equal Employment Practices, 1997; contbr. articles to profl. jours. Bd. dirs. Union Orthodox Jewish Congregations Am., N.Y.C., 1973-74, West Side Instl. Synagogue, 1987-98, Amalgamated Dwellings, Inc., 1992-96; bd dirs. Harry and Jane Fischel Found., 1977—; nat. pres. YAVNEH, N.Y.C., 1973-74; mem. youth commn. Am. Jewish Congress, 1973-76. Mem. ABA, NY State Bar Assn. (various coms.), Am. Soc. Access Profls. (founder, 1st chmn. NY chpt.), Nat. Jewish Commn. on Law and Pub. Affairs (family law com.), Yeshiva U. Alumni Assn. (exec. com. 1971-87, editor-in-chief Bull. 1974-78). Avocations: writing, baseball, tennis, compiling proverbs. Home: 83-28 Abingdon Rd Kew Gardens NY 11415-1714 Office: Adminstr Harry and Jane Fischel Found Suite 1701 875 Avenue of the Americas New York NY 10001

REICHEL, WALTER EMIL, advertising executive; b. Irvington, NJ, Dec. 12, 1935; s. Walter Edwin and Flora Maria (Pfister) R.; m. Priscilla Tedesco, Feb. 1, 1969; 1 son, Bradley Joseph. BA, Columbia U., 1959; MA., NYU, 1971, M Philosophy, 1989, postgrad., 1989—. With Benton & Bowles, NYC, 1959-67, v.p., 1965-67, asso. media dir., 1965-67; with Ted Bates & Co., Inc. NYC, 1967-87; sr. v.p. Ted Bates & Co., Inc., NYC, 1973-82, exec. dir. media and programs, 1974-82, exec. v.p., 1982-87, dir.; cons., 1987-91; mng. ptnr. A.S. Link Inc., NYC, 1991-2000; sr. v.p., dir. client svcs. KSL Media, 2000—01; prof. advt. and comm. Fashion Inst. of Tech., 2002—; ptnr. Media Trust, 2007—. Ptnr. Media Trust, 2007—. Home and Office: 449 1/2 Henry St Brooklyn NY 11231-3011 E-mail: aslreichel@aol.com.

REICHELDERFER, BRENDA L., manufacturing executive; b. May 29, 1958; BSEE, Ohio No. Univ. Joined ITT Corp. (predecessor to ITT Industries), 1982; various engring., ops. positions ITT Defense & Electronics, 1982—97; v.p., engring., electrical sys. group, automotive divsn. ITT Industries, 1997—98, pres., fluid specialty group, 1998—2001, pres., motion & flow control group, 2001—03, pres., electronic components group, 2003—05, sr. v.p., chief tech. officer White Plains, NY, 2005—. Bd. dirs. Fed. Signal Corp., 2006—. Office: ITT Industries 4 W Red Oak Ln West Harrison NY 10604 Office Phone: 914-641-2000. Office Fax: 914-696-2950.

REICHENBACH, LINDA LOUISE, mathematician, language educator; b. Joliet, Ill., Dec. 3, 1946; d. Frank James and Mary Lavonne Kachelhoffer; m. Michael Joseph Reichenbach, July 19, 1969; children: Heidi Marie, Brian Joseph. BS in Math. with honors, Ill. State U., 1968; MS with honors, U. St. Francis, Joliet, Ill., 1997. Tchr. math Joliet Cath. Acad., Ill.; tchr. math. Lockport Twp. HS, Ill.; chair dept. math. Aurora Ctrl. Cath. HS, Ill.; instr. math. tutoring ctr. Joliet Jr. Coll., 2007—. Inclusive tchr. REI Level One Tng., Ill., 1997—98; dir. program for acad. excellence Aurora Ctrl. Cath. H.S., Ill.; mem. Diocesan-wide math. assessment com. Joliet Diocese, Ill.; local, regional and state sci. fair judge, Ill., 1988—2005. Life mem. Cantigny VFW Ladies Aux., 1968. Named Tchr. of Yr., Aurora Ctrl. Cath. HS, 2002—03. Mem.: Math. Assn. Am., Nat. Coun. Tchrs. Math., Girl Scouts Am. (life Nat. Appreciation award Trailways Coun., Ill.). Avocations: writing, antique cars, gardening, art. Personal E-mail: reichenmom@hotmail.com.

REICHERT, CHRISTINE EDWARDS, academic administrator; b. St. Joseph, Mich., May 25, 1949; d. Jerome Calvin Patterson and Jane Edna Wohl; children: Jennifer Elizabeth, Rachel Ariana. BA in English Lit., with hon., Baldwin-Wallace Coll., Berea, Ohio, 1985; MA in English Lit., with hon., U. Toledo, Ohio, 1998. Bureau chief The Morning Journal, Lorain, Ohio, 1987—99, regional editor, 1988—89, reporter, 1985—87; instr. U. Toledo, Monroe County, Toledo, 1997—99; dir. acad. svcs. Lourdes Coll., Sylvania, Ohio, 1999—, dir. of retention, 2004—05. Chair Policy and Procedure Ctr., Sylvania, Ohio, 2003—05; mem. Student Success Task Force Lourdes Coll., 2007—. Editor: The Learning Assistance Review, 2007; contbr. articles to profl. jours. Recipient Outstanding Tchg. award, U. Toledo, 1998, Staff Excellence award, Lourdes Coll., 2007. Mem.: Nat. Coll. Learning Ctr. Assn., Coll. Reading Learning Assn., Nat. Tutoring Assn., Modern Lang. Assn. Avocations: art, music, theater, reading. Office: Lourdes Coll 6832 Convent Blvd Toledo OH 43615 Office Phone: 419-824-3759. Business E-Mail: creichert@lourdes.edu.

REICHERT, DAVID, lawyer; b. Cin., Nov. 23, 1929; s. Victor E. and Louise F. Reichert; m. Marilyn Frankel, May 31, 1959; children— James G., Steven F., William M. BA, Bowling Green State U., Ohio, 1951; JD, U. Cin., 1954. Bar: Ohio 1954, US Supreme Ct. 1963. Of counsel Porter, Wright, Morris & Arthur, formerly sr. ptnr. Reichert, Strauss & Reed and predecessors, Cin. Dir. numerous corps. Monthly columnist: Scrap Age mag, 1966-74; bd. editors: U. Cin. Law Rev, 1953-54. Pres. brotherhood Rockdale Temple, Cin., 1960-61, temple treas., 1973-75, v.p., 1975-79, pres., 1979-81; mem. Amberley Village Planning Commn. & Zoning Bd. Appeals, 1972-79, Ohio Solid Waste Adv. Group, 1974; treas. Contemporary Arts Ctr., Cin., 1973-75, pres., 1976-77, trustee, 1982-88; trustee Cin. Art Mus., 1978-93, v.p., 1992-93, chmn. vis. com. for contemporary art, 1990-92; trustee Jewish Publ. Soc., 1980-86, Cin. Sculpture Coun., 1984-87; mem. acquisitions com. Miami U. Art Mus., 1982-85. Mem. Cin. Print and Drawing Cir. (pres. 1974-76), The Literary Club (sec. 1988-91, v.p. 1991-92, pres. 1992-93), Losantiville Country Club (bd. govs. 1985-92, sec. 1986-90, pres. 1990-92), ISRI 20th Century Club (hon. 1998), Omicron Delta Kappa, Sigma Tau Delta, Phi Delta Phi, Zeta Beta Tau. Office: Porter Wright Morris & Arthur 250 E 5th St Ste 2200 Cincinnati OH 45202-5118

REICHERT, DAVID G. (DAVE REICHERT), congressman; b. Detroit Lakes, Minn., Aug. 29, 1950; m. Julie Reichert; 3 children. AA, Concordia Lutheran Coll., Portland, Oreg., 1970. Police officer Sheriff's Office King County, Wash., 1972—97, sheriff Wash., 1997—2004; mem. US Congress from 8th Wash. dist., 2005—, mem. sci. com., mem. transp. and infrastructure com., vice chmn. Coast Guard and maritime transp. subcommittee, mem. homeland security com., chmn. emergency preparedness, sci. and tech. Author: Chasing the Devil: My Twenty Year Quest to Capture the Green River Killer, 2004. Co-chmn. Wash. State Partners in Crisis; mem. adv. bd. Criminal Justice Coun., King County, Wash., Domestic Violence Coun., King County, Wash. Served in Res. USAF, 1971—76, served in USAF, 1976. Named Sheriff of Yr., Nat. Sheriffs Assn., 2004; recipient

Champion of Freedom award, Wash. Policy Ctr., 2 Medal of Valor awards, King County, Wash. Sheriff's Office. Mem.: Wash. Assn. Sheriffs & Police Chiefs (mem. exec. bd.), Wash. State Sheriffs Assn. (past pres.). Republican. Lutheran. Office: US Ho Reps 1223 Longworth Ho Office Bldg Washington DC 20515-4708 Office Phone: 202-225-7761. *

REICHERT, LEO EDMUND, JR., biochemist, department chairman, endocrinologist; b. NYC, Jan. 9, 1932; s. Leo and Anne (Holsten) R.; m. Gerda Sihler, July 20, 1957; children: Leo, Christine, Linda, Andrew. BS, Manhattan Coll., NYC, 1955; PhD, Loyola U., Chgo., 1960. Asst. prof. biochemistry Emory U. Med. Sch., Atlanta, 1960-66, assoc. prof., 1966-72, prof., 1972-79; prof., chmn. dept. biochemistry Albany (N.Y.) Med. Coll., 1979-88, prof. biochemistry and molecular biology, 1988-99; dir. Tucker Endocrine Rsch. Inst., LLC, Atlanta, 2000—. Dir. human and animal hormone isolation lab. (NIH), Emory U. Med. Sch., 1960-75; mem. med. adv. bd. Nat. Pituitary Agy., 1971-74; com. on glycoprotein hormones Nat. Hormone and Pituitary Program, 1968-86; mem. reproductive biology study sect. NIH, 1971-75; mem. adv. panel on cellular physiology NSF, 1983-86, divsn. of integrative and neuro biology, 1992; mem. WHO Expert Adv. Panel on Biol. Standardization, 1984-2006, Nat. Bd. Med. Examiners, Part I, 1989-91. Mem. editl. bd. Endocrinology, 1967-75, Molecular and Cellular Endocrinology, 1977-83, 90-94, Biology of Reproduction, 1968-70, 86-90, Andrology, 1983-86, Molecular Andrology, 1989-99; contbr. more than 275 articles to profl. jours.; patentee in field. With USMC, 1949—52. Listed among 75 endocrinologists, 1000 scientists most cited, 1965-78. Mem.: Soc. for Study of Reprodn., Andrology Soc. (coun. 1983—87), Endocrine Soc. (ethics adv. com. 2000—01, Ayerst award 1970), Am. Soc. Biol. Chemists. Home: 1974 Mountain Creek Dr Stone Mountain GA 30087-1018 Office Phone: 770-491-8436. Personal E-mail: lerjr@aol.com.

REICHERTZ, PETER STUART, lawyer; b. Dallas, Sept. 28, 1950; s. Paul Peter and Clara Stuart (Robinson) Reichertz. AB, Brown U., 1972; JD with honors, George Washington U., 1975. Bar: DC 1976, US Supreme Ct. 1984. Atty. US Rlwy. Assn., Washington, 1975-78; assoc. McMurray & Pendergast, Washington, 1978-79, Hamel, Park, McCabe & Saunders, Washington, 1979-81, ptnr., 1981-83, McMurray & Pendergast, 1983; assoc. Arent Fox Kintner Plotkin & Kahn, Washington, 1983-86, ptnr., 1987—2002, Sonnenschein Nath & Rosenthal LLP, Washington, 2002—, head food and drug law group, 2002—. Mem.: ABA, Internat. Trademark Assn., Fed. Cir. Bar Assn. Office: Sonnenschein Nath & Rosenthal LLP Ste 600, E Tower 1301 K St NW Washington DC 20005 Office Phone: 202-408-9222. Office Fax: 202-408-6399. Business E-Mail: preichertz@sonnenschein.com.

REICHGOTT, MICHAEL JOEL, medical educator, dean, physician; b. Newark, July 26, 1940; s. Leo and Gertrude (Millman) R.; m. Lynn Gay Haar, Dec. 22, 1962; children: Jay Howard, Seth Alan, Douglas Jordan. AB, Gettysburg Coll., Pa., 1961; MD, Albert Einstein Coll. Medicine, 1965; PhD, U. Calif., San Francisco, 1973. Diplomate Am. Bd. Internal Medicine. Fellow in clin. pharmacology U. Calif., 1969-72; asst. prof. medicine U. Pa., Phila., 1973-81, assoc. prof., 1981-84, Albert Einstein Coll. Medicine, Bronx, N.Y., 1984-94, prof., 1994—, assoc. dean of students and grad. med. edn., 1989-99, assoc. dean clin. affairs and grad. med. edn., 1999—; med. dir. Bronx Mcpl. Hosp. Ctr., 1984-89. Mem. Liaison Com. on Med. Edn., 2002—; presenter in field. Contbr. articles to profl. jours. V.p. Larchmont (N.Y.) Temple, 1990-92, pres., 1992-94. Maj. M.C., U.S. Army, 1967-69, Vietnam. Fellow ACP (com.); mem. Assn. Am. Med. Colls. (com. 1990—), N.Y. Acad. Medicine, Phila. Acad. Medicine, Soc. for Gen. Internal Medicine (com.). Avocations: camping, gardening, print collector. Office: Albert Einstein Coll of Medicine 1300 Morris Park Ave Bronx NY 10461-1926 Office Phone: 718-430-4282. E-mail: reichgot@aecom.yu.edu.

REICHGOTT JUNGE, EMBER DARLENE, retired senator, lawyer, writer, broadcast commentator, radio personality, communications executive; b. Detroit, Aug. 22, 1953; d. Norbert Arnold and Diane (Pincich) Reichgott; m. Michael Junge. BA summa cum laude, St. Olaf Coll., Minn., 1974; JD, Duke U., 1977; MBA, U. St. Thomas, 1991. Bar: Minn. 1977, D.C. 1978. Assoc. Larkin, Hoffman, Daly & Lindgren, Bloomington, Minn., 1977-84; counsel Control Data Corp., Bloomington, Minn., 1984-86; ptnr. The Gen. Counsel, Ltd., 1987—; mem. Minn. State Senate, 1983-2000, chmn. legis. com. on econ. status of women, 1984-86, vice chmn. senate edn. com., 1987-88, senate majority whip, 1990-94, chmn. property tax divsn. senate tax com., 1991-92, chmn. senate judiciary com., 1993-94, senate asst. majority leader, 1995-2000, chmn. spl. subcom. on ethical conduct; pres. Ember Comm., Inc. Dem. endorsed candidate Minn. Atty. Gen., 1998; instr. polit. sci. St. Olaf Coll., Northfield, Minn., 1993; bd. dirs. Citizens Ind. Bank, St. Louis Park, Minn. Host cable TV monthly series Legis. Report, 1985-92. Cand. US Congress, 2006; state co-chair Clinton/Gore Presdl. Campaign, Minn. Dem. Farmer-Labor Party, 1992, 1996; del. Nat. Dem. Conv., 1984, 1992, 1996; pres. Minn. Women's Polit. Caucus, 2002—04; trustee, bd. dirs. N.W. YMCA, New Hope, Minn., 1983—88, United Way Mpls., 1989—, Greater Mpls. ARC, 1988—2004, chair, 2001—03. Recipient Woman of Yr. award North Hennepin Bus. and Profl. Women, 1983, award for contbn. to human svcs. Minn. Social Svcs. Assn., 1983, Clean Air award Minn. Lung Assn., 1988, Disting. Svc. award Mpls. Jaycees, 1984, Minn. Dept. Human Rights award, 1989, Myra Bradwell award Minn. Women Lawyers, 1993, Disting. Alumnae award Lake Conf. Schs., 1993, Disting. Alumnae award St. Olaf Coll., 1998, awards for leadership Am. Lung Assn., 1999, Am. Heart Assn., 1997, Everyday Hero award Up with People, 1995, Unsung Hero award United Way of Mpls., 1999, 2000 Innovations in Am. Govt. award Harvard U. and Ford Found., others; 1st recipient of award named in her honor for prevention of sexual assault, 2000; charter inductee Robbinsdale H.S. Hall of Fame, 2000; named One of ten Outstanding Young Minnesotans, Minn. Jaycees, 1984, Policy Adv. of Yr., NAWBO, 1988, Woman of Achievement, Twin West C. of C., 1989, Marvelous Minn. Woman, 1993. Mem. Minn. Bar Assn. (bd. govs. 1992-96, Pro Bono Publico Atty. award 1990), Hennepin County Bar Assn., Corp. Counsel Assn. (v.p. 1989-96). Home: 500 E Grant St #1308 Minneapolis MN 55404 Personal E-mail: ember@visi.com.

REICHL, PETER, computer scientist, researcher; BA, Philos U., Munich, 1991; MSc, U. Cambridge, UK, 1992; diploma in Math., U. Tech., Munich, 1994; PhD in Computer Sci., U. Tech., Aachen, Germany, 1999. Acad. guest Bell Labs, Murray Hill, NJ, 1998; guest rschr. Swiss Fed. Inst. Tech., Zurich, 1998—2001; key rschr. Telecomm. Rsch. Ctr., Vienna, 2001—. Dist. lectr. U. Tech., Graz, Austria, 2007. Contbr. articles to numerous profl. jours. and confs. Mem.: IEEE. Achievements include research in next generation networks and internet economics; human-computer interaction. Address: Forschungszentrum Telekomm Wien Donaucity Str 1 1220 Wien Austria

REICHL, RUTH MOLLY, editor-in-chief; b. NYC, Jan. 16, 1948; d. Ernst and Miriam and (Brudno) R.; m. Douglas Wilder Hollis, Sept. 5, 1970 (div. 1985); m. Michael Singer, 1985; 1 child, Nicholas Singer. BA, U. Mich., 1968, MA in history of art, 1970. Chef, co-owner The Swallow Restaurant, Berkeley, Calif., 1974—77; food writer, editor New West mag., San Francisco, 1977—84; editor restaurant column LA Times, 1984-93, food editor, 1990-93; restaurant critic NY Times, 1993-99; editor-in-chief Gourmet Mag., 1999—. Lectr. in field. Author: Mmmm: A Feastiary, 1972, The Contest Book, 1977, Tender at the Bone: Growing Up at the Table, 1998, Comfort Me with Apples: More Adventures at the Table, 2001; editor: Modern Library Food Series, 2000—, Endless Feasts: Sixty Years of Writing from Gourmet, 2002, Remembrance of Things Paris, 2004, The Gourmet Cookbook, 2004, Garlic and Sapphires, 2005, Tanner Lectures on Human Values, 2005. Recipient James Beard Award for journalism, 1994, James Beard Award for restaurant criticism, 1996, 1998. Office: 4 Times Sq New York NY 10036-6518 Business E-Mail: ruth.reichl@gourmet.com.

REICHLE, RALPH L., radiologist; b. Lakeview, Mich., May 18, 1961; s. Ralph L. and Betty Jean Reichle; m. Caroline Amy Berry, Jan. 2, 1999; children: Charles Laper, Henry Mills. BS in Elec. Engring., Mich. State U., E.Lansing, 1979—83; MD, U. Mich., Ann Arbor, 1983—88. Diplomate U. Mich., 1988, in diagnostic radiology Am. Bd. Radiology, 1993, cert. interventional radiology Am. Bd. Radiology, 1998. Surg. intern Butterworth Hosp., Mass. Stat U., Grand Rapids, 1988—89; radiology resident Johns Hopkins Hosp., Balt., 1989—92, chief radiology resident, 1992, interventional radiology fellow, 1993—94; staff radiologist Mt. Auburn Hosp., Cambridge, Mass., 1994—; clin. instr. Harvard Med. Sch., Cambridge, 1994—; staff radiologist med. dept. MIT, Cambridge, 1994—. Mem.: Soc. Uroradiology, Radiol. Soc. N.Am., Am. Coll. Radiology, Soc. Interventional Radiology, Alpha Omega Alpha. Independent. Avocations: skiing, golf. Office: Mount Auburn Hosp Dept Radiology 330 Mount Auburn St Cambridge MA 02238 Home Phone: 978-287-4663. Office Fax: 617-499-5649. Business E-Mail: rreichle@mah.harvard.edu.

REICHLEY, A. JAMES, political scientist; b. St. Clair, Pa., Mar. 3, 1929; s. Grant G. and Mary (Thompson) R.; m. Mary Donohue, Apr. 15, 1961; children: Douglas G., Richard J., Susan M. BA, U. Pa., 1950; MA, Harvard U., 1956. Reporter Pottsville (Pa.) Republican, 1957-61; legis. asst. Senator Kenneth Keating, Washington, 1961-62; legis. sec. Gov. William Scranton, Harrisburg, Pa., 1962-67; polit. editor Fortune, NYC, 1967-76; spl. asst. Pres. Gerald Ford, Washington, 1976; sr. fellow Brookings Instn., Washington, 1977-91, Georgetown U., Washington, 1992—2003. Author: Conservatives in an Age of Change, 1981, Religion in American Public Life, 1985 (Benchmark award 1986), The Life of the Parties, 1992, rev. edit., 2000, The Values Connection, 2001, Faith in Politics, 2002; others; editor: Elections American Style, 1987; contbr. articles to profl. jours. Served with U.S. Army, 1951-53. Congl. fellow, 1959. Mem. Am. Polit. Sci. Assn., Cosmos Club. Republican. Presbyterian. Home: 11912 Gregerscroft Rd Potomac MD 20854-2145 E-mail: j.reichley@worldnet.att.net.

REICHLIN, SEYMOUR, endocrinologist, educator; b. NYC, May 31, 1924; s. Henry and Celia (Rosen) R.; m. Elinor Thurman Dameshek, June 24, 1951; children: Seth David, Douglas James, Ann Elise. Student, CCNY, 1940-41; AB, Antioch Coll., 1945; MD, Washington U., St. Louis, 1948; PhD, U. London, 1954. Intern N.Y. Hosp., 1948-49; asst. resident Barnes Hosp., St. Louis, 1949-50, N.Y. Hosp., 1950-51; chief resident Barnes Hosp., 1951-52; research fellow physiology dept. Maudsley Hosp., London, Eng., 1952-54; instr. psychiatry Washington U., 1954-55, asst. prof. psychiatry and medicine, 1955-60; asso. prof. medicine U. Rochester, 1960-66, prof., 1966-69; prof., head dept. med. and pediatric spltys. Sch. Medicine U. Conn., 1969-71, prof., head dept. physiology, 1971-72; prof. medicine Tufts U., 1972-97, prof. emeritus, 1997—; rsch. prof. U. Ariz., 1994-2000. Sr. physician New Eng. Med. Ctr., 1972-93, sr. endocrinologist, 1993-96; mem. endocrinology study sect. NIH, 1966-70; mem. adv. panel FDA, 1977-79; mem. coun. Nat. Inst. Kidney, Diabetes, Digestive Diseases, 1987-90. Mem. editl. bd. Endocrinology, 1969-74, New Eng. Jour. Medicine, 1976-79, Jour. Psychoneuroendocrinology, 1979-83, Brain, Behavior and Immunity, 1990—; contbr. articles to profl. jours. Bd. dirs. Founds. Fund, New Haven, 1968-70; med. adv. bd. Med. Found., Boston, adv. bd. MacArthur Found., 1988. Served with AUS, 1943-44. Recipient Rebecca Rire award Antioch Coll., Horace Mann Alumni award Antioch Coll., Alumni award Wash. U.; fellow Commonwealth Fund, 1952-54, Lowell M. Palmer fellow, 1954-56. Master ACP-Am. Soc. Internal Medicine (award 2002); fellow AAAS, Am. Acad. Arts and Scis.; mem. Ctrl. Soc. Clin. Rsch., Am. Soc. Clin. Investigation, Assn. Am. Physicians, Am. Physiol. Soc., Endocrine Soc. (Eli Lilly award 1972, Disting. Leadership award 1986, pres. 1975-76), Brit. Soc. Endocrinology, Am. Psychosomatic Soc., Am. Thyroid Assn., Internat. Brain Orgn., Assn. for Rsch. in Nervous and Mental Disease (pres. 1976), Pituitary Soc. (pres. 1994-95), Sigma Xi, Alpha Omega Alpha. Home: 685 S LaPosda Cir GH 3402 Green Valley AZ 85614 Personal E-mail: reichlin@wildblue.net. Business E-Mail: reichlin@laposadagv.net.

REICHMAN, LEE BRODERSOHN, physician; b. NYC, June 25, 1938; s. Theodore and Elinore (Brodersohn) R.; m. Rose Ehrinpreis, Oct. 9, 1965; children: Daniel Mark, Deborah Gur. AB, Oberlin Coll., Ohio, 1960; MD, NYU, 1964; MPH, Johns Hopkins U., Balt., 1971. Intern Bellevue Hosp., I Med. Divsn., NYC, 1964-65, resident, 1967-68, Harlem Hosp. Ctr., NYC, 1968-69, fellow in pulmonary medicine, 1969-70; dir. Bur. Tb, Bur. Chronic Disease, N.Y.C. Health Dept., 1971-73, asst. commr. health, 1973-74; assoc. prof. medicine U. Medicine and Dentistry N.J. Med. Sch., Newark, 1974-78; prof. medicine N.J. Med. Sch., Newark, 1978—, prof. preventive medicine, cmty. health, 1993—; dir. pulmonary div. U. Medicine and Dentistry N.J.-N.J. Med. Sch. Univ. Hosp., 1974-92; founding exec. dir. N.J. Med. Sch. Nat. Tb Ctr., 1993—2006, N.J. Med. Sch. Global Tubercular Inst., 2006—. Cons. CDC, Atlanta, 1970—; prin. investigator pulmonary complications of HIV infection NHLBI, 1987—95; prin. investigator Model Tb Ctr. CDC, 1993—2003, prin. investigator Nat. Tb Trials Consortium, 1994—99, adv. coun. for elimination of Tb, 2002—; prin. investigator Regional Tng. & Med. Conv. Ctr. CDC, 2003—; sr. advisor WHO Stop TB Partnership Group, 2007—. Editor: Tuberculosis-A Comprehensive International Approach, 2d edit., 2000; author: Timebomb-The Global Epidemic of Multi-Drug Resistant Tuberculosis, 2002; contbr. articles to profl. jours. Bd. dirs. Art Ctr. No. N.J., 1979-86; chmn. N.J. Commn. on Smoking of Health, 1986-87; mem. N.J. TB Adv. Coun., 1976—, chmn. 1991—; chair Nat. Coalition for Elimination of Tb, 1992—2004; mem. N.J. Clean Air Coun., 1987. With USPHS, 1965-67. Recipient Nat. Heart Lung and Blood Inst., Pulmonary Acad. career award, 1975-80, Preventive Pulmonary Acad. career award, 1987-92, Tb Acad. career award, 1993—98, 1st prize trade category Am. Med. Writers Assn., 2002, Solomon A. Berson Med. Alumni Achievement award NYU, 2003. Fellow ACP, Am. Coll. Chest Physicians (gov. 1984-90, pres. N.J. chpt. 1982-84, Simon Rodbard Meml. lectr. 2000); mem. Am. Thoracic Soc. (hon. life), Internat. Union Against Tb and Lung Disease (exec. com. 1982-92, vice chair exec. com. 1989-91, N.Am. Region Disting. Svc. award 2001), Am. Lung Assn. (hon. life, nat. bd. dirs. 1980-94, pres. elect 1991-92, pres. 1992-93, past pres. 1993-94, Will Ross medalist 1999), N.J. Thoracic Soc. (pres. 1982-84), Am. Lung Assn. N.J. (hon. life, bd. dirs. 1976—86, pres. 1984-86), Global Alliance for Tb Drug Devel. Stakeholders Assn. (pres., 2004-05, bd. dirs., 2006—) Office: PO Box 1709 225 Warren St Newark NJ 07101-1709 Home Phone: 201-541-4020; Office Phone: 973-972-3270. E-mail: reichmlb@umdnj.edu.

REICHMANIS, ELSA, chemist; b. Melbourne, Victoria, Australia, Dec. 9, 1953; arrived in U.S., 1962; d. Peteris and Nina (Meiers) R.; m. Francis Joseph Purcell, June 2, 1979; children: Patrick William, Elizabeth Anne, Edward Andrew, Thomas Alexander. BS in Chemistry, Syracuse U., 1972, PhD in Chemistry, 1975. Postdoctoral intern Syracuse (N.Y.) U., 1975-76, Chaim Weizmann rsch. fellow, 1976-78; mem. tech. staff AT&T Bell Labs., Murray Hill, NJ, 1978-84, supr. radiation sensitive materials and applications, 1984-94, head organic and polymer materials, 1994-95; head polymer and organic materials Lucent Techs., Bell Labs., New Providence, NJ, 1996—2000, dir. materials rsch., 2001—. Panel on advanced materials. Japanese Tech. Evaluation Prog., NSF, Washington, 1986, com. to survey materials. rsch. opportunities and needs for electronic industry Nat. Rsch. Coun., 1986, Nat. Materials Adv. Bd., 1993-98, U.S. Nat. Com. for Internat. Union for Pure and Applied Chemistry, 1996-2001, co-chair bd. on chem. sci. and tech., 2005-07, bur., 2006—. Editor: The Effects of Radiation on High Tech Polymers, 1989, Polymers in Microlithography, 1989, Irradiation of Polymer Materials, 1993, Microelectronics Technology: Polymers for Advanced Imaging and Packaging, 1995, Micro and Nano Patterning Polymers, 1998; patentee in field; assoc. editor Chemistry of Materials, 1996—; contbr. numerous articles to profl. jours. Recipient Soc. Women Engrs. Achievement award, 1993, Engring. Materials award ASM, 1996, Arents Pioneer medal Syracuse U., 2001. Fellow: AAAS; mem.: IEEE, Soc. Women Engrs., Am. Phys. Soc., Soc. for Photo-optical Engrs., Soc. Chem. Industry (Perkin medal 2001), Am. Chem. Soc. (mem.-at-large 1986—90, sec. 1991—92, polymer materials sci. and engring. divsn. 1991—, vice chair 1993, chair-elect 1994, chmn. 1995, pres.-elect 2002, pres. 2003, award in applied polymer sci. 1999), Nat. Acad. Engring. (elected mem.). Avocations: music, reading, needlepoint.

REICHMANN, PÉTER IVÁN, mathematics professor; b. Budapest, Hungary, Feb. 10, 1942; came to US, 1959; s. Rezso Rudolf and Margit (Grünberger) Reichmann. BSEE, Ill. Inst. Tech., Chgo., 1967, MS in Math., 1973, PhD in Math., 1986; BFA in Digital Design Visual Comm. cum laude, Am. Internat. U., online, 2006. Elec. engr. Zenith Military and Motorola Comm. and Govt. divsns., various cities, 1967—69; instr. math. and elec. engring. depts. Chgo. Tech. Coll., 1973—74; asst. prof. math. Cath. U. Am., Washington, 1987—89; ind. distbr. Brain Garden Co., American Fork, Utah, 2001—04; instr. math. Star Sch. Technol. U., Laguna, N.Mex., 2004—; chief mathematician Psitronics Group Sys. Internat., 2002—04. Grantee NASA, 1982. Achievements include research on the introduction of a novel geometry for individual cell for negative Poisson's ratio foam and computing its volume. Home and Office: 1305 Coloma Way Roseville CA 95661-4604 Personal E-mail: pireichmann@hotmail.com, pireichmann@msn.com.

REICHS, KERRY E., lawyer; b. Bethesda, Md., Nov. 17, 1970; BA, Oberlin Coll., 1993; MA in Pub. Policy, Duke U., 2000, JD, 2000. Bar: DC, NC. Assoc. Arent Fox Kintner Plotkin & Kahn PLLC, Washington, Sonnenschein Nath & Rosenthal LLP, Washington.

REICIN, RONALD IAN, lawyer; b. Chgo., Dec. 11, 1942; s. Frank Edward and Abranita (Rome) R.; m. Alyta Friedland, May 23, 1965; children: Eric, Kael. BBA, U. Mich., 1964, MBA, 1967, JD cum laude, 1967. Bar: Ill. 1967, U.S. Tax Ct. 1967; CPA, Ill. Mem. staff Price Waterhouse & Co., Chgo., 1966; ptnr. Jenner & Block, Chgo., 1967—. Bd. dirs. Nat. Kidney Found., Ill., 1978-2003, v.p., 1992-95, pres., 1995-98, life trustee, 2004—; bd. dirs. Ruth Page Found., 1985—, v.p., 1990—; bd. dirs. Scoliosis Assn. Chgo., 1981-90, Kohl Children's Mus., 1991-95, River North Chgo. Dance Co., 1999—. Mem.: Ill. State Bar Assn., Chgo. Mortgage Attys. Assn., Chgo. Bar Assn., ABA, Lawyers Club (Chgo.), Exec. Club, Beta Alpha Psi, Beta Gamma Sigma, Phi Kappa Phi. Office: Jenner & Block LLP 330 N Wabash Ave Fl 40 Chicago IL 60611-3586 Home Phone: 847-831-5969; Office Phone: 312-923-2687. Personal E-mail: rreicin@jenner.com.

REID, ANDREW ERNEST, composer; b. Camden, NJ, Nov. 21, 1960; s. Ernest William and Elena Francolino Reid; m. Juli Anne Robbins Canter, Dec. 8, 1961; stepchildren: Nicole Marie Robbins, Jason Alan Robbins. MusB, Stetson U., Deland, Fla., 1983. Choir dir. & organist St. Benedict's Episcopal Ch., Plantation, Fla., 2002—; owner Santares Music People, Inc., Plantation, 2005—. Tchr. Broward County Schs., Ft. Lauderdale, Fla., 1986—. Composer: (classical music) The Fifeth of July. Sec. Libertarian Party Broward County, Fort Lauderdale, Fla., 2006. Mem.: Am. Guild Organists (assoc.). Libertarian. Avocations: raising birds, barbershop quartets. Office Phone: 954-584-8621. Personal E-mail: andrewereid@saintbenedicts.org. Business E-Mail: santaresmusicpeople@earthlink.net.

REID, ANDY (ANDREW WALTER REID), professional football coach; b. LA, Mar. 19, 1958; m. Tammy Reid; children: Garrett, Britt, Crosby, Drew Ann, Spencer. Student, Brigham Young U., 1979—81. Coach Brigham Young U., 1982, San Francisco State, 1983—85; head coach No. Ariz. U., 1986, Tex.-El Paso U., 1987—88; asst. coach U. Mo., Columbia, 1989—91, Green Bay Packers, 1992-99; head coach Phila. Eagles, 2000—, exec. v.p. football ops., 2001—. Named NFL Coach of the Yr., Sporting News, 2000, 2002, Maxwell Football Club, 2000, 2002, Pro Bowl Football Weekly, 2002, AP, 2002. Achievements include asst. coach Super Bowl XXXI Champion Green Bay Packers, 1997. Office: Philadelphia Eagles Nova Care Complex 1 Nova Care Way Philadelphia PA 19145-5298 *

REID, ANTONIO (L.A. REID), music company executive; b. June 7, 1956; m. Perri Reid (div.); 1 child, Aaron. With musical group The Deele; co-founder La Face Records, 1989; chmn. & CEO Hitco Music Pub., Atlanta, 1996—; pres., CEO Arista Records, NYC, 2000—04; chmn. Island Def Jam Music Group, 2004—. Songwriter with Kenny Edmonds, also occasionally with Darryl Simmons. Songs include Girlfriend, 1987, Rock Steady, 1987, Two Occasions, 1987, Don't Be Cruel, 1988, Love Saw It, 1988, Lover In Me, 1988, Every Little Step, 1988 (Grammy award nomination for R&B Song of Yr. 1989), Dial My Heart, 1988, Way You Love Me, 1988, Secret Rendezvous, 1988, Superwoman, 1988, Roses Are Red, 1988, Can't Stop, 1989, My Kinda Girl, 1989, It's No Crime, 1989, On Our Own, 1989, Ready or Not, 1989, Tender Lover, 1989, Giving You the Benefit, 1990, I'm Your Baby Tonight, 1990, Shock Dat Monkey, 1992, End of the Road, 1996. Recipient three Grammy awards; named one of Most Influential Black Americans, Ebony mag., 2006 Office: Island Def Jam Music Group 825 8th Ave, 28th fl New York NY 10019 *

REID, CHARLES ADAMS, III, lawyer; b. Plainfield, NJ, Apr. 21, 1947; s. Charles Adams Jr. and Gertrude C. (Egan) R.; m. Teresa Keenan, May 11, 1974. BA, Colgate U., 1969; JD, Columbia U., 1974. Bar: N.Y. 1974, N.J. 1976, U.S. Ct. Appeals (3d cir.) 1983, U.S. Ct. Appeals (fed. cir.) 1989, U.S. Ct. Appeals (2d cir.) 1991, U.S. Ct. Appeals (9th cir.) 2002, Calif. 2002. Law clk. to hon. John R. Bartels U.S. Dist. Ct. (ea. dist.) N.Y., Bklyn., 1974-75; assoc. Coudert Bros., NYC, 1975-77, Shanley & Fisher, Newark, 1977-82, ptnr. Newark and Morristown, N.J., 1983-99, Drinker Biddle & Reath LLP, Florham Park, NJ, 1999—. Mem. planning bd. Peapack-Gladstone, N.J., 1984-88, chmn., 1987-88; bd. dirs. Morris Ctr. YMCA, Cedar Knolls, N.J., 1986-93. Served with U.S. Army, 1970-72, Vietnam. Mem. ABA (litigation sect.), N.J. Bar Assn., Morris County Bar Assn., Essex County Bar Assn., Calif. State Bar, Park Avenue Club (Florham Park). Home: PO Box 716 Gladstone NJ 07934 Office: Drinker Biddle & Reath LLP 500 Campus Dr Florham Park NJ 07932-1047 Office Phone: 973-360-1100. Business E-Mail: Charles.Reid@dbr.com.

REID, DAVID G., lawyer; b. NYC, Oct. 28, 1948; s. Donald D. and Charlotte A. (Marois) Reid. BA, McGill U., Montreal, 1970; JD, Boston U., 1973. Bar: Vt. 1973, U.S. Dist. Ct. Vt. 1973, Mass. 1977, U.S. Supreme Ct. 1978, U.S. Ct. Appeals (2d cir.) 1978, U.S. Dist. Ct. Mass. 1991. Pub. defender Orleans, Caledonia, Essex counties, St. Johnsbury, Vt., 1973-75, Bennington (Vt.) County, 1975-79, Windham County, Brattleboro, Vt., 1979-89; ptnr. Reid & Rodgers, Brattleboro, 1989—. Office: Reid & Rodgers 47 Williston St Brattleboro VT 05301-3202 Office Phone: 802-257-7887. E-mail: reidrodg@sover.net.

REID, DONNA JOYCE, small business owner; b. Springfield, Tenn., June 25, 1954; d. Leonard Earl Reid and Joyce (Robertson) Kirby; m. Kenneth Bruce Sadler, June 26, 1976 (div. Apr. 1980); m. John Christopher Moulton, Oct. 18, 1987 (div. Dec. 1992); m. Peter Leatherland, Apr. 3, 1993. Student, Austin Peay State U., Clarksville, Tenn., 1972-75. Show writer, producer WTVF-TV (CBS affiliate), Nashville, 1977-83, promotion producer, 1983-85, on-air promotion mgr., 1985-86; gen. mgr. Steadi-Film Corp., Nashville, 1986-90; co-owner Options Internat., Nashville, 1990—2003, Shanti's, Inc., Hermitage, 2003—. Big sister Buddies of Nashville, 1981-87. Named to Honorable Order of Ky. Cols. John Y. Brown, Gov., 1980; recipient Significant Svc. award ARC, 1982, Clara Barton Communications award, 1983. Mem. NAFE, Nat. Assn. TV Arts and Scis., Nat. Film Inst., Nat. Assn. Broadcasters, Internat. Platform Assn., Am. Soc. Prevention of Cruelty to Animals, Humane Soc. U.S. Methodist. Avocations: reading, outdoor sports, travel. Office: 15277 Lebanon Rd Old Hickory TN 37138 Office Phone: 615-773-8133. Personal E-mail: donnaoptionspj@aol.com.

REID, EDWARD SNOVER, III, lawyer; b. Detroit, Mar. 24, 1930; s. Edward S. Jr. and Margaret (Overington) Reid; m. Carroll Grylls, Dec. 30, 1953; children: Carroll Reid Highet, Richard Gerveys, Jenny Reid McTigue, Margaret Reid Boyer. BA, Yale U., 1951; LL.B. magna cum laude (Sheldon fellow), Harvard U., 1956. Bar: Mich. 1957, N.Y. 1958, D.C. 1982, Gaikokuho jimu-bengoshi, Tokyo 1991-96. Asso. Davis, Polk & Wardwell, NYC, 1957-64, partner, 1964-95, sr. counsel, 1996—; dir. Gen. Mills, Inc., 1974-89. Mem. N.Y.C. Bd. Higher Edn., 1971—73; trustee Bklyn. Inst. Arts and Scis., 1966—93, chmn., 1974—79; trustee Bklyn. Mus. Art, 1973—93, 1994—; bd. dirs. Bklyn. Bot. Garden Corp., 1977—92, 1996—, Bargemusic Ltd., 1990—93. Active duty USMCR, 1951—53. Mem. ABA, N.Y. State Bar Assn., Assn. of Bar of City of N.Y., Am. Law Inst., Internat. Bar Assn., Heights Casino Club, Rembrandt Club, Century Assn. Club, Yale Club, Quoque Beach Club, Shinnecock Yacht Club, Quoque Field Club. Home: PO Box 39 Quogue NY 11959-0039 Office: Davis Polk & Wardwell 450 Lexington Ave New York NY 10017-3982 E-mail: ereid@dpw.com.

REID, FRANCES A., music educator; d. Arthur Walter and Frances Ellen Schenk; m. Dale David Reid, Dec. 19, 1964; 1 child, Ryan David. MusB, U. Wash., Seattle, 1967. Pvt. music instr., Seattle, 1959—. Mem. found. bd. Highline CC, Des Moines, 1995—2001; coach Hi-liners Theatre Group, Burien, 1983—. Mem.: Wash. Music Tchr. Assn., Nat. Assn. Tchrs. Singing (cert.). Lutheran. Home: 3527 S 194th St Seattle WA 98188 Office: Fran Reid Music 3527 S 194th St Seattle WA 98188

REID, FRANCES EVELYN KROLL, freelance/self-employed cinematographer, film director, communications executive; b. Oakland, Calif., Mar. 25, 1944; d. William Farnham and Marion Storm (Teller) Kroll. BA, U. Oreg., 1966. Tchr. secondary sch., Los Angeles, 1968-69; sound recordist Churchill Films, Los Angeles, 1971; freelance sound recordist Los Angeles, 1972-75; freelance dir., prodr., 1975—; freelance cinematographer Berkeley, Calif., 1978—; dir. Iris Films, Berkeley, 1977—; lectr. U. Calif. Grad. Sch. Journalism, 2005. Vol. Peace Corps, Malawi, Africa, 1969-70. Producer/dir. Long Night's Journey Into Day, 2000 (Grand Jury award Sundance 2000, Acad. award nominee 2001); dir. (film) In The Best Interests of the Children, 1977 (Blue Ribbon Am. Film Festival 1978), The Changer: A Record of the Times, 1991, The Faces of AIDS, 1992, Skin Deep, 1995, Talking About Race, 1994, Straight from the Heart, 1994 (Acad. award nominee 1995); cinematographer: (film) The Times of Harvey Milk, 1984 (Oscar 1985), Living with AIDS, 1986 (Student Acad. award 1987), Common Threads: Stories from the Quilt, 1989 (Oscar award 1990), Complaints of a Dutiful Daughter, 1994 (Acad. award nominee 1995). Mem. Film Arts Found., Assn. Ind. Video and Filmmakers, Acad. Motion Picture Arts and Scis. Office: Iris Films 2600 10th St Berkeley CA 94710-2522 Office Phone: 510-845-5414.

REID, GERALDINE WOLD (GERALDINE REID SKJERVOLD), artist; b. Apr. 11, 1944; d. Alden Elroy and Verna (Kocinski) Wold BA in Fine Art, Calif. State U., Sacramento, 1972, MFA, 1975; postgrad., Ind. U. - Purdue U. Instr. dental aux. edn. U. Minn., 1966-70, anthropol. rsch. asst., 1976-78; mng. editor Nat. Arts Guide, Chgo., 1978-80; freelance artist Chgo., 1981-94; pres. Chgo. Art Emerging Inc., 1983-85; graphic artist Reid Design & Illustration, Chgo., 1981-94; dir. show coordination Circle Fine Art, Chgo., 1981. Instr. comm. art and design Alexandria Tech. Coll., Minn., 1994—; seminar lectr., 1977, 86; lectr., art and math. Dept. Math. U. Ill., 1987—88; guest lectr. women's art history AAUW, Alexandria, 1997; lectr. on drawing approaches, 2005. One-woman shows include Artists' Coop. Gallery, Santa Fe, 1976, Artlink, Ft. Wayne, Ind., 1979, 84—, D.E.O. Fine Arts, Inc., Chgo., 1982-83, Union League Gallery, Chgo., 1989, Brodsky Gallery, 1993, Second Floor Gallery, Cen. Square, Glenwood, Minn., 1999, Ann Bickle Heritage House, Glenwood, 2000, Pope County Mus., Glenwood, 2004, Pope Art, Ter. Mill, Minn., 2005; group exhbns. include Crocker Art Mus., Sacramento, 1975, Ft. Wayne Mus. Art, 1978, Artists Guild Chgo., 1982, Charles A. Wustum Mus., Racine, Wis., 1983, Limelight, Chgo., 1986, 87, 88, Neville-Sargent Gallery, 1986, 87, Beacon Street Hull House Gallery, 1988, McDonalds Corp., Chgo., 1988, Prairie Ave. Gallery, Chgo., 1990, Peace Mus., Chgo., 1990, Hyde Park Art Ctr., Chgo., 1990, Lettuce Entertain You Enterprises, Inc., 1990, Olive Tree Gallery, Daley Coll., Chgo., 1991, Crown Ctr. Gallery, Loyola U., Chgo., 1992, Agora Syndicate, Inc., 1992, Kieffer-Nolde/TIC, 1992, Flora '92, 1992, Chgo. Bot. Garden, 1992, Open Spectrum, David Adler Cultural Ctr., 1994, August House Studio, Chgo., 1994—, Upper West Gallery, Alexandria Tech. Coll., Minn., 1995, Plains Art Mus., Fargo, ND, 1997, Regional Art Exhibit, New York Mills, Minn., 1997, Runestone Mus., Alexandria, 1997-98, Art on the Plains, 3d Ann. Regional Exhbn., Plains Art Mus., Fargo, 31st Ann. Fergus Falls CC Invitational Art Show, Minn., 2002-03, Pope County Artists Exhibit, Lake Region Arts Coun. Gallery, Fergus Falls, Minn., 2002, 06, Prairie Renaissance Cultural Alliance Gallery, Morris, Minn., 2002-03, 07, Celebration of Lake Region Arts Coun., Fergus Falls, 2002-03, New York Mills (Minn.) Ann. Regional Exhbn., 2003, Minn. State Cmty. and Tech. Coll., Fergus Falls, 2004, Minn. State Colls. and Univs., 2005-07, Three Havens Art Gallery, Alexandria, Minn., 2006-07; contbr. artwork to 2 ann. 1994 calendars; artwork selected for inclusion in Alex Tech Coll. greeting card suite, 2005. Mem. New York Mills Cultural Ctr., Mpls. Art Inst., Am. Inst. Graphic Arts, Mpls. Inst. Arts, Glacial Ridge Artists. Business E-Mail: gerrir@alextech.edu.

REID, HARRY MASON, senator; b. Searchlight, Nev., Dec. 2, 1939; s. Harry and Inez Jaynes Reid; m. Landra Joy Gould; children: Lana, Rory, Leif, Josh, Key AS, Southern Utah State U., 1959; BS in Hist. and Polit. Sci., Utah State U., 1961; JD, George Washington U., 1964; LLD (hon.), U. So. Utah, 1984. Bar: Nev. Bar 1963. Police officer US Capitol, Washington, 1961—64; city atty. City of Henderson, Henderson, Nev., 1964—66; mem. Nev. State Assembly, 1969—70; lt. gov. State of Nev., 1971—75; chmn. Nev. Gaming Commn., 1977—81; US rep. from Nev. Washington, 1983—87; US Senator from Nev., 1987—; minority whip US Senate, 1998—2001, majority whip, 2001—02, minority whip, 2002—03, asst. minority leader, 2003—04, minority leader, 2004—07, majority leader, 2007—. Mem. select cm. intelligence US Senate, mem. com. appropriations; vice chmn. US Senate Commn. Art. Author: Searchlight: The Camp that Didn't Fail, 1998. Bd. dirs. Am. Cancer Soc., Legal Aid Soc., Young Men's Christian Assn.; bd. trustees So. Nev. Meml. Hosp., 1967—69. Recipient Humanitarian award, Nat. Asthma Ctr. and Nat. Jewish Hosp., 1984, Public Svc. award, Am. Found. Suicide Prevention, 1999, Friend of Zion award, The Jerusalem Fund, 2000, MLA award disting. public svc., 2002, Award of Merit, The Military Coalition, 2002, Arthur T. Marix award, Military Officers Assn. Am., 2003, Disting. Svc. award, Am. Public Works Assn., 2003, Inspirational Leadership award, Military Order of Purple Heart, 2003, Nat. Landscape Conservation Sys. Champion award, NLCS Coalition, 2004, Pick and Gravel award, Assn. Am. State Geologists, 2004, TechNet Founders Cir. award, 2005. Mem.: Nev. Athletic Commn., Nat. Conf. Lt. Governors, Am. Bd. Trial Advocates, Clark County Bar Assn., Nev. Bar Assn., ABA. Democrat. Lds Ch. Office: US Senate 528 Hart Senate Office Bldg Washington DC 20510-0001 also: Lloyd D George Bldg Ste 8016 333 Las Vegas Blvd South Las Vegas NV 89101 Office Phone: 202-224-3542, 702-388-5020. Office Fax: 202-224-7327, 702-388-5030. *

REID, HELEN VERONICA, provost; b. Reading, Eng., Sept. 25, 1956; d. Alan A. and Teresa H. (Thatcher) Ware; m. Gary B. Reid, May 29, 1976; children: Robert, Jennifer, Kristen. BA in Biology, U. Tex., 1976; BSN, U. Tex., Arlington, 1978; MSN, Tex. Women's U., 1983; EdD, U. North Tex., 2000. CCRN, 1980, cert. CPR instr. Asst. nurse coord., staff nurse, float pool nurse Parkland Meml. Hosp., Dallas, 1979—83, float pool nurse, 1987—93; instr. Trinity Valley CC, Kaufman, Tex., 1983—86, leader freshman team, 1986—90, dean health occupations, 1990—2006; provost Health Sci. Ctr., 2007—. Mem.: Tex. Assn. Deans and Dirs. for Profl. Nursing Programs (treas. 2005—), Tex. C.C. Tchrs. Assn., Nat. Orgn. ADN (pub. rels. dir. 1998—2002, treas. 2006—), Tex. Orgn. for ADN (sec. 1988—92, nominating com. chair 1995—96, pres.-elect 2002—03, pres. 2003—05, past pres. 2005—06), Tex. Assn. Vocat. Nurse Educators, Phi Kappa Phi, Sigma Theta Tau. Office Phone: 972-932-4309. Business E-Mail: reid@tvcc.edu.

REID, INEZ SMITH, lawyer, educator, judge; b. New Orleans, Apr. 7, 1937; d. Sidney Randall Dickerson and Beatrice Virginia (Bundy) Smith. BA, Tufts U., 1959; LLB, Yale U., 1962; MA, UCLA, 1963; PhD, Columbia U., 1968; LLM in Jud. Process, U. Va., 2004. Bar: Calif. 1963, N.Y. 1972, D.C. 1980. Assoc. prof. Barnard Coll. Columbia U., NYC, 1972-76; gen. counsel youth divsn. State of N.Y., 1976-77; dep. gen. counsel HEW, Washington, 1977-79; inspector gen. EPA, Washington, 1979-81; chief legis. and opinions, dep. corp. counsel Office of Corp. Counsel, Washington, 1981-83; corp. counsel D.C., 1983-85; counsel Laxalt, Washington, Perito & Dubuc, Washington, 1986-90, ptnr., 1990-91; counsel Graham & James, 1991-93, Lewis, White & Clay, P.C., 1994-95; assoc. judge D.C. Ct. Appeals, 1995—. William J. Maier, Jr. vis. prof. law W.Va. U. Coll. Law, Morgantown, 1985-86. Contbr. articles to profl. jours. and publs. Trustee emeritus Lancaster Sem., Pa., 2002—; bd. dirs. Homeland Ministries bd. United Ch. of Christ, NYC, 1978—83, vice chmn., 1981—83; chmn. bd. govs. Antioch Law Sch., Washington, 1979—81; chmn. bd. trustees Antioch U., Yellow Springs, Ohio, 1981—82; trustee Tufts U., Medford, Mass., 1988—98, trustee emeritus, 1999—; trustee Lancaster (Pa.) Sem., 1988—2001; bd. govs. D.C. Sch. Law, 1990—96, chmn., 1991—95. Recipient Emily Gregory award Barnard Coll., 1976, Arthur Morgan award Antioch U., 1982, Service award United Ch. of Christ, 1983, Disting. Service (Profl. Life) award Tufts U. Alumni Assn., 1988. Office: DC Ct Appeals 500 Indiana Ave NW Fl 6 Washington DC 20001-2138

REID, IVONNE FIGUEROA, language educator; b. Santiago, Chile, May 25, 1938; d. Hector Francisco Figueroa and Uberlinda Eulojia Cristi; m. Roderic Eugene Reid, June 13, 1963; children: David Alan, Nancy Gail. B in English, U. Chile, 1960; MS in Edn., U. So. Calif., 1963, PhD in Edn., 1972. Rschr. Inst. Statistical Rsch. U. Chile, 1959—63; prof. statistics Family Edn. Inst. Cath. U., Santiago, Chile, 1960—61; rsch. assoc. in evaluation art in elem. edn. rsch. project U. SC, 1975—80; intermediate sch. tchr. Montebello Unified Sch. Dist., Bell Gardens, 1981—89, h.s. Spanish tchr., 1989—99, literacy facilitator, 1999—2002, cons., 2002—05; vol. cons., 2005—. Presenter Calif. Edn. Rsch. Assn., 1972, 77, 78, Calif. Assn. of Bilingual Edn., 1997—99, 2003. Named High Sch. Tchr. of the Yr., Calif. Bilingual Edn. Assn., Montebello Chapt., 1997; Fulbright scholarship, Dept. State, U. So. Calif., 1961—62. Mem.: Montebello Teachers Assn., Calif. Teachers Assn., Nat. Edn. Assn., Calif. Assn. Bilingual Edn., Am. Ednl. Rsch. Assn. Avocations: travel, music, art, reading. Personal E-mail: ivonnereid@earthlink.net.

REID, JACKSON BROCK, psychologist, educator; b. Honea Path, SC, Sept. 18, 1921; s. Alexander Mack and Ann Orr (Brock) R.; m. Avis Boykin Long, Jan. 12, 1947; step-children: Jules Heywood Long, Barbara Banning Long. BS, The Citadel, 1942; postgrad., Ariz. State Coll., Flagstaff, 1948; PhD, UCLA, 1951, postgrad., summer 1951. Cert., lic. psychologist, Tex. Asst. prof. ednl. psychology U. Tex., Austin, 1951-55, assoc. prof., 1955-59, prof., 1959-93, prof. emeritus, 1993—, assoc. dean for grad. studies in edn., 1965-73; coordinator ESEA programs U.S. Office Edn., 1969—, chmn. dept. ednl. psychology, 1972-84. Cons. in field. Served to capt. U.S. Army, 1942-47. Office Edn. grantee, 1966-73 Fellow Am. Psychol. Assn. (exptl. and ednl. divs.); mem. AAAS, Am. Ednl. Research Assn., Interam. Soc. Psychology, AAUP, Southwestern Psychol. Assn. (sec.-treas. 1965-66, pres. 1967-68), Tex. Psychol. Assn., Ret. Officers Assn., Nat. Psoriasis Found., ACLU, Common Cause, Fund for Peace, Planned Parenthood of Am., Sigma Xi. Clubs: U. Tex. Faculty Center; Lighthouse Resort and Club (Sanibel Island, Fla.). Achievements include research, publs. in learning theory, behavioral effects of radiation and drugs, child and adolescent behavior, programmed instn., computer-assisted instrn. Home: 3801 Westlake Dr Austin TX 78746-1617 Office: U Tex Dept Ednl Psychology Austin TX 78712 *The principal goal in my career has been to preserve psychology as an academic discipline devoted to objective inquiry into the etiology of behavior on the basis of logically directed empirical investigation as opposed to rationalistic - mystical - doctrinaire approaches.*

REID, JOHN MITCHELL (JACK REID), biomedical engineer, researcher, consultant; b. Mpls., June 8, 1926; s. Robert Sherman and Meryl (Mitchell) R.; m. Virginia Montgomery, Dec. 31, 1949 (div.); children: Donald, Kathryn, Richard; m. Shadi Wang, June 30, 1983. BS, U. Minn., 1950, MS, 1957; PhD, U. Pa., 1965. Engring. assoc. U. Minn., Mpls., 1950-54; rsch. engr. St. Barnabas Hosp., Mpls., 1954-57; assoc. U. Pa., Phila., 1957-66; rsch. asst. prof. U. Wash., Seattle, 1966-72; rsch. engr. Providence Hosp., 1972-74; dir. bioengring. Inst. of Applied Physiology & Medicine, 1973-81; Calhoun prof. Drexel U., Phila., 1981-94, prof. emeritus, rsch. prof., 1994—. Adj. prof. radiology Thomas Jefferson Med. Sch., Phila., 1982—; affiliate prof. U. Washington, 1995—; cons. Inst. Applied Physiology and Medicine, Seattle. Contbr. numerous articles to profl. jours.; 5 U.S. patents on devel. of ultrasonic med. imaging. Scoutmaster Boy Scouts Am., Mpls., 1955-57, Phila., 1960-65, cub and scoutmaster, Seattle, 1965-70. With USN, 1944—46. Recipient Pioneer award Soc. Vascular Technologists, 1994; grantee NIH; Professorship in his named established at Drexel U. Sch. Biomed. Engring. and Health Sys., Phila., 2004. Fellow IEEE, Am. Inst. Ultrasound in Medicine (bd. govs., Pioneer award), Acoustical Soc. Am., IEEE Engring. in Medicine and Biology Soc. (Lifetime Achievement award 1993), Am. Inst. Med. and Biol. Engrs.; mem. World Fedn. Ultrasound in Medicine and Biology (hon.). Home: 16711 254th Ave SE Issaquah WA 98027-6973 Business E-Mail: jmreid@u.washington.edu.

REID, JOHN PHILLIP, law educator; b. Weehawken, NJ, May 17, 1930; s. Thomas Francis and Teresa Elizabeth (Murphy) R. BSS., Georgetown U., 1952; LLB, Harvard U., 1955; MA, U. N.H., 1957; LLM, NYU, 1959, JSD, 1962. Bar: N.H. 1955. Law clk. U.S. Dist. Ct. N.H., 1956; instr. NYU, NYC, 1960-62, asst. prof. law, 1962-64, assoc. prof., 1964-65, prof. Sch. Law, 1966—2003, prof. emeritus, 2003—. Author: Chief Justice: The Judicial World of Charles Doe, 1967, A Law of Blood: The Primitive Law of the Cherokee Nation, 1970, In a Defiant Stance, 1977, In a Rebellious Spirit, 1979, Law for the Elephant: Property and Social Behavior on the Overland Trail, 1980, In Defiance of the Law, 1981, Constitutional History of the American Revolution: The Authority of Rights, 1986, Constitutional History of the American Revolution: The Authority to Tax, 1987, The Concept of Liberty in the Age of the American Revolution, 1988, The Concept of Representation in the Age of the American Revolution, 1989, Constitutional History of the American Revolution: The Authority to Legislate, 1991, Constitutional History of the American Revolution: The Authority of Law, 1993, Policing the Elephant: Crime, Punishment, and Social Behavior on the Overland Trail, 1997, Patterns of Vengeance: Crosscultural Homicide in the North American Fur Trade, 1999, Contested Empire: Peter Skene Ogden and the Snake River Expeditions, 2002, Controlling the Law: Legal Politics in Early National New Hampshire, 2004, Rule of Law: The Jurisprudence of Liberty in the Seventeenth and Eighteenth Centuries, 2004, The Ancient Constitution and the Origins of Anglo-American Liberty, 2005. Fellow Guggenheim Found., 1980, Huntington Library-NEH, 1980, 84; hon. fellow Am. Soc. Legal History, 1986. Fellow Am. Acad. Arts and Scis. Republican. Roman Catholic. Office: NYU Law Sch 40 Washington Sq S New York NY 10012-1099 Home Phone: 603-734-2877; Office Phone: 212-998-6230. Business E-Mail: john.reid@nyu.edu.

REID, KAREN DENISE, aerospace transportation executive, writer; b. Memphis, Jan. 17, 1961; d. L.C. and Shirley (Spencer) Reid. BS in Edn., Memphis State U., 1992; postgrad., Webster U., 2007. Journeyman trainee Memphis Pub. Co., 1977—2000; exec. sec., treas., trustee Raleigh Ch., Memphis, 1985—94; acctg. clk. Nat. Hardwood Lumber Assn., Memphis, 1996—98; customer svc. agt. Pinnacle Airlines divsn. Northwest Airlines, Memphis, 1998—; owner K.K.'s Express Boutique, 1998—. Author: From Mistress to Ministry, 2003, The Transformation of a Pastor's Mistress, 2007. Bd. dirs., CEO Twin Ministries, 2000—. Avocations: travel, bowling, writing. Home and Office: Twin Ministries PO Box 752613 Memphis TN 38175 Office Phone: 901-634-2667. Personal E-mail: thetwinministries@yahoo.com.

REID, KATHERINE LOUISE, artist, educator, writer; b. Port Arthur, Tex., Mar. 25, 1941; d. Clifton Commodore and Helen Ross (Moore) Reid. BA, Baylor U., 1963; postgrad. in design and illustration, Kans. City Art Inst., 1964; MEd, U. Houston, 1973; cert. supervision, U. Houston-Clear Lake City, 1980; postgrad., San Jacinto Coll., 1982. Litho reprodn. artist Hallmark Cards, Kansas City, Mo., 1963-64; tchr. art high sch. Pasadena (Tex.) Ind. Sch. Dist., 1964-77, supr. art, gifted and talented and photography, 1977-85, supr. art and photography InterAct, 1985-90, instrnl. specialist, 1990-2000, photography and art, 1990-93, instrnl. specialist in art and spl. programs, 1993-96, rsch. planning, data disaggregation, 1996-2000; internet tchr. recruiter, 2001—02; mural artist Old Car Barn, Edna, Tex., 2000—. 4 MAT learning styles trainer DuPont Leadership Devel. Process Trainer, Selective Rsch., Inst., tchr. perceiver specialist, performance quality sys. trainer, coop. learning trainer, outcome based edn. trainer, integrated unit devel. and authentic assessment trainer Greater Gulf Coast Adminstr. Assessment Project, Assessor, 1990-2000; head crafts, asst. dir., dir. summer, winter discovery program-ski camp Cheley Colo. Camps, Denver, Estes Park, 1967-75; awards com. John Austin Cheley Found., 1990-92; staff artist, media workshop Tex. Edn. Agy., Austin, 1961; art enrichment tchr. Port Arthur Ind. Sch. Dist. (Tex.), 1961; head crafts Camp Waluta, Silsbee, Tex., 1960; mem. Tex. Edn. Agy., Art Leadership Inst., 1989-90, Tracking Rsch. Com., 1991, Core Strategic Planning Team, 1992-2000, Outcome Based Edn. Dist. Planning Com., 1991-92, Quality Sys. Improvement Team, 1991-92, Outcome Based Edn. Com. Exit Outcomes, 1991; Region IV data disk trainer, 1998-2000, target teach coord., 1993-2000, multiple intelligence trainer, 1997-2000, data disaggregation trainer, 1997-2000, supt.'s rsch. com., 1999. Author: Through Their Eyes, 1989. Mem. Friends of Fine Arts-Baylor U., Waco, Tex., 1981—, Scholastic Art awards Regional Bd., Houston, 1978-84; bd. dirs. Houston Coun. Student Art Awards, Inc., 1984-90, Pasadena Ind. Sch. Dist. Edn. Found., 2005—; mem. Baylor U. Endowed Scholarship Soc., Baylor U. Old Main Scholarship Soc., 2003—. Named Outstanding Secondary Educator of Am., 1975, Tex. Art Educator of Yr., 1985, Outstanding Vol., City of Pasadena, 2004. Mem. ASCD, Tex. ASCD, Tex. Art Edn. Assn. (rep. editor newsletter 1982-85, chmn. supervision divsn. 1982-83, v.p. membership 1978-80, chmn. pub. info. com., regional chmn. youth art month 1980-82; regional chmn. membership com. 1976-78, pres. elect 1986, sec. 1991-93, Disting. Fellows award 2004), Tex. Alliance for Arts Edn. (bd. vice chmn. 1984-86, treas. 1988-90), Nat. Art Edn. Assn. (conv. com. 1977, 85), Tex. Assn. Sch. Adminstrs., Houston Art Edn. Assn. (sec. 1969), Tex. Ret. Tchrs. Assn. (Dist. IV historian 2001-03), Pasadena Area Ret. Sch. Employees (parliamentarian 2002-04), Delta Kappa Gamma (2d v.p. 1984-86, pres. 2002-2004, state leadership devel. chpt. pres. com., 2003-2005, state banner com., 2004, State Leadership Seminar 2005, area III coord. 2005-07, Internat. Golden Gift Leadership Seminar 2006, state rsch. com. 2007—). Baptist. Achievements include patents for pet car seat. Home: 106 Ravenhead Dr Houston TX 77034-1520 Personal E-mail: klreid@academicplanet.com.

REID, LANGHORNE, III, merchant banker; b. Dallas, Apr. 3, 1950; s. Langhorne Jr. and Mary Anne (Beasley) R.; m. Sally Wolf, Dec. 26, 1972 (div. Aug. 1977); m. Eve Catherine Murphy, Sept. 6, 1986 (div. 1996); 1 child, Claire Hart Reid; m. Vera Anderson Reid, 1999. BA in Psychology, U. Tex., 1972, JD, 1975; MBA, U. Pa., 1977. Bar: Tex. 1975. V.p. Dillon, Read & Co., Inc., NYC, 1977-82; mng. dir. Drexel Burnham Lambert Inc., NYC, 1982-87; co-dir. mergers and acquisitions Paine Webber Group, NYC, 1987-89; ptnr. Gordon Investment Inc., NYC, 1989-93; pres. Beacon Advisors, Inc., Dallas, 1993-99. Bd. dirs. Windmill Holdings; pres. Partnership Svcs., 1992-93; chmn. Cedco Sys., Inc., 1997—, Amtex Holdings, Inc., 1996—, Garland Broadcast Investors, Inc., 1997—, Pogesa SA, 2002-. Trustee, treas. Animal Med. Ctr., N.Y.C., 1981—; trustee St. Mark's Sch. of Tex., 2002-. Mem. Tex. Bar Assn. Home: 4109 Windsor Pkwy Dallas TX 75205-1670 Office: Arcady Capital Inc Ste 330 100 Highland Park Village Dallas TX 75205-2726

REID, LORENE FRANCES, middle school educator; b. St. Louis, May 28, 1946; d. Frank Bernard and Marcella Marie (Froechtenigt) Niemeyer; m. Patrick Joseph Reid, Aug. 11, 1967; 1 child, Christina Marie. BA in Spanish, Maryville U., 1968; MEd in Secondary Edn., U. Mo., St. Louis, 1990; PhD in Edn., St. Louis U., 1995; MA in English, S.E. Mo. State U., 1996. Cert. Spanish, social studies, ESL tchr., reading specialist K-12, sch. psychologist, Mo.; cert. early adolescence/English lang. arts Nat. Bd. for Profl. Tchg. Stds. Spanish tchr. Rosary H.S., Spanish Lake, Mo., 1968-69, Taylor Sch., Clayton, Mo., 1969-70, Roosevelt H.S., St. Louis, 1988-89, Cleve. Jr. Naval Acad., St. Louis, 1989-90, Thomas Dunn Meml. Adult Edn., St. Louis, 1992-95; social studies tchr. St. Luke's Sch., Richmond Heights, Mo., 1981-88; ESL tchr. Grant Mid. Sch., St. Louis, 1990-92, Fanning Mid. Sch., St. Louis, 1992-98; tchr. leader Mid. Sch. Initiative, 1998-99; Schs. for Thought coord. MEGA Magnet Cluster, St. Louis, 1999-2000; psychol. examiner Student Support Svcs.-Gifted and Talented, St. Louis, 2000—03, sch. psychologist, 2003—04; sch. psychologist/psychol. examiner Ft. Zumwalt Sch. Dist., 2004—. Adj. prof. U. Mo.-St. Louis, 2000—; tutor Sylvan Learning Ctr., Crestwood, Mo., 1990-92; mem. St. Louis Ednl. Leadership Inst., 1994-97. Mem. Cmty. Leadership Program for Tchrs., St. Louis, 1993-94. Recipient Emerson Electric Excellence in Teaching award, 1994; named Tchr. of Yr., St. Louis Pub. Schs., 1994-95; named as one of 60 tchrs. recognized by Disney Channel Salutes the Am. Tchr., 1995-96. Mem. ASCD, Tchrs. English to Spkrs. of Other Langs., Nat. Coun. Tchrs. English, Midam. Tchs. English to Spkrs. of Other Langs., Internat. Reading Assn., Nat. Assn. Sch. Psychologists, Mo. Assn. Sch. Psychologists, Phi Delta Kappa. Home: 12208 Applerock Dr O Fallon MO 63368 Personal E-mail: lorenereid@sbcglobal.net.

REID, MARGARET ELIZABETH, elementary school educator, secondary school educator; b. Tampa, Fla., Feb. 8, 1934; d. James Byron and Zella Mae (Thompson) Bruce; m. Arthur M. Reid Jr., Dec. 28, 1955 (div. Dec. 1982); children: Laura Jean, Nancy Ann. BS in Edn., SUNY, Potsdam, 1956; postgrad., SUNY, Stony Brook, 1975—78; MS in Spl. Edn., L.I. U., 1979, postgrad., 1989—. Cert. spl. edn. tchr., N.Y. Tchr. Harborfields Sch. Dist., Greenlawn, NY, 1956—61; tchr. Project Able Three Village Sch. Dist., Stony Brook, 1971—72; substitute tchr. spl. edn. Smithtown Sch. Dist., 1972—75, substitute tchr., 1972—75, Shoreham Sch. Dist., NY, 1974—76, Mt. Sinai Sch. Dist., NY, 1974—79, Middle Island Sch. Dist, NY, 1974—79; tchr. resource rm. Hempstead Sch. Dist., NY, 1979—96. Tchr. rep. spl. edn. com. Hempstead Sch. Dist., 1985—. Mem. N.Y. Pub. Interest Rsch. Group, N.Y.C. 1987—, Citizens Campaign for the Environment, 1988—, Arthur Murray Sch. Dance (V.I.P. Hon. Student award 2002). NSF grantee Stevens Inst. Tech., 1959. Mem. N.Y. Assn. for Learning Disabled, Hempstead Classroom Tchrs. Assn., Coun. for Exceptional Children, N.Y. Branch Orton Dyslexia Soc., Kappa Delta Pi Republican. Methodist. Avocations: music, art, drama. Home: 64 Walter Ave Hauppauge NY 11788-3425

REID, ROBERT LELON, engineering educator, dean; b. Detroit, May 20, 1942; s. Lelon Reid and Verna Beulah (Custer) Menkes; m. Judy Elaine Nestell, July 21, 1962; children: Robert James, Bonnie Kay, Matthew Lelon. ASE, Mott C.C., Flint, Mich., 1961; BChemE, U. Mich., 1963; MME, So. Meth. U., 1966, PhDME, 1969. Registered profl. engr., Tenn., Tex., Wis. Asst. rsch. engr. Atlantic Richfield Co., Dallas, 1964-65; assoc. staff engr. Linde Divsn., Union Carbide Corp., Tonawanda, NY, 1966-68; from asst. to assoc. prof. U. Tenn., Knoxville, 1969-75; assoc. prof. Cleve. State U., 1975-77; from assoc. to full prof. U. Tenn., Knoxville, 1977-82; prof., chmn. U. Tex., El Paso, 1982-87; dean Coll. Engring., Marquette U., Milw., 1987-98, prof. mech. engring., 1998-2001; dean emeritus, 2001. Summer prof. NASA Marshall Space Ctr., Huntsville, Ala., 1970, EXXON Prodn. Rsch., Houston, 1972, 73, NASA Lewis Space Ctr., Cleve., 1986; cons. Oak Ridge Nat. Lab., 1974-75, TVA, 1978, 79, State of Calif., Sacramento, 1985, Tex. Higher Edn. Coordinating Bd., Austin, 1987. Contbr. articles 100 articles on heat transfer and solar energy. Grantee NSF, DOE, TVA, NASA, DOI, 1976-87; named Engr. of Yr. Engring. Socs. El Paso, 1986. Fellow ASME (Centennial medallion 1980, chmn. cryogenics com. 1977-81, chmn. solar energy divsn. 1983-84, chmn. Rio Grande sect. 1985-87, John Yellott award, 1997, Dedicated Svc. award 1998); mem. ASHRAE, Engrs. and Scientists Milw. (bd. dirs. 1988-93, v.p. 1989-90, pres. 1991-92), Wis. Assn. Rsch. Mgmt. (pres. 1996-97). Lutheran. Avocations: travel, classic car restoration. Business E-Mail: bobreid@umich.edu.

REID, ROSEMARY ANNE, insurance agent; b. Portland, Maine, June 15, 1951; d. Kenneth Bruce and Mary (Hollywood) R.; m. Ronald E. Walls, May 7, 1977 (div. Mar. 1986); children: Rachel A., Tate A. BS in Edn., U. South Maine, Portland, 1973. V.p. ins. Gruntal and Co., Inc., Portland, 1987-91; pvt. practice Portland, 1973—. Mem. Cape Elizabeth Town Coun., 1990, 95-99; mem. Cape Elizabeth Sch. Bd., 1991-94, fin. chair, 1992-93. Recipient 10 Yrs. Nat. Quality, 10 Yrs. Nat. Sale Achievement award, 1979-89, Nat. Assn. of Life Underwriters, 1974—, Am. Hometown Leadership award WalMart, 1998. Mem. Million Dollar Round Table (life and qualifying mem., Top of Table 1984, 86), South Maine Assn. Life Underwriters (bd. dirs. 1985-91, officer 1987-91, pres. 1989-90, regional v.p., pub. svc. chair, others), Life Underwriter Tng. Coun. (chair 1986-87), Maine Assn. Life Underwriters (bd. dirs. 1988-92, v.p. 1991-92, pres. elect 1992). Roman Catholic. Avocations: skiing, swimming, biking. Office: PO Box 927 Portland ME 04104-0927

REID, RUST ENDICOTT, lawyer; b. N.Y.C., Dec. 31, 1931; s. Thorburn and Mary (Newhall) R.; m.. Jeanne Inge, Aug. 5, 1955; children: Dorothy, Elizabeth, Margaret, Mary. BA, U. Va., 1954, LLB, 1960. Bar: Tex. 1960, Va. 1960. Bd. cert. in estate planning, probate. Assoc. Thompson & Knight, Dallas, 1960-65, 2003-06, ptnr., 1965—; lectr. SW Grad. Sch. Banking, Dallas, 1978-88; adj. prof. So. Meth. U., Dallas, 1980-86. Contbg. author: Texas Estate Administration, 1975. Trustee Child Care, Dallas, 1968-72, pres. 1970-72, Hockaday Sch., Dallas, 1972-82 (chmn. 1976-78), Texas coun. Girl Scouts U.S., 1982-83; trustee Vis. Nurse Assn., Dallas, 1984—, treas. 1986-89, v.p. 1989-91, pres., 1991-93; pres. Dallas Estate Planning Coun., 1988-89; trustee Dallas Children's Advocacy Center (v.p. 1993—). Lt. (j.g.) USNR, 1954-57. Fellow Am. Trust and Estate Counsel; mem. Tex. Bar Found. Presbyterian. Office: Thompson & Knight 1700 Pacific 1700 Pacific 3300 Dallas TX 75201 Home: 6715 Golf Dr Dallas TX 75205-1213 Home Phone: 214-360-0155; Office Phone: 214-969-1483.

REID, SUE TITUS, law educator; b. Bryan, Tex., Nov. 13, 1939; d. Andrew Jackson Jr. and Lorraine (Wylie) Titus. BS with honors, Tex. Woman's U., 1960; MA, U. Mo., 1962, PhD, 1965; JD, U. Iowa, 1972. Bar: Iowa 1972, U.S. Ct. Appeals (D.C. Cir.) 1978, U.S. Supreme Ct. 1978. From instr. to assoc. prof. sociology Cornell Coll., Mt. Vernon, Iowa, 1963-72; assoc. prof., chmn. dept. sociology Coe Coll., Cedar Rapids, Iowa, 1972-74; assoc. prof. law. U. Wash., Seattle, 1974-76; exec. assoc. Am. Sociol. Assn., Washington, 1976-77; prof. law U. Tulsa, 1978-88; dean, prof. Sch. Criminology, Fla. State U., Tallahassee, 1988-90; prof. pub. adminstrn. and policy Fla. State U., 1990—. Acting chmn. dept. sociology Cornell Coll., 1965-66; vis. assoc. prof. sociology U. Nebr., Lincoln, 1970; vis. disting. prof. law and sociology U. Tulsa, 1977-78, assoc. dean 1979-81; vis. prof. law U. San Diego, 1981-82; mem. People-to-People Crime Prevention Del. to People's Republic of China, 1982; George Beto Vis. Disting. Prof. criminal justice Sam Houston U., Huntsville, Tex., 1984-85; lecture/study tour of Criminal Justice systems of 10 European countries, 1985; cons. Evaluation Policy Rsch. Assocs., Inc., Milw., 1976-77, Nat. Inst. Corrections, Idaho Dept. Corrections, 1984, Am. Correctional Inst., Price-Waterhouse. Author (with others): Bibliographies on Role Methodology and Propositions Volume D - Studies in the Role of the Public School Teacher, 1962, The Correctional System: An Introduction, 1981, Crime and Criminology, 11th edit., 2006; author: Criminal Justice, 7th edit., 2006, Criminal Law, 7th edit., 2007; editor (with David Lyon): Population Crisis: An Interdisciplinary Perspective, 1972; contbr. articles to profl. jours. Recipient Disting. Alumni award Tex. Woman's U., 1979; named One of Okla. Young Leaders of 80's Oklahoma Monthly, 1980. Mem. ABA, Am. Soc. Criminology, Acad. Criminal Justice Scis., Soc. Criminal Jus. Assn. Avocations: walking, reading, cooking, skiing. Office: Fla State Univ Dept Pub Adminstrn Tallahassee FL 32306 Personal E-mail: suetreid@adelphia.net. E-mail: suetreid@roadrunner.com.

REID, S.W., language educator; b. Neptune, NJ, Nov. 24, 1943; s. Sidney Webb and Mary Cook (Bennett) R.; m. Judith Wright, Aug. 22, 1969; 1 child, Laura. BA, Duke U., 1965; MA, U. Va., 1966, PhD, 1972. Grad. tchg. fellow U. Va., Charlottesville, 1968-70; asst. prof. English, Kent (Ohio) State U., 1970-75, assoc. prof., 1975-84, prof., 1984—, dir. Inst. Bibliography and Editing, 1985—. Vis. fellow Clare Hall, Cambridge (Eng.) U., 1992-93, life mem., 1993—. Textual editor Bicentennial Edition of Charles Brockden Brown, 6 vols., 1977-87; editor-in-chief: (Cambridge edits. of Joseph Conrad) The Secret Agent, 1990, Almayer's Folly, 1994, Notes on Life and Letters, 2004. NDEA fellow U. Va., 1965-68; Rsch. grantee NEH, 1977-84. Office: Kent State University Inst Bibliography-Editing 1118 Library Kent OH 44242-0001 Office Phone: 330-672-2092.

REID, WILLIAM HILL, mathematics professor; b. Oakland, Calif., Sept. 10, 1926; s. William Macdonald and Edna Caroline (Hill) R.; m. Elizabeth Mary Kidner, May 26, 1962; 1 child, Margaret Frances. BS, U. Calif., Berkeley, 1949, MS, 1951; PhD, Cambridge U., Eng., 1955, ScD (hon.), 1968; AM (hon.), Brown U., 1961. Lectr. Johns Hopkins U., Balt., 1955-56; NSF fellow Yerkes Observatory, Williams Bay, Wis., 1957-58; asst. prof. Brown U., Providence, 1958-61, assoc. prof., 1961-63, U. Chgo., 1963-65, prof., 1965-89, prof. emeritus, 1989—; prof. Ind. U.-Purdue U., Indianapolis, 1989—. Cons. research labs. Gen. Motors Corp., Warren, Mich., 1960-73. Author (with P.G. Drazin): Hydrodynamic Stability, 1981; author: 2d edit., 2004; contbr. articles to profl. jours. Served with U.S. Mcht. Marine, 1945-47, with AUS, 1954-56. Fulbright Rsch. scholar, Australian Nat. U., 1964—65. Fellow Am. Phys. Soc., Cambridge Philos. Soc.; mem. Am. Math. Soc., Am. Meteorol. Soc., Sigma Xi. Office: Ind U-Purdue U Dept Math Scis 402 N Blackford St Indianapolis IN 46202-3216 Home: 10900 Lightship Ct Fishers IN 46038-2651

REID, WILLIAM JAMES, mining executive; b. Cowdenbeath, Scotland, Jan. 18, 1941; arrived in U.S., 1968; s. William and Sheila (Davidson) Reid; m. Thelma Rear, Sept. 27, 1969; children: Judith, Robert. Nat. cert. Mining Engring, Ashington County Tech. Coll., Northumberland, Eng., 1961. Student apprentice Brit. Coal, England, 1958-63; sales engr. Huwood Ltd., England, 1964-68; mining engr. Huwood-Irwin Co., Irwin, Pa., 1968-71, mgr. mining sales, 1971-74, gen. sales mgr., 1974-77, v.p., 1977-79; internat. sales dir. Huwood Ltd., England, 1979-81; exec. v.p. Am. Longwall Mining Corp., Abingdon, Va., 1981-83, pres., 1983-95, Am. Longwall Face Conveyors Inc., Abingdon, 1993-95, Internat. Longwall Cons., Abingdon, 1996-98, Internat. Entertainment Assocs., 1996-98; v.p. mktg. Long Airdox Co., Blacksburg, Va., 1998-99; pres. Eimco LLC, Bluefield, W.Va., 1999-2001, Internat. Longwall Cons., Bluefield, 2001—. Apptd. to Nat. Coal Coun. by Sec. Energy, 1994—; dir. Ea. Coal Coun., 1994—2002. Editor (mng.): Coal Leader, 2001—04; editor: (mng., pub.) Coal News, 2004—. Trustee Sullins Acad., Bristol, Va., 1984. Recipient Overseas medal, Brit. Instn. Mining Engrs., 1992. Mem.: AIME (treas. 1978), Nat. Mining Assn. (bd. govs. mfrs. divsn. 1991—96, 1999—2001), N. Eng. Inst. Mining and Mech. Engrs. (assoc.), Greater Irwin Area C. of C. (bd. dirs. 1977). Presbyterian. Avocations: travel, tennis. Home and Office: Coal News Inc 106 Tamarack St Bluefield WV 24701-4573 Office Phone: 304-327-6777. Personal E-mail: billreid007@comcast.net.

REID, WILLIAM R., agricultural studies educator; b. Morristown, NJ, Jan. 21, 1956; s. Roger A. and Helen L. Reid; m. Brenda L Olcott, June 11, 1977; children: Catherine G., Sarah J., Michael W. BS in Hort. Sci., Rutgers U., New Brunswick, NJ, 1978; MS in Soil Sci., N.C. State U., 1980; PhD in Entomology, Okla. State U., 1993. Rsch. and ext. specialist Kans. State U., Chetopa, 1981—. Contbr. articles to profl. jours. Grantee Nut Tree Ext. in Mo., U. of Mo., 1996—. Mem.: Am. Phytopathol. Soc., Am. Pomological Soc., Entomol. Soc. of Am., Am. Soc. for Hort. Sci., Kans. Nut Growers Assn. (life; sec./treas. 1983—), No. Nut Growers Assn. (life). Achievements include research in Development of new pecan cultivars and novel production techniques. Office: Pecan Experiment Field PO Box 247 Chetopa KS 67336-0247 Office Phone: 620-597-2972. E-mail: wreid@ksu.edu.

REID-ANDERSON, JAMES, diagnostic equipment company executive; BS in Commerce with honors, U. Birmingham, Eng.; MBA, Rutgers U. Exec. level positions with Pepsico Inc., Grand Met. PLC, Mobil Oil Corp.; COO, chief adminstrv. officer Wilson Sporting Goods, Chgo., 1994-96; exec. v.p., CFO Dade Behring, Deerfield, Ill., 1996-97, exec. v.p., CFO, chief adminstrv. officer, 1997-99, pres., COO, 1999—2000, pres., CEO, 2000—02, chmn., pres., CEO, 2002—. Fellow Chartered Assn. Cert. Accts. Office: Dade Behring Corp Hdqrs 1717 Deerfield Rd Deerfield IL 60015-3977 *

REIDENBERG, MARCUS MILTON, physician, educator; b. Phila., Jan. 3, 1934; m. June Wilson, July 14, 1957; children: Bruce, Joel, Julie. Student, Cornell U., 1951-54; MD, Temple U., 1958. Diplomate Am. Bd. Internal Medicine. Intern Community Gen. Hosp., Reading, Pa., 1958-59; resident Temple U. Hosp., Phila., 1962-65; from instr. to assoc. prof. Temple U. Med. Sch., Phila., 1962-75; assoc. prof. Cornell U. Med. Coll., NYC, 1975-76, prof. pharmacology, head div. clin. pharmacology, 1976—, prof. medicine, 1980—, prof. pub. health, 2002—, acting assoc. dean, 1981-82, asst. dean, 1988—; attending physician N.Y. Hosp., 1980—2006. Vis. physician Rockefeller U. Hosp., NYC, 1980—99; mem. project adv. group FDA, Rockville, Md., 1977-82; vice chmn. Joint Commn. on Prescription Drug Use, Washington, 1977-80; mem. study sect. NIH, Bethesda, Md., 1980-86; del. US Pharmacopeal Conv., 1975-80. Author: Renal Function and Drug Action, 1971; editor: various books, Clin. Pharmacology and Therapeutics, 1985—2001; contbr. articles to profl. jours. Served to lt. M.C., USNR, 1960-62. Recipient Research Career Devel. award NIH, 1970, Julius Sturmer award Phila. Coll. Pharmacy and Sci., 1982. Fellow ACP; mem. Am. Soc. Clin. Investigations, Assn. Am. Physicians, Am. Soc. Clin. Pharmacology and Therapeutics (pres. 1984-85, Rawls Palmer award 1981), Am. Soc. Pharmacology and Exptl. Therapeutics (award 1983, Harry Gold award 1999), Internat. Union Pharmacology (vice chmn. sect. clin. pharmacology 1984-87, chmn. 1987-89), World Health Organization Expert Com. on the Selection and Use of Essential Drugs (vice chmn. essential drugs com. 2003, 05, chmn. essential medicine com. 2007). Office: Cornell U Med Coll Dept Clin Pharmacology 1300 York Ave New York NY 10021-4805 Office Phone: 212-746-6227.

REID ENGLISH, CRISTEN, bank executive; married; 3 children. BS, Kalamazoo Coll., 1990; JD, Univ. Toledo, 1992; MBA, Univ. Mich., 1995. V.p. Access Bidco; positions including exec. v.p., gen. counsel & chief adminstrv. officer Capitol Bancorp Ltd., Lansing, Mich., 1997—2005, bd. dir., 2002—, COO, 2005—. Named one of 25 Women to Watch, US Banker mag., 2006. Office: Capitol Bancorp 200 Washington Sq N Lansing MI 48933

REIDER, SUZIE, Internet company executive, marketing professional; With Ziff-Davis Pub., 1988—2002; sr. v.p. sales and mktg. CNET, 2002—06, gen. mgr. entertainment, 2006; chief mktg. officer YouTube Inc., 2006—. Office: YouTube Inc 1000 Cherry Ave #200 San Bruno CA 94066

REIDER, VICTORIA A., state agency administrator; Grad. cum laude, Mercyhurst Coll.; JD, Dickinson Sch. Law. Bar: Pa. Supreme Ct., US Dist. Ct. (mid. dist. Pa.). With Pa. Commn. Crime and Delinquency; hearing examiner Pa. Dept. Revenue; exec. policy specialist, Gov.'s staff liaison to export-import bank US Gov.'s Office Policy Devel., Pa.; chief counsel, dep. chief counsel Pa. Ins. Dept.; ind. legal cons.; chief counsel Pa. Dept. Banking, 2004—06, acting sec., 2006—. Chmn. bd. dirs. Pa. Housing Fin. Agy., 2006—; bd. dirs. Pa. Indsl. Devel. Authority, Pa. Econ. Devel. Financing Authority, Pa. Minority Bus. Devel. Authority, Pa. Cmty. Devel. Bank Operational Com., Pa. Energy Devel. Authority, Commonwealth Financing Authority. Mem.: Am. Corp. Counsel Assn., Pa. Bar Assn., ABA. Office: Pa Dept Banking 17 N Second St Ste 1300 Harrisburg PA 17101-2290 Office Phone: 717-783-7151. Office Fax: 717-787-8773. E-mail: vareider@state.pa.us.

REIDY, CAROLYN KROLL, publisher; b. Washington, May 2, 1949; d. Henry August and Mildred Josephine (Mencke) Kroll; m. Stephen Kroll Reidy, Dec. 28, 1974. BA, Middlebury Coll., 1971; MA, Ind. U., 1974, PhD, 1982. Various positions to mgr. subs. rights Random House, Inc., NYC, 1975-83, assoc. pub., 1987-88; dir. subs. rights William Morrow & Co., NYC, 1983-85; v.p., assoc. pub. Vintage Books, NYC, 1985-87, pub., 1987-88, Anchor Books, Doubleday & Co., NYC, 1988; pres., pub. Avon Books, NYC, 1988-92; pres., pub. trade divsn. Simon & Schuster, NYC, 1992—2001, pres. adult publ. divsn., 2001—. Bd. dirs. NAMES Project, 1994—98, Literacy Partners, Inc., 2000—, Nat. Book Found., 2001—. Mem.: NY Women in Comm. (recipient Matrix award 2003), Pubs. Lunch Club. Office: Simon & Schuster 1230 Avenue Of The Americas New York NY 10020-1586 Business E-Mail: carolyn.reidy@simonandschuster.com.

REIDY, DANIEL EDWARD, lawyer; b. Chgo., Nov. 21, 1949; s. Francis W. and Ann E. (Harrington) R.; m. Elizabeth Gamble, Aug. 21, 1971; children: David, Patrick, Kevin, Jean. BA in Polit. sci., cm laude, Loyola U., 1971; JD magna cum laude, U. Mich., 1974. Bar: Ill. 1974, US Dist. Ct. (no. dist.) Ill. 1974, Supreme Ct., Ill., 1974, US Ct. Appeals (7th cir.) 1975, US Ct. Appeals (11th cir.) 1992, US Ct. Appeals (fed. cir.) 1994, US Dist. Ct. (ctrl. dist.) Ill. 1995, US Dist. Ct. (so. dist.) Ill. 2002, US Ct. Appeals (1st cir.), 2004. Law clk. to Hon. Walter J. Cummings U.S. Ct. Appeals (7th cir.), Chgo., 1974-75; asst. US atty. US Atty.'s Office, Chgo., 1975—85; first asst. US atty. No. Dist. of Ill., Chgo., 1985—87; ptnr. Jones Day Chgo., 1987—. Litig. group coord., Chgo. & nat. chair, Corp. Criminal Investigation Practice; mem. commn. adminstrn. justice Ill. Supreme Ct., Chgo., 1992-93. Fellow Internat. Acad. Trial Lawyers, Am. Coll. Trial Lawyers; mem. ABA, Chgo. Bar Assn.(sec. 2001-2005), Fed. Bar Assn., Chgo. Coun. Lawyers, Chgo. Inn Ct. Office: Jones Day 77 W Wacker Ste 3500 Chicago IL 60601-1692 Office Phone: 312-782-3939. Business E-Mail: dereidy@jonesday.com.

REIDY, MAUREEN J., fashion industry executive; b. 1970; Grad., U. Md., Coll. Park. With Price Waterhouse; staff auditor Trump Org.; pres. Miss Universe Org.; COO NYC Host Com. 2004; pres., CEO NYC Big Events, Inc.; COO IMG Fashion, NYC, 2007—; CPA. Named to 40 Under 40 list, Crain's NY Bus. Office: IMG Fashion 420 W 45th St New York NY 10036 Business E-Mail: fashionweeksponsorship@imgworld.com. *

REIDY, THOMAS MICHAEL, financial executive; b. Elmira, NY, Dec. 22, 1951; s. Bernard Thomas and Betty Pauline Reidy; m. Rosemarie Stella, June 12, 1982; 1 child, Carla. AS, Corning C.C., 1971; BA, St. John Fisher Coll., 1973; Cert. in Exec. Leadership, Cornell U. Cert. fin. planner. Exec. br. dir. YMCA, Rochester, N.Y., 1975-84; fin. planner IDS/Am. Express, Rochester, 1984-86; pres., CEO TMR Adv. Group, Rochester, 1986-95; divsn. mgr. Waddall & Reed, Rochester, 1995-98; pres. Morgan & Alexander Ltd., Rochester, 1998—. Pres. CPA/Bus. Forum, Rochester, 1988—90; prin. Sandler Sales Inst., Pittsford, NY, 2002—. Author: (tng. manual) The NOW Client System, 1996, The True Wealth Revolution, 1999, Quality Life Management System, 1999, Winning and Losing It, 2005. Recipient Outstanding Young Man Am. Jaycees, 1979, Businessman of Yr. Nat. Rep. Congrl. Com., 2003. Mem. Rotary Club, C. of C. Profl. Sales Soc. (bd. dirs. 1988-89). Office Phone: 585-249-9189. Business E-Mail: tom@thomasreidy.com.

REIDY, VALERIE J., principal, educator; 2 children. BS, PhD, Coll. Mt. St. Vincent; MS, Fordham U. Fellow Roswell Park Cancer Rsch. Inst., Buffalo; tchr. sci. Jr. HS High School 117, Bronx, NY, 1974—78; tchr. biology, head Biology Dept. Bronx HS of Sci., NY, 1978—2001, prin. NY, 2001—. Office: Bronx HS Sci 75 W 205 St Bronx NY 10468 Office Phone: 718-817-7700. E-mail: reidy@bxscience.edu. *

REIF, DAVID (FRANK DAVID REIF), artist, educator; b. Cin., Dec. 14, 1941; s. Carl A. and Rachel L. (Clifton) R.; m. Ilona Jekabsons, July 30, 1966; 1 child, Megan Elizabeth. BFA, Art Inst. Chgo., 1968; MFA, Yale U., 1970. Asst. prof. art U. Wyo., Laramie, 1970-74, assoc. prof., 1974-81, U. Mich., Ann Arbor, 1980-81; prof. U. Wyo., Laramie, 1981—2004, acting head dept. art, 1986—87, Disting. prof. emeritus, 2004—; prin., owner Reif Artworks & Design Consulting, Laramie, Wyo., 2005—. Selection cons. Ucross Found. Residency Program, Wyo., 1983—; exhibit juror Artwest Nat., Jackson, Wyo., 1986; panelist Colo. State U., Ft. Collins, 1981; lectr. U. Mich., 1980; apptd. Wyo. Arts Coun., 1993-96; vis. artist lectr. Colo. State U., 1996; vis. artist Colo. State U., Ft. Collins, 1996; 3-D juror, art exhbn. Colo. State Fair, Pueblo, 2001. One-man shows include U. Wyo. Art Mus., 1993, Dorsky Galleries, NYC, 1980, No. Ariz. U., 1977, 87, U. Mich., 1980-81, One West Ctr. Contemporary Art, Ft. Collins, 1991, West Wyo. C.C., Rock Springs, 1999, Casper Coll. Goldstein Gallery, 2003; exhibited in group shows at First, Second and Third Wyo. Biennial Tour, 1984-88, U.S. Olympics Art Exhbn., LA, 1984, Miss. Mus. Art and NEA Tour, 1981-83, LA Invitational Sculpture Tour Exhbn., 1991-92, Nicolaysen Art Mus., Casper, Wyo., 1994, Jackson Hole Ctr. Arts, Wyo., 2006, Gene Siskel Film Ctr. Gall, Art Inst. Chgo., 2006. Apptd. chair Wyo. Arts Coun., 1995-96. With USAR, 1963-69. Recipient F.D. Pardee award Yale U., 1970; Best Sculpture award Joslyn Art Mus. Omaha, 1978; grantee Nat. Endowment Arts, 1978-79, Wyo. Basic Rsch., 1983-84, 86-87; Tchg. Excellence grantee U. Wyo., 1996-97. Mem. Coll. Art Assn., Internat. Sculpture Ctr. Democrat. Home: 3340 Aspen Ln Laramie WY 82070-5702 Office: U Wyo Dept Art PO Box 3138 Laramie WY 82071-3138 Home Phone: 307-745-3110; Office Phone: 307-745-3110.

REIF, DEBORAH, manufacturing executive; Grad., Univ. Bridgeport; MBA, Univ. Conn. Fin. positions Gen. Electric, 1973—82; fin. analyst GE Capital, 1982—85; risk mgr. GE Comml. Equipment Fin., 1985—89; chief risk officer GE Vendor Fin. Services, 1990—98; sr. risk officer telecom equipment GE Capital, 1998—99, v.p. global asset mgmt., 2000—01; CEO GE Fin. Guaranty Ins. Co., 2001—03; exec. v.p. fin. restructuring NBC Universal Digital Media, 2004, pres., 2004—05; pres., CEO GE Equipment Services, Fairfield, Conn., 2005—. Office: General Electric 3135 Easton Turnpike Fairfield CT 06828 *

REIF, L. RAFAEL, academic administrator, engineering educator; m. Christine Reif; children: Jessica, Blake. BS, Universidad de Carabobo, Venezuela, 1973; MS, Stanford U., 1975, PhD, 1979. Asst. prof. Universidad Simon Bolivar, Caracas, Venezuela, 1973—74; faculty mem. MIT, Cambridge, 1980—, Maseeh Professor of Emerging Tech., dir. Microsystems Tech. Labs., 1990—99, assoc. head electrical engring., 1999—2004, head Dept. Electrical Engring. and Computer Sci., 2004—05, provost, 2005—. Recipient US Presdl. Young Investigator Award, 1984, Aristotle Award, Semiconductor Rsch. Corp., 2000. Fellow: IEEE; mem.: Am. Physical Soc., Electrochemical Soc., Tau Beta Pi. Office: MIT Rm 38-403 77 Massachusetts Ave Cambridge MA 02139-4307 Office Phone: 617-253-4601. E-mail: reif@mtl.mit.edu.

REIF COHEN, JESSICA, broadcast executive; m. Bob Cohen; children: AJ, Marisa Rachel. BS in Mktg., NYU, MBA in Fin. and Internat. Bus. Securities analyst, mng. dir. Oppenheimer & Co, Inc.; securities analyst First Boston Corp., Credit Lyonnais, Arnhold & S. Bleichroeder; mng. dir. and sr. media & entertainment analyst Merrill Lynch & Co., 1994, first v.p. rsch., media and global securities. Named one of 100 Most Powerful Women in Entertainment, Hollywood Reporter, 2006. Mem.: Nat. Assn. Television Program Execs., Mus. Television and Radio, Internat. Radio and Television Soc., Media and Entertainment Analysts NY, Beta Gamma Sigma. Office: Merrill Lynch & Co 4 World Financial Ctr New York NY 10080 *

REIFF, JAY, political organization worker; b. Lancaster County, 1968; Grad., Am. U. Head Dem. Gov. Michael Easley Campaign, 2000, 2004, SC Gov. Jim Hodges Campaign, 2002. Spl. adv. Gov. Easley; dir. of comm. Gov. Jim Hodges. *

REIFF, LAURA FOOTE, lawyer; b. Goldsboro, NC, July 21, 1964; BA in Legal Inst., Econ., Govt., Am. Univ., 1986; JD with honors, George Washington Univ., 1989. Bar: Md. 1989, DC 1990, US Ct. of Internat. Trade. Shareholder, co-chair bus. immigration group Greenberg Traurig LLP, McLean, Va. Co-recipient Outstanding Young Lawyers award, Am.

Immigration Law Assn., 1996; recipient Albert Arent Pro Bono award for Cmty. Svc., 1991. Mem.: ABA, Fed. Bar Assn., DC Bar Assn., Md. Bar Assn., Am. Immigration Law Found., Am. Immigration Lawyers Assn. Office: Greenberg Traurig LLP 12th Fl 1750 Tysons Blvd Mc Lean VA 22102-4202 Office Phone: 703-749-1372. Office Fax: 703-714-8372. Business E-Mail: reiffl@gtlaw.com.

REIFF, PATRICIA HOFER, space physicist, educator; b. Oklahoma City, Mar. 14, 1950; d. William Henry and Maxine Ruth (Hoffer) R.; m. Thomas Westfall Hill, July 4, 1976; children: Andrea Hofer Hill, Adam Reiff Hill, Amelia Reiff Hill. Student, Wellesley Coll., 1967-68; BS, Okla. State U., 1971; MS, Rice U., 1974, PhD, 1975. Cert. secondary tchr., Okla., Tex. Resident rsch. assoc. Marshall Space Flight Ctr., Huntsville, Ala., 1975-76; rsch. assoc. space physics and astronomy dept. Rice U., Houston, 1975, asst. prof. space physics and astronomy dept., 1978-81, asst. chmn. space physics and astronomy dept., 1979-85, assoc. rsch. sci., 1981-87, sr. rsch. scientist, 1987-90. Adj. asst. prof. Rice U., 1976-78, disting. faculty fellow, 1990-92, prof. 1992—, chmn. dept. space physics and astronomy, 1996-99, dir. Rice Space Inst., 1999—; mem. sci. team Atmosphere Explorer Mission, Dynamics Explorer Mission; co-investigator Global Geospace Sci. Mission, ESA/Cluster Mission, IMAGE Mission, Men's Mission; prin. investigator The Public Connection NASA, Mus. Tchg. Planet Earth Immersive Earth; cons. Houston Mus. Natural Sci., 1986—; adv. com. on atmospheric scis. NSF, Washington, 1988-92; mem. stategic implementation study panel NASA, Washington, 1989-91; mem. space sci. adv. com. NASA, 1993-98, mem. space sta. utilization subcom., 1995-98; mem. adv. com. Los Alamos Non-Proliferation Divsn., 1998-2001; univ. rep. U. Space Rsch. Assn., Washington, 1993—, chair Coun. of Instns., 2001-04; exec. com. George Observatory, Houston, 1989-92, others. Designer Cockrell Sundial/Solar Telescope, 1989; editor EOS (sci. newspaper), 1986-89; contbr. articles to profl. jours. Trustee, Citizens' Environ. Coalition, Houston, 1978-98, pres. 1980-85, adv. com. 1998-2000; mem. air quality com. Houston/Galveston Area Coun., 1980-83, Green Ribbon Com., City of Houston, 1981-83; active coms. Macedonia United Meth. Ch., 1988—. Named rsch. fellow NAS/NRC., 1975, an Outstanding Young Woman Am., 1977, '80, to Houston's Women on the Move, 1990; named Outstanding Aerospace Educator, Women in Aerospace, 1999; NASA grantee 1993-95, 98, 99, 2001-06; recipient NASA Group Achievement award. Fellow Am. Geophys. Union (fin. com. 1980-82, editor search com. 1992, pub. edn. com.); mem. Cosmos Club, Wellesley Club, Internat. Union of Geodesy and Geophysics (del. 1975, 81, 83, 89, 91, 93, 95, chair working group 2F, 1991-95). Avocations: organic gardening, beef ranching, scouting. Office: Rice U Dept Physics and Astronomy 6100 S Main St Houston TX 77251 Business E-Mail: reiff@rice.edu.

REIFFEL, LEONARD, physicist, consultant; b. Chgo., Sept. 30, 1927; s. Carl and Sophie (Miller) R.; m. Judith Eve Blumenthal, 1952 (div. 1962); children— Evan Carl, David Lee; m. Nancy L. Jeffers, 1971. B.Sc., Ill. Inst. Tech., 1947, M.Sc., 1948, PhD, 1953. Physicist Perkin-Elmer Corp., Conn., 1948; engring. physicist U. Chgo. Inst. Nuclear Studies, 1948-49; with Ill. Inst. Tech. Research Inst., Chgo., 1949-65, dir. physics research, 1956-63, v.p., 1963-65; cons. to Apollo program NASA Hdqrs., 1965-70; pvt. practice cons., 1970—; tech. dir. manned space flight expts. bd. NASA, 1966-68; chmn. bd. Instructional Dynamics, Inc., 1966-81, Interand Corp., 1969-91, Telestrator Industries, Inc., 1970-73; sci. editor Sta. WBBM-CBS radio, Chgo.; sci. cons./commentator WBBM-TV, 1971-72; host Backyard Safari, 1971-73; sci. feature broadcaster WEEI-CBS radio, Boston, 1965-75; syndicated newspaper columnist World Book Ency. Sci. Service, Inc. (later Universal Sci. News, Inc.), 1966-72, Los Angeles Times Syndicate, 1972-76; sci. cons. CBS Network, 1967-71; chmn., CEO Exelar Corp., Chgo., 1991—; chmn. bd., pres., CEO Ameraine Corp., Chgo., 1992-95; bd. overseers Armour Coll., bd. advisors engring. depts. Ill. Inst. Tech., 1995—; founder, chmn. Luxelar Corp., 2001—; founder Exelar Med. Corp., 2004, chmn., chief tech. officer, 2004—; founder, chmn., chief tech. officer Iron Mount Corp., 2005—07; chief tech. officer CAPTR Corp., 2007—. Cons. Korean Govt. on establishment atomic energy rsch. program; mem. adv. com. isotope and radiation devel. AEC; com. rsch. reactors NAS, 1958-64; cons. U.S. Army, 1976—; chmn. Reiffel Technologies, LLC; mem. advanced tech. adv. com. Children's Meml. Rsch. Ctr. Chgo., 2005-. Author: (book) The Contaminant, 1979; author numerous sci. papers; patentee in field. Bd. dirs. Student Competitions on Relevant Engring. Named Outstanding Young Man of Year Chgo. Jr. C. of C., 1954, 61; recipient Merit award Chgo. Tech. Socs., 1968, Peabody award, 1968, IR-100 award Telestrator CBS Chalkboard, 1970, award Aviation Writers Assn., 1971, IR-100 award, 1972, 73, 85, Disting. Alumni Achievement award Ill. Inst. Tech., 1974, Third Annual High Tech Entrepreneur award, 1986, Emmy award, 2004; named to Hall of Fame IIT, 1984. Fellow Am. Phys. Soc.; mem. AAAS, Chgo. Literary Club, Sigma Xi, Tau Beta Pi, Eta Kappa Nu. Achievements include being responsible for world's 1st indsl. nuclear reactor, 1956. Home: 602 W Deming Pl Chicago IL 60614-2618 Office Phone: 773-871-0171. Personal E-mail: lreiffel@aol.com.

REIFLER, STEWART, lawyer; b. Poughkeepsie, NY, May 5, 1954; s. Aaron and Sally Reifler; m. Sheryl Louise Perry, Sept. 19, 1982; 1 child, Jonathan Perry. Student, McGill U., 1972—75; BA, Bard Coll., 1979; JD magna cum laude, NY Law Sch., 1992. Bar: N.Y. 1992, Conn. 1992, U.S. Tax Ct. 1992, U.S. Supreme Ct. 2004. Assoc. Law Offices of Joseph E. Bachelder, NYC, 1992—95, Weil, Gotshal & Manges, 1995—98; dir. PricewaterhouseCoopers, 1998—2001; ptnr., shareholder, head N.Y. exec. compensation group Vedder, Price, Kaufman & Kammholz, 2001—. Steering com. mem., exec. compensation AICPA. Co-author: Compensation Committee Handbook, 2d edit., 2004; contbr. articles to profl. jours. Trustee Westport Pub. Libr., Conn. Recipient Outstanding Editl. Contbn., NY Law Sch. Law Rev., 1991, Law Rev., NY Law Sch., Am. Jurisprudence award, 1991. Mem.: ABA, N.Y. State Bar Assn., Conn. State Bar Assn., Assn. of Bar City of N.Y., WorldatWork, Nat. Assn. Stock Plan Profls., Rockefeller Club, Minuteman Yacht Club, Penn Club. Home: 8 Brightfield Ln Westport CT 06880 Office: Vedder Price Kaufman & Kammholz 1633 Broadway New York NY 10019 Office Phone: 212-407-7700. E-mail: sreifler@vedderprice.com.

REIFSNIDER, KENNETH LEONARD, metallurgist, educator; b. Balt., Feb. 19, 1940; s. David Leonard and Daisy Pearl (Hess) R.; m. Loretta Lieb, June 15, 1963; children: Eric Scott, Jason Miles. BA, Western Md. Coll., 1963; BS in Engring., Johns Hopkins U., 1963, MS in Engring., 1965, PhD, 1968. Jr. instr. Johns Hopkins U., Balt., 1966-67; asst. prof. Va. Poly Inst. and State U., Blacksburg, 1968-72, chmn. materials engring. sci. Ph.D. program, 1974-92, assoc. prof., 1972-75, prof., 1975-83, Reynolds Metals prof. engring. sci. and mechanics, 1983-90, Alexander Giacco prof., 1990—2002; chmn. adminstrn. bd. Ctr. Composite Materials and Structures, 1984, 1994-97; Pratt and Whitney Chair prof. design and reliability U. Conn., 2002—; dir. Conn. Global Fuel Cell Ctr., Storrs. Dir. Va. Inst. for Material Systems, 1988-2001, Conn. Global Fuel Cell Ctr., 2004-, assoc. provost for interdisciplinary programs, 1996-2001; engr. Lawrence Livermore Nat. Lab., 1981; mem. Nat. M aterials Adv. Bd., 1996—; cons. in materials sci. NATO, 1969, 75. Editor in chief Internat. Jour. of Fatigue; assoc editor Internat. Jour. of Fuel Cell Science and Technology, 2003-; editor, co-editor, author books, book chpts, articles for profl. publs. Mem. troop 44 com. Boy Scouts Am., Blacksburg, Va. Recipient Va. Acad. Sci. J. Shelton Horsley award, 1978, Va. Poly Inst. Alumni award, 1982, Disting. Rsch. award Am. Soc. Composites, 1992. Fellow ASTM (founder Jour. of Composites Tech. and Rsch., vice chmn. standing com. on publs., award of merit 1982); mem. ASME, NAE, Coun. on Engring. Home: 13 Quail Run Rd Storrs Mansfield CT 06268-2768 Office: Conn Global Fuel Cell Ctr 44 Weaver Rd, Unit 5233 Storrs Mansfield CT 06269-5233 also: 262 United Technologies Bldg 191 Auditorium Rd, Unit 3139 Storrs Mansfield CT 06269-3139 Office Phone: 860-486-5360, 860-486-3139. Office Fax: 860-486-8378, 860-486-5088. E-mail: reifsnid@engr.uconn.edu.

REIG, JUNE WILSON, scriptwriter, television director and producer; b. Schenectady, NY, June 1, 1933; d. Wallace John and Lillian Lucy (Gay) Wilson; m. Robert Maxwell, Nov. 26, 1969. BA summa cum laude, N.Y. State U., 1954; MA in Dramatic Arts, NYU, 1962. Instr. NYU, NYC, 1962—67; prodr., dir. NYU Theater, NYC, 1963—67; dir.-prodr., writer news and pub. affairs NBC TV Network, NYC, 1963—67; dir., writer, prodr. divsn. entertainment NBC-TV Network, NYC, 1967—73; pres. Bunny/Chord Prodns., NYC, 1972—97. Author: (book) Dairy of the Boy King Tut-Ankh-Amen, Charles Scribner's Sons, 1978; writer: (music spl.) The Heart of Christmas with Skitch Henderson, Robert Shaw Chorale and NBC Symphony, 1965; An Afternoon at Tanglewood with Erich Leinsdorf and the Boston Symphony Orch. (Peabody award); writer, dir. (with Johnny Carson) (TV spl.) Stuart Little, 1966 (Peabody award, Prix Jeunesse); writer The Reluctant Dragon, 1968 (Brotherhood award); writer, dir., prodr. (with Burl Ives) Rabbit Hill, 1966 (ALA award); writer, dir., prodr. Bill Cosby As I See It, 1970 (Ohio State award); A Day with Bill Cosby, 1971; Jennifer & Me, 1972; prodr., writer (with Edward Villella and Joanne Woodward) Little Women, the ballet, 1976; prodr., writer (with Orson Welles) Tut, the Boy King, 1978 (Peabody award); writer, dir., prodr.: (TV series) Watch Your Child - The Me Too Show, 1973 (Action for Children's TV Achievement award); films in permanent collections Mus. Broadcasting, N.Y.C. Nominee Emmy award, 1966, 1976; recipient Christopher award. Mem.: NATAS, Dirs. Guild Am., Writers Guild Am., Audubon Soc., NYU Alumni Assn., Internat. Soc. Animal Rights, Friends of Animals, Alan Devoe Bird Club (Old Chatham, N.Y.). Avocations: photography, music, animals. Office: Resnick Druckman Group LLC 469 Seventh Ave Ste 1300 New York NY 10018 *Whether I am working on a teleplay or book, I write about things I believe children are interested in: feelings, aspirations, caring, animals, loving. As I see it, too much of the fare for young people gives them a distorted view of how much violence there is in the world, and I want to counteract that impression. I want to write about things that create a sense of worth, warm security, and an absence of unnecessary anxiety. When I do write about the darker things that happen in life, it is to help the young person understand himself and the world a little better.*

REILEY, T(HOMAS) PHILLIP, consultant; b. Ft. Lewis, Wash., May 5, 1950; s. Thomas Phillip and Anne Marie (Russick) R. BSc in Biophysics, Pa. State U., 1973; postgrad. in Bus. Adminstrn., Rutgers U.; MBA, NYU, 1991. Cert. prodn. and inventory mgmt., cert. integrated resource mgmt. Inventory supr. Leland Tube Co., South Plainfield, NJ, 1973-76; prodn. inventory control supr. Bomar Crystal Co., Middlesex, NJ, 1976-79; prodn. control mgr. Codi Semiconductor Inc., Linden, NJ, 1979-81; mfg. systems analyst Western Union Info. Systems, Mahwah, NJ, 1981-85; bus. analyst Nabisco Brands Biscuit Divsn., Parsippany, NJ, 1985-91, sr. systems analyst, 1991-94, tech. advisor, 1994-97; applications cons. SAP Am., Newton Square, Pa., 1997—. Mem. Am. Prodn. and Inventory Control Soc. (past chmn. edni. com. Raritan Valley chpt.), NY Acad. Scis., Coun. Logistics Mgmt., Am. Inst. Mgmt. Accts., Mensa. Republican. Home: 1308 Centennial Ave #111 Piscataway NJ 08854 Office: 3999 West Chester Pike Newtown Square PA 19073 Office Phone: 610-661-7603. Business E-Mail: phillip.reiley@sap.com, preiley@world.std.com.

REILLEY, DENNIS H., retired chemicals executive; b. Feb. 25, 1953; m. Cindy Reilley; children: Jason, Michael. BS in Fin, Okla. State U., 1975. With Conoco, 1974-80, mgr. adminstrn. surface transp. Houston, 1980-81, exec. asst. to pres. petroleum ops., 1981-83, gen. mgr. planning and adminstrn. N.Am. mktg., 1983-84; v.p. ops. Kayo Oil Co., Chattanooga, 1984-87; pres., mng. dir. Conoco, 1987-89; dir. ops. white pigment and mineral products divsn. DuPont, 1989-91, v.p., gen. mgr. white pigment and mineral products, 1991-95, v.p., gen. mgr. specialty chems., 1995-96, v.p., gen. mgr. Lycra/Terathane, 1996-97, sr. v.p., 1997-99, exec. v.p., COO, 1999-2000; pres. Praxair, Inc., Danbury, Conn., 2000—06, CEO, 2006, chmn., 2006—07. Mem. electricity adv. bd. US Dept. Energy; past chmn. Am. Chemistry Council; bd. dirs. Entergy Corp., The Conservation Fund; bd. dir. Marathon Oil Co., 2002—; bd. dirs. H. J. Heinz Co., 2005—. *

REILLEY, JAMES CLARK, artist, cartoonist, small business owner; b. Detroit, Nov. 4, 1919; s. James Aloyisus and Lillian May (Cole) R.; m. Beatrice C. Clemente, May 10, 1952 (dec.); children: James A. (dec.), Anthony Francis, Beatrice Anita. Grad., Art Inst. of Pitts., 1948. Artist Banner Advt., Phila., 1948-49; layout artist Lit Bros. Dept. Store, Phila., 1949; comic book illustrator John Prentice, LI, 1950; artist DuPont Co., Wilmington, Del., 1950-59; artist/owner Jim Reilley Studio, Wilmington, 1959-94; ret. Link trainer instr.; jazz harmonica soloist various radio programs and shows, Chanutefield, Ill., Walla Walla, Wash. Cartoon series, This is the Life, Hornepipe. Sgt. USAAF, 1942-45. Inducted to Penns Grove H.S. Personal Achievement Hall of Fame, 1996. Roman Catholic. Avocations: fishing, music, sports. Home: 110 N Broad St Penns Grove NJ 08069-1269

REILLY, ANNE HUEDEPOHL, university educator, researcher; b. Chgo., Sept. 16, 1957; d. E. Bradley and Lynne (Swanson) Huedepohl; m. John J. Reilly, Aug. 12, 1978; children: Kristine Anne, Meghan Lynne, Caroline Hannah. BA in Econs. and Bus. Adminstrn. summa cum laude, Knox Coll., 1978; MBA in Finance, U. Iowa, 1980; PhD in Organizational Behavior, Northwestern U., 1989. Banking officer spl. industries Cont. Ill. Nat. Bank, Chgo., 1980-82; asst. v.p. corp. banking Lloyds Bank Internat., Chgo., 1983-84; lectr. bus. adminstrn. U. Iowa, 1979-80; teaching asst. Northwestern U., Evanston, 1987; asst. prof. mgmt. Loyola U., Chgo., 1988-95, assoc. prof. mgmt., 1995—2000, prof. mgmt., 2000—. Presented numerous papers in field; contbr. articles to profl. jours. including Jour. Orgnl. Behavior, Acad. Mgmt. Jour., Sloan Mgmt. Rev., Orgn. Sci., Indsl. Crisis Quar., Jour. Mgmt. Studies, Jour. Vocat. Behavior, Jour. Mgmt. Edn., Strategic Mgmt. Jour.; book and textbook reviewer. Trustee Knox Coll., Galesburg, Ill., 2000—06. Rsch. grantee Northwestern U. Banking Rsch. Ctr., 1987, 88, Nat. Ctr. for Mgmt. R&D, Can., 1989-90, Employee Relocation Coun., 1989-90, Loyola U. Summer Rsch., 1990, Abbott Labs., 1997-99, Loyola U. Family Bus. Ctr., 2006. Mem. Acad. Mgmt., Orgnl. Behavior Teaching Soc., Phi Beta Kappa, Beta Gamma Sigma, Phi Beta Delta. Democrat. Lutheran. Avocations: travel, reading, swimming. Office: Loyola U Chgo 820 N Michigan Ave Chicago IL 60611-2147 Home Phone: 847-835-2946; Office Phone: 312-915-6537. Business E-Mail: areilly@luc.edu.

REILLY, CHARLES EDMUND, JR., communications executive; b. Phila., Nov. 4, 1928; s. Charles Edmund, Sr. and Kathryn (McHugh) Reilly; m. Joan Emily Hunter; children from previous marriage: Lynn, Susan, Kathryn, Charles III. BS in Bus., St. Joseph's U., Phila., 1950; postgrad., U. Pa., 1955; MA in Liberal Studies, Villanova U., 2002. Med. rep. Stuart Pharms., Phila., 1954-56; mgr. newsstand promotion TV Guide Mag., Radnor, Pa., 1956—64, rep. ea. coast NYC, 1959—63; asst. to v.p., dir. corp. relations Young & Rubicam Inc., NYC, 1964-66; exec. dir. Nat. Cath. Office for Radio-TV, NYC, 1966-71; exec. v.p. Patrick Carr Assocs., NYC, 1971-72; corp. exec. J. Walter Thompson, NYC, 1972-74; v.p. Ogilvy and Mather, NYC, 1975-76; founder In-Person Communications Inc., NYC, 1976—2007. Cons. Pontifical Commn. Social Comm., Vatican City, 1968—71; adj. assoc. prof. St. John's U., NYC, 1971—72; mem. vis. com. Loyola U., New Orleans, 1987—2007. Author: You Speak.They Listen, 1984, You and A Life of Reilly, 1987, Special Delivery, 1998, Korea 1950-1953--The War That Never Was, 2000, In the Wings of Show Business, A Personal Memoir, 2006, others; newspaper columnist Suburban and Wayne, 1991—, Main Line Life, 1994—. Lt. col. Valley Forge Mil. Coll., 1995—2003. 1st lt. US Army, 1950—53. Named to Hall of Fame, Inf. Sch., Ft. Benning, Ga., 1996. Mem.: St. Davids Golf Club (Wayne, Pa.), Merion Cricket Club (Haverford, Pa.). Republican. Personal E-mail: crinperson@aol.com.

REILLY, CHARLES JAMES, lawyer, educator, accountant; b. Pawtucket, RI, Oct. 10, 1950; s. Thomas Joseph and Florence Marie (McKenna) R.; m. Barbara Bouffard, Aug. 7, 1971 (div. July 2004); children: Kristen, Elizabeth. BSBA, Providence Coll., 1972; JD, Suffolk U., 1979. Bar: R.I. 1979, U.S. Dist. Ct. R.I. 1979, U.S. Ct. Appeals (1st cir.) 1979, U.S. Supreme Ct. 1984, U.S. Ct. Claims, 1985; CPA, R.I. Agt. IRS, Providence, 1972-75; appellate conferee U.S. Dept. Treasury, Boston, 1976-81; ptnr. Arcaro & Reilly, Providence, 1981-91, Reilly Law Assocs., Providence, 1991—. Assoc. prof. Grad. MST program Bryant Coll., Smithfield, R.I., 1983—. Mem. AICPA, R.I. Soc. CPAs, ABA, R.I. Bar Assn. (chair tax sect. 1996-2000). Clubs: R.I. Country. Democrat. Roman Catholic. Avocation: golf. Office: Reilly Law Assocs 1040 Turks Head Bldg Providence RI 02903 Home Phone: 401-247-0716; Office Phone: 401-861-1120. Business E-Mail: reillylaw1@aol.com.

REILLY, DANIEL PATRICK, retired bishop; b. Providence, May 12, 1928; s. Francis E. and Mary (Burns) R. Student, Our Lady of Providence Sem., 1943—48, Grand Seminaire, St. Brieuc, France, 1948—53, Harvard U., 1954—55, Boston Coll., 1955—56; D (hon.), Providence Coll., St. Michael's Coll., Holy Apostles Coll. and Sem., Salve Regina Coll., Our Lady of Providence Coll., Sacred Heart U., Assumption Coll., 1995, Anna Maria Coll., 1995, Holy Cross Coll., 1996. Ordained priest Roman Cath. Ch., 1953. Asst. pastor Cathedral Saints Peter and Paul, Providence, 1953—54; asst. chancellor Diocese of Providence, 1954—56, sec. to bishop, 1956—64; became monsignor, 1964; chancellor Diocese of Providence, 1964—72, adminstr., 1971—72, vicar gen., 1972—75; consecrated bishop, 1975; bishop Norwich, Conn., 1975—94; Conn. state chaplain K.C., 1976—94; Episcopal moderator Nat. Cath. Cemetery Corp., 1977—87; bishop of Worcester Mass., 1994—2004. Ad hoc mem. to aid ch. in Ea. Europe, adminstrv. com. mem. NCCB/U.S. Cath. Conf., 1976—86, 1992—; pro-life com. mem. NCCB, 1989—92, chmn. 10th anniversary peace pastoral com., 1992—93, chmn. internat. policy com., 1993; mem. Priestly Life and Ministry Commn., 1991—94; past pres. New Eng. Consultation Ch. Leaders; drafting com. mem. U.S. Cath. Conf. Pastoral Letter on Peace, 1983, mem. com. on coms.; active Holy See Pontifical Coun.-Cor Unum, 1984—89. Trustee Cath. Mut. Relief Soc., Omaha, 1979—, St. John's Sem., Brighton, Mass., 1987—, Am. Coll., Louvain, Belgium, St. Mary's Sem., Balt.; chmn. bd. Cath. Relief Svcs. Cath. Relief Svcs., 1978—86; mem. fin. and budget com. U.S. Cath. Conf. U.S. Cath. Conf., 1985—87; chancellor Holy Apostles Coll. and Sem., Cromwell, Conn., 1982—94; pres. Conn. Interfaith Housing, 1975—94; cons. Pontifical Coun. Justice and Peace, 1995; bd. dirs. United Way Southeastern Conn., 1976—94, Conn. Drug and Adv. Coun., 1978—80. Mem.: KC (R.I. state chaplain 1964—75), Rotary. Roman Catholic. Office: St Paul Cathedral Rectory 38 High St Worcester MA 01609 Home Phone: 508-799-0999; Office Phone: 508-799-4193. Personal E-mail: vocdir@aol.com. Business E-Mail: breilly@worcesterdiocese.org. *If you would make a true success of your life for time and for eternity, never forget that it will be achieved by your willingness to make countless efforts that will be known only to God.*

REILLY, DAVID HENRY, retired university dean; b. Paterson, NJ, Nov. 7, 1936; s. David Henry and Ethel Taylor (Alt) R.; m. Jean Lockwood, July 2, 1960; children— David Scott, Chris Robert, Sandra Jean. BA, U. Vt., 1959; Ed.M., Rutgers U., 1962, Ed.D., 1965. Diplomate: Am. Bd. Profl. Psychology. Remedial reading instr. Drake Sch. of N.J. Neuro-Psychiat. Inst., Princeton, 1959-62, jr. fellow psychol. services at inst., summer 1962-63; research asst. N.J. Bur. Research Neurology and Psychiatry; also sch. psychologist Woodbridge (N.J.) sch. system, 1962-63; clin. psychologist, then research asso. N.J. Bur. Research Neurology and Psychiatry, 1963-64, 65; sch. and research psychologist Woodbridge sch. system, 1964-65; post doctoral fellow clin. child psychology Devereux Found., Devon, Pa., 1965-66; mem. faculty U. N.C., Chapel Hill, 1966-74, prof. psychology, 1974—, chmn. dept. sch. psychology program, 1966-74; dean U. N.C. (Sch. Edn.), Greensboro, 1974-86; dean Coll. of Grad. and Profl. Studies The Citadel, Charleston, 1992—. Mem. N.C. Bd. Examiners Practicing Psychologists, 1973—, treas., 1975, chmn., 1976 Contbr. articles to profl. jours. Research grantee NIMH, 1963; Fulbright Vis. scholar Republic of Cyprus, 1986-87, USSR, 1990. Fellow APA; mem. Am. Acad. Sch. Psychology (pres.-elect 1996-97, pres. 1997-98), Southeastern Psychol. Assn., N.C. Psychol. Assn. (pres. 1980-81), N.C. Assn. Coll. Tchr. Edn. (pres. 1981), N.C. Sch. Psychology Assn. (pres. 1976-77), S.C. Grad. Deans Assn. (pres. 1998-99). Home: 3311-Seven Lakes W Seven Lakes NC 27376 Personal E-mail: skipreilly@aol.com.

REILLY, DAVID N. (NICK REILLY), automotive executive; b. Wales, 1949; Diploma, U. Cambridge, 1971. Gen. ops. mgr. GM Svc. Parts Ops., 1984—86, dir. mfg., 1986—87; v.p. ops. GM, Isuzu, IBC, Luton, England, 1987—90; dir. mfg. Vauxhall Port Plant, Ellesmere, 1990—94; v.p. GM Europe, Zurich, Switzerland, 1994—96; chmn. mng. dir. Vauxhall Motors, 1996—2001; v.p. GM Corp., 1997—; v.p. sales, mktg. GM Europe, 2001—02; pres., CEO GE Daewoo Auto and Tech. Co., Republic of Korea, 2002—06; pres. GM Asia Pacific divsn, 2006—. Mem. Asia Pacific Strategy Bd. GM. Recipient Cmdr. Order British Empire, 2000. Mem.: Soc. Motor Mfgs. and Traders (pres. 2001—02).

REILLY, EDWARD ARTHUR, lawyer; b. NYC, Dec. 17, 1943; s. Edward Arthur and Anna Marguerite (Sautter) R.; children: M. Teresa, Edward A. AB, Princeton U., 1965; JD, Duke U., 1968. Bar: NY 1969, NC 1971, Fla. 1979, Conn. 1983. Asst. dean law sch. Duke U., 1970-72; assoc. Shearman & Sterling, NYC, 1972-80, ptnr., 1980-87, Harlow, Reilly, Derr & Stark, Rsch. Triangle Park, NC, 1988-90; counsel Morris & McVeigh, NYC, 1991-93, ptnr., 1993—. Pres. Am. Friends Paris Opera Ballet, Inc.; sec. Camille and Henry Dreyfus Found., Inc.; sec. Owen Cheatham Found. Decorated Knight of Order of Arts and Letters, French Govt.-Ministry of Culture and Comm., 1992. Fellow Am. Coll. Trust & Estate Counsel; mem. NY State Bar Assn., Fla. Bar Assn., Conn. Bar Assn. Episcopalian. Office: Morris & McVeigh 767 3rd Ave New York NY 10017-2023 Home: 5 Old Field Pl Norwalk CT 06853-1116

REILLY, EDWARD FRANCIS, JR., federal agency administrator, former state senator; b. Leavenworth, Kans., Mar. 24, 1937; s. Edward F. and Marian C. (Sullivan) R. BA, U. Kans., 1961. V.P. Reilly & Sons, Inc., Leavenworth, 1967-92; pres. Yllier Lake Estates, Inc., Easton, Kans., 1965-89; mem. Kans. Ho. Reps., 1963-64, Kans. State Senate, 1964-92, asst. majority leader, 1977-80, vice-chmn. govtl. orgn., chmn. ins. subcom., chmn. fed. and state affairs com.; mem. U.S. Parole Commn., U.S. Dept. Justice, 1992—, chmn., 1992—97, 2001—. Commr. Nat. Commn. on Accreditation of Law Enforcement Agys., 1982-96; adv. mem. Am. Justice Inst. fed. and state prisons; mem. cmty. liaison com. U.S. Penitentiary Lansing, Kans. Commr. ex officio U.S. Sentencing Commn., Washington; del. to Rep. Nat. Conv., Miami Beach, Fla., 1968; chmn. Leavenworth County Radio Free Europe Fund, 1972; bd. dirs. St. John's Hosp., Leavenworth, 1970-79, sec.; bd. dirs. Leavenworth Assn. for Handicapped, 1968-69, ARC, Leavenworth chpt., Kans. Blue Cross/Blue Shield, 1969-72; apptd. by Pres. Reagan Nat. Hwy. Safety Adv. Com.; active Trinity Nat. Leadership Roundtable, Cath. Campaign Am., Kans. Adv. Bd. Juvenile Offenders, Nat. Com. Cmty. Corrections. Recipient Cmty. Leaders of Am.,

1971, 85, 86, Hallpac Pub. Svc. award, 1988, Am. Police Hall of Fame award, 1990, Good Samaritan award Order of Michael the Arch Angel Police Legion, 1990, Commendation award mayor and city commn. of Leavenworth, Kans., 1990, Carnegie Hero Fund Commn. award and medallion, 1991, Silver Angel award Kans. Cath. Conf., 1992; named Outstanding Young Men Am., 1965-76. Mem. Nat. Criminal Justice Assn., Nat. Inst. Corrections (adv. bd.), Advisory Bd., Dept. of Philosophy, Catholic Univ. of America, Am. Paroling Authorities Internat., Am. Correctional Assn., Am. Probation and Paroling Assn., Leavenworth C. of C. (hon. dir. 1970-73), No. Assn. Chiefs Police, Assn. U.S. Army (Henry Leavenworth award 1960), Kansas City (Kans.) C. of C., Leavenworth Hist. Soc. (dir. 1968-73), John Carroll Soc., Native Sons of Kansas City, Ancient Order of Hibernians, U.S. Supreme Ct. Hist. Soc., Kiwanis (dir. 1969-70, Connelly award 1991, Legion of Honor award 1996), K.C., Elks, Eagles, Order of Malta, Equestrian Order Holy Sepulchre Jerusalem, Sacred Military Constantinian Order of Saint George. Republican. Roman Catholic. Office: US Parole Commn 5550 Friendship Blvd Ste 420 Chevy Chase MD 20815-7201 *

REILLY, EDWARD T., JR., advertising executive; b. NYC, Oct. 21, 1946; s. Edward Thomas and Dorothy (Comba) R.; m. Susan M. Brooke, June 28, 1969; children: Kristen, Greg. BBA, St. Francis Coll., NYC, 1968. Editor-in-chief Gregg div. McGraw Hill Book Co., NYC, 1974-76; controller CTB, Monterey, Calif., 1976-78; gen. mgr. Instructo, Palli, Pa., 1978-79; group v.p. for Europe, Africa, Mideast McGraw Hill U.K. Ltd., Maidenhead, U.K., 1980-83; exec. v.p. McGraw-Hill Internat. Book Co., NYC, 1983-84; sr. v.p. fin., planning and adminstrn. McGraw-Hill Broadcasting Co., NYC, 1985-86, exec. v.p., chief operating officer, 1986-87, pres., 1987—; CEO Big Flower Holdings, 1997-2000. Mem. corp. adv. council Nat. Council La Raza; mem. local carriage task force Nat. Assn. Broadcasters; mem. adv. com. on local excellence in TV programming Mus. of Broadcasting; bd. dirs. Internat. Radio and TV Found., Nat. Assoc. of Broadcasters, 1990-94, TV Bur. of Advt., 1988-95, chmn. 1990-93, assoc. of Max Svc. TV, 1987—, chmn. 1994—, Gov.- ABC TV network affiliates assoc., chmn. gov. rel., 1993-95. Chmn. Monterey County Overall Econ. Devel. Com., Monterey, Calif., 1977; bd. govs. Carmel Unified Sch. Dist. (Calif.), 1977. Fellow Inst. Dirs. Great Britain Office: Big Flower Holdings Inc 345 Park /ave New York NY 10154-0004

REILLY, ELIZABETH ANN, law educator, dean; b. South Bend, Ind., Sept. 9, 1951; d. Edward Leo and Barbara (Nolan) Reilly; m. Scott Robert Piepho, Dec. 30, 1994; children: Chloe, Naomi. AB, Princeton U., NJ, 1973; JD, U. Akron, Ohio, 1978. Bar: Ohio State Supreme Ct. Atty. Whitaker and Reilly, Akron, 1978—84; asst. prof. U. Akron Sch. Law, 1984—88, assoc. prof., 1988—92, prof., 1992—99, C. Blake McDowell Jr. prof. law, 1999—, assoc. dean, 1995—. Fellow constl. ctr. U. Akron Sch. Law, 1998—; chair juvenile rules subcom., adv. com. Ohio Supreme Ct., Columbus, 1999—2002; chair pres. commn. on equity U. Akron, 1999—2002, fellow symposium tchg. assessment and learning, 2002—03. Contbr. articles to profl. jours. Pres. Unitarian Universalist Ch. Akron, Fairlawn, 2007—. Recipient Outstanding Tchr. Scholar award, U. Akron, 2004, Outstanding Alumna award, Akron Sch. Law, 2006. Fellow: Akron Bar Foun.; mem.: Am. Bar Assn., Ohio State Bar Assn. (mem. section bd. govs. of women in profession 1999—), Akron Bar Assn. (trustee 2000—03). Avocations: photography, hiking, reading. Office: Univ Akron Sch Law Akron OH 44325-2901

REILLY, FRANK KELLY, business educator; b. Chgo., Dec. 30, 1935; s. Clarence Raymond and Mary Josephine (Ruckrigel) R.; m. Therese Adele Bourke, Aug. 2, 1958; children: Frank Kelly III, Clarence Raymond II, Therese B., Edgar B. BBA, U. Notre Dame, 1957; MBA, Northwestern U., 1961, U. Chgo., 1964, PhD, 1968; LLD (hon.), St. Michael's Coll., 1991. CFA. Trader Goldman Sachs & Co., Chgo., 1958-59; security analyst Tech. Fund, Chgo., 1959-62; asst. prof. U. Kans., Lawrence, 1965-68, assoc. prof., 1968-72; prof. bus., assoc. dir. divsn. bus. and econ. rsch. U. Wyo., Laramie, 1972-75; prof. fin. U. Ill., Champaign-Urbana, 1975-81; Bernard J. Hank prof. U. Notre Dame, Ind., 1981—, dean Mendoza Coll. Bus. Ind., 1981-87. Bd. dirs., chmn. UBS Funds, Assn. Investment Mgmt. and Rsch.; past chmn. Inst. Chartered Fin. Analysts; past chmn. bd. dirs. NIBCO Corp.; bd. dirs. Internat. Bd. CFPs, Discover Bank, chmn. Ft. Dearborn Income Securities, Battery Park High Yield Fund., Morgan Stanley Trust Fed. Savs. Bank (FSB). Author: Investment Analysis and Portfolio Management, 1979, 8th edit., 2006, Investments, 1982, 7th edit., 2006; co-editor: Ethics and the Investment Industry, 1989; editor: Readings and Issues in Investments, 1975, High Yield Bonds: Analysis and Risk Assessment, 1990; assoc. editor Fin. Mgmt., 1977-82, Quar. Rev. Econs. and Bus, 1979-87, Fin. Rev., 1979-87, 92—, Jour. Fin. Edn., 1981—, Jour. Applied Bus. Rsch., 1986—, Fin. Svcs. Rev., 1989-96, Internat. Rev. Econs. and Fin., 1992—, European Jour. Fin., 1994—. Arthur J. Schmidt Found. fellow, 1962-65; U. Chgo. fellow, 1963-65; recipient faculty award U. Notre Dame, 1999. Fellow Fin. Mgmt. Assn. (pres. 1983-84, chmn. 1985-91, bd. dirs.); mem. Midwest Bus. Adminstrn. Assn. (pres. 1974-75), Am. Fin. Assn., Western Fin. Assn. (exec. com. 1973-75), Ea. Fin. Assn. (exec. com. 1979-84, pres. 1982-83), Midwest Fin. Assn. (pres. 1993-94; Lifetime Achievement award 2007), Fin. Analysts Fedn., Acad. Fin. Svcs. (pres. 1990-91), Inst. Chartered Fin. Analysts (coun. of examiners, rsch. and edn. com., edn. steering com.), Internat. Assoc. Fin. Planners (ednl. resource com., bd. dirs.), Assn. of Investment Mgmt. and Rsch. (C. Stewart Sheppard award 1991, Daniel J. Forrestal III Leadership award for profl. ethics 2001), CFA Soc. Chgo. (bd. dirs. 1988-89), Beta Gamma Sigma. Roman Catholic. Office: U Notre Dame Mendoza Coll Bus Notre Dame IN 46556-5646 Business E-Mail: reilly.1@nd.edu. *Any success I have enjoyed is due to the talents God has given me and my belief that I have an obligation to maximize the output from those talents by hard work, while never forgetting that my family comes first because they have always provided me with the love and support necessary for success and happiness.*

REILLY, JILL MARLENE, school system administrator; b. Chgo., Jan. 27, 1951; d. Jack Louis and Leah M. Cappels; m. Patrick Duane Reilly, May 29, 1971; children: Elizabeth M. Brama, Joseph D., Heather von Mering. BA in English, U. Cin., 1974; MA in Curriculum, U. Minn., 1985; D in Edn. Leadership, U. St. Thomas, St. Paul, 1992. Co-ptnr. Featherstone-Reilly Ednl. Cons., Apple Valley, Minn., 1984-95; mentor program coord. Intermediate Sch. Dist. # 917, Apple Valley, 1985-93; sr. cons. Honeywell, Inc., Mpls., 1993-95; adj. asst. prof. St. Mary's U., Mpls., 1994—; pres. Acad. Holy Angels, Richfield, Minn., 1995—. Bd. govs. Sch. Engrng. U. St. Thomas, 2007—. Author: Mentorship: The Essential Guide for Schools and Business, 1992; co-author: College Comes Sooner Than You Think, 1987. Bd. dirs. guidance divsn. Nat. Assn. Gifted Children, Mpls., 1988-93, Min. Women's Econ. Roundtable, 2007-; bd. dirs., chair elect Minn. Coun. Gifted and Talented, Mpls., 1991-94. Office: Acad Holy Angels 6600 Nicollet Ave Richfield MN 55423-2498 Home Phone: 952-431-2530; Office Phone: 612-798-2611. Business E-Mail: jreilly@ahastars.org.

REILLY, JOHN B., lawyer; b. Bangor, Maine, Sept. 12, 1947; s. Louis J. and Evelyn I. (Lindsay) R.; children: Carolyn, Bridget. BA, U. R.I., 1970; JD cum laude, Suffolk U., 1976. Bar: R.I. 1976, Mass. 1985, U.S. Dist. Ct. R.I. 1976, U.S. Dist. Ct. Mass. 1985, U.S. Dist. Ct. Conn. 1995, U.S. Claims Ct. 1980, U.S. Ct. Appeals (1st and 2d cirs.) 1984, U.S. Ct. Appeals (3d cir.) 1985, U.S. Supreme Ct. 1983; cert. fraud examiner. Sole practice, Providence, 1976-81, Warwick, RI, 1981-83; sr. ptnr. John Reilly & Assocs. and predecessor firms, Warwick, RI, 1984—99, 2002—, Reilly & Nikolyszyn, LLP, Warwick, RI, 2000—01. Mem. Gov.'s Automobile Ins. Task Force, 1992-93. Mem. ABA, R.I. Bar Assn., Def. Rsch. Inst., R.I. Assn. Auth Theft and Arson Investigators (sec. 1995-96, pres. 1997—), Trucking Ind. Def. Assn., Pi Sigma Alpha, Phi Kappa Psi. Home: 80 Paterson Ave Warwick RI 02886-9110 Office: John Reilly & Assocs 300 Centerville Rd Warwick RI 02886-0200 Office Phone: 401-739-1800. E-mail: jreilly@lawyers-online.us.

REILLY, JOHN C., actor; b. Chgo., May 24, 1965; m. Alison Dickey, 1992; 2 children. BFA, DePaul U., 1987. Actor: (films) Casualties of War, 1989, We're No Angels, 1989, Days of Thunder, 1990, State of Grace, 1990, Shadows and Fog, 1992, Out on a Limb, 1992, Hoffa, 1992, What's Eating Gilbert Grape, 1993, The River Wild, 1994, Georgia, 1995, Dolores Claiborne, 1995, Hard Eight, 1996, Boys, 1996, Boogie Nights, 1997, The Thin Red Line, 1998, Never Been Kissed, 1999, For Love of the Game, 1999, Magnolia, 1999 (Nat. Bd. Rev. award for Best Ensemble, 1999), The Settlement, 1999, The Perfect Storm, 2000, The Anniversary Party, 2001, Frank's Book, 2001, The Good Girl, 2002, Gangs of New York, 2002 (Las Vegas Film Critics Award for Best Supporting Actor, 2003), Chicago, 2002 (Golden Globe for Best Supporting Actor, Acad. award nomination for Best Actor, Las Vegas Film Critics Award for Best Supporting Actor, 2003), The Hours, 2002 (Las Vegas Film Critics Award for Best Supporting Actor, 2003), Anger Management, 2003, Piggie, 2003, Criminal, 2004, The Aviator, 2004, Are You the Favorite Person of Anybody?, 2005, Dark Water, 2005, A Prairie Home Companion, 2006, Talladega Nights: The Ballad of Ricky Bobby, 2006; (plays) True West, 2000 (Spl. Outer Critics Cir. Award, 2000), Streetcar Named Desire, 2005. Roman Catholic.

REILLY, KATHLEEN C., director, retired secondary school educator; b. Bridgeport, Conn., Mar. 24, 1937; d. John J. and Lillian (Higgins) Collins; m. Donald Reilly, Aug. 21, 1988; children: Robert L., John, Maura Williams. BS, Boston U., 1958; MA in Teaching, Manhattanville Coll., Purchase, NY, 1973; postgrad., Teachers Coll. Columbia U., 1983; CAS, Wesleyan U., 1985. Cert. permanent-English tchr., grades 7-12, N.Y. English tchr. Sch. of Holy Child, Rye, NY, Edgemont High Sch., Scarsdale, NY; ret., 2000; dir. of tng. Tri-State Consortium. Adj. prof. Hofstra U., Hempstead, N.Y., 1991. Grantee Am. Studies Consortium, NEH, SUNY Tchr. Rsch., 1991, Nat. Coun. Tchrs. English, 1990.; recipient Scarsdale-Westchester Phi Beta Kappa award, N.Y. State Educator of Excellence award, 1996; named Edgemont High Sch. Tchr. Yr.; finalist N.Y. State Tchr. of Yr. Mem. Nat. Coun. Tchrs. of English (tchr. researcher grant). Home: 211 Newtown Tpke Wilton CT 06897-4713

REILLY, KENNETH JAMES, lawyer; b. Elizabeth, NJ, Jan. 19, 1949; s. James Arthur and Lucille (Vernon) R.; m. Mary Jane Stanley, Mar. 17, 1973; children: Lauren V., Kristopher L., Peter D. BA, Trinity U., 1970; JD, U. Tex., 1973. Bar: Colo. 1973, Kans. 1974, U.S. Dist. Ct. Kans. 1974, U.S. Supreme Ct. 1978, Mo. 1990, U.S. Dist. Ct. (we. dist.) Mo. 1990. Assoc. Boddington & Brown, Kansas City, Kans., 1974-90, McDowell, Rice & Smith, Overland Park, Kans., 1990-95, Shook, Hardy & Bacon, Kansas City, Mo., 1995—, assoc. to mng. ptnr. Miami, Fla., 1998—. Office: Shook Hardy & Bacon LLP 201 S Biscayne Blvd Ste 2400 Miami FL 33131-4313 Office Fax: 305-358-7470. E-mail: kreilly@shb.com.

REILLY, KEVIN, broadcast executive; Pres. Brad Grey TV; pres. entertainment FX, 2000—03; pres. NBC Entertainment, 2003—07; pres. entertainment Fox Broadcasting Co., 2007—. Office: Fox Broadcasting Co 10201 W Pico Blvd Los Angeles CA 90035 Office Phone: 310-369-3553. *

REILLY, KEVIN P., academic administrator; BA, U. Notre Dame, 1971; MA, U. Minn., 1974, PhD in English, 1979. Teaching asst. dept. English U. Minn., Mpls., 1974-79, asst. to dir. undergrad. study dept. English, 1976-77; coord. project on ednl. advisement in the work setting N.Y. State Bd. Regents, 1979-80, dir. Teaching and Beyond project, 1983-84, dir. nat. program non-coll. sponsored instrn., 1979-84, dir. div. coll. and univ. evaluation, 1984-92; assoc. provost for acad. programs, sec. of the univ. SUNY Sys., Albany, 1992—96; also sr. fellow in univ./sch. rels. SUNY Systems, Albany, 1992—96; provost, vice-chancellor U. Wis.-ext., 1996—2000, chancellor, 2000—04, U. Wis. System, Madison, 2004—. Mem. vis. del. Am. educators to rev. sch. system in No. Ireland, 1990; lectr. and presenter in field. Editor: (with Carol Wolfe) A Guide to Educational Programs in Noncollegiate Organizations, 1983, (with Sheila Murdick) Teaching and Beyond: Nonacademic Career Programs for Ph.D.'s, 1984; contbr. numerous articles to profl. jours. Tutor, Literacy Vols. of Am., Schenectady, 1988-90. Recipient Mgmt. Performance awards N.Y. State, 1989, 90; recipient fellowships at U. Minn. Mem. MLA, Am. Assn. for Higher Edn., Am. Conf. for Irish Studies, Am. Ednl. Rsch. Assn., Assn. for Continuing Higher Edn., Irish Am. Cultural Inst. Office: U Wis System 1720 Van Hise Hall 1220 Linden Dr Madison WI 53706-1557 E-mail: kreilly@uwsa.edu.

REILLY, MICHAEL ATLEE, finance company executive, venture capital investor; b. Ft. Worth, Dec. 10, 1948; s. Thomas William and Alma Margaret (Cox) R.; m. Beverly Ann Yates, Dec. 27, 1974; children: Atlee Michael, Asher Yates, Anson Marcus, Austin Thomas, Axton Carter. BA, U. Tex., 1971. Ptnr. Michael A. Reilly Co., Dallas, 1971—80; pres., CEO Ryan Cos., Arlington, Tex., 1980—90, Reilly Bros., Arlington, 1990—. Trustee Childrens Trust Fund State of Tex; vice chmn. Troy Aikman Found. Mem.: Urban Land Inst. Office: Reilly Bros Property Co 1017 So F M Rd 5 Aledo TX 76008-5169

REILLY, NANCY (ANNE CAULFIELD REILLY), painter; b. Bryn Mawr, Pa., Mar. 29, 1927; d. Ralph Caulfield and Claire Helena (Roesch) Goodman; m. Donald Elliott Reilly, May 14, 1949; children: Kevin Caulfield, William Stockbridge, Peter Elliott. Studies with Samuel E. Brown, Westport, Conn., 1955-63; studies with Mimi Jennewein, Larchmont, NY, 1964-65. Lectr., demonstrator portrait painting Bridgeport (Conn.) Art League, Milford (Conn.) Art League, Pen and Brush Club, New Haven, Conn. Classic Arts Assn., Allied Artists Am., Kent (Conn.) Art Assn., SCAN, Newtown, Conn. Exhibited in group shows at Nat. Acad. Design, N.Y.C., 1964, 1965, 1969, 1970, Stamford (Conn.) Mus., 1965, Wadsworth Antheum, Hartford, Conn., 1966, 1972, Nat. Acad. Arts and Letters, N.Y.C., 1971, Mus. Sci. and Industry, Bridgeport, 1972, Salmagundi Club, N.Y.C., Nat. Arts Club, Butler Inst. Am. Art, Youngstown, Ohio, 2001, New Britain (Conn.) Mus. Am. Art, 2001, exhibitions include invitational travelling exhbn. Allied Artists Am., 2003—05, exhibitions include Bennington Ctr. Arts, 2007; included in slide collection Smithsonian Instn., Washington, U. Conn. Health Ctr., Farmington. Vol. artist rehab. unit Norwalk Hosp., 1984—95. Recipient Gold medal for oil painting, Catherine Lorillard Wolfe Art Club, 1965, Silver medal for oil painting, Nat. Arts Club, 1969, George Height award for portrait, 1969, Blanche Farr award, 1991. Fellow: Am. Artists Profl. League (Claude Parsons Meml. award 2003, Leila Gardin Sawyer Meml. award 2005); mem.: Conn. Pastel Soc. (signature, Honors award 2003, 2004, J.D. Altobello Meml. award), Artists' Fellowship N.Y., Kent Art Assn. (Best in Show 1991, Gordon C. Aymar award for oil 1993, Mabel Rowe Aiken award for oil 1995, Frances B. Townley award for portrait 1998, 1999, James H. Aiken award Best Pastel 2006), Hudson Valley Art Assn. (Bronze medal for oil painting 1981, Thora M. Jensen Portrait award 1989, 2005), Pastel Soc. Am. (CPS award 2005), Nat. Arts Club (Silver medal for oil painting 1969, Bruce Stevenson award for portrait 1971, 1988, 1991, First prize 106th Annual Exhibiting Artist Mems. Exbhn. 2005), Allied Artists Am. (bd. dirs. 1991—99, participant in travelling exhbn. 2003—05), New Haven Paint and Clay Club (Merit award 1992, 1997). Home: 9 Marilane Westport CT 06880-1008 Office Phone: 203-227-6729.

REILLY, PAUL J., electronics executive; b. Jan. 13, 1957; BS, St. John's U., Queens, NY, 1979. CPA. Audit mgr. KPMG Peat Marwick, NYC, 1979-90; dir. reporting, asst. contr. Arrow Electronics, Inc., Melville, NY, 1991—96, corp. v.p., 1996—99, v.p. fin., 1999—2001, v.p., CFO, 2001—05, sr. v.p., CFO, 2005—. Lectr. St. John's U., Pace U. Office: Arrow Electronics Inc 50 Marcus Dr Melville NY 11747-4210 Office Phone: 631-847-2000. *

REILLY, RICHARD R., lawyer; b. Montclair, NJ, Dec. 22, 1951; BA, Rutgers U., 1973; JD, Fordham U., 1980; LLM, NYU, 1984. Bar: NJ 1980, NY 1981, US Dist. Ct. (NJ dist.) 1980. Ptnr., head Global Employment & Employee Benefits practice Coudert Bros. LLP, NYC. Mem.: ABA, NY State Bar Assn. Office: Coudert Bros LLP 1114 Ave of the Americas New York NY 10036 Office Fax: 212-626-4468, 212-626-4120. Business E-Mail: reillyr@coudert.com.

REILLY, ROBERT FREDERICK, investment banker; b. NYC, Oct. 3, 1953; s. James J. and Marie (Griebel) Reilly; m. Janet H. Steiner, Apr. 16, 1975; children: Ashley Lauren, Brandon Christopher, Cameron Courtney. BA in Econs., Columbia U., 1975, MBA in Fin., 1976. CPA Ohio, Ill., cert. mgmt. acct.; CFA, cert. real estate appraiser, rev. appraiser, gen. appraiser Ill., Va., Utah, Oreg., NY, bus. appraiser, accredited bus. valuator, valuation cons. Sr. cons. Booz, Allen & Hamilton, Cin., 1975-76; dir. corp. planning Huffy Corp., Dayton, Ohio, 1976-81; v.p. Arthur D. Little Valuation, Inc., Chgo., 1981-85; ptnr., nat. dir. valuation svcs. Deloitte & Touche, Chgo., 1985-91; mng. dir. Willamette Mgmt. Assocs., Chgo., 1991—. Adj. prof. acctg. U. Dayton Grad. Sch. Bus., 1977—81; adj. prof. econs. Elmhurst Coll., Ill., 1982—87; adj. prof. fin. Ill. Inst. Tech. Grad. Sch. Bus., Chgo., 1985—91; adj. prof. taxation U. Chgo. Grad. Sch. Bus., 1985—87. Co-author: (book) Valuing Small Businesses and Professional Practices, 1993, 4th edit., 2000, Business Valuation Video Course, 1993, Valuing a Business, 1995, Valuing Accounting Practices, 1997, Valuing Professional Practices--A Practitioner's Approach, 1997, Valuing Intangible Assets, 1998, Handbook of Advanced Business Valuation, 1999, Handbook of Business Valuation and Intellectual Property Analysis, 2004, Guide to ESOP Valuation, 2007; editor, columnist: Ohio CPA Jour., 1984—86, 1991—2001, Small Bus. Taxation, 1989—90, Bus. Valuation Rev., 1989—90, Jour. Real Estate Acctg. and Taxation, 1991—93, Jour. Property Taxation Mgmt., 1993—, Jour. Am. Bankruptcy Inst., 1993—, Valuation Strategies, 2003—; co-editor: (book) Financial Valuation-Valuation of Business and Business Interests, 1997; contbr. articles to profl. jours. Mem.: AICPA (mem. ABV exam. com. 2002—06, mem. bus. valuation com. 2006—), Appraisal Inst., Nat. Assn. Bus. Economists, Am. Econ. Assn., Am. Bankruptcy Inst., Inst. CFAs, Chgo. Soc. Investment Analysts, Bus. Valuation Assn., Accreditation Coun. Accountancy (accredited fed. income taxation), Ohio Soc. CPAs (chpt. dir. 1978—81), Ill. Soc. CPAs, Inst. Property Taxation, Inst. Cert. Mgmt. Accts. (chpt. dir. 1976—), Nat. Assn. Real Estate Appraisers, Am. Soc. Appraisers (mem. bd. examiners 1985—89), Inst. Bus. Appraisers (life). Home: 310 Algonquin Rd Barrington IL 60010-6109 Office: 8600 W Bryn Mawr Ave Chicago IL 60631-3579 Office Phone: 773-399-4300.

REILLY, ROBERT JOSEPH, counselor; b. Spokane, Wash., Mar. 7, 1936; s. John Francis and Vivian Helen (White) R.; m. Joan Steiner, June 20, 1960; children: Sean Michael, Patrick Joseph, Bridget Colleen. BA in Psychology, Seattle U., 1985; postgrad., Infantry Officer Candidate Sch., Ft. Benning, 1960, EOAC, Ft. Belvoir, 1968, Leadership Inst. Seattle/City U., 1991—92. Ordained Congl. Ch. Practical Theology, 1992. Enlisted U.S. Army, 1953, advanced through grades to maj., 1981, served in Republic of Korea, 1961-62, Vietnam, 1966-67, 69-70, ret., 1981; counseling supr. Schick Shadel Hosp., Seattle, 1984-89; dir. Canyon Counseling, Puyallup, Wash., 1987-92, 95—; social worker Wash. State Employee Adv. Svc., Olympia, 1992-99. Exec. v.p. Coll. Therapeutic Hypnosis, Puyallup, 1989-94; mem. adj. faculty Pierce Coll., Tacoma, 1991-92; mem. Wash. State Chem. Dependency Counselor Cert. Bd., sec., 1995—. Editor: The Update, 2003—05. Ombudsman Office of Asst. Sec. of Def. Res. Affairs; mem. vestry St. Luke's Episcopal Ch., Wenatchee, 2003—06; pres. Irish Cultural Club, Tacoma, 1983—85, 1993—94; sec. Tacoma chpt. Ret. Officers Assn., 1983—87, pres., 1993—96, bd. dirs., 1982—97, Tacoma Mus. Playhouse Theater Co., 1997—2000, adv. bd., 2000—06, Friends of the Ctrl. Highlands, Vietnam, 1999—2005. Decorated Vietnamese Cross of Gallantry with silver star, Bronze Star with oak leaf cluster, Meritorious Svc. medal, Army Commendation medal with 2 oak leaf clusters; recipient Nobel Fredspris, United Peacekeeping Forces, 1988; named Profl. of Yr. Chem. Dependency Profls. Wash., 1994. Mem.: Assn. Addiction Profls., The Ret. Enlisted Assn. (pres. Wehatchee chpt. 2001—02, chaplain 2002—, editor Appleland 86er), Mil. Officers Assn. Am., Nat. 4th Inf. Divsn. Assn. (sec.-treas. NW chpt. 1993—2003, chpt. pres. 2002—03, nat. svc. officer 2004—), Army Engrs. Assn., Nat. Assn. Tobacco Addiction Counselors, Am. Congress Hypnotist Examiners, Nat. Assn. Alcohol and Drug Abuse Counselors (del. Russia and Czech Republic 1996), Nat. Guild Hypnotists, Nat. Bd. Hypnotherapy and Hypnotic Anesthesiology (pres. Wash. chpt. 1991—94, v.p. 1991—97, Mem. of Yr. 1994), Internat. Conf. War Vet. Mins., La Soc. des Quarante Hommes et Huit Chevaux (Aumonier 2001—04, chef de gare 2004—05), Wash. West Home Owners Assn. (pres. 2001—02). Avocations: symphony music, theater. Personal E-mail: joans.bob@charter.net.

REILLY, THOMAS F., former state attorney general; b. Springfield, Mass. m. Ruth Reilly; 3 children. BA, Am. Internat. Coll., 1964; JD, Boston Coll., 1970. Atty. Civil Rights divsn. Atty. Gen.'s Office; dist. atty. Middlesex County Dist. Atty. Office, 1991—99; atty. gen. State of Mass., Springfield, 1999—2006. Founder The Cmty. Based Justice Program. Democrat. Mailing: 60 Palfrey St Watertown MA 02472 *

REILLY, WILLIAM FRANCIS, media company executive; b. NYC, June 8, 1938; s. William F. and Genevieve Reilly; m. Ellen Chapman, Nov. 19, 1966; children: Anthony Chapman and Jane Wasey (twins). AB cum laude, U. Notre Dame, 1959; MBA, Harvard U., 1964. Mgr. fin. analysis W.R. Grace & Co., NYC, 1964-67, asst. to Chmn., 1969-71, CEO Bekaert Textile Divsn., 1971-74, v.p., pres., 1978; pres., CEO Herman's World of Sporting Goods, Carteret, NJ, 1974-77, Home Ctr. Div., 1979-80; pres., COO Macmillan, Inc., NYC, 1980-90; founder, chmn., CEO Primedia Inc., NYC, 1989—2001, Aurelian Comm., LLC, NYC, 2001—06; chmn. F&W Publications, Inc., Cin., 2002—05; chmn., CEO Summit Business Media, LLC, Seven Hills, Ohio, 2006—. Dir. FMC Corp., Chgo., 1992-, Barnes & Noble.com, F&W Publishing Co., LLC, Harvard Bus. Sch. Publications; trustee WNET, Channel 13, NYC. Trustee U. Notre Dame, South Bend, Ind.; dir., Citymeals-on-Wheels; co-chmn., Cardinal Hayes HS Endowment Fund. 1st lt. US Army, 1959—61. Named to Sales Exec. Hall of Fame, min's b2b mag., 2007. Mailing: 7 Sutton Sq New York NY 10022-2407 Office: Summit Business Media LLC 375 Park Ave Ste 1909 New York NY 10152 Office Phone: 212-752-2415, 216-328-8926, 212-752-2495. Office Fax: 212-752-2749. *

REILLY, WILLIAM KANE, former government official, educator, lawyer, conservationist; b. Decatur, Ill., Jan. 26, 1940; s. George P. and Margaret (Kane) M.; m. Elizabeth Buxton; children: Katherine, Megan. BA in History, Yale U., 1962; JD, Harvard U., 1965; MS in Urban Planning, Columbia U., 1971. Bar: Ill., Mass. 1965. Atty. firm Ross & Hardies, Chgo., 1965; assoc. dir. Urban Policy Center, Urban Am., Inc., also Nat. Urban Coalition, Washington, 1969-70; sr. staff mem. Pres.'s Council Environ. Quality, 1970-72; exec. dir. Task Force Land Use and Urban Growth, 1972-73; pres. Conservation Found., Washington, 1973-89, World Wildlife Fund, Washington, 1985-89; adminstr. U.S. EPA, Washington, 1989-93; Payne vis. prof. Stanford U., 1993-94, vis. prof., 1994-97; CEO

Aqua Internat. Ptnrs., Tex. Pacific Group, San Francisco, 1997—. Chmn. Natural Resources Coun. Am., 1982-83; head U.S. del. Earth Summit, 1992; head U.S. del. to negotiate Amendments to Montreal Protocol on the Ozone Layer, 1990, 92; bd. dirs. E.I. DuPont de Nemours and Co., Am. Acad. in Rome, Evergreen Holdings, Inc., Ionics Inc., Nat. Geog. Soc., World Wildlife Fund, Presidio Trust; mem. internat. adv. bd., Lafarge; chair adv. bd. Goldman Sch. Pub. Policy U. Calif. at Berkeley. Editor: The Use of Land, 1973, Environment Strategy America, 1994-96; author articles in field, chpts. in books. Served to capt., CIC U.S. Army, 1966-67; bd. dirs. David and Lucile Packard Found. Fellow: Am. Acad. Arts & Scis.; mem.: University (Washington), Univ. (N.Y.C.). Office: Aqua Internat Ptnrs 345 California St Ste 1770 San Francisco CA 94104-2606 *

REILLY, WILLIAM THOMAS, lawyer; b. Passaic, NJ, Feb. 25, 1949; s. Thomas Edwin and Edna May (Dorritie) R.; m. Sheila Mary Brogan, Aug. 1, 1981; children: Kathleen Anne, Brendan Thomas, Timothy John. BS, Boston Coll., 1971; JD, Harvard U., 1974. Bar: N.J. 1974, U.S. Dist. Ct. N.J. 1974, U.S. Supreme Ct. 1979, U.S. Ct. Appeals (3rd cir.) 1984, U.S. Ct. Claims, 1996, U.S. Ct. Appeals (fed. cir.) 1997. Assoc. McCarter & English LLP, Newark, 1974-81, ptnr., 1982—. Trustee United Hosps. Med. Ctr., Newark, 1983-89, One-to-One/N.J., Inc., 1990-97, chmn., 1993-97. Mem. ABA, N.J. State Bar Assn., Harvard Law Sch. Assn., Eastward Ho Country Club. Avocation: golf. Home: 302 Kensington Dr Ridgewood NJ 07450-1822 Office: McCarter & English LLP Four Gateway Ctr 100 Mulberry St Newark NJ 07102-4004 Office Phone: 973-622-4444. Business E-Mail: wreilly@mccarter.com.

REIMAN, DONALD HENRY, language educator; b. Erie, Pa., May 17, 1934; s. Henry Ward and Mildred Abbie (Pearce) R.; m. Mary, 1958 (div. 1974); one child, Laurel Elizabeth Reiman Henneman; m. Hélène (Liberman) Dworzan, Oct. 3, 1975. BA, Coll. of Wooster, 1956; MA, U. Ill., 1957, PhD, 1960; LittD., Coll. of Wooster, 1981. Instr. English, Duke U., Durham, NC, 1960—62, asst. prof., 1962—64; assoc. prof. U. Wis., Milw., 1964—65; adj. assoc. prof. grad. program in English City Univ. of N.Y., 1967—68; adj. prof. Columbia U., NYC, 1969—70, sr. rsch. assoc. in English, 1970—73; vis. prof. St. John's U., Jamaica, NY, 1974—75; editor Shelley and His Cir., Carl H. Pforzheimer Libr., NYC, 1965—86, N.Y. Pub. Libr., 1986—92; with Carl and Lily Pforzheimer Found., 1992—. Vis. lectr. U. Ill., 1963; vis. prof. U. Wash., Seattle, 1981, N.Y. U., 1992; Lyell reader in bibliography Oxford U., 1988-89; adj. prof. English, U. Del., 1992-; cons. Harvard U. Press, Yale U. Press, Princeton U. Press, Johns Hopkins U. Press, Garland Pub., Inc., W.W. Norton, Oxford U. Press, others. Author: Shelley's The Triumph of Life, A Critical Study, 1965, 2d edit., 1979, Percy Bysshe Shelley, 1969, 2d edit., 1990, (with D.D. Fischer) Byron on the Continent, 1974, English Romantic Poetry, 1800-1835, 1979, Romantic Texts and Contexts, 1987, Intervals of Inspiration: The Skeptical Tradition and the Psychology of Romanticism, 1988, The Study of Modern Manuscripts, 1993; editor: Shelley and His Circle, Vols. V-VI, 1973, Vols. VII-VIII, 1986, (with D.D. Fischer) IX-X, 2002, The Romantics Reviewed: Contemporary Reviews of English Romantic Writers, 9 vols., 1972, (with S.B. Powers) Shelley's Poetry and Prose: A Norton Critical Edit., 1977, (with Neil Fraistat) 2nd rev. edit., 2002, The Romantic Context: Poetry, 128 vols., 1976-79, (with M.C. Jaye and B.T. Bennett) The Evidence of the Imagination, 1978; gen. editor: Manuscripts of the Younger Romantics, 1985-98; I The Esdaile Notebook: A Facsimile, 1985, II The Mask of Anarchy: Facsimiles, 1985, III Hellas, 1985, V The Harvard Shelley Poetic Manuscripts, 1991; (with M. O'Neill) VIII Fair-Copy Manuscripts of Shelley's Poems, 1997; editor-in-chief: The Bodleian Shelley Manuscripts, 1986-99, I Peter Bell The Third and the Triumph of Life, 1986, VII Shelley's Last Notebook and Other MSS, 1990, (with M.J. Neth) XVI The Hellas Notebook, 1994, (with N. Fraistat) The Complete Poetry of Percy Bysshe Shelley Vol. I, 2000, Vol. II, 2004; mem. editl. com. adv. bd. Keats Shelley Jour., 1968-73, Milton and the Romantics, 1975-80, Studies in Romanticism, 1977—, Romanticism Past and Present, 1980-86, Text, 1981—, Nineteenth Century Literature, 1986—, Nineteenth Century Contexts, 1987-90; co-founder, editor (with others) Romantic Circles. Website; contbr. articles to encyclopedias, books, and profl. journals. Active in Common Cause. Am. Coun. Learned Soc. Fellow, 1963-64, Wesleyan Ctr. Advanced Studies Fellow, 1963-64, NEH Fellow, 1978; grantee Am. Coun. Learned Soc., 1961, NEH, 1983-2003, 07—. Mem. AAUP, MLA (life), Modern Humanities Rsch. Assn. (life), Wordsworth Coleridge Assn. Am. (founder), Byron Soc. (Am. com. 1973—, treas. 1999-2002, pres. 2003-05), Keats Shelley Assn. Am. (bd. dir., treas. 1973-91, v.p. 1991-2005, Disting. Scholar Award 1987), Soc. Textual Scholarship (exec. com. 1981-93, pres. 2005-06), Charles Lamb Soc., Assn. Documentary Editing, N.Am. Soc. Study of Romanticism. Democrat. Presbyterian. Business E-Mail: dhreiman@udel.edu.

REIMANN, ARLINE LYNN, artist; b. St. Louis, Nov. 25, 1937; d. Albert Robbins and Bess (Kagan) Miller; m. Hans Reimann, Feb. 24, 1957; 1 child, Robert. BA, Rutgers U., NJ, 1974; MA, Montclair State U., NJ, 1980. Exhibited in group shows at Hunterdon Art Ctr., Clinton, NJ, 1982, 96, Galeria San Jeronimo, San Juan, P.R., 1987, Nat. Arts Club, NYC, 1988, 90—, Interch. Ctr., NYC, Butler Inst. Am. Art, Youngstown, Ohio, 1989, 395 West Broadway Gallery, NYC, 1994, 420 West Broadway Gallery, Soho, NY, 1995, Lever House Gallery, NYC, 1995, Art Ctr. Municipality of Athens, Greece, 1996, West Beth Gallery, Montclair in Manhattan, NYC, 1996, ISE Art Found. NYC, 1996, Soc. Am. Graphic Artists, New Rochelle, NY, 1997, Gallery Art 54, NYC, 1997, Jane Voorhees Zimmerli Art Mus., New Brunswick, NJ, 1998-99, Old Print Shop, NYC, 2004, 07, Art Students League of NY, NYC, 2005, Worldwide Feminist Expo, Balt., 2000, Nat. Assn. Women Artists, UN, 2002, Salmagundi Club, NYC, 2005, 06, 07, Ringling Mus. Sch. Art, Sarasota, Fla., 2006, Goggleworks Ctr. Arts, Reading, Pa., 2006, Venezuelan Consulate, NYC, 2006, Longview Mus. Fine Arts, Tex., 2007, Monroe Ctr. for Arts, Hoboken, NJ, 2007; represented in permanent collections at Jane Voorhees Zimmerli Art Mus., New Brunswick, NJ, Newark Pub. Libr. Fine Print Collection, Newark, Montclair (NJ) State U., Bailey Matthews Mus., Sanibel, Fla., Black Hills Inst., Hill City, SD. Recipient Best in Show award Salute to Women in Arts, Lincoln Ctr., N.Y.C., 1981, Hon. mention award Nat. Juried Exhbn. Small Works Montclair State U., N.J., 1995. Aida Whedon Meml. award Nat. Assn. Women Artists, 1996. Mem. Nat. Assn. Women Artists (bd. dirs., chair traveling print exhbn. 1984-89, printmaking jury 1987-89, 95-97), Audubon Artists (bd. dirs., rec. sec. 1991-97), Soc. Am. Graphic Artists, Phi Beta Kappa. Home: 546 Hillrise Pl Walnut Creek CA 94598-4064

REIMER, CHARLES WILSON, curator, consultant; b. Indpls., May 14, 1923; s. Charles Louis Reimer and Cora Morton-May Wilson; m. Reba Marjorie Fines, Jan. 2, 1944 (div. June 1976); children: Bruce W., Kurt L.; m. Jacquelyn Gayle White, Nov. 13, 1976; children: Laura E., Emilie G. BA, Butler U., 1946, MA, 1948; PhD, Mich. State U., 1952. Instr. Butler U., Indpls., 1946-48, DePauw U., Greencastle, Ind., 1950-51, Mich. State U., East Lansing, 1951-52; from asst. curator to curator Acad. Nat. Scis., Phila., 1952-91, curator proprius, 1991—. Adj. prof. Drexel U., Phila., 1965-72; vis. prof. Iowa Lakeside Lab., Milford, Iowa, 1966-90, Jinan U., Guangzhow, China, 1983, U. Concepcion, Chile, 1984. Co-author: Diatoms of the U.S. vol. I, 1966, vol. II, 1975. With U.S. Army, 1942-45, ETO. Decorated Purple Heart, Combat Infantryman's badge; recipient Spl. Recognition award Biennial N.Am. Diatom Symposium, 1993. Mem. Phycol. Soc. Am., Ind. Acad. Sci., Sigma Xi. Avocations: fishing, chess. Home: 458 Woodcrest Ln Media PA 19063-4835 Office: Acad Natural Scis 19th & The Parkway Philadelphia PA 19103

REIMER, DENNIS J., retired career military officer; b. Medford, Okla., July 12, 1939; m. Mary Jo Powers; 2 children. BS, U.S. Mil. Acad., 1962; MS, Shippensburg State Coll. Gen. U.S. Army, Ft. McPherson, Ga., chief of staff Washington, 1995—99; ret., 1999; dir. Nat. Meml. Inst. for Prevention of Terrorism, Oklahoma City, 2000—. Bd. mem. Plato Learning Inc., Minn. Decorated Def. Disting. Svc. medal, DSM, two Legions of Merit, DFC, six Bronze Star medals, Purple Heart, Combat Infantryman badge, Parachutist badge, Aircraft Crewman badge, Ranger Tab; recipient Nat. Vets. award, 1999. Office: Nat Meml Inst for Prevention of Terrorism Chief of Staff PO Box 889 Oklahoma City OK 73101-0889

REIMER, JUDY MILLS, pastor, religious executive; m. George G. Reimer, 1964; children: Todd, Troy. BA, Emory and Henry Coll., 1962; MDiv, Bethany Theol. Sem., 1994. Ordained into Set Apart Ministry, Ch. of the Brethren, 1994. Vol. Brethren Vol. Svc. NIH, Bethesda, Md., 1962-64, Hessish Lichtenau, Germany, 1964-65; elem. sch. tchr. Pub. and Private Schs., various cities, 1965-76; deacon Ch. of the Brethren, 1966—; mem Virlina Dist. Bd., 1978-90; chair of nurture com. Ch. of the Brethren Virlina Dist., 1979-82, chair of outdoor ministry, 1983-84, conf. speaker, 1992; founding pastor Ch. of the Brethren, Smith Mountain Lake, Va., 1996-98, gen. bd. exec. dir., 1998—2003; owner, sr. v.p. Harris Office Furniture Co., Roanoke, Va., 1976—. Co-chair and vice-chair of two Virlina Fin. Campaigns, Ch. of the Brethren, 1980s, mem. Gen. Bd., Ch. of Brethren, 1977-90; mem. PTA, United Way Allocation Com., Roanoke Valley Women Owners Assn. (charter mem.); adult advisor Nat. Youth Cabinet. 1991, 92; worship coord. Nat. Youth Conf. 1994 numerous other coms. for Ch. of Brethren; official observer for Nat. Coun. of Chs. at Nicaraguan Election, Feb., 1990; rep. of Ch. of the Brethren, 1989. Atlanta, The Torch of Conscience Campaign to sensitize congregation to the campaign to abolish death penalty; workshop leader across the denomination on leadership devel., pastor/spouse retreats, women's rallies, etc.; ann. conf. moderator elect, 1993-94. Mem. Inst. Indsl. Comml. Chaplains (chmn. bd. dirs. local unit, asst. treas. nat. bd.). Office: Church of the Brethren General Offices 1451 Dundee Ave Elgin IL 60120-1694

REIMS, CLIFFORD WALDEMAR, music educator; b. Bklyn., May 1, 1924; s. Sven Waldemar and Jenny Helen (Nelson) R.; m. Georgette Louise Howell, May 30, 1952; children— Kathryn Louise, Karen Helen, Eric Howell. AB in Music, Bucknell U., 1949; M.Mus. in Voice, Ind. U., 1951; D.MA in Opera, U. So. Calif., 1971. Asst. prof. Auburn U., 1952-57; asst. prof., dir. opera Ohio U., 1957-60, U. So. Miss., 1961-63, Ohio State U., 1963-66; asso. prof., dir. opera theater Calif. State U. at Fullerton, 1966-71; prof., chmn. voice dept., dir. opera theatre Roosevelt U., Chgo., 1972-86, prof. emeritus, 1986—. Lang. coach Mobile (Ala.) Opera, 1986—; opera cons. U. South Ala., 1986—. Gen. dir., Hattiesburg (Miss.) Civic Opera, 1961-62, artistic adviser, Springfield (Ohio) Civic Opera, 1963-66, opera, recital and oratorio singer, 1947—; dir., condr. various opera and little theater groups, 1953—; bd. dirs., artistic adv., resident designer, Hinsdale Opera Theater, 1977—; Contbr. articles to profl. jours.; translator operas. Served with AUS, 1943-46. Decorated Purple Heart; named Outstanding Grad. in Opera U. So. Calif., 1971; scholar Opera Leadership Sch., Tanglewood, Mass., 1958 Mem. Nat. Opera Assn. (dir. 1965—, pres. 1970-72), Nat. Assn. Tchrs. Singing, Oprill (charter, pres. 1980), Phi Eta Sigma, Omicron Delta Kappa, Phi Mu Alpha, Sigma Alpha Epsilon. *It has always been my intent to develop not only those students who will become performers in the musical arts, but to promote an enthusiastic understanding among those who will become the audiences of our artistic future. With the gradual shortening of our work week, the necessity of a strongly developed artistic life becomes more and more visible. If I have been able to develop both professional and competent amateur talent for operatic performances and the audiences necessary to maintain them, I will consider my job well done.*

REIN, BERT WALTER, lawyer; b. Bklyn., Feb. 7, 1941; s. Moe and Florence (Fishman) Rein; m. Jennifer Christine Bulson, July 11, 1966 (dec. Mar. 1989); children: Joanna, Benjamin, Samantha; m. Barbara Jean Kahn, Oct. 18, 1992. BA, Amherst Coll., 1961; LLB, Harvard U., 1964. Bar: DC 1965, U.S. Dist. Ct. DC 1965, U.S. Ct. Appeals (DC cir.) 1968, U.S. Ct. Appeals (2d cir.) 1973, U.S. Ct. Appeals (8th cir.) 1974, U.S. Ct. Appeals (4th cir.) 1976, U.S. Ct. Appeals (11th cir.) 1982, U.S. Supreme Ct. 1982. Law ck. to Justice John M. Harlan U.S. Supreme Ct., Washington, 1966-67; assoc. Kirkland & Ellis, Washington, 1967-69, ptnr., 1973-83; spl. asst. U.S. Dept. State, Washington, 1969-70, dep. asst. sec., 1970-73; ptnr. Wiley, Rein & Fielding, Washington, 1983—2006, Wiley Rein, Washington, 2007—. Bd. dirs., chmn. govt. and regulatory affairs com. U.S. C. of C., 1986—90; bd. dirs. Nat. Chamber Litig. Ctr.; advisor Reagan Dept. Justice Transition, Washington, 1980; mem. adv. com. U.S. Sentencing Commn., 1988—89; edn. gen. counsel Cmty. Learning and Info. Network, 1992—. Contbr. articles to profl. jours. Mem. capitol area adv. bd. Salvation Army. Capt. USAR, 1964—68. Mem.: ABA, Internat. Trade Commn. Trial Lawyers Assn. (pres. 1990—91), Am. Law Inst., Aviation Club. Republican. Jewish. Home: 6423 Shadow Rd Chevy Chase MD 20815-6613 Office: Wiley Rein 1776 K St NW Washington DC 20006-2304 Office Phone: 202-719-7080. Business E-Mail: brein@wileyrein.com.

REIN, CATHERINE AMELIA, insurance company executive, lawyer; b. Lebanon, Pa., Feb. 7, 1943; d. John and Esther (Scott) Shultz. BA summa cum laude, Pa. State U., 1965; JD magna cum laude, NYU, 1968. Bar: NY 1968, US Supreme Ct. 1971. Assoc. Dewey, Ballantine, Bushby, Palmer & Wood, NYC, 1968-74; with Continental Grp., Stamford, Conn., 1974-85, sec., sr. atty., 1976-77, v.p., gen. counsel, 1980-85; sec., asst. gen. counsel Continental Diversified Ops., 1978-80; v.p. human resources Met. Life Ins. Co., NYC, 1985-88, sr. v.p. human resources, 1988-89, exec. v.p. corp. and profl. svcs. dept., 1989—98, sr. exec., v.p. bus. svcs. grp. and corp. svcs., 1998-99; pres., CEO Met. Life Auto and Home, Warwick, RI, 1999—2004; sr. exec. v.p., chief adminstrv. officer Met. Life Inc., 2004—. Bd. dirs. Bank of NY, First Energy Corpn. Trustee NYU Sch. Law Found. Mem.: ABA, Assn. Bar City of NY. Episcopalian. Avocations: decorating, restoration, cooking. Office: Met Life Inc One Metlife Plz 27 01 Queens Plz North Long Island City NY 11101 Office Phone: 212-578-2115. Business E-Mail: crein@metlife.com.

REIN, JEFFREY A., retail executive; b. Feb. 28, 1952; BS in Acctg., U. Ariz., 1974, BS in Pharmacy, 1980. Asst. mgr. Walgreen Co., Deerfield, Ill., 1982—84, store mgr., 1984—90, dist. mgr., 1990—96, divisional v.p., treas., 1996—2000, v.p. mktg. systems svcs., 2000—01, exec. v.p. mktg., 2001—03, COO, 2003—06, pres., 2003—07, CEO, 2006—, chmn., 2007—. Office: Walgreen Co 200 Wilmot Rd Deerfield IL 60015 *

REIN, STANLEY MICHAEL, lawyer; b. St. Paul, Apr. 15, 1946; s. Clayton George Rein and Rose Gertrude (Mintz) Brown; m. Linda. R. Arnold; children: Gabriel Todd, Leah Suzanne. BA, U. Minn., 1968; JD cum laude, Harvard U., 1973. Bar: Minn. 1973, U.S. Tax Ct. 1973. Assoc. Dorsey & Whitney, LLP, Mpls., 1973-78; ptnr. Dorsey & Whitney LLP, Mpls., 1979—. Mem. planned giving adv. coun. ARC Mpls. chpt., 1986, 88, planned giving adv. com. Minn. Pub. Radio, 1988-89; bd. dirs. South Metro Airport Action Council, Mpls., 1986, 87. With U.S. Army, 1968-70, Vietnam. Named Best Lawyers in Am., 1995-2007, Who's Who in Am. Law, 1995-2006, Minn. Law & Politics Super Lawyers, 2000-2006. Fellow Am. Coll. of Trust and Estate Counsel; mem. Minn. Bar Assn. & Hennepin County Bar Assn. (probate and trust law sect.), Phi Beta Kappa, Wax & Seal Com. Jewish. Avocations: reading, travel. Office: Dorsey & Whitney LLP 50 S 6th St Ste 1500 Minneapolis MN 55402-1498 Office Phone: 612-340-2912. Office Fax: 612-340-8827. Business E-Mail: rein.stan@dorsey.com. E-mail: rein.stan@dorseylaw.com.

REINA, CARRILLO JOSÉ GABRIEL, physician, surgery educator; b. Caqueza, Cundinamarca, Colombia, May 15, 1937; s. Hernández Santos Reina and Reina Evidalia Carrillo; m. Uriz María Encarnación Rivas, Dec. 12, 1958; 1 child, Rivas María Teresa. MD, Universidad Javeriana, 1965. Attending vascular surgeon Caprecom, Bogotá, 1970—75; instr. gen. surgery Universidad del Rosario, Bogotá, Colombia, 1973—76, prof. gen. surgery, 1977—78; chief gen. surgery Hosp. Ctrl. de la Policia Nacional, Bogotá, 1975—77; chief dept. surgery Clínica Hosp. Juan N. Corpas, Bogotá, 1977—2005. Author: (book) Nociones de Cirugía General, Nutrición Parenteral. Recipient Medalla al Mérito, Policía Nacional, 1996. Fellow: ACS, Sociedad Colombiana de Cirugía Vascular, Sociedad Colombiana de Gastroenterología, Colegio Colombiano de Cirujanos, Real Colegio Español de Médicos, Internat. Soc. Surgeons. Católica. Avocation: magic. Home: Calle 61 No 9 - 38 Apt 902 Cundinamarca Bogotá Colombia Office: Fundación Universitaria Juan N Corpas Cra 111 No 157 - 45 Cundinamarca Bogotá Colombia Home Phone: 57-1-2482037; Office Phone: 57-1-6845063. Business E-Mail: gabriel.reina@juanncorpas.edu.co.

REINARDY, SCOTT ROBERT, science educator; s. Marlin and Marlene Reinardy; m. Cindy Reinardy; 1 child, Trent Robert. BSc, SD State U., Brookings, 1987; MA, U. Mo., Columbia, 2003, PhD, 2005. News editor Columbia Missourian, 2000—05; asst. prof. Ball State U., Muncie, Ind., 2005—.

REINECKE, MANFRED G., chemistry professor; b. Milw., May 19, 1935; s. Fritz Wilhelm and Erna (Rittmeyer) R.; m. Marlene Zwisler, June 15, 1957; children: Kurt, Kryn, Claire. BS in Chemistry, U. Wis., 1956; PhD in Organic Chemistry, U. Calif., 1960. Asst. prof. U. Calif., Riverside, 1959-64, Tex. Christian U., Ft. Worth, 1964-68, assoc. prof., 1968-73, prof., 1973—2006, Cecil and Ida Green disting. emeritus tutor, 2006—. Chmn. health professions adv. com. Tex. Christian U., 1974-91; mem. sci. adv. bd. Univera Pharm., Inc., 1996-2002; vis. prof. U. Tubingen, Germany, 1971-72, U. B.C., Vancouver, Can., 1987; cons. in field. Contbr. more than 85 articles on natural product, organic chemistry and chem. edn. to profl. jours. Recipient W.T. Doherty award Ft. Worth, Dallas sect. Am. Chem. Soc., 1984; NSF Tchg.fellow, 1971-72, NAS fellow, 1979, 90. Mem. Am. Chem. Soc. (chmn. Ft. Worth, Dallas sect. 1976), So. Assn. Advisors Health Professions (bd. dirs. 1986-89), Alpha Epsilon Delta (dir. SW region 1985-2002). Office: Tex Christian Univ Dept of Chemistry PO Box 298860 Fort Worth TX 76129-0001 Business E-Mail: m.reinecke@tcu.edu.

REINEMUND, STEVEN S., retired food products executive; b. Queens, NY, Apr. 6, 1948; s. Ott and Dora (Kramer) R.; m. Gail Timbers, Dec. 14, 1974; children: Steven S. Jr., Jonathan Craig. BS in Naval Sci., U.S. Naval Acad., 1970; MBA, U. Va., 1978. Commd. 2d lt. USMC, 1970, advanced through grades to capt., 1974, resigned, 1975; mktg. rep. IBM Corp., 1975-76; v.p., gen. mgr. Marriott-Roy Rogers, 1978-84; sr. v.p., field operator Pizza Hut, Inc., Wichita, Kans., 1984-86, exec. v.p., 1986, pres., CEO, 1986—92, Frito-Lay N.Am., 1992—96; chmn., CEO Frito-Lay, 1996—99; pres., COO PepsiCo, 1999—2001, chmn., CEO, 2001—07. Bd. dir. Johnson & Johnson, Marriott Internat., Am. Express, ExxonMobil, 2007—. Chmn. Nat. Minority Supplier Develop. Council; trustee U.S. Naval Acad. Found.; bd. dir. U. Va., Darden Sch. Alumni Assn. Named one of Outstanding Young Men Am. Republican Presbyterian. Avocations: tennis, running. Office: PepsiCo 700 Anderson Hill Rd Purchase NY 10577 *

REINER, CARL, director, actor, writer; b. Bronx, NY, Mar. 20, 1922; s. Irving and Bessie (Mathias) R.; m. Estelle Lebost, Dec. 24, 1943; children: Robert, Sylvia A., Lucas. Student, Sch. Fgn. Service, Georgetown U., 1943. Appeared on Broadway and with road co.: Call Me Mister, 1947-48; on Broadway in:Inside U.S.A, 1948-49, Alive and Kicking, 1950; TV actor, 1950—; appeared: Your Show of Shows, 1950-54, Caesar's Hour, 1954-58 (Emmy award 1956, 57); master ceremonies: Keep Talking, 1958-59; writer-actor: Dinah Shore Show, 1960; producer, writer: The Dick Van Dyke Show (Emmy awards as writer 1962, 63, 64, as producer 1965, 66), The New Dick Van Dyke Show, Enter Laughing, written 1958, directed 1967, The Comics, 1968; dir.: (films) Enter Laughing, The Comic, 1967, The Comic, 1969, Where's Poppa, 1970, Oh, God!, 1977, The One and Only, 1978, The Jerk, 1979, Dead Men Don't Wear Plaid, 1982, The Man With Two Brains, 1983, All of Me, 1984, Summer Rental, 1985, Summer School, 1987, Bert Rigby, You're a Fool, 1989, Sibling Rivalry, 1990, Fatal Instinct, 1993, Ocean's Eleven, 2001, The Majestic, 2001, Ocean's Twelve, 2004, Ocean's Thirteen, 2007; appeared in: movie Happy Anniversary, 1959, The Gazebo, 1960, Gidget Goes Hawaiian, 1961, It's a Mad, Mad, Mad, Mad World, 1963, The Russians Are Coming, 1966, The End, 1978, Dead Men Don't Wear Plaid, 1982, (TV movies) Danny Kaye: A Legacy of Laughter, 1996, The Right to Remain Silent, 1996, The Slums of Beverly Hills, 1998, The Adventures of Rocky and Bullwinkle, 2000, Good Boy!, 2003; writer, dir.: Something Different, 1967; writer: Sid Caesar, Imogene Coca, Carl Reiner, Howard Morris Special (Emmy award, 1967); producer: TV series Good Heavens, 1976 (recipient Emmy award 1957, 58, 62, 63); Author: (novels) Enter Laughing, 1958, All Kinds of Love, 1993, Continue Laughing, 1995, NNNNN, 2005; (memoir) My Anecdotal Life, 2003; short stories; (screenplay) The Thrill of It All; (with Mel Brooks) albums The 2000 Year Old Man, The 2001 Year Old Man, The 2013 Year Old Man; exec. producer: film Heaven Help Us, 1976; dir. The Man with Two Brains, 1983. Served with AUS, 1942-46. Recipient Guest Actor in a Comedy Series Emmy award for Mad About You, 1995, Mark Twain Prize for Am. Humor, Kennedy Center, 1999, 2006 Hon. Life Mem. award, Directors Guild of Am. Achievements include receiving the greatest number of Emmys (12) for any individual. Office: care George Shapiro Shapiro-West 141 S El Camino Dr Ste 205 Beverly Hills CA 90212-2718 *

REINER, GARY M., diversified technology and services company executive; BA, Harvard U., 1976, MBA, 1980. Rsch. analyst Boston Consulting Group, 1980—86, ptnr., 1986—91; v.p. corp. bus. devel. GE, Fairfield, Conn., 1991-96, sr. v.p., chief info. officer, 1996—. Office: GE 3135 Easton Tpke Fairfield CT 06431-0002 *

REINER, JOHN, cartoonist; b. NYC, Nov. 9, 1956; s. Allen and Mildred Reiner. BA, SUNY, Stony Brook, 1978. Freelance illustrator Joe Simon, Editor, Stony Brook, 1974-80, Marvel Comics Group, NYC, 1978-84, Mort Drucker, Woodbury, NY, 1984-87, Bill Hoest/Wm. Hoest Enterprises, Lloyd Neck, NY, 1985—. Freelance illustrator for various mags., newspaper, advt. agys., also others, 1978—. Cartoonist syndicated daily comic strips Lockhorns, 1986—, Agatha Crumm, 1986-96, What A Guy!, 1986-96; cartoons appear in Parade mag., 1986—. Mem. Nat. Cartoonists Soc. (nat. rep. 1985-87, Best Gag Cartoonist awad 1994), Graphic Artists Guild. Avocation: bibliophile. Office: Wm Hoest Enterprises 27 Watch Way Huntington NY 11743-9707 E-mail: wmhoest@aol.com.

REINER, ROB, film director, actor; b. Bronx, NY, Mar. 6, 1947; s. Carl and Estelle (Lebost) R.; m. Penny Marshall, 1971 (div. 1979), m. Michele Singer, May 19, 1989; 3 children. Student, UCLA. Co-founder Castle Rock Entertainment, Beverly Hills, Calif. Actor: (TV series) All In the Family, 1971-78 (Emmy award 1974, 78), (TV movies) Thursday's Game, 1974 (films) Enter Laughing, 1967, Halls of Anger, 1970, Summertree, 1971, The Jerk, 1979, This is Spinal Tap, 1984, Throw Momma From the Train, 1987, Postcards From the Edge, 1990, The Spirit of '76, 1990, Sleepless in Seattle, 1993, Bullets Over Broadway, 1994, Mixed Nuts, 1994, Bye Bye, Love, 1995, First Wives Club, 1996, Mad Dog Time, 1996, I Am Your Child (TV), 1997, Primary Colors, 1998, EDtv, 1999, The Muse, 1999, The

Story of Us, 1999, (voice) The Majestic, 2001, Dickie Roberts: Former Child Star, 2003, (voice) Everyone's Hero, 2006, (theatre) The Roast, 1980; actor, writer: (films) Halls of Anger, 1970, Where's Pappa?, 1970, Summertree, 1971, Fire Sale, 1971; actor, co-writer, prodr. (TV) More Than Friends, 1978, Million Dollar Infield, 1982; actor, co-writer, dir. (film) This Is Spinal Tap, 1984; dir. (films) The Sure Thing, 1985, Stand By Me, 1986, Rumor Has It, 2005; dir. prodr. (films) The Princess Bride, 1987, When Harry Met Sally, 1989, Misery, 1990, A Few Good Men, 1992, North, 1994, The American President, 1995, Ghosts of Mississippi, 1996, The Story of Us, 1999, Alex & Emma, 2003, The Bucket List, 2007; co-creator (TV series) The Super, 1972; co-creator, actor (TV series) Free Country, 1977-78. Mem. SAG, AFTRA, Dir. Guild Am., Writers Guild Am. Office: Castle Rock Entertainment 335 N Maple Dr Ste 135 Beverly Hills CA 90210-3867

REINER, THOMAS KARL, manufacturing executive, engineering scientist; b. Budapest, Hungary, Dec. 29, 1931; came to U.S., 1959; s. Pál and Jozefa (Keller) R.; m. Joyce Kramer (div.); children: Paul A., Reneé K. Hedsand; m. Eleanor Ruth Aldridge (div.); m. Bonnie Sherman, 1995. Diploma optics trade sch., Budapest, 1952; MSME, Tech. U., Budapest, 1955; postgrad., London Coll., 1958, U. Pitts., Carnegie Inst. Tech., 1964; PhD, U. Wexford, England, 2001. Shift charge engr. Power Sta., Hungary, 1954-56; test engr. Blaw-Knox Co., London, 1956-57; sr. engr. Eubank & Ptnrs., London, 1957-59; rsch. engr. Pitts. Plate Glass Co., 1959-60, product mgr. Copes-Vulcan divsn., 1960-62; chief engr. J.W. Fecker divsn. Am. Optical Co., 1962-66; product mgr. Carco Electronics, Calif., 1966-68; chief engr. Fairchild Camera Space and Def. Divsn., Calif., 1968-70; dir. engring. Templeton, Kenly & Co., 1970-72; gen. mgr. Foremark Corp., Calif., 1972-74; owner Kinetron, Inc., Calif., 1974-76, GRW, Inc., Calif., 1977-97; pres. Renmark-Pacific Corp., Calif., 1998—2003; chief engring. scientist Integrated Def. Sys., The Boeing Co., Calif., 2004—. Adj. prof. math. Tech. U., Budapest, 1951-54. Pres. Peacock Ridge Homeowners Assn., Calif. Lt. Hungarian Army, 1951-57. Mem. Internat. Soc. Weighing and Measurements. Achievements include patents for concrete post tensioning device, air bearing and slave connector for Satellite Attitude Control Space Simulator; synchronization of hydraulic jacking systems to raise the Freemont Street Bridge in one piece; bending of automotive side windows; invention of a tug/barge latching system, membrane type PANCAKE loadcells, ultra low profile industrial scales, air cargo direct loading device. Home: 14110 Valley Vista Blvd Sherman Oaks CA 91423 Office Phone: 310-367-9997. Personal E-mail: t-reiner@pacbell.net.

REINERT, JAMES A., entomology educator; b. Enid, Okla., Jan. 26, 1944; s. Andrew J. and Emma Reinert; m. Anita Irwin; children: Travis J., Gina N., Mindy K., Melanie B., Gregory W., Teresa J. BS, Okla. State U., Stillwater, 1966; MS, Clemson U., SC, 1968, PhD, 1970. Asst. state entomologist U. Md., College Park, 1970; asst. prof. entomology to prof. entomology Ft. Lauderdale Rsch. and Edn. Ctr., U. Fla., 1970-84; resident dir., prof. entomology Tex. A&M Univ. Sys., Dallas, 1984-94, prof. entomology, 1994—2003, prof. entomology, Tex. agrl. experiment sta. faculty fellow, 2004—, regents fellow, 2005—. Contbr. over 420 articles to profl. jours. Grantee, NDEA, 1968. Mem. Inter-Turfgrass Soc., Entomol. Soc. Am. (S.W. br. sec.-treas. 1998, pres. 2000, chair sec. sect. F 2005, award in urban entomology 2002), So. Nurserymen's Assn. (Porter Henegar Meml. award 1982), Fla. Entomol. Soc. (v.p. 1983, pres. 1984, Entomologist of Yr. 1985), Fla. State Hort. Soc. (v.p. 1982), S.C. Entomol. Soc. (J.H. Cochran award 2002, Rsch. Ctr. Adminstrs. Soc. (v.p. 1994, state rep. 1991-92, sec. 1993), Dallas Agr. Club (bd. dirs. 1989, v.p. 1990, pres. 1991). Roman Catholic. Home: 3805 Covinton Ln Plano TX 75023-7731 Office: Tex A&M Univ Rsch and Ext Ctr 17360 Coit Rd Dallas TX 75252-6599 Office Phone: 972-231-5362. Business E-Mail: j-reinert@tamu.edu.

REINERT, NORBERT FREDERICK, lawyer, retired chemicals executive; b. Hamilton, Ohio, Apr. 12, 1928; s. Fred F. and Jennie A. R.; m. Ida Elizabeth Barickman, Jan. 26, 1956; children: Matthew W., Paul H. B.Ch.E., Ohio State U., 1951; LL.B., Cleve.-Marshall Law Sch., 1959. Bar: Ohio 1959, D.C. 1961. Patent agt. Standard of Ohio, Cleve., 1957-59, patent lawyer, 1959-60, E.I. duPont de Nemours & Co., Wilmington, Del., 1960-91, dir. investor relations, 1981-84, mng. counsel, 1985-91; v.p., gen. counsel Endo Labs, Inc. subs. DuPont, Garden City, NY, 1971-73, exec. v.p., 1973-77, pres., 1977-81; pvt. practice patent law, 1991—2002. Served with Chem. Corps AUS, 1955-56. Mem. Am. Patent Law Assn., Tau Beta Pi. Republican. Roman Catholic. Home: PO Box 311 Mendenhall PA 19357-0311

REINERTSEN, NORMAN, retired air transportation executive; b. Bklyn., Mar. 27, 1934; s. Berthin and Malene Katherine (Dahl) R.; m. Elizabeth T. O'Shea, Aug. 30, 1958 (dec. 2003); children: Michael, Christopher, Katherine. BEE, CCNY, 1960; postgrad., Harvard U., 1982. Registered profl. engr., Calif. Various positions Grumman Aerospace Corp., 1960-75; gen. mgr. Grumman Aerospace Corp. (Great River ops.), 1975-77; v.p. automotive Grumman Allied Industries, Melville, NY, 1977-83, sr. v.p. vehicle div., 1983-94; sr. v.p. Olson Bodies, Inc., 1977-79; exec. v.p. Grumman Flexible, Delaware, Ohio, 1979-82; pres. Grumman Olson, Mellville, 1983-85; sr. v.p. Vehicle div. Grumman Allied, 1985-87; v.p. quality ops. Grumman Aircraft Sys. div. Northrop Grumman, 1987-94; ret., 1994. With U.S. Army, 1955-57. Mem. Air Force Assn., Northport Yacht Club. Home: 7 Oleander Dr Northport NY 11768-3438

REINFELD, GEORGE, retired communications educator; b. Newark, Dec. 24, 1927; s. Abe and Grace Reinfeld; children: Larry, Grace Lubin. BA, Montclair State Tchrs. Coll., 1950, MA, 1954. Tchr. Westwood (NJ) HS, 1950—54, North Arlington (NJ) HS, 1954—56; prof. Glassboro (NJ) State Coll., 1956—2002, founder dept. comms. Contbr. numerous articles to profl. publs. With Air Corp USN, 1945—46. Avocations: piano, backgammon, reading. Home: 16 Monroe Ave Pitman NJ 08071-1563

REINFELDT, MIKE (MICHAEL RAY REINFELDT), professional sports team executive, former professional football player; b. Baraboo, Wis., May 6, 1953; m. Susan Reinfeldt; children: Jared Michael, Elise Marie. BA in Mktg., U. Milwaukee-Wis., 1975; MBA in Mgmt. & Fin., Houston Baptist U., 1985. Safety Oakland Raiders, Calif., 1976, Houston Oilers, Tex., 1976—83; CFO LA Raiders, 1985—87; assoc. athletic dir. U. So. Calif., 1988—90; CFO Green Bay Packers, 1991—98, v.p. admin., 1994—98; sr. v.p. Seattle Seahawks, 1999—2004, consul., v.p. football admin., 2005—07; gen. mgr., Tenn. Titans, 2007—. Named NFL Defensive Player Yr., 1979; named to NFL All-Pro Team, 1979, Am. Football Conf. Pro Bowl Team, 1979. Office: Tenn Titans One Titans Way Nashville TN 37213 *

REINGLASS, MICHELLE ANNETTE, lawyer, mediator, arbitrator; b. LA, Dec. 9, 1954; d. Darwin and Shirley (Steiner) R. Student, U. Calif., Irvine, 1972-75; BSL, Western State U., 1977; JD, Western State U., Coll. Law, 1978. Bar: Calif. 1979, U.S. Dist. Ct. (ctrl. dist.) Calif. 1979, U.S. Ct. Appeals (9th cir.) 1981, U.S. Dist. Ct. (so. dist.) Calif. 1990. Pvt. practice employee litig., Laguna Hills, Calif., 1979—. Instr. Calif. Continuing Edn. of Bar, 1990—, Western State Coll., 1991, Rutter Group, 1994—; chmn. magistrate selection com. ctrl. dist. US Dist. Ct.,Calif., LA, 1991, 93-95, com. mem., 1994-97, 2003-06, lawyer rep. to 9th cir. jud. conf.; lectr. in field. Contbr. articles to profl. jours. Pres., bd. dirs. Child or Parental Emergency Svcs., Santa Ana, Calif., 1982-92; bd. dirs. Pub. Law Ctr., Santa Ana, Coalition for Justice, Working Wardrobes; mem. exec. com. and cast CHOC Follies. Recipient Jurisprudence award Anti-Defamation League, 1997; named to Western State U. Hall of Fame, 1993; named one of Top 100 Most Influential Lawyers in Calif., LA Daily Jour., 2001; one of Top 30 Female Litigators in Calif., LA Daily Jour., 2002; one of Top 50 Female Litigators, LA Daily Jour., 2003-04; named to Super Lawyers, LA Mag., 2004-07. Fellow Coll. Labor and Employee Lawyers; mem. State Bar Calif., Assn. Bus. Trial Lawyers (bd. dirs.), Orange County Bar Assn. (del. to state conv. 1980-94, bd. dirs. 1983-94, chmn. bus. litigation sect. 1989, sec. 1990, treas. 1991, pres.-elect 1992, pres. 1993), Nat. Employee Lawyers Assn., Calif. Employee Lawyers Assn. (com. mem., chair 2005-07), Orange County Trial Lawyers Assn. (bd. dirs. 1987-89, Bus. Trial Lawyer of Yr. award 1995, Employee Trial Lawyer of Yr. 2004), So. Calif. Mediation Assn., Orange County Women Lawyers (Lawyer of Yr. award 1996), Vols. in Parole (chmn. adv. com. 1990-91), Peter Elliot Inns Ct. (master), Am. Bd. of Trial Advocates. Avocations: distance running, skiing. Office: 23161 Mill Creek Dr Ste 170 Laguna Hills CA 92653-1650 E-mail: michelle@reinglasslaw.com.

REINGOLD, ARTHUR LAWRENCE, epidemiologist, educator; b. Chgo., Oct. 31, 1948; married AB, U. Chgo., 1970, MD, 1976. Diplomate Am. Bd. Internal Medicine. Resident in internal medicine Mount Auburn Hosp., Cambridge, Mass., 1976-78; instr. dept. medicine (epidemiology) U. Conn., Hartford, 1979; epidemic intelligence svc. officer Conn. State Dept. Health Svcs., Hartford, 1979-80; epidemic intelligence svc. officer spl. pathogens br., bacterial diseases divsn. Ctr. Disease Control, Atlanta, 1980-81, resident in preventive medicine, 1980-82, asst. chief respiratory & spl. pathogens epidemiology br. Ctr. Infectious Disease, 1981-85, liaison officer, 1985-87; vis. lectr. dept. biomed. and environ. health scis. (epidemiology) U. Calif., Berkeley, 1985-87, prof. epidemiology, 1987—, head epidemiology program, 1990—, prof. dept. epidemiology & biostatistics San Francisco, 1989—, clin. prof. dept. medicine, 1991—; dir. UCB-UCSF Fogarty Internat. AIDS Training Program; co-dir. Calif. Emerging Infections Program. Cons. in field. Contbr. articles to profl. jours. Fellow Am. Coll. Epidemiology, Infectious Disease Soc. Am.; mem. ACP, Am. Epidemiological Soc., Am. Soc. Microbiology, Soc. Epidemiologic Rsch., Sigma Xi, Inst. Medicine. Office: UC Berkeley Sch Pub Health 140 Warren Hall 7360 Berkeley CA 94720-7360 Office Phone: 510-642-0327. Office Fax: 510-643-5163. E-mail: reingold@berkeley.edu.

REINGOLD, DAVID AMI, sociologist, educator; b. Chgo., Oct. 30, 1968; s. Haim and Badonna Reingold. BA in Sociology and Social Welfare, U. Wis., 1990; MA in Sociology, U. Chgo., 1992, PhD in Sociology, 1996. Asst. prof. Ind. U., Bloomington, 1997—2003, assoc. prof., 2003—; dir. rsch. and policy devel. Corp. for Nat. and Cmty. Svc., Washington, 2002—04; dir. pub. affairs and doctoral pub. policy programs Ind. U. Sch. Pub. and Environ. Affairs, 2006—. Rsch. assoc. Ctr. for the Study of Urban Inequality, Chgo., 1990—94; program assoc. Govs. Task Force on Human Svcs. Reform, Chgo., 1993; rsch. assoc. Dept. Children and Family Svcs., Chgo., 1996; field assoc. Rockefeller Inst. Govt., Albany, NY, 1996—98. Contbr. articles to profl. jours. Family self sufficiency com. Bloomington Housing Authority, 1997—2002, chmn. family self-sufficiency com., 1998—2002; housing commr. Bloomington Housing Authority Bd., 1999—2002, vice chmn., 2000—02; task force for disadvantaged youth White House, 2002—03; chmn. Ind. Commn. on Cmty. Svc. and Volunteerism, 2005—; pres. bd. dirs. South Ctrl. Ind. Cmty. Action Program, 2006—. Fellow fellwship on race, poverty and social policy, NSF/U. Chgo., 1992—96; grantee rsch. grantee, Ind. Family Social Svcs. Adminstrn., The Joyce Found., Ind. Twp. Assn., 1998—2000, The Joyce Found., 2001—02; scholar Century scholar, U. Chgo., 1990—92. Mem.: Assn. for Pub. Policy Analysis and Mgmt. (policy com. 2003—), Urban Affairs Assn., Am. Sociol. Assn. Office: Ind Univ, Sch Pub & Environ Affairs 1315 E 10th St Bloomington IN 47405 Office Phone: 812-855-5971. Business E-Mail: reingold@indiana.edu.

REINHARD, CHRISTOPHER JOHN, merchant banker, venture capitalist, biotechnologist, director; b. Bridgeport, Conn., Nov. 11, 1953; s. Warren John and Marian Louise (Dutter) R.; m. Maureen Francis, Sept. 24, 1977; 1 child, Griffin John. BS, Babson Coll., 1976, MBA, 1977. Sr. fin. analyst Gen. Motors Corp., Detroit and NYC, 1977-81; asst. sec. Wheelabrator-Frye Inc., NH, 1981-83; asst. sec., asst. treas. The Signal Cos., Inc., La Jolla, Calif., 1983-86; mng. dir., v.p. The Henley Group, Inc., La Jolla, 1986-90; mng. dir. Fisher Sci. Group, Inc., La Jolla, 1986-90; mng. dir., v.p. Wheelabrator Tech. Inc., Henley Mfg. Corp., 1987-90; founder, pres. Colony Group Inc., Rancho Santa Fe, 1990—, Reinhard Assocs., Rancho Santa Fe, 1990-95; founder, v.p., CFO Advanced Access, Inc., San Diego, 1995-97. Pres. Direct Feedback, Inc., 1990, Dairy Queen Ventures, 1990-94, Winsor Sport Fencing, 1993—; CEO, founder, pres. Collateral Therapeutics Inc., 1995-2005; gen. ptnr. Cabrillo Ventures, 1995-96; founder, pres. ihumon, 2000—; exec. chmn. Artes Med., Inc., 2004—; exec. chmn., CEO, founder Cardium Therapeutics Inc., 2003—. Mem. Boston Athenaeum, N.Y. Athletic Club, San Diego Polo Club, Rancho Santa Fe Polo Club. Office: Cardium Therapeutics 3611 Valley Ctr Dr Ste 525 San Diego CA 92130

REINHARD, JAMES RICHARD, judge; b. Pollock, Mo., July 7, 1929; s. Virgil and Meltha (Anspach) R.; m. Shari L. Horton, Dec. 30, 1958; 1 child, James K. Student, N.E. Mo. State U., 1947-50; AB, U. Mo., 1951, JD, 1953. Bar: Mo. 1953. Pros. atty. Sullivan County, Mo., 1955-57, Monroe County, Mo., 1959-65; spl. asst. atty. gen. State of Mo., 1967-68; judge 10th Jud. Circuit, 1973-77, Mo. Ct. Appeals (ea. dist.), St. Louis, 1977-97, chief judge, 1984-85, sr. judge, 2003—; pvt. practice Milan, Mo., 1955-57, Paris, Mo., 1957-73, Hannibal, Mo., 1997—2003. Bd. regents N.E. Mo. State U. (now Truman State U.), Kirksville, 1965-73, bd. pres., 1967-73, now mem. found. bd.; trustee State Hist. Soc. Mo. Sgt. U.S. Army, 1953-55. Mem. ABA, 10th Jud. Bar Assn. (pres. 1972), Mo. Bar Assn. (bd. govs. 1965-69), Met. Bar Assn. St. Louis, Lawyers Assn. St. Louis, Mo. Bd. Cert. Ct. Reporter Examiner (vice chmn. 1988-90), Mo. Press-Bar Commn., Judicial Fin. Commn. (chmn. 1990-94). Home: Box 1218 Hannibal MO 63401-1903

REINHARD, JOAO PEDRO, chemicals company executive; b. Sao Paulo, Brazil, Aug. 4, 1945; BA, MBA, Escola de Administração de Empresas, da Fundação Getulio Vargas, Sao Paulo, Brazil, 1967; completed postgraduate studies at the U. Cologne, Germany and Stanford U. Fin. planning supr. Squibb do Brazil, Sao Paulo, 1968; credit mgr. Dow Quimica, Sao Paulo, 1970-72; fin. asst. Dow Latin Am., Miami, Fla., 1973; treas. Latin Am. Dow Lepetit Latin Am., Miami, Fla., 1974-76; corp. fin. planning mgr. Dow Chem. Co., Midland, Mich., 1976-77, treas., 1988—96, v.p., 1990—95, fin. v.p., 1995—96, CFO, 1995—2005, exec. v.p., 1996—2005, sr. advisor, 2005; fin. dir. Dow Quimica S.Am., Sao Paulo, Brazil, 1978-80, Dow Europe, Horgen, Switzerland, 1981-85, asst. treas., 1984, v.p., 1985-87; mng. dir. Dow Italy, Milan, 1985—88. Bd. dirs. Royal Bank of Canada, 2000-, Dow Corning Corp., 1995-2007, Sigma-Aldrich Corp., 2001-, Coca-Cola Co., 2003-06, Colgate-Palmolive Co., 2006-, Liana Ltd., Midland, Mich., Dorinco Reinsurance Co., Midland, Dow Chem. Internat. BV, Midland, DCOMCO Inc., Midland, Dow Chm. Inter-Am. Ltd., Midland, Dow Chem. Internat. Inc. (Panama), Midland, Dow Chem. Internat. Ltd., Midland, Midland Pipeline Corp., Dow Chem. Overseas Capital NV, Midland, Bank Mendes Gans NV, Amsterdam, The Netherlands; mem. Environment Health & Safety Com., Dow Chemical Co. Mem. Fin. Execs. Inst., Fin. Mgmt. Assn., Nat. Assn. Corp. Treasurers, Corp. Fin. Inst. *

REINHARD, KEITH LEON, advertising executive; b. Berne, Ind., Jan. 20, 1935; s. Herman L. and Agnes V. R.; m. Rose-Lee Simons, Nov. 7, 1976; children: Rachel, Elizabeth; children by previous marriage: Christopher, Timothy, Matthew, Geoffrey, Jacqueline. Student public schs., Berne. Comml. artist Kling Studios, Chgo., 1954-56; mgr. tech. comm. dept. Magnavox Co., Ft. Wayne, Ind., 1957-60; creative/account exec. Biddle Co., Bloomington, Ill., 1961-63; jr. copywriter Needham, Harper & Steers, Chgo., 1964, named creative dir., 1975, pres., 1980, chmn., 1982; chmn., CEO DDB Needham Worldwide & DDB Worldwide Inc., 1986—2001; chmn. DDB Worldwide Inc., 2001—06, chmn. emeritus, 2006—. Episcopalian. Office: DDB Worldwide Inc 437 Madison Ave New York NY 10022-7001

REINHARD, PHILIP GODFREY, federal judge; b. LaSalle, Ill., Jan. 12, 1941; s. Godfrey and Ruth R.; m. Virginia Reinhard; children: Bruce, Brian, David, Philip. BA, U. Ill., Champaign, 1962, JD, 1964. Asst. state atty. Winnebago County, 1964-67; atty. Hyer, Gill & Brown, 1967-68; state atty. Winnebago County, 1968-76; judge 17th Jud. Cir., Ill., 1976-80, 2nd Dist. Ct. Appeals, Ill., 1980-92, US Dist. Ct. (no. dist.) Ill., 1992—2007, sr. judge, 2007—. Mem. Am. Acad. Jud. Edn., Winnebago County Bar Assn. Office: US Courthouse 211 S Court St Rockford IL 61101-1219 Office Phone: 815-987-4480. *

REINHARDT, BENJAMIN MAX, lawyer, arbitrator, mediator; b. NYC, Dec. 29, 1917; s. Meyer and Miriam (Fischer) R.; children: Dennis, Dixie, Sara, Shawn; m. Rosa Reinhardt. BA, Harvard U., 1940; JD magna cum laude, Southwestern U., LA, 1956. Bar: Calif. 1956, U.S. Supreme Ct. 1960. Pvt. practice, Van Nuys, Calif., 1957-87, Palm Desert, Calif., 1987—. Chief legal counsel Northridge (Calif.) Hosp. Found., 1965-75; atty. Calif. Psychol. Assn., San Francisco, 1965-70; tchr. law Los Angeles County Bd. Edn., L.A., 1965-73; instr. law U. So. Calif., L.A., 1963-69, Coll. of Desert, Palm Desert, Calif., 1992-94; arbitrator Superior Ct. Calif., Palm Springs, 1994—; atty. Sr. T.V., Indian Wells, Calif., 1992—. Mem. Palm Desert Police Adv. Com., 1993-98; mem. adv. bd. Ret. Sr. Vol. Program, Palm Desert, 1994-96; instr. law Elderhostel, Indian Wells, Calif., 1993-98. Capt. U.S. Army, 1941-46. Mem. State Bar Calif., Desert Bar Assn. Republican. Avocations: golf, reading. Office: Palm Desert Greens 38-101 Story Creek Dr Palm Desert CA 92260-8617 Fax: 760-346-0936. E-mail: reino81@earthlink.net.

REINHARDT, DANIEL SARGENT, lawyer; b. Orange, NJ, Jan. 27, 1949; s. Warren Irwin and Winifred Ruth (Sargent) R.; m. Elizabeth Ann Johnson, June 11, 1982; 1 child, Meredith Alexandra. BA, Duke U., 1971; JD, Georgetown U., 1974. Bar: Ga. 1975, U.S. Dist. Ct. (no. dist.) Ga. 1975, U.S. Ct. Appeals (5th and 11th cirs.) 1981, U.S. Dist. Ct. (so. dist.) Ga. 1984, U.S. Dist. Ct. (mid. dist.) Ga. 1985, U.S. Ct. Appeals (4th cir.) 1985. Assoc. Troutman Sanders LLP, Atlanta, 1974—79, ptnr., 1980—, mem. exec. com. Dep. asst. atty. gen. State of Ga., 1975-79. Named a Super Lawyer, Atlanta Mag., 2004. Mem. ABA, Ga. Bar Assn., Atlanta Bar Assn., fellow, Am. Coll. Trial Lawyers, Lawyers Club. Avocation: sports. Office: Troutman Sanders LLP 600 Peachtree St Atlanta GA 30308-2265 Office Phone: 404-885-3206. Office Fax: 404-885-3900. Business E-Mail: daniel.reinhardt@troutmansanders.com.

REINHARDT, DEBORAH ANN, music educator; d. James Willard Reinhardt and Wilma Ruth Gibler. MusB in Edn., Baldwin-Wallace Coll., Berea, Ohio, 1973; MusM, Ithaca Coll., NY, 1987; PhD in Music Edn., Case Western Res. U., Cleve., 1990. Music tchr. A.B. Hart Jr. High Cleve. Pub. Schs., 1973—77; music tchr. Kenston Pub. Schs., Chagrin Falls, Ohio, 1977—80, Busby Sch. of No. Cheyenne Tribe, Busby, Mont., 1980—82, Jonesport (Maine) Elem. Sch., 1982—85; asst. prof. music edn. U. Nebr., Lincoln, 1995—2000, Ball State U., Muncie, Ind., 1990—95; assoc. prof. music edn., dir. music edn. Calif. State U., Chico, 2000—. Author: (monograph) A Rich Tapestry: The Music Of Nebraska; contbr. articles to profl. jours. Coord. h.s. honor choir Calif. State U., Chico, 2002—05. Mem.: Calif. Coun. Music Tchr. Educators (chair 2004—), Am. Orff-Schulwerk Assn. (collegiate rep. 2003), Coll. Music Soc., Calif. Assn. Music Edn. (treas. no. sect. 2003—, coord. solo and ensemble festival, coord. large group choral festival 2002). Achievements include research in relationship between creative activities, music learning and curriculum. Avocations: folk dancing, swimming. Home: 5 Delaware Dr Chico CA 95973 Office: Calif State U Chico 103 Performing Arts Ctr Chico CA 95929-0806 Home Phone: 530-342-7030; Office Phone: 530-898-4639. Fax: 530-898-4082. E-mail: dreinhardt@csuchico.edu.

REINHARDT, ELIZABETH A., mathematics educator; d. Jose V. and Lupita M. Sandoval; m. Carl W. Reinhardt, Jr., Oct. 9, 1976; children: Carl III, Daniel, Lisa Marie. BS in Elem. Edn. summa cum laude, U. N.Mex., Gallup, 1999, MA in Literacy and Lang., 2002; postgrad., WNM U., Gallup, 2007. 5th grade tchr. McKinley County Schs., Gallup, 1997—2002, 2nd grade tchr., 2001—02, ednl. math. specialist, 2002—03, ednl. reading specialist, 2003—05, head tchr., 2003—05, instrnl. support tchr., 2005; ednl. math. specialist BIA-Boca Cmty. Sch., Prewitt, N.Mex., 2006—. U. N.Mex. head tutor U. N.Mex.-CASA, Gallup, 1997—2002; co-coord. Four Corners Writing Project, Gallup, 2002. Nominee Disney Tchr. of Yr., 2001; named Employee of Month, Gallup McKinley County Schs., 2002; Nat. Hispanic scholar, Nat. Hispanic Assn., 1998, 1999. Mem.: Assn. for Women in Math., Nat. Coun. Tchrs. Math. Office: BIA Baca Cmty Sch Hwy I-40 South Exit 63 Prewitt NM 87045

REINHARDT, GEORGE ROBERT, lawyer; b. Tifton, Ga., Mar. 1, 1954; BBA magna cum laude, U. Ga., 1975; JD, U. Va., 1978. Bar: Ga. 1979. Atty. Reinhardt, Whitley, Wilmot, Summerlin & Pittman, PC, Tifton, Ga. Mem.: Tifton Bar Assn., State Bar Ga. (bd. govs. 1992—, state disciplinary bd. review panel 1993—98, chmn. 1996—98, fin. com. 1996—, program com. 1998—, exec. com. 1998—, chair fin. com. 1999—2000, treas. 2000—01, pres.-elect 2003—, pres. 2004), Sphinx Soc. Office: Reinhardt Whitley Wilmot et al PO Drawer 1287 1001 N Central St Tifton GA 31794 *

REINHARDT, JOHN EDWARD, former international affairs specialist; b. Glade Spring, Va., Mar. 8, 1920; s. Edward Vinton and Alice (Miller) R.; m. Carolyn Lillian Daves, Sept. 2, 1947; children: Sharman W. Reinhardt Lancefield, Alice N., Carolyn C. Reinhardt Fenstermaker. AB, Knoxville Coll., 1939; MS, U. Wis., 1947, PhD, 1950. Prof. English Va. State Coll., Petersburg, 1950-56; cultural affairs officer USIS, Manila, 1956-58; dir. Am. Cultural Ctr., Kyoto, Japan, 1958-63; cultural attache USIS, Tehran, Iran, 1963-66; dep. asst. dir. Office East Asia and Pacific, USIA, Washington, 1966-68, 70-71, asst. dir. Office for Africa, 1968-70; ambassador to Nigeria, 1971-75; asst. sec. state for pub. affairs, 1975-77; dir. USIA, Washington, 1977-78, U.S. Internat. Communication Agy., Washington, 1978-81; acting dir. Smithsonian Mus. African Art, Washington, 1981-83; asst. sec. for history and art Smithsonian Instn., Washington, 1983-84, dir. directorate internat. activities, 1984-87; prof. polit. sci. U. Vt., Burlington, 1987-90, prof. emeritus, 1990—. Served as officer AUS, 1942-46. Mem. MLA, Am. Fgn. Svc. Assn. (v.p. 1969-71). Clubs: Cosmos. Methodist. E-mail: john.reinhardt3@verizon.net.

REINHARDT, JOHN W., dean, dental educator; b. Nashville, Ill. m. Claudia Reinhardt. B in biology, Ill. Wesleyan U., 1971; DDS, Loyola U., 1975; MS in operative dentistry, U. Iowa, 1979; MPH in health services rsch., Harvard U., 1988. Diplomate Am. Bd. Operative Dentistry. With US Army Dental Corps; asst. prof. U. Iowa Coll. Dentistry, 1980—84, assoc. prof., 1984—90, head dept. operative dentistry, 1988—2000, prof., 1990—2000; dean U. Nebr. Med. Ctr. Coll. Dentistry, 2000—, prof. dept. adult restorative dentistry, 2000—. Rschr. in field; cons. NIH, ADA, US Navy, Am. Dental Edn. Assn., Consortium Operative Dentistry Educators, Internat. Assn. Dental Rsch., others.; chair Children's Amalgam Trial Data and Safety Monitoring Bd. Nat. Inst. Dental and Craniofacial Rsch., 1997—; mem. bd. dirs. Friends of the Nat. Inst. of Dental and Craniofacial Rsch., 2005—. Contbr. articles to profl. pubs., scientific papers, chapters to books. Fellow: Internat. Coll. Dentists, Am. Coll. Dentists; mem.: ADA, Am. Bd. Operative Dentistry, Acad. Operative Dentistry (pres. 1997, chair. bd. dirs. founder's fund 2000—, Award of Excellence 2002). Office: U Nebr Med Ctr Coll Dentistry 40th and Holdrege Streets Box 830740 Lincoln NE 68583-1301 Office Phone: 402-472-1344. Office Fax: 402-472-6681. Business E-Mail: jreinhardt@unmc.edu.

REINHARDT, STEPHEN ROY, federal judge; b. NYC, Mar. 27, 1931; s. Gottfried and Silvia (Hanlon) Reinhardt; children: Mark, Justin, Dana. BA cum laude, Pomona Coll., 1951; LLB, Yale, 1954. Bar: Calif. 1958. Law clk. to Hon. Luther W. Youngdahl US Dist. Ct., Washington, 1956—57; atty. O'Melveny & Myers, LA, 1957—59; ptnr. Fogel Julber Reinhardt Rothschild & Feldman LC, LA, 1959—80; judge US Ct. Appeals (9th cir.), LA, 1980—. Adj. prof. Loyola Law Sch., LA, 1988—90. Pres. LA Recreation and Parks Commn., 1974—75; active Coliseum Commn., 1974—75, LA Police Commn., 1974—78, pres., 1978—80; sec., exec. organizing com. LA Olympics, 1980—84; exec. com. Dem. Nat. Com., 1969—72; nat. Dem. committeeman State of Calif., 1976—80; bd. dirs. Amateur Athletic Found. LA, 1984—92. 1st lt. USAF, 1954—56. Mem.: ABA (labor law coun. 1975—77), Calif. Bar Assn., LA County Bar Assn. Office Phone: 213-894-3639. *

REINHARDT, UWE ERNST, economist, educator; b. Osnabrueck, Germany, Sept. 24, 1937; came to U.S., 1964; s. Wilhelm and Edeltraut (Kehne) R.; m. Tsung-mei Cheng, May 25, 1968; children— Dirk, Kara, Mark B.Comm. in Econs. with honors, U. Sask., Saskatoon, Can., 1964; MA in Econs., Yale U., 1965, M.Ph. in Econs., 1967, PhD, 1970; DSc (hon.), Med. Coll. of Pa., 1987, CUNY, 1994, SUNY, 1998. Asst. prof. econs. and pub. affairs Princeton (N.J.) U., 1968-74, assoc. prof., 1974-79, prof., 1979—, James Madison prof. polit. economy, prof. econs., 1984—. Bd. dirs. McAllister Holdings; trustee Tchrs. Ins. and Annuity Assn., 1978-93, H&Q Health Fund; cons. Urban Inst., Washington, 1971-75, HEW, 1974—, HHS, Math., Inc., Princeton, 1970-80, AT&T, Basking Ridge, N.J., 1976-82, Nat. Westminster Bank USA, N.Y.C., 1979—, mem. Nat. Leadership Commn. Health Care, 1986—; mem. spl. adv. bd. VA, 1981-85; mem. U.S. Physicians' Payment Rev. Commn., U.S. Congress, 1986—; pres. Assn. for Health Svcs. Rsch., 1989-90, Found. Health Svcs. Rsch., 1990-91; mem. bd. advisors Nat. Inst. Healthcare Mgmt., 1993—, Pew Health Professions Commn., 1997—; mem. Coun. Econ. Impact Health Reform, 1994—; mem. external adv. panel health and nutrition World Bank, 1997—; chair coordinating com. Commonwealth Fund Internat. Program Health Policy, 1998—; commr. Kaiser Commn. Medicaid and Uninsured; trustee Duke U. Health Sys., Triad Hosps., Inc., Medcast/WebMD. Author: Physician Productivity and the Demand for Health Manpower, 1975; mem. editorial bd. Health Affairs, 1982—, New Eng. Jour. Medicine, 1989-92, Health Mgmt. Quar., Health Policy and Edn., Milbank Meml. Quar., Jour. AMA, 1991—; assoc. editor Jour. Health Econs., 1980-85, mem. editorial bd., 1981-83; contbr. articles to profl. jours. Bd. dirs. Nat. Acad. Aging, 1993—. Mem. Nat. Inst. Health Care Mgmt., Inst. Medicine Nat. Acad. Scis. (gov. council 1979-82) Office: Princeton U Woodrow Wilson Sch Prof of Economics & Public Affairs 412 Robertson Hl Princeton NJ 08544-0001

REINHARDT, WILLIAM PARKER, chemical physicist, educator; b. San Francisco, May 22, 1942; s. William Oscar and Elizabeth Ellen (Parker) R.; m. Katrina Hawley Currens, Mar. 14, 1979; children: James William, Alexander Hawley. BS in Basic Chemistry, U. Calif., Berkeley, 1964; AM in Chemistry, Harvard U., 1966, PhD in Chem. Physics, 1968; MA (hon.), U. Pa., 1985. Instr. chemistry Harvard U., 1967-69, asst. prof. chemistry, 1969-72, assoc. prof., 1972-74; prof. U. Colo., Boulder, 1974-84, chmn. dept. chemistry, 1977-80; prof. chemistry U. Pa., Phila., 1984-91, chmn. dept., 1985-88, D. Michael Crow prof., 1987-91; prof. chemistry U.Wash., Seattle, 1991—, assoc. chmn. undergrad. program, 1993-96. Adj. prof. physics U. Wash., Seattle, 1998—; vis. fellow Joint Inst. for Lab. Astrophysics of Nat. Bur. Stds. and U. Colo., 1972, 74, fellow, 1974-84; dir. Telluride Summer Rsch. Ctr., 1986-89, treas., 1989-93; com. on atomic, molecular and optical scis. NRC, 1988-90; sub com. Internat. Union Pure and Applied Physics, Atomic Molecular Physics, 2002—05; vis. scientist Nat. Inst. Stds. and Tech., summers 1993—, Harvard-MIT Ctr. Ultra-Cold Atoms, 2005; vis. prof. chemistry U. Paris VI, 1991, U. Melbourne, Australia, 1997, Harvard U., 1998, Davidson lectr. U. Kans., 2000; Kohler lectr. U. Calif., Riverside, 2002; R.S. Berry pub. lectr. Telluride, Colo., 2004, Bertman Meml. lectr. Wesleyan U., Middletown, Conn., 2005. Mem. edit. bd. Phys. Rev. A, 1979-81, 05-, Chem. Physics, 1985-94, Jour. Chem. Physics, 1987-89, Jour. Physics B. (U.K.), 1992-2004, Internat. Jour. Quantum Chemistry, 1994-2001, Digital Libr. of Math. Functions, 1999-; rschr. theoretical chem. physics, theoretical atomic and molecular physics for numerous publs Recipient Camille and Henry Dreyfus Tchr. Scholar award, 1972; Alfred P. Sloan fellow, 1972; J.S. Guggenheim Meml. fellow, 1978; Coun. on Rsch. and Creative Work faculty fellow, 1978; Wilsmore fellow U. Melbourne (Australia), 1997; J.W. Fulbright sr. scholar, Australia, 1997; Cougar scholar, 2007. Fellow AAAS, Am. Phys. Soc., Inst. Physics (U.K.), Phi Beta Kappa; mem. Am. Chem. Soc., Sigma Xi (nat. lectr. 1980-82), Phi Lambda Upsilon (Fresenius award 1977), Phi Beta Kappa (vis. scholar 2002-03, disting. fellow lectr., 2004-, Comper lectr. 2006-07). Office: U Wash Dept Chemistry Box 351700 Seattle WA 98195-1700 Office Phone: 206-543-0578. Business E-Mail: rein@chem.washington.edu.

REINHART, ANNE CHRISTINE, special education educator, consultant; b. Detroit, Mar. 9, 1950; m. Charles Reinhart; children: Kim Meredith, Theodore Justin. BS, Ea. Mich. U., 1972; MA, U. Detroit, 1977. Cert. spl. edn. Mich. Spl. edn. tchr. for emotionally impaired State of Mich. Hosp., Pontiac, Berkley Sch. Dist, Mich., 1976—. Co-chair ASSET, Birmingham, Mich., 1996—98; com. mem. Mich. Dept. of Edn., Office Spl. Edn.; participant Mich. Pilot Study grant Quality Assurance Rev., 2000—03. Grantee, Dept. Spl. Edn., Mich., 2000—03. Mem.: Kappa Delta Pi. Avocation: writing. Home: 25925 Romany Way Franklin MI 48025-1909

REINHART, CHARLES LAWRENCE, performing company executive; b. Summit, NJ, Dec. 5, 1930; s. Albert and Rose Belle (Goldstein) R.; m. Molly Moore, Jan., 1967 (div. 1974); children: Taylor, Adam; m. Stephanie Reinhart, July, 1987; 1 child, Ariane; m. Patricia Reinhart, 1953 (div. 1962); 1 child, Scott. BA, Rutgers U., 1952; postgrad., U. Copenhagen, 1955-56; DFA (hon.), Duke U., 2003. Pres. Am. Dance Festival, Durham, NC, 1968—, co-dir., 1993—2002; co-artistic dir. for dance Kennedy Ctr., Washington, 1996—2002, artistic dir. for dance, 2002—04. Mem. dance panel Guggenheim Found., 1973-85; producer numerous NYC dance events including City Ctr. Spring Dance Festival, 1969-73, dance seasons at Anta Theater & City Ctr. for Music and Drama, 1968-73, Dance Repertory Season at Billy Rose Theatre, 1969; developer, nat. coord. NEA Dance Touring Program, 1967-78, NEA Artists-in-Schs. program, 1970-81; organizer cultural presentation program U.S. Dept. State, 1966; mem. adv. com. Asia Soc. Performing Arts program, 1970; dir. Jacob's Pillow Dance Festival, 1974; bd. dirs. Theatre Devel. Fund, Anglo-Am. Contemporary Dance Found., Internat. Theatre Inst., Japan Soc. Performing Arts Com.; co-exec. prodr. PBS Series Free to Dance: The African American Presence in Modern Dance, 2001 (Emmy award, 2001). Cpl. U.S. Army, 1952-53, Korea. Decorated officer Order Arts and Letters comdr. Order Arts and Letters (France); recipient Morrison award, 1985, Dance/USA Honors for lifetime achievement in dance, 1994, Capezio Dance award, 1996, Diaghilev award, 1997, Dance Notation Bur. Svc. award, 1999, Dance Mag. award, 2003.

REINHART, DIETRICH THOMAS, academic administrator, social studies educator; b. Mpls., May 17, 1949; s. Donald Irving and Eleanor Therese (Noonan) R. BA in History, St. John's U., Collegeville, Minn., 1971; AM in History, Brown U., 1976, PhD in History, 1984. Benedictine monk St. John's Abbey, 1971—; prof. history St. John's U., 1981—, dean of the coll., 1988-91, pres., 1991—. Dir. liturgy St. John's Abbey, 1983-88. Bd. dirs. Minn. Pvt. Coll. Coun., 1991—, George A. MacPherson Fund, 1991—, Hill Monastic Manuscript Library, 1991—, Inst. for Ecumenical and Cultural Rsch., 1991—, First Am. Nat. Bank St. Cloud., 1992—; bd. overseers St. John's Prep. Sch., 1990—. Home: St Johns Abbey Collegeville MN 56321 Office: St John's U Office of Pres Collegeville MN 56321

REINHART, JOHN BELVIN, retired child and adolescent psychiatrist, educator; b. Merrill, Wis., Dec. 22, 1917; s. Dabney Belvin and Ann (Toomey) R.; m. Helen Elsen Reinhart, Jan. 3, 1949; children: Peter, Catherine, Ann, John, Frederick, Andrew. BA, Duke U., 1939; MD, Bowman Gray Sch. Medicine, Winston-Salem, NC, 1943. Diplomate Am. Bd. Pediatrics, Am. Bd. Psychiatry in child and adolescent psychiatry. Instr. pediatrics Bowman Gray Sch. Medicine, Winston-Salem, 1950-52; asst. prof., assoc. prof., prof. pediatrics and psychiatry U. Pitts. Sch. Medicine, 1956-83, emeritus prof. pediatrics, 1983—; clin. prof. psychiatry Bowman Gray Sch. Medicine, Winston-Salem, 1986-99, ret., 1999—. Co-Author: A Baby's First Year, 1956. Capt. M.C. AUS, 1946-48. Roman Catholic. Avocations: reading, golf, tennis, travel. Home: 34 Hunters Ln Hendersonville NC 28791-1665

REINHART, KELLEE CONNELY, journalist; b. Kearney, Nebr., Dec. 15, 1951; d. Vaughn Eugene and Mary Jo (Mullen) Connely; m. Stephen Wayne Reinhart, June 15, 1974; children: Keegan Connely, Channing Mullen. BA, U. Ala., 1972, MS, 1974. Advt. copywriter Stas. WTBC-AM, WUOA-FM, 1970-72; asst. mgr. Ala. Press Assn., 1972-74; asst. to the editor Antique Monthly mag., 1974-75, mng. editor, 1975-77; editorial dir. Antique Monthly and Horizons mags., 1977-89; dir. univ. rels. U. Ala. Sys., Tuscaloosa, 1989—2004, vice chancellor for sys. rels., 2004—. Editor: Wild Birds of America: The Art of Basil Ede, 1991, Centennial Memories, Millennial Hopes, 2000, The People's City, 2003. Bd. dirs. Ala. Humanities Found.; bd. dirs. Ala. Writers Forum, pres., 1999—2001. Recipient Druids Arts award, 1995, Betsy Plank Disting. Achievement award U. Ala., 2006. Mem. Soc. Profl. Journalists, Am. Soc. Mag. Editors, Newcomen Soc. U.S., Art Table, XXI/U. Ala. Women's Hon. Soc. Office: 401 Queen City Ave Tuscaloosa AL 35401-1551 Business E-Mail: kreinhar@uasystem.ua.edu.

REINHART, PETER SARGENT, lawyer; b. Mineola, NY, May 17, 1950; s. Charles Woodham and Martha Way (Sargent) R.; m. Susan Stockwell, Aug. 29, 1970 (div. Jan. 1976); 1 child, Amy Lynn; m. Gale McElroy, Oct. 16, 1976 (div. May 1985); 1 child, James Gharrett; m. Carol O. Gaffney, Jan. 4, 1992 (div. Jan. 2001); m. Nancy Jean Byrne, Nov. 4, 2006. BA, Franklin and Marshall Coll., 1971; JD, Rutgers U., 1975. Bar: N.J. 1975. Atty. Pillsbury and Russell, Atlantic Highlands, NJ, 1975-78; corp. counsel K. Hovnanian Enterprises, Inc., Red Bank, NJ, 1978-81, sr. v.p., gen. counsel, 1981—; also bd. dirs. Pres. Inst. Multi-Family Housing, Plainsboro, N.J., 1989-90. Trustee, mem. editorial bd. Housing N.J. mag., 1991—. Trustee Cmty. Assns. Inst., Arlington, Va., pres. NJ chpt., 1988; trustee Assn. for Children of NJ, Newark, 1988-93, Keep Middlesex Moving, New Brunswick, 1990-93, Bayshore Cmty. Hosp., Holmdel, NJ, 1992-01, v.p., 1995, chmn., 1997, Meridian Hosp. Corp., 2002—, vice chmn., 2007; chmn. Jersey Shore Partnership, 2003-; pres. Greater Red Bank Jaycees, 1978-79, Atlantic Highlands Rep. Club, 1978; v.p. Monmouth coun. Boy Scouts Am., Oakhurst, NJ, 1987-94, pres., 1994-95; v.p. Garden State Games, Edison, NJ, 1991-94; mem. Coun. Affordable Housing, Trenton, NJ, 1993-04. Named to Community Assns. Inst. Hall of Fame, 1988; named Jaycee of Yr. Greater Red Bank Jaycees, 1977. Mem. N.J. State Bar Assn., N.J. Shore Builders Assn. (pres. 1989-90, Builder of Yr. 1987, Hall of Fame 1991), Nat. Assn. Indsl. and Office Parks (bd. dirs. 1990-92), N.J. Builders Assn. (v.p. 1992-94, pres. 1995-96, Builder of Yr. award 1995, Shore Athletic Club (Oakhurst), Ea. Monmouth C. of C. (trustee 1992-98, Vol. of Yr. 1995). Avocations: road racing, marathon running, golf. Office: Hovnanian Enterprises Inc PO Box 500 110 West Front St Red Bank NJ 07701-5902

REINHART, RICHARD PAUL, lawyer; b. Cleve., Sept. 1, 1954; s. Richard A. and Carole F. (Kaspar) R.; m. Debra Rae Hitchcock, June 20, 1976; children: Geoffrey, Richelle Marie. BA with honors, Rollins Coll., 1976; JD with distinction, Emory U., 1979. Cert. circuit civil mediator: 2005. Ptnr. Morris, Manning & Martin, Atlanta, 1979-89; officer McMillen Reinhart and Voght, P.A., Orlando, Fla., 1989—2005; ret., 2005. Mem. Fla. Bar Assn., Ga. Bar Assn., Acad. Fla. Trial Lawyers, Order of Coif, Omicron Delta Kappa. Personal E-mail: richard.reinhart@gmail.com.

REINHART, ROBERT ROUNTREE, JR., lawyer; b. Chgo., Oct. 21, 1947; s. Robert Rountree and Ruth (Duncan) R.; m. Elizabeth Aileen Plews, July 26, 1969; children: Andrea Jean, Jessica Elizabeth, Rebecca Jill. BA, Northwestern U., 1968; JD, U. Mich., 1971. Bar: Ill. 1971, Mich. 1972, Minn. 1973, U.S. Supreme Ct. 1976. Law clk. to judge U.S. Dist. Ct. (we. dist.) Mich., Grand Rapids, 1971-73; assoc. Oppenheimer Wolff & Donnelly, Mpls., 1973-77, ptnr., 1978-96, chair labor and employment bus. group, 1985-92; ptnr. Dorsey & Whitney, Mpls., 1996—, chair labor and employment practice group, 2000—. Co-chmn. Upper Midwest Employment Law Inst., Mpls., 1984—; gen. counsel Minn. Empoyment Law Coun., 1990—. Mem. ABA (labor and employment, civil litigation sects.), Minn. Bar Assn. Office: Dorsey & Whitney Ste 1500 50 S 6th St Minneapolis MN 55402-1498 Office Phone: 612-340-7835. Office Fax: 612-340-2868. E-mail: reinhart.robert@dorseylaw.com.

REINHARZ, JEHUDA, academic administrator, history educator; b. Haifa, Israel, Aug. 1, 1944; came to U.S., 1961; s. Fred and Anita (Weigler) R.; m. Shulamit Rothschild, Nov. 26, 1967; children— Yael, Naomi BS, Columbia U., 1967; BRE, Jewish Theol. Sem., 1967; MA, Harvard U., 1968; PhD, Brandeis U., 1972; LHD (hon.), Hebrew Union Coll., 1995; DHL (hon.), Jewish Theol. Soc. Am., 1996, Fairfield U., 1999. Prof. modern Jewish history U. Mich., Ann Arbor, 1972—82; Richard Koret prof. modern Jewish history Brandeis U., Waltham, Mass., 1982—84, dir. Tauber Inst. Study of European Jewry, 1984—94; provost, sr. v.p. for acad. affairs Brandeis U., Waltham, Mass., 1992—94; pres. Brandeis U., Waltham, Mass., 1994—. Mem. internat. acad. bd. Annenberg Rsch. Inst., 1986-90; bd. dirs. Yad Chaim Weizmann, 1990-2000, Internat. Editl. Bd. Pardès, 1996—; pres. Israel Prize, 1990, Akiba award, Am.-Jewish Com., 1996. Author: Fatherland or Promised Land: The Dilemma of the German Jew 1893-1914, 1975, Chaim Weizmann: The Making of a Zionist Leader, 1985 (Present Tense Literary award 1985, Kenneth B. Smilen Literary award 1985, Nat. Jewish Book award 1986, Shazar prize in history Israel, 1988), (in Hebrew) Hashomer Hazair in Germany, 1931-39, 1989, Chaim Weizmann: The Making of a Statesman, 1993 (Nat. Jewish Book award 1994); also numerous articles in French, German, Hebrew and English; co-author: Zionism and the Creation of a New Society, 1998, 2d edit., 2000, The Era of Political Zionism, 2000; gen. editor: Studies in Jewish History, 1984, European Jewish History, 1985; co-editor: The Jew in the Modern World, 1980, 2d edit. 1995, Mystics, Philosophers and Politicians, 1982, Israel in the Middle East 1948-83, 1984, The Jewish Response to German Culture, 1985, The Jews of Poland Between Two World Wars, 1989, The Impact of Western Nationalisms, 1992, Zionism and Religion, Hebrew edit., 1994, Essential Papers on Zionism, 1996; editor: The Letters and Papers of Chaim Weizmann, 1918-20, 1977, Dokumente zur Geschichte des deutschen Zionismus, 1882-1933, 1981, Living with Antisemitism, 1987. Bd. govs. United Israel Appeal/Jewish Agy., 1994, 2000; bd. dirs., mem. exec. com. Am. Joint Distbn. Com., 1994-2002; mem. acad. com. U.S. Holocaust Mus., 1990-2003, mem. com. on conscience nat. adv. forum, 1996—; mem. Presdl. Adv. Commn. on Holocaust Assets in U.S., 1998-2000; mem. Commn. on Israel-Diaspora Rels., 1996-97; trustee Am. Hebrew Acad., Greensboro, N.C., 2000—. Recipient Akiba award, Am. Jewish Com., 1996. Fellow Leo Baeck Inst., Royal Hist. Soc., Am. Acad. Jewish Rsch., Am. Acad. Arts and Scis.; mem. Yad Vashem Soc. (adv. bd. 1983), Nat. Coun. Shazar Ctr., Assn. for Jewish Studies (sec. 1986-88, treas./sec., 1988-94), Coun. on Fgn. Rels. Home: 66 Beaumont Ave Newton MA 02460-2331 Office: Office Of The Pres Irving Enclave 113 415 South St # Ms100 Waltham MA 02453-9110 E-mail: jreinharz@brandeis.edu. *

REINHERZ, HELEN ZARSKY, social worker, researcher; b. Boston, Aug. 4, 1923; d. Zachary and Anna (Cohen) Zarsky; m. Samuel E. Reinherz, Aug. 29, 1943; 1 son, Ellis. AB magna cum laude, Wheaton Coll., 1944; MS, Simmons Coll., 1946; S.M., Harvard U., 1962, Sc.D., 1965. Social worker Newton Family Service, Mass., 1946-49, Mass. Gen. Hosp., Boston, 1949-51; supr. psychiat. social work State Hosp., Waltham, Mass., 1958-61; faculty mem. Simmons Coll., Boston, 1965—, prof. methods rsch., 1972—, dir. research Sch. Social Work, 1968-93, dir. PhD program, 1993-96. Prin. investigator Identifying Children at Risk, 1976—84, Adaption in Adolescence, 1987—93, Adult Rsch. Project, 1998—2001, Early Adulthood Rsch. Project, 1993—97, Simmons Longitudinal Study, 2001—, Study Adolescent Drug Abuse, 1971—73; rsch. cons. Dept. Mental Health, 1970—80; chmn. Gov.'s Adv. Coun. on Mental Health and Retardation, 1972; mem. adv. com. Mental Health Manpower fo Fed. Govt., 1980—82. Author (with H. Wechler, D. Dobbins): Social Work Research in the Human Services, 1976; author (with M. Heywood, J. Camp) A Community Response to Drug Abuse, 1976; cons., assoc. editor: Jour. Prevention, 1980—91, mem. fed. adv. com.: Rsch. in Prevention Rev., 1984—87, editl. bd.: Jour. Early Adolescence, cons. editor: NASW Jour.; contbr. articles to profl. jours. Recipient Maida H. Solomon award, Simmons Coll. Alumni, 1961, Disting. Career award, Soc. Social Work and Rsch., 2005, Rsch. Achievement award, NASW, 2005; grantee, Grant Found., 1963, Med. Found., 1967—69, NIMH, 1975—84, 1987—; NIH tng. fellow, 1961—65. Fellow Am. Orthopsychiat. Assn.; mem. Acad. Cert. Social Workers, Am. Pub. Health Assn., Coun. Social Work Edn., Harvard Sch. Pub. Health Alumni Assn. (sec.-treas. 1965-68), Phi Beta Kappa, Delta Omega. Home: 17 Corey Rd Malden MA 02148-1116 Office: Simmons Sch Social Work 300 The Fenway Boston MA 02115 Home Phone: 781-322-0228. Business E-Mail: helen.reinherz@simmons.edu, reinherz@simmons.edu. *As a teacher and researcher my efforts have been directed towards encouraging students to formulate the right questions about human problems as a first step to understanding and change.*

REINHOLD, JUDGE (EDWARD ERNEST REINHOLD JR.), actor; b. Wilmington, Del., May 21, 1957; m. Carrie Frazier, 1986 (div.); m. Amy Miller, Jan. 8, 2000. Student, Mary Washington Coll., N.C. Sch. of the Arts. Actor: (feature films) Running Scared, 1979, Stripes, 1981, Thursday the Twelfth, 1982, Pandemonium, 1982, Fast Times at Ridgemont High, 1982, Gremlins, 1984, Beverly Hills Cop, 1984, Roadhouse, 1985, Ruthless People, 1986, Head Office, 1986, Off Beat, 1986, Beverly Hills Cop II, 1987, Vice-Versa, 1988, Rosalee Goes Shopping, 1990, Daddy's Dyin'...Who's Got the Will, 1990, Zandalee, 1991, Beverly Hills Cop III, 1994, The Santa Clause, 1994, Last Lives, 1997, Homegrown, 1998, Floating Away, 1998, Big Monster on Campus, 1998, Wild Blue, 1999, (voice) Robots of Mars, 1999, Redemption High, 1999, Puss in Boots, 1999, My Brother the Pig, 1999, Walking Across Egypt, 1999, NewsBreak, 2000, Ping!, 2000, Wild Blue, 2000, Betaville, 2001, No Place Like Home, 2001, Hollywood Palms, 2001, Whacked!, 2002, The Santa Clause 2, 2002, (voice) Clifford's Really Big Movie, 2004, The Hollow, 2004, Checking Out, 2005, Crab Orchard, 2006, The Santa Clause 3: The Escape Clause, 2006; (TV episodes) Wonder Woman, Magnum P.I., Seinfeld, 1993 (Emmy nomination, Guest Actor - Comedy Series, 1994); (TV films) The Survival of Dana, 1979, Brothers and Sisters, A Step Too Slow, The Wilmar Eight, Booker, Promised a Miracle, Dad, the Angel, and Me, 1995, Right to Remain Silent, 1996, Runaway Car, 1997, Coming Unglued, 1999, NetForce, 1999, Dead in a Heartbeat, 2002, Thanksgiving Family Reunion, 2003; (TV series) Secret Service Guy, 1997. Mem. Screen Actors Guild, AFTRA. *

REINHOLD, RICHARD LAWRENCE, lawyer; b. Buffalo, Feb. 24, 1951; s. Richard J. and Ann J. R.; m. Beth Stacey Grossman, May 11, 1991; children: Elizabeth Jane, Eleanor Terese, Rebecca Hope. AB, Cornell U., 1973; JD, SUNY, Buffalo, 1976. Bar: NY 1977, Fla. 1977. With office of tax legis. counsel US Dept. Treasury, Washington, 1982-84; ptnr., chair tax dept. Willkie Farr & Gallagher LLP, NYC. Adj. faculty Sch. Law NYU. Contbr. articles to profl. jours. Bd. dirs. NYU Internat. Tax Program; mem. dean's adv. coun. sch. of law SUNY, Buffalo. Fellow Am. Coll. Tax Counsel; mem. ABA, NY State Bar Assn. (chair tax sect. 1996-97, mem exec. com. 1985-), Internat. Fiscal Assn., Tax Forum, Tax Club, Am. Alpine Club. Office: Willkie Farr & Gallagher 787 Seventh Ave New York NY 10019-6099 Office Phone: 212-728-8292. Office Fax: 212-728-9292. E-mail: rreinhold@willkie.com.

REINIGER, DOUGLAS HAIGH, lawyer; b. Mt. Kisco, NY, Nov. 8, 1948; s. Haigh McDiarmid and Virginia (Munson) R.; m. Margaret Vrablic, Aug. 31, 1968 (div. Jan. 1983); 1 child, Brian Christopher; m. Anne Fanning, Aug. 5, 1984. BA, Iona Coll., 1970; MSW, Fordham U., 1974, JD, 1980. Bar: NY 1981, Wyo. 1996, US Dist. Ct. (so. dist.) NY 1982, US Dist. Ct. (ea. dist.) NY 1991, US Dist. Ct. Wyo. 2006, US Supreme Ct 1986. Psychiat. aide St. Vincent's Psychiat. Hosp., Harrison, N.Y., 1968-69; child care worker Cardinal McCloskey Home for Children, White Plains, N.Y., 1969-71, social worker, 1971-75, dir. legal affairs, 1975-81; pvt. practice NYC, 1981-83; ptnr. Rosin & Reiniger, NYC, 1983—2002; assoc. prof. Sch. Social Work Columbia U., NYC, 1991-99, coord. law minor program, Sch. Social Work, 1994-99; ptnr. The Reiniger Law Firm, 2002—. Lectr. appellate divsn. NY Supreme Ct., NYC, 1985, 99, Fedn. Protestant Welfare, NYC, 1987-91, Ct. Apptd. Spl. Advs., NYC, 1987-94, 2007, Practicing Law Inst., NYC, 1988, 1999-01, 2004-07; chair PLI Adoption Law Inst., 2004, 05, 06, 07. Mem. ABA (family law sect., com. on adoption, com. on custody 1992-01), NY State Bar Assn. (lectr. 1988, 99, family law sect., com. on family ct., com. on adoption), Assn. Bar City NY (lectr. 1995, 99, com. on family law and family ct. 1985-88, com. on juvenile justice 1989-91, com. on children and the law 1993-97), Wyo. State Bar Assn. (family law sect. 2000-), Am. Acad. Adoption Attys. (lectr. 1995-96, 00-01, 06, 07, chmn. adoption agy. com. 1998-01, trustee 2000-05, pres.-elect 2002-03, pres. 2003-04), NY State Foster and Adoptive Parents Assn. (bd. dirs. 1992-01, lectr. 1992-01), NY County Lawyers Assn. (lectr. 1994-01). Roman Catholic. Office: 25 S Gros Ventre St Jackson WY 83001-1215 also: 630 Third Ave New York NY 10017 Office Phone: 307-690-6625. Business E-Mail: d.reiniger@adoptionattorneys.org.

REINIKE, IRMA, retired civilian military employee, writer, artist, poet, lyricist; b. White Harbor, Long Beach, Miss., Oct. 20, 1927; d. Chester Henry and Edna Claire (Latille) Reinike; children: Harvey Franklin Linn Shows Jr., George David Shows, Thelma Jewell Shows Hoffman. Student, St. Mary's Dominican Coll.; grad., North Light Art Sch., Cin., 1996, 97, 99. Freelance writer, student Famous Writers Sch., Westport, Conn., 1965—69; editor Seabee Courier, writer US Naval Contrn. Battalion Ctr., Gulfport, 1969—71; adminstr. US Army Corps. Engrs.; ret., 1994. Author: Mystery, 1940—41, Long Beach Movie Personality, 1949, My Beach, 1990, Thelma, 1991, (poetry) My Lady of Medjugorje, 1987—88, Irma Reinike Poetry-Book 1, 2002, I Love My Flag, 2000; columnist Round the

Town, Long Beach, Miss., 1963—66, The Illustrated Press, Irma Reinike's Personality Parade, New Orleans, 1952; composer: (songs) See You Tomorrow, 1995—96, Days of Love, 1997, The Blue of Your Eyes, 1997, I Am An American, 2006, No Tear Big Enough for Katrina, 2006, (plays) Ethel Chichester, Peg O' My Heart, Kaye Hamilton, Stage Door, 1949, Song, Dance Dixieland Minstrel and Variety Artists, 1950—52, Charity Performer, Le Petit Theatre de Vieux Carre' Sunday Salon, 1996, Destruction by Hurricane Camille, Times Picayune, 1970; Introduction Camille Book-Hurricane, 1969, Ten Acres, 1970—71, Sunrise Lake Ponchartrain, exhibitions include St. Thomas Parish, Long Beach, Miss., Baton Rouge Gallery, Le Petite Theatre, New Orleans, Mandeville, La., City Long Beach, Miss., 2005, Represented in permanent collections Nat. D-Day Museum, New Orleans, prin. works include Enjoying My Beach, The Road to... No. 1, The Road to... No. 2. Mem. La. Libr. Found. New Orleans Friends Pub. Libr., 1994—96; charter mem. World War II Monument Meml., Washington; mem. Nat. Rep. Senatorial Com., 1994—97, Nat. Rep. Congl. Com., 2000, Rep. Presdl. Task Force, 2007. Named Honored Author, La. Libr. Assn., 1994, 1996, La. State Libr., 1995, Friends Fest New Orleans Pub. Libr., 1994—96, Patron, Le Petit Theatre de Vieux Carre, 1996. Mem.: New Orleans Mus. Art. Republican. Roman Catholic. Avocations: fine arts, songwriting, poetry, lyricist, philosophy.

REININGHAUS, RUTH, retired artist; b. NYC, Oct. 4, 1922; d. Emil William and Pauline Rosa (Lazarik) R.; m. George H. Morales, Feb. 20, 1944; children: George James, Robert Charles; m. Allan Joseph Smith, May 28, 1960. Student, Hunter Coll., NYU, Nat. Acad. Sch. of Design, 1960-61, Frank Reilly Sch. of Art, 1963, Art Students League, 1964-68; studied oil painting, with Robert Beverly Hale and Robert Philips, with Morton Roberts and Frank Reilly, Robert Maione, with Rudy Colao. Instr. art Banker's Trust, N.Y.C., 1971-77, 79-99, Kittredge Club for Women, N.Y.C., 1971-98. Exhibited in group shows at Berkshire Art Mus., 1970s, Hammer Galleries, Inc., N.Y.C., 1974, Far Gallery, N.Y.C., 1974, Mufalli Gallery, N.Y. and Fla., 1983-90, Pen and Brush Club, 1985—, Petrucci Gallery, Saugerties, N.Y., 1988-94, Pastel Soc. Am., 1988—, John Lane Gallery, Rhinebeck, N.Y., 1992-97, Regianni Gallery, N.Y.C., 1994, Catherine Lorillard Wolfe Club, Salmagundi Club, Allied Artists Am., Heidi Newhoff Gallery, N.Y.C., Hudson Valley Art Assn., Knickerbocker Artists, N.Y.C., Pen & Brush Club Inc., Pastel Soc. Am., Heritage Mus.; represented in permanent collections at US Navy Art, US Coast Guard Art Program, Hon. Murtogh D. Guinness, Salmagundi Club; contbr. to popular mags. Active Navy Art Coop. and Liaison, Coast Guard Art Program. Recipient 3d prize in Oils, Murray Hill Art Show, 1959, 69; Washington Sq. Outdoor Art Exhibit scholar Nat. Acad., 1962, Frank Reilly Sch. Art, 1963, NYU, 1963, Talens award, 1963, Robert Lehman award, 1968, Richtone Artists award, 1968, Baker Brush award, 1969, Silver medal Excellence in Pastel Art Spirit Found., 2006, Helen G. Oehler award, 2006; Salmagund scholar, 1969; subject NBC TV show You Are an Artist, 1950s. Fellow: Hudson Valley Art Assn. (Claude Parson's Meml. award 1974), Am. Artists Profl. League (Claude Parsons Meml. award 1974, 2d prize oils 1992, 3d prize pastel 1993, Pres. award 1994, Hon. Mention award 2004); mem.: Navy Art Coop. and Liaison, Knickerbocker Artists (Flora B. Giffuni PSA Pres.' award 1990), Oil Pastel Assn. (Pen and Brush award 1987, Strathmore award 1989, Pen and Brush award 1990, Salmagundi Club award 1991), Allied Artists Am. (assoc.), Washington Sq. Outdoor Art Assn. (bd. dirs. 1983—90), Nat. Arts Club (Reciprocal) Artists Fellowship, Soc. Illustrators (hon. 1983—87), Pastel Soc. Am. (bd. dirs. 1988—90, J. Giffuni purchase award 1988, Pastel Soc. of West Coast award 1997), Coast Guard Art Program, Salmagundi Club N.Y. (pres. 1983—87, curator 1989—97, 2003—04, Philip Isenberg award 1974, Salmagundi Club prize 1985, Franklin B. Williams Fund prize 1987, Tom Picard award 1987, Mortimer E. Freehof award 1988, John N. Lewis award 1988—89, Medal of Honor 1989, Philip Isenberg award 1989—90, Helen S. Coes award 1990, Flora B. Giffuni Pres. award 1990, Thomas Moran award 1990, Samuel T. Shaw award 1990, Alphaeus Cole Meml. award 1991, Salmagundi award 1991, Alice B. McReynolds Meml. award 1991, Philip Isenberg award 1992, 1995, Harry Ballinger Meml. award 2000—01, Philip Isenberg award 2001, Jane Impastato award 2003, 1st prize John N. Lewis award 2004, John N. Lewis award 2004, Best in Show award 2004, Mortimer Freehof award 2005, Art Spirit Found. Silver medal for Excellence in Pastel 2006, 2d prize for Pastel 2006), Pen and Brush Club (Helen Slotman award 1986, OPA Internat. award 1987, Gene Alden Walker award 1988, Pen and Brush Solo award 1992, Margaret Sussman award 1996, 1998, Merit award 2000), Catharine Lorillard Wolfe Art Club (bd. dirs. 1987—97, Anna Hyatt Huntington award 1978, Coun. Am. Artists award 1985, Pastel award 1992, Still Life award 1993, 1st prize 2001, 2d prize in Pastel 2007), Alpha Delta Pi. Lutheran. Avocations: travel, technical illustration, oil, pastel and watercolor painting, collecting antique music boxes and watches. Home: 222 E 93rd St Apt 26A New York NY 10128-3758 Personal E-mail: reininghaus@netzero.com.

REINISCH, JOHN FERDINAND, plastic surgeon, educator; b. Holyoke, Mass., July 4, 1944; married; 4 children. AB, Dartmouth Coll., 1966, BS, 1968; MD, Harvard U., 1970. Intern U. Mich., Ann Arbor, 1970-71, resident, 1971-73, Tulane U., New Orleans, 1975-76, U. Va., Charlottesville, 1976-78; asst. prof. U. Mo., Columbia, 1978-82, U. So. Calif., LA, 1983-85, chmn., divsn. plastic surgery, 1984—94, assoc. prof., 1985—; head, plastic surgery divsn. Children's Hosp. LA. Examiner, Am. Bd. Plastic Surgery. Contbr. articles to profl. jours., chpts. to books. Recipient Leonard R. Rubin award, Am. Assn. Plastic Surgeons, 2004; Named one of LA's Best Doctors, LA mag. Fellow ACS. Featured in Vogue, Self, NY Times, McCalls, and on CNN, Leeza, NY Views, and Medical Miracles. Office: Plastic Surgery Children's Hosp LA 4650 W Sunset Blvd Los Angeles CA 90027-6062 also: 414 Camden Dr Ste 800 Beverly Hills CA 90210 Office Phone: 323-669-4544. Office Fax: 323-669-4106. *

REINISCH, JUNE MACHOVER, psychologist, educator, researcher; d. Mann Barnett and Lillian (Machover) R. BS cum laude, NYU, 1966; MA, Columbia U., 1970, PhD with distinction, 1976. Cert. in childhood edn. NY. Asst. prof. psychology Rutgers U., New Brunswick, N.J., 1975-80, assoc. prof. psychology New Brunswick, N.J., 1980-82, adj. assoc. prof. psychiatry, 1981-82; prof. psychology Ind. U., Bloomington, 1982-93, dir. Kinsey Inst. Rsch. in Sex, Gender, and Reprodn., 1982-93; prof. clin. psychology Sch. Medicine, Indpls., 1983-93; dir. emeritus Kinsey Inst., 1993—. Dir., prin. investigator Prenatal Devel. Projects, Copenhagen, 1976—, sr. rsch. fellow, trustee The Kinsey Inst., 1993—; pres. R2 Sci. Comms., Inc., Ind., NY, 1985—; vis. sr. rschr. Inst. of Preventive Medicine, Copenhagen Health Svcs., Kommunehospitalet, Copenhagen, 1994—; cons. SUNY; sr. cons. Mus. of Sex, NYC, 1998, dir. acquisitions and new exhbns., 2003-, v.p. sci. affairs, 2003; exec. dir. Health and Sci. Adv. Bd., 2004-. Author: The Kinsey Institute New Report on Sex, 1990, 94, pub. 8 fgn. edits.; editor, contbr. books Kinsey Inst. series; syndicated newspaper columnist: The Kinsey Report; contbr. rsch. reports, revs., articles to profl. jours.; appeared on TV shows including PBS, BBC, ABC and NBC sci. spls., Discovery, A&E, ABC & NBC Science Spls., 20/20, Oprah Winfrey, Geraldo Rivera, Charles Grodin, Montel Williams, Sally Jessy Rafael, Good Morning Am., Today Show, CBS This Morning; guest host TV shows including CNBC Real Personal, TalkLive, also fgn. appearances. Founders day scholar NYU, 1966; NIMH trainee, 1971-74; NIMH grantee, 1978-80, Ford Found. grantee, 1973-75, Nat. Inst. Edn. grantee, 1973-74, Erikson Ednl. Found. grantee, 1973-74, grantee Nat. Inst. Child Health and Human Devel., 1981-88, Nat. Inst. on Drug Abuse, 1989-95; recipient Morton Prince award Am. Psychopath. Assn., 1976, medal for 9th Dr. S.T. Huang-Chan Meml. Lectr. in anatomy Hong Kong U., 1988, Dr. Richard J. Cross award Robert Wood Johnson Med. Sch., 1991, Award First Internat. Conf. on Orgasm, New Delhi, 1991, Disting. Alumnae award Tchrs. Coll. Columbia U., 1992, award for su contbn. Profl. al Conocimiento dela Sexualidad Humana, Assn. Mexicana de Sexologia, Mexico City, 1996; named Regents lectr. UCLA, 1999. Fellow AAAS, APA, Am. Psychol. Soc., Soc. for Sci. Study Sex; mem. Internat. Acad. Sex Rsch. (charter), Internat. Women's Forum, NY Women's Forum Inc., Am. Assn. Sex. Educators, Counselors and Therapists, Sigma Xi. Avocations: travel, scuba diving, flying, skydiving. Office: Kinsey Inst Prenatal Devel Project Ind U Bloomington IN 47405 also: Mus Sex 233 Fifth Ave Ste 3B New York NY 10016 Office Phone: 212-689-6337, 718-373-2221. Business E-Mail: jreinisch@museumofsex.com.

REINISH, GLORIA BROOKS, electrical engineer, educator; b. Bklyn., July 23, 1925; d. Julius Benjamin and Celia Glickman Brooks; m. Martin David Reinish, 1948; children: Nancy Reinish Passow, Julie Brook Askins, James Charles. BSEE, Columbia U., NY, 1945, MSEE, 1948, D of Engring Sci. in Bioengineering, 1974. Mem. tech. staff Bell Telephone Lab., NYC, 1945—46; project. engr. Sperry Gyroscope Co., Lake Success, 1946—51; prof. elec. engring. Fairleigh Dickinson U., Teaneck, NJ, 1962—. Chair elec. engring. dept. Fairleigh Dickinson U., 1975—78, chair bioengring. program; cons. Medical Devices Panel FDA, 1976—86; dir. Matrix Instruments, Orangeburgh, NY, 1980—85. Contbr. numerous articles to profl. jours. Grantee Project Kaleidoscope grant, 2001. Fellow: Soc. Women Engrs.; mem.: Inst. Elec. & Electronic Engrs. (life), Tau Beta Pi (Women's Badge 1945), Sigma Xi. Achievements include patents for a new method of precision ranging; research in electrical stimulation of bone growth; being first woman to earn an engineering degree from Columbia University. Avocations: tennis, golf, piano, bridge, crossword puzzles. Office: Fairleigh Dickinson Univ 1000 River Rd Teaneck NJ 07666

REINIUS, MICHELE REED, executive recruiter; b. San Diego, Jan. 17, 1948; d. Wallace Alvin Reed and Dorothy Louise Austin; m. Robin Patric Reinius, Aug. 4, 1990; 1 child, Joselyn Ann Andrews. Supr. Asosa Personnel, Tucson, 1981-83; recruiter TAD Tech., Tucson, 1983-85; co-owner Migar Personnel, Tucson, 1985-90; mgr. Temps by Encore, Tucson, 1990-2000; pres. Ariz. Recruiting Source, Tucson, 2000—. Democrat. Jewish. Avocations: reading, swimming. Office: Ariz Recruiting Source 7483 E Broadway Tucson AZ 85710 Home Phone: 520-749-0298; Office Phone: 520-751-0067. Business E-Mail: michelereinius@reinius.com.

REINKE, DORIS MARIE, retired elementary school educator; b. Racine, Wis., Jan. 12, 1922; d. Otto William Reinke and Louise Amelia Goehring. BS, U. Wis., 1943, MS, 1967. Tchr. kindergarten Elkhorn Area Sch. Sys., Wis., 1943—69, prin. bldg., 1968—70, dir. summer sch., 1974—75, tchr. grade 2, 1970—84, chmn. primary dept., 1967—84, administrv. asst., supervising tchr., 1957—83, student tchr., 1984, ret., 1984; tchr. oriented experience Program Area Sch. Sys., Elkhorn, 1966. Pres. Elkhorn Edn. Assn., 1949-50; rep. dist. State Kindergarten Conf., Oshkosh, Wis., 1966; participant early edn. conf. State Early Edn. Conf., Eagle River, Wis., 1968; tchr. Covenant Harbor Elderhostel, 1997, 98; established Doris M. Reinke Resource Ctr., 2002. Author: Bit of History-Walworth County Historical Society Legacy, 1992—; author: (with Charlotte and William Gates) Guide to Beckwith's History of Walworth County, 2000; author: Images of America-Elkhorn, 2004; contbr. weekly newspaper column Webster Notes, 1989, monthly column in The Week, 1991. Chmn. Sch. Centennial, Elkhorn, 1987; mem. Elkhorn Hist. Preservation Com., 1991—; chmn. Sesquicentennial com., 1997—; dir. Webster House Mus., 1991—; mem. Walworth County Sesquicentennial Com., 1997—98; mem. sesquicentennial com. Walworth County Fair, 1998—; archivist Sugar Creek Luth. Ch., 1992—, mem. ch. coun., 2003, sec., 2005; choir mem. Luth. Ch., 1995—2001; del. dist. constn. conv. Evang. Luth. Ch. Am., Beloit, Wis., 1987; com. mem. Luth. Ch., Elkhorn, 1987, sec., 2005; RSVP Vol. Food Pantry, Elkhorn, 1985—2002, bd. dirs., 1985—88, 1995—. Recipient Wis. Edn. Rsch., West Bend, Wis., 1966, Outstanding Elem. Tchrs., Wash., 1973, Wis. Dept. Edn., Madison, 1980, Local History award State Hist. Soc. Wis., 1993, Outstanding Sr. Citizen award Walworth County Fair, 1999, Cmty. Svc. award Masons, 2000, Disting. Svc. award Rotary, 2004; named one of 50 Who Matter, Janesville Gazette, 2006, Vol. of Yr., Walworth County Area Ret. Educators Assn., 2006, DAR medal of Honor, 2007. Mem.: Walworth County Ret. Tchrs. Assn. (v.p. 1988, pres. 1991), Nat. Ret. Tchrs. Assn., Walworth County Geneal. Soc. (bd. dirs. 1991—92), Walworth County Hist. Soc. (treas. 1985—89, v.p. 1990—91, pres. 1991—96, v.p. 1999—2000, pres. 2000—05), Elkhorn Women's Club (sec. 1999—2000, v.p. 2003, pres. 2005—), Alpha Delta Kappa (state pres. 1968—70, 1976—78, chpt. pres. 2002—03). Avocations: reading, baseball, bird watching, travel. Home: 516 N Wisconsin St Elkhorn WI 53121-1119 Office Phone: 262-723-4248. Personal E-mail: walcohistory@elknet.net.

REINKE, MARK KEVIN, otolaryngologist; b. July 16, 1956; m. Katherine A. Reinke; children: Rhiannon, Robin, Rebecca, Rochelle, Ryan. BS, U. ND, Grand Forks, 1979; MD, Rush U., Chgo., 1992. Diplomate Am. Bd. Otolaryngology, 1998. Intern in gen. surgery U. Ill., Chgo., 1992—93, resident in otolaryngology, head and neck surgery, 1993—97; physician, owner NEW ENT, Green Bay, Wis., 1997—. Chmn. EENT surgery Bellin Hosp., St. Vincent Hosp., 1998—2002. Vol. Big Bros., ND and Calif., 1983—86; mem. Green Bay Symphony/Green Bay Youth Symphony, 1999—, Green Bay Area Salvation Army, 2001—; vol. ARC, 2002—; mem. coun. Ascension Luth. Ch., 2000—03. Capt. USAF, 1980—86. Recipient Suggestion award, USAF, 1985. Fellow: ACS, Am. Acad. Otolaryngologic Allergy, Am. Rhinologic Soc., Am. Bd. Otolaryngology; mem.: Wis. State Soc. Otolaryngology, Am. Laryngological, Rhinological and Otologic Soc., Am. Acad. Facial Plastic and Reconstructive Surgery, Mensa. Office: 923 Eliza St Green Bay WI 54301 Home: 807 Broadway De Pere WI 54115

REINKE, RALPH LOUIS, retired academic administrator; b. Elmhurst, Ill., June 22, 1927; s. Louis Fred and Malinda Marie (Beckmann) R.; m. Lois Hermine Borneman, Aug. 28, 1948 (dec. Mar. 1984); children: Janice Reinke Eisenloeffel, Stephan, Sharon Reinke Holaway; m. Carole Louise Rediehs, June 14, 1986 Student, U. Ill., 1945—46; BS, Concordia U., River Forest, Ill., 1949; MA, Northwestern U., 1952; postgrad., U. Chgo., 1956—63; LittD, Concordia Sem., 1972. Prin. St. John Elem. Sch., Houston, 1949-56; assoc. prof. psychology and edn. Concordia U., River Forest, Ill., 1956-68, CEO, 2003—04; pres., chief exec. officer Concordia Pub. House, St. Louis, 1968-86; pres. Concordia U., Seward, Nebr., 1986—90; ret., 1990; CEO Concordia U., Ill., 2002—04. Author: Christian Spelling Series, 2d edit, 1971. Mem. sch. bd. selecting com., Oak Park, Ill., 1965-67, chmn. lit. commn. Mo. Synod Luth. Ch., 1967-69; bd. dirs. Concordia U., 1992-2004, chair, 1999-2002. With USNR, 1944-46. Mem. Protestant Ch. Owned Pubs. Assn. (dir. 1969-84, pres. 1982-84), St. Louis Printing Assn. (bd. dirs. 1975-77), Am. Assn. Indsl. Mgmt. (bd. dirs. 1981-85), Assn. Ind. Colls. and Univs. of Nebr. (pres. 1988-89), Luth. Edn. Assn. (pres. 1967-69), Rotary, Phi Delta Kappa. Lutheran. Personal E-mail: rlreinke@aol.com. *Life is a most precious and finite gift of God to man. Those who would lead must make a commitment to devote their full energies and intellects to the improvement of the quality of life of their fellowmen. In the highest sense, leadership is the integrity to heed the quiet voice of conscience from within in the quest of that quality.*

REINKE, STEFAN MICHAEL, lawyer; b. Concord, Calif., May 7, 1958; s. Albert Richard and Patricia Eleanor (Stefan) R.; m. Lisa Elaine Williams, June 7, 1997. AA, Bakersfield Coll., 1978; AB, U. So. Calif., 1981; JD, U. Calif., Davis, 1984. Bar: Hawaii 1984, U.S. Dist. Ct. Hawaii 1984, U.S. Ct. Appeals (9th and Fed. cirs.) 1985. Assoc. Carlsmith, Wichman, Case, Mukai & Ichiki, Honolulu, 1984-86; dir. Lyons, Brandt, Cook & Hiramatsu, Honolulu, 1986—. Lectr. Windward C.C., 1995-98; lawyer rep. 9th Cir. Jud. Conf., 1995; lawyer rep. Jud. Conf. for the U.S. Dist. Ct. Hawaii, 1996-98, 2002-2004. Bd. dirs. Hawaii Ctrs. for Ind. Living, Honolulu, 1985-91, Prevent Child Abuse Hawaii, 1995-, v.p., 1999-2000, pres., 2000-2001. Mem. ABA, FBA (pres. Hawaii chpt. 1994-96, 98-99), Hawaii Bar Assn. (mem. jud. adminstrn. com.), Def. Rsch. Inst., Hawaii State Cycling Assn. (bd. dirs. 1998-2001), Phi Beta Kappa, Phi Alpha Delta. Office: Lyons Brandt Cook & Hiramatsu 841 Bishop St Ste 1800 Honolulu HI 96813-3992 Office Phone: 808-524-7030. Business E-Mail: sreinke@lbchlaw.com.

REINKE, SUSSANAH HOPE, music educator, coach; b. Oshkosh, Wis., May 17, 1981; d. Steven Edwin and Holly Elizabeth Reinke. MusB in Edn. magna cum laude, Northwestern Coll., St. Paul, Minn., 2004. Lic. vocal and classroom music K-12 tchg. Minn. Dept. Edn., initial-in-state choral and classroom music K-12 tchg. Wis. Dept. Edn. Volleyball coach Mahtomedi Area Volleyball Assn., Minn., 2001—05; voice and piano tchr. Son-Sheim Music Sch., Spring Lake Park, Minn., 2005—06, Keynote Sch. of Music, Shawano, Wis., 2006—; choral and gen. music educator Clintonville Mid. Sch., Wis., 2006—; varsity head volleyball coach Clintonville HS, Wis., 2006—. Piano accompanist, vocalist, Wis., 1999—; ch. musician Maranatha Bapt. Ch., Navarino, Wis., 2006—. Composer: (rec.) Breathe, 2005. Vol. mentor/tutor for underprivileged youth Kaleidoscope, Mpls., 2003; counselor, activist Minn. Citizens Concerned for Life, St. Paul, 2000—05; mission team vol. to orphanages in Jamaica Woodland Hills Ch., St. Paul, 2000; youth group leader, mentor Clintonville, 2006. Named to Volleyball Regional Champion Team, Wis. Interscholastic Athletic Assn., 2006; recipient Principles of Learning and Tchg. Recognition of Excellence award, ETS, 2004. Mem.: Nat. Assn. for Music Edn. (licentiate), Wis. Volleyball Coaches Assn. (assoc.). Avocations: travel, poetry, beach sand volleyball. Office: Clintonville Pub Sch Dist 255 N Main St Clintonville WI 54929-1154 Home Phone: 715-823-6661; Office Phone: 715-823-7215 2452. Business E-Mail: sureinke@clintonville.k12.wi.us.

REINKE, WILLIAM JOHN, lawyer; b. South Bend, Ind., Aug. 7, 1930; s. William August and Eva Marie (Hein) R.; m. Sue Carol Colvin, 1951 (div. 1988); children: Sally Sue Taelman, William A., Andrew J.; m. Elizabeth Beck Lockwood, 1991. AB cum laude, Wabash Coll., 1952; JD, U. Chgo., 1955. Bar: Ind. 1955. Assoc. Barnes & Thornburg and predecessors, South Bend, Ind., 1957-61, ptnr., 1961—, of counsel, 1996—, former chmn. compensation com. Mem. mgmt. com. Barnes & Thornburg and predecessors. Trustee Stanley Clark Sch., 1969-80, pres., 1977-80; life mem. adv. bd. Salvation Army, 1973—, pres., 1990-92; bd. dirs. NABE Mich. chpt., 1990-94, pres. 1993-94, Isaac Walton League, 1970-81; bd. dirs. United Way, 1979-81; pres. South Bend Round Table, 1963-65; trustee First Meth. Ch., 1976-70, 2005; bd. dirs. So. Bend Civic Theatre, 1997-2003. With U.S. Army, 1955-57. Recipient Outstanding Local Pres. award Ind. Jaycees, 1960-61, Boss of Yr. award, 1979, South Bend Outstanding Young Man award, 1961. Mem. ABA, Ind. State Bar Assn., St. Joseph County Bar Assn., Ind. Bar Found. (patron fellow), Am. Judicature Soc., Summit Club (founders com.), Rotary (bd. dirs. 1970-73, 94-97). Home: 51795 Waterton Square Cir Granger IN 46530-8317 Office: Barnes & Thornburg 1st Source Bank Ctr 100 N Michigan St Ste 600 South Bend IN 46601-1632 Office Phone: 574-233-1171.

REINKER, MARY STEFANICH, musician, educator; b. Joliet, Ill., Aug. 12, 1947; d. Anthony Edward and Mary Vidmar Stefanich; m. Myron Edward Reinker, Oct. 20, 1984; children: Meryt Antonia Reinker Dean, Molly Elizabeth. MusB, U. St. Francis, Joliet, IL, 1969; MusM, Roosevelt U., Chicago, Ill., 1971. Teaching Certificate Chgo. Bd. of Edn., 1972. Organist St. John's Ch., Joliet, Ill., 1958—65; tchr. Chgo. Pub. Schools, 1971—84; pianist/organist St. Edward's Ch., Dana Point, Calif., 1989—94, Gloria Dei Ch., Dana Point, Calif., 1985—89, St. Frances Cabrini Ch., Littleton, Colo., 1994—, St. Mary's Ch., Littleton, Colo., 2004—; private piano instr. Laguna Beach & Dana Point, 1984—94; founder/dir. Forte Acad. of Music, Littleton, Colo., 1997—, Centennial, Colo., 2004—; organist St. Mary's Chamber Orchestra, 2005—. Clinician & pedagogy advisor Colo. State Music Teachers Assn., Colo., 1996—, Forte Acad. of Music, Littleton, Colo., 1997—. Musician: (performance) Requiem by John Rutter; musician: (organist/pianist) St. Peter's Basilica, Rome, Salzburg Music Festival (Medal, 2002), St. Mark's Cathedral, Notre Dame, Chartres; organist (performance) Cathedrals of Madrid and Barcelona. Vol. St. Frances Cabrini Ch., Littleton, Colo., 1994—2004; vol. for local retirement and nursing homes Littleton, Colo., 1995—2004. Scholar Ill. State Scholarship, State of Ill., 1965. Mem.: Music Teachers Assn. of Calif., Colo. State Music Teachers Assn., Music Teachers Nat. Assn., Delta Mu Theta Music Honor Soc. Avocations: horseback riding, travel, reading. Office: Forte Acad Music 10143 W Chatfield Ave Ste 15 Littleton CO 80127 Home Phone: 303-978-9363; Office Phone: 303-948-9221 ext. 305. Personal E-mail: maryreinker@qwest.net. Business E-Mail: forteacademy@att.net.

REINKING, ANN H., dancer, actress; b. Seattle, Nov. 10, 1949; d. Walter Floyd and Francis Holmes (Harrison) R.; m. Larry Small, 1970; m. Herbert A. Allen; Aug. 25, 1982; (stepchildren): Leslie, Christie, Herbert, Charlie. Student public schs. Guest tchr. NYU, Duke U., Durham, N.C., Rutgers, N.J., Harvard, Cambridge, Mass.; choreographer Pal Joey, Goodman Theater, Chgo., 1988. Broadway appearances include Coco, 1970, Wild and Wonderful, 1972, Pippin, 1973, Over Here, 1974, Goodtime Charlie, 1975, Chicago, 1977, A Chorus Line, 1976, Dancin', 1978, Sweet Charity, 1986-87; TV appearances include Ellery Queen, Doug Henning: Magic on Broadway, 1982, Parade of Stars, 1983, American Treasury, 1985, Salute to Jules Styne, Broadway Salutes Washington, An Introduction to the Dance Gala of the Stars; film appearances include Movie, Movie, 1978, All That Jazz, 1979-80, Annie, 1982, Micki and Maude, 1984; play Ann Reinking-...Music Moves Me, 1984; actor, choreographer Broadway shows: Chicago, 1996 (Tony award 1997), Annie Get Your Gun, 1999 (Tony award 1999), Fosse, 2001; choreographer Broadway shows: Annie Get Your Gun, 1999, Look of Love, 2003 Recipient Clarence Derwent award, 1974, Outer Critics Circle award, 1974, Theatre World award, 1974, Dance Educators Am. award, 1979, Harkness Dance award, 1979, two Tony award nominations, Tony award for Choregraphy, 1997; Ford Found. scholar, 1964-66, Hero With a Heart award Nat. Marfan Found., 2007; Robert Joffery scholar, 1967; Harkness scholar; Nat. Dance Educators award. Mem. Actors Equity, AFTRA, Stage Actors Guild. Avocations: horseback riding, skiing, swimming, hiking. also: Steps Contemporary & Classical Dance 2121 Broadway Fl 3 New York NY 10023-1786 *

REINLEITNER, KATHERINE MINDLIN, psychologist, foundation administrator; b. Scarsdale, NY, May 10, 1948; m. Theodore B. Day, Aug. 25, 1968 (div. Sept. 1980); children: Eleanor Day, T. Eugene Day, Jennifer Day, David A.; m. Lee A. Reinleitner, Sept. 15, 1990; children: Mark A., Paul H. BA, Barnard Coll., 1967; MA, Columbia U., 1968; PhD, U. Wash., 1974. Diplomate Am. Bd. Psychopharmacology and Forensic Psychology, Am. Bd. Advanced Practice Psychologists. Intern Astor Home for Children, Reinbeck, NY; psychologist Children's Hosp., Seattle, 1974-83; pvt. practice, Mercer Island and Bellevue, 1976-2000; pvt. practice Bainbridge Island, 1983—2000; adminstr. The Mindlin Found., Bellevue, 1994—. Lectr., asst. prof. U. Wash., 1975-83; gov.'s coun. on abuse and neglect State of Wash., Olympia, 1978-80; bd. dirs. Prescribing Psychologists Register, 1996—, curriculum com., 1996—. Author childrens books; author: What To Do After You've Seen the Zoo, 1983. Tng. fellowship I and IV, VA, 1970-71, 73-74, NIMH, 1969-70. Mem. AAAS, Internat. Coll. of Prescribing Psychologists, Am. Psychol. Assn., Wash. State Psychol. Assn. Achievements include patents for (with Michael Harrington) water sanitizing system. Office Phone: 425-246-8584. Personal E-mail: drkathyday@aol.com.

REINMAN, GLENN D., computer scientist, educator; b. Miami, Fla., Sept. 1, 1974; s. Raymond Rodney and Helene Reinman; m. Terry Soossani Reinman, July 7, 2002. BS in Computer Sci. and Engring., MIT, Cambridge, 1996; MS in Computer Sci., U. Calif., San Diego, 1999, PhD in Computer Sci., 2001. Prof. dept. computer sci. UCLA, LA, 2001—. Contbr. articles to profl. jours. Recipient TA Excellence award, U. Calif. San Diego, 1996—97, CAREER Award, NSF, 2001—06, Excellence in Tchg. award, Northrop Grumman, 2004; grantee ITR: Reconfigurable Fabric, NSF, 2002—05; Microarchitectural Evaluation with Phys. Planning grantee, U. Calif. Micro, 2003—04. Mem.: IEEE. Achievements include patents pending for. Office: UCLA Computer Science Dept 4731 D Boelter Hall Los Angeles CA 90095 Business E-Mail: reinman@cs.ucla.edu.

REINOEHL, RICHARD LOUIS, artist, scholar, martial artist; b. Omaha, Oct. 11, 1944; s. Louis Lawrence and Frances Margaret (Robinson) R.; 1 child, Joy Margaret Iroff-Reinoehl. BS in Sociology, Portland State U., 1970; MSW, U. Minn., Duluth, 1977; postgrad., Cornell U., 1984-88. Acting dir. Vanguard Group Homes, Virginia, Minn., 1976-77; dir. Minn. Chippewa Tribe Group Home, Duluth, 1978, Human Devel. Consortium, Minn., N.Y., Ohio, 1978—; coord. NE Ohio Green Libertarian Partys' Vote Recount Observation Teams, 2004. Faculty Social Work Program U. Wis., Superior, 1981-84, Bohecker Coll., 2005—; adv. bd. Computers in Social Svcs. Network, 1982-85; mem. Com. on Internat. Social Welfare Edn., 1982-86, Am. Evaluation Assn., 1986-89; affiliate scholar Oberlin Coll., 1991—; artist-in-residence Ohio Arts Coun., 1996-97. Editor: Computer Literacy in Human Services Education, 1990, Computer Literacy in Human Services, 1990, Men of Achievement, 16th edit., 1993; mem. editl. bd. Computers in Human Svcs., 1983-96, 99, Jour. Technology in Human Svcs., 1999—; assoc. editor book rev., 1996-99; contbr. numerous articles to profl. jours. Mem. Legis. Task Force Regional Alcoholism Bd., 1972-73, Assn. Drug Abuse, Prevention and Treatment, 1973-74, Minn. Pub. Health Assn., 1976-78, Minn. Social Svc. Assn., 1976-83, Wis. Coun. Social Work Edn., 1983-84, N.Y. State Coun. Family Rels., 1986-89, Nat. Coun. Family Rels., 1986-89; exec. bd. Duluth Community Action Program, 1982-83; Dem. precinct chair, Portland, Oreg., 1972-74; precinct vice-chair Dem. Farmer-Labor Party, Duluth, 1979-81, chair, 1981-83, 2d vice-chair exec. bd., 1981-83; mem. Zoning Appeals Bd., New Russia Twp., Ohio, 1996—; mem. art edn. com. Fireland Assn. Visual Arts, 1996-99; mem. land use planning com. New Russia Twp., Ohio, 1998—; chair Lorain County Comprehensive Plan Growth Mgmt. Com., 1999—; mem. Smart Devel. Coalition of Lorain County, 1998—, Lorain County Multi-Modal Transp. Planning Steering Com., 2000—, airport subcom., 2000—, roadways sub-com., 2000—, transit subcom., 2000—, info. tech. sub-com., 2000—; field spl. projects field coord., nat. coord. rural issues Kucinich for Pres. campaign, 2003-; chmn. Smart Devel. Coalition Lorain County, 1996-98, Lorain County Growth Mgmt. Com., mem. Environ. Sub.-Com., 1997-98; mem. Lorain County Multi-Modal Transp. Plan Steering Com., sub-coms. transit, roadways, airports, rail, and info. tech., 1999-2001, New Russia Township Zoning Bd. Appeals, 1995-2000, New Russia Township Land Use Planning Com., 1996-98; coord. Ohio Voters Reform, 2005—. Mem. NASW (exec. com., chair program com. Arrowhead Region Minn. chpt., 1980-81, co-chair task force on computers in social work, 1981-82), Acad. Cert. Social Workers, Cornell U. Sailing Club (pres. 1990). Avocations: canoeing, antique volkswagens, wilderness hiking. Office Phone: 440-315-0121. *It's noteworthy that the most sought-after items in a society cannot be bought or sold. Included are wisdom, respect, generosity, truthfulness, and the love of family and friends.*

REINOLD, CHRISTY DIANE, school counselor, consultant; b. Neodasha, Kans., July 21, 1942; d. Ernest Sherman and Faye Etta (Herbert) Wild; m. William Owen Reinold, Dec. 20, 1964; children: Elizabeth, Rebecca. BA Edn., Calif. State U., Fresno, 1964, MA in Edn. and Psychology, 1964. Cert. counselor, Family Wellness instr.; lic. mental health counselor, Fla. Tchr. Clovis (Calif.) Unified Sch. Dist., 1965-66, Santa Clara (Calif.) Unified Sch. Dist., 1966-67, Inst. Internat. Chateaubriand, Cannes, France, 1968-69; tchr., vice prin. Internat. Sch., Sliema, Malta, 1969-70; elem. sch. counselor Duval City Schs., Jacksonville, Fla., 1977-82, Lodi (Calif.) Unified Sch. Dist., 1982—2004. Cons. Calif. Dept. Edn.; mem. Calif. Commn. on Tchr. Credentialing, Sacramento, 1986—2004, mem. adv. panel, 1998—2004; mem. stds. rev. com. Nat. Bd. Cert. Sch. Counselors, 2002—. Co-author: The Best for Our Kids; Counseling in the 21st Century; contbr. articles. Chmn. bd. dirs. Oak Crest Child Care Ctr., Jacksonville, 1979-81. Named Anne Upton Sch. Counselor of Yr. for Calif., Calif. Sch. Counselor's Assn., 1995; named to H.B. McDaniel Hall of Fame, Stanford U., 2003; recipient H.B. McDaniel Individual award, 1986, James Saum Legis. award, Calif. Sch. Counselor's Assn., 1991, Donald Hayes Lifetime Achievement award, Assn. Calif. Sch. Counselors, 2002. Mem.: AAUW (3rd v.p. 1974, 1st v.p. 1980, by-laws chmn. 1990, chmn. pub. policy 1991—93, pres. 1993), Lodi Pupil Pers. Assn. (pres. 1986—87), Calif. Alliance Pupil Svcs. Orgns. (bd. dirs. 1988—95), Fla. Sch. Counselors Assn., Calif. Assn. Counseling and Devel., Calif. Sch. Counselor Assn. (legis. chmn. 1985—90, pres. 1991), Am. Sch. Counselor Assn. (govt. rels. specialist 1993—94). Republican. Avocations: history, travel, politics. Home: 1772 Le Bec Ct Lodi CA 95240 Personal E-mail: creinold@earthlink.net.

REINSCH, WILLIAM ALAN, association executive, educator; b. Evanston, Ill., Jan. 15, 1946; s. Bert and Kathleen (Penn) R.; m. Susan Polley Reinsch, Jan. 3, 1970; children: Andrew, Christian. BA, Johns Hopkins U., 1968; MA in Internat. Rels., Johns Hopkins U.-Sch. Advanced Internat. Studies, 1969. Legis. asst. Congressman Gilbert Gude, Washington, 1973-76, Congressman Richard Ottinger, Washington, 1976; chief legis. asst. Senator John Heinz, Washington, 1977-91; legis. asst. Senator John D. Rockefeller IV, Washington, 1991-93; cons., under sec. for export adminstrn. Dept. Commerce, Washington, 1994-2001; pres. Nat. Fgn. Trade Coun., Washington, 2001—; mem. U.S.-China Econ. and Security Rev. Commn., 2001—. Tchr. Landon Sch., Bethesda, Md., 1968-73; acting staff dir. Environ. Study Conf. U.S. Ho. Reps., 1976; bd. dirs. KHI Svcs. Contbr. articles to profl. jours. Bd. dirs. Middle East Inst. Mem. Phi Beta Kappa, Omicron Delta Kappa, Alpha Delta Phi. Democrat. Presbyterian. Office: Nat Fgn Trade Coun 1625 K St NW Ste 200 Washington DC 20006 E-mail: breinsch@nftc.org.

REINSCHMIDT, KENNETH FRANK, engineering and construction executive, educator; b. Cin., Mar. 26, 1938; s. Christian Edward and Martha Marie (Kellerman) R.; m. Marlene Faye Taub, Dec. 16, 1967. BSCE, MIT, 1960, MSCE, 1962, PhD in Engring., 1965. Assoc. prof. civil engring. MIT, Cambridge, 1965-75; sr. v.p. Stone & Webster Engring. Corp., Boston, 1975-93, also bd. dirs.; pres. Stone & Webster Advanced Systems Devel. Svcs., Boston, 1988-96; bd. dirs. Stone & Webster Advanced Tech. Applications Inc., NYC, 1990-94; sr. v.p. Stone & Webster, Inc., 1993-96; ind. cons., 1996—2001; prof. civil engring., J.L. Frank/Marathon Ashland Petroleum LLP chair in engring. project mgmt. Tex. A&M U., College Station, 2001—; J.L. Frank/Marathon Ashland Petroleum LLC chair in engring. project mgmt. Tex. A & M U., 2001—. Chmn. com. on oversight of Ctr. for Bldg. Tech., Nat. Inst. Standards and Tech., Gaithersburg, Md., 1986-89; adj. prof. civil engring. Tex. A&M U., College Station, 1997-98, vis. prof., 1998-99; chmn. com. to assess policies and procedures of Dept. Energy to design, manage and procure environ. restoration, waste mgmt. and other constrn. projects NRC, 1998-99, Nat. Rsch. coun. com. on oversight and assessment U.S. Dept. Energy Project Mgmt., 2000—. Author: Stress: A User's Manual, 1963; editor: Systems Building, 1974; contbr. numerous articles to profl. jours. Capt. U.S. Army, 1966-67. Decorated Legion of Merit; NSF fellow, 1962. Fellow AAAS; mem. NAE, ASCE, INFORMS. Office: Tex A&M U Dept Civil Engring CE/TTI Bldg Rm 702A 3136 TAMU College Station TX 77843-3136 Office Phone: 979-845-8599. Business E-Mail: kreinschmidt@civil.tamu.edu.

REINSDORF, JERRY MICHAEL, professional sports team owner, real estate company executive, accountant, lawyer; b. Bklyn., Feb. 25, 1936; s. Max and Marion (Smith) Reinsdorf; m. Martyl F. Rifkin, Dec. 29, 1956; children: David Jason, Susan Janeen, Michael Andrew, Jonathan Milton. BA, George Washington U., 1957; JD, Northwestern U., 1960. CPA Ill., registered mortgage underwriter; bar: DC, Ill. 60; cert. specialist real estate securities, rev. appraiser. Atty. staff regional counsel IRS, Chgo., 1960—64; assoc. law firm Chapman & Cutler, 1964—68; ptnr. Altman, Kurlander & Weiss, 1968—74; of counsel Katten, Muchin, Gitles, Zavis, Pearl & Galler, 1974—79; gen. ptnr. Carlyle Real Estate Ltd. Partnerships, 1971—72; chmn. bd. Balcor Co., 1973—87; mng. ptnr. TBC Films, 1975—83; chmn. Chgo. White Sox, 1981—, Chgo. Bulls, 1985—; ptnr. Bojer Fin., 1987—. Lectr. John Marshall Law Sch., 1966—68; bd. overseers Inst. Civil Justice, 1996—98; lectr. real estate, sports and taxation. Author (with L. Herbert Schneider): Uses of Life Insurance in Qualified Employee Benefit Plans, 1970. Mem. Chgo. region bd. Anti-Defamation League, 1986—2001; mem., trustee Ill. Inst. Tech., 1991—96; mem. Ill. Commn. on African-Am. Males, 1992—; bd. dirs. Chgo. Youth Success Found., 1992—, Corp. for Supportive Housing, 1995—; nat. trustee Northwestern U., 1993—2005, bd. govs., 1993—2005, Hugh O'Brian Youth Found.; mem. internat. adv. bd. Barrow Neurol. Found., 1996—97; active Chgo. Baseball Cancer Charities, 1994, 1998; bd. trustees Equity Office Properties, 1997—2004. Named Sportsman of Yr., Nat. Italian-Am. Sports Hall of Fame, 2006; named to B'nai B'rith Nat. Jewish Am. Sports Hall of Fame, 1994, Chgo. Sports Hall of Fame, 1997; recipient Hallmark award, Chgo. Baseball Cancer Charities, 1986, Corp. Superstar award, Ill. chpt. Cystic Fibrosis Found., 1988, Sportsman of Yr. award, 1994, Chicagoan of Yr. award, Chgo. Park Dist., 1990, Kellogg Excellence award, 1991, Cmty. Hero award, Interfaith Organizing Project, 1991, Operation Push Bridgebuilder award, 1992, Alumni Merit award, Northwestern U., 1992, Ellis Island Medal of Honor award, Nat. Ethnic Coalition of Orgns., 1993, Lifetime Achievement award, March of Dimes, 1994, Hallmark Hall of Fame Civic award, Ind. Sports Charities, 1994, Am. Spirit award, USAF, 1995, Alpha Epsilon Pi Arthur and Simiteich Outstanding Alumnus award, 1995, Order of Lincoln, 1997, Mayor's medal Hon., 1997, Bklyn. Businessman of Yr., 1997, Guardian of Children award, Jewish Coun. for Youth Svc., 1998, Amb. award, Keshet, 2005, Nat. Humanitarian award, Nat. Conf. Cmty. and Justice, 2006, Merit award, Decalogue Soc., 2007, History Maker award, Chgo. Hist. Soc., 2007. Mem.: FBA, ABA, Nat. Sports Lawyers Assn., Chgo. Bar Assn., Ill. Bar Assn., Northwestern U. Law Sch. Alumni Assn. (bd. dirs.), Order of Coif, Comml. Club Chgo., Omega Tau Rho. Achievements include owner, MLB World Series Champions, 2005. Office: Chgo White Sox 333 W 35th St Chicago IL 60616-3651 Office Phone: 312-674-5200.

REINSDORF, JUDITH A., lawyer; b. 1963; BA in Polit. Sci., magna cum laude, U. Rochester; JD, Cornell U. Bar: NY 1990. With Crowell & Morling, Washington; asst. gen. counsel to chief legal counsel Monsanto Co.; v.p., assoc. gen. counsel Pharmacia Corp., 2000—03; v.p., corp. sec. Tyco Internat. Ltd., Princeton, NJ, 2003—04; v.p., gen. counsel, corp. sec. C.R. Bard, Inc., Murray Hill, NJ, 2004—. Mem.: ABA. Office: CR Bard Inc 730 Central Ave New Providence NJ 07974

REINSTEIN, JOEL, lawyer; b. NYC, July 23, 1946; s. Louis and Ruth Reinstein; children: Lesli, Louis, Mindy. BSE, U. Pa., 1968; JD cum laude, U. Fla., 1971; LLM in Taxation, NYU, 1974. Bar: Fla. 1971, U.S. Tax Ct. 1973, U.S. Dist. Ct. (so. dist.) Fla. 1976. Atty., office of chief counsel IRS, 1971-74; ptnr. Capp, Reinstein, Kopelowitz and Atlas, P.A., Ft. Lauderdale, Fla., 1975-85; dir., ptnr. Greenberg, Traurig, Hoffman, Lipoff, Rosen & Quentel, P.A., Ft. Lauderdale, 1985-92; gen. counsel Internat. Magnetic Imaging, Inc., Boca Raton, Fla., 1992-94; prin. Law Offices of Joel Reinstein P.A., Boca Raton, 1993—. Lectr. Advanced Pension Planning, Am. Soc. C.L.U.s; lectr. in field. Mem. editl. bd. U. Fla. Law Rev. 1970-71; contbr. articles to profl. jours. Mem. Fla. Bar Assn. (tax sect.), ABA (tax sect.), Order of Coif, Phi Kappa Phi, Phi Delta Pi. Office: 925 S Federal Hwy Ste 325 Boca Raton FL 33432 Office Phone: 561-393-6714. E-mail: joel@reinsteinlaw.com.

REINSTEIN, ROBERT J., dean, law educator; b. Balt., Mar. 17, 1945; m. Mary Taylor Aspinwall; children: Ellen, Thomas. BS in Engring. Physics with distinction, Cornell U., 1965; JD cum laude, Harvard U., 1968. Bar: Md. 1969, Pa. 1982, U.S. Supreme Ct. 1971. Law clk. to Hon. Frank A. Kaufman U.S. Dist. Ct. Md., 1968-69; from asst. prof. to assoc. prof. Sch. Law Temple U., Phila., 1969-73, prof. Sch. Law, 1973—; sr. atty. appellate sect. Civil Rights Divsn., U.S Dept. Justice, 1977-78, chief litigation sect., 1979-80; chief legal officer Temple U., 1982-89, dean Sch. Law, 1989—. Vis. prof. law Hastings Coll. Law, San Francisco, 1975, Georgetown U., 1978-79; cons. atty. NAACP Spl. Contbn. Fund, 1970-77. Contbr. articles to profl. jours. Chair civil rights com. B'nai Brith Anti-Defamation League, Phila. Recipient Friendship Award, People's Rep. China, 2002. Mem. ABA, Pa. Bar Assn. Office: Temple U Sch Law 1719 N Broad St Philadelphia PA 19122-6002 E-mail: robert.reinstein@temple.edu.

REINTHALER, RICHARD WALTER, lawyer; b. NY, Feb. 27, 1949; s. Walter F. and Maureen C. (Tully) R.; m. Mary E. Maloney, Aug. 8, 1970; children: Brian, Scott, Amy. BA in Govt. magna cum laude, U. Notre Dame, 1970, JD summa cum laude, 1973. Bar: N.Y. 1974, U.S. Dist. Ct. (so. and ea. dists.) N.Y. 1974, U.S. Ct. Appeals (2d cir.) 1974, U.S. Ct. Appeals (9th cir.) 1976, U.S. Supreme Ct., 1977, U.S. Ct. Appeals (5th cir.) 1978, U.S. Ct. Appeals (11th cir.) 1981, U.S. Ct. Appeals (1st cir.) 2004, U.S. Ct. Appeals (3d cir.) 2005. Assoc. White & Case, NYC, 1973—81, ptnr., 1981—95, Dewey Ballantine LLP, NYC, 1995—, co-chmn. litigation dept., 2002—03. Mem. adv. group U.S. Dist. Ct. (ea. dist.) N.Y., 1992-2004, chairperson subgroup on ethics, 1993-2000. Contbr. articles to profl. jours. Served to 1st lt. US Army, 1974. Fellow Am. Bar Found.; mem. ABA (2d cir. chmn. discovery com. 1982-87, program coord. 1986, ann. meeting litigation sect., vice chmn. com. on fed. procedure 1988-89, co-chmn. com. on profl. responsibility 1989-92, vice chmn. securities litigation com. 1993-94, vice chair Hong Kong meeting 1995, co-chair energy litigation com. 1996-97, co-chair antitrust litigation com. 1997-2000, mem. Ethics 2000 task force 1999-2000), N.Y. State Bar Assn., Assn. of Bar of City of N.Y. (mem. com. to enhance diversity in the profession 1990-95, mem. Orison S. Marden Meml. Lectrs. com. 1994-2000, chair 1997-2000, spl. com. on mergers, acquisitions and corp. control contests 1995-2002), Scarsdale Golf Club (Hartsdale, N.Y., bd. govs. 1994—2003, pres. 2002-2003), Capital Hill Club (Washington). Republican. Roman Catholic. Avocations: golf, tennis. Office: Dewey Ballantine LLP 1301 Avenue Of The Americas New York NY 10019-6022 Office Phone: 212-259-6090.

REINTZEL, WARREN ANDREW, trust company executive; b. Phila., Jan. 4, 1945; s. Warren H. and Lorna (Geibel) R.; m. Susan Rodgers, Dec. 20, 1969; children: Lisa S., Kurt W. BA with high honors, U. Del., 1967; MA in History, Rutgers U., 1968; JD, U. Pa., 1971. Trust adminstrn. trainee First Pa. Bank, Phila., 1971, trust adminstr., 1972-73, trust officer, 1973-79, sr. trust officer, 1979-81; v.p. Provident Nat. Bank, Phila., 1981-86; v.p., head trust adminstrn. dept. Glenmede Trust Co., Phila., 1986—, sr. v.p., 1994—. Trustee Wanamaker Inst., Phila., 1986—, 1st v.p., 1995-2000, pres., 2000-; trustee Meml. Fund, Luth. Ch. of our Saviour, Haddonfield, N.J., 1989-2000, Haddonfield Hist. Soc., 1997—, Haddonfield Cmty. Found., 1998-. Mem. Phila. Bar Assn., Phila. Fin. Assn. (treas. bd. trustees 1987-89), Phila. Estate Planning Coun. (trustee 1991, sec. 1994-95, treas. 1995-96, v.p. 1996-97, pres. 1997-98), Corp. Fiduciaries Assn. Phila. (mem. personal trust com. 1986-89, pres. 1996-98), Phi Beta Kappa. Republican. Office: Glenmede Trust Co 1650 Market St Ste 1200 Philadelphia PA 19103-7391 E-mail: warren_reintzel@glenmede.com.

REINUS, JOHN F., hepatologist, medical educator; b. NYC, Jan. 4, 1949; s. Francis Z. Reinus and Helene Reinus Margulies; m. Enid L. Leikin, June 1, 1980; children: Frances Rebecca, John Leikin, Zoe Ann. AB, Amherst Coll., Mass., 1970; MD, Cornell U., NYC, 1981. Diplomate Am. Bd. Internal Medicine, 1985, Am. Bd. Gastroenterology, 1988, Am. Bd. Transplant Hepatology, 2006. Assoc. prof. medicine Albert Einstein Coll. Medicine, Bronx, NY, 1995—; dir. hepatology Montefiore Med. Ctr., Bronx, 1996—. Editor: (textbook) Clinical Practice of Gastroenterology. Fellow: Am. Coll. Gastroenterology. Office: Montefiore Med Ctr 111 E 210th St Bronx NY 10467 Office Phone: 718-920-6033.

REIS, DON, publishing executive; b. NYC, Nov. 19, 1927; m. Barbara Weinberg, 1949; children: Robert, Richard. AB, Princeton U., 1947; MA, NYU, 1955. Rsch. editor Bantam Books, 1952-55, edn. editor, 1955-66; editor-in-chief Washington Square Press Divsn. Simon & Schuster, 1966-68; v.p., editorial dir. Ednl. Directions Inc., Westport, Conn., 1968-85; mng. editor Barron's Ednl. Series, 1985-87; gen. and ednl. editor Barron's, 1987-93, sr. cons. editor, 1993-99; editorial dir. Reis Assocs., Forest Hills, NY, 1993—. Author (with A. Butman and D. Sohn) Paperback Books in the Schools, 1962; editor The Collected Essays of Aldous Huxley, 1958. Home and Office: 57 Summer St Forest Hills NY 11375-6035 Personal E-mail: donjreis@yahoo.com.

REIS, LESLIE ANN, lawyer, educator; b. Plainfield, NJ, Apr. 21, 1958; BS cum laude, Syracuse Univ., 1981; JD, John Marshall Law Sch., Chgo., 1996. Bar: Ill. 1996. Broadcast journalist, 1981—96; legal fellow Reporters Com. for Freedom of the Press, 1996—97; adj. prof. John Marshall Law Sch., 1997—, dir. Ctr. for Info. Tech. & Privacy Law, 1997—. Supr. Jour. of Computer and Info. Law; contbr. articles to prof. jours. Mem. Fed. Info. Security & Privacy Adv. Bd. Mem.: Am. Judicature Soc. (past dir., Ctr. for Judicial Independence). Office: Ctr Info Tech and Privacy Law John Marshall Law Sch 315 S Plymouth Ct Chicago IL 60604 Office Phone: 312-987-1425. Business E-Mail: 7reis@jmls.edu. *

REISBERG, BARRY, geriatric psychiatrist, neuropsychopharmacologist; b. Bklyn., Dec. 3, 1947; s. Harry and Claire (Cohen) R.; m. Rosalie DePaola, Feb. 23, 1974 (dec. Oct. 1975); m. Nancy A. Minich, May 7, 1988. BA, CUNY, Bklyn., 1968; MD, N.Y. Med. Coll., 1972. Diplomate Am. Bd. Psychiatry and Neurology, Am. Bd. Geriatric Psychiatry. Intern NY Med. Coll./Met. Hosp., NYC, 1972—73, resident in psychiatry, 1972-75; fellow dept. psychiatry Middlesex Hosp. Med. Sch. U. London, 1975; staff psychiatrist Franklin D. Roosevelt VA Hosp., Montrose, NY, 1975-78; staff psychiatrist Neuropsychopharmacology Rsch. Unit NYU Med. Ctr., NYC, 1978-80, asst. attending psychiatrist, 1978—2001, clin. dir. William and Sylvia Silberstein Aging and Dementia Rsch. Ctr., 1978—, attending psychiatrist, 2002—. Adj. prof. Ctr. for Studies in Aging McGill U., Montreal, Que., 1993—; clin. instr. dept. psychiatry N.Y. Med. Coll., Valhalla, 1975—78; asst. prof. NYU Sch. Medicine, NYC, 1978—84, assoc. prof., 1984—90, prof., 1990—; rsch. collaborator, vis. clinician Brookhaven Nat. Labs., Upton, NY, 1979—90; dir. clin. core NIMH Clin. Rsch. Ctr., 1989—93, Nat. Inst. Aging Alzheimer's Disease Ctr., 1990—; dir. Zachary and Elizabeth M. Fisher Alzheimer's Disease Edn. and Resources Program NYU Sch. Medicine, 1995—; med. and sci. adv. bd. Alzheimer's Assn., Chgo., 1993—97; med. and sci. panel Alzheimer's Disease Internat., 1997—; cons. psychiatrist N.Y. VA Hosp., 1980—89; chmn. work group WHO, Copenhagen, 1984; mem. aging sect. NIH, 1986—90; vis. prof. Palmerston North Postgrad. Med. Soc., New Zealand, 1991; rsch. adv. bd. WHO Project on Alzheimer's Disease, 1995; Bayer vis. prof. St. Louis U. Sch. Medicine, 1999; vis. prof. Georgetown U. Med. Ctr., 2004; vis. prof. in geriatrics Stony Brook U. Health Scis. Ctr., 2005. Author: Brain Failure, 1981; editor: Alzheimer's Disease, 1983; editor: (with others) Diagnosis and Treatment of Senile Dementia, 1989; guest editor Drug Devel. Rsch., Internat. Psychogeriat., mem. editl. bd. Jour. Am. Aging Assn., 1985—2004, Alzheimer's Disease and Associated Disorders, 1985—2004, Jour. Geriat. Psychiatry and Neurology, 1986—, Am. Jour. Alzheimer's Disease, 1986—, Internat. Psychogeriat., 1989—96, Am. Jour. Geriat. Psychiatry, 1992—2001, Rsch. and Practice in Alzheimer's Disease, 1999—, Middle East Jour. of Age and Aging, 2004—, Polish Jour. Geriatric Psychiatry, 2005—, assoc. editor Psychiat. Quar., 2007—; contbr. over 250 articles to med. and sci. jours. and books. Recipient Home Care award Vis. Nurse Svc. NY, 1985, Disting. Svc. award, Internat. Psychogeriatric Assn., 2001, Ann. Barry Reisberg Lectr. award Hearthstone Alzheimer's Family Found., 2002-, Lifetime Achievement award Alzheimer's Assn. and 9th Internat. Conf. on Alzheimer's Disease and Related Disorders, 2004; fellow NSF, 1963, Coun. on Internat. Ednl. Exch.-Japan Soc., Tokyo, 1968; grantee NIH, 1979-85, 87-2003, 90-95, NIMH, 1983-85, Adminstrn. on Aging, 1998-2003, 2004—. Fellow: Am. Aging Assn. (bd. dris. 1990—92), Am. Psychiat. Assn.; mem.: Am. Coll. Neuropsychopharmacology, Alzheimer's and Related Disorders Soc. India (hon.), Am. Assn. Geriat. Psychiatry (sec. 1991—92, bd. dirs. 1992—96), Internat. Psychogeriat. Assn. (bd. dirs. 1985—93, treas. 1993—95, pres.-elect 1995—97, pres. 1997—99, Disting. Svc. award 2001). Achievements include patents for assessment of dementia; patents in field; Alzheimer's medications. Office: NYU Sch Medicine William and Sylvia Silberstein Aging and Dementia Rsch Ctr 550 1st Ave New York NY 10016-6402 Office Phone: 212-263-8550. Business E-Mail: barry.reisberg@med.nyu.edu.

REISCHAUER, ROBERT D., research organization executive; AB, Harvard U., 1963; MIA, Columbia U., 1966, PhD, 1971. Spl. asst. to dir., dep. dir., asst. dir. human resources and cmty. devel. Congl. Budget Office, 1975-81, dir., 1989-95; sr. v.p. Urban Inst., 1981-86, pres., 2000—; chmn. bd. trustees MDRC (formerly Manpower Devel. Rsch. Corp.), 1999—2000; vice chair payment adv. commn. Medicare, 2001—06. Author: (with Henry J. Aaron) Countdown to Reform: The Great Social Security Debate, 2001 (revised and updated); editor: Setting National Priorities: Budget Choices for the Next Century, 1997; co-editor: Medicare: Preparing for the Challenges of the 21st Century, 1998, Setting National Priorities: The 2000 Election and Beyond, 1999; contbr. articles to profl. jours., chpts. to books. Sr. Fellow econ. studies Brookings Inst., 1970-75, 86-89, 95-2000. Office: Urban Inst 2100 M St NW Washington DC 20037 Office Phone: 202-261-5400. Business E-Mail: rreischa@ui.urban.org.

REISER, MORTON FRANCIS, psychiatrist, educator; b. Cin., Aug. 22, 1919; s. Sigmund and Mary (Roth) R.; m. Lynn B. Whisnant, Dec. 19, 1976; children: David E., Barbara, Linda. BS, U. Cin., 1940, MD, 1943; grad., N.Y. Psychoanalytic Inst., 1960. Diplomate Am. Bd. Psychiatry and Neurology. Intern King's County Hosp., Bklyn., 1944; resident Cin. Gen. Hosp., 1944-49; practice medicine, specializing in psychiatry Cin., 1947-52, Washington, 1954-55, NYC, 1955-69; mem. faculty Cin. Gen. Hosp., also U. Cin. Coll. Medicine, 1949-52, Washington Sch. Psychiatry, 1953-55; faculty Albert Einstein Coll. Medicine, Yeshiva U., NYC, 1955-69, prof. psychiatry, 1958-69, dir. research dept. psychiatry, 1958-65; chief div. psychiatry Montefiore Hosp. and Med. Center, NYC, 1965-69; chmn. dept. psychiatry Yale Med. Sch., 1969—, prof., 1969-78, chmn. dept., 1969-86, Charles B.G. Murphy prof., 1978-86, Albert E. Kent prof., 1986-90, Albert E. Kent prof. emeritus, 1990—. Cons. Walter Reed Army Inst. Research, 1957-58, WHO, 1963; mem. clin. program projects rev. com. NIMH, 1970—, chmn., 1973-74. Author: (with H. Leigh) The Patient: Biological, Psychological, and Social Dimensions of Medical Practice, 1980, Mind, Brain, Body: Toward a Convergence of Psychoanalysis and Neurobiology, 1984; (with H. Leigh) The Patient, 3d edit., 1992; Memory in Mind and Brain: What Dream Imagery Reveals, 1990; editor: American Handbook of Psychiatry, vol. IV, 1975; editor in chief Psychosomatic Medicine, 1962-72; mem. editorial bd. AMA Archives of Gen. Psychiatry, 1961-71, (with H. Leigh) Psychiatry Medicine and Primary Care, 1978; contbr. articles to profl. jours. and books. Fellow Am. Coll. Psychiatrists, Am. Psychiat. Assn. (Seymour Vestermark award 1986); mem. Am. Soc. Clin. Investigation, Am. Psychosomatic Soc. (pres. 1960-61), Am. Fedn. Clin. Research, Am. Assn. Chairmen Depts. Psychiatry (exec. com. 1971—, pres. 1975-76), Acad. Behavioral Medicine Research (exec. council 1978), Am. Psychoanalytic Assn. (pres.-elect 1980-82, pres. 1982-84), Internat. Psycho-Analytical Assn., Assn. Psychophysiol. Study of Sleep, Internat. Coll. Psychosomatic Medicine (pres. 1975), Psychiat. Research Soc., A. Graeme Mitchell Undergrad. Pediatric Soc., Benjamin Rush Soc., Rapaport-Klein Study Group, World Psychiat. Assn. (organizing com. sect. psychosomatic medicine 1967), Sigma Xi, Phi Eta Sigma, Pi Kappa Epsilon, Alpha Omega Alpha. Home: PO Box 187039 Hamden CT 06518-7017 Personal E-mail: mdmreiser@comcast.net.

REISER, RICHARD SCOTT, lawyer; b. Chester, SD, Apr. 8, 1946; s. Kinney S. and Edna E. (Sweet) R.; m. Mary Lynn Durrie, Aug. 24, 1968; children: Todd S., Sally A. BS, U. Nebr., 1968, JD, 1972. Bar: Iowa 1972, Nebr. 1972, U.S. Dist. Ct. Nebr. 1972, U.S. Ct. Appeals (8th cir.) 1989. Assoc. Nelson & Harding, Omaha, 1972-75, ptnr., 1975-84; dir. Gross & Welch, P.C., Omaha, 1984-92; v.p., gen. counsel Werner Enterprises, Inc., Omaha, 1993—96, exec. v.p., gen. counsel, 1996—. Com. mem. Nebr. Transp. Efficiency Task Force, Lincoln, 1995. Bd. dirs., treas. Fontenelle Forest Assn., Omaha, 1988-94; pres. 2d lt. USAR, 1968-74. Mem. Am. Corp. Counsel Assn., Transp. Lawyers Assn., Omaha Bar Assn. (bd. dirs., exec. com.), Nebr. State Bar Assn. (mem. task force on civil justice sys. 1994-95), Iowa State Bar Assn, Nebr. State Hwy. (comm Dist.2, 2001-), Nebr. Trucking Assn. (bd. dir., sec., 2003-), Am. Trucking Assn. (bd. dir., 1999-). Democrat. Presbyterian. Avocations: hunting, skiing, motorcycling. Office: Werner Enterprises Inc PO Box 45308 Omaha NE 68145-0308

REISERT, CHARLES EDWARD, JR., realtor, real estate developer; b. New Albany, Ind., Apr. 5, 1941; s. Charles Edward, Jr. and Jane W. (Wilcox) Reisert; m. Mary Lynn Nunemacher, Nov. 9, 1963; children: Perry G., Heidi L. BS in Edn., Ind. U., 1963, MA, 1968. Tchr. Ind. Pub. Schs., 1963-67; mgr. Ind. Bell Tel. Co., Indpls., 1967-70; trust officer Ind. Nat. Bank, Indpls., 1970-72; ptnr. R.F.R. Prodns. Inc., Zionsville; dir. Wichita (Kans.) Art Assn., 1972-73; mng. ptnr. Century 21 Realty Group-Reisert, Jeffersonville, Ind., 1973—. Chmn. Ind. Real Estate Commn., 1982—90, pres. Ind., 1990; past pres. Clark County Youth Shelter; bd. dirs., past pres. United Way Clark County; bd. dirs. New Hope, Inc., Sagamore of Wabash; mem. Leadership So. Ind., Leadership Louisville; v.p. Clark County Redevel. Commn.; pres. Jeffersonville Housing Authority; trustee, past pres. Clark Meml. Hosp. Found. Recipient Pinnacle award, Sales Mgmt. and Mktg. Assn. Louisville, Servant Leader award, Leadership So. Ind., 2006. Mem.: Realtors Nat. Mktg. Inst., Ind. Assn. Realtor, Nat. Assn. Realtors, So. Ind. Realtors Assn. (past pres., past bd. dirs., Realtor of Yr. 1983, Realtor Hall of Fame 1998), So. Ind. C. of C. (Profl. Person of Yr. 1990), Rotary (past pres., Paul Harris fellow). Roman Catholic. Home: 14 Abby Chase Jeffersonville IN 47130-9762 Office: Century 21 Realty Group-Reisert 1302 E 10th St Jeffersonville IN 47130-4299 Office Phone: 812-285-5000.

REISING, RICHARD P., lawyer; BA, Stanford U.; JD, U. Mo. Bar: Ill. 1970. Asst. gen. counsel, sec. Archer-Daniels-Midland Co., Decatur, Ill., v.p., sec., gen. counsel, 1991-97, sr. v.p., 1997—. Office: Archer-Daniels-Midland Co 4666 E Faries Pky Decatur IL 62526-5666

REISKE, STEVEN ROBERT WARREN, human services manager; b. Grand Forks, Nd, July 10, 1964; s. Terry Michael Reiske and Kathleen Niegelsen; life ptnr. Timothy A. Nehring. BA in Philosophy, Marquette U., Milw., 1986, BA in Latin, 1986. Vice-chancellor, sec. to the bishop Roman Catholic Diocese of Fargo, ND, 1993—2002, chancellor, 2002—03; rector Basilica of St. James, Jamestown, ND, 2003—04; human resources and bus. mgr. Old Meeting Ho. Ice Cream, Tampa, Fla., 2004—; exec. asst. Hoffman Family Found., Tampa, 2004—. Scholar ROTC, USN, 1981. Mem.: Am. Guild Organists (assoc.), Eta Sigma Phi (life). Liberal. Roman Catholic. Avocations: organ performance, fine cuisine. Office: Old Meeting House Ice Cream 4004 S MacDill Ave Tampa FL 33611 Home Phone: 813-385-5361.

REISLER, HELEN BARBARA, public relations executive; b. NYC, June 21; d. George and Elizabeth Lois (Schultz) Gottesman; m. Melvin Reisler, June 5, 1955; children: Susan O'Brien, Karen Reisler, Keith James. BS in Edn., NYU, 1954; MS in Edn. and Reading, L.I. U., 1978. Elem. tchr., NYC, 1954-78; instr. grad. sch., adj. lectr. L.I. U., Bklyn., 1978; acct. exec. N.Y. Yellow Pages, Inc., NYC, 1979, personnel mgr., 1979, adminstrv. dir., 1980-83, v.p. personnel, 1983-84, v.p. adminstrn./personnel, 1984-85, also dir.; staff specialist sales and market support Southwestern Bell Publs., 1985-88; N.Y. mgr. pub. rels. and recruitment N.Y. Yellow Pages/Mast Advt. and Publs., Inc. of Southwe. Bell, 1988; cons. human resources devel. and product promotion, 1989—. Recruiter N.E. Region, N.Y. area cmty. rels. rep.; moderator weekly cable TV show New York Business Forum, N.Y.C., 1983-85. Founder Firefighters Vacation com., 2001—02; bd. dirs. Park Slope Geriatric Ctr., 2002—, Heritage Hills Condo. Assn., 2000—. Named Ptnr. in Edn., NYC Bd. Edn., 1984, Heritage Hills Theatre Group, 2004, Golden Poets Award; Paul Harris award, 2000-03, 05-07. Mem. Internat. Assn. Sales and Mktg. Exec. (bd. dirs. 1993-94), UN Assn., Sales Execs. Club NY (bd. dirs., reception, membership and mem. rels. coms., chmn. youth edn., v.p. 1987-88, chmn. internal com. 1989), Execs. Assn. Greater NY (chmn. com. Sec. Day), Heritage Hills Country Club Westchester (bd. dir. 2000—), Sales Exec. Club (v.p.), NY Rotary (chmn. environ. com. 1991—, bd. liaison to pub. rels. and membership coms. 1994—, interviewing com. scholarship candidates 1993-2003, mentor Japanese amb. scholars, 1992-93, divsn. chmn. cmty. svcs., chmn. pub. rels. com., bd. liaison 1996-2001, 03, bd. dirs., co-chmn. advt. com. chmn. pub. rels. 1996-04, coord. Gift of Life, 2d v.p. bd. dirs. 1998—, 1st v.p., bd. dirs. 1999—, pres. 2001-02, trustee dist. 7230 2002-05, bd. dirs. 100 club 2006-07, trustee found. 2003—, prodr. cable TV series NY Rotary-A Club That Works, exec. prodr. Gift of Life-A Child's Story, apptd. media liaison to NY 1998—, creator 9/11 disaster fund 2001-02, chmn. 9/11 adv. com. 2001-04, chmn. publicity and pub. rels., dist. leadership com. 2002-04, #7230 dist. gov.-elect, 2004, #7230 dist. gov., 2005—, pres. NY 2001-02, alt. liaison UN 2007—, trustee NY Found. 2003-, vice chair found. 2007-, Paul Harris Soc. fellow 1992, 2001, 03, 05-06, Disting. Pres. award 2001-02, Pub. Rels. award, 1905 Silver Nickel award 2003, Dist. Centennial Project award, "Response to 9/11", 2004, Global History fellowship, bd. dir. 2003-, 4x Dist. P.R. award, Svc. Above Self award, Centennial Project award Rotary Zone 32, profiled in 100th hist. edit. The Rotarian Mag. 2005), Dutch Treat Club, 100 Club (bd. dirs. 2006). Office: 47 Plaza St W Brooklyn NY 11217-3905 Personal E-mail: helenbreisler@aol.com.

REISLER, MARC S., lawyer; b. NYC, Nov. 19, 1960; BA, McGill U., 1984; MA, Syracuse U., 1988, JD cum laude, 1988. Bar: NY 1990. Ptnr., co-head Tech. Practice, Corp. Dept. Katten Muchin Zavis Rosenman, NYC. Mem.: Copyright Soc. of USA. Office: Katten Muchin Zavis Rosenman 575 Madison Ave New York NY 10022 Office Phone: 212-940-6456. Office Fax: 212-940-8776. E-mail: marc.reisler@kmzr.com.

REISMAN, ANDREW LOUIS, information technology executive, lawyer; b. Memphis, Tenn., Nov. 24, 1969; s. John Mark and Margo Sue Reisman; m. Polina Shadkin Shadkin, July 27, 1997; 1 child, Elijah Nathaniel. BS, Ill. State U., Normal, Ill., 1990; JD, U. Ill. Coll. of Law, Champaign, Ill., 1993. Bar: Supreme Ct. of Ill. 1993. Jud. clk. Hon. Harlington Wood, Jr., U.S. Ct. of Appeals, 7th Circuit, Springfield, Ill., 1993—94; assoc. Mayer, Brown & Platt, Chgo., 1994—97; gen. counsel Internat. Save the Children Alliance, Geneva, 1997—98; ptnr. Foley & Lardner, Chgo., 1998—2003, Enterprise Law Group, LLP, Chgo., 2003—; pres. Elijah Tech., Ltd., Chgo., 2003—. Pres. Internat. Info. Systems Forensics Assn., Chgo. Chpt., Chgo., 2004—. Dir. Internat. Info. Systems Forensics Assn., Chgo. Chpt., Chgo., 2004. Recipient Outstanding Recent Alumni Award for Pub. Svc., U. Ill. Coll. of Law Recent Alumni Adv. Bd., 2001. Mem.: Assn. Corp. Counsel (dir. Chgo. chpt. 2005—), Internat. Info. Systems Forensics Assn. (dir. 2005—). Achievements include patents for Self-Generating Elevator Emergency Power Source. Office: Elijah Tech Ltd 70 W Madison St Ste 740 Chicago IL 60602 Home: 395 Brownville Highland Park IL 60035 Office Phone: 866-354-5240. Office Fax: 866-354-5240. Business E-Mail: andy@elijahtechnologies.com.

REISMAN, ELLEN KELLY, lawyer; b. Oct. 24, 1959; BA summa cum laude, Boston Coll., 1981; JD cum laude, U. Chgo., 1984. Bar: DC 1984, US Dist. Ct., DC 1985, Calif. 1996. Assoc. Arnold & Porter LLP, Washington, 1984, ptnr., 1992—99; assoc. gen. counsel, v.p. legal divsn. Wyeth-Ayerst Pharmaceuticals, 1999—2001; ptnr., Product Liability Practice Group Arnold & Porter LLP, LA, 2001—. Named one of Top 50 Women Litigators, The Nat. Law Jour., 2001, The Top 45 Under 45, The Am. Lawyer, 2003. Office: Arnold & Porter 777 S Figueroa St 44th Flr Los Angeles CA 90017-2513 Office Phone: 213-243-4111. Office Fax: 213-243-4199.

REISMAN, JUDITH ANN GELERNTER, media communications executive, educator; b. Hillside, NJ, Apr. 11, 1935; MA in Speech Comm., Case Western Res. U., 1976, PhD in Speech Comm., 1980. Faculty dept. anthropology and sociology Haifa U., Israel, 1981—83; rsch. prof. sch. edn. Am. U., Washington, 1983—85; founder, pres. Inst. Media Edn., 1985—. Cons., reviewer grant proposals audio-visual drug programs for youth Dept. Edn., 1987; rsch. design cons. Alcohol and Tobacco Media Analysis in Mainstream Mags., Dept. HHS, 1987—90; cons., field reviewer Drug Free Youth Sch. Candidates Dept. Edn., 1988; lectr., adj. prof. George Mason U., Va., 1990; expert witness Pres.'s Commn. on Assignment of Women in Armed Forces, 1992, U.S. Atty. Gen. Commn. on Pornography, 1985—86, U.S. Atty. Gen. Task Force on Domestic Violence, Washington, 1985, Mapplethorpe Trial, Cin., 1990, Australian Parliament, 1992, Ga. State Senate, 1992; nominated to panel on sex harassment in the Air Force U.S. Inspector Gen., 2003; sci. advisor Protective Parents Assn.; subcom. junk sci. Am. Legis. Exchange Coun. Edn. Task Force, 1999—2004. Author: Images of Children, Crime and Violence in Playboy, Penthouse and Hustler, 1989, Kinsey, Sex and Fraud, 1990, Softport Plays Hardball, 1991, Kinsey, Crimes and Consequences, 1998, 2003; contbr. preme Ct. cases to profl. jours. Co-recipient Scholastic Mag. awards, Dukane award, 1982; recipient Gold Camera award, 1982, Silver Screen award, 1982, Filmstrip of Yr. award, 1981—82, Silver Plaque award, 1982, Family Svc. Assn. Am. 1st pl. award local TV series, 1974, Best of 1965 award, 1965, Scientist of Yr. for Children award, 1993; U.S. Dept. Justice grantee. Mem.: AAAS, Women in Neurosci., Nat. Black Child Devel. Inst., Soc. Sci. Study Sex, N.Y. Acad. Scis., Internat. Comm. Assn., Am. Statis. Assn., Am. Assn. Composers, Authors and Pubs., Nat. Assn. Scholars. E-mail: jareisman@cox.net.

REISMAN, ROBERT E., allergist, educator; b. Buffalo, Nov. 1, 1932; s. Harry S and Jessie (Goldberg) Reisman; m. Rena Estry, Sept. 5, 1954; children: Jeanne, Linda, Nancy, David. MD, SUNY-Buffalo, 1956; Dr.h.c., U. Montpellier, France, 1982. Diplomate Am. Bd. Internal Medicine, Am. Bd. Allergy and Clin. Immunology. Intern Buffalo Gen. Hosp., 1956-57, resident in medicine, 1957-59; practice medicine specializing in allergy and clin. immunology Buffalo, 1961—; co-dir. Allergy Rsch. Lab., Buffalo Gen. Hosp., 1970—90; clin. prof. pediatrics and medicine SUNY, Buffalo, 1978—. Mem. panel allergenic extracts Bur. Biologists FDA; bd. dirs. Am. Bd. Internal Medicine, 1984—86, Am. Bd. Allergy and Clin. Immunology, 1981—86, chmn., 1985. With US Army, 1968—69. Master: ACP; fellow: Am. Acad. Allergy (pres 1980—81). Home: 113 Carriage Cir Buffalo NY 14221-2163 Office: 295 Essjay Rd Williamsville NY 14221-8216 also: 85 High St Buffalo NY 14203-1149 Office Phone: 716-630-1130. Business E-Mail: rreisman@buffalomedicalgroup.com.

REISMAN, ROSEMARY MOODY CANFIELD, writer, humanities educator; b. Des Moines, Nov. 18, 1927; d. V. Alton and Lois Gloria (Slee) Moody; m. Michael Ellison Canfield, Sept. 6, 1952 (div. May 1961); children: Michael, John Charles, Celia Catherine, Christopher James; m. Maurice Reisman, May 10, 1986 (dec. 1990). BA in English, U. Minn., 1949, MA in English, 1952; PhD in English, La. State U., 1971. Reporter Ames Tribune, Iowa, summer 1944; writer, actor Sta. WOI Pub. Radio, Ames, 1944-48; dir., writer children's plays Sta. KASI, Ames, 1949; tchg. asst. U. Minn., 1949-52; writer Sta. WOI-TV, Ames, summer 1952; writer, show host Sta. WDGY, Mpls., 1952-54; instr. La. State U., 1961-69, NDEA fellow, 1969-71; asst. prof. English Troy State U., 1971-80, assoc. prof., 1980-90, chairperson dept. English, 1985-90, prof., 1990-94. Honors coun. Troy State U., 1985-94, honors faculty, 1986-94, acad. coun., 1989-92, faculty adv. coun., 1990-92, Rhodes scholar instnl. rep., 1987-91; adj. prof. Charleston So. U., 1996-99, vis. prof., 1999—; humanities scholar Richland County Libr., S.C., 2002—; coord. sr. honors seminar Coll. of Charleston, 1996-98; prodr., writer Perspectives project films Ala. ETV, 1977-80; chmn. conf. sessions South Ctrl. Soc. for 18th-Century Studies, 1988, Southeastern Am. Soc. for 18th Century Studies, 1991, 93, workshop Ala. Coun. Tchrs. English, 1987; grant writer, project dir. Ala. Humanities Found., 1980, 89, asst. project dir. summer grad. course, 1990; grant writer, project dir. Ala. Pub. Libr. Sys., 1977-80; presenter, lectr., cons. in field. Author: Perspectives: The Alabama Heritage, 1978; co-author: Contemporary Southern Women Fiction Writers, 1994, Southern Men Fiction Writers, 1998; editor, course writer Coastal C.C., Calif., 2002—; chair editl. adv. bd. Ala. Lit. Rev., 1986-94; mem. editl. bd. Biog. Guide to Ala. Lit., 1985-89; guest editor spl. issue Ala. English 7, 1995; contbr. articles to profl. jours. Baldwin County Humanities scholar Ala. Humanities Found., 1983-84. Mem.: AAUW (past br. pres., mem. steering com.), NEA, Thomas Cooper Soc. (bd. dirs. 2001—04), English Spkg. Union (bd. dirs. Charleston 1997—98, pres. 1998—2002, Sourcelist spkr. 1999—2000, pres. 2006—07, bd. dirs. 2007—), Troy State U. Edn. Assn. (pres. 1990—93), Ala. Edn. Assn., Assn. Coll. English Tchrs. Ala., Assn. Depts. English (state pres. 1986—88), South Atlantic MLA, Soc. of Mary, Confrat. of the Blessed Sacrament, Gamma Beta Phi (nat. pres. 1978—79, cert. of merit 1979), Phi Beta Kappa (del. to nat. triennial coun. 1991, alt. 1994, pres. Low Country Assn. 1996—98, del. 1997, bd. dirs. 1998—2001, alt. del. 2000, bd. dirs. 2003—05, past pres. S.E. Ala. assn.). Anglican. Home and Office: 121 Innisbrook Bend Summerville SC 29483-5084 Personal E-mail: creisman@bellsouth.net.

REISMAN, SHARYL A., lawyer; b. NYC, 1967; AB magna cum laude, Dartmouth Coll., 1989; JD cum laude, U. Mich., 1992. Bar: Ill. 1992, NY 1998. Ptnr., environmental law Jones Day (formerly Jones,Day, Reavis & Pogue), NYC. Office: Jones Day 222 E 41st St New York NY 10017-6702 Office Phone: 212-326-3939. Office Fax: 212-755-7306. Business E-Mail: sareisman@jonesday.com.

REISMAN, WILLIAM MICHAEL, lawyer, educator; b. 1939; LL.B., Hebrew U., 1963; LL.M., Yale U., 1964, J.S.D., 1965. Bar: Conn. 1964. Assoc. prof. Yale U. Law Sch., New Haven, 1969-72, prof., 1972-82, Hohfeld prof. jurisprudence, 1982-98, McDougal prof. internat. law, 1998—. Mem. Inter-Am. Commn. on Human Rights, 1990—95, chmn., 1994—95; vice-chmn. Policy Scis. Ctr., Inc., 1992—; assoc. Inst. Droit Internat., 1999; pres. Arbitration Tribunal Bank for Internat. Settlements, 2001—; mem. Eritrea-Ethiopia Boundary Commn., 2001—; pres. Anglo-Irish OSPAR Convention Tribunal, 2001—03. Author: Nullity and Revision, 1971, Art of the Possible: Diplomatic Alternatives in Middle East, 1970, Puerto Rico and the International Process, 1974, Folded Lies: Bribery, Crusades and Reforms, 1979, (with Weston) Toward World Order and Human Dignity, 1976, (with McDougal) International Law in Contemporary Perspective, 1981, (with McDougal) International Law Essays, 1981, (with McDougal) Power and Policy in Quest of Law: Essays in Honor of Eugene V. Rostow, 1985, (with Schreiber) Jurisprudence: Understanding and Shaping Law, 1986, (with Willard) International Incidents: The Law that Counts in World Politics, 1988, (with James E. Baker) Regulating Covert Action: Practices, Contexts and Policies of Covert Coercion Abroad in International and American Laqw, 1991, Systems of Control in International Adjudication and Arbitration: Breakdown and Repair, 1992, (with Westerman) Straight Baselines in International Maritime Boundary Delimitation, 1992, (with C. Antoniou) The Laws of War, 1994, The Suspervisory Jurisdiction of the International Court of Justice: International Arbitration and International Adjudication, 1997, (with L. Craig W. Park and J. Paulsson) International Commercial Arbitration: Cases, Materials and Notes on the Resolution of International Business Disputes, 1997, Law in Brief Encounters, 1999, Jurisdiction in International Law, 1999, (with M. Arsanjani, S. Wiessner and G. Westerman) International Law in Contemporary Perspective, 2004; editor-in-chief Am. Jour. Internat. Law, 1998-2003, (with R. Doak Bishop and James Crawford) Foreign Investment Disputes: Cases, Materials and Commentary, 2005. Decorated 1st class Order of Bahrain; Fulbright grantee, 1966-67 Mem. Fgn. Policy Assn. (bd. dirs. 1997—), Coun. Fgn. Rels, Am. Soc. of Internat. Law (Manley O. Hudson Medal). Office: Yale U Law Sch PO Box 208215 New Haven CT 06520-8215 Fax: 203-432-7247. E-mail: michael.reisman@yale.edu.

REISMANN, HERBERT, engineer, educator; b. Vienna, Jan. 26, 1926; s. Henrik and Olga (Pokorny) R.; m. Edith Falber, Aug. 14, 1952; children: Sandra Jean, Barbara Anne BS Aero. Engring., Ill. Inst. Tech., 1947, MS, 1949; PhD Engring., U. Colo., 1962. Project engr. Convair, Ft. Worth, 1951—53; prin. structures engr. Republic Aviation Corp., Hicksville, NY, 1954—56; chief engr. sys. analysis, chief solid mechanics Martin Marietta Corp., 1957—64; prof., dir. aerospace engring. SUNY, Buffalo, 1964—2001, prof. emeritus, 2002—. Cons. NASA, Bell Aero Sys. Corp. Co-author: Elastokinetics, 1974, Elasticity, 1980; author: Elastic Plates, 1988; contbr. articles to profl. jours Assoc. fellow AIAA (Best Tech. Paper award 1962, Outstanding Aerospace Achievement award 1987); mem. ASME, AAUP, Internat. Assn. Bridge and Structural Engring., Sigma Xi, Tau Beta Pi Home: 71 Chaumont Dr Buffalo NY 14221-3511 Office: SUNY-Buffalo 605 Furnas Hall Buffalo NY 14260-4200 Office Phone: 716-634-5862. Personal E-mail: herreis@msn.com.

REISNER, ANDREW DOUGLAS, psychologist; b. Ithaca, NY, Dec. 28, 1955; s. Gerald Seymour and Estelle Ruth (Siegel) R.; m. Deborah Kay Dermen, Aug. 1, 1981; children: David Aaron, Alyssa Danielle. BA, Allegheny Coll., Meadville, Pa., 1977; MA, Edinboro U., Pa., 1978; D of Psychology, Baylor U., Waco, Tex., 1987. Lic. psychologist, Ohio. Psychology asst. Tiffin Devel. Mental Health Ctr., 1979—80, Cmty. Counseling Svcs., Galion, Ohio, 1980—83, chief clin. officer, 1990—99; pvt. practice, 1996—99; intern in clin. psychology Mich. State U., East Lansing, 1986—87; postdoctoral tng. in clin. psychology Harding Hosp., Worthington, Ohio, 1987—88; psychologist Ctr. for Individual Family Svcs., Mansfield, Ohio, 1988—90, Appalachian Behavioral Healthcare, Cambridge, Ohio, 1999—. Cons. MedCtrl. Crestline Hosp., Ohio, 1989-99, Forensic Diagnostic Ctr., Byesville, Ohio, 1999—; mem. adj. faculty Ashland U., 1993-96. Contbr. chpt. to book, articles to profl. jours. Mem. APA, Ohio Psychol. Assn. Office: Appalachian Behavioral Healthcare 66737 Old 21 Rd Cambridge OH 43725-9298 Office Phone: 740-439-1371. Business E-Mail: reisnera@mh.state.oh.us.

REISNER, LORIN L., lawyer; b. Bklyn., Dec. 30, 1961; s. Ira Aaron and Roberta Goldglit. AB in Politics, Brandeis U., 1983; JD, Harvard U., 1986. Bar: N.Y. 1987, U.S. Dist. Ct. (so. dist.) N.Y. 1987, (ea. dist.) N.Y. 2000, U.S. Ct. Appeals (2d cir.) 1991, (11th cir.) 1995, (4th cir.) 2001, (7th cir.) 2002, U.S. Supreme Ct. 2003. Law clk. to judge U.S. Dist. Ct. (so. dist.) N.Y., NYC, 1986-87; assoc. Debevoise & Plimpton LLP, NYC, 1987-90; asst. U.S. atty. for so dist. N.Y. U.S. Atty.'s Office, NYC, 1990—94; assoc. Debevoise & Plimpton LLP, 1994—96, ptnr., 1996—. Author: (with Bruce P. Keller) Trademark Related Causes of Action and Defenses, 2000; contbr. articles to law revs. and jours. Mem. alumni admissions coun. Brandeis U., 1987—. Mem. ABA, Assn. of Bar of City of N.Y. Democrat. Jewish. Office: Debevoise & Plimpton LLP 919 Third Ave New York NY 10022 Office Phone: 212-909-6191. Office Fax: 212-909-6836. Business E-Mail: llreisner@debevoise.com.

REISS, CRAIG KEITH, cardiologist, educator; b. St. Louis, Mo., May 29, 1959; BS, U. Mo., Kansas City, 1979; MD, U. Mo. Kansas City Sch. Medicine, Kansas City, 1983. Cert. Internal Medicine, Cardiovascular Disease. Intern, internal medicine Brigham and Women's Hosp., Boston, 1983—84, resident, jr. asst. internal medicine, 1985, resident, sr. asst. internal medicine, 1986, chief resident, internal medicine, 1989, fellow, cardiology, 1989; chief resident, medicine West Roxbury VA Hosp., Boston, 1986; cardiology cons. Barnes-Jewish Hosp., St. Louis; asst. prof. Wash. U., St. Louis, assoc. prof., prof. medicine; dir. Wash. U. Cardiology Consultants, St. Louis, Heart Care Inst., St. Louis. Contbr. articles to profl. jours. Named one of Consumers Guide to the Top Doctors in the US, 1999, 2001, 40 Under 40 award, St. Louis Bus. Jour., 1999, America's Top Doctors, Castle Connolly Med. Ltd., 2002—06, Best Doctors in Am., Best Doctors Inc., 2002, 2003, 2005, 2006. Office: Wash U Sch Medicine Cardiovascular Divsn 666 S Euclid Campus Box 8086 Saint Louis MO 63110 Address: Heart Care Inst 1020 N Mason Rd 100 Saint Louis MO 63141 Office Phone: 314-362-1291. Office Fax: 314-996-3268. *

REISS, DALE ANNE, corporate financial executive; b. Sept. 3, 1947; d. Max and Nan (Hart) R.; m. Jerome L. King, Mar. 5, 1978; children: Matthew Reiss, Mitchell, Stacey. BS, Ill. Inst. Tech., 1967; MBA, U. Chgo., 1970. CPA, Fla., Ill., Mich., Mo. Cost acct. First Nat. Bank, Chgo., 1967; asst. contr. City Colls. of Chgo., 1967-71; dir. fin. Chgo. Dept. Pub. Works, 1971-73; prin. Arthur Young & Co., Chgo., 1973-80; sr. v.p., contr. Urban Investment & Devel. Co., Chgo., 1980-85; mng. ptnr. Ernst & Young LLP, Chgo., 1985-98, Ernst & Young, NYC, 1998-99; global dir. real estate, hospitality and constrn. Ernst & Young LLP, NYC, 1999—. Bd. dirs. Ill. Inst. Tech., Urban Land Inst.; adv. bd. Kellogg Real Estate, Northwestern U., U. Chgo. Grad. Sch. of Bus. Mem. AICPA, Fin. Execs. Inst., Pension Real Estate Assn., Chgo. Network (bd. dirs.), Econ. Chgo. Club, Met. Club, Chgo. Yacht Club, NY Athletic Club. Office: Ernst & Young 5 Times Sq 16th Fl New York NY 10036-6530 E-mail: dale.reiss@ey.com.

REISS, GEORGE RUSSELL, JR., physician; b. Phila., Dec. 25, 1928; s. G. Russell Sr. and Mary Ellen (Brogan) R.; m. Rosemarie Theresa Curcillo, Sept. 19, 1959; children: Mary Elizabeth, Stephanie, G. Russell III, Charlene. BA, LaSalle U., 1953; MD, Temple U., 1957. Diplomate Am. Bd. Pediatrics. Intern Misericordia Hosp., Phila., 1957-58; resident pediatrics St. Christopher Hosp. for Children, Phila., 1958-60; pvt. practice Glenside, Pa., 1960—. With USCG, 1946-49. Mem. Montgomery County

Med. Soc., Pa. Med. Soc., Am. Acad. Pediatrics, AMA, Am. Assn. Pro-Life Pediatricians. Roman Catholic. Office: 2220 Mount Carmel Ave Glenside PA 19038-4610 Office Phone: 215-884-7861. Personal E-mail: grcreissjr@aol.com.

REISS, HOWARD, chemistry professor; b. NYC, Apr. 5, 1922; s. Isidor and Jean (Goldstein) R.; m. Phyllis Kohn, July 25, 1945; children: Gloria, Steven. AB in Chemistry, NYU, 1943; PhD in Chemistry, Columbia U., 1949. With Manhattan Project, 1944-46; instr., then asst. prof. chemistry Boston U., 1949-51; with Ctrl. Rsch. Lab., Celanese Corp. Am., 1951-52, Edgar C. Bain Lab. Fundamental Rsch., U.S. Steel Corp., 1957, Bell Telephone Labs., 1952-60; asso. dir., then dir. rsch. div. Atomics Internat., div. N.Am. Aviation, Inc., 1960-62; dir. N.Am. Aviation Sci. Ctr., 1962-67, v.p. co., 1963-67; v.p. rsch. aerospace systems group N.Am. Rockwell Corp., 1967-68; vis. lectr. chemistry U. Calif. at Berkeley, summer 1957; vis. prof. chemistry UCLA, 1961, 62, 64, 67, prof., 1968-91, prof. emeritus, 1991—2003, disting. prof. emeritus, 2003—; vis. prof. U. Louis Pasteur, Strasbourg, France, 1986, U. Pa., 1989; vis. fellow Victoria U., Wellington, New Zealand, 1989. Vis. fellow Princeton (N.J.) Materials Inst., 1996; vis. sci., Hebrew U., Jerusalem, 1998; cons. to chem.-physics program USAF Cambridge Rsch. Labs., 1950-52; chmn. editor Procs. Internat. Conf. Nucleation and Interfacial Phenomena, Boston; mem. USAF Office Sci. Rsch. Physics and Chemistry Rsch. Evaluation Groups, 1966—, Oak Ridge Nat. Lab. Reactor Chemistry Adv. Com., 1966-68; adv. com. math. and phys. scis. NSF, 1970-72, ARPA Materials Rsch. Coun., 1968—; chmn. site rev. com. NRC Associateships Program, Naval Rsch. Lab., 1989. Author: Methods of Thermodynamics, 1965, republished, 1996; author articles; editor in field.; editor: Progress in Solid State Chemistry, 1962-71, Jour. Statis. Physics, 1968-75, Jour. Colloid Interface Sci; mem. editorial adv. bd. Internat. Jour. Physics and Chemistry of Solids, 1955, Progress in Solid State Chemistry, 1962-73, Jour. Solid State Chemistry, 1969, Jour. Phys. Chemistry, 1970-73, Ency. of Solid State, 1970, Jour. Nonmetals, 1971—, Jour. Colloid and Interface Sci., 1976-79, Langmuir, 1985—. Guggenheim Meml. fellow, 1978; Howard Reiss chair in chemistry and biochemistry established named in his honor, UCLA, 1999. Fellow AAAS, Am. Phys. Soc. (exec. com. div. chem. physics 1966-69); mem. NAS, Am. Chem. Soc. (chmn. phys. chemistry sect. N.J. sect. 1957, Richard C. Tolman medal 1973, Kendall award in colloid and surface chemistry 1980, J.H. Hildebrand award in theoretical and exptl. phys. chemistry of liquids 1991, Van Arkel hon. chair in chemistry U. Leiden, The Netherlands, 1994), Am. Assn. for Aerosol Rsch. (David Sinclair award 1997), Phi Beta Kappa, Sigma Xi, Phi Lambda Upsilon. Office: U Calif Dept Chemistry And Biochemis Los Angeles CA 90095-0001 Office Phone: 310-825-3029. Business E-Mail: reiss@chem.ucla.edu.

REISS, IRA LEONARD, retired sociology educator, writer; b. NYC, Dec. 8, 1925; s. Philip and Dorothy (Jacobs) R.; m. Harriet Marilyn Eisman, Sept. 4, 1955; children: David, Pamela, Joel. BS cum laude, Syracuse U., 1949; MA, Pa. State U., 1951, PhD, 1953. Instr. in sociology Bowdoin Coll., Brunswick, Maine, 1953-55; asst. prof. sociology Coll. William and Mary, Williamsburg, Va., 1955-59; asst. prof. Bard Coll., Annandale-On-Hudson, N.Y., 1959-61; assoc. to full prof. U. Iowa, Iowa City, 1961-69; prof. U. Minn., Mpls., 1969-96, prof. emeritus, 1996—. Rsch. evaluator U.S. Dept. Edn. and Nat. Inst. Child Health and Human Devel., Washington, 1966-78; rsch. dir. Family Study Ctr., U. Minn., 1969-74; ednl. advisor Kimberly-Clark Corp., Neenah, Wis., 1971-75; chair planning com. and bd. dirs. Inst. for Child, Adolescent Sexual Health, 1992-93; vis. prof. Uppsala Univ., Sweden, 1975-76; lectr. in field. Author: Premarital Sexual Standards in America, 1960, The Social Context of Premarital Sexual Permissiveness, 1967, Family Systems in America, 1971, 4th edit., 1988, Journey into Sexuality: An Exploratory Voyage, 1986, An End to Shame: Shaping Our Next Sexual Revolution, 1990, Solving America's Sexual Crises, 1997, At the Dawn of the Sexual Revolution: Reflections on a Dialogue, 2002, An Insider's View of Sexual Science Since Kinsey, 2006; editor: 3 textbooks; contbr. over 150 papers to jours. and textbooks in field. Mem. ACLU, 1948—, Planned Parenthood, 1960—, Nat. Abortion Rights Action League 1975—, Amnesty Internat., 1984—. With U.S. Army, 1944-46, ETO. Mem. Midwest Sociol. Soc. (pres. 1971-72), Am. Sociol. Assn. (chair family sect. 1975-76), Nat. Coun. on Family Rels. (pres. 1979-80, Reuben Hill award 1980, E.W. Burgess award 1984), Polish Acad. Sexual Sci. (hon., Internat. Sexual Sci. award 1989), Soc. for Sci. Study Sex (pres. 1980-81, Disting. Sci. Achievement award 1982, Alfred Kinsey award 1990), Internat. Acad. Sex Rsch. (pres. 1984-85), Am. Assn. Sex Educators, Counselors and Therapists (leadership award 1993). Democrat. Jewish. Home: 5932 Medicine Lake Rd Minneapolis MN 55422-3328 E-mail: irareiss@comcast.net.

REISS, JEROME, retired lawyer; b. Bklyn., Dec. 7, 1924; s. William and Eva (Marenstein) Reiss; m. Naomi Betty Plutzik, June 15, 1947; children: Robert Scott, Harlan Morgan, Andrea Ellen, Samantha Glynis. BA, Bklyn. Coll., 1948; JD, Harvard U., Cambridge, Mass., 1951. Bar: NY 1951, US Dist. Ct. (so. dist.) NY 1954, US Ct. Claims 1960, US Dist. Ct. (ea. dist.) NY 1964, DC 1967, US Dist. Ct. (we. dist.) NY 1979, US Supreme Ct. 1989. Staff atty. civil br. Legal Aid Soc., NYC, 1951—54; asst. corp. counsel City of N.Y., 1954—58; assoc. Max E. Greenberg, 1958-67; sr. ptnr. Max E. Greenberg, Trayman, Cantor, Reiss & Blasky, 1967-80, Max E. Greenberg, Cantor & Reiss, NYC, 1980-88, Thelen, Marrin, Johnson & Bridges, NYC, 1989-97, Thelen, Reid & Priest, 1997-2000, ret., 2000; gen. counsel Kiska Constrn. Co.-USA, Inc., 2004—. Arbitrator Small Claims Ct., 1960—88; bd. adv. Fed. Pub., Inc.; chmn. bd. AMT-Pacific, Israel, 2000—02; former mem. Am. Judges Assn.; rep. various Japanese, British, Turkish, Israeli internat. contractors; lectr. in constrn. field; drafter renovation contracts Statue of Liberty; drafter expansion contracts Met. Mus. of Art; drafter construction contracts NYC Conv. Ctr. Contbr. articles to profl. jours., chapters to books. Trustee Brownsville Boys Club Alumni Assn.; gen. counsel Artist Fellowship, Inc. With USAAF, 1943—46. Fellow: Am. Coll. Constrn. Lawyers (founding mem.); mem.: Wash. (DC) Bar Assn., NY Bar Assn., Internat. Bar Assn., Jacob K. Javits Conv. Ctr. Oper. Corp. (bd. dirs.), Mcpl. Assist. Corp. City NY (bd. dirs.), Am. Arbitrators Assn.

REISS, JOHN BARLOW, lawyer; b. London, Aug. 29, 1939; arrived in U.S., 1963; s. James Martin and Margaret Joan (Ping) R.; m. Mary Jean Maudsley, Aug. 6, 1967 (div. 1978); m. Kathleen Strouse, Aug. 2, 1979; 1 child, Juliette Blanche. BA with honors, Exeter U., Devon, Eng., 1961; AM, Washington U., St. Louis, 1966, PhD, 1971; JD, Temple U., 1977. Bar: Pa. 1977, N.J. 1977, U.S. Dist. Ct. N.J. 1977, D.C. 1980, U.S. Supreme Ct. 1981, U.S. Dist. Ct. D.C. 1982. Economist Commonwealth Econ. Com., London, 1962-63; asst. prof. Allegheny Coll., Meadville, Pa., 1967-71; assoc. prof. Stockton State Coll., Pomona, NJ, 1971-75; asst. health commr. State of N.J., Trenton, 1975-79; dir. office of health regulation U.S. Dept. HHS, Washington, 1979-81; assoc. Baker & Hostetler, Washington, 1981-82, Dechert Price & Rhoads, Phila., 1982—93, ptnr., 1986-93, asst. chair health law group, 1984-91, chmn. health law group, 1991-93; ptnr. Saul Ewing LLP, Phila., 1993—, chmn. health law dept., 1995—2002, chmn. health law practice group, 2002—07. Mem. editl. bd. Topics in Hosp. Law, 1985-86, Hosp. Legal Forms Manual, 1985-2002, Jour. Health Care Tech., 1984-86; contbr. Hosp. Contracts Manual, 1983-2002; contbr. articles to profl. jours., chpts. to books. Bd. dirs. Gateway Sch. Little Children, Phila., 1986-99, ECRI, Plymouth Meeting, Pa., 1994—, chmn. bd., 2001—; mem. bd. vestry All Saints Ch., Wynnewood, Pa., 1993, 96-2001; treas. The U. BC 1871 Found., 2006-07. Pub. Health Svc. fellow, 1979-81, English Speaking Union fellow, 1963-66, Econ. Devel. Adminstr. fellow Washington U., 1966-67. Mem. Nat. Health Lawyers Assn., Phila. Bar Assn., Brit. Am. C. of C. of Greater Phila. (bd. dirs. 1991), Health Care Fin. Mgmt. Assn. (bd. dirs. NJ chpt. 2005-), Union League Phila., U. Barge Club (sec. 2007—), Brit. Officers Club Phila. (1st v.p. 2003—04, pres. 2005-06), Phila. Club. Avocations: gardening, house restoring, reading, sculling. Home: 415 Wister Rd Wynnewood PA 19096-1808 Office: Saul Ewing LLP 3800 Centre Sq W Philadelphia PA 19102 Home Phone: 610-649-4434; Office Phone: 215-972-7124. Business E-Mail: jreiss@saul.com.

REISS, LENORE ANN, language educator, retired secondary school educator; b. Bklyn., Apr. 17, 1936; d. Morris and Alice Shestack; m. Edward Lawrence Reiss, Sept. 13, 1959 (dec. June 5, 2000); children: Stephanie Lynne, Jonathan David. BA cum laude, Boston U., 1957; postgrad., Middlebury Coll., 1956, NYU, 1974—76, U. Miami, 1979. Tchr. Spanish and French Martin Van Buren HS, Queens Village, NY, 1957—59; pvt. tutor NYC, 1960—77; pvt. sch. tchr. Studio on Eleventh St., NYC, 1970—77; tchr. The Livingston Sch., NYC, 1977—78, Chiaravalle Montessori Sch., Evanston, Ill., 1986—87; pvt. tutor Evanston, 1990—95; ret., 1995. Author: White-Robed Recluse: A Study of Emily Dickinson, 1993, Genius of Darkness: A Study of Edgar Allan Poe, 1994, The Good Lady of Nohant: A Study of George Sand, 1995, numerous poems; contbr. articles to profl. jours. Avocations: reading, music, dance, antiques, theater. Home: 2025 Sherman Ave Evanston IL 60201 also: 136 E 76th St New York NY 10021

REISS, MITCHELL B., academic administrator, law educator, former ambassador; b. Dayton, Ohio, June 12, 1957; s. Martin H. and Rhea E. (Cohen) R.; m. Elisabeth M. Reiss, Oct. 25, 1986; children: Mathew A., Michael E. BA, Williams Coll., 1979; postgrad., Fletcher Sch., 1982; PhD, Oxford U., Eng., 1985; JD, Columbia U., 1988. Bar: D.C. Spl. asst. to nat. security adv. NSC, Washington, 1988-89; assoc. Covington & Burling LLP, Washington, 1989—94; asst. exec. dir. Korean Peninsula Energy Devel. Orgn. (KEDO), 1994—99; dir., Wendy & Emery Reves Ctr. for Internat. Studies Coll. William & Mary, Williamsburg, Va., 1999—2003, dean for internat. affairs, 1999—2003; prof. law & govt. Marshall-Wythe Law Sch., Williamsburg, Va., 1999—, vice provost for internat. affairs Wiliamsburg, Va., 2005—; dir. policy planning US Dept. State, Washington, 2003—05, spl. presidential envoy to No. Ireland, 2004—07. Guest scholar Woodrow Wilson Ctr., 1992-95 Author: Without the Bomb: The Politics of Nuclear Non-proliferation, 1988, Bridled Ambition: Why Countries Constrain Their Nuclear Capabilities, 1995; co-editor: Nuclear Proliferation after the Cold War, 1994, The Nuclear Tipping Point: Why States Reconsider Their Nuclear Choices, 2004. Presdl. Commn. on White House fellows, 1988. Avocations: tennis, squash. Office: William & Mary Sch Law PO Box 8795 Williamsburg VA 23187-8795

REISS, PAUL J., academic administrator; b. Lake Placid, NY, Aug. 10, 1930; s. Julian J. and Daisy M. (Smith) R.; m. Rosemary A. Donohue, June 25, 1955; children: Catherine, Paul, Gregory, Mark, Julia, David, Steven, Martha, John. BS, Holy Cross Coll., 1952; MA, Fordham U., 1954; PhD, Harvard U., 1960; LHD (hon.), Showa U., 1994; LLD (hon.), Middlebury Coll., 1996; LHD (hon.), St. Michael's Coll., 2005. Tutor Harvard U., 1954-57; instr., asst. prof. Marquette U., 1957-63, chmn. dept. sociology, 1961-63; asso. prof. sociology Fordham U., Bronx, NY, 1963-75, prof., 1976-85, chmn. dept. sociology and anthropology, 1964-68; dean Fordham U. (Liberal Arts Coll.), 1968-69, v.p. acad. affairs, 1969-75, exec. v.p., 1975-85; pres. St. Michael's Coll., Colchester, Vt., 1985-96, pres. emeritus, 1996—. Editor: Sociological Analysis: A Journal in the Sociology of Religion, 1961-68; contbr. articles to profl. jours. Chmn. bd. dir. Julian Reiss Found., Lake Placid, NY; trustee Wadhams Hall Sem. Coll.; St. Edmund's Retreat, bd. dirs. Lake Placid Sinfonietta, Mercy Care for Adirondacks; mem. Nat. Assn. Ind. Colls., Assn. Cath. Colls. and Univs., Assn. Vt. Ind. Colls. (pres.), Vt. Higher Edn. Coun. (pres.), Vt. Bus. Roundtable, Vt. World Trade Office (chmn.). Fellow Am. Sociol. Assn.; mem. Assn. Sociology Religion (pres.). Democrat. Roman Catholic. Home: 48 Daisy Way Lake Placid NY 12946 Personal E-mail: proreiss@aol.com.

REISS, ROBERT FRANCIS, physician; b. Watertown, NY, Dec. 11, 1938; s. Ernest Paul and Elizabeth Munk (Clark) R.; m. Giovanna Dora Bassi, Mar. 18, 1964; children: Carroll, Christian, Mark, Dylan. AB, Syracuse U., 1959; MD, U. Bologna, Italy, 1965. Diplomate Am. Bd. Pathology (hematology, transfusion medicine). Dir. lab. hematology and blood bank State U. Hosp., Bklyn., 1975-77; asst. prof. pathology SUNY Downstate Med. Ctr., Bklyn., 1975-77; dir. Hudson Valley Blood Svc., Valhalla, NY, 1978-85; assoc. prof. pathology and medicine N.Y. Med. Coll., Valhalla, 1978-88; med. dir. N.Y. Blood Ctr., NYC, 1985-88; dir. lab. hematology and transfusion medicine Columbia-Presbyn. Med. Ctr., NYC, 1988-98; prof. clin. pathology and clin. medicine Columbia U. Coll. Physicians and Surgeons, NYC, 1988—; v.p., chief med. officer N.Y. Blood Ctr., NYC, 1998—2001, 2006—. Chmn. steering com. Hudson Valley Blood Resources Assn., Valhalla, 1981-85; chief examiner blood banking N.Y.C. Dept. Health, 1980-86, mem. adv. com. on blood banking, 1988-90; mem. instnl. rev. bd. N.Y. Blood Ctr., N.Y.C., 1991-2001. Editor, co-author: Clinical Laboratory Medicine, 1992; contbr. more than 40 articles to med. jours., chpts. to books. Bd. mgrs. camping plus N.Y.C. Mission Soc., 1975-78; scout leader Boy Scouts Am., N.Y.C., 1975-80. Col. U.S. Army, 1966-69, USAR, 1988—2005. Fellow Assn. Clin. Scientists (vice chair sect. on hematology and transfusion medicine, 1999—; mem. Am. Assn. Blood Banks (dist. advisor 1982-88, mem. editl. bd. Ann. Clin. Labs. Sci. 1999—), Coun. Hosp. Blood Bank Dirs. Greater N.Y. (bd. dirs. 1989-98), Am. Soc. Hematology. Avocations: travel, running, stamps. Home Phone: 718-446-2739; Office Phone: 212-570-3407. Business E-Mail: rfr1@columbia.edu.

REISS, STEVEN ALAN, lawyer, educator; b. NYC, Dec. 18, 1951; s. Louis and Ruth (Harrow) R.; m. Mary A. Mattingly; children: Alexandra Mattingly Reiss, Tyler Brennan Reiss. BA, Vassar Coll., 1973; JD, Stanford U., Calif., 1976. Bar: N.Y., D.C., Calif. Law clk. to John Minor Wisdom U.S. Ct. Appeals for 5th Cir., New Orleans, 1976-77; law clk. to justice William J. Brennan U.S Supreme Ct., Washington, 1977-78; assoc. Miller, Cassidy, Larroca & Lewin, Washington, 1978-80; vis. prof. Georgetown U. Law Ctr., Washington, 1981; asst. prof. Law Sch., NYU, 1981-83, assoc. prof., 1984-87, prof., 1987-91; ptnr. Weil, Gotshal & Manges, NYC, 1990—. Editor-in-chief White Collar Crime Reporter, 1987-91, contbg. editor, 1991—. Trustee Vassar Coll. Poughkeepsie, N.Y., 1978-82; bd. dirs. NYU Cmty. Fund, 1984-87, Concert Artists Guild, 1991-94, Lyrics Chamber Music Soc., 2000--; gen. counsel Brennan Ctr. for Justice, 1996—; bd. trustees Vols. of Legal Svcs. Mem. N.Y. State Bar Assn., D.C. Bar Assn., Calif. Bar Assn., Assn. of Bar of City of N.Y. (fed. legis. com. 1981-87), 2d Jud. Conf. (reporter 1984—). Home: 25 E 86th St New York NY 10028-0553 Office: Weil Gotshal & Manges 767 5th Ave Fl Conc1 New York NY 10153-0119 E-mail: steven.riess@weil.com.

REISS, SUSAN MARIE, editor, writer; b. Washington, Sept. 14, 1963; m. Paul L. Roney Jr., May 25, 1991. BA in English Lit., U. Va., 1985; MA in English, George Mason U., 1989. Editl. asst. Water Pollution Control Fedn., Alexandria, Va., 1985-87; freelance writer, editor Arlington, Va., 1987-90; staff writer George Mason U., Fairfax, Va., 1988-90, Optical Soc. Am., Washington, 1990-91, news editor, 1991-93, mng. editor, 1993-96; editor On Campus With Women Assn. Am. Colls. and Univs., 1996—2000; freelance writer, editor Arlington, 1996—. Newsletter editor: Arlington County Tennis Assn., 1990-91; contbr. articles to profl. jours. and mags. Mem. Am. Soc. Laser Medicine and Surgery, Nat. Assn. Science Writers, Nat. Press Club, Washington Ind. Writers, D.C. Sci. Writers Assn., Sigma Tau Delta (founding mem. U. Va. chpt.). Avocations: tennis, piano, cross country skiing. Home and Office: 6814 30th Rd N Arlington VA 22213-1602

REISTER, RAYMOND ALEX, retired lawyer; b. Sioux City, Iowa, Dec. 22, 1929; s. Harold William and Anne (Eberhardt) R.; m. Ruth Elizabeth Alkema, Oct. 7, 1967 AB, Harvard U., 1952, LLB, 1955. Bar: N.Y. 1956, Minn. 1960. Assoc. Paul, Weiss, Rifkind, Wharton & Garrison, NYC, 1955-56; ptnr. Dorsey & Whitney LLP, Mpls., 1959-92; ret., 1993. Instr. U. Minn. Extension Divsn., 1964-66. Editor (with Larry W. Johnson): Minnesota Probate Administration, 1968. Trustee Mpls. Soc. Fine Arts, 1981-87; mem. exec. coun. Minn. Hist. Soc., 1984-2002; bd. dirs. Mpls. Athenaeum, 1992—, pres., 1998-2001; bd. dirs. Minn. Humanities Commn., 1997—. 1st lt. U.S. Army, 1956-59. Mem. Minn. Bar Assn., Hennepin County Bar Assn. Home: 93 Groveland Ter Minneapolis MN 55403-1142 Office: Dorsey & Whitney LLP Ste 1500 50 South 6th Street Minneapolis MN 55402-1498

REITAN, BERNT, metal products executive; b. Norway, Apr. 11, 1948; married; 2 children. M in Civil Engring., Tech. U. Trondheim, Norway. Various civil enging. project positions, Stavanger and Lillehammer, Norway, 1972—79; plant mgr. Rodsand magnetite mine Elkem, Norway, 1980—83, gen. mgr. Elkem Chems. Ltd. England, 1983—84, plant mgr. Fiskaa silicon plant Norway, 1985—87, bus. unit mgr. ferro alloys divsn., 1987, sr. v.p. materials and tech., mng. dir. Elkem Aluminium ANS, 1988—2000; gen. mgr. World Alumina Chems. Alcoa, Inc., 2000, pres. World Chems., 2000—01, pres. Alcoa World Alumina and Chems., v.p., 2001—03, pres. Primary Metals, 2003, group pres. Global Primary Products, exec. v.p. NYC, 2004—. Bd. mem. Internat. Primary Aluminium Inst., European Aluminium Assn., Norwegian Employers Fedn., Norwegian Process and Mfg. Assn.; chmn. bd. Norwegian Metall. Industry Assn., 1990—92; bd. dirs. Royal Caribbean Cruise Lines. Office: Alcoa Inc 390 Park Ave New York NY 10022 Office Phone: 212-836-2600. *

REITAN, DANIEL KINSETH, electric and computer engineering educator; b. Duluth, Minn., Aug. 13, 1921; s. Conrad Ulfred and Joy Elizabeth R.; m. Marian Anne Stemme, July 18, 1946; children: Debra Leah, Danielle Karen. BSEE, ND State U., Fargo, 1946; MSEE, U. Wis., Madison, 1949, PhD, 1952. Registered profl. engr., Wis. Control engr. GE, Schenectady, NY, 1946-48; transmission line engr. Gen. Telephone Co., Madison, Wis., 1949-50; mem. faculty Coll. Engring. U. Wis., Madison, 1952-85, prof. elec. and computer engring., 1962-85; cons. Energy Industries, 1985-95; dir. power sys. simulation lab. Coll. Engring. U. Wis., 1968-84, also dir. wind power rsch. Energy Ctr. Coll. Engring. Cons. Nat. Inst. Sci. and Tech. (formerly U.S. Nat. Bur. Stds.); dir. electric network calculator lab. Wis. Utilities, 1959-68. Author: Interstellar Space Travel at Near Light Speed, 1995, The Visual Appearance of Relativistically Moving Objects, 1999; contbr. articles to profl. jours.; patentee in field. With US Army, World War II. Recipient Outstanding Tchr. award Polygon Engring. Council., Gov.'s citation for service to State of Wis. Fellow IEEE (Centennial medal and cert. for outstanding achievement 1984, Centennial medal and cert. dept. ECE U. Wis., 1991, IEEE power Engring., Computer Control Indsl. Applications and Edn. Soc.), Conf. Internat. des Grand Reseaux Electriques a Haute Tension, Am. Soc. Engring. Edn., Wis. Acad. Scis., Am. Wind Energy Assn., The Planetary Soc., Sigma Xi, Tau Delta Pi, Tau Beta Pi, Eta Kappa Nu, Kappa Eta Kappa. Lutheran. Achievements include research and study of the cosmos. Home: 1200 Harwood Dr Apt 322 Fargo ND 58104-6294 Personal E-mail: dkreitan@cableone.net. *I believe that in one's career professionalism and perseverance are key factors in success. In one's personal life, the family should be the center, but not the circumference, about which all activities revolve.*

REITAN, PAUL HARTMAN, retired geologist, educator; b. Kanawha, Iowa, Aug. 18, 1928; s. John Olsen and Anna (Meldahl) R.; m. Reidun Engebretsen, Sept. 28, 1962; children: Kirsten Berit, Eric Hartmann. AB (Salisbury fellow), U. Chgo., 1953; PhD, U. Oslo, Norway, 1959. Instr. U. Ill., Chgo., 1955; geologist U.S. Geol. Survey, 1953-56; state geologist Geol. Survey of Norway, 1956-60; asst. prof. mineralogy Stanford U., 1960-66; mem. faculty SUNY, Buffalo, 1966-98, dean, 1975-79, prof. emeritus dept. geology, 1998—. Guest scientist Centre for Geol. Sci., Acad. Sci., Warsaw, Poland, Geol. Survey Prague, Czechoslovakia., Geol. Survey, Norway, Nat. Geophys. Rsch. Inst. and Geol. Survey, India Author: (with Davis and Pestrong) Geology, 1976; contbr. articles to profl. jours. Served with U.S. Army, 1946-49. Fulbright fellow, Norway, 1955-56; NATO sr. fellow in sci., 1972; G. Unger Vetlesen fellow, 1973; Fulbright sr. lectr., India, 1986; Norwegian Marshall Fund grantee, 1986, 93. Fellow AAAS, Geol. Soc. Am., Mineral. Soc. Am.; mem. Internat. Assn. Geochemistry and Cosmochemistry, Royal Norwegian Soc. Scis. and Letters (fgn.), Norsk Geologisk Forening (life), Sigma Xi. Home: 120 Walton Dr Buffalo NY 14226-4556 Office: U Buffalo Dept Geology Buffalo NY 14260-3050 Office Phone: 716-645-6800 3988. E-mail: preitan@buffalo.edu.

REITAN, RALPH MELDAHL, clinical neuropsychologist, former educator; b. Beresford, SD, Aug. 29, 1922; s. John O. and Anna (Meldahl) Reitan; m. Lucille Ann Kirsch, Feb. 14, 1952 (dec. July 1985); children: Ellen, Jon, Ann, Richard, Erik. BA, Ctrl. YMCA Coll., Chgo., 1944; PhD, U. Chgo., 1950. Cert. in clin. psychology and clin. neuropsychology Am. Bd. Profl. Psychology. Instr. U. Chgo., 1948-51; asst. prof. Roosevelt U., Chgo., 1950-51; from asst. prof. to prof. Ind. U. Med. Sch., Indpls., 1951-70; prof. U. Wash., Seattle, 1970-77, U. Ariz., Tucson, 1977-86; pres. Reitan Neuropsychology Labs., Tucson, 1981—. Cons. NIH, Bethesda, Md., 1960—71, VA, Washington, 1955—84, NASA, Washington, 1964—66. Author: Traumatic Brain Injury, 1985, Neuropsychological Evaluation of Older Children, 1992, The Halstead-Reitan Neuropsychological Test Battery, 1993, Detection of Malingering and Invalid Test Results, 1998, Mild Head Injury: Intellectual, Cognitive and Emotional Consequences, 2000, 15 others; contbr. articles to profl. jours. Trustee Easter Seal Rsch. Found., Chgo., 1974—83. With US Army, 1942—43. Fellow: APA, Nat. Acad. Neuropsychology; mem.: Reitan Soc., Coalition Clin. Neuropsychology Practitioners, Am. Acad. Neurology (affiliate), Am. Neurol. Assn. Avocations: walking, birdwatching. Home: 4831 N Via Serenidad Tucson AZ 85718-5715 Office: Reitan Neuropsychology Labs PO Box 66080 Tucson AZ 85728-6080 Office Phone: 520-299-5725. Personal E-mail: reitanlabs@aol.com.

REITER, DAVID S., engineering company executive, lawyer; b. St. Louis, 1967; m. Susie Reiter; children: Garrett, Audrey. BA, U. Notre Dame, 1989; JD, U. Southern Calif., 1993, M in Internat. Rels.; MBA, U. Sheffield, UK. Sr. counsel Compaq Computer Corp.; v.p., gen. counsel 724 Solutions Inc.; co-founder, ptnr. Phillips & Reiter, PLLC, 2003—; v.p., gen. counsel, corp. sec. Luminex Corp., Austin, Tex., 2003—. Mem.: Tex. Bar Assn., ABA (chair, Law Dept. Mgmt. subcommittee). Avocations: tennis, bicycling. Office: Luminex Corp 12212 Technology Blvd Austin TX 78727 Office Phone: 512-219-8020. Office Fax: 512-219-5195. *

REITER, GLENN MITCHELL, lawyer; b. NYC, Feb. 1, 1951; s. Bernard Leon and Helene (Edson) R.; m. Marilyn Beckhorn, Sept. 5, 1976; children: Benjamin, Diana, Julie. BA, Yale U., 1973, JD, 1976. Bar: N.J. 1976, Pa. 1977, D.C. 1978, N.Y. 1979. Law clk. to judge U.S. Ct. Appeals, Phila., 1976-77; assoc. Schnader, Harrison, Segal & Lewis, Phila., 1977-78, Simpson Thacher & Bartlett LLP, NYC, 1978-84, ptnr., 1984—, resident ptnr. London, 1986-90. Mem.: Phi Beta Kappa. Office Phone: 212-455-3358.

REITER, JESSE MATTHEW, lawyer; b. Maliga, Spain, Sept. 7, 1961; came to US, 1961; s. Charles Jules Reiter and Ann (Amenta) Long; m. Susan Lynn Nebroski, Aug. 27, 1988. BA, U. Mich., 1984; JD, DePaul U., 1987. Bar: Mich. 1987, Ohio 2007, US Dist. Ct. (ea. dist.) Mich. 1987, US Supreme Ct. 2006. Assoc. Kitch, Saurbier, Drutchas, Wagner & Kenney,

P.C., Detroit, 1987-89, Turner & Turner, P.C., Southfield, Mich., 1989-97; shareholder Gregory & Reiter, P.C., Farmingham Hills, Mich., 1997—. Adj. prof. legal writing Coll. Law, U. Detroit, 1989-90; mem. Million Dollar Advocates Forum. Named Lawyer of Yr., Mich. Weekly, 2006; fellow, Am. Assn. for Justice Coll. Advocacy. Mem. ABA, Am. Assn. for Justice (mem. birth trauma litigation group), Mich. Bar Assn. (mem. coun. negligence law com. 1998-99), Oakland Country Bar Assn. (chairperson negligence com. 1991-92), DC Bar Assn., Mich. Trial Lawyers Asn. (pres. 2006-07), State Bar Mich., Acad. for Trial Advocacy. Avocations: running, biking, reading. Office: Gregory & Reiter PC 122 Concord Rd Bloomfield MI 48304-2920 Business E-Mail: jreiter@abclawcenters.com.

REITER, JOSEPH HENRY, lawyer, retired judge; b. Phila., Mar. 21, 1929; s. Nicholas and Barbara (Hellmann) Reiter; m. Beverlee A. Bearman, Nov. 8, 1993. AB, Temple U., 1950, LLB, 1953. Bar: D.C. 1953, Pa. 1954. Atty. advisor U.S. Army, 1955—61; asst. U.S. atty. Ea. Dist. Pa., 1961—63, asst. U.S. atty. in charge of civil div., 1963—69; chief organized crime and racketeering strike force Western N.Y. State U.S. Dept. Justice, 1969—70, sr. trial atty. tax divsn., 1970—72, regional dir. office of drug abuse law enforcement, 1972—73; dep. atty. gen., dir. Drug Law Enforcement Office of Pa., 1973—77; ptnr. Stassen, Kostos and Mason, Phila., 1978—85, Kostos Reiter & Lamer, 1985—89; judge Armed Svcs. Bd. of Contract Appeals, Falls Church, Va., 1989—95; of counsel Kostos & Lamer, Phila., 1995—. Mem. adv. com. Joint State Commn. on Procurement; lectr. in field. Contbr. articles to profl. jours. With US Army, 1953—55. Recipient Meritorious Svc. award, U.S. Atty. Gen. Clark, 1967, Spl. Commendation, Asst. U.S. Atty. Gen. Tax Divsn., 1969, Outstanding Performance award, U.S. Atty. Gen. Richardson, 1973. Mem.: ABA, Phila. Bar Assn., D.C. Bar Assn., Fed. Bar Assn., Pan Am. Assn. Phila., Vesper Club, Am. Legion. Office: Kostos & Lamer 1608 Walnut St Ste 1300 Philadelphia PA 19103-5407 Home Phone: 305-867-0465.

REITER, LUIS, lawyer; b. Lima, Peru, 1956; BA magna cum laude, U. Miami, 1977, JD, 1980. Bar: Fla. 1980. Ptnr. Squire, Sanders & Dempsey LLP, Miami, co-chmn., Project Fin. Practice Group. Mem.: Fla. Bar, Nat. Assn. Bond Lawyers. Fluent in Spanish. Home: Squire Sanders & Dempsey LLP 200 S Biscyne Blvd Ste 4000 Miami FL 33131 Office Phone: 305-577-7710. Office Fax: 305-577-7001. Business E-Mail: lreiter@ssd.com.

REITER, STANLEY, economist, educator; b. NYC, Apr. 26, 1925; s. Frank and Fanny (Rosenberg) R.; m. Nina Sarah Breger, June 13, 1944; children: Carla Frances, Frank Joseph. AB, Queens Coll., 1947; MA, U. Chgo., 1950, PhD, 1955. Rsch. assoc. Cowles Commn., U. Chgo., 1948-50; mem. faculty Stanford U., 1950-54, Purdue U., 1954-67; prof. econs. and math. Northwestern U., 1967—, now Morrison prof. econs. and math. Weinberg Coll. Arts and Scis., Morrison prof. managerial econs. and decision scis. Kellogg Sch. Mgmt. Dir. Ctr. for Math. Studies in Econs. and Mgmt. Sci.; cons. in field. Trustee Roycemore Sch., Evanston, Ill., 1969-71, treas., 1970-71. Served with inf. AUS, 1943-45. Decorated Purple Heart. Fellow Econometric Soc., AAAS; mem. Soc. Indsl. and Applied Math., Inst. Mgmt. Scis., Ops. Rsch. Soc. Am., Am. Math. Soc., Math. Assn. Am., Am. Acad. of Arts and Scis. Home: Apt 4B 838 Michigan Ave Evanston IL 60202 Office: Northwestern U Ctr for Math Studies 2001 Sheridan Rd Evanston IL 60208-0814 Office Phone: 847-491-3527. Business E-Mail: s-reiter@northwestern.edu.

REITMAN, IVAN, film director, producer; b. Komarmo, Czechoslovakia, Oct. 27, 1946; came to Can., 1951; s. Leslie and Clara R.; m. Genevieve Robert, Sept. 12, 1976; children: Jason, Catherine, Caroline. MusB, McMaster U., 1969. Judge FOCUS Nissan-Datsun, NYC, 1981-83. Theatrical prodr.: The Magic show, 1974, The National Lampoon Show, 1975, Merlin, 1983 (also dir.); films include: (dir., exec. prodr.) Cannibal Girls, 1973; (prodr.) They Came From Within (aka Shivers), 1975, Death Weekend (aka The House by the Lake), 1977, Blackout, 1978, National Lampoon's Animal House, 1978, Heavy Metal, 1981, Stop! Or My Mom Will Shoot, 1992, Space Jam, 1996, Private Parts, 1996, Father's Day, 1997, Six Days and Seven Nights, 1998, Doomsday Man, 1999, Evolution, 2001; (prodr., dir.) Foxy Lady, 1971, Meatballs, 1979, Stripes, 1981, Ghostbusters, 1984, Legal Eagles, 1986, Twins, 1988, Ghostbusters II, 1989, Kindergarten Cop, 1990, Dave, 1993, Junior, 1994; (exec. prodr.) Rabid, 1976, Spacehunter: Adventures in the Forbidden Zone, 1983, Big Shots, 1987, Casual Sex?, 1988, Feds, 1988, Beethoven, 1992, Beethoven's 2nd, 1993, Commandments, 1996, Road Trip, 2000, Killing Me Softly, 2002, Old School, 2003, Eurotrip, 2004, That Guy, 2006, Trailer Park Boys: The Movie, 2006, Disturbia, 2007; (dir.) My Super Ex-Girlfriend, 2006; TV series: (prodr., dir.) Delta House, 1978; TV films exec. prodr. The Late Shift, 1996, Fathers Day, 1997. Mem. Dirs. Guild Am. also: Bldg 489 100 University City Plz Universal City CA 91608-1002 *

REITMAN, JERRY IRVING, advertising agency executive; b. Phila., Jan. 9, 1938; s. Benjamin and Ruth (Eisenberg) R.; m. Monica Birgitta Hall, Oct. 27, 1968; children: Jennifer Sharon, Sarah Beth. BS in Fin., Pa. State U., 1961. Exec. v.p., CEO Brit. Pubs., NYC and London, 1965-69; pres., pub. Acad. Media, Sherman Oaks, Calif., 1969-73; v.p. Pubs. Clearing House, Port Washington, NY, 1973-78; exec. v.p. Ogilvy & Mather, NYC, 1978-81; with Scali, McCabe, Sloves, Inc., NYC, 1981-86; pres. Scali, McCabe, Sloves Direct, NYC; chmn. bd. dirs. The Reitman Group, 1986; exec. v.p. The Leo Burnett Co., Chgo., 1986-96; pres., CEO, vice chair Internat. Data Response Corp., Chgo., 1996—. Dir. Scandinavian Airlines Sys. Pub./Distbn. Svcs.; mem. adv. bd. Ill. Dept. Trade and Tourism, 1988—; internat. awards chmn., bd. dirs. John Caples Internat., 1989—; mem. Internat. Direct Mktg. Symposium, Zürich, Switzerland; dir. Catylst Direct, Goliath Solutions, LLC. Author: A Common Sense Approach to Small Business, 1968, Beyond 2000: The Future of Direct Marketing, 1994; contbr. articles to profl. jours. Trustee Locust Valley Libr. Assn., NY, 1982—; exec. com. mem. Pub. Hall of Fame, 1987—; bd. govs. Children's Miracle Network, 1992-, vice chmn., chmn. bd. govs., 1998—, 1999-2001, chmn. 2002-04, dir.; bd. dirs. Children's Meml. Found. Telethon, The Direct Mktg. Ednl. Found., exec, dir., 1996—. Anderson scholar, 1960; recipient Key to City, New Orleans, 1959, Silver Apple award N.Y. Direct Mktg. Club, 1989, Ed Mayer award Ednl. Found., 1996, Charles S. Downs award, 1997, Direct Marketer of Yr. award. Fellow Psychiat. Re-Edn. Assn.; mem. Am. Mktg. Assn. (at-large mem., 2000, bd. dirs.), Direct Mktg. Assn. (bd. mem. ethics com. 1984), Creative Guild (dir. 1984), Internat. Direct Mktg. Assn. (bd. dirs. 1981-82), Publ. Hall of Fame (exec. com. 1988—), Direct Mktg. Club N.Y. (pres. 1983-84), Beta Gamma Sigma. Avocations: tennis, auto restoration, woodworking. Home and Office: Callahan Group LLC 2204 N Leavitt St Chicago IL 60647-3204 Home (Summer): Ringso 237 Nasbyviken 64061 Stallanholmen Sweden Office Phone: 773-342-1973. Personal E-mail: jireitman@aol.com.

REITMAN, ROBERT STANLEY, management consultant, not-for-profit advisor; b. Fairmont, W.Va., Nov. 18, 1933; s. Isadore and Freda A. (Layman) R.; m. Sylvia K. Golden, Dec. 24, 1955; children: Scott Alan, Alayne Louise. BS in Acctg., W.Va. U., 1955; JD, Case Western Res. U., 1958. Bar: Ohio 1958. Mem. firm Burke, Haber & Berick, Cleve., 1958-60, ptnr., 1960-68; exec. v.p., vice chmn. Tranzonic Cos. (formerly AAV Cos.), Pepper Pike, Ohio, 1968-70, pres., vice-chmn., 1970-73, chief exec. officer, pres., vice chmn., 1973-82, pres., chmn., CEO, 1982-98, chmn. emeritus, bd. dirs., 1998—; prin. Riverbend Advisors, 1998—. Bus. adv. com. Mandel Ctr. for non-profit Orgn. Case We. Res. U., 1995-99, vis. com. Weatherhead Sch. of Bus., 1995-03, vis. com. Sch. of Law, 1998-03, chmn. dean's nat. adv. com., Sch. of Law, 1997-98; pvt. banking adv. bd. Key Bank, N.A., 1997-2007; dean's adv. com. Sch. Medicine, 2004-06. Mem. Rep. fin. com., Cuyahoga County, 1968-78; mem. Com. for Econ. Growth for Israel, Cleve., 1977-80, pres., 1978-80; adv. coun. Cleve. Mus. Nat. History, 1982-85, Cleve. Opera, 1977—; del. Coun. of Jewish Fedns., NYC, 1981-97; gen. co-chmn. Jewish Welfare Fund, Cleve., 1975-78, 81-85, gen. vice chmn., 1985-89, gen. chmn., 1989-91; sect. and divsn. chmn., team capt. United Way Svcs., 1974-97, del. assembly, 1976-85, trustee, 1977-2000, v.p., 1985-88, chmn. nominating. com., 1988-90, campaign chmn., 1993, chair fund raising planning com., 1994-97, chair bd. trustees, 1997-2000, life trustee, 2000—; employment com. Jewish Vocat. Svc., Cleve., 1974-83; bd. dirs. Capital for Israel, Inc., NYC, 1986-87; nat. vice chmn. United Jewish Appeal, 1987-92, nat. allocations chmn., 1987-90, trustee, 1988-94, chair retirement fund com., 1994-97; trustee B'nai B'rith Hillel Found., 1975-81, Cleve. Jewish News, 1976-79, Ideastream, Cleve., 1976-99, vice chmn. 1986-90, chmn. bd., 1990-97, immediate past chair, 1997-99, chair emeritus, 1999—; trustee, pres. Bus. Volunteerism Coun., 1994-96, chmn. 1996-97; trustee Jewish Cmty. Fedn. Cleve., 1983-98, 1999-03, treas., 1991-94, v.p., 1995-97, life trustee, 2003—, Jewish Edn. Ctr. of Cleve., 1993-96, Cleve. Zool. Soc., 1972—, pres., 1979-87, chmn., 1987-92, chmn. emeritus, 1992—, chmn. JDC-Brookdale Inst. of Gerontology and Human Devel., Israel, 1995; trustee Am. Jewish Joint Distbn. Com., 1988—, United Israel Appeal, 1987-94, Mt. Sinai Med. Ctr., Cleve., 1976-96, chmn., 1982-85; trustee Cleve. State U. Devel. Found., 1988-91, Greater Cleve. Roundtable, 1991-04, The Wilds, 1995-99, adv. bd., 1999-02, trustee Mt. Sinai Health Care Found., 1995-04, life trustee, 2004—, vice chair 1998-2001, chair, 2001-04; trustee Univ. Hosps. Health Sys., 1999-04, 05-, Univ. Hosps. Cleve., 1999-2007; trustee, chair Heather Hill, Inc., 2001—; coun. mem. Village of Gates Mills, Ohio, 1997-00, clk., 2000-07. Mem. The 50 Club Cleve., Case We. Res. Univ. Sch. of Law Soc. Benchers, Am. Kennel Club (regional del. 1960-75), We. Res. Kennel Club (officer, trustee 1959-75), Beechmont Club (fin. com. 1972-80, house com. 1974), Pepper Pike Club, Union Club, Carambola Golf Club, Masons, Zeta Beta Tau, Tau Epsilon Rho. Avocations: golf, swimming. Office: Riverbend Advisors 2087 Chagrin River Rd Gates Mills OH 44040-9740 Home Phone: 440-423-1515. Business E-Mail: rsrform@core.com.

REITNAUER, ANDREW RICHARD, forensic specialist; b. Pottstown, Pa., Aug. 1, 1977; s. Richard Gerald and Cheryl Ann Reitnauer; m. Gina Ann Longobardi, Dec. 6, 2003. B in Criminal Justice, York Coll., Pa., 1999; M in Forensic Exam., Touro Coll., Bay Shore, NY, 2004; B in Biology, Stony Brook U., NY, 2005. Coord. security svcs. York Coll., Pa., 2000—03; criminalist Boston Police Dept. Latent Print Unit, 2005—. Team mem. Am. Cancer Soc., Pottstown, Pa., 2000—03, co-chair, team capt. Port Jefferson Station, NY, 2004—05. Mem.: New England Assn. Identification, Am. Acad. Forensic Scis., Northeastern Assn. Forensic Scientists (assoc.), Internat. Assn. Identification (assoc.). Office: Boston Police Department 1 Schroder Plz Boston MA 02120 Office Phone: 617-343-5580. Personal E-mail: areitnau@hotmail.com. E-mail: reitnauera.bpd@ci.boston.ma.us.

REITSEMA, HAROLD JAMES, aerospace engineer; b. Kalamazoo, Jan. 19, 1948; s. Robert Harold and Bernice Jean (Hoogsteen) R.; m. Mary Jo Gunnink, Aug. 6, 1970; children: Ellen Celeste, Laurie Jean. BA, Calvin Coll., 1972; PhD, N.Mex. State U., 1977. Rsch. assoc. U. Ariz., Tucson, 1977-79, sr. rsch. assoc., 1979-82, vis. scientist, 1987—; sr. mem. tech. staff Ball Aerospace, Boulder, Colo., 1982-85, prin. systems engr., 1985-88, program mgr., 1988-89, staff cons., 1989-96, dir., 1996—. Cons. Aerospace Tech., 1987—. Contbr. articles to profl. jours. including Astrophys. Jour., Aston. Jour., Nature, Sci., Icarus. Bd. dirs. EE Barnard Obs., Golden, Colo., 1984-91. Fellow AIAA (assoc., tech. com. chair 1991, Engr. of Yr. Colo. region 1990); mem. Am. Astron. Soc. (planetary sci. com. 1991-94), Internat. Astron. Union. Achievements include discovery of Larissa, fifth satellite of Neptune; co-discovery of Telesto, seventeenth satellite of Saturn; patents for Optically-coupled Shaft Angle Encoder. Home: 4795 Hancock Dr Boulder CO 80303-1103 Office: Ball Aerospace 1600 Commerce St Boulder CO 80301-2734 E-mail: hreitsema@ball.com.

REITZ, BRUCE ARNOLD, cardiac surgeon, educator; b. Seattle, Sept. 14, 1944; BS, Stanford U., 1966; MD, Yale U., 1970. Diplomate: Am. Bd. Surgery, Am. Bd. Thoracic Surgery. Intern Johns Hopkins Hosp., Balt., 1970-71, cardiac surgeon-in-charge, 1982-92; resident Stanford U. Hosp., Calif., 1971-72, 74-78; clin. assoc. Nat. Heart Lung Blood Inst., NIH, Bethesda, Md., 1972-74; asst. prof. Stanford U. Sch. Medicine, 1977-81, assoc. prof., 1981-82; prof. surgery Johns Hopkins U. Sch. Medicine, Balt., 1982-92; prof., chmn. Sch Medicine Stanford (Calif.) U., 1992—2005; prof. Stanford U. Sch. Medicine, 2005—. Developer heart-lung transplant technique, 1981. Office: Stanford U Sch Medicine Dept Cardiothoracic Surgery Stanford CA 94305-5407 Office Phone: 650-725-4497. Business E-Mail: breitz@stanford.edu.

REITZ, CHRISTOPHER M., lawyer, gas industry executive; Corp. counsel Blackwell Sanders Peper Martin LLP, Sprint Corp., Cerner Corp.; joined Aquila, Inc., Kansas City, Mo., 2000, asst. gen. counsel, interim gen. counsel, corp. sec., 2005, sr. v.p., gen. counsel, corp. sec., 2005—. Office: Aquila, Inc 20 W Ninth St Kansas City MO 64105 Office Phone: 816-467-3611. E-mail: christopher.reitz@aquila.com. *

REITZ, CURTIS RANDALL, lawyer, educator; b. Reading, Pa. s. Lester S. and Magdalene A. (Crouse) R.; m. Virginia R. Patterson, Dec. 19, 1953 (div.); children— Kevin R., Joanne E., Whitney A.; m. Judith N. Renzulli, Sept. 18, 1983 BA, U. Pa., 1951, LL.B., 1956. Bar: Pa. 1957, U.S. Supreme Ct. 1959. Law clk. to Chief Justice Earl Warren U.S. Supreme Ct., 1956-57; mem. faculty law U. Pa., Phila., 1957—, asst. prof. law, 1957-60, assoc. prof., 1960-63, prof., 1963—, provost, v.p., 1971—73, Algernon Sydney Biddle prof. law, 1985—. Trustee Internat. House Ctr. Phila.; bd. mgrs. Glen Mills Schs., Pa. Served to 1st lt. U.S. Army, 1951-53 Life Mem. Am. Law Inst., Mem., Nat. Conf. Commrs. on Uniform State Laws, Order of Coif Office: U Pa Law Sch 3400 Chestnut St Philadelphia PA 19104-6204 Business E-Mail: creitz@law.upenn.edu.

REITZ, JENNIFER LEE, financial company managing partner; b. Fresno, Calif., Mar. 17, 1976; d. Donald Lee and Mary Teresa McClellan, June Ellen McClellan (Stepmother); m. Scott Kelly Reitz, Apr. 8, 2000; children: Breana Dominique, Mason Alexander. Office mgr. Bulldog Brewing Co., Fresno, Calif., 1998—99; exec. asst. Venture Resources Group, LLC, Fresno, Calif., 1998—2000, Mike Rozell - Realtor, Renton, Wash., 2007—; mng. ptnr. NW Investment Group, LLC, Renton, Wash., 2005—. Various positions Oasis Seattle, Renton, Wash., 2004—07. Mem.: Am. Inst. Profl. Bookkeepers (assoc.). Office: Mike Rozell Realtor 14201 SE Petrovitsky Rd #A3-188 Renton WA 98058 Office Phone: 206-799-3414.

REITZAS, JOSHUA T., lawyer, venture capitalist; b. Fall River, Mass., July 9, 1974; s. Richard Arthur Reitzas and Donna Lee Haas. BA, Bowdoin Coll., Brunswick, Maine, 1998; JD, Benjamin N. Cardozo Sch. Law, 2001. Bar: NY 2002, NJ 2002, US Dist. Ct. (3d cir.) NJ 2002, US Dist. Ct. (so. dist.) 2005, US Dist. Ct. (ea. dist.) 2005. Assoc. Rockefeller & Co., Inc., NYC, 1999—2000, Bear Stearns & Co., Inc., NYC, 2001—02, Jaffe & Asher LLP, NYC, 2002—. Adv. bd. Beacon Capital LLC, Martinsville, 2004—; founder ModernFetch, Inc., NYC, 2002—. Fundraiser Metrolacrosse, Boston, 2003—04; alumni interviewer Phillips Exeter Acad., Exeter, NH, 2004. Mem.: ABA (assoc.), NY State Bar Assn. (mem. com. atty. professionalism), Harvard Club Private Equity and Hedge Fund Group. Achievements include patents pending for in Business and E-commerce. Office: Jaffe & Asher LLP 600 Third Ave New York NY 10016 Home Phone: 212-253-8980; Office Phone: 212-687-3000. Office Fax: 212-687-3601. Business E-Mail: jreitzas@jaffeandasher.com.

REITZFELD, ALAN D., lawyer; b. Bklyn., Mar. 13, 1951; s. William and Jeanette (Winzelberg) Reitzfeld; m. Lois Carol Goldfinger, June 24, 1973; children: Jordan Lawrence, Stacey Elyse. BA, Syracuse U., 1973; JD, Hofstra U., 1976. Bar: NY, 1977, US Dist. Ct. (So. and Ea. Dists. NY), 1977, US Ct. of Internat. Trade, 1978, US Ct. of Military Appeals, 1978, US Dist. Ct. (No. and Western Dists. NY), 1979, US Ct. of Appeals (2nd and 4th Circs.), 1979, US Ct. of Appeals (7th Cir.), 1980, US Supreme Ct., 1980, US Dist. Ct. (Ea. Dist. Wis.), 1988, US Ct. of Appeals (6th Cir.), 1993, US Ct. of Appeals (8th Cir.), 1997, US Ct. of Appeals (9th Cir.), 2001, US Ct. of Appeals, DC Cir., 2004. Dir. First Yr. Legal Rsch. and Advisement Fellows Program, Hofstra U., 1975—76; assoc. Martin, Van de Walle & Sawyer, Great Neck, NY, 1976—77, Haight, Gardner, Poor & Havens, 1978—97; ptnr. Holland & Knight LLP (previously Haight, Gardner, Poor & Havens), NY, 1997—. Mem. firmwide tech. com. Holland & Knight LLP, NYC, 2003—, chmn., 2003—07, firmwide tech. ptnr., 2003—07; lectr. in field; spkr. in field. Mem. Hofstra Law Review, 1974—76, rsch. editor, 1975—76; contbr. articles to profl. jours. Mem.: Internat. Tech. Law Assn., Def. Rsch. Inst., Nassau County Bar Assn., Internat. Assn. Def. Counsel (vice chair newsletters, aviation and space law com. 2007—), Fed. Bar Coun., Assn. of the Bar City of NY (aero. law com. 2002—06), Internat. Bar Assn. (vice-chair tech. and e-Commerce law com. 2004—06), NY State Bar Assn. (mem. bus. law sect. exec. com. 1996—2006, chmn. bus. law sect. internet and tech. law com. 1998—2001, del. Ho. of Dels. 2002—06, mem. bus. law sect. exec. com. 2007—), Zeta Beta Tau (pres. 1972—73). Office: Holland & Knight LLP 195 Broadway 24th Fl New York NY 10007 Office Phone: 212-513-3400. Business E-Mail: alan.reitzfeld@hklaw.com.

REJAI, MOSTAFA, political science professor; b. Tehran, Iran, Mar. 11, 1931; came to U.S., 1954; s. Taghi and Forough (Lashgari) R. AA, Pasadena City Coll., 1957; BA, Calif. State U., LA, 1959, MS, 1961; PhD, UCLA, 1964. Teaching fellow UCLA, 1963-64; asst. prof. polit. sci. Miami U., Oxford, Ohio, 1964-67, assoc. prof., 1967-70, prof., 1970-83, Disting. prof., 1983—. Vis. scholar Ctr. for Internat. Affairs, Harvard U., 1972, Hoover Instn. on War, Revolution and Peace, Stanford U., 1973, Inst. Internat. Studies, Iran, 1974-75; vis. prof. Western Coll., Oxford, 1971, 72. Author: World Miltary Leaders: A Collective and Comparative Analysis, 1996, The Strategy of Political Revolution, 1973, The Comparative Study of Revolutionary Strategy, 1977, Comparative Political Ideologies, 1984; (with Kay Phillips) Leaders of Revolution, 1979, World Revolutionary Leaders, 1983, Loyalists and Revolutionaries: Political Leaders Compared, 1988, Political Ideologies: A Comparative Approach, 1991, 2d edit., 1995, Demythogizing an Elite: American Presidents in Empirical, Comparative, and Historical Perspectives, 1993, World Military Leaders: A Collective and Comparative Analysis, 1996, Leaders and Leadership: An Appraisal of Theory and Research, 1997, The Young George Washington in Psychobiographical Perspective, 2000, Concepts of Leadership in Western Political Thought, 2002; editor, contbr.: Democracy: The Contemporary Theories, 1967, Decline of Ideology?, 1971; editor: Mao Tse-Tung on Revolution and War, 1969, rev. edit., 1970; assoc. editor Jour. Polit. and Mil. Sociology, 1973—; contbr. articles to profl. jours., book chpts. Recipient Outstanding Teaching award Miami U., 1970. Mem. Am. Polit. Sci. Assn. (polit. psychology sect.), Am. Sociol. Assn. (polit. soc. sect.), Internat. Polit. Sci. Assn., Internat. Soc. Polit. Psychology, Internat. Studies Assn., Inter-Univ. Seminar on Armed Forces and Soc., Conf. for Study Polit. Thought, Midwest Polit. Sci. Assn., So. Polit. Sci. Assn., Wesetern Polit. Sci. Assn., Pi Gamma Mu, Pi Sigma Alpha. Office: Miami U Dept of Political Science Oxford OH 45056

REJENT, MARIAN MAGDALEN, retired pediatrician; b. Toledo, Aug. 12, 1920; d. Casimir Stanley and Magdalen (Szymanowski) R. BS, Mary Manse Coll., 1943; MD, Marquette U., 1946; MPH, U. Mich., 1960. Diplomate Am. Bd. Pediatrics. Intern St. Vincent Med. Ctr., Toledo, 1946-47; resident communicable diseases City Hosp., Cleve., 1947-48; resident pediatrics Childrens Hosp., Akron, Ohio, 1948-50; pvt. practice Toledo, 1950-54; chief div. maternal child health Toledo Bd. Health, 1953-64; dir. pediatrics Maumee Valley Hosp., Toledo, 1964-69; assoc. prof. pediatrics Med. Coll. Ohio, Toledo, 1969-76; med. dir. State Crippled Childrens Program, Columbus, Ohio, 1976-78; attendant pediatrician St. Vincent Med. Ctr., Toledo, 1978-80, 87-99; chief pediatric svcs. Wake County Health Dept., Raleigh, NC, 1980-87; ret. clin. prof. pediatrics Med. Coll. Ohio, 1998; ret., 1999. Exec. com. March of Dimes, 1988-92. Mem. AMA, APHA, Am. Acad. Pediatrics, Am. Med. Women's Assn., Ohio PHA, Ohio State Med. Assn., NW Ohio Pediatric Assn., Acad. Medicine Toledo, Alpha Omega Alpha. Republican. Roman Catholic. Avocations: travel, photography, painting. Home: The Woodlands Apt 401 4030 Indian Rd Toledo OH 43606

REKATE, ALBERT C., physician; b. Buffalo, June 12, 1916; s. Gustave E. and Fannie (Hummell) R.; m. Elizabeth Foster, June 12 1943 (dec. 1985); 1 child, Suzanne (Mrs. R. Willis Post); m. Linda Ann Holt, Aug. 1, 1992. MD, U. Buffalo, 1940. Diplomate Am. Bd. Internal Medicine. Intern E.J. Meyer Meml. Hosp., Buffalo, 1940-41, med. resident, 1941-44; asst. prof. medicine SUNY-Buffalo, 1954-61, assoc. prof., 1961-65, prof., 1965-86, prof. emeritus, 1986—; dir. rehab. medicine SUNY, Buffalo, 1965-72, acting dean Sch. Health Related Professions, 1965-66, assoc. dean, 1966-74, acting chmn. dept. rehab. medicine, 1972-75; assoc. dir. medicine E.J. Meyer Meml. Hosp., Buffalo, 1957-63, head dept. rehab. medicine, 1964-69, dir. primary rehab. center, 1965-69, acting head cardiology, 1966-69, dir., 1970-72. Bd. dirs. Buffalo Hearing and Speech Ctr., 1973-99; mem. adv. bd. Coastal Empire Mental Health Ctr., S.C., 1980-81, bd. dirs., 1981-93; mem. dean's adv. coun. SUNY-Buffalo Sch. Medicine and Biomed. Scis., 1995—, med. emeritus faculty group steering con., 2000—. Contbr. articles to profl. jours. Served with M.C. AUS, World War II. Mem. Am. Heart Assn., Western N.Y. Heart Assn. (pres. 1954-55), Assn. Am. Med. Colls., N.Y. State Heart Assembly, N.Y. Acad. Scis., Med. Union (pres. 1974-75), Buffalo Acad. Medicine (pres. 1969-70), Erie County Med. Soc., Med. Alumni Assn. U. Buffalo (pres. 1960-61), Beaufort-Jasper Mental Health Assn. (dir. 1980-86). Home and Office: 52 Hampton Hill Dr Williamsville NY 14221-5840 Personal E-mail: lre1832886@aol.com.

REKLAITIS, GINTARAS VICTOR, chemical engineer, educator; b. Oct. 20, 1942; BS, Ill. Inst. Tech., 1965; MS, PhD, Stanford U., Calif., 1969. Edward W. Comings prof. chem. engring. Purdue U., West Lafayette, Ind., 1970—; co-dir. Pharm. Tech. & Edn. Ctr., 2006—; dep. dir. NSF Engring. Rsch. Ctr. Structured Organic Composites, 2006—. Contbr. articles to sci. jours. Mem.: NAE. Office: Purdue U Sch Chem Engring Forney Hall Chem Engring 480 Stadium Mall Dr West Lafayette IN 47907-2100 Office Phone: 765-494-9662. Office Fax: 765-494-0805. E-mail: reklaiti@purdue.edu. *

RELIAS, JOHN ALEXIS, lawyer; b. Chgo., Apr. 2, 1946; s. Alexis John and Marie Helen (Metos) R.; m. Linda Ann Pontious, Nov. 27, 1971; children: Anne, Alexandra. BA, Northwestern U., Evanston, 1968; LLB, Northwestern U., Chgo., 1972. Bar: Ill., 1972, U.S. Dist. Ct. (no. dist.) Ill. 1972, U.S. Ct. Appeals (9th cir.) 1981, U.S. Ct. Appeals (7th cir.) 1983, U.S. Supreme Ct. 1997. Assoc. Vedder, Price, Kaufman & Kammholz, Chgo., 1972-78, ptnr., 1979-94, Franczek, Sullivan, Mann, Crement, Hein & Relias, Chgo., 1994—. Mem. bd. edn. Wilmette (Ill.) Sch. Dist. 39, 1989-97, 2001—, pres., 1992-93, 1995-96. Mem. Nat. Assn. Sch. Attys., Ill. Assn. Sch. Attys., Order of the Coif, Phi Beta Kappa. Greek Orthodox. Home: 2500 Kenilworth Ave Wilmette IL 60091-1337 Office: Franczek Sulian Mann Crement Hein & Relias 300 S Wacker Dr Chicago IL 60606-6680 Office Phone: 312-786-6160. Business E-Mail: jar@franczek.com.

RELL, M. JODI, governor; b. Norfolk, Va., June 16, 1946; m. Lou Rell; children: Meredith, Michael. Student, Old Dominion U., Western Conn. State U.; LLD (hon.), U. Hartford, 2001. Mem., dep. minority leader Conn. Ho. Reps., 1984-94; lt. gov. State of Conn., 1995—2004, gov., 2004—. Past vice chmn. Brookfield Rep. Town Com., appt. chair of the Hartford Econ. Devel. Adv. Group, (HEDAG), 1998; trustee YMCA Western Conn; played a key role in raising funds for the Conn. Firefighters Meml.; estab. the Lt. Gov.'s Comm. on State Mandate Reform, Lt. Gov.'s Conn. Treasures award. Named Melvin Jones Fellow, Lions Club Internat. Found., 2003; recipient Leadership award, Nat. Order of Women Legislators (NOWL), Impact award, Conn. Tech. Coun., 2001, First Kids 2001 Policy Leadership award, Conn. Voices for Children, Arnold Markle Public Service award. Mem. Nat. Order Women Legislators (past nat. pres., former v.p., treas., corr. sec.), Women Execs. in State Govt., Brookfield Rep. Women's Club (past pres.), Brookfield Bus. and Profl. Women's Club, Prison and Jail Overcrowding comm., Governor's Law Enforcement Coun., Yale Corp., State Finance Advisory Com. Republican. Office: Office Gov Exec Chambers 210 Capitol Ave Hartford CT 06106 E-mail: Governor.Rell@po.state.ct.us. *

RELLE, FERENC MATYAS, chemist; b. Gyor, Hungary, June 13, 1922; came to U.S., 1951, naturalized, 1956; s. Ferenc and Elizabeth (Netratics) R.; m. Gertrud B. Tubach, Oct. 9, 1946; children: Ferenc, Ava, Attila. BSChemE, MS, Jozsef Nador Poly. U., Budapest, Hungary, 1944. Lab. mgr. Karl Kohn Ltd. Co., Landshut, Germany, 1947-48; resettlement officer Internat. Refugee Orgn., Munich, 1948-51; chemist Farm Bur. Coop. Assn., Columbus, Ohio, 1951-56; indsl. engr. N.Am. Aviation, Inc., Columbus, 1956-57; rsch. chemist Keever Starch Co., Columbus, 1957-65, Ross Labs. divsn. Abbott Labs., Columbus, 1965-70, rsch. scientist, 1970-89; cons. in field. Congl. sci. counselor, 1971—81. Chmn. Columbus and Ctrl. Ohio UNWeek, 1963; pres. Berwick Manor Civic Assn., 1968; trustee Stelios Stelson Found., 1968-69; deacon Brookwood Presbyn. Ch., 1963-65, 92-93, trustee, 1990-91. Decorated knight St. Ladislaus Order. Mem. Am. Chem. Soc. (emeritus; alt. councilor 1973, chmn. long range planning com. Columbus sect. 1972-76, 78-80), Am. Assn. Cereal Chemists (life; chmn. Cin. sect. 1974-75), Ohio Acad. Sci., Arpad Acad. (gold medal mem.), Internat. Tech. Inst. (adv. dir. 1977-82), Nat. Intercollegiate Soccer Ofcls. Assn., Am. Hungarian Assn., Hungrian Cultural Assn. (pres. 1978-81), Ohio Soccer Ofcls. Assn., Columbus Mannerchor, Germania Singing and Sport Soc., Civitan (gov. Ohio dist. 1970-71, dist. treas. 1982-83, pres. Ea. Columbus 1963-64, 72-73, gen. sec. for Hungary 1991-92, Ea. European growth mgr. 1993-94, amb. at large 1994—, established 1st Civitan club in Hungary 1991, Ukraine, 1992, Slovakia 1994, Internat. Gov. of Yr. award 1971, Internat. Honor Key 1992, Internat. Found. fellow 2000, master club builder award 1992, various other awards); World Fedn. Hungarian Engrs. Home and Office: 2983 Melford Rd Upper Arlington OH 43221-2822

RELMAN, ARNOLD SEYMOUR, physician, editor, educator; b. NYC, June 17, 1923; s. Simon and Rose (Mallach) Relman; m. Harriet Morse Vitkin, June 26, 1953; children: David Arnold, John Peter, Margaret Rose. AB, Cornell U., 1943; MD, Columbia U., 1946; LLD (hon.), U. Pa.; ScD (hon.), Med. Coll. Wis., Union U., Med. Coll. Ohio, CUNY; DMSc (hon.), Brown U.; DLH (hon.), SUNY; LittD (hon.), Temple U. Diplomate Am. Bd. Internal Medicine. House officer New Haven Hosp., Yale, 1946—49; NRC fellow Evans Meml., Mass. Meml. hosps., 1949—50; practice medicine, specializing in internal medicine Boston, 1950—68, Phila., 1968—77; asst. prof., prof. medicine Boston U. Sch. Medicine, 1950—68; dir. Boston U. Med. Services, Boston City Hosp., 1967—68; prof. medicine, chmn. dept. medicine U. Pa.; chief med. services Hosp. of U. Pa., 1968—77; editor New Eng. Jour. Medicine, Boston, 1977—91, editor emeritus, 1991—; sr. physician Brigham and Women's Hosp., Boston, 1977—; prof. medicine and social medicine Harvard Med. Sch., 1977—93, prof. medicine and social medicine emeritus, 1993—95, prof. emeritus, 1995—. Cons. NIH, USPHS; mem. bd. registration in medicine Commonwealth of Mass., 1995—2001. Author: A Second Opinion, 2007; editor: Jour. Clin. Investigation, 1962—67; editor: (with F.J. Ingelfinger and M. Finland) Controversy in Internal Medicine, Vol. 1, 1966, Controversy in Internal Medicine, Vol. 2, 1974; contbr. articles to profl. jours. Trustee Columbia U., 1990—96; bd. dirs. Hastings Ctr., 1981—83. Recipient Columbia Alumni Gold medal, 1980, Disting. Svc. award, Am. Coll. Cardiology, 1987, McGovern award, Cosmos Club Washington, 1991, John Peters award, Am. Soc. Nephrology, 1992, George Polk award in journalism, 2003. Master: ACP (John Phillips medal 1985); fellow: Am. Acad. Arts and Scis.; mem.: AMA, Am. Fedn. Clin. Rsch. (past pres.), Am. Soc. Clin. Investigation (past pres.), Inst. of Medicine of NAS (coun. 1979—82), Mass. Med. Soc., Am. Physiol. Soc., Assn. Am. Physicians (coun., pres. 1983—84, Kober medal 1993), Alpha Omega Alpha, Phi Beta Kappa (senator 1991—98). Office: Brigham and Women's Hosp Dept Medicine 181 Longwood Ave Fl 5 Boston MA 02115-5804

RELWANI, NIRMAL MURLIDHAR (NICK RELWANI), mechanical engineer; b. Bombay, Aug. 9, 1954; came to the U.S., 1976; m. Prema Vasandani; children: Karuna, Daksh. BS in Mech. Engring., U. Baroda, 1976; student, U. Nebr., 1977-78; MS in Mech. Engring., U. Wis., Milw., 1980. Registered profl engr., Wis., Ill. Rsch. asst. dept. mech. engring. U. Nebr., Lincoln, 1978; design engr. Allis Chalmers Corp., Milw., 1978-80; engring. cons. Bombay, 1980-86; assoc. engr. IIT Rsch. Inst., Chgo., 1986; mech. engr. Gen. Energy Corp., Oak Park, Ill., 1987-89, Arrowhead Environ. Control, Chgo., 1989-90; environ. engr. Ill. Dept. Pub. Health, Bellwood, 1990-92; sr. environ. protection engr. field ops. sect. bur. air Ill. EPA, Maywood, 1992—. Recipient Cert. of appreciation Ill. EPA, 1993, 94. Mem. ASME, ASHRAE (energy conservation award 1991), Assn. Energy Engrs. (sr.). Home: 1806 Marne Rd (River Bend) Bolingbrook IL 60490-4589 Office: Ill EPA 9511 W Harrison St Des Plaines IL 60016 Office Phone: 847-294-4030.

RELYEA, CARL MILLER, retired hydrologist; b. Claverack, NY, Dec. 29, 1912; s. Charles Miller Croswell and Edna (Pulver) R.; m. Harriet Watson, Sept. 6, 1946 (dec. Nov. 1982); children: Richard, Deborah, Cornelia. Grad., Inst. Musical Art, 1933; AB, Columbia Coll., 1935; MA, Columbia U., 1938; postgrad., MIT, 1943. Organist, choirmaster Morrow Meml. Ch., Maplewood, NJ, 1937-41; meteorologist Air Corps, Pan Am., Weather Bur., Bermuda, 1946-48, Weather Bur., JFK Internat. Airport, NY, 1948-50; hydrologist Ohio River Forecast Ctr., Cin., 1950-65, hydrologist-in-charge, 1965-77; ret., 1977; dep. dir. Hamilton County Emergency Mgmt. Agy., Cin., 1979-2000. Contbr. articles to profl. jours. Organist Highland United Meth. Ch., Fort Thomas, Ky., 1962-99, now organist emeritus; clk. of vestry Grace Episcopal Ch., Cin. Capt. U.S. Army Air Corps, 1943-46. Recipient Pub. Svc. cert. Hamilton County Disaster Coun., Cin., 1990. Mem. Ret. Engrs. and Scientists Cin. (chmn. 1984-86), N.Y. Acad. Scis., Columbia U. Club N.Y., Downtown Kiwanis Club. Republican. Avocations: travel, music, organist, home maintenance. Home: 1346 Teakwood Ave Cincinnati OH 45224-2126

RELYEA, HAROLD CLARENCE, political scientist, writer; b. Oneida, NY, Apr. 5, 1944; s. Clyde Frederick and Pauline Elizabeth R.; children: Jennifer L., Stephen F. AB, Drew U., 1966; PhD, American U., 1971. Specialist in Am. nat. govt. Congrl. Rsch. Svc. Libr. Congress, Washington, 1971—. Author: A Brief History of Emergency Powers in the United States, 1974, The Evolution and Organization of the Federal Intelligence Function: A Brief Overview 1776-1975, 1988, Silencing Silence: National Security Controls and Scientific Communication, 1994; co-author: Presidential Staffing-A Brief Overview, 1978, United States Government Information: Policies and Sources, 2002; editor, contbg. author: The Presidency and Information Policy, 1981, Striking a Balance: National Security and Scientific Freedom, 1985, The Executive Office of the President, 1997; co-editor, contbg. author: Freedom of Information Trends in the Information Age, 1983, United States Government Information Policies: Views and Perspectives, 1989, Comparative Perspectives on E-Government, 2006; bd. editors Presdl. Studies Quar., 1979-99, Govt. Publs. Rev., 1981-83, Transnational Data Report, 1982-89, Jour. Media Law and Practice, 1982-95, Govt. Info. Quar., 1984—, Internat. Jour. E-Govt. Rsch., 2004—, Jour. E-Govt., 2004-07; contbr. articles to profl. jours. Mem. adv. bd. Coll. Info. Studies, U. Md., 2004—07. Named Expert's Expert on U.S. Freedom Info. Act, The Economist of London, 1981; recipient Exec. Bd. award for superior pub. svc. Am. Soc. Access Profls., 1983, The Best of 1983 award for essay selection Libr. Lit. 14, 1984, Blue Pencil award Nat. Assn. Govt. Communicators, 1984; named to Freedom of Info. Act Hall of Fame, Freedom Forum, 1996. Mem. Pi Sigma Alpha. Office: Libr Congress CRS 101 Independence Ave SE Washington DC 20540-7470

REMAR, ROBERT BOYLE, lawyer; b. Boston, Nov. 19, 1948; s. Samuel Roy and Elizabeth Mary (Boyle) R.; m. Victoria A. Greenhood, Nov. 11, 1979; children: Daniel A.G., William B.G. BA, U. Mass., 1970; JD, Boston Coll., 1974. Bar: Ga. 1974, Mass. 1975, US Ct. Appeals (5th cir.) 1978, US Ct. Appeals (11th cir.) 1981, US Ct. Appeals (2d cir.) 1995, US Supreme Ct. 1981. Staff atty. Ga. Legal Svcs. Program, Savannah, 1974-76, Western Mass. Legal Svcs., Greenfield, 1976-77; sr. staff atty. Ga. Legal Svcs. Program, Atlanta, 1977-82; ptnr. Remar & Graettinger, Atlanta, 1983-95, Kirwan, Parks, Chesin & Remar PC, Atlanta, 1993-96, Rogers & Hardin, Atlanta, 1996—. V.p., mem. exec. com., bd. dirs. ACLU, NYC, pres. Ga. chpt., 1985-87, gen. counsel, 1980-83; hearing officer Ga. Pub. Svc. Commn., Atlanta, 1985-98; adj. prof. Ga. State U., Atlanta, 1984-98, spl. asst. atty. gen., 1990-2003; bd. experts Lawyers Alert, Boston, 1985-94; pres. bd. dirs. Fed. Defender Program. Mem. Ga. Energy Regulatory Reform Commn., Gov. of Ga., 1980-82, Ga. Consumer Adv. Bd., 1981-82, City Atl. Bd. Ethics, AAA Comml. Panel; pres. Ga. Consumer Ctr. Inc., 1988-91; bd. dirs., exec. com. Ga. Resource Ctr.; v.p. Ga Ctr. Law Pub. Inst., 1991-94; bar coun. U.S.D.C. N.D.G., 1996-99. Fellow Am. Coll. Trial Lawyers; mem. ABA (chmn. individual rights access to civil justice com. 1988-99), Ga. Bar Assn. (chmn. individual rights sect. 1981-83, co-chmn. consumer rights and remedies com. 1979-83, chmn. death penalty re. com. 1993—, mem. legis. adv. com. 1994-97, mem. indigent def. com. 2000—), Atlanta Bar Assn., Lawyers Club Atlanta, Lamar Inn of Ct. (master of the bench). Democrat. Avocations: golf, gardening. Home: 1714 Meadowdale Ave NE Atlanta GA 30306-3114 Office: Rogers & Hardin Internat Tower Peachtree Ctr 229 Peachtree St NE Ste 2700 Atlanta GA 30303-1638 Office Phone: 404-420-4031. Business E-Mail: rbr@rh-law.com.

REMBOLT, JAMES EARL, lawyer; b. Nov. 13, 1943; s. Earl Lester and Dorothy Elouise (Mehring) Rembolt; m. Marilyn Sue Schmadeke, July 16, 1972; children: Tami Anne, Michelle Sue. BBA, U. Nebr., 1965; MA in Bus. Orgn. and Mgmt., 1967, JD with distinction, 1972. Bar: Nebr. 1972, U.S. Dist. Ct. Nebr. 1972, U.S. Tax Ct. 1978, U.S. Ct. Claims 1978. Pres. Nebr. Moot Ct. Bd., 1972; pilot Nebr. Air Nat. Guard, Lincoln, 1969-74; lecr. legal writing U. Nebr. Coll. Law, 1973-74; ptnr. Rembolt, Ludtke LLP, Lincoln, 1976—. Chmn. bd. trustees YWCA, Lincoln, 1982—83; mem., past pres. Lincoln/Lancaster Sr. Ctrs. Found., Inc., bd. dirs., 1988—90; mem., past chair bd. dirs. Madonna Found., Inc., 1989—91; trustee, past bd. dirs. U.Nebr. Found.; past bd. dirs., pres. Nebr. Continuing Legal Edn., Inc.; bd. elders Eastridge Presbyn. Ch., Lincoln, 1979—82. Fellow: ABA, Nebr. State Bar Found., Am. Coll. Trust and Estate Counsel; mem.: Lincoln Estate Planning Coun. (past pres.), Lincoln Probate Discussion Group (charter mem.), Nebr. State Bar Assn. (pres. 2002—03), Lincoln Bar Assn., U. Nebr. Lincoln Coll. Bus. Adminstrn. Alumni Assn. (past pres.). Office: Rembolt Ludtke LLP 1201 Lincoln Mall Ste 102 Lincoln NE 68508-2839 Office Phone: 402-475-5100. Business E-Mail: jrembolt@remboltludtke.com.

REMELE, LEWIS ALBERT, JR., lawyer; b. Mpls., Nov. 25, 1948; s. Lewis Albert Sr. and Mary Elizabeth (Ryan) R.; m. Constance Ann Bauser, June 26, 1982; 1 child, Lewis Albert III. BA magna cum laude, Harvard U., 1970; JD cum laude, Creighton U., 1975. Bar: Minn. 1975, U.S. Dist. Ct. Minn. 1976, U.S. Ct. Appeals (8th cir.) 1978, U.S. Supreme Ct. 2004. Law clk. Judge Miles W. Lord, U.S. Dist. Ct., Minn., Mpls., 1975-77; assoc. Simonson & Bartsh, Mpls., 1977-78; ptnr. Rider, Bennett, Egan & Arundel, Mpls., 1978-88; ptnr., gen. & comml. litig., past CEO Bassford, Lockhart, Truesdell & Briggs (now Bassford Remele), Mpls., 1989—. Mem. bd. dir. & vol. atty. Legal Advice Clinics; dir. Pillsbury Neighborhood Svcs; trustee William Mitchell Coll. Law 2001-. Named Minn. Super Lawyer, Mpls. St. Paul mag. & Minn. Law & Politics mag., 2000-04. Fellow Am Bar Found., Am. Bd. Trial Advs., Am. Coll. Trial Lawyers, Internat. Soc. Barristers; mem. ABA, Minn. Bar Assn. (sec. 1992-93, treas. 1993-94, pres. 1995-96), Hennepin County Bar Assn. (pres. 1989-90, sec. 1986-87, treas. 1987-88), Hennepin County Bar Found. (dir. 1986-), Def. Rsch. Inst., Minn. Def. Lawyers Assn., Harvard & Radcliffe Club Minn. (pres. 1984-85). Office: Bassford Remele Ste 3800 33 S 6th St Minneapolis MN 55402 Office Phone: 612-376-1601. Office Fax: 612-333-8829. Business E-Mail: lewr@bassford.com.

REMES, ROBIN EVA, secondary school educator, cartographer; d. Jeremiah and Sarah Remes; m. Fredrick Biddle; 1 child, Patrick Biddle. BS, William Paterson U., 1974; MS, U. South Fla. Cert. tchr. Tex., NJ. World culture studies educator Houston Ind. Sch. Dist., 2004—, reading educator, reading specialist, ESL educator, English educator, chmn. reading dept.; assoc. educator Pinellas County Schools; oil exploration cartographer; computer cartographer Property Appraiser. Elem. sch. tutor, NJ. Author: Cartography Curriculum and H.S. Math Review. Rep. Young Dems., NJ, 1970. State scholar, NJ, 1971—74. Mem.: Houston Fedn. Tchrs. (bldg. steward, Membership Recruiter award 2001). Avocation: travel. Home Phone: 713-943-5700; Office Phone: 713-943-5700.

REMICK, FORREST JEROME, JR., former university official; b. Lock Haven, Pa., Mar. 16, 1931; s. Forrest Jerome Sr. and Ruth Betsy (Saiers) R.; m. Grace Louise Grove, June 7, 1953; children: Beth Ann Remick Gillio, Eric Forrest; m. Soon Ja Cho, Dec. 8, 1995. BSME, Pa. State U., 1955, MSME, 1958, PhD in ME, 1963; diploma, Oak Ridge Sch. Reactor Tech., Tenn., 1956. Engr. Bell Telephone Labs., Whippany, NJ, 1955—56; dir. nuclear reactor facility Pa. State U., University Park, 1959—65, dir. Inst. Sci. Engring., 1967—79, acting dir. Ctr. Air Environ. Studies, 1976—78, dir. intercoll. research programs, 1979—85, asst. v.p. research, grad. studies, 1979—84, assoc. v.p. research, 1985—89; dir. Curtiss Wright Nuclear Research Lab., Quehanna, Pa., 1960—65; chief tng. sect. dept. tech. assistance IAEA, Vienna, 1965—66. Mem. Nat. Nuclear Accrediting Bd., Inst. Nuclear Power Ops., Atlanta, mem. adv. coun., 1995—; mem. Sci. Adv. Com. Idaho Nat. Engring. Lab., Idaho Falls, 1984-89, Reactor Safety Adv. Com., Savannah River Lab., Aiken, S.C., 1986-89, chmn., 1989; mem. Adv. Com. on Reactor Safeguards, Washington, 1982, vice chmn., 1987-88, chmn., 1989; commr. U.S. Nuclear Regulatory Commn., 1989-94, cons., 1994—; bd. dir. Pub. Svc. Enterprise Group, Pub. Svc. Electric and Gas, 1995-2001; mem. adv. bd. Applied Rsch. Lab., Pa. State U., 1994-97. Served to sgt. U.S. Army, 1951-52. Named Outstanding Engring. Alumnus, Pa. State U., 1993; recipient Thomas P. Hamrick award for contbns. to tng. of nuclear facility pers., 1995. Fellow Am. Nuclear Soc. (bd. dir. 1995-98, meml. lectr. award 1971, disting. speaker award 1983); mem. ASME, Am. Soc. Engring. Edn., Nuclear Accrediting Bd. Republican. Lutheran. Home and Office: Canterbury Crossing 439 Brandywine Dr State College PA 16801-7984

REMICK, SCOT CLIFTON, oncologist, clinical investigator, educator; b. New Rochelle, NY, Oct. 16, 1956; s. Robert Merrick and Marjorie Allis (Stamm) R. BA, SUNY, Oswego, 1978; MD, N.Y. Med. Coll., Valhalla, 1982. Resident Johns Hopkins Hosp., Balt., 1982-85; fellow Clin. Cancer Ctr. U. Wis. Clin. Cancer Ctr., Madison, 1985-88; assoc. prof. Dept. Medicine Albany (N.Y.) Med. Coll., 1988-96; with Case Western Res. U., Cleve., 1996—, assoc. prof. dept. medicine, dir. devel. therapeutics divsn. hematology/oncology, prof. medicine. Prin. investigator numerous oncology and HIV/AIDS clin. trials, Albany, 1988—. Contbr. over 100 papers, textbook chpts. and abstracts. Active Am. Cancer Soc. (Career Devel. award 1991), Albany. Fellow Am. Coll. Physicians; mem. Am. Assn. for Cancer Rsch., Am. Soc. Clin. Oncology, N.Y. Acad. Sci., Alpha Omega Alpha. Office: Univ Hosps of Cleve Divsn Hematol/Oncol 11100 Euclid Ave Cleveland OH 44106-1736 Office Phone: 216-844-5412. Office Fax: 216-844-5234. Business E-Mail: scr@po.cwru.edu. *

REMILLARD, JEAN D., medical association administrator; b. Verdun, Quebec, Canada, July 22, 1958; s. Francis Amos Remillard; m. Laura Chuoke, Oct. 19, 1985; children: Daniel Francis, Marielle Erin, Chantal Annick. MD, Tex. Tech. U., Lubbock, 1985. Cert. Am. Bd. Ob-gyn., 1991. Physician First Step Clinic, Las Cruces, N.Mex., 1989—91, Los Alamos Women's Heath Svcs., N.Mex., 1991—2002; chief med. officer, chief quality officer Gila Regional Med. Ctr., Silver City, N.Mex., 2004—. Fellow: ACS, ACOG. Office: Gila Regional Medical Center 1313 32nd St Silver City NM 88061

REMINE, WILLIAM HERVEY, JR., retired surgeon; b. Richmond, Va., Oct. 11, 1918; s. William Hervey and Mabel Inez (Walthall) ReM.; m. Doris Irene Grumbacher, June 9, 1943; children: William H., Stephen Gordon, Walter James, Gary Craig. BS in Biology, U. Richmond, 1940, D.Sc. (hon.), 1965; MD, Med. Coll. Va., Richmond, 1943; MS in Surgery, U. Minn., Mpls., 1952. Diplomate Am. Bd. Surgery. Intern Doctor's Hosp., Washington, 1944; fellow in surgery Mayo Clinic, Rochester, Minn., 1944-45, 47-52; instr. surgery Mayo Grad. Sch. Medicine, Rochester, Minn., 1954-59, asst. prof. surgery, 1959-65, assoc. prof. surgery, 1965-70, prof. surgery, 1970-83, prof. surgery emeritus, 1983—. Surg. cons. to surgeon gen. U.S. Army, 1965-75; surg. lectr., USSR, 1987, 89, Japan, 1988, 90, Egypt, 1990; lectr. Soviet-Am. seminars, USSR, 1987, 89. Sr. author: Cancer of the Stomach, 1964, Manual of Upper Gastro-intestinal Surgery, 1985; editor: Problems in General Surgery, Surgery of the Biliary Tract, 1986; mem. editorial bd. Rev. Surgery, 1965-75, Jour. Lancet, 1968-77; contbr. 200 articles to profl. jours. Served to capt. U.S. Army, 1945-47 Recipient St. Francis surg. award St. Francis Hosp., Pitts., 1976, Disting. Svc. award Alumni Coun., U. Richmond, 1976, Dist. Alumnus award Mayo Found., Priestley Soc. Mayo Clinic Surg. Alumni Legacy award, 2004; named one of Am. Top Surgeons, 2007. Mem. ACS, AAAS, Am. Assn. History of Medicine, AMA, Am. Med. Writers Assn., Am. Soc. Colon and Rectal Surgeons, Soc. Surgery Alimentary Tract (v.p. 1983-84), Am. Surg. Assn., Assn. Mil. Surgeons U.S., Internat. Soc. Surgery, Digestive Disease Found., Priestley Soc. (pres. 1968-69, Legacy award 2004), Central Assn. Physicians and Dentists (pres. 1972-73), Central Surg. Assn., Soc. Med. Cons. Armed Forces, Mayo Clinic Surg. Soc. (chmn. 1964-66), Soc. Head and Neck Surgeons, Soc. Surg. Oncology, So. Surg. Assn., Western Surg. Assn. (pres. 1979-80), Minn. State Med. Assn., Minn. Surg. Soc. (pres. 1966-67), Zumbro Valley Med. Soc., Sigma Xi; hon. mem. Colombian Coll. Surgeons, St. Paul Surg. Soc., Flint Surg. Soc., Venezuelan Surg. Soc., Colombian Soc. Gastroenterology, Dallas So. Clin. Soc., Ga. Surg. Soc., Soc. Postgrad. Surgeons Los Angeles County, Japanese Surg. Soc., Argentine Surg. Digestive Soc., Bassanese Surg. Assn. (Italy), Tex. Surg. Soc., Mayo Clinic Surg. Alum Assn., Omicron Delta Kappa, Alpha Omega Alpha, Beta Beta Beta, Kappa Sigma (pres. 1939-40). Methodist. Avocations: hunting, fishing, golf, photography, boating, music. Home: Sawgrass Players Club 8212 Seven Mile Dr Ponte Vedra Beach FL 32082-3129

REMINGER, RICHARD THOMAS, lawyer, artist; b. Cleve., Apr. 3, 1931; s. Edwin Carl and Theresa Henrietta (Bookmyer) Reminger; m. Billie Carmen Greer, June 26, 1954; children: Susan Greer, Patricia Allison, Richard Thomas. AB, Case-Western Res. U., 1953; JD, Cleve. State U., 1957. Bar: Ohio 1957, Pa. 1978, U.S. Supreme Ct. 1961. Pers. and safety dir. Motor Express, Inc., Cleve., 1954-58; founder, mng. ptnr. Reminger & Reminger Co., L.P.A., Cleve., 1958-90. Mem. nat. claims coun. adv. bd. Comml. Union Assurance Co., 1980—90; lectr. transp. law Fenn Coll., 1960—62; lectr. bus. law Case Western Res. U., 1962—64; lectr. products liability U. Wirtschaft at Schloss Gracht, Erfstadt-Liblar, Germany, 1990—91, Bar Assn. City of Hamburg, Germany, 1990; mem. faculty Nat. Inst. Trial Advocacy, 1992. Trustee Cerebral Palsy Assn., 1984—87, Andrew Sch., 1984—96, Meridia Huron Hosp., Cleve., 1978—96, Cleve. Sch. Blind, 1987—88, Intracoastal Health Sys., Palm Beach, Fla., 1992—2000; mem. joint com. Cleve. Acad. Medicine-Greater Cleve. Bar Assn.; v.p. Cleve. Zool. Soc., 1984—87. With AC USNR, 1950—58. Mem.: FBA, ABA (profl. responsiblity com. 1977—90, com. law and medicine), Palm Beach County Bar Assn., Internat. Ins. Law Soc., Am. Coll. Law and Medicine, Maritime Law Assn., Def. Rsch. Inst., Am. Judicature Soc., Ohio Assn. Civil Trial Attys., Soc. Ohio Hosp. Attys., Am. Soc. Hosp. Attys., Cleve. Assn. Civil Trial Attys., Transp. Lawyers Assn., Cleve. Bar Assn. (prof. liability com. 1977—90, chmn. med. legal com. 1978—79), Pa. Bar Assn., Ohio Bar Assn. (coun. dels. 1987—90, internat. law com. 1990—91), Internat. Bar Assn., Fedn. Ins. and Corp. Counsel, 8th Jud. Bar Assn. (life), Internat. Soc. Marine Painters (v.p.), Oil Painters Am., Soc. Four Arts, Cleve.-Marshall Law Alumni Assn. (hon. trustee 1980—), Univ. Club (N.Y.C.), Salmagundi Club (N.Y.C.), Rolling Rock Club (Pa.), Kirtland Country Club (Cleve.), Everglades Club (Fla.), Lost Tree Club (Fla.) (bd. govs. 1991—94), Hermit Club (Cleve.) (pres. 1973—75), Mayfield Country Club (Cleve.) (pres. 1980—82), Case Res. Athletic Club (life). Office: Reminger & Reminger Co LPA 1400 Midland Bldg 101 Prospect Ave W Cleveland OH 44115-1093 Office Phone: 216-687-1311.

REMINGTON, DEBORAH WILLIAMS, artist; b. Haddonfield, NJ, June 25, 1935; d. Malcolm Van Dyke and Hazel Irwin (Stewart) R. BFA, San Francisco Art Inst., 1955. Adj. prof. art Cooper Union, NYC, 1973—97, NYU, 1994—98; tchr. Nat. Acad. Sch., NYC, 2003—. One-woman shows include Dilexi Gallery, San Francisco, 1962, 63, 65, San Francisco Mus. Art, 1964, Bykert Gallery, NYC, 1967, 69, 72, 74, Galerie Darthea Speyer, Paris, 1968, 71, 73, 92, Pyramid Gallery, Washington, 1973, 76, zola-Leiberman Gallery, Chgo., 1976, Hamilton Gallery, NYC, 1977, Portland Ctr. Visual Arts, Oreg., 1977, Michael Berger Gallery, Pitts., 1979, Mary Ryan Gallery, NYC, 1982, Ramon Osuna Gallery, Washington, 1983, Newport Harbor Art Mus., 1983, Oakland Mus., Calif., 1984, Jack Shainman Gallery, NYC, 1987, Shoshana Wayne Gallery, LA, 1988, Mitchell Algus Gallery, NYC, 2001; group shows include Whitney Mus. Am. Art, NYC, 1965, 67, 72, San Francisco Mus. Art, 1956, 60, 61, 63, 64, 65, Lausanne Mus., Switz., 1966, Fondation Maeght, St. Paul de Vence, France, 1968, Smithsonian Am. Art Mus., Washington, 1968, Art. Inst., Chgo., 1974, Inst. Contemporary Art, Boston, 1975, Nat. Gallery Modern Art, Lisbon, Portugal, 1981, Toledo Mus. Art, 1975, The 6 Gallery, 1954-57, Natsoulas Gallery, Davis, Calif., 1990, 1st Trienale des Ameriques Maubeuge, France, 1993, Tamarind Inst. Retrospective, 2000, Worcester Art Mus., Mass., 2001, San Jose Mus. Art, Calif., 2002, Nat. Acad. Mus. Annuals, NY, 2001, 03, 05, 07, numerous others; represented in permanent collections Whitney Mus. Am. Art, Smithsonian Am. Art Mus., Washington, Art Inst., Chgo., Centre d'Art et de Culture Georges Pompidou, Paris, Carnegie Mus., Pitts. Recipient Hassam and Speicher Purchase award Am. Acad. and Inst. Arts and Letters, 1988; NEA fellow, 1979-80; Tamarind Inst. fellow, 1973; Guggenheim fellow, 1984; Pollock-Krasner Found. grantee, 1999. Mem. NAD (Benjamin Altman prize for painting 178th Ann. Exhbn. 2003). Home: 309 W Broadway New York NY 10013-5325 Office Phone: 212-925-3037. Personal E-mail: deborahremington@aol.com. *Be aware of yourself, aware of what makes you distinctive from others, and make those individual characteristics part of your work, whatever that may be. Read philosophy. Develop your own. This gives you ballast when the pendulum swings too far in one direction.*

REMINI, LEAH, actress; b. Bklyn., June 15, 1970; m. Angelo Pagan, July 19, 2003; 1 child, Sofia Bella. Actress: (TV series) Living Dolls, 1989, Saved By The Bell, 1991, The Man in the Family, 1991, Getting Up and Going Home, 1992, King of Queens, 1999-2007, (voice) Gabriel Knight: Sins of the Fathers, 1994, (voice) Phantom 2040: The Ghost Who Walks, 1994, The First Time Out, 1995, Glory Daze, 1996, Fired Up, 1997, Follow Your Heart, 1998, guest appearances, including Head of the Class, 1988, Who's the Boss?, 1989, Valerie, 1990, Paradise, 1991, Cheers, 1991 & 1993, Blossom, 1992, Evening Shade, 1993, The Commish, 1994, Renegade, 1994, Diagnosis Murder, 1995, Friends, 1995, NYPD Blue, 1996; (TV movies) Legend of the Lost Tribe, 2002 (voice), Hooves of Fire, 1999 (voice); (films) Follow Your Heart, 1998, Old School, 2003. Office: Gold Marchak & Liedtke 3500 W Olive Ave Ste 1400 Burbank CA 91505-5512

REMINI, ROBERT VINCENT, historian; b. NYC, July 17, 1921; s. William Francis and Lauretta (Tierney) R.; m. Ruth Theresa Kuhner, Oct. 9, 1948; children: Elizabeth Mary, Joan Marie, Robert William. BS, Fordham U., 1943; MA, Columbia U., 1947, PhD, 1951; LHD (hon.), Gov.'s State U., 1989; LittD (hon.), Ea. Ky. U., 1992, Fordham U., 1993, Columbia Coll. Chgo., 2000, So. Ill. U., 2004. Prof. history, emeritus prof. U. Ill. Chgo., 1965—, historian, 1997—, U.S. Ho. of Reps., 2005—; life dir. Ill. Humanities Coun., 2007—. Prof. Fordham U., 1947—65, Columbia U., 1959—60, Jilin U. Tech., China, 1986, U. Richmond, 1992, U. Notre Dame, 1995, 96, Wofford Coll., 1998; Walter Lynwood Fleming lectr. La. State U., 1984. Author: Martin Van Buren and the Making of the Democratic Party, 1959, The Election of Andrew Jackson, 1963, Andrew Jackson, 1966, Andrew Jackson and the Bank War, 1968, The Revolutionary Age of Andrew Jackson, 1976 (award of merit Friends of Am. Writers), Andrew Jackson and the Course of American Empire, 1767-1821, 1977, Andrew Jackson and the Course of American Freedom, 1822-1832, vol. II, 1981 (George Washington medal of Honor, Freedoms Found.), Andrew Jackson and the Course of American Democracy, 1833-1845, vol. III, 1984 (Nat. Book award for non-fiction 1984, Chgo. Found. for Lit. award 1985, English Speaking Union U.S. Ambassador of Honor award 1985); The Legacy of Andrew Jackson: Essays on Democracy, Indian Removal and Slavery, 1988, The Life of Andrew Jackson (abridgement of 3-vol. biography), 1988 (Carl Sandburg Lit. award for non-fiction 1989), The Jacksonian Era, 1989, Henry Clay: Statesman for the Union, 1991 (award for biography Soc. Midland Authors 1992), Daniel Webster: The Man and His Time, 1997, The Battle of New Orleans, 1999, Andrew Jackson and His Indian Wars, 2001, (Am. Hist. Assn. award for scholarly dist., 2001, Western Writers of Am. award, 2002, John Hope Franklin Hist. Maker award, Chgo. Hist. Soc., 2003), John Quincy Adams, 2002, Joseph Smith, 2002 (Freedom award Capitol Hist. Soc. 2004), The House: The History of the House of Representatives, 2006 (George Pendleton award Soc. History in Fed. Govt. 2007); co-author: We the People: A History of the United States, 1975, The Era of Good Feelings and the Age of Jackson, 1816-1841, 1979, The American People: A History, 1981, Andrew Jackson: A Bibliography, 1991; also articles, chpts. in books.; editor: The Decline of Aristocracy in the Politics of New York, 1965, The Presidency of Andrew Jackson, 1967, The Age of Jackson, 1972; spl. editor Am. history, Crowell-Collier Co., 1960-68, 72-73; mem edit. bd. Jour. Am. History, 1969-72; editl. cons. Papers of Andrew Jackson, 1972—. Lt. USNR, 1943—46. Recipient Encaenia award Fordham U., 1963; Silver Circle award U. Ill., Chgo., 1981, Univ. Scholar award, 1986; grantee Am. Coun. Learned Socs., 1964, Am. Philos. Soc., 1966, 80; Guggenheim fellow, 1978-79. Mem. Am. Hist. Assn. (council 1979-82), So. Hist. Assn., Orgn. Am. Historians. Roman Catholic. Office: Univ Ill at Chgo Office of Historian 815 W Van Buren Chicago IL 60607

REMKUS, CONNIE ELAINE, nutritional consultant; d. Charles Edward and Phyllis Mary Remkus. BSBA in Acctg., San Francisco State U., 1986. Registered nutritional cons. Sch. of Nutritional Sci., San Jose. Flight attendant United Air Lines, Chgo., 1966—2002; self-employed property and investment mgr. Chgo., 1973—2003; tax preparer David Nitz & Assocs., San Mateo, Calif., 1975; nutritional cons., ind. distbr. Diamite Corp., San Carlos, Calif., 1988—95; field v.p. Symmetry Direct, Chgo., 1995—. Mem. South Loop Neighbors, Chgo., 2001—05; vol. SPCA, San Mateo, 1984—87. Recipient United Airlines award of Merit, 1987. Mem.: Airline Flight Attendants Union (membership chair grievance com. 1967—70), Bus. Networking Internat. (sec. 2001—03, asst. dir., amb. 2002—03). Avocations: travel, real estate, health and wellness. Home Phone: 312-583-1147; Office Phone: 312-455-2850.

REMMELE, RICHARD L., JR., research scientist, director; s. Richard L. Remmele, Sr. and Esther Remmele. BS, Oral Roberts U., Tulsa, 1978; MS, Calif. Poly. U., Pomona, 1983; PhD, Ariz. State U., Tempe, 1988. Postdoctoral fellow Colo. State U., Fort Collins, 1988—93, U. Colo. Sch. Pharmacy, Denver, 1993; formulations chemist Immunex Corp., Seattle, 1993—2002; biotherapeutics formulations scientific dir. Amgen, Thousand Oaks, Calif., 2002—. Editor: Current Pharmaceutical Biotechnology; contbr. articles to sci. jours., chapters to books. Recipient DAAD scholarship, Karlsruhe Tech. Inst. of Phys. and Electrochemistry. Mem.: AIChE, Am. Chem. Soc., Am. Assn. of Pharm. Sci., Phi Lambda Upsilon (treas. 1985—86), Alpha Chi Sigma. Achievements include patents for increased recovery of active proteins; Polypeptide Formulation; research in liquid formulation development using differential scanning calorimetry, Real-time in situ monitoring lysozyme during lyophilization using infrared spectroscopy; dehydration stress in the presence of sucrose; designing proteins that work using recombinant technologies, Biophysical characterization of a soluble CD40 ligand (CD154) coiled-coil trimer; low-temperature infrared spectroscopy reveals four stages of water loss during lyophilization of hen egg-white lysozyme. Office: Amgen One Amgen Center Dr Thousand Oaks CA 91320-1799 Office Phone: 805-447-5534. Business E-Mail: remmeler@amgen.com.

REMNICK, DAVID J., journalist, editor-in-chief; b. Hackensack, NJ, Oct. 29, 1958; s. Edward C. and Barbara (Seigel) Remnick; m. Esther B. Fein; children: Alexander, Noah, Natasha. BA in comparative lit., Princeton U., 1981. Reporter The Washington Post, 1982—88, Moscow (Russia) corr., 1988—92; staff writer The New Yorker, NYC, 1992—98, editor, 1998—. Author: (book) Lenin's Tomb: The Last Days of the Soviet Empire, 1993 (Pulitzer Prize for gen. non-fiction, 1994, George Polk award, 1994), Resurrection, 1997, The Devil Problem (and other True Stories), 1997, King of the World: Muhammad Ali and the Rise of an American Hero, 1998, Life Stories: Profiles from The New Yorker, 2000, Reporting: Writings from The New Yorker, 2006. Named Editor of Yr., Advt. Age Mag., 1999; recipient Livingston award, 1991, Helen Bernstein award, N.Y. Pub. Libr., 1994. Fellow: Am. Acad. Arts & Sciences. Office: The New Yorker 4 Times Sq New York NY 10036-6561 Office Phone: 212-286-5774. *

REMPT, RODNEY P., retired academic administrator, career military officer; b. Burbank, Calif., June 13, 1945; married. BS, U.S. Naval Acad., 1966; MS in Sys. Analysis, Stanford U.; M.Security and Strategic Studies, Naval War Coll. Commd. ensign USN, advanced through grades to vice admiral; comdr. USS Antelope, Naples, Italy; exec. officer USS Dahlgren; initial project officer MK 41 vertical launch sys. Naval Sea Sys. Command; program coord. AEGIS weapons sys. Chief Naval Officer; adminstrv. asst., aide Vice Chief of Naval Ops.; comdr. USS Callaghan, USS Bunker Hill, Yokosuka, Japan; dir. PCO/PXO dept. Surface Warfare Officers Schs. Command, Newport, R.I.; dir. anti-air warfare requirements divs. Staff of Dep. Chief Naval Ops., Naval Warefare; head surface ships and combat sys. Staff of Chief of Naval Ops.; dir. Theater Air Def., 1994-96, program exec. officer, 1996-98; dep. asst. sec. theater combat sys. USN, Washington, 1998—2001; pres. Naval War Coll., Newport, RI, 2001—03; supt. US Naval Acad., Annapolis, Md., 2003—07. Decorated Disting. Svc. medal, Legion of Merit (3 awards), Meritorious Svc. medal (3 awards), Navy Commendation medal with combat V (3 awards). *

REMSEN, JAMES F., JR., biology educator; b. Oceanside, NY, Oct. 17, 1964; s. James F. and Ethel M. Remsen; m. Angela G. Pepe, June 25, 2000. AS, Nassau C.C., 1982—84; BS, Hofstra U., 1982—86, MA, 1988—91; PhD, NY U., 1993—2000. Substitute asst. prof. NYC Coll. of Tech., Bklyn., 2001—03, asst. prof., 2003—. Contbr. chapters to books, articles to profl. jours. Com. chair South Shore Audubon Soc., Freeport, NY, 1988—2004, pres., 1992—94, v.p., 1990—92, mem., 1973—2004. Recipient Gladys Mateyko award for Excellence in Biology, NY U. Dept. of Biology, 1999; Grad. Rsch. Tech. Initiative, CUNY, 2004, Grad. Assistantship, NY U., 1993—2000, South Shore Audubon Soc. Scholarship, South Shore Audubon Soc., 1989, Hofstra U. Grad. scholarship, Hofstra U., 1988—89, Hofstra U. Academic scholarship, 1984, NY State Regents scholarship, NY State Bd. of Regents, 1982—86. Mem.: Met. Assn. of Coll. and U. Biologists. Achievements include research in systematics of drosphilidae; systematics of phyllostomid bats; character congruence in systematics; role of developmental programs in evolution. Avocations: birdwatching, films, travel. Office: NYC Coll of Tech 300 Jay St Brooklyn NY 11201 Home Phone: 631-957-0949; Office Phone: 718-260-5960. E-mail: jremsen@citytech.cuny.edu.

REN, CHRISTINE, surgeon; b. 1966; BS, Holy Cross Coll., Worcester, Mass., 1988; MD, Tufts Univ. Sch. Med., Boston, Mass. Surg. residency NYU Med. Ctr.; founder, dir. prog. surg. weight-loss NY Univ. Sch. Med. Faculty mem. Mt. Sinai Med. Ctr.; assoc. prof. surgery NYU Sch. Med.; chmn., ins. com. Am. Soc. for Bariatric Surgery; nominated counilman-at-large Exec. Coun. of the Am. Soc. for Bariatric Surgery. Named one of Woman's Achievement award, YWCA, 2003, NY Rising Stars, Crain's Bus. Mag., 2005; fellow advanced laparoscopic surgery, Mt. Sinai Med. Ctr. Office: New York Univ Sch Med 530 First Ave New York NY 10016 *

REN, CLEMENT L., immunologist, researcher; MD, U. Chgo., 1987. Cert. allergist and immunologist Am. Bd. Allergy and Immunology, 1993, pediatrician Am. Bd. Pediat., 1990, sub-bd. pediats. Am. Bd. Pediat., 1996. Cystic fibrosis ctr. co-director U. Rochester, NY, 2001—, assoc. prof. pediat., 2001—07, chief, divsn. pediat. pulmonology, 2001—. Resident pediat. Children's Hosp., Harvard Med. Sch., Boston, 1987—90, fellow immunology, 1990—93; fellow in pediat. pulmonology St. Christopher's Hosp Children, Phila., 1994—96. Contbr. articles to profl. jours. Mem.: Cystic Fibrosis Found. (mem. ctr. com. 2006—), Am. Coll. Chest Physicians (mem. pediat. network 2004—), Am. Thoracic Soc. (program chair 2005—06). Office: Univ Rochester 601 Elmwood Ave Rochester NY 14642 Office Phone: 585-275-2464. Office Fax: 585-275-8706. Business E-Mail: clement_ren@urmc.rochester.edu.

REN, JIAN-GUO, cell biologist, researcher; BS in Zoology, Lanzhou U., China, 1993, MS in Biochemistry and Biophysics, 1996; PhD, Tsinghua U., Beijing, China, 2001. Postdoctoral fellow, Willmer Eye Inst. Johns Hopkins U., Balt., 2001—04; rsch. fellow med. sch. Harvard U., Boston, 2004—. Mem.: Am. Soc. Biochemistry Molecular Biology (assoc. Travel award 2006). Office: Harvard Med Sch 20 Shattuck St Thorn 530 Boston MA 02115 Office Phone: 617-732-6839. Office Fax: 617-278-6921. Personal E-mail: renjg98@yahoo.com.

REN, JIANHUA, education educator; d. Shumin (Zhang) and Shanhou Ren; m. Bogdan Bogdanov, Mar. 18, 2006. PhD, Purdue U., West Lafayette, Ind., 1999. Asst. prof. U. of the Pacific, Stockton, Calif., 2002—. Recipient Petroleum Rsch. Fund Type-G grant, Am. Chem. Soc., 2006—. Achievements include research in phys. organic chemistry. Office: Univ of the Pacific Dept of Chemistry 3601 Pacific Ave Stockton CA 95211 Home Phone: 209-473-3023; Office Phone: 209-946-2393. Office Fax: 209-946-2607. Business E-Mail: jren@pacific.edu.

REN, WEI, control systems educator; m. Fei Cheng, Jan. 10, 2002. BS, Hohai U., 1997; MS, Tongji U., 2000; PhD, Brigham Young U., 2004. Rsch. assoc. U. Md., College Park, 2004—05; asst. prof. Utah State U., Logan, 2005—. Contbr. articles to profl. jours., chapters to books. Taitan scholar, Guanghua scholar. Mem.: AIAA, IEEE. Achievements include research in coordinated control of multiple fully or partially autonomous systems, autonomous control technologies for unmanned air, ground, or underwater vehicles, nonlinear control theory and applications. Office: Utah State U Dept Electrical & Computer Engring Logan UT 84322 Home Phone: 435-797-5982; Office Phone: 435-797-2831. Office Fax: 435-797-3054; Home Fax: 435-797-3054. Business E-Mail: wren@engineering.usu.edu.

REN, XING JIAN, physician; b. Shanghai, June 27, 1961; s. Yun Feng Ren and Xin Yi Zhang; m. Bei Xie, June 27, 1990; 1 child, Oriana Leigh. MD, Shanghai First Med. Coll., 1984. Diplomate internal medicine and geriatric medicine Am. Bd. Internal Medicine. Resident in surgery Shanghai Ruhui Hosp., China, 1984-85; resident Ft. Wayne (Ind.) Med. Edn. Program, 1993-94; resident, intern in medicine Loyola U. of Chgo., Maywood, Ill., 1994-97; fellow in medicine Harvard Med. Sch., Boston, 1997-99; staff physician Scripps Clinic Found., La Jolla, Calif., 1999—; asst. clin. prof. medicine U. Calif. Sch. Medicine, 2003—. Co-author: Virology, 1986; contbr. articles to profl. jours. Fellow Harvard Med. Sch., 1998; recipient 1st prize Nat. Med. Student Competition for Knowledge of Med. Lit., 1983, grad. student scholarship U. N.C., Chapel Hill, scholarship Carolina Biotechnolgoy Ctr., others. Fellow ACP; mem. AMA, Mass. Med. Soc., Am. Geriatrics Soc., Fell. Am. Coll. Physician. Home Phone: 858-794-9284; Office Phone: 858-268-9500, 858-554-8077.

RENARD, MEREDITH ANNE, marketing and advertising professional; b. Newark, Apr. 12, 1952; d. W. Edward and Lois E. (Velthoven) Young; m. Robert W. Renard, Nov. 11, 1995. BA, Caldwell Coll., 1974. Advt., pub. rels. asst. Congoleum Corp., Lawrenceville, NJ, 1974—77; account mgr. Saatchi & Saatchi Compton, NYC, 1977—82; dir. advt., sales promotion Singer Sewing Co., Edison, NJ, 1982—86, dir. product mktg., 1986—88, dir. nat. accounts, 1988—90; sr. mktg. rep. Walt Disney World Co., Lake Buena Vista, Fla., 1990—91; divsn. mktg. rep. Vista Advt., Walt Disney World Co., 1991—92; mgr. advt. Walt Disney World Co., 1992—94, mgr. Fla. tourist mktg., 1994—97; mgr. spl. events Disney Cruise Vacations, Celebration, Fla., 1997—; mgr. ops. integration Disney Cruise Line, Celebration, Fla., 2000—02, dir. youth activities and ops. integration, 2002—06, dir. ops. integration, 2006—. Contbr. articles to profl. jours. Vol. North Brunswick Dem. Orgn., 1985—87; pub. rels. mgr. Cultural Arts Com., North Brunswick, 1986—87; props chair Adult Drama Group, North Brunswick, 1986—87; mem. mktg. com. Vol. Ctr. Ctrl. Fla., 1993—94. Mem.: Ctrl. Fla. Direct Mktg. Assn. (bd. dirs. 1990—92), Fla. Direct Mktg. Assn. Episcopalian. Avocations: cross stitch, reading. Office: Disney Cruise Line 210 Celebration Pl Ste 400 Celebration FL 34747-4978 Office Phone: 407-566-3651.

RENARD, PAUL STEVEN, music educator; b. NYC, May 5, 1934; s. Joseph Maurice and Elsie (Wolpow) R. Student, Miami (Fla.) Conservatory, 1947-48, Sch. of Am. Music, 1950-51; cert., Ida Elkan Sch. of Music, 1958. Staff concert organist Hammond Organ Co., NYC, 1950-74; staff organist various TV stas., NYC, 1952-61, King Records and Riverside Records, NYC, 1955-64; staff organist, ednl. dir. Lyon-Healy Music Co., Chgo., 1962-72; founder, dir. Paul Renard's Music Dynamics, Chgo., 1972—. Cons. in field. Co-inventor first electric piano, Wurlitzer Mus. Instruments Co., 1953-54; author (software) Paul Renard's Music Dynamics, 1999; author numerous piano and organ texts; contbr. articles to profl. jours. Home Phone: 706-736-3263; Office Phone: 312-609-0061, 706-736-1565.

RENARD, RONALD LEE, allergist; b. Chgo., July 31, 1949; s. Robert James and Dorothy Mae (Fruik) R.; m. Maureen Ann Gilmore, Aug. 5, 1972 (div. Mar. 1992); children: Jeffrey, Stephen, Justin, Leigh Ellen; m. Catherine L. Walker, Apr. 1, 1992; children: Morgan, Michal, Luke. Degrees in Lang., U. de Montepellier, France, 1970; BS in French, U. San Francisco, 1971; MD, Creighton U., 1976. Dir. med. ICU, lt. U.S. Army Hosp., Ft. Leonard Wood, Md., 1980-81; dir. respiratory therapy, asst. chief allergy svc. Walter Reed Med. Ctr., Washington, 1981-84; staff allergist Chico (Calif.) Med. Group, 1984-86; allergist pvt. practice Redding, Calif., 1986—. Dir. ACLS program Enloe Hosp., Chico, 1988-91; bd. dirs. Am. Lung Assn. Calif., 1989-91, med. dir. asthma camp, Chico, Redding, 1986-95; asst. prof. medicine USPHS, Bethesda, Md., 1982-84; asst. prof. family medicine U. Calif. Davis Med. Sch., Redding, 1990-94; Shasta County Planning Commr., 1994-95. Contbr. articles to profl. jours. Fellow Am. Acad. Allergy and Immunology, Am. Coll. Allergists; mem. Assn. Mil. Allergists, Calif. Thoracic Soc., Alpha Omega Alpha. Republican. Roman Catholic. Avocations: hunting, biking. Office: 1505 Victor Ave Redding CA 96003 Home Phone: 530-246-8843; Office Phone: 530-226-5325. Home Fax: 530-246-8856. Personal E-mail: rlr@reddingallergy.com.

RENAUD, BERNADETTE MARIE ELISE, author; b. Ascot Corner, Que., Can., Apr. 18, 1945; d. Albert and Aline (Audet) R. Diploma, Présentation de Marie, Granby, Que., 1962-64. Librarian asst. Schs. of Waterloo, Que., 1964-67, tchr. primary schs. Que., 1967-70; adminstrv. sec. Assn. Medi-Tech-Sci., Montreal, Que., 1972-76. Author: Emilie La Baignoire A Pattes, 1976 (Can. Coun. Children's Lit. prize, 1976, Assn. Advancement of Scis. and Technics of Documentation award, 1976), 2d edit., 2002, Le Chat de l'Oratoire, 1978, Emilie la baignoire á pattes album, 1978, La maison tête de pioche, 1979, La révolte de la courte pointe, 1979, La dépression de l'ordinateur, 1981, Une boîte Magique Très Embêtante, 1981, La grande question de Tomatelle, 1982, Comment on fait un livre?, 1983, The Cat in the Cathedral, 1983, The Computer Revolts, 1984, (book and movie) Bach et Bottine, 1986 (awards for movie, 19 awards across the world, transl. ino 8 langs., subtitled into 18 langs.), Bach and Broccoli, 1986, (short movie) Quand l'accent devient grave, 1989, (novels) Un Homme Comme Tant d'Autres, tome 1, 1992, tome, II, 1993, tome, III, 1994, Prix Germaine Guévremont, 1995, Gala des Arts du Bas-Richelieu (QC); dir., coord.: Ecrire pour la jeunesse, 1990; author: short stories, adaptations of 8 children's classics, 1977—79, La quête de Kurweena, 1997; dir., coord.: album and CD Le petit violon muet, 1997, Héritiers de l'éternité, 1998, Les Funambules D'un Temps Nouveau, 2001, Les Chemins d'Eve Tome I, 2002, Les Chemins d'Eve Tome II, 2002, Grand Prix du Livre de la Monteregie, 2001, 2002, Émilie, la baignoire à pattes, rééd, 2002, Drôle de nuit pour Miti, 2004, Les gros bisous, 2004, Pas de chouchous, 2004, Les chemins d'Ève Tome III, 2005, Casimir, le maladroit, 2006, Mon chat zoo, 2006, Les chemins d'Eve, tome 4, 2006.

RENBAUM, BARRY JEFFREY, lawyer; b. Balt., Feb. 26, 1948; s. David and Leah (Cohen) R.; m. Carol Barbash, June 22, 1980. BS magna cum laude, Rider U., Princeton, NJ, 1970; postgrad., NYU, 1973; JD, Georgetown U., Washington, DC, 1973. Bar: Md. 1973, US Dist. Ct. Md. 1998. Jud. clk. to Hon. John C. Eldridge, Md. Ct. Appeals, 1974-75; asst. pub. defender State of Md., 1975-79; exec. v.p., gen. counsel Custom Savs. Bank, Tmple Fin. Co., Balt., 1980-91; pvt. practice Glyndon, Md., 1991—. Mem. ATLA, Md. Bar Assn., Alpha Epsilon Zeta. Office: Brydonwood Glyndon MD 21071-0326 Business E-Mail: brydonwood@earthlink.net.

RENCHER, NATALIE R., library director; married; 2 children. BS in Child Devel., San Diego State U.; MLS, San Jose State U., Calif. Libr. technician San Diego County Libr., 1978, libr. capital projects mgr., dep. dir., interim dir., 2005; with San Diego Pub. Libr., San Jose Pub. Libr.; dir. libr. svcs. Stockton-San Joaquin County Pub. Libr., Calif., 2005—. Office: Stockton San Joaquin County Pub Libr 605 N El Dorado St Stockton CA 95202 Office Phone: 209-937-8365. Office Fax: 209-937-8683. E-mail: nrencher@ci.stockton.ca.us.

RENDA, LARREE M., retail executive; Joined Safeway, Inc., 1974, exec. v.p. retail ops., human resources, pub. affairs, labor and govtl. rels. Pleasanton, Calif., 1999—. Office: Safeway Inc 5918 Stoneridge Mall Rd Pleasanton CA 94588 *

RENDALL, DONALD JAMES, JR., lawyer; b. Phila., Jan. 31, 1956; s. Donald James and Mary (Hough) R.; m. Sandra Smallwood, July 28, 1979; children: Samuel, Katherine, Ann. AB summa cum laude, Dartmouth Coll., 1978; JD, Duke U., 1981. Bar: Ill. 1982, U.S. Dist. Ct. (no. dist.) Ill. 1983, U.S. Dist. Ct. Vt. 1984, Vt. 1985, U.S. Ct. Appeals (2d cir.) 1986. Law clk. to Hon. James S. Holden U.S. Dist. Ct. for Vt., Rutland, 1981-82; assoc. Jenner & Block, Chgo., 1982-84; asst. US atty. US Attorney's Office for Dist. Vt., Rutland, Vt., 1984-87; assoc. Sheehey Furlong Rendall & Behm PC, Burlington, Vt., 1987, ptnr., 1988—2002; v.p. & gen. counsel, sec. Green Monster Power Corp., 2002—. Mem. ABA, Vt. Bar Assn.(pres. 2002-03), Chittenden County Bar Assn., Order of Coif, Phi Beta Kappa. Office: Green Mountain Power Corp 163 Acorn Ln Burlington VT 05446-6611 E-mail: rendall@greenmountainpower.bix.

RENDELL, EDWARD GENE, governor, retired mayor, lawyer; b. NYC, Jan. 5, 1944; s. Jesse T. and Emma (Sloat) R.; m. Marjorie Osterlund, July 10, 1971; 1 son, Jesse Thompson. BA in Polit. Sci., U. Pa., 1965; JD, Villanova U., 1968. Bar: Pa. 1968, U.S. Supreme Ct. 1981. Asst. dist. atty., chief homicide unit Office Dist. Atty., Phila., 1968-74; dep. spl. prosecutor Phila., 1976; dist. atty., 1978-86; mayor City of Phila., 1992—2000; gov. Commonwealth of Pa., Harrisburg, 2003—. Gen. chmn. Dem. Nat. Com., 1999—2000. 2d lt. USAR, 1968—74. Recipient Man of Yr. award VFW, 1980, Am. Cancer League, 1981, Disting. Pub. Svc. award Pa. County Detectives Assn., 1981. Mem. ABA, Pa. Dist. Attys. Assn. (legis. chmn. 1979—), Phila. Bar Assn., B'nai B'rith, United Jewish Orgns., Jewish War Vets. Democrat. Jewish. Office: Governor's Office Rm 225 Main Capitol Bldg Harrisburg PA 17120 Office Phone: 717-787-2500. Office Fax: 717-772-8284. *

RENDELL, KENNETH WILLIAM, rare and historical documents dealer, consultant; b. Boston, May 12, 1943; s. Harry H. and Pauline (Walsh) R.; m. Diana J. Angelo, June 3, 1967 (div. 1985); children: Jeffrey H., Jason J. (dec.); m. Shirley L. McNerney, July 14, 1985; 1 child, Julia Louise. Student, Boston U., 1961-63. Pres. Kingston Galleries, Inc., Somerville, Mass., 1960-67, Kenneth W. Rendell, Inc., Newton, Mass., 1967—, Kenneth W. Rendell, Ltd., London, 1970—, Kenneth W. Rendell Gallery, Inc., NYC, Tokyo, 1985—, Mus. World War II. Bd. dirs. John Wilson Autographs Ltd., London, 1961-75, Charles Ede Gallery Ltd., London, 1976-92; chmn. New England Antiquarian Booksellers Assn., 1975-77; pres. Internat. League Autograph and Manuscript Dealers, 1975-77; cons. numerous univ. librs., govtl. and media orgns. Author: The

Fundamentals of Autograph Collecting, 1976, Tax Appraisals of Manuscript Collections, 1983, Changing Concepts of Value and Rarity, 1985, The Hitler Diaries: Bad Forgeries But a Great Hoax, 1986, The Mormon Conman, Forger and Killer, 1987, Other People's Mail: 30 Years As a Dealer in Historical Documents, 1988, The One Hundred Americans Who Have Made America What it is Today, 1989, The Detection of Forged Historical Letters and Documents, 1990, With Weapons and Wits: Propaganda and Psychological Warfare in World War II, 1991, Forging History: The Detection of Fake Historical Letters and Documents, 1994, History Comes to Life, !995, The Western Pursuit of the American Dream, 2005; co-editor: Autographs and Manuscripts: A Collector's Manual, 1978 (Outstanding Reference Book award ALA); contbr. numerous articles in field to mags. and profl. jours. Trustee D-Day Mus., New Orleans, 1998, Youth Enrichment Svcs., Boston, 1998, William J. Donovan Meml., N.Y., 1998, Churchill Mus., London, 2000. Recipient Dept. Justice award, 1991. Fellow Manuscript Soc. (bd. dirs. 1968-74, pres. 1972-74); mem. Assn. Internat. de Bibliophilie Paris, Grolier Club, Army and Navy Club, Am. Antiquarian Soc., Bohemian Club (San Francisco), Appalachian Mountain Club (trustee 2000), Explorers Club, Saville Club (London), Spl. Forces Club (London). Avocation: ski racing. Office: Kenneth W Rendell Inc 46 Eliot St Natick MA 01760-6042 also: 989 Madison Ave New York NY 10021-1825

RENDELL, MARJORIE O., federal judge; b. 1947; m. Edward G. Rendell, 1971; 1 child, Jesse. BA, U. Pa., 1969; postgrad., Georgetown U., 1970—71; JD, Villanova U., 1973; LLD (hon.), Phila. Coll. Textile and Sci., 1992. Ptnr. Duane, Morris & Heckscher, Phila., 1972—93; judge US Dist. Ct. (ea. dist.) Pa., 1994—97, US Ct. Appeals (3d cir.), Phila., 1997—. Mem. Am. Jud. Soc., Fed. Judges Assn. Asst. to dir. ann. giving Dept. Devel. U. Pa., 1973—78; mem. adv. bd. Chestnut Hill Nat. Bank/East Falls Adv. Bd.; mem. alternative dispute resolution com. mediation divsn. Ea. Dist. Pa. Bankruptcy Conf.; active Acad. Vocal Arts, Market St. East Improvement Assn., Pa.'s Campaign for Choice, Phila. Friends Outward Bound; vice chair Ave. of Arts, Inc.; vice chair bd. trustees Vis. Nurse Assn. Greater Phila.; bd. mem. Alumni Trust, U. Penn. Mem.: ABA, Phila. Bar Found. (bd. dirs.), Phila. Bar Assn. (bd. dirs. young lawyers sect. 1973—78), Pa. Bar Assn., Am. Bankruptcy Inst., Internat. Women's Forum, Forum Exec. Women, Phi Beta Kappa. Office: US Courthouse 601 Market St Rm 21613 Philadelphia PA 19106-1715 *

RENDICH, ANA, painter, collage artist; arrived in U.S., 1988; d. Ernesto Pedro Rendich and Maria Elena Romero de Rendich; m. Glenn D. Millis, Dec. 31, 1993; children: Sara C. Millis, Amy C. Millis, Sophie A. Millis. Student, Sch. Art U. Salvador, Buenos Aires, 1979—81, Inst. Superior del teatro Colon, 1980—81; master classes with, Victor Callegery, Buenos Aires, 1981; after the master classes with, Franco Zeffirelli, NYC, 1996. Exhibitions include Cork Gallery Lincoln Ctr., NYC, 2003, 2004, 2005, Brush Strokes Art Gallery, Fredericksburg, Va. Mem.: Art First Gallery, Nat. Coll. Soc. Roman Catholic. Achievements include being the first South American painter to specialize in miniature painting. Avocations: art, opera. Personal E-mail: ana_rendich@brushstrokesfredericksburg.com.

RENDLEN, CHARLES EARNEST, III, (SKETCH RENDLEN), federal judge, lawyer; b. Hannibal, Mo., Aug. 17, 1950; s. Charles Earnest and Shirley Anne (Raible) R.; m. Susan L. David, Aug. 14, 1976; 1 child, Lindsey D. BS magna cum laude, William Jewell Coll., 1972; JD, U. Mo., 1976. Bar: Mo., U.S. Ct. Claims, U.S. Dist. Ct. (ea. and we. dists.) Mo., U.S. Tax Ct., U.S. Ct. Appeals (8th and Fed. cirs.), U.S. Supreme Ct. Assoc. The Rendlen Law Firm, P.C. (formerly Rendlen, Rendlen, Redington & Bastian, P.C.), Hannibal, Mo., 1976—79, ptnr., 1979—91, mng. ptnr, 1991—2003; US trustee, Reg. 13, Exec. Office US Trustees US Dept. Justice, 2003—06; judge US Bankruptcy Ct. (ea. dist.) Mo., St. Louis, 2006—. Mem. com. for jud. redistricting Mo. Supreme Ct., 1991-92, civil rules com., 1990-92; vice-chmn. worker compensation sect. Mo. Bar, 1992—. Co-author: Hedonics, 1992. Coord. Danforth for Senator, Marion County, 1976, 82, 88; chmn. Marion County Rep. Com., 1976-80, state com. 1992—; field worker Re-Elect the Pres., Mo., 1972; bd. dirs. Mennonite Home Assn., Inc., v.p., 1986—; v.p., bd. dirs. Beth Haven Terrace, Inc., 1986—, Beth Haven Group Homes, 1988—, Beth Haven Mgmt. Svcs., 1986—; bd. dirs. Hannibal Regional Hosp., sec., 1987-89. Mem. Rotary (pres. 1985-86). Avocations: golf, sailing. Office: Thomas F Eagleton US Courthouse 111 S Tenth St Rm 4380 Saint Louis MO 63102

RENDL-MARCUS, MILDRED, artist, economist; b. May 30, 1928; d. Julius and Agnes (Hokr) Rendl; m. Edward Marcus, Aug. 10, 1956. BS, NYU, 1948, MBA, 1950; PhD, Radcliffe Coll., 1954. Economist GE, 1953-56, Bigelow-Sanford Carpet Co., Inc., 1956-58; instr. econs. Hunter Coll. CUNY, 1959-60, Columbia U., 1960-61, rschr., 1961-63; sr. economist Nat. Indsl. Conf. Bd., 1963-66; asst. prof. Pace Coll., 1964-66; assoc. prof. Borough of Manhattan C. of C. CUNY, 1966-71, prof., 1972-85. Lectr. econs. CCNY, 1953-58; vis. prof. Fla. Internat. U., 1986; bd. dirs. N.Y.C. Coun. on Econ. Edn.; coun. mem. Harvard Mus. Natural History, 2002-04; assoc. mem. Allied Artists Am., Inc., 2004—; cons. in field. Exhibited group shows at in New Canaan Art Show, 1982-85, Am. Soc. Bus. and Behavioral Scis., 1990-96, New Cannan Soc. for Arts Ann., 1983, 85, New Canaan Arts, 1985, Silvermine Galleries, 1986, Stamford Art Assn., 1987, Phoenix Gallery, 1988, N.Y.C., Parkview Point Gallery, 1982-89, Miami Beach, Fla., 1982-89, Art Complex, New Canaan, Miami Beach, 1985—, Lever House, N.Y.C., 1990, Cork Gallery, Lincoln Ctr., N.Y.C., 1990, Women's Caucus for Art, San Antonio, 1990, Artist's Equity, Broome St. Gallery, N.Y.C., 1991, Greater Hartford Architecture Conservancy, 1991, N.H. Arts Ctr., 1997, Just Originals Art Web, Albuquerque, 1999, Ward-Nasse Gallery, N.Y.C., 2000—, Art Complex Gallery, Las Vegas, 2000-, Liliana Fine Art Gallery, Lenox, Mass., 2003—, Artists Gallery, Chelsea, N.Y.C., 2003, Nat. Assn. Women Artists, 2003—, 115-Yr. Anniversary Show, World Trade Ctr., N.Y.C., 2004, Pen and Brush Non-Mem. Show, 2004, Allied Artists Am., N.Y.C., 2005, Nat. Assn. Women Artists, N.Y.C., 2005, Catherine Lorillard Wolfe Art Club, 2005 (Rendl Drawing award 2006), Audubon Artists, N.Y.C., 2005, Real Art Ways Gallery, Hartford, 2005, 06, 07, Karpeles Mus., N.Y., 2006, Port of Call Gallery, Warwick, N.Y., 2006; author (with E. Marcus) Investment and Development of Tropical Africa, 1959, International Trade and Finance, 1965, Monetary and Banking Theory, 1965, Economics, 1969, Economic Progress and the Developing World, 1970, Economics, 1978, Fine Art with Many Equilibrium Prices, 1995; editor Women in the Arts Found. Newsletter, 1986-92; contbr. articles to profl. jours. Founder Rendl Fund for Slavic Art, Mus. of Modern Art, NYC, 1999—, Harvard U. Art Mus. Fund for Slavic Art, Cambridge, 2000—, Harvard Mus. Natural History, Peabody Mus. Archeology and Ethnology, Rendl Fund for the Conservation of Slavic Artifacts, 2000—, Rendl Fund for the Conservation of the Ware Collection of Blaschka Glass Models of Plants, 2001—; mem. mus. coun. Harvard Mus. Natural History, 2001—; founder Rendl Fund for Czech Art, 2006—, Met. Mus. Art, NYC. Recipient Merit award Manhattan Arts Internat., 1998, Excellence award 1998, Artist Showcase award Manhattan Arts Internat., 1999; Dean Bernice Brown Cronkhite fellow Radcliffe Coll., 1950-51, Anne Radcliffe Econ. Rsch. Sub-Sahara Africa fellow, 1958-59; fellow Gerontol. Assn. Mem. AAUW, Internat. Schumpeter Econs. Soc. (founding), Met. Econ. Assns. (sec. 1954-56), Indsl. Rels. Rsch. Assn., Women's Econ. Roundtable (program planning com.), N.Y.C. Women in Arts, Allied Social Sci. Assn. (artist 1994), Allied Artists Am. Inc. (assoc.), NYU Grad. Sch. Bus. Adminstrn. Alumni (sec. 1956-58), Radcliffe Club, Women's City Club (art and landmarks com.), Met. Mus. Arts.

RENDOCK, MARY KAY, elementary school educator; b. Conn. m. Doug Rendock; 2 children. AA in Early Childhood Edn., Becker Jr. Coll., 1983; BA in Elem. Edn., Ea. Conn. Univ., 1985; MS in Ednl. Tech. and Media, Ctrl. Conn. State Univ., 1996. Tchr. Bloomfield (Conn.) Sch. Sys., 1985—, J. P. Vincent Elem. Sch., Bloomfield Mid. Sch.; now tchr., fifth grade team leader Carmen Arace Intermediate Sch., Bloomfield, Conn. Named Conn. Tchr. of Yr., 2006. Office: Carmen Arace Intermediate Sch 390 Park Ave Bloomfield CT 06002 E-mail: mkrendock@sbcglobal.net. *

RENDU, JEAN-MICHEL MARIE, mining executive; b. Tunis, Tunisia, Feb. 25, 1944; s. Paul C. and Solange M. (Krebs) R.; m. Karla M. Meyer, Aug. 18, 1973; children: Yannick P., Mikaël P. Ingénieur des Mines, Ecole des Mines St. Etienne, France, 1966; MS, Columbia U., 1968, D of Engring. Sci., 1971. Mgr. ops. rsch. Anglovaal, Johannesburg, 1972-76; assoc. prof. U. Wis., Madison, 1976-79; assoc. Golder Assocs., Denver, 1979-84; dir. tech. and sci. systems Newmont Mining Corp., Danbury, Conn., 1984-88; v.p. Newmont Gold Co., Denver, 1988-93, Newmont Mining Corp., Denver, 1993-2001; ind. cons. Denver, 2001—. Author: An Introduction to Geostatistical Methods of Mineral Evaluation, 1978, 81; contbr. tech. papers to profl. jours. Fellow South African Inst. Mining and Metallurgy (corr. mem. of coun.), Australasian Inst. Mining and Metallurgy; mem. NAE, Soc. Mining, Metallurgy and Exploration (bd. dirs. 1998—2005, Jackling award 1994, Pres.'s citation 1993, 2004), Sigma Xi. Roman Catholic. E-mail: JMRendu@aol.com.

RENEE, LISABETH MARY, small business owner, glass artist; b. Bklyn., July 28, 1952; d. Lino P. and Elizabeth M. (Dines) Rivano; m. John S. Witanowski, May 15, 1982. Student, U. Puget Sound, 1972-74; BA in Art, SUNY, Buffalo, 1977; MFA, L.I. U., 1982; EdD, U. Ctrl. Fla., 1996. Cert. art tchr., Fla. Adj. faculty L.I. U., Greenvale, N.Y., 1980-82, Rollins Coll., Winter Park, Fla., 1982; art tchr. Phyllis Wheatley Elem. Sch., Apopka, Fla., 1983-85, McCoy Elem. Sch., Orlando, Fla., 1985-86, Lake Howell H.S., Winter Park, Fla., 1986-93; adj. faculty U. Ctrl. Fla., 1994-95, vis. instr., coord. art edn., 1995-96; gallery dir., prof. West Campus Valencia (Fla.) C.C., 1996-98; owner, designer Nartique, 2002—; dir. Renée Studios (now Nartique Glass), Casselberry, Fla., 2000—. Adj. faculty Valencia C.C., 1995-96; dir. So. Artists Registry, Winter Park, 1984-87; cons. Fla. Dept. Edn., 1989-90, mem. curriculum writing team for arts edn. program; mem. com. Fla. Bd. Edn. Task Force for Subject Area Subtest of Fla. Tech. Cert. Exam.; visual arts dir. Very Spl. Arts Ctr. Fla. Fest, 1996; presenter at profl. confs. Author: The Phenomenological Significance of Aesthetic Communion, 1996, Co-operative Art, 1991; editor: Children and the Arts in Florida, 1990. Visual arts dir. Very Spl. Arts Ctrl. Fla. Festival, 1995; mem. local Sch. Adv. Coun., Winter Park, 1992. Grantee Found. for Advancement of Cmty. Through Schs., 1991, Divsn. Blind Svcs. Invision, 1995, Tangelo Park Project, 1995; ACE scholar Arts Leadership Inst., 1993-96; recipient Tchr. Merit award Walt Disney World Co., 1990. Mem. NEA, ASCD, Nat. Art Edn. Assn., Fla. Art Edn. Assn. (regional rep. 1989-94), Seminole County Art Edn. Assn., Coll. Art Assn., Caucus on Social Theory and Art Edn., Women's Caucus for Art, Phi Kappa Phi, Kappa Delta Pi. Home and Office: Nartique 20 Cobblestone Ct Casselberry FL 32707-5410 Office Phone: 407-921-0257. Business E-Mail: liz@nartiqueglass.com.

RENEHAN, EDWARD JOHN, writer; b. NYC, Aug. 7, 1956; s. Edward John Renehan and Joan Margaret Salvesen; m. Christa Elizabeth Bartkovick, Aug. 24, 1985; children: William James, Katherine Eleanor. BA in Polit. Sci., SUNY, New Paltz, 1980. Author: John Burroughs: An American Naturalist, 1992, The Secret Six: The True Tale of the Men Who Conspired with John Brown, 1995, The Lion's Pride: Theodore Roosevelt and His Family in Peace and War, 1998, The Kennedys at War, 2002, Dark Genius of Wall Street: The Misunderstood Life of Jay Gould, King of the Robber Barons, 2005, Commodore: The Life of Cornelius Vanderbilt, 2007; tech. cons. film John Kennedy and PT-109, 2003; contbr. columns to papers; contbr. articles to jours. Dir. So. R.I. Conservation Dist., Warwick, 2000-05; del. R.I. Conservation Com., 2000-05. Mem. PEN, Theodore Roosevelt Assn. (trustee 2000-04), Nat. Arts Club, Hudson River Sloop Clearwater, Inc. (dir. 1976-80), Boston Atheneaum, Pi Sigma Alpha. Avocations: hiking, sailing. Office: Chris Calhoun/Sterling Lord Literistic 65 Bleecker St New York NY 10012

RENEHAN, RICHARD WILLIAM, lawyer; b. Boston, Dec. 30, 1933; s. Francis Xavier and Mary (Sullivan) R.; m. Mary B. Brophy, Feb. 17, 1962; children: Anne M., Joan F., Richard W., Jr., Mark D. BA, Boston Coll., 1955; LLB, Harvard U., 1958. Bar: Mass. 1958, U.S. Dist. Ct. Mass. 1959, U.S. Ct. Appeals (1st cir.) 1964, U.S. Supreme Ct. 1971. Assoc. Peabody, Koufman & Brewer, Boston, 1959-64; ptnr. Hill & Barlow, Boston; dir., profl. liability, securities litig. Goulston & Storrs, Boston. Mem. Gov's Select Com. on Jud. Needs, Boston, 1978-79, Joint Bar Com. on Jud. Appointments, 1979-84, Gov's Jud. Nominating Coun., Boston, 1987-90. Mem. Milton (Mass.) Housing Authority, 1979-86, chmn., 1981-85. Fellow Am. Bar Found, Am. Coll. Trial Lawyers; mem. ABA, Mass. Bar Assn., Boston Bar Assn. (pres. 1985-86). Office: Goulston & Storrs 400 Atlantic Ave Boston MA 02110-3333 Office Phone: 617-574-4024. Office Fax: 617-574-7593. Business E-Mail: rrenehan@goulstonstorrs.com.

RENEKER, MAXINE HOHMAN, librarian; b. Chgo., Dec. 2, 1942; d. Roy Max and Helen Anna Christina (Anacker) Hohman; m. David Lee Reneker, June 20, 1964 (dec. Dec. 1979); children: Sarah Roeder, Amy Johannah, Benjamin Congdon. BA, Carleton Coll., 1964; MA, U. Chgo., 1970; DLS, Columbia U., 1992. Asst. reference libr. U. Chgo. Libraries, 1965-66; classics libr. U. Chgo. Libr., 1967-70, asst. head acquisitions, 1970-71, personnel libr., 1971-73; personnel/bus. libr. U. Colo. Libr., Boulder, 1978-80; asst. dir. sci. and engring. div. Columbia U., NYC, 1981-85; assoc. dean of univ. librs. for pub. svcs. Ariz. State U. Libr., Tempe, 1985-89; dir. instrnl. and rsch. svcs. Stanford (Calif.) Univ. Librs., 1989-90; assoc. provost for libr. and info. resources Naval Postgrad. Sch., Monterey, Calif., 1993—2005, prof. emerita, 2005—. Acad. libr. mgmt. intern Coun. on Libr. Resources, 1980-81; chmn. univ. librs. sect. Assn. Coll. and Rsch. Librs., 1989-90. Contbr. articles to profl. jours. Trustee Monterey Pub. Libr. Rsch. grantee Coun. on Library Resources, Columbia U., 1970-71, fellow, 1990-92. Mem. ALA, Am. Soc. Info. Sci., Sherlockian Scion Soc., Phi Beta Kappa, Beta Phi Mu. Home: 740 Dry Creek Rd Monterey CA 93940-4208 E-mail: mreneker@pacbell.net.

RENFER, JAMES ALLEN, elementary school educator; b. Kingston, Pa., May 11, 1975; s. Merle Joseph and Ellen Renfer; m. Christine B. Mulhern, Aug. 19, 2000; children: Lamont, Latoya, Justin. AS in Edn., Luzerne County C.C., Nanticoke, Pa., 1996; BS in Elem. Edn., Coll. Misericordia, Dallas, Pa., 1999. Cert. tchr. grades K-6 Pa., Cath. sch. tchr. Substitute tchr. Wyoming Area Cath., Exeter, Pa., 1999; 6th grade English tchr. Sacred Heart of Jesus, Dupont, Pa., 1999—. Mem. Sacred Heart Cons. Group, Dupont, 2006—; forensic coach Scranton Diocese Cath. Elem. Sch.; mission moderator Holy Childhood Assn., Diocese Scranton. Mem.: Pa. State Edn. Assn., Nat. Cath. Edn. Assn., Nat. Coun. Tchrs. English. Roman Catholic. Avocation: piano. Home: 1440 Suscon Rd Pittston Township PA 18640

RENFREW, ANDREW COLIN (LORD RENFREW OF KAIMSTHORN), archaeologist, educator, director; b. July 25, 1937; s. Archibald and Helena Douglas (Savage) R.; m. Jane Margaret Ewbank, Apr. 21, 1965; children: Helena Margaret, Alban Robert, Magnus Archibald. BA, St. John's Coll., Cambridge U., 1962, MA, 1964, PhD, 1965, ScD, 1976. Lectr. archaeology U. Sheffield, 1965-72; prof. U. Southampton, 1972-81; Disney prof. archaeology Cambridge U., 1981—2004; dir. McDonald Inst. Archeol. Rsch., 1990—2004. Vis. lectr. UCLA, 1967; fellow St. John's Coll., 1981-86, hon. fellow 2004-; master Jesus Coll., Cambridge, 1986-97, fellow, 1997-04, hon. fellow, 2004—; George Grant McCurdy lectr. Harvard U., 1977; Patten lectr. Ind. U., 1982; field excavations in Saliagos, 1961-64, Sitagroi, 1968-70, Quanterness, Orkney, 1972-74, Phylakopi, Melos, 1974-76, Dhaskalio Karos Keras, 2006-07. Author (with J. D. Evans): Excavations at Saliagos Near Antiparos, 1968 in Orkney, 1979; author: Problems in European Prehistory, 1979; author: (with J. M. Wagstaff) An Island Polity, 1982; author: Approaches to Social Archaeology, 1984, The Prehistory of Orkney, 1985, The Archaeology of Cult, 1985, Archaeology and Language, 1987; author: (with G. Daniel) The Idea of Prehistory, 1988; author: The Cycladic Spirit, 1991; author: (with P. Bahn) Archaeology, 1991; author: Loot, Legitimacy and Ownership: The Ethical Crisis in Archaeology, 2000, Figuring It Out, 2003, Prehistory, 2007; editor: The Explanation of Culture Change, 1973, British Prehistory, 1974, Transformations: Mathematical Approaches to Culture Change, 1979, Theory and Explanation in Archaeology, 1982; presenter (TV films) The Tree That Put the Clock Back, 1970, Islands Out of Time, 1973, Orkney Underground, 1974, Aphrodite's Other Island, 1977, Bronze Age Blast Off, 1978, Lost Kings of the Desert, 1980, The Emperor's Immortal Army, 1981, City of the Dead, 1982, Who Built Stonehenge, 1986. Trustee Brit. Mus., 1991-01. With RAF, 1956-58. Recipient European Sci. Found. Latsis Prize, 2003, Rivers Meml. medal Royal Anthrop. Inst., 1979, Huxley Meml. medal, 1991, Balzan prize, 2004; named Fgn. Assoc. NAS, 1996; elevated to peerage, 1991. Fellow Brit. Acad., Soc. Antiquaries London, Royal Soc. Edinburgh (hon.), Austrian Acad. Sci., German Archeol. Inst.; mem. Am. Philos. Soc. (fgn.), Athenaeum. Office: Dept Archaeology Downing St Cambridge CB2 3DZ England also: House of Lords London SW1A 0PW England Office Phone: 01223-333521. Business E-Mail: des25@cam.ac.uk.

RENFREW, CHARLES BYRON, lawyer; b. Detroit, Oct. 31, 1928; s. Charles Warren and Louise (McGuire) R.; m. Susan Wheelock, June 28, 1952 (div. June 1984); children: Taylor Allison Ingham, Charles Robin, Todd Wheelock, James Bartlett; m. Barbara Jones Orser, Oct. 6, 1984; 5 stepchildren. AB, Princeton U., 1952; JD, U. Mich., 1956. Bar: Calif. 1956. Assoc. Pillsbury, Madison & Sutro, San Francisco, 1956-65, ptnr., 1965-72, 81-82; U.S. dist. judge No. Dist. Calif., San Francisco, 1972-80; dep. atty. gen. U.S. Washington, 1980-81; instr. U. Calif. Boalt Hall Sch. Law, 1977-80; v.p. law Chevron Corp. (formerly Standard Oil Co. Calif.), San Francisco, 1983-93, also bd. dirs.; ptnr. LeBoeuf, Lamb, Greene & McRae, San Francisco, 1994-97; pvt. practice San Francisco, 1998—. Mem. exec. com. 9th Cir. Jud. Conf., 1976-78, congl. liaison com. 9th Cir. Jud. Council, 1976-79, spl. com. to propose standards for admission to practice in fed. cts. U.S. Jud. Conf., 1976-79; chmn. spl. com. to study problems of discovery Fed. Jud. Ctr., 1978-79; mem. council on role of cts. U.S. Dept. Justice, 1978-83; mem. jud. panel Ctr. for Pub. Resources, 1981—; head U.S. del. to 6th UN Congress on Prevention of Crime and Treatment of Offenders, 1980; co-chmn. San Francisco Lawyers Com. for Urban Affairs, 1971-72, mem., 1983—; bd. dirs. Internat. Hospitality Ctr., 1961-74, pres., 1967-70; mem. adv. bd. Internat. Comparative Law Ctr., Southwestern Legal Found., 1983-93; trustee World Affairs Council No. Calif., 1984-87, 94—, Nat. Jud. Coll., 1985-91, Grace Cathedral, 1986-89. Contbr. articles to profl. jours. Bd. fellow Claremont U., 1986-94; bd. dirs. San Francisco Symphony Found., 1964-80, pres., 1971-72; bd. dirs. Coun. Civic Unity, 1962-73, pres., 1971-72; bd. dirs. Opportunity Through Ownership, 1969-72, Marin County Day Sch., 1972-74, No. Calif. Svc. League, 1975-76, Am. Petroleum Inst., 1984—, Nat. Crime Prevention Coun., 1982—; alumni trustee Princeton U., 1976-80; mem. vis. com. u. chgo. Law Sch., 1977-79, u.Mich. Law Sch., 1977-81; bd. visitors J. Reuben Clark Law Sch., Brigham Young U., 1981-83, Stanford Law Sch., 1983-86; trustee Town Sch. for Boys, 1972-80,pres. 1975-80; gov. San Fransciso Symphony Assn., 1974—; mem. nat. adv. bd. Ctr. for Nat. Policy, 1982—; bd. dirs. Nat. Coun. Crime and Deliquency, 1981-82,NAACP Legal Def. and Edn. Fund, 1982—; parish chancellor St. Luke's Episcopal Ch., 1968-71, sr. warden, 1974-76; mem. exec. coun. San Francisco Deanery, 1969-70; mem. diocesan coun. Episcopal Diocese of Calif., 1970; chmn. Diocesan Conv., 1977, 78, 79. Served with USN, 1946-48, 1st lt. U.S. Army, 1952-53. Fellow Am. Bar Found.; mem. ABA (coun. mem. sect. antitrust law 19778-82, vice c hmn. sect. antitrust law 1982-83), San Francisco Bar Assn. (past bd. dirs.), Assn. Gen. Counsel, State Bar Calif., Am. Judicature Soc., Am. Coll. Trial Lawyers (pres. 1995-96), Am. Law Inst., Coun. Fgn. Rels., Order of Coif, Phi Beta Kappa, Phi Delta Phi. Office: 710 Sansome St San Francisco CA 94111-1704

RENFREW, MALCOLM MACKENZIE, chemist, educator; b. Spokane, Wash., Oct. 12, 1910; s. Earl Edgar and Elsie Pauline (MacKenzie) R.; m. Carol Joy Campbell, June 26, 1938. BS, U. Idaho, 1932, MS, 1934, D.Sc., 1976; PhD, U. Minn., 1938. Asst. physics U. Idaho, 1932-33, Asst. chemistry, 1933-35, U. Minn., 1935-37, duPont fellow, 1937-38; research chemist plastics dept. duPont Co., 1938-44, supr. process devel., 1944-46, supr. product devel., 1946-49; head chem. research dept., research labs. Gen. Mills, Inc., 1949-52, dir. chem. research, 1952-53, dir. chem. research and devel., 1953-54; dir. research and devel. Spencer Kellogg & Sons, Inc., 1954-58; phys. sci. div. head, prof. chemistry U. Idaho, 1959-73, prof., 1973-76, emeritus, 1976—; dir. U. Idaho (Coll. Chem. Cons. Service), 1969-76. On leave as sr. staff assoc. Adv. Coun. Coll. Chemistry, Stanford, 1967-68; mem. materials adv. bd. Nat. Rsch. Coun., 1963-67; exec. v.p. Idaho Rsch. Found., 1977-78, patent dir., 1978-88. Editor: Safety in the Chemical Laboratory, Vol. IV, 1981, (with Peter Ashbrook), Safe Laboratories: Principles and Practices for Design and Remodeling, 1991; safety editor: Jour. Chem. Edn, 1977-91; Contbr. to tech. and trade publs. on plastics, coatings, safety, chem. edn. Recipient Excellence in Teaching award Chem. Mfrs. Assn., 1977, Outstanding Achievement award U. Minn., 1977, Disting. Idahoan award U. Idaho Alumni Assn., 2006; named to U. Idaho Hall of Fame, 1977, Idaho Hall of Fame, 1996. Fellow AAAS, Am. Inst. Chemists; mem. Am. Chem. Soc. (councilor 1948, 59, 67-89, chmn. paint varnish and plastics div. 1949, chmn. chem. mktg. and econs. div. 1958-59, chmn. chem. health and safety div. 1982, James Flack Norris award 1976, Chem. Health and Safety award 1985, Mosher award 1986), Am. Inst. Chem. Engrs., Soc. Chem. Industry, Phi Beta Kappa, Sigma Xi, Phi Kappa Phi, Sigma Pi Sigma, Phi Gamma Delta (dising. Fiji 1986). Presbyterian. Home: 1271 Walenta Dr Moscow ID 83843-2426 Office: U Idaho Coll Sci Dept Chemistry PO Box 442343 Moscow ID 83844-2343 Business E-Mail: renfrew@uidaho.edu.

RENFRO, CHARLES GILLILAND, economist; b. Paris, Tex., Nov. 23, 1943; s. Charles G. and Virginia Armstrong (Dawsey) R.; m. Patricia Elise Candlin, June 21, 1969; children: Rebecca Elise, James Lawrence. BA, U. of York, Eng., 1966; MSc, London Sch. Econs., U. London, 1968; MA, U. Pa., 1971, PhD, 1976. Rsch. asst. Indsl. Manpower Project London Sch. Econs., 1967-68; rsch. asst. Brookings Instn., Washington, 1968-70; econ. rsch. fellow U. Pa.-Wharton Econometric Forecasting Assocs., Phila., 1970-71; instr. econs. U. Pa., 1971-73; lectr. dept. econs. Swarthmore (Pa.) Coll., 1972-73; rsch. assoc., asst. prof. econs. U. Ky., Lexington, 1973-77, assoc. dir. econ. studies and analysis, 1975-81, dir. ctr. for Applied Econ. Rsch., 1979-81; dir. regional forecasting, chief regional economist Chase Econometric Assocs. Inc., Bala Cynwyd, Pa., 1981-83; pres. C.G. Renfro & Assocs., Bala Cynwyd, 1978—, Alphametrics Corp., Bala Cynwyd, 1984—. Pres. Sparks Agribus. Info. Systems, Inc., Bala Cynwyd and Memphis, 1989-92; bd. dirs. Alphametrics Ltd., Cambridge, Eng.; former bd. dirs. Integrated Modelling Applications Ltd., Cambridge, Eng., 1985-90; econ. advisor office budget and mgmt. State of Ohio, 1980, 82-83, permanent subcom. investigations, com. govt. ops. U.S. Senate, 1974-75, State Govt. Pa., 1981-83, environ. protection agy. State of N.J., 1982-83, State of Conn., 1982-83, State of Tex., 1982-83, dept. of taxation State of North Dakota, 1981-83, State of Mo., 1982-83; assoc. dir. Ky. Coun. Econ. Advisors, 1977-79, exec. dir., 1979-81; econ. advisor State of Va., 1982-83; info. systems advisor small bus. subcom. U.S. Ho. Reps., 1979-80; cons. Merrill Lynch Econs. Inc., 1986-87, Data Resources Inc., 1985-90,

Wharton Econometric Forecasting Assocs., Inc., 1984-86, Chase Econometric Assocs., 1983, 85-87, Humana, Inc., 1981, Dames & Moore, 1980-81, Gen. Telephone Co., Ky., 1977-81, 1st Security Nat. Bank and Trust Co., 1979-81, Elsevier Sci. Publ. Co., Inc., 1980-87, Townsend-Greenspan & Co., Inc., 1986-88; cons., mem. sci. adv. com. Pitagora Spa, Rome, 1990-93, M & DR Cons. Srl, Milan, 1990-93, Ibermetrics S.A., Madrid, 1987—. Author and developer computer software systems, first PC-based comml. econ. forecasting svc., principally MODLER Statis. Info. and Modeling System, 1970, DATAVIEW Statis. Info. System, 1982; author: Computational Econometrics: Its Impact on the Development of Quantitative Economics, 2004, The Practice of Econometric Theory, 2007; co-author: MODLER BLUE Advanced Econometric Estimation System, 1985-86, MODLER MBA Bus. Decision Support and Forecasting System, (co-author) Wharton PC-Mark 7/MODLER Microcomputer-based Econometric Modelling System and Quar. Model of U.S. Economy, 1984, POWERSTATION, MAESTRO; MODLER systems used worldwide by internat. orgns. such as UN, EEC, govts., major econ. forecasting firms; editor Rev. of Public Data Use, 1980-84, Jour. Econ. and Social Measurement, 1985—; editl. adv. bd. Computers and the Social Sciences, 1985-87; contbr. articles to profl. jours.; founder, prin. developer Ky. Econ. Info. System, 1973-81; designer, developer Online Retrieval and Computation Lang. for Economists (Oracle), 1976. Mem. Am. Econ. Assn., Am. Statis. Assn., Southeastern Econ. Analysis Conf. (program chmn. 1977, exec. com. 1977-81), Early English Text Soc., Soc. for Computational Econs., Nat. Assn. Bus. Economists, Penn Club (N.Y.C.).

RENFRO, JOHN M., human resources specialist; b. Collinsville, Ill., Dec. 31, 1959; BS, So. Ill. U., 1982. V.p. human resources A.C. Nielson Internat.; v.p. human resources consumer mktg. info. group Asia-Pacific, Latin Am. and Africa ops. Dun & Bradstreet; v.p. human resources and adminstrn. small bus. svcs. divsn. Ameritech, Chgo.; sr. v.p. human resources and adminstrn. Zenith Electronics Corp., Chgo.; v.p. corp. human resources to sr. v.p. human resources Gateway, San Diego, 1998—2002; sr. v.p., chief human resources officer Walt Disney Co., Burbank, Calif., 2002—06; v.p. human resources HP Imaging and Printing Group (IPG) Hewlett-Packard, 2006—. Mem. external adv. bd. coll. bus. adminstrn. So. Ill. U.; bd. dirs. LA Urban League; mem. external adv. bd. So. Ill. U., Carbondale. Mem. exec. com. United Way, San Diego, mem. Alexis de Tocqueville Soc. Office: HP Imaging and Printing Group 3000 Hanover St Palo Alto CA 94304 Office Phone: 818-560-1000. Office Fax: 818-560-1930.

RENFRO, NORM, energy executive; BS in Biology, S.W. Tex. State U.; BS in Chemistry, Corpus Christi State U. With Kerr McGee Corp., Okla. City, Southwestern Refining Co., Corpus Christi, Tex.; v.p. environ. and safety affairs Valero Energy Corp., San Antonio, 1997, v.p. health, safety and environ. Office: Valero Energy Corpn 1 Valero Way San Antonio TX 78292-0500

RENFRO, PATRICIA ELISE, library director, academic administrator; b. Nelson, Lancashire, Eng. d. Henry Lawrence and Maud (Thompson) Candlin; m. Charles Gilliland Renfro, June 21, 1969; children: Rebecca Elise, James Lawrence. BA in English and History with honors, U. York, Eng., 1966; acad. postgrad. diploma, U. London, 1968; MA in History, U. Ky., 1981. Libr. asst. Holborn br. London Borough of Camden Pub. Librs., London, 1966-67, sr. asst. libr., 1968-69; dep. acquisitions libr. Folger Shakespeare Libr., Washington, 1969-70; cataloger Libr. Co. of Phila., 1970-72; reference libr. U. Pa. Librs., 1972-73, U. Ky. Librs., 1975-76, head of reference svcs., 1976-78; exec. sec. U. Ky. Libr. Assocs., U. Ky., 1979-80; reference libr. U. Pa., 1982-83, head circulation svcs. Van Pelt Libr., 1983-85, asst. dir. librs. for pub. svcs., 1985-89, assoc. dir. librs., 1989—2000; dep. univ. libr. Columbia U., NYC, 2000—. Mem. programs adv. com. Rsch. Librs. Group, 1991-92; mem. circulation interchange com. NISO 1999-2002; bd. dirs. N.Y. State Higher Edn. Initiative, 2004—. Contbr. articles to profl. jours. Mem. ALA, Assn. Coll. and Rsch. Librs. (rsch. com. 1992-94, ULS program com. 2005). Office Phone: 212-854-2226.

RENFRO, WILLIAM LEONARD, futurist, lawyer, inventor, entrepreneur; b. West Palm Beach, Fla., Sept. 9, 1945; s. Ernest Leonard and Oine Warren (McAdams) R. BS in Physics, Rensselaer Poly. Inst., 1967, MS in Nuclear Engring., 1972; postgrad., Yale U., 1967-68; JD, U. Conn., 1972. Bar: Conn. 1973, U.S. Ct. Fed. Claims, Fed. Ct. Appeals (D.C. cir.) 2002. Physicist Compustion Engring., Windsor Locks, Conn., 1968-69; pvt. practice law, Hartford, Conn., 1973-74; sr. rsch. assoc. The Futures Group, Glastonbury, Conn., 1973-76; analyst futures rsch. Congl. Rsch. Svc., U.S. Congress, Washington, 1976-80; pres. Policy Analysis Co., Inc., Washington, 1980—. Vis. fellow Ark. Inst.; guest lectr. Georgetown U., Brookings Inst., Nat. War Coll.; adj. prof. George Washington U., Indsl. Coll. Armed Forces Nat. Def. U.; mem. nat. foresight network U.S. Congress. Author: (with others) The Futures Research Handbook, 1997, Anticipatory Democracy, 1978, The Public Affairs Handbook, 1983, The Legislative Role of Corporations, 1982, Applying Methods and Techniques of Futures Research, 1983, Future Research and the Straegic Planning Process, 1985, Non-Extrapolative Forecasting in Business, 1988, Futures Research Methodology: The UN Millennium Project, 1999; author: Issue Management in Stratetic Planning, 1993, Vision-2020, 1999; editor Futures Rsch. Quar. World Futures Soc., 1980-1991; issues mgmt. editor the Futurist, 1982—, Tech. Analysis and Strategic Mgmt. Mem. long range planning com. United Way; trustee World Tech. Found., Am. Friends of Romania, 2002—; lic. pastoral vis. lay eucharistic min. Wash. Diocese; Atlantic Coun, 2004—. Named Alumni of 2003, Rensselaer Alumni Assn.; named one of Alumni of Yr., Rensselaer Poly. Inst., 2003. Mem.: ABA, Nat. Rep. Lawyers Assn., Washington Choral Ensemble (trustee 2004—06), Russian Am. Student Exch. (chmn., founder), Georgetown Hist. Structures Preservation Soc. (co-founder), People to People Internat., Hartford County Bar Assn., Conn. Bar Assn., Internat. Pub. Rels. Assn., Assn. Former Intelligence Officers, World Futures Soc., Issues Mgmt. Assn. (bd. dirs. 1981—98, v.p. 1986—88, pres. 1988—96), Pub. Rels. Soc. Am., Women Impacting Pub. Policy (charter), English Speaking Union (trustee, v.p. internat. programs Washington br.), Federalist Soc., St. Andrews Soc., Clan Hamilton Soc., Women's Nat. Dem. Club. Episcopalian. Achievements include patents in field. E-mail: counsel_for_the_future@apanet.org.

RENFRO, ZOE VAUGHAN, principal; b. Conroe, Tex., Aug. 30, 1954; d. Roy Ray and Kathryn Walding Vaughan; m. Gordon Dewayne Renfro, Dec. 21, 1997; stepchildren: Laura Renfro Phillips, Zach, Matthew. BBA, Sam Houston State U., Huntsville, Tex., 1977; MEd, San Houston State U., Huntsville, Tex., 1981; MDiv, Tex. Christian U., Ft. Worth, 1998. Ordained min. Christian Ch. (Disciples of Christ); cert. tchr., adminstr., counselor Tex., Tenn. Tchr., counselor New Caney Ind. Sch. Dist., Tex., 1978—84, tchr., adminstrv. asst. prin., 1985—88; counselor Coldspring-Oakhurst Cmty. Ind. Sch. Dist., Coldspring, Tex., 1988—90, Montgomery Ind. Sch. Dist., Tex., 1991—97; asst. prin. Waco Ind. Sch. Dist., Tex., 1990; pastor Christian Ch. (Disciples of Christ), Tex. and Tenn., 1995—2003; prin., adult edn. supr. Bradley County Schs., Cleveland, Tenn., 2004—. Cons. Christian Ch. (Disciples of Christ), Nashville, 2003—06; chaplain Crockett County Sheriff's Office, Alamo, Tenn., 2001—03, res. dep., 2001—03. Pres. Crockett County Care Coun., Alamo, 2001—02. Scholar, Christian Ch. Found., Abilene, Tenn., 1996—98. Mem.: Tenn. Assn. Adult and Continuing Edn. Avocations: singing, crocheting, piano. Office: Bradley County Schs 800 S Lee Hwy Cleveland TN 37311

RENICK, JAMES CARMICHAEL, educational association administrator, former academic administrator; b. Rockford, Ill., Dec. 8, 1948; s. Constance Renick; m. Peggy Renick; 1 child, Karinda. BA, Ctrl. State U., Ohio, 1970; MSW, Kans. U., 1972; PhD in public adminstrn., Fla. State U., 1980. Cmty. mental health counselor; asst. prof social work U. West Fla., 1975—81; assoc. prof. pub. adminstrn. U. South Fla., 1981—85, asst. to pres., 1983—85; asst. dean adminstrn. U. South Fla., Grad. Sch., 1985—88; founding edn. chair Exec. Fellows Prog. Inst. of Govt., U. South Fla., 1985—88, dir. pub. adminstrn. prog., 1988; assoc. provost & dir. Early Identification Prog. George Mason U., 1989—91, vice provost academic initiative & external affairs, 1991—93; chancellor U. Mich., Dearborn, 1993—99; prof polit. sci. NC A&T State U., 1999—, chancellor, 1999—2006; sr. v.p. programs and rsch. Am. Coun. Edn., Washington, 2006—. Cons. in edn. field nat. and internat.; mem. President's Bd. Adv. on Historically Black Coll. and Univ., NC Bd. of Sci. and Tech., Bus.-Higher Edn. Forum; bd. trustees JSTOR; bd. dirs. Microelectronics Ctr. of NC, Piedmont Triad Ctr. for Adv. Mfg., Piedmont Triad Partnership. Contbr. articles to profl. jours. Mem. James Lawrence Found., Parrin J. Mitchell Found.; mem. hon. edn. coun. Nat. Minority Military Mus. Found.; bd. dirs. Greater Greensboro C. of C; pres. Greensboro Merchants Assn. Named to Donald K. Anthony Achievement Hall of Fame, Ctrl. State U., Ohio, 1993; recipient President's Medallion, U. Mich., Exemplary Award for Pub. Service, Am. Assn. for Higher Edn. Black Caucus. Office: Am Coun Edn One Dupont Circle NW Washington DC 20036 Office Phone: 202-939-9300.

RENICK, KYLE, artistic director; b. St. Louis, Apr. 24, 1948; s. Mark Allen and Annabelle (Myers) R. BA magna cum laude, Tufts U., 1970. Sr. fund acct. New Eng. Mchts. Nat. Bank, Boston, 1970-73; fund acct. Fidelity Mgmt. and Rsch. Corp., Boston, 1973; bus. mgr. Am. Pl. Theatre, NYC, 1973-78; producing dir. WPA Theatre, NYC, 1977-82, artistic dir., 1982—; pres. WPA Prodns., Inc., NYC, 1987—. Trustee Alliance of Resident Theatres-N.Y., 1982-92; cons. N.Y. State Council on Arts, 1982-85, Nat. Endowment for Arts, 1986. Producer Steel Magnolias, 1987, The Lady in Question, 1989; contbr. articles to profl. publs. Recipient spl. award for outstanding achievement Drama Desk Assn., 1983. Mem.: Neue Bachgesellschaft, Nev. Hist. Soc., Film Music Soc., Wildlife Conservation Soc., The Packard Club, Phi Beta Kappa. Avocations: early music, record collecting, ghost town photography. Home: 2 Bethune St Apt 4B New York NY 10014-1862 E-mail: wpatheatre@msn.com.

RENKES, GREGG D., former state attorney general; b. 1958; m. Maureen Renkes; 2 children. BA, Vassar Coll.; MS, Yale U.; JD, U. Colo. Bar: Alaska 1987. Law clk., magistrate State Alaska Ct. Sys.; chief of staff, chief counsel to U.S. Senator Frank Murkowski; majority staff dir. U.S. Senate Com. on Energy and Natural Resources, 1995—98; pres. The Renkes Group, Ltd.; atty. gen. State of Alaska, Juneau, 2002—05. Spkr. in field. Contbr. articles to profl. jours. Mem. Campaign to Re-elect Senator Frank Murkowski, 1992, 1998, Murkowski 2002 Alaska Gubernatorial Campaign; active Rep. Nat. Conv. Platform Com., 1996. Republican.

RENKIEWICZ, MARTIN, federal agency administrator; married; 2 children. Grad., U. RI, 1976. With Immigration & Naturalization Svc. US Dept. Justice; with US Nat. Ctrl. Bur. INTERPOL, 1992—, sr. rep. from US Dept. Justice, asst. dir. Alien Fugitive Divsn., 2002—03, dep. dir., 2003—06, dir., 2006—. Office: INTERPOL US Nat Ctrl Bur 1301 New York Ave NW 4th Fl Washington DC 20530 Office Phone: 202-616-7820. Office Fax: 202-616-1048. E-mail: martin.renkiewicz@usdoj.gov. *

RENKIS, ALAN ILMARS, plastics formulating company executive; b. Preili, Latvia, Apr. 16, 1938; arrived in U.S., 1950, naturalized, 1958; s. Joseph and Malvine (Sturitis) R.; m. Inara Balodis, July 15, 1961; children: Martin Alan, Laura Alise. BSChemE, Pa. State U., State College, 1960. Staff product devel. and tech. svc. divsn. Diamond Alkali Co., Painesville, Ohio, 1960-63; tech. dir. G.S. Plastics Co., Cleve., 1963; founder, pres. Thermoclad Co., Erie, Pa., 1963—, Riverside, Calif., 1972-80, Ocala, Fla., 1985—. Developer comml. PVC resins for formulating fluidized bed and electrostatic coating powders; formulations and compounding techniques. Mem. World Pres. Orgn., Am. Latvian Assn., Erie Yacht Club, Kahkwa Club, Sigma Pi, Fraternitas Metropolitana. Home: 214 Crystal Point Dr Erie PA 16505 Office: Thermoclad Co 361 W 11th St Erie PA 16501-1703 Office Phone: 814-456-1243. Business E-Mail: arenkis@thermoclad.com.

RENNE, PAUL A., lawyer; b. Mpls., Nov. 2, 1930; AB, Univ. Minn., 1956; JD, Harvard Univ., 1959. Bar: DC 1959, NY 1961, Calif. 1964, US Supreme Ct. 1964. Law clk. Judge Edwin D. Steel, Jr., US Dist Ct. (Del.), 1959—60; assoc. Haight Gardner Poor & Havens, NYC, 1960—61; atty. U.S. Dept. Justice, civil rights div., Washington, 1961—62; asst. U.S. atty. U.S. Dept. Justice, DC dist., 1962—64; sr. counsel, litigation dept. Cooley Godward LLP, San Francisco, 1964—. Adj. prof. Golden Gate Univ.; lectr. Calif. CLE; mediator Assn. San Francisco, US Dist. Ct. Contbr. articles to profl. jours. Pilot USAF, 1951—56. Mem.: ABA, Am. Coll. Trial Lawyers (state chmn., no. Calif.), Am. Arbitration Assn. (mem. com. panel), Bar Assn. San Francisco. Office: Cooley Godward Llp 101 California St Fl 5 San Francisco CA 94111-5800 Office Phone: 415-693-2073. Office Fax: 415-951-3699. Business E-Mail: prenne@cooley.com.

RENNE, PAUL F., retired food products executive; b. Pitts. BS in Acctg., St. Vincent Coll. CPA. With acctg. firm, 1965-73; fin. analyst H.J. Heinz Co., Pittsburgh, Pa., 1973-75, dir. fin. rels., 1975-81, v.p. fin. Heinz Can., 1981-84, corp. treas. Heinz World Hdqrs., 1984-86, v.p., treas., 1986-1996, v.p. fin., treas., 1989—, CFO, 1996—2001, sr. v.p. fin. to exec. v.p., 1997—2001, spl. advisor, fin., 2002.

RENNER, ANDREW IHOR, surgeon; b. Buenos Aires, Aug. 1, 1951; came to U.S., 1956; s. Vladimir and Emelia R.; m. Cristina Sasyk, Apr. 17, 1982. MD, Albert Einstein Coll. Medicine, 1975. Diplomate Am. Bd. Surgery. Pvt. practice gen. surgery, Burbank, Calif.; chief of staff Providence-St. Joseph Med. Ctr., 2005, 2006. Chmn. dept. surgery St. Joseph Hosp., Burbank, 1995-97, vice chief of staff Providence St. Joseph Med. Ctr., Burbank, 2003-04, chief of staff, 2005-06. Fellow ACS, Internat. Coll. Surgeons; mem. Am. Soc. Gen. Surgeons, L.A. Surg. Soc. Office: 2701 W Alameda Ave Ste 300 Burbank CA 91505-4408 Office Phone: 818-843-1492. Office Fax: 818-843-5283.

RENNER, WILLIAM SCOTT, retired military officer; b. Washington, Pa., Apr. 26, 1935; s. Albert Conrad and Ruth Estel (Tombaugh) Renner; m. Sara Elisabeth Donahue, Apr. 4, 1959; children: Michael Paul, Mandy Jane. BA in Finance, Pa. State U., State College, 1958; grad., Naval War Coll., Newport, RI, 1973. Comd. ensign USNR, 1958; rose to capt. US Navy, 1980; anti-submarine pilot HS-9, Quonset Point, RI, 1959—63; flight instr. HS-1, Key West, Fla., 1963—66, 1968—70, Jacksonville, Fla., 1973—74; asst. navigator USS Independence CV-62, Norfolk, Va., 1966—68; ASW pilot and ops. officer HS-5, Quonset Point, 1970—72; commanding officer HS-15, Jacksonville, 1974—76; enlisted rating coord. Chief of Naval Pers., Washington, 1976—79; head ASW manpower and tng. Chief of Naval Ops., Washington, 1979—82; commanding officer US Naval Support Facility Diego Garcia, Indian Ocean, 1982—83; dir. adminstrn. Naval Mil. Pers. Command, Washington, 1983—86; commander program support divsn. Def. Logistics Agy., Washington, 1986—90; ret. US Navy, 1990. Mem. mil. adv. bd. Pa. Senator Piccola, Harrisburg, 1996—. Constrn. leader Habitat for Humanity, Harrisburg, 1998—; pres. Kensington Pl. Cmty. Assn., Harrisburg, 2004—. Recipient Winged S award, Sikorsky Aircraft, 1961, 1975—76, Meritorious Svc. award, Sec. of Navy, 1982, 1989, Legion of Merit, 1983, Def. Superior Svc. medal, Sec. of Def., 1990, Humanitarian award, Habitat for Humanity of Greater Harrisburg, 2002, Chuck Dorsey Humanitarian award, 2007. Mem.: Mil. Officers of Am. Assn., Navy Helicopter Assn., Pi Kappa Alpha (Beta Alpha social chmn.). Republican. Avocations: woodworking, gardening, travel. Home: 4309 S Victoria Way Harrisburg PA 17112 E-mail: salsctoren@aol.com.

RENNERT, IRA LEON, manufacturing executive; b. 1934; married; 3 children. BA, Bklyn. Coll., 1954; MBA, NYU, 1956. Credit analyst M. Lowenstein Corp., NYC, 1956-57; salesman Underwood Corp., NYC, 1957-58; registered rep. Francis I. Dupont & Co., NYC, 1958-60; established I.L. Rennert & Co., Inc. (formerly Rubin, Rennert & Co., Inc.), NYC, 1960-64; cons. NYC, 1964-75; pres. Consolidated Sewing Machine Corp., NYC, 1975—; pres., CEO, chmn. Renco Grp., Inc., NYC, 1980—; CEO WCI Steel Inc., Warren, Ohio, 1988—. Chmn. bd. Am. Gen. Corp., South Bend, Ind., 1992. Named one of 400 Richest Ams., Forbes mag., 2006. Office: Renco Grp 30 Rockefeller Plz New York NY 10112

RENNERT, OWEN MURRAY, pediatrician, geneticist, educator; b. NYC, Aug. 8, 1938; s. David Rennert and Frieda (Weinsteiner) Sommer; m. Sandra Serota, Mar. 22, 1964; children: Laura, Rachel, Ian. BS, BA, U. Chgo., 1957, MD, 1961, MS in Biochemistry, 1963. Diplomate Am. Bd. Pediatrics, Am. Bd. Genetics, Am. Bd. Med. Genetics. Assoc. prof. pediatrics U. Fla. Coll. Medicine, Gainesville, 1968—70, assoc. prof. biochemistry, 1970—71, head instl. divsn. genetics, endocrinology and metabolism, 1970—78, prof. pediatrics, biochemistry and neurosci., 1971-78; prof. biochemistry, prof. and head dept. pediatrics U. Okla., Oklahoma City, 1977-88; chief pediatrics svc. and head genetics, sect. endocrinology and metabolism Okla. Children's Mem. Hosp., Oklahoma City, 1977-88; prof., chmn. dept. pediatrics Georgetown U. Sch. Medicine, Washington, 1988-98, prof. dept. biochemistry and molecular biology, 1995—98, prof. emeritus, 1998—2000; spl. asst. to dir. ctr. rsch. mothers and children Nat. Inst. Child Health Human Devel., NIH, Bethesda, Md., 1998—2000, dir. Ctr. Rsch. Mothers and Children, 2000, sci. dir. divsn. intramural rsch., 2000—. Co-author: Metabolism of Trace Metals in Man: Developmental Biology and Genetic Implications (2 vols.), 1984; contbr. articles to profl. jours. Bd. dirs. Children's Med. Rsch., Oklahoma City, 1984-88. Served to sr. surgeon USPHS, 1964-66. Named Clin. Scientist of Yr., Am. Assn. Clin. Scientists, 1978. Mem. Am. Pediatric Soc., Am. Acad. Pediatrics, Soc. Pediatric Research, Am. Coll. Clin. Nutrition, Biochem. Soc., Am. Soc. Molecular Biology and Biochemistry, Am. Coll. Med. Genetics, Am. Soc. Human Genetics. Office: NICHD/NIH Divsn Intramural Rsch 31 Center Dr Bldg 31 Rm 2A46 Bethesda MD 20892-2425 Home Phone: 301-299-6174; Office Phone: 301-594-5984. Business E-Mail: rennerto@mail.nih.gov.

RENNEY, TOM, professional hockey coach; m. Glenda Renney; children: Jessica, Jamie. Head coach Kamloops Blazers (WHL), 1991—93, Team Can., 1993—96, Vancouver Canucks, 1996—97; v.p. hockey Can. Nat. Team, 1998—99, head coach, v.p., 1999—2000; dir. player pers. NY Rangers, 2000—02, asst. coach, 2003—04, v.p. player devel., 2003—, head coach, 2004—. Head coach Team Canada, Lillehammer Olympic Games, 1992. Office: c/o NY Rangers 2 Pennsylvania Plaza New York NY 10121

RENNIE, JOHN, editor-in-chief; b. 1959; BS in Biology, Yale U., 1981. With Harvard Med. Sch.; sci. writer various publs.; mem. bd. editors Sci. Am., 1989—94, editor-in-chief, 1994—, Sci. Am. Presents, 1998—. TV appearances include ABC World News Hour, ABC News Overnight, The Newshour with Jim Lehrer, Fox News Channel, Entertainment Tonight, Science Friday (National Public Radio), CBS Early Show; contbr. articles to profl. publications including The Economist, The New York Times, Longevity. Recipient Sagan award, Coun. Sci. Soc. Presidents, Navigator award, Potomac Inst. Policy Studies. Avocation: Karate. Office: Sci Am 415 Madison Ave New York NY 10017-1111 Office Phone: 212-754-0550. Business E-Mail: editors@sciam.com.

RENNIE, PAUL STEVEN, research scientist, surgeon; b. Toronto, Ont., Can., Feb. 9, 1946; m. Carol Andrews, 1968; 1 child, Jan. BSc, U. Western Ont., 1969; PhD in Biochemistry, U. Alta., Can., 1973. Rsch. assoc. U. Alta., 1975-76, asst. prof. medicine, 1976-79, assoc. prof., 1979; rsch. scientist B.C. Cancer Agy., Canada, 1979-92, dir. rsch., 1992-97; prof. surgery U. B.C., 1986—, dir. prostate rsch. lab., 1998—. Med. Rsch. Coun. rsch. fellow Imperial Cancer Rsch. Fund, 1973-75; rsch. scholar Nat. Cancer Inst. Can., 1976-79. Achievements include research on biochemical control of growth in androgen responsive organs and neoplasms; genetic markers in prostate cancer. Office: Prostate Ctr Jack Bell Rsch Ctr 2660 Oak St Vancouver BC Canada V6H 3Z6 Home Phone: 604-275-5030. Business E-Mail: prennie@interchange.ubc.ca.

RENNINGER, MARY KAREN, retired librarian; b. Pitts., Apr. 30, 1945; d. Jack Burnell and Jane (Hammerly) Gunderman; m. Norman Christian Renninger, Sept. 3, 1965 (div. 1980); 1 child, David Christian. BA, U. Md., 1969, MA, 1972, M.L.S., 1975. Tchr. English West Carteret High Sch., Morehead City, NC, 1969-70; instr. in English U. Md., College Park, 1970-72; head network services Nat. Libr. Svc., Libr. of Congress, Washington, 1974-78, asst. for network support, 1978-80; mem. fed. women's program com. Libr. of Congress, Washington, 1978-80; chief libr. divsn. Dept. Vets. Affairs, Washington, 1980-90; chief serial and govt. publs. divsn. Libr. of Congress, Washington, 1991—2006, mem. fed. libr. com., 1980-90, mem. exec. adv. bd., 1985-90; ret., 2006. Mem. USBE pers. subcom., 1982-84; bd. regents Nat. Libr. of Medicine, 1986-90, mem. outreach panel, 1988-89; fed. libr. task force for 1990 White House Conf. on Librs., 1986-90; liaison to The White House Conf. Med. Libr. Assn., 1989-90. Recipient Meritorious Svc. award Libr. of Congress, 1974, Spl. Achievement award, 1976, Performance award VA, ann. 1982-89, Adminstr.'s Commendation, 1985, Spl. Contbn. award, 1986. Mem. ALA (Govt. Documents Roundtable), Libr. Tech. Assn., Med. Libr. Assn. (govt. rels. com. 1985—), DC Libr. Assn., Soc. Applied Learning Tech., Med. Interactive Videodisc Consortium, Govt. Documents Roundtable, Knowledge Utilization Soc., Nat. Multimedia Assn. Am., US Tennis Assn., Phi Beta Kappa, Alpha Lambda Delta, Beta Phi Mu. Home: 840 College Pky Rockville MD 20850-1931 Personal E-mail: KarenRenninger@comcast.net.

RENO, JANET, former United States attorney general; b. Miami, Fla., July 21, 1938; d. Henry and Jane (Wood) R. AB in Chemistry, Cornell U., 1960; LL.B., Harvard U., 1963. Bar: Fla. 1963. Assoc. Brigham & Brigham, 1963-67; ptnr. Lewis & Reno, 1967-71; staff dir. judiciary com. Fla. Ho. of Reps., Tallahassee, 1971-72; cons. Fla. Senate Criminal Justice Com. for Revision Fla.'s Criminal Code, spring 1973; adminstrv. asst. state atty. 11th Jud. Circuit Fla., Miami, 1973-76, state atty., 1978-93; ptnr. Steel Hector and Davis, Miami, 1976-78; US atty. gen. Dept. Justice, Washington, 1993-2001. Mem. jud. nominating commn. 11th Jud. Circuit Fla., 1976-78; chmn. Fla. Gov.'s Council for Prosecution Organized Crime, 1979-80. Exec. prodr.: (albums) Song of America, 2007. Recipient Women First award YWCA, 1993. National Women's Hall of Fame, 2000. Mem. ABA (Inst. Jud. Adminstrn. Juvenile Justice Standards Commn. 1973-76), Am. Law Inst., Am. Judicature Soc. (Herbert Harley award 1981), Dade County Bar Assn., Fla. Pros. Atty.'s Assn. (pres. 1984-86). Democrat. *

RENO, JOSEPH HARRY, retired orthopedist; b. Allentown, Pa., Mar. 5, 1915; s. Harvey Luther and Olive May (Wilson) R.; m. Maude Olivia Mutchler, June 27, 1942; children: Joseph David, Sally Jo, Diana Jane, Deborah Marion. Student, Temple U., 1934-37, MD, 1941. Intern. Chester (Pa.) Hosp., 1941-42; resident Tex. Scottish Rite Hosp. for Crippled Children, Dallas, 1942-43, 44-45, Robert Packer Hosp., Sayre, Pa., 1943-44; assoc. Homer Stryker, M.D., Kalamazoo, 1945-46; pvt. practice Bethlehem, Pa., 1946-71, Flagstaff, Ariz., 1971-93; team physician Lehigh

U., Bethlehem, 1946-70, No. Ariz. U., Flagstaff, 1971-77, Ariz. State U., Tempe, 1977-84. Chief surg. staff Flagstaff Hosp., 1975. Contbr. articles to profl. jours.; prodr. surg. films for Am. Acad. Ortho. Surgeons and others, 1952-70. Pres. Coconino County Easter Seal Soc., 1973; bd. dirs., med. advisor Ariz. Easter Seal Soc., 1974-84. Recipient Pioneer award Ariz. Med. Assn., 1981, Cert. of Appreciation, Pa. Dept. Health Crippled Children's Div., 1971; Dr. Joseph Reno Sports Medicine award named in honor, No. Ariz. State U. and Blue Cross Blue Shield, 1986. Fellow Am. Acad. Ortho. Surgeons, Am. Assn. for Surgery of Trauma, Am. Coll. Sports Med., Am. Coll. Surgeons (chmn. Lehigh Valley subcom. on trauma 1954-66, Ea. Pa. chpt. pres. 1969); mem. NRA, Am. Bd. Ortho. Surgery (cert., diplomate 1948), Babcock Surg. Soc., Mason, Phi Chi, Alpha Tau Omega.

RENO, OTTIE WAYNE, former judge; b. Pike County, Ohio, Apr. 7, 1929; s. Eli Enos and Arbannah Belle (Jones) Reno; m. Janet Gay McCann, May 22, 1947; children: Jennifer Lynn, Lorna Victoria, Ottie Wayne II. A in Bus. Adminstrn., Franklin U., 1949; LLB, Franklin Law Sch., 1953; JD, Capital U., 1966; grad. Coll. Juvenile Justice, U. Nev., 1973. Bar: Ohio 1953. Practiced in Pike County; recorder Pike County, 1957-73, common pleas judge probate and juvenile divsn., 1973-79. Author: Story of Horseshoes, 1963, Pitching Championship Horsehoes, 1971; 2d rev. edit., 1975; author: The American Directory of Horseshoe Pitching, 1983, Ohio vs. Smith, Murder, 1990, Reno and Apsaalooka Survive Custer, 1996. Del. Dem. Nat. Conv., 1972, 1996; mem. Camp Creek precinct Dem. Ctrl. Com., 1956—72, 1983—90, 1999—2002; sec. Pike County Dem. Exec. Com., 1971—72, 1983—90, 1983—87, chmn., 1971—72, 1988—90; mem. Ohio Dem. Ctrl. Com., 1969—70; Dem. candidate 6th Ohio dist. U.S. Ho. of Reps., 1966; Dem. candidate 88th Ohio dist. Ohio Ho. of Reps., 1992; pres. Scioto Valley Local Sch. Dist., 1962—66. Named to Nat. Horseshoe Pitchers Hall of Fame, 1978; recipient Disting. Svc. award, Ohio Youth Commn., 1974, 6 Outstanding Jud. Svc. awards, Ohio Supreme Ct., 17 times Ala. horseshoe pitching champion. Mem.: Pike County Bar Assn., Nat. Coun.Juvenile Ct. Judges, Ohio Bar Assn., Am. Legion. Mem. Ch. Of Christ In Christian Union. Home: 148 Reno Rd Lucasville OH 45648-9580

RENO, ROGER, lawyer; b. Rockford, Ill., May 16, 1924; s. Guy B. and Hazel (Kinnear) R.; m. Janice Marie Odelius, May 17, 1952 (dec. Aug. 2005); children: Susan Marie, Sheri Jan Reno-Rudolph, Michael Guy. Student, Kenyon Coll., 1943-44, Yale U., 1944, U. Wis., 1946; AB, Carleton Coll., 1947; LL.B., Yale U., 1950. Bar: Ill. 1950. Practiced in Rockford, 1950; assoc. firm Reno, Zahm, Folgate, Lindberg & Powell, 1950-56, partner, 1956-84; of counsel Reno & Zahm LLC, 1984—. Chmn. Amcore Fin. Inc., 1982-95; atty. Rockford Bd. Edn., 1955-64. Past pres., bd. dirs. Childrens Home Rockford; trustee Swedish-Am. Hosp. Assn., 1967-77, Keith Country Day Sch. Served to 1st lt. USAAF, 1943-46. Mem. ABA, Ill. Bar Assn., Winnebago County Bar Assn. (pres. 1979-80) Clubs: Forest Hills Country (Rockford). Methodist. Home: 2515 Chickadee Trl Rockford IL 61107 Office: 2902 McFarland Rd #400 PO Box 4353 Rockford IL 61110 Home Phone: 815-877-0810. Office Fax: 815-961-4092.

RENO, RUSSELL RONALD, JR., lawyer; b. Gary, Ind., Nov. 28, 1933; s. Russell Ronald Sr. and Katherine Narcissus (White) R.; m. Mary Ellen Klock, Jan. 30, 1956 (dec. June 5, 2004); children: Mary Hall, Russell III, William, Elizabeth. AB, Haverford Coll., 1954; JD, U. Pa., 1957. Bar: Md. 1957, D.C. 1983. Assoc. Venable, Baetjer & Howard, Balt., 1958-66, ptnr., 1966—; asst. atty. gen. State of Md., Balt., 1962-64. Author: Maryland Real Estate Law-Practice, 1983. Bd. dirs. Balt. Choral Arts Soc., 1966—; trustee Goucher Coll., Balt., 1978-98, trustee emeritus, 1998—; chancellor Episcopal Diocese of Md., Balt., 1985—; bd. mgrs. Haverford Coll., 1990-2002. Fellow Am. Bar Found., Md. Bar Found.; mem. ABA, Md. State Bar Assn., Am. Coll. Real Estate Lawyers, Hamilton St. Club, Wednesday Law Club. Home: 224 Grindall St Baltimore MD 21230 Office: Venable Baetjer & Howard 2 Hopkins Plz Ste 2100 Baltimore MD 21201-2982 Office Phone: 410-244-7480. E-mail: rrreno@venable.com.

RENOUF, ANNE, corporate financial executive, consultant; Diploma, Emma Willard Sch., 1954; student, Inst. World Affairs, 1957; AB magna cum laude, honors in Anthropology, Columbia U., 1959; MA, Yale U., 1962, PhD, 1966; JD with honors, Am. U., 1978; postgrad., Duke U. Asst. prof. U. N.C., Chapel Hill, 1966-71; sr. profl. cons. U.S. Govt., Washington, 1972-75; pvt. practice fin. cons. Washington, 1976—; vis. assoc. prof. George Washington U. Sch. Bus. Adminstrn., Washington, 1983-84; gen. ptnr., v.p. Tech. Mgmt. Corp., Montgomeryville, Pa., 1986-88; chmn. Pivot, Inc., 1988—90; founding prin. SaraTech Fin. Inc., 1990-92; pvt. practice fin. cons. Founding dir., chmn. bd., CFO/bd. treas. Initiatives in Industry, Inc., 1996-02; corp. dir.; dir. fin. devel. Ctr. for Space and Advanced Tech., 1990; cons. The Brookings Instn., Washington, 1966, U.S. Dept. State, Washington, 1967, World Bank, 1992—; mem. Pres.'s Commn. Grad. Edn., 1967-68, Nat. Chamber Found. Task Force on Space Commercialization, Washington, 1983-86; vis. scholar Carnegie Endowment for Internat. Peace, N.Y.C., 1968-69; fellow U.S. Dept. State, EUR/RPE, 1967; northeastern dir. Va. Advanced Tech. Assn., 1984-88; fin. and tech. spkr.; mem. Coun. on Competitiveness, 1998—2003, Tech. Coun. Washington, 1998—; mem. Greater Washington Bd. Trade, The Potomac Conf., 1999-2001; mem. The World Bank, The Global Devel. Network, 1998— Contbr. articles on tech. commercialization and fin. to profl. jours. Co-chair, charter mem. U.S./China Capital Cities Coun., Washington, 1985-95; advisor Greater Washington D.C. Bd. Trade, 1985-86, Internat. Red Cross, 1987-90; mem. Mayor's Adv. Coun. on Trade and Investment, 1987-91; mem. adv. coun. Ctr. for Internat. Bus. Edn. U. Alaska, Fairbanks, 1990-91, co-chmn. World Trade Day, 1989; bd. dirs. Nat. Symphony Orch., 1990-99, Greater Washington Met. Boys and Girls Clubs, 1992-2000; dir. Initiatives in Industry, Inc., 1996-02. Recipient citation, Washington D.C. Mayor's Office, 1986; Woodrow Wilson fellow, 1958, Bushnell fellow, Yale U., 1964, Hon. Officer-Faculty fellow, U.S. Dept. State, 1967. Fellow Washington Acad. Scis.; mem. Am. Soc. Internat. Law, Internat. Forum U.S. C. of C., Internat. Energy Seminar-Johns Hopkins Sch. for Advanced Internat. Study, Corcoran Gallery of Art (nat. coun.), Washington Internat. Trade Assn., Assn. for Corp. Growth, Phi Beta Kappa. Business E-Mail: arenouf@indevone.com.

RENOUF, EDDA, artist; b. Mexico City, June 17, 1943; d. Edward and Catharine Smith; m. Alain Middleton, Sept. 20, 1977; 1 child, Mélisande. BA, Sarah Lawrence Coll., 1965; M.F.A., Columbia U., 1971. One-woman shows include Yvon Lambert Gallery, Paris, 1972, 1974, 1976, 1978, 1980, 1982, 1984, 1993, Konrad Fischer Gallery, Düsseldorf, Germany, 1974, 1979, Blum-Helman Gallery, N.Y.C., 1978, 1980, 1982, 1985, 1987, 1989, U. Mich. Mus. Art, 1995, Elisabeth Kaufmann Gallery, Basel, Switzerland, 1994, 1996, Galerie Sollertis, Toulouse, France, 1994, 1996, 2007, 1998, Staatliche Kunsthalle Karlsruhe, Germany, 1997, Galerie Hubert Winter, Vienna, Austria, 1998, Galerie Liesbeth Lips, Rotterdam, 1998, 2001, Joseph Helman Gallery, N.Y.C., 2001—02, 2002, Nat. Mus. Women in the Arts, Washington, D.C., 2004, Brenan U. Galleries, Gainesville, Ga., 2004, Arnaud Lefebvre Gallery, Paris, 2006, New Arts Gallery, Litchfield, Conn., 2006, Galeria Charpa, Valencia, Spain, 2007, exhibited in group shows at Mus. Modern Art, N.Y.C., 1973, 1990, 1998, Stedelijk Mus., Amsterdam, 1974, 8th Paris Biennale, 1973, Whitney Mus. Am. Art, N.Y.C., 1979, 1985, Centre Georges Pompidou, Paris, 1979, 2002, Met. Mus. Art, N.Y.C., 1982, Serpentine Gallery, 1984, Galerie Denise René, Paris, 1985, Tel Aviv Mus., 1986, 1998, Mus. Fridericianum, Kassel, Germany, 1988, Mus. d'Art Moderne de Lille, France, 1992, Bibliothèque Nationale, Paris, 1992, Nat. Gallery Art, Washington, 1993—94, Harvard U. Straus Gallery, 1996, Yokohama (Japan) Mus. Art, 1998, Yale U. Art Gallery, 1998, Cabinet des Estampes et des Dessins, Liege, Belgium, 1999, Brit. Mus., London, 2000, 2004, Corcoran Gallery, Washington, 2001, Neue Galerie, Graz, Austria, 2001—02, Ctr. Georges, Pompidon, Paris, 2002, Riva Yares Gallery, Santa Fe, N.Mex., 2004, Brit. Mus., London, 2004, 2007, Staatliche Kunsthalle, Karlsruhe, Germany, 2004, New Arts Gallery, Litchfield, Conn., 2005, Addison Gallery Am. Art, Andover, Mass., 2005, Hayward Gallery and Brit. Mus., 2006—07, Represented in permanent collections Mus. Modern Art, Whitney Mus. Am. Art, Met. Mus. Art, Centre Georges Pompidou, Paris, Chgo. Art Inst., Mus. of Contemporary Art, Chgo., Phila. Art Mus., Yale U. Art Gallery, Neuberger Mus., Australian Nat. Gallery, Cin. Mus. Art, St. Louis Art Mus., Tel Aviv Mus., La. Mus., Denmark, Walker Art Ctr., Washington, BibliotequeNationale Paris, Bklyn. Mus. Am. Art, Dallas Mus. Fine Art, Detroit Mus. Art, Mus. Contemporary Art, L.A., High Mus., Atlanta, Corcoran Gallery, Washington, Staatliche Kunsthalle, Karlsruhe, Nat. Gallery Art, Washington, Kunstmuseum Winterthur, Switzerland, Neue Galerie, Graz, Nat. Mus. of Women in the Arts, Washington. Nat. Endowment Arts grantee, 1976-77, Pollock-Krasner Found. Inc. grantee, 1990-91, Ctr. Nat. Arts Plastiques grantee, 1996. Address: 37 rue Volta 75003 Paris France Home Phone: 01-42-78-36-49; Office Phone: 33-01-42-78-3649. Personal E-mail: eddarenouf@mac.com.

RENOUF, HAROLD AUGUSTUS, retired transportation executive; b. Sandy Point, Nfld., Can., June 15, 1917; s. John Robert and Louisa Maud (LeRoux) R.; m. Janet Dorothy Munro, June 16, 1942; children: Janet Dorothy, Ann Louise Petley-Jones, John Robert, Susan Elizabeth Thompson. B.Commerce, Dalhousie U., 1938, LL.D. (hon.), 1981. N.S.C.A., Halifax, 1942 C.M.A., 1950. With H.R. Doane and Co., Halifax, N.S., Can., 1938-75, ptnr., 1942-75, ptnr. in charge New Glasgow, N.S., Can., 1947-62, ptnr. in charge mgmt. svcs. Halifax, 1963-67, chmn., 1967-75; bd. dirs. Associated Acctg. Firms Internat., NYC, 1967-75; commr. Anti-Inflation Bd., Ottawa, Ont., 1975-77, chmn., 1977-79, Petroleum Monitoring Agy., Ottawa, 1980-82, VIA Rail Can. Inc., Montreal, Que., 1982-85; pres. Fundy Industries Ltd., Halifax, 1990-94; ret., 1996. Cons. to N.S. Provincial Mcpl. Fact-Finding Com., 1967-70; pres. Can. Inst. Chartered Accts., 1974-75. Contbr. articles to profl. publs. Chmn. adv. commn. Dalhousie U. Grad. Sch. Bus. Adminstrn., 1978-86. Recipient Queen's medal, Queen's Golden Jubilee medal, 2002, Commemorative medal for 125th anniversary of Can. Confedn., 1992; decorated officer Order of Can.; named to Acctg. Hall of Fame St. Mary's Univ., N.S., 1993. Fellow Inst. Chartered Accts. N.S. (pres. 1948); mem. Can. Inst. Chartered Accts. (pres. 1974-75), Can. Tax Found. (gov. 1969-71), Soc. Mgmt. Accts. N.S., Dalhousie U. Alumni Assn. (hon. chmn. 1987-89), Halifax Club, Saraguay Club (treas. 1972-75), Waegwaltic Club. Liberal. Mem. United Ch. Can. Avocations: boating, fishing. Home: 6369 Coburg Rd Apt 1605 Halifax NS Canada B3H 4J7

RENOUX, ANDRÉ, physicist, researcher; b. Courbevoie, France, Oct. 27, 1937; s. Robert and Jeanne (Noël) R.; divorced; children: Vincent, Nathalie. Lic. Sci., Faculty Scis. Paris, 1958, D 3d cycle, 1961, D, 1965. Asst. Faculty Scis., Paris, 1959—61, master asst., 1961—66; prof. faculty scis. U. Tunis, Tunisia, 1966—69, U. Brest, France, 1969—80; prof. U. Paris, 1980—2003, dir. lab. phys. aérosols et transfert des contaminations, 1980—, dir. DESS (3d cycle) sci. des aerosols-génie de l'Aérocontamination, 1981—2003, prof. emeritus, 2003—. Gen. chmn. European Aerosol Conf., Blois, France, 1994; del. Internat. Coun. for Engrng. and Tech., UNESCO, 2000-; adminstr. Maisons Maternelles, 2005-. Author: (with D. Boulaud, Lavoisier, Ed.) Les Aérosols, Physique et Métrologie, 1998; mem. editl. bd. Idojaras, 1979—, Pollution Atmosphérique, 1979-2003, Aerosol Sci. & Tech., 1992-2000, Revue Salles Propres, 2000-02; contbr. over 300 articles to profl. jours. Gen. sec. Syndicat d'initiative, Brest, 1973-77; mem. Cons. Com. Univs., France, 1973-77. Mem. Am Assn. Advancement Rsch., N.Y. Acad. Scis., Com. Regional Anti-Pollution Brest (pres. 1973-80), Soc. France for Nuclear Energy idFNE (pres. 1987-91), Am. Assn. Aerosol Rsch., Gesellschaft Aerosolforschung, Hungarian Meteorol. soc. (hon.), French Aerosol. Rsch. Assn. (pres. 1983-2000, hon. pres. 2000—), European Aerosol Assembly (co-founder, pres. 1998-2000), Office Professionnel de qualification des Entreprises de l'Utrapropreté (pres. 1995—), Chevalier des Dames du vin et de la Table, Ordre de l'Echarpe. Avocations: tennis, opera, photography. Home: 11 Sq de L'eau Vive 94000 Creteil France Office: Univ Paris XII Lab Phys Aerosols Ave Gal de Gaulle 94000 Creteil France Office Phone: 06-84211880. Business E-Mail: renoux.andre@numericable.fr.

RENSBERGER, BOYCE, science journalism fellowship program administrator; b. 1942; BS in Zoology and Journalism, U. Miami; MS in Mental Health Comm., Syracuse U. Sci. editor Detroit Free Press, 1966—71, NY Times, 1971—79, Washington Post, 1984—98; dir. Knight Sci. Journalism Fellowship program Mass. Inst. Tech., Cambridge, 1998—. Co-dir. summer sci.writing fellowships program Marine Biol. Lab, Woods Hole, Mass. Head writer: TV series 3-2-1 Contact; author: (book) The Cult of the Wild, 1977, How the World Works: A Guide to Science's Greatest Discoveries, 1986, Instant Biology: From Single Cells to Human Beings, and Beyond, 1996, Life Itself: Exploring the Realm of the Living Cell, 1997. Alicia Patterson Fellow, 1973—74. Mem.: AAAS (sr. editor Science Mag. 1981—84, chmn. com. on pub. understanding sci. and tech., two-time sci. writing award recipient). Office: Mass Inst Tech Knight Sci Journalism Fellowships 77 Massachusetts Ave E19-307 Cambridge MA 02139-4307 E-mail: boyce@mit.edu.

RENSHAW, AMANDA FRANCES, retired physicist, nuclear engineer; b. Wheelwright, Ky., Dec. 10, 1934; d. Taft and Mamie Nell (Russell) Wilson; divorced; children: Linda, Michael, Billy. BS in Physics, Antioch Coll., 1972; MS in Physics, U. Tenn., 1982, MS in Nuclear Engring., 1991. Rsch. asst. U. Mich., Ann Arbor, 1970-71; teaching asst. Antioch Coll., Yellow Springs, Ohio, 1971-72; physicist GE, Schenectady, N.Y., 1972-74, Union Carbide Corp., Oak Ridge, Tenn., 1974-79; rsch. assoc. Oak Ridge Nat. Lab., 1979-91, mgr. strategic planning, 1991-92, liaison for environ. scis., 1993-96; ret., 1996. Asst. to counselor for sci. and tech. Am. Embassy, Moscow, 1990; asst. to dir. nat. acid precipitation assessment program Office of Pres. U.S., 1993-94. Contbr. articles to profl. jours. Mem. AAUW, Am. Nuclear Soc. (Oak Ridge chpt.), Soc. Black Physicists Avocations: reading, travel. Home: 1850 Cherokee Bluff Dr Knoxville TN 37920-2215

RENSHAW, CHARLES LUCIUS, retired surgeon; b. Ft. Worth, Tex., Apr. 2, 1935; s. Horace Stephen and Carol Jim Renshaw; m. Sally Marie Tull, June 22, 1957; children: Stephen Vance, Lisa Carol, Lucius Scott, Julie Kay. BA, Tex. Christian, Ft. Worth, 1957; MD, Johns Hopkins, Balt., 1961; Degree in Ranch Mgmt., Tex. Christian, 1989. Diplomate Tex. Bd. Med. Examiners, 1961, Am. Bd. Orthop. Surgery, 1969. Orthop. surgeon US Army, Ft. Ord, Calif., 1967—69; pvt. practice orthop. surgeon All Saints Hosp., Ft. Worth, 1969—89; stock farmer Wise County, Tex., 1989—. Chief med. staff All Saints Hosp., 1983—85. Maj. US Army, 1967—69, Ft. Ord. Mem.: Alpha Omega Alpha, Phi Beta Kappa. Avocation: sport shooting. Personal E-mail: lrfarms@aol.com.

RENT, CLYDA STOKES, academic administrator; b. Jacksonville, Fla., Mar. 1, 1942; d. Clyde Parker Stokes Sr. and Edna Mae (Edwards) Shuemake; m. George Seymour Rent, Aug. 12, 1966; 1 child, Cason Rent Lynley. BA, Fla. State U., 1964, MA, 1966, PhD, 1968; LHD (hon.), Judson Coll., 1993. Asst. prof. Western Carolina U., Cullowhee, NC, 1968-70, Queens Coll., Charlotte, NC, 1972-74, dept. chair, 1974-78, dean Grad. Sch. and New Coll., 1979-84, v.p. for Grad. Sch. and New Coll., 1984-85, v.p. acad. affairs, 1985-87, v.p. cmty. affairs, 1987-89; pres. Miss. U. for Women, Columbus, 1989—2001; disting. prof. sociology Miss. State U. Mem. adv. bd. Nat. Women's Hall of Fame; cons. Coll. Eb. N.Y.C., 1983-89; sci. cons. N.C. Alcohol Rsch. Authority, Chapel Hill, 1976-89; bd. mem. So. Growth Policies Bd., 1992-94; adv. bd. Nat. Women's Hall of Fame, Trustmark Nat. Bank, 1991-97; rotating chair Miss. Instns. Higher Learning Pres. Coun., 1990-91; commn. govtl. rels. Am. Coun. Edn., 1990-93; mem. adv. bd. Entergy/Miss., 1994-97, Freedom Forum 1st Amendment Ctr., 1996-2001; mem. Miss. adv. bd. Trustmark Nat. Bank, 1991-97; mem. Mary Baker Eddy Adv. Group, 2000—; mem. Rhodes Scholar selection com. of Miss., 1996-98; mem. Free Sprit Awards selection com., 1996—; mem. ACE Commn. on Women in Higher Edn., 1999—. Mem. editl. bd. Planning for Higher Education, 1995; contbr. articles to profl. jours.; speeches pub. in Vital Speeches; mem. editl. bds. acad. jours. Trustee N.C. Performing Arts Ctr., Charlotte, 1988-89, Charlotte County Day Sch., 1987-89; bd. visitors Johnson C. Smith U., Charlotte, 1985-89; exec. com. bd. dirs. United Way Allocations and Rev., Charlotte, 1982-88; bd. advisors Charlotte Mecklenburg Hosp. Authority, 1985-89; bd. dirs. Jr. Achievement, Charlotte, 1983-89, Miss. Humanities Coun., Miss. Inst. Arts and Letters, Miss. Symphony, Miss. Econ. Coun.; chair Leadership Miss. and Collegiate Miss.; chmn. bd. dirs. Charlotte/Mecklenburg Arts and Sci. Coun., 1987-88; Danforth assoc. Danforth Found., St. Louis, 1976-88, Leadership Am., 1989; mem. golden triangle adv. bd. Bapt. Meml. Hosp., 1999—; pres. So. Univs. Conf., 1994-95; mem. commn. govt. rels. Am. Coun. Edn., 1990-93; mem. alumni bd. First United Meth. Ch., 1996—. Recipient Grad. Made Good award Fla. State U., 1990, medal of excellence Miss. U. for Women, 1995, Women Who Make a Difference award IWF, 2000; named Prof. of Yr., Queens Coll., 1979, One of 10 Most Admired Women Mgrs. in Am., Working Women mag., 1993, One of 1000 Women of the 90's, Mirabella mag., 1994; Ford Found. grantee, 1981; Paul Harris fellow, 1992; OWHE fellow, 1999—. Mem. Am. Assn. State Colls. and Univs. (bd. dirs. 1994-96, 99), Sociol. Soc., So. Assn. Colls. and Schs. (mem. commn. on colls. 1996-98), N.C. Assn. Colls. and Univs. (exec. com. 1988-89), N.C. Assn. Acad. Officers (sec.-treas. 1987-88), Soc. Internat. Bus. Fellows, Miss. Assn. Colls. (pres. 1992), Newcomen Soc. U.S., Internat. Women's Forum, Univ. Club, Rotary. Achievements include 1st female pres. of Miss. U. for Women (1st pub. coll. for women in Am.).

RENTER, LOIS IRENE HUTSON, retired librarian; b. Lowden, Iowa, Oct. 23, 1929; d. Thomas E. and Lulu Mae (Barlean) Hutson; m. Karl A. Renter, Jan. 3, 1948; children: Susan Elizabeth, Rebecca Jean, Karl Geoffrey. BA cum laude, Cornell Coll., 1965; MA, U. Iowa, 1968. Tchr. Spanish Mt. Vernon High Sch., 1965-67; head libr. Am. Coll. Testing Program, Iowa City, Iowa, 1968-89, ret., 1989. Vis. instr. U. Iowa Sch. Library Sci., 1972-82. Mem. Phi Beta Kappa. Methodist. Home: 1308 Brendel Hill Dr NW Cedar Rapids IA 52405-1566 E-mail: thisislois@mchsi.com.

RENTERIA, EDGAR, professional baseball player; b. Barranquila, Columbia, Aug. 7, 1975; Short stop Fla. Marlins, 1996—98, St. Louis Cardinals, 1999—2004, Boston Red Sox, 2005, Atlanta Braves, 2005—. Named to NL All-Star Team, 1998; recipient NL Gold Glove award, MLB, 2002—03, NL All-Star Team, 2000, 2003, 2004. Achievements include world series champion, 1998. Office: Turner Field 755 Hank Aaron Dr Atlanta GA 30315

RENTON, HOLLINGS C., health products executive; BS Maths., Colo. State U.; MBA, U. Mich. Pres., COO Cetus Corp., 1981—91; pres., Chiron Corp., 1991—92; chmn., pres., CEO Onyx Pharms. Inc., Emeryville, Calif., 1993—. Office: Onyx Pharms Inc 2100 Powell St Emeryville CA 94608

RENTOUMIS, ANN MASTROIANNI, psychotherapist; b. New Haven, Apr. 27, 1928; d. Luigi Mastroianni and Marion Dallas; m. George Rentoumis, June 27, 1959; children: Michael, Mary, Anne. BA in Psychology, Vassar Coll., 1949; postgrad., Boston U. Med. Sch., 1949-50; MS in Social Work, Columbia U., 1952. Diplomate Am. Bd. Social Work, Am. Psychotherapy Assn.; lic. cert. social worker; lic. marriage and family therapist. Child and adolescent therapist Bklyn. Psychiat., 1952-55; family therapist Community Svc. Soc., NYC, 1955-58; psychotherapist Bleuler Psychotherapy Ctr., LI, N.Y., 1958-60, Adolescent Psychiat. Clinic, Tex. Children's Hosp., Houston, 1975-76; pvt. practice Houston, 1976-77, Lauderdale Psychiat. Group, Ft. Lauderdale, Fla., 1978-90, Pompano Beach, Fla., 1990-93, Ft. Lauderdale, 1993—. Bd. dirs. Envirodyne, Inc., 1989—2000. Pres. Pine Crest Sch. Mothers Club, 1985-86; v.p. Opera Soc., 1987-88, bd. dirs., 1998—, parliamentarian 2000-02, parlimentarian, 2006-07; bd. govs., v.p. exec. bd. Fla. Philharm Orch., 1988-91, bd. dirs., 1990-2003; pres. Ft. Lauderdale Philharm. Soc., 1988-90; bd. dirs. Goodwill Ambassadors, 2003-2006. Recipient Golden Rule award J.C. Penney Co., 1990; named Woman of Yr., Am. Cancer Soc., 1989, Woman of Style and Substance, Ft. Lauderdale Philharm. Soc., 1998. Fellow Am. Psychotherapy Assn., Am. Orthopsychiat. Assn.; mem. Am. Assn. Marriage and Family Therapists, Am. Group Therapy Assn., Royal Dames of Cancer Rsch., Inc. (trustee 2006—, dir. 2006—), Harbor Beach Surf Club (v.p. 1986-90). Avocations: piano, tennis, swimming. Home: 2200 S Ocean Ln Ph 6 Fort Lauderdale FL 33316-3836 Office: 1326 SE 3d Ave Fort Lauderdale FL 33316-1260 Office Phone: 954-767-0048.

RENUART, VICTOR EUGENE, JR., (GENE RENUART), career military officer; b. Nov. 26, 1949; s. Victor Eugene and Ruthann Wigglesworth Renuart; m. Jill Colleen Jenner; children: Ryan Victor, Andrew John. BS in Prodn. and Indsl. Mgmt., Ind. U., 1971; MA in Psychology, Troy State U., 1975; Disting. grad., Squadron Officer Sch., Maxwell AFB, Ala., 1977; Grad., Air Command & Staff Coll., 1979, Army War Coll., 1992, Sr. Officers in Nat. Security Program, 1997. Commd. 2d. lt. USAF, 1973, advanced through grades to gen., 2007; instr., pilot Craig AFB, 1973-76; asst. prof. aerospace studies U. Notre Dame, South Bend, Ind., 1976-79; A-10 instr. pilot, flight comdr. to ops. officer 81st Tactical Fighter Wing, RAF Bentwaters, Eng., 1980-84; ops. inspector Office of the Inspector Gen. Hdqrs. USAF Europe, Ramstein AB, West Germany, 1984-85, exec. officer to inspector gen., 1985-86; chief wing inspections 23rd Tactical Fighter Wing, England AFB, La., 1986-91, ops. officer to comdr., 1986-91, dir. assignments, 1992-93; comdr. support group Allied Air Forces Ctrl. Europe, England AFB, 1993-94, asst. chief of staff, ops., sr. U.S. rep., 1994-95; dir. ops. plans NATO Combined Air Ops. Ctr. 5th Allied Tactical AF, Vicenza, Italy, 1994-95; asst. dir. ops. Hdqrs. USAF Europe, Ramstein, Germany, 1995-96; comdr. 52nd Fighter Wing, Spangdahlem AB, Germany, 1996-98, 347th Wing, Moody AFB, Ga., 1998—2000; comdr. Joint Task Force-Southwest Asia, comdr. 9th Air & Space Expeditionary Task Force-Southwest Asia US Ctrl. Command, Riyadh, Saudi Arabia, 2000—01; dir. ops. (J-3) US Ctrl Command, MacDill AFB, Fla., 2001—03; vice comdr. Pacific Air Forces, Hickam AFB, Hawaii, 2003—05; dir. strategic plans & policy (J-5) Joint Staff, The Pentagon, Washington, 2005—06; sr. mil. asst. to sec. US Dept. Def., Washington, 2006—07; comdr. N.Am. Aerospace Def. Command (NORAD), Peterson AFB, Colo., 2007—, US No. Command, Peterson AFB, 2007—. Decorated Def. Disting. Svc. medal with oak leaf cluster, Disting. Svc. medal, Def Superior Svc. medal with oak leaf cluster, Meritorious Svc. medal with four oak leaf clusters, Aerial Achievement medal with three oak leaf clusters, Air Force Commendation medal with oak leaf cluster, Air Force Achievement medal with oak leaf cluster, Legion of Merit with oak leaf cluster, Air medal with two oak leaf clusters. Office: US Northern Command 250 Vandenberg Ste B016 Colorado Springs CO 80914 *

RENWICK, EDWARD S., lawyer; b. LA, May 10, 1934; AB, Stanford U., 1956, LLB, 1958. Bar: Calif. 1959, U.S. Dist. Ct. (cen. dist.) Calif. 1959, U.S. Ct. Appeals (9th cir.) 1963, U.S. Dist. Ct. (so. dist.) Calif. 1973, U.S. Dist. Ct. (no. dist.) Calif. 1977, U.S. Dist. Ct. (ea. dist.) Calif. 1981,

U.S. Supreme Ct. 1985. Ptnr. Hanna and Morton LLP, LA. Mem., bd. vis. Stanford Law Sch., 1967-69; mem. environ. and natural resources adv. bd. Stanford Law Sch. Bd. dirs. Calif. Supreme Ct. Hist. Soc. Fellow Am. Coll. Trial Lawyers, Am. Bar Found.; mem. ABA (mem. sect. on litigation, antitrust law, bus. law, chmn. sect. of nat. resources, energy and environ. law 1987-88, mem. at large coord. group energy law 1989-92, sect. rep. coord. group energy law 1995-97, Calif. del. legal com., interstate oil compact com.), Calif. Arboretum Assn. (trustee 1986-92), L.A. County Bar Assn. (chmn. natural resources law sect. 1974-75), The State Bar of Calif., Chancery Club (pres. 1992-93), Phi Delta Phi. Office: Hanna and Morton LLP 444 S Flower St Ste 1500 Los Angeles CA 90071-2922 E-mail: erenwick@hanmor.com.

RENWICK, GLENN M., insurance company executive; b. May 22, 1955; B in Math. & Econs., U. Canterbury, Christchurch, New Zealand; MS in Engring., U. Fla., Gainesville, 1978. With Progressive Corp., 1986—, chief info. officer, 1998—2000, CEO ins. ops., 2000, pres., CEO, 2001—; CEO, ins. ops. and bus. tech. process leader Progressive Casualty Ins. Co., 1998—2000, pres., chmn., CEO, 2000—04. Bd. dirs. Fiserv Inc. Office: Progressive Corp 6300 Wilson Mills Rd Cleveland OH 44143-2109 Office Phone: 440-461-5000. *

RENWICK, SCOTT, lawyer; BA, Purdue U., 1974; JD, Northwestern U., 1977. Corp. sec., counsel Unitrin, Inc., 1991—95, gen. counsel, corp. sec., 1995—2002, sr. v.p., sec., gen. counsel, 2002—. Office: Unitrin Services Co One E Wacker Dr Chicago IL 60601 *

RENYI, THOMAS A., bank executive; b. 1946; m. Elizabeth Renyi; children: Christopher, Caroline, Timothy. BA in Bus. Adminstrn., Rutgers U., 1967, MBA, 1968. With Bank of NY Co Inc., 1971—, pres., COO, 1992—, vice chmn., 1992-98, chmn., CEO, 1998—2007; exec. chmn. Bank of NY Mellon Corp., NYC, 2007—. Mem. Fin. Services Roundtable; chmn. BITS; bd. dirs. Public Svc. Enterprise Group, The Clearing House; pres. Fed. Advisory Coun. Fed. Reserve Bd. Trustee Rutgers U., Bates Coll.; bd. dirs. United Way NY, Lincoln Ctr. Performing Arts; bd. managers NY Botanical Gardens; bd. dirs. World Trade Ctr. Meml. Found. First lt. M.I. US Army, 1968—70, Vietnam. *

RENZ, CHRISTOPHER P., lawyer; BA, St. Olaf Coll., 1998; JD, U. Minn. Law Sch., 2001. Bar: Minn. 2001, US Dist. Ct. (dist. Minn.) 2002. Pros. atty. City of Edina and the Met. Airports Commn.; atty. Thomsen & Nybeck, P.A., Edina, Minn. Legal writing instr. U. Minn. Law Sch., 2003—. Contbr. articles to profl. publs. Named a Rising Star, Minn. Super Lawyers mag., 2006. Mem.: Assn. Trial Lawyers of Am., Hennepin County Bar Assn., Minn. State Bar Assn., ABA. Office: Thomsen & Nybeck PA 3300 Edinborough Way Ste 600 Edina MN 55435 Office Phone: 952-835-7000. E-mail: crenz@tn-law.com. *

RENZETTI, PHYLLIS JEAN, retired technical editor; b. Kingman, Ind., Feb. 3, 1925; d. Claude and Helen (Duchene) A.; divorced; 1 child, Jeanne. BA, Wheaton Coll., Ill., 1947; MA, Columbia U., 1950; PhD, Ind. U., 1961. Tchr. Wheaton Coll., 1948-49; tech. editor U.S. Geol. Survey, Reston, Va., Menlo Park, Calif., 1963-94, ret., 1994. Mem. AAAS, Paleontological Soc. Home: 3266 Hanover Dr Lafayette IN 47909-3852

RENZI, RICK (RICHARD GEORGE RENZI), congressman; b. Sierra Vista, Ariz., June 11, 1958; s. Gene Renzi; m. Roberta Renzi; 12 children. BS in Criminal Justice, No. Ariz. U., 1980; JD, Cath. U., 2002. Owner Renzi & Co.; staff mem. to Senator Jon Kyl US Senate; mem. US Congress from 1st Ariz. dist., 2003—, former mem. fin. svc. com., nat. resources com., permanent select com. on intelligence, resources com. Named to No. Ariz. U. Hall of Fame, 1998; recipient Friends of Affordable Housing award, Fed. Home Loan Bank San Francisco, 2004, Unsung Hero award, Ariz. Am. Legion, 2004. Republican. Roman Catholic. Office: 418 Cannon Ho Office Bldg Washington DC 20515-0301 also: 1420 1st Ave Ste 100 Safford AZ 85546 *

REOCK, ERNEST C., JR., retired social studies educator, director; b. Belleville, NJ, Oct. 13, 1924; s. Ernest C. and Helen Rutan (Evans) R.; m. Jeanne Elizabeth Thomason, Jan. 25, 1953; children: Michael, Thomas, Kathleen. BS, Swarthmore Coll., 1945; AB, Rutgers U., 1948, MA, 1950, PhD, 1959. Rsch. assoc. bur. govt. rsch. Rutgers U., New Brunswick, N.J., 1950-59, asst. prof., dir., 1960-63, assoc. prof., dir., 1963-68, prof., dir., 1968-92. Cons. N.J. Constnl. Conv., New Brunswick, 1966, N.J. State and Local Revenue and Expenditure Commns., 1986-88. Author: Handbook for New Jersey Assessors, 1962, School Budget Caps in New Jersey, 1981 (Govtl. Rsch. Assn. award, 1983), Unfinished Business: The New Jersey Constitutional Conv. of 1966, 2003; editor: New Jersey Legislative District Data Book, 1972—92. Chmn. Middlesex County Charter Study Commn., New Brunswick, 1973—74; cons. State Apportionment Commn., 1981, 1991, 2001, various mcpl. charter commns., 1965—; mem. NJ Property Tax Conv. Task Force, 2004. Lt. USN, 1943—46, lt. USN, 1951—53. Recipient Gov.'s award for Pub. Svc., 1997. Mem.: Am. Soc. Pub. Adminstrn. (Pub. Adminstr. Yr. 1982), Am. Ednl. Fin. Assn. Avocations: sailing, swimming. Home: 7 Kendall Rd Kendall Park NJ 08824-1010 Office: Rutgers U Ctr Govt Svcs 33 Livingston Ave New Brunswick NJ 08901-1900 Office Phone: 732-932-3640 633.

REPHAN, JACK, lawyer; b. Little Rock, Mar. 16, 1932; s. Henry and Mildred (Frank) R.; m. Arlene Clark, June 23, 1957; children: Amy Carol, James Clark. BS in Commerce, 1954; LLB, U. Va., 1959. Bar: Va. 1959, D.C. 1961. Assoc. Kanter & Kanter, Norfolk, Va., 1959-60; law clk. to Judge Sam E. Whitaker, U.S. Ct. Claims, Washington, 1960-62; assoc. Pierson, Ball & Dowd, Washington, 1962-64; ptnr. Danzansky, Dickey, Tydings, Quint & Gordon, Washington, 1964-77; mem. Braude, Margulies, Sacks & Rephan, Washington, 1977-87; ptnr. Porter, Wright, Morris & Arthur, Washington, 1987-88, Sadur, Pelland & Rubinstein, Washington, 1988-93; counsel Hofheimer Nusbaum P.C., Norfolk, Va., 1993-00; principal Rephan Lassiter PLC, Norfolk, 2001—. Mem. Nat. Panel Arbitrators Am. Arbitration Assn., Nat. Panel Mediators Am. Arbitration Assn., NASD Bd. Arbitrators; lectr. joint com. continuing legal edn. State Bar Va. Contbr. articles to legal jours. Pres. Patrick Henry PTA, Alexandria, Va., 1968-69, Linkhorn Bay Condominium Assn., 2000—; treas. John Adams Mid. Sch. PTA, Alexandria, 1970-71; pres. Seminary Ridge Citizens Assn., 1976-77; Dem. candidate for Alexandria City Com., 1969. 1st lt. AUS, 1955-57. Mem. ABA (chmn. subcom. on procurement of jud. remedies pub. contract sect. 1973-74), Va. Bar Assn. (govt. sect. constrn. law 1979-81, 99—, vice chmn. 1980-81, 2006-, chmn. 1981-82, 2007—), D.C. Bar Assn., Assoc. Gen. Contractors, Hampton Roads Utility and Heavy Contractors Assn. (gen. counsel), Cavalier Golf and Yacht Club, Kiwanis (pres. Landmark Club 1969). Jewish. Home: 1276 Laskin Rd Ste 402 Virginia Beach VA 23451-5272 Office: 500 E Main St Ste 1200 Norfolk VA 23510 Home Phone: 757-491-5599; Office Phone: 757-274-0045. Business E-Mail: jrephan@rephanlassiter.com.

REPINE, JOHN EDWARD, internist, educator; b. Rock Island, Ill., Dec. 26, 1944; married, 1969, 88; 6 children. BS, U. Wis., 1967; MD, U. Minn., 1971. Instr., then assoc. prof. internal medicine U. Minn., Mpls., 1974-79; asst. dir divsn. exptl. medicine Webb-Waring Inst. Biomedical Rsch., Denver, 1979-89; prof. medicine, pres. and dir. Webb-Waring Inst. Cancer, Aging & Antioxidant Rsch., Denver, 1989—; prof. medicine U. Colo., Denver, 1979—, James J. Waring prof. medicine, 1996—, prof. pediatrics, 1981-96. Mem. rsch. com., co-chmn. steering com. Aspen Lung Conf., 1980, chmn., 1981; assoc. dean for student advocacy Nat. Heart and Lung Inst., 1990—. Young Pulmonary Investigator grantee Nat. Heart & Lung Inst., 1974-75; recipient Basil O'Connor Starter Rsch. award Nat. Found. March of Dimes, 1975-77. Mem. AAAS, Am. Assn. Immunologists, Am. Soc. Clin. Investigation, Am. Heart Assn. (established investigator award 1976-81), Am. Thoracic Soc., Assn. Am. Physicians. Achievements include research in role of phagocytes and oxygen radicals in lung injury and host defense (ARDS). Office: Webb Waring Inst Cancer Aging & Antioxidant Rsch Box C322 4200 E 9th Ave Denver CO 80220-3706

REPINSKI, SARA, library director; d. Stephen Charles and Sharon Ann Gilles; m. Jeffrey Lawrence Repinski, Dec. 10, 1998. BS in History and Art, U. Wis., La Crosse, 1998; MLIS, U. S.C., 2002. Libr. dir. So. Meth. Coll., Orangeburg, SC, 2002—06; catalog libr. Coleman Karesh Law Libr., U. S.C., Columbia, 2006—. Mem. accreditation team Transnat. Assn. Christian Colls. and Schs., Lynchburg, Va., 2002—. Mem.: SC Libr. Assn., Assn. Christian Librs., Civil War Preservation Trust. Avocations: scrapbooks, music, Green Bay Packer football.

REPKO, WILLIAM CLARKE, banker; b. New Haven, June 25, 1949; s. John Edward Jr. and Beatrice Jane (Martin) R.; m. Susan Sillcox, Oct. 29, 1983; children: John Edward III, Meaghan Ann, Andrew Spotswood, Parker Yates, Thomas Strong, Nathaniel Russell. Student, Lehigh U., 1973. Rep. Mfrs. Hanover Trust Co., NYC, 1975, asst. sec., 1976-77, v.p., 1980-85, sr. v.p., 1985-89, mng. dir., 1989-91; v.p. European Am. Bank, NYC, 1978-79; mng. dir. Chem. Banking Corp., NYC, 1991-96, The Chase Manhattan Bank, NYC, 1996—99, JP Morgan, 1999—2005; sr. mng. dir. Encore Ptnrs. Inc., NYC, 2005—. Dir. Turnaround Mgmt. Assn. Dir. The Stanwich Club. Republican. Office: Evercore Ptnrs Inc 55 E 52nd St New York NY 10055

REPLOGLE, DAVID ROBERT, publishing executive; b. Chgo., Feb. 24, 1931; s. Homer Mock and Helen (Fluke) R.; m. Jeanne Lonnquist, Nov. 4, 1954; children: William T., Bruce R., Stewart D., James M., John B. AB, Dartmouth Coll., 1953; postgrad., Princeton U., 1957-58. V.p., gen. mgr. Doubleday & Co., Inc., NYC, 1958-70; pres., chmn. bd. G. & C. Merriam Co., Springfield, Mass., 1970-75; pres. Praeger Publishers, NYC, 1970-75; exec. v.p., dir. Houghton Mifflin Co., Boston, 1975-91; pres. DR&A Inc., Cohasset, Mass., 1992—; pres., publ. Hot House Press, Cohasset. Dir. L.I. Replogle Found., Chgo., 1982—; trustee South Shore Health and Ednl. Found, 2000—. Served to lt. USNR, 1953-57. Mem. Cohasset Golf Club, Plantation Golf and Country Club. Home: 84 Gammons Rd Cohasset MA 02025-1406 Office: David Replogle & Assocs 760 CJ Cushing Hwy Cohasset MA 02025-2124 Office Phone: 781-383-8360. Personal E-mail: drreplogle@aol.com.

REPLOGLE, ROBERT LEE, cardiovascular surgeon, thoracic surgeon; b. Ottumwa, Iowa, Sept. 30, 1931; s. Ralph Ruby and Edith Dorothy (Swartz) R.; m. Carol A. Heeschen, Aug. 24, 1958; children: Robert E., Jennifer Bremer, Edith Sheffer. MD cum laude, Harvard U., 1960; DSc (hon.), Cornell Coll., 1972. Diplomate Am. Bd. Surgery, Am. Bd. Thoracic Surgery, Am. Bd. Pediat. Surgery. Intern in surgery U. Minn. Hosp., 1960-61; asst. resident in surgery Peter Bent Brigham Hosp., Boston, 1961-63, Mass. Gen. Hosp., Boston, 1965-66; sr. resident in surgery Children's Hosp. Med. Ctr., Boston, 1966; asst. in surgery Children's Hosp. Med. Ctr. and Harvard Med. Sch., Boston, 1966-67; asst. prof. surgery Pritzker Sch. Medicine U. Chgo., 1967-70, assoc. prof. surgery and head, sect. pediat. surgery, 1970-73, prof. surgery and head, sect. pediat. surgery, 1973-74, prof. surgery and head, sect. cardiac surgery, 1973-80, prof. surgery, sect. cardiac surgery, 1973-90; med. dir. cardiac surgery unit Ingalls Meml. Hosp., 1989-98; chief divsn. cardiac surgery Columbus Hosp., Chgo., 1987-97; pres. CTS Net Inc., Chgo., 1998—. Vis. prof. Albany Med. Coll., 1974, Dalhousie Sch. of Medicine, Halifax, 1975, Walter Reed Army Med. Ctr., 1978, U. Miami Med. Sch., 1992, Philippine Heart Ctr. for Asia March, 1979, Health Inst. Japan, Tokyo, 1982, Creighton Med. Sch., 1988, Brooke Army Med. Ctr., 1993, U. Heidelberg, 1995, Kerkoff Clinic/Max Planct Inst., Bad Nanheim, Germany, 1995, German Heart Ctr., Munich, 1995, Peter Bent Brigham Hosp. Harvard Med. Sch., 1996; mem. surgery and bioengring. study sect. HHS, NIH, 1979-83; mem. ad hoc adv. com. bypass angioplasty revascularization investigation, NIH, 1993-94; mem. subcom. on quality N.Y. State Dept. Health, 1989-96, mem. subcom. on resources and facilities, 1993—, mem. cardiac adv. com., 1989—; pres. Ctsnet.org, Inc., 1999—. Author: (with others) Microcirculation, Perfusion, and Transplantation of Organs, 1970, The Critically Ill Child, 1972, Surgical Clinics in North America, 1976, Biprosthetic Cardiac Valves, 1979, Year Book of Nuclear Medicine, 1981, among others; mem. editl. bd. Jour. Cardiac Surgery, 1982-99; contbr. more than 125 articles to profl. jours. With USN, 1951-54. Recipient Merit award Philippine Heart ctr. for Asia, Manila, 1985, Friendship award Shanghai Chest Hosp., 1987. Mem. AMA (diagnostic and therapeutic tech. assessment panel 1995—, ho. of dels. 1992—, joint rev. com. on ednl. programs for physicians assts. 1979-84), ACS (com. on allied health pers. 1979-84, chmn. 1983-84, com. on med. motion pictures 1979-85, com. on membership 1988—, residency rev. com. for thoracic surgery of the accreditation com. for grad. med. edn. 1992-95, 96—), Ill. State Med. Soc., Chgo. Med. Soc., Am. Surg. Assn., European Assn. for Cardiothoracic Surgery, Soc. for Vascular Surgery, Am. Heart Assn. (adv. coun. cardiovasc. surgery 1968-71), Soc. Univ. Surgeons, Internat. Cardiovasc. Soc., Societe Internationale de Chirurgie (N.Am. chpt.), Am. Assn. for Thoracic Surgery (del. AMA 1992—, com. on soc. responsibility 1991—), Soc. Thoracic Surgeons (program com. 1978-81, chmn. 1981, com. on medico-legal affairs, chmn. 1985-88, ad hoc fin. adv. com. 1987-89, ad hoc exhibitors adv. com. 1988-89, ad hoc com. on social responsibility 1992-95, ad hoc database liaison com. 1993-94, database liaison com. 1994—, ad hoc com. on physician-specific mortality for cardiac surgery 1993-96, stds. and ethics com. 1984-88, treas. 1986-92, exec. com. 1986—, pres.-elect. 1995-96, pres. 1996-97, rep. to the coun. of med. specialty socs. 1990—, annals of thoracic surgery liaision com. 1992—, com. on grad. edn. in thoracic surgery 1992—, com. on major issues in thoracic surgery 1993, chmn. 1994, 95, pres.-elect coun. med. splty. socs. 1997-98, pres. coun. med. specialty socs. 1998-99), Coun. of Med. Specialty Socs., German Cardiac Surgery Soc. (hon. mem.). Avocations: wine collecting, photography, travel. Address: CTS Net Inc 1160 E 56th St Chicago IL 60637-1541

REPNIKOVA, MARIA, international migration scholar; b. Latvia; BS in Internat. Polit., Georgetown Univ., 2006; MPhil student in Migration Studies, Oxford Univ., 2007—. Contbr. articles to China Bus. Rev. Fulbright Scholar in China, 2006, Rhodes Scholar. Fluent in English, Russian, Mandarin, Latvian, French and Spanish. *

REPP, PAGE W., JR., construction executive; b. 1974; Owner, pres. Repp Enterprises Inc., Tucson, 1995—. Steering com. vice-chair West Side Weed and Seed. Pres. Barrio Blue Moon Neighborhood Assn. Named one of 40 Under 40, Tucson Bus. Edge, 2006. Office: Repp Design & Construction 422 W Speedway Tucson AZ 85705 Office Phone: 520-791-7035. Office Fax: 520-791-7075.

REPPER, GEORGE ROBERT, lawyer; b. Topeka, Dec. 22, 1954; s. George Vincent Jr. and Maria Magdalena (Bullert) R.; m. Helen Linda Zeichner, Aug. 23, 1981; children: Brian Lawrence, Kevin Michael, Michelle Suzanne. BS, SUNY, Albany, 1977; JD, Albany Law Sch., 1981. Bar: N.Y. 1982, D.C. 1982, U.S. Patent and Trademark Office 1984, U.S. Ct. Appeals (fed. cir.) 1989. V.p. Rothwell, Figg, Ernst & Manbeck, Washington, also bd. dirs. Contbr. articles to profl. jours. including Patent World. Mem. ABA (patents, trademarks and copyrights sect.), D.C. Bar Assn. (patents, trademarks and copyrights sect.), Am. Intellectual Property Law Assn., Internat. Intellectual Property Assn., Internat. Fedn. Indsl. Property Attys., Intellectual Property Owners, Internat. Trademark Assn. Office: Rothwell Figg Ernst & Manbeck 1425 K St NW Ste 800 Washington DC 20005

REPPERT, RICHARD LEVI, lawyer; b. Phila., Nov. 6, 1948; s. William Downing and Angela R. (Schmid) R.; m. Faith Simpson, Dec. 30, 1972 (div. Aug. 1992); 1 child, Richard Jacob; m. Jeanette T. deHaven, Apr. 10, 1994. BA, Lehigh U., 1970; JD, Villanova U., 1974. Bar: Ohio 1974, U.S. Dist. Ct. (no. dist.) Ohio 1974, Pa. 1993. Assoc. Thompson, Hine and Flory, Cleve., 1974-82, ptnr., 1982-89, Jones Day, Cleve., 1989—. Mem. ABA, Am. Coll. Real Estate Lawyers, Ohio State Bar Assn., Cleve. Bar Assn. Office: Jones Day North Point 901 Lakeside Ave Cleveland OH 44114-1190 E-mail: rreppert@jonesday.com.

REPPERT, SIBLEY PUTNAM, lawyer; b. Lancaster, Pa., July 4, 1945; s. Reppert Miller Charles and Charlotte Putnam Reppert; m. Christine Ann Vezetinski, May 10, 1980; children: Victoria Charlotte, Catherine Abigail Burke. BA summa cum laude with highest honors, Wesleyan U., 1967; BPhil, Oxford U., Eng., 1969; JD, Harvard U., 1975. Bar: Mass. 1975. Ptnr. Posternak, Blankstein & Lund, Boston, 1990—94, Herrick & Smith, Boston, 1994—95, Goodwin Procter & Hoar, Boston, 1995—2000, Samuels, Gauthier, Stevens & Reppert, Boston, 1995—98; pres., CEO LawRisk, Inc., Boston, 1998—2000, Incogno Corp., Boston, 2000—02; ptnr. Lahive & Cockfield, LLP, Boston, 2002—. Dir. Coalition for Buzzards Bay, Marion, Mass., 1990—94. Lt. USN, 1969—72. Keasbey fellow, Keasbey Meml. Found., 1967—69, Hon. fellow, Woodrow Wilson Found., 1967. Mem.: ABA, New Bedford Yacht Club (dir. 2000—). Avocations: sailing, rowing. Home: PO Box 14 Westport Point MA 02791 Office: Lahive & Cockfield LLP One Post Office Sq Boston MA 02109-2127 Home Phone: 508-636-8110; Office Phone: 617-227-7400. Office Fax: 617-742-4214. Business E-Mail: spr@lahive.com.

REPPERT, STEVEN MARION, pediatrician, research scientist, educator; b. Sioux City, Iowa, Sept. 4, 1946; s. Ray Fred and Norma Grace (Coppock) R.; m. Mary Alice Herman, Dec. 28, 1968; children: Jason Steven, Katherine Mary, Christina Marie. BS, U. Nebr., Lincoln, 1973; MD with distinction, U. Nebr., Omaha, 1973; MA (hon.), Harvard U., 1993. Diplomate Nat. Bd. Med. Examiners. Intern Mass. Gen. Hosp., Boston, 1973-74, resident in pediatrics, 1974-76, asst. in pediatrics, 1979-80, asst. pediatrician, 1980-85, dir. lab devel. chronobiology, 1983-2001, assoc. pediatrician, 1985-2000, pediatrician, 2000-2001. Clin. assoc. NIH, Bethesda, Md., 1976-79; instr. pediatrics Harvard Med. Sch., Boston, 1979-81, asst. prof., 1981-85, assoc. prof., 1985-93, prof., 1993—, Higgins family prof. neurosci., 2001—; vis. scientist Lab. Molecular Neurobiology, Mass. Gen. Hosp., 1989-90; prof., chair dept. neurobiology U. Mass. Med. Sch., 2001—. Editor: Development of Circadian Rhythmicity and Photoperiodism in Mammals, 1989; co-editor: Suprachiasmatic Nucleus: The Mind's Clock, 1991; mem. editl. bd. Neuron, 1997—; contbr. articles to sci. jours., chpt. to books. Mem. adv. com. Charles H. Hood Found., 1993-98. Recipient E. Mead Johnson award, 1989, NIH Merit award, 1992; Regents scholar U. nebr., 1971; Pfizer Labs. Med. scholar, 1971; Charles King Trust rsch. fellow, 1981-83; grantee NIH, 1981—, Nat. Found./March of Dimes, 1981-88. Mem. Am. Pediatric Soc., Am. Physiol. Soc., Am. Soc. for Clin. Investigation, Endocrine Soc., Soc. for Pediatric Rsch., Soc. for Neurosci., Soc. for Rsch. on Biol. Rhythms (adv. com.), Am. Heart Assn. (established investigator 1985-90), Lepidopterists Soc., Cambridge Entomol. Club, Alpha Omega Alpha. Democrat. Office: Mass Gen Hosp 32 Fruit St Boston MA 02114-2620

REPPUCCI, NICHOLAS DICKON, psychologist, educator; b. Boston, May 1, 1941; s. Nicholas Ralph and Bertha Elizabeth (Williams) R.; m. Christine Marlow Onufrock, Sept. 10, 1967; children: Nicholas Jason, Jonathan Dickon, Anna Jin Marlow Chapman. BA with honors, U. N.C., 1962; MA, Harvard U., 1964, PhD, 1968. Lectr., rsch. assoc. Harvard U., Cambridge, Mass., 1967-68; from asst. prof. to assoc prof. Yale U., New Haven, 1968-76; prof. psychology U. Va., Charlottesville, 1976—, dir. grad. studies in psychology, 1984-95, 97-98. Originator biennial conf. on community rsch. and action, 1986. Author: (with J. Haugaard) Sexual Abuse of Children, 1988; (with P. Britner and J. Woolard) Preventing Child Abuse and Neglect Through Parent Education, 1997; editor: (with J. Haugaard) Prevention in Community Mental Health Practice; (with E. Mulvey, L. Weithorn and J. Monahan) Mental Health, Law and Children, 1984; assoc. editor Law and Human Behavior, 1986-96, mem. editl. bd., 1996—; mem. editl. bd. Am. Jour. Cmty. Psychology, 1974-83, 88-91; contbr. articles to profl. jours., chpts. in books. Adv. bd. on prevention Va. Dept. Mental Health, Mental Retardation and Substance Abuse Svcs., Richmond, 1986-92. Recipient Disting. Scholar in psychology award Va. Assn. Social Sci., 1991, Outstanding Psychology Tchg. award, U. Va., 2005, Mentoring and Tchg. award Am. Psychology and Law Soc., 2007. Fellow APA (chmn. task force on pub. policy 1980-84), Am. Psychol. Soc., Soc. for Cmty. Rsch. and Action (pres. 1986, Disting. Contbn. award in theory and rsch. 1998, Inaugural award for ednl. mentoring 1999), Phi Beta Kappa. Office: U Va Dept Psychology PO Box 400400 Charlottesville VA 22904-4400 Office Phone: 434-924-0662. E-mail: ndr@virginia.edu.

RERYCH, STEPHEN KARL, surgeon; b. Phila., Pa., May 14, 1946; s. Henry and Gloria (French) Rerych; 1 child from previous marriage, Stephanie Karen. BS, NC State U., Raleigh, 1969; MD, Columbia U. Coll. Physicians and Surgeons, NYC, 1974. Cert. Bat. Bd. Med. Examiners, 1975, Am. Bd. Surgery, 1993, lic. physician NY, W.Va. Surg. tng. Duke U. Med. Ctr., Durham, NC, 1974—86, asst. clin. prof. surgery, 1986—; pvt. practice Biltmore Surg., Asheville, 1988—2006; clin. instr. surgery Marshall U. Pleasant Valley Hosp., Point Pleasant, W.Va., 2006—. Chief surgery Meml. Mission Hosp. Systems, Asheville, 2005—06. Named to Sports Hall of Fame, NC, NJ, All-Am. Swimming Team, NCAA, 1964—68; recipient Gold Medals (2), Mex. City Olympics, 1968, Runner-Up Youg Investigator award, Am. Coll. Cardiology, 1979. Mem.: Am. Acad. Cosmetic Surgery, Rotarty. Republican. Episcopal. Avocation: golf. Home: 18 Ridgewood Dr Point Pleasant WV 25550-9745 Office: Pleasant Valley Hosp 2520 Valley Dr Point Pleasant WV 25550

RESCH, EDWARD J., investment company executive; BS, Lehigh U.; MBA, Rutgers U. Sr. positions Salomon Brothers Inc., Price Waterhouse, Procter & Gamble; CFO, capital markets group Donaldson, Lufkin & Jenrette, Inc., mng. dir., chief acctg. officer; mng. dir., CFO Pershing; exec. v.p., CFO State Street Corp., Boston, 2002—. Office: State Street Corp 225 Franklin St Boston MA 02110 *

RESCH, JOSEPH ANTHONY, neurologist; b. Milw., Apr. 29, 1914; s. Frank and Elizabeth (Zetsch) R.; m. Rose Catherine Ritz, May 25, 1939; children— Rose, Frank, Catherine. Student, Milw. State Tchrs. Coll., 1931-34; BS, U. Wis., Madison, 1936, MD, 1938. Intern St. Francis Hosp., LaCrosse, Wis., 1938-39; gen. practice medicine Holmen, Wis., 1939-40; med. fellow in neurology U. Minn., 1946-48, clin. instr. neurology, 1948-51, clin. asst. prof., 1951-55, clin. assoc. prof., 1955-62, assoc. prof., 1962-65, prof., 1965-84, prof. emeritus, 1984—, head dept. neurology, 1976-82, asst. v.p. health sci., 1970-79, prof. lab. medicine and pathology, 1979-84; practice medicine specializing in neurology Mpls., 1948-62. Contbr. articles and abstracts to profl. jours., chpts. to books. Served to lt. col. M.C. U.S. Army, 1940-46; col. Med. Res. 1946-53. Mem. Hennepin County Med. Soc., Minn. Med. Assn., AMA, Minn. Soc. Neurol. Scis., Am. Acad. Neurology, Am. Neurol. Assn., Am. Assn. Neuropathologists, Am. Clin. Neurophysiol. Soc., Am. Epilepsy Soc. Home: 1609 Pleasant St Apt 307 Lauderdale MN 55108

RESCH, RITA MARIE, retired music educator; b. Minot, ND, Dec. 26, 1936; d. Clement Charles and Magdalena Marie (Zeltinger) Resch. BS in Edn., Minot State U., 1957; MM in Music Lit., Eastman Sch. Music, Rochester, NY, 1960; MA in English Lit., U. N.D., 1967; MFA in Voice, U. Iowa, 1973, DMA in Piano Chamber Music/Accompanying, 1974. Music tchr. (vocal) Biwabik Sch. Dist., Minn., 1957—58, S. Redford Twp., Detroit, 1958—59; instr. music Fontbonne Coll., St. Louis, 1960—63; asst. prof. music Wis. State U., Stevens Point, 1965—68, U. Ctrl. Mo. (formerly Ctrl. Mo. State U.), Warrensburg, 1974—79, assoc. prof., 1979—89, prof., 1989—2005, prof. emerita, 2005—. Adjudicator for vocal music Mo. State High Sch. Activities Assn., Columbia, Kans. State High Sch. Activities Assn., Topeka, other orgns., 1976—. Author (with Judith E. Carman, William K. Gaeddert, Gordon Myers): Art Song in the United States: An Annotated Bibliography, 1976, 2001. Assoc. organist Sacred Heart Cath. Ch., Warrensburg, 1980—. Mem.: Mo. Music Tchrs. Assn. (v.p. auditions 1995—98), Music Tchrs. Nat. Assn., Nat. Assn. Tchrs. Singing, Pi Kappa Lambda, Sigma Alpha Iota. E-mail: resch@cmsul.cmsu.edu.

RESCHER, NICHOLAS, philosopher, author, educator; b. Hagen, Westphalia, Germany, July 15, 1928; arrived in US, 1938, naturalized, 1944; s. Erwin Hans and Meta Anna Rescher; m. Dorothy Henle, Feb. 10, 1968; children: Mark, Owen, Catherine; 1 child from previous marriage, Elizabeth. BS in Math., Queens Coll., 1949; PhD, Princeton U., 1951; LHD (hon.), Loyola U., Chgo., 1970, Lehigh U., 1993; Dr. honoris causa (hon.), U. Córdoba, Argentina, 1992, U. Constance, Germany, 1995; DS (hon.), CUNY, 1999; PhD (hon.), Fern U., Hagen, 2001; Dr.rer.pol.hc, Helsinki, 2006; LHD (hon.), Cleve. State U., 2007. Instr. philosophy Princeton (N.J.) U., 1951-52; mathematician RAND Corp., 1954-56; assoc. prof. philosophy Lehigh U., Bethlehem, Pa., 1957-61; univ. prof. philosophy U. Pitts., 1961—, chmn. Ctr. for Philosophy of Sci., 1988—. Trustee St. Edmunds Acad., Pitts., 1980—85; nonresident mem. Corpus Christi Coll., Oxford; disting. vis. lectr., Oxford, Salamanca, Munich, Konstanz; cons. in field. Author: The Coherence Theory of Truth, 1973, Methodological Pragmatism, 1977, Scientific Progress, 1978, The Limits of Science, 1985, Luck, 1995, Predicting the Future, 1997, Complexity, 1998, Nature and Understanding, 2000, Paradoxes, 2000, Philosophical Reasoning, 2001, Fairness, 2002, Epistemic Logic, 2004, Epistometrica, 2006; exec. editor: Am. Philos. Quar., 1961—; mem. editl. bd. 15 jours.; contbr. articles to profl. jours. Sec. gen. Internat. Union History and Philosophy Sci. UNESCO, 1969—72. With USMC, 1952—54. Recipient Alexander von Humboldt Humanities prize, 1983, Prix Mercier, 2005; Ford Found. fellow, 1959—60, Guggenheim Found. fellow, 1970—71. Mem.: Acad. Europaea, Academie Internat. de Philosophie des Scis., Inst. Internat. de Philosophie, C. S. Perice Soc. (past pres.), G. W. Leibniz Soc. Am. (past pres.), Royal Soc. Can., Royal Asiatic Soc., Am. Metaphys. Soc. (past pres.), Am. Cath. Philos. Assn. (past pres.), Am. Philos. Assn. (past pres., Aquinas medal 2007). Roman Catholic. Avocation: reading. Home: 1033 Milton Ave Pittsburgh PA 15218 Office: U Pitts Dept Philosophy 1012 Cathedral Pittsburgh PA 15260 Office Phone: 412-624-5950. Business E-Mail: rescher@pitt.edu.

RESCHKE, MICHAEL W., real estate company officer; b. Chgo., Nov. 29, 1955; s. Don J. and Vera R. (Helmer) R.; children: Michael W. Jr., Tiffanie G., Taylor N. BS summa cum laude with univ. honors, No. Ill. U., 1977; JD summa cum laude, U. Ill., 1980. Bar: Ill. 1980; CPA, Ill. Assoc. Winston & Strawn, Chgo., 1980-82; pres., CEO The Prime Group, Inc., Chgo., 1981, chmn. bd. dirs., CEO, 1981—. Mem. Chgo. Devel. Coun., 1987—. Mem. ABA, Ill. Bar Assn., Urban Land Inst., Chgo. Econ. Club, Real Estate Roundtable (dir.), Order of Coif, Phi Delta Phi, Beta Alpha Psi. Business E-Mail: mreschke@primegroupinc.com.

RESCHLY, DANIEL J., education educator, psychologist; b. Wayland, Iowa, Dec. 30, 1943; married; 3 children. BS, Iowa State U., 1966; MA, U. Iowa, 1968; PhD, U. Oreg., 1971. Lic. sch. psychologist Iowa, Oreg., Ariz.; nat. cert. sch. psychologist, cert. secondary edn. educator Iowa. Sch. psychologist Louisa County Schs., Wapello, Iowa, 1967—69; dir. summer head start program Louisa County, Iowa, 1969; sch. psychology intern Albina Youth Opportunity Ctr. and Portland (Oreg.) Pub. Schs., 1970—71; asst. prof. U. Ariz., Tucson, 1971—75; assoc. prof. Iowa State U., 1975—80, prof., 1980—91, disting. prof. liberal arts and sciences, 1991—98, dir. Sch. Psychology Program, interim assoc. dean Coll. Edn., 1996—98, dir. Rsch. Inst. for Studies in Edn., 1996—98; prof. edn. and psychology Vanderbilt U., Nashville, 1998—, chair dept. spl. edn., 1998—2006. Presenter in field; editor Sch. Psychology Rev., 1979—81, mem. editl. bd., 1974—2000, Jour. Sch. Psychology, 1982—96, Sch. Psychology Quarterly, 1984—90, Jour. of Psychoeducational Assessment, 1983—88, Canadian Jour. Sch. Psychology, 1990—, Jour. of Learning Disabilities, 1998—. Contbr. chapters to books, articles to profl. jours. Recipient Award for outstanding contributions to the develop. of sch. psycholgy, NJ Assn. Sch. Psychologists, 1983, James B. Stroud award, Iowa Sch. Psychologists Assn., 1989, Dorthy H. Hughes Meml. award for disting. svc. in edn. and sch. psychology, NYU Dept. Applied Psychology, 1994, Outstanding Alumnus awrad, U. Ore. Coll. Edn., 1996, Award for Exemplary Effort in Support of the University's Commitment to Promoting Opportunities for Persons with Disabilities, Vanderbilt U., 2004. Fellow: APA (fellow Sch. Psych. Divsn. 1985, fellow Edn. Psychology Divsn. 1990); mem.: Am. Psychol. Soc. (charter fellow 1989), Learning Disabilities Assn., Tenn. Assn. Sch. Psychologists, Internat. Sch. Psychology Assn., Coun. for Exceptional Children, Am. Assn. on Mental Retardation, Am. Ednl. Rsch. Assn., Iowa Acad. Edn. (charter), Nat. Assn. Sch. Psychologists (pres., editor Sch. Psychology Rev., chair grad. program approval, Disting. Svc. award 1980, 1987, 1990, Lifetime Achievement award 2000, Legends award 2007). Office: Vanderbilt Univ Box 328 Peabody College Nashville TN 37203-5701 Office Phone: 615-322-8150. Office Fax: 615-343-1570. *

RESCORLA, ROBERT ARTHUR, psychology professor; b. Pitts., May 9, 1940; s. Arthur R. and Mildred J. (Jenkins) Rescorla; m. Shirley Steele; children: Eric, Michael. BA, Swarthmore Coll., 1962; PhD, U. Pa., 1966; MA, Yale U., 1974; PhD (hon.), Ghent U., Belgium, 2006. Successively asst. prof., assoc. prof., prof. Yale U., New Haven, 1966—80; prof. psychology U. Pa., Phila., 1981—, James Skinner prof. sci., 1986—2000, Christopher Browne disting. prof. psychology, 2000—, dean of coll. Sch. Arts and Scis., 1994—97. Author: Pavlovian Second-Order Conditioning, 1980; editor: Animal Learning and Behavior, 1995—97; contbr. articles to profl. jours. Recipient Ira Abrams Tchg. award, 1999, Horsley Grant award, Pavlovian Soc., 2005. Mem.: AAAS (pres. sect. J., psychology 1988—89), NAS, APA (pres. divsn. 3 1985, Disting. Sci.Contbn. award 1986), Psychonomic Soc. (mem. governing bd. 1979—85, chmn. publ. bd. 1985—86), Ea. Psychol. Assn. (bd. dirs. 1983—86, pres. 1986—87, Warren medal 1991), Soc. Exptl. Psychologists, Am. Psychol. Soc. (William James fellow). Office: U Pa Dept Psychology 3720 Walnut St Philadelphia PA 19104-3604

RESDEN, RONALD EVERETT, medical devices product development engineer; b. Littleton, NH, Oct. 27, 1944; s. Lawerence A. and Rita Mae (Bowen) R.; m. Dee Kronenburg, Apr. 20, 1974 (div.); children: Philip, Alison; m. Louise Simons, June 18, 1994. Cons. Franklin Mfg. Co., Norwood, Mass., 1984—, Boston Sci. Co., Watertown, Mass., 1985—, Via Med, Easton, Mass., 1986—, White Marsh Labs., Balt., 1989—, Spectraphos Malmo Sweden, 1991—, Vision Scis. Inc., Natick, Mass., 1991—, Cordis Corp., Miami, Fla., 1993—; cons. Cardiology Catheter Lab. Mass. Hosp. Cardiology, Boston, 1993—; cons. Boston Med. Products, Inc., Westborough, Mass., 1998—. Active MIT Enterprise Forum. Author: Hologram Control Transfer, 1984; inventor, patentee in field. Elected official Town of Guildhall, Vt.; com. mem. Lancaster Fair, NH. Mem. NRA (life), Soc. Plastics Engrs. (mem. med. plastics and biomaterials mag. rev. bd.), Soc. Mfg. Engrs., Nat. Geog. Soc., Mass. Chiefs of Police Assn., Citizens for Ltd. Taxation. Home and Office: Mt View Med PO Box 145 Guildhall VT 05905 Office: Ron Resden Gunsmith Box 145 3545 Fellows Rd Guildhall VT 05905-0145 Office Phone: 802-328-2765. Office Fax: 802-328-4451. Personal E-mail: rresden@yahoo.com.

RESEK, ROBERT WILLIAM, economist; b. Berwyn, Ill., July 2, 1935; s. Ephraim Frederick and Ruth Elizabeth (Rummele) R.; m. Lois Doll, July 9, 1960; 1 child, Richard Alden. BA, U. Ill., 1957; AM, Harvard U., 1960, PhD, 1961. Asst. prof. econs. U. Ill., Urbana, 1961-65, assoc. prof., 1965-70, prof., 1970—2005, prof. emeritus, 2005—; vis. scholar MIT, Cambridge, 1967-68; dir. Bur. Econ. and Bus. Rsch., 1977-89, acting v.p. for acad. affairs, 1987-89, v.p. for acad. affairs, 1989—94, v.p. emeritus, 1995—; prof. Inst. Govt. and Pub. Affairs, 1994—2005, prof. emeritus, 2005—. Tchg. fellow Harvard U., 1959-61; vis. prof. U. Colo., 1967, 74-76, 82, Kyoto (Japan) U., 1976; cons. GM, 1964-66, U.S. Congress Joint Econ. Com., 1978-80, ABA, 1980-82; vis. scholar UCLA, 1994-95; co-dir. Midwest Economy: Issues and Policy, Midwest Govs. Conf., 1981; bd. dirs. Midwest U. Consortium Internat. Activities, 1989-94, v.p., 1991-94; mem. Ill. Gov.'s Econ. Policy Coun., 1999-2003. Co-author: Environmental Contamination by Lead and Other Heavy Metals--Synthesis and Modeling, 1978, Special Topics in Mathematics for Economists, 1976, A Comparative Cost Study of Staff Panel and Participating Attorney Panel Prepaid Legal Service Plans, 1981, Illinois Higher Education: Building the Economy, Shaping Society, 2000; editor: Illinois Economic Outlook, 1982-87, Illinois Economic Statistics, 1981, Economic Edge, 1996-2004; co-editor: The Midwest Economy: Issues and Policy, 1982, Frontiers of Business and Economic Research Management, 1983, Illinois Statistical Abstract, 1987, 2002-04. Mem. exec. com. Assn. Univ. Bus. and Econ. Rsch., 1977-89, v.p., 1978-82, pres., 1982-83. Woodrow Wilson fellow, 1957; Social Sci. Rsch. Coun. grantee, 1964; NSF fellow, 1967-69, grantee, 1974-77; U.S. Dept. State scholar, Japan, 1976; grantee Ill. Bd. Higher Edn., 1998-99. Mem. Econometric Soc., Beta Gamma Sigma, Phi Kappa Phi. Home: 201 E Holmes St Urbana IL 61801-6612 Office: Univ Ill 211 IGPA 1007 W Nevada St Urbana IL 61801-3812 Business E-Mail: resek@uiuc.edu.

RESHCHIKOV, MICHAEL A., physics professor, researcher; b. Leningrad, Russia, June 11, 1959; s. Alexander Pavlovich Reshchikov and Oktyabrina Grigorievna Reshchikova; m. Elena Nikolaevna Petrova, Nov. 25, 1983; children: Paul, Alexander. MSEE, St. Petersburg Poly. Inst., St. Petersburg, Russia, 1976—82; PhD in physics, Ioffe Physico-Technical Inst., St. Petersburg, Russia, 1982—89. Rsch. scientist Ioffe Physico-Technical Inst., St. Petersburg, Russia, 1982—97, Northwestern U., Evanstone, Ill., 1997—99, Dept. of Elec. Engring., Va. Commonwealth U., 1999—2004; asst. prof. Dept. of Physics, Va. Commonwealth U., 2004—. Contbr. more than 100 articles to profl. jours. Mem.: Va. Acad. Scis., Am. Phys. Soc., Materials Rsch. Soc. (assoc.). Achievements include research in deep defects in semiconductors, mostly by luminescence methods. Identification of point defects in GaN, GaAs, InSb, Ge. Avocations: swimming, diving, reading. Office: Dept Physics Virginia Commonwealth Univ 1020 West Main St Richmond VA 23284 Home Phone: 804-754-3272; Office Phone: 804-828-1613. Office Fax: 804-828-7073. Business E-Mail: mreshchi@vcu.edu.

RESHETNYAK, YANA K., physics professor; d. Guili Dumbadze and Konstantin Reshetnyak; m. Oleg A. Andreev, Aug. 30, 2001; 1 child, Stefania Andreev. MS with honors, St. Petersburg U., Russia, 1993; PhD with honors, Russian Acad. Sci., Pushchino, Russia, 2000. Asst. prof. U. RI, Kingston, 2004—. Recipient G. Weber Internat. prize, 2001; fellow Wood/Whelean, Internat. Unit Biochemistry and Molecular Biology, 1997—98. Achievements include patents pending for selective delivery of molecules into cells in diseased tissue regions using environmentally sensitive transmembrane peptide insertion; research in theory of protein fluorescence. Office: Univ RI Physics 2 Lippitt Rd Kingston RI 02881 Home Phone: 401-282-0970; Office Phone: 401-874-5586. Office Fax: 401-874-2380.

RESHOTKO, ELI, aerospace engineer, educator; b. NYC, Nov. 18, 1930; s. Max and Sarah (Kalisky) R.; m. Adina Venit, June 7, 1953; children: Deborah, Naomi, Miriam Ruth. BS, Cooper Union, 1950; MS, Cornell U., 1951; PhD, Calif. Inst. Tech., 1960. Aero. research engr. NASA-Lewis Flight Propulsion Lab., Cleve., 1951-56, head fluid mechanics sect., 1956-57; head high temperature plasma sect. NASA-Lewis Research Center, 1960-61, chief plasma physics br., 1961-64; asso. prof. engring. Case Inst. Tech., Cleve., 1964-66, dean, 1986-87; prof. engring. Case Western Res. U., Cleve., 1966-88, chmn. dept. fluid thermal and aerospace scis., 1970-76, chmn. dept. mech. and aerospace engring., 1976-79, Kent H. Smith prof. engring., 1989-98, Kent H. Smith prof. emeritus, 1999—. Susman vis. prof. dept. aero. engring. Technion-Israel Inst. Tech., Haifa, Israel, 1969-70; cons. Inst. Def. Analyses, Dynamics Tech. Inc., Wyle Labs., Rockwell Sci. Ctr.; adv. com. fluid dynamics NASA, 1961-64; aero. adv. com. NASA, 1980-87, chmn. adv. subcom. on aerodynamics, 1983-85; chmn. U.S. Boundary Layer Transition Study Group, NASA/USAF, 1970—2001, steering com., 2001-; U.S. mem. fluid dynamics panel AGARD-NATO, 1981-88; chmn. steering com. Symposium on Engring. Aspects of Magneto-hydro-dynamics, 1966, Case-NASA Inst. for Computational Mechanics in Propulsion, 1985-92, USRA/NASA ICASE Sci. Coun., 1992; Joseph Wunsch lectr. Technion-Israel Inst. Tech., 1990 Contbr. articles to tech. jours. Chmn. bd. govs. Cleve. Coll. Jewish Studies, 1981-84 (life trustee); bd. govs. Technion-Israel Inst. Tech., Haifa, Israel, 1999-2005; mem. NRC Air Force Studies bd., 2000-06. Guggenheim fellow Calif. Inst. Tech., 1957-59. Fellow ASME, AAAS, AIAA (Fluid and Plasma Dynamics award 1980, Dryden lectr. in rsch. 1994), Am. Phys. Soc. (vice-chmn. divsn. fluid dynamics 1998, chair-elect 1999, chair 2000, Otto Laporte award in fluid dynamics 1999), Am. Acad. Mechanics (pres. 1986-87); mem. NAE, Ohio Sci. and Engring. Roundtable, Sigma Xi, Tau Beta Pi, Pi Tau Sigma. Home: 1200 Humboldt St Apt 601 Denver CO 80218-2454

RESIDANTE, EL (RENÉ PÉREZ), singer, composer; b. Hato Rey, PR, Feb. 23, 1978; Co-founder & lead singer Calle 13; signed to White Lion records. Singer: (albums) Calle 13, 2005 (Latin Grammy award for Best Urban Music Album, 2006), (songs) Atrévete Te, Te!, 2005 (Latin Grammy award for Best Short Form Music Video, 2006), (with Nelly Furtado) No Hay Igual, 2006. Recipient Best New Artist award, Best Urban Album & Best Short Music Video, Latin Grammy Awards, 2006. Office: White Lion Records Inc Urb Ocean Park 2072 Cacique Santurce PR 00911-1514 *

RESIKA, PAUL, artist; b. NYC, Aug. 15, 1928; Student, Sol Wilson, NYC, 1940—44, Hans Hofmann Sch., 1945—47, Sch. Venice, Italy, 1950—52, Sch. Venice, Rome, 1953. Adj. prof. art Cooper Union, 1966-78; instr. Art Students League, 1968-69; faculty Skowhagen Sch. Painting and Sculpture, 1973, 76; chmn. M.F.A. program Parsons Sch. Design, 1978-89. Dartmouth Coll. 1972 Artist in Residence. One-man shows include George Dix Gallery, NYC, 1948, Peridot Gallery, 1965, 1967, 1968, 1969, 1970, Washburn Gallery, 1971, 1973, Hopkins Ctr. Dartmouth Coll., 1972, Graham Gallery, 1976, 1979, 1981, 1983, 1985, Longpoint Gallery, Provincetown, Mass., 1979, 1981, 1989, 1992, 1995, 25-yr. survey Artists Choice Mus., 1985, Merideth Long Gallery, Houston, 1986, 1997, 2005, Walker-Kornbluth Gallery, Fair Lawn, N.J., 1986, 1995, 1997, Crane Kalman Gallery, London, 1986, Graham/Modern Gallery, 1987—88, 1990, Salander-O'Reilly Galleries, NYC, 1993, 1994, 1995, 1999, 2001, 2002, 2005, Benucci, Rome, 2005, Vered Gallery, East Hampton, N.Y., 1995, 2003, 2004, Gerald Peters Gallery, Santa Fe, 1996, Provincetown Art Assn. and Mus., 1997, Lori Bookstein Gallery, N.Y.C., 1998, 2001, Berta Walker Gallery, Provincetown, 1998, 2001, 2003, Provincetown, Mass., 2004, 2005, Bertha Walker Gallery, 2005, 2006, Lizan Tops Gallery, East Hampton, N.Y., 1998, Hackett Freedman, San Francisco, 1998, Hackett-Freedman, 1999, 2000, 2002, 2006, Metta Galleria, Madrid, 2000, Camino Real Gallery, Boca Raton, Fla., 2003, Benucci Gallery, Rome, 2005, Lori Bookstein Gallery, 2006. Represented in permanent collections Nat. Mus. Am. Art, Washington, Muson-Williams-Proctor Inst. Mus. Art, Utica, N.Y., U. Nebr. Art Gallery, Indpls. Mus. Art, Chase Manhattan Bank, N.Y.C., Neuberger Mus., SUNY, Purchase, U. Wyo., Laramie, Met. Mus. Art, N.Y., Colby Coll., NAD, Owensboro (Ky.) Mus. Art, U. Ariz., William Benton Mus. Art, Hood Mus., Dartmouth Coll., Hanover, N.H., Tucson Mus. Art, Crackow Mus. Art, Poland, Parish Art Mus., Southampton, N.Y., Heckscher Mus., Huntington, N.Y., Mills Coll. Mus., Oakland, Calif., Meml. Art Gallery, Rochester, Whitney Mus., NYC, Mus. Modern Art, also pvt. collections. Recipient award Am. Acad. Arts and Letters, 1977; Altman prize NAD, 1982, 91, 97, 2003, Obrig prize, 1996; Louis Comfort Tiffany grantee, 1959, Ingram Merrill grantee, 1969; John Simon Guggenheim Meml. fellow, 1984. Mem. NAD, Am. Acad. Arts and Letters. Office: Salander Oreilly Galleries 22 E 71st St New York NY 10021-4975

RESKE, STEVEN DAVID, lawyer, writer; b. Mpls., May 31, 1962; s. Albert Edgar Reske and Florence Mae Altland. BA with distinction, St. Olaf Coll., Northfield, Minn., 1985; JD cum laude, Boston U., 1988. Bar: Ill. 1988, Minn. 1989, U.S. Dist. Ct. Minn. 1991, U.S. Ct. Appeals (5th cir.) 1989, U.S. Ct. Appeals (7th and 8th cirs.) 1992, U.S. Supreme Ct. 1993, DC 1998, U.S. Ct. Appeals (DC cir.) 1998. Intern U.S. Senator Durenberger, Washington, 1981-82, Citizens for Ednl. Freedom, Washington, 1981-82, Abbott-Northwestern Hosp., Mpls., 1984, U.S. Dist. Ct. Judge Magnuson, St. Paul, 1986; summer assoc. Faegre & Benson, Mpls., 1987; assoc. Sidley & Austin, Chgo., 1988; law clk. to Hon. Judge Politz U.S. Ct. Appeals 5th Cir., Shreveport, La., 1988-89; pvt. practice, 1989—. Contbr. CD Rev., 1993-95, JAZZIZ, 1996—, Skyway News, 1997—, City Pages, 2000—; contbr. articles to profl. jours.; mem. Am. Jour. Law and Medicine, 1986-87, editor, 1987-88; legal editor-at-large Law and Politics, 1998—; columnist Twin Cities Revue, 1998—. Recipient Minn. Super Lawyer award, 1998, Am. Jurisprudence award, 1988; Edward F. Hennessey scholar, 1988, G. Joseph Tauro scholar, 1986. Mem. ABA (antitrust divsn.), Minn. State Bar Assn., Hennepin County Bar Assn., Am. Econ. Assn., Am. Philos. Assn. Office: 3021 Devon Ln Mound MN 55364-9325 Personal E-mail: sreske@hotmail.com.

RESKIN, BARBARA F., sociologist; b. St. Paul; Student, Reed Coll., Portland, Oreg.; BA in Sociology, U. Wash., 1968, MA in Sociology, 1970, PhD in Sociology, 1973. Acting asst. prof. sociology U. Calif., Davis, 1972—73; asst. to assoc. prof. sociology Indiana U., Bloomington, 1973—83; prof. sociology and women's studies U. Mich., Ann Arbor, 1983—85; prof. sociology, dir. grad. studies U. Ill., Urbana, 1985—91; prof. sociology Ohio State U., 1991—97, Harvard U., 1997—2002; S. Frank Miyamoto prof. sociology U. Wash., 2002—. Study dir. com. women's employment and related social issues Nat. Rsch. Coun./NAS, Washington, 1981—82; vis. scholar Stanford U. Inst. Rsch. Women and Gender, 1987; fellow Ctr. Advanced Study in Behavioral Scis., 1987—88; chair dept. sociology Ohio State U., 1993—95. Contbr. articles to profl. jours., chapters to books; assoc. editor: Am. Sociol. Rev., 1979—81, Rsch. in Social Stratification and Mobility, 1988—, Work and Occupations, 1995—; author: Sex Differences in the Profl. Life Chances of Chemists, 1980, Realities of Affirmative Action, 1998; editor: Sex Segregation in the Workplace: Trends, Explanations, Remedies, 1984; co-author: Women's Work, Men's Work: Sex Segregation on the Job, 1986, Job Queues, Gender Queues: Explaining Women's Inroads into Male Occupations, 1990, Women and Men at Work, 1994, Mng. Work and Family: Nonstandard Work Arrangements Among Mgrs. and Profls., 1997, Nonstandard Work, Substandard Jobs: Flexible Work Arrangements in the U.S., 1997; adv. editor: Gender & Soc., 1986—88, assoc. editor:, 1990—93, mem. editl. bd.: Social Forces, 1992—95, Gender, Work and Orgns., 1993—. Recipient SWS Mentorship award, Sociologists for Women in Soc., 1998. Fellow: NAS, Am. Acad. Arts and Scis.; mem.: Sociol. Rsch. Assn., Am. Sociol. Assn. (chair sect. on occupations, orgns. and work 1997—98, pres. 2001—02, v.p. 1990—91, Disting. Scholar award, sect. on sex and gender 1995). Office: Dept Sociology U Wash Box 353340 Seattle WA 98195-3340 E-mail: reskin@u.washington.edu.

RESMAN-TARGOFF, BETH HOLLY, pharmacist, educator; d. Norman M. and Rowena Resman; m. Ira N. Targoff, June 14, 1981; 1 child, Deborah Judith Targoff. BS in Pharmacy, SUNY, Buffalo, 1973, PharmD, 1976. Registered pharmacist NY, 1974, Okla., 1991. Clin. coord., asst. dir. pharmacy The Buffalo Gen. Hosp., 1976—81; clin. instr. SUNY, 1976—81; clin. prof. U. Okla., Oklahoma City, 1981—. Mem. adv. bd. Annals Pharmacotherapy, 1989—. Contbr. chapters to books. Fellow: Am. Coll. Clin. Pharmacy; mem.: Am. Assn. Colls. Pharmacy, Okla. Pharmacists Assn., Am. Pharmacists Assn., Okla. Soc. Health-Sys. Pharmacists, Am. Soc. Health-Sys. Pharmacists, Phi Kappa Phi, Rho Chi (Outstanding Faculty Mem., U. Okla. Chpt. 1992—2006). Avocations: travel, photography. Office: U Okla Coll Pharm PO Box 26901 Oklahoma City OK 73190

RESNECK-SANNES, HELEN, psychologist; b. Marion, Ind., Dec. 14, 1947; d. William and Charlotte Resneck; m. Larry David Sannes, June 20, 1976; children: Aaron Sannes, Myrrhia. PhD, U. Wis., Madison, 1974. Lic. psychologist Bd. of Med. Quality Assurance, 1975. Pvt. psychotherapy practice Helen Resneck-Sannes, Ph.D., Santa Cruz, Calif., 1977—; tchr. trainer Internat. Inst. for Bioenergetic Analysis, NYC, 1997—. Asst. prof. Antioch Coll., Monterey, Calif., 1977—77; prof. U. Calif., Santa Cruz, 1989; presenter in field. Author: (memoir) Father's Rooms, 2004; contbr. articles to profl. jours. Recipient medal, Phi Kappa Phi Hon. Soc., 1969; Work study grant, Western Interstate Commn. for Higher Edn., 1968, fellowship, NIMH, 1970-1974, grant to establish a women's therapy ctr., Wis. Psychol. Assn., 1972. Mem.: APA, Monterey Bay Psychol. Assn., Calif. Psychol. Assn., Internat. Inst. for Bioenergetic Analysis (bd. of trustees 2002—03, co-editor jour. 2003). Home and Office: 216 Suburbia Ave Santa Cruz CA 95062 Office Phone: 831-426-2768. Personal E-mail: helenrs@aol.com.

RESNIC, BURTON S., lawyer; s. Samuel and Theresa Babe Resnic; m. Marjoie C. Meyer, July 1, 1961; children: Laura J. Brounstein, Joanne H. Lippman. BA, Washington U., St. Louis, 1950; LLB, Harvard U., Cambridge, Mass., 1953. Bar: Mass. 1954, D.C. 1954. Ptnr. Resnic, Beauregard, Waite & Driscoll, Holyoke, Mass., 1955—. Spkr. in field, 1975—2005. Contbr. articles to profl. jours. Past pres. Pioneer Valley Coun. Boy Scouts Am., Hampden County, Mass.; past bd. dirs. Jewish Nursing Home, Longmeadow, Mass., Jr. Achievement, Holyoke; vol. Law Day spkr. various Sr. Citizen Couns.; past. bd. dirs. StageWest; del. Rep. Nat. Conv., 1976, 1980; bd. dirs., pro bono legal counsel Congregation Sons of Zion, Holyoke. With US Army, 1953—55. Recipient Recognition for Successful Major Capital Campaign, Holyoke Hosp., 1986—87. Avocations: golf, tennis, skiing. Home: 20 Longfellow Rd Holyoke MA 01040 Office: Resnic Beauegard Waite & Driscoll 330 Whitney Ave Ste 400 Holyoke MA 01040 Office Phone: 413-536-0653. Office Fax: 413-536-4074. Business E-Mail: kstdenis@rbwd.com.

RESNICK, ADRIENNE JO, clinical social worker, psychotherapist; b. NYC, July 19, 1954; d. Martin and Molly Starkman; m. Paul Resnick, Sept. 30, 1978; 1 child, Elana. BA, NYU, 1975, MSW, 1981. Psychotherapist Stamford Child Guidance Clinic, Conn., 1981—83; group facilitator YWCA, White Plains, NY; psychotherapist pvt. practice, Sleepy Hollow, 1983—. Author: Sometimes I Feel Blue, 2002, Food Play, 2002. Recipient

Founders Day award, NYU, N.Y.C., 1975. Mem.: NASW (diplomate), Am. Soc. Trial Cons., Acad. Cert. Social Workers, Soc. Clin. Social Work. Avocations: writing, travel, yoga. Office: 229 N Broadway Sleepy Hollow NY 10591 Office Phone: 914-633-3389. Personal E-mail: agres719@aol.com.

RESNICK, ALICE ROBIE, retired state supreme court justice; b. Erie, Pa., Aug. 21, 1939; d. Adam Joseph and Alice Suzanne (Spizarny) Robie; m. Melvin L. Resnick, Mar. 20, 1970 PhB, Siena Heights Coll., 1961; JD, U. Detroit, 1964; LLD (hon.), Heidelberg Coll., 1999, U. Akron, 1994. Bar: Ohio 1964, Mich. 1965, U.S. Supreme Ct. 1970. Atty. priv. practice, 1964—75; asst. county prosecutor Lucas County Prosecutor's Office, Toledo, 1964-75, trial atty., 1965-75; judge Toledo Mcpl. Ct., 1976-83, 6th Dist. Ct. Appeals, State of Ohio, Toledo, 1983-88; instr. U. Toledo, 1968-69; justice Ohio Supreme Ct., 1988—2006. Co-chairperson Ohio State Gender Fairness Task Force. Trustee Siena Heights Coll., Adrian, Mich., 1982—; organizer Crime Stopper Inc., Toledo, 1981—; mem. Mayor's Drug Coun.; bd. dirs. Guest House Inc. Named to Ohio Women's Hall of Fame, 1995; recipient Gertrude W. Donahey award, Ohio Democratic Party, 1999, Woman of Toledo award, St. Vincent Mercy Medical Ctr., 1999. Mem. ABA, Toledo Bar Assn., Lucas County Bar Assn., Ohio State Bar Assn. (Nettie Cronise Lutes award 1995), Nat. Assn. Women Judges (Making A Difference award 1996), Am. Judicature Soc., Toledo Women's Bar Assn., Ohio State Women's Bar Assn. (Alice Robie Resnick Outstanding Lawyer award 1998), Toledo Mus. Art, Internat. Inst. Toledo. Roman Catholic. Personal E-mail: icenick@aol.com.

RESNICK, DONALD IRA, lawyer; b. Chgo., July 19, 1950; s. Roland S. and Marilyn B. (Weiss) R.; m. Jill Allison White, July 3, 1977; children: Daniel, Allison. BS with high honors, U. Ill., 1972; JD, Harvard U., 1975. Bar: Ill. 1975, U.S. Dist. Ct. (no. dist.) Ill. 1975. Assoc. Arvey, Hodes, Costello & Burman, Chgo., 1975-80, ptnr., 1981-83; sr. ptnr. Nagelberg & Resnick, Chgo., 1983-89, Levenstein & Resnick, Chgo., 1989-91; chmn. real estate dept. Jenner & Block, Chgo., 1992—. Mem. mgmt. com. Jenner & Block, Chgo. Mem. ABA, Birchwood (Highland Park, Ill.) Club. Office: Jenner & Block 1 E Ibm Plz Fl 4000 Chicago IL 60611-7603 E-mail: dresnick@jenner.com.

RESNICK, IDRIAN NAVARRE, foundation administrator; b. Wichita, Kans., Apr. 24, 1936; s. Herbert and Virginiae Miriam (Goldsmith) Speer; m. Jane Letham Riley (div. 1980); children: Michael Mosi, David Shaka; m. Louise LaMontagne, 1996. BA, Clark U., 1958; MA, Boston U., 1961, PhD, 1966. Lectr. dept. econs. Boston U., 1962-63; asst. prof. econs. Howard U., Washington, 1963-64; lectr. econs. U. Dar es Salaam, Tanzania, 1964-67; vis. prof. econs. Princeton (N.J.) U., 1967-68; asst. prof. econs. Columbia U., NYC, 1968-70; sr. economist Ministry Econ. Planning, Dar es Salaam, 1970-72; exec. dir. Econ. Devel. Bur., New Haven, 1974-81; pres. Resnick Devel. Svcs., Branford, Conn., 1985—; exec. dir. Assn. Am. Indian Affairs, NYC, 1985—89, Action for Corp. Accountability, New Haven, 1991—94; fiction writer, 1995—; tchr. ESL, 1998—2006. Prof. Cornell U., Ithaca, N.Y., 1982-84; cons. Govt. of Nicaragua, Managua, 1979-81, Govt. of the Netherlands, The Hague, 1977, Govt. of Somalia, Mogodishu, 1985. Author: The Long Transition: Building Socialism in Tanzania, 1981, Controlling Consulting, 1989; editor: Tanzania: Revolution by Education, 1968; video producer (in the Lakota lang.) AIDS, 1989; contbr. articles to profl. jours. Organizer Namibia Com., New Haven, 1977-79, Conn. Task Force on Cen. Am., 1985; mem. Pledge of Resistance, U.S., 1985-89; vol. adviser AIDS Interfaith Network, New Haven, 1990. Nat. Edn. scholar U.S. Govt., 1959-62; Albert Schweitzer Resh fellow Columbia U., 1969-70. Avocations: chess, theater, travel, tennis, golf. Home: 16 Old Pawson Rd Branford CT 06405-5117 Office Fax: 203-481-4802.

RESNICK, IRVEN MICHAEL, philosophy educator; b. Rochester, NY, Nov. 22, 1952; s. William Resnick and Mary Eskenazi; m. Elizabeth Anne Scofield, May 28, 1989; children: Austin Scofield, Matthew Scofield, Ariel Resnick. BA, Tulane U., 1974; MA, Cath. U. Am., 1980; PhD, U. Va., 1983. Asst. prof. La. State U., Baton Rouge, 1987-90; prof. Dept. Philosophy and Religion U. Tenn., Chattanooga, 1990—. Chair of excellence in Judaic studies; sr. assoc. Oxford Ctr. for Hebrew and Jewish Studies, 2003—. Author: Divine Power and Possibility in St. Peter Damian's De Divina Omnipotentia, 1992, Two Theological Treatises of Odo of Tournai, 1994; co-author, translator: Albertus Magnus On Animals, 1999, An Annotated Bibliography of Albert the Great (1900-2000), 2004, The Letters of Peter Damian, 121-150, 2004, The Letters of Peter Damian, 151-180, 2005, Petrus Alfonsi's Dialogue against the Jews, 2006. Jerusalem Trust fellow Oxford Ctr. for Hebrew Std., Yarnton, Eng., 1995, corr. fellow Ingeborg Rennert Ctr., Bar-Ilan U., Israel, 1996, C.G. Found. Jerusalem Project, Bar-Ilan U., 1996; named disting. vis. fellow Queen Mary, U. London, 2006. Mem.: Medieval Acad. Am., Assn. for Jewish Studies, Soc. for Medieval and Renaissance Philosophy, Oxford Ctr. for Hebrew and Jewish Studies (sr.). Home: 204 Slayton St Signal Mountain TN 37377-2285 Office: U Tenn Chattanooga 615 Mccallie Ave Chattanooga TN 37403-2504 Office Phone: 423-425-4446. Office Fax: 423-425-4153. Business E-Mail: Irven-Resnick@utc.edu.

RESNICK, JEFFREY I., plastic surgeon; b. Jersey City, Mar. 2, 1954; s. Victor and Regina (Bistritz) R.; m. Michele Gail Zinger, July 12, 1981; children: Andrew Gregory, Daniel Zachary. BS, Yale U., 1975; MD, U. Pa., 1980. Diplomate Am. Bd. Surgery, Am. Bd. Plastic Surgery. Resident in surgery Mass. Gen. Hosp., Boston, 1980—85, resident in plastic surgery, 1985—87; asst. clin. prof. plastic surgery UCLA, 1987—, fellow in craniofacial surgery, 1987—88; full time asst. prof. clin. surgery U. So. Calif, Santa Monica, 1998—. Contbr. articles to profl. jours. Surgeon Interplast, Vietnam, Nepal, Myanmar. Mem. Am. Assn. Plastic Surgeons., Am. Soc. Plastic Surgeons, Am. Soc. Maxillofacial Surgeons, Am. Cleft Palate-Craniofacial Assn., Plastic Surgery Ednl. Found., Sigma Xi, Alpha Omega Alpha. Office: 1301 20th St Ste 470 Santa Monica CA 90404-2082 Home Phone: 310-471-3532; Office Phone: 310-315-0222. Business E-Mail: jresnick@ucla.edu.

RESNICK, KENNETH, photography director; b. NYC, May 11, 1934; s. Reuben and Helen (Edelson) R.; m. Marijke Koch, Aug. 1960 (div. Aug. 1974); children: Sonya, Paul, Karen; m. Karen louise Matthesius, July 23, 1977; children: Margaret Rose, Charles Andrew. Student, Trinity Coll., 1952—56. Dir. photography Ga. Ctr., U. Ga., Athens, 1960-61; cameraman, editor Milner and Fenwick, Inc., Balt., 1961-63; film maker US Info. Agy., Washington, 1963-66; producer Nat. Ednl. TV, NYC, 1965; cameraman, asst. cameraman NBC-TV, Washington, 1967-68; chief photographer Md. Ctr. for Pub. Broadcasting Sta. WMPB-TV, Owings Mills, 1968-69; cameraman, asst. dir. BF&J Prodns., Balt., 1969-72; news film cameraman Sta. WTTG-TV, Metromedia Prodns., Washington, 1972-78; producer, videographer Cable News Network, Atlanta, 1981-82; video producer Wang Labs., Inc., Lowell, Mass., 1986-90; freelance dir. photography. Instr. Md. Inst. Coll. of Art, Balt., 1968-73; guest lectr. Goucher Coll, Towsen, Md., 1969-70, Caselton (Vt.) State Coll., 1985; conf. participant Arts and Soc., Morgan State Coll, Balt., 1966. Co-produced, co-directed, cinematographer Sunday on the River, 1962 (Bronze medal, Silver Gondola award humanitarian idealism in film Venice Internat. Documentary Film Festival 1962, An Outstanding Film of Yr. Brit. Film Inst. and London Film Festival 1962, Golden Eagle award Council Internat. Nontheatrical Events 1962, 63, work inducted in the Mus. Modern Art Film Archives 1991); produced, directed, photgraphed Men, Marble and Machines, 1984 (Bronze medal Internat. Film and TV Festival of NYC 1984, Golden Eagle award, 1984 Chris plaque Columbus Film Festival 1985, Emmy award 1987); photographed Now and in the Future (Silver Plaque INTERCOM 1988); producer, dir., photographer A Celebration of Architecture (Gold Camera award, 3 Silver Screen awards, U.S. Indsl. Film and Video Festival 1989, Gold CINDY award, Rose Layos Green Meml. award 1989, Chris award Columbus Film Festival 1989, Silver Plaque INTERCOM, 1989, 2 Silver Medals Internat. Film & TV Festival N.Y. 1990, Golden Eagle award 1990). Mem. World Wildlife Found., Wilderness Soc., Nature Conservancy. Recipient First Prize Gen. News Class award, 1973, Spot News Class award, 1976, 78, White House News Photographer's Assn., First Place Spot News award Nat. Press Photographer's Assn., 1978, Emmy news film photography Washington Chpt. Nat. Acad. TV Arts and Scis., Inc., 1978. Mem. Internat. Photographers of Motion Picture and TV Industries (local 600), Sierra Club. Democrat. Unitarian Universalist. Home: 73 Washington St Concord NH 03301-4172

RESNICK, KIRSTEN FAY MARKUSON, history professor; b. Torrance, Calif., Aug. 22; d. Daniel Maxwell Gluck and Miriam Priscilla Anne Sheridan; m. William David Crook, Mar. 11, 2000; children: Micah James Resnick Crook, Kira Danielle Resnick Crook. Student, UCLA, 1980—81; BA, U. Calif., Santa Barbara, 1985, MA, 1994; adult edn. credential, Calif. State U. Dominguez Hills, Carson, 1998. Cert. adult edn. tchr. Calif. Tchr. various elem and HS, Mombasa, Kenya, 1981—91; tchr. asst. black studies U. Calif., Santa Barbara, 1991, tchg. asst. history of western civilization, 1992—94; tchr. Met. Sch. Ctr., LA, 1997—2000, County Clerical Cert. Program, LA, 1998—2001; adj. prof. history Coll. of Canyons, Santa Clarita, Calif., 2001—, El Camino Coll., Torrance, Calif., 2002—, Chapman Coll., Manhattan Beach, Calif., 2007. Spkr. in field; tchr. adults various vol. orgns., 1980—; cons. to home-schooling families. Author written/oral expression curriculum. Advisor homeless adolescents, Hollywood, Calif., 1986—88; presch. tchr. El Segundo, 2002—. Recipient Achievement award, Nat. Assn. Counties, 2000, award, 14th Ann. Productivity and Quality Awards Projects, LA County, 2000. Mem.: Orgn. Am. Historians, Western Assn. Women Educators. Avocations: wedding coordinating, collecting vintage clothing.

RESNICK, LYNDA, corporate financial executive; Co-owner, vice chmn. Franklin Mint; co-owner Roll Internat. Chmn. Teleflora. Chmn. mktg. com. Conservation Internat.; bd. dirs. Assn. for Cure of Cancer of the Prostate, CaP CURE, Milken Family Found.; mem. exec. com., trustee, chmn. acquisitions com. L.A. County Mus. Art; mem. com. on sculpture and decorative arts Met. Mus. Art; trustee Phila. Mus. Art. Recipient Gold Effie award, 1983; named one of Top 50 U.S. Women Bus. Owners, Working Women, #1 L.A.-based woman Bus. Owner, L.A. bus. Jour., one of top 100 U.S. art collectors Art & Antiques mag. Office: Roll Internat Corp 11444 W Olympic Blvd Los Angeles CA 90064-1549

RESNICK, MARTIN I., urologist, educator; b. Bklyn., Jan. 12, 1943; s. Daniel and Bertha (Becker) R.; m. Victoria Klein, July 4, 1965; children: Andrew Howard, Jeffrey Scott. BA, Alfred U., NYC, 1964; MD, Bowman Gray Sch. Medicine, Winston-Salem, NC, 1969; MS, Northwestern U., Evanston, Ill., 1973. Diplomate Am. Bd. Urology. Instr. urology Northwestern U., Chgo., 1974-75, Bowman Gray Sch. Medicine, 1974-77, asst. prof., 1977-79, assoc. prof., 1979-81; prof., chmn. dept. urology Case Western Res. U., Cleve., 1981—, prof. oncology, 1987—. NIH awardee. Mem. Am. Urol. Assn. (pres. 2003-04), Am. Bd. Urology (pres. 2002-03), Alpha Omega Alpha. Jewish. Avocation: running. Office: 11100 Euclid Ave Cleveland OH 44106-5046 Office Phone: 216-844-3011. Business E-Mail: martin.resnick@case.edu.

RESNICK, MYRON JAY, retired insurance company executive, lawyer; b. Louisville, July 13, 1931; s. Harry C. and Sybil G. (Glick) R.; m. Alicia M. Ward, Dec. 16, 1967; children— Hugh, Clay, David. BS in Econs., U. Pa., 1953; JD, U. Mich., 1956. Various positions Allstate Ins. Co., Northbrook, Ill., 1959-88, sr. v.p., treas. bd. dirs., 1959-95; chmn. bd. Federated Ins. Co. Ltd. (UK), Sale, Cheshire, England, 1979-81; ret., 1995. Dir. Allstate Ins. Co. Ltd. (U.K.), Sale; pres. Allstate Investment Mgmt. Co.; mem. adj. faculty John Marshall Law Sch., Chgo., 1996-98. Chmn. Chgo. exec. com. Anti-Defamation League, 1975—; bd. dirs. Chgo. Urban League, 1987-2001, St. Scholastica High Sch., Chgo., 1977-79; trustee George Williams Coll., Downers Grove, Ill., 1981-93, chmn. bd. trustees, 1991-93; trustee Aurora U., 1993—; bd. advisors Inst. Law and Econs. U. Pa., 1994—. With U.S. Army, 1956-58. Mem. ABA, Chgo. Bar Assn., Ill. Bar Assn., Assn. Life Ins. Counsel, Chgo. Mortgage Attys. Assn. (bd. dirs. 1965-75), Reform Club (London). E-mail: amresnick@aol.com.

RESNICK, PHILLIP STANLEY, lawyer; b. Mpls., July 19, 1944; s. Sidney L. and Rae J. (Barres) Resnick; children: Allison, David. BA, U. Minn., 1967; JD, William Mitchell Coll., 1971. Bar: Minn. 1971, U.S. Dist. Ct. Minn. 1972, U.S. Ct. Appeals (8th cir.) 1972, U.S. Supreme Ct. 1977. Pres. Phillip S. Resnick & Assocs., Mpls. Mem.: ABA, Hennepin County Bar Assn., Minn. Assn. Criminal Def. Lawyers (bd. dirs., pres. 1995—), Minn. Trial Lawyers Assn., Minn. Bar Assn., Nat. Assn. Criminal Def. Lawyers. Address: Phillip S Resnick & Assocs 527 Marquette Ave Ste 1925 Minneapolis MN 55402-1334

RESNICK, RHODA BRODOWSKY, psychotherapist; b. Mar. 22, 1930; d. Isador and Rose (Wasserman) Brodowsky; m. Jack H. Resnick, May 21, 1950; children: Steven E., Caryn B. BS, CCNY, 1951; MS, Queens Coll., 1973; postgrad., Hunter Coll. Tchr. N.Y.C. Bd. Edn., 1960—80, guidance counselor, 1980—; psychotherapist L.I. Cons. Ctr., 1973—77; pvt. practice psychotherapy, 1975—. Fellow, L.I. Inst. Mental Health, 1975. Mem.: PGA, United Fedn. Tchrs., Am. Pers. and Guidance Assn., PGA Hole in One Club, Am. Contract Bridge League (Bronze life). Home: 340 E 64th St New York NY 10021-7503 E-mail: xrojac@hotmail.com.

RESNICK, ROBERT, physicist, researcher; b. Balt., Jan. 11, 1923; s. Abraham and Anna (Dubin) R.; m. Mildred Saltzman, Oct. 14, 1945; children— Trudy, Abby, Regina. AB, Johns Hopkins U., 1943, PhD (Pres.'s Fund scholar 1946-49), 1949. Physicist NACA, Cleve., 1944-46; asst. prof., assoc. prof. physics U. Pitts., 1949-56; assoc. prof., prof. physics Rensselaer Poly. Inst., Troy, NY, 1956-93; prof. emeritus, 1993—; chmn. interdisciplinary sci. curriculum Rensselaer Poly. Inst., Troy, NY, 1973-88, Edward P. Hamilton Disting. prof. sci., 1975-93; hon. research fellow Harvard U., 1964-65; Fulbright prof. Peru, 1971. Hon. vis. prof. Peoples Republic of China, 1981, 85; mem. Commn. on Coll. Physics, 1960-68; commencement speaker Rensselaer Poly. Inst., 1993; mem. U.S. adv. bd. Quantum Joint USSR/USA sci. mag., 1989-93. Author: A Manual for Laboratory Physics, 1954, (with D. Halliday) Physics, 1960, 3d edit., 1978, 4th edit., 1991, 5th edit., 2000, (with Halliday and Krane) extended version, 1986, 2d edit. extended version, 1991, 3rd edit., 2000, 5th edit., 2003, (with Halliday and Krane) Introduction to Special Relativity, 1968, (with R. Eisberg) Notes on Quantum Theory, 1968, Notes on Modern Physics, 1969, Quantum Physics of Atoms, Molecules, Solids, Nuclei and Particles, 1974, 2d edit., 1985, (with D. Halliday) Fundamentals of Physics, 1970, 5th edit., 1996, extended version, 1988, 2d edit., 1993, 3rd edit., 1996, 4th edit., 1999, (with J. Walker and D. Halliday) 7th edit., 2004, (with others) Student Study Guide for Physics, 1970, 6th edit., 2001, Basic Concepts in Relativity and Early Quantum Theory, 1972, 2d edit., 1985, Basic Concepts in Relativity, 1991; author: (with others) Sourcebook for Programmable Calculators, 1978, (with E. Derringh) Solutions to Physics Problems, 1980, 5th edit., 1996, (with K. Brownstein) Tests for Physics, 1987, (with J. Walker and D. Halliday) CD Physics, 1993, 3rd edit., 2000; books translated into numerous fgn. langs; So You Want to Write a Textbook, 1999 (video); mem. adv. bd., project staff: Physical Science for Non-Scientists, 1964-68, pub., 1968; co-dir.: Project Physics Demonstration Experiments, 1962-70; pub. project, 1970, Workshop on Apparatus for College Physics, 1964-65, 66, Videotapes in Physics Instruction, 1975-78; dir. Physics Demonstration and Laboratory Apparatus Workshop, 1960-61; adv. editor: John Wiley & Sons, Inc., 1967-89, Macmillan Pubs., 1990-94. Recipient Disting. Svc. citation Am. Assn. Physics Tchrs., 1967, Hans Christian Oersted medal, 1974, Disting. Alumnae award Johns Hopkins U., 2005; named to Hall of Fame, Balt. City Coll., 1989, Rensselaer Poly. Inst., 2003; Robert Resnick Ctr. for Physics established at Rensselaer Poly. Inst., 1993, Robert Resnick Ann. Sci. Lectr. series endowed, 1993. Fellow AAAS, Am. Phys. Soc.; mem. AAUP, Am. Assn. Physics Tchrs. (v.p. 1986, pres.-elect 1987, pres. 1988), Am. Soc. Engring. Edn., Am. Inst. Physics (governing bd. 1987-90, mem. coun. Ctr. for History of Physics 1997—), Philosophic Soc. South Fla. (exec. bd. 1997-2000), Textbook Author Assn. (coun. 1990-93), Phi Beta Kappa, Sigma Xi. Achievements include rsch. publs. in aerodynamics, nuclear physics, atomic physics, upper atmosphere physics, history of physics, physics edn. Home: 5757 Bartlett St Pittsburgh PA 15217 Personal E-mail: resnir@aol.com.

RESNICK, SCOTT N., real estate company executive; s. Burton P. Resnick. Grad., NYU. With Sonnenblick-Goldman Co.; joined Jack Resnick & Sons Inc., NYC, 1989, named v.p., 1991, mng. dir., exec. mng. dir. leasing & mgmt., 1995—2000, pres & COO, 2000—. Dir. comml. bd. Realty Adv. Bd. on Labor Rels. Inc. Bd. trustees Whitney Mus. Am. Art, NYC, The Phipps Housing Group; bd. dirs. Grand Ctrl. Partnership. Mem.: Real Estate Bd. NY (bd. governors). Office: Jack Resnick & Sons Inc 110 E 59th St New York NY 10022 Office Phone: 212-421-1300. Office Fax: 212-758-2948.

RESNICK, STEPHANIE, lawyer; b. NYC, Nov. 12, 1959; d. Diane Gross. AB, Kenyon Coll., 1981; JD, Villanova U., 1984. Bar: Pa. 1984, N.J. 1984, U.S. Dist Ct. (ea. dist.) Pa. 1984, U.S. Dist Ct. N.J. 1984, N.Y. 1990, U.S. Ct. Appeals (3d cir.) 1993, U.S. Dist. Ct. (so. dist.) N.Y. 1996, U.S. Dist. Ct. (ea. dist.) N.Y. 2001, U.S. Supreme Ct. 1998. Assoc. Cozen and O'Connor, Phila., 1984-87, Fox, Rothschild LLP, Phila., 1987-92, ptnr., 1992—. Mem. exec. com. Fox, Rothschild LLP, 2003—06, co-chair litigation dept., 2007—. Mem.: ABA, Am. Law Inst., Womens Way (vice-chair 2002, chair 2003—04), N.Y. Bar Assn., N.J. Bar Assn., Phila. Bar Assn. (investigative divsn. Commn. on Jud. Selection and Retention 1988—94, profl. guidance com. 1992—96, profl. responsibility com. 1992—2000, women in the profession com. 1993—, women's rights com. chair 1995—96, Comm. on Jud. Selection and Retention 1995—2001, chair 1997, fed. cts. com. 2000—, chair 2002—03, bd. govs. 2006—07, vice chair 2007), Pa. Bar Assn. (disciplinary bd. and study com. 1989—91, prof. liability com. 1991—92, commr. on Women in the Profession 1997). Office: Fox Rothschild LLP 2000 Market St Ste 10 Philadelphia PA 19103-3231 Home: 233 S 6th St Apt 2107 Philadelphia PA 19106-3756 Office Phone: 215-299-2082. E-mail: sresnick@foxrothschild.com.

RESNICK, STEWART ALLEN, diversified company executive; b. Jersey City, Dec. 24, 1936; s. David and Yetta (Goldmaker) R.; children from previous marriage: Jeffrey Brian, Ilene Sue, William Jay; m. Lynda Rae Harris, Nov. 26, 1972; children: Jonathan Charles Sinay, Jason Daniel Sinay. BS, UCLA, 1959, LLB, 1962. Co-chmn., CEO, pres. Roll Internat. Corp., LA; chmn., CEO The Franklin Mint, Aston, Pa., 1985—; co-chmn., CEO Teleflora, LA; pres. Paramount Farms, Inc., LA; other subsidiaries of Roll Internat. Corp. include Paramount Citrus, Fiji Water, POM Wonderful. Bd. trustees J. Paul Getty Trust, LA, 2005—; mem. bd. Caltech, Bard Coll., Conservation Internat. Avocation: health and fitness related activities. Office: Roll Internat Corp 10th Fl 11444 W Olympic Blvd Los Angeles CA 90064 Office Phone: 310-966-5700. Office Fax: 310-914-4747.

RESNICOW, NORMAN JAKOB, lawyer; b. NYC, July 23, 1947; s. Herbert and Melly (Engelberg) R.; m. Barbara Jane Roses, June 14, 1970; children: Daniel Ilan, Joel Ethan. BA summa cum laude, Yale U., 1969, JD, 1972. Bar: N.Y. 1973, U.S. Dist. Ct. (so. and ea. dists.) N.Y. 1973. Assoc. Baker & McKenzie, NYC, 1972-79, ptnr., 1979-98, Piper, Marbury Rudnick & Wolff, NYC, 1998-2000, Fox Horan & Camerini, NYC, 2000—. Term mem. Council Fgn. Relations, N.Y.C., 1976-81; exec. com., vice chair, v.p., treas., bd. dirs. Hebrew Immigrant Aid Soc., N.Y.C., 1981—; mem. nat. young leadership cabinet United Jewish Appeal, N.Y.C., 1978-83. Recipient Young Leadership award United Jewish Appeal-Fedn. Jewish Philanthrophies, 1978. Mem. ABA (corp. bus. and banking law, internat. law sects.), Assn. of Bar of City of N.Y. (internat. trade com. 1987-89, com. nuclear law and tech. 1992-98), N.Y. State Bar Assn. (internat. law com. 1985-87, internat. employement law com. 1997-99), Phi Beta Kappa. Democrat. Avocation: international political relations. Office: Fox Horan & Camerini LLP 825 Third Ave New York NY 10022 Home: 71 Washington PL Apt 1A New York NY 10011-9184 Office Phone: 212-709-0281. Business E-Mail: njresnicow@foxlex.com.

RESNIK, HARVEY LEWIS PAUL, psychiatrist; b. Buffalo, Apr. 6, 1930; s. Samuel and Celia (Greenberg) R.; m. Audrey Ruth Frey, Aug. 30, 1964 (dec. 1993); children: Rebecca Gabrielle, Henry Seth Maccabee, Jessica Ruth. BA magna cum laude, U. Buffalo, 1951; MD, Columbia, 1955; grad., Phila. Psychoanalytic Inst., 1967. Diplomate: Am. Bd. Psychiatry and Neurology. Intern Phila. Gen. Hosp., 1955-56, resident in surgery, 1956-57; resident in psychiatry Jackson Meml. Hosp., Miami, Fla., 1959-61; fellow U. Pa. Hosp., 1961-62, mem. staff, 1962-67; instr; Sch. Medicine, U. Pa., 1962-66; instr. med. hypnosis Sch. Medicine, U. Pa. (Grad. Sch. Medicine), 1963-65; clin. dir. psychiatry E. J. Meyer Meml. Hosp., Buffalo, 1967, dir. psychiatry, 1968; from assoc. prof. to prof., dep. chair Sch. Medicine, SUNY at Buffalo, Buffalo, 1968—70; chief Nat. Center for Studies of Suicide Prevention, NIMH, 1969-74, chief mental health emergencies sect., 1974-76; with Reproductive Biology Rsch. Found., St. Louis, 1971; clin. prof. psychiatry and behavioral sci. Sch. Medicine, George Washington U., 1969—2002, prof. emeritus clin. psychiatry and behavioral scis., 2002—; dir. Human Behavior Found., 1975—; lectr. Sch. Medicine, Johns Hopkins, Balt., 1969-74; adj. lectr. Johns Hopkins U. Sch. Pub. Health, Balt., 1981-82. Prof. cmty. health Fed. City Coll., 1971-75; med. dir. Johns Hopkins U. Compulsive Gambling Ctr., 1981-83; med. dir. alcohol and substance abuse program, College Park, 1986-2000; vis. prof. Katholieke U., Leuven, Belgium, 1986-93; cons. to Sec.-Gen. Ministry of Health, Belgium, 1986-90, NATO fellow, 1986-87; cons. various hosps. and orgns., Medicare, Pa. Blue Shield, 1984-96, Trailblazer Health, 1996-99, Blue Cross/Blue Shield S.C., 1999; sr. attending Suburban Hosp., Bethesda, Md., 1976—, psychiatry chair, 2006—. Author: Suicidal Behaviors: Diagnosis and Management, 1968, 2d edit., 1994, (with M. E. Wolfgang) Treatment of the Sexual Offender, 1971, Sexual Behaviors: Social, Clinical and Legal Aspects, 1972, (with B. Hathorne) Suicide Prevention in the Seventies, 1973, (with H.L. Ruben) Emergency Psychiatric Care, 1974, (with others) The Prediction of Suicide, 1974, Emergency and Disaster Management, 1976; (with J.T. Mitchell) Emergency Response to Crisis, 1981; editor: Bull. Suicidology, 1969-74; contbr. articles to profl. jours. Mem. Addictions Adv. Bd. Prince Georges County, 1980-85. Served to capt. USAF, 1957-59, ETO-Middle East; capt. USNR; ret. Decorated officer Order of Crown (Belgium), 1989. Fellow Am. Coll. Mental Health Adminstrs. (life), Am. Coll. Psychiatrists (life), Am. Psychiat. Assn. (life); mem. Med-Chi of Md., Prince Georges County Med. Soc. (co-chair joint com. with Bar Assn. 1996-2001), Montgomery County Med. Soc., Washington Psychiatry Soc., Am. Acad. Psychiatry and Law (suicidology com. 1998-2000), Phila. Psychoanalytic Soc., NIH Alumni Assn., Columbia U. Med. Alumni Assn. (bd. dirs. 1993-95), Cosmos Club (Washington), Phi Beta Kappa, Beta Sigma Rho (grand vice warden 1963). Jewish. Office: 4209 Bradley Ln Chevy Chase MD 20815-5234

RESNIK, ROBERT, medical educator; b. New Haven, Dec. 7, 1938; s. Nathan Alfred and Elsie (Hershman) R.; m. Lauren Brahms, Oct. 29, 1966; children: Andrew Scott, Jamie Layne. BA, Yale U., 1960; MD, Case Western Res. U., 1965. Intern in internal medicine Mt. Sinai Hosp., Cleve., 1965-66; resident in ob-gyn. Yale U. Sch. Medicine, 1966-70; asst. prof. Sch. Medicine U. Calif., San Diego, 1974-78, assoc. prof., 1978-82, prof. reproductive medicine, 1982—, chmn. dept., 1982-95, dean clin. affairs, 1988-90, dean admissions, 1995—2003. Cons. Nat. Heart, Lung and Blood Inst. NIH, Washington, 1987; mem. exec. com. Coun. Residency Edn. Ob-Gyn, Washington, 1988-94, residency rev. com., 1988-94. Editor: (textbook) Maternal-Fetal Medicine: Principles and Practice, 1984, 5th edit., 2004; contbr. numerous articles to profl. jours. Major U.S. Army, 1970-72. Recipient Lifetime Achievement award, Soc. Maternal Fetal Medicine, 2004, Mentor of Yr., U. Calif. San Diego, 2005; Rsch. grantee, Nat. Found., NIH. Fellow: Royal Coll. Obstet. Gynecologists (ad eundem), N.W. Obstet. Gynecological Soc., Pacific Coast Obstet. and Gynecol. Soc., Am. Coll. Ob-Gyn. (vice chmn. obs. practice com. 1998—2000), New England Obstet. Gynecological Soc.; mem.: San Diego Gynecol. Soc. (pres. 1982), Am. Gynecologic and Obstet. Soc. (treas. 2003—), Perinatal Rsch. Soc. (pres. 1985), Soc. Gynecologic Investigation (coun. 1983—88), Yale Club, Am. Gynecol. Club (pres. 2002—03). Office: UCSD Med Ctr 200 W Arbor Dr 8433 San Diego CA 92103-8433 Business E-Mail: rresnik@ucsd.edu.

RESO, ANTHONY, geologist, educator, earth resources economist; b. London, Eng., Aug. 10, 1931; arrived in US, 1940, naturalized, 1952; AB, Columbia Coll., 1954; MA, Columbia U., 1955; postgrad., U. Cin., 1956—57; PhD, Rice U., 1960; postgrad., Grad. Sch. Bus. U. Houston, 1964—68. Instr. geology Queens Coll., Flushing, NY, 1954; geologist Atlantic Richfield Corp., Midland, Tex., 1955—56; asst. prof. geology and curator invertebrate paleontology Pratt Mus., Amherst Coll., Mass., 1959—62; staff rsch. geologist Tenneco Oil Co., Houston, 1962—86; mgr. geol. Peak Prodn. Co., Houston, 1986—, v.p., 1988—, bd. dirs., 2000—. Cons. in geol. rsch. Tenn. Gas and Oil Co., 1960—61; lectr. U. Houston, 1962—65; vis. prof. Rice U., 1980; mem. bd. advisers Gulf Univs. Rsch. Corp., Galveston, Tex., 1967—75, chmn., 1968—69. Contbr. articles to profl. jours. Grantee Rsch., Eastman Fund, 1962, NSF fellow, 1958—59. Fellow: AAAS, Geol. Soc. Am. (com. investments 1984—95, chmn. 1985—92, budget com. 1993—95, found. trustee 1999—2004, Rsch. grantee 1958, Disting. Svc. award 1996); mem.: English-Speaking Union U.S. (dir. Houston br. 1978—, v.p. 1982—88, mem. scholarship com. 1988—97, chmn. 1991—97, pres. 1997—98), Houston Geol. Soc. (v.p. 1973—75, pres. 1975—76, chmn. constn. revision com. 1981, Disting. Svc. award 1985), Paleontol. Rsch. Instn., Am. Assn. Petroleum Geologists (life; com. convs. 1977—83, gen. chmn. nat. conv. 1979, chmn. 1980—83, com. investments 1982—88, chmn. com. group ins. 1986—88, treas. 1986—88, found. trustee assoc. 1991, Rsch. grantee 1958, 1959, Disting. Svc. award 1985), SEPM Soc. for Sedimentary Geology (com. investments 1990—2004, chmn. 1992—95, treas. SEPM Found. 1997—2003, Disting. Svc. award 2003), Paleontol. Soc., Varsity C Club, Beta Theta Pi, Sigma Gamma Epsilon, Sigma Xi. Episcopalian. Home: 1805 Brun St Houston TX 77019-5712 Office: care Peak Prodn Co PO Box 130785 Houston TX 77219-0785 Personal E-mail: aresogeo@swbell.net.

RESOR, RANDOLPH RICHARDSON, transportation consultant; b. White Plains, NY, Sept. 3, 1952; s. Robert Reuben and Julie Houston (Harper) R.; m. Carol Diane Wahl, June 8, 1991; children: Joy Patricia, Robert Randolph. BA, U. Chgo., 1975. Spl. asst. exec. dept. Assn. Am. RRS., Washington, 1977-78; analyst maintenance of way U.S. Railway Assn., Washington, 1978-80; mem. profl. staff Dynatrend, Inc., Arlington, Va., 1980; sr. systems analyst Advanced Tech., Inc., McLean, Va., 1981; project mgr. Met. Transp. Authority, NYC, 1982-84; asst. dir. planning N.Y.C. Transit Authority, Bklyn., 1984-87; dir. costing and pricing Zeta-Tech. Assocs., Inc., Cherry Hill, N.J., 1987-92, v.p. costing and econ. analysis, 1992—. Contbr. articles to profl. jours. Recipient Rail Transp. award ASME, 1992, Special Act award, FRA, 2001. Mem. Transp. Rsch. Forum (Cost Analysis Rsch. award, 1992), Rotary Internat. Republican. Methodist. Avocations: bicycling, rowing, hist. rsch. Office: Zeta-Tech Assocs Inc 900 Kings Hwy N Ste 208 Cherry Hill NJ 08034-1516 Office Phone: 856-779-7795. Business E-Mail: resor@zetatech.com.

RESOR, STANLEY ROGERS, retired lawyer; b. NYC, Dec. 5, 1917; s. Stanley Burnet and Helen (Lansdowne) Resor; m. Jane Lawler Pillsbury, Apr. 4, 1942 (dec.); children: Stanley R., Charles P., John L., Edmund L., William B., James P., Thomas S.; m. Louise Mead Walker, May 1, 1999. BA, Yale U., 1939, LLB, 1946. Bar: N.Y. 1947. From assoc. to ptnr. Debevoise & Plimpton, NYC, 1946-65, 71-73, 79-87, of counsel, 1988-90; undersec. Dept. Army, 1965, sec., 1965-71, amb. negotiations Mut. and Balanced Force Reductions in Ctrl. Europe, 1973-78; undersec. policy Dept. Def., 1978-79; ret., 1990. Fellow Yale Corp., 1979—86. Served to maj. US Army, 1942—45. Decorated Silver Star US Army, Bronze Star, Puple Heart; recipient George C. Marshall award, Assn. U.S. Army, 1974, Sylvanus Thayer award, Assn. Graduates U.S. Mil. Acad., 1984. Mem.: ABA, Internat. Inst. Strategic Studies, Lawyers Alliance World Security, Coun. Fgn. Rels., Arms Control Assn. (chmn. bd. dirs. 1994—2000), Atlantic Coun., Assn. Bar City of N.Y., UN Assn. U.S.A. Republican. Episcopalian. Home: 809 Weed St New Canaan CT 06840-4023

RESPELIERS, PATRICK J., lawyer; s. John Joseph and Lucille Ann Respeliers; m. Monica Jeanne Demma, May 29, 1987; children: Emily, Madeline, John Patrick. BSBA in Acctg., Creighton U., Omaha, 1984; JD, So. Meth. U., Dallas, 1987. Bar: Tex. 1987, Mo. 1996. Assoc. Akin Gump Strauss Hauer & Feld, Dallas, 1982—95; ptnr. Stinson Morrison Hecker LLP, Kansas City, Mo., 1995—. Mem.: aba, Mo. Bar Assn., Tex. Bar Assn. Avocations: remodeling, woodworking, reading, cycling. Office: Stinson Morrison Hecker LLP 1201 Walnut Kansas City MO 64106

RESS, CHARLES WILLIAM, management consultant; b. Columbus, Ohio, Aug. 6, 1933; s. George Leonard and Martha (Lake) R.; m. Virginia M. Beck, Aug. 28, 1954; children: Beverly Beck, Suzanne E., Charles W. Jr., Linda Perrins Foxworth, Jennifer Laurel Brulé. BS, Miami U., 1955; MA in Psychology, Rutgers U., 1969. Buyer The Higbee Co., Cleve., 1956-59; asst. to gen. mdse. mgr. The Halle Bros. Co., Cleve., 1959-64; research dir. The Associated Mdse. Corp., NYC, 1964-73; v.p. Mgmt. Horizons, Columbus, 1973-76; founder, chmn. bd. C.W. Ress & Assoc., Inc., Columbus, 1976-90; gen. mgr. Levi Strauss & Co., Columbus, 1990-94, mgmt. cons., 1994—. Lectr. in field. Author: Future Trends in Retailing, 1983, Trans National Retailing, 1988, Retailing 2000, 1991; contbr. articles to profl. jours. Republican. Avocations: cooking, wine tasting. Office: 3860 Lyon Dr Columbus OH 43220-4907 Office Phone: 614-457-8885. E-mail: ressandress@wowway.com.

RESSA, GREGORY JOHN, lawyer; b. Rockville Centre, NY, Oct. 3, 1962; s. Ames D. and Roslyn Maguire Ressa; 1 child, Margo Avallone. BA, Tufts U., 1984; JD, Fordham U., 1987. Bar: NY 1987. Assoc. Simpson Thacher & Bartlett LLP, NYC, 1987—95, ptnr., 1995—. Named a Dealmaker of Yr., Am. Lawyer mag., 2007. Mem.: Assn. Bar City NY. Office: Simpson Thacher & Bartlett 425 Lexington Ave New York NY 10017-3954 Office Phone: 212-455-7430. Office Fax: 212-455-2502. Business E-Mail: gressa@stblaw.com.

RESSEL, TERESA MULLETT, diversified financial services company executive, former federal agency administrator; BS in Engring., MS in Engring., U. Del.; MBA, Rensselaer Poly. Inst., 1990. V.p., chief compliance officer Kaiser Found. Health Plan, Inc., Kaiser Found. Hosps., Inc.; prin. dep. asst. sec. for mgmt. & budget US Dept. Treasury, Washington, 2001—02, asst. sec. for mgmt. & CFO, 2003—04; COO UBS Investment Bank, 2004—; CEO UBS Securities LLC, 2007—. Recipient Presdl. Citation for Outstanding Alumni Achievement, U. Del., 1996, Disting. Svc. award, US Dept. Treasury, 2003. Office: UBS Securities LLC UBS Warburg Ctr 677 Washington Blvd Stamford CT 06901 *

RESTANI, JANE A., federal judge; b. San Francisco, Feb. 27, 1948; d. Roy J. and Emilia C. Restani. BA, U. Calif., Berkeley, 1969; JD, U. Calif., Davis, 1973. Bar: Calif., 1973. Trial atty. U.S. Dept. Justice, Washington, 1973-76, asst. chief comml. litigation sect., 1976-80, dir. comml. litigation sect., 1980-83; judge U.S. Ct. Internat. Trade, NYC, 1983—2003, chief judge, 2003—. Mem. Order of Coif. Office: US Ct Internat Trade 1 Federal Plz New York NY 10278-0001

RESTIVO, JAMES JOHN, JR., lawyer; b. Pitts. s. James J. and Dorothy (Ardolino) R.; m. Gail Sharon Hackenburg, July 11, 1970; 4 children. BA in History, U. Pa., 1968; JD, Georgetown U., 1971. Bar: Pa. 1971, U.S. Dist. Ct. (we. and ea. dists.) Pa. 1971, U.S. Ct. Appeals (3d cir.) 1971, U.S. Supreme Ct. 1979. Ptnr. Reed Smith, Pitts., 1979—; head litig. dept. Reed, Smith, Shaw & McClay, Pitts., 1986-97. Mem. editl. bd.: Georgetown Law Rev., 1970—71. Bd. dirs. Rebuilding Together-Greater Pitts., Pitts. Regional Alliance. Fellow Am. Coll. Trial Lawyers; mem. Acad. Trial Lawyers Allegheny County, Allegheny County Bar Assn., Pa. Economy League (We. divsn.), Def. Rsch. Inst. Home: 209 Deer Meadow Dr Pittsburgh PA 15241-2253 Office: Reed Smith 435 6th Ave Ste 2 Pittsburgh PA 15219-1886 Home Phone: 412-835-2283; Office Phone: 412-288-3122. Business E-Mail: jrestivo@reedsmith.com.

RESTREPO, RUBEN DARIO, physician, educator; b. Medellin, Antioquia, Colombia, June 6, 1963; s. Jose Ignacio Restrepo and Maria Alma Panesso; m. Lorena Maria Fernandez, Dec. 1, 2002; children: Andrea, Natalia, Simon Usuga. MD, Universidad Pontificia Bolivariana, Medellin, Colombia, 1987; BS, Ga. State U., Atla., 1994. Primary care physician Comedal, Medellin, 1988—90; pediatric outreach program coord. St. Joseph's Hosp., Atla., 1991—92; pediatric ICU therapist Children's Healthcare of Atla., 1994—2005; clin. instr. Ga. State U., Atla., 1997—98, adj. faculty, 1998—99, asst. prof., 1999—2005; assoc. prof. U. Tex. Health Sci. Ctr., San Antonio, 2005—. Contbr. chapters to books, articles to profl. jours. Usher St. Matthew Cath. Ch., San Antonio, 2005—06; bd. mem. and vol. Habitat for Humanity, San Antonio; bd. mem. Office of Family Concerns, Atlanta, 1995—2002. Recipient Respiratory Therapy award, Am. Lung Assn., 1992, Academic Excellence award, Ga. State U., 1994, Berneice Castella Allied Health Aging Rsch. award, U. Tex. Health Sci. Ctr. San Antonio, 2006—; scholar James Ancil Lewis award, Ga. Soc. for Respiratory Care, 1992. Mem.: Am. Assn. for Respiratory Care, Am. Thoracic Soc., Am. Coll. Chest Physicians, Lambda Beta Soc. Catholic. Achievements include development of Educational CD. Avocations: travel, sports, computer technology. Office: Univ TexHealth Scis Ctr 7703 Floyd Curl Dr San Antonio TX 78229 Office Phone: 210-567-8858. Business E-Mail: restrepor@uthscsa.edu.

RESWICK, JAMES BIGELOW, former government official, biomedical engineer; b. Ellwood City, Pa., Apr. 16, 1922; s. Maurice and Katherine (Parker) R.; children: James Bigelow, David Parker (dec.), Pamela Reswick; m. Irmtraud Orthlies Hoelzerkopf, Dec., 27, 1973. SBME, MIT, 1943, SM, 1948, ScD, 1952; DEng (hon.), Rose Poly. Inst., 1968. Asst. prof., then assoc. prof., head machine design and graphics div. MIT, 1948-59; Leonard Case prof. engring., dir. Engring. Design Ctr., Case Western Res. U., 1959-70; prof. biomed. engring. and orthopaedics U. So. Calif., also dir. of rsch. dept. orthopaedics, 1970-80; assoc. dir. tech. Nat. Inst. Handicapped Rsch., U.S. Dept. Edn.; dir. VA Rehab. R & D Evaluation Unit VA Med. Ctr., Washington, 1984-88; dir. rsch. scis. Nat. Inst. on Disability and Rehab. Rsch. U.S. Dept. Edn., Washington, 1989—94; ret., 1994; acting dir. Nat. Inst. Disability and Rehab. Rsch., Washington, 1989-91. Engring. cons. on automatic control, product devel., automation and bio-med. engring. Mem. com. prosthetics R & D Nat. Acad. Scis., 1962-; chmn. design and devel. com.; mem. bd. rev. Army R & D Office, 1965-; mem. applied physiology and biomed. engring. study sect. NIH, 1972-. Author: (with C.K. Taft) Introduction to Dynamic Systems, 1967; also articles.; Editor: (with F.T. Hambrecht) Functional Electrical Stimulation, 1977; series on engring. design, 1963-; inventor, patentee in field. Chmn. Mayor's Commn. for Urban Transp., Cleve., 1969. Served to lt. (j.g.) USNR, 1943-46, PTO. Decorated officer Yugoslav Flag with golden wreath medal (Yugoslavia), 1990; recipient Product Engring. Master Designer award, 1969, Isabelle and Leonard H. Goldenson award United Cerebral Palsy Assn., 1973; NSR sr. postdoctoral fellow Imperial Coll., London, 1957. Fellow IEEE, Am. Inst. Med. and Biological Engring. (founder); mem. ASME (honor award for best paper 1956, sr. mem.), Am. Soc. Engring. Edn., Instrument Soc. Am., Biomed. Engring. Soc. (sr. mem., pres. 1973, dir.), Am. Acad. Orthopedic Surgeons (assoc.), Inst. Medicine of NAS, NAE, Internat. Soc. Orthotics and Prosthetics, Orthopaedics Rsch. Soc., Rehab. Engring. Soc. N.Am. (founding pres.), Sigma XI. Home: 1834 Calf Mountain Rd PO Box 549 Crozet VA 22932 Personal E-mail: jimreswick@ntelos.net.

RETALLACK, GREGORY JOHN, geologist, educator; b. Hobart, Australia, Nov. 8, 1951; arrived in U.S., 1977; s. Kenneth John Retallack and Moira Wynn (Dean) Gollan; m. Diane Alice Retallack, May 31, 1981; children: Nicholas John, Jeremy Douglas. BA, Macquarie U., Sydney, 1973; BSc with honors, U. New Eng., 1974, PhD, 1978. Vis. asst. prof. No. Ill. U., DeKalb, 1977—78; vis. scholar Ind. U., Bloomington, 1978—81; asst. prof. U. Oreg., Eugene, 1981—86, assoc. prof., 1986—92, prof., 1992—. Author: Late Eocene and Oligocene Paleosols from Badlands National Park, South Dakota, 1983, Soils of the Past, 1990, 2d edit., 2001, Miocene Paleosols and Ape Habitats in Pakistan and Kenya, 1991, Colour Guide to Paleosols, 1997; contbr. articles to profl. jours. Grantee, NSF, 1979—, Wenner-Gren Found., 1983. Fellow: AAAS, Geol. Soc. Am.; mem.: Soc. Econ. Paleontologists and Mineralogists, Oreg. Acad. Sci. (pres. 1986), Paleontology Soc. (pres. Pacific sect. 1986), Bot. Soc. Am., Geol. Soc. Australia, Sigma Xi (pres. U. Oreg. chpt. 1983—84). Home: 2715 Elinor St Eugene OR 97403-2513 Office Phone: 541-346-4558. Business E-Mail: gregr@uoregon.edu.

RETALLICK, MICHAEL S., agricultural studies educator, director; b. Lancaster, Wis., Jan. 27, 1971; s. Steven F. and Jaquelyn J. Retallick; m. Dawn M. Johnson, July 27, 1991; children: Danielle Marie, Alex Michael. PhD in Agrl. Edn., Iowa State U., 2005. Cert. C.C. tchr. Agrl. edn. instr. Maquoketa (Iowa) Cmty. Schools, 1993—2001; coord. academic advising Iowa State U., Ames, 2001—03, coord. undergraduate programs, 2003—06, sci. with practice co-coordinator, 2005—06, asst. prof. agrl. edn., 2006—, dir. undergrad. edn., 2006—, dir. sci. with practice, 2006—. Tt-ball and soccer coach Story City (Iowa) Recreation Dept., 2004—05; adv. com. mem. Indian Hills C.C., Centerville, Iowa, 2005—06, Des Moines Area C.C., Ankeny, Iowa, 2003—06. Named Sam Walton Bus. Leader of the Yr., Maquoketa Area C. of C., 1999; recipient Rsch. Excellence award, Iowa State U., 2005, Exceptional Support Recognition award, 2005, Friends of Agr. Outstanding Pub. Svc. award, Maquoketa Area C. of C. and Maquoketa Rotary, 2000. Mem.: N.Am. Colls. and Tchrs. Agr., Iowa Assn. Agrl. Educators (v.p. 1999—2000, Outstanding Young Mem.), Am. Assn. Agrl. Educators, Am. Edn. Rsch. Assn., Assn. Career and Tech. Edn. Rsch., Acad. of Career and Tech. Tchr. Edn., US Assn. Small Bus. and Entrepreneurship, Nat. FFA Alumni (life Hall of Fame 2001), Iowa FFA Alumni (life), Gamma Sigma Delta. Office: Iowa State U 206 Curtiss Hall Ames IA 50011 Home Phone: 515-733-9257; Office Phone: 515-294-4810. Office Fax: 515-294-0530. Personal E-mail: rplace@iowatelecom.net. Business E-Mail: msr@iastate.edu.

RETHORE, BERNARD GABRIEL, manufacturing and mining company executive, consultant; b. May 22, 1941; s. Francis Joseph and Katharine Eunice (MacDwyer) Rethore; m. Marilyn Irene Watt, Dec. 1, 1962 (div. Apr. 2002); m. Shirley Ann Michels, July 7, 2007; children: Bernard Michael, Tara Jean, Kevin Watt, Alexandra Marie, Rebecca Ann, Christopher Philip, Abigail Lyn. BA, Yale U., 1962; MBA, U. Pa., 1967. Assoc. McKinsey & Co., Inc., Washington, 1967—73, sr. assoc., 1973; v.p., gen. mgr. Greer div. Microdot, Inc., Darien, Conn., 1973—77, v.p. ops. connector group, 1977—78, pres. bus. devel. group, 1978—82, pres. fastening sys. and sealing devices groups, 1982—84; pres. Microdot Industries, Darien, Conn., 1984—87, pres., CEO, 1988; pres. Microdot Europe Ltd., Darien, Conn., 1984—88; sr. v.p. Phelps Dodge Corp., Phoenix, 1989—95; group exec. Phelps Dodge Industries, Phoenix, 1989—90, pres., 1990—95; pres., CEO, bd. dirs. BW/IP Internat., Inc., Long Beach, Calif., 1995—97, chmn., 1997; CEO, chmn. bd. dirs. Flowserve Corp., Dallas, 1997—2000, chmn. emeritus, 2000—; chmn. McDyre & Spendley, Ltd., 2000—. Bd. dirs. Belden, Inc., Dover Corp., Walter Industries, Inc., Mueller Water Products, Inc.; cons. U.S. Govt., UN; dean's adv. bd. Wharton Sch. Bus., U. Pa., 1972—80. Elected mem. bd. fin. Town of Westport, Conn., 1986-90; trustee Ballet Ariz., 1989-95, vice chmn., 1991-95; bd. dirs. Boys Hope of Phoenix, 1989-95, Franciscan Renewal Ctr., 2005—, vice chair 2006—; trustee Phoenix Country Day Sch., 1992-2003, adv. trustee, 2003-; mem. global bus. coun. Thunderbird Sch. Global Mgmt., 1990—, chmn., 1991—, trustee, 1994—, vice chmn., 2004—. Served to capt. inf. US Army, 1962—65. Decorated Bronze Star. Mem. Nat. Assn. Mfrs. (bd. dirs. 1994-95, 96-99), Yale Club (N.Y.C.), Union League (Chgo.), Nat. Assn. Corp. Dirs. (blue ribbon com. on bd. role in strategic plan 2000), Gainey Ranch Club (Scottsdale, Ariz.). Home: 7010 East Avenida El Alba Paradise Valley AZ 85253 Office: McDyre & Spendley Ltd Ste 4C N Hayden Rd Scottsdale AZ 85250 Office Phone: 480-368-8033. Personal E-mail: bgreth@aol.com.

RETHORE, BERNARD M., lawyer; b. Ft. Bragg, NC; BA, LeMoyne Coll., 1985; JD, Pa. State U. Dickinson Sch. Law, 1988. Bar: Conn. 1988, Pa. 1988, Ariz. 1993. Founding ptnr., mem. estate planning grp. Graves & Rethore, P.C., Phoenix. Named one of Top 100 Attys., Worth mag., 2005. Mem.: Esperti Peterson Inst. Advanced Studies for Estate and Wealth Planning, Pa. State Bar Assn., Conn. State Bar Assn., Maricopa County Bar Assn., Ariz. State Bar Assn. Office: Graves & Rethore PC 5060 N 40th St Ste 112 Phoenix AZ 85018 Office Phone: 602-381-6253. Office Fax: 602-381-6260.

RETTIG, DWIGHT W., lawyer; b. July 6, 1960; BA, Ind. U., 1982; JD, U. Houston, 1986, MBA, 1993. Bar: Tex. 1986. Chief legal officer NATCO Group, Inc., 1997—98; gen. counsel Distbn. Svcs. Group Nat. Oilwell Varco, Houston, 1998—99, v.p., gen. counsel, 1999—. Mem.: Houston Bar Assn., ABA, State Bar Tex. (mem. Corp., Internat., Banking and Bus. Law Sect.). Office: Nat Oilwell, Inc 10000 Richmond Ave Houston TX 77042 Office Phone: 713-346-7550. E-mail: dwight.rettig@natoil.com. *

RETTIG, JAMES R., university librarian, library association executive; b. Chgo., Nov. 11, 1950; m. Monica Rettig; children: Chris, Tony, Katie. BA cum laude, Marquette U., 1972, MA, 1974; MLS, U. Wis., Madison, 1975. Asst. reference libr. Murray State U. Libr., Ky., 1976—77, head reference libr. Ky., 1977—78; reference libr. Roesch Libr., U. Dayton, Ohio, 1978—83; head reference libr. U. Ill., Chgo., 1983—87; asst. dean univ. librs. for reference & info. svcs. Earl Gregg Swem Libr., Coll. William & Mary, Williamsburg, Va., 1988—98; univ. libr. Boatwright Meml. Libr., U. Richmond, Va., 1998—. Mem. reference svcs. adv. com. Online Computer Libr. Ctr. (OCLC), 1992—95. Author: (columns) Current Reference Books, for Wilson Libr. Bull., Rettig on Reference. Recipient Info. Authorship award, Info. Access Corp., 1997, Faculty Recognition award, Earl Gregg Swem Libr., 1998, Richard A. Mateer Quality of Life award, U. Richmond Student Govt., 2005, Disting. Alumnus award, U. Wis.-Madison Sch. Libr. & Info. Studies, 2006; fellow sr. fellow, UCLA Dept. Info. Studies, 2001. Mem.: ALA (chair pub. com. 1997—99, chair orgn. com. 2000—03, exec. bd. 2003—06, pres. elect 2007—08, G.K. Hall award for Libr. Literature 1993), Assn. Coll. Rsch. Librs. (chair news editl. bd. 1986—88), Reference & User Svcs. Assn. (past pres., Mudge Citation 1988, Louis Shores-Oryx Press award 1995). Office: Univ Libr Boatwright Meml Libr U Richmond Richmond VA 23173 Office Phone: 804-289-8456. Office Fax: 804-287-1840. E-mail: jrettig@richmond.edu. *

RETTIG, PAM, literature educator; b. Williston, ND, Mar. 11, 1964; d. Vincent Gregory and Agnes Caroline Rettig. BS, Minot State U., 1986; MS in ednl. psychology, U. of Mary, 1994. Tchr. Burke Ctrl. Sch., Lignite, ND, 1986—89; tchr., prin. Manning Sch., Bismarck, ND, 1989—92; reading specialist Bismarck Pub. Sch., Bismarck, ND, 1992—; adj. prof. U. of Mary, Bismarck, 1998—. Internat. tchr. trainer Internat. Reading Assn., Newark, 2004—; trainer of assessors Nat. Bd. of Tchg. Certification, Clemson, SC, 2004; ednl. cons. U. of Mary, Bismarck, 2000—. Co-author: ND Lang. Arts Standards, 1996—2000. Recipient Milken award, Milken Family Found., 2000, Constance McCullough award, Internat. Reading Assn., 2004; Fulbright scholar, Fulbright Meml. Fund Found., 2001. Mem.: South Ctrl. Reading Assn., ND Reading Assn. Office: Bismarck Public School 1227 N 35th St Bismarck ND 58504 Office Phone: 701-224-1784 x 119. Office Fax: 701-250-1172. Business E-Mail: pam_rettig@educ8.org.

RETTMANN, ROBERT D., corporate communications specialist; s. John F. and Carol J. Rettmann; m. Jennifer Ann Meissner, July 9, 1995; children: Katherine Ann, Madeline Althea. BA in Comm., Marquette U., Milw., 1998. Editor Horicon Reporter, Wis., 1998—2002; rsch. & comm. svcs. coord. Crisis Prevention Inst., Brookfield, Wis., 2002—. Pres. Horicon Hist. Preservation Commn., 1999—2002. Drill sgt. USAR, 1986—, sfc. US Army, 2005—06, Iraq. Decorated Bronze Star US Army; recipient Best Spot Photography award, Wis. Newspaper Assn., 2000, Best Local Column award, 2001. Mem.: VFW. Democrat-Npl. Achievements include research in reducing physical restraint; best practices in human services. Avocations: travel, rock climbing. Home: 215 N Clark St Horicon WI 53032 Office: Crisis Prevention Inst 3315-H N 124th St Brookfield WI 53005 Business E-Mail: rrettmann@crisisprevention.com.

RETZ, WILLIAM ANDREW, naval consultant, retired naval officer; b. Blauvelt, NY, June 3, 1940; s. Andrew Macmillan and Katherine (Deyoe) R.; m. Julia Irene Patterson, Sept. 23, 1989; children: Andrew, Gregory, Mark, Alyse Reavis, Mark Rogers. Student, Tex. A&M U., Coll. Sta., 1957; BS in Mech. Engring., U. N.Mex., Albuquerque, 1963; MS, George Wash. U., Washington, DC, 1971; grad., Naval War Coll., Newport, RI, 1972. Commd. ensign USN, 1963, advanced through grades to rear adm., 1991, patrol officer river div. 511 Vietnam, 1968-69, flag sec. to comdr. Amphibious Group Two Norfolk, Va., 1972-74, exec. officer USS Ainsworth, 1974-76, commanding officer USS Stump, 1980-82, commodore Destroyer Squadron 22, 1985-87, dep. for ops. US Ctrl. Command Tampa, Fla., 1987—90; comdr. Naval Base Pearl Harbor, 1992-94, Naval Surface Group Mid. Pacific, 1992-94; commanded and closed Naval Base Phila., 1994-95; ret. USN, 1995; v.p. govt. svcs. Aramark Corp., Phila., 1996-99; ind. cons., 1999; CEO Nofire Techs., Inc., 2000—03; exec. dir. Am. Competitiveness Inst., Phila., 2003—05; ind. cons. Retz & Assoc., 2005—; with Def. Solutions, Washington, 2005—. Active Episcopal Ch.; bd. dirs. Indus. Denison Devel. Found., St. Luke's Sch.; adv. bd. U. Tex., Dallas; chmn. Texoma Tech. Enterprise Coun., Denison, Tex. Decorated Disting. Svc. medal, Legion of Merit, Def. Disting. Svc. medal, Meritorious Svc. medal, Bronze Star, Purple Heart. Mem. Surface Navy Assn., Nat. Def. Indsl. Assn. (bd. dirs.). Avocations: gardening, sailing. Office: Def Solutions 1725 1st NW Ste 300 Washington DC 20006 Personal E-mail: retzw@comcast.net.

RETZER, MARY ELIZABETH HELM, retired librarian; b. Balt. d. Francis Leslie C. and Edna (Smith) Helm; m. William Raymond Retzer, June 28, 1945; children: Lesley Elizabeth, April Christine. BA, Western Md. Coll., Westminster, 1940; MA, Columbia U., NYC, 1946; postgrad., George Washington U., 1941, Ind. U., 1952, U. Ill., 1958-59, Ill. State U., Normal, 1964-66, Bradley U., Peoria, Ill.; PhD, Western Colo. U., 1972. Faculty Rockville Bd. Edn., Md., 1940-47, elem. supr. Md., 1945-47; staff Peoria Pub. Libr., 1957-63, homebound libr., 1961-63; cons., organizer libr. Bergan High Sch., 1964-67; condr. libr. sci. course in reference Bradley U., 1966-83. Libr. Hines Elem. Sch., 1963-66, Roosevelt Jr. H.S., 1966-69; head media ctr. Manual H.S., Peoria, Ill., 1969-83. Instr. water safety courses ARC, 1938-93; pres. Entre Nous, 1949-51; pres. women's bd. Salvation Army, 1952-54; pres. Peoria Nursery Sch. Assn., 1953-54; mem. legis. action com. Ill. Congress PTA, 1955-56; mem. Crippled Children's Adv. Com., Peoria, 1957-60; active various community drives; women's adv. bd. Peoria Jr. Star, 1970-73; vol. Sarasota Internat. Airport, 1990-98. Mem. AAUW (life), NEA, ALA (life), Ill. Edn. Assn. (life), Peoria Edn. Assn. (life), Ill. Libr. Assn., Ill. Valley Librs. Assn. (pres. 1971-72), Ill. Assn. Media in Edn. (cert. com. 1973-80), Ill. Audiovisual Assn., Internat. Platform Assn., Order Ea. Star (life), Ill. State U. Adminstrs. Club, Willowknolls Country Club, Sarasota Yacht Club, Ladies Oriental Shrine. Republican. Presbyterian. Home: 3240 Lake Pointe Blvd Unit 101 Sarasota FL 34231

RETZER, MICHAEL L., political association executive; Mem. Rep. Nat. Com., Miss., 1996; chmn. Miss. State Rep. Party, 1996; US amb. to Tanzania Dept. State, 2005—. Del. Rep. Nat. Conv. Mailing: DOS Amb 2140 Dar Es Salaam Pl Washington DC 20521-2140 *

REUBEN, ALVIN BERNARD, communications and entertainment executive; b. Harrisburg, Pa., Aug. 11, 1940; s. Maurice and Lillian (Katzef) R.; m. Barbara Ann Harrison, Mar. 18, 1968; 1 dau., Mindee Jill. BS in Commerce, Rider U., 1962. Buyer Pomeroy's div. Allied Stores Corp., Harrisburg, 1962-67; sales rep. Random House, Inc., NYC, 1967-74; dir. mktg. Ballantine Books, Inc. (div. Random House), NYC, 1974-76; v.p. sales Simon & Schuster, NYC, 1976-79, sr. v.p. sales Pocket Books div., 1979-81, sr. v.p. mktg., 1981-82, pres. ref. and promotional pub. group, 1982-83, exec. v.p. electronic pub. div., 1983-85; exec. v.p. Prentice Hall div. Simon & Schuster, 1985-86; sr. v.p. mktg., sales and distbn. Vestron, Inc., 1986-89; sr. v.p. St. Martin's Press, NYC, 1989-91; sr. v.p. sales, mktg. Sony Music Video, NYC, 1991-92; sr. v.p. spl. markets Sony Music, NYC, 1992-95; sr.v.p. video and interactive sales and distbn. BMG Entertainment, 1995-97; pres. BMG Video, 1997-99. Instr. edn. in pub. program, grad. program SUNY. With USAFR, 1963-69. Mem. Tau Kappa Epsilon. Home and Office: 5 Tyler Ln Bluffton SC 29909-5028 Home Phone: 843-705-2531. Personal E-mail: alreubenschh@aol.com.

REUBEN, DON HAROLD, lawyer; b. Chgo., Sept. 13, 1928; s. Michael B. and Sally (Colucci) R.; m. Evelyn Long, Aug. 27, 1948 (div.); children: Hope Reuben Boland, Michael Barrett, Timothy Don, Jeffrey Long, Howard Ellis; m. Jeannette Hurley Haywood, Dec. 13, 1971; stepchildren: Harris Hurley Haywood, Edward Gregory Haywood. BS, Northwestern U., 1949, JD, 1952. Bar: Ill. 1952, Calif. 1996, U.S. Supreme Ct. 1957. With firm Kirkland & Ellis, Chgo., 1952-78, sr. ptnr., Reuben & Proctor, Chgo., 1978-86, Isham, Lincoln & Beale, Chgo., 1986-88; sr. counsel Winston & Strawn, Chgo., 1988-94; of counsel Altheimer & Gray, Chgo., 1994—2003, Fioretti, Lower & Carbonara, Ltd., Chgo., 2007—. Spl. asst. atty. gen. State of Ill., 1963—64, 1969, 84; gen. counsel Tribune Co., 1965—88, Chgo. Bears Football Club, 1965—88, Cath. Archdiocese of Chgo., 1975—88; counsel spl. session Ill. Ho. of Reps., 1964, for Ill. treas. for congl., state legis. and jud. reapportionment, 1963; spl. fed. ct. master, 1968—70; mem. citizens adv. bd. to sheriff County of Cook, 1962—66, jury instrn. com., 1963—73; past mem. pub. rules com. Ill. Supreme Ct., 1963—73; past mem. pub. rels. com. Nat. Conf. State Trial Judges; com. study caseflow mgmt. in law divsn. Cook County Cir. Ct., 1979—88; adv. implementation com. U.S. Dist. Ct. No. Dist. Ill., 1981—82; mem. Chgo. Better Sch. Com., 1968—69, Chgo. Crime Commn., 1970—80; supervisory panel Fed. Defender Program, 1971—78; sec. gen. counsel, chair audit com. Palm Springs Air Mus., 1998—. Bd. dirs. Lincoln Pk. Zool. Soc., 1972—84; trustee Northwestern U., 1977—; mem. vis. com. U. Chgo. Law Sch., 1976—79; bd. dirs. Blood Bank of the Desert, 1999—2004, vice-chmn., 2003—04; chmn. gen. plan adv. com. City of Rancho Mirage, 1994—; dir., sec. Friends of the Animal Campos, 2004—. Recipient Northwestern U. Law Sch. Alumni Merit award, 2002. Fellow: Am. Bar Found., Internat. Acad. Trial Lawyers; mem.: ABA (standing com. on fed. judiciary 1973—79, standing com. on jud. selection, tenure and compensation 1982—85), Desert Bar Assn., Calif. Bar Assn., Am. Arbitration Assn. (nat. panel arbitrators 1998—), Am. Coll. Trial Lawyers (Rule 23 com. 1975—82, judiciary com. 1987—91), Am. Law Inst., Chgo. Bar Assn. (chmn. subcom. propriety and regulation of contingent fees com. devel. 1966—69, subcom. on media liaison 1980—82, com. on profl. info. 1980—82), Ill. Bar Assn., Mission Hills Country Club, Casino Club, Mid-Am. Club, Com. of 25 Palm Springs, Chgo. Club, Tamarisk Country Club (hon.), Order of Coif, Beta Gamma Sigma, Beta Alpha Psi, Phi Eta Sigma. Office: 1100 Glendon Ave 10th fl Los Angeles CA 90024 also: 74-900 Hwy 111 Ste 21 Indian Wells CA 92210 also: 222 S Riverside Plz Ste 1550 Chicago IL 60606-6000 Home: 222 S Riverside Plz Ste 1550 Chicago IL 60606-6000 Office Phone: 312-726-2322. Personal E-mail: dreuben456@aol.com.

REUBEN, GLORIA, actress, singer; b. Toronto, Ont., June 9, 1964; m. Wayne Isaak, 1999. T.V. and movie actress; backup singer and dancer Tina Turner's World Tour, 2000. Actress (films) Immediate Family, 1989, Wild Orchid II: Two Shades of Blue, 1992, The Waiter, 1993, Time Cop, 1994, Nick of Time, 1995, David and Lola, 1999, Macbeth in Manhattan, 1999, Bad Faith, 2000, Pilgrim, 2000, Happy Here and Now, 2002, Kettle of Fish, 2005, The Sentinel, 2006, (TV films) The Day They Came to Arrest the Book, 1987, Shadowhunter, 1993, Percy & Thunder, 1993, Confessions: Two Faces of Evil, 1994, Dead Air, 1994, Johnny's Girl, 1995, Indiscreet, 1998, Sara, 1999, Deep in My Heart, 1999, Sole Survivor, 2000, The Agency, 2001, Feast of All Saints, 2001, Little John, 2002, Salem Witch Trials, 2002, host (TV series) Polka Dot Door, 1985, actress ER, 1995—99, The Agency, 2001—02, actress, composer, prodr. 1-800-Missing, 2003—04, appearances in Alfred Hitchcock Presents, 1987, 21 Jump Street, 1988, The Flash, 1990—91, Silk Stalkings, 1993, Homicide: Life on the Street, 1995, The District, 2002, Law & Order: Special Victims Unit, 2002, Numb3rs, 2005, actress (plays) Stuff Happens, 2005 (Lucille Lortel award outstanding lead actress, 2007), A Nervous Smile, 2006; singer: (albums) Just for You, 2004; back-up singer Twenty Four Seven, Tina Turner's World Tour, 2000. Recipient SAG Awards, 1998, 99, Q Award, 1997, 98; named one of 50 Most Beautiful People in World, People mag., 1996. Mailing: c/o Elise Konialian/ Untitled Mgmt Floor 3 23 East 22nd St New York NY 10010 Office Phone: 212-777-1214. *

REUBEN, LAWRENCE MARK, lawyer; b. Akron, Ohio, Apr. 5, 1948; s. Albert G. and Sara I. (Rifkin) R. Student, London Sch. Econs., 1969; BS, Ind. U., 1970; JD, Ind. U., Indpls., 1973. Bar: Ind. 1973, U.S. Dist. Ct. (so. dist.) Ind. 1973, U.S. Dist. Ct. (no. dist.) Ind. 1975, U.S. Ct. Appeals (7th cir.) 1975, U.S. Supreme Ct. 1976, U.S. Ct. Appeals (9th cir.) 1978, U.S. Ct. Appeals (D.C. cir.) 1994, U.S. Ct. Appeals (fed. cir.) 1999. Ptnr. Atlas, Hyatt & Reuben, Indpls., 1976-87, Atlas & Reuben, Indpls., 1987-90; chief counsel Ind. Dept. Ins., 1990-91; gen. counsel Ind. Dept. Transp., 1991-93; chief deputy Ind. Atty. Gen., Indpls., 1993-94; gen. counsel State Lottery Commn. Ind., Indpls., 1994-97; pvt. practice Indpls., 1997—. V.p. Ind. Civil Liberties Union, 1975-84; sec., bd. dirs. Indpls. Humane Soc., 1974-85; fellow Indpls. C. of C.-Lacey Leadership Program, 1982; sec., v.p., bd. dirs. Julian Ctr., Inc., 1983-89; mem. ch.-state commn. Nat. Jewish Community Relations Adv. Council, N.Y.C., 1982-89; bd. dirs. Indpls. Consumer Credit Counseling Bur., 1983-89; pres. Bur. Jewish Edn., 1984-86; parliamentarian Ind. State Dem. Party, 1985-86; mem. Indpls. Police Community Relations Rev. Com., 1983. Recipient Robert Risk award Ind. Civil Liberties Union, 1981, David M. Cook Meml. award Indpls. Jewish Community Rels. Coun., 1982; L.L. Goodman Leadership award, Jewish Fed. Indpls., 1989. Mem. Am. Trial Lawyers Assn., Ind. State Bar Assn., Indpls. Bar Assn., Nat. Employment Lawyers Assn., Am. Collectors Assn. (mem. atty. program). Office: 136 E Market St Ste 200 Indianapolis IN 46204-3671 Office Phone: 317-634-2200. Business E-Mail: lmr@reubenlaw.net.

REUBER, GRANT LOUIS, banking insurance company executive; b. Mildmay, Ont., Can., Nov. 23, 1927; s. Jacob Daniel and Gertrude Catherine (Wahl) R.; m. Margaret Louise Julia Summerhayes, Oct. 21, 1951 (dec. Feb. 1998); children: Rebecca, Barbara, Mary. BA, U. Western Ont., 1950; AM, Harvard U., 1954, PhD, 1957; LLD (hon.), Wilfred Laurier U., 1983, Simon Fraser U., 1985, U. Western Ont., 1985, McMaster U., 1994; postgrad., Cambridge U., 1954-55. Mem. research dept. Bank Can., Ottawa, 1950-52; mem. Can. Dept. Finance, Ottawa, 1955-57; asst. prof. econ. U. Western Ont., London, 1957-59, assoc. prof., 1959-62, prof., head dept., 1963-69, 1963-69; mem. bd. govs. U. Western Ont., London, 1974-78, acad. v.p., provost, 1975-78, chancellor, 1988-92; sr. v.p., chief economist Bank of Montreal, Que., Canada, 1978-79, exec. v.p., 1980-81, dep. chmn., dep. chief exec. officer, 1981-83, dir., mem. exec. com., 1981-89, pres., chief operating officer, 1983-87, dep. chmn., 1987-89; dep. minister fin. Can., 1979-80; chmn. Can. Deposit Ins. Corp., 1993-99; sr. adv., dir. Sussex Circle, 1999—. Staff mem. Royal Commn. Banking and Fin., Toronto, 1962—63; chmn. Ont. Econ. Coun., 1973—78; cons. Can. Internat. Devel. Agy., 1968—69; hon. rsch. assoc. in econs. Harvard U., 1968—69; cons. devel. ctr. OECD, 1969—73; lectr. U. Chgo. Sch. Bus., 1992—93. Author: Private Foreign Investment in Development, 1973, Canada's Political Economy, 1980; contbr. articles. Bd. dirs. Can. Merit Scholarship Found., 1994—2000; bd. govs. Royal Ont. Mus., 2000—02; chmn. Can. Ditchley Found., 1981—. Decorated officer Order of Can. Fellow: Royal Soc. Can. Home Phone: 416-924-4971; Office Phone: 416-867-3614.

REUBISH, GARY RICHARD, English language educator; b. Breckenridge, Minn., Jan. 6, 1946; s. Irving Earl and Genevieve Loretta (Miller) R. AA, N.D. State Coll. Sci., Wahpeton, 1969; BS, Valley City State Coll., 1971. Cert. tchr., N.D. Tchr. English Wolford Pub. Sch., ND, 1971-72, Lake Benton Pub. Sch., Minn., 1972-76, Wahpeton Pub. Sch., ND, 1976—2001. With USAF, 1965-71. Mem. N.D. Edn. Assn. Home: PO Box 181 Wahpeton ND 58074-0181

REUM, JAMES MICHAEL, lawyer; b. Oak Park, Ill., Nov. 1, 1946; s. Walter John and Lucy (Bellegay) R. BA cum laude, Harvard U., Cambridge, Mass., 1968, JD cum laude, 1972. Bar: NY 1973, DC 1974, US Dist. Ct. (so. dist.) NY 1974, Ill. 1979, US Dist. Ct. (no. dist.) Ill. 1982. Assoc. Davis Polk & Wardwell, NYC, 1973-78; assoc. Minority Counsel Com. on Judiciary US Ho. of Reps., Washington, 1974; ptnr. Hopkins & Sutter, Chgo., 1979-93, Winston & Strawn, Chgo., 1994—. Dir. Great Books Found., 2007—; Midwest advance rep. Nat. Reagan Bush Com., 1980; nominee commr. Securities and Exchange Comm., Pres. Bush, 1992; mem. fin. com. G.W. Bush, 2000; mem. Lawyers for Bush, 2004. Served to SP4 USAR, 1969—75. Recipient Harvard U. Honorary Nat. Scholarship, 1964-72. Mem.: Monte Carlo Country Club (Monaco), Univ. Club (NYC), Racquet Club Chgo. Republican. Home: 12 E Scott St Chicago IL 60610-2320 Office: Winston & Strawn 35 W Wacker Dr Ste 4200 Chicago IL 60601-1695 Office Phone: 312-558-5644. Business E-Mail: jreum@winston.com.

REUM, W. ROBERT, manufacturing executive; b. Oak Park, Ill., July 22, 1942; m. Sharon Milliken. BA, Yale U., 1964; JD, U. Mich., 1967; MBA, Harvard U., 1969. Dir. investment analysis City Investing Co., NYC, 1969-72; v.p. corp fin. Mich. Nat. Corp., Bloomfield Hills, Mich., 1972-78; v.p., treas. White Motor Corp., Cleve., 1978-79; v.p. fin., CFO, Lamson & Sessions, Cleve., 1980-82, The Interlake Corp., Oak Brook, Ill., 1982-88, exec. v.p., 1988-90, chmn., pres., CEO, 1991-99, Amsted Industries Inc., Chgo., 2001—, also bd. dirs. Bd. dirs. Lindberg Corp. Contbr. articles to Harvard Bus. Rev. Bd. dirs. Morton Arboretum, Lisle, Ill.; trustee Elgin (Ill.) Acad. Mem. Chgo. Golf Club, Chgo. Club, Rolling Rock Club (Ligonier, Pa.). Office: AMSTED Industries Inc 205 N Michigan Ave 44th Fl Chicago IL 60601

REUPKE, WILLIAM ALBERT, engineer; b. Chgo., Jan. 22, 1940; BA, Northwestern U., Chgo., 1961; AM, Ind. U., Bloomington, 1967; MS, Ga. Inst. Tech., Atlanta, 1973, PhD, 1977. Gen. physicist NASA, Cleve., 1963-64; staff physicist Aerospace Rsch. Applications Ctr., Bloomington, Ind., 1965-67; rsch. engr. Lockheed Missiles and Space Co., Sunnyvale, Calif., 1967-68; engring. physicist Stanford (Calif.) Linear Accelerator Ctr., 1968-71; staff mem. Los Alamos (N.Mex.) Nat. Lab., 1977-82; sr. engr. Computer Scis. Corp., Lanham-Seabrook, Md., 1983-95, Sci. Applications Internat. Corp., Seabrook, Md., 1996—2006, Perot Sys. Govt. Svcs., Fairfax, Va., 2006—. Recipient Group Achievement award NASA, 1987, 91, 93, 2001, Dr. Robert H. Goddard Hist. Essay award Nat. Space Club, 1991. Fellow Brit. Interplanetary Soc.; mem. AIAA (sr.), Am. Phys. Soc. Achievements include development of new method of adjusting neutron cross sections to improve fit of measured and calculated reaction rates in nuclear fusion integral experiments and application of that method to show that a neutron cross section important for fusion energy production is significantly smaller than was previously believed. Office: NOAA Satellite Ops Facility 4231 Suitland Rd Suitland MD 20746 Business E-Mail: reupke@mailaps.org.

REUTER, FRANK THEODORE, historian, educator; b. Kankakee, Ill., Mar. 18, 1926; s. Frank Theodore and Evelyn Marie (Scott) R.; m. Kathleen Ann Pester, June 16, 1951; children: Mark, Stephen, Christopher, Ann, Katherine. BS, U. Ill., 1950, MA, 1959, PhD, 1960. Instr. West Liberty (W. Va.) State Coll., 1960-62; asst. prof. Texas Christian U., Fort Worth, 1962-66, assoc. prof., 1966-71; prof. history Tex. Christian U., 1971-92, dean Grad. Sch., 1970-75, chmn. dept. history, 1980-83, prof. emeritus, 1992—. Vis. prof. Pázmány Péter Cath. U., Budapest, Hungary, 1999. Author: West Liberty State College: The First 125 Years, 1963, Catholic Influence on American Colonial Policies, 1898-1904, 1967, Trials and Triumphs: George Washington's Foreign Policy, 1983; co-author: Injured Honor: The Chesapeake-Leopard Affair, 1996. Served with USNR, 1944-46. U. Durham Rsch. fellow, 1991. Mem. Orgn. Am. Historians, Am. Hist. Assn., Soc. Historians Early Republic, Soc. Historians Am. Fgn. Relations, Phi Beta Kappa, Phi Alpha Theta. Roman Catholic. Home: 3617 Winifred Dr Fort Worth TX 76133-2126 Office: Tex Christian U Dept History Fort Worth TX 76129-0001 Office Phone: 817-257-7288. E-mail: rfkreuter@sbcglobal.net.

REUTER, MARK F., lawyer; b. South Bend, Ind., Sept. 13, 1971; BA, U. Notre Dame, 1992; JD, U. Notre Dame Law Sch., 1996. Bar: Ohio 1996. Ptnr. Keating Muething & Klekamp PLL, Cin. Mem., Bd. Trustees First Step Cleaning Co.; mem., Deal Maker Awards Nomination Com. Greater Cin. Assn. for Corp. Growth. Named one of Ohio's Rising Stars, Super Lawyers, 2005, 2006. Fellow: Cin. Acad. Leadership for Lawyers; mem.: Ohio State Bar Assn. (mem., Corp. Law Com.), Cin. Bar Assn. Office: Keating Muething & Klekamp PLL One E Fourth St Ste 1400 Cincinnati OH 45202 Office Phone: 513-579-6400. Office Fax: 513-579-6457.

REUTER, STEWART RALSTON, retired radiologist; b. Detroit, Feb. 14, 1934; s. Carl H. and Grace M. R.; m. Marianne (Ahfeldt), June 6, 1966. BA, Ohio Wesleyan U., 1955; MD, Case Western Res. U., 1959; JD, U. San Francisco, 1980. Diplomate: Am. Bd. Radiology, Am. Bd. Legal Medicine. Bar: Tex., 1981. Intern U. Calif., San Francisco, 1959—60, resident in radiology, 1960—63; instr. radiology Stanford U., Calif., 1963—64; asst. prof. U. Mich., Ann Arbor, 1966—69; assoc. prof. U. Calif., San Diego, 1969—72; prof. U. Mich., Ann Arbor, 1972—76, U. Calif., San Francisco and Davis, 1976—80; prof., chmn. dept. radiology Health Sci. Ctr., U. Tex., San Antonio, 1980—2001, prof. emeritus, 2001. Co-author: Gastrointestinal Radiology, 3d edit., 1986; mem. editorial bd. Am. Jour. Roentgenology, 1975-91, Iatrogenics, 1990-93; contbr. articles to profl. journals. Picker Fellow, 1964-66. Fellow: Soc. Interventional Radiologists (pres. 1978, Gold medal 2004), Am. Coll. Legal Medicine (bd. gov. 1985—91, 1992—94, sec. 1994, pres. elect 1995, pres. 1996), Am. Heart Assn., Am. Coll. Radiology (councillor 1996—99, fellow emeritus 2000); mem.: Am. Roentgen Ray Soc., Assn., Soc. Gastrointestinal Radiologists, Tex. Radiol. Assn. (trustee 1989—92, pres. 1994, trustee 1995—98, Gold medal 2000), Assn. Univ. Radiologists, Am. Bd. Legal Medicine, Tex. Bar Assn. Home: 3923 Morgans Creek San Antonio TX 78230-1945 Office: U Tex Health Sci Ctr Dept Radiology 7703 Floyd Curl Dr San Antonio TX 78284-6200 Business E-Mail: reuter@uthscsa.edu.

REUTHER, DAVID LOUIS, retired children's book publisher, writer; b. Detroit, Nov. 2, 1946; s. Roy Louis and Fania (Sonkin) Reuther; m. Margaret Alexander Miller, July 21, 1973; children: Katherine Anna, Jacob Alexander. BA with honors, U. Mich., 1968. Tchr. Lewis-Wadhams Sch., Westport, NY, 1969-71; asst. dir. Children's Book Coun., NYC, 1971-73; editor children's books Macmillan Pub. Co., NYC, 1973-76; sr. editor Four Winds Press-Scholastic Inc., NYC, 1976-82; sr. v.p., pub. Morrow Jr. Books, NYC, 1982-98; co-founder Baseball Ink, Inc., 1986-90; pub. Lothrop Lee & Shepard, NYC, 1996-98, Beech Tree Books, NYC, 1997-98; pres., pub. SeaStar Books, NYC, 1999—2002, North-South Books, NYC, 1999—2002. Chmn., bd. dirs. Children's Book Coun. Author (with Roy Doty): Fun to Go, A Take-Along Activity Book, 1982; author: Save-the-Animals Activity Book, 1982; author: (with John Thorn and Pete Palmer) The Hidden Game of Baseball, 1984; author: Total Baseball, 1989, The Whole Baseball Catalog, 1990, Total Baseball II, 1991; editor (with John Thorn): The Armchair Quarterback, 1982, The Armchair Aviator, 1983, The Armchair Mountaineer, 1984, The Armchair Book of Baseball, 1985, The Armchair Angler, 1986, The Amrchair Book of Baseball II, 1987, The Armchair Traveler, 1988. Bd. dirs. Clinton-Essex-Franklin County Libr. Sys., 2007—; treas., bd. dirs. Smith House Family Health Ctr., 2006—. Mem.: NSTA (children's book coun. joint com. 1982—85), ALA (co-chmn. children's book coun. joint com. 2000—02), Champlain Valley Film Soc. (pres. bd. dirs. 2003—), Am. Bookseller Assn. (childrens book coun. joint com. 1990—93). Home: Box 337 Willsboro NY 12996

REUTHER, RONALD THEODORE, museum director; b. Dec. 29, 1929; s. Frederick and Grace (Roehll) R.; m. Mary B. Howard, 1956 (div. 1981); children: Catherine Virginia, Paul Douglas, Jon Frederick, Victoria Grace; m. Alla Elkus, Aug. 4, 2006. BA, U. Calif., 1951, postgrad., 1953, U. Ariz., 1952. Mgr. Micke Grove Zoo, 1957-62; gen. curator Cleve. Zoo, 1958-62, asst. dir., 1964-66; dir. Indpls. Zoo, 1962-64, San Francisco Zoo, 1966-73; pres., exec. dir. Phila. Zoo, 1973-78; dir. corp. devel. Exploratorium, San Francisco, 1980-81; founder, pres. Western Aerospace Mus., Oakland, Calif., 1980—88, exec. dir., 1995-99; field rep. Bell & Howell Edn. Corp./DeVry Inst. Tech., 1983-88; exec. dir. Whale Ctr., Oakland, 1988-89; edn. cons. Sierra Acad. Aeronautics, Oakland, 1989-92; lectr. Golden State U., San Francisco, 1992. Co-founder Pt. Reyes Bird Obs., Calif., 1968-70; v.p. Del. Valley Mus. Coun., 1976-78. Author zoo guidebooks, Wings Over San Francisco Bay, 1997; co-author: San Francisco Bay Area Aviation, 2007. Mem. exec. com. Greater Phila. Cultural Alliance, 1976-78; owner, moderator internet Amelia Earhart Rsch. Discussion Group, 2000-03. 1st lt. USAF, 1953-57; with USARNG, 1958-66; lt. col. USAR, 1966-81, ret. Mem. The Explorers Club (chmn. No. Calif. chpt. 1990-95), Tamalpais Conservation Club (life mem.), Aero Club No. Calif. (bd. dirs. 2004-06), Ox-5 Pioneers (bd. govs. Golden Gate chpt. 1996—05, editor newsletter), Silver Wings Frat. (pres. No. Calif. chpt. 2003—06). E-mail: reuther@comcast.net.

REUTIMAN, ROBERT WILLIAM, JR., lawyer; b. Mpls., June 4, 1944; s. Robert William and Elsbeth Bertha (Doering) R.; m. Virginia Lee Traxler, June 25, 1983; children: Robert James, Joseph Lee. BA magna cum laude, U. Minn., 1966, JD, 1969. Bar: Minn. 1969, U.S. Ct. Mil. Appeals 1969, U.S. Dist. Ct. Minn. 1973, U.S. Ct. Appeals (8th cir.) 1976, U.S. Tax. Ct. 1979. Mem. Armstrong, Phleger, Reutiman & Vinokour, Ltd., Wayzata, Minn., 1973-76; ptnr. Phleger & Reutiman, Wayzata, 1976-81; pvt. practice Wayzata, 1981—. Chmn. Spring Pk. Planning Commn., 1978; city ct. judge, Hopkins and Minnetonka, Minn. Capt. U.S. Army, 1969-73. Decorated Army Commendation medal. Mem. Minn. Bar Assn., Hennepin County Bar Assn., Phi Beta Kappa. Lutheran. Avocations: fishing, gardening. Home: 11610 3rd Ave N Plymouth MN 55441-5919 Office: PO Box 367 Wayzata MN 55391 Office Phone: 952-473-7328. Business E-Mail: billreutiman@lycos.com.

REUTTER, EBERHARD EDMUND, JR., education and law educator; b. Balt., May 28, 1924; s. Eberhard Edmund and Irene Louise (Loewer) R.; m. Bettie Marie Lytle, Aug. 16, 1947; 1 son, Mark Douglas. BA, Johns Hopkins U., 1944; MA, Columbia U., 1948, PhD, 1950. Dir., Tokyo Army Edn. Program Sch., 1945-47; head math. dept. Barnard Sch., NYC, 1947-49; mem. faculty Tchrs. Coll., Columbia U., 1950—, prof., 1957-96, prof. emeritus, 1996—. Vis. prof. U. Alaska, 1960, 66, U. P.R., 1954, U. So. Calif., 1960; speaker, cons. Coordinator spl. edn. projects NAACP Legal Def. Fund, 1965-68 Author: The School Administrator and Subversive Activities, 1951, Schools and the Law, 5th edit., 1981, (with W.S. Elsbree) Staff Personnel in the Public Schools, 1954, (with R.R. Hamilton) Legal Aspects of School Board Operation, 1958, (with W.S. Elsbree) Principles of Staff Personnel Administration in Public Schools, 1959, (with L.O. Garber) The Yearbook of School Law, 1967, 68, 69, 70, Legal Aspects of Control of Student Activities by Public School Authorities, 1970, The Law of Public Education, 4th edit., 1994, The Courts and Student Conduct, 1975, The Supreme Court's Impact on Public Education, 1982; also articles, chpts. in books. Chmn. citizens adv. com. Emerson (N.J.) Bd. Edn., 1954-57. Served from pvt. to 1st lt. inf. AUS, 1943-46. Recipient Marion A. McGhehey award for outstanding service in field edn. law, 1986. Mem. NEA, AAUP, Nat. Orgn. Legal Problems of Edn. (pres. 1967), Am. Assn. Sch. Adminstrs., Am. Assn. Sch. Pers. Adminstrs., Internat. Pers. Mgmt. Assn., Phi Beta Kappa, Kappa Delta Pi, Phi Delta Kappa. Home: 316 Grand Blvd Emerson NJ 07630-1157 Office: Columbia Univ Tchrs Coll New York NY 10027

REUTTY, MICHELE MARIE, library director; b. Passaic, NJ, Oct. 17, 1949; d. Charles Hugo and Jean Cammarano Reutty; children: David Lavern Walters Jr., Jennifer Walters McCoy, Cristian Michael Maiullo. AA, Bergen County C.C., Paramus, NJ, 1979; B in English, Montclair State Coll., NJ, 1987; MLS, Rutgers U., New Brunswick, NJ, 1989. Cert. ESL tutor Bergen County Coop. Libr. Systems/N.J., 1989. Reference libr. Elmwood Pk. Pub. Libr., 1987—88; asst. dir. Cresskill Pub. Libr., NJ, 1988—89; dir. Free Pub. Libr. Hasbrouck Heights, NJ, 1989—2006, Oakland Libr., NJ, 2006—. Editor-in-chief, contbg. author: history book Remembering the Past, Looking Toward the Future, 1996. Sec. Kelley Found., New Brunswick, NJ, 2005—. Named Citizen of the Yr., Mayor and Coun., Hasbrouck Heights, 1992; recipient Downs Intellectual Freedom award, U. Ill., Campaign-Urbana, 2006; fellow Snowbird Leadership Inst., Salt Lake City, Utah, Rutgers U., 1991. Mem.: ALA (assoc.), Rutgers Sch.

Communication, Info. and Libr. Studies (mem. exec. bd. 2006—07), NJ Libr. Assn. (assoc.; second v.p./chair adminstrn. and mgmt. com. 2004—05, v.p., pres.-elect 2006—07), Spokes-Women Motorcycle Club. Democrat. Roman Catholic. Avocations: creative writing, motorcycling, pysanky writing. Home: 189 Lincoln Ave Elmwood Park NJ 07407 Office: Oakland Pub Libr 2 Municipal Plaza Oakland NJ 07436 Office Phone: 201-337-3742. E-mail: xlibris@optonline.net.

REVEAL, ERNEST IRA, III, retired lawyer; b. Chgo., Oct. 19, 1948; s. Ernest Ira Jr. and Hazel (Holt) R.; m. Katherine Trennerry, Nov. 24, 1979; children: Genevieve, Adrienne, Danielle. BA, Cornell U., 1970; JD cum laude, U. Mich., 1973. Bar: Minn. 1973, U.S. Dist. Ct. Minn. 1973, U.S. Ct. Appeals (8th cir.) 1974, U.S. Dist. Ct. S.D. 1976, U.S. Ct. Claims 1976, U.S. Ct. Appeals (7th cir.) 1984, U.S. Dist. Ct. (ctrl. dist.) Calif. 1991, U.S. Ct. Appeals (9th cir.) 1991, U.S. Supreme Ct., 1991, U.S. Cir. Ct. Appeals (fed. cir.)2001. Assoc. Robins, Kaplan, Miller & Ciresi, Mpls., 1973—79, ptnr., 1979—2002, mediator, arbitrator, 2003—; temp. judge Orange County Superior Ct., 2007—. Atty. settlement officer US Dist. Ct.; panel mem. Am. Arbitration Assn., Nat. Arbitration Forum. Author: Public Sector Labor Law, 1983. Pro tem mem. Civil Svc. Commn., St. Paul, 1976; chmn. regional adv. com. So. Calif. Pub. Radio. Mem. ABA, Minn. Bar Assn. (past chair labor and employment law sect.), Calif. State Bar Assn. (adv., past exec. com., antitrust and unfair competition sect.), Cornell Club of Minn. (past pres.), LA Theatre Works (bd. dir.). Democrat. Presbyterian. Avocations: history, travel. Office Phone: 949-589-1276. Personal E-mail: ernest.reveal@cox.net.

REVEL, JEAN-PAUL, biology professor; b. Strasbourg, France, Dec. 7, 1930; arrived in U.S., 1953; s. Gaston Benjamin and Suzanne (Neher) Revel; m. Helen Ruth Bowser, July 27, 1957 (div. 1986); children: David, Daniel Neher, Steven Robert; m. Galina Avdeeva Moller, Dec. 24, 1986 (dec. 2004); 1 stepchild, Karen (dec.). BS, U. Strasbourg, 1949; PhD, Harvard U., 1957. Rsch. fellow Cornell U. Med. Sch., NYC, 1958-59; from instr. to prof. Harvard Med. Sch., Boston, 1959-71; prof. Calif. Inst. Tech., Pasadena, 1971—, emeritus, 2006—, AB Ruddock chair in biology, 1978—2006, dean of students, 1996—2005, emeritus, 2006—. Mem. sch. advisors bd. Nat. Insts. Aging, Balt., 1977-80; mem. ad hoc adv. biology NSF, Washington, 1982-83; mem. Nat. High Voltage Microscopy Adv. Group, Bethesda, Md., 1983, Nat. Rsch. Resources Adv. Coun., 1986-90. Author: (with E.D. Hay) Fine Structure of Developing Avian Cornea, 1969, over 150 publs., 1952-99; editor: Cell Shape and Surface Architecture, 1977, Science of Biological Specimen Preparation, 1986; mem. editl. bd. Jour. Cell Biology, 1969-72, Internat. Rev. Cytology, 1970, Cell and Tissue Rsch., 1979—, Molecular and Cell Biology, 1983-91; editor in chief Jour. Microscopy Soc. Am., 1994-96. Fellow AAAS (leader biol. scis. sect. 1991-92, Gordon conf. cell adhesion); mem. Am. Soc. Cell Biology (pres. 1972-73), Electron Micros. Soc. Am. (pres. 1988, Disting. Scientist award 1993), Soc. Devel. Biology. Avocations: watercolors, photography. Office: Calif Inst Tech # 114-96 Pasadena CA 91125-0001 Home Phone: 626-796-0701; Office Phone: 626-395-4986. Business E-Mail: revelj@caltech.edu.

REVELEY, WALTER TAYLOR, III, dean, law educator; b. Churchville, Va., Jan. 6, 1943; s. Walter Taylor and Marie (Eason) R.; m. Helen Bond, Dec. 18, 1971; children: Walter Taylor IV, George Everett Bond, Nelson Martin Eason, Helen Lanier. AB, Princeton U., 1965; JD, U. Va., 1968. Bar: Va. 1970, D.C. 1976. Asst. prof. law U. Ala., 1968-69; law clk. to Justice Brennan U.S. Supreme Ct., Washington, 1969-70; fellow Woodrow Wilson Internat. Ctr. for Scholars, 1972-73; internat. affairs fellow Coun. on Fgn. Rels., NYC, 1972-73; assoc. Hunton & Williams, Richmond, Va., 1970-76, ptnr., 1976-98, mng. ptnr., 1982-91, cons., 1998—; dean William and Mary Law Sch., 1998—, law prof. Lectr. Coll. William and Mary Law Sch., 1978—80; cons. in field. Author: War Powers of the President and Congress: Who Holds the Arrows and Olive Branch, 1981; mem. editl. bd. Va. Law Rev., 1966-68; contbr. articles to profl. jours. Trustee Princeton U., 1986-90, 91-2001, Presbyn. Ch. (U.S.A.) Found., 1991-97, Va. Hist. Soc., 1991-96, 2003—, Union Theol. Sem., 1992-2000, Andrew W. Mellon Found., 1994—, JSTOR, 1995—, Va. Mus. Fine Arts, 1995-2005, pres. 1996-99, St. Christopher's Sch., 1996-01, 2004—, Carnegie Endowment for Internat. Peace, 1999—; bd. dirs. Fan Dist. Assn., Richmond, Inc., 1976-80, pres., 1979-80; bd. dirs. Richmond Symphony, 1980-92, pres., 1988-90, pres. symphony coun., 1994-99; bd. dirs. Presbyn. Outlook Found., 1985-2003, 2004-, pres., 1992-95; bd. dirs. Va. Mus. Found., 1990-99; bd. dirs. New Covenant Trust Co., 1997-99, Va. Found. Humanities, 2001—. Mem. ABA, Va. Bar Assn., D.C. Bar Assn., Am. Bar Found., Va. Bar Found., Princeton Assn. Va. (bd. dirs. 1981—, pres. 1983-85), Va. State Bar (Edn. Lawyers sect. bd. govs. 1992—, chmn. 1992-95), Raven Soc., Phi Beta Kappa, Omicron Delta Kappa. Home: 2314 Monument Ave Richmond VA 23220-2604 Office: William and Mary Law Sch PO Box 8795 Williamsburg VA 23187-8795 Office Phone: 757-221-3790. Business E-Mail: taylor@wm.edu.

REVELL, HENRY, JR., social services administrator, retired education educator; b. Selma, NC, Apr. 13, 1932; s. Henry William Sr. and Flora (Vinson) Revell; m. Carolyn Yvonne L. Revell (dec.); children: Gary, Keith, Kevan Croper. BS, NC A&T State U., Greensboro, 1974. Facilitator, pres. Family Strengths, Greensboro, NC, 1980—; pres., CEO Kent-FJHB, Inc., Selma, NC, 1989—; owner, dir. Revell's Enrichment Ctr., Greensboro, 2002—. State 4-H youth coord. NC A&T State U., Greensboro, 1974—87; program dir. Another Chance Recovery Ctr., Greensboro, 2002—; presenter in field. Author: 4-H in Public Housing Communities. Pres., bd. dirs. Triad Sickle Cell Reg., Greensboro, 1987—91, Daniel Godfrey Meml. Fund, Greensboro, 1988—; past pres. RH Family Orgn.; deacon Providence Bapt. Ch., Greensboro, 1981—. With US Army, 1956—58. Grantee, Cmty. Found., Greensboro, 2000. Mem.: NACCP (parlimentarian 1990—), Epsilon Sigma Phi (life). Democrat. Baptist. Avocations: baseball, basketball, football, walking, dance. Home: 3316 S Elm-Eugene St Greensboro NC 27406 Personal E-mail: revellh@bellsouth.net.

REVELLE, DONALD GENE, manufacturing and health care company executive, consultant; b. Cape Girardeau, Mo., July 16, 1930; s. Lewis W. and Dorothy R.; m. Jo M. Revelle, Aug. 1, 1954; children— Douglas, David, Daniel, Dianne BA, U. Mo., 1952; JD, U. Colo., 1957; grad., Harvard U. Bus. Sch., 1971. Dir. employee relations Westinghouse Corp., Pitts., 1957-65; asst. to v.p. Diebold Corp., 1966; v.p. human resources TRW Corp., Cleve., 1967-84; sr. v.p. human resources Black and Decker Co., Towson, Md., 1984-86; exec. v.p. corp. rels. Montefiore Acad. Med. Ctr., Bronx, 1987-98; pres., CEO Syzygy, Inc., 1998—. Univ. lectr.; cons. Duerba Ship, Blue Cross N.Y., Windsor Hosp., Salvation Army Contbr. articles to profl. jours. Mem. sch. bd. State of N.Y. Lt. USNR, 1952-54 Mem.: ABA (labor law com.), Human Resource Planning Soc., Fed. Bar Assn., Colo. Bar Assn., MBA Assn., Rotary. Methodist. Home and Office: Syzygy Inc 29903 Baywood Ln Wesley Chapel FL 33543-9744 Home Phone: 813-994-3403; Office Phone: 813-994-3403.

RE VELLE, JACK B(OYER), statistician, consultant; s. Mark A. and Myril (Bubes) Re V.; m. Brenda Lorraine Newcombe, Aug. 2, 1968; 1 child, Karen Alyssa. BSChemE, Purdue U., 1957; MS in Indsl. Engring. and Mgmt., Okla. State U., 1965, PhD in Indsl. Engring. and Mgmt., 1970. Adminstrv. asst. Gen. Dynamics, Ft. Worth, 1970-71; cons. engr. Denver, 1971-72; chmn. decision scis. U. Nebr., Omaha, 1972-77; dean Chapman U. Sch. Bus. and Mgmt., Orange, Calif., 1977-79; sr. staff engr. McDonnell Douglas Space Systems, Huntington Beach, Calif., 1979-81; head mfg. tng. and devel. Hughes Aircraft Co., Fullerton, Calif., 1981-82, sr. statistician, 1982-86, corp. mgr. R & D LA, 1986-88, corp. chief statistician, 1988-93; leader continuous improvement Raytheon Missile Systems Co., Tucson, 1994-97; dir. Ctr. for Process Improvement GenCorp Aerojet, Azusa, Calif., 1998-99; consulting statistician Santa Ana, Calif., 1999—. Mem. bd. examiners Malcolm Baldrige nat. quality award Nat. Inst. Stds. and Tech., U.S. Dept. Commerce, Washington, 1990, 93; judge Ariz. Quality Alliance, Phoenix, 1994-96, Rochester Inst. Tech.-USA Today Quality Cup Competition, 1994-2001, Def. Contract Mgmt. Command-Commdrs. Cup, 1995-2000; cons., presenter, lectr. in field. Author: Safety Training Methods, 1980, 2d edit., 1995, The Two-Day Statistician, 1986, The New Quality Technology, 1988, Policy Deployment, 1993, What Your Quality Guru Never Told You, 2000, Quality Essentials, 2004; (with others) Quest for Quality, 1986, Mechanical Engineers Handbook, 1986, 2d edit., 1998, 3d edit., 2005, Production Handbook, 1987, Handbook of Occupational Safety and Health, 1987, A Quality Revolution in Manufacturing, 1989, Quality Engineering Handbook, 1991; co-author: Quantitative Methods for Managerial Decisions, 1978, The Executive's Handbook on Quality Function Deployment, 1994, From Concept to Customer, 1995, The Quality Function Deployment Handbook, 1998, Manufacturing Handbook of Best Practices, 2001; (software) TQM ToolSchool, 1995, QFD/Pathway, 1998. Bd. dirs. Assn. for Quality and Participation, Cin., 1985-86; mem. adv. bd. dept. indsl. and mech. engring. Calif. Poly. State U., Pomona, 1985-2000; mem. adv. bd. dept. indsl. and sys. engring. Ohio U., Athens, 2000—05; mem. SCORE Santa Ana, 2005—, 2d vice chair, 2006-07, 1st vice chair, 2007, chair, 2007—. 2d lt. to maj. USAF, 1957—68, served in Japan USAF, 1957—59, served in Vietnam USAF, 1966—67, joint svc. assignment Defense Nuclear Agy., 1967—68, Wash., DC. Recipient Disting. Econs. Devel. award Soc. Mfg. Engrs., 1990, Taguchi Recognition award Am. Supplier Inst., 1991, Akao prize QFD Inst., 1999, Melvin R. Lohmann medal Okla. State U. Coll. Engring., Arch. and Tech., 2006; named to Purdue U. ROTC Hall of Fame, 2006. Fellow Am. Soc. for Quality (co-chair total quality mgmt. com. 1990-92), Inst. Advancement Engring., Inst. Indsl. Engrs. (regional v.p. 1982-84, treas. 1992-93, sr. v.p. 1993-94); mem. Aerospace and Def. Divsn. (dir. 1997-99). Office: The Wizard of Odds A Consulting Statistician Re Velle Solutions LLC PO Box 10315 Santa Ana CA 92711-0315 Home Phone: 714-633-1077; Office Phone: 714-289-1664. Personal E-mail: cactus_statman@yahoo.com.

REVENKOVA, EKATERINA, biologist, researcher; b. Moscow, May 22, 1962; arrived in U.S., 2000; d. Vladimir Preobrazhensky and Natalia Alekhina; 1 child, Anton Revenkov. MS in Genetics, Moscow State U., 1984; PhD in Molecular Biology, V.A.Engelhardt Inst. Molecular Biology, Moscow, 1993. Rsch. scientist Ctr. of Bioengineering, Moscow, 1989—94; postdoctoral rsch. fellow Friedrich Miescher Inst., Basel, Switzerland, 1995—99; scientist Basel Inst. for Immunology, 1999—2000; instr. Mt. Sinai Sch. Medicine, NYC, 2001—04, asst. prof., 2004—. Contbr. articles to profl. jours. Mem.: Am. Soc. for Cell Biology. Office: Mount Sinai School of Medicine 1 Gustave L Levy Pl New York NY 10029 Home Phone: 201-592-0193; Office Phone: 212-659-8248.

REVENS, JOHN COSGROVE, JR., state legislator, lawyer; b. Providence, Jan. 29, 1947; s. John C. and Rita M. (Williams) R.; m. Susan L. Shaw, Aug. 31, 1974; children: Leigh Elizabeth, Marcie Greene, Emily May. AA, C.C. of RI, 1966; BA, Providence Coll., 1969; JD, Suffolk U., 1973. Bar: RI 1973. Mem. RI Ho. of Reps., Providence, 1968-74, sec. house steering com., 1971-74, mem. edn. and welfare com., 1968—78; pres. Revens, Revens & St. Pierre, Warwick, RI, 1977—; mem. RI Senate, Dist. 31, Providence, 1990—. Mem. RI Senate, 1974-89, 1991—, fin. svs., tech. and regulatory issues, mem. jud. and labor coms., 1974, chmn. jud. com., 1980-83, majority whip, 1977-80, Senate majority leader, 1983-89; Senate pres., pro tempore, 1993-95, 2001—; dir. New Eng. Bd. Higher Edn., 1975-83, chmn., 1977-81; chmn. RI Children's Code Commn., 1979-83; bd. dirs. C.C. of RI Found., Vols. of Warwick Schs., RI Acad. Decathlon Assn.; mem. Commn. on Jud. Tenure and Discipline, 1982-84, Family Ct. Bench Bar Com., 1980-82, Women and Infants Hosp. Corp., 1983—; commr. Uniform State Laws, 1982-84. Bd. dirs. Senate Presidents' Forum. Mem. RI Bar Assn., Kent County Bar Assn., Am. Arbitration Assn. (panel of arbitrators 1980-), State Legis. Leaders Found. (pres. senate forum, bd. dirs.), KC. Democrat. Roman Catholic. Office: 946 Centerville Rd Warwick RI 02886-4398

REVER, GEORGE WRIGHT, psychiatrist, health facility administrator; b. Balt., May 18, 1928; s. William Benjamin and Amy Blanche (Wright) R.; m. Bridget Valerie Hanley, 1961 (dec. 1988); children: Kurt, Maeve Rever Raedle; m. Ann Roe, Feb. 4, 1994. BS, U. Md., 1950; MD, U. Md., Balt., 1957. Rotating intern Mercy Hosp., Balt., 1957-58; resident psychiatry and neurology VA Hosp., Boston, 1958-60; fellow Harvard Med. Sch., Cambridge, Mass., 1960-64, clin. instr. psychiatry, 1964—2004; psychiatrist divsn. legal medicine Cambridge Ct., 1960-71; psychiatrist Cambridge Ct. Clinic Divsn. of Legal Medicine, Mass., 1960-71; pvt. practice Cohasset, Mass., 1963-90, Easton, Md., 1990-93; psychiatric cons. Travelers Aid Soc., Boston, 1966-74; psychiatrist Eunice Kennedy Shriver Ctr., Waltham, Mass., 1967-90; fellow child psychiatry Mass. Gen. Hosp., Boston, 1960-61, 62-63, fellow community mental health, 1963-64, staff psychiatrist, 1964-90, dir. child psychiatry tng. program neuropsychiatry devel. disabilities sect., 1967-90, asst. pediatrician, 1969-71, psychiat. cons. social svc. dept., 1970-74, psychiatrist Chelsea Health Ctr., 1974-77, hon. psychiatrist, 1991—2004; med. dir. Brockton (Mass.) Family and Community Rsch., 1979-90; child and adolescent psychiatrist Wicomico County Health Dept., Salisbury, Md., 1990-91, Queen Anne County Mental Health Center, Centreville, Md., 1990-92, Talbot County Mental Health, Easton, 1990-92, med. dir., 1992—2002, Regional Mid-Shore Mental Health Svcs., 1998—2005, Caroline County Mental Health Clinic, 2005—, Bay Hundred Behavioral Health Svcs./Choptank Cmty. Health Svcs., 2005—; psychiatric cons. Benedictine Sch., Ridgely, Md., 1990—. Part-time fellow child psychiatry Mass. Gen. Hosp., Boston, 1961-62, James Jackson Putnam Children's Ctr., Roxbury, Mass., 1961-62; cons. Am. Heritage Dictionaries, 1992; fleet surgeon Miles River Yacht Club, 2000—04. Editl. cons. The Am. Jour. of Child and Adolescent Psychiatry, 1994—. Sgt. U.S. Army, 1950-52, Korea. Decorated Bronze Star medal; Recipient Talbot County Assn. Retarded Citizens award, 1993. Fellow: Am. Psychiat. Assn. (life Disting.), Am. Coll. Forensic Examiners (life); mem.: AMA, Am. Soc. Clin. Psychopharmacology, Soc. Biol. Psychiatry, Assn. Child Psychology and Psychiatry, Am. Neuropsychiat. Assn., Talbot County Med. Soc., Med. and Chururg. Faculty Md., Md. Psychiat. Soc., Am. Assn. Mental Retardation, Am. Assn. Cmty. Psychiatrists, Am. Acad. Child and Adolscent Psychiatry. Home: 8627 North Bend Cir Easton MD 21601-7327 Business E-Mail: rever@shore.intercom.net.

REVERCOMB, HORACE AUSTIN, III, judge; b. Richmond, Va., Sept. 22, 1948; s. Horace Austin Jr. and Mary Virginia (Kelley) R.; m. Annie S. Anthony, July 10, 1976; children: Brian Austin, Suzanne Melanie. BA, Pembroke State U., 1971; JD, George Mason U., 1977. Bar: Va. 1978. Pvt. practice law, King George, Va., 1978-82; ptnr. Revercomb & Revercomb, King George, 1982-90; judge Gen. Dist. Cts. of 15th Jud. Dist. Va., 1990-99, Cir. Cts. 15th Jud. Cir. Va., 1999—. Mem. Va. Bar Assn. Methodist. Avocation: music. Home: PO Box 216 King George VA 22485-0216 Personal E-mail: HRevercomb@aol.com.

REVERDIN, BERNARD J., lawyer; b. Baden, Switzerland, June 21, 1919; came to U.S., 1948, naturalized, 1954; s. Jean and Germaine Reverdin; m. Marcelle Coicou Reverdin; children: Caroline Reverdin Flanagan, Brigitte, Nathalie. LLB, U. Geneva, 1942; postgrad., Harvard Law Sch., 1949. Bar: Switzerland 1945, N.Y. 1955. Atty., legal asst. Geneva Govt., 1945-48; assoc. Sullivan & Cromwell, NYC, 1949-51; assoc., ptnr. Lovejoy, Wasson & Ashton, NYC, 1951-84; ptnr., counsel Hunton & Williams, NYC, 1984-88; ptnr. Eaton & Van Winkle, NYC, 1988-97, sr. counsel intern, 1998—. Dir. subs. of European corps. Contbr. articles to profl. jours.; lectr. in field V.p. LCM Found. on European Affairs Inc. Mem. N.Y. State Bar Assn. (chair com. internat. trust and estate 1988-90), Am. Fgn. Law Assn. (past pres.), Consular Law Soc. (past pres.), Internat. Law Assn., Union Internat. des Avocats, Swiss Soc. N.Y., German Am. Law Assn. Office: Eaton & Van Winkle LLP 3 Park Ave Fl 16 New York NY 10016-5902 E-mail: breverdin@evw.com.

REVERE, VIRGINIA LEHR, psychologist; b. Long Branch, NJ; d. Joseph and Essie Lehr; m. Robert B. Revere; children: Elspeth, Andrew, Lisa, Robert Jr. PhB, U. Chgo., 1949, MA, 1959, PhD, 1971. Lic. cons. clin. psychologist, Va. Intern, staff psychologist Ea. Mental Health Reception Ctr., Phila., 1959-61; instr. Trenton (N.J.) State Coll., 1962-63; psychologist Trenton State Hosp., 1964-65, Bucks County Psychiat. Ctr., Phila., 1965-67; assoc. prof. Mansfield (Pa.) State U., 1967-77; clin. rsch. psychologist St. Elizabeth Hosp., Washington, 1977-81, tng. psychology coord., 1981-83, psychologist, 1985-91; child psychologist Cmty. Mental Health Ctr., Washington, 1983-85; pvt. practice Alexandria, Va., 1980—. Cons., lectr. in field. Author: Applied Psychology for Criminal Justice Professionals, 1982; contbr. articles to profl. jours. Recipient Group Merit award St. Elizabeth's Hosp., 1983, Community Svc. award D.C. Psychol. Assn., 1978, Outstanding Educator award, 1972; traineeship NIH, USPHS, Chgo., 1963-65; fellow Family Svcs. Assn., 1958-59. Mem. APA, No. Va. Soc. Clin. Psychologists, Va. Acad. Clin. Psychologists. Office: 3801 Buckman Rd Alexandria VA 22308-2733 Office Phone: 703-780-4872. Personal E-mail: rrevere923@aol.com.

REVES, JOSEPH GERALD (JERRY REVES), anesthesiology educator, dean; b. Charleston, SC, Aug. 14, 1943; s. George Everett and Frances (Masterson) R.; m. Virginia Cathcart, Jan. 05, 1945; children: Virginia Masterson, Christine Frances, Elizabeth Cathcart. BA, Vanderbilt U., 1965; MD, Medical Coll. S.C., 1969; MS, U. Ala., Birmingham, 1973. Lic. anesthesiologist S.C., Ala., Md., N.C.; Diplomate Am. Coll. Anesthesiology, Am. Bd. Anesthesiology. Rsch. asst., dept pharmacology Med. Coll. S.C., 1965, 66 (summers); intern U. Ala. Hosp. and Clinics, Birmingham, Ala., 1969-70, resident in anesthesiology, 1970-72; post-doctoral, dept. anesthesia and physiology U. Ala. Med. Sch., 1972; instr., dept anesthesiology U. Ala. Hosp. and Clinics, 1973; dept. tng. staff, anesthesiology Nat. Naval Med. Ctr., Bethesda, Md., 1973-75; clin. instr., dept. anesthesiology George Washington U. Sch. Med., Washington, 1973-75; assoc. prof., dept. anesthesiology U. Ala. Hosp. and Clinics, 1975-78; dir., div. anesthesiology rsch. U. Ala., 1977-84, prof. anesthesiology, 1978-84; clin. anesthesia coord. UAB Cardiac Transplant Program, Birmingham, 1982-84; prof. anesthesiology, dir. cardiothoracic anesthesia Duke U. Med. Ctr., Durham, NC, 1984-1991; dir. Duke Heart Ctr., Duke Med. Ctr., Durham, NC, 1987-97; interim chmn., dept. anesthesiology Duke U. Med. Ctr., 1990-91, prof. and chmn., dept. anesthesiology, 1991—2001; dean, v.p. for med. affairs Med. U. S.C. Coll. Medicine, Charleston, 2001—. Cons. Hoffman-LaRoche, Somatogen, Abbott/Oximetric. Contbr. to numerous profl. jours., refereed jours., chpts. in books, published scientific reviews, selected abstracts, editorials, films, audio visual presentations, letters, positions and background papers; author: Acute Revascularization of the Infracted Heart, 1987, Common Problems in Cardiac Anesthesia, 1987, Intravenous Anesthesia and Analgesia, 1988, Anesthesiology Clinics of North America, 1988, Anesthesia, 1990, International Anesthesiology Clinics, 1991; Cardiac Anesthesia, Privileges and Practice, 1994; editor: Anesthesia and Analgesia, 1984—, cardiovascular sect. editor 1991—; editorial bd. Society Cardiovascular Anesthesia Monograph Series (chmn. 1986-89), Current Opinion in Anaesthesia 1987—, American Antec Newsletter 1989—; co-editor in chief: Current Opinion in Anaesthesiology 1990—. Dir. Clairmont Ave Hist. Preservation Com. 1976-78; Am. Heart Assn. (Durham chpt. pres. 1988-90, com. mem. anesthesiology, radiology and surgery rsch. study com. 1988-91). Grantee NIH 1991—, Janssen Pharmaceutica 1991-93, Anaquest 1989-92, Diprivan Ednl. grant ICI Pharmaceuticals Group 1991-92. Fellow Am. Coll. Cardiology; mem. AMA, Durham County Medical Soc., Internat. Soc. on Oxygen Transport to Tissue, N.C. Soc. Anesthesiologist (edn. com. 1992—), N.C. State Medical Soc., Birmingham Vanderbilt Club (bd. dirs. 1975-80, 1st v.p. 1979, pres. 1980), Southern Med. Assn. (chmn. elect. anesthesiology sect. 1976-77, chmn. 1977-78, chmn. 1988-89), Southern Soc. Anesthesiologists (v.p. 1978-79, pres. elect 1979-80, pres. 1980-81), Soc. Cardiovascular Anesthesiologists (pres. 1979-80), Assn. Univ. Anesthetists (elected to mem. 1980), Assn. Cardiac Anesthesiologists (elected to mem. 1982, pres. 1990), Soc. for Neuroleptanalgesia (bd. dirs. 1988), U. Ala. Birmingham Nat. Alumni Soc. (dist. dir., bd. dirs. 1991-93), Internat. Anesthesia Rsch. Soc. (bd. Trustees 1992—), Am. Soc. Anesthesiologists (com. sub-specialty representation 1980—, subcommittee on clin. circulation 1992—, com. geriatric anesthesia 1992—), Sigma Xi, Alpha Omega Alpha. Achievements include research on effects of age on neurologic response to cardiopulmonary bypass; cerebral blood flow and metabolism during cardiac surgery; automated delivery system of intravenous anesthetic drugs; pathophysiology of cardiopulmonary bypass; redesign of medical education. Office: Med U SC PO Box 250617 96 Jonathan Lucas St Ste 601 Charleston SC 29425 Office Phone: 843-792-2842. Business E-Mail: revesj@musc.edu.

REVESZ, RICHARD LUIS, dean, law educator; b. Buenos Aires, May 9, 1958; BSE in Civil Engring. summa cum laude, Princeton U., 1979; MS, MIT, 1980; JD, Yale U., 1983. Bar: NY 1986, DC 1986, US Supreme Ct. 1989, US Ct. Appeals DC Cir. 1986, US Dist. Ct. So. Dist. NY 1986. Jud. clerk to Chief Judge Wilfred Feinberg US Ct. Appeals 2nd Cir., NYC, 1983-84; jud. clerk to Justice Thurgood Marshall US Supreme Ct., 1984-85; asst. prof. NYU Sch. Law, 1985-88, assoc. prof., 1988-90, prof., 1990—2001, Lawrence King prof. law, 2001—, dir. Program on Environ. Regulation, 1996—, dean, 2002—. Vis. prof. U. Geneva Sch. Law, 1995, Harvard Law Sch., 1995-96, Yale Law Sch., 2001; Shelby Cullum Davis vis. prof. Grad. Inst. Internat. Studies, Geneva, 1995; vis. prof. pub. & internat. law Princeton U., 2002; pro-bono rep. Natural Resources Def. Coun., 1987; term mem. Coun. Fgn. Rels., 1989-94; cons. Environ. Economics Adv. Com. of Sci. Advisory Bd. EPA, 1998-99, mem., 1999-; cons. dept. tech. coop. for devel. UN, 1980-81, Adminstrv. Conf. of US, 1986-89, 1991-92, Carnegie Commn. Sci., Tech., and Govt., 1989-90; mem. internat. adv. bd. Yearbook European Environ. Law, 1998-. Author: Foundations of Environmental Law and Policy, 1997; editor: Distinctive Practices of the Second Circuit, 1989; co-editor: Analyzing Superfund: Economics, Science, and Law, 1995, Environmental Law, the Economy, and Sustainable Development: The United States, the European Union, and the International Community, 2000. Mem. ABA (vice chmn. com. jud. review sect. adminstrv. law 1988-98, chair, 1998—), Am. Law Inst., Assn. Bar City of NY (chmn. com. adminstrv. law 1988-91, sec. com. second century 1986-88, mem. com. environ. law 1986-88), Am. Law and Economics Assn. (bd. dirs. 1999-), Phi Beta Kappa, Sigma Xi, Tau Beta Pi (prize winner); fellow Am. Acad. Arts & Scis. Office: NYU Sch Law Vanderbilt Hall Ste 406 40 Washington Sq S New York NY 10012-1099 Office Phone: 212-998-6000. Office Fax: 212-995-3150. E-mail: richard.revesz@nyu.edu. *

REVILLE, ROBERT T., economist; PhD, Brown U. Economist RAND Inst. Civil Justice, 1995—99, rsch. dir., 1999—2003, dir., 2003—; co-dir. RAND Ctr. for Terrorism Risk Mgmt. Policy. Author of books & articles on workers compensation issues. Mem.: Nat. Acad. Social Insurance (mem. Workers' Compensation Steering Com.). Office: RAND Institute for Civil Justice 1776 Main St PO Box 2138 Santa Monica CA 90407-2138 Office Phone: 310-393-0411. E-mail: reville@rand.org. *

REVIS, DON RAY, JR., plastic surgeon; b. Greenwood, SC, Oct. 16, 1966; BS in Zoology, Duke U.; MD, Med. U. S.C., 1992. Cert. Am. Bd. Surgery 1999, Am. Bd. Plastic Surg. 2001, lic. Fla. Founder So. Fla. Plastic

Surgery Assocs. Intern, gen. surgery George Washington U. Med. Ctr., Washington, 1992—93, residency, gen. surg., 1993—98; residency, plastic & reconstructive surg. U. Fla., Gainesville, 1998—2000; fellowship, cosmetic surgery Plastic Surgery Assocs., Miami, Fla., 2000; cons. staff, divsn. plastic reconstructive surgery Univ. Fla. Coll. Medicine. Vol. Interplast, Honduras, Project Senegal, Senegal. Nominee Exec. Com., Candidates and Assocs. Soc., Am. Coll. Surgeons, mem. editl. adv. bd., Obesity Help Magazine, Ethics Com., eMedicine Online Med. Textbook, 2000—, Ho. of Dels., Fla. Med. Assn., 2001; named Disting. Physician, Best Plastic Surgeon and Best Physician, Coral Springs Forum, The Jewish Jour. newspapers, 2002—03, Up and Coming Physician of Year, Fla. Med. Bus. Jour., to symposium com., Am. Soc. Aesthetic Plastic Surg. and Aesthetic Soc. Education and Rsch. Found., among America's top surgeons, Consumer Rsch. Coun. of Am., 2001; recipient Physician's Recognition award, Am. Med. Assn., 1998; grantee Rsch. fellow, Nat. Insts. Health, Bethesda, Md., 1995—96. Fellow: ACS; mem.: AMA, Duke U. Alumni Assn., Better Bus. Bureau, Lipoplasty Soc., Wound Healing Soc., Fla. Med. Assn., Internat. Coll. Surgeons, Broward County Med. Assn., Internat. Fedn. Surgery of Obesity, Am. Soc. Bariatric Surgery, Broward County Soc. Plastic Surgeons, Am. Soc. Aesthetic Plastic Surgery, Am. Soc. Plastic Surgeons, Med. Univ. So. Carolina Alumni Assn. (life), Monterey Bay Sea Otter Rsch. and Conservation Program, Nat. Trust Historic Preservation, Iron Dukes, Rotary Club Internat. Achievements include numerous speaking engagements; tv appearances include Healthy Living, 2001, The Maury Povich Show, 2004, Channel 10 News, WPLG, 2004; Author of numerous publications including author of 26 chptrs. of an online medical textbook: emedicine.com. Office: So Fla Plastic Surgery Assocs 2500 N Federal Hwy Ste 301 Fort Lauderdale FL 33305 Office Phone: 954-630-2009. *

REVIS-PYKE, ROBIN LYNN, director; b. Orlando, Fla., Feb. 16, 1962; d. Ed Revis and Carol Joan Rogers; m. Scott Douglas Pyke; children: Robert Stevin Revis Pyke, Spencer Douglas Pyke, Barrett Harper Pyke. BS in Comm., Trinity Internat. U., Miami; MS in Higher Edn. Adminstrn., Barry U., Miami, post graduate studies in Edn. Preschool tchr. Miami Shores Baptist Ch., 1996—97, fin. asst., 1997—2000; media comm. coord. Archdiocese of Miami, 2000—01; assoc. dir. admission and fin. aid Miami Country Day Sch., Miami, 2001—06; dean of admission Montverde Acad., Fla., 2006—. Assoc. editor The Admission Review. Chair Miami Shores Village Fine Arts Commn., Fla., 1997—2002; mem. Philanthropic Educators Orgn., 1999—2002; exec. bd. mem. Shores Performing Arts Theater, Miami Shores, 2002—04; mem. pres. bd. advisors St. Thomas U.; chair Miami Shores Village Mayors Task Force, Fla., 1998—2001. Mem.: Assn. Ind. Sch. Admission Profls., Secondary Sch. Admission Test Bd., Nat. Coun. Measurement in Edn., Nat. Assn. Independent Schs., Am. Ednl. Rsch. Assn. (grad. student coun. camps liaison 2005—), Am. Assn. U. Women, Phi Delta Kappa, Kappa Delta Pi. Republican. Baptist. Avocations: yoga, cooking, reading, boating, snorkeling. Home: 912 Sunset Shores Dr Minneola FL 34715 Office: Montverde Academy 17235 Seventh St Montverde FL 34756 E-mail: robin@revispyke.net.

REVKIN, ANDREW C., writer, reporter; married; 2 children. B in Biology, Brown Univ.; M in Journalism, Columbia Univ. Staff writer LA Times; sr. writer Science Digest; sr. editor Discover mag.; reporter New York Times, 1995—. Lectr. on writing and environment; appearances on Today Show, Good Morning America, NPR, CNN; adj. prof. Columbia U. Sch. Journalism, NYC. Author: (books) The Burning Season (Sidney Hillman Foundation Book prize, Robert F. Kennedy Book award, New York Times Notable Book of Yr.), 1990, Global Warming: Understanding the Forecast, 1992. Recipient AAAS Journalism award, 2002, Investigative Reporters & Editors award. Avocations: guitar, songwriting. Office: Environmental Writer New York Times 229 W 43rd St New York NY 10036

REVNEW, THOMAS RICHARD, lawyer; b. 1968; BBA with distinction, U. Mich., Ann Arbor, 1991; JD, Marquette U. Law Sch., 1994. Bar: Wis. 1994, Minn. 1999. Shareholder Seaton, Beck & Peters, P.A., Mpls. Contbr. articles to profl. publs.; assoc. editor: Marquette Law Rev. Named a Rising Star, Minn. Super Lawyers mag., 2006. Mem.: ABA, Minn. State Bar Assn., Milw. Bar Assn. Office: Seaton Beck & Peters PA 7300 Metro Blvd Ste 500 Minneapolis MN 55439 Office Phone: 952-921-4622. E-mail: trevnew@seatonlaw.com. *

REVOILE, CHARLES PATRICK, lawyer; b. Jan. 15, 1934; s. Charles Patrick and Olga Lydia (Zecca) R.; m. Sally Cole Gates, Nov. 8, 1963. BA, U. Md., 1957, LLB, 1960. Bar: Md. 1962, U.S. Dist. Ct. Md. 1962, U.S. Supreme Ct. 1970, U.S. Ct. Claims 1976, U.S. Ct. Appeals (fed. cir.) 1982. Legis. counsel Nat. Canners Assn., Washington, 1960-64; asst. counsel Deco Electronics Inc., Washington, 1964-67; divsn. counsel Westinghouse Electric, Leesburg, Va., 1967-71; v.p., gen. counsel Stanwick Corp., Arlington, Va., 1971-85; sr. v.p., gen. counsel, sec. CACI Internat. Inc., 1985-92, bd. dirs., 1992—, chmn. compensation com., 1995—, exec. com., 1999—, mem. investor rels. com., 2001—, mem. corp. governance com., 2003—. Mem. regional adv. coun. NASD, 1989-92, mem. nominating com., 2004—; lectr., panelist, advisor. Active in Md. Ednl. Found., College Park, 1974-98; assoc. Nat. Symphony Orch., Washington, 1972-93, Smithsonian Instn., 1980-93, M Club Found., 1985-98; lawyer, lobbyist various non-profit orgns., Washington, 1984-98; mem. exec. com. ann. bus. campaign Gallaudet U., 1989-91; chmn. various coms. Kemper Open Championships, 1980-86; exec. com. 1995 USGA Sr. Open, 1997 USGA Open Championships; gen. counsel, mem. exec. com. 1995, 96, 97 Kemper Open Championship. Mem. Md. Bar Assn., Washington Corp. Counsels Assn., Am. Corp. Counsels Assn., Nat. Assn. Corp. Dirs., USGA, Mid. Atlantic Golf Assn. (exec. com. 1989-99, v.p., pres. 1998), Roger Howell Soc. U. Md. Sch. Law (charter), Congl. Country Club (com. chmn. 1966-92, bd. govs. 1987-93, Bethesda, Md.), Ocean Forest Golf Club (Sea Island, Ga.), Sea Island Club (founder), Sea Island Srs. Golf Assn. (pres. 2003), Sea Island Property Owners Ass. (bd. dirs. 2006—). Home: PO Box 31223 Sea Island GA 31561-1223

REW, LAWRENCE BOYD, lawyer; b. Eugene, Oreg., June 22, 1936; BA, Whitman Coll., 1958; JD, Willamette U., 1961. Bar: Oreg. 1961. Ptnr., of counsel Corey, Byler, Rew, Lorenzen & Hojem, LLP, Pendleton, Oreg., 1965—2005; ret., 2005. Fellow Am. Bar Found.; mem. ABA, Oreg. State Bar Assn. (pres. 2000, Pub. Svc. award 1991, bd. bar examiners 1975-79, bd. govs. 1996-2000). Home Phone: 541-276-4801. Personal E-mail: lbrew01@yahoo.com.

REWAK, WILLIAM JOHN, retired academic administrator, clergyman; b. Syracuse, NY, Dec. 22, 1933; s. William Alexander and Eldora Venetia (Carroll) R. BA, Gonzaga U., 1957, MA in English, 1958; MA in Theology, Regis Coll., Toronto, Ont., Can., 1965; PhD in English, U. Minn., 1970. Joined S.J., 1951, ordained priest Roman Cath. Ch., 1964. Tchr. English Bellarmine Coll. Prep. Sch., 1958-61; asst. prof. English Santa Clara (Calif.) U., 1970-71, pres., 1976-88; rector Jesuit Community, 1971-76; pres. Spring Hill Coll., Mobile, Ala., 1989-97; ret., 1997. Bd. dirs. Gulf Coast Broadcasting Inc., Badger-Stonewall Ins. Co., Marine Environ. Scis. Consortium. Contbr. articles to theol. and critical jours., poetry, short stories to lit. jours. Bd. dirs. Mobile Bay Area Partnership for Youth, Mercy Med. Ctr.; mem. Ala. Ind. Colls., Coun. for Advancement Pvt. Colls. in Ala.; bd. trustees Loyola U. New Orleans. Mem. MLA, Coll. English Assn., Bienville Club. Democrat. Home and Office: Spring Hill Coll Office of Pres 4000 Dauphin St Mobile AL 36608-1780

REWCASTLE, NEILL BARRY, neuropathologist; b. Sunderland, Eng., Dec. 12, 1931; arrived in Can., 1955; s. William Alexander and Eva (Coapes) R.; m. Eleanor Elizabeth Barton Boyd, Sept. 27, 1958 (dec. Jan. 1999); 4 children. MB, BChir cum laude, U. St. Andrews, Scotland, 1955; MA, U. Toronto, 1962. Licentiate Med. Coun. Can., 1957; cert. in gen. pathology, 1962, cert. in neuropathology, 1968 Royal Coll. Physicians, Can. Rotating intern Vancouver Gen. Hosp., 1955-56; resident in pathology Shaughnessy Hosp., Vancouver, 1956-57, U. Toronto, Ont., Canada, 1957-60, demonstrator dept. pathology, 1964-65, lectr., acting head divsn. neuropathology, dept. pathology, 1965—69, assoc. prof., 1969-70, prof., head divsn. neuropathology, 1970—81; fellow Med. Rsch. Coun. Can., 1960-64; prof. & head dept. pathology U. Calgary, 1981-91, prof., 1981-2000, prof. emeritus pathology, lab. medicine, clin. neuroscis., 2000—, mem. neurosci. rsch. group, 1982—2003; sr. pathologist Toronto Gen. Hosp., 1970—81. Dir. dept. histopathology Foothills Hosp., Calgary, 1981-91, pathologist, 1981—, cons. neuropathology, 1981-2003; spl. acad. adv. to dean faculty medicine U. Calgary, 1995-97; presenter in field. Contbr. over 146 articles to profl. jour., chpts. to books. Recipient Queen Elizabeth Silver Jubilee medal, 1977. Fellow: Royal Coll. Physicians; mem. Can. Assn. Neuropathologists (ret. mem., sec. 1965-69, pres. 1976-79), Am. Assn. Neuropathologists (sr.), Sunshine Coast Power and Sail Squadron (bd. dirs., comdr. 2007), Gibsons Curling Club (bd. dirs.) Sunshinre Cost Golf and Country Club. Avocations: gardening, philately, golf, curling, sailing. Personal E-mail: rewcastb@telus.net.

REX, JIM, school system administrator; m. Sue Rex; children: Adam, Jeff, Nathan, Siri. Dean edn. Winthrop U., Coastal Carolina U.; pres. Columbia Coll.; v.p. devel. and alumni rels. U. SC, v.p. univ. advancement; supt. edn. SC Dept. Edn., Columbia, 2007—. Cons. Nat. Inst. Edn., SC Educator Improvement Task Force. Contbr. articles to profl. jours. Chair Clean Water SC; bd. dirs. Palmetto Conservation Found. Office: SC Dept Edn Ste 1006 1429 Senate St Columbia SC 29201 Office Phone: 803-734-8500. Office Fax: 803-734-3389. *

REX, LONNIE ROYCE, religious organization administrator; b. Caddo, Okla., May 11, 1928; s. Robert Lavern and Lennie Cordy (Gilcrease) R.; m. Betty Louise Sorrells, Apr. 8, 1949; children: Royce DeWayne, Patricia Louise, Debra Kaye. MusB, Oklahoma City U., 1950; DD (hon.), Am. Bible Inst., 1970; LLD (hon.), Wesley Synod, NYC, 1999, Meth. Wesley Synod, Toledo, 1999; LittD, Wesley Synod, 2000. Advt. mgr. Oral Roberts Evang. Assn., Tulsa, 1955-57; bus. mgr. T.L. Osborn Found., Tulsa, 1957-69; gen. mgr. Christian Crusade, Tulsa, 1969-80; sec.-treas. David Livingstone Missionary Found., Tulsa, 1970-80, pres., 1980—98. Dep. dir. gen. Internat. Biog. Assn.; bd. dirs. Intra-Ch. Pension Fund, Bethany, Okla.; spkr. internat. confs. Eng., Hungary, Korea, Singapore, Spain, N.Y.C., Congress of Arts and Comms., Oxford U., 1997; invited Pyongyang, North Korea to meet as an NGO with Peace Com. and med. aid, 1996, 97; participant peace conf. Carter Ctr. between North Korea and South Korea, 1997. Author: Never a Child, 1989. Mem. Internat. PHC Loan Fund; bd. dirs. Armand Hammer United World Coll. of Am. West, 1993—; bd. mem. Internat. Humanitarian Centre Russia, Moscow, 2000. Recipient Merit award Korea, 1975, Moran medal Republic of Korea, Humanitarian award Senator Hugh Scott, 1983, Svc. to Mankind award Internat. Biog. Congress, Spain, 1987, Internat. Lions Club award, UN award, medal Gen. Ground Forces USSR, 1990, World Humanitarian Leadership award by M. Susan Savage Mayor of Tulsa, 1998, Roseland Cook Bronze award David Livingstone Found., 1998; knighted in Moscow, 1993; Lonnie Royce Rex Day named in his honor by Gov. Keating of Okla., Jan. 24, 1998. Mem. Knights of Malta (Sword of Svc. 1996), Phi Beta Kappa. Home: 7914 Oxfordshire Dr Spring TX 77379-4668 Personal E-mail: lonnierrex@sbcglobal.net. *In my work among the starving in Ethiopia, I walked into a tent of over 100 mothers, lying on mats, who had given birth during the last three days. It was silent! Morbid silence! That haunting silence lives with me since that moment. I asked why? I was informed the babies did not have the strength to cry. I have given my life to "cry out" for those in need that did not have the strength to "cry".*

REXFORD, JOHN H., information technology company executive; BA, MBA, So. Meth. U. V.p. Citicorp, Citibank, Continental Ill. Corp.; sr. v.p. Affiliated Computer Svcs., Inc. (ACS), Dallas, 1996—2001, exec. v.p., 2001—, CFO, bd. dirs., 2006—. Office: ACS 2828 N Haskell Dallas TX 75201 Office Phone: 214-841-6111. *

REY, ROBERT M., plastic surgeon; b. São Paolo, Brazil; arrived in US, 1974; m. Hayley Rey; children: Sydney, Robby. BA in Chemistry, Ariz. State U., 1983; M in Health Policy, Harvard U., 1990; MD, Tufts U. Sch. Medicine, 1990. Diplomate Nat. Bd. Med. Examiners. Resident, gen. surgery Harbor-UCLA Med. Ctr., 1995; resident, plastic surgery U. Tenn. Med. Ctr., 1997; aesthetic and breast reconstruction fellowship Harvard Med. Sch., 1998; private practice Beverly Hills, Calif. Former health policy writer Office of the US Surgeon General. Contbr. articles to med. and plastic surgery jours.; cons. (films) Seven, featured on Dr. 90210, 2004—, featured in CBS, WB, E! Channel, Elle Mag. and fgn. media, featured doctor (DVD series) Rey's Anatomy: The Sensual Body (Vol. I, II, & III). Recipient Am. Assn. Clin. Anatomist Student award for original anatomy and biomechanics rsch., Southeastern Soc. Plastic Surgeons Resident's award. Mem.: AMA, SAG. Avocations: Eagle Scout, martial arts. Office: 436 North Bedford Dr Ste 304 Beverly Hills CA 90210 Office Phone: 310-205-3107. Office Fax: 310-205-8822.

REYELTS, PAUL C., chemical company executive; MBA, Harvard U. V.p. corp. fin. dept. Piper, Jaffray & Hopwood; sr. v.p. fin., CFO Valspar Corp., Mpls. Office: Valspar Corp 1101 Third St South Minneapolis MN 55415

REYER, STEVEN E., engineering educator; s. Elliott and Jean Reyer; m. Linda Philipps, May 21, 1989. BSEE, U. of Wis., Milw., 1972, MSEE, 1973; ABD, U. of Ill., Urbana, 1975; PhD, Marquette U., 1978. Registered profl. engr., Wis. Asst. prof. elec. engring. U. Wis., 1978—84; prof. elec. engring. Milw. Sch. Engring., 1984—. Cons. numerous cos. Contbr. articles to tech. publs., photographs to contests (numerous nat. photo contest awards). Recipient univ. fellowship, U. of Ill., 1973—75, F. R. Bacon fellowship, Marquette U., 1977—78, rsch. grant, ANR Pipeline Co., 1988, 1991, 3M Co., 1988, 1990, 1992, 1994; fellow F. R. Bacon fellowship, U. Wis.-Milw., 1972—73. Mem.: ASEE, IEEE (dir. Milw. sect. 1981—84), Mensa, Sigma Xi, Phi Eta Sigma, Phi Kappa Phi, Eta Kappa Nu, Tau Beta Pi. Achievements include development of First FM Stereo Radio Transmitter based on Digital Signal Processing. Avocation: photography. Office: Milw Sch Engring 1025 N Broadway Milwaukee WI 53202 Home Phone: 262-242-4553; Office Phone: 414-277-7347. E-mail: reyer@msoe.edu.

REYES, ANNA MARIA, broadcast executive; b. Phoenix, Aug. 21, 1957; d. Perfecto C. and Esperanza (Del Castillo) R. BA in Fin., Ariz. State U., 1983. Radio-Tel. operators permit FCC; notary public, Ariz. Traffic/continuity dir. First Media Corp./KOPA AM and FM, Scottsdale, Ariz., 1978-81, music dir., air talent, 1981-83; bus. mgr., asst. sta. mgr. Cook Inlet Radio Ptnr. KSLX-FM and KOPA-AM, 1983-92; sta. contr., asst. gen. mgr. Jacor/Citicasters KSLX AM/FM, Phoenix, 1992-96; gen. mgr. Jacor Comm. KSLX AM/FM, Phoenix, 1997—. Interviewer KSLX FM/KOPA AM, Scottsdale, 1990. Co-author: INXS Newsletter, 1994. Spokeswoman campaign against radio for men format KSLX FM/KOPA AM, Scottsdale, 1988. Recipient Cert. for Announcing, City of Phoenix-Hello Phoenix, 1985, Bus. Mgr. award Corp. Chain Contest, Phoenix, 1990-92. Mem. AAUW, Am. Women in Radio and TV, Broadcast Cable Fin. Mgmt., Univ. Women London. Democrat. Roman Catholic. Avocations: european travel, ballet, reading, music. Home: 12340 W Elwood St Avondale AZ 85323-9618 Office: KSLX Radio FM/AM 4343 E Camelback Rd Ste 200 Phoenix AZ 85018-8306

REYES, CZARINA SUZANNE, mathematics educator; d. Suzanne Paulette Reynolds. BA in Math., So. Meth. U., 1998, MA, 2001; attended in Higher Edn., U. N. Tex. Cert. tchr. Tex., 1999. Math. tchr. Creekview HS, Carrollton, Tex., 1999—2000; faculty math. Dallas County C.C. Dist.-Brookhaven Coll., Farmers Branch, Tex., 2000—. Mem. Tex. Instruments CC Math. Adv. Panel, 2007—08. Recipient LENs award Focusin Excellence, Brookhaven Coll., 2006. Mem.: AAUW, Tex. CC Tchrs. Assn., Math. Assn. Am., Phi Kappa Phi, Nat. Scholars, Phi Theta Kappa (Outstanding Student Honor Soc. 2004). Office: Brookhaven Coll 3939 Valley View Ln Farmers Branch TX 75244 Home Phone: 214-868-0925; Office Phone: 972-860-4338. Office Fax: 972-860-4151. Business E-Mail: creyes@dcccd.edu.

REYES, GEORGE, information technology executive; BA in Acctg., U. South Fla.; MBA, Santa Clara U. Various fin. roles Sun Microsystems Inc., Santa Clara, Calif., 1994—2001; interim CFO ONI Systems, 2002; sr. v.p., CFO Google Inc., Mountain View, Calif., 2002—. Dir. Symantec Corp., BEA Systems Inc., Chordiant Software. Office: Google Inc 1600 Amphitheatre Pky Mountain View CA 94043 Office Phone: 650-623-4000. Office Fax: 650-618-1499. *

REYES, J. CHRISTOPHER, food products distribution executive; BS in Finance, U. Maryland, 1975. Co-founder, CEO Reyes Holdings, Lake Forest, Ill., 1976—. Bd. dirs. Fortune Brands Inc., Wintrust Financial Corp., 1991—, Allstate Corp., Tribune Co., 2005—. Bd. dirs. Lyric Opera of Chgo., Mus. Sci. and Industry, Northwestern Meml. Found., U. Notre Dame. Mem.: Old Elm, Onwentsia. Office: Reyes Holdings LLC 9500 W Bryn Mawr Ave Ste 700 Rosemont IL 60018 Office Fax: (847) 604-9972. *

REYES, JOSE BERNABE, professional baseball player; b. Villa Gonzalez, Dominican Republic, June 11, 1983; s. Jose Manuel and Rosa Reyes. Shortstop NY Mets, 2003—. Named to Nat. League All-Star Team, Maj. League Baseball, 2006—07; recipient Silver Slugger award, 2006. Achievements include leading the Nat. League in triples, 2005 (17), 2006 (17), and stolen bases, 2005 (60), 2006 (64). Office: New York Mets Shea Stadium 123-01 Roosevelt Ave Flushing NY 11368-1699 *

REYES, RAUL GREGORIO, surgeon; b. Tegucigalpa, Morazan, Honduras, June 18, 1928; came to U.S., 1939; s. Julio Gregorio and Mercedes Ofelia (Mazzoni) Reyes-Zelaya; m. Mildred Dane Smith, 1951 (dec. May 1990); children: Tyra, Kimberly; stepchildren: Javier, Christian; m. Blanca Lidia Milla, Apr. 2, 1993. BS, Georgetown U., 1945; MD, George Washington U., 1950. Diplomate Nat. Bd. Med. Examiners, Am. Bd. Surgery. Intern Charity Hosp., New Orleans, 1950-51; resident Emergency Hosp./George Washington U., Washington, 1951, Charity Hosp., New Orleans, 1952-55; chief thoracic surgery San Felipe Hosp., Tegucigalpa, 1955-56; assoc. to ptnr. Browne-McHardy Clinic, New Orleans, 1955-60, 60-73; med. dir. New Orleans Indsl. Clinic, 1956-58; chief of surgery and orthopedics Lallie Kemp Regional Hosp., Independence, La., 1987-89, med. dirs., 1988-89; owner, pres. Raul G. Reyes, A Med. Corp., New Orleans, 1973—. Owner, pres. Internat. Maritime Med. Svcs., New Orleans, 1978—, Catracho Enterprises, New Orleans, 1975—. Phys. Therapy Svcs. of New Orleans, 1975—; faculty La. State Univ. Sch. Medicine, 1953—, others. Inventor in field; contbr. articles to profl. jours. Chmn. Rep. Hispanic Assembly, New Orleans, 1983; pre-cand. Nat. Party, Honduras, 1985; founder Literacy Ctrs. of Honduras, 1991; presdl. candidate Christian Dem. Party of Honduras, 1994. Named to Hon. Consul of Honduras, Hon. Citizen, City of New Orleans. Mem. ACS, AMA, So. Med. Assn., La. State Med. Soc., Orleans Parish Med. Soc., Colegio Medico de Honduras. Roman Catholic. Avocations: tennis, reading, writing, social progs. Office: PO Box 15379 New Orleans LA 70175-5379 Office Phone: 225-766-5050.

REYES, SILVESTRE, congressman; b. Canutillo, Tex., Nov. 10, 1944; m. Carolina Gaytan; children: Monica, Rebecca, Silvestre Jr. Student, U. Tex., Austin, 1964—65, U. Tex., El Paso, 1965—66; AA, El Paso CC, 1976. Agt. US Immigration and Naturalization Svc. Border Patrol, 1969, asst. regional commr. Dallas, sector chief, 1984-95; mem. US Congress from 16th Tex. Dist., 1997—, mem. armed svcs. com., vets. affairs com., chmn. permanent select com. on intelligence, 2007—, founder Missing and Exploited Children's Caucus. Served in US Army, 1966—68, Vietnam. Recipient Moving Forward award, El Paso Hispanic C. of C., Presdl. award, Outstanding Svc., Mex. Am. Bar Assn., Outstanding Leadership award, Hispanic Assn. Colls. and Univs., Disting. Cmty. Health Defender award, Nat. Assn. Cmty. Health Ctr., Chmn.'s award, US Hispanic C. of C., Govt. Bus. Adv. of Yr. award, Pres.'s award, League of United Latin Am. Citizens, Govt. Hispanic Bus. Adv. of Yr. award, Tex. Assn. Mex. Am. Cs. of C., Border Health Hero award, Pan Am. Health Orgn., Susan. G. Hadden Pioneer award, Alliance for Pub. Tech., Nat. Congl. award, Nat. Pks. Conservation Assn., L. Medel Rivers award, Legis. Excellence, Air Force Sgts. Assn., Century Coun. Congl. award, Elected Ofcl. of Yr. award, Rio Grande Coun. Govts. Democrat. Office: US Congress 2433 Rayburn Ho Office Bldg Washington DC 20515 also: 310 N Mesa St Ste 400 El Paso TX 79901-1301 Office Phone: 202-225-4831. *

REYES, VICTOR H., lawyer; b. Mexico, Apr. 28, 1964; BA Polit. Sci., Loyola Univ., 1987; JD, DePaul Univ., 1990. Bar: Ill. 1990. Asst. to Mayor City of Chgo., 1989—95, dir. Mayor's Off. Intergovernmental Affairs, 1995—2002; shareholder, governmental and adminstrv. law dept. Greenberg Traurig LLP, Chgo., 2002—. Bd. dir. Park Fed. Savings. Bd. dir. Rehabilitation Inst. Chgo.; bd. overseers Chgo.-Kent Coll. of Law. Mem.: Ill. Inst. Technology (bd. trustees). Office: Greenberg Traurig LLP Ste 2500 77 W Wacker Dr Chicago IL 60601-1732 Office Phone: 312-456-8400. Office Fax: 312-456-8435. Business E-Mail: reyesv@gtlaw.com.

REYES-CUBIDES, WILLIAM, language educator, researcher, writer, actor; b. Bogotá, Colombia, Dec. 21, 1969; arrived in U.S., 1992; s. Alvaro Reyes and Patricia Cubides. BA, Nat. Pedagogical U., Bogotá, 1990; MA in Applied Linguistics, Nat. U., Bogotá, 1992; PhD, Boston Coll., 2006. Fgn. langs. lectr. Goucher Coll., Towson, Md., 1995—96, Towson U., Towson, Md., 1996—99; Romance langs. tchg. fellow Boston Coll., Chestnut Hill, Mass., 1999—2006; lectr. Spanish and fgn. langs. MIT, 2005—; asst. prof. dept. cultural studies U. Mass., Lowell, 2005—06. Editor-in-chief Romance Rev., Boston, 2000—02; conf. dir. Internat. Congress on Romance Studies, Boston, 2000—02. Scriptwriter: pedagogic video Impresiones, 2002. Dir. Colombia's March for Peace, Boston, 1999. Recipient Donald J. White Tchg. Excellence award, Boston, 2003; grantee U.S. Dept. Edn., 2003. Fellow: Internat. Alliance of Tchr.-Scholars; mem.: ACTFL, MLA, L.Am. Studies Assn., Romance Langs. Grad. Assn. (pres. Boston 2002—04). Office: MIT 77 Massachusetts Ave 14N-426 Cambridge MA 02139 Business E-Mail: reyescw@mit.edu.

REYES ROBBINS, ANN MARIE, lawyer, researcher, educator, former magistrate judge; b. LA, Mar. 9, 1966; d. Raymond Alexander and Flora (Sanchez) Reyes; m. Jeffrey Warren Schroeder, Sept. 20, 1986 (div. July 22, 1997); 1 child, Andrew Nicholas Reyes Schroeder; m. Bruce Anthony Robbins, Nov. 7, 1997. BA in Am. Lit. and Bus. minor with honors, U. So. Calif., LA, 1994; attending, U. So. Calif., 2005—; JD, U. Mich., Ann Arbor, 1998; AA in Social and Behavioral Scis., Mt. San Antonio Coll., Walnut, Calif., 2004, AA in Fine Arts and Humanities, 2004, AA in Lang. Arts and Communication, 2005. Bar: Ind. 1999, US Dist. Ct. (so and no. dists.) Ind. 1999, cert.: Ind. Jud. Ctr. (probation officer) 1998, Ind. (domestic rels. mediator) 1998, Ind. Bar Assn. (family law specialist) 2002. Edn. track liaison, title IV-E waiver coord. Allen Superior Ct. Family Rels.

Divsn., Fort Wayne, Ind., 1998, asst. chief juvenile probation officer, adminstrv. divsn., 1999—99; assoc. atty. Avery & Van Gilder, Fort Wayne, Ind., 1999—2000; assoc. atty., jr. ptnr. Blume Connelly Jordan & Stucky, LLP, Fort Wayne, Ind., 2000—01, ptnr., 2002; magistrate judge Allen Superior Ct. Family Rels. Divsn., Fort Wayne, Ind., 2003; family law specialist Mallor, Clendening, Grodner & Bohrer LLP, Bloomington, Ind., 2003—04; tchr. Elite Ednl. Inst., Rowland Heights, Calif., 2004—05; sr. pub. adminstrv. analyst, dept. social welfare Children and Families Rsch. Consortium, Inter-U. Consortium Social Work Schs., U. Calif., LA, 2006—; rsch. asst., ctr. rsch. crime and social control U. So. Calif., 2006—. Trial atty. Allen County Divsn. Children and Family Svcs., Ft. Wayne, 1999—2000; continuing legal edn. tchr., Ind., 2000—04; gen. counsel Allen County Apptd. Spl. Advs., 2001—02; com. mem. Ind. 3rd Dist. Pro Bono Commn., Fort Wayne, 2002—03; lectr. in field; cons. in field. Latino/Hispanic liaison Allen County Dem. Party, Fort Wayne, Ind., 2001, vice chair, 2002; bd. dirs. Assn. Hispanic Profls. Edn., LA, 1992—95, vice chair fin., 1994—95; v.p. League of United Latin Am. Citizens, Fort Wayne, Ind., 1999—2000; bd. dirs. United Hispanic Ams., Fort Wayne, 1999—2001, Ind. Minority Health Coalition, 2001—02, Vol. Lawyers Program, Fort Wayne, 2002—04; pres. Allen County Minority Health Coalition, Fort Wayne, 2001—02; mem. parent adv. com. Diabetech, Inc., Dallas, 2003—. Fellow Kellogg/Bergstom Child Welfare Law Summer Fellow, U. Mich. Law Sch., 1997, Mexican Am. Legal Def. and Edn. Fund, Pub. Interest Law Initiative (PILI), 1997, Hispanic Lawyers Assn., 1997; scholar Juan Luis Tienda scholarship, U. Mich. Law Sch., 1996. Fellow: Ind. Bar Found.; mem.: Soc. Social Work and Rsch., Coun. Social Work Edn., Nat. Ct. Apptd. Spl. Advs., Nat. Assn. of Counsel for Children, Ind. State Bar Assn. (civil rights of children, Latino affairs, diversity profession coms.), Allen County Bar Assn. (women lawyers sect. co-chair 2000), Hispanic Nat. Bar Assn., U. Mich. Alumni Assn., UCLA Anderson Sch. Mgmt. Riordan Fellows Alumni Assn., U. So. Calif. Mexican Am. Alumni Assn. Office: University Southern California Ctr Research Crime and Social Control AHF B61 University Pk Los Angeles CA 90089-0375 Office Phone: 213-740-4285. Office Fax: 213-740-8077. Personal E-mail: childlaw@sbcglobal.net. Business E-Mail: reyesrob@usc.edu.

REY-GIRAUD, AGNÈS, health products executive; m. Chris Rey-Giraud; children: Charlotte, Julie. MBA, U. Chgo.; M in Engring., Ecole Nationale d'Ingenieurs de Saint-Etienne, France; M of Ops. Mgmt., ESC, Lyon, France. Various mgmt. positions in mktg., gen. mgmt., ops., sales, fin. and info. systems in US and Europe Xerox; v.p., gen. mgr. eBusiness Express Scripts, Inc., Md. Heights, Mo., 2000—02, sr. v.p. prog. devel., 2002—03, sr. v.p. product mgmt., 2003—06, sr. v.p. strategy and bus. devel., 2006—, sr. v.p. supply chain orgn., 2006—. Office: Express Scripts Inc 13900 Riverport Dr Maryland Heights MO 63043 Office Phone: 314-770-1666. *

REY-HERNANDEZ, CESAR A., school system administrator; BA, MA Polit Sc. and Internat. Rels., Nat. Autonomous U., Mex., PhD in Sociology, Sec. edn. PR Dept. Edn., San Juan, 2001—. Office: Puerto Rico Dept Edn PO Box 190759 San Juan PR 00919-0759

REYNA, CLAUDIO, professional soccer player; b. Springfield, NJ, July 20, 1973; m. Danielle Egan, 1997; 2 children. Student, U. Va. Midfielder Bayer Leverkusen, Germany, 1994—97, VfL Wolfsburg, Germany, 1997—99, Glasgow Rangers, Scotland, 1999—2000, Sunderland FC, England, 2001—03, Manchester City FC, England, 2003—. 109 caps, 8 goals U.S. Nat. Soccer Team, 1994—, capt., 1999—; mem. U.S. World Cup Team, 1994, 98, 2002, 06. Named Nat. H.S. Player of the Yr., Parade Mag., 1989—90, N.J. H.S. Player of the Yr., 1990, Gatorade H.S. Player of the Yr., 1990, Freshman of Yr., Soccer Am., 1991, 3-time first-team All-Am., Nat. Soccer Coaches Assn. Am., 1991—93; recipient Player of Yr. award, Mo. Athletic Club, 1992, 1993. Office: US Soccer Fedn 1801 S Prairie Ave Chicago IL 60616-1319

REYNARD, MURIEL JOYCE, lawyer; b. Miami Beach, Fla., May 20, 1945; d. Hyman and Faye (Feinstein) Friedkin; m. Brian Patrick Delaney, Nov. 27, 1983; children: Kelly, Charlotte. BA, SUNY, Stony Brook, 1967, MS, 1973; JD cum laude, Yeshiva U., 1983. Bar: N.Y. 1984, U.S. Dist. Ct. (so. and ea. dists.) N.Y. 1984. Health planner Nassau-Suffolk RMP/CHP, Centereach, NY, 1972-74; adminstr. NYC Health and Hosps. Corp., 1974-75; health planner AFSCME Dist. Coun. 37, NYC, 1975-76; adminstr. Inst. Emergency Medicine Albert Einstein Coll. Medicine, NYC, 1977-80; asst. atty. US Atty.'s Office (so. dist.) N.Y., NYC, summer 1982; assoc. Skadden, Arps, Slate, Meagher & Flom, NYC, 1983-85, Paskus, Gordon & Mandel, NYC, 1985-86; v.p., sr. assoc. counsel The Chase Manhattan Bank, N.A., NYC, 1986-96; v.p. assoc. gen. counsel Citicorp Credit Svcs. Inc., NYC, 1997—2002, sr. v.p., assoc. gen. counsel, 2002, sr. v.p., dep. gen. counsel, 2006. Notes and comments editor Cardozo Law Rev.; contbr. numerous articles to law jours. Mem. ABA, N.Y.C. Bar Assn., N.Y. State Bar Assn. Office: Citicorp Credit Services Inc One Court Square New York NY 11120

REYNAUD-ROEPKE, SUZANNE, psychologist; b. Kansas City, Kans., Mar. 26, 1954; d. Raymond Lucien and Donna Jean Reynaud; m. Carl Frank Roepke, Jr., Dec. 22, 1985; children: Peter Hague Roepke II, Lucienne Marie Roepke. BA in Psychology, U. Calif., Santa Barbara, 1976; MEd in Spl. Edn., U. Nev., Reno, 1985; MSEd in Counseling Psychology, U. So. Calif., LA, 1989, PhD in Psychology, 1995. Cert. clear pupil pers. credential sch. psychology Calif., clear pupil pers. credential Calif., clear specialist credential in learning handicapped Calif., clear multiple subjects credential Calif., sch. psychologist endorsement Nev. Student intern Linda Mar Elem. Sch., Pacifica, Calif., 1978—79; pvt. practice ednl. therapy Gardnerville, Nev., 1984—85; grad. intern Douglas County Sch. Dist., 1984—85; grad. asst. ind. ednl. programs educationally handicapped U. Nev., Reno, 1984—85; psychol. intern Julia Ann Singer Children's Psychiatric Ctr., LA, 1986—87; outreach L.A. Jewish Orthodox Cmty., 1986—88, Focus on Youth L.A. Unified Sch. Dist., 1988—89; sch. counselor Multnomah St. Magnet Sch., East Los Angeles, 1988—89; psychol. intern Hollywood Counseling Ctr., 1988—89; predoctoral intern Alvarado Parkway Inst., La Mesa, 1991—92; resource specialist North Ter. Elem. Sch., Oceanside, 1994, The Rhoades Sch., Encinitas, 1995; pvt. practice psychology The Dennison Clinic, Carlsbad, 1995—99; NIMH post doctoral rsch. fellow Geriatric Psychiatry Clin. Rsch. Ctr. U. Calif. San Diego Sch. Medicine, 1996—99; sch. psychologist Inyo and Mono Counties Sch. Dists., Calif., 2000—. Doctoral com. mem. LaVerne Coll., Calif.; field work supr. Calif. State U., San Bernardino; spl. edn. cons. region 10 Calif. Preschool Instrnl. Network Spl. Edn. Divsn. Calif. Dept. Edn., 2000—; contract psychologist Cal-Works Dept. Health and Human Svcs., 2000—; presenter to profl. meetings. Co-author (with J. McQuaid, R. Scinta and P. Cutler): Cognitive Behavioral Therapy for Thought Disorder, 1998; co-author: (with J. McQuaid, E. Granholm and F.S. McClure) Group Therapy Manual for Cognitive Behavioral Skills Training (CBSST) for Older Persons with Schizophrenia, 1999; contbr. scientific papers, articles to profl. jours. Task force mem. southwest dist Luth. Ch. (Mo. Synod), Irvine; bd. mem. Bishop (Calif.) Swim Team, 2002—03. Fellow, NIMH, 1996—99; grantee, Am. Assn. Geriatric Psychiatry; Educare scholarship award, U. So. Calif. Sch. Edn., 1985. Mem.: Nat. Assn. Sch. Psychologists, USA Swimming (nat. cert. swim official 1994—), Am. Paint Horse Assn., Phi Delta Kappa (scholarship award 1988). Republican. Lutheran. Avocations: trail riding, photography, cross country skiing, hiking, yoga. Home: 398 Mt Tom Rd Bishop CA 93514-2122 Office: Bernasconi Edn Ctr Big Pine CA 93513 Office Phone: 760-938-2633.

REYNIK, ROBERT JOHN, materials scientist, consultant, science educator; b. Bayonne, NJ, Dec. 25, 1932; m. Georgiana M. Walker, Apr. 12, 1959; children: Michael, Christopher, Jonathan, Katherine, Steven, Kevin. BS in Math. and Physics, U. Detroit, 1956; MSEE, U. Cin., 1960, PhD in Phys. Chemistry, 1963. Rsch. assoc. Sch. Metall. Engring. U. Pa., Phila., 1963-64, asst. prof., 1964-67; assoc. prof. Drexel U., Phila., 1967-70; assoc. dir. engring. materials program NSF, Washington, 1970-71, dir. engring. materials program, 1971-74, dir. metallurgy program, 1974-82, head metallurgy, polymers, ceramics and electronic materials, 1983-90, head office spl. programs in materials, 1990-94, sr. staff scientist divsn. materials rsch. Arlington, Va., 1994-96; exec. sec. and cognizant program dir. US-USSR Internat. Agreement in Sci. and Tech., Washington, 1974-79; NSF liaison rep. Nat. Materials Adv. Bd., Washington, 1985-94; math. and phys. sci. directorate coord. Integration of Rsch. and Edn., 1996-97; sr. scientist Office of Sci. and Tech. Infrastructure, 1997-98, sr. staff scientist divsn. materials rsch., 1998-99, grantsmanship cons., 1999—2002. Dir. electrometallurgy and materials, corrosion, program US-USSR internat. agreement sci. and tech., 1974-80; mem. First U.S. Metall. Del. People's Republic China, 1978;bd. dirs. 1980-81; vis. prof. materials sci. and engring. U. Pa., 1982-83; tech. coord. Sci. & Tech. Ctrs. in Materials Sci. & Engring., 1990-94; co-chair Fed. Coord. Coun. for Sci., Engring. and Tech. joint com. edn. and tng. Office of Sci. and Tech. Policy, 1992-93; co-chair task group edn. and tng. Aeronautics Materials and mfg. Techs. Working Groups Nat. Sci. and Tech. coun., Office of Vice Pres. of U.S., 1994; tech. mgr. rsch. grants mfg. devel. and mfg. Tech. Reinvestment Project, Fed. Govt., 1994-96. Vol. income tax assistance and tax counseling for the elderly programs IRS, 2001—. Fellow Am. Soc. Materials Internat. (mem.-at-large materials sci. coun. 1990-96, mem.-at-large materials sci. tech. sector coun. 1993-96, fed. affairs com. 1996-99, gold medal selection com.); mem. AAAS, AIME (chmn. govt. pub. affairs com. 1994-96), Am. Chem. Soc., Am. Assn. Engring. Socs. (honors and awards com.), The Metals, Minerals and Materials Soc. (mem. and chmn. tech. coms., Leadership award 2004), Materials Rsch. Soc., Sigma Xi (past chpt. pres., exec. counselor), Tau Beta Pi. Office Phone: 856-428-4336. Office Fax: 856-428-4336. E-mail: rreynik@comcast.net.

REYNOLDS, ALBERT BARNETT, nuclear engineer, educator; b. Lebanon, Tenn., Feb. 1, 1931; s. George Lazenby and Marion (Barnett) R.; m. Helen Buck, Sept. 6, 1954; children— Albert Jr., Charlotte, Marion Student, U. of South, 1948-51; S.B. in Physics, MIT, 1953, S.M. in Nuclear Engring., 1955, Sc.D. in Chem. Engring., 1959. Physicist-mgr. Gen. Electric Co., San Jose, Calif., 1959-68; prof. nuclear engring. U. Va., Charlottesville, 1968-96, chmn. dept. nuclear engring. and engring. physics, 1991-92, prof. emeritus, 1996—. Cons. NRC, Washington, 1970-84, U.S. Dept. Energy, 1987-89 Author: Bluebells and Nuclear Energy, 1996; co-author: Fast Breeder Reactors, 1981; contbr. numerous articles to profl. jours. Fellow Am. Nuclear Soc. (exec. com. div. nuclear reactor safety 1980-83, chair Va. sect. 1986-87); mem. ASME, IEEE, Am. Soc. Engring. Edn., Sigma Xi, Tau Beta Pi Achievements include research in liquid metal reactor safety, electric cable aging. Home: 2228 Shepherds Ridge Rd Charlottesville VA 22901-0674 Personal E-mail: hareyn@aol.com.

REYNOLDS, BARBARA C., retired mental health educator, dean; b. Syracuse, NY; d. Robert J. Clark; m. George L. Reynolds, June 9, 1962 (dec.); children: George L. III, Katherine C.; m. George Barnard, Apr. 17, 2004. BSN, Syracuse U., 1952; MPH, U. Minn., 1968, PhD, 1990. Asst. prof. U. Cin., 1968-75; ind. human resources cons. Cin., 1975-76; asst. prof. sch. pub. health U. Minn., 1976-82; asst. prof. Vanderbilt U., Nashville, 1986-90, N.Y. Med. Ctr. Sch. Nursing, 1964—69, Coll. Mt. St. Joseph, 1973—75; dean sch. nursing Tenn. Tech. U., Cookeville, 1991-98. Contbr. articles to profl. jours. Mem. Leadership Putnam Alumni Assn. (pres. 1995-96), Rotary (Cookeville chpt., bd. dirs.), Sigma Theta Tau, Phi Kappa Phi. Home: 1750 Heathrow Dr Cookeville TN 38506

REYNOLDS, BURT, actor, film director; b. Waycross, Ga., Feb. 11, 1936; s. Burt R.; m. Judy Carne (div. 1965); m. Loni Anderson, Apr. 29, 1988 (div. 1994). Ed., Fla. State U., Palm Beach Jr. Coll. Owner ranch, Jupiter, Fla. Actor numerous stage prodns. including The Rainmaker; movie appearances include: Angel Baby, 1961, Armored Command, 1961, Operation CIA, 1965, Navajo Joe, 1967, Impasse, 1969, 100 Rifles, 1969, Sam Whiskey, 1969, Skullduggery, 1970, Shark, 1970, Deliverance, 1972, Fuzz, 1972, Everything You've Always Wanted to Know about Sex But Were Afraid to Ask, 1972, Shamus, 1973, The Man Who Loved Cat Dancing, 1973, White Lightning, 1973, The Longest Yard, 1974, At Long Last Love, 1975, W.W. and the Dixie Dance Kings, 1975, Hustle, 1975, Lucky Lady, 1975, Silent Movie, 1976, Nickelodeon, 1976, Smokey and the Bandit, 1977, Semi-Tough, 1977, Hooper, 1978, Starting Over, 1979, Rough Cut, 1980, Smokey and the Bandit II, 1980, Cannonball Run, 1981, Paternity, 1981, The Best Little Whorehouse in Texas, 1982, Best Friends, 1982, Stroker Ace, 1983, The Man Who Loved Women, 1983, City Heat, 1984, Cannonball Run II, 1984, Stick, 1985, Uphill All The Way, 1986, Rent A Cop, 1987, Heat, 1987, Malone, 1987, Switching Channels, 1988, Physical Evidence, 1989, Breaking In, 1989, Modern Love, 1990, Cop and a Half, 1993, also voice in All Dogs Go To Heaven, 1989, The Maddening, 1996, Striptease, 1996, Ravin, 1996, Mad Dog Time, 1996, Frankenstein and Me, 1996, Citizen Ruth, 1996, Meet Wally Sparks, 1997, Crazy Six, 1997, Boogie Nights, 1997, Raven, 1997, Waterproof, 1998, Mystery Alaska, 1998, The Hunter's Moon, 1998, Without a Paddle, 2004, The Librarians, 2004, Grilled, 2005, Forget About It, 2005, The Longest Yard, 2005, The Dukes of Hazzard, 2005, Broken Bridges, 2006, Deal, 2007; dir., actor: Gator, 1976, The End, 1978, Sharkey's Machine, 1981; TV appearances include: M Squad, 1959, Alfred Hitchcock Presents, 1960, Zane Grey Theater, 1961, Route 66, 1962, Perry Mason, 1962, The Twilight Zone, 1963, Branded, 1965, Flipper, 1965, Twelve O'Clock High, 1965, The Carol Burnett Show, 1967, The FBI, 1968, Love American Style, 1970, The Golden Girls, 1986, Dolly, 1987, Beverly Hills, 90210, 1993, The Larry Sanders Show, 1993, Hope & Gloria, 1995, Cybill, 1995, (voice) King of the Hill, 1997, The X Files, 2002, Hollywood Squares, 2002, Ed, 2003, Dinner for Five, 2004, The King of Queens, 2005; regular appearances on Gunsmoke, 1962-65; star series Hawk, 1966, Dan August, 1970-71, B.L. Stryker, 1989, ABC Saturday Mystery Movie, 1988, Evening Shade, 1990-94, (TV movie) The Cherokee Kid, 1996. Recipient Emmy award as Outstanding Lead Actor in a Comedy Series ("Evening Shade") Nat. Acad. TV Arts and Scis., 1991. Mem. Dirs. Guild Am. Office: Jeffrey Lane & Assocs 8380 Melrose Ave Ste 206 Los Angeles CA 90069-5498

REYNOLDS, C. LEWIS, JR., materials scientist, educator; b. Roanoke, Va., Dec. 16, 1948; s. Claude Lewis and Lois Anne Reynolds; m. Judith Ann Grenko, May 11, 2002; children: Karen Marie, Brian Lewis, Kristin Marie. BS, Va. Mil. Inst., Lexington, Va., 1970; MS, PhD, U. Va., Charlottesville, Va., 1974. Sr. scientist U. Va., Charlottesville, 1974—75; rsch. assoc. physics U. Ill., Urbana, Ill., 1975—77; sr. project engr. Union Carbide Corp., Indpls., 1977—80; disting. mem. tech. staff AT&T Bell Labs., Reading, Pa., 1980—92, Agere/Lucent Bell Labs., Breinigsville, Pa., 1992—2002; rsch. prof. NC State U., Raleigh, 2003—, tchg. asst. prof., 2004—. Contbr. more than 120 articles to profl. jours. Mem.: IEEE, Am. Assn. Physics Tchrs., Materials Rsch. Soc., Am. Phys. Soc., Sigma Xi. Independent. Methodist. Achievements include 8 patents in field. Avocations: reading, running, hiking. Office: NC State Univ Dept Materials Sci Engring 911 Partners Way Raleigh NC 27695-7907 Home Phone: 919-303-1376; Office Phone: 919-515-7623. Office Fax: 919-515-7724. Business E-Mail: lew_reynolds@ncsu.edu.

REYNOLDS, CHARLES PATRICK, pediatric oncologist, researcher; b. El Paso, Tex., Aug. 8, 1952; s. Charles Albert and Lallah Elizabeth (Munro) R.; m. Debra Dawn Adams, Feb. 3, 1979; children: Amy Elizabeth, Jennifer Ann. BA in Biology, U. Tex., 1974; MD, U. Tex. Southwestern Med. Sch., Dallas, 1979; PhD, U. Tex., 1979. Lic. Tex., Calif., Ga. Postdoctoral fellow U. Tex. Southwestern Med. Sch., Dallas, 1979-80; pediatric intern Nat. Naval Med. Ctr., Bethesda, Md., 1980-81; battalion surg. Third Marine Div., Okinawa, Japan, 1981-82; rsch. med. officer Naval Med. Rsch. Inst., Bethesda, 1982-87; asst. prof. UCLA, 1987-89; assoc. prof. U. So. Calif., LA, 1989-2000, prof., 2000—; head devel. therapeutics sect. divsn. hematology-oncology Children's Hosp. L.A., LA, 1993—; co-dir. develpmental therapeutics program U. So. Calif. Norris Comprehensive Cancer Ctr., 2000—; dir. devel. therapeutics program U. So. Calif.-Children's Hosp. L.A. Inst. for Pediat. Clin. Rsch., 2003—. Dir. Neuroblastoma Marrow Purging Lab. Childrens Cancer Group, L.A., 1988-99; team physician U.S. Shooting Team, 1991—; dir. neuroblastoma purging lab. Children's Oncology Group, L.A., 2000—; mem. FDA Pediat. Subcom. of Oncologic Drug Adv. Com., 2000—. Patentee in field; contbr. articles to profl. jours. Mem. 1992 USA Olympic Shooting Team, Barcelona, Spain. Grantee Nat. Cancer Inst. Mem. Am. Soc. Clin. Oncology, Am. Assn. Cancer Rsch., Soc. Analytical Cytology, AAAS, Children's Oncology Group, Internat. Soc. for Pediat. Oncology. Roman Catholic. Avocations: filmmaking, guitar playing. Office: Childrens Hospital of LA PO Box 27980 Los Angeles CA 90027-0980 Business E-Mail: preynolds@chla.usc.edu.

REYNOLDS, CLARK WINTON, economist, educator; b. Chgo., Mar. 13, 1934; m. Nydia O'Connor Viales; children: Rebecca, C. Winton III, Matthew, Camila. AB, Claremont Coll., Calif., 1956; student, MIT, 1956—58, Harvard U. Div. Sch., 1957—58; MA, U. Calif., Berkeley, 1960, PhD in Econs., 1962. Asst. prof. Occidental Coll., LA, 1961-62; from asst. to assoc. prof. dept. edn. and econ. growth Yale U., New Haven, 1962-67; sr. fellow The Brookings Inst., Washington, 1975-76; prof. econs., prin. investigator, founding dir. Americas program Stanford U., Calif., prof. emeritus econs. Calif., 1996—. Vis. prof. Nat. U. Mex., Chapingo, 1966, El Colegio de Mex., Mexico City, 1964, 65, 79, Hopkins-Nanjing Ctr. for Chinese and Am. Studies, Nanjing, China, 1999-2002, China Europe Internat. Bus. Sch., Shanghai, 2002, 03; vis. lectr. in econs. Stockholm U. Econs., 1968; fellow St. Antony's Coll., Oxford, 1975; vis. rsch. scholar Internat. Inst. for Applied Systems Analysis, Laxenburg, Austria, 1978; Fulbright chair in internat. econs. U. Viterbo, Italy, 2001; prof. Stanford Continuing Studies, 2007. Author: The Mexican Economy, 1970, The New Regionalism: How Globalization Reorders the Three Worlds of Development, 2006; co-author: (with C. Tello) Essays on the Chilean Economy, 1965, (with Donald Nichols) Economic Principles, 1970, U.S.-Mexican Relations: Economic and Social Aspects, Las Relaciones Mexico Estados Unidos, 1983, Dynamics of North American Trade, 1991, North American Labor Market Interdependence, 1992, Open Regionalism in the Andes, 1996. Mem. Presdl. Commn. to Latin Am., Rockefeller Commn., 1969; founding dir. Monticello West Found., 1980-2003. Woodrow Wilson Found. fellow, 1956-57, Rockefeller Found. fellow, 1957-58, Doherty Found. fellow, 1960-61, Inst. Internat. Studies fellow Stanford U., 1990-2000; grantee Social Sci. Rsch. Coun., Ford Found., Hewlett Found., Rockefeller Found., Mellon Found., MacArthur Found., Tinker Found. Mem. Am. Econ. Assn. Avocations: travel, photography, journalism. Personal E-mail: reynolds@stanford.edu.

REYNOLDS, CLAYTON S., lawyer; b. White Plains, NY, June 18, 1955; s. Charles Wesley and Ota (Thomas) R. BA, Trinity Coll. Camgridge U., Eng., 1976, MA, 1982; JD magna cum laude, Harvard U., 1979; LLM taxation, NYU, 1987. Assoc. Sullivan & Cromwell, NYC, 1979-84; assoc. then ptnr. Bachner, Tally, Polevoy, Misher & Brinberg, NYC, 1984-86; ptnr. Mudge, Rose, Guthrie, Alexander & Ferdon, NYC, 1987—, Orrick, Herrington & Sutcliffe LLP, NYC. Contbr. articles to profl.journs. Roman Catholic. Office: Orrick Herrington & Sutcliffe LLP 666 5th Ave New York NY 10103 Office Phone: 212-506-5173. Office Fax: 212-506-5151. Business E-Mail: creynolds@orrick.com.

REYNOLDS, CRAIG W., research scientist; PhD. Dir. office sci. ops. Nat. Cancer Inst.; project officer SAIC Frederick, Inc., Data Mgmt. Svcs. Inc., Wilson Info. Svcs. Corp.; assoc. dir. Nat. Cancer Inst. at Frederick, Frederick, Md., 2002—. With NCI-Frederick's ednl. outreach program. Achievements include research in the development and production of vaccines for treatment of patients with leukemia and myeloma. Office: NCI-Frederick Bldg 427 Rm 1 PO Box B Frederick MD 21702-1201 Business E-Mail: reynoldsc@ncifcrf.gov.

REYNOLDS, DAVID SPENCER, humanities educator, writer; b. Providence, Aug. 30, 1948; s. Paul Ripley and Adelaide (Koch) R.; m. Suzanne Nalbantian, July 23, 1983; 1 child, Aline Elizabeth. BA, Amherst Coll., Mass., 1970; PhD, U. Calif., Berkeley, 1979. Asst. prof. Northwestern U., Evanston, Ill., 1980-83; vis. prof. Barnard Coll., NYC, 1983-84; assoc. prof. Rutgers U., Camden, N.J., 1986-89; prof. Dept. English Baruch Coll. and Grad. Sch. CUNY, NYC, 1989-96, disting. prof. dept. of English, 1996—. Author: Faith in Fiction: The Emergence of Religious Literature in America, 1981, Beneath the American Renaissance: The Subversive Imagination in the Age of Emerson and Melville, 1988 (Christian Gauss award 1988), Walt Whitman's America: A Cultural Biography, 1995 (Bancroft award 1996), A Historical Guide to Walt Whitman, 1999, Walt Whitman, 2005, John Brown, Abolitionist, The Man Who Killed Slavery, Sparked The Civil War, and Seeded Civil Rights, 2005. Recipient Christian Gauss award Phi Beta Kappa, Washington, 1988, Bancroft award Columbia U., N.Y.C., 1996, Ambassador Book award English-Speaking Union, N.Y.C., 1996, Gustavus Myers Outstanding Book award, 2005. Fellow: Am. Antiquarian Soc., Soc. Am. Historians. Avocations: musical performance (singing, playing guitar and piano), tennis, swimming. Office: English Dept Baruch Coll 17 Lexington Ave New York NY 10010-5518 Office Phone: 646-312-3942. E-mail: rey.sn@juno.com.

REYNOLDS, DON WILLIAM, geologist; b. Centerburg, Ohio, Apr. 6, 1926; s. Loren William and Charlotte Lones (Hunt) R.; m. Betty Jeannette Spears, Sept. 4, 1953; children: Don William Jr., Richard Allen (dec.), Brenda Gay. BS, Ohio State U., 1952. Registered profl. geologist Calif., 1970, environ. assessor Calif. Mgr. Geochem. Engring., Inc., Midland, Tex., 1950-52; geologist Union Oil Co. Calif., Midland, 1953-66, dist. exploration geologist Anchorage, 1966-68, area geologist Bakersfield, Calif., 1968-76, dis. devel. geologist Ventura, Calif., 1976-86, dis. devel. geologist mid-continent divsn. Oklahoma City, 1986-89, regional mgr. mid-continent devel., 1989-90, advisor geology, 1990-92. Gen. ptnr. Reynolds Farm, 1979—; sec. ASF Inc., IFP Inc., Austin, 1989—; chmn. bd. Future Petroleum Corp., 1992-98, bd. dirs., 2001-2004; ptnr. Alianza Solutions, LP, 2004—, bd. advisors, 2004— Pres. Park Stockdale Civic Assn., Bakersfield, 1970, Clearpoint Homeowner's Assn., Ventura, 1980-86; chmn. Kern County Freeway Com. Bakersfield, 1970-73. Served with USAF, 1944-45. Mem. Am. Assn. Petroleum Geologists, West Tex. Geol. Soc. (sec. 1965-66), Kans.-Okla. Oil and Gas Assn. (nomenclature com. 1987-92), San Joaquin Geol. Soc. (treas. 1974-75), Am. Assn. Petroleum Geologists (sec. Pacific sect. 1975-76). Republican. Methodist. Home: 5009 Reynolds Rd Centerburg OH 43011 Office Phone: 805-644-7676. E-mail: don_wm_reynolds@compuserve.com.

REYNOLDS, DONALD MARTIN, art historian, foundation administrator, educator; b. Kansas City, Mo., Jan. 11, 1931; s. James Martin and Mary Helen (Hughes) Reynolds; m. Nancy Zlobik, June 5, 1970. Student, Amarillo Coll., 1949-51; BA, Assumption Sem., San Antonio, 1955, Columbia U., 1968, MA, 1970, PhD, 1975. Announcer Sta. KGNC

Radio/TV, Amarillo, Tex., 1949-51; account exec. Monte Rosenwald & Assocs., Amarillo, 1957-59; copy writer, account rep., account supr. J. Walter Thompson, NYC, C.Am., 1959-61; mgr. Ctrl. Am., Young & Rubicam Advt., NYC, Panama, 1961-62; advt. mgr., mktg. dir. Colgate-Palmolive Co. Western Hemisphere Divsn., 1962-64; founder, dir. Image, Internat. Mktg. Agy., NYC, 1964-66; mus. educator in charge Dept. Pub. Edn. Met. Mus. Art, 1977-79; curator pks. Dept. Pks. and Recreation, NYC, 1986-88; founder, coord. Ann. Symposium Pub. Monuments, NYC, 1991—; founder, dir. Monuments Conservancy, Inc., NYC, 1992—. Adj. prof. art history Columbia U., NYC, 1970—, Fairfield (Conn.) U., 1981—; adj. asst. prof. Hunter Coll., 1972—81; asst. prof. Coll. Mt. St. Vincent, 1973—77, Manhattan Coll., 1973—77; cons. Corps of Discovery monument Kemper Found., Kansas City, Mo., 2000; designer sculpture program Our Mother of Africa Chapel, Nat. Shrine of the Immaculate Conception, Nat. Black Cath. Congress, Washington, 2001. Author: (book) The Ideal Sculpture of Hiram Powers, 1977, The Architecture of New York City: Histories and Views of Important Structures, Sites, and Symbols, 1984, The Architecture of New York City: Histories and Views of Important Structures, Sites, and Symbols, rev. edit., 1994, Nineteenth-Century Art, 1985, Manhattan Architecture, 1988, Monuments and Masterpieces: Histories and Views of Public Sculpture in New York City, 1988, Nineteenth Century Architecture, 1992, Masters of American Sculpture, The Figurative Tradition from American Renaissance to the Millennium, 1993; editor, compiler: book The Impact of Non-European Civilizations on the Art of the West: Selected Lectures of Rudolf Wittkower, 1989; co-author: MacMillan Ency. Archs., 1982. With US Army, 1952—61. Mem.: Authors Guild, Coll. Art Assn., Nat. Sculpture Soc.

REYNOLDS, ERIC WILLIAM, medical educator; b. Frankfort, Ky., Jan. 20, 1971; s. Gary and JoAnn Reynolds; m. Melanie Avent Reynolds, June 26, 1993; 3 children. BS, U. Louisville, 1993, MD, 1997. Resident N.E. Ohio U. Coll. Medicine Children's Hosp., Youngstown, Ohio, 1997—2000; mem. faculty U. Ky., Lexington, 2003. Chmn. rsch. grant com. Assn. Postgrad. Physician Asst. Programs, 2006—; mem. k-30 scholars programs U. Ky., 2003—05. Contbr. articles to profl. jours. Fellow, U. Md., Balt., 2000—02, U. Ky., 2002—03. Fellow: Am. Acad. Pediatrics; mem.: Ky. Pediatric Soc., So. Soc. Pediatric Rsch. (coun. mem. 2007—), Southeast Assn. Neonatologists, Ky. Perinatal Assn. (bd. dirs. 2007—), Physician Asst. Edn. Assn. Office: U Ky 800 Rose St MS 477 Lexington KY 40536 Business E-Mail: ereyn2@uky.edu.

REYNOLDS, ERNEST WEST, retired internist, educator; b. Bristow, Okla., May 11, 1920; s. Ernest West and Florence (Brown) R. BS, U. Okla., 1942, MD, 1946, MS, 1952. Diplomate: Am. Bd. Internal Medicine. Intern Boston City Hosp., 1946-47; resident Grady Meml. Hosp., Atlanta, 1949-50; practice medicine Tulsa, Okla., 1953-54; prof. medicine U Mich., 1965-72; prof. medicine, dir. cardiology U. Wis., 1972-90, prof. emeritus, 1991—. Dir. Kellogg Found. Comprehensive Coronary Care Project, 1967-72; chmn. NIH Cardiovascular Study Sect. A, 1972-73 Mem. editorial bd.: Am. Heart Jour; Contbr. articles to profl. jours. Served to capt. AUS, 1947-49. Mem. Am. Heart Assn. (fellow coun. clin. cardiology), Ctrl. Soc. Clin. Rsch. Home: 17 Red Maple Trl Madison WI 53717-1515 Personal E-mail: ernest_reynolds@yahoo.com. *In the academic environment, research oriented toward the solution of human problems is more productive in career advancement than the pursuit of applications of new technology. In the private sector applied research which solves real problems rather than copies or improves existing technology is met with surprising sales success and few failures.*

REYNOLDS, FRANK MILLER, retired government agency administrator; b. Tulsa, Jan. 8, 1917; s. Frank Miller and Grace (Shields) R.; m. Barbara G. MacWilliams, Dec. 7, 1946; children: Susan G., Ellen M., Frank M. AB, LL.B., U. Okla., 1939; LL.M., George Washington U., 1942; BS, Georgetown Sch. Fgn. Service, 1946. Bar: Okla. 1940. Mem. firm Flippo & Reynolds, Tulsa, 1940; elec. engr. Bur. Ships, Dept. of Navy, 1942-43; with Office Gen. Counsel, Dept. of Navy, 1946; chief negotiator, dep. dir. contract div. Office Naval Research, 1947-54; dep. dir., dir. resources div. Office Asst. Sec. Def., 1954-57; asst. sec. Inst. for Defense Analyses, 1957-61; sec., treas. Logistics Management Inst., Washington, 1961-65, v.p., 1966-76; dir. adminstrv. affairs Uniformed Services U. Health Scis., Bethesda, Md., 1976-78, dir. resource mgmt., 1978-82, exec. sec. bd. regents, 1978-83; dir. patient relations Sibley Meml. Hosp., 1983-84, cons., 1984-87. Professorial lectr. mgmt. research George Washington U. Sch. Engring., 1956—; cons. Nat. Exec. Service Corps., United Srs. Health Coop., 1984—. Served with radio divsn. Naval Research Lab., 1944-46. Mem. Okla. Bar Assn., Congl. Country Club, Delta Upsilon. Personal E-mail: frank17re@verizon.net.

REYNOLDS, FREDRIC G., broadcast executive; b. Miami, Fla. married; 4 children. BBA in Fin., U. Miami, 1972. CPA. Tax cons., staff auditor Touche Ross & Co., 1972, prin.; v.p. fin. Burger King Internat. divsn. Pillsbury Co.; various positions to sr. v.p., CFO Frito-Lay unit PepsiCo Foods Internat., 1981-94, CFO KFC, PepsiCola Internat., Pizza Hut units; exec. v.p., CFO Westinghouse Electric Corp., 1994-96; CFO CBS Inc., NYC, 1996—97; exec. v.p., CFO CBS Corp., NYC, 1997-2000, 2005—, Viacom Inc., NYC, 2000—01; pres., CEO Viacom TV Stations Group, 2001—05; pres., COO, CFO Evercore Ptnrs. Inc., 2005. Office: CBS Corp 51 W 52nd St New York NY 10019-6188 Office Phone: 212-975-4321. *

REYNOLDS, GEORGE ANTHONY, JR., engineering executive; b. Columbia, SC, May 5, 1961; s., George Anthony and Flora Mae (La Coste) R.; m. Katherine Alison Albea, Apr. 14, 1984; children: Amanda Kate, William Anthony. BSME, Clemson U., 1983; postgrad., U. Ala., Huntsville, 1985. Design engr. Motorola, Plantation, Fla., 1983-85; sr. engr. Chrysler, Huntsville, Ala., 1985-88; prin. engr. NCR, Liberty, S.C., 1988-91, project leader, 1991-94; mgr. mech. engring. Sensormatic Electronics, Boca Raton, Fla., 1994-96, dir. product engring., 1996-98, dir. active products, 1998-2000, v.p. hard tag and product line engring., 2000—02; v.p. electronic article surveillance Tyco Internat., Boca Raton, Fla., 2002, v.p. radio frequency identification, 2002—05; v.p. worldwide sales and mktg., radio frequency identification Avery Dennison, Atlanta and Clinton, SC, 2006—. Mem. editl. quality audit panel Electronic Packaging & Prodn. Mag., N.Y.C., 1992. Advisor Clemson U. Mech. Engring. Endowment Fund; elder, mem. ednl. dir. search com., chair Christian edn. com., nominating com., chair stewardship campaign 1st Presbyn. Ch., Delray Beach, Fla.; pres. Seagate Neighborhood Assn., 1996-97; team mgr. Caloosa Park Girls Fast Pitch Softball Assn.; mem. adv. bd. ID World, Rome. Italy, 2005-07. Finalist S. Fla. Up and Comers award, 1997. Mem. ASME (life), NRA (life; Legion of Honor), S.E. Pro/Engr. User Group (pres. 1992-93), S. Fla. Clemson Alumni Club, Clemson Alumni Assn., Nature Conservancy, Ducks Unltd., Fla. Sheriff's Assn. (life), Tau Beta Pi, Phi Kappa Phi, Alpha Tau Omega (alumni adv. bd. Eta Pi chpt. 1993-94). Republican. Presbyterian. Avocations: genealogy, hunting, fishing. Office: Avery Dennison RFID Co Atlanta Tech Ctr 4350 Avery Dr Flowery Branch GA 30542 Office Phone: 770-561-6942. Business E-Mail: george.a.reyonlds@excite.com.

REYNOLDS, GLENN HARLAN, law educator, blogger; b. Birmingham, Ala., Aug. 27, 1960; s. Charles Harlan Reynolds and Glenda Lorraine (Teal) Childress; m. Helen Smith; one child. BA, U. Tenn., 1982; JD, Yale U., 1985. Bar: Tenn. 1985, D.C. 1986. Law clk. U.S. Ct. Appeals, Nashville, 1985-86; assoc. Dewey, Ballantine, Bushby, Palmer & Wood, Washington, 1986-89; assoc. prof. law U. Tenn., Knoxville, 1989-96; Beauchamp Brogan Disting. prof. law U. Tenn. Coll. Law, Knoxville, Tenn., 1996—. Author: Outer Space: Problems of Law and Policy, 1989, 97, An Army of Davis:How Markets and Technology Empower Ordinary People to Beat Big Media, Big Government, Business and Society, 2006; co-author (with Peter W. Morgan) The Appearance of Impropriety: How the Ethics Wars Have Undermined American Government, Business and Society, 1997; supervising exec. editor, Pajamas Media; contbg. editor, TechCentralStation.com; maintains blog site, Instapundit.com.; co-founder (record co.) WonderDog Records. Recipient Outstanding Svc. award Space Cause, Wash., 1990, Harold C. Warner Outstanding Faculty award, Space Pioneer award by Nat. Space Soc., 1991, W. Allen Separk Outstanding Faculty Scholarship award, 1998; nominee WIRED mag. RAVE award, 2005; named one of Top 25 Web Celebs, Forbes mag. 2007. Mem. AAAS, Nat. Space Soc. (chair legis. com. 1989-93, CEO 1994-95), Gov. Juvenile Justice Reform Commn., 1997-99, White House Adv. Panel on Space Policy. Avocation: music. Office: U Tenn Coll Law 1505 W Cumberland Ave Knoxville TN 37996 Office Phone: 865-974-2521. Office Fax: 865-974-6595. Business E-Mail: reynolds@libra.law.utk.edu. *

REYNOLDS, HELEN ELIZABETH, management consultant; b. Minerva, NY, Aug. 30, 1925; d. Henry James and Margurite Catherine (Gallagher) McNally; m. Theodore Laurence Reynolds, Feb. 27, 1948; children: Laurence McBride, David Scott, William Herbert. BA, SUNY, Albany, 1967; MA, Union Coll., Schenectady, NY, 1971. Cert. realtor Realtors Inst., N.Y. Owner, mgr. Schafer Studio, Schenectady, 1970—73; co-owner, v.p. Reynolds Chalmers Inc., Schenectady, 1971—97; program coord. Schenectady County, 1980—81; adminstr. Wellspring House Albany, NY, 1981—94; pres. HR Mgmt. Cons., Port Charlotte, Fla., 1994—2002; ret. Cons., examiner N.Y. State Civil Svc., Albany, 1971—81; mem. adv. coun. SBA, Washington, 1978—80. Planning bd. Town of Niskayuna, NY, 1977—81, town councilwoman, 1986—94; co-chair Great N.E. Festival Mohawk River, 1989—90; bd. dirs. HAVEN, Schenectady YWCA; mem. N.Y. State Commn. Capital Region, 1994—98, Acad. Women Achievement, Schenectady, 1994; pres. Photo Arts Group Charlotte County, 1998—2003, Buena Vista Property Owners Assn., Port Charlotte, 1998—2003; bd. mem. Charlotte Symphony Orch. Named Woman Vision, 1986—87, Today's Woman, Schenectady YWCA, 1987. Mem.: Assn. Adminstrs. Ind. Housing, Charlotte County Art Guild, Union Coll. Alumni Assn., Charlotte Symphony League (pres.), Antique and Classic Boat Soc. (bd. dirs. 1974—89, Disting. Svc. award 1979), Charlotte Harbor Yacht Club, Zonta (pres. 1981—82). Avocations: photography, reading, golf, skiing, canoeing. Home and Office: 104 Leland St SW Port Charlotte FL 33952-9131

REYNOLDS, HERBERT YOUNG, internist; b. Richmond, Va., Aug. 20, 1939; s. George Audney and Pearle Maupin (Young) R.; m. Anne Browning Leavell, July 11, 1964; children: Nancy, George, William Stuart. BA in English, U. Va., 1961, MD, 1965; MA (hon.), Yale U., 1979. Diplomate Am. Bd. Internal Medicine, Am. Bd. Allergy and Immunology. Intern NY Hosp., Cornell Med. Ctr., NYC, 1965—66, asst. physician, fellow in medicine, 1966—67; clin. assoc., lab. clin. investigation Nat. Inst. Allergy, Infectious Diseases, NIH, Bethesda, Md., 1967—70, chief clin. assoc., lab. clin. investigation, 1968—69; chief resident, instr. medicine U. Hosp. U. Wash., Seattle, 1970—71; sr. investigator, lab. clin. investigation Nat. Inst. Allergy, Infectious Diseases, NIH, Bethesda, 1971—76; assoc. prof. internal medicine, head pulmonary divsn. Yale U. Sch. Medicine, New Haven, 1976—79, prof., 1979—88; J. Lloyd Huck prof. medicine, chmn. dept. Pa. State U., Milton S. Hershey Med. Ctr., 1988—2002; assoc. chmn. divsn. medicine Pa. State Geisinger Health Sys., 1997—2000, chief medicine ops. Hershey Med. Ctr. Region, 1997—2000; med. officer Lung Biology and Disease br., divsn. lung diseases NHLBI/NIH, Bethesda, 2002—; prof. medicine emeritus Pa. State U. Coll. Medicine, 2002—. Adj. prof. medicine Uniformed Svcs. U. Health Scis., Bethesda, 2003—; mem. exec. com. Coll. Medicine Pa. State U.-Hershey Med. Ctr., 1988-2002, exec. bd. U. Hosp., 1988-2002, fin. bd. acad. enrichment fun, 1988-95, dean's adv. com., 1988-97, diversity task force, 1995-2002, physicians faculty practice plan exec. com. 1996-97, human resources team leader, 2000-02; dept. chair rep. Milton S. Hershey Med. Ctr. Bd., 2000-2002; cons. in infectious diseases Nat. Naval Med. Ctr., NIH, Bethesda, 1971-76, clin. rsch. com., 1971-76, chmn., 1974-76, pulmonary disease adv. com. divsn. of lung diseases NHLBI, 1978-82, sci. counselors bd., 1984-88, data and safety monitoring bd. registry of patients with deficiency of Alpha-1 Antitrypsin, 1989-96. Mem. editl. bd. Lung, 1978-2005, Am. Jour. Medicine, 1979-89, Jour. Clin. Investigation, 1980-86, Am. Rev. Respiratory Diseases, 1980-87, Jour. Applied Physiology, 1981-89, Resident Physician, 1981-95; contbr. more than 305 articles to profl. jours. and med. textbooks. Parent com. Troop 1 Boy Scouts Am., Madison, 1979-82; bd. dirs. Neighborhood Music Sch., Guilford, Conn., 1978-87; Music at Gretna, 1994-2002; bd. dirs. Harrisburg Symphony, 1996-2000; active All Saints Episc. Ch., Hershey; pulmonary infections com. Cystic Fibrosis Found., Bethesda, 1980-86; mem. coun. sci. advisors Parker B. Francis Found., Kansas City, Kans., 1983-87; internat. com. World Orgn. for Sarcoidosis and other Granulomatous Disorders, 1987-95; bd. dirs., mem. coun. Am. Lung Assn., 1989-93, bd. govs. 1990-93, com. mem., 1990-93; coach Guilford Soccer League, 1985-88; vol. Mercy Health Clinic, Gaithersburg, Md., 2003—. Surgeon USPHS, 1967-70. John Edward Nobel fellow, 1961-65; named Outstanding Med. Specialist in USA, Town and Country Mag., 1989, 97, The Best Med. Specialists, Town & Country mag., 1995, One of 400 Best Drs. in U.S. Good Housekeeping Mag., 1991, Best Drs. in Am., 2005-2006. Fellow ACP (coun. subsplty. socs. 1989-2000, gov. Pa. Ea. Region 1, 2000-02), Am. Coll. Chest Physicians (program com. 1978-84), Infectious Disease Soc. Am., Coll. Physicians Phila.; mem. Am. Thoracic Soc. (sec.-treas. 1987-88, bd. dirs. 1989-93, v.p. 1988-89, pres. 1991-92), Am. Soc. Clin. Investigation, Assn. Am. Physicians, Am. Assn. Immunologists, Am. Fedn. Clin. Rsch., Am. Clin. and Climatol. Assoc. (v.p. 2001-02, pres. 2002-03), Acad. Medicine Wash., Interurban Clin. Club (emeritus 1989), Hershey Country Club, Farmington Country Club, Raven Soc., Phi Beta Kappa, Alpha Omega Alpha, Omicron Delta Kappa. Republican. Avocations: tennis, violin. Home: 226 E Caracas Ave Hershey PA 17033-1309 Office: NHLBI/NIH Divsn Lung Diseases 6701 Rockledge Dr Rm 10180 Bethesda MD 20892-7952 Office Phone: 301-435-0218. Business E-Mail: reynoldh@nhlbi.nih.gov.

REYNOLDS, JAMES, management consultant; s. Richard James and Esther (Nikander) R.; m. Joanne M.J. BA in Econs., NYU, 1965, postgrad., 1965-66. Cons. to pres. Rothrock, Reynolds & Reynolds Inc., NYC, 1966-70; sr. v.p. health, med. div. Booz, Allen & Hamilton, NYC, 1970-80; pres. Reynolds & Co. (mgmt. cons.), San Francisco, NYC, Washington, 1981—. Developer Combining Pay for Performance with Gain Sharing to align incentives, Leap Frog Group, 2007; bd. dirs. Booz, Allen & Hamilton, 1977-79; chmn. bd. J.X. Reynolds Fine Arts, Ltd., 1979—; lectr. Harvard Sch. Pub. Health; faculty mem. Am. Coll. of Healthcare Execs.; bd. dirs. Health Ctr. Mgmt. Inst., Richmond, Va., 1977; mem. health adv. bd. Hunter Coll., 1980—. Mem. editl. bd. Physicians Fin. News. Recipient NYU Founders award, 1965 Mem. Am. Pub. Health Assn., Am. Mgmt. Assn., Assn. Am. Med. Colls., Am. Hosp. Assn., Hosp. Mgmt. Systems Soc., Hosp. Fin. Mgmt. Assn., Asia Soc., China Inst., Phi Beta Kappa, Guggenheim Mus., Mus. Modern Art, Met. Mus. Art, Met. Opera Guild (NYC) Episcopalian. Home and Office: Reynolds & Co 333 E 51st St New York NY 10022-6702 Home: 333 E 51st St New York NY 10022-6702 Office Phone: 212-826-1818. Business E-Mail: jreynolds@jxreynolds.com.

REYNOLDS, JEAN EDWARDS, publishing executive; b. Saginaw, Mich., Dec. 11, 1941; d. F. Perry and Katharine (Edwards) R.; m. Cary Wellington, Sept. 10, 1975 (div. 1982); children, Bradley, Abigail, Benjamin; m. Jon Haddon, Nov. 8, 1997. BA, Wells Coll., 1963; postgrad., CCNY, 1965-67. Asst. editor, sr. editor trade book div. Prentice-Hall, Englewood Cliffs, NJ, 1963—66, dir. children's books, 1966—69, McCall Pub. Co., NYC, 1969—71; sr. v.p., editorial dir. Franklin Watts Inc., NYC, 1971—75; pres. Pet Projects Inc., Ridgefield, Conn., 1975—81; editor in chief young people's publs. Grolier Inc., Danbury, Conn., 1981—89; founder, pub., exec. v.p. The Millbrook Press, Brookfield, Conn., 1989—2004; assoc. pub. Lerner Publs., Mpls., 2004—06, exec. editor, 2006—. Bd. dirs. Jewish Fedn. Greater Danbury; chair Conn. Ctr. for the Book, 1991-94. Mem. Bd. of Govs. for Higher Edn., State of Conn., 2004—; pres. Jewish Fedn. Greater Danbury, 1991—93, 2003—; bd. dirs. Jewish Home for the Elderly, Fairfield, Conn., 1989—90, 1999, Book Industry Study Group, 1991—98, The Wooster Sch., Danbury, Conn., 1992—, chair headmaster search, 2002—; bd. dirs. Temple Shearith Israel, Ridgefield, Conn., 1994—97, chair Kehila campaign, 2002; bd. dirs. The Children's Book Coun., 1996—2000, vice chair, 1997—98, chair, 1998—99; bd. dirs. Ridgefield Symphony, 2006—. Mem. ALA, Children's Book Coun., Mensa. Jewish. Avocations: skiing, sailing, needlecrafts. Home and Office: 33 Corntassle Rd Danbury CT 06811-3208

REYNOLDS, JEFF, men's college basketball coach; m. Janet Montgomery. Part-time asst. James Madison U., Harrisonburg, Va., 1981; coach Randolph-Macon Coll., Ashland, Va., 1982—85, Winthrop Coll., Rock Hill, SC, 1986—90; head coach NC Wesleyan Coll., Rocky Mount, 1985—86, Wingate U., NC, 1997—2000; asst. coach U. NC, Wilmington, 1991—95, Greensboro, 1995—97, Tulane U., New Orleans, 2000—04, Air Force Acad., Colo., 2005—07, head coach, 2007—. Named South Atlantic Conf. Coach of Yr., 1999. Office: Air Force Acad Mens Basketball 2169 Field House Dr U S A F Academy CO 80840-9500 Office Phone: 719-333-3519. E-mail: Jeff.Reynolds.ctr@usafa.af.mil.

REYNOLDS, JEFFREY WARREN, music educator; b. Tuscaloosa, Ala., Jan. 5, 1961; s. John Edward Reynolds and Betty Francis Rainwater; 1 child, Jennifer. MusB, Samford U., Birmingham, Ala., 1982; MusM, Southwestern Sem., Ft. Worth, Tex., 1985; D of Mus. Arts, U. Ill., Champaign/Urbana, 1990. Dir. choral activities, coord. of music Brevard C.C., Melbourne, Fla., 1989—97; dir. choral activities U. Ark., Monticello, 1997—98, U. Ala., Birmingham, 1998—, chmn. dept. music, 2000—. Condr. Brevard Symphony Youth Orch., 1993—96; music dir., condr. Internat. Cathedral Music Festival, England, 1998—; min. of arts Southside Bapt. Ch., Birmingham, Ala., 2005—. Contbr.: chpt. Maurice Durufle-The Last Impressionist, 2001. Recipient Disting. Educator award, Brevard C.C., 1991, Tchg. Excellence award, Nat. Inst. for Staff and Orgnl. Devel., 1992. Mem.: Music Educators Nat. Conf., Am. Choral Dirs. Assn. (life). Baptist. Avocations: bicycling, kayaking, gardening, cooking, photography. Home: 1575 Oak Park Dr Helena AL 35080 Office: 240 Hulsey Ctr Birmingham AL 35209 Office Phone: 205-934-8782. Office Fax: 205-975-1931. Business E-Mail: jwr@uab.edu.

REYNOLDS, JERALD M., music educator; b. Dallas, May 21, 1934; s. Austin Jesse Reynolds and Carmen Edith Hines; 1 child, Anthony. BA, Pepperdine Coll., LA, 1957; MusM, U. Oreg., Eugene, 1962; postgrad., Akadamie Musik und Darstelende Kunst, Graz, Austria, 1964—66. Baritone Graz Opera, 1964—66; prof. music U. South Fla., Fla. Bd. dirs. Tarpon Springs Manors, Fla., 1988—. With US Army, 1957—59. Scholar, Fulbright Found., 1964—66. Mem.: Nat. Assh. Tchrs. Singing (treas. 1980—2004). Home: 11723 Primrose Ln Temple Terrace FL 33637

REYNOLDS, JERRY (GERALD A.), federal agency administrator; BA, CUNY York Coll.; JD, Boston U. Atty. Schatz & Schatz, Conn., Ribicoff & Kotkin; legal analyst Ctr. Equal Opportunity, 1995—97; pres., legal counsel Ctr. New Black Leadership, 1997—98; sr. regulatory counsel Kansas City Power & Light Co., 1998—2002; asst. sec. civil rights US Dept. Edn., Washington, 2002—04; chmn. US Comm. on Civil Rights, Washington, 2004—. Mem. editl. bd.: Am. Jour. Law and Medicine. Office: US Commn on Civil Rights 624 Ninth St NW Ste 700 Washington DC 20425

REYNOLDS, JERRY OWEN, professional sports team executive; b. French Lick, Ind., Jan. 29, 1944; m. Dodie Reynolds; children: Danielle, Jay. Student, Vincennes U.; grad., Oakland City Coll., Ind., 1966; student, Ind. U.; M in Phys. Edn., Ind. State U., 1970. Coach Rockhurst Coll., Kansas City, Mo., 1975—84, Pittsburg State U., Kans., 1984—85; asst. coach Sacramento Kings, 1985—88, head coach, 1987, 1988—89, dir. player pers., 1990—92, 1994—, gen. mgr., 1992—93; gen. mgr, v.p. WNBA Sacramento Monarchs, 1998—2003. Mem. USA Basketball Women's Sr. Nat. Team Com., 2001—04. Office: Sacramento Kings 1 Sports Pkwy Sacramento CA 95834-2300 *

REYNOLDS, JOHN FRANCIS, insurance company executive; b. Escanaba, Mich., Mar. 29, 1921; s. Edward Peter and Lillian (Harris) R.; m. Dorothy Gustafson, May 1, 1946; children; Lois, Margaret, Michael. BS, Mich. State U., 1942. Claims and assoc. surety mgr. Hartford Ins. Co., Escanaba, Mich. and Chgo., 1946-55; asst. v.p., bond mgr. Wolverine Ins. Co., Battle Creek, Mich., 1955-64, v.p. underwriting, 1964-69; Midwest zone underwriting mgr. Transamerica Ins. Co. (Wolverine Ins. Co.), Battle Creek, Mich., 1969-74; pres., gen. mgr. Can. Surety Co. subs. Transamerica Ins. Co., Toronto, Ont., Canada, 1974-75; v.p. midwestern zone mgr. Transamerica Ins. Group, Battle Creek, Mich., 1975-83, pres., chief operating officer Los Angeles, 1983-84, chmn., chief exec. officer, 1984-85; apptd. spl. dep. ins. commr., dep. conservator Cadillac Inc. Co., 1989. Pres. Underwriting Exec. Council Midwest, 1967; dir. Underwriters Adjustment Bur., Toronto, 1974, Underwriters Labs. of Canada, Montreal, 1974; chmn. Mich. Assn. Ins. Cos., Lansing, 1976, Mich. Basic Property Ins. Assn., Detroit, 1973. Commr. City of Battle Creek, 1967-69; dir. Urban League, Battle Creek, 1969, 70, dir. Mich. Ins. Fedn., Lansing, 1975-83. Served to sgt. U.S. Army, 1942-45; New Guinea Roman Catholic. Avocations: golf, fishing. Home: 14037 N Cameo Dr Sun City AZ 85351-2903 Personal E-mail: reynolds213@yahoo.com.

REYNOLDS, JOHN R., hospital executive; Joined Hosp. for Special Surgery, NYC, 1985, CFO, 1985—97, co-CEO, 1997—99, pres., CEO, 1999—. Office: Hosp for Special Surgery 535 East 70th St New York NY 10021 Office Phone: 212-606-1000.

REYNOLDS, JOHN TERRENCE, oil industry executive; b. Madison, Wis., Oct. 2, 1944; s. John Francis and Evelyn Ruth (Straus) R.; m. Diane Marie Princl-Reynolds, Sept. 3, 1966; 1 child, Channing. BSME, U. Wis., 1967, MS in Metallurgical Engring., 1968. Engr. Shell Chem. Co., Denver, 1968-70, Royal Dutch/Shell, The Hague, The Netherlands, 1970-72; sr. engr. Shell Devel. Co., Houston, 1972-75, Shell Oil Co., Houston, 1975-78, staff engr. Deer Park, Tex., 1978-81, engring. mgr. Anacortes, Wash., 1981-87, engring. cons. Houston, 1987—92, Shell GS, Houston, 1992—. Chmn. inspection codes com., 1989—, inspection subcommittee, 1993-96, Am. Petroleum Inst., Washington. Author: Mechanical Integrity of Refinery Equipment, 1993, The New In-Service Piping Inspection Code, 1993, Risk-based Inspection for Petroleum and Petrochemical Industry, 1997, 101 Essential Elements of Pressure Equipment Integrity, 2001. Recipient certificates of appreciation. Mem. ASME, Am. Soc. for Metals, Nat. Assn. Corrosion Engrs., Am. Petroleum Inst., Nat. Petroleum Refiners Assn. Avocations: mountain climbing, backpacking, kayaking, rafting, fishing. Office: Shell Oil Co 3333 Highway 6 S Houston TX 77082-3101 Business E-Mail: john.reynolds@shell.com.

REYNOLDS, JUDITH AMY, nutritionist, consultant, animal scientist, educator; d. Jacob Alen and Mary Emeline Lundgren; m. Rodney Roger Reynolds, Aug. 28, 1971; children: Andrea Mary Rickards, James Christopher. AA summa cum laude, Anoka Ramsey CC, 1988; BS summa cum laude, St. Cloud State U., 1990; MS, Tex. A&M U., 1993, PhD, 1997. Cert.

Profl. Animal Scientist Am. Registry Profl. Animal Scientists, 1995. Co-owner, mgr. Reynolds Quarter Horses, Palmyra, Mo., 1978—; grad. asst. rschr. Tex. A&M U., College Station, 1990—91, grad. asst. tchr., 1991—95; long term substitute tchr. biology, anatomy physiology, chemistry Princeton and Elk River Pub. Sch. Sys., Minn., 1997—98; divisional equine tech. specialist Archer Daniels Midland Animal Health Nutrition and MoorMan's Inc., Quincy, Ill., 1998—2001; equine nutritionist Archer Daniels Midland Alliance Nutrition Inc., Quincy, 2001—. Asst. prof. William Woods U., Fulton, Mo., 1995—97; assoc. faculty John Woods CC, Quincy, Ill., 2004—; spkr. in field; ofcl. reviewer Nat. Rsch. Coun., Nutrient Requirements of Horses, 2006; mem. Equine Sci. Soc. Nutrition Com., 2006—. Author: (online source) Equine Nutrition in the 21st Century (1st Pl. Online Svc. To Reader, 2003); contbr. articles in to profl. jours. Vol. Princeton Pub. Schools, Princeton, Minn., 1983—90; vol. leader; horse sci., horse bowl, horse advancement, vet. sci. Isanti County 4-H, Minn., 1983—90; vol. leader horse judging, market steers, poultry Bryan HS Future Farmers of Am., Tex., 1992—94; vol. horse judge Brazos County, College Station, Tex., 1991—94, Tex. A&M U., College Station, 1991—95; vol. horse bowl team coach Mo. State 4-H, 1996—97; vol. 4-H horse judge Audrain and Calloway Counties, Fulton, Mo., 1996—97. Recipient High Point All Around Horse, Minn. Quarter Horse Assn., 1980, Two Register of Merit Horses, Am. Quarter Horse Assn., 1980, 1982, Four High-Point and Res. Performance Gelding awards, Five State Champions, Five Res. State Champions, Minn. Quarter Horse Assn., 1980-1983, One Performance Horse Qualified, Outstanding Horses of World, World Equine Rsch. Inst., 1983; Mensa scholarship, Am. Mensa, 1987, Alliss scholarships, Alliss, 1987-1990, Academic scholarships, Anoka Ramsey CC, 1987-1988, St. Cloud State U., 1988-1990. Mem.: Am. Registry Profl. Animal Scientists, Equine Sci. Soc. (nutrition com. 2006—), Am. Quarter Horse Assn., Nat. Reining Horse Assn., Phi Kappa Phi, Psi Chi, Kappa Delta Pi, Phi Theta Kappa, Gamma Sigma Delta. Achievements include development of equine feeds and supplements, SENIORGLO, MOORGLO, PRO-VITA-MIN 20 supplement tubs, FORAGE FIRST Horse Rewards, MOORGLO Canadian formula, GROSTRONG QuadBLOCK Canadian formula; StaySTRONG Metabolic Mineral Pellets, JUNIORGLO. Avocations: horses, reading, writing, cooking. Office: ADM Alliance Nutrition 1000 N 30th St Quincy IL 62305 Home Phone: 573-439-5632. Office Fax: 217-222-9060. Business E-Mail: judy_reynolds@admworld.com.

REYNOLDS, KAREN ANN, retired elementary school educator; b. Mpls., Jan. 20, 1944; d. Herbert Laverne and Doris Emma (Olson) Hinrichs; m. Kenneth Allen Reynolds, Aug. 2, 1975; stepchildren: Terri Lynn Winberry, Sheri Lee DeMaagd, Robert Scott. BS in Elem. Tchr. Edn. cum laude, So. Oreg. Coll., Ashland, 1966, MS in Elem. Tchr. Edn., 1974. Std. tchg. cert. State of Oreg. Tchr. elem. sch. Riddle Sch. Dist., Oreg., 1966—70, Ashland Sch. Dist. # 5, 1970—80; substitute tchr. Coos Bay and North Bend Sch. Dists., Oreg., 1981, Williston Sch. Dist., ND, 1982—83; tchr. County and City Schs. and pvt. kindergarten, Klamath Falls, Oreg., 1983—90; tchr. elem. sch. Klamath Falls City Schs. Dist. 1, Klamath Falls, 1990—98. Dir. Christmas Program Trenton K-12 Sch., ND, 1984; vol. dist.-sponsored program, mentor Conger Elem. Sch., 1990—91. Sunday sch. and Bible sch. tchr. Grace Luth. Ch., Ashland, 1959—65, tchr. confirmation class, 1972—74; children's message presenter Zion Luth. Ch., Klamath Falls, 2000—05, mem. altar guild, altar server, banner artist, 2002—, asst. to sec., e-mail prayer chain, 2005—, mem., 2007—; active Luth. Women's Missionary League, 2007; mem./sponsor Good Shepherd Luth. Home, Hillsboro, Oreg., 2007—. Named Best Student in a Survey Class in Am. History, Faculty of So. Oreg. Coll., 1964, Best Student in Prins. of Econs. Survey Class, 1965, Best Student in a Survey Course in Geography, Faculty So. Oreg. Coll., 1964, Co-Salutatorian of Graduating Class, Ashland Sr. H.S., 1962; recipient State Bd. Full Tuition scholarship, State of Oreg., 1962—65. Mem.: Ashland Edn. Assn. (mem. salary negotiation team 1972—73), Klamath Falls Edn. Assn. (treas. 1996—98), Riddle Edn. Assn. (v.p. 1967—68, pres. 1968—69, salary negotiations team 1968—69). Lutheran. Avocations: digital photographic art works, genealogy, writing, back country jeeping.

REYNOLDS, LEWIS DAYTON, pastor; b. Charleston, W.Va., July 26, 1937; s. James Shelby and Sybil Catherine (Lanham) R.; m. Ann Kathryn Combs, Aug. 25, 1962; children: John Mark, Daniel Adam. BBA, Marshall U., 1959; BTh, Aurora U., 1961; MDiv, Evang. Theol. Sem., Naperville, Ill., 1962. Ordained to ministry Advent Christian Ch., 1962. Pastor Mendota (Ill.) Advent Christian Ch., Mendota, Ill., 1961-64, Clendenin (W.Va.) Advent Christian Ch., Clendenin, W.Va., 1964-72, New Covenant Fellowship, Penfield, NY, 1972-89; gen. overseer Elim Fellowship, Lima, NY, 1989-97; sr. pastor Faith Christian Fellowship, Clarksburg, W.Va., 1997—2002, Charismatic Episcopal Ch. of the Transfiguration, Sterling, Va., 2002—; dir. Appalachian Highlands mission, eastern province Charismatic Episcopal Ch., 2003—. Mem. Phi Eta Sigma. Republican.

REYNOLDS, LINDA ANN, elementary school educator; b. Teheran, Iran, Jan. 1, 1959; d. John Kendrick and Fatemah Nikou Reynolds; 1 adopted child, Derek. BS in Elem. Edn., Auburn U., Ala., 1991, MEd, 1995, Edn. Specialist degree, 2000. LCSW. Med. transcriptionist St. Margaret's Hosp., Montgomery, Ala., 1980—84, Drs. Reynolds, Little and Thomas, Montgomery, 1981—87; typing instr. Riley Coll., Montgomery, 1987—88; tchr. 5th grade Davis Elem. Sch., Montgomery, 1991—92; edn. instr. Fews Elem. Sch., Montgomery, 1995, tchr. 5th grade, 2000—01. Ednl. instr. CAP Program, Montgomery, 1995. Vol. city crime prevention unit Montgomery Police Dept.; vol. Montgomery Area Food Bank; active Rainbow Com. Recipient Tchr. of Yr., 1991—92. Mem.: Chi Sigma Iota. Home: PO Box 153 Coosada AL 36020-0153 Personal E-mail: lindaannreynolds@yahoo.com.

REYNOLDS, MARSHALL TRUMAN, printing company executive; b. Logan, W.Va., Feb. 21, 1937; s. Douglas Vernon and Dorothy Lee (Dingess) R.; m. Shirley Ann Earwood, Mar. 24, 1968; children: Jack Marine, Douglas Vernon. Student, Marshall U., 1956-58. Sales mgr. Chapman Printing Co., Huntington, W.Va., 1960-61, gen. mgr., 1961-64, pres., gen. mgr. Huntington, Parkersburg and Charleston, W.Va., Lexington, Ky., 1964—. Chmn. bd. McCorkle Machine & Engring., Huntington, KYOWVA Corrugated Container, Huntington, Stationers, Inc., Huntington, Charleston, Radisson Hotel, Huntington, Huntington Indsl. Corp., Champion Industries Inc., Am. Babbit Bearing Inc.; bd. dirs. Guyan Machinery, Huntington, United Huntington Industries, Persinger Supply Co., Prichard, W.Va., First Guaranty Bank, Hammond, La., Banc One WV Corp., Charleston, W.Va. Bd. dirs. W.Va. Roundtable, Huntington, 1989—, W. Va. Bus. Found., Huntington, 1989—, Boys and Girls Club, Huntington, 1989—, Huntington United Way, 1989—; mem. Gov.'s Task Force on Children, Youth and Families, 1989—; guest lectr. various high schs. on free enterprise. Named Outstanding Small Businessman of Yr., Huntington Jaycees, 1983, Business Man of Yr. Jaycess, 1988. Mem. Huntington C. of C., Western Star Lodge (Guyandotte, W.Va.). Republican. Baptist. Avocation: raising cattle. Home: 1130 13th St Huntington WV 25701-3632 Office: Chapman Printing Co 2450 1st Ave Huntington WV 25703-1218

REYNOLDS, NANCY REMICK, writer, researcher, editor; b. San Antonio, July 15, 1938; d. Donald Worthington and Edith (Remick) R.; m. Brian Rushton, June 25, 1983; 1 child: Ehren P. Student, Sch. Am. Ballet, NYC, 1951, student, 1953—61, Juilliard Sch. Music, 1957, Martha Graham Sch. Contemporary Dance, 1959, U. Sorbonne, Paris, 1962; BA in Art History, Columbia U., NYC, 1965; postgrad., Goethe Inst., Prien, 1972, U. Chgo., 1974—77, Sarah Lawrence Coll., Bronxville, NY, 1974—77. Dancer NYC Ballet, 1956—61; editor Praeger Pubs., NYC, 1965—71; dir. rsch. book Choreography by George Balanchine: A Catalogue of Works, 1979—82; dir. rsch. pub. TV spl. Balanchine, NY, 1983—84; assoc. editor Internat. Ency. of Dance, 1998; dir. rsch. The George Balanchine Found., NYC, 1994—. Co-pub. Twentieth-Century Dance in Slides, 1978-93. Author: Repertory in Review: Forty Years of the New York City Ballet, 1977 (De la Torre Bueno prize 1977), The Dance Catalog: A Complete Guide to Today's World of Dance, 1979, co-author: In Performance, 1980, Dance Classics, 1991 (rec. for teen age NY Pub. Libr.), No Fixed Points: Dance in the Twentieth Century, 2003, Remembering Lincoln, 2003; editor: Movement and Metaphor: Four Centuries of Ballet (Lincoln Kirstein), 1970, Dance as a Theatre Art: Source Readings in Dance History from 1581 to the Present (Selma Jeanne Cohen), 1974, School of Classical Dance (V. Kostrovitskaya and A. Pisarev), 1978; contbr. (book) Ballet: Bias and Belief, "Three Pamphlets Collected" and Other Dance Writings of Lincoln Kirstein, 1983; contbr. articles to profl. jours Ford Found. Travel and Study grantee, 1974; Mary Duke Biddle Found. grantee, 1990. Mem. Dance Critics Assn. (pres. 1986-87), Soc. Dance History Scholars, Soc. for Dance Rsch., Am. Soc. for Theatre Rsch., European Assn. Dance Historians, Internat. Fedn. for Theatre Rsch. in affiliation with Societe Internat. des Bibliotheques et Musees des Arts du Spectacle, Phi Beta Kappa. Home: 9 Prospect Park W Brooklyn NY 11215-1758 Home Phone: 718-783-4265.

REYNOLDS, PATRICIA ELLEN, artist; b. Apr. 6, 1934; d. Edwin and Anna (Pacewicz) Steeg; m. Carlyle Reynolds, Oct. 4, 1953 (div. 1991); children: Clifford, Stephanie. Student, SUNY, Plattsburg, 1951-52, Moon Bus. Sch., NYC, 1953; studied with Robert Whitney, studied with Mario Cooper. Watercolor painter, Willsboro, N.Y. Condr. workshops in field, mem. art juries. One-woman shows include Gallerie Camille Renaud, Paris, 1979, Hollsworthy Gallery, London, 1980, Ctr. Modern Design, Riyadh, Saudi Arabia, 1981-83, 25 Yr. Retro Art Mus., SUNY, Plattsburgh, Remington Mus., 1996, North Country Cultural Ctr., Plattsburgh, NY, 2005; exhibited in group shows at Schenectady Mus., SUNY, Plattsburgh, St. Lawrence U., Canton, N.Y., Ctr. Music, Drama and Arts, Lake Placid, N.Y., 1980, Audubon Artists Ann., 1980, 94, Fleming Mus. Burlington, Vt., Am. Watercolor Soc., 1982, 87 (Traveling Shows awards, Lena Newcastle award), Salmagundi Club (Gold Medal award), 1983, 88-89, 91-92 (awards 1983, 88), Nat. Works Paper, 1982 (award), Nat. Exhbn. Am. Watercolors, 1983-84, 87 (award), Allied Trusts Exhbn., 1987, 91, 93, Watercolor West, 1988, Mid-West Watercolor Soc., 1983, 89, 92, Nat. Watercolor Soc., 1991. Recipient Best of Show arad No. Vt. Artists, 1970-71, 76, 78-79, Adirondack Art Exhbn. award, 1973, Outstanding Woman Artist award Am. Pen Women, 1975, Benedictine Nat. award, 1975, Lena Newcastle award Am. Watercolor Soc., 1987, Travel Exhbn. award Am. Watercolor Soc., 1987, William Kowalsky Meml. award, 1991, Adirondack Pk. Centennial award, 1992, Multi-Focus award, 1992, Adirondack Art Assn. award, 2003 Mem. Transparent Watercolor Soc. Am. (Signature Mem. award 1992, North Country award), Allied Artist Am. (assoc.), Nat. Watercolor Soc. (assoc.), Ctrl. N.Y. Watercolor Soc. (signature), Adirondack Art Assn. Office Phone: 518-963-8356. Fax: 518-963-8382.

REYNOLDS, PAUL L., lawyer, bank executive; b. Covington, Ky., May 29, 1961; BS cum laude, No. Ky. U., Highland Heights, 1983; JD, U. Ky. Coll. Law, Lexington, KY., 1986. Bar: Ohio 1986, US Dist. Ct. (so. dist. Ohio) 1986, Ky. 1987. Gen. counsel, asst. sec. Fifth Third Bank, 1995, asst. sec., 1995, sr. v.p., 1997; exec. v.p. Fifth Third Bancorp, Cin., 1999—, gen. counsel, sec., 2002—. Recipient Am. Jurisprudence award, Constl. Law, Am. Jurisprudence award, Corp. Fin. Law. Mem.: Ky. Bar Assn., Cin. Bar Assn., Ohio State Bar Assn. Office: Fifth Third Bancorp 38 Fountain Square Plz Cincinnati OH 45263 *

REYNOLDS, PAULA ROSPUT See ROSPUT REYNOLDS, PAULA

REYNOLDS, PETER JAMES, physicist; b. NYC, Nov. 19, 1949; s. Rudolph and Lydia Mary (Schanzer) R.; m. Louise Perini, Aug. 7, 1982. AB in Physics, U. Calif., Berkeley, 1971; PhD, MIT, 1979. Rsch. assoc., lectr. Boston U., 1978, asst. rsch. prof., 1979-83; mem. sci. staff Nat. Resource for Computation in Chemistry Lawrence Berkeley Lab., U. Calif., 1980-81, mem. rsch. staff materials and chem. scis. divsn., 1982-88; vis. scientist NEC Fundamental Rsch. Lab., Kawasaki, Japan, 1986; vis. rsch. chemist U. Calif., Berkeley, 1988; adj. assoc. prof. dept. chemistry San Francisco State U., 1988-91; program mgr. Office Naval Rsch., 1988—2003, Army Rsch. Office, 2003—, assoc. dir. head physics, 2004—06, divsn. chief, 2006—. Vis. scientist Inst. Theoretical Physics, Santa Barbara, 1994, Univ. Insubria, Como, Italy, 2001, 2002; rsch. prof. Georgetown U., Washington, 1996-2005; lectr. and rschr. in field of statis., chem. and computational physics and Monte Carlo Methods; program mgr. atomic and molecular physics, laser cooling and trapping, Bose-Einstein condensates, quantum degeneracy, optical lattices, quantum coherence and control, atom lasers, quantum computing. Editor: On Clusters and Clustering: From Atoms to Fractals, 1993; co-author: Monte Carlo Methods in Ab Initio Quantum Chemistry, 1994; contbr. articles to profl. jours., also rev. articles, book chpts. NATO lectr., NSF fellow, 1971-74, IBM fellow, 1975; Lawrence Berkeley Lab. grantee, 1982-83. Fellow Am. Phys. Soc. (chmn. membership com. 1998, nominating com. Divsn. Computational Physics and Forum on Physics and Soc. 1996-97, exec. com. Divsn. Computational Physics 1992-96, 2002-04, mem. editl. bd. Am. Jour. Physics 2002-04); mem. Materials Rsch. Soc., Optical Soc. Am., N.Y. Acad. Scis., Phi Beta Kappa, Sigma Xi. Office: Army Research Office Physics Divsn PO Box 12211 Research Triangle Park NC 27709

REYNOLDS, ROBERT, artist, educator; b. San Luis Obispo, Calif., Mar. 7, 1936; s. Agee Grady and Viola Elizabeth (Curran) R.; m. Sharon Ardelle Bodley, June 17, 1962 (div. 1979); children: Robert Scott, Richard Lance, Jill Elizabeth; m. Patricia Lee Smith, Oct. 5, 1981. BPA with honors, Art Ctr. Coll. Design, LA, 1963; MA, Calif. Poly. U., 1970. Artist Creative Arts Studio, San Luis Obispo, 1955-56; freelance artist/illustrator L.A., San Luis Obispo, 1957—; staff artist Calif. Poly. U., San Luis Obispo, 1964—, assoc. prof. architecture, 1970-75, prof. art & design, 1980-81, dept. chair art & design, 1984-86, acting head dept. art, 1983-84. Artist Ford Times mag., Dearborn, Mich., 1971-79; instr. Cuesta Coll., San Luis Obispo, 1972-76; artist, tchr., co-founder High Sierra Watercolor Workshop, 1975—, Asilomar Watercolor Workshop, Pacific Grove, Calif., 1980-83; free-lance illustrator for variousi studios, Calif., 1972—; painting instr. Robert Reynolds Workshop, high Sierra, 1973-2007; resident dir. London Study Program Calif. Poly. U., London, 1986, 91; art. acquisitions com. mem. Calif. Poly. State U., 1997—, performing arts adv. com., 1995—; London Study Program Com., 1986—. One-man shows include San Luis Obispo Art Ctr., 1975, 2007, Calif. State U. Hdqrs./Gallery, 1979, Allan Hancock Coll., Santa Maria, Calif., 1981, Olive Tree Gallery, Santa Maria, 1983, Johnson Gallery, 1998-2002, Harbinger Gallery, 1998-2006, Elverhoj Mus. Art and History, Solvang, Calif. 2004; group shows include Calif. Survey Drawing and Watercolor, Humboldt, 1982, U. Gallery, Calif. Poly. State U., 1985; exhibitions include Florence Biennale Internat. Art Exhbn., Italy, 2003; represented in permanent collections at City of Stockton, Calif., City of San Luis Obispo, Santa Barbara Mus. Natural history, Calif. State U. and CSU Collection, Long Beach, Mid-State Fair Assn., others; works include design of San Luis Obispo bicentennial symbol and coin, design of ofcl. seal County of San Luis Obispo, ofcl. painting 1984 Mozart Festival, San Luis Obispo; designer U.S. Commemorative Postcard Stamp, 1987, Annual Bear Valley Music Festival Poster, Calif., 2004; design (book): Splash9: Best of Watercolor, 2006; author: Painting Nature's Peaceful Places, 1993, The Art of Robert Reynolds: Quiet Journey, 2006; executed mural Mus. Nat. History, Calif., 1983; commd. to do poser for Morro Bay Nat. Estuary Program, 2001. Mem. San Luis Obispo Design and Rev. Bd., 1970-73; chmn. San Luis Obispo Glad Design Competition, 1973. With USNR, 1955-63. Recipient Disting. Teaching award Calif. Poly. State U., 1986, Pres. Art award, 1993, Bronze award Nat. Painting Competition Artist mag., 1996, finalist 1999, 2000, Gold medal Art Inst. Calif., 1994, Alumni award Calif. Poly. State U., 2005; Purchase prize IronStone Vineyards Nat Art Competition, 1999; named Calif. Ctrl. Coast Wine Classic Commemorative Artist, 2002; subject of article Ctrl. Coast Mag., 2004. Mem. San Luis Obispo Art Assn. (past pres. 1970-71), Ctrl. Coast Watercolor Soc. (co-founder 1978, pres. 1980-81). Achievements include artwork featured in over 20 art books in the US and England. Office Phone: 805-275-1850. Personal E-mail: rgreynolds@charter.net.

REYNOLDS, ROBERT A., JR., electric distributor executive; Degree in bus., Stonehill Coll., 1972. Joined Graybar Electric Co., St. Louis, 1972, various mgmt. positions, v.p. commn./data divsn., 1991, pres., CEO, 2000—, chmn., 2001—. Mem.: Nat. Assn. Wholesaler-Distributors (sec., vice chmn. 2002—05, chmn. elect 2005—). Office: Graybar Electric 34 N Meramec Ave Saint Louis MO 63105 *

REYNOLDS, ROBERT EDGAR, academic administrator; b. Pontiac, Mich., June 3, 1938; s. Arthur James and Jean Lucille (Thompson) R.; m. Barbara Fisher, June 11, 1961 (div. May 1980); children: Jennifer Robin, Lisa Anne; m. Erika Renate Forte, July 25, 1981; children: Timothy William, Julia Renate. BA, Yale U., 1960; MD, Harvard U., 1964; MPH, Johns Hopkins U., 1967, DrPH, 1970. Med. dir. Chronic Disease Hosp., Balt. City Hosps., 1968-70; assoc. prof. medicine and cmty. medicine, assoc. dean Med. Coll. Ga., Augusta, 1970-73; med. dir. br. hosps. Rush Presbyn. St. Lukes Med. Ctr., Chgo., 1973-81, assoc. prof. internal medicine, prof. preventive medicine, 1973-81, med. dir., 1975-81; assoc. dean, assoc. prof. medicine Johns Hopkins U. Sch. Medicine, Balt., 1981-88; sr. assoc. v.p. for health scis., prof. medicine U. Va. Health Sci. Ctr., Charlottesville, 1988—; prof. health evaluation scis. U. Va., Charlottesville, 1995—, dir. divsn. clin. info., 1997—2000, vice provost for health scis., 1995—99, v.p., chief info. officer, 1999—2006, acting chmn. pub. health sci., 2006—. Sec.-treas. Med. Adminstrs. Conf., 1979-80, pres., 1981. Served to capt. USAR, 1965-73. Fellow ACP, Am. Coll. Preventive Medicine; mem. AMA, Assn. Am. Med. Colls. (assoc., chmn. group on instnl. planning 1988-89), Found. for Health Svcs. Rsch. (nat. adv. com.), Assn. for Health Svc. Rsch., Nat. Libr. Medicine (biomed. rev. com. 1992-95), Computer-based Patient Record Inst. (bd. dirs. 1992—). Office: Univ Va PO Box 800717 Charlottesville VA 22908-0717 Office Phone: 434-924-6532. Office Fax: 804-924-8437. Business E-Mail: rreynolds@virginia.edu.

REYNOLDS, ROBERT HUGH, lawyer; b. St. Louis, Jan. 3, 1937; s. Leslie A. and Rebecca (McWaters) R.; m. Carol Jemison, Apr. 8, 1961; children: Stephen H., Cynthia C., Laura M. BA, Yale U., 1958; JD, Harvard U., 1964. Assoc. Barnes & Thornburg, Indpls., 1964—70, ptnr., 1970—2004, chmn. bus. dept., 1983—91, chmn. internat. practice group, 1992—2004, of counsel, 2005—; vice-chmn. TerraLex, 1996—2003, chmn., 2003—06, chmn. emeritus, 2007—. Co-chmn., editor Comml. Real Estate Financing for Ind. Attys., 1968; vice-chmn., co-editor Advising Ind. Businesses, 1974; chmn., editor Counseling Ind. Businesses, 1981, The Purchase and Sale of a Business, 1987. Bd. dir. Crossroads Am. Coun. Boy Scouts Am., v.p., 1971—75, pres., 1987—89, v.p. Area 4 Ctrl. Region, 1989—92, pres., 1992—93, pres. Ctrl. Region, 1993—96, nat. exec. bd., 1993—; bd. dir. Family Svc. Assn. Indpls., 1974—81, pres., 1978—80; bd. dir. Family Svc. Am., 1979—88, Greater Indpls. Fgn. Trade Zone, 1987—2000, Indpls. Conv. and Visitors Assn., 1989—2000, Indpls. Econ. Devel. Corp., 1983—99, Greater Indpls. Progress Com., 1986—2000, exec. com., vice chmn.; trustee Children's Mus. Indpls., 1988—96, chmn., 1992—94; bd. dirs. Indpls. Downtown Inc., chmn., 1996—99; bd. govs. Legacy Fund, 1992—, vice chmn., 2000—03, chmn., 2004—06; bd. dir. Noyes Meml. Found., pres., 2004—; bd. dir. Japan-Am. Soc. Ind., pres., 1994—2005, pres. emeritus, 2005—; bd. dir. Ctrl. Ind. Cmty. Found., 2003—; bd. dirs. Indpls. Symphony Orch. Found., 2004—. With USN, 1958—61, lt. comdr. USNR, 1961—78. Named hon. Consul Gen. of Japan, 1999—, hon. trustee, Children's Mus. Indpls., 1997—; recipient Silver Buffalo award, Boy Scouts Am., Charles L. Whistler award, Greater Indpls. Progress Com., Sagamore of the Wabash award, Gov. Ind. Fellow Ind. Bar Found., Indpls. Bar Found.; mem. ABA, Ind. Bar Assn. (chmn. corp., banking and bus. law sect. 1981-82, chmn. internat. sect. 1994-96), Internat. Bar Assn., Indpls. Bar Assn., Greater Indpls. C. of C. (bd. dirs., sec. 2000-05, dir. emeritus 2005—), Econ. Club Indpls. (bd. dirs. 1995-2004), Kiwanis. Republican. Office: Barnes & Thornburg LLP 11 S Meridian St Indianapolis IN 46204-3535 Office Phone: 317-231-7227. Business E-Mail: rreynolds@btlaw.com.

REYNOLDS, ROBERT JOEL, economist, consultant; b. Indpls., May 13, 1944; s. Joel Burr and Betty (Schimpf) R.; m. Lucinda Margaret Lewis, May 27, 1979; children: Joel, Sarah. BSBA in Fin., Northwestern U., Evanston, Ill., 1965, PhD in Econs., 1970. Asst. prof. econs. U. Idaho, Moscow, 1969—73, assoc. prof., 1973—75; asst. dir, sr. economist econ. policy office Dept. Justice, Washington, 1973—81; sr. economist, v.p. ICF Inc., Washington, 1981—87, sr. v.p., 1987—91; exec. v.p., prin. Econsult Corp., Washington, 1991—96; chmn., exec. v.p. Econsult of D.C., Inc., Washington, 1997; chmn. Competition Econs., Inc., Washington, 1997—2007; prin. Brattle Group, 2004—. Vis. assoc. prof. U. Calif., Berkeley, 1976-77, Cornell U., Ithaca, N.Y., 1981. Reviewer: NSF, Rand Jour. of Econs., Internat. Econ. Rev., Internat. Jour. Indsl. Orgn., Jour. Indsl. Econs., Am. Econ. Rev.; mem. editl. bd. Managerial and Decision Econs.; contbr. articles to profl. jours. Recipient Dow Jones award Wall St. Jour., 1965; AT&T grantee, 1971-72, Brookings Instl. grantee, 1968-69; NDEA fellow, 1965-69. Mem. AAAS, IEEE (computer sect.), SIAM, Am. Math. Assn., Am. Econ. Assn., Econometric Soc., Royal Econ. Soc., Am. Statis. Assn., European Assn. for Rsch. in Indsl. Econs., Soc. for the Promotion of Econ. Theory, Math. Assn. Am. Congregationalist. Home: PO Box 59712 Potomac MD 20859-9712 Office: Brattle Group 1850 M St NW Ste 1200 Washington DC 20036 Home Phone: 301-765-3370; Office Phone: 202-955-5050. Personal E-mail: rjrcei@aol.com.

REYNOLDS, ROGER LEE, composer, educator; b. Detroit, July 18, 1934; s. George Arthur and Katherine Adelaide (Butler) Reynolds; m. Karen Jeanne Hill, Apr. 11, 1964; children: Erika Lynn, Wendy Claire. BSE in Physics, U. Mich., 1957, MusB in Music Lit., 1960, MusM in Composition, 1961. Assoc. prof. U. Calif. San Diego, La Jolla, 1969—73, founding dir. Ctr. Music Expt. and Related Rsch., 1972—77, prof., 1973—; George Miller prof. U. Ill., 1971—. Vis. prof. Yale U., New Haven, 1981; sr. rsch. fellow ISAM Bklyn. Coll., 1985; Valentine prof. Amherst (Mass.) Coll., 1988; Rothschild composer in residence Peabody Conservatory of Music, 1992—93; pub. Peters Music Pubs.; mgr. Graham Hayter, Contemporary Music Promotions. Author: MIND MODELS: New Forms of Musical Experience, 1975, A Searcher's Path: A Composer's Ways, 1987, A Jostled Silence: Contemporary Japanese Musical Thought, 1992—93, Form and Method: Composing Music, 2002; first Dolby Digital 5.1 DVD release of custom-designed, multichannel classical compositions: WATERSHED, Mode Records, 1998; contbr. numerous articles and revs. to profl. jours. Mem. bd. govs. Inst. Current World Affairs; co-founder ONCE festivals, 1960; bd. dirs. Am. Music Ctr., Meet the Composer; bd. dirs. Fromm Found. Harvard U. Named sr. fellow, Inst. Studies in Am. Music, 1985, fellow, Inst. Current World Affairs, Rockefeller Found., Guggenheim Found., Fulbright scholar; recipient Koussevitzky Internat. Rec. Award, 1970, Nat. Inst. Arts and Letters award, 1971, NEA awards, 1975, 1978, 1979, 1986, Pulitzer prize for music, 1989. Office: U Calif San Diego Dept Music 0326 La Jolla CA 92093 Office Phone: 858-534-3230.

REYNOLDS, RONALD J., astronomer, educator; b. Chicago Heights, Ill., May 17, 1943; s. James Lonnie and Elsie Gerhardt Reynolds; m. Carla Strohmeyer Reynolds; children: Julie Elizabeth, Suzanne Emilie. BS, U. of

Illinoinois, Champaign, IL, 1965; MS, U. of Wis., Madison, WI, 1967, PhD, 1971. NAS-NRC rsch. assoc. Goddard Space Flight Ctr., Greenbelt, Md., 1971—73; rsch. assoc. U. Wis., Madison, Wis., 1973—76, asst. scientist, 1976—81, assoc. scientist, 1981—87, sr. scientist physics, 1987—96, prof. astronomy, 1996—; prof. emeritus. Recipient Kellett Faculty Rschr. award, U. Wis., Madison; Rsch. Grants, NASA, 1974—, NSF, 1974—. Mem.: Internat. Astron. Union, Am. Astron. Soc. (Beatrice M. Tinsley prize 2004). Achievements include first to develop unique high sensitivity spectrometers for astronomy; detected and characterized the diffuse ionized component of our galaxy's interstellar hydrogen. Office: U Wis Dept Astronomy 475 N Charter St Madison WI 53706

REYNOLDS, RUTH CARMEN, school administrator, secondary school educator; b. Dec. 30; d. Jim and Beulah Eliza (Woods) R. BS in Math., Chgo. State U., 1973, BS in Acctg., 1983, MS in Edn., 1986; MA in Math. Edn., DePaul U., 1991. Cert. tchr., high sch. math., gen. adminstrv. Tchr. Chgo. Pub. Schs., 1973—; adminstrv. asst. South Shore Cmty. Acad., Chgo., 1995-96, registrar, 1995-96, dir. scheduling, grade coord., 1995-96; dir. scheduling, registrar Phillips H.S. Acad., Chgo., 1996-97; adminstrv. asst. Harper H.S., Chgo., 1997—2000; program officer, grade coord. and registrar, adminstrv. asst. Collins H.S., Chgo., 2000—. Adj. prof. Columbia Coll., Chgo., 1988-89; program officer Lindblom Tech. H.S., Chgo., 1985-95; mem. symposium com. Chgo. Pub. Schs. Student Sci. Fair, Inc.; mem. Ill. Jr. Sci. Fair, Inc. Contbr. articles to profl. jours. Treas. Chgo. Chpt. NAAF, 1988, nat. phone contact. Frye Found. Math. fellow U. Chgo., 1991. Mem. ASCD, Nat. Coun. Tchrs. Math., Ill. Coun. Tchrs. Math. (del. to Japan 1988), Nat. Coun. Suprs. Math., Notaries Assn. Ill., Benjamin Banneker Assn., Andover-Dartmouth Urban Tchr. Inst., Exeter Math. Inst., Nat. Geneaological Soc., Afro-Am. Geneal. and Hist. Soc. Chgo. (bd. dirs., v.p. 2000-2001, treas. 2001-2002), Met. Math. Club Chgo., Daus. of Union Vets. of the Civil War 1861-1865 (mem. Sarah M.W. Sterling Tent # 3, nat. sec. 2002-), U.S. Colored Troops Inst. for Local History and Family Rsch., Internat. Soc. of Sons and Daus. of Slave Ancestry, Phi Delta Kappa, Chgo. Women's Golf Club, (treas. 2002), NAIC, (regional dir. 1998, treas. 2001-02). Avocations: reading mystery novels, travel, genealogy, golf. Home: 2901 S King Dr Apt 1802 Chicago IL 60616-3315 Office: Collins HS 1313 S Sacramento Blvd Chicago IL 60623

REYNOLDS, SCOTT WALTON, academic administrator; b. Summit, NJ, July 15, 1941; s. Clark Leonard and Shirley (Hill) R.; m. Margaret Ann Johnson, July 5, 1969; children: Jane, Amy, David. BA, Trinity Coll., Hartford, Conn., 1963; MBA, Harvard U., 1965. Mng. dir. corp. staff Bankers Trust Co., NYC, 1967-94; asst. to the pres. St. Peter's Coll., Jersey City, 1994-96, Trinity Coll., Hartford, Conn., 1996-98, sec., 1998—, interim v.p. fin., treas., 2004—05. Chmn. fund campaign Montclair (N.J.) ARC, 1974; chmn. bus. and fraternal group Montclair Bicentennial Com., 1976; bd. fellows Trinity Coll., 1982-88, trustee, 1992-96, sec., exec. com., 1993-96. 1st lt. U.S. Army, 1965-67. Recipient 150th Anniversary award Trinity Coll., 1978, Alumni medal for Excellence, 1988, Pres.' Leadership medal, 1993. Mem. Montclair Jaycees (treas. 1973), Trinity Coll. Alumni Assn. N.Y. (pres. 1972-73) Clubs: Harvard (N.Y.C.). Episcopalian. Office: Trinity Coll Office of Pres 300 Summit St Hartford CT 06106-3100 Office Phone: 860-297-2093. Business E-Mail: scott.reynolds@trincoll.edu.

REYNOLDS, SHERI, writer; b. Conway, SC, 1967; BA in English, Davidson Coll., 1989; MFA in creative writing, Va. Commonwealth U., 1992. Assoc. prof., Ruth and Perry Morgan Chair So. Lit. Old Dominion U., Norfolk, Va. Adj. instr. English Va. Commonwealth U., Richmond, 1992. Author: Bitterroot Landing, 1994, The Rapture of Canaan, 1996, A Gracious Plenty, 1997, The Firefly Cloak, 2006, (plays) Orabelle's Wheelbarrow, 2005 (Women Playwrights' Initiative playwriting competition, 2005). Recipient Outstanding Faculty award, State Coun. Higher Education Va., 2003; grantee, Va. Commn. for the Arts in playwriting, 2005. Mailing: Old Dominion U University Village 02 Norfolk VA 23529 *

REYNOLDS, STEPHEN PHILIP, utility company executive; b. Berkeley, Calif., Jan. 5, 1948; s. Philip Elmore and Annette (Medefind) R.; m. Sharon Ann Rudd, Sept. 6, 1969; 1 child, Matthew. BA in Econs., U. Calif., Berkeley, 1970; MBA in Prodn. Mgmt., U. Oreg., 1972. Various mktg./rate positions Pacific Gas and Electric Co., San Francisco, 1967-75, sr. rate engr., 1975-77, supervising rate engr., 1977-80, mgr. rate dept., 1980-84, v.p. rates, 1984-87; pres., CEO Pacific Gas Transmission Co. (subs. Pacific Gas and Electric), 1987—98, Reynolds Energy Internat., 1998—2002; chmn., pres., CEO Puget Energy, Bellevue, Wash., 2002—. Bd. dirs. UNOVA Inc., Oregon Steel Mills Inc., InfrastruX Group,, Interstate Gas of Am., Interstate Gas of Am. Found., Assn. of Northwest Gas Utilities. Contbr. numerous articles to trade publs. and profl. symposiums on rate issues. Served with Calif. Army N.G., 1970-76. Mem. Pacific Coast Gas Assn., Nat. Planning Assn. (Canadian-American Com.), Calif. Found. on Environment & Economy, San Francisco World Affairs Coun., San Francisco Engrs. Club, Commonwealth Club, World Trade Club. Office: Puget Energy 10885 NE 4th St PO Box 97034 Bellevue WA 98009-9734 *

REYNOLDS, STEPHEN ROBERT, lawyer; b. Orange, NJ, Sept. 20, 1958; s. James Edward and Jane (McDonough) R.; m. Julia Dunn Herndon, Sept. 17, 1983; children: Matthew Thomas, John James, Stephen Bennett, William Douglas. BA in History, Princeton U., 1980; JD, Fordham U., 1983. Bar: N.Y. 1984, N.J. 1986; U.S. Dist. Ct. (ea. dist.) N.Y. 1984, U.S. Dist. Ct. (so. dist.) N.Y. 1985, U.S. Dist. Ct. N.J. 1980. Assoc. Haight, Gardner, Poor & Havens, NYC, 1983-85, Crummy, Del Deo, Dolan, Newark, 1985-90; ptnr. Crummy, Del Deo, Dolan, Griffinger & Vecchione, Newark, 1990-97, Gibbons, Del Deo, Dolan, Griffinger & Vecchione, Newark, 1988—2003; v.p., chief litig. counsel Aventis SA, 2004—06; dep. gen. counsel, chief litig. counsel Lucent Techs., Inc., 2006—07; gen. counsel Alcatel Lucent, 2007—. Chief asst. adminstr. Exxon-Valdez claims, Trans-Alaska Pipeline Liability Fund, Anchorage, 1991—. Editor Fordham Internat. Law Jour., 1982-83. Adminstr. Pro Bono program. Mem. ABA (mem. litigation com. 1987—, RICO sub-com. 1991—), N.J. State Bar Assn., Essex County Bar Assn., N.Y. State Bar Assn. Roman Catholic. Office: Alcatel Lucent 54 rue la Boétie 75008 Paris France *

REYNOLDS, TERRY RAY, curator, anthropologist, educator; d. Raymond Roberts and Harriet Pearl Reynolds. BA, U. Colo., 1962; MA, Stanford U., 1965; PhD, U. BC, 1979. Instr. Calif. State U., Northridge, 1965—68, 1972—74; sessional lectr. U. BC, Vancouver, Canada, 1968—69; dir. mus. studies U. Denver, 1989—98; curator N.Mex. State U., Las Cruces, 1998—. Cons., rschr., Boulder, Denver and Las Cruces, 1979—89. Editor: A Place as Wild as West Ever Was, 2004. Fellow, Can. Coun., 1969—72. Mem.: Am. Soc. Ethnohistory, Am. Assn. Museums (chair profl. standing com. 1994—98). Avocations: dogs, antiques. Office: NMex State U Mus PO Box 30001 MSC 3564 Las Cruces NM 88003 Office Phone: 505-646-4056. Office Fax: 505-646-1419. Business E-Mail: tereynol@nmsu.edu.

REYNOLDS, THOMAS M., congressman; b. Springville, NY, Sept. 3, 1950; m. Donna Reynolds; 4 children. Student, Kent State U., Ohio, 1968—69. Pres. TM Reynolds Ins. Agy.; mem. to dep. supr. Concord Town Bd., 1974—82; mem. Erie County Legislature, 1982—88, NY State Assembly from Dist. 147, 1988-98, Rep. leader, 1995—98, chmn. minority affordable housing task force; mem. corrections com. N.Y. State Assembly; mem. US Congress from 26th NY dist., 1999—, mem. ways and means com., chmn. Nat. Rep. Congl. Com. Rank up to sgt. NY Air Nat. Guard, 1970-76; exec. asst. Staff of NY State Assemblyman Ronald Tillis; clk. Erie County Legislature; legis. asst. to minority Rep. leader, 1987; Erie County Rep. chmn., 1990-96. Named a Friend of Law Enforcement, NY State Sheriff's Assn.; named Legislator of Yr., Am. Legis. Exch. Coun., Shooters Com. Polit. Edn.; recipient Golden Apple award, US Apple Assn. Mem. Am. Legion, NRA, Southtown Walleye Assn., Masons. Republican. Presbyterian. Office: US House Reps 332 Cannon House Office Bldg Washington DC 20515-3226 Office Phone: 202-225-5265. Office Fax: 202-225-5910. *

REYNOLDS, VIRGINIA EDITH, sociologist, anthropologist, educator, artist; b. Lafayette, Ind., July 3, 1941; d. Ira Hubert and Harriet G. (Robertson) Reynolds; m. Antonio G. Arroyo, 1961 (div. 1974); children: Mary-Jane R. Arroyo Young, Joanne R. Arroyo Shirley. BS with hons. in Sociology, Columbia U., 1965, MA in Sociology, 1967; postgrad., Pa. State U., 1974—84. Rsch. asst. demographic divsn. Population Coun., NYC, 1968; tchr. CUNY Borough Manhattan C.C., NYC, 1969; asst. prof. sociology and anthropology Lycoming Coll., Williamsport, Pa., 1970—75, Indiana U. Pa., 1975—2001; ret., 2001. Mem. exec. com. Assn. for Asian Studies Mid-Atlantic Region, 1997—99; Tai Chi tchr. Solo show, Indiana County Hist. Mus., Indiana, Pa., 2007, exhibited in group shows at Old Courthouse Office Gallery, 2002 (Hon. Mention award, 2002), 2003 (2d Pl. award, 2003), Centennial of the Union Street Sanctuary, 2004, Presbyn. Ch. of Punxsutawney, 2004. Singer Indiana County Singers and Ch. Choir; elected Indiana County Dem. Com., Pa., 2001—07. Mem.: AAUW (chair nat. conv. 2005), Touchstone Ctr. for Crafts, Indiana (Pa.) Art Assn., Pitts. Ctr. for the Arts. Episcopalian. Avocations: tai chi, community theater musicals, international folk dancing, Chinese painting, Tibetan Buddhism. Home and Studio: 1699 Church St Indiana PA 15701 Office Phone: 724-349-4952. Personal E-mail: veren77@yahoo.com.

REYNOLDS, WILLIAM BRADFORD, lawyer; b. Bridgeport, Conn., June 21, 1942; s. William Glasgow and Nancy Bradford (DuPont) R.; m. Marguerite Lynn Morgan, June 27, 1964 (div. Feb. 1987); children: William Bradford Jr., Melissa Morgan, Kristina DuPont, Wendy Riker; m. Clare Alice Conroy, Aug. 29, 1987 (div. June 2000); 1 child, Linda Matisan; m. Barbara Lynn Wooster, July 15, 2000; children: Courtney Enright, Brooke Ashley. BA, Yale U., 1964; LLB, Vanderbilt U., 1967. Bar: N.Y. 1968, D.C. 1973, U.S. Supreme Ct. 1971. Assoc. Sullivan and Cromwell, NYC, 1967-70; asst. to Solicitor Gen. U.S. Dept. Justice, Washington, 1970-73; ptnr. Shaw, Pittman, Potts & Trowbridge, Washington, 1973-81; asst. atty. gen. Civil Rights div. U.S. Dept. Justice, Washington, 1981-88, counselor to Atty. Gen., 1987-88; ptnr. Ross & Hardies, 1989-91, Dickstein, Shapiro & Morin, 1991-94, Collier, Shannon, Rill & Scott, 1994-2000, Howrey LLP, Washington, 2000—. Chmn. Archtl. Transp. Barriers Compliance Bd., 1982-84. Editor-in-chief Vanderbilt Law Rev., 1966. Disting. scholar Free Congress Found., 1989-93, Disting. fellow Nat. Legal Ctr. for Pub. Interest, Washington, 1989-90. Mem. ABA, Fed. Bar Assn., D.C. Bar Assn., Order of Coif. Republican. Episcopalian. Home Phone: 703-556-0559; Office Phone: 202-383-6912. Business E-Mail: reynoldsw@howrey.com.

REYNOLDS, WILLIAM FRANCIS, mathematics professor; b. Boston, Jan. 31, 1930; s. William Leo and Grace Regina (Devlin) R.; m. Pauline Jane Fitzgerald, Aug. 5, 1962; children: Nancy Elizabeth, Jane Anele. AB summa cum laude, Holy Cross Coll., 1950; A.M., Harvard, 1951, PhD, 1954. Instr. Holy Cross Coll., Worcester, Mass., 1954-55; instr. Mass. Inst. Tech., Cambridge, 1955-57; asst. prof. math. Tufts U., Medford, Mass., 1957-60, assoc. prof., 1960-67, prof., 1967-98, Walker prof. math., 1970-98, prof. emeritus, 1998—. Contbr. articles to math. jours. Mem. Am. Math. Soc. Achievements include research on modular and projective representations of finite groups. Home: 3 Preble Gardens Rd Belmont MA 02478-3460 E-mail: wfr@post.harvard.edu.

REYNOLDS, WILLIAM LEROY, lawyer, educator; b. Balt., July 26, 1945; s. Austin Leroy and Doris (Hill) R.; m. Theodora Hoe, Sept. 3, 1966; children: William, Megan, Sarah. AB, Dartmouth Coll., Hanover, NH, 1967; JD, Harvard U., Cambridge, Mass., 1970. Bar: Md. 1972, US Supreme Ct. 1975. Clk. to judge U.S. Dist. Ct. Md., 1970-71; asst. prof. law U. Md., 1971-74, assoc. prof., 1974-77, prof., 1977—; of counsel DLA Piper, LLP, Balt., 1992—. Bd. dirs. Md. Jud. Inst. Author: Judicial Process in a Nutshell, 1980, 3d edit., 2002, Understanding the Conflict of Laws, 1984, 3d edit., 2002, Cases and Materials on Conflict of Laws, 1990, 2d edit., 2003, The Full Faith and Credit Clause, 2005. Mem. Am. Law Inst., Md. State Bar Assn., Am. Judicature Soc. Clubs: Serjeants' Inn, Wranglers (Balt.); St. Regis Yacht (Paul Smiths, NY), Hamilton St. Office: U Md Sch Law 500 W Baltimore St Baltimore MD 21201-1701 Office Phone: 410-706-7279. Business E-Mail: wreynolds@law.umaryland.edu.

REYNOLDS COOCH, NANCY D., sculptor; b. Greenville, Del., Dec. 28, 1919; d. Eugene Eleuthere and Catherine Dulcinea (Moxham) duPont; m. William Glasgow Reynolds, May 18, 1940 (dec. Jan. 1987); children: Katherine Glasgow Reynolds, William Bradford Reynolds, Mary Parminter Reynolds Savage, Cynthia duPont Reynolds Farris.; m. Edward W. Cooch, Jr., Sept. 6, 2003. Student, Goldey-Beacom Coll., Wilmington, Del., 1938. One-woman shows include Caldwell Inc., 1975, Nat. Museum of Women in Arts, 1998; exhibited in group shows at Corcoran Gallery, Washington, 1943, Soc. Fine Arts, Wilmington, 1937-38, 40-41, 48, 50, 62, 65, Rehoboth Art League, Del., 1963, NAD, NYC, 1964, Pa. Mil. Coll., Chester, 1966, Del. Art Ctr., 1967, Del. Art Mus., Wilmington, Wilmington Art Mus., 1976, Met. Mus. Art, NYC, 1977, Lever House, NYC, 1979, Nat. Mus. Women in the Arts, Washington, 1998; represented in permanent collections Wilmington Trust Co., E.I. duPont de Nemours & Co., Children's Home, Inc., Claymont, Del., Children's Bur., Wilmington, Stephenson Sci. Ctr., Vanderbilt U., Nashville, Lutheran Towers Bldg., Travelers Aid and Family Soc. Bldg., Wilmington, bronze fountain head Longwood Gardens, Kennett Square, Pa., bronze statue Brookgreen Gardens, Murrells Inlet, S.C., bronze sculpture "Veiled Lady", Nat. Mus. Women in Arts, Washington, 1998, bronze sculpture U. Del., Newark, 2001, bronze sculpture Biggs Mus., Dover, Del., 2002; contbr. articles to profl. jours. Organizer vol. svc. Del. chpt. ARC, 1938-39; chmn. Com. for Revision Del. Child Adoption Law, 1950-52; pres., bd. dirs. Children Bur. Del.; pres., trustee Children's Home, Inc.; del., past regent Gunston Hall Plantation, Lorton, Va.; mem. adv. com. Longwood Gardens, Kennett Sq., Pa.; garden and grounds com. Winterthur (Del.) Mus.; mem. rsch. staff Henry Francis DuPont Winterthur Mus., 1955-63; mem. archtl. com. U. Del., Newark. Recipient Confrerie des Chevaliers du Tastevin Clos de Vougeot-Bourgogne France, 1960; Hort. award Garden Club Am., 1964, medal of Merit, 1976, Dorothy Platt award Garden Club of Phila., 1980, Alumni medal of merit Westover Sch., Middlebury, Conn., Medal of Distinction, U. Del., 1999. Mem. Pa. Hort. Soc., Wilmington Soc. Fine Arts, Mayflower Descs., Del. Hist. Soc., Colonial Dames, League Am. Pen Women, Nat. Trust Hist. Preservation. Garden Club of Wilmington (past pres.), Garden Club of Am. (past asst. zone 4 chmn.), Vicmead Hunt Club, Greenville Country Club, Chevy Chase Club (Washington), Colony Club (NYC). Episcopalian. Address: PO Box 3919 Greenville DE 19807-0919

REYNOLDSON, WALTER WARD, retired judge, lawyer; b. St. Edward, Nebr., May 17, 1920; s. Walter Scorer and Mabel Matilda (Sallach) Reynoldson; m. Janet Aline Mills, Dec. 24, 1942 (dec. 1986); children: Vicki, Robert; m. Patricia A. Frey, June 3, 1989. BA, State Tchrs. Coll., 1942; JD, U. Iowa, Iowa City, 1948; LLD (hon.), Simpson Coll., Indianola, Iowa, 1983, Drake U., Des Moines, 1987. Bar: Iowa 1948. Justice Iowa Supreme Ct., 1971-78, chief justice, 1978-87, sr. judge, 1989-93; of counsel Reynoldson Law Firm, Osceola, Iowa, 1993—. County atty. Clark County, Iowa, 1953—57; adj. prof. law Drake U., 1989—93. Co-author: (book) Trial Handbook, 1969. Pres. Nat. Ctr. State Cts.; trustee Drake U., 1987—2000. With USNR, 1942—46. Recipient Osceola Cmty. Svc. award, 1968. Fellow: Am. Bar Found.; mem.: Am. Coll. Trial Lawyers, Conf. Chief Justices (pres. 1984—85), Acad. Trial Lawyers, Am. Judicature Soc. (bd. dirs. 1983—87, Herbert Harley award 1990), Iowa Bar Assn. (chmn. com. legal edn. and admission to bar 1964—71). Office: Reynoldson Law Firm 200 W Jefferson St Osceola IA 50213-1413 Home Phone: 515-242-0231.

REYNOLDS-SAKOWSKI, DANA RENEE, science educator; b. Centralia, Ill., June 28, 1968; d. David Lavern and Betty Lou (Shelton) Reynolds; m. Jason Bielas Sakowski, Oct. 8, 1994. BS in Edn., U. No. Colo., 1991, MEd in Middle Sch. Edn., 1996. Tchr. life sci. and math. Ken Caryl Mid. Sch., Littleton, Colo., 1991-92; tchr. sci. Moore Mid. Sch., Arvada, Colo., 1992-93, tchr. life sci., 1993—. Mem. Nat. Wildlife Fedn., Colo. Assn. Sci. Tchrs., Colo. Biology Tchrs. Assn., Sierra Club, World Wildlife Fund, Nat. Parks and Conservation Assn., Natural Resources Def. Coun., Audubon Soc., Nature Conservancy. Avocations: camping, poetry, hiking, singing. Office: Mandalay Mid Sch 9651 N Pierce St Westminster CO 80020

REYNVAAN, MICHAEL THOMAS, lawyer; b. Bremerton, Wash., Sept. 26, 1953; s. Theodore Thomas Reynvaan and Clara Anne (Malinowski) Reynvaan-Graves; m. Gale Arlene Beegle; children: Amanda, Angela, Matthew. Student, Whitman Coll., 1971-73; BA in Polit. Sci, Lewis and Clark Coll., 1976; JD, U. Puget Sound, 1982. Bar: Wash. 1982, US Dist. Ct. (We. Dist.) Wash. 1983, US Ct. Appeals (9th Cir.) 1983, US Dist. Ct. (Ea. Dist.) Wash. 1985. Mill worker Internat. Telephone & Telegraph/Rayonier Inc., Hoquiam, Wash., 1976-77, 79; legal asst. Bogle & Gates, Seattle, 1979; law clk. to chief justice Wash. State Supreme Ct., Olympia, 1982-83; assoc. Perkins Coie, Seattle, 1983—, ptnr., mem. mgmt. com. & exec. com. Active Alki Found., Seattle, 1988, Leadership Tomorrow, 1988—; campaign treas. Callow for Supreme Ct., Seattle, 1984; del. Kitsap County Dem. Conv. Mem. ABA (YLD labor law com., vice-chair 1988-89, chmn. 1989—), Seattle-King County Bar Assn. (young lawyers div., bd. trustees), Wash. State Bar Assn., Wash. Athletic Club. Episcopalian. Office: Perkins Coie LLP 1201 3rd Ave Fl 40 Seattle WA 98101-3029 Office Phone: 206-359-8469. Office Fax: 206-359-9000. Business E-Mail: mreynvaan@perkinscoie.com.

REZA, ALI HAJMOHAMMAD, cardiologist; b. Tehran, Iran, Apr. 14, 1957; came to U.S., 1988; s. Tayeb Hajmohammad and Fakhri (Mohajer) R.; m. Elizabeth Gheisari; children: Tara, Arteen. MD, Nat. U. Iran, Tehran, 1982. Diplomate Am. Bd. Internal Medicine, Am. Cardiovasc., Am. Bd. Interventional Cardiology; bd. cert. nuclear cardiology, bd. cert. in vascular medicine, 2005, endovascular medicine, 2005. Rsch. asst. in pathology Rush Med. Sch., Chgo., 1988-89; resident in internal medicine SUNY, Buffalo, 1989-93, fellow in nephrology, 1992-93; fellow in cardiology Tulane U., New Orleans, 1993-96; pvt. practice, Chalmette, La., 1996—; pvt. practice Oschner Cardiovascular Inst., 2001—. Mem. ACP, AMA, Am. Coll. Cardiology. Muslim. Home: 1804 Octavia St New Orleans LA 70115 Office: 5701 Deerpark Blvd New Orleans LA 70127

REZA, SHAHED, electrical engineer; Scientist Philips Med. Sys., Gainesville, Fla., 2003—. Achievements include research in nanotechnology. Home Phone: 352-846-5867. Personal E-mail: sreza@ieee.org.

REZANKA, THOMAS W., lawyer; b. Plainfield, NJ, Mar. 3, 1954; s. William L. and Helen G. Rezanka; m. Karen T. Rezanka, May 21, 1977. BA, Montclair State U., Upper Montclair, NJ, 1976; JD, Stetson U., 1980. Bar: Fla. 1980, U.S. Ct. Appeals (5th and llth cirs.) 1980. Pvt. practice, Palm Harbor, Fla., 1980—. Presenter Joint Conf. on Law and Aging, Washington, 1995. Columnist Tropical Breeze, 1995-2001, Countryside Cougar, East Lake Eagle, Palm Harbor Panther, 1995-2005, Dunedin Highlander, 2001-05; author: The Catholic Challenge: A Question of Conscience, 2004. Adv. com. Countryside HS, Clearwater, Fla., 1998-99; bd. dirs. Tampa Bay Area Planned Giving Coun., Tampa, 2001. Mem. ABA, Nat. Acad. Elder Law Atty., Fla. Bar Assn. (former mem. legis. drafting com. real property, probate and trust law sect.) exec. coun. elder law sect. 1995-99, faculty counseling your Fla. client seminar for out-of-state atty. 1999, faculty elder law bd. cert. rev. course 1998, editor The Advocate newsletter 1996-97, elder law sect.), Clearwater Bar Assn. (estate planning columnist 1996-97, 2000-01, probate, guardianship and trust practice com.), Pinellas County Estate Planning Coun. (bd. dir. 1995-99). Office: 2672 Westlake Rd Palm Harbor FL 34684 Office Phone: 727-787-3020.

REZEK, FRANCISCO, former judge, former supreme court justice; b. Cristina, Brazil, Jan. 18, 1944; s. Elias and Baget Rezek; m. Myreia de Palma Castro, Jan. 14, 1971; children: Adriana, Veronica, Francisco, João Paulo. LLB, U. Minas Gerais, Belo Horizonte, 1966; LLD, U. Paris-Sorbonne, 1970; diploma in law, Oxford U., England, 1979. Atty. Rep. of Brazil, 1972-79, dep. atty. gen., 1979-83, justice Supreme Ct., 1983—90, 1992—97; fgn. min. Dept. State, Brasilia, 1990-92; dean faculty of law U. Brasilia, 1978-79; judge Intl. Ct. of Justice, The Hague, Netherlands, 1997—2006. Prof., internat. law and constl. law, Univ. Brasilia, 1971-97 (chmn., dept. of law, 1974-76, dean, faculty of social studies, 1978-79); prof., internat. law, Rio Branco (diplomatic) Inst., 1976-97; lecturer, The Hague Acad. of Internat. Law, 1986, Inst. of Internat. Public Law and Internat. Rels., Thessaloniki, 1989; mem., Permanent Ct. of Arbitration, 1987-; chief justice at the High Electoral Ct., Brasilia, 1989. Author: Law of Treaties, 1984, International Law, 1989, 4th edit., 1994, others. Recipient Grand Cross Orders of Brazil, Argentina, Chile, Colombia, Lebanon, Tunisia, Korea, Portugal, Spain, and Italy, 1986-92. Roman Catholic.

REZK, NASER LABEEB, biochemist, researcher; b. Meet Masoud, Egypt, Feb. 21, 1961; s. Labeeb Hasan and Atyate Hasanan Rezk; m. Nesrin Salah Shrsher, Sept. 1, 1991; children: Salma Abdelnaser, Omar Abdelnaser, Ali Abdelnaser. BSc in Chemistry, Monofia U., Egypt, 1983, MSc in Biochemistry, 1994; PhD, Tanta U., Egypt, 2007. Formulation scientist Trimeris Biopharmaceuticals, Durham, NC; from rsch. tech. to rsch. assoc. prof. U. NC, Chapel Hill, 2000—07, rsch. assoc. prof., 2007—. Recipient Chancellor's award, U. NC, 2006, Excellence Innovation award, NC Gov., 2006, Innovation award, 2006. Mem.: ACS (assoc. Membership award 2005), Egyptian Chem. Soc. (assoc. Membership award 2000), Toastmasters. Home: 6220 Dawn Dr Hurdle Mills NC 27541 Office: Univ NC 2405 Kerr Hall CB 7360 Chapel Hill NC 27599 Home Phone: 919-245-0393; Office Phone: 919-843-0596. Office Fax: 919-962-0644; Home Fax: 919-962-0644. Personal E-mail: nascr21@gmail.com. Business E-Mail: naser2@unc.edu.

REZKALLA, LAURENCE, internist; b. Asyut, Egypt, Mar. 9, 1958; arrived in U.S., 1990; s. Lamie Rezkalla Rophael and Eniat William Basaly; m. Evette Wadie Kamel, Apr. 15, 1990; children: Paul, Peter, John, Mary. ND, Asyut Med. Sch., 1982; ob-gyn. specialist, Ain Shams Med. Sch., Cairo, 1988. Cert. Am. Bd. Internal Medicine. Intern Asyut U. Hosp., 1983—84; ob-gyn resident El-Iman Gen. Hosp, Asyut, 1986—88; ob-gyn. physician Oasis Gen. Hosp., El-Wahat El-Bahria, Egypt, 1989, Sahelsleem (Egypt) Hosp., 1989—91; internal medicine resident Kingsbrook Jewish Med. Ctr., Bklyn., 1995—98; physician St. Barnabas's Hosp., East Elmhurst, NY, 1998—2000, Woodull Hosp., Bklyn., 1999—, N.Y. Meth. Hosp., 2002—, Victory Meml. Hosp., 2004—. Pres. Bay Ridge Med. Svcs., Bklyn., 2001—; mem. exec. com. Kingsbrook Hosp., 1996—2003. Author: (book) 10 Cases of Ob/Gyn, 1988. Leader youth meetings Salvation Soc., Asyut, 1973—81; founder Arab 2000 Inc., Bklyn., 1997—2000; ptnr. Internat. Resource Ctr., Johannesburg, 1997—2000. With med. svcs. Egyptian Army, 1984—86. Scholar Full scholar, Egyptian Govt., Asyut U.,

1976. Mem.: ACP, AMA, Egyptian Med. Syndicate, Com. of Internal Residents (del. 1996—97). Avocations: travel, reading, painting. Home: 124 86th St Brooklyn NY 11209 Office: Bay Rige Med Svcs 124 86th St Brooklyn NY 11209 Office Phone: 718-921-1977.

REZNICK, RICHARD HOWARD, pediatrician; b. Chgo., Oct. 31, 1939; s. Louis and Mae Reznick; m. Barbara Ann Glantz, June 20, 1965; children: Steven L., Alicia T., Scott M., Stacey R. BS, U. Ill., 1961; MD, Loyola U., Chgo., 1965. Diplomate Am. Bd. Pediatrics. Resident in pediat. Michael Reese Hosp., Chgo., 1966-68; pediatrician USAF, Homestead AFB, Fla., 1968-70; pediatrician pvt. practice Winnetka, Ill., 1970—71, Scottsdale, Ariz., 1971—. Pres. med. staff Phoenix Children's Hosp., 1990-93, bd. dirs. 1990-94. Capt. USAF, 1968-70. Fellow Am. Acad. Pediatrics (treas. Ariz. chpt. 1982-84); mem. Ariz. Med. Assn., Phoenix Pediatric Soc. (treas. 1976-77), Maricopa County Med. Soc. Avocations: aerobics, bicycling, gardening, classical music, collecting stamps. Office: Papago Buttes Pediatric Ctr 8573 E San Alberto Ste E100 Scottsdale AZ 85258-4318 Office Phone: 480-778-1732.

REZNICK, STEVEN MICHAEL, orthopedic surgeon, educator; b. Washington, 1954; 3 children. BS, U. Md., 1975; MD, George Washington U., 1979; MBA, Columbia U., 2000. Diplomate Am. Bd. Orthopedic Surgery. Resident in gen. surgery George Washington U., 1979-81; resident in orthop. surgery U. Mich., Ann Arbor, 1981-84; clin. instr. orthopedic surgery UCLA Sch. Medicine, 1988-94. Sr. aviation med. examiner FAA, 1985-87; talk show host KGIL-Radio, L.A., 1987-90. Mem. Calif. Rep. Party, Calif. Rep. Assembly, bd. dirs. Palm Springs chpt., 1996-98. Fellow Internat. Coll. Surgeons, Am. Coll. Surgeons, Am. Acad. Orthopedic Surgeons, Beta Gamma Sigma Honor Soc. Avocation: commercial pilot. Home: PO Box 101 Somers NY 10589 E-mail: smr50@columbia.edu.

REZNIKOV, ANDREY, linguist, educator; BA MA in English and Lang. Lit., St. Petersburg U., Russia, 1978, PhD in Linguistics, 1984. Assoc. prof. Karelian State Pedagogical U., Petrozavodsk, Karelia, Russia, 1978—2004; asst. prof. Black Hills State U., Spearfish, SD, 2004—. Prin. translator and interpreter Russian Am. Rule Law Consortium, Burlington, Vt., 1992—. Recipient Excellent Tchr. Russian Fedn. award, Ministry of Edn. Russia, 1996, Honored Educator award, Govt. Republic of Karelia, Russia, 2003; Fulbright Sr. Rsch. grant, Fulbright Found., 2000. Mem.: Linguistic Soc. Am. Office: Black Hills State Univ 1200 University St Spearfish SD 57799-9128 Home Phone: 605-722-4054; Office Phone: 605-642-6249. Office Fax: 605-642-6715. Business E-Mail: andreyreznikov@bhsu.edu.

REZNIKOV, LEV, process engineer, researcher; arrived in US, 1992, naturalized; s. Efim Lvovich Reznikov and Polina Yakovlevna Reznikova. BS in Mech. Engring. with honors, Inst. Tech., Odessa, 1972; MS in Mech. Engring. with honors, Inst. Tech., 1972, PhD in Engring., 1988. Sr. rsch. assoc. Cryogenic Corp. Kislorodmach, Odessa, 1977—92; rsch. engr. APD Cryogenics, Allentown, Pa., 1993; cons. Transnow, Inc., Yonkers, NY, 1994—99; sr. cryogenic engr. Virtis, Inc., Gardiner, NY, 2000—01; prin. investigator Beltran, Inc., Bklyn., 2001—; sr. cryogenic process engr. Gas Equipment Engring. Co., Milford, Conn., 2005—06, Voltaix, Inc., NJ, 2007. Cons. Acad. Refrigeration, Odessa, 1997—2005, Ind. State U., Indpls., 2002—, Soro, LLC, NYC, 2004—06; reviewer Jour. Pressure Vessel Tech., Indpls., 2004—; cons. Beltran, Inc., 2006—. Contbr. articles to profl. jours. Mem.: Cryogenic Soc. Am. (assoc.). Achievements include 50 patents in cryogenics, thermodynamics, heat transfer, process improvements, measurements and control, machines and apparatuses; patents for cryogenic in-transit refrigeration; invention of eco-thermal management for aerospace; high-performance refrigeration for first compact cryogenic freeze-dryer; new methods for temperature control and isothermal storage of cryogen products; inert atmosphere for effective fire suppression; technologies for storage of cryogen products; development of new methods for refrigerant blend express testing; thermodynamic concept for direct measurement of p—v—t and process parameters of refrigerants. Avocations: bicycling, swimming, travel. Home: 1510 Ocean Pky Apt A17 Brooklyn NY 11230 Office: Beltran Inc 1133 E 35th St Brooklyn NY 11210 Personal E-mail: l.reznikov@yahoo.com. Business E-Mail: lyres@netzero.net.

REZNIKOV, VLADIMIR LVOVICH, historian, playwright; b. Donetzk, Ukraine, May 26, 1937; s. Lev Davidovich Reznikov and Sofia Semyonovna Baskina; m. Natalya Klueva, Nov. 4, 1994; children: Lev, Michael, Sonya. MS in History, Moscow State Pedagogic U., 1962; PhD in History, Russain Acad. Scis., 1972; MS in Screenplay Writing (hon.), State Inst. Cinematography, Moscow, 1973. Sci. editor Oriental Book Publishers, Moscow, 1962—69; dept. editor Asia and Africa Today, Moscow, 1977—81; sr. rsch. fellow Inst. Oriental Studies of Russian Acad. of Scis., Moscow, 1969—97, 1981—97; freelance playwright scholar of art history, 1997—. Author: (screenplays) Encounter, 1971, Forgive me, Vietnam, 1971, Personal Case, 1971, Nature and Society, 1980, Voice of the Centuries, 1975, Use of Isotope Control Devices in Automatization of Production Processes, 1975, (plays) True Story of Buratino or the Song of Triumphant Love, 2006, (books) Policy of Caeser's Germany in Oceania, 1975; editor: India - Country and People, 1967 (Hon. Diploma Geog. Soc. of USSR, 1973). Mem.: Journalist Soc. of Russia, Am. Taekwondo Assn. (2d Degree Black belt). Avocation: Tae Kwon Do. Personal E-mail: nklueva@yahoo.com.

RHAMES, VING (IRVING), actor; b. NYC, May 12, 1961; m. Valerie Scott, 1994 (div. 1999); m. Deborah Reed, Dec. 25, 2000; children: Tiffany, Rainbow, Freedom. Grad., Julliard Sch. Drama. Actor (Broadway plays) The Winter Boys, 1984; (films) Native Son, 1986, Patty Hearst, 1988, Casualties of War, 1989, The Long Walk Home, 1990, Jacob's Ladder, 1990, Flight of the Intruder, 1991, Homicide, 1991, Stop! Or My Mom Will Shoot, 1992, The People Under the Stairs, 1992, Dave, 1993, The Saint of Fort Washington, 1993, Bound By Honor Blood In Blood Out, 1993, Pulp Fiction, 1994, Drop Squad, 1994, Kiss of Death, 1995, Ed McBain's 87th Precinct, 1995, Mission: Impossible, 1996, Striptease, 1996, Con Air, 1997, Rosewood, 1997, Dangerous Ground, 1997, The Split, 1998, Out of Sight, 1998, Body Count, 1998, Entrapment, 1999, Bringing Out the Dead, 1999, Mission Impossible II, 2000, (voice) Final Fantasy: The Spirits Within, 2001, Baby Boy, 2001, Lilo & Stitch (voice only), 2002, Dark Blue, 2002, Undisputed, 2002, (voice) Stitch! The Movie, 2003, Back in the Day, 2004, Dawn of the Dead, 2004, Mission: Impossible III, 2006, Idlewild, 2006, Animal 2, 2007, I Now Pronounce You Chuck and Larry, 2007; (TV films) Go Tell It On the Mountain, 1985, Rising Son, 1990, When You Remember Me, 1990, Amerique en otage L', 1991, Terror on Track 9, 1992, Deadly Whispers, 1995, Don King: Only in America, 1997 (Golden Globe for best performance by an actor in a mini-series or motion picture made for TV 1998), American Tragedy, 2000, Holiday Heart, 2000, Little John, 2002, RFK, 2002, Sins of the Father, 2002; (TV series) Another World, 1986, Men, 1989, UC: Undercover, 2001; TV appearances include Miami Vice, 1985, 87, Crime Story, 1986, Tour of Duty, 1987, Spenser: For Hire, 1988, The Equalizer, 1989, ER, 1994, 95, 96, New York Undercover, 1995, The District, 2002, 03, The Adventures of Jimmy Neutron: Boy Genius, 2003. Office: William Morris Agy 151 S El Camino Dr Beverly Hills CA 90212-2775

RHEA, JERRY DWAINE, consumer lending director; b. Knoxville, Tenn., Dec. 11, 1950; s. Paul Edward and Pearl (Cornett) R.; m. Lamara Hurt, Aug. 22, 1973; children: Kathryn, Jerry. BS in Acctg., Tenn. Wesleyan Coll., Athens, 1973. Corp. credit adminstr. G.E. Capital, Stamford, Conn., 1973-88; exec. v.p., consumer lending officer, dir. Chase Fin., Cleve., 1988-97; exec. v.p. ops. So. Pacific Funding Corp., Lake Oswego, Oreg., 1997-98; pres. Financial Ptnrs., Portland, Oreg., 1998—. Avocations: photography, boating.

RHEAMS, ANNIE ELIZABETH, education educator; b. Lake Providence, La. d. Curtis Kleinpeter Sr. and Annie Augusta (Webb) Kleinpeter; 1 child, Darryl Jemall Rheams. BA, Grambling U., La., 1971; MS, Ala. A&M U., Normal, 1975; PhD, U. Wis., Milw., 1989. Cert. tchr. in exceptional edn., adminstrn. Tchr. Ala. A&M U., Normal, 1971-79, adminstr., 1977-79; acad. specialist U. Wis., Milw., 1979-82, Parkside, 1982-84; tchr. diagnostician, adminstr. Milw. Schs., 1984-89; asst. prof. dept. edn. Marquette U., Milw., 1989-96; asst. prin. North Divsn. H.S., Milw., 1996—, Marshall H.S., Milw., 1997—99, tchr. exceptional edn. cognitively disabled, consumer math., 1999—, adminstr., asst. prin., 1999. Career counselor Madison County Career Counseling Svcs., Huntsville, 1975; adj. prof. Oakwood SDA Coll., Ala., 1975-78; tchr. Gateway to Engring. Program, Milw., 1984-88; cons. pub. schs./Wee Care Day Care, Milw., 1992-96; condr. workshops in field. Author: P.A.C.E.: A Thematic Approach to Developing Essential Experiences, 1996. Voter registrar/poll watcher NAACP, Lake Providence, 1966; v.p. Work for Wis., Inc., Milw., 1993-94, Messmer H.S. Bd., Milw., 1990-94; com. chmn. Citizen's Rev. Bd., Milw., 1980-82, Met. Milw. Alliance Black Sch. Educators, 1994-95. Assoc. fellow Ctr. for Great Plains Studies, U. Nebr.-Lincoln, 1995; named Outstanding Tchr. Educator, Am. Assn. for Coll. Tchr. Educators Directory, 1995. Mem. Zonta Internat., Alpha Kappa Alpha, Phi Delta Kappa. Avocations: tennis, sewing, ceramics, horseback riding, biking. Home: PO Box 90681 Milwaukee WI 53209-0611 Office Phone: 414-902-8497. Office Fax: 414-902-8315. Business E-Mail: rheams@hotmail.com.

RHEAULT, KEITH W., school system administrator; m. Denise Rheault; 4 children. BS, ND State U., 1976, MS in Agrl. Edn., 1980; PhD in Agrl. Edn., Iowa State U., 1985. With Nev. Dept. Edn., 1986—, agriculture edn. cons., state FFA adv., asst. dir. to dir. Office of Occupational and Continuing Edn., dep. supt. for Instructional, Rsch. and Evaluative Svcs., supt. pub. instrn., 2004—. Adj. prof. Agrl. Engring. Dept. Iowa State U. Officer USAR, 1977—85. Office: Nev Dept Edn 700 E Fifth St Carson City NV 89701-5096 Office Phone: 775-687-9217. Office Fax: 775-687-5660, 775-687-9101. E-mail: krheault@doe.nv.gov. *

RHEE, MOOWEON, business educator; arrived in U.S., 1997; s. Seoung-Bae Rhee and Young-Ja Han; m. Mihyang Ahn, Dec. 24, 1995; children: Yoojin, Jennifer. BBA, Yonsei U., Seoul, 1991, MBA, 1993; PhD, Stanford U., 2003. Air traffic contr. Korean Army, Wontong, Republic of Korea, 1993—95; rsch. assoc. POSCO, Seoul, 1995—96; instr. Seoul Nat. U. Tech., 1997; rsch. asst. UCLA, LA, 1997, Stanford (Calif.) U., 1998—2003; co-dir. Stanford Project on Entrepreneurial Edn., Stanford, 2003; asst. prof. U. Hawaii, Honolulu, 2004—. Cons. Hyundai Semicondr., San Jose, 2001, F-Net, Seoul, 2002, Hyundai Motors Am., LA, 2003. Contbr. articles to profl. jours. Recipient Student Writing Competition award, IRRA, 1999, William Miller award, Stanford U., 1999. Mem.: Am. Sociol. Assn., Acad. Mgmt. (Most Pub. Pact Paper award 2003). Office: U Hawaii 2404 Maile Way Honolulu HI 96822

RHEE, SOKWOO, mechanical engineer; BS in Mech. Engring., Seoul Nat. U., Korea, 1995; MS in Mech. Engring., MIT, 1997, PhD in Mech. Engring., 2000. Postdoctoral rschr. MIT, 2000—02; chief tech. officer Millennial Net, Inc., 2000—. Contbr. articles to profl. jours. Named one of Top 100 Young Innovators, MIT Tech. Review, 2004; recipient Douglas H. Annin award, Instrumentation, Systems, and Automation Soc., 2004. Achievements include 4 US patents issued or pending. Office: Millennial Net Inc 2 Fourth Ave Burlington MA 01803

RHEIN, ARTHUR, computer company executive; V.p. mktg. Harvey Electronics, 1983—86; sr. v.p. mktg. Pioneer, 1986; from v.p. mktg. to pres., CEO Agilysys, Inc., Boca Raton, Fla., 1986—2002, pres., CEO, 2002—03, chmn., pres., CEO, 2003—. Office: Agilysys Inc Ste 301E 2255 Glades Rd Boca Raton FL 33431 *

RHEIN, JOHN HANCOCK WILLING, III, publishing executive; b. Richmond, Va., Aug. 8, 1931; s. John Hancock Willing Jr. and Margaret (Packard) R.; m. Phyllis Betz, June 13, 1953; children: Susan Rhein Dubowski, Deborah B., John Hancock Willing IV. BA, Hobart Coll., 1953. With rsch. dept. Benton & Bowles Advt., NYC, 1956; sales mgmt. asst. to pub. Forbes Mag., NYC, 1956—71; sr. v.p., assoc. pub. Fin. Mag., NYC, 1971-73, Fin. World Mag., NYC, 1973-81; pres. Nat. Bus. Confs., NYC, 1975-81; sr. v.p. dir. sales and mktg. Sat. Rev. Mag., NYC, 1980-81, View Mag., NYC, 1980-81; pub. Equities Mag. (formerly OTC Rev.), NYC, 1981-93; CEO Am. Depository Receipt Assn., 1993—2005. Pub. CapitalistForum.com, 2000—05; chmn. bd. W.R. Keegan Corp., Focus the Nat. HS News Mag., 1994—2006; pres. The Investor Intelligence Group, Garden City, NY, 1981—; dir. Top Tier Writers, Inc., 2000—03; mng. dir. Green Rhino Pixelbooks, 2003—, Creative Resources Adv. and Pub. Rels., 1995—. Author: Dr. Kane: Hero Hypster or Both, 2003, Kane's Arctic: A Graphic Experience, 2004, Who Is Col. Chambers?, 2005, The Explorer and the Spiritualist, 2005. Office: Investor Intelligence Group 96 10th St Garden City NY 11530-1560 Personal E-mail: John_Rhein3@yahoo.com.

RHEINS, CARL JEFFREY, historian, director; b. Cin., Sept. 17, 1945; s. Joseph Melvin and Gertrude (Mandell) R.; m. Brenda Dale Gevertz, July 8, 1979; children: Jason Gabriel, Jaclyn Gail. BS with distinction, U. Wis., 1967; MA, SUNY, Albany, 1970; PhD, SUNY, Stony Brook, 1978. Lectr. Judaic studies SUNY, Stony Brook, 1974-78, asst. to provost, 1978-80, 81-86; dir. acad. affairs Nat. Found. Jewish Culture, NYC, 1980-81; asst. dean Adelphi U., Garden City, NY, 1986-87, assoc. dean, 1987, exec. asst. to pres., 1987-90, dean student life and devel., 1990-92, v.p. student life and devel., 1992-97, v.p. external affairs and comty. rels., 1997—99; exec. dir., CEO Yivo Inst. for Jewish Rsch., NYC, 1999—. Bd. dirs. Coalition on Higher Edn., Jewish Cmty. Rels. Coun., NYC; Delegate (NGO) Vilinius Internat. Forum on Holocaust-Era Looted Cultural Assets, 2000. Contbg. author: Yearbook of the Leo Baeck Inst., 1978, 80, 81; co-editor: Jewish Almanac, 1980 (dual main selection Jewish Book Club Am. 1981). Mem. nat. governing coun. Am. Jewish Congress, NYC, 1986-87, 1st v.p. Suffolk County, NY, 1985-87; bd. govs. LI region Am. Jewish Com., NY, 1984-85; judge Nat. Jewish Book Awards, 1993, 94, 2005—. Summer fellow NEH, 1987; recipient Frank Cassell Meml. award, 1994. Mem. Garden City C. of C. (bd. dirs. 1997—99), Phi Kappa Phi, Phi Alpha Theta, Alpha Epsilon Pi, Sigma Beta. Home: 424 West End Ave New York NY 10024-5782 Office: YIVO Inst for Jewish Rsch 15 W 16th St New York NY 10011-6301 Office Phone: 212-294-6126. Business E-Mail: crheins@yivo.cjh.org.

RHEINSTEIN, PETER HOWARD, healthcare company executive, physician, lawyer; b. Cleve., Sept. 7, 1943; s. Franz Joseph Rheinstein and Hede Henriette (Neheimer) Rheinstein Lerner; m. Miriam Ruth Weissman, Feb. 22, 1969; 1 child, Jason Edward. BA with high honors, Mich. State U., 1963, MS, 1964; MD, Johns Hopkins U., 1967; JD, U. Md., 1973. Bar: Md. 1973, DC 1980, U.S. Supreme Ct. 2000; diplomate Am. Bd. Family Medicine; cert. added qualifications in geriatric medicine. Intern USPHS Hosp., San Francisco, 1967-68; resident in internal medicine USPHS Hosp. (now Homewood Hosp. Ctr.), Balt., 1968-70, lt., 1967—68, lt. comdr., 1968—70; instr. internal medicine U. Md., Balt., 1970-73; med. dir. extended care facilities CHC Corp., Balt., 1972-74; dir. drug advt. and labeling divsn. FDA, Rockville, Md., 1974-82, acting dep. dir. Office Drugs, 1982-83, acting dir. Office Drugs, 1983-84, dir. Office Drug Stds., 1984-90, dir. medicine staff Office Health Affairs, 1990-99; sr. v.p. for med. and clin. affairs Cell Works, Inc., Balt., 1999—2004; pres. Severn Health Solutions, 2000—. Bd. dirs. Marnac, Inc., Dallas, 2003-; chmn. FDA Bur. Drugs Com. on Advanced Sci. Edn., 1978-86, Rsch. in Human Subjects Com., 1990-92; adj. prof. forensic medicine George Washington U., 1974-76; WHO cons. on drug regulation Nat. Inst. for Control Pharm. and Biol. Products, China, 1981-90; advisor on essential drugs WHO, 1985-90; FDA del. to U.S. Pharmacopeial Conv., 1985-90, coord. com. for assessment and transfer of tech. NIH, 1990-99, mem. health care fin. adminstrn. tech. adv. com., 1990-98, Nat. Adv. Coun. on Healthcare Policy, Rsch. and Evaluation, 1990-99, Healthy People 2000/2010 Steering Com., 1990-99, US Preventive Svcs. Task Force, 1990-96, CDC Nat. Task Force on Cmty. Preventive Svcs., 1996-99, Nat. Task Force on CME Industry/Provider Collaboration, 1992—, ann. meeting chmn., 2003, mem. com. chmn., 2002-05, US Adopted Names Coun. Rev. Bd., 2004-05, US Adopted Names Coun., 2006—; cons. in legal medicine and regulatory affairs, 1999—. Co-author: Human Organ Transplantation, 1987; spl. editl. advisor Good Housekeeping Guide to Medicine and Drugs, 1977-80; mem. editl. bd. Legal Aspects Med. Practice, 1981-89, Drug Info. Jour., 1982-86, 91-95; pub. Discovery Medicine, 2001-; contbr. articles to profl. jours. V.p. Intercultural Friends Found., 1998—. Recipient Commendable Svc. award, FDA, 1981, Group award of merit, 1983, 1988, Group Commendable Svc. award, 1989, 1992—93, 1995, 1999, Commr.'s Spl. citation, 1993; NIH Nat. Cancer Inst. SBIR grant, 2001. Fellow: Am. Acad. Family Physicians, Am. Coll. Legal Medicine (bd. govs. 1983—93, chmn. fin. com. 1985—88, chmn. publs. com. 1988—93, chmn. fin. com. 1990—91, treas. 1985—88, jud. coun. 1993—95, treas. 1990—91, Pres.'s awards 1985, 1986, 1989—91, 1993, Gold medal 2003); mem.: APHA, AMA (life; ho. of dels. 2002—), ABA, Assn. Clin. Rsch. Profls., Acad. Medicine Wash., Math. Assn. Am., Md. Bar Assn., Johns Hopkins Med. and Surg. Assn., Soc. Indsl. and Applied Math. (life), Balt. City Med. Soc., Md. State Med. Soc., Fed. Bar Assn. (chmn. food and drug com. 1976—79, Disting. Svc. award 1977), Drug Info. Assn. (bd. dirs. 1982—90, pres. 1984—85, v.p. 1986—87, pres. 1988—89, chmn. ann. meeting 1991, steering com. Ams. 1991—2004, chmn. ann. meeting 1994, Outstanding Svc. award 1990), Am. Bd. Legal Medicine (treas. 2003—), Acad. Pharm. Physicians and Investigators (trustee 1999—2003, pres. Washington-Balt. chpt. 1999—2003, v.p. AMA rels. 1999—), FDA Alumni Assn., Johns Hopkins U. Alumni Assn. (life), U. Md. Alumni Assn. (life), Mensa (life), Fed. Exec. Inst. Alumni Assn. (life), Mich. State U. Alumni Assn. (life), Mich. State U. Honors Coll. Alumni Assn. (bd. dirs. 1998—2001, pres. 2000—01), John Hopkins Club, Annapolis Yacht Club, Chartwell Golf and Country Club, Delta Theta Phi (life). Achievements include development of precedents for FDA regulation of prescription drug promotion, initiated FDA's first patient medication information program; implemented Drug Price Competition and Patent Term Restoration Act of 1984, authored medication goals for Healthy People 2000 and 2010. Avocations: boating, exercise, real estate. Home and Office: 621 Holly Ridge Rd Severna Park MD 21146-3520 Home Phone: 410-647-9501; Office Phone: 410-647-9500. Office Fax: 410-647-6135. Personal E-mail: phr@jhu.edu.

RHENEY, SUSAN O., paper company executive; MBA, Harvard Univ. CPA. Public acctg. auditor Deloitte & Touche; prin. Sterling Group LP (parent co., Mail-Well), 1992—2001; dir. Mail-Well, 1993—97; interim chmn. Cenveo (formerly Mail-Well), 2005—. Bd. dir. Genesis Energy LP, Cenveo, 2003—. Office Phone: 303-790-8023. Office Fax: 303-566-7466.

RHETT, HASKELL EMERY SMITH, educational association administrator; b. Evanston, Ill., Aug. 29, 1936; s. Haskell Smith and Eunice Campbell (Emery) R.; m. Roberta Teel Oliver, Sept. 9, 1961 (div. 1973); children: Kathryn Emery, Cecily Coffin; m. Anita Leone, May 30, 1983 (div. 1993); m. Janet Lee Rollings, Nov. 15, 1997. Diploma, Gov. Dummer Acad., 1954; AB, Hamilton Coll., 1958; MA, Cornell U., 1967, PhD, 1968. Asst. to the pres. Hamilton Coll., Clinton, NY, 1961-64; rsch. asst. Cornell U., Ithaca, NY, 1964-66; rsch. assoc. U. London, 1966-67; dir. program devel. Ednl. Testing Svc., Princeton, NJ, 1967-73; asst. chancellor NJ Dept. Higher Edn., Trenton, 1973—85; v.p. The Coll. Bd., NYC, 1985-90; pres. The Woodrow Wilson Nat. Fellowship Found., Princeton, NJ, 1990—97, pres. emeritus, 1997—. Author: Going to College in New Jersey, 1978; contbg. author: Government's Role in Supporting College Savings, 1990. Commr. NJ Pub. Broadcasting Authority, Trenton, 1983—85; mem. Nat. Task Force on Student Aid Problems, Washington, 1974—75, Gov.'s Adv. Panel on Higher Edn. Restructuring, State of NJ, 1994; trustee Dominican U. of Calif., San Rafael, 1990—99, 2001—07, William Alexander Procter Found., 1998—2002, The Coll. of NJ, 1992—97, vice-chmn., 1995—97, chmn., 1997; trustee The Gov.'s Acad., Mass., 1993—, Heartland Edn. Cmty., Ohio, 1992—97, Forums Inst. for Pub. Policy, NJ, 1999—, treas. NJ, 2000—05, chmn. NJ, 2005—; del. Dem. Nat. Conv., Miami, 1972; sr. warden Trinity Episcopal Ch., Princeton, 1988—92, vestryman, 1979—82, 1987—88, 2001—04; dep. Gen. Conv., Detroit, 1988, Phoenix, 1991; mem. standing com. Episcopal Diocese of NJ, 1992—97; bd. dirs. Reach the World, Inc., NYC, 1998—2001, Trenton After Sch. Program, 1989—93, 2001—04. Lt. USNR, 1958—61, Heavy Attack Squadron 5 (VAH-5), USS Forrestal. Nat. Def. fellow US Govt., 1966-67, Eliot-Winant fellow Brit.-Am. Assocs., 1982, fellow Kennedy Sch. Harvard U., 1985, Wilson Coll., Princeton U., 1993-97. Mem. Nat. Assn. State Scholarship and Grant Programs (pres. 1976-78), Princeton Officers Soc., Springdale Golf Club. Avocations: travel, tennis, golf, sailing, classic automobiles. Home: 80 Province Line Rd Skillman NJ 08558-1102 Personal E-mail: hrhett@patmedia.net.

RHEW, PERRY JAMES, federal judge; BS in Psychology/Biology, Southeast Mo. State U., Cape Girardeau, 1980; JD, UMKC Sch. Law, Kansas City, 1983. Lic. Mo., 1983. Pub. defender State of Mo., Kennett, 1983-84; asst. prosecuting atty. Dunklin County, Kennett, Mo., 1985-86; prosecuting atty., 1986-90; adjunct prof. Bus. Law Southeast Mo. State U., Cape Girardeau, 1987-89; assoc. circuit judge 35th Judicial Circuit, Kennett, Mo., 1990; US adminstrv. law judge Social Security Adminstrn., Cleve., 1997—2005; mng. adminstrv. law judge Office of Medicare Hearings and Appeals, US Dept. Health & Human Services, Cleve., 2005, acting chief adminstrv. law judge, 2005—06, chief U.S. adminstrv. law judge, 2006—. Bd. dirs. Family Counseling Ctr., Kennett, Mo., 1986-90, Stapleton Detoxification Ctr., Kennett, Mo., 1986-90, Ctr. for Family Resources, Malden, Mo., 1986-90, Cmty. Caring Counsel, Kennett, Mo., 1993-2005. Author: eight published plays. Elected prosecuting atty., 1986, elected assoc. circuit judge, Dunklin Co. Mo., Kennett, 1990, 94. Recipient Young Alumni Merit award Southeast Mo. State U., Cape Girardeau, Mo., 1993, Denman Dist. Evangelism award United Meth. Ch., 1993. Mem. Mo. Bar Assn., Dunklin County Bar, Lions Club Internat. Mem. United Meth. Ch. Avocations: writing, composer, singing, cooking. Office: Cleveland Regional Office Office of Medicare Hearings & Appeals 200 Public Sq PB Tower Suite 1300 Cleveland OH 44112 Office Phone: 216-615-4000. Office Fax: 216-615-4115.

RHIM, JOHNG SIK, physician, medical researcher; b. Kwang Ju, Korea, July 24, 1930; came to U.S., 1958; s. Hac Woon and Moo Duc (Choi) R.; m. Mary Margaret Lytle, Aug. 24, 1962; children: Jonathan, Christopher, Peter, Andrew, Michael, Kathleen. MD, Seoul U., Republic of, 1957. Intern Seoul Nat. U. Hosp., 1958; rsch. fellow Children's Hosp. Rsch. Found., Cin., 1958-60, Baylor U. Coll. Medicine, Houston, 1961; rsch. assoc. Grad. Sch. Pub. Health, U. Pitts., 1962, La. State U. Acad. Medicine, New Orleans, 1962-64; vis. scientist Nat. Inst. Allergy and Infectious Diseases, NIH, Bethesda, Md., 1964-66; project dir. cancer rsch. Microbiol. Assocs., Bethesda, Md., 1966-78; sr. investigator Nat. Cancer Inst., NIH, Bethesda, 1978-98; assoc. dir., prof. surgery Ctr. Prostate Disease Rsch., Uniformed Svcs. U. of the Health Sci., Bethesda, 1999—; rsch. prof. dept. surgery Uniformed Svcs. U. Health Scis., Bethesda, 2000—. Adj. prof. Georgetown

U. Med. Ctr., Washington, 1988—. Editor: Neoplastic Transformation in Human Cell Culture, 1991, 1995, 1999, 2003; mem. editl. bd.: Internat. Jour. Oncology Prostate Cancer and Prostate Disease, Cancer Therapy; contbr. articles to profl. jours., chapters to books. Mem. AAAS, AMA, Am. Assn. Cancer Rsch., Am. Soc. Virology, Soc. Exptl. Biology and Medicine, Internat. Assn. Leukemia Rsch. Achievements include patents in field. Home: 11455 S Glen Rd Potomac MD 20854-1851 Office: CPDR Dept Surgery Uniformed Svcs Univ Health 4301 Jones Bridge Rd Bethesda MD 20814-4712 Office Phone: 301-319-8223. Business E-Mail: jrhim@cpdr.org.

RHIMES, SHONDA, producer, director, writer; b. Chgo., Jan. 13, 1970; 1 adopted child, Harper. BA in English, Dartmouth U., 1991; MFA, U. So. Calif., 1994. Dir., writer: (films) Blossoms and Veils, 1998; writer Crossroads, 2002; The Princess Diaries 2: Royal Engagement, 2004; exec. prodr., writer: (TV series) Grey's Anatomy, 2005— (Norman Felton Prodr. of Yr. Award in Episodic TV, Prodrs. Guild of Am., 2007, Writing in Drama Series, NAACP Image Awards, 2007, Best Drama TV Series Golden Globe, 2007). Named one of the World's Most Influential People, Time Magazine, 2007, 40 Under 40, Advt. Age, 2007. Office: c/o ABC TV 500 S Buena Vista St Burbank CA 91521-4551 *

RHIND, JAMES THOMAS, lawyer; b. Chgo., July 21, 1922; s. John Gray and Eleanor (Bradley) R.; m. Laura Haney Campbell, Apr. 19, 1958; children: Constance Rhind Robey, James Campbell, David Scott. Student, Hamilton Coll., 1940-42; AB cum laude, Ohio State U., 1944; LL.B. cum laude, Harvard U., 1950. Bar: Ill. bar 1950. Japanese translator U.S. War Dept., Tokyo, 1946-47; congl. liaison Fgn. Operations Adminstrn., Washington, 1954; atty. Bell, Boyd & Lloyd, Chgo., 1950-53, 55—, ptnr., 1958-92, chmn. exec. com., 1976—88, of counsel, 1993—. Bd. dirs. Kewaunee Scientific Corp., Statesville, NC. Commr. Gen. Assembly United Presbyn. Ch., 1963; life trustee Ravinia Festival Assn., Hamilton Coll., Clinton, N.Y., U. Chgo.; Northwestern Univ. Assocs.; chmn. Cook County Young Republican Orgn., 1957; Ill. Young Rep. nat. committeeman, 1957-58; v.p., mem. bd. govs. United Rep. Fund Ill., 1965-84; pres. Ill. Childrens Home and Aid Soc., 1971-73, life trustee; bd. dirs. E.J. Dalton Youth Center, 1966- 69; governing mem. Chgo. Symphony Orch., Chgo.; mem. Ill. Arts Council, 1971-75; mem. exec. com. div. Met. Mission and Ch. Extension Bd., Chgo. Presbytery, 1966-68; trustee Presbyn. Homes, W. Clement and Jessie V. Stone Found., U. Chgo. Hosps. Served with M.I. AUS, 1943-46. Mem. ABA, Ill. Bar Assn., Chgo. Bar Assn. (bd. mgrs. 1967-69), Fed. Bar Assn., Chgo. Coun. on Fgn. Rels., Japan Am. Soc. Chgo., Lawyers Club Chgo., Phi Beta Kappa, Sigma Phi. Clubs: Chicago, Glen View (Ill.), Commercial (Chgo.), Mid-Day Club (Chgo.), Economic (Chgo.). Home: 830 Normandy Ln Glenview IL 60025-3210 Office: Bell Boyd & Lloyd 3 First National Plz 70 W Madison St Ste 3200 Chicago IL 60602-4244 Office Phone: 312-372-1121. Business E-Mail: jrhind@bellboyd.com.

RHINESMITH, STEPHEN HEADLEY, management consultant; b. Mineola, NY, Dec. 13, 1942; s. Homer Kern and Winifred Headley (Long) Rhinesmith; m. Kathleen Alys Law, Aug. 28, 1965; children: Christopher Law, Colin Headley. BA (Baker scholar), Wesleyan U., 1965; M in Pub. and Internat. Affairs, (Heinz fellow), U. Pitts., 1966, PhD (NDEA fellow), 1972. Dir. internat. svcs. McBer and Co., Cambridge, Mass., 1969-71; pres. AFS Intercultural Programs, NYC, 1972-80, 87-89, Holland Am. Cruises, NYC, 1980-82, Moran, Stahl, Boyer, NYC, 1982-84, Rhinesmith & Assocs. Inc., West Chatham, Mass., 1984—; ptnr. CDR Internat., 1998—2004; sr. ptnr. Oliver Wyman Delta Orgn. and Leadership, 2004—. Named amb., coord. Pres.'s U.S.-Soviet Exch. Initiative, 1986—87; chmn. dept. orgnl. sociology Moscow State U., 1991—96. Author: Bring Home the World: A Management Guide to Community Leaders of International Programs, 1975, 1985, A Manager's Guide to Globalization: Six Skills for Success in a Changing World, 2d edit., 1996; co-author: Head Heart and Guts: How the World's Best Companies Develop Complete Leaders, 2006. Mem.: ASTD (chair 1994), Eastward Ho! Country Club, Met. Club (Washington). Home and Office: 86 Capri Ln Chatham MA 02633 Home Phone: 508-945-5092. E-mail: SHRglobal@aol.com.

RHOAD, RICHARD E., manufacturing executive; m. Marlaine J. Walker; children: Scott R., Bradley R., Nicholas W. BS, Ind. U.; MBA, U. Notre Dame. Cert. mem. Am. Coll. Med. Practice Execs., 1995, diplomate Am. Coll. Healthcare Execs., 1995. Sales mgmt. Xerox Corp., Los Angeles, Calif., 1971—82; exec. v.p. and gen. mgr. North Am. Van Lines, Fort Wayne, Ind., 1982—91; healthcare exec. mgmt. Allied Profl. Services, LLC, 1991—2001; CEO Ft. Wayne Orthopaedics, Fort Wayne, Ind., 2001—04; CFO Family and Social Svcs. Adminstrn., State of Ind., Indpls., 2005—06; pres. ICON Internat., Ft. Wayne, Ind., 2006—. Dir. Luth. Hosp., Fort Wayne, Ind. Author: (refereed literature) Strategic Approach to the Income Statement (award Inst. Mgmt. Accts., 2002); contbr. articles Mgmt. Acctg. Quar. Trustee U. St. Francis; coun. mem. Trinity English Luth. Ch.; bd. mem. Early Childhood Alliance, Anthony Wayne Svcs. Mem.: Gulf Harbour Yact & Country Club (corr.), Ft. Wayne Country Club (corr.). Republican. Lutheran. Office: ICON Internat 8333 Clinton Park Dr Fort Wayne IN 46825 Office Phone: 260-466-1382.

RHOADES, EVERETT RONALD, medical educator; b. Lawton, Okla., Oct. 24, 1931; s. Lee Joseph and Dorothy Apasha Rhoades; m. Bernadine Herwona Toyebo, Oct. 22, 1931; children: Lee Charles, Melanie Cheryl Campos, Melinda Sue Yoder, Dorothy Alison, Lisa Patricia. MD, U. Okla., 1956. Diplomate Am. Bd. Internal Medicine, 1963. Chief infectious diseases sect. USAF Hosp., Lackland Air Force Base, Tex., 1961—66; prof. medicine U. Okla. Health Scis. Ctr., Oklahoma City, 1966—92, chief infectious diseases sect., 1966—82; asst. surgeon gen. USPHS, Rockville, Md., 1982—93; dir. Indian Health Svc., 1982—93; assoc. dean cmty. affairs U. Okla. Health Scis. Ctr., 1993—2000; dir. of edn. initiatives Ctr. Am. Indian and Alaska Native Rsch., Balt., 1993—2000; sr. cons. Ctr. Am. Indian Health Rsch., 2000—; dir. Native Am. Prevention Rsch. Ctr., 2000—03; prof. emeritus of medicine U. Okla. Health Scis. Ctr., 2005—. Coun. Nat. Inst. Allergy and Infectious Diseases, Bethesda, Md., 1971—75, Nat. Inst. Deafness and Other Comm. Disorders, 1996—2000, Nat. Ctr. Complementary and Alt. Medicine, 1997—2001; adv. con. Nat. Ctr. Vital and Health Stats., Washington, 1978—82; cons. Nat. Libr. Medicine, Bethesda, 1974, U. Saigon Sch. Medicine, Saigon, Vietnam, 1970—72; adj. prof. internat. health Johns Hopkins Sch. Pub. Health, Balt., 1993—2000. Editor: (text book) American Indian Health - Innovations in Health Care, Promotion and Policy; contbr. scientific papers. Founder, mem., pres. Assn. Am. Indian Physicians, Oklahoma City, 1972—2005. Maj. USAF, 1957—66. Decorated Commendation medal USPHS, Meritorious Svc. medal, DSM, Commendation medal, Surgeon General's Exemplary Svc. award; named Outstanding Am. Indian, Am. Indian Expn., 1996; named to Kiowa Tribal Hall Fame, Kiowa Tribe Okla., 1997; recipient Recognition Achievement award, 1988, St. Martin-Beaumont Rsch. award, Indian Health Svc., 1993, Establishment of Everett R. Rhoades prize, U. Okla. Coll. Medicine, 1995, Child Advocacy award, Am. Acad. Pediat., 1995; fellow, John Hay Whitney Found., 1952—56; scholar, Zeta Psi Frat., Lafayette Coll., 1949—52, John and Mary Markle Found., 1967—72; Sequoyah fellow, Am. Indian Sci. and Engring. Soc., 1992. Fellow: Infectious Diseases Soc. Am., Am. Coll. Physicians; mem.: Assn. Am. Indian Affairs (bd. dirs.), Am. Fedn. Clin. Rsch., Kiowa Tribal Bus. Com. (vice chmn. 1978—80), Nat. Congress Am. Indians, Assn. Am. Indian Physicians (pres. 2004—05, Excellence award 1980), Commd. Officers Assn., Assn. Mil. Surgeons US, Alpha Omega Alpha, Phi Beta Kappa, Kiowa Gourd Clan (life), Kiowa Blacklegging Soc. (life; sr. counsellor 1970—2005). Methodist. Avocations: hunting, fishing, cave exploring. Home: 1808 Dorchester Dr Oklahoma City OK 73120 Office: U Okla Health Scis Ctr 801 NE 13th St Oklahoma City OK 73104 Home Phone: 405-848-2508.

RHOADES, MARYE FRANCES, paralegal; b. Ft. Defiance, Va., Jan. 29, 1937; d. Silas Caswell Sr. and Mary Ann Frances (James) Rhodes; m. Minter James Rowe, May 1964 (div. 1968); children: Margaret Frances Omar, James Robert Rowe; m. Robert Charles Rhoades Jr., July 25, 1980. Student, Mountain State U., 1956-58, 68, U. Charleston, 1962-63, 74, 89, Antioch U., 1972-73; grad., Mike Tyree Sch. Real Estate, 1984, Evans Coll. Legal Studies, 1990. Educator Nicholas County Sch. Sys., Summersville, W.Va., 1958-61; edit. staff, columnist, staff writer, reporter, photographer Beckley Newspapers Corp., 1962-76; educator Raleigh County Bd. Edn., Beckley, W.Va., 1967-68; exec. editor, columnist Local News Jour., Whitesville, W.Va., 1976-77; libr. bookmobile, asst. ref. libr., outreach coord. Raleigh County Pub. Libr., Beckley, 1977-78; agt. Combined Ins. Co., Chgo., 1978-79; legal sec., paralegal W.Va. Legal Svcs. Inc., Beckley, 1979-82; paralegal Applachian Rsch and Defense Fund Inc., Beckley, 1982-83; exec. dir., owner Rhoades and Rowe, Beckley, 1983—85; paralegal patient advocate Comty. Health Sys. Inc., Beckley, 1986-96; pvt. practice Beckley, 1996—. Contbr. articles to mags. State bd. dirs., pub. resl. LWV, Beckley; pub. rels., various coms. Raleigh County Dem. Women, Beckley; sec., pub. rels. Orchard Valley Women's Club, Crab Orchard, W.Va.; trustee Fraternal Order Eagles; pub. rels., various coms. Loyal Order Moose, Beckley, Beckley Profl. Bus. Women; com. mem. Nat. Coalition to Save the New River; sales rep. So. U.S. Rep. to U.S. Mil. Acad., West Point, N.Y.; active Am. Legion Aux., Mullens, W.Va. Mem. NEA, Classroom Tchrs. Assn., Nat. Paralegal Assn., Nat. Fedn. Paralegals Assn., Nat. Ind. Paralegals Assn., Nat. Com. Save Soc., Sec. Medicare, Nat. Legal Aid and Def. Assn., Nat. Orgn. Social Security Claimants Reps., State Soc. Sec. Task Force, Nat. Vets. Legal Svcs. Project Inc., W.Va. U. Alumni Assn., Community AIDS Edn. Com., W.Va. Edn. Assn., Am. Disability Repr. Specs. Assn. Democrat. Mem. Ch. of God. Avocations: creative arts and music, walking, nascar, doll collecting, writing. Home: PO Box 2173 Beckley WV 25802 Office: Benefit Services PO Box 7265 Beckley WV 25802 Home Phone: 304-252-8431; Office Phone: 304-252-8431. Office Fax: 304-252-1098. E-mail: tv65000@charter.net.

RHOADES, RODNEY ALLEN, physiologist, educator; b. Greenville, Ohio, Jan. 5, 1939; s. John H. and Floris L. Rhoades; m. Judith Ann Brown, Aug. 6, 1961; children: Annelisa, Kirsten. BS, Miami U., 1961; MS, 1963; PhD, Ohio State U., 1966. Asst. prof. Pa. State U., State College, 1966-72, assoc. prof., 1972-75; rsch. scientist NIH, Bethesda, Md., 1975-76; prof. Ind. U. Sch. Medicine, Indpls., 1976-81, 81—, chmn., 1981—2003. Dir. Indpls. Ctr. for Advanced Rsch. Author: Physiology, 1984; contbr. articles to profl. jours. Fellow NASA, 1964-66; recipient Rsch. Career Devel. award NIH, 1975-80. Mem. Am. Physiol. Soc, AHA, Am. Thoracic Soc., Biophysics Soc., Sigma Xi. Home: 1768 Spruce Dr Carmel IN 46033-9025 Office: Ind U Sch Medicine 635 Barnhill Dr Indianapolis IN 46202-5126

RHOADS, GERALDINE EMELINE, editor, consultant; b. Phila., Jan. 29, 1914; d. Lawrence Dry and Alice Fegley (Rice) R. AB, Bryn Mawr Coll., 1935. Publicity asst. Bryn Mawr (Pa.) Coll., 1935-37; asst. Internat. Students House, Phila., 1937-39; mng. editor The Woman mag., NYC, 1939-42; editor Life Story mag., 1942-45, Today's Woman mag., NYC, 1945-52, Today's Family Mag., NYC, 1952-53; lectr. Columbia U., 1954-56; assoc. editor Readers Digest, 1954-55; producer NBC, 1955-56; assoc. editor Ladies Home Jour., 1956-62, mng. editor, 1962-63; exec. editor McCall's mag., 1963-66; editor Woman's Day mag., 1966-82, editorial dir., 1982-84, Woman's Day Resource Center, 1984-89; v.p. Woman's Day mag., 1972—84, CBS Consumer Publs., 1977-84; cons. Woman's Day, NYC, 1989-91. Editorial cons., dir. Nat. Mag. Awards, 1991-94. Author: (with others) Woman's Day Help Book, 1988. Mem. journalism awards com. James Beard Found., 1993-2001. Recipient award for profl. achievement Diet Workshop Internat., 1977; Elizabeth Cutter Morrow award YWCA Salute to Women in Bus., 1977; Recipient Econ. Equity award Women's Equity Action League, 1982; March of Dimes Women Editor's citation, 1982 Mem.: Women's Forum (bd. dirs. 1985—87), Advt. Women in N.Y. (bd. govs. 1983—85, 2d v.p. 1985—87, 1st v.p. 1987—89, bd. dirs. 1989—90, Pres.'s award 1987), N.Y. Women in Comm. (Matrix award 1975), Am. Soc. Mag. Editors (chmn. exec. com. 1971—73), Fashion Group (bd. govs. 1977—79, chmn. bd. govs. 1978—80, bd. dirs. Found. 1980—81, treas. bd. govs. 1983—85, bd. govs. 1987—88), Nat. Press Club (dir.), Bryn Mawr Coll. Alumni Assn. (bd. dirs. 1989—94), Turtle Bay Assn. (bd. dirs. 1989—92), Literacy Vols. of N.Y.C. (bd. dirs. 1986—93), YWCA Acad. Women Achievers, Bryn Mawr Club of N.Y.C. (bd. dirs. 1994—2000), Women's City Club of N.Y. (bd. dirs. 1996—, chair comm. 2001—04, Honoree of Yr. 2004). Home: 185 W End Ave Apt 21A New York NY 10023-5548 Personal E-mail: rhoadsge@aol.com.

RHOADS, JAMES BERTON, archivist, consultant, federal official, educator; b. Sioux City, Iowa, Sept. 17, 1928; s. James Harrison and Mary (Keenan) R.; m. S. Angela Handy, Aug. 12, 1947 (dec. Jan. 8, 2007); children: Cynthia Patrice Neven, James Berton, Marcia Marie MacKellar. Student, Southwestern Jr. Coll., 1946-47, Union Coll., Lincoln, Neb., 1947-48; BA, U. Calif.-Berkeley, 1950, MA, 1952; PhD, Am. U., 1965. With GSA-Nat. Archives and Records Service, Washington, 1952-79, asst. archivist for civil archives, 1965, dept. archivist U.S., 1966-68, archivist U.S., 1968-79; chmn. Nat. Archives Trust Fund Bd., 1968-79; chmn. adminstrv. com. Fed. Register, 1968-79; chmn. Nat. Hist. Publs. and Records Commn., 1968-79; mem. Fed. Council on Arts and Humanities, 1970-79; pres. Rhoads Assos. Internat., 1980-84; dir. grad. program in archives and records mgmt. Western Wash. U., Bellingham, 1984-94, prof. history, 1987-94, dir. Ctr. for Pacific N.W. studies, 1994-97; prof. emeritus, 1994—. Trustee Woodrow Wilson Internat. Center for Scholars, 1969-79; v.p. Intergovtl. Coun. UNESCO Info. Program, 1977-79; mem. adv. bd. Wash. State Hist. Records, 1990-97. Recipient Meritorious and Disting. Service awards GSA, 1966, 68, 79 Fellow Soc. Am. Archivists (pres. 1974-75); mem. Internat. Coun. Archives (pres. 1976-79), Am. Antiquarian Soc., Am. Coun. Learned Socs. (com. Soviet-Am. archival coop. 1986-91), Mass. Hist. Soc. (corr.), Wash. State Hist. Soc. (trustee 1986-95), Acad. Cert. Archivists (pres. 1992-94).

RHOADS, JONATHAN EVANS, JR., surgeon, medical educator; b. Phila., Sept. 20, 1938; s. Jonathan Evans and Teresa Folin Rhoads; m. Julia Gleason, Apr. 2, 1967; children: Mary Teresa, Ruth Anne, Margaret Paxson. BA, Haverford Coll., 1960; MD, Harvard U., 1964. Diplomate Am. Bd. Surgery, Am. Bd. Thoracic Surgery. Rotating intern Cin. Gen. HOsp., 1964-65; resident in surgery U. Cin., 1965-69, resident in thoracic surgery, 1971-72, chief resident in surgery, 1972-73; asst. prof. surgery Med. Coll. Pa., Phila., 1974-77, assoc. prof. surgery, 1977-85, clin. assoc. prof. surgery, 1985—. Residency program dir. York (Pa.) Hosp., 1985-91, chmn. surgery, 1985-97; clin. prof. surgery U. Pa., Phila., 1986—, Pa. State U., Hershey, 1987—. Sch. com. mem. Germantown Friends Sch., Phila., 1979-90, 2000—; bd. mgrs. Haverford (Pa.) Coll., 1994—. Lt. comdr. USPHS, 1969-71. Fellow ACS (bd. govs. 1998—), S.E. Surg. Congress (trustee 1995-2000); mem. Pa. Med. Soc. (spkr. ho. dels. 1989-93, v.p. 1993-94, pres.-elect 1994-95, pres. 1995-96), Phi Beta Kappa. Mem. Soc. Of Friends. Avocation: chess. Office: Wellspan Surgical Assocs Apple Hill Medical Ctr 25 Monument Rd Ste 120 York PA 17403

RHOADS, MARK B., lawyer; b. Mar. 1, 1959; BA, Coll. William and Mary, 1981; JD, U. Richmond, 1985. Bar: Pa. 1985, Va. 1988, US Dist. Ct. Ea. Dist. Pa. 1985, US Dist. Ct. Ea. Dist. Va. 1988. With Montgomery McCracken Walker & Rhoads, Pa., 1985—88, McCandlish Holton (formerly Mezzullo McCandlish), Richmond, Va., 1988—2003; ptnr., practice group leader bus. immigration group Reed Smith LLP, Richmond, Va., 2003—. Editor: US Immigration Law Handbook, A Guide for Foreign Business. Office: Reed Smith LLP Riverfront Plz - West Tower 901 E Byrd St, Ste 1700 Richmond VA 23219-4068 Office Phone: 804-344-3422. Office Fax: 804-344-3410. Business E-Mail: mrhoads@reedsmith.com.

RHOADS, MICHAEL DENNIS, sales executive; b. Vinton, Iowa, June 25, 1949; s. Lloyd and Marilyn Mae (Appleton) Rhoads. BS in Indsl. Edn., Iowa State U., 1973; MBA, York Coll. of Pa., 1984. Order detailer, sales rep. Fisher Controls Inc., Marshalltown, Iowa, 1973-75; inside sales engr. Proconex, King of Prussia, Pa., 1975-79, outside sales engr. York, Pa., 1979-85, br. mgr., 1985-87, v.p. process instrumentaion sales King of Prussia, Pa., 1987-90, v.p., sales mgr., 1990—, sr. v.p., 1992—2005, COO, 2005—. Instr. Continuing Adult Edn., Marshalltown, 1973—75. Youth group leader Meth. Ch., Center Square, Pa., 1977—79. With USN, 1968—70, Vietnam. Mem.: VFW, Instrument Soc. Am. (v.p. 1984—86, pres. 1986—87, Best Sect. Pres. award 1987, Old Shoe award 1990), Am. Legion. Lutheran. Avocations: woodworking, carpentry, hunting, boating, sailing. Office: Proconex 101 Enterprise Dr Royersford PA 19468 Home: 435 SR 1005 Tunkhannock PA 18657 Business E-Mail: mike.rhoads@proconexdirect.com.

RHOADS, NANCY GLENN, lawyer; b. Washington, Oct. 15, 1957; d. Donald L. and Gerry R. R.; m. Robert A. Koons, June 23, 1984. BA, Gettysburg Coll., 1980; JD, Temple U., 1983. Bar: Pa., U.S. Dist. Ct. (ea. dist.) Pa. 1983. Rsch. asst. Prof. Mikochick, Phila., 1982-83; law clk. Phila. Ct. of Common Pleas, 1983-85; assoc. Post and Schell P.C., Phila., 1985-90, Sheller, Ludwig and Badey, Phila., 1990—2005, The Beasley Firm, Phila., 2005—. Co-author: Aging and the Aged: Problems, Opportunities, Challenges, 1980. Vol. Spl. Olympics. Mem. ATLA, Phi Beta Kappa Avocations: classical piano, horticulture, swimming. Home: 401 Audubon Ave Wayne PA 19087-4006 Office: The Beasley Firm 1125 Walnut St Philadelphia PA 19107 Office Phone: 215-931-2678. E-mail: ngr@bcaskyfirm.com.

RHOADS, STEVEN ERIC, political science professor; b. Abington, Pa., May 12, 1939; s. John Reginald and Barbara Ann (Dugan) Rhoads; m. Diana Cabanis Akers, May 17, 1944; children: Christopher, Nicholas, John. BA, Princeton U., 1961; MPA, Cornell U., 1965, PhD, 1972. Mem. staff Office Mgmt. and Budget, Washington, 1965—66; asst. prof. dept. politics U. Va., Charlottesville, 1970—76, assoc. prof., 1977—86, prof., 1986—. Author: Policy Analysis in the Federal Aviation Administration, 1974, Valuing Life: Public Policy Dilemmas, 1980, The Economist's View of the World: Government, Markets and Public Policy, 1985, Incomparable Worth: Pay Equity Meets the Market, 1993, Taking Sex Differences Seriously, 2004; contbr. articles to profl. jours. Lt. (j.g.) USN, 1961—63. Fellow, Sloan NEH, Inst. Ednl. Affairs, Bradley Found., Olin Found. Mem.: Assn. Pub. Policy and Mgmt., Am. Polit. Sci. Assn. Home: 3190 Dundee Rd Earlysville VA 22936-9621 Office: U Va Dept Politics Cabell Hall 232 Charlottesville VA 22903 Office Phone: 434-924-7866.

RHODA, JANICE TUCKER, writer, educator, musician; b. Lynn, Mass., Mar. 24, 1955; d. Robert Samuel and Cecilia Mary Ann (DiTroia) Tucker; m. David Michael Cleary, Jan. 21, 2001. BMus, New Eng. Conservatory Music, Boston, 1989; Suzuki Tchr. Tng., Ithaca Coll., NY, 1980—81. Pvt. violin tchr., 1975—; violin tchr. Wakefield Pub. Schs., 1979—80, Newton Pub. Schs., 1979—81, All-Newton Music Sch., 1980—84, McGill U., 1982, 1983, Boston Ctr. for Adult Edn., 1992—95, 1997—98, New Eng. Conservatory of Music, Boston, 2000, Cambridge Ctr. for Adult Edn., Mass., 2003—; dir., tchr. Suzuki program Longy Sch. Music, Cambridge, Mass., 1980—87, Brookline Music Sch., Mass., 1992—94; clinician The ABCs of Strings, 1998—, Penn. State U., 2002, Royal Conservatory Music, Toronto, 2004, 2005, Vancouver Acad. Music, Canada, 2004—, others. Author: (book series) The ABCs of Strings; concertmistress North-Eastern Dist. Orch., 1972—73, Mass. All-State Orch., 1972; actor: (DVD) The ABCs of Violin for the Absolute Beginner, 2006. Mem.: Nat. Assn. for Music Edn., Am. String Tchrs. Assn., Suzuki Assn. of Ams., Mu Phi Epsilon. Office: The ABCs of Strings PO Box 400428 Cambridge MA 02140 Personal E-mail: abcsofstrings@comcast.net.

RHODE, ALFRED SHIMON, finance educator; b. Vienna, July 31, 1928; came to U.S., 1940, naturalized, 1949; s. Aron and Olga (Schwarz) Rothkirch; m. Phyllis Mazur, Dec. 28, 1959; children: Yael, Tamar, Yvette, Liane. BCE, CUNY, 1950; MEA, George Washington U., 1959; PhD, Am. U., 1973. Registered profl. engr., Md. Engr. Bur. of Reclamation, Sacramento, 1950—52; various engring. positions U.S. Govt., 1954—63; head logistics rsch. Navy Supply Sys. Command, Washington, 1963—68; head support forces, manpower and logistics br. Navy Program Planning Office, Washington, 1968—75; sr. v.p. nat. security analysis and warfare support group Info. Spectrum, Inc., Arlington, Va., 1976—89, cons., 1989—92; professorial lectr. George Washington U., Washington, 1969—75; adj. faculty Sch. Mgmt. George Mason U., Fairfax, Va., 1990—2002; adj. faculty Sch. Bus. Adminstrn. Georgetown U., Washington, 1998—. Exec. dir. Montgomery County Retail Security and Loss Prevention Assn. Contbr. articles to profl. jours. Capt. USAF, 1952-54. Congl. fellow, 1962. Fellow Mil. Ops. Rsch. Soc. (1st v.p., dir.); mem. Inst. Ops. Rsch. and Mgmt. Scis. (chmn. mil. applications sect.), Washington Inst. for Ops. Rsch. and the Mgmt. Scis. Home: 8305 Fox Run Potomac MD 20854-2576 Home Phone: 301-299-6307. Personal E-mail: arhode@verizon.net. E-mail: arhode@comcast.net.

RHODE, DEBORAH LYNN, law educator; b. Jan. 29, 1952; BA, Yale U., 1974, JD, 1977. Bar: D.C. 1977, Calif. 1981. Law clk. to judge U.S. Ct. Appeals (2d cir.), NYC, 1977-78; law clk. to Hon. Justice Thurgood Marshall U.S. Supreme Ct., Washington, 1978-79; asst. prof. law Stanford U., Calif., 1979-82, assoc. prof. Calif., 1982-85, prof. Calif., 1985—; dir. Inst. for Rsch. on Women and Gender, 1986-90, Keck Ctr. of Legal Ethics and The Legal Profession, 1994—2003; sr. counsel jud. com. Ho. of Reps., Washington, 1998. Trustee Yale U., 1983-89; pres. Assn. Am. Law Schs., 1998; Ernest W. McFarland prof. Stanford Law Sch., 1997—; sr. counsel com. on the jud. U.S. Ho. of Reps., 1998; dir. Stanford Ctr. on Ethics. Author: Justice and Gender, 1989, (with Geoffrey Hazard) the Legal Profession: Responsibility and Regulation, 3d edit., 1993, (with Annette Lawson) The Politics of Pregnancy: Adolescent Sexuality and Public Policy, 1993, (with David Luban) Legal Ethics, 2005, 4th edit., 2004, Speaking of Sex, 1997, Professional Responsibility: Ethics by the Pervasive Method, 1998, In the Interests of Justice, 2000 (with Geoffrey Hazard, Jr.) Professional Responsibility and Regulation, 2002; editor: Theoretical Perspectives on Sexual Difference, 1990, Ethics in Practice, 2000, The Difference Difference Makes: Women and Leadership, 2002, Access to Justice, 2004, Pro Bono in Principle and in Practice, 2005, (with Katherine Bartlett) Gender and Law, 2005, (with Carol Sanger) Gender and Rights, 2005, Moral Leadership: The Theory and Practice of Power, Judgment and Policy, 2006, In Pursuit of Knowledge: Scholars, Status, and Academic Culture, 2006, Women and Leadership: The State of Play and Strategies for Change, 2007; contbr. articles to profl. jours. Mem.: ABA (chmn. commn. on women 2000—02). Office: Stanford U Law Sch Crown Quadrangle Stanford CA 94305

RHODE, EDWARD ALBERT, veterinary medicine educator, veterinary cardiologist; b. Amsterdam, NY, July 25, 1926; s. Edward A. and Katherine (Webb) R.; m. Dolores Bangert, 1955; children: David E., Peter R., Paul W., Robert M., Catherine E. DVM, Cornell U., 1947. Diplomate Am. Coll. Veterinary Internal Medicine. Prof. emeritus vet. medicine U. Calif., Davis,

1964—, chmn. dept. vet. medicine, 1968-71; assoc. dean instrn. U. Calif. Sch. Vet. Medicine, Davis, 1971-81, dean, 1982-91. Mem. AAAS, Nat. Acad. Practices, Am. Coll. Vet. Internal Medicine, Am. Vet. Medicine Assn., Basic Sci. Coun., Am. Heart Assn., Am. Acad. Vet. Cardiology, Am. Physiol. Soc., Calif. Vet. Medicine Assn. Office: U Calif Sch Vet Med Davis CA 95616 E-mail: earhode@ucdavis.edu.

RHODES, ALAN CHARLES, minister; b. Plattsburgh, NY, July 25, 1951; s. Charles Oliver and Lillian Mary (Cromie) R.; m. Holly C. Craver, June 14, 1975 (div. June 1987); m. Nancy Lichtenhan, June 18, 1988. BA, Lycoming Coll., Williamsport, Pa., 1973; MDiv, Boston U., 1976; DMin, Bangor Theol. Sem., Maine, 1997. Ordained to ministry United Meth. Ch. as deacon, 1974, as elder, 1977. Assoc. pastor Shenendehowa United Meth. Ch., Clifton Park, NY, 1976-79; pastor Ft. Plain and Freysbush United Meth. Chs., NY, 1979-83, St. Paul's United Meth. Ch., Castleton-on-Hudson, NY, 1983-87, Grace United Meth. Ch., Ravena, NY, 1987-98, North Main St. United Meth. Ch., Gloversville, NY, 1998—2002, Mechanicville United Meth. Ch., NY, 2002—. Trustee Troy Ann. Conf., 1993—; bd. dirs. Captain Youth and Family Svcs., Inc. Founder, former co-chair R.C.S. Task Force Against Domestic Violence; bd. dirs. Mechanicville Cmty. Ctr. Mem.: Rotary Club (pres. Champlain Canal 2004—05, gov. aide dist. 7190 2007—). Republican. Home: 148 S 2d Ave Mechanicville NY 12118-2200 Office: Mechanicville United Meth Ch 7 N Main St PO Box 429 Mechanicville NY 12118-2200 Office Phone: 518-664-3095. Personal E-mail: arhodes1@nycap.rr.com.

RHODES, ALICE GRAHAM, lawyer, not-for-profit community development consultant; b. Phila., June 15, 1941; d. Peter Graham III and Fannie Isadora (Bennett) Graham; m. Charles Milton Rhodes, Oct. 14, 1971 (div. Apr. 21, 1997); children: Helen, Carla, Shauna. BS, East Stroudsburg U., Pa., 1962; MS, U. Pa., Phila., 1966, LLB, 1969, JD, 1970, cert. program exec. adminstrn. non-profit, 2004. Bar: NY 1970, US Dist. Ct. (so. and ea. dists.) NY 1971, US Ct. Appeals (2d cir.) 1971, Ky. 1983, US Dist. Ct. (ea. dist.) Ky. 1985. Staff atty. Harlem Assertion Rights, Mobilization for Youth Office Econ. Opportunity, NYC, 1969-70, coord. Cmty. Action Legal Svcs., 1970-72; assoc. dir. in charge of civil representation HUD Model Cities Cmty. Law Offices, NYC, 1972-73; resource assoc. Commn. on Edn. & Employment of Women, NC Dept. Adminstrn., Raleigh, 1975; mgr. policies and procedures Div. for Youth, NC Dept. Human Resources, Raleigh, 1976; in-house counsel, petroleum transactional atty. Ashland, Inc. (formerly Ashland Oil, Inc.), 1980-82; corp. atty. core group Ashland, Inc., 1985-87, 88-91; mem. Ashland City Commn. Human Rights, 1993-99; mem. bd. regents Ea. Ky. U., 1994—2000; asst. county atty. Jefferson County, 1999—2000; atty.-advisor EEOC, 2001. Mem. Property Valuation Appeals Commn., Greenup County, 1994, Pub. Mems. Fgn. Svc.; cons. pub. mem. selection and performance stds. review bd. Fgn. Svc., US Dept. State, 1995, Fgn. Agrl. Svc. USDA, 1997; prison program planner, cons. NY City Dept. Corrections, 1971; lectr. NYC Corrections Acad., Riker's, 1971; lectr. juvenile justice NC Law Enforcement Acad., Salemburg, 1976. Vol. Meals on Wheels, 1983—91, Am. Heart Assn., 1982—91; mem. adv. com. task force post secondary edn. Gov. of Ky.; mem. Ky. Gov.'s Conf. on Postsecondary Edn., 1999; active Global Interdependence Ctr. U. Pa., 2003—; bd. dirs. exec. com. Boyd County Dem. Women, 1996—2000; mem. missionary soc., scholarship com. St. Matthew AME Ch., St. Matthew Lay Orgn., SC Club; bd. dirs. YWCA Ashland, 1983—84, Ashland Heritage Pk. Commn., 1983—85, Negro Baseball Hall of History; bd. dirs., budget com. United Way, Greenup County, Ky., 1988—92; found. bd. dirs. Franciscan Sisters of the Poor, Ky. Health Sys. Found., Inc., 1996—99; mem. presdl. search com. Ea. Ky. U., 1997—98. Recipient Cmty. Svc. award Queens Community Coll., NYC, 1972, Ashland C.C., 1986, Cmty. Svc. award NAACP, Ky.; NSF fellow, 1964, 65; faculty friends of Penn scholar U. Pa. Law Sch., 1966-69, Reginald Heber Smith postgrad. law and cmty. econ. devel. fellow, 1969-71; named to Hon. Order of Ky. Cols., 1989. Fellow Ky. Bar Found.; mem. NAFE, AAUW (bd. dirs. Phila. chpt. 1963-65), NAACP (life), NY Bar, Ky. Bar Assn. (mem. edn. law, corp. house counsel, law sects.), Pilot Club (exec. bd. Ashland 1983), Links, Inc., Penn Club (charter mem.), Assn. Gov. Bds. Colls. and Univs., Fgn. Svc. USA, (pub. mem., cons. to fgn. svc. bds.), Global Interdependence Ctr., Phila. Sr. Ctr. (life mem.), Pyramid Club Phila., U. Pa. Edn. Alumni Assn. (bd. dirs.), SC Club (Ann. Day program chair 2006). Democrat. Avocations: interior decorating, sports, dance, gourmet cooking, gardening. Address: 658 N 65th St Philadelphia PA 19151

RHODES, ARTHUR DELANO, benefits administrator; b. Philadelphia, Miss., Nov. 26, 1960; s. A.D. and Mary (McNair) R.; m. Angela Marie Jolly, May 21, 1988. AA, Miss. Delta Jr. Coll., Moorhead, 1980; BA in Polit. Sci., Millsaps Coll., 1982; JD, U. Miss., 1985. Bar: Miss. 1985, U.S. Dist. Ct. (no. and so. dist.) Miss. 1985. Intern asst. dist. atty. Dist. Atty's Office, Hernando, Miss., 1985; counsel Child Support Unit, Dept. of Human Svcs., Brookhaven, Miss., 1985-87; assoc. Prewitt & Bradley, Jackson, Miss., 1987-88; chief of staff Congressman Mike Parker, Washington, 1988-98; pres., CEO The Benefits Bd., Inc., Cleveland, Tenn., 1999—. Republican. Mem. Ch. Of God. Avocations: travel, reading. Home: 2014 Woodchase Way NE Cleveland TN 37311-1461 Office: The Benefits Bd PO Box 4608 Cleveland TN 37320-4608 Office Phone: 423-478-7131. Business E-Mail: artrhodes@benefitsboard.com.

RHODES, BETTY FLEMING, rehabilitation services professional, nurse; b. Franklin, Pa., Nov. 28, 1920; d. John and Twyla Odella (Callen) Fleming; m. Donald Muir Cain, Dec. 31, 1952 (div.); m. Lee Chester Rhodes, June 23, 1962 (dec. Apr. 1997). RN, Allegheny Gen. Hosp., Pitts., 1942. Lic. phys. therapist, Pa. Phys. therapist Office of D.T. Watson, Pitts., 1947, Ky. Soc. for Crippled Children, Louisville, 1947-51, St. Anthony Hosp., Louisville, 1953-78. Nurse U.S. Army, 1943-45; capt. Army Nurse Corps, 1951-52. Decorated Bronze Star. Mem. Am. Phys Therapy Assn. (pres. Ky. chpt.). Roman Catholic. Home: Providence Retirement Home 4915 Charleston Rd Apt 312 New Albany IN 47150

RHODES, DAISY CHUN, writer, researcher, historian; b. Kahuku, Hawaii, Nov. 16, 1933; d. Pyung Chan Chun and Shin Ai Park; children: Joseph, Carmella, Thomas Francese. BA in Creative Writing, Eckerd Coll., 1995. Info. specialist Reconstrn. Devel. Corp., Washington, 1970; specialist indigent funding George Washington U. Hosp., Washington, 1971-74; mgr. hosp. assistance Alexandria (Va.) Hosp., 1975-79; asst. editor Employee Futures Rsch., Luray, Va., 1980-84; editor Inside Negotiations, Rochester, NY, 1985-87, Educators Negotiating Svc., New Port Richey, Fla., 1987-89; novelist, writer New Port Richey, 1989-95; rschr., oral historian Honolulu, 1994; writer Colorado Springs, 1995—; rschr., cons. Donna Ladd, Writer, Colorado Springs, 1996. Rschr., cons. Donna Ladd, Writer, Colorado Springs, 1996; presenter Asian Studies Conf., Honolulu; presenter scholarly and abstract Korean Picture Brides We. Asian Studies Conf., Boulder, Colo., 1997; lectr. Ctr. for Korean Studies U. Hawaii, 1998. Author: Forever Long-Never End, 1990, Wahaiawa Red Dirt, 1991, At Crossroads of Inspiration, 1993, Shirley Temple Feet, 1993, Remembering the Fallen, 1994, Passages to Paradise: Early Korean Immigrant Narratives from Hawaii, 1998; author: (play) I Know About Olympus, 1993; author: (scholarly and abstract) How Oral History of the First Koreans in America Advances Archival Research, 1996; author: Eye of the Dragon, 1994 (finalist Hemingway 1st Novel Competition, 1994), My Father's Voice, Echoes Upon Echoes, 2002, A Place of Noise, 2003, A Literary Lei, 2004. Pres. Colorado Springs Friends of Aquatics, 1997—; bd. dirs. All Souls Unitarian Ch.; mem. adv. bd. City of Colorado Springs Pks. and Recreation, 2004—. Recipient Work Study award for profls., Rotary Internat. Found., South Korea, 1998—99. Mem.: Korean Am. Women's Soc. Greater Washington (pres. 1983—84, bd. dirs., Commendation), Korea Soc., Assn. for Asian Studies, West Pasco Kiwanis (pres. 1990—92). Home: 1912 Eastlake Blvd # 502 Colorado Springs CO 80910 E-mail: dyschun@msn.com.

RHODES, DAVID, academic administrator; s. Silas H. Rhodes. BA in philosophy, Wesleyan Coll.; attended, Columbia U. Pres. Sch. Visual Arts, NYC, 1978—. Mem.: Commn. Higher Edn. Middle States Assn. Coll. & Sch. (appointment 2003—04), Regants Adv. Coun. Instl. Accreditation, Commn. Higher Edn., Assn. Proprietary Coll. (bd. trustees 1989—, chmn. fed. affairs com. 1989—). Office: School of Visual Arts Office of the President 209 East 23 St New York NY 10010 *

RHODES, DEBORAH JEAN JOHNSON, prosecutor; b. 1958; BA with high honors, Wheaton Coll.; JD with honors, Rutgers U. Law clk. to Hon. J. William Ditter US Dist Ct. (ea. dist.) Pa; mem. Organized Crime & Racketeering sect., Phila. Strike Force US Dept. Justice, Phila., asst. US atty. San Diego, 1990—2004, counselor to asst. atty. gen., criminal divsn. Washington, 2004—05, US atty. (so. dist.) Ala. Ala., 2005—. Ex-officio commr. US Sentencing Commn., 2003—. Editor (in chief): Rutgers Law Jour. Office: US Attys Office Southern District of Alabama 63 S Royal St Ste 600 Mobile AL 36602 *

RHODES, DONALD ROBERT, musicologist, educator, retired electrical engineer; b. Detroit, Dec. 31, 1923; s. Donald Eber and Edna Mae (Fulmer) R.; children: Joyce R. Holbert, Jane E., Roger C., Diane R. Herran. BEE, Ohio State U., 1945, MEE, 1948, PhD, 1953. Research assoc. Ohio State U., Columbus, 1945-54; research engr. Cornell Aero. Lab., Buffalo, 1954-57; head basic research dept. Radiation, Inc., Orlando, Fla., 1957-61, sr. scientist Melbourne, Fla., 1961-66; Univ. prof. N.C. State U., Raleigh, 1966-94, univ. prof. emeritus, 1994—. Author: Introduction to Monopulse, 1959, 2d edit., 1980, Synthesis of Planar Antenna Sources, 1974, A Reactance Theorem, 1977. Co-founder Central Fla. Community Orch., Winter Park, 1961, pres., 1961-62. Recipient Benjamin G. Lamme medal Ohio State U., 1975; Eminent Engr. award Tau Beta Pi, 1976; named to N.C. State U. Acad. Outstanding Tchrs., 1980. Fellow AAAS, IEEE (John T. Bolljahn award 1963, pres. Antennas and Propagation Soc. 1969); mem. Am. Musicological Soc. Home: Apt 101 625 Centennial Pkwy Raleigh NC 27606-3255 Office: PO Box 7911 Raleigh NC 27695-7911

RHODES, ERIC FOSTER, employee relations consultant, writer; b. Luray, Va., Feb. 5, 1927; s. Wallace Keith and Bertha (Foster) R.; m. Barbara Ellen Henson, Oct. 19, 1946; children: Roxanne Jane, Laurel Lee (dec.); m. Lorraine Eridresen, July 29, 1972; m. Daisy Chun, May 31, 1980; m. Barbara Rhodes, Oct. 19, 2004. AA, George Washington U., 1949, AB, 1950, MA, 1952, EdD, 1967. Tchr. high sch., Arlington, Va., 1950-52; counselor Washington Lee High Sch., Arlington, Va., 1952-53, dir. publs., 1953-54, chmn. dept. English, 1954-55; exec. sec. Arlington Edn. Assn., Arlington, Va., 1952-53, Montgomery County Edn. Assn., Rockville, Md., 1955-57; lectr. edn. George Washington U., Washington, 1955-60, 65-70; salary cons. NEA, Washington, 1957-58, asst. dir. membership div., 1958-60; dir. N.Y. regional office, NYC, 1960-64; ednl. cons. Ednl. Rsch. Svcs., White Plains, N.Y., 1964-65; pres. Ednl. Svc. Bur., Inc., Arlington, Va., 1965-72, chmn. bd., 1972-80; pres. Negotiations Consultation Svcs., Inc., Arlington, 1969-80, Eastern States Advt. Inc., Arlington, 1970-79, EFR Corp., Arlington, 1972-90; exec. dir. Assn. Negotiators and Contract Adminstrs., 1981-89; area coord. U.S. Legal Protection Co., 1989-95; pres. Employee Futures Rsch., New Port Richey, Fla., 1980—, Waterfront Only Real Estate, New Port Richey, Fla., 1988-92, Inst. for Negotiations Tng., New Port Richey, 1989-95, Asset Protection Co., 1991—; asst. supt. for adminstrn. Brighton Schs., Rochester, N.Y., 1983-88; owner Frederick Foster Galleries, Arlington, 1974-80. Cons. Va. Dept. Community Colls., Richmond, 1965-77; vice chancellor Va. Community Coll. System, 1970-71; employee rels. ofcl. City of Orlando, 1980-83; lectr. edn. Frostburg (Md.) State Coll., 1967 Author: Negotiating Salaries, 41 Ways to Cut Budget Costs, Making Good Things Happen Through Negotiation; editor: Inside Negotiations, Wages and Benefits, Employers' Negotiating Service. Mem. Civil Rights Commn., Franklin Twp., N.J., 1962-64; mem. Sr. victim assistance team Colorado Springs Police Dept., 1997-2003; mem. Franklin Twp. Bd. Edn., 1964-65; mem. adv. bd. Keep Am. Beautiful, 1964-75, nat. chmn., 1968; bd. dirs., v.p. Unitarian-Universalist Ch., Tarpon Springs, Fla., 1990-95, pres., 1994-95, bd. dirs., dir. summer programs, 2005—, v.p. 2007-; mem. Land Devel. Rev. Bd., New Port Richey, Fla., 2005—. With U.S. Army, 1945-47. Mem. Am. Assn. Sch. Adminstrs., Internat. Assn. Sch. Bus. Ofcls., NEA, Edn. Press Assn., Nat. Assn. Ednl. Negotiators (exec. dir. 1971-81), Am. Arbitration Assn. (labor arbitrator), Indsl. Rels. Rsch. Assn., United C. of C. of Pasco County (sec., treas. 1989-90, exec. dir. 1990-91), Am. Legion, Fed. Schoolmen's Club, N.Y. Schoolmen's Club, Lions (v.p. N.Y.C. club 1964-65), Kiwanis (pres. West Pasco club 1991-93, treas. 2004-06), Order of St. John of Jerusalem, Phi Delta Kappa (chpt. pres. 1959-60). Home: 5547 Richey Dr New Port Richey FL 34652 Office: PO Box 1178 New Port Richey FL 34656 Office Phone: 727-849-9484. E-mail: ericrhodes@netzero.com.

RHODES, FRANK HAROLD TREVOR, academic administrator, geologist; b. Warwickshire, Eng., Oct. 29, 1926; came to US, 1968, naturalized, 1976; s. Harold Cecil and Gladys (Ford) R.; m. Rosa Carlson, Aug. 16, 1952; children: Jennifer, Catherine, Penelope, Deborah. BSc, U. Birmingham, 1948, PhD, 1950, DSc, 1963; LLD (hon.), Wooster Coll., Ohio, 1976, Nazareth Coll., Rochester, NY, 1979, Skidmore Coll., Saratoga Springs, NY, 1989, U. Mich., 1990, Clemson U., SC, 1991, Dartmouth Coll., Hanover, NH, 1993, U. Birmingham, Eng., 1999, Fla. Internat. U., Miami, 2000, Trinity Coll., U. Dublin, 2001; LHD (hon.), Colgate U., Hamilton, NY, 1980, Johns Hopkins U., Balt., 1982, Wagner Coll., SI, 1982, Hope Coll., Holland, Mich., 1982, Rensselaer Poly Inst., Troy, NY, 1982, LeMoyne Coll., 1984, Pace U., NYC, 1986, Alaska Pacific U., Anchorage, 1987; LHD, Hamilton Coll., 1987; LHD, DSc, Fla. Atlantic U., Boca Raton, 1996; LHD (hon.), Coll. St. Rose, Albany, NY, 2002; DSc (hon.), U. Wales, Eng., 1981, Bucknell U., Lewisburg, Pa., 1985, U. Ill., 1986, Reed Coll., Portland, 1988, Elmira Coll., NY, 1989, U. Southampton, Eng., 1989, U. Sydney, Australia, 1995, U. Durham, Eng., 1995, Millsaps Coll., 1996; DLitt (hon.), U. Nev., 1982; EdD (hon.), Ohio State U., 1992; D (hon.), U. Stirling, Eng., 1994; LHD (hon.), U. NC, 2003, Ariz. State U., Tempe, 2006. Post-doctoral fellow, Fulbright scholar U. Ill., 1950-51, vis. lectr. geology, summers 1951, 52; lectr. geology U. Durham, 1951-54; asst. prof. U. Ill., 1954-55, assoc. prof., 1955-56; dir. U. Ill. Field Sta., Wyo., 1956; prof. geology, head geology dept. U. Wales, Swansea, 1956-68, dean faculty of sci., 1967-68; prof. geology and mineralogy Coll. Lit., Sci. and Arts, U. Mich., 1968-77, dean, 1971-74, v.p. for acad. affairs, 1974-77; pres., prof. geology Cornell U., Ithaca, NY, 1977-95, pres emeritus, 1995—. Gurley lectr. Cornell U., 1960; Bownocker lectr. Ohio State U., 1966; Case lectr. U. Mich., 1976; Jefferson lectr. U. Calif., Berkeley, 1996-98; dir. NSF, Am. Geol. Inst., summer field inst., 1963; Australian vice-chancellors' visitor to Australian univs., 1964; vis. fellow Clare Hall, Cambridge, 1982; Bye fellow Robinson Coll., Cambridge, 1986-87; Am. Fulbright Disting. fellow, Kuwait, 1987, scholar in residence, Bellagio study and conf. ctr., 1995. Author: The Evolution of Life, 1962, 2d edit., 1976, Fossils, 1963, Geology, 1972, Evolution, 1974, Language of the Earth, 1981, Creation of the Future: The Role of the American University, 2001; author numerous articles and monographs on sci. and edn.; editor, contbr.: Successful Fund Raising for Higher Edn., 1997. Trustee Carnegie Found. for Advancement Tchg., 1978-86, vice chmn., 1983-85, chmn. 1985-86; trustee The Freedom Forum, 1983-93, Com. for Econ. Devel., 1984-93; prin. Washington Adv. Group, 1997—; bd. dirs. KMI Continental, Inc., 1985-86, Tompkins County Trust Co., 1984-98, Gen. Electric Co., 1984-2002, NBC, 1986-2002, H. John Heinz III Ctr. Sci., Econs. & Environ., 1996-98, Am. Coun. on Edn., 1983-88, vice chair, 1985-86, chair, 1986-88, The Johnson Found., 2000—, Atlantic Philanthropies, 1995—, chmn., 2000—; bd. dirs. Goldman Sachs Found., 2000—; bd. overseers Meml. Sloan-Kettering Cancer Ctr., 1979-91, Koç U., Turkey, 1996—; chmn. adv. bd. Freedom Forum Media Studies Ctr., 1984-93; mem. Nat. Sci. Bd., 1987-98, chair, 1994-96, Internat. Exec. Svc. Corps Coun., 1984-95; v.p. Dyson Charitable Trust, 1996-98; bd. mem. The Johnson Found., 2000—. Recipient Clark Kerr medal U. Calif., Berkeley, 1995, Reginald Wilson Diversity Leadership award Am. Coun. Edn., 2003; Sr. Vis. Rsch. fellow NSF, 1965-66; scholar U. Calif., Berkeley, 1995. Fellow Am. Acad. Arts and Scis., Geol. Soc. London (coun. 1963-66, Bigsby medal 1967); mem. Am. Philos. Soc. (pres. 1999-2005), Palaeontol. Assn. (v.p. 1963-68), Brit. Assn. Advancement Sci., Geol. Soc. Am., Am. Assn. Petroleum Geologists, Soc. Econ. Paleontologists and Mineralogists, Phi Beta Kappa. Office: Cornell U Office of President Emeritus 3104 Snee Hall Ithaca NY 14853-1504 Office Phone: 607-255-6233.

RHODES, LAWRENCE, artistic director; b. Mt. Hope, W.Va., Nov. 24, 1939; Studied with Violette Armand. Joined Ballet Russe de Monte Carlo, 1958-60; from dancer to prin. dancer Joffrey Ballet, NYC, 1960-64; prin. dancer Harkness Ballet, 1964-68, dir., prin. dancer, 1968-70; tchr. dance dept. NYU, 1978—, prin. ballet tchr., 1981—, chmn. dance dept., 1981-91; ballet master, choreographer, tchr., artistic dir. Les Grands Ballets Canadiens, Montreal, 1989-99; dir. dance divsn. The Juilliard Sch., 2002—. Guest artist Het Nationale Ballet, Amsterdam, 1970—71, Pa. Ballet, 1971—76, Feld Ballet, NYC, 1973—75; free-lance master ballet tchr., coach. Danced with Makarova, Hayden and Fracci, danced for Butler, Joffrey, Ailey, Lubovitch, Harkarvy, Nault, Van Dantzig and Mac Donald, featured dancer (TV films) A Dancer's Vocabulary, PBS's Dance Am. series, CBS's Camera Three. Office Phone: 212-799-5000 x 255. E-mail: llrhodes@worldnet.att.net.

RHODES, LINDA JANE, psychiatrist; b. San Antonio, May 23, 1950; d. George Vernon and Lucy Agnes (O'Dowd) R. BA, Trinity U., 1972; MD, U. Tex. Med. Br., 1975. Diplomate Am. Bd. Pediat.; bd. certified, Am. Bd. Psychiatry and Neurology. Resident in pediat. U. Tex. Med. Br., Galveston, 1975-78; fellow in ambulatory pediat. U. Tex. Health Sci. Ctr., Houston, 1978-80, resident in psychiatry San Antonio, 1990-92, child and adolescent psychiatrist, fellow in biol. psychiatry, 1992-95, asst. prof. psychiatry, 1995—2004; pediatrician Kelsey Seybold Clinic, P.A., Houston, 1980-95. Pediat. rep. Tex. Lay Midwifery Bd. Tex. Dept. Health, Austin, 1994-95. Active San Antonio Conservation Soc., San Antonio Herb Soc., Nat. Trust for Hist. Preservation, San Antonio Mus. Assn., Trinity U. Assocs., 1992-95, Witte Mus. Assn.; mem. McNay Art Inst.; bd. dirs. Mind. Sci. Found., 1995-2000., Tex. Found. Psychiatric Edn. & Rsch., 1997—, sec., 1998-99, treas., 1999-2004; chair Tex. Found. for Psychiat. Edn. and Rsch., 2007—. Fellow Am. Acad. Pediat.; mem. Am. Psychiat. Assn., Am. Acad. Child and Adolescent Psychiatry (past gifts and endowments com., child abuse and neglect com.), Ambulatory Pediat. Assn., Tex. Pediat. Soc., Tex. Soc. Psychiat. Physicians, Tex. Acad. Child and Adolescent Psychiatry, Am. Med. Women's Assn., Am. Soc. Clin. Psychopharmacology, Tex. Med. Assn. (com. on child and adolescent health), AMA, Bexar County Psychait. Soc. (sec. 2000-01, pres. 2002-2003, past pres. 2003-2004), Baxter County Med. Soc.

RHODES, MELVIN FRANK, minister, writer; b. Grimsby, Lincolnshire, Eng., Jan. 25, 1951; (parents Am. citizens); s. Frank Rhodes and Grace Evison; m. Diane Claire Hoot, Oct. 12, 1975; children: Alexandra Victoria Claire Kubik, Kurt Melvin George, Pallas Marion Grace. BA, Amb. Coll., Bricket Wood, Herts, Eng., 1974. Ministerial trainee Worldwide Ch. God, Bulawayo, 1976—78, ch. pastor Accra, Ghana, 1978—90, United Ch. God, Lansing, 1990—, writer Cin., 1995—, sr. editor, world news & prophecy, 1995—, regional pastor for Ghana, W. Africa, 1999—. Writer, editor World News & Prophecy, Anchor Magazine, writer Good News Magazine, Lansing State Journal; author: (booklet) The Middle East in Prophecy.

RHODES, MICHAEL E., biologist, educator; b. Greensburg, Pa., June 1, 1971; s. Edward C. and Gloria L. Rhodes; m. Lee Ann Kosakowski, Oct. 11, 1997; children: Katelyn Frances, Justin Michael. BS, St. Vincent Coll., Latrobe, Pa., 1993; MS, Duquesne U., Pitts., 1995; PhD, Duquesne U., 1997. Part-time assoc. prof. Duquesne U., Pitts., 1997—2006; rsch. asst. prof. Allegheny-Singer Rsch. Inst., Allegheny Gen. Hosp., Pitts., 1997—2005; part-time assoc. prof. Carlow Coll., Pitts., 1995—2005; asst. prof. of biology St. Vincent Coll., Latrobe, Pa., 2005—. Contbr. more than 25 articles to profl. jours. Recipient Best Prof. award, Nat. Cmty. Pharmacy Assn., 1998, Internat. Jr. Investigator award, Internat. Coll. of Geriatric Psychoneuropharmacology, 2003; grantee, Royal Soc. Of Edinburgh, 1999, Commonwealth Of Pa. Tobacco Settlement Fund, 2004—06, Allegheny Gen. Aux. Grant Program, 2002—04; Rafaelsen fellow, Collegium Internat. Neuropsychopharmacologium, 2002. Mem.: Internat. Coll. of Geriatric of Psychoneuropharmacology (assoc.), Soc. for Neurosci. (assoc.), Am. Soc. of Pharmacology and Exptl. Therapeutics (assoc.). Independent. Methodist. Achievements include patents for novel memory-enhancing drugs. Avocations: fishing, golf, woodcarving. Office: Saint Vincent College 300 Fraser Purchase Rd Latrobe PA 15650 Office Phone: 724-805-2360. E-mail: michael.rhodes@email.stvincent.edu.

RHODES, PETER EDWARD, label company executive; b. Rochester, NY, Sept. 25, 1942; s. Robert A. and Anne (Ward) R.; m. Cassandra Durkee, May 26, 1962 (div. Sept. 1991); children: Tamara, Amy, Brian; m. Nancy Lewis, Aug. 16, 2002. BS, Rochester Inst. Tech., 1964, MBA, 1970. With Touche Ross & Co., Rochester, 1962-69, sr. auditor, to 1969; with Xerox Co., Rochester, 1969, Fay's Drug Co., Inc., Liverpool, NY, 1970-87, exec. v.p., 1974-87, also dir.; pres. Syracuse Label Co., Inc., Liverpool, 1987—2002, 2002—, also bd. dirs. Bd. dirs. Byrne Dairy Inc. Mem.: AICPA, NY State Soc. CPAs, Bellevue Country Club.

RHODES, RAMONA LAGIERS, medical educator, researcher; d. Jim and Linda Rhodes. BS, Xavier U. La., New Orleans, 1996; MD, U. Ark., Little Rock, 2000; MPH, Brown U., Providence, RI, 2006. Diplomate in geriatrics Am. Bd. Internal Medicine. Intern/resident Case Western Res. U./MetroHealth Med. Ctr., 2000—03; geriatric medicine fellow Brown U./Rhode Island Hosp., Providence, 2003—06; postdoctoral rsch. fellow Brown U. Ctr. Gerontology and Health Care Rsch., Providence, 2004—06; asst. prof. medicine Brown Med. Sch., Providence, 2006—. Assoc. med. dir. Home and Hospice Care of R.I., Providence, 2006—, mem. diversity task force, 2006—; mem. fellowship exec. com. Brown Med. Sch., divsn. Geriat., Providence. Author: (book chpt.) The Elderly Female Patient; co-author (book chpt.) Pain Management in the Geriatric Patient, (article) Jour. Palliative Medicine, (review) Medicine and Health Rhode Island. Recipient James and Susan Carter Humanitarian award, Dept. Internal Medicine, MetroHealth Med. Ctr., 2003, Haffenreffer award in Fellowship Excellence, R.I. Hosp., Grad. Med. Edn., 2006, Chancellor's List, Nat. Academic Affairs, 2004—06, Tannenbaum Scholarship, U. Ark. for Med. SciS., 1996-2000; grantee, Agy. for Healthcare Rsch. and Quality, 2004—06. Mem.: Am. Acad. Hospice and Palliative Medicine, Am. Geriat. Soc., Nat. Med. Assn., Delta Sigma Theta Sorority, Inc. (mentor 2005). Baptist. Avocations: piano, singing, tennis, travel. Office: Brown Univ Ctr for Gerontology 2 Stimson Ave Box GS-311 Providence RI 02912 Home Phone: 401-270-7135.

RHODES, RANDI, radio personality; b. Bklyn. d. Loretta; m. Jim Robertson, 1994 (div. 2004). Jobs at Radio Stations, Seminole, Tex., Mobile, Ala., NY, Dallas, Milw.; former sec., waitress, trucker and US Air Force aircraft mechanic; public relations job then weekend disc jockey WSHE, Coast 97.3 FM, 1987—92; radio talk show host WIOD AM,

Miami, Fla., 1992—94, WJNO, West Palm Beach, Fla., 1994—2004, The Randi Rhodes Show, Air Am. Radio, NYC, 2004—. With USAF, 1977. Named Most Outstanding Woman in the Air Force, 1979; recipient Am. Women in Radio and Television award. Mailing: care Carmen Shamwell 4th Fl 641 Sixth Ave New York NY 10019 Office: Air America Radio 641 Avenue Of The Americas Fl 4 New York NY 10011-2038 E-mail: rrhodes@airamericaradio.com.

RHODES, RICHARD (LEE), writer; b. Kansas City, Kans., July 4, 1937; s. Arthur and Georgia Saphronia (Collier) R.; children: Timothy James, Katherine Hampton; m. Ginger Kay Untrif, Oct. 3, 1993. BA cum laude, Yale U., 1959; LHD (hon.), Westminster Coll., Fulton, Mo., 1988. Author: The Inland Ground, 1970, The Ungodly, 1973, The Ozarks, 1974, Holy Secrets, 1978, Looking for America, 1979, The Last Safari, 1980, Sons of Earth, 1981, The Making of the Atomic Bomb, 1986, Farm, 1989, A Hole in the World, 1990, Making Love, 1992, Nuclear Renewal, 1993, How to Write, 1995, Dark Sun, 1995, (with Ginger Rhodes) Trying to Get Some Dignity, 1996, Deadly Feasts, 1997, Visions of Technology, 1999, Why They Kill, 1999, Masters of Death, 2002, John James Audubon: The Making of an American, 2004. Trustee Andrew Drumm Inst., Independence, Mo., 1991-, Atomic Heritage Found., DC, 2004-, Cypress Found., DC, 2005-. Recipient Nat. Book Critics Cir. award for nonfiction, Nat. Book award for nonfiction, 1987, Pulitzer prize, 1988; Guggenheim fellow, 1974-75, fellow Nat. Endowment for Arts, 1978-79, Ford Found., 1981-83, Sloan Found., 1985, 89, 91, 92, 2002-, MacArthur Found., 1990-91. Office: c/o Janklow & Nesbit Assoc 445 Park Ave New York NY 10022-2606

RHODES, ROSAMOND, medical educator, philosophy educator; b. NYC, Mar. 19, 1946; d. Michael S. and Helen Rhodes; m. Joe Robert Fitschen, Nov. 0, 1992; children: Keli Ann Rosenberg, David Gabriel Rosenberg. PhD, CUNY, NYC, 1990. Prof. med. edn. Mt. Sinai Sch. Medicine, NYC, 1988—; prof. philosophy The Grad. Ctr., CUNY, NYC, 1998—. Editor, newsletter on philosophy and medicine Am. Philosophic Assn., Newark, 1990—; mem. Wadsworth Ctr. working group in bioethics N.Y. Dept. Health, Albany, 2005—. Editor: (book, edited collection) Physician Assisted Suicide: Expanding the Debate, Medicine and Social Justice: Essays on the Distribution of Health Care, The Blackwell Guide to Medical Ethics. Recipient Spl. Recognition award for Achievement in Med. Edn., The Mt. Sinai Alumni, 2005. Mem.: Internat. Hobbes Assn. (program com. 1998—2006), Am. Soc. for Bioethics And Humanities (bd. 2005—06), Am. Philos. Assn. (ex officion 1990—2006, com. on philosophy and medicine). Office: Mount Sinai School of Medicine One Gustave Levy Pl New York NY 10029 Home Phone: 718-549-5503; Office Phone: 212-241-3757. Office Fax: 212-241-5028. E-mail: rosamond.rhodes@mssm.edu.

RHODES, SAMUEL, violist, educator; b. Long Beach, NY, Feb. 13, 1941; s. Bernard and Martha (Ephraim) R.; m. Hiroko Yajima, Dec. 30, 1968; children— Amy, Harumi. BA, Queen's Coll., CUNY, 1963; M.F.A., Princeton U., 1967; D.F.A. (hon.), Mich. State U., 1984; MusD (hon.), Jacksonville U., 1986, San Francisco Conservatory, 1996. Mem. faculty Juilliard Sch., NYC, 1969—, Mich. State U., East Lansing, 1977-85, SUNY-Purchase, 1982-86; violist Marlboro Festival, 1960-68, 78-81, 91—, Galimir String Quartet, 1961-68, Juilliard String Quartet, 1969—; mem. faculty Tanglewood Music Ctr., 1988—. Office: Juilliard Sch Music Lincoln Ctr New York NY 10023

RHODES, STEPHEN MICHAEL, poultry company executive; b. Harrisonburg, Va., Mar. 12, 1949; s. Trovilla Geil and Ogretta (Dove) R.; m. Judy Ann Higgs, June 19, 1971; children: Jeremy, Meridith. AA, Shenandoah Coll., 1969; BA in Biology, Madison Coll., 1971. Mgr. quality control Rocco Farm Foods, Inc., Edinburg, Va., 1971-95, wastewater/environ. mgr., 1996—. V.p., bd. dirs. Plains Youth Baseball League, Va., 1989-91, coach 1984-90; coach pony league, 1991; 1st lt., pres. Broadway Emergency Squad, 1971-77; chmn. coun. on Ministries Sunset Dr. United Meth. Ch., Broadway, 1991, 94-96, 99—, vice chmn., 1997-98; mem. PPR com., 1994-95; coach Timberville Midget League Football, 1985-89; bd. dirs. Community Pk. Bd., Broadway, 1984-86; mem. Rockingham County Recreation Commn., 1990-97; pres. Broadway H.S. Athletic Booster Club, 1994-96, v.p., 1996-97. Mem. Va. Poultry Industry Lab. (chmn. bd. dirs. 1983, 87), Southeastern Poultry and Egg Fedn. (sci. adv. com. 1983-91). Avocations: hunting, fishing, swimming. Home: 199 3rd St Broadway VA 22815-9511 Office: Rocco Farm Foods Inc 19992 Senedo Rd Edinburg VA 22824-3172

RHODES, THOMAS WILLARD, lawyer; b. Lynchburg, Va., Mar. 9, 1946; s. Howard W. and Ruth R.; m. Ann Bloodworth, May 31, 1975; children: Mildred, Andrew. AB, Davidson Coll., NC, 1968; JD, U. Va., 1971. Bar: Ga. 1971. Assoc. Smith, Gambrell & Russell and predecessor firms, Atlanta, 1971-76, ptnr., 1976—. Dir., pres. Atlanta Vol. Lawyers Found., 1984-89; dir. Fed. Defender Program, Atlanta, 1988-92, 2003—, pres., 1991-92. Contbr. profl. jours. and textbooks; editor: Nonprofit News. Capt. USAR, 1968—72. Recipient Heiner award Atlanta Vol. Lawyers Found., 1989, Anderson Lecture award Am. Acad. Facial Plastic and Reconstructive Surgery, 2004. Fellow Am. Law Inst.; mem. ABA, Ga. Bar Assn. (past chmn. antitrust law sect.). Office: Smith Gambrell & Russell Promenade II 1230 Peachtree St NE Ste 3100 Atlanta GA 30309-3592

RHODES, WILLIAM C., III, automotive executive; B in Acctg., U. Tenn.; MBA, U. Memphis. CPA. With Ernst & Young, 1988—94, Autozone Inc., Memphis, 1994—, v.p., 1997—99, sr. v.p., 1999—2002, exec. v.p., 2002—05, pres., CEO, 2005—07, chmn., pres., CEO, 2007—. Bd. mem. Memphis Tomorrow; treas. Nat. Civil Rights Mus.; mem. partners bd. FedEx Inst. Tech. Office: Autozone Inc 123 S Front St Memphis TN 38103 *

RHODES, WILLIAM REGINALD, banker; b. NYC, Aug. 15, 1935; s. Edward R. and Elsie Rhodes; divorced; 1 child, Elizabeth. BA in History, Brown U., 1957, degree (hon.), 2005. Joined Citibank, 1957, served in several sr. positions in Latin Am. and Caribbean, 1957—77; from sr. officer internat. banking group-L.Am. and Caribbean to vice-chmn. Citibank, N.A., NYC, 1977—91, vice-chmn., 1991—2001, sr. vice chmn., 2001—03, chmn., 2003—05, chmn., pres., CEO, 2005—; sr. vice chmn. Citigroup, Inc., 1999—; chmn., CEO Citicorp Holdings, Inc., 2003—05, chmn., pres., CEO, 2005—. First vice chmn. Inst. Internat. Fin.; mem. Met. Mus. Bus. Com., U.S.-Russia Bus. Coun.; past chmn. adv. com. Export-Import Bank of US; past chmn. U.S. sect. Venezuela-U.S. Bus. Coun.; founding mem. U.S. Nat. Adv. Coun. to the Internat. Mgmt. Ctr., Budapest; active U.S.-Egyptian Pres. Coun.; bd. dirs. ConocoPhillips, Pvt. Export Funding Corp. Chmn. Northfield-Mt. Hermon Sch., Hong Kong-U.S. Bus. Coun.; bd. dirs., gov., trustee NY and Presbyn. Hosp.; bd. overseers Watson Inst. for Internat. Studies, Brown U.; active Lincoln Ctr. Corporate Leadership Com.; vice-chmn. Metropolitan Mus. Art Bus. Com. and chmn. com.; bd. dirs. Africa-Am. Inst.; vice chmn. bd. Nat. Com. on U.S.-China Rels.; hon. chmn., Sister City Program of City of NY. Decorated comdr. and grand officer Nat. Order of the So. Cross (Brazil); officer Legion of Honor (France); Orden de Mayo (Argentina); officer Order Francisco Miranda 1st and 3rd classes, Order Merito en el Trabajo 1st class (Venezuela); Order of Diplomatic Svc., Heung-In medal, Korea; comdr. Order of Distinction (Jamaica); recipient Am.'s award, 1997, African Bus. Devel. award African Am. Inst., 1998, Banker's Lifetime Achievment award Arab Bankers Assn. N.Am., 1999, Stephen P. Duggan award for Internat. Understanding, Inst. for Internat. Edn., 1999, William I. Spencer award NY Blood Ctr., 1999. Mem. Americas Soc. (chmn. bd. dirs.), Coun. of Ams. (chmn. bd. dirs.), Bankers Assn. Fin. and Trade (past pres., Banker of Yr. award 2004), Coun. Fgn. Rels., Venezuelan-Am. C. of C. (past pres.), Fgn. Policy Assn. (bd. dirs.). Avocations: jogging, swimming, archeaology, reading. Office: Citigroup Inc 399 Park Ave New York NY 10043-0001 *

RHODY, RONALD EDWARD, bank, communications executive; b. Frankfort, Ky., Jan. 27, 1932; s. James B. and Mary M. (Clark) R.; m. Patricia Schupp, Apr. 23, 1955; children: Leslie K., Mary M., Virginia K., Ronald C. Student, Georgetown Coll., Ky., 1950-52, U. Ky., 1953-55. Pub. rels. dir. Kaiser Aluminum & Chem. Corp., Ravenswood, W.Va., 1959-62, NYC, 1962-67, corp. v.p. Oakland, Calif., 1967-83; sr. v.p. corp comm. Bank of Am. NT&SA, San Francisco, 1983—, exec. v.p., 1992-94; CEO Rhody, Inc., 1994—. Author: The CEO's Playbook, 1999, Wordson Thing, 2006; contbr. articles to profl. jours. Founding chmn. adv. bd. San Francisco Acad. Named Pub. Rels. Profl. of Yr., Pub. Rels. News, 1981; recipient Hall of Fame award Page Soc., 1997. Fellow Pub. Rels. Soc. Am.; mem. Pub. Rels. Soc. Am. (accredited, pres.'s adv. coun. Rex Harlow award), Internat. Assn. Bus. Communicators (Gold Quill award 1980), Pub. Rels. Roundtable San Francisco (mem. bd. govs., awards 1980, 85). Home: 2725 Pontiac Dr Walnut Creek CA 94598-4437 Office: Rhody Inc 2725 Pontiac Dr Walnut Creek CA 94598-4437 E-mail: ron.rhody@att.net.

RHONE, ELVIE SUE, educational administrator; b. La., Oct. 06; d. Henry and Clara (McWright) Turner; m. Samuel Rhone, Apr. 24, 1964; children: Debra Lynn, Nedra Lanae. BS, So. U., Baton Rouge, 1962; MEd, Loyola U., Chgo., 1974; MS, Chgo. State U., 1986; EdD, Nova Southeastern U., Ft. Lauderdale, Fla., 1993. Lic. adminstr., supr., guidance, counseling and math. Instr. Cook County Sch. Nursing, Chgo., 1963-65; cons., supr. Cook County Dept. Pub. Aid, Chgo., 1965-66; tchr. Chgo. Pub. Schs., 1966-76, resource tchr., 1976-88, counselor, asst. prin., 1989-94, adminstr. Ctrl. Office Ctr., 1994—. Cons. math. textbook Houghton Mifflin Co., Dallas, 1987. Candidate for alt. del. to nat. conv., Chgo., 1980; bd. dirs. Cmty. Mental Health Coun., Inc.; mem. Referral Counselors Real Estate Connection. Recipient Outstanding Svc. award nat. legislation Nat. Cmty. Edn. Assn.; named Outstanding Educator PTA, Chgo., 1987; grantee Ill. State Bd. Edn., Springfield, 1992-94. Mem. ASCD, Nat. Sch. Bd., Assn. for Counselors, Chgo. Area Reading Assn., Phi Delta Kappa (Educator of Yr. 1994). Avocations: writing, gardening, travel, reading. Home: 7027 S Bennett Ave Chicago IL 60649-2007 Office Phone: 773-779-7300. Personal E-mail: phd612@aol.com.

RHONE, SYLVIA MARIE MILLER, recording industry executive; b. Phila., Mar. 11, 1952; BS in Econs. (hon.), U. Pa., 1974; Degree (hon.), Adelphi U., LHD (hon.), 1996. Comml. lending trainee Bankers Trust Co., NYC; sec. Buddha Records, 1974, nat. promotion coord., Bareback Records; regional promotions mgr. ABC Records, 1976—78, Ariola Records, 1978—79; N.E. regional promotions mgr./special markets Elektra Records, 1980—83, dir. mktg./special markets, 1983—85; dir. nat. black music promotion Atlantic Records, NYC, 1985—88, v.p., gen. mgr. black music ops., 1988—88, sr. v.p., gen. mgr. black music ops., 1988—90; CEO, co-pres. EastWest Records America, NYC, 1990—91; chmn., CEO EastWest/Atco Records, NYC, 1991—94; chair/CEO Elektra Entertainment, NYC, 1994—2004; exec. v.p. Universal Records, 2004—06; pres. Motown Records, 2004—06, Universal Motown Records, 2006—. Mem., bd. dirs. Alvin Ailey Am. Dance Theatre, The RIAA, Rock n' Roll Hall of Fame, Jazz at Lincoln Ctr., R&B Found., Studio Mus. of Harlem; bd. dirs. NARAS. Alumni trustee U. Pa., 2001—. Named an Most Influential Black Americans, Ebony mag., 2006; named one of 100 Most Powerful Women in Entertainment, Hollywood Reporter, 2006; recipient Whitney M. Young Svc. Award, Boy Scouts of Am., 1992, New Music Seminar Joel Webber Prize for Excellence in Music and Bus. award, 1993, Sony Soul of Am. Music Excellence Award, 1993, Legacy Life Mem. award, Nat. Coun. of Negro Women, 1995, Urban Network Exec. Yr. Award, 1995, Herbert H. Wright award, Nat. Assn. Market Developers, 1995, Studio Mus. Corp. award, 1996, Creative Spirit Award, Black Alumni of Pratt Inst., Echo Awards, Trumpet Awards, Turner Broadcasting, 2004. Achievements include became 1st African American and first woman chairman and CEO of a major record company, 1994. Office: Univeral Motown Records 1755 Broadway # 6 New York NY 10019 *

RHOTEN, KENNETH DALE, writer; b. Hammond, Ind., Dec. 28, 1950; s. James Edward and Helen Louise (Wasson) R.; m. Virginia Haynie (div.); m. Linda Robin Damron (div.); m. Josephine Meese (dec.). Draftsman Hahn, Inc., Evansville, Ind., 1973—75; laborer Inland Steel Works, 1975; draftsman N.W. Ind. Regional Planning Com., Highland, 1975—76; draftsman, artist graphic sys. divsn. Rockwell Internat., Cicero, Ill., 1977—78; designer Roper Outdoor Products (in cooperation with Espo Engring.), Bradley, 1978—79; draftsman Fedders Corp., Effingham, 1982—83; freelance writer, inventor, 1983—. Author, editor: Dark Twist of Fate, 1995, 3d edit., 2003, Dark Twist of Fate and Other Works, 1999; author: A Voice From Beyond, 1999, The Complete Works of Kenneth D. Rhoten, 1999, Mathematical Equivalents, 2006; composer pub. songs; patentee automatic brewing apparatus, 1984. Rep. candidate Ill. House of Reps., 1986. Achievements include successful redevelopment of the Edison storage cell and development of new secondary cell; deduced mechanism of Bessler's wheel and constructed model; development of mechanical advantage gravity motors. Home and Office: PO Box 225 Stoy IL 62464-0225

RHOTON, ALBERT LOREN, JR., neurosurgeon, educator; b. Nov. 18, 1932; s. Albert Loren and Hazel Arnette (Van Cleve) R.; m. Joyce L. Moldenhauer, June 23, 1957; children: Eric L., Albert J., Alice S., Laural A. BS, Ohio State U., 1954; MD cum laude, Washington U., St. Louis, 1959. Diplomate Am. Bd. Neurol. Surgery (bd dirs. 1985-91, vice-chmn. 1991). Intern Columbia Presbyn. Med. Ctr., NYC, 1959; resident in neurol. surgery Barnes Hosp., St. Louis, 1961-65; cons. neurol. surgery Mayo Clinic, Rochester, Minn., 1965-72; chief divsn. neurol. surgery U. Fla., Gainesville, 1972-80, R.D. Keene prof., 1980—, chmn. dept. neurol. surgery, 1980-2000, chmn. emeritus, 2000—. Developer microsurg. tng. ctr.; hon. v.p. World Congress of Neurosurgery, 2005-; hon. prof. Beijing (China) Capital U., 2005—; lectr. in field. Author: The Orbit and Sellar Region: Microsurgical Anatomy and Operative Approaches, 1996, Cranial Anatomy and Surgical Approaches, Chinese and English edits., 2003, Millenium issue Neurosurgery, 25th Anniversary issue; designed more than 200 microsurgery instruments; mem. editl. bd. Neurosurgery, Jour. Microsurgery, Surg. Neurology, Jour. Fla. Med. Assn., Am. Jour. Otology, Skull Base Surgery; contbr. articles to profl. jours. Bd. dirs. Neurosurgery Edn. and Rsch. Found. Recipient Disting. Faculty award, U. Fla., 1981, Alumni Achievement award, Washington U. Sch. Medicine, 1985, Jones award for outstanding spl. med. exhibit of yr., Am. Assn. med. Illustrators, 1969, Jameison medal, Neurosurg. soc. Australasia, 1997, Outstanding Achievement award, World Congress of Skull Base Surgery, 2000, medal of honor, World Fedn. Neurosurg. Socs., 2001, medal, Neurosurg. Soc. Am., 2001, endowed professorship named in his honor, U. Fla., Lifetime Achievement award, Wall of Fame Honoree, Honorary Alumnus award, 2001, medal of honor, Neurosurg. Soc. of Am., 2001, Bucy award, U. Chgo., 2002; grantee NIH, VA, Am. Heart Assn. Mem. ACS (bd. govs. 1978-84), AMA (Billings Bronze medal 1969), Congress Neurol. Surgeons (pres. 1978, Exceptional and Disting. Svc. award 2004, honored guest 1993, Founders Laurel award 2006), Nat. Found. Brain Rsch. (bd. dirs. 1990-94), Nat. Coalition for Rsch. in Neurol. Disorders (bd. dirs. 1990-94), Neurol. Soc. Am. (medal 2001), Internat. Congress Meningiomas (hon. pres. 2000), Neurosurg. Soc. Brazil (hon., honored guest 2004), Neurosurg. Soc. Japan (hon., Honored guest 2002), Neurosurg. Soc. Mex. (hon.), Neurosurg. Soc. Can. (hon.), Neurosurg. Soc. Uruguay (hon.), Neurosurg. Soc. Venezuela (hon.), Neurosurg. Soc. Turkey (hon.), Korean Neurol. Soc. (hon.), Neurosurg. Soc. Tex. (hon.), Neurosurg. Soc. Okla. (hon.), Neurosurg. Soc. Wis. (hon.), Neurosurg. Soc. Ga. (hon.), Neurosurg. Soc. Rocky Mountain (hon.), Neurosurg. Soc. China (hon.), Neurosurg Soc. Argentina (hon.), Latin Am. Neurosurg. Soc. (hon.), Neurosurg. Soc. Chili (hon.), Fla. Neurosurg. Soc. (pres. 1978), Am. Assn. Neurol. Surgeons (chmn. vascular sect., treas. 1983-86, v.p. 1987-88, pres. 1989-90, exec. com. 1993, Cushing medal 1998), Soc. Neurol. Surgeons (treas. 1975-81, pres. 1993), So. Neurol. Soc. (v.p. 1976), Alachua County Med. Soc. (exec. com. 1978), Fla. Med. Assn., Am. Surg. Assn., Soc. Univ. Neurosurgeons, Am. Heart Assn. (stroke coun., Outstanding Achievement award 1971), N.Am. Skull Base Soc. (pres. 1993-94, honored guest 2001, Lifetime Achievement award 2005), Am. Acad. Neurol. Surgery, Acoustic Neuroma Assn. (med. adv. bd. 1983-2000, chmn. 1992-2001, chmn. emeritus 2001—), Trigeminal Neurol. Assn. (med. advisor bd. 1992—), Hemifacial Spasm Assn. (med. adv. bd. 2002—), Internat. Interdisciplinary Congress on Craniofacial and Skull Base Surgery (pres. 1996-97), Internat. Soc. Neurosurg. Tech. and Instrument Invention (pres. 1997—), Japanese Skull Base Soc. (hon. pres. 2000), Internat. Soc. for Microsurgery Anatomy (hon. pres. 2002, 04), World Fedn. Neurosurg. Soc. (hon. v.p. 2005—) Achievements include fundraising for 11 endowed chairs at University of Florida. Home: 2505 NW 22d Ave Gainesville FL 32605-3819 Office: U Fla Dept Neurosurgery PO Box 100265 100 S Newell Dr Gainesville FL 32610 Office Phone: 352-273-7788. Business E-Mail: rhoton@neurosurgery.ufl.edu.

RHUE, MONIKA RIVERA, archivist; d. Ernest and Gloria Williams, Roy Payne; m. Stephen Eric Short, July 12, 2003. MLIS, U. NC, Greensboro, 2002. Monika R. Rhue NC Pub. Libr. Bd., 2004. Libr. asst. II Pub. Libr. Charlotte Mecklenburg County, 1995—99; archivist Johnson C. Smith U., Charlotte, 1999—. CEO Preserve Pro, Inc., Charlotte, 2005—; adv. bd. mem. NC Exploring Cultural Heritage Online, Raleigh; exec. bd. mem. Charlotte Black Heritage Grp. Recipient Rsch. grant, Arts & Sci. Emerging Artist, 1993. Mem.: ALA, Afro-Am. Hist. and Geneal. Soc., Soc. NC Archivists (program chair, pres. 2005—07). D-Conservative. Pan African. Avocations: dance, writing. Home: 7419 Balancing Rock Ct Charlotte NC 28262 Office: Johnson C Smith Univ 100 Beatties Ford Rd Charlotte NC 28216 Office Fax: 704-378-3524. Business E-Mail: mrhue@jcsu.edu.

RHYNE, JAMES JENNINGS, condensed matter physicist; b. Oklahoma City, Nov. 14, 1938; s. Jennings Jefferson and Clyde Margaret (Russell) R.; m. Susan Margaret Watson, May 26, 1990; children: Nancy Marie, Edward Paxton. BS in Physics, U. Okla., 1959; MS in Physics, U. Ill., 1961; PhD in Physics, Iowa State U., 1965. Rsch. scientist Naval Ordnance Lab., White Oak, Md., 1965-75; rsch. physicist Nat. Inst. of Stds. and Tech., Gaithersburg, Md., 1975-90; prof. physics U. Mo., Columbia, 1991—2003, dir. Rsch. Reactor Ctr., 1991-96; dep. group leader Lujan Ctr., Los Alamos Nat. Lab., 2003—. Adv. editor Jour. of Magnetism and Mag. Materials, 1990—; editl. bd. Jour. Applied Physics, 1986-89; co-editor procs. Fellow: Neutron Scattering Soc. Am. (pres. 1999—2002), Am. Phys. Soc. Home Phone: 505-661-8629; Office Phone: 505-665-0071. Personal E-mail: jrhyne@los-alamos.net. Business E-Mail: rhyne@lanl.gov.

RHYNE, SIDNEY WHITE, retired lawyer; b. Charlotte, NC, Apr. 2, 1931; s. Sidney White and Ruth (Dry) R.; m. Rosemarie Kennedy, July 11, 1959; children: Patricia Ruth, Kendall Sidney, Randall Sylvanus. AB, Roanoke Coll., 1952; LLB, U. Pa., 1955; LLM, Georgetown U., 1961. Bar: Pa. 1955, D.C. 1957, U.S. Supreme Ct. 1959, Md. 1987. Assoc. Rhyne, Mullin, Connor and Rhyne, Washington, 1957—60; mem. Mullin, Rhyne, Emmons and Topel, Washington, 1961—97; individual practice law Washington, 1997—2005; ret., 2005. Lectr. law ctr. Georgetown U., Washington, 1964-70. Trustee Luth. Theol. Sem. at Phila., 1988-93, pres. coun., 1993—. With U.S. Army, 1955-57. Prettyman fellow Georgetown U., 1960-61. Fellow Am. Bar Found. (life); mem. ABA (house of dels. 1972-73, 75, 76-78, 98-2001), Bar Assn. D.C. (bd. dirs. 1969-73, 92-94, 98-02, trustee Found., v.p. 1990-91, presdl. award 2000-01), Fed. Comm. Bar Assn. (exec. com. 1988-96, treas. 1991-92, Disting. Svc. award 1992, pres. 1994-95), Legal Aid Soc. of D.C. (pres. 1976-78, trustee, 1968-80, pres. coun., 1991—, 75th anniversary Servant of Justice award 2007). Independent. Lutheran. Home Phone: 202-244-6248; Office Phone: 202-244-6248. Business E-Mail: swrhyne@abanet.org.

RHYS-MEYERS, JONATHAN, actor; b. Dublin, July 27, 1977; Actor: (films) A Man of No Importance, 1994, Michael Collins, 1996, Lengua asesina, La, 1996, The Disappearance of Finbar, 1996, The Maker, 1997, Telling Lies in America, 1997, Velvet Goldmine, 1998, The Governess, 1998, B. Monkey, 1998, The Loss of Sexual Innocence, 1999, Ride with the Devil, 1999, Titus, 1999, Happy Now, 2001, Prozac Nation, 2001, Tangled, 2001, Bend It Like Beckham, 2002, The Tesseract, 2003, Octane, 2003, I'll Sleep When I'm Dead, 2003, The Emperor's Wife, 2003, Vanity Fair, 2004, Alexander, 2004, Match Point, 2005; (TV films) Samson and Delilah, 1996, The Tribe, 1998, The Lion in Winter, 2003; (TV miniseries) Gormenghast, 2000, Elvis, 2005 (Golden Globe award for Best Actor in a Mini-Series or Motion Picture Made for TV, Hollywood Fgn. Press, 2006). Office: c/o United Talent Agency, Inc 9560 Wilshire Blvd Beverly Hills CA 90212

RIALL, TAYLOR SOHN, surgeon, researcher; b. Edison, NJ, Aug. 16, 1971; d. Richard Steven and Alexsandra Sohn; m. Charles Cole Riall, June 5, 2004. BA, Rutgers U., New Brunswick, NJ, 1992; MD, Johns Hopkins U., Balt., 1996. Cert. gen. surgery Am. Bd. Surgery, 2005. Intern, resident Johns Hopkins U., Balt., 1996—2004, instr., 2004—05; asst. prof. U. Tex. Med. Br., Galveston, 2005—. Rsch. fellow Johns Hopkins U., Balt., 1999—2004. Contbr. articles to profl. jours. Recipient Upjohn Clin. Rsch. award, Johns Hopkins U., 1998, 1999, 2000, A. McGehee Harvey Rsch. award, Johns Hopkins U. Sch. Medicine, 2002, Outstanding Tchr. Yr., U. Tex. Med. Br., 2005—06; scholar, Rutgers U. Douglas Campus, 1989—92, Barry M. Goldwater Scholarship and Excellence in Edn. Found., 1991—92; Disting. scholar, State NJ., 1989—92, Rsch. grant, Niarchos Found., 1999—2002. Fellow: ACS; mem.: Am. Cancer Soc. (Rsch. grant 2006), Soc. U. Surgeons (Wyeth Clin. scholar 2007—), Am. Geriatric Soc. (Dennis W. Jahnigen Clin. Scholars Career Devel. award 2007—), Am. Assn. Cancer Rsch., Assn. Acad. Surgeons, Am. Hepato-Pancreato-Biliary Assn. (Rsch. award 2000), Soc. Surgery of Alimentary Tract, Pancreas Club, Phi Beta Kappa (life), Alpha Omega Alpha (life). Achievements include research in defining the management of periampullary adenocarcinoma/pancreatic adencarcinoma; defining the surgical managment of intraductal papillary mucinous neoplasms of the pancreas. Avocations: ballroom dancing, running, golf, swimming, diving. Office: Univ Tex Med Br 301 University Blvd Galveston TX 77555-0542 Office Phone: 409-772-1846. Office Fax: 409-747-2253. Business E-Mail: tsriall@utmb.edu.

RIASANOVSKY, NICHOLAS VALENTINE, retired historian, educator; b. Harbin, China, Dec. 21, 1923; arrived in U.S., 1938, naturalized, 1943; m. Arlene Ruth Schlegel, Feb. 15, 1955; children: John, Nicholas, Maria. BA, U. Oreg., 1942; AM, Harvard U., 1947; DPhil, Oxford U., Eng., 1949. Mem. faculty U. Iowa, 1949-57, U. Calif., Berkeley, 1957—, prof. history, 1961—, Sidney Hellman Ehrman prof. European history, 1969—2003, ret., 2003. Vis. rsch. prof. USSR Acad. Scis., Moscow, 1969, Moscow and Leningrad, 1974, 79. Author: Russia and the West in the Teaching of the Slavophiles: A Study of Romantic Ideology, 1952, Nicholas I and Official Nationality in Russia, 1825-1855, 1959, A History of Russia, 1963, 7th edit. (with Prof. Mark Steinberg), 2005, The Teaching of Charles Fourier, 1969, A Parting of Ways: Government and the Educated Public in Russia, 1801-1855, 1976, The Image of Peter the Great in Russian History and Thought, 1985, The Emergence of Romanticism, 1992, Collected Writings 1947-94, 1993, Russian Identities, a Historical Survey, 2005; co-editor: California Slavic Studies, 1960—; editl. bd.

Russian rev., Zarubezhnaia Periodicheskaia Pechat' na Russkom Iazyke, Simvol; contbr. articles to profl. jours. Trustee Nat. Coun. Soviet and East European Rsch., 1978—82; mem. Kennan Inst. Acad. Coun., 1986—89. 2d lt. AUS, 1943—46. Decorated Bronze Star; recipient Silver medal Commonwealth Club Calif., 1964; Rhodes scholar, 1947-49; Fulbright grantee, 1954-55, 74, 79; Guggenheim fellow, 1969; sr. fellow NEH, 1975; Fulbright sr. scholar, sr. fellow Ctr. Advanced Studies in Behavioral Scis., 1984-85; sr. fellow Woodrow Wilson Internat. Ctr. for Scholars, 1989-90. Mem. Am. Assn. Advancement Slavic Studies (pres. 1973-76, Disting. Contbr. award 1993), Am. Hist. Assn. (award for Scholarly Distinction 1995), Am. Acad. Arts and Scis.

RIBA, SHIRLEY, artist; d. Arthur Roy and Idell Carolina Riba. BFA, Calif. Coll. Arts and Crafts, Oakland, 1977. Sales/dept. display Gumps Oriental Antique Dept., San Francisco, 1979—90; owner ARTRIBA, Laporte, Colo., 1995—. Exhibitions include Corcoran Sch. Art, Washington, D.C., 1977—78, Calif. Coll. of Arts & Crafts, San Francisco, 1977, E.B. Crocker Kingsley, Sacramento, 1979, Gump's Gallery, San Francisco, 1979—90, 1981, 1986, Represented in permanent collections Bohemian Found., Calif., prin. works include Mural After Parrish, 2002, represented in pvt. collections. Home: PO Box 800 Laporte CO 80535 Office Phone: 970-221-2023.

RIBARY, URS, neuroscientist, educator; b. Lucerne, Switzerland, Nov. 24, 1955; came to U.S., 1988; m. Evelyne Dahinden, July 11, 1986; 1 child, Samanta R. MS, Swiss Fed. Inst. Tech., Zurich, 1981, DSc, 1985. Rsch. asst. prof. NYU Med. Ctr., NYC, 1988—93, dir. ctr. neuromagnetism, 1989—2005, assoc. prof., 1993—2007; prof. Simon Fraser U., Vancouver, BC, Canada, 2007—. Vis. asst. prof. Simon Fraser U., Can., 1986-88; endowed leadership chair Cognitive Neurosci. Childhood Health and Devel., BC, Can., 2007-. Cons. (Time Life series) The Brain, 1990; contbr. articles to profl. jours. Co-founder, chmn. Samanta S. Ribary Found. Inc. Mem. AAAS, Am. Soc. Neurosci., N.Y. Acad. Scis., European Neurosci. Assn., Soc. Cognitive Neuroscience. Achievements include rsch. on using functional brain imaging techniques, to study quantal sequences of dynamic network connectivity in humans during normal cognitive processing, and its alterations in neurological and neuropsychiatric patients. Home: 1068 Sugar Mountain Way Anmore BC V3H 4Y7 Canada Business E-Mail: urs.ribary@med.nyu.edu.

RIBBANS, GEOFFREY WILFRID, language educator; b. London, Apr. 15, 1927; came to U.S. 1978; s. Wilfrid Henry and Rose Matilda (Burton)R.; m. Magdalena Willmann, Apr. 21, 1956; children: Madeleine Elizabeth, Helen Margaret, Peter John. BA with 1st class hons., Kings Coll., U. London, 1948, MA, 1953. Asst. lectr. U. Sheffield, Eng., 1954-56, lectr., 1956-61, sr. lectr. Spanish, 1961-63; Gilmour prof. Spanish U. Liverpool, Eng., 1963-78; vis. Mellon prof. Spanish U. Pitts., 1970-71; Wm. R. Kenan Jr. U. prof. Spanish Brown U., Providence, 1978-99, chmn. dept., 1981-84, prof. emeritus, 1999—. Editor Bull. Hispanic Studies, 1964-78; vis. prof. U. Salamanca, Spain, 1995. Author: Catalunya i Valencia al Segle XVIII, 1955, 2d edit., 1993, Niebla y Soledad: Aspectos de Unamuno y Machado, 1971, Galdós: Fortunata y Jacinta, 1977, Spanish transl., 1988; editor: Antonio Machado, Soledades, Galerias, Otros Poemas, 1984, rev. 16th edit., 2000, Campos de Castilla, 1989, 14th edit., 2003, History and Fiction in Galdós's Narratives, 1993, 2d edit., 1995, Conflicts and Conciliations: The Evolution of Galdós's "Fortunata y Jacinta", 1997. Decorated La Encomienda de la Orden de Isabel la Catolica Spain; recipient prize for excellence in Galdos studies, Las Palmas, 1997, Batista i Roca prize, Barcelona, 2000; Hispanic studies in his honour, Liverpool, 1992, Symposium on Modernism and Modernity in his honor, Brown U., 1998. Mem. MLA, Internat. Assn. Hispanists (v.p. 1974-80), Internat. Assn. Galdós Scholars (pres. 1988-89), N.Am. Catalan Soc. (hon.). Office: Brown U Dept Hispanic Studies PO Box 1961 Providence RI 02912-1961 Business E-Mail: Geoffrey_ribbans@brown.edu.

RIBBLE, JOHN CHARLES, medical educator; b. Paris, Tex., July 26, 1931; s. Elbert Alfred and Dorothy (Pyeatt) R.; m. Anne Blythe Hoerner; 1 stepchild Helen Blythe Strate Kielty. MD, U. Tex., 1955. Diplomate Am. Bd. Internal Medicine. Asst. prof. medicine Cornell U., NYC, 1962-66, assoc. prof. pediatrics, 1966-78, assoc. dean, 1974-78, Med. Sch., U. Tex., Houston, 1978-86, dean, 1986-95; vis. scholar The Health Inst. New Eng. Med. Ctr., Boston, 1995-96; prof. medicine U. Tex., Houston, 1996—. Mem. Nat. Adv. Coun. Gen. Med. Scis. NIH, Bethesda, Md., 1988-91. Episcopalian. Home: 6200 Willers Way Houston TX 77057-2808 Office: U Tex Med Sch 6431 Fannin St Houston TX 77030-1501 Office Phone: 713-500-6709. E-mail: jribble@houston.rr.com.

RIBBLE, RONALD GEORGE, psychologist, educator, writer, behavioral consultant; b. West Reading, Pa., May 7, 1937; s. Jeremiah George and Mildred Sarah (Folk) Ribble; m. Catalina Valenzuela Torres, Sept. 30, 1961; children: Christina, Timothy, Kenneth. BSEE cum laude, U. Mo., 1968, MSEE, 1969, MA, 1985, PhD, 1986. Bd. cert. forensic examiner, diplomate in behavioral sci. Am. Bd. Psychol. Spltys., Am. Coll. Forensic Examiners; cert. in homeland security. Enlisted USAF, 1956-60, advance through grades to lt. col., 1976—81; rsch. dir. Coping Resources, Inc., Columbia, Mo., 1986; pres., co-owner Towers and Rushing Ltd. (Pubs. and Psychol. Cons., Troubadour 1997-2001), San Antonio, 1986—; referral devel. Laughlin Pavilion Psychiat. Hosp., Kirksville, Mo., 1987; program dir. Psychiat. Insts. of Am., Iowa Falls, Iowa, 1987-88; lead psychotherapist Gasconade County Counseling Ctr., Hermann, Mo., 1988; sr. lectr. U. Tex., San Antonio, 1989—2002; lectr. Trinity U., San Antonio, 1995-96; assessment clinician Afton Oaks Psychiat. Hosp., San Antonio, 1989-91; ret. from tchg., 2002. Faculty cons. Edn. Testing Svc., 1997; psychologist Olmos Psychol. Svcs., Inc., San Antonio, 1991—93; vol. assessor Holmgreen Children's Shelter, San Antonio, 1992—93; founder Ruth Bohn Weissman Scholarship in Creative Writing U. Tex., San Antonio, 1994—2004; co-sponsor Lyric Recovery Festival, Carnegie Hall, 2000; condr. seminars, revs. for maj. publs.; founding mem. U. Mo.-Columbia Bd. Psychology Leaders, 2007. Author: (book) Apples, Weeds, and Doggie Poo, 1995, Dont' Eat the Snake!, 1999; contbr. essays to psychol. refernce books, poetry to anthologies periodicals, lyrics to popular music; interviewer: celebrities in performing and lit. arts, 1995—, columnist: Feelings, 1993—97; pub. access TV appearances, 1991—. Founding cabinet mem. World Peace and Diplomacy Forum; vol. announcer pub. radio sta., Colombia, 1993; vol. Cath. Family and Children's Svc., San Antonio, 1989—91; chpt. advisor Rational Recovery Program for Alcoholics, San Antonio, 1991—92; mem. Pres. Leadership Cir., 1994—2002; contbg. mem. Dem. Nat. Com., 1983—, Presdl. Congl. Task Force, 1994; del. Boone County (Mo.) Dem. Conv., 1984. Recipient Roberts Meml. prize in Poetry, 1995, DaVinci Diamond award, 2004, Internat. Peace prize, United Cultural Conv., U.S.A., 2002, Am. medal Hon., 2004. Fellow: Am. Coll. Forensic Examiners; mem.: ACLU, USN Inst., Internat. Found. for Protection Officers, Internat. Soc. Genetic Genealogists, MENSA, Am. Psychol. Soc., World Affairs Coun. San Antonio, London Diplomatic Acad., Academic Coun., Internat. Soc. Polit. Psychology, Human Behavior and Evolution Soc., Acad. Polit. Sci., Soc. for the Psychol. Study of Social Issues, The Jefferson Coun. (founder, dir. 2002), Physicians for Social Responsibility (leadership cir.), So. Poverty Law Ctr. (leadership coun. for tchg. tolerance), Soc. Profl. Journalists, Interfaith Alliance, Mil. Officers Assn., Air Force Assn., Internat. Platform Assn. (Poetry award 1995). Independent. Deist. Avocations: running and fitness, poetry, singing, public speaking. Home: 14023 N Hills Village Dr San Antonio TX 78249-2534 Address: Towers and Rushing Ltd San Antonio TX 78249 Office Phone: 210-558-1393. Business E-Mail: ronribble@usa.net.

RIBLEY-BORCK, JOAN GRACE, medical/surgical rehabiliation nurse; b. Schenectady, NY, Jan. 5, 1939; d. Harry Jacob and Lillian Josephine (Cheney) Ribley; m. Walter Carl Borck Jr., Oct. 24, 1964; 1 child, Constance Maria. Diploma, Ellis Hosp. Sch. Nursing, Schenectady, 1960; BSN, Russell Sage Coll., Troy, NY, 1981. RN, NY. Staff nurse operating room Columbia Meml. Hosp., Hudson, NY, 1960-63, staff nurse rusk rehab., 1963-64; staff nurse cardiovascular operating room U. Md. Hosp., Balt., 1965-66; staff nurse, evening charge nurse St. Peters Hosp., Albany, NY, 1968-89; substitute staff nurse Wildwood Program, Schenectady, NY, 1989-96, 2001—02, 2002—03; staff nurse Apria Health Care (formerly Homedco Home Care), 1984—; substitute staff, nurse South Colonie Ctrl. Sch., 1996—; staff nurse Gentiva Health Svcs., Schenectady, 2006—. Ind. provider in nursing Medicaid Mgmt. Info. Sys, NY, 2004—. Mem. ANA, NY State Nurses Assn., Albany Coun. Cath. Nurses. Roman Catholic. Home: PO Box 11214 2 Charming Ln Loudonville NY 12211-1818 E-mail: jborck@nycap.rr.com.

RIBMAN, JAMES W., lawyer; b. NYC, Jan. 17, 1970; BS, Georgetown U., 1992; JD, U. Houston Law Ctr., 1996. Bar: Tex. 1996, US Dist. Ct. (no. and so. dists. Tex.). Atty., dir. Dallas office Looper, Reed & McGraw, P.C. Named a Rising Star, Tex. Super Lawyers mag., 2006. Mem.: Dallas Bar Assn. Office: Looper Reed & McGraw 4100 Thanksgiving Tower 1601 Elm St Dallas TX 75201 Office Phone: 214-237-6349. E-mail: jribman@lrmlaw.com.

RIBONSON-SMITH, SONIA ANTHONETTE, counselor, mental health services professional; d. Allen Anthony and Violet Hawkins Robinson; m. Llewellyn W. Smith, July 23, 1983; children: Ashley Smith-Bigson, Ashton Avery Smith. BA in Sociology, So. U., New Orleans, 1976; MA in Guidance Counseling, Xavier U., New Orleans, 1993. Counseling supr. New Orleans Job Corps; guidance counselor Delgado C.C., New Orleans; case mgr. United Meth. Recovery Ctr., New Orleans; case worker Ctrl. City Mental Health Clinic, New Orleans. Usher Thomas United Meth. Ch., Kenner, La.

RICAPITO, JOSEPH VIRGIL (GIUSEPPE RICAPITO), literature educator; b. Giovinazzo, Bari, Italy, Oct. 30, 1933; came to U.S., 1935; s. Frank and Filomena (Cervone) R.; m. Carolyn Sue Kitchen, Apr. 7, 1958; children: Frank Peyton, Maria Avadna. BA, CUNY, Bklyn., 1955; MA, U. Iowa, Iowa City, 1956; PhD in Romance Langs., U. Calif., LA, 1966. From instr. to asst. prof. Pomona Coll., Claremont, Calif., 1962-70; from assoc. prof. to prof. Ind. U., Bloomington, Ind., 1970-80; prof. La. State U., Baton Rouge, 1980—, chmn. dept., 1980-85, Joseph Yenni disting. prof. Italian studies, 1999. Author: Bibliografia Razonada y anotada, 1980; editor: La Vida de Laz de Tormes, 1976; translator: Dialogue of Mercury and Charon, 1986, Cervantes's Novelas ejemplares: Between History and Creativity, 1996. Pres. Greater Baton Rouge Am.-Italian Assn., 1984-85. With U.S. Army, 1957-59. Grantee NEH, 1981; named Knight Order of Merit, Republic of Italy, 1988, Knight Order of Queen Isabel, Govt. of Spain, 1990; named Disting. Rsch. Master La. State U., 2001, Cervantes Lectr., Fordham U., 2004. Mem. MLA, Renaissance Soc. Am., Am. Comparative Lit. Assn., Am. Assn. Tchrs. Spanish and Portuguese, Cervantes Soc. Am. Avocations: music, photography, films. Office: La State U 309 Hodges Hall Baton Rouge LA 70803-0001 Home Phone: 225-769-2762; Office Phone: 225-578-6616. Business E-Mail: ricapito@lsu.edu.

RICARD, JOHN H., bishop, educator; b. Baton Rouge, Feb. 29, 1940; s. Maceo and Albanie (St. Amant) R. BA, St. Joseph Sem., 1962, MA, 1968; MS, Tulane U., 1970; D, Cath. U. Am., Washington, DC, 1984. Ordained priest Roman Cath. Ch., 1968. Pastor Holy Redeemer Ch., Washington, 1972—75, Holy Comforter Ch., Washington, 1975—84; ordained titular bishop of Rucuma, 1984; aux. bishop Balt., 1984—97; assoc. prof. Cath. U. Am., Washington, 1973—; bishop of Pensacola-Tallahassee Fla., 1997—. Mem. priest's senate Archdiocese of Washington, 1974—, mem. sch. bd., 1976—. Pres. Cath. Relief Svcs. USCC, 1995—, chair, 1995—2002; mem. Pontifical Coun., COR UNUM, 1996—; Chmn. Com. on Social Devel. and World Peace, Domestic Social Devel., 1992—95. Mem.: Secretariat of Black Caths. Office: 11 N B St Pensacola FL 32501

RICARDO-CAMPBELL, RITA, economist, educator; b. Boston, Mar. 16, 1920; d. David and Elizabeth (Jones) Ricardo; m. Wesley Glenn Campbell, Sept. 15, 1946; children: Barbara Lee, Diane Rita, Nancy Elizabeth. BS, Simmons Coll., 1941; MA, Harvard U., 1945, PhD, 1946. Instr. Harvard U., Cambridge, Mass., 1946—48; asst. prof. Tufts U., Medford, Mass., 1948—51; labor economist U.S. Wage Stabilization Bd., 1951—53; economist Ways and Means Com. U.S. Ho. of Reps., 1954; economist, 1957—60; prof. San Jose (Calif.) State U., 1960—61; sr. fellow Hoover Instn. on War, Revolution, and Peace, Stanford, Calif., 1968—95, sr. fellow emerita, 1995—. Lectr. health Stanford U. Med. Sch., 1973—78; bd. dirs. Watkins-Johnson Co., Palo Alto, Calif., Gillette Co., Boston; mgmt. bd. Samaritan Med. Ctr., San Jose. Author: Voluntary Health Insurance in the U.S., 1960, Economics of Health and Public Policy, 1971, Food Safety Regulation: Use and Limitations of Cost-Benefit Analysis, 1974, Drug Lag: Federal Government Decision Making, 1976, Social Security: Promise and Reality, 1977, The Economics and Politics of Health, 1982, 2d edit., 1985, Resisting Hostile Takeovers: The Case of Gillette, 1997, Chinese transl., 2004; co-editor: Below-Replacement Fertility in Industrial Societies, 1987, Issues in Contemporary Retirement, 1988; contbr. articles to profl. jours. Mem. Western Interstate Commn. for Higher Edn. Calif., 1967-75, chmn., 1970-71; mem. Pres. Nixon's Adv. Coun. on Status of Women, 1969-76; mem. Pres. Ford's Adv. Coun. on Status of Women, 1976-79; mem. task force on taxation Pres.'s Coun. on Environ. Quality, 1970-72; mem. Pres.'s Com. Health Svcs. Industry, 1971-73, FDA Nat. Adv. Drug Com., 1972-75; mem. Pres. Reagan's Econ. Policy Adv. Bd., 1981-90, Pres. Reagan's Nat. Coun. on Humanities, 1982-89, Pres. Reagan's Nat. Medal of Sci. com., 1988-91, Pres. Bush's Nat. Medal of Sci. com., 1991-94; bd. dirs. Ind. Colls. No. Calif., 1971-87; mem. com. assessment of safety, benefits, risks Citizens Commn. Sci., Law and Food, Rockefeller U., 1973-75; mem. adv. com. Ctr. Health Policy Rsch., Am. Enterprise Inst. Pub. Policy Rsch., Washington, 1974-80; mem. adv. coun. on social security Quadrennial Health and Human Svcs., 1974-75; bd. dirs. Simmons Coll. Corp., Boston, 1975-80; mem. adv. coun. bd. assocs. Stanford Librs., 1975-78; mem. coun. SRI Internat., Menlo Park, Calif., 1977-90. Mem. Am. Econ. Assn., Mont Pelerin Soc. (bd. dirs. 1988-92, v.p. 1992-94), Harvard Grad. Soc. (coun. 1991-94), Phi Beta Kappa. Home: Classic Residence Hyatt 620 Sand Hill Rd Apt 308D Palo Alto CA 94304 Office: Stanford U Hoover Instn Stanford CA 94305-6010 Personal E-mail: rricardocampbell@sbcglobal.net.

RICCA, GREGORY J., broadcast executive, management consultant; BA, George Washington U., 1970; JD, U. Calif. Hastings Coll. Law, 1973. Bar: Calif., NY. Assoc. Fulop & Hardee, NYC, 1976—77; assoc. gen. counsel Ednl. Broadcasting Corp., NYC, 1973—76, Madison Sq. Garden Corp., NYC, 1977—81; chief legal counsel Westinghouse Broadcasting & Cable, NYC, 1981—82; assoc. gen. counsel Viacom Internat., NYC, 1982—86; exec. v.p. & gen. counsel Viacom Networks/MTV, 1986—94; exec. v.p. MTV Networks, 1994—96, MTV Networks US, 1994—2003; COO MTV Networks Internat., 1996—2003; pres. & CEO Discovery Networks Internat., 2007—. Office: 450 Park Ave Ste 2100 New York NY 10022 also: 1140 Ave of the Americas Ste 1700 New York NY 10036 *

RICCARDI, VINCENT MICHAEL, pediatrician, educator, entrepreneur; b. Bklyn., Oct. 14, 1940; s. Gabriel John and Frances Mary (Novak) R.; m. Susan Leona Bogda, July 27, 1967; children: Angela M., Ursula M., Mikah F. AB, UCLA, 1962; MD, Georgetown U., 1966; MBA, U. LaVerne, 1993. Intern, resident in medicine U. Pitts., 1966-68; fellow in genetics Harvard Med. Sch., Boston, 1968-70, 72; asst. prof. medicine U. Colo. Med. Ctr., Denver, 1973-75; assoc. prof. medicine, pediatrics Med. Coll. Wis., Milw., 1975-77; prof. medicine, pediatrics Baylor Coll. Medicine, Houston, 1977-90; med. dir. The Genetics Inst., Pasadena, Calif., 1990-92; clin. prof. pediatrics UCLA, 1991—; founder, CEO Am. Med. Consumers, La Crescenta, 1992. Dir. The Neurofibromatosis Inst., La Crescenta, Calif., 1985—. Author: Genetic Approach to Human Disease, 1977, Communication and Counseling in Health Care, 1983, Neurofibromatosis, 1986, rev. edit., 1992, 99. Maj. U.S. Army, 1970-71. Fellow ACP, AAAS, Am. Coll. Med. Genetics; mem. Am. Soc. Human Genetics, Am. Coll. Physician Execs. Avocations: creative writing, acting. Office: Am Med Consumers 5415 Briggs Ave La Crescenta CA 91214-2205 Home Phone: 818-957-4926; Office Phone: 818-957-3508. Business E-Mail: riccardi@medcomsumer.com.

RICCARDS, MICHAEL PATRICK, academic administrator; b. Hillside, NJ, Oct. 2, 1944; s. Patrick and Margaret (Finelli) Riccards; m. Barbara Dunlop, June 6, 1970; children: Patrick, Catherine, Abigail. BA, Rutgers U., 1966, MA, 1967, MPhil, 1969, PhD, 1970. Spl. asst. to chancellor Dept. Higher Edn., Trenton, NJ, 1969-70; from asst. prof. to assoc. prof. SUNY, Buffalo, 1970-77; dean U. Mass., Boston, 1977-82; provost Hunter Coll. CUNY, NY, 1982—83, prof., 1982-86; pres. St. John's Coll., Santa Fe, 1986-89, Shepherd Coll., Shepherdstown, W.Va., 1989-95, Fitchburg State Coll., Mass., 1995—2002; pub. policy scholar-in-residence Coll. Bd., Washington, 2002—05; exec. dir. Hall Inst. Pub. Policy, Trenton, NJ, 2005—. Mem. joint commn. tchr. preparation, 1999—2000. Author: (book) The Making of the American Citizenry, 1973, A Republic, If You Can Keep It, 1987, The Ferocious Engine of Democracy, 2 vols., 1995, 2002, Vicars of Christ, 1998, The Presidency and the Middle Kingdom, 2000, The Odes of DiMaggio, 2001, The Papacy and the End of Christendom, 2003, The Myth of American Miseducation, 2005, The State of the Garden State, 2006. Chmn. N.Mex. Endowment Humanities, 1989; trustee Albuquerque Acad.; mem. Coun. Humanities W.Va., Nat. Skills Stds. Bd., 1993—98; mem. nat. adv. com. Ctr. Study Presidency, 1987—89. Fulbright fellow, 1973, Huntington Libr. fellow, 1974, NEH fellow, Princeton U., 1976—77. Home: 32 Kingston Blvd Hamilton NJ 08690 Office: Hall Inst Pub Policy 130 W State St Trenton NJ 08630

RICCI, CHRISTINA, actress; b. Santa Monica, Calif., Feb. 12, 1980; Appeared in films Mermaids, 1990, The Hard Way, 1991, The Addams Family, 1991, The Cemetery Club, 1993, Addams Family Values, 1993, Casper, 1995, Now and Then, 1995, Gold Diggers: The Secret of Bear Mountain, 1995, Bastard Out of Carolina, 1996, The Last of the High Kings, 1996, That Darn Cat, 1996, Ice Storm, 1997, Little Red Riding Hood, 1997, Souvenir (voice) 1998, Pecker, 1999, I Woke Up Early When I Died, 1998, Fear and Loathing in Las Vegas, 1998, Desert Blue, 1998, Buffalo 66, 1998, The Opposite of Sex, 1998, Small Soldiers (voice only), 1998, Souvenir (voice only), 1998, 200 Cigarettes, 1999, No Vacancy, 1999, Sleepy Hollow, 1999, Bless the Child, 2000, The Man Who Cried, 2000, All Over the Guy, 2001, Prozac Nation (also co-prodr.), 2001, The Laramie Project, 2002, Pumpkin (also prodr.), 2002, Miranda, 2002, The Gathering, 2002, Anything Else, 2003, I Love Your Work, 2003, Monster, 2003, Cursed, 2005, Penelope, 2006, Black Snake Moan, 2006, Home of the Brave, 2006; TV appearances include H.E.L.P., 1990, The Simpsons (voice only), 1996, Ally McBeal, 2002, Malcolm in the Middle, 2002, Joey, 2005, Grey's Anatomy, 2006. Office: ICM 8942 Wilshire Blvd Beverly Hills CA 90211-1934 *

RICCI, LISA A., geneticist, researcher; b. Ft. Wayne, Ind., Oct. 21, 1980; d. William J. and Nancy A. Ricci. BS in Biology, Ind. U., Bloomington, 2003; MFS, The George Wash. U., Wash., 2005. Lab. asst. Foster Microbiology Lab., Bloomington, 2001—03; rsch. contractor US Secret Svc., Washington, 2003—04; dna analyst ii Bode Tech., Lorton, Va., 2005—. Fundraiser Food & Friends, Washington, 2005; docent Corcoran Gallery Art, Washington, 2006. Fernandus & Elizabeth Payne scholarship, Ind. U. Dept. Biology, 2002. Mem.: Am. Acad. Forensic Scis. (assoc.), Internat. Assn. Identification (assoc.), Kappa Delta Sorority (life; v.p. membership 2002—03, named Outstanding Pledge 2000). Independent. Roman Catholic. Avocations: bicycling, running, travel. Office: Bode Technology 10430 Furnace Rd Ste 107 Lorton VA 22079 Home Phone: 260-413-1580; Office Phone: 703-646-9785. Personal E-mail: lisa.a.ricci@gmail.com. Business E-Mail: lisa.ricci@bodetech.com.

RICCIARDI, J.P., professional sports team executive; m. Diane Ricciardi; 2 children. Baseball coach minor league N.Y. Yankees, 1982—84, Milw. (Minn.) Brewers, 1985; from scout to dir. player pers. Oakland (Calif.) Athletics, 1986—99, dir. player pers., 1999—2001; sr. v.p. Toronto (Can.) Blue Jays, 2001—, gen. mgr., 2001—. Office: 1 Blue Jays Way Ste 3200 Toronto ON Canada M5V 1J1

RICCIARDI, LOUIS MICHAEL, brokerage house executive; b. Worcester, Mass., 1959; s. Michael Joseph and Mary Theresa Ricciardi; m. Cynthia Anne Booth. BA, Bridgewater State Coll., 1981. Account exec. Shearson/Am. Express, Brockton, Mass., 1981-83; v.p. Thomson McKinnon, Taunton, Mass., 1983-87; sr. v.p. Morgan Stanley Dean Witter, Taunton, Mass., 1988—2002, UBS Paine Webber, Taunton, 2002—. Bd. corporators Bristol County Savs. Bank, Taunton, Mass., 1985—, bd. trustees, 1992—; trustee Taunton Devel. Corp., 1994—, v.p., treas. 1995—. Weekly investment columnist, 1983-2004. Bd. corporators Morton Hosp., Taunton, 1987—, trustee, 1994—, treas., 2002—; pres. Heart of Taunton (Mass.) Revitalization Corp., 1988-89, 2004—; trustee Bridgewater (Mass.) State Coll., 1989-99, 2004—, chmn. 1990-94, 2006—; trustee Bridgewater Found., 1989—, chmn. 1996-2004; bd. dirs. Taunton Boys & Girls Club, 1999—. Recipient Rondileau award for Outstanding Profl. Achievement and Cmty. Svc., 1999, Disting. Svc. award Bridgewater State Coll., 2002, Good Scout award Boy Scouts Am., 2003. Mem. Taunton Rotary Club (Paul Harris fellow 2000, pres. 1991-92), Bridgewater Coll. Alumni Assn. (treas. 1992-95). Avocations: guitar, coin collecting/numismatics, baseball, community service, Coca Cola Memorabilia. Home: PO Box 228 Taunton MA 02780-0228 Home Phone: 866-528-6528.

RICCIARDI, SALVATORE, wholesale distribution executive; Pres., CEO Purity Wholesale Grocers, Boca Raton, Fla. Office: Purity Wholesale Grocers Ste 100 5400 Broken Sound Blvd NW Boca Raton FL 33487-3511

RICCIARDONE, FRANCIS JOSEPH, JR., ambassador; b. Boston; m. Marie Dunn Ricciardone; 2 children. BS summa cum laude, Dartmouth Coll., 1973. Tchr., Iran, 1976—78; with US Fgn. Svc., 1978—, with Bur. Intelligence and Rsch. Washington, sr. mgmt. positions under dir. gen., chief civilian observer unit Multinational Force and Observers in Egypt Sinai Desert, 1989—91, polit. adv. to U.S. and Turkish commanding gens. Operation Provide Comfort; dep. chief of mission and charge d'affaires US Embassy, Ankara, Turkey, 1995—99; spl. coord. for transition of Iraq US Dept. State, Washington, 1999—2001, US amb. to Philippines and Palau Manilla, 2002—05, US amb. to Egypt Cairo, 2005—. Office: DOS Amb 7700 Cairo Pl Washington DC 20521-7700 also: American Embassy Garden City 8 Kamal El Din Salah St Cairo Egypt

RICCIO, ANGELA, science educator; b. Kankakee, Ill., Dec. 13, 1976; d. Daniel and Patricia Riccio. BS in Elem. Edn., Ill. State U., Normal, 2000; M Sci. Edn., Nat. Louis U., Wheeling, Ill., 2005. Cert. Am. sport edn. program Ill. Sci. tchr. Jefferey C. Still Mid. Sch., Aurora, Ill., 2000—06, Gordan Gregory Mid. Sch., Naperville, Ill., 2006—. Athletic scholar, Ill. State U., 1996—2000. Mem.: NSTA. Home Phone: 630-726-1202.

RICCIO, FELIX, professional sports team owner; m. Moira Riccio; children: Thomas, Andrew, Catherine, Nicholas. Grad., Princeton U., NJ; law degree, U. Va. Investment banker Morgan Stanley & Co., NYC; atty. Goodwin, Procter & Hoar, LLP, Boston; bd. mgrs. Atlanta Spirit, LLC (parent co. of NBA Atlanta Hawks and NHL Atlanta Thrashers); sr. v.p. corp. devel. Trans Nat. Grp. Mailing: Atlanta Spirit LLC Ste 1900 101 Marietta St NW Atlanta GA 30303 *

RICCIO, FRANK JOSEPH, lawyer, educator; b. Somerville, Mass. BS, Boston Coll., 1973; JD, Suffolk U., 1985; D of Dental Medicine, Boston Coll., 1986. Bar: Mass. 1985, U.S. Dist. Ct. Mass. 1986, U.S. Ct. Appeals (1st cir.) 1986. Dentist, Lowell, Mass., 1977-83, Metheun, Mass., 1983-84; assoc. Sugarman & Sugarman, Boston, 1985-87; pvt. practice Braintree, Mass., 1987. Clin. instr. oral medicine Harvard U., Boston, 1995—. Mem. alumni bd. Boston U., 2004—. Dental extern USPHS, 1976. Named one of Mass. Super Lawyers, Boston Mag., 2005, 2006. Fellow Am. Coll. Legal Medicine; mem. Am. Assn. Trial Attys., Nat. Bd. Trial Attys. (cert. civil trial specialist 2005), Mass. Bar Assn. (co-chmn. health law coun.), Mass. Acad. Trial Attys., Million Dollar Advs. Forum. Office: 25 Braintree Hill Park Ste 208 Braintree MA 02184-8702 Office Phone: 781-380-4373. Business E-Mail: fjriccio@socialaw.com.

RICCITIELLO, JOHN S., interactive software/gaming executive, venture capitalist; b. Erie, Pa., Aug. 3, 1959; BS cum laude in Mktg., Economics and Finance, U. Calif. Berkeley, 1981. Brand mgr. The Clorox Co., Oakland, Calif., 1981—84; mktg. mgr. Henkel GmbH, Germany, 1984—85; mktg. & sales dir. 17 country Middle East/Greece regions Pepsi-Cola Co., Cyprus, 1985—89, group mktg. dir. then bus. devel. dir.; joined Hagen-Dazs, 1989, London, mng. dir. internat. divisions Paris; pres., CEO Wilson Sporting Goods Co., Chgo., 1993—96; pres., CEO Sara Lee bakery worldwide divsn. Sara Lee Corp., Chgo., 1996—97; pres., COO Electronic Arts, Inc., Redwood City, Calif., 1997—2004, CEO, 2007—; co-founder Elevation Partners, Menlo Park, Calif., 2004—. Bd. dirs. Hyperion Solutions, Forbes Media LLC. Office: Electronic Arts Inc 209 Redwood Shores Pkwy Redwood City CA 94065 *

RICCO, DONNA, fashion designer; Pres. Donna Ricco Inc., NYC.

RICCO, EDWARD ROBERT, lawyer; b. Teaneck, NJ, Jan. 17, 1950; s. Leopold Joseph and Rose Mary (Lotito) R.; m. Mary Ann Sweeney, Feb. 2, 1974; children: Alanna Catherine, Susanna Maria. BS, Stevens Inst. Tech., 1971; MA, Columbia U., 1973; JD, U. N.M., 1980. Bar: N.Mex. 1980, U.S. Dist. Ct. N.Mex. 1980, U.S. Ct. Appeals (10th cir.) 1981, U.S. Supreme Ct. 1984, U.S. Ct. Appeals (D.C. cir.) 1992, U.S. Ct. Appeals (9th cir.) 2004. Law clk. to chief judge U.S. Dist. Ct., Albuquerque, 1980-81; assoc. Rodey, Dickason, Sloan, Akin & Robb P.A., Albuquerque, 1981-87, ptnr., 1987—. Mem. com. uniform jury instrns. in civil cases N.Mex. Supreme Ct., Albuquerque, 1986-98, mem. com. rules of appellate procedure, 1999-04; adj. prof. law U. N.Mex. Lead articles editor Natural Resources Jour., 1979-80. Served to capt. USAF, 1973-77. Mem. ABA (sect. antitrust law, sect. litigation), Am. Acad. Appellate Lawyers, Albuquerque Bar Assn., State Bar Assn. N.Mex. (chmn. health law sect. 1987-88, chmn. appellate practice sect. 1997-98). Office: Rodey Dickason Sloan Akin & Robb PA PO Box 1888 201 3rd St NW Ste 2200 Albuquerque NM 87103-1888 Office Phone: 505-768-7314. Business E-Mail: ericco@rodey.com.

RICCOBONO, RICHARD M., bank executive, former federal administrator; b. Bklyn., Sept. 15, 1957; Grad., SUNY, Albany; JD, Western New Eng. Sch. Law; postgrad., Boston U. With Deloitte & Touche, Fed. Home Loan Bank Boston; regional dep. dir. Office of Thrift Supervision, US Dept. Treasury, Washington, 1990-98, dep. dir., 1998—2005, acting dir., 2005; exec. v.p., COO Fed. Loan Bank Seattle, 2005—07, pres., CEO, 2007—. Bd. dirs. FDIC, 2005. Office: Fed Home Loan Bank 1501 4th Ave Ste 1800 Seattle WA 98101-1693 *

RICE, BARBARA LYNN, stage manager; b. Hartford, Conn., Nov. 9, 1955; d. Joe Roger and Betty Barbara (Baxter) R. BA in Theatre and French, Ind. U., 1978; MFA in Directing, U. Cin., 1982. Freelance stage mgr., NYC; dir. The Open Eye: New Stagings, NYC, 1989; prodn. stage mgr. Belmont Italian-Am. Playhouse, NYC, 1994, 95; prodn. assn. Silence, Cunning, Exile, NYC, 1995; asst. stage mgr. The Merry Wives of Windsor, NYC, 1995; stage mgr. The Message of Peace, NYC, 2005. Dir. The Open Eye: New Stagings, N.Y.C., 1989; stage mgr. 20 Years Ago Today, Cin., 1989, Fourscore & 7 Years Ago, Paramus, N.J., 1989-90, Hanging the President, N.Y.C., 1990, Message of Peace (Lotus Music and Dance), N.Y.C., 2004; prodn. asst. Kiss of the Spiderwoman, Purchase, N.Y., 1990, (off-Broadway) Beau Jest, N.Y.C., 1992, Belmont Italian-Am. Playhouse, N.Y.C., 1994, 95, Transformations, 1997; listings editor Back Stage, 1998; contbg. writer The Headset, 2005; stage manager The Message of Peace, Lotus Music and Dance, NYC, 2005. Mem. Actors' Equity Assn., Stage Mgrs. Assn. Presbyterian. Avocations: music, history, art, reading, languages. Home: 412 W 56th St Apt 10 New York NY 10019-3647 E-mail: cincydame@aol.com.

RICE, CHARLES LANE, surgeon, educator; b. Atlanta, May 22, 1945; s. Marion Jennings and Molly Black (Moore) R.; m. Lynn Carol Inscoe, Dec. 27, 1968 (div. 1976); m. Judith Josephine Bousha, July 9, 1977; children: Aaron Nicholas, Patrick Marion. AB, U. Ga., 1964; MD, Med. Coll. Ga., 1968. Commd. ensign USN, 1966, advanced through grades to comdr., 1976, ret., 1977; intern Bowman Gray Sch. Medicine, Winston-Salem, NC, 1968-69; resident Nat. Naval Med. Ctr., Bethesda, Md., 1969-73; asst. prof. surgery U. Chgo., 1977-80, assoc. prof. surgery, 1980-84; dir. intensive care unit Michael Reese Hosp., Chgo., 1977-84; prof., vice chmn. dept. surgery U. Wash., Seattle, 1985-92; surgeon-in-chief Harborview Med. Ctr., Seattle, 1985-92; Dr. Lee Hudson- Robert R. Penn prof., chmn., divsn. gen. surgery U. Tex. Southwestern Med. Ctr., Dallas, 1992-93; prof. surgery U. Ill., Chgo., 1993—2005, prof. physiology and biophysics, 1996—2005, vice dean Coll. Medicine, 1994-99, vice chancellor health affairs, 1999—2004; prof. surgery, pres. Uniformed Svcs. U. of Health Scis., Bethesda, Md., 2005—. Robert Wood Johnson Health Policy fellow, 1991-92; legis. asst. to U.S. senator Tom Daschle, 1991-92. Assoc. editor Jour. of Surg. Rsch., 1983-90; contbr. articles to profl. jours. Rep. Accrediting Coun. Grad. Med. Edn., chair elect, 2001—02, chair, 2002—04. Capt. USNR, 1989—2003. Decorated Legion of Merit. Fellow ACS (gov. 1992-98, vice chmn. com. on trauma 1992-93), Am. Surg. Assn., Am. Assn. for Surgery of Trauma (com. chair 1989-91); mem. Soc. Univ. Surgeons, Am. Physiol. Soc., Shock Soc. (pres. 1991-92), Ctrl. Surg. Assn., Pacific Coast Surg. Assn., So. Surg. Assn. Democrat. Episcopalian. Office: Uniformed Svcs U Health Sci Office of Pres 4301 Jones Bridge Rd Bethesda MD 20814-4799 Home Phone: 301-530-0885; Office Phone: 301-295-3013. Business E-Mail: crice@usuhs.edu.

RICE, CHARLES M., virologist, educator; BS in Zoology, U. Calif., Davis, 1974; PhD in BioChemistry, Calif. Inst. Tech., 1981. Postdoctoral rsch. fellow Calif. Inst. Tech., 1981—85; asst. prof. Washington U. Sch. Medicine, prof. dept. molecular microbiology, 1995; head lab. virology and infectious disease Rockefeller U., NYC, 2000—, Maurice R. and Corinne P. Greenberg chair virology, 2000—. Achievements include research in molecular genetics; virology. Office: Rockefeller U 1230 York Ave New York NY 10021

RICE, CLARE I., electronics company executive; b. Rice Lake, Wis., Nov. 3, 1918; s. Chris Nilson and Ingeborg (Haug) R.; m. Virginia M. Bateman; children: Karen Rice, Carol Rice Brannon, David Alan. BSEE, U. Wis., 1943; BS in Law, St. Paul Coll. Law, 1950; DEngring, Rose-Hulman Inst. Tech., 1979. Registered profl. engr., Minn., D.C. Supr. aircraft radio engring. Northwest Airlines, Inc., Mpls., 1946-51; staff engr. Aero. Radio, Inc., Washington, 1951-53; aviation sales mgr., gen. mgr. Bendix Avionics Divsn., Balt., 1953-62; pres. Sunbeam Electronics, Inc., Ft. Lauderdale, Fla., 1962-66; v.p. Nova U., Ft. Lauderdale, 1966-68; asst. v.p., v.p., sr. v.p. Collins Radio Co., pres. Collins Avionics group Rockwell Internat. Corp., Cedar Rapids, Iowa, 1968-83. Dir. Rockwell-Collins Internat., Inc., Dallas. Chmn. United Way, Cedar Rapids, 1973-74; trustee Coe Coll., 1979-83, Hoover Presdl. Libr.; eminent fellow Wisdom Hall of Fame; bd. dirs. St. Luke's Hosp., 1976-82, Mchts. Nat. Bank, 1977-83; chmn. Mcpl. Airport Commn., Cedar Rapids, 1980-84; charter mem. Aviation Hall of Fame; capt. Hon. Dep. Sheriffs Assn., 1987—; pres. Sales and Mktg. Execs. Balt., 1960-61, Cmty. Assn. Bernardo Heights, 1988-91; dir. Rancho Bernardo Cmty. Found. Lt. comdr. USNR, 1943-46. Recipient Disting. Svc. citation U. Wis., 1979, 84; Pioneer award Milw. Sch. Engring., 1981. Sr. mem. IEEE; mem. Iowa Mfrs. Assn. (bd. dirs. 1975-81), Gen. Aviation Mfrs. Assn. (dir. 1970-81, chmn. 1979), U. Wis. Alumni Assn. (chmn. 1981-82, pres. 1980-81, Disting. Svc. award 1984). Clubs: Wings (N.Y.C.); Nat. Aviation (Washington); Rancho Bernardo Heights Country. Lodges: Royal Order of Jesters (dir. 1979). Republican. Presbyterian. Home: The Remington Club 16925 Hierba Dr # 219 San Diego CA 92128

RICE, CLARETHA MAYES, medical/surgical nurse, educator; d. Fred Dossie and Luethisa Mayes; children: William Eugene Mayes, Carisa Denise Brewster. Assoc. in Gen. Studies, C.C. of Phila., 1988. Lic. practical nurse, Pa. Staff nurse Albert Einstein, Phila., 1973—; charge nurse Maplewood Manor, Phila., 1980—84, Stapely Health Care Ctr., Phila., 1984—94; tchr. Sch. Dist. of Phila., 1992—2004. Bereavement counselor Canaan Bapt. Ch., Phila., 1999—. Musician: Canaan Baptist Church Daycare Song (Recommedation from dir. of day care, 1995). Mem. xec. com. Stenton Ave. and Partnership Com., Phila., 1990—2006; tchr. Sunday sch. Disciples of Christ Ch., Phila., 1958—70, Canaan Bapt. Ch., Phila., 1980—2006, deaconess, Bible tchr., 1997—2006, bereavement facilitator and counselor, 1999—2006; coord. women's conf. Canaan Bapt. Ch., Enon Bapt. Ch., Keystone Mercy, 2005. Recipient Cert. of Achievement, Phillippian Bapt. Church-New Hope Ministry, 1999—2006, Cert. of Recognition, Greater Phila. Area Sunday Sch. Assn., Retirement Cert. of Recognition, Am. Fedn. of Tchrs., Cert. of Attendance, Ctr. for Grieving Children, Teens and Families, Cert. of Completion of Mission Study Course, Lott Carey Bapt. Fgn. Mission Conv. of Am.-44Shaw Div. Sch., Name placed on the Wall of Tolerance-So. Poverty Law Ctr., Nat. Campaign for Tolerance, 2005. Democrat. Baptist. Avocations: travel, reading, music, gardening, writing. Home Phone: 215-848-1692. Personal E-mail: crice63808@aol.com.

RICE, CONDOLEEZZA, secretary of state, former national security advisor; b. Birmingham, Ala., Nov. 14, 1954; d. John Wesley and Angelena Ray Rice. BA cum laude, U. Denver, 1974, PhD, 1981; MA, U. Notre Dame, 1975; PhD (hon.), Morehouse Coll., 1991, U. Ala., 1994, U. Notre Dame, 1995, Nat. Def. U., 2002, Miss. Coll. Sch. of Law, 2003, U. Louisville, 2004, Mich. St. U., 2004; degree (hon.), Boston Coll., 2006. Intern, Bur. of Ednl. & Cultural Affairs US Dept. State, Washington, 1977; intern Rand Corp., Santa Monica, Calif., 1978; polit. sci. cons. Stanford U., 1980—81, asst. prof. polit. sci., 1981—87, assoc. prof., 1987—93, prof., 1993—99; provost Stanford U., 1993-99; spl. asst. to dir. of the Joint Chiefs of Staff US Dept. Def., Washington, 1986; spl. asst. to the Pres. for nat. security affairs NSC, 1989-91, dir. to sr. dir. Soviet & East European Affairs, 1989—91; sr. fellow Hoover Inst., Stanford, Calif., 1991—93; nat. security cons. George W. Bush presdl. campaign, 2000; asst. to the Pres. for nat. security affairs NSC, Washington, 2001—05; sec. US Dept. State, Washington, 2005—. Cons. ABC News, Washington; mem. spl. advisory panel to comdr. and chief strategic air commd.; mem. gov. ind. advisory redistricting the state of Calif.; mem. U.S. Delegation to 2+4 Talks on German Unification; former mem. bd. dirs. Chevron Corp., Charles Schwab Corp., Internat. Advisory Coun. of J.P. Morgan, William & Flora Hewlett Found., U. Notre Dame. Author: Uncertain Allegiance: The Soviet Union and the Czechoslovak Army, 1984; co-author (with Alexander Dallin): The Gorbachev Era, 1986; co-author: (with Philip Zelikow) Germany Unified and Europe Transformed, 1995. Ex officio trustee Nat. Gallery Art. Named one of The World's Most Influential People, TIME mag., 2005—07, 100 Most Influential People, Time mag., 2006, 100 Most Powerful Women, Forbes mag., 2005—06, The 10 Most Fascinating People of 2005, Barbara Walters Special, Most Influential Black Americans, Ebony mag., 2006; recipient Sch. of Humanities and Scis. Dean's award for Disting. Tchg., Stanford U., 1993, Walter J. Gores award for Excellence in Tchg., 1984, Pres. award, NAACP Image Awards, 2002. Mem. Coun. Fgn. Rels. Republican. Office: US Dept State 2201 C St NW Washington DC 20520 Office Phone: 202-647-4000. *

RICE, DAVID LEE, university president emeritus; b. New Market, Ind., Apr. 1, 1929; s. Elmer J. and Katie (Tate) R.; m. Betty Jane Fordice, Sept. 10, 1950; children: Patricia Denise Rice Dawson, Michael Alan. BS, Purdue U., 1951, MS, 1956, PhD, 1958; degree (hon.), U. Evansville, 1994, U. So. Ind., 1995; LHD, U. Evansville, 1994; LLD, U. So. Ind., 1995. Dir. prof. research Ball State U., Muncie, Ind., 1958-66; v.p. Coop. Ednl. Research Lab., Inc., Indpls., 1965-67; research coordinator, bur. research HEW, Washington; dean campus Ind. State U., Evansville, 1967-71, pres. campus, 1971-85; pres. U. So. Ind., Evansville, 1985-94, pres. emeritus, 1994—. Adminstrv. asst. Gov.'s Com. on Post High Sch. Orgn. Contbr. articles to profl. jours. Past mem. State Citizens Adv. Bd. Title XX Social Security Act; bd. dirs., past pres. bd. commrs. Evansville Housing Auth.; pres. Leadership Evansville, 1978-79; bd. dirs., past pres. S.W. Ind. Pub. TV, 1972—; chair Indian Pub. Broadcasting Sts., 1990-93; bd. dirs. Villages Inc.; mem. Buffalo Trace Coun. Boy Scouts Am., 1963—, New Harmony Commn., 1989-94; chair So. Ind. Rural Devel. Project., Inc.; bd. trustees Rapp Granary-Owen Found.; bd. dirs. So. Ind. Higher Edn. Inc., U. So. Ind. Found. With inf. U.S. Army, 1951-53. Decorated Bronze Star, Combat Infantryman's Badge; recipient Svc. to Others award Salvation Army, 1974, Citizen of Yr. award Westside Civitan Club, 1972, Boss of Yr. award Am. Bus. Women's Assn., 1976, Disting. Citizen of Yr. award Ivy Tech State Coll., 1994; David L. Rice Libr./U. So. Ind. named in his honor, 1994. Mem. DAR (medal of honor for cmty. svc. 1998), Am. Assn. Higher Edn., Am. Ednl. Rsch. Assn., Am. Assn. State Colls. and Univs., Nat. Soc. Study Edn., Met. Evansville C. of C. (dir.), Evansville Kennel Club, Rotary (civic award Evansville club 1985, life), Alpha Kappa Psi, Alpha Zeta, Phi Delta Kappa. Methodist. Home: 335 W Church St Box 400 New Harmony IN 47631 Office: Neef Lesueur House 404 Church St New Harmony IN 47631

RICE, DENIS TIMLIN, lawyer; b. Milw., July 11, 1932; s. Cyrus Francis and Kathleen (Timlin) R.; children: James Connelly, Tracy Ellen. AB, Princeton U., 1954; JD, U. Mich., 1959. Bar: Calif. 1960. Practiced in, San Francisco, 1959—; assoc. firm Pillsbury, Madison & Sutro, 1959-61, Howard & Prim, 1961-63; prin. firm Howard, Rice, Nemerovski, Canady, Falk & Rabkin, 1964—. Bd. dirs. Anabas, Inc.; chmn., mng. com. San Francisco Inst. Fin. Svcs., 1983—92. Councilman, City of Tiburon, Calif., 1968-72, mayor, 1970-72; dir. Marin County Transit Dist., 1970-72, 77-81, chmn., 1979-81; supr. Marin County, 1977-81, chmn., 1979-80; commr. Marin Housing Authority, 1977-81; mem. San Francisco Bay Conservation and Devel. Commn., 1977-83; bd. dirs. Planning and Conservation League, 1981-2006, Marin Symphony, 1984-92, Marin Theatre Co., 1987-97, Marin Conservation League, 1995-2000, Digital Village Found., 1995—, pres., 1997—; mem. Met. Transp. Commn., 1980-83; mem. bd. visitors U. Mich. Law Sch. 1st lt. AUS, 1955-57. Recipient Freedom Found. medal, 1956 Fellow Am. Bar Found.; mem. ABA (fed. regulation of securities com., chair Asia-Pacific Bus. Law Com., chmn. subcom. on internat. venture law), State Bar Calif. (editor 1978-80, vice-chair sect. bus. law 1978-80, chair com. adminstrn. justice 1997-98, chair com. cyberspace law 1997-2001), San Francisco Bar Assn., Am. Judicature Soc., Internat. Tech. Law Assn. (bd. dirs.), Am. Internat. Property Law Assn., Inter-Pacific Bar Assn. (vice-chmn. securities com.). South End Rowing Club, Tiburon Peninsula Club, Pacific Union Club, Olympic Club, Order of Coif, Phi Beta Kappa, Phi Delta Phi. Office: 3 Embarcadero Ctr Ste 700 San Francisco CA 94111-4003 Office Phone: 415-434-1600. Business E-Mail: drice@howardrice.com.

RICE, DERICA W., pharmaceutical executive; b. Decatur, Ala., 1965; m. Robin Rice; 3 children. BSEE, Kettering U. (formerly GMI Engring. and Mgmt. Inst.), Flint, Mich., 1988; MBA, Ind. U., 1990. Internat. treasury assoc. Eli Lilly and Co., 1990—92, various positions including sales rep., mgr. global fin. planning and analysis for med. devices divsn., global planning mgr. pharms., fin. dir., CFO Can., 1995—97, exec. dir., CFO European ops. London, 1997—2000, gen. mgr. UK and Republic of Ireland, 2000—03, mem. Diversity Leadership Coun., v.p., contr. Indpls., 2003—06, sr. v.p., CFO, 2006—, mem. policy and strategy and ops. coms. Bd. dirs. Clarian Health North. Bd. govs. Indpls. Mus. Art. Office: Eli Lilly and Co Lilly Corp Ctr Indianapolis IN 46285 Office Phone: 317-276-2000. *

RICE, DONALD BLESSING, corporate executive, former federal official; b. Frederick, Md., June 4, 1939; s. Donald Blessing and Mary Celia (Santangelo) R.; m. Susan Fitzgerald, Aug. 25, 1962; children: Donald Blessing III, Joseph John, Matthew Fitzgerald. BSChemE, U. Notre Dame, 1961, DEng (hon.), 1975; MS in Indsl. Mgmt., Purdue U., 1962, PhD in Econs., 1965, D (hon.) in Mgmt., 1985; LLD (hon.), Pepperdine U., 1989; LHD (hon.), West Coast U., 1993; D in Pub. Policy (hon.), Rand Grad. Sch., 1995. Dir. cost analysis US Dept. Def., Washington, 1967-69, dep. asst. sec. for resource analysis, 1969-70; asst. dir. Office Mgmt. and Budget, Exec. Office of the Pres., Washington, 1970-72; pres., CEO The Rand Corp., Calif., 1972-89; sec. USAF, Washington, 1989-93; pres., COO Teledyne, Inc., LA, 1993-96; chmn. Scios, Inc., Sunnyvale, Calif., 1998—2003; chmn., pres., CEO Agensys, Inc., Santa Monica, Calif., 1996—. Bd. dirs. Vulcan Materials Co., Wells Fargo & Co., Chevron Corp.; mem. nat. adv. com. oceans and atmosphere Dept. Commerce, 1972-75; mem. Nat. Sci. Bd., 1974-86; mem. adv. coun. Coll. Engring., U. Notre Dame, 1974-88; chmn. Nat. Commn. Supplies and Shortages, 1975-77; mem. adv. panel Office Tech. Assessment, 1976-79; mem. Def. Sci. Bd., 1977-83, sr. cons., 1984-88; dir. for sec. def. and Pres. Def. Resource Mgmt. Study, 1977-79; mem. U.S. Commn. Nat. Security/21st Century, 1998-2001; trustee RAND, 2001-, chmn. grad. sch. bd. govs., 1999—. Author articles. Served to capt. AUS, 1965-67. Recipient Sec. Def. Meritorious Civilian Svc. medal, 1970, Def. Exceptional Civilian Svc. medal, 1993, Forrestal award, 1992; Ford Found. fellow, 1962-65. Fellow AAAS, Nat. Acad. of Pub. Adminstrn.; mem. Inst. Mgmt. Scis. (past pres.), Tau Beta Pi. Office: Agensys Inc 1545 17th St Santa Monica CA 90404 Office Phone: 310-820-8029 ext. 210. Business E-Mail: drice@agensys.com.

RICE, DONALD SANDS, lawyer; b. Bronxville, NY, Mar. 25, 1940; s. Anton Henry and Lydia Phipps (Sands) R.; m. Edgenie Higgins, Aug. 27, 1966; children: Alice Higgins, Edgenie Rice Thomas. AB magna cum laude, Harvard U., Cambridge, Mass., 1961, LLB/JD cum laude, 1964; LLM in Taxation, NYU, 1965. Bar: NY 1964, US Ct. Claims 1965, US Supreme Ct. 1981. Law clk. judge US Ct. Claims, 1965-67; assoc. Barrett, Smith, Schapiro & Simon, NYC, 1967-71; ptnr. Barrett, Smith, Schapiro, Simon & Armstrong, NYC, 1971-86; vice chmn. bd. Bowery Savs. Bank, NYC, 1986-88; ptnr. Chadbourne & Parke, NYC, 1988-96; mng. dir., prin. Ravitch Rice & Co. LLC, NYC, 1996—; ptnr. Rice & Ravitch LLP, NYC, 1996—. Chmn. Yaddo, 1987—2003; co-chmn. Russian-Am. Banking Law Working Group, 1991—99; v.p., treas., bd. dirs. Soviet Bus. Comml. Law Edn. Found., 1991—96; mem. nat. com. Am. fgn. policy study group dels. to China, Taiwan, 1996, 2000—01; roundtable US China Policy Cross-Strait Rels., 1996—; nat. com. Am. for Pol. Ctrl. Asia Project, 2004—; real estate adv. bd. NY State Comptr., 1987—93; bd. advisors Am.-Russian Investment Forum, 1999—2002; lectr. in field. Contbr. articles to profl. jours. Trustee Nat. Com. Am. Fgn. Policy, 1994—, sr. v.p., 1996—; trustee Chapin Sch., 1980—91, v.p., 1989—91; trustee Marimed Found., 1984—97, Hackley Sch., 1974—81, St. Philip's Episcopal Ch., Mattapoisett, Mass., 1987—, Old Dartmouth Hist. Soc.-New Bedford Whaling Mus., 2006—; pres. Quadequina Co./Mattapoisett Casino, 2001—04; mem. adv. bd. Shorenstein Ctr. on Press, Politics and Pub. Policy, JFK Sch. Govt., Harvard U., 2003—; bd. dirs. African Med. Rsch. Found., 1978—2002. Mem. Coun. Fgn. Rels., NY State Bar Assn., Assn. Bar City NY, Century Assn., Harvard Club NY, NY Yacht Club, Bay Club, Beverly Yacht Club, Mattapoisett Casino. Office: Ravitch Rice & Co LLC 610 5th Ave Rm 420 New York NY 10020-2403 Home: 45 E 89th St Apt 18F New York NY 10128-0144 Office Phone: 212-218-7880. Personal E-mail: ravricellc@aol.com.

RICE, DOROTHY PECHMAN, medical economist; b. Bklyn., June 11, 1922; d. Gershon and Lena (Schiff) Pechman; m. John Donald Rice, Apr. 3, 1943; children: Kenneth D., Donald B., Thomas H. Student, Bklyn. Coll., 1938—39; BA, U. Wis., 1941; DSc (hon.), Coll. Medicine and Dentistry N.J., 1979. With hosp. and med. facilities USPHS, Washington, 1960—61; med. econs. studies Social Security Adminstrn., 1962—63; health econs. br. Community Health Svc., USPHS, 1964—65; chief health ins. rsch. br. Social Security Adminstrn., 1966—72, dep. asst. commr. for rsch. and statistics, 1972—75; dir. Nat. Ctr. for Health Stats., Rockville, Md., 1976—82; prof. Inst. Health & Aging U. Calif., San Francisco, 1982—94, prof. emeritus, 1994—. Developer, mgr. nationwide health info. svcs.; expert on aging, health care costs, disability, and cost-of-illness. Contbr. articles to profl. jours. Recipient Social Security Adminstrn. citation, 1968, DSM, HEW, 1974, Jack C. Massey Found. award, 1978, UCSF medal, 2002. Fellow: Am. Statis. Assn.; mem.: LWV, APHA (domestic award for excellence 1978, Sedgwick Meml. medal 1988), Assn. Health Svc. Rsch. (President's award 1988), Inst. Medicine. Office: Univ Calif Sch Nursing 3333 California St Ste 340 San Francisco CA 94118 Office Phone: 415-476-2771. Business E-Mail: dorothy.rice@ucsf.edu.

RICE, FERILL JEANE, writer; b. Hemingford, Nebr., July 4, 1926; d. Derrick and Helen Agnes (Moffatt) Dalton; m. Otis LaVerne Rice, Mar. 7, 1946; children: LaVeria June McMichael, Larry L. Student, U. Omaha, 1961. Dir. jr. and sr. choir Congl. Ch., Tabor, Iowa, 1952-66; tchr. Fox Valley Tech. Inst., Appleton, Wis., 1970-77; activity dir. Family Heritage Nursing Home, Appleton, Wis., 1972-75; dir. activity Peabody Manor, Appleton, Wis., 1975-76. Editor: Moffatt and Related Families, 1981; asst. editor (mag.) Yester-Year, 1975-76; contbr. articles to profl jours. Chmn. edn. Am. Cancer Soc., Fremont County, 1962-64; founder, 1st pres. Mothers Club Nishna Valley chpt. Demolay for Boys. Mem. DAR, Heisey Collectors Am., Iowa Fedn. Women's Clubs (Fremont county chmn. 1964, 65, 66, 67, 7th dist. chmn. libr. svcs. 1966-67), Tabor Women's Club (pres. 1962, 63, 64), Jr. Legion Aux. (founder, 1st dir. 1951-52), Fenton Art Glass Collectors Am. (co-founder 1977, sec., editor newsletter 1976-86, editor/sec. 1988-93, pres./editor 1993-95, treas. 1995-96, pres. 2000-01), Mayflower Soc., John Howland Soc., Ross County Ohio Geneal. Soc., Dallas County Mo. Geneal. Soc., Imperial Collectors Am., Clay County (Ind.) Geneal. Soc., Fenton Finders of Wis. (chpt. #1 pres. 1988-90). Republican. Methodist. Lodges: Order Ea. Star (worthy matron 1956, 64), Rainbow for Girls (bd. dirs. 1964), Internat. Order Job's Daus. (honored queen 1945).

RICE, FUHRMAN D. (RUNT RICE), retired paper company executive; b. June 12, 1927; s. Robert Fulton and Carrie Ann (Whitaker) R.; m. Marie Mayben, 1967; 1 child, Kathleen Ann. Forest ranger Ala. Forestry Commn., Marshall County, 1951-74; procurement agent Paperboard Divsn. Mead Corp., Stevenson, Ala., 1974-91. Pres. Grant Conservation Club, 1964-73; chmn. Marshall County Rep. Exec. Com., Ala., 1995-99; bd. dirs. Ala. Wildlife Fedn., 1961-77 (Conservationist of Yr. 1970); mem. Boy Scouts of Am. (Dist. Scouters award 1964, Silver Beaver award 1974); v.p. soc. Ala. Retirees, Guntersville, 1999, Alder Springs Cmty. Assn., Marshall County, 1999, 2003; mem. Alder Springs Vol. Fire Dept. Home: 831 Ham Rd Albertville AL 35951-4321 E-mail: runt@hiwaay.net.

RICE, GARY RUSSELL, retired special education educator; b. Franklin, Pa., Oct. 11, 1951; s. Robert Russell and Della Elizabeth Rice. Grad. cum laude, Cleve. State U., 1973. Cert. polit. sci. tchr., learning disabilities, behavioral disorders, Ohio. Substitute tchr. Lakewood, Rocky River, Westlake (Ohio) Schs., 1973—77; instr. West Side Inst. Tech., Cleve., 1977—78; spl. edn. tchr. Parma (Ohio) City Sch. Dist., 1978—2005, ret., 2005. Learning disabilities tutor, Lakewood, 1974-75; guitar cons. Rock and Roll Hall of Fame and Mus., Cleve. Asst. scoutmaster, leader Boy Scouts Am., Cleve.; former Sunday sch. tchr. local chs., Lakewood; author, columnist, spkr. to various groups on Exceptional Children, the Holocaust and Native Americans; charter mem. U.S. Holocaust Meml. Mus. Recipient Outstanding Spl. Educator award Parma PTA Spl. Edn. com., 1985, Thanks to Tchrs. award Sta. TV-8 WJW, Cleve., 1994, dist. award of merit Boy Scouts Am., 1997, Daniel Carter Beard Masonic Scouter award, 2005. Mem. Parma Edn. Assn., Cleve. Fedn. Musicians, DeMolay (active Legion of Honor 1996), Masons, Shriners. Avocations: music, photography.

RICE, GEORGE LAWRENCE, III, (LARRY), lawyer; b. Jackson, Tenn., Sept. 24, 1951; s. George Lawrence, Jr. and Judith W. (Pierce) Rice; m. Joy Gaia, Sept. 14, 1974; children: George (Nick) Lawrence IV, Amy Colleen. Student british studies, Oxford U., 1972-73; BA with honors, Rhodes Coll., Memphis, 1974; JD, U. Memphis, 1976, Nat. Coll. Advocacy, ATLA, 1978. Bar: Tenn. 1977, US Supreme Ct. 1980. Assoc. Rice, Admundsen & Capenton LLPC, 1976—, ptnr., 1981—. Cert. family law trial advocate NBTA and Family Law Specialist by Tenn. Author: Divorce Practice in Tennessee, 1987, Family Law, 1988, Winning for Your Client, 1988, Divorce Practice A to Z, 1989, Divorce Lawyer's Handbook, 1989, (video) Divorce: What You Need to Know When It Happens to You, 1990, Rice's Divorce Practice Manual, 1990, Child Custody in Tennessee, 1992, Divorce Trial Tribulations, Tactics and Triumphs, 1993, The Complete Guide to Divorce Practice, 1993, 3d edit., 2005, Divorce Practice Made Easier, 1993, Divorce Practice, 1994, Visual Persuasion, AIDS 1996 Clients, Prenuptial Agreements, 1996, The Ethical Effective Lawyer, 1996, Wiley Family Law Update, Discovery Supplement, 1997, Tennessee Evidence Workshop Handbook, 1997, Hot Topics in Family Law, 1997, Child Custody and Visitation in Tennessee, 1998, Larry Rice on Divorce: How to Run an Efficient and Effective Divorce Practice and Improve Client Satisfaction, 1998, Client Communications, 1998, Post Nuptial Agreement a Proposal for Consideration, 1998, Larry Rice of Divorce, 1998; mem. bd. editors Matrimonial Strategist, 1995—2002, Hunt, Hide Shoot -- a Guide to Paintball, 1996, AboutDivorce.com, 2003; contbr. articles to profl. jours. Founding chmn. Student Legal Assistance Program, 1975; active Supreme Ct. Child Support Guidelines Commn., 1989, Family Law Revision Commn., 1990—91, 1998—2001; mem. Timberwolves Paintball Team, 1988—2000; exec. com. Rhodes Coll. Red and Black Soc., 1999—2002, chmn., 2001—01; treas. Rocky Mountain Elk Found., Memphis, 2001. Named Outstanding Intern Supr., Rhodes Coll.; named one of Best Lawyers in Am., 1993, 1994; recipient Excellence in Edn. award, PESI, 1997, Mentor award, Rhodes Coll., 1997—98, award, Amicus Curi Family Laws Sect. Wilson-Wilson, 1997—98. Mem.: ATLA, ABA (7 time conv. lectr.), Tenn. Trial Lawyers Assn., Memphis Bar Assn. (founding chmn. family law sect.), Tenn. Bar Assn. (chmn., co-founder family law sect. 1987—88). Office: Rice Admundsen Rogers PLLC 275 Jefferson Memphis TN 38103-2251 Office Phone: 901-526-6701. Business E-Mail: larry@ricelaw.com.

RICE, JAMES BRIGGS, JR., lawyer; b. Kansas City, Mo., Dec. 31, 1940; s. James Briggs and Oma J. R.; m. Carolyn Ryan, Aug. 11, 1962 (div.); children: James Briggs III, Cynthia L.; m. Beverly Sue, Oct. 24, 1980. AB, U. Mo., 1962, JD, 1965. Bar: Mo. 1965, U.S. Dist. Ct. (we. dist.) Mo. 1968. Assoc., Rogers, Field & Gentry, Kansas City, 1967-72; ptnr. Wesner, Wesner & Rice, Sedalia, Mo., 1972-75, Rice & Romines, Sedalia, 1975-80; pvt. practice, Sedalia, 1980—; atty. Sedalia Area Devel. Corp., 1976-79. Chmn., Police Pers. Bd., Sedalia, 1976. Served as capt. U.S. Army, 1965-67; Vietnam. Mem. ABA, Mo. Bar Assn., Pettis County Bar Assn. (pres. 1975),, Am. Judicature Soc., Mo. Assn. Trial Atty.'s, VFW, Vietnam Vets. of Pettis County. Republican. Methodist. Lodges: Kiwanis (pres. 1975), Noon-day Optimist, Masons, Shriners. Office: 701 S Ohio Ave Sedalia MO 65301-4415 Home: 1940 Ashwood Cir Sedalia MO 65301-9296 Office Phone: 660-827-1631.

RICE, JERRY LEE, retired professional football player; b. Starkville, Miss., Oct. 13, 1962; s. Joe Nathan and Eddie Rice; m. Jackie Rice; children: Jaqui, Jerry Jr. Student, Miss. Valley State U., 1981—84. Wide receiver San Francisco 49ers, 1985—2000, Oakland Raiders, 2001—04, Seattle Seahawks, 2004—05, Denver Broncos, 2005. Celebrity dancer Dancing With the Stars, 2006; co-author (with Brian Curtis): Go Long!: My Journey Beyond Fame and the Game, 2007. Named MVP, NFL, 1987, Super Bowl XXIII, 1989, AP/NFL/Sports Illustrated Offensive Player of Yr., 1993; named to Sporting News Coll. All-Am. team, 1984, Pro Bowl team, 1986—96, 1998, 2002; recipient Pro Bowl MVP, 1995. Achievements include holds NFL career records for most touchdowns, receptions, touchdown receptions; having the most consecutive games with one or more touchdowns (13), 1987; holds the NFL single-season record for most touchdown receptions (22), 1987; shares NFL single-game record for most touchdown receptions (5), 1990; holds NFL record of 274 consecutive games with a reception, 1985-2004; led NFL in receptions, 1990, 1996; led NFL in recieving touchdowns, 1986, 1987, 1989-1991, 1993; led NFL in recieving yards, 1986, 1989, 1990, 1993-1995; being a member of SuperBowl XIX, XXIII, XXIV, XXIX Champion San Francisco 49ers.

RICE, JERRY MERCER, biochemist, consultant, pathologist; b. Washington, Oct. 3, 1940; s. John Earle Rice and Leona (Mercer) Greiner; m. Mary Jane Janocha, Jan. 10, 1978; children: Stacey Lynn, Stephen Mark. BA, Wesleyan U., 1962; PhD, Harvard U., 1966. Commd. officer USPHS, 1966, ret., 1996; rsch. scientist Nat Cancer Inst., Bethesda, Md., 1966-81, chief Lab. of Comparative Carcinogenesis Frederick, Md., 1981-94, 96, assoc. dir. Frederick Cancer Rsch. and Devel. Ctr., 1994-95, acting dir. divsn. cancer etiology, 1994-95, ret., 1996; sr. scientist WHO, 1996—2002, ret., 2002; chief unit of carcinogen identification and evaluation Internat. Agy. for Rsch. on Cancer, Lyons, France, 1996—2002, cons. in toxicology, 2003—; Disting. prof. dept. oncology Georgetown U., Washington, 2003—. Editor: Perinatal Carcinogenesis, 1979; co-editor: Organ and Species Specificity in Chemical Carcinogenesis, 1983, Perinatal and Multigeneration Carcinogenesis, 1989, The Use of Short and Medium Term Tests for Carcinogens and Data on Genetic Effects in Carcinogenic Hazard Evaluation, 1999, Species Differences in Thyroid, Kidney and Urinary Bladder Carcinogenesis, 1999, Mech. of Carcinogenesis-contributions of molecular epidemiology, 2004,; contbr. rsch. articles and revs. in mechanisms of chem. carcinogenesis to profl. jours.; dir. emeritus IARC monographs on the evaluation of carcinogenic risks to humans. Mem. Internat. Soc. Differentiation (emeritus), Soc. Toxicology, European Assn. Cancer Rsch., Am. Assn. Cancer Rsch. (emeritus), Phi Beta Kappa, Sigma Xi. Avocations: viticulture, tropical orchids. Home: 3213 Coquelin Ter Bethesda MD 20815-4840 Personal E-mail: jmricewas@aol.com. Business E-Mail: jr332@georgetown.edu.

RICE, JIM, state supreme court justice; b. Ramore AFB, Ont., Canada, Nov. 15, 1957; (parents Am. citizens); BA in Polit. Sci., Mont. State U., 1979; JD U. Mont., 1982. Former firefighter Mont. Dept. of Natural Resources & Conservation; former legal intern Missoula City Atty. Office, Lewis and Clark County Atty. Office; former pub. defender Lewis and Clark County; mem. Mont. House Reps., 1989—95, house majority whip, 1993; ptnr. Jackson & Rice, Helena, Mont., 1985—2001; assoc. justice Mont. Supreme Ct., 2001—. Active in Montana Hope Project, Kiwanis; mem. Governor's Council on Food and Nutrition. Recipient Thomas McHugh Disting. Community Service award, Helena Jaycees, 1993. Mem.: Mont. Bar Assn. Office: Justice Bldg Rm 323 PO Box 203003 Helena MT 59620-3003 *

RICE, JOHN D., agricultural products executive; BS, Univ. Ill., 1977. Plant mgmt. positions A.E. Stanley Mfg. Co., 1977—85; mgmt. positions Archer Daniels Midland Co., Decatur, Ill., 1985—90, v.p., dir. corp. transp., 1990—93, v.p., pres. ADM-Transp., 1993—96, v.p., pres. food oils divsn., 1996—2000, group v.p., pres. N.Am. oilseed processing divsn., 1999—2000, sr. v.p. corn processing and food specialties, 2000—05, exec. v.p. global mktg. & risk mgmt., 2005—. Office: Archer Daniels Midland Co 4666 Faries Pkwy Decatur IL 62526 *

RICE, JOHN G., diversified technology and services executive; BA in Econs., Hamilton Coll. Mem. fin. mgmt. program GE, 1978-81, mem. corp. audit staff, 1981-84; mgr. materials GE Appliances, 1984-86, mgr. quality control prodn. engring. and materials ops., 1986-87; pres. GEM Products, Inc., Garden Grove, Calif., 1987-90; gen. mgr. material resources GE Appliances, 1990-92; pres., COO Camco, Inc., Canada, 1992-94; head corp. audit staff GE, 1994-95; pres. GE Plastics Pacific, Singapore, 1995-97; pres., CEO GE Transp. Sys., Erie, Pa., 1997—2000, GE Energy, Fairfield, Conn., 2000—05; vice chmn., pres., CEO GE Industrial, Fairfield, Conn., 2005—06, GE Infrastructure, Fairfield, Conn., 2006—. Chmn. U.S. Energy Assn. Chmn. elect Metro Atlanta C. of C.; trustee Hamilton Coll., Woodruff Arts Ctr., Walker Sch.; mem. adv. bd. Ga. Tech. Univ.; dir. Emory Healthcare. Mailing: General Electric Co 3135 Easton Tpke Fairfield CT 06828

RICE, JOHN S., lawyer; b. Evanston, Ill., Apr. 15, 1938; BA, Roosevelt U., 1962; JD cum laude, Northwestern U., 1967. Bar: Ill. 1967, Tex. 1978. Shareholder Jenkens & Gilchrist, P.C., Dallas, firm leader ERISA practice group. Mem.: ABA, Dallas Pension Soc., Chgo. Bar Assn., Dallas Bar Assn., Ill. State Bar Assn., Tex. State Bar Assn. Office: Jenkens & Gilchrist PC Ste 3200 1445 Ross Ave Dallas TX 75202-2799 Office Phone: 214-855-4327. Office Fax: 214-855-4300. Business E-Mail: jrice@jenkens.com.

RICE, JOHN THOMAS, architecture educator; b. New London, Conn., Feb. 4, 1931; s. Clarence Benjamin and Emily (Gudal) R. BS in Engring., U. Conn., 1952; MSME, Newark Coll. Engring., 1954; D.Sc. in Engring., Columbia U., 1962. Registered profl. engr., N.Y. Test equipment designer propeller div. Curitss-Wright Corp., Caldwell, NJ, 1952-54; stress analyst Wright Aeronautical div. Curtiss-Wright Corp., Woodridge, NJ, 1954-59; chief structural mechanics Gen. Dynamics/Electric Boat, Groton, Conn., 1962-64; asst. prof. mech. engring. Pratt Inst., Bklyn., 1964-66, assoc. prof., 1966-74, prof., 1974—, chmn. dept. mech. engring., 1981-90. Mem. ASME (chmn. mech. engring. dept. heads com. region II 1987-89, chmn. profl. devel. region II 1989-93, mem. exec. com. met. sect. 1990—, vice chmn. 1991-92, chmn. 1992-93, sec. region II 1993-96, treas. met. sect. 1999—), Pi Tau Sigma, Tau Beta Pi. Office: Pratt Inst Dept of Architecture 200 Willoughby Ave Brooklyn NY 11205-3899

RICE, JOSEPH ALBERT, retired bank executive; b. Cranford, NJ, Oct. 11, 1924; s. Louis A. and Elizabeth J. (Michael) R.; m. Katharine Wolfe, Sept. 11, 1948; children: Walter, Carol, Philip, Alan. B in Aero. Engring., Rensselear Poly. Inst., 1948; M in Indsl. Engring., NYU, 1952, MA, 1968. With Grumman Aircraft Engring. Corp., 1948-53, IBM, NYC, 1953-65, mgr. ops., real estate, constrn. divsns., 1963-65; dep. group exec. N.Am. comml. telecom. group, pres. telecom. divsn. ITT, NYC, 1965-67; sr. v.p. Irving Trust Co., NYC, 1967-69, exec. v.p., 1969-72, sr. exec. v.p., 1972-73, vice chmn., 1973-74, pres., 1974-83, chmn., 1984-88, ret., 1988. Exec. v.p. Irving Bank Corp., 1971-74, vice chmn., 1974-75, pres., 1975-83, chmn. bd., CEO, 1984-88. Chmn., trustee John Simon Guggenheim Meml. Found., 1997-2007; trustee Blanton-Peale Inst., 1989-2007, Hist. Hudson Valley, 1998-2007, vice chmn., 1998-2007. Mem. Coun. Fgn. Rels., NY Acad. Scis., Univ. Club, Links, Union League Club. Office Phone: 212-572-6348.

RICE, JOSEPH LEE, III, lawyer; b. Bklyn., Feb. 24, 1932; s. Joseph Lee Jr. and Frances (Plunkett) R.; m. Franci Blassberg, Jan. 4, 1992; children: Kimberley, Daniel, Lee Ann. BA, Williams Coll., Williamstown, Mass., 1954; LLB, Harvard U., 1960. Assoc. Sullivan & Cromwell, NYC, 1960-66; v.p. Laird Inc., NYC, 1966-68, McDonnell & Co., NYC, 1968-69; founding ptnr. Gibbons, Green & Rice, NYC, 1969-78; founder, chmn. Clayton, Dubilier & Rice, Inc., NYC, 1978—. Trustee, Williams Coll., 1988-92. Lt. USMC, 1954-57. Mem. Maidstone Club, The Links Club, River Club. Office: Clayton Dubilier & Rice Inc 375 Park Ave New York NY 10152-0002 E-mail: jrice@cdr-inc.com.

RICE, JOY KATHARINE, psychologist, education educator; d. Joseph Theodore and Margaret Sophia (Bednarik) Straka; m. David Gordon Rice, Sept. 1, 1962; children: Scott Alan, Andrew David. BFA with high honors, U. Ill., 1960; MS, U. Wis., 1962, MS, 1964, PhD, 1967. Lic. clin. psychologist. USPHS predoctoral fellow dept. psychiatry Med. Sch. U. Wis., Madison, 1964-65, asst. dir. Counseling Ctr., 1966-74, dir. Office Continuing Edn. Svcs., 1972-78, prof. ednl. policy studies and women's studies, 1974-95, clin. prof. psychiatry, 1995—; pvt. practice psychology Psychiat. Svcs., S.C., Madison, 1967—. Mem. State Wis. Ednl. Approval Bd., Madison, 1972—73; mem. Adult Edn. Commn. U.S. Office Career Edn., Washington, 1978; co-chmn. Wis. Lt. Gov.'s Task Force on Women and Depression, 2005—. Author: Living Through Divorce, A Developmental Approach to Divorce Therapy, 1985, 2d edit., 1989, Transforming Leaderships Diverse Visions and Women's Voices, 2007; mem. editl. bd. Lifelong Learning, 1979—86; cons. editor: Psychology Women Quar., 1986—88, assoc. editor:, 1989—94, cons. editor: Handbook of Adult and Continuing Education, 1989, Encyclopedia of Women and Gender, 2001, Handbook of Girls' and Women's Psychological Health, 2005; contbr. articles to profl. jours. Pres. Big Bros. Big Sisters Dane County, 2002, bd. dirs.; co-chair Wis. Lt. Gov.'s Task Force on Women and Depression, 2005—06. Recipient Disting. Achievement award, Ednl. Press Assn. Am., 1992, John Fritschler Jr. award for Disting. Achievement, 2004; Knapp fellow, U. Wis., Madison, 1960—62, Tchg. fellow, 1962—63. Fellow: APA (exec. bd. psychology women divsn. 1994—, internat. psychology divsn. 1998—, exec. bd. 1998—, chair internat. com. women 2000—02, chair com. internat. rels. psychology 2005, divsn. pres. 2006, Disting. Leadership award 2000—02); mem.: Am. Assn. Continuing and Adult Edn. (Meritorious Svc. award 1978—80, 1982), Internat. Coun. Psychologists (bd. dir. 1998—2001, sec. 2002—04, bd. dir. 2004—), Nat. Assn. Women Edn. (editl. bd. jour. 1984—88, cons. editor Initiatives 1988—91), TEMPO Internat. (bd. dir., sec. 2000—03, 2006—), Rotary, Phi Delta Kappa. Avocations: interior decorating, painting, gardening, travel. Home: 4230 Waban Hl Madison WI 53711-3711 Office: 2727 Marshall Ct Madison WI 53705-2255 Office Phone: 608-238-9354.

RICE, JULIAN CASAVANT, lawyer; b. Miami, Fla., Dec. 31, 1923; s. Sylvan J. and Maybelle (Casavant) R.; m. Dorothy Mae Haynes, Feb. 14, 1958; children— Scott B., Craig M. (dec.), Julianne C., Linda D., Janette M. Student, U. San Francisco, 1941-43; JD cum laude, Gonzaga U., 1950. Bar: Wash. 1950, Alaska 1959, U.S. Tax Ct. 1988. Pvt. practice law, Spokane, 1950-56, Fairbanks, Alaska, 1959—; prin. Law Office Julian C. Rice (and predecessor firms), Fairbanks, 1959, Salcha, Alaska, 1999. Founder, gen. counsel Mt. McKinley Mut. Savs. Bank, Fairbanks, 1965-99, chmn. bd., 1979-80; v.p., bd. dirs., gen. counsel Skimmers, Inc., Anchorage, 1966-67; gen. counsel Alaska Carriers Assn., Anchorage, 1960-71, Alaska Transp. Conf., 1960-67. Mayor City of Fairbanks, 1970-72. Served to maj. USNG and USAR, 1943-58. Decorated Bronze Star, Combat Infantryman's Badge. Fellow Am. Bar Found. (life); mem. ABA, Wash. State Bar Assn. (50-Yr. mem. award 2000), Alaska Bar Assn., Transp. Lawyers Assn., Alternative Dispute Resolution Com., Am. Arbitration Assn. (mem. transp. comml., transp. panel), Spokane Exch. Club (pres. 1956). Home and Office: 10104 Salcha Dr Salcha AK 99714-9624 E-mail: j.c.rice@att.net.

RICE, KAY DIANE, elementary school educator, consultant; d. Ray H. and Patricia Quibell; 1 child, Brooke Elise; m. F. Scott Rice. AA in Gen. Edn., Shasta Coll., Redding, 1972; BA in Liberal Studies, Calif. State U., Chico, 1975; EdM in Policy and Govt., U. Wash., 1991. Cert. tchr., Calif., Wash., cert. prin., Wash. Tchr. grade 3 Anderson (Calif.) Schs., 1976-79; tchr. grades 1, 2, and 3 Redding (Calif.) Elem. Schs., 1979-81, tchr. grade 1, 1981-83, tchr. grade 5, 1986-87; tchr. grade 2 Bellevue (Wash.) Pub. Schs., 1987-88; tchr. grade 4 Lake Wash. Sch. Dist., Kirkland, Wash., 1988-89; tchr. grades 3-4 Bellevue (Wash.) Pub. Schs., 1989-90; prin. intern Bellevue (Wash.) and Mercer Island (Wash.) Schs., 1990-91; tchr. grades K-1 Bellevue (Wash.) Pub. Schs., 1991-93, tchr. grades 1-2, 1993—. Mem. early childhood assessment project Bellevue Pub. Schs., 1993-99; presenter in field. Vol. ZEST Sch. Dist. Vol. Program, Bellevue, 1991-93. Recipient Pres.'s Merit award Parent Student Tchr. Assn., 1988, U.S. Presdl. EPA award, 1987; grantee Bellevue Schs. Found., 1987, 95-96, 96-97, 98-2006, Danforth Edn. Leadership grantee Bellevue Pub. Schs., 1990-91, Shunju Club, Japanese Bus. People Wash., 1994, Seattle Chinese Sch., 2004. Mem. ASCD, NEA, AAUW (hospitality com. 1982), PTSA, Wash. Orgn. for Reading Devel., PEO. Avocations: cooking, outdoor sports, reading, writing, religious studies. Home: 6818 205th Ave NE Redmond WA 98053-4721 Office: Somerset Elem Sch 14100 Somerset Blvd SE Bellevue WA 98006-2399

RICE, KENNER CRALLE, medicinal chemist; s. Kenner Cralle Jr. and Annie Grace Rice. BS, Va. Mil. Inst., 1961; PhD, Ga. Inst. Tech., 1966. Sr. scientist Ciba-Geigy Corp., Summit, 1969—72; sr. staff fellow NIH, Bethesda, Md., 1972—76, rsch. chemist, 1977—86; chief sect. drug design and synthesis Nat. Inst. Diabetes, Digestive and Kidney Diseases, Bethesda, Md., 1987—88; chief lab. medicinal chemistry NIDDK, NIH, Bethesda, Md., 1989—2006; chief chem. biology rsch. br. Nat. Inst. on Drug Abuse, 2006—. Adj. prof. pharmacology U. Md., Balt., 1985—; mem. Fed. Sr. Exec. Svc., Bethesda, 1989—98, Fed. Sr. Biomed. Rsch. Svc., 1998—; affiliate prof. Va. Commonwealth U., Richmond, 1995—; vis. prof. pharmacology U. Ill., Peoria, 1995—; adj. prof. medicinal chemistry Comprehensive Drug Rsch. Ctr. U. Miami, 1995—. Author (with others): Pharmacological Reviews, 1987; editor: NIDA Research Monograph 96, 1990; contbr. more than 500 rsch. papers to profl. jours. Capt. US Army, 1966—68. Recipient Internat. Sato Meml. award, Japanese Pharm. Soc., 1983, Rsch. Achievement award, Am. Pharm. Assn., 1987, Hillebrand prize, Chem. Soc. Washington, 1986, Divsn. Medicinal Chemistry award, Am. Chem. Soc., 1996, Rsch. Achievement award, Am. Assn. Pharm. Scientists, 1998, Chem. Pioneer award, Am. Inst. Chemists, 2000, Nathan B. Eddy award, Coll. Problems of Drug Dependence, 2001, Bristol-Myers Squibb Smissman award, Am. Chem. Soc. Divsn. Medicinal Chemistry, 2007. Fellow: Coll. on Problems of Drug Dependence (bd. dirs. 1988—92, 1997—2001); mem.: Am. Coll. Neuropsychopharmacology, Cosmos Club. Achievements include 42 patents in organic chemical synthesis and pharmacology of drugs of abuse; development of NIH opiate total synthesis as first practical synthesis of opium alkaloids and derivatives as narcotics and narcotic antagonists. E-mail: kr21f@nih.gov.

RICE, LACY I., JR., lawyer; b. Martinsburg, W.Va., Dec. 29, 1931; s. Lacy Isaac and Anna (Thorn) R.; m. Linda Watkins, Mar. 2, 1957; children: Anne W., Lacy I. III, William T. BA, Princeton U., 1953; LLB, U. Va., 1956. Bar: W.Va. 1956, U.S. Dist. Ct. (No. Dist.) W.Va. 1956, U.S. Cir. Ct. Appeals (3rd and 4th cirs.) 1968, W.Va. Supreme Ct. Appeals. Ptnr. Lacy I. Rice Sr. law firm & Rice, Hannis & Rice & successors, Martinsburg, 1956-89; sr. ptnr. Bowles, Rice, McDavid, Graff & Love LLP, Martinsburg, 1989—. Pres. Old Nat. Bank of Martinsburg, 1978, chmn. bd.; chmn., One Valley Bank-East N.A.; vice chmn. One Valley Bancorp, Inc.; pres. Suburban Nat. Bank Martinsburg; past chmn., CEO Moutaineer Bankshares of W.Va., Inc.; bd. dir. Bell Atlantic W.Va., Continental Brick Co. Sec. bd. dirs., State Coll. Sys. W.Va.; dir., past pres. W.Va. C. of C., W.Va. U. Found., W.Va. Edn. Fund. Mem. W.Va. Bar Assn. (pres. 1984-85); W.Va. Golf Assn.(dir., treas.) Home: 600 N Tennessee Ave Martinsburg WV 25401-9281 Office: Bowles Rice McDavid Graff & Love LLP PO Drawer 1419 101 S Quenn St Martinsburg WV 25401-1419

RICE, LESTER, electronics company executive; b. Detroit, Feb. 23, 1927; s. Carvel Lester and Irene R.; m. Barbara Helen Winston, June 27, 1957; children— Scott W., Jody I., Jeffrey C., Judy A., Timothy D. BSE.E., U. Mich., 1951. Gen. sales mgr. Westinghouse Semicondr. Div., Youngwood, Pa., 1951-68; pres. Airco Speer Elec. div. Airco Inc., Bradford, Pa., 1968-80; vice chmn., dir. KOA Speer Electronics, Inc., Bradford, 1980-98; chmn. KOA Europe GMBH, 1998—; vice chmn. KOA Speer Electronics Inc., Bradford, Pa., 2001—. Bd. dirs. DeFond No. Am. Inc.; chmn. bd. Lester Rice, Inc., Bradford, 1980—. Adv. bd. U. Pitts. With USN, 1945-46. Mem. IEEE, Electronics Industries Assn. (bd. govs.), Am. Legion, Masons. Republican. Home: 2 Vista Avenue Ext Bradford PA 16701-2759 Office: PO Box 547 Bradford PA 16701-0547 Business E-Mail: lrice@koaspeer.com.

RICE, LINDA JOHNSON, publishing executive; b. Chgo., Mar. 22, 1958; d. John J. and Eunice Johnson; m. Andre Rice, 1984, 1 child, Alexa Christine; m. Mel Farr Sr. BA Journalism, Univ. Southern Calif., LA, 1980; MBA, Northwestern Univ., Evanston, Ill., 1987. With Johnson Pub. Co., 1980—, past v.p. and asst. to pub., COO, 1987—2002; pres. Johnson Pub. Co., Inc., Chgo., 1987—, CEO, 2002—; pres. Fashion Fair Cosmetics, Ill., 1987—. Named one of 100 Most Powerful Women in Chgo., Chgo. Sun-Times, Chicago's 40 Under 40, Crain's Chgo. Bus.; recipient Women of Power award, Nat. Urban League, Trumpet award, Turner Broadcasting, Alumni Merit award, Univ. So. Calif., Alumni of the Year award, Kellogg Grad. Sch. Mgmt.,stern University. Mem.: Exec. Club Chgo., Econ. Club Chgo., Young Presidents Orgn., Nat. Assn. Black Journalists, Fashion Group Internat., Comml. Club Chgo. Office: Johnson Pub Co Inc 820 S Michigan Ave Chicago IL 60605-2191 *

RICE, LOIS DICKSON, retired computer company executive; b. Portland, Maine, Feb. 28, 1933; d. David A. and Mary D. Dickson; m. Alfred B. Fitt, Jan. 7, 1978 (dec. 1992); children: Susan, John Rice. AB magna cum laude, Radcliffe Coll., 1954; postgrad. (Woodrow Wilson fellow), Columbia U., 1954—55; LLD (hon.), Brown U., 1981, Bowdoin Coll., 1984. Dir. counseling services Nat. Scholarship Service and Fund for

Negro Students, NYC, 1955-59; with The Coll. Bd., NYC and Washington, 1959-81, v.p. Washington, 1973-81; sr. v.p. govt. affairs Control Data Corp., 1981-91. Guest scholar The Brookings Inst., Washington, 1991—; bd. dirs. McGraw Hill, Inc., 1987—2003, Internat. Multifoods, 1991—2003, UNUM/Provident Corp., 1992—2003; overseer Tuck Sch. Mgmt. Dartmouth Coll., 1990—94; mem. Pres.'s Fgn. Intelligence Adv. Bd., 1993—2001; trustee George Washington U., 1992—98, trustee Mgmt. Leadership for Tomorrow, 1994—; trustee CNA Corp. Pub. Agenda Found., Harry Frank Guggenheim Found., 1994—. Contbr. articles on edn. to profl. publs.; editor: Student Loans: Problems and Policy Alternatives, 1977. Mem. adv. bd. to dir. NSF, 1981—89, chair, 1986—89; mem. Gov.'s Commn. on Future of Postssecondary Edn. in N.Y. State, 1976—77, Carnegie Coun. on Higher Edn., 1975—80; trustee Radcliffe Coll., 1969—75, Stephens Coll., Mo., 1976—78, Beauvoir Sch., Washington, 1970—76, Children's TV Workshop, 1970—73; bd. dirs. Potomac Inst., 1977—92, German Marshall Fund, 1984—94, Joint Ctr. Polit. and Econ. Studies, 1991—94, Reading is Fundamental, 1991—2004. Recipient Disting. Service award HEW, 1977 Mem. Cosmos Club, Phi Beta Kappa. Episcopalian. Home: 2332 Massachusetts Ave NW Washington DC 20008 Office: The Brookings Instn 1775 Massachusetts Ave NW Washington DC 20036-2103

RICE, LUANNE, writer; b. 1955; B in Humane Letters, Conn. Coll., 1977, degree (hon.), 2002. Author: Angels All Over Town, 1985, Crazy in Love, 1988, Stone Heart, 1990, Secrets of Paris, 1991, Blue Moon, 1994, Home Fires, 1996, Cloud Nine, 2000, Follow The Stars Home, 2001, Firefly Beach, 2001, Dream Country, 2002, Summer Light, 2002, True Blue, 2002, Safe Harbor, 2003, The Secret Hour, 2003, The Perfect Summer, 2003, Dance With Me, 2004, Summer's Child, 2005. Mailing: c/o Andrea Cirillo Jane Rotrosen Agency 318 E 51st St New York NY 10022

RICE, MARK P., dean, management educator; BS, Rensselaer Poly. Inst., MS in Mech. Engring., PhD in Mgmt. Co-founder, pres. Power Kinetics, Inc.; dir. Incubator Program Rensselaer Poly. Inst., co-founder, dir. Severino Ctr. for Tech. Entrepreneurship; Murata dean, Jeffry A. Timmons prof. entrepreneurial studies at F. W. Olin Grad. Sch. Bus., Babson Coll., Babson Park, Mass., 2001—; prof. tech. entrepreneurship Olin Coll. Engring., Babson Coll. Co-author: Growing New Ventures, Creating New Jobs: Principles and Practices of Successful Business Incubation, 1995, Radical Innovation: How Mature Companies Can Outsmart Upstarts, 2000; contbr. articles to profl. jours. Recipient Edwin M. and Gloria W. Appel Entrepreneurship in Edn. Prize, 2002. Mem.: Nat. Bus. Incubation Assn. (former dir. and chmn., Founder's Award 1998). Office: FW Olin Grad Sch Bus Babson Coll 231 Forest St Babson Park MA 02457-0310 Office Phone: 781-239-5237. E-mail: mrice@babson.edu.

RICE, MARY ESTHER, biologist; b. Washington, Aug. 3, 1926; d. Daniel Gibbons and Florence Catharine (Pyles) R. AB, Drew U., 1947; MA, Oberlin Coll., 1949; PhD, U. Wash., 1966. Instr. biology Drew U., Madison, NJ, 1949-50; rsch. assoc. Columbia U., NYC, 1950-53; rsch. asst. NIH, Bethesda, Md., 1953-61; curator invertebrate zoology and dir. Smithsonian Marine Sta., Smithsonian Instn., Washington, 1966—2002, sr. rsch. scientist emeritus, 2002—. Mem. adv. panel on systematic biology NSF, Washington, 1977-78; mem. com. on marine invertebrates Nat. Acad. Sci., 1976-81; mem. overseers com. on biology Harvard U., Cambridge, Mass., 1982-88. Assoc. editor Jour. Morphology, Ann Arbor, Mich., 1985-91, Invertebrate Biology, 1995—; editor: (with M. Todorovic) Biology of Sipuncula and Echiura, 1975, 2nd vol., 1976, (with F.S. Chia) Settlement and Metamorphosis of Marine Invertebrate Larvae, 1978, (with F.W. Harrison) Microscopic Anatomy of Invertebrates, Vol. 12, 1993; contbr. articles to profl. jours. Recipient Drew U. Alumni Achievement award in sci., 1980. Fellow AAAS; mem. Am. Soc. Zoologists (pres. 1979), Am. Microscopical Soc. (pres. 1999), Phi Beta Kappa. Office: Smithsonian Marine Sta 701 Seaway Dr Fort Pierce FL 34949-3140

RICE, MICHELLE, communications executive; b. 1968; Degree in Journalism, Temple U.; MA in Comm. Mgmt., U. Southern Calif. Mgr., Special Markets and Can. BET, Inc.; dir., Affiliate Sales and Special Markets NBC Cable Networks; northeast regional v.p., Affiliate Rels. and Nat. Accounts iNDemand, 2001—04; v.p., Distbn. Strategy and Ops. TV One, 2004—06, sr. v.p., Nat. Accounts and Affiliate Mktg., 2006—. Named one of 40 Executives Under 40, Multichannel News, 2006. Office: TV One 1010 Wayne Ave Silver Spring MD 20910 Office Phone: 301-755-0400.

RICE, NANCY E., state supreme court justice; b. Denver, June 2, 1950; 1 child. BA cum laude, Tufts U., 1972; JD, U. Utah, 1975. Law clerk U.S. Dist. Ct. of Colo., 1975-76, dep. state pub. defender, appellate divn., 1976-77; asst. U.S. atty. Dist. of Colo., 1977-87; dep. chief civil divn. U.S. Attorney's Office, 1985-88; judge Denver Dist. Ct., 1988-98; justice Colo. Supreme Ct., 1998—. Adjunct prof. law, trial advocacy U. Colo. Sch. of Law, 1987—. Contbr. articles to profl. jours. Mem. Denver Bar Assn. (Judicial Excellence award 1993), Colo. Bar Assn. (bd. govs. 1990-92, exec. coun., 1991-92), Women's Bar Assn., Rhone-Brackett Inn of Ct. (master 1993-97), Women Judges Assn. (co-chair nat. conf. 1990). Office: Colo Supreme Ct Colo State Jud Bldg 2 E 14th Ave Fl 4 Denver CO 80203-2115 *

RICE, NORMAN B., bank executive, former mayor; b. Denver, May 4, 1943; m. Constance Rice; 1 child, Mian. BA in Comm., U. Wash., MPA. Past mgr. corp. contbns. and soc. policy Rainier Nat. Bank; past dir. govt. svcs. Puget Sound Coun. Govts.; past asst. dir. Seattle Urban League; past reporter KIXI Radio; past editor, writer KOMO TV; with govt. City of Seattle, 1978—, city councilman, 1978-89, mayor, 1990-97; pres., chief exec. officer Fed. Home Loan Bank of Seattle, 1999—. Pres. U.S. Conf. of Mayors, 1995; bd. dirs. Safeco Corp. Office: Fed Home Loan Bank 1501 4th Ave Ste 1900 Seattle WA 98101-1693

RICE, PAMELA ANN, marriage and family therapist; d. Charles Jefferson Rice, Jr. and Helen Ann (Larsen) Rice. B. of Bibl. Studies, Friends Internat. Christian U., 1983, M. of Bibl. Counseling, 1985, Dr. of Ministry, 1988; MA in Marriage, Family, Child Counseling, Calif. Christian Inst., 1991. Lic. marriage and family therapist Calif., 2000. Program dir. clin. psychiat. unit Van Nuys Cmty. Hosp., Calif., 1991—93; self-employed marriage and family therapist LA, 2000—. Pastoral staff tng. counselor Vineyard Christian Fellowship, Santa Monica, 1981—86; exec. dir. Homes Of Hope, Hollywood, 1987—89; adminstrv. cons. City of Santa Monica, 1987—89; case mgr. clin. psychiat. unit Buena Pk. Cmty. Hosp., Calif., 1988—91; exec. dir. Mental Health Rehab. Facility, Palmdale, Calif. Recipient Outstanding Achievement award, City of Santa Monica, 1989. Mem.: EMDRIAN (assoc.), Calif. Assn. Marriage and Family Therapists (assoc.). Born-Again Christian. Achievements include receiving a commendation from President Ronald Regan for the development of the Homes of Hope outreach. Avocations: skiing, travel, decorating, poetry. Office: 1460 7th St Ste 306 Santa Monica CA 90401 Home Phone: 310-553-2203; Office Phone: 310-553-2203.

RICE, PATRICIA JANE, journalist; b. St. Louis, Oct. 20, 1942; d. Canice T. and Jane Elizabeth Tobin) R. BA, Maryville Coll., Tenn., 1964; postgrad., St. Louis U., 1965—66. Copywriter Wohl Co., St. Louis, 1964-67; free-lance journalist Paris, 1967; copywriter D'Arcy Advt. Co., St. Louis, 1968; feature writer, columnist St. Louis Post, 1969-94, religion editor, 1994—2004, South reporter, 2004—05; freelance writer, 2005—. Moderator Rutgers U./Eagleton Ctr. Women in Politics Conf., 1980, 82, 84; lectr. in field. Author: City House, 1968, The Eclectic Shopper, 1973, A Catholic Funeral, 2005; co-author: In the Running: The New Political Woman, 1981 V.p. The St. Louis Forum, 1997-2002; bd. dirs. Leadership St. Louis, 1985-90. Recipient Quest award Mo. Press Women's, 1998; Knight Ctr. fellow U. Md., College Park, 1996, 2004. Mem. Journalism Found. Met. St. Louis (pres. 1984-91), St. Louis Newspaper Guild (treas. 1977-87), Soc. Profl. Journalists (mem. St. Louis Regional Arts Commn. grants com.). Avocations: gardening, skiing. Office: Rice Assoc 1221 Locust St Ste 800 Saint Louis MO 63103 Office Phone: 314-241-8000.

RICE, PATRICIA OPPENHEIM LEVIN, retired special education educator, consultant; b. Detroit, Apr. 5, 1932; d. Royal A. and Elsa (Freeman) Oppenheim; m. Charles L. Levin, Feb. 21, 1956 (div. Dec. 1981); children: Arthur David, Amy Ragen, Fredrick Stuart; m. Howard T. Rice, Dec. 16, 1990 (div. Apr. 1994). AB in History, U. Mich., 1954, PhD, 1981; MEd, Marygrove Coll., 1973. Cert. elem. tchr., Mich. Tchr. reading and learning disabled, cons., Detroit Pub. Schs., 1967-76; assoc. prof., coord. spl. edn., Marygrove Coll., 1976-86; adj. prof. Oakland U., 1987-90, U. Miami, 1989-95, ret.; edn. curriculum cons. Lady Elizabeth Sch., Jávea (Alicante) Spain, 1988-91; v.p. Machpelah Non-profit Cemetery Bd., Ferndale, Mich., 1978-87, co-pres., 1987—; adv. bd. Eton Acad., Birmingham, Mich., 1991-93; workshop presenter Dade City Schs., 1992-97; presenter in field. Mem. Mich. regional bd. ORT, 1965-68; mil. affairs and youth svcs. SE Mich. chpt. ARC Bd., 1973-79; v.p. exec. bd. Women's Aux. Children's Hosp. Mich., 1968-73; bd. dirs. women's com. United Cmty. Svcs., 1968-73; judge Dade County Schs. for Tchr. Grants, 1996—2004; bd. dirs. Detroit Grand Opera Assn., 1970-75; com. chair morning of music benefits Detroit Symphony Orch.; torch drive area chmn. United Found., 1967-70; benefactor Fla. Grand Opera, 1990-2001, grand benefactor, 2002—, guild exec. bd., 1992-, v.p., 1998-99, co-pres. 2000-02, chair, found. bd. dirs., 2000-01; guild exec. bd. Miami City Ballet, 1996-2000, Choreographers Cir., 1990-; chair Lincoln Rd. Walk, 1996, co-chair All Star Luncheon, 1996, Ball Com., 1992; active Diabetes Rsch. Inst. & Found. Love & Hope Com., Fla. Concert Assn. Cresendo Soc., 1993-97, Villa Maria Angel, 1996—, v.p. angel bd. 1998—2005, co-pres. Angels of Villa Maria, 2005-, found. bd. dirs. 2000—; v.p. Miami Children's Hosp., 2004-, co-pres., 2005—; panel judge Dade County Cultural Affairs Coun., 2002-04; v.p., amb. Mt. Sinai Hosp. Alzheimer's Bd. Mem. NAACP (life), Navy League, Greater Miami Social Register, Citizens Interested in the Arts (charter, grant chair, exec. bd. 1997—), Williams Island Club, Miami Shores Country Club, Surf Club, Phi Delta Kappa, Pi Lambda Theta.

RICE, PAUL JACKSON, lawyer, educator; b. East St. Louis, July 15, 1938; s. Ray Jackson and Mary Margaret (Campbell) Rice; m. Carole Jeanne Valentine, June 6, 1959; children: Rebecca Jeanne Ross, Melissa Ann Hansen, Paul Jackson Jr. BA, U. Mo., 1960, JD, 1962; LLM, Northwestern U., 1970; student, Command and Gen. Staff Coll., 1974-75, Army War Coll., 1982-83. Bar: Mo. 1962, Ill. 1969, U.S. Dist. Ct. (no. dist.) Ill. 1970, U.S. Supreme Ct. 1972, U.S. Ct. Appeals (DC cir.) 1991, DC 1993, U.S. Dist. Ct. DC 2000. Commd. 1st lt. U.S. Army, 1962, advanced through grades to col., 1980; asst. judge advocate 4th Armored Div., Goeppingen, Germany, 1966-69; dep. staff judge advocate 1st Cavalry Div., Vietnam, 1970-71; inst., prof. Judge Adv. Gen. Sch., Charlottesville, Va., 1971-74, commdt., dean, 1985-88; br. chief Gen. Law Br., Pentagon, 1975-78; chief adminstrv. law div. Office Judge Adv. Gen., Pentagon, Washington, 1978-79; staff judge adv. 1st Inf. Div., Ft. Riley, Kans., 1979-82, V Corps U.S. Army, Frankfurt, Germany, 1983-85, USACAC, Ft. Leavenworth, Kans., 1989-90; faculty Indsl. Coll. Armed Forces, 1988-89; chief counsel Nat. Hwy. Traffic Safety Adminstrn., Washington, 1990-93; ptnr. Arent Fox PLLC, Washington, 1993—. Contbr. articles to profl. jours. Recipient Granted Legal Svc. award, State of Hessen, Germany, 1985, cert. of merit, U. Mo. Alumni Assn., 1987. Mem.: Ctr. Law and Nat. Security, Mo. Bar Assn., Lion Tamers, Phi Delta Phi. Methodist. Avocations: writing, reading, golf. Home: 7835 Vervain Ct Springfield VA 22152-3107 Office: Arent Fox PLLC 1050 Connecticut Ave NW Washington DC 20036-5339 Office Phone: 202-857-6009. Business E-Mail: ricepj@arentfox.com.

RICE, PHILIP L., bank executive; BBA, U. Akron, Ohio; MBA, Case Western Res. U., Cleve. Mgmt. trainee Nat. City Corp., Cleve., 1980, mng. dir. Nat. City Venture, mgr. regional and nat. comml. real estate businesses, pres. Ohio for Corp. Banking bus. unit, corp. exec. v.p., pres., CEO Nat. City Bank. Bd. dirs., chmn. bd. trustees Cleve. Devel. Advisors. Mem. corp. cabinet Harvest for Hunger; mem. vis. com. Case Western Res. U. Weatherhead Sch. Mgmt.; bd. dirs., vice chairperson, exec. com. mem. Cuyahoga Cmty. Coll. Found. Office: Nat City Corp Nat City Ctr 1900 E Ninth St Cleveland OH 44114-3484 Office Phone: 216-222-2000. *

RICE, REGINA KELLY, marketing executive; b. Yonkers, NY, July 11, 1955; d. Howard Adrian and Lucy Virginia (Butler) Kelly; m. Mark Christopher Rice, Sept. 11, 1981; children: Amanda Kelly, Jaime Brannen. BS in Cmty. Nutrition, Cornell U., 1978. Account exec. J. Walter Thompson Co., NYC, 1978—79; sr. account exec. Ketchum, MacLeod & Grove, NYC, 1979—80; supr. Burson Marstellar, Hong Kong, 1981—83; v.p., dep. dir. food and beverage unit, creative dir. N.Y. office Hill and Knowlton, NYC, 1983—91; mktg. cons. Rice & Rohr, NYC, 1991—93; sr. v.p., dir. consumer mktg. practice Manning, Selvage & Lee, NYC, 1993—97, sr. v.p. global tng. dir., 1999—; chief inspiration officer, dir. corp. devel. Internat. Pub. Rels. Assn., 1999—2001. Writer Fast and Healthy Mag., 1991-2000. Mem. Pub. Rels. Soc. Am. Roman Catholic. Avocation: collecting Provence pottery. Home: 31 Wrangler Ln Bell Canyon CA 91307 Office: Manning Selvage & Lee 6500 Wilshire Blvd Los Angeles CA 90048-4920 Office Phone: 323-866-6023.

RICE, RICHARD LEE, retired architect; b. Raleigh, NC, May 4, 1919; s. Robert Edward Lee and Grace Lucille (Betts) R.; m. Cora Belle Stegall, Apr. 12, 1946; children— Richard Lee, Westwood Carter, David Sinclair. BS in Archtl. Engring., N.C. State U., 1941; grad., U.S. Army Command and Gen. Staff Coll., 1961. Assoc. Cooper-Shumaker, Architects, Raleigh, 1946-47; prin. Richard L. Rice, Architects, Raleigh, 1947-48; assoc. Cooper, Haskins & Rice and predecessor firm, Raleigh, 1948-52, ptnr., 1953-54, Haskins & Rice, Architects, Raleigh, 1954-85; prin. Haskins, Rice, Savage & Pearce, Architects, 1985-91, pres., 1985-91. V.p. N.C. Design Found., 1973; pres. N.C. Archtl. Found., 1975; mem. Raleigh Arts Commn., 1978-82, Raleigh Hist. Properties Commn., 1990-92, Raleigh Hist. Dists. Commn., 1991-92. Archtl. works include renovations, Raleigh Meml. Auditorium, 1964, 78, 91 (SE Regional AIA award of merit 1964), Auditorium, 4 high schs. and 13 elem. schs., Raleigh Civic Ctr., stack addition Wilson Libr. U. N.C., Chapel Hill, 1977, Reidsville, N.C. Jr. High Sch.; assoc. architect Raleigh Radisson Hotel, 1980, One Hanover Sq. Office Bldg., 1985, Two Hannover Sq. Office Bldg., 1990, additions and renovations to Raleigh Meml. Auditorium, 1989, 3 indsl. plants, 7 bldgs., Wake Tech. C.C., 50 chs. Pres. Wake County (N.C.) Hist. Soc., 1973-74; mem. N.C. Gov.'s Com. for Facilities for Physically Handicapped, 1970-73; arbitrator Am. Arbitration Assn. With inf. and C.E. U.S. Army, 1941-46, ETO; col. USAR; ret. Decorated Silver Star.; Legion of Merit; Bronze Star; Purple Heart. Fellow AIA (pres. N.C. chpt. 1970, Disting. Svc. award N.C. chpt. 1975); mem. Raleigh Council Architects (pres. 1950), Nat. Trust for Hist. Preservation, N.C. State Art Soc., Ret. Officers Assn. U.S. (pres. Triangle chpt. 1983), N.C. State U. Gen. Alumni Assn. (pres., chmn. bd. 1960-61, pres. Class 1941, 1986-91), Carolina Country Club, Lions, Torch Club (pres. 1982-83), Phi Eta Sigma, Phi Kappa Phi. Democrat. Baptist. Office Phone: 919-782-0122.

RICE, RICK BLACKBURN, application developer, systems analyst; b. Louisville, Sept. 17, 1954; s. Blackburn M. and Alice Jane (Walker) R.; m. Peijuan Miao, June 23, 1989; children: Richard J., Franklin W. BA in Psychology, U. Mich., 1978; MS in Computer Systems Mgmt., U. Md., 1997. Mem. computing staff Hughes Aircraft Co., El Segundo, Calif., 1980-84; programmer, analyst Candle Corp., LA, 1984-86; sr. programmer, analyst Computer Assocs., LA, 1986-88; fgn. expert Shaanxi Inst. Fin. and Econs., Xi'an, People's Republic of China, 1989-90; sr. programmer, analyst Disclosure, Inc., Bethesda, Md., 1988-96; info. sys. specialist IBM, Gaithersburg, Md., 1996—97; sr. programmer analyst Sci. Applications Internat. Corp., Falls Church, Va., 1998—2003. Avocation: sinology. Home: 714 Sligo Ave # 210 Silver Spring MD 20910 E-mail: rick_rice@hotmail.com.

RICE, RONALD JAMES, hospital administrator; b. Springfield, Mo., Feb. 5, 1944; s. Glen Elwood and Alice Jeanett (Robinson) R. BSBA, Cen. Mo. State U., 1966, MABA, 1969, Specialist, 1972. Lic. nursing home adminstr.; lic. risk mgr. Unit mgr. Bapt. Med. Ctr., Kansas City, Mo., 1970-71; dir. unit mgmt. Ind. Health Ctr., Independence, Mo., 1971-72; adminstrv. officer Meth. Hosp., Jacksonville, Fla., 1972-73, dir. personnel, 1973-74; assoc. adminstr. Humana Hosp. Orange Park (Fla.), 1974-77; adminstr. Cathedral Rehab. Hosp., Jacksonville, 1977-79, Marion County Gen. Hosp., Hamilton, Ala., 1979-80, Nassau Gen. Hosp., Fernandina Beach, Fla., 1980-85, Reception Med. Ctr., Lake Butler, Fla., 1985-91; regional adminstr. health svcs. Dept. Corrections, Gainesville, Fla., 1991—; sr. health svc. adminstr. Columbia Correctional Instn., 1999—2006. Cons. Clay Meml. Hosp., Green Cove Springs, Fla., 1976-77, Allied Health Care, Jacksonville, 1989. Mem. Polit. Action Com., Fla. Hosp. Assn., 1990, Coun. on Crime and Delinquency, Gainesville, 1990, Human Resources Com., Orlando, 1991; active Orange Park Presbyn. Ch. With U.S. Army, 1967-69. Decorated Army Commendation medal. Fellow Am. Coll. Health Care Execs.; mem. Am. acad. Med. Adminstrs., Am. Coll. Health Care Adminstrs., Am. Soc. Personnel Adminstrs., Fla. Hosp. Assn., Rotary (pres. 1984-86). Democrat. Avocations: boating, collecting model cars, antique juke box collecting, reading. Home: 1744 Horton Dr Orange Park FL 32073-2757 Personal E-mail: ricerjq45@aol.com.

RICE, ROSE ANN M., secondary school educator; b. Washington, Mo., Nov. 9, 1948; d. Martin Henry and Mary Ann Kraft; m. Frank William Rice, July 1, 1995. B in Chemistry and Math, Notre Dame Coll., St. Louis, 1971; MS in Edn., Creighton U., 1981. Cert. tchr. Mo., FAST 1 and FAST 2 sci. tchr. Sci. tchr. St. Gabriel Sch., St. Louis, 1971—75, Hannibal Cath. Sch., Mo., 1975—84, St. Aloysius Sch., St. Louis, 1984—88, Immaculate Conception Sch., Union, Mo., 1991—95, Notre Dame HS, St. Louis, 2001—; sci. and math. tchr. St. Cecilia Sch., St. Louis, 1995—97, St. Dominic Savlo Sch., St. Louis, 1997—2001; prin., sci. and math. tchr. St. Anthony's Sch., Sullivan, Mo., 1988—91. Regional sci. coord. East Ctrl. Coll., Union, 1991—95; tutor Sylvan Learning Ctr., Fenton, Mo., 2002—04, Notre Dame Tutorial Ctr., St. Louis, 2004—05; speech coach, judge in field; moderator sch. sci. fairs. Bd. dirs. Phoenix Homeless Shelter, Washington, Mo., 1992—94; mem. ch. coun. Hannibal (Mo.) Cath. Ch., 1980—84, Mary Mother Ch., St. Louis, 2000—01. Recipient ribbons for needlework and crafts, Washington Town & Country Fair; grantee, Litzinger Ctr., Mo. Bot. Gardens, St. Louis, 1998—2001. Mem.: NSTA, Sci. Tchrs. Mo. Roman Catholic. Avocations: needlecrafts, reading, walking, golf, travel. Office: Notre Dame HS 320 E Ripa Ave Saint Louis MO 63125 Business E-Mail: ricer@ndhs.net.

RICE, STANLEY ARTHUR, biology professor; b. Cushing, Okla., May 30, 1957; s. Arthur John and Nina Irene (Hicks) R.; m. Althea Lisette Clarkston, June 9, 1984; 1 child, Anita. BA, U. Calif., Santa Barbara, 1979; PhD, U. Ill., 1987. Vis. teaching specialist U. Ill., Urbana, 1986-87; asst. prof. The King's Coll., Briarcliff Manor, NY, 1987-90; vis. faculty Sarah Lawrence Coll., Bronxville, NY, 1989-90; asst. prof. Huntington (Ind.) Coll., 1990-93, S.W. State U., Marshall, Minn., 1993-98, S.E. Okla. State U., Durant, 1998—2003, assoc. prof., 2003—. Vis. faculty mem. Wheaton (Ill.) Coll. Sci. Sta., 1993—, Taylor U., Upland, Ind., 1993. Author: Encyclopedia of Evolution, 2006; contbr. articles to profl. jours. including Internat. Jour. Plant Sci., Am. Biol. Tchr., Jour. Coll. Sci. Tchg., Oecologia, Perspectives on Sci. and Christian Faith, Nat. Ctr. for Sci. Edn. Reports, Jour. Entomol. Sci. Predoctoral fellow NSF, U. Ill., 1980. Mem. Ecol. Soc. Am., British Ecol. Soc., Bot. Soc. Am., Am. Sci. Affiliation, Am. Biol. Tchrs. Office: Dept Biol Sci SE Okla State Univ Durant OK 74701 Office Phone: 580-745-2688. E-mail: srice@sosu.edu.

RICE, STEPHEN GARY, pediatrician, sports medicine physician, educator; b. Bklyn., Dec. 21, 1945; s. Abraham S. Rice and Anne (Shelling) Rice-Brown; m. Hilary Jo Turett, May 10, 1987; children: Adam, Bryan. AB, Columbia Coll., 1967; MD, PhD, NYU, 1974; MPH, U. Wash., 1983. Diplomate in pediat. and sports medicine Am. Bd. Pediat. Intern, resident Children's Hosp. and U. Wash., Seattle, 1974-77; faculty mem. sports medicine U. Wash., Seattle, 1977-96; program dir. primary care sports medicine fellowship Jersey Shore Univ. Med. Ctr., Neptune, NJ, 1996—; clin. assoc. prof. pediat. Robert Wood Johnson Med. Sch. U. Medicine and Dentistry NJ, New Brunswick, 1999—. Team physician U. Wash., 1977-81, Georgian Ct. U., 1997-; developer, dir. Athletic Health Care Sys., 1978—; dir. Jersey Shore Sports Medicine Ctr., 1997-; med. cons., NJ Youth Soccer Olympic Devel. Program, 2002-; cons. in field. Author: Athletic Health Care System, 1988. Mem. Alumni Representative Com., Columbia Coll., 1974-, Concussion in Sports Steering Com., Brain Inquiry Assn. NJ, 2005-. Named Top Doctor in Sports Medicine, NJ, NJ Mag., 2001, 2003, 2005, Top Doctor in Greater NY Metro. Area, Castle Connelly, 2002—06; recipient Commendation award, Washington State Interscholastic Activities Assn., 1981, 1995, Vol. Faculty Tchg. award, UMDNJ-Robert Wood Johnson Med. Sch., 2000, Silvio O. Conte award, Brain Injury Assn. NJ, 2006. Fellow: Am. Coll. Sports Medicine (sec. Greater NY regional chpt. 1997—2002, chmn. health and sci. policy com. 2000—, trustee 2007—, mem. bd. trustees 2007—), Am. Acad. Pediat. (chmn. sports medicine com. NJ chpt. 1999—, chmn. govt. affairs com. NJ chpt. 2000—06, sec.-editor NJ chpt. 2002—04, exec. com. of sports medicine and fitness coun. 2003—, treas. NJ chpt. 2004—06, v.p.-elect NJ chpt. 2006—); mem.: AAHPERD, Med. Soc. NJ, Am. Med. Soc. Sports Medicine, Nat. Strength and Conditioning Assn. Avocations: sports, cooking, gardening, gilbert & sullivan, chess. Home: 6 Wildflower Ct Manalapan NJ 07726-2861 Office: Jersey Shore Univ Med Ctr Dept Pediat PO Box 397 Neptune NJ 07754-0397 Office Phone: 732-776-2384. Business E-Mail: srice@meridianhealth.com.

RICE, STEVEN WILLIAM, ophthalmologist; BA, St. Mary's U., Winona, Minn., 1979; MD, Mayo Med. Sch., Rochester, Minn., 1983. Diplomate Am. Bd. Ophthalmology, 1988. Ophthalmologist St. Cloud Eye Clinic, Minn., 1987—. Fellow: ACS; mem.: AMA, Minn. Med. Assn., Am. Acad. Ophthalmology, Minn. Acad. Ophthalmology. Office: 2055 N 15th St Saint Cloud MN 56303

RICE, STUART ALAN, chemist, educator; b. NYC, Jan. 6, 1932; s. Harry L. and Helen (Rayfield) Rice; m. Marian Ruth Coopersmith, June 1, 1952 (dec. June 1994); children: Barbara, Janet; m. Ruth O'Brien, Sept. 27, 1997; 1 child, David Lawrence. BS, Bklyn. Coll., 1952; MA, Harvard, 1954, PhD, 1955. Jr. fellow Harvard, 1955—57; faculty U. Chgo., 1957—60, prof. chemistry, 1960—69, Louis Block prof. phys. scis., 1969—77, chmn. dept. chemistry, 1971—76, Frank P. Hixon disting. service prof., 1977—, dean phys. scis. div., 1981—95, dir. Inst. Study Metals, 1957—59; Newton Abraham prof. Oxford U., 1999—2000. Mem. Nat. Sci. Bd., 1980—86. Author: Polyelectrolyte Solutions, 1961, Statistical Mechanics of Simple Liquids, 1965, Physical Chemistry, 1980, 2d edit., 2000, Optical Control of Molecular Dynamics, 2000; contbr. articles to profl. jours. Named Falk-Plautt lectr., Columbia U., 1964, Riley lectr., Notre Dame U., 1964, U. lectr. chemistry, U. Western Ont., 1970, Seaver lectr., U. Soc. Calif, 1972, Noyes lectr., U. Tex., 1975, Foster lectr., SUNY, 1976, Frank T. Gucker lectr., Ind. U., 1976, Fairchild lectr., Calif. Inst. Tech., 1979, Baker lectr., Cornell U., 1985—86, Centenary lectr., Royal Soc. Chemistry, 1986—87, Nat. lectr., Phi Beta Kappa, 1994—95, Kennedy lectr., Washington U., 2002, Noyes lectr., U. Oreg., 2002; recipient Centennial medal, Harvard U., 1997, Nat. Medal of Sci., 1999, Hirschfelder award for Theoretical Chemistry, 2002; fellow, Guggenheim, 1960—61, Sr. Postdoctoral fellow, NSF, 1965—66, USPHS Spl. Postdoctoral fellow, U. Copenhagen, 1970—71. Fellow: Royal Irish Acad. Scis., Am. Philos. Soc.; mem.: AAAS, Danish Acad. Sci. and Letters, N.Y. Acad. Scis. (A. Cressy Morrison prize 1955), Faraday Soc. (Marlowe medal 1963), Am. Phys. Soc., Am. Acad. Sci. (Hirschfelder award for theoret. chemistry 2002, Willis Lamb medal 2004), Nat. Acad. Sci., Am. Chem. Soc. (Pure Chemistry award 1963, Leo Hendrik Baekland award 1971, Peter Debye award 1985, Hildebrand award 1987). Office Phone: 773-702-7199. Business E-Mail: s-rice@uchicago.edu.

RICE, SUE ANN, retired dean, psychologist; b. Ponca City, Okla., Sept. 17, 1934; d. Alfred and Helen (Revard) R. BS in Edn., U. Okla., 1956; MA, Cath. U., 1979, PhD, 1988. Ensign USN, 1956, advanced through grades to comdr., 1973; ednl. svcs. officer 9th Naval Dist., Great Lakes, Ill., 1956-58; adminstr., asst. staff, comdr. in-chief Pacific Fleet, Honolulu, 1958-61; head edn. div. Naval Air Sta., Lemoore, Calif., 1961-63; instr., acad. dir. Women Officers' Sch., Newport, R.I., 1963-66; head. tng. div. Naval Command Systems Support Activity, Washington, 1966-70; head, ops. support sec. staff, comdr.-in-chief Lant, Norfolk, Va., 1970-74; sr. U.S. rep. NATO, subgroup 5 orgn. JCS, Washington, 1974-77; ret. USN, 1977; head vocation office Archdiocese of Washington, 1977-78; cons. Notre Dame Inst., Arlington, Va., 1989-97, dean of students, 1990-95; ret., 1995. Lectr. Cath. U. Am., Washington, 1983-84; bd. dirs. Villa Cortona Apostolic Ctr., Bethesda, 1984-94. Tech. reviewer Personnel Administration, 1964; editor (newsletter) Vocation News, 1978. Conoco scholarship Continental Oil Co., 1952-56; recipient Meritorious Svc. medal Pres. of U.S., 1977, rsch. grant Cath. U., Sigma Xi, 1986. Mem.: Lay Women's Assn. (internat. v.p.), Cath. War Vets. (nat. membership task force com., nat. youth act com., nat. co-chmn. pub. rels. com.), Gamma Phi Beta, Kappa Delta Pi. Roman Catholic. Avocations: travel, music, gardening, woodworking. Home: PO Box 2742 Ponca City OK 74602-2742

RICE, SUSAN ELIZABETH, foreign policy analyst, former federal agency administrator; m. Ian Cameron; children: John D. Rice-Cameron, H. Maris Rice-Cameron. BA in History, Stanford U., 1986; MPhil, Oxford U., 1988, DPhil, 1990. Mgmt. cons. McKinsey and Co., Toronto, Ont., Canada, 1991-93; dir. internat. orgns. and peacekeeping NSC, Washington, 1993-95, spl. asst. to the Pres., sr. dir. African affairs, 1995-97; asst. sec. state African affairs US Dept. State, Washington, 1997—2001; mng. dir., prin. Intellibridge Internat., Washington, 2001—02; sr. fellow fgn. policy The Brookings Instn., Washington, 2002—. Fgn. policy aide Dem. Pres. Campaign, Boston, 1988 Harry S. Truman scholar, 1984, Rhodes scholar, 1986; recipient Walter Frewen Lord prize, Royal Commonwealth Soc., 1990, Assn. prize, Chatham House-British Internat. Studies, 1992, Samuel Nelson Drew Meml. award, NSC, 2000. Mem. Phi Beta Kappa. Office: The Brookings Instn 1775 Massachusetts Ave NW Washington DC 20036

RICE, THOMAS CHARLES, lawyer; b. NYC, Jan. 18, 1956; s. Thomas P. and Laura T. (Hage) R.; m. Cheryl A. Christman, Sept. 15, 1984; children: Thomas Christman, Matthew David. BA in math. magna cum laude, St. John's U., 1978, JD, 1981. Bar: US Dist. Ct. (so. dist.) NY, US Dist. Ct. (ea. dist.), NY, US Dist Ct. (we. dist.) NY, US Dist. Ct. (no. dist.) NY, US Dist. Ct. (no. dist.) Tex., US Dist. Ct. Colo., US Dist Ct. (no. dist.) Okla., US Ct. Appeals (2nd cir.) (U.S. Ct. Apeals), US Ct. Appeals (3rd cir.), US Ct. Appeals (5th cir.), US Supreme Ct, US Dist. Ct. (ea. dist.), Mich. Assoc. Simpson Thacher & Bartlett, NYC, 1981-88, ptnr., 1989—, mem. exec. com. Contbr. articles to profl. jours. Mem. ABA (litigation sect.), N.Y. State Bar Assn., Assn. Bar City of N.Y. (Judiciary Comm.) Office: Simpson Thacher & Bartlett LLP 425 Lexington Ave Fl 15 New York NY 10017-3954 Office Phone: 212-455-3040. Office Fax: 212-455-2502. Business E-Mail: trice@stblaw.com.

RICE, THOMAS HILARY (SPEEDY RICE), lawyer; b. Richmond, Va., Apr. 10, 1954; s. Spencer Victor and Kathleen Francis (Reney) R.; m. Judy Clare Clarke, Dec. 31, 1975. BA in Sociology, Furman U., Greenville, SC, 1976; JD summa cum laude, Calif. Western Sch. Law, San Diego, 1986. Bar: Calif. 1986, Wash. 1994, US Supreme Ct., US Ct. Appeals (9th cir.). Travel cons. TMT Travel, La Jolla, Calif., 1977; mgr. TLC Travel, San Diego, 1977-80; mgr. passenger/interline sales Pinehurst Airlines, Greenville, SC, 1980-81; gen. mgr. Mission Airlines, El Cajon, Calif., 1981-82; customer svc. and pub. rels. coord. Balboa Travel, San Diego, 1982-83; assoc. Luce, Foreward, Hamilton & Scripps, San Diego, 1983-89; of counsel Robinson & Phillips, San Diego, 1989—90; pvt. practice atty. Law Office of Speedy Rice, San Diego, 1989—95. Aviation cons. Calif. Air Express, Marina del Ray, 1982; instr. Nat. U., San Diego, 1982-83, San Diego Cmty. Coll. Dist., 1979-80; dir. externship prog., trial advocacy instr. Gonzaga U. Sch. Law, 1993-2002. Contbr. articles to profl. publs. Trustee Calif. Western Sch. Law; mem., sec. Internat. Aerospace Hall of Fame; bd. dirs. US-USSR Hist. Aircraft Search. Mem. NACDL, Am. Trial Lawyers Assn., ABA, San Diego Trial Lawyers Assn., Calif. Trial Lawyers Assn. Democrat. Roman Catholic. Avocations: flying, photography, bicycling. Mailing: PO Box 80188 San Diego CA 92138

RICE, THOMAS HOWARD, healthcare educator; b. Washington, Apr. 21, 1954; s. John Donald and Dorothy Pechman R.; m. Katherine Anne Desmond, Oct. 21, 1953; children: Clara, Daniel. BA, U. N.C., 1976; MA, U. Calif., Berkeley, 1979, PhD, 1982. Sr. health economist SRI Internat., Menlo Park, Calif., 1979—83; assoc. prof. U.N.C. Sch. Pub. Health, Chapel Hill, 1983—91; prof. UCLA Sch. Pub. Health, 1991—, vice chancellor for academic personnel, 2006—. Chmn. bd. dir. Acad. Health, Washington, 2005—06; editor Med. Care Rsch. and Rev., Thousand Oaks, Calif., 1994—2000; chair Dept. Health Svcs., UCLA Sch. of Pub. Health, 1996—2000. Author: Economics of Health Reconsidered, 2003; editor: Changing the U.S. Health Care System, 2006. Recipient Young Investigator of the Yr. award, Assn. Health Svcs. Rsch., 1988, Thompson prize, Assn. U. Programs in Health Adminstrn., 1992, Article of the Yr. award, Assn. Health Svcs. Rsch., 1998. Mem.: Inst. of Medicine. Office: 2138 Murphy Hall Los Angeles CA 90095-1405 Office Phone: 310-206-9345. Business E-Mail: trice@conet.ucla.edu.

RICE, SIR TIMOTHY MILES BINDON, lyricist; b. Amersham, Eng., Nov. 10, 1944; s. Hugh Gordon and Joan Odette (Bawden) Rice; m. Jane McIntosh, Aug. 19, 1974; children: Eva Jane Florence, Donald Alexander Hugh. Student, Lancing Coll., Sussex, 1958—62. Solicitor's articled clk. Pettit & Westlake, London, 1963—66; mgmt. trainee E.M.I. Records Manchester Sq., London, 1966—68; record prodr. Norrie Paramor Orgn., London, 1968—69; ind. writer, record producer London, 1969—; broadcaster BBC Radio and TV, Ind. TV, England, 1973—; formed label EP Records with Elaine Paige, 1981. Founder, dir. GRRR Books, 1978—, Pavilion Books, 1981—97; mem. of pop group Aardvarks, 1961—63, Whang and the Cheviots. Host (TV) Friday Night Saturday Morning, Musical Triangles, Disco; lyricist for: Marvin Hamlisch, Rick Wakeman, Vangelis, Paul McCartney, Mike Batt, Francis Lai, John Barry, Freddie Mercury, Richard Kerr, Graham Gouldman, lyricist stage musicals (with music by Andrew Lloyd Weber: Joseph and the Amazing Technicolor Dreamcoat, 1968, Joseph and the Amazing Technicolor Dreamcoat, rev., 1973 (Tony award nominations best book of musical and best original score, 1982, Grammy award nomination best cast show album, 1982), Jesus Christ Superstar, 1970 (Grammy award nomination album of the year, 1971, Tony award nomination best original score, 1972), lyricist: The Likes of Us, 1965, Evita, 1976, rev., 1978 (Tony awards best book of musical and best original score, 1980, Grammy award best cast show album, 1980), Heathcliff, 1995, Cricket, 1986, King David, 1997, Aida, 1998, Andrew Lloyd Webber: Masterpiece, 2002, Mickey's Philhar Magic, 2003, Michelle Kwan: Princess on Ice, Michelle Kwan Skates to Disney's Greatest Hits, Aladdin on Ice, Stuart Little, The Road to El Dorado, Connie and Carla, 2004, lyricist for film musicals (with music by Elton John): The Lion King, 1994, lyricist with music by Stephen Oliver: Blondel, 1983, lyricist with music by Benny Andersson and Björn Ulvaeus: Chess, 1984, rev., 1986, 1988, 1995—96, 2002, lyricist with music by Michel Berger: Tycoon, 1992, lyricist with music by Alan Menken: Beauty and the Beast, 1994, lyricist for film musicals (with music by Menken): Aladdin, 1992, lyricist for songs (from Aladdin, with Menken): A Whole New World, 1992 (Academy award best original song, 1992, Grammy award song of the year, 1993), lyricist for songs from The Lion King with John: Can You Feel the Love Tonight, 1994 (Academy award best original song, 1994), Circle of Life, 1994 (Academy award nomination best original song, 1994), Hakuna Matata, 1994 (Academy award nomination best original song, 1994); prodr.: (stage musical) Anything Goes, 1989; author: Heartaches Cricketers' Almanack (yearly), 1975—, script for 15 part series on the hisotry of Western Pop Music; author: (with others) The Guiness Book of British Hit Singles, 1977, The Guiness Book of Hits of the Seventies, 1980, Treasures of Lord's, 1989, The Complete Eurovision Song Contest Companion, 1998; editor: Lord Taverners Sticky Wicket Book, 1980; actor: Joseph and the Amazing Technicolor Dreamcoat, The Survivor, 1980, Three More Men in a Boat, 1982, Cricket, 1986. Chmn. Stars Orgn. for Spastics, 1983—85, Shaftesbury Ave. Centenary Com., 1984—86, Found. for Sport and the Arts, 1991—; pres. Lord's Taverners, 1988—90, 2000; bd. dir. The Really Useful Group, 1986—88. Inducted Songwriters Hall of Fame, 1999, as a Disney Legend, Walt Disney Studios Park, Paris, 2002; knighted, 1994; recipient 12 Ivor Novello awards. Mem.: Music Industry Forum (mem. 1998—), Garrick, Saints and Sinners Club, Heartaches Cricket Club (mem. 1973—), Marylebone Cricket Club (mem. 1969—, pres. 2002—03). Mailing: Attn: Michael Sissons PFD Drury House 34-43 Russell St London WC2B 5HA England

RICE, WAYNE, artist, educator, small business owner; b. Chgo., Ill., Jan. 13, 1950; s. Raymond and Genevieve (Kocol) Rice; 1 child, Conor Raymond. Student, U. Calif. Berkeley, 1968—70, Northern Ill. U., 1971; BA in art studio, U. N.Mex., 1980; cert. in tchg., U. Colo., 1988. Cert. tchr. cert. K-12 U. Colo., 1988. Graphic artist Webb-Pantaleoni Design, Taos, N.Mex., 1980—81; art dir. Artlines Inc., Taos, 1981—84; graphic designer Westview Press Inc., Boulder, Colo., 1985—87; designer, mus. educator Mus. of N. Mex., Office of Statewide Programs and Edn., Santa Fe, 1989—92; curator of edn. Mus. of N. Mex., Palace of Gov., Santa Fe, 1992; creative dir., owner Design Arts, 1984—; visual info. specialist The Imagination Team, US Dept. of Interior, Bur. Land Mgmt., Anasazi Heritage Ctr., Dolores, Colo., 1992—2007, Dolores Pub. Lands Ctr., 2007—. Cons. Design Arts, Boulder, Colo., 1986—2007; staff designer, edn. divsn. Mus. of N.Mex., Santa Fe, 1989—91; curator of edn. Mus. of N.Mex., Palace of the Gov. Mus., Santa Fe, 1991—92. Numerous group shows including, exhibited in group shows at Internat. Art Competition, LA, 1984, Palo Alto Cultural Ctr., Calif., 1986, Gallery at the Rep, Santa Fe, N.Mex., 1989, Richmond Art Ctr., Calif., 1997, Ctr. Visual Arts, Chautauqua, NY, 2000, Mus. Contemporary Art, Ft. Collins, Colo., 2004, one-man shows include Harwood Found. U. N.Mex., Taos, N.Mex., 1981, The Bridge Gallery Boulder Pub. Libr., Colo., 1985, Art and Crafts Cooperative, 1986, Tybie Davis Satin Gallery Santa Fe Pub. Libr., N.Mex., 1992, Centennial Savings Bank, Durango, Colo., 1996, prin. works include mural Four Corners Child Advocacy Ctr., Cortez, Colo., mural Neonatal Intensive Care Unit Holy Cross Hosp., Taos, N.Mex., Represented in permanent collections City Cortez Pub. Libr., Taos Coutny Assn. Retarded Citizens. Finalist Nat. Forest Sys. Stamp Contest, USDA, 1992; recipient Design award, N. Mex. Route 66 Assn., Shadow Ridge Corp., Town of Taos Adminstrn., Leopold's Records, U. Calif., Artist-in-residence, Nat. Pk. Svc., USDA Forest Svc., Colo., Wy., N. Mex., Silver award, Nat. Assn. Interpretation, 2005; grantee, N.Mex. Arts Divsn., 1982, 1983. Mem.: Colo. Arts Assn., Four Corners Club-Toastmasters Internat. (pres.), Nat. Assn. for Interpretation. Avocations: visual arts, creative writing, hiking, walking, bicycling. Mailing: PO Box 746 Dolores CO 81323 Personal E-mail: desarts@gmail.com.

RICE, WILLIAM EDWARD, journalist; b. Albany, NY, July 26, 1938; s. Harry Edward, Jr. and Elizabeth (Lally) R.; m. Carol Timmon, June 3, 1978 (div.); m. Jill Van Cleave, Aug. 20, 1983. BA in History, U. Va., 1960; MS with honors, Columbia U., 1963. Reporter, editorial writer, critic Washington Post, 1963-69; student LeCordon Bleu, Paris, 1969-70; dir. L'Ecole de Cuisine, Bethesda, Md., 1971-72; freelance writer, restaurant critic Washingtonian Mag., 1971-72; exec. food editor Washington Post, 1972-80; editor-in-chief Food and Wine Mag., NYC, 1980-85; food and wine columnist Chgo. Tribune, 1986—2003. Dining In columnist Gentlemen's Quarterly, 1987-89; chmn. restaurant awards com. James Beard Found., 1993-2003, chmn. who's who food and beverage in Am. com., 2005—. Author: Feasts of Wine and Food, 1986, Steak Lovers Cookbook, 1997; editor: (with others) Where to Eat in America, 1978, 2d edit., 1980, 3d edit., 1987. Served with USN, 1960-62. Recipient Vesta award as outstanding newspaper food editor, 1979, Ordre du Merite Agricole (France), 1983 Home: 655 W Buena Ave Chicago IL 60613-2201 Office Phone: 773-975-6685. Personal E-mail: wricechicago@yahoo.com.

RICE, WINSTON EDWARD, lawyer, priest; b. Shreveport, La., Feb. 22, 1946; s. Winston Churchill and Margaret (Coughlin) R.; m. Barbara Reily Gay, Apr. 16, 1977; 1 child, Andrew Hynes; children by previous marriage: Winston Hobson, Christian MacTaggart. Student, Centenary Coll. La., 1967; JD, La. State U., 1971. Bar: La. 1971, Colo. 1990, Tex. 1992; ordained to priesthood Episcopal Ch., 2005. Cons. geologist, Gulfport, Miss., 1968-70; ptnr. Phelps, Dunbar, New Orleans, 1971-88; sr. ptnr. Rice, Fowler, New Orleans, Houston, Miami, Fla., London and Bogota, 1988-2000; gen. mgr. Winston Edw. Rice LLC, Covington, La., 2000—. Instr. law La. State U., Baton Rouge, 1970-71. Assoc. editor La. Law Rev., 1970-71. Asst. rector Christ Ch., Covington, La., 2005—. Mem.: Trucking Industry Def. Assn., Ctr. Transp. Law and Policy, Soc. Ins. Trainers and Educators, Assn. Average Adjusters (U.K.), Assn. Average Adjusters U.S., Maritime Law Assn. U.S. (chmn. subcom. on offshore exploration and devel. 1985—88, vice chmn. com. internat. law of the sea 1988—91, chmn. 1991—95, membership sec. 1998—2002), Com. Maritime Internat. (titulary mem.), Fedn. Ins. and Corp. Counsel, La. Assn. Def. Counsel, New Orleans Assn. Def. Counsel, Can. Transp. Lawyers Assn., New Orleans Bar Assn., Tex. State Bar, Colo. State Bar Assn., La. Bar Assn., Stratford Club, Boston Club, Mariners Club (treas. 1974—75, 1978—79, sec. 1975—76, v.p. 1976—77, pres. 1977—78), Kappa Alpha, Phi Kappa Phi, Phi Delta Phi, Order of Coif. Republican. Episcopalian. Office: 512 E Boston Ave Covington LA 70433-2943 Home Phone: 985-893-8934; Office Phone: 985-893-8949. Business E-Mail: rice@ricellc.com.

RICH, ADRIENNE, poet; b. Balt., May 16, 1929; d. Arnold Rice and Helen Elizabeth (Jones) R.; m. Alfred H. Conrad (dec. 1970); children: David, Paul, Jacob. AB, Radcliffe Coll., Cambridge, Mass., 1951; LittD (hon.), Wheaton Coll., Norton, Mass., 1967, Smith Coll., Northampton, Mass., 1979, Brandeis U., Waltham, Mass., 1987, Coll. Wooster, Ohio, 1988, CCNY, Harvard U., Cambridge, Mass., 1990, Swarthmore Coll., Pa., 1992. Tchr. workshop YM-WHA Poetry Ctr., NYC, 1966-67; vis. lectr. Swarthmore Coll., 1967-69; adj. prof. writing divsn. Columbia U., 1967-69; lectr. CCNY, 1968-70, instr., 1970-71, asst. prof. English, 1971-72, 74-75; Fannie Hurst vis. prof. creative lit. Brandeis U., 1972-73; prof. English Douglass Coll., Rutgers U., 1976-79; Clark lectr., disting. vis. prof. Scripps Coll., 1983-84; A.D. White prof.-at-large Cornell U., 1981-87; disting. vis. prof. San Jose State U., 1984-85; prof. English and feminist studies Stanford U., 1986-93. Marjorie Kovler vis. lectr. U. Chgo., 1989. Author: Collected Early Poems, 1950-1970, 1993, Diving into the Wreck, 1973, The Dream of a Common Language, 1978, A Wild Patience Has Taken Me This Far, 1981, Your Native Land, Your Life, 1986, Time's Power, 1989, An Atlas of the Difficult World, 1991, Dark Fields of the Republic, 1995, Midnight Salvage, 1999, Fox, 2001, The Fact of a Doorframe: Selected Poems 1950-2001, 2002, The School Among the Ruins, 2004 (Nat. Book Critics Cir. prize poetry, 2005, Telephone Ringing in the Labyrinth, 2007; (prose) Of Woman Born: Motherhood as Experience and Institution, 1976, 10th anniversary edit., 1986, On Lies, Secrets and Silence, 1979, Blood, Bread and Poetry, 1986, What Is Found There: Notebooks on Poetry and Politics, 1993, 2d edit., 2003, Arts of the Possible: Essays and Conversations, 2001, Poetry and Commitment, 2007; editor: Muriel Rukeyser, Selected Poems, 2004. Mem. nat. adv. bd. Nat. Writers Union, Rosenberg Fund for Children. Recipient Yale Series of Younger Poets award, 1951, Nat. Inst. Arts and Letters award in poetry, 1961, Eunice Tietjens Meml. prize, 1968, Shelley Meml. award, 1971, Nat. Book award, 1974, Fund for Human Dignity award Nat. Gay Task Force, 1981, Ruth Lilly Poetry prize, 1986, Brandeis U. Creative Arts medal for Poetry, 1987, Nat. Poetry Assn. award, 1989, Elmer Holmes Bobst award arts and letters NYU, 1989, MacArthur fellowship, 1994-99, Dorothea Tanning award Acad. Am. Poets, 1996, others; chancellor Acad. Am. Poets, 1999-2001, Lannan Found. Lifetime Achievement award, 1999, Bollingen prize, 2003, Nat. Found. Jewish Culture award, 2003, Nat. Book Found. medal for Disting. Contribution, 2006. Mem. PEN, Nat. Writers Union, A Jewish Voice for Peace. Office: c/o W W Norton Co 500 5th Ave New York NY 10110-0002

RICH, ALAN, music critic, writer; b. Boston, June 17, 1924; (parents Am. citizens); s. Edward and Helen (Hirshberg) R. AB, Harvard, 1945; MA, U. Calif-Berkeley, 1952. Alfred Hertz Meml. Traveling fellow in music, Vienna, Austria, 1952-53; Asst. music critic Boston Herald, 1944-45, N.Y. Sun, 1947-48; contbr. Am. Record Guide, 1947-61, Saturday Rev., 1952-53, Mus. Am., 1955-61, Mus. Quar., 1957-58; tchr. music U. Calif. at Berkeley, 1950-58; program and music dir. Pacifica Found., FM radio, 1953-61; asst. music critic N.Y. Times, 1961-63; chief music critic, editor N.Y. Herald Tribune, 1963-66; music critic, editor N.Y. World Jour. Tribune, 1966-67; contbg. editor Time mag., 1967-68; music and drama critic, arts editor N.Y. mag., 1968-81, contbg. editor, 1981-83; music critic, arts editor Calif. (formerly New West mag.), 1979-83, contbg. editor, 1983-85; gen. editor Newsweek mag., NYC, 1983-87; music critic L.A. Herald Examiner, 1987-89, L.A. Daily News, 1989-92, L.A. Weekly, 1992—. Tchr. New Sch. Social Rsch., 1972-75, 77-79, U. So. Calif. Sch. Journalism, 1980-82, Calif. Inst. Art, 1982-94, UCLA, 1990-91; artist-in-residence Davis Ctr. Performing Arts CUNY, 1975-76. Author: Careers and Opportunities in Music, 1964, Music: Mirror of the Arts, 1969, Listeners Guides to Classical Music, Opera, Jazz, 3 vols., 1980, The Lincoln Center Story, 1984, Play-by-Play: Bach, Mozart, Beethoven, Tchaikovsky, 4 vols., 1995, American Pioneers, 1995, So I've Heard: Notes of a Migrating Music Critic, 2006; author: (interactive CD-ROM computer programs): Schubert's Trout Quintet, 1991, So I've Heard: Bach and Before, 1992, So I've Heard: The Classical Ideal, 1993, So I've Heard: Beethoven and Beyond, 1993; contbr. articles to entertainment mags. Recipient Deems Taylor award ASCAP, 1970, 73, 74 Mem. Music Critics Circle N.Y. (sec. 1961-63, chmn. 1963-64), N.Y. Drama Critics Circle, Am. Theatre Critics Assn., Music Critics Assn., PEN. Democrat. Avocations: gardening, cooking. Home: 2925 Greenfield Ave Los Angeles CA 90064-4019 Office Phone: 310-475-5102. Office Fax: 310-694-0115. Personal E-mail: alanrich1@mac.com.

RICH, ANDREA LOUISE, museum administrator; BA, UCLA, 1965, MA, 1966, PhD, 1968. Asst. prof. comms. studies UCLA, LA, 1976, asst. dir. office learning resources, 1976, acting dir. Media Ctr., 1977, dir. office of instructional devel., 1978-80, asst. vice chancellor office of instructional devel., 1980-86, asst. exec. vice chancellor, 1986-87, vice chancellor acad. adminstrn., 1987-91, exec. vice chancellor, 1991-95; pres., CEO L.A. County Mus. of Art, 1995—, pres., Wallis Annenberg dir., 2003—. Office: LA County Mus Art 5905 Wilshire Blvd Los Angeles CA 90036-4597

RICH, CHARLES ANTHONY, hydrogeologist, consultant; b. London, Nov. 5, 1951; came to U.S., 1955; s. Eric Hebert and Ilse (Renard) R.; m. Linda Christine Johnson, June 23, 1984; 1 child, Oliver Sandor. BS in Geology, Syracuse U., 1973; MA in Geology, CUNY, 1975. Cert. in dispute resolution; cert. profl. geologist. Hydrologic technician U.S. Geol. Survey, Mineola, NY, 1973—75; hydrogeologist H2M Corp., PC, Melville, NY, 1975—76, Geraghty & Miller, Inc., Port Washington, NY, 1976—79; prin.-in-charge Dames and Moore, Cranford, NJ, 1979—82; pres. C.A. Rich Cons., Inc., Plainview, NY, 1982—. Expert witness Nat. Forensic Ctr., 1989; environ. cons., spkr. in field. Bd. dirs. L.I. Real Estate Practitioners Inst., 2001—, vice chmn. white paper com., chmn., 2003—. Mem. ASTM (stds. com., environ. audits for real property transfer com., environ. monitoring com. water supply exploration and devel.), Am. Inst. Profl. Geologists (pres. N.E. sect. 1981-92, nat. govt. affairs com. 1983—, chair N.E. U.S. membership screening bd. 2000—), Am. Water Resources Assn., Am. Water Works Assn., Nat. Ground Water Assn. (cons. com.), N.Y. Water Pollution Control Assn., Am. Geol. Inst./Geol. Soc. Am., Nat. Forensic Ctr. (expert writer) Cons. Bus. and Industry Assn., Conn. Ground Water Assn., N.Y. State Coun. Profl. Geologists (v.p.), L.I. Assn., L.I. Geologists (govt. affairs liaison 2003—). Home: 168 Baldwin Ave Locust Valley NY 11560-1920 Office: CA Rich Cons 17 Dupont St Plainview NY 11803-1602 Office Phone: 516-576-8844. E-mail: crich@carichinc.com.

RICH, CLAYTON, retired academic administrator, educator; b. NYC, May 21, 1924; s. Clayton Eugene and Leonore (Elliot) R.; m. Mary Bell Hodgkinson, Dec. 19, 1953 (div. May 1974); 1 son, Clayton Greig; m. Rosalind Morgan-Jones, Apr. 6, 1987. Grad., Putney Sch., 1942; student, Swarthmore Coll., 1942-44; MD, Cornell U., 1948. Diplomate Am. Bd. Internal Medicine. Intern Albany Hosp., NY, 1948-49, asst. resident, 1950-51; rsch. asst. Cornell U. Med. Coll., 1949-50; asst. Rockefeller U., 1953-58, asst. prof., 1958-60; asst. prof. medicine U. Wash. Sch. Medicine, 1960-62, assoc. prof., 1962-67, prof., 1967-71, assoc. dean, 1968-71; chief radioisotope service VA Hosp., Seattle, 1960-70, assoc. chief staff, 1962-71, chief of staff, 1968-70; v.p. med. affairs, dean Sch. Medicine; prof. medicine Stanford U., 1971-79, Carl and Elizabeth Naumann prof., 1977-79; chief staff Stanford U. Hosp., 1971-77, CEO, 1977—79. Sr. scholar Inst. Medicine, Nat. Acad. Sci., Washington, 1979-80; Mem. gen. medicine B study sect. NIH, 1969-73, chmn., 1972-73; mem. spl. med. adv. group VA, 1977-81; provost U. Okla. Health Scis. Ctr., Oklahoma City, 1980-92—, v.p. for healh scis., 1983-92; also exec. dean, prof. U. Okla. Coll. Medicine, 1980-83, emeritus Regents prof. and provost U. Okla., 1993—. Editorial bd.: Calcified Tissue Research, 1966-72, Clin. Orthopedics, 1967-72, Jour. Clin. Endocrinology and Metabolism, 1971-72; Contbr. numerous articles to med. jours. Bd. dirs. Children's Hosp. at Stanford, Stanford U. Hosp., 1974-79; chmn. Gordon Research Conf. Chemistry, Physiology and Structure of Bones and Teeth, 1967; bd. dirs. Okla. Med. Research Found.; bd. dirs. Leadership Oklahoma City, 1981-92, v.p., 1985-92; bd. dirs. Okla. Blood Inst., 1982-92, Oklahoma City chpt. ARC, 1983-92. Lt. USNR, 1951-53. Fellow ACP, AAAS; mem. Assn. Am. Physicians, Western Assn. Physicians, Am. Soc. Mineral and Bone Research (adv. bd. 1977-80), Am. Soc. Clin. Investigation, Assn. Am. Med. Colls. (exec. council 1975-79), Inst. of Medicine, Western Soc. Clin.

Research (v.p. 1967-68), Endocrine Soc., Assn. Acad. Health Ctrs. (bd. dirs. 1984-88, chmn. 1987-88), Sigma Xi, Alpha Omega Alpha. Home: 13450 64th Ter NE Kirkland WA 98034-1656 Personal E-mail: claytrich@earthlink.net.

RICH, DANIEL HULBERT, retired chemistry professor; b. Fairmont, Minn., Dec. 12, 1942; married, 1964; 2 children. BS, U. Minn., 1964; PhD in Organic Chemistry, Cornell U., 1968. Rsch. assoc. organic chemist Cornell U., Ithaca, NY, 1968; rsch. chemist Dow Chem. Co., 1968—69; rsch. assoc., organic chemist Stanford U., Palo Alto, Calif., 1969—70; asst. prof. pharm. chemistry U. Wis., Madison, 1970—75, assoc. prof., 1975—81, prof. dept. med. chemistry, 1981—2006, prof. dept. organic chemistry, 1988—2006, Ralph F. Hirschmann prof. medicinal and organic chemistry, 1994—2006, emeritus prof. chemistry and organic chemistry, 2006—. Cons. biorganic natural product study sect., NIH, 1981-85, chmn., 1985. Recipient H.I. Romnes award, 1980, Vincent du Vigneaud award, 1990, Hitchings award for innovative methods in drug design, 1992, Alexander von Humboldt award, 1993, E. Volwiler award Am. Assn. Colls. Pharmacy, 1995, Outstanding Achievement award U. Minn., 2004; fellow NIH, 1968. Fellow AAAS, Am. Chem. Soc. (Ralph F. Hirschmann award in peptide chemistry 1993, divsn. medicinal chemistry award 1991, A.C. Cope scholar 1999, E. Smissman award, 2005), Am. Assn. Pharm. Sci. (rsch. achievement award 1992), Am. Assn. Coll. Pharmacy (Volwiler award 1995). Am. Peptide Soc. (R.B. Merrifield award 1999). Achievements include research in synthesis in peptides and hormones, inhibition of peptide receptors and proteases, characterization, synthesis and mechanisms of action of peptide natural products. Office: U Wis Dept Med Chemistry 7109 Rennebohm Hall 777 Highland Ave Madison WI 53705-2222

RICH, DOROTHY KOVITZ, educational association administrator, writer; BA in Journalism and Psychology, Wayne U.; MA, Columbia U.; EdD, Catholic U. Founder, pres. The Home and Sch. Inst., Inc., Washington, 1964—. Adv. coun. Nat. Health Edn. Consortium; adv. com. Ctr. for Workplace Prep. and Quality Edn., US C. of C.; mem. readiness to learn task force US Dept. Edn., urban edn. team Coun. Gt. City Schs.; legislative nat. initiatives including work on Family/Sch. Partnership Act, 1989, Improving America's Edn. Act, 1994; formulator New Partnerships for Student Achievement program, 1987; creator MegaSkills Edn. Ctr. The Home and Sch. Inst. Inc., 1990; designer MegaSkills Leader Tng. for Parent Workshops, 1988, MegaSkills Essentials for the Classroom, 1991, Learning and Working program for sch.-to-work initiatives, 1996, Career Megaskills, 1999, New MegaSkills Bond Tchr./Parent Partnership, 1994, Career MegaSkills materials and tng., 1998, Adult MegaSkills for Profl. Growth, 1999, MegaSkills Behavior Mgmt. Kit, 2002; developer NEA/MegaSkills nat. mentor tng. initiative, 2000-06, MegaSkills for the Job, 2002, Adult MegaSkills and MegaSkills for Teachers, 2002-06, MegaSkills for Teachers Video Programs, 2003, edn. columns McClatchy Ridder News Svc., 2004-07; bd. mem. Doubleday Children's Book of Month, 2007; guest columnist EducationNews.org, 2006-07; selected commentary Edn. Wk., 2007. Author: MegaSkills in School in Life: The Best Gift You Can Give Your Child, 1988, rev. edit., 1992, What Do We Say? What Do We Do? Vital Solutions for Children's Educationsl Success, 1997, MegaSkills, 3d edit., 1997, 18 tng. books, MegaSkills: Building Children's Achievement for the Information Age, new and expanced edit., 1998, Improving Student Teaching through MegaSkills, All Around the House (early childhood literacy curriculum), 2005, The MegaSkills Way to Reading for Preschool, 2005, New MegaSkills Infancy/Toddler Curriculum, 2006, New MegaSkill Respect, 2006; TV appearances include The Learning Channel, NBC Today Show, Good Morning Am.; subject of videos nat. ednl. programs in Thailand, Singapore and China: Families and Schools: Teaming for Success, Survival Guide for Today's Parents. Recipient Am. Woman Leader award, Citation US Dept. Edn., Nat. Gov.'s Assn., Alumni Achievement award in edn. Cath. U., 1992, Golden Apple award for MegaSkills Tchrs. Coll., Columbia U., 1996; grantee John D. and Catherine T. MacArthur Found.; named Washingtonian of Yr., Adv. Bd. of McNeil-Lehrer NewsHour, 2004. Mem. Nat. Press Club. Office: MegaSkills Edn Ctr Home and Sch Inst Inc 1500 Massachusetts Ave NW Washington DC 20005-1821 Office Phone: 202-466-3633, 202-362-7889. Business E-Mail: edstaff@megaskills.org.

RICH, FRANK HART, journalist, writer; b. Washington, June 2, 1949; s. Frank Hart Rich and Helene Bernice (Aaronson) Fisher; m. Alexandra Rachelle Witchel, 1991; children from previous marriage: Nathaniel Howard, Simon Hart. BA in Am. History and Lit. with honors, Harvard U., 1971. Co-editor Richmond (Va.) Mercury, 1972-73; sr. editor, film critic New Times mag., NYC, 1973-75; film critic NY Post, NYC, 1975-77; film and TV critic Time mag., NYC, 1977-80; chief drama critic NY Times, NYC, 1980-93; columnist NY Times Sunday Mag., NYC, 1993; Op-Ed columnist NY Times, NYC, 1994—2003, 2005—, assoc. editor, columnist, 2003—05. Author: (with others) The Theatre Art of Boris Aronson, 1987, Hot Seat: Theater Criticism for the New York Times 1980-93, 1998, Ghost Light, 2000, The Greatest Story Ever Sold, 2006. Assoc. fellow Jonathan Edwards Coll., Yale U., 1998—; recipient George Polk award for commentary, 2006. Office: The NY Times 620 Eighth Ave New York NY 10018-1405

RICH, FREDERIC CARL, lawyer; b. Elizabeth City, NC, 1956; AB, Princeton U., 1977; JD, U. Va., 1981. Bar: NY 1982. Ptnr., head global project fin. group Sullivan & Cromwell, NYC, 1981—, now co-mng. ptnr. corp. practice group. Chmn. Scenic Hudson; bd. dir. Boscobel Restoration, Inc., Hudson River Found. Sci. and Rsch., Inc., Scenic Hudson, Inc., Friends of Palisades Interstate Pk. Commn., Inc. Keasby fellow King's Coll., Cambridge, Eng., 1978. Office: Sullivan & Cromwell 125 Broad St Fl 28 New York NY 10004-2489 Office Phone: 212-558-4000. Office Fax: 212-558-3588.

RICH, HARRY EARL, corporate financial executive; b. Wichita, Kans., Mar. 5, 1940; s. Hubert E. and Lorene (Sadler) R.; m. Elfreda Elizabeth Babcock, Aug. 8, 1964; children: Lisa G., Carey E., Ashley H. BA, Harvard U., 1962, MBA, 1968. Pres. instrumentation divsn. Baxter Travenol, Deerfield, Ill., 1977-78; group v.p. Mallinckrodt, Inc., St. Louis, 1978-83; sr. v.p., chief fin. officer Brown Group, Inc., St. Louis, 1983-88, exec. v.p., chief fin. officer, 1988-00, also bd. dirs. Bd. dirs. Gen. Am. Capital Co. divsn. GenAm. Bd. dirs. Repertory Theatre, 1984-90, 1998—, pres. bd. dirs.,1988-90; treas., v.p. Fair Found., 1985-88; bd. trustees Mary Inst., 1986-90, Mary Inst./St. Louis Country Day Sch., 1990-97, chmn., 1995-97. Lt. USN, 1962-66. Avocations: tennis, jogging, sailing. Home: 101 Fair Oaks Saint Louis MO 63124-1579

RICH, JEFFREY A., former information technology company executive; b. 1960; BA, U. Mich., 1982. Asst. v.p. Interfirst Bank Dallas, 1982-86; v.p. Citibank, 1986-89; sr. v.p., CFO Affiliated Computer Svcs., Inc., Dallas, 1989-95, COO, 1995—2001, pres., 1995—2002, CEO, 1999—2005. Dir. Pegasus Solutions Inc. Dir. US C. of C., Edn. is Freedom Found.; mem. Young President's Orgn., Dallas Citizen's Coun.; bd. gov. Dallas Symphony Orchestra.

RICH, JOHN HUBBARD, JR., news correspondent; b. Cape Elizabeth, Maine, Aug. 5, 1917; s. John Hubbard Rich and Alma Estella Glidden Rich; m. Doris Lee Halstead, Sept. 2, 1954; children: Barb, John III, Whitney, Nathaniel. AB, Bowdoin Coll., 1939, LittD (hon.), 1974. News reporter Daily Kennebec Jour., Augusta, Maine, 1939—40, Portland (Maine) Press Herald, 1941—42; reporter, fgn. corr. Internat. News Svc., Tokyo, 1945—50; fgn. corr. NBC News, Tokyo, 1950—54; fellowship Coun. on Fgn. Rels., NYC, 1954—55. Maj. USMCR, 1943—45, PTO. Decorated Bronze star; recipient Peabody award, 1974. Mem.: Tokyo Fgn. Corrs. Club, Overseas Press Club (award 1974), Sigma Delta Chi. Avocations: tennis, sailing. Home: 13 Rocky Point Ln Cape Elizabeth ME 04107

RICH, JOHN MARTIN, humanities educator, researcher; b. Tuscaloosa, Ala., Dec. 14, 1931; s. Emanuel Morris and Bertha (Rose) R.; m. Martha Elaine Schur, June 6, 1955 (div. June 1966); children— Jeffrey Brian, Suzanne Elon; m. Joyce Ann Stegemoller, Aug. 28, 1967 (div. Mar. 1985); m. Audrey Faye Arnold, Aug. 1, 1987. BA, U. Ala., 1954, MA, 1955; PhD, Ohio State U., 1958. Grad. asst. Ohio State U., Columbus, 1955, asst. instr. edn., 1956-58; asst. prof. edn. U. Tenn.-Martin, 1958-60; assoc. prof. edn. Coll. SUNY-Oneonta, 1960-61; from asst. prof. to assoc. prof. Iowa State U., Ames, 1961-66; assoc. prof. social and philos. studies U. Ky., Lexington, 1966-69; prof. cultural founds. edn. U. Tex., Austin, 1969-96, prof. emeritus, 1996—, chmn. dept. cultural founds. edn., 1969-75. Vis. lectr. Nat. Kaohsiung (Taiwan) Normal U., 1993. Author: (books) Education and Human Values, 1968, Humanistic Foundations of Education, 1971, Portuguese translation, 1975, Korean translation, 1985, Challenge and Response, 1974, New Directions in Educational Policy, 1974, Discipline and Authority in School and Family, 1982, Professional Ethics in Education, 1984, Innovative School Discipline, 1985, Foundations of Education, 1992; co-author: Theories of Moral Development, 1985 (named an Outstanding Book of 1985-86 Choice mag.), 2d edit., 1994, Korean translation, 1999, Helping and Intervention, 1988, Competition in Education, 1992, The Success Ethic, Education, and the American Dream, 1996, Korean translation, 1998; editor: Readings in the Philosophy of Education, 1966, 2d edit., 1972, Conflict and Decision, 1972, Innovations in Education, 6th edit., 1992; co-editor, editl. adv. bd. Ednl. Studies, 1970-74, 77-80, 89-91; bd. contbg. editors Rev. Edn., 1977-85; editl. bd. Focus on Learning, 1980-84, Educational Foundations, 1985-91; bd. cons. Jour. Rsch. and Devel. in Edn., 1982-96, Ednl. Theory, 1991-95; contbr. articles to profl. jours., U.S., Can., Eng., Australia. Recipient Faculty Research Assignment award Univ. Research Inst., Austin, Tex., 1983-84; vis. scholar U. London, 1977; Univ. Research Inst. grantee, 1981-82, 84-85 Mem. North Central Philosophy of Edn. Soc. (pres. 1966-67), Ohio Valley Philosophy of Edn. Soc. (pres. 1967-68), Philosophy of Edn. Soc. (exec. bd. 1967-68, 80-82, Cert. Significant Svc.), Am. Ednl. Studies Assn. (exec. council 1972-74, pres. 1975-76) Home: 1801 Lavaca St Apt 8M Austin TX 78701-1312 Office: U Tex Edn Bldg 406 Austin TX 78712 E-mail: john1931@webtv.net.

RICH, JOHN TOWNSEND, lawyer; b. Lansing, Mich., Mar. 10, 1943; s. Townsend and Jean (Trembley) R.; m. Charlotte Pia Mahon, Nov. 25, 1978; children: Anna-Sophie, Lucia Danforth. BA, Harvard U., 1965, postgrad., 1965-66; LLB, Yale U., 1969; postgrad., U. Coll., Oxford, Eng., 1969-70. Bar: N.Y. 1970, D.C. 1972. Law clk. to Hon. David L. Bazelon U.S. Ct.Appeals D.C. Cir., 1970-71; law clk. to Hon. Harry A. Blackmun U.S. Supreme Ct., Washington, 1971-72; assoc. Shea & Gardner, Washington, 1972-76, ptnr., 1976—2004, Goodwin Procter LLP, Washington, 2004—. Adj. prof. Georgetown U. Law Ctr., 1972-75; spl. master U.S. Dist. Ct. for No. Dist. Tex., 1985-88. Home: 6309 Kenhowe Dr Bethesda MD 20817-5419 Office: Goodwin Procter LLP 901 NY Ave NW Washington DC 20001 Business E-Mail: jrich@goodwinprocter.com.

RICH, KEITH M., neurosurgeon; b. Indpls., Sept. 16, 1951; BA, Taylor U., Upland, Ind., 1974; MD, Ind. U. Sch. Medicine, Indpls., 1977. Asst. prof. neurol. surgery Wash. U. Sch. Medicine, St. Louis, 1984—95, asst. prof. neurobiology, 1988—95, assoc. prof. neurol. surgery, 1995—, assoc. prof. neurobiology, 1995—. Co-med. dir. St. Louis Gamma Knife Ctr., 2006—; mem. joint sect. on tumors Am. Assn. Neurol. Surgeons and Congress Neurol. Surgeons. Contbr. articles to profl. jours. Grantee, Accelerated Brain Cancer Cure, 2006—07, Alvine Pharm., 2005—06, Barnes-Jewish Hosp. Found., 2004—06. Mem.: AAAS, St. Louis Soc. Neurol. Sciences, Internat. Stereotactic Radiosurgery Soc., Soc. Neuroscience, Rsch. Soc. Neurol. Surgeons, Congress Neurol. Surgeons, Am. Assn. Neurol. Surgeons, Soc. Neurol. Surgeons. Achievements include patents for transglutaminase inhibitors and methods of use. Office: Washington Univ Med Ctr 660 S Euclid Ave Campus Box 8057 Saint Louis MO 63110 Office Phone: 314-362-3566. Office Fax: 314-362-2107. Business E-Mail: richk@nsurg.wustl.edu.

RICH, LAURA, columnist; Grad., DePauw Univ. Writer Adweek mag., Inside Media mag.; sr. writer Industry Standard mag.; contbg. editor fastcompany.com; columnist New York Times. Author: The Accidental Zillionaire: Demystifying Paul Allen, 2003; contbr. articles to Entertainment Weekly, Hollywood Reporter.

RICH, MARC DAVID, commodities trader; b. Antwerp, Belgium, Dec. 18, 1934; arrived in US, 1941; s. David Rich and Paula Rich-Wang; m. Denise Eisenberg, Oct. 1966 (div. 1992); children: Ilona, Gabrielle(dec.), Danielle. With Philipps Bros., NYC, 1954—64, Phibro office mgr. Madrid, 1964—74; co-founder Marc Rich + Co AG (name changed to Glencore Internat., 1994), Zug, Switzerland, 1974—97, Marc Rich + Co Holding AG, Zug, Switzerland, 1987. Co-founder Rich Foundations; chmn. Marc Rich Found. Edn., Culture & Welfare, Gabrielle Rich Found. Leukemia Rsch., Swiss Found. for the Doron Prize. Named one of 400 Richest Americans, Forbes, 2000—, World's Richest People, 2001—, The Famous 15: America's Most Fascinating Tycoons, 2001. Office: Glencore Internat AG Baarermattstrasse 3 CH-6340 Baar Switzerland Office Phone: 41-41-709-2000. Office Fax: 41-41-709-3000. E-mail: info@glencore.com.

RICH, MARVIN P., health association executive; Formerly with CalFed Bank, Carter Hawley Hale Stores, Inc., Dart Industry; former exec. v.p., fin. and info. svcs. Wellpoint Health Networks/Blue Cross of Calif.; exec. v.p. strategic planning, fin. and adminstrn. K-Mart, Troy, Mich., 1994-98; CEO, exec. v.p. Oxford Health, Norwalk, Conn., 1998—99; pres., CEO CareInsight, 2000; pres. WebMD, Elmwood Park, NJ, 2000—01; exec. v.p., fin. and ops. Health Net, Inc., Woodland Hills, Calif., 2002—. Office: Health Net Life Insurance Co 21281 Burbank Blvd Woodland Hills CA 91367-6607

RICH, MICHAEL DAVID, think-tank executive, lawyer; b. LA, Jan. 23, 1953; s. Ben Robert and Faye (Mayer) Rich; m. Debra Paige Granfield, Jan. 12, 1980; children: Matthew, William. AB, U. Calif., Berkeley, 1973; JD, UCLA, 1976. Bar: Calif. 1976. Extern law clk. to judge U.S. Dist. Ct., Boston, 1975; staff mem. RAND, Santa Monica, Calif., 1976—85, dir. resource mgmt. program, 1980—85, dep. v.p., 1986, v.p. nat. security rsch. and dir. Nat. Def. Rsch. Inst., 1986—93, sr. v.p., 1993—95, exec. v.p., 1995—. Co-chmn. bd. overseers Rand-Qatar Policy Inst., 2003—. Author: numerous classified and unclassified reports and articles. Bd. dirs. WISE Sr. Svcs., Coun. Aid to Edn., chmn., 1996—2005; mem. bd. councillors UCLA Found., 2000—; mem. fin. oversight com. Santa Monica-Malibu Unified Sch. Dist., 2000—04; bd. advisers Santa Monica-UCLA Med. Ctr.; mem. adv. coun. Everychild Found.; chmn. bd. trustees The Comm. Inst., 2003—. Mem.: Intenrat. Inst. Strategic Studies (mem. governing coun. 2001—07, chmn. bd. trustees IISS-US 2004—), Coun. Fgn. Rels. Office: RAND PO Box 2138 1776 Main St Santa Monica CA 90407-2138 Office Phone: 310-451-6934. E-mail: mrich@rand.org.

RICH, MICHAEL JOSEPH, lawyer; b. NYC, June 19, 1945; s. Jesse and Phyllis (Sternfeld) R.; m. Linda Christine Kubis, July 19, 1969; children: David Lawrence, Lisa Diane. BA, Gettysburg Coll., 1967; JD, Am. U., 1972. Bar: Del. 1973, U.S. Dist. Ct. Del. 1973, U.S. Supreme Ct., 1976, Pa., 1981. Law clk. Del. Supreme Ct., Georgetown, 1972-73; assoc. Tunnell & Raysor, Georgetown, 1973-76; ptnr. Dunlap, Holland & Rich, P.A., Georgetown, 1976-80; gen. counsel Pearlette Fashions, Inc., Lebanon, Pa., 1981-83; assoc. Morris, Nichols, Arsht & Tunnell, Georgetown, 1983-86; ptnr., 1987-91, Twilley, Street, Rich Braverman & Hindman, P.A., Dover, Del., 1991-95; state solicitor, 1995-2001; dep. atty. gen., 2001—. Mem. Bd. Bar Examiners, Del., 1986-97, chmn., 1996-97;minority counsel Del. Ho. of Reps., Dover, 1977-79; mem. Del. Gov's Magistrate Commn., 1980, 83-86; sec. Del. Gov's. Jud. Nominating Commn., 1986-89. Bd. dirs. People's Place II, Inc., Milford, Del., 1973-77; pres. Bi-County United Way, Inc., Milford, 1977-78; mem. Partnership Greater Milford Commn., 1987-89, Friends Milford Library. Served to 1st lt. U.S. Army, 1967-69, Vietnam. Dean's fellow Am. U., 1971-72. Mem. Del. Bar Assn. (pres. 1990-91), Sussex County Bar Assn. (pres. 1987-89). Republican. Office Phone: 302-674-7326. Business E-Mail: michael.rich@state.de.us.

RICH, NANCY JEAN, lawyer; b. Chgo., June 11, 1959; d. John Keith and Phyllis Vallerie (Delaney) R. AB with honors, Loyola U., Chgo., 1981, JD, 1984. Bar: Ill. 1984, U.S. Dist. Ct. (no. dist.) Ill. 1984. Asst. atty. gen. environ. control div. Ill. Atty. Gen.'s Office, Chgo., 1984-87; assoc. Isham, Lincoln & Beale, Chgo., 1987-88, Sidley & Austin, Chgo., 1988-89, Bell, Boyd & Lloyd, Chgo., 1989-91, ptnr., 1992, Katten Muchin Zavis Rosenman, Chgo. Bd. dirs. Pub. Interest Law Initiative. Contbr. to Loyola Consumer Law Reporter, 1991. Adminstrv. asst. Hartigan for Atty. Gen. Campaign, Chgo., 1982; bd. dirs. Suburban Area Agy. on Aging, 1990-2004, pres. bd. dirs., 1999-2001, chmn. resource devel. com., 1991—. Mem. ABA, Ill. Bar Assn., Chgo. Bar Assn. (environ. law com.). Office: Katten Muchin Zavis Rosenman 525 W Monroe St Chicago IL 60661 Home Phone: 708-749-8130; Office Phone: 312-902-5536. Office Fax: 312-577-8676. Business E-Mail: nancy.rich@kattenlaw.com. E-mail: nancy.rich@kmzr.com.

RICH, NORMAN MINNER, surgeon; b. Ray, Ariz., Jan. 13, 1934; s. George and Leona LuVerne Minner R.; m. Ann Lois Rich, June 20, 1959; children: Suzanne, Alison, David, Bethany. BA, Stanford U., 1956, MD, 1960, Cath. U., Santiago, Chile, 1977; MD (honoris causa), Mayab U., 2000. Diplomate Am. Bd. Surgery, Med. Care Catastrophes; cert. ATLS instr. Rotating intern Tripler Gen. Hosp., Honolulu, 1960-61; gen. surgery resident Letterman Gen. Hosp., San Francisco, 1961-65; chief surg. svc. 2d Surg. Hosp., Fort Bragg, NC, 1965-66, Vietnam, 1965—66; chief vascular surgery svc. Walter Reed Army Med. Ctr., Washington, 1967-78, dir., vascular fellowship program, 1967-78; vascular rsch. coord. Armed Forces Inst. of Pathology, Edgewood Arsenal, Md., 1966-76; cons. in vascular surgery The Surgeon Gen. of the Army, Washington, 1970-82; chmn. dept. of surgery Uniformed Svcs. U. of Health Scis., Bethesda, Md., 1977—2002, prof. surgery, 1976—, mil. medicine, 1983—. Leonard Heaton and David Packard Prof., 1999—; lectr. in field worldwide, including Scudder Oration/Am. Coll. Surgeons, Mitchiner Meml. Lectr./Royal Army Med. Coll.; Emile Holman lectr. Stanford U.; cons. to nat. and internat. activities and mem. govt./specialty socs. Author/co-author books in field, including: (with Frank C. Spencer) Vascular Trauma, 1978; mem. 10 editl. bds. jours. in field. Decorated Legion of Merit, Bronze Star, Meritorious Svc. award, Vietnam medals, Medaille D'Honneur, France, others; recipient J.E. Wallace Sterling Lifetime Alumni Achievement award Stanford Med. Alumni Assn., 1999, Carol Johns medal Uniformed Svcs. U. Health Scis., 2003, DeBakey award Michael E. DeBakey Internat. Surg. Soc., 2004. Fellow ACS (Surgeons award for service to safety 2003, Leriche prize 2003, Frank Berry prize 2006), Am. Surg. Assn.; mem. Am. Assn. Surgery for Trauma, Am. Soc. for Vascular Surgery, Apothecaries of London, Austrian Vascular Soc. (hon.), Am. Venous Forum, Assn. Acad. Surgery, Mexican Acad. Surg., French Surg. Assn., Chesapeake Vascular Soc., Ea. Vascular Soc., Halsted Soc., Hellenic Surg. Soc., Internat. Soc. for Cardiovascular Surgery, Soc. of Univ. Surgeons, Soc. for Vascular Surgery, So. Assn. for Vascular Surgery, So. Surg. Assn., Royal Belgian Soc. of Surgery (assoc.), Royal Australian Coll. Surgeons (vascular sect.), German Surg. Soc. (hon.), Alpha Omega Alpha, numerous others. Office Phone: 301-295-3155. E-mail: nrich@usuhs.mil.

RICH, NORMAN S., food service executive; From mem. staff to pres., CEO Weis Markets, Sunbury, Pa., 1964—2002, pres., 2002—, CEO, 2002—. Dir. Food Mktg. Inst.; bd. trustees Evang. Cmty. Hosp.; bd. dirs. Weis Markets. Office: Weis Markets 1000 S Second St Sunbury PA 17801 *

RICH, PHILIP DEWEY, publishing executive; b. Nashua, NH, Feb. 1, 1940; s. John Parker and Olive Frances (Hussey) R.; m. Leslie Ann Burke, June 14, 1974 (div. 1982). AB magna cum laude, Harvard U., 1961; MA, NYU, 1962; postgrad., Princeton U., 1962. Editor Houghton Mifflin Co., Boston, 1964-73; asst. mng. editor UpCountry Mag. Berkshire Eagle, Pittsfield, Mass., 1976-77; editor Book Creations Inc., Canaan, NY, 1977-80, editor-in-chief, 1980-91, v.p., exec. editor, 1991-92; cons. editor Berkshire Ho. Publs., Lee, Mass., 1992-93, mng. editor, 1993-96, mng. editor and prodn. editor, 1996-99, editl. dir., prodn. dir., 1999—2003; editl. cons. Pittsfield, Mass., 2003—. Office: 18 Boylston St Pittsfield MA 01201-6748 Office Phone: 413-443-1737. Personal E-mail: prich@bcn.net.

RICH, R(OBERT) BRUCE, lawyer; b. NYC, Oct. 28, 1949; s. John J. and Sylvia (Berkenblit) R.; m. Melissa Jo Saxe; children— Megan, Alexander. AB, Dartmouth Coll., 1970; JD, U. Pa., 1973. Bar: NY 1974, US Dist. Ct. (so. and ea. dists.) NY 1974, US Ct. Appeals (2d cir.) 1980, US Supreme Ct. 1980, US Ct. Appeals (D.C. cir.) 1985. Assoc. firm Weil, Gotshal & Manges, NYC, 1973-81, ptnr., 1981-. Mem. bd. overseers U. Pa. Law Sch., 2002-, bd. dirs. Expeditionary Leaning Outward Bound, 2002-, Appleseed Found., 2003-. Contbg. author: Cultivating the Wasteland: Can Cable Put the Vision Back in TV?, 1983, The International Libel Handbook, 1995. Contbr. articles to profl. jours.; co-editor: Business and Legal Guide to Online-Internet Law, 1997. Mem. ABA (antitrust law sect., forum com. on communications law), Assn. Bar City NY (com. on trade regulation 1982-85, communications law com. 1985-88), Phi Beta Kappa. Office: Weil Gotshal & Manges 767 5th Ave Fl Concl New York NY 10153-0119

RICH, ROBERT E., JR., frozen foods company executive; b. 1941; s. Robert E. Rich Sr. and Janet Rich; m. Mindy Rich. BA, Williams Coll., 1963; MBA, U. Rochester, 1969; Ph.D (hon.), St. Bonaventure U., Niagra U., Johnson & Wales U. Pres. Rich Products Corp., Buffalo, 1978—, chmn., 2006—. Co-founder Western NY United Against Drug & Alcohol Abuse, Inc., 1986; chmn. Nat. Grocery Mfrs. Assn., 1999—, Students in Free Enterprise, 2003—06, Nat. Frozen & Refrigerated Foods Assn., 2006—. Author: Fish Fights: A Hall of Fame Quest, 2001, The Fishing Club, 2006. Named a Diplomat, Nat. Restaurant Assn., 2000; named Citizen of the Yr., Buffalo News, 1983, Buffalo/Niagra Frontier Sales & Mktg. Exec. of the Yr., 1984, Exec. of the Yr., Am. Assn., 1986, Triple-A Exec. of the Yr., The Sporting News, 1988, Exec. of the Yr., Refrigerated & Frozen Foods mag., 1996; named to, Nat. Frozen Food Ind. Hall of Fame, 1996, Buffalo Baseball Hall of Fame, S. Fla. Fishing Hall of Fame, 1999, Greater Buffalo Sports Hall of Fame, Nat. Restaurant Assn. Ednl. Found. Coll. Diplomats, 2000; recipient Peter Medaille medal, Outstanding alumni award, U. Rochester. Office: Rich Products Corp One Robert Rich Way Buffalo NY 14213

RICH, ROBERT EDWARD, lawyer; b. Corbin, Ky., Feb. 4, 1944; s. Edward Bluch and Marjorie Brooks (Wentworth) R.; m. Janet Sue Shearer, May 14, 1966; children: Susan M., Christopher R., David E., Sarah M. AB, U. Ky., 1966; JD, Harvard U., 1969. Bar: Ohio 1970. Jud. clk. U.S. Ct. Appeals for 6th Cir., Louisville, 1969-70; assoc. Taft, Stettinius &

Hollister, Cin., 1970, ptnr., 1978—. Pres. Lighthouse Youth Svcs., Inc., Cin., 1985, Ky. YMCA Youth Assn., Frankfort, 2001; mem. exec. bd. Ky. Hist. Soc.; pres. Cin. Bar Found., 1991. Mem. ABA, Cin. Bar Assn. Republican. Presbyterian. Home: 215 Hilltop Ln Wyoming OH 45215-4121 Office: 1800 US Bank Tower 425 Walnut St Cincinnati OH 45202-3923 Office Phone: 513-357-9355. E-mail: rich@taftlaw.com.

RICH, ROBERT F., law educator, political science professor; married; 3 children. BA in Govt. with honors, Oberlin Coll., 1971; student, Free U. of Berlin, 1971-72; MA in Polit. Scis., U. Chgo., 1973, PhD in Polit. Scis., 1975. Project dir., asst. rsch. scientist Ctr. for Rsch. on Utilization Sci. Knowledge, Inst. Social Rsch., U. Mich., lectr. dept. polit. sci., 1975-76; asst. prof. politics and pub. affairs Princeton U., 1976-82, coord. domestic and urban policy field Woodrow Wilson Sch., 1976-82; assoc. prof. polit. sci., pub. policy and mgmt. Sch. Urban and Pub. Affairs, Carnegie-Mellon U., 1982-86; prof. U. Ill., Urbana, 1986—, dir. Inst. Govt. and Publ. Affairs, 1986-97, 2005—, acting head med. humanities and social scis. program Urbana-Champaign, 1988—97; fellow Johns Hopkins U. Ctr. for Study of Am. Govt., Washington, 1993-95; Mercator prof. Humboldt U., Berlin, 2002—03. Cons. U.S. Dept. Health and Human Svcs., Carnegie-Mellon U., 1986—, MacArthur Found., NIMH, 1988-89, Food, Drug and Law Inst., HHS, 1989, Am. Career Soc., 1996-97; disting. lectr. German Marshall Fund, Hamburg, Germany, 1997. Author: Social Science Information and Public Policy Making: The Interaction Between Bureaucratic Politics and the Use of Survey Data, 1981; co-author: Government Information Management: A Counter-Report of the Commission on Federal Paperwork, 1980; editor: Translating Evaluation into Policy, 1979, The Knowledge Cycle, 1981, Knowledge, Creation, Diffusion, Utilization, 1979-88, 88-91; co-editor: Competitive Approaches to Health Policy Reform, 1993, Health Policy, Federalism and the Role of the American States, 1996; assoc. editor Society, 1984-88, Evaluation Rev., 1985-89; mem. editl. bd. Policy Studies Rev. Series, 1980-83, Evaluation and Change, 1979-82, Law and Human Behavior, 1983-87; contbr. articles to profl. jours., book chpts. Recipient Emil Limbach Teaching award Carnegie-Mellon U., Sch. Urban and Pub. Affairs, 1985; fellow German Acad. Exch. Program, Fed. Republic Germany, 1971-72, Nat. Opinion Rsch. Ctr. fellow, 1972-73, German Govt. fellow, 1974, Russel Sage Found. Rsch. fellow, 1974-75; vis. scholar Hastings Ctr. for Society, Ethics and Life Scis., 1982. Mem. APA (task force on victims of crime and violence 1982-84), Soc. for Traumatic Stress Studies (bd. dirs. 1980—), World Fedn. for Mental Health (chmn. com. on mental health needs of victims 1985—, vice chmn. 1981-83, Robert F. Rich rsch. ann. award established in his honor, sci. com. on mental health needs of victims 1983), Howard R. Davis Soc. for Knowledge Utilization and Planned Change (pres. 1986-89), Polit. Sci. 400, Policy Studies Assn. (Aaron Wildausky award 1994), Phi Beta Kappa, Sigma Xi, Phi Kappa Phi. Office: U Ill Inst Govt & Pub Affairs 1007 W Nevada St # 204 Urbana IL 61801-3812 also: 815 W Van Buren St Chicago IL 60607-3506 Office Phone: 217-244-8550. Business E-Mail: rfrich@uillinois.edu.

RICH, ROBERT REGIER, physician, medical educator, immunologist; b. Newton, Kans., Mar. 7, 1941; s. Eldon Stahly and Margaret Joy (Regier) R.; m. Susan Jepsen Solliday, Mar. 22, 1974; children from previous marriage: Kenneth Eldon, Cathryn Louise; 1 stepchild, Lynn Solliday Todorov. AB, Oberlin Coll., 1962; MD, U. Kans., 1966. Diplomate Am. Bd. Internal Medicine (bd. dirs. 1990-93), Am. Bd. Allergy and Immunology (bd. dirs. 1987-93, chmn. 1991); cert. spl. qualification Diagnostic Lab. Immunology. Intern, resident in internal medicine U. Wash., Seattle, 1966-68; clin. asso., chief clin. asso., sr. staff fellow NIH, Bethesda, Md., 1968-71; research asso. Harvard Med. Sch., Boston, 1971-73; asst. in medicine Peter Bent Brigham Hosp., 1972-73; asst. prof., assoc. prof. microbiology, immunology and internal medicine Baylor Coll. Medicine, Houston, 1973-78, prof., 1978-95, Disting. Svc. prof., 1995—2002, head immunology sect., 1978-98, chief clin. immunology, 1979-91, v.p., dean rsch., 1990-98; exec. assoc. dean, prof. medicine & microbiology/immunology Emory U. Sch. Medicine, 1998—2004; sr. v.p. for medicine, dean Sch. Medicine U. Ala., Birmingham, 2004—, prof. medicine and microbiology, 2004—. Investigator Howard Hughes Med. Inst., Bethesda, Md., 1977-91; mem. immunobiology study sect. NIH, 1977-81; mem. transplantation biology and immunology com. Nat. Inst. Allergy and Infectious Disease, 1982-86, chmn., 1984-86; mem. nat. ctr. grants com. Arthritis Found., 1983-86, chmn., 1984-86, nat. rsch. com., 1984-89, chmn., 1986-89, ho. of dels., 1985-91, Blue Ribbon com. on rsch. 2000-01; mem. rsch. adv. com. Nat. Multiple Sclerosis Soc., 1989-94, chmn., 1993-94; adv. panel on rsch. Assn. Am. Med. Coll., 1990—, shared responsibility advocacy com., 1997-98; chmn. ctrs. working group Nat. Inst. Arthritis Musculoskeletal Skin Diseases, 1996-97; mem. nat. human rsch. protections adv. com., dept. health and human svcs., 2000-02; vice chmn. UAB Health Sys., 2004—, bd. dirs.; bd. dirs. Ctr. Infectious Diseases Rsch., Zambia, 2006—. Assoc. editor: Jour. Immunology, 1978-82, sect. editor, 1991-96, deputy editor, 1997-2002, editor-in-chief, 2003—; assoc. editor: Jour. Infectious Diseases, 1984-88; adv. editor: Jour. Exptl. Medicine, 1980-84; mem. editl. bd. Jour. Clin. Immunology, 1989-96, Clin. and Exptl. Immunology, 1995-2000; editor-in-chief Clin. Immunology: Principles and Practice, 1996, 2d edit., 2001; contbr. articles to profl. jours. With USPHS, 1968—70. Recipient Rsch. Career Devel. award, NIH, 1975—77, Merit award, 1987. Fellow ACP, Am. Acad. Allergy, Asthma, and Immunology (chmn. basic and clin. immunology interest sect. 1992-93, chmn. profl. edn. coun. 1996-98, v.p. 2001-2002), Infectious Diseases Soc. Am.; mem. AMA, AAAS, Am. Bd. Internal Medicine (diplomate, bd. dirs. 1990-93), Am. Bd. Allergy and Immunology (diplomate, bd. dirs. 1987-93, chmn. bd. 1992), Assn. Am. Physicians, Am. Soc. Clin. Investigation, Am. Assn. Immunologists (chmn. pub. affairs com. 1994-2000, Disting. Svc. award 1999), Am. Assn. Investigative Pathology, Am. Soc. Microbiologists, Am. Fedn. Med. Rsch., Am. Clin. Climatological Assn. (councillor 2001-05), Fedn. Am. Socs. for Exptl. Biology (bd. dirs. 1998-2003, pres. and chmn. bd. dirs. 2001-02), Clin. Immunology Soc. (coun. 1990-96, pres. 1995), Nat. Assn. Biomed. Rsch. (bd. dirs. 2002-05), Assn. for Assessment and Accreditation of Lab. Animal Care Internat. (trustee 2003-05), Alpha Omega Alpha, Sigma Xi. Office: Univ Ala Birmingham Sch Medicine 1530 3d Ave S Birmingham AL 35294-3412 Business E-Mail: rrich@uab.edu.

RICH, ROBERT STEPHEN, lawyer; b. NYC, Apr. 30, 1938; s. Maurice H. and Natalie (Priess) R.; m. Myra N. Lakoff, May 31, 1964; children: David, Rebecca, Sarah. AB, Cornell U., 1959; JD, Yale U., 1963. Bar: N.Y. 1964, Colo. 1973, U.S. Tax Ct. 1966, U.S. Supreme Ct. 1967, U.S. Ct. Claims 1968, U.S. Dist. Ct. (so. dist.) N.Y. 1965, U.S. Dist. Ct. (ea. dist.) N.Y. 1965, U.S. Dist. Ct. Colo. 1980, U.S. Ct. Appeals (10th cir.) 1978; conseil juridique, Paris, 1968. Assoc. Shearman & Sterling, NYC, Paris, London, 1963-72; ptnr. Davis, Graham & Stubbs, Denver, 1973—. Adj. faculty U. Denver Law Sch., 1977—; mem. adv. bd. U. Denver Ann. Tax Inst., 1985—, global bus. and culture divsn., U. Denver, 1992—, Denver World Affairs Coun., 1993—; mem. Colo. Internat. Trade Coun., 1985—; mem. Rocky Mt. Dist. Export Coun., US Dept. Commerce, 1993—; tax adv. com. US Senator Hank Brown; bd. dirs. Clos du Val Wine Co. Ltd., Danskin Cattle Co., Ouray Ranch, Areti Wines, Ltd., Taltarni Vineyards, Christy Sports, others. Contbr. articles to profl. jours. Actor, musician N.Y. Shakespeare Festival, 1960; sponsor Am. Tax Policy Inst., 1991—; adv. bd. Middle Park Land Trust, Granby, Colo., 2003—; pres. So. Boulder Park Ecol. Assn., 1999—; sec. Bhutan Found.; sec., treas. Citizens for Arts to Zoo; bd. dirs. Alliance Francaise, 1977—, Copper Valley Assn., Denver Internat. Film Festival, 1978—79, Anschutz Family Found.; trustee, sec. Denver Art Mus., 1982—; pres., bd. dirs. Ouray Ranch, Granby, Colo., 2001—; bd. dirs. Aspen Music Festival and Sch., 2004—. Capt. US Army, 1959—60. Fellow Am. Coll. Tax. Coun. (bd. regents 10th cir. 1992—), Soc. Fellows Aspen Inst.; mem. ABA, Internat. Bar Assn., Colo. Bar Assn., NY State Bar Assn., Assn. Bar City of NY, Asia-Pacific Lawyers Assn., Union Internat. des Avocats, Internat. Fiscal Assn. (pres. Rocky Mt. br. 1992—, US regional v.p. 1988—), Japan-Am. Soc. Colo. (bd. dirs. 1989—, pres. 1991-93), Confrerie des Chavaliers du Tastevin, Rocky Mt. Wine and Food Soc., Meadowood Club, Denver Club, City Club Denver, Mile High Club, Cactus Club Denver, Yale Club, Denver Tennis Club. Office: Cherry Creek Sta PO Box 61429 Denver CO 80206-8429 also: Antelope Co 555 17th St Ste 2400 Denver CO 80202-3941 Home Phone: 303-321-4965; Office Phone: 303-299-1230. Personal E-mail: robertrich@tac-denver.com. E-mail: robertrich@aya.yale.edu.

RICH, S. JUDITH, public relations executive; b. Chgo., Apr. 14; d. Irwin M. and Sarah I. (Sandock) R. BA, U. Ill., 1960. Staff writer, reporter Economist Newspapers, Chgo., 1960—61; asst. dir. pub. rels. and communications Coun. Profit Sharing Industries, Chgo., 1961—62; dir. advt. and pub. rels. Chgo. Indsl. Dist., 1962—63; account exec., account supr., v.p., sr. v.p., exec. v.p. and nat. creative dir. Edelman Pub. Rels. Worldwide, Chgo., 1963—85; exec. v.p., dir. Ketchum Pub. Rels. Worldwide, Chgo., 1985—89, exec. v.p., exec. creative dir. USA, 1990—97, exec. v.p., chief creative officer worldwide, 1998—2001; pres. Rich Rels. A Creativity Consultancy, Chgo., 2002—. Frequent spkr. on creativity and brainstorming; workshop facilitator. Contbr. articles to popular mags. Mem. pub. rels. adv. bd. U. Chgo. Grad Sch. Bus., Roosevelt U., Chgo., DePaul U., Chgo., Gov.'s State U. Recipient Pub. Rels. All-Star award for Creativity, Inside PR mag., 1999. Mem. Pub. Rels. Soc. Am. (Silver Anvil award, judge Silver Anvil awards), Counselors Acad. of Pub. Rels. Soc. Am. (exec. bd.), Chgo. Publicity Club (8 Golden Trumpet awards). Avocations: theater, swimming, bicycling, racquetball. Office: Rich Rels A Creative Consultancy Ste 2603 2500 N Lakeview Ave Chicago IL 60614

RICH, SHARON LEE, financial planner; b. Houston, Sept. 7, 1956; d. Hershel Maurice and Hilda R.; children: Mariah, Sophie. BA, Cornell U., 1977; MAT, U. Chgo., 1978; diploma in fin. planning, Boston U., 1985; EdD, Harvard U., 1986. Registered investment advisor, Mass. High sch. tchr. Clear Lake High Sch., Houston, 1978-80; rschr. Harvard U., Cambridge, Mass., 1981-86; fin. planner, pres. Womoney, Belmont, Mass., 1984—. Instr. Cambridge Ctr. for Adult Edn. Co-author: The Challenges of Wealth, 1988; co-editor: Women's Experience and Education, 1985. Conf. organizer Haymarket People's Fund, Jamaica Plain, Mass., 1988—96; spkr. Pub. Edn. Svcs., Boston, 1984—; organizer, mem. The Consortium, Boston, 1991—99; referral for battered women B'nai Brith Women's Connection Card, Boston, 1991—95; co-founder Pride Planners; treas. Beth El Temple Ctr., Belmont, 1999—2001, trustee, 1999—, chair social action com., budget com.; bd. dirs. Boston Women's Fund, 1988—90, Arsenal Ctr. for Arts, 2004—07. Named One of Ams. Top Fin. Advisors, Worth Mag., 1994, 96. Mem.: Nat. Assn. Personal Fin. Advisors, Fin. Planners Assn. Avocation: parenting. Office: Womoney 76 Townsend Rd Belmont MA 02478-3435 Business E-Mail: sharon.rich@womoney.com.

RICH, TRACY LEON, lawyer, insurance company executive; b. Nesmith, SC, Jan. 31, 1952; BA in Political sci., Union Coll., 1974; JD, NYU Sch. of Law, 1977; LLM in Taxation, Boston U. Sch. of Law, 1985. Bar: NY 1978, Conn. 1981, Mass. 1997. Trial atty. office of chief counsel IRS, NYC, 1977—81; atty. Robinson and Cole, Hartford, Conn., 1981—82; v.p., gen. counsel Conn. Mutual, Hartford, Conn., 1982—96; sr. v.p., dep. gen. counsel Mass. Mutual Life Insurance Co., Springfield, Mass., 1996—2000; sr. v.p., gen. counsel Phoenix Life (div. of The Phoenix Co., Inc.), Hartford, Conn., 2000—02; exec. v.p., gen. counsel, sec. The Phoenix Co., Inc., Hartford, Conn., 2002—. Lecturer U. Conn. Law Sch., 1998—2000. Mem.: ABA, Tax Club of Hartford. Office: The Phoenix Co Inc PO Box 5056 One Am Row Hartford CT 06102-5056

RICH, TYVIN ANDREW, radiation therapist; b. Trenton, NJ, Feb. 6, 1948; s. Jospeh Anthony and Mary Virginia R.; m. Christine Schmiel, June 5, 1977; children: Andrew, Karina, Alexander, Austin. BA, Rutgers U., 1969; MD, U. Va., 1973. Instr. Joint Ctr., Boston, 1979-82; asst. prof. Harvard Med. Sch., Boston, 1982-84, M.D. Anderson Cancer Ctr., Houston, 1984-85, assoc. prof., 1986-92, dir. clinics, 1988-90, prof., 1992—; chmn. dept. radiation oncology U. Va. Health Scis. Ctr., prof. dept. radiation oncology. Chmn. GI com. Radiation Therapy Oncology Group, Phila., 1990—; mem. editl. bd. Jour. Infusional Chemotherapy, Ontario, Can., 1991—, M.D. Anderson Cancer Ctr., Oncology, Houston, 1990—, Internat. Jour. GI Cancer, London, 1991—. Recipient Nat. Rsch. Svc. award Nat. Cancer Inst., 1978. Mem. AMA, Am. Coll. Radiology, Am. Soc. Clin. Oncology, Soc. for Surgical Oncology, Am. Radium Soc., Am. Soc. for Therapeutic Radiology and Oncology, New Eng. Cancer Soc., Tex. Radiol. Soc. Office: U Va Health Cancer Ctr Dept Radiation Oncology Box 800383 Jefferson Park Ave Charlottesville VA 22908 Office Phone: 808-924-5564. *

RICH, WALTER GEORGE, railroad transportation executive; b. Oneonta, NY, Jan. 9, 1946; s. George C. and Dorretta (Gregg) R.; m. Karine Schmook, July 14, 1990; children: Derik, Stephanie. BA, Syracuse U., NY, 1968, JD, 1971. Gen. mgr. Delaware Otsego Corp., Oneonta, 1966-68, v.p., gen. mgr., 1968-71, chmn., pres., CEO Cooperstown, NY, 1971—, N.Y. Susquehanna & Western Rwy., Cooperstown, NY, 1980—. Bd. dir. Delaware Otsego Corp., Cooperstown, Security Mut. Life Ins. Co. of N.Y., Energy East Corp., Crucible Materials; mem. N.Y. Pub. Transp. Safety Bd., 1993—; chmn. bd. dirs. Am.Shortline and Regional R.R. Assn., 1999—2004; bd. dirs. Crucible Materials, 2005—. Commr. of elections Delaware County, 1971-78; mem. N.Y. Gov. George Pataki's transition team, 1994; bd. dirs. N.Y. Bus. Devel. Corp., 1995—. Mem. Nat. Rwy. Hist. Soc., Lexington Group in Transp., Ft. Orange Club (Albany), Union League Club (Phila.), Met. Club (N.Y.C.), Binghamton (N.Y.) Club. Episcopalian. Republican. Home: One Lake St Cooperstown NY 13326-1016 Office: NY Susquehanna & Western Rwy 1 Railroad Ave Cooperstown NY 13326-1110 Office Phone: 607-547-2555. E-mail: wrich@nysw.com.

RICH, WILLIS FRANK, JR., banker; b. Ft. Dodge, Iowa, July 26, 1919; s. Willis Frank and Agnes Reed (Paterson) R.; m. Jo Ann Rockwell, Apr. 12, 1947; children: Ronald Rockwell, Roxanne, Andrew Paterson. BA, Princeton U., 1941. Credit analyst Northwestern Nat. Bank, Mpls., 1947-52, asst. cashier, 1952-55, asst. v.p., 1955, v.p., 1955-57; pres. N.W. Nat. Bank, Bloomington-Richfield, Minn., 1952-58, v.p., cashier, 1957-60, v.p. div. A, 1960-68, sr. v.p. nat. and internat. divs., 1968-73, exec. v.p. Mpls., 1973-81, vice chmn. bd. dirs., chief credit officer, 1981-84; fin. cons., 1984—. Dir. Advance Acceptance Corp., 1985-2000. Pres. Viking coun. Boy Scouts Am., 1970-71, trustee found., 1971-86; mem. exec. bd. Minn. Cmty. Rsch. Coun., 1969-77; dir. Minn. Zoo, 1987-95; trustee St. Martin's Found., 1986-90; vestry mem. St. Martin's-By-The-Lake Ch. With AUS, 1941-46. Decorated Bronze Star. Mem. Robert Morris Assocs. (nat. pres. 1977-78), Mpls. Suburban Gyro Club. Clubs: Woodhill, Swan Lake Country. Episcopalian. Home: 378 Waycliffe N Wayzata MN 55391-1390 Personal E-mail: WFRJR@msn.com.

RICHARD, ALISON FETTES, anthropology educator, academic administrator; b. Great Britain, Mar. 1, 1948; BA, Cambridge U., 1969; PhD, London U., 1973; PhD (hon.), U. Peking, 2004. Asst. prof. anthropology Yale U., New Haven, 1972-76, assoc. prof. anthropology, 1976-85, prof. anthropology, 1985—2003, provost, 1994—2002, Franklin Muzzy Crosby prof., 1998—2002, prof. emeritus, 2003—; vice-chancellor Univ., Cambridge, 2003—. Dir. Yale Peabody Mus. Natural History, 1990-94. Bd. dir. Yale-New Haven Health Svc., 1994-2002, World Wildlife Fund, 1995-2004. Decorated officer Nat. Order Madagascar. Mem. Am. Primatological Soc., Am. Assn. Phys. Anthropologists, Am. Anthrop. Assn., Brit. Ecol. Soc., Primate Soc. Gt. Britain, Zool. Soc. London, Cambridge Philosophical Soc. Office: Office of the Vice Chancellor Univ of Cambridge The Old Schools CB2 1TN Cambridge England Office Phone: 44 1223 332290. E-mail: v-c@admin.cam.ac.uk.

RICHARD, BARRY, lawyer; b. Miami Beach, Fla., Mar. 28, 1942; BA, U. Miami, 1964, JD, 1967. Bar: Fla. 1967, N.Y., D.C., U.S. Dist. Ct. (no., mid., and so. dists.) Fla, U.S. Ct. Appeals (5th, 11th, and D.C. cirs.), U.S. Ct. Mil. Appeals, U.S. Supreme Ct. Atty. Judge Advocate Gen.'s Corps USN; pvt. practice Miami; asst. atty. gen., dep. atty. gen. State of Fla.; shareholder Roberts, Baggett, LaFace & Richard, Tallahassee, 1978-91, Greenberg, Traurig, Tallahassee, 1991—. Spl. counsel Gov. Fla., Fla. Legis., Fla. Atty. Gen., Fla. Sec. of State, Fla. Ins. Comms. Contbr. articles to Nat. Law Jour. Named a Super Lawyers, Fla. Super Lawyers Mag., 2006; named Lawyer of the Yr., Nat. Law Jour., 2001, Disting. Lectr., U. Miami Sch. Law, 2002; named one of Legal Elite, Fla. Trend Mag., 2004, 2005, 2006, Leading Litigators in Am., Lawdragon 500, 2006, 100 Most Influential Lawyers, Nat. Law Jour., 2006; recipient Traditions of Excellence Award, Fla. Bar, 2005. Fellow: Internat. Acad. of Trial Lawyers, Am. Coll. of Trial Lawyers; mem.: Am. Acad. of Appellate Lawyers (founding mem.), Fla. Acad. of Trial Lawyers, Fla. Bar Assn. (gen. litig. counsel). Office: Greenberg Traurig PA PO Drawer 1838 101 E College Ave Tallahassee FL 32301

RICHARD, CANDACE L., music educator; d. James S. and Nelda M. (Northrup) Terrill; m. Loren D. Richard, July 20, 1974; children: Christopher L., Colby A. MusB in Edn., Emporia State U., 1970; MusM, Kans. State U., 1993. Cert. tchr. Kans. Vocal music tchr. Unified Sch. Dist. 322, Onaga, Kans., 1970—73, Unified Sch. Dist. 457, Garden City, Kans., 1973—76; vocal and instrumental music tchr. Trinity Cath. HS, Hutchinson, Kans., 1982—84; applied vocal music instr. Cloud County CC, Concordia, Kans., 1985—2000; vocal music tchr. Unified Sch. Dist. 333, Concordia, 1990—2000, Unified Sch. Dist. 480, Liberal, Kans., 2000—. Choral clinician, adjudicator, Kans. Bd. dirs. Cmty. Concert Assn., Concordia, 1987—2000, Liberal, 2000—04, Live on Stage II, 2004—. Mem.: NEA, Music Edn. Nat. Conf., Seward County Hist. Soc., DAR, PEO, Delta Kappa Gamma. Lutheran. Avocation: genealogy.

RICHARD, EDWARD H., manufacturing executive, retired municipal official; b. Mar. 15, 1937; s. Henry and Ida Richard. BA, Antioch Coll., 1959. Pres., chmn., bd. dirs. Magnetics Internat. Inc., Maple Heights, Ohio, 1967-86; exec. v.p. Stearns Magnetics S.A., Brussels, Belgium, 1974-77; prin. Edward H. Richard & Assocs., Cleve., 1967-96; pres., treas. David Round & Son, Inc., Cleve. Chmn. Cleve. dist. adv. council Small Bus. Adminstrn., 1975-79; past nat. adv. council Dept. Treasury; cons. and advisor in field; del. world trade fairs. Former trustee Regional Econ. Devel. Coun., Met. Cleve. Jobs. Coun., Cleve. Devel. Found., Cleve. BBB; former trustee Hiram House, Antioch U., former treas., 1972-77; N.E. Ohio Regional Sewer Dist., Greater Cleve. Domed Stadium Corp., Greater Cleve. Conv. and Visitor Bur.; former trustee, vice-chmn. Cleve. Ctr. Econ. Edn.; former pres. Bratenahl Condominium Assn.; chmn. fin. com. Bratenahl Bd. Edn., 1971-75; former trustee, chmn. nominating com., exec. com. La Jolla Playhouse; CFO Mainly Mozart Festival, 1998—; CFO, chmn. bd. orch. rels. com., exec. com., fin. com., trustee San Diego Symphony Orch.

RICHARD, ELLEN, theater executive; b. Bridgeport, Conn., Dec. 12, 1957; d. Laurent and Anne (Markham) R. Bus. mgr. Atlas Scenic Studio, Bridgeport, 1977-82; theater mgr. Stamford (Conn.) Ctr. for Arts, 1980-83; bus. mgr. Westport (Conn.) Country Playhouse, 1982-84; gen. mgr. Roundabout Theatre Co. Inc., NYC, 1983—; dir. design and constrn. Am. Airlines Theatre, Studio 54, Harold and Mirium Steinberg Ctr. Theatre, Laurel Pels Theatre, various Broadway Theatres. Dir. design and constrn. Am. Airlines Theatre, Studio 54, Harold and Miriam Steinberg Ctr. for Theatre, Laura Pels Theatre, Broadway theatres. Mng. dir.: (Broadway plays) A View From the Bridge, 1997-98 (Tony award Revival of a Play 1998), Cabaret, 1998-2004 (Tony award Revival of a Musical 1998), The Deep Blue Sea, 1998, Side Man, 1998-99 (Tony award Best Play 1999), Little Me, 1998-1999, Death of a Salesman, 1999, The Lion in Winter, 1999, The Rainmaker, 1999-2000, Uncle Vanya, 2000, The Man Who Came to Dinner, 2000, Betrayal, 2000-01, Design for Living, 2001, Major Barbara, 2001, The Women, 2001-02, An Almost Holy Picture, 2002, The Crucible, 2002, The Man Who Had All the Luck, 2002, An Evening with Mario Cantone, 2002, The Boys from Syracuse, 2002, Tartuffe, 2003, A Day in the Death of Joe Egg, 2003, As Long As We Both Shall Laugh, 2003, Nine, 2003 (Tony award Best Revival of a Musical, 2003), The Look of Love, 2003, "MASTER HAROLD"...and the boys, 2003, Big River, 2003, The Caretaker, 2003-04, Twentieth Century, 2004, Assassins, 2004 (Tony award Best Revival of a Musical, 2004); prodr.: Sideman, 1999 (Tony award New Play). Mem. NY Cycling Club. Avocations: bicycling, antiques, art, sailing. Office: 203 Brewster St Bridgeport CT 06605-3112 Personal E-mail: ellrch2@aol.com.

RICHARD, HOWARD M., lawyer; b. Oak Park, Ill., Sept. 20, 1944; BA, Cornell U., 1965; LLB, Harvard U., 1968. Bar: Ill. 1968. Ptnr. Katten Muchin Rosenman, Chgo. Bd. editors Harvard Law Rev., 1967-68. Mem. ABA (sect. real property, probate and trust law), Chgo. Bar Assn. Office: Katten Muchin Rosenman 525 W Monroe St Ste 1900 Chicago IL 60661-3693 Home Phone: 847-432-7924; Office Phone: 312-902-5219. Office Fax: 312-577-8670. E-mail: howard.richard@kattenlaw.com.

RICHARD, LOREN DRU, bank executive; b. Ellsworth, Kans., Feb. 12, 1947; s. Loren Clarence and Drucilla Ruth Richard; m. Candace Leigh Terrill, July 20, 1974; children: Christopher Loren, Colby Alexander. BS, Kans. State U., Manhattan, 1970. HS agr. instr., Garden City, Kans., 1972—75; field rep. Evans Grain Co., Garden City, 1975—76; asst. v.p. Fidelity State Bank, Garden City, 1977—80; agr. loan officer Hutchinson Nat. Bank, Kans., 1980—84; sr. v.p. UMB Bank, Concordia, Kans., 1984—2000, Cmty. Bank, Liberal, Kans., 2000—. Pres. Kans. Assn. Bank Agr. Reps., 1984—85; chmn. agr. com. Kans. Bankers Assn., 1984—85; mem. adv. bd. UMB, Concordia, 1998—2000. Chmn. agr. com. C. of C., Liberal, 2003—04; v.p. Crossroads Ctr., Liberal, 2005—06; chmn. Luth. Ch. Coun., Liberal, 2005—06. 1st lt. US Army, 1970—72. Mem.: Kans. Agr. Bankers, Panhandle Team Penning Assn., Fellowship Christian Cowboys (sr.), Am. Quarter Horse Assn., Lions (Liberal club 2006, pres. Concord Club 1988). Office: The Cmty Bank Liberal KS 67905 Office Phone: 620-624-6898. Office Fax: 620-624-2381. E-mail: dru@communitybankliberal.com.

RICHARD, ROBERT CARTER, retired psychologist; b. Waterloo, Iowa, Apr. 4, 1938; s. Quentin Leroy and Adeline Pauline (Halverson) R.; m. Shirley Ruth Jones, Aug. 25, 1962 (div. Mar. 1999); children: David, John; m. Jacqueline J. Mendes, Feb. 19, 2000; stepchildren: Julianne Mendes, Katherine Mendes. BA Wheaton (Ill.) Coll., 1960; BD, Fuller Theol. Sem., 1963, PhD, 1973; STM, Andover Newton Theol. Sch., 1964. Ordained to ministry Am. Bapt. Conv., 1963; lic. psychologist, Calif. Pastor Peninsula Bapt. Ch., Gig Harbor, Wash., 1965-68; marriage, family counselor Glendale Family Svc., Calif., 1970-71; psychol. asst. Oakland and Pleasant Hill, Calif., 1972—73; psychologist Rafa Counseling Ctr., Pleasant Hill, 1974—2006; ret., 2006. Mem. faculty John F. Kennedy U., Orinda, Calif., 1975-78; adj. faculty mem. New Coll., Berkeley, Calif, 1986; mem. dean's nat. adv. coun. Sch. Psychology, Fuller Theol. Sem., 2005—; co-founder, bd. dirs. New Directions Counseling Ctr., 1974-81; rschr. assertiveness tng., lay counselor tng., psychotherapy and religious experience, treatment of adults abused as children. Author: (with Deacon Anderson) The Way Back: A Christian's Journey to Mental Wholeness, 1989; contbr. articles to profl. publs. Recipient Integration of Psychology and Theology award, 1973. Mem.: APA, Christian Assn. Psychol. Studies, Calif. Psychol. Assn. Republican. Avocations: boating, astronomy, photography, art, tennis. Personal E-mail: robertcrichard@cs.com.

RICHARD, ROBERT JOHN, library director; b. Oakland, Calif., Sept. 20, 1947; s. John Argyle and Vern Elizabeth (Bauer) R.; m. Anne Elizabeth Terrell, June 8, 1968 (div. 1982); children: Jennifer Lynn, Laura Ellen, Constance Anne, Andrea Lee. Student, Fullerton Coll., 1965—67; BA in Biology, Chapman Coll., Orange, Calif., 1972; MLS, Calif. State U., Fullerton, 1973. Cert. county libr., Calif. Audiovisual specialist Fullerton Pub. Libr., 1969-72, asst. to city libr., 1972-73, libr., 1973-76; br. libr. Orange County Pub. Libr., 1976-78, regional adminstr., 1979-80; assoc. dir. Long Beach Pub. Libr., Calif., 1980-81; dir. Sacramento Pub. Libr., 1981-86, Santa Ana Pub. Libr., Calif., 1986—. Mem. ALA, Pub. Libr. Execs. Assn So. Calif., Calif. Libr. Assn., Libr. Adminstrn. and Mgmt. Assn., Libr. Info. and Tech. Assn., Pub. Libr. Assn. Office: Santa Ana Pub Libr 26 Civic Center Plz Santa Ana CA 92701-4078 Office Phone: 714-647-5250.

RICHARD, STEPHEN O., sports association executive; BS in Acctg., Northeastern U., Boston; MBA in Fin., Columbia Bus. Sch., NYC. Sr. audit mgr. Deloitte & Touche, LLP; dist. mgr. fin. planning & analysis AT&T; v.p., region dir. corp. audit grp. Citibank N.A.; sr. v.p. fin. NBA, NYC, 1998—. Mem.: Nat. Assn. Black Accts. (pres. no. NJ chpt.), NJ Soc. CPA, AICPA. Office: NBA Olympic Tower 645 5th ave Fl 10 New York NY 10022-5986 *

RICHARD, VIRGINIA RYNNE, lawyer; b. Mt. Vernon, NY, Aug. 6, 1943; m. Peter L. Richard. BA, Manhattanville Coll., 1965; LLB, NYU, 1969. Bar: N.Y. 1969, Colo. 1973, U.S. Supreme Ct. 1992. Pvt. practice, Denver, 1973-75; assoc. Kane, Dalsimer, Sullivan, NYC, 1970-72, 76-82, ptnr., 1982—99, Winston & Strawn LLP, NYC, 1999—, mem. exec. com., chair IP practice group. Chmn. trademark appeals com. Fed. Cir. Bar Assn., 1991-93; spkr. in field. Mem. editl. bd. Trademark Reporter, 1988-89; contbr. articles to profl. jours. Mem. ABA, Internat. Trademark Assn., U.S. Trademark Assn. (trademark reporter, mem. editorial bd., chmn. subcom. 1982-87), N.Y. Patent, Trademark and Copyright Lawyers Assn., NY Intellectual Property Law Assn. (chair copyright law com. 1994-96). Office: Winston & Strawn LLP 200 Park Ave New York NY 10166-4193 Office Phone: 212-294-4639. Office Fax: 212-294-4700. Business E-Mail: vrichard@winston.com.

RICHARDS, ALAN EDWARD, lawyer; b. Chgo., Mar. 7, 1949; s. Robert E. and Ann R. (Ekhart) R.; m. Meridee G. Johnson, June 13, 1970; children: Kate Elizabeth, Zachary Stephen. B.A., Carthage Coll., Kenosha, Wis., 1970; J.D., Marquette U., 1976. Bar: Wis. 1976, Ill. 1977, U.S. Dist. Ct. (no. dist.) Ill. 1977. Ptnr. Richards & Ralph, Chartered, Libertyville, Ill., 1977-87, Richards, Ralph & Schwab Chartered, Vernon Hills, Ill., 1987-. Editor Marquette U. Law Rev., 1975-76. Mem. ABA, Ill. Bar Assn., Lake County Bar Assn. Office: Richards Ralph & Schwab Chartered 175 E Hawthorne Pkwy Vernon Hills IL 60061-1463 E-mail: arichards@rrs-chartered.com.

RICHARDS, (A)LBERT DEWEY, retired physician, medical educator, writer; b. industry, Maine, Mar. 4, 1927; s. Albert Dodge and Nellie (Booker) Richards; m. Loretta Maychild, Sept. 7, 1992; stepchildren: Andrea Tilden, Julie Tilden, Sarah Warner, Robin Tilden; m. Emily Ricker Gamage (dec. June 7, 1989); children: Susan Finch, Michael, Donna Cotton, Catherine Hill, John. BS with honors, U. Maine, Orono, 1956; MD, Tufts U. Sch. Medicine, Boston, 1960. Cert. Am Bd. Family Practice, 1985. Intern Maine Med. Ctr., Portland, 1960, 1961; rsch. assoc. Dartmouth Med. Sch., Hanover, NH, 1973—75; asst. prof. Tufts U. Sch. Medicine, Boston, 1975—78, assoc. prof., 1978—80; prof. Ea. Va. Med. Sch., Norfolk, 1980—85, chmn. dept. family medicine, 1980—85; ret. Pres. No. Cumberland Meml. Hosp., Bridgton, Maine, 1974; residency dir. EMMC Family Practice, Bangor, Maine, 1975—80; chief FP svc. Ea. Maine Med. Ctr., Bangor, 1975—80; residency assistance program cons. Am Acad. Family Practice, Kansas City, Mo., 1977—84; exec. com Norfolk Gen. Hosp., 1975—80; founder and pres. Mednow Urgent Care Ctrs., Orono, 1985—95, Hartland, Maine, 1985—95, Ellsworth, Maine, 1985—95, Saco, Maine, 1985—95, Salsbury, Maine, 1985—95. Author: (books) Solutions, 2002, Wide Swath, 2003, Detective's Apprentice, 2003, Live Lively Longer, 2004, Just My Luck, 2005. Cpl. 82nd airborne divsn. US Army, 1946—48, Ft. Bragg, NC. Fellow: Am. Acad. Family Practice. Home (Summer): 37 Brady Brook Ln Ellsworth ME 04605

RICHARDS, AUSTIN AMES, physicist, artist; s. Peter Ames Richards and Virginia Youngren, William Thomas Harvey Youngren (Stepfather) and Caroline Frick Richards; m. Victoria Charters, Apr. 14, 2006. PhD, U. Calif., Berkeley, 1995. Prin. scientist Wyatt Tech. Corp., Santa Barbara, Calif., 1998—99; sr. rsch. scientist FLIR Systems, Indigo Ops., Goleta, 1999—. Adj. prof. Brooks Inst. Photography, Santa Barbara, Calif., 2004—. Author: (non-fiction book) Alien Vision: Exploring the Electromagnetic Spectrum with Imaging Technology (Book Pub. by SPIE Optical Engring. Press as a tech. monograph, 2001). Libertarian. Achievements include patents pending for Extending dynamic range of NIR/SWIR infrared cameras. Home Phone: 805-284-5757.

RICHARDS, BERNARD, investment company executive; b. NYC, July 12, 1927; s. Charles and Sadie (Rubin) R.; m. Arlene Kaye, Dec. 23, 1948; children: Carol Leslie, Patricia Ellen, Lori Gale. BBA, Baruch Coll., 1949. CPA, NY. Acct. Eisner & Lubin, NYC, 1949-53, S.D. Leidesdorf, NYC, 1953-56; from contr. to treas. to v.p. fin. to pres. Slattery Group Inc., NYC, 1956-87; pres. Slattery Investors Corp., NYC, 1988—; chmn. bd. dirs. Slattery Assocs., Inc., NYC, 1968-87. Trustee Temple Sinai, Roslyn, NY, 1969-89; bd. dirs. Variety Boys Club, Queens, NY, 1972-96; bd. dirs. NYC Indsl. Devel. Bd., 1973-76; bd. dirs. Baruch Coll. Fund, NYC, 1975—, pres., 1996-98. Recipient Heavy Constrn. award United Jewish Appeal, 1980, Pres.'s medal Baruch Coll., 1989; named Oustanding Alumnus of Yr. Baruch Coll., 1979, Man of Yr. United Jewish Appeal, 1980, March of Dimes, 1983, Man of Yr. Baruch Coll. Fund, 1972; Wood fellow Baruch Coll., 1979. Mem. AICPA, N.Y. State Soc. CPAs, Moles, Beavers (bd. dirs. 1982-96), Shelter Rock Tennis Club. Republican. Jewish. Avocations: tennis, travel, bicycling, swimming, hiking. Home: 18 Applegreen Dr Old Westbury NY 11568-1203 Office: Slattery Investors Corp 1 Hollow Ln Ste 311 New Hyde Park NY 11042-1215

RICHARDS, BRAD, professional hockey player; b. Murray Harbour, Prince Edward Island, May 2, 1980; Player Rimouski Oceanic (QMJHL), 1998—2000, Tampa Bay Lightning, 2000—. Player Team Can., World Championships, 2001; mem. Team Can., World Cup of Hockey, 2004. Named to, NHL All-Rookie Team, 2000; recipient Conn Smythe Trophy, 2004, Lady Byng Trophy, 2004. Achievements include being a member of Stanley Cup Champion Tampa Bay Lightning, 2004; being a member of World Cup Champion Team Canada, 2004. Office: c/o Tampa Bay Lightning 401 Channelside Dr Tampa FL 33602

RICHARDS, BRIAN F., lawyer; b. Oaklawn, Ill., Jan. 23, 1967; BS in Finance with highest honors, U. Ill., 1989; JD, U. Va., 1992. Bar: Ill. 1992. Atty. Winston & Strawn, Chgo.; v.p., gen. counsel sofware devel. co.; ptnr., co-chair Mergers and Acquisitions Practice Katten Muchin Zavis Rosenman, Chgo. Mem. Children's Inner City Edn. Fund, Chgo., Holy Angels Adv. Bd., Chgo.; mem. bd. trustees Cristo Rey Jesuit High Sch.; mem. adv. coun. to bd. trustees Holy Trinity High Sch.; active Philo J. Carpenter Elem. Sch., Chgo. Recipient Armour Scholar, U. Va. Sch. Law. Mem.: Order of the Coif. Office: Katten Muchin Zavis Rosenman 525 W Monroe St Chicago IL 60661-3693 Office Phone: 312-902-5234. Office Fax: 312-577-8764. E-mail: brian.richards@kattenlaw.com. *

RICHARDS, CARLYLE EDWARD, lawyer; b. Deadwood, SD, July 21, 1935; BA, Northwestern U., 1957; LLB, U. S.D., 1960. Bar: S.D. 1960. Law clk. to judge U.S. Dist. Ct., 1960-61; pvt. practice Aberdeen, SD, 1961—; U.S. magistrate, 1971-2000. Mem. S.D. Bar Assn., Brown County Bar Assn. Office: 222 Midwest Bldg Aberdeen SD 57401 Address: PO Box 114 Aberdeen SD 57402-0114

RICHARDS, CARMELEETE A., computer company executive, network administrator, consultant; b. Springport, Ind., Feb. 8, 1948; d. Gordon K. and Virginia Christine (New) Brown; 1 child, Annasheril. AA in Elem. Edn., No. Okla. Coll., 1969; BS in Edn., Southwestern State Coll., Weatherford, Okla., 1971; postgrad., Ashland U., Ohio, 1981—, U. Phoenix, 1994—; MEd in Instrnl. Design, Am. Intercontinental U., 2004. Cert. tchr. Ohio. 6th grade tchr., Scott City, Kans., 1971; salesperson, customer svc. Jafra Cosmetics, 1979-81; br. asst. mgr. Barclays Am. Fin., Columbus, Ohio, 1981—84; tng. mgr., ednl. dir. Computer Depot, Columbus, 1984—85; corp. trainer, exec. sales Litel Telecomm., Worthington, Ohio, 1985—87; comm. cons. Telemarketing Comm. Columbus, Ohio, 1988—89; corp. computer tng. O/E Learning, Troy, Mich., 1989-98; corp. computer trainer ETOP Cols., Ohio, 1989—; dist. asst. network adminstr. Bexley Sch. Dist., 1998-99; dir. tech., computer instr. MCS, 2001—02; info. tech. specialist, trainer Franklin County Common Pleas Ct., 2002—07; instr. IT tech. edn. Vorys, Sater, Seymour, and Pease LLP, Columbus, Ohio, 2007—. Pres. PTA, 1981—82. Recipient Outstanding Participation award Dorothy Carnegie Pub. Speaking; winner Ms. Ohio Beauties of Am. Pageant, 1991. Mem. IEEE, NAFE, Am. Soc. for Tng. and Devel., Columbus Computer Soc., Kappa Delta Pi. Baptist. Avocations: western square dancing, bowling, boating, reading, hiking. Personal E-mail: bkar10@yahoo.com.

RICHARDS, CAROL ANN RUBRIGHT, retired editor, journalist; b. Buffalo, Sept. 24, 1944; d. Jesse Bailey and Emma Amanda (Fisher) Rubright; m. Clay F. Richards, Aug. 12, 1967; children: Elizabeth Amanda, Rebecca Diana. BA, Syracuse U., 1966. Reporter Rochester (N.Y.) Times-Union, 1966; legis. corr. Gannett News Svc., Albany, NY, 1967-73, White House corr. Washington, 1974-76, regional/nat. editor, 1979-84; founding editor USA Today, Arlington, Va., 1982, mem. editl. bd., 1985-87; dep. editor editl. page Newsday, Melville, NY, 1987—2006; ret., 2006. Adj. prof. journalism Hofstra U., Hempstead, NY, 2006—; freelance editor. Pres. Washington Press Club, 1981-82; trustee Northport Historical Soc. and Mus. Mem.: Women's Press Club N.Y. (named to Hall of Honor 2003), Nat. Press Club. Episcopalian. Home and Office: 352 Scudder Ave Northport NY 11768-3021 Office Phone: 631-896-4571. Business E-Mail: carol.richards@yahoo.com, carol.richards@hofstra.edu.

RICHARDS, CECILE, healthcare network executive; b. 1957; d. Ann Richards; married; 3 children. Grad., Brown U., 1980. Dep. chief of staff to Rep. Nancy Pelosi US Ho. Reps., Washington; founder, pres. America Votes, Washington, 2003—06; pres. Planned Parenthood Fedn. of Am., Inc., NYC, 2006—. Bd. dirs. NARAL Pro-Choice Am., Planned Parenthood Action Fund; founder, bd. dirs. Tex. Freedom Network, 1995. Democrat. Office: Planned Parenthood Fedn Am Inc 434 W 33rd St New York NY 10001-2601 Office Phone: 212-541-7800. Office Fax: 212-245-1845.

RICHARDS, CHRISTINE P., delivery service executive, lawyer; b. Amityville, NY, Jan. 8, 1955; BA magna cum laude, Bucknell U., 1976; JD, Duke U., 1979. Bar: Tenn. 1987, NC 1980. Joined FedEx Corp., 1984, corp. v.p. customer and bus. transactions & gen. counsel FedEx Corp. Services, exec. v.p., gen. counsel, sec., 2005—. Office: FedEx Corp 942 S Shady Grove Rd Memphis TN 38120 Office Phone: 901-818-7500. Office Fax: 901-395-2000. *

RICHARDS, DARRIE HEWITT, investment company executive; b. Washington, May 31, 1921; s. George Jacob and Esmee (MacMahon) R.; m. Patricia Louise Moses, Jan. 1, 1947; children: Hilary Wade, Craig Hewitt, Lynn Cotter. Student, Brown U., 1937-39; BS, U.S. Mil. Acad., 1943; MS, Princeton U., 1949. Commd. 2d lt. U.S. Army, 1943, advanced through grades to maj. gen., 1970; mem. Army Gen. Staff Logistics, 1962-66; brigade comdr., logistics staff officer Europe, 1966-68; comdr. Qui Nhon (Vietnam) Support Command, 1968-69, Western Area Mil. Traffic Mgmt. Command, 1969-70; asst. dep. chief staff for logistics Dept. Army, 1970-73; dep. dir. Def. Logistics Agy., 1973-74, ret., 1974; v.p. Capital Resources Inc., Washington, 1974-75; asso. Devel. Resources, Inc., Alexandria, Va., 1975-79; pres. the Montgomery Corp., Alexandria, 1976-84; mng. gen. ptnr. Craighill Co., Alexandria, 1980—; pres., chmn. Montgomery Group, Inc., 1987—. Author publs. on devel allied strategy in World War II, also nat. transp. policy. Decorated D.S.M. with oak leaf cluster, Legion of Merit with 3 oak leaf clusters, Bronze Star, Air medal with 3 oak leaf clusters; Order Chung Mu (Republic of Korea); Disting. Svc. Order; Honor medal 1st class (Vietnam). Mem. Def. Mgmt. Assn. (v.p. 1973-74), Am. Def. Preparedness Assn. (nat. council 1974-76), Assn. U.S. Army (pres. Heidelburg chpt. 1967-68), alumni assns. U.S. Mil Acad., Princeton U., Brown U. Episcopalian. Home: Apt 709 1250 S Washington St Alexandria VA 22314-4455 Office: 300 Montgomery St # 200 Alexandria VA 22314-1516

RICHARDS, DAVID A.J., law educator; b. 1944; AB, Harvard U., 1966, JD, 1971; PhD in Moral and Polit. Philosophy, Oxford U., Eng., 1970. Bar: NY, 1972. Assoc. Cleary, Gottlieb, Steen & Hamilton, NYC, 1971-74; assoc. prof. Fordham U., NYC, 1974-77; vis. assoc. prof. philosophy Barnard Coll., NYC, 1974-77; assoc. prof. law NYU Sch. Law, 1977-79, prof. law, 1979—, Edwin D. Webb prof. law, 1994—. Author: A Theory of Reasons for Action, 1971, The Moral Criticism of Law, 1977, Sex, Drugs, Death and the Law, 1982, Toleration and the Constitution, 1986, Foundations of American Constitutionalism, 1989, Conscience and the Constitution, 1993, Women, Gays and the Constitution, 1998, Italian American: The Racializing of an Ethnic Identity, 1999, Identity and the Case for Gay Rights, 1999, Free Speech and the Politics of Identity, 1999. Rockefeller grantee Austinian Soc. and Ctr. for Study of Law and Soc., Berkeley, Calif., 1974; Knox Meml. Fellow, 1966-68; Humanities Fellow Aspen Inst., 1979. Fellow NYU Soc. Fellows; mem. Soc. for Philosophy and Pub. Affairs (bd. dirs. NY chpt. 1975-76), Am. Soc. Polit. and Legal Philosophy (v.p. 1984), Austinian Soc. (pres. 1974) Clubs: Tuesday Evening. Office: NYU Sch Law Vanderbilt Hall Rm 421 40 Washington Sq S New York NY 10012-1099 Office Phone: 212-998-6251. E-mail: david.richards@nyu.edu.

RICHARDS, DAVID ALAN, lawyer; b. Dayton, Ohio, Sept. 21, 1945; s. Charles Vernon and Betty Ann (Macher) R.; m. Marianne Catherine Del Monaco, June 26, 1971; children: Christopher, Courtney. BA summa cum laude, Yale U., 1967, JD, 1972; MA, Cambridge U., Eng., 1969. Bar: N.Y. 1973. Assoc. Paul, Weiss, Rifkind, Wharton & Garrison, NYC, 1972-77, Coudert Bros., NYC, 1977-80, ptnr., 1981-82; ptnr., head real estate group Sidley & Austin, NYC, 1983-2000; ptnr. McCarter & English, NYC, 2001—, mng. ptnr. N.Y. office, 2002—06. Gov. Anglo-Am. Real Property Inst. U.S./U.K., 1983-88, chair, 1993; mem. Chgo. Title N.Y. Realty Adv. Bd., 1992—. Author: Rudyard Kipling: The Books I Leave Behind, 2007; co-editor: Kipling and His First Publisher, 2001; co-author: The Commercial Office Lease Handbook, 2003; contbr. articles to profl. jours. Trustee Scarsdale Pub. Libr., 1984-89, pres., 1988-89; co-chair N.Y. Lawyers for Clinton/Gore, 1996. Fellow Am. Bar Found.; mem. ABA (real property, probate and trust sect., coun. 1982-88, chair 1991-92), Am. Coll. Real Estate Lawyers (gov. 1987-93), Assn. of Bar of City of N.Y. (real property com. 1978-80, 84-87), Century Assn., Kipling Soc. (N.Am. rep., v.p. 2005—), Assn. Fellows of Morgan Libr., Shenorock Shore Club (Rye, N.Y.), The Grolier Club (N.Y.C., coun. 2003—, sec. 2006-), Yale Club (N.Y.C.), Yale Libr. Assn. (trustee 2003—). Democrat. Home: 18 Forest Ln Scarsdale NY 10583-6464 Office: McCarter & English 245 Park Ave Fl 27 New York NY 10167 Office Phone: 212-609-6817. Personal E-mail: darichards21@aol.com. Business E-Mail: drichards@mccarter.com.

RICHARDS, DAVID GLEYRE, German language educator; b. July 27, 1935; s. Oliver L. and Lilian Marie (Powell) R.; m. Annegret Horn, Sept. 3, 1959 (div. 1992); 1 child, Stephanie Suzanne; m. Friederike Hensler, Oct. 11, 1997. BA, U. Utah, 1960, MA, 1961; PhD, U. Calif., Berkeley, 1968. Asst. prof. German SUNY, Buffalo, 1968, assoc. prof., 1974—84, prof., 1984—99, chair dept., 1986—92, prof. emeritus, 1999—. Author: Georg Buchners Woyzeck, 1975, George Buchner and the Birth of the Modern Drama, 1976, The Hero's Quest for the Self: An Archetypal Approach to Hesse's Demian and other Novels, 1987; editor: (with H. Schulte) Crisis and Culture in Post-Enlightenment Germany: Essays in Honor of Peter Heller, 1993, Exploring the Divided Self: Hermann Hesse's Steppenwolf and its Critics, 1996, Georg Buchner's Woyzeck: A History of Its Criticism, 2001. SUNY grantee, 1973; NEH grantee, 1977-78, Fulbright Commn. grantee, 1980. Rsch. Found. of SUNY fellow, 1982. Democrat. Avocation: photography. Personal E-mail: dgrich@nc.rr.com.

RICHARDS, DENISE, actress; b. Downers Grove, Ill., Feb. 17, 1971; m. Charlie Sheen, June 15, 2002 (div. Nov. 17, 2006); children: Sam, Lola Rose. Former model. Actor: (films) Loaded Weapon 1, 1993, Nowhere, 1997, Starship Troopers, 1997, Wild Things, 1998, Lookin' Italian, 1998, Drop Dead Gorgeous, 1999, The World is Not Enough, 1999, Tail Lights Fade Away, 1999, Valentine, 2001, Good Advice, 2001, Empire, 2002, Undercover Brother, 2002, The Third Wheel, 2002, You Stupid Man, 2002, Love Actually, 2003, Scary Movie 3, 2003, Elvis Has Left the Building, 2004, Edmond, 2005; (TV films) 919 5th Avenue, 1995, In the Blink of an Eye, 1996, Pier 66, 1996, I Do (But I Don't), 2004, (guest appearances): (TV series) Spin City, Melrose Place. Office: 722 Elvira Ave #A Redondo Beach CA 90277 *

RICHARDS, ERIC ALBERT STEPHAN, lawyer; b. Detroit, Jan. 1, 1965; s. June Hill. BA, Yale Coll., 1986; JD cum laude, Harvard U., 1989. Bar: Calif. 1989, US Ct. Appeals (9th Cir.) 1989, US Dist. Ct. (Ctrl. Dist. Calif.) 1989. With O'Melveny & Myers, LA, 1989—, assoc., ptnr., mem. policy com., mem. project development practice group, mem., 1940 Act Practice group, active with joint venture and corp. combinations. Mem.: LA County Bar Assn., Nat. Bar. Assn., ABA. Office: O'Melveny & Myers LLP 400 S Hope St Los Angeles CA 90071-2899

RICHARDS, FEMI SOYINKA, lawyer; b. Pontiac, Mich., Aug. 29, 1971; s. Josephus and Laura Richards; m. Nettie Mahone, Mar. 23, 2002. Master of Pub. Policy, Harvard U., Cambridge, MA, 1997—99; JD, U. of Conn. Sch. of Law, Hartford, CT, 1994—97; BA, U. of Mass. - Amherst, Amherst, MA, 1989—94. Connecticut Bar: Conn. 1997, District of Columbia Bar: DC 2002. Assoc. Holland & Knight, LLP, Washington, 2001—; sr. policy analyst Ct. Services and Offender Supervision Agy. for the DC, Washington, 1999—2001. Contbr. journal Multiculturalism and the Democratic State: Three Frameworks for Social Equity. Public Integrity. Spring 2000. Volume 2. Number 2, journal Sports and the Socialization of Women. Five College Journal of Law and Society. Spring 1993. Volume 1. Number 2. Recipient Outstanding Performance Award, Ct. Services and Offender Supervision Agy., 2000, Manuel C. Carballo Meml. Prize, John F. Kennedy Sch. of Govt., Harvard U., 1999, Cali Excellence for the Future Award, U. of Conn. Sch. of Law, 1997, Round Robin Moot Ct. Competition Best Brief, Nova Southeastern U. Sch. of Law, 1997, Best Oral Adv., Alva P. Loiselle Moot Ct. Competition, U. of Conn. Sch. of Law, 1995, Academic Achievement Award, U. of Mass., Black Student Union, 1993. Mem.: Acad. of Polit. Sci. (assoc.), ASPA (assoc.), Conn. Bar Assn. (assoc.), DC Bar Assn. (assoc.), ABA (assoc.), Harvard Club of Wash., DC (assoc.). D-Liberal. Avocations: basketball, travel. Home: 98 East Wayne Avenue Silver Spring MD 20901 Office: Holland & Knight LLP 2099 Pennsylvania Avenue NW Washington DC 20006 Personal E-mail: frichards_mpp99@post.harvard.edu. E-mail: fsrichar@hklaw.com.

RICHARDS, GALE LEE, communications educator; b. Long Run, W.Va., July 31, 1918; s. Robert Amaziah and Edna Jane (Scott) R.; m. Barbara Lee Neely, Apr. 19, 1944; children: Robin Lee, Wendell Scott, Jeffrey Marshall. BA (Pixley scholar), U. Akron, O., 1940; MA (C.S. Knight Meml. scholar), U. Ia., 1942, PhD, 1950. Instr. speech U. Akron, 1941-42; asst. prof. speech Drake U., 1947-48; asst. prof. English U. Nev., 1948-52; asst. prof. speech U. Wash., 1952-58; assoc. prof. speech U. So. Calif., 1958-65; prof. communication Ariz. State U., Tempe, 1965—, chmn. dept. speech and theatre, 1965-73. Pub. relations cons. Red Feather campaign United Fund, Los Angeles, 1955-58; mgmt. and tng. cons. various profl. and comml. orgns., 1955— Cons. editor: Western Speech, 1957-61, 62-65, 69-72, Jour. of Communication, 1961-67; Contbr. articles profl. jours. Bd. dirs. Phoenix Little Theatre. Served to lt. USNR, 1942-45, PTO. Recipient Distinguished Alumni award Radio Sta. WSUI, 1942 Mem. We. States Communication Assn. (adminstrv. coun., legis. coun., chair commn. on Am. Parliamentary procedure, 1988, emeritus 1991), Internat. Communication Assn. (adminstrv. coun.), Am. Inst. Parliamentarians, Western States Communication Assn. (2d v.p. 1956, 71, pres. Execs. club 1975, Disting. Svc. award 1989), Ariz. Communication and Drama Assn. (pres. 1967, editor jour. 1984-87), Blue Key, Phi Kappa Phi, Delta Sigma Rho. Democrat. Presbyterian. Home: 614 E Bishop Dr Tempe AZ 85282-2325 E-mail: galeri@imap3.asu.edu.

RICHARDS, GEORGE ALVAREZ, psychiatrist, educator; b. La Paz, Bolivia, May 11, 1934; came to U.S., 1952; s. John Joseph and Matilde (Alvarez) R.; m. LaClaire Lissetta Jones, July 26, 1958; children: Leslie Rosario Richards-Yellen, Lia Mercedes Richards Palmiter. BA, Hastings Coll., 1957; MD, U. Autonoma Guadalajara, Jalisco, Mex., 1970. Lic. physician, S.D. Lang. asst. Hastings (Nebr.) Coll., 1953-57; nursing asst. Hastings State Hosp., 1952-57; tchr. lang. and sci. Knoxville (Iowa) Pub. Sch., 1960-65; rotating intern Regina (Sask., Can.) Gen. Hosp., 1970-71; gen. med. officer Dept. Vets. Affairs, Knoxville, 1974; resident psychiatrist Mental Health Inst., Cherokee, Iowa, 1974-77; acting chief, adminstrv. chief, staff psychiatrist Royal C. Johnson Vets. Meml. Hosp., Sioux Falls, S.D., 1977—; asst. prof. psychiatry U. S.D. Sch. Medicine, Sioux Falls, 1977—. Mem. planning and health coms. Multi-Cultural Ctr., Sioux Falls, 1996—; mem. NAACP, Sioux Falls, 1980—. Recipient Exemplary Psychiatrist award Nat. Alliance for Mentally Ill, 1996—. Fellow Interam. Coll. Physicians and Surgeons; mem. AMA (Hispanic Physicians), Am. Psychiat. Assn. (Nancy C. A. Roeske, MD, Cert. of Excellence 1998), S.D. State Med. Assn., S.D. Psychiat. Assn., 7th Dist. Med. Assn. Avocations: languages, mentoring, music, reading, jogging. Office: Royal C Johnson Vets Meml Hosp 2501 W 22d St Sioux Falls SD 57117

RICHARDS, GERALD THOMAS, lawyer, educator, writer; b. Monrovia, Calif., Mar. 17, 1933; s. Louis Jacquelyn Richards and Inez Vivian (Richardson) Hall; children: Patricia M. Richards Grauf, Laura J., Dag Hammarskjold; m. Mary Lou Richards, Dec. 27, 1986. BS magna cum laude, Lafayette Coll., Easton, Pa., 1957; MS, Purdue U., 1963; JD, Golden Gate U., San Francisco, 1976. Bar: Calif. 1976, US Dist. Ct. (no. dist.) Calif. 1977, US Patent Office 1981, US Ct. Appeals (9th cir.) 1984, US

Supreme Ct. 1984. From computational physicist to asst. lab. counsel Lawrence Livermore Nat. Lab., Calif., 1967—84, asst. lab. counsel, 1984—93; sole practice Livermore, Calif., 1976-78, Oceanside, Calif., 1994-97; emeritus atty. pro bono participant Calif. State Bar, 1998—; staff atty. Contra Costa Sr. Legal Svcs., Concord, 1998—. Constrn. law instr. Contrs. State License Schs., Van Nuys, Calif., 1998; mem. exec. com., policy advisor Fed. Lab. Consortium for Tech. Transfer, 1980-88; panelist, del. White House Conf. on Productivity, Washington, 1983; del. Nat. Conf. on Tech. and Aging, Wingspread, Wis., 1981. Author: (novel) Jimmy, 2003. Commr. Housing Authority, City of Livermore, 1977, vice chmn., 1978, chmn., 1979; mem. Bd. Administrn. Appeals, City of Antioch, Calif., 2003-2005, Contra Costa Count Adv. Coun. on Aging, 2005—, sec., 2007—; sec. Contra Costa for Every Generation, 2006-; pres. Housing Choices, Inc., Livermore, 1980-84; bd. dirs. Valley Vol. Ctr., Pleasanton, Calif., 1983, pres., 1984-86; staff Calif. Boys' State Am. Legion, 1996—. Maj. U.S. Army, 1959-67 Recipient Engring. award GE, 1956. Mem. ABA, Calif. State Bar (conv. alt. del. 1990-92, del. 2000, 04-, mem. com. sr. lawyers 2002-05), Alameda County Bar Assn., Contra Costa County Bar Assn., Ea. Alameda County Bar Assn. (sec. 1978, bd. dirs. 1991-92, chair lawyers referral com. 1992-93), LA County Bar Assn., Santa Barbara County Bar Assn., San Diego County Bar Assn., Bar Assn. No. San Diego County, San Francisco Bar Assn., Phi Beta Kappa (No. Calif. chpt. bd. dirs., newsletter chair 2001-07), Tau Beta Pi, Sigma Pi Sigma. Home: 1099 Baywood Ln Hercules CA 94547-2739 Personal E-mail: hesiod@calbears.com.

RICHARDS, GLENORA, artist; b. Feb. 18, 1909; d. Tracy Henry and Bertha (Huber) Case; m. Walter DuBois Richards, June 20, 1931 (dec. May 2006); children: Timothy, Henry Tracy(dec.). Student, Cleve. Sch. Art, 1927-30. Exhibited in group shows at Nat. Collection Fine Arts (Smithsonian Inst.), NAD, Portraits, Inc., N.Y.C., Phila., Pa. Soc. Miniature Painters, L.A., Royal Soc. Miniature Painters, Sculptors and Gravers, R.W.S. Galleries, London, 1958, 95, IBM Gallery Arts and Scis., N.Y.C., 1966; represented in permanent collection Phila. Mus. Arts, Smithsonian Inst., Worcester (Mass.) Art Mus., Yale Mus. Fine Arts; contbr. articles to profl. jours.; designer commemorative stamp of Edna St. Vincent Millay, 1981, of Dr. Mary Walker, 1982. Recipient Pa. Soc. prize Pa. Soc. Miniature Painters, 1947. Mem. Am. Soc. Miniature Painters (Levantia White Boardman Meml. medal 1947), Nat. Assn. Women Artists (medal of honor 1953, 74, Aileen O. Webb prize 1971), Miniature Painters, Sculptors and Gravers Soc. Washington (Elizabeth Muhlhoffer award 1956, 57, 61, hon. award for miniature portrait 1969, Levantia White Boardman Meml. prize 1979, 81), Miniature Art Soc. N.J. (Best on Ivory 1974, 77), Miniature Soc. Fla. (Richard B. Baumgardner award 1989). Home: 87 Oak St New Canaan CT 06840-5840

RICHARDS, HERBERT EAST, retired minister, commentator; b. Hazleton, Pa. m. Lois Marcey, Jan. 1, 1942; children: Herbert Charles, Marcey Lynn, Robyn Lois, Fredrick East, Mark Allen. AB, Dickinson Coll., 1941; BD, Drew U., 1944; MA, Columbia, 1944; DD, Coll. of Idaho, 1953; postgrad., Union Theol. Sem., 1941-48, Bucknell U., 1943-44. Accredited news reporter Nat. Assn. Broadcasters. Ordained to ministry Methodist Ch., 1944; pastor in Boiling Springs, Pa., 1937-40, West Chester, Pa., 1940-41, Basking Ridge, NJ, 1941-47; mem. faculty Drew U. and Theol. Sem., 1944-51, assoc. prof. homiletics and Christian criticism, chmn. dept., asst. dean, 1947-51; spl. lectr. religion Howard U., 1947; minister 1st Meth. Cathedral, Boise, Idaho, 1951-69, 1st United Meth. Ch., Eugene, Oreg., 1969-78, Tabor Heights United Meth. Ch., Portland, Oreg., 1978-86, minister emeritus, 1986—. Weekly radio broadcaster Sta. KBOI, Sta. KIDO, 1941—; weekly TV broadcaster CBS, 1945—, ABC, 1969—, NBC, 1973; pres. Inspiration, Inc., TV Found., 1965—, TV Ecology, 1973; producer Life TV series ABC, 1974-85, PBS TV, 1968-85, also BBC, Eng., Suise Romande, Geneva; chmn. Idaho bd. ministerial tng. Meth. Conf., 1954-60, TV, Radio and Film Commn., 1954-62, Oreg. Coun. Public Broadcasting, 1973; del. Idaho Conf. Meth. Gen. Conf., 1956, Jurisdictional Conf., 1956, World Meth. Coun., 1957, 81, World Meth. Conf., 1981, mem. Gen. Conf., 1956-60, Jurisdictional Conf., 1956, 60; meml. chaplain Idaho Supreme Ct., 1960; chaplain Idaho Senate, 1960-68; mem. Task Force on TV and Ch., 1983 Author: In Time of Need, 1986, Faith and the Pursuit of Healing, 1996; contbr. articles to religious publs.; composer: oratorios Prophet Unwilling, 1966, Meet Martin Luther, 1968, Dear Jesus Boy, 1973. Mem. Commn. on Centennial Celebration for Idaho, 1962-63; committeeman Boy Scouts Am.; bd. dirs. Eugene chpt. ARC, 1954-73; trustee Willamette U., Cascade Manor Homes; adv. bd. Medic-Alert Found. Recipient Alumni citation in religious edn. Dickinson Coll., 1948, Golden Plate award Am. Acad. Achievement, 1965, Jason Lee Mass Media TV award, 1983, Disting. Citizen award Idaho Statesman Newspaper, 1964, Disting. Alumnus award Drew U., 1965, disting. Eagle award Boy Scouts Am.; named Clergyman of Yr., Religious Heritage Am., 1964. Mem. AAUP, CAP (chaplain Idaho wing, lt. col.), Am. Acad. Achievement (bd. govs. 1967—), Am. Found. Religion and Psychiatry (charter gov.), Idaho Found. Medicine and Biology (charter), Greater Boise Ministerial Assn. (pres.), Eugene Ministerial Assn. (pres. 1978), Masons (33 degree, editor Pike's Peak Albert That Is), Shriners, Elks, Rotary (editor Key and Cog, pres. dist. 510 Pioneer Club), Kappa Sigma (Grand Master of Beta Pi). *When a person presses his face against the window pane of life, he becomes as a child waiting for his father's return; simple, trusting and infinitely wiser. In our present time of growth/conflict, such a face-pressing is essential to get us safely from where we are to where we ought to be.*

RICHARDS, JAY CLAUDE, photographer, publishing executive, historian; b. Glen Ridge, NJ, Apr. 6, 1954; s. Jacob Tilghman and Joan Louise (Walsh) Richards. Student, Tenn. Wesleyan Coll., Athens, 1972-73. Various positions armed security work, 1973-75; reporter, photographer Press Publs.: The News, Belvidere, NJ, 1977-98; pres. J.C. Richards Assocs., Harmony Twp., NJ, 1980—; owner Poor Richards' Brit. Gun Shop, Harmony Twp., 1976—; freelance ct. reporter The Morning Call, Allentown, Pa., 1986—; reporter The Knowlton News, 1998—2002, NorthWarren News, 2002—04. Photography judge Warren County 4-H, Belvidere, 1990—; press officer Warren County Office Emergency Mgmt, Belvidere, 1989—98; news corresp WRNJ-News, 1991—, NJN Pubs, The News, 2001—02. Author: Penn, Patriots and the Pequest: The History of Pre-Victorian Belvidere, 1716-1845, 1995, Flames Along the Delaware, 1996 (NJ Frontier Guard's Book Award, 1997), Bugles, Battles & Belvidere: The History of Warren County, N.J. in the Civil War, 1997, Officers and Men of Warren County, N.J. Civil War, 1998, More Bugles, Battles and Belvidere: Warren County, N.J. Civil War Letters to Home, 1999, Following the Hand of Franklin: Warren County, N.J. and the Search for the North Pole, 2000, Warren, Warriors & The World: Warren County, New Jersey In the Plains Indians Wars & The Spanish-American War 1865-1902, 2002, 1903 Flood Centennial Souvenier Book, 2003, Officers and Men of Warren County in the Civil War, expanded edit., 2005, Fighting Fascism for Freedom: Warren County, NJ in World War 2, Book 1, 2006, Just Another Dog Face Fighting Fascism for Freedom, 2007; contbr. art work Hackettstown, NJ "Billy Yank" Civil War Monument, 2001. Mem Hazardous Materials Adv Coun, Warren County, NJ, 1989—98, Joint Emergency Mgmt Coun, Belvidere/White Township, NJ, 1989—98, Warren County Arts Adv Coun, Warren County War Mem Comt, 1997—98; trustee Warren County War Mem Corp, 1999—; consult Harmony NJ Hist Preservation Commn., 2000—; mem Warren County Purple Heart Monument Construction Com., 2000; mem. Statue of Liberty - Ellis Island Found.; participant foreign policy leadership George Washington Univ., 1999, 2003, 2005; Civil War monument project Hackettstown, NJ, 2001; mem. Glamour Photographers Internat., 2003—04. Nominee Legion of Honor award, Chapel of Four Chaplains, 2007; named hon. mem., Boy Scout Troop 141, Belvidere, 1993; recipient Outstanding Cmty. Svc. award, Am Legion Post 131, 1994. Mem.: Nat Indian Wars Asn, Oxford NJ Hist Soc, US Naval Inst, Sr Army Res Comdrs Asn, Res Officers Asn US, Soc Profl Journalists, Nat Press Photographers Asn, NRA, Forks of the Del. Hist. Arms Soc., Frederick A. Cook Soc., Sigma Delta Chi. Episcopalian. Avocations: gourmet cooking, gardening, herbal medicine, military antiques, making leather and canvas gear for re-enacters. Home and Office: 3110 Belvidere Rd Phillipsburg NJ 08865-9515 E-mail: jayrichards@enter.net.

RICHARDS, JODY, state legislator, communications educator, small business owner; b. Columbia, Ky., Feb. 20, 1939; m. Neva Richards; 1 child, Roger. BA in English, Ky. Wesleyan Coll., Owensboro; MA in Journalism, U. Mo., 1962. Mem. faculty in journalism Western Ky. U., from 1962; owner Superior Books, Bowling Green, Ky.; mem. Ky. Ho. of Reps., 1976—, speaker, 1995—; vice chair So. Legislative Conf., 1998—. Mem. adv. bd. dirs. Republic Savs. Bank. Pres. bd. dirs. So. Ky. Fair; bd. dirs. Bowling Green Girls Club, United Way, Warren County (Ky.) Drug Abuse Task Force. Recipient Disting. Svc. award Nat. Art Edn. Assn., 1992. Mem. Bowling Green C. of C., Bowling Green Noon Rotary Club. Office: Ky Ho of Reps State Capitol Rm 309 Frankfort KY 40601

RICHARDS, JOHN PICKFORD, musician, educator; b. St. Matthews, Ky., Feb. 27, 1980; s. Robert Manor Richards and Sherrie Pickford. MusB, Eastman Sch. of Music, U. of Rochester, NYC, 2002; MusM, Eastman Sch. of Music, U. of Rochester, 2004. Founding mem., violist, and libr. Alarm Will Sound, NY, 2001—; founding mem. and violist Payton MacDonald Ensemble, JACK Quartet, 2004—; profl. freelance musician. Musician: (recording) Jeff Manookian: Concertos, Improvisations on Armenian Folk Songs for Viola and Orchestra performed by John Pickford Richards and the Armenian Philharmonic Orchestra, TROY581, Steve Reich: Tehillim and The Desert Music performed by Alarm Will Sound and Ossia, CA21009, Acoustica: Alarm Will Sound performs Aphex Twin, CA21028, (dvd recording) Reich at the Roxy performed by Alarm Will Sound, Sweetspot Productions. Mem.: Chamber Music Am. Office Phone: 717-422-6359.

RICHARDS, KEITH, musician; b. Dartford, Kent, Eng., Dec. 18, 1943; s. Bert and Doris (Dupree) R.; children with Anita Pallenberg: Marlon, Angela (Dandelion), Tara (dec. 1976); m. Patti Hanson, Dec. 18, 1983, children: Hansen, Theodora, Alexandra Student, Sidcup Art Sch. Guitarist The Rolling Stones, 1962—. Guitarist (albums with The Rolling Stones) England's Newest Hitmakers: The Rolling Stones, 1964, 12 X 5, 1964, The Rolling Stones, Now!, 1964, Out of Our Heads, 1965, December's Children (And Everybody's), 1965, Big Hits, High Tide, & Green Grass, 1966, Aftermath, 1966, Got Live if You Want It!, 1966, Between the Buttons, 1967, Flowers, 1967, Their Satanic Majesties Request, 1967, Beggars Banquet, 1968, Through the Past, Darkly (Big Hits Vol. II), 1969, Let It Bleed, 1969, Get Yer Ya-Yas Out !: The Rolling Stones in Concert, 1970, Hot Rocks, 1964-1971, 1971, Sticky Fingers, 1971, More Hot Rocks: Big Hits and Fazed Cookies, 1972, Exile on Main Street, 1972, Goats Head Soup, 1973, It's Only Rock and Roll, 1974, Metamorphosis, 1975, Made in the Shade, 1975, Black and Blue, 1976, Love You Live, 1977, Some Girls, 1978, Emotional Rescue, 1980, Sucking in the Seventies, 1981, Tattoo You, 1981, "Still Life" (American Concert, 1981), 1982, Undercover, 1983, Rewind (1971-1984), 1984, Dirty Work, 1986, Singles Collection: The London Years, 1989, Steel Wheels, 1989, Flashpoint, 1991, Jump Back: The Best of The Rolling Stones, 1993, Voodoo Lounge, 1994 (Grammy award for Best Rock Album, 1994), Stripped, 1995, Bridges to Babylon, 1997, No Security, 1999, Forty Licks, 2002, Singles: 1965-1967, 2004, Live Licks, 2004, A Bigger Bang, 2005, Rarities 1971-2003, 2005, singer, guitarist (solo albums) Talk Is Cheap, 1988, Keith Richards & The X-Pensive Winos Live At The Hollywood Palladium, 1991, Main Offender, 1992; performer: (films) Gimme Shelter, 1970, Sympathy for the Devil, 1970, Ladies and Gentlemen: The Rolling Stones, 1974, Let's Spend the Night Together, 1983, 25 X 5: The Continuing Adventures of the Rolling Stones, 1989, At the Max, 1991, Voodoo Lounge, 1994, The Rolling Stones Rock 'N' Roll Circus, 1996, The Rolling Stones Bridges to Babylon Tour '97-98, 1997; performer, musical dir. (films) Hail! Hail! Rock & Roll, 1987; actor: (films) Pirates of the Caribbean: At World's End, 2007. Named to Rock and Roll Hall of Fame (as mem. of The Rolling Stones), 1989; recipient Living Legend award Internat. Rock, Nordoff Robbins Silver Clef award, 1982, Grammy award for Lifetime Achievement, 1986, Ivor Novello award for Outstanding Contribution to British Music, 1991, Greatest Touring Band of All Time, World Music Awards, 2006. Office: Virgin Records 5750 Wilshire Blvd Ste 300 Los Angeles CA 90036 *

RICHARDS, LEONARD MARTIN, investment executive, consultant; b. Phila., June 4, 1935; s. Leonard Martin and Marion Clara (Lang) R.; m. Phyllis Janelle Mowrey, Aug. 26, 1961 (div. Aug. 1978); children: Lisa, David Reed. BS, Pa. State U., 1957; MBA, U. Pa., 1963; MTh, Universal Sem., 1996, ThD, 2000. Asst. to sr. ptnr. Van Cleef, Jordan & Wood, NYC, 1963-68; v.p., portfolio mgr. Bernstein-Macaulay, Inc., NYC, 1968-72; ptnr. G. H. Walker, Laird Co., NYC, 1972-74; v.p., trust officer, mgr. instnl. funds group Republic Bank N.A., Dallas, 1974-77; v.p., sr. investment officer, mem. exec. com. Variable Annuity Life Ins. Co., Houston, 1977-88; v.p., sr. investment officer Am. Gen. Series Portfolio Co., 1985-88; pres. L.M. Richards & Co., Houston, 1982—, also bd. dirs.; mem. adv. bd. Trinity Life Ctr., Houston, 1996-2000; pres. Lenan Holdings, Inc., Houston, 2005—. Pres., bd. dirs. Sand Dollar, Inc., Houston, 1985—96; trustee Post Oak Sch., Houston, 1997—99, Universal Sem., 1997—2000, pres., 2001—; mem., bd. dir. Capital Institutional Services, Dallas, 1991—99; trustee PAIRS Found., Weston, Fla., 2004—06; bd. dirs. Houston Chorale, 1988—90. Capt. US Army, 1957—65. Mem. ACFA Inst., Houston Soc. Fin. Analysts, Wharton Club (Houston), Houstonian Club Republican. Avocations: skiing, travel, scuba. Home: 9023 Briar Forest Dr Houston TX 77024-7220 Office: LM Richards & Co 1900 St James Pl Ste 800 Houston TX 77056 Office Phone: 713-961-0400. Business E-Mail: lrichards@enhancementinstitute.com.

RICHARDS, MARTA ALISON, lawyer; b. Mar. 15, 1952; d. Howard Jay and Mary Dean (Nix) Richards; m. Richard Peter Massony, June 16, 1979 (div. Apr. 1988); 1 child, Richard Peter Massony Jr. Student, Vassar Coll., 1969-70; AB cum laude, Princeton U., 1973; JD, George Washington U., 1976. Bar: La. 1976, U.S. Dist. Ct. (ea. dist.) La. 1976, U.S. Ct. Appeals (5th cir.) 1981, U.S. Supreme Ct. 1988, U.S. Dist. Ct. (mid. dist.) La. 1991. Assoc. Phelps, Dunbar, Marks, Claverie & Sims, New Orleans, 1976-77; assoc. counsel Hibernia Nat. Bank, New Orleans, 1978; assoc. Singer, Hutner, Levine, Seeman & Stuart, New Orleans, 1978-80, Jones, Walker, Waechter, Poitevent, Carrere & Denegre, New Orleans, 1980-84; ptnr. Montgomery, Barnett, Brown, Read, Hammond & Mintz, 1984-86, Montgomery, Richards & Ballin, 1986-89, Gelpi, Sullivan, Carroll and Laborde, 1989; gen. counsel Maison Blanche Inc., Baton Rouge, 1990-92, La. State Bond Commn., 1992-97; pvt. practice, cons., 1998—. Lectr. paralegal inst. U. New Orleans, 1984-89, adj. prof., 1989; of counsel Sanford & Assocs. Law Firm, 2004—. Contbr. articles to legal jours. Treas. alumni coun. Princeton U., 1979-81. Mem. ABA, La. State Bar Assn., New Orleans Bar Assn., Baton Rouge Bar Assn., Nat. Assn. Bond Lawyers, Princeton Alumni Assn. New Orleans (pres. 1982-86), Princeton Alumni Assn. Baton Rouge (pres. 2002—). Episcopalian. Home: 4075 S Ramsey Dr Baton Rouge LA 70808-1653 Office: 5800 One Perkins Pl Ste 5F Baton Rouge LA 70808 Home Phone: 225-344-2746; Office Phone: 225-761-9600. Personal E-mail: marta73@alumni.princeton.edu. Business E-Mail: mrichards@sanfordlaw.org.

RICHARDS, MARTIN, theatrical producer; m. Mary Lea Johnson (dec.). Co-founder Prodr. Circle, 1976—. Prodr. plays including Chicago (11 Tony nominations Best Musical London and L.A.), The Norman Conquests (Outer Critics Circle award), On the Twentieth Century (5 Tony awards), Sweeney Todd (8 Tony awards including Best Musical), Crimes of the Heart (Pulitzer prize), Foxfire, La Cage aux Folles (6 Tony awards including Best Musical), Grand Hotel (5 Tony awards), The Will Rogers Follies (6 Tony awards including Best Musical), Sally Marr... and Her Escorts, Dylan (Obie award), March of the Falsettos (Outer Critics Circle award Best Musical), Mayor, The Best of Friends, 1971, The Life, films include The Boys From Brazil, 1978, The Shining, 1980, Fort Apache the Bronx, 1981, Chicago, 2002 (Best Picture Academy award, 2003). Trustee Trust for Cultural Resources of City of N.Y.

RICHARDS, MICHAEL, actor, comedian; b. Culver City, Calif., July 24, 1949; 1 child. Stand-up comedian, 1999—. TV appearances include Fridays, 1980-82, Marblehead Manor, 1987, Seinfeld, 1990-1999 (Emmy award, Outstanding Supporting Actor in a Comedy Series, 1993, 94), The Michael Richards Show, 2000, David Copperfield, 2000; films include Young Doctors in Love, 1982, Transylvania 6-5000, 1985, Whoops Apocalypse, 1986, UHF, 1989, Problem Child, 1990, Coneheads, 1993, So I Married and Axe Murderer, 1994, Airheads, 1994, Unstrung Heroes, 1995, Trial ad Error, 1997; TV movie London Suite. *

RICHARDS, NORMAN BLANCHARD, lawyer; b. Melrose, Mass., May 27, 1924; s. Henry Edward and Annie Jane (Blanchard) R.; m. Diane Maionchi, July 9, 1977; children— Terri, Jeffrey. BS, Bowdoin Coll., 1945; JD, Stanford U., 1951. Bar: Calif. bar 1951. Mem. firm McCutchen Doyle Brown & Enersen, San Francisco, 1951—, partner, 1960—. Mem. faculty Tulane Admiralty Law Inst., Hastings Coll. Advocacy. Bd. visitors Stanford Law Sch. With USN, 1943-46. Fellow Am. Coll. Trial Lawyers; mem. ABA, Calif. State Bar, San Francisco Bar Assn., Maritime Law Assn. U.S. Home: 85 Platt Ave Sausalito CA 94965-1897 Office: Bingham McCutchen 3 Embarcadero Ctr San Francisco CA 94111-4003 Home Phone: 415-332-0894; Office Phone: 415-393-2030.

RICHARDS, PAUL GRANSTON, seismologist, geophysics educator; b. Cirencester, Eng., Mar. 31, 1943; came to U.S., 1965; s. Albert George and Kathleen Margaret (Harding) R.; m. Jody Margaret Porterfield, June 1, 1968; children: Mark, Jessica, Gillian. BA, Cambridge U., Eng., 1965; MS, Calif. Inst. Tech., Pasadena, 1966, PhD, 1970. Prof. geol. scis. Columbia U., NYC, 1971—, chmn. dept. geol. scis., 1980-83. Co-author: Quantitative Seismology, 2 vols., 1980, 2nd edit., 2002. Guggenheim Found. fellow, 1977-78, MacArthur Found. fellow, 1981-86. Fellow Royal Astron. Soc.; mem. Am. Geophys. Union (Macelwane award 1976), Coun. Fgn. Rels. Episcopalian. Office: Lamont-Doherty Earth Obs 61 Rte 9W Palisades NY 10964 E-mail: richards@ldeo.columbia.edu.

RICHARDS, PHYLLIS ANDERSON, nurse, health service executive; b. Stuart, Iowa, Sept. 9. 1929; d. John Edward and Verna Mae (Hully) Anderson; m. Herbert Montaque, Mar. 16, 1956; children— Pamela, Herbert, III, Patricia, John. B.S. in Nursing, U. Wash., 1948-53. Surgery nurse Swedish Hosp., Seattle, 1953-54, 1954-56; delivery nurse Kapiolani, Honolulu, 1954; nurse Hawaii Prep. Acad., Kamuela, 1969-90, dir. health services, 1983-90; bd. dirs. Hawaii Island Hosp. Council, 1960-70, Lucy Henriques Med. Center, Kamuela, 1981—96, North Hawaii Cmty. Hosp, 1996—. Bd. dirs., ARC, 1970-83, instr. 1970-88; bd. dirs. Girl Scouts council Pacific Hawaii, 1969—. Recipient Alumni award Hawaii Prep. Acad. Alumni, 1983, Thanks award Girls Scouts U.S.A. Mem. Am. Nurses Assn. Club: Hawaiian Republican. Home: Kahua Ranch PO Box 837 Kamuela HI 96743-0837 Office: Hawaii Preparatory Acad Kamuela HI 96743 Home Phone: 808-882-4424; Office Phone: 808-882-4646.

RICHARDS, PRISCILLA ANN, medical/surgical nurse; b. Providence, Nov. 10, 1949; d. Frank L. Thornton and Dorothy A. Maker; children: Tanya Rene, Jason Edward. Assoc. Degree Nursing, Lincoln Land C.C., Springfield, Ill., 1980. RN Ill., 1980, R.I., 1997. Cert. nursing asst. Meml. Med. Ctr., Springfield, 1971—73, lic. practical nurse, 1973—80, RN, 1980—97, South County Nursing and Subacute Ctr., North Kingstown, RI, 1997—2000, Elmhurst Extended Care, Providence, 2000—05, Maxim Health Care, Providence, 2005—. Sgt. USAF, 1968—71. Baptist. Avocations: reading, swimming, yard work. Home: 71 Wells Ave Warwick RI 02889 Personal E-mail: paramanri@aol.com.

RICHARDS, SHANA NATALIE, physical therapist; b. Kingston, Jamaica, June 22, 1976; BS in Biology, Lehman Coll., Bronx, NY, 1998; BS in Health Sci., Upstate Med. U., Syracuse, NY, 2002; MS in Phys. Therapy, Upstate Med. Ctr., 2002. Lic. phys. therapist NY, 2002. Phys. therapist James J. Peter's Veterans Affairs Med. Ctr., Bronx, 2002—. With subacute rehab. svcs. Rehab. Medicine Program, James J. Peter's VA Med. Ctr., 2002—, with amputee svcs., 2006—. Contbr. articles to profl. jours. Vol. homeless Time Sq. Ch., NYC, 2004—05. Mem.: Golden Key (assoc.). Avocations: travel, exercise. Home: 51 Cross St Bronxville NY 10708 Office: James J Peters VA Med Ctr 130 W Kingsbridge Rd 3D-06 Bronx NY 10468 Office Fax: 718-741-4701. Personal E-mail: sshana76@aol.com. Business E-Mail: shana.richards@va.gov.

RICHARDS, STANFORD HARVEY, advertising agency and design studio executive; b. Phila., Nov. 8, 1932; s. Jack and Ruth (Stein) R.; m. Betty Jo Pugh, July 12, 1957; children— Grant Leonard, Bradford Craig Student, Pratt Inst., 1950-53. Creative dir. Bloom Advt., Dallas, 1954-55; owner Stan Richards & Assocs., Dallas, 1955-75; owner, pres. The Richards Group, Inc., Dallas, 1975—; also bd. dirs. Instr. E. Tex. State U., Commerce, 1976-77; assoc. bd. mem. Cox Sch. Bus., So. Meth. U., Dallas, 1980-84, 88—. Author: Hobo Signs, 1965 Trustee Dallas Symphony, 1978, Dallas Ballet, 1978; bd. dirs. Episcopal Sch., Dallas, 1981—, Dallas Arboretum, 1984-86, The Sci. Pl., 1987-90; mem. Dallas Citizens Council, adv. council Salvation Army Adult Rehab. Ctr., 1986—, adv. bd. Dallas County Salvation Army, 1987—; exec. com. United Way, 1990—; bd. dirs. YMCA, 1990—. Named Top Creative, AdWeek, Entrepreneur of Yr., Inc Mag.; named one of Wall Street Jours. Giants of our Time; recipient Alumni Achievement award, Pratt Inst., Bklyn., 1985, Reddick award, U. Tex. Mem.: Aerobic Activity Ctr. Avocations: deep sea fishing, running, skiing. Office: The Richards Group 8750 N Central Expy Ste 1200 Dallas TX 75231-6436 Business E-Mail: stan_richards@richards.com.

RICHARDS, STEPHEN HAROLD, engineering educator; b. Austin, Tex., July 19, 1952; s. Harold Richards Jr. and Janice Valerie (Mahone) Jackson; m. Mary Kathryn King Coleman, Aug. 15, 1974 (div. July 1981); 1 child, Adam King; m. Elizabeth "Jeannie" Stevens, Apr. 5, 2006. BSCE, U. Tex., 1976; MCE, Tex. A&M U., 1977; PhDCE, U. Tenn., 1989. Registered profl. engr., Tenn., Tex. Rsch. asst. Tex. Transp. Inst., Tex. A&M U., 1976-77, engring. rsch. assoc., 1977-81, asst. rsch. engr., 1982-84; asst. dir. transp. ctr. U. Tenn., Knoxville, 1984-87, acting dir. transp. ctr., 1987-89, dir. transp., 1989—, assoc. prof. civil engring., 1989—; traffic engring. cons. Ctr. Transp. Rsch., 1976—. Engr., mgr. Walton & Assocs./Cons. Engrs., Inc., Houston, 1981-82; lectr. in civl engring. U. Houston, 1982, Tex. A&M U., 1978-81, 83-84; instr. Tex. Engring. Extension Svc., Tex. A&M U., 1978-84; Dwight D. Eisenhower Fellowship Rev. Com., Tenn. State U., 1993, N.C. A&T Univ., 1992; Bicentennial planning Com. U. Tenn., 1993, dir. program for minority student recruitment into transp. careers, 1992—, coll. engring. awards com., 1991—, chmn. spl. events traffic planning com., 1985—. Contbr. numerous articles to profl. jours. Mem. Cumberland Gatewaa Com., 1993—; edn. com. Southeastern Transp. Ctr., 1992—; exec. dir. Southeastern Consortium of

U. Transp. Ctrs., 1992—; chmn. Knoxville Transp. Authority, 1992-94, vice-chmn., 1990-92, commr., 1989-93; rep. Coun. of Univ. Transp. Ctrs. U. Tenn., 1987—, bd. dirs. 1992—, sec., 1994-95, v.p., 1995-96, pres., 1996—; adv. com. Ga. State U. Transp. Ctr., 1989—; traffic control device subcom. Transp. Rsch. Bd., 1989-91, traffic control devices, 1991—, many other coms. Hwy. Safety fellowship Fed. Hwy. Adminstrn., U.S. Dept. Transp., 1976-77. Mem. ASCE, Inst. of Transp. Engrs. (chmn. tech. com. Tenn. sect. 1988—, area coord. Tex. sect. 1982-84, guidelines for driveway design and location), Transp. Rsch. Bd., Soc. Profl. Engrs., Am. Road and Transp. Builders Assn. (edn. com. 1988—), Phi Kappa Phi, Chi Epsilon. Office: Ctr Transp 600 Henley St Ste 309 Knoxville TN 37996-4133 Home Phone: 865-382-0123; Office Phone: 865-974-5255. Personal E-mail: shrichards@tds.net.

RICHARDS, SUZANNE V., lawyer; b. Columbia, SC, Sept. 7, 1927; d. Raymond E. and Elise C. (Gray) R. AB, George Washington U., 1948, JD with distinction, 1957, LLM, 1959. Bar: D.C. 1958. Sole practice, Washington, 1974—. Mem. D.C. Jud. Conf., 1975—2007; lectr. in family and probate law. Bd. dirs. Coun. for Ct. Excellence. Recipient John Bell Larner award George Washington U., 1958; named Woman Lawyer of Yr., Women's Bar Assn. D.C., 1977. Mem. ABA (ho. of dels. 1988-90), Bar Assn. D.C. (pres. 1989-90, named Lawyer of Yr. 2002), Women's Bar Assn. (pres. 1977-78), Trial Lawyers Assn. of D.C. (bd. govs. 1978-82, 85-2001, treas. 1982-85), D.C. Bar. Home: 530 N St SW Washington DC 20024-4546 Office: PO Box 65466 Washington DC 20035-5466

RICHARDS, THOMAS E., telecommunications industry executive; m. Mary Beth Richards; 2 children. BA in Econs., U. Pitts.; MS in Mgmt., MIT, Cambridge. Exec. v.p. Ameritech; pres., CEO, chmn. Clear Comm.; exec. v.p. bus. markets group Qwest Comm. Internat., Inc., Denver, 2005—. Bd. dirs. Nat. Alliance Bus., Tele Danmark (TDK). Mem. Pitts. coun. Boy Scouts Am.; bd. dirs. Pa. Econ. League, Pa. SW Econ. Devel. Assn., Pitts. C. of C. Office: Qwest Comm Internat Inc 1801 California St Denver CO 80202 Office Phone: 303-992-1400. Office Fax: 303-896-8515. *

RICHARDS, VINCENT PHILIP HASLEWOOD, librarian; b. Sutton Bonington, Nottinghamshire, Eng., Aug. 1, 1933; arrived in Can., 1956, naturalized, 1961; s. Philip Haslewood and Alice Hilda (Moore) R.; m. Ann Beardshall, Apr. 3, 1961; children: Mark, Christopher, Erika. ALA, Ealing Coll., London, 1954; BLS with distinction, U. Okla., 1966. Cert. profl. libr., B.C. Joined Third Order Mt. Carmel, Roman Cath. Ch., 1976; with Brentford and Chiswick Pub. Librs., London, 1949-56; asst. librarian B.C. (Can.) Pub. Libr. Commn., Dawson Creek, 1956-57; asst. dir. Fraser Valley Regional Libr., Abbotsford, B.C., 1957-67; chief librarian Red Deer Coll., Alta., Canada, 1967-77; dir. librs. Edmonton (Alta.) Pub. Libr., Edmonton, 1977-89; libr. and book industry cons. Victoria, Canada, 1990—. Pres. Faculty Assn. Red Deer Coll., 1971-72, bd. govs., 1972-73; pres. Libr. Assn. Alta., 1984-85. Contbr. articles to profl. jours. V.p. Jeunesses Musicales, Red Deer, 1969-70; bd. dirs. Red Deer TV Authority, 1975-76; dir. Alta. Found. Lit. Arts, 1984-86. Served with Royal Army Ednl. Corps, 1951-53. Home and Office: 105 1049 Costin Ave Victoria BC Canada V9B 2T4 Home Phone: 250-391-9892; Office Phone: 250-391-9892. Personal E-mail: v.p.h.richards@gmail.com. *Dedication to public service, in spite of its frustrating aspects, diversity of experience, people and places, and the avoidance of overspecialization are great contributors to an enjoyable working life.*

RICHARDS-KORTUM, REBECCA RAE, biomedical engineering educator; b. Grand Island, Nebr., Apr. 14, 1964; d. Larry Alan and Linda Mae (Hohnstein) Richards; m. Philip Ted Kortum, May 12, 1985; children: Alexander Scott, Maxwell James, Zachary Alan. BS, U. Nebr., 1985; MS, MIT, 1987, PhD, 1990. Prof. U. Tex., Austin, 1990—, and Robert M. and Prudie Leibrock Endowed Prof., Engring., and assoc. chair, rsch., biomedical engring. dept. Prof. Howard Hughes Med. Inst., 2002—. Named Presdl. Young Investigator NSF, Washington, 1991; NSF presdl. faculty fellow, Washington, 1992; recipient Career Achievement award Assn. Advancement Med. Instrumentation, 1992, Dow Outstanding Young Faculty awd., Am. Soc. for Engring. Edn., 1992, Y.C. Fung Young Investigator award, Bioengring. Divsn., Am. Soc. of Mechanical Engrs., Howard Hughes Med. Inst. grantee in biomedical engring., 2002. Mem. AAAS, Am. Soc. Engring. Edn. (Outstanding Young Faculty award 1992), Optical Soc. Am., Am. Soc. Photobiology. Achievements include research in photochemistry, photobiology, applied optics and bioengring. Office: Dept Biomed Engring U Texas 1 U Station C0800 Austin TX 78712-0238 Office Phone: 512-471-3604. Business E-Mail: kortum@mail.utexas.edu.

RICHARDSON, ALBERT EDWARD, chemistry professor, researcher; b. Lovelock, Nev., Feb. 4, 1929; s. James Harold and Mary Lorraine Richardson; m. Shirley Arlene Richardson, June 10, 1959 (dec. Apr. 1997); children: Anne Ikard, John (dec.), Stephen; stepchildren: Corinne Jameson, Elisabeth Anderson, David Beckman, Margaret Chambers. BS in Chemistry, U. Nev., 1950; PhD, Iowa State U., 1956. Accredited profl. chemist Am. Inst. Chemists. Rsch. chemist Ames (Iowa) Lab. of the Atomic Energy Commn., 1950—55; asst. prof. chemistry N.Mex. State U., Las Cruces, 1955—60, radiation safety officer, 1957—75, assoc. prof. chemistry, 1960—91, assoc. prof. emeritus, 1991—. Vis. scientist N.Mex. secondary schs., 1960—91; vis. prof. chemistry Adams State Coll., Alamosa, Colo., 1963; summer rschr. Ames Lab. Atomic Energy Commn., 1964, Lawrence Livermore (Calif.) Nat. Lab., 1979; cons. White Sands (N.Mex.) Missile Range, 1965—71, contractor, 1973—74, chemist, 1981—82, 1984—92; vis. staff mem. Los Alamos (N.Mex.) Nat. Labs., 1975—80; summer faculty Sandia Nat. Lab., Albuquerque, 1983; owner, mgr. Timberline Bed and Breakfast, Cedaredge, Colo., 1992—98. Contbr. over 20 articles to profl. jours. Mem. founding cabinet The World Peace and Diplomacy Forum, 2003—; bus. mgr. Coll. Cmty. Chorus, Las Cruces, 1956—57; pres. U. Park Toastmaster's Club, Las Cruces, 1961; dir. Southwestern N.Mex. Regional Sci. Fair, Las Cruces, 1967—68; vol. reading aide to elem. schs. Las Cruces, 2000—03. Rsch. grantee NASA, 1966, Equipment grantee Atomic Energy Commn., 1968; postdoctoral rsch. fellow Atomic Energy Commn., 1968-69. Mem. Am. Chem. Soc. (chmn. so. N.Mex. sect. 1962, chmn. Rio Grande Valley sect. 1977), World Peace and Diplomacy Forum (charter), Sigma Xi, Phi Kappa Phi (pres. N.Mex. State U. chpt. 1972-73), Phi Lambda Upsilon, Sigma Pi Sigma. Democrat. Avocations: photography, collecting coins and CD's, travel, gardening, cultural activities. Home: 1185 Villita Loop Las Cruces NM 88007 Personal E-mail: aerinlc@earthlink.net.

RICHARDSON, ALFONSO AUSTIN, accountant, financial services executive; b. St. Nicholas, Aruba, W.I., Feb. 29, 1932; came to U.S., 1951; s. Ashley A. and Elvia H. Richardson; m. Florence C. St. Hilaire, Sept. 7, 1957 (dec. Nov. 17, 1998); children: Paula, Kathy, Peter, Steven, Edward, Vernon; m. Jennifer Harrypersad Dec., 24, 2002; stepchildren: Nicholas Binda, Devon Binda. BS, L.I. U., 1959. Cert. internat. financier. V.p., treas. Node 4 Assocs., Inc., Bklyn., 1970-71; asst. contr. Kings County Hosp. Ctr., Bklyn., 1971-74; owner Richardson Mgmt. Assoc., 1971—; contr. Kings County Hosp. Ctr., Bklyn., 1974-79; contr., CFO Harlem Hosp. Ctr., NYC, 1979-95; CFO L.B.J. Health Complex, Inc., Bklyn., 1996-98; pres., CEO Accudata Sys. Svcs., Inc., NYC, 1997—. Owner Empire Trading Co., 2002. Contbr. articles to profl. publs. Dir., treas. Bklyn. Local Econ. Devel. Corp., 1965-70, L.B.J. Health Complex, Inc., Bklyn., 1991-96; mem. Pub. Citizens. Sgt. U.S. Army, 1952-55. Mem. Healthcare Fin. Mgmt. Assn. (Follmer Bronze Merit award 1996), Nat. Soc. Accts., Ind. Assn. Accts. Bklyn., Caribbean Am. C. of C., Oxford Club, VFW, Disabled Am. Vets., Contrs. Orgn. (past pres.), Internat. Assn. Fin. Planning, Internat. Soc. Financiers; Am. Legion. Avocations: bowling, Scrabble, stamp collecting/philately, coin collecting/numismatics, bicycling. Home: 704 Empire Blvd Brooklyn NY 11213-5309

RICHARDSON, ANN BISHOP, foundation executive, lawyer; b. New Rochelle, NY, Dec. 15, 1940; d. Erwin Julius and Mary Frances (Stuart) Heilemann; children: Timothy William, Lynn Patricia, Melanie Elizabeth. BA summa cum laude, Georgetown U., 1977; JD, George Washington U., 1984; cert., Oxford U., Eng., 1986. Bar: Md. 1988, DC 1989. Student counselor Amideast, Beirut, 1967-68, program specialist, 1970-73; adminstrv. asst. UN Devel. Program, Yaounde, Cameroon, 1968-70; adminstrv. mgr. Antioch Sch. Law, Washington, 1977-79; chief adminstrv. officer for internat. ops. Peace Corps, Washington, 1980-84; dir. adminstrn. and fin. African Devel. Found., Washington, 1984-87; atty. Karr and McLain, Washington, 1987-92; v.p., gen. counsel Time Dollar, Inc., Washington, 1992-98; adj. prof. law DC Sch. Law, Washington, 1994-98; prof., acad. dean U. DC David A. Clarke Sch. Law, Washington, 1998—. Bd. dirs. Bur. Rehab., Inc. Active Neighbors, Inc., Washington, 1976—, Time Dollar, Inc. Recipient Spl. Achievement award Peace Corps, 1981, 82, African Devel. Found., 1986. Mem. ABA, ACLU, DC Bar Assn., Am. Women Univ. Grads., Soc. for Internat. Devel., Phi Beta Kappa. Office: David A Clarke Sch Law 4200 Connecticut Ave NW Washington DC 20008-1122

RICHARDSON, ANNE WORSHAM, art gallery owner, artist; b. Turbeville, SC, Oct. 22, 1922; d. George Talbert and Jessie Phillips Worsham; m. Marvin D. Richardson, 1946 (dec.); 1 child, Marvin D. Jr. (dec.); m. John Peter Paszek, 1972 (dec. 2005). Student, Rice Bus. Coll., Charleston, SC, 1938. Artist, gallery owner Birds I View Gallery, Charleston, 1972—. Lectr. in field. Exhibitions include Ga. Ornithological Soc., 1949, Carolina Bird Club, Lake Mattamuskeet, NC, 1950, Kennedy Gallery, NYC, 1958, East Clarendon HS, Turbeville, 1958, Dock St. Theatre Green Rm., Charleston, 1962, Wilson Ornithological Soc., Charleston Mus., 1963, The Gibbes Mus. Art, Charleston, 1965, Bob Jones U., Greenville, SC, 1966, The Berkshire Mus., Pittsfield, Mass., 1966, Columbia Mus. Art, 1967, Calif. State Mus., LA, 1970, 1972, 1977, Harbour Town Mus., Hilton Head Island, SC, 1971, St. Louis Art and Sci. Mus., 1974, The Sumter Art Gallery, SC, 1974, Nat. Wildlife Fedn., Washington, 1975, Nat. History Mus., Anniston, Ala., 1976, Vt. Art Ctr., Manchester, Vt., 1977, The Arts Club of Washington, 1978, Schloss Glueecksburg, Germany, 1978, Morton Arboretum Mus., Chgo., 1991, York County Natural History Mus., Rockhill, SC, 1991, Darlington Garden Club, SC, 2003, Delta Kappa Gamma, Florence, SC, 2004, Florence Mus., Represented in permanent collections SC State Ho., Columbia. Named to SC Fedn. Women's Clubs Hall of Fame, 1978, SC Hall of Fame, Myrtle Beach, 1991; recipient award, Summerville Art Guild, 1959, Medway Art Festival 1st award purchase prize, Gibbes Mus. Art, 1959, Commendation award, Calif. State Mus., LA, 1972, commendation for conservation, Dept. of Interior, Washington, 1985, Lifetime Svc. award, Horry County Literacy Coun., 2002; grantee, Charleston Cultural and Sci. Found., 1962. Mem.: Charleston Artists Guild, Nat. Wildlife Fedn. (Art Print of Yr. award 1970), Nat. Audubon Soc., Cornell Ornithological Soc., USN League (life), Alpha Kappa Gamma (hon.), Delta Kappa Gamma (hon.). Office: Birds I View Gallery 119-A Church St Charleston SC 29401 Office Phone: 843-723-1276. Personal E-mail: 4awr@bellsouth.net.

RICHARDSON, ARTHUR WILHELM, lawyer; b. Glendale, Calif., Apr. 3, 1963; s. Douglas Fielding and Leni (Tempelaar-Lietz) R.; m. Noriko Satake, Nov. 14, 1998. Student, London Sch. Econs., 1983; AB, Occidental Coll., 1985; JD, Harvard U., 1988. Bar: Calif. 1989, Ohio 2002. Assoc. Morgan, Lewis and Bockius, LA, 1988—90; staff lawyer U.S. SEC, LA, 1990—92, br. chief, 1992—96, sr. counsel, 1996—2001; of counsel Arter and Hadden, Columbus, Ohio, 2002—03. Mem. ABA, Calif. Bar Assn., L.A. County Bar Assn., Town Hall Calif., L.A. World Affairs Coun., Phi Beta Kappa. Presbyterian.

RICHARDSON, BETTY H., lawyer, former prosecutor; b. Oct. 3, 1953; BA, U. Idaho, 1976; JD, Hastings Coll. Law, 1982. Staff aide U.S. Senator Frank Church, 1976-77; tchg. asst. Hastings Coll. Law, 1980-82, 1980-82; legal rsch. asst. criminal divsn. San Francisco Superior Ct., 1982-84; jud. law clk. Chamber of Idaho Supreme Ct. Justice Robert C. Huntley Jr., 1984-86; atty. U.S. Dept. Justice, Boise, Idaho, 1993-2001, Richardson & O'Leary, Eagle, Idaho, 2001—; jud. law clk. Chamber of Chief U.S. Dist. Ct. Judge B. Lynn Winmill, Idaho, 2003—. Instr. Boise State U., 1987, 89; mem. U.S. Atty. Gen.'s Adv. Com. subcoms. on environ., civil rights and native Am. issues, others, 1993-2001; mem. hon. adv. bd. for Crime Victims Amendment in Idaho, 1994; mem. Dist. of Idaho Judges and Lawyer Reps. com., gender fairness com., Civil Justice Reform Act com. and criminal adv. com., 1993-2001; Dem. nominee Dist 1 Idaho, U.S. Ho. of Reps., 2003; adj. prof. constnl. law Boise State U., 2004; program planner Idaho State Bar and Law Found., 2004—. Mem. Idaho Indsl. Commn., 1991-93, chmn., 1993; mem. adv. bd. Family and Workplace Consortium, 1995-2001; bd. dirs. Tony Patino Fellowship. Recipient Harold E. Hughes Exceptional Svc. award Nat. Rural Inst. on Alcohol and Drug Abuse, 1999; Tony Patino fellow Hastings Coll. Law, 1982. Mem. FBA, Idaho Bar Assn. (governing coun. govt. and pub. sectors lawyers sect. 1999-01, Pro Bono Svc. award 1988), Idaho State Bar (alt. dispute resolution sect.), Idaho Women Lawyers (Kate Feltham award 2006), Idaho Legal Hist. Soc. Ptnrs. for Justice, Assistance League Boise, YMCA, City Club Boise. Office: Richardson & O'Leary 515 N 27th Boise ID 83702 Office Phone: 208-938-7900.

RICHARDSON, BILL (WILLIAM BLAINE RICHARDSON III), governor; b. Pasadena, Calif., Nov. 15, 1947; s. William Blaine & María Luisa López-Collada Márquez Richardson; m. Barbara Flavin, 1972. BA, Tufts U., Medford, Mass., 1970; MA, Fletcher Sch. Law and Diplomacy, 1971. Mem. staff US Congress, 1971-72, US Dept. State, 1973-75; mem. staff fgn. relations com. US Senate, 1975-78; exec. dir. N. Mex. State Democratic Com., 1978, Bernalillo County Democratic Com., 1978; businessman Santa Fe, 1978-82; mem. US Congress from 3rd N.Mex. dist., Washington, 1982-96; permanent US rep. UN, NYC, 1997-98; sec. US Dept. Energy, Washington, 1998-2001; sr. mng. dir. Kissinger McLarty, Washington, 2001—02; gov. State of N. Mex., Santa Fe, 2003—. Ranking minority mem. Resources Com. on Nat. Pks., Forests and Lands; mem. Select Com. on intelligence, Helsinki Commn.; adj. prof. pub. policy Harvard U., 2001; cons. Salomon Smith Barney Author (with Michael Ruby): Between Worlds: The Making of an American Life, 2005. Vice chair Dem. Nat. Com.; active Big Bros.-Big Sisters, Santa Fe. Named one of 25 Most Influential Hispanics, Time Mag., 2005. Mem. Santa Fe Hispanic C. of C., Santa Fe C. of C., Council Fgn. Relations, NATO 2000 Bd., Congl. Hispanic Caucus, Am. G.I. Forum Democrat. Catholic. Office: Office of the Gov State Capitol Rm 400 Santa Fe NM 87501 Office Phone: 505-476-2200. Office Fax: 505-476-2226. *

RICHARDSON, CAMPBELL, retired lawyer; b. Woodland, Calif., June 18, 1930; s. George Arthur and Mary (Hall) R.; m. Patricia Packwood, Sept. 3, 1957 (dec. Oct. 1971); children: Catherine, Sarah, Thomas; m. Carol Tamblyn, June 1975 (div. Dec. 1977); m. Susan J. Lienhart, May 3, 1980; 1 child, Laura. AB, Dartmouth Coll., 1952; JD, NYU, 1955. Bar: Oreg. 1955, U.S. Dist. Ct. Oreg. 1957. Ptnr. Stoel Rives LLP, Portland, 1964-2000; ret., 2000—. Co-author: Contemporary Trust and Will Forms for Oregon Attorneys, 2003, and for Idaho Attorneys, 2001; contbr. articles to profl. jours. Mem. Portland/Metro Govt. Boundary Commn., 1976; mem. Oreg. Adv. Com. to U.S. Commn. on Civil Rights, 1976-84; bd. dirs. Ctr. for Urban Edn., Portland, 1980-84, Dorchester Conf., Inc., 1982, Oreg. Zoo Found., 1993-2003; chmn. planned giving com. St. Vincent Med. Found., 1988-98; mem. planned giving coun. Oreg. Health Scis. Found., 1994-2003; trustee Met. Family Svc. Found., 1990-98; bd. dirs. Elders in Action, Portland, 2000-06. Served with U.S. Army, 1955-57. Mem. ABA, Oreg. Bar Assn., Multnomah County Bar Assn., Estate Planning Coun. Portland (pres. 1978), Am. Coll. Trust and Estate Counsel, City Club, Multnomah Athletic Club (Portland). Republican. Home: 1500 SW 5th Ave Unit 1701 Portland OR 97201-5410 Office: Stoel Rives LLP 900 SW 5th Ave Ste 2300 Portland OR 97204-1229 Office Phone: 503-294-9337. E-mail: crichardson@stoel.com.

RICHARDSON, CHARLES CLIFTON, biochemist, educator; b. Wilson, NC, May 7, 1935; s. Barney Clifton and Florence Elizabeth (Barefoot) R.; m. Ute Ingrid Hanssum, July 29, 1961; children: Thomas Clifton, Matthew Wilfrid BSM., Duke U., 1959, MD, 1960; A.M. (hon.), Harvard U., 1967. Intern dept. medicine Duke U., Durham, NC, 1960-61; postdoctoral fellow dept. biochemistry Stanford U. Med. Sch., Calif., 1961-63; asst. prof. biol. chemistry Harvard Med. Sch., Boston, 1964-67, assoc. prof., 1967-69, prof. biol. chemistry, 1969—, chmn. dept. biol. chemistry, 1978-87, Edward S. Wood prof., 1979—. Physiol. chemistry study sect. NIH, 1970-74; mem. Fachbeirat of Max-Planck Inst. für Moleculare Genetik, Berlin, Fed. Republic Germany, 1980-89; sci. adv. com. U.S. Biochem. Corp., Cleve., 1983-93, Genetics Inst., Cambridge, Mass., 1986-99, NYCOMED-Amersham, U.K., 1998-2000; mem. Nat. Bd. Med. Examiners, 1973-76; nucleic acids and protein adv. com., Am. Cancer Soc. Inst., 1975-78; vis. com. Boston Biomed. Rsch. Found., 1985—; assoc. Helicon Found., San Diego, 1983-2000; sci. adv. bd. Amersham Life Sci. Inc., 1994-98. Assoc. editor: Ann. Rev. Biochemistry, 1973-82, editor, 1983-2003; mem. editl. bd. Jour. Biol. Chemistry, 1968-73, 84-88, Jour. Molecular Biology, 1976-79. Recipient Career Devel. award, NIH, 1967—76, Merit award, 1986, Herbert Tabor lectureship award, Jour. Biol. Chemistry, 2006. Fellow Am. Acad. Arts and Scis., Inst. of Medicine; mem. Nat. Acad. Scis., Am. Chem. Soc. (Eli Lilly Co. biol. chem. award 1968), Am. Soc. Biol. Chemists (mem. nominating com. 1974-75, 1983-84), Am. Cancer Soc. (coun. for rsch. and clin. investigation 1989-92), Am. Soc. Biochemistry and Molecular Biology (Merck award in biochemistry and molecular biology 1996, Herbert Tabor/Jour. Biol. Chemistry Lectureship award 2006). Business E-Mail: ccr@hms.harvard.edu.

RICHARDSON, DANA ROLAND, technology consultant; b. Mason City, Iowa, Jan. 11, 1945; s. Dana Roland Richardson and Louise Marion (Duke) Sarles; m. Sandra Anderson, June 12, 1966; children: Patricia Nan, Dana Roland, Jr. BS, UCLA, 1966, MBA, 1967. CPA, Calif., N.Y. Staff acct. Arthur Young, LA, 1967—72, mgr., 1972—76, prin. NYC, 1976—78; ptnr. Ernst & Young, NYC, 1978—94; founder, ptnr. Dream Street Prodns., New Canaan, Conn., 1994—2002; pres. Richardson Media & Tech. LLC, 2003—. Author: A Manager's Guide to Computer Timesharing, 1975, Audit and Control of Information Systems, 1987. Staff sgt. Reserves USANG, 1967-73. Named one of Techology 100 Top 100 Achievers in Techn. in Am., Tech. Mag., 1982, Top 100 Influential People in Acctg., Acctg. Today mag., 2005; recipient Nat. Videographer award, Nat. Videography Assn., 1998, 1999, Telly award, 1999. Mem. AICPA (Lifetime Achievement award 2003), Calif. Soc. CPA's, Conn. Soc. CPA's. Republican. Episcopalian. Avocations: boating, fishing, music, videography, multimedia. Office: Richardson Media & Tech LLC 24 Blueberry Ln Canton CT 06019 Home: 24 Blueberry Ln Canton CT 06019-4503 Business E-Mail: rick@richardson-media-tech.com.

RICHARDSON, DAVID L., lawyer; b. Washington, 1954; BA with high distinction, U. Va., Charlottesville, 1975, JD, 1978. Bar: Va. 1978. Ptnr. McGuireWoods LLP, Richmond, Va., chair firm fin. services dept., head firm pub. fin. group. Fellow: Healthcare Fin. Mgmt. Assn.; mem.: Va. Govt. Fin. Officers Assn., Va. Hosp. & Healthcare Assn., Local Govt. Attorneys of Va., Nat. Assn. Bond Lawyers. Office: McGuireWoods LLP One James Ctr 901 E Cary St Richmond VA 23219-4030 Office Phone: 804-775-1030. Office Fax: 804-698-2148. Business E-Mail: drichardson@mcguirewoods.com.

RICHARDSON, DAVID WALTHALL, cardiologist, educator, consultant; b. Nanking, China, Mar. 22, 1925; s. Donald William and Virginia (McIlwaine) R.; m. Frances Lee Wingfield, June 12, 1948; children: Donald, Sarah, David. BS, Davidson Coll., 1947; MD, Harvard U., 1951. Diplomate Am. Bd. Internal Medicine, Am. Bd. Cardiology. Intern, resident Yale New Haven Hosp., 1951-53; resident, fellow Med. Coll. Va., Richmond, 1953-56, assoc. prof. to prof. medicine, 1962-95, prof. emeritus, 1995—2007, prof. medicine, 2007—. Chmn. divsn. cardiology, 1972-87; interim chmn. dept. medicine, 1973-74; chief cardiology, assoc. chief staff for rsch. VA Hosp., Richmond, 1956-61, dir. cardiology tng. program, 1990-95; vis. scientist Oxford U., Eng., 1961-62; vis. prof. U. Milan, Italy, 1972-73. Contbr. articles to profl. jours. Moderator Hanover Presybery, Presbyn. Ch. U.S., Richmond, 1970; chmn. events com., NHLBI Cardiac Arrhythmia Suppression Trial, 1983-92, NHLBI Anti-Arrhythmics versus Implantable Defibrillators Trial, 1993-97. Served with USN, 1944-46. Fellow Am. Coll. Cardiology (gov. VA 1970-72), Am. Heart Assn. (coun. clin. cardiology and high blood pressure rsch.); mem. Am. Soc. Clin. Investigation, Am. Clin. and Climatol. Assn. Democrat. Presbyterian. Home: 1500 Westbrook Ct CYA 1105 Richmond VA 23227-3366 Home Phone: 804-200-1256; Office Phone: 804-200-1256. Personal E-mail: dwr1@wcrichmond.org.

RICHARDSON, DEAN WHEELER, equine surgeon, veterinary educator; b. Aug. 30, 1953; married; 1 child. BS, Dartmouth Coll., Hanover, NH, 1974; DVM, Ohio State U., Coll. Vet. Medicine, 1975—79. Internship surgical residency training prog., U. Pa., 1979; with New Bolton Ctr., U. Pa. Sch. Vet. Medicine, Kennett Sq., Pa., 1979—, Charles W. Baker prof. equine surgery, chief of Large Animal Surgery. Mem. editl. bd. Specialty Mag. in the Sci. Biol. Chemicals, mem. adv. editl. bd. Zeitschrift für Metallkunde. Recipient Norden Disting. Teaching award, Disting. Alumni award, Coll. Vet. Medicine, Ohio State U., 2005. Mem.: Osteosynthesis Soc., Grayson-Jockey Club (mem. scientific adv. bd.). Achievements include recognized for teaching AO Veterinary in North America and Switzerland; leading authority in orthopedic surgery and long bone fractures in horses; renown for performing life saving surgery on Kentucy Derby winner Barbaro, 2006. Avocations: horseback riding, basketball, golf, birdwatching. Office: School Vet Medicine U Pa 382 W St Rd Kennett Square PA 19348 Office Phone: 610-444-5800. Office Fax: 610-925-8100.

RICHARDSON, DENNIS MICHAEL, lawyer, educator; b. LA, July 30, 1949; s. Ralph Lee and Eva Catherine (McGuire) R.; 1 child from previous marriage, Scott Randol; m. Catherine Jean Coyl, July 27, 1973; children: Jennifer Eve, Valerie Jean, Rachel Catherine, Nicole Marie, Mary Rose, Marie Christina, Laura Michelle, Alyssa Rose. BA, Brigham Young U., 1976, JD, 1979. Bar: Oreg. 1979. Owner Law Firm of Dennis Richardson, P.C., Central Point, Oreg., 1979—; pvt. practice law Central Point, Oreg., 1979—; mem. Oreg. House of Reps., 2003—, spkr. pro tem, 2005—07. Guest lectr. in field. Contbr. articles to profl. jours. Bd. dirs. Oreg. Lung Assn., 1980, Shakespearean Festival, Ashland, 1981, Jackson County Legal Services, 1982; chmn. GOP Oreg. 2d. Congl. Dist., 1996-2000, treas. GOP Oreg. Exec. Com., 1996-2002; councilman Ctrl. Point City, 2001-2002. Served as helicopter pilot U.S. Army, 1969-71, Vietnam. Decorated Vietnamese Cross Gallantry. Republican. Office: Law Firm of Dennis Richardson PC 55 S 5th St Central Point OR 97502-2474 Office Phone: 541-664-6622. Business E-Mail: dennis@justiceonline.com.

RICHARDSON, DESMOND, dancer; b. Sumter, NC; Ed., Alvin Ailey Am. Dance Ctr., 1983—86, Internat. Sommer Acad. Tanz, Koln, Germany, 1984—85. Dancer Alvin Ailey Repertory Ensemble, Alvin Ailey Am. Dance Theater, 1987-93; soloist Frankfurt Ballet, Germany, 1994-96; prin.

dancer Am. Ballet Theatre, NYC, 1997—; co-artistic dir. (with Dwight Rhoden) Complexions Contemporary Ballet, 1994—. Dancer (Broadway plays) Fosse, 1999, Moving Out, 2002, The Look of Love, 2003, (ballets) Soul Possessed, 1999, Othello, 2003, (solo show choreographed by Taye Diggs) Loose Change, 2007; actor: (films) One Last Dance, 2003, Chicago, 2002, Light and the Sufferer, 2004; dancer (films) Across the Universe, 2007, (TV films) Mosè e Faraone, o Il passaggio del Mar Rosso, 2003. Recipient Presdl. Scholar Arts award, 1986, Bessie award, 1991, Monarch award, Apex award, Alvin Ailey Sch., 2006. *

RICHARDSON, DOT (DOROTHY GAY), former Olympic softball player, physician; b. Orlando, Fla., Sept. 22, 1961; m. Bob Pinto. Student, Western Ill. U.; BS in Kinesiology, UCLA; M in Exercise, Adelphi U.; MD, U. Louisville; PhD (hon.), Western Ill. U., 2003, St. Leo Coll., 2004, Adelphi U.; LLD (hon.), Phila. Coll. Osteo. Medicine, 2005. Mem., capt. US Olympic Softball Team, 1996, 2000; resident in orthopedic surg. U. Calif. Med. Ctr.; med. dir. Nat. Tng. Ctr., Clermont, Fla., 2001—. Recipient Gold medal Pan. Am. Games, 1979, 87, 95, 99, ISF Women's World Championship, 1982, 86, 90, 94, 98, South Pacific Classic, 1994, Superball Classic, 1995, Atlanta Olympics, 1996, Sydney Olympics, 2000, Medal of Honor DAR, 2005; ERV Linda Best Defensive Player in Nation award (7 times), Flo Hyman award, 2002; named All-Am. Am. Softball Assn. (16 times), MVP Am. Softball Assn. (3 times), Major Fast Pitch Nat. Championship, Player of Decade for 80s NCAA. Office: Nat Tng Ctr 1099 Citrus Tower Blvd Clermont FL 34711 E-mail: dot.richardson@orhs.org.

RICHARDSON, EDWARD R., former academic administrator; b. Pensacola, Fla., Jan. 24, 1939; s. Edward H. and Doria (Parker) R.; m. Nell C.; children: Merit Lynn Richardson Smith, Laura Leigh. BS, Auburn U., 1962, MEd, 1967, EdD, 1972. Sci. tchr. Montgomery Pub. Schs., Montgomery, Ala., 1962-64, prin., 1967-70, Andalusia High Sch., Andalusia, Ala., 1972-80; asst. prof. Auburn U., Montgomery, Ala., 1980-82, interim pres., 2004—06, pres., 2006—07; supt. Auburn City Schs., Auburn, Ala., 1982-95; supt. edn. State of Ala., Montgomery, Ala., 1995—2004. Bd. mem. So. Regional Edn. Bd., Atlanta, 1989—; co-dir. Ala. Mgmt. Inst. Sch. Leaders, Montgomery, 1980-82. Ednl. advisor Gov. Guy Hunt, Montgomery, 1987—; active Landmarks Found., Montgomery, 1968-69. Named Supt. of Yr., State PTA, Montgomery, 1986-87, Educator of Yr., Andalusia Jaycees, 1973-74. Mem. Ala. Assn. Secondary Sch. Adminstrs. (pres. 1978-79), Ala. Assn. Sch. Adminstrs. (pres. 1986-87), Rotary (Auburn chpt. pres. 1987-88), Capitol Lions Club (pres. 1968-69), Phi Delta Kappa (Auburn U. chpt. pres. 1971-72). Republican. Methodist. Avocations: tennis, reading, gardening. Office Phone: 334-844-4650. E-mail: president@auburn.edu. *

RICHARDSON, EMILIE WHITE, manufacturing, investment company executive, educator; b. Chattanooga, July 08; d. Emmett and Mildred Evelyn (Harbin) White; 1 child, Julie Richardson Milunic. BA, Wheaton Coll. With Christy Mfg. Co., Inc., Fayetteville, N.C., Ft. Lauderdale, Fla., 1952—, sec., 1956-66, v.p., 1967-74, exec. v.p., 1975-79, pres., CEO, 1980—. V.p. E. White Investment Co., 1968-83, pres., 1983—; cons. Aerostatic Industries, 1979—; v.p. Gannon Corp., 1981—; cons. govt. contacts and offshore mfg., 1981—; lectr., spkr. in field. V.p. pub. rels. Ft. Lauderdale Symphony Soc., 1974-76, v.p. membership, 1976-77, adv. bd., 1978—; active Atlantic Found., Ft. Lauderdale Mus. Art, Beaux Arts, Freedoms Found.; mem. East Broward Women's Rep. Club, 1968—, Americanism chmn., 1971-72. Mem. Internat. Platform Assn., Nat. Spkrs. Assn., Fla. Spkrs. Assn., Toastmasters, Coral Ridge Yacht Club. Methodist. Home: 1531 NE 51st St Fort Lauderdale FL 33334-5709 Office: 3311 Fort Bragg Rd Fayetteville NC 28303-4763 Personal E-mail: emilier@mindspring.com.

RICHARDSON, ERIC W., lawyer; b. Fort Thomas, Ky., 1973; BA, Thomas More Coll., 1993; JD, U. Cin., 1996. Bar: Ohio 1996, Ky. 1997, US Supreme Ct., US Ct. of Appeals Sixth Cir., US Ct. of Appeals Fed. Cir., US Dist. Ct. Southern Dist. Ohio, US Dist. Ct. Eastern Dist. Ky., US Dist. Ct. Western Dist. Ky. Law clerk Hon. R. Guy Cole, Jr., US Ct. of Appeals Sixth Cir., 1996—97; ptnr. Vorys, Sater, Seymour and Pease LLp, Cin. Named one of Ohio's Rising Stars, Super Lawyers, 2006. Mem.: Ky. Bar Assn., Cin. Bar Assn., Order of Coif, Delta Epsilon Sigma. Office: Vorys Sater Seymur and Pease LLP Atrium Two Ste 2000 221 E Fourth St PO Box 0236 Cincinnati OH 45202-0236 Office Phone: 513-723-4019. Office Fax: 513-852-7885. E-mail: ewrichardson@ussp.com.

RICHARDSON, EVERETT VERN, hydraulic engineer, educator, administrator, consultant; b. Scottsbluff, Nebr., Jan. 5, 1924; s. Thomas Otis and Jean Marie (Everett) R.; m. Billie Ann Kleckner, June 23, 1948; children: Gail Lee, Thomas Everett, Jerry Ray. BS, Colo. State U., 1949, MS, 1960, PhD, 1965. Registered profl. engr., Colo. From hydraulic engr. to project chief US Geol. Survey, Wyo., 1949—52, Iowa, 1952—56, rsch. hydraulic engr. Wyo., 1956—63, project chief Ft. Collins, Colo., 1963—68; adminstr. Engring. Rsch. Ctr. Colo. State U., Ft. Collins, 1968—88, dir. Egypt water use project, 1977-84, prof. in charge of hydraulic program, 1982-88, dir. hydraulic lab. Engring. Rsch. Ctr., 1982-88, prof. emeritus, 1988—, dir. Egypt irrigation improvement project, 1985-90; dir. Egypt Water Rsch. Ctr. Project, Ft. Collins, 1988-89; sr. assoc. Ayers Assocs. Inc. (formerly Resource Cons./Engr., Inc.), Ft. Collins, 1989—. Dir. Consortium for Internat. Devel., Tucson, 1972-87; developer stream stability and scour at hwy. bridges course for State Dept. Transps. for NHI, FHWA; investigator for NTSB 1987 I-90 bridge failure, NY, 1997, railroad bridge failure, Ariz., CALTRAN 1995 I-5 bridge failure; chmn. peer rev. panel Turnefairbanks Rsch. Ctr. Hydraulics Lab., 2004; cons. in field; lectr. in field. Sr. author Highways in the River Environment: Hydraulic and Environmental Considerations, FHWA, 1975, 1990, Evaluating Scour at Bridge, FHWA, 1991, 1993, 1995, 2001, FHWA Hydr. Design Series No. 6: River Engineering for Highway Encroachments, 2001, Civil Engring. Handbook, 1995; co-author: Engring. Handbook, 1995, 2003; contbr. Handbook of Fluid Dynamics and Fluid Machinery, 1996, Water Resources-Environmental Planning, Management and Development, 1996, more than 200 articles to profl. jours. Mem. Ft. Collins Water Bd., 1969-84; mem. NY State Bridge Safety Assurance Task Force, 1988-91. Decorated Bronze Star, Purple Heart, Combat Infantry Badge; named hon. diplomate Am. Acad. Water Resources Engring. 2005; U.S. Govt. fellow MIT, 1962-63. Fellow: ASCE (chair task com., bridge scour rsch. 1990—96, editor Compendium of Stream Stability and Scour Papers 1991—98, vice chair 1997—2002, J.S. Stevens award 1961, hydraulics divsn. task com. excellence award 1993, Hans Albert Einstein award 1996); mem.: Am. Acad. Water Resource Engrs. (hon. diplomate 2005), Internat. Congress for Irrigation and Drainage (bd. dirs.), Sigma Xi, Sigma Tau, Chi Epsilon. Home: 824 Gregory Rd Fort Collins CO 80524-1504 Office: Ayres Assocs PO Box 270460 Fort Collins CO 80527-0460 Office Phone: 970-223-5556. Personal E-mail: mudih2o@aol.com. Business E-Mail: richardsone@ayresassociates.com.

RICHARDSON, FRANK ELMER, III, investor; b. Pitts., Aug. 19, 1939; s. Frank Elmer Jr. and Rosamund (Fitch) R.; m. Nancy McCarthy, June 8, 1973 (div.); children: Philip T., Carolina Sherman, Isabelle Payne; m. Kimba Wood, 1998. BA, Princeton U., 1961; MA, Oxford U., 1964; JD, Harvard U., 1967. Mng. dir. Dean Witter Reynolds, NYC, 1977-81; gen. ptnr., head merger, acquisitions dept. Bear Stearns & Co., NYC, 1982-84; dir., exec. v.p. Wesray Capital Corp., NYC, 1984, pres., 1986—95; chmn. F. E. Richardson & Co., Inc., NYC, 1995—. Bd. dirs. Gemini Industries, Clifton, N.J., Wilson Sporting Goods Corp., Chgo. Trustee Met. Mus. Art; dir. Met. Opera Guild. Mem.: Brook, Racquet and Tennis (N.Y.C.). Republican. Christian Scientist. Office: 245 Park Ave 41st Fl New York NY 10167 *

RICHARDSON, GERALD B., hearing officer, lawyer; b. June 21, 1950; BA magna cum laude, U. N.Mex., 1972; JD, U. N.Mex., Albuquerque, 1975. Bar: N.Mex. 1975, US Supreme Ct. N.Mex. Atty. N.Mex. Human Svcs. Dept., Santa Fe, 1978—79, N.Mex. Taxation and Revenue Dept., Santa Fe, 1979—86, chief hearing officer, 1986—2002; contract adminstrv. law judge, settlement facilitator Jud. Dist. Ct., 2002—. Trustee bd. Mus. N.Mex. Found., 1991—, chair, 1992—93, vice chair, 1992—93. Named N.Mex. Pub. Lawyer of Yr., pub. law sect. State Bar N.Mex., 2002. Personal E-mail: jerryrich4@msn.com.

RICHARDSON, GRACE ELIZABETH, consumer products company executive; b. Salem, Mass., Nov. 22, 1938; d. George and Julia (Sheridan) R.; m. Ralph B. Henderson, Mar. 3, 1979. BS, Simmons Coll., 1960; MS, Cornell U., 1962; MBA, NYU, 1981. Textile technologist Harris Rsch. Lab., Washington, 1962-65; instr. Simmons Coll., Boston, 1965-66; dir. consumer edn. materials J.C. Penney, NYC, 1966-73; dir. residential conservation Con Edison, NYC, 1974-81; dir. consumer affairs Chesebrough-Ponds, Greenwich, Conn., 1981-85; v.p. global consumer affairs Colgate Palmolive, NYC, 1985—2004; chmn. of bd. YMCA of N.Y.C., 2004—. Chair Simmons Coll. Leadership Coun., 1993—97; mem. com. Juilliard Sch., 1996—; bd. dirs. SOCAP, 1996—99, Nat. Coalition Consumer Edn., 1983—93; mem. Cornell U. Coun., chair pub. rels. com., 1988—97; bd. mem. UNIFEM, 2002—. Named Nat. Bus. Home Economist of Yr., Home Economists in Bus., 1979. Mem. Women's Forum, Cornell Club N.Y.C. (bd. dirs. 1989-96). Home: 180 E 79th St New York NY 10021-0437

RICHARDSON, HERBERT HEATH, retired mechanical engineer, educator, dean, academic administrator; b. Lynn, Mass., Sept. 24, 1930; s. Walter Blake and Isabel Emily (Heath) R.; m. Barbara Ellsworth, Oct. 6, 1973. SB, SM with honors, MIT, 1955, ScD, 1958. Registered profl. engr., Mass., Tex. Rsch. asst., rsch. engr. Dynamic Analysis and Control Lab. MIT, 1953-57, instr. dept. mech. engring., 1957-58, mem. faculty, 1958-84, prof. mech. engring., 1968-85, head dept., 1974-82, assoc. dean engring., 1982-84; disting. prof. engring. Tex. A&M U. Sys., Coll. Sta., 1984—2006, regents prof., 1993—2006, dean, vice chancellor engring., 1984-85, dep. chancellor, dean, dir. Tex. Engring. Expt. Sta., 1985-91, chancellor, 1991-93, assoc. vice chancellor engring., assoc. dean engring., dir. Tex. Transit Inst., 1993—2006, dir. emeritus Tex. Transp. Inst., 2006—, disting. prof. engring. emeritus, chancellor emeritus, 2006—. With Ballistics Rsch. Lab. Abderdeen Proving Ground, Md., 1958; chief scientist U.S. Dept. Transp., 1970-72; chmn. adv. com. for engring. NSF, 1987-89, adv. com. basic energy scis. U.S. Dept. Energy, 1987-91. Author: Introduction to System Dynamics, 1971; contbr. articles to profl. publs. Trustee S.W. Rsch. Inst. Officer U.S. Army, 1968. Recipient medal Am. Ordnance Assn., 1953, Gold medal Pi Tau Sigma, 1963, Meritorious Svc. award and medal Dept. Transp., 1972, Disting. Svc. award Coun. U. Transp. Ctrs., 2006. Fellow AAAS, ASME (Moody award fluid engring. divsn. 1970, Centennial medallion 1983, Rufus Oldenberger medal 1984, Meritorious Svc. medal 1986, Disting. Svc. award 1986, hon. mem. 1987), Transp. Rsch. Bd. (Roy Crumm award 2007); mem. NAE (coun. 1986-92, com. on engring. edn.), Am. Soc. Engring. Edn. (Disting. Svc. medal 1993, Lamme award 1997), Nat. Rsch. Coun. (gov. bd. 1986-92, chmn. transp. rsch. bd. 1988-89), Nat. Acads. (nat. assoc., life), Sigma Xi, Tau Beta Pi. Office: Tex A&M U Sys MS 3135 College Station TX 77843-3135 Home Phone: 979-846-7179. E-mail: herbert-richardson@tamu.edu.

RICHARDSON, J. WILLIAM, hotel executive; Acting pres. Interstate Hotels Corp., Pitts., 1999—, vice chmn., CFO, 1999—. Office: Interstate Hotels Corp Foster-Plaza Ten 680 Andersen Dr Pittsburgh PA 15220-2700 also: Interstate Hotels & Resorts 4501 Fairfax Dr Arlington VA 22203-1656

RICHARDSON, JAMES, chef; Line cook Boca, sous chef, 1997; owner, head chef Atomic Café, 1998; chef Berns; line cook Bergamot Café, LA, 2001, co-exec. chef; co-owner, exec. chef Nook Bistro, LA. Named one of LA's Rising Stars, StarChefs.com, 2006. Office: Nook Bistro 11628 Santa Monica Blvd Los Angeles CA 90025 Office Phone: 310-207-5160. *

RICHARDSON, JAMES DAVID, surgeon; b. Morehead, Ky., 1945; MD, U. Ky., 1970. Diplomate Am. Bd. Surgeons, Am. Bd. Vascular Surgery, Am. Bd. Thoracic Surgery, Am. Bd. SCC. Intern U. Ky. Med. Ctr., Lexington, 1970, resident, 1971-72, U. Tex., San Antonio, 1972-76; surgeon Norton Hosp., Louisville, 1977—; prof. surgery U. Louisville, 1979—; pres. Am. Bd. Surgery, 1998-99. Past pres. So. Surg. Assn., Western Surg. Assn. Editor: (jour.) Am. Surgeon, 2005—. Fellow ACS (bd. regents); mem. AMA, Am. Assn. Surgery of Trauma, Soc. Surgergy Alimentary Tract, Alpha Omega Alpha. Office: U Louisville Dept Surgery 550 S Jackson St Louisville KY 40202-1622 Office Phone: 502-583-8303, 502-852-5452.

RICHARDSON, JASON ANTHONEY, professional basketball player; b. Jan. 20, 1981; Student, U. Mich. Profl. basketball player Golden State Warriors, Oakland, Calif., 2001—. Named to, NBA All-Rookie First Team, 2002; recipient Winners award, NBA All-Star Slam Dunk Contest, 2002—03. Achievements include member of NCAA championship team, 2000; won NBA Slam Dunk Contest, 2002, 2003. Office: Golden State Warriors 1011 Broadway Oakland CA 94607

RICHARDSON, JEFFREY CARL, public relations executive; b. Camden, NJ, May 7, 1953; s. Robert C. and Marguerite (Hayes) R. BA with honors, Rutgers U., 1975; postgrad., Temple U. Instr. Temple U., Phila., 1976-79; editor, reporter Gannett Newspapers, 1978-82; dir. pub. relations Meritor Fin. Group, Phila., 1982-86; v.p. communications Independence Bancorp, Doylestown, Pa., 1986-88; dir. worldwide pub. relations Rorer Group, Inc., Ft. Washington, Pa., 1988—. Trustee Ctr. for Literacy, Phila., 1988—. Contbr. speeches to Vital Speeches mag., 1989. Recipient First Pl. Writing award, United Way of Southeastern Pa., Phila., 1983, Excellence award Communications Arts Mags., 1988. Mem. Pub. Rels. Soc. Am. (accredited, bd. dirs. Phila. chpt., award 1989), Phila. Pub. Rels. Assn., Del. Valley Round Table.

RICHARDSON, JEROME LYNN (JERRY RICHARDSON), secondary school educator; b. Greensboro, NC, Aug. 22, 1946; s. Frank C. and Doris (Mitchell) Richardson; children from previous marriage: Victoria, Heather. MA, Pepperdine U., Malibu, Calif., 1975. Tchr., Lagunitas, Calif., 1980—91; dressage trainer U.S.D.F. C.D.F. Marin County, Calif., 1980—. 3-day tchr. U.S.C.T.A., Marin, 1980—; pres. Marin Horse Counsel, Nicasio, Calif., 1985—95; tutor, Nicasio, 1991—. Child advocate YMCA Marin County, 1982—95; mem., coach US Combined Tng. Team. Master: Los Altos Hunt Club; mem.: Mid. Marin Hunt Pony Club (dist. commr. 1980—). Democrat. Avocations: model building, hunting, Go. Home: PO Box 435 60 Rockridge Rd Woodacre CA 94973 Office: Two Bridges Farm 700 Nicasio Blvd Nicasio CA 94946

RICHARDSON, JOHN, retired international relations executive; b. Boston, Feb. 4, 1921; s. John and Hope (Hemenway) R.; m. Thelma Ingram, Jan. 19, 1945; children: Teren de Cossy, Hope Gravelly, Catherine Munch, Hetty L AB, Harvard U., 1943, JD, 1949. Bar: NY 1949. Assoc. Sullivan & Cromwell, NYC, 1949-55; with Paine, Webber, Jackson & Curtis, NYC, 1955-69, gen. ptnr., 1958-61, ltd. ptnr., 1961-69; pres., chief exec. officer Free Europe, Inc. (Radio Free Europe), 1961-68; asst. sec. for ednl. and cultural affairs Dept. State, 1969-77, also acting asst. sec. state for pub. affairs, 1971-73; exec. dir. for social policy Ctr. for Strategic and Internat. Studies; rsch. prof. internat. comm. Sch. Fgn. Svc., Georgetown U., Washington, 1977-78; pres., chief exec. officer Youth for Understanding, Inc., 1978-86, bd. dirs., 1986-98; counselor US Inst. of Peace, 1987-90. Spl. advisor Aspen Inst. Humanistic Studies, 1977—80. Founder Polish Med. Aid Project, 1957—61; co-founder, chmn. bd. Am. Com. to Aid Poland, 1989—95; pres. Internat. Rescue Com., 1960—61, bd. dirs., 1958—61, 1978—2004, bd. overseers, 2004—; chmn. Am. Coun. for UN U., 1977—87, Consortium for Internat. Citizens Exch., 1980—84, Delphi Internat., 1995—99, bd. dirs., 1999—2001; chmn., bd. dirs. Nat. Endowment for Democracy, 1984—88, 1991—92, chmn. emeritus, 1992—; bd. dirs. Freedom House, 1963—69, pres., 1977—84; mem. Coun. Fgn. Rels., 1957—; Citizens Commn. on S.E. Asian Refugees, 1978—85; bd. dirs. Fgn. Policy Assn., 1958—68, 1977—86, Japan-US Friendship Commn., 1976—77; chmn. NYC Met. Mission United Ch. of Christ, 1966—69; bd. dirs. Kennedy Ctr. for the Performing Arts, 1970—77, Inter-Am. Found., 1970—77, East-West Ctr., 1975—77, Am. Forum for Global Edn., 1977—, Social Sci. Found., U. Denver, 1992—2004, World Learning, 2001—05, Meridian House Internat., 1978—83, Atlantic Coun. U.S., 1982—84, Fgn. Student Svc. Coun., 1978—82, Coun. for Advancement of Citizenship, 1991—96, Coun. Cmty. of Democracies, 1996—, chmn., 1999—2001, chmn. emeritus, 2001—. With paratroops USAR, WWII. Decorated Bronze Star with v device, Japan Order of the Sacred Treasure, Gold and Silver Star; Germany Order of Merit, Commdr.'s Cross, Poland Order of Merit, Knight Cross. Home: 9707 Old Georgetown Rd Apt 1104 Bethesda MD 20814-1746

RICHARDSON, JOHN CARROLL, lawyer, financial consultant; b. Mobile, Ala., May 3, 1932; s. Robert Felder and Louise (Simmons) R.; m. Cicely Tomlinson, July 27, 1961; children: Nancy Louise, Robert Felder III, Leslie. BA, Tulane U., 1954; LLB cum laude, Harvard U., 1960. Bar: Colo. 1960, N.Y. 1965, D.C. 1972. Assoc. Holland & Hart, Denver, 1960-64; legal v.p. Hoover Worldwide Corp., NYC, 1964-69; v.p., gen. counsel Continental Investment Corp., Boston, 1969; dep. tax legis. counsel U.S. Dept. Treasury, Washington, 1970-71, tax legis. counsel, 1972-73; ptnr. Brown, Wood, Ivey, Mitchell & Petty, NYC, 1973-79, LeBoeuf, Lamb, Leiby & MacRae, NYC, 1979-88, Morgan, Lewis & Bockius, NYC, 1988-93; ret., 1993. Tax legis. cons., Orford, N.H., 1993—; adj. prof. Law Sch. Fordham U., 1990-94. Served to lt. comdr. USN, 1954-58. Mem. ABA (chmn. com. adminstrv. practice tax sect. 1984-86), N.Y. State Bar Assn. (exec. com. tax sect. 1975-84), D.C. Bar Assn., Am. Coll. Tax Counsel, N.Y. Athletic Club, Royal Automobile Club. Office Phone: 603-353-4608.

RICHARDSON, JOHN THOMAS, academic administrator, clergyman; b. Dallas, Dec. 20, 1923; s. Patrick and Mary (Walsh) R. BA, St. Mary's Sem., Perryville, Mo., 1946; S.T.D., Angelicum U., Rome, Italy, 1951; MA, St. Louis U., 1954. Prof. theology, dean studies Kenrick Sem., St. Louis, 1951-54; lectr. Webster Coll., 1954; dean Grad. Sch. DePaul U., Chgo., 1954-60, exec. v.p., dean faculties, 1960-81, pres., 1981-93; prof. DePaul U. Coll. Law, Chgo., 1955; chancellor DePaul U., Chgo., 1993—. Vis. mem. theology faculty Christ the King Major Sem., Nyeri, Kenya, East Africa, 1997—. Trustee DePaul U., Chgo., 1954-93, life trustee, 1993-. Office: De Paul U 1 E Jackson Blvd Chicago IL 60604-2287

RICHARDSON, JOHN VINSON, JR., library and information science professor; b. Columbus, Ohio, Dec. 27, 1949; s. John Vinson Sr. and Hope Irene (Smith) R.; m. Nancy Lee Brown, Aug. 22, 1971. BA, Ohio State U., 1971; MLS, Peabody Coll., 1972; PhD, Ind. U., 1978. Asst. prof. UCLA, 1978-83, assoc. prof., 1983-98, editor The Libr. Quar., 1994—2003, prof., 1998—, assoc. dean grad. divsn., 2002—07, mem. editl. bd., The Libr. Quar., 2004—. Faculty coord. UCLA-St. Petersburg State Acad. of Culture Exch. Program, 1996—; fellow advanced rsch. Inst. U. Ill., 1991; pres. Info. Transfer, Inglewood, Calif., 1988—; vis. fellow Charles Sturt U. NSW Australia, 1990; vis. scholar ALISE Russia Project, St. Petersburg and Moscow, 1996; vis. disting. scholar OCLC Inc., Dublin, Ohio, 1996-97; presidential scholar, Libr. Sys. & Svcs., LLC, 2002—03; chmn. Calif. Pacific Ann. Conf. Com. on Archives and History, 1992-96; Henderson lectr. U. N.C., Chapel Hill, 1997; mem. UCLA Privilege and Tenure, 1999-2000, chair, 2000-02; Fulbright sr. specialist Vladivostok State U. Econ. and Svc., Russia, 2005.; cons. to U.S. Dept of State, Vladivostok, 2000, Uganda and Zambia, 2001, Eritrea, 2003, Turkmenistan, 2005. Author: Spirit of Inquiry, 1982, Gospel of Scholarship, 1992, Knowledge-based Systems for General Reference Work, 1995, Understanding Reference Transactions, 2002; mem. editl. bd. Ref. Svcs. Rev., Ann Arbor, Mich., 1991—, Jour. Govt. Info., Oxford, Eng., 1975-2005, Index to Current Urban Documents, Westport, Conn., 1987—, U. Calif. Press Catalogues and Bibliographies series, 1994-97, Jour. Edn. for Libr. and Info. Sci., 2005-07. Mem. UCLA Grad. Coun., 1992-96, chair, 1995-96; mem. U. Calif. systemwide coord. com. on grad. affairs, 1993-96; pres. Wesley Found., L.A., 1981-87; lay del. Cal-Pac Conf. United Meth. Ch., 1985, 86, 92-96, chair conf. commn. on archives and history, 1992—96. Rsch. grantee Coun. on Libr. Resources, 1985, 90, Assn. Libr. and Info. Sci. Educators rsch. grantee, 1984, 87, 98, Online Computer Libr. Ctr. Libr. and Info. Sci. rsch. grantee, 1999; Harold Lancour scholar Beta Phi Mu, 1986, 99, Kaliper Sr. scholar U. Mich., 1998-99, Presdl. scholar Libr. Systems and Svcs. LLC, 2002—03; recipient Louise Maxwell award Ind. U. Alumni Assn., 1995. Mem. ALA (Justin Winsor prize 1990, Ref. and Adult Svcs. divsn. Outstanding Paper award 1992), AAAS, Assn. Libr. and Info. Sci. Educators (rsch. paper prize 1986, 91, rsch. grants 1984, 87, 98), Am. Soc. for Info. Sci. (Best Info. Sci. book 1995), Am. Assn. Adv. Slavic Studies, Sigma Xi. Democrat. Avocations: wine tasting, bread baking, reading, foreign travel. Office: UCLA GSE&IS DIS Campus Box 951520 Los Angeles CA 90095-1520 Office Phone: 310-206-9369. Business E-Mail: jrichard@ucla.edu. *By our common action, we can bend the flow of history.*

RICHARDSON, JOHN W., telecommunications industry executive; m. Rose Richardson; children: Anne Marie, Jake. BBA, Ohio U., Athens, 1967. CPA Ohio. Mgmt. positions through v.p. fin. N.Am. tire bus. Goodyear Tire & Rubber Co., 1967—2002; sr. v.p., contr. Qwest Comm. Internat., Inc., Denver, 2003—04, sr. v.p., chief acctg. officer, 2004—07, exec. v.p., CFO, 2007—. Bd. dirs. Ashworth, Inc. Mem. adv. bd. Ohio U. Sch. Accountancy. Office: Qwest Comm Internat Inc 1801 California St Denver CO 80202 Office Phone: 303-992-1400. Office Fax: 303-896-8515. *

RICHARDSON, JOSEPH HILL, physician, medical educator; b. Rensselaer, Ind., June 16, 1928; s. William Clark and Vera (Hill) R.; m. Joan Grace Meininger, July 8, 1950; children: Lois N., Ellen M., James K. MS in Medicine, Northwestern U., 1950, MD, 1953. Diplomate Am. Bd. Internal Medicine. Intern U.S. Naval Hosp., Great Lakes, Ill., 1953-54; physician internal medicine, hematology pvt. practice, Marion, Ind., 1959-67, Ft. Wayne, Ind., 1967—. Assoc. clin. prof. medicine Ind. U. Sch. Medicine, 1993—; founding mem. The Reviewing Physician Group, 2001—. Contbr. articles to profl. jours. Fellow in medicine Cleve. Clinic, 1956-59. Fellow: AAAS, ACP; mem.: AMA, Masons. Home and Office: 8726 Fortuna Way Fort Wayne IN 46815-5725 Office Phone: 260-485-1391.

RICHARDSON, JUDY MCEWEN, investment banker, consultant, cartoonist; b. Appleton, Wis., June 3, 1947; d. John Mitchell and Isabel Annette (Ruble) McEwen; m. Larry Leroy Richardson, Mar. 19, 1972 (div. Oct. 1983). BA in English, Stanford U., 1968, MA in Edn., 1969; PhD in Higher Edn., U. Wash., 1975. Dir. ednl. rsch. St. Olaf Coll., Northfield, Minn., 1975-79; evaluation specialist Northwest Regional Ednl. Laboratory, Portland, 1980-82; legis. rsch. analyst Ariz. State Sen., Phoenix, 1982-87; dir. sch. fin. Ariz. Dept. Edn., Phoenix, 1987-92, assoc. supt.,

1992-94; ednl. cons. Scottsdale, Ariz., 1994-96; exec. dir. Ariz. State Bd. for Sch. Capital Facilities, Phoenix, 1996-98; sch. fin. cons. Peacock, Hislop, Staley & Given, Phoenix, 1998—2002; v.p. Stone & Youngberg, Phoenix, 2002—. Cartoonist for the Ariz. Capitol Times, 1995-96. Office: Stone & Youngberg LLC 2555 E Camelback Rd Ste 280 Phoenix AZ 85016 Office Phone: 602-794-4012. Business E-Mail: jrichardson@syllc.com.

RICHARDSON, K. SCOTT, sales executive; b. Laurens, Iowa, Nov. 3, 1951; s. Kenneth and Lanore R.; m. Theresa Ann Fitzsimmons, Aug. 31, 1974; children: Seth Ian, Aaron Paul, Evan Scott, Claire Elizabeth, Anna Christine. BS in Radiologic Tech., Creighton U., Omaha, 1974; MS, U. Nebr., Omaha, 1976. Spl. procedures tech. Med. Coll. Va., Richmond, 1974-75; chief spl. procedure tech. St. Vincent Hosp., Sioux City, Iowa, 1975; inservice coordinator to radiology mgr. Nebr. Meth. Hosp., Omaha, 1975-78; sales rep. to sr. sales rep. Philips Med. Systems, Inc., Omaha, 1978-81; adminstrv. dir. radiology The Meth. Hosp., Houston, 1981-83; reg. mgr. R.P. Kincheloe Co., Dallas, 1983-84, mgr. sales and svc., 1984-87, v.p. sales and svc., 1987-98, sr. v.p. sales and svc., 1998—2003; COO Perkins Electronics, Dallas, 2000—; regional sales mgr. Philip Med. Systems N.Am., 2003—04; exec. v.p. Celebrations Mgmt., 2004—, also bd. dirs., 2004—; pres. Life's a Beach Grill, 2004—; dir. sales Sirtex Med., Inc., 2007—. Bd. dirs. Strategic Med. Svcs., Inc., Strategic Med. Svcs. San Antonio, SMS Acquisition #1. Eucharistic min., svc. min., lector, tchr. continuing Cath. edn., chmn. fin. com., chmn. bldg. steering com. St. Philips Ch.; T-ball coord. Braeburn Little League, 1989—; coach YMCA Indoor Soccer League, 1987—, Highland Village Area Baseball and Softball Assn., 1998—; mgr. Lewisville Baseball Assn., 1990—, team sponsor, 1990—, bd. dirs., commr., 1992—; active ARC, Glenshire Soccer Club, Braeburn Valley West Swim Team; chmn. City of Highland Village Parks and Recreation Bd.; mem. City of Highland Village Tree Bd., Highland Village Cmty. Ctr. Com.; bd. dirs. Louisville Baseball Assn. Mem. Am. Registry Radiologic Technologists, Iowa Soc. Radiologic Technologists, Assn. Univ. Radiology Technologists, Tex. Soc. Radiologic Technologists. Republican. Roman Catholic. Avocations: fishing, travel, swimming, golf, basketball, collecting wine. Home: 2415 Silverthorne Ct Highland Village TX 75077-3109 Home Phone: 972-317-6527; Office Phone: 972-768-6600. E-mail: ksr2531@aol.com.

RICHARDSON, LAURA A., congresswoman; b. Apr. 1962; m. Anthony W. Batts (div.). BA in Polit. Sci., UCLA, 1984; MBA, U. So. Calif., 1996. With Xerox Corp., 1987—2007; field dep. to Congresswoman Juanita Millender-McDonald US Congress, 1997; staff mem. to Councilwoman Doris Topsy-Elvord Long Beach City Coun., mem., 2000—06; So. Calif. dir., Office Lt. Gov. State of Calif., 2001—05; mem. Calif. State Assembly from Dist. 55, 2006—07, asst. spkr. pro tempore Leadership Team, mem. Budget, Human Svcs., Utilities & Commerce, Govt. Orgn., and Joint Legis. Budget Coms.; mem. US Congress from 37th Calif. dist., 2007—. Mem.: Calif. Mfg. and Tech. Assn. (bd. mem.). Democrat. Office: US Congress 2233 Rayburn House Office Bldg Washington DC 20515 also: PO Box 50080 Long Beach CA 90815 *

RICHARDSON, M. CATHERINE, lawyer; b. Syracuse, NY, July 14, 1941; d. George Lynch and Margaret (Mansfield) R. BS, SUNY, 1963; MA, U. No. Colo., 1969; JD magna cum laude, Syracuse U., 1977; LLD (hon.), SUNY, 2005. Bar: NY 1978, US Dist. Ct. (no. dist.) NY 1978, NY Ct. Appeals (2d cir.) 1982. Math. tchr. Westhill HS, NY, 1963-67, Jamesville-Dewitt (NY) HS, 1969-74; lawyer Bond, Schoeneck & King, PLLC, Syracuse, 1977—2003; ret., 2003. Mem. com. on profession and the cts. and profl. edn. project Chief Judge State NY With St. Camillus Health and Rehab. Ctr.; Frank H. Hiscock Legal Aid Soc. (pres. 1994-96, bd.dir.); mem. Syracuse Rsch. Corp. Recipient Take the Lead award Ctrl. NY Girl Scout Coun., 1988, Athena award Greater Syracuse C. of C. Small Bus. Bur., 1989, Spirit of Am. Women award Girls Inc. of Ctrl. NY, 1994, Syracuse Law Rev.'s Alumni Achievement award, 1995; named Outstanding Alumni SUNY Oswego, 1995; Kate Stoneman award, Albany Law Sch., 1996. Fellow ABA (bd. govs.; 2003-06), Am. Bar Found., NY State Bar Found. (bd. dirs. 1992—, Ruth G. Shapiro award 2002); mem. NY State Bar Assn. (pres. 1996-97), NY State Jud. Inst., Hist. Soc. Cts. State NY, Onondaga County Bar Assn. (pres. 1987, Pro Bono award), Onondaga County Bar Found. (bd. dirs.), Am. Law Inst., Nat. Health Lawyers Assn., Am. Acad. Hosp. Attys., NY State Assn. Sch. Attys., Lambda Sigma Tau, Kappa Delta Pi, Delta Kappa Gamma, Phi Kappa Phi, Justinian Hon. Law Soc., Ordr of Coif. Office: Bond Schoeneck & King LLP One Lincoln Ctr Syracuse NY 13202 Home Phone: 315-428-0521; Office Phone: 315-218-8230. Business E-Mail: crichardson@bsk.com.

RICHARDSON, MARGARET ANN, art historian, educator; d. Charles E. and Barbara S. Richardson; m. Jeffrey S. Plassman, June 16, 2001. BA in Painting and English, Mary Baldwin Coll., Staunton, Va., 1998; MA in Art History, Va. Commonwealth U., Richmond, 2000, PhD in Art History, 2005. Asst. coord., photographic resources Va. Mus. Fine Arts, Richmond, 2005—06; asst. prof. art history George Mason U., Faifax, Va., 2006—. Adj. instr. art history Christopher Newport U., Newport News, Va., 2000—01, Va. Commonwealth U., Richmond, 2002—06, Coll. William and Mary, Williamsburg, Va., 2003—05; adj. instr. art history and Asian studies Mary Baldwin Coll., Staunton, Va., 2001—. Fellow, Dept. Art History, Va. Commonwealth U., 2001—02; grantee, Sch. Arts and Dept. Art History, Va. Commonwealth U., 2004—05; scholar, Va. Commonwealth U., 2002—03. Mem.: Coll. Art Assn. (grantee 2007), Phi Alpha Theta, Phi Beta Kappa. Home Phone: 804-864-4795; Office Phone: 703-993-1250. Personal E-mail: margaretr1@hotmail.com. Business E-Mail: mricharа@gmu.edu.

RICHARDSON, MARGARET MILNER, retired lawyer; b. Waco, Tex., May 14, 1943; d. James W. and Margaret Wiebusch Milner; m. John L. Richardson, July 22, 1967; 1 child, Margaret Lawrence. AB in Polit. Sci., Vassar Coll., 1965; JD with honors, George Washington U., 1968. Bar: Va. 1968, D.C. 1968, U.S. Dist. Ct. D.C. 1968, U.S. Ct. Appeals (4th, 5th, D.C. and Fed. cirs.) 1968, U.S. Claims Ct. 1969, U.S. Tax Ct. 1970, U.S. Supreme Ct. 1971. Clk. U.S. Ct. Claims, Washington; with Office Chief Counsel IRS, Washington, 1969-77; with Sutherland, Asbill and Brennan, Washington, 1977-80, ptnr., 1980-93; commr. IRS, Washington, 1993-97; ptnr. Ernst & Young, Washington, 1997—2003. Mem. commr.'s adv. group IRS, 1988-90, chair, 1990; bd. advisors George Washington Law Sch.; mem. D.C. Bar Commn. on Multidisciplinary Practice, Presdl. Commn. on Holocaust Assets; bd. dirs. Legg Mason, Inc., JacksonHewitt, Eurasia Found., USA4 UNHCR. Contbr. articles to profl. jours. Assisted Clinton 1992 primary and gen. election campaign; served as team leader Justice Dept./Civil Rights Cluster during Presdl. Transition; mem. bd. Mayor's Transition Team, 1998, Women's Campaign Fund, Nat. Cathedral Sch., Hosp. for Sick Children; trustee Eurasia Found., USA for UNHCR, Woodrow Wilson Coun., U.S.-Russia Bus. Coun., 1999-03; mem. bd. dirs. Nat. Mus. Women in the Arts. Mem. ABA, D.C. Bar Assn. (tax sect.), Va. State Bar, Fed. Bar Assn. (com. taxation), Fin. Women's Assn. N.Y., Washington Women's Forum, Internat. Alliance, U.S. Russia Bus. Coun., Woodrow Wilson Ctr. Avocations: travel, antiques, needlepoint, gardening. Home Phone: 540-364-0241. Personal E-mail: margaretrichardson@yahoo.com.

RICHARDSON, MARK P., protective services official, educator; b. St. Paul, June 27, 1962; m. Mary K Sanford, Oct. 8, 1988; children: Lara S., Sonja S. BS, St. Cloud State U., Minn., 1992; Med, St. Mary's U., Minn., 1998; JD, William Mitchell Coll. of Law, Minn., 2004. Tchr. Ind. Sch. Dist. #728, Elk River, Minn., 1993—; firefighter Elk River Fire Dept., Minn., 1997—. E-5 staff sargeant USAF, 1982—86, Ramstein Airbase, Germany. Avocations: Karate, scuba diving, horseback riding, travel. Office: Ind Sch Dist #728 900 School St Elk River MN 55330 Home Phone: 763-241-1077; Office Phone: 763-241-1077 2173. E-mail: mrichardson@elkriver.k12.mn.us.

RICHARDSON, MARY L., psychotherapist; b. Topeka, Oct. 4, 1953; d. Darrell and Beverly Nutter; m. Kenneth T. Richardson Jr. children: Shad Martin, Cheralyn Pasbrig, Kenneth T. Richardson III, Russ Richardson. BS in Addictions Counseling, Westbrook U., W.Va., 2001. Cert. behavioral health examiner, addictions counselor, Ariz., Hawaii; cert. Nat. Assn. of Alcolism and Drug Abuse Counselors; lic. ind. substance abuse counselor, Ariz. Behavioral Health. Counselor Compcare Alcoholism Ctr. The Meadows Treatment Ctr., Phoenix, 1986-88; co-founder Co-Dependents Anonymous, 1986—; co-dir. Phoenix Cons. & Counseling Assocs., Ariz., 1989—; co-founder Co-Dependents Anonymous, 1986—. Founder, adminstr. The Orion Found., Ariz.; project mem. The Hutoomkhum Com. and Support Program, Hopi Reservation, Ariz.; cons. Baywood Hosp., 1988-89; faculty instr. The Recovery Source, 1989-90; chair Nat. Conv. Women, 1992; facilitator Your Healing Journey Workshop, 2002-; co-founder, v.p., treas. The U. of Creative Arts and Scis., 2005-. Author: Women's Acts of Power, 1991-93, Relationship Recover, 1992—, Women's Empowerment, 1992—, Body, Mind & Spirit, 1994—. Mem. Am. Mental Health Counselors, Am. Counseling Assn., Nat. Assn. Alcoholism & Drug Abuse Counselors, Nat. Reciprocity Consortium. Avocations: writing, sculpting, dance, herbology. Home: 6841 E Gelding Dr Scottsdale AZ 85254 Home Phone: 480-621-7345; Office Phone: 602-230-8994. E-mail: believe1610@cox.net.

RICHARDSON, MIRANDA, actress; b. Lancashire, Eng., Mar. 3, 1958; Studied, Drama Program Bristol. Stage performances include Moving, All My Sons, Who's Afraid of Virginia Woolf, The Life of Einstein, A Lie of the Mind, Edmond, Insignificance, Aunt Dan & Lemon, The Changeling, Mountain Language, Educating Rita, The Maids, The Designated Mourner, Etta Jenks; actor(TV appearances): The Hard Word, Sorrel and Son, A Woman of Substance, Underworld, Death of the Heart, The Scold's Bridle, 1998, Merlin, 1998, Alice, 1999,: (TV series) Black Adder II & III, Sweet as You Are, The Life and Times of Vivian Vyle, 2007; (TV miniseries) Die Kinder, The James Bond Story, 1999, (voice): The Miracle Maker, 2000,: (films) Dance with a Stranger, 1985, The Innocent, 1986, Empire of the Sun, 1987, Eat the Rich, 1987, Twisted Obsession, 1990, The Bachelor, 1991, Enchanted April, 1992 (Golden Globe award), Damage, 1992 (B.A.F.T.A. award for Best Supporting Actress, Acad. award nominee for Best Supporting Actress), The Crying Game, 1992, Fatherland, HBO, 1994 (Golden Globe award), Tom & Viv, 1994 (Acad. award nominee for best actress, 1995), La Nuit et Le Moment, 1994, Kansas City, 1996, The Evening Star, 1996, Swann, 1996, Saint-Ex, 1997, The Apostle, 1997, The Designated Mourner, 1997, All for Love, 1998, Jacob Two Two and the Hooded Fang, 1998, Sleepy Hollow, 1999, Blackadder Back and Forth, 1999, Get Carter, 2000, Spider, 2001, The Hours, 2001, Rage on Placid Lake, 2002, Young Victoria, 2007, The Lost Prince, 2002, Chicken Run, 2000, Snow White, 2000, The Actors, 2002, Falling Angels, 2003, The Prince and Me, 2003, Phantom of the Opera, 2003, Churchill The Hollywood Years, 2003, Wah-Wah, 2004, Harry Potter and the Goblet of Fire, 2005, Gideon's Daughter, 2005, Provoked, 2005, Merlin's Apprentice, 2005, Final Chance To Save, 2005, Southland Tales, 2005, Spinning Into Butter, 2006, Puffball, 2006, Fred Claus, 2006. Address: c/o Paul Lyon Maris 76 Oxford St London W1D 1BS England Office Phone: 0207 636 6565.

RICHARDSON, PATRICIA, actress; b. Bethesda, Md., Feb. 23, 1951; d. Laurence Baxter and Elizabeth (Howard) R.; m. Raymond Baker, June 20, 1982; children: Henry, Roxanne, Joseph. BFA, So. Meth. U., 1972. Appearences include (Broadway) Gypsy, Loose Ends, The Wake of Jamie Foster; (off-Broadway) The Collected Works of Billy the Kid, The Frequency, Vanities, The Coroner's Plot, Hooters, Company, Fables for Friends, The Miss Firecracker Contest, Cruise Control; (regional theatre) King Lear, The Killing of Sister George, Relatively Speaking, The Importance of Being Earnest, Of Mice and Men, The Philadelphia Story, Room Service, Fifth of July, About Face; (nat. tours) Gypsy, Vanities; (films) Gas, 1972, You Better Watch Out, Lost Angels, 1988, In Country, 1988, Ulee's Gold, 1997; (TV) Double Trouble, 1984, Eisenhower & Lutz, 1988, FM, 1989-90, Home Improvement, 1991-99 (Lead Actress in a Comedy Series Emmy award nominee, 1994, Golden Globe award nominee, 1993, 94), Sophie and the Moonhanger, 1995, Undue Influence, 1996, Viva Las Nowhere, 2000. Office: William Morris Agy care Jonathon Howard 151 S El Camino Dr Beverly Hills CA 90212-2775

RICHARDSON, PAUL JOSEPH, economist; b. Pincourt, Que., Can., Oct. 26, 1965; s. Donald Herbert and Denise Marie Richardson; m. Julia Louise Adams, July 6, 1996; children: Cameron Forbes, Emily Adams. Diploma in Bus. Adminstrn., John Abbott Coll., Ste. Anne de Bellevue, Can., 1987; BA in Econs., Concordia U., Montreal, Can., 1991; M Internat. Econs. and Mgmt., Bocconi U., Milan, 1994. English tchr. Prime Acad. English, Osaka, Japan, 1991—92; mortgage banker Love Funding Corp., Washington, 1992—93; rschr. UN Econ. Commn. for Africa, Addis Ababa, Ethiopia, 1994—94; fin. analyst UN Indsl. Devel. Orgn., Milan, 1995—96, head St. Helens, England, 1996—99; dir. internat. programs U.S. C. of C., Washington, 1999—2003; dir. new bus. World Vision, Washington, 2003—05; fgn. svc. officer U.S. Agy. for Internat. Devel., Washington, 2005—. Author: (research) Africa: An Overview of the Manufacturing and Agricultural Sectors and the Factors Impeding their Export Promotion. Mem.: Black Watch Assn. (life), Izaack Walton League Am. (corr.). Office: US C of C 1615 H St Washington DC 20062

RICHARDSON, PAUL JOSEPH, food scientist, researcher; b. Lincoln, Nebr., Jan. 6, 1975; s. Adam Nathaniel and Rose Anne (Schoener) Richardson; m. Alison Leigh Spinner, Feb. 18, 2002; children: Eric William, Adam Joseph. BS in Consumer Food Sci., Iowa State U., Ames, 1997, MS in Food Sci. and Tech., 1999, D in Food Sci. and Tech., 2003. Rschr. asst. Iowa State U., Ames, 1997—99, tchg. asst., 1999—2003; food scientist Meriks Labs., Coralville, Iowa, 2003—. Adj. prof. U. Iowa, 2004—. Contbr. scientific papers to profl. pubs. Recipient Best Paper award, Jour. Food Sci., 2004. Mem.: Am. Coun. Sci. and Health, Am. Pub. Health Assn. Democrat. Lutheran. Achievements include research in field. Avocations: exercise, hiking, skiing.

RICHARDSON, RICHARD JUDSON, retired political science professor; b. Poplar Bluff, Mo., Feb. 16, 1935; s. Jewell Judson and Naomi Fern (Watson) R.; m. Sammie Sue Cullum, Dec. 29, 1961; children: Jon Mark, Anna Cecile, Ellen Elizabeth, Megan Leigh. BS, Harding Coll., Searcy, Ark., 1957; cert., U. Dublin, Ireland, 1958; MA, Tulane U., New Orleans, 1961, PhD, 1967. Instr. Tulane U., 1962—65; 67asst. prof. polit. sci. Western Mich. U., Kalamazoo, 1965, assoc. prof., 1967—69; vis. assoc. prof. U. Hawaii, 1967—68; from asso. prof. to v.p. acad. affairs U. N.C., Chapel Hill, 1969—91, assoc. v.p. acad. affairs univ. gen. adminstrn., 1991—92. Adj. prof. Duke U., Durham, 1972-74; provost, vice chancellor acad. affairs U. N.C., 1995-2000; cons. in field. Author: (with Kenneth Vines) The Politics of Federal Courts, 1971, (with Darlene Walker) People and the Police, 1973, (with Marian Irish, James Prothro) The Politics of American Democracy, 1981. Del. County Dem. Conv., 1972, 83; vice chmn. Dem. Party Precinct, 1983-85; chmn. bldg. fund YMCA, 1976; chmn. Carolina Challenge for endowment U. N.C., Chapel Hill, 1979-80; chmn. U. N.C. Bicentennial Observance, 1991-94; chmn. United Way, 1983, pres., 1985; pres. PTA County Coun., 1984. Recipient Edward S. Corwin award Am. Polit. Sci. Assn., 1967, Tanner Disting. Teaching award U. N.C., 1972, Univ. award for Outstanding Teaching, 1981, Thomas Jefferson award, 1987, James Johnston Disting. Tchg. award, 1993, Alumni Faculty Disting. Svc. award, 1994, Disting. Eagle Scout award Boy Scouts Am., 1998, Laura Thomas award, 1999, C. Knox Massey award, 2000, Disting. Svc. medal U. N.C. Alumni Assn., 2001, William Richardson Davie award, 2005; named life regent Boy Scouts Am., 1998; Edgar Stern fellow, 1959-61; NEH grantee, 1970. Mem. N.C. Polit. Sci. Assn. (pres. 1978-79), Am. Polit. Sci. Assn., So. Polit. Sci. Assn., ACLU (bd. dirs. local chpt. 1985-88, state bd. dirs. 1988-89), Order of Janus, Order of the Long Leaf Pine, Order of Golden Fleece, Order of the Grail. Home: 234 Terrells Creek Ln Pittsboro NC 27312-5145

RICHARDSON, ROBERT, cinematographer; b. Hyannis, Mass., 1955; m. Monica Wali; 2 children. Cinematographer: (films) An Outpost of Progress, 1982, Salvador, 1986, Platoon, 1986 (Academy award nomination best cinematography 1986), Wall Street, 1987, Dudes, 1987, Eight Men Out, 1988, Talk Radio, 1988, Born on the Fourth of July, 1989 (Academy award nomination best cinematography 1989), City of Hope, 1991, The Doors, 1991, JFK, 1991 (Academy award best cinematography 1991), A Few Good Men, 1992, Heaven and Earth, 1993 (also dir. photography), Natural Born Killers, 1994, Casino, 1995, Nixon, 1995, U-Turn, 1997, Fast, Cheap & Out of Control, 1997, Wag the Dog, 1997, The Horse Whisperer, 1998, Snow Falling on Cedars, 1999, Bringing Out the Dead, 1999, The Hire: Power Keg, 2001, The Four Feathers, 2002, Kill Bill: Vol. 1, 2003, Kill Bill:Vol. 2, 2004 (also dir. photography), The Aviator, 2004 (Academy award best cinematography, 2005), (TV spl.) To the Moon, Alice, 1990 (also camera operator, visual cons.); cameraman: (films) Repo Man, 1984, Making the Grade, 1984; cinematographer, photographer Mr. Death: The Rise and Fall of Fred A. Leuchter, Jr., 1999; exec. prodr. The Wind Effect, 2003

RICHARDSON, ROBERT ALLEN, retired lawyer, educator; b. Cleve., Feb. 15, 1939; s. Allen B. and Margaret C. (Thomas) R.; m. Carolyn Eck Richardson, Dec. 9, 1968. BA, Ohio Wesleyan U., 1961; LLB, Harvard U., 1964. Bar: Ohio 1964, Hawaii 1990. Ptnr. Caffee, Halter & Griswold, Cleve., 1968-89; counsel Mancini, Rowland & Welch (formerly Case & Lynch), Maui, Hawaii, 1990—2001; lectr., affirmative action officer, atty., exec. com. Maui (Hawaii) C.C., 1989—2001; ret., 2001. Chmn. gov. fin. dept., chmn. cmty. svc. com., mem. oper. com. Caffee, Halter & Griswold; past lectr. Sch. Law Cleve. State U.; counsel Maui C. of C., Kahului, 1994-98. Pres., trustee Big Bros./Big Sisters of Maui, 1990-94; v.p., trustee, pres. Ka Hole A Ke Ole Homeless Resource Ctr., 1990—; trustee Maui Acad. Performing Arts, 1990-97, Maul Counseling Svc., 1990-96, Kapalua Music Festival, Friends of Children Advocate Ctr., Legal Aid Soc. Hawaii, pres., 1998-88; trustee Hui Noeur Visual Arts Ctr., 2004—; mem. land use com. Maui Coastal Land Trust, 2004; v.p., trustee, chmn. devel. com. Cleve. Playhouse, 1984-89; trustee, mem. exec. com., program chmn. Cleve. Coun. World Affairs, 1970-89; past model UN chmn. Cleve. Com. on Fgn. Rels.; trustee, mem. exec. com., budget chmn. Neighborhood Ctrs. Assn., 1980-89; trustee Maui Symphony, 1995-98, v.p., 1999—. Recipient T.S. Shinn award Maui C. of C., 2000. Mem. Rotary Club of Maui, Maui Country Club, Rowfant Club (adv.), Cleve. Skating Club. Home: 1365 Lower Kula Rd Kula HI 96790-9724

RICHARDSON, ROBERT COLEMAN, physics professor, researcher; b. Washington, June 26, 1937; s. Robert Franklin and Lois (Price) R.; m. Betty Marilyn McCarthy, Sept. 2, 1962; children: Jennifer, Pamela. BS in Physics, Va. Poly. Inst. and State U., 1958, MS, 1960; PhD in Physics, Duke U., 1966; PhD (hon.), Ohio State U., 2000. Research assoc. Cornell U., Ithaca, NY, 1966-67, asst. prof., 1968-71, assoc. prof., 1972-74, prof., Low Temp. Physics, 1975—86, Floyd R. Newman prof. physics, 1987—, dir., Lab. of Atomic and Solid State Physics, 1990—97, vice provost for rsch. Ithaca, NY, 1998—. Chmn. Internat. Union Pure and Applied Physics Commn. (C-5), 1981-84; mem. bd. assessment Nat. Bur. Standards, 1983—; vis. scientist Bell Labs., Murray Hill, N.J., 1984; mem. adv. panel for MIT v.p. rsch., 1998-; mem. NASA Life and Microgravity Sci. and Applications Adv. Panel, 1999-; mem. Internat. Space Station Mgmt. and Cost Evaluation Task Force, NASA, 2001-02; trustee Duke U., 1997—, exec. com. bd. trustees, 2001—; bd. dirs. Brookhaven Sci. Assocs.; mem. ecec. com. of sr. rsch. officers, Am. Assn. Univs., 2002-. Author: Experimental Techniques in Condensed Matter Physics at Low Temperatures, 1988, (videotape lectr.); College Physics, 2003; mem. editorial bd. Jour. of Low Temperature Physics, 1984—. Served to 2d lt. U.S. Army, 1959-60. Guggenheim fellow 1975-76, 82-83; recipient Simon Meml. prize Brit. Phys. Soc., 1976, Dinting. Grad. Sch. Alumnus Award, Va. Polytechnic Inst. and State U.; co-recipient Nobel prize in physics, 1996; commendation, Va. Gen. Assembly, 1988. Fellow AAAS (bd. dirs. 2000—), Am. Phys. Soc. (Oliver E. Buckley prize 1981), Am. Philos. Soc, Am. Acad. Arts & Scis.; mem. NAS, Nat. Sci. Bd. (exec. com. 2000—); Finnish Acad. Sci. & Letters. Achievements include research in experimental low temperature physics, especially the properties of liquids and solids at sub-millikelvin temperatures. Avocations: photography, gardening. Office: Cornell U Lab of Atomic and Solid Physics 529A Clark Hall Ithaca NY 14853-2501

RICHARDSON, ROBERT DALE, JR., language educator; b. Milw., June 14, 1934; s. Robert Dale and Lucy Baldwin (Marsh) R.; m. Elizabeth Hall, Nov. 7, 1959 (div. 1987); m. Annie Dillard, Dec. 10, 1988; children: Elisabeth, Anne, Rose. AB magna cum laude in English, Harvard U., 1956, PhD in English Lit., 1961; DHL (hon.), Meadville-Lombard Theol. Sch., 2003. Instr. English Harvard U., Cambridge, Mass., 1961-63; asst. prof. English U. Denver, 1963-68, assoc. prof., 1968-72, prof., 1972-87, Lawrence C. Phipps prof. humanities, 1979-82, chmn. dept., 1968-73, pres. Univ. senate, 1972-73, assoc. dean grad. studies, 1975-76; prof. English, U. Colo., Boulder, 1987; vis. prof. letters Wesleyan U., Middletown, Conn., 1989-94. Vis. prof. Harvard U., summer 1976, CUNY, 1978, Sichuan U., 1983, U. N.C., Chapel Hill, 2002, 05; vis. fellow Huntington Libr., 1973-74; vis. instr. Yale U., 1988; bd. dirs. David R. Godine Pub., Key West Literary Seminar. Author: Literature and Film, 1969, Henry Thoreau: A Life of the Mind, 1986 (Melcher award, 1986), Emerson: The Mind on Fire, 1995 (Parkman prize, 1995, Melcher award, 1995, Washington Irving award, 1995), Myth and Literature in the American Renaissance, 1978; author: (with Burton Feldman) The Rise of Modern Mythology 1680-1860, 1972; author: (with Allen Mandelbaum) Three Centuries of American Poetry, 1999; author: William James: In the Maelstrom of American Modernism, 2006 (Bancroft prize, 2006). Trustee Meadville-Lombard Theol. Sch., 1981-87. Fellow Guggenheim Found., 1990, Nat. Humanities Ctr., 1999-00; recipient Acad. award in lit. Am. Acad. Arts and Letters, 1998. Mem. Soc. Am. Hist., Author's Guild, Thoreau Soc., Emerson Soc., Assn. Lit. Scholars and Critics, William James Soc. Democrat. Unitarian Universalist. Personal E-mail: rrchardson@gmail.com.

RICHARDSON, R(OSS) FRED(ERICK), insurance company executive, consultant; b. Renfrew, Ont., Can., Feb. 4, 1928; came to U.S., 1980; s. Garfield Newton and Grace Mary (MacLean) R.; m. Betty Blanche Betts, Feb. 4, 1972; children by previous marriage: Sheri Joan, Robert John, Paul Frederick. BA in Math. and Physics with honors, Queens U., 1950. Actuarial asst. Empire Life Ins. Co., Kingston, Ont., Canada, 1950-55; sec. Maritime Life Ins. Co., Halifax, N.S., Canada, 1955-59, dir. sales, 1959-65, chief exec. officer, 1967-72; mng. dir., chief exec. officer Abbey Life Ins. Co., England, 1972-80; group gen. mgr. Hartford Europe Group, 1975-80; sr. v.p., dir. worldwide life ins. ops. Hartford Ins. Group, Conn., 1980-83, dir. worldwide life ins. ops. Conn., 1983-88; pres., COO, Hartford Life Cos., 1983-88; pvt. ins. cons., Boca Raton, Fla., 1988; pres., CEO, Crown Life Ins. Co., 1988-93; cons. INSCE, Boca Raton, 1993—. Fellow Soc. Actuaries, Can. Inst. Actuaries. Home and Office: 300 SE 5th Ave Apt 1090 Boca Raton FL 33432-6093 Office Phone: 561-417-9390. E-mail: richar_f@bellsouth.net.

RICHARDSON, SALLY KEADLE, academic administrator; b. Mar. 2, 1933; d. Okey P. and Viola Miriam (Graybeal) Keadle; m. Don Rule Richardson, Dec. 15, 1961; children: Miriam Paige, Ruth Evan. AB, Vassar Coll., 1954. Regional pub. info. rep. Columbia Gas Sys., Charleston, W.Va., 1958-62; dir. Children's Mus., Charleston, 1963; coord. space-related sci. project Kanawha County Schs., Charleston, 1967-68; vol. dir. Rockefeller for Gov. Campaign, Charleston, 1972, program dir., 1976, 80; dir. admissions W.Va. Wesleyan Coll., Buckhannon, 1974-75; spl. asst. Office of Gov. State of W.Va., 1977, dep. commr. dept. welfare, 1978-79, dep. dir. dept. health, 1979-83; chmn. W.Va. Health Care Cost Rev. Authority, Charleston, 1983-85. Health care cons., Charleston, 1985-89; dir. W.Va. Pub. Employees Ins. Agy., Charleston, 1989-93; vice-chmn. W.Va. Health Care Planning Task Force, 1992-93; mem. White House Health Care Reform Task Force, Washington, 1993; dir. Medicaid Bur., Health Care Financing Adminstrn., U.S. DHHS, Balt., 1993-96; acting dep. adminstr. HCFA, U.S. DHHS, Washington, 1996-97; dir. HCFA Ctr. for Medicaid and State Ops., 1997-99; mem. U.S. DHHS Governing Coun. on Children and Youth, 1993-97, co-chmn. U.S. DHHS Children's Health Initiative, 1997-99; co-chmn. U.S. DHHS Home and Cmty. Based Svcs. Task Force, 1996-99; mem. U.S. DHHS Pub. Health Coun.'s D.C. Task Force, 1994-99; mem. Nat. Adv. Com. on Rural Health, DHHS, 2000-04; bd. dirs. Molina Healthcare, Inc. W.Va. rep. Task Force on So. Children, So. Growth Policies Bd., 1978-79; co-chmn. exec. com. W.Va. Internat. Yr. of Child, 1979; staff mem. Com. on Human Resources Nat. Gov. Assn., 1983-85; trustee U. Charleston, 1994-; bd. dirs. Children's Home Soc., Charleston, 1999—. Mem. Acad. Health, Nat. Rural Health Assn. Democrat. Office: WVa U Inst Health Policy Rsch 3110 Maccorkle Ave SE Rm 3015 Charleston WV 25304-1210

RICHARDSON, SCOTT, federal official, researcher, writer; s. Stewart and Jeanne Richardson; m. Leighann Lowley, Nov. 12, 1994; 1 child, Evan Stewart. BA, Thomas Edison Coll., Trenton, NJ, 1981. Cert. in public health Bloomberg Sch. Public Health, Johns Hopkins U., Balt., 2001. Project mgr., coord. Nat. Evaluation Sys., Amherst, Mass., 1981—88; project dir. Nat. Evaluation Systems, Inc., Austin, Tex., 1988—90; mgr. bur. of labor stats. programs Tex. Workers' Compensation Commn., 1991—94, chief safety info. sys, 1994—99; dir. office of stats. Occupl. Safety and Health Adminstrn., Washington, 1999—2000; program mgr. census of fatal occupl. injuries Bur. Labor Stats., Washington, 2000—. Contbr. articles to profl. jours., chapters to books. Sr. warden, vestry Christ Our Lord Ch., Woodbridge, Va., 2004—06. Mem.: APHA. Anglican. Office: Bureau of Labor Statistics 2 Massachusetts Ave Washington DC 20212 Business E-Mail: richardson.scott@bls.gov.

RICHARDSON, SELMA KATHERINE, retired library and information scientist; b. McCandless, Pa., Oct. 23, 1931; d. John J. and Laura Ingrid Richardson. BM, St. Olaf Coll., Northfield, Minn., 1953; MA, U. Mich., Ann Arbor, 1959, MALS, 1962, PhD, 1969. Tchr. Berkley Sch. Dist., Mich., 1953—60; libr. Oak Park Sch. Dist., Mich., 1960—69; prof. Ball State U., Muncie, Ind., 1969—70; libr. Oak Park-River Forest Sch. Dist., 1970—74; prof. libr. sci. U. Ill., Urbana, 1974—95, prof. emeritus, 1995—. Author: Periodicals for School Media Programs, 1978, Magazines for Children, 1983, 2d edit., 1991, Magazines for Young Adults, 1984; editor: Children's Services of Public Libraries, 1978, Study and Collecting of Historical Children's Book, 1979, Research About Nineteenth-Century Children and Books, 1980; contbr. articles to profl. jours. and mags., chapters to books. Named Disting. Alumnus, Sch. Libr. Sci. U. Mich., 1978. Mem.: ALA (mem. coun. 1972—76), Beta Phi Mu, Pi Lambda Theta, Phi Kappa Phi. Avocation: travel. Home: 814 Phoenix Dr Champaign IL 61820 Office: U Ill Sch Libr and Info Sci 501 E Daniel St Champaign IL 61820

RICHARDSON, SHIRLEY MAXINE, editor; b. Rising Sun, Ind., May 3, 1931; d. William Fenton and Mary (Phillips) Keith; m. Arthur Lee Richardson, Feb. 11, 1950; children: Mary Jane Hunt, JoDee Mayfield, Steven Lee Richardson. Pers. mgr. Mayhill Pubs., Knightstown, Ind., 1967-87, prodn. mgr., 1975-87, editor, 1967-87; info. staff, assoc. editor Ind. Farm Bur., Inc., 1987-89, dir. info. and pub. rels., 1989-94; genealogy editor AntiqueWeek, 1996-2001; exec. editor Knightstown Banner, 2001—. Avocations: travel, reading, boating, quilting. Home: 366 E Carey St Knightstown IN 46148-1208 Office: 24 N Washington St Knightstown IN 46148-1242 Office Phone: 765-345-2292.

RICHARDSON, THOMAS A., lawyer; b. Flint, Mich., Sept. 4, 1945; BA, Mich. State U., 1966; JD, Harvard U., 1970. Bar: Colo. 1970. Ptnr. Holmes Roberts & Owen, Denver, 1970—. Mem. ABA, Colo. Bar Assn., Denver Bar Assn. Office: Holme Roberts & Owen 1700 Lincoln St Ste 4100 Denver CO 80203-4541 Office Phone: 303-861-7000. Office Fax: 303-866-0200. Business E-Mail: thomas.richardson@hro.com.

RICHARDSON, THOMAS ANDREW, business executive, educator; b. Providence, Aug. 31, 1955; s. Edward Ferris and Olive Elizabeth (Lynaugh) R.; m. Patricia Ann Mundie, Dec. 30, 1982; children: Michael Edward, Lauren Elizabeth, Kristen Mundie. AS in Oceanography, Fla. Inst. Tech., 1977, BS in Environ. Sci., 1979, MBA, 1985; EdD, Nova Southeastern U., 2003. Asst. prof., div. head sch. marine and environ. tech. Fla. Inst. Tech., Jensen Beach, 1979-85; tng. mgr. PADI Internat., Santa Ana, Calif., 1985-88, dir. tng. and edn., 1988-90, sr. v.p., 1991—2003; pres. PADI Worldwide, 2003—; v.p. Capital Investment Ventures Corp., 1991—2003; pres., COO Emergency First Response Inc., 2003—; pres. Current Publs., 2003—. Dir. lakefront City of Evanston, Ill., 1980-82; bd. dirs. CIVCO; chmn. bd. dirs. Project AWARE Found., Santa Ana; pres. DSAT Inc., Santa Ana, 1989—, DSAT Worldwide, 2003—; pres., CEO, Emergency First Responce Corp., 2003—; guest faculty Duke Med. Sch. continuing edn., Durham, N.C., 1992. Editor in chief: Open Water Diver Manual, 1988, Rescue Diver Manual, 1988, Divemaster Manual, 1990, Undersea Journal, 1987, Adventures in Diving; Open Water Diving video, Adventures in Diving video, Peak Performance video; contbr. articles to profl. jours. CPR and first aid instr. Martin County Sch. Dist., Stuart, Fla., 1982-83. Recipient Diver of Yr. award Divers Alert Network/Rolex, Inc., 1992, Craig Hoffman Meml. award for diving safety, Undersea and Hyerbaric Med. Soc., 2000; scholar Nova Southeastern U., 1998. Mem. Am. Mgmt. Assn., Am. Soc. Training and Devel., Am. Soc. Assn. Exec., Undersea and Hyperbaric Med. Soc., South Pacific Undersea Med. Soc., Sierra Club, Nat. Audubon Soc., Emergency Med. Planning Inc., Am. Acad. Underwater Scis., Nat. Assn. Search and Rescue, PADI Diving Soc. (pres. 1998—). Avocations: photography, music, woodworking, scuba diving. E-mail: drewr@padi.com.

RICHARDSON, TOM (EDWARD THOMPSON RICHARDSON), artist; b. Upper Darby, Pa., Aug. 12, 1948; s. Edward Thompson and Elizabeth Catherine (Fredericks) R.; m. Margaret Reed Colvin, July 1, 1972; 1 child, Edward Thompson III. BFA, U. Pa., 1974, MFA, 1975. Scenic artist San Francisco Opera Assn., 1979-84, San Francisco Ballet Assn., 1982-84; scenic designer music dept. Stanford U., Calif., 1980-84; scenic designer San Jose Opera Assn., Calif., 1985; lead scenic artist FM Prodn., Brisbane, Calif., 1984-87, artist-in-charge, 1987-93. Scenic artist: (films) James and the Giant Peach; Down Periscope; Phenomenon; A Smile Like Yours; Rainmaker; Flubber; What Dreams May Come; The Horse Whisperer; Mumford; Bicentennial Man; Invisible Circus; A Woman on Top; Boys and Girls; Bartleby; Sweet November; Forty Days and Forty Nights; High Crimes; The Matrix Reloaded; Revolutions; Twisted; The Assassination of Richard Nixon; (TV series) Nash Bridges; (films) Bee Season; Starwars Episode 3; RENT: Pursuit of Happyness; The Kite Runner; scenic artist (films) The Heartbreak Kid; scenic artist: (TV series) Partners. Mem. Internat. Alliance Theatrical Stage Employees (Bay area bus. rep. 1984-88, Bay area field rep. 2000—, pres. 1998—). Home: 87 Roosevelt Cir Palo Alto CA 94306-4219

RICHARDSON, VERNAL EDWARD, retired music educator; b. Bloomington, Ind., May 20, 1932; s. Edgar Lee and Olive Mae Richardson; m. Elpha Ernestine Patton, Aug. 10, 1958; children: Ernest Todd, Patricia Beth Niemann, Edward Scott. MusB, Ind. U., Bloomington, 1950—55, MusM, 1959—63; PhD in Musical Arts, Cath. U. Am., DC, 1970—77. Cert. orch. tchr. Ga., 1989. Orch. dir. Manatee Pub. Schs., Bradenton, Fla., 1985—89, Atlanta Pub. Schs., 1989—2004. First violin sect. Atlanta Symphony Orch., 1955—56; pilot USAF, Lincoln AFB, Nebr., 1956—59; asst. prof., music David Lipscomb Coll., Nashville, 1959—63, Southeastern La. U., Hammond, 1963—65, Harding Coll., Searcy, Ark., 1965—68, Towson State U., Md., 1968—79; assoc. prof., music Lebanon Valley Coll., Annville, Pa., 1979—82, Moorhead State U., Minn., 1982—85. 1st lt. USAF, 1956—59, Lincoln, Nebr. Mem.: Am. Fedn. Musicians. Democrat. Methodist. Avocations: aviation, photography, music. Home: 5968 Brasstown Creek Estates Young Harris GA 30582 Office: Richardson String Studios 5968 Brasstown Creek Estates Young Harris GA 30582 Home Phone: 706-379-2711; Office Phone: 706-379-2711. E-mail: verned@alltel.net.

RICHARDSON, VETA TERESA, professional society administrator, lawyer; b. Phila., Aug. 4, 1962; d. William Alfred and Teresa Richardson. BS in Bus. Mgmt., U. Md., 1983, JD, 1986. Bar: Pa. 1986, N.Y. 1995, D.C. 1988. Corp. and securities counsel Sunoco, Inc., Phila., 1986-97; v.p. Assn. Corp. Counsel, Washington, 1997-2000; exec. dir. Minority Corp. Counsel Assn., Washington, 2001. Dir. publs. Diversity and the Bar mag., Washington, 2001—; mem. adv. bd. Georgetown Law Sch. Corp. Counsel Inst., Washington, 2000—06. Trustee Prince George's Arts Coun., 1997—03; mem. steering com. Lawyers for One Am., Washington, 1999-2000. Mem. Nat. Bar Assn., Assn. Corp. Counsel, Am. Soc. Assn. Execs., Alpha Kappa Alpha. Avocation: african american art collector.

RICHARDSON, W. C., painter; Exhibitions include W.C. Richardson: New Paintings, Kiang Gallery, Atlanta, 2004, one-man shows include, Loyola U., Baltimore, 2004, Fusebox Gallery, Washington DC, 2002, 2003, Baumgartner Gallery, NYC, 2000, displayed in, Hirshhorn Twenty-five: Celebrating Modern & Contemporary Art, Hirshhorn Mus. & Scuplture Garden, 1999, two painted triptychs, reproduced in porcelanized steel, North Terminal, Ronald Reagan Nat. Airport; co-curator with Paula Crawford (exhibitions) Recent Paintings, Projectspace, Washington DC, 1998. Grantee Individual Artist Award, Md. State Arts Coun., 2002, Visual Arts Fellowship, 2002, 1998, 1987, 1981Md. State Arts Coun. Office: U Maryland 1211 Art/Sociology Bldg College Park MD 20742-1311 Office Phone: 301-405-1460. Office Fax: 301-314-9740. E-mail: wr8@umail.umd.edu.

RICHARDSON, WALTER JOHN, architect; b. Long Beach, Calif., Nov. 14, 1926; s. Walter Francis and Ava Elizabeth (Brown) R.; m. Marilyn Joyce Brown, June 26, 1949 (div. 1982); children: Mark Steven, Glenn Stewart; m. Mary Sue Sutton, Dec. 4, 1982. Student, UCLA, 1944—45, Long Beach City Coll., 1946; BA, U. Calif., Berkeley, 1950. Registered arch., Ala., Ariz., Calif., Colo., Fla., Hawaii, Ill., Kans., Md., Mass., Nev., N.J., N.Y., Okla., Oreg., Tex., Utah, Vt., Va., Wash. Draftsman Wurster, Bernardi, Emmons, San Francisco, 1950-51, Skidmore, Owings & Merrill, San Francisco, 1951; designer Hugh Gibbs Arch., Long Beach, 1952-58; ptnr. Thomas & Richardson Archs., Long Beach, Costa Mesa, 1958-70; pres. Walter Richardson Assocs. Archs., Newport Beach, Calif., 1970-74; chmn. bd. Richardson, Nagy, Martin Archs. and Planners, Newport Beach, 1974—2000, RNM Architecture-Planning, Newport Beach, 2000—. Co-author: The Architect and the Shelter Industry, 1975. Chmn. Planning Commn., City of Orange, Calif., 1967-68. With USAF, 1945. Recipient over 200 Gold Nugget Design awards Pacific Coast Builders Conf., San Francisco, 1969-96, 12 Builders Choice Design awards Builder Mag.; named Arch. of Yr. Profl. Builder mag., 1986; named to Hall of Fame Builder Mag., 2005 Fellow AIA (pres. Orange County chpt. 1970, chmn. nat. housing com. 1976, 77 design awards); mem. Nat. Assn. Home Builders, Nat. Coun. Archtl. Registration Bds., Urban Land Inst., Alpha Tau Omega. Republican. Avocations: photography, downhill skiing, travel. Office: RNM Design 4611 Teller Ave Ste 100 Newport Beach CA 92660-2104 Office Phone: 949-752-1800.

RICHARDSON, WILLIAM CHASE, retired foundation executive; b. Passaic, NJ, May 11, 1940; s. Henry Burtt and Frances (Chase) R.; m. Nancy Freeland, June 18, 1966; children: Elizabeth, Jennifer. BA, Trinity Coll., 1962; MBA, U. Chgo., 1964, PhD, 1971; PhD (hon.), from 11 Univs. including, U. Mich., 2006. Rsch. assoc., instr. U. Chgo., 1967-70; asst. prof. health services U. Wash., 1971-73, assoc. prof., 1973-76, prof., 1976-84, chmn. dept. health services, 1973-76, assoc. dean Sch. Pub. Health, 1976-81, acting dean, 1977, 78, dean Grad. Sch., vice provost, 1981-84; exec. v.p., provost, prof. dept. family and community medicine Pa. State U., 1984-90; pres. Johns Hopkins U., Balt., 1990-95, pres., prof. emeritus, 1995, prof. dept. health policy, mgmt., 1990-95, prof. emeritus, 1995—; pres., CEO W.K. Kellogg Found, Battle Creek, Mich., 1995—2005; prof. policy Kalamazoo Coll., 2005—. Cons. in field; bd. dir. CSX Corp., Bank of NY, Exelon Corp.; chmn., bd. dir. Coun. on Founds.; chmn. Kellogg Trust, 1996-2006. Author: books, including Ambulatory Use of Physicians Services, 1971, Health Program Evaluation, 1978; contbr. articles to profl. jours. Mem. adv. com. Rand Corp. Kellogg Coll. fellow, Oxford U., 1965—. Mem.: Nat. Acad. Arts and Scis., Nat. Acad. Scis., Inst. Medicine, Am. Public Health Assn.

RICHARDSON, WILLIE FORREST, JR., physician, consultant; s. Willie Forrest Richardson and Linda Lou Cummings. BS in Biology (hon.), Pembroke State U., 1996; MD, East Carolina U., 2000. Diplomate Am. Bd. Dermatology, lic. dermatologist N.Mex., Fla. Intern in internal medicine Med. U. S.C., Charleston, 2000—01; resident indermatology U. N.Mex. Health Scis. Ctr., Albuquerque, 2001—04; staff dermatologist Gallup Indian Med. Ctr., N.Mex., 2003—; dermatologist Presbyn. Med. Group-Kaseman Dermatology, Albuquerque, 2004—05; staff dermatologist Broward Gen. Med. Ctr., Ft. Lauderdale, Fla., 2005—; dermatologist Las Olas Dermatology, Ft. Lauderdale, Fla., 2005—. Author: (textbook) Native American Skin Disease, 2005; contbr. articles to profl. jours. Recipient Indian Health Svc. scholarship, U.S. Dept. HHS, 1994—96, Premedical scholarship, Indian Health Svc., 1993-1996, Outstanding Clin. Excellence award, Gallup Indian Svc. Divsn., 2003. Fellow: Am. Soc. Mohs Surgery; mem.: AMA, Broward County Dermatology Soc., Broward County Med. Assn., Am. Acad. Dermatology, Alpha Chi. Achievements include research in Native American skin disease. Home Phone: 505-301-5469; Office Phone: 954-763-4331. Personal E-mail: nativehealer@aol.com.

RICHARDSON-BOWMAN, LEQUETTA DEVERA, finance company executive, consultant; d. Edward Richardson and Lonzetta Beatrice Townsend-Richardson; life ptnr. Thomas Michael Sellers; m. Michael Jerome Bowman, Mar. 24, 1987 (div. June 31, 1989); m. Ray Alexander, Dec. 27, 1963 (div. Dec. 13, 1967); children: Malik (Ray) Edward Shakur (Alexander), Briant Leonard Alexander. BA in Psychology magna cum laude, Langston U., 1995; MBA, Okla. City U., 1998. Cost risk analysis course, Dept. Def. Logistics Mgmt. Coll., sys. acquisition funds mgmt. courses, Dept. Def. Sys. Mgmt. Coll., Md., contractor performance measurement course, Dept. Def. Sys. Mgmt. Coll., Md., fed. appropriation law, Grad. Sch. USDA, Okla., federal budget process, Grad. Sch. USDA, Okla., cert. acquisition profl. level I in fin. mgmt., Dept. of Air Force, Ohio, budget estimating techniques, US Office of Pers. Mgmt., Tex., budget formulation, US Office of Pers. Mgmt., Tex., budget execution, US Office of Pers. Mgmt., Tex.; aeronautics Dept. Transp., FAA, Okla., ISO 9000 implementation and documentation workshop Hartley Group Performance Paradigms, Inc., Okla., ISO 9000 internal quality auditor workshop Hartley Group-Performance Paradigm, Inc., Okla., Outclass the Competition PRO-TOCOL PLUS through Protocol Sch. of Washington, Profl. Devel. Inst. Symposium Sequoyah chpt. Am. Soc. of Mil. Comptrs., cert. acquisition profl. level I in acquisition logistics Dept. of the Air Force, Ohio, fgn. mil. sales internat. budget workshop Pentagon and Wright-Patterson AFB, appropriations law update in mgmt. field of study Learning Curve Tng. Group, Inc., Okla., cert. acquisition profl. level I in program mgmt. Dept. of Air Force, Ohio, quality participation for employees USAF, quality leadership for mgrs. USAF. Alterations bookkeeping clk. alterations dept. Al Rosenthal's, Oklahoma City, 1966—67; sec.-receptionist ITT Continental Baking Co., Wonder Bread Regional Sales-Svc. Bus. Office, Oklahoma City, 1967—69; teller Tinker Field Credit Union, Tinker AFB, Okla., 1969; sales-svc. sec. West Coast regional sales svc. office Reynolds Metals Co., LA, 1969—70; purchasing technician purchasing dept. Memorex Corp., Santa Clara, Calif., 1970—72; pers.-payroll clk. Unit Parts Co.-Borg Warner Corp., Oklahoma City, 1972—73; teller Tinker Field Credit Union, Tinker AFB, Okla., 1972; payroll technician acctg. divsn., C.G. Payroll Br. FAA Mike Monroney Aero. Ctr., Oklahoma City, 1974—81; payroll clk. divsn. WR Grace Petroleum, Bus. Office, payroll sect. TRG Drilling, Oklahoma City, 1981—83; payroll clk. civilian pay Dept. Def., USAF Acctg. Br., Civilian Payroll Sect., Tinker AFB, 1973—74; mgr., supr. Cmty. Day Care Presch., Bus. Office, Pers. & Payroll, Oklahoma City, 1981; travel clk. FAA, Mike Monroney Aero. Ctr., Acctg. Divsn., Travel Br., Travel Adminstrn. Sect., Oklahoma City, 1983—83; acctg. technician FAA Mike Monroney Ctr., Acctg. Divsn., Accounts Payable Br., Oklahoma City, 1983—85; air traffic control specialist pre-developmental student flight svcs. trainee Dept. Transp., FAA, Ea. Region, Jamaica, N.Y., Oklahoma City, 1986; mgr.-supr. family bus. Cmty. Day Care PreSch. Bus. Office, Oklahoma City, 1986—87; shipment clk. Def. Logistics Agy., Billing OS & D Sect. (Inbound), Tinker AFB, 1988—90; transp. control clk. Def. Logistics Agy., Freight Terminal Br., Tinker AFB, 1988; customer svc. rep. ATT Sales-Svc. Office, Oklahoma City, 1988; child devel. ctr. supr. HQ 72nd Air Base Wing, 72 Svcs. Divsn., Child Devel. Ctr.-West, Tinker AFB, 1990—91; budget analyst 552 Airborne Computer Squadron, Tinker AFB, 1991—93; budget asst. Okla. City-Air Logistics Ctr., Commodities Mgmt. Directorate, Fin. Mgmt. Br., Tinker AFB, 1991—92; budget analyst Okla. City-Air Logistics Ctr., Tech. and Indsl. Support Directorate, Resource Mgmt. Divsn., Funds Mgmt. Br., Tinker AFB, 1992—97, Okla. City-Air Logistics Ctr., Fin. Mgmt. Directorate Workloading Sect., Tinker AFB, 1998—2001, Okla. City-Air Logistics Ctr., Fin. Mgmt. Directorate, Fin. Analysis Divsn., Tinker AFB, 2001—03. Leader participant League of Black Women, Flossmoor, Ill., 2005; treas. US Green Bldg. Coun., Oklahoma City, 2005; cons. OCU Women As Servant Leaders, Oklahoma City, 2005—06. Named to Vice President's Honor Roll, Rose State Coll., 1991, President's Honor Roll, 1991, 1992; recipient Acad. Achievement award, Langston U., 1994, Spl. Act award, FAA Mike Monroney Aero. Ctr., 1979, Svc. award, 1983, Performance award, Okla. City-Air Logistics Ctr., Tech. and Indsl. Directorate, Resource Mgmt. Divsn., Funds Mgmt. Sect., 1996, Okla. Scholar-Leadership Enrichment Program' Elizabeth George Seminar fellowship, Okla. State Regents for Higher Edn. through the U. of Okla., 1995. Mem.: Friends Earth, Nat. Wildlife Fedn., Price Tower Arts Ctr., League Black Women, Sustainable OKC, T&L Golf Club. Episcopalian. Avocations: cooking, gardening, hiking, yoga, reading.

RICHARDSON-MELECH, JOYCE SUZANNE, music educator, singer; b. Perth Amboy, NJ, Nov. 15, 1957; d. Herbert Nathaniel and Fannie Elaine (Franklin) Richardson; m. Gerald Melech, July 28, 1990. MusB, Westminster Choir Coll., 1979, MusM, 1981; postgrad., Rutgers U., 1999—. Cert. music tchr. NJ, supr. NJ. Musical play dir. Perth Amboy HS, 1989-92, asst. band dir., 1984-94; music tchr. Perth Amboy Bd. Edn., 1981—, gifted and talented music tchr., 1992-96; vocal soloist NYC. Vocal soloist NY Philharm. and Westminster Symphonic Choir, 1977, United Moravian Ch., NYC, 1980-81, Ctrl. Jersey Concert Orch., Perth Amboy, 1994-96, St. Peters Episcopal Ch., Perth Amboy, 2006; mezzo-soprano soloist in The Messiah, John Hus Moravian Ch., Bklyn., 1998, St. Peter's Episcopal Ch., Perth Amboy, NJ; master tchrs. collaborative with NJ Symphony Orch., 2000-01, 2003, 2005. Contbg. author: Teacher's Resource Book, 2000, 2001, 2003, 2005, illustrator: The Peacock of Half-Way Tree: A Caribbean Fable, 2004; actor: Perth Amboy Adult Cmty. Theatre, 1983. Participant Perth Amboy Adult Cmty. Theatre, 1983; del. to Russia Dwight D. Eisenhower People to People Amb. Program, 2007. Recipient award for excellence in tchg., NJ Symphony Orch., 2000, 2001, 2003, 2005, Lois Bailey Glenn award for tchg. excellence, Nat. Music Found., 2004; grantee, Am. Music Edn. Initiative for Programmatic Ragtime, 2004. Mem. NAACP, Am. Fedn. Tchrs., Am. Fedn. Musicians (local 204-373), Music Educators Nat. Conf., Orgn. Am. Kodaly Educators, Am. Mus. Natural History (assoc.), Kodaly Educators, Alliance for Arts Edn. NJ, Ctrl. Jersey Music Educators, NJ Music Educators Assn., Alpha Phi Omega. Democrat. Episcopalian. Avocations: travel, Art Deco antiques, needlecrafts, knitting, crocheting. Home: 148 Carson Ct Somerset NJ 08873-4790 Office: Anthony V Ceres Sch 445 State St Perth Amboy NJ 08861-3205 Office Phone: 732-376-6020.

RICHARDSON-WENINEGAR, LORETTA LYNNE, biologist, educator; b. Ft. Riley, Kans., Sept. 19, 1954; d. Woodrow and Florence Myrtle Denton; children: Jennifer Lynne Weninegar-Canady, Jessica Leigh Weninegar, James Christopher Weninegar. BS in Biology and Secondary Edn./Minor Psychology, U. Mobile, 1976, MSEd in secondary edn./biology, 1993; MS in biology, Jacksonville State U., 2002. Cert. Tchr. #252735, Type B Ala., 1976, Tchr. #252735, Type A Ala., 1993. Sci. tchr. Arnold Sch. of Ala., Mobile, 1976, Berney Points Sch., Birmingham, Ala., 1977—79, Hueytown H.S., Ala., 1995—98, Jacksonville H.S., Ala., 1990—91; grad. tchg. asst., biology Jacksonville State U., Ala., 1993, adj. instr. biology, 1993—98; asst. project dir. Ala. Sci. in Motion Ala. A&M U., Huntsville, 1998—; tchr. of sci. Columbia H.S., 2006—. Field technician, botanist Natural Resource Conservation Svc., Ala., 1996; chmn., pers. com. Berney Points Sch., Birmingham, 1979—81; asst. dir. Chattooga river environ. edn. and water quality project Jacksonville State U., Ala., 1994—95, facilitator environ. edn. From Awareness to Action, 1993, staff, Little River Field Sch., 1993—97; trainer Ala. Water Watch Ala. A&M U., Huntsville, 1998—; adj. instr. Biology Calhoun C.C., Decatur/Huntsville, Ala., 2004—; mem. Ala. Invasive Plant Coun., 2007. Spkr. hike leader The Land Trust of Huntsville and North Ala.; strategic planning com. Columbia HS, Huntsville, 2005—; outdoor amb. Ala. Bur. Tourism and Travel, 2006; spkr. Ala. Wildflower Soc., Huntsville. Grantee Toyota Tapestry 10K grant, 2007. Mem.: NEA, Ala. Invasive Plant Coun., Nat. Sci. Tchr. Assn., Nat. Assn. Biology Tchrs., Ala. Edn. Assn., The LandTrust of Huntsville and North Ala. (speaker's bur., hike leader), Beta Beta Beta, Delta Kappa Gamma (membership chmn. 2002—04). Achievements include research in water quality analysis of Cane Creek in Calhoun County, Ala; STS-106 Atlantis; Vascular Flora of Choccolocco Creek, Calhoun, Cleburne, and Talladega Counties, Ala. Avocations: hiking, camping, gardening, birdwatching, dance. Home: 9507 Hemlock Dr SE Huntsville AL 35803-1161 Office Phone: 256-428-7576 ext 157. Personal E-mail: bcdh@aol.com.

RICHARDS-VITAL, CLAUDIA, small business owner, recreational facility executive; b. Banes, Oriente, Cuba, May 18, 1935; arrived in U.S., 1951; d. Vasper Zacharia Richards and Ana Louisa Coombs - Vital; m. Eugene Blackman, July 22, 1956 (div. Apr. 20, 1965); children: Emery, John, Veronica. AA in Bus. Adminstrn./English, Havana Bus. Acad., 1951;

diploma in Early Childhood Devel., Miami Dade C.C., 1972. Pvt. practice nanny, Miami Beach, Fla., 1951—56; seamstress Playboy Club, Miami, Fla., 1961—65; prodn. supr. So. Bakery, 1965—69; care mother James E. Scott Cmty. Agy., 1970—75; nurse asst. North Shore Hosp., 1970—75; home health aide Total Care Home Health Agy., 1975—85; site dir. YMCA, 1985—95; sole propr. Veronica's Boutique, 1982—89, Claudia's Formal Wear, 1989—. Pres. Local #249 Am. Bakery and Confectionery Workers Internat. AFL-CIO, Fla., 1966—69. Named Parent of Yr., Metro Dade County, 1993; recipient Diamond Pendant, Queen Elizabeth II, 1965, cert. of Appreciation, YMCA of Miami, Fla., 1990. Mem.: NAFE, NAACP. Democrat. Roman Catholic. Avocations: sewing, decorating, gardening, babysitting, animals. Home: 1915 NW 49 St Miami FL 33142 Office Phone: 305-637-2090. Personal E-mail: claudia@claudiaformalweareleganza.com.

RICHBURG, BILLY KEITH, healthcare manager, consultant, entrepreneur; b. Memphis, Tex., Dec. 16, 1946; s. Byron C. and Marjorie Mae (Draper) R.; children: Gretchen, Jeremy; m. Paula Anita Mason, July 27, 1990. BA, U. Alaska, Anchorage, 1974; MS in Health Care Adminstrn., Trinity U., San Antonio, 1978. Exec. dir. Med. Park Hosp. (Am. Med. Internat.), Hope, Ark., 1979-84; asst. adminstr. Columbia (Mo.) Regional Hosp. (Am. Med. Internat.), 1984-85, v.p., CFO, 1985-96; exec. dir. VNA Ctrl. Mo., Columbia, 1996-98; gen. mgr. Coram Healthcare, Earth City, Mo., 1999-2000; dir. govt. programs and compliance IMACS, Ltd., Dallas, 2001—. Founder MPTC Svcs. With USAF, 1969-76. Fellow Healthcare Fin. Mgmt. Assn.; mem. Mensa. Episcopalian. Avocations: motorcycles, on-line computing. Home Phone: 469-287-2081.

RICHE, ROBERT S., research and development company executive; b. Great Lakes, Ill., Apr. 11, 1953; m. Lynn Riehl, June 5, 1975; children: Jennifer Van Horn, Michelle. BSc, US Naval Acad., Annapolis, Md., 1975, Naval Postgraduate Sch., Monterey, Calif., 1981; MA, Naval War Coll., Newport, RI, 1988, Salve Regina, 1988; MSc, Nat. Def. U., Washington, 1997. Commd. ensign USN, 1975, advanced through grades to capt., ret., 2004, commdg. officer USS Curtis Wilbur, dep. dir. joint theater air and missile def. orgn., 1997—99, comdr. destroyer squadron 23, 2000—02, exec. asst. bur. naval pers., 2003—04; dir. bus. devel. Lockheed Martin, Washington, 2004—. Contbr. articles to profl. jours. Mem.: AIAA, U.S. Naval Inst., Army Navy Country Club. Episcopalian. Avocation: history. Office: Lockheed Martin 300 M St SE Washington DC 20003 Office Phone: 202-863-3392. Business E-Mail: robert.riche@lmco.com.

RICHELS, JOHN, energy executive, lawyer; BA, York Univ.; LLB, Univ. Windsor, 1978. Mng. ptnr., COO, mem. exec. com. Bennett Jones; bd. dir. Northstar Energy Corp., 1993—96, exec. v.p., CFO, 1996—98; pres., CEO Devon Canada, 1998—2001; sr. v.p. Canadian div. Devon Energy Corp., Oklahoma City, 2001—04, pres., 2004—. Gen. counsel XV Olympic Winter Games, Calgary, 1986—88. Office: Devon Energy Corp 20 N Broadway Oklahoma City OK 73102-8260 *

RICHELSON, PAUL WILLIAM, curator; b. Montpelier, Idaho, Sept. 27, 1939; s. Paul Newton and June (Quayle) R. BA, Yale U., 1961; MFA, Princeton U., 1967, PhD, 1974. Asst. prof. Lawrence U., Appleton, Wis., 1970-77, U. Denver, 1977-84; asst. dir., curator Trisolini Gallery of Ohio U., Athens, 1984-87; chief curator Grand Rapids (Mich.) Mus., 1987-91; curator of Am. art Mobile Mus. Art, Mobile, Ala., 1991-97, asst. dir., chief curator, 1997—. Author: (book) Studies in the Personal Imagery Collection of 20th Prints Ohio University, 1985, (catalogue) The Golden Age 19th Century Prints by David Roberts, 1988, Lee Loring: A Southern Sophisticate, 1992, Modernism and American Painting of the 1930s, 1993, ThirtySomething, 1994, Alabama Impact: Contemporary Artists with Alabama Ties, 1995, Louise Lyons Heustis (1965-1951): A Retrospective, 1995, The French Connection: Jean Simon Chaudron Returns To Mobile, 1996, John Roderick Dempster MacKenzie (1865-1941): A Retrospective, 1997, Celebrating the Creative Spirit, 1998, Contemporary Southeastern Furniture, 1998, Coming Home: American Paintings, 1930-1950, from the Schoen Collection, 2003. Lt. (j.g.) USN, 1961-63. Recipient Elizabeth B. Gould Rsch. award Mobile Hist. Devel. Commn., 1997; Fulbright-Hays fellow to Italy, 1967-69; Mus. Purchase Plan grantee Nat. Endowment for the Arts, 1991; grantee Mus. Loan Network, 2002. Mem. Southeastern Museums Conf. Home: 6427 Grelot Rd Apt 405 Mobile AL 36695-2630 Office: Mobile Museum of Art 4850 Museum Dr Mobile AL 36608-1917 Home Phone: 251-633-8596; Office Phone: 251-208-5215. Fax: 251-208-5201. E-mail: prichelson@mobilemuseumofart.com.

RICHENHAGEN, MARTIN H., manufacturing executive; b. July 1, 1952; married; 3 children. Grad., Univ. Bonn, Germany, 1975. Vice-pres. field ops. Schindler Aufzugefabrik GmbH, Germany, 1995—98; group pres. GLAAS KgaA mbH, Germany, 1995—2003; group exec. vice-pres. Forbo Internat. SA, 2003—04; pres., CEO AGCO Corp., Duluth, Ga., 2004—06, chmn., pres., CEO, 2006—. Bd. dir. PPG Industries, 2007—. Office: AGCO Corp 4205 River Green Pkwy Duluth GA 30096 Office Phone: 770-813-9200. *

RICHER, MARC-HANS, marketing executive; Account dir. DDB, Chgo.; joined GM, Detroit, 1998; chief mktg. officer Harley-Davidson, Inc., Milw., 2007—. Named one of Mktg. 50, Advt. Age, 2004. Office: Harley-Davidson, Inc 3700 W Juneau Ave Milwaukee WI 53208 Office Phone: 414-342-4680. *

RICHERSON, HAL BATES, internist, allergist, immunologist, educator; b. Phoenix, Feb. 16, 1929; s. George Edward and Eva Louise (Steere) R.; m. Julia Suzanne Bradley (dec. 1996), Sept. 5, 1953; children: Anne, George, Miriam, Julia, Susan. BS with distinction, U. Ariz., 1950; MD, Northwestern U., 1954. Diplomate Am. Bd. Internal Medicine, Am. Bd. Allergy and Immunology, Bd. Diagnostic Lab. Immunology; lic. physician, Iowa. Intern Kansas City (Mo.) Gen. Hosp., 1954-55; resident in pathology St. Luke's Hosp., Kansas City, 1955-56; trainee in neuropsychiatry Brooke Army Hosp., San Antonio, 1956; resident in medicine U. Iowa Hosps., Iowa City, 1961-64, fellow in allergy and immunology, 1964-66; fellow in immunology Mass. Gen. Hosp., Boston, 1968-69; instr. internal medicine U. Iowa Coll. Medicine, Iowa City, 1964-66, asst. prof., 1966-70, assoc. prof., 1970-74, prof., 1974-98, prof. emeritus, 1998—; acting dir. divsn. allergy/applied immunology U. Iowa Hosps. and Clinics, Iowa City, 1970-72, dir. allergy and clin. immunology sect., 1972-78, dir. divsn. allergy and immunology, 1978-91; gen. practice, asst. to Gen. Surgeon Ukiah, Calif., 1958; gen. practice medicine Holbrook, Ariz., 1958-61. Vis. lectr. medicine Harvard U. Sch. Medicine, Boston, 1968-69; vis. prof., rsch. scientist U. London and Brompton Hosp., 1984; prin. investigator Nat. Heart, Lung and Blood Inst., 1971-94, mem. pulmonary diseases adv. com., 1983-87; prin. investigator Nat. Inst. Allergy and Infectious Diseases, 1983-94; dir. Nat. Inst. Allergy and Infectious Diseases' Asthma and Allergic Diseases Ctr., U. Iowa, 1983-94; mem. VA Merit Rev. Bd. in Respiration, 1981-84; mem. com. NIH Gen. Clin. Rsch. Ctrs., 1989-93; mem. rev. reserve NIH, 1993-98; mem. bd. sci. advisors Merck Inst., 1990-94; presenter lectures, seminars, continuing edn. courses; mem. numerous univ., coll. and hosp. coms., 1970—; cons. Merck Manual, 1982, 87, 92, 96-97. Contbr. numerous articles and revs. to profl. jours., chpts. to books; reviewer Sci., Jour. Immunology, Jour. Allergy and Clin. Immunology, Am. Rev. Respiratory Disease, New Eng. Jour. Medicine, Ann. Internal Medicine. Served to capt. U.S. Army, 1956-58. NIH fellow 1968-69. Fellow ACP (Laureate award 1996), Am. Acad. Allergy Asthma & Immunology (Disting. Clinician award 1998); mem. AMA (mem. residency and rev. com. for allergy and immunology; mem. accreditation coun. for grad. med. edn. 1980-85, vice-chmn. 1984-85), AAAS, Iowa Med. Soc., Iowa Thoracic Soc. (chmn. program com. 1964-65, 69-71, pres. 1972-73, mem. exec. com. 1972-74), Am. Thoracic Soc. (bd. dirs. 1981-82, councilor assembly on allergy and immunology 1980-81, mem. nominating com. 1988-90), Iowa Clin. Med. Soc., Am. Fedn. Clin. Rsch., Am. Assn. Immunologists, Ctrl. Soc. Clin. Rsch. (chmn. sect. on allergy-immunology 1980-81, mem. coun. 1981-84), Alpha Omega Alpha. Avocations: reading, trombonist, swimming, scuba diving. Home: 331 Lucon Dr Iowa City IA 52246-3300 Office: U Iowa Health Care Dept Internal Medicine 200 Hawkins Dr Iowa City IA 52242-1009 Personal E-mail: richersonh@mchsi.com. Business E-Mail: hal-richerson@uiowa.edu.

RICHERT, JOHN ROLIN, neuroimmunologist, educator; b. Boston, June 9, 1945; s. Daniel Arnold and Esther (Beamer) Richert; m. Nancy Dembeck, July 5, 1969. BA, Cornell U., 1966; MD, U. Rochester, 1970. Diplomate Am. Bd. Med. Examiners, Am. Bd. Psychiatry and Neurology. Intern, resident in medicine Strong Meml. Hosp. U. Rochester, NY, 1970-72; resident in neurology Mayo Clinic, Rochester, Minn., 1974-77; fellow Nat. Multiple Sclerosis Soc. NIH, Bethesda, Md., 1977-80; rsch. asst. prof. neurology Georgetown U. Med. Ctr., Washington, 1980-83, asst. prof. neurology, 1983-89, assoc. prof. neurology, 1989-93, prof. neurology, 1993—2005, prof., chair dept. microbiology and immunology, 1997—2005; v.p. rsch. and clin. programs Nat. Multiple Sclerosis Soc., NYC, 2005—07, exec. v.p. rsch. and clin. programs, 2007—; mem. data and safety monitoring bd. Acorda Therapeutics, Hawthorne, NY, 2005—07, Novartis, Basel, Switzerland, 2005—06; mem. data and safety monitoring com. Biogen Idec, Cambridge, 2007—. Mem. physician adv. bd. Biogen Inc., Cambridge, Mass., 1994-2000; cons. Immunex, Inc., Seattle, 1998-2000; external adv. com. VA Multiple Sclerosis Ctr. of Excellence, U. Md. Multiple Sclerosis Ctr., Balt., 2003-2005; sci. adv. bd. TolerGenics, Inc., Rockville, Md., 2001-2005; cons. Health Sci. Ctr. for Continuing med. Edn., NY, 2003; mem. med. adv. com. Multiple Sclerosis Soc. Can., 2006—. Mem. editl. bd.: NeuroRx. Mem. immunol. scis. study sect. NIH, 1989, mem. mental health AIDS and immunology rsch. study sect., 1992, mem. neurol. disorders program project com., 2003, Brain Disorders and Clin. Neuroscience spl. emphasis panel, 2003-2004. Maj. USAF, 1972-74. Fellow Am. Acad. Neurology; mem. Internat. Soc. Neuroimmunology, Nat. Multiple Sclerosis Soc. (med. adv. bd. 1988-91, 93-96, profl. adv. com. 1988-2005, sci. peer rev. com. 1993-98), Am. Neurol. Assn., Am. Assn. Immunologists, Am. Soc. for Biochemistry and Molecular Biology, Am. Soc. for Exptl. Neurotherapeutics (pub. com. 2006—), N.Y. Acad. Scis., Assn. Med. Sch. Microbiology and Immunology Chairs (pub. policy com., 2002-05, chair 2004-05) Alpha Omega Alpha. Avocations: tennis, golf, skiing. Office: Nat Multiple Sclerosis Soc 733 3d Ave New York NY 10017 Home Phone: 301-654-6293; Office Phone: 212-476-0423. Business E-Mail: john.richertj@nmss.org.

RICHERT, PAUL, law educator; b. Elwood, Ind., Aug. 31, 1948; m. Catherine George Stanton, June 24, 1972; children: John, William. AB, U. Ill., Urbana, 1970, MS, 1971; JD, Tulane U., New Orleans, 1977. Bar: Ohio 1977. Asst. law libr. U. Akron, 1977-78, law libr., asst. prof. law, 1978-83, assoc. prof., 1983-87, prof. law, 1987—. Local bd. dirs. Selective Svc. sys. Co-author: Searching the Law, 3d edit., 2005. Mem. United Chs. of Christ. With U.S. Army, 1971-74. Mem. Am. Assn. Law Librs., Akron Bar Assn., ABA. Home: 2030 Ganyard Rd Akron OH 44313-6050 Office: Univ Akron Sch Law Library 302 Buchtel Common Akron OH 44325-2902 Home Phone: 330-867-8272; Office Phone: 330-972-7330. Business E-Mail: richert@uakron.edu.

RICHESON, HUGH ANTHONY, JR., lawyer; b. Aberdeen, Md., Apr. 22, 1947; s. Hugh Anthony Sr. and Mary Evelyn (Burford) R.; m. Melissa Anne Baum, Apr. 4, 1970; children: Hugh Anthony III, Heidi E., Holly K., Hagin G., Herald Joshua. BS in Bus. Adminstrn., U. Richmond, 1969; JD, U. Fla., 1973; student, St. Catherine's Coll., Oxford U., Eng., summer 1973. Bar: Fla. 1974, US Dist. Ct. (mid. dist.) Fla. 1975, U.S. Supreme Ct. 1992. Assoc. Bryant, Dickens, Rumph, Franson & Miller, Jacksonville, Fla., 1974—76, ptnr., 1977, Smith, Hallowes & Richeson, Orange Park, 1982—83; sole practice Orange Park, Fla., 1977—82, Palm Harbor, Fla., 1984—98; of counsel Carey & Hilbert, Clearwater, Fla., 1998—2005, Florin Roebig P.A., Palm Harbor, Fla., 2005—. Author: Legally Yours, 2002. Pres. Full Gospel Bus. Men's Fellowship Internat., Orange Park, 1983-84, Palm Harbor, 1985-92, field rep., 1987—; bd. dirs. Religious Freedom Coalition, Washington. Mem. Fla. Coun. Bar Assn. Pres. (life), Gideons Internat., Phi Delta Phi, Sigma Phi Epsilon. Republican. Methodist. Office: Florin Roebig PA 777 Alderman Rd Palm Harbor FL 34683 Office Phone: 727-785-5858. Personal E-mail: hariia@aol.com.

RICHESON, JAMES GRADY, JR., dentist; m. Nancy Richeson; 1 child, Suzanne. DDS, Georgetown U. Dentist, Washington. Recipient Disting. Svc. award, Georgetown Dental Alumni, 2003. Fellow: Pierre Fauchard Acad., Am. Coll. Dentists, Acad. Gen. Dentistry (pres.-elect 2001—02, pres. 2002—03, v.p., treas., bd. trustee, budget and fin. com., regional dir., Found. bd. dirs.); mem.: ADA (alt. del. 2001—, del. 2004), DC Dental Soc. (The Sterling V. Meade award 2004), DC Acad. Gen. Dentistry (past pres.), Georgetown U. Alumni Club of Met. Washington (past pres.). Office: 4400 Jenifer St NW Ste 340 Washington DC 20015-2113 Office Phone: 202-364-5246. Business E-Mail: richeson@agd.org.

RICHESON, JENNIFER ANNE, psychology professor, researcher; b. Sept. 1972; ScB, Brown U., 1994; PhD in Social Psychology, Harvard U., 2000. Asst. prof. psychol. and brain scis. Dartmouth Coll., Hanover, NH, 2000—05; assoc. prof. Dept. Psychology Northwestern U., Evanston, 2005—, faculty fellow Inst. for Policy Rsch., 2005—. Vis. fellow Rsch. Inst. for Comparative Studies in Race and Ethnicity, Stanford U., 2004—05. Contbr. articles to profl. jours. Grantee Ford Found. Odyssey Grant, 1993, NIMH Individual Rsch. Svc. Award, 1999—2000, Walter and Constance Burke Rsch. Initiation Award, 2000—06, NIMH B/START Grant, 2002—04, NSF, 2002—05; MacArthur Fellow, John D. and Catherine T. MacArthur Found., 2006. Mem.: Soc. for Psychol. Study of Social Issues, Soc. for Personality and Social Psychology, Am. Psychol. Soc., Am. Psychol. Assn. Office: Dept Psychology Northwestern U 2029 Sheridan Rd Evanston IL 60208-2710 Office Phone: 847-467-1331. E-mail: jriches@northwestern.edu.

RICHEY, CYNTHIA K., library director; BA, MLS, Univ. Pitts. Libr. positions through head children's services Mt. Lebanon Pub. Libr., Pitts., 1983—96, dir., 1996—. Bd. dir. Allegheny County Libr. Assn.; chair. internet access com. Allegheny County Elect. Info. Network, 1997—. Recipient Libr. award, NY Times, 2006. Mem.: Pa. Libr. Assn. (past pres., Disting. Svc. award), Assn. Libr. Svc. to Children (past pres.). Office: Mt Lebanon Pub Library 16 Castle Shannon Blvd Pittsburgh PA 15228-2252 Office Phone: 412-531-1912. Business E-Mail: richeyc@einetwork.net.

RICHEY, ELLEN, credit card company executive; BA summa cum laude, Harvard U.; JD, Stanford U. Law clk. Hon. Lewis F. Powell, Jr. U.S. Supreme Ct.; law clk. Hon. Charles B. Renfrew U.S. Dist. Ct. (no. dist.); ptnr. Farella, Braun & Martel, San Francisco, 1980—94; from gen. counsel, sec. Providian Fin. Corp., San Francisco, 1995—, exec. v.p., 1997—99, vice chmn. Enterprise Risk Mgmt., 1999—.

RICHEY, LUKE MERRITT, otolaryngologist, researcher; b. Wilmington, NC, Sept. 28, 1976; s. Michael James Richey and Nancy Richey Barnett. BA in Philosophy and Religion, U. NC, Wilmington, 2002; MD, U. NC, Chapel Hill, 2007. Rsch. fellow Holderness Med. Found., Chapel Hill, 2003—04; Doris Duke clin. rsch. fellow sch. medicine U. NC, Chapel Hill, 2005—. Pres. wellness com. sch. medicine U. NC, Chapel Hill, 2002—05, tutor sch. medicine, 2006—07. Contbr. articles to profl. jours. Vol. hospice patient care Lower Cape Fear Hospice, Wilmington, 2000—02; vol. patient care Free Health Clinic, Carrboro, NC, 2005—06. Scholar, NC Bd. Govs., 2002—07. Mem.: ACP, AMA, John B. Graham Rsch. Soc., Am. Med. Student Assn., Physicians Human Rights. Achievements include research in clinical cancer research and cancer epidemiology. Office: PO Box 313 Wilmington NC 28401 Home Phone: 919-923-4308; Office Phone: 919-923-4308. Personal E-mail: richeyl@gmail.com.

RICHEY, MARY ELLEN, lawyer; b. Boston, Mar. 16, 1949; BA summa cum laude, Radcliffe Coll., 1970; JD, Stanford U., 1977. Bar: Calif. 1978. Law clk. to Hon. Charles B. Renfrew U.S. Dist. Ct. (no. dist.) Calif., 1977-78; law clk. to Hon. Lewis F. Powell, Jr., assoc. justice U.S. Supreme Ct., 1979-80; with Farella, Braun & Martel, San Francisco; assoc. Providian Fin. Corp., San Francisco, 1980—85, ptnr., v.p., sec., 1985—93, gen. counsel, 1985—, vice chmn., 2001—. Symposium editor Stanford Law Rev., 1976-77. Mem. ABA (bus. law sect., real property probate and trust law sect.), State Bar Calif. (bus. law sect., real property law sect.), Bar Assn. San Francisco, Phi Beta Kappa, Order of Coif.

RICHEY, P. JEROME, lawyer, energy executive; b. Pitts., Feb. 23, 1949; BA, U. Pa., 1971, JD cum laude, 1974. Bar: Pa. 1974. Shareholder Buchanan Ingersoll, PC, Pitts.; v.p., gen. counsel CONSOL Energy Inc., Pitts., 2005—. Mem. ABA (individual rights and responsibilities in the workplace com. 1984—), Allegheny County Bar Assn. Office: CONSOL Energy 1800 Washington Rd Pittsburgh PA 15241 Office Phone: 412-831-4000.

RICHGELS, GLEN WILLIAM, mathematics professor; b. Madison, Wis., Aug. 5, 1949; s. Marion Urban and Eudelma Rosena (Bomkamp) R.; m. Sharon Rae Hart, Aug. 14, 1976; children: Amber Rae, Erin Ellen, Erik Glen. BA, U. Wis., 1971, MA, 1976, PhD, Cert. tchr. math./computer sci. Tchr. math. Woodstock (Ill.) Cmty. H.S., 1973-76; tchr. math. and computer sci. Beloit (Wis.) Pub. Schs., 1976-82, Baraboo (Wis.) Pub. Schs., 1982-93; prof. math. Bemidji (Minn.) State U., 1993—, dir. summer math. insts., 1993—. Computer cons. Custom Data Svcs., Baraboo, 1984—. Author: Individualized Planning Program, 1990. Named Regional Basketball Coach of Yr., Wis. Basketball Coaches Assn., 1984, Basketball MVP, U. Wis.-Madison, 1971. Mem. Nat. Coun. Tchrs. Math., Math. Assn. Am., Wis. Math. Coun. Avocations: computer programming, fishing, basketball, football. E-mail: grichgels@bemidjistate.edu.

RICHIE, BOYD LYNN, lawyer; b. Breckenridge, Tex., July 11, 1945; s. Bradie Eugene adn Billie June (Robinson) R.; m. Betty Zoe Furr, May 28, 1966; children: Christophber Robin, Tracy Lynn. BA in Polit. Sci. and History, Midwestern State U., 1967; JD, Tex. Tech. U., 1970. Bar: Tex. 1970, U.S. Dist. Ct. (no. dist.) Tex. 1975. Trial atty. Fed. Power Commn., Washington, 1970-71; assoc. John Bradshaw, Graham, Tex., 1971-72; sole practice Graham, 1972-77; dist. atty. 90th Jud. Dist., Graham, 1977-80; asst. dist. atty. Wichita County, Wichita Falls, Tex., 1980-81; ptnr. Neal, Neal, Richie & Hill, Graham, 1981—; atty. Young County, Tex., 1996—. Co-op, Inc, Bluegrove, Tex., 1979-83, Ft. Belknap Electric Coop., Inc., Olney, Tex., 1984—. Mem. State Bar Tex., Young County Bar Assn. (pres. 1972-73). Democrat. Episcopalian. Home: 1307 Roanoake Dr Graham TX 76450-4037 Office: Young County Courthouse Rm 102 PO Box 390 Graham TX 76450-0390 E-mail: ycatty@wf.net, brichie@wf.net.

RICHIE, JEROME PAUL, surgeon, educator; b. San Antonio, 1944; MD, U. Tex., 1969. Surg. intern UCLA, 1969—70, resident in gen. surgery, 1970—71, resident in urology, 1971—75, lectr. surg. urology, 1974—75; asst. clin. prof. U. Calif., San Diego, 1975—77; asst. prof. urology Harvard U., 1977—80, assoc. prof., 1980—86, prof., 1986—, Elliott C. Cutler prof. surgery, 1987—, chmn. program in urology, 1987—. Chief urol. Brigham and Women's Hosp., Boston, 1977—; cons. Dana Farber Cancer Ctr., Boston, 1977—. Lt. comdr. M.C. USN, 1975—77. Mem.: ACS, Am. Surg. Assn., Am. Soc. (Clin.) Oncology, Assn. Acad. Surgery, Am. Urol. Assn., Am. Assn. Gerito-Urinary Surgeons. Office: Brigham & Womens Hosp 45 Francis St # 3 Boston MA 02115-6105 E-mail: jrichie@parnters.org.

RICHIE, NICOLE, television personality; b. Berkeley, Calif., Sept. 21, 1981; d. Lionel and Brenda Harvey Richie. Co-star: (TV series) The Simple Life, 2003; The Simple Life 2: Road Trip, 2004; The Simple Life 3: Interns, 2005; The Simple Life 4: 'Til Death Do Us Part, 2006; The Simple Life 5: Goes to Camp, 2007; guest appearance Punk'd, 2003; Mad TV, 2004; Rock Me Baby, 2004; Six Feet Under, 2004; actor: (films) Kids in America, 2005; author: The Truth About Diamonds, 2005 (Publishers Weekly hardcover fiction bestseller list). Office: Creative Artists Agy 9830 Wilshire Blvd Beverly Hills CA 90212 *

RICHIE, RODNEY CHARLES, critical care and pulmonary medicine physician; b. Big Springs, Tex., Aug. 17, 1946; s. Howard Mouzon and Gloria (Hollingshead) R.; m. Sara Lee Dilley, July 13, 1968; children: Megan Kathryn, Paul Nathan. BA in Chemistry, So. Meth. U., 1968; MD cum laude, Baylor Coll., 1972. Diplomate in Internal Medicine, Pulmonary, Crit. Care and Ins. Medicine. Resident in medicine Baylor Affiliated Hosps., Houston, 1973-75, chief med. resident, 1975, fellow in pulmonary medicine, 1976-77; pres. Waco (Tex.) Lung Assocs., 1977—2007; assoc. clin. prof. cmty. medicine Heart of Tex. Cmty. Health Ctr./U. Tex. S.W. Med. Sch., 2004—. Med. dir. Tex. Life Ins., Waco, 1985—, Cmty. Hospice of Waco, 1996—, EMSI, Waco, Tex., 1997—. Chmn. med. staff Hillcrest Bapt. Med. Ctr., Waco, 1993; chmn. bd. dirs. GH Pape Found., Waco, 1993. Fellow: ACP, Am. Coll. Chest Physicians; mem.: AMA, Am. Thoracic Soc., Am. Acad. Internal Medicine (del. to AMA), Tex. Club Internists. Episcopalian. Avocations: skiing, writing, reading. Home: 3509 Lake Heights Dr Waco TX 76708-1005 Office: Waco Med Group 7125 New Sanger Rd Ste B Waco TX 76712 Office Phone: 254-741-1688. E-mail: rcrichie@earthlink.net.

RICHIERI, KENNETH A., lawyer, publishing executive; b. Jersey City, June 5, 1951; m. Kathryn Obler; children: Julia, Camille, Peter. AB, Brown U., 1973; JD cum laude, Harvard U., 1976. Bar: 1977. Assoc. Cahill Gordon & Reindel, 1976—82; legal counsel The NY Times Co., NYC, 1983—89, sr. counsel, 1989—93, asst. gen. counsel, 1993—2001, dep. gen. counsel, 2001—05, v.p., 2005—, gen. counsel, 2006—, NY Times Digital, 1999—2004. Office: The NY Times Co 229 W 43rd St New York NY 10036 *

RICHLAND, KENT LEWIS, lawyer; b. Nov. 1946; m. Barbara Sue Circle, 1969; children: Justin Blake, Sara Circle. AB, U. Calif., Berkeley, 1968; JD, UCLA, 1971. Bar: Calif. 1972, US Supreme Ct. 1975, US Ct. Appeals (9th cir.) 1972, US Dist. Ct. (ctrl. dist.) Calif. 1972. Supervising dep. atty. gen. Calif. State, 1972—76; supervising atty. for Calif. State Pub. Defender, 1976—78; sr. rsch. atty. to Presiding Justice Otto M. Kaus Calif. Ct. Appeals, 1978—79; atty. Horvitz & Greines, 1980—83; founding mem. Greines, Martin, Stein & Richland LLP, LA, 1983—. Trustee state appellate jud. evaluation com., 1998—2000; chair appellate cts. com., 1985—88, Calif. jud. sys. com., 1988—90, jud. appts. com., 2001—03; adj. prof. law Southwestern Sch. Law, 1986—87; guest lectr. U. So. Calif. Law Ctr., UCLA Sch. Law, U. West LA Sch. Law. Bd. editors LA Bar Jour. and LA Lawyer, 1973—78, articles editor and mng. editor, 1977—78, bd. advisors Hastings Constl. Law Quarterly, 1978—88; contbr. articles to law jours. Fellow: Am. Acad. Appellate Lawyers; mem.: ABA (co-chair Nat. Inst. on Med. Malpractice 1989—90, mem. appellate adv. com. 2001—, mem. torts and ins. practice sect. appellate advocacy com.), Calif. Judicial Coun., LA County Bar Assn. (trustee 1998—2000), Calif. Acad. Appellate Lawyers (pres. 1995—96), Calif. Supreme Ct. Hist. Soc. (bd. dirs. 1998—, pres. 1999—2005). Achievements include successful arguing Marshall versus Marshall (Anna Nicole Smith case) in the United States Supreme Court, 2006. Office: Greines, Martin, Stein & Richland LLP Ste 375 5700 Wilshire Blvd Los Angeles CA 90036-3697 Office Phone: 310-859-7811. Office Fax: 310-276-5261. Business E-Mail: krichland@gmsr.com.

RICHLEN, SCOTT LANE, federal government program administrator; b. Ames, Iowa, July 23, 1949; s. Ellsworth Mark and Betty Jane (Wegner) R.; m. Deborah Lou Dick, Feb. 6, 1971; children: Mindy Lou, Gwendolyn Anne. BSME, Mont. State U., 1972; M.Engring. in Mech. Engring., U. Idaho, 1982; grad. exec. potential program, Office Pers. Mgmt., 1995. Assoc. engr. Thiokol Chem. Corp., Brigham City, Utah, 1973-75; rsch. engr. EG&G Idaho, Inc., Idaho Falls, 1975-79, sr. program specialist, 1979-84; program mgr. indsl. heat pumps U.S. Dept. Energy, Washington, 1984-87, program mgr. advanced heat exchangers, 1984-94, program mgr. continuous fiber ceramic composites, 1990-95, team leader steel industry R&D, 1995-99, integrated delivery sys. devel. team, 1998-99, dir. Office Indsl. Techs., 2000—03, team leader advanced process sys., 2003—05; supr. Indsl. Tech. Program, 2005—. Lectr. profl. ext. U. Wis., Madison, 1982—83; lectr. Nat. Air & Space Mus., Smithsonian Instn., Washington, 2005—06. Author: (reference text) ASM, Engineered Materials, 1992, Ceramics Information Analysis Center/American Ceramic Society Handbook on Continuous Fiber Reinforced Ceramic Matrix Composites, 1993; editor (conf. procs.) Industrial Heat Exchangers, 1985. Vol. Martha's Table, Washington, 1986—; v.p. Aid Assn for Lutherans, Br. 2792, Annandale, Va., 1988-92. Mem. Precision Aerobatics Model Pilots Assn., No. Va. Control-line Assn. (pres. 1987-89, 91-92, 2000-04, 2007-, youth com. chmn. 2005-06), Mont. State Soc. Mont. State U. Alumni Assn. (life). Achievements include patents for corrosive resistant heat exchanger. Avocations: woodworking, martial arts, control-line model airplanes, gardening, readings in psychology, history and law. Office: US Dept Energy 1000 Independence Ave SW Washington DC 20585-0001

RICHLOVSKY, THOMAS ANDREW, bank executive; b. Cleve., July 26, 1951; s. Simon Andrew and Arline Miriam (Uresh) R.; m. Rhonda Marie Dolens, June 30, 1973; children: Paul, Abbey, Jill. BBA in Acctg., Cleve. State U.; grad., Stonier Grad. Sch. Banking. CPA. Audit supr. Ernst & Whinney, Cleve., 1973-78; v.p., treas. Nat. City Corp., Cleve., 1978, sr. v.p., treas. Bd. dirs. Banic Adminstrn. Inst., Cleve., 1982-84. Treas. Urban Cmty. Sch., Cleve., 1974, bd. trustees; mem. vis. com. Cleve. State U., Coll. Bus., 1985-86.; mem. fin. com. Magnificat HS; bd. dirs., treas. Jesuit Retreat House. Mem. AICPA, Fin. Execs. Inst., Nat. Investor Rels. Inst. (bd. dirs. Cleve. chpt.), Bank Adminstrn. Inst., Ohio Soc. CPAs, Greater Cleve. Growth Assn. Roman Catholic. Avocation: running. Office: Nat City Corp Nat City Ctr 1900 E 9th St Cleveland OH 44114-3484 Office Phone: 216-222-2000. *

RICHMAN, ALAN, magazine editor, educator; b. Bronx, NY, Nov. 12, 1939; s. Louis and Sonia (Carity) R.; m. Kelli Shor, June 21, 1964; children: Lincoln Seth Shor, Matthew Mackenzie Shor. BA, Hunter Coll., 1960. Reporter Leader-Observer, NYC, 1960-61; asst. editor Modern Tire Dealer, NYC, 1962-64; assoc. editor ASTA Travel News, NYC, 1964-65; pub. rels. rep. M.J. Jacobs, Inc., NYC, 1965-66; mng. editor Modern Floor Coverings, NYC, 1966-68; editor Bank Systems & Equipment, NYC, 1968-79, Health Care Product News, NYC, 1976; from assoc. pub. to pub. Bank Systems & Equipment, NYC, 1969-79; editorial dir. Nat. Jeweler, NYC, 1979-81; editor Health Foods Bus.; editorial dir. Army/Navy Store and Outdoor Merchandiser, 1981-88, The Pet Dealer, 1983-88; editor Cabinet Mfg. and Fabricating KBC Publs., 1988-94; comm. cons., freelance writer Alan Richman Comm. Svcs., 2007—. Program dir. Cabinet Mfg. Fair, 1989-94; adj. faculty NYU, 1989—, Brookdale C.C., 1992—, Bergen County C.C., 1994—. Exec. editor: Kitchen and Bath Design News, 1992-93; editor-in-chief Wood Digest, PTN Pub. Co., 1992-94; editor: Whole Foods, 1994-2007; author: Czechoslovakia in Pictures, 1969, A Book on the Chair, 1968. With AUS, 1961-62. Recipient Jesse H. Neal certificate merit Am. Bus. Press, 1973.

RICHMAN, DAVID PAUL, neurologist, educator, researcher; b. Boston, June 9, 1943; s. Harry S. and Anne (Goodkin) R.; m. Carol Mae von Bastian, Aug. 31, 1969; children: Sarah Ann, Jacob Charles. AB, Princeton U., 1965; MD, Johns Hopkins U., 1969. Diplomate Am. Bd. Psychiatry and Neurology. Intern, then asst. resident in medicine Albert Einstein Coll. Medicine, NYC, 1969-71; resident in neurology Mass. Gen. Hosp., Boston, 1971-73, chief resident, 1973-74; instr. neurology Harvard U. Med. Sch., Boston, 1975-76; asst. prof. neurology U. Chgo., 1976-80, assoc. prof., 1981-85, prof., 1985-91, Straus prof. neurol. Scis., 1988-91; prof. neurology U. Calif., Davis, 1991—, chmn. dept., 1991-97. Mem. com. Nat. Inst. Aging, NIH, 1984-85, mem. immunogical scis. study sect., 1986-90. Mem. AAAS, Am. Assn. Immunologists, Am. Acad. Neurology, Am. Neurol. Assn., Phi Beta Kappa, Sigma Xi. Office: U Calif Davis Dept Neurology 1515 Newton Ct Davis CA 95616-4859 Office Phone: 530-752-5013. Business E-Mail: dprichman@ucdavis.edu.

RICHMAN, DOUGLAS DANIEL, medical virologist, educator, internist; b. NYC, Feb. 15, 1943; s. Daniel Powell and Louise Kohnstamm (Woolf) R.; m. Eva Acquino, June 21, 1965; children: Sara, Matthew. AB cum laude, Dartmouth Coll., 1965; MD, Stanford U., 1970. Diplomate Am. Bd. Internal Medicine, Am. Bd. Infectious Diseases, Am. Bd. Med. Examiners. Intern Stanford Med. Sch., Calif., 1970—71, resident, 1971—72; rsch. assoc. LID/NIAID NIH, Bethesda, Md., 1972—75; fellow Beth Israel and Children's Hosps., Harvard Med. Ctr., Boston, 1975—76; asst. prof. depts. pathology and medicine U. Calif., San Diego, 1976—82, assoc. prof., 1982—88, prof., 1988—, Florence Seeley Riford chair in AIDS rsch., 2004—. Vis. prof. Hubei Med. Coll., Wuhan, People's Republic of China, 1987, Tokyo Med. and Dental U., Kumamoto U. Sch. Medicine, Inst. for Virus Rsch. at Kyoto U., St. Marianna U., Tokyo, Inst. Med. Rsch., Tokyo, Fukishima Prefecture Med. Sch., Japan, 1990; vis. fellow Clare Hall, U. Cambridge, 1984-85; mem. U. Calif. Pres.'s Cancer Rsch. Coord. Com., 1984-89, NIH AIDS Rsch. Rev. Com., 1987-90; cons. FDA Ctr. for Drugs and Biologics, 1986-89; dir. U. Calif.-San Diego Ctr. for AIDS Rsch., AIDS Rsch. Inst. Co-editor: Clin. Virology, —; mem. editl. bd.: Antimicrobial Agts. and Chemotherapy, 1987—, Jour. of AIDS, 1988—, Antiviral Agts., 1988—, AIDS, 1990—, AIDS Alert, 1990—, Antiviral Drug Resistance, 1996—, Virology, 1997—, others; contbr. more than 520 articles to profl. jours. Recipient Lowell Rantz award in infectious diseases, 1970, AMA Physicians Recognition award, 1976, 79, 82, 85, 88, William S. Middleton award Dept. Vet. Affairs, 2002; John Simon Guggenheim fellow, 1984. Fellow: ACP, AAAS, We. Assn. Physicians, Am. Assn. Physicians, Infectious Diseases Soc. Am.; mem.: Am. Clin. and Climatologic Assn., VA Soc. for Physicians in Infectious Diseases, Internat. AIDS Soc., Internat. Soc. Antiviral Rsch., Am. Soc. for Virology, Am. Fedn. for Clin. Rsch., Am. Soc. for Microbiology. Office: U Calif San Diego Dept Pathology & Medicine 9500 Gilman Dr La Jolla CA 92093-0679

RICHMAN, HAROLD ALAN, social welfare policy educator; b. Chgo., May 15, 1937; s. Leon H. and Rebecca (Klieman) R.; m. Marlene M. Forland, Apr. 25, 1965; children: Andrew, Robert. AB, Harvard U., 1959; MA, U. Chgo., 1961, PhD, 1969. Asst. prof., dir. Ctr. for Study Welfare Policy, Sch. Social Svc., U. Chgo., 1967-69, dean, prof. social welfare policy, 1969-78, Hermon Dunlap Smith prof., 1978—, dir. of ctr., 1978-81, dir. Children's Policy Rsch. Project, 1978-84, dir. Chapin Hall Ctr. for Children, 1985—2002, faculty assoc. Chapin Hall Ctr. for Children, 2002—, chmn. univ. com. on pub. policy studies, 1974-77. Chmn. Univ. Lab. Schs., 1985-88; cons. to gov. State of Ill., Edna McConnell Clark Found., 1984-95, Lilly Endowment, 1987-90, Ford Found., 1987-89; co-chair Aspen Roundtable on Cmty. Change, 1993—. Chmn. editl. bd. Social Svcs. Rev., 1970-79; contbr. articles to profl. jours. Bd. dirs. Chgo. Com. Fgn. and Domestic Policy, 1969-78, S.E. Chgo. Commn., 1970—, Jewish Fedn. Met. Chgo., 1970-75, Ill. Facilities Fund, 1989-94, Welfare Coun. Met. Chgo., 1970-72, Erikson Inst. Early Childhood Edn., 1972-79, Nat. Urban Coalition, 1975-86, Family Focus, 1980-89, Jewish Coun. Urban Affairs, 1982-87, Ctr. for Study Social Policy, 1983-92, chmn., 2003—; bd. dirs. Nat. Family Resource Coalition, 1990-93, Pub./Pvt. Ventures, 1992-98, Benton Found., 1994-2004; bd. dirs. Israel Ctr. on Children, chmn., 1995-04; bd. dirs. Info. and Rsch Ctr., Amman, Jordan, 2001—, Michael Reese Health Trust, 2002—, bd. dirs. U. Capetown Childen's Inst., dep. chair, 2002—; mem. adv bd. John Gardner Ctr., Stanford U., 2003—; bd. dirs. Brookdale Inst., Jerusalem, 2004—, Interfaith Youth Core, 2005—, SEED Found., 2005-, Bull. Atomic Scientists, 2006—. White House fellow, Washington, 1965-66; recipient Disting. Svc. citation U.S. Dept. Health, Edn. & Welfare, 1970, Quantrell award U. Chgo., 1990. Mem. White House Fellows Assn. (v.p. 1976-77), Am. Pub. Welfare Assn. (bd. dirs. 1989-92). Home: 5715 S Dorchester Ave Chicago IL 60637-1726 Office: U Chgo Chapin Hall Ctr for Children 1313 E 60th St Chicago IL 60637-2830 Office Phone: 773-256-5176. Business E-Mail: hrichman@chapinhall.org.

RICHMAN, JOEL ESER, lawyer, arbitrator, mediator; b. Brockton, Mass., Feb. 17, 1947; s. Nathan and Ruth Miriam (Bick) R.; m. Elaine R. Thompson, Aug. 21, 1987; children: Shawn Jonah, Jesse Ray, Eva Rose. BA in Psychology, Grinnell Coll., 1969; JD, Boston U., 1975. Bar: Mass. 1975, U.S. Dist. Ct. Mass. 1977, U.S. Supreme Ct. 1980, U.S. Ct. Appeals (1st cir.) 1982, Hawaii 1985, U.S. Dist. Ct. Hawaii 1987. Law clk. Richman & Perenyi, Brockton, Mass., 1973-75, atty., 1975-77; pvt. practice Provincetown, Mass., 1977-82, Paia, Hawaii, 1985—. Pres. Jewish Congregation Maui (Hawaii), 1989-97, dir. 1997-; bd. dirs., 1984-89; bd. dirs. Pacific Primate Ctr., 1991, pres., 1994. Mem.: Maui Kitesurfing Cmty. (pres. 2006—). Avocations: windsurfing, youth soccer, t'ai chi, kite surfing. Office: PO Box 791539 Paia HI 96779-0046 Office Phone: 808-572-6293. Business E-Mail: jer@haikulaw.com.

RICHMAN, JOHN MARSHALL, lawyer, food products executive; b. NYC, Nov. 9, 1927; s. Arthur and Madeleine (Marshall) R.; m. Priscilla Frary, Sept. 3, 1951; children: Catherine Richman Wallace, Diana H. BA, Yale U., 1949; LLB, Harvard U., 1952. Bar: N.Y. 1953, Ill. 1973. Assoc. Leve, Hecht, Hadfield & McAlpin, NYC, 1952-54; mem. law dept. Kraft, Inc., Glenview, Ill., 1954-63, gen. counsel Sealtest Foods div., 1963-67, asst. gen. counsel, 1967-70, v.p., gen. counsel, 1970-73, sr. v.p., gen. counsel, 1973-75, sr. v.p. adminstrn., gen. counsel, 1975-79, chmn. bd., chief exec. officer, 1979, Dart & Kraft, Inc. (name changed to Kraft, Inc. 1986), Glenview, 1980; chmn. Kraft Gen. Foods, Glenview, Ill., 1988-89; counsel Wachtell, Lipton, Rosen & Katz, Chgo., 1990-98. Life bd. dirs. Evanston Northwestern Healthcare. Life trustee Chgo. Symphony Orch., Northwestern U.; bd. dirs. Chgo. Coun. Global Affairs, Lyric Opera Chgo., Norton Mus. Art, West Palm Beach. Fla. Mem. Coun. Ret. Chief Exec., Comml. Club, Chgo. Club, Casino Club (Chgo.), Westmoreland Country Club (Wilmette, Ill.), Old Elm Club (Highland Park, Ill.), Lost Tree Club (N. Palm Beach, Fla.), Racquet Club of Chgo. Congregationalist. Office: 179 E Lake Shore Dr Chicago IL 60611-1306 E-mail: johnrichman@att.net.

RICHMAN, JOSEPH HERBERT, retired public health service officer; b. Balt., Aug. 13, 1941; s. Samuel and Beatrice Richman. BS, Howard U., 1962, MD, 1966; MPH, Johns Hopkins U., 1974. Intern Maimonides Med. Ctr., Bklyn., 1966-67; resident in pediat. Sinai Hosp. of Balt., 1967-69; chief sch. health P.G. Health Dept. of Md., Cheverly, Md., 1972-75; dir. area health svcs. Montgomery County Health Dept., Bethesda, Md., 1975-82; county chief pub. health physician State of Del., Dover, 1982-99; ret., 2000. Capt. USAF, 1969—71. Recipient Outstanding Svc. award, Delaware Health and Soc. Svc., 1999. Fellow Am. Acad. Pediatrics (emeritus), Am. Coll. Preventive Medicine; mem. AMA, Masons, Phi Beta Kappa. Democrat. Jewish. Avocations: golf, photography. Home: PO Box 880852 Boca Raton FL 33488-0852 Home Phone: 561-482-3154. Personal E-mail: joefortsedgwick@aol.com.

RICHMAN, KEITH, communications executive; b. 1973; married. BA in Internat. Policy Studies, MA in Internat. Policy Studies, Stanford. Dir., Corp. Planning Walt Disney Co.; mgr. Excite, Classifieds2000; dir., Bus. Devel. Billpoint Inc.; co-founder, CEO Break.com. Named one of 40 Executives Under 40, Multichannel News, 2006. Office: Break.com 311 N Robertson Blvd Ste 917 Beverly Hills CA 90211

RICHMAN, LAWRENCE I., lawyer; b. Chgo., Aug. 8, 1954; s. Jack and Reggie (Heller) R. BA magna cum laude, Columbia U., 1974; JD, U. Chgo., 1977. Bar: Ill. 1977. Atty. McDermott Will & Emery, Chgo., 1977-80, Neal Gerber & Eisenberg, Chgo., 1980—. Named one of Top 100 Attys., Worth mag., 2006. Mem. ABA (generation shipping transfer tax com. 1990, recipient cert. of appreciation 1989), Chgo. Bar Assn. (chmn. trust law com. 1988-89), Am. Technion Soc. (bd. dirs. 1987), Phi Beta Kappa. Avocation: skiing. Office: Neal Gerber & Eisenberg LLP 2 N LaSalle St Ste 2200 Chicago IL 60602-3801 Office Phone: 312-269-8070. Office Fax: 312-750-6460. E-mail: lrichman@ngelaw.com.

RICHMAN, MARC HERBERT, engineer, forensic specialist, educator; b. Boston, Oct. 14, 1936; s. Samuel and Janet (Gordon) R.; m. Ann Raeshel Yoffa, Aug. 31, 1963. BS, MIT, 1957, ScD, 1963; MA, Brown U., 1967. Registered profl. engr., Conn., Mass., R.I.; cert. forensic examiner. Cons. engr., 1957—; engr. shipbldg. div. Bethlehem Steel Corp., Quincy, Mass., 1957; instr. metallurgy MIT, Cambridge, 1957-60, research asst. dept. metallurgy, 1960-63; instr. metallurgy div. univ. extension Commonwealth of Mass., 1958-62; asst. prof. engring. Brown U., Providence, 1963-67, assoc. prof., 1967-70, prof., 1970-98, dir. central electron microscopy facility Materials Research program, 1971-86, dir. undergrad. program in engring., 1991-98; prof. emeritus, 1998—; pres. Ednl. Aids of Newton Inc., Providence, 1968-71, Marc H. Richman Inc., Providence, 1981—. Guest scientist Franklin Inst., Phila., 1959; vis. prof. U. R.I., Kingston, 1970-71; biophysicist dept. medicine Miriam Hosp., Providence, 1974-87; biogengr. dept. orthopaedics R.I. Hosp., 1979-93; prof. emeritus Brown U., Providence, 1998—. Author: Introduction to Science of Metals, 1967; also articles; editor Soviet Physics: Crystallography, 1970-94; mem. editl. adv. bd. Materials Characterization, 1970—98, Jour. Forensic Engring., 1985-88. Served to maj. Ordnance Corps, U.S. Army, 1963. Recipient Engr. of Yr. award R.I. Soc. Profl. Engrs., 1993. Fellow Nat. Acad. Forensic Engrs. (cert.), Am. Coll. Forensic Examiners (cert.), Am. Inst. Chemists, Inst. Materials (U.K.); mem. ASCE, AIME, NSPE, ASEE (Outstanding Young Faculty award 1969), NAFE (bd. cert. diplomate in forensic engring.), Am. Soc. Metals (sec.-treas. 1965-68, chmn. R.I. chpt. 1968-69, Albert Sauveur Meml. award 1968, 69), Providence Engring. Soc. (pres. 1991-92, Freeman award for engring. achievement 1989), B'nai B'rith, Sigma Xi, Tau Beta Pi. Home: 291 Cole Ave Providence RI 02906-3452 Office: One Richmond Sq Providence RI 02906 Office Phone: 401-751-9656. Personal E-mail: mhrichman@aol.com.

RICHMAN, MARTIN FRANKLIN, lawyer; b. Newark, Feb. 23, 1930; s. Samuel L. and Betty E. (Goldstein) R.; stepson Doris (Bloom) R.; m. Florence E. Reif, May 6, 1962; children— Judith, Andrew. BA magna cum laude, St. Lawrence U., 1950; LL.B. magna cum laude, Harvard U., 1953. Bar: N.Y. 1953. Law clk. to Judge Calvert Magruder and Chief Justice Earl Warren, 1955-57; assoc., mem. firm Lord Day & Lord, Barrett Smith (and predecessors), NYC, 1957-66, 69-94; of counsel Kirkpatrick & Lockhart Preston Gates Ellis LLP, NYC, 1994—; dep. asst. atty. gen. Office Legal Counsel, Dept. Justice, Washington, 1966-69. Public mem. Adminstrv. Conf. U.S., 1970-76; bd. dirs. Community Action for Legal Services, 1977-80 Trustee St. Lawrence U., 1979-95, trustee emeritus, 1995—, vice chmn. bd., 1988-95; bd. dirs. Friends of Law Libr. of Congress, 1992-99. Recipient Alumni citation St. Lawrence U., 1972 Fellow Am. Bar Found., N.Y. Bar Found.; mem. ABA (chmn. sect. adminstrv. law 1983-84), N.Y. State Bar Assn. (ho. of dels. 1981-84), Assn. of Bar of City of N.Y. (sec. and mem. exec. com. 1976-79, chmn. com. fed. legislation 1972-75, com. lawyer's pro bono obligations 1977-81), Am. Law Inst. Office: Kirkpatrick & Lockhart Preston Gates Ellis LLP 599 Lexington Ave New York NY 10022-6030 Office Phone: 212-536-3945. E-mail: martin.richman@klgates.com.

RICHMAN, MICHAEL PAUL, lawyer; b. New Rochelle, NY, Mar. 12, 1953; m. Elizabeth Fried, July 10, 1977; children: Joseph, Peter. AB, Vassar Coll., 1975; JD, Columbia U., NYC, 1979. Bar: DC 1979, US Dist. Ct. DC 1980, US Ct. Appeals (DC cir.) 1980, NY 1985, US Ct. Appeals (so. and ea. dist.) NY 1985, US Ct. Appeals (2d cir.) 1989, US Ct. Appeals (9th cir.) 1992, US Dist. Ct. Ariz. 1995, US Dist. Ct. (no. dist.) Ill. 1996, US Dist. Ct. (we. dist.) Mich. 1998. Assoc. Covington & Burlng, Washington, 1979-84, Shoeman, Marsh, Updike & Welt, NYC, 1984-86, Rosenman & Colin, NYC, 1986-89, Mayer, Brown & Platt, NYC, 1989-92, partner, 1993—2006, Foley & Lardner LLP, NYC, 2006—. Dir. Am. Bankruptcy Inst., Alexandria, Va., 1996—, mem. exec. com., 2001-, pres., 2004-05, founding mem. Indubitable Equivalents Contbg. editor: Am. Bankruptcy Inst. Jour.; columnist Daily Bankruptcy Review. Named NY Super Lawyer, Law & Politics Media, Inc., 2006; named one of 12 Outstanding Restructuring Lawyers, Turnarounds & Workouts, 2004. Mem. ABA, NY State Bar Assn., Assn. of Bar City of NY Avocations: music, running, tennis. Home: 17 Eck Pl New Rochelle NY 10804-4605 Office: Foley & Lardner LLP 90 Park Ave New York NY 10016 *

RICHMAN, MURRAY, lawyer; b. Bronx, NY, Oct. 3, 1937; children from previous marriage: Stacey Gayle, Nicole; m. Rene Arias, Sept. 22, 2002. BA, CCNY, 1959; JD, N.Y. Law Sch., 1964. Bar: U.S. Dist. Ct. (so. dist.) NY 1969, U.S. Dist. Ct. (ea. dist.) NY 1969, U.S. Ct. Internat. Trade 1982, U.S. tax Ct. 1979, U.S. Ct. Appeals (2d cir.) 1975, U.S. Supreme Ct. Sole practice, Bronx, 1964—. Numerous TV appearances. Recipient Humanitarian award Black Econ. Survival Assn., 1976, Honor award Borough Pres. Bronx County, 1972, Lawyer of Yr. award United Jewish Appeal, 1985, Man of Yr. award Black Bar ASsn., 2005, Thurgood Marshall award, 2005; named Man of Yr., Am. Jewish Congress, 1972. Mem. Bronx Bar Assn. (bd. dirs.), Bronx Criminal Bar Assn. (v.p., Humanitarian award 1981), NY Assn. Criminal Def. Lawyers, B'nai B'rith. Subject of profile New Yorker mag., 2001; subject of book A Cold Case by Philip Gurevich; subject of other articles. Office: 2027 Williamsbridge Rd Bronx NY 10461-1605 Office Phone: 718-892-8588. Personal E-mail: mrichman_mr@msn.com.

RICHMAN, PAUL, semiconductor industry executive, educator; b. NYC, Nov. 17, 1942; s. Harry and Molly (Armel) Richman; m. Ellen Margaret Kleiman, July 3, 1966; children: Lee Stuart, Alyson Michelle, Daniel Noah. BSEE, MIT, 1963; MSEE, Columbia U., 1964. V.p. R & D Standard Microsystems Corp., Hauppauge, NY, 1971-76, pres., 1976-81, pres., chief exec. officer, 1981-83, pres., chmn. bd., chief exec. officer, 1983-2000; co-founder Toyo Microsystems Corp., Tokyo, 1987—. Pres Consortium Technology Licensing Ltd, Nissequogue, NY, 1994—99, chmn bd dirs, CEO, 1999—; vis prof elec eng SUNY, Stony Brook, 1976—85; mem vis comt elec eng and computer sci dept MIT, 1996—; adj. prof. elec. engring. CUNY, 1973—75; bd. dirs. Wi-LAN, Inc., Ottawa, Canada, 2007—. Author: (book) Characteristics and Operation of MOS Field Effect Devices, 1967, MOS Field Effect Transistors and Integrated Circuits, 1974. Named one of 30 Most Important Contributors in the World to Devel Integrated Circuit Technology, Elec Eng Times/Elec Buyer's News/VLSI Sys Design, 1988; recipient Ann Award Achievement in Electronics, Electronics Mag, 1978. Fellow: IEEE (Award for Outstanding Technical Achievement 1980, Third Millennium Medal 2000). Achievements include invention of COPLAMOS technology. Personal E-mail: richman.paul@gmail.com. E-mail: paul_consortium@verizon.net.

RICHMAN, PETER, electronics executive; b. NYC, Nov. 7, 1927; s. Emil H. and Janet (Seidler) R.; m. Vivian Hoffman, July 29, 1951; children: Meredith, Jeremy. BS, MIT, 1946; MS, NYU, 1953. Asst. chief engr. Reeves Instrument Corp., Garden City, NY, 1948-58; chief engr. Epsco, Inc., Cambridge, Mass., 1959-60; v.p., co-founder Rotek Instrument Corp., Watertown, Mass., 1960-64; v.p. Weston-Rotek, Lexington, Mass., 1964-67; cons. electronics engr. Lexington, 1967—. Bd. dirs. Thermo Voltek Corp, Thermo Sentron Corp.; founder, pres. KeyTek Instrument Corp., 1975-93; mem. NRC/NAS/Nat. Acad. Engring. Evaluation Panel for electricity divsn. Nat. Bur. Standards; mem. sci. adv. groups for several indsl. and sci. orgns. Patentee in precision electronic instrumentation; pioneer in precision dc and audio-frequency measurements, surge electrostatic discharge generation and electrostatic discharge measurements; author: The Insider's Guide to Growing a Small Business, 1996; contbr. articles to profl. jours. Mem. bd. overseers Boston Mus. Sci. Fellow IEEE; mem. Electromagnetics Acad., Instrument Soc. Am. (sr.), Sigma Xi, Tau Beta Pi.

RICHMAN, PETER MARK, actor, painter, film producer; b. Phila., Apr. 16, 1927; s. Benjamin and Yetta Dora (Peck) Richman; m. Theodora Helen Landess, May 10, 1953; children: Howard Bennett, Kelly Allyn, Lucas Dion, Orien, Roger Lloyd. BS in Pharmacy, U. of the Scis., 1951; student of Lee Strasberg, NYC, 1952-54; mem., Actors' Studio, NYC, 1954—. Registered pharmacist Pa., NY. Actor: (plays), 1946—51, Have I Got a Girl for You, 1963, Ctr. Theater Group, 1965, Grove Theater, 1952, Westchester Playhouse, 1953, Drury Ln., 1957, Strand, 1957, Capri, 1959, Ongonquit Playhouse, 1955—62, 1955, 1953—55, 1955, 1962, 1955—62, Phila. Playhouse in Pk., 1962—63; (Broadway plays) End as a Man, 1953, Hatful of Rain, 1956—57, Masquerade, 1959; (plays) End as a Man, 1953, The Dybbuk, 1954, The Zoo Story, 1960—61, Rainmaker, Private Lives, Angel Street, Arms and the Man, Rose Tattoo, Liliorn, Funny Girl, Owl and the Pussycat, Hold Me, Equus, Night of the Iguana, Blithe Spirit, Twelve Angry Men, 1985, Babes in Toyland, 1988, Ray Bradbury's Next in Line, 1992, numerous others, stage, radio, TV, 1948—65; writer, performer: 4 Faces, 1995 (Drama-Logue Critics Performance award, 1996), 1996; The Actors Studio, 1996; others; actor: 7 Circles of Life: A Subud Cantata, 1997, 2005, A Lincoln Portrait, 2004; (films) Friendly Persuasion, 1956, The Strange One, 1956, Black Orchid, 1958, The Dark Intruder, 1965, Agent for HARM, 1965, For Singles Only, 1967, Judgement Day (formerly The Third Hand), 1988, Friday the 13th, Part 8: Jason Takes Manhattan, 1989, Naked Gun 2 1/2: The Smell of Fear, 1991, Pool Hall Junkies, 2003; prodr., writer, actor: 4 Faces, 2000; actor: (TV series) Cain's Hundred, 1961—62, David Chapter III, 1966, Longstreet, 1971—72, Three's Company, 1978—79, Heroes of the Bible, 1979, Dynasty, 1981—84, Santa Barbara, 1984, Defenders of the Earth, 1986, My Secret Summer (formerly Mystery of the Keys), 1991; guest actor: Hotel; Dallas; Hart to Hart; Fantasy Island; Murder She Wrote; Nothing Sacred; Three's Company; Knight Rider; Star Trek: The Next Generation; Matlock; Beverly Hills 90210; others; actor: (TV films) House on Greenapple Road, 1968, McCloud, 1969, Yuma, 1970, Nightmare at 43 Hillcrest, 1974, Mallory, 1975, The Islander, 1978, Greatest Heroes of the Bible, 1979, Blind Ambition, 1979, The PSI Factor, 1981, Dynasty, 1981, Dempsey, 1983, City Killer, 1984, Bonanza: The Next Generation, 1988; one-man shows include Am. Masters Gallery, LA, 1967, Orlando Gallery, 1966, McKenzie Gallery, 1969, 1973, Hopkins Gallery, 1971, Goldfield Gallery, 1979, Galerie des Stars, 1968, Crocker Mus., Sacramento, 1967, Parkhurst

Gallery, Seal Beach, Calif., 1991, Henley Gallery, Chapman U., Orange, Calif, 1996, exhibited in group shows at Bednarz Gallery, LA, 1968, Dohan Gallery, 1966, Celebrity Art Exhibits, 1964—65; author: (plays) Heavy, Heavy What Hangs Over?, 1971, A Medal for Murray, 1991, 4 Faces, 1995 (Commendation award Prism Film Festival, 2002); dir.: (plays) Apple of His Eyes, 1954, Glass Menagerie, 1954; author: Hollander's Deal, 2000, The Rebirth of Ira Masters, 2001; performer: (albums) Twilight Zone, 2005. Trustee Motion Picture and TV Fund. With USN, 1945—46. Recipient Silver medallion, Motion Picture TV Fund, 1990, Sybil Brand Humanitarian award, Jeffrey Found., 1990, Spl. award, 1997, Golde Halo Eagle award, So. Calif. Motion Picture Coun., 1997, Lifetime Achievement award, 2004. Mem.: AFTRA, SAG, Acad. TV Arts and Scis., Acad. Motion Picture Arts and Scis., Assn. Can. TV and Radio Artists, Actors Equity Assn. Office: 4 Faces Prodns 19528 Ventura Blvd Ste 385 Tarzana CA 91356 Office Phone: 818-623-6476. Personal E-mail: office@petermarkrichman.com. *I have always been grateful to be able to work in more than one medium. In a way they are all related, each solidifying and nurturing the other. I have a strong belief in God...and spiritual values. This, along with my marriage, children, and family life, has helped me enormously to express my own individuality as an artist.*

RICHMAN, SOPHIA, psychologist; b. Lwow, Poland, Jan. 28, 1941; arrived in US, 1951; d. Leon and Dorothy Weiss Richman; m. Spyros D. Orfanos, Nov. 25, 1976; 1 child, Lina Joanna Orfanos. BA in Psychology, CCNY, 1962, MS in Psychol. Svcs., 1965; PhD in Psychology, NYU, 1970, cert. in psychoanalysis, 1975. Lic. psychologist N.Y., 1972, N.J., 1993, diplomate in psychoanalysis Am. Bd. Profl. Psychology. Testing asst. Hunter Coll., NYC, 1965—68; rsch. assoc. Harvard U., Boston, 1967—68; counselor to students NYU, NYC, 1968—72; clin. psychologist SS Rockaway (N.Y.) Mental Health, 1972—74, Student Ctr. Roosevelt Hosp., NYC, 1974—75; cons. psychologist Diocese of Bklyn., 1974—80; pvt. practice psychotherapy and psychoanalysis NY, 1972—, NJ, 1991—93. Adj. prof. Fordham U., Baruch Coll., NYC, 1986, NYC, 87; supervising analyst ICP, CCAPS, NY, 1986—, NJ, 1995—; supr. postdoctoral program NYU, NY, 2003—. One-woman shows include Cornelia St. Café, 2005; author: A Wolf in the Attic: The Legacy of a Hidden Child of the Holocaust, 2002; contbr. articles to profl. jours., chapters to books. Holocaust testimony Fortunoff Video Archive, Yale U., Conn., 1990, Survivors of the Shoah Visual History Found., LA, 1998; pub. edn. spkr. on the holocaust various elem. and middle schs. NJ, 1994—95. Recipient scholarship, Jewish Women's Caucus of Assn. Women in Psychology, 2003; Fellowship grant, Meml. Found. for Jewish Culture, 2000—01. Fellow: Acad. Psychoanalysis; mem.: APA (divsn. 39 sect. 3 and 5 treas.), The Pen and Brush Club. Avocations: painting, writing, music. Office: Ste 5 303 Second Ave New York NY 10003 Office Phone: 212-533-3383. Personal E-mail: sophiarichman@aol.com.

RICHMAN, STEPHEN ERIK, retired lawyer, consultant; b. Austin, Tex., Mar. 10, 1945; s. Allen A. and Erika (Zimmerman) Richman; m. Frances Ellen Sharpe, Aug. 29, 1971; children: Joshua Eric, Wendy Michelle. BA magna cum laude, Amherst Coll., Mass., 1967; JD cum laude, Harvard U., Cambridge, Mass., 1970. Bar: Wis. 1972. Assoc. Webster Sheffield, NYC, 1970-72, Quarles & Brady, Milw., 1972-78, ptnr., 1978—2006; ret., 2006. With Richman Nonprofit Strategies, LLC, 2005. Pres. Milw. Youth Symphony Orch., 1985—87; bd. dirs. Milw. Symphony Orch., 1995—2004, chmn., 2000—02; bd. dirs. Jewish Cmty. Found., Milw., 1992—; chmn. steering com. Milw. Youth Arts Ctr., 2003—05; pres. Milw. Jewish Fedn., 1996—98. Mem.: Phi Beta Kappa. Home and Office: 1611 W Eastbrook Ct Mequon WI 53092

RICHMAN, STEPHEN I., lawyer; b. Washington, Pa., Mar. 26, 1933; m. Audrey May Gefsky. BS, Northwestern U., 1954; JD, U. Pa., 1957. Bar: Pa. 1958, U.S. Dist. Ct. (we. dist.) Pa. Assoc. McCune Greenlee & Richman, 1960—63, Greenlee Richman Derrico & Posa, 1963—84; ptnr. Richman, Smith Law Firm, PA, Washington, 1985—2005; of counsel Webber, Gallagher, 2005—. Lectr. U. South Fla. Sch. Medicine, Mine Safe Internat. Chamber of Mines of We. Australia, W.Va. U. Med. Ctr. Grand Rounds, Am. Coll. Chest Physicians, Pa. Thoracic Soc., Am. Thoracic Soc., The Energy Bur., Coll. Am. Pathologists, Allegheny County Health Dept., APHA, Internat. Assn. Ind. Accident Bds. and Commns., Indsl. Health Found., Nat. Coun. Self-Insurers Assn., Am. Iron and Steel Inst., Can. Thoracic Soc., I.L.O./N.I.O.S.H., Univs. Associated for Rsch. and Edn. in Pathology, Am. Ceramics Soc., Nat. Sand Assn.; mem. adv. com. U.S. Dist. ct. We. Dist. Pa., 1994—. Author: Meaning of Impairment and Disability, Chest, 1980, Legal Aspects for the Pathologist, in Pathology of Occupational and Environmental Lung Disease, 1988, A Review of the Medical and Legal Definitions of Related Impairment and Disability, Report to the Department of Labor and the Congress, 1986, Medicolegal Aspects of Asbestos for Pathologists, Arch. Pathology and Laboratory Medicine, 1983, Legal Aspects of Occupational and Environmental Disease, Human Pathology, 1993, Impairment and Disability in Pneunoconiosis, State of the Art Reviews in Occupational Medicine-The Mining Industry, 1993, House Bills 2103 and 885; co-author: Act 44 and 57 amending Pa. Workmen's Compensation act. Mem. legal com. Indsl. Health Found., Pitts.; bd. dirs. Pitts. Opera Soc., Pitts. Jewish Fedn., 1994—97; dir. Jewish Family and Children's Svc., Pitts., 1995—2001. Mem.: ATLA, ABA (former vice chair workers compensation and employers liability law com, toxic and hazardous substance and environ. law com., lectr.), Pa. Chamber Bus. and Industry (worker's compensation com., chmn. subcom. on legis. drafting, lectr.), Pa. Bar Assn. (former coun. worker's compensation sect., contbr. bar assn. quar. 1992, 1993). Home: 820 E Beau St Washington PA 15301-2906 Office: Washington Trust Bldg Ste 200 Washington PA 15301 Office Phone: 724-222-5100. Personal E-mail: steve2633@aol.com.

RICHMOND, ALICE ELENOR, lawyer; b. NYC; d. Louis A. and Estelle (Muraskin) R.; m. David L. Rosenbloom, July 26, 1981; 1 child, Elizabeth Lara. BA magna cum laude, Cornell U., 1968; JD, Harvard U., 1972; grad. Owners and Pres.'s Mgmt. Program, Harvard U., Harvard Bus. Sch., 2001; DLH (hon.), North Adams State U., 1987. Bar: Mass. 1973, U.S. Dist. Ct. Mass. 1975, U.S. Ct. Appeals (1st cir.) 1982, U.S. Supreme Ct. 1985. Law clk. to justices Superior Ct., Boston, 1972-73; asst. dist. atty. Office of Dist. Atty., Boston, 1973-76; spl. asst. atty. gen. Office of Atty. Gen., Boston, 1975-77; asst. prof. New Eng. Sch. of Law, Boston, 1976-78; assoc. Lappin, Rosen, Boston, 1978-81; ptnr. Hemenway & Barnes, Boston, 1982-92, Deutsch, Williams, Boston, 1993-95, Richmond, Pauly & Ault, Boston, 1996—2003; prin. Richmond & Assocs., Boston, 2003—. Asst. team leader, faculty Trial Advocacy Course, 1978—82; examiner Mass. Bd. Bar Examiners, Boston, 1983—; trustee Mass. Continuing Legal Edn., Inc., Boston, 1985—96, Boston, 1998—2004; treas. Nat. Conf. Bar Examiners, 1995—2005, chmn., 2003—04; analyst CBS TV WBZ, 1991—; v.p., bd. dirs. Am. Bar Ins., Inc., 1995—; bd. dirs. Valora Tech., Inc. Conbr. chpts. to book; contbr. articles to profl. jours. Mem. Pres. Adv. Com on the Arts, 1995—99; bd. overseers Handel & Haydn Soc., 1985—94, bd. govs., 1994—, v.p., 1996—2002; mem. Boston 2000 Millennium Comm., 1997—98; sec., dir. Boston 2000, Inc., 1998—2001; mem., pres. Coun. of Cornell Women, Cornell U. Coun.; trustee Red Auerbach Youth Found., Fund for Justice and Edn., 1997—2002; mem. adv. bd. Ctrl. and Ea. European Law Initiative, 1998—2002; mem. Angell Meml. Hosp. Coun. of Fellows, 2001—. Named one of Outstanding Young Leaders, Boston Jaycees, 1982; Sloan Found. Urban fellow, N.Y.C., 1969. Fellow: Am. Coll. Trial Lawyers; mem.: NOW, Legal Def. and Edn. Fund (trustee 1995—2002, sec. 1998—2002), ABA (ho. of dels. 1980—, vice chmn. com. on rules and calendar 1986—88, bd. govs. 2002—05, task force on gats 2003—, standing com. on audit 2005—, treas.-elect 2007—), Latin Am. Legal Initiatives Coun., Mass. Bar Found. (pres. 1988—91), Mass. Bar Assn. (pres. 1986—87), Am. Law Inst., Bostonian Soc. (dir.), Boston Club, Harvard Club. Office: Richmond & Assocs 39 Brimmer St Boston MA 02108 Home Phone: 617-523-0331; Office Phone: 617-523-8187. Business E-Mail: arichmond@rpalaw.com.

RICHMOND, ANTHONY HENRY, sociologist, emeritus educator; b. Ilford, Essex, Eng., June 8, 1925; s. Henry James and Ellen Bertha R.; m. Freda Williams, Mar. 29, 1952; 1 dau., Glenys Catriona Richmond Troth. BSc in Econs., London Sch. Econs., 1949; MA, U. Liverpool, Eng., 1951; PhD, U. London, 1965. Rsch. officer U. Liverpool, 1949-51; lectr. dept. social study U. Edinburgh, Scotland, 1952-63; reader in sociology Bristol (Eng.) Coll. Sci. and Tech., 1963-65; prof. sociology York U., Toronto, Ont., Canada, 1965-89, prof. emeritus, sr. scholar, 1989—; dir. York U. (Inst. Behavioral Rsch.), 1979-82. Social rsch. cons.; vis. prof. Australian Nat. U., Canberra, 1971, 77, St. Antony's Coll., Oxford, Eng., 1984-85. Author: Colour Prejudice in Britain, 1954, 2d edit., 1971, The Colour Problem: A Study of Racial Relations in Britain, Africa and the West Indies, 1955, rev. edit., 1961, Post-War Immigrants in Canada, 1967, (with others) Immigrant Integration and Urban Renewal in Toronto, 1973, Migration and Race Relations in an English City, 1973, (with W. E. Kalbach) Factors in the Adjustment of Immigrants and Their Descendants, 1980, Immigration and Ethnic Conflict, 1988, Caribbean Immigrants: A Demoeconomic Analysis, 1989, Global Apartheid: Refugees, Racism and the New World Order, 1994; editor: Readings in Race and Ethnic Relations, 1972, (with D. Kubat) Internal Migration: The New World and the Third World, 1976; contbr. chpts. to books, articles to profl. jours. Recipient research grants and scholarships. Fellow Royal Soc. Can.; mem. Can. Sociology and Anthropology Assn. (Outstanding Contbrn. award 2001), Can. Population Soc. Mem. Soc. Of Friends. Avocations: classical music, photography. E-mail: richmond@yorku.ca.

RICHMOND, EERO, composer, music librarian; b. Tacoma, Wash., Jan. 5, 1938; s. Orin August and Esther Maija (Johnson) R. BA in Music, U. Wash., 1961, MLS, 1966. Music libr. N.Y.C. Pub. Libr., 1966-68, head music cataloger, 1969-80; dir. info. svcs. Am. Music Ctr., NYC, 1982-93, head music cataloger, 1994-95, coord. info. svcs., 1995-99. Pianist Slavic Arts Ensemble, N.Y.C., 1985—, Inoue Chamber Ensemble, N.Y.C., 1993—. Composer musical works performed throughout U.S., Europe, South Am., Japan; contbr. articles to profl. jours. Mem. ASCAP, Internat. Soc. for Contemporary Music (v.p. 1986-90), Sibelius Soc. (v.p. 1985—), Phi Mu Alpha Sinfonia, Beta Phi Mu. Democrat. Lutheran. Avocations: travel (especially berlin), reading. Home: 152 Kent St Brooklyn NY 11222-2142 Office Phone: 718-389-6030. E-mail: kafka333@aol.com.

RICHMOND, GAIL LEVIN, law educator; b. Gary, Ind., Jan. 9, 1946; d. Herbert Irving and Sylvia Esther (Given) Levin; children: Henry, Amy. AB, U. Mich., 1966, MBA, 1967; JD, Duke U., 1971. Bar: Ohio 1971, U.S. Claims Ct. 1986, U.S. Ct. Mil. Appeals, 1994; CPA, Ill. Acct. Arthur Andersen & Co., Chgo., 1967-68; assoc. Jones, Day, Cleve., 1971-72; asst. prof. Capital U. Law Sch., Columbus, Ohio, 1972-73, U. N.C. Law Sch., Chapel Hill, 1973-78; vis. asst. prof. U. Tex. Law Sch., Austin, 1977-78, Nova U. Law Ctr., Ft. Lauderdale, Fla., 1979-80, assoc. prof., 1980-81, assoc. prof., assoc. dean, 1981-85, prof., assoc. dean., 1985-93, 95—, prof., acting dean, 1993-95. Author: Federal Tax Research, 7th edit., 2007; co-author: Tax Planning for Lifetime and Testamentary Dispositions, 1997, A Complete Introduction to Corporate Taxation, 2006, Florida Wills, Trusts and Estates: Cases and Materials, 2007; contbr. articles to profl. jours. Pres. Greater Ft. Lauderdale Tax Coun., 1987-88; trustee Law Sch. Admission Coun., 1994-99, chair audit com., 1991-93, chair svcs. and programs com., 1997-99. Mem. ABA (chair commn. on individual income, tax sect. 2001-03, supervising editor News Quar. 2006—, chair AMT task force 2003-2004, chair adj. com., legal edn. sect. 2002-05), Am. Assn. Atty.-CPAs (dir. Fla. chpt. 1992-98), Assn. Am. Law Schs. (chmn. audit com. 1992, chair sect. adminstrn. of law schs. 1996, pres. S.E. chpt. 1993-94, sec. S.E. chpt. 1995-2002), S.E. Assn. Law Schs. (pres. 2002-03, sec. 2004—). Office: Nova Southeastern U Shepard Broad Law Ctr 3305 College Ave Fort Lauderdale FL 33314-7721

RICHMOND, GERALDINE LEE, chemist, educator; BS in Chemistry magna cum laude, Kansas State U., 1975; PhD in Phys. Chemistry, U. Calif., Berkeley, 1980. Rsch. and teaching asst. Kans. State U., 1973-76, U. Calif., Berkeley, 1976-80; asst. prof. chemistry Bryn Mawr Coll., 1980-85; assoc. prof. chemistry U. Oreg., Eugene, 1985-91, dir. rsch. experience for undergrad. program, 1987—2004, dir. chem. phys. inst., 1991-95, prof. chemistry, 1991—, Knight prof. liberal arts and sci., 1998—2001, Richard M. and Patricia H. Noyes prof. chemistry, 2001—. Mem. adv. bd. Chemistry, NSF, 1986-89, Materials Sci., 1989-92; mem. adv. bd. Accounts of Chem. Rsch., 1991-94, Analytical Chemistry, 1992-95; chair, founder Com. Advancement Women Chemists (COACh), 1998-2005; mem. governor's sci. adv. bd., State of Oreg., 1986-89; mem., Basic Energy Sci. Adv. Com. Dept. Energy, 1995-2003, chair, 1998-2003; regent Oregon State Bd. Higher Edn. (Gov. Kitzhabor appointee), 1999-2003, system atrategic planning com., 1999-2000, Budget and Fin. Com., 2000-03, regent, v.p. (Gov. Kulongoski appointee), 2002-, mem. exec. com., 2003-05, v.p. and interim pres., 2004, chair, chancellor's office reorganization com., 2004-05; mem. Coun. on Chem. Sciences, Dept. Energy 1996-2001; mem. bd. chem. sci. and tech. matter, NAS/NRC, 1989-92, mem.bd. on solid state sciences, 1991-94, mem. chem. sci. roundtable 2003-;chair, NAS Frontiers in Sci. Symposium, 1993-94, Women Faculty Resource Network, U. Oreg., 1992-2004;lectr. in field. Mem. editl. bd. Critical Reviews and Surface Anatomy, 1991-95, Analytical Chemistry, 1992-95, Accounts of Chemical Research, 1991-94, Vibrational Spectroscopy, 1990-94, Jour. Physical Chemistry, 1989-1994, Applied Spectroscopy, 1993-96, Langmuir, 2001-03; adv. bd. mem. Chemical and Engineering News, 2002-04; assoc. editor, Annual Review of Physical Chemistry, 2005-; contbr. articles to profl. jours. King Meml. scholar, 1973-75; Alfred P. Sloan rsch. fellow, 1985-89; recipient Rosalyn Schwartz award, 1982, NSF Presdl. Young Investigator award, 1985-90, Camile and Henry Dreyfus Tchr. award, 1986-90, Chemistry Dept. Alumni award, Kansas State U., 1986, Women Scientists and Engrs. Faculty award, NSF, 1991-96, Rsch. Creativity award, NSF, 1991, Agnes Faye Morgan Rsch. award, 1993, Coll. Arts & Sciences Alumni award, Kansas State U., 1997, Presdl. award Excellence Sci. and Engring. Mentoring White House, 1997, Women Helping Women award Soroptomist Internat., 1998, Rsch. Creativity award, NSF, 2000, Advance Leadership award, NSF, 2001, Oregon Outstanding Sci. award Oregon Acad. Sci., 2001, Spiers medal, Royal Soc. Chemistry (UK) Faraday divsn., 2004 Fellow AAAS, Am. Phys. Soc.(mem. adv. com. laser sci. topical group, 1990-95), Am. Acad. Arts & Sciences; mem. Am. Chem. Soc. (Analytical Chemistry award 1973, Francis P. Garvan medal, 1996, Women Chemist Com. Regional award Diversity, 2002, Spectrochemical Analysis award, 2002, award for Encouraging Women into Careers in Chem. Sci. 2005), Assn. Women in Sci., Coblentz Spectroscopy Soc. (mem. exec. com., 1988-91, award 1989), Electrochem. Soc., Soc. Applied Spectroscopy, Western Spectroscopy Assn. (exec. bd. mem. 1986-1989) Office: Dept Chemistry 1274 Univ Oregon Eugene OR 97403 Office Phone: 541-346-4635. Office Fax: 541-346-5859. Business E-Mail: richmond@uoregon.edu.

RICHMOND, HAROLD NICHOLAS, lawyer; b. Elizabeth, NJ, Apr. 5, 1935; s. Benjamin I. and Eleanor (Turbowitz) R.; m. Elaine Zemel, June 16, 1957 (div. Nov. 1972); children: Bonnie J. Ross, Michele Weinfeld; m. Marilyn A. Wenrich, Aug. 26, 1973; children: Eric L., Kacy L. BA, Tulane U., 1957; LLB, NYU, 1961, LLM in Taxation, 1965. Estate tax examiner IRS, Newark, 1963-65; tax mgr. Puder & Puder/Touche Ross & Co., CPAs, Newark, 1965-73; ptnr. Sodowick Richmond & Crecca, Newark, 1973-84; prin. Harold N. Richmond, West Orange, N.J., 1984-86; ptnr. Wallerstein Hauptman & Richmond, West Orange, 1986-91, Hauptman & Richmond, West Orange, 1992—. With US Army, 1959—60. Mem. ABA (tax sect. closely held bus. com., real property and probate sect.), N.J. Bar Assn. (tax, real property and probate sects.), Essex County Bar Assn. (chmn. tax com. 1989, real property and probate sect.). Avocations: running, tennis. Office: Hauptman & Richmond 100 Executive Dr Ste 330 West Orange NJ 07052-3309 Office Phone: 973-731-1100. Business E-Mail: hnr@hrlawfirm.com.

RICHMOND, JAMES ELLIS, retired restaurant company executive; b. Chgo., Feb. 16, 1938; s. Kenneth E. and Irene M. (Anderson) R.; m. Karen Ann Ryder, Oct. 6, 1956; children: Scott, Brian, Ann, Susan. BBA, Case Western Res. U., 1960. CPA, Ohio. Sr. auditor Ernst & Ernst, Cleve., 1960-64; treas. Cook United, Inc., Cleve., 1964-75, Fairmont Foods Co., Houston, 1975-80, v.p. ops., 1980-82; v.p., treas. U-tote-M, Inc., 1982-84; mktg. exec. Circle K Convenience Stores, 1984-86; v.p. Consol. Products, Inc., Indpls., 1986-2000; ret. Lutheran. Home: 331 Wild Turkey Blvd Boerne TX 78006- E-mail: jkrich@gvtc.com.

RICHMOND, JAMES GLIDDEN, lawyer; b. Sacramento, Feb. 20, 1944; s. James Gibbs and Martha Ellen (Glidden) R.; m. Lois Marie Bennett, Oct. 22, 1988; 1 child, Mark R. BS in Mgmt., Ind. U., 1966, postgrad., 1966-69, JD, 1969. Bar: Ind. 1969, Ill. 1991, U.S. Dist. Ct. (no. dist.) Ind. 1971, U.S. Dist. Ct. (so. dist.) Ind., 1969, U.S. Ct. Appeals (7th cir.) 1975, U.S. Tax Ct. 1980. Spl. agent FBI, 1970-74; spl. agent Criminal Investigation Divsn. IRS, 1974-76; asst. U.S. atty. no. dist. U.S. Atty. Office, Ind., 1976-80; assoc. Galvin, Stalmack & Kirschner, Hammond, Ind., 1980-81; pvt. practice Highland, Ind., 1981-83; ptnr. Goodman, Ball & Van Bokkelen, Highland, Ind., 1983-85; U.S. atty. no. dist. State of Ind., Hammond, 1985-91; spl. counsel to dep. atty. gen. of the U.S. U.S. Dept. Justice, Washington, 1990-91; mng. ptnr. Ungaretti and Harris, Chgo., 1991-92, ptnr., 1995—2002; exec. v.p., gen. counsel Nat. Health Labs., 1992-95; shareholder Greenberg Traurig, Chgo., 2002—. Practitioner-in-residence Ind. U. Sch. Law, Bloomington, 1989, 2003. Minority counsel senate republicans October Surprise Hearings, 1992. Named one of Best Lawyers Am., 2006—07. Fellow Am. Coll. Trial Lawyers; mem. Chgo. Inn of Ct. (pres., 2007—). Avocation: fly fishing. Office: Greenberg Traurig 77 W Wacker Dr Ste 2500 Chicago IL 60601 Home Phone: 630-910-8191; Office Phone: 312-456-5204. Business E-Mail: richmondj@gtlaw.com.

RICHMOND, JOHN REVERE, physician, educator; b. Burger, Tex., Nov. 24, 1949; s. Henry B. Richmond Jr. and Irene D. Richmond; m. Carol Ann Richmond, Nov. 5, 1977; children: Marian Boone, Sarah Olivas, John David, Michael, Luke, Jasmine. BS, So. Meth. U., Dallas, 1972; MS, U. Ill., Chgo., 1976. Diplomate Am. Bd. Family Medicine, lic. Tex. Med. Bd., 1977. Resident in family medicine Meml. Med. Ctr., Corpus Christi, 1976—79; family physician Family Physician Assoc., Dallas, 1979—92; assoc. dir. Corpus Christi Family Medicine Residency Program, 1992—94, dir., 1994—95; assoc. dir. SW family medicine residency program U. Tex., Dallas, 1995—2004, dir. SW family medicine residency program, 2004—. Chmn. resident student conf. Tex. Acad. Family Physicians, Austin, 1993—; Stanley Gilbert MD prof. U. Tex., SW Med. Sch., Dallas, 2004, faculty advisor family medicine interest group, 2005—. Leader Boy Scouts Am., Dallas, 1988—; vol. physician N. Dallas Shared Ministries, 2000—. Named Family Physician of Yr., Tex. Acad. Family Physicians, 2007; recipient Eagle Scout, Boy Scouts Am., 1962, Silver Beaver, Circle Ten Coun., Boy Scouts Am., 2007. Roman Catholic. Avocations: camping, fishing, history. Office: Univ Tex SW Family Medicine Residency Program 6263 Harry Hine Blve Dallas TX 75390-9067 Office Phone: 214-645-3900. E-mail: john.richmond@utsouthwestern.edu.

RICHMOND, JULIUS BENJAMIN, retired pediatrician, former Surgeon General of the United States, health policy educator; b. Chgo., Sept. 26, 1916; s. Jacob and Anna (Dayno) Richmond; m. Rhee Chidekel, June 3, 1937 (dec. Oct. 9, 1985); children: Barry J., Charles Allen; m. Jean Rabow, Jan. 11, 1987; 1 child, Dale Keith (dec.). BS, U. Ill., 1937, MS, MD, 1939; DSc (hon.), Ind. U., 1978, Rush-Presbyn.-St. Luke Med. Ctr., 1978, U. Ill., 1979, Georgetown U., 1980, SUNY, Syracuse, 1986, U. Ariz., 1991; DMS (hon.), Med. Coll. Pa., 1980; D in Pub. Svc. (hon.), Nat. Coll. Edn., Evanston, Ill., 1980; DHL (hon.), Tufts U., 1980; DMS (hon.), Yale U., 1999; DEd (hon.), Wheelock Coll., 2000; DSci, Harvard U., 2002. Intern Cook County Hosp., Chgo., 1939—41, resident, 1941—42, 1946, Mcpl. Contagious Disease Hosp., Chgo., 1941; faculty U. Ill. Med. Sch., Chgo., 1946—53, prof. pediat., 1950—53; dir. Inst. Juvenile Rsch., Chgo., 1952—53; prof., chmn. dept. pediatrics Coll. Medicine, SUNY at Syracuse, 1953—65, dean med. faculty, chmn. dept. pediatrics, 1965—70; prof. child psychiatry and human devel., prof., chmn. dept. preventive and social medicine Harvard Med. Sch., 1971—77, prof. health policy, 1981—88, dir. divsn. health policy rsch. and edn., 1983—88, prof. health policy emeritus, 1988—; asst. sec. health, surgeon gen. US Dept. Health & Human Services, Washington, 1977—81. Psychiatrist-in-chief Children's Hosp. Med. Ctr., Boston, 1971—77, adv. on child health policy, 1981—; dir. Judge Baker Children's Ctr., Boston, 1971—77; mem. Pres.'s Commn. on Mental Health, 1977. Author: Pediatric Diagnosis, 1962, Currents in American Medicine, 1969, The Health Care Mess, 2005. Nat. dir. Project Head Start; dir. Office Health Affairs, OEO, 1965—66. Flight surgeon U.S. Army Air Force, 1942—46. Recipient Agnes Bruce Greig Sch. award, 1966, Parents Mag. award, 1966, Disting. Svc. award, Office Econ. Opportunity, 1967, Family Health Mag. award, 1977, Myrdal award, Assn. for Evaluation Rsch., 1977, award for disting. sci. contbn., Soc. for Rsch. in Child Devel., 1979, Dolly Madison award, Inst. on Clin. Infants Programs, 1979, Pub. Health Disting. Svc. award, HEW, 1980, Illini Achievement award, U. Ill. Alumni Assn., 1982, Cmty. Svc. award, Health Planning Coun. Greater Boston, 1985, Lemuel Shattuck award, Mass. Pub. Health Assn., 1985, 1st Ann. Ronald McDonald Children's Charities award for Outstanding Contbns. to Child Health and Welfare, 1986, David E. Rogers award, Assn. Am. Med. Colls., 1997, A.L. Ellis award, Children's Home Soc. Fla., 1997, John Stearns award, N.Y. Acad. Medicine, 1999, Heinz Family Found. award. Fellow: Am. Psychiat. Assn. (disting.), Am. Orthopsychiat. Assn. (Ittleson award 1994); mem.: APHA (Martha May Eliot award 1970, Sedgwick medal 1992), AMA (AMA-ERF award in health edn. 1988), Am. Psychosomatic Soc., Soc. Pediatric Rsch., Am. Acad. Child Psychiatry (hon.), New Eng. Coun. Child Psychiatry (assoc.), Am. Acad. Pediat. (C. Anderson Aldrich award 1966, ann. award sect. on cmty. pediat. 1977, Outstanding Contbn. award sect. cmty. pediat. 1978, Job Lewis Smith award 2000), Am. Pediatric Soc. (John Howland award 1990), Inst. Medicine of NAS (1st ann. Gustav O. Lienhard award 1986, McDermott medal 2002), Phi Eta Sigma, Alpha Omega Alpha, Sigma Xi. Office Phone: 617-432-1410.

RICHMOND, LYLE L., judge; BA, Wesleyan U., 1952; LLB, Yale U., 1955. Dep. dist. atty., San Diego, 1959—64; pvt. practice Calif., 1964—70; dist. atty. Truk/Ponape dists., 1970—73; head legal divsn. atty.'s gen. office Trust Territory of the Pacific Islands, Saipan, 1973—75; atty. gen. American Samoa, 1975—77; legal counselor to American Samoa govs. Peter T. Coleman and A. P. Lutali, 1978—89; adminstr., legal mgr. Samoa Packing Co., Pago Pago, American Samoa, 1989—91; assoc. justice High Ct., Pago Pago, American Samoa, 1991—. With USN, 1955—58, capt. JAGC USNR, ret., 1984. Office: Courthouse PO Box 309 Pago Pago AS 96799 Office Phone: 684-633-1261. Business E-Mail: lylerichmond72@hotmail.com.

RICHMOND, MARILYN SUSAN, lawyer; b. Bethesda, Md., Oct. 19, 1949; d. Carl Hutchins Jr. and Elizabeth Adeline (Saeger) R. BA with honors, U. Fla., 1971; JD, Georgetown U., 1974. Bar: Md. 1974, D.C. 1975. Atty. Office of Gen. Counsel, FTC, Washington, 1974-77, antitrust atty. Bur. of Competition, 1977-81; counsel, consumer subcom. of com. on commerce, sci. and transp. U.S. Senate, Washington, 1981-85; assoc. Heron, Burchette, Ruckert & Rothwell, Washington, 1985-87, ptnr., 1987-90; dep. asst. sec. for govtl. affairs U.S. Dept. Transp., Washington, 1990-91, acting asst. sec. for govtl. affairs, 1991-92; cons. Raffaelli, Spees, Springer & Smith, Washington, 1993-94; asst. exec. dir. govt. rels. APA Practice Orgn., 1995—. Lectr. Brookings Instn. Ctr. for Pub. Policy Edn., Washington, 1985-88. Active Lawyers for Bush-Quayle, Washington, 1988. Mem. ABA (antitrust, adminstrv. law sect., vice chair transp. industry com. antitrust sect. 1992-99). Republican. Methodist. Avocations: horseback riding, tennis. Home: Apt 601 2725 Connecticut Ave NW Washington DC 20008-5305 Office Phone: 202-336-5889.

RICHMOND, NANCY MASON, retired state agency administrator; b. Buxton, Maine, Mar. 14, 1933; d. Ansel Robert and Kate Douglas (Libby) M. Grad., Bryant Coll., Providence, RI, 1952; BA, U. Mass., Boston, 1977; postgrad., Inst. Governmental Services, Boston, 1985, The Auditor's Inst., 1988. Asst. to chief justice Mass. Superior Ct., Boston, 1964-68; cmty. liaison Action for Boston Cmty. Devel., Boston, 1968-73; mgmt. cons. East Boston Cmty. Devel. Assn., Boston, 1973-78; asst. dir. Mass. Office of Deafness, Boston, 1978-86; dir. of contracts Mass. Rehab. Commn., Boston, 1986-98; ret., 1998. Cons. Jos. A Ryan Assocs., Boston and Orleans, Mass., 1981-86, Radio Sta. WFCC, Chatham, Mass., 1987-91, Networks, Inc., 2003-05. Author: Bromley-Heath Security Patrols, 1974, Reorganization of East Boston Community Development Corporation, 1976, How to Start Your Own Small Business, 1981. Bd. dirs. Deaf-Blind Contact Ctr., Boston, 1988-91; vol. Am. Cancer Soc., Winchester, Mass., 1986-93, Tax Equity Alliance Mass., 1994; treas. Sunset Bay Condo Assn., 1998-99, bd. dirs. 1998-2001, Highland Cemetery Assn., 2002-; mem. vestry Trinity Episc. Ch., Saco, Maine, 2005-07. Recipient Good Citizen award DAR, 1950, Community Svc. award Northeastern U., 1986, Gov.'s citation for outstanding performance, 1993; named to Outstanding Young Women of Am., 1965. Mem. NOW, Mass. State Assn. Deaf, Mass. Rehab. Commn. Statewide Cen. Office Dirs. (chair 1995-98, MRC procurement mgmt. team 1997-98, co-chair Take Your Daughters to Work Day 1998-99), Red Hat Soc. Democrat. Episcopalian. Avocations: reading, music, swimming, sign language. Home: 12315 SR 674 #34 Lithia FL 33547-1417

RICHOZ, JOAN KATHRYN, real estate agent, retired school nurse; b. Elgin, Ill., Apr. 20, 1944; d.William Arnold and Elsie Bertha (Hamm) Gavelek; m. Arthur Vernon Richoz, Jan. 26, 1964; children: Kimberli Ellen Richoz Wiemer, Suzon Michelle Kowalski. BSN, No. Ill. U., DeKalb, 1966, MS, 1989. RN, Ill.; lic. realtor, Ill.; lic. vision and hearing screening technician, Ill.; cert. sch. nurse, Ill. Staff nurse obsetetrics DeKalb Pub. Hosp., 1966-68; clin. supr. No. Ill. U. Sch. Nursing, DeKalb, 1968-70; staff and rehab. nurse DeKalb County Nursing Home, 1967-70; staff nurse pediatrics Kishwaukee Hosp., DeKalb, 1977-80; real estate sales agt. DeKalb County and Ill. Bd. Realtors, 1994—; nurse DeKalb Cmty. Unit Sch. Dist. #428, 1970—2000. Founder sch. health adv. com.; health adv. bd. Cmty. Coordinated Child Care, DeKalb, 1986-96, Kishwaukee Family Ctr. Child Devel. Clinic, DeKalb, 1993-96; instr. ARC, DeKalb, 1992-96; adv. com. No. Ill. U. Sch. Nursing, 2002. Mem. Family Svc. Agy., DeKalb, 1990-96, First Congl. Ch., United Ch. of Christ, DeKalb, 1966-96; mem. Spiritual Frontiers Fellowship Internat., 1984-96; pastoral care asst. 1st Congl. Ch., 1984-86; mem., svc. chairperson Am. Cancer Soc., 1975-79; mem. adv. bd. Dolores Ruland Cancer Found., 2004—. Recipient awards of recognition Ill. State Bd. Edn., Springfield, 1991-92, Ill. Assn. Sch. Nurses, 1991-92. Mem. Am. Holistic Nurses Assn., Nat. Assn. Realtors, Ill. Assn. Sch. Nurses (pres. northeastern divsn., sec., legislation chmn.), Am. Fedn. Tchrs., Ill. Fedn. Tchrs., DeKalb Classroom Tchrs. Assn., Ill. Sch. Health Assn., Ill. Assn. Realtors, DeKalb Area Assn. Realtors, No. Ill. U. Sch. Nursing Alumni Assn. Avocations: mind/body-complementary health studies, piano playing, singing, walking, reading. Office: Richoz Sullivan Real Estate 100 E Locust St Dekalb IL 60115 Office Phone: 815-748-4663.

RICHT, MARK, college football coach; b. Feb. 18, 1960; m. Katharyn Francis; children: Jonathan, David, Zach, Anya. Graduate, Univ. Miami, 1982. Asst. coach Ea. Carolina Univ., 1989; quarterbacks coach FSU, 1985—2000, Offensive Coord., 1994—2000; head football coach Univ. Ga., 2000—. Recipient SEC Coach Yr., 2002, 2005. Office: Sanford Stadium PO Box 1472 Sanford Dr at Reed St Athens GA 30602

RICHTEL, MATT (THERON HEIR), reporter, cartoonist; BA, Univ. Calif., Berkeley; M in journalism, Columbia Univ. Reporter & editor Peninsula Times Herald; reporter Oakland Tribune; telecommunications reporter New York Times, 2000—. Co-author (with Darrin Bell, under pen name Theron Heir): (syndicated comic strip) Rudy Park. Office: New York Times 201 Spear St San Francisco CA 94105 Office Phone: 415-836-6700. Business E-Mail: mattr@nytimes.com.

RICHTER, BURTON, physicist, educator; b. NYC, Mar. 22, 1931; s. Abraham and Fanny (Pollack) Richter; m. Laurose Becker, July 1, 1960; children: Elizabeth, Matthew. BS, MIT, 1952, PhD, 1956; degree in physics (hon.), U. Pisa, 2001. Research assoc. Stanford U., 1956—60, asst. prof. physics, 1960—63, assoc. prof., 1963—67, prof., 1967—2006, Paul Pigott prof. phys. sci., 1980—2005, tech. dir. Linear Accelerator Ctr., 1982—84, dir. Linear Accelerator Ctr., 1984—99; dir. emeritus, 1999—2006. Loeb lectr. Harvard U., 1974; DeShalit lectr. Weizmann Inst., 1975; pres. Internat. Union of Pure and Applied Physics, 1997; Astor vis. lectr. Oxford U., 2000; cons. NSF, 1999—2002, advisor, chair NERAC subcom. adv. nuc. transmutation tech., 2002—; sec., bd. dirs. AREVA Enterprises, Inc., Litel Instruments. Contbr. over 300 articles to profl. publs. Recipient E.O. Lawrence medal, Dept. Energy, 1976, Nobel prize in Physics, 1976. Fellow: AAAS, Am. Acad. Arts and Scis., Am. Phys. Soc. (pres. 1994, chmn. energy efficiency study group); mem.: NAS, Nat. Rsch. Coun. (mem. bd. physics and astronomy, chair 2003—), Internat. Coun. Sci. (mem. exec. bd. 2002—05), Regents Mercersbury Acad. (hon.), Nat. Climate Change Assessment (PCAST rev. panel), Am. Phil. Soc. (bd. dirs.). Achievements include research in elementary particle physics. Office: SLAC 2575 Sand Hill Rd Menlo Park CA 94025

RICHTER, DONALD PAUL, lawyer; b. New Britain, Conn., Feb. 15, 1924; s. Paul John and Helen (Racoske) R.; m. Jane Frances Gumpright, Aug. 10, 1946; children: Christopher Dean, Cynthia Louise. AB, Bates Coll., 1947; LL.B., Yale U., 1950. Bar: NY 1951, Conn. 1953. Assoc. Winthrop, Stimson, Putnam & Roberts, NYC, 1950-52; ptnr. Murtha, Cullina, Richter and Pinney, Hartford, Conn., 1954-94; counsel Murtha Cullina LLP, Hartford, Conn., 1994—. Trustee Bates Coll., 1962-94, Manchester (Conn.) Meml. Hosp., 1963-94, Hartford Sem., 1973-85; trustee Suffield Acad., 1974—, pres., 1982-89; bd. dirs. Met. YMCA Greater Hartford, 1970-94, pres., 1976-81, trustee, 1994—; mem. nat. coun. YMCA, 1978-82; bd. dirs. Church Homes, 1967-81; trustee, v.p., Silver Bay Assn., 1971-96. With USNR, 1943-46. Fellow Am. Coll. Trust and Estate Counsel; mem. ABA, Conn. Bar Assn., Univ. Club, Hartford Club, 20th Century Club, Rotary (Paul Harris fellow 1996), Phi Beta Kappa, Delta Sigma Rho. Congregationalist. Home: 140 Boulder Rd Manchester CT 06040-4508 Office: Murtha Cullina LLP City Place I 185 Asylum St Hartford CT 06103-3469 Home Phone: 860-643-6024; Office Phone: 860-240-6003.

RICHTER, FRANK M., geophysicist, educator; b. Dominican Republic; naturalized, US, 1974; Profl. engring. degree, Colo. Sch. Mines, 1965; MS, U. Chgo, 1971; PhD, U. Chgo., 1972. Rsch. assoc. dept. earth and planetary sci. MIT, 1972—74; asst. prof. dept. geophys. scis. U. Chgo., 1975—78, assoc. prof., 1978—81, prof., 1981—, Sewel L. Avery Disting. Svc. prof. geophys. scis., 1994—. Chmn. dept. geophys. scis. U. Chgo., 1985—94. Contbr. articles to sci. jours. Named a Fairchild Disting. Scholar, Calif. Inst. Tech., 1978, Green Scholar, Inst. Geophysics and Planetary Physics, La Jolla, Calif., 1979; recipient George Woollard award, Geol. Soc. Am., 1999, Arthur L. Day medal, 2006; grantee John Simon Guggenheim fellowship, 1974, Royal Soc. Rsch. fellowship, 1981. Fellow: Am. Geophys. Union (Norman L. Bowen award 1995), Am. Acad. Arts & Scis.; mem.: NAS. Office: Dept Geophys Scis U Chgo 5734 S Ellis Ave HGS 549 Chicago IL 60637 E-mail: richter@geosci.uchicago.edu.

RICHTER, GERHARD, artist; b. Dresden, Germany, Feb. 9, 1932; m. Isa Genzken, 1982; 1 child, Betty. Student, Hochschule fur Bildende Kunste, Dresden, 1952-57; studied with, Karl-Otto Gotz Staatliche Kunstakademie, Dusseldorf, 1961-64. Scenery painter Stadttheatre Zittau, East Germany, 1949-50; commercial artist numerous firms Zittau, 1950-51; photolab. technician Dresden, 1957-60; painter Dusseldorf, 1963—; visual artist Staatliche Kunstakademie, Germany. Prof. Staaliche Kunstakademie, Dusseldorf, 1971; lectr. in field. One man shows include Mobelhaus Berges, Dusseldorf, 1963, Galerie Heiner Friedrich, Munich, 1964, 67, 70, 72, Galerie Rene Block, 1965, 69, 74, White Wide Space Gallery, Antwerp, 1967, Galerie Ricke, Kassel, 1968, Galleria del Naviglio, 1969, Palais des Beaux-Arts, Brussels, 1970, Galerie Konrad Fischer, Dusseldorf, 1970, 72, 75, 83, Mus. Folkwang, Essen, 1970, 80, Kunstverein, Dusseldorf, 1971, Galerie Thomas Borgmann, Cologne, 1971, 84, Galerie Rudolph Zwirner, Cologne, 1972, Galerie Seriaal, Amsterdam, 1973, Onnasch Gallery, NY, 1973, Galleria La Bertesca, Milan, 1973, Galerie Rolf Preisig, Basle, 1975, Nova Scotia Coll. Art, Halifax, 1978, Whitechapel Art Gallery, London, 1979, Sperone-Westwater-Fischer, NY, 1980, 83, Kunsthalle, Dusseldorf, 1981, Galerie Hetzler, 1982, Padiglione d'Arte Contemporanea, Milan, 1982, Galleria Lucio Amelio, Naples, 1983, Galleria Maria Pieroni, Rome, 1983, Musée d'Art et d'Industrie, St. Etienne, France, 1984, Marian Goodman Gallery, NY, 1985, Sperone-Westwater, NY, 1985, Anthony d'Offay Gallery, London, 1988, Art Gallery Ont., 1988, others; exhibited in group shows at Whitechapel Art Gallery, London, Stedelijk Mus., Amsterdam, Kunsthalle, Royal Acad. London, LA County Mus. Art; represented in permanent collections Kunstmuseum, Dusseldorf, Neue Gallery, Mus. Folkwang, Nationalgalerie, Berlin, Kunstmuseum, Basle, Guggenheim Mus., NY; author: Bericht uber eine Demonstr., 1963, Gerhard Richter: Atlas von de fot., 1972, Gerhard Richter: Atlas der Fotos, Collgen und Skizzen, 1976. Recipient Kunstpreis Junger Westen, Recklinghausen, 1967, Arnold Bode prize, Kassel, 1982, Wolf prize in arts (painting) Wolf Found., 1994/5 Mem.: Am. Acad. Arts and Sciences (hon. fgn.). Mailing: Staatliche Kunstakademie Eiskellerstraße 1 Alstadt Germany

RICHTER, GLENN, retail executive; BBA, George Washington U.; MBA, Duke U. Various exec. level positions with Frito-Lay Co., McKinsey and Co.; pres., CEO Specialty Foods Corp., 1994—97; sr. v.p., corp. contr. Dade Behring, Deerfield, Ill., 1997-99, CFO, 1998—99; exec. v.p., CFO St. Paul Companies Inc., 1997—2000; v.p., controller Sears Roebuck, Hoffman Estates, Ill., 2000—02, senior v.p., CFO, 2002—05, exec. v.p., CFO, 2005—. Office: Sears Roebuck 3333 Beverly Rd Schaumburg IL 60179

RICHTER, HARVENA, retired literature educator, poet; b. Reading, Pa., Mar. 13, 1919; d. Conrad Michael and Harvena Maria (Achenbach) R. BA, U. N.Mex., 1938; MA, NYU, 1955, PhD, 1967. Advt. copyrighter Saks 5th Ave., NYC, 1942-43, R.H. Macy, NYC, 1944-46; copy chief Elizabeth Arden, NYC, 1946-47; advt. dir. I. Miller, NYC, 1947-48; European corr. various newspapers, 1948-49; lectr. NYU, NYC, 1952-66, U. N.Mex., 1969-89. Author: The Human Shore, 1959, Virginia Woolf: The Inward Voyage, 1970, Writing to Survive: The Private Notebooks of Conrad Richter, 1988, The Yaddo Elegies and Other Poems, 1995, Green Girls, Poems Early and Late, 1996, The Innocent Island, 1999, Frozen Light, the Crystal Poems, 2002, The Golden Fountains, Sources of Energy and Life, 2002, Passage to Teheran, 2004; author numerous poems; short stories to Sat. Eve. Post, New Am., Blue Mesa Rev.; essays to Atlantic, Modern Fiction Studies, C.S. Monitor, others. AAUW fellow, 1964-65; grantee Yaddo, 1963-64, MacDowell Colony, 1965-66, Wurlitzer Found., Taos, N.Mex., 1968, 73-75, Va. Ctr. for Creative Arts, 1983, 85, Ragdale Found., 1990. Mem. Author's Guild, Virginia Woolf Soc., Kappa Kappa Gamma. Avocation: gardening. Home and Office: 1932 Candelaria Rd NW Albuquerque NM 87107

RICHTER, JOHN CHARLES, prosecutor; Grad., Emory U.; JD, U. Va. Law clk. to Hon. J. Owen Forrester US Dist. Ct. (no. dist.) Ga.; asst. dist. atty. Cobb County, Ga., 1998; chief of staff, criminal divsn. US Dept. Justice, 1998, acting asst. atty. gen. criminal divsn., acting US atty. (we. dist.) Okla., 2005—06, US atty., 2006—. Office: US Attys Office 210 W Park Ave Ste 400 Oklahoma City OK 73102 *

RICHTER, JUDITH ANNE, pharmacologist, educator; b. Wilmington, Del., Mar. 4, 1942; d. Henry John and Dorothy Madelyn (Schroeder) R. BA, U. Colo., 1964; PhD, Stanford U., 1969. Postdoctoral fellow Cambridge (Eng.) U., 1969-70, U. London, 1970-71; asst. prof. pharmacology Sch. Medicine Ind. U., Indpls., 1971-78, assoc. prof. pharmacology and neurobiology, 1978-84, prof., 1984—. Vis. assoc. prof. U. Ariz. Health Sci. Ctr., Tucson, 1983; mem. biomed. rsch. rev. com. Nat. Inst. on Drug Abuse, 1983-87. Mem. editl. bd. Jour. Neurochemistry, 1982-87; contbr. numerous articles to sci. jours. Fellow, Wellcome Trust, 1969—71; scholar, Boettcher Found., 1960—64. Mem. AAAS, Am. Soc. for Pharmacology and Exptl. Therapeutics (exec. com. neuropharmacology div. 1989-91), Am. Soc. for Neurochemistry, Internat. Soc. for Neurochemistry, Soc. for Neurosci., Women in Neurosci., Assn. Women in Sci., Phi Beta Kappa, Sigma Xi. Achievements include research in neuropharmacology, especially barbiturates, neurobiology of mutant mice and dopaminergic systems, and regulation of sensory neuron glutamate release. Office: Ind U Sch Medicine 635 Barnhill Dr Indianapolis IN 46202-5126 Home Phone: 317-291-9222; Office Phone: 317-274-7593. Business E-Mail: jrichter@iupui.edu.

RICHTER, PETER CHRISTIAN, lawyer; b. Opava, Czechoslovakia, June 13, 1944; came to U.S., 1951; s. Hanus and Alzbeta (Kindlarova) R.; m. Leslie Diane Rousseau, Nov. 25, 1967; children: Timothy Jason, Lindsey Berta. BS, U. Oreg., 1967, JD, 1971. Bar: Oreg. 1971, U.S. Dist. Ct. 1972, U.S. Ct. Appeals (9th cir.) 1972, U.S. Supreme Ct. 1983. Assoc. Veatch, Lovett & Stiner, Portland, Oreg., 1971-73; ptnr. Miller Nash LLP, Portland, 1978—. Adj. prof. law trial advocacy Northwestern Sch. of Law, Lewis and Clark Coll., Portland, 1986—; pro tempore judge Multnomah County Cir. Ct., Portland, 1985—1998, Oreg. State Bar Trial Advocacy Seminars, 1988—; trial advocacy coll. planner, instr. Oreg. State Bar, 1998—. Author: (handbook) Oregon State Bar, 1987, 88, 89; co-author: (chpt. in book) Oregon State Bar Damage Manual, 1985, 90; editor, program planner Sales: The Oregon Experience, 1989. Trustee, bd. dirs. Parry Ctr. for Children, Portland, 1990; former bd. dir. Boy Scouts of Am., Columbia Pacific Coun., Portland, Nat. Conf. Christians and Jews, Portland, 1983; bd. advisers Pacific Crest Outward Bound, 2000. With Oreg. Army N.G., 1967-75. Recipient Cert. of Appreciation Northwestern Sch. of Law, 1990; named one of ten Best Litigators in Oreg., Nat. Bar Jour. Fellow Am. Bar Found.; mem. ABA (trial techniques com.), Fed. Bar Assn. (Oreg. chpt.), Am. Bd. Trial Advocates (advocate), Internat. Assn. of Def. Counsel, Oreg. Bar Assn. (lectr. trial advocacy seminars 1988—, mem. jud. adminstn. com, bus. lit. sec. exec. comm.), Multnomah Bar Assn. (former bd dirs.), Oreg. Assn. Def. Counsel (cert. of appreciation 1987, 89) Inns of Ct., Multnomah Athletic Club (trustee, pres.), Arlington Club. Avocations: squash, tennis, skiing, golf, reading, motorcycling riding. Office: Miller Nash LLP 111 SW 5th Ave Ste 3500 Portland OR 97204-3699 Office Phone: 503-224-5858. Business E-Mail: peter.richter@millernash.com.

RICHTER, ROBERT C., retired automotive executive; V.p.- admin. Dana Corp., Toledo, 1997—98, v.p.- fin. and admin., 1998—99, v.p., CFO, 1999—2006; chmn. Dana Credit Corp., 2002.

RICHTER, STUART M., lawyer; b. Bethlehem, Pa., July 17, 1961; BS, U. Va., 1983; JD summa cum laude, Pepperdine U., 1986. Bar: Calif. 1986, US Ct. Appeals, 9th Cir., US Dist. Ct., Dist. Ariz., US Dist. Ct., Ctrl. Ea. No. and So. Dists. Calif. Ptnr., co-head Litig. Practice Katten Muchin Zavis Rosenman, LA. Mem.: LA County Bar Assn. Office: Katten Muchin Zavis Rosenman Ste 2600 2029 Century Park E Los Angeles CA 90067 Office Phone: 310-788-4582. Office Fax: 310-712-8434. E-mail: stuart.richter@kmzr.com.

RICHTER, W.D., screenwriter, director, producer; b. New Britain, Conn., Dec. 7, 1945; s. Walter Oswald and Hedwig (Duch) R.; m. Susan Booth, June 22, 1968. BA, Dartmouth Coll., 1968; postgrad., U. So. Calif., 1968-70. Freelance writer, producer, director, 1973—. Screenwriter: Slither, 1973, Peeper, 1975, Nickelodeon, 1976, Invasion of the Body Snatchers, 1978, Dracula, 1979, Brubaker, 1980 (Academy award nomination best original screenplay 1980), All Night Long, 1981, Hard Feelings, 1982, Big Trouble in Little China, 1986, Needful Things, 1993, Home for The Holidays, 1995, Stealth, 2005; prodr., dir.: (films) Buckaroo Banzai, 1984, Late for Dinner, 1991. Mem. Writers Guild Am., Dirs. Guild Am.

RICHTMAN, JACK, French language educator; b. NYC, Mar. 15, 1927; s. Fred and Rose (Blumenfeld) R BA, Bklyn. Coll., 1959; MA, Columbia U., 1961, PhD, 1969. Prof. French studies SUNY, Albany, 1962—95, prof. emeritus, 1995—. Assoc. dean Coll. of Humanities SUNY, Albany, 1992-94 Author: Adrienne Lecouvreur: The Actress and the Age, 1971; contbr. articles to profl. jours Fulbright fellow Fulbright Commn., 1961-62 Mem. MLA (editor Lesbian and Gay Studies Newsletter, 1999-2004), Les Amis de Jean Cocteau (Am. corr. 2002—) Home: 484 W 43d St Apt 12R New York NY 10036 Personal E-mail: jack.richtman@rcn.com.

RICK, ROSELEEN P., lawyer; b. NYC, 1941; BA, Va. Commonwealth Univ., 1976; JD, Univ. Richmond, 1980. Bar: Va. 1980. Ptnr., practice group leader, multi-family housing Troutman Sanders LLP, Richmond, Va. Mem.: ABA, Nat. Assn. Women Bus. Owners, Va. Bar Assn., Richmond Bar Assn. Office Phone: 804-697-1462. Office Fax: 804-698-6007. Business E-Mail: roseleen.rick@troutmansanders.com.

RICKABAUGH, RENÉ LANE, principal; b. Newcastle, Wyo., Sept. 1, 1957; d. James Austin and Patricia Lee (Baumgartner) Lane; m. Ronald J. Rickabaugh, Aug. 1, 1981. BA in Elem. and Spl. Edn. cum laude, U. Wyo., Laramie, 1979, MA in Spl. Edn., 1989. Spl. summer program dir. Assn. for Retarded Citizens Weston County, Newcastle, 1979; spl. edn. tchr. Natrona County Sch. Dist. 1, Casper, Wyo., 1979—84, ednl. resource specialist, cons. for instrn., curriculum and materials for handicapped students, 1984—92, prin. spl. edn., 1992—94; elem. prin., Title I dir. Bar Nunn Sch., 1994—. Mem. Wyo. state com. North Ctrl. Assn. Edn. chmn. First United Meth. Ch., chair staff/parish rels. com. Recipient Medallion Excellence award, NCSD, 2005. Mem. NEA, AAUW, Wyo. Assn. Elem. Prins. (past treas., pres.-elect 2005, pres. 2006), Nat. Assn. Elem. Prins., Coun. Exceptional Children (past membership chmn.), Assn. Direct Instrn., Assn. Retarded Citizens (past sec. N.C. chpt.), U. Wyo. Alumni Assn., PEO (past pres. chpt.), Omicron Delta Kappa, Kappa Delta Pi (past v.p.), Phi Delta Kappa (past chpt. pres.), Phi Kappa Phi. Home: 80 Magnolia St Casper WY 82604-4063 Home Phone: 307-266-5526; Office Phone: 307-577-4507. Personal E-mail: rener_9@msn.com.

RICKARD, DAVID B., retail executive; b. Oneida, NY, 1946; BS, Cornell U., 1969; MBA, Harvard U., 1971. From internat. acct. to fin. control mgr. U.S. mktg. S.C. Johnson Wax, Inc., 1971-74; with Gen. Foods Corp., fin. dir. internat.; dir. investor rels. Kraft Gen. Foods; v.p. fin. and strategy Kraft USA; sr. v.p., CFO Grand Metropolitan, 1991-94, group contr. London, 1994-95; fin. dir. Internat. Distillers and Vintners, Ltd., 1995-96; exec. v.p. Internat. Distillers and Vintners-Americas, 1996-97; sr. v.p., CFO RJR Nabisco, NYC, 1997-99; exec. v.p., CFO, chief adminstrv. officer CVS Corp., Woonsocket, RI, 1999—2007; exec. v.p., CFO, CAO CVS/Caremark Corp., Woonsocket, RI, 2007—. Bd. dirs. Harris Corp., May Dept. Stores. Mem.: Worldwide Retail Exchange, Financial Acctg. Standards Advisory Coun. (mem. steering comt.). Office: CVS Caremark Corp 1 CVS Dr Woonsocket RI 02895 *

RICKARD, LISA ANN, lawyer; b. Englewood, NJ, Oct. 22, 1955; d. Joseph Mitchell and Ann Marie (Samen) Moore; m. J. Scott Rickard, June 18, 1977; children: Jack Taylor, Justin Moore. BA in Govt. and French, Lafayette Coll., 1977; JD, Am. U., 1982. Legis. asst. Bank of Am., Washington, 1977-78; spl. asst. and press asst. to Sen. Richard Stone, Washington, 1978-80; legis. asst. to Sen. Frank Murkowski, Washington, 1981; assoc. and ptnr. Akin, Gump, Strauss, Hauer & Feld, Washington, 1982-93; v.p. federal affairs Ryder System, Inc., Washington, 1993-97, sr. v.p. govt. affairs, 1997; v.p. fed. & state govt. affairs Dow Chemical Co.; pres. U.S. C. of C. Inst. for Legal Reform, Washington. Bd. dirs., mem. corp. adv. coun. Women's Rsch. and Edn. Inst., Washington, 1991—. Diplome D'Etudes Francaises Cours Moyen, Deuxieme Degres, U. Strasbourg, France, 1976. Mem. ABA, D.C. Bar Assn. Episcopalian. Avocation: travel. Office: Institute for Legal Reform 1615 H St NW Washington DC 20062-2000 Office Phone: 202-463-3107. E-mail: lrickard@uschamber.com.

RICKARD, MARGARET LYNN, library director, consultant; b. Detroit, July 31, 1944; d. Frank Mathias and Betty Louise (Lee) Sieger; m. Cyriac Thannikary, Nov. 13, 1965 (div. Feb. 1973); 1 child, Luke Anthony Thannikary; m. Marcos T. Perez, Mar. 1973 (dec. Oct. 1973); m. Lui Gotti, Dec. 23, 1984 (dec. Aug. 1997); m. William A. Rickard, Aug. 22, 1998 (dec. Aug. 21, 2005). AB, U. Detroit, Mich., 1968; MLS, Pratt Inst., Bklyn., 1969; postgrad., NYU, 1976—77. Cert. libr. N.Y. Sr. libr. Queens Pub. Libr., Jamaica, NY, 1969-77; libr. dir. El Centro (Calif.) Pub. Libr., 1977-99; ret., 1999. Vice chmn., chmn. Serra Coop. Libr. Sys., San Diego, 1980—82; libr. cons., 1998—; county libr./cons. Imperial County Free Libr., 1993—99. Pres. Hist. Site Found., El Centro, 1988—99, 1992, sec., 1989, trustee, 1989—99, v.p., 1991—92; mem. Downton El Centro Assn., mem. arches bus. improvement dist.; mem. comm. and arts task force Imperial County Arts Coun.; coord. arts and culture com. City of El Centro Strategic Plan; fin. sec. St. Elizabeth Luth. Ch., El Centro, 1988. Recipient Disting. Svc. award, El Dorado County ACSA, 2004, El Dorado County Disting. Employee Svc. award, ACSA, 2004; Title IIB fellow, Pratt Inst., 1968—69. Mem.: AAUW (v.p. El Centro 1988), ALA, Calif. County Librs. Assn., Calif. Libr. Assn., Toastmasters, El Centro C. of C., Women of Moose (sr. regent El Centro 1988—89, ednl. advancment chmn. 1999—2000), Soroptomists (life; v.p. El Centro 1978, corr. sec. 1990—91, 1st v.p. 1991—92, pres. 1992—93, 2d v.p. 1995—96, 1998—99, rec. sec. 1997—98). Democrat. Lutheran. Home and Office: 6169 Terrace Dr PO Box 232 Pollock Pines CA 95726 E-mail: rickmeg@worldnet.att.net.

RICKARD, RUTH DAVID, retired history and political science professor; b. Fed. Republic Germany, Feb. 20, 1926; came to U.S., 1940; d. Carl and Alice (Koch) David; m. Robert M. Yaffe, Oct. 1949 (dec. 1959); children: David, Steven; m. Norman G. Rickard, June 1968 (dec. 1988); 1 stepson, Douglas. BS cum laude, Northwestern U., Evanston, Ill., 1947, MA, 1948. Law editor Commerce Clearing House, Chgo., 1948; instr. history U. Ill., Chgo., 1949-51, instr. extension program Waukegan, 1960-67; instr. history Waukegan Schs., 1960-69; original faculty, prof.

western civilization, polit. sci. Coll. of Lake County, Grayslake, Ill., 1969-92. Mem. Inter-Univ. Seminar on Armed Forces and Soc.; mem. Hospitality Info. Svc. for Diplomatic Residents and Families affiliate Meridian Internat. Ctr.; spkr. in field. Author: History of College of Lake County, 1987 (honored by city of Waukegan 1987), (poem) I Lost My Wings, 1989, Au Revoir from Emeritusdom, 1993, Where are the Safety Zones, 1994; contbg. author: History of National Press Club: Reliable Sources, 1997; contbr. articles to profl. jours. Mem. Econ. Devel. Com., Waukegan, 1992-93; working with homeless through Samaritans of Greater Washington area, 2000—. Scholar Freedoms Found. Am. Legion, Valley Forge, Pa., 1967. Mem. AAUW (pres. Waukegan chpt. 1955-57, scholarship named for her 1985, program co-chair McLean chpt. 1997-2000), LWV (charter, v.p. Waukegan chpt.), Nat. Press Club D.C., Northwestern U. Alumni Washington (bd. dirs.). Avocations: writing, travel, lecturing, reading, theater.

RICKEL, ANNETTE URSO, psychology and psychiatry researcher, educator; b. Phila. d. Ralph Francis and Marguerite (Calcaterra) Urso; 1 child, John Ralph Rickel. BA, Mich. State U., 1969; PhD, MD, U. Mich., 1972. Lic. psychologist, Mich. Faculty early childhood edn. Merrill-Palmer Inst., Detroit, 1967-69; adj. faculty U. Mich., Ann Arbor, 1969-75; asst. dir. N.E. Guidance Ctr., Detroit, 1972-75; asst. prof. psychology Wayne State U., Detroit, 1975-81; vis. assoc. prof. Columbia U., NYC, 1982-83; assoc. prof. psychology Wayne State U., 1981-87, asst. provost, 1989-91, prof. psychology, 1987-95; Am. Coun. on Edn. fellow Princeton and Rutgers Univs., 1990-91; clin. prof. dept. psychiatry Georgetown U., Washington, 1995—2000; program officer Rockefeller Found., 2000—03; pres. Annette Urso Rickel Found., 2003—; prof. Weill Cornell Med. Sch., 2005—. AAAS and APA Congl. Sci. fellow on Senate Fin. Subcom. on Health and Pres.'s Nat. Health Care Reform Task Force, 1992—93; prof. Weill Cornell Med. Sch., 2005. Cons. editor Jour. of Cmty. Psychology, Jour. Primary Prevention; co-author: Social and Psychological Problems of Women, 1984, Preventing Maladjustment..., 1987; author: Teenage Pregnancy and Parenting, 1989, Keeping Children From Harm's Way, 1997, High Risk Sexual Behavior, 1998, Understanding Managed Care, 2000, Attention Deficit Hyperactivity Disorder in Children and Adults, 2006, Chronic Illness in Children and Adolescents, 2007; contbr. articles to profl. jours. Mem. Pres.'s Task Force on Nat. Health Care Reform, 1993; bd. dirs. Children's Ctr. of Wayne County, Mich., 1989—, The Epilepsy Ctr. of Mich., 1984-92, Nat. Symphony Orch., 1997—, Reading is Fundamental, 2000—, Chamber Music Soc. of Lincoln Ctr., 2002—, Soc. Meml. Sloan Kettering Cancer Ctr., 2002—, The Kellogg Found., 1996-97, The John D. and Catherine T. MacArthur Found., 1998-99. Grantee NIMH, 1976-86, Eloise and Richard Webber Found., 1977-80, McGregor Fund, 1977-78, 82, David M. Whitney Fund, 1982, Katherine Tuck Fund, 1985-90, NIH, 2000; recipient Career Devel. Chair award, 1985-86. Fellow APA (div. pres. 1984-85); mem. Internat. Women's Forum, Soc. for Rsch. in Child Devel., Soc. for Rsch. in Child and Adolescent Psychopathology, Internat. Assn. of Applied Psychologists, Sigma Xi, Psi Chi. Roman Catholic. Office Phone: 212-659-7760. Personal E-mail: rickelau@aol.com.

RICKELS, KARL, psychiatrist, educator; b. Wilhelmshaven, Germany, Aug. 17, 1924; came to U.S., 1954, naturalized, 1960; s. Karl E. and Stephanie (Roehrhoff) R.; m. Rosalind Wilson, June 27, 1964; children: Laurence Arthur, PhD, Stephen W., Michael R. MD, U. Muenster, 1951. Intern Dortmund (Germany) City Hosp., 1951-52; postgrad. tng. U. Erlangen, U. Frankfurt, City Hosp. Kassel, 1952-54; resident in psychiatry Mental Health Inst., Cherokee, Iowa, 1954-55, Hosp. U. Pa., Phila., 1955-57; from instr. to assoc. prof. U. Pa., Phila., 1957-69, prof. psychiatry, 1969—, prof. pharmacology, 1976-98, Stuart and Emily B.H. Mudd prof. human behavior, 1977—, chief mood and anxiety disorders program, 1964—, chmn. com. on studies involving human beings Phila., 1985-98. Chief psychiatry Phila. Gen. Hosp., 1975-77. Editor, author 9 books; contbr. over 550 articles to profl. publs. Fellow Am. Coll. Neuropsychopharmacology (life; charter), Am. Soc. Clin. Psychopharmacology, Am. Psychiat. Assn. (life), Coll. Physicians Phila., Collegium Internat. Neuro-Psychopharmacologicum; mem. Psychiat. Rsch. Soc., European Coll. Neuropsychopharmacology (corr.). Home: 1324 Youngsford Rd Gladwyne PA 19035 Office: U Pa Dept Psychiatry Ste 670 3535 Market St Philadelphia PA 19104-3515 Home Phone: 610-649-4838; Office Phone: 215-746-6417. Business E-Mail: krickels@mail.med.upenn.edu.

RICKERT, ANTHONY H., lawyer; b. Salisbury, Md., May 28, 1955; BA cum laude, Univ. Md., 1977; JD magna cum laude, Georgetown Univ., 1981. Bar: DC 1982, Md. 1982. Law clk. Judge J. Dudley Digges, Md. Ct. Appeals; ptnr., chmn. pvt. equity practice group DLA Piper, Washington. Contbr. articles to profl. jours. Office: DLA Piper 1200 19th St NW Washington DC 20036-2412 Office Phone: 202-861-3894. Office Fax: 202-689-7604. Business E-Mail: anthony.rickert@dlapiper.com.

RICKERT, JEANNE MARTIN M., lawyer; b. Cambridge, Mass., May 13, 1953; d. Robert Torrence and Margaret (Mutchler) Martin; m. Scott Edwin Rickert, Aug. 19, 1978. BA, Cornell U., 1975; JD, Case Western U., 1978. Bar: Ohio 1980, admitted to practice: US Dist. Ct. (No. Dist.) Ohio 1980. Law clk. to Judge Leroy J. Contie Jr. U.S. Dist. Ct. Ohio, Akron, 1978-80; assoc. Jones, Day, Reavis & Pogue, Cleve., 1980-86; ptnr. Jones & Day, Cleve., 1987—. Author: The Limited Liability Company in Ohio: 1994 Senate Bill 74, with Commentary and Practice Pointers, 1994; co-author (with John Currivan): Ohio Limited Liability Companies, 1999. Mem.: ABA, Ohio State Bar Assn. (corp. law com. 1985—), Cleve. Bar Assn., Order of the Coif. Office: Jones Day Reavis & Pogue N Point 901 Lakeside Ave E Cleveland OH 44114-1190 Office Phone: 216-586-7220. Office Fax: 216-579-0212. Business E-Mail: jmrickert@jonesday.com.

RICKERT, JONATHAN BRADLEY, retired foreign service officer; b. Washington, July 23, 1937; s. Van Dusen and Margaret Eleanor (Bradley) R.; m. Ulla Gerd Margareta Granstrand, June 20, 1969; children: Ulla Margaret, Jonathan Bernt. AB cum laude, Princeton U, 1959; diploma Russian lang., U.S. Army Lang. Sch., 1962; student, Harvard U., 1976-77; MA, George Washington U., 1982. Rotational jr. officer Exec. Sec. State Dept., 1963-65; consular officer Embassy, London, 1965-66, staff aide to amb., polit. officer Moscow, 1966-68; exchanges officer Office Soviet and Eastern European Exchanges State Dept., 1969-70, with Romanian Lang. Tng. FSI, 1971; consular officer Embassy Bucharest, 1971-73, polit. officer, 1973-74; spl. asst. to U.S. Rep. U.S. Delegation MBFR, Vienna, 1974-76; polit./labor officer Embassy Port of Spain, 1977-80; desk officer Trinidad, Guyana, Suriname, acting dep. dir. Office Caribbean Affairs State Dept., 1980-82, desk officer Romania, Office Eastern European and Yugoslav Affairs, 1982-84, with Bulgarian Lang. Tng., 1984-85; dep. chief mission Embassy Sofia, 1985-88; chief European Assignments divsn. State Dept., 1988-90; legis. asst. to Sen Bob Packwood, 1990-91; dep. chief mission Embassy Bucharest, 1991-95; dir. Office of N. Cen. European Affairs State Dept., 1995-98, program officer Office of the Coord. for U.S. Assistance to Europe and Eurasia, 1998—2005, pub. diplomacy officer Bur. European and Eurasian Affairs, 2006—; bd. dirs. Project on Ethnic Rels., Princeton, N.J., 1999. With U.S. Army, 1961-62. Mem. Am. Fgn. Svc. Assn. Episcopalian. Personal E-mail: therickets@hotmail.com.

RICKETSON, MARY E., former dean, lawyer; m. Nathan Ben Coats. JD, U. Denver, 1978. Asst. atty gen., Colo.; dep. dist. atty. Colo.; pvt. practice specializing in employment dispute mediation; exec. dir. Colo. Lawyer's Com.; dean, univ. prof. U. Denver Sturm Coll. Law, 2000—06. Affiliated Jud. Arbitrators and Mediators. Trustee Dian Fossey Found. Internat.; co-chair Mayor Wellington Webb's 2025 Commn., 2002. Recipient Women of Distinction award, Mill High Girl Scouts, 2004, Edwin Wolf award, Lawyers Com. Civil Rights Under Law, 2004, Mile High Coun. Girl Scouts award, 2004. Mem.: Am. Bar Found., Am. Law Inst., Colo. Hispanic Bar Assn. (Cmty. Svc. award 2003), Colo. Profl. Soc. on Abuse of Children (former pres.), Colo. Women's Bar Found. (former pres.), Colo. Women's Bar Assn. (former pres., Mary Lathrop award 2003).

RICKETT, CAROLYN KAYE MASTER, artist, small business owner; b. Ft. Worth, Apr. 24, 1941; d. Lester Buford and Dorothy Minerva (Whittington) Master; m. David Franklin Rickett, May 3, 1981; 1 child, Julia Beth Allen. BFA, Tex. Christian U., Ft. Worth, 1993; MFA, Tex. Woman's U., 1997; M in Criminology, U. Tex., Arlington, 2001, student in History, 2002—. Artist, owner StarMaster Graphic Design and Fine Art, Ft. Worth, 1988—; represented by Downstairs Gallery, Dallas, Marriane Garrah, Jasper, Alberta, 2005—. Presenter in field. Represented in permanent collections Jasper Mus., Nat. Women's Caucus Arts Archives, also pvt. collections, one-woman shows include Jasper Mus., Alta., Can., 1994, Downstairs Gallery, Jasper, 1994, Del Bello Gallery, Toronto, Ont., Can., 1996, Jasper Artists Guild, Jasper Mus. Satellite Gallery, 2005, exhibitions include Tex. Christian U., Ft. Worth, 1991, 1995, 1997, UN 4th Conf. Women, Beijing, 1995, Greater Denton Coun. Arts., Tex., 1994—96, Bass Mus., Miami Broward C.C., Davie, Fla., 1996, San Jacinto Coll., Houston, 1996, Aisling Studio, Durango, Colo, 1996, U. Tex., Arlington, 1998, World Trade Ctr., Dallas, 1998, exhibitions include traveling show Beijing and Beyong, NY, 1998—2000; co-prodr.:, one-woman shows include Jasper Mus., 2005. Grantee, Tex. Christian U., 1990—93; scholar, 1991—93, Ray and Bertha Lakey Meml., 1994—96. Mem.: Am. Soc. Crime, Tex. Art Educators Assn., Nat. Trust for Hist. Preservation, Mus. Women in Arts, Am. Soc. Criminology, Am. Criminal Justice Scis.

RICKETTS, JOHN JOE, securities company executive; b. Nebr. City, Nebr., July 16, 1941; s. Donovan Platte and Florence Marie (Erhart) R.; m. Marlene Margaret Volkmer, June 15, 1963; children: J. Peter, Thomas, Laura. BA, Creighton U., 1969. Counselor Father Flannagan's Boys Home, Boys Town, Nebr., 1967—68; with sales dept. Dean Witter & Co., Omaha, 1968—74; investment counselor Ricketts & Co., Omaha, 1974—75; pres. Ameritrade Inc., Omaha, 1975—82, CEO, 1982—99, co-CEO, 1999—. Named one of Forbes' Richest Americans, 2006. Republican. Roman Catholic. Office: Ameritrade Holding Corp 4211 S 102d St Omaha NE 68127

RICKETTS, SONDRA LOU, librarian; b. McFall, Mo., Aug. 4, 1941; d. Jewell E. and Daisie Glenn (Weller) Rainey; m. Rex Errol Ricketts, June 14, 1964; children: Chad Errol, Trina Rae, Neysa Carrie. BS, U. Mo., 1963—. Cert. tchr., Mo. Libr. East Ladue Jr. High Sch., Ladue, Mo., 1963-65; adminstrv. asst. Jacksonville (Ill.) Pub. Libr., 1965; reference libr. Ill. Coll., Jacksonville, 1965-66; cataloger Stephens Coll., Columbia, Mo., 1966-69; libr. Clark (Mo.) Elem. Sch., 1981-95, Middle Grove Elem. Sch., 1996—2003. Sun. sch. tchr. Presbyn. Ch., Columbia, 1977-84; mem. Hallsville (Mo.) Sch. bond com., 1980; cmty. leader Hallsville 4-H, 1980-82, mem. state com., Columbia, 1985, project leader Hallsville 4-H, 1980-85, 94-2000; bd. dirs. 4-H Found., Columbia, 1991—, sec., 1997-2000; mem. Boone County 4-H Auction com., 1994-2000; mem. ways and means com., hallsville PTA, 1980, publicity com., 1981; co-chmn. Hallsville H.S. All Night Sr. party, 1985, 90. Conf. honoree AIJCA, 1991. Mem. Am. Internat. Charolais Assn., Mo. Assn. of Sch. Librs., Mid.-Mo. Regional Assn. Sch. Librs., Mo. Univ. Alumnae Assn., Boone County Alumnae Assn., Alpha Chi Omega Alumni Assn., U. Mo. Jefferson Club, Pi Lambda Theta. Avocations: crafts, swimming, reading, dance, genealogy. E-mail: rex.ricketts@gte.net.

RICKETTS, VIRGINIA LEE, historian, researcher; b. Jamestown, Kans., Jan. 12, 1925; d. Roy Earl Eastman and Alma Anna Hunter; m. Clair Keith Ricketts, June 3, 1944; children: Keith Alan, Dennis Lee, Donald Gene. Grad. H.S., Filer, Idaho. Clk. dist. ct., auditor, recorder Jerome County, Idaho, 1972—79; pvt. practice historian, rschr. Jerome, 1979—. Mem. Idaho State Hist. Records Adv. Bd., Boise, 1976-2002; pres. Idaho Assn. Recorders and Clks., 1977-78; cons. Idaho State Supreme Ct., Boise, 1979-81; tour dir., instr. Coll. So. Idaho, Twin Falls, 1984-97; mem. Bur. Land Mgmt. Adv. Bd., Shoshone, Idaho, 1989-95, Upper Snake River Ecosystem Adv. Bd., Idaho, 1995-98; Internat. Toastmistress communicator, 1988; lectr. in field Author: The History of the North Side-The First 75 Years, 1982, Greater Twin Falls Historical Guide, 1988, A History of the Middle Snake River, 1996, Then and Now in Southern Idaho, 1998, Shoshone Falls the Magnificent Spectacle, 2005 Organizer Friends St. Stricker Ranch, Inc., Twin Falls, 1984 Recipient Cert. of Commendation, Am. Assn. for State and Local History, 1984, Cert. of Resolution of Appreciation, Idaho State Bd. Edn., 1998, Esto Perpetua award Idaho State Hist. Soc., 2004; named Idaho Disting. Citizen, Idaho Statesmen, 1988, Centennial Citizen, Citizens of Jerome County Idaho, 1990 Mem. Idaho State Hist. Soc. (trustee 1987-99, chair bd. trustees 1991-98), Oreg. Calif. Trails Assn. (organizer Idaho chpt. 1984, treas. 1985-99), Jerome County Hist. Soc., Inc. (co-organizer 1984, former pres., curator 1985-2004), Idaho Assn. Mus. (Outstanding Svc. award 1998), Soroptimist Internat. Am. (Woman of Distinction 1999), PEO (historian Ea. Idaho chpt. 1987-98) Republican. Presbyterian. Avocations: needlecrafts, gardening, sports, family activities. Home: 516 E 300 S Jerome ID 83338-6747

RICKLEFS, DALE LYNNE, library director; b. Chgo., July 29, 1953; d. Glenn Harley and Eleanor Clara Rogers; 1 child, Reyhan. BA, Ill. Wesleyan U., 1974; MLS, U. Tex., 1977. Libr. Radian Corp., Austin, Tex., 1975—80; libr. dir. City of Round Rock, Tex., 1980—. Mem. ex officio Friends Round Rock Pub. Libr., 1983—, Round Rock Pub. Libr. Found., 1991—; bd. dirs. Round Rock Cmty. Choir, 1998—2003; pres. United Way Greater Williamson Co., Round Rock, 2003—05; boy scout dist. cub trainer Boy Scouts Am. Tomahawk Dist., Austin-Georgetown, Tex., 1991—92; pres. Main St. Quilt Guild, 2002—03. Recipient Dist. Cub-scouter of Yr., Boy Scouts Am. Tomahawk Dist., Texas, 1992. Mem.: ALA, Texas Mcpl. League Libr. Dir.'s Divsn. (pres. 1988—89), Tex. Libr. Assn. (chmn. dist. 3 1984—85). Avocations: machine embroidery, old house renovations, painting, quilting. Office: City Round Rock Pub Libr 216 E Main St Round Rock TX 78664 Office Phone: 512-218-7010. Business E-Mail: dale@round-rock.tx.us.

RICKLES, DONALD JAY, comedian, actor; b. LI, NY, May 8, 1926; s. Max S. and Etta (Feldman) R.; m. Barbara Sklar, Mar. 14, 1965; children: Mindy Beth, Lawrence Corey. Grad., Am. Acad. Dramatic Arts, NYC. Appeared in TV shows The Don Rickles Show, 1971-72, C.P.O. Sharkey, 1976-77, Foul-Ups, Bleeps and Blunders, 1984, Daddy Dearest, 1993; appeared in movies Run Silent, Run Deep, 1958, The Rat Race, 1960, Kelly's Heroes, 1992, Casino, 1995, Toy Story, 1995, Quest for Camelot, 1998, Toy Story 2, 1999, The Wool Cap, 2004, others; Reno and Lake Tahoe, Nev., Golden Nugget, Las Vegas, Resorts Atlantic City, numerous other nightclubs; numerous appearances TV variety shows; rec. albums include Don Rickles Speaks, Hello Dummy; author: Rickles Book, 2007 (NY Times Bestseller). With USN, 1943—45. Named Entertainer of Yr. Friars Club, 1974, Entertainer of Yr., Am. Gaming Assn., 2004, Las Vegas Comedian of Yr., Las Vegas Conv. and Visitor's Authority, 2004; awarded star on Hollywood Walk of Fame, 2000; recipient Pinnacle award US Comedy and Arts Festival, 2007. Office: care Shefrin Co 808 S Ridgeley Dr Los Angeles CA 90036-4727

RICKMAN, ALAN, actor; b. Hammersmith, London, England, Feb. 21, 1946; Student, Royal Acad. of Dramatic Art. Stage appearances: The Seagull, Mephisto, Les Liaisons Dangereuses, 1985, 87 (Tony nominee Best Actor 1987), Tango at the End of Winter, 1991, Hamlet, 1992, Anthony and Cleopatra, 1998, Private Lives (Tony nominee, Best Stage Actor award Variety Club Show Bus. Awards 2002); (TV movies) Romeo and Juliet, Masterpiece Theater, 1978, Therese Raquin, 1980, Barchester Chronicles, 1984, Spirit of Man, 1989, Revolutionary Witness, 1989, Victoria Wood's All Day Breakfast, 1992, Fallen Angels, 1993, Rasputin, 1996 (Golden Globe, Emmy and SAG awards for Best Actor), Victoria Wood with All the Trimmings, 2000, We Know Where You Live, 2001, Something the Lord Made, 2004; (films) Die Hard, 1988, The January Man, 1989, Robin Hood: Prince of Thieves, 1991, Quigley Down Under, 1990, Truly, Madly, Deeply, 1991, Closet Land, 1991, Close My Eyes, 1991, Bob Roberts, 1992, Mesmer, 1993, An Awfully Big Adventure, 1994, Sense and Sensibility, 1995, Michael Collins, 1996, Judas Kiss, 1998, Dogma, 1998, Dark Harbor, 1998, Galaxy Quest, 1999, Play, 2000, Blow Dry, 2001, Harry Potter and the Sorcer's Stone, 2001, Search for John Gissin, 2001, (also exec prodr.) Willows, 2001, Harry Potter and the Chamber of Secrets, 2002, Love Actually, 2003, Harry Potter and the Prisoner of Azkaban, 2004, (voice) The Hitchhiker's Guide to the Galaxy, 2005, Harry Potter and the Goblet of Fire, 2005; writer, dir.: The Winter Guest, 1997 (Best Film award Chgo. Film Festival). Office: Oxford House 76 Oxford St London W1N 0AX England

RICKS, JOHN ADDISON, III, history professor; b. Charlotte, NC, Aug. 18, 1939; s. John Addison Jr. and Mamye Snow (Turner) R.; m. Nancy Elaine Ricks, Apr. 23 1966; children: Elizabeth Anne, John Addison IV. BA, Davidson Coll., 1961; MA, Tulane U., 1963; PhD, U. N.C., 1974. Instr. history Montreat- Anderson Coll., NC, 1966-68; from instr. to prof. Valdosta State U., Ga., 1968-88; prof. history, chmn. social sci. edn., bus. adminstrn. div. Mid. Ga. Coll., Cochran, 1988—2003. Contbr. articles to jour., newspapers. Pres. Friends of the Libr., Cochran, 1989-90; clk. of session, elder First Presbyn. Ch., Eastman, 1990-93; 1998-2001, scoutmaster Boy Scouts Am., Valdosta, 1982-84; mem. Valdosta Bd. Edn., 1976-80. 1st lt. US Army, 1963-65. Fulbright Found. grantee, 1992, 97. Mem.: Cochran C. of C., Ga. Assn. Historians (pres. 1994—95), So. Assn. Secondary Sch. and Coll. (vis. team 1979), So. Assn. Coll. and Sch. (vis. team 1990), Rotary (pres. 1993—94, asst. gov. Dist. 6920 2005—, Rotarian of Yr. 1997, Paul Harris fellow 2001), Kiwanis (treas. 1980—82, Kiwanian of Yr. 1979). Presbyterian. Avocations: piano, weightlifting, nordic track exercise, reading, chess. Home: 201 E Beech St Cochran GA 31014 Office: Cochran Better Hometown Inc 318 Second St Cochran GA 31014 Home Phone: 478-934-0017; Office Phone: 478-934-0017. E-mail: jricks39@yahoo.com.

RICKS, JOYCIA CAMILLA, retired lawyer; b. Atlanta, Feb. 17, 1949; d. George Palmer and Johnnie Mae (Ricks) Redd. BBA, Albany State Coll., 1971; MS, Ga. State U., 1977; JD, Woodrow Wilson Coll. Law, Atlanta, 1979, LLM, 1987. Bar: Ga. 1979, US Dist. Ct. (no. dist.) Ga. 1979, US Ct. Appeals (5th cir.) 1979. Acctg. clk. Gulf Oil Corp., Atlanta, 1971; clk. EEOC, Atlanta, 1971-73, paralegal specialist, 1973-79, investigator, 1979-91, supervisory investigator, 1992-2000; complaints mgr. CDC, Atlanta, 2000—03; gen. counsel Albany State U. Alumni Assn., 1986—90, 2005—. Recipient Presdl. citation award Equal Opportunity in Higher Edn., Washington, 1981. Mem. ATLA, Atlanta Bar Assn., Albany State Coll. Alumni Assn. (pres. Atlanta chpt. 1983-85), Ga. State U. Alumni Assn., State Bar Ga., Women of the Ch. Presbyn. (hon. life), Am. Bus. Women's Assn. (Woman of Yr., Tara chpt. 1985, 91, Peach chpt. 2003), Spreading Oak Cmty. Club. Democrat. Baptist.

RICKS, MARK G., former lieutenant governor, former state senator; b. Rexburg, Idaho, July 4, 1924; s. Peter J. and Emily E. (Arnold) R.; m. Evelyn Tonks, Aug. 9, 1944; children: Michael T., Gary M., Alan D., Adele Ricks Nielsen, Glen L., Kathie Ricks Tensmeyer, Grant H., Merle K., Douglas T. AS in Agr., Ricks Coll. Mem. Idaho State Senate, 1979-94, majority leader, 1983-88, chmn. reapportionment com., 1982, chmn. senate commerce and labor commn., 1981-82, vice chmn. senate fin. com., 1989-94, state affairs com., chmn., 1989-94, chmn. revenue and projection com., 1989-94, chmn. reapportionment com., 1990-94, lt. gov., State of Idaho, 2006-07; Mem. exec. and adv. bd. council Boy Scouts Am. Named to Eastern Idaho Agrl. Hall of Fame, 1989, Idaho Blue Ribbon Task Force, 2002; named One of Ten Outstanding Legislators Nat. Rep. Legislators Assn., 1987; recipient Community Svc. Prodn. and Example award Rexburg C. of C., 1976, Outstanding Svc. award Madison Sch. Dist., 1987, Distinguished Alumni award Ricks Coll., 1988. Mem. Nat. Conf. State Legis. (exec. com. 1985-87, chmn. nominating com. 1988, mem. rsch. and grants com., vice chmn. fed. taxation com., vice chmn. trade and econ. devel. com., mem. budget and rules com., co-chmn. reapportionement com. 1989, vice chmn. state fed. assembly 1988), Coun. State Govts. (exec. com., budget com. 1989-90, chmn. western legislative conf. 1988-89, chmn. ann. meeting com. 1989-90), Idaho Wheat Growers, Nat. Fedn. Ind. Bus., Rexburg C. of C. (maj. gifts com. Ricks Coll.). Republican. Mormon.

RICKS, THOMAS AARON, real estate developer; b. Boise, Idaho, June 2, 1972; s. Thomas Mecham Ricks and Laura Faye Hodge; m. Ann Marie Baker, Aug. 26, 2003; 1 child, Thomas Jacob. BA, Albertson Coll., Caldwell, Idaho, 1995; MBA, N.W. Vazarene U., Nampa, Idaho, 2007. Aviation cert. Naval Postgrad. Sch., Monterey, Calif., 2004, cert. comml. piolot FAA, multi-engine airplanes and helicopters US Dept. Def., flight instr., lic. real estate. Rancher, farmer Ricks Ranches, Eagle, Idaho, 1985—; asst. Office Gov., Boise, 1995—96; dir. devel. Spur Devel., Eagle, 2005—; owner, CEO Lineage Homes, Eagle, 2005—. Mem. Albertson Coll. Idaho, 1996—, Idaho Young Reps. Capt. USMC, 1997—2005, San Diego. Decorated 5 Strike Flight Air medals USMC, Commendation awards; recipient Eagle Scout award, Boy Scouts Am., Idaho, 1989. Mem.: DAV, VFW, Albertson Coll. Idaho Alumni Bd. Dirs., Boise Young Profls., Am. Legion, Aircraft Owners and Pilots Assn., Marine Corps Assn., Cattlemen's Beef Assn. Avocations: horseback riding, fishing, hunting, running. Office: 1560 N Park Ln Eagle ID 83616

RICKS, THOMAS EDWIN, journalist, writer; b. Beverly, Mass., Sept. 25, 1955; s. David Frank and Anne (Russell) R.; m. Mary Catherine Giblin, Oct. 10, 1981, 1 child BA, Yale U., 1977. Instr. Lingnan Coll., Hong Kong, 1977-79; asst. editor Wilson Quar., Washington, 1979-81; reporter Wall St. Jour., Atlanta, Miami, 1982-86, dep. bur. chief Miami, 1986, reporter Washington, 1987-89, feature editor, 1989-92, Pentagon corr., 1992—99; mil. corr. Washington Post, 2000—. Author: Making the Corps, 1997, FIASCO: The American Military Adventure in Iraq, 2006, A Soldier's Duty, 2001. Co-recipient Pulitzer prize for Nat. Reporting, 2000, 2002. Office: The Washington Post 1150 15th St NW Washington DC 20071

RICKS, THOMAS MILLER, historian, academic administrator; b. Lafayette, Ind., Oct. 15, 1938; s. Michael T. and Veronica K. (Jordan) R.; m. Janice D. Grasso, Aug. 26, 1967; children: Cynthia C., Laila M. BA, U. Notre Dame, 1961; MA, Ind. U., 1968, PhD, 1975. Tchr. history Tehran Internat. Sch., 1972-73; instr. history Macalester Coll., St. Paul, 1974-75; asst. prof. history Georgetown U., Washington, 1975-83; asst. dir. Ctr. for Arab and Islamic Studies Villanova U., Pa., 1985-91, dir. internat. studies Pa., 1985—2002; lectr. history U. Pa., 2002—05. Adj. assoc. prof. history Ctr. for Arab and Islamic Studies, Villanova U., 1985-2002; vis. asst. prof. history Birzeit U., Palestine, 1983-85; mem. Am. Friends Svc. Com., Mid. East Panel, 1996-2006. Editor, compiler, author: (bibliography) Persian Studies: A Bibliography, 1970, Iran: Contemporary Persian Literature, 1974, Critical Perspectives on Persian Literature, 1976; co-author: (textbook) Middle East: Past and Present, 1986; co-founder, co-editor: (jour.) Rev. of Iranian Polit. Economy and History, 1976-80, Birzeit Rsch. Rev., 1985-90; assoc. editor: Frontiers: An Interdisciplinary Jour. of Study Abroad, 1994—. Vol. Iran III program Peace Corps, Mashhad and Mahabad, Iran, 1964-66. Scholar, Ind. U., 1966-67, Birzeit U., 1983-84, Fulbright Found., 1993-95, Gest scholar Haverford Coll., 2003, Spencer Found., 2005-06; Nat. Def. Edn. Act grant US Dept. Edn., 1967-70, grantee

Fulbright-Hays Found., 1971-72, NEH, 1976, 91, Social Sci. Rsch. Coun., 1977, US Dept. Edn., 1988-90, Pa. Dept. Edn., 1990-94, Palestinian Am. Rsch. Ctr., 2003, Spencer Found. fellow, 2005-06. Mem. Coun. for Internat. Ednl. Exch. (bd. dirs. 1997-2000), Coun. for Internat. Exch. of Scholars (bd. dirs. 1996-04), Pa. Coun. for Internat. Edn. (bd. dirs. 1994-03, pres. 1994-99), Mid. East Studies Assn. (co-editor jour. 1980-82), Ctr. for Iranian Rsch. and Analysis (bd. dirs. 1997-2000), Soc. for Iranian Studies (treas. 1974-76), Mid. East Inst., Am. Hist. Assn., Oral History Assn., Hist. Soc. Pa., Presbyn. Hist. Soc., Sons of the Union Vets. of the Civil War, Palestinian Am. Rsch. Ctr. Democrat. Roman Catholic. Avocations: civil war living history/reenactment, musician. E-mail: tmricks@sas.upenn.edu.

RICOL, RENE JEAN, accountant; b. Lyon, France, Dec. 26, 1950; s. Benoit and Marie Antoinette (Mercier) R.; children: Raphaelle, Stephane, Matthieu, Antoine, Arthur, Victor. MBA in Econs., Lyon U., France, 1973. Ptnr. Calan Ramolino Ricol, Paris, 1978—80, mng. ptnr., 1980—86; pres. Ricol-Lasteyrie & Assocs., Paris, 1986—; hon. pres. France Defi, Paris, 1989-97, Euro Defi, 1991-94. Pres. Compagnie Regionale Des Commissaires Aux Comptes, 1982-84, Compagnie Nationale Des Commissaires Aux Comptes, 1985-89, Conseil Superieur de l'Ordre des Experts-Comptables, 1994-98, Internat. Fedn. Accts., NY, 2002-04, France Investments, 2006-. Decorated comdr. Legion of Honor, comdr. Nat. Order of Merit (France). Office: Ricol-Lasteyrie & Associes 2 Ave Hoche 75008 Paris France Business E-Mail: rr@ricol-lasteyrie.fr.

RICORDI, CAMILLO, surgeon, researcher; b. NYC, Apr. 1, 1957; m. Valerie A. Grace, Aug. 8, 1986; children: M. Caterina, Eliana G., Carlo A. MD, Milan U., Italy, 1982. Trainee in gen. surgery San Raffaele Inst., Milan, 1982-85; NIH trainee Washington U. Sch. Medicine, St. Louis, 1985-88; attending surgeon San Raffaele Inst., Milan, 1988-89; asst. prof. to assoc. prof. surgery U. Pitts., Pa., 1989-93; prof. surgery and medicine, pathology, microbiology and immunology, chief divsn. cellular transpl. Diabetes Rsch. Inst., U. Miami, Fla., 1993—, sci. dir., chief acad. officer Fla., 1996—, Stacy Joy Goodman chair in Diabetes Rsch., 1998—. Reviewer of applications for grants Can. and Am. Diabetes Assns., Juvenile Diabetes Found., NIH; chmn. First and Third Internat. Congresses of Cell Transplant Soc., Pitts., 1992, Miami, 1996, 5th Internat. Congress on Pancreas and Islet Transplantation, Miami, 1995, others; mem. editl. bd. Transplantation, Cell Transplantation, Transplantation Procs., Jour. Tissue Engring. Editor: Pancreatic Islet Cell Transplantation, 1992, Methods in Cell Transplantaion, 1995; co-editor-in-chief Cell Transplantation, Graft; assoc. editor Am. Jour. Transplantation, 2003—; contbr. numerous chpts. to books and articles to jours. including Immunology Today, Jour. Clin. Investigation, New Eng. Jour. Medicine, Hepatology, Diabetes, Transplantation, Endocrinology, Procs. NAS, USA, Am. Jour. Physiology, Surgery, Nature, Nature Genetics, Lancet, Nature Immunology Rev. Grantee Juvenile Diabetes Found. Internat., 1988—, NIH, 1993—; recipient Nessim Habif World prize of surgery, 2001. Mem. AAAS, Cell Transplant Soc. (founder, pres. 1992-94), Am. Soc. Transplant Surgeons, Internat. Pancreas and Islet Transplant Assn. (v.p. 1979-99, pres. 1999-2001), The Transplantation Soc., Am. Diabetes Assn. (councillor, 2003-, Outstanding Sci. Achievement award 2002). Achievements include patents in cellular biotechnologies. Office: U Miami Diabetes Rsch Inst PO Box 016310 Miami FL 33101-6310 Business E-Mail: ricardi@miami.edu.

RIDD, BRIAN V., chemicals executive; With Huntsman Corp., Salt Lake City, 1984—, v.p. purchasing Huntsman Chem. Corp. subs., v.p. purchasing Huntsman Petrochemical Corp. subs., v.p. Olympus Oil subs., v.p. purchasing, 1995—2000, sr. v.p. purchasing, 2000—. Office: Huntsman Corp 500 Huntsman Way Salt Lake City UT 84108 Office Phone: 801-584-5700. *

RIDDELL, STEPHEN W., lawyer; b. Quincy, Mass., 1959; BA magna cum laude, Univ. SC, 1981; JD with honors, Univ. NC, 1985. Bar: Ga. 1985, cert.: Am. Arbitration Assn. (arbitrator) 1993. Assoc. Troutman Sanders LLP, Atlanta, 1985—93, ptnr., labor, employment, 1993—, mng. ptnr., Atlanta office, and mem. exec. com. Named a Super Lawyer, Atlanta Mag., 2004—05, Legal Elite in labor/employment, Ga. Trend Mag., 2004—05; named one of Leading Lawyers for Bus., Chambers USA, 2004—05. Mem.: ABA, State Bar Ga., Phi Beta Kappa. Office: Troutman Sanders LLP Ste 5200 600 Peachtree St NE Atlanta GA 30308-2216 Office Phone: 404-885-3408. Office Fax: 404-962-6668. Business E-Mail: stephen.riddell@troutmansanders.com.

RIDDER, PAR, publishing executive; b. 1969; s. Tony Ridder; m. Sara Ridder; 2 children. BA, U. Wash., 1990; MBA, U. Mich., 1996. Retail sales rep. Washington Post, 1990—94; circulation zone mgr. Akron Beacon Jour., 1996—97; recruitment mgr. Contra Costa Times, 1996—97; pub. San Luis Obispo (Calif.) Tribune, 2001—04, v.p. & advt. dir., 1997—99; pub. & pres. St. Paul Pioneer Press, St. Paul, 2004—07; pub. & CEO Star Tribune, Mpls., 2007—. Recipient Alvah H. Chapman award, San Luis Obispo Tribune, 2003. Office: Star Tribune 425 Portland Ave Minneapolis MN 55488 Office Phone: 612-673-1708. E-mail: publisher@startribune.com. *

RIDDER, P(AUL) ANTHONY, newspaper company executive; b. Duluth, Minn., Sept. 22, 1940; s. Bernard H. and Jane (Delano) Ridder; m. Constance Louise Meach, Nov. 6, 1960; children: Katherine Lee Pennoyer, Linda Jane, Susan Delano Cobb, Paul Anthony Jr. BA in Econs., U. Mich., 1962. With Aberdeen Am. News, SD, 1962—63; With Pasadena Star News, Calif., 1963—64; with San Jose Mercury News, Calif., 1964—86, bus. mgr., 1968—75, gen. mgr., 1975—77, pub., 1977—86, pres., 1979—86, Knight-Ridder Inc., Miami, Fla., 1989—95, pres., chmn., CEO, 1995—. Bd. dirs. Seattle Times, Knight-Ridder, Inc.; adv. bd. Stanford U. Grad. Sch. Bus. Bd. trustees Santa Clara U. Named Calif. Pub. of Yr., 1983, Newspaper Exec. of Yr., Ad Week, 1991. Mem.: San Francisco Golf Club, Pine Valley Golf Club, Cypress Point Club. Office: Knight-Ridder Inc Ste 1500 50 W San Fernando St San Jose CA 95113-2413

RIDDICK, DANIEL HOWISON, obstetrician, gynecologist, priest; b. Lynchburg, Va., Dec. 12, 1941; s. Joseph Henry and Nancy Eloise (Gordon) R.; m. Louisa McIntosh Spruill, June 9, 1963; children: Ellen, Daniel. BA, Duke U., 1963, MD, 1967, PhD in Physiology, 1969. Diplomate Am. Bd. Ob-Gyn, Am. Bd. Reproductive Endocrinology; ordained priest Episc. Ch., 1969. Asst. prof. physiology Duke U., Durham, NC, 1973-74; asst. prof. ob-gyn U. Conn. Sch. Medicine, Farmington, 1974-76, dir. reproductive endocrinology and infertility, 1974-85, assoc. prof. ob-gyn, 1976-81, prof. ob-gyn, 1981-85; prof., chmn. ob-gyn dept. U. Vt., Burlington, 1985-97, assoc. dean grad. med. edn., 1987-88. Editor: Reproductive Endocrinology in Clinical Practice, 1987; editor: (with others) Pathology of Infertility, 1987. Mem. ACOG, Am. Fertility Soc. (pres. 1992-93), Am. Gynecol. and Obstet. Soc. Avocation: sheep-raising. Home: 680 Mayo Rd Huntington VT 05462-9410 Office: Fletcher Allen Health Care Dept of Obstetrics & Gynecology 111 Colchester Ave Burlington VT 05401-1416 Office Phone: 802-847-1400. E-mail: dan.riddick@vtmednet.org.

RIDDICK, FRANK ADAMS, JR., physician, healthcare administrator; b. Memphis, June 14, 1929; s. Frank Adams and Falba (Crawford) Riddick; m. Mary Belle Alston, June 15, 1952; children: Laura Elizabeth Dufresne, Frank Adams III, John Alston. BA cum laude, Vanderbilt U., 1951, MD, 1954. Diplomate Am. Bd. Internal Medicine. Intern Barnes Hosp., St. Louis, 1954—55, resident in medicine, 1957—60; fellow in metabolic diseases Washington U., St. Louis, 1960—61; staff Ochsner Clinic (Ochsner Found. Hosp.), New Orleans, 1961—, head sect. endocrinology and metabolic disease, 1976—83, asst. med. dir., 1968—72, assoc. med. dir., 1972—75, med. dir., 1975—92; CEO Alton Ochsner Med. Found., New Orleans, 1992—2001; CEO emeritus Ochsner Clinic Found., 2001—. Bd. govs. Am. Bd. Internal Medicine, 1973—80; clin. prof. Tulane U., New Orleans, 1977—; trustee Alton Ochsner Med. Found., 1973—, CEO, 1991—; chmn. bd. Ochsner Health Plan, 1983—92; pres. Orleans Svc. Corp., 1976—80, South La. Med. Assocs., New Orleans, 1978—; dir. Brent House Corp., New Orleans, 1980—; chmn. Accreditation Coun. on Grad. Med. Edn., 1986—87, v.p. nat. resident matching program, 1986—90, mem. accreditation coun. on med. edn., 1988—90. Bd. govs. Isidore Newman Sch., New Orleans, 1987—93; trustee St. Martin's Protestant Episc. Sch., Metairie, La., 1970—84. Recipient Tchg. award, Alton Ochsner Med. Found., 1969, Disting. Alumnus award, Castle Heights Mil. Acad., 1979, Physician Exec. award, Am. Coll. Med. Group Adminstrs., 1984, Disting. Alumnus award, Vanderbilt U. Sch. Medicine, 1988. Master: ACP; fellow: Am. Coll. Physician Execs. (pres. 1987—88); mem.: NAS Inst. Medicine, AMA (ho. dels. 1971—92, chmn. coun. on med. edn. 1983—85, coun. on jud. and ethical affairs 1995—2002, chair 2001—02, Disting. Service award 2003), Am. Group Practice Assn. (pres. 1992—94), Soc. Med. Adminstrs. (pres. 1995—), Am. Diabetes Assn., Endocrine Soc., Am. Soc. Internal Medicine (trustee 1970—76, Disting. Internist award), Cosmos Club, New Orleans Country Club, Boston Club. Office: Ochsner Clinic 1516 Jefferson Hwy New Orleans LA 70121-2429 Home: 150 Broadway 709 New Orleans LA 70118-7610 Office Phone: 504-842-4019. Business E-Mail: friddick@ochsner.org.

RIDDICK, WINSTON WADE, SR., lawyer; b. Crowley, La., Feb. 11, 1941; s. Herbert Hobson and Elizabeth (Wade) Riddick; m. Patricia Ann Turner, Dec. 25, 1961; 1 child, Winston Wade. BA, U. Southwestern La., 1962; MA, U. N.C., 1963; PhD, Columbia U., 1965; JD, La. State U., 1973. Bar: La. 1974, U.S. Dist. Ct. (so., mid. and we. dists.) La., U.S. Ct. Appeals (5th cir.), U.S. Supreme Ct. Asst. prof. gov., dir. Inst. Gov. Rsch. La. State U., Baton Rouge, 1966-67; dir. La. Higher Edn. Facilities Commn., Baton Rouge, 1967-72; exec. asst. state supt. La. Dept. Edn., Baton Rouge, 1972-73; law ptnr. Riddick & Riddick, Baton Rouge, 1973—; asst. commr., gen. counsel La. Dept. Agr., Baton Rouge, 1981-82. Cons. Riddick & Assoc., Baton Rouge, 1973—; part-time law faculty mem. Southern U. Law Ctr., Baton Rouge, 1974—95, assoc. prof., 1995—99, prof. law, 1999—; real estate investor, property mgr., 1975—; exec. asst. atty. gen. State of La., 1977—91. Spl. asst. to Gov. John McKeithen on Nat. Ctr. Edn. Politics Fellowship, 1966—67; state campaign mgr. Gillis W. Long for Gov., Baton Rouge, 1971; mem. East Baton Rouge Parish Dem. Exec. Com., 1981—84. Mem.: La. Trial Lawyers Assn. (bd. govs. 1978—80). Presbyterian. Office: Riddick & Assocs Inc 1563 Oakley Dr Baton Rouge LA 70806-8622 Home Phone: 225-925-9364; Office Phone: 225-771-4900 x203. Business E-Mail: wriddick@sulc.edu.

RIDDIFORD, LYNN MOORHEAD, biologist, educator; b. Knoxville, Tenn., Oct. 18, 1936; d. James Eli and Virginia Amalia (Berry) Moorhead; m. Alan W. Riddiford, June 20, 1959 (div. Jan. 1966); m. James William Truman, July 28, 1970. AB magna cum laude, Radcliffe Coll., 1958; PhD, Cornell U., 1961. Rsch. fellow in biology Harvard U., Cambridge, Mass., 1961-63, 65-66, asst. prof. biology, 1966—71, assoc. prof., 1971—73; instr. biology Wellesley Coll., Mass., 1963—65; from assoc. prof. to prof. zoology U. Wash., Seattle, 1973—2003, prof. biology, 2003—07, prof. biology emeritus, 2007—, Virginia and Prentice Bloedel prof., 2000—05, assoc. chmn., 2003—04; sr. fellow Janelia Farm Howard Hughes Med. Inst., Ashburn, Va., 2007—. Mem. study sect. tropical medicine and parasitology NIH, Bethesda, Md., 1974—78, 1997; mem. Competitive Grants panel USDA, 1979, 89, 95; mem. regulatory biology panel NSF, 1984—88, 2001, 05, 07, mem. biol. adv. com., 1992—95; mem. governing coun. Internat. Ctr. for Insect Physiology and Ecology, 1985—91, chmn. program com., 1989—91; chmn. adv. com. SeriBiotech, Bangalore, India, 1989; mem. coun. Internat. Cong. Entomology, 1988—, pres., 2000—04; mem. coun. Internat. Fedn. Comparative Endocrine Socs., 1996—, pres., 2001—05. Mem. editl. bd. profl. jours.; contbr. articles to profl. jours. Bd. dirs. Entomol. Found., 1998—2001, chmn., 2001; bd. dirs. Whitney Lab., 2000—04, chmn., 2004. Recipient Gregor J. Mendel award, Czech Republic Acad. Scis., 1998, Ann. Dinner honors, Entomol. Found., 2006; fellow, NSF, 1958—60, 1961—63, NIH, 1960—61, John S. Guggenheim Found., 1979—80, NIH, 1986—87; grantee, NSF, 1964—65, 1967—, Rockefeller Found., 1970—79, USDA, 1978—82, 1989—2006, NIH, 1975—. Fellow: AAAS, Entomol. Soc. Am. (Recognition award in insect physiology, biochemistry and toxicology), Royal Entomol. Soc., Am. Acad. Arts and Sci.; mem.: Soc. Exptl. Biology, Soc. Devel. Biology, Am. Soc. Biochem. and Molecular Biology, Soc. Integrative and Comparative Biology. Methodist. Office: Janelia Farm Howard Hughes Med Inst 19700 Helix Dr Ashburn VA 20147 Home: 40733 Manor House Dr Leesburg VA 20175 Business E-Mail: riddifordl@janelia.hhmi.org.

RIDDLE, CHARLES ADDISON, III, district attorney, former state legislator; b. Marksville, La., June 8, 1955; s. Charles Addison Jr. and Alma Rita (Gremillion) R.; m. Margaret Susan Noone, Mar. 24, 1978; children: Charles Addison IV, John H., Michael J. BA, La. State U., 1976, JD, 1980. Bar: La. 1980, U.S. Dist. Ct. (mid. and we. dists.) La. 1983, U.S. Ct. Appeals (5th cir.) 1988, U.S. Supreme Ct. 1991, U.S. Ct. Vets. Appeals 1994. Ptnr. Riddle & Bennett LLC, Marksville, 1980; pvt. practice Marksville, 1981—2004; mem. La. Ho. of Reps., Baton Rouge, 1992—2003; reelected La. House of Reps., Baton Rouge, 1995—99, 1999—2003; dist. atty. Avoyelles Parish 12th Jud. Dist., 2003—. Elected La. State Dem. Cen. com., Avoyelles Parish, 1983-87, Parish Exec. Demo. Com. 1987-91. Mem. Avoyelles Bar Assn. (pres. 1987-88), Bunkie Rotary (bd. dirs.), Marksville Lions, Marksville C. of C. (pres. 1988-92). Office: PO Box 608 208 E Mark St Marksville LA 71351-2416 Office Phone: 318-253-4551. Personal E-mail: criddle777@aol.com.

RIDDLE, MICHAEL LEE, lawyer; b. Oct. 7, 1946; s. Joy Lee and Francis Irene (Brandes) R.; m. Suzan Ellen Shaw, May 25, 1969 (div.); m. Carol Jackson, Aug. 13, 1977; 1 child, Robert Andrew. BA, Tex. Tech U., 1969, JD with honors, 1972. Bar: Tex. 1972, U.S. Dist. Ct. (no. dist.) Tex. 1972, U.S. Ct. Appeals (5th cir.) Tex. 1972, U.S. Supreme Ct. 2007. Assoc. Geary Brice Barron & Stahl, Dallas, 1972-75; ptnr. Baker Glast Riddle Tuttle & Elliott, Dallas, 1975-80; ptnr., mng. ptnr. Middleburg, Riddle & Gianna, 1980—; chmn., CEO MRG Document Techs., 2000—. Bd. dirs. Dallas Opera. Bd. dirs. U.S.A. Film Festival, pres., 1984-86, North Tex. Pub. Broadcasting, 1992-97; chmn., bd. dirs. Provident Bancorp Tex., 1987-90. Mem. ABA, Tex. Bar Assn., Dallas Bar Assn., Coll. of State Bar of Tex., Lakewood Country Club, Crescent Club. Democrat. Lutheran. Office: 717 N Harwood Ste 2400 Dallas TX 75201 Office Phone: 214-220-6300. Personal E-mail: mriddle@midrid.com.

RIDDLE, VERYL LEE, lawyer; b. Campbell, Mo., Dec. 6, 1921; s. Elvis Lloyd and Etter Whitehead (Wood) R.; m. Mary J. Riggs, Jan. 15, 1941 (div. 1967); children— Kay, Jo, Janet, Veryl Lee, Jr.; m. Janet Lewis, Nov. 24, 1985. Student, Southeast Mo. U., 1939-41; student, U. Buffalo, 1942, 45-46; JD, Washington U., St. Louis, 1948. Bar: Mo. 1948, US Dist. Ct. (ea. and we. dists.) Mo. 1949, US Ct. Appeals (8th cir.) 1949, US Supreme Ct. 1969, US Ct. Appeals (7th cir.) 1970, US Ct. Appeals (5th cir.) 1974, US Ct. Appeals (3d cir.) 1975. Agt. US Dept. Justice, NY, Ohio, Tex., Mex., 1942-43; US atty. Eastern Dist. Mo. Dept. Justice, St. Louis, 1967-69; ptnr. Riddle, Baker & O'Herin, Malden, Mo., 1948-67; sr. ptnr. Bryan Cave, St. Louis, 1969—. Pros. atty. Dunklin County, Mo., 1950-53; chmn. merit selection panel for US Magistrate, St. Louis, 1983-84 Del., Nat. Democratic Conv., Chgo., 1956, Los Angeles, 1960. With US Army, 1943-45, European Theatre, Military Intelligence. Recipient Disting. Alumni award Washington U. Sch. Law, 1993. Fellow Am. Coll. Trial Lawyers, Internat. Acad. Trial Lawyers; mem. Acad. Mo. Squires. Clubs: Bellerive Country, Noonday, Round Table (St. Louis). Baptist. Office: Bryan Cave 211 N Broadway Saint Louis MO 63102-2733 Office Phone: 314-259-2235. Business E-Mail: vlriddle@bryancave.com.

RIDE, SALLY KRISTEN, physics professor, research scientist, retired astronaut; b. LA, May 26, 1951; d. Dale Burdell and Carol Joyce (Anderson) R.; m. Steven Alan Hawley, July 26, 1982 (div.). BA in English, Stanford U., 1973, BS in Physics, 1973, PhD in Physics, 1978. Tchg. asst. Stanford U., Palo Alto, Calif., rschr. dept. physics, sci. fellow, 1987-89; astronaut candidate, trainee NASA, 1978-79, astronaut, 1979-87, on-orbit capsule communicator STS-2 mission Johnson Space Ctr. Houston, on-orbit capsule communicator STS-3 mission, mission specialist STS-7, 1983, mission specialist STS-41G, 1984; dir. Calif. Space Inst. U. Calif. San Diego, La Jolla, 1989—96, pres. space com., 1999-2000; prof. dept. physics U. Calif. San Diego, 1989—. Mem. Presdl. Commn. on Space Shuttle Challenger Accident, 1986, World Resources Inst. Global Coun., 1993—, Presdl. Com. Advisors on Sci. and Tech., 1994—, U. Calif. Oversight Com. for Nat. Labs, Pacific Coun. on Internat. Policy; pres., CEO Space web site, 1999—2000, Imaginary Lines, Inc., 2001—; intiated NASA EarthKAM project; bd. dir. Nat. Rsch. Coun. Space Studies, Congressional Office of Tech. Assessment, Carnegie Instn. Washington; past bd. dir. NCAA Found.; bd. trustee Caltech; lectr. in field. Author: (with Susan Okie) To Space and Back, 1986, (with T.O'Shaughnessy) Voyager: An Adventure to the Edge of the Solar System, 1992, The Third Planet: Exploring the Earth From Space, 1994, (revised 2004), The Mystery of Mars, 1999, Exploring Our Solar System, 2003. Named to The Nat. Women Hall of Fame, 1988, Astronaut Hall of Fame, Kennedy Space Center, 2003; recipient Jefferson award for Pub. Svc., Nat. Spaceflight medal (twice), Von Braun award, Lindbergh Eagle award, Silver Anniversary award, NCAA, 1998, Golden Plate award, Acad. Achievement, 2004, Theodore Roosevelt award, NCAA, 2005. Fellow: Am. Physical Soc. Achievements include becoming the first American woman to orbit Earth when she flew aboard Space Shuttle Challenger, June, 18 1983. Avocations: tennis, running, volleyball, softball, stamp collecting. Office: U Calif San Diego Dept Physics 0426 La Jolla CA 92093-0426 Address: Sally Ride Science 9191 Towne Centre Dr San Diego CA 92122

RIDEN, MICHAEL DAVID, nuclear engineer; b. Maryville, Tenn., July 2, 1947; s. William Walter and Grace Ella (Elrod) R.; m. Perry Dene Thyberg, Mar. 28, 1970; children: Chad Michael, Kirk David, Eric Wesley. Cert. nuc. weapons specialist, Lowry Tng. Ctr., Denver, 1968; cert. nuc. weapons technician, Gen. Electric Co. Tng. Program, King of Prussia, Pa., 1969; BS, U. Tenn., Knoxville, 1974. Cert. regional judge, Duck Town, Tenn., 1995. Asst. engr. Duke Power Co. Oconee Nuclear Sta., Seneca, SC, 1974-78; reactor insp. Nuc. Regulatory Commn., Glen Ellyn, Ill., 1978-79; gen. mgr. Chgo. Barra Corp. Am., Inc., Wheaton, Ill., 1979-82; reg. mgr. Watpro, Inc., Orland Park, Ill., 1982-83; pres. ETs, Glen Ellyn, 1983-87; engring. assurance engr. TVA Watts Bar Nuc. Plant, Spring City, Tenn., 1987-88, Sequoyah Nuc. Plant, Soddy-Daisy, Tenn., 1988-89; supervising engr. United Energy Svcs. Corp., Palo Verde Nuc. Power Plant, Wintersburg, Ariz., 1989-90; nuc. engr. Sigma Sci. Browns Ferry Nuc. Plant, Athens, Ala., 1990-93; lead auditor SECORE Svcs. Inc., Trans-Alaska Pipeline, Anchorage, 1994; plant ops. and betterment I&C cons. engr. Raytheon Engrs. and Constructors Inc. TVA Watts Bar Nuclear, Spring City, Tenn., 1994-95; cons. nuc. engr. Sci. Applications Internat. Corp. TVA Sequoyah Nuc. Plant, Soddy-Daisy, Tenn., 1995-96; sports staff mem. Atlanta com. Olympic Games, Cherokee Nat. Forest, Tenn., 1996; cons. nuc. engring. environ. qualification Cooper Nuc. Station, Brownville, Nebr., 1996-97; sys. engring. mentor Duke Engring. & Svc. Resources, Inc., Two Rivers, Wis., 1997-98; maintenance commitment project mgr. Cook Nuc. Plant Cook Nuc. Plant, Duke Engring. & Svcs. Resources, Inc., Sun Tech. Svcs., Inc. and S&L, Bridgman, Mich., 1998-2001; agt. Ednl. Tng. Svcs., Riceville, Tenn., 2000—, elec. field engr., 2000—01; elec. supt. Newberg, Perini, Stone and Webster, Braceville, Ill., 2001—02; nuc. engr. Sun Tech. Svcs. and SWCI, Browns Ferry Nuc. Plant, Athens, Ala., 2003—. Re-entry system evaluation team mem. minuteman III missile USAF, Minot, N.D., 1969-71. Deacon Presbyn. Ch. US, Seneca, 1976-77; lay spkr. United Meth. Ch. Holston Conf., 1991-2001. Sgt. USAF, 1967-71. Recipient Outstanding Achievement in Poetry During the 20th Century award Internat. Libr. of Poetry, 2000. Mem. Am. Nuc. Soc. Sovereign American.

RIDENHOUR, MARILYN HOUSEL, retired accountant; b. Madison, Nebr., July 12, 1931; d. Kenneth Virgil Housel and Edna Christina Reese Housel; m. Henry Clifton Ridenhour, Apr. 25, 1954 (dec.); children: Keith James, Susan Marie Ridenhour Redelfs, Jill Housel Ridenhour Cortese. Student, Nebr. Wesleyan U., 1949—50; BS in Bus. Adminstrn. with distinction, U. Nebr., 1953. CPA Mo., 1957. CPA Price Waterhouse & Co., St. Louis, 1953—54, Adolph Kahn, St. Louis, 1954—57; ptnr., CPA Adolph Kahn & Co., St. Louis, 1957—61, Kahn, Ridenhour & Co., St. Louis, 1961—65, Ridenhour Hylton & Co., St. Louis, 1965—91; cons. Baird Kurtz & Dobson, St. Louis, 1991—92, ret., 1992. Citizen leader Chesterfield, Mo. 2d Congl. Dist., 2005. Mem.: Rep. Leadership Found. (founding mem.), Am. Women's Soc. CPA, Am. Soc. Women Accts. (charter pres. 1959), Dawn Hope Soc., Soaring Eagle, Nat. Law Enforcement (founding mem. 2005), Century Soc., U. Nebr. Alumni Assn., St. Labre Indian Sch. Ednl. Assn., Chancellors Club U. Nebr., Beta Gamma Sigma, Phi Chi Theta, Alpha Lambda Delta, Delta Delta Delta. Republican. Methodist. Personal E-mail: hermhr@wchtv.net.

RIDENOUR, AMY MORITZ, research center administrator; b. Pitts., Nov. 9, 1959; d. Karl Berkoben and Carol Lee (Riley) M. B or Econs., U. Md., 1981. Exec. dir. Nat. Ctr. for Pub. Policy Rsch., Washington, 1982-88, trustee, 1986—; pres. The Nat. Ctr. for Pub. Policy Research, Washington, 1988—; formerly host Scoop!, Nat. Empowerment Television, Washington; nationally sundicated columnist UPI and Knight-Ridder Tribune, 1998—. Chmn. Liberty Inst., Washngton. Assoc. pub. Cath. Study Coun. Bull.; editor Nat. Policy Watch Jour., Liberation Bull.; exec. editor Liberty Letter; contbr. articles to Policy Rev. and other profl. jours. Regional coord. Reagan-Bush Nat. Campaign, Washington, 1980; bd. dirs., v.p. Internat. Youth Yr. Commn. for U.S., 1985; chmn. Md. Fedn. Coll. Rep. Clubs, 1978-80. Mem. Accuracy in Academia (adv. bd.). Lutheran. Avocations: skiing, books, history. Office: Nat Ctr for Pub Policy Rsch 501 Capitol Court Washington DC 20002

RIDER, KATHLEEN MARY, dietician; b. Bronx, NY, Mar. 21, 1953; d. William Anthony and Elizabeth Catherine (Gavin) Browne; m. David York Rider, Oct. 15, 1983; children: Kathleen M., Colleen M., David Y., Elizabeth A., Erin M. AAS, Maria Coll., 1976; BS, Empire State Coll., 1978; M of Profl. Studies, SUNY, New Paltz, 1982; cert. alternative & complimentary health, Marist Coll., 1999. Cert. dietitian/nutritionist, N.Y. Food svc. dir./dietitian Lovely Hill Nursing Home, Pawling, N.Y., 1979-81; adminstrv. dietitian Hudson River Psychiat. Ctr., Poughkeepsie, N.Y., 1981-82; cmty. svc. dietitian Wassaic (N.Y.) Developmental Ctr., 1982-83; ind. cons. dietitian, 1981—. Cons. Bapt. Home, Hospice Inc., Campball Hall Rehab. Ctr., Greystone Inc., Mountainview Nursing Ctr., Victory Lake Care Ctr., Campbell Hall Rehab. Ctr., Assn. for Retarded Citizens, Ulster and Orange Counties, Home Care, Alcohol Rehab. Ctr., various other orgns.; advisor Mid Hudson Food Svc. Mgrs. Assn., Poughkeepsie. Vol. nutrition educator area parochial schs., Dutchess County, 1996; instr. religious edn. St. Peter's Ch., Poughkeepsie, 1981-84; team mem. engaged encounter Cath. Engaged Encounter, Dutchess County, 1986-89. Soroptomist scholar, Schenectady, N.Y., 1976. Fellow Am. Dietetic Assn. (del. 1999, Flora Wishart Davies Meml. award for Outstanding Caregiver 1994,

Outstanding Svc. award); mem. N.Y. State Dietetic Assn. (state profl. recruitment coord. 1976—, scholar 1976), Mid Hudson Dietetic Assn. (pres. 1992-94). Democrat. Home and Office: 13 Edna Dr Hyde Park NY 12538-2939

RIDER, ROGER ALAN, lawyer; b. Sweickley, Pa., May 28, 1945; s. Joseph W. and Evelyn M. (Kuntzman) R.; m. Nancy Lucille Huston, May 8, 1982; children: Matthew Huston, Zachary Alan Huston. BS in Psychology, U. Houston, 1971, JD magna cum laude, 1974. Bar: Tex. 1974; cert. in civil trial, Tex. Bd. Legal Specialization, Nat. Bd. Trial Advs. Assoc. Butler, Binion, Rice, Cook & Knapp, Houston, 1974-80, ptnr., 1980-82; founding ptnr. Mayor Day & Caldwell, Houston, 1982-90; founder Rider & Assocs., Houston, 1990-96; ptnr. Doyle, Rider, Restrepo, Harvin & Robbins, 1996—2000; pvt. practice, 2000—. Sec., treas., v.p., pres.-elect, pres. Houston Young Lawyers Assn., 1976-81; speaker, instr. U. Houston Law Ctr., 1991, 92; faculty Tex. Legal Svcs. Ctr., 1993. Editor Houston Law Review, 1974. Mem. steering com. numerous judicial election campaigns, Houston, 1991—; mgr., coach youth sports YMCA, Houston, 1987-93; mgr. youth sports United Ch. Athletic League, Houston, 1993—; mgr., coach youth baseball West Univ. Little League, Houston, 1990—. Cpl. USMC, 1966-68, Vietnam. Named a Tex. Super Lawyer, 2003, 2004, 2006; named one of Houston's Top Lawyers, H Tex. Mag., 2004, 2006. Fellow Houston Bar Found. (life), Tex. Bar Found. (life); mem. ABA (torts and ins. practice sect. 1985-94), Tex. Bar Assn. (Cert. of Merit 1986), Houston Bar Assn. (sec. 1987-89, dir. 1981-85, 90, Pres.'s award 1980, 90, 91), Inns of Ct. (chmn. bd. dirs. 1990-92), Order of Barons (pres. 1974). Avocations: coaching youth sports, physical fitness, skiing. Home: 2064 Timber Ln Houston TX 77027-4118 Office: 5300 Memorial Dr Ste 950 Houston TX 77007 Home Phone: 713-805-5001; Office Phone: 713-400-1777. Business E-Mail: rrider@rogerrider.com.

RIDGE, DAVY-JO STRIBLING, retired school librarian; b. Westminster, SC, Jan. 16, 1932; d. David Warren and Thelma Josephine (Braselton) Stribling; m. George Ross Ridge, June 9, 1956 (div. Dec. 1964). BA, Queens Coll., 1954; MLN, Emory U., 1955. Catalog libr. U. Ga., Athens, 1955—56; head ref. libr. Dekalb Regional Libr., Decatur, Ga., 1956—64; ref. libr. U. S.C., Columbia, 1965—66, head ref. dept., 1967—74, asst. dir. libr., 1975—76, assoc. dir. libr., 1977—88, ret., 1988. Author: A Load of Gratitude: Audubon and South Carolina, 1985, A South Carolina Family in Wartime, 2003. Mem.: S.C. Libr. Assn. (chmn. legis. & pub.), S.C. Libr. Soc. (life), Thomas Cooper Libr. Soc. (life), S.E. Libr. Assn. (life; chmn. constrn. & bylaws 1980—84). Episcopalian. Avocations: gardening, reading, cats.

RIDGE, TOM (THOMAS JOSEPH), former secretary of homeland security, governor; b. Munhall, Pa., Aug. 26, 1945; s. Thomas Regis Ridge and Laura A. Sudimack; m. Michele Moore, 1979, children, Lesley, Tommy. BA in govt. studies, Harvard U., 1967; JD, Dickinson Sch. Law, Carlisle, Pa., 1972. Bar: Pa. 1972. Pvt. practice, Erie, Pa., 1972-82; asst. dist. atty. Erie County, Pa., 1979-82; mem. US Congress from Pa. 21st dist., Washington, 1983—95; mem. Banking, Fin., Urban Affairs com., subcoms. Econ. Growth and Credit Formation, Housing and Community mem. banking, Devel., Veteran's Affairs com.; gov. State of Pa., Harrisburg, 1995—2001; dir. U.S. Dept. Homeland Security, Washington, 2001—02, sec., 2003—05. Bd. dirs. The Home Depot, Inc., Atlanta, 2005—, Exelon Corp., Chgo., 2005—. Staff Sergeant, U.S. Army, 1968-70, Vietnam; Awarded a Bronze Star for Bravery. Republican.

RIDGELY, HENRY DUPONT, state supreme court justice; b. Dover, Del., May 31, 1949; s. Henry Johnson and Mary Lil (Berry) R.; m. Barbara Shepard, Mar. 17, 1973; children: Daniel, Michael. BS in Business Administration, Syracuse U., 1971; JD, Cath. U. Am. Columbus Sch. Law, 1973; LLM in Corp Law, George Washington U. Nat. Law Ctr., 1974. Atty. Ridgely and Ridgely, Dover, 1974—84, Del. State Senate, Dover, 1981—84; judge Superior Ct. Del., Dover, 1984—2004; justice Del. Supreme Ct., Dover, 2004—. Recipient Chief Justice's Annual award for Outstanding Judicial Service, 1997, Judicial Professionalism and Civility award, Am. Bd. Trial Advocates- Del. Chapter, 2000. Fellow: Am. Bar Found.; mem.: ABA (co-chair Ct. Technology Com. 2003—), Terry-Carey Am. Inn of Ct. (pres. 1996—98, bd. dirs. 2007—), Nat. Assn. for Ct. Mgmt., Am. Judicature Soc. (bd. dirs. 2003—05). Republican. Episcopalian. Office: Del Supreme Ct 502 S State St Dover DE 19901

RIDGEWAY, JAMES FOWLER, journalist; b. Auburn, NY, Nov. 1, 1936; s. George L. and Florence (Fowler) Ridgeway; m. Patricia Carol Dodge, Nov. 1966; 1 child, David Andrew. AB, Princeton U., 1959. Assoc. editor New Republic, Washington, 1962-68, contbg. editor, 1968-70; editor Hard Times, 1968-70, Elements, 1974-78; assoc. editor Ramparts, 1970-75; assoc. fellow Inst. for Policy Studies, 1973-77; mem. Pub. Resource Center, 1977—; staff writer Village Voice, 1973—2006; corr. Washington Ulather Jones, 2006—. Author: (book) The Closed Corporation, 1969, Politics of Ecology, 1970, The Last Play, 1973, New Energy, 1975; author: (with Alexander Cockburn) Smoke, 1978; author: Political Ecology, 1979, Energy-Efficient Community Planning, 1979, Who Owns the Earth, 1980, Powering Civilization, 1983, Blood in the Face, 1991, The March to War, 1991; author: (with Jean Casella) To Cast a Cold Eye, 1991; author: The Haiti Files, 1994; author: (with Jasmika Udovicki) Yugoslavia's Ethnic Nightmare, 1995; author: (with Sylvia Plachy) Red Light, 1996; author: (with Jeffrey St. Clair) Environmental Bad Guys, 1999; author: (with Kevin Rafferty, Fran K. Kerandren) Who Wants to Be President; prodr., dir. (with Anne Bohlen, Kevin Rafferty): (films) Blood in the Face, 1990; prodr., dir. (with Kevin Rafferty) Feed, 1992; cons. prodr. Awful Truth, 1999; author: It's All For Sale, 2004, The 5 Unanswered Questions about 9/11, 2005, Baghdad Burning, 2005; editor (founder): Video website. With N.G. US Army, 1959. Home: 3103 Macomb St NW Washington DC 20008-3325 Personal E-mail: jridgew@yahoo.com.

RIDGLEY, THOMAS BRENNAN, lawyer; b. Columbus, Ohio, Apr. 29, 1940; s. Arthur G. and Elizabeth (Tracy) R.;); children: Elizabeth, Jennifer, Kathryn; m. Lisa Lester, Nov. 27, 1999. BA, Princeton U., NJ, 1962; JD with honors, U. Mich., 1965. Bar: Pa. 1965, Ohio 1968, U.S. Dist. Ct. (so. and no. dists.) Ohio, U.S. Dist. Ct. (ea. dist.) Pa., U.S. Ct. Appeals (6th, 3d and 10th cirs.), U.S. Supreme Ct. Assoc. Dechert, Price and Rhoades, Phila., 1965-67; ptnr. Vorys, Sater, Seymour and Pease LLP, Columbus, 1967—. Author: Interstate Conflicts and Cooperation, 1986, (with others) Fending Off Corporate Raiders, 1987. Bd. dirs., mem. exec. com. United Way of Franklin County, Columbus, 1986-98; bd. dirs. Cmty. Shelter Bd., 1992-98, pres. 1997-98; bd. dirs. Columbus Bar Found., 1992-99, pres., 1998. Fellow Am. Coll. Trial Lawyers. Office: Vorys Sater Seymour and Pease LLP 52 E Gay St Columbus OH 43215-3161 Office Phone: 614-464-6229. Business E-Mail: tbridgley@vssp.com.

RIDGWAY, DELISSA ANNE, federal judge; b. Kirksville, Mo., June 28, 1955; d. Kenneth Driggs and Margaret Anne (Warner) R. BA with honors, U. Mo., 1975, postgrad., 1976; JD, Northeastern U., 1979. Bar: DC Ct. Appeals 1979, US Dist. Ct. DC 1980, US Ct. Appeals (DC cir.) 1980, US Supreme Ct. 1983, US Ct. Appeals (1st cir.) 1988. Law clk. to presiding justice U.S. Dist. Ct. D.C., Washington, 1979; assoc. Shaw, Pittman, Potts & Trowbridge, Washington, 1979-88, counsel, internat. practice group, 1988—94; chair, US Fgn. Claims Settlement Commn. US Dept. Justice, Washington, 1994—98; judge US Ct. Internat. Trade, NYC, 1998—. Lectr. nuclear and environ. law to various orgns. Mem. Women's Legal Def. Fund. Recipient: Hardin-Craig fellow U. Mo., Columbia, 1974, Frederick B. Abramson award, DC Bar Assn., 1996, Earl W. Kintner award, Fed. Bar Assn., 2000, Woman Lawyer of The Year, Washington, 2001. Mem. ABA, Women's Bar Assn. (sec. 1989-90), Fed. Bar Assn. (chair adminstrv. law sect. com. agy. adjudication 1985-89, chair adminstrv. law sect. com. regulatory reform 1984-85), Am. Law Inst., Fellow, Am. Bar Found. Roman Catholic. Office: US Ct Internat Trade One Federal Plz New York NY 10278-0001 *

RIDGWAY, JAMES MASTIN, retired government agency administrator; b. Sedalia, Mo., Mar. 14, 1917; s. Amelius Biddle and Maude Anna (Brandt) R.; m. Lillian Belle Shaneyfelt, May 25, 1941; children: Duressa, Richard (dec.), Cheryl. BSBA, U. Mo., 1939, MA, 1940; PhD, U. Chgo., 1953. Tchr. High Schs., Mo., Kans., 1940-44, prin. Butler, Mo., 1944-45; instr. Southwest & Ctrl. Mo. State U., Springfield, Warrensburg, Mo., 1945-47; chmn. dept. edn. Carroll Coll., Waukesha, Wis., 1949-55; instr. dept. head Nat. Civil Def. Coll., Battle Creek, Mich.; 1955-62, dir., 1958-62; deputy asst. dir. tng. & edn. Office Civil Def., Def. Civil Preparedness Agy., Washington, 1963-73; edn. advisor DCPA/DOD and FEMA, Washington, 1973—80. Cons. in field. Contbr. articles to profl. jours. Mem. Am. Strategic Def. Assn., Internat. Assn. Emergency Mgrs., Am. Civil Def. Assn., Heritage Found. Avocation: stamp collecting/philately.

RIDGWAY, MARCELLA DAVIES, veterinarian; b. Sewickley, Pa., Dec. 24, 1957; d. Willis Eugene and Martha Ann (Davies) R. BS, Pa. State U., 1979; VMD, U. Pa., 1983; MS, U. Ill., 1997. Diplomate Am. Coll. Vet. Internal Medicine. Intern U. Ill., Urbana, 1983-84, resident in small animal internal medicine, 1984-87; small animal vet. Vet. Cons. Svcs., Savoy, Ill., 1987-97; clin. asst. prof. small animal vet. medicine U. Ill., Urbana, 1997—. Contbr. articles to profl. jours. Mem. Am. Vet. Med. Assn., Acad. Vet. Clinicians, Ea. Ill. Vet. Med. Assn. (pres. 2000-2001), Savoy Prairie Soc. (pres. 1989—), Grand Prairie Friends (bd. dirs. 1993-96), Sangamon Valley Conservancy (bd. dirs. 1995-2005 Avocations: prairie conservation activities, hiking, canine collectibles, running, dog obedience training. Office: U Ill Vet Med Teaching Hosp 1008 W Hazelwood Dr Urbana IL 61802-4714 Home: 808 Indigo Savoy IL 61874

RIDGWAY, ROZANNE LEJEANNE, corporate director, retired ambassador; b. St. Paul, Aug. 22, 1935; d. H. Clay and Ethel Rozanne (Cote) R.; m. Theodore E. Deming. BA, Hamline U., 1957, LLD (hon.), 1978, George Washington U., 1986, Elizabethtown Coll., 1990, U. Helsinki, 1992; LLD in Pub. Svc. (hon.), Coll. of William and Mary, 1994; DHL (hon.), Hood Coll., 1994; LLD (hon.), Albright Coll.; DHL in Pub. Adminstrn. (hon.), The Citadel, 2003; DHL (hon.), Ill. Coll., 2003. Career diplomat U.S. Fgn. Svc., 1957-89, amb. at large for oceans and fisheries, 1975-77, US amb. to Finland Helsinki, 1977—80; counselor State Dept., 1980—81, spl. asst. to sec., 1981, amb. to German Dem. Republic, 1982-85, asst. sec. Europe and Can., 1985-89; pres. Atlantic Coun. US, 1989-92, co-chmn., 1993-96; chmn. Baltic-Am. Enterprise Fund, Washington, 1994—. Bd. dirs. 3M Corp., Emerson Electric Co., Boeing Co., Sara Lee Corp., Manpower, Inc., New Perspective Fund, Europacific Fund, New World Fund. Life trustee Hamline U.; trustee Nat. Geog. Soc., Ctr. Naval Analyses. Decorated Grand Cross Order of the Lion (Finland); recipient Profl. awards Dept. State, Presdl. Disting. Performance awards, Joseph C. Wilson Internat. Rels. Achievement award, 1982, Sharansky award Union Couns. Soviet Jewry, 1989, U.S. Presdl. Citizens medal, 1989; named Person of Yr. Nat. Fisheries Inst., 1977, Knight Comdr., Order of Merit, Germany; inducted into Nat. Women's Hall of Fame, 1998. Fellow Nat. Acad. Pub. Adminstrn.; mem. Am. Acad. Diplomacy, Army-Navy Country Club.

RIDING, RANDY LYNN, welder; b. Granger, Utah, July 25, 1963; s. Thomas J Riding and Velda Hamblin; m. Lesa Marie Wark, Apr. 22, 1994; children: Gene Albert Zufelt, Heather Valerio, Cheyenne Nichole, Kaitlynn Marie, Miranda Hope, Alexis J'Lynn, Sierra Paige. City works Delta City, Utah, 1983—91; mechanic welder ipsc, Delta, Utah, 1991—. Composer: (creative poetry) The Awesome Beauty of Death (Grand Champion, 2006), (childerens book) The Bubblegum Machine (Sterling scholar, 1981). Hunters safety instr. Utah Dept. Wildlife, Hinckley, 1994—2006. Mem.: Lions Club (assoc.; pres. 2004—05). Liberal. Lsd Ch. Office: Ipsc Brush Wellman Hwy Hinckley UT 84635 Home Phone: 435-864-1829; Office Phone: 435-864-4414. Personal E-mail: rriding1@yahoo.com.

RIDINGS, DOROTHY SATTES, former association executive; b. Charleston, W.Va., Sept. 26, 1939; d. Frederick L. and Katharine E. (Backus) Sattes; m. Donald Jerome Ridings, Sept. 8, 1962 (dec. June 1997); children: Donald Jerome Jr., Matthew Lyle. Student, Randolph-Macon Woman's Coll., 1957-59; BSJ, Northwestern U., 1961; MA, U. N.C., 1968; D.Pub. Svc. (hon.), U. Louisville, 1985; LHD (hon.), Spalding U., 1986; LLD (hon.), U. Charleston, 1999. Reporter Charlotte Observer, NC, 1961-66; instr. U. N.C. Sch. Journalism, 1966-68; freelance writer Louisville, 1968-77; news editor Ky. Bus. Ledger, Louisville, 1977-80, editor, 1980-83; communications cons./ editor, 1983-86; mgmt. assoc. Knight-Ridder Inc., Charlotte, NC, 1986-88; pres., pub. Bradenton Herald, Fla., 1988-96; pres., CEO Coun. on Founds., Washington, 1996—2005. Adj. prof. U. Louisville, 1982-83; v.p. Nat. Mcpl. League, 1985-86; bd. dirs. com. on Constl. Sys., Nat. Com. Against Discrimination in Housing, 1982-87, Com. Study of Am. Electorate, 1982—; bd. dirs. Ind. Sector, 1983-88, 92-97; mem. exec. com. Leadership Conf. Civil Rights, 1982-86; mem. Accrediting Coun. on Edn. in Journalism and Mass Comm., 2000-06. Pres. LWV U.S., 1982-86, 1st v.p., 1980-82, human resources dir., 1976-80, chair edn. fund, 1982-86, 1st vice chair, 1980-82, trustee, 1976-80, pres. Louisville/Jefferson County, 1974-76, bd. dirs., 1969-76; chmn., bd. dirs. Nat. Civic League, 2000-04; trustee Louisville Presbyn. Theol. Sem., 1992—, chmn., 2000—; trustee Ford Found., 1989-96, Manatee C.C., 1992-96; bd. dirs. Benton Found., 1989-96, Fla. Press Assn., 1994-96, Leadership Ky., 1984-87, Leadership Louisville, 1983-86, Louisville YWCA, 1978-80, Jr. League Louisville, 1972-74; mem. ABA Accreditation Com., 1987-93, ABA coun. legal edn. and admissions to bar, 1997-03, Gov.'s Coun. Ednl. Reform, 1984-85; chair Prichard Com. Acad. Excellence, 1985-86; mem. Gov.'s Commn. Full Equality, 1982-83; mem. state adv. coun. U.S. Commn. Civil Rights, 1975-79; mem. steering com. Task Force for Peaceful Desegregation, 1974-75; elder 2d Presbyn. Ch., 1972-75, 78-81; mem. adv. coun. on ch. and soc. United Presbyn. Ch. in USA, 1978-84; mem. bd. visitors U. N.C., 1993-96; mem. Nat. Commn. on Presdl. Debates, 1997—; mem. Urban Librs. Coun. Exec. Bd., 2005—; bd. dirs. Editl. Projects in Edn., 2004—. Recipient Northwestern U. award of merit, 1994, Disting. Alumna award U. N.C., 1995, Leadership award Nat. Assn. Cmty. Leadership Orgns., 1986, Alumnae Achievement award Randolph-Macon Woman's Coll., 1985, Disting. Citizen award Nat. Mcpl. League, 1983; inducted into Northwestern U. Medill Sch. Journalism Hall of Fame, 1996, U. N.C. Journalism Hall of Fame, 1997.

RIDKER, PAUL M., cardiologist, medical educator; b. St. Louis, Oct. 2, 1959; BS, Brown U., Providence, 1981; MD, Harvard Med. Sch., 1986; MPH, Harvard Sch. Pub. Health, 1992. Cert. internal medicine 1989. Resident internal medicine Brigham and Women's Hosp., Boston, 1989, assoc. physician, dir. Ctr. Cardiovasc. Disease Prevention; co-dir. Leducq Ctr. Cardiovasc. Rsch. Brigham and Women's Hosp. and Harvard Med. Sch.; chief med. resident Vets. Adminstrn. Boston Health Care, 1989; Eugene Braunwald prof. medicine Harvard Med. Sch., Boston, Reynolds investigator, co-dir. Reynolds Ctr. Cardiovasc. Rsch., 2003—; cons. cardiologist So. Jamaica Plain Health Ctr., Boston. Simon Dack vis. prof. Mt. Sinai Med. Ctr., 2000. Contbr. articles to profl. jours., chapters to books; consulting editor: Circulation. Named one of Am.'s Ten Best Rschrs. in Sci. and Medicine, Time mag., 2001, 100 Most Influential People, 2004; recipient Clinician Scientist award, Am. Heart Assn., 1992—97, Established Investigator award, 1997—2002, SmithKline Beecham Faculty Devel. award, 1997—99, Disting. Clin. Scientist award, Doris Duke Charitable Found., 2000, Linus Pauling Lecture and 2000 Prevention award, Am. Coll. Advancement in Medicine, 2000. Fellow: Am. Coll. Cardiology; mem.: Am. Assn. Physicians, Am. Soc. Clin. Investigation, Am. Epidemiol. Soc. Achievements include one of the world's leading experts on arterial inflammation, an immune-system reaction that is the most powerful contributor after cholesterol to heart attacks; pioneering work on cardiovascular inflammation and C-reactive protein. Office: Divsn Preventive Medicine Brigham and Womens Hosp 900 Commonwealth Ave E 3rd Fl Boston MA 02215 Office Phone: 617-732-8790. Office Fax: 617-734-1508. E-mail: pridker@partners.org. *

RIDLEN, SAMUEL FRANKLIN, agriculture educator; b. Marion, Ill., Apr. 24, 1916; s. Will and Leoma Josephine (Sneed) R.; m. Helen Louise Camp, Apr. 17, 1946; children: Judith Elaine, Barbara Jo, Mark Ellis. BS, U. Ill., 1940; MS, Mich. State U., 1957. Agr. instr. Westville (Ill.) Twp. High Sch., 1940-43; gen. mgr. Honegger Breeder Hatchery, Forrest, Ill., 1953-56; assoc. prof. poultry sci. U. Conn., Storrs, 1957-58; from asst. prof. to prof. poultry extension U. Ill., Urbana-Champaign, 1946-86, prof. emeritus poultry extension, 1986—, asst. head dept. animal scis., 1978-86. Author: An Idea and An Ideal-Nabor House Fraternity 1939-1989, 1989; poultry editorial cons. Successful Farming, Wonderful World Ency., 1960; poultry editor Am. Farm Youth, 1949-53, Ill. Feed Folks, 1949-53. Founding mem., charter mem. Nabor House Frat. Recipient Superior Svc. award U.S. Dept. Agr., 1982, Paul A. Funk Recognition award Coll. Agr., U. Ill., 1983, numerous others. Fellow Poultry Sci. Assn.; mem. World's Poultry Sci. Assn., Ill. State Turkey Growers Assn., Ill. Poultry Industry Coun., Ill Egg Market Devel. Coun. (adv. mem.), Ill. Animal Industry Coun., Coun. for Agr. Sci. and Tech., Ill. Alumni Assn. (life), DAV (life), Alpha Tau Alpha, Epsilon Sigma Phi, Gamma Sigma Delta (pres. 1982-83). Home: 1901 Lakeside Dr Unit C Champaign IL 61821-5997

RIDLEY, BETTY ANN, theology studies educator; b. St. Louis, Oct. 19, 1926; d. Rupert Alexis and Virginia Regina (Weikel) Steber; m. Fred A. Ridley, Jr., Sept. 8, 1948; children: Drue Alexis, Clay Kent. BA, Scripps Coll., Claremont, Calif., 1948. Christian Sci. practitioner, Oklahoma City, 1973—. Tchr. Christian Sci., 1983—; mem. Christian Sci. Bd. Lectureship, 1980-85. Trustee Daystar Found., 1990-; mem. First Ch. of Christ Scientist, Boston, 1956-2005, Fifth Ch. of Christ Scientist, Oklahoma City. Mem. Jr. League Am. Home: 2933 Lansdowne Ln Oklahoma City OK 73120-4343 Office: Suite 100-G 3000 United Founders Blvd Oklahoma City OK 73112 Office Phone: 405-848-7565. E-mail: baridley@aol.com.

RIDLEY, CAROLYN FLUDD, retired social studies educator; b. Nashville, Jan. 21, 1942; d. Quitman Daniel and Glennora Elizabeth (Cannon) F.; m. Raymond Bennett, June 23, 1962 (div. 1984); 1 child, Karen Elizabeth Bennett Moore; m. Cornelius Theodore Ridley, July 16, 1988; stepchildren: Constance Maria Ridley Smith, William Keith. BA, CUNY, 1973; MEd, Tenn. State U., 1985. Cert. tchr., prin., Tenn., N.Y. Tchr. N.Y.C. Bd. Edn., 1973-75, Dickson (Tenn.) County Bd. Edn., 1976-77, Hickman County Bd. Edn., Centerville, Tenn., 1977-86, Met. Nashville Bd. Edn., 1986—2003; ret, 2003. Dir. Hickman County Career Day, 1982-83; bd. dirs. Assn. Retarded Citizens, Centerville, 1982-86; adv. com. Hickman County Bicentennial Com., Centerville, 1984-86, initiator commemorative quilt; participant NEH lectr. Author: A Black History of Hickman County, 1985. Campaign worker Met. Nashville Bd. Edn., 1991; campaigner Met. Nashville Edn., Assn., 1992; attendant Dem. Socialization Meeting, Nashville, 1992; participant Nat. Endowment for the Humanities Summer Inst. Furman U., Greenville, SC, 1995; mem. Nashville Symphony Orch. League, 2005; bd. dirs. Hall of Champions/Tenn. Secondary Schs. Athletic Assn., 2005. Grantee Mid. Tenn. State U., Murfreesboro, 1990, Tenn. State U., Nashville, 1992; James R. Stokeley Inst. fellow U. Tenn., 1993; participant NEH Summer Inst. at Furman U., Greenville, SC, 1995; named Tchr. of Yr., 1997, 2002-03. Fellow Taft Inst. (cert. 1992, tchr. of yr. 1997, 2002-03); mem. AAUW, NEA, NASA Space Inst. (cert. 1990), Met. Nashville Edn. Assn. (campaign worker and assn. rep.), Smithsonian Instn., Internat. Platform Assn., Nat. Historic Preservation Soc., Nat. Geographic Soc., Nat. Coun. Social Studies, Internat. Platform Assn., Holocaust Meml. Mus. (charter mem.). Democrat. Mem. Ch. of Christ. Avocations: travel, reading, music, studying quilting folk art. Home: 4348 Setters Rd Nashville TN 37218-1839 Personal E-mail: CTRidley@comcast.net.

RIDLEY, CLARENCE HAVERTY, retail executive; b. Atlanta, June 3, 1942; s. Frank Morris Jr. and Clare (Haverty) R.; m. Eleanor Horsey, Aug. 22, 1969; children: Augusta Morgan, Clare Haverty. BA, Yale U., 1964; MBA, Harvard U., 1966; JD, U. Va., 1971. Bar: Ga. 1971. Ptnr. King & Spalding, Atlanta, 1977—2000, chmn., policy com., 1995—97; chmn. bd. Haverty Furniture Cos., Inc., 2001—. Bd. dirs. Crawford & Co., Inc.; bd. trustees STI Classic Funds and Variable Trusts, 2001—. Co-author: Computer Software Agreements, 1987, 3d edit., 2003; exec. editor Va. Law Rev., 1970-71. Chmn., bd. trustees St. Joseph's Health Sys., 2003—; founding trustee Atlanta Girls Sch., 2000-2003; chmn., bd. visitors Emory U., 1999-2000; dir. Atlanta Ballet Co., 1993-2003; bd. councilors Carter Ctr., 2000-2001; mem. Atlanta bd. Am. Red Cross, 2002—. Lt. US Army, 1967—68, Korea. Mem.: Atlanta Rotary Club. Roman Catholic. Home: 2982 Habersham Rd NW Atlanta GA 30305-2854 Office: Haverty Furniture Companies Inc 780 Johnson Ferry Rd Atlanta GA 30342

RIDLEY, HARRISON, JR., history professor; b. Phila., Oct. 22, 1938; s. Harrison and Janet Collins Ridley; m. Jade Ridley, July 18, 1986. Cert. in Radio Tele-Type, U.S. Army, 1962. Instr. Temple U., Phila., 1975—. Host radio WRTI 90 FM Temple U., Phila., 1976—; master ceremonies African Am. Cultural Mus., Phila., 1990—2000; discographer Libr. Congress, Washington, 1992; spkr. in field; cons. in field. Specialist US Army, 1961—63. Named a Day in his hon., Mayor John F. Street, Phila., Pa., 2001; nominee Excellence in Jazz Broadcasting award, Jazz Journalists Assn., 2002; recipient Master Tchr. award, Temple U., 1989, Preserving Jazz Heritage award, Vols. Am. Del. Valley, 1996, Jazz Studies citation, Commonwealth Pa. Ho. Reps., 1996, 20 Yrs. Broadcasting award, Temple U., 1996, Preservation African-Am. Music award, Nat. Assn. Negro Musicians, 1997, numerous others. Mem.: Duke Ellington Soc., Clef Club (discographer 2000, historian, rschr. 1997—2002, 25 Yrs. Radio Broadcasting award 2001). Avocations: basketball, collecting recordings, books. Home: 243 N Wanamaker St Philadelphia PA 19139 Office: Phila School Dist 734 Schuylkill Ave Philadelphia PA 19146

RIDLEY, JOHN A., lawyer; b. Jersey City, Oct. 27, 1943; AB, St. Peter's Coll., 1965; LLB, U. Va., 1968. Bar: Va. 1968, N.J. 1968, U.S. Supreme Ct. 1979. Law sec. to Hon. Lawrence A. Whipple U.S. Dist. Ct. N.J., 1968-70; mem. Gibbons, Del Deo, Dolan, Griffinger & Vecchione, Newark, 1970—2002; ptnr., co-chair human resources law practice group Drinker Biddle & Reath LLP, Florham Park, 2002—. Mem. ABA (labor and employment law, litigation, tort and ins. practice sects.), N.J. State Bar Assn., Essex County Bar Assn. Office: Drinker Biddle & Reath LLP 500 Campus Dr Florham Park NJ 07932-1047 Office Phone: 973-549-7030. Office Fax: 973-360-9831. Business E-Mail: john.ridley@dbr.com.

RIDOLFI, DOROTHY PORTER BOULDEN, nurse, real estate broker; b. SI, NY, Jan. 24, 1937; d. David Porter and Helen Marie (McCloskey) Boulden; m. Edward Benjamin Ridolfi, Aug. 16, 1958; children: Edward Brian, Judyann Nixon, Jacqueline Ryan. RN, St. Francis Hosp., 1957; student, Seton Hall U., South Orange, NJ, 1958, Mercer C.C., 1974, student, 1984, Thomas Edison Coll., 1979—84. Cert. coronary and critical care nurse; real estate cert. South Jersey Sch. Profl. Bus., 1976, lic. real estate instr. NJ, broker NJ, sales person NJ, cert. residential broker, residential specialist. Owner Stay 'N Play Day Camp, 1963—65; nurse Princeton Med. Ctr., NJ, 1972—73; pres., broker Ridolfi Realty Inc., Trenton, NJ, 1977—91; nurse Hamilton Hosp., NJ, 1982—85; instr. real estate Mercer County CC and Career Devel. Sch. Trustee NJ Assn. Realtors Edn. Found., No. Regional Adv. Bd. Bank Mid Jersey. Corr. sec. Hist. Soc., Hightstown, NJ, 1971—72; bd. dirs. Campfire Girls and Boys, 1984; committeewoman Burlington County Dem. Com., Willingboro, NJ, 1966—67, Mercer County Dem. Com., East Windsor, NJ, 1969—72. Mem.: TREND, Mercer County Multiple Listing, Nat. Assn. Realtors, Nat. Fedn. Ind. Bus. (RPAC chmn. 1989), NJ Assn. Realtors (bd. dirs., v.p. 5th dist. 1989, Make Am. Better award 1982), Mercer County Bd. Realtors (bd. dirs. 1981—83, treas., v.p., pres. 1988—, 1997), Soroptomist Internat. of Am. and NJ, Mercer County C. of C. Roman Catholic. Avocations: genealogy, travel, reading. Home Phone: 609-954-8924. Personal E-mail: dotridolfi@aol.com.

RIDOLFI, PATRICK MURPHY, music educator, tenor; b. San Francisco, Calif., July 29, 1954; s. Joseph Oreste Ridolfi and Lillian Ruth Scott; m. Margie Gayatin, May 22, 1993; 1 child, Justin Robert; m. Barbara Ridolfi, Sept. 20, 1980 (dec. Nov. 6, 1989); 1 child, Joseph Patrick. BA, U. of Calif. at Santa Barbara, Santa Barbara, CA, 1977; BM, Calif. State U. at Northridge, Northridge, CA, 1987. Free-lance operatic tenor LA Opera, LA Master Chorale, Long Beach Opera, Carnegie Hall, Roger Wagner Chorale, 1981—; elem. tchr. LA Unified Sch. Dist., 1991—2007, elem. music tchr., 1995—. Grantee ELSA Grant, Fed. Arts Grant, 1999, 2000. Mem.: UTLA, MENC. Avocations: swimming, snorkeling, travel. Office Phone: 818-620-6515.

RIDOUT, SUSAN RAMP, education educator; b. Peoria, Ill., Nov. 3, 1955; d. Wayne Samuel and Dorothy Bowers Ramp; m. Kyle Royce Ridout, Oct. 2, 1983; children: Patrick, Emily. MA, Murray State U., 1976; PhD, Ind. U., 1983. Tchr. S.W. Elem. Sch., Murray, Ky., 1977—81; instr. So. Ill. U., Carbondale, 1980; grad. asst. Ind. U., Bloomington, 1981—83; asst. prof. edn. Ind. U. S.E., New Albany, 1983—89, assoc. prof. edn., 1989—95, prof. edn., 1995—. Cons. Perry County Schs., Leopold, Ind., 2001—, Springs Valley Schs., French Lick, Ind., 2002—06; mem. Action Team, Success by Six, Floyd County, Ind., 2005. Contbr. articles to profl. jours. Bd. dirs. Cmty. Action (Head Start), New Albany, Ind., 1996—; parent vol. Renaissance PTO/Theatre, Floyds Knobs, Ind., 1999—2006; v.p. Philanthropic Ednl. Orgn., New Albany, Ind., 1975—. Named one of Outstanding Young Women of Am., 1988; recipient Tchg. Excellence Recognition award, Ind. U., 1998, 1999, Master Tchr. award, Ind. U. Southeast, 2002, Trustees' Tchg. award, 2003, Woman of Achievement award, Bus. and Profl. Women's Club, 2003. Mem.: Ind. Profs. of Reading, Internat. Reading Assn., Phi Delta Kappa (various positions 1982—). Avocations: watching theatrical productions, reading, spending time with family.

RIECKEN, CLAUDIA, researcher, director; b. São Paulo, Brazil, Nov. 8, 1966; d. Gottfried Kurd Riecken and Maria Auxiliadora (Zuquim) Lia De Paoli; life ptnr. Jacy Martins Lage; children: Liliane Riecken (Caldeira), Isabella Riecken (Calvo), Luanna Riecken (Calvo) stepchildren: Rodrigo Rasia Lage, Tiago Rasia Lage, Carolina Souza Lage. Degree in Neurol. Behavioral Studies, Inst. Systematic Psychology of Ocident & Quantum Leap, Guadalajara, Mex., 1998. Cert. Fed. Therapy Counsel, 1995. Chair woman Quantum Assessment, São Paulo, 1987—. Customer rels. dir. Editora Três, 1989—93. Author: (book) Empowerment to Win, 1999, Alive Winner's Story, 2006. Sponsor searcher Brazilian Assn. Multiple Sclerosis, São Paulo, 2003—07. Mem.: Endeavor (assoc.). Avocations: ice skating, dance, horseback riding, motorcycling, travel. Office: Quantum Assessment Av Brig Faria Lima 2894 conj 73 & 81 São Paulo 01451902 Brazil Office Phone: 5511 37093388. Home Fax: 5511 37093398. Personal E-mail: elaclau@hotmail.com. Business E-Mail: claudia@metodoquantum.com.br.

RIEDEL, ALAN ELLIS, manufacturing executive, lawyer; b. Bellaire, Ohio, June 28, 1930; s. Emil George and Alberta (Shafer) R.; m. Ruby P. Tignor, June 21, 1953; children: Ralph A., Amy L., John T. AB magna cum laude, Ohio U., 1952, LLD (hon.), 1994; JD, Case Western Res. U., 1955; grad., Advanced Mgmt. Program, Harvard, 1971. Bar: Ohio 1955, Tex. 1968. Assoc. Squire, Sanders & Dempsey, Cleve., 1955-60; from gen. counsel to sec. Cooper Industries Inc. (formerly Cooper Bessemer Co.), Mt. Vernon, Ohio, 1960-68; from sec. to v.p. indsl. rels. Cooper Industries Inc., Mt. Vernon, Ohio, 1963-73; from sr. v.p. adminstrn. to vice chmn. Cooper Industries, Inc., Houston, 1973-94. Dir. Factory Mut. Ins., 1999-2000; bd. dirs. Belden Inc., St. Louis, 1993-2000, Gardner Denver Inc., Quincy, Ill., 1994-2000, chmn. bd. dirs., 1994-98; of counsel Squire, Sanders & Dempsey, Houston, 1994-2000. Past chmn. bd. dirs. Jr. Achievement of S.E. Tex.; trustee, past chmn. bd. trustees Ohio U. Endowment Found. Mem. Order of Coif, Phi Beta Kappa, Omicron Delta Kappa, Delta Tau Delta. Home: Bunker Hill Village 4 Heritage Ct Houston TX 77024 Personal E-mail: aeriedel@swbell.net.

RIEDER, ERIC, lawyer; BA, Columbia U., 1976, JD, 1985. Bar: NY 1987, US Dist. Ct. (so. and ea dists.) NY, US Ct. Appeals (2d cir.). Ptnr., leader Securities Enforcement, Compliance Litig. Group, Bryan Cave LLP, NYC. Office: Bryan Cave LLP 1290 Ave of the Americas New York NY 10104 Office Phone: 212-541-2057. E-mail: erieder@bryancave.com.

RIEDER, KEITH LEE, psychologist; b. Warren, Pa., Aug. 12, 1951; s. Emerson Neil and Betty May Rieder; m. Linda L. Dixon, June 22, 1974; children: Erik, Joshua, Sara Lynne Rieder Bennett. BS, Edinboro State U., Pa., 1973; MDiv, Wesley Theol. Sem., Washington, 1977; MS, Duquesne U., Pitts., 1986; EdD, W.Va. U., Morgantown, 1991. Pastor United Meth. Ch., Pa., 1974—93; assoc. dir. Morgantown Pastoral Counseling Ctr., 1993—2007; assoc. prof. Waynesburg Coll., Pa., 2007—. Intern in psychology W.Va. U., Morgantown, 1990—91; sr. cons. Duquesue U., 1991—92; psycho-therapist Cleanfield-Jefferson Mental Health, Pa., 1992—93; adj. asst. prof. Fairmont State U., W.Va., 1996—2007. Author: Being Ministry, 2006; contbr. articles to profl. jours. Mem.: Am. Assn. Pastoral Counselors (regional chair 2001—05, 2007—). Avocations: photography, travel, philosophy. Office: Morgantown Pastoral Counseling Ctr 1062 Maple Dr Ste 1 Morgantown WV 26505

RIEDER, NAOMI, artist; b. Bklyn., Mar. 12, 1937; d. Jacob and Pearl Rieder; children: Mara Yolken, Thea Clark. BA, Bklyn Coll., 1958; MA, Columbia U., NYC, 1967. Instr. fine arts Bd. Edn., NYC, 1966—75; substitute instr. sculpture and drawing Ft. Mason Art Ctr., San Francisco, 1977—80; instr. life sculpture Conn. Coll., New London, 1985, Ft. Mason Art Ctr., 1980—81. Ceramic forms. Mem.: Woodstock Artists Assn. (fundraiser 2002—04). Avocations: gardening, crossword puzzles, homemade marshmallows. Home: PO Box 134 Glenford NY 12433-0134 Personal E-mail: naomirdr@aol.com.

RIEDESEL, LAUREEN FALK, library director; b. Wakefield, Nebr., June 1, 1951; d. Arlyn Dale and Glaura Milly (Harry) Falk; m. Charles Paul Riedesel, May 25, 1973; children: Aprilla Florentine Lynnae, Amerilla Maye Falk. BA, Wheaton Coll., 1973; MA in Libr. Sci., U. Mo., 1974. Cert. libr. level V, Nebr. Youth svcs. libr. Dunklin County Libr., Kennett, Mo., 1974-77; dir. Beatrice (Nebr.) Pub. Libr., 1977—. Instr. Nebr. Libr. Commn., Lincoln, 1988-92; spkr. Nebr. Humanities Coun. Spkrs. Bur., 1993—. Editor: Nebraska Writers, Nebraska Readers, 1995; contbr. articles to profl. jours. Incorporator, exec. bd. Gage County Heritage Preservation, Inc., Beatrice, 1987—97, 1999—; alt. del. White House Conf. on Librs., Washington, 1991; hist. preservation rep. City Plan Coordinating Com., Beatrice, 1991—92, 1999—2001; apptd. mem. Gov.'s Task Force on Hist. Preservation, Nebr., 1992—94; co-dir. Nebr. Lit. Festival, 2000; Gov.'s appointee representing librs. to State Records Bd., 2002—; Gov.'s appointee Nebr. State Hist. Records Adv. Bd., 2003—; bd. dirs. Nebr. State Hist. Soc. Found., 2003—. Named Outstanding Genealogist, Nebr. State Genealogical Soc., 1992, Woman of the Yr., Beatrice Bus. and Profl. Women, 1993, Outstanding Cmty. Leader, Beatrice Jaycees, 1993, Citizen of the Yr., Beatrice C. of C., 1995, Sower award Nebr. Humanities Coun., 1998. Mem.: ALA, Nat. Libr. Assn. (pres. 1989, Excalibur Outstanding Libr. award pub. libr. sect. 1991, Meritorious Svc. award 1998), Nat. Mgmt. Assn. (exec. bd. mem. 1993, 1998—99, charter, pres. 2007—), Friends of Homestead Nat. Monument of Am. (pres. 1999—), Nebr. Lit. Heritage Assn. (bd. mem. 2001—), S.E. Nebr. Genealogical Soc. (charter, Hall of Fame 1982), S.E. Nebr. Coords. for Literacy (charter), Nebr. Ctr. for the Book (exec. bd. 1992—99, pres. 1998). Democrat. Mem. Church of the Brethren. Avocations: reading, history, genealogy, doll collecting, antiques. Home: 721 Grant St Beatrice NE 68310-2939 Office Phone: 402-223-3584.

RIEDL, GEORGE J., retail executive; BS, Univ. Ill., 1983. Pharmacist, dist. supr. Walgreen Co., Deerfield, Ill., 1982—91, mgmt. positions through gen. mdse. mgr., 1991—2001, divisional v.p., 2001—03, sr. v.p., 2003—06, exec. v.p. mktg., 2006—. Office: Walgreen Co 200 Wilmot Rd Deerfield IL 60015 *

RIEDL, JOHN ORTH, retired university dean; b. Milw., Dec. 9, 1937; s. John O. and Clare C. (Quirk) R.; m. Mary Lucille Priestap, Feb. 4, 1961; children: John T., Ann E., James W., Steven E., Daniel J. BS in Math. magna cum laude, Marquette U., Milw., 1958; MS in Math., U. Notre Dame, 1960, PhD in Math., 1963; postgrad., Northwestern U., 1963; degree (hon.), MedCentral Coll. Nursing, 2003. Asst. prof. math. Ohio State U., Columbus, 1966-70, assoc. prof., 1970—2003, asst. dean Coll. Math. and Phys. Sci., 1969-74, assoc. dean, 1974-87, acting dean, 1984-86, spl. asst. to provost, 1987—2003, dean, dir. Mansfield (Ohio) Campus, 1988—2003, exec. dean regional campus, 1988—2003, assoc. prof. emeritus, 2003—; ret., 2003; interim pres. MedCentral Coll. Nursing, 2007—. Panelist sci. edn. NSF, 1980-91; cons. Ohio Dept. Edn., 1989, Ohio bd. regents subsidy cons., 1991, 95, 97, 99, 2001, 03; bd. dirs. Richland County Univ. and Coll. Access Network, 2001—, pres. Richland County bus. adv. coun., 2004—; trustee Mansfield Meml. Homes, 2007—. Pres., v.p. exec. com. Univ. Cmty. Assn., Columbus, 1970-78; mem. edn. commn. St. Peter's Schs., Mansfield, 1989-95; trustee Rehab. Svc. N. Ctrl. Ohio, Mansfield, 1990-99, v.p., 1993-94, pres., 1995-97; pres. Ohio Assn. Regional Campuses, 1993-94; co-chair capital campaign St. Peter's Schs., 1998. Recipient Faculty Svc. award, Nat. U. Continuing Edn. Assn., 1988, Creative Programming award, 1988; NSF grad. fellow, 1960—62. Mem. Math. Assn. Am. (chair com. on minicourse 1981-87), Downs Am. Chestnut Found. of Ohio (bd. dirs. 2001-04), Rotary Internat. (bd. dirs., pres.-elect, pres.) C. of C. (bd. dirs.). Democrat. Roman Catholic. Avocations: fishing, woodworking, gardening. Home: 789 Clifton Blvd Mansfield OH 44907-2284 Office: Ohio State U 1680 University Dr Mansfield OH 44906-1547 Business E-Mail: riedl.1@osu.edu.

RIEDLINGER, STEPHEN C., federal judge; b. 1950; BA, La. State U., 1971, JD, 1977. Bar: La. 1977, U.S. Dist. Ct. (ea. dist.) La. 1979, U.S. Dist. Ct. (mid. dist.) 1978, U.S. Ct. Appeals (5th cir.) 1983. Law clk. U.S. Dist. Ct. La., 1977-78; pvt. practice Baton Rouge, 1978-86; magistrate judge U.S. Dist. Ct. (mid. dist.) La., Baton Rouge, 1986—. With USNR, 1971-77. Office: Russell B Long Fed Bldg & Courthouse 777 Florida St Ste 260 Baton Rouge LA 70801-1717 Office Phone: 225-389-3584. Office Fax: 225-389-3585.

RIEDMAN, MARY SUZANNE, lawyer; b. June 1951; JD, Yale U. Bar: Wash. 1980, DC 1983, Calif. 1988. Various positions Beverly Enterprises Inc., Forth Smith, Ark.; counsel Vencor Inc., Louisville, 1995—96, assoc. gen. counsel, 1996—97, v.p., assoc. gen. counsel, 1997—98, Vencor Inc. (renamed Kindred Healthcare Inc. in 2001), Louisville, 1998—99, sr. v.p., gen. counsel, 1999—. Office: Kindred Healthcare Inc 680 S 4th St Louisville KY 40202-2412

RIEDY, MARK JOSEPH, finance educator; b. Aurora, Ill., July 9, 1942; s. Paul Bernard and Kathryn Veronica R.; m. Erin Jeanne Lynch, Aug. 29, 1964; children: Jennifer Erin, John Mark. BA in Econs. maxima cum laude, Loras Coll., 1964; MBA, Washington U., St. Louis, 1966; PhD, U. Mich., 1971. Asst. prof. bus. adminstrn. U. Colo., Boulder, 1969-71; sr. staff economist Council of Econ. Advisers, Washington, 1971-72; spl. asst. to chmn. Fed. Home Loan Bank Bd., Washington, 1972; v.p., dir. research PMI Investment Corp., San Francisco, 1973; v.p., chief economist Fed. Home Loan Bank of San Francisco, 1973-77; exec. v.p., chief operating officer Mortgage Bankers Assn. of Am., Washington, 1978-84; pres., chief operating officer Fed. Nat. Mortgage Assn., Washington, 1985-86, cons., 1986-87; pres., chief operating officer J.E. Robert Cos., Alexandria, Va., 1987-88; pres., chief exec. officer Nat. Coun. Community Bankers, Washington, 1988-92, also bd. dirs.; prof. real estate fin. U. San Diego, 1993—, exec. dir. Burnham-Moores Ctr. Real Estate, 1993—. Mem. adv. coun. Credit Rsch. Ctr., Purdue U., 1981-82; bd. dirs. Fed. Nat. Mortgage Assn., Continental Savs. Bank, AccuBanc Mortgage Corp., Pan Pacific Retail Properties, Inc., Am. Mortgage Network, Inc., Bio-Med. Realty Trust, Noble Broadcast Group, Drayton Ins. Cos., Perpetual Savs. Bank, Ctr. for Fin. Studies; chmn., bd. dirs., Neighborhood Bancorp; mem. San Diego Mayor's Renaissance Commn. Bd. dirs. Lambda Alpha Internat. Woodrow Wilson scholar, 1964; Nat. Def. scholar, 1964-66; U.S. Steel Found. fellow, 1966-68; Robert G. Rodkey Found. fellow, 1966-69; Earhart Found. fellow, 1968-69 Mem. Am. Econ. Assn., Am. Fin. Assn., Nat. Assn. Bus. Economists, Am. Soc. Assn. Execs., Urban Land Inst. Office: U San Diego Sch Bus Adminstrn 5998 Alcala Park San Diego CA 92110-2492 Business E-Mail: mriedy@sandiego.edu.

RIEF, MICHELLE M., cultural studies educator; b. Council Bluffs, Iowa, Oct. 8, 1972; d. Thomas L. and Jeanne A. Rief; m. David F. Carpio, Aug. 16, 2003. BS, Fla. State U., 1993; MA, Temple U., 1996, PhD, 2003. Exec. dir. Thresholds in Del. County, Media, Pa., 1999—2003; asst. prof. Borough of Manhattan C.C., NYC, 2003—06; ind. writer/scholar, 2006—. Faculty fellow publs. program, CUNY, 2005. Mem.: Nat. Women's Studies Assn., Nat. Coun. Black Studies, Am. Hist. Assn., Assn. for Study of African Am. Life and History. Unitarian Universalist. Avocations: travel, films. E-mail: mrief@comcast.net.

RIEFF, DAVID SONTAG, editor, writer, critic; b. Boston, Sept. 28, 1952; s. Philip and Susan (Sontag) R. Student, The Lycee Francais de NY, New Lincoln Sch., B.A., Princeton U., 1978. Dir. publs. N.Y. Inst. for Humanities, 1980-85, program dir., 1984—85, now fellow; sr. editor Farrar, Straus & Giroux Inc., N.Y.C., 1979—89. vis. prof., creative writing, City Univ. NY, 1985-86; writing faculty, Empire State Summer Writing Program, Skidmore Coll., 1990-95; freelance writer, 1989-, dep. editor, World Policy Jour., 1998-; contbg. editor, The New Republic, 1990-, Author: Texas Boots, 1979, Going to Miami: Exiles, Tourists, and Refugees in the New America, 1987, Los Angeles: Capital of the Third World, 1991, The Exile: Cuba in the Heart of Miami, 1993, Slaughterhouse: Bosnia and the Failure of the West, 1995, A Bed for the Night: Humanitarianism in Crisis, 2002, At the Point of a Gun: Democratic Dreams and Armed Intervention, 2005; contbr. numerous articles, short stories to various publs. Club: Princeton (N.Y.C.). Office: Pentagram Design 204 5th Ave New York NY 10010-2103 Address: c/o Wylie Agy Ste 2114 250 W 57th St New York NY 10107 E-mail: davidrieff@compuserve.com.

RIEFLER, DONALD BROWN, financial consultant; b. Washington, Nov. 10, 1927; s. Winfield W. and Dorothy (Brown) R.; m. Patricia Hawley, Oct. 12, 1957; children: Duncan, Linda, Barbara. BA, Amherst Coll., 1949. With J.P. Morgan & Co. Inc., NYC, 1952-91; v.p. Morgan Guaranty Trust Co. of N.Y., 1962-68, sr. v.p., 1968-77, chmn. sources and uses of funds com., 1977—88, chmn. market risk com., 1989—91; fin. mkts. cons., 1991—. With U.S. Army, 1950-52. Mem. John's Island Club, Riomar Country Club, Quail Valley River Club, Birchwood Farms Club, Harbor Point Club, Creek Club. Home: 512 Bay Dr Vero Beach FL 32963-2107

RIEGEL, BYRON WILLIAM, ophthalmologist; b. Evanston, Ill., Jan. 19, 1938; s. Byron and Belle Mae (Huot) Riegel; m. Marilyn Hills, May 18, 1968; children: Marc William, Ryan Marie, Andrea Elizabeth. BS, Stanford U., 1960; MD, Cornell U., 1964. Diplomate Nat Bd Med Examiners, Am Bd Ophthalmology 2007. Intern King County Hosp., Seattle, 1964-65; asst. resident in surgery U. Wash., Seattle, 1965; resident in ophthalmology U. Fla., Fla., 1968-71; pvt. practice medicine specializing in ophthalmology Sierra Eye Med. Group, Inc., Visalia, Calif., 1972—. Mem staff Kaweah Delta Dist Hosp, chief staff, 1978—79, bd dirs, asst secy, 1983—90; asst med dir Sierra Ambulatory Surg Ctr, Visalia, Calif., 2000—. Flight surgeon USN, 1966—68. Co-recipient Fight-for-Sight Citation for rsch. in retinal dystrophy, 1970. Fellow: ACS, Am. Acad. Ophthalmology; mem.: AMA, Am. Soc. Cataract and Refractive Surgery, Calif. Acad. Ophthalmology (v.p. 3d party liaison 1994—96, dir. 1996—98), Tulare County Med Asn, Calif. Med. Assn. (del. 1978—79), Rotary. Roman Catholic. Home: 3027 Keogh Ct Visalia CA 93291-4228 Office: 2830 W Main St Visalia CA 93291-4331 Office Phone: 559-636-1000. Personal E-mail: briegel@pacbell.net. Business E-Mail: briegel@sierraeye.com.

RIEGER, JAMES A., plastic surgeon; m. Linda M. Rieger; children: Katrina, Andrew, Claire. BS in Chem. Engring. magna cum laude, SUNY, Buffalo, 1983; MD, St. Louis U., 1987. Cert. Am. Bd. Plastic Surgery, Am. Bd. Otolaryngology, lic. physician Kansas, Calif. Resident, otolaryngology US Naval Hosp., Oakland, Calif., 1992; resident, plastic surgery Providence Hosp. Med. Ctrs., Southfield, Mich., 2001; sole practitioner Aesthetic Plastic Surgery PA, Wichita, Kans. Mem.: Am. Soc. Plastic Surgery, Am. Soc. Aesthetic Plastic Surgery. Avocations: gardening, bicycling, hiking, travel. Office: Aesthetic Plastic Surgery Ste 204 9300 E 29th St N Wichita KS 67226-2183 *

RIEGER, JULIE, marketing executive; Media dir. Sicola Martin, Austin, 1997; sr. v.p., global media dir. Hewlett-Packard Co.; exec. v.p., mng. dir. West Coast ZenithOptimedia, San Francisco. Named a Woman to Watch, Advt. Age, 2007. Office: ZenithOptimedia 2001 The Embarcadero San Francisco CA 94133 *

RIEGER, MICHAEL IRA, lawyer; b. NYC, Oct. 19, 1952; s. Joseph and Adrienne R. BA in Sociology, SUNY, Buffalo, 1973; JD, George Mason U., 1977. Bar: Va. 1977. Pvt. practice, Fairfax, Va., 1977—. Lectr. in field. Mem. Va. State Bar Assn., Fairfax Bar Assn. co-chmn. com. law related edn. 1996-97, co-chmn. com. continuing legal edn. 1995-96, chmn. subcom. gen. dist. ct. criminal law 1993-95, com. mem.) Office: Ste 301-B 10623 Jones St Fairfax VA 22030 Office Phone: 703-352-1400. Business E-Mail: riegerlaw@aol.com.

RIEGER, MITCHELL SHERIDAN, lawyer; b. Chgo., Sept. 5, 1922; s. Louis and Evelyn (Sampson) Rieger; m. Rena White Abelmann, May 17, 1949 (div. 1957); 1 child, Karen Gross Cooper; m. Nancy Horner, May 30, 1961 (div. 1972); stepchildren: Jill Levi, Linda Hanan, Susan Perlstein, James Geoffrey Felsenthal; m. Pearl Handelsman, June 10, 1973; stepchildren: Steven Newman, Mary Ann Moseley, Nancy Halbeck. *Wife, Pearl H. Rieger, born in Chicago (1928), received a B.A. degree in Speech and Language Pathology from the University of Michigan (1948) and an M.A. degree in Educational Psychology from the University of Chicago (1974). Since then she has been in private practice as a psychoeducational diagnostician. In January, 1997 she became a consultant at the Rush Neurobehavioral Center, Skokie, Illinois. In 1997, the Center established the Pearl H. Rieger award to honor a pioneer in the field of neurobehavioral disorders in children. On November 13, 1997 Pearl Rieger became the first recipient of the award named after her.* AB, Northwestern U., 1944; JD, Harvard U., 1949. Bar: Ill. 1950, U.S. Dist. Ct. (no. dist.) Ill. 1950, U.S. Supreme Ct. 1953, U.S. Ct. Mil. Appeals 1953, U.S. Ct. Appeals (7th cir.) 1954. Legal asst. Rieger & Rieger, Chgo., 1949-50, assoc., 1950-54; asst. U.S. atty. No. Dist Ill., Chgo., 1954-60, 1st asst., 1958-60; assoc. gen. counsel SEC, Washington, 1960-61; ptnr. Schiff Hardin & Waite, Chgo., 1961—. sr. counsel, 1998—. Instr. John Marshall Law Sch., Chgo., 1952—54. *Notable cases: before federal court juries (Chicago) for U.S. convictions in 1st vote fraud trial (U.S. v Louis Nathan, 1955), and last income tax evasion trial involving post WWII sale of new automobiles for unreported amounts exceeding price control (U.S. v. Leonard Bernard, 1959); for SEC first judicial opinion interpreting SEC's then Statement of Policy about literature used in mutual fund shares sales (Boruski v. SEC, U.S. Court Appeals, 2nd Circuit, 1961); successfully represented 35 investment banking firms in one of 1st class action jury trials involving legality of initial public offering (Bisgeier v. Fotomat Corp., (federal court, San Diego, 1976).* Contbr. articles to profl. jours. Mem. Chgo. Crime Commn., 1964—, bd. dirs., 1998—; pres. Park View Home Aged, 1969—71; bd. dirs. Spertus Mus. Judaica, 1987—91, mem. vis. com., 1991—2005; Rep. precinct committeeman Highland Park, Ill., 1964—68. Served to lt. (j.g.) USNR, 1943—46, PTO. Fellow: Am. Coll. Trial Lawyers; mem.: FBA (pres. Chgo. chpt. 1959—60, nat. v.p. 1960—61), ABA, 7th Cir. Bar Assn., Am. Judicature Soc., Ill. Bar Assn., Chgo. Bar Assn., Vail Racquet Club, Lawyers Club Chgo., Standard Club, Phi Beta Kappa. Jewish. Avocations: photography, skiing, sailing. Office: SchiffHardin LLP 6600 Sears Tower Chicago IL 60606 Office Phone: 312-258-5644. Personal E-mail: msheridanr@aol.com. Business E-Mail: mrieger@schiffhardin.com.

RIEGLER, ALAN MARTIN, bank technology consultant; b. Cleve., Aug. 30, 1946; s. Martin and Caroline (Bartsche) R. BS, Case Western Res. U., 1968; MBA, Xavier U., 1970; JD, No. Ky. U., 1978. Bar: Ohio 1978, Tenn. 1979; cert. systems profl. Sr. systems analyst Proctor & Gamble, Cin., 1968-72; systems and processing mgr. Automatic Data Processing, Cin., 1972-78; v.p. MIS Leader Fed. Savs. & Loan, Memphis, 1978-81; v.p. systems First Tenn. Bank, Memphis, 1982-85; dir. fins. svcs. consulting Price Waterhouse, Charlotte, N.C., 1985-86; Atlanta, 1986-87; LA, 1987--. Editorial advisor Small Systems World, Chgo., 1981-83; bd. dirs. Hogan Systems User Group, Inc., 1984-85. Contbr. articles to profl. jours. Mem. The Computer Soc. Home: 1111 Crown Dr Pasadena CA 91107-5912 Office: Price Waterhouse Coopers 350 S Grand Ave # 49 Los Angeles CA 90071-3406

RIEGSECKER, MARVIN DEAN, pharmacist, state senator; b. Goshen, Ind., July 5, 1937; s. Levi and Mayme (Kauffman) R.; m. Norma Jane Shrock, Aug. 3, 1958; children: Steven Scott, Michael Dean. BA in Pharmacy, U. Colo., 1967. Pharmacist Parkside Pharmacy, Goshen, Ind., 1967-73, Walgreens, Goshen, 1994-96, Meijer, Goshen, 1998—2004; pharmacist, mgr. Hooks Drugs, Inc., Goshen, 1973-94; coroner Elkhart County, Goshen, 1977-84; mem. Ind. Senate from 12th dist., Indpls., 1988—; pharmacy cons., 2003—. Bus. affairs cons. Goshen Health Sys., 1997-98. Rep. commr. Elkhart County, 1985-88; bd. commrs. pres., 1987-88; past adv. bd. dirs. Oaklawn Hosp.; past chmn. Michiana Area Coun. of Govts. Mem. Ind. Pharm. Assn. Republican. Mennonite. Avocation: jogging. Home: 1814 Kentfield Way Goshen IN 46526-5610 Office: Ind Senate Statehouse 200 W Washington St Indianapolis IN 46204-2728

RIEHECKY, JANET ELLEN, writer; b. Waukegan, Ill., Mar. 5, 1953; d. Roland Wayne and Patricia Helen (Anderson) Polsgrove; m. John Jay Riehecky, Aug. 2, 1975; 1 child, Patrick William. BA summa cum laude, Ill. Wesleyan U., 1975; MA in Comm., Ill. State U., 1978; MA in English, Northwestern U., 1983. Tchr. English Blue Mound (Ill.) H.S., 1977-80, West Chicago (Ill.) H.S., 1984-86; editor Child's World Pub. Co., Elgin, Ill., 1987-90; freelance writer Elgin, 1990—. Author: Dinosaur series, 24 vols., 1988, UFOs, 1989, Saving the Forests, 1990, Irish Americans, 1995, The Mystery of the Missing Money, 1996, The Mystery of the UFO, 1996, Stegosaurus, 1998, Triceratops, 1998, Tyrannosaurus, 1998, Velociroptor, 1998, A Ticket to China, 1999, Greece, Sweden, 2000, George Lucas, 2001, The Emancipation Proclamation, 2002, The Osage Nation, 2002, The Cree Nation, 2002, Indonesia, 2002, The Plymouth Colony, 2002, The Settling of Jamestown, 2002, The Settling of St. Augustine, 2002, The Siege of the Alamo, 2002, Benjamin Franklin, 2003, Daniel Boone, 2003, The Wampanoag, 2003, Ulysses S. Grant, 2004, William McKinley, 2005, Respect, 2005, Citizenship, 2005, Cooperation, 2005, Iguanodon, 2006, Diplodocus, 2006, Pteranodon, 2006, Megalodon, 2006, Cave Bear, 2007, Sabertooth Cat, 2007, Tasmanian Tiger, 2007. Nat. dir. Kids Love a Mystery, 1999-2004. Recipient Summit award for best children's nonfiction Soc. Midland Authors, 1988. Mem. Soc. Am. Magicians, Soc. Children's Book Writers and Illustrators (network rep. 2006), Mystery Writers Am. (midwest bd. dirs. 2000-04), Sisters in Crime, Phi Kappa Phi. Democrat. Baptist. Avocations: reading, hiking, dinosaur hunting. Office Phone: 847-695-9781. Personal E-mail: jr@janetriehecky.com.

RIEHL, CHRISTINA PAULINE, ecologist; b. New Orleans, Apr. 27, 1983; d. Robert Ellison Riehl and Christina Vella. BA, Harvard U., Cambridge, Mass., 2005; postgrad., Princeton U., NJ, 2005—. Tchr. Princeton U., Princeton, 2005—. Curatorial asst. Harvard U., Mus. Comparative Zoology, Cambridge, Mass., 2001—05; editl. asst. Assn. Field Ornithologists, 2006—. Cello tchr. NJ. Pub. Schs., Princeton, 2005—06, 2005—06. Fellow, Smithsonian Tropical Rsch. Inst., 2007; scholar, Barry M. Goldwater Scholarship and Excellence in Edn. Program, 2005; Grad. Rsch. fellow, NSF, 2005. Mem.: Wilson Ornithol. Soc., Raptor Rsch. Found., Assn. of Field Ornithologists, Cooper Ornithol. Soc., Am. Ornithologist's Union. Avocations: music, reading, birdwatching. Office: Princeton Univ Dept EEB 107A Guyot Hall Princeton NJ 08544 Home Phone: 504-891-9858; Office Phone: 609-651-3439. Business E-Mail: criehl@princeton.edu.

RIEHL, JANE ELLEN, education educator; b. New Albany, Ind., Oct. 17, 1942; d. Henry Gabbart Jr. and Mary Elizabeth Willham; m. Richard Emil Riehl, June 15, 1968; 1 child, Mary Ellen. BA in Elem. Edn., U. Evansville, 1964; MS, Ind. U., Bloomington, 1966; postgrad., Spalding U., 1979, Ind. U. S.E., New Albany, 1991—2002. Cert. 1-8 and kindergarten tchr., Ind.; lic. profl. elem adminstrn., reading minor kindergarten tchr., Ind. Elem. tchr. Clarksville (Ind.) Cmty. Sch., 1964-68, 70-75, 81-82, tchr. kindergarten, 1975-81; elem. tchr. Chapelwood Sch. Wayne Twp., Indpls., 1968-70; lectr. edn. Ind. U. S.E., 1988-97, dir. tchg. and rsch. project, 1990-91, 92-93, dir. field and career placement, cert./lic. grad advisor New Albany, 1998, coord. elem./spl. edn. field and career placement, license and grad. advisor, 1998—. Cons. Riehl Assocs., Jeffersonville, Ind., 1995—. Co-author: An Integrated Language Arts Teacher Education Program, 1990, The Reading Professor, 1992, Multimedia: HyperStudio and Language Education, 1996, Technology: Hypermedia and Communications, 1997, others; author procs. Parent vol. Girl Scouts U.S.A., Jeffersonville, 1988-95; mem. adminstrtv. bd. Wall Street United Meth. Ch., Jeffersonville, 1993-95; mem. women's health adv. coun. Clark Meml. Hosp., Jeffersonville, 1995—; bd. dirs. Clark Meml. Hosp. Found., vice chair, 1999, chair 2000, sec. 2002-03; team mem. People to People Citizen Amb. Program, 1993, 95, 96; chair internat. bylaws Altrusa Internat., Inc., 2001—. Named Young Career Woman of Yr. Bus. and Profl. Women New Albany and Dist. 13 Ind., 1966; tchg. and rsch. grantee Ind. U. S.E., 1990, 94, 95, 96, 97, 2000; recipient Disting. Tchg. award Ind. U. S.E., 1997, Tchg. Excellence Recognition award, 1997. Mem. Nat. Coun. Tchrs. English, Profs. Reading Tchr. Edn., Ind. State Med. Assn. Alliance (v.p. so. area 1999-2000), Clark County Med. Soc. Alliance (pres.-elect 1997-98, pres. 1998-99), Altrusa Internat. Inc. (internat. bd. 1993-95, dist. gov. 1993-95, svc. award 1995), Phi Delta Kappa (v.p. 1991-92, pres. 1997—, svc. award 1991), Kappa Kappa Kappa (pres. Jeffersonville 1975-76, 90-91, Outstanding Mem. award 1987). Avocations: travel, reading, crafts, decorating. Home: 1610 Fox Run Trl Jeffersonville IN 47130-8204 Office: Ind U SE 4201 Grant Line Rd New Albany IN 47150-2158

RIEHL, JOYCE K., veterinarian; b. Manila, Philippines, June 7, 1974; arrived in US, 1987; d. James Leslie and Maria Ana Riehl. BA, Stanford U., Palo Alto, Calif., 1997; DVM, PhD, U. Calif., Davis, 2006. Rsch. asst. Stanford U., Palo Alto, 1996—2001; vet. asst. South Peninsula Vet. Emergency Clinic, Palo Alto, 1999—2005; vet. VCA Miller-Robertson Animal Hosp., West Hollywood, Calif., 2006—. Contbr. articles to profl. jours. Recipient Award for Rsch. Excellence by a Trainee, Associated Profl. Sleep Socs., 1997—98, Bayer Animal Health award for clin. proficiency, Bayer, 2006, Eli Lilly Travel award, 2005, Achievement Rewards for Coll. Scientists scholarship, ARCS Found., 2003, Award for Rsch. Excellence by a Trainee, Sleep Rsch. Soc., 1999, Vet. Scientist Tng. Program fellowship, U. Calif., Davis, 2002—06; scholar Wilds award for rsch. proficiency, 2006. Mem.: AVMA, Soc. Toxicology (3d Pl. award grad. student poster presentation 2005), Biophys. Soc., Calif. Vet. Med. Assn., Phi Sigma. Office: VCA Miller-Robertson Animal Hosp 8807 Melrose Ave West Hollywood CA 90069 Home Phone: 310-209-4927; Office Phone: 310-657-7050.

RIEHLE, B. HUDSON, trade association executive; b. Cin., Sept. 10, 1953; s. Robert Arthur Riehle and Lois W. Hudson; m. Eileen Patricia Betit, Aug. 2, 1986; children: B. Hudson Jr., Bradley Patrick. BA, Skidmore Coll., 1975; MBA, U. Pa., 1986. Rsch. cons. Avmark, Inc., Washington, 1976-78; rsch. analyst Airline Pilots Assn., Washington, 1978-81, supr. econ. analysis, 1981-84; rsch. mgr. Nat. Restaurant Assn., Washington, 1986-91, sr. rsch. mgr., 1991-95, dir. rsch., 1995-97, sr. dir. rsch., 1997-99, v.p. rsch. & info. svcs., 1999-2000, sr. v.p. rsch. and info. svcs., 2000—; bd. dirs. Alexandria Econ. Devel. Partnership, 2002—04. Bus. rsch. adv. coun. Bureau of Labor Stats., 2003—. Editor: Comml. Airline Fleets, 1976—78, Restaurant Industry Ops. Report, 1986—; contbr. Airline Pilot, 1978—84, Restaurants USA, 1986-2002; reviewer: Cornell Hotel and Restaurant Adminstrn. Qrly., 2007—. Mem., bd. dirs., 1st v.p. Fairlington Meadows, Arlington, 1990—92. Mem.: Alexandria Conv. and Visitors Assn. (vice chmn. bd. govs. 2001—02, chmn. bd. govs. 2002—04, treas. 2004—05). Avocations: geology, cross country skiing, photography. Home: 2431 Davis Ave Alexandria VA 22302-3209 Office: Nat Restaurant Assn 1200 17th St NW Ste 700 Washington DC 20036-3006 Office Phone: 202-331-5962. E-mail: hriehle@dineout.org.

RIEKE, MARCIA J., astronomer, educator; BS in Physics, MIT, 1972, PhD, 1976. Prof. astronomy Univ. Ariz., Tucson. Fellow: Am. Acad. Arts & Scis.; mem.: NSF (math, phys. sci. adv. com. 2006—07), NAS, Am. Astronomical Soc. Office: Steward Observatory 262 Univ Ariz PO Box 210065 Tucson AZ 85721 Office Phone: 520-621-2731. Office Fax: 520-621-1532. Business E-Mail: mrieke@as.arizona.edu. *

RIEKE, PAUL VICTOR, lawyer; b. Seattle, Apr. 1, 1949; s. Luvern Victor and Anna Jane (Bierstedt) R.; m. Judy Vivian Farr, Jan. 24, 1974; children: anna Katharina, Peter Johann. BA, Oberlin Coll., 1971; postgrad., U. Wash., 1971, Shoreline C.C., 1972-73; JD, Case Western Res. U., 1976. Bar: Wash, 1976, U.S. Dist. Ct. (we. dist.) Wash. 1976, U.S. Tax Ct. 1978. Assoc. Hatch & Leslie, Seattle, 1976-82, ptnr., 1982-91, Foster, Pepper & Shefelman, PLLC, 1991—. Exec. notes editor Case Western Res. U. Law Rev., 1975-76. Mem. exec. bd. dist. coun. N. Pacific dist. Am. Luth Ch., Seattle, 1978-83, coun. pres., 1983, Am. Luth. Ch. pub. bd., 1984-87; v.p. Northwest Wash. Synod of Evangelical Luth. Ch. Am., Seattle, 1988-90, mem. Synod Coun., 1990-92, del. ELCA Nat. Assembly, 1991, ELCA Northwest Synod Regional Rep., 1992-96, region one coun. pres., 1994-96. Mem. ABA, Wash. State Bar Assn., Seattle-King County Bar Assn., Order of Coif. Lodges: Seattle Downtown Central Lions. Democrat. Home: 321 NE 161st St Shoreline WA 98155-5741 Office: Foster Pepper & Shefelman PLLC 34th Fl 1111 3rd Ave Seattle WA 98101 E-mail: RiekP@Foster.com.

RIEKELS, LYNDA MARIE, materials engineer; d. Carl Herman and Shirley Jean (Page) Piethe; m. Bruce Warren Riekels, Mar. 27, 1971; children: Ryan, Robyn. BS in Geology cum laude, Mich. Tech. U., Houghton, 1971; MS in Geology, U. Ill. Chgo., 1973; PhD in Materials and Sci. Engring., Northwestern U., Evanston, Ill., 1979. Engr., rsch. engr.,sr. rsch. engr. Inland Steel Co., East Chicago, Ind., 1973-82; pres. Geomet Tech., Longview, Tex., 1982-84; dir. R&D, v.p. tech. ops., v.p. quality and tech. Lone Star Steel, Tex., 1984-89; from sr. rsch. engr. to engring. cons. Mobil R&D Co., Dallas, 1989-95; group mgr. materials and corrosion Mobil Tech. Co., Dallas, 1995-98; tech. mgr. Mobil de Venezuela, Caracas, 1998-99; sr. engr. cons. Mobil Tech. Co., 2000-01; sr. bus. cons. IPA, Chgo., 2001—02; v.p. bus. devel. and forging ops. Delfasco, Inc., 2002—07; hot mill metallurgist SeverCorr, Columbus, Miss., 2007—. Mem. adv. bd. North Tex. Rsch. Inst., Dallas, 1993-96. Patentee in field; contbr. articles to profl. jours. Mem. Am. Soc. Metals, Nat. Assn. Corrosion Engrs., Am. Soc. Quality Control, Soc. Petroleum Engrs., The Metals Soc., Am. Assn. Iron and Steel Engrs., Phi Kappa Phi, Tau Beta Pi (hon.), Alpha Sigma Mu (hon.). Avocations: painting, drawing, rock collecting, sailing, gardening. Home: 500 Mallory Ln Apt 29J Starkville MS 39759 Office Phone: 662-848-0992 Ext. 0302. Personal E-mail: lriekels@bellsouth.net. Business E-Mail: lriekels@severcorr.com.

RIEKKI, LEE WILLIAM, musician, educator; BS, U. Wis., Green Bay, 1995; MSW, Washington U., St. Louis, 1999; BA, Webster U., St. Louis, 2006; postgrad. in Music, U. Mo., Kansas City, 2006—. Intern St. Louis Effort AIDS, 1997—99; psychosocial/spiritual support Doorways Supportive Housing, St. Louis, 2001—02; substitute organist, cathedral choir accompanist Cathedral Basilica St. Louis, 2003—04; asst. to canon precentor Christ Ch. Cathedral, St. Louis, 2003—06; substitute univ. organist Washington U., 2005—06; mem. faculty Cathedral Acad. Music, St. Louis, 2005—. Curdy Organ scholar Grace and Holy Trinity Cathedral, Kansas City, Mo., 2007—. Recipient Talent scholarship, Conservatory of Music, U. Mo., 2006—. Applied Music scholarship, 2006—; Internat. Travel grantee, Inst. for Study Abroad, 1993, Music Dept. scholar, Christ Ch. Cathedral, 2003—06, Finlandia Found. scholar, Finlandia Found., 2005—06. Mem.: Presbyn. Assn. Musicians, Organ Hist. Soc., Assn. Anglican Musicians, Am. Guild Organists, Blue Key, Phi Theta Kappa. Episcopalian. Avocations: music, travel, reading, walking.

RIELLY, JOHN EDWARD, educational association administrator; b. Rapid City, SD, Dec. 28, 1932; s. Thomas J. and Mary A. (Dowd) R.; m. Elizabeth Downs, Dec. 28, 1957 (marriage annulled 1976); children: Mary Ellen, Catherine Ann, Thomas Patrick, John Downs; m. Irene Diedrich, Aug. 1, 1987. BA, St. John's U., Collegeville, Minn., 1954; postgrad. (Fulbright scholar), London Sch. Econs. and Polit. Sci., 1955-56; PhD, Harvard U., 1961. Faculty dept. govt. Harvard U., 1958-61; with Alliance for Progress programs Dept. State, Washington, 1961-62; fgn. policy asst. to Sen. then Vice Pres. Hubert Humphrey, Washington, 1963-69; cons. office European and internat. affairs Ford Found., NYC, 1969-70; sr. fellow Overseas Devel. Council, Washington, 1970-71; exec. dir. Chgo. Council on Fgn. Relations, 1971-74, pres., 1974—2001. Adj. prof. Northwestern U., 2001—; vis. prof. Grad. Sch. Internat. Rels. U. Calif., San Diego, 2003-; cons. NSC; adv. bd. Grad. Sch. Arts and Scis., Harvard U. Alumni Assn.; bd. dirs. Am. Coun. on Germany, Nat. Com. on U.S.-China Rels., China Coun. of Asia Soc., Am. Ditchley Found., Trilateral Commn., commn. on U.S.-Brazilian Rels.; past pres. Nat. Coun. Comty. World Affairs Orgns. Contbr. articles to profl. jours.; editor: American Public Opinion and U.S. Foreign Policy, 1975, 2d edit., 1979, 83, 87, 91, 95, 99; editl. bd. Fgn. Policy Quar., 1974—. Former trustee St. John's U. Recipient Legion d'Honneur, France, Distinguished Service Cross, Germany, Commendatore of the Italian Republic, Bernardo O'Higgins Award, Chile, The Golden Decoration, Austria, European Friendship Award, European Union, Order of Leopold (Belgium), Nat. Hon. Southern Cross, Brazil. Mem.: Council on Fgn. Relations, N.Y.C. Home: 2021 Kenilworth Ave Wilmette IL 60091-1519 Office: Ctr for Internat & Comparative Studies 1902 Sheridan Rd Evanston IL 60208 Office Phone: 847-467-4409.

RIELLY, J(OHN) P., corporate financial executive; Ptnr. Ernst & Young; v.p., controller, chief acctg. officer Amerada Hess Corp., NYC, 2001—04, sr. v.p., CFO. Office: Amerada Hess Corp 1185 Avenue of the Americas New York NY 10036 Office Phone: 212-997-8500. Office Fax: 212-536-8390. *

RIELY, CAROLINE ARMISTEAD, gastroenterologist, educator; b. Washington, Feb. 1, 1944; d. John William and Jean Roy (Jones) Riely. AB, Mt. Holyoke Coll., 1966; MD, Columbia U., 1970. Diplomate Am. Bd. Internal Medicine. Med. intern Presbyn. Hosp., NYC, 1970-71, resident in medicine, 1971-73; fellow in liver disease Yale U., New Haven, 1973-75, asst. prof., 1975-80, assoc. prof., 1980-88; prof. medicine U. Tenn., Memphis, 1988—. Fellow ACP, Am. Coll. Gastroenterology; mem. Am. Assn. Study Liver Disease, Internat. Assn. Study Liver, N.Am. Soc. for Pediatric Gastroenterology and Nutrition. Home: 1756 Central Ave Memphis TN 38104-5116 Office: U Tenn 951 Court Ave Rm 555D Memphis TN 38103-2813

RIEMER, MICHAEL PAUL, educational association administrator; b. Dallas, Feb. 28, 1978; s. William Donald Riemer and Susan D'ann Dublin. BBA in Mktg. and Info. Sys., Baylor U., 2001. Co-owner Anvil Web Pub., Waco, Tex., 2001—03. Named Eagle Scout, Cir. Ten Coun., 1996. Mem.: Phi Kappa Chi. Independent. Baptist. Office: Baylor Univ Waco TX 76706 Home Phone: 254-710-1011. Business E-Mail: michael_riemer@baylor.edu.

RIEMKE, RICHARD ALLAN, nuclear engineer; b. Vallejo, Calif., Oct. 11, 1944; s. Allan Frederick and Frances Jewell (O'Brien) R. BA in Physiology, U. Calif., Berkeley, 1967, MA in Physiology, 1971, PhD in Engring. Sci., 1977. Postdoctoral fellow U. So. Calif., LA, 1977-78; rsch. engr. Del Mar Avionics, Irvine, Calif., 1979; staff fellow NIH, Bethesda, Md., 1980; nuc. engr. Battelle Energy Alliance, Idaho Nat. Lab., Idaho Falls, 1980—. With USAR, 1969—75. Mem. AAAS, ANS, ASME, Biomed. Engring. Soc., Soc. Computer Simulation, Soc. Math. Biology, Soc. Engring. Sci., Order of Golden Bear, Alpha Sigma Phi. Republican. Roman Catholic. Avocations: swimming, surfing. Home: 1727 Grandview Dr # 4 Idaho Falls ID 83402-5016 Office: Battelle Energy Alliance Idaho Nat Lab Idaho Falls ID 83415-3890

RIENDL, ROBIN WENDY, wealth advisory specialist, financial advisor; b. Madison, Wis., Feb. 8, 1966; d. Jim McCaslin and Dean Naomi Brown; m. Paul Alex Riendl, Feb. 4, 1994. B in Natural Resources Mgmt., U. Alaska, Fairbanks, 1988; MBA, U. Alaska, 1991. Field investigator Harding Lawson Assocs., Anchorage, 1988—89; rsch. asst. U. Alaska, Fairbanks, 1989; planner Fairbanks N. Star Borough, 1989—90; forestry tech. Environ. Rsch. Inst., 1989—90; environ. analyst State of Alaska Dept. Transportation, Anchorage, 1992—96; fin. advisor Morgan Stanley, 1996—2002, Smith Barney, 2002—. Recipient Outstanding Young Woman of Am., 1997. Mem.: Fin. Planning Assn., U. Alaska Fairbanks Alumni Assn. Avocations: martial arts, skiing, scuba diving. Office: Smith Barney 2550 Denali St 17th Fl Anchorage AK 99503

RIENHOFF, WILLIAM FRANCIS, III, retired surgeon, thoracic surgeon; b. Balt., July 10, 1925; s. William Francis and Frances Young Rienhoff; m. Grace Cover Symington; children: William, Grace, Stuart. BA, U. Va., Charlottesville; MD, Johns Hopkins U., Balt. Bd. cert. gen. surgery and thoracic surgery. Resident surgery Johns Hopkins Hosp., 1949—58, Halsted fellow pathology, 1953—54, instr. surgery, 1958—63, asst. prof. surgery, 1963—96; attending surgeon Union Meml. Hosp., Balt., 1958—96, Greater Balt. MD Ctr., 1958—96; cons. Vets. Adar, Petty Point, Md., 1958—75. Med. bd. Greater Balt. MD Ctr., 1965—75, Union Meml. Hosp., 1975—88; bd. dirs. Johns Hopkins Hosp., 1970—80. 1st lt. med. US Army, 1951—59. Avocations: travel, hunting, fishing. Home: 24425 Smithville Rd Worton MD 21678

RIEPENHOFF-TALTY, MARIE, retired virologist; b. Ohio, Aug. 7, 1935; d. Harry Leo Riepenhoff and Phyllis Marie Meyer; m. Joseph Thomas Gallagher, Dec. 27, 1961 (div. Jan. 0, 1978); children: Phyllis Louise Gallagher, Joseph Thomas Gallagher, Julius Nyerere Gallagher, Anna Nzinga Gallagher; m. Thomas George Talty, Oct. 10, 1980. BSN, St. Marys Notre Dame, Ind., 1958; MSN, St. Louis U., 1961; PhD, SUNY, Buffalo, 1978. RN Bd. Nursing Edn., 1956. Campus nurse St. Mary's Notre Dame, 1955—58; outpatient sister St. Bartholomew's Hosp., London, 1958; disaster nurse ARC, Meknes, Morocco, 1960—61; nursing arts instr. Boston Coll., 1961—62; biology instr. Songea Secondary Sch., Tanzania, 1965—69; virology lab. dir., rsch. scientist Children's Hosp. Buffalo, 1977—2005; ret., 2005. Achievements include research in rotavirus-induced hepatitis is mice. Home: 313 Whisperlodge Ct Roseville CA 95747

RIES, CHARLES P., ambassador; b. 1951; BA, Johns Hopkins U., 1972, MA, 1973. Dep. asst. U.S. Trade Rep. for N.Am. Affairs Office of the U.S. Trade Rep., Washington, 1990—92; min. counselor for econ. affairs U.S. Mission to the European Union, Brussels, 1992—96, U.S. Embassy, London, 1996—2000; prin. dept. asst. sec. of state for European and Eurasian affairs Dept. of State, Washington, 2000—04, U.S. amb. to Greece, 2004—.

RIES, EDWARD RICHARD, petroleum geologist, consultant; b. Freeman, SD, Sept. 18, 1918; s. August and Mary F. (Graber) R.; m. Amelia D. Capshaw, Jan. 24, 1949 (div. Oct. 1956); children: Rosemary Melinda, Victoria Elise; m. Maria Wipfler, June 12m 1964. AB magna cum laude, U. S.D., 1941; MS, U. Okla., 1943, PhD, 1951; postgrad., Harvard U., 1946-47, Harvard, 1946-47. Asst. geologist Geol. Survey S.D., White River area, 1941; geophys. interpreter Robert Ray Inc., Western Okla., Okla., 1942; jr. geologist Carter Oil Co., Mont., Wyo., 1943-44; geologist Standard Vacuum Oil Co., Mont., Wyo., Colo., India, 1944-49, sr. geologist Asam, Tripura, Bangladesh, India, 1951-53; sr. regional geologist NY Standard Vacuum Petroleum, Maatschappij, NY, Indonesia, 1953-59, geol. advisor Far East and Africa White Plains, NY, 1959-62, Oceania, Mobile Petroleum Co., NYC, 1962-65; geol. advisor Europe, Far East Mobil Oil Corp., NYC, 1965-71, sr. regional explorationist Far East, Australia, New Zealand, 1971-73, sr. regional explorationist Asia-Pacific, Dallas, 1973-76, sr. geol. advisor Rsch. Geology, 1976-79; assoc. geol. advisor Geology-Geophysics, Dallas, 1979-82; sr. geol. cons., 1982-83. Ind. internat. petroleum geol. cons. Europe, Africa, Sino-Soviet and S.E. Asia, 1986—; grad. asst., teaching fellow U. Okla., 1941-43, Harvard, 1946-47. Contbr. numerous domestic and internat. proprietary and pub. hydrocarbon generation and reserve evaluations, reports and profl. papers. With AUS, 1944-46. Warden-Humble fellow, U. Okla., 1951. Mem. AAAS, Am. Inst. Econ. Rsch., Am. Assn. Petroleum Geologists (assoc. editor 1978-83, 50 Yr. Mem. Svc. award 1993, 60 Yr. Mem. Svc. award 2003), Geol. Soc. Am., Am. Geol. Inst., Nat. Wildlife Fedn., Nat. Audubon Soc., NY Acad. Sci., Soc. Exploration Geophysicists, Wilderness Soc., Am. Legion, Harvard Club (Dallas), Phi Beta Kappa, Sigma Xi, Sigma Gamma Epsilon. Republican. Mennonite. Home and Office: 810 E 6th St Freeman SD 57029

RIES, WILLIAM CAMPBELL, lawyer; b. Pitts., Apr. 8, 1948; s. F. William and Dorothy (Campbell) R.; m. Mallory Burns, Oct. 26, 1968; children: William Sheehan, Sean David. AB, Cath. U. Am., 1970; JD, Duquesne U., 1974; cert. Grad. Sch. Indsl. Adminstrn., Carnegie Mellon U., 1980. Bar: Pa. 1974, U.S. Dist. Ct. (we. dist.) Pa. 1974, U.S. Supreme Ct. 1979. Atty., then mng. counsel trust and investment svc. Mellon Bank, N.A., Pitts., 1974-90; ptnr. Dickie, McCamey and Chilcote, Pitts., 1990-98; mem. Sweeney, Metz, Fox, McGrann & Schermer, LLC, 1998-2001; shareholder Tucker Arensberg, 2001—. Mem. adv. com. decedents' estates and trust law Pa. Joint State Govt. Commn., 1981—; adj. prof. Duquesne U., 1984—; mem. risk mgmt. adv. group Bank Adminstrn. Inst., 2003—. Author: The Regulation of Investment Management and Fiduciary Services West, 1997. Pres. McCandless Twp. Civic Assn., Pitts., 1981—, McCandless Town Coun., chair pub. safety com., vice chair fin com.; sec. McCandless Indsl. Devel. Auth.; liaison McCandless zoning hearing bd. Fellow Am. Bar Found.; mem. ABA (chmn. fiduciary svcs. subcom.), Pa. Bar Assn., Allegheny County Bar Assn., Pitts. Estate Planning Coun., Am. Bankers Assn. (co-chmn. nat. conf. lawyers and corp. fiduciaries, chmn. trust counsel com.), Pa. Bankers Assn. (trust com., trust legis. com.), Rivers Club, Treesdale Golf and Country Club. Republican. Avocations: golf, sailing, cross country skiing, exercise. Home: 9602 Fawn Ln Allison Park PA 15101-1737 Office Phone: 412-594-5646. Business E-Mail: wries@tuckerlaw.com.

RIESEBERG, LOREN, botanist, educator; BA, Southern Coll., Tenn., 1981; MS, U. of Tenn., Knoxville, 1984; PhD., Wash. State. u., 1987. Rsch. scientist Rancho Santa Ana Botanic Garden, Claremont, Calif., 1987—93; asst. prof. Claremont Grad. Sch., 1987—93; assoc. prof. biology Ind. U., Bloomington, Ind., 1993—97; dir. Plant Sci. Program, 1996—; prof. biology Ind. U., Bloomington, Ind., 1997—. Contbr. scientific papers more than 150 articles; editor (chief): (text book) Molecular Ecology, 1999. Recipient George R Cooley award in Plant Systematics, 1990, David Starr Jordan award in Evolution, Ecology, and Organismal Biology, 1998; grantee MacArthur Found. Fellowship, 2003. Fellow: Am. Acad. Arts & Sciences; mem.: Am. Genetics Assn. Office: Ind U dept of Biology 1001 E 3rd St Jordan Hall Bloomington IN 47405

RIESEL, SHEILA GINSBERG, lawyer; b. Bklyn., Oct. 5, 1944; BA, Vassar Coll., 1966; JD, Fordham U., 1969. Bar: NY 1969, US Supreme Ct., US Ct. Appeals (2nd cir.), US Dist. Ct. (ea. dist. NY), US Dist. Ct. (so. dist. NY). With Legal Aid Soc.; ptnr. Blank Rome, LLP, NYC. Adj. prof. law, appellate advocacy and legal writing Fordham Law Sch., 1976—82. Mem. Matrimonial Commn., 2005. Named one of Top 100 Attys., Worth mag., 2006, 2007. Mem.: Women's Bar Assn., NY State Bar Assn., NYC Bar Assn., Fed. Bar Coun. Office: Blank Rome LLP Chrysler Bldg 405 Lexington Ave New York NY 10174-0208 Office Phone: 212-885-5535. Office Fax: 212-885-5002. E-mail: SRiesel@BlankRome.com. *

RIESENBERGER, JOHN RICHARD, science administrator; b. NYC, Sept. 25, 1948; s. Richard Raymond and Marie Teresa (Long) R.; m. Patricia Ann Casey, Nov. 23, 1974; children: Christine, Jennifer. BS in Econs. and Bus., Hofstra U., 1970, MBA in Mgmt., 1975; cert. internat. sr. mgmt. program, Harvard U., 1989. Customer svc. supr. Chase Manhattan Bank, 1970-72; gen. sales rep. various regions Upjohn Co., Bklyn., 1972-75, sales rep., sales mgr. various locations, N.Y., 1976-81, profl. tng. and devel. officer Kalamazoo, 1981-83, dir. Chgo. sales area, 1983-87; v.p., group mgr. Upjohn Co. of Can., Toronto, Ont., 1987-89; exec. dir., worldwide med. scis. liaison Upjohn Co., Kalamazoo, 1989-92, exec. dir. worldwide strategic mktg., 1992-95; exec. dir. corp. info. tech. Pharmacia & Upjohn, Inc., Kalamazoo, 1995, v.p. bus. info., 1996-97; v.p. global bus. mgmt. Pharmacia & Upjohn Inc., Bridgewater, N.J., 1998-99; pharm. cons., 1999—; exec.-in-residence Mich. State U., 2000—; pres. Consilium Ptnrs. Inc., 2000—; exec. v.p. Shaw Sci. Ptnrs., Atlanta, 2000—. Chmn. industry adv. bd. dirs. SEI Ctr. Advanced Studies in Mgmt., Wharton Sch., U. Pa.; mem. Global Adv. bd. Am. Mktg. Assn., 1999; mem. edtl. review bd. Jour. Internat. Mktg.; Ciber adv. bd. Mich. State U. Author: (with Robert T. Moran) The Global Challenge: Building the New Worldwide Enterprise, 1994, Global Business Strategies for the Year 2000, 1995. Mem. ciber adv. bd. Mich. State U. Mem. Am. Mgmt. Assn., Am. Mktg. Assn., Strategic Mgmt. Soc., Pharm. Rsch. Mfrs. Am. (chmn. mktg. practices com.), The Planning Fom, Internat. Soc. for Strategic Planning and Mgmt., Harvard Bus. Sch. Club, Pharm. Bus. Intelligence and Rsch. Group, European Pharm. Market Rsch. Assn., Harvard Bus. Sch. Health Industry Alumni Assn. Avocation: golf. Home: 42 Independence Dr Basking Ridge NJ 07920-3815

RIESER, JOSEPH A., JR., tax specialist; b. Pitts., Aug. 28, 1947; s. Joseph Alexander and Ruth Margaret (Piper) R.; m. Susan Jean Irving, Feb. 28, 1976; 1 child, Alexander H.I. AB, Princeton U., 1969; JD, MPP, Harvard U., 1974. Bar: Pa. 1974, D.C. 1976, U.S. Supreme Ct. 1979. Assoc. Reed Smith LLP, Pitts. and Washington, 1974-82, ptnr. Washington, 1983—2003; mem. Arent Fox LLP, Washington, 2003—. Mem. D.C. Office of Tax and Revenue Adv. Group, 1997-2001. Chmn. nat. alumni assn. Kennedy Sch. Govt., Cambridge, Mass., 1979-82; bd. dirs. Harvard U. Alumni Assn., 1982-84; gen. counsel 1984 Dem. Nat. Conv., Washington, 1983-84; gen. counsel Nat. Dem. Party, Washington, 1985-89; spl. counsel Clinton/Gore '92, Inc.; mem. Clinton-Gore 1992 Presdl. Transition Team. Mem. D.C. Bar (chmn. bus. related taxes com. 1989-92, tax policy steering com., chmn. D.C. Bar Nat. Fed. Tax Inst. 1991, 92, 2000, chmn. state and local taxes com. 1994-97, tax sect. steering com. 1997-2003, co-chair tax sect. 1998-2001), Ctr. for Nat. Policy Bd. Advisors, Harvard-Yale-Princeton Pitts. Club, Cosmos Club. Presbyterian. Home: 3517 Davis St NW Washington DC 20007-1426 Office: Arent Fox LLP 1050 Connecticut Ave NW Washington DC 20036 Office Phone: 202-857-8964.

RIESS, ADAM GUY, astronomer, educator; b. Dec. 16, 1969; BS in Physics, MIT, 1992; AM in Astrophysics, Harvard U., 1994, PhD in Astrophysics, 1996. Undergraduate rsch. asst. MIT, 1990—92, sr. thesis student, 1991—92; rsch. assoc. Lawrence Livermore Nat. Lab., 1992; doctoral student Harvard U., 1992—96; Miller Fellow U. Calif., Berkeley, 1996—99; asst. astronomer Space Telescope Sci. Inst., Balt., 1999—2001, assoc. astronomer, 2001—; assoc. adj. prof. John Hopkins U., 2002—06, prof., physics and astronomy, 2006—. Tchg. fellow, physics dept., The Physics of Sports MIT, 1992; tchg. fellow, astronomy Harvard U., 1993, 94; co-taught, Hot Topics in Astrophysics, astronomy and physics dept. John Hopkins U., 2003; invited spkr. in field. Contbr. articles to profl. jours.; guest appearance Quirks and Quarks, CPR, 1998, News, BBC, 1998, Science Friday, NPR, 1998, 2001, Headline News, CNN, 1998, Jim Lehrer News Hour, PBS, 1998, Sound Prints, NPR, 2000, NOVA, PBS, 2000, 60 Minutes, CBS, 2003, Scientific American Frontiers, PBS, 2004. Co-recipient Shaw prize in Astronomy, Shaw Found., Hong Kong, 2006; finalist Innovator award, Discover Mag., 2003; recipient Nat. Merit Scholar, 1988, Trumpler award, Astronomical Soc. Pacific, 1999, AURA Sci. award, 2000, Innovator award, Time Mag., 2000, Bok prize, Harvard U., 2001, Helen B. Warner prize, Am. Astronomical Soc., 2003, Best and Brightest award, Esquire Mag., 2003, Raymond and Beverly Sackler prize, Tel-Aviv U., 2004; Margaret Weyerhaeuser Jewett Meml. Fellowship, 1993, Harvard GSAS Merit Fellow, 1995. Mem.: Phi Beta Kappa. Achievements include design of Space Shuttle, Leap Frog Toys, children's educational astronomy toy, 1997-98; published the first evidence that the expansion of the Universe was accelerating % filled with Dark Energy, as a result, Science Magazine called this the Breakthrough Discovery of the Year in 1998. Avocations: bicycling, coin collecting/numismatics, home improvement. Office: Space Telescope Sci Inst 3700 San Martin Dr Baltimore MD 21218 Office Phone: 410-338-4509. Office Fax: 410-338-5090. Business E-Mail: ariess@stsci.edu.

RIESS, GORDON SANDERSON, management consultant; b. Thessaloniki, Greece, Feb. 25, 1928; came to U.S., 1932; s. Lewis William and Dorothy Onward Riess; m. Priscilla Rich, June 2, 1951; children: Mark C., Kimberly A., Blake G. AB with highest honors, Whitman Coll., 1949; MBA cum laude, Harvard U., 1951. Cert. mgmt. cons.; registered profl. cons.; accredited profl. cons. With Ford Internat. Div., NYC, 1951-53; asst. fin. mgr. Ford Motor Co., Mid. East, Alexandria, Egypt, 1953-57; gen. sales mgr. Ford Motor Co., Rome, Italy, 1957-60; regional fin. mgr. Ford Motor Co., Scandinavia, Copenhagen, Denmark, 1960-62; gen. mgr. Ford Motor Co., European, Brussels, Belgium, 1962-67; v.p. Internat. Paper Co., Zurich, Switzerland, 1967-71; exec. v.p. Cinema Internat. Corp., London, 1971-75; chmn., pres. Stewart-Riess Labs. Inc., Tarzana, Calif., 1976-83; pres., CEO Intercontinental Enterprises Ltd., Beverly Hills, Calif., 1983—. Chmn. Vis. Nurse Found., L.A., 1985-87; bd. dirs., chmn. Vis. Nurse Assn., L.A., 1976-97; bd. dirs. Beverly Found., Pasadena, Calif., 1990-97; vice-chmn. of bd. Witman Coll., Walla Walla, Wash., 1985-96. Author: Confessions of a Corporate Centurion--Tales of International Adventures, 2000, From Communism to Capitalism, 2001, Passports to Adventure, 2005; inventor/patentee pre-fillable hypodermic syringe. Chmn. Inter-Community Sch. Zurich, 1968-71; trustee Am. Sch. London, 1972-75; vice chmn. Krafterliner Mfgs. Assn., Zurich, 1968-71; bd. dirs. Vols. in Tech. Assistance, Arlington, Va., 1986-93; bd. overseers Muhlenberg Coll., 1993—; internat. bd. Czechoslovak Mgmt. Ctr., 1992—. Sgt. U.S. Army, 1946-47. R.H. Macy scholar, Harvard Bus. Sch., 1949. Mem. Am. Assn. Profl. Cons., Am. Cons. League, Asia Acad. Mgmt., Hollywood Radio & Television Soc., Inst. Mgmt. Cons., Lic. Execs. Soc. Avocations: skiing, scuba diving. Home: PO Box 2912 Beverly Hills CA 90213-2912 Personal E-mail: g.riess@sbcglobal.net.

RIESZ, PETER CHARLES, marketing educator, consultant; b. Orange, NJ, Apr. 30, 1937; s. Kolman and Ellen (Wachs) R.; m. Elizabeth Strider Dunkman, Dec. 28, 1968; children: Sarah Kathleen BS, Rutgers U., 1958; MBA, Columbia U., 1963, PhD, 1971. From asst. prof. to assoc. prof. U. Iowa, Iowa City, 1968-80, prof. mktg., 1980—, chmn. dept. mktg., 1981-87, Williams prof. tchg., 1994-97. Vis. prof. Boston U., 1974-75, Duke U., Durham, N.C., 1984-85; guest prof. Meiji U., Japan, summer 2004; cons. in field. Contbr. articles to profl. jours. Recipient Teaching Excellence award HON Industries, 1989; named MBA Prof. of Yr., 1990; Old Gold fellow U. Iowa, 1972. Mem. Am. Chem. Soc., Am. Mktg. Assn. Democrat. Presbyterian. Avocation: photography. Home: 2411 Tudor Dr Iowa City IA 52245-3638 Office: U Iowa Dept Mktg Tippie Coll Bus Adminstrn Iowa City IA 52242 Office Phone: 319-335-0937. Business E-Mail: peter-riesz@uiowa.edu.

RIETSCHEL, ROBERT LOUIS, dermatologist; b. New Orleans, Oct. 9, 1946; s. Frederick Arnt and Estelle Marie (Fleckinger) R.; m. Connie Joanne Dent, Sept. 3, 1966; children: Eric, Penny. BA, North Tex. State U., 1968; MD, U. Tex., Galveston, 1972. Diplomate Am. Bd. Dermatology. Intern Letterman Army Med. Ctr., San Francisco, 1972-73, dermatology rschr., 1973-74; resident in dermatology Brooke Army Med. Ctr., San Antonio, 1974-77, staff dermatologist, 1977-79; assoc. prof. dermatology Emory U. Sch. Medicine, Atlanta, 1981-85, acting chmn. dept. dermatology, 1984-85; assoc. chmn. dept. dermatology Ochsner Clinic, New Orleans, 1985-88, chmn. dept. dermatology, 1988—2004; chief dermatology sect. So. Ariz. VA Health Care Sys., Tucson, 2004—; prof. medicine (dermatology) U. Ariz. Sch. Medicine, 2004—. Contbr. articles to profl jours. Cubmaster Boy Scouts Am., Decatur, Ga., 1983-84. Maj. U.S. Army, 1971-79. NIOSH grant, 1981-84. Fellow Am. Acad. Dermatology, Soc. for Investigative Dermatology; mem. Am. Dermatol. Assn., N.Am. Contact Dermatitis Group (sec. 1985-93), Am. Contact Dermatitis Soc. (sec. 1989-93, pres. 1993-95). Republican. Lutheran. Avocation: sailing. Office: So Ariz VA Health Care Sys 3601 S 6th Ave Tucson AZ 85723 E-mail: Robert.Rietschel@va.gov.

RIEW, K. DANIEL, cervical spine surgeon; b. Seoul, Republic of Korea, July 28, 1958; arrived in U.S., 1966; s. C. Keith and H. Kim Riew; m. Mary Kahng, Sept. 12, 1992. MD, Case Western Res. U., 1984. Diplomate Am. Bd. of Orthopaedic Surgery. Asst. attending physician, instr. medicine Cornell U. Med. Ctr., NYC, 1987—89; resident gen. surgery Beth Israel Med. Ctr., NYC, 1989—90; resident orthop. surgery George Washington U. Hosp., Washington, 1990—94; fellow spine surgery U. Hosps. Cleve./Case We. Res. U.; from asst. prof. to prof. Washington U. Sch. Medicine, St. Louis, 1995—2005, Mildred B. Simon disting. prof. orthop. surgery, prof. neurol. surgery, 2006—, chief cervical spine surgery, dir. Orthopedic-Rehab. Inst. for Cervical Spine Surgery. Contbr. articles to profl. jours. (Cervical Spine Rsch. Soc. Outanding Basic Sci. Rsch. award, 2000, Mayfield award for basic sci. Am. Assn. of Neurol. Surgeons, 2000, North Am. Spine Soc. Outstanding Paper award, 2000, Russell S. Hibbs Basic Sci. award Scoliosis Rsch. Soc., 2000). Recipient C. Richard Bowman award, N.Y. Hosp., Cornell Med. Ctr., 1987, Caring Spirit award, Barnes-Jewish Hosp., 2001, Best Paper award, Am. Soc. Spine Radiology, 2005, Mentor award, 2006, Excellence in Tchg. award, 2007; grantee, Orthopaedic Rsch. and Edn. Found., 2002—05. Fellow: Am. Acad. Orthop. Surgeons; mem.: Mo. State Orthop. Assn., Mid. Am. Orthop. Assn., Am. Orthop. Assn., Scoliosis Rsch. Soc., Orthop. Rsch. Soc., N.Am. Spine Soc. (CME com. and surg. care com. 2000, Outstanding Paper award 2003), Cervical Spine Rsch. Soc. (clin. outcomes com. 2001, Outstanding Clin. Rsch. award 2004, Clin. Poster award 2005, Outstanding Clin. Rsch. award 2006, Outstanding Clin. Poster award 2006). Avocations: skiing, golf. Office: Washington U Sch of Medicine ste 11300 One Barnes-Jewish Hosp Plz Saint Louis MO 63110

RIFENBURGH, RICHARD PHILIP, investment company executive; b. Syracuse, NY, Mar. 3, 1932; s. Russell D. and Edna (MacKenzie) R.; m. Doris Anita Hohn, June 24, 1950; children: David, Susan, Robert. Student, Wayne State U. With Mohawk Data Scis. Corp., Herkimer, NY, 1964-74, pres., 1970-74, chmn., 1974, Moval Mgmt. Corp., Herkimer, 1968—; CEO, GCA Corp., Andover, Mass., 1986-87; gen. ptnr. Hambrecht and Quist Venture Ptnrs., 1987-90; chmn. Miniscribe Corp., Longmont, Colo., 1988-91, Ironstone Group Inc., 1988-91, St. G Crystal Ltd., Jeannette, Pa., 1985—, Paradise Music and Entertainment Inc., 2000—. Chmn. Tristar Corp., 1992—2002. With USAF, 1951-55. Address: Moval Mgmt Corp PMB 133 2637 E Atlantic Blvd Pompano Beach FL 33062-4939 Office Phone: 954-941-9182. Personal E-mail: dickrif@gmail.com.

RIFF, LAWRENCE P., lawyer; BA in History with highest honors and high distinction, U. Mich., 1978; JD, U. Oreg., 1982. Bar: Calif. 1982, Oreg. 1985, Washington 1987. Lawyer So. Pacific Transp. Co., San Francisco, 1982—86; mng. ptnr., toxic tort, transp. & litig. depts. Steptoe & Johnson LLP, LA, 1997—. John Williams Fellowship. Mem.: Am. Bd. Trial Advocacy, LA County Bar Assn. (Litig. Sect.), Internat. Moot Ct. Team, Jessup Competition. Office: Steptoe & Johnson LLP 633 W 5th St Ste700 Los Angeles CA 90071 Office Phone: 213-439-9494. Office Fax: 213-439-9599. Business E-Mail: lriff@steptoe.com.

RIFFEL, KAREN SHEFFER, music educator; b. Ft. Lauderdale, Fla. d. Thomas Fox and Frances McGaffick Sheffer; m. Keith Allen Riffel; children: Christopher, Kyle, Kathryne, Kirk, Carlton, Carolyn. BS in Music Edn., Bob Jones U., 1976. Tchr. elem. music Silver State Bapt. Schs., Lakewood, Colo., 1976—77, 1978—87, Schaumburg (Ill.) Christian Sch., 1987—, pvt. piano/voice tchr., 1987—. Dir. children's choir Bethel Bapt. Ch., Schaumburg. Mem.: Am. Coll. Musicians. Republican. Baptist. Avocations: stamping, crafts. Office: Schaumburg Christian Sch 200 N Roselle Rd Schaumburg IL 60194 E-mail: riffelkeith@sbcglobal.net.

RIFFEL, LOREN DARREL, retired entrepreneur; b. Shattuck, Okla., Mar. 3, 1936; s. Charles F. and Fern L. Riffel; m. Betty Lou Hawthorne, 1963. Gen. mgr. Best Western Inn, Woodward, Okla., 1965—84, dist. mgr., 1984—87; motel owner Motel Group, Inc., Oklahoma City, 1987—91; restaurant owner J.B. & Twin Oak Inc., Woodward, 1991—2005. Author: Country Schools, 2002, In the Shadows of the Law & Beyond, 2004. Pres. Junior Woodward C. of C., Woodward, Okla., 1971; bd. mem. Woodward C. of C., Woodward, Okla., 1975—2005, Kids Inc., Woodward, Okla., 1974—78, pres., 1978—79. Private first class US Army, 1958—60, Germany. Recipient Best Restaurant award, Woodward, 1997, 1998, 1999, 2001, 2002, 2003, 2004. Mem.: Lions Club (pres. 1978—79). Republican. Avocation: history writing. Home: 4805 Cedardale Woodward OK 73801 Office: JBs Steak House 225 E Main PO Box 351 Woodward OK 73801 Office Phone: 580-256-4845.

RIFFENBURGH, GERRYE H., artist, educator; d. Herman Harvey and Mary (Beryl) Harlow; m. Robert Harry Riffenburgh, Nov. 22, 1952; children: Robin, Scott, Marc, Karen, Douglas. BS, Coll. William and Mary, 1951, MS, 1955; BA summa cum laude, San Diego State U., 1979. Exhibiting artist and instr. San Diego Adult Coll., 1978—81; exhibiting artist The Hague, Netherlands, 1982—86, La Spezia, Italy, 1986—89, San Diego, 1990—. Rep. exhibitor Cosmopolitan Fine Arts Gallery, La Jolla, Calif., 2001—, Timmons Courtyard Gallery, Encinitas, Calif., 2001—. Author: (article on color choice) Jour. of Gen. Psychol.; over 45 juried exhibitions, Europe, U.S. Vol. Coastal Planning Coun., San Diego, 1971—73; leader Girl Scouts, San Diego, 1968—74, Girl Guides, Pembrokeshire, Wales, 1974—77; vol. polit. groups, San Diego, 1978—81; fund raiser vol. COTA, San Diego, 1978—82. Named hon. mention, Associazione Artisti Versiliese, Italy, 1989; named to Gold Medal Exhbn., Salon d'Automne/Pasadena, Calif., 2002; recipient 1st pl., Pembrokeshire Artists Assn., UK, 1974, hon. mention, Nat. Annual Galleon Exhibit, London, 1975, 3d pl., Congressgebouw, Netherlands, 1984, Cenacolo Buttini, Italy, 1988, 1st pl., Maurice Braun Meml. Plein Air Exhbn., Calif., 2000, cert. merit, LaJolla Art Assn., 2001, 3d pl., Offtrack Gallery, Leucadia, Calif., 2002, William Schultz award, Am. Impressionist Soc., Fla., 2002, 2d pl., Mcpl. Art Gallery, Escondido, Calif., 2003, spl. merit, Coos Mus. Art, Oreg., 2003, Nat. Arts Club, N.Y.C., 2003—05, Spl. Merit award, Internat. Mus. Contemporary Masters Fine Art, San Antonio, 2004—05, Arts for the Pks. award for excellence, 2005, cert. merit, LaJolla Art Assn., 2006. Mem.: Internat. Plein Air Painters (signature mem.), Am. Soc. Marine Artists (juried artist mem.), Artists' Guild San Diego Mus. Art, Oil Painters Am., Plein Air Painters Assn. San Diego (founder), Am. Impressionists Soc. (signature mem.), La Jolla Art Assn. (life; treas., bd. dir. 1996—2001), Calif. Art Club (juried artist mem.). Avocations: photography, piano, walking, tennis, yoga. E-mail: gerryeriff@yahoo.com.

RIFFENBURGH, ROBERT HARRY, biostatistician, researcher; b. Christiansburg, Va., June 19, 1931; s. Harry Buchholz and Ada Swallow Riffenburgh; m. Gerrye Harlow, Nov. 22, 1952; children: Robin, Scott, Marc, Karen, Douglas. BS, Coll. William and Mary, Richmond, Va., 1951, MS, 1953; PhD, Va. Poly. Inst., Blacksburg, 1957. Asst. prof. math. Va. Poly. Inst., Blacksburg, 1955—57, U. Hawaii, Honolulu, 1957—61; prof., head dept. stats. U. Conn., Storrs, 1962—70; prof. stats. San Diego State U., 1968—74, 1979—82, 1990—93, prof. stats, 2006—; head, biomedical program Naval Undersea Ctr., San Diego, 1970—73; scientist Naval Facility, Brawdy, Wales, 1974—77; math. statistician Naval Ocean Systems Ctr., San Diego, 1977—82; leader, naval ops. rsch. NATO SHAPE Tech. Centre, The Hague, Netherlands, 1982—86; head, ops. rsch. NATO SACLANT Undersea Rsch. Centre, La Spezia, Italy, 1986—90; chief biostats. Naval Med. Ctr. San Diego, San Diego, 1991—. Pres. and ceo Gen. Systems Analysis Co., Storrs, Conn., 1963—70. Author: Statistics in Medicine; contbr. more than 140 articles to profl. jours. Capt. NATO, 1982—89. Decorated Navy Commendation Medal; Predoctoral fellow, NIH, 1954-1956. Fellow: Am. Statis. Assoc., Royal Statis. Soc. (life); mem.: Internat. Biometrics Soc., Phi Kappa Phi, Sigma Xi. Office Phone: 619-532-9414.

RIFKA, JUDY, artist, educator; b. Bklyn., Sept. 25, 1945; d. Irving David Tenenbaum and Pearl Fessler; children: John Reed, Matthew Lenski. BA, SUNY, Old Westbury, 1993; MA, Adelphi U., 1994. Asst. prof. SUNY, Rochester, NY, 1974; artist-in-residence Princeton U., NJ, 1976, Tamarind Inst., N.Mex., 1983, Columbia U., NY, 1994, Md. Inst. Mt. Royal, Balt., 1985, Skowkegan Sch., Maine, 1989, Tandem Press, Madison, Wis., 1991. Grants juror NY State Coun. Arts, NYC, 1983, Mass. Coun. Arts, Boston, 1984, Nat. Found. Arts, 1988. One-woman shows include numerous others, 1974—2001, Brooke Alexander Gallery, 1982—85, Galerie de France, Paris, 1984, Anna Friebe Gallery, Cologne, Germany, 1985—86, Brooke Alexander Gallery, 1987—88, Tobias Hirschmann, Frankfurt, Germany, 1988, Pyramide Arte Contemporeane, Florance, 1989, Brooke Alexander Gallery, 1991, Hofstra U., 1996, prin. works include murals Madison Sq. Garden, 1989, Union Sq. Cafe, NY, 2004; author: Opera of Worms, 1984; Exhibited in group shows at Brooke Alexander Editions, 2004, N.Y. Studio Sch., 2005, Austin Mus., Tex., 2006, Andy Warhol Mus., 2006, Berkely Art Mus., Calif., 2006, Grey Gallery NYU, 2006. Jewish. Office Phone: 212-285-1532. Personal E-mail: jrifka@nyc.rr.com.

RIFKIN, ARNOLD, film company executive; b. Bklyn. m. Rita George; two children. BA, U. Cin. Founder Rifkin-David, 1974-80; merged to form Rifkin/David/Kimble/Parseghian, 1980-81, DHKPR, 1981-84; head motion picture dept. Triad Artists, Inc., 1984-92, founding ptnr.; exec. v.p., worldwide head motion picture divsn. William Morris Agy., Beverly Hills, Calif., 1992-96; pres. William Morris Talent and Lit. Agy., Beverly Hills, Calif., 1996-2000; CEO Cheyenne Enterprises, LLC, Santa Monica, Calif., 2000—. Bd. dirs. Am. Cinematheque; faculty, co-chair UCLA Sch. Theatre, Film & TV; lecturer Yale Law Sch., Harvard Sch. Bus., 2002-. Bd. councillors U. So. Calif. Office: Cheyenne Enterprises 406 Wilshire Blvd Santa Monica CA 90401-1410

RIFKIN, BARRY R., dean, dental educator, researcher; b. Trenton, NJ, Mar. 30, 1940; s. Samuel H. and Ida M. Rifkin; m. Harriet Smith, Mar. 1960 (div. Sept. 1981); children: Avery, Carl; m. Linda Ruth Rosenberg, Nov. 1993; 1 child, Hannah. BS, Ohio State U., 1961; MS, U. Ill., 1964; DDS, Temple U., 1968; PhD, U. Rochester, 1974. Andrew Mellon fellow U. Rochester Med. Ctr., 1974; assoc. pathologist Strong Meml. Hosp., 1974—80; assoc. prof. NYU, NYC, 1980—84, chmn. dept. oral medicine, 1980—87, prof., 1984—91, chmn. dept. oral medicine and pathology, 1987—91, head divsn. basic scis., 1991—98, prof. emeritus, 1998—; prof. oral biology and pathology, dean SUNY Stony Brook Health Sciences Ctr. Sch. Dental Medicine, 1998—. Rschr. in field; bd. mem. Friends of the Nat. Inst. of Dental and Craniofacial Rsch., 2005—. Sr. editor Biology and Physiology of the Osteoclast, 1992; mem. editl. bd.: Jour. Dental Rsch.; contbr. articles and abstracts to profl. jours. Fellow: Am. Coll. Dentists; mem.: AAAS, Am. Soc. Bone and Mineral Rsch., Internat. Assn. Dental Rsch., Am. Soc. Cell Biology, N.Y. Acad. Scis., Am. Assn. Oral Biologists (pres. 1992—93), Sigma Xi, Omicron Kappa Upsilon. Office: Stony Brook Univ Sch Dental Medicine 160 Rockland Hall Stony Brook NY 11794-8700 Office Phone: 631-632-8950. Office Fax: 631-632-9105. E-mail: barry.rifkin@stonybrook.edu.

RIFKIN, MATTHEW D., radiologist; b. NYC, Mar. 26, 1949; m. Susan Greenberg, 1971; children: Adam, Jason. BA, Brandeis U., 1971; MD, Albert Einstein Coll., 1974. Intern in medicine Montefiore Hosp. and Med. Ctr., Bronx, NY, 1974—75, resident in diagnostic radiology, 1975—78; fellow in ultrasound/CT Johns Hopkins Hops. and Med. Ctr., Balt., 1978—79; instr. radiology Johns Hopkins Hosp. and Med. Sch., Balt., 1978—79; clin. asst. prof. radiology U. Miami Sch. Medicine, Fla., 1979—81, Jefferson Med. Coll., Thomas Jefferson U., Phila., 1981—83, asst. prof. radiology, 1983—85, assoc. prof. radiology, 1983—86, prof. urology, 1985—91, prof., assoc. chair dept. radiology, 1986—91; clin. prof. Coll. Allied Health Sci., Thomas Jefferson U., Phila., 1984—91, 1991; chair dept. radiology Albany Med. Coll., 1991—98, prof. radiology, 1991—98, prof. surgery, 1995—99; prof., vice chmn., chief diagnostic radiology SUNY Sch. Medicine, Stony Brook, 1999—2003, prof. urology, 1999—2003; chmn. radiology Good Samaritan Hosp., West Islip, NY, 2002—; dir. radiology St. Catherine of Siena Hosp., Smithtown, NY, 2004—, St. Charles Hosp., Port Jefferson, NY, 2005—, Mather Hosp., Port Jefferson, 2007—. Cons. radiology VA, Perry Point, Md., 1978—79; staff radiologist Johns Hopkins Hosp., Balt., 1978—79, Plantation Gen. Hosp., Fla., 1979—80, St. Mary's Hosp., West Palm Beach, Fla., 1980—81; med. and edn. dir. med. sonography St. Mary's Hosp. Sch. Diagnostic, West Palm Beach, 1980—81; staff radiology Thomas Jefferson Univ. Hosp., Phila., 1981—91; dir. radiology rsch. Jefferson Med. Coll., Thomas Jefferson U. Hosp., 1986—91; dir. divsn. magnetic resonance imaging, 1986—91; med. svc. dir. dept. radiology Albany Med. Ctr. Hosp., 1996—98, chief radiologist, 1991—98; vice chair, chief diagnostic radiology, chief clin. ops., chief abdominal radiology SUNY Health Sci. Ctr., Stony Brook, 1999—2003; presenter in field. Contbr. scientific papers and articles to profl. jours.; author: Diagnostic Imaging of the Lower Genitourinary Tract, 1985, Handbook of Normal Ultrasound Anatomy, 1985; author: (editor) Intraoperative and Endoscopic Ultrasound, 1987; author: Ultrasound of the Prostate, 1988, 1997, Ultrasound, 1991; editor: Ultrasound of the Urinary Tract, 1991; co-editor: Interventional Radiology of the Genitourinary Tract, 1993; co-author: Pocket Atlas of Normal Ultrasound Anatomy, 2001, Diagnostic Imaging of the Scrotum and External Male Genitalia, 2002. Fellow: Phila. Coll. Physicians, Am. Coll. Radiology, Am. Inst. Ultrasound Medicine; mem.: Soc. Uroradiology. Home: 198 Field Rd East Setauket NY 11733 Office: Good Samaritan Hosp and Med Ctr Dept Radiology 1000 Montauk Hwy West Islip NY 11795 Office Phone: 631-376-4030. E-mail: matthew.rifkin@chsli.org.

RIFKIN, NED, museum director; b. Florence, Ala., Nov. 10, 1949; s. Arthur Robert and Ina Blanche (Steinberg) R.; children: Moses Kleinman, Amos Kleinman. BA, Syracuse U., 1972; MA in Art History, U. Mich., 1973, PhD in Art History, 1976. Asst. prof. dept. art U. Tex., Arlington, 1977-80; curator, asst. dir. New Mus. Contemporary Art, NYC, 1980-84; curator contemporary art Corcoran Gallery Art, Washington, 1984-86; chief curator exhbns. Hirshhorn Mus. and Sculpture Garden, Washington, DC, 1986-90, chief curator, 1990-91, dir., 2002—05; Nancy and Holcombe T. Green Jr. dir. High Mus. Art, Atlanta, 1991—99; dir. Menil Collection and Found., Houston, 2000—01, Smithsonian Internat. Art Mus. Div., 2004—; under sect. for art Smithsonian Institution, 2004—. Address: Smithsonian Institution Bldg 1000 Jefferson Dr SW MRC 041 Washington DC 20560-0001 *

RIFKIN, RON, actor; b. NYC, Oct. 31, 1939; m. Iva Rifkin, 1966. Actor: (films) Flareup, 1969, Devil's 8, 1969, Silent Running, 1971, Rabbit Test, 1978, The Big Fix, 1978, The Chosen, 1981, The Sting II, 1983, Kidco, 1984, JFK, 1991, Husbands and Wives, 1992, Manhattan Murder Mystery, 1993, Wolf, 1994, Last Summer in the Hamptons, 1995, The Substance of Fire, 1996, I'm Not Rappaport, 1996, L.A. Confidential, 1997, The Negotiator, 1998, Sam the Man, 1999, The Boiler Room, 2000, Keeping the Faith, 2000, The Majestic, 2001, Tadpole, 2002, Dragonfly, 2002, The

Sum of All Fears, 2002, Just a Kiss, 2002, Pulse, 2006; (TV films) The Sunshine Boys, 1975, The Dream Makers, 1975, The Night that Panicked America, 1975, In the Glitter Palace, 1977, A Question of Guilt, 1978, Columbo: Make Me a Perfect Murder, 1978, Mrs. R's Daughter, 1979, Day the Bubble Burst, 1981, Another Woman's Child, 1983, The Ratings Game, 1984, Concealed Enemies, 1984, Do You Remember Love, 1985, Courage, 1986, Dress Gray, 1986, Conspiracy: The Trial of the Chicago 8, 1987, Sunset Gang, 1991, W.S.H., 1994, Norma Jean and Marilyn, 1996, Flowers for Algernon, 2000, Deliberate Intent, 2000, The Warden, 2001; (TV series) Adam's Rib, 1973, When Things Were Rotten, 1975, Husbands, Wives & Lovers, 1978, One Day at a Time, 1980—81, Falcon Crest, 1983—84, Evergreen, 1985, Leaving L.A., 1997, Alias, 2001—06, Brothers & Sisters, 2006; Broadway actor Cabaret, 1998 (Tony award featured actor in a musical, 1998), The Paris Letter, 2005, TV guest appearances include The Bob Newhart Show, 1972, Mary Tyler Moore Show, 1970, The Rockford Files, 1974, Hill Street Blues, 1981, Law & Order, 1990, ER, 1994, The Outer Limits, 1995.

RIFKIN, STEPHEN, nephrologist; s. Morris and May Rifkin; children: Steven, Laura. AB, U. Rochester, 1963, MD, 1967. Diplomate in internal medicine and in nephrology Am. Bd. Internal Medicine. Pvt. practice nephrology, Tampa, Fla., 1980—; assoc. prof. medicine U. South Fla. Coll. Medicine, Tampa, 1999—. Chief of staff Tampa Gen. Hosp., 1988—90, chief nephrology sect., 2002—; pres. Fla. End Stage Renal Disease Network #7, Tampa, 1990—92, bd. dirs., 1999—2004. Capt. U. S. Army, 1969—71. Recipient Exemplary Practice award for nephrology, Nat. Kidney Found. of Fla., 1996. Fellow: ACP; mem.: Fla. Soc. Nephrology, Am. Soc. Internal Medicine, Am. Soc. Nephrology. Avocations: tennis, travel. Personal E-mail: sirifkin@hotmail.com.

RIFKIND, ARLEEN B., pharmacologist, researcher, educator; b. NYC, June 29, 1938; d. Michael C. and Regina (Gottlieb) Brenner; m. Robert S. Rifkind, Dec. 24, 1961; children: Amy, Nina. BA, Bryn Mawr Coll., 1960; MD, NYU, 1964. Resident Bellevue Hosp., NYC, 1965; clin. assoc. Endocrine br. Nat. Cancer Inst., 1965—68; rsch. assoc., asst. resident physician Rockefeller U., 1968—71; from asst. prof. to assoc. prof. Weill Med. Coll. Cornell U., NYC, 1971—83, prof. pharmacology Weill Med. Coll., 1983—, chmn. Gen. Faculty Coun. Weill Med. Coll., 1984—86. Mem. Nat. Inst. Environ. Health Scis. Rev. Com., 1981-85, chmn., 1985-86; mem. toxicology study sect. NIH, 1989-91, chmn., 1991-93; bd. sci. counselors USPHS Agy. for Toxic Substances and Disease Registry, 1991-95; adv. com. FDA, Spl. Studies Relating to the Possible Long-Term Health Effects of Phenoxy Herbicides and Contaminents, 1995-99; external adv. bd. Environ. Health Scis. Ctr., Wayne State U., 1999—. Assoc. editor Drug Metabolism and Disposition, 1997-2005; mem. editl. bd. Toxicology and Applied Pharmacology, 1996-2002, Biochem. Pharmacology, 1996—2003; contbr. articles to profl. jours. Chair Friends of Libr., Jewish Theol. Sem. Am., 1984-86; trustee Dalton Sch., 1986-92; bd. govs. Am. Jewish Com., 1999—; bd. dirs. N.Y. chpt. Am. Jewish Com. Recipient Andrew W. Mellon Tchr.-Scientist award, 1976-78, Tchg. Excellence award Weill Med. Coll. Cornell U., 2004 Mem. AAAS, Internat. Soc. Study Xenobiotics, Am. Soc. Clin. Investigation, Am. Soc. Pharmacology and Exptl. Therapeutics, Endocrine Soc., Soc. Toxicology. Office: Cornell U Med Coll Dept Pharmacology 1300 York Ave New York NY 10021-4805 Business E-Mail: arifkind@med.cornell.edu.

RIFKIND, ROBERT S., lawyer; b. NYC, Aug. 31, 1936; s. Simon H. and Adele (Singer) R.; m. Arleen Brenner, Dec. 24, 1961; children: Amy, Nina. BA, Yale U., 1958; JD, Harvard U., 1961; LHD (hon.), Jewish Theol. Sem. Am., 1998. Bar: N.Y. 1961, U.S. Supreme Ct. 1965. Asst. to solicitor gen. Dept. Justice, 1965-68; assoc. firm Cravath, Swaine & Moore LLP, NYC, 1962-65, 68-70, ptnr., 1971—2001, sr. counsel, 2002—. Trustee Dalton Sch., N.Y.C., 1975-83, hon. trustee, 1983—, pres., 1977-79; trustee Brandeis U., 1998—, The Loomis Inst., 1987-95; bd. dirs. Charles H. Revson Found., 1991-2005, chmn., 1997-2003; bd. dirs. Jewish Theol. Sem. Am., 1983—, Jerusalem Found., 1998-2006, Leo Baeck Inst., 1999—, Benjamin N. Cardozo Sch. Law, 1984-89, UN Assn., 2006—; pres. Am. Jewish Com., 1994-98; chmn., adminstr. coun., Jacob Blaustein Inst. Advancement of Human Rights, 1999-2007. Fellow Am. Coll. Trial Lawyers, Am. Bar Found.; mem. ABA, Coun. Fgn. Rels., Am. Law Inst., Assn. of Bar of City of N.Y., The Century Assn., Phi Beta Kappa. Democrat. Office: Cravath Swaine & Moore LLP Worldwide Pla 825 8th Ave Fl 40 New York NY 10019-7475 Office Phone: 212-474-1450. Business E-Mail: rrifkind@cravath.com.

RIGALI, JUSTIN FRANCIS CARDINAL, archbishop; b. LA, Apr. 19, 1935; s. Henry Alphonsus and Frances Irene (White) Rigali. B in Sacred Theology, Cath. U. Am., 1961; Lic. in Canon Law, Gregorian U., Rome, 1963, D in Canon Law, 1964; LHD (hon.), St. Louis U., 1995. Ordained priest Roman Cath. Ch., 1961, ordained bishop 1985, elevated to cardinal 2003. Served at Apostolic Nunciature, Madagascar, 1966—70; named Papal Chamberlain to Pope Paul VI, 1967; titular archbishop of Bolsena, 1985—94; sec. Congregation for Bishops Holy See, Vatican City, 1989—94, sec. Coll. of Cardinals, 1990—94; archbishop Archdiocese of St. Louis, St. Louis, 1994—2003, Archdiocese of Philadelphia, Pa., 2003—; dir. English-lang. sect. Vatican Secretariat of State. Pres. Pontifical Ecclesiastical Acad., 1985—89. Office: Archdiocese of Philadelphia 222 N 17th St Philadelphia PA 19103

RIGAS, JOHN NICHOLAS, lawyer; b. Muncie, Ind., Feb. 24, 1949; s. Nicholas Peter and Edna (Krestakos) Rigas; m. Rosemary Ann Dzienis, May 19, 1979; children: Margaret Rosemary, Nicholas John. BA, Mich. State U., 1971; MA in history and polit. sci., U. Mich., 1972; JD, U. Conn., 1979. Bar: Mich. 1979, US Dist. Ct. Mich. 1979. Joined Dow Corning Corp., 1982; sr. internat. atty. Dow Corning Europe, Brussels, 1988-91; mng. counsel for bus. and comml. law Dow Corning Corp., Midland, Mich., 1992-94, sr. mng. counsel for litigation and claimant law, 1994—99; dep. gen. counsel litig. Armstrong World Industries Inc., 1999—2000, sr. v.p., gen. counsel, sec., 2001—, Armstrong Holdings Inc., Lancaster, Pa., 2000—. Dir. Armstrong Found. Bd. dirs. Lancaster C. of C. and Industry, 2000—03. Mem. ABA, State Bar Mich., Am. Corp. Counsel Assn., Internat. Bar Assn., Midland Country Club (bd. dirs.). Office: Armstrong Holdings Inc PO Box 3001 Lancaster PA 17604-3001 *

RIGAUD, EDWIN JOSEPH, museum administrator; b. New Orleans, June 25, 1943; m. Carole Rigaud; children: Simone, Edwin, Eric. BS in Chemistry, Xavier U., Louisiana, 1965; MA in BioChemistry, U. Cincinnati, Ohio, 1972; LHD (hon.), Saint Joseph Coll., N. Kentucky U. Joined Procter & Gamble, 1965, v.p., gen. mgr. food and beverage products, 1992—95, v.p. govt. relations, 1996—2001; exec. dir. Nat. Underground Railroad Freedom Ctr., Cincinnati, 1996—2001, pres., 2001—; pres., CEO Enova Tech., LLC. Trustee emeritus Nat. Conference for Community & Justice, Cincinnati; bd. mem. Amistad Rsch. Ctr., Tulane U.; bd. dirs. Hebrew Union Coll., Tofa Bus. Consulting. Bd mem. Internat. Youth Inst.; adv. coun. Ohio River Way; bd. dirs. Knowledge Funding Ohio. Recipient Annual YMCA Black Achiever award, 1980. Mem.: Queen City Club (bd. dirs.), Jr. League Cin. (mentor). Office Phone: 513-557-5311.

RIGBY, JOSEPH M., utilities executive; B in acctg., Rutgers Univ.; MBA, Monmouth Univ. CPA NJ. Mgmt. positions Pepco Holdings Inc. & subsidiaries, 1979—; v.p., gen. mgr. gas delivery Atlantic City Elec., v.p., gen. mgr. elec. delivery, pres., 2002—04; sr. v.p., pres. Connectiv power delivery Pepco Holdings Inc., Washington, 2002—04, sr. v.p., CFO, 2004—07, exec. v.p., COO, 2007—. Mem. exec. adv. bd. Rutgers-Camden Sch. Bus.; mem. cabinet United Way Del.; mem. adv. bd. Girl Scouts Chesapeake bay. Mem.: Am. Inst. CPAs, NJ Soc. CPAs. Office: Pepco Holdings Inc 701 9th St NW Washington DC 20068 *

RIGBY, PERRY GARDNER, medical association administrator, internist, medical educator; b. East Liverpool, Ohio, July 1, 1932; s. Perry Lawrence and Lucille Ellen (Orin) R.; m. Joan E. Worthington, June 16, 1957; children: Martha, Peter, Thomas, Matthew. BS summa cum laude, Mt. Union Coll., 1953, D.Sc. hon., 1976; MD, Western Res. U., 1957. Diplomate: Am. Bd. Internal Medicine. Intern in medicine U. Va. Hosp., Charlottesville, 1957-58, asst. resident in medicine, 1958-60; research fellow in hematology Mass. Meml. Hosp., Boston, 1960-62; clin. asst. in medicine Boston City Hosp., 1961-62; research assoc. in medicine Mass. Meml. Hosp., Boston U. Med. Ctr., 1961-62; asst. prof. internal medicine and anatomy U. Nebr., Omaha, 1964-66, assoc. prof. internal medicine and anatomy, 1966-69, prof. internal medicine, 1969-78, prof. anatomy, 1969-74, prof. med. edn., 1973-74, head sect. hematology Eugene C. Eppley Inst. for Research in Cancer and Allied Diseases, 1964-68, dir. hematology div., 1968-74, asst. dean for curriculum Coll. Medicine, 1971-72, assoc. dean for acad. affairs, 1972-74, dir. office ednl. services, 1972-74, acting assoc. dean for allied health professions, 1973-74, vice chmn. dept. med. and ednl. adminstrn., 1974, dean, 1974-78, chmn. dept. med. and ednl. adminstrn., 1974; prof. internal medicine La. State U., Shreveport, 1978—, assoc. dean acad. affairs Sch. Medicine, 1978-81, acting dean, 1981-82, dean, 1982-85, chancellor, 1985-94, dir. Health Care Systems New Orleans, 1994—, mem. clin. bd. Univ. Hosp., 1978-94, chmn. clin. bd., 1981-85, program dir. biomed. research support grant program, 1980-81; chmn. dean's com. VA Hosp., 1978-85; mem. courtesy staff Immanuel Med. Ctr.; bd. dirs. Health Planning Council of Midlands, Omaha, 1976-78; cons. WHO, Kabul, Afghanistan, 1976. Bd. dirs. Fontenelle Forest, Omaha, 1976-78; bd. dirs. River Cities High Tech. Group, Shreveport, 1982-85. Served as capt. M.C. U.S. Army, 1962-64. Markle scholar, 1965 Fellow ACP; mem. Am. Fedn. Clin. Research (councillor 1971), AMA (del.), Am. Soc. Hematology, N.Y. Acad. Scis., Am. Assn. Med. Colls. (council of deans of Midwest-Gt. Plains 1974-78, chmn. Midwest-Gt. Plains 1976), Am. Assn. Cancer Research, AAAS, Am. Heart Assn., Central Soc. Clin. Research, Internat. Soc. Hematology, Health Edn. Media Assn., Am. Assn. Physicians' Assts., So. Soc. Clin. Investigation, Shreveport C. of C. (dir. 1982-85), Sigma Xi, Alpha Omega Alpha, Phi Rho Sigma

RIGDON, DAVID TEDRICK, military officer, geneticist, director; b. Laurel, Miss., Jan. 27, 1948; s. James T. and Marie T. (Taylor) R.; m. Elizabeth Sue Jones, June 1, 1973; children: Angela Denise, Michael David. BS in Biology, U. Ala., 1970; MD cum laude, U. Miss., 1975. Diplomate Am. Bd. Pediats., Am. Bd. Med. Genetics. Commd. USAF, 1975, advanced through grades to col., 1991; intern in pediats. USAF Med. Ctr., Keesler AFB, Miss., 1975-76, resident in pediats., 1976-78; fellow in med. genetics U. Ala., Birmingham, 1978-80; med. geneticist USAF Med. Genetics Ctr., Keesler AFB, 1980-85, dir. Air Force Med. Genetics Ctr., 1985—. Cons. Surgeon Gen. USAF, Miss. State Dept. Health; clin. asst. prof. pediats. Uniformed Svcs. Univ. of Health Scis., F. Edward Herbert Sch. Medicine, Bethesda, Md. Contbr. articles to profl. jours. Recipient Physician's Recognition awards AMA. Fellow Am. Acad. Pediats.; mem. Am. Soc. Human Genetics, So. Genetics Group, Alpha Omega Alpha. Republican. Methodist. Avocations: boating, fishing. E-mail: david.rigdon@keesler.af.mil, drigdon@bellsouth.net.

RIGDON, KEVIN LEIGH, theater educator, lighting designer, set designer; b. Pontiac, Mich., Feb. 17, 1956; s. Donald Lee and Arlene Mae Rigdon; m. Patricia Patrick, June 21, 1998. Student, Drake U., Des Moines, Iowa, 1974—75. Resident designer Steppenwolf Theatre Co., Chgo., 1976—97; from vis. prof. to prof. U. Houston, 1997—2001, prof., 2001—. Adj. faculty The Theater Sch. De Paul U., 1991—96; assoc. dir. design The Alley Theater, Houston, 1998—. Lighting designer (plays) Steppenwolf Theatre, 1980 (The Joseph Jefferson award, 1980), Remains Theatre, 1982 (The Joseph Jefferson award, 1981, 1982), Glengarry Glen Ross, 1984, Speed the Plow, 1988, Ghetto, 1989, Our Town, 1989 (nominated Drama Desk award, 1989), The Grapes of Wrath, Broadway, 1990 (nominated Drama Desk award, 1990, Am. Theatre Wing Design award, 1990, nominated Tony award, 1990), A Streetcar Named Desire, 1992, Steppenwolf Theatre, 1994 (The Joseph Jefferson award, 1994), The Rise and Fall of Little Voice, 1994, Buried Child, 1996, Mark Taper Forum, 1997 (Drama-Logue Critic's award, 1997), One Flew Over the Cuckoo's Nest, 2001, Lincoln Ctr. Theater (Am. Theatre Wing Design award, 1985, nominated Drama Desk award, 1985, 1985, Am. Theatre Wing Design award, 1985), A Clockwork Orange (The Joseph Jefferson award, 1997), Goodman Theatre (The Joseph Jefferson award, 1988), Remains Theatre, scenic designer, lighting designer The Caretaker, 1986, The Song of Jacob Zulu, 1993, Coast Playhouse, 1994 (The L.A. Weekly award, 1994, LA Weekly award, 1994), The Old Neighborhood, 1997, designer (over 300 other plays off-Broadway plays). Recipient Outstanding Faculty award, The Houston Alumni Orgn., 2003. Mem.: United Scenic Artists. Home: 2115 Runnels St Apt 5308 Houston TX 77003 Office: Univ Houston 133 Cynthia Woods Mitchell Houston TX 77204-4016 Home Phone: 713-236-0990; Office Phone: 713-743-2816. Home Fax: 713-236-0986. Personal E-mail: rigdondesign@sbcglobal.net. Business E-Mail: krigdon@uh.edu.

RIGG, CAROL MARGARET ELIZABETH RUTH, retired art educator; b. Pitts., Dec. 14, 1928; d. Carl Hazlett and Ruth Standish (Massey) Rigg. BA, Fla. State U., Tallahassee, 1951; MA, Presbyn. Sch. Christian Edn., 1955; MFA, Chgo. Art Inst., Ill., 1963. Art. dir. bd. publs. Fla. State U., Tallahassee, 1950-53; art editor Motive Mag., Nashville, 1954-65; artist-in-residence Fla. Presbyn. Coll., St. Petersburg, 1965-66; prof. visual arts Eckerd Coll., St. Petersburg, 1967-93, prof. emerita, 1999—. Founder Possum Press, St. Petersburg, 1969; lectr. Princeton Div. Sch., 1972; vis. art lectr. Harvard Div. Sch., 1982; lectr. in field. Calligraphy featured on CBS-TV, 1969, 1971; one-woman shows include Cultural Olympics, Seoul, 1987, exhibited in group shows at CBS News TV, 1969, 1971; author: Calligraphy of the Americas, 1977-95. Pres. Nashville Artists Guild, 1960—62. Fulbright grantee, 1972. Mem.: Am. Calligraphic Arts Assn., Fla. Artist Group, Fla. Gulfcoast Soc. Scribes (founder, pres. 1976—78). Mem. Religious Soc. Friends. Home Phone: 727-867-1131; Office Phone: 727-864-7380.

RIGG, CHARLES ANDREW, pediatrician; b. Hamilton, Victoria, Australia, Oct. 18, 1926; arrived in U.S., 1963; s. Arthur Oscar and Mary Eileen (Wingrove) Rigg. B Medicine, Surgery with honors, Sydney U., 1951. Registrar pediat. unit St. Mary's Hosp., London, 1956, 1958; registrar professorial unit Children's Hosp., Sydney, 1954—56, fellow adolescent medicine Boston, 1963—64, staff adolescent medicine, 1964—65; asst. prof. pediat. Georgetown U. Med. Sch., 1965—67; chief dept. adolescent medicine Children's Nat. Med. Ctr., Washington, 1967—80, Boston City Hosp., 1981—83; med. dir. Outer Cape Health, Provincetown, Mass., 1983—88; pediatrician, med. dir. Medicenter Five, Harwich, Mass., 1988—95, pediatrician, 1995—97; cons. pediatrician May Ctr. Child Devel., Chatham, Mass., 1990—; pediatrician Harwich Town Pub. Sch. Sys., 1997—. Cons. Nat. Naval Med. Ctr., Bethesda, Md., 1973—80, Walter Reed Army Med. Ctr., Washington, 1973—80; courtesy staff medicine Children's Hosp., Boston, 1983—2005, emeritus mem. courtesy staff, 2005—; vis. prof. Philippine Pediat. Soc., 1978, 9th Congress Brazilian Med. Assn., 1979, 16th Internat. Congress Pediat., Barcelona, 1980; from asst. prof. to assoc. prof. child health George Washington U. Med. Sch., 1967—80; assoc. prof. pediat. Boston U., 1981—83. Editor: Adolescent Medicine Present and Future Concepts, 1980; contbr. articles to profl. jours. Mem. Shakespeare Libr., Washington, Nat. Trust Hist. Preservation, Nat. Trust Australia, Tasmania, Royal Oak Soc. Maj. M.C. Royal Australian Army, 1951—60, lt. col. USAR, 1985—91. Model Tng. Program Adolescent Medicine grantee, Maternal and Child Health Svcs.-U.S. Govt., 1967—80, Comprehensive health Svcs. Adolescent Ctr. grantee, Mass. Dept. Pub. Health, 1981—83. Fellow: Royal Australasian Coll. Physicians, Am. Acad. Pediatrics (life); mem.: Soc. Adolescent Medicine (Washington, DC chpt. pres. 1974—76, New Eng. chpt. pres. 1982—84, charter, treas., chmn., legis. com.), Folger Shakespeare Libr., Royal Sydney Golf Club. Episcopalian. Avocations: historic preservation, gardening, theater, music, walking. Office Phone: 508-945-1147.

RIGG, DAME DIANA, actress; b. Doncaster, Yorkshire, Eng., July 20, 1938; d. Louis and Beryl (Helliwell) R.; m. Menahem Gueffen, July 6, 1973 (div. Sept. 1976); m. Archibald Hugh Stirling, Mar. 25, 1981 (div. Apr. 1993); 1 child, Rachael Atlanta. Grad., Fulneck Girls' Sch., Pudsey, Yorkshire; student, Royal Acad. Dramatic Art, London; D (hon.), Stirling U., Eng., 1988, Leeds U., 1992, Southbank U., 1996. Prof. of theater studies Oxford U., 1998—. Stage debut as Natella Abashwilli in The Caucasian Chalk Circle, Theatre Royal, York, Eng., 1957; joined Royal Shakespeare Co., Stratford-on-Avon, 1959, debut as Andromache in Troilus and Cressida, 1960; London debut as Philippe Trincant in The Devils, London, 1961; numerous repertory appearances; joined Nat. Theatre, 1972; appeared in Jumpers, Macbeth, 1972, The Misanthrope, 1973, Pygmalion, 1974, Phaedra Britannica, 1975, Night and Day, 1978, Colette, 1982, Heartbreak House, 1983, Little Eyolf, 1985, Antony and Cleopatra, 1985, Wildlife, 1986, Follies, 1987, Love Letters, 1990, All for Love, 1991, Putting It Together, 1992, Berlin Bertie, 1992, Medea, 1992 (Tony award, Broadway prod., 1994, Eve. Standard award, Variety Club award), Mother Courage and Her Children, 1995, Who's Afraid of Virginia Wolf, 1996, Humble Boy, 2001, Honour, 2006; film appearances include A Midsummer Night's Dream, 1968, The Assassination Bureau, 1969, On Her Majesty's Secret Service, 1969, Julius Caesar, 1970, The Hospital, 1971, Theatre of Blood, 1973, A Little Night Music, 1977, The Great Muppet Caper, 1981, Evil Under the Sun, 1982, A Good Man in Africa, 1994, Parting Shots, 1998, Heidi, 2005, All About My Mother, 2007; co-starred as Emma Peel in Brit. TV miniseries: Charles II: The Power and the Passion, 2003. TV series The Avengers, 1965-67; star TV series Diana, 1973-74; numerous TV movies including This House of Brede, 1975, Hedda Gabler, 1981, Little Eyolf, 1982, Witness for the Prosecution, 1982, King Lear, 1983, Bleak House, 1984, A Hazard of Hearts, 1987, Worst Witch, 1987, Unexplained Laughter, 1989, Mother Love (Broadcasting Guild Award, BAFTA), 1989, Genghis Cohn, 1994, Zoya, 1995, The Haunting of Helen Walker, 1995, Moll Flanders, 1996, Samson and Delilah, 1996, Rebecca, 1997 (Emmy award, 1997); host PBS series Mystery, 1989—, Mrs. Bradley Mysteries, 1999—, In the Beginning, 2000, The American, 2000, Victoria & Albert, 2001; author: No Turn Unstoned, 1982, U.S. edit., 1983, So To The Land, 1994. Decorated comdr. Brit. Empire; created dame, 1994; recipient Tony award nomination as best actress in Abelard and Heloise and The Misanthrope; Plays and Players award for Phaedra Britannica and Night and Day; Variety Club Gt. Britain award for best actress for Evil Under the Sun; Brit. Acad. Film and TV Arts award for best TV actress in Mother Love, 1989, Award for Women in TV & Film, 2001. Mem. United Brit. Artists (co-founder, dir. 1982—). Address: c/o Lionel Larner Ltd 119 W 57th St New York NY 10019-2303 *

RIGG, LYLE D., headmaster; m. Sharon Creech; 2 children. BA, Miami U.; MA, W.Tex. State U.; EdM, Harvard U. Former headmaster & English teacher Am. Sch. in Switzerland (TASIS) England Am. Sch.; headmaster Pennington Sch., Pennington, NJ, 1999—2006.

RIGGENBACH, JEFF, journalist; b. Highland Park, Mich., Jan. 12, 1947; s. Frank Riggenbach and Dorothy Jane Miller; m. Suzanne Hoy Riggenbach, Mar. 10, 1996; m. Leslee J. Newman, Sept. 5, 1976 (div. 1989); m. Patricia Streeter, Mar. 29, 1967 (div. 1973); children: Max Rigman, Blaine Streeter. BS in Liberal Studies, Excelsior Coll. (formerly Regents Coll.); MA in humanities, Calif. State U., 2004. Anchor/newswriter KNUZ Radio, Houston, 1966—72; anchor/book critic/cultural affairs reporter KFWB All News Radio, LA, 1972—78; editor The Castalian (mag.), LA, 1972—74; instr. (journalism) Pierce Coll., LA, 1977—78; freelance writer L.A. Times, 1977—86; reporter, prod. Pub. Affairs Broadcast Group, Los Angeles, 1977—79; exec. editor The Libertarian Rev., San Francisco, 1978—82; exec. prodr., Byline Cato Inst., Washington, 1979—90; contbg. editor Inquiry mag., Washington, 1982—85; freelance writer San Jose (Calif.) Mercury News, 1983—88, U.S.A. Today, 1983—95; editl. writer Oakland Tribune, Calif., 1984—85; contbg editor Reason mag., LA, 1984—90; editl. writer/columnist Orange County Register, Santa Ana, Calif., 1985—87; daily economics commentator CNN Radio, Atlanta, 1985—87; prodr./program host KFAC Classical Radio, LA, 1987—89; mng. editor Pacific Bus. Rev., San Francisco, 1992—93; prodr./program host KKHI Classical Radio, San Francisco, 1993—94; instr. (liberal arts) Acad. of Art Coll., San Francisco, 1996—2000; contbg. editor Liberty mag., Port Townsend, Wash., 2001—. Co-founder, vice chair Free Press Assn., Columbus, Ohio, 1983—87; sr. fellow Randolph Bourne Inst., Redwood City, Calif., 2005—. Author: (book) In Praise of Decadence; books columnist: Rational Review.com, 2005—. Mem.: Orgn. of Am. Historians. Home: 5622 Allendale Rd Houston TX 77017 Personal E-mail: jriggenbach@bigfoot.com.

RIGGINS, WILLIAM G., electric power industry executive; b. 1958; BS, U. Kansas; MS, U. Mo., Kansas City; JD, U. Kansas. Bar: Mo. 1984. Atty. Great Plains Energy, Inc., Kansas City, Mo., 1991—92, staff atty., 1992—94, sr. atty., 1994—96, mng. atty., 1996, asst. gen. counsel, 1996—98, asst. chief legal officer, 1998—2000, gen. counsel, corp. sec., 2000—. Bd. mem. vice chmn. Swope Health Found. Office: Great Plains Energy Inc PO Box 418679 1201 Walnut St Kansas City MO 64141 *

RIGGIO, KERRY KERSTIN, elementary school worker, researcher; d. Patrick Peter and Giedre Grazina (Lisauskas) Riggio. BA in Econs., Pa. State U., University Park, 1993. Cert. United Animal Nations Emergency Rescue Svc., EMT NJ. Patient care rep. Hunterdon Med. Ctr., Flemington, NJ, 1998—2000; statis. analyst A.M. Best, Oldwick, NJ, 2000; aftercare asst. Immaculate Conception Sch., Annandale, NJ, 2003—. Author: Calls of the Tame: Dog Sounds Explained, 1999. Pet therapy vol. St. Hubert's Geralda, Madison, NJ, 1994; CCD aide Immaculate Conception Ch., 2004. Recipient award for slogan, Mellon Bank, 1992; scholar, Garden State, Lithuanian Am. Club No. NJ. Mem.: Am. Mensa Ltd. Roman Catholic. Avocations: collecting Sleeping Beauty memorabilia, ceramics. E-mail: savekoala@aol.com.

RIGGIO, LEONARD, book store company executive; b. 1941; married; 3 children. Student, NYU; D (hon.), CUNY Baruch Coll., Bentley Coll. Mdse. mgr. NYU Bookstore, NYC, 1962—65; pres., CEO, bd. dirs. Barnes & Noble Bookstores, Inc., 1965—86; founder, CEO, pres., treas. Barnes & Noble Inc., NYC, 1986—2002, chmn. bd., 1986—; chmn. bd., prin. beneficial owner Software Etc. Stores, Inc., Mpls., MBS Textbook Exch. Inc., Columbia, Mo. Chmn. bd. Dia Art Found., 1998—2006, bd. mem., 2006—; bd. dirs. Children's Def. Fund, Black Children's Cmty. Crusade, Bklyn. Tech Found., Italian Am. Found. Named one of Top 200 Collectors, ARTnews mag., 2003—06; named to Acad. of Disting. Entrepreneurs, Babson Coll., Retailing Hall of Fame, Tex. A&M U., 2005; recipient Ellis Island Medal of Honor, Frederick Douglas Medallion, Americanism award, Anti-Defamation League, 2002. Avocation: collecting contemporary art. Office: Barnes & Noble Inc 4th Fl 122 5th Ave Fl 4 New York NY 10011-5605 *

RIGGIO, STEPHEN, book store company executive; married; 3 children. BA in Anthropology, Bklyn. Coll., 1974. Buying, mktg. areas Barnes & Noble Bookstores, Inc., NYC, 1974-78, gen. mdse. mgr., 1978-81, head direct mail bus., 1981-86, exec. v.p. merchandising, 1986-90, exec. v.p., chief oper. officer, 1990—97; vice-chmn. & acting CEO barnesandnoble-.com, 2000—02; vice-chmn. Barnes & Noble, Inc., 1997—, CEO, 2002—. Originator Children With Special Needs collection books about and for children with learning disabilities. Bd. dirs. N.Y. chpt. Assn. Help Retarded Children. Office: Barnes & Noble, Inc 122 5th Ave New York NY 10011-5605 *

RIGGLE, BLAIR ANDREW, educational association administrator, consultant, psychologist, educator; b. Springfield, Ohio, Apr. 16, 1962; s. Margaret Elaine and Loren Robert Riggle; m. Jennifer Sue Riggle, Aug. 16, 1986. BS in Psychology, Wright State U., Ohio, 1984, MA in Sch. Psychology, 1987; PhD in Ednl. Leadership, U. Dayton, 2001. Cert. supr., edn. of the handicapped, elem. prin., H.S. prin., sch. psychologist, asst. supt. Ohio, 1987. Sch. psychologist Del. County Bd. of Edn., Delaware, Ohio, 1987—91; dir., planning, rsch. & testing, evaluation Westerville City Schs., Ohio, 1991—95; dir., assessment intervention, sch. improvement Hilliard City Schs., Ohio, 1995—. Adj. prof. U. Dayton, 1997—. Vestry mem. St. Matthews Episcopal Ch., Westerville, 2001—02. Mem.: NASP (assoc.), Phi Delta Kappa (assoc.), Nat. Assn. of Test Dirs. (assoc.), Kappa Delta Pi (assoc.), Assn. for Suprs.and Curriculum Devel. (assoc.), Am. Ednl. Rsch. Assn. (assoc.). Achievements include design of School Improvement Template; Assessment Analysis Procedures. Home: 5558 Lynbrook Ln Westerville OH 43082 Office: Hilliard City Sch Dist 5323 Cemetery Rd Hilliard OH 43026 Home Phone: 614-657-8288; Office Phone: 614-771-4273. Office Fax: 614-777-2424. Personal E-mail: arigglebar@aol.com. Business E-Mail: andy_riggle@fclass.hilliard.k12.oh.us.

RIGGS, ARTHUR D., health facility administrator, research scientist; b. Modesto, Calif., Aug. 8, 1939; s. John Arlis and Nelly Laura Riggs; m. Jane Merill, June 12, 1960; children: Karen, Lynelle, Derrick. AB in Chemistry, U. Calif., Riverside, 1961; PhD in Biochemistry, Calif. Inst. Tech., Pasadena, 1966. Predoctoral fellow biology dept. Calif. Inst. Tech., 1961—66; postdoctoral fellow Salk Inst. for Biol. Studies, La Jolla, Calif., 1966—69; assoc. rsch. scientist dept. molecular biology City of Hope Nat. Med. Ctr., Duarte, Calif., 1969—74, sr. rsch. scientist, 1974—83, assoc. chmn. divsn. biology, 1979—81, chmn. divsn. biology, 1981—83, assoc. dir. rsch., 1998—99; adj. prof. U. So. Calif., Los Angeles, 1978—; assoc. dir. for lab. rsch. City of Hope Cancer Ctr., 1981—87, dir. shared resources, 1993—95; chmn. divsn. biology Beckman Rsch. Inst. City of Hope, 1983—87, 1994—2000, dir., 1999—, 2000—; founding dean City of Hope Grad. Sch., Duarte, 1994—98. Contbr. articles to profl. jours. Recipient Rsch. award, Juvenile Diabetes Found., 1979, Disting. Alumnus award, U. Calif., Riverside, 1988, Tech. Leadership award, 2004. Mem.: NAS. Achievements include first human protein produced in bacteria; first man-designed and man-made gene; discovery of new type of genetics. Avocations: hiking, kayaking, mountain biking. Office: Beckman Rsch Inst City of Hope 1450 E Duarte Rd Duarte CA 91010

RIGGS, ARTHUR JORDY, retired lawyer; b. Nyack, NY, Apr. 3, 1916; s. Oscar H. and Adele (Jordy) R.; m. Virginia Holloway, Oct. 15, 1942 (dec.); children: Arthur James (dec.), Emily Adele Riggs Freeman, Keith Holloway, George Bennett; m. Priscilla McCormack, Jan. 16, 1993. AB, Princeton U., 1937; LLB, Harvard U., 1940. Bar: Mass. 1940, Tex. 1943; cert. specialist in labor law. Assoc. Warner, Stackpole, Stetson & Bradlee, Boston, 1940-41; staff mem. Solicitors Office U.S. Dept. Labor, Washington, Dallas, 1941-42; mem. Johnson, Bromberg, Leeds & Riggs, Dallas, 1949-81; of counsel Geary & Spencer, Dallas, 1981-91. Mem. ABA, State Bar Tex., Phi Beta Kappa. Avocations: maya archeology, history, photography. Home and Office: 2110 Antibes Dr Carrollton TX 75006-4326

RIGGS, BARBARA, federal agency administrator; b. Albany, NY; B in Internat. Studies, Cornell U., 1974. With U.S. Secret Svc., 1975—, assigned to field office LA, NY, with presdl. protective divsn. Washington, asst. dir. office protective rsch., head tech. security divsn, head Nat. Threat Assessment Ctr., 1998, chief of staff, dep. dir., 2004—. Mem. White House Security Rev., 1995. Recipient Meritorious Exec. Presdl. Rank award, 2002. Achievements include first female supervisory agent assigned to presdl. protective divsn.; first female to serve as dep. dir. Office: US Secret Svc US Dept Homeland Security 245 Murray Dr Bldg 410 Washington DC 20223

RIGGS, DONALD EUGENE, librarian, academic administrator; b. Middlebourne, W.Va., May 11, 1942; m. Jane Vasbinder, Sept. 25, 1964; children: Janna Jennifer, Krista Dyonis. BA, Glenville State Coll., 1964; MA, W.Va. U., 1966; MLS, U. Pitts., 1968; EdD, Va. Poly. Inst. and State U., 1975. Head libr., tchr. sci. Warwood HS, W.Va., 1964-65, head libr., audiovisual dir., 1965-67; sci. and econs. libr. California State Coll. of Pa., 1968-70; dir. libr. and learning ctr. Bluefield State Coll., 1970-72; dir. librs. and media svcs. Bluefield State Coll., Concord Coll., Greenbrier C.C., and So. campus W.Va. Coll. of Grad. Studies, 1972-76; dir. librs. U. Colo., Denver, Met. State Coll., and C.C. of Denver- Auraria Campus, 1976-79; univ. libr. Ariz. State U., 1979-88, dean univ. librs., 1988-90; prof. info. and libr. sci., dean univ. libr. U. Mich., Ann Arbor, 1991-97; prof., v.p. for info. svcs., univ. libr. Nova Southeastern U., Ft. Lauderdale, Fla., 1997—. Adj. prof. Calif. State Coll., 1968-70, W.Va. U., 1970-72, U. Colo., 1977-79, U. Ariz., 1985, Emporia State U., 1996—, U. South Fla., 1997—; fed. rels. coord. Am. and W.Va. Libr. Assns., 1970-75; chmn. bd. dirs. Ctrl. Colo. Libr. Sys., 1976-79; chmn. Colo. Coun. Acad. Librs., 1977-78; mem. exec. bd. Colo. Alliance Rsch. Librs., 1978-79; cons. to librs.; fgn. assignments in Xi'an, China, 1988, Guadalajara, Mex., 1990, Budapest, Hungary, 1991, 95, Hong Kong, 1992, 94, San Juan, PR, 1993, Melbourne, Australia, 1994, Eupatory, Republic Crimea, Ukraine, 1995, London, 1996, Prague, Czech Republic, 1996, Beijing, China, 1996, 98, Pretoria, South Africa, 1996, others; del. Users Coun. Online Computer Libr. Ctr., Dublin, Ohio, 1987-91, pres.-elect, 1990-91, chair artificial intelligence and expert systems nat. group, 1987-88; bd. govs. Rsch. Librs. Group, Inc., Mountain View, Calif., 1991-92; vice chmn. mgmt. com. William L. Clements Libr., 1991-97. Editor: W.Va. Librs., 1973-75, Libr. Hi Tech, 1993-96, Coll. & Rsch. Librs., 1996-2002; founding editor: Libr. Adminstrn. and Mgmt., 1987-89; assoc. editor: Southeastern Libr., 1973-75; contbg. editor: Libraries in the Political Process, 1980, Options for the 80's, 1982, Library and Information Technology: At the Crossroads, 1984; contbg. author, editor: Library Leadership: Visualizing the Future, 1982; author: Strategic Planning for Library Managers, 1984, (with Helen Gothberg) Time Management in Academic Libraries, 1986, (with Gordon Sabine) Libraries in the 90's: What the Leaders Expect, 1988, Creativity, Innovation and Entrepreneurship in Libraries, 1989, Library Communication: The Language of Leadership, 1991, (with Rao Aluri) Expert Systems in Libraries, 1990, Cultural Diversity in Libraries, 1994; editl. bd. Am. Librs., 1987-89, Jour. Libr. Adminstrn., 1987-97, Coll. and Rsch. Librs., 1990-96, Coll. and Rsch. Librs. News, 1996-2002. Trustee Mesa Pub. Libr., Ariz., 1980-86, chmn., 1985-86; mem. Ariz. State Libr. Adv. Coun., 1981-84; bd. dirs. Documentation Abstracts, Inc., 1986-90. Recipient Alumnus of Yr. award Glenville State Coll., 1992; named Outstanding Young Educator, Ohio County Schs., 1966; Coun. on Libr. Resources grantee, 1985; sr. fellow UCLA, 1989. Mem. ALA (councilor-at-large 1982-86, 89-93, chmn. coun.'s resolutions com. 1985-86, pub. com. 1988-92, Hugh Atkinson award 1991), Ariz. Libr. Assn. (pres. coll. and univ. divsn. 1981-82, pres. 1983-84, Spl. Svc. award 1986, Disting. Svc. award 1990), Colo. Libr. Assn. (pres. 1978-79), W.Va. Libr. Assn. (pres. 1975-76), Assn. Coll. and Rsch. Librs. (pres. Tri-State chpt. 1972-74, pres. Ariz. chpt. 1981-82), So. Libr. Assn. (chmn. coll. and univ. sect. 1982-83), Assn. Rsch. Librs. (100th meeting planning com. 1982, mgmt. of rsch. libr. resources com. 1990-93, rsch. collections com. 1993-96), AMIGOS Bibliograph Coun. (trustee 1986-90, chmn. bd. trustees 1988-89), Libr. Adminstrn. and Mgmt. Assn. (bd. dirs. 1987-89, pres.-elect 1993-94, pres. 1994-95), Libr. Info. and Tech. Assn. (bd. dirs. 1989-93), Ctr. for Rsch. Librs. (councilor 1979-97), Fla. Libr. Assn. (chair leadership devel. com. 2003-2004), Mountain Plains Libr. Assn. (bd. dirs. 1987-90, pres.-elect 1990-91), S.E. Fla. Libr. Info. Network (exec. com., bd. dirs. 1997—, pres. 1998-99), Beta Phi Mu, Chi Beta Phi, Phi Delta Kappa, Phi Kappa Phi. Office: Nova Southeastern U Alvin Sherman Libr Rsch & Info Tech Ctr Ray Ferrero Jr Blvd Fort Lauderdale FL 33314-7721 Office Phone: 954-262-4640. Business E-Mail: driggs@nova.edu.

RIGGS, FLETCHER EUGENE, economist, consultant; b. Kansas City, Mo., Dec. 21, 1923; s. Fletcher and Martha Mae (Pitcher) Riggs; m. Frances Maude Cooley, Feb. 5, 1944 (dec.); children: Fletcher Vincent, Roger Eugene, Keturah Ann, Russell Craig. BS in Agrl. Econs., Kans. State U., Manhattan, 1948, MS in Agrl. Econs., 1949; PhD in Econs., Vanderbilt U., Nashville, 1956. Asst. prof. agrl. econs. Kans. State U., 1951—56; agrl. economist, regional econ. analyst Tenn. Valley Authority, 1956—64; agrl. economist, regional econ. analyst, dep. chief rural devel. divsn. AID, Republic of Korea, 1964—70, asst. dir. agr. and rural devel. Thailand, 1970—75, chief. agr. and rural devel. bur. Asia Washington, 1975—77, dep. assoc. asst. adminstr. bur. devel. support, 1977—78, chief agr. and rural devel. New Delhi, 1978—81; cons., 1981—91; housing constrn. and land developer Costa Rica, 1991—2000; exotic hardwood mfr., Peru, 2000—07. Co-author: Economics of Watershed Planning, 1961. With US Army, 1942—46, ETO. Decorated Most Noble Order of Crown of Thailand Royal Thai Govt.; recipient Disting. Career Svc. award, Agy. Internat. Devel., 1975, 1979. Avocations: sculpting, painting. Office: Mar de Sueños LLC 852 1st Ave S Naples FL 34102 Home: 1100 13th Sr N Naples FL 34102

RIGGS, FRED WARREN, retired political science professor; b. Kuling, China, July 3, 1917; (parents Am. citizens); s. Charles H. and Grace (Frederick) R.; m. Clara-Louise Mather, June 5, 1943; children: Gwendolyn, Ronald (dec.). Student, U. Nanking, China, 1934-35; BA, U. Ill., 1938; MA, Fletcher Sch. Law and Diplomacy, 1941; PhD, Columbia U., 1948. Lectr. CUNY, 1947-48; rsch. assoc. Fgn. Policy Assn., 1948-51; asst. dir. Pub. Adminstrn. Clearing House, NYC, 1951-55; Arthur F. Bentley prof. govt. Ind. U., 1956-67; dir. Social Sci. Rsch. Inst. U. Hawaii, 1970-73, prof. polit. sci., 1967-87; prof. emeritus, 1987. Vis. asst. prof. Yale U., 1955-56; vis. lectr. Nat. Officials Tng. Inst., Korea, 1956; vis. prof. U. Philippines, 1958-59, MIT, 1965-66, CUNY, 1974-75; vis. scholar Inst. Soc. Studies, The Hague, 1972; sr. specialist East-West Ctr. U. Hawaii, 1962-63. Author: Pressures on Congress: A Study of the Repeal of Chinese Exclusion, 1950, reprinted, 1973, Formosa under Chinese Nationalist Rule, 1952, reprinted, 1972, The Ecology of Public Administration, 1961 (pub. in Portuguese, 1964), Administration in Developing Countries: The Theory of Prismatic Society, 1964 (pub. in Korean, 1966, Portuguese, 1968), Thailand: The Modernization of a Bureaucratic Polity, 1966, Organization Theory and International Development, 1969, Administrative Reform and Political Responsiveness: A Theory of Dynamic Balancing, 1971, Prismatic Society Revisited, 1973 (pub. in Korean, 1987), Applied Prismatics, 1978, (with Daya Krishna) Development Debate, 1987; author: (with others) Contemporary Political Systems: Classifications and Typologies, 1990, Handbook of Comparative and Development Public Administration, 1991, Terminology: Applications in Interdisciplinary Communication, 1993, Parliamentary vs. Presidential Government, 1993, Public Administration in the Global Village, 1994, Comparing Nations: Concepts, Strategies, Substance, 1994, Handbook of Bureaucracy, 1994, Standardizing and Harmonizing Terminology, 1995, Korea in the Era of Post-Development and Globalization, 1996, Designs for Democratic Stability, 1997, Modernity and Bureaucracy, 1997, Presidentialism vs. Parliamentarism, 1998, Public Administration in America, 1998, The Modernity of Ethnic Identity and Conflict, 1998, Beyond Area Studies, 1998, Impeachment vs. Harassment, 1999; Ethnic Diversity, Nationalism and Constitutional Democracy, 2000, The Para-Modern Context of Ethnic Nationalism, 2000, Globalization, Ethnic Diversity and Nationalism, 2002, Globalization and Faith, 2002, Electronic Nomenclators, 2002, A Comparativist's Sojourn, 2003, American Myth as Global Model, 2004, In Response to Globalization, 2004, Manifesto: The Vicious Cycle and How to Reverse It, 2005, Turbulent World, 2005, Globalization and Religion on the Web, 2005, Trends in Bureaucracy, Democracy, and Representation, 2006, Impact of Globalization on Public Administration, 2006; co-author, editor: Frontiers of Development Administration, 1971, Tower of Babel: On the Definition and Analysis of Concepts in the Social Sciences, 1975. Dir. INTERCOCTA project Internat. Social Sci. Coun., 1970-93; chair UNESCO com. INTERCONCEPT project, 1977-79; chair Comm. on Conceptual and Terminological Analysis (COCTA), Internat. Polit. Sci. Assn., Internat. Sociol. Assn. and Internat. Social Sci. Coun., 1973-79; co-chair N.AM. roundtable on cooperation Social Sci. Info. Mpls., 1979; chair lexicographic terminology com. Dictionary Soc. N.Am., 1983-86; co-chair Com. on Viable Constitutionalism (COVICO), 1993—. Decorated Order of White Elephant, King of Thailand, 1986; fellow com. comparative politics Social Sci. Rsch. Coun., 1957-58, Ctr. Advanced Study in Behavioral Scis., 1966-67; recipient Disting. Ret. Faculty award U. Hawaii, 2005; honoree Eastern Regional Orgn. Pub. Adminstrn. Conf., 1983. Mem. Am. Soc. Pub. Adminstrn. (chair comparative adminstrn. group 1960-71, Dwight Waldo award 1991), Am. Polit. Sci. Assn., Internat. Studies Assn. (chair comparative interdisciplinary studies sect. 1970-74, v.p. 1970-71, co-chair ethnicity, nationalism and migration sect. 1994-95), Internat. Polit. Sci. Assn., Internat. Sociol. Assn., Assn. Asian Studies (chair com. rsch. materials S.E. Asia 1969-73), Soc. Comparative Rsch. (co-founder 1994—), Faculty Retirees Assn, U. Hawaii. (pres. 2007—). Home: 3920 Lurline Dr Honolulu HI 96816-4006 Office: U Hawaii Political Science Dept 2424 Maile Way Honolulu HI 96822-2223 Business E-Mail: fredr@hawaii.edu.

RIGGS, GEORGE E., newspaper publishing executive; m. Elise Riggs. With Contra Costa (Calif.) Times, 1985—2004, pub.; CEO, 1991—2004; chmn., pub. San Jose Mercury News, Calif., 2004—07; pres. & CEO Calif. Newspaper Partnership, 2006—. Bd. dir. Tony LaRussa's Animal Rescue Found., John Muir Hosp. Found., Calif. Symphony; corp. adv. com. St. Mary's Coll. Mem.: Calif. Newspaper Pub. Assn. (past pres.). Office: San Jose Mercury News 750 Ridder Pk Dr San Jose CA 95190 Office Phone: 650-688-7500. *

RIGGS, GREGORY LYNN, lawyer; b. Columbus, Ohio, Apr. 21, 1948; s. Roy Albert and Edith Myrtle (Riggins) R.; m. Janet Kaye Adams, June 26, 1982; children: Caroline Ashley, Kristen Nicole. BA, U. NC, 1971; BA in jurisprudence, Oxford U., 1976; JD, Emory U., 1979. Bar: Ga. 1979, US Dist. Ct. No. Dist. Ga. 1979, US Ct. Appeals 7th cir. 1982, US Ct. Appeals 11th cir. 1985, US Ct. Appeals 5th cir. 1986. Atty. Delta Air Lines, Atlanta, 1979-84, sr. atty., 1984-92, asst. gen. counsel, 1992-94, assoc. gen. counsel, 1994-98, v.p., dep. gen. counsel, asst. sec., 1998—2003, sr. v.p., gen. counsel, 2003—04, sr. v.p., gen. counsel, chief corp. affairs, 2004—05; chmn. exec. com., corp. counsel sect. State Bar Ga., 2005—. Mem.: Atlanta Vol. Lawyers Found. (bd. dirs. 2000—04), Am. Corp. Counsel Assn. (chair law dept. mgmt. com. 1995—96, bd. dirs. Ga. chpt. 1998), State Bar of Ga. (access to justice com. 1999, chair exec. com. corp. counsel sect. 2005—). Office: Delta Air Lines Inc Dept Law Hartsfield Internat Airport Atlanta GA 30320 E-mail: greg.riggs@comcast.net.

RIGGS, HENRY EARLE, academic administrator, engineering educator; b. Chgo., Feb. 25, 1935; s. Joseph Agnew and Gretchen (Walser) Riggs; m. Gayle Carson, May 17, 1958; children: Elizabeth, Peter, Catharine. BS, Stanford U., 1957; MBA, Harvard U., 1960; Doctorate (hon.), Harvey Mudd Coll., 2006, Kech Grad. Inst., 2007. Indsl. economist SRI Internat., Menlo Park, Calif., 1960—63; v.p. Icore Industries, Sunnyvale, Calif., 1963—67, pres., 1967—70; v.p. fin. Measurex Corp., Cupertino, Calif., 1970—74; prof. engrng. mgmt. Stanford U., Calif., 1974—88, Ford prof. Calif., 1986—88, Ford prof. emeritus Calif., 1990, v.p. for devel. Calif., 1983—88; pres. Harvey Mudd Coll., Claremont, Calif., 1988—97, pres. emeritus, 1997; pres. Keck Grad. Inst., Claremont, 1997—2003, pres., trustee emeritus, 2003—. Bd. dirs. Capital Rsch. Group, 1989—; dir. Inst. for Sys. Biology, 2006—, F.W. Olin Sch. Engrng., 2006—. Author: Accounting: A Survey, 1981, Managing High-Tech Companies, 1983, Financial and Economic Analysis, 1994, 2d edit., 2004, Understanding the Financial Score, 2007; contbr. articles to profl. jours. Recipient Gores Tchg. award, Stanford U., 1980; Baker scholar, Harvard Bus. Sch., 1959. Mem.: Stanford U. Alumni Assn. (bd. dirs. 1990—94, chmn. 1993), Palo Alto Club, Sunset Club, Calif. Club, Tau Beta Pi, Phi Beta Kappa. Home: 24 Peter Coutts Circle Stanford CA 94305 Personal E-mail: henryriggs@comcast.net.

RIGGS, JACK TIMOTHY, emergency physician, retired lieutenant governor; b. Coeur d'Alene, Idaho, Oct. 1, 1954; BS summa cum laude, U. Idaho, 1976; MD, U. Wash., 1980. Diplomate Am. Bd. Emergency Medicine. Intern Deaconess Med. Ctr., Spokane, Wash., 1980-81; mem. Idaho Senate, Dist. 4, Boise, 1996-2000; owner North Idaho Immediate Car Ctrs., 1985—; lt. gov. State of Idaho, 2001—03. Fellow Am. Coll. Emergency Physicians; mem. AMA, Am. Coll. Physician Execs., Idaho Med. Assn., Am. Coll. Occupl. and Environ. Medicine. Address: 927 E Polston Post Falls ID 83854

RIGGS, KENNETH P., JR., real estate company executive; BBA in Real Estate and Fin., Kent State U.; MBA in Fin. and Statistics, Univ. Chgo. Founder and ptnr. Houston Property Consultants; dir. and sr. mgr. real estate consulting Deloitte & Touche; CEO Real Estate Rsch. Corp., 1991. Spkr. in field; editor-in-chief RERC Real Estate Report; pub. RERC/CCIM Investment Trends Quarterly; co-pub. Expectations & Market Realities in Real Estate. Named one of Real Estate's 25 Most Influential Thought Leaders, Realtor Mag., 2006. Mem.: Nat. Assn. Realtors (comml. real estate rsch. subcom.). Office: Real Estate Research Corp 980 N Michigan Ave Ste 1110 Chicago IL 60611 Office Phone: 312-587-1800. Office Fax: 312-587-0357. *

RIGGS, KRISTA DYONIS, music educator, librarian; b. Aurora, Colo., June 17, 1977; d. Donald Eugene and Jane (Vasbinder) Riggs. MusB summa cum laude, Ariz. State U., 1999; MusM, Ind. U., 2000, MLS, 2004, MusD with high distinction, 2004. Libr. Woodward Park Regional Libr., Fresno, Calif., 2004—; tchr. oboe and music theory Calif. State U., Fresno, 2006—. Invited spkr. World Conf. Internat. Soc. Music Edn., Internat. Symposium on Philosophy of Music Edn., Nat. Conf. Coll. Music Soc.; invited peformer recital Internat. Double Reed Soc. Author: (articles) Double Reed Jour., Philosophy of Music Edn. Rev. Recipient Nina Neal merit scholarship, Ind. U., 2000—04. Mem.: Internat. Double Reed Soc., Coll. Music Soc., Internat. Soc. Philosophy of Music Edn. Office: Calif State Univ Music Dept 2380 Keats Ave M/S 77 Fresno CA 93740 Business E-Mail: kdriggs@csufresno.edu.

RIGGS, LEW, foundation executive; b. Indpls., Apr. 1, 1937; s. Frank Lloyd Riggs and Marie Loretta (Shaner) Ellis; m. Christine Marie Stiemke, Dec. 2, 2000. BS in Bus. Adminstrn., U. Ariz., 1961, EdD, 1976; MBA, George Washington U., 1964. Mktg. adminstr. TRW Systems, LA, 1964-67; assn. exec. Electric League Ariz., Phoenix, 1967-68; pub. affairs adminstr. Ariz. Regional Med. program Coll. of Medicine, U. Ariz., Tucson, 1968-73; dir. community affairs Tucson Med. Ctr., 1973-82; dir. pub. rels. Good Samaritan Med. Ctr., Phoenix, 1982-85; pres. The Lew Riggs Co., Phoenix, 1985-88; chief exec. officer Tucson Osteo. Med. Found., Tucson, 1988—. Adj. prof. U. Ariz. Coll. Edn., Tucson, mem. internat. adv. bd., 1996-99, pres., 2000; cons. to hosps. and physicians in group practice nationally; presenter in field. Editor: Public Relations Handbook, 1982; co-author booklets; contbr. articles to profl. jours. Chmn. pub. rels. Nat. Arthritis Found., Atlanta, 1985-87; participant Ariz. Strategic Planning and Econ. Devel., 1991-92. Lt. col. USAFR, 1987. Recipient IABC gold quill award, Silver Anvil award Pub. Rels. Soc. Am., Golden Mike award Am. Legion Aux., MacEachern citation Acad. Hosp. Pub. Rels., Pres.'s citation Pub. Rels. Soc. Mem. Pub. Rels. Soc. Am. (trustee 1999—), Nat. Assn. Osteo. Founds. (pres. 1991-93), Student Osteo. Med. Assn. (found. bd. dirs. 1990—), Soc. Assn. Execs. (bd. dirs. 1995—), Rotary. Republican. Presbyterian. Home: 4566 E Camino De Oro Tucson AZ 85718-4475 E-mail: lriggs@tomf.org.

RIGGS, LORRIN ANDREWS, psychologist, educator; b. Harput, Turkey, June 11, 1912; parents Am. citizens; s. Ernest Wilson and Alice (Shepard) R.; m. Doris Robinson, 1937 (dec.); children: Douglas Rikert, Dwight Alan; m. Caroline Cressman, 1994. AB, Dartmouth Coll., 1933; MA, Clark U., 1934, PhD, 1936; DSc, Brown U., 2001. NRC fellow biol. scis. U. Pa., 1936-37; instr. U. Vt., 1937-38, 39-41; with Brown U., 1938-39, 41—, from asst. to assoc. prof., 1938-51, prof., 1951—, L. Herbert Ballou prof., 1960-68, E.J. Marston Univ. prof., 1968-77, prof. emeritus, 1977—; Guggenheim fellow U. Cambridge, 1971-72. Author sci. articles on vision, physiol. psychology. Recipient Kenneth Craik award Cambridge U., 1979, Prentice medal Am. Acad. Optometry, 1973 Mem. AAAS (chmn., v.p. sect. 1 1964), APA (div. pres. 1962-63, Disting. Sci. Contn. award 1974), Eastern Psychol. Assn. (pres. 1975-76), Optical Soc. Am. (Tillyer medal 1969, Ives medal 1982), Nat. Acad. Scis., Am. Physiol. Soc., Internat. Brain Rsch. Orgn., Soc. for Neurosci., Soc. Exptl. Psychologists (Howard Crosby Warren medal 1957), Assn. Rsch. in Vision and Ophthalmology (pres. 1977, Friedenwald award 1966), Am. Acad. Arts and Scis., Am. Psychol. Soc. (William James fellow 1989), Sigma Xi (chpt. pres. 1962-64). Home: Kendal at Hanover Apt 1018 80 Lyme Rd Hanover NH 03755-1225 Personal E-mail: clriggs@valley.net.

RIGGS, MICHAEL DAVID, editor, writer; b. Frankfort, Ky., Apr. 30, 1951; s. Homer David and Helen Marion (Webber) R.; m. Elizabeth Susan Borman, Apr. 24, 1983; children: David B., William B. AB, Washington U., 1973. Chief trader Thomte & Co., Boston, 1975-77; tech. writer Saddlebrook Corp., Cambridge, Mass., 1977-79; assoc. editor Mini-Micro Systems Mag., Boston, 1979-80; editor High Fidelity Mag., NYC, 1980-89; exec. editor Stereo Review Mag., NYC, 1989-95; editor-in-chief Audio Mag., NYC, 1995-2000; ind. technology writer, editor, cons. Westfield, NJ, 2000—. Author: Understanding Audio and Video, 1989; sr. contbg. editor: Sound and Vision Mag., 2001—04, sr. editor:, 2004—05, online editor:, 2006—. Mem. Audio Engring. Soc., Boston Audio Soc. Office Phone: 212-767-6028. E-mail: michael@riggsnet.com.

RIGGS, R. WILLIAM, retired state supreme court justice; Grad., Portland State U., 1961; JD, U. Oreg., 1968. Atty. Willner Bennett & Leonard, 1968—78; judge circuit ct. 4th Jud. Dist., 1978—88; judge Oreg. Ct. of Appeals, 1988—98, presiding judge, 1995—98; judge Oreg. Supreme Ct., 1998—2006. Vice-chair exec. com. Oreg. Jud. Conference, 1996—98; mem. Council on Ct. Procedures, 1986—89; founder Oreg. Acad. of Family Law Practitioners. Active mem. Cmty. Law Project; founder Integra Corp. Capt. USNR. Mem.: Oreg. Trial Lawyers Assn.

(pres. 1973—74), Oreg. Appellate Judges Assn. (pres. 1993—94, 2001—02), Oreg. State Bar Assn. (founding mem., chair Family Law Section 1979). Office: Lewis & Clark Law Sch 10015 SW Terwilliger Blvd Portland OR 97219 *

RIGGS, ROBERT MELDRUM, French educator; b. Washington, Aug. 1, 1932; s. Theodore Scott and Phillis Wey (Symmonds) R.; B.A. with distinction, George Washington U., 1955; Fulbright scholar, U. Toulouse (France), 1955-56; M.A. (Miller fellow), U. Ill., 1957, postgrad., 1957-62. Grad. asst. U. Ill., 1957-62; instr. French, then asst. prof. George Washington U., 1964-70, asst. to chmn. dept. Romance langs., 1963-70; assoc. prof. French, Frostburg (Md.) State Coll., 1970—94, prof. emeritus, 1994, chmn. dept. fgn. langs., 1984-88. Bd. dirs. Allegany County Mental Health Assn., 1975-81; trustee Cumberland Theatre, 2000-05; bd. mem. Cumberland Cultural Found., 2007; bd. mem. Cumberland Bicentennial Com.; layreader, chmn. Christian edn. com. Emmanuel Episcopal Ch., Cumberland, 1979—, vestryman, 1981-85, 2004-07. Mem. Am. Assn. Tchrs. of French, Soc. War 1812, Nat. Trust Hist. Preservation, Denison Soc., Gallup Family Assn., Allegany County Hist. Soc. (curator 1976-78, 1st v.p. 1978-80, trustee 1980-82), Phi Beta Kappa, Phi Kappa Phi, Omicron Delta Kappa, Pi Delta Epsilon, Pi Delta Phi, Sigma Delta Pi, Acacia. Democrat. Home: 101 Washington St Cumberland MD 21502-2966 E-mail: rmriggs264@hotmail.com.

RIGGS, RORY B., pharmaceutical executive; b. Orange, NJ, May 5, 1953; d. Thomas Jeffries and Virginia (Griggs) R. BA, Middlebury Coll.; MBA, Columbia U. Mng. dir. PaineWebber, Inc.; CEO RF&P Corp.; mng. dir. Pharma Ptnrs. LLC; pres. Biomatrix Inc., Ridgefield, N.J., 1995—. Bd. dirs. Biomatrix, Inc. 1990—; bd. mem. Fibrogen Corp., Spartan Corp., Pharma Ptnrs, LLC. Mem. Young Pres. Orgn. Office: Biomatrix Inc 65 Railroad Ave Ste 3 Ridgefield NJ 07657-2176

RIGGS, TIMOTHY ALLAN, museum curator; b. New Haven, Feb. 15, 1942; s. Douglas Shepard and Robin (Palmer) R.; divorced; 1 child, Emma; m. Carolyn P. Coolidge, June 25, 1995. BA, Swarthmore Coll., 1964; MA, Yale U., 1966, PhD, 1971. Rschr. Print Coun. Am., 1970-73; asst. curator Worcester (Mass.) Art Mus., 1973-76, curator prints and drawings, 1976-84; asst. dir. Ackland Art Mus., Chapel Hill, N.C., 1984—, acting dir., 1986, 94. Adj. prof. U. N.C., Chapel Hill, 1984-2003, curator of collections, 2003—. Contbr. catalogs. Mem. Print Coun. Am. (bd. dirs. 1981-84), Historians Netherlandish Art. Office: Ackland Art Mus CB #3400 UNC-CH Chapel Hill NC 27599-3400

RIGGS, WAYNE, artist, photographer; b. Long Beach, Calif., Sept. 30, 1949; s. Harry W. and Katherine C. Riggs. Student, Parsons Coll., Fairfield, Iowa, 1972—74; BFA in Photography, So. Ill. U., Carbondale, 1976. Dir. photography Callanwolde Arts Ctr., Atlanta, 1980—81; lectr. Mus. Arts and Scis., Daytona Beach, Fla., 1989, Cornell Fine Arts Mus., Winter Park, Fla., 1990; guest critic RI Inst. Design, Rome, 1997. One-man shows include Davenport City Gallery and Mus., Cornell Fine Arts Mus., Winter Park, UN, Rome, La Mama Galleria, Spoleto, Italy, Brit. Embassy, Rome, Antigua, Crocker's Mark Gallery, Raleigh, NC, exhibitions include Artspace, Richmond, Va., Represented in permanent collections Met. Mus. Art, NYC, High Mus. Art, Atlanta, LA Mcpl. Art Gallery, Muse Des Beaux-Arts, Le Havre, France, Tampa Mus. Art, Fla. Radioman petty officer 2nd class USN, 1968—72. Grantee, Nat. Endowment Arts, 1981—83, Nat. Endowment Arts and Atlanta Bur. Cultural Affairs, 1983. Home: 20 Mayo St G3 Raleigh NC 27603 Home Phone: 919-755-6346.

RIGGS, WILLIAM W., social sciences educator; b. Decatur, Ill., Apr. 26, 1945; d. William and Doris Mae Riggs; m. Karen Sue Henderson, May 19, 1998 (div.); children: William, Christopher. BA, The Citadel, 1967; MS, U. So. Miss., 1989; PhD, U. New Orleans, 1999. Commd. 2d lt. USMC, 1967, advanced through grades to maj., ret., 1987; tchr. Coast Episcopal High Sch., Pess Christian, Miss., 1987—89; asst. prof. polit. sci. Tex. A&M Internat. U., Larado, 2001—04, chair dept. social scis., 2004—. Vis. prof. U. West Ala., Livingston, 1989—90; external reviewer N.W. State U., Nachitoles, La., 2004; presenter in field. Contbr. chapters to books. Chair Logistics Cmty. Anchorage Sch. Dist., 2000—01; bd. dirs. Anchorage Mus., 1998—2001. Fellow, TAMU. Mem.: NEH, Am. Soc. Pub. Adminstrn. (v.p. 2004—). Avocations: golf, bridge, travel. Office: Tex A&M Internat U 5201 Univ Blvd Laredo TX 78041

RIGGSBY, DUTCHIE SELLERS, education educator; b. Montgomery, Ala., Oct. 26, 1940; d. Malcolm Sellers and Marcelia Sellers Dickman; m. Ernest Duward Riggsby, Aug. 25, 1962; 1 child, Lyn. BS, Troy State Coll., 1962, MS, 1965; postgrad., George Peabody Coll., 1963; EdD, Auburn U., 1972. Cert. tchr., Ala., Ga.; cert. libr., Ga. Tchr. Montgomery Pub. Schs., 1962—63, Troy City Schs., 1963—67; instr. Auburn U., Ala., 1968—69, dir. media svcs., 1972—77; asst. prof. Columbus Coll., Ga., 1972—77, assoc. prof., 1978—83, prof., 1983—. Vis. prof. U. P.R., Rio Piedras, 1972—73; leader various workshops, 1989, 1993—; sorfware reviewer NSTA; chmn. publicity Ga. Ednl. Tech. Conf., 1997—, bd. dirs.; bridal cons. Hist. Moments, Inc., 1998—2001, v.p., 1998—2001; chair scholarship com. Ga. Ednl. Consortium, 1999—; coord. instrnl. Tech. Sch. Edn., 1996—97; coord. program Ednl. Founds., 2001—04. Contbr. more than 90 articles on state, regional, nat., and internat. programs to profl. jours., 1968—. Active Internal Aerospace Edn. CAP, Maxwell AFB, 1980-90; dir. Air and Space Camp for Kids, 1990-98; apptd. selection com. Coll. Edn. Columbus State U. Hall of Fame, 2005— Recipient STAR Tchr. award NSTA, 1968; named to Lee H.S. Hall of Fame, Montgomery, 1997. Mem.: Ga. Assn. Instrnl. Tech. (bd. dirs. 1982—84), World Aerospace Edn. Orgn. (v.p. for Ams. 1996—98, pres. for Ams. 1998—, pres. 1999—), Nat. Congress on Aviation and Space Edn. (dir. spl. promotions 1986—90), Assn. for Ednl. Commn. and Tech. (awards com. 1994—96, non-periodical publs. com. 1994—99, chair meml. awards com. 1996—99), Phi Delta Kappa (pres. Chattahoochee Valley chpt. 1986—87, membership v.p. 2005—06, pres. Chattahoochee Valley chpt. 2006—, Svc. award 1989, Svc. Key award 1993). Baptist. Avocations: photography, mining for gemstones. Office: Columbus State U Coll Edn 4225 University Ave Columbus GA 31907-5679 Office Phone: 706-565-7802.

RIGHINI, MARILOU MAUSTELLER, editor, consultant; b. Savannah, Ga., June 17, 1937; d. John Ellis and Ethel Mae Mausteller; m. Massimo A. Righini, May 5, 1962; children: Giovanna, John Paolo. BA in Polit. Sci. magna cum laude, Mich. State U., East Lansing, 1958; attended, Johns Hopkins U., Bologna, Italy, 1958—60; MA in Internat. Rels., Johns Hopkins U., Washington, DC, 1963. Editor Internat. Legal Materials Am. Soc. Internat. Law, Washington, 1968—97, dir. pubs., 1992—97; editor, mem. editl. bd. Transnational Pubs., Inc., Ardsley, NY, 1998—, aquisitions editor, cons., 1998—2001. Translator IBM, Milan, 1960—61; tchr. polit. sci., internat. law, am. lit. Istituto Ugo Foscolo, Bologna, Italy, 1961—62; rschr., editl. asst. Washington Ctr. Fgn. Policy Rsch., 1963—68; program chmn. Internat. Devel. Conf., Washington, 1977; program coord. Washington Fgn. Law Soc., 1980—81, bd. govs., 1980—82; chmn. Coun. Washington Reps. UN, 1983—85; tchr. internat. law and orgn. Trinity Coll., Washington, 1985; elected com. rep. DC Dem. State Com., Ward 1, 1988—92; chmn., nominating com. Worldwise 2000, 1989, bd. dirs., 1989—91; ann. mtg. roundtable chair Am. Soc. Internat. Law, 1991, ann. mtg. panel chair, 92; program developer Am. Assn. Law Librs., 1999, 2000. Mem.: Mich. State U. DC Study Devel. Coun., Am. Soc. Internat. Law, UN Assn. U.S.A., Meridian Internat. Ctr., Delta Gamma.

RIGHTER, KATHLEEN ANNE, language educator; d. Frederick Arthur and Theresa Jeanne Ingram; m. Robert Lin Righter, Feb. 28, 1976; children: Kaitlin, Sarah. BA, Penn. State U., State Coll., 1972; attended, Arcadia U., Glenside, Pa., 1992—93. Tchr. Upper Perkioman Sch. Dist., Red Hill, Pa., 1972—73, N. Penn. Sch. Dist., Lansdale, Pa., 2000—; bus. mgr. Fredericks Bridal Salon, Norristown, Pa., 1972—80, bus. owner, 1980—2000. Com. mem. rep. Dem. Party, Horsham, Pa., 2000—06; libr. bd. mem. Arcadia U., 1993—96. Mem.: NEA. Avocations: sewing, quilting.

RIGHTER, WALTER CAMERON, retired bishop; b. Phila., Oct. 23, 1923; s. Richard and Dorothy Mae (Bottomley) R.; m. Nancy Ruth DeGroot, Aug. 22, 1992; children: Richard, Rebecca. *Walter is a ninth generation descendent of Peter Righter, one of the earliest German settlers in the Philadelphia, Pennsylvania area. He is also a descendent of Abraham Tunis, head of one of the original 13 families from Krefeld, Germany. Abraham was invited by William Penn to join him in settling his colony where they founded Germantown, now a part of Philadelphia. Currently in the city there is a Righter's Ferry Road and Righter's Mill Road. Fellow descendants include Authors, Astrologers, inventors, lawyers, veterans and scientists. Walter's brother, Richard, is an active architect in the Pittsburgh area.* BA, U. Pitts., 1948; MDiv, Berkeley Div. Sch., New Haven, 1951, DD, 1972; DCL, Iowa Wesleyan U., 1982; DD, Seabury Western Sem., 1984. Ordained priest Episcopal Ch., 1951, consecrated bishop, 1972; lay missioner St. Michael's Ch., Rector, Pa., 1947-48; priest-in-charge All Saints Ch., Aliquippa, Pa., 1951-54, St. Luke's, Georgetown, Pa., 1952-54; rector Ch. of Good Shepherd, Nashua, NH, 1954-71; bishop Diocese of Iowa, Des Moines, 1972-89; asst. bishop Dio. of Newark, 1989-91; interim rector St. Elizabeth's, Ridgewood, NJ, 1991; assisting bishop Diocese of Mass., 2000—03; ret. Mem. exec. coun. Protestant Episcopal Ch. U.S.A., 1979-85; spl. adv. NH Cursillo, 1994-96; interim rector Emmanuel, Rockford, Ill., 1989. *Following military service in World War II Walter pursued his dream of entering Holy Orders in the Episcopal Church. He was a leader in the move to ordain women, liturgical reform, the use of marketing research and techniques, and in inclusivity for gay and lesbian persons. In 1995 Walter was targeted by the ultra-conservative element within the church of "Heresy" for ordaining Barry Stopfel, a partnered gay man, to the Deaconate. The case was dismissed by the Church Court as having violated no Core Doctrine or Christian teaching. His book A Pilgrim's Way was published by Knopf in 1998.* Author: A Pilgrim's Way, 1998. Mem. N.H. com. White House Conf. on Youth, 1962, Regional Crime Commn., Hillsboro County, N.H., 1969-71; trustee Nashua Libr., 1968-71, Seabury Western Sem., 1986-89; founding trustee The Morris Fund, Des Moines; planning com. Town of Alstead, N.H., 1993-96. Fellow Coll. Preachers, Washington Cathedral. Episcopalian. Personal E-mail: wcrighter@alltel.com.

RIGHTMIRE, GEORGE PHILIP, anthropology educator; b. Boston, Sept. 15, 1942; s. Brandon Garner and Marcia (Ham) R.; m. Berit Johansson, Aug. 20, 1966; children: Anna Marcia, Eric Philip. AB, Harvard U., 1964; MS, U. Wis., 1966, PhD, 1969. Asst. prof. SUNY, Binghamton, 1969-73, assoc. prof., 1973-82, prof., 1982—2002, chmn., 1976-78, disting. prof., 2002—; rsch. assoc. Harvard U., 2006—. Vis. in archaeology U. Cape Town, South Africa, 1975-76; rsch. fellow in osteology U. Stockholm, Sweden, 1973. Author: The Evolution of Homo erectus, 1990; contbr. articles to profl. jours., chpts. to books and encyclopedias. Fellow Nat. Inst. Gen. Med. Scis., 1973; rsch. grantee NSF, 1975—, Nat. Geographic Soc., 1978-79, L.S.B. Leakey Found., 1990-91, 1992-93, 1995-96, 98-99. 2001-2003, 2006—, Am. Philos. Soc., 2003-04. Fellow AAAS; mem. Am. Assn. Phys. Anthropologists, Human Biology Assn., Paleoanthropology Soc., Sigma Xi Achievements contributions to systematics of genus Homo, research and field work in paleoanthropology, fossil evidence for hominid evolution examined in East Africa, South Africa, Europe, the Near East, the Caucasus, China and Southeast Asia. Office: Harvard Univ Dept Anthropology Peabody Mus Cambridge MA 02138 Home: 24 Whittier Dr Scituate MA 02066-2436 Office Phone: 617-495-5703. Business E-Mail: gprightm@fas.harvard.edu.

RIGHTS, GRAHAM HENRY, retired minister; b. Winston-Salem, NC, Jan. 14, 1935; s. Douglas LeTell and Cecil Leona (Burton) R.; m. Sybil Critz Strupe, Sept. 7, 1963; children: Susan Elizabeth, John Graham. BA, U. N.C., 1956; BD, Yale U., 1959; postgrad., Moravian Theol. Sem., 1959-60, DHL (hon.), 1997; postgrad., U. Edinburgh, Scotland, 1965-66; DD (hon.), Wofford Coll., 1989. Ordained to ministry Moravian Ch., 1960. Pastor Union Ch., Managua, Nicaragua, 1960-63, Managua Moravian Ch., 1960-65, Mayodan (N.C.) Moravian Ch., 1966-72, Messiah Moravian Ch., Winston-Salem, 1972-81; exec. dir. Bd. World Mission Moravian Ch., Bethlehem, Pa., 1981-83, pres. exec. bd. so. province Winston-Salem, 1983-95, pres. exec. bd. world-wide, 1991-94; pastor First Moravian Ch., Greensboro, NC, 1995-2000; ret. Bd. dirs. Crisis Control Ministry, Forsyth County, 1976-, Ecumenical Inst.of the Carolinas, 1995-, Wachovia Hist. Soc., 2004-, CareNet Counseling, 2005—. Mem. N.C. Soc. Mayflower Descendants (elder 2000—). Mem. Moravian Ch. Home: 553 Steeple View Ct Winston Salem NC 27101-5850

RIGOLOSI, ELAINE LA MONICA, lawyer, educator; b. Astoria, NY, Oct. 12, 1944; d. Richard Anthony La Monica and Caroline La Monica; m. Robert Salvatore Rigolosi, June 15, 1997. BS, Columbia Union Coll., Takoma Park, Md., 1964; MN, U. Fla., 1967; EdD, U. Mass., 1975; JD, Benjamin N. Cardozo Sch. Law, NYC, 1993. Bar: N.J. 1994, N.Y. 1994, D.C. 1995; RN, N.Y. Chair dept. nursing edn. Tchrs. Coll., Columbia U., NYC, 1988-91, prof. nursing edn., 1982-96, acting chair dept. nursing edn., 1994-96, prof. dept. orgn. and leadership, 1996—; health care mgmt. cons. in pvt. practice, NYC, 1974—. Bd. dirs. Hooper Holmes, Inc., Basking Ridge, N.J., 1989—; cons. Delaware Valley Transplant Program, Phila., 1998, U. Tenn. Coll. Pharmacy, Memphis, 1995-98. Author: The Nursing Process: A Humanistic Approach, 1979 (Am. Jour. Nursing Book of Yr. 1979), Management in Health Care, 1994, Management and Leadership in Nursing and Health Care, 2005. Dept. HHS grantee, 1977-80, 80-83. Fellow Am. Acad. Nursing; mem. ABA, Assn. Bar City N.Y. (com. on health law 1994-97), Am. Health Lawyers Assn., Am. Assn. Nurse Attys., Am. Coll. Legal Medicine, Sigma Theta Tau. Avocations: tennis, needlepoint, interior design. Home: 158 Summit Dr Paramus NJ 07652-1312 Office: Tchrs Coll Columbia U 525 W 120th St New York NY 10027-6625

RIGOR, BRADLEY GLENN, lawyer; b. Cheyenne Wells, Colo., Aug. 9, 1955; s. Glenn E. and Lelia (Teed) R.; m. Twyla G. Helweg, Sept. 4, 1983; children: Camille, Brent, Tiffany, Lauren. BS in Mktg., Ft. Hays State U., 1977; JD, Washburn U., 1980. Bar: Kans. 1980, U.S. Dist. Kans., 1980, U.S. Tax Ct. 1981, U.S. Ct. Appeals (10th cir.) 1982, U.S. Supreme Ct. 1986, Colo. 1990, Tex. 1991, U.S. Dist. Ct. Colo. 1991, Mo. 1993, Fla. 1998; cert. trust and fin. advisor Inst. Cert. Bankers; cert. fin. planner. Ptnr. Zuspann & Rigor, Goodland, Kans., 1980—82, Fairbanks, Rigor & Irvin, P.A., Goodland, 1982—93, Bond Schoeneck & King P.A., Naples, 1998—2005, Quarles & Brady LLP, Naples, 2005—; city atty. Goodland, 1981—82, Sharon Springs, 1983—84; asst. county atty. Wallace County, Sharon Springs, Kans., 1982—84, county atty., 1984; judge Mcpl. Ct., Goodland, 1988—93; v.p., mgr. personal trusts Mcht. Bank, St. Joseph, Mo., 1993—96; sr. v.p., mgr., personal trust adminstr. SunTrust Bank, Naples, Fla., 1996—98. Mem. Estate Planning Coun., Naples. Mem. Kans. Bar Assn., Tex. Bar Assn., Mo. Bar Assn., Colo. Bar Assn., Fla. Bar Assn., Collier County Bar Assn. (trust and estates sect.). Republican. Baptist. Office: 1395 Panther Ln Ste 300 Naples FL 34109 Home Phone: 239-594-7067; Office Phone: 239-659-5032, 239-659-5032. Business E-Mail: brigor@quarles.com.

RIGSBY, LINDA FLORY, lawyer, director; b. Topeka, Dec. 16, 1946; d. Alden E. and Lolita M. Flory; m. Michael L. Rigsby, Aug. 14, 1963; children: Michael L. Jr., Elisabeth A. MusB, Va. Commonwealth U., 1969; JD, U. Richmond, 1981. Bar: Va. 1981, D.C. 1988. Assoc. McGuire, Woods, Battle & Boothe, Richmond, Va., 1981-85; dep. gen. counsel and corp. sec. Crestar Fin. Corp., Richmond, 1985-99, gen. counsel, 1999-2000; mng. atty. Sun Trust Banks Inc., 2000—05, deputy gen. coun., 2006; ret., 2007. Mem. audit com. Bon Secours Health Systems, Richmond, 1999—. Bd. dirs. Commonwealth Cath. Charities, 2004-. Recipient Disting. Svc. award U. Richmond, 1987; named Vol. of Yr. U. Richmond, 1986, Woman of Achievement, Met. Richmond Women's Bar, 1995. Mem. Va. Bar Assn. (exec. com. 1993-96), Richmond Bar Assn. (bd. dirs. 1992-95), Va. Bankers Assn. (chair legal affairs 1992-95), U. Richmond Estate Planning Coun. (chmn. 1990-92). Roman Catholic. Avocations: music, gardening. Home: 163 W Square Pl Richmond VA 23238-6157 Office: Williams Mullen Law Firm PO Box 1320 Richmond VA 23218-1320 Home Phone: 804-784-7479; Office Phone: 804-783-6404. Personal E-mail: mlrigsby163@comcast.net.

RIGSBY, MARY SUE, retired elementary school educator, adult education educator; b. Big Stone Gap, Va., June 22, 1936; d. Sherman Coomer and Jenelle Kilbourne; m. Hobert Herchel McElyea (div. 1978); children: Gary A. McElyea, Tammy Sue McElyea, Jeffrey Earl McElyea; m. Elmer Virgil Rigsby Jr., June 1, 1985 (dec. July 12, 2000). BS, East Tenn. State U., Johnson City, 1979, MEd, 1989. Cert. postgrad. profl. Va., early edn., mid. edn., learning disabilities tchr., reading specialist Va. Tchr. aide Lee County Schs., Pennington Gap, Va., 1971—74; tchr. Tazewell County Pub. Schs., Tazewell, Va., 1979—86, Rogersville City Schs., Tenn., 1988—89, Scott County Pub. Schs., Gate City, Va., 1989—2004; ret., 2004; part-time tchr. adult edn. Scott County Pub. Schs., Weber City, Va., 2004—06, substitute tchr., 2006—. Home: 101 Milton Ct Kingsport TN 37664-3570

RIHANNA, (ROBYN RIHANNA FENTY), singer, actress; b. St. Michael, Barbados, Feb. 20, 1988; d. Ronald and Monica Fenty. Model, spokesperson Covergirl. Singer: (albums) Music of the Sun, 2005 (Album of Yr., Barbados Music Awards, 2006), A Girl Like Me, 2006 (Album of Yr., Barbados Music Awards, 2007), Good Girl Gone Bad, 2007, (songs) Pon de Replay, 2005 (Best Dance Single Song of Yr., Barbados Music Awards, 2006), SOS, 2006 (Best New Video Artist, MTV Video Music Awards Japan, 2006), Unfaithful, 2006 (Best R&B Single, Song of Yr., Barbados Music Awards, 2007); actor: (films) Bring It On: All or Nothing, 2006. Recipient Best Internat. Artist award, MuchMusic Video Awards, 2006, Female Breakout Artist award, Teen Choice Awards, 2006, Choice R&B Artist award, 2006, Best R&B award, MTV Europe Music Awards, 2006, Female Artist of Yr. award, Billboard Music Awards, 2006, Female Hot 100 Artist of Yr., 2006, Pop 100 Artist of Yr., 2006, 7 awards, including Best New Artiste, Female Artiste of Yr., Best-Selling Female Artiste of Yr., and Entertainer of Yr., Barbados Music Awards, 2006, 7 awards, including Worldwide Best-Selling Recording Artiste, Female Entertainer of Yr., and Entertainer of Yr., 2007, Barbados Music Awards ring, 2007. *

RIHN, RICHARD JOHN, retired physician; b. Richmond, Calif., Mar. 20, 1925; s. John Percy and Mary Alma Rihn; m. Patricia Louise Mackay, July 26, 2003; m. June Evelyn Hall, June 26, 1949 (dec. Aug. 19, 2002); children: Patricia Mackay Abramson, James McIntosh Mackay, Donald Sage Mackay, Sally June Campbell, Daniel Richard, Margery Susan James. MD, Boston U., 1951. Diplomate Am. Bd. Med. Examiners, 1952, Am. Bd. Family Practice, 1974; lic. master flight instr. Nat. Assn. Flight Instrs., 2003. Fund raiser Missionary Aviation Fellowship, Nampa, Idaho. Decorated Bronze Star medal US Army; recipient Frank Price Cup award, Internat. Aerobatic Club, 1997. Mem.: Exptl. Aircraft Assn. (flight leader young eagles 2000—04). Republican. Presbyterian. Avocations: aerobatic competition, aviation. Home: 1101 Scots Ln Walnut Creek CA 94596 Home Phone: 925-938-4236.

RIJKEN, PIETER, medical association administrator; arrived in US, 1982; s. Adriaan Marinus Rijken and Hendrika Johanna Voor de Poorte; m. Lynn Marie Keenan; 1 child, Nicolaas. AA, Miami Dade C.C., 1983; BA, Fla. State U., Tallahassee, 1986; MBA, Erasmus U., Rotterdam, Netherlands, 1988. Lic. managed healthcare profl. Health Ins. Assn. Am., Wash., 1996. Cons. healthcare RWB Unternehmensgruppe, Muenster, Germany, 1990—93; network cons. Neighborhood Health Plan, Fla. Health Choice, Delray Beach, Fla., 1994—96; v.p. so. region Multiplan, Ft. Lauderdale, Fla., 1996—2001; nat. cons. Medsolutions, Franklin, Tenn., 2001—02; regional mgr. Allianz AG, Munich, 2002—04; lectr. Ludwig Maximilian U., Munich, 2004—05; mgr. physician contracting and ctrl. svcs. AvMed Healt Plans, Orlando, Fla., 2006—. Mem. adv. coun. bus. liason Wendell Watson Elem. Sch., Lakeland, Fla., 2006—; trainer Amerikahaus Munich, Munich, 2003—05; cons. Primo, Breda, Netherlands, 1988—90. Cpl. Royal Dutch Mil. Police, 1981—82. Mem.: Netherlands Assn. So. Fla. (dir. 1993—95), Toastmasters Internat. (assoc.), Mensa (assoc.). Avocations: golf, bicycling, travel. Office: AvMed Health Plans 541 S Orlando Ave Ste 205 Maitland FL 32751 Home Phone: 863-409-2879; Office Phone: 407-975-1642. Personal E-mail: prijken@ft1988.rsm.nl. Business E-Mail: pieter.rijken@avmed.org.

RIKARD, WILLIAM L., JR., lawyer; b. Canton, NC, Apr. 7, 1945; BA, Davidson Coll., 1967; JD, Vanderbilt U., 1970. Bar: N.C. 1970, US Dist. Ct. (NC), US Ct. Appeals (4th cir.), US Supreme Ct. Ptnr., chmn litig. dept. Parker Poe Adams & Bernstein, Charlotte, NC. Bd. dir. Charlotte Merchants' Found.; mem. Charlotte Mecklenburg Bd. Edn., 1988—, vice chmn., 1990—. 1st lt. adj. gen. corps U.S. Army, 1970-72. Mem. ABA, NC Bar Assn., Mecklenburg County Bar Assn. (mem. exec. com. 1985-88), Omicron Delta Kappa. Office: Parker Poe Adams & Bernstein LLP Ste 3000 3 Wachovia Ctr 401 S Tryon St Charlotte NC 28202-1935 Office Phone: 704-335-9011. Office Fax: 704-335-9689. Business E-Mail: williamrikard@parkerpoe.com.

RIKKERS, LAYTON FREDERICK, surgeon; b. Fond du Lac, Wis., Jan. 31, 1944; s. Judson John and Dorothy (Layton) R.; m. Diane Lynn Foster, Aug. 20, 1966; children: Steven, Kristin. BS, U. Wis., 1966; MD, Stanford U. Sch. Medicine, 1970. Diplomate Nat. Bd. Med. Examiners, Am. Bd. Surgery. Intern U. Utah Sch. Medicine, Salt Lake City, 1970-71, surgical resident, 1971-76; instr. surgery Emory U. Sch. Medicine, Atlanta, 1976-77; from asst. prof. surgery to acting chmn. div. gen. surgery U. Utah Sch. Medicine, Salt Lake City, 1977-84; prof., chmn. dept. surgery U. Nebr. Med. Ctr., Omaha, 1984-96, U. Wis., Madison, 1996—. Interim dean Coll. Medicine, U. Nebr. Coll. Medicine, 1991-93, M.M. Musselman prof. surgery, 1990—; cons. Omaha Vet. Adminstrv. Ctr., 1984-86, NIH, 1992, Gov.'s Blue Ribbon Coalition on Health Care, Nebr., 1993-94. Editor: Surgical Clinics of North America, 1990; editor-in-chief Annals of Surgery, 1996—; contbr. articles to profl. jours. Mem. Am. Surgical Assn., Am. Coll. Surgeons (com. chair 1993-95), Am. Bd. Surgery (clin. chmn. 1994-95), Soc. Clin. Surgery (pres. 1994-95), Soc. Surgery Alimentary Tract (pres. 2000), Halsted Soc. (pres. 2000). Episcopalian. Avocations: hiking, reading, skiing, travel. Office: U Wis H4/710 Clin Sci Ctr 600 Highland Ave Madison WI 53792-3284

RIKON, MICHAEL, lawyer; b. Bklyn., Feb. 2, 1945; s. Charles and Ruth (Shapiro) R.; m. Leslie Sharon Rein, Feb. 11, 1968; children: Carrie Rachel, Joshua Howard. BS, NY Inst. Tech., 1966; JD, Bklyn. Law Sch., 1969; LLM, NYU, 1974. Bar: NY 1970, U.S. Dist. Ct. (so. and ea. dists.) NY 1971, U.S. Ct. Appeals (2d cir.) 1972, U.S. Supreme Ct. 1973, U.S. Ct. Appeals (5th and 11th cirs.) 1981. Asst. corp. counsel City of NY, 1969-73; law clk. NY State Ct. Claims, 1973-80; ptnr. Rudick and rikon, P.C., NYC,

1980-88; pvt. practice NYC, 1988-94; ptnr. Goldstein, Goldstein Rikon & Gottlieb PC, NYC, 1994—. Contbr. articles to profl. jours. Pres. Village Greens Residents Assn., 1978-79; chmn. bd. Arden Heights Jewish Ctr., S.I., NY, 1976-77; pres. North Shore Rep. Club., 1977; mem. cmty. bd. S.I. Borough Pres., 1977. With SSGT 99th Signal Batallion USAR. Nominee Best Lawyers in Eminent Domain and Condemnation Law, NY, 2006; recipient Bus. Leadership award, NYIT Alumni Fed., 2006. Fellow Am. Bar Found.; mem. ABA (chair com. Condemnation) NY State Bar Assn. (spl. com. of condemnation law), Suffolk County Bar Assn., NY County lawyers Assn. (chair condemnation com.), Assn. Bar City of NY (condemnation com.), Owners Counsel Am. (dir.). Republican. Jewish. Avocations: collecting stamps, photography, collecting miniature soldiers. Office: 80 Pine St New York NY 10005-1702 Home: 105 East 29th St New York NY 10016-8014 Home Phone: 201-445-4608; Office Phone: 212-422-4000 23.

RIKOON, JONATHAN J., lawyer; b. 1955; AB cum laude, U. Pa., 1976; JD cum laude, NYU, 1979. Bar: NY 1980. Assoc., prin. atty. Paul, Weiss, Rifkind, Wharton & Garrison; of counsel Mudge, Rose, Guthrie, Alexander & Ferdon; counsel to ptnr. Debevoise & Plimpton, LLP, NYC, 1995—. Prin. author: Essential Facts: Estate Planning and Family Wealth Transfers, 1995, Stocker and Rikoon on Drawing Wills and Trusts, 2000; contbr. articles to profl. publs. Named one of Top 100 Attys., Worth mag., 2005. Fellow: Am. Coll. Trust and Estate Counsel; mem.: NY State Bar Assn. (privilege subcommittee 1992—95, mem. estate litig. com. 1992—, fees subcommittee 1995—, tax aspects of settling probate litig. subcommittee 1998—99, chair estate liitg. com. 2003—06, exec. com. 2003—, first dist. rep. 2007—, trusts and estates sect.), Assn. of Bar of the City of NY (estate and gift taxation com. 1993—96, chair allocation of estate taxes subcommittee 1993—96, chair dead man statute subcommittee 1996, estates, trust & surrogate's ct. com. 1996—, chair working grp. on prin. and income 1998—). Office: Debevoise & Plimpton LLP 919 Third Ave New York NY 10022-3904 Office Phone: 212-909-7217. Office Fax: 212-521-7212. E-mail: jjrikoon@debevoise.com.

RIKOSKI, RICHARD ANTHONY, electrical engineering executive; b. Kingston, Pa., Aug. 13, 1941; s. Stanley George and Nellie (Gober) R.; m. Giannina Batchelor Petrullo, Dec. 18, 1971 (div. 1979); children: Richard James, Jennifer Anne; m. Carol Westbrook. BEE, U. Detroit, 1964; MSEE, Carnegie Inst. Tech., 1965; PhD, Carnegie-Mellon U., 1968; postdoctoral fellow, Case-Western Res. U./NASA, 1971. Registered profl. engr., Ill., Mass., Pa. Engr. 1st communication satellite systems Internat. Tel. & Tel., Nutley, NJ, 1961-64; engr. Titan II ICBM program Gen. Motors, Milw., 1964; trainee NASA, 1964-67; instr. Carnegie-Mellon U., Pitts., 1966-68; asst. prof. U. Pa., Phila., 1968-74; assoc. prof., dir. hybrid microelectronics lab., chmn. ednl. TV com. IIT, Chgo., 1974-80, chmn. ednl. TV com., 1974-80; rsch. engr. nuclear effects ITT Rsch. Inst., Chgo., 1974-75; pres. Tech. Analysis Corp., Chgo., 1980—. Engr. color TV colorimetry Hazeltine Rsch., Chgo., 1969; engr. Metroliner rail car/roadbed ride quality dynamics analysis US Dept. Transp., ENSCO, Inc., Springfield, Va., 1970; pres. Tech. Analysis Corp., Chgo., 1978-91; contractor analysis of color TV receiver safety hazards US Consumer Product Safety Commn., 1977, analysis heating effect in aluminum wire Beverly Hills Supper Club Fire, Covington, Ky., 1978; engr. GFCI patent infringement study 3M Corp., St. Paul, 1979-81; elec. systems analyst Coca-Cola Corp., Atlanta, 1983-91; fire investigator McDonald's Corp., Oak Brook, Ill., 1987-90; engring. analyst telephone switching ctrs. ATT, Chgo., 1990-91; expert witness numerous other govtl. and corp. procs.; evaluator Accreditation bd. Engring. and Tech., 2000—. Author: Hybrid Microelectronic Circuits, 1973; editor: Hybrid Microelectronic Technology, 1973; contbr. articles to profl. jours. Officer Planning Commn., Beverly Shores, Ind., 1987-93, trustee town coun., 1992—, police liason 1993-96, dir. emergency mgmt., 1998, coun. pres., 1999-2000; mem. Chgo. Coun. Fgn. Rels., USAF SAC Comdrs. Disting.is. Program; adv. coun. Nat. Park Svc. Ind. Dunes Nat. Lake Shore, 1993—. NASA fellow, 1964-67, 70. Mem. IEEE (sr. ednl. activities bd. NYC 1970-74, USAB career devel. com. 1972-74, editor Soundings 1973-75, Cassette Colloquia 1973-74, del. Popov Soc. Tech. Exch. USSR, mgr. Dial Access Tech. Edn. program 1972), Assn. for Media Based Continuing Engring. Edn. (bd. dirs.), Nat. Fire Protection Assn., Sigma Xi, Tau Beta Pi, Eta Kappa Nu. Republican. Avocations: sailing, travel. Home: One E Lakefront Dr Beverly Shores IN 46301-0444 Office: 211 E Ontario St Chicago IL 60611 Office Phone: 773-883-1333. Personal E-mail: rikoski@earthlink.net.

RILEY, BARBARA POLK, retired librarian; b. Roselle, N.J., Nov. 21, 1928; d. Charles Carrington and Olive Bond P.; AB, Howard U., 1950; BS, N.J. Coll. Women, 1951; MS, Columbia U., 1955; m. George Emerson Riley, Feb. 23, 1957 (dec.); children: George E., Glenn C., Karen O.; m. William I. Scott, Oct. 6, 1990 (div. 1998). Asst. librarian, Fla. A&M U., 1951-53; with Morgan State Coll., 1955; with Dept. Def., 1955-57, S.C. State Coll., 1957-59, U.Wis., 1958-59; asst. librarian Atlanta U., 1960-68; asst. dir. Union County Anti Poverty Council, 1968; librarian Union County Tech. Inst., Scotch Plains, N.J., 1968-82, Plainfield campus Union County Coll., 1982-95; ret., 1995. Contbr. articles in Past and Promise, 1990, Ency. NJ. Mem. Roselle Bd. Edn., 1976-78; bd. dirs. Union County Anti Poverty Council, 1969-72; mem. Roselle Human Relations Commn., 1971-73, Plainfield Sci. Center, 1974-76, Union County Psychiat. Clinic, 1980-83, Pinewood Sr. Citizens Council, 1981-85; bd. dirs. Project, Women of N.J, 1985-93, Pinewood Sr. Citizen Housing, 1981-85, Black Women's History Conf., 1985-92, pres., 1989-91; Mem. Heard A.M.E. Ch. Mem. N.J. Library Assn., Council Library Tech., ALA (Black caucas), N.J. Coalition of 100 Black Women, African Am. Women's Polit. Caucus, N.J. Black Librarians Network (bd. dirs.), Links, Inc. (North Jersey chpt.), Black Women's History Conf., Alpha Kappa Alpha. Club: Just-A-Mere Lit. Home: 76 Hana Rd Edison NJ 08817-2037

RILEY, BETTY ANNE, psychologist, educator; d. James Andrew Riley and Elizabeth Riley Deurloo; m. Ronald Robert Teed, June 14, 1997. BA in Music, Wheaton Coll., 1969, MA in Christian Edn. with highest honors, 1971, MA in Counseling Psychology, 1985; PsyD in Clin. Psychology, Ill. Sch. Profl. Psychology, 1992. Lic. clin. psychologist Ill., 1993. Dir. of Christian edn. Naperville Bible Ch. (now called Grace Pointe), Ill., 1971—78; vis. instr. Wheaton Coll., Wheaton, Ill., 1980—81; writer and editor Scripture Press Pubs. Inc., Wheaton, Ill., 1971—76; pre-primary dept. mgr. Scripture Press Pubs., Inc., Wheaton, 1976—83; clin. psychologist Psychotherapy & Consultation Svcs., Wheaton, 1985—97; founder and dir., clin. psychologist Bethel Ctr. for Psychotherapy, Wheaton, 1997—. Vol. cons. Solomon Klein Orphanage, Cochabamba, Bolivia, 1988; provide respite for refugee ctr. workers The Alpenland Life Ctr., Crikvenica, Croatia, 1995—95; lectr. in field. Author: (leader's guide) Leader's Guide for Building Stronger Families; co-author (with Mary Lebar): You Can Teach 4s and 5s; editor, composer (song book) Let's Sing! for 4s and 5s; prodr.: (cassettes) Motions 'N Music 1; Motions 'N Music 2; Let's Sing! for 4s and 5s; contbr. chapters to books. Youth ministries bd. Evangel Bapt. Ch., Wheaton, Ill., 2002—03; co-founder (with husband) and co-pastor Village Ch. of Wheaton, Wheaton, Ill., 2003—. Recipient Rech award in Psychol. Studies, Wheaton Coll., 1985. Mem.: Christian Assn. for Psychol. Studies, Am. Assn. for Marriage and Family Therapy, APA, Christians for Bibl. Equality. Christian Evangelical. Avocations: attending concerts, cooking, golf. Office: Bethel Center for Psychotherapy 213 W Wesley St Ste 204 Wheaton IL 60187 Home Phone: 630-665-4479; Office Phone: 630-681-1900.

RILEY, BOB (ROBERT RENFROE RILEY), governor; b. Ashland, Ala., Oct. 3, 1944; m. Patsy (Adams) Riley; children: Rob, Jenice, Minda, Krisalyn. Degree in bus. administrn., U. Ala. Past poultry and egg bus. co-owner, Ala.; past owner automobile dealership, Ala.; owner trucking co., Ala.; past owner grocery store and local pharmacy, Ala.; mem. Ho. of Reps. from 3d Ala. dist., 1996—2002, asst. whip, mem. house armed svcs. com., mem. house banking and fin. svcs. com., mem. house agr. com., house-senate conferee on FY 1998 Def. Authorization bill, 1997, mem. ho. agrl. com.; gov. State of Ala., 2003—. Past chmn. fin. com. Clay County Hosp.; mem. First Baptist Ch., men's Sunday sch. tchr., past chmn. bd. trustees; pres., Ala. State Bd. Edn, 2003-. Named Pub. Official of Yr., Governing mag., 2003. Mem. Masons, Shriners, Jaycees (past pres. Ashland chpt.). Republican. Baptist. Office: Office of the Gov State Capitol 600 Dexter Ave Montgomery AL 36130 Office Phone: 334-242-7100. Office Fax: 334-242-0937. *

RILEY, CARROLL LAVERN, anthropology educator; b. Summersville, Mo., Apr. 18, 1923; s. Benjamin F. and Minnie B. (Smith) R.; m. Brent Robinson Locke, Mar. 25, 1948; children: Benjamin Locke, Victoria Smith Evans, Cynthia Winningham AB, U. N.Mex., 1948, PhD, 1952; MA, UCLA, 1950. Instr. U. Colo., Boulder, 1953-54; asst. prof. U. N.C., Chapel Hill, 1954-55, So. Ill. U., Carbondale, 1955-60, assoc. prof., 1960-67, prof., 1967-86, Disting. prof., 1986-87, Disting. prof. emeritus, 1987—, chmn. dept., 1979-82, dir. mus., 1972-74; rsch. assoc. lab. anthropology Mus. N.Mex., 1987—. Rsch. collaborator Smithsonian Instn., 1988—; adj. prof. N.Mex. Highlands U., 1989—. Author: The Origins of Civilization, 1969, The Frontier People, 1982, expanded edit., 1987, Rio del Norte, 1995, Bandelier, 1996, The Kachina and Cross, 1999, 2003, Becoming Aztlan, 2005; editor: American Historical Anthropology, 1967, Man Across the Sea, 1971, Southwestern Journals of Adolph F. Bandelier, 4 vols., 1966, 70, 75, 84, Across the Chichimec Sea, 1978, A Zuni Life, 1998, The Casas Grandes World, 1999, others; contbr. numerous articles to profl. jours. Served in USAAF, 1942-45 Decorated 4 battle stars; grantee Social Sci. Rsch. Coun., NIH, Am. Philos. Soc., Am. Council Learned Socs., NEH, others. Home and Office: 1106 6th St Las Vegas NM 87701 E-mail: criley@desertgate.com.

RILEY, CHERYL, artist, educator; b. Houston, Dec. 1, 1952; d. Bennie Riley and Gladys Mae DuBois. AA in Fashion Fine Art, Columbia Coll., 1973. Advt. exec. Levi Strauss & Saatchi Saatchi, San Francisco, 1979—84; instr. mixed media Penland (N.C.) Sch. Crafts, 2004; instr. wood decorative surfaces Haystack Mountain Sch. Crafts, Deer Isle, Maine, 2003; instr. mixed media Arrowmont Sch. Arts and Crafts, Gatlinburg, Tenn., 2001; instr. visual concepts N.Y. Sch. Interior Design, NYC, 2001—05; artist, furniture designer Right Angle Designs, San Francisco, 1986—99; artist, designer NYC, 2000—. Designer, cons. selected site art and graphics San Francisco Redevel. Agy., 1992; designer, think tank cons. Design Revival, Rock Hill (S.C.) Art Coun., 1999, 2000; conceptualist, think tank cons. Alternative Design for Walt Disney Industries, Jersey City and Orlando, Fla., 1998; keynote spkr. ann. conf. Furniture Soc. Am., Purchase, NY, 1997; artist, comty. facilitator Mosaic Mural on Exterior of 911 Emergency Ctr., San Francisco, 1994—98; artist, civic artist Lifetime Cultural Achievement from San Francisco Bus. and Profl. Women, Inc., 1997. Included in book and panel, Women Designers in the USA, 1900-2000, 2000. Bd. dirs. Mus. Arts and Design, NYC, 2000—06, chair membership com., 2000—06; bd. dirs., chair SECA aux. San Francisco Mus. Modern Art, 1996—99; bd. dirs., exec. bd. sec. Am. Craft Coun., NYC, 1992—97; bd. dirs., exec. bd. dirs., chair Capp St. Project, San Francisco, 1990—97; fundraiser Ndebele tribe-inspired wall panels for Carver Acad. Elem. Sch. and Bayview Police Sta.'s Comty. Conf. Rm., San Francisco. Design Arts Individual grant, NEA, 1994, Visual Art grant, Fleishacker Found. and Tamarack Found., 1997. Mem.: Bead Soc., Orgn. of Black Designers (panel discussion participant 1997), Furniture Soc. Avocations: reading, swimming, walking, fine dining, opera, gallery and museum visits. Office: 150 Bay St #824 Jersey City NJ 07302 Office Phone: 646-230-7222 ext 211. E-mail: mail@cherylriley.com.

RILEY, CHERYL M., prosthodontist, military officer; b. Biloxi, Miss., Aug. 4, 1963; d. William Richard and Gloria Lucille Morgan; m. Kevin Gerard Riley; 1 stepchild, Jared Nolan. BS in Chemistry magna cum laude with high honors, Millsaps Coll., 1985; RDH, U. Ala., 1987, DMD, 1989; MS in Oral Scis., SUNY, Buffalo, 1993. Diplomate Am. Bd. Prosthodontics. Dental specialist Miss. Army N.G., 1983—85; dental hygienist Ala. Army N.G., 1985—87; NBC officer, phys. tng. officer, retention officer La. Army N.G., 1987—89; dental officer, NBC officer N.Y. Army N.G., 1989—90; resident in prosthodontics SUNY, Buffalo, 1990—93; NBC officer USAFR, NY, 1990—93; tng. officer, divsn. officer, chmn. children's dental health care month USN, Quantico, 1993—96, head prosthodontic dept., weapons officer Palms, 1996—97; chief prosthodontics, PROFIS officer U.S. Army, Ft. Bragg, NC, 1997—2003, chief prosthodontic mentor, 2004—05; comdr. 257th Med. Detachment. Part-time instr. SUNY, Buffalo, 1991—93. Decorated Bronze Star, Army Commendation medal, Navy Commendation medal, NATO medal Bosnia Theater, others; Merit scholar, Millsaps Coll., 1981—82, Acad. scholar, 1982—83, 1983—84, 1984—85, Ruth Cushman scholar, 1984—85, Emma Lou Ohsburg scholar, U. Ala., 1986—87, Dorothy Perkins Campbell scholar, SUNY, Buffalo, 1991—92. Fellow: Am. Coll. Prosthodontics (diplomat); mem.: Aircraft Owners and Pilots Assn., U.S. Parachute Assn., Tri Chi, Beta Beta, Omicron Delta Kappa, Phi Eta Sigma, Eta Sigma, Alpha Epsilon Delta (pres.), Theta Nu Sigma (v.p.), Phi Mu. Personal E-mail: aeropros@aol.com. Business E-Mail: cheryl.riley@us.army.mil.

RILEY, DAVID RICHARD, retired management consultant, military officer; b. Spokane, Wash., Mar. 28, 1940; s. Lee James and Louise Elizabeth (Duncan) R.; m. Anna Maria Formigoni, July 6, 1963; children: David Scott, Michelle Andrea. BS in Naval Sci., USN Acad., 1963; MS in Applied Math., USN Post Grad. Sch., 1972; postgrad., Armed Forces Staff Coll., 1975. Navy ops. mgmt. specialist, Navy aerospace engring. specialist, Navy material specialist, Navy weapon sys. mgmt. specialist. Ensign USN, 1963, advanced through grades to capt., 1984, antisubmarine warfare/antisubmarine rocket officer Mayport, Fla., 1963-65, pilot trainee Pensacola, Fla., 1965-67, designated naval pilot San Diego, 1967, with antisubmarine/antiair warfare, 1967-74, maintenace officer, 1976-78, officer in charge Nerra Naples, Italy, 1978-81; exec. officer Naval Aviation Depot, Alameda, Calif., 1981-84, comdg. officer Pensacola, 1987-90; aviation depot program mgr. Navairsyscom Hdqrs., Washington, 1984-87; ret., 1990; cons. bus. planning and organizational devel., internat. commerce Chula Vista, Calif., 1990-94; pres., COO Speco Corp., Springfield, Ohio, 1994-95; pres. David Riley Assocs., Inc., 1998—. Mem. Assn. Naval Aviation, Ret. Officers Assn., Am. Legion, Naval Helicopter Assn. Republican. Presbyterian. Avocation: golf. Home: 115 Eastwick Ct Dayton OH 45440-3647 Personal E-mail: dave.riley@earthlink.net.

RILEY, FAITH LYNCH, retired historian, writer; b. Lockesburg, Ark., Sept. 16, 1940; d. Lester Doss and Nina Pettigrew-Doss Shuffield; m. Bryan Riley, Mar. 12, 1962; children: Reed Lynch, Costa Lynch, Alex Lynch. BS of Edn., Henderson State Tchrs. Coll., Arkadelphia, Ark., 1962. Tchg. Ark. Dept. of Edn., 1962. Dir. SW Ark. Regional Archives, Washington, Ark., 2002—; flight attendant Delta Airlines, Dallas, 1963—64; tchr. Crawfordsville H.S., Ark., 1962—63; columnist Mena Star Newspaper, Mena, Ark., 1980—92; writer, owner Riley Publications, Wickes, Ark., 1994—, ret. Author (publisher): (oral history) Legacy of Arkanas, Somewhere The Sun Is Shining: Eyewitness Accounts of the Great Depression, To Do Or Die: Ouachita Mountain Men Remember World War II; editor: (non-fiction) 25 Years at Southwest Archives: True Stories From the Collections of Southwest Arkansas Regional Archives, Washington, Arkansas. Chmn. Rich Mountain CC, Mena, Ark., 1988—89, mem., 1983—2000. Baptist. Achievements include research in History of Schools Since 1836 in Twelve SW Arkansas Counties. Avocations: working on the ranch, fishing/hunting, piano playing, nature photography, four wheeling in the back woods and trails near the Cossatot River. Home: 740 Hwy 278 Wickes AR 71973 Home Phone: 870-385-7747. Personal E-mail: faithriley@alltel.net.

RILEY, HELENE MARIA KASTINGER, Germanist; b. Vienna, Mar. 11, 1939; came to U.S., 1959; d. Josef and Helene (Friedl) Kastinger; m. Edward R. Riley, Nov. 6, 1957 (div. May 1970); children: India Helene, John Edward, Jesse Dale, Michael Rutledge; m. Darius G. Ornston, May 11, 1983. Grad., bus. coll., Vienna, 1955; BA in Music, North Tex. State U., 1970; MA in Germanics, Rice U., Houston, 1973, PhD in Germanics, 1975. Tchg. asst. Rice U., Houston, 1971—75; asst. prof. German Yale U., New Haven, 1975—79, head summer lang. inst., 0979—1981, assoc. prof., 1979—85; chmn. Dept. Fgn. Langs. Wash. State U., Pullman, 1981—82; head Dept. Langs. Clemson U., SC, 1985—86, prof., 1985—95, alumni Disting. prof., 1996—, chmn. alumni disting. assoc. prof., 2006—. Guest prof. Middlebury Coll., Vt., 1976; speaker in field. Author: Achim von Arnim, 1979, Virginia Woolf, 1983, Clemens Brentano, 1985, Die Weibliche Muse, 1986, Max Weber, 1991, Hildegard von Bingen, 1997, John Adam Treutlen: The European Heritage of Georgia's First Governor, 1999, Clemson University, 2002; editor: Germanic Notes and Reviews, 2005—; prodr., dir. traveling exhibit Cultural Contbns. of German-speaking Settlers in SC, 1996—; others; contbr. articles to profl. jours. Recipient German-Am. Friendship award Consul Gen. of the German Fed. Republic, 1989; grantee Griswold Found., 1975-76, 78, SC Dept. Edn., 1986, NEH, 1986, Provost's award Clemson U., 1989, 96, Hilles Fund, 1976, 79, 82, SC Humanities Coun., 1996; NDEA fellow, 1972, 73, Rice fellow, 1971, 74, Morse fellow, 1977-78, Deutscher Akademischer Austausch-Dienst fellow, 1979, Yale U. sr. faculty fellow, 1981-82, Holland Fund fellow, 1982, Deutsche Forschungsgemeinschaft fellow, 1982, Mesda fellow, 1993, Davenport Coll. fellow Yale U. Mem. AAUP (v.p. 1987-88, pres. 1988-89), MLA, Am. Assn. Tchrs. German, So. Comparative Lit. Assn., others. Democrat. Avocations: reading, writing, sports, needlecrafts, painting. Office: Clemson U Dept Langs 717 Strode Twr Clemson SC 29634-0001 Business E-Mail: rhelene@clemson.edu.

RILEY, HENRY CHARLES, banker; b. Newton, Massachusetts, Mar. 23, 1932; s. Charles Matthew and Marion Anna (Armstrong) R.; m. Patricia Ann (Buchanan), Mar. 3, 1962; children: Lauren Elizabeth, Carolyn Ann, Julie Louise. BA, Yale U., 1954; MBA, Boston Coll., 1965. With BayBank Harvard Trust Co., Cambridge, Mass., 1958—89, treas., sec., 1967—70, sr. v.p., sec., 1972—82, exec. v.p., 1982—87; mng. dir. cmty. banking BayBank Systems Inc., Waltham, Mass., 1987—90; exec. v.p., dir. cmty. banking BayBank Boston, 1990—92; exec. v.p. BayBank Systems, Inc., Waltham, Mass., 1992—97; bd. dir. BayBank F.S.B., BayBank N.A., Waltham, Mass., 1995—96. Mem. pvt. banking adv. com. Fleet Boston, Sarasota, Fla., 2000-04. Trustee, treas. Longy Sch. Music, 1970-92; bd. dir. Richard Warren Surg. Rsch. and Ednl. Fund Inc., 1984—; bd. dir., pres. Cambridge Econ. Devel. Corp., 1982-87; corporator, past asst. treas. Mt. Auburn Hosp.; mem. exec. bd. Gettysburg Coll. Parents Assn.; treas. St. John's Episcopal Ch., sr. warden, Westwood, Mass., 1982-85; mem. St. Paul's Cathedral chpt., Boston, 1990-93. Served in USNR, 1956-57. Mem. Am. Bankers Assn. (chmn. 1991-92, exec. com. br. adminstrv. divsn. 1992, chmn. nat. retail banking conf. 1990), Nat. Br. Adminstr. Roundtable, Boston Coll. Sch. Mgmt. Alumni Assn. (past dir., pres.), Harvard Sq. Bus. Assn. (past dir.), Cambridge C. of C. 1975-87 (past dir., past treas., v.p.) Rotary (club dir. 1976-80, pres. 1979-80), Yale Club, Yale Club of the Suncoast (bd. dir. 2001—, v.p., 2004), Harvard Club, Dennis Yacht Club (mem. bd. govs., treas. 1993-94), The Meadows Country Club, Ivy League Club, The Club at Yarmouthport. Episcopalian. Home: 33 York Way Westwood MA 02090-2633 also: PO Box 1192 240 New Boston Rd Dennis MA 02638-2121 also: 5284 Huntingwood Ct Sarasota FL 34235-5600 Personal E-mail: Marshwind@aol.com.

RILEY, JAMES B., JR., lawyer; b. Evanston, Ill., 1954; BA magna cum laude, U. Ill., 1976; JD cum laude, George Wash. U., 1979. CPA; bar: Ill. 1979, US Dist. Ct. No. Dist. Ill. 1979, US. Ct. Fed. Claims. Ptnr. Ross & Hardies (merged with McGuireWoods LLP in 2003), Chgo., 1985—2003, McGuireWoods LLP, Chgo., 2003—, co-chair firm health care dept., 2003—. Bd. dirs. Christmas in Apr. - North Suburban Chgo., past pres.; bd. dirs., pres. Rebuilding Together North Suburban Chgo. Mem.: ABA (health law sect.), Ill. Assn. Hosp. Attorneys, Am. Health Lawyers Assn., Ill. Bar Assn. Office: McGuireWoods LLP Ste 4100 77 W Wacker Dr Chicago IL 60601-1815 Office Phone: 312-750-8665. Office Fax: 312-920-6133. Business E-Mail: jriley@mcguirewoods.com.

RILEY, JAMES CLIFFORD, military career officer; b. Montacello, Calif., Nov. 13, 1946; m. Linda Jean Axtater. BS, U. Nebr., 1971; MA, Webster U., 1978; grad., Command and Gen. Staff Coll., 1980, U.S. Army War Coll., 1987. Drafted U.S. Army, 1965, commd. 2d lt., 1966, advanced through grades to lt. gen., 1999, co. comdr., S4 and Battalion Maintenance Officer 1st Bn., 6th Inf., 1st Armored Divsn. Illesheim, Germany, 1972-75, dep. G3 1st Armored Divsn., exec. officer 1st Bn., 52d Inf., S3, 3d Brigade Bamberg, Germany, 1981-83, comdr. 2d Bn., 7th Cavalry, 1st Cavalry Divsn. Ft. Hood, Tex., 1983-86, G3 and chief of staff 2d Armored Divsn. (forward) Garlstedt, Germany, 1987-89, comdr. 3d Brigade, 3d Infantry Divsn. Aschaffenburg, Germany, 1989-90, with 1st Armored Divsn. Saudi Arabia, Iraq & Kuwait, 1990-91, chief European divsn., J-5, the Joint Staff, Joint Chiefs of Staff rep. for European security matters Washington, Vienna, Austria, 1992-94, asst. divsn. comdr. for support, 1st Armored Divsn. Hanau, Germany, 1994-95, chief U.S. Mil. Tng. Mission Saudi Arabia, 1995-97, comdr. 3d Inf. Divsn. (Mechanized) Ft. Stewart, Ga., 1997-99. Decorated Def. Disting. Svc. medal, Disting. Svc. medal, Def. Superior Svc. medal, Legion of Merit with oak leaf cluster, Bronze Star medal with oak leaf cluster, Meritorious Svc. medal with four oak leaf clusters, Army Commendation medal.

RILEY, JAMES KEVIN, lawyer; b. Nyack, NY, July 21, 1945; s. Charles A. and Mary Lenihan R.; m. Joan Leavy Riley, Oct. 4, 1969; children: Carolyn, Tara, Sean. AB, Fordham Coll., 1967; JD, Rutgers U., 1970. Bar: N.Y. 1971, N.J. 1983, U.S. Supreme Ct. 1984; cert. fin. planner; accreditated real estate planner. Asst. dist. atty. Rockland County, New City, NY, 1973-74; ptnr. Amend & Amend, NYC, 1974-78, O'Connell & Riley, Pearl River, NY, 1978—. Pub., pres. 1099 Express Software, 1099 Express Ltd., Pearl River, 1987-97; adj. prof. estate planning Pace Univ., White Plains, N.Y.; town atty. Town of Orangetown; adj. prof. pub. edn. law LI U., Sparkill, NY. Bd. dirs. United Way of Rockland County, N.Y., 1974-80, Rockland Family Shelter for Victims of Domestic Violence, 1981-85, Literacy Vols. Rockland County, 1989-99; chmn. bd. dirs. New Hope Manor, Barryville, N.Y., 1985-88. Mem. ABA, Am. Soc. Hosp. Attys., Nat. Coun. Sch. Dist. Attys., N.Y. State Bar Assn. (ho. of dels. 1988-92, 2000-04), Rockland County Bar Assn. (bd. dirs. 1986—, pres. 1997-98), Nat. Acad. Elder Law Attys., Rotary Club of Pearl River (pres. 1999-2000). Democrat. Roman Catholic. Home: 145 Franklin Ave Pearl River NY 10965-2510 Office: O'Connell & Riley 144 E Central Ave Pearl River NY 10965 also: 103 Chestnut Ridge Rd Montvale NJ 07645

RILEY, JENNIFER BELL, finance educator; d. Dalton and Doris E Bell; m. Christopher D Riley, Oct. 22, 2004; 1 child, Micah Dalton. BS, Lubbock Christian U., Tex., 1991; MSA, Tex. Tech U., Lubbock, 1997. Internat. tax cons. KPMG, Dallas, 1996—2000; tax and fin. cons. Ernst & Young LLP, Dallas, 2000—03; ind. tax, fin. cons. Lubbock, 2003—04; dir. devel. rsch. svcs. Tex. Tech U., Lubbock, 2004—. Mem.: Am. Fundraising Profls., APRA Internat. (sw chpt. bd. of dirs. 2005), CASE. R-Liberal. Office: Texas Tech U Sys PO Box 45025 Lubbock TX 79409 Office Phone: 806-742-4024. Business E-Mail: jennifer.riley@ttu.edu.

RILEY, JESSICA, lawyer; b. Seattle, Mar. 30, 1976; BA, Univ. Calif., Berkeley, 1998; JD, Seattle Univ. Sch. Law, 2002. Bar: Wash. 2002. Ptnr. atty., criminal defense Law Offices of John Henry Brown, P.S., Seattle, 2002—. Contbr. articles to numerous profl. jours. Named Wash. Rising Star, SuperLawyer Mag., 2006. Office: Law Office John Henry Browne PS Ste 2100 821 Second Ave Seattle WA 98104

RILEY, LYNNE F., lawyer; b. Boston, Oct. 31, 1959; BA cum laude, U. Mass., 1981; JD cum laude, Suffolk U. Law Sch., 1992. Bar: Mass. 1992, U.S. Dist. Ct. Mass. 1993, U.S. Ct. Appeals First Ct. 1993. Ins. agent Fidelity Nat. Title Ins. Co., Lawyers Title Ins. Co. Title examiner Mass. Land Ct., 1994—. Author: Recent First Cir. Devel. & Persisting Problems Regarding Avoidance of Impairing Liens, 1999. Named an top Boston lawyers, Boston Mag., 2004. Mem.: U.S. Panel Bankruptcy Trustees Dist. Mass. (mem. 1995), Mass. Conveyancer's Assn., Internat. Women's Insolvency & Restructuring Confederation (network chairperson), Am. Bankruptcy Inst., Women's Bar Assn. Mass., Boston Bar Assn. (bankruptcy sect.). Office: Riley & Esher LLP 69 Thorndike St Cambridge MA 02141 Office Phone: 617-876-3755. Office Fax: 617-876-3155.

RILEY, MARGARET FOSTER (MIMI), law educator; b. NYC, 1959; AB in History and Polit. Sci., magna cum laude, Duke U., 1981; JD, Columbia U., 1985. Bar: NY 1986, Pa. 1988. Assoc. Rogers & Wells, NYC, 1985—88, Pepper, Hamilton & Scheetz, Phila., 1988—92; asst. prof. U. Va. Sch. Law, 1992—98, named assoc. prof., 1998, now prof., co-dir. Legal Rsch. and Writing Program, 1992—. Office: U Va Sch Law 580 Massie Rd Charlottesville VA 22903-1789 Office Phone: 434-924-4671. E-mail: mf9c@virginia.edu.

RILEY, MARK RICHARD, biochemical engineer, educator; b. Dearborn, Mich., Mar. 16, 1969; s. Richard A. and Mary Alice Stella (Malaski) R.; m. Jill Susan Bonita Riley, Oct. 7, 1995. BSE in Chem. Engring. cum laude, U. Mich., 1990; MS in Chem. and Biochemical Engring., Rutgers U., 1994, PhD in Chem. and Biochemical Engring., 1995; Post Doctoral in Biochemical Engring. and Analytical Chemistry, U. Iowa, 1997. Undergraduate rsch., cellular bioengineering lab., dept. chemical engring. U. Mich., 1989—90; grad. dissertation rsch., dept. chemical and biochemical engring. Rutgers U., NJ, 1992—95; postdoctoral rschr., dept. chemical and biochemical engring. and dept. chemistry U. Iowa, Iowa City, 1995-97; faculty mem. of grad. interdisciplinary program in biomedical engring. U. Ariz., Tucson, 1997, chair, activities subcommittee, 1999—, asst. prof. dept. agrl. and biosystems engring. and program in biomedical engring., 1997—2003, assoc. prof., dept. agrl. and biosystems engring., biomedical engring., 2003—, assoc. prof., chemical and environ. engring., 2004—, assoc. prof., materials sci. and engring., 2005—, assoc. prof., Bio5 Inst., 2005—. Undergraduate tchg. asst. for self-paced biochemistry class, dept. biochemistry U. Mich., 1990; tchg. asst. for grad. and undergraduate classes in transport phenomena, dept. chemical and biochemical engring. Rutgers U., 1993—94, Merck Excellence fellow, NJ, 1993—95, instructor of undergraduate class in momentum transport phenomena, dept. chemical and biochemical engring., NJ, 1994; tchg. of several workshops/seminars for small groups of students U. Ariz., 1997—2001; indsl. intern Ortho Pharma., Raritan, NJ, 1991, Exxon Rsch. and Engring., Annandale, NJ, 1993, Annandale, 94. Refereed articles for peer-reviewed jours.; contbr. chapters to books; editor for patents and lit. reviews Applied Biochemistry and Biotechnology, 1998—, biol. engring. representative to resource mag. editl. bd., 2004—06. Recipient Nat. Assn. Coll. anf Teachers of Agr., Tchg. award of merit, U. Ariz, Coll. Agr. and Life Sciences, 2002; U. Ariz. Dean of Students Faculty Fellow, 2001—. Mem. Am. Chem. Soc. (membership chair for biochemical tech. divsn. 1998-2002), Biomed. Engring. Soc., AIChE, Am. Soc.Agrl. Engring. (chair, biol. engring. divsn., 1999-2000, assoc. editor, Transactions, 2005-), Am. Soc. of Engring. Soc., Inst. Biol. Engring. (councilor, 2000-02, 2003-04), Alpha Epsilon. Achievements include development of methods to predict the rates of nutrient transport and reaction in immobilized cell systems; developed near infrared spectroscopic techniques for bioreactor monitoring; invented a sticker that can tell consumers if a fruit or vegetable is ripe. Office: Dept Agrl and Biosystems Engring U Ariz Shantz Bldg Rm 403 Tucson AZ 85721-0038 Office Phone: 520-626-9120. Office Fax: 520-621-3963. Business E-Mail: riley@ag.arizona.edu.

RILEY, MARY JANE, computer scientist; b. Raleigh, NC, May 26, 1946; d. Charles William and Geraldine Lucile (Adams) Hampton; m. William Walter Schubert, Dec. 30, 1967 (div. June 1979); children: Kristen, Stephen, Betsy, Kathryn; stepchildren: Lee, Scott; m. Jim Riley, Oct. 17, 1998. BA in Math., Park Coll., 1967. Cert. IBM exec. project mgr. Programmer U. Mo. Med. Ctr., Columbia, 1968-72, City and County of Denver, 1979-80; sr. sys. programmer Citicorp Person to Person, Denver, 1980-82; sys. support rep. Software AG, NA, Denver, 1982-83; prin. info. sysm. specialist Idaho Nat. Engring. Lab., EG&G, Idaho Falls, 1983-89; adv. svcs. specialist IBM Profl. Svcs., Albuquerque, 1989-91; field mgr. IBM Svc., Boulder, Colo., 1991-93; project mgr. IBM Global Svcs., Denver, 1993-99; exec. project mgr. IBM Global Svcs. Healthcare, 1999—2002; delivery project exec. IBM Global AMS, Boulder, Colo., 2002—03, IBM, NYC, 2003—06, Calif., 2006—. Presenter career workshop for girls No. Colo. U., Greeley, 1993. Leader Girl Scout Am., Pocatello, Idaho, Columbia, Mo., 1969-79, Idaho Falls, 1986-89, cluster leader, Rigby, Idaho, 1988-89; active Albuquerque Civic Chorus, 1990-91, Luth. Ch. Coun., 1994-96; bd. dirs. LWV, Pocatello, 1977-79, 84-85, 2003—, pres., 1978-79; bd. dirs. Luth. Ch. Women, Pocatello, 1978-79; youth advisor Luth. Ch., Idaho Falls, 1984-89; tchr. Sunday sch. local ch., Albuquerque, 1990-91; youth com. chair local ch., Boulder, Colo., 1994-96; tchr. 7th and 8th grade Sunday sch., 1993-96, mem. ch. choir, 1995-96; mem. Denver Art Mus., Denver Nat. History Mus. Mem. AAUW, LWV. Episcopalian. Avocations: youth work, reading, choir, photography, swimming. Home: PO Box 2030 112 Palmers Dr Silverthorne CO 80498-2030 E-mail: mjriley@us.ibm.com.

RILEY, MARY JANE STEWART, secondary school educator; d. Norman Stewart and Martha Veronica Venzuch; m. Richard Michael Riley, Jan. 11, 1980 (div. Mar. 23, 1987); children: Megan Stewart, Erin Courtney Stewart. BS, We. Mich. U., Kalamazoo, 1967—71; MA in Tchg., Oakland U., Rochester, Mich., 1971—77. Profl. edn. cert. Mich. Guest tchr. Birmingham Pub. Schs., Mich., 1993—95; HS tchr. Ferndale Pub. Schs., Ferndale, Mich., 1995—96; HS tchr. in adult edn. Royal Oak Pub. Schs., Mich., 1995—97; mid. sch. tchr. Sch. Dist. Pontiac, Mich., 1996—. Exec. bd. mem. Mich. Coun. Social Studies (MCSS), Ann Arbor, Mich., 1996—98, state conf. chmn., 1999—2005; state contest judge Mich. Social Studies Olympiad (MSSO), Shelby Twp., Mich., 1996—; tech. writer for curriculum Pontiac Public Schs., 1996—; mem. social studies steering com. Mich. Dept. Edn., 2001—; mem. tchr. del. to Kusatsu, Japan. Chmn. Marine Safety Edn. Commn., Lansing, Mich., 1989—90; mem. house dels. Nat. Coun. Social Studies, 2002. Recipient Top Fellow award, Goethe Inst., 2002. Mem.: Pontiac Edn. Assn. (dir. 2006—, contract labor negotiator, Pontiac Public Schs. 2006—07). Independent Thinkers. Achievements include writing a senate bill in 1989 for boating safety that passed the Michigan state legislature, and signed into law by former Governor James Blanchard, causing boating regulations in other states. Avocations: golf, travel, reading, photography, karaoke. Office: Madison Mid Sch 1275 N Perry St Pontiac MI 48340 Office Phone: 248-451-8010.

RILEY, MONICA, microbiologist, educator; b. New Orleans, Oct. 4, 1926; d. Chauncey Wesley and Maude (Kemper) R.; children: Adam, Christine (dec.), Katherine. BA, Smith Coll., 1947; PhD, U. Calif.-Berkeley, 1960. Asst. prof. U. Calif., Davis, 1960-66; assoc. prof. SUNY-Stony Brook, 1966-75, prof. and provost biol. scis., 1975-78, prof. biochemistry, 1975-89, acting chmn., 1984-85, emeritus prof., 1989—; sr. scientist Marine Biol. Lab., Mass., 1989-06; vis. prof. U. Paris-Sud-Orsay, 1991, 94; mem. program com. for meeting Engineered Organisms in the Environment, 1985; mem. rev. panel NSF; organizer Conf. on Orgn. Bacterial Chromosome, 1988; chair Gordon Rsch. Conf. on Population Biology of Microorganisms, 1989; mem. Recombinant DNA Adv. Com. NIH, 1988-91; lectr. Found. for Microbiology, 1987-88; co-organizer 1st Internat. Conf. on E coli Genome, 1992, organizer 3d conf., 1993-94; organizer Internat. Workshops Annotation Ecoli genome, 2003, 05. Editor: The Bacterial Chromosome, 1990; co-editor: Escherichia coli and Salmonella typhimurium, 2d edit.; contbr. articles to profl. jours., chpts. to books. Bd. dirs. Brookhaven chpt. LWV, N.Y., 1982-87, Falmouth chpt., Mass., 1990-00. Grantee NIH, 1960-00, 05, NSF, 1960-90, DOE, 1999-06. Fellow Am. Acad. Microbiologists; mem. Am. Soc. Microbiology (chmn. com. genetic and molecular microbiology of pub. and sci. affairs bd. 1984-88), Phi Beta Kappa, Sigma Xi. As a graduate student at the University of California at Berkeley in the 1950s, Ms. Riley's work on how genes make protein helped forge the field of Molecular Biology. When the complete DNA sequence of the bacterium Escherichia coli was determined in the mid 1990s, she played an important role by interpreting gene functions from their sequences. As a leader in the field, she organized international workshops in 2003 and 2005 to update the annotation of this model organism, which was a major step toward learning how all the genes of a cell work. Business E-Mail: mriley@mbl.edu.

RILEY, NANCY C., state legislator; b. Tulsa, Okla., June 20, 1958; m. Jerry A. Riley; children: Dan, Robin, Patrick stepchildren: Steve, Phil. Student, Okla. Christian U., 1976-79; BSE, UCT Langston, 1985. Tchr. Tulsa Pub. Schs., 1986—; mem. Okla. Senate from 37th dist., Oklahoma City, 2001—. Active PTA, Berryhill Hoover, S.W. Tulsa Chamber, Sand Springs Chamber, Bixby Chamber, Green Country Campfire Adv. Coun., Interagency Coun. Early Childhood Intervention, Okla. Fedn. Rep. Women, Okla. First Ladies, Tulsa Rep. Men's Club, After Five Rep. Women's Club, Tchr. Recruitment Com. for Minorities. Mem. Tulsa Classroom Tchrs. Assn. (del. 1986-2000), Rolling Oaks Homeowners Assn. (past pres. 1999-2000), Delta Kappa Gamma (sec. 1994-97). Republican. Mailing: State Capitol Bldg Rm 528A 2300 N Lincoln Blvd Oklahoma City OK 73105 E-mail: Rileyn@lsb.state.ok.us.

RILEY, PATRICK JAMES, professional basketball coach, professional sports team executive; b. Rome, NY, Mar. 20, 1945; s. Leon R.; m. Chris Riley; children: James Patrick, Elisabeth Marie. Grad., U. Ky., 1967. Guard San Diego Rockets, 1967-70, Phoenix Suns, 1975-76, LA Lakers, 1970-75, asst. coach, 1979-81, head coach, 1981-90, NY Knicks, 1991-95, Miami Heat, 1995—2003, 2005—, pres. basketball ops., 2003—; broadcaster LA Lakers games Sta. KLAC and Sta. KHJ-TV, 1977-79; broadcaster NBC Sports, 1990-91. Author: Show Time: Inside the Laker's Breakthrough Season, 1988, The Winner Within: A Life Plan for Team Players, 1993. Named NBA Coach of Yr., 1990, 93, 97 Head coach, NBA Champions, LA Lakers, 1982, 85, 87, 88, NBA Champions, Miami Heat, 2006. Achievements include setting the NBA record for most playoff wins (137). Office: Miami Heat Am Airlines Arena 601 Biscayne Blvd Miami FL 33132 *

RILEY, REBECCA MICHELLE, music educator; b. Carthage, Mo., June 23, 1974; d. Russell and Ruby Richmond; m. Ben Lee Riley; children: Raecancia Ann, Matthew Lee. BS in Edn. and Music, Mo. So. State U., 1997; M, William Woods U., Fulton, Mo., 2003. Cert. tchr. Mo. Elem. music tchr. Diamond Elem. Sch., Mo., 1997—2000; music tchr. Jasper HS, Mo., 2000—02, Noel Sch., Mo., 2002—06; music and HS choral tchr. Seneca, Mo., 2006—. Mem.: Mo. State Tchrs. Assn. (assoc.), Music Educators Nat. Conf. (assoc.), Mo. Music Educators Assn. (assoc.). Home Phone: 417-439-8288. Business E-Mail: rriley@seneca.k12.mo.us.

RILEY, RICHARD WILSON, lawyer, former secretary of education; b. Greenville, SC, Jan. 2, 1933; s. Edward Patterson and Martha Elizabeth (Dixon) Riley; m. Ann Osteen Yarborough, Aug. 23, 1957; children: Richard Wilson, Anne Y., Hubert D., Theodore D. BA, Furman U., 1954; JD, U. S.C., 1959. Bar: S.C. 1960. Ptnr. Riley & Riley, Greenville, 1959—78, Nelson, Mullins, Riley & Scarborough, Greenville and Columbia, 1987—93, Greenville, 2001—; gov. State of S.C., 1979—87; sec. U.S. Dept. Edn., Washington, 1993—2001; disting. univ. prof. U. S.C., Columbia, 2001—; disting. prof. govt., politics, and pub. policy Furman U., 2001—. Spl. asst. to subcom. U.S. Senate Jud. Com., 1960; mem. S.C. Ho. of Reps., 1963—66, S.C. Senate from Greenville-Laurens Dist., 1966—76; sr. adv. and chair Richard W. Riley Inst. Govt., Politics and Pub. Leadership, Furman U., 2001—; bd. dirs. ACT (Am. Coll. Testing Program), Laureate Edn., Inc.; bd. trustees Knowledge Works Found., 2001—; trustee Carnegie Corp. N.Y., 2004—, Furman U., 2001—; former bd. dirs. Pub. Broadcasting Svc. (PBS). Lt. (j.g.) USNR, 1954—56. Recipient Dist. Svc. award, Coun. Chief State Sch. Officers, 1994, James Bryant Conant award, Edn. Comm. of the States, 1995, T.H. Bell award for outstanding edn. advocacy, Com. for Edn. Funding, 1996, Dist. Svc. award, Am. Coun. on Edn., 1998; disting. sr. fellow, NAFSA: Assn. Internat. Educators, Wash., D.C. Mem.: Greenville Bar Assn., S.C. Bar Assn., Rotary, Phi Beta Kappa. Office: Nelson Mullins Riley & Scarborough Poinsett Plaza Ste 900 104 S Main St Greenville SC 29601 Office Phone: 864-250-2300. Business E-Mail: dick.riley@nelsonmullins.com.

RILEY, ROBERT BARTLETT, landscape architect; b. Chgo., Jan. 28, 1931; s. Robert James and Ruth (Collins) R.; m. Nancy Reeves Mills, Oct. 5, 1956; children: Rebecca Hill, Kimber Bartlett. PhB, U. Chgo., 1949; BArch, MIT, 1954. Chief designer Kea, Shaw, Grimm & Crichton, Hyattsville, Md., 1959-64; prin. partner Robert B. Riley (A.I.A.), Albuquerque, 1964-70; campus planner, asso. prof. architecture, dir. Center Environ. Research and Devel., U. N.Mex., 1966-70; prof. landscape architecture and architecture U. Ill., Urbana-Champaign, 1970—, head dept. landscape architecture, 1970-85, dir. PhD program, 1999—; vis. prof. Harvard U., 1996-97; prof. emeritus, dir. joint PhD program U. Ill., 1997—. Sr. fellow landscape architecture studies Dumbarton Oaks/Harvard U., 1992—, chmn. fellows, 1996—; mem. rev. panel landscape architects Fed. Civil Service-Nat. Endowment Arts. Assoc. editor Landscape mag., 1967-70; editor Landscape Jour., 1987—. Served with USAF, 1954-58. Nell Norris fellow U. Melbourne, Australia, 1977; project fellow Nat. Endowment Arts, 1985 Fellow Am. Soc. Landscape Architects (Nat. Honor award 1979); mem. Coun. of Educators in Landscape Architecture, pres. 1984-85, chmn. bd. dirs. 1985-86, Outstanding Educator award 1992, Pres.'s award 1994, chmn. editl. adv. bd. Landscape Architecture 1996-99), AIA (Design award Md. 1962, N.Mex. 1968, Environ. Svc. award N.Mex. 1970), Environ. Design Rsch. Assn. (chmn. bd. 1990-91, Career award 2003), Phi Beta Epsilon. Unitarian Universalist. Office: Univ Ill 101 Temple Buell Hall 611 E Lorado Taft Dr Champaign IL 61820-6921 Home: 407 E George Huff Dr Urbana IL 61801-6703 Business E-Mail: rbriley@uiuc.edu.

RILEY, ROBERT H., lawyer; BA, Denison U., 1975; JD, U. Chgo., 1978. Bar: Ill., Wis., U.S. Ct. Appeals (3d and 7th cir.), U.S. Dist. Ct. (no. and ctrl. dist.) Ill. Ptnr., chmn. Schiff Hardin LLP, Chgo. Mem.: ABA, State Bar Wis., Chgo. Bar Assn. Office: Schiff Hardin LLP 233 S Wacker Dr Ste 6600 Chicago IL 60606 Office Phone: 312-258-5664. Office Fax: 312-258-5600. E-mail: rriley@schiffhardin.com. *

RILEY, ROBERT SHEAN, writer, publishing executive, retired army officer; b. West Point, Ky., Oct. 16, 1929; s. Niram Brooks and Nan Estelle (Shean) R.; m. Matsuko Uechi, Mar. 24, 1955; children: Elizabeth Mae, Robert Jr. BS in Engring., U.S. Mil. Acad., 1952; MPA, U. Okla., 1974; M in Internat. Affairs, Columbia U., 1975. Commd. 2d lt. U.S. Army, 1952, advanced through grades to col.; writer, pub. Lawton, Okla., 1978—. Author: History of Shumate Family, 1992, Our European Origins, 1992, History O'Ferrall-Shaen Family, 1994, History of Ditto Families, 1996, The Colonial Riley Families of the Tidewater Frontier, 1999, Marc Hardouin (Mark Hardin) and Descendants, 2003, History of the Woolfolk Family, 2005. Decorated Bronze Star medal with 3 oak leaf clusters, Air medal, Joint Svc. Commendation medal, Meritorious Svc. medal with 1 oak leaf clusters, Army Commendation medal. Mem. Mil. Order of World Wars, West Point Soc., TEXOMA. Home: 6102 NW Lincoln Ave Lawton OK 73505-1319 E-mail: rsriley29@sbcglobal.net.

RILEY, SALLY JEAN, science educator; b. Pasadena, Calif., Feb. 24, 1941; d. Richard Dunlap Hopping and Nelle Bernice Webb-Hopping; m. Robert William Riley, Sept. 27, 1977; children: Stacie Lynn Scripter, Derrick Wayne, Stefanie Lyn Campbell. BA, Calif. State U., LA, 1963; Tchg. Credential, U. Calif., Irvine, Calif., 1982. Social worker County of LA, Covina, Calif., 1967—71, County of Orange, Santa Ana, Calif., 1974—76; sci. tchr. Irvine Unified Sch. Dist., Irvine, Calif., 1982—. Mem. Sch. Site Coun., Irvine, Calif., 1995—. Vol. Pacific Wildlife Orgn., Laguna Niguel, Calif., 2000—04. Mem.: NEA, Calif. Tchrs. Assn., Irvine Tchrs. Assn. R-Liberal. Christian Scientist. Achievements include Dean's List - Univ. Calif., Irvine. Avocations: genealogy, gardening, reading, travel. Office: Venado Mid Sch 4 Deerfield Irvine CA 92604 Home Phone: 949-857-0435; Office Phone: 949-936-6856. Business E-Mail: sriley@iusd.org.

RILEY, THOMAS EDWARD, lawyer; BA, SUNY, Binghamton, 1976; JD, NYU, 1979. Bar: NY 1980, US Dist. Ct. (so. dist.) NY 1983, US Dist. Ct. (ea. dist.) NY 1983, US Dist. Ct. Ariz. 1992, US Ct. Appeals (4th cir.) 1995, US Ct. Appeals (6th cir.) 1998, US Dist. Ct. (no. dist.) NY 2002, US Ct. Appeals (3rd cir.) 2004, US Ct. Appeals (2nd cir.) 2004. Staff atty. Mfrs. Hanover Trust Co., NYC, 1979-80; law clk. to presiding justice US Dist. Ct. (We. Dist.) NY, Buffalo, 1980-82; with Chadbourne & Parke LLP, NYC, 1982—, ptnr., head litig. dept., mem. mgmt. com. Staff mem. NYU Jour. Internat. Law & Politics, 1977—78, rsch. editor, 1978—79; contbr. articles to profl. jours. Bd. dirs. U. Settlement Soc. of NY, 1992—2004. Mem.: ABA (product liability com., litigation sect.), Internat. Assn. Def. Counsel (mem. Amicus Curiae com.), NY State Bar Assn. Office: Chadbourne & Parke LLP 30 Rockefeller Plz Fl 31 New York NY 10112-0129 Office Phone: 212-408-5408. Office Fax: 212-541-5369. Business E-Mail: triley@chadbourne.com.

RILEY, THOMAS JOSEPH, anthropologist, academic administrator; b. Portland, Maine, Nov. 2, 1943; s. Joseph Gerard and Virginia C. (Cunningham) R.; m. Karma Jean Ibsen, July 10, 1967 (div. 1985); children: Kirsten, Katharine, Erin; m. Carol Ann, Nov. 21, 1989; 1 child, Julia Wade. BA, Boston Coll., 1965; MA, U. Hawaii, 1970, PhD, 1973. Asst. prof. NYU, 1972—74; from asst. prof. to prof. anthropology U. Ill., Urbana, 1974—96; dean Coll. Arts, Humanities/Social Scis., prof. anthropology N.D. State U., Fargo, 1996—. Acad. adv. bd. SALT Ctr., Portland, 1980-96; assoc. dean Grad. Coll. U. Ill., 1983-86, head dept. anthropology, 1986-93, chmn. senate coun., 1995-96; dir. N.D. Inst. Regional Studies, 1996—. Co-author: Prehistoric Agriculture, 1972; mem. editl. bd. Ency. World Cultures, 1993-96, Ency. Cultural Anthropology, 1994-95, Ency. World Pre-history, 1996-2001; contbr. over 100 articles to profl. jours Chmn. bd. Devel. Svcs. Ctr., Champaign, 1986—89, Human Rels. Area Files at Yale U., 1985—96, v.p., 1995, pres., 1996; sec. bd. C-U Independence, Champaign, 1987—96; bd. dirs. Disabled Citizens Found., Champaign, 1988—96, Ill. Assn. Retarded Citizens, Chgo., 1988—94, Champaign County Mental Health Bd., 1993—96, Prairie Pub. Broadcasting, 1999—2005, Plains Art Mus., Fargo, vice-chair, 2001—05, chair, 2005—06; bd. dirs. ND State Hist. Soc. Found., 2001—, Ill. State Hist. Sites Adv. Coun., 1986—89, United Way Cass-Clay, 2001—. Fellow, NSF, 1978—79; grantee, 1978—99. Mem. AAAS, Am. Assn. State and Local History, Am. Anthropology Assn., Ill. Archeol. Survey, Soc. Am. Archaeology, Soc. Archeol. Scis. (treas. 1982-83), Sigma Xi (chpt. v.p. 1987-88, chpt. pres. 1988-91) Roman Catholic. Office: ND State U 221 Minard Hall Fargo ND 58105 Office Phone: 701-231-8338. Business E-Mail: thomas.riley@ndsu.edu.

RILEY, TOM JOSEPH, lawyer; b. Cedar Rapids, Iowa, Jan. 9, 1929; s. Joseph Wendell and Edna (Kyle) R.; m. Nancy Evans, Jan. 21, 1952; children: Pamela Chang, Peter, Lisa Thirnbeck, Martha Brown, Sara Riley, Heather Mescher. BA, U. Iowa, 1950, JD, 1952. Bar: Iowa 1952, U.S. Dist. Ct. (no. dist.) Iowa 1952, U.S. Ct. Appeals (8th cir.) 1960, U.S. Ct. Appeals (7th cir.) 1977, U.S. Ct. Appeals (9th cir.) 1996, U.S. Supreme Ct. 1966. Assoc. Simmons, Perrine, Allbright & Ellwood, Cedar Rapids, 1952-60, ptnr., 1960-80; pres. Tom Riley Law Firm, P.C., Cedar Rapids, 1980—. Adj. prof. trial advocacy Coll. Law, U. Iowa, Iowa City, 1979. Author: Proving Punitive Damages, 1981, The Price of a Life, 1986, Trial Handbook for Iowa Lawyers (Civil), 1997, Iowa Practice: Civil Litigation Handbook, 2003, 5th rev. edit., 2007. Active Iowa Ho. of Reps., 1960-64, Iowa Senate, 1965-74. First lt. USAF, 1952-54. Named Outstanding Freshman Legislator, Des Moines Press and Radio Club, 1961. Fellow Iowa Acad. Trial Lawyers (bd. govs. 1982-91); mem. Iowa Trial Lawyers Assn. (bd. govs. 2000-2002), Cedar Rapids Country Club. Democrat. Presbyterian. Avocations: tennis, sailing. Home: 5300 Lakeside Rd Rural Route Marion IA 52302 Office: 4040 1st Ave NE Cedar Rapids IA 52402-3143 Home Phone: 319-377-6512; Office Phone: 319-363-4040. Business E-Mail: ellena@trlf.com.

RILEY, WAYNE JOSEPH, academic administrator, medical educator; b. New Orleans, May 3, 1959; s. Emile E. Jr. and Jacqueline Jean (Cerf) R.; m. Charlene Maria Dewey, May 1, 1959; children: Erin Elizabeth, Alexis Camille. BA in Med. Anthropology, Yale U., New Haven, 1981; MPH in Health Systems Mgmt., Tulane U., 1988; MD, Morehouse Sch. Medicine, Atlanta, 1993; MBA, Rice U., 2002. Adminstrv. asst. to mayor City New Orleans, 1981—86, exec. asst., 1986; instr. sect. gen. internal medicine to v.p., vice dean health affairs and govtl. rels. and assoc. prof. medicine Baylor Coll. Medicine, Houston, 1996—2006, asst. dean edn., 2000—04; asst. chief medicine, practicing gen. internist Ben Taub Gen. Hosp., Houston; mem. med. staff, attending physician Michael E. DeBakey Vet. Affairs Med. Ctr., Meth. Hosp., St. Luke's Episcopal Hosp.; pres. Meharry Med. Coll., Nashville, 2007—. Adv. bd. La. State U., 1993; adj. prof. mgmt. Rice U. Jesse H. Jones Grad. Sch. Mgmt.; chmn. Harris County Hosp. Dist. Med. Bd., 2003. Mem. Am. Coll. Physicians (assoc., vice chair coun. assocs. 1995-96, health & pub. policy com. 1996), Yale Club Houston, Morehouse Sch. Medicine Nat. Alumni Assn., Alpha Phi Alpha. Roman Catholic. Avocations: jazz, golf, reading. Office: Meharry Med Coll 1005 Dr DB Todd Jr Blvd Nashville TN 37208-3599 Office Phone: 615-327-6904. Office Fax: 615-327-6540. *

RILEY, WILLIAM JAY, federal judge; b. Lincoln, Nebr., Mar. 11, 1947; s. Don Paul and Marian Frances (Munn) R.; m. Norma Jean Mason, Dec. 27, 1965; children: Brian, Kevin, Erin. BA, U. Nebr., 1969, JD with distinction, 1972. Bar: Nebr. 1972, US Dist. Ct. Nebr. 1972, US Ct. Appeals (8th cir.) 1974; cert. civil trial specialist Nat. Bd. Trial Advocacy, 1994-2004. Law clk. US Ct. Appeals (8th cir.), Omaha, 1972-73; assoc. Fitzgerald, Schorr Law Firm, P.C., LLO, Omaha, 1973-79; shareholder Fitzgerald, Schorr Law Firm, Omaha, 1979—2001; judge US Ct. Appeals (8th cir.), 2001—. Adj. prof. trial practice Creighton U. Coll. Law, Omaha, 1991—. Nebr. Law Sch., Lincoln, 2006-; chmn. fed. practice com. Fed. Ct., 1992-94; mme. criminal law com. Jud. Conf. US, 2005—. Scoutmaster Boy Scouts Am., Omaha, 1979—89, scout membership chair Mid. Am. coun., 1995—98, trustee, 2001—. Recipient Silver Beaver award Boy Scouts Am., 1991. Fellow Am. Coll. Trial Lawyers (chair state com.

1997-99), Nebr. State Bar Found.; mem. Am. Bd. Trial Advs. (Nebr. chpt. pres. 2000), Nebr. State Bar Assn. (chmn. ethics com. 1996-98, ho. of dels. 1998—, profl. com. 2002—), Omaha Bar Assn. (treas. 1997-98, pres. 2000-01), Robert M. Spire Inns of Ct. (master 1994—2001, counselor 1997-98, 2007-, jud. mem. 2001-07), Order of Coif, Phi Beta Kappa. Republican. Methodist. Avocations: reading, hiking, bicycling. Office: Roman L Hruska US Courthouse 111 S 18th Plaza Ste 4303 Omaha NE 68102-1325 Office Phone: 402-661-7575. *

RILEY, WILLIAM JOHN, neurologist; b. Seattle, Oct. 24, 1930; s. William John and Virginia (McCarthy) R.; m. Joan Marie Weismann, 1956 (div. 1976); children: Sean, Kevan, Megan, Janeen, Michael; m. Margit Mary Winstrom, 1976; children: Britta, Shane, Timothy. MS in Anatomy, U. Chgo., 1958, MD, 1960; PhD, U. Minn., 1965. Intern Mpls. Gen. Hosp., 1961-62; resident U. Minn. Hosps., 1962-65; asst. chief neurology Mpls. Gen. Hosp., 1965-69; chief neurology St. Luke's Episcopal Hosp., Houston, 1970-85; pres., CEO Tex. Neurol. Clinic Assn., Houston, 1969—. Staff sgt. USAF, 1951-55. Recipient Disting. Tchg. award Minn. Med. Found., Mpls., 1969. Fellow: ACP, Tex. Neurol. Soc. (pres. 2002—, Lifetime Achievement award 2005), Am. Acad. Neurology; mem.: Alpha Omega Alpha, AMA, Tex. Med. Assn. (pres. 9th dist. 1991), Sigma Xi. Roman Catholic. Avocation: ranching. Office: Tex Neurol Clinic Assn 4126 SW Freeway # 1210 Houston TX 77027-7306 Office Phone: 713-621-9291. Personal E-mail: wjrileymd@earthlink.net.

RILLING, DAVID CARL, surgeon; b. Phila., Oct. 10, 1940; s. Carl Adam and Elizabeth Barbara (Young) R.; m. Karina Sturman, Mar. 25, 1972; children: Jonathan David, Alexander Valentine, Claudia Carla. BS with honors in Biology, Dickinson Coll., Carlisle, pa., 1962; MD, Hahnemann U., 1966. Diplomate Am. Bd. Surgery. Intern Hosp. of U. Pa., Phila., 1966-67; resident Abington (Pa.) Meml. Hosp., 1967-68, 70-73; surgeon Pennridge Surg Assocs., Sellersville, Pa., 1973—. Active staff Grand View Hosp., Sellersville, Pa., chmn. dept. surgery, 1985-89, pres. med. staff, 1995. Lt. col. U.S. Army, 1968-70, Vietnam, USARMC. Decorated Bronze Star medal, Nat. Def. Svc. medal, Vietnam Svc. medal. Fellow Am. Coll. Surgeons; mem. AMA, Soc. Clin. Vascular Surgery, Pa. Med. Soc., Bucks County Med. Soc., Vietnam Vascular Registry. Achievements include one of the first surgeons to successfully re-attach a completely severed upper arm in 1974. Avocations: paleontology, tennis, skiing. Office: Pennridge Surg Assocs 670 Lawn Ave Sellersville PA 18960-1571 Office Phone: 215-257-3697.

RILLING, JOHN ROBERT, history professor; b. Wausau, Wis., Apr. 28, 1932; s. John Peter and Esther Laura (Wittig) R.; m. Joanne Marilyn McCrory, Dec. 21, 1953; children: Geoffrey Alan, Andrew Peter. BA summa cum laude, U. Minn., 1953; AM, Harvard U., 1957, PhD, 1959. Asst. prof. history U. Richmond, Va., 1959-62, assoc. prof. history, 1962-68, prof. history, 1968-99, prof. English history emeritus, 1999—, chmn. dept. history, 1977-83, Westhampton Coll., 1965-71. Pres. Faculty Senate of Va., 1975—77. Contbr. articles to profl. jours. Elder, Ginter Park Presbyn. Ch., 1973-83. Served with U.S. Army, 1953-55. Recipient U. Richmond Disting. Educator award, 1975, 76, 77, 80, 87, Prof. of Yr. finalist Coun. for Advancement and Support of Edn., 1981. Woodrow Wilson fellow, 1955-59; Harvard U. travelling fellow, 1958; Coolidge fellow, 1955-56; Folger Libr. fellow, 1960. Mem.: Agecroft Assn. (bd. dir.), Am. Hist. Assn., Omicron Delta Kappa (Prof. of Yr. 1995), Phi Beta Kappa. Avocations: hiking, bicycling, enology. Home: 1507 Wilmington Ave Richmond VA 23227-4429 Office: U Richmond Dept History Richmond VA 23173 Business E-Mail: jrilling@richmond.edu.

RIMA, INGRID HAHNE, economics professor; b. Germany; d. Max F. and Hertha G. (Grunsfeld) Hahne; m. Philip W. Rima; children: David, Eric. BA with honors, CUNY, 1945; MA, U. Pa., 1946, PhD, 1951. Prof. econs. Temple U., Phila., 1967—. Author: Development of Economic Analysis, 1967, 6th edit., 2000, Labor Markets Wages and Employment, 1981, The Joan Robinson Legacy, 1991, The Political Economy of Global Restructuring, Vol. I, Production and Organization, Vol. II, Trade and Finance, 1993, Measurement, Quantification and Economic Analysis, 1994, Labor Markets in a Global Economy, 1996. Fulbright Disting. Lectr., Lingnan U., China, 2000. Fellow Ea. Econ. Assn.; mem. Am. Econ. Assn., History of Econs. Soc. (pres. 1993-4), Phi Beta Kappa (pres. chpt. 2006). Office: Temple U Broad & Montgomery Ave Philadelphia PA 19122 Personal E-mail: irima@aol.com.

RIMEL, IRA WESLEY, writer, US Navy supply officer, real estate specialist, real estate appraiser, real estate broker; b. Wibaux, Mont., Jan. 10, 1921; s. Ira Dice and Hazel Barbara (Webber) Rimel; m. Mary Mackinlay, Dec. 13, 1943 (div.); children: Patricia, Valerie, Linda, David, Glenn. Basic sci./engring, Mont. Sch. Mines, 1943—44; BA in mgmt./acctg., U. Wash., 1943—47; Navy supply, acctg. grad., Harvard Grad. Sch. Bus., 1945—46; nat. security, econ., Indust. Coll. Armed Forces, 1965. Tech. writer Military Manuals Co., Renton, Wash., 1952—55; indsl. agent No. Pacific Railway, Seattle, 1955—58; right of way agent/supr. Mont. Hwy. Dept., Helena, 1958—65; right of way agent Lane County, Eugene, Oreg., 1965—86; columnist Fishing & Hunting News, Seattle, 1992—95; freelance writer, 1956—. Ensign, reserve, supply, disbursing, acctg. officer U.S. Navy Naval Prison, Norfolk, Va., 1946; LTJG supply officer liaison U.S. Navy, Republic of Korea, 1950—51. Author: (short stories) Dynamic Tension, 1990 (First Prize, 1990), Lucky Man, 2002 (Best of Show/Class, 2002), Winter Travel, 2002 (First Prize, 2002). Adj., publicity officer/comdr. Disabled Am. Vet., Renton, Wash., 1952—58, Wash. publicity officer Seattle, 1953—58; lifetime mem. VFW, Marcola, Oreg., 1960—2003. Lt. jr. grade USN, 1942—46, WWII, Korea, lt. jr. grade USN, 1950—51, WWII, Japan, selected for V-12 Coll. Prog. USN. Named rep. to Rep. Korea, Yokosuka, Japan, Celebration of Commissioning Frigates to Korea, U.S. Navy, 1950; recipient corr., Mont. Sports Outdoors, Missoula, 1959, Author "Lady Gets Her Buck", 1959. Mem.: DAV. Avocations: hunting, fishing, boating, horseback riding, gardening.

RIMEL, REBECCA WEBSTER, foundation administrator; b. 1951; BS, U. Va., 1973; MBA, James Madison U., 1983. Head nurse, emergency dept. U. Va. Hosp., Charlottesville, 1973-74, coord. med. out-patient dept., 1974-75, nurse practitioner dept. neurosurgery, 1975-77, instr. in neurosurgery, 1975-80, asst. prof., 1981-83; program mgr. health Pew Charitable Trusts, Phila., 1983-84; asst. v.p. Glenmede Trust Co., Pew Charitable Trusts, Phila., 1984-85; v.p. for programs Pew Charitable Trusts, Phila., 1985-88, exec. dir., 1988-94, pres., CEO, 1994—. Mem. Coun. on Founds., Washington; prin. investigator dept. neurosurgery U. Va., 1981—83; adv. com. Boxing U.S. Olympics, 1983—86; adv. coun. Nat. Inst. of Neurol. Disorders and Strokes, 1988—91, bd. dirs., Thomas Jefferson Meml. Found., Deutsche Banc Flag Investors Fund, VIASYS Healthcare Inc., 2007—. Contbr. chpts. in books, articles and abstracts to profl. jours. Recipient Disting. Nursing Alumni award, U. Va., 1988; fellow Kellogg Nat. fellow, 1992. Mem.: APHA, ANA, Va. State Nurses Assn. (membership and credentials com. 1982—86), Emergency Dept. Nurses Assn., Am. Assn. Neurosurg. Nurses, Am. Acad. Nursing. Address: The Pew Charitable Trusts 2005 Market St Ste 1700 Philadelphia PA 19103-7017 *

RIMER, BARBARA K., health facility administrator, educator, dean; b. Wilkes Barre, Pa., Jan. 14, 1949; married. BA in English, U. Mich., 1970, MPH in Med. Care Adminstrn. and Health Edn., 1973; PhD in Health Edn., Johns Hopkins Sch. of Hygiene and Public Health, 1981. Instr. Wayne State U. Sch. Medicine, Detroit, 1973-75; program dir. Nat. Cancer Inst., Bethesda, Md., 1975-77; intervention coord. Johns Hopkins Oncology Ctr., Balt., 1977-79; rsch. assoc. Johns Hopkins Sch. Hygiene and Public Health, Balt., 1977-79; sr. health educator Fox Chase Cancer Ctr., Phila., 1981-87, dir. health comms. rsch., 1981-87, dir. behavioral rsch., 1987-91, dir. population sci. for behavioral rsch., 1990-91; dir. cancer prevention, detection and ctrl. rsch. Duke Comprehensive Cancer Ctr., Durham, NC, 1991-97; sr. fellow Aging Ctr. Duke U. Med. Ctr., Durham, NC, 1991-97, assoc. prof. in cmty. and family medicine, 1991-93, prof. cmty. and family medicine, 1993-97; acting dep. dir. Duke Comprehensive Cancer Ctr., Durham, NC, 1995-96; dir. cancer ctrl. and population scis. Nat. Cancer Inst., Rockville, Md., 1997—2002; dep. dir., population sciences, Lineberger Cancer Ctr. UNC, Chapel Hill, 2003—05, alumni disting. prof., Dept. Health Behavior & Health Edn., 2003—, dean, Sch. Pub. Health, 2005—. Adj. assoc. prof. dept. health behavior and health edn. U. N.C. Sch. of Public Health, Chapel Hill, NC, 1992-97; adj. mem. Fox Chase Cancer Ctr., Phila., 1992-97; preceptor, lectr. Temple U., 1983-91; guest lectr. Duke U. Med. Ctr., 1991-97, U. N.C. Sch. Public Health, 1991-93; Judith P. Schlager vis. prof. Dana-Farber Cancer Inst., 1995; disting. vis. lectr. Harvard U., 1998; mem. institutional review bd. Fox Chase Cancer Ctr., 1983-88, vice chair, 1988-91; proposal review, site visitor Nat. Cancer Inst., 1985-95; chairperson tech. advisory com. Am. Lung Assn., 1987; external advisory com. Vermont Regional Cancer Ctr., 1988-89; advisory com. Brown U., U. R.I. Cancer Prevention Rsch. unit, 1988-95; mem. Am. Assn. Retired Persons task force on smoking, 1989-91, Health Promotion adv. bd. Wesley Found., 1990-91, program com. annual mtg. Am. Soc. Preventive Oncology, 1990-93, chair, 1993 mtg., expert adv. com. AMC Cancer Rsch. Ctr./Ctrs. for Disease Ctrl. Coop. Agreement, 1991, adult edn. subcom. and tobacco materials review group Am. Cancer Soc., 1991; mem. Nat. Task Force on Breast Cancer Ctrl. Am. Cancer Soc., 1992, chair Nat. and State (NC) Task Force on Breast Cancer Ctrl., 1992; mem. Pub. Edn. subcom. on Adult Edn. Am. Cancer Soc., 1992; mem. adv. bd. Office of Cancer Comms., NCI, 1992; mem. Clin. Cancer com. Duke U. Med. Ctr., 1992-95; mem. Cancer Ctrs.' Support com. NCI, 1993-94, Recruitment and Adherence com. Office of Women's Health NIH, 1993, Report com. Internat. Workshop on Screening for breast cancer NCI, 1993, Detection and Treatment subcom. on Breast Cancer Am. Cancer Soc., 1993, 94, Nominating com. Soc. Behavioral Medicine, 1993-96, adv. com. on cancer coordination and ctrl. State of NC, 1993-97; invited participant and com. chair Frontiers of Behavioral Medicine mtg., Chantilly, Va., 1993; invited co-chair Sec. Shalala's Mtg. to develop nat. strategic plan for breast cancer, Bethesda, Md., 1993; chair, mem. Nat. Cancer Adv. Bd. (presdl. appointment), 1994-97; bd. dirs. Am. Family Life Assurance Corp., 1995—; fellowship selection com. Am. Assn. Cancer Rsch., 1996; mem. exec. com. Acad. Behavioral Medicine Rsch., 1998, Charles S. Mott Selection com. of Gen. Motors Cancer Rsch. Found., 1999, Inst. Medicine com. effective health comm. and behavior change strategies for diverse populations, 2000. Editor: special cancer issue Health Education Research, 1998-89; editl. bd. Health Education Quarterly, 1985-87, guest editl. bd. 1983; editl. bd. Jour. of Compliance in Health Care, 1989-90, Health Edn. Rsch., 1990-98, Cancer Prevention, Epidemiology and Biomarkers, 1990—, Patient Edn. and Counseling, 1994—, Breast Diseases, 1998—, Cancer Causes and Control, 1998—, Effective Clin. Practice, 2000—; assoc. editor: Preventive Medicine, 1990—; reviewer Am. Jour. Preventive Medicine, Am. Jour. Public Health, Annals of Internal Medicine, Health Edn. Quarterly, Health Services Research, Jour. of Am. Med. Assn., Jour. Nat. Cancer Inst., Milbank Quarterly, Women's Health, 1986—; contbr. numerous articles, papers to profl. pubs. Fellow Johns Hopkins Sch. of Hygiene and Public Health, 1979-81, Soc. of Behavioral Medicine, 1997; recipient Mayhew Derryberry award Am. Public Health Assn., 1992, Best Visual Presentation of Session award Soc. of Behavioral Medicine, San Diego, 1995, Citation award Soc. Behavioral Medicine, 1996, Disting. Achievement award Am. Soc. Preventive Oncology, 1997, Herbert J. Block Leadership award Ohio State U., 1997, John P. McGovern award in Health Promotion U. Tex. Sch. Public Health, 1999. Office: Sch Public Health Univ North Carolina 170 Rosenau Hall Campus Box 7400 Chapel Hill NC 27599-7400 Office Phone: 919-966-3215. Office Fax: 919-966-7678. E-mail: brimer@unc.edu.

RIMER, JOHN THOMAS, language educator, academic administrator, writer; b. Pitts., Mar. 2, 1933; s. John T. and Naomi (Bowser) R.; m. Laurence E. Mus., Apr. 18, 1964; children: John, Mark. BA, Princeton U., 1954; MA, Columbia U., 1969, PhD, 1971. Asst. cultural officer USIA, Laos, Japan; then dir. Am. Cultural Ctr. Kobe, Japan, 1958-67; assoc. prof., then prof. Japanese lang. and lit. Washington U., St. Louis, 1973-83, chmn. dept. Chinese and Japanese, 1973-83; chief Asian div. Library of Congress, Washington, 1983-86; chmn. Hebrew and East Asian langs. and lits. U. Maryland, College Park, 1986-91; chmn. East Asian langs. and lits. U. Pitts., 1991—2005; ret., 2005. Author: Toward a Modern Japanese Theatre, 1974, Traditions in Modern Japanese Fiction, 1978; translator: stories Mori Ogai, 2 vols., 1977, Mask and Sword: Two Plays for the Contemporary Japanese Theatre, 1980, On the No Drama, 1983, Pilgrimages, 1988, A Reader's Guide to Japanese Literature, 1988; editor: Multiple Meanings, 1987; editor, contbr.: Culture and Identity, Japanese Intellectuals during the Interwar Years, 1990, Shisendo, 1991, Youth and Other Stories by Mori Ogai, 1994, Kyoto Encounters, 1995, A Hidden Fire: Russian and Japanese Cultural Encounters, 1868-1929, 1995, The Blue-eyed Tarōkaja: Essays by Donald Keene, 1996, Nara Encounters, 1997, The Voyage of Japanese Theatre: Theatre Criticism of Senda Akihiko, 1997, Poems to Sing: The Wakan Rōeishū, 1997; (with Jonathan J. Mayo) War, Occupation, and Creativity: Japan and East Asia 1920-1960, 2001, Collected Writings of J. Thomas Rimer, 2004; (with Van Gessel) The Columbia Anthology of Modern Japanese Literature, vol. 1, 2005, vol. 2, 2007; (with Stephen Addiss and Gerald Groemer) Traditional Japanese Arts and Cultures: An Illustrated Sourcebook, 2006. Served with U.S. Army, 1955-58. NEH fellow France, 1976-77; NEH grantee, 1979-81; recipient Order of the Sacred Treasure award Japanese Govt., 1997. Episcopalian. Home: 4319 Redwood #1 Marina Del Rey CA 90292-7643

RIMKUNAS, BARBARA, historian, educator; b. May 4, 1963; BA in History, U. Maine, Orono, 1985; Ma in History, U. NH, Durham, 1993. Field rsch. asst. archaeology U. Maine, 1984; tchr. social studies Catherine McAuley HS, Portland, Maine, 1986—89, Newmarket HS, NH, 1997—99; curator Exeter Hist. Soc., NH, 2000—. Author: (column) Historically Speaking, 2004—, (book preface) Exeter - Squamscott River of Many Uses, 2004—, Exeter Newsletter, 2004—. Bd. trustees NH Archives Group, 2003—, 1st Unitarian Soc. Exeter, 2004—. Office: Exeter Hist Soc PO Box 924 Exeter NH 03833-924

RIMLAND, LISA PHILLIP, writer, composer, lyricist; b. Stamford, Conn., Mar. 27, 1954; d. Maurice Louis and Eva (Kreiz) R. BA, U. Conn., 1978. Owner Ph Rimland Press, Storrs, Conn., 1991—. Composer numerous songs, including Your Heart or Mine, 1990, Drive Me Crazy, 1991, Send Me an Angel, 1992, Geography of Heaven, 1990, 2002, The Winds of Time (The Cloning Song), 2003; author: The Candida Manual: Candida Overgrowth and the Quest for Human Wellness, 1999, Voices From the Farm, 1999, Machronomarker Observations Conducted During the First Three Months of the Life of a Cloned Heifer Dairy Calf, 2000, An Evaluation of Machronomarker Observations, 2001, Amy and Aspen: Behavioral Observations of a Cloned Holstein Cow and Her Genetic Donor Living Together In Pasture, 2003, Betty and Cathy With Aspen In Summer, 2004, Behavioral Observations of Two Cloned Holstein Cows and Their Genetic Donor Living Together in Pasture, 2006; contbr. articles, poems, essays to profl. jours. Vol. dairy barn U. Conn., 1992—, vol. photographer Morgan horse facility, 1982-91. Recipient DAR award, 1969, Soc. Women Engrs. award, 1971, Editor's Choice award Nat. Libr. Poetry, 1995, 96; Nat. Merit scholar, 1972. Mem. ASCAP. Avocations: film and drama, art, poetry, athletics, morgan horses. Home: PO Box 408 Storrs Mansfield CT 06268-0408

RIMLER, ANITA A., former state official; b. 1944; m. George W. Rimler. Campaign aide, legis. asst. former Del. Rob James, 1975; asst. to atty. gen. Mary Sue Terrry State of Va., Richmond, 1985—91; dir. fin. ops. Terry for Gov. campaign, 1993, Robb for Senate campaign, 1994, Warner's U.S. Senate campaign, 1996; sr. advisor, dir. fin. ops. Warner for Gov. campaign; sec. of state State of Va., Richmond, 2002—06. Democrat.

RIMOIN, DAVID LAWRENCE, medical geneticist; b. Montreal, Nov. 9, 1936; s. Michael and Fay (Lecker) Rimoin; m. Mary Ann Singleton, 1962 (div. 1979); 1 child, Anne; m. Ann Piilani Garber, July 27, 1980; children: Michael, Lauren. BSc, McGill U., Montreal, 1957, MSc, MD, CM, 1961; PhD, Johns Hopkins U., 1967; LHD (hon.), Finch U., 1997. Asst. prof. medicine, pediat. Washington U., St. Louis, 1967—70; assoc. prof. UCLA, 1970—73, prof., 1973—, chief med. genetics, Harbor-UCLA Med. Ctr., 1970—86; chair dept. pediat., dir. Med. Genetics and Birth Defects Ctr. Cedars-Sinai Med. Ctr., LA, 1986—2004, Steven Spielberg chair, 1989—, dir. Med. Genetics Inst., 2004—. Chmn. coun. Med. Genetics Orgn., 1993. Co-editor: Emory and Rimoin's Principles and Practice of Medical Genetics, 1983, 5th edit., 2007; contbr. chapters to books, articles to profl. jours. Recipient E. Mead Johnson award, Am. Acad. Pediat., 1976, Col. Harland Saunders award, March of Dimes, 1997, Pioneer in Medicine award, Cedars Sinai Med. Ctr., 2001, Extraordinary Merit award, UCLA Med. Alumni Assn., 2005, Legends Harbor award, LA Biomed. Found., 2006, Leadership award, Am. Soc. Human Genetics, 2006. Fellow: Am. Coll. Med. Genetics (pres. 1991—96, bd. dirs. 1996—2000), AAAS, ACP; mem.: Inst. of Medicine, Assn. Am. Physicians, Am. Pediat. Soc., Am. Soc. Human Genetics (pres. 1984, Leadership award 2006), Am. Bd. Med. Genetics (pres. 1979—83), Western Soc. Pediat. Rsch. (pres. 1995, Ross Outstanding Young Investigator award 1976), Western Soc. Clin. Rsch. (pres. 1978), Am. Fedn. Clin. Rsch. (sec.-treas. 1972—75), Am. Coll. Med. Genetics Found. (pres. 1999—2002, bd. dirs. 2002—), Johns Hopkins Soc. Scholars. Office: Cedars Sinai Med Ctr 8700 Beverly Blvd Los Angeles CA 90048-1865 Office Phone: 310-423-4461. Business E-Mail: david.rimoin@cshs.org.

RIMPEL, AUGUSTE EUGENE, JR., management and technical consulting executive; b. St. Thomas, V.I., Aug. 25, 1939; s. Auguste Eugene and Leah Eudora (Harris) R. B.A. magna cum laude, Inter-Am. U. P.R., 1957; M.S. in Ch.E., MIT, Cambridge, Mass., 1961; Ph.D., Carnegie Inst. Tech., 1964; M.B.A., Columbia U., NYC, 1964-65; m. Maria Czernetski, Sept. 23, 1966; children: Nicole, Christopher. Research chem. engr. Am. Cyanamid Co., Stamford, Conn., 1961-62; with Arthur D. Little, Inc., Cambridge, Mass., 1965-75, sr. staff mem., 1973-75; commr. of commerce, spl. advisor to gov. for econ. affairs Govt. U.S. V.I., St. Thomas, 1975-78; mem. corp. spl. staff Arthur D. Little, Inc., Cambridge, 1978-81, also v.p. Arthur D. Little Internat., Inc.; v.p. Booz-Allen and Hamilton, Inc., 1981-83; v.p., ptnr., Price Waterhouse, 1983-98, ptnr. Price Waterhouse Coopers, 1998—. sr. partner Boston Global Partners, 2001-; Bd. dirs. Caribbean/Lat. Am. Action, 1979-; chair, bd. dirs. U. V.I., 1997—; mem. subcoms. on internat. econ. devel. US C. of C., 1980-83; bd. dirs. travel adv. bd. U.S. Dept. Commerce, 1977-78; pres. Caribbean Tourism Assn., 1977-78; bd. dirs., mem. exec. com. Caribbean Tourism Research Center, 1976-78. Mem. Am. Inst. Chem. Engrs., Am. Chem. Soc., Am. Inst. Chemists, Soc. Internat. Devel., Sigma Xi. Office: Ste 400 283 Franklin St Boston MA 02103-1195 Personal E-mail: arimpel@aol.com.

RIMSZA, SKIP, former mayor; b. Chgo. m. Kim Gill; children: Brian, Jenny, Alexander, Taylor, Nicole. Mem. Phoenix City Coun., 1990-94; vice mayor City of Phoenix, 1993, mayor, 1994—2003. Former pres. Bd. Realtors. Mem. several cmty. bds.

RINACA, JAMES M., lawyer; b. Harrisonburg, Va., Dec. 12, 1950; BS in Nuclear Engring. with highest distinction, Univ. Va., 1973, JD, 1976. Bar: Va. 1976. Ptnr., regulated industries, govtl. rels.; co-head, energy, telecom. team Hunton & Williams LLP, Richmond, Va. Mem.: ABA, Va. Engring. Found. (past pres., bd. dir.), Va. State Bar Assn., Richmond Bar Assn., Raven Soc., Omicron Delta Kappa, Tau Beta Pi. Office: Hunton & Williams LLP Riverfront Plz East Tower 951 Byrd St Richmond VA 23219-4074 Office Phone: 804-788-8334. Office Fax: 804-788-8218. Business E-Mail: jrinaca@hunton.com.

RINAKER, SAMUEL MAYO, JR., retired utilities executive; b. Chgo., Sept. 29, 1922; s. Samuel Mayo and Marjorie (Horton) R.; m. Alice Benthey, Dec. 17, 1949 (div. 1974); children: Elizabeth Cherry, Samuel M. III, Laura Frazier, Mary Clark. Student, UCLA, 1941-42. Farmer, Nebr. and Ill., 1946-49; exec. sec. to atty. gen. Olympia, Wash., 1949-52; news dir. Sta. KTNT-TV, Tacoma, Wash., 1952-57, Sta. KIRO-TV, Seattle, 1957-60; assoc. news dir., news anchor Sta. KGTV, San Diego, 1960-75; dir. pub. policy San Diego Gas & Electric Co., 1976-84. Bd. dirs. 1st Nat. Bank, Beatrice, Neb., 1976-93. Maj. U.S. Army Air Corps, 1942-46, ETO. Mem. Rotary (bd. dirs. 1965-67), La Jolla Beach Tennis Club. Republican. Presbyterian. Avocation: golf. Home: 5935 Rutgers Rd La Jolla CA 92037-7834 E-mail: smr11@san.rr.com.

RINALDI, JAMES J., federal agency administrator; BA in computer sci., U. North Fla. Various positions ending as sr. v.p. info. resources, ops. and services Marriott Corp., Bethesda, Md.; dir. e-Govt. program office, chief info. tech. services IRS, Washington; chief info. officer FDA, Rockville, Md., NASA Jet Propulsion Lab., Pasadena, Calif., 2005—. Named one of Premier 100 IT Leaders, Computerworld, 2005. Office: Jet Propulsion Lab 4800 Oak Grove Dr Pasadena CA 91109 Office Phone: 818-354-4321.

RINALDO, PETER MERRITT, publishing executive; b. Evanston, Ill., June 21, 1922; s. Philip Sidney and Harriet Huntington (Beach) R.; m. Dorothy Hastings Warren, July 20, 1946; children: David, Marjory, John. BA, Bowdoin Coll., 1943; BS, MIT, 1944, MS, 1947. Chem. engr. Dewey & Almy Chem. Co., Cambridge, Mass., 1947-54; v.p. overseas chem. divsn. W.R. Grace & Co., Cambridge, Mass., 1954-65, v.p. indsl. chem. group NYC, 1965-77, v.p. gen. indsl. prodn. group, 1977-82; pres. Dorpete Press, Briarcliff Manor, N.Y., 1982—. Chmn. bd. Flexible Steel Lacing Co., Downers Grove, Ill., 1984-96; cons. Nat. Exec. Svc. Corps., N.Y.C., 1982-85. Author: The Five-day Week End, 1989, Unnecessary Wars?, 1993, Marrying the Natives, 1996, The Great Reindeer Caper, 1997, Nature, Nurture, and Chance, 1998, Atheists, Agnostics, and Deists in America, 2000. Pres. Briarcliff Vol. Fire Dept., Briarcliff Manor, N.Y. 1983-85; pres. bd. trustees Ossinining (N.Y.) Pub. Libr., 1990-92. Lt. USN, 1944-46. Mem. Am. Chem. Soc., Am. Inst. Chem. Engineers. Avocations: hiking, canoeing, nordic skiing. Home: 428 Savage Farm Dr Ithaca NY 14850 E-mail: prinaldo@twcny.rr.com.

RINAMAN, JAMES CURTIS, JR., lawyer; b. Miami, Fla., Feb. 8, 1935; s. James Curtis and Ruth Marie (Rader) R.; m. Gloria Margaret Kaspar; children: James, Mark, Christine, Karen BA, U. Fla., 1955, JD, 1960. Bar: Fla. 1960, U.S. Dist. Ct. (so. dist.) Fla. 1960, U.S. Ct. Appeals (5th cir.) 1960, U.S. Supreme Ct. 1963, U.S. Dist. Ct. (mid. dist.) Fla. 1967, U.S. Dist. Ct. (no. dist.) Fla. 1981, U.S. Ct. Appeals (11th cir.) 1981, U.S. Ct. Claims 1991, U.S. Ct. Mil. Appeals 1994; cert. civil trial lawyer Fla. Bar. With Marks, Gray, Conroy & Gibbs, P.A., Jacksonville, Fla., 1960—. Gen. counsel Fla. Bd. Architecture, 1965-79, City of Jacksonville, 1970-71, Jacksonville C. of C., 1973-76, 90; adj. prof. Coll. Architecture, U. Fla., 1975-90; dir. gen. The Southern Acad. Letters, Arts and Scis., 1997—. Pres. Jacksonville Cmty. Coun. Inc., 1985. Leadership Jacksonville, Inc., 1987; mem. Jacksonville Transp. Authority, 1971-80, Jacksonville Base Realignment and Closure Commn., 1993-95. Jacksonville Cecil Field Devel. Commn., 1994-96; chmn. N.E. Fla. chpt. ARC, 1996. With U.S. Army,

1955-57, Fla. NG, 1957-92. ret. brig. gen., 1992. Named to U. Fla. Hall of Fame. Fellow Am. Coll. Trial Lawyers, Am. Bar Found., Fla. Bar Found. (bd. dirs. 1982-87, 88, Disting. Svc. award 1983, 86, Medal of Honor 1988); mem. ABA (ho. of dels. 1982-86), Jacksonville Bar Assn. (pres. 1972-73, Lawyer of Yr. 1994), The Fla. Bar (pres. 1982-83), Def. Rsch. Inst. (so. regional v.p. 1980-83, bd. dirs. 1976-78, 83-87), Am. Judicature Soc. (Herbert Harley award 1987), Fla. Coun. Bar Pres. (Outstanding Past Pres. award 1989), Lawyers for Civil Justice (pres. 1989-91, chmn. bd. dirs. 1991-94), Vol. Lawyers Resource Ctr. of Fla., (pres. 1984-89, chmn. bd. dirs. 1989-93), So. Conf. of Bar, Nat. Conf. of Bar, Assn. Def. Trial Attys. (internat. pres. 1976-77), Internat. Assn. Def. Counsel, Jacksonville Assn. Def. Counsel, Fla. Defense Lawyers Assn. (pres. 1973), Fla. C. of C., Jacksonville C. of C. (chmn. 1994), Meninak Civic Club (pres. 1986), Jacksonville Commodores League, The Army War Coll. Alumni Assn. (life), Fla. Blue Key, San. Jose Country Club, River Club, Phi Gamma Delta (bd. trustees ednl. found. 1995—), Phi Alpha Delta. Republican. Methodist. Office: Marks Gray Conroy & Gibbs 1200 Riverplace Blvd Ste 800 Jacksonville FL 32207-1805 also: PO Box 447 Jacksonville FL 32201-0447 Office Phone: 904-398-0900. E-mail: jrinaman@marksgray.com.

RINDE, ANDREA J., mathematics educator; d. John Wesley Frysinger and Angela Ashcraft; m. Paul A. Rinde, June 22, 2006; children: Dillon Russell, Amanda Russell, Aarika Baker, Chelsea, Kailee, Corey. AA in Liberal Studies, Moorpark Coll., Calif., 1993; BA in Bus. Adminstrn., Calif. Luth. U., Thousand Oaks, 1995, MEd, 2006. Multiple subject tchg. credential Calif., elem. cert. Ariz. Math. tchr. Prescott H.S., Ariz., 2006—. Advisor Nat. Honor Soc. Prescott H.S., 2006—. Dr. Phyllis Jane Nusz scholar, Calif. Luth. U., 1995. Mem.: Prescott H.S. PTA, Nat. Coun. Tchr. Math., Kappa Delta Pi. Avocations: reading, hiking, camping, power walking, yoga. Office: Prescott HS 1050 N Ruth St Prescott AZ 86301

RINDEN, DAVID LEE, clergyman; b. Lake Mills, Iowa, Aug. 1, 1941; s. Oscar Henry and Iva (Stensrud) R.; m. Gracia Elizabeth Carlson, Sept. 11, 1966; children: Jonathan, Elizabeth, Amy. BA, Moorhead State U., 1964; diploma, Luth. Brethren Sem., 1966; postgrad., Seattle Pacific U., 1973. Ordained to ministry Luth. Ch., 1967. Pastor Bethesda Luth. Ch., Eau Claire, Wis., 1968-72, Maple Pk. Luth. Ch., Lynnwood, Wash., 1972-79; v.p. Ch. of the Luth. Brethren of Am., Fergus Falls, Minn., 1991—; editor Faith & Fellowship, Fergus Falls, Minn., 1979-2000; exec. dir. Faith and Fellowship Press Ch. of the Luth. Brethren of Am., Fergus Falls, 1979-2000; pastor Gethsemane Lutheran Ch., Rochester, Minn., 2000—. Chmn. com. on commitment Ch. of Luth. Brethren, Fergus Falls, 1981-82, com. on role of women in ch., 1984-86, chmn. com. on 90th anniversary, chmn. bd. publs., 1968-78. Editor: Explanation of Luther's Small Catechism, 1988; author: Biblical Foundations, 1981. Founding com. JAIL, Inc., Fergus Falls, 1991; pres. bd. dirs. Fergus Falls Fed. Community Credit Union, 1987-2000. Mem. Fergus Falls Ministerial Assn. (sec. 1989-90, v.p. 1991-92, pres. 1992-93), Kiwanis (pres. 1994-95, lt. gov. 1996-97). Home: 1925 Century Valley Rd NE Rochester MN 55906-7705 Office: Gethsemane Lutheran Ch 2204 22d St NW Rochester MN 55901

RINDFUSS, RONALD RICHARD, social studies educator; b. Buffalo, Dec. 11, 1946; married Aug. 1968; 2 children. BA, Fordham U., 1968; PhD, Princeton U., 1974. Rsch. asst. Nat. Fertility Study, Office Population Rsch., Princeton U., 1971-73; rsch. assoc. Ctr. Demography and Ecology U. Wis., Madison, 1973-76; asst. prof. sociology U. N.C., Chapel Hill, 1976-79, assoc. prof., 1979-84, prof. sociology, 1984-2000, Robert Paul Ziff Disting. prof., 2000—; dir. Carolina Population Ctr., Chapel Hill, 1992-97; sr. fellow East-West Ctr., Honolulu, 2006—. Cons. in field Assoc. editor Social Forces, 1976—; cons. editor Am. Jour. Sociology, 1977-80; contbg. editor Sociol Biology, 1974; mem. editl. bd. Deomography, 2007—; referee for numerous jours.; contbr. numerous articles to profl. jours. Recipient NIH traineeship, 1968—71, 1st place Erdas award for best sci. paper on remote sensing, 2000. Fellow: AAAS (mem. nominating com. sect. K 2001—03); mem.: Sociol. Rsch. Assn., Coun. on Family Rsch., So. Sociol. Soc., So. Regional Demographic Group, Nat. Coun. on Family Rels., Internat. Union for Sci. Study Population, Population Assn. Am. (bd. dirs. 1984—87, Mindel C. Sheps award com. 1990, pres. 1991), Am. Sociol. Assn. (publs. com. 1983—84, chmn. sociology of population sect. 1989—90). Office: Carolina Population Ctr CB # 8120 University Sq 123 W Franklin St Chapel Hill NC 27516-2524 Office Phone: 919-966-7779. E-mail: Ron_Rindfuss@unc.edu.

RINDONE, JOSEPH PATRICK, clinical pharmacist, educator; b. Santa Fe, Oct. 4, 1954; s. Guido Salvatore and Elizabeth Ann (Murphy) R.; m. Diane Marie Rollins, June 23, 1991; children: Jacqueline, Alexandra. BS, U. Nebr., 1977; PharmD, Creighton U., 1978. Lic. pharmacist, Nebr., Calif. Staff pharmacist Bergan Mercy Hosp., Omaha, 1978, Phoenix (Ariz.) VA Med. Ctr., 1978-81, clin. resident, 1981; clin. pharmacist Tucson VA Med. Ctr., 1982-93; assoc. prof. U. Ariz., Tucson, 1982—; clin. pharmacist Prescott (Ariz.) VA Med. Ctr., 1993—, rsch. coord., 1994—. Author: Therapeutic Monitoring of Antibiotics, 1991; contbr. articles to Arch. Internal Medicine, Pharmacotherapy, Clin. Therapeutics, Am. Jour. Cardiology, Am. Jour. Therapeutics, Chest, West Jour. Medicine, Am. Jour. Health Sys. Pharm., Fereral Practioner, Jour. AMA. Regents scholar U. Nebr., 1976. Avocations: sports, photography, bridge, astronomy. E-mail: JosephRindone@med.va.gov.

RINEBOLD, ALICE JUNE, environmental scientist; b. Fostoria, Ohio, June 24, 1953; d. Rex Gene and Hilma Alice (Huff) Rinebold; 1 child, Nicholas Jeremy. AA, USAF C.C., 1982; BA in Psychology and Biol. Sci., U. No. Colo., 1983. Cert. Nat. Environ. Health Trainer NEHA, 2003, Administr. Profl. Excellence APEX, 2005. Vet. food insp. WAC, Ft. Carson, Colo., 1972—75; environ. health specialist Weld County Health Dept., Greeley, Colo., 1986—91; environ. specialist Environ. Health, City and County Denver, 1991—. Trainer Nat. Environ. Health Assn., Denver; environ. medicine tech. Master sgt. USAF Reserves, Colorado, ret., 1998. Recipient Outstanding Achievement Humanitarian award, USAF Caledonia, San Blas Islan. Mem.: Colo. Environ. Health Assn. (Honary award 1993), Nat. Environ. Health Assn. Achievements include being one of the first 5 women food inspectors in the US Army in 1972. Home Phone: 303-371-1829.

RINEHART, JAMES FORREST, political science professor, department chairman; b. Kansas City, Mo., Dec. 1, 1950; s. Kenneth Perry and Eleanor Louise (Lane) R.; m. Betty Keller, Feb. 3, 1973; children: Erica Christine, Andrew James. BA, U. Fla., Gainesville, 1972; M of Social Sci., Syracuse U., NY, 1991, PhD, 1993. Vis. prof. internat. rels. U. Tenn., Chattanooga, 1993-95; dir., prof. grad. program in internat. rels. U.S. Army John F. Kennedy Spl. Warfare Sch. Troy U., 1995—2001, lectr. regional studies program, 1996—2001; prof., chair dept. polit. sci. Troy U., Ala., 2001—, dir. grad. program in internat. rels., 2001—. Author: Revolution and the Millennium: China, Mexico and Iran, 1997, Apocalyptic Faith and Political Violence: Prophets of Terror, 2006; contbr. articles to profl. jours. Mem. Coun. on Peace Rsch. in History, 1992-94; active Program on Analysis and Resolution of Conflict, Syracuse U., 1991-93; bd. dirs. Ulster Project Chattanooga, 1993-94. Capt. USAR, 1972-80. Recipient Cert. of Achievement U.S. Army JFK Spl. Warfare Ctr. and Sch., 1996. Mem. Am. Polit. Sci. Assn., Internat. Studies Assn. (exec. cou. South 2002-05, treas. 2005—), Internat. Soc. Polit. Psychology, Am. Radio Relay League, Fla. Blue Key Soc., Phi Gamma Delta. Democrat. Presbyterian. Home: 201 Hampton Ave Troy AL 36081-4045

RINEHART, NEIL, financial consultant; b. Mt. Ayr, Iowa, May 9, 1951; s. Park and Joan Rinehart; m. Sheila Kay Funderburgh, Sept. 3, 1977; children: Allison Rinehart Billodeau, Matthew. MBA, U. Iowa, 1975. Fin. cons. E.F. Hutton, Dallas, 1977—90; sr. v.p. investments Smith Barney, Inc., Plano, Tex., 1990—2004; sr. v.p. investments, sr. portfolio mgr. UBS Financial Svc., Dallas, 2004—. Author: It's All The Same Game: The Sports Fan's Guide to Success in the Stock Market, 2003, Finding Your "A" Game: Golf, Investing and Life, 2005. Mem.: Assn. Authors and Pubs., U. Iowa Alumni Assn. Avocations: sports, sports psychology, travel. Office: UBS Fin Svc 5080 Spectrum Dr Ste 1000-W Addison TX 75001 Office Phone: 972-450-4367. E-mail: neil.rinehart@ubs.com.

RINES, ROBERT HARVEY, lawyer, educator, physicist, composer; b. Boston, Aug. 30, 1922; s. David and Lucy (Sandberg) R.; m. Carol Williamson, Dec. 29, 1972 (dec. 1993); 1 son, Justice Christopher; children by previous marriage: Robert Louis, Suzi Kay Ann; m. Joanne Hayes, June 2, 1996; 1 stepchild, Laura Ellen Hayes-Heuer. BS in Physics, MIT, 1942; JD, Georgetown U., 1947; PhD, Nat. Chiao Tung U., 1972; DJ (hon.), New Eng. Coll. Law, 1974; DSc (hon.), Notre Dame Coll., 1994; LLD (hon.), Franklin Pierce Law Ctr., 2004. Bar: Mass. 1947, D.C. 1947, N.H. 1974, Va. 1983, U.S. Supreme Ct., FCC, Tax Ct., U.S. and Can. patent offices; Registered profl. engr., Mass. Asst. examiner U.S. Patent Office, 1946; partner Rines & Rines, Boston, NH, 1947—; pres., founder, chmn. emeritus, prof. Franklin Pierce Law Ctr., 1973-97. Pres. Jura Corp., 1996-; bd. dirs. Megapulse, Inc., Nat. Inventors Hall of Fame Found., 1997-99, New Eng. Fish Farming Enterprises-D.E. Salmon Inc., 1983-99, Acad. Applied Sci.-Project Orbis Bangladesh and Singapore Opthamology Programs and Loch Ness Rsch. Program, 1972—, Seagull Tech., Inc., 1994-98, New Eng. Aquarium, 1973-75, Albavision Ltd. U.K., Promotion of Am. Chinese Tech., Knox Mt. Licensors Inc., Ctr. Broadcasting Corp. of N.H., Accelerated Genomics Inc., 2001-04, Sotti Records; Gordon McKay lectr. patent law Harvard, 1956-58; lectr. inventions and innovation MIT, 1962—; commerce tech. adv. bd. Dept. Commerce, 1963-67, nat. inventors coun., 1963-67, 81—; mem. N.H. Gov.'s Crime Study Com., 1976-78; trustee Mass. Eye and Ear Infirmary, 2001. Author: A Study of Current World-Wide Sources of Electronic and Other Invention and Innovation; Computer Jurisprudence: Create or Perish--The Case for Patents and Inventions; patentee in field of radar and sonar, fish farming and plant nutrients; composer music for on and off broadway prodns. including Drums Under the Windows (S. O'Casey, P. Shyre), Different, Long Voyage Home (E. O'Neil, P. Shyre), Strindberg's Creditors, Whitman Portrait, Blasts and Bravos (H.L. Menken), Hizzoner the Mayor (Emmy winning tv prodn.), 1-800-Save Me and Friendly Acquaintances (Jack Betts), Bob's Dream Ballet, Lincoln Ctr., 1999, Life at MIT suite, (films) Search at Loch Ness, 2002, Irish Eyes, 2002-2004. Campaign chmn. United Fund, Belmont Mass., 1960; mem. adv. bd. Harvard-MIT Biomed. Engring. Ctr., 1976-80; bd. dirs. Allor Found. Capt. AUS, 1942-46, European and Pacific Theaters, WWII, Brevet Col., 1994, U.S. Army Signal Corps. Named to Nat. Inventors Hall of Fame, 1994, Wall of Fame U.S. Army Signal Corps, 1994; recipient Inventions citation Pres. Carter and U.S. Dept. Commerce, 1980, N.H. High Tech. Entrepreneur award, 1989, Beyond Peace award, 1989, Disting. Svc. award Bangladesh, 1990, 96, honors Town of Inverness, Scotland, 2003, Dinsdale award Soc. Sci. Exploration, 2004, Disting. Lifetime award Boston Patent Law Assn., 2004; Robert H. Rines Bldg. dedication at Franklin Pierce Law Ctr., 1993, Distance Learning Ctr. Bldg. dedication MIT, 1997. Fellow Internat. Soc. Cryptozoology; mem. IEEE (sr.), AAAS, ABA, Acad. Applied Sci. (pres., founder, Medal of Honor 1989), Am. Patent Law Assn. (Disting. Lifetime Achievement award Boston chpt. 2004), Sci. Rsch. Soc. Am., Aircraft Owners and Pilots Assn., Nat. Acad. Engring. (patent com. 1969-80, cons. to exec. officer 1979-80), Explorers Club, Harvard Club, Chemists Club, MIT Faculty Club, Nat. Lawyers Club, Capitol Hill Club, Highland Club, Commonwealth Club, Sigma Xi. Unitarian Universalist. Address: Harbor Towers Boston MA 02110

RING, ALICE RUTH BISHOP, retired preventive medicine physician; b. Ft. Collins, Colo., Oct. 11, 1931; d. Ernest Otto and Mary Frances Bishop; m. Wallace Harold Ring, July 26, 1956 (div. 1969); children: Rebecca, Eric, Mark; m. Robert Charles Diefenbach, Sept. 10, 1977. BS, Colo. State U., 1953; MD, U. Colo., 1956; MPH, U. Calif., Berkeley, 1971. Diplomate Am. Bd. Preventive Medicine. Physician cons. Utah State Divsn. Health, Salt Lake City, 1960—65; med. dir., project head start Salt Lake City Cmty. Action Program, 1965—70; resident Utah State Divsn. Health, 1969—71; asst. assoc. regional health dir. USPHS, San Francisco, 1971—75, med. cons. Atlanta, 1975—77, dir. primary care, 1977—84; dir. divsn. diabetes control Ctrs. Disease Control, Atlanta, 1984—88; dir. WHO Collabor Ctr., Atlanta, 1986—91; dir. preventive medicine residency Ctrs. Disease Control, Atlanta, 1988—93; exec. dir. Am. Bd. Preventive Medicine, 1993—98. Trustee Am. Bd. Preventive Medicine, 1990—92; lectr. Emory U. Sch. Pub. Health, 1988—94; bd. dirs. Redwood Coast Med. Svcs., v.p., 1994—2004; mem. adv. com. Shamli Hospice, Gualala, Calif.; mem. adv. coun. Sonoma County Area Agy. on Aging, Santa Rosa, Calif., 2001—07, sec., 2004—06, v.p., 2006—07; bd. dirs. Alliance Rural Cmty. Health, Calif., 2002—04. Co-author: Clinical Diabetes, 1991; author: History of the American Board of Preventive Medicine, 2002. Bd. dirs. Diabetes Assn. Atlanta, 1985—90. Recipient Disting. Svc. award, Am. Bd. Med. Splties, 2004. Fellow: Am. Coll. Preventive Medicine (bd. dirs. 1990—94, Spl. Recognition award 1998); mem.: AMA (grad. med. edn. adv. com. 1993—97), Steering Com. Environ. Commons, Am. Bd. Med. Specialists (Disting. Svc. award 2004), Am. Acad. Pediat., Assn. Tchrs. Preventive Medicine. Office: PO Box 364 Gualala CA 95445-0364 Business E-Mail: ard@mcn.org.

RING, ALVIN MANUEL, pathologist, educator; s. Julius and Helen (Krolik) R.; m. Cynthia Joan Jacobson, Sept. 29, 1963; children— Jeffrey, Melinda, Heather. BS, Wayne State U., 1954; MD, U. Mich., 1958. Intern Mt. Carmel Hosp., Detroit, 1958-59; resident in pathology Michael Reese Hosp., Chgo., 1960-62; asst. pathologist Kings County Hosp., Bklyn., 1962-63; assoc. pathologist El Camino Hosp., Mountain View, Calif., 1963-65; chief pathologist, dir. labs. St. Elizabeth's Hosp., Chgo., 1965-72, Holy Cross Hosp., Chgo., 1972-87, Silver Cross Hosp., Joliet, Ill., 1990—. Instr. SUNY, 1962-63, Stanford U., 1963-65; asst. prof. pathology U. Ill., Chgo., 1966-69, assoc. prof., 1969-78, prof., 1978—; adj. clin. prof. No. Ill. U., 1981-87; adj. prof. med. edn. U. Ill. Coll. Medicine, 1988—; chmn. histotech. Nat. Accrediting Agy. for Clin. Lab Scis., 1977-81; mem. spl. adv. com. Health Manpower, 1966-71; pres. Spear Computer Users Group, 1981-82; mem. adv. com. Mid-Am. chpt. ARC, 1979-85; pres. Pathology and Lab Cons., Inc., 1985—; adj. prof., med. dir. Med. Tech., Moraine Valley C.C., 1994—; originator, coord. pathology, med. decision-making courses Nat. Ctr. for Advanced Med. Edn., 1981—, others; co-coord. computer courses Midwest Clin. Conf., 2000—. Author: Laboratory Correlation Manual, 1968, 82, 86, Laboratory Assistant Examination Review Book, 1971, Review Book in Pathology, Anatomic, 1986, Review Book in Pathology, Clinical, 1986; mem. editorial bd. Lab. Medicine, 1975-87; contbr. articles to med. jours. Fellow: Am. Soc. Clin. Pathology, Coll. Am. Pathology (insp. 1973—, ins. com. 2002—06, membership com. 2005—06, PathPac bd. dirs. 2007—, adv. com. on health care delivery); mem.: AMA, Assn. Brain Tumor Rsch. (cons.), Am. Assn. Blood Banks, Chgo. Pathol. Soc. (censor 1980—88, exec. com. 1985—89, program com. 1987—), Ill. Pathol. Soc. (trustee 1997—), Chgo. Med. Soc. (alt. councilor 1980—85), Ill. Med. Soc., Exec. Svc. Corps (exec. cons. 1988—), Phi Lambda Kappa (chpt. pres.). Home: 100 Graymoor Ln Olympia Fields IL 60461-1213 Office: Silver Cross Hosp 1200 Maple Rd Joliet IL 60432-1497

RING, GERALD J., real estate developer, insurance company executive; b. Madison, Wis., Oct. 6, 1928; s. John George and Mabel Sarah (Rau) R.; m. Armella Marie Dohm, Aug. 20, 1949; children: Michael J., James J., Joseph W. Student public schs., Madison. With Sub-Zero Freezer Co., Madison, 1948-70, mfr.'s rep., 1954-70; founder, chmn. bd. Parkwood Hills Corp., Madison, from 1965; founder, pres. Park Towne Devel. Corp., Madison, from 1969, Ring Devel. Co., 1992—. Bd. dirs. CUNA Mut. Ins. Soc., CUNA Mut. Ins. Group, CUNA Mut. Investment Corp., CUDIS Ins. Soc., all Madison, 1968-98, exec. com., 1973-83, chmn. bd., 1979-81; bd. dirs. CUMIS Ins. Soc., mem. exec. com., 1973-83, chmn. bd., 1977-79; bd. dirs. CMCI Corp., mem. exec. com., 1974-83, chmn. bd., 1981-83; treas. CUNADATA Corp., 1974-81; bd. dirs. Wis. Credit Union League, 1958-79, pres., 1965-67; mem. Wis. Credit Union Rev. Bd., 1967-83, chmn., 1973-76, 82-83; bd. dirs. CUNA Credit Union Nat. Assn., Inc., 1964-81, League Life Ins. Co., League Gen. Ins. Co., Southfield, Mich., CUNA Mut. Fin. Svcs. Corp., Century Ins. Co. Am., Waverly., Iowa. Chmn. Greater Madison C. of C., 1980, bd. dirs., 1976-89, v.p. econ. devel., 1983-85, v.p. govtl. affairs, 1985-89, mem. capital fund raising com., 1983—, chmn. 1983-86; mem. Mayor's Emergency Housing Com., 1984-85; chmn. fin. com. St. Patrick's Congregation, 1983-89; bd. dirs. Cath. Charities of Madison, 1995—, pres., 1996-99; bd. dirs. Future Madison Housing Fund, 1997—, pres, 2005—. Served with USMC, 1951-53. Mem. Aircraft Owners and Pilots Assn. Lodges: Rotary. (bd. dirs. 1981-83). Roman Catholic. Home: 607 Farwell Dr Madison WI 53704-6029 Office: 402 S Gammon Rd Madison WI 53719-1002

RING, HERBERT EVERETT, retired management executive; b. Norwich, Conn., Dec. 19, 1925; s. Herbert Everett and Catherine (Riordan) R.; m. Marilyn Elizabeth Dursin, May 21, 1955 (dec. Jan. 1994); children: Nancy Marie, Herbert Everett. BA, Ind. No. U., 1971, MBA, 1973; AMP, Harvard U., 1981. V.p. ops. Ogden Foods, Inc., Toledo, 1963-74, sr. v.p. Boston, 1974-75; v.p. concessions SportSvc. Corp., Buffalo, 1976-78, sr. v.p., 1978-80, pres., 1980-83, bd. dir.; pres. Universal Mgmt. Concept Counseling, Sylvania, Ohio, 1983—2003; prin. Hysen Group II, Livonia, Mich., 1991-95. Counselor L.A. Olympic Concessions Food Svc., 1984, Phila. Meml. Stadium, 1985, Del. North Cos. Internat. London Eng., 1985-86, Chgo. Stadium Corp., 1989-92, Buffalo Sabres N.Y., 1992, Fine Host Inc. Greenwich Ct., 1993, Delaware North of Australia Ltd., 1994, Temp DNC Health Support Ltd., Wellington, New Zealand, 1995, Fanfare Enterprises, 1997, Geneva Lakes Kennel Club, Delavan, Wis., 1997, St. Francis Health Care Ctr., Greenspring, Ohio, 1998, Detroit Opera House, 2000; bd. dirs. Greenfield Restaurant Co., Inc., Letheby and Christopher Ltd., Reading, Berkshire, Eng., Air Terminal Svcs., Inc., The Aud Club, Inc., Bluegrass Turf Svc., Inc., Concession Suppliers, Inc., Cosel Drive-In Theatre, Inc., G&H Sports Concessions, Inc., Hazel Park Parking, Inc. Mem. Toledo Mus. Art., 1985-92. Sgt. Air Corps U.S. Army, 1944-46, ETO, USAF, 1950-51. Mem.: N.W. Ohio Restaurant Assn. (bd. dirs. 1990—93), Internat. Assn. Auditorium Mgrs., Am. Culinary Fedn. Inc. Roman Catholic. Home and Office: 5540 Radcliffe Rd Sylvania OH 43560-3740

RING, JAMES WALTER, physics professor; b. Worcester, NY, Feb. 24, 1929; s. Carlyle Conwell and Lois (Tooley) R.; m. Agnes Elizabeth Muir, July 18, 1959; 1 son, Andrew James. AB, Hamilton Coll., 1951; PhD (Root fellow), U. Rochester, 1958. Asst. prof. physics Hamilton Coll., Clinton, NY, 1957—62, assoc. prof., 1962—69, prof., 1969—75, Winslow prof., 1975—2003, chmn. dept. physics, 1968—80, 1987—88, 1991—92, radiation safety officer, 1964—84, engring. liaison officer, 1969—2002, prof. emeritus, 2003—. Attached physicist Atomic Energy Rsch. Establishment, Harwell, Eng., 1965-66; vis. physicist Phys. Chemistry Lab., Oxford (Eng.) U., 1973; vis. fellow Ctr. for Energy and Environ. Studies, Princeton U., 1981; vis. scientist Lab. for Heating and Air Conditioning, Danish Tech. U., Copenhagen, 1987. Contbr. articles to profl. jour. and books in physics, chemistry, solar energy, environ. sci., health physics, archaeology, and engring. Recipient prize Acad. Edn./Devel., 1980, medal for outstadig achievements in physics Hamilton Coll., 2005; NSF grantee, 1959-66; NSF sci. faculty fellow, 1965-66. Mem. AAUP (chpt. pres. 1987-92), Am. Phys. Soc., Am. Assn. Physics Tchrs., Phi Beta Kappa, Sigma Xi. Achievements include solar house design and testing; indoor air studies in radon dangers and thermal comfort; study of the use of solar energy by the Romans during the Roman Empire; analysis of experimental evidence for the validity of continuous spontaneous localization theory as an alternative to standard quantum mechanics; detection of Pb210 gamma radiation to establish geochronology for sediment core samples taken in antarctic peninsula bay and straits; to study global warming. Avocations: reading, cross country skiing, landscape painting, visiting wine country, studying architecture. Office: Hamilton Coll Dept Physics Clinton NY 13323 Office Phone: 315-859-4366. Business E-Mail: jring@hamilton.edu.

RING, JUDITH A., state librarian; BS in Elem. Edn., Edinboro Coll., Pa., BLS; MLS, Clarion U., Pa. Exec. dir. Erie County Libr. System, Pa.; dep. divsn. dir. Lee County Libr. System, interim libr. dir.; asst. divsn. dir. Divsn. Libr. and Info. Services, Tallahassee, 2001—03, state libr., 2003—. Mem. adv. com. Fla. Book Awards, 2007. Mem.: Chief Officers of State Libr. Agys., Fla. Libr. Assn. (mem. exec. bd. 2007—08). Office: Fla State Libr RA Gray Bldg 500 South Bronough St Tallahassee FL 32399-0250 Office Phone: 850-245-6600. Office Fax: 850-245-6735. Business E-Mail: jring@dos.state.fl.us. *

RING, NANCY GAIL, artist, writer, art educator; b. Irvington, NJ, Dec. 24, 1956; d. Frank and Dorothy (Kasoff) R. Student, Sch. of Mus. of Fine Arts, Boston, 1975-76; BFA, Syracuse U., 1978. Food history columnist, feature food article contbr. N.J. Star Ledger, Newark, 1998—2004; art educator Far Brook Sch., NJ, 2004—. Muralist pvt. commns., 2000—. Author (and illustrator): Walking on Walnuts, 1996; exhibitions include Iandor Fine Art Gallery, Newark, 2005, New Door Creative Gallery, Balt., 2005. Recipient Drawing award Barbara Chase Burke, 1978; fellow Mid-Atlantic Arts Found., 1988, N.Y. Found. for Arts, 1987, Montalvo Ctr. for Arts, 1987. Avocations: baking, cooking, exercise, travel, reading.

RING, RAY, editor; No. Rockies editor High Country News, Colo. Author: (novels) Telluride Smile, 1988, Peregrine Dream, 1990, Arizona Kiss, 1991. Recipient Journalism award, Investigative Reporters and Editors Scroll, 1982, Am. Planning Assn., 2006, award, Soc. Environ. Journalists, 2003, 2004, 2005, George Polk award for Political Reporting, 2007. Office: High Country News 119 Grand Ave PO Box 1090 Paonia CO 81428 Office Phone: 970-527-4898. E-mail: rayring@hcn.org.

RING, RENEE ETHELINE, lawyer; b. Frankfurt, Germany, May 29, 1950; arrived in U.S., 1950; d. Vincent Martin and Etheline Bergetta (Schoolmeesters) Ring; m. Paul J. Zofnass, June 24, 1982; children: Jessica Renee, Rebecca Anne. BA magna cum laude, Catholic U. Am., 1972; JD, U. Va., 1976. Bar: NY 1977. Assoc. Whitman & Ransom, NYC, 1976-83, Carro, Spanbock, Fass, Geller, Kaster & Cuiffo, NYC, 1983-86, ptnr., 1986, Finley Kumble Wagner et. al., NYC, 1987; of counsel Kaye, Scholer, Fierman, Hays & Handler, NYC, 1988; ptnr. Kaye, Scholer, Fierman, Hays & Handler, LLP, NYC, 1989-97, Hunton & Williams, NYC, 1997—2002, McKee Nelson LLP, NYC, 2006—. Trustee The Spence Sch., 2001—02; advisor WestWind Found., 2001—; mem. exec. com. Lawyers for Clinton, Washington, 1991—92; team capt. Clinton Transition Team, Washington, 1992—93; mem. Nat. Lawyers Coun. Dem. Nat. Com., 1993—98; trustee The Clinton Legal Expense Trust, 1998—2002, Pound Ridge Land Conservancy, 2003—; mem. alumni coun. U. Va. Sch. of Law, 1997—2005, 2d v.p., 2000—01, 1st v.p., 2001—03, pres., 2003—05. Mem.: ABA, Queens Bot. Garden Soc. (trustee 2003—, v.p. 2005—, mem. exec. coun. 2005—, vice chmn. 2007—, sec. 2005—). Democrat. Roman Catholic. Office Phone: 917-777-4527.

RING, TIMOTHY MICHAEL, human services administrator, pharmaceutical executive; b. Buffalo, Sept. 30, 1957; s. Roger Michael and Leone Ann (Reitmeier) R.; m. Mary Lou Mauro, June 10, 1984; children: Christina and Alexandra (twins). BS in Indsl. Labor Relations, Cornell Univ., 1979. Coll. grad. in tng. GM, Detroit, 1979-80, labor relations rep., 1980, salaried personnel rep., 1980-81, sr. salaried personnel rep., 1981-82, sr. labor relations rep., 1982-83; div. personnel mgr. Abbott Labs., North Chicago, Ill., 1983-84, regional personnel mgr., 1984-86, dir. personnel Pacific, Asian and African ters., 1986-87, dir. personnel Pacific, Asian, African and European ters., 1987—92; corp. v.p., human resources CR Bard Inc., New Providence, NJ, 1992—93, group v.p.-internat., 1993—97, group pres.-coronary vascular products, 1997—99, group pres.-electrophysiology, peripheral vascular products, 1999—2003, chmn, CEO, 2003—. Advisor Midwest Personnel Forum U. Ill., Champaign. Mem. European Pharm. Mfg. Assn. Personnel, Pacific Area Personnel Assn., Human Resource Assn. Chgo. (chmn. internat. human relations com. 1986-88), Cornell U. Indsl. and Labor Relations Assn., Delta Upsilon. Republican. Roman Catholic. Avocations: real estate investments, tennis, golf, sailing. Office: CR Bard 730 Central Ave New Providence NJ 07974 Office Phone: 908-277-8000. *

RINGEL, DEAN, lawyer; b. NYC, Dec. 12, 1947; m. Ronnie Sussman, Aug. 24, 1969; children: Marion, Alicia. BA, Columbia Coll., 1967; JD, Yale U., 1971. Bar: NY 1972, US Ct. Appeals (6th cir.) 1972, US Ct. Appeals (2d and DC cirs.) 1974, US Supreme Ct. 1976, US Ct. Appeals (10th cir.) 1982, US Ct. Appeals (11th cir.) 1997, US Ct. Appeals (9th cir.) 2000. Law clk. to Judge Anthony J. Celebrezze U.S. Ct. Appeals (6th cir.), 1971—72; assoc. Cahill Gordon & Reindel, NYC, 1972—79; ptnr. Cahill, Gordon & Reindel LLP, NYC, 1979—. V.p. def. coun. sect. Media Law Resource Ctr., 2006—. Mem.: ABA (vice chmn. com. on freedom of speech and press 1978—79), Pub. Edn. Assn. (trustee, sec. 1997—2000, trustee CEI-PEA 2000—), Assn. Bar City NY (commn. comm., fed. litigation, antitrust and trade regulation), NY State Bar (chmn. antitrust litigation com., sect. comml. and fed. litigation 1994—96, co-chmn. fed. judiciary com. 1997—2001, co-chair newsgathering com. Media Law Resource Ctr. 2001—05). Office: Cahill Gordon & Reindel LLP 80 Pine St 17th Fl New York NY 10005-1790 Office Phone: 212-701-3521.

RINGEL, FAYE JOYCE, literature educator; b. Norwich, Conn., Aug. 17, 1951; d. Harold L. and Toube Marilyn (Barsky) Ringel; m. E. Paul Hazel, 1990 (div. 1993). AB in Comparative Lit. summa cum laude, Brandeis U., Waltham, Mass., 1972; PhD in Comparative Lit., Brown U., Providence, 1979. Instr. English Ea. Conn. State U., Nillimantic, Conn., 1981—84, Three Rivers C.C., Norwich, Conn., 1981—85; prof. English dept. humanities USCG Acad., New London, Conn., 1985—. Author: New England's Gothic Literature, 1995; singer, pianist: CD recording Hot Chestnuts, 2002. Founding pres. Norwich Arts Coun., 1987; pres., bd. mem. Norwich chpt. Hadassah, 1998—; bd. mem. Beth Jacob Synagogue, Norwich, 1999—. Recipient Hand of Healing award, Conn. Region Hadassah, 2006, Disting. Faculty award, Coast Guard Acad. Alumni Assn., 2006. Mem.: Nat. Coun. Tchrs. English, Internat. Assn. for the Fantastic in the Arts, NE Popular Culture Assn. (area chair 1999—), Internat. Gothic Assn. (editl. bd. mem. 1996—), New Eng. Assn. Tchrs. English (exec. bd., sec. 1994—, Charles Swain Thomas award 2005), Phi Beta Kappa. Jewish. Avocations: vocal and instrumental music, theater. Home: 6 Taylor Dr Norwich CT 06360 Office: USCG Acad Dept Humanities 27 Mohegan Ave New London CT 06320

RINGEL, JUDY G., writer; b. Cleve., Aug. 31, 1940; d. Leo and Ernestine F. Greenberger; m. Neil E. Ringel, June 30, 1960; children: Elizabeth Ringel Saslawsky, James M., Jonathan L. Student, Goucher Coll., 1958—60; BA magna cum laude, Cast Western Res. U., 1962. Assoc. editor Memphis Mag., 1982—86, sr. editor, 1986—91, assoc. pub., 1991—92; freelance writer Memphis, 1992—. Author: Children of Israel, 2004 (cert. of commendation Am. Assn. State and Local History, 2005); contbr. numerous articles to mags. Chmn. bd. dirs. Memphis Planned Parenthood, Memphis, 1995—97; pres. Jewish Fedn. Women's Divsn., Memphis, 1976—77. Mem.: Memphis Jewish Hist. Soc., West Tenn. Hist. Soc., Am. Assn. for State and Local History, Phi Beta Kappa. Avocations: golf, gardening, jogging, reading.

RINGEL, ROBERT LEWIS, academic administrator; b. NYC, Jan. 27, 1937; s. Benjamin Seymour and Beatrice (Salis) R.; m. Estelle Neuman, Jan. 18, 1959; children— Stuart Alan, Mark Joseph. BA, Bklyn. Coll., 1959; MS, Purdue U., 1960, PhD, 1962. cert. speech pathologist. Rsch. scientist, laryngeal rsch. lab. Ctr. Health Scis., UCLA, 1962-64; asst. prof. communication disorders U. Wis., 1964-66; from mem. faculty to provost Purdue U., 1966—91, provost, 1991—2001, prof. speech, lang. & hearing scis., Donald S. Powers disting. univ. adminstr., 2001—. Vis. prof. Inst. Neurology and Nat. Hosps. Coll. Speech Scis., U. London, 1985; cons. NIH, NEH, Bur. Edn. Handicapped of U.S. Office Edn.; bd. dirs. Indpls. Ctr. for Advanced Rsch., 1988-92; hon. prof. Coll. of Computer Scis. and Mgmt., Rzeszów, Poland, 2000—; bd. dir., faculty adv. Hillel Found. Purdue U., 2000-. Author sci. articles; contbr. to monographs and textbooks; cons. editor Chapman & Hall, London. Bd. dirs. Lafayette Home Hosp., 1978-87, Lafayette Symphony Orch., 1983-85. Recipient Rsch. Career Devel. award Nat. Inst. Dental Rsch., 1967-70, Award for highest merit for sci. article Jour. Speech and Hearing Rsch., 1979, Disting. Alumnus award Bklyn. Coll., 1985; Para-Rabbi fellow Hebrew Union Coll., 2001—; Robert L. Ringel Art Gallery at Purdue U. named in his honor. Fellow Am. Speech and Hearing Assn. (v.p. Found. 1990—, honors 1998); mem. Nat. Assn. State Univs. and Land Grant Colls. (exec. com. 1988-91, rsch. policy and grad. edn., exec. com. coun. on acad. affairs 1991-2001, com. on instnl. coop., exec. com. provosts instn. coop. com. 1991-2001), Sigma Xi (v.p. 1986-90). Office: Purdue U Speech Lang & Hearing Scis 1353 Heavilon Hall G-12B West Lafayette IN 47907-1353 Home: 208 Rosebank Ln West Lafayette IN 47906-8613 Business E-Mail: rringel@purdue.edu.

RINGENBERG, DONNA LOU, music educator, conductor; b. Mt. Joy, Pa., Jan. 22, 1954; d. Robert George Landvater and June Kathleen Wenger; m. Paul David Ringenberg, July 2, 1977; children: Rebekah, Ruth, Rachel, Paul Jr., Rose, Rosalyn, Peter, Priscilla. BS in Music Edn., Bob Jones U., 1976, student in Elem. Edn.; student, Converse Coll., 1998—99, Furman U., summer sessions. Cert. tchr. S.C. Tchr. music, dir. chorus Goldsboro (N.C.) Christian Sch., 1976—77; tchr. Southgate Christian Sch., Augusta, Ga., 1977—78; tchr. music, dir. orch. Acad. Arts, Taylors, SC, 1991—93; pvt. music instr. Greenville, SC, 1991—; tchr. music Hampton Park Christian Sch., Greenville, 1997—99. Music dir. Camp of Nations, South Gibson, Pa., 1976; dir. home schooling string orch. Pecknel Music, Greenville, SC, 1997—; judge various competitions. Musician: Greenville (S.C.) Cmty. Chamber Orch., 2001. Organist Tabernacle Bapt. Ch., Clayton, Ga., 1977—81; pianist, dir. children's choir Colonial Hills Bapt. Ch., Taylors, SC, 1991—93; dir. children's choir Hampton Pk. Bapt. Ch., Greenville, 1998—99; musician Greenville (S.C.) Rescue Mission, 1995—. Recipient Musicianship award, Park Hills Elem. Sch., 1966, Bus. award, Southwestern H.S., 1972. Mem.: Nat. Guild Piano Tchrs., Suzuki Assn. Am. Republican. Bapt. Avocations: sewing, crafts. Home: 16 Brookview Cir Greenville SC 29605 Personal E-mail: ringenberg9@juno.com.

RINGER, DARRELL WAYNE (DAN), lawyer; b. Elizabeth, NJ, Apr. 14, 1948; s. Darrell Wayne and Elva (Brown) R.; m. Rebecca Ruth Bonner, Feb. 23, 1979; children: Daniel Benjamin, Darren Wayne. BS in Physics, W.Va. U., 1971; MBA, U. N.D., 1975; JD, W.Va. U., 1978. Bar: W.Va. 1978, U.S. Dist. Ct. (no. and so. dists.) W.Va. 1978. Assoc. Jones, Williams, West & Jones, Clarksburg, W.Va., 1978-80, Moreland & Ringer, Morgantown, W.Va., 1980-83, Reeder, Shuman, Ringer & Wiley, Morgantown, 1983-91, Ringer Law Offices, Morgantown, 1991—. 1st asst. prosecutor Monongalia County, W.Va., 1985-87; host W.Va. Pub. TV, PBS Pub. Affairs Programming, 1991—. Bd. dirs. Monongalia County (W.Va.) Mental Health Assn., Morgantown, 1981-83; mem. W.Va. U. Animal Care and Use Com., 1985-2003. Capt. USAF, 1971-75. Named W.Va. Bar Found. Lawyer Citizen of Yr., 1996. Fellow W.Va. Bar Found.; mem. ABA (named Sole Practitioner of Yr., 2000), ATLA, W.Va. State Bar (pres. 1999-2000), Monongalia County Bar Assn. (sec. 1980-92, pres. 2001), W.Va. Trial Lawyers Assn. (bd. govs. 1982-91, Pres.'s award 2001). Democrat. Avocation: amateur radio. Office: 823 Fairmont Rd Morgantown WV 26501-3812 Home Phone: 304-296-1718; Office Phone: 304-292-1999. Business E-Mail: dringer@ringerlaw.com.

RINGER, PAULA DENISE HOLLENSHEAD, secondary school educator; b. Urania, La., Sept. 15, 1961; d. Feldor Herold and Betty Jane Hollenshead; m. William Craig Ringer, June 14, 1986; 1 child, William Chase. BA in Tchg., Sam Houston State U., Huntsville, Tex., 1984. Cert. tchr. in math. and computer info. sys. Tex., 1984. Tchr. Hull-Daisetta Ind. Sch. Dist., Tex., 1994—2000, Hardin Ind. Sch. Dist., Tex., 2000—. Participant Conf. for the Advancement of Math. Tchg., Tex., 1988—; tchr. Brazos-Sabine Connection, Daisetta, Tex., 1996—2000; math. textbook panel mem. Tex. Edn. Agy., Austin, 2006. Mem. Hardin United Meth. Ch., 1988. Mem.: Assn. of Tex. Profl. Educators (assoc.). Home: PO Box 383 Hardin TX 77561 Office: Hardin Ind Sch Dist PO Box 330 Hardin TX 77561 Office Phone: 936-298-2112. Personal E-mail: pringer@esc5.net.

RINGGOLD, FAITH, artist; b. NYC, Oct. 8, 1930; BS, CCNY, 1955, MA, 1959; DFA (hon.), Moore Coll. Art, Phila., 1986, Coll. Wooster, Ohio, 1987, Mass. Coll. Art, Boston, 1991, CCNY of CUNY, 1991, RI Sch. Design, 1994, Russell Sage Coll., NY, 1996, Parsons Sch. Design, 1996, Marymount Coll., 1999, Mary Grove Coll., 2000, William Patterson U., 2001, Chgo. Art Inst., 2001, Bloomfield Coll., 2005; DSc (hon.), Brockport State U., NY, 1992, Calif. Coll. Arts and Crafts, Oakland, 1993; DHL (hon.), Malloy Coll., 1997, Bank St. Coll., 1999, William Patterson U., 2001, St. Joseph Coll., 2004; DEd (hon.), Wheelock Coll., 1997. Art tchr. NY Pub. Schs., 1955-73; lectr. Bank St. Coll. Grad. Sch., NYC, 1970-80; prof. art U. Calif., San Diego, 1984—2002, prof. emeritus, 2002—, ret., 2002. Solo exhbns. include Bernice Steinbaum Gallery, 1991, ACA, 2000, Spectrum Gallery, NYC, 1967, 70 10 year retrospective, Studio Mus. in Harlem, NYC, 1984, Bernice Steinbaum Gallerym NYC, 1987-88, Balt. Mus., Deland Mus., Fla., Faith Ringgold 25 Yr. Survey Fine Arts Mus. LI, Hempstead, 1990-93, Textile Mus., Washington, 1993, Children's Mus. of Manhattan, NYC, 1993-95, Hewlett-Woodmere Pub. Libr., Hewlett, NY, 1993-94, St. Louis Art Mus., 1994, Athenaeum, La Jolla, Calif., 1995, A.C.A. Gallery, NYC, 1995, 98, Ind. U. of Pa., 1995, Bowling Green State U., Ind., 1996, New Mus. Contemporary Art, NYC, 1998; exhibited in group shows at Harlem Cultural Coun., NYC, 1966, Meml. Exhibit for MLK, Mus. Modern Art NYC, 1968, Chase Manhattan Bank Collection, Martha Jackson Gallery, NYC, 1970, Am. Women Artists, Gedok, Kunstalle, Hamburg, Ger., 1972, Jubliee, Boston Mus. Fine Arts, 1975, Major Contemporary Women Artists, Suzanne Gross Gallery, Phila., 1984, Committed to Print Mus. Modern Art, NYC, 1988, The Art of Black Am. in Japan, Terada Warehouse, Tokyo, Made in the USA, Art in the 50s and 60s U. Calif. Berkeley Art Mus., Craft Today Poetry of the Physical, Am. Craft Mus., NYC, Portraits and Homage to Mothers Hecksher Mus. Huntington, 1987, NJ State Mus., Trenton, 1992-94, Fukui Fine Art Mus., Fuki, Japan, 1992, Takushima Modern Art Mus., Japan, 1993, Otani Meml. Art Mus., Japan, 1993, Salina Art Atr., Kans., 1993, Bruce Watkins Ctr. Kansas City, Mo., 1993, Barton County CC, Great Bend, Kans., 1993, Del. State Coll. Arts Ctr. Gallery, Dover, 1993-94, Roswell Mus. and Art Ctr., N.Mex., 1994, Aknaton Gallery, Cairo, Alexandria, Egypt, Exit Art, NYC, 1994, New Mus. Contemporary Art, NYC, 1996, Spellman Coll. Mus., Atlanta, 1996, Whitney Mus., NYC, 1996, Centre Georges Pompidou, Paris, 1997, Mus. Art, Ft. Lauderdale, Fla., 1997, NJ Ctr. Arts, Summit, NJ, 1997, Trout Gallery Dickenson Coll., Carlisle, Pa., numerous others; represented in collections at Chase Manhattan Bank, NYC, Philip Morris Collection, NYC, Children's Mus., Bklyn., Newark Mus., The Women's House of Detention, Rikers Island, NY, The Studio Mus., NYC, High Mus., Atlanta, Guggenheim Mus., Met. Mus. Art, Boston Mus. Fine Arts, MOMA, AARP, Washington, Am. Craft Mus., NYC, Clark Mus., Williamstown, Mass., ARCO Chem., Phila., Coca-Cola, Atlanta, Ft. Wayne Mus. Fine Art, Ind., Harold Washington Libr. Ctr., Chgo., Lang Comm. Corp., Coll., Phila. Mus. Art, Pub. Art Pub. Schs., P.S. 22, Bklyn., Spenser Mus. Lawr., Kans., St. Louis Mus. Art, Balt. Mus., Nat. Mus., Washington, Woman's Mus., Washington, Eugenio Maria de Hostos CC, NYC, MTA 125th St. IRT subway sta. installation, NYC, numerous others; author: Tar Beach, 1991, Aunt Harriet's Underground Railroad in the Sky, 1992 (Picture Book award 1993, Best Children's Book of Yr. 1993), Dinner at Aunt Connie's House, 1993 (Reading Magic award 1993), We Flew Over the Bridge: Memoirs of Faith Ringgold, 1995, Talking to Faith Ringgold, 1995, Bonjour Lonnie, 1996, My Dream of Martin Luther King, Jr., 1996, The Invisible Princess, 1999, If a Bus Could Talk: The Story of Rosa Parks, 1999, Counting to Tar Beach, 1999, Cassie's Colorful Day with Daddy, 1999, Cassie's Word Quilt, 2000, O Holy Night, 2004, Three Witches, 2006; author: (video prodn.) Goodnight Moon: and Other Sleepy Time Tales, Tar Beach, 2000; contbr. articles to profl. jours. Recipient AAUW travel award to Africa, 1976; John Simon Guggenheim Meml. Found. Fellowship (painting), 1987, NY Found. for Arts award (painting), 1988, Nat. Endowment Arts award (sculpture), 1978, (painting) 1989, La Napoule Found. award (painting in So. of France), 1990, Video and Software award Calif. children's book, 1991, Parent's Choice Gold award, 1991, Artist award Studio Mus., Harlem, 1991, Artist of Yr. award Sch. Art League NY, 1991, Coretta Scott King award for illustration, 1992, Dist. Artist award Nat. Coun. Art Adminstrs., 1992, award, 1993, Arts Internat. award (travel to Morocco), 1992, Honors award for outstanding achievement in the visual arts Woman's Caucus Arts, NY, 1994, Towsend Harris medal City Coll. Alumni Assn., 1995, NJ Artist of Yr. award NJ Ctr. Visual Arts, 1997, 31st NAACP Image award, 1999, Visionary Woman award, Moore Coll. Art & Design, 2005. Home: PO Box 429 Englewood NJ 07631-0429 Office: ACA Galleries 529 W 20th St Fl 5 New York NY 10011-2800 Office Phone: 858-576-0397. Personal E-mail: ringgoldfaith@aol.com.

RINGKAMP, STEPHEN H., lawyer, educator; b. St. Louis, Nov. 14, 1949; s. Aloysius G. and Melba Ann (Finke) Ringkamp; m. Patricia Sue Fuse, July 5, 1971; children: Christa, Angela, Laura, Stephen M., Kara. BSEE, St. Louis U., 1971, JD cum laude, 1974. Bar: Mo. 1974, U.S. Dist. Ct. (ea. dist.) Mo. 1974, U.S. Ct. Appeals (8th cir.) 1974, U.S. Supreme Ct. 1990. Law clk. 22d Jud. Cir. Mo., St. Louis, 1974-75; mng. prin. The Hullverson Law Firm, St. Louis, 1976—. Chmn., mem. com. on civil instrns. Mo. Supreme Ct., 1981—; adj. prof. law St. Louis U., 1983—1997; mem. faculty Mo. Jud. Coll., 1993-2004; lectr. legal seminars. Contbr. articles to legal jours. Recipient Trial Lawyer award Mo. Bar Found. 1983, Smithson award for Excellence, 1996. Mem. ABA, ATLA, Mo. Bar Assn. (vice chmn. civil practice com. 1983-84), Mo. Assn. Trial Attys. (pres. 1991), Bar Assn. Met. St. Louis, Lawyers Assn. St. Louis. Office: The Hullverson Law Firm 1010 Market St Ste 1550 Saint Louis MO 63101-2091 Home Phone: 314-849-3403; Office Phone: 314-421-2313. E-mail: sringkamp@hullverson.com.

RINGLE, BRETT ADELBERT, lawyer, oil and gas industry executive; b. Berkeley, Calif., Mar. 17, 1951; s. Forrest A. and Elizabeth V. (Darnall) R.; m. Sue Kinslow, May 26, 1973. BA, U. Tex., 1973, JD, 1976. Bar: Tex. 1976, US Dist. Ct. (no. dist.) Tex. 1976, US Supreme Ct. 1980, US Ct. Appeals (5th cir.) 1984. Ptnr. Shank, Irwin & Conant, Dallas, 1976-86, Jones, Day, Reavis & Pogue, Dallas, 1986-96; v.p. Hunt Petroleum Corp., Dallas, 1996—. Adj. prof. law So. Meth. U., Dallas, 1983. Author: (with J.W. Moore and H.I. Bendix) Moore's Federal Practice, 2d edit., Vol. 12, 1980, Vol. 13, 1981, (with J.W. Moore) Vol. 1A, 1982, Vol. 1A Part 2, 1989. Mem. Dallas Bar Assn. Home: 3514 Gillon Ave Dallas TX 75205-3220 Office: Hunt Petroleum Corp Ste 4700 1601 Elm St Dallas TX 75201 Office Phone: 214-922-1004. Business E-Mail: bar@huntpetroleum.com.

RINGLE, PHILIP HAMILTON, JR., lawyer; b. Portland, Oreg., Mar. 23, 1931; s. Philip Hamilton and Audrey Louise (Smallhouse) R.; children: James B., Sara Louise; m Marva Fabien, June 6, 2000. BA, Willamette U., 1953, JD, 1956. Bar: Oreg. 1957, US Dist Ct. (9th cir.) Oreg. Assoc. Green, Richardson, Green & Griswold, Portland, Oreg., 1958-63, Hibbard, Jacobs, Caldwell & Kincart, Oregon City, Oreg., 1963-65, Misko, Njust & Ringle, Oregon City, 1965-67; ptnr. Ringle & Herndon, Gladstone, Oreg., 1968-76; pres. Ringle, Herndon & Beck, P.C., Gladstone, Oreg., 1976-85, Ringle & Herndon, P.C., 1985-86; sole practice, Gladstone, 1986-98, Oregon City, 1999—; Mcpl. ct. judge City of Gladstone, 1965—; ptnr. Ringle & Son Tree Farms, 1986-. Chmn. Nat. Caterpillar Show, Brooks, Oreg., 2006. Named Caterpillar 2006 Man of Yr. Mem. ABA, Oreg. Trial Lawyers Assn., Oreg. State Bar Assn., Clackamas County Bar Assn., Multnomah Bar Assn., Oreg. Mcpl. Judges Assn. (pres. 1975-77), Schnee Vögeli Ski (Portland) (pres. 1960-61), Elks, Rotary, Oregon City Club (pres. 1970-71), Oreg. Old Time Fiddlers Assn., Pacific N.W. Christmas Tree Assn. Co-editor: Oregon Special Court Bench Book, 1978. Democrat. Presbyterian (elder). Office: 1001 Molalla Ave Ste 214 Oregon City OR 97045-3769 Office Phone: 503-656-0879. Personal E-mail: cat60@juno.com.

RINGLEE, ROBERT JAMES, retired consulting engineering executive; b. Sacramento, Apr. 23, 1926; s. Francis and Marie N. R.; m. Helen Laura Carleton, Aug. 27, 1949; children— Sarah N., Jane C., Robert K. BSEE, U. Wash., Seattle, 1946, MSEE, 1948; PhD in Mechanics, Rensselaer Poly. Inst., Troy, NY, 1964. With advanced engring. program Gen. Electric Co., 1948-51, advanced devel. engr., power transformer dept., 1951-55, supr. power transformer design, 1955-60, sr. analytical engr., 1960-65, mgr. system and equipment reliability, 1965-69; prin. engr. dir. Power Technologies, Inc., Schenectady, 1969-86, prin cons., 1986-93; TAG assoc. Power Techs., Inc., 1993-94, assoc. cons., 1994-98. Contbr. articles to profl. pubs.; patentee in field. Active Schalmont Bd. Edn., 1966—70, pres., 1968—69; environ. adv. coun. NYISO, 2004—; sec. Friends of the Pine Bush Cmty. Inc., 2005—. With USNR, 1944—46. Recipient Managerial award Gen. Electric Co., 1953 Fellow IEEE (3 prize paper awards), AAAS; mem. Internat. Conf. on High Voltage Power Systems (expert advisor, Attwood Assoc.), Adirondack Mountain Club (pres. 1990-93, acting exec. dir. 1994). Democrat. Unitarian Universalist. Home and Office: 315 Juniper Dr Schenectady NY 12306-1705

RINGLER, JAMES M. (JAMES M. RINGLER), computer services company executive; b. 1945; BS, U. Buffalo, 1967, MBA, 1968. Mgr., cons. Arthur Andersen & Co., 1968-76; v.p. appliance group Tappan Co., Mansfield, Ohio, 1976-78, gen. v.p., mgr. appliance div., 1978-87, pres., COO, 1987-90, also bd. dirs., 1987-90; exec. v.p. Premark Internat., Inc., Deerfield, Ill., 1990-92, pres., COO, 1992-96, pres., CEO, 1996—99, chmn., 1997—99; vice chmn. Ill. Tool Works, Inc., Glenview, 1999—2004; interim CEO NCR Corp., Dayton, Ohio, 2005, chmn., 2005—. Bd. dir. Union Carbide Corp., 1996—2001, Dow Chemical Co., 2001—, Corn Products Internat., 2001—, FMC Tech., 2001—, Autoliv Lic., 2002—, NCR Corp., 2003—. Bd. mem. Lyric Opera Chgo.; trustee Boys & Girls Club of No. Am., Midwest region. Office: NCR Corp 1700 S Patterson Blvd Dayton OH 45479 *

RINGLER, KENNETH J., JR., former state agency administrator; b. May 29, 1948; m. Marty DeLaney; 3 children. Grad., Siena Coll. Chmn. planning bd. Town of Bethlehem, Albany County, NY, 1988—89, supr. NY, 1990—93; first dep. sec. state State of NY, 1996—99, commr. gen. svcs., 2001—04; exec. dep. commr. NY State Dept. Motor Vehicles, 1999—2001; exec. dir. The Port Authority of NY & NJ, NYC, 2004—07. Former chmn. Emergency Fin. Control Bd., City of Yonkers; bd. mem. Capitalize Albany Transp. Com., Com. on Open Govt., Coun. of Contracting Agencies, Gov. Nelson A. Rockefeller Empire State Plaza - Performing Arts Ctr. Corp., Gov.'s Seventh Regiment Armory Adv. Coun., Nat. Emergency Repatriation, Police Officers Meml. Adv. Coun., NY State Procurement Coun., Purchase Coun. for State and Local Govt. Procurement Officers, State Civil Defense Commn., State Commn. on Restoration of Capital, State Interagency Coun. on Mental Hygiene Property Utilization. Mem.: Nat. Assn. State Purchasing Officers, Nat. Assn. of State Chief Adminstr., NY State Heritage Commn., Am. Commodity Distribution Assn., Exec. Mansion Preservation Soc. Office Phone: 212-435-7000.

RINGLESBACH, DOROTHY LOUISE, retired nurse, writer; b. Ft. Wayne, Ind., Aug. 14, 1925; d. Paul Frederich and Elizabeth Barbara Preusser; m. Robert J. Salisbury, 1946 (div.); children: David, Claudia Ann, Evelyn, Claude, Jane; m. John C. Ringlesbach, July 5, 1980. RN, Wishard Meml. Hosp., 1947. RN Ind., Ky., Va. RN staff Mary Chiles Hosp., Mt. Sterling, Ky., 1958—60; interperter Colonial Williamsburg, Williamsburg, Va., 1968—73; house supr. Williamsburg Cmty. Hosp., Williamsburg, Va., 1973—80, 1985—93; ret. Author: OSS Stories that can Now Be Told, 2005; contbr. articles pub. to profl. jour. Mem. US Cadet Nurse Corps., 1944—47; state pres. Aux. to Kymedical Assn., Louisville, 1965—66, rec. sec., 1962—65. Cadet nurse corps, 1944—47. Mem.: OSS Com. Vets, OSS Soc. Luth. Avocations: reading, raise orchids, travel, writing. Home: 303 Farmville Ln Williamsburg VA 23188 Office Phone: 757-564-8299. Personal E-mail: esp22693@widomaker.com.

RINGWALD, MOLLY, actress; b. Sacramento, Feb. 18, 1968; d. Bob and Adele Ringwald; m. Valery Lameignère, July 28, 1999 (div. Nov. 2002); life ptnr. Panio Gianopoulos; 1 child, Mathilda Ereni. Grad. high sch., Los Angeles. Actress: (stage prodns.) The Glass Harp, 1973, Annie, 1977, Cabaret, 2001, Enchanted April, 2004, When Harry Met Sally, 2004, Sweet Charity, 2006;(feature films) Tempest, 1982, Spacehunter: Adventures in the Forbidden Zone, 1983, Sixteen Candles, 1984, The Breakfast Club, 1985, Pretty in Pink, 1986, The Pick-Up Artist, 1987, For Keeps, 1988, Betsy's Wedding, 1990, Seven Sunday, 1994, Office Killer, 1996, Kimberly, 1999, Requiem For Murder, 1999, Teaching Mrs. Tingle, 1999, Cut, 2000, In the Weeds, 2000, Ring of Fire, 2000, Not Another Teen Movie, 2001, The Tulse Luper Suitcases: The Moab Story, 2003; (TV movies) Packin' It In, 1983, P.K. and the Kid, Something to Live For: The Alison Gertz Story, 1992, Twice Upon a Time, 1998, Since You've Been Gone, 1998, The Big Time, 2002; (TV mini-series) The Stand, 1994; regular (TV series) The Facts of Life, 1979-80, Townies, 1996; guest-star: (TV shows) Diff'rent Strokes, The Merv Griffin Show; (Album) Molly Sings, 1974. Office: William Morris Agy 151 S El Camino Dr Beverly Hills CA 90212-2775

RINI, JOEL, language educator, linguist; b. Cleve., Dec. 4, 1957; s. Joseph Charles and Virginia Ann Rini; m. Pamela Jean De Vries; children: Christopher Michael, Marcus Joel. BS in Edn., Kent State U., 1981; PhD, U. Mich., 1987. Asst. prof. Spanish linguistics U. Va., Charlottesville, 1987—93; assoc. prof. Spanish linguistics, 1993—2000, prof. Spanish linguistics, 2000—, chmn. Spanish, Italian and Portuguese, 1998—2004. Author: (books) Motives for Linguistic Change in the Formation of the Spanish Object Pronouns, 1992, Exploring the Role of Morphology in the Evolution of Spanish, 1999; contbr. articles to profl. jours. Home: 1039

Hayrake Ln Charlottesville VA 22903 Office: Univ Virginia 115 Wilson Hall Charlottesville VA 22904 Office Phone: 434-924-4657. Personal E-mail: jrini@adelphia.net. E-mail: jr6b@virginia.edu.

RINI, JOSEPHINE NANCY, nuclear medicine physician; b. Astoria, NY, Apr. 29, 1964; d. Joseph Anthony and Nancy Rini; m. Gary Limoncelli, Sept. 7, 1996; 1 child, Grace Ann Limoncelli. MD, Mayo Med. Sch., Rochester, MN, 1989. Diplomate Am. Bd. Nuc. Medicine, 1998, Am. Bd. Internal Medicine, 1996. Staff physician divsn. of nuc. medicine L.I. Jewish Med. Ctr., New Hyde Park, NY, 1999—. Mem.: SNM, Acad. of Molecular Imaging, RSNA. Achievements include research in PET and lymphoma, PET of FDG labeled WBC. Office: LI Jewish Med Ctr 270-05 76th Ave New Hyde Park NY 11040 Office Phone: 718-470-7080. Personal E-mail: rinlim2@aol.com. E-mail: rini@lij.edu.

RINK, WESLEY WINFRED, retired bank executive; b. Hickory, NC, June 14, 1922; s. Dewey Lee and Mabel E. (Yount) R.; m. Patricia A. Jones, Aug. 19, 2000; children from previous marriage: Rebecca S., Christopher L BS in Accountancy, U. Ill., 1947, MS, 1948. Acct., Glidden Co., Chgo., 1948-58; adminstrv. mgr. Central Soya Co., Chgo., 1958-65; v.p., comptroller State Nat. Bank, Evanston, Ill., 1965-71; exec. v.p., dir. Pioneer Trust & Savs. Bank, Chgo., 1971-76; corp. v.p. Exchange Bancorp., Inc., Tampa, 1977-82; sr. v.p. NCNB Nat. Bank Fla., Tampa, 1982-86; fin cons. Temple Terrace, Fla., 1986-2001; ret., 2001. Served to capt. USAAF, 1942—46. Home: 11402 Robles Del Rio Pl Temple Terrace FL 33617-2627

RINKENBERGER, RICHARD KRUG, physical scientist, geologist, consultant; b. Gridley, Ill., May 15, 1933; s. Burl E. and Olive J. (Krug) R.; m. Marilyn Ruth Ratliff, Feb. 19, 1960; children: Janice L., Ginger R., Rebekah P. BA in Geology, U. Colo., Boulder, 1959. Dir. prospecting Grubstake Assn., Sask., Can., 1958-59; engr. Martin-Marietta Aerospace Co., Denver, 1960-75; geologist U.S. Geol. Survey, Denver, 1975; geologist remote sensing U.S. Mine Safety and Health Adminstrn., Denver, 1975-79; pres., exploration geologist Banner Set, Ltd., Denver, 1980-84; pres., cons. geologist R.K. Rinkenberger & Assocs., Aurora, Colo., 1979-87; phys. scientist U.S. Dept. Energy, Germantown, Md., 1987-97; cons. geologist, rsch. geologist Denver, Rockville, Md., 1988—. Educator prospecting Denver Sch. Prospecting, 1968-71, U. Colo., Denver, Boulder, 1970-75; rsch. geochemist Heritage Chem. Co., Englewood, 1984-86; prospecting researcher, gold and silver prospector R.K. Rinkenberger & Assocs., 1965—. Contbr. articles to profl. jours. Mem. parent adv. bd, supt. of schs. Westminster, Colo., 1982-83. Grantee Sask. Dept. Mineral Resources, 1958, 59; remote sensing grantee U.S. Geol. Survey, 1978. Mem. Denver Mining Club, Sigma Gamma Epsilon. Mem. Ch. of the Nazarene. Achievements include geological theory and experimentation, research on animal and plant killing mechanisms responsible for dinosaur extinction and other mass plant and animal extinctions. Office: 12183 Monaco Dr Brighton CO 80602-9603

RINO, BARBARA ELIZABETH, musician, educator; b. Lincoln, Nebr., Jan. 14, 1945; d. Howard Gillette and Elizabeth Lucille Cook; m. Louis Stanislaus Rino, Dec. 22, 1974 (dec. Aug. 31, 2004); 1 child, John Gaspare. MusB (with distinction), Nebr. Wesleyan U., Lincoln, 1966; violin study, Harold Wippler, Denver, Colo., 1974—77. Lic. tchr. Colo., 1967. Violinist Lincoln Symphony Orch., Lincoln, Nebr., 1962—66; music educator Denver Pub. Sch., Denver, 1966—68; orch. dir. Adams County Sch. Dist. 50, Westminster, Colo., 1969—78, Adams County Sch. Dist. 12 Five Star Schs., Thornton, Colo., 1988—2001; pvt. studio tchr. self employed, Westminster, Colo., 1971—; concertmaster Brico Symphony Orch., Denver, 1972—74; dir. orch. Denver Youth Musicians Inc., 1973—77, 1984—89; free lance violinist Denver Musicians Assn., Denver, 1973—95; orch. clinician, adj. Solo and Group Competitions Youth Orch. Chair Auditions, Colo., 1973—; concertmaster Rocky Mountain Chamber Orch., 1985—87. Conductor: Colo. Music Educators State Conf., 1972, 1975; musician: Disneyland and Universal Studios, Kennedy Arts Ctr., 1976, Expo '86; author (curriculum): Dist. Orch. grades 6-12, 1990. Music activities Westminister United Meth. Ch., Colo., 1980—. Recipient Outstanding Alumni award, Nebr. Wesleyan U. Dept. Music, 2006. Mem.: Music Tchrs'. Nat. Assn., Am. String Tchrs. Assn. (Colo. Outstanding Tchr. of the Yr. 2003), Music Educators Nat. Conf., Phi Kappa Phi, Kappa Delta Pi. Meth. Achievements include pvt. violin and viola students consistently chosen to participate in Colo. All State HS Orch., Western States Honor Orch., Denver Young Artist Orch., MTNA divsn., Nat. solo competitions.

RINSCH, MARYANN ELIZABETH, occupational therapist; b. LA, Aug. 8, 1939; d. Harry William and Thora Analine (Langlie) Hitchcock; m. Charles Emil Rinsch, June 18, 1964; children: Christopher, Daniel, Carl. BS, U. Minn., 1961. Registered occupational therapist Calif., lic. Calif., 2003. Staff occupl. therapist Hastings State Hosp., Minn., 1961-62, Neuropsychiat. Inst., LA, 1962-64; staff and sr. occupl. therapist Calif. Children's Svcs., LA, 1964-66, head occupl. therapist, 1966-68; rschr. A. Jean Ayres, U. So. Calif., LA, 1968-69; pvt. practice neurodevel. and sensory integraton Tarzana, Calif., 1969-74; pediat. occupl. therapist neurodevel. & sensory integration St. Johns Hosp., Santa Monica, Calif., 1991-95; pvt. practice, cons. Santa Monica-Malibu Unified Sch. Dist., 1994-2001; pvt. practice, 2001—. Mem. alliance bd. Natural History Mus., LA County, 1983—, pres., 1998-99; cub scouts den mother Boy Scout Troop 474, Sherman Oaks, Calif., 1986-88, advancement chair Boy Scout Troop 474, 1989-92; mem. Vol. League San Fernando Valley, Van Nuys, Calif., 1985-93; trustee Viewpoint Sch., Calabasas, Calif., 1987-90; bd. dirs. Valley Women's Ctr., 1990-91. Mem. Am. Occupl. Therapy Assn., Calif. Occupl. Therapy Assn. Home: 430 S Oakhurst Dr Beverly Hills CA 90212 Personal E-mail: merinsch@sbcglobal.net.

RINSKY, ARTHUR C., lawyer; b. Cin., July 10, 1944; AB with honors, U. Cin., 1966; JD cum laude, U. Mich., 1969; LLM in Taxation, NYU, 1974. Bar: Fla. 1969, Calif. 1975, US Tax Ct. 1974, Tex. 2004; cert. tax specialist, Calif. Ptr. DLA Piper US LLP, Palo Alto, Calif., 1975—. Mem. ABA, State Bar Calif., Phi Beta Kappa, Phi Eta Sigma. Office: DLA Piper US LLP 2000 University Ave East Palo Alto CA 94303

RINSKY, JOEL CHARLES, lawyer; b. Bklyn., Jan. 29, 1938; s. Irving C. and Elsie (Millman) R.; m. Judith L. Lynn, Jan. 26, 1963; children: Heidi M., Heather S., Jason W. BS, Rutgers U., 1961, LLB, 1962, JD, 1968. Bar: NJ 1963, U.S. Dist. Ct. NJ 1963, U.S. Supreme Ct. 1967, U.S. Ct. Appeals (3d cir.) 1986. Sole practice, Livingston, NJ, 1964—97; sr. ptnr. Rinsky & Marley L.L.C., Livingston, 1997—98; of counsel Poles, Tublin, Stratakis, Gonzalez and Weichert LLP, Livingston, 1999—. Committeeman Millburn-Short Hills (N.J.) Dem. Com., 1982-97, vice chmn., 1983-87; trustee Student Loan Fund, Millburn, 1983-91. Fellow Am. Acad. Matrimonial Lawyers; mem. N.J. Bar Assn., Essex County Bar Assn. (exec. com. sect. family law). Jewish. Avocations: tennis, chess, golf, piano. Home: 87 Sullivan Dr West Orange NJ 07052-2262 Office: 127 E Mount Pleasant Ave Livingston NJ 07039-3005 Office Phone: 973-669-8687. Personal E-mail: rinsky3@aol.com. Business E-Mail: rinsky2@comcast.org. E-mail: jrinsky@polestublin.com.

RINSKY, JUDITH SUE LYNN, foundation administrator, consultant, educator; b. Sept. 12, 1941; d. Allan A. and Sophie (Schwartz) Lynn; m. Joel C. Rinsky, Jan. 29, 1963; children: Heidi Mae Schnapp, Heather Star Maxon, Jason Wayne. BA in Home Econs., Montclair State U., 1963. Tchr. home econs. Florence Ave. Sch., Irvington, NJ, 1963—66; substitute tchr. Millburn-Short Hills Sch. Sys., Millburn Twp., NJ, 1978—82, Millburn-Short Hills Sch. Sys., Milburn Twp., 1990—98; sr. citizen coord. Millburn-Short Hills Sch. Sys., Millburn Twp., 1982—87; coord. respite care Essex County Divsn. on Aging, East Orange, NJ, 1988—90; pvt. practice educator Short Hills, NJ, 1990—98; tchr. basic skills Millburn H.S., 1998—. Bd. mem. adv. com. gerontology Seton Hall U., 1984—90; coord. Mayor's Adv. Bd. Sr. Citizens, Millburn-Short Hills, 1982—87; home instrn. Millburn-Short Hills Sch. Sys., 1997—98; tchr. adv. Millburn H.S. Interart Club, 2000—. Pres. Deerfield Sch. PTA, 1979-80, Millburn H.S. PTA, 1983-85; co-chmn. dinner dance Charles T. King Student Loan Fund, 1981; active Handicapped Access Study Com., 1983-85; bd. dirs. Coun. on Health and Human Svcs., 1985-90, 94-97; acting dir. B'nai Israel Nursery Sch., 1994. Mem. Lake Naomi Assn. (chmn. sailing com. 1981), N.J. Home Econs. Assn., Am. Home Econs. Assn., Rotary (hon., pres. Millburn-Short Hills club 1992-93, bd. dirs. 1992-2000, advisor Millburn interact club 1987-98, 2000-04, chmn. internat. interact dist. 7470 1993-95, advisor 1995-98). Home and Office: 87 Sullivan Dr West Orange NJ 07052-2262 Home Phone: 973-669-8687; Office Phone: 973-376-3600. Personal E-mail: jsr_07041@yahoo.com. Business E-Mail: rinsky@millburn.org.

RION, JOHN HAYES, lawyer; b. Dayton, Ohio, Aug. 4, 1943; s. Paul West and Vera E. (Spitler) R.; m. Barbara Smith, July 31, 1965; children: Stacey, Jennifer, Jon Paul. BA, Ohio State U., 1965; JD, U. Toledo, 1969. Bar: Ohio 1970, U.S. Dist. Ct. (so. dist.) Ohio 1970, U.S. Ct. Appeals (6th cir.) 1983, U.S. Supreme Ct. 1977; cert. Criminal Trial Advocate, Nat. Bd. Trial Advocacy. Ptnr., Rion, Rion & Rion, Dayton, Ohio, 1969-78; v.p. Rion, Rion & Rion, L.P.A., 1978-88; pres. John H. Rion & Assocs., 1988-97; ptnr., chmn. Rion, Rion & Rion, L.P.A., Inc., Dayton, 1997—; lectr. in field. Contbr. articles to profl. jours. Mem. jud. selection com. Republican Com., 1974. Mem. NACDL (life), ABA, Ohio State Bar Assn. (faculty 1983, chmn. criminal justice com. 1989-91, mem. setting standards for bd. cert. com. 1999), Dayton Bar Assn. (Outstanding Service award 1977, 80, chmn. bar briefs 1975), Ohio Assn. Criminal Def. Lawyers (life, pres. 1989, chmn. 1990), Montgomery County Trial Lawyers (v.p. 1989-90, mem. bd. trustees 1990), Calif. Def. Lawyers Assn., Ohio Trial Lawyers Assn. Republican. Methodist (pres. Grace United Ch. Ushers Club 1982-84). Clubs: Dayton Racquet, Comos (pres. 1982-84), Briarwood Sportsman. Lodges: Masons (32 degree), Shriners. Avocations: fly fishing, tennis. Office: Rion Rion and Rion Ste 2150 (21st Fl) 130 W Second St Ltd Dayton OH 45402 Office Phone: 937-223-9133. E-mail: info@rionlaw.com. *

RIORDAN, GEORGE NICKERSON, investment banker; b. Patchogue, NY, May 16, 1933; s. E. Arthur and Constance E. (Whelden) R.; m. Ann Wiggins, Jan. 4, 1958; children— Susan M., Peter G. BS, Cornell U., 1955; MBA, Harvard U., 1960. Vice-pres. Lehman Bros., NYC, 1960-71; mng. dir. Blyth Eastman Paine Webber, Los Angeles and NYC, 1971-81, Prudential-Bache Securities, Los Angeles, 1981-88, Bear Stearns & Co., Inc., LA, 1988-89, Dean Witter Reynolds Inc., 1989-91. Chmn. bd. MSC Software, Inc., 1997-99; bd. dirs. MSC Software, Inc., L.A. Served to capt. USAF, 1955-57 Mem. Calif. Club, Quoque Field Club (L.I., N.Y.), Athenaeum Club, Valley Hunt Club (Pasadena, Calif.). Office: 815 Colorado Blvd Ste 104 Los Angeles CA 90041-1720 Business E-Mail: george.riordan@mscsoftware.com.

RIORDAN, JOHN A., retired food products executive; b. NYC, Oct. 23, 1933; s. John J. and Margaret M. Riordan; m. Mary P. Riordan, Feb. 27, 1963; 1 child, Mary P. BA, Iona Coll., NYC. Food sales rep. Procter & Gamble, Cin.; food sales rep., asst. mgr. Harvey Corp., NYC; ret. Fundraiser Dept. Vets. Affairs. Staff sgt. US Army, 1953—55, Korea. Mem.: VFW (svc. officer, fund raiser), Am. Legion (svc. officer, fund raiser). Democrat. Roman Catholic. Avocations: golf, woodworking, building. Home: 323 Shadowlawn Dr Neptune NJ 07753-2868

RIORDAN, JOHN THOMAS, trade association executive, consultant; b. Newark, June 5, 1937; s. Daniel Francis and Kathleen May (Hanan) R.; m. Mary Theresa Fleming, Sept. 10, 1966; children: Sheila, Patrick, Aidan, Meghan, Brendan, Caitlin. BA, Montclair St. Coll., 1959; MA, Laval U., Que., Can., 1963; postgrad., Harvard U., 1980. Tchr. Princeton (N.J.) Pub. Schs., 1959-64; instr. SUNY, Cortland, 1965; editor McGraw-Hill Book Co., St. Louis, 1966; assoc. examiner Ednl. Testing Svc., Princeton, 1967-68; mgr. Houghton Mifflin Co., Boston, 1968-73, editl. dir., 1973-74; v.p. Hougton Mifflin Co., Boston, 1974-75, dir., 1975, sr. v.p., 1975-81; dir. programs Internat. Coun. Shopping Ctrs., NYC, 1982-83, gen. mgr., 1983-85, exec. v.p., 1986-96, pres., CEO, 1997—2001, vice chmn., 2001—03, lifetime trustee, 2003. Cons., leader Experiment in Internat. Living, Brattleboro, Vt., 1961-64; mem. adv. bd. Sch. Internat. Tng., Brattleboro, 1971-79, Real Estate Ctr. U. Pa., 1991—, Ctr. for Real Estate MIT, 1992—; mem. fin. adv. bd. City of Georgetown, Mass., 1972-75, chmn. 2001-03; trustee The Pike Sch., Andover, Mass., 1973-76; bd. trustees Travel Bus. Roundtable; mem. adv. bd. Baruch Coll., adv. bd. MIT ctr. for real estate, adv. bd. U Pa. real estate ctr.; bd. dirs. Gen. Growth Properties, 2003—. Mem.: Am. Soc. Assn. Execs. (bd. dirs. Ivanhoe/Cambridge 2005—). E-mail: jtriordan@aol.com.

RIORDAN, RICHARD J., former state official, former mayor; b. Flushing, NY, 1930; m. Eugenia Riordan; 6 children (2 dec.); m. Jill Riordan; m. Nancy Daly Riordan; 3 children. Attended, U. Calif., Santa Clara; grad., Princeton U., 1952; JD, U. Mich., 1956. With O'Melveny & Myers, LA; owner, operator Original Pantry Cafe; founder Total Pharmaceutical Care, Tetra Tech; atty. Riordan & McKinzie, 1970—2003; mayor LA, 1993—2001; sec. of edn. State of Calif., Sacramento, 2003—05. Co-founder LEARN, 1991; sponsor Writing to Read computer labs Riordan Found.; active Eastside Boys and Girls Club. Lt. U.S. Army, Korea.

RIORDAN, RICK, writer; b. San Antonio, Tex. married; 2 children. Graduate, Univ. Tex., Austin. Former English, history tchr., Calif. and Tex. Author: (novels) Big Red Tequila, 1997 (Anthony award for best original paperback novel, Shamus award for best first private eye novel), Widower's Two-Step, 1998 (Edgar Allen Poe award for best original paperback novel, 1999), Last King of Texas, 2000, Devil Went Down to Texas, 2001, Cold Springs, 2003 (One of top 10 suspense novels, Am.Libr. Assn., 2003), South Town, 2004 (Edgar award, 2004), Mission Road, 2005, (childrens books) Percy Jackson & the Olympians: The Lightning Thief, 2005, Percy Jackson & the Olympians: The Sea of Monsters, 2006, Percy Jackson & the Olympians: The Titan's Curse, 2007. Inducted into Tex. Inst. Letters, 2003. Mailing: c/o Nancy Gallt Lit Agy 273 Charlton Ave South Orange NJ 07079 Address: c/o Gina Maccoby Lit Agy PO Box 60 Chappaqua NY 10514 E-mail: rick@rickriordan.com. *

RIORDAN, ROBERT P., lawyer; b. Milw., Feb. 6, 1958; AB, Duke Univ., 1980, JD, 1984. Bar: Ga. 1984. Ptnr., head, labor and employment group Alston & Bird LLP, Atlanta. Mem.: ABA, Henry L. Lumpkin Am. Inn of Ct., Atlanta Bar Assn., Ga. Bar Assn. Office: Alston & Bird LLP One Atlantic Ctr 1201 W Peachtree St NW Atlanta GA 30309-3424 Office Phone: 404-881-7682. Office Fax: 404-881-7777. Business E-Mail: briordan@alston.com.

RIORDAN, THOMAS J., lawyer, chemicals executive; BA, Loyola U., 1972, MBA, 1975; JD, No. Ill. U., 1979. Bar: Ill. With Trane Co., 1972—75; employee rels. mgr., atty. UOP, 1975—89, chief litig. counsel; joined Laporte, 1989; v.p. law and adminstrn. Rockwood Holdings, Inc., Rockwood Specialties Group, Inc., Princeton, NJ, 1992—2000, sr. v.p. law and adminstrn., sec., 2000—. Mem.: ABA. Office: Rockwood Holdings, Inc 100 Overlook Ctr Princeton NJ 08540 Office Phone: 609-514-0300. *

RIORDAN, THOMAS J., manufacturing executive; BS, Northwestern Univ.; MS, Purdue Univ. Mgmt. positions Borg-Warner Automotive, J.I. Case; pres. Consolidated Sawmill Machinery Internat.; mgmt. positions through exec. v.p., COO SPX Corp., 1997—2006; pres., COO TEREX Corp., Westport, Conn., 2007—. Office: TEREX Corp 500 Post Rd E Westport CT 06880 *

RIOS, ELENA, health association administrator; BA, Stanford U., 1977; M in Health Policy and Planning Analysis, UCLA, 1980, MD, 1987. With State of Calif. Office of Statewide Health Planning and Devel.; mem. Nat. Health Care Reform Task Force; coord. outreach groups for White House; advisor regional and minority women's health U.S. Dept. Health and Human Svcs., 1994—98; pres., CEO Nat. Hispanic Med. Assn. Primary care health svcs. rsch. fellow UCLA, 1990; CEO Hispanic-Serving Health Professions Schools, Inc.; bd. dirs. Nat. Hispanic Leadership Agenda, Women's Policy Inc., Partnerships for Prevention; co-chair Hispanic Health Coalition; mem. advisory panel Medicare Edn.; lectr. in field. Named one of Top 10 Latinos in Healthcare, LatinoLeaders mag., 2004. Office: Nat Hispanic Med Assn 1411 K St NW Ste 1100 Washington DC 20005

RIOS, EVELYN DEERWESTER, columnist, musician, artist, writer; b. Payne, Ohio, June 25, 1916; d. Jay Russell and Flossie Edith (Fell) Deerwester; m. Edwin Tietjen Rios, Sept. 19, 1942 (dec. Feb. 1987); children: Jane Evelyn, Linda Sue Rios Stahlman. BA with honors, San Jose State U., 1964, MA, 1968. Cert. elem., secondary tchr. Calif. Lectr. in music San Jose (Calif.) State U., 1969-75; from bilingual cons. to assoc. editor Ednl. Factors, Inc., San Jose, 1969-76, mgr. field rsch., 1977-78; writer, editor Calif. MediCorps Program, 1978-85; contbg. editor, illustrator Cmty. Family Mag., Wimberly, Tex., 1983-85; columnist The Springer, Dripping Springs, Tex., 1985-90. Author, illustrator, health instr. textbooks elem. schs., 1980—82. Author: The Best of It Seems To Me, 2002. Chmn. Dripping Springs Planning and Zoning Commn., 1991—93; music dir. Cambrian Park (Calif.) Meth. Ch., 1961—64; choir dir. Bethel Luth. Ch., Cupertino, Calif., 1965—66, 1968—83; dir. music St. Aban's Ch., Bogota, Colombia; organist Holy Spirit Episcopal Ch., Dripping Springs, 1987—94. Mem.: Am. Guild Organists (dean 1963—64), Phi Kappa Phi (pres. San Jose chpt. 1973—74). Avocations: weaving, stitching, painting. Home: PO Box 3175 Atascadero CA 93423-3175

RIOTTO, SCOTT M., secondary school educator; b. Ft. Campbell, Ky., July 28, 1968; BA in History, U. Pa., Phila., 1990; MEd, U. Pa., 1991; MA in Am. History, Rutgers U., Newark, NJ, 2002. History tchr. SESIS, Fairview, NJ, 1991—93, NVRHS, Demarest, NJ, 1993—94, Montville Twp. HS, NJ, 1994—. History prof. County Coll. Morris, Randolph, NJ, 2003—. Mem.: OAH, NCHE, NJCHE, NCSS, NJCSS, NEA, NJEA, MCEA, MTEA. Office: Montville Twp HS 100 Horseneck Rd Montville NJ 07045 Office Fax: 973-334-0753. Business E-Mail: sriotto@montville.net.

RIOU, JEAN-PIERRE ALAIN, plastic surgeon; b. NYC, Nov. 21, 1962; s. Marcel Henri and Marie-Louise Riou; m. Lori Beth Sehneider, Apr. 30, 1989; children: Jessica Nicole, Justin Taylor. BA, NYU, NYC, 1983, MD, 1987. Diplomate Am. Bd. Surgery, 1993, Am. Bd. Plastic Surgery, 1996, Nat. Bd. Med. Examiners. Intern NYU Sch. Medicine, NYC, 1987—88; resident Yale U. Sch. Medicine, New Haven, 1992—94; hand surgeon Hartford Hosp., Hartford, 1994—. Instr. in surgery Yale U. Sch. Medicine, New Haven, 1992—94. Contbr. articles to profl. jours. Fellow: ACS; mem.: AMA, Yale Plastic Surgery Alumni Soc., Iredell Med. Soc. (program dir. 1996), NC Med. Soc., Am. Soc. Plastic and Reconstructive Surgeons. Roman Catholic. Avocations: boating, tennis, waters sports. Office: Harborview Plastic Surgery 19615 Liverpool Pkwy Cornelius NC 28031

RIOULT, FABIEN ANDRE, research scientist; s. Antoine Serge and Beatrice Annick Rioult; m. Laura Suzanne Steele, Nov. 1, 2006. MS in Chem. and Process Engring., Ecole des Mines, Saint-Etienne, France, 2002, PhD in Chem. and Process Engring., 2005. Rschr. Alcan, Voreppe, Isere, France, 2002—05; rsch. assoc. U. Wis., Madison, 2005—. Contbr. articles to profl. jours. Office: U Wis 1500 Engineering Dr Madison WI 53706 Home Phone: 1-608-257-2526. Personal E-mail: fabien.rioult@laposte.net. E-mail: frioult@cae.wisc.edu.

RIOUX, PIERRE AUGUST, psychiatrist; b. Hartford, Conn., Sept. 2, 1953; s. Berchmans and Mary (Sauter) R. BA, Concordia Coll., 1975; MD, U. N.D., 1981. Diplomate Am. Bd. Psychiatry and Neurology. Intern U. Mich., 1981-82, resident, 1982-85; asst. prof. dept. psychiatry Emory U., Atlanta, 1985-86; attending physician VA Med. Ctr., Atlanta, 1985-86; staff physician UniMed Med. Ctr., Minot, ND, 1986-87, med. dir. adult partial hospitalization program, 1988-98, dir. behavioral health svcs., 1990—2001; med. dir. North Ctrl. Human Svc. Ctr., Minot, 1987-98; med. dir. stress unit Austin Med. Ctr., 2001—; med. dir. behavioral health Mayo Health Sys., Austin, 2003—06, med. dir. dept. psychiatry and psychology, 2006—; instr. Mayo Med. Sch., 2003—. Cons. North Ctrl. Human Svc. Ctr., 1986—2001; mem. chem. dependency unit UniMed Med. Ctr, 1986—; mem. adv. bd. UniMed Med. Ctr., 1998—2001; clin. prof. neurosci. U. N.D. Sch. Medicine, 1986—96; mem. family practice residence adv. bd. com. U. N.D., 1987—95; physician advisor N.D. Health Care Rev., Inc., 1987—2001; dir. psychiat. svcs. Dakota Boys Ranch, Minot, 1990—94; med. dir. Rural Mental Health Consortium, 1999—2001; instr. Mayo Med. Sch., 2003—. Bd. Am. Coll. of Heraldry, 2003; comsumer rsch. coun. America's Top Psychiatrists, 2002—. Recipient Nat. Alliance for the Mentally Ill Exemplary Psychiatrist award, 1993, Top Psychiatrists in Am. award Consumers Rsch. Coun. Am., 2003. Fellow Am. Coll. Forensic Examiners (life); mem. AMA, Am. Psychiat. Assn. (pres. N.D. dist. br. 1993-96, dep. rep. area IV coun. 1993-98, mem. psychiat. svcs. achievement awards bd. 1996-97, chmn. 1998, fellowship award 1996, disting. fellowship award 2003), Assn. Am. Physicians and Surgeons, Am. Soc. Clin. Psychopharmacology, N.D. Psychiat. Assn. (dist. br. exec. coun. 1997-2001), N.D. Med. Assn. (mem. commn. on socio-econ. affairs 1997-2001), Internat. Soc. for Philos. Enquiry (pres.2002-05) Avocation: art. Office: PO Box 188 Austin MN 55912-0188

RIPA, KELLY MARIA, television personality, actress; b. Stratford, NJ, Oct. 2, 1970; d. Joseph and Esther Ripa; m. Mark Consuelos, 1996; children: Michael Joseph, Lola Grace, Joaquin Antonio. Student, Camden CC, NJ. Co-host Live with Regis and Kelly, NY, 2001—. Dancer (TV series) Dance Party USA, 1986; actor: (TV series) All My Children, 1990—2002 (Soap Opera Digest award, 1996, 1998, 2000, 3 Daytime Emmy nominations); (films) Marvin's Room, 1996, The Stand-In, 1999 (Best Actress award N.Y. Internat. Ind. Film and Video Festival, 1999), It's a Very Merry Muppet Christmas Movie, 2002, Cheaper by the Dozen, 2003; (TV films) Someone to Love, 2001; voice: (films) Kim Possible: A Stitch in Time, 2003; Batman: Mystery of the Batwoman, 2003; actor: (TV series) Hope & Faith, 2003—. Nominee Outstanding Talkshow Host award, Daytime Emmy; named one of 25 Most Intriguing People, People Mag., 2001, Top 20 Entertainers of Yr., E! Entertainment. Office: Live with Regis and Kelly 7 Lincoln Sq New York NY 10023

RIPERT, ERIC, food service executive; b. Antibes, France, Mar. 2, 1965; married. Grad., Culinary Sch., Perpignan, France, 1982. Apprentice La Tour D'Argent, Paris; with Jamin; sous chef Watergate Hotel, Washington, 1989—91, Bouley, NYC; exec. chef Le Bernardin, NYC, 1991—94, chef., 1994—, co-owner. Chair City Harvest's Food Coun.; pres. Jean-Louis

Palladin Found. Author: (cookbooks) A Return to Cooking, 2002; co-author: Le Bernardin. Recipient Top Chef in NYC award James Beard Found., 2003. Avocations: eating, travel, skiing. *

RIPERT, JEAN-MAURICE, ambassador; b. June 22, 1953; married; 1 child. Grad., Inst. Polit. Studies, Paris, 1973, Nat. Sch. Adminstrn., 1980. With legal affairs divsn. French Ministry Fgn. Affairs, 1980—82, with econ. and fin. affairs divsn., 1982—83, tech. advisor, mem. staff of the min. for cooperation and devel., 1983—84, tech. advisor, mem. staff of the min. for European affairs, 1984, tech. advisor, mem. staff of the min., 1984, 2nd counselor Washington, 1986—88, tech. advisor, mem. staff of the prime min., 1988—90, diplomatic advisor to prime min., 1991, chief of staff to sec. state for humanitarian action, 1991—92, advisor to min. health and humanitarian action, 1992—93, consul gen. LA, 1993—96, dep. dir. UN and Internat. Orgns. desk, 1996—97, diplomatic advisor to prime min., 1997—2000, amb. to Greece, 2000—03, dir. UN and Internat. Orgns. desk, 2003—05, amb., permanent rep. to UN Geneva, 2005—07, NYC, 2007—. Office: French Mission to UN 245 E 47th St New York NY 10017 Office Phone: 212-308-5700. Office Fax: 212-355-2763.

RIPKEN, CAL (CALVIN EDWIN RIPKEN JR.), retired professional baseball player; b. Havre de Grace, Md., Aug. 24, 1960; s. Calvin and Viola Ripken; m. Kelly Geer, Nov. 13, 1987; children: Rachel, Ryan. Played for minor league teams, Bluefield, Miami, Charlotte, Rochester, 1978—81; shortstop Balt. Orioles, 1981—2001; pres., CEO Ripken Baseball Group, 1999—; spl. sports envoy US Dept. State, Washington, 2007—. Co-founder The Cal Ripken Sr. Found., 2001—; baseball analyst TBS Network, 2007—. Author: The Only Way I Know, 1997, Get in the Game: Eight Elements of Perseverance That Make the Difference, 2007, (children's books) Parenting Young Athletes the Ripken Way: Ensuring the Best Experience for Your Kids in Any Sport, 2006, The Longest Season, 2007; co-author (with Bill Ripken): Play Baseball The Ripken Way: The Complete Illustrated Guide to the Fundamentals, 2004. Named Am. League MVP, 1983, 1991, MLB All-Star Game MVP, 1983, 2001, Sportsman of Yr., SI mag., 1995, Male Athlete of Yr., AP, 1995; named to Am. League All-Star Team, 1983—2001, MLB All-Century Team, 1999, Nat. Baseball Hall of Fame, 2007; recipient Am. League Rookie of Yr. award, 1982, Am. League Silver Slugger award, 1983—86, 1989, 1991, 1993—94, Am League Golden Glove award, 1991—92, Lou Gehrig Meml. award, 1992. Achievements include being a holder of the major league record for consecutive games played; breaking Lou Gehrig's record of 2131 consecutive games played, 1995; maj. league record home runs by shortstop; highest single season fielding percentage (.996), 1990; most consecutive errorless games at shortstop (95); led Am. League in Runs (121), Hits (211), 1983. Office: Ripken Baseball 1427 Clarkview Rd Ste 100 Baltimore MD 21209 *

RIPLEY, AFA, JR., attorney general; b. 1949; BBA, MBA, Kans. State Teachers Coll., Emporia, Kans.; JD, Calif. Western Sch. Law, San Diego, 1978. Dep. atty. gen. Atty. Gen. Office, Hawaii, 1978; dep. pros. atty. City and County of Honolulu, 1979—80, dep. corp. counsel, trial divsn., 1980—82; atty. Minn & Ripley, Hawaii, 1982—89; chmn., bd. mem. Am. Samoa Power Authority; lawyer pvt. practice; atty. gen. Am. Samoa, 2007—. Office: American Samoa Govt Exec Office Bldg Utulei Territory of American Samoa Pago Pago AS 96799 Office Phone: 684-633-4163. *

RIPLEY, CHARLENE A., lawyer; BA, U. Alta.; JD, Dalhousie U., Nova Scotia. Counsel Amoco Can. Petroleum Co. Ltd., 1990—97; sr. counsel Norcen Energy Resources Ltd. (predecessor to Anadarko Can. Corp.), 1997—98, v.p., gen. counsel, corp. sec., 1998—2003; v.p., gen. counsel Anadarko Petroleum Corp., 2003—, corp. sec., 2004—. Mem.: Can. Bar Assn., Law Soc. Alta., Assn. Corp. Counsel, Tex. Gen. Counsel Grp., API Gen. Com. on Law, Alta. Arbitration & Mediation Soc., Tex. State Bar. Office: Anadarko Petroleum Corp 1201 Lake Robbins Dr The Woodlands TX 77380-1046 Office Fax: 832-636-8220, 832-636-1000. *

RIPLEY, JUDITH G., state agency administrator; Student, U. Cin.; LLB, Ind. U., Indpls., 1981. Mem. Ind. Utility Regulatory Commn., 1998—2005; dir. Ind. Dept. Fin. Instns., 2005—. Mem. fed.-state joint bd. jurisdictional separations FCC, 2003. Adv. coun. N.Mex. State U. Ctr. Pub. Utilities. Mem.: Conf. State Bank Suprs. (vice chmn. dist II, vice chmn. legis. com.). Office: Dept Fin Instns Ste 300 30 S Meridian St Indianapolis IN 46204 Office Phone: 317-232-3955.

RIPLEY, RANDALL BUTLER, political scientist, educator; b. Des Moines, Jan. 24, 1938; s. Henry Dayton and Aletha (Butler) R.; m. Grace A. Franklin, Oct. 15, 1974; children: Frederick Joseph, Vanessa Gail. BA, DePauw U., 1959; MA, Harvard U., 1961, PhD, 1963. Tchg. fellow Harvard, 1960-62; mem. staff Brookings Inst., Washington, 1963-67, rsch. asst., 1963-64, rsch. assoc., 1964-67; intern Office Dem. Whip, US Ho. of Reps., Washington, 1963; assoc. prof. dept. polit. sci. Ohio State U., Columbus, 1967-69, prof., 1969—2005, prof. emeritus, 2005, chmn., 1969-91, dean Coll. Social and Behavioral Scis., 1992—2004. Lectr. Cath. U., Washington, 1963-64; professorial lectr. Am. U., Washington, 1964-67; vis. prof. U. Okla., 1969-91. Author: Public Policies and Their Politics, 1966, Party Leaders in the House of Representatives, 1967, Majority Party Leadership in Congress, 1969, Power in the Senate, 1969, The Politics of Economic and Human Resource Development, 1972, Legislative Politics U.S.A, 1973, American National Government and Public Policy, 1974, Congress: Process and Policy, 1975, 4th edit., 1988, Policy-making in the Federal Executive Branch, 1975, Congress, the Bureaucracy, and Public Policy, 1976, 5th edit., 1991, National Government and Policy in the United States, 1977, A More Perfect Union, 1979, 4th edit., 1989, Policy Implementation and Bureaucracy, 1982, 2d edit., 1986, CETA: Politics and Policy, 1973-82, 1984, Policy Analysis in Political Science, 1985, Readings in American Government and Politics, 1989, 2d edit. 1993, 3d edit., 1999, Congress Resurgent, 1993, U.S. Foreign Policy After the Cold War, 1997, American Labor Unions in the Electoral Arena, 2001; contbr. articles to profl. jours. Bd. govs. Stratford Festival, Ont., Can., 1994-98. Woodrow Wilson fellow, 1959-60; Danforth fellow, 1959-63; recipient Sumner prize Harvard, 1963 Mem. Am. Polit. Sci. Assn. (sec. 1978), Phi Beta Kappa. Democrat. Home: 11465 Cable Rd SW Pataskala OH 43062-8809 Home Phone: 740-964-6977; Office Phone: 614-292-4392. Personal E-mail: ripley.1@osu.edu.

RIPMA, MARY, librarian; b. St. Johns, Mich., Aug. 7, 1952; d. Charles William and Vera Elizabeth Austin; m. Mark Gale Ripma, Apr. 29, 1978; children: Lee, Tye, Clay. BA, Mich. State U., 1974; MLS, San Jose State U., Calif., 1977; cert. in bus. mgmt., Cañada Coll., Redwood City, Calif., 2000. Dir. editl. Info. Access Corp., Redwood City, 1977—83; info. advisor Mothers with Babies, Menlo Park, Calif., 1983—88; reference libr. Menlo Park Pub. Libr., 1988—92; bus. specialist Dialog Inc., Mountain View, Calif., 1992—98; mgr. Menlo Park Rsch. Inc., 1998—2001; mgr., owner www.yourgetawayhouse.com, Santa Cruz, Calif., 2001—. Vol. libr. Kristin Sch., Albany, New Zealand, 2004—; music program organizer, rm. mother PTA, Menlo Park, 1987—2004. Seeburg scholar, San Jose State U., 1977. Mem.: AAUW, Forest & Bird, Warkworth Quilters, Collie Club of Am. Democrat. Unitarian. Avocations: quilting, swimming. Home: 217 Goatley Rd Warkworth 1241 New Zealand Mailing: 849 Almar Ave Ste C 190 Santa Cruz CA 95060 E-mail: ripma@hotmail.com.

RIPOLL, SHAKIRA ISABEL MEBARAK See SHAKIRA

RIPOSO, JOSEPH, music educator, director; b. Syracuse, NY, Aug. 5, 1933; s. Joseph and Leona Riposo; m. Joann Riposo, Jan. 27, 1956; children: Joe, David, Marc, Todd. MusB in Music Edn., Syracuse U., NY, 1956; MusM in Music Edn., Syracuse U., 1969. Cert. amdinstrn. in music edn. NY State Edn. Dept., 1969, woodwind adjudicator NY State Sch. Music Assn., state jazz adjudicator NY State Sch. Music Assn. Chief instr. Sch. Music Ft. Dix, NJ, 1956—58; dir. music edn. Liverpool Ctrl. Sch. Dist., NY, 1960—91; jazz studies program Onondagot C.C., Syracuse, 1974—85; jazz coord. Cultural Resources Coun., Syracuse, 1976—84; dir. jazz studies Syracuse U., 1985—. Mem. adv. com. Onondaga C.C., Syracuse, 1980—90; presenter in field. Author: Jazz Improv A Whole Brain Approach, 1989, LMI Recorder Method, 1998. Mem. adv. com. PAC Program in the Arts, Liverpool, 1968—91, Students in the Arts, Liverpool, 1968—91. Staff sgt. US Army, 1956—59, Korea. Named to Music Hall of Fame, Sammys, 1997, Fine Arts Hall of Fame, Liverpool Schs., 2003; recipient Citation of Excellence, State Edn. Dept., Liverpool Ctrl. Sch. Dist., 1983. Mem.: ASCAP, Internat. Assn. Jazz Edn. (North Ea. region coord. 1990—95, pres. NY state unit 1980—85).

RIPP, JOSEPH ALLEN, information technology executive; b. NYC, Nov. 29, 1951; m. Virginia Nolan. BA, Manhattan Coll.; MBA, Bernard M. Baruch Coll. CUNY, 1980. Mgr. Ernst & Whinney, NYC, 1973-82; asst. contr. Time Inc., NYC, 1982-85, v.p. fin., 1985-90, v.p., CFO, 1990-92, sr. v.p., CFO, 1992-94, exec. v.p., CFO, 1994-99, Time Warner Inc., NYC, 1999-01; CFO America On-Line, Inc., 2001—03, vice chmn., 2002—04; sr. v.p. media & comm. group Time Warner Inc., 2004—05; pres., COO Dendrite Internat. Inc., Bedminster, NJ, 2005—. Bd. dirs. Greenfield Online Inc. Trustee Manhattan Coll.; bd. dir. Advt. Edn. Found; bd. dir., mem. exec. com., chmn. fin. com. Ad Council Office: Dendrite Internat Inc 1405-1425 Rt 206 S Bedminster NJ 07921

RIPPERT, ERIC THEODORE, oral and maxillofacial surgeon, health-care consultant; b. Ft. Devens, Mass., Feb. 22, 1942; s. Jacob Kopf and Kathleen (Faughnan) R.; m. Mary Ellen Dormer, Nov. 25, 1965; children: Thomas, Kathleen. AB, Holy Cross Coll., 1964; DMD, U. Pa., 1968. Diplomate Am. Bd. Oral and Maxillofacial Surgery. Intern Phila. Gen. Hosp., 1968-69, resident, 1973-76; dental officer U.S. Navy, 1965-95; asst. prof. oral and maxillofacial surgery U. Nebr., Lincoln, 1996-99; asst. prof. U. Pitts., 1999-2000; assoc. prof. Med. Coll. Va., Richmond, 2000—02; assoc. prof., dir. residency tng., oral and maxillofacial surgery Med. Coll. Ga., Augusta, Ga., 2002—05; cons. in health care, 2005—. Clin. asst. prof. Med. Coll. Va., Richmond, 1979-81; adj. assoc. prof. Temple U., Phila., 1984-87; asst. prof. U. Calif., San Francisco, 1991-93. Fellow Am. Assn. Oral and Maxillofacial Surgeons, Am. Coll. Dentists, Internat. Coll. Dentists; mem. Varsity Club Coll. Holy Cross, Delta Sigma Delta. Republican. Roman Catholic. Avocations: tennis, skiing, speech and dialogue, writing. Office Phone: 706-836-0781. Personal E-mail: etrippert@yahoo.com.

RIPPETEAU, DARREL DOWNING, retired architect; b. Clay Center, Nebr., Jan. 14, 1917; s. Claude LaVerne and Eva (Downing) R.; m. Donna Doris Hiatt, Jan. 8, 1939 (dec. 1988); children: Bruce Estes, Darrel Downing, Jane Upson Heffron; m. Joyce Spencer, May 18, 1991. BA in Architecture, U. Nebr., 1941. Staff architect FHA, Omaha, 1941-42; project mgr., mng. ptnr. Sargent-Webster-Crenshaw & Folley, Archs. and Engrs., Watertown, Buffalo, Syracuse, NY, Burlington, Vt, Bangor, Maine, 1946-81; treas., dir. Empire Forest System, Albany, N.Y., 1984-89; ret., 1990. Bd. dirs. Archtl. Corp. Atlanta, Key Bank No. N.Y., Watertown, Assn. Island Recreational Corp.; commr. N.Y. State Coun. Architecture, 1975-85; mem. N.Y. State Forest Practice Bd., 1980-2000, chmn., 1994-98; nat. adv. bd. mem. Remington Art Mus., Ogdensburg, N.Y., 1983-95. Prin. works include Justice Bldg, Albany, N.Y. State Office Bldg Watertown, Toomey Abbott Towers Syracuse, State U. N.Y. Cortland, U.S. P.O. Facility Syracuse. Mem. nat. fin. com. Rep. Party, 1971-73; bd. trustees The Antique Boat Mus., Clayton, N.Y., 1973-99, Glenn Curtiss Mus., Hammondsport, N.Y. Maj. U.S. Army, 1942-46; lt. col. Corps of Engrs. retired, 1977. Recipient North Country citation St. Lawrence U., Canton, N.Y., 1971; Sears-Roebuck scholar, 1936-37; U. Nebr. Dept. Architecture grantee, 1940-41; Nebr. master U. Nebr., 1971; Disting. Alumni award Coll. of Architecture Alumni Assn., U. Nebr., 1996. Fellow AIA (nat. dir. 1969-73, trustee AIA Found. 1970-73); mem. Greater Watertown C. of C. (past pres.), NY State Assn. Indsl. Devel. Agys. (past v.p.), N.Y. State Assn. Architects (pres. 1968-69, polit. action com. 1980-98, James Kideney award 1987), Bldg. Rsch. Inst., Res. Officers Assn. (past pres.), Am. Tree Farm Assn., Jefferson County Hist. Soc. (dir. 1974-78), OX-5 Aviation Pioneers (chpt. pres.), Assn. US Army (Ft. Drum NNY chpt. pres. 1985-86). Republican. Presbyterian. Home: 1011 NW 3rd Ave Delray Beach FL 33444-2938

RIPPLE, KENNETH FRANCIS, federal judge; b. Pitts., May 19, 1943; s. Raymond John and Rita (Holden) Ripple; m. Mary Andrea DeWeese, July 27, 1968; children: Gregory, Raymond, Christopher. AB, Fordham U., 1965; JD, U. Va., 1968; LLM, George Washington U., 1972, LLD (hon.), 1992. Bar: Va. 1968, NY 1969, US Supreme Ct. 1972, US Supreme Ct. 1972, DC 1976, Ind. 1984, US Ct. Appeals (7th cir.), US Ct. Mil. Appeals, US Dist. Ct. (no. dist.) Ind. Atty. IBM Corp., Armonk, NY, 1968; legal officer US Supreme Ct., Washington, 1972—73, spl. asst. to chief justice Warren E. Burger, 1973—77; prof. law U. Notre Dame, 1977—; judge US Ct. Appeals (7th cir.), South Bend, 1985—. Reporter Appellate Rules Com., Washington, 1978—85; commn. on mil. justice US Dept. Def., Washington, 1984—85; cons. Supreme Ct. Ala., 1983, Calif. Bd. Bar Examiners, 1981, Anglo-Am. Jud. Exch., 1977; adv. com. Bill of Rights to Bicentennial Constn. Commn., 1989; adv. com. on appellate rules Jud. Conf. US, 1985—90, chmn., 1990—93; chmn. adv. com. on appellate judge edn. Fed. Jud. Ctr., 1996—2003; mem. jud. conf. adminstrv. office US Cts. Com., 2003—06; mem. faculty Law Clerkship Inst., Pepperdine U., 2001—04; mem. vis. com. U. Chgo. Sch. Divinity, 2005—, U. Chgo. Sch. Law, 2005—; mem. com. on jud. resources Jud. Conf. U.S., 2006—. Author: Constitutional Litigation, 1984. With JAGC USN, 1968—72. Mem.: ABA, Am. Law Inst., Phi Beta Kappa. Office: US Ct of Appeals 208 US Courthouse 204 S Main St South Bend IN 46601-2122 also: Fed Bldg 219 S Dearborn St Ste 2660 Chicago IL 60604-1803 *

RIPPLINGER, GEORGE RAYMOND, JR., lawyer; b. East St. Louis, Apr. 19, 1945; s. George Raymond and Virginia Lee (Toupnot) R. AB, U. Ill., 1967, JD, 1970. Bar: Ill. 1970, U.S. Dist. Ct. (so. dist.) Ill. 1970, U.S. Ct. Appeals (7th cir.) 1970, U.S. Dist. Ct. (ctrl. dist.) Ill. 1972, U.S. Tax Ct. 1971, U.S. Claims Ct. 1973, U.S. Ct. Mil. Appeals 1985, U.S. Supreme Ct. 1973, U.S. Ct. Internat. Trade 1973, U.S. Dist. Ct. (ea. dist.) Mo. 1977, U.S. Ct. Appeals (8th cir.) 1977. Assoc. Meyer & Meyer, Belleville and Greenville, Ill., 1970-72; assoc. Meyer & Kaucher, 1972—73; sole practice Belleville, 1974; ptnr. Ripplinger & Walsh, Clayton, Mo., 1974-76, Ripplinger, Dixon & Johnston, Belleville, Ill., St. Louis, Scott AFB, and Bellvue, Neb., 1976-94; prin. George Ripplinger & Assocs., Belleville, 1994—2005; mng. mem. Ripplinger & Zimmer LLC, Belleville, 2006—. Mem. com. minimum continuing legal edn. Ill. Supreme Ct., 2005—. Bd. visitors Coll. Law U. Ill., 1979-86, pres., 1983-84; pres., bd. dirs. Ill. Legal Aid on Line, 2006—, bd. dirs. 2005—. Col. USAR, 1970-2001. Recipient Disting. Alumnus award, U. Ill., Coll. Law, 2006. Fellow Am. Bar Found., Ill. Bar Found. (bd. dirs. 1988-2004, treas. 1998-2004); mem. ABA (ho. of dels. 1989-93, 95-99, chmn. workers compensation com. 1985-88, divsn. dir. 1988-89, 95-99, mem. coun. 1989-93, 99-2003, sec. 1999-2000, vice-chmn. 2000-2001, chmn. 2001-02, gen. practice/solo and small firm divsn.), ATLA, Lawyers Trust Fund Ill. (bd. dirs. 1988-94), Ill. Bar Assn. (bd. govs. 1981-83, 87-93, sec. 1991-92), St. Clair County Bar Assn., Bar Assn. Met. St. Louis, Mo. Bar Assn., Ill. Trial Lawyers Assn. (bd. advs. 1993—), Land of Lincoln Legal Assistance Found. (bd. dirs. 1982-88, vice-chmn. 1987-88), Res. Officers Assn. Democrat. Office: Ripplinger and Zimmer LLC 2215 W Main St Belleville IL 62226-6668 Home Phone: 618-398-6112; Office Phone: 800-733-8333. Business E-Mail: george@ripplingerlaw.com.

RIPS, LANCE JEFFREY, psychology professor; b. Omaha, Dec. 19, 1947; s. Norman Julian and Barbara (Taxman) R.; m. Julie West Johnson; 1 child, Eve Clare Johnson. BA, Swathmore Coll., Pa., 1970; PhD, Stanford U., 1974. Asst. prof. U. Chgo., 1974-80, assoc. prof., 1980-91, prof., 1991-93, Northwestern U., Evanston, Ill., 1993—. Author: Psychology of Proof, 1994, Psychology of Survey Response, 2000; mem. editl. bd. Cognition; contbr. articles to profl. jours. James McKeen Cattell fellow, 1989-90, Fulbright fellow, 2004-2005. Fellow APA, Am. Psychol. Soc.; mem. Psychonomic Soc., Soc. Exptl. Psychologists, Cognitive Sci. Soc., Phi Beta Kappa. E-mail: lrips@attglobal.net.

RISCASSI, ROBERT W., communications systems company executive, retired military officer; Comdr. Combined Arms Ctr. US Army, dep. chief of staff Ops. and Plans, dir. joint staff Joint Chief of Staff, vice chief of staff, comdr. in chief UN Command/Korea; positions up to v.p. land systems Washington ops. Loral Corp., 1993—96; v.p. land systems C3I and Systems Integration Sector Lockheed Martin; sr. v.p. Washington ops. L-3 Comm. Holdings, Inc. Office: L-3 Comm Holdings Inc 1215 S Clark St Ste 1205 Arlington VA 22202 Office Phone: 703-412-7190. *

RISCH, JIM (JAMES E.), lieutenant governor, former governor, state legislator; b. Milw., May 3, 1943; s. Elroy A. and Helen B. (Levi) R.; m. Vicki L. Choborda, June 8, 1968; children: James E., Jason S., Jordan D. BS in Forestry, U. Idaho, 1965, JD, 1968. Dep. pros. atty. Ada County, Idaho, 1968-69, chief dep. pros. atty. Idaho, 1969-70, pros. atty. Idaho, 1971-75; mem. Idaho Senate, Dist. 18, Boise, 1974—88, 1995—2002, majority leader, 1977—82, 1997—2002, pres. pro tem, 1983-88; ind. counsel to Gov. State of Idaho, Boise, 1996; ptnr. Risch Goss & Insinger, Boise, 1975—; lt. gov. State of Idaho, Boise, 2003—06, 2007—, acting gov., 2006, gov., 2006—07. Prof. law Boise State U., 1972-75. Bd. dirs. Nat. Dist. Attys. Assn., 1973, Idaho Co., 1992-94, State Legis. Leaders Found., 2002; chmn. bd. dirs. Am. Trailer Mfg. Co., 1995—; pres. Idaho Pros. Attys., 1970-74; chmn. George Bush Presdl. Campaign, Idaho, 1988; gen. counsel Idaho Rep. Party, 1991-2002. Mem. ABA, Idaho Bar Assn., Boise Bar Assn., Ducks Unlimited, Nat. Rifle Assn., Nat. Cattlemans Assn., Idaho Cattlemans Assn., Am. Angus Assn., Idaho Angus Assn., Am. Legis. Exch. Coun., Boise Valley Angus Assn., Phi Delta Theta, Xi Sigma Pi Republican. Roman Catholic. Avocations: hunting, fishing, skiing. Office: Office Lt Gov State Capitol Rm 225 Boise ID 83720 Office Phone: 208-345-9974.

RISDON, MICHAEL PAUL, manufacturing executive; BS, Iowa State U., Ames, 1967, U. Ky., Lexington, 1968; MBA, U. Pitts., 1971. Sr. acct. Ernst & Young, Indpls., 1971-75; audit supr. Ashland Oil, Inc., Ky., 1975—77; v.p. fin. and sys. Diesel ReCon Co., Memphis, 1982-86; budget analyst Cummins Engine Co., Columbus, Ind., 1969-70, mgr. corp. audit, 1977-78, dir. corp. and EDP audit, 1978-82, dir. fin. and planning power sys. group, 1987-88; v.p. Cummins Power Generation, Columbus, 1989; v.p. fin., CFO Metal Powder Products Co., Inc., Indpls., 1989-99; pres. MPM LLC, Carmel, Ind., 1998-99; pres., CEO The Cumbernauld Group, 1999—; exec. v.p., chief adminstrv. officer PiezoTech, LLC, Indpls., 1999—2003; v.p. Alpha Natural Resources, 2007—. V.p. Columbus Child Care Ctr., 1981-82; vol. Big Sisters Ctrl. Ind., 1994-98; trustee Barter Theatre. Mem. AICPA, Ind. CPA Soc., Metal Powder Industry Fedn. (fin. com. 1991-98, chmn. 1994-98), APMI Internat., Fin. Execs. Internat. (sec. 1997-98, v.p. 1998, pres. 1999), Inst. Mgmt. Accts. (nat. bd. dirs. 1981-87, v.p. 1985), Kiwanis (v.p. Columbus 1981). Roman Catholic. Avocations: bicycling, hiking, sports.

RISEBROUGH, DOUG, professional sports team executive; b. 1954; m. Marilyn Risenbrough; children: Allison, Lindsay. Former player Montreal Canadiens, for 8 years, Calgary Flames, for 5 years, former asst. coach, 1987-89, asst. gen. mgr., 1989-90, head coach, 1990-92, gen. mgr., 1992—95; v.p. hockey ops. Edmonton Oilers, 1996—99; gen. mgr. Minn. Wild, 1999—; pres. Minn. Sports & Entertainment (MSE), 2003—. Office: Minn Wild 317 Washington St Saint Paul MN 55102

RISEN, JAMES E., journalist; b. Cin., Apr. 27, 1955; married; 3 children. BA in history, Brown U., 1977; MS in journalism, Northwestern U., 1978. Reporter Detroit Free Press, 1981—84; bur. chief LA Times, Detroit, 1984—90, chief econ. corr. Washington, 1990—95, nat. sec. & intelligence corr., 1995—98; investigative corr. NY Times, Washington, 1998—. Recipient Pulitzer Prize for nat. reporting, 2006. Fellow: Am. Acad. Arts & Scis. Office: NY Times Washington Bur 7th Fl 1627 I St NW Washington DC 20006 Office Phone: 202-862-0355. Office Fax: 202-862-0340. Business E-Mail: risenj@nytimes.com. *

RISHEL, JAMES BURTON, manufacturing executive, director; b. Omaha, Apr. 27, 1920; s. James Blaine and Elizabeth Helen (Kerr) R.; m. Alice Jane Snyder, June 30, 1945; children: James Richard, Sara Jane Rishel Fields. BSME, U. Nebr., 1946. Profl. engr., Ohio. Pres. Corp. Equipment Co., Cin., 1962-82; chmn. bd. Systecon Inc., Cin., 1982-2000; cons. Pumping Solutions LLC, 2000—. Author: The Water Management Manual, 1994, HVAC Pump Handbook, 1996, 2d edit., 2006, Water Pumps and Pumping Systems, 2002; patentee hydraulic systems; contbr. numerous articles to profl. jours. Capt. USAF, 1942-46, 51-52. Fellow ASHRAE. Avocations: philanthropy, walking. Home: 6470 Post Rd Apt 305 Dublin OH 43016-5200 E-mail: burt@tekworx.us.

RISHEL, RICHARD CLINTON, retired bank executive; b. Oreland, Pa., June 7, 1943; S. Herbert Beale and Evelyn (Lauer) R.; m. Carol Staub, Apr. 3, 1965; children: Christian Daniel, Peter James. BA, Pa. State U., 1965; postgrad., Drexel Inst. Tech., 1965-66. Credit analyst 1st Pa. Banking & Trust Co., Phila., 1965-69; comml. lending officer Nat. Bank of Chester County, West Chester, Pa., 1969; asst. v.p. Continental Bank of Norristown, Pa., 1969-70, sec., 1970-71, v.p., 1971-73, sr. v.p., chief fin. officer, 1973-75, exec. v.p., chief fin. officer, 1975-81, vice chmn., 1981-83, pres., chief adminstrv. officer, 1984-89, also dir.; pres., chief exec. officer Continental Bank, Continental Bancorp, 1990-92; vice chmn. bd. Continental Bank, 1981-84; pres. parent co. Continental Bancorp., 1981-92; dir. Barnett Inst. U. North Fla., 1993-94; sec. of banking Commonwealth of Pa., 1995-99; ret., 1999.

RISHER, JAMES A., electronics executive; b. 1943; MS in Econs. and Stats., U. Tex., 1943. With IBM Corps., 1969-80; v.p. Wang Labs., 1980-84; sr. v.p. Motorola Computer Systems, Inc., 1984-86; pres., CEO Exide Electronics Group, Inc., Raleigh, NC, 1986—98, chmn., 1997—98; mng. ptnr. Lumina Group LLC, 1998—; chmn., CEO Blue Star Battery Systems Internat., 2001—02; CEO Del Global Technologies, Valhalla, NY, 2006—. Bd. dir. SL Industries Inc, New Century Equity Holdings Corp. Office: Exide Electronics Corp 8609 Six Forks Rd Raleigh NC 27615-2966

RISHER, WILLIAM HENRY, cardiothoracic surgeon, educator; b. New Orleans, Oct. 3, 1958; m. Michele Helene Van Kuren, July 11, 1981; children: Amelia Alexandra, Jordan Prescott, Olivia Leigh. Student, U. New Orleans, 1981; BS in Biomed. Engring., Tulane U., 1981; MD, La. State U., 1985. Diplomate Am. Bd. Surgery, Am. Bd. Thoracic Surgery; lic. surgeon, N.Y.; cert. ACLS, advanced trauma life support, pediatric advanced life support provider, basic life support provider. Resident in gen.

surgery Alton Ochsner Med. Found., New Orleans, 1985-90, chief resident, 1989-90, resident and fellow in cardiovascular surgery, 1990-92, chief resident, 1991-92; flight care physician Ochsner Flight Care, 1986-92; assoc. prof. cardiothoracic surgery Med. Ctr. U. Rochester, NY, 1992—2002; chief St. Luke's Regional Heart Program, Bethlehem, Pa., 2002—. Presenter in field. Contbr. over 20 articles to med. and sci. jours. T.H. Harris scholar Tulane U, 1977-79, full scholar, 1979-81. Fellow ACS, Am. Coll. Cardiology (assoc.); mem. AMA, Am. Coll. Chest Physicians, Soc. Thoracic Surgeons, Internat. Soc. Heart and Lung Transplantation, S.E. Surg. Congress, Med. Assn., Med. Soc. County Monroe, Rochester Acad. Medicine, Rochester Cardiovascular Soc., Upstate Soc. Thoracic Surgeons, Rochester Surg. Soc., Assn. for Advancement of Med. Instrumentation, Alton Ochsner Med. Soc., Tau Beta Pi, Alpha Omega Alpha. Home: 1875 Augusta Dr Center Valley PA 18034-8924 Office Phone: 610-954-3990. Personal E-mail: mbaj05@aol.com.

RISHWAIN, JAMES MICHAEL, JR., lawyer; b. Stockton, Calif., Apr. 28, 1959; BA with honors, UCLA, 1981; JD cum laude, Pepperdine U., 1984. Bar: Calif. Co-mng. ptnr. Pillsbury Winthrop Shaw Pittman LLP, Century City, Calif., 2001—04, L.A., 2004—06, chmn., co-leader real estate group, 2007—. Editor (Note & Comment): Pepperdine Law Rev. Mem. adv. bd. LA City Coun. for Holmby Pk., Calif. Coalition for Adequate Sch. Housing, Jonathan Club; bd. mem. Bldg. Owners and Mgrs. Assn.; bd. experts Internat. Real Estate Trade Orgn., mem. pres.'s cir. Named Best Lawyer Am., 2005—06; named one of Calif. Super Lawyers, 2004, 2005, 2006; recipient Calif. Lawyer of Yr. award, 2004, 2005. Mem.: ABA, State Calif. Bar Assn., LA County Bar Assn., Urban Land Inst. Office: Pillsbury Winthrop Shaw Pittman LLP Ste 2800 725 S Figueroa St Los Angeles CA 90017-5406 Office Phone: 213-488-7111. Office Fax: 213-488-7400. E-mail: jrishwain@pillsburylaw.com. *

RISHWORTH, SUSAN KNOKE, archivist, researcher; b. Appleton, Wis., Aug. 25, 1945; d. Leland Leonard and Gertrude Helen Martha Posselt Knoke; m. Clarence Douglas Rishworth, Apr. 7, 1971; children: Corey Adam, Benjamin Tobey, Amelia Marzieh. BA, U. Wis., Madison, 1967; MLS, Ind. U., Bloomington, 1968; MA, U. Md., College Park, 1998. Cert. archivist Modern Archives Inst., 1994. Libr. African studies Mich. State U., East Lansing, 1968—70; Africana bibliographer Libr. Congress, 1970—74; libr. to libr. dir. Southeastern U., 1983—90; interim dir. libr. svcs. U. Md. U., College Park, 1985; history libr., archivist Am. Coll. Ob/Gyns, 1990—2001; archivist ACS, Chgo., 2001—. Founder Chgo. Area Med. Archivists, 2002—; co-initiator Lone Arrangers Roundtable SAA, Birmingham, Ala., 2002—; presenter in field. Co-founder Ann. Martin Luther King Tribute, College Park, 1991—2001; facilitator Human Rels. Com. Race Study Circles, Prince George's County, Md., 1996—2000; Baha'i travel tchr. Nat. Spiritual Assembly of Baha'is of US, Wilmette, Ill., 1972—73; Baha'i pioneer Nat. Spiritual Assembly of Leeward Islands, Antigua and Barbuda, 1981—83; Baha'i travel tchr. Nat. Spiritual Assembly of Baha'is of Cameroon, Yaounde, 1998; sec. Spiritual Assembly of Baha'i, College Park, 1973—2001; facilitator study circles Baha'i, Chgo., 2002—. Recipient 10 Yr. Svc. on MLK tribute award, City of Coll. Pk., 1991—2001, Murray Gottlieb prize, Med. Libr. Assn., 1994; fellow Wood Found. History of Women in Medicine award, Coll. Physicians Phila., 2005—06. Mem.: Midwest Archives Conf., Soc. Am. Archivists, Am. Assn. for History Medicine (shryock award com. 2005—06), Archivists and Librs. in History of Health Sci. (sec., steering com. 1994—95, 2004—06), Assn. Bahai Studies. Baha'I. Office: Am Coll Surgeons 633 N St Clair St Chicago IL 60611

RISI, LOUIS JAMES, JR., manufacturing executive; b. Highland Park, Ill., July 2, 1937; s. Louis J. and Ann E. Risi; m. Mary Jean Anson, Jan. 15, 1958; children: Steven, Janet, Andrew. BS, Bradley U.; MBA, U. Chgo. Pres. and CEO, bd. dirs., mem. exec. com. Norin Corp., Miami, Fla., 1969-81; exec. com. dir. Maple Leaf Mills Ltd., Toronto, Can., 1970-81, Corp. Foods, Inc., 1970-81; chmn. bd. dirs. Louis Sherry, Inc., 1976-81; chmn. bd., CEO Nat. Investors Fire & Casualty Co., 1975-77; exec. com. dir. Investors Equity Life Ins. Co. of Hawaii, 1970-75; pres., dir. The Abbey, Lake Geneva, 1970-75; exec. com., dir. Upper Lakes Shipping, Ltd., Toronto, Can., 1970-76; pres., dir. The Pioneer, Lake Oshkosh, 1971-76; exec. com., dir. Port Weller and St. Lawrence Dry Dock, Ltd., St. Catharines, Can., 1971-76; pres., dir. Homosassa Springs, Fla., 1971-78, Ivan Tors Films Inc., Culver City, Calif., 1971-78, Ivan Tors Studios Inc., Miami, Fla., 1976-80; exec. com. dir. Midland Nat. Bank, 1976-80; pres., dir. Norris Grain Co., 1980-82; chmn. bd., CEO CTC Corp., 1981-83. Exec. com. Nat. Investors Life Ins. Co., 1970-77; chmn. bd., pres. Victory Industries, Inc.; chmn. bd. dirs. Red Wing Co., Oklawaha Farms, Inc., Assured Security Co.; dir. Breckinridge Group; exec. v.p. Ft. Worth Red Wings Hockey Club, Inc., 1975-78, Detroit Red Wings Hockey Club, Inc., 1976-82, Adirondack Red Wings Hockey Club, Inc., 1976-82; bd. govs. Nat. Hockey League, 1976-82; bd. dirs. Chgo. Rock Island and Pacific R.R.; exec. com. AfriAir Corp., 1972-79, Southeastern Airlines, Inc., 1972-78; exec. com., bd. dirs. Peter Bowden Drilling Ltd., Bankmgrs. Corp.; U.S. rep. Grain negotiations with USSR; U.S. rep. Feedstuffs negotiations with China; adv. coun. Am. Stock Exch.; mem. Agril. Processors Liaison com. FTC; adv. bd. Nat. Millers Assn.; bd. govs. Internat. Hockey League, 1978-82, Am. Hockey League, 1975-79; pres., chmn. bd. dirs. Kinnard Body Works, Inc., 1970-73. Trustee Fairchild Tropical Garden, Miami, Fla. Lt. comdr. USNR, 1959—67. Mem. Ocean Reef Yacht Club (Key Largo, Fla.), Santa Rosa (Calif.) Country Club, Riviera Country Club (Coral Gables, Fla.), Lake Toxaway Country Club (Lake Toxaway, NC), Coral Reef Yacht Club (Miami, Fla.), Anabelle's Club (London), St. James Club (London). Office: 9200 S Dadeland Blvd Miami FL 33156-2715

RISIN, JACK See BUTCHER, JACK

RISIN, SEMYON AARON, pathologist, educator; b. Belarus; m. Diana Risin; 1 child, Michael. MD, PhD, Minsk State Med. Inst., Belarus, 1964. Diplomate Am. Bd. of Pathology, 2003. Physician, physician-in-chief Village Hosp., Khominka, Belarus, 1964—66; rschr. Minsk State Med. Inst., 1971—79, prof., 1979—89; rsch. prof. U. Tex. M. D. Anderson Cancer Ctr., Houston, 1990—97; resident physician dept. pathology & lab. medicine U. Tex.-Houston Med. Sch., 1997—2001, prof. dept. pathology & lab. medicine, 2001—. Med. cons. Am. Biomed, Houston, 1990—91; med. interpretor and cons. Johnson Space Ctr., NASA, Houston, 1996—97. Avocation: travel. Office: UT-Houston Medical School 6431 Fannin Street MSB 2290 Houston TX 77030 Home Phone: 713-668-2487; Office Phone: 713-500-5320. Office Fax: 713-500-0730.

RISING, KEVIN D., lawyer; BA in Criminology, Law and Society, U. Calif., Irvine, 1997; JD, U. Calif., Los Angeles, 2000. Bar: Calif., US Ct. of Appeals, 9th Circuit, US Dist. Ct. (So., Ea., Central & No. dist.), DC. Assoc., litigation dept. Akin Gump Strauss Hauer & Feld LLP, Los Angeles, Calif., 2001—. Recipient Award for Excellence in Preparation for Trial Practice of the Law, Am. Bd. of Trial Advocates. Office: Akin Gump Strauss Hauer & Feld LLP 2029 Century Park E Ste 2400 Los Angeles CA 90067 Office Phone: 310-229-1000. Office Fax: 310-229-1001. Business E-Mail: krising@akingump.com.

RISINGER, BETH N., elementary school educator; b. New Orleans, June 24, 1959; d. Merrill J. and Betty Nunez; m. Kurt Risinger, May 21, 1983; children: Kristofer, Kevin. BA in Elem. Edn., Nicholls State U., 1982. Life cert. in elem. edn., grades 1-8. Sci. tchr. St. Bernard Parish Schs., Chalmette, La., 1982—83; 4th and 5th grade tchr. West Ascension Elem., Donaldsonville, La., 1986—92; 3rd and 4th grade tchr. G.W. Carver Primary, Gonzales, La., 1992—. Vol. Children's Miracle Network. Named Tchr. of Yr., Carver Primary, 1996—97. Mem.: La. Fedn. Tchrs., Nat. Coun. Math. Tchrs., Internat. Reading Assn. Home: 13668 Parwood Ave Baton Rouge LA 70816-1473

RISINGER, D. MICHAEL, lawyer, educator; b. Kansas City, Mo., Mar. 31, 1945; s. Homer D. and Madeline F. Risinger; m. Celia A. Defensor, Oct. 17, 1977 (div. Jan. 1990); children: Ariel Michelle, Michael R. Defensor, Jonathan Marshall; m. Barbara B. Comerford, Jan. 1991; 1 child, Caroline Violet Comerford. BA magna cum laude in Polit. Sci, Yale U., 1966; JD cum laude, Harvard U., 1969. Bar: Pa. 1973, N.J. 1978, N.Y. 1983. Asst. counsel Mass. Joint Legis. Com. on Drugs and Drug Abuse, 1969; tchr. N.Y.C. Public Schs., 1969-71; law clk. to hon. Clarence C. Newcomer US Dist. Ct. (ea. dist.) Pa., 1972-73; asst. prof. law Seton Hall U., Newark, 1973-76, assoc. prof., 1976-79, prof., 1979—. Vis. sr. fellow Nat. U. Singapore, 1985-86; mem. faculty Nat. Jud. Coll., 1988; lectr. on evidence N.J. Inst. Continuing Legal Edn., N.J. Jud. Coll., N.J. Adminstrv. Law Inst., N.Y. Practising Law Inst., N.Y.C.; trial adv. trainer Nat. Legal Services Corp.; mem. N.J. Supreme Ct. Com. on Evidence. Author: (with Mark P. Denbeaux) Trial Evidence, 1978; co-author of Trial Evidence, Continuing Legal Education Casebook, contbr. articles to profl. jours. Grantee Dean's Rsch. Fellows, Seton Hall's, 2002—04. Mem. ABA, Am. Law Inst., past chair Assn. Am. Law Sch., chair-elect AALS Sect., mem. NJ Supreme Ct. Com. Office: Seton Hall U 1 Newark Center Newark NJ 07102-5206 Office Phone: 973-642-8834. Office Fax: 973-642-8876. Business E-Mail: risingmi@shu.edu.

RISINGER, FRED OWEN, pharmacologist; b. Shreveport, Aug. 12, 1954; s. Reggie and Margaret Risinger; m. Deborah Christman; children: Stewart, Lynn. BS, La. State U., 1978; MS, PhD, U. of La., 1987. Postdoctoral fellow Oreg. Health Sciences U., Portland, 1988—91, asst. prof., 1991—2002; assoc. prof. Idaho State U., Pocatello, 2002—. Grantee, Alcoholic Beverage Med. Rsch. Found., 1995, NIH, 1993—95. Mem.: Rsch. Soc. on Alcoholism, Soc. Neurosci., APA (assoc.), Psi Chi, Rho Chi, Omicron Delta Kappa. Avocation: reading, cooking, camping. Home: 11780 SW Ebberts Ct Beaverton OR 97008 Office: Dept Pharma Scis CollPharmacy Idaho State Univ Pocatello ID 83209 Home Phone: 503-524-7426. Business E-Mail: risinger@ohsu.edu. *

RISKIN, VICTORIA, former trade association administrator; d. Robert Riskin and Fay Wray; m. David Rintels. Pres. Writers Guild Am., West, 2001—04. Author: (TV films) My Antonia, 1995; prodr.: (TV films) The Last Best Year, 1990, A Town Torn Apart, 1992, World War II: When Lions Roared, 1994, The Member of the Wedding, 1997.

RISKO, VICTORIA J., language educator; BS, U. Pitts., 1966; MS, W.Va. U., 1969, EdD, 1971; postgrad., U. London, 1975. Fellow Learning Disabilities Inst. W.Va. U., 1969—70; tchr. Johnstown (Pa.) Pub. Sch. Sys., 1967—68; tchr. remedial reading Johnstown (Pa.) Pub. Sch. Dist., 1967; instr. home econs. W.Va. U., 1968—69, instr., supr. reading clinic, 1969; rschr.-tchr. Robert F. Kennedy Youth Ctr., Morgantown, W.Va., 1969—70; tchr.-cons. inservice edn. of tchrs. Belair-Manchester Schs. of Mandeville, Jamaica, 1974—75; instr., asst. prof., assoc. prof., dir. reading clinic programs, mem. grad. faculty SUNY, Fredonia, 1970—75; rsch. scientist Learning Tech. Ctr., mem. faculty interdisciplinary team Child Study Ctr., Kennedy Ctr. Peabody Coll., Vanderbilt U., Nashville, 1978—89, assoc. prof., 1975—94, prof. lang. and learning, 1994—. Vis. prof. reading W.Va. U., 1971. Recipient Disting. Svc. and Leadership award, Coll. Reading Assn., 1995, Disting. Rsch. in Tchr.'s Edn. award, Assn. Tchr. Educators Conf., 1992. Office: Vanderbilt U Peabody Coll 367 Wyatt Ctr Box 330 Nashville TN 37203

RISKOWSKI, GERALD LEE, engineering educator; b. Loup City, Nebr., Feb. 26, 1952; s. Stanley George and Rose Marie (Eurek) R.; m. Janet Ann Riskowski, June 19, 1976; 1 child, Ryan Lee. BS in Agrl. Engring., U. Nebr., 1974, MS in Agrl. Engring., 1976; PhD in Agrl. Engring., Iowa State U., 1986. Registered profl. engr., Ill., Iowa, Wis. Design engr. Lesters Bldgs., Lester Prairie, Minn., 1976-77; product engr. Wick Bldg. Systems, Mazomanie, Wis., 1977-80; instr. Iowa State U., Ames, 1980-86; prof. dept. agrl. engring. U. Ill., Urbana, 1986—2001; prof., head biol. and agrl. engring. dept. Tex. A&M U., College Station, 2002—. Swine facilities cons. Am. Tech. Products, Savoy, Ill., 1997-2002; pres. Internat. Air Technologies, Savoy, 1994-2003. Author: Designing Facilities for Pesticide and Fertilizer Containment, 1991 (Am. Soc. Agrl. Engrs. Blue Ribbon 1992); editor: Swine Housing and Equipment Handbook, 1983 (Am. Soc. Agrl. Engrs. Blue Ribbon 1984), Livestock Waste Facilities, 1985, Farm Buildings Wiring Handbook, 1986 (Am. Soc. Agrl. Engrs. Blue Ribbon 1987). Named to Rural Builders Hall of Fame, 1998. Mem. ASHRAE (TC.2 Handbook chair 1993-2000), Am. Soc. Agrl. Engrs. (S&E program chair, stds. chair, Henry Giese award 2001). Office: Tex A&M U 2117 TAMU College Station TX 77843-2117 E-mail: riskowski@tamu.edu.

RISLEY, GREGORY BYRON, retail executive, interior designer; b. Vincennes, Ind., Feb. 2, 1949; s. Jack Byron and Elizabeth Louise (Rockwell) R.; children: Christopher Byron, Timothy Neal. BS, Oakland City Coll., Ind., 1973; postgrad., Butler U., 1973—74, Oxford Worcester Coll. Pres. Risley Furniture & Design, Bicknell, Ind., 1974—, Risley Enterprises Inc., Bicknell, Ind., 1979—. Co-author: Preview IV The Home Furnishings Store. Pres. Better Bicknell Club, 1971; coach Pee Wee League, Bicknell, 1975-77; leader cub pack Boy Scouts Am., Bicknell, 1977; chmn. Queen Pageant, Bicknell, 1978-85. Mem. Nat. Home Furnishings Assn. (chmn. nat. execs. 1978-80), Am. Contract Bridge League (life master, unit sec. 1986-88, v.p. 1989, pres. 1991-92, bd. dirs. unit 193, 1993-95), Bicknell Mchts. Assn., Interior Design Soc. (outstanding rm. design award 1980), Knox County Assn. Retarded Citizens, French Club, Masons, Scottish Rite, Old Town Players (charter), Elks (past exalted ruler Bicknell 1976-77). Avocations: bridge, golf, reading. Office: 114 S Main St Bicknell IN 47512-2626 Home Phone: 812-735-3109; Office Phone: 812-735-2016. Business E-Mail: riz2222@charter.net.

RISLEY, ROD ALAN, educational association administrator; b. Hutchinson, Kans., Oct. 17, 1954; s. Ralph Edward and Patricia Ann (Gaulding) R. AA, San Jacinto Coll., Tex., 1975; BBA, Sam Houston State U., Huntsville, Tex., 1982; AA (hon.), Austin Community Coll., Tex., 1991; MBA, Millsap Coll., 1995; PhD (hon.), Highpoint U., 1996, Mt. Ida Coll., Newton Centre, Mass., 1996, Landmark Coll., Putney, Vt., 2003; ABD, Miss. State U., 2003. Dir. alumni affairs Phi Theta Kappa, 1976-82; assoc. dir. Phi Theta Kappa Internat. Hdqrs., Jackson, Miss., 1982-85, exec. dir., 1985—. Chmn. bd. dirs. Miss. Humanities Coun.; bd. dirs. Jack Kent Cooke Found., CC Transfer Initiative; chmn. bd. devel. com. Miss. Ctr. Non-Profit Orgns., Am. Soc. Assn. Execs.; grant reviewer NSF, CC Humanities Assn., NEH; mem. adv. bd. Horne CPA Group. Judge Truman Scholarship Found., 1993, 94, Coca-Cola Scholars Found., 2001-04, USA Today's All-USA Acad. Team HS, 2003-04, Jack Kent Cooke Found., 2004-06, Nat. Assn. C.C. Tchr. Edn. Program, 2004-07. Named one of Outstanding Young Men Am., 1982, 83, 84, 85, 86, 87, 88, 89, Top Bus. Leaders Miss., 1994, Disting. Alumnus, San Jacinto Coll., 1997; Mid South Found. C.C. fellow, 2001. Mem. Am. Assn. of Cmty. Colls. (commr. coun. for acad., student and cmty. devel., grant reviewer, Disting. Alumnus award 1996), Am. Soc. Assn. Execs., Phi Theta Kappa (sec., pub. jour.), Phi Kappa Phi. Episcopalian. Office: Phi Theta Kappa Soc PO Box 13729 Jackson MS 39236-3729 Office Phone: 601-984-3518. Business E-Mail: rod.risley@ptk.org.

RISLEY, TODD ROBERT, psychologist, educator; b. Palmer, Alaska, Sept. 8, 1937; s. Robert and Eva Lou (Todd) R.; 1 child, Todd Michael; m. Cheryl Thomas, Mar. 30, 1996. AB with distinction in Psychology, San Diego State Coll., 1960; MS, U. Wash., 1963, PhD, 1966. Asst. prof. psychology Fla. State U., Tallahassee, 1964-65; rsch. assoc. Bur. Child Rsch., U. Kans., Lawrence, 1965-77, sr. scientist, 1977—2003, emeritus, 2003—, asst. prof. dept. human devel., 1967-69, assoc. prof., 1969-73, prof., 1973-84; prof. psychology U. Alaska, Anchorage, 1982—2003, prof. emeritus, 2003—. Pres. Ctr. for Applied Behavior Analysis, 1970-82; dir. Johnny Cake Child Study Ctr., Mansfield, Ark., 1973-74; vis. prof. U. Auckland (N.Z.), 1978; acting dir. Western Carolina Ctr., Morgantown, N.C., 1981; dir. Alaska Div. Mental Health and Devel. Disabilities, 1988-91; cons. in field to numerous orgns. and instns. Co-author: The Infant Center, 1977, Shopping with Children: Advice for parents, 1978, The Toddler Center, 1979, Meaningful Differences, 1995, The Social World of Children, 1999; editor: Jour. Applied Behavior Analysis, 1971-74; mng. editor: Behavior Therapy, The Behavior Therapist, Behavioral Asessment, 1977-80; assoc. editor: Jour. Positive Behavior Support, 1998--; mem. editl. bds. of numerous profl. jours.; contbr. revs. and numerous articles. Co-chmn. Fla. task force on use of behavioral procedures in state programs for retarded, 1974—; mem. resident abuse investigating com. div. retardation Fla. Dept. Health and Rehab. Services, 1972—; mem. adv. com. Social Research Inst., U. Utah, 1977—; mem. Alaska Gov.'s Council on Handicapped and Gifted, 1983-88, NIH Mental Retardation Research Com., 1987-88, Alaska Mental Health Bd., 1988. Grantee NIMH, 1971-72, 72-73; rsch. grantee Nat. Ctr. Health Services, 1976-79; grantee Nat. Inst. Edn., 1973, NIH, 1967-86; grantee U.S. Dept. Edn., 1997-2002. Fellow APA (coun. of reps. 1982-85, pres. div. 25, 1989, Edgar Doll award 2000), Am. Psychol. Soc.; mem. AAAS, Am. Assn. Mental Deficiency (Rsch. award 2000), Assn. Advancement of Behavior Therapy (dir. 1975-80, pres. 1976-77, chmn. profl. rev. com. 1977—, series editor Readings in Behavior Therapy 1977—), Soc. Behavioral Medicine, Assn. Behavior Analysis, Sigma Xi. Home Phone: 907-746-6509; Office Phone: 907-745-4360. Business E-Mail: risley@alaska.net.

RISMAN, MICHAEL, lawyer, real estate developer, broker; b. Everett, Mass., Apr. 2, 1938; s. Morris Charles and Doris (Rosenbaum) R.; m. Rebecca R. Fuchs, Mar. 23, 1974; 1 stepchild, Ian Carlton Murray; children: Matthew Craig, Deborah Risman Kyle, Jared Evan. BA, U. Mich., 1960; LLB, Georgetown U., 1964. Bar: D.C. 1964. Staff mem. Democratic Nat. Com., Washington, 1964; atty. U.S. Fgn. Claims Settlement Commn., Washington, 1964-66, SEC, Washington, 1966-67; counsel Seaboard Planning Corp., Beverly Hills, Calif., 1967-72, pres., 1970-72; v.p. Seaboard Corp., Beverly Hills, 1970-72; sec. B.C. Morton Realty Trust, 1967-71; with Arlington Investments Corp., Santa Monica, Calif., 1979-86; founder The Quincey Group, 1986; owner, pres. Armstrong Kitchens, San Francisco, 1988-90; sr. v.p. AFC Am. Housing Corp., LA, Calif., 1991-97; mng. dir. Hollingsworth & Lord, LA, 1997—; ptnr. Dorama, L.L.C., 2002—. Bd. dirs. Competitive Capital Fund, Income Fund Boston, Inc., Admiralty Fund. Named Businessperson of Yr., Desert Hot Springs C. of C., 2007. Home: 1133 Centinela Ave Santa Monica CA 90403-2316 Office Phone: 310-890-6011. Personal E-mail: mrisman02@aol.com.

RISOM, JENS, furniture designer, consultant, manufacturing executive; b. Copenhagen, May 8, 1916; came to U.S., 1939; naturalized, 1944; s. Sven J. and Inger Risom; m. Iben Haderup, Dec. 12, 1939 (dec. Jan. 1977); children: Helen Ann, Peggy Ann, Thomas Christian, Sven Christian; m. Henny Panduro, May 12, 1979. Student, Krebs, Denmark, 1922-27, St. Annae, 1927-32, Niels Brock Bus. Coll., 1932-34, Sch. for Arts and Indust., Denmark, 1935—37; DFA (hon.), R.I. Sch. Design, 2003. With design and decorating divsn. Nordiska Kompanet, Stockholm, Inge Westin, Stockholm, 1934-35, Ernst Kühn, Arch., Copenhagen and NYC, 1937-38; with Dan Cooper, Inc., N.Y., 1939-41; freelance furniture designer, 1941-46; founder, pres. Jens Risom Design Inc., 1946-71; pres. Jens Risom Design, Inc. (became subs. Dictaphone Corp. 1971); v.p. Dictaphone Corp., 1971-73; pres. Design Control, New Canaan, Conn., 1973—. Cons. design, mktg., space planning. Trustee RISD, New Canaan Libr., Indsl. Design Soc. Am. With U.S. Army, 1943-45, ETO. Decorated Danish Knight's Cross (Denmark); recipient awards Archtl. League, Am. Inst. Internat. Design, Lifetime Achievement award Bklyn. Mus. Art, 1994, Russell Wright Manitoga Design award RI Sch. Design, 2004, numerous Danish and Am. design awards. Home and Office: 24 Parade Hill Ln New Canaan CT 06840-4119 also: PO Box 596 Block Island RI 02807-0596

RISS, ERIC, psychologist; m. Miriam Barbara Schoen; children: Arthur, Suzanne, Wendy. BA, Bklyn. Coll., 1950; PhD, NYU, 1958. Diplomate Am. Bd. Psychotherapy. Pvt. practice psychotherapy, family therapy and marriage counseling, NYC, 1952; sr. psychologist N.Y.C. Diagnostic Ctr., 1954-57; with Marriage and Family Life Inst., NYC, 1956-92, cons., 1956-58, dir. pub. edn., 1960-73, chmn. bd. dirs., 1961-73, dir., 1973-92; mem. attending staff, supr. psychotherapy and family therapy Payne Whitney Psychiat. Clinic, N.Y. Hosp., NYC, 1971-78; clin. instr. psychology and psychiatry Cornell U. Med. Coll., 1971-72, clin. asst. prof., 1973-78; dir. Inst. for Exploration of Marriage, 1976-84; chief psychologist Artists, Writers and Performers Psychotherapy Ctr., 1978-92. Sr. psychologist N.Y.C. Diagnostic Center, 1954-57; with Marriage and Family Life Inst., N.Y.C., 1956-92; cons., 1956-58, dir. pub. edn., 1960-73, chmn. bd. dirs., 1961-73, dir., 1973-92; mem. attending staff, supr. psychotherapy and family therapy Payne Whitney Psychiat. Clinic, N.Y. Hosp., N.Y.C., 1971-78; clin. instr. psychology and psychiatry Cornell U. Med. Coll., 1971-72, clin. asst. prof., 1973-78; dir. Inst. for Exploration of Marriage, 1976-84; chief psychologist Artists, Writers and Performers Psychotherapy Center, 1978-92; lectr. Bklyn. Coll., 1955-62; cons. Fordham Hosp., 1956-68; psychotherapist N.Y. Neuropsychiat. Center, 1958-60; psychotherapist Community Guidance Service, N.Y.C., 1958-61; founder, head Natural Psychotherapy Internat., 1999—; webmaster www.naturalpsychotherapy.com. Contbr. numerous articles to profl. jours. Mem. APA, N.Y. State Psychol. Assn., Am. Acad. Psychotherapy, N.Y. State Marriage, Family and Child Counseling Assn. (pres. 1971-72), Acad. Family Psychology. Office: 174 E 73rd St New York NY 10021-4352 Office Phone: 212-988-4700. E-mail: eriss@naturalpsychotherapy.com, eriss@npsy.com.

RISS, RICHARD MICHAEL, research economist, church history educator; b. Rochester, NY, May 22, 1952; s. Walter and Barbara Ann (Johnson) R.; m. Kathryn Janet Grieser, Mar. 3, 1979. BA, U. Rochester, 1974; MCS, Regent Coll., Vancouver, B.C., Can., 1979; MA, Trinity Evang. Div. Sch., Deerfield, Ill., 1988; MPhil, Drew U., 2002. Instr. ch. history Christian Life Coll., Mt. Prospect, Ill., 1980-83; data base mgr. Systems and Mgmt. Infor. Svcs. 1st Chgo. Corp., 1980-85; rsch. assoc. to chief economist Prudential Securities, NYC, 1988-91, C.J. Lawrence/Deutsche Bank Securities Corp., NYC, 1991-96; assoc. prof. ch. history Somerset Christian Coll., 1989—. Author: The Evidence for the Resurrection of Jesus Christ, 1977, Latter Rain, 1987, A Survey of Twentieth Century Revival Movements in North America, 1988, A History of the Worldwide Awakening, 1992-95, 1995, A Defense of the Revival, 1996, Images of Revival, 1997; also articles to New International Dictionary of Pentecostal and Charismatic Movements, Ency. Hanoverian Eng. and The Library of Christian Worship. Mem. Soc. for Pentecostal Studies, Conf. on Faith and History, Evang. Theol. Soc., Soc. Christian Philosophers, Am. Soc. Ch. History, Wesleyan Theol. Soc. Avocation: playing violin. Home: 290 River Rd Apt M-1 Piscataway NJ 08854-7516

RISSE, GUENTER BERNHARD, physician, historian, educator; b. Buenos Aires, Apr. 28, 1932; s. Francisco B. and Kaete A. R.; m. Alexandra G. Paradzinski, Oct. 14, 1961; children— Heidi, Monica, Alisa. MD, U.

Buenos Aires, 1958; PhD, U. Chgo., 1971. Intern Mercy Hosp., Buffalo, 1958-59; resident in medicine Henry Ford Hosp., Detroit, 1960-61, Mt. Carmel Hosp., Columbus, Ohio, 1962-63; asst. dept. medicine U. Chgo., 1963-67; asst. prof. dept. history of medicine U. Minn., 1969-71; asso. prof. dept. history of medicine and dept. history of sci. U. Wis., Madison, 1971-76, prof., 1976-85, chmn. dept. history of medicine, 1971-77; prof. dept. history health scis. U. Calif., San Francisco, 1985-99, prof. dept. anthropology, history and social medicine, 1999-2001, prof. emeritus, 2001—, dept. chair, 1985—99; affiliate prof. dept med. history and ethics Univ. Wash. Sch. of Medicine, Seattle, 2002—. Mem. project com. Ctr. for Photog. Images in Medicine and Health Care. Author: Paleopathology of Ancient Egypt, 1964, Hospital Life in Enlightenment Scotland, 1986, Mending Bodies-Saving Souls: A History of Hospitals, 1999, New Medical Challenges During the Scottish Enlightenment, 2005; editor: Modern China and Traditional Chinese Medicine, 1973, History of Physiology, 1973, Medicine Without Doctors, 1977, AIDS and the Historian, 1991, Culture, Knowledge and Healing, Historical Perspectives of Homeopathic Medicine in Europe and North America, 1998; mem. editl. bd. Jour. History of Medicine, 1971-74, 90-93, Clio Medica, 1973-88, Bull. History of Medicine, 1980-94, Medizinhistorisches Jour., 1981—, Med. History, 1989-95, NTM Internat. Jour. of History, Ethics, Medicine, 1992—, History of Philos. Life Scis., 1993—, Asclepio, 1995—, Health and History, 1998—. With Argentine Armed Forces, 1955. Recipient NIH grants, 1971-73, 82-84, WHO grant, 1979, named Logan Campbell Disting. Lectr., New Zealand, 1994, Karl Sudhoff Meml. Lectr., Germany, 2000; grantee Nat. Lib. Medicine, 2006—. Mem. Am. Assn. History of Medicine (pres. 1988-90, William H. Welch medal 1988, Lifetime Achievement award 2005), History Sci. Soc., Deutsche Gesellschaft fur Geschichte der Medizin, European Assn. History of Medicine and Health, Internat. Network for History of Pub. Health, Mex. Soc. History and Philosophy of Medicine, Peruvian Assn. Med. Ethnology and History, Brit. Soc. for Social History of Medicine, Argentine Ateneo de Historia de la Medicina, AIDS History Group (co-chair 1988-94), Internat. Network for History of Hosps. (convenor 1995—), Bay Area Med. Hist. Club (pres. 1994-96). Home: 2612 SW 167th St Burien WA 98166-3228 Business E-Mail: risseg@u.washington.edu.

RISSER, JAMES VAULX, JR., journalist, educator; b. Lincoln, Nebr., May 8, 1938; s. James Vaulx and Ella Caroline (Schacht) R.; m. Sandra Elizabeth Laaker, June 10, 1961; children: David James, John Daniel. BA, U. Nebr., 1959, cert. in journalism, 1964; JD, U. San Francisco, 1962. Bar: Nebr. 1962. Pvt. practice law, Lincoln, 1962-64; reporter Des Moines Register and Tribune, 1964-85, Washington corr., 1969-85, bur. chief, 1976-85; dir. John S. Knight fellowships for profl. journalists, prof. communication Stanford U., 1985-2000. Lectr. Wells Coll., 1981; mem. com. on agrl. edn. in secondary schs. Nat. Acad. Scis., 1985-88. Trustee Reuter Found., 1989-00, Am. Conservatory Theater, 2000-03, Oreg. Shakespear Fest., 2003—, Jefferson Pub. Radio, 2003-; mem. Pulitzer Prize Bd., 1990-99; mem. journalism adv. com. Knight Found., 2000-06. Profl. Journalism fellow Stanford U., 1973-74; recipient award for disting. reporting public affairs Am. Polit. Sci. Assn., 1969; Thomas L. Stokes award for environ. reporting Washington Journalism Center, 1971, 79; Pulitzer prize for nat. reporting, 1976, 79; Worth Bingham Found. prize for investigative reporting, 1976; Raymond Clapper Meml. Assn. award for Washington reporting, 1976, 78; Edward J. Meeman award for Conservation Reporting, 1985. Mem.: Com. Concerned Journalists, Soc. Profl. Journalists (Disting. Svc. award 1976), Soc. Environ. Journalists, Gridiron Club. Home: 71 Water St 206 Ashland OR 97520 E-mail: jimrisser@earthlink.net.

RISSER, PAUL GILLAN, academic administrator, botanist; b. Blackwell, Okla., Sept. 14, 1939; s. Paul Crane and Jean (McCluskey) R.; children: David, Mark, Stephen, Scott. BA, Grinnell Coll., 1961; MS in Botany, U. Wis., 1965, PhD in Botany and Soils, 1967. From asst. prof. to prof. botany U. Okla., 1967-81, also asst. dir. biol. sta., chmn. dept. botany and microbiology, 1977-81; dir. Okla. Biol. Survey, 1971-77; chief Ill. Natural History Survey, 1981-86; program dir., ecosystem studies NSF; provost and v.p. acad. affairs U. N.Mex., 1989-92; former pres. Miami U., Oxford, Ohio; pres. Oreg. State U., 1996—2002; chancellor Okla. Sys. Higher Edn., 2003—. Author: (with Kathy Cornelison) Man and the Biosphere, 1979, (with others) The True Prairie Ecosystem, 1981; research, numerous publs. in field. Trustee Pioneer Multi-County Library Bd. Mem. Am. Acad. Arts and Scis., Ecol. Soc. Am. (pres.), Brit. Ecol. Soc., Soc. Range Mgmt., Southwestern Assn. Naturalists (pres.), Am. Inst. Biol. Sci. (pres.), Torrey Bot. Club. Presbyterian. Address: OK State Regents Higher Edn Off Chancellor 655 Rsch Pky Ste 200 Oklahoma City OK 73104

RISSETTO, HARRY A., lawyer; b. Dec. 1, 1943; AB, Fairfield U., 1965; JD, Georgetown U., 1968. Bar: N.Y. 1969, D.C. 1970, U. S. Supreme Ct. Law clk. to Hon. John J. Sirica US Dist. Ct. D.C., 1968-69; law clk. to Chief Justice Warren E. Burger US Supreme Ct., 1969-70; sr. counsel Morgan, Lewis & Bockius, Washington. Adj. prof. Law Ctr., Georgetown U., 1986-89. Mem. ABA (co-chmn. railway labor act com. sect. of labor and employment law 1987-89), Coll. Labor & Employment Lawyers. Office: Morgan Lewis & Bockius 1111 Pennsylvania Ave NW Washington DC 20004 Home Phone: 703-241-0442; Office Phone: 202-739-5130. Business E-Mail: hrissetto@morganlewis.com.

RISSMAN, BURTON RICHARD, lawyer; b. Chgo., Nov. 13, 1927; s. Louis and Eva (Lyons) R.; m. Francine Greenberg, June 15, 1952; children: Lawrence E., Thomas W., Michael P. BS, U. Ill., 1947, JD, 1951; LLM, NYU, 1952. Bar: Ill. 1951, U.S. Dist. Ct. (no. dist.) Ill. 1954, U.S. Ct. Appeals (7th cir.) 1978, U.S. Supreme Ct. 1982. Assoc. Schiff, Hardin & Waite, Chgo., 1953-59, ptnr., 1959—2003, mem. mgmt. com., 1984-92, chmn. mgmt. com., 1986-90; ret., 2003. Mem. faculty Practicing Law Inst. Bd. editor U. Ill. Law Forum, 1949-51; contbr. articles to profl. jours. 1st lt. JAGC USAF, 1952—53. Food Law fellow, 1951. Mem. ABA, Ill. Bar Assn., Chgo. Bar Assn., Chgo. Coun. Lawyers, Carlton Club.

RISTAU, JACOB ROBERT, art educator, graphics designer; b. Lawrence, Kans., Jan. 3, 1978; s. Mel H. and Jacque A. Ristau; m. Melissa Dawn Sheldon, July 15, 2000. BFA, Abilene Christian U., Tex., 2000; MFA in Visual Comm., Sch. Art Inst. Chgo., 2005. Asst. artist Mel Ristau Design/Media Garden, Inc., Ft. Collins, Colo., 1998—; designer Richards, Brock, Miller, Mitchell and Assoc., Dallas, 2000—03; freelance artist and designer, 2003—; instr. Sch. Art Inst. Chgo., 2005; asst. prof. dept. art and art history U. Redlands, Calif., 2005—. Exhibited in group shows at Virginia Shore Gallery Abilene Christian U., Tex., 2001, one-man shows include Peppers Art Gallery U. Redlands, 2007, exhibitions include Grad. Thesis Exhbn. at Gallery 2, Sch. Art Inst. Chgo., 2005, 45th Ann. Dallas Show, 2003, Faculty Exhbn. Peppers Art Ctr., Redlands, Calif., 2005, Peppers Art Gallery, U. Redlands, Calif., 2007, illustrations, The Business of Holidays, edited by Maud Lavin, 2004, appearing in collections and trade publs. Recipient Graphic Designer of Yr., Abilene Christian U., 1998, awards of excellence (4), Houston Art Dirs. Club, 2002. Mem.: Coll. Arts Assn. Avocations: linguistics, word games, board games, card games. Office: Univ Redlands Dept Art and Art History 1200 E Colton Ave Redlands CA 92373

RISTAU, MARK MOODY, lawyer, consultant; b. Warren, Pa., Mar. 21, 1944; s. Harold J. and Eleanor K. (Moody) Ristau. BA, Pa. Mil. Coll., 1966, Widner Coll., 1966; JD, Case Western Res. U., 1969. Bar: Pa. 1970, D.C. 1972, U.S. Supreme Ct. 1973, N.Y. 1982. Pvt. practice, Warren, Pa., 1970—85, Warren and Vancouver, B.C., Canada, 1976—85, Jamestown, NY, 1982—85; sr. ptnr. Ristau & McKeirnan, Warren, 1986—2002; sr. dir. Pa. Allied Oil Prodrs., 1972—78; atty. Pa. Field Prodrs., 1981—85; ptnr. SAR Devel., 1984—91, Slagle Almendinger & Ristau, 1983—89. Counsel United Refining Co., Pennbank, Enhanced Oil Recovery, Consol. Svcs., 1982—84; chmn. bd. Comml. Svc. Corp., U.S. interim trustee, 1979—88, bankruptcy trustee, 1988—98; CEO Silicon Electro-physics Corp., Inc., 1988—91, Phoenix Materials Corp., Inc., 1988—91; dirs. Warren Industries, Inc., 1991—94, CEO, 2003—; bd. dirs. Petrex, Inc., A & A Metal Fabricating; U.S. counsel Brazilian Promotions, Inc. of Brazilian Govt., 1981—85; v.p. Daytona Apts., Inc., Daytona Beach, Fla.; case reporter Legal Intelligencer, 1972—79. Contbr. articles to profl. jours. Sec. Daytona Devel. League; mem. Warren County Bd. Pub. Assistance, 1970—71, chmn., 1971—72; mem. Broward County (Fla.) Devel. League, 1981—83, Fla. Profl. Recruitment Assn., 1980—83. Recipient Tate Meml. award, 1981, Sambas award, 1981. Mem.: ATLA, Warren County Bar Assn. (past pres.), Am. Arbitration Assn., Conewango (Warren), Ipanema (Brazil), Eagles (life). Home and Office: PO Box 885 Warren PA 16365-0885 Office Phone: 814-723-2050. Personal E-mail: ristaulaw@penn.com.

RISTER, GENE ARNOLD, humanities educator; b. Merkel, Tex., Apr. 18, 1943; s. Jettie William and Mary Evelyn (Scott) R.; m. Janet Kathleen Ledermann, Jan. 21, 1967. BA summa cum laude, McMurry U., 1965; MA, Tex. Christian U., 1966; PhD, U. Wis., 1972; postgrad., U. Ariz., 1990, No. Ariz. U., 1990. Prof., divsn. chmn. McMurry U., Abilene, Tex., 1970-81, East Ctrl. U., Ada, Okla., 1981-83, Paradise Valley Coll., Maricopa C.C., Phoenix, 1983—. Adj. prof. No. Ariz. U., Phoenix, 1994—; del. Nat. Inst. Higher Edn. for Mex.-Ams., Albuquerque, 1975. Author: (poems) Canticles I, 2002, Canticles II, 2003, Canticles III, 2004, Rumors of Unruh, 2006; book reviewer Tex. Rev., 1985; illustrator Tex. Rev. and Tex. Anthology, 1979-82; contbr. articles to profl. jours.; contbr. numerous poems to jours., anthologies. Regional cons. Human Rels. Coun., Midland; moderator, dir. West Tex. Coun. Govts.; mem. Tex. Com. for Humanities and Pub. Policy, 1975-81; ECU rep. Intertribal Coun., Five Nations, Sulphur, Okla., 1981; co-sponsor Tex. Reading Cir. Consortium of Univs., 1977-79. Recipient Faculty Recognition award Consortium for C.C. Devel., 1996; named Innovator of the Yr. Maricopa CCD/League for Innovation, 1988, Outstanding Faculty Employee award Maricopa C.C. Dist., 1985, 89, 92; NDEA Title VI fellow, 1965-67, Am. Grad. Sch. Internat. Mgmt. fellow, 1995, East-West Ctr. fellow, 1994, Japan Found. fellow, 1995; U.S. Dept. Edn. Title VIA grantee, 1996-98. Mem. C.C. Humanities Assn. (Ariz. state rep. to nat. bd. 1992). Democrat. Baptist. Avocations: archaeology, art, movies, music, travel. Home: 14407 N 60th St Scottsdale AZ 85254-5540 Office: Paradise Valley Cmty Coll 18401 N 32nd St Phoenix AZ 85032-1210 Home Phone: 480-991-6501; Office Phone: 602-787-6575. E-mail: gene.rister@pvmail.maricopa.edu.

RISTICH, MIODRAG, psychiatrist; b. Belgrade, Yugoslavia, July 19, 1938; arrived in US, 1967; s. Teodosije and Gordana (Isailovic) Ristich; m. Yvonne Muriel Cunliffe, May 6, 1967; children: Katharine Alexandra, Elizabeth Victoria. MD, U. Belgrade, 1962. Resident psychiatry Manhattan Psychiat. Ctr., NYU, 1980-83; med. dir. Cambridge (Minn.) State Hosp., 1967-72; dir. Willowbrook State Sch., Staten Island, NY, 1972-74; med. dir. DeWitt Rehab. Nursing Ctr., NYC, 1976—; clin. asst. prof. psychiatry NYU Med. Sch., 1996—. Pvt. practice psychiatry, NYC, 1973—. Mem.: AMA, Royal Coll. Psychiatrists, Am. Assn. Geriatric Psychiatry, Am. Psychiat. Assn. Republican. Avocation: tennis. Home: 37 Sunrise Ln Upper Saddle River NJ 07458-1631 Office: 201 E 79th St Apt 7J New York NY 10075-0835 Home Phone: 201-934-5513; Office Phone: 212-737-6990. E-mail: mristich@yahoo.com.

RISTOW, GEORGE EDWARD, neurologist, educator; b. Albion, Mich., Dec. 15, 1943; s. George Julius and Margaret (Beattie) R.; 1 child, George Andrew Martin. BA, Albion Coll., 1965; DO, Coll. Osteo. Medicine/Surgery, Des Moines, 1969. Diplomate Am. Bd. Psychiatry and Neurology. Intern Garden City Hosp., 1969-70; resident Wayne State U., 1970-74; fellow U. Newcastle Upon Tyne, 1974-75; asst. prof. dept. neurology Wayne State U., Detroit, 1975-77; assoc. prof. Mich. State U., East Lansing, 1977-83, prof., 1983-84, 95—, prof., chmn., 1984-95, prof. emeritus, 2001—. Fellow Am. Acad. Neurology, Royal Soc. Medicine; mem. AMA, Am. Osteo. Assn., Pan Am. Med. Assn., World Fedn. Neurology, Am. Coll. Neuropsychiatrists (sr.). Home: 6149 Bridgewater Cir East Lansing MI 48823 Office Phone: 517-374-7600. Personal E-mail: gristow@cimamed.com.

RISTOW, THELMA FRANCES, retired elementary school educator; b. Plymouth, Wis., Sept. 9, 1938; d. Ambrose J. and Marie A. (Lauby) Enders; m. William A. Ristow, Nov. 7, 1964; children: James, Lora, Kim Marie, Robert, Donald. BS, U. Wis., Oshkosh, 1960, MS in Edn., 1995. Cert. elem. tchr. Peer coach Oshkosh Area Sch. Dist., 2000—. Contbr. chapters to books; co-author (with Dr. Ava McCall): Teaching State History: A Guide to Developing a Multicultural Curriculum. Mem. Internat. Reading Assn. (state coord.), Wis. State Reading Assn., Ctrl. Wis. Reading Coun., Mid-East Reading Coun., Wolf River Reading Coun., Fox Valley Reading Coun., Headwaters Reading Coun., Menominee Indian Reading Coun., Phi Delta Kappa, Kappa Delta Pi. Home: 1600 Northpoint St Oshkosh WI 54901-3119 Personal E-mail: tfristow@sbcglobal.net.

RISUKHIN, VLADIMIR NIKOLAYEVICH, aeronautical engineer, educator; b. Verkhnyaya Pokrovka, Ukraine, Dec. 26, 1946; arrived in U.S., 2001; s. Nikolay Ostapovich Risukhin and Nina Josephovna (Linevich) Risukhina; m. Tatyana Vasilyevna Chernysh, July 12, 1969; children: Dmitry, Ekaterina. BS in Radio Comm., Coll. Elec. Comm., 1965; BS in Flight Ops., Coll. Civil Aviation, 1968; MS in Aeronautical Engring., Acad. Civil Aviation, 1974, PhD in Aeronautical Engring., 1988. Radio tech. Airport, Lugansk, Ukraine, 1964—65; pilot Regoinal Adminstrn. Civil Aviation, Yakutsk, 1968—77; flight ops. mgr. Ctrl. Adminstrn. Internat. Airline, Moscow, 1977—83; flight tng. mgr. Min. Aviation Industry, 1983—90; sr. instr. pilot Aepoflot-Russian Airlines, 1990—2002; assoc. prof. Coll. Aviation, Western Mich. U., Battle Creek, 2002—. Cons. Internat. Air Transp. Assn., Montreal, 2000—. Author: Controlling Pilot Error: Automation, 2001. Mem.: AIAA, Univ. Aviation Assn. (profl.). Avocations: photography, tennis. Office: Coll Aviation Western Mich U 237 N Helmer Rd Battle Creek MI 49015 Home Phone: 269-381-4262. E-mail: vladimir.risukhin@wmich.edu.

RITACCO, PATSY RICHARD, sales executive; b. Newark, Aug. 27, 1956; s. Michael Patsy and Adelaide (Caruso) Ritacco; m. Linda La Falce, Nov. 5, 1978; children: Michael A., Patsy Richard Jr. B in History, William Paterson Coll., 1978. Notary pub. N.J. Tchr. Belleville (N.J.) HS, 1978-82; bd. pneumatics Robert Tool, Saddle Brook, NJ, 1983-94; dist. sales mgr. Std. Abrasives, Simi Valley, Calif., 1994—2007, regional sales mgr., 2007—. Concert promotion dir. edn. groups 50s and 60s Bklyn. Bridge, Coasters, 1980—; scholar bd. Unico Nat., Nutley, NJ, 1995—, treas., 1998—99, v.p., 2000—, chpt. pres., 2005—; guest lectr. in field. Contbr. poetry to anthologies; contbg. writer: Italian Tribune. Fellow bdlgs. and grounds pub. rels. Christ Ch. Sch. Bd., 1985—88; chmn. com. Nutley Hall of Fame, 2002—; chmn. Ferraro Found., 2004; mem. planning bd. Township of Nutley, 2005; mem. Nutley Planning Bd., 2005—; coun. mem. NIAF; assoc. mem. Mus. Natural History. Named in Greatest Poets and Poems of the 20th Century, 1999; recipient Editor's Choice award "Riddle of the Rose", Internat. Libr. of Poetry, Color of Heart, 2000, Poetry's Elite: The Best Poets, 2000, Unican of the Yr. award, Nutley chpt. Unico Nat., 2002, Poetry's Elite: The Best Poet, 2001, 2002, 2003, 2004, Outstanding Achievement award, Ferraro Found., 2003, Cmty. Svc. award, 2003, Parable of Time Editor's Choice award, 2003, Civic award, Nutley Jaycees, 2006. Mem.: Internat. Soc. Poets, Platers Assn. (contbg.), Soc. Engrs. (contbg.), Am. Softball Assn. (assoc.). Roman Catholic. Avocations: reading, cooking, music, sports. Office: Standard Abrasives 4201 Guardian St Simi Valley CA 93063-3372 Office Phone: 800-423-5444. Personal E-mail: BaBiBard@aol.com. Business E-Mail: pritacco@standardabrasives.com.

RITCH, KATHLEEN, diversified financial services company executive; b. Harbor Beach, Mich., Jan. 23, 1943; d. Eunice (Spry) R. BA, Mich. State U., 1965; student, Katharine Gibbs Sch., 1965—66. Exec. sec., adminstrv. asst. to pres. Katy Industries, Inc., NYC, 1969-70; exec. sec., adminstrv. asst. to chmn. Kobrand Corp., NYC, 1970-72; adminstrv. asst. to chmn. and pres. Ogden Corp., NYC, 1972-74, asst. sec., adminstr. office svcs., asst. to chmn., 1974-81, corp. sec., adminsr. office svcs., 1981-84, v.p., corp. sec., adminstr. office svcs., 1984-92, v.p. corp. sec., 1992-2000; freelance executive NYC, 2000—. Co-owner Unell Mfg. Co., Port Hope, Mich., 1966-87. Bd. dir. Young Concert Artists, Inc. Home: 500 E 77th St New York NY 10162-0025

RITCH, ROBERT HARRY, ophthalmologist, educator; b. New Haven, May 14, 1942; s. Edward Lewis and Minerva (Grosberg) R. BA cum laude, Harvard U., 1965, MA, 1967; postgrad., Rice U., 1967—68; MD, Albert Einstein Coll. Medicine, 1972. Diplomate Am. Bd. Ophthalmology, Am. Bd. Laser Surgery. Intern St. Vincent's Med. Ctr., NYC, 1972-73; resident in ophthalmology Mt. Sinai Sch. Medicine, NYC, 1973-75, chief resident, 1975-76, Heed Ophthalmic Found. fellow, 1976-77, NIH-Nat. Rsch. Svc. fellow, 1976-78, asst. clin. ophthalmologist, 1976-77, instr., 1977-78, asst. prof., 1978-80, assoc. prof., 1980-82; attending ophthalmologist Beth Israel Med. Ctr., NYC, 1978—. Cons. ophthalmologist VA Hosp., Bronx, 1978—82, Manhattan Eye, Ear & Throat Hosp., 1989—; dir. glaucoma svc. Elmhurst Hosp., 1978—82, acting dir. dept. ophthalmology, 1979—82; chief glaucoma svc. NY Eye and Ear Infirmary, NYC, 1983—, surgeon dir., 1991—; adj. sr. scientist Singapore Eye Rsch. Inst., 1997; adj. prof. Mt. Sinai Sch. Medicine, 2005—; prof. clin. ophthalmology N.Y. Med. Coll., Valhalla, 1983—; Arthur Bedell Meml. lectr. Wills Eye Hosp., Phila., 1995; John Edwin Brown Meml. lectr. Ohio State U., Columbus, 1996; Schoenburg Meml. lectr. Ill. Eye and Ear Infirmary, Chgo., 1996; Schlaegel lectr. U. Ind., Indpls., 1996; Gerasimos Frenimopoulos Meml. lectr. Duke U., 1997, Joseph M. Bryan Meml. lectr., 97; Roger P. Mason Meml. lectr. Howard U., 1997; Abraham S. Ticho lectr., Jerusalem, 98; Anagnostakis-Trantus lectr., Athens, 98; Sanford Gifford Meml. lectr., Chgo., 98; Annie Wong lectr. Chinese U., Hong Kong, 1999; Arthur Lim lectr., Hong Kong, 2001; Am. Glaucoma Soc. Subspecialty Day lectr. Am. Acad. Ophthalmology, New Orleans, 2001; King Khaled Meml. lectr., Riyadh, 03; Chew Sek-Jin Meml. lectr., Hong Kong, 03; Irving Leopold Meml. lectr., Irvine, Calif., 04; Francis Proctor Meml. lectr., San Francisco, 05; Julius Silver Meml. lectr., NY, 06; Irving Leopold Meml. lectr., NY, 06; Robert Shaffer lectr. Am. Acad. Opthalmology, 2007; program chmn. East Coast Glaucoma Symposium, NY, 2000; cons. Sukhumvit Hosp., Bangkok, 1994; pres. Internat. Eye Cons., Ltd., 1995—, N.Y. Glaucoma Rsch. Inst., 1996; mem. adv. bd. Dr. to Dr., Berkeley, Calif., 1995—; sec., treas., chmn. sci. adv. bd. Glaucoma Found., 1984—; med. dir., chmn., grant rev. com.; med. dir. Children's Right to Sight, prin. investigator Collaborative Initial Glaucoma Treatment Study, 1993—2003; mem. adv. bd. Sturge-Weber Found., 1996; mem. glaucoma adv. com. Nat. Soc. to Prevent Blindness, 1986—; organizing chmn. Bangkok Ophthal. Congress, 1985—93, Optic Nerve Rescue & Restoration Think Tank, NY, 1994—2003, First Internat. Think Tank on Exfoliation Syndrome, NY, 1999, Myanmar Internat. Ophthal. Congress, 1997, 99, 2003; internat. sci. com. Internat. Congress of Ophthalmology, Sydney, 2002; sci. organizing com. mem. 4th Internat. Glaucoma Congress, Barcelona, 2003; external assessor U. Malaya, 1988—96; cons. Tun Hussein Onn Nat. Eye Hosp., Kuala Lumpur, Malaysia, 1996—; internat. adv. bd. 4th Internat. Symposium of Ophthalmology, Shantou, China, 2002; mem. steering com. Assn. Internat. Glaucoma Soc., 2002—; internat. advisor Tianjin Med. Ctr., China, 2002—; hon. pres. Chinese Internat. Glaucoma Congress, Beijing, 2004; mem. sci. organizing com. 5th Internat. Glaucoma Congress, Capetown, South Africa, 2005; chmn. sci. organizing com. glaucoma sect. World Congress Ophthalmology, Sao Paulo, Brazil, 2006; organizing chmn. Kazakhstan Ophthalmological Congress, Almaty, 2006, ARVO/AAO Symposium on Nanotech., Am. Acad. Ophthalmology, 2007; organizing com. World Glaucoma Congress, Singapore, 2007; bd. dirs. Helen Keller Internat. Author (with M.B. Shields): The Secondary Glaucomas, 1982, The Glaucomas, 1988, 1996; author: (with R. Caronia) Classic Papers in Glaucoma, 2000; spl. sect. editor: Jour. Glaucoma, 1991—98, mem. editl. bd.: Sightsaving, 1981—86, Opthalmic Laser Therapy, 1984—88, Ophthalmic Resident, 1992—95, Ophthalmic Surgery and Lasers, 1995—, Microsurgery, 1994—2004, Ophthalmology Times, 1996—2001, Jour. Glaucoma, 1998—, Internat. Glaucoma Rev., 1999—, Archives Ophthalmology, 2004—, BMC Ophthalmology, 2005—, Expert Rev. Ophthalmology, 2005—, Asian Jour. Ophthalmology, 2006—, contbg. editor: Ophthalmic Practice, 1993—; contbr. to films on laser therapy, over 1100 articles and abstracts in field. Bd. dirs. Dooley Found./Intermed. U.S.A., 1991—, UN, Southeastern Nigeria Eye Care Outreach Coll. Med. Scis. U. Calabar, Nigeria, 1996—; vol. Devel. Coun., 1991-93; chmn. bd. dirs. I-Med. Devel Corp., 1991-94; sci. adv. bd. Singapore Eye Rsch. Inst.; bd. govs. Internat. Soc. for Imaging of the Eye, 2002—; adv. com. Internat. Coun. Ophthalmology, 2002—. Hon. scholar, Harvard U., 1965, NSF fellow, 1966—67, Harvard Traveling fellow, Rice U., 1967—68; recipient Acad. Investigator award, NIH, 1978—81, Disting. Svc. award, Internat. Ctr. NY, 1981, Exec. Dirs. award, 1985, Founders award, Nat. Exhibits by Blind Artists, 1985, Gold medal of Merit and Honor, Greek Glaucoma Soc., 1998, Ophthalmology Times Achievement in Ophthalmology award, 1998, Louis Rudin award for rsch. in glaucoma, 1999, Decorated comdr. Grace Sovereign Order of Orthodox Knights Hospitalier of St. John of Jerusalem; named spl. honoree, Helen Keller Found., 2000, Glaucoma Found., 2000; Jesse H. Neal award for editl. achievement, 2000, John Kearny Rodgers Physician of Yr. award, NY Eye and Ear Infirmary, 2005; Albion O. Bernstein award, Med. Soc. State of NY Fellow Am. Acad. Ophthalmology (edn. distbn. subcom. 1994-97, book/jour. link subcom. 1994-97, distbn. adv. subcom. 1997-2000, chmn. subcom., 2001—, Honor award, 1985, sr. honor award 1995), Heed Ophthalmic Found. (ophthalmologist of Yr. 1996), Am. Ophthalmol. Soc. (program com. 2002-2004), NY Acad. Medicine, Royal Coll. Ophthalmologists (U.K.), ACS, Internat. Coll. Surgeons, Am. Soc. Laser Surgery Medicine (chmn. ophthalmology sect. 1991-92, moderator and program chmn. joint sci. symposium on glaucoma 1991), NY Acad. Medicine (sec. sect. on ophthalmology 1991-92, chmn. 1993-94, Charles May Meml. Lectr. 1991, bd. trustees 2003—); mem. AMA, AAAS, NY State Med. Soc., NY County Med. Soc., Assn. Rsch. in Vision and Ophthalmology (program com., glaucoma sect. 1991-93, program chmn. 1993-94, internat. com. 2003—, bd. trustees 2003—, v.p. 2007-), Am. Assn. Ophthalmology, Ophthal. Soc. U.K., Internat. Assn. Ocular surgeons, Internat. Congress Ophthalmology (glaucoma com. 1994—), NY Intra-Ocular Lens Implant Soc., Manhattan Ophthal. Soc., Assn. Internat. Glaucoma Soc., Internat. Soc. Eye Rsch., Soc. Clin. Trials, Pan-Pacific Anterior Segment Soc. (v.p. 1985-88), Internat. Coun. Ophthalmology (adv. com.), NY Acad. Sci., Ophthalmic Laser Surgery Soc. (sec.-treas. 1982-98, 2000-, pres. 1998-2000), NY Soc. Clin. Ophthalmology (rec. sec. 1988-90, program chmn. 1990-91, pres. 1991-92), NY Glaucoma Rsch. Inst. (pres. 1996—), Am. Soc. Cell Biology, Am. Telemed Assn., Internat. Soc. On-Line Ophthalmologists (mem. orgn. com., chmn. glaucoma sect. 1995—), Internat. Fedn. Cell Biologists, Philippine Soc. Ophthalmology (hon.), Thailand Ophthal. Soc. (hon.), Italian Assn. for Study of Glaucoma (hon.), La.-Miss. Ophthal. and Otolarygol. Soc. (hon.), Can. Implant Soc. (hon). Home: 455 E 57th St # 14D New York NY 10022-3065 Office: NY Eye and Ear Infirmary 310 E 14th St New York NY 10003-4201 Home Phone: 212-980-7187; Office Phone: 212-477-7540. Personal E-mail: ritchmd@earthlink.net.

RITCHEY, KENNETH WILLIAM, social services administrator; b. Washington, June 7, 1947; s. Conrad Monroe and Katherine Costance (Sheris) (dec. 2004) R.; m. Nancy Jayne Kirk, Aug. 22, 1970; children: Kirk Damon, Erin Kathryn (dec. Apr. 1988). BS in Edn., Shippensburg U., 1969; MEd in Spl. Edn., U. Va., 1972; MS in Ednl. Adminstrn., U. Dayton, 1980; grad. sr. execs. in state & local govt. program, Harvard U., 1992. Spl. edn. tchr. Shippensburg Area Sch. Dist., Pa., 1969-71; head cross country and track coach Shippensburg U., 1970-74; master tchr., coord. work experience program Lincoln Intermediate Unit, New Oxford, Pa., 1971-76; adult edn. tchr. Franklin County Prison, Chambersburg, Pa., 1972-76; asst. supt. mgmt. svcs. Montgomery County Bd. Mental Retardation & Devel. Disabilities, Dayton, Ohio, 1977-83, supt. bd., 1983-99; dir. Ohio Dept. Mental Retardation and Devel. Disabilities, Columbus, 1999—2007; asst. commr. divsn. devel. disabilities NJ Dept. Human Svcs., 2007—. Mem. part-time faculty edn. dept. U. Dayton, 1983-97; mem., vice-chair cmty. and mil. adv. com. ARC, 1986-95, needs and priorities com. Human Svcs. Levy Coun., 1982-84, 87-99; trustee Ohio Polit. Action Com., Brighter Tomorrow Found., 1990-2000, County Corp., 1992-98, Leadership Dayton, 1991. Former editor statewide newsletter for tchrs. and profls. in Work Experience. Vol. mem. cmty. and agys. resources coun. United Way, 1986—98; v.p. HelpLink Bd., pres.; mem. Gov.'s Vision Com., Ill., 1997—2000, Gov.'s Cabinet; bd. dirs. Ohio Pub. Images, Inc., past pres. Recipient Harold Hilty Humanitarian award, United Cerebral Palsy Rehab. Svcs., 1994, Robert Weaver Disting. Svc. award, Montgomery County Bd. Mental Retardation and Devel. Disabilities, 1999, Svc. award, Profl. Assn. on Retardation, 2002, Chair's Recognition award, Wright State U. Dept. Psychiatry, 2005, Cmty. Star award, Franklin County, 2006, Ray Ferguson Advocacy award, ARC, Ohio, 2007; honored by, Ohio Assn. County Bds., 2005. Mem.: Ohio Self Determination Assn. (Catalyst award 2003), Nat. Assn. State Dirs. Devel. Disabilities Svcs. (chair nat. policy work group 2002, bd. trustees 2004, sec.-treas. 2005—, v.p./pres. elect 2007), Supts. Assn. (exec. com.), Ohio Supts. County Bds. Mental Retardation (v.p., pres.), Am. Assn. Mental Retardation, Phi Beta Kappa. Democrat. Methodist. Home: 86 Lochatorg Rd Ewing NJ 08628 Office: Division Devel Disabilities PO Box 726 Trenton NJ 08025 Home Phone: 609-882-4648; Office Phone: 609-987-0864. Personal E-mail: k1ritchey@aol.com.

RITCHEY, PATRICK WILLIAM, lawyer; b. Pitts., July 9, 1949; s. Joseph Frank and Patricia Ann (Giovengo) R. BA high honors english lit., Haverford Coll., 1971; JD, Yale U., 1974. Bar: Pa, US Dist. Ct. (we. dist.) Pa. 1974, US Ct. of Appeals (3d. cir.) 1976, US Supreme Ct. 1980, US Ct. of Appeals (4th cir.) 1981, US Ct. of Appeals (6th cir.) 1982, US Dist. Ct. (ea. dist.) Wis. 1987, US Ct. of Appeals (7th cir.) 1991, US Ct. of Appeals (DC cir.) 1993, US Ct. of Appeals (8th cir.) 1993, US Dist. Ct. (no. dist.) Ind., State Supreme Ct. Pa. Assoc. Reed Smith Shaw & McClay, Pitts., 1974-82, ptnr., 1982—, Reed Smith LLP, Pitts., 1974—. Mem. Pitts. Personnel Assn., Pitts., 1982—, U.S. Dist. Ct. Rules Task Force, Pitts., 1988. Bd. dirs. Pitts. Opera. Recipient Who's Who in Am. Law, Best Lawyers in Am. Mem. Fed. Bar Assn. (labor and employment sect.), Allegheny County Bar Assn. (labor law and fed. ct. sects.), Harvard-Yale-Princeton Club, Duquesne Club. Office: Reed Smith LLP James H Reed Bldg 435 6th Ave Ste 2 Pittsburgh PA 15219-1886 Office Phone: 412-288-3072. Office Fax: 412-288-3063. Business E-Mail: pritchey@reedsmith.com.

RITCHEY, SAMUEL DONLEY, JR., retired retail executive; b. Derry Twp., Pa., July 16, 1933; s. Samuel Donley and Florence Catherine (Litsch) R.; m. Sharon Marie Anderson, Apr. 6, 1956; children: Michael Donley, Tamara Louise, Shawn Christopher. BS, San Diego State U., 1955, MS, 1963; postgrad., Stanford U., 1964. With Lucky Stores Inc., 1951-61, 64-86, pres., chief operating officer, 1978-80, pres., chief exec. officer, 1980-81, chmn., chief exec. officer, 1981-85, chmn. bd., 1981-86. Bd. dirs. The McClatchy Co., De La Salle Inst., John Muir Health; grad. mgr. San Diego State U., 1961-63; lectr. in field; past chmn. Calif. Power Exch., mem. adv. coun. Grad. Sch. Bus., Stanford U. Sloan Found. fellow. Mem. Mex. Am. Legal Def. and Edn. Fund, Western Assn. Food Chains (bd. dirs., pres.), Food Mktg. Inst. (bd. dirs., vice chmn.), Sloan Alumni Assn. (adv. bd., pres.).

RITCHIE, ALBERT, lawyer; b. Charlottesville, Va., Sept. 29, 1939; s. John and Sarah Dunlop (Wallace) R.; m. Jennie Wayland, Apr. 29, 1967; children: John, Mary. BA, Yale U., 1961; LLB, U. Va., 1964. Bar: Ill. 1964, Tenn. 2000. Assoc. Sidley & Austin, Chgo., 1964-71, ptnr., 1972-99, ret., 1999. Bd. dirs. Erie Neighborhood House, Chgo., 1978-88; bd. dirs. United Charities of Chgo., 1979-90; trustee U. Va. Law Sch. Found., 1997-99. Capt. U.S. Army, 1965-67. Mem. ABA, Am. Coll. Real Estate Lawyers, Chgo. Legal Aid Soc., Legal Club Chgo. (pres. 1986-87), U. Va. Law Sch. Alumni Assn. (v.p. 1989-93, pres. 1993-95), Cherokee Country Club, Hillsboro Club. Episcopalian. Home: 436 Boxwood Sq Knoxville TN 37919-6627 Personal E-mail: ritchiea@bellsouth.net.

RITCHIE, ALEXANDER BUCHAN, lawyer; b. Detroit, Apr. 19, 1923; s. Alexander Stevenson and Margaret (May) R.; m. Sheila Spellacy, June 1998; 1 child, Barbara Ritchie Drolshagen. BA, Wayne State U., 1947, JD, 1949. Bar: Mich. 1949. Pvt. practice, Detroit, 1949-52, 84—; asst. gen. counsel, asst. v.p. Maccabees Mutual Life Ins. Co., Detroit, 1952-65, v.p., sec., gen. counsel Southfield, Mich., 1977-84; sec., house counsel Wayne Nat. Life Ins. Co., Detroit, 1966-67; ptnr. Fenton, Nederlander, Dodge & Ritchie, Detroit, 1967-77. Spl. asst. atty. gen. State Mich., 1974-77. Bd. mem. Detroit Bd. Edn., 1971-77, Detroit Ctrl. Bd. Edn., 1971-73; bd. Police Commrs., Detroit, 1974-77; bd. dirs. Doctor's Hosp., Detroit, 1974-89. With U.S. Army, 1943-46. Recipient Key to the City of Detroit, Mayor Coleman Young, 1977. Mem. Mich. State Bar Assn. Avocations: reading, golf, theater, gourmet. Home: 29255 Laurel Woods Dr Apt 201 Southfield MI 48034-4647

RITCHIE, COY DOYLE, management consultant; b. Blythe, Calif., Dec. 30, 1937; s. Coy Doyl Ritchie and Carolyn Helen Schwacofer; m. Juanita Pacita Domingo, June 13, 1959; children: Coy C., Harold M. BSBA, Roosevelt U., Chgo., 1965; MBA, City U., Bellevue, Wash., 1984; D of Mgmt., Colo. Tech. U., Colorado Springs, 1996. Dir., officer-in-charge Navy Elec. Tng. Sch., Norfolk, Va., 1975—78; dir., area mgr. ITT Tech. Inst., Portland, Oreg., 1978—86; v.p. acad., dean Colo. Tech. Coll., 1986—88; dir. ITT Tech. Inst., Sacramento, 1988—91, Aurora, Colo., 1991—96; v.p., chancellor Colo. Tech. U., 1997—2002; pres. Ritchie Mgmt. Svcs., Aurora, 2003—. Author: Digital Computers, 1965. Treas. Spring Creek Homeowners Assn., Aurora, 2003—; sec. Colo. Pvt. Sch. Assn., Denver, 1994—95; chmn. edn. com. Aurora C. of C., 1995—96. Mem.: Mil. Order of the World Wars, Navy League US (Denver coun. bd. dirs. 2006—07), Mile High Mil. Officers Assn., Beta Gamma Sigma. Republican. Roman Catholic. Avocations: genealogy, gardening, classic automobiles. Home: 4198 S Kirk Ct Aurora CO 80013-6022 Office Phone: 303-981-5519. Personal E-mail: coyritchie@aol.com.

RITCHIE, DORIS LEE, executive secretary; b. Oak Park, Ill., May 18, 1926; d. Joseph Bulicek and Janette Louise Whitmire; m. H. R. Ritchie, Nov. 7, 1947 (dec.); children: H. Russell III, Jane Lee, Dara Kim. AA, Harper Coll., Palatine, Ill., 1972; BA, Elmhurst Coll., Ill., 1975; MS, Northern Ill. U., 1979; EdD, No. Ill. U., 1987. Exec. sec. Motorola, Chgo., 1943—45, Englander Bedding, Chgo., 1945—48, Pioneer Press, Oak Park, Ill., 1949—50, ABC, Chgo., 1948—49; tchr. Rolling Meadows Ill. Sch. Dist., 1979—81; vol. cons. Palatine, Ill., 1980—83. Spkr. in field. Sr. commr. City of Carlsbad, 1986—91, housing commr., 2000—06. Recipient Woman of Distinction, Soroptimist Club, 1990, DAR, 2000, Rookie of Yr., Hi Noon Rotary Club, 1989. Mem.: Hospice of North Coast, Belleek Collector's Soc., Country Friends (life), Widows and Widowers Club. Avocations: antiques, reading, bridge. Home: 3379 Garibaldi Pl Carlsbad CA 92010 Personal E-mail: dl-ritchie@sbcglobal.net.

RITCHIE, GEORGE G., JR., retired psychiatrist; b. Richmond, Va., Sept. 25, 1923; s. George Gordon Ritchie and Katherine Elizabeth Dabney; m. Marguerite Shell Ritchie; children: Bonnie Louise Ritchie DeHaven, John Coleman. Grad., U. Richmond, 1943; MD, Med. Coll. Va., 1943. Intern Med. Coll. Va., 1950—51; pvt. family practice Richmond, 1951—64; resident psychiatry U. Va., 1964—67, instr. psychiatry, 1967—68; pvt. gen. psychiatry practice Charlottesville, Va., 1968—77; chief psychiatry Towers Hosp., Charlottesville, 1971—72; pvt. practice psychiatry White Stone, Va., 1977—80. Attending and cons. psychiatrist Martha Jefferson Hosp., 1968—77; med. exec. bd. Towers Hosp., 1971—72, chief psychiatry, 1971—72; chmn. bd. Arlington House Hosp., 1972—73; treas. Ctrl. Va. Psychiat. Assn., Inc., 1973—77; cons. psychiatrist Rappahanock Gen. Hosp., 1977—80, No. Neck Mental Health Clinic, 1978, Hopesville Boys Ranch, Dutton, Va., 1978—80, No. Neck Mental Health Clinic, 1979; med. exec. bd. NE Ala. Regional Med. Ctr. Hosp., 1980—82, chief psychiatry, 1980—82; cons. staff Stringfellow Hosp., Anniston, Ala., 1982, Johnston-Willis Hosp., Richmond, 1983—87; attending staff Westbrook Hosp., Richmond, 1983—87. Author: Return From Tomorrow, My LIfe After Dying; contbr. articles to profl. jours. Founder Offender Aid and Restoration, Charlottesville, Va.; founder, pres. Universal Youth Corps Inc. Va., 1957—83; elder East Hanover Presbytery, 1951—54; mem. adminstrv. bd. First United Meth. Ch., Charlottesville, Va., Centenary United Meth. Ch., Richmond, White Stone United Med. Ch., Va.; trustee, mem. commn. on edn. First United Meth. Ch., Anniston, Ala. With US Army, 1943—46, ETO. Recipient William James Rsch. award, U. Va. Dept. Psychiatry, 1967. Mem.: No. Neck Med. Assn., Neuropsychiatric Soc. Va., Va. Med. Soc. Home: 32 Lancaster Rd #621 Irvington VA 22480-2002

RITCHIE, KEVIN, electronics executive; BSEE, U. Dayton, Ohio, 1978. Product engr. def. bus. Tex. Instruments Inc., 1978—80, with semiconductor group, 1980—90, wafer fab mgr., 1990—96, mgr. worldwide application-specific products mfg. ops., 1996—2000, sr. v.p. worldwide mfg. ops., tech. and mfg. group Dallas, 2000—. Office: Tex Instruments Inc PO Box 660199 Dallas TX 75266-0199 Office Phone: 972-995-2011. Office Fax: 972-995-4360. *

RITCHIE, MARK, state official; b. 1951; m. Nancy Gaschott; 1 child, Rachel Gaschott (dec.). Grad., Iowa State U., 1971. Founder League of Rural Voters, 1986—2005; founder, pres. Inst. Agr. and Trade Policy, Mpls., 1986—2005; founder, nat. coord. Nat. Voice NOVEMBER 2 Campaign, 2003—04; founder, coord. Internet Resources on Election Protection, 2003—; founder, vol. leader Ctr. Civic Participation, 2004—05; sec. state State of Minn., St. Paul, 2007—. Recipient Activist of Yr. award, Minn. Alliance for Progressive Action, 2004, Progressive Campaign award to Voting Rights Coalition, 2005, Nat. Progressive Leadership award, US Action, 2005. Office: Office Sec State 180 State Office Bldg 100 Rev Dr Martin Luther King Jr Blvd Saint Paul MN 55155-1299 *

RITCHIE, RICHARD LEE, media company executive; b. Grand Rapids, Mich., July 20, 1946; s. Robert George and Gertrude (Dryer) R.; m. Marlene Barton, Nov. 16, 1969; children: Gabrielle Gay, Steven Barton. BA, Mich. State U., 1968, MBA, 1972; P.MD, Harvard U., 1982. C.P.A., Mich. Sr. acct. Peat, Marwick, Mitchell & Co., Detroit, 1968-69, 72-74; mgr. corp. acctg. Grand Trunk Western R.R., Detroit, 1974-76, treas., 1976-79, asst. v.p., treas., 1980-83; v.p., treas. James River Corp., Richmond, Va., 1984-86; sr. v.p. fin., chief fin. officer Harte Hanks Communications, San Antonio, 1987-96; exec. v.p., CFO Big Flower Holdings, Inc., NYC, 1997-2000. Prof. Oakland Community Coll., Farmington, Mich. Served with AUS, 1969-71. Mem. AICPA, Mich. Assn. CPAs, Am. Acctg. Assn., Beta Alpha Psi, Beta Gamma Sigma. Jewish. Office: Bice Mercato 551 Madison Ave #1601 New York NY 10022-3261

RITCHIE, ROBERT JAMES See KID ROCK

RITCHIE, ROBERT OLIVER, materials science educator, department chairman; b. Plymouth, Devon, Eng., Jan. 2, 1948; arrived in US, 1974, naturalized, 1990; s. Kenneth Ian and Kathleen Joyce (Sims) Ritchie; m. Connie Olesen (div. 1978); 1 child, James Oliver; m. HaiYing Soong, 1991; 1 child, Duncan Soong. BA with honors, U. Cambridge, Eng., 1969, MA, PhD, 1973, ScD, 1990. Cert. engr., UK. Goldsmith's rsch. fellow Churchill Coll. U. Cambridge, 1972-74; Miller fellow in basic rsch. sci. U. Calif., Berkeley, 1974-76, prof., 1981—, chair Materials Sci. and Engring. Dept., 2005—; assoc. prof. mech. engring. MIT, Cambridge, 1977-81; dep. dir. Materials Scis. Divsn. Lawrence Berkeley Nat. Lab., Cambridge, 1990-94, dir. Ctr. for Advanced Materials, 1987-95, head structural Materials Dept., Materials Scis. Divsn., 1995—. Cons. Alcan, Allison, Applied Materials, Boeing, Chevron, Cordis, Exxon, GE, GM, Grumman, Guidant, Instron, Northrop, Rockwell, Westinghouse, Baxter, Carbomedics, Med. Inc., Shiley, St. Jude Med.; Van Horn Disting. lectr. Case Western U., 1997. Editor: 18 books; contbr. more than 550 articles to profl. jours. Named one of Top 100 Scientists, Sci. Digest mag., 1984; recipient G. R. Irwin medal, ASTM, 1985, Mathewson gold medal, TMS-AME, 1985, Curtis W. McGraw Rsch. award, Am. Soc. Engring. Educators, 1987, Rosenhain medal, Inst. Materials London, 1992, Wohler medal, European Structural Integrity Soc., 2006, Van Horn Disting. Lectr. award, Case Western U., 1997. Fellow: Royal Acad. Engring. (London), Minerals, Materials and Metals Soc. (Mathewson Gold medal 1985, Disting. Structural Materials Scientist/Engr. award 1996), Am. Soc. Metals Internat. (Marcus A. Grossman award 1980), Internat. Congress on Fracture (pres. 1997—2001), Inst. Materials (London, AA Griffith medal 2007); mem.: NAE, ASME (NADAI medal 2004), Am. Acad. Arts and Scis., Am. Ceramic Soc., Materials Rsch. Soc. Avocations: skiing, hiking, antiques, orchids. Home: 590 Grizzly Peak Blvd Berkeley CA 94708-1238 Office: U Calif Dept Materials Sci and Engring Berkeley CA 94720-1760 Office Phone: 510-486-5798. Business E-Mail: roritchie@lbl.gov.

RITCHIE, WALLACE PARKS, JR., retired surgeon, educator; b. St. Paul, Nov. 4, 1935; s. Wallace Parks and Alice Ransome (Otis) R.; m. Barbara Carey Jewell, Aug. 10, 1960; children: Stephanie, David, Jessica. BA, Yale U., 1957; MD, Johns Hopkins U., 1961; PhD, U. Minn., 1971. Diplomate Am. Bd. Surgery. Intern, resident in surgery Yale U., New Haven, 1961-63; resident in surgery U. Minn. Hosps., Mpls., 1963-69, instr. in surgery, 1969-70; from asst. prof. to prof. surgery U. Va. Sch. Medicine, Charlottesville, 1973-83; prof., chmn. dept. surgery Temple U. Sch. Medicine, Phila., 1983-93; exec. dir. Am. Bd. Surgery, Phila., 1994—2002; ret. Editor textbook: Essentials of Surgery, 1994; contbr. over 160 sci. articles to profl. jours. Lt. col. M.C., U.S. Army, 1970-73. USPHS grantee, 1974-85. Office: Am Bd Surgery Inc 1617 John F Kennedy Blvd Philadelphia PA 19103-1821 Office Phone: 215-525-3809. E-mail: wallace.ritchie@verizon.net.

RITCHIE, WILLIAM PAUL, lawyer; b. Columbus, Ohio, June 3, 1946; s. Austin Everett and Helen (Drake) R.; m. Diane Smith, Aug. 2, 1969; 1 child, Elizabeth Drake. BS in Bus. Adminstrn., Ohio State U., 1968, JD, U. Va., 1971. Bar: Ohio 1971, Calif. 1973, Ill. 1987. Assoc. Jones, Day, Reavis & Pogue, Cleve., 1971-77, ptnr., 1977—, ptnr.-in-charge, Chgo., 1987—. Served to lt. USAR, 1972. Mem. ABA, Ohio Bar Assn., Calif. Bar Assn., Chgo. Bar Assn., Mayfield Country Club (Cleve.), Chgo. Club. Republican. Office: Jones Day 77 W Wacker Dr Fl 35 Chicago IL 60601-1662 Office Phone: 312-782-3939. Office Fax: 312-782-8585. Business E-Mail: wpritchie@jonesday.com.

RITER, ROBERT C., JR., lawyer; b. Pierre, SD, July 8, 1948; BS, U. SD, 1970, JD, 1973. Bar: SD 1973. Asst. city atty., 1973—; with Riter, Rogers, Wattier & Brown, LLP, Pierre, SD, 1973—, ptnr. Lectr. in field. Contbr. articles to profl. jours. Fellow: Am. Bar Found., Am. Bd. Trial Advocates, Am. Coll. Trial Lawyers; mem.: ABA, Def. Rsch. Inst. (state rep. 1994—99, bd. dirs. 1999—2003), Am. Counsel Assn., SD Def. Lawyers Assn. (pres. 1994—95), State Bar SD (chmn. adminstrv. law com. 1979—81, continuing legal edn. com. 1981—84, ethics com. 1986—89, commr. 1992—95, pres. 2005—06), Phi Delta Phi. Office: Riter Rogers Wattier & Brown LLP Profl and Exec Bldg 319 S Coteau St PO Box 280 Pierre SD 57501 Office Phone: 605-224-5825. Office Fax: 605-224-7102. E-mail: r.riter@riterlaw.com. *

RITER, STEPHEN, academic administrator, electrical engineer; b. Providence, Mar. 7, 1940; s. Max and Jeannette (Finn) R.; m. Eve R. Hirsch, Aug. 11, 1963; children— Heidi L., Theodore H. BA, Rice U., Houston, 1961, BS in Elec. Engring, 1962; MS, U. Houston, 1967, PhD, 1968. Registered profl. engr., Tex. Dir. Center Urban Programs, Tex. A&M U., 1974-76, mem. univ. faculty, 1968-80, prof. elec. engring., 1976-80; dir. Tex. Energy Extension Service, 1976-79; prof. elec. engring., chmn. dept. elec. engring. and computer sci. U. Tex., El Paso, 1980-89, dean engring., 1989-95, dir. Ctr. for Environ. Resource Mgmt., 1989-95, interim v.p. acad. affairs, 1995-96, provost, v.p., 1996—2005, v.p. info. rsch. and planning, 2005—. Active El Paso Pub. Svc. Bd., El Paso Utility Regulatory Bd., 1982-89; cons. in field. Author papers in field.; Editor: Trans. Geosci. Electronics, 1972-76. Mem. policy adv. com. Tex. Dept. Community Affairs, 1979-81; Tex. Border Health and Environ. Issues Task Force, 1990—95. Served with U.S. Army, 1962-64. Mem. IEEE, Am. Soc. Engring. Edn. Home: 836 Cherry Hill Ln El Paso TX 79912-3325 Office: U Tex Info Rsch and Planning El Paso TX 79968-0001 Office Phone: 915-747-5216. Business E-Mail: sriter@utep.edu.

RITMAN, BARBARA ELLEN, counselor; b. LA, Oct. 19, 1946; d. Jack and June Harriett (Marcus) R. AA, Long Beach City Coll., 1969; BA (magna cum laude), Calif. State U., Long Beach, 1974; MA, Chapman Coll., 1976. Lic. marriage, family and child counselor. Instr. Mt. San Antonio Coll., Walnut, Calif., 1976-78; mental health worker Orange County (Calif.) Mental Health, 1978-80; therapist Family Svc., Long Beach, Calif., 1980-82; clin. dir. Neighborhood Youth Assn., Wilmington, Calif., 1981-88; head psychology svcs. Bellflower (Calif.) Med. Group, 1988-89; chem. dependency counselor Kaiser Permanent, Orange, Calif., 1990—. Cons. Child Abuse Info. Ctr., L.A., 1976-78, Action Seminars for Progress, Santa Monica, Calif., 1976-82. Vista vol., Salt Lake City, Houston, 1967—68. Fellow mem. Calif. Assn. Marriage & Family Therapists. Avocations: film, music, theater, photography.

RITSCH, FREDERICK FIELD, academic administrator, historian; b. Covington, Va., Nov. 25, 1935; s. Frederick Field and Harriet Curtis (Miller) R.; m. Jeannette McClung, June 14, 1957 (dec.); children: Frederick Field III, Lise Catherina; m. Debra Ronning, Dec. 21, 1991; 1 child, Anne Ronning. BA, U. Va., 1956, MA, 1959, PhD, 1962; student, Univ. de Strasbourg, France, 1957-58. Instr. Randolph-Macon Women's Coll., Lynchburg, Va., 1959; vis. lectr. Sweet Briar (Va.) Coll., 1959-60; from asst. prof. to prof. Dana history and humanities Converse Coll., Spartanburg, SC, 1960-83, dir. ctr. for humanities, head div. humanities; dean of faculty Elizabethtown (Pa.) Coll., 1984-85, provost, 1986-96, prof., 1997—2003, prof. and provost emeritus, 2004—. Cons. Ednl. Svcs., Inc., Washington, 1975-77; vice chmn. Comm. Svcs., Inc., Spartanburg, 1978-82; dir. Ctr. for Study Contemporary Humanities, Spartanburg, 1972-81. Author: French Left and European Idea, 1967; author, editor: Issues and Commitment, 1976; editor: (with M. Goldberg) Probes and Projections, 1974; contbr. articles to profl. jours. and collections. Elder Donegal Presbyn. Ch., Mt. Joy, Pa.; sch. bd. EASD, 2005—. Fulbright fellow, 1957-58; NEH grantee, 1969; recipient Cert. Merit, Inst. Internat. Edn., 1978. Mem. Am. Hist. Assn., Pa. Acad. Deans Conf. (program chmn. 1984), So. Humanities Conf. (editor jour. Humanities in the South 1971-83, chmn. 1984), Phi Beta Kappa. Home: 102 Meadowbrook Ln Elizabethtown PA 17022-2239 Business E-Mail: ritschf@etown.edu.

RITSON, SCOTT CAMPBELL, management consultant; b. New London, Conn., July 20, 1945; s. Ian Douglas and Ann Breyer (Maxwell) R.; m. Dianne Kischitz, May 16, 1966 (div. Oct. 1977); children: Mark Douglas (dec.), Carrie Stewart; m. Donna Dianne Nietschmann, Feb. 25, 1978; 1 child, Evan Ray-Bernard. Student, U. Vt., 1963-65. Field engrs. asst. Gilbane Bldg. Co., Providence, 1966-67; project control engr. Olin Corp., Stamford, Conn., 1967-73; v.p. Reed Corp., Roxbury, Conn., 1973-76; pres. Ritson & Assocs., Lake Forest, Ill., 1976—; sr. project engr. Abbott Labs., North Chicago, Ill., 1990-95. Pres. treas. Axeman Island, Ltd., Gananoque, Ont., Can., 1990—, v.p., 1979-90, dir., 1981-90; pres. Ritson, Ryan Inc., Gurnee, Ill., 1983-86; sr. program mgr. Project Leadership Group, Inc., Libertyville, Ill., 2001—. Charter mem. Congrl. Adv. Com., Washington, 1982. Can. nat. sailfish champion, 1961. Mem. Internat. Assn. Profl. Planners and Schedulers (charter mem.), Chgo. Yacht Club, Lake Forest Yacht Club. Home: 1084 Old Colony Rd Lake Forest IL 60045-3898 Office: Unit 2 14045 Petronella Dr Libertyville IL 60048-9699 Office Phone: 847-996-6962. Business E-Mail: sritson@plginc.net.

RITT, ROGER MERRILL, lawyer; b. NYC, Mar. 26, 1950; m. Mimi Santini, Aug. 25, 1974; children: Evan Samuel, David Martin. BA, U. Pa., 1972; JD, Boston U., 1975, LLM, 1976. Bar: Mass. 1977, Pa. 1975, U.S. Tax Ct. Sr. ptnr. Wilmer Cutler Pickering Hale and Dorr LLP, Boston, 1984—. Adj. prof. grad. tax program Boston U., 1979-92; panelist Am. Law Inst., Mass. Continuing Legal Edn., World Trade Inst., NYU Inst. on Fed. Taxation; mem. exec. com. Fed. Tax Inst. New Eng. Treas. Found. for Tax Edn. Mem. ABA (tax sect.), Boston Bar Assn. Office: Wilmer Cutler Pickering Hale and Dorr 60 State St Boston MA 02109-1816 Office Phone: 617-526-6475. Business E-Mail: roger.ritt@wilmerhale.com.

RITTENHOUSE, NANCY CAROL, elementary school educator; b. Humeston, Iowa, May 26, 1941; d. Myrl Matthews and Opal L. (McCartney) Hixson; m. J. Kent Rittenhouse, Dec. 18, 1960 (div. Mar. 1984); children: Brenda L. Carroll, J. Aaron, Timothy K. Grad., Kirksville State Tchrs. Coll., 1960; student, St. Mary of the Plains Coll., 1984-87; degree in elem. edn., Ft. Hays State Coll., 1989. Cert. tchr., Kans. Reading instr. Sacred Heart Sch., Dodge City, Kans., 1984; elem. tchr. Miller Sch., Dodge City, Kans., 1985-86, Washington Sch., Hays, 1987; city-county recreation dir. Sherman County, Goodland, 1988; elem. tchr. Northside Sch., Larned, 1989-90; with Great Bend (Kans.) Tribune. Artist numerous paintings; author poetry. Mem. Menninger Found., Topeka, 1984—; hon. mem. Boy Scouts Am., 1978; camp instr. Spl. Olympics Blind Found., Junction City, Kans., 1985-90, Dodge City, 1984; leader Girl Scouts USA, 1975-77. Recipient Hon. award Spl. Olympics, 1984, 1st pl. poetry award, 1990, watercolor award, 1990, oils award, 1988, pen and ink award, 1984. Mem. AAAS, Nat. Trust for Hist. Preservation, Nat. Geog. Soc., Planetary Soc., Smithsonian Assn., MIT. Republican. Avocations: painting, drawing, walking, swimming, writing prose. Home: PO Box 1872 Great Bend KS 67530-1872 Office: Great Bend Tribune 2012 Forest Ave Great Bend KS 67530-4014

RITTENMEYER, RONALD ALLEN, information technology executive; b. Wilkes-Barre, Pa., May 22, 1947; s. Harold E. and Shirley A. (Hitchner) R.; m. Hedy A. Wrightson; children: Christopher, Ashley. BS in Commerce & Fin., Wilkes U., 1972; MBA, Rockhurst U., 1984. Fin. officer U.S. HUD, Washington, 1972-74; shipping mgr. Frito-Lay, Inc., Kirkwood, NY, 1974-76, distbn. mgr. Fall River, Mass., 1976-77, Louisville, 1977-78, Charlotte, NC, 1978-80, prodn. mgr., 1980-82, ops. analyst Dallas, 1982, plant mgr. Topeka, 1982-85, v.p. zone ops. Dallas, 1985-86, v.p. sales and strategic planning, v.p. ops.; v.p. Mid. Ea. & worldwide ops. PepsiCo Food Internat.; pres., COO Merisel; COO Ryder TRS, 1997-98; pres., CEO RailTex, Inc., San Antonio, 1998—2000; chmn., pres., CEO Safety-Kleen Inc., 2001—04; mng. dir. The Cypress Group L.L.C., 2004—05; exec. v.p. global svc. delivery Electronic Data Systems Corp., Plano, Tex., 2005—06, co-COO, 2005—06, pres., COO, 2006—07, pres., CEO, 2007—. Bd. mem. U.S. C. of C., Am. Heart Assn., No. Tex. Kidney Assn.; mem. exec. bd. Cox Sch. Bus. So. Methodist Univ. Recipient Outstanding Achievement award U.S. HUD, 1974. Avocations: diving, aviation. Office: Electronic Data Systems Corp 5400 Legacy Dr Plano TX 75024 E-mail: ron.rittenmeyer@eds.com. *

RITTER, ANN MARIE, pediatric neurosurgeon; b. Bryn Mawr, Pa., May 27, 1964; d. Thomas F. Ritter and Mae Groover; m. Albert S Diradour, May 23, 1998; children: Cannon A Diradour, Madelyn O Diradour. BS in Nutrition with honors, U. Tex., Austin, 1986; MD, Baylor Coll. Medicine, Houston, 1991. Diplomate neurological surgeons Am. Bd. Neurol. Surgeons, 2004, pediatric neurosurgeons Am. Bd. Pediatric Neurosurgeons, 2007. Intern Baylor Coll. Medicine, 1991—93; resident Med. Coll. Va., 1993—99; fellow U. Tex., Dallas, 1999—2000; pediatric neurosurgeon, chief pediatric neurosurgery U. NC, Chapel Hill, 2000—05; pediatric neurosurgeon A. I. duPont Hosp. for Children, Wilmington, 2005—. Lectr. Houston C.C., 1989—94, Baylor Coll. Medicine-Neuroanatomy, Houston, 1994, U. NC, 2000—05. Contbr. articles various profl. jours., chapters to books, numerous medical presentations. Chmn. Pedal for Pediat., Chapel Hill, 2003—05. Mem.: AMA, Richmond Acad. Medicine, Women in Neurosurgery, Am. Acad. Pediat., Va. Med. Soc., Am. Soc. Pediatric Neurosurgeons, Am. Assn. Neurol. Surgeons, Congress Neurol. Surgeon. Avocations: scuba diving, gardening. Home Phone: 804-353-1551; Office Phone: 302-651-5993. Business E-Mail: amritter@nemours.org.

RITTER, BILL (AUGUST WILLIAM RITTER JR.), governor, former prosecutor; b. Aurora, Colo., Sept. 6, 1956; s. August William and Ethel Ritter; m. Jeannie L. Ritter; children: August, Abe, Sam, Tally. BA, Colo. State U., 1978; JD, U. Colo. Sch. Law, 1981. Dep. dist. atty. City of Denver, 1981—84, chief dep. dist. atty., 1984—87, 1992—93, dist. atty. Denver, 1993—2005; asst. US atty. criminal divsn. Dist. Colo. US Dept. Justice, Denver, 1990—91; coord. Mongu Nutrition Grp., Zambia, 1987—90; gov. State of Colo., Denver, 2006—. Bd. mem. Nat. Assn. Drug Ct. Profls., 1995—2002; v.p. Nat. Dist. Attys. Assn., 1995—2004; chmn. Am. Prosecutors Rsch. Inst., 1998—2004; pres. Colo. Dist. Attys. Coun., 1999—2000, 2003—04. Bd. chair Project PAVE (Promoting Alternatives to Violence through Edn.), 1992—2003; bd. mem. Mile High United Way, 1999—2004. Roman Catholic. Office: Office Gov 136 State Capitol Denver CO 80203-1792 *

RITTER, C. DOWD, diversified financial services company executive; b. Birmingham; m. Susan; 2 children. BA, Birmingham-Southern Coll., 1969; grad., Sch. Banking of South, L.S.U. With AmSouth Bancorporation and AmSouth Bank, Birmingham, Ala., 1969—2006, exec. v.p., 1980-88, sr. exec. v.p., 1988-93, vice chmn. bd., 1993-94, pres., COO, 1994-96, chmn., pres., CEO, 1996—2006; pres., CEO Regions Fin. Corp., Birmingham, Ala., 2006—. Bd. dirs. Ala. Power Co., Protective Life Corp. Bd. trustees Tuskegee Inst., Bus. Council Ala., Ala. Econ. Develop. Partnership, Region 2020 Inc., Birmingham Mus. Art, Burmingham-Southern Coll., Leadership Birmingham, adv. bd. Birmingham Crime Commn., Juvenile Diabetes Found., bd. visitors U. ala. Coll. Commerce and Bus. Adminstrn., campaign co-chmn. Am. Cancer Soc. Five Points South Ctr. and Hope Lodge, campaign steering com. YWCA Birmingham, pres's. coun. U. Ala., campaign chmn. United Way Central Ala., 1993. Named Ala. Outstanding Young Banker 1984. Mem. Ala. Young Bankers (past pres.), Birmingham Festival Arts (past pres.). Office: Regions Fin Corp 417 20th St N Birmingham AL 35203 *

RITTER, DALE WILLIAM, obstetrician, gynecologist; b. Jersey Shore, Pa., June 17, 1919; s. Lyman W. and Weltha B. (Packard) Ritter; m. Winnie Mae Bryant, Nov. 13, 1976; children: Eric, Lyman, Michael, Gwendolyn, Daniel. AB, UCLA, 1942; MD, U. So. Calif., 1946. Diplomate Am. Bd. Ob-Gyn. Intern Los Angeles County Hosp., 1945—46, resident, 1948—52, admitting room resident, 1948—52; pvt. practice Chico, Calif., 1952—98; founder, mem. staff, past chmn. bd. dirs. Chico Cmty. Meml. Hosp. Guest lectr. Chico State Coll., 1956—; staff Enole Hosp., Chico, 1952—, Glenn Gen. Hosp., Willows, Calif., 1953-98, Gridley Meml. Hosp., Calif., 1953-80; spl. cons. obs. Calif. Dept. Pub. Health, No. Calif., 1958-70. Contbr. articles to profl. jours. Bd. dirs. No. dist. Children's Home Soc., Chico, 1954-70. With AUS, 1943-45, M.C., AUS, 1946-48. Recipient Pro-Life award Calif. KC. Fellow ACS, Am. Coll. Ob-Gyn; mem. AMA, AAAS, DAV, Calif. Med. Assn., Internat. Soc. Hypnosis, Am. Soc. Clin. Hypnosis, Am. Fertility Soc., Pacific Coast Fertility Soc., Assn. Am. Physicians and Surgeons, Pvt. Drs. Am., Butte-Glenn County Med. Soc. (past pres.), Am. Cancer Soc. (past bd. dirs. Butte County), Christian Med. Soc., Am. Assn. Pro-life Obstetricians and Gynecologists, Butte-Glenn County Tumor Bd., Anthrop. Assn. Am., Archaeol. Inst. Am., Soc. Calif. Archaeology, Oreg. Archaeology Soc., Archeol. Survey Assn., Southwestern Anthrop. Soc., Am. Rock Art Rsch. Assn. (Pioneer award), Calif. Hist. Soc., Calif. Oreg. Trails Assn., Australian Rock Art Rsch. Assn., Internat. Assn. for Study of Prehistoric and Ethnologic Religions, Fretted Instrument Guild Am. (dir. Banjo Kats 'n Jammers), North Valley Banjo Band, Am. Philatelic Soc., Am. Horse Coun., Peruvian Paso Horse Registry of N.Am., Assn. Owners Breeders Peruvian Paso Horses, Sons of Am. Revolution, Am. Legion, Am. Vets. WWII, Rotary (Paul Harris fellow), Gideons Internat., Phi Chi, Lambda Sigma, Zeta Beta Sigma. Republican. Home: PO Box 156 975 East Ave Chico CA 95926-1308

RITTER, DANIEL BENJAMIN, lawyer; b. Wilmington, Del., Apr. 6, 1937; s. David Moore and Bernice Elizabeth (Carlson) R.; m. Shirley F. Sether, Jan. 29, 1971 (dec. Jan. 1998); 1 child, Roxane Elise. AB with honors, U. Chgo., 1957; LLB, U. Wash., 1963. Bar: Wash. 1963, U.S. Dist. Ct. (we. dist.) Wash. 1963, U.S. Tax Ct. 1965, U.S. Ct. Appeals (9th cir.) 1963. Assoc. Davis, Wright Tremaine LLP (formerly Davis, Wright and Jones), 1963-69, ptnr., 1969—2006; ret., 2006. Lectr. Bar Rev. Assocs. Wash., Seattle, 1964—86; chmn. internat. dept. Davis, Wright and Jones, Seattle, 1984—85, chmn. banking dept., 1986—89. Casenote editor U. Wash. Law Rev., 1962-63; editor-in-chief, contbg. author Washington Revised Article 9 Deskbook, 2003; contbg. author: Washington Commercial Law Desk Book, 1982, rev. edit., 1987, Washington Community Property Desk Book, 1977. Trustee Cathedral Assoc., Seattle, 1980-86; legal counsel Wash. State Reps., Bellevue, 1983-92; bd. dirs. U. Chgo. Club Puget Sound, Seattle, 1982-95, pres., 1984-86; bd. dirs. Am. Lung Assn. Wash., Seattle, 1983-92; mem. vis. com. U. Wash. Law Sch., 1984-88; trustee U. Wash. Law Sch. Found., 1989-92; chmn. alumni rels. coun. U. Chgo., 1986-88; mem. statute law com. State of Wash., 1978-87; bd. dirs. Seattle Camerata, 1991-93; bd. dirs. Early Music Guild, Seattle, 1993-96. Mem. ABA (bus. law sect.), Wash. State Bar Assn. (chmn. bus. law sect. 1988-89, uniform comml. code com. 1980—, chmn. 1980-86, chmn. internat. law com. 1979-81, jud. recommendations com. 1991-93), Seattle-King County Bar Assn. (chmn. internat. and comparative law sect. 1980-82), Rainier Club, Order of Coif. Republican. Lutheran. Avocations: reading, theater, early music. Home: 907 Warren Ave N Apt 202 Seattle WA 98109-5635 Business E-Mail: danritter@dwt.com.

RITTER, ELISE DAWN, therapist, clinical social worker, writer, artist, photographer; b. Balt., Aug. 14, 1952; d. Nelson Fred and Marjorie Jean (Corke) Ritter; m. Philip Anthony Gibson, Apr. 7, 1979 (div. Feb. 1990); 1 child, Christopher Ritter Gibson; m. Victor Wayne Clough, Jr., Mar. 3, 1990; stepchildren: Wesley T., Lindsay, Sharon. Student, Austro-Am. Inst., Vienna, Austria, 1973; BS, U. Kans., 1974; M Psychiatric Social Work, Va. Commonwealth U., 1998. LCSW. Rschr. impeachment inquiry staff U.S. Ho. of Reps., Washington, 1974; rschr. APA, Washington, 1975; editor prodn. The New Republic Mag., Washington, 1976-77; copy editor Time-Life Books, Alexandria, Va., 1977-79, assoc. editor, 1979-83, adminstrv. editor, 1983-87, asst. dir. editl. resources, 1988-90; dir. editl. resources Time Warner, Time-Life Books, Alexandria, 1990-94; pvt. practice therapist, 2000—04. Juried show, Summer Memories, Yates House Gallery, 2000 (1st and 2d prize), exhbn. juried shows, Yates House, 2004 (honorable mention), Poetry Art Show, 2006 (2d prize, 2006), dirs. show, Rappahannock Art League Studio Gallery, Va., 2005, Mathews Art Group, 2005—. With Arlingtonians Ministering to Emergency Needs-AMEN, 1995; vol. Mental Health Program, Visiting Nurse Assn., 1996, Women's Ctr., Vienna, Va., 1997-99, PsychologyNetwork.com, 2000-02, DiscoveryHealth.com, 2002-03. Recipient 1st prize, Urbanna Oyser Festival Poster Contest, 2006.

RITTER, JASON, actor; b. LA, Calif., Feb. 17, 1980; s. John Ritter and Nancy Morgan. Attended, NYU. Actor: (TV series) Joan of Arcadia, 2003—05, The Class, 2006—; (TV films) The Dreamer of Oz, 1990, Who's Your Momma?, 2004; (films) Mumford, 1999, PG, 2002, Swimfan, 2002, Smash the Kitty, 2003, Freddy vs. Jason, 2003, Raise Your Voice, 2004, Perceptions, 2005, Happy Endings, 2005, Our Very Own, 2005, Placebo, 2005, The Wicker Man, 2006, (off-Broadway) The Beginning of August; (plays) The Distance from Here, Third, 2005 (Clarence Derwent award, Actors' Equity Found., 2006). Mailing: c/o The Burstein Co Ste 208 15304 Sunset Blvd Pacific Palisades CA 90272

RITTER, JODI GOTTESFELD, lawyer; b. Bklyn., May 1966; BA cum laude, SUNY, Albany, 1988; JD, NY Law Sch., 1992. Bar: NY 1993, Conn. 1993, US Dist. Ct. So. Dist. NY, US Dist. Ct. Ea. Dist. NY, US Supreme Ct. Asst. dist. atty. Kings County Dist. Atty.'s Office, NY, Spl. Narcotics Prosecutor's Office; ptnr. Wilson, Elser, Moskowitz, Edelman & Dicker LLP, NYC. Mem.: NY State Bar Assn. Office: Wilson Elser Moskowitz Edelman & Dicker LLP 23rd Fl 150 E 42nd St New York NY 10017-5639 Office Phone: 212-490-3000 ext. 2245. Office Fax: 212-490-3038. Business E-Mail: ritterj@wemed.com.

RITTER, NADINE M., research scientist; AS, San Jacinto Coll., Pasadena, Tex., 1976—78; BS, U. Houston, Clear Lake, Tex., 1980—84; MS, PhD, Rice U., Houston, 1984—88. Principle cons. NMRBiotech Cons. Svcs., Germantown, Md., 2001—; sr. cmc cons. Biologics Cons. Group, Alexandria, Va., 2005—. Home: 13613 Anndyke Pl Germantown MD 20874 Office: Biologics Cons Group 13613 Anndyke Pl Germantown MD 20874 Home Phone: 301-528-7840; Office Phone: 240-372-4898. Personal E-mail: nmrbiotech@ritterward.com. E-mail: nritter@bcg-usa.com.

RITTER, RENEE D., theater educator; b. Knoxville, Tenn., May 10, 1975; d. Kenneth, Jr. Frost and Paula Hinton; m. Wesley E. Ritter (div.); children: Cole W., Savannah R. BS in theater, Middle Tenn. State U., Murfreesboro, 1998. Theater tchr. Hendersonville HS, Tenn., 1999—2002, Station Camp. HS, Gallatin, Tenn., 2002—. Dir. Portland Arts Council, Tenn., 1994; tchr. Hendersonville Arts Council, Tenn., 2001—03; dir. Theatre of Summer County, Gallatin, Tenn., 2001. Grantee, Hendersonville C. of C., 2001, 2002. Republican. Baptist. Avocations: theater, dance, music, art. Home: 152 Putter Point Dr Gallatin TN 37066 Office: Station Camp HS 1040 Bison Trail Gallatin TN 37066 Personal E-mail: ritterr@k12tn.net.

RITTER, ROBERT T., diversified financial services company executive; BBA in Acctg., Coll. William and Mary, 1973. Various fin. positions Am. Cyanamid Co.; CFP WLR Foods, Inc.; v.p., CFO The Pittston Co., Glen Allen, Va., 1998—. Mem. AICPAs. Office: The Pittston Co 1801 Bayberry Ct PO Box 18100 Richmond VA 23226

RITTER, ROBERT THORNTON, lawyer; b. NYC, Nov. 4, 1956; s. Robert J. and Barbara W. (Foust) R.; m. Rebecca L. Grubbs, July 25, 1981; children: Sarah, Luke, Robert R. BA, Duke U., 1979; JD, Washington U., 1984. Bar: Mo., 1984, U.S. Dist. Ct. (ea. dist.) Mo., 1985. Assoc. William Brown, Atty. at Law, Bridgeton, Mo., 1984-85, Kopsky & Vouga, Chesterfield, Mo., 1986; pvt. practice Clayton, Mo., 1987-89, St. Charles, Mo., 2003—; ptnr. Ritter & Gusdorf, Clayton, 1990-96; mem. Ritter & Gusdorf L.C., Clayton, 1997—2002; ptnr. Belz & Jones, P.C., Clayton, 2002—03. Treas. Campaign Election of State Rep. Steve Moore, 1988. Mem.: St. Louis Assn. Christian Attys. (pres.), Bar Assn. Met. St. Louis, Mo. Bar Assn. Republican. Avocations: tennis, guitar. Office: 566 First Capitol Dr Saint Charles MO 63301 Home Phone: 636-947-2350; Office Phone: 636-255-0000. Business E-Mail: rob@ritterlaw.com.

RITTERBAND, ARNOLD B., internist; b. NYC, July 21, 1926; s. Max Ritterband and Sara Abelson; m. Phyllis Rosenthal Ritterband, Aug. 3, 1957; children: Alan, Vicki, David. AB, Columbia Coll., NYC, 1945; MD, Columbia Coll. Physicians and Surgeons, NYC, 1950. Cert. Am. Bd. Internal Medicine. Intern Mt. Sinai Hosp., NYC, 1950—51, asst. to chief resident medicine, 1952—55, fellow pathology, 1952—55; asst. resident neurology Neurol. Inst. Columbia-Presbyn. Med. Ctr., NYC, 1951—52; fellow rheumatology NYU Goldwater Meml. Hosp., NYC, 1955—56; fellow epidemiology Columbia U. Sch. Pub. Health, NYC, 1956—61; med. dir. St. Clare's Hosp., Schenectady, 1959—60; pvt. practice Schenectady, 1959—2004; co-founder, co-med. dir. Schenectady Free Clinic, 2003—. Clin. prof. medicine Albany Med. Sch., NY, 2007—. Contbr. articles to profl. jours. Founder, chmn. Schenectady County Commn. Health Care Issues, 1986. With USNR, 1945—46, PTO. Recipient Sen. Edward J. Speno award, NY State Fedn. Profl. Health Educators, 1998. Democrat. Jewish. Achievements include research in coronary heart disease. Office: Schenectady Free Health Clinic 600 Franklin St Schenectady NY 12305 Home: 915 Northumberland Dr Schenectady NY 12309

RITTERSKAMP, DOUGLAS DOLVIN, lawyer; b. St. Louis, July 7, 1948; s. James Johnstone Jr. and Linn M. (Dolvin) R.; m. Linda S. Vansant, Mar. 23, 1974; 1 child, Tammy. AB, Washington U., 1970, JD, 1973; LLM in Taxation, NYU, 1978. Bar: N.Y. 1974, Mo. 1979. Assoc. Patterson, Belknap, Webb & Tyler, NYC, 1974-78; jr. ptnr. Bryan Cave LLP (and predecessors), St. Louis, 1978-82; ptnr. Bryan Cave LLP, St. Louis, 1983—2004, of counsel, 2005—. Trustee Scottish Rite Clinic for Childhood Lang. Disorders of St. Louis, Inc., 1987-97, St. Louis Mission and Ch. Ext. Soc., United Meth. Ch., 1987-97, Mo. United Meth. Found., 1994—2003, pres., 2000—03; trustee The Coll. Sch., 1995-2001. Served to capt. USAR, 1970—79. Mem. ABA (employee benefits com. sect. taxation 1987-91, 96—), Bar Assn. Met. St. Louis (steering com. employee benefits 1989—), Masons (32d degree, knight comdr. ct. of honor), Shriner. Methodist. Home: 5223 Sutherland Ave Saint Louis MO 63109-2338

RITTMANN, BRUCE EDWARD, environmental engineering educator, researcher; b. St. Louis, Nov. 17, 1950; s. Albert and Ruth (Schulz) R. BS, MS, Washington U., St. Louis, 1974; PhD, Stanford U., 1979. Engr. Sverdrup & Parcel, St. Louis, 1974-75; asst. prof. U. Ill., Urbana, 1980-84, assoc. prof., 1984-88, prof., 1988; John Evans prof. Dept. Civil and Environ. Engring. Northwestern U. Mem. adv. bd. critical engr. systems NSF, Washington, 1987-90; cons. Wastewater Tech. Ctr., Burlington, Ont. Can., 1988-91. Contbr. articles to profl. jours. NSF awardee, 1984; U. Ill. scholar, 1987. Mem. NAE, Am. Soc. for Microbiology, Am. Water Works Assn., Am. Soc. Civil Engrs., Water Pollution Control Fedn., Assn. Environ. Engring. Profs. (pres. 1990-91). Office: Northwestern U Dept Civil and Environ Engring A228 Technol Inst 2145 Sheridan Rd Evanston IL 60208-3109 Office Phone: 847-491-8790. Office Fax: 847-491-4011. E-mail: b-rittmann@northwestern.edu.

RITVO, HARRIET, historian; b. Cambridge, Mass., Sept. 19, 1946; d. Martin and Zelma R. AB, Harvard U., 1968, PhD, 1975; student, U. Cambridge, Eng., 1968-69. Staff assoc. AAAS, Boston, 1976-79; from asst. prof. to prof. MIT, Cambridge, 1979—, assoc. dean humanities and social scis., 1992-95, Arthur J. Conner prof. of history, 1995—, head history faculty, 1999—2006. Author: The Animal Estate, 1987, The Platypus and the Mermaid, 1997; co-editor: Macropolitics of 19th Century Literature, 1991. Rsch. fellow Stanford Humanities Ctr., 1985-86, fellow NEH, 1989, Guggenheim fellow, 1990, sr. fellow Nat. Humanities Ctr., 1990, 2002-03; recipient Whiting Writer's award Whiting Found., 1990. Fellow: Am. Acad. Arts and Scis. Office: MIT E51-285 Cambridge MA 02139 Office Phone: 617-253-6960. Business E-Mail: ritvo@mit.edu.

RITZ, DAVID M., photographic retail company executive; Various positions Ritz Camera, Beltsville, Md., 1969-74, mgmt. positions to pres., 1974—, former pres., now CEO; also chmn. Ritz Interactive, Irvine, Calif. Past pres. PMA Internat. Recipient PMA Hall of Fame award. Office: Ritz Camera 6711 Ritz Way Beltsville MD 20705-1318 also: Ritz Interactive 2010 Main St Ste 400 Irvine CA 92614

RITZ, GEORGE F., forester, consultant; s. George Augustus and Ethel Maria Ritz; m. Sylvia J. Brackett, Aug. 26; children: Jeremy, Andrea. BS, U. Maine, 1971, MS, 1972. Lic. forester Maine. Forester Peace Corps, Chile, 1968—71; cons. forester self, Bradford, Maine, 1971—82, 1987—90; assoc. dir. U.S. Peace Corp., Asuncion, Paraguay, 1982—87; forester Maine Dept. Conservation, Old Town, Maine, 1990—; coord. Andrea Ritz Clinics, Paraguay, 1997—. Co-author: Los Arboles Comunes del Paraguay. Selectman Town of Bradford (Maine), 1987—93. Recipient Spl. Achievement award, Peace Corps, 1982, 1985, Outstanding Achievement award, Paraguaym Soc. Foresters, 1985. Mem.: Internat. Soc. Tropical Foresters, Soc. Am. Foresters (Outstanding Field Forester award for Northeast US area 2006, Austin Cary award 2007). Home: 572 Main Rd Bradford ME 04410 Office: Maine Dept Conservation PO Box 415 Airport Rd Old Town ME 04468

RITZ, STEPHEN MARK, lawyer; b. Midland, Mich., Aug. 23, 1962; s. Alvin H. and Patricia M. (Padway) R. BA, Northwestern U., 1985; JD, Ind. U., 1989. Bar: Ill. 1990, U.S. Dist. Ct. (no. dist.) Ill. 1990, Ind. 1996. Atty. Chapman & Cutler, Chgo., 1990-93; CEO Newport Pension Mgmt. LLC, Indpls., 1993—97, atty., 1997—. Office: 1445 N State Pkwy Chicago IL 60610

RITZ, THORSTEN, biophysics professor; b. Hanau, Germany, Apr. 17, 1971; s. Dietmar and Seol-Ok Ritz; m. Brooke Ritz. Diploma, JW Goethe U., Frankfurt, Germany, 1996; PhD, U. Ulm, Germany, 2001. Rsch. assoc. Va. Tech, Blacksburg, 2001—03; asst. prof. U. Calif., Irvine, 2003—. Author: The Quantum Physics of the Bacterial Photosynthetic System. Recipient Disting. Asst. Prof. Rsch., U. Calif. Irvine, 2007—; fellow in molecular biology, Alfred P Sloan Found., 2005; Cottrell scholar, Rsch. Cooperation, 2006. Fellow: Inst. of Physics (UK), German Nat. Merit Found.; mem.: Am. Phys. Soc. Mem. Lds Ch. Office: Dept Physics and Astronomy U Calif Irvine 4129 Frederick Reines Hall Irvine CA 92697-4575 Office Phone: 949-824-4345. Office Fax: 949-824-2174. E-mail: tritz@uci.edu.

RITZEN, HORST REINHOLD, retired pharmacist; b. Hanau, Germany, June 22, 1923; s. John Henry and Wilhelmina Marie (Rix) Ritzen; m. Dolores Ann Ritzen, Sept. 18; 1 child, Tina Marie Ritzen Gibson; children: Karla Ann, Bryce David, Amanda Elizabeth Gibson, Colleen Renee Gibson. Student, Midlane Luth. Coll., Fremont, Nebr., 1941—43; BS in Pharmacy, U. Tex., Austin, 1950. Owner, chief pharmacist North Main Pharmacy, Houston, 1950—91; ret., 1991. Treas., pres. Linkwood Civic Club, Houston; mem. coun. Luth. Ch., Houston. Staff sgt. Signal Corps US Army, 1942—46, PTO, staff sgt. Med. Corps US Army, 1950—51, Korea. Avocation: woodworking. Home: 115 Guenther St Sugar Land TX 77478

RIVADENEIRA, DAVID EDWARD, colon and rectal surgeon, researcher; b. NYC, Dec. 27, 1969; s. Eduardo and Manuela Rivadeneira; m. Anabela Alves, June 3, 1995; children: Sophia Bella, Gabriella. MD, Howard U., Washington, 1995. NIH rsch. fellow Cornell Med. Sch., NYC; surgery resident Meml. Sloan-Kettering Cancer Ctr., NYC, 1995—2002, NY Presbyn. Hosp.-Cornell Med. Ctr., NYC, 1995—2001, surgery chief resident, 2001—02; fellow Lahey Clinic, Burlington, Mass., 2002—03; asst. prof. surgery Stony Brook U. Med. Ctr., NY, 2003—. Contbr. articles to profl. jours. Recipient Scholar award, Am. Assn. Cancer Rsch., 1995, Outstanding Academic Achievement award, Lahey Clinic Med. Ctr., 2003. Fellow: ACS (licentiate; diplomate), Am. Soc. Colon and Rectal Surgeons (diplomate); mem.: Assn. for Academic Surgery, NY Surg. Soc. (licentiate), Soc. Am. Gastrointestinal Endoscopic Surgeons (licentiate), Soc. for Surgery of the Alimentary Tract (licentiate). Home Phone: 631-692-7161; Office Phone: 631-444-8086. Personal E-mail: drivad@aol.com. Business E-Mail: drivadeneira@notes.cc.sunysb.edu.

RIVARA, FREDERICK PETER, pediatrician, educator; b. Far Rockaway, NY, May 17, 1949; s. Frederick P. and Mary Lillian (Caparelli) R.; m. J'May Bertrand, May 17, 1975; children: Matthew, Maggie. BA, Holy Cross Coll., 1970; MD, U. Pa., 1974; MPH, U. Wash., 1980. Diplomate Am. Bd. Pediatrics. Intern Children's Hosp. and Med. Ctr., Boston, 1974-75, resident, 1975-76, Seattle, 1978-80; RWJ clin. scholar U. Wash., Seattle, 1978-80, assoc. prof. pediatrics, 1984-89, prof. pediatrics, head divsn. gen. pediatrics, 1990—; mem. staff Nat. Health Svc. Corps, Hazard, Ky., 1976-78; asst. prof. pediatrics U. Tenn., Memphis, 1981-84. Editor Archives of Pedatrics and Adolescent Medicine. Fellow Am. Acad. Pediatrics; mem. Ambulatory Pediatrics Assn., Internat. Assn. Child, Adolescent and Injury Prevention (pres. 1993-2000), Inst. Medicine. Office: Harborview Med Ctr 325 9th Ave PO Box 359960 Seattle WA 98195-9960 Business E-Mail: fpr@uwashington.edu.

RIVARD, ROBERT, newspaper executive; b. Nov. 17, 1952; m. Monika Maeckle, Sept. 19, 1981; children: Nicolas, Alex. BA in Polit. Sci., U. Tex., San Antonio, 1996; postgrad., Northwestern U., 1996. Sportswriter Brownsville Herald, 1977-78; news reporter Corpus Christi (Tex.) Caller, 1978-79; reporter Dallas Times Herald, 1979-81, Ctrl. Am. bur. chief, 1981-83, Newsweek, 1983-85, sr. editor, chief corrs. NYC, 1985-90; dep. mng. editor San Antonio Light, 1990-93; mng. editor Express News, San Antonio, 1993-97, editor, sr. v.p., 1997—. Author: (non-fiction) Trail of Feathers: Searching for Philip True, 2005. Named Editor's and Pub.'s Editor of Yr., 2000. Mem.: Soc. Profl. Journalists (Disting. Svc. award 1982). Office: San Antonio Express-News 301 Ave E San Antonio TX 78205 Office Phone: 210-250-3111. E-mail: rrivard@express-news.net. *

RIVER, SANDRA A., university librarian; BA, Minn. State U., Mankato; MA, Tex. Tech. U.; MSLS, U. North Tex. Current periodicals/microforms libr. Tex. Tech. U. Libris., Lubbock, Tex., architecture & humanities libr., 2003—. Mem.: Tex. Libr. Assn. (Continuing Edn. & Devel. com.), Assn. Coll. & Rsch. Librs. (Women's Studies sect., WSS Career Achievement award 2007). Office: Tex Tech U Librs 18th St & Boston Ave MS 40002 Lubbock TX 79409-0002 Office Phone: 806-742-8058. Office Fax: 806-742-2855. E-mail: sandy.river@ttu.edu.

RIVERA, CHITA (CONCHITA DEL RIVERO), actress, singer, dancer; b. Wash., Jan. 23, 1933; d. Pedro Julio Figuerva del Rivero; m. Anthony Mordente. Student, Am. Sch. Ballet, NYC. Broadway debut: Call Me Madam, 1952; appeared on stage in: Guys and Dolls, Can-Can, Seventh Heaven, Mister Wonderful, West Side Story, Father's Day, Bye Bye Birdie, Three Penny Opera, Flower Drum Song, Zorba, Sweet Charity, Born Yesterday, Jacques Brel is Alive and Well and Living in Paris, Sondheim-A Musical Tribute, Kiss Me Kate, Ivanhoe, Chicago, Bring Back Birdie, Merlin, Jerry's Girls, 1985, The Rink, 1984 (Tony award 1984), Can-Can, 1988, Kiss of the Spider Woman (Tony award, Best Actress in a musical), 1993, The Dancer's Life, 2005; performs in cabarets and nightclubs around world; starred in: film Sweet Charity, 1969; numerous TV appearances include Kojak and the Marcus Nelson Murders, 1973, The New Dick Van Dyke Show, 1973-74, Kennedy Ctr. Tonight-Broadway to Washington!, Pippin, 1982, The Mayflower Madam, 1987, Sammy Davis Jr.'s 60th Birthday Celebration, 1990, Ira Gershwin at 100: A Celebration at Carnegie Hall, 1997, Venecia, 2001, Anything Goes, 2000, The Visit, 2001. Recipient Best Actress, Outer Critics Circle award, 1993, Drama League award, Spider Woman, 1993, Best Leading Actress in a Musical, Tony award, Ellis Island Medal of Honor, 2000, Kennedy Center Honor, 2002—02, Rolex Dance award, Career Transition for Dancers, 2006. Mem. AFTRA, SAG, Actors Equity Assn. Office: William Morris Agy c/o Samuel Liff 1325 Ave of the Ams New York NY 10019 *

RIVERA, GERALDO, television personality, journalist; b. NYC, July 4, 1943; s. Cruz Allen and Lillian (Friedman) R.; m. Sheri Rivera (div. 1984); m. C.C. Dyer, 1987 (div. 2002); children: Gabriel, Cruz, Isabella, Simone, m. Erica Levy, 1 child, Solita Liliana. BS, U. Ariz., 1965; JD, Bklyn. Law Sch., 1969; postgrad., U. Pa., 1969, Sch. Journalism, Columbia U., 1970. Bar: NY 1970. Mem. anti-poverty neighborhood law firms Harlem Assertion of Rights and Community Action for Legal Svcs., NYC, 1968-70; with Eyewitness News, WABC-TV, NYC, 1970-75; reporter Good Morning America program ABC-TV, 1973-76, corr., host Good Night America program, 1975-77, corr., sr. producer 20/20 Newsmag., 1978-85; host syndicated talk show The Geraldo Rivera show, NYC, 1987-98; host investigative show on cable CNBC Rivera Live, NYC, 1994—2001; host nightly news show on cable CNBC Upfront Tonight, NJ, 1998—2000; spl. corr. Fox News Channel, 2001—; host weekend show on cable At Large with Geraldo Rivera; contbr. Fox newsmag. The Pulse; host Fox News Channel, NYC, 2001—. Author: Willowbrook, 1972, Island of Contrasts, 1974, Miguel, 1972, A Special Kind of Courage, 1976, Exposing Myself, 1991; host numerous syndicated TV spls.; film appearances: The Bonfire of the Vanities, 1990; television movie: Perry Mason: The Case of the Reckless Romeo. Recipient 7 Emmy awards, Peabody award, Kennedy Journalism award, 1973, 75, numerous others; named Broadcaster of Yr. N.Y. State AP, 1971, 72, 74; Smith fellow U. Pa., 1969, 2000 Robert F. Kennedy journalism award, Scripps Howard Found. nat. journalism award, George Foster Peabody award. Jewish. Office: Fox News Channel 2nd fl 1211 Ave of Ams New York NY 10036 Office Phone: 212-301-3000. Office Fax: 212-301-8588. Business E-Mail: foxnewsonline@foxnews.com. *

RIVERA, JOSE DE JESUS, lawyer; b. Zacatecas, Mex., 1950; m. Nina Rivera; 5 children. BA, No. Ariz. U.; JD, Ariz. State U. Atty. civil rights divsn. Dept. of Justice, 1976—77; asst. U.S. atty. Dist. Ariz., 1977—81; with Langerman, Begam, Lewis and Marks, 1981—84; ptnr. Rivera, Scales and Kizer, 1984—98; atty. City of El Mirage, U.S. Atty., Dist. of Ariz., 1998—2001; with Haralson, Miller, Pitt & McAnally PLC, Phoenix, 2001—. Vice-chair adv. com. civil rights Atty. Gen. Ariz. dist., 1998-2001, adv. com. Native Am. issues, domestic terrorism subcom., 1998-2001, chair subcom. no Mem. com. Los Abogados; bd. dirs. Inst. for County Initiatives, 1996-98; with N.G. Mem. Ariz. State Bar. (bd. govs. 1995-98, bd. officer, sec. treas. 1996, 2d v.p. 1997-98, exec. dir. search com. 1996-97, chair appointments com. 1997-98), Hispanic Bar Assn., Los Abogados Bar Assn. (bd. dirs. 1981-83). Democrat. Avocation: reading. Office: Haralson Miller Pitt Feldman & McAnally PLC 2800 N Ctrl Ste 840 Phoenix AZ 85004 Home Phone: 602-279-5687; Office Phone: 602-266-5557. Business E-Mail: jrivera@hmpmlaw.com.

RIVERA, LIONEL, mayor; b. El Paso, Tex. B in Microbiology, Tex. Tech. U.; MBA, Jacksonville State U., 1986. V.p. investments UBS Fin. Svc.; mem. Colorado Springs City Coun., Colo., 1997—2001; vice mayor City of Colorado Springs, Colo., 2001—03, mayor Colo., 2003—. Founder, past pres. Colorado Springs Hispanic C. of C.; trustee United Way; mem. exec. com., co-chair The Springs Cmty. Action Plan; mentor Big Bros.-Big Sisters. Capt. US Army, 1979—87. Office: PO Box 1575 Colorado Springs CO 80901 Office Phone: 719-385-5986. Office Fax: 719-385-5495. E-mail: lrivera@ci.colospgs.co.us. *

RIVERA, MARIANO, professional baseball player; b. Panama City, Panama, Nov. 29, 1969; Baseball player N.Y. Yankees, 1995—. Named World Series MVP, 1999, ALCS MVP, 2003; named to Am. League All-Star Team, 1997, 1999—2002, 2004; recipient Am. League Rolaids Relief Award, 1999, 2001. Achievements include mem. of World Series Champions New York Yankees, 1996, 1998, 1999, 2000; led Am. League in saves (45), 1999, (50), 2001, (53), 2004. Office: New York Yankees Yankee Stadium East 161St and River Ave Bronx NY 10451

RIVERA, MILUKA, actress, journalist, poet; b. San Juan, Mar. 24, 1953; d. Francisco and Fidelina (Rabell) R.; m. Paul Navarre Matlovsky, Sept. 28, 1981; children: Élan Lixander, Miluette Nalin Matlovsky. Student, Inter-Am. U., Hato Rey, PR, 1971-74; diploma in pub. rels., U. P.R., Rio Piedras, 1974; student in writing and journalism, UCLA, 1986. Lic. in real estate, Calif. Model Polianna/Barbizon, San Juan, 1968-74; instr. modeling, advisor, co-founder Barbizon Sch. of Modeling, San Juan, 1971-74; freelance dir., 1994—; hostess Buena Vista Cable TV, LA, 1997—; instr. acting, modeling and etiquette Creative Arts Ctr., Burbank, Calif., 1998—2004; co-founder, artistic dir., instr. Kumaras Ctr. Arts and Etiquette, 2004—. Appeared in T.V. shows including Kojak, Nurse and General Hospital; films include Taxi Driver, All That Jazz, Fort Apache: The Bronx; prodr. documentaries; author (poems), "Unequaled Raul Julia", Hollywood Latinos Offspring, 1998; contbr. articles to profl. publs. Founder, pres. Alliance of Latin Artists, N.Y.C., 1982-84. Recipient Governor Mario Cuomo's Citation award for service, N.Y.C., 1984, Excellent Svc. award Assn. Cronistas Espectaculo, N.Y.C., 1996, Best of Burbank award Kumaras Ctr. for Arts Etiquette, 2005, 06. Mem. AFTRA, SAG (nat. bd. dirs. 1992-93, chair com., 1998—), Actors Equity Assn. Avocations: poetry, drawing, ballroom dancing, horseback riding, skiing. Office: Kumaras Ctr for Arts & Etiquette 1616 W Magnolia Blvd Burbank CA 91506 Home Phone: 818-606-5536; Office Phone: 818-848-9333. Business E-Mail: kumarascenter@aol.com.

RIVERA, OSCAR R., lawyer, educator; b. Havana, Cuba, Dec. 8, 1956; s. Alcibiades R. and Marian (Fernandez) R.; children: Peter, Taylor. BBA, U. Miami, 1978; JD, Georgetown U., 1981. Bar: Fla. 1981, US Dist. Ct. (so. dist.) Fla. 1982, US Tax Ct. 1982. Assoc. Corrigan, Zelman & Bander P.A., Miami, Fla., 1981-83; ptnr. Siegfried, Rivera, Lerner De La Torre & Sobel P.A., Miami, 1984—. Adj. prof. law U. Miami, 1987—. Asst. mgr. campaign to elect Michael O'Donovan, Miami, 1976; mem. youth adv. bd., Miami, 1975-78, youth planning council Dade County, Miami, 1975-78. Mem. ABA, Cuban Am. Bar Assn., Internat. Coun. Shopping Ctrs. (pres. Fla. polit. action com., v.p. Fla. govtl. affairs com., state dir. Fla.), Little Havana Kiwanis, Orange Key, Omicron Delta Kappa, Phi Kappa Phi. Avocations: photography, skiing. Home Phone: 305-448-8449; Office Phone: 305-442-3334. Business E-Mail: orivera@siegfriedlaw.com.

RIVERA, RICHARD EDWIN, former restaurant chain executive; b. Jan. 6, 1947; m. Leslie Suzanne Pliner, Nov. 18, 1984. BA, Washington & Lee U., 1968. Credit analyst Nat. Bank Commerce, Dallas, 1970-71; from mgmt. trainee to exec. v.p., dir. Steak and Ale Restaurants of Am., Dallas, 1971-80; pres. restaurant div. El Chico Corp., 1980-82; exec. v.p., chief operating officer T.J. Applebee's and Taco Villa Mexican Restaurant, Dallas, 1982-87; exec. v.p. ops. TGI Friday's Inc., Dallas, 1987-88, pres., CEO, 1988-94, RARE Hosp. Internat., Inc., Atlanta, 1994-97, Chart House Restaurants, Inc., 1997; pres. Red Lobster Restaurants, Orlando, Fla., 1997—2002, 2003—04; vice-chmn. Darden Restaurants, Inc., Orlando, Fla., 2002; interim pres. Bahama Breeze Restaurants, 2002—03; pres., COO Darden Restaurants, Inc., 2003—04.

RIVERA, SALVADOR, JR., history and sociology educator, researcher; b. Glendale, Calif., Aug. 14, 1957; s. Salvador Joseph Rivera and Mary Rodriguez; m. Rosina A. Pezzati, Apr. 8, 1995. BA, Calif. State U., LA, 1985, MA, 1987; PhD, SUNY, Albany, 2003. Prof. history and sociology SUNY, 1992—. Mem. coun. Zion Luth. Ch., Cobleskill, 1996—99. Grad. fellow, SUNY at Albany, 1996. Mem.: Soc. Historians for Am. Fgn. Rels. Baptist. Achievements include research in concerning US efforts to promote European and Latin American economic integration; efforts of former New York Senator Jacob K. Javits to promote Latin American economic integration. Avocations: sailing, swimming, ice hockey, lacrosse. Home: 203 Elm St # 5 Cobleskill NY 12043 Office: SUNY Rt 7 Cobleskill NY 12043 Home Phone: 518-234-7883; Office Phone: 518-255-6238. Office Fax: 518-255-5113. Business E-Mail: riveras@cobleskill.edu.

RIVERA, WALTER, lawyer; b. NYC, Jan. 18, 1955; s. Marcelino and Ana Maria (Reyes) R. BA, Columbia U., 1976; JD, U. Pa., 1979. Bar: N.Y. 1980. Law clk. to cen. legal research staff N.Y. State Ct. Appeals, Albany, 1979-81; asst. atty. gen. State of N.Y., NYC, 1981-85; pvt. practice NYC, 1985-88; shareholder Rivera & Muniz, P.C., NYC, 1988-93, Law Offices of Walter Rivera P.C., 1994-97; ptnr. Rivera, Hunter and Colon, LLP, NYC, 1998—. Chmn. Third World Lawyers Caucus, N.Y. State Atty. Gen.'s Office, N.Y.C., 1984; arbitrator City Ct. N.Y.C., 1985. Mem. adv. bd. Andrew Glover Youth Program, 2006—. Mem. ABA, Puerto Rican Bar Assn., Nat. Hispanic Bar Assn., N.Y. State Bar Assn., Assn. Bar City N.Y. (past chmn. com. on small law firm mgmt.), Sch. of Visual Arts (bd. dirs.). Avocations: golf, travel. Home: 19 Orchard Ln Elmsford NY 10523 Office: Rivera Hunter & Colon LLP 61 Broadway Rm 1030 New York NY 10006-2701 Office Phone: 212-269-2091. Business E-Mail: wrivera@rhclegal.com.

RIVERA-DOMINGUEZ, ALBERTO, mathematician, educator, mechanical engineer; b. Vega Baja, PR, June 17, 1958; s. Angel Rivera-Delgado and Concepcion Dominguez-Suarez; m. Elli Reyes-Grote, Jan. 6, 1985; 1 child, Albert Vincent Rivera-Reyes. BSME magna cum laude, U. P.R., 1981; MSME, La. Tech. U., 1990. Engr. Boeing Comml. A/P Co., Seattle, 1981-82; lectr. U. P.R., Mayaguez, P.R., 1983-84, asst. to the assoc. dean of engring., 1984; tchg. asst. La. Tech. U., Ruston, 1985-86; mech. engr. U.S. Army, Fort Buchannan/San Juan, P.R., 1987-90, USN/AFWTF, Ceiba, P.R., 1990-91; gen. engr. USN - NUWC, Newport, R.I., 1991-95; engr. Breeze-Eastern, Union, NJ, 1995—2001; tchr. h.s. math NJ, 2001—. Lectr. U. P.R., 1983-84. Contbr. articles to profl. jours. Recipient tuition award MIT, Cambridge, Mass., 1982, 84, Panam. Surety Assn. scholarship La. Tech. U., Ruston, 1986; inductee Nat. Honor Roll's Outstanding Am. Tchr., 2005-06. Mem. ASME, NSPE, Am. Soc. for Composites, Colegio de Ingenieros Y Agrimensores de P.R. Achievements include research on viscoelastic characterization of composite materials; theoretical rsch. findings include: co-established the prin. of virtual equillibrium state of viscoelasticity; devel. a generalized predictive creep response formulation suitable for composite materials; developed algorithm and techniques for performance and reliability prediction of assembled products. Home: PO Box 868 Matawan NJ 07747-1370

RIVERA-MARTINEZ, SOCORRO, retired elementary school educator, assistant principal; b. Mayagüez, PR, Apr. 19, 1942; d. Sotero R. and Rafaela Martinez; m. Carmelo Torres, Dec. 26, 1965; 1 child, Yolivette. AEd, Catholic U., 1963, BA in Elem. Edn., 1980. Cert. tchr., mentor tchr. Tchr. 1-6 grades P.R. Dept. Edn., Mayagüez, 1962-93; auxilliary administr. Colegio San Agustin, Cabo Rojo, P.R., 1993-94, asst. principal, 1994-98. Tchr. in charge Rio Hondo Sch. Mayagüez, 1964-70, 73-93, gifted children club, 1990-91, dir.'s resource for tng., 1985-93; math and sci. counselor Rio Hondo, Sch., Castillo Sch., 1971-93. Co-leader troop 384 Girl Scouts Am., Rio Hondo Sch., Mayagüez, P.R., 1975-79; vol. leader Catholic Ch. Summer camp, Cabo Rojo, P.R., 1990-92. Recipient Presidential award Excellence in Sci. and Math. Tchg. The White House, 1993, State award Excellence in Math. Nat. Coun. Math. Tchrs., 1993, Excellence in Math. award Dept. Edn., 1993; named Tchr. of the Year Dept. Edn., 1975, 82. Mem. Educadores Puertorriqueños en Acción, Coun. Elem. Sci. Internat., Coun. Presidential Awardees. Roman Catholic. Avocations: reading, poetry, writing, wire craft, gardening. Home: L22 Calle 3 Borinquen Cabo Rojo PR 00623-3324 Office: Colegio San Agustin Cabo Rojo PR 00623

RIVERA PÉREZ, EFRAÍN E., judge; b. Mayaguez, PR, July 15, 1951; s. Efrain Rivera Padilla and Irene Perez Camacho; m. Border Mariluz; 1 child, Mariela Mariluz. B in Adminstrn. of Cos., U. P.R., 1971; JD, Pontifica Caht. U., 1975. Dist. judge Judicial Region Mayaguez, 1982—84, superior judge, 1984—85; pvt. practice law Maguayez, 1985—92; chmn. U. Enclosure Mayaguez U. P.R., 1986—92; dir. office of commn. Judicial Reformation; judge Ct. Cir. Appeals, 1995—2000; assoc. justice PR Supreme Ct., 2000—. Office: PO Box 902 2392 San Juan PR 00902-2392 *

RIVERA-SOTO, ROBERTO A., state supreme court justice; b. NYC, 1954; m. Mary Catherine Mullaney; 3 children. Grad., Colegio Nuesra Senora Del Pilar, Rio Piedras, PR, 1970, Haverford Coll., 1974; JD, Cornell U. Sch. of Law, 1977. Asst. US atty. criminal divsn. US Atty. Office, Pa., 1978—80; litigation assoc. Fox Rothschild, O'Brien & Frankel, 1980—83; v.p., gen. counsel, corp. sec. Sands Hotel Casino, Atlantic City, 1984—94, Caesars World, Las Vegas, 1994—99; ptnr. Fox Rothschild, Princeton, NJ, 1999—2004; justice NJ Supreme Ct., 2004—. Former instructor trial advocacy Rutgers Sch. of Law; certified mediator U.S. Dist. Ct. for Dist. of N.J.; mem., chair N.J. Supreme Ct. Dist. VII Ethics Com. Former mem. bd. dirs. Please Touch Museum, N.J. Devel. Authority for Small Bus., Minorities and Women's Enterprises. Recipient Director's award for superior performance as asst. U.S. atty., U.S. Dept. Justice, 1980. Office: NJ Supreme Ct PO Box 970 Trenton NJ 08625 *

RIVERA-VELAZQUEZ, MARIA, marketing professional; BA in Econs. cum laude, U. P.R., San Juan, 1993; MA in Econs., U. Wis., Milw., 1995. Statistician Blue Shield P.R., San Juan, 1996—97; rsch. analyst Info. Resources, Inc., Chgo., 1998—2001; sr. rsch. analyst Northwestern Mut., Milw., 2001—04, mgr. corp. and market rsch., 2004—. Spkr. Wis. SAS Users Group Conf., Milw., 2003. Vol. Vecinos Unidos Pro Macun, Toa Baja, PR, 1996—97; vol. United Way campaign Northwestern Mut. Friends, Milw., 2001—; pres. Young Dems. Macun, Toa Baja, PR, 1990—94. Scholar, NEA-P.R. chpt., 1994—95. Mem.: Am. Mktg. Assn. Office: Northwestern Mutual 720 E Wisconsin Ave Milwaukee WI 53202

RIVERO, DENNIS P., orthopedist; b. Albuquerque, Mar. 11, 1952; MD, Ctrl. U. Venezuela, Caracas, 1981. Chief sect. adult reconstrn. U. N.Mex., Albuquerque, 1992—. Author: (with others) Surgical Infections, 1995. Mem. Am. Acad. Orthopaedic Surgeons, Am. Assn. Hip and Knee Surgeons. Office: U NMex Sch Med Dept Orthopaedics Albuquerque NM 87131-5296 Office Phone: 505-272-4107. Business E-Mail: drivero@salud.unm.edu.

RIVERO, LUIS RAUL, aerospace physician, military officer; b. San Juan, July 7, 1968; s. Luis Raul Rivero and Ana Luisa Marin de Rivero; m. Maria Judith Stillwell, Dec. 19, 1993. BS in Biology, Georgetown U., Washington, 1990; MD cum laude, U. Ctrl. Caribbean Sch. Medicine, Bayamon, PR, 1994; MPH, U. Tex. Med. Br., Galveston, 2005. Lic. PR, 1995, cert. preventive and aerospace medicine Am. Bd. Preventive Medicine, 2007. Intern surgery U. Dist. Hosp. U. PR, San Juan, 1994—95; gen. med. officer US Army Health Clinic Darmstadt, Germany, 1995—97; emergency med. treatment physician 212th Mobile Army Surg. Hosp. Operation Joint Endeavor, Bosnia-Herzegovina, 1996—97; gen. med. officer Rodriguez Army Health Clinic, Fort Buchanan, PR, 1997—2000; bn. field surgeon 296th Brigade Support Bn., 3rd BDE, 2nd ID, Fort Lewis, Wash., 2000—02; flight surgeon Raymond W. Bliss Army Health Clinic, Fort Huachuca, Ariz., 2002—03; bn. flight surgeon 5th Bn., 158th Rgt., 12th Aviation BDE Operation Iraqi Freedom, 2003—04; resident aerospace medicine Naval Aerospace Med. Inst., Pensacola, Fla., 2004—06, asst. chief resident, 2006—07; stationed at Schofield Barraks, Hawaii, 2007—. Dep. comdr. Rodriguez Army Health Clinic, Fort Buchanan, 1997—99; chief dept. mil. medicine Raymond W. Bliss Army Health Ctr., Fort Huachuca, 2003. Author: (research) A Study of the 1993 Healthcare Reform in Puerto Rico; contbr. scientific papers, articles to profl. jours. Lt. col. US Army, 1994—. Decorated Bronze Star US Army, Nat. Def. Svc. medal with Bronze Star, Global War on Terrorism Svc. medal, Global War on Terrorism Expeditionary medal, Meritorious Svc. medal with Oak Leaf Cluster, Army Commendation medal with 2 Oak Leaf Clusters, Armed Forces Svc. medal, Armed Forces Expeditionary medal, Humanitarian Svc. medal, NATO medal, Army Superior Unit award, Army Presdl. Unit citation. Mem.: Am. Coll. Preventive Medicine, Aerospace Medicine Student and Resident Orgn. (mil. liaison 2006—07), Aerospace Med. Assn., Coll. Physicians and Surgeons of PR, Soc. US Army Flight Surgeons (life). Roman Catholic. Avocation: travel. Home: 26445 Misty Ridge Pl Canyon Country CA 91387 Home Phone: 409-939-4355. Personal E-mail: luis.r.rivero@us.army.mil.

RIVERO, MARILYN ELAINE KEITH, state legislator; b. Burlington, Vt., Aug. 22, 1942; d. Kenneth Charles and Irene (Haskell) Keith; m. Victor Paul Rivero, Sr., 1966; children: Lina, Mita, Victor Jr., Amy, Nicholas. BS, U. Vt., 1964, MS, 1988; postgrad., Middlebury Coll., 1973, St. Michaels Coll., 1986. Vol. Peace Corps., 1964-66; mem. Vt. Ho. of Reps., 1991—; mem. health and welfare com., 1991—. Recipient Beyond War award. Mem. ANA, Vt. Nurses Assn., Returned Peace Corps. Vol., Am. Assn. Retired People. Roman Catholic. Home: PO Box 37 Milton VT 05468-0037 E-mail: m149rivero@aol.com.

RIVERS, BEVERLY D., former district secretary; b. 1965; JD U. Ala. Sch. Law; BS in bus. mgmt., Oakwood Coll., Huntsville, Ala. Sec. D.C.; spl. asst. CFO; chief legis. asst. State Senator Henry L. Marsh, Richmond, Va.; atty. Hill Tucker Firm, Marsh Firm; acting sec. of dist. D.C. Govt., 1999, sec. of dist., 1999—2003. Mem.: Nat. Forum Black Pub. Adminstr., Wash. Bar Assn., Ala. Bar Assn., D.C. Bar Assn.

RIVERS, CHRISTINE D., academic administrator; d. John L. Irvin, Jr. and Maxine D. McConnell Irvin; m. Ernest L. Rivers, Jr., June 24, 1972; 1 child, Wendy L. BA, U. Mo., Kansas City, 1972; cert. in nonprofit bus. adminstrn., La. State U., Shreveport, 2003. Cert. archival studies Western Archive Inst., Calif., 1994. Translator Black & Veatch, Overland Park, Kans., 1973—76; accounts receivable analyst Robbie Mfg. Inc., Lenexa, Kans., 1977—78; translator BMI, Kansas City, 1978—80; cost acctg. supr. Baghouse Accessories Co., Kansas City, 1980—81; office mgr. Diocese of Alexandria-Shreveport, La., 1982—89; vice chancellor, archivist Diocese of Shreveport, La., 1990—2002, chancellor, corp. officer, 2003—. Bd. officer, mem. La. Cath. Fed. Credit Union, Shreveport, 1999—2005, Holy Angels Residential Facility, Shreveport, 2003—06. Editor: Guided by the Spirit, 2006. Named Mem. of Yr., ARMA Internat. Ark.-La.-Tex. Chpt., 2001; recipient medal of honor, Diocese of Shreveport, 1998. Mem.: Assn. Records, Mgrs. and Adminstrs., Assn. Cath. Diocesan Archivists (bd. mem. 1999—2003), Soc. Am. Archivists, Nat. Assn. Lay Ministry. Roman Catholic. Office: 2903 E Linton Rd Benton LA 71006

RIVERS, DOC (GLENN ANTON RIVERS), professional basketball coach; b. Maywood, Ill., Oct. 13, 1961; m. Kris Rivers, 1987; children: Jeremiah, Callie, Austin, Spencer. Student, Marquette U., 1980-83, grad., 1985. Player Atlanta Hawks, 1983-91, LA Clippers, 1991-92, NY Knicks, 1992-94, San Antonio Spurs, 1994-96; sports analyst Turner Sports, 1996—99, ABC Sports, 2003—04; head coach Orlando Magic, 1999—2003, Boston Celtics, 2004—. Asst. coach U.S.A. Men's Basketball Team Goodwill Games, Brisbane, Australia, 2001. Named Coach of Yr., NBA, 2000, Male Coach of Yr., Rainbow Sports Awards, 2000; named to NBA All-Star Team, 1988; recipient J. Walter Kennedy Basketball Citizenship award, Pro Basketball Writers, 1990. Office: Boston Celtics 226 Causeway St 4th Fl Boston MA 02114-4720 *

RIVERS, EMANUEL P., emergency physician, medical educator; b. Detroit; m. Kandis Rivers; 2 children. BS, MD, MPH, U. Mich., Ann Arbor. Cert. Emergency Medicine, Internal Medicine, Critical Care Medicine. Dir. rsch., dept. emergency medicine & surg. critical care Henry Ford Hosp., Detroit, asst. prof. internal medicine & surgery, sr. staff attending physician. Assoc. prof. emergency medicine Case Western Reserve U., Cleveland. Internat. lectr.; contbr. articles, scientific papers. Recipient Outstanding Contbn. in Rsch. award, Am. Coll. Emergency Physicians (ACEP), 2005, Teacher of Yr. award, Emergency Medicine Resident's Assn. (Mich. chpt.), Clin. Sci. Faculty award, Soc. Academic Emergency Medicine. Fellow: Am. Acad. Emergency Medicine, Am. Coll. Chest Physicians; mem.: AMA, Soc. Critical Care, Am. Coll. Emergency Physicians, Soc. Academic Emergency Medicine, Inst. Medicine. Achievements include patents for Selective Aortic Arch Perfusion & Oxygenation; development of Early Goal Directed Therapy (EGDT). Office: Henry Ford Hosp 2799 W Grand Blvd Detroit MI 48202 Office Phone: 313-916-1801, 313-916-7437. E-mail: erivers1@hfhs.org.

RIVERS, JOAN, entertainer; b. NYC, June 8, 1937; d. Meyer C. Molinsky; m. Edgar Rosenberg, July 15, 1965 (dec.); 1 child, Melissa. BA, Barnard Coll., 1958. Formerly fashion coordinator Bond Clothing Store; founder Joan Rivers Classics Collection, 1990, Joan Rivers Worldwide Enterprises, 1996—. Debut entertaining, 1960; mem. From Second City, 1961-62; TV debut Tonight Show, 1965; Las Vegas debut, 1969; nat. syndicated columnist Chgo. Tribune, 1973-76; creator: CBS TV series Husbands and Wives, 1976-77; host: Emmy Awards, 1983; guest hostess: Tonight Show, 1983-86; hostess The Late Show Starring Joan Rivers, 1986-87, Hollywood Squares, 1987, (morning talk show) Joan Rivers (Daytime Emmy award 1990), 1989-93, Can We Shop? Home Shopping Network, 1994, (radio) The Joan Rivers Show, 1997-2002, (TV series) E! Pre-awards Show, 1995-2004, red carpet events, TV Guide Channel,

2005-07; originator, screenwriter TV movie The Girl Most Likely To, ABC, 1973; other TV movies include: How to Murder A Millionaire, 1990, Jackie Collins' Lady Boss, 1992, Tears and Laughter: The Joan and Melissa Rivers Story, 1994; cable TV spl. Joan Rivers and Friends Salute Heidi Abromowitz, 1985; film appearances include The Swimmer, 1968, Uncle Sam, The Muppets Take Manhattan, 1984; co-author, dir.: (films) Rabbit Test, 1978 (also acted), Spaceballs, 1987, Serial Mom, 1994 Goosed, 1998, L'Intern, 2000, Shrek 2, 2004; actress: theatre prodn. Broadway Bound, 1988, Sally Marr...and her escorts, 1994; recs. include: comedy album What Becomes a Semi-Legend Most, 1983; author: Having a Baby Can be a Scream, 1974, The Life and Hard Times of Heidi Abromowitz, 1984, (autobiography with Richard Meryman) Enter Talking, 1986, (with Richard Meryman), Still Talking, 1991, From Mother to Daughter: Thoughts and Advice on Life, Love and Marriage, 1998, Don't Count the Candle, Just Keep the Fire Lit, 1999; debuted on Broadway (play) Broadway Bound, 1988, creator Seminar You Deserve To Be happy, 1995; columnist (magazines) She Says/She Says, McCall's mag. (with daughter Melissa), 1999-2000, Star Mag. Fashion column (with daughter Melissa), 2002-03. Nat. chmn. Cystic Fibrosis, 1982—, benefit performer for AIDS, 1984. Recipient CLIO awards for commls., 1976, 82, Jimmy award for best comedian, 1987, 91, Accessories Coun. award of Excellence, 1997, Rebekah Kohut award for Svc. in Cmty., 2004; named Hadassah Woman of Yr., 1983, Harvard Hasty Pudding Soc. Woman of Yr., 1984. Mem. Phi Beta Kappa. Office: William Morris Agy 151 S El Camino Dr Beverly Hills CA 90212-2775 also: JR Worldwide 150 E 58th St New York NY 10155-0002 *

RIVERS, ROBERT ALFRED, microwave company executive; b. Phillipston, Mass., Sept. 5, 1923; s. Frank Allen and Marie Ange (Pelchat) R.; m. Priscilla Bradford, Oct. 8, 1944; children: Lucy Marie, Rosalind Dolley, Robert Bradford. BSEE, MIT, 1953. Registered profl. engr., NH. Flight radio officer Pan Am. Airways, various locations, 1942-50; design engr. Gen. Electronic Labs., Boston, 1953-54; pres. Aircom, Inc., various cities, 1954—. Editor Tech. Employment and Engring. Manpower Newsletter, 1989-2002; contbr. articles to profl. jours. Inventor wideband cavity resonator; designer over 1300 microwave components, portable and desktop microcomputer systems. Fellow IEEE (life, bd. dirs. 1975-76, mem. numerous coms. and bds., ethics rev. panel 1982-88, Centennial medal 1984, US Activities Bd. citation of hon., Profl. Achievement award 1992, Haradan Pratt award 1997); mem. IEEE Microwave Theory and Techs. Soc. (pres. 1974, mem. numerous coms., chmn. Boston chpt. 1958-59, digest editor 1967, MTT Disting. Svc. award 1978), Eta Kappa Nu, Tau Beta Pi. Republican. Avocations: gardening, travel, reading. Office: Aircom Inc 334 E Main St Orange MA 01364

RIVERS, WILGA MARIE, language educator; b. Melbourne, Australia, Apr. 13, 1919; arrived in U.S., 1970; d. Harry and Nina Diamond (Burston) Rivers. BA, U. Melbourne, 1939, diploma in Edn., 1940, MA, 1948; Licence es L., U. Montpellier, France, 1952; PhD, U. Ill., 1962; MA (hon.), Harvard U., 1974; PhD of Langs. (hon.), Middlebury Coll., 1989. H.S. tchr., Victoria, Australia, 1940-48; asst. in English lang. France, 1949-52; tchr. prep. schs., 1953-58; asst. prof. French No. Ill. U., DeKalb, 1963-64; assoc. prof. Monash U., Australia, 1964-69; vis. prof. Columbia U., 1970-71; prof. French U. Ill., Urbana-Champaign, 1971-74; prof. Romance langs. and lit., coord. lang. instrn. Harvard U., 1974-89, prof. emerita, 1989—. Cons. NEH, Ford Found., Rockefeller Found., others; lectr 44 countries and throughout U.S.; mem. adv. bd. Modern Lang. Ctr., Ont. Inst. for Studies in Edn., Nat. Fgn. Lang. Ctr., Lang. Acquire Rsch. Ctr., San Diego. Author: The Psychologist and the Foreign-Language Teacher, 1964, Teaching Foreign-Language Skills, 1968, 2d edit., 1981, Speaking in Many Tongues, 1972, 3d edit., 1983, A Practical Guide to the Teaching of French, 1975, 2d edit., 1988, 3d edit. (on Web), 2001, Opportunities for Careers in Foreign Languages, 1993; co-author: A Practical Guide to the Teaching of German, 1975, 2d edit., 1988, A Practical Guide to the Teaching of Spanish, 1976, 2d edit., 1988, A Practical Guide to the Teaching of English as a Second or Foreign Language, 1978, Communicating Naturally in a Second Language, 1983, Teaching Hebrew: A Practical Guide, 1989, others; editor, contbr. Interactive Language Teaching, 1978, Teaching Languages in College: Curriculum and Content, 1992, Down Under/Up Top: Creating a Life, 2004; writing translated into 11 langs.; editl. bd. Studies in Second Language Acquisition, Applied Linguistics, Language Learning, Mosaic, System; adv. com. Can. Modern Lang. Rev.; contbr. articles to profl. jours. Decorated chevalier des Palmes Académiques; recipient Disting. Fgn. Lang. Leadership award N.Y. State Assn. Fgn. Lang. Tchrs., 1974, Disting. Alumni award U. Ill., 1999, Dean's Disting. Svc. award Harvard Continuing Edn., 2004. Mem. MLA, Am. Assn. Applied Linguistics (charter pres.), Am. Coun. on Tchg. Fgn. Langs. (Florence Steiner award 1977, Anthony Papalia award 1988), Mass. Fgn. Lang. Assn. (Disting. Svc. award 1983), Tchrs. of English to Spkrs. of other Langs., Am. Assn. Tchrs. French, Linguistic Soc. Am., Am. Assn. Univ. Suprs. and Coords. Fgn. Lang. Programs Northeast Conf. (Nelson Brooks award 1983), Internat. Assn. Applied Psycholinguistics (v.p. 1983-89), Japan Assn. Coll. English Tchrs. (hon.), Am. Assn. Tchrs. German (hon.), Internat. Assn. Lang. Labs. (hon.). Episcopalian. Home and Office: 84 Garfield St Watertown MA 02472-4916 Personal E-mail: wmrivers@comcast.net.

RIVES, JACK L., judge, career military officer; BA in Polit. Sci., U. Ga., Athens, 1974, JD, 1976; postgraduate student, Squadron Officer Sch., 1982, Air Command and Staff Coll., 1983, Nat. Security Mgmt., 1985, Air War Coll., 1990; disting. grad., Naval War Coll., Fort Lesley J. McNair, Washington, 1993. Advanced through ranks to maj. gen. USAF, 2002, 2nd lt., 1974—77; asst. staff judge adv. Griffiss AFB, NY, 1977, area def. counsel NY, 1977—78; dep. staff judge adv. Kunsan Air Base, Republic of Korea, 1978—79; asst. staff judge adv. Hellenikon Air Base, Greece, 1979—81; cir. def. counsel (Pacific cir.) Clark Air Base, Philippines, 1981—83; judge adv. air staff tng. officer The Pentagon, Washington, 1983—84, dep. legal counsel to Chmn. Joint Chiefs of Staff, 1993—95; staff judge adv. Plattsburgh AFB, NY, 1984—86; chief officer br., judge adv. profl. devel. divsn. Office of JAG, Washington, 1986—90; appellate judge USAF Ct. Mil. Rev., Bolling AFB, DC, 1990—92; comdt. Air Force JAG Sch., Maxwell AFB, Ala., 1995—98; chief Air Force Exec. Issues Team Office of Sec. of Air Force, Washington, 1998—2000; staff judge adv. Hdqrs. Air Combat Command, Langley AFB, Va., 2000—02; dep. JAG USAF, Washington, 2002—06, JAG, 2006—. Decorated Legion of Merit with oak leaf cluster, Def. Superior Svc. Medal, Meritorious Svc. Medal with silver and bronze oak leaf clusters, Air Force Commendation Medal, DSM. Office: JAG 1420 Air Force Pentagon Washington DC 20330 *

RIVES, STANLEY GENE, retired academic administrator; b. Decatur, Ill., Sept. 27, 1930; s. James A. and Frances (Bunker) R.; m. Sandra Lou Belt, Dec. 28, 1957; children: Jacqueline Ann, Joseph Alan. BS, Ill. State U., 1952, MS, 1955; PhD, Northwestern U., 1963; EdD (hon.), Lincoln Coll., 1998. Instr. W.Va. U., 1955-56, Northwestern U., 1956-58; prof. Ill. State U., Normal, 1958-80, Am. Coun. on Edn. Fellows Program, 1969-70, assoc. dean faculties, 1970-72, dean undergrad. instrn., 1972-80, assoc. provost, 1976-80, acting provost, 1979-80; provost, v.p. acad. affairs, prof. Eastern Ill. U., Charleston, 1981-83, pres., 1983-92, pres. emeritus, 1992—. Vis. prof. U. Hawaii, 1963—64. Author: (with Donald Klopf) Individual Speaking Contests: Preparation for Participation, 1967, (with Gene Budig) Academic Quicksand: Trends and Issues in Higher Education, 1973, (with others) Academic Innovation: Faculty and Instructional Development at Illinois State University, 1979, The Fundamentals of Oral Interpretation, 1981; contbr. articles to profl. jours. Bd. dirs. Ill. State Univs. Ret. Sys., 1992-2005, treas., 1995-2001, pres., 2001-05; bd. dirs. Ea. Ill. Univ. Found., 1993-98, also pres., 1996-98, East Ctrl. Ill. Devel. Corp., 1983-92, Charleston Area Econ. Devel. Found., 1986-92, Coles Together, 1988-92; mem. pres. commn. NCAA, 1986-91; trustee Nat. Debate Tournament, 1967-75. With U.S. Army, 1952-54. Named to Co. of Edn. Hall of Fame; recipient Alumni Achievement award, Ill. State U., 1998. Mem. Am. Assn. State Colls. and Univs., Ill. State C. of C. (bd. dirs. 1990-92), Charleston C. of C. (bd. dirs. 1985-88), Theta Alpha Phi, Phi Kappa Delta, Pi Gamma Mu, Alpha Phi Omega, Alpha Zeta, Sigma Phi Epsilon (hon.). Home: 2231 Andover Pl Charleston IL 61920-3807 Personal E-mail: srives@consolidated.net.

RIVEST, RONALD L., engineer; BS, Yale Univ., 1969; PhD, Stanford Univ., 1974. Andrew and Erna Viterbi prof. elec. engring. and computer sci. Mass. Inst. Tech., 1974—; mem. MIT Computer Sci. and Artificial Intelligence Lab (CSAIL). Dir., founding inventor Peppercorn Corp.; founder RSA Data Security, Inc. Recipient ACM Turing award, 2002, Secure Computing Lifetime Achievement award, ACM Paris Kanallakis award, 1996. Fellow World Tech. Network; mem. NAS, IEEE (Koji Kobayashi Computers and Comm. award 2000), Nat. Acad. Engr., Assn. Computer Mach., Internat. Assn. Cryptographic Rsch., Am. Acad. Arts and Scis. Office: CSAIL 32 Vassar St Rm 32-G692 Cambridge MA 02139 E-mail: rivest@mit.edu.

RIVET, DENNIS JAMES, neurosurgeon; b. Bkln., Dec. 1968; s. Dennis James and Kathleen Eleanor Rivet; m. Emily Burke Diskin, Sept. 2003. BS with distinction, US Naval Acad., Annapolis, Md., 1992; MD, Dartmouth Med. Sch., Hanover, NH, 1997. Lic. Mo. Bd. Healing Arts, 1999, neurosurgeon Am. Bd. Neurol. Surgery, 2003. Fellow Mallinckrodt Inst. Radiology, St. Louis, 2003—05; sr. inventor Intellectual Ventures, Bellevue, Wash., 2006—. Lt. comdr. USN. Bear Cub Venture Capital Funding grant, Wash. U., 2004. Mem.: Am. Soc. Interventional and Therapeutic Neuroradiology. Achievements include patents pending for multiple medical devices. Office Phone: 757-953-9390.

RIVET, DIANA WITTMER, lawyer, farmer; b. Auburn, NY, Apr. 28, 1931; d. George Wittmer and Anne (Jenkins) Wittmer Hauswirth; m. Paul Henry Rivet, Oct. 24, 1952; children: Gail, Robin, Leslie, Heather, Clayton, Eric. BA, Keuka Coll., 1951; JD, Bklyn. Law Sch., 1956. Bar: N.Y. 1956, U.S. Dist. Ct. (ea. and so. dists.) N.Y. 1975; cert. organic NOFA, 2001. Sole practice, Orangeburg, NY, 1957—2000; farmer Danny's Backyard Organic Farm, Orangeburg, 2000—. County atty. Rockland County (N.Y.), 1974-77; asst. to legis. chmn. Rockland County, 1978-79; counsel, adminstr. Indsl. Devel. Agy., Rockland County, 1980-91, Rockland Econ. Devel. Corp., 1981-90; counsel, exec. dir. Pvt. IndustryCoun. Rockland county, 1980-90; pres., CEO Environ. Mgmt. Ltd., Orangeburg, 1980-98; mem. air mgmt. adv. com. N.Y. State Dept. Environ. Conservation 1984-92, Orangetown Planning Bd., 1993-2000, master plan com., 2000-03. Pres. Rockland County coun. Girl Scouts U.S., 1981-84; chmn. Rockland County United Way, 1996-97, mem. campaign com., 1983-84, 88-89, 93, sec., 1997-99, bd. dirs., 1988-94, 95-2004, adv., nominating com., 2004-06, cmty. investment com. 2007—; mem. Leadership Rockland, 1991-94. Recipient Cmty. Svc. award Keuka Coll., 1965, Disting. Svc. award Town of Orangetown, 1970, Disting. Svc. award Rockland County, 1989, Econ. Devel. award Rockland Econ. Devel. Corp., 1990, Retirement award Keuka Coll., 2006; named Businessperson of Yr. Jour. News, Rockland County, 1982.E Mem. ABA, N.Y. State Bar Assn. (mcpl. law sect. exec. com. 1976-83, environ. law sect. exec. com. 1974-86), Rockland County Bar Assn. (chair environ. law com. 1994-96), Rockland Bus. Assn. (bd. dirs. 1981-97, small bus. adv. com. 1998, gov. affairs com. 1998-2004), Rockland Computer Users' Group (bd. dirs. 1998-99). Democrat. Mem. Religious Soc. of Friends. Home: 1 Lester Dr Orangeburg NY 10962-2316 Office Phone: 845-359-1515. Personal E-mail: ydannyy@verizon.net.

RIVET, JEANNINE M., health insurance company executive; BS in Nursing, Boston Coll.; MPH, Boston U. Sch. Public Health. V.p. grp. ops. Prudential Ins. Co. Am.; v.p. health svc. ops. to CEO United HealthCare, Minnetonka, Minn., 1990-98, CEO, 1998—2000, Ingenix; exec. v.p. UnitedHealth Grp., 2000—. Office: UnitedHealth Group 9900 Bren Rd E Minnetonka MN 55343-9664 *

RIVETTE, FRANCIS ROBERT, lawyer; b. Syracuse, NY, May 1, 1952; s. Francis Patrick and Barbara Parker (Smith) R.; m. Judith A. La Manna, 1993. BA, Allegheny Coll., 1974; JD, Syracuse U., 1977. Bar: N.Y. 1978, D.C. 1980, U.S. Dist. Ct. (no. dist.) N.Y. 1978, U.S. Supreme Ct. 1993. Ptnr. Rivette & Rivette P.C., Syracuse, 1978—2006; corp. counsel Nicom Techs., Inc., 1995—2006, Group 52, Inc., 2002—. Corp. counsel Fangand Enterprises Ltd., 1978—; co-founder Apex Racing. Mem. ATLA, NY State Acad. Trial Lawyers, Syracuse Corvette Club (pres. 1985-86), Sportscar Vintage Racing Assn., Nat. Corvette Restorers Soc. (nat. judge 1985, 88, 95, 97), Historic Sportscar Racing Ltd., Phi Delta Phi, Phi Gamma Mu. Republican. Home: 200 Old Liverpool Rd Liverpool NY 13088-6354 Office: Rivette & Rivette PC 224 Harrison St Ste 306 Syracuse NY 13202-3067 Office Phone: 315-478-1122. Business E-Mail: rrivette@rivette.us.

RIVIERE, JIM EDMOND, JR., pharmacologist, toxicologist, educator; b. New Bedford, Mass., Mar. 3, 1953; s. Raymond R. Riviere and Gertrude E. Pelletier-Riviere; m. Nancy Ann Monteiro-Riviere, May 31, 1976; children: Christopher, Brian, Jessica. BS, MS, Boston Coll., 1976; DVM, PhD, Purdue U., 1980, DSc (hon.), 2007. Lic. vet. medicine; diplomate Am. Bd. Forensic Medicine, Acad. Toxicological Sci. From asst. prof. to assoc. prof. NC State U., Raleigh, 1981-88, prof., 1988-92, Burroughs-Wellcome disting. prof. pharmacology, 1992—, dir. Ctr. Chem. Toxicology Rsch. and Pharmacokinetics, 1989—, dir. Biomath. Program, 2005—. Cons. for govt. and pharm. cos.; mem. com. on revision US Pharmacopeia; mem. sci. bd. FDA. Author, editor 10 books, author over 410 rsch. manuscripts. Recipient Ebert prize Am. Pharm. Assn., 1991, Disting. Alumni award Purdue U., 1991, Outstanding Rsch. award NC State U. Alumni Assn., 1993, Harvey Wiley medal, 1997, FDA Commrs. Spl. citation, 1997, O. Max Gardner award U. NC Sys., 1999; numerous rsch. grants. Fellow Am. Acad. Vet. Pharmacology and Therapeutics (editor 1989-92, 99—, First Rsch. award 1998), Inst. Medicine Nat. Academies (elected); mem. Am. Assn. Pharm. Scientist, Soc. Toxicology, Am. Vet. Med. Assn., Am. Coll. Forensic Examiners. Achievements include 5 patents in field. Avocations: baseball, boating, beachcombing. Office: NC State U 4700 Hillsborough St Raleigh NC 27606-1428 Home Phone: 919-881-9219. Business E-Mail: Jim_Riviere@ncsu.edu.

RIVIN, EUGENY (EUGENE) I., engineering educator, researcher, consultant; b. Moscow, Russi, June 11, 1932; came to U.S., 1979; s. Izrail Borisovich and Frida Mikhailovna Rivin; m. Irina Rivin, Dec. 30, 1958; children: Igor, Natasha. MS in Mech. Engring., Moscow Machine Tool Inst., 1954; PhD, Moscow Machine Tool. Inst., 1962; DSc, USSR Supreme Attestation Bd., 1972. Registered profl. engr., Ont., Can. Sr. engr. Moscow Profl. Motion Cameras Plant, 1954—57; sr. rschr. Rsch. Inst. Machine Tools, Moscow, 1957—68; had. lab. Rsch. Inst. Standardization, Moscow, 1968—75; prin. staff engr. Ford Motor Co., Dearborn, Mich., 1976—81; prof. Wayne State U., Detroit, 1981—. Co-prin. The TRIZ Group, West Bloomfield, Mich. Author: Dynamics of Machine Drives, 1966, Mechanical Design of Robots, 1988, The Science of Innovation, 1997, Stiffness and Damping in Mechanical Design, 1999, Passive Vibration Isolation, 2003, Innovation on Demand, 2005; author 13 books/monographs; editor 10 books; contbr. some 150 articles to profl. jours.; holder more than 60 patents. Bd. mem. Inst. Individual and Group Therapy, Farmington Mills, Mich., 2002—. Recipient Shingo prize for excellence in mfg. Shingo Found., 1992, DeVlieg Rsch. awards Wayne State U., 1987-89; Eminent Scholar Invitation, Loughborough Univ. Tech., 1995. Fellow ASME, Soc. Mfg. Engrs., Internat. Acad. for Prodn. Engring. (membership com. 1990). Achievements include over 60 patents in field. Office: Wayne State Univ 5050 Anthony Wayne Dr Detroit MI 48202 Office Phone: 313-577-3898.

RIVKIN, DAVID WOLFE, lawyer; b. NYC, Oct. 17, 1955; s. Donald H. and Lois (Herman) R.; m. Marilyn Aloi, Sept. 13, 1981; children: Jessica, Catherine. BA, Yale U., 1977, JD, 1980. Bar: NY 1981. Law clk. to Hon. Luther M. Swygert US Ct. Appeals (7th cir.), Chgo., 1980-81; assoc. Debevoise & Plimpton, NYC, 1982-88, ptnr., 1988—. Author: (with others) Stockbroker Supervision: Managing Stockbrokers and Surviving Sanctions, 1990, Commercial Arbitration for the 1990's, 1991, Competition and Arbitration Law, 1993; contbr. articles to profl. publs. Mem. ABA (co-chmn. internat. litigation com. litigation sect. 1990—, task force on liaison with internat. profl. assns. 1989—, task force on broker-dealer supervision and compliance 1987-89), Inter-Am. Bar Assn., Am. Arbitration Assn. (panel comml. arbitrators 1986—, internat. arbitration, arbitration practice and corp. counsel coms. 1988—), Assn. Bar City NY (com. on US in global economy 1991—, com. on internat. trade 1984-89), London Ct. Internat. Arbitration, N.Am. Users' Coun. (sec. 1992—), Inst. for Transnat. Arbitration (adv. bd. dirs. 1988—), Internat. Bar Assn. (internat. litigation com., com. on procedures for settling disputes, sect. on bus. law), Internat. Law Assn. (chmn. com. on internat. arbitration Am. br. 1989—). Home: 62 Park Rd Scarsdale NY 10583-2140 Office: Debevoise & Plimpton LLP 919 Third Ave New York NY 10022 Office Phone: 212-909-6671, 212-909-6836. E-mail: dwrivkin@debevoise.com.

RIVKIN, WILLIAM B., physicist; b. Latvia, Jan. 6, 1921; arrived in US, 1931; s. Oscar W. and Fannie Mary Rivkin; m. Dolores Cohan Rivkin; children: Francine, Debra Rivkin Haggarty. BSEE, Ill. Inst. Tech., 1945; postgrad., Northwestern U., Evanston, Ill., 1960—61. V.p., gen. mgr. Health Physics Assoc., Northbrook, Ill., 1959—86; physicist Vets. Adminstrn. Hosp., Hines, Ill., 1961—75; v.p., gen. mgr. Isotope Measurements Labs., Northbrook, 1969—87, Mobsce Imaging, Inc., Northbrook, 1970—93; health physicist U. Ill., Chgo., 1970—76; CEO Medx, Inc., Wooddale, Ill., 1993—98, Arlington Heights, Ill., 2003—. Field engr. Tracerlab, Inc., Boston, 1953—57; criticality engr. Westinghouse Electric Co., Creswick, Pa., 1957—58; cons. Imaging Concepts, Inc., Highland Park, Ill., 1980—2003. Bd. dirs. Northbrook Symphony Orch., 1980—2003, Am. Nuc. Soc., Washington, 1980—85. With Signal Corps. US Army, 1940—42. Mem.: Am. Assn. Physics in Medicine (com. mem. 1965—), Soc. Nuc. Medicine (com. mem. 1970—), Health Physics Soc. (pres. 1970—74), Rotary. Democrat. Jewish. Avocations: sailing, travel. Home: 1190 Ridge Rd Highland Park IL 60035 Office: Medx Inc 3456 N Ridge Ave Arlington Heights IL 60004

RIVLIN, ALICE MITCHELL, economics professor, former federal official; b. Phila., Mar. 4, 1931; d. Allan C. G. and Georgianna (Fales) Mitchell; m. Lewis Allen Rivlin, 1955 (div. 1977); children: Catherine Amy, Allan Mitchell, Douglas Gray; m. Sidney Graham Winter, 1989. AB, Bryn Mawr Coll., 1952; MA, Radcliffe Coll., 1955, PhD, 1958; LLD (hon.), U. Mich., 1975, U. Md., 1975; DSc (hon.), U. Ind., 1976; LLD (hon.), Yale U., 1984; DSc (hon.), N.J. Inst. Tech., 1998; LLD (hon.), U. Dist. of Columbia, 1999, Harvard U., 2001. Mem. staff Brookings Instn., Washington, 1957-66, 69-75, 83-93; dir. econ. studies Brookings Inst., 1983-87; dir. Congl. Budget Office, 1975-83; prof. pub. policy George Mason U., 1992—93; dep. dir. Office Mgmt. & Budget, Exec. Office of the Pres., Washington, 1993-94, dir., 1994-96; mem. bd. govs. Fed. Res. Sys., 1996—99, vice chmn. Washington, 1996-99; chair Fin. Assistance and Mgmt. Authority, 1998—2001; sr. fellow, econ. studies program Brookings Instn., Washington, 1999—; Henry J. Cohen prof. New Sch. U., 2001—; co-dir. Greater Wash. Rsch. Program, Brookings Instn., 2001—. Dep. asst. sec. program coordination HEW, Washington, 1966-68, asst. sec. planning and evaluation, 1968-69; mem. Staff Adv. Commn. on Intergovtl. Rels., 1961-62; bd. dirs. NY Stock Exch., 2005-06, NYSE Group, Inc., 2006-, BearingPoint, Inc., Washington Post Co. Author: The Role of the Federal Governemnt in Financing Higher Education, 1961, (with others) Microanalysis of Socioeconomic Systems, 1961, Systematic Thinking for Social Action, 1971, (with others) Economic Choices 1987, 1986, (with others The Swedish Economy, 1987, (with others) Caring for the Disabled Elderly: Who Will Pay?, 1988, Reviving the American Dream, 1992, The Economic Payoff from the Internet Revolution (co-edited with Robert E. Litan), 2001, Beyond the Dot.Coms: The Economic Promise of the Internet (with Robert E. Litan), 2001. MacArthur fellow, 1983-87, Elliot J. Richardson prize for excellence in pub. svc., 2002, Barnard medal of distinction, Barnard Coll., 2002. Mem. Am. Econ. Assn. (nat. pres. 1986), Nat. Acad. Pub. Adminstrn., Nat. Acad. of Social Insurance, Coun. on Fgn. Rels., Women's Econ. Roundtable Office: Brookings Instn 1755 Massachusetts Ave Washington DC 20036 also: NYSE Group Inc 11 Wall St New York NY 10005

RIVLIN, BENJAMIN, political science professor; b. Bklyn., July 10, 1921; s. Moses and Esther (Ribnick) R.; m. Leanne Green, July 9, 1957; 1 child, Marc Alexander. BA, Bklyn. Coll., 1942; MA, Harvard U., 1947, PhD, 1949. With OSS, 1943-45; teaching fellow Harvard U., 1948; mem. trusteeship dept. UN Secretariat, 1948, 50, 52; research assoc. Hoover Commn., 1948; mem. faculty Bklyn. Coll. of CUNY, 1949-75, prof. polit. sci., 1962-70, chmn. dept., 1966-70; mem. Grad. Sch. faculty CUNY, 1970-85, exec. officer polit. sci. Ph.D. program, 1970-75, dean research and univ. programs Grad. Sch. and Univ. Center, 1975-78, prof. emeritus, 1985—, dir. Ralph Bunche Inst. on UN, 1984—91, dir. emeritus, 1991—. Vis. lectr. Johns Hopkins Sch. Advanced Internat. Studies, 1956; vis. prof. African and Middle East Insts., Columbia U., 1963-68; co-chair Ralph Bunche Centenary Commemoration com., 2001-04; mem. bd. advisors Nat. Com. Am. Fgn. Policy. Author: The United Nations and The Italian Colonies, 1950, Self-Determination and Dependent Areas, 1955, (with J.S. Szyliowicz) The Contemporary Middle East: Tradition and Innovation, 1965, Ralph Bunche: The Man and His Times, 1990, (with Leon Gordenker) The Challenging Role of the UN Secretary-General, 1993; also articles. Served with AUS, 1942-45. Grantee Social Sci. Research Council, 1951, 54, 64; Fulbright scholar France and N. Africa, 1956-57 Fellow Middle East Studies Assn.; mem. Internat. Studies Assn. (pres. Middle Atlantic region 1978-80), Am. Polit. Sci. Assn., Acad. Coun. on UN System (vice chair 1990-91). Office: CUNY Grad Ctr 365 5th Ave New York NY 10016-4334 Office Phone: 212-817-2100. E-mail: brivlin@gc.cuny.edu.

RIVLIN, GARY, writer, reporter; b. NYC, June 20, 1958; s. Kenneth and Naomi Rivlin. Staff writer Chgo. Reader, 1985—89; reporter Conta Costa Times, 1990—91; editor East Bay Express, 1999; sr. writer & editor Industry Standard, 2000—01; contbg. editor Wired mag., 2001—04; tech. reporter NYTimes, 2004—. Author: Fire on the Prairie, 1992 (Nonfiction Book of the Yr., Chgo. Tribune, 1992, Carl Sandburg award, 1992), Drive-By, 1995 (one of NY Times' notable books of the yr., 1995, non-fiction book of yr. finalist, San Francisco Bay Area Book Reviewers Assn., 1995, non-fiction finalist for Pen-WEST Best of West, 1995), The Plot to Get Bill Gates, 1999, The Godfather of Silicon Valley, 2001; contbr. to magazines such as NY Times Magazine Newsweek, Fortune, The New Republic, Parada and GQ. Named best writer non-daily newspaper, Calif. Newspaper Pub. Assn., 1993; recipient print journalism prize, San Francisco Bay Area Media Alliance, 1993, Best Enterprise reporting award, Soc. Profl. Journalists, 1993, Gold Medallion award, Calif. Bar Assn.,

1996, Gerald Loeb award for disting. bus. & fin. journalism in the mag. category, 2001, Gerald Loeb award, 2005. Office: New York Times 201 Spear St San Francisco CA 94105 Office Phone: 415-836-6700. Business E-Mail: rivlin@nytimes.com.

RIVLIN, RACHEL, lawyer; b. Bangor, Maine, Sept. 1, 1945; d. Lawrence and A. Sara (Rich) Lait. BA, U. Maine, 1965; MA, U. Louisville, 1968; JD, Boston Coll., 1977. Bar: Mass. 1977, U.S. Dist. Ct. Mass. 1978, U.S. Ct. Appeals (1st cir.) 1983, U.S. Supreme Ct. 1985. Audiologist Boston City Hosp., 1969-72; dir. audiology Beth Israel Hosp., Boston, 1972-74; atty. Legal Sys. Devel., Boston, 1977-78, Liberty Mut. Ins., Boston, 1978-82; counsel, sec. Lexington Ins. Co., Boston, 1982-85, v.p., assoc. gen. counsel, sec., 1985—. Mem. task force fin. literacy students U.S. Bankruptcy Ct. and Boston Bar Assn., 2004—05. Mem. civil rights com. Anti-Defamation League, Boston, 1982—2005; bd. dirs. Dance Art, Inc., Boston, 1985—92. Mem.: ABA (mem. ins. regulation com. 1980, vice chair internat. ins. law com. 1983—84, internat. ins. law com. 1985—86, sr. vice chair nat. inst. insurer insolvency 1987—88, sr. vice chair pub. regulation of ins. 1987—90, nat. inst. reins. collections and insolvency 1988, chair excess surplus lines and resins. com. 1988—89, nat. inst. insurer insolvency 1989, internat. ins. law com. 1997—2005, task force ins. and corp. counsel interests and involvement 1999—2003, vice chair corp. counsel com. 2003—07), Boston Bar Assn. (mem. coun. 1983—86, chmn. corp. counsel 1987, steering com. corp. bus. law and fin. sect. 1987—89, chmn. ins. law. com. 1987—90, nominating com. 1988, edn. com. 1989, 1990—91, chmn. ins. com. 1990—93, ethics com. 1993—2005, edn. com. 1994, multi-disciplinary practice task force 2000—02, comprehensive revision Mass. corp. law 2000—02, mem. coun. 2002—05, edn. com. 2003, mem. task force fin. literacy students 2004—05), Boston Coll. Law Sch. Alumni Assn. (ann. fund com. 1981—89, chmn. telethon com. 1989—94, nominating com. 1990, search com. for dean 1993, search com. for law sch. fund dir. 1993, leadership gifts exec. com. 1994—98, search com. for dir. instl. advancement 1995, reunion com. 2002, Father James Malley award 1996). Office Phone: 941-870-3326. Business E-Mail: rachelrivlin@aol.com.

RIVLIN, RICHARD SAUL, internist; b. Forest Hills, NY, May 15, 1934; s. Harry Nathaniel and Eugenie (Graciany) R.; m. Barbara Melinda Pogul, Aug. 28, 1960 (div.); children: Kenneth Stewart, Claire Phyllis; m. Rita Klausner, Feb. 29, 1976; children: Michelle Elizabeth, Daniel Elliott. AB cum laude in Biochem. Scis., Harvard U., 1955, MD cum laude, 1959. Diplomate Am. Bd. Internal Medicine. Intern Bellevue Hosp., NYC, 1959-60; asst. resident medicine Johns Hopkins U. Hosp., Balt., 1960-61, 1963—64; fellow dept. physiol. chemistry, medicine Johns Hopkins U. Sch. Medicine, 1964-66, lectr. clin. medicine, 1965-66; clin. assoc. endocrinology br. Nat. Cancer Inst., NIH, Bethesda, Md., 1961-63; assoc. in medicine Columbia U. Coll. Physicians and Surgeons, NYC, 1966-67, asst. prof. medicine, 1967-71, assoc. prof. medicine, 1971-79; mem. Inst. Human Nutrition, 1972-79; chief endocrinology, asst. physician Francis Delafield Hosp., NYC, 1966-75; asst. physician Presbyterian Hosp., NYC, 1966-73, assoc. attending physician, 1973-79; chief nutrition service Meml. Sloan-Kettering Cancer Ctr., NYC, 1979-90; prof. medicine Cornell U. Med. Coll., 1979—; chief div. nutrition dept. medicine NY Hosp. -Cornell Med. Ctr., 1979—2001; NIH Nutrition Study Sec., 2000—02; vis. prof. Creighton U., 1974, U. Guadalajara, Mexico, 1974, NJ Coll. Medicine, East Orange VA Hosp., 1974, 1976, 1983; Upjohn vis. prof. in nutrition Med. Coll. Ga., 1976; vis. prof. Syracuse U., 1980; Nat. Dairy Coun. vis. prof. in nutrition U. Mich., Ann Arbor, 1982; vis. prof. Washington U.-Jewish Hosp., St. Louis, 1983; external examiner in physiology Calcutta U., India; prin. investigator VIH clin. nutrition rsch. unit Strang Cancer Rsch. Lab., NYC, 1980—, dir. Anne Fisher Nutrition Ctr., 2004—; sr. v.p. med. affairs, Naylor-Dana chair in nutrition Inst. Cancer Prevention, NYC, 2001—04; vis. prof. UCLA, 2000, Emory U., 2002, Purdue U., 2002. Sydenstricker lectr. Med. Coll. Ga., 1989; mem. rsch. program oversight com. Am. Inst. Cancer Rsch., 1995—, chmn., 2006- Editor: Riboflavin, 1975; referee numerous profl. jours.; contbr. articles to profl. jours. Served with USPHS, 1961-63. Recipient Grace A. Goldsmith Lectr. award Am. Coll. Nutrition, 1981, Lifetime Achievement award, 2001. Fellow ACP, AAAS; mem. Am. Soc. Nutrition (v.p. 1992-93, pres. 1993-94), Am. Fedn. Clin. Rsch., Endocrine Soc., Am. Thyroid Assn., Am. Physiol. Soc., Am. Soc. Clin. Investigation, Soc. Exptl. Biology and Medicine. Home: 30 Farragut Rd Scarsdale NY 10583-7206 Office: Strang Cancer Prevention Ctr Weill Cornell Med Coll 428 E 72 St Ste 600 New York NY 10021

RIZK, MAGED, cardiologist, researcher; b. Cairo, Apr. 12, 1961; s. Mostafa Rizk; m. Magda Rashad, May 25, 1992; children: Ahmed, Rahma. MD, Ain Shams U., 1985; PhD in Pharmacology and Toxicology, U. Medicine and Dentistry NJ, 1992. Cert. Am. Bd. Internal Medicine, 1996, ABIM Bd. Cert. in Cardiology 2000, Bd. Cert. in Echocardiography 2001. Instr., dept. medicine NY Med. Coll., Valhalla, NY, 1995—97, cardiology fellow, 1997—2000; asst. prof. cardiology St. Louis U., 2000—01; cardiology cons. Cardiovascular Cons., PC, Sterling Heights, Mich., 2001; dir. noninvasive cardiology St. John Macomb Hosp., 2006. Pres. Grad. Student Assn. UMDNJ, Newark, 1990—91; instr. of medicine NY Med. Coll., Valhalla, 1995—96; pres., CEO Medcom Am. Inc., Elmsford, NY, 1995—97; dir. Cardiology So. Ill., Herrin, 2000—01. Doctorate fellowship, UMDNJ, 1987. Mem.: ACP, Am. Soc. Nuc. Cardiology, Am. Soc. Echocardiography, Am. Heart Assn., Am. Assn. Univ. Profs., Am. Coll. Cardiology. Achievements include patents for Anticoagulant effect of aspirin and salicylamide, 1992. Avocation: tennis. Office: Cardiovascular Cons PC 37771 Schoenherr Ste 101 Sterling Heights MI 48312 Home: 2221 Custer Dr Troy MI 48085-6728 Office Phone: 586-274-2450. Personal E-mail: maged@sbcglobal.net.

RIZK, TOUFIC ASSAAD, vascular surgeon; b. Beirut, Nov. 8, 1960; arrived in US, 1979; s. Assaad Toufic and Colette Rizk; m. Anne Jacquinot, Sept. 29, 1990; children: Nina, Michael, Emma, Catherine. French Baccalaureat, Coll. Stanislas, Paris, 1978; BS in Biology magna cum laude, Syracuse U., NY, 1982; MD, SUNY, Syracuse, 1986. Diplomate Nat. Bd. Med. Examiners, Am. Bd. Surgery in gen. and vascular surgery. Resident in gen. surgery Guthrie Clinic, Sayre, Pa., 1991; rsch. fellow Albany Med. Ctr., NY, 1993; fellow in vascular surgery SUNY, Buffalo, 1994; attending surgeon Rochester Vascular Surgery Assocs., NY, 1994—2001, Rochester Vascular Surgery Assn., NY, 2003—, Rizk Hosp., Beirut, 2001—03. Mem.-at-large med. exec. com. Unity Hosp., Rochester, 2005—; lectr. in field. Contbr. articles to profl. jours. Mem. parish coun. Queen of Peace Ch., Rochester, 2005—. Recipient Stanley Conklin award, Guthrie Clinic, Sayre, Pa., 1989; postdoctoral rsch. fellow, NIH, 1991—93. Fellow: ACS; mem.: Soc. Clin. Vascular Surgery, Ea. Vascular Soc. Roman Catholic. Avocations: reading, sailing, skiing, walking, music. Office: Rochester Vascular Surgery Assocs 3525 Buffalo Rd Rochester NY 14624 Personal E-mail: rizk56@hotmail.com.

RIZOWY, CARLOS GUILLERMO, lawyer, educator, political analyst; b. Sarandi Grande, Uruguay, Mar. 5, 1949; arrived in U.S., 1973, naturalized, 1981; s. Gerszon and Eva (Visnia) R.; m. Charlotte Gordon, Mar. 14, 1976; children: Brian Isaac, Yael Deborah, Michal Evie. BA, Hebrew U., Jerusalem, 1971; MA, U. Chgo., 1975, PhD, 1981; JD, Chgo. Kent Coll. Law, Ill. Inst. Tech., 1983. Bar: Ill. 1983, U.S. Dist. Ct. (no. dist.) Ill. 1983, U.S. Ct. Appeals (7th cir.) 1983. Asst. prof. polit. sci. Roosevelt U., Chgo., 1982-89, chmn. dept. polit. sci., 1983-86, dir. internat. studies program, 1986-89; mng. ptnr. Ray, Rizowy & Fleischer, Chgo., 1983-90; ptnr. corp. law dept. Gottlieb and Schwartz, 1990-92; ptnr. Levenfeld, Eisenberg, Janger, Glassberg, Samotny & Halper, 1993-94; of counsel Sonnenschein, Nath & Rosenthal, 1994—2004; internat. bus. cons., 2004—. Hon. consul of Uruguay, Chgo., 1994—; adj. assoc. prof. Spertus Coll. Judaica, Chgo., 1984—; weekly polit. analyst on Mid. East, internat. law and fgn. policy, resource specialist Sta. WBEZ Pub. Radio and BBC L.Am.; mem. panel of arbitrators of Mediation and Arbitration Ctr., Internat. Arbitration Ct. for Mercosur Bolsa de Comercio, Uruguay, 1999—; gen. counsel Assn. Iberoamerican Consuls, 2003-; internat. bus. cons., 2004-; spkr. and presenter to CEOs on Am. fgn. policy. Author: May 17, Elections in Isreal, National Stragey Forum, 1999, Guidelines for US Mideast Policy, National Strategy Forum, 2001; co-editor: Latin American Business Cultures-Crossing Cultural Barriers, Prentice Hall, 2005; contbr. articles to profl. jours. V.p., resource specialist to exec. com. Orgn. Children of Holocaust Survivors, Chgo., 1982; pres. Assn. Children Holocaust Survivors, 1986-91; pres. bd. dirs. Soviet Jewry Legal Advocacy Ctr., 1986-88; rsch. com. Nat. Strategy Forum, bd. dirs. UN Assn. U.S., 1985-89; cmty. rels. com. Jewish Fedn. Met. Chgo., 1983-84; adv. bd., chmn. internat. affairs commn. Am. Jewish Congress, Chgo., 1983-85, chmn. subcom. for Israel, 1986-88; mem. Nat. Spkrs. Bur. United Jewish Appeal, Nat. Spkrs. Bur. Devel. Corp. for Israel; spkr. to CEOs The Exec. Com., 1980-; adv. bd. Chgo. Action for Soviet Jewry, 1983-85; bd. dirs. Am. Friends of Hebrew U., Chgo., 1984-86, Florence Heller Jewish Cmty. Ctr., 1986-88; human rights com. Anti-Defamation League, 1986, bd. dirs., 1989—; bd. dirs. Bd. Jewish Edn., 1989-91, Hispanic Coalition for Jobs, 1991-94; chmn. univ. educators divsn. Jewish United Fund, 1988-90; consular corp. adv. bd. Internat. Vis. Ctr. Chgo., 1995—, com. fgn. affairs Chgo. Coun. Fgn. Rels., 1994—. Scholar Hebrew U., 1967-72, U. Chgo., 1972-78, Hillman Found., 1978, Peter Volid Found., 1980; recipient Globalist award Heritage Internat. Trade Assn., 1997. Mem. ATLA, ABA (chmn. bus. com. 1993-95), Assn. Ibero-Am. Consuls of Chgo., Ill. State Bar Assn., Chgo. Bar Assn. (internat. trade com.), Latin Am. Bar Assn., Nat. Hispanic Bar Assn., Am. Immigration Lawyers Assn., Am. Polit. Sci. Assn., Am. Judicature Soc., Exec. Club Chgo., Internat. Platform Assn., Wexner Heritage Found., Am. Forum, Latin Am. C. of C. (bd. dirs. 1991—, gen. counsel 1992—), Anshe Emet Congregation, Masons. Office Phone: 312-371-5531. Personal E-mail: crizowy49@hotmail.com.

RIZZELLO, JOSEPH SAMUEL, stock exchange executive; b. Phila., Mar. 5, 1947; s. Samuel Joseph and Helen (Calabree) R.; m. Daria Catherine Sawicky; children: Damien Joseph, Justin Michael, Marcus Samuel. Ops. mgr. Drexel Burnham, Phila., 1970-74; asst. v.p. ops. and sales Thomson McKinnon Securities, Phila., 1974-80, v.p., br. mgr., 1980-85; sr. v.p. mktg. Phila. Stock Exchange, 1985-89, exec. v.p. bus. devel. mktg., new product devel., 1994—98; pres. Phila Bd. Trade subs. Phila. Stock Exchange, 1989; principal Vanguard Brokerage Services, Malvern, Pa., 1998—2000; mng. dir., mem. exec. com. Pershing LLC, 2001; pres. Pershing Trading Co.; bd. dirs. NSX Holdings, Inc., Chgo., 2002—04, special advisor to CEO and bd. dirs., 2004—06, chmn., 2006—; CEO Nat. Stock Exchange, 2006—. Bd. dirs. Internat. Cons. and Investment Techs., Inc., Calif., Found. for Rsch. Internat. Banking and Fin., Calif. With U. S. Army, 1966-67. Mem. Nat. Futures Assn. (bd. dirs. 1989—), Investment Traders Assn. Phila. (bd. dirs. 1987—). Roman Catholic. Office: NSX Holdings 440 S LaSalle St Ste 2600 Chicago IL 60605 *

RIZZETTA, DONALD P., aerospace engineer; s. Pasquale C. and Dora Rizzetta. BS in Aviation, We. Mich. U., Kalamazoo, 1962—66; MS in Aeronautics and Astronautics, Purdue U., W.Lafayette, 1966—69; PhD in Aeronautical and Astron. Engring., Ohio State U., Columbus, 1970—76. Design engr. Pratt & Whitney Aircraft, W.Palm Beach, Fla., 1969—70; grad. rsch. assoc. Ohio State U., Columbus, 1970—76; vis. scientist Air Force Flight Dynamics Lab., Wright-Patterson AFB, Ohio, 1976—77; sr. specialist engr. Boeing Mil. Airplane Co., Seattle, 1977—82; sr. rsch. aerospace engr. Air Force Rsch. Lab., Wright-Patterson AFB, Ohio, 1982—. Fellow: AIAA (assoc.). Office: USAF 2210 Eighth St Wright Patterson Afb OH 45433-7512 Business E-Mail: donald.rizzetta@wpafb.af.mil.

RIZZI, JOSEPH VITO, banker; b. Berwyn, Ill., Dec. 5, 1949; s. Joseph and Mary Catherine (Mancini) R.; m. Candace Kunz, June 24, 1972; children: Jennifer, Joseph, Sammantha. BS in Commerce summa cum laude, DePaul U., 1971; MBA, U. Chgo., 1973; JD magna cum laude, U. Notre Dame, 1976. Bar: Ill. 1976. Law clk. to judge US Dist. Ct. (no. dist.) Ill., 1976—77; exec. v.p. T.B.R. Enterprises, Inc., Downers Grove, Ill., 1977—83; mng. dir. ABN AMRO, NYC, 1983—. Mem. Delta Epsilon Sigma. Roman Catholic. Home: 287 Bartram Rd Riverside IL 60546-1886 Office: ABN AMRO Bank 135 S LaSalle St Chicago IL 60661 Office Phone: 312-904-6366. Business E-Mail: joe.rizzi@abnamro.com.

RIZZO, CHRISTIE J., psychologist; b. Dorchester, Mass., June 14, 1977; d. Ronald C. Rizzo and Deborah J. Gorman-Sprague. BA, Barnard Coll., NYC, 1999; PhD, U. So. Calif., LA, 2000—05. Lic. psychologist Rhode Island. Predoctoral psychology internship McLean Hosp., Harvard Med. Sch., Belmont, Mass., 2004—05; postdoctoral rsch. assoc. Brown Med. Sch., Providence, 2005—. Contbr. articles to profl. jours. Recipient Tchg. Asst. Mentor award, U. So. Calif., 2003; grantee 5-Yr. Coll. Merit fellowship, 2000, Wallis Annenberg fellowship, Annenberg Family, U. So. Calif., 2002. Mem.: APA, Soc. Clin. Child & Adolescent Psychology, Soc. Rsch. Adolescence, Assn. Behavior and Cognitive Therapies, Soc. Sci. Clin. Psychology, Phi Kappa Phi. Achievements include research in national institutes of health pediatric loan repayment program. Office: Brown Med Sch DPHB Box G 5121 8 Providence RI 02906 Business E-Mail: christie_rizzo@brown.edu.

RIZZO, JEFFREY F., corporate financial executive; BA in Econ., Fairfield U., Conn.; post grad. studies, NYU, NYC. Mng. dir. pub. fin. dept. Moody's Investors Svc., NYC, 1976—95; dir. fin. Met. Transportation Authority, NYC, 1995—97; mgmt. cons. NYC, 1997—2000; controller Marble Collegiate Ch., NYC, 2001—04; v.p. fin. and adminstrn., CFO Cmty. Svc. Soc. NY, NYC, 2004—. Mem. Calif. Debt & Investment Adv. Com., Mcpl. Analysts Group, NY, Nat. Coun. Pub.-Pvt. Partnerships, US Conf. Mayors, All Am. Mcpl. Analysts Team. Bd. treas. United Charities, Friends of R.S.V.P.; mem. Mayors Leadership Inst. Mem.: Nat. Fedn. Mcpl. Analysts, Govt. Fin. Officers Assn.

RIZZO, JOHN ANTHONY, lawyer; b. 1947; BA, Brown U., 1969; JD, George Washington U., 1972. Bar: 1973. Acting gen. counsel CIA, Washington, 2004—. Office: Office of General Counsel Central Intelligence Agy Washington DC 20505 Office Phone: 703-482-1951.

RIZZO, RONALD STEPHEN, lawyer; b. Kenosha, Wis., July 15, 1941; s. Frank Emmanuel and Rosalie (Lo Cicero); m. Mary Rizzo; children: Ronald Stephen Jr., Michael Robert. BA, St. Norbert Coll., 1963; JD, Georgetown U., 1965, LLM in Taxation, 1966. Bar: Wis. 1965, Calif. 1967, Ill. 1999. Assoc. Kindel & Anderson, LA, 1966-71, ptnr., 1971-86, Jones & Day, LA, 1986—93, Chgo., 1993—2004, of counsel, 2005—. Bd. dirs. Guy LoCicero & Son Inc., Kenosha, Bristol Oaks Country Club Enterprises, Bristol, Wis. Contbg. editor ERISA Litigation Reporter, 1994-99; mem. internat. adv. editl. bd. Jour. Pensions Mgmt. and Mktg. Schulte zur Hausen fellow Inst. Internat. and Fgn. Trade Law, Georgetown U., 1966. Fellow Am. Coll. Tax Counsel, Am. Coll. Employee Benefits Counsel (charter); mem. ABA (chmn. com. on employee benefits sect. on taxation 1988-89, vice chair com. on govt. submissions 1995-99), Los Angeles County Bar Assn. (chmn. com. on employee benefits sect. on taxation 1977-79, exec. com. 1977-78, 90-92), State Bar Calif. (co-chmn. com. on employee benefits sect. on taxation 1980), West Pension Conf. (steering com. L.A. chpt. 1980-83). Avocations: reading, golf, travel. Home: 1040 N Lake Shore Dr #19C Chicago IL 60611-6164 Office: Jones Day 77 W Wacker Ste 3500 Chicago IL 60601-1692 Home Phone: 312-415-1941; Office Phone: 312-269-1568. Business E-Mail: rsrizzo@jonesday.com.

RIZZO, STEPHEN WAYNE BURTON, secondary school educator, music minister; s. Fredrick Stephen and Betty Burton Rizzo; m. Kristi Lynn Longsworth; children: Olivia Lynnea, Nicholas Stephen Martin. BA in Music, Jacksonville State U., Ala., 1987; MA in Edn. in English, U. Ala., Birmingham, 1989; MusM, Samford U., Birmingham, 1997. Instr., devel. studies dept. chair Bevill State C.C., Sumiton, Ala., 1995—. Mem. ministerial staff Living Water Cmty. Ch. of God, Fultondale, Ala., 2005—. Editor: (newsletter) Music in Ministry; contbr. articles to profl. jours. and presentations. Vol. Am. Cancer Soc., Sumiton, Ala., 2002—05; mem. state music com. Ch. of God, Birmingham, 1986—95. Recipient Svc. award, Warrior River Chpt., SAR, 2002. NEA, Ala. Edn. Assn., Internat. Trumpet Guild, Music Tchrs. Nat. Assn., Music Educators Nat. Conf., Nat. Assn. Devel. Edn., Contessa Entellina Heritage Assn. (New Orleans), Order Sons of Italy in Am., Italian-Am. Progressive Lodge. Conservative. Mem. Church Of God. Achievements include research in the relationship between types/learning styles and developmental placement of rural two-year college students. Avocation: genealogy. Home: PO Box 1408 Sumiton AL 35148 Office: Bevill State CC PO Box 800 101 State St Sumiton AL 35148 Home Phone: 205-648-2380.

RIZZUTO, KATHERINE, publishing executive; married; 3 children. B, Rutgers Coll., New Brunswick, NJ. Advt. dir. Fitness, v.p.; assoc. pub. Brides Condé Nast, 1997—2000, pub. Brides, Modern Bride, Elegant Bride and Your Prom, 2006—; v.p., pub. Marie Claire, 2000—04, Radar and Radaronline.com, 2004—06. Office: Brides Conde Nast 750 Third Ave 4th Fl New York NY 10017 Office Phone: 212-630-3976. E-mail: Katherine_Rizzuto@condenast.com. *

RO, WON WOO, engineering educator, researcher; b. Daegu, Republic of Korea, Mar. 2, 1972; permanent resident, 2003; s. Il Young Ro and Kwang Soon Park; m. Yun Jung Kim, Dec. 22, 2001; 1 child, Avery Jaehee. PhD, U. So. Calif., LA, 2004. Asst. prof. Calif. State U., Northridge, 2004—. Contract software engr. ARM Inc. Mem.: ASEE, IEEE, KSEA. Office: Calif State Univ ECE Dept 18111 Nordhoff St Northridge CA 91330 Home Phone: 323-206-1740; Office Phone: 818-677-7002.

ROACH, ADRIENNE J., lawyer; b. London, Ohio, Nov. 30, 1971; BA, U. Richmond, 1993; JD, U. Cin. Coll. Law, 1996. Bar: Ohio 1996, Ky. 1998. Ptnr. Keating Muething & Klekamp PLL, Cin. Mentor Oyler Elem. Sch., Help One Student to Succeed Prog.; mem., Bd. Dirs. Art Machine, Inc. Named one of Ohio's Rising Stars, Super Lawyers, 2005, 2006. Fellow: Cin. Acad. Leadership for Lawyers; mem.: Ohio State Bar Assn. (Family Law Sect.), Northern Ky. Bar Assn., Northern Ky. Collaborative Grp., Inc., Ky. Bar Assn. (Family. Law Sect.), Collaborative Family Lawyers Cin., Cin. Bar Found. (trustee 2006—), Cin. Bar Assn. (sec. 2002—04, CLE chair 2004—06, vice chair, Domestic Rels. Com. 2004—06, chairperson, Domestic Rels. Com. 2006—), ABA (Family Law Sect.). Office: Keating Muething & Klekamp PLL One E Fourth St Ste 1400 Cincinnati OH 45202 Office Phone: 513-579-6400. Office Fax: 513-579-6457.

ROACH, CAROLE HYDE, music educator; d. Clyde Eugene Hyde and Mary Evelyn Springer; m. Samuel Frederick Roach, Nov. 14, 1970. BMus, Ga. State U., 1962; MusM, Fla. State U., 1963; postgrad., U. Ga., 1974. Nat. cert. voice and piano Tchrs. Nat. Assn., 1974, cert. piano & voice Music Tchrs. Nat. Assn., 1985. Voice & piano tchr. Mary Hardin-Baylor Coll., Belton, Tex., 1964—65, Kennesaw State U., Ga., 1967—70, Perimeter Coll., Decatur, Ga., 1970—71; choral dir. Jerusalem Ave. Jr. HS, North Bellmore, NY, 1965—67; choir dir. Ch. of Ascension, Cartersville, Ga., 1993—96, St. Teresa's Episcopal Ch., Acworth, Ga., 2000—; mezzo-soprano soloist Peachtree Presbyterian, Atlanta, 1967—84, Peachtree Meth., Atlanta, 1984—86. Soloist Fletcher Wolfe Chorale, Atlanta, 1968—71, state vocal auditions chmn., 2003, Atlanta, 04; soloist Atlanta Chamber Opera, 1968—71; musical dir. Canton Theatre, Canton, Ga., 2004. Actress: Gooch (Best Supporting Actress, 1991); Bloody Mary (Best Supporting Actress, 1995); dir.: Fantasticks (Best Dir., 1998), Lend Me a Tenor (Best Dir., 1999), I Hate Hamlet (Best Dir., 2000). Pres., treas. Pumphouse Players, Cartersville, Ga., 1990—2003. Mem.: Music Tchrs. Nat. Assn., Ga. Music Tchrs. Assn., Greater Marietta Music Tchrs. Assn. (pres. 2003—), Cobb County Music Tchrs. Assn. (pres. 1975—76, state chair for vocal auditions). Democrat. Episcopalian. Avocations: theater, travel, dog breeding, dog showing, dog rescue. Office: Music Acad So Keyboards 1898-B Leland Dr Marietta GA 30067

ROACH, DANIEL T., JR., (TAD ROACH), headmaster; BA, Williams Coll.; MA, Middlebury Coll. English teacher, dorm parent, and coach in 1979 St. Andrew's Sch., Middletown, Del., 1979—84, various positions including dean of students, asst. headmaster for student life, academic dean, and asst. headmaster for academic affairs, 1984—97, headmaster, 1997—. Mem. bd. trustees St. Andrew's Sch. Office: St Andrew's Sch 350 Noxontown Rd Middletown DE 19709-1605 Office Phone: 302-378-9511. Office Fax: 302-378-7120. *

ROACH, JAMES CLARK, federal agency administrator; b. Charleston, W. Va., Sept. 29, 1943; m. Susan Roelke Roach, June 27, 1970; children: Edward J., Andrew A. BA in Social Studies and History, W. Va. Wesleyan Coll., 1965; MA in Am. History, W. Va. U. Historian Harpers Ferry (W. Va.) Nat. Hist. Pk., 1967-68, 70-72; chief interpretation resource mgmt. Ft. Frederica Nat. Monument, St. Simons Island, Ga., 1972-74; asst. chief interpretation visitor svcs. Colonial Nat. Hist. Pk., Yorktown, Va., asst. chief interpretation, visitor svc. Jamestown, Va.; chief interpretation visitor svcs. Gettysburg (Pa.) Nat. Mil. Pk., Eisenhower Nat. Hist. Site, 1981-94; site mgr. Eisenhower Nat. Hist. Site, 1995—2001; sch.-to-work coord. Adams County Bus. Edn. Partnership, Gettysburg, Pa., 2001—. Sec., past bd. dirs. Gettysburg Peace Celebration Commn. Inc.; sec. Adams County Econ. Edn. Found.; vice chair Blue and Grey dist. coms. York Adams coun. Boy Scouts Am.; bd. dirs. Adams County Hist. Soc. With US Army, 1968—70, Vietnam. Recipient Freeman Tilden award Mid-Atlantic Region Interpreter of Yr., 1984, Ea. Superior Performance award Nat. Park and Monument Assn., 1985, Spl. Events award GETT Travel Coun. award, 1986, 87. Mem. Assn. Nat. Pk. Rangers, Lincoln Fellowship Pa. (sec., past pres.), Adams County Torch Club (past pres.), Rotary (bd. dirs. Gettysburg club). Lutheran. Avocations: gardening, reading, fishing, stamp collecting/philately. Home: 84 Knoxlyn Orrtanna Rd Gettysburg PA 17325-7215 Office: Adams County Bus Edn Partnership 18 Carlisle St Ste 203 Gettysburg PA 17325 Office Phone: 717-338-0861. Business E-Mail: acbep@gettysburg-chamber.org.

ROACH, JAMES ROBERT, retired political science professor; b. Rock Rapids, Iowa, Aug. 25, 1922; s. Paul Ramsey and Doris (Kline) R. BA, U. Iowa, 1943; AM, Harvard U., 1948, PhD, 1950. Mem. faculty, adminstrn. U. Tex., Austin, 1949—, prof. govt., 1965-95, prof. emeritus, 1995—, dir. spl. programs, 1965-69, vice provost, dean interdisciplinary programs, 1971-72, dean divsn. gen. and comparative studies, 1972-74; counselor for cultural affairs Am. embassy, New Delhi, 1974-78. Fulbright vis. lectr. polit. sci. Rajasthan U., India, 1961-62; mem. bd. Fgn. Scholarships, 1965-74, chmn., 1969-71; mem. U.S. Commn. for UNESCO, 1966-69.

With USNR, 1943-46. Fulbright rsch. grantee, Australia, 1951-52, Ford Found. fgn. fellow, India, 1956-57. Mem. Phi Beta Kappa, Kappa Tau Alpha, Phi Kappa Psi. Democrat. Congregationalist. Home: 8604 Dorotha Ct Austin TX 78759-8113

ROACH, JAMES W., orthopedist, surgeon; b. Norfolk, Va., Mar. 22, 1947; s. James W. and Evelyn N. Roach; m. Elizabeth T. Schwarz, May 19, 1973; children: Sarah Todd, Mary Lowe. BA in Chemistry, Tex. Tech. U., 1965—70; MD, Georgetown U., Washington, 1974; MBA, Duke U., Durham, NC, 2001. Lic. Am. Bd. Orthop. Surgery, 1979. Intern Tripler Army Med. Ctr., 1974—75, resident, 1975—78; fellow Tex. Scottish Rite Hosp., Dallas, 1980—81, asst. chief staff, 1985—93; dir. orthops. Cook Children's Med. Ctr., Fort Worth, 1993—2001; chief staff Shriners Hosp. Children, Intermountain, Salt Lake City, 2001—. Assoc. clin. prof. orthop. surgery U. Tex. S.W. Med. Ctr., Dallas, 1988—2001; bd. examiner Am. Bd. Orthop. Surgery, 1989—90, 1992, 95; prof. orthops. U. Utah Sch. Medicine, Salt Lake City, 2001—. Maj. US Army, 1979—80. Mem.: AMA, Am. Orthop. Assn., Scoiliosis Rsch. Soc., Am. Acad. Orthop. Surgeons, Pediatric Soc. N.Am. (treas. 2003, chmn. edn. coun. 2002—), Alpha Omega Med. Scholastic Hon. Frat. Office Phone: 801-536-3600.

ROACH, JOHN C., state supreme court justice; b. Frankfort, Ky., 1967; m. Maria Roach; 3 children. BA, Washington & Lee Univ.; JD with high distinction, Univ. Ky. Bar: Ky. Supreme Ct., Kentucky Ct. of Appeals, US Ct. of Appeals (6th Cir.). Law clk. to Hon. Pierce Lively, sr. judge US Ct. Appeals (6th cir.); atty. Akin Gump Strauss Hauer & Feld LLP, Washington; ptnr. Ransdell Roach & Wier PLLC, Lexington, Ky., 1996—2001; gen. counsel to gov. State of Ky., 2001—05; assoc. justice Ky. Supreme Ct., 2005—. Articles editor Kentucky Law Jour. Office: Ky Supreme Ct Ste 200 155 E Main St Lexington KY 40507-1332 Office Phone: 859-246-2220. *

ROACH, JOHN D., building products company executive; b. West Palm Beach, Fla., Dec. 3, 1943; s. Benjamin Browning and Margaret (York) R.; m. Dec. 29, 1967 (div. Aug. 1981); children: Vanessa, Alexandra; m. Betty Lou (Elizabeth Louise) Phillips, Aug. 28, 1982; children: Bruce Phillips, Bryce Phillips, Brian Phillips. BS in Indsl. Mgmt., MIT, 1965; MBA, Stanford U., 1967. Dir. mgmt. acctg. and info. sys. Ventura divsn. Northrop Corp., Thousand Oaks, Calif., 1967—70; co-founder, mgr. Northrop Venture Capital, Century City, Calif., 1970—71; v.p., dir. Boston Consulting Group, Boston and Menlo Park, Calif., 1971—80; v.p., world-wide strategic mgmt. practice mng. officer Booz, Allen, Hamilton, San Francisco, 1980—82, Houston, 1982—83; vice chmn., mng. dir. Braxton Assocs., Houston, 1983—87; sr. v.p., CFO Manville Corp., Denver, 1987—88, exec. v.p. ops., 1988-91; pres. Manville Bldg. Products Group, Denver, 1988-90, Manville Mining and Minerals Group, Denver, 1990-91, Celite Corp., Denver, 1990-91; chmn., pres., CEO Fibreboard Corp., Walnut Creek, Calif., 1991—97, Stonegate Resources, Dallas, 1997—2001; founder, chmn., pres., CEO Builders FirstSource, Inc., Dallas, 1998—2001; chmn., CEO Stonegate Internat., Dallas, 2001—; chmn. Unidare U.S., Muskogee, Okla., 2002—06. Bd. dirs. PMI Group, Kaiser Aluminum, URS Corp., Mat. Scis., NCI Bldg. Systems, Wash. Internat., Am. Stock Exch., Thompson PBE, Magma Power, Fibreboard Corp., Builders First Source. Author: Strategic Management Handbook, 1983. Bd. dirs. Opera Colo., Denver, 1987-91, Bay Area Coun., San Francisco, 1991-96, Dallas Symphony, 1996-03, mem. exec. com., 1996-03; bd. trustees Alta Bates Med. Ctr.; mem. exec. com. San Francisco Opera Assn. Mem.: MIT Alumni Club, Stanford Grad. Sch. Bus. Club, Dallas Country Club, Cordillera Country Club (Colo.), Beaver Creek (Colo.) Country Club, Red Sky Golf Club (Wolcott, Colo.), Preston Trail Golf Club (Dallas), Cherry Hills Country Club (Englewood, Colo.). Avocations: golf, skiing, hunting. Home: 4278 Bordeaux Ave Dallas TX 75205-3718 Office: Stonegate Internat 100 Crescent Ct 7th Fl Dallas TX 75201 Office Phone: 214-459-3460. Personal E-mail: johndcroach@aol.com.

ROACH, JOHN HENDEE, JR., bank and financial services executive, investment banker; b. NYC, Oct. 24, 1941; s. John Hendee and Julia (Casey) R.; m. Joan Hayden Muchmore, Sept. 23, 1972; children: Hayden, Cameron, John, Lauriston, Schuyler. BA, Washington and Jefferson Coll., 1964; postgrad., Aspen Inst., 1987, Harvard U., 1989. With Chem. Bank, NYC, 1968-71, sr. v.p. corp. bank, 1972-87, mng. dir. corp. fin., 1987-92, ret., 1992; sr. mng. dir., vice chmn. Geneva Cos., NYC, 1992-94; sr. mng. dir., client mgmt. and mktg. Am. Internat. Group, NYC, 1994-97; sr. mng. dir. Reliance Nat., NYC, 1998-99, JP Morgan Pvt. Bank, Greenwich, Conn., 2000—01, Jamison Prince Asset Mgmt., 2003—06; sr. mng. dir., head pvt. banking and wealth mgmt. Commerce Bank Pvt. Banking, Westchester, Conn., 2007—. Bd. dirs. Strategic Capital Resources Inc., Boca Raton, Fla., PrivaTechnologies, Arlington, Va., MBAs 4 N.Y.C. Capt. U.S. Army, 1964-66. Mem. Round Hill Club. Republican. Roman Catholic. Home: 16 Oakwood Ln Greenwich CT 06830-3909 Office: 3020 Westchester Ave Purchase NY 10577 Office Phone: 914-922-2820. E-mail: casey.roach@yesbank.com.

ROACH, JOHN VINSON, II, retail company executive; b. Stamford, Tex., Nov. 22, 1938; s. John V. and Agnes M. (Hanson) R.; m. Barbara Jean Wiggin, Mar. 31, 1960; children: Amy, Lori. BA in Physics and Math., Tex. Christian U., 1961, MBA, 1965. V.p. Radio Shack, 1972-75, Radio Shack Mfg., 1975-78; exec. v.p. Radio Shack, 1978-80; gen. mgr. data processing Tandy Corp., Ft. Worth, 1967-73, pres., from 1980, CEO, from 1981, chmn., 1982—99, Roach Enterprises, 1999—. Chmn. bd. Justin Ind., 1999—2001. Bd. dirs. Van Cliburn Found.; former chmn. bd. Tex. Christian U. Mem. Ft. Worth Club, City Club, Colonial Country Club. Office: 777 Taylor St PII-J Fort Worth TX 76102 Office Phone: 817-347-3214.

ROACH, JON GILBERT, lawyer; b. Knoxville, Tenn., June 17, 1944; s. Walter Davis and Lena Rose (Chapman) R.; m. Mintha Marie Evans, Oct. 22, 1977; children: Jon G., II, Evan Graham. BS, U. Tenn., 1967, JD, 1969. Bar: Tenn. 1970, D.C. 1981, U.S. Ct. Appeals (6th cir.); bd. cert. civil trial specialist, 2001. Assoc. Stone & Bozeman, Knoxville, 1970—71; pvt. practice Knoxville, 1971—75; delinquent tax atty. Sevier County, 1971—76; city atty., dir. of law City of Knoxville, 1976-83; ptnr. Peck, Shaffer & Williams, Knoxville, 1983-90, Watson, Hollow & Reeves, PLC, Knoxville, 1990—2005, Watson & Hollow, P.L.C., Knoxville, 2002—05, Watson, Roach, Batson, Rowell & Lauderback, P.L.C., 2005—. City atty. City of Plainview, 1999—, City of Maynardville, 2000—, City of Harrogate, 2007—; faculty Knoxville Bus. Coll., 1973-74; mem. Tenn. Commn. on Continuing Legal Edn. and Specialization of Tenn. Supreme Ct., 1995-2000. Hearing officer Civil Svc. Merit Bd., Knoxville, 2003-; mem. Tenn. Petroleum Underground Storage Tank, 2005—. Mem. ABA, Tenn. Bar Assn., Knoxville Bar Assn. (bd. govs., 2006—), D.C. Bar Assn., Internat. Mcpl. Lawyers Assn., Kiwanis (East Knoxville). Democrat. Baptist. Home: 722 Cheowa Cir Knoxville TN 37919-6676 Office: Watson Roach Batson Rowell & Lauderback PLC PO Box 131 1500 Riverview Tower Knoxville TN 37901-0131 Office Phone: 865-637-1700. E-mail: jroach@watsonroach.com.

ROACH, LONNIE CALVIN, social studies educator; b. Brewster, Wash., Aug. 3, 1951; s. Nolen Calvin and Berta Ellen (Lackey) Roach; m. Vickie Lynn Johnson, 1976 (div. Jan. 1994); children: Megan Bridget, Cameron Holt. BS in Edn., U. Ark., Fayetteville, 1972, MEd, 1978, EdS, 1987, EdD, 1995. Cert. global studies tchr., K-12 ESL tchr., K-12 curriculum specialist, 6-12 social studies tchr., tchr. trainer, K-12 gifted and talented tchr. Tchr. math. Huntsville Mid. Sch., Ark., 1973; photo collector Shiloh History Mus., Springdale, Ark., 1983—85; tchr. observer Ark. Dept. Edn.; job counselor U.S. Dept. Labor, Ark., 1990—95, Ark., 1997—98; gifted & talented/advanced placement tchr./facilitator Hunstville HS, 1987—2006, tchr. social studies, 1973—. Adj. prof. N. Ark. Coll., Harrison, 2004—06; mem. approval team U. Ark. Ark. Dept. Edn., 1998. Co-author: No Smoke, No Soot, No Clinkers, 1974; author: Arkansas in a Changing World: A Global Studies Historical Approach, 1986. Coord. Huntsville Centennial, 1977; chmn. Madison County Ark. Reps., Huntsville, 1984—86; commr. Madison County Ark. Election Commn., 1984—86; active Huntsville Ch. of Christ; co-founder AEA Dist. 10 Fed. Credit Union, Ark., 1977; pres. Hunstville Jaycees, 1980; chmn. scholarship com. Madison County Med. Mentors. Named Ark. HS Tchr. of Yr., VFW, 2000—01, Outstanding Young Man of Am., Am. Mensa, Ltd.; recipient Svc. award, Am. Legion, 1998. Mem.: Ark. Ret. Tchrs. Assn., Global Assn. Tchrs. Econs., Ark. Geog. Alliance. Republican. Avocations: history, genealogy, writing, sci. fiction, reading. Home: PO Box 134 635 Hwy 412B Huntsville AR 72740 Office: Huntsville Mid Sch 133 School Dr PO Box G Huntsville AR 72740 Office Phone: 479-738-6520.

ROACH, MARGARET, publishing executive; b. 1954; Editor., mgr. NY Times; garden columnist Newsday Newspapers; creative developer Martha Stewart Living Omnimedia, 1995; gardening editor Martha Stewart Living; mgr. devel. and execution marthastewart.com; editor-in-chief Martha Stewart Living, NYC, 2001—05, editl. dir., 2005—. Author: A Way to Garden, 1998 (Garden Writers Assn. Am. Best Book, 1998). Mailing: Martha Stewart Living 11 West 42nd St 25th Floor New York NY 10036 *

ROACH, MARGOT RUTH, retired biophysicist, educator; d. Robert Dickson and Katherine Roach; m. Franklyn St. Aubyn House, Dec. 20, 1994 (wid. Feb. 2000). B.Sc. in Math. and Physics with honors, U. N.B., Fredericton, Can., 1955; MD, C.M. cum laude, McGill U., Montreal, Can., 1959; PhD in Biophysics, U. Western Ont., Can., 1963; D.Sc. (hon.), U. N.B., St. John, Can., 1981. Jr. intern Victoria Hosp., London, Ont., Can., 1959-60, fellow in cardiology, 1962-63, asst. resident in medicine, 1963-64, Toronto Gen. Hosp., 1964-65; mem. faculty, dept. biophysics U. Western Ont., London, 1965—98, head dept. biophysics, 1970-78, prof., 1971-98, asst. prof. medicine, 1965-72, assoc. prof., 1972-78, prof., 1978-98, prof. emeritus Biophysics & Med., 1998. Mem. staff dept. medicine Victoria Hosp., 1967-72, U. Hosp., London, 1972-98; Commonwealth vis. sci., dept. applied math. theoretical physics Cambridge U., 1975; vis. sci. Bioengring. Inst., Chonqing U., People's Republic of China, 1991; mem. bioengring. grants com. Med. Rsch. Coun. Can., 1993-96; cons. and lectr. in field. Mem. editl. bd.: Imprints, 2003—06, Can. Jour. General Internal Medicine, 2007—. Active civic orgns. and coms. including Univ. Rsch. Coun., 1976-79; mem. interview bd. London Conf. of United Ch., 1967-90; steward United Ch. of Can., 1967-73, elder, 1973-82, mem. com. on ministry vocations, 2004-06, chair unified bd. Tatamagouche Pastoral Charge, 2001-07; chmn. stewardship devel. com. Colborne St. United Ch., 1990-93. Recipient A. Wilmer Duff prize in physics U. N.B., 1955, Cushing prize in pediatrics, 1959, Ciba Found. award for research in aging, 1959, Teaching award Faculty of Medicine U. Western Ont., 1990, Dean's award, 1997, Women of Distinction award YWCA, 1997; Med. Research Council fellow U. Western Ont., 1960-62, Arthur Guyton award Internat. Soc. Cardiovascular Medicine and Sci., 1997; numerous other fellowships and grants in medicine. Fellow Royal Coll. Physicians (Can.), Am. Coll. Cardiology (Young Investigator's award 1963); mem. Can. Physiol. Soc., Can. Cardiovascular Soc. (of council), Can. Clin. Investigation Soc. (council 1980-84), Can. Soc. Internal Medicine. Address: RR #1 104 Sea Shore Dr Tatamagouche NS Canada B0K 1V0 Personal E-mail: mroach@pchg.net.

ROACH, MAUREEN S., primary school educator; B, Boston U.; M, U. Mass. Primary sch. educator Lyndon Pilot Sch., West Roxbury, Mass. Presenter Nat. Bd. Insts.; mem. bd. dir. Nat. Bd. Profl. Tchg. Standards, 2005. Mem.: Nat. Bd. for Profl. Tchg. Stds. (bd. mem.). Avocations: cross country skiing, reading. Office: Patrick Lydon School 20 Mount Vernon St West Roxbury MA 02132-2809

ROACH, PAM, state legislator; m. Jim Roach; 5 children. BA in History, Brigham Young U., 1970. Mem. Wash. Legislature, Olympia, 1991—, mem. govtl. ops. and election com., mem. internat. trade and econ. devel. com., mem. ways and means com., mem. sentencing guidelines commn. Past mem. Gov.'s Juvenile Issues Task Force; mem. local coun. Boy Scouts Am.; past mem. adv. com.; founder, dir. Escuela de Esperenza; mem. Joint Com. Vets. and Mil. Affairs; mem. Sentencing Guidelines Commn. Mem. Wash. Policy Coun., Rotary. Republican. Office: 202 Irving Newhouse Bldg Olympia WA 98504-0001 also: PO Box 40431 Olympia WA 98504 Office Phone: 360-786-7660. Business E-Mail: roach-pam@leg.wa.gov.

ROACH, ROBERT MICHAEL, JR., (RANDY), lawyer; b. Bronxville, NY, May 27, 1955; s. Robert M. and Mary Dee R. BA, Georgetown U., 1977; JD, U. Tex., 1981. Bar: Tex. 1981, U.S. Dist. Ct. (so. dist.) Tex. 1982, U.S. Ct. Appeals (5th cir.) 1982, U.S. Dist. Ct. (we. dist.) Tex. 1984, U.S. Supreme Ct. 1986, U.S. Dist. Ct. (ea. dist.) 1986, U.S. Dist. Ct. (no. dist.) Tex. 1988. Assoc. Vinson & Elkins, Houston, 1981-83, Ryan & Marshall, Houston, 1983, Mayor, Day & Caldwell, Houston, 1983-88; ptnr. Mayor, Day, Caldwell & Keeton, Houston, 1989-93; founding ptnr. Cook & Roach LLP, Houston, 1993—; dir. appellate advocacy U. Houston Law Ctr., 1994—; adj. prof. U. Tex., 2000—; ptnr. RBS Napa Winery, 2000—. Adj. prof. law U. Houston, 1990-; lectr. continuing legal edn. U. Houston Law Ctr., 1989—; lectr. continuing legal edn. State Bar Tex., U. Tex., U. Houston, South Tex. Coll. Law, So. Meth. U., ABA; rschr., editor U.S. Senate Com. on Nutrition, 1975, 76, 77; rschr. U.S Supreme Ct., Washington, 1977; mem. Tex. Law Rev., 1979-81. Editor Def. Counsel Jour., 1990-93. Mem. Product Liability Adv. Coun., Internat. Assn. Def. Counsel, Fedn. Defense and Corp. Counsel, Def. Rsch. Inst., Tex. Assn. Def. Counsel, State Bar Tex. (appellate sect. chmn. 2006-07, chair of coun. chairs, grievance com., insurance section judicial liaison), Houston Bar Assn. (former chmn., appellate sect.), Meadowood of NAPA Valley, Coronado Club, Houston Racquet Club. Avocations: oenology, music, travel, tennis. Office: Cook & Roach LLP Heritage Plaza Ste 2650 1111 Bagby St Houston TX 77002-2543 Home Phone: 713-459-5550; Office Phone: 713-652-2032. Business E-Mail: rroach@cookroach.com.

ROACH, STEPHEN S., economist; B in Economics, U. Wis.; MA, NYU, 1970, PhD, 1973. Rsch. fellow Brookings Instn., Washington; with rsch. staff Fed. Reserve Bd., 1972—79; v.p. econ. analysis Morgan Guaranty Trust Co., NYC; with Morgan Stanley, NYC, 1982—, sr. economist, mng. dir., chief economist, dir. gloal econ. analysis NYC, chmn. Asia Hong Kong, 2007—. Contbr. articles to profl. jours. Recipient Grad. Sch. Arts and Sciences Alumni Achievement award, NYU, 2006. Mem.: NAS (com. study impact info. tech. on performance of service activities 1994). Office: Morgan Stanley 3 Exchange Sq 30th fl Central Hong Kong Office Phone: (852) 2848-5200. *

ROACH, SUSAN, literature educator; b. Ruston, La., Oct. 25, 1947; d. Max and Nell Colvin Roach. BA in English, La. Tech U., Ruston, 1969; MA in English, U. Ark., Fayetteville, 1971, PhA in English, 1973; PhD in Anthropology, U. Tex., Austin, 1986. From asst. prof. to prof. english La. Tech U., 1989—99, prof. english, 1999—. Folklorist La. Regional Folklife Program, Ruston, 1998—. Author (curator, editor): (exhibition and catalog) On My Way: The Arts of Sarah Albritton (Eli Kongas Maranda award Am. Folklore Soc. women's sect., 1999); author: (project dir., editor) The Louisiana Quilt Documentation Project; contbr. essays to anthologies. Mem. La. Folklife Commn., Baton Rouge, 1988—2007, chmn., 1993—2001; active Autrey Ho. Mus., Dubach, La., 1990—2007; pres. North Ctrl. La. Arts Coun., Ruston, La., 1988—90, 1996—99; mem. bd. La. Folklife Festival, Monroe, La., 1994—2005. Recipient Spl. Humanities award, La. Endowment Humanities, 1999; grantee, 1983—84, 1998—99, La. Divsn. Arts, 1983—84, 1998—2007. Mem.: Am. Folklore Soc. (co-chmn. program com. 2004—05). Avocations: tai chi, photography, reading. Office: La Regional Folklife Program La Tech Univ Ruston LA 71272 Home Phone: 318-255-4831; Office Phone: 318-257-2728. Office Fax: 318-257-4376. Business E-Mail: msroach@latech.edu.

ROACH, WESLEY LINVILLE, lawyer, insurance executive; b. Norlina, NC, Oct. 8, 1931; s. Joseph Franklin and Florence G. (Sink) R.; m. Mary Jon Gerald, Aug. 13, 1955; children: Gerald, Mary Virginia. BS, Wake Forest U., 1953, JD, 1955. Bar: N.C. 1955. With Pilot Life Ins. Co., Greensboro, NC, 1958-86, also bd. dirs.; sr. v.p., gen. counsel Jefferson-Pilot Life Ins. Co., Greensboro, 1986-88; sec. Great Ea. Lif. Ins. Co., 1975-85; of counsel Smith, Anderson, Blount, Dorsett, Mitchell & Jernigan, Attys. at Law, Raleigh, NC, 1988—. Former chmn. bd. dirs. N.C. Life and Accident and Health Ins. Guaranty Assn., Va. Life, Accident and Health Guaranty Assn., S.C. Life, Accident and Health Guaranty Assn.; sec. JP Investment Mgmt. Co., Jefferson-Pilot Equity Sales, Inc., Spl. Services Agy., Inc., 1974-84; mem. exec. com., bd. dirs. N.C. Ins. Edn. Found., 1978—; trustee In-Home Care, Inc., 1999—, chmn., 2001. Mem. fin. com. Greensboro United Fund, 1964-65; mem. fin. com. Greensboro 1st Bapt. Ch., 1963-66, 83-86, chmn., 1983-85, chmn. bd. deacons, 1974-76, 80-81; nat. chmn. alumni coun. coll. fund Wake Forest U., 1971-76, pres. nat. alumni coun., 1975-76, trustee univ., 1978-82, emeritus trustee, 1999—; trustee So. Bapt. Theol. Sem., Louisville, 1973-84; trustee Bapt. Retirement Homes N.C., Inc., 1992-2000, chmn., 1993-94, emeritus trustee, 2001-; trustee In Home Care, Inc., 1997—, chmn., 2001; trustee Bapt. Retirement Homes Found. 2001-. With USNR, 1955-58. Mem. ABA, N.C. Bar Assn., Raleigh Bar Assn., Assn. Life Ins. Counsel (bd. govs. 1984-88), Greensboro C. of C. (chmn. nat. legis. com. 1973—), Nat. Orgn. Life Guaranty Assn. (bd. dirs. 1982-87). Democrat. Home: PO Box 1690 601 Selma Rd Wendell NC 27591-8648 Office: 2500 First Union Capitol Ctr PO Box 2611 Raleigh NC 27602-2611 Office Phone: 919-821-6630.

ROACHE, PATRICK MICHAEL, JR., management consultant; b. Elizabeth, NJ, Oct. 8, 1946; s. Patrick Michael and Rose Marie (Remite) R. BS, St. Peter's Coll., 1969. Adminstrv. aide to a state assemblyman N.J. Assembly, NJ, 1969-71; supr. acctg. Dept. Pub. Works Newark, Newark, 1971-78, asst. to dir. pub. works, 1978-79, mgr. div. motors, 1979-84; mgmt. specialist Dept. Gen. Svcs., Newark, 1985-86, 2002; pvt. practice as mgmt. and fin. cons. Brick, NJ, 1986—. Mem. Lions (treas. 1983-86, pres. 1988-89). Republican. Roman Catholic. Home and Office: 170 Binnacle Rd Brick NJ 08723-6704 Home Phone: 732-477-7036; Office Phone: 732-477-9162. E-mail: proache@haywardnet.com.

ROADARMEL, STANLEY BRUCE, civilian military employee; b. Albion, NY, May 5, 1937; s. Kenneth A. and Catherine Louise (Bobel) R.; m. Carole Ann Hayes, Nov. 26, 1959; children: Karen Marie, Ann Catherine, William Hayes, Oscar Pacific. Student, Purdue U., 1956—58; BA, Syracuse U., 1962; grad., Squadron Officer Sch., 1965, Air Command Staff Coll., 1976, Indsl. Coll. Armed Forces, 1976; postgrad., Golden Gate U., 1976—78. Commd. 2d lt. USAF, 1962, advanced through grades to maj.; adminstrv., security and recruiting ops. officer Air Tng. Command, Tex. and W.Va., 1962—69; chief field maintenance Titan II ICBM Strategic Air Command, Davis Monthan AFB, Ariz., 1969—71, chief Hq SAC's 3901st Titan II maintenance evaluation team Vandenberg AFB, Calif., 1971—74, logistics staff officer, 1974—77, contract specialist, 1977—82, U.S. Air Forces Europe, Adana, Turkey, 1980—81; ret. USAF, 1982; launch complex constrn. contract negotiator, adminstr. NASA/USAF Space Shuttle Program, Lompoc, Calif., 1983—89, USAF Titan IV Space Booster, Vandenberg AFB, 1991—92; constrn. and maj. svcs. contract negotiator, adminstr. 30th Contracting Squadron USAF Space Command, Vandenberg AFB, 1992—2001; ret. active fed. svc., 2001. With Ctrl. Coast Profls., Mut. Profl. Counseling/Placement, Santa Maria, Calif., 1990-91. Author manual: Man Lifting Crane Operations, 1976 (Air Force Commendation award 1977); revision officer Air Force Manual 66-1 Maintenance Management, 1976 (Air Force Commendation award 1977); contbr. Strategic Air Command Manual 66-12 ICBM Maintenance Mgmt. Spkr. World Orgn. Ovulation Method, Calif., 1987—; pro life adv., activist Am. Life League, Nat. Right to Life, 1980—; mem. and vol. Rep. Party, 1992—; marriage preparation instr. Cath. Archdiocese of L.A., Santa Maria, 1995—; professed to Pauline Holy Family Inst., Roman Cath. Ch., 2006—. Mem. NRA, Air Force Assn. (life), Mil. Officers Assn. Am. (life), Disabled Am. Vets. (life), Assn. Air Force Missileers (life), Am. Legion, Couple to Couple League, The Heritage Found., Exptl. Aircraft Assn. Avocations: aviation, music, marksmanship, travel, literature. Home and Office: 4532 Glines Ave Santa Maria CA 93455-4313 Personal E-mail: csroadarmel@earthlink.net.

ROADEN, ARLISS LLOYD, retired academic administrator; b. Bark Camp, Ky., Sept. 27, 1930; s. Johnie Samuel and Ethel Nora (Killian) R.; m. Mary Etta Mitchell, Sept. 1, 1951; children: Janice Arletta Roaden Skelton, Sharon Kay Roaden Vogt. Grad., Cumberland Coll., 1949; AB, Carson Newman Coll., 1951; MS, U. Tenn., 1958, EdD, 1961; PhD (hon.), Cumberland Coll., 1986; DLitt (hon.), Tusculum Coll., 1992. With Oak Ridge Inst. Nuclear Studies, 1957-59, Auburn U., 1961-62; mem. faculty Ohio State U., 1962-74, prof. edn., 1967-74, acting dean Coll. Edn., 1968-70, vice provost for research, dean Grad. Sch., 1970-74; pres. Tenn. Tech. U., 1974-85, pres. emeritus, 1985—; dir. Tenn. Higher Edn. Commn., Nashville, 1985-95, exec. dir. emeritus, 1995—. Summer vis. prof. Marshall U., 1961, U. So. Calif., 1964, Ind. U., 1967; cons. ednl. instns., 1961—; pres. Tenn. Coll. Assn., 1978; chmn. sci. and tech. com. Am. Assn. State Colls. and Univs., 1980; chmn. task force on program and instl. assessment State Higher Edn. Exec. Officers', 1987, pres. 1993-94, chmn. coun. postsecondary accreditation liaison com., 1986-88, exec. com., 1988-95, pres. elect 1992-93; mem. exec. bd. trustees Southern Assn. Colls. and Schs., 1986—, chair communications com., 1990—, mem. task force, 1990—; mem. Southern Regional Edn. Bd., 1985—, chmn. procedures com. for reviewing bylaw changes and revisions, 1988-89; mem. exec. com., state rep., treas., chair Internal Audit Com., 1990-91, Edn. Commn. States, 1987-90; mem. Tenn. Econ. Cabinet Coun., 1988—, chmn.m 1988-91, bd. dirs. 1988—, Fgn. Lang. Inst.; treas., chair Internal Audit Com., 1990-91; mem. Performance Standards in Vocat.-Tech. Edn. Working Group, U.S. Dept. Edn., 1990. Co-author: The Research Assistantship: Recommendations for Colleges and Universities, 1975, Cultures of the States: A Handbook on the Effectiveness of State Governments, 2003; editor: Problems of School Men in Depressed Urban Areas, 1967; contbr. articles to profl. jours. State chmn. Tenn. Cancer Soc. Crusade, 1986-88, bd. dirs., 1987—; mem. exec. bd., commr. Mid. Tenn. coun. Boy Scouts Am., 1987-88, mem. nat. coun., 1988—, chmn. scouts membership rels. com.; mem. Phi Delta Kappa Found., 1965—, past chmn. bd. govs., mem. futures and diamond jubilee coms., 1989—; chmn. Blue Ribbon Com. To Respond to Edn. Goals, 1990; bd. dirs. Nat. Project 714, 1986—, pres.-elect, 1987-88, chmn., 1988-89; pres. alumni assn. bd. Cumberland Coll., 1987-88, chmn. devel. bd., 1994—; adult Sunday sch. tchr. Woodmont Bapt. Ch., chmn. pers. com., 1989—, chmn. deacons, ch. moderator, 1998-99. With U.S. Army, 1951-53. Rsch.grantee Phi Delta Kappa Internat., 1968; named Disting. Alumnus Cumberland Coll., 1970; recipient Disting. Alumni and Faculty Centennial medallion Coll. Edn., 1970, Disting. Service award Coun. Grad. Students, 1974, both Ohio State U.; recipient Silver Beaver award Boy Scouts Am.; named Rotarian of Yr., 1984; Eagle Scout honoree Middle Tenn. Coun. Boy Scouts Am., 1989, others. Fellow Oxford Soc. Scholars; mem. AASA, Am. Assn. Higher Edn., Acad. Polit. and Social Scis., Am. Ednl. Rsch. Assn. (chmn. publs. com.

1979-80), Nat. Soc. Study Edn., Nat. Assn. State Colls. and Land Grant Univs., Lions (bd. dirs. Nashville 1988-90, pres. 1991-92, zone chmn. 1992-93, dist. gov. 1996), Rotary (bd. dirs.), Order of Lion and Eagle, Phi Kappa Phi, Phi Delta Kappa (Disting. Svc. award Ohio State U. chpt. 1974), Kappa Phi Kappa, Kappa Delta Pi. Baptist.

ROADMAN, JOSEPH PETER, engineering consultant; b. Mount Pleasant, Pa., Oct. 15, 1980; s. Joseph R. and Cheryl Lynn Roadman; m. Jennifer Michele Smitley, July 30, 2005. BS in Computing and Info. Sci., St. Vincent Coll., Latrobe, Pa., 2004; postgrad., Colo. Tech. U., Colorado Springs, 2005—. Network tech. Mt. Pleasant Area Sch. Dist., Pa., 2002—04, Norwin Sch. Dist., North Huntingdon, Pa., 2004—06; rep. The Logic Ho., Inc., Pitts., 2006—. Network cons. The Logic Ho., Inc, 2006—, network engring. and design, 2006—, fed. funding k-12 ednl. instns. cons., 2006—. Mem.: Assn. Ednl. Comm. and Tech. (corr.). Conservative. Avocations: music, travel, motocross. Home: 513 East Main St Mount Pleasant PA 15666 Home Phone: 724-547-0709; Office Phone: 724-454-2219. Personal E-mail: jroadman@verizon.net.

ROAF, ANDREE LAYTON, judge; b. Mar. 31, 1941; m. Clifton G. Roaf; 4 children. BS in Zoology, Mich. State U., 1962; JD with high honors, U. Ark., 1978; LLD (hon.), Mich. State U., 1996. Bar: Ark. 1978. Bacteriologist Mich. Dept. Health, Lansing, 1963—65; rsch. biologist FDA, Washington, 1965—69; staff asst. Pine Bluff (Ark.) Urban Renewal Agy., 1971—75; biologist Nat. Ctr. for Toxicological Rsch., Jefferson, Ark., 1978—79; assoc. Walker, Roaf, Campbell, Ivory & Dunklin, Little Rock, 1979—86, ptnr., 1986—95; assoc. justice Ark. Supreme Ct., Little Rock, 1995—96; appellate judge Ark. Ct. Appeals, 1997—. Editor: Ark. Law Rev. Mem. PTA bd. Forest Park Elem. Sch., 1972—74, 34th Ave. Sch., 1974—76, 1980—83, Southeast Jr. High, 1976—77; mem. ad hoc com. for voter registration Jefferson County, 1972—73; bd. trustees Southeast Ark. Arts and Scis. Ctr., 1972—75, sec., 1974—75, Pine Bluff OIC Bd., 1972—78, Pine Bluff Police-Cmty. Rels Task Force, 1973; mem. Jefferson County Com. on Black Adoptions, 1973—75, chmn., 1974—75; mem. Ark. Code of Ethics Commn., 1987, Friends of Sta. KRLE-FM, 1982—88, 1990—94, pres., 1985—86; trustee Winthrop Rockefeller Found., 1990—94; mem. Jefferson County Dem. Com., 1980—82; mem. vestry Grace Episcopal Ch., 1995—; bd. dirs. Ark. Coun. on Human Rels., 1972—73, Ark. for Arts, 1983, Ark. Student Loan Authority, 1977—81, Vocals, 1989—. Named Gayle Pettus Pontz outstanding Ark. woman lawyer, 1996; named to Ark. Black Hall of Fame, 1996; recipient disting. alumni award, Mich. State U., 1996. Mem.: ABA, W. Harold Flowers Law Soc., Jefferson County Bar Assn., Pulaski County Bar Assn. (chmn. hist. com. 1986—87), Ark. Bar Assn. (chmn. youth edn. com. 1979—80). Office: Justice Bldg 625 Marshall St Ste 1230 Little Rock AR 72201-1052

ROALES, ROBERT R., natural science educator; b. N.Y.C., July 17, 1944; s. John and Gertrude (Buxo) R.; m. Francoise A. Galland, Nov. 29, 1969; 1 child, Nicole. BS, Iona Coll., 1966; MS, NYU, 1969, PhD, 1973. Asst. prof. Ind. U.-Kokomo, 1974-79, assoc. prof., 1979—, coordinator natural sci., 1981-87, chairperson dept. biol. and physical scis., 1987-96, coord. allied health scis., 1987-91, asst. dean. Sch. Allied Health Scis., Sch. Medicine, 1992-2002, chair dept. natural, info. and math. scis., 1996—, acting dean of arts and sci., 1990, dir. informatics, 2006—. Contbr. articles to profl. jours. Mem. AAAS, Nat. Assn. Advisors for Health Professions, Am. Inst. Biol. Sci., Sigma Xi. Avocations: photography, gardening, computers. Home: 1001 N Hickory Ln Kokomo IN 46901-6420 Office: Ind U 2300 S Washington St PO Box 9003 Kokomo IN 46904-9003 Business E-Mail: rroales@iuk.edu.

ROALKVAM, DONALD L., library and information scientist; BA in Political Sci., Luther Coll., 1970. Mem. bd. trustees Indian Trails Pub. Libr., Wheeling, Ill., 1995—, pres. bd. trustees, 2005—; pres. bd. dirs. North Suburban Libr. Sys., 2001—03. Mem.: Ill. Libr. Assn. (mem. 2006 conf. prog. com. 2005), Assn. for Libr. Trustees and Advocates (bd. dirs. 2001—, divsn. councilor 2003—05, second v.p. bd. dirs. 2005—06, pres.-elect 2006—07, pres. 2007—), ALA (chmn. 2006 conf. prog. coordinating team 0200—4200, mem. nominating com. 2005—06). Office: Board Trustees Indian Trails Public Library 355 S Schoenbeck Rd Wheeling IL 60090 E-mail: droalkva@allstate.com.

ROAN, FORREST CALVIN, JR., lawyer; b. Waco, Tex., Dec. 18, 1944; s. Forrest Calvin and Lucille Elizabeth (McKinney) Roan; m. Vickie Joan Howard, Feb. 15, 1969 (div. Dec. 1983); children: Amy Katherine, Jennifer Louise; m. Leslie D. Hampton, Jan. 2, 1999. BBA, U. Tex., Austin, 1973, JD, 1976. Bar: Tex. 1976, US Dist. Ct. (we. dist.) Tex. 1977, US Dist. Ct. (so. dist.) Tex. 1998, US Ct. Appeals (5th cir.) 1977, US Supreme Ct. 1979, US Ct. Appeals (11th cir.) 1981, US Ct. Appeals (fed. cir.) 1998, US Ct. Internat. Trade 1998. Prin. Roan & Assocs., Austin, 1969-71; counsel, com. dir. Tex. Ho. of Reps., 1972-75; assoc. Heath, Davis & McCalla, Austin, 1975-78; prin. Roan & Gullahorn, P.C., Austin, 1978-85, Roan & Autrey (formerly Roan & Simpson), P.C., 1986-99; sr. ptnr. Cantey, Hanger, Roan & Autrey, 1999—2003; shareholder Winstead, P.C. (formerly Winstead, Sechrest & Minick, P.C.), Austin, 2003—. Trustee Safeplace Found.; mem. leadership coun. Am. Lung Assn.; bd. dirs. Lawyers Credit Union, chmn., 1982—83; bd. dirs. pub. law sect. State Bar Tex., 1980—84; mem. Littlefield Soc. and Chancellor's Coun. U. Tex. With Tex. N.G. US Army, 1966—74. Fellow: Austin Bar Found. (founding fellow), Am. Bar Found. (life), Tex. Bar Found. (life); mem.: ABA, Tex.-Mex. Bar Assn., Austin Bar Assn., Def. Rsch. Inst., Tex. Assn. Bank Counsel, Tex. Assn. Def. Counsel, Austin C. of C., Tex. Lyceum Assn. (v.p., bd. dirs. 1980—87), Mensa (life), Headliners Club, Austin Club, Shriners (Parons Masonic master 1976—77), Masons, Knights of the Symphony (Lord Chancellor 2003—04). Methodist. Office: Winstead PC 401 Congress Ste 2100 Austin TX 78701 Home Phone: 512-502-8777; Office Phone: 512-370-2999. E-mail: froan@winstead.com.

ROANE, DAVID JAMES, JR., information technology auditor; b. Petersburg, Va., Nov. 11, 1960; s. David James Roane, Sr. and Anne (Vest) Savage; m. Bonnie L. Dear, Dec. 3, 1983; two children. BS, Va. Commonwealth U., 1984. CPA, Va.; cert. info. systems auditor. Audit intern Continental Fin. Services Co., Richmond, Va., 1983-84, staff auditor, 1984-85; EDP auditor Life Ins. Co. of Va., Richmond, 1985-86, Fort James Corp., Richmond, Va., 1986-88, sr. EDP auditor, 1990-2000; technologies group specialist Mgmt. Info. Systems, 1989-90; info. tech. audit cons. Ft. James Corp./Ga. Pacific, 2000-01; info. tech. audit supr. The Brink's Co., Richmond, Va., 2001—06, info. tech. audit mgr., 2006—. Treas. Civic Assn., Chester, Va., 1985-91; chmn. fin. com. Matoaca United Meth. Ch., 1990-92, 1997-98, chmn. adminstrv. bd., 1993-95. Methodist. Avocation: micro computers. Home: 3148 Talleywood Ln Chester VA 23831-7036 Office Phone: 804-289-9649. Business E-Mail: droane@brinkscompany.com.

ROARK, BARBARA ANN, librarian; b. Evanston, Ill., July 24, 1958; d. Edward B. and Ann H. Rowe; m. Paul E. Roark, Sept. 18, 1982; children: Sarah, John. BA in History, U. Ky., 1981, MLS, 1982. Dir. Hopkins County Madisonville (Ky.) Pub. Libr., 1983-85; ops. mgr. Wurzburg Inc., Nashville, 1985-91; dir. Spies Pub. Libr., Menominee, Mich., 1991-98, Franklin (Wis.) Pub. Libr., 1998—. V.p. adv. coun. Mid-Peninsula Libr. Coop., Mich., 1993-95, sec. adv. coun., 1991-93; chair tech. adv. com. Milwaukee County Federated Libr. Sys., 2001—; dir. Libr. Coun. Southeastern Wis.; chair Libr. Dirs. Adv. Coun., 2007—. Grant writer Title II, 1994, Title I, 1995. Treas. Franklin Area Jr. Woman's Club. Recipient Cert. of Excellence Libr. of Mich., 1995, Cert. of Appreciation Menominee Area C. of C., 1998. Mem. ALA, Wis. Libr. Assn. (pers. and profl. concerns com. 1999—, Muriel Fuller award 2002), Spies Pub. Libr. Found., PEO, Order Ea. Star, U. Ky. Alumni Assn., Franklin Area Jr. Women's Club (treas. 1999—), Kiwanis (pres. Milw. suburban S.W. chpt. 2002—), Zeta Tau Alpha. Methodist. Avocations: golf, reading, cross stitching, travel. Home Phone: 414-427-8397; Office Phone: 414-425-8214. E-mail: barbara.roark@mcfls.org.

ROARK, TERRY PAUL, astronomer, educator; b. Okeene, Okla., June 11, 1938; s. Paul J. and Erma K. (Morrison) R.; m. Beverly Brown, Sept. 7, 1963; 1 child, David. C. BA in Physics, Oklahoma City U., 1960; MS in Astronomy, Rensselaer Poly. Inst., 1962, PhD in Astronomy, 1966. Asst. provost for curricula Ohio State U., Columbus, 1977-79, assoc. provost for instrn., 1979-83; prof. physics Kent (Ohio) State U., 1983-87, v.p. acad. and student affairs, 1983-87, provost, 1985-87; pres. U. Wyo., Laramie, 1987-97, prof. physics and astronomy, 1987-2001; interim pres. Mont. State U., Bozeman, 2000. Bd. dirs. Rocky Mountain Fed. Savs. Bank, chmn. audit com., 1989-93; commr. Western Interstate Commn. for Higher Edn., 1987-97, chmn., 1991; bd. dirs. Associated Western Univs., 1987-94, chmn., 1991, bd. trustees, 1994-97, chmn. 1996; adv. bd. Wyo. Geol. Survey, 1987-97; mem. Warren AFB Civilian Adv. Coun., 1987-97; bd. dirs. First Interstate Bank of Wyo.; bd. dirs. Albany County Hosp. Dist., chmn. 2006. Mem., treas. Ctr. for Pub. Edn., Columbus, 1980-83; mem. fin. adv. com. LWV, Kent, 1986; mem. long range planning com. Cleve. Urban League, 1985-86; mem. adv. com. Battelle youth sci. program Columbus and Ohio Pub. Schs., 1982; bd. dirs. Ivinson Hosp. Found., 1987-97, 2005—. Mem. Am. Astron. Soc., Internat. Astron. Union, Nat. Assn. State Univs. and Land Grant Colls. (bd. dirs. 1994-96, chair commn. on intenat. affairs 1995), Astron. Soc. Pacific, Sigma Xi, Phi Kappa Phi, Omicron Delta Kappa. Avocations: photography, music, hiking. Office: U Wyo Dept Physics & Astronomy Dept No 3905 1000 E University Ave Laramie WY 82071-3905

ROARKE, MICHAEL CHARLES, medical educator, nuclear medicine physician; b. Albany, NY, May 8, 1959; s. Charles Augustus and Joan Ann Roarke; m. Maria Giuliani, June 25, 1988; 1 child, Michael Andrew. BS, SUNY, Albany, 1981, MS, 1982; MD, U. Rochester Sch. Medicine, NYC, 1990. Cert. Am. Bd. Radiology, 1995, Am. Bd. Nuc. Medicine, 1996. Chemistry tchr. Albany Acad. Boys, NY, 1982—86; intern internal medicine St. Mary's Hosp., Rochester, 1990—91; resident diagnostic radiology Mallinckrodt Inst. Radiology, St. Louis, 1991—95, fellow nuc. medicine, 1995—96; asst. prof. radiology U. Tex. Med. Ctr., Houston, 1996—97, Mayo Med. Sch., Scottsdale, 1997—. Sect. head nuc. radiology Mayo Clinic Ariz., Scottsdale, Ariz., 1997—, med. dir. nuc. radiology, 1997—. Named one of Best Doctors in Am., 2003—06, America's Top Physicians, Consumer's Rsch. Coun., 2005; recipient Best Intern award, St. Mary's Hosp. Internal Medicine Program, 1991, Tchr. Recognition award, White House Commn. on Presdl. Scholars, 1985; Klingenstein Summer Tchg. fellow, Columbia U., 1983. Mem.: Acad. Molecular Imaging (assoc.), Soc. Nuc. Medicine (assoc.), Radiol. Soc. N.Am. (assoc.), Am. Coll. Radiology (assoc.), Beta Beta Beta, Alpha Omega Alpha (life). Avocations: music, composing, mineral photography. Office: Mayo Clinic Ariz 13400 East Shea Blvd Scottsdale AZ 85259 Office Phone: 480-301-8016. E-mail: mroarke@aol.com.

ROBAK, KIM M., lawyer; b. Columbus, Nebr., Oct. 4, 1955; m. William J. Mueller; children: Katherine, Claire. BS with distinction, U. Nebr., 1977, JD with highest distinction, 1985. Tchr. Lincoln Pub. Schs., Nebr., 1978—82; clerk Cline Williams Wright Johnson & Oldfather, 1983; summer assoc. Cooley Godward Castro Huddleson & Tatum, San Francisco, 1984, Steptoe & Johnson, Washington, 1985; ptnr. Rembolt Ludtke Parker & Berger, Lincoln, 1985—91; legal counsel Gov. E. Benjamin Nelson/State of Nebr., 1991—92, chief of staff, 1992—93; lt. gov. State of Nebr., 1993—98; v.p. external affairs, corp. sec. U. Nebr., 1999—2004; with Ruth Mueller Robak, LLC, Lincoln, Nebr., 2004—. Chair Prairie Fire Internat. Symposium on Edn., 1986; bd. dirs. Fiserv, Inc., First Ameritas Life Ins. Corp. NY, Union Bank & Trust Co. Program com. Leadership Lincoln, 1987—90; chair program com. Leadership Lincoln Alumni Assn., 1987, selection com., 1990; mem. Toll Fellowship Program, 1995; chair Nat. Conf. Lt. Govs., 1996; hon. chair Daffodil Day Campaign An, Cancer Soc.; hon chair Walktoberfest Am. Diabetes Assn.; hon. chair Prevent Blindness Campaign, Nebr.; hon. mem. Red Ribbon Campaign Mothers Against Drunk Driving, 1994—95; active Groundwater Found., 1997, Medicaid Managed Care Commn., 1993—98; bd. dirs. Nebr. Health Sys., 1997—2004, Nat. Found. Women Legislators Found., 1997—98; chair Nebr. Info. Tech. Commn., 1997—98; hon. Christmas chair Salvation Army, 1997; cert. program chair Nat. Order Women Legislators, 1997; mem. Martin Luther Home Soc., 1999—2001, Dem. Gen. Counsel, Nebr., 1985—92; bd. dirs. women's ministries First Congl. Ch., 1988—91, trustee, 1991—99, asst. moderator, 1999—; trustee Plymouth Congl. Ch., 1998—; bd. dirs. Doane Coll., 1997—, Lincoln Pub. Sch. Found., 1998—2004, Lincoln Partnership for Econ. Devel. Bd., 2000—, Nebr. Found. for the Humanities, 2003—, Lincoln Cmty. Found., 2004—, United Way of Lincoln and Lancaster County, 2000—, Strategic Air and Space Mus., 2006—, Exec. Women's Golf Assn., 2005—. Named Notable Woman, First Plymouth Congl. Ch.'s Bd. Women's Ministries, 1996; fellow, Leadership Lincoln, 1986—87. Mem.: ABA (steering com. 1997—), Lincoln Bar Assn., Nebr. State Bar Assn. (ethics com. 1987—92, chair com. yellow pages advt. 1988, vice chair com. pub. rels. 1988—92, ho. of dels. 1988—95), Nat. Inst. Trial Advocaty, Alzheimers Assn. (hon. chair Lincoln-Greater Nebr. chpt. 1996—98), Updowntowners, Exec. Women's Golf Assn. (trustee 2005—), Order of Coif, U. Nebr. Coll. Alumni Assn. (bd. dirs. 1986—89). Office: Ruth Mueller Robak LLC 530 S 13th St Ste 110 Lincoln NE 68508 Business E-Mail: robak@ruthmueller.com.

ROBARDS, THOMAS FREDERICK, banker; b. Sewickley, Pa., June 10, 1946; s. Woodford Lee and Elizabeth Jane (Linscheid) R.; m. Karen Ann Puskarz, June 19, 1976; children: David Woodford, Christopher Joseph, Katherine Elizabeth. BA, Brown U., 1968; MBA, Harvard Bus. Sch., 1976. Asst. treas. Republic N.Y. Corp., NYC, 1976-82, 1st v.p., treas., 1983-85, sr. v.p., treas., 1985-87, exec. v.p., treas., 1987—; asst. v.p. J. Aron div. Goldman Sachs, NYC, 1982-83; CFO Republic New York Corp., NYC, 1995—, Datek Online Holding Corp., Iselin, N.J., 2000—. Bd. dirs. Nat. Down Syndrome Soc., N.Y.C., 1986-87. Served to 1st lt. U.S. Army, 1968-72. Mem.: Harvard (N.Y.C.). Avocations: cross-country skiing, reading, racquet sports.

ROBART, JAMES LOUIS, federal judge, lawyer; AB, Whitman Coll., 1969; JD, Georgetown U., 1973. Bar: Wash. 1973, U.S. Dist. Ct. (we. dist.) Wash. 1973, U.S. Supreme Ct. 1977, U.S. Ct. Appeals (9th cir.) 1978, U.S. Dist. Ct. (ea. dist.) Wash. 1981, Alaska 1985, U.S. Dist. Ct. Alaska 1985, U.S. Ct. Appeals (fed. cir.) 1985. Assoc. Lane Powell Moss Miller LLP, Seattle, 1973—79, ptnr., 1980—90, Lane Powell Spears Lubersky LLP, 1990—98; co-mng. ptnr. Lane Powel Spears Lubersky, 1998—2002, mng. ptnr., 2003—04; judge US Dist. Ct. (we. dist.) Wash., 2004—. Trustee Children's Home Soc., 1991-92, Seattle Children's Home, pres., 1984, Whitman Coll., bd trustees, 2000-, bd. overseers, 1988-2000. Mem. Fed. Cir. Bar Assn. (trustee 1985-88). Office Phone: 206-370-8920.

ROBB, CHUCK (CHARLES SPITTAL), law educator, former senator; b. Phoenix, June 26, 1939; s. James Spittal and Francis Howard (Wooley) R.; m. Lynda Bird Johnson, Dec. 9, 1967; children: Lucinda Desha, Catherine Lewis, Jennifer Wickliffe. BBA, U. Wis., 1961; JD, U. Va., 1973. Bar: Va. 1973, U.S. Supreme Ct. 1976. Law clk. to Hon. John D. Butzner U.S. Ct. Appeals (4th Dist.), 1973—74; atty. Williams & Connolly, 1974-77; lt. gov. State of Va., 1978—82, gov., 1982—86; ptnr. Hunton & Williams, 1986—88; U.S. Senator from Va., 1989—2001; former mem. armed svcs. com., intelligence com., senate Dem. policy com., senate Dem. tech. and comm. com., subcom. on readiness, subcom. on seapower; disting. prof. law & pub. policy George Mason U., Fairfax, Va., 2001—. Chmn. Nat. Conf. Lt. Govs., 1979-80, Am. Coun. Young Polit. Leaders Dels. to Peoples Republic of China, 1979, Edn. Commn. of the States, 1984-85; vis. prof. pub. affairs George Mason U., spring 1987; co-chmn. Commn. on the Intelligence Capabilities of the US Regarding Weapons of Mass Destruction, 2004, mem. Iraq Study Group, 2006 Chmn. Jobs for Am.'s Grads. Inc., 1985-90, Dem. Leadership Coun., 1986-88; gov. Atlantic Inst. for Internat. Affairs, 1987. With USMC, 1961—70. Decorated Bronze Star, Vietnam Service medal with 4 Stars; Vietnamese Cross of Gallantry with Silver Star; recipient Raven award, 1973, Seven Soc. award U. Va. Mem. ABA, Va. Bar Assn., So. Govs. Assn. (chmn., 1983-85), Dem. Govs. Assn. (chmn., 1984-85), Coalition for Dem. Majority, Res. Officers Assn., USMC Res. Officers Assn., U.Fa. La. Alumni Assn. (bd. dirs. 1974-85), Am. Legion, Raven Soc., Navy League U.S., Coun. on Fgn. Rels., Omicron Delta Kappa. Democrat. Episcopalian. Office: George Mason U Sch Law 3301 N Fairfax Dr Rm 409 Arlington VA 22201-4498 *

ROBB, GARY CHARLES, lawyer; b. Kansas City, Mo., May 17, 1955; m. Anita Candace Porte, Apr. 30, 1983. BA with distinction, U. Mo., Kansas City, 1977, MA in Econs., 1978; JD cum laude, U. Mich., 1981. Bar: Ill. 1981, U.S. Dist. Ct. (no. dist.) Ill. 1981, Mo. 1982, U.S. Dist. Ct. (we. dist.) Mo. 1982, U.S. Ct. Appeals (8th cir.) 1982. Assoc. Mayer, Brown & Platt, Chgo., 1981—82, Shughart, Thomson & Kilroy, Kansas City, Mo., 1982—84; ptnr. Robb & Robb LLC, Kansas City, Mo., 1984—. Adj. prof. law U. Mo., Kansas City; lectr., program chmn. Nat. Conf. on Products Liability Law, Chgo., 1983, lectr., 84. Contbg. author: Tort Law, Missouri Bar Handbook, 1982, Products Liability, 1984; editor: U. Mich. Jour. Law Reform, 1980—81; contbg. editor: Products Liability, 1983; mem. bd. editors: Products Liability Newsletter, 1982—, mem. bd. experts: Lawyers Alert Newsmag.; contbr. articles. Mem.: ATLA (tort and aviation sects.), ABA (tort and ins. practice 1981—, trial evidence com. 1981—, sect. litigation, chmn. future programs and projects subcom., products, liability and consumer law com., co-chmn.Aviation Litig. Com., Sect. of Litig., 2004-2005), Lawyers Assn. Kansas City, Mo. Bar Assn. (fed. practice com.), Kansas City Bar Assn., Mo. Assn. Trial Attys. (bd. govs. 1993—, pres. elect), Univ. Mo.-Kansas City Alumni Assn. (chmn. career planning com.), Pi Sigma Alpha (pres. 1977—78), Omicron Delta Epsilon, Phi Kappa Phi. Republican. Office: Robb & Robb LLC One Kans City Pl Ste 3900 1200 Main St Kansas City MO 64105-2100

ROBB, GEOFFREY LAWRENCE, plastic surgeon; b. El Paso, Tex., May 28, 1946; s. Giles Anthony and Mary Jo (Lawrence) R.; m. Cathy Jean Cross, May 31, 1974; children: Tiffany, Kimberly, Courtney, Carly, Melaney, Mary. BS, U. Miami, 1969, MD, 1974. Diplomate Am. Bd. Otolaryngology. Commd. ensign USNR, 1970-92; advanced through grades to capt., 1989; resident in otalaryngology, mem. staff US Naval Hosp., San Diego, 1974-79, otolaryngologist Orlando, Fla., 1979-83; plastic surgeon USN Sponsorship at U. Pitts., 1983-85, microvascular surgeon, 1985; plastic surgeon U.S. Naval Hosp., Portsmouth, Va., 1985-88; ret., 1992; chief plastic surgery U.S. Naval Hosp., Portsmouth, Va., 1988-92; vice chmn. plastic surgery M.D. Anderson Cancer Ctr., Houston, 1992-97, chmn. plastic surgery, 1997—, dep. chmn. divsn. surgery, 1994—, dir. postgrad. med. edn., 1992—, med. dir. plastic surgery clinic, 1992—, assoc. med. dir. skin cancer ctr., 1996. Contbg. author: Reconstructive Plastic Surgery for Cancer, 1995, Endoscopic Plastic Surgery, 1995, Advanced Skin Cancer of Head and Neck, 1995; contbr. articles to profl. jours. Fellow ACS, Am. Soc. Plastic Reconstructive Surgeons, Am. Soc. Reconstructive Microsurgeons, Am. Assn. Plastic Surgeons; mem. Internat. Soc. Reconstructive Microsurgery, Tex. Soc. Plastic Surgeons, Houston Soc. Plastic Surgeons, KC. Avocations: physical fitness, weightlifting, tennis, running. Office: MD Anderson Cancer Ctr 1515 Holcombe Blvd # 443 Houston TX 77030-4009 E-mail: grobb@mdanderson.org. *

ROBB, JAMES ALEXANDER, lawyer; b. Huntingdon, Que., Can., May 3, 1930; s. Alexander George and Irma Mary (Martin) R.; m. Katherine Ann Teare, June 26, 1960; children: Laura, John, Andrew. BA, McGill U., 1951, B.C.L., 1954; postgrad., U. Montreal, 1961-63. Bar: Que. 1955, queen's counsel 1970. Lectr. comml. law and taxation Sir George Williams U., 1958-60; ptnr. Stikeman Elliott LLP and predecessor firm Stikeman, Elliott, Tamaki, Mercier & Robb, Montreal, 1967—2002, ret., 2003. Pres. Que-Japan Bus. Forum, 1993—95; bd. dirs. Itochu Can. Ltd., YKK Can. Inc., NGK Spark Plugs Can. Ltd., Western Life Assurance Co., Bank West. Mem. Protestant Sch. Bd. Greater Montreal, 1971-75; chmn. bd. trustees Martlet Found., 1967-69; v.p. Que. Liberal Party, 1976-79; mem. adv. com. McGill Ctr. for Study of Regulated Industries; bd. dirs. Montreal Mus. Fine Arts, 1987-90; bd. govs. McGill U., 1991-95. Mem.: Consumers Assn. Can. (past chmn. regulated industries program), Bar Que. (chmn. multidisciplinary com. 1998—2001), Can. C. of C. (internat. arbitration com.), McGill Alumni Assn. (pres. 1996—98), Hillside Tennis Club, Royal Montreal Curling Club (pres. 1999—2000), Kanawaki Golf Club (Que.), Univ. Club (pres. 1988—89), Can. Club Montreal (pres. 1990—91). Home: 9 Renfrew Ave Westmount PQ Canada H3Y 2X3 Office: 1155 Renè Lèvesque Blvd W 40th Fl Montreal PQ Canada H3B 3V2 Office Phone: 514-397-3086. Personal E-mail: jrobb@stikeman.com.

ROBB, JAMES WILLIS, romance languages educator; b. Jamaica, NY, June 27, 1918; s. Stewart Everts and Clara Johanna (Mohrmann) R.; m. Cecilia Uribe-Noguera, 1972. Student, Inst. de Touraine, Sorbonne, 1937-38; BA cum laude, Colgate U., 1939; postgrad., U. Nacional de Mex., 1948; MA, Middlebury Coll., 1950; PhD, Cath. U. Am., 1958. Instr. romance langs. Norwich U., 1946-50; from asst. prof. to prof. romance langs. George Washington U., Washington, 1950-88, prof. emeritus, 1988—. Corr. mem. Academia Mexicana de la Lengua, 1998. Author: El Estilo de Alfonso Reyes, 1965, 78, Repertorio Bibliográfico de Alfonso Reyes, 1974, Prosa y Poesía de Alfonso Reyes, 1975, 84, Estudios sobre Alfonso Reyes, 1976, Por los Caminos de Alfonso Reyes, 1981, Imágenes de América en Alfonso Reyes y en Germán Arciniegas, 1990, Más Páginas Sobre Alfonso Reyes, 1996-97; contbr. articles to profl. jours. With USNR, 1942—44, Brazil, with USNR, 1944—46, PTO. Recipient Alfonso Reyes Internat. Lit. prize, 1978; Lit. Diploma of Merit, State of Nuevo León and City of Monterrey, Mex., 1979; OAS grantee, 1964; Am. Philos. Soc. grantee, 1977 Mem. MLA, Internat. Assn. Ibero-Am. Lit., Am. Assn. Tchrs. Spanish and Portuguese, Assn. Colombianistas, Phi Beta Kappa. Office: George Washington U Romance Langs Dept Washington DC 20052-0001

ROBB, JOHN WESLEY, religion educator; b. LA, Dec. 1, 1919; s. Edgar Milton and Alta (Boger) R.; m. Ethel Edna Tosh, June 13, 1942; children: Lydia Joan Robb Durbin, Judith Nadine Robb Eggerman. AB, Greenville Coll., 1941; Th.M., U. So. Calif., 1945, PhD, 1952; L.H.D., Hebrew Union Coll.-Jewish Inst. Religion, 1977. Asst. prof. philosophy and religion Dickinson Coll., Pa., 1948-51; fellow Fund for Advancement Edn., 1951-52; asso. prof. U. So. Calif., LA, 1954-62, chmn. dept. religion, 1954-67, assoc. dean humanities Coll. Letters, Arts and Scis., 1963-68, Leonard K. Firestone prof., 1974-75, prof., 1962-87, prof. emeritus, 1987—, prof. Sch. Medicine, 1981-87; coun. mem. Inst. of Lab. Animal Resources Nat. Acad. Scis. Nat. Rsch. Coun., 1986-93. Vis. disting. prof. USAF Med. Ctr., Wilford Hall, Tex., 1985; mem. rev. com. NIH Guide for the Care and Use of Lab. Animals, NRC, NAS, 1993-96; advisor/tutor Med. Quality Assurance Commn., Dept. Health, State of Wash., 1994-2001; mem. ethics com. Swedish Med. Ctr., N.W. Hosp., Seattle, 1992-2002; adj. prof. bioethics Sch. Medicine, U. So. Calif., 1989-91, adj. prof. emeritus, 1991—. Author: Inquiry Into Faith, 1960; co-editor: Readings in Religious Philosophy; The Reverent Skeptic, 1979. Served as lt. (j.g.)

USNR, 1945—47, o lt., 1952—54. Recipient award for excellence in tchg. U. So. Calif., 1960, 74, Dart award for acad. innovation, 1970, Raubenheimer Disting. Faculty award divsn. humanities, 1980, Robert Fenton Craig award Blue Key, 1980, Outstanding Faculty award Student Senate, 1981, Disting. Emeritus award, 1995, Educator of Yr. award Swedish Med. Ctr., Providence, Seattle, 2002. Fellow Soc. for Values in Higher Edn.; mem. Am. Acad. Religion (v.p. 1966, pres. 1967), Am. Philos. Assn., AAUP (v.p. Calif. Conf. 1977, pres. 1978-79), Phi Beta Kappa (hon.), Phi Kappa Phi, Phi Chi Phi. United Methodist. Home: 12507 Green Wood Ave N A-405 Seattle WA 98133

ROBB, KATHY MCCLESKEY, lawyer; b. Bklyn., Nov. 14, 1954; BA cum laude, spl. honors, Plan II, Univ. Tex., 1976; JD, Univ. Va., 1980. Bar: Va. 1982, NY 1989, US Dist. Ct. (ea. and so. dists.) NY, US Supreme Ct. Law clk. to Hon. Glen M. Williams US Dist. Ct. (we. dist.) Va., 1980—81; ptnr. resources, regulatory and environ. law Hunton & Williams LLP, NYC, 1988—. Adv. bd. BNA's Environ. Due Diligence Guide. Fellow: ABA; mem.: Assn. of City Bar of NY. Office: Hunton & Williams LLP 200 Park Ave New York NY 10166 Office Phone: 202-995-1128, 212-309-1128. Office Fax: 202-309-1100. Business E-Mail: krobb@hunton.com.

ROBB, LYNDA JOHNSON, writer; b. Washington, Mar. 19, 1944; d. Lyndon Baines and Claudia Alta (Taylor) Johnson; m. Charles Spittal Robb, Dec. 9, 1967; children: Lucinda Desha, Catherine Lewis, Jennifer Wickliffe. BA with honors, U. Tex., 1966. Writer McCall's Mag., 1966-68; contbg. editor Ladies Home Jour., 1968-80; lectr., bd. dirs. Reading Is Fundamental, 1968—, Lyndon B. Johnson Family Found., 1969-95. Past mem. Va. State Coun. on Infant Mortality, Va. Maternal & Child Health Coun.; mem. Nat. Commn. to Prevent Infant Mortality, 1987-93; chmn. Pres.'s Adv. Com. for Women, 1979-81; pres. bd. dirs. Nat. Home Libr. Found.; chmn. Va. Women's Cultural History Project, 1982-85; chmn. Reading is Fundamental, 1996-2001. Mem.: Zeta Tau Alpha. Office: Reading is Fundamental Ste 400 1825 Connecticut Ave NW Washington DC 20009-5708

ROBBERT, LOUISE BUENGER, retired historian; b. St. Paul, Aug. 18, 1925; d. Albert and Myrtle (Rubbert) Buenger; m. George S. Robbert, Sept. 17, 1960; 1 child, George Harold. BA, Carleton Coll., 1947; MA, U. Cin., 1948, B. Edn., 1949; PhD, U. Wis., 1955. Instr. history Smith Coll., Northampton, Mass., 1954-55, Hunter Coll., NYC, 1957-60; asst. prof. history Tex. Tech U., Lubbock, 1962-63, assoc. prof. history, 1964-75; vis. assoc. prof. history U. Mo., St. Louis, 1978-79, assoc. prof. history, 1979-91, prof. history, 1991—2000, ret., 2001. Author: Venetian Money Market in: Studi Veneziani, 1971, Venice and the Crusades in: The Crusades V., 1985, Il sistema monetario in: Storia di Venezia, II l'eta del comune, 1995. Officer Wednesday Club, St. Louis, 1981-83, 87-90, 94-96, v.p., 1997—99, pres., 1999-2001. Scholar Fulbright Commn., 1955-57; grantee A.C.L.S., 1960, Gladys Krieble Delmas Found., 1983, 87. Mem. Medieval Acad. Am., Soc. for Study of Crusades & the Latin East, Midwest Medieval History Conf. (pres.). Lutheran. Home: 162 Ameren Way #402 Ballwin MO 63021

ROBBINS, ALICE ELIZABETH, musician; b. NYC, Aug. 29, 1950; d. Jacob and Jean Robbins; m. Gregory Hayes (div.); m. Walter Denny. AB in Renaissance Music Performance, Ind. U., 1973; grad. degree, Schola Cantorum Basiliensis, Switzerland, 1977. Adj. faculty Boston U., 1990—2002, Five Coll. Early Music Program, Northampton, Mass., 1979—. Musician (cello, viola da gamba): Concerto Castello, 1980—85, Smithsonian Chamber Players, 1979—82, 1986—91, 2005; musician: (cello, basse de violon) Boston Early Music Festival Orch., 1997—; musician: (viola da gamba) Oberlin Consort of Viols, 1979—; musician: (prin. cello, viola da gamba) Wash. Bach Consort, 1996—; musician: (cello) Handel and Haydn Soc., 1987—; musician: (prin. cello, viola da gamba) Arcadia Players, 1988—; musician: (CD) Electrola, 1975, Arabesque, 1990, Centaur, 2000. Mem.: Early Music Am., Viola da Gamba Soc. of Am., Boston Musicians Assn. E-mail: arobbins@smith.edu.

ROBBINS, ALLEN BISHOP, physics professor; b. New Brunswick, NJ, Mar. 31, 1930; s. William Rei and Helen Grace (Bishop) R.; m. Shirley Mae Gernert, June 14, 1952 (div. 1978); children: Catherine Jean, Marilyn Elizabeth, Carol Ann, Melanie Barbara; m. Alice Harriet Ayars, Jan. 1, 1979. Student, Oberlin Coll., 1948—49; BS, Rutgers U., 1952; MS, Yale U., 1953, PhD, 1956. Rsch. fellow U. Birmingham (Eng.), 1957-58, lectr., 1960-61; instr. physics Rutgers U., New Brunswick, 1956-57, asst. prof. physics, 1957-60, assoc. prof., 1960-68, prof., 1968-97, prof. emeritus, 1997—, chmn. dept. physics and astronomy, 1979-95. Contbr. articles on nuc. physics to profl. jours. Recipient Lindbach Christian and Mary F. Lindbach Found., Rutgers U., 1975. Fellow Am. Phys. Soc.; mem. Am. Assn. Physics Tchrs., AAAS, Phi Beta Kappa, Sigma Xi. Office: Rutgers U Dept Physics and Astronomy 136 Frelinghuysen Rd Piscataway NJ 08854-8019 Personal E-mail: allenbrobbins@aol.com.

ROBBINS, ANNE FRANCIS See REAGAN, NANCY

ROBBINS, ARNIE, editor-in-chief; m. Terrie Robbins. Grad., Northwestern U. Medill Sch. Journalism, 1975. Sports reporter & editor Suburban Tribune, 1975—78; copy editor, dep. sports editor Chgo. Sun-Times, 1978—84; exec. sports editor, asst. mng. editor, features & change editor Mpls. Star Tribune, 1984—97; dir. news staff & orgnl. devel. St. Louis Post-Dispatch, 1997, dep. editor, 1997—99, mng. editor, 1999—2005, editor, 2005—. Office: St Louis Post-Dispatch 900 N Tucker Blvd Saint Louis MO 63101 Office Phone: 314-340-8130. E-mail: arobbins@post-dispatch.com. *

ROBBINS, AUDREY, county employee; b. Chgo., Mar. 1, 1932; d. Philip I. and Manya Lehr; children: Dana Merfeld, Cindy Buss. BA, DePaul U., Chgo., 1993. Mfrs. rep. Museum Reprodns. - Marwall Industries, NYC, 1969—79; asst. to chief counsel Arthur Andersen & Co., Chgo., 1979—98; mem. staff Office of Chief Judge, Cook County Cir. Ct., Chgo., 1999—. Author: Goldblatt's Galloping Gourmets, 1974 (Tribune award, 74). Vol. intensive care infants Northwestern Meml. Hosp., Chgo., 1979—80; vol. Art Inst. Chgo., 1984—86; touring docent Terra Mus. Am. Art, Chgo., 1999—2004, Clarke/Glessner House, 2005—, Loyola U. Mus. Art, 2005—; bd. dirs., sec., pres. Nathan & Francis Goldblatt Soc. for Cancer Rsch., 1955—83. Mem.: Golden Key (life). Avocations: art history, watercolors, cooking. Home: 910 N Lake Shore Dr # 718 Chicago IL 60611 Office: Cir Ct Cook County 50 W Washington Chicago IL 60602

ROBBINS, CHRISTIANE PATRICIA, media director, artist, designer, educator; b. Montclair, NJ, Jan. 9, 1956; d. Frederick James Nabkey and Eleanor Maroon; m. Andrew Richard Magdanz (div. Feb. 1984); 1 child, Justin; m. K.C. Lambert, Oct. 5, 1987; 1 child, John. BA with honors, U. Wis., 1975; MFA with highest honors, Calif. Inst. Arts, 1989. Design prin. Western Influence Studios, Berkeley, Calif., 1976—80; assoc. curator Art Mus. Assn. of Am., San Francisco, 1977—81; prin. Max Almy Prodns., Oakland, Calif., 1981—84, Robbins Design, San Francisco, 1981—89; exec. editor, pub. G.A.S. Jour., Corning, NY, 1984—88; creative dir. Digifilm, Oakland, 1988—90; lectr. U. Calif., Berkeley, 1989; asst. prof. TFNM Sch. of Comm., San Diego State U., 1997—99; assoc. prof. Roski Sch. of Fine Art, U. Southern Calif., LA, 1999—; prin. Jetztzeit Studios, 1999—. Cons. fine arts and design, San Francisco, 1981—, Calif. Arts Coun., Sacramento, 1981—, Craft and Folk Art Mus., LA, 1985; vis. asst. prof. creative arts San Francisco State U., 1990—96, Mills Coll., 1994—97; co-dir. ICATA, 1990; exec. co-dir. New Langton Arts, 1993—96, 1995. Numerous internat. pub. and pvt. collections, exhibitions, lectures, and publications, including SFMOMA, Banff Ctr. for the Arts, the Getty Mus., MOMA, NYC. Bd. dirs. New Langton Arts, CONSTRUCT; bd. advisors Session Gallery, San Francisco; chair, artist com. San Francisco Art Inst. Recipient 1st place Calif. State Art Exhibn., 1982, 1st place Women Design Internat., NYC, 1982-83, Best of Video, 27th SF Internat. Film Festival, 1984; Video Artist award, Long Beach Mus. of Art, 1991, Ind. Filmmaker award, Film Arts Found., 1991, Banff Ctr. fellowship, CAN, 1997; named Notable Alumni, CalArts, 2000-; Artist fellowship award, City of LA, 2002-03; Rsch. fellowship, Stanford U., 2006. Mem. AAUP, AAUW, AFI, BAVC, CAA, Film Arts Foundation, Norman Lear Center for the Study of Entertainment, Rhizome, X-Factor (co-founder), Glass Art Soc. (bd. dirs. 1984-88), Image Techs. (bd. advisors 1986-91), Commonwealth Club of Calif.

ROBBINS, CORNELIUS (CORNELIUS VAN VORSE), educational administration educator; b. Wilmington, Del., Nov. 2, 1931; s. Cornelius V. and Irene (Tatman) R.; m. Janet Porter, Aug. 1953; children: Eva Robbins Burke, Laurel Robbins, Susan Robbins, Melissa Robbins Beegle. BA in Polit. Sci, U. Del., 1953, MEd in Social Scis, 1961; EdD in Ednl. Adminstrn, U. Pa., 1964. Asst. mgr. Robbins & Clark Hardware, 1953-57; asst. provost U. Del., 1957-58, 1964—65; tchr. Marshallton (Del.) Sch. Dist., 1958-60, Mt. Pleasant (Del.) Sch. Dist., 1960-62; asst. to dir. sch. study councils U. Pa., 1962-64; dir. mgmt. sys. U. Del., 1964—65; dean instrn. Ocean County Coll., 1965-67; dean of coll. C/C. of Delaware County, Pa., 1967-69; sr. assoc., coll. div. dir. McManis Assocs., Washington, 1969-70; pres. Genesee C.C., 1970-75; assoc. chancellor for community colls. SUNY, 1975-85; acting pres. Potsdam State Coll. (N.Y.), 1982-83; pres. Cobleskill (N.Y.) Coll. Agr. & Tech., 1985-92; prof. edn. adminstrn. SUNY, Albany, NY, 1992—. Cons. Middle States Assn. Colls.; area liaison officer U.S. Mil. Acad., 1971-75; chmn. SUNY West Pres.'s Council and mem. Chancellor's Council, 1973-91. Contbr. articles to profl. publs. Served with U.S. Army, 1954-56; maj. USAR ret. Recipient Outstanding Educator's award N.Y. State Assn. Jr. Colls., 1975, Disting. Svc. award Faculty Coun. Community Colls., 1988. Mem. Am. Assn. Higher Edn., State Dirs. of Community Colls. Assn., Phi Delta Kappa. Office: SUNY Albany Ed 322 Albany NY 12222-0001 Home Phone: 518-372-3035; Office Phone: 518-442-5085. Business E-Mail: crobbins@uamail.albany.edu.

ROBBINS, DARREN J., lawyer; b. San Bernardino, Calif., 1966; BS in Economics, MS in Economics, U. Southern Calif., 1990; JD, Vanderbilt U., 1993. Bar: Calif. 1993, US Dist. Ct., Ctrl. Dist. Calif. 1994, US Dist. Ct., Northern Dist. Calif. 1994, US Dist. Ct., Southern Dist. Calif. 1994. Co-founder, ptnr. Lerach Coughlin Stoia Geller Rudman & Robbins LLP, San Diego, 2003—. Named one of Litigation's Rising Stars, The Am. Lawyer, 2007. Office: Lerach Coughlin Stoia Geller Rudman & Robbins LLP 655 W Broadway Ste 1900 San Diego CA 92101-4297 Office Phone: 619-231-1058. Office Fax: 619-231-7423. *

ROBBINS, ELLEN SUE, lawyer; b. Chgo., Mar. 15, 1967; d. Sheldon Neal and Barbara Lynn (Corenman) R. BS in Bus. Adminstrn. summa cum laude, U. Ill., 1988; JD magna cum laude, Harvard U., 1991. Bar: Ill. 1991. Jud. clk. to Judge Charles P. Kocoras U.S. Dist. Ct., Chgo., 1991-92; ptnr. Sidley & Austin, Chgo., 1999—. Adj. prof. law DePaul Coll. Law, Chgo. Mem. ABA, Chgo. Bar Assn. Avocations: jogging, golf, sports. Office: Sidley & Austin One South Dearborn Chicago IL 60603 Office Phone: 312-853-2931. E-mail: erobbins@sidley.com. *

ROBBINS, EMMALEE ELIZABETH, theater director, speech professional; b. Kingstree, SC, Mar. 29, 1941; d. Thomas Earl and Elizabeth Eloise (Payne) Gaddy; children: Alicia Rhett Howard, Christopher Michael. BA in speech and drama, Columbia Coll., 1963; MFA in theatre, U. N.C., Greensboro, NC, 1977. Cert. teaching 1965. Dance instr. Columbia Coll., 1961—63; dir. Christian youth activities Kingstree Meth. Ch., 1962; dir. Christian edn. Main St. Meth. Ch., Columbia, SC, 1963—64; dir., prod., choreographer Charleston County Playhouse, Summer Playhouse and St. Andrew's Parish H.S., 1969—72; tchg. asst. U. N.C., Greensboro, 1972—74; hostess Today's Woman CBS, 1972—74; dir., prod., choreographer Charleston County Playhouse, Summer Playhouse and St. Andrew's Parish H.S., 1974—79; tchr. Charleston Southern U., 1969—70; guest, choreographer ABC, 1977; theatre dir. Town Theatre, Columbia, SC, 1979—97; instr. Newberry Coll., Newberry, SC, 1979—80; dir. Young Town Players and Young People's Theatre, 1985—97; tchr. Buckley Sch. of Pub. Speaking, Camden, SC, 1998—. Vol., tchg. character edn. Lugoff Elem. Sch., Camden, SC, 2002—03; vol, tchg. character edn. Carolina Care Plan, 2003. Author: (9 story books on character edn.) The Lighthouse Learning Express. Recipient Career Achievement award, Columbia Coll., 1990. Mem.: SC Theater's Assn., Daughters of Am. Colonists. Republican. Presbyterian. Avocations: ballroom dancing, travel, reading, writing, pilates. Home: 30 Royal Gate Columbia SC 29223 Home Phone: 803-736-1555; Office Phone: 803-736-1555. E-mail: eer_productions@msn.com.

ROBBINS, ETTA JO, music educator; b. Fayetteville, Ark., Dec. 29, 1951; d. Memo Conrad and Dena Neva Robbins; children: Timothy Morris, Jessica Mitchell, Benjamin Morris. BA, Ark. Tech. U., Russellville, 1974, MEd, 1979. Instr. choir and band Yellville- Summit H.S., Yellville, Ark., 1974—75, Mountain Burg H.S., 1991—93; instr. band Westside H.S., Coal Hill, 1993—96; instr. choir and band Augusta H.S., 1996—98, Concord H.S., 1999—2001, West Side H.S., Greers Ferry, 2001—. Mem.: Ark. Sch. Band and Orch. Assn., Ark. Choral Dirs. Assn., Ark. Women Band Dirs. Assn. Baptist. Avocations: church choir, handbells, community band. Office: West Side HS 7295 Greers Ferry Rd Greers Ferry AR 72067-9416

ROBBINS, HENRY ZANE, public relations and marketing executive; b. Winston-Salem, NC, Jan. 17, 1930; s. Romulus Mayfield and Vera Ethel (Daniel) R.; m. Barbara Anne Brown, Jan. 19, 1955; children: Zane Scott, Jill Stewart, Gail Ruth. AB, U. N.C., 1952; student, Emory U., 1952. Reporter Atlanta Constn., 1952; exhibit specialist Gen. Electric Co., Schenectady, 1952, employee relations specialist Cin., 1955, editor Schenectady, 1955, account supr. Winston-Salem, 1956-58, group supr. Schenectady, 1958-60; v.p., gen. mgr. Burson-Marsteller, Pitts. and Chgo., 1960-70, sr. v.p., 1970; pres., chief exec. officer SL&H-Robbins Inc., Chgo., 1970-72; also dir.; pres., chief exec. officer Beveridge Kraus Robbins & Manning, Chgo., 1973-75; also dir.; pres., dir., chief exec. officer Beveridge and Robbins Inc., Chgo., 1975-77; pres., chief exec. officer Financial Advt. of Ill., Inc., Chgo.; mng. dir. Sports Mgmt. Group, Chgo., 1975-77; dir. communications Arthur Andersen & Co., Chgo. and Geneva, Switzerland, 1977-81, dir. mktg. support services, 1981-89, dir. mktg. and comms., 1989-91; mem. Worldwide Alpha Group, 1991-96, exec. dir. global markets program, 1995—2000; prin. Arthur Andersen & Co., 1980—2000; cons. Exec. Svc. Corps, 2004—. Mem. journalism adv. com. Harper Coll., Palatine, Ill., exec. svc. corp.; dir. Evanston Environ. Assn.; mem. Ladd Arboretum Commn., Evanston, Ill.; pub. rels. com. Chgo. Met. Crusade Mercy; mem. Nat. Task Force on Environment; cons. sec. Dept. Health, Edn. and Welfare, 1970; chmn. pub. rels. com. Honor Am. Day Com., 1970. Author: Vision of Grandeur, 1988, Globalizing the Enterprise, 2000, Tradition of Excellence, 2001; contbr. articles to profl. jours. Counselor Council of Mojave, 1972-74; gen. chmn. Chgo. Children's Classic Golf Tournament, 1974-77; chmn. Chgo. fin. com. Am.'s Freedom Train, 1976; chmn. fund devel. com. Presbytery of Chgo., 1977-83, maj. mission fund, 1977-79; dist. commr. Boy Scouts Am., 1976-79, chmn. Wildcat dist., 1980-83; mem. exec. bd. N.E. Ill. council, 1980-85; mem. Republican Citizens Com. Ill., 1960-61, Allegheny County (Pa.) Rep. Com., 1962-65; Trustee Roycemore Sch., Evanston, 1971-74; trustee, v.p. devel. Child and Family Services Chgo.; bd. dirs. Fellowship of Christian Athletes, U. N.C. Alumni Ill., Stockbrokers Assn. Chgo.; chmn. devel. com. Potawatomie Dist., 2000, chmn. fin. com., 2001; bd. dirs. Evanston Environ. Ctr., Ladd Arboretum, North Shore Nature Ctr., 2001-; mem. Ctr. for the Rehab. of Wildlife; bd. visitors U. N.C., 2004-. Served to 1st lt. AUS, 1952-54. Elected to N.C. Pub. Rels. Hall of Fame, 1994. Mem.: Chgo. Assn. Commerce and Industry, Environ. Writers Assn. Am., Am. Mgmt. Assn., Pub. Rels. Counselors Roundtable, Chgo. Ednl. TV Assn., Midwest Travel Writers Assn., Nat. Investor Rels. Inst., Pub. Rels. Soc. Am., Art Inst. Chgo., Sunset Ridge Country Club, OptimistClub of Wilmette (pres. 2005—), Univ. Club, Chi Psi. Republican. Presbyterian. Home: 2759 Broadway Ave Evanston IL 60201-1556 Personal E-mail: hzrobbins@sbcglobal.net.

ROBBINS, HULDA DORNBLATT, artist, printmaker; b. Atlanta, Oct. 19, 1910; d. Adolph Benno and Lina (Rosenthal) Domblatt. Student, Phila. Mus's. Sch. Indsl. Art, 1928-29, Prussian Acad., Berlin, 1929-31, Barnes Found., Merion, Pa., 1939. Poster designer and maker ITE Circuit Breaker Co. Inc., Phila., 1944; instr. serigraphy Nat. Serigraph Soc. Sch., NYC, 1953-60; instr. creative painting Atlantic County Jewish Cmty. Ctrs., Margate, Atlantic City, NJ, 1960-67. Represented by William P. Carl, Fine Prints, Boston, Picture Store, Boston. One-woman shows include Lehigh U. Art Galleries, 1933, ACA Galleries, Phila., 1939, 8th St. Gallery, N.Y.C., 1941, Serigraph Gallery, 1947, Atlantic City Art Ctr., 1961, 1971, exhibited in group shows at 2d Nat. Print Ann. Bklyn. Mus., Carnegie Inst., Libr. of Congress, LaNapoule Art Found., Am. Graphic Contemporary Art, Represented in permanent collections Met. Mus. Art, N.Y.C., Mus. Modern Art, Biblioteque Nationale, Smithsonian Instn., Art Mus. Ont., Can., Victoria and Albert Mus., London, U.S. embassies abroad, Lehigh U., Princeton Print Club, 6 prints, Phila. Mus. Art. Recipient Purchase prize, Prints for Children, Mus. Modern Art, N.Y.C., 1941, prize, 2d Portrait Am. Competition, 1945, 2d prize, Paintings by Printmakers, 1948. Mem.: Serigraph Soc. (mem. founding group, charter sec., Ninth Ann. prize 1948, 1949), Graphics Soc., Print Club, Am. Color Print Soc. Home and Office: 16 S Buffalo Ave Ventnor City NJ 08406-2635 Office Phone: 609-823-7314. *To cherish and express living through devotion to art.*

ROBBINS, JANET LINDA, language educator; b. LaJunta, Colo., Jan. 16, 1947; d. Richard Carl and Ruth Janet Robbins. B in Music Edn., Drake U., Des Moines, Iowa, 1969; BA, U. Minn., Mpls., 1974. Cert. life office mgmt. ins. cos., Iowa, 1970, tchg. music K-12, psychology 9-12 Iowa, 1969. Acctg. clerk Ctrl. Life Assurance Co., Des Moines, 1970; reader, tutor, intern Minn. State Svcs. for the Blind, St. Paul, 1973—74, 1975; tng. asst. psychology Mankato State U., Minn., 1974—75; intern mentally retarded St. Peter State Hosp., Minn., 1975; tchr. bi-lingual (Spanish and English) So. Minn., 1976; substitute tchr. pvt. students St. Louis Park Pub. Schs., Minn., 1977—81; care of aged and child care Okaloosa, Iowa, 1981—; instr. ESL Indian Hills C.C., Okaloosa, 1987—. Intern pvt. co., Washington, 1977; tchr. Sunday Sch. Presbyn. Friends, Meth. Chs.; owner Janet L. Robbins Bookkeeping and Ednl. Svcs., 1987—. Violinist: Des Moines Symphony, 1965—69; author: numerous newspaper articles and poetry. Vol. some Dem. Party campaigns; youth asst. 1st Bapt. Ch., Okaloosa, 1987—88. Recipient Vol. award, Gov. Iowa, 1993, 2000, Ten County Literacy Tutor award, IHCC, 2001. Mem.: Iowa Life Long Learning Assn., U. Minn. Alumni Assn., Drake U. Alumni Assn., Peale Ctr. Positive Thinkers Club, Peale Ctr. Bible Club. Democrat. Methodist. Avocations: piano, writing, tutoring, composing music. Mailing: PO Box 576 Oskaloosa IA 52577

ROBBINS, JEFFREY HOWARD, media consultant, research writer, educator; b. NYC, Mar. 29, 1941; s. Stanley Samuel and Miriam (Cooper) R.; m. Marsha Sue Rimler, Nov. 3, 1984 (div. Dec. 1996); 1 child, Nina Camille. BSME, Carnegie Mellon U., 1962; MS in Physics, U. N.Mex., 1966, ABD in Physics, 1967; postgrad., U. Calif., Berkeley and LA, 1963-64. Summer rsch. assoc. Linde Co., Tonawanda, NY, 1961; rsch. engr. N.Am. Aviation (Rockwell), Downey, Calif., 1962—64; summer rsch. assoc. Los Alamos Nat. Lab., N.Mex., 1965; sr. engr. Radio Engring. Labs., LI, NY, 1968—70; engring. cons. PRD Electronics, Syosset, NY, 1972—73; sr. cons. Bendix Corp., Teterboro, NJ, 1974—76; sr. engr. Giordano Assocs., Franklin Lakes, NJ, 1977—81; sr. applications engr. Racal-Redak, Mahwah, NJ, 1981—83; tech. media cons. Allied Signal Corp., Teterboro, 1983—92, U.S. Army, Picatinny Arsenal, NJ, 1992; tech. cons. Ford Motor Co., Lansdale, Pa., 1992—98, Visteon Automotive Electronics, Markham, Ont., Canada, 1998; adj. prof. Rutgers U., New Brunswick, NJ, 2002—. Cons. Tyco Internat., Clark, N.J., 1998-2002; tech. cons., rsch. writer media literacy programs Packer Collegiate Inst., Bklyn., N.Y.C., 1992-93, On TV, Inc., N.Y.C., 1992; initiator, moderator Media Literacy Forum, 1995; evening sch. instr. New Sch. for Social Rsch., N.Y.C., 1979-85; presenter in field. Author: On Balance and Higher Education, 1970; contbr. articles to profl. jours. and G. Altmann's Festschrift. Organizer, co-moderator Future Impact of Artificial Intelligence, Robotics Forum, 1984. Recipient 1st prize for essay The World and I Mag., 1990; nominee Grawemeyer award in Edn., 1988; NDEA fellow, 1966-67, others; feature essay premier issue Plain mag., 1994; contbr. essays to publs. Mem. IEEE (presenter Internat. Symposium in Tech. and Soc. 1993, 96, 98, 2006, 07, Internat. Soc. Sys. Scis. Conf. 1993, 95, 97, 99, 2000, 02, initiator, moderator, media literacy forum Packer Collegiate Inst. 1995, presenter World Order Conf., Toronto 1999, 2001, 02, 04, judge sci. engring. fair 2003-07, spkr.), N.Y. Acad. Scis., Sigma Xi, Phi Kappa Phi, Pi Tau Sigma. Home and Office: PO Box 335 Long Beach NY 11561-0335 E-mail: jhrobbins@erols.com.

ROBBINS, JERRY HAL, educational administration educator; b. DeQueen, Ark., Feb. 28, 1939; s. James Hal and Barbara I. (Rogers) R. BA in Math, Hendrix Coll., 1960; M.Ed., U. Ark., 1963, Ed.D., 1966. Tchr. math. and music Clinton (Ark.) pub. schs., 1960-61; prin. Adrian (Mo.) High Sch., 1961-63; exec. sec. Ark. Sch. Study Council, Fayetteville, 1963-65; mem. faculty U. Miss., University, 1965-74, prof. ednl. adminstrn., 1970-74, chmn. dept. ednl. adminstrn., 1970-74; dean Coll. Edn., U. Ark., Little Rock, 1974-79; asso. v.p. for acad. affairs Ga. State U., Atlanta, 1979-84, dean Coll. Edn., 1984-90, prof. ednl. adminstrn., 1990-91; dean. Coll. Edn. Ea. Mich. U., Ypsilanti, 1991—2004, prof. ednl. leadership, 2004—05. Co-author: (with S. B. Williams Jr.) Student Activities in the Innovative School, 1969, School Custodian's Handbook, 1970, Administrator's Manual of School Plant Administration, 1970. Mem. NEA, Am. Assn. Sch. Adminstrs., Am. Assn. Colls. Tchr. Edn. (dir. 1979-82, 2000-04), Nat. Assn. Secondary Sch. Prins., So. Regional Council Ednl. Adminstrn. (pres. 1970-71), Tchr. Edn. Coun. State Colls. and Univs. (pres. 1998-99), Phi Delta Kappa, Kappa Delta Pi (v.p. chpt. devel. 1978-80, pres. elect 1980-82, pres. 1982-84, past pres. 1984-86) Mem. United Meth. Ch. Home and Office: 3384 Bent Trail Dr Ann Arbor MI 48108-9316 E-mail: jerry.robbins@emich.edu.

ROBBINS, JOHN BENNETT, medical researcher; b. Bklyn., Dec. 1, 1932; BA, NYU, 1956; MD (hon.), U. Goteborg, Sweden, 1959. Intern, resident Children's Med. Svc. Mass. Gen. Hosp., Boston, 1959—60; rsch. fellow dept. pediat. U. Fla., 1961—64; guest scientist dept. chem. immunology Weizmann Inst. Sci., Rehovot, Israel, 1965—66; asst. prof. pediat. and microbiology U. Fla., Gainesville, 1964—67; from asst. prof. to assoc. prof. pediat. Albert Einstein Coll. Medicine, 1967—70; clin. dir. Nat. Inst. Child Health and Human Devel. NIH, 1970—72; chief devel. immunology br. NIH, 1971—74; dir. divsn. bacterial products FDA, 1974—83; chief lab. devel. and molecular immunity Nat. Inst. Child Health and Human Devel. NIH, 1983—. Henry Bale Meml. lectr. Nat. Inst. Biol. Stds. and Control, 1979; Erwin Neter Meml. lectr. U. Buffalo, 1984; Henry L. Barnett lectr. Albert Einstein Coll. Medicine, 1985; Maxwell Finland lectr. Infectious Disease Soc. Am., 1989; Louis Weinstein lectr.

Tufts U., 1989. Recipient E. Mead Johnson award, Am. Acad. Pediat., 1975, Albert Lasker Clin. Med. Rsch. award, Albert and Mary Lasker Found., 1996. Fellow: Am. Acad. Microbiology; mem.: NAS, Am. Philos. Soc., Nat. Inst. Medicine, Am. Assn. Immunologists, Assn. Am. Physicians, Am. Soc. Clin. Investigation, Soc. Infectious Disease, Soc. Pediatric Rsch. Achievements include development of first effective typhoid fever vaccine for children. Office: Nat Inst Child Health & Human Devel 9000 Rockville Pike Rm 424 Bethesda MD 20892-0001

ROBBINS, JOHN CLAPP, management consultant; b. Cleveland, Jan. 22, 1921; s. John Clapp and Esther Turner (Holland) R.; m. Louise Severance Nash, Jan. 10, 1951 (div. Oct. 1974); children: Anne Millikin, Julia Severance, John Nash; m. Beatrice Blair, Aug. 2, 1975 (dec. July 1994); m. Sylvia Hordosch, Dec. 20, 2000. AB, Harvard U., 1942. Copy boy, reporter, writer, promotion editor Cleve. Press, 1946-57; exec. internat. div. Mobil Oil Corp., NYC, Istanbul, 1957-70; chief exec. officer Planned Parenthood/World Population, NYC, 1970-75; prin. mgmt. cons. Stanford Research Inst., 1976-83; v.p. GPA Inc., NYC, 1983—; pres. John Robbins Assocs. Spl. fin. cons. Internat. Helsinki Fedn., Vienna, Parkinson Disease Found., N.Y.C., Alan Guttmacher Inst., N.Y.C. Author: Too Many Asians, 1959. Bd. dirs., pres. Am. Hosp. Istanbul; treas. Harvard Libr. in N.Y.C. Capt. AUS, 1942-45. Decorated Bronze Star, Purple Heart; Reid fellow, 1953 Mem. Internat. Planned Parenthood Fedn. London, N.Y. State Rep. Pro-Choice Alliance. Unitarian Universalist. Home and Office: 115 E 87th St New York NY 10128-1136 Office Phone: 212-369-9800. E-mail: johnrobbin@aol.com.

ROBBINS, LANNY ARNOLD, chemical engineer; b. Wahoo, Nebr., Apr. 3, 1940; s. Earl Willard and Mildred Irene (Hanson) R.; m. Connie Lou Polich, Feb. 24, 1962; children: James Alan, Debra Renea. BS, Iowa State U., 1961, MS, 1963, PhD, 1966. Rsch. engr., project leader Dow Chem. Co., Midland, Mich., 1966-73, rsch. specialist, 1973-76, assoc. scientist, 1976-83, rsch. scientist, 1983-88, sr. rsch. scientist, 1988-97, rsch. fellow, 1997—2003; cons. Larco Techs., LLC, Midland, Mich., 2003—, GANTEC Inc. Adj. prof. Va. Poly. Inst., Blacksburg, 1973—76, Mich. State U., Lansing, 1983; mem. indsl. adv. bd. Iowa State U., Ames, 1994—2000. Author (chpt.) Schweitzer's Handbook of Separation Techniques, 1997, Perry's Chemical Engineer's Handbook, 1997. Recipient H.H. Dow medal, 1993. Mem.: NAE, AIChE. Republican. American Baptist. Achievements include patents for AquaDetox Aqueous Purification stripping devices and process, Sorbathene pressure swing adsorption vent emission control processes, liquid distributors for packed distillation, distillation process control and optimization. Home: 4101 Old Pine Trl Midland MI 48642-8892

ROBBINS, N. CLAY, foundation administrator; b. Indpls., May 30, 1957; m. Amy Robbins; 3 children. BA, Wabash Coll., Crawfordsville, Ind., 1979; JD, Vanderbilt U., 1982; LLD (hon.), Ind. State U., 2004; LHD (hon.), Rosc-Hulman Inst. Tech., 2006. Exch. assoc. European Econ. Cmty. law dept. Rycken Burlion Bolle & Houben, Brussels, 1985-86; assoc. Baker & Daniels, 1982-85, ptnr., 1988—92; v.p. cmty. devel. Lilly Endowment Inc., Indpls., 1993-94, pres., 1994—. Mem. drafting com. Ind. Nonprofit Corp. Act 1991. Past dir., pres. Indpls. Chamber Orch.; past dir. Damar Homes, Inc.; bd. dirs., exec. com. Ctrl. Ind. Corp. Partnership; bd. dirs. United Way Ctrl. Ind. Mem. Ind. State Bar Assn., Indpls. C. of C. Methodist. Office: Lilly Endowment Inc 2801 N Meridian St PO Box 88068 Indianapolis IN 46208-0068

ROBBINS, NANCY SLINKER, volunteer; b. New Kensington, Pa., Jan. 28, 1923; d. Charles Morris and Nancy Grace (Moore) Slinker; m. James Bingham Murray, Aug. 1, 1946 (div. 1959); m. Daniel Harvey Robbins, Nov. 21, 1964; children: Nancy Caroline, Christina Chapman. BA, Westminster Coll., 1945; grad., U. Pitts., 1946. Cert. tchr., Pa. Tchr. Lower Burrell Sch., New Kensington, 1945-48; asst. buyer Gimbel's, Pitts., 1951-53, buyer, 1953-57, La Salle's, Toledo, 1957-61, Sibley's, Rochester, N.Y., 1961-66. Editor: Fan Fare, 1980-81. Pres. bd. Woman's Edn. and Indsl. Union, Rochester, 1973-76, Women's Coalition for Downtown, Rochester, 1982-84; pres. bd. Ronald McDonald House, Rochester, 1986-90, adminstr. grants program, 1996—2004; chmn. Pub. TV Auction, Rochester, 1980. Recipient Jefferson award Am. Inst. Pub. Svc., 1988, Forman Flair award for outstanding volunteerism, 1990, DeWitt Clinton award for pub. svc. Masons, 1989, Miracle Maker award Golisano Children's Hosp., 2005. Avocations: antiques, travel, cooking. Home: 35 Schoolhouse Ln Rochester NY 14618-3231 E-mail: nandan35@frontiernet.net.

ROBBINS, NORMAN NELSON, lawyer; b. Detroit, Sept. 27, 1919; s. Charles and Eva (Gold) R.; m. Pamela Anne Eldred, April 22, 1946; children: Susan, Aimee. LLB, JD, Wayne State U., 1943. Bar: Mich. 1943. Pvt. practice, Birmingham, Mich., 1943—. Chmn. Mich. Bd. for Marriage Counselors, 1971-75; lectr. Inst. Continuing Legal Edn. Editor Mich. Family Law Jour., 1974—; mem. editorial bd. Am. Jour. Family Law; co-editor: Michigan Family Law, 2 vols., 1988; contbr. 600 articles to legal publs. Chmn. Wayne County unit Am. Cancer Soc., Detroit, 1971-76, Mich. Dept. Vets. Trust Fund, 1977-78. Capt. USMCR, 1943-46, PTO. Recipient Gov.'s award State of Mich., Cert. of Appreciation, Gov. of Mich., Cert. of Recognition, Detroit Common Coun. award Mich. Assn. Marriage Counselors, Lifetime Achievement award Mich. Family Law Sect. Mem. ABA (mem. family law coun. 1993-95, sr. editor ABA Family Adv. 1991—), Mich. Bar Assn. (chmn. family law sect. 1974-75), Oakland County Bar Assn., Am. Acad. Matrimonial Lawyers (pres. Mich. chpt. 1982), Am. Legion (judge adv. Mich. dept. 1968-69, comdr. Detroit chpt. 1970-71). Office Phone: 248-737-9168.

ROBBINS, OREM OLFORD, insurance company executive; b. Mpls., Feb. 5, 1915; s. Douglas Ford and Grace (Rorem) R.; m. Annette Strand Scherer, May 17, 1992; children: Ford M., Ross S., Gail R. Tomei, Cynthia R. Rothbard. BBA with distinction, U. Minn., 1936; BS in Law, William Mitchell Coll. Law, 1946, JD, 1948. Comml. rep. NW Bell Telephone Co., Mpls., 1936-48; dep. dir. US Treas. Dept., Mpls., 1948-49; sales rep. Conn. Gen. Life Ins. Co., Mpls., 1949-56; founder, chmn. Security Life Ins. Co. Am., Mpls., 1956—. Bd. dirs., past pres. Family and Children's Svcs., Mpls., 1968—; bd. govs., past chmn. Meth. Hosp., Mpls., 1960-90; past treas., bd. dirs. Goodwill/Easter Seals, St. Paul, 1958-68, 75-88; life trustee Hamline U., St. Paul, 1979—, chmn. bd. trustees, 1990-91. Col. US Army, 1941-46. Decorated Legion of Merit; recipient Outstanding Achievement award U. Minn., 2001; named Disting. Eagle Scout, 2000. Fellow Life Mgmt. Assn.; mem. Am. Soc. CLU (pres. Mpls. chpt. 1959), Health Underwriters Assn., Chartered Fin. Cons., Am. Legion, Skylight Club (Mpls.), Naples Yacht Club, Mpls. Club, Officer's Club, Masons. Republican. Methodist. Office: Security Life Ins Co Am 10901 Red Circle Dr Minnetonka MN 55343-9304 Home Phone: 239-261-4295. E-mail: oorobbins@securitylife.com.

ROBBINS, RACHEL F., stock exchange executive, lawyer; b. Trenton, NJ, Oct. 30, 1950; 2 children. BA, Wellesley Coll., 1972; JD, NYU, 1976. Bar: N.Y. 1977. Assoc. Milbank Tweed Hadley & McCloy, 1976—80; atty. J.P. Morgan & Co., Inc., NYC, 1981—96, gen. counsel, corp. sec., 1996—2001; founding ptnr. Blaqwell, Inc., 2001—03; gen. counsel Citigroup Internat., 2003—04; strategic adv. Axiom Legal Solutions, 2004—06; exec. v.p., gen. counsel NYSE Group, Inc., NYC, 2006—07, NYSE Euronext, NYC, 2007—. Mem. Fed. Regulation Com. Securities Industry Assn., 1987—2001, Legal Adv. Com. on NYSE, 1992—95, Exec. Com. Securities Regulation Inst., 1994—2001, US Treasury Adv. Com. on Fin. Services, 1996; chmn., pres Am. Bankers Assn. Securities Assn., 1997—2000. Mng. editor Ann. Survey Am. Law. Bd. trustees NYU Sch. Law. Named a Woman of Achievement, YMCA, 2003; named one of 100 Most Influential Lawyers, Nat. Law Jour., 1997, 2000, The 50 Most Influential Women Lawyers in Am., 2007. Mem. ABA, Assn. of the Bar of the City of N.Y., N.Y. State Bar Assn., Order of the Coif. Office: NYSE Euronext 11 Wall St New York NY 10005 *

ROBBINS, RAY C., retired manufacturing executive; b. Syracuse, NY, Sept. 15, 1920; s. Frederick and Mary Elizabeth (Field) R.; children: Sandra Robbins Jannetta, Ray Charles Jr., Eric L. With Lennox Internat. Inc. (formerly Lennox Co.), 1940-48; asst sales mgr. Lennox Industries Inc., Syracuse, 1948-52, gen. mgr. new factory and sales office, Toronto, Ont., Canada, 1952-67; dir. Lennox Can. and Timeplan Fin. Co. Ltd., 1953-65; pres. Lennox Can., 1965-69, chmn. bd., 1976-92; exec. v.p. Lennox Internat. Inc., 1969-70, pres., CEO, 1970-77, chmn. bd., chief exec. officer, 1977-80, chmn. bd., 1980-91, chmn. emeritus, 1991—. Bd. dirs. Lennox Internat., First Interstate of Iowa, Inc., Hawkeye Security Ins. Co., Des Moines, Fin. Security Group, Inc., Des Moines, Q-Dot, Garland, Tex.; pres., founder, bd. dirs. Exec. Inst., Inc., Dallas, 1983—; cons. Internat. Exec. Svc. Corp., 1992—, bd. adv., 1993-. Bd. dirs. Metro Toronto Big Bros., 1964-69, Queensway Gen. Hosp., 1957-69, Texx Found., 1979-81, Bus. Industry Polit. Action Com.; bd. govs., mem. exec. com. Iowa Coll. Found., 1975-78; v.p., mem. exec. bd. Mid-Iowa County Boy Scouts Am., 1972-78; mem. Pres.' Phys. Fitness Council, from 1979; exec. bd. Circle 10 council Boy Scouts Am., from 1979; mem. Dallas Citizens Council; bd. of govs. Nat. Women's Econ. Alliance Found.; bd. dirs. North Tex. Commn.; fellow Legacy for Pub. Opinion, 2001—. Served with AUS, 1942-45, PTO. Mem. ASHRAE (life), Am. Refrigeration Inst. (bd. dirs. 1973-74, 78, life from 1979, v.p. 1975-76, chmn. 1977), NAM (bd. dirs. 1974-75, dir. at large 1976, dir. State of Iowa 1977-78, dir. State of Tex. 1979-92), Nat. Mgmt. Assn. (exec. adv. com. 1979-92), Gas Appliance Mfrs. Assn. (past bd. dirs.), Can. Gas Assn. (pres.), Can. Mfg. Assn. (chmn. Toronto dist.), U.S. C. of C. (Can.-U.S. sect.), Bus.-Industry Polit. Action Com. (bd. dirs. 1991). Clubs: Park Cen., Landmark Athletic, Cooper Fitness Ctr. (Dallas); Canyon Creek Country (Richardson, Tex.).

ROBBINS, REGINALD L., mathematician, educator; b. Jasper, Ala., Aug. 11, 1964; s. Cherry I. Clemons; m. Lisa A. Hudson, Oct. 26, 1996; children: Kyle L., Kynnadi J. BS, Tenn. State U., Nashville, 1988. Substitute tchr. Norfolk Pub. schs., Va., 1989—95; supr. Craative Plastering, Chesapeake, Va., 1994—2004; tchr. math. Virginia Beach Friends Sch., Va., 2004—; pres. Snibor Tutoring & Learning, Chesapeake, 2006—. Curriculum devel. coord. Virginia Beach Friends Sch., 2005—; project coord. Creative Plastering, 2000—04; pres., instr. tutor Snibbor Tutoring and Learning Ctr., Cheasaoeaje, Va., 2006—. Author short stories. Mem.: Nat. Coun. Tchrs. Math., Phi Mu Alpha. Democrat. Baptist. Avocations: music, poetry. Office: Virginia Beach Friends Sch 1537 Laskin Rd Virginia Beach VA 23451 Office Phone: 757-822-4022.

ROBBINS, ROBERT CLAYTON, surgeon; b. Laurel, Miss., Nov. 20, 1957; MD, U. Miss., 1983. Cert. cardiothoracic surgery Am. Bd. Thoracic Surgery, gen. surgery Am. Bd. Surgery. Intern U. Miss. Med. Ctr., 1983—84, resident, 1984—88; fellow Stanford U., 1989—91, asst. prof. then assoc. prof., 1993—, prof., chmn. dept. cardiothoracic surgery, 2005—; dir. Inst. Cardiovasc. Medicine, 2004—. Mem.: Western Thoracic Surgical Assn., Am. Assn. Thoracic Surgery, Cardiothoracic Surgery Network. Office: Falk Cardiovasc Rsch Ctr 300 Pasteur Dr CVRB MC 5407 Stanford CA 94305 Office Phone: 650-725-3828.

ROBBINS, SHERRI LYNN, quality assurance professional; b. Charlotte, Mich., Nov. 20, 1975; adopted d. Clifford Nowell and Laura Sue Anderson, d. Cynthia Lee Waterbury; m. Peter Norman Robbins, June 18, 1999; 4 children. BS in Microbiology, Weber State U., Ogden, Utah, 1998. Cert. specialist microbiology Am. Soc. Microbiology, 2005. Study dir. Nelson Laboratories, Inc., Salt Lake City, 1999—2000, quality assurance specialist, 2000—01, quality assurance mgr., 2001—. Presenter in field. Young women's leader LDS Ch., Lehi, Utah, 2006—07. Mem.: Am. Soc. Quality (local chpt. sec. 2004—05, cert. quality engr. 2005, cert. quality auditor 2002). Independent. Avocations: fly fishing, sewing, watercolor painting, gardening. Office: Nelson Labs Inc 6280 S Redwood Rd Salt Lake City UT 84123 Home Phone: 801-768-4472; Office Phone: 801-963-2600.

ROBBINS, STEPHEN J. M., lawyer; b. Seattle, Apr. 13, 1942; s. Robert Mads and Aneita Elberta (West) R.; m. Nina Winifred Tanner, Aug. 11, 1967; children: Sarah E.T., Alicia S.T. AB, UCLA, 1964; JD, Yale U., 1971. Bar: D.C. 1973, U.S. Dist. Ct. D.C. 1973, U.S. Ct. Appeals (D.C. cir.) 1973, U.S. Ct. Appeals (3d cir.) 1973, U.S. Dist. Ct. (ea. and no. dists.) Calif. 1982, U.S. Dist. Ct. (cen. dist.) Calif. 1983, Supreme Ct. of Republic of Palau, 1994. Pres. U.S. Nat. Student Assn., Washington, 1964-65; dir. scheduling McGovern for Pres., Washington, 1971-72; assoc. Steptoe & Johnson, Washington, 1972-75; chief counsel spl. inquiry on food prices, com. on nutrition and human needs U.S. Senate, Washington, 1975; v.p., gen. counsel Straight Arrow Pubs., San Francisco, 1975-77; dep. dist. atty. City and County of San Francisco, 1977-78; regional counsel U.S. SBA, San Francisco, 1978-80; spl. counsel Warner-Amex Cable Communications, Sacramento, 1981-82; ptnr. McDonough, Holland and Allen, Sacramento, 1982-84; v.p. Straight Arrow Pubs., NYC, 1984-86; gen. legal counsel Govt. State of Koror, Rep. of Palau, Western Caroline Islands, 1994-95; pvt. practice law, 1986—. Adj. prof. govt. Calif. State U., Sacramento, 1999-05. Staff sgt. U.S. Army, 1966-68. Fellow Acad. Polit. Sci.; mem. ABA (sect. urban, state and local govt.), DC Bar, State Bar Calif., Urban Land Inst., Am. Hist. Assn., Supreme Ct. Hist. Soc. Democrat. Unitarian. Avocations: theater, art, hiking. Office: PO Box 390 Middlebury VT 05753

ROBBINS, SUSAN PAULA, social work educator; b. Bklyn., Aug. 15, 1948; d. Harold Jess and Rose (Bernstein) R. AA, Manhattan C.C., 1972; BA summa cum laude, Hamline U., 1974; MSW, U. Minn., 1976; PhD, Tulane U., 1979. Adj. instr. dept. sociology and social work Augsburg Coll., Mpls., 1975-76; part-time instr. women's studies program U. Minn., Mpls., 1976; rsch. and grant cons. Seminole Tribe of Fla., Hollywood, 1978-79, child and adolescent caseworker, program planning cons., 1979-80; coord. criminal justice/corrections program St. Mary's Dominican Coll., New Orleans, 1979-80; asst. prof. social work New Orleans Consortium, 1978-80, U. Houston, 1980-86, assoc. prof., 1986—, assoc. dean acad. affairs, 1998-2000. Cons. ABA Multi Door Program, Houston, Cmty. Svc. Option Program, Houston; mediator Dispute Resolution Ctrs., Houston, 1982—; trainer Tex. Dept. Protective Svcs. Tng. Inst., 1995—. Author (with others): Encyclopedia of Social Work, Social Workers' Desk Reference; contbr. articles and book chpts. to profl. jours. Women's Club of Mpls. fellow, 1975, Nat. Inst. of Mental Health fellow, 1976-78; recipient Nat. Faculty Excellence award Univ. Continuing Edn. Assn., 1998. Mem. NASW, Coun. on Social Work Edn., Social Welfare Action Alliance, Assn. for Cmty. Orgn. and Social Adminstrn., So. Sociol. Soc., Phi Kappa Phi (sec. Houston chpt. 1984—). Democrat. Jewish. Office: Univ Houston 4800 Calhoun Rd Houston TX 77204-4013 Office Phone: 713-743-8103. Business E-Mail: srobbins@uh.edu.

ROBBINS, THOMAS EUGENE, writer; b. Blowing Rock, NC, 1936; m. Terrie Hemingway (div.); m. Alexa d'Avalon, 1995; 1 child, Fleetwood Starr. Student, Washington and Lee U., 1954-56, U. Wash., 1963; degree in social sci., Va. Commonwealth U., 1959. Former copy editor Richmond (Va.) Times-Dispatch, 1959—62, Seattle Post-Intelligencer, 1967—69; art critic Seattle Times, 1962—65. Author: Guy Anderson, 1965, Another Roadside Attraction, 1971, Even Cowgirls Get the Blues, 1976 (Best Am. Short Story 1977), Still Life with Woodpecker, 1980, Jitterbug Perfume, 1984, Skinny Legs and All, 1990, Half Asleep in Frog Pajamas, 1994, Fierce Invalids Home from Hot Climates, 2000, Villa Incognito, 2003, Wild Ducks Flying Backward, 2005. With USAF. Named one of 100 Best Writers of 20th Century, Writer's Digest. Office: PO Box 338 La Conner WA 98257-0338

ROBBINS, THOMAS LANDAU, researcher, editor; b. NYC, Oct. 13, 1943; s. Manuel Lee and Elly (Landau) R. AB, Harvard U., 1965; MA, U. N.C., 1968, PhD in Sociology, 1973. Instr., asst. prof. Queens Coll., 1971-78; instr. Cen. Mich. U., 1982-83; NIMH postdoctoral trainee in sociology Yale U., New Haven, 1979-81; sr. rsch. assoc. Santa Barbara (Calif.) Ctr. for Humanistic Studies, 1990—. Author: Cults, Converts and Charisma, 1988; co-editor: In Gods We Trust, 1981, 2d edit., 1990, Cults, Culture and the Law, 1985, Church-State Relations, 1987, Millennium, Messiahs and Mayhem, 1997, Misunderstanding Cults, 2004, New Religious Movements in the 21st Century, 2000; assoc. editor Sociol. Analysis, 1984-90; editl. cons. Nova Religio, 1997—; contbr. articles to profl. jours. Mem. Soc. for the Sci. Study of Religion (exec. coun. 1988-91), Assn. for the Sociology Religion, (exec. coun. 1985-87), Am. Sociol. Assn., Soc. for the Study of Social Problems. Meher Baba. Home and Office: 936 41st NW Apt C-116 Rochester MN 55901 Personal E-mail: tomrobbins427@aol.com. *I am becoming concerned these days about threats to freedom of religion in the United States and Europe.*

ROBBINS, TIM (TIMOTHY FRANCIS ROBBINS), actor, film director; b. West Covina, Calif., Oct. 16, 1958; s. Gil Robbins; life ptnr. Susan Sarandon; children: John Henry, Miles 1 stepchild, Eva Maria. BA with honors, UCLA, 1981. Founder, artistic dir. The Actor's Gang, 1981—. Actor: (films) No Small Affair, 1984, Toy Soldiers, 1984, Fraternity Vacation, 1985, The Sure Thing, 1985, Howard the Duck, 1986, Top Gun, 1986, Five Corners, 1987, Bill Durham, 1988, Tapeheads, 1989, Eric The Viking, 1989, Miss Firecracker, 1989, Cadillac Man, 1990, Twister, 1990, Jacob's Ladder, 1990, Jungle Fever, 1991, The Player, 1992 (Best Actor award Cannes Film Festival 1992), Short Cuts, 1993, The Hudsucker Proxy, 1994, The Shawshank Redemption, 1994, Ready to Wear (Prêt-à-Porter), 1994, I.Q., 1994, Nothing to Lose, 1997, Arlington Road, 1999, Austin Powers: The Spy Who Shagged Me, 1999, Mission to Mars, 2000, High Fidelity, 2000, Antitrust, 2001, Human Nature, 2001, The Truth About Charlie, 2002, The Day My God Died (voice), 2003, Mystic River, 2003 (Golden Globe for best supporting actor in a drama, 2004, Screen Actors Guild Award for best supporting actor, 2004, Acad. Award for best supporting actor in a drama, 2004), Code 46, 2004, Anchorman: The Legend of Ron Burgundy, 2004, War of the Worlds, 2005, The Secret Life of Words, 2005, Zathura: A Space Adventure, 2005, Catch a Fire, 2006, Tenacious D: The Pick of Destiny, 2006; (TV movies) Quarterback Princess, 1983, Malice in Wonderland, 1985; (TV appearances) St. Elsewhere, 1982, Legmen, 1984, Hardcastle and McCormick, 1984, Hill Street Blues, 1984, Moonlighting, 1985, Amazing Stories, 1986, (voice) The Simpsons, 1999, Jack & Bobby, 2005; actor, dir., writer, composer: Bob Roberts, 1992; dir., writer, prodr.: Dead Man Walking, 1995 (Golden Globe nomination for best dir. of film 1996, Acad. Award nomination for best dir. 1996), The Cradle Will Rock, 1999; exec. prodr., The Typewriter, the Rifle, and the Movie Camera, 1994, The Spectre of Hope, 2000; dir. (plays) Ubu Roi (L.A. Weekly Dir. award), A Midsummer's Night Dream, Methusalem, the Eternal Bourgeois, The Good Woman of Setzuan (L.A. Drama Critics Circle nominee), and others, (TV series) Queen's Supreme, 2003; co-writer: (plays) Alagazam...After the Dog Wars, Violence: The Misadventures of Spike Spangle, Farmer, Carnage, a Comedy, Embedded, and others. Recipient Tribute to Ind. Vision Award, Sundance Film Festival, 1997. Office: ICM c/o Elaine Goldsmith Thomas 40 W 57th St New York NY 10019 *

ROBBINS, TONY (ANTHONY ROBBINS), writer; b. Glendora, Calif., Feb. 29, 1960; m. Becky Robbins, 1985 (div. 2001); 3 children; m. Sage Bonnie Humphrey, Oct. 14, 2001; 1 child. Founder The Anthony Robbins Found. Author: (book) Awaken the Giant Within: How to Take Immediate Control of Your Mental, Emotional, Physical, and Financial Destiny, 1992, Giant Steps: Small Changes to Make a Big Difference, 1994, Unlimited Power: The New Science of Personal Achievement, 1997, (audio programs) Lessons in Mastery, 2002, Personal Power II, Get the Edge; actor: (films) Shallow Hal, 2001, (guest appearances): (TV series) Roseanne, 1997, The Sopranos, 2004. Achievements include invention of the neuro-linguistic programming based motivational technique "neuroassociative conditioning". Office: Anthony Robbins Companies 9888 Carroll Centre Rd San Diego CA 92126

ROBBINS-WILF, MARCIA, educational consultant; b. Newark, Mar. 22, 1949; d. Saul and Ruth (Fern) Robbins; 1 child, Orin. Student, Emerson Coll., 1967-69, Seton Hall U., 1969, Fairleigh Dickinson U., 1970; BA, George Washington U., 1971; MA, NYU, 1975; postgrad., St. Peter's Coll., Jersey City, 1979, Fordham U., 1980; MS, Yeshiva U., 1981, EdD, 1986; postgrad., Monmouth Coll., 1986. Cert. elem. tchr., N.Y., N.J., reading specialist, N.J., prin., supr., N.J., adminstr., supr., N.Y. Tchr. Sleepy Hollow Elem. Sch., Falls Church, Va., 1971-72, Yeshiva Konvitz, NYC, 1972-73; intern Wee Folk Nursery Sch., Short Hills, NJ, 1978-81, dir. day camp, 1980-81, tchr., dir., owner, 1980-81; adj. prof. reading Seton Hall U., South Orange, NJ, 1987, Middlesex County Coll., Edison, NJ, 1987-88; asst. adj. prof. L.I. U., Bklyn., 1988, Pace U., NYC, 1988—. Ednl. cons. Cranford High Sch., 1988; presenter numerous workshops; founding bd. dirs. Stern Coll. Women Yeshiva U., N.Y.C., 1987; adj. vis. lectr. Rutgers U., New Brunswick, N.J., 1988. Chairperson Jewish Book Festival, YM-YWHA, West Orange, N.J., 1986-87, mem. early childhood com., 1986—, bd. dirs., 1986—; vice chairperson dinner com. Nat. Leadership Conf. Christians and Jews, 1986; mem. Hadassah, Valerie Children's Fund, Women's League Conservative Judaism, City of Hope; assoc. bd. bus. and women's profl. divsn. United Jewish Appeal, 1979; vol. reader Goddard Riverside Day Care Ctr., N.Y.C., 1973; friend N.Y.C. Pub. Libr., 1980—; life friend Millburn (N.J.) Pub. Libr.; pres. Seton-Essex Reading Coun., 1991-94. Co-recipient Am. Heritage award, Essex County, 1985; recipient Award Appreciation City of Hope, 1984, Profl. Improvement awards Seton-Essex Reading Council, 1984-86, Cert. Attendance award Seton-Essex Reading Counci, 1987. Mem. N.Y. Acad. Scis. (life), N.J. Council Tchrs. English, Nat. Council Tchrs. English, Am. Ednl. Research Assn., Coll. Reading Assn. (life), Assn. Supervision and Curriculun Devel., N.Y. State Reading Assn. (council Manhattan), N.J. Reading Assn. (council Seton-Essex), Internat. Reading Assn., Nat. Assn. for Edn. of Young Children (life N.J. chpt., Kenyon group), Nat. Council Jewish Women (vice chairperson membership com. evening br. N.Y. sect. 1974-75), George Washington U. Alumni Club, Emerson Coll. Alumni Club, NYU Alumni Club, Phi Delta Kappa (life), Kappa Gamma Chi (historian). Clubs: Greenbrook Country (Caldwell, N.J.); George Washington Univ. Avocations: reading, theater. Home: 242 Hartshorn Dr Short Hills NJ 07078-1914 E-mail: dr.mrw349@aol.com.

ROBBOY, STANLEY J., pathologist, educator; s. John and Sarah (Shapiro) R.; m. Anita Wyzanski, July 21, 1968 (div. 1981); children: Elizabeth, Caroline; m. Marion Meyer, June 14, 1990. Student, U. Mich., 1958-61, MD, 1965. Diplomate Am. Bd. Pathology, Am. Bd. Med. Mgmt. Intern Mt. Sinai Hosp, Cleve., 1965-66; resident to chief in pathology Mass. Gen. Hosp., 1966-70, asst. in pathology, 1972-73, asst. pathologist, 1973-76, assoc. pathologist, 1976-84; resident in pathology Boston Hosp. for Women, 1970; instr. Tufts Med. Sch., 1968-69; asst. prof. pathology Harvard Med. Sch., Boston, 1972-76, assoc. prof., 1976-84; prof. pathology U. Medicine and Dentistry N.J.-N.J. Med. Sch., Newark, 1984—92, chmn. dept., 1984-89, prof. ob-gyn, 1990—92, pathologist-in-chief, 1984-89, dir. faculty practice service, 1985-89; prof., vice chmn. dept. pathology Duke U., 1992—. Cons. pathologist St. Joseph Hosp., Paterson, NJ,

1985—92, St. Barnabas Hosp., Livingston, NJ, 1985—92, Beth Israel Hosp., Newark, 1985—92, VA Med. Ctr., Durham, 1992-, Durham Reg. Hosp., 2003-, Raleigh Com. Hosp., 2003-; pathologist (DES) Registry Rsch. Transplacental Hormonal Carcinogenesis (formerly Clear-Cell Adenocarcinoma Registry), 1972-83; pathologist, prin. investigator Nat. Collaborative Diethylstilbestrol project, 1974-82; vis. scientist New Eng. Primate Ctr., 1973-84; vis. prof. U. Shiraz Med. Sch., Iran, 1976; commr. NJ Commn. on Cancer Rsch., 1987-92; sr. advisor East Asia Cons. Group, Boston, LA and Tokyo, 1984-85; reference panel for diagnostic and therapeutic tech. AMA, 1982—99; mem. nat. med. com. Planned Parenthood Fedn. Am., 1990-93, vice chmn. com. on oncology, 1993; mem. DES steering com. Nat. Cancer Inst., 1995—; mem. exec. editl. bd. ArchPathhab Med, 2005-; bd. dir. Pamet Sys. Inc. Mem. editorial bd. Human Pathology, 1980-90, Cervix and the Low Female Genital Tract, 1983-94, Internat. Jour. Gynecologic Pathology, 1985-; editor: Informatics in Pathology, 1985-88, Pathology Rsch. and Practice, 1990-, Gynecologic Oncology, 1997-2004, InsSciht, 1998-; sect. editor Functional Biomarkers in Disease, 2005-; contbr. articles to profl. jours. Trustee Am. Pathology Found., 1984—86; NJ commn. Cancer Rsch., 1987—92; co-pres. Chapel Hill Kehillah, 2005—. Maj. US Army, 1970—72. Recipient Jr. Faculty award Am. Cancer Soc., 1972-75, Found. prize Am. Coll. Ob-Gyn, 1975; Pardee fellow U. Mich., 1961, Lederle Lab. fellow, 1962, Eliza Howell fellow, 1964, Ford Found. fellow, 1964-65; clin. fellow Am. Cancer Soc., 1967-68. Fellow Am. Soc. Clin. Pathologists (chmn. pathology telecommunications network com. 1983, task force on computers 1980-83, council on med. informatics 1983-84, planning and scope com. 1983-84, co-chmn. pathology communication network 1983-87, coun. anat. pathology, 1995-2001, future directions, 1995-98), Coll. Am. Pathologists (alt. Mass. del. to house dels. 1981-84, co-chmn. pathology comm. network 1983-85, alt. NJ del. to house dels. 1985-92, exec. com. and advisor nomenclature and classification of disease 1975-80, editl. bd. Systematized Nomenclature Medicine 1976-80, gov. 1999-2005, mem. reimbursement com., 1992-94, profl. and econ. affairs com., 1995-97, outcomes com., 1999-2000, vice chmn. coun. on pub. affairs 1999-2005, coun. of govt. prof. affairs, 2000-2004, credentials com., 2000-04, spokesperson, 2001—, performance measurement com. 2000, nat. meeting planning com. 2003—, vice chmn. election oversight com. 2006—, leadership devel. com. 2006—), Soc. Gynecologic Oncologists Assocs.; mem. Arthur Purdy Stout Soc. Surg. Pathology (membership com. 1980-86, treas. 1993-2001, pres.-elect 2001-03, pres. 2003-05), Internat. Acad. Cytology, Internat. Acad. Pathology (edn. com. 1979-83), Internat. Soc. Gynecologic Pathologists (chmn. membership com. 1982-84), Mass. Soc. Pathology (3d party relations 1978-84, chmn. computer com. 1981-84), NC Med. Soc., NC Soc. Pathology, NJ Med. Soc., NJ Soc. Pathology (edn. and profl. rels. coms. 1984-92, exec. com. 1985-92), Chapel Hill Kehillah (co-pres. 2004—). Jewish. Office: Duke U Med Ctr PO Box 3712 Durham NC 27710-0001 Home Phone: 919-968-9773; Office Phone: 919-684-3656. Business E-Mail: stanley.robboy@duke.edu.

ROBE, THURLOW RICHARD, retired engineering educator, dean; b. Petersburg, Ohio, Jan. 25, 1934; s. Thrulow Scott and Mary Alice (McKibben) R.; m. Eleanora C. Komyati, Aug. 27, 1955; children: Julia, Kevin, Stephen, Edward. BSC.E., Ohio U., 1955, MS in Mech. Engring., 1962; PhD in Applied Mechanics, Stanford U., 1966. Engr. Gen. Electric Co., Niles, Ohio, Cleve., Erie, Pa., Evendale,Ohio, 1954-60; instr. Ohio U., Athens, 1960-63; asst. prof to prof., assoc. dean U. Ky., Lexington, 1965-80; dean Ohio U., Athens, 1980-96, Cruse W. Moss prof. Engring. Edn., 1992-96, dir. Innovation Ctr. Authority, 1983-96; dean emeritus, Moss prof. emeritus Russ Coll. Engring. and Tech., Ohio U., Athens, 1996—; pres., chmn. bd. Q.E.D. Assocs., Inc., Lexington, 1975-83. Trustee Engring. Found. Ohio, 1988-94; bd. govs. Edison Materials Tech. Ctr., 1987-96; founding dir. T. Richard and Eleanora K. Robe Leadership Inst., Ohio U., 1997-2005; mem. adv. bd. Robe Leadership Inst., 2005—; liaison engring. accreditation commn. Accreditation Bd. Engring. and Tech., 1989-91; mem. Russ Prize Selection Com., NAE, 2000—. Contbr. articles to profl. jours.; patentee trailer hitch. Bd. dirs. Athens County Cmty. Redevel. Corp., 1980-86; treas. South Lexington Little League, 1976-80; vice chmn. Thoroughbred dist., Boy Scouts Am., 1975-77; mem.-at-large Oconee Dist. Boy Scouts Am., 2007—; pres. Tates Creek H.S. PTA, Lexington, 1975-76; bd. dirs. U. Ky. Athletics Ass.n, 1975-80; trustee Ohio U. Found., 1998-2007, trustee emeritus, 2007—. Maj. USAF Res., 1955-85. Recipient Alumni medal of merit Ohio U., 1993; named Am. Coun. on Edn. Adminstrn. fellow, 1970-71, Ohio U. Alumnus of Yr., 1996, inductee Acad. Disting. Grads., Russ Coll. Engring. & Tech., 2001. Mem. ASME, NSPE (profl. engring. in edn. exec. bd., ctrl. region vice-chmn. 1987-89), Am. Soc. Engring. Edn. (Outstanding Contbn. in Rsch. award 1966), Athens Reading Club, Athens Symposiarchs, Rotary, Sigma Xi, Tau Beta Pi, Omicron Delta Kappa, Alpha Lambda Delta Personal E-mail: robe@ohio.edu.

ROBECK, MILDRED COEN, retired education educator, writer; b. Walum, ND, July 29, 1915; d. Archie Blain and Mary Henrietta (Hoffman) Coen; m. Martin Julius Robeck, Jr., June 2, 1936; children: Martin Jay Robeck, Donna Jayne Robeck Thompson, Bruce Wayne Robeck. BS, U. Wash., 1950, MEd, 1954, PhD, 1958. Ordnance foreman Sherman Williams, U.S. Navy, Bremerton, Wash., 1942-45; demonstration tchr. Seattle Pub. Schs., 1946-57; reading clinic dir. U. Calif., Santa Barbara, 1957-64; rsch. cons. State Dept. Edn., Sacramento, 1964-67; prof., head early childhood edn. U. Oreg., Eugene, Oreg., 1967-86; vis. scholar West Australia Inst. Tech., Perth, 1985; v.p. acad. affairs U. Santa Barbara, Calif., 1987-95; ret., 1989. Vis. prof. Victoria Coll., B.C. Can., summer 1958, Dalhousie U., Halifax, 1964; trainer, evaluator US Office Edn. Head Start, Follow Thru, 1967-72; cons., evaluator Native Am. Edn. Programs, Sioux, Navajo, Umatilla, 1967-86; cons. on gifted Oreg. Task Force on Talented and Gifted, Salem, 1974-76; evaluator Early Childhood Edn., Bi-Ling. program, Petroleum and Minerology, Dhahran, Saudi Arabia, 1985. Author: Materials KELP: Kgn. Evaluation Learning Pot, 1967, Infants and Children, 1978, Psychology of Reading, 1990, Oscar: His Story, 1997, 2d edit., 2000; contbr. articles to profl. jours. Evaluation cons. Rosenburg Found. Project, Santa Barbara, 1966-67; faculty advisor Pi Lambda Theta, Eugene, Oreg. 1969-74; guest columnist Oreg. Assn. Gifted and Talented, Salem, Oreg., 1979-81; editorial review bd. ERQ, U.S. Calif., L.A., 1981-91. Recipient Nat. Dairy award 4-H Clubs, Wis., 1934, NYA and U. Wis. scholar, Madison, 1934-35, Faculty Rsch. grant U. Calif., Santa Barbara, 1958-64, NDEA fellow Retraining U.S. Office Edn., U. Oreg., 1967-70. Mem. APA, Am. Ednl. Rsch. Assn., Internat. Reading Assn., Phi Beta Kappa, Pi Lambda Theta. Democrat. Achievements include research in high IQ children who had severe difficulties learning to read and then doing a follow up study of 30-40 year olds. Avocations: dyslexia research, historical research, writing. Home: 95999 Highway 101 S Yachats OR 97498-9714 Office Phone: 541-547-3967. Personal E-mail: mrobeck@casco.net.

ROBEK, MARY FRANCES, business education educator; b. Superior, Wis., Jan. 30, 1927; d. Stephen and Mary (Hervert) R. BE, U. Wis., 1948; MA, Northwestern U., 1951; MBA, U. Mich., 1962, PhD, 1967. Tchr. Bergland (Mich.) High Sch., 1948, Tony (Wis.) High Sch., 1948-50, Sch. Vocat. and Adult Edn., Superior, 1950-58; prof. bus. edn. and office tech. Ea. Mich. U., Ypsilanti, 1958-93; instr. Jazyckova Gymnasium, Banská, Stiavnica, Slovakia, 1994. Author: Information and Records Management, 1995. Assn. of Records Mgrs. and Adminstrs. fellow, 1992. Mem. Assn. Records Mgrs. and Adminstrs. (life), Inst. Cert. Mgrs. (pres. 1980-81, Emmett Leahy award 2000), Cath. Daus. Am., Delta Pi Epsilon, Delta Kappa Gamma, Pi Lambda Theta. Republican. Roman Catholic. Home: 515 Clough Ave Superior WI 54880 Home Phone: 715-394-5400. Personal E-mail: RobekMary@aol.com. *Opportunity to do creative and innovative things without infringing on the rights of others is limited only by priorities set considering people and technology.*

ROBEL, LAUREN, dean, law educator; b. Dec. 1953; BA high honors, Auburn U., 1978; JD summa cum laude, Ind. U., 1983, postgrad., 1985. Bar: US Supreme Ct., Ind., Ill. Law clk. to Hon. Jesse Eschbach, U.S. Ct. Appeals (7th cir.), 1983—85; assoc. dean Ind. U. Sch. Law, Bloomington, Ind., 1991—2002, Val Nolan prof. law, 1999—, acting dean, 2002—03, dean, 2003—. Vis. faculty U. Panthenon-Assas, Paris; reporter rules com. U.S. Dist. Ct. (so. dist.) Ind.; mem. rules com. Ind. Supreme Ct. Author: Les États des Noirs: Federalisme et question raciale aux États-unis, 2000, Federal Courts: Cases and Materials on Judicial Federalism and The Lawyering Process, 2005; contbr. articles to profl. jours. Recipient Leon Wallace Teaching Award, 1997, Teaching Excellence Recognition Award, Ind. U. Sch. Law, 1997, 1999, Leonard D. Fromm Public Interest Award, 1999, 2002. Mem.: Ind. State Bar Women (Law Recognition award 2000), Ind. Bar Found. (Pro Bono Publico award 1997), Order of Coif. Office: Ind Univ Sch Law 211 S Indiana Ave Bloomington IN 47405 Home Phone: 812-334-8844; Office Phone: 812-855-8885. Business E-Mail: lrobel@indiana.edu. *

ROBELOT, JANE, anchor; b. Greenville, SC, Oct. 9, 1960; married; 1 child. BA in Econs., Clemson U. News and sports dir., reporter WCCP-AM Radio, Clemson, SC; anchor, reporter WSPA-TV, CBS affiliate, Spartanburg, SC, 1983—90; gen. assignment reporter WCAU-TV, Phila., 1990—92, co-anchor 6:00 PM news, 1991—92, co-anchor 11:00 PM news, 1992—95; co-anchor CBS Morning News, NYC, 1995; news reader This Morning CBS News, NYC, 1995—96, co-anchor This Morning, 1996—99, co-anchor CBS Atlanta News, 1999—. Office: WGCL TV 46 Meredith Corp 425 14th St NW Atlanta GA 30318-7965

ROBENALT, JOHN ALTON, lawyer; b. Ottawa, Ohio, May 2, 1922; s. Alton Ray and Kathryn (Straman) R.; m. Margaret Morgan Durbin, Aug. 25, 1951 (dec. July 1990); children: John F., William A., James D., Robert M., Mary K., Margaret E., Thomas D.; m. Nancy Leech Kidder, Sept. 21, 1991. BA, Miami U., 1943; LL.B., JD, Ohio State U., 1948. Bar: Ohio 1948. Asst. atty. gen., Ohio, 1949-51; practice in Lima, Ohio, 1951-59; acting municipal judge Lima Municipal Ct., 1955-59; partner Robenalt, Daley, Balyeat & Balyeat, 1959-82; ptnr. Robenalt, Kendall & Robenalt, 1983-85, Robenalt, Kendall, Rodabaugh & Staley, 1985-92, Robenalt & Robenalt, 1993—. Chmn. Lima March of Dimes, 1957-58; Bd. dirs. Lima Civic Center, pres., 1971-72; bd. dirs. Lima Rotating Fund; trustee Allen County Regional Transit Authority, Lima, pres., 1975—. Served with AUS, 1943-45. Mem. ABA, Ohio Bar Assn., Allen County Bar Assn. (pres. 1969-70), Am. Legion, Lima Automobile Club (bd. dirs., pres. 1975-82), Shawnee Country Club (pres. 1968-70), Ohio Automobile Club (trustee 1982-2002, chmn. 1995-97), Elks (bd. trustees 1991-97), Rotary, Delta Tau Delta, Phi Delta Phi. Home: 1755 Shawnee Rd Apt 700 Lima OH 45805-3857 Office Phone: 419-229-0054. Personal E-mail: jarobenalt@wcoil.com.

ROBERSON, BRUCE HEERDT, lawyer; b. Wilmington, Del., Mar. 7, 1941; s. A. L. and Virginia Amelia (Heerdt) R.; m. Mary E. Abrams; children: Cheryl Anne, David B., Douglas M. BS cum laude, Washington and Lee U., 1963; JD, U. Va., 1966. Bar: Del. 1966, Fla. 1969. Assoc. Morris, Nichols, Arsht & Tunnell, Wilmington, 1966-67; assoc. Holland & Knight LLP, Tampa, Fla., 1969-74, ptnr., 1975—. Contbg. editor Pratt's Banking and Lending Institution Forms, 1992—. Capt. U.S. Army, 1967-69 Decorated Bronze Star. Fellow Am. Bar Found. (life), Fla. Bar Found.(life), Am. Coll. Consumer Fin. Svcs. Lawyers; mem. ABA (bus. law sect. com. on consumer fin. svcs. 1976—, banking law com. 1980—, savs. instns. com. 1989-96), Am. Judicature Soc., Fla. Bar Assn. (corp. banking and bus. law sect. exec. coun. 1978-86, chmn. banking law com. 1982-84), Hillsborough County Bar Assn., Univ. Club, Tampa Yacht and Country Club, Lambda Chi Alpha. Republican. Methodist. Office: Holland & Knight LLP PO Box 1288 Tampa FL 33601-1288 Office Phone: 813-227-8500. Business E-Mail: bruce.roberson@hklaw.com.

ROBERSON, JAMES O., foundation executive; m. Rita Quinn; children: Melanie Merrill, Sharyl Shatz, James Jr., Trisha, Joel. AB in Journalism, Baylor U., 1956; student Indsl. Devel. Inst., U. Okla.; student Inst. Orgnl. Mgmt., U. Houston. Cert. econ. developer. Dir. info. West Tex. C. of C., Abilene, 1956-59; area devel. mgr. Mo.-Kans.-Tex. R.R., 1959-63; exec. dir. Albuquerque Indsl. Devel. Svc., 1963-65; dir. N.Mex. Dept. Devel., Santa Fe, 1965-69; mgr. Forward Metro Denver, 1969-72; dir. R.I. Dept. Econ. Devel., Providence, 1972-77; v.p., dir. new bus. devel. Howard Rsch. and Devel. Corp. subs. Rouse Co., Columbia, Md., 1977-79; sec. Md. Dept. Econ. and Community Devel., Annapolis, 1979-83; pres. Louisville C. of C., 1983-88; pres., CEO Rsch. Triangle Found. N.C., 1988—. Chmn. bd. dirs. Charlotte br. Fed. Res. Bank Richmond; cons., speaker in field. Editor West Tex. Today mag., 1956-59. Trustee, vice chmn. Wake Tech. C.C.; bd. dirs. N.C. Biotech. Ctr. Fellow Am. Econ. Devel. Coun. (past chmn.); mem. Indsl. Devel. Rsch. Coun., Nat. Assn. State Devel. Agys. (past pres.), Assn. Univ. Related Rsch. Parks (pres.).

ROBERSON, ROBERT S., investment company executive; b. Mt. Kisco, NY, 1942; m. Barbara Drane, 1967; children: Elizabeth de V., Merritt B., Barbara D. BS, NYU, 1964; MBA, Coll. William and Mary, 1973. Various positions in fin. and bldg. industries, 1964—67; mem. NY Produce Exchange, 1965—66; with Weaver Bros., Inc., Newport News, Va., 1967—, now pres., dir. Former dir. Peninsula unit Am. Cancer Soc., Newport News; former dir. Heritage Coun. Girl Scouts USA, Hampton; former trustee Newport News Pub. Libr., former trustee Va. Living Mus., Newport News; former trustee, chmn. com. on devel. Hampton Roads Acad., Newport News; former mem. bd. visitors to George Washington's Mt. Vernon Nat. Shrine; hon. dep. chief NYC Fire Dept.; trustee, pres., chief curator Golf Mus., Newport News; mem., chmn. Newport News Arts Commn.; trustee, former pres. Va. War Mus. Found., Newport News; former mem. bd. visitors, mem. exec. com., chmn. com. on devel. and alumni affairs Coll. William and Mary, Williamsburg, Va.; trustee, former vice chmn. NY Geneal. and Biog. Soc., NYC; former mem. bd. visitors, mem. exec. com. Richard Bland Coll., Petersburg, Va. Decorated officer Order of St. John (England); recipient Patrick Henry award Commonwealth of Va. Mem. Newcomen Soc. US, Hon. Fire Officers Assn., US Golf Assn. (former nat. com. mem. mus. and libr.), Gen. Soc. Colonial Wars, St. Nicholas Soc. City NY, Colonial Order Acorn, Sovereign Mil. Order Temple of Jerusalem (knight comdr.), Squadron A Assn., Pilgrims US/UK, Union Club, The Brook (libr. and arts com.), Church Club (NYC), Southampton Club (NY), Farmington Country Club (Charlottesville, Va.), Cypher Soc. of William and Mary (exec. com.), James River Country Club, Hampton Roads German Club (past pres.), Hampton Roads Assembly, The Hundred Club (Newport News, Va.), NY Yacht Club (libr. com.), Fishers Island Yacht Club (NY), Rotary Internat. (Paul Harris fellow), Blue Key, Delta Sigma Pi. Republican. Episcopalian. Home: PO Box 3 Williamsburg VA 23187-0003

ROBERSTON, NANCY R., state librarian; BA, Coll. of Wooster, Ohio; MA in English Lit., U. Ill.; MLIS, Drexel U. With State Libr. of Mich., 1995—, dep. state libr. internal ops., acting state libr., 2005, state libr., 2005—. Mem.: Chief Officers of State Libr. Agencies, Mich. Libr. Assn. (mem. bd. dirs.). Office: Mich State Library 702 W Kalamazoo St Lansing MI 48909 Office Phone: 517-373-5504. Office Fax: 517-373-4480. Business E-Mail: nrobertson@michigan.gov. *

ROBERT, DAVILA R., academic administrator; b. Calif. m. Donna Robert. BA in Edn., Gallaudet U., 1953; MS in Spec. Edn., Hunter Coll., 1963; PhD in Ednl. Tech., Syracuse U., 1972; PhD (hon.), Stonehill Coll., Mass., Rochester Inst. Tech., Hunter Coll., Gallaudet U. Prof. Dept. Edn., acting dean Model Secondary Sch. for Deaf, dir. Kendall Sch., and v.p. pre-coll. programs Gallaudet U., Washington, 1978—89, interim pres., 2006—07, pres., 2007—; asst. sec. spl. edn. and rehab. services US Dept. Edn., Washington, 1989—93; headmaster NY Sch. Deaf, White Plains, 1993—96; v.p. and CEO Nat. Tech. Inst. Deaf, Rochester, NY, 1996—2004; bd. dirs. Comm. Svc. for Deaf, 2004, sr. v.p., 2004, spl. asst. to CEO, 2004—05. Mem. adv. bd. Nat. Inst. on Deafness and Other Communicative Disorders NIH, 1996—2000; mem. Universal Design Com. Verizon Telephone Co.; bd. mem. Nat. Theatre of Deaf; program adv. com., Tng. Leadership Acad. NY State Edn. Dept.; program adv. com. NY State Rehab. Coun.; adv. bd. Inst. Disabilities Rsch. and Tng.; vice chmn. bd. trustees Hillside Children's Ctr.; chmn. bd. trustees NY Sch. Deaf, White Plains; pres. Coun. on Edn. of Deaf, Conv. Am. Instr. of Deaf., Conf. Ednl. Adminstr. Serving the Deaf. Named to Hall of Fame for Persons with Disabilities, 1987, Alumni Hall of Fame, Hunter Coll., 1991. Achievements include becoming the first and only deaf person to hold the post of asst. sec. for Spec. Edn. and Rehab. Services at US Dept. of Edn. Office: Office of President Gallaudet Univ 800 Florida Ave NE Washington DC 20002 *

ROBERTS, ALAN SILVERMAN, orthopedic surgeon; b. Apr. 20, 1939; s. Joseph William and Fannie (Margolies) S.; children: Michael Eric, Daniel Ian. BA, Conn. Wesleyan U., Middletown, 1960; MD, Wesleyan U., Phila., 1966. Rotating intern Lankenau Hosp., Phila., 1966—67; resident in orthop. Tulane U. Med. Coll., 1967—71; pvt. practice specializing in orthop. and hand surgery LA, 1971—. Clin. faculty UCLA Med. Coll., LA, 1971—76. Contbr. articles to profl. jours. With AUS, 1961. Riordan Hand fellow, 1969, Boyes Hand fellow, 1971. Mem. AMA, ACS, Am. Acad. Orthop. Surgeons, Calif. Med. Assn., LA County Med. Assn., We. Orthop. Assn., Riordan Hand Soc. Republican. Jewish. Office Phone: 310-276-7748. Personal E-mail: arobertsmd@earthlink.net.

ROBERTS, ALBERT DEE, internist; b. Ft. Worth, Mar. 7, 1930; s. Albert D. and Irene Burnett (Lewis) R.; m. Diane Truett, Dec. 22, 1952; children: Truett, Hillary. BS, So. Meth. U., 1951; MD, U. Tex. Southwestern, Dallas, 1954. Diplomate Am. Bd. Internal Medicine, Am. Bd. Nephrology. Pvt. practice, Dallas, 1960-75, 88-91; assoc. dean, prof. medicine U. Tex. Southwestern, 1975-88, prof. medicine, 1991—, Hartman prof. medicine, 1995—2004, prof. medicine, 2005—. Mem. ACP (master, gov. 1977-81, regent 1981-87, vice chair 1986-87), AMA, Am. Soc. Nephrology, Internat. Soc. Nephrology, Tex. Med Assn., Dallas County Med. Assn. Avocations: reading, music, tennis, travel.

ROBERTS, ANDREW C., air transportation executive; married; 2 children. Grad. with honors in Engring. Prodn., U. Birmingham, Eng.; grad. in Mfg., Coventry City Poly., Eng. Various engr. and maintenance positions Lucas Industries; gen. mgr. engine repair Aviall, Inc., Dallas; gen. mgr. Columbus engine ctr. Pratt & Whitney, Columbus, Ga.; mng. dir. Mpls./St. Paul engine ops. NW Airlines Corp., 1997, v.p. materials mgmt. ops., sr. v.p. tech. ops., 2001—04, exec. v.p. ops. Chmn. bd. Aeroxchange. Bd. mem. Spl. Olympics Minn. Office: NW Airlines Corp 2700 Lone Oak Pky Eagan MN 55121 Office Phone: 612-726-2111. *

ROBERTS, BILL GLEN, retired protective services official; b. Deport, Tex., June 2, 1938; s. Samuel Westbrook and Ann Lee (Rhodes) R.; m. Ramona Ryall, June 1, 1963 (dec. Nov. 1988); 1 child, Renee Ann; m. Johana R. Caines, Oct. 14, 2000. Student, So. Meth. U., 1968, North Tex. State U., 1974; grad. paramedic course, U. Tex. Southwestern Med. Sch., 1974; grad. Exec. Program for Fire Service, Tex. A&M U., 1978; AAS, El Centro Jr. Coll., Dallas, 1980; grad. exec. fire officer program, Nat. Fire Acad., 1989. With Dallas Fire Dept., 1958-82, lt., 1964-67, capt., 1967-71, div. fire chief, 1971-79, asst. fire chief, 1979-83; fire chief Austin (Tex.) Fire Dept., 1983-94. Tech. bd. dirs. Found. Fire Safety, Washington, 1982-85; adj. faculty Nat. Fire Acad., 1981-86; aft. State Life of Indpls., Dallas, 1962; owner Personnel Testing Lab., Dallas, 1963; real estate salesman Dale Copus Realtor, Dallas, 1963-66; salesman intercommunications equipment Chandler Sound, Dallas, 1966-67; field engr. IBM Corp., Dallas, 1968; cons. U. Tenn., 1974, Ga. Inst. Tech., 1974, Tex. Dept. Health Resources, 1973-78, Rand Corp., Washington, Mission Rsch., Santa Barbara, Calif., Macro Author: EMS Dallas, 1978; (with others) Anesthesia for Surgery Trauma, 1976, EMS Measures to Improve Care, 1980; contbr. articles to periodicals. Com. chmn. Dallas Jaycees, 1962-65; mem. task force Am. Heart Assn., Austin, 1973-83; bd. dirs. Brackenridge Hosp., 1989, Rehab. Hosp. Austin, 1992-94, Austin Police Pensions Bd., 1989, Capitol Area coun. Boy Scouts Am., 1989-92. Recipient John Stemmons Service award Dallas Fire Dept., 1979; Internat. Assn. Fire Chiefs scholar, 1967. Mem. Internat. Assn. Fire Chiefs, Am. Heart Assn., North Tex. Coun. of Govts. (regional emergency svc. adv. coun. 1973-79), Found. Fire Safety (tech. bd. dirs. 1982-85), Tex. Assn. Realtors, Rotary. Methodist. Home: 192 Hunter's Ridge Rd Canton NC 28716 Office Phone: 828-648-4345. E-mail: bglenrob@aol.com.

ROBERTS, BRIAN L., communications executive; b. Phila., June 28, 1959; s. Ralph J. and Suzanne F. Roberts; m. Aileen Kennedy, Dec. 28, 1985; children: Sarah, Tucker, Amanda. BS, U. Pa., 1981. V.p. ops. Comcast Cable Communications, Inc., Phila., 1985-86; exec. v.p. Comcast Corp., 1986-92, pres., 1992—97, pres., CEO, 1997—2004, chmn., pres., CEO, 2004—. Bd. dirs. The Bank of NY; bd. trustees Simon Wiesenthal Ctr.; founding co-chair Phila. 2000; dir., exec. com. CableLabs, 1999, now chmn. bd. dir. Vice chmn. The Walter Katz Found. Named one of Am. Top CEOs, Inst. Investor mag., 2004—07; named to Cable TV Hall of Fame, 2006; recipient Steven J. Ross Humanitarian award, UJA Fedn NY, 2003, Humanitarian Award, Simon Wiesenthal Ctr., 2004. Mem.: Nat. Cable & Telecommunications Assn. (chmn. 1995—96, 2005—). Avocation: squash (All-American, silver medal with U.S. team 1981, 85 and 97). Office: Comcast Corp Fl 35 East Twr 1500 Market St Fl 33 Philadelphia PA 19102-2100 *

ROBERTS, BRIAN MICHAEL, professional baseball player; b. Durham, NC, Oct. 9, 1977; s. Mike Roberts. Student, U. NC, U. SC. Draft pick Balt. Orioles, 1999, player, 2001—. Named a Second Team All-Am., Baseball Am., 1999; named Freshman of Yr., 1997; named to Am. League All-Star Team, 2005, 2007. Mailing: Balt Orioles Oriole Park at Camden Yards 333 W Camden St Baltimore MD 21201 *

ROBERTS, BURTON BENNETT, lawyer, retired judge; b. NYC, July 25, 1922; s. Alfred S. and Cecelia (Schanfein) R.; m. Gerhild Ukryn. BA, NYU, 1943, LL.M., 1953; LL.B., Cornell U., 1949. Bar: NY 1949. Asst. dist. atty., New York County, 1949-66; chief asst. dist. atty. Bronx County, Bronx, NY, 1966-68, acting dist. atty., 1968-69, dist. atty., 1969-72; justice Supreme Ct. State NY, 1973-98, adminstrv. judge criminal br. Bronx County 12th Jud. Dist., 1984-98, adminstrv. judge civil br. Bronx County 12th Dist., 1988-98; ret., 1998; counsel Fischbein, Badillo, Wagner & Harding, 1999—2005, Dreier LLP, 2005—. Pres. Bronx div. Hebrew Home for Aged, 1967-72. With US Army, 1943-45. Decorated Purple Heart, Bronze Star with oak leaf cluster, Combat Infantry badge Mem. Assn. Bar City NY, Am. Bar Assn., NY Bar Assn., Bronx County Bar Assn., NY State Dist. Attys. Assn. (pres. 1971-72) Jewish (exec. bd. temple). Home: 215 E 68th St Apt 19A New York NY 10021-5727 Office: Dreier LLP 499 Park Ave New York NY 10022 Business E-Mail: broberts@dreierllp.com.

ROBERTS, CARL GEOFFREY, lawyer; b. Boston, June 17, 1948; s. Simon Matthew and Ruth (Gorfinkle) Roberts; m. Sharon Ash, Mar. 24, 1979 (div. June 19, 2002); 1 child, Dennis; m. Susan Busch, Dec. 28, 2002. BA, Harvard U., 1970; JD, U. Pa., 1974. Bar: Pa. 1974, U.S. Dist. Ct. (ea. dist.) Pa. 1974, U.S. Ct. Appeals (3d cir.) 1978, U.S. Supreme Ct. 1980, U.S. Ct. Claims 1980, U.S. Dist. Ct. (mid. dist.) Pa. 1986. Law clk. U.S. Dist. Ct. (ea. dist.) Pa., Phila., 1974-76; assoc. Dilworth, Paxson, Kalish & Kauffman, Phila., 1978-82, ptnr., 1982-92, Ballard, Spahr, Andrews & Ingersoll, Phila., 1992—. Bd. dirs. Phila. Chamber Ensemble, sec., 1977-92, pres., 1992-95; mem. Hillel com. U. Pa., 1999—, chair 2001-05; bd. dirs. Hillel of Greater Phila., 2000-06. Mem.: ABA (law practice mgmt. sect. sec. 2002—03, vice chmn. 2003—04, chmn.-elect 2004—05, SCOTIS 2004—07, chmn. 2005—06), Phila. Bar Assn. (bd. govs. 2007—, co-chair law practice mgmt. divsn. 2007—). Office: Ballard Spahr Andrews & Ingersoll 1735 Market St Fl 51 Philadelphia PA 19103-7599 Office Phone: 215-864-8120. Business E-Mail: cgroberts@ballardspahr.com.

ROBERTS, CARTER S., environmental services administrator; married; 3 children. AB, Princeton U., 1982; MBA, Harvard U., 1988. Led mktg. and mgmt. teams at Procter & Gamble and Gillette; Mass. state dir. Nature Conservancy, 1990—96, dir., strategic planning, divsn. v.p., C.Am., v.p., dir., strategic planning and global priorities; chief conservation officer, COO World Wildlife Fund, Washington, 2004—05, pres., CEO, 2005—.

ROBERTS, CECIL EDWARD, JR., labor union administrator; b. Oct. 31, 1946; s. Cecil Edward and Evelyn Roberts; m. Carolyn Sue Stewart; children: Kyle Edward, Melissa Dawn. Student, Beckley Jr. Coll.; grad., W.Va. Technical Coll., 1987; HHD (hon.), W.Va. U. Tech. Gen. inside laborer, shuttle car operator, unitrack operator, greaser, beltman & mechanic Carbon Fuels Mine, Winifred, W.Va., 1971-77; v.p. dist. 17 United Mine Workers of Am., 1977-82, v.p., 1982-95, pres., 1995—. Mem. Com. Employer Support Vet. Employment, 1985, 86; pres. Nat. Coun. Holmes Safety Assn., 1985; mem. W. Va. Employment Opportunities and Econ. Devel. Commn. Gen. v.p. Nat. Coun. Sr. Citizens; adv. bd., Inst. Labor Studies and Rsch. W.Va. U., 1996; bd. dir. Blue Cross and Blue Shield So. W.Va., Cabin Creek Clinic, W.Va.; mem. adv. com. Black Lung Program. With US Army, 1966—67, Vietnam. Recipient Martin Luther King award, Rainbow Coalition. Mem.: Vietnam Vets. of Am., Am. Legion, VFW (life). Office: United Mine Workers of Am Internat Union 8315 Lee Hwy Fairfax VA 22031-2215 *

ROBERTS, CELIA ANN, librarian; b. Bangor, Maine, Feb. 6, 1935; d. William Lewis and Ruey Pearl (Logan) Roberts. AA, U. Hartford, 1957, BA, 1961; postgrad., So. Conn. State Coll., 1963—. With catalog, acquisition and circulation depts. U. Hartford Libr., 1956-65; libr. Simsbury Free Libr., Simsbury, Conn., 1965-69; reference libr. Simsbury Pub. Libr., 1969—. Tchr. ballet, 1965—66; tchr. genealogy, 1977—; ballet mistress Ballet Soc. Conn., Inc., 1968—70; with corps de ballet Conn. Opera Assn., 1963—64; active in prodns. Simsbury Light Opera Assn., 1964—69. Contbr. articles to profl. jours. Vol. Family History Ctr., 1970—. Mem.: DAR (Abigail Phelps chpt.), AAUW (past pres. Greater Hartford br.), ALA, Simsbury Hist. Soc., Conn. Libr. Assn., Denison Soc., Inc., Daus. of Scotia, Simsbury Geneal. and Hist. Rsch. Libr., Chateauguay Valley Hist. Soc., New Brunswick Geneal. Soc., Conn. Hist. Soc., Dance Masters Am. (Conn. Dance Tchrs. Club chpt.), Soc. Mayflower Descs. Conn., Conn. Soc. Genealogists (registrar Hartford 1983), Pro Dance, New Eng. Historic Geneal. Soc., Ont. Geneal. Soc. Unitarian Universalist. Office: Simsbury Public Libr 725 Hopmeadow St Simsbury CT 06070-2243 Business E-Mail: croberts@simsburylibrary.info.

ROBERTS, CHARLES BREN, lawyer; b. Washington DC, Oct. 28, 1949; s. Ray Oliver and Ruth B. (Barlow) R.; children: Elisha Ruthanne, Jacquelyn Celene. BS, Wright State U., 1974; JD, U. Dayton, 1978; postgrad., Ohio State U., 1980, Harvard Law Sch., 1984. Bar: Ohio 1978, D.C. 1983, Va. 1986, U.S. Supreme Ct. 1987, U.S. Dist. Ct. (ea. dist.) Va., 1988, U.S. Ct. Appeals (4th cir.) 1990. Legal intern U.S. Atty's Office, Dayton, Ohio, 1977-78; law clk. Ohio Supreme Ct., Columbus, Ohio, 1978-80; congl. intern U.S. Gen. Acctg. Office, Washington, summer 1977, atty. advisor, 1980-86; sr. ptnr. Charles B. Roberts and Assocs. P.C., Woodbridge, Va., 1986—. Mem. bus. adv. coun. Nat. Rep. Congl. Com. With USN, 1971—77. Recipient Disting. Svc. award Washington Songwriter's Assn., 1986, Acad. scholarship U. Dayton Law Sch., 1977, 78, Registry of America's Outstanding Profs. Award. Mem. ABA, Va. Trial Lawyers Assn., Fairfax County Bar Assn., Prince William County Bar Assn., Woodbridge C. of C., Republican Nat. Congressional Com. Bus. Adv. Coun. Avocations: racquetball, running. Office: Charles B Roberts & Assocs PC 1308 Devils Reach Rd Ste 303 Woodbridge VA 22192 E-mail: info@charlesrobertslaw.com.

ROBERTS, CHARLES MURRAY, retired publishing executive, writer; b. New Haven, Conn., Mar. 30, 1937; s. Samuel S. and Bertha L. Roberts; m. Sally Miller, June 19, 1960; children: Susan Hilary, Julie Handel. BA, U. Pa., 1958. V.p. field sales dir. western region Simon & Schuster, NYC, 1960—2002; pres. Author Escort & Media Svcs., Houston, 2002—. PBR Mag. Bd. trustees Congregation Beth Israel, Houston, 1972—74. With Air N.G., 1961—64. Mem.: Houston Forum. Avocations: tennis, travel, walking. Home: 49 Briar Hollow Ln #1002 Houston TX 77027 Home Phone: 713-629-1556. Home Fax: 713-572-5785. Personal E-mail: charles@authortours.net.

ROBERTS, CHARLES PATRICK (PAT ROBERTS), senator; b. Topeka, Kans., Apr. 20, 1936; m. Frankie Fann, 1969; children: David, Ashleigh, Anne-Wesley. BA in Journalism, Kans. State U., 1958. Pub. Litchfield Park, Ariz., 1962-67; adminstrv. asst. to U.S. Senator Frank Carlson, U.S. Senate, Washington, 1967-68; adminstrv. asst. to U.S. Congressman Keith Sebelius U.S. Ho. of Reps., Washington, 1968-80; mem. 97th to 104th Congresses from Kans. 1st Dist., Washington, 1980-96; US Senator from Kansas, 1997—. Com. agr. US Senate, com. armed services, com. health, edn., labor and pensions, select com. ethics, chmn. select com. intelligence. Served with USMC, 1958—62. Recipient Am. Farmer award, Future Farmers of Am., 1986, Disting. Leadership award, Prodn. Credit Assn., Disting. Svc. award, Kans. Farm Bur., Wheat Man of Yr., Assn. Wheat Growers, 1993, Public Svc. award, Am. Chem. Soc., 2001, John H. Chafee award public svc., Rep. Main Street Partnership, 2003. Republican. Methodist. Office: US Senate 109 Hart Senate Off Bldg Washington DC 20510-1605 also: District Office Ste 203 100 Military Plz Dodge City KS 67801 Office Phone: 202-224-4774, 620-227-2244. Office Fax: 202-224-3514, 620-227-2264. *

ROBERTS, CHRIS, strategy and finance educator, researcher; b. New Castle, Pa., July 16, 1954; s. Samuel Bruce and Jan Roberts, Della V. Roberts (Stepmother), Sheldon S. Smith (Stepfather). BS in Mgmt., U. Utah, 1975, BS in Fin., 1981; MBA, U. Phoenix, Salt Lake City, 1986; PhD in Mgmt., U. Mass., 1995. Supr. Holiday Inns Reservation Ctr., Memphis, Utah, 1972—78; product mgr. Mountain Bell/Qwest Comms., Salt Lake City, 1978—89; prof. Isenberg Sch. Mgmt. U. Mass., Amherst, 1993—, assoc. dept. head Isenberg Sch. Mgmt., 2001—07. Contbr. articles to profl. jours.; editor: Jour. Hospitality and Tourism Edn. Mem.: Acad. Mgmt., Strategic Mgmt. Soc., Coun. Hotel, Restaurant & Instnl. Edn. (chair symposium com. 1998—2002, dir. publs. and info., Outstanding Peer Reviewer 1999), Phi Beta Lambda, Beta Gamma Sigma. Avocations: contract bridge, international travel. Home: PO Box 4 Millers Falls MA 01376 Office: U Mass Flint 206 90 Campus Center Way Amherst MA 01003-9247 Office Phone: 413-545-4411. Personal E-mail: q@qutah.com. Business E-Mail: q@ht.umass.edu.

ROBERTS, CHRISTOPHER WAYNE, psychologist, educational consultant; b. Richmond, Va., June 5, 1974; s. Eddie Donald and Patricia Walker Roberts; m. Robin Lee Reinert, Aug. 14, 2005; 1 child, Tatum Grace. BS in Psychology cum laude, Va. Poly. Inst. and State U., 1996; MS in Psychology, Radford U., Va., 1998, EdS in Sch. Psychology, 1999; postgrad., Ariz. State U., 2002—. Nat. cert. sch. psychologist, cert. sch. psychologist Ariz. Dept. Edn., Calif. Dept. Edn., NC Dept. Edn., Va. Dept. Edn. Tchr. The Children's Ho., Chesterfield, Va., 1991—96; svc. provider New River Valley Cmty. Svcs., Radford, 1996—98; sch. psychologist Cumberland County Pub. Schs., Fayetteville, NC, 1998—2000; psychologist, diagnostician Piedmont Psychol. Svcs., Farmville, Va., 2000—01; sch. psychologist Dept. Correctional Edn., Richmond, 2001—02; contract sch. psychologist Phoenix 1 Elem. Sch. Dist., 2002—, Whittier Area Coop. Spl. Edn. Program, Calif., 2002—, Balsz Elem. Sch. Dist., Phoenix, 2004—05, Ariz. Dept. Juvenile Corrections, Phoenix, 2004—; pres. Valley Ednl. Specialists, Phoenix, 2004—. Camp counselor, svc. provider Camp Baker, Chesterfield, Va., 1995—96; substitute tchr. Montgomery County Pub. Schs., Christiansburg, Va., 1996—97, Chesterfield County Pub. Schs., 2000; intern Montgomery County Pub. Schs., 1997—98; mem. local arrangements com. 19th Internat. Conf. on Learning Disabilities, Washington, 1997; grad. counselor Disability Resource Office, Radford U., 1997—98; adj. prof. gen. psychology, developmental psychology and behavior modification Fayetteville Tech. CC, 1998—2000; evaluator Maricopa County Juvenile Probation/Vocat. Rehab. Program, Ariz. State U., Phoenix, 2002, 03; mem. conf. com. 26th Ann. Conf. on Severe Behavior Disorders of Children and Youth, Tempe, Ariz., 2002; rsch. asst. Nat. Ctr. on Edn., Disability and Juvenile Justice, Ariz. State U., Tempe, 2002—03; intern, co-instr. Ariz. State U., 2003, instr., 2003—05; presenter in field. Recipient Tara Reilly Meml. Scholarship award, Behavioral Inst. for Children and Adolescents, 2004. Mem.: Tchr. Educators for Children with Behavior Disorders, Nat. Assn. Sch. Psychologists (nat. cert.), Coun. Exceptional Children (divsn. learning disabilities, coun. for children with behavioral disorders), Pi Lambda Phi. Avocations: racing, exercise, movies, football. Home and Office: Valley Ednl Specialists Inc 418 E Beth Dr Phoenix AZ 85042 Office Phone: 602-690-1502. Fax: 602-304-9332. E-mail: skoolpsyco@aol.com.

ROBERTS, COKIE (CORINNE BOGGS ROBERTS), newscaster; b. New Orleans, Dec. 27, 1943; d. Thomas Hale and Corinne Morrison (Claiborne) Boggs; m. Steven V. Roberts, Sept. 10, 1966; children: Lee Harriss, Rebecca Boggs. BA in Polit. Sci., Wellesley Coll., 1964; degree (hon.), Amherst Coll., Columbia Coll., Loyola U. of the South, Manhattanville Coll., Gonzaga U., Boston Coll., Hood Coll., Chestnut Hill Coll., Miss. Women's U., Notre Dame U., Duke U. Assoc. prodr., host Altman Prodns., Washington, 1964—66, prodr. LA, 1969—72; reporter, editor Cowles Comm., NYC, 1967; prodr. Sta. WNEW-TV, NYC, 1968, Sta. KNBC-TV, LA, 1972—74; reporter CBS News, Athens, Greece, 1974—77; sr. news analyst. Nat. Pub. Radio, Washington, 1977—; corr. MacNeil/Lehrer Newshour, Washington, 1984—88; spl. Washington corr. ABC News, Washington, 1988—92; interviewer, commentator This Week With David Brinkley, Washington, 1992—96; co-anchor This Week with Sam Donaldson & Cokie Roberts, 1996—2002; chief congrl. analyst ABC News, 1998—; polit. commentator, analyst ABC News, World News Tonight and other ABC News broadcasts. Lectr. in field. Co-host weekly pub. TV program on Congress The Lawmakers, 1981—84, prodr., host pub. affairs program Sta. WRC-TV, Washington; prodr.: Sta. KNBC-TV Serendipity (award for excellence in local programming, Emmy nomination for children's programming); author: We Are Our Mother's Daughters, 1998, Founding Mothers: The Women Who Raised Our Nation, 2004; contbr. articles to newspapers, mags.; writer of a weekly column along with husband for newspapers around the country by United Media; contbg. editor (with husband): USA Magazine; co-author: From this Day Forward. Bd. dir. Presidential Commn. on Service and Civic Participation, Dirksen Ctr., Pekin, Ill., 1988—95, Fgn. Students Svc. Ctr., Washington, 1990—, Manhattanville Coll., Purchase, NY, 1991—99, Children's Inn at NIH, Bethesda, Md., 1992—. Named one of 50 Greatest Women in the History of Broadcasting, Am. Women in Radio and Television; named to Broadcasting Hall of Fame, Cable Hall of Fame; recipient Broadcast award, Nat. Orgn. Working Women, 1984, Distinguished Alumnae Achievement awards, Wellesley Coll., 1985, Everett McKinley Dirksen disting. reporting of Congress, 1987, Weintal award, Georgetown U., 1987, Corp. Pub. Broadcasting award, 1988, Edward R. Murrow award, Corp. Pub. Broadcasting, 1990, Broadcast award, Nat. Women's Polit. Caucus, 1990, David Brinkley Comm. award, 1991, Mother of Yr. award, Nat. Mother's Day Com., 1992, Emmy award news and documentary, 1991. Mem.: Radio-TV Corrs. Assn. (pres. 1981—82, bd. dirs. 1980—94), U.S. Capitol Hist. Soc. Roman Catholic. Mailing: 1717 DeSales St NW Washington DC 20036

ROBERTS, CURTIS CREED, minister, writer; b. Lenox, Ga., Nov. 20, 1920; s. Walter C. Roberts and LeeAnnie Goodwin; m. Pauline Powell Roberts (dec.); children: Don Wayne, Marcus Carroll, Randy Curtis. BA, Valdosta State Coll., Ga., 1967. Co-owner Roberts Furniture Co., Lenox, Ga., 1947—58, Bradenton, Fla., 1958—60; pastor United Meth. Ch., Ga., 1963—2001; bookkeeper Roberts Reliant Property Mgmt., Tifton, Ga., 1988—. Co-author: (book) The Leesburg Methodist Story, 1974; author: More Precious Than Gold, 2002, Korn on the Kob, 2006. Ordained elder United Meth. Ch., 1970. Sgt. US Army, 1942—45. Decorated EAMET Svc. medal U.S. Army, Am. Theatre Ribbon, World War II Victory medal. Methodist. Avocations: art, woodworking. Home: 88 Richards Dr Apt A-5 Tifton GA 31793 Office: Roberts Reliant Property Mgmt 1015 E 12th St Tifton GA

ROBERTS, DAVID A., manufacturing executive; b. Dec. 8, 1947; m. Susan Roberts; 2 children. BS, Purdue Univ., 1974; MBA, Indiana Univ., 1978. Mgmt. positions Budd Co., Detroit, 1969—83; v.p., gen. mgr. Pitney Bowes, Stamford, Conn., 1983—93; div. gen. mgr. FMC Corp., Chgo., 1993—95; pres. AM Internat., Mt. Prospect, Ill., 1995—96; group v.p. Marmon Group, Chgo., 1996—2001; pres., CEO Graco Inc., Mpls., 2001—07, chmn., 2006—07; chmn., pres., CEO Carlisle Companies Inc., Charlotte, NC, 2007—. Bd. dir. Franklin Elec. Co., Arctic Cat Inc. Served USMC, 1967—69. Office: Carlisle Companies Inc Ste 400 13925 Ballantyne Corp Pl Charlotte NC 28277 *

ROBERTS, DAVID E., JR., oil industry executive; BS in Min. Engring., Univ. Alabama, Tuscaloosa, Ala. Engr., oil and gas ops. Texaco No. Am., 1983—96, regional mgr., 1997, dir. strategic mgmt., worldwide ops., 1999—2001; adv. to vice-chmn. Chevron Texaco Corp., 2001—03; exec. v.p., mng. dir. BG Group, 2003—06; sr. v.p. bus. devel. Marathon Oil Corp. Office: Marathon Oil Co 5555 San Felipe St Houston TX 77056

ROBERTS, DAVID GLEN, prospector, investor; b. Plainview, Tex., Feb. 8, 1952; s. Doris Glen and Anna Grace (Mathis) R. Student, Tex. A&M U., 1970-71, Dallas Bapt. Coll., 1971-75; BA in Comm., U. Tex. Permian Basin, 1987. Lic. minister Bapt. Ch.; cert. profl. landman. Profl. stuntman, actor, 1972-76; mgr. Channel 100, Midland, Tex., 1976-78; pub., owner Basin Voice newspaper, 1987—; owner Diamond Developers Fire and Enviro-Safety Co., Midland, 1989—; regional mktg. dir. Nochar Inc.-Region 11, Midland, Tex., 1990-96; owner D.G. Roberts Land Mgmt., Midland, Tex., 1978—2004; CEO Permian Basin Diamond Developers, Inc., Skelly Oil Co., Inc., Heart of Tex. Quik Internet., Inc., 2004—. Cons. EPA, Indpls., 1991—. Appeared in film Giovanni & Ben, 1974, Drive In, 1976; theatre appearance at Globe Theatre, Odessa, Tex., 1975, Shakespeare in the Park, Dallas, 1976. Past chair Midland County Libertarian Party; past mem. exec. com. Dist. 31 Tex. Libertarian Party; organizer Sons of Liberty, Midland, 1990—; candidate US Congress Dist. 21, Tex., 2002. Mem. Am. Assn. Petroleum-Landmen, Five Aces, NRA, Tex. State Rifle Assn., Permian Basin Landman's Assn., N.O.R.M.L., Rep. Nat. Com. (libertarian), Harley Owner's Group, Col. Commemorative AF (life). Avocations: golf, motorcycling, travel, shooting, poker. Home Phone: 432-230-1812; Office Phone: 432-520-0012. Business E-Mail: dgroberts@skellyoil.com.

ROBERTS, DAVID LOWELL, journalist, educator; b. Lusk, Wyo., Jan. 12, 1954; s. Leslie James and LaVerne Elizabeth (Johns) R. BA, U. Ariz., 1979; MA, U. Nebr., 1997. Founder, editor, publisher Medicine Bow (Wyo.) Post, 1977-88; journalism instr. U. Wyo., Laramie, 1987-92; adviser U. Wyo. Student Publs., Laramie, 1987-92; gen. mgr. Student Media Corp U No. Colo., Greeley, 1995-98; founder, publisher Hanna Herald, Wyo., 1979-80; asst. prof. mass comm. Missouri Valley Coll., Marshall, Mo., 2001—. Exch. reporter The Washington Post, 1982; freelance reporter Casper (Wyo.) Star-Tribune, 1978-83, various publs.; freelancer, 1977—. Co-author: (book) The Wyoming Almanac, 1988, 90, 94, 96, 2001; author: (book) Sage Street, 1991; columnist Sage Street, 1989-92; editor: The Missouri Almanac, 2006. Chmn. Medicine Bow Film Commn., 1984; treas. Friends of the Medicine Bow Mus., 1984-88; pres. Medicine Bow Area C. of C., 1984; dir. Habitat for Humanity of Albany County, Laramie, 1991-92. Recipient Nat. Newspaper Assn. awards, over 40 Wyo. Press. Assn. awards, Five Editorial awards U. Wyo., Citizen of Yr. award People of Medicine Bow, 1986, Student Publs. awards U. Wyo., 1990, 92. Mem. Friends of Medicine Bow Mus. Mem. Green Party. Methodist. Avocations: writing, golf, visiting museums, photography. Business E-Mail: robertsd@moval.edu.

ROBERTS, DELMAR LEE, editor; b. Raleigh, NC, Apr. 9, 1933; s. James Delmer and Nellie Brockelbank (Tyson) R. BS in Textile Mgmt., NC State U., 1956; postgrad., Inst. Polit. Studies, U. Paris, 1963; MA in Journalism, U. SC, 1974. Product devel. engr. U.S. Rubber Co. (Uniroyal), Winnsboro, SC, 1959—63; process improvement engr. Allied Chem. Co., Irmo, SC, 1965-67; assoc. editor S.C. History Illustrated Mag., Columbia, 1970; editor-in-chief, editl. v.p. Sandlapper-The Mag. of S.C., Columbia, 1968-74; mng. editor, art dir. Legal Econs. mag. of the ABA, Chgo., 1975-89, Law Practice Mgmt. mag. of the ABA, Chgo., 1990-2000, editor emeritus, 2000—. Editor: The Best of Legal Economics, 1979; freelance editor and/or designer of over 35 books. Active World Affairs Coun. Columbia, 1997-; 1st v.p. English-Speaking Union, 1996-97, v.p., 2005—, pres. 1997-2003, bd. dirs. 2003—. With U.S. Army, 1956-58. Hon. fellow Coll. of Law Practice Mgmt., Golden, Colo., 1995—. Mem. Soc. Profl. Journalists, Capital City Club (Columbia), Phi Kappa Tau, Kappa Tau Alpha. Avocations: travel, turkish carpet/kilim collecting, antiques.

ROBERTS, DENNIS WILLIAM, construction executive; b. Chgo., Jan. 7, 1943; s. William Owen and Florence Harriet (Denman) R. BA in Journalism, U. N.Mex., 1968; MA in Legal Studies, Antioch U., 1982; MA, St. John's Coll., 1984. Gen. assignment reporter Albuquerque Pub. Co., 1964, sports writer, 1960-64, advt. and display salesman, 1967-68; dir. info. N.Mex. bldg. br. Asso. Gen. Contractors Am., Albuquerque, 1968-79, asst. exec. dir., 1979-82, dir., 1982—. Adj. prof. civil engring. U. N.Mex., 2004—06. Active United Way, Albuquerque, 1969-78; chmn. Albuquerque Crime Prevention Coun., 1982; bd. dirs. Rio Grande chpt. ARC, 1992-95, Albuquerque Lit. Coun., 1998-2004, Luth. Campus Ministry, U. N.Mex., 2003—; mem. cmty. adv. coun. Albuquerque Jobs Corps. Recipient Pub. Rels. Achievement award Assoc. Gen. Contractors Am., 1975, 78. Mem. N.Mex. Pub. Rels. Conf. (chmn. 1975, 82-83), Pub. Rels. Soc. Am. (accredited, pres. N.Mex. chpt. 1981, chmn. S.W. dist. 1984, chmn. sect. 1988), Constrn. Specifications Inst. (Outstanding Industry Mem. 1974, Outstanding Com. Chmn. 1978), Am. Soc. Safety Engrs., Toastmasters Club (dist. gov. 1977-78, Disting. Dist. award 1978, Toastmaster of Yr. 1979-80), Masons, Shriners, Sigma Delta Chi (pres. N.Mex. chpt. 1969). Republican. Lutheran. Home: Apt 21 1410 Girard NE Albuquerque NM 87106 Office: Assn Gen Contractors 1615 University Blvd NE Albuquerque NM 87102-1717 Office Phone: 505-842-1462. Business E-Mail: dennisr@agcnm.org. *Personal philosophy: Set your priorities in life, then your goals. In pursuing your goals, visualize their accomplishment. Be persistent, and you will accomplish what you set out to accomplish. Learn to be fair to others and empathetic.*

ROBERTS, DONALD JOHN, economics, business professor, consultant; b. Winnipeg, Man., Can., Feb. 11, 1945; came to U.S., 1967; s. Donald Victor and Margaret Mabel R.; m. Kathleen Eleanor Taylor, Aug. 26, 1967 (dec. 2006). BA with honors, U. Man., 1967; PhD, U. Minn., 1972. Instr. dept. managerial econs. and decision scis. J.L. Kellogg Grad. Sch. Mgmt., Northwestern U., Evanston, Ill., 1971—72, asst. prof., 1972—74; assoc. prof. J. L. Kellogg Grad. Sch. Mgmt., Northwestern U., Evanston, Ill., 1974—77; prof. J.L. Kellogg Grad. Sch. Mgmt., Northwestern U., Evanston, Ill., 1977—80, Grad. Sch. Bus., Stanford (Calif.) U., 1980, Jonathan B. Lovelace prof., 1980—2001, assoc. dean, dir. rsch., 1987—90, dir. exec. program in strategy and orgn., 1992—, dir. global mgmt. program, 1994—, sr. assoc. dean, 2000—, John H. Scully prof., 2001—; dir. Ctr. for Global Bus. and the Economy, 2003—. Prof. (by courtesy) dept. econs. Stanford U., 1986—; vis. rsch. faculty U. Catholique de Louvain, Belgium, 1974-75; inaugural Clarendon lectr. mgmt. studies Oxford U., 1997; cons. bus., econs. and antitrust, 1976—; vis. fellow All Souls Coll., Oxford U., 1995, Nuffield Coll., Oxford U., 1999-00; vis. acad. fellow in leadership and orgn. McKinsey & Co., London, 1999-00. Author The Modern Firm: Organizational Design for Performance and Growth, 2004; co-author: Economics, Organization and Management, 1992; assoc. editor Jour. Econ. Theory, 1977-92, Econometrica, 1985-87, Games and Economic Behavior, 1988-; mem. editl. bd. Am. Econ. Rev., 1991-95, Jour. Econs. and Mgmt. Strategy, 1991-98, Orgns. and Markets Abstracts, 1996-; contbr. articles to profl. jours. NSF grantee, 1973-93; rsch. fellow Ctr. Ops. Rsch. and Econometrics, Heverlee, Belgium, 1974, fellow Ctr. for Advanced Study in the Behavioral Scis., 1991-92. Fellow Am. Acad. Arts and Scis., Econometric Soc. (coun. 1994-96); mem. Am. Econ. Assn., Beta Gamma Sigma. Home: 835 Santa Fe Ave Stanford CA 94305-1022 E-mail: roberts_john@gsb.stanford.edu.

ROBERTS, DONALD MUNIER, retired banker, trust company executive; b. Paterson, NJ, Aug. 3, 1935; s. Edward and Dorothy (Munier) R.; m. Sally D. Ingram, Sept. 6, 1958 (dec. Feb. 1978); 1 dau., Sarah M.; m. Mary Ayer Gordon, June 23, 1978; children: Edward (dec.), John, Martha. BS, Yale U., 1957; MBA, NYU, 1961. Exec. v.p., 1979-90; vice chmn., treas. U.S. Trust Co. N.Y., NYC, 1990-95; retired, 1995. Bd. dirs. Burlington Resources, Inc. Mem. N.Y. Road Runners Club Inc. (bd. dirs., past chmn.), Tau Beta Pi. Clubs: Links (N.Y.C.). Republican. Office: 18th Fl 645 Fifth Ave New York NY 10022-5910

ROBERTS, DONALD WILSON, pathologist, consultant; b. Phoenix, Jan. 20, 1933; s. Alpha Wilson and Rubye Clotilde R.; m. Mae Astrid Strand, June 17, 1959; children: Marc Donald, Sara Judith Roberts Roundy. BS, Brigham Young U., 1957; MS, Iowa State U., 1959; PhD, U. Calif., Berkeley, 1964. Postdoctoral Swiss Fed. Inst. Tech., Zurich, 1964—65; insect pathologist Boyce Thompson Inst. for Plant Rsch., Ithaca, NY, 1965—96; insect pathologist, rsch. prof. dept. biology Utah State U., Logan, 1997—. Cons. WHO, Kaduna, Nigeria, 1974, 76, Empresa Brasileira de Pesquisa Agropecuraria, Brasilia, Brazil, 1978, 79, 80, 94, 96; mem. sci. adv. bd. EcoSci. Corp., Worcester, Mass., 1990-95; project reviewer UN Devel. Program, Africa and South Am., 1993-96, USAID Africa, 1991-96; adj. prof. dept. entomology Cornell U., Ithaca, N.Y., 1993-2000, adj. prof. dept. plant pathology, 1994-99. Editor: (3 books) Diseases of Medically Important Arthropods, 1977, 80, 83, Invasion Processes of Fungi, 1983, Biotechnology in Pest Control, 1989; contbr. over 250 articles to profl. jours. Recipient Fulbright Sr. Rsch. scholarship

Fulbright Found., Australia, 1985; named Family of Yr., Utah State U. Internat. Students, 1999. Mem. Soc. for Invertebrate Pathology (hon. 1998, founding mem., pres. 1988-90, Founder's Lectr. 1996, Svc. to Brazilian Insect Pathology award 2002), Entomol. Soc. Am. (Ea. br., Ciba-Geigy Recognition award 1985, 86, L.O. Howard Disting. Achievement award 1989), Am. Soc. Microbiology, Mycol. Soc. Am., Brazilian Entomol. Soc. (hon., recognition award 1996). Avocation: ballroom and swing dance. Office: Utah State U Dept Biology Logan UT 84322-5305 Office Phone: 435-797-0049. Business E-Mail: dwroberts@biology.usu.edu.

ROBERTS, DORIS, actress; b. St. Louis, Nov. 4, 1930; d. Larry and Ann (Meltzer) R.; m. Michael E. Cannata, June 21, 1950; 1 child, Michael R.; m. William Goyen, Nov. 10, 1963 (dec.). Student, NYU, 1950-51; studies with, Sanford Meisner, Neighborhood Playhouse, NYC, 1952-53, Lee Strasberg, Actors' Studio, 1956. Ind. stage, screen and TV actress, 1953—. Profl. stage debut, Ann Arbor, Mich., 1953; appeared in summer stock Chatham, Mass., 1955; Broadway debut in The Time of Your Life, 1955; other Broadway and off-Broadway appearances include The Desk Set, 1955, The American Dream, 1961, The Death of Bessie Smith, 1961, The Office, 1965, The Color of Darkness, 1963, Marathon 33, 1963, Secret Affair of Mildred Wilde, 1972, Last of the Red Hot Lovers, 1969-71, Bad Habits, 1973 (Outer Circle Critics award 1974), Cheaters, 1976, Fairie Tale Theatre, 1985, The Fig Tree, 1987, It's Only a Play, 1992, Bye Bye Birdie, 2004; movie debut Something Wild, 1961, film appearances include: Barefoot in the Park, 1968, No Way to Treat a Lady, 1973, A Lovely Way to Die, 1969, Honeymoon Killers, 1969, A New Leaf, 1970, Such Good Friends, 1971, Little Murders, 1971, Heartbreak Kid, 1972, Hester Street, 1975, The Taking of Pelham, One, Two, Three, 1974, The Rose, 1979, Good Luck, Miss Wyckoff, 1979, Rabbit Test, 1979, Ordinary Hero, 1986, #1 with a Bullet, 1987, For Better or for Worse-Street Law, 1988, National Lampoon's Xmas Vacation, 1989, Used People, 1992, The Night We Never Met, Momma Mia, 1994, Walking to Waldheim, 1995, The Grass Harp, 1995, A Fish in the Bathtub, 1997, My Giant, 1998, All Over the Guy, 2001, Dickie Roberts-Child Star, 2003, Lucky 13, I Can See You.Com, Grandma's Boy, 2005; TV debut on Studio One, 1958, Mary Hartman, Mary Hartman, 1975, Mary Tyler Moore Hour, 1976, Soap, 1978-79, Angie, 1979-80, Remington Steele, 1984-88, Lily Tomlin Comedy Hour, Barney Miller, Alice, Full House, Perfect Strangers, Sunday Dinner, A Family Man, The Fig Tree (PBS), 1987, (TV films) The Story Teller, 1979, Ruby and Oswald, 1978, It Happened One Christmas, 1978, Jennifer: A Woman's Story, 1979, The Diary of Anne Frank, 1982, A Letter to Three Wives, Blind Faith, 1989, A Mom For Christmas, 1990, The Sunset Gang, 1990, Crossroads, 1993, Dream On, 1993, The Boys, 1993, A Time To Heal, 1994, A Thousand Men and a Baby, 1997, One True Love, 2000, Sons of Miseltoe, 2001, A Time to Remember (Hallmark channel) 2003, Raising Waylon, (CBS) 2003, Lucky 13, 2004, (Hallmark channel) Our House, 2005, Grandma's Boy, 2005, Keeping Up With The Sterns, 2006; (TV series) include St. Elsewhere, 1982 (Emmy award best sup. actress drama) Murder She Wrote, 1990, Step By Step, 1994, Burk's Law, 1994, Walker Texas Ranger, 1995, High Society, 1996, Everybody Loves Raymond, 1996-05 (Amer. Comedy award, 1999, Emmy award outstanding supporting actress in a comedy series, 2001, 02, 03, 2005, Gracie Allen award, 2004), Law and Order, Criminal Intent, 2007. Recipient People's Choice award, 2006. Mem. SAG (Ensemble award 2002), AFTRA, Actors Equity Assn., Dirs. Guild Am.

ROBERTS, DWIGHT LOREN, engineering consultant, writer; b. San Diego, June 3, 1949; s. James Albert and Cleva Lorraine (Conn) R.; B.A., U. San Diego, 1976, M.A., 1979; m. Phyllis Ann Adair, Mar. 29, 1969; children: Aimee Renee, Michael Loren, Daniel Alexandr. Engring. aide Benton Engring. Inc., San Diego, 1968-73; pres. Robert's Tech. Research Co., also subs. Marine Technique Ltd., San Diego, 1973-76; pres. Research Technique Internat., 1978—; freelance writer, 1979—; owner Agrl. Analysis, 1985-88; constrn. mgr. Homestead Land Devel. Corp., 1988-92; sr. engr. cons. Morrison Knudson, 1992-95; sr. soils analyst Geotechnics, Inc., 1995-98; offsite field supt. coastal divsn. Kaufman and Broad, 1998—. Served with U.S. Army, 1969-71. Mem. ASTM, AAAS, Nat. Inst. Sci., N.Y. Acad. Scis., Nat. Inst. Cert. in Engring. Techs., Soil and Found. Engr. Assn., Phi Alpha Theta. Baptist. Author: Geological Exploration of Alaska, 1898-1924, Alfred Hulse Brooks, Alaskan Trailblazer, Papaveraceae of the World, Demarchism, Arid Regions Gardening, Visions of Dame Kind: Dreams, Imagination and Reality, Antal's Theory of the Solar System, Science Fair-A Teacher's Manual, Common Ground: Similarities of the World Religions, Black Sheep-Scientific Discoveries From the Fringe, After Manhattan, The Christofilos Effect; and others; contbr. articles to profl. jours. Office: 3111 E Victoria Dr Alpine CA 91901-3679 *Personal philosophy: Honesty and ethical behavior at all times. Trueness of being throughout my life. Love of my wife and children makes my life worth living and is always a light when there is darkness. God watches over my shoulder.*

ROBERTS, E. F., law educator; b. 1930; m. Alice A. Dunn, July 4, 1955; children: Martha, Ernest III, Michael, Marianne. BA, Northeastern U., Boston, 1952; LL.B., Boston Coll., 1954. Bar: Mass. 1954. Asst. prof. law Villanova U., Pa., 1957-59, assoc. prof. law Pa., 1959-60, prof. law Pa., 1960-64, Cornell U., Ithaca, NY, 1964-96, Edwin H. Woodruff prof. law, emeritus prof., 1996. Vis. prof. Nottingham U., Eng., 1962-63, Harvard U., 1983. Author: Public Regulation of Title Insurance, 1960, Land Use Planning, 2d edit., 1975, Law and the Preservation of Agricultural Land, 1982, (with Broun et al) McCormick on Evidence, 6th edit., 2006. Mem. Am. Law Inst. (life). Office: Cornell U Sch Law Ithaca NY 14853 Home Phone: 607-257-6298; Office Phone: 607-255-2356. Business E-Mail: efr4@cornell.edu.

ROBERTS, EDWARD BAER, technology management educator; b. Chelsea, Mass., Nov. 18, 1935; s. Nathan and Edna (Podradchik) Roberts; m. Nancy Helen Rosenthal, June 14, 1959; children: Valerie Jo Friedman, Mitchell Jonathan, Andrea Lynne. BSEE, MSEE, MIT, 1958, MS in Mgmt., 1960, PhD in Econs., 1962. Founding mem. system dynamics program MIT, 1958-84, instr., 1959-61, asst. prof., 1961-65, assoc. prof., 1965-70, prof., 1970—, David Sarnoff prof. mgmt. of tech., 1974—, assoc. dir. research program on mgmt. of sci. and tech., 1963-73, chmn. tech. and health mgmt. group, 1973-88, chmn. mgmt. of tech. and innovation, 1988-99, founder, chmn. MIT Entrepreneurship Ctr., 1992—94, 1997—, co-dir. internat. ctr. rsch. mgmt. tech., 1993-2000, dir. mgmt. of tech. program, 1980-89, co-chmn., 1989-99, chmn. mgmt. tech. innovation and entrepreneurship group, 1999—2003, chair, entrepreneurship & innovation MBA program, 2006—. Co-founder, dir. Med. Info. Tech., Inc., Westwood, Mass., 1969—; co-founder, gen. ptnr. Zero Stage Capital Group, 1981—99; co-founder, dir. SOHU.com, Inc., Beijing, 1996—; bd. dirs. PR Restaurants, LLC, Andover, Mass., 1995—, Interactive SuperComputers Inc., Waltham, Mass., 2005—, Visible Measures, Inc., Boston, 2006, DynaoMedia Corp, Beijing, 2006—. Author: (books) The Dynamics of Research and Development, 1964, Systems Simulation for Regional Analysis, 1969, The Persistent Poppy, 1975, The Dynamics of Human Service Delivery, 1976, Entrepreneurs in High Technology, 1991; prin. author, editor: books Managerial Applications of System Dynamics, 1978; editor (with others): Biomedical Innovation, 1981; editor: Generating Technological Innovation, 1987, Innovation, 2002; mem. editl. bd. IEEE Trans. on Engring. Mgmt., Jour. Engring. and Tech. Mgmt., Sloan Mgmt. Rev., Tech. Forecasting and Social Change, Internat. Jour. Entrepreneurship and Innovation, Internat. Jour. Product Devel., Internat. Jour. Tech. Mgmt. Bd. gov. Combined Jewish Philanthropies, Boston; bd. dirs. N. Country Chamber Players, Littleton, NH, Littleton Mus. Fine Arts, NH. Mem.: IEEE, Tau Kappa Alpha, Eta Kappa Nu, Tau Beta Pi, Sigma Xi. Republican. Jewish. Office: MIT E52-535 50 Memorial Dr Cambridge MA 02142-1347 Office Phone: 617-253-4934. Business E-Mail: eroberts@mit.edu.

ROBERTS, EDWARD GRAHAM, librarian; s. Samuel Noble and Frances Johnson (Boykin) R.; m. Anna Jean Walker, Nov. 12, 1949; children: Galer Walker, Edward Graham, John Boykin. BA, U. South, 1943; BA in Library Sci., Emory U., 1948; PhD, U. Va., 1950. Curator manuscripts Duke U., Durham, NC, 1948-52; dir. libraries (Drake U.), Des Moines, 1952-56; dir. Southeastern Interlibrary Research Facility, Atlanta, 1956-59; asst. prof. info. sci. Ga. Inst. Tech., Atlanta, 1963-66, assoc. prof., 1966-69, prof., 1969-73, assoc. dir. libraries, 1966-71, dir. libraries, 1971-84, dir. emeritus, 1984—. Chmn. info bank com. Ga. Tech. Service Program, Atlanta, 1965-67; mem. exec. bd. Southeastern Library Network, Atlanta, 1973-74; library cons. So. Regional Edn. Bd., Atlanta, 1958-59 Compiler, editor: Southeastern Supplement to the Union List of Serials, 1959; author: Literature of Science and Engineering, 1966, 2d edit.,1969. Served with U.S. Army, 1942-43. Mem. ALA, Southeastern Library Assn., Ga. Library Assn. Democrat. Episcopalian. Home: 1639 Adelia Pl NE Atlanta GA 30329-3807

ROBERTS, EDWIN ALBERT, JR., editor, journalist; b. Weehawken, NJ, Nov. 14, 1932; s. Edwin Albert and Agnes Rita (Seuferling) R.; m. Barbara Anne Collins, June 14, 1958; children: Elizabeth Adams, Leslie Carol, Amy Barbara, Jacqueline Harding. Student, Coll. William and Mary, 1952-53, NYU, evenings 1955-58; AA in Coll. & Cmty. Svc., St. Petersburg Jr. Coll., 1994. Reporter N.J. Courier, Toms River, 1953-54, Asbury Park (N.J.) Press, 1954-57; reporter Wall Street Jour., NYC, 1957, editorial writer, 1957-63; news editor Nat. Observer, Silver Spring, Md., 1963-68, columnist, 1968-77; editorial writer, columnist Detroit News, 1977-78, editorial page editor, 1978-83; editor editorial page Tampa Tribune, 1983—2003, ret., 2003. Author: Elections, 1964, 1964, Latin America, 1965, The Smut Rakers, 1966, Russia Today, 1967; Editor anthology: America Outdoors, 1965. Recipient Disting. Reporting Bus. award U. Mo., 1969; Pulitzer prize for distinguished commentary, 1974 Business E-Mail: ededitor@tampabay.rr.com.

ROBERTS, ELIZABETH H., lieutenant governor, former state legislator; b. Washington, Apr. 17, 1957; m. Thomas H. Roberts; children: Kathleen, Nora. BA, Brown U., 1978; MBA, Boston U., 1984. Mem. RI Senate, Dist. 11, Providence, 1996—2006; lt. gov. State of RI, 2007—. Mem. fin. com. RI State Senate, health, edn. and welfare com. Mem. bd. dirs. Childrens Mus. RI, Southside Cmty. Land Trust. Democrat. Office: Lieutenant Governor State House Rm 115 Providence RI 02903 Office Phone: 401-222-2371. Office Fax: 401-222-2012. *

ROBERTS, EMMA ROSE, actress; b. Rhinebeck, NY, Feb. 10, 1991; d. Eric Roberts and Kelly Cunningham, Eliza Roberts (Stepmother). Model nat. ad campaign Dooney & Bourke, 2006. Actress (films) BigLove, 2001, Blow, 2001, Grand Champion, 2002, Spymate, 2006, Aquamarine, 2006, Nancy Drew, 2007, (TV series) Drake & Josh, 2004, Unfabulous, 2004—07, appearances include The Late Show with David Letterman, 2004, The Ellen DeGeneres Show, 2005, Teen Choice Awards, 2005, Live with Regis and Kelly, 2005—07, Nikelodeon Kids' Choice Awards, 2006—07; singer: (albums) Unfabulous and More: Emma Roberts, 2005. Named Female Star of Tomorrow, ShoWest, 2007. Office: Sweeny Mgmt 8033 Sunset Blvd Ste 1048 Los Angeles CA 90046 *

ROBERTS, ERIC, actor; b. Biloxi, Miss., Apr. 18, 1956; m. Eliza Roberts, 1992; 1 child, Emma. Student, Royal Acad. Dramatic Art, London, 1973-74, Am. Acad. Dramatic Art, NYC. Appeared in stage prodns. Rebel Women, Streetcar Named Desire, others; TV appearances include Another World; films include King of the Gypsies, 1978, Raggedy Man, 1981, Star 80, 1983, The Pope of Greenwich Village, 1984, The Coca-Cola Kid, 1985, Runaway Train, 1985, Nobody's Fool, 1986, Rude Awakening, 1989, Blood Red, 1989, The Best of the Best, 1989, Final Analysis, 1992, The Best of the Best 2, 1993, Babyfever, 1994, The Specialist, 1994, It's My Party, 1996, The Cable Guy, 1996, American Strays, 1996, The Shadow Men, 1997, Most Wanted, 1997, The Prophecy II, 1998, La Cucharacha, 1998, Facade, 1998, Death Valley, 1998, Dead End, 1998, Bittersweet, 1998, TripFall, 1999, Hitman's Run, 1999, The Beat Nicks, 2000, Dirk and Betty, 2000, No Alibi, 2000, Luck of the Draw, 2000, Facade, 2000, The Alternate, 2000, Cecil B. DeMented, 2000, Two Shades of Blue, 2000, TripFall, 2000, The King's Guard, 2000, Mercy Streets, 2000, Sol Goode, 2001, Wrong Number, 2001, Mindstorm, 2001, Fast Sofa, 2001, Endangered Species, 2002, Fool Proof, 2002, Spun, 2002, Wolves of Wall Street, 2002, Intoxicating, 2003, National Security, 2003, The Long Ride Home, 2003, Graves End, 2004, Killer Weekend, 2004, Miss Cast Away, 2004, Six: The Mark Unleashed, 2004, The Last Shot, 2004, Border Blues, 2004, Sister's Keeper, 2005, (voice) Geppetto's Secret, 2005, Comedy Hall, 2005, Sledge: The Untold Story, 2005, Break a Leg, 2005, Split, 2005, The Civilization of Maxwell Bright, 2005, The Double, 2005, Light Years Away, 2006, 8 of Diamonds, 2006, Phat Girlz, 2006, A Guide to Recognizing Your Saints, 2006, DOA: Dead or Alive, 2006. Aurora, 2006, 4-Bidden, 2007, One Way, 2007; TV films include Paul's Case, Miss Lonelyhearts, A Time to Heal, 1988, Love, Honor & Obey: The Last Mafia Marriage, 1993, Love, Cheat and Steal, 1993, In Cold Blood, 1996, The Odyssey, 1997, Heaven's Fire, 1999, Purgatory, 1999, Lansky, 1999, Heaven's Fire, 1999, Race Against Time, 2000, Sanctimony, 2000, Strange Frequency, 2001, Stiletto Dance, 2001, Walking Shadow, 2001, The Flying Dutchman, 2001, Rough Air: Danger on Flight 534, 2001, Roughing It, 2002, Christmas Rush, 2002, L.A. Confidential, 2003, Southern Comfort, 2006, Fatal Desire, 2006, Pandemic, 2007, others; Broadway plays include Burn This, 1988 (Theatre World award 1988); appeared in TV series C-16:FBI, 1997—98, Less Than Perfect, 2002-05; TV guest appearances include The Tomorrow People, 1973, Frasier, 1993, The Drew Carey Show, 1995, Oz, 1997, Falcone, 2004, The King of Queens, 2001, Law & Order: Special Victims Unit, 2001, Strange Frequency, 2001, Witchblade, 2002, Border Blues, 2003, (voice) Justice League, 2002-04, CSI: Miami, 2005, Heroes, 2007. Office: Innovative Artists Ste 2850 1999 Avenue Of The Stars Los Angeles CA 90067-4612 *

ROBERTS, ERNST EDWARD, marketing consultant; b. Wheeling, W.Va., Dec. 19, 1926; s. Charles Emmitt and Virginia Mae (Stephenson) R.; m. Donna Clare Davis, Dec. 27, 1949; children: Ernst Edward II, Carol Lee Roberts Gaydac. BS, U.S. Mil. Acad., 1949; MBA, Xavier U., Cin., 1954; MS in Mech. Engring., U. So. Calif., 1957; grad. with distinction, Air War Coll., 1970. Commd. 2nd lt. U.S. Army, 1949, advanced through grades to brig. gen., 1971, served as officer in combat Korea, 1950-52; prof. mil. sci. Xavier U., 1952-54; mgmt. asst. to asst. comdt. U.S. Army Air Def. Sch., Fort Bliss, Tex., 1957-60; admissions officer U.S. Mil. Acad., West Point, NY, 1961-62, asst. to supt. (pres.), 1962-64, dir. admissions, 1964-65; comdg. officer 3d Missile Bn., 71st Arty., Fed. Republic of Germany, 1965-67; staff officer Gen. Staff U.S. Army, Washington, 1968-70; commdg. officer NATO Air Def. Arty. Group, Germany, 1970-71; commdg. gen. 38th Air Def. Arty. Brigade, Korea, 1971-72; dep. commanding gen. U.S. Army Air Def. Sch. and Ctr., Fort Bliss, 1972-74; ret. U.S. Army, 1974; v.p. bldg. and property mgr. El Paso (Tex.) Nat. Bank and Corp., 1974-79, sr. v.p., dir. pers. and tng., 1979-83, exec. v.p., dir. mktg., 1983-92; mktg. cons., 1992—. Mem. exec. mgmt. com. Tex. Commerce Bank, El Paso, 1983-92; vis. lectr. mktg. Webster U. Mem. bd. advisors SBA; mem. mayor's Citizens Com. on Police Dept. Matters, El Paso; mem. Task Force to Evaluate Mgmt. of Sheriff's Dept.; head bond-issue campaign, El Paso; adv. dir. Armed Svcs. YMCA, past pres.; adv. dir. nat. bd. dirs. Armed Svcs. YMCA, El Paso Cmty. Found.; past pres. U. Tex.-El Paso Eldorados; mem. bd. dirs., trustee Found. Lighthouse for Blind; chmn. adv. bd. dirs. El Paso Bus. Com. for Arts; chmn. capital fund drive com. Rio Grande Girl Scouts Am., Plz. Theatre-Plz. Park Restoration bd.; past mem. campaign cabinet United Way El Paso County; chmn. Capital Fund Drive, Air Def. Arty. Mus., Ft. Bliss; bd. dirs. City of El Paso, mem. steering com. Safe 2000; bd. dirs. Crimestoppers of El Paso. Decorated D.S.M., Legion of Merit, Silver Star, Meritorious Svc. medal; recipient Pro Eclesio Et Pontifice, Vatican, 1971; Conquistador award City of El Paso, Liberty Bell award Legal Cmty. El Paso, 1988. Mem. Am. Inst. Banking, Assn. U.S. Army (Gen. Army Omar N. Bradley chpt.), El Paso C. of C. (mem. armed forces com., chmn. spl. task force to evaluate chamber mgmt.), Mil. Order World Wars (chpt. chmn. citizen of yr. award 1996-2001), U.S. Army Air Def. Arty. Assn. (past pres., named Disting. Korean War Vet. 2004), El Paso Club (past pres., bd. dirs.), Rotary (past pres.). Republican. Roman Catholic. Home: 8212 Antero Pl El Paso TX 79904-2401

ROBERTS, FLETCHER, editor; Arts & Leisure sect. writer, editor NY Times, 1987—. Office: NY Times 229 W 43rd St New York NY 10036 Office Phone: 212-556-4260.

ROBERTS, FRANCIS STONE, advertising executive; b. Scranton, Pa., Aug. 15, 1944; s. Gordon Link and Eleanor Swartz (Stone) R.; m. Julie Ann Dolan; children: Francis Stone, Link McGregor. BA, Grove City Coll., Pa., 1966; A.M.P., U. Chgo., 1984. With media dept., then account exec. Compton Advt. Inc., NYC, 1966-69; account exec. Tatham-Laird & Kudner Advt., NYC, 1969-70; account supr., v.p. SSC&B Advt. Inc., NYC, 1970-78, sr. v.p., mgmt. supr., 1994; group exec. v.p. SSC&B: Lintas Advt. Worldwide, 1987-89; COO, pres. Lintas, NY, 1990-94; mem. policy and ops. coms., chmn. strategy rev. bd. Lintas N.Y.; also dir. Lintas N.Y. and U.S.A.; CEO, chmn. The CEO-Gotham Grp., NYC, 1994-95; chmn., CEO Gotham Inc., NYC, 1995—2004; mng. dir. Gotham Ltd., London, 1996—2004; CEO, pres. Carlson & Ptnrs., NYC, 2004—05, Roberts & Tarlow, NYC, 2005. Mem. bd. dirs. Am. Assn. Advertising Agencies, Am. Advertising Fedn., The Ad Coun.; bd. trustees Pro Ad PAC. Alumni coun. Grove City Coll., 1999—. Mem. William Penn Charter Alumni Assn. (pres. N.Y. chpt. 1984-88), Ad Club N.Y., The Union League N.Y. Clubs: New Canaan Field, New Canaan Winter, New Canaan Country, Congl. Country. Republican. Presbyterian. Home: 28 Landing Dr Dobbs Ferry NY 10522 Office: Roberts and Tarlow 437 Madison New York NY 10022 Office Phone: 646-289-7301. Business E-Mail: stone@robertsntarlow.com.

ROBERTS, FRANK ALAN, periodontist, researcher, dental educator; b. Ill. s. Glynn W. and Joanna B. Roberts; m. Laura J. Theobald; children: Hannah L., Elizabeth G. BS, Davidson Coll., NC, 1986; DDS, U. Tenn., 1990; PhD, U. Ala., Birmingham, 1996; cert. in Periodontics, U. Ala., 1996. Diplomate Am. Bd. Periodontology, 2002. Assoc. prof. U. Wash., Seattle, 1996—; staff periodontist Vets. Healthcare Sys., Seattle, 1997—. Infection control cons. Dental Quality Assurance Bd. State of Wash. and Wash. State Medicaid Program, Olympia, Wash., 2002—; infection control cons. Dept. of Labor and Industries State of Wash. and Wash. Indsl. Safety and Health Act, Olympia, 2002—; reviewer Jour. Periodontology, Chgo., 1998—, Jour. Periodontal Rsch., Oxford, 1998—, Jour. Dental Rsch., Washington, 2005—. Contbr. articles to profl. jours. Grantee, Nat. Ctr. Minority and Minority Health Disparities, 2002—, NIH, 1999—. Fellow: Am. Acad. Periodontology (Tarrson fellowship 2000—03); mem.: ADA (accreditation site visitor 2002—), Internat. Assn. Dental Rsch. Office: Univ Wash HSB D580C Box 357444 Seattle WA 98195-7444 Office Phone: 206-685-9046.

ROBERTS, GARY, professional hockey player; b. North York, Ont., Can., May 23, 1966; Left wing Calgary Flames, 1987—97, Carolina Hurricanes, 1997—2000, Toronto Maple Leafs, 2000—05, Fla. Panthers, 2005—07, Pitts. Penguins, 2007—. Player NHL All-Star Game, 1992, 93, 2004. Named to NHL All-Star team, 1992, 1993, 2004; recipient Bill Masterton Trophy, NHL, 1996. Achievements include being a member of Stanley Cup Champion Calgary Flames, 1989. Office: c/o Pitts Penguins 66 Mario Lemieux Pl Pittsburgh PA 15219 *

ROBERTS, GENE, newspaper executive; Pres., exec. editor Phila. Inquirer; managing editor New York Times, NYC. Spkr. in field. Coauthor: (History Book) The Race Beat, 2006 (Pulitzer Prize for History, 2007). Office: New York Times 229 W 43rd St New York NY 10036-3959 *

ROBERTS, GEORGE BERNARD, JR., management and government relations consultant, former state legislator; b. Andover, Mass., June 13, 1939; s. George Bernard and Helene F. (Eversen) R.; m. Margaret Fay Edmunds, Aug. 26, 1967; children: Abigail Emerson, Jessica Swift. BS, U. N.H., 1964, M.P.A., 1967. Ptnr. Roberts Real Estate Assocs., Gilmanton, NH, 1966—; mem. N.H. Ho. of Reps., 1967-80, majority leader, 1971-74, speaker, 1975-76, 77-78, 79-80; pres. Policy Mgmt. Assocs., Concord, NH, 1980—. Pres. and treas. Concord, Concord Coach Soc. Del. Nat. Rep. Conv., 1972-76; mem. N.H. Constl. Conv., 1974, 84, N.H. Rep. Party Fin. Com.; pres. Nat. Conf. State Legislatures, 1979-80; chmn. exec. com. 1st Congl. Soc. Gilmanton. Mem. Nat. Rep. Legislators Assn. (founding, past pres.), Masons, Shriners, Scottish Rite, Historic Dist. Commn. Gilmanton, Sigma Alpha Epsilon. Republican. Office: Concord Policy Mgmt Assocs 4 Park St Ste 100 Concord NH 03301-6313

ROBERTS, GEORGE R., investment banker; b. Houston, Tex., 1945; m. Leanne Bovet Roberts (dec.); children: Eric, Mark, Courtney. BA, Claremont McKenna Coll., 1966; JD, U. Calif. Hastings Law Sch., San Francisco, 1969; LLD (hon.), Claremont McKenna Coll., 2003. Joined corp. fin. dept. to partner Bear Stearns & Co., New York, 1969—79; founding sr. ptnr. Kohlberg, Kravis, Roberts, San Francisco, 1976—. Dir. Accel-KKR, Safeway, Inc., DPL, Inc., KinderCare Learning Centers, Inc., Owens-Illinois, Inc. and PRIMEDIA Inc. Bd. San Francisco Symphony, San Francisco Ballet, Fine Arts Mus., San Francisco, Claremont McKenna Coll. Named one of Forbes' Richest Americans, 2006; recipient Man of Yr. award, Culver Ednl. Found., 2006. Achievements include historic billion dollar buyout of Wometco Companies in 1984; $25 billion RJR Nabisco buyout in 1989. Office: Kohlberg Kravis Roberts & Co 2800 Sand Hill Rd Ste 200 Menlo Park CA 94025-7055

ROBERTS, GREGORY, educational association administrator; BSc, MS, Ind. U., Bloomington; Ednl. Specialist degree, U. Mo., Kansas City. Cert. ednl. mgmt. Harvard U. Grad. Sch. Edn. V.p. student affairs U. St. Thomas, Minn., 1992—2003; exec. dir., sr. oper. officer Am. Coll. Pers. Assn., Washington, 2003—. Contbr. articles to profl. publs. Mem.: Phi Delta Kappa, Omicron Delta Kappa. Office: Am Coll Pers Assn One Dupont Cir NW Ste 300 Washington DC 20036-1188 Office Phone: 202-835-2272 ext. 613. Office Fax: 202-296-3286. Business E-Mail: groberts@acpa.nche.edu.

ROBERTS, HARRY MORRIS, JR., lawyer; b. Dallas, June 10, 1938; s. Harry Morris and La Frances (Reilly) R.; m. Nancy Beth Johnson, Mar. 7, 1964; children: Richard Whitfield, Elizabeth Lee. BBA, So. Meth. U., 1960; LLB, Harvard U., 1963. Bar: Tex. 1963, U.S. Dist. Ct. (no. dist.) Tex. 1964, U.S. Ct. Appeals (5th cir.) 1972, U.S. Supreme Ct. 1971. Assoc. Thompson & Knight, Dallas, 1963-69, ptnr., 1970-75, sr. ptnr., 1975—. Chmn. real estate, probate and trust law sect. State Bar Tex., 1984-85; vis. scholar U. Tex. Law Sch., 1986; adj. prof. So. Meth. U. Law Sch., 2007. Contbr. articles to profl. jours. Trustee Shelter Ministries of Dallas, 1982—, chmn. bd. trustees, 1992-95, 2004-05. Mem. ABA, Dallas Bar Assn.

(chmn. real estate sect. 1981), Am. Bar Found., Tex. Bar Found., Dallas Bar Found., Am. Coll. Real Estate Lawyers, Tex. Coll. Real Estate Attys., Salesmanship Club (Dallas), Dallas Country Club. Episcopalian. Office: Thompson & Knight 1700 Pacific Ave Ste 3300 Dallas TX 75201-4693 Office Phone: 214-969-1616. Business E-Mail: harry.roberts@tklaw.com.

ROBERTS, HOWARD H., JR., transportation executive; b. 1940; Grad., West Point; M in Pub. Affairs, Princeton U., M in Engring. V.p., fin. and adminstrn. NYC Transit, 1981—83, v.p., COO, surface transit, 1983—86, pres., Met. Transp. Authority NYC, 2007—; dep. gen. mgr. Southeastern Pa. Transp. Authority, 1989—97. Served in US Army, 1961—81. Office: Met Transp Authority 347 Madison Ave 5th Fl New York NY 10017-3739 *

ROBERTS, J. BERRY, elementary school educator, sports official; s. James Berry Roberts III and Edith Hartle Carhart Roberts; 1 child, James Berry V. BA in Math., Western Wash. U., Bellingham, 1969. Tchr. Shuksan Mid. Sch., Bellingham, 1966—71, Utterback Mid. Sch., Tucson, 1971—93, Univ. H.S., Tucson, 1993—. Sports ofcl. Wash. State Officials Assn., 1966—71, Ariz. Interscholastic Assn., 1971—. Deacon Presbyn. Ch. USA, Tucson, 1970. Recipient Excellence in Edn. award, US Dept Edn., 1983; grantee, NSF, 1967—69, 1990, 1992. Office: Univ HS 421 North Arcadia Ave Tucson AZ 85711 Home Phone: 520-885-5799; Office Phone: 520-232-5903. Office Fax: 520-232-5901. Personal E-mail: uhspenguin118@cox.net. Business E-Mail: berry.roberts@tusd1.org.

ROBERTS, JAMES ALLEN, retired urologist, educator; b. Beach, ND, May 31, 1934; s. Earl Fernando and Maria Ellen Roberts; m. Hilda Peachy Roberts, Nov. 29, 1986; children from previous marriage: Jennifer Lou Roberts Walsh, Mary Ellen Roberts Wargo, Thomas Jay. MD, U. Chgo., 1959. Diplomate: Am. Bd. Urology. Intern U. Chgo. Sch. Medicine, 1959-60, resident in urology, 1961-65; from mem. faculty to prof. Tulane U. Med. Sch., New Orleans, 1971-99, prof. urology, 1999—, assoc. chmn., 1986—99; sr. research scientist, head dept. urology Tulane Regional Primate Research Center, Covington, 1972-99; prof. emeritus, 1999—; fellow Fogarty Sr. Internat. NIH, 1984; ret., 2005. Mem. editorial bd. Am. Jour. Kidney Diseases and Urol. Rsch.; contbr. articles to profl. jours. Bd. dirs. Highland Park Hosp., 1985-87. With USN, 1965—67. Recipient grants NIH, Original Rsch. award Southern Med. Assn., 1990, Cert. Achievement Am. Urological Assn., 1997; Fulbright Sr. scholar, 1999-2000. Fellow ACS; mem. St. Tammany Parish Med. Soc. (pres. 1979), Soc. Rsch. on Calculous Kinetics, La. Urol. Soc., Am. Urol. Assn., Soc. Univ. Urologists, Nat. Kidney Found., Soc. Exptl. Biology and Medicine, Nat. Inst. Health (SAT study sect. 1995-99), Sigma Xi. Office: 83 Towne Place Dr Hendersonville NC 28792 Personal E-mail: jrhr285@mchsi.com.

ROBERTS, JAMES BRIAN, engineer; b. Milw., Aug. 25, 1954; s. Phillip Wallace and Betty Ann Roberts, Walter Punko (Stepfather); m. Julie Joanne Wenzler, Aug. 5, 1978; children: Phillip Carl, Jamie Joanne. BS, U. Wis., Madison, 1976. Hull designer and test driver Ski Boats Inc. -Cobra Jet Divsn., Menomonee Falls, Wis., 1976—77; mgr. fleet operation Sherwin Williams Automotive Divsn., Chgo., Afghanistan, 1977—79; v.p. customer svcs. W.B. Combustion Inc., Milw., 1980—85; mgr. application engring. Eclipse Combustion Inc., Rockford, Ill., 1985—99, dir. global metals accts., 1999—. Charter mem. Penn State Ctr. Advanced Materials, Ctr. Heat Treating Excellence, Worcester Poly Tech. Inst., Mass. Contbr. articles to profl. jours. Named to Hall of Fame, Am. Gas Assn., 1998. Mem.: Metal Treating Inst. (assoc.; trustee, bd. dirs. 2005—), Sigma Chi (life). Liberal. Avocations: skiing, golf, writing, sports. Office: Eclipse Combustion Inc 1665 Elmwood Rd Rockford IL 61103 Home Phone: 815-623-2311; Office Phone: 815-637-7217. Business E-Mail: jroberts@eclipsenet.com.

ROBERTS, JAMES HAROLD, III, lawyer; b. Omaha, Aug. 11, 1949; s. James Harold Jr. and Evelyn Doris (Young) R.; m. Marilyn Novak, June 29, 1974; children: Jessica Noël, Meredith Caitlin. BA, U. Notre Dame, 1971; JD, St. Louis U., 1974. Bar: Iowa 1974, U.S. Ct. Mil. Appeals 1974, U.S. Supreme Ct. 1979, D.C. 1981. US govt. atty. US Army, Kans., 1974—78, Ala., 1974—78, Washington, 1978-83; govt. contract atty. US Dept. Treasury, Washington, 1983-88; pvt. practice Van Scoyoc Kelly PLLC, Washington, 1988—. Editor St. Louis U. law rev., 1973-74. Lt. col. JAGC, U.S. Army, 1974-78, USAR/NG, 1978-99. Mem. ABA (pub. contract law sect.), D.C. Bar Assn., Fed. Bar Assn. Roman Catholic. Home: 308 N Monroe St Arlington VA 22201-1736 Office: Van Scoyoc Kelly PLLC Ste 665E 101 Constitution Ave NW Washington DC 20001-1737 Office Phone: 202-898-1898. Business E-Mail: jroberts@vsklaw.com.

ROBERTS, JAMES MCGREGOR, retired trade association administrator; b. Moncton, NB, Can., Nov. 24, 1923; came to U.S., 1949, naturalized, 1956; s. Roland M. and Edith M. (Shields) R.; m. Thelma E. Williams, May 6, 1944; 1 dau., Jana M. B.Commerce, U. Toronto, Ont., Can., 1949. Auditor Citizens Bank, Los Angeles, 1949-54; auditor Acad. Motion Picture Arts and Scis., Hollywood, Calif., 1954—, controller, 1956-71, exec. dir., 1971-89, exec. sec. acad. found., 1971-89, exec. cons. Hollywood, Calif., 1989-92, 1990-93; ret., 1994. Served as pilot Royal Can. Air Force, World War II. Home: 16925 Hierba Dr Apt 112 San Diego CA 92128 Personal E-mail: jmr-ter@cox.net.

ROBERTS, JEANNE ADDISON, retired literature educator; b. Washington; d. John West and Sue Fisher (Nichols) Addison; m. Markley Roberts, Feb. 19, 1966; children: Addison Cary Steed Masengill, Ellen Carraway Masengill Coster. AB, Agnes Scott Coll., 1946; MA, U. Pa., 1947; PhD, U. Va., 1964. Instr. Mary Washington Coll., 1947-48; instr., chmn. English Fairfax Hall Jr. Coll., 1950-51; tchr. Am. U. Assn. Lang. Center, Bangkok, Thailand, 1952-56; instr. Beirut (Lebanon) Coll. for Women, 1956-57, asst. prof., 1957-60, chmn. English dept., 1957-60; instr. lit. Am. U., Washington, 1960-62, asst. prof., 1962-65, asso. prof., 1965-68, prof., 1968-93. Dean faculties Am. U., 1974; lectr. Howard U., 1971-72; seminar prof. Folger Shakespeare Libr. Inst. for Renaissance and 18th Century Studies, 1974; dir. NEH Summer Inst. for HS Tchrs. on Tchg. Shakespeare, Folger Shakespeare Libr., 1984-86; dir. NEH summer inst. Va. Commonwealth U. 1995-96 Writings By and About Women in The English Renaissance; study group leader Inst. Learning in Retirement, Am. U., 1999-, mem. study groups. Author: Shakespeare's English Comedy: The Merry Wives of Windsor in Context, 1979, The Shakespearean Wild: Geography, Genus and Gender, 1991; editor: (with James G. McManaway) A Selective Bibliography of Shakespeare: Editions, Textual Studies, Commentary, 1975; (with Peggy O'Brien) Shakespeare Set Free, vol. 1, 1993, vol. 2, 1994, vol. 3, 1995, (with Georgianna Ziegler) Shakespeare's Unruly Women, 1997; contbr. articles to profl. jours. and scholarly collections. Danforth Tchr. grantee, 1962—63, Folger Sr. fellow, 1969—70, 1988. Mem. MLA (chmn. Shakespeare divsn. 1981-82), Renaissance Soc. Am., Milton Soc., Shakespeare Assn. Am. (trustee 1978-81, 87-89, pres. 1986-87), AAUP (pres. Am. U. chpt. 1966-67), Southeastern Renaissance Conf. (pres. 1981-82), English Speaking Union (bd. dirs. 2005-07), Mortar Board, Phi Beta Kappa, Phi Kappa Phi. Episcopalian. Home: 4931 Albemarle St NW Washington DC 20016-4359 Personal E-mail: jeannerobe@aol.com.

ROBERTS, JEANNE DELORES, lawyer; b. St. Louis, Oct. 31, 1978; d. Michael Victor and Jeanne Gore Roberts. BS in Math., Spelman Coll., Atlanta, 2001; JD, Pepperdine U., Malibu, Calif., 2004. Assoc. Gallop, Johnson & Newman, St. Louis. Hon. campaign chair Monsanto Family YMCA, St. Louis, 2006; sec. bd. dirs. Christmas in St. Louis, 2005—. Office: Gallop Johnson & Newman 101 S Hanley Rd Ste 1700 Saint Louis MO 63105

ROBERTS, JIM, editor; m. Debby Krenek, Feb. 1987; 2 children. Grad, Univ. N.C., 1977. Reporter Richmond Times Dispatch; copy editor Baltimore News American; news editor Dallas Times Herald; copy editor, dep. metro. editor, nat. policital editor New York Times, 1987—2001, dep. nat. editor, 2001—02, nat. editor, 2002—05, sr. editor, nat. desk, 2005—06, editor, digital news, 2006—. Office: New York Times 229 W 43d St New York NY 10036

ROBERTS, JOHN, news anchor; b. Toronto, Ont., Nov. 15, 1956; Student, U. Toronto. Anchor, corr. several broadcasts City TV, Toronto, 1979—89; anchor, corr. WCIX TV (now WFOR-TV), Miami, Fla., 1989—90; co-anchor Can. A.M., 1990—92, CBS Morning News, 1992, WCBS-TV, NYC, 1994—95; anchor CBS Evening News Sunday, NYC, 1995—2006; chief White House corr. CBS News, NYC, 1999—2006; sr. nat. corr. CNN, Washington, 2006—. Recipient Emmy award for best newscast (live coverage of the 1994 elections), New York Press Club award. Office: CNN Bldg 820 First St NE Washington DC 20002

ROBERTS, JOHN, II, television producer, writer; s. Robert Benjamin Roberts and Mary Pauline Ross; m. Elizabeth Ann Levandoski, May 18, 1996; 1 child, John B. III. BA in Fine Arts, U. Calif., Irvine, 1973; BA in Philosophy, Politics & Econs., Oxford U., Eng., 1978, MA in Philosophy, Politics & Econs., 2002. Cert. Witch's Rock Surf Camp, 2007. Asst. to exec. dir. Citizens for Republic, Santa Monica, Calif., 1978—79; press spokesman Reagan-Bush Campaign, Arlington, Afghanistan, 1980; dir. news & info. Presdl. Inaugural Com., Washington, 1980—81; dir. editl. policy & svcs. US Dept. Edn., Office of Legislation and Pub. Affairs, Washington, 1981—83; assoc. dir. Office of Planning & Evaluation The White House, 1983—84, assoc. dir. Office of Polit. & Govtl. Affairs, 1984—86; sr. internat. v.p. Russo Watts & Rollins, Inc., Washington, 1986—89; ptnr. Roberts Comm., Colorado Springs, Colo., 1989—; dir. comm. Nat. Rep. Campaign Com., Washington, 1990—91; sr. v.p. Bozell Worldwide, DC, 1991—94. Speech writing cons. The White House, Washington, 1981; dep. dir. comm. Rep. Nat. Com., Washington, 1981; policy dir. Reagan-Bush Re-election Campaign, 1984; various positions Am. Coun. Young Polit. Leaders, Washington; bd. mem. Am. Coun. of Young Polit. Leaders, Washington, 1988—94, Inst. Rsch. on Small Arms in Internat. Security, Washington, 1991—; war game participant rex 82 bravo US Dept. of Def., Arlington, Va., 1982—83; del. US Dept. of State, Washington, 1986, Am. participant, Chile, 89, Argentina, 89, Mexico, 91; expert lectr. Nat. Endowment for Democracy, Argentina, 1986—90, Internat. Rep. Inst., Washington, 1991, 92, 1992—94; cons. US Sec. Labor, Washington, 1987—89, Chilean Fgn. Ministry, Santiago, Chile, 1993—94; advisor Bush-Quayle '88 Campaign, Washington, 1988—89, Chief Min. of Punjab, Lahore, Pakistan, 1989—90; mng. dir. Sawyer/Miller Group, Washington, 1991—92; polit. advisor Internat. Rep. Inst., Washington, 1991—93; advisor Inkatha Freedom Party, South Africa, 1992—93. Prodr.: (television programs) McLaughlin Group (Emmy nomination), McLaughlin's One on One, McLaughlin Special Report, McLaughlin, (video documentary) Smithsonian Institution's Civil War Uniforms, 1990; author: (book) Rating the First Ladies: The Women Who Influenced the Presidency, 2003, (novel) Hemingway's Suitcase, 2007; editor: (mags.) Handgunner, Ltd., 1980—96. Mem., sec. edns. task force on adult literacy US Dept. Edn., Washington, 1982—83; adv. mem. Tahoe re-green healthy forest com. US Forest Svc., Calif., 1999—2001. Named an Outstanding Young Man of Am., 1981, 1982, 1983, 1984. Mem.: Brit. Alpine Rifles, London Practical Rifle Club (life; founder 1980), UK Practical Shooting Assn. (life; founder 1977). Buddhist. Avocations: backpacking, skiing, drawing, painting. Home and Office: Roberts Comm 1331 W Pike's Peak Ave Colorado Springs CO 80904 Office Phone: 719-473-7688.

ROBERTS, JOHN CHARLES, law educator; b. Aberdeen, SD, Feb. 29, 1940; s. Jacob John Schmitt and Leona (Blethen) Blake; m. Kathleen Kelly (div. 1985); children: Katherine, John Charles Jr.; m. Lynn Dale Friedman, Dec. 22, 1985; 1 child, Emily Sara. BS, Northwestern U., 1961; LL.B., Yale U., 1968. Bar: U.S. Dist. Ct. D.C. 1969, Mich. 1981. Assoc. Covington & Burling, Washington, 1968-71; assoc. dean, lectr. Yale U. Law Sch., New Haven, 1971-77; gen. counsel U.S. Senate Com. on Armed Services, 1977-80; adj. prof. law Washington Coll. Law, Am. U., 1978-80; dean, prof. law Wayne State U. Law Sch., Detroit, 1980-86; prof., dean Law Sch. DePaul U., Chgo., 1986-96, v.p. for univ. advancement, 1996-97, prof. law, 1997—. Mem. exec. com. Inst. for Continuing Legal Edn., Chgo., 1988-91. Mem. adv. com. Mich. Psychiat. Soc., 1980-86; bd. dirs. Constl. Rights Found., 1992-96. Lt. USN, 1961-65. Mem. ABA, Assn. Am. Law Schs. (mem. exec. com., chmn. sect. instn. advancement 1987-88, chmn., sec. adminstrn. law schs. 1993-94), Order of Coif. Democrat. Avocation: collecting modern first editions. Office: DePaul U Coll Law 25 E Jackson Blvd Chicago IL 60604-2289 Office Phone: 312-362-8776. Business E-Mail: jroberts@depaul.edu.

ROBERTS, JOHN D., chemist, educator; b. LA, June 8, 1918; s. Allen Andrew and Flora (Dombrowski) Roberts; m. Edith Mary Johnson, July 11, 1942; children: Anne Christine, Donald William, John Paul, Allen Walter. AB, UCLA, 1941, PhD, 1944; D in Natural Scis. (hon.), U. Munich, 1962; DSc (hon.), Temple U., 1964, Notre Dame U., 1993, U. Wales, 1993, Scripps Rsch. Inst., 1996. Instr. chemistry UCLA, 1944—45; NRC fellow chemistry Harvard U., 1945—46, instr. chemistry, 1946, MIT, 1946, asst. prof., 1947—50, assoc. prof., 1950—52; vis. prof. Ohio State U., 1952, Stanford U., 1973—74; prof. organic chemistry Calif. Inst. Tech., 1953—72, inst. prof. chemistry, 1972—88, inst. prof. chemistry emeritus, lectr., 1988—, dean of faculty, v.p., provost, 1980—83, lectr., 1988—, chmn. divsn. chemistry and chem. engring., 1963—68, acting chmn., 1972—73. Bd. dirs. Huntington Med. Rsch. Insts., 1984—99, Organic Syntheses Inc.; Robert Noyce vis. prof. sci. Grinnell Coll., 2001. Author: Basic Organic Chemistry Part I, 1955, Nuclear Magnetic Resonance, 1958, Spin-Spin Splitting in High-Resolution Nuclear Magnetic Resonance Spectra, 1961, Molecular Orbital Calculations, 1961; author: (with M.C. Caserio) Basic Principles of Organic Chemistry, 1964, 2d edit., 1977, Modern Organic Chemistry, 1967; author: (with R. Stewart and M.C. Caserio) Organic Chemistry-Methane To Macromolecules, 1971; author: At The Right Place at the Right Time, 1990, ABCs of FT-NMR, 2000; contbg. editor: McGraw-Hill Series in Advanced Chemistry, 1957—60; editor: Organic Syntheses, Vol. 41, 1961; Spectroscopy, mem. editl. bd.: Organic Magnetic Resonance in Chemistry. Trustee L.S.B. Leakey Found., 1983—92; bd. dirs. Coleman Chamber Music Assn.; adv. com. Calif. Competitive Tech., 1989—92. Co-recipient Robert A. Welch award, 1990; named Hon. Alumnus, Calif. Inst. Tech., 1990, SURF dedicatee, 1992; named one of Most Influential Chemists of Last 75 yrs., Chem. and Engring. News, 1998; recipient Alumni Profl. Achievement award, UCLA, 1967, Nichols medal, 1972, Tolman medal, 1975, Michelson-Morley award, 1976, Norris award, 1978, Pauling award, 1980, Theodore Wm. Richards medal, 1982, Willard Gibbs Gold medal, 1983, Golden Plate award, Am. Acad. Achievement, 1983, Priestley medal, 1987, Madison Marshall award, 1989, Nat. Medal Sci., NSF, 1990, Glenn T. Seaborg medal, 1991, Award in nuclear magnetic resource, 1991, Svc. to Chemistry award, 1991, History Maker award, Pasadena Hist. Soc., 1994, Pauling Legacy award, 2006;, Guggenheim fellow, 1952—53, 1955—56. Mem.: AAAS (councillor 1992—95), NAS (councillor 1980—83, com. on sci. and engring. pub. policy 1983—87, Chem. Scis. award 1999), Am. Acad. Arts and Scis., Am. Philos. Soc. (coun. mem. 1983—86), Am. Chem. Soc. (chmn. organic chemistry divsn. 1956—57, award pure chemistry 1954, Harrison Howe award 1957, Roger Adams award in organic chemistry 1967, Arthur C. Cope award 1994, Chem. Pioneer award 1994, Nakanishi prize 2001, Auburn Kosolapoff award 2003), Phi Lambda Upsilon, Sigma Xi. Office: Calif Inst Tech Crellin Lab Pasadena CA 91125-0001

ROBERTS, JOHN DERHAM, lawyer; 1 child. Cert., Richmond Coll., Va., 1960; BS, Hampden-Sydney Coll., Va., 1964; LLB, Washington & Lee U., 1968. Bar: Va. 1968, Fla. 1969, U.S. Supreme Ct. 1969, U.S. Ct. Customs and Patent Appeals 1970, U.S. Tax Ct. 1970, U.S. Ct. Appeals (5th cir.) 1970, U.S. Ct. Appeals (9th cir.) 1974, U.S. Supreme Ct. 1969. Law clk. U.S. Dist. Ct., Jacksonville, Fla., 1968-69; assoc. Phillips, Kendrick, Gearhart & Aylor, Arlington, Va., 1969-70; asst. U.S. Atty. mid. dist. Fla. U.S. Dept. Justice, Jacksonville, 1970-74, Dist. of Alaska, Anchorage, 1974-77, U.S. magistrate judge, 1977—. Bd. dirs. Teen Challenge Alaska, Anchorage, 1984-93; chmn. Eagle Scout Rev. Bd., 1993—; bd. dirs. Alaska Youth for Christ, 1993-96; govs.'s Prayer Breakfast Com., 1994—, vice-chair, 1998—. Recipient Citizenship award DAR, Anchorage, 1984, plaque, U.S. Navy, Citizen Day, Adak, Alaska, 1980, Silver Beaver award, 2004. Mem. ABA, Nat. Conf. Spl. Ct. Judges (exec. bd. 1985-92), 9th Cir. Conf. Magistrate Judges (exec. bd. 1982-85, chmn. 1984-85, 2005—), Alaska Bar Assn., Anchorage Bar Assn., Chi Phi, Psi Chi, Phi Alpha Delta. Republican. Office: US Magistrate Judge 222 W 7th Ave Unit 46 Anchorage AK 99513-7504 Office Phone: 907-677-6255.

ROBERTS, JOHN GLOVER, JR., United States Supreme Court Chief Justice; b. Buffalo, Jan. 27, 1955; s. John Glover and Rosemary (Podrasky) R.; m. Jane Marie Sullivan Roberts, July 27, 1996; children Jack, Josie. AB summa cum laude, Harvard U., 1976, JD magna cum laude, 1979. Bar: DC 1981, US Ct. Appeals (Fed. Cir.) 1982, US Ct. Appeals (DC, 5th, 9th Cirs.) 1988, US Ct. Appeals (3rd, 7th, and 10th Cirs.) 1996, US Ct. Claims 1982, US Supreme Ct. 1987. Law clk. to Hon. Henry Friendly US Ct. Appeals (2nd Cir.), NYC, 1979-80; law clk. to Assoc. Justice William H. Rehnquist US Supreme Ct., Washington, 1980-81; spl. asst. to US Atty. Gen. William French Smith US Dept. Justice, Washington, 1981-82; assoc. counsel to Pres. Ronald Reagan The White House, Washington, 1982-86; assoc. Hogan & Hartson, LLP, Washington, 1986-87, ptnr., 1988—89, 1993—2003; prin. dep. solicitor gen. US Dept. Justice, Washington, 1989-93; judge US Ct. Appeals (DC Cir.), Washington, 2003—05; initially nominee for assoc. justice US Supreme Ct., Washington, 2005, chief justice, 2005—. Editor: Harvard Law Rev., 1977-79 Named one of The World's Most Influential People, TIME mag., 2006—07. Mem. Am. Law Inst., Am. Acad. Appellate Lawyers, Edward Coke Appellate Inn of Ct., Supreme Ct. Hist. Soc., Lawyers Club, Met. Club, Robert Trent Jones Golf Club, Phi Beta Kappa; fellow Am. Acad. Arts & Sciences Republican. Argued 39 cases before the US Supreme Court. Office: US Supreme Ct One First St SE Washington DC 20543 *

ROBERTS, JOHN ROBERT, cardiothoracic surgeon, consultant; b. Athens, Tenn., Apr. 5, 1959; s. Doyle Ford and Frankie Howard Roberts; children: Amanda, Timothy, John Anthony, Thomas. AB summa cum laude, Duke U., 1981; MD with honors, Yale U., 1985; MBA, Auburn U., 2003. Bd. cert. gen. surgery Am. Bd. Surgery, bd. cert. thoracic surgery Am. Bd. Thoracic Surgery, lic. med. practice Tenn. Resident surgeon Johns Hopkins Hosp., Balt., 1986—92, fellow in surg. oncology, 1992—93; fellow in thoracic surgery Brigham and Women's Hosp., Boston, 1993—95; asst. prof. U. Pa., Phila., 1995—97; chief gen. thoracic surgery Vanderbilt U., Nashville, 1997—2003; thoracic surgeon The Surg. Clinic, Nashville, 2003—. Ingram Prof. Cancer Rsch. Vanderbilt U., 1997; lectr. in field. Reviewer: jours. CHEST, Annals of Thoracic Surgery, Jour. Thoracic and Cardiovasc. Surgery; contbr. articles to profl. jours. Capt. USAR, 1999—2003. Recipient Resident Rsch. award, Johns Hopkins Hosp., 1986, grants in field. Fellow: ACS (scholarship for health policy 2004), Am. Coll. Chest Physicians; mem.: Am. Coll. Surgeons Workforce on Health Policy, Reform and Advocacy, So. Thoracic Surg. Assn., Soc. Thoracic Surgeons, Am. Soc. Clin. Oncology, So. Assn. for Oncology, Soc. Cell and Tissue Kinetics, Phi Kappa Phi. Avocation: Tae Kwon Do. Office: The Surg Clinic #356 24th Ave Nashville TN 37203 Office Phone: 615-327-4808, 615-327-4809. Personal E-mail: johnbob999@msn.com. Business E-Mail: jroberts@tsclinic.com.

ROBERTS, JUDITH MARIE, librarian, educator; b. Bluefield, W.Va., Aug. 5, 1939; d. Charles Bowen Lowder and Frances Marie (Bourne) Lowder Alberts; m. Craig Currence Johnson, July 1, 1957 (div. 1962); 1 child, Craig Jr.; m. Milton Rinehart Roberts, Aug. 13, 1966 (div. 1987). BS, Concord State Tchrs. Coll., 1965. Libr. Cape Henlopen Sch. Dist., Lewes, Del., 1965—91; with Lily's Gift Shop, St. Petersburg, Fla., 1991—. Pres. Friends of Lewes Pub. Libr., 1986—90; chmn. exhibits Govs. Conf. Librs. and Info. Svcs., Dover, Del., 1978; mem. Gov.'s State Libr. Adv. Coun., 1987—91. Mem.: NEA, ALA, Del. Learning Resources Assn. (pres. 1976—77), Del. Library Assn. (pres. 1982—83), Sussex Help Orgn. for Resources Exch. (pres. 1984—85), Del. State Edn. Assn. Methodist. Home Phone: 727-864-0051; Office Phone: 727-867-7974. Business E-Mail: judyoffice2003@yahoo.com.

ROBERTS, JULIA FIONA, actress; b. Smyrna, Ga., Oct. 28, 1967; d. Betty and Walter Roberts; m. Lyle Lovett, Jun. 25, 1993 (div. March 22, 1995); m. Daniel Moder, July 4, 2002; children: Hazel Patricia, Phinnaeus Walter, Henry Daniel. Actress: (films) Blood Red, 1986, Satisfaction, 1987, Mystic Pizza, 1988, Steel Magnolias, 1989 (Acad. Award nominee, Golden Globe award), Pretty Woman, 1990 (Acad. Award nominee, Golden Globe Award), Flatliners, 1990, Sleeping With the Enemy, 1991, Hook, 1991, Dying Young, 1991, The Player, 1992, The Pelican Brief, 1993, I Love Trouble, 1994, Ready to Wear (Prêt-à-Porter), 1994, Something To Talk About, 1995, Mary Reilly, 1996, Everybody Says I Love You, 1996, Michael Collins, 1996, My Best Friend's Wedding, 1997, Conspiracy Theory, 1997, Stepmom, 1998, Notting Hill, 1999, Runaway Bride, 1999, Erin Brockovich, 2000 (Acad. award for Best Actress, Golden Globe for Best Performance by an Actress), The Mexican, 2001, America's Sweethearts, 2001, Ocean's Eleven, 2001, Full Frontal, 2002, Confessions of a Dangerous Mind, 2002, Mona Lisa Smile, 2003, Closer, 2004, Ocean's Twelve, 2004, (voice only) The Ant Bully, 2006, (voice only) Charlotte's Web, 2006; (TV films) Baja Oklahoma, 1988, (narrator) Before Your Eyes: Angelie's Secret, 1995; (TV appearances) Crime Story, 1987, Miami Vice, 1988, Friends, 1996, Murphy Brown, 1998, Sesame Street, 1998, AFI's 100 Years...100 Movies, 1998, In the Wild, 1998, Law & Order, 1999; Broadway plays include Three Days of Rain, 2006. Involved with UNICEF; lent celebrity name to help raise money for research to develop a cure for Rett Syndrome. Recipient People's Choice awards Favorite Motion Picture Actress, 1991, 98, Favorite Comedy/Dramatic Motion Picture Actress, 1992, Favorite Dramatic Motion Picture Actres, 1994; recipient Woman of Yr. award Hasty Pudding Theatricals, 1997, Spl. award Internat. Star of Yr., ShoWest Conv., 1998,; Named Female Star of the Yr., Nat. Assn. Theatre Owners, 1991, Am. Cinematheque award, 2007; named one of '50 Most Beautiful People in the World, People Mag., 1990, 1991, 50 Most Beautiful List', People Mag.(USA), 2000, 2002, '25 Most Intriguing People, People Mag., 2001, Top Entertainers, E!, 2001.; named one of 50 Most Powerful People in Hollywood Premiere mag., 2002-06, 100 Most Powerful Celebrities, Forbes.com, 2007. One of the most popular and sought-after talents in Hollywood; highest paid actress in film history. Office: c/o Kevin Huvane Creative Artists Agency 9830 Wilshire Blvd Beverly Hills CA 90212-1825 *

ROBERTS, KATHARINE ADAIR, retired bookkeeper; b. Columbus, Ga., June 4, 1930; d. William Lynn and Ella Miller (Adair) R. BA, U. Redlands, 1955; postgrad., San Bernardino Valley Coll., 1971—74, Calif. State U., San Bernardino, 1975—78. Bookkeeper Rettig Machine Shop,

Inc., Redlands, Calif., 1970-97, ret., 1997. Pres. Dem. Study Club, San Bernardino, 1967-68, Redlands Dem. Club, 1976, Wilsonian Club, San Bernardino, 1986; chair Redlands/San Bernardino chpt. Citizens for Global Solutions, 1987—, San Bernardino leader ptnrs. for global change program; active San Bernardino County Dem. Ctrl. Com., treas. 1977-80. Named one of 63 Women of Distinction, 63rd Assembly Dist., Calif., Assemblyman Bill Emmerson, 2005; recipient Citizen Achievement award, LWV, 1989. Mem. Dem. Luncheon Club (George E. Brown Amb. of Peace award 2000), Humane Soc. of San Bernardino Valley, Redlands Humane Soc., Redlands Dem. Club (treas.), LWV, Inland Empire Debating Soc. (treas.). Democrat. Home: 798 W 18th St San Bernardino CA 92405-4235

ROBERTS, KATHLEEN JOY DOTY, secondary school educator; b. Jamaica, NY, Apr. 19, 1951; d. Alfred Arthur and Helen Caroline (Sohl) Doty; m. Robert Louis Roberts, Nov. 24, 1974; children: Robert Louis, Michael Sean, Kathleen Meagan. BA in Edn., CUNY, 1972, MS in Spl. Edn., 1974; cert. advanced study in ednl. adminstrn., Hofstra U., 1982; Ednl. Specialist, Nova Southeastern U., 2003, PhD Computing Tech. in Edn., 2004. Cert. sch. adminstrn., tchr. math., N.Y.; cert. N.Y. Dept. Mental Hygiene; lic. spl. edn. supr., ednl. adminstr., N.Y. Tchr. health conservation Woodside (N.Y.) Jr. H.S., 1973-77; coord. spl. edn. dept. Ridgewood (N.Y.) Jr. H.S., 1977-81; adminstrv. asst., health, compliance and mainstream coord., grant writer Grover Cleveland H.S., Ridgewood, 1981—2004, also coord. transition linkage, resource tchr. mentor, 1981—2004; tech. staff developer Region 4, N.Y.C. Dept. Edn., 2004—06; collaborative team tchr. Queens H.S. of Tchg., 2006—. Instr. Grad. Sch. U. Phoenix. Author: Closed Circuit TV and Other Devices for the Partially Sighted, 1971, Nat. Soc. Colonial Daughters of the Seventeenth Century Lineage Book (Centennial Remembrance edit.), 1999, Infusing Online Components Into the Academic Coursework of High Schools in the State of New York Using HSTOR-E, 2003; contbr. articles to profl. jours. Legis. chmn. Fairfield Jr. and Sr. H.S. PTA and Massapequa coun., 1987-92. Mem.: ACM, DAR, NEA, Internat. Soc. Tech. in Edn., N.Y. State Tchrs. Assn., Colonial Dames of the XVII Century, Colonial Daus. of the XVII Century (pres. 1985—91, nat. chmn. hist. activities com. 1988—91, registrar, historian Founders chpt. 1991—94, nat. councillor, publicity chmn. 1991—94, centennial com. 1994—96, registrar gen. nat. soc. 1997—2000, pres. 2000—), Pilgrim Edward Doty Soc. Republican. Home: 52 Hicksville Rd Massapequa NY 11758-5843 Office: AHST 74-20 Commonwealth Blvd Bellerose NY 11426 E-mail: DrKathyRoberts@aim.net.

ROBERTS, KATHLEEN MARY, retired school system administrator; b. Syracuse, NY, Apr. 15, 1947; d. Casimer and Lorrayne Arletta (Molloy) Piegdon; m. James C. Roberts, June 29, 1968 (div. Sept. 1988). BA, Cen. State U., Edmond, Okla., 1968, MEd, 1971; PhD, U. Okla., 1977. Cert. tchr., prin., supt., Okla.; cert. supt., N.Y. Tchr. Putnam City Schs., Oklahoma City, 1960-72; reading specialist Moore (Okla.) Pub. Schs., 1973-74, Crooked Oak Pub. Schs., Oklahoma City, 1974-77, 1990-95; rsch. assoc. Oklahoma City Pub. Schs., 1977-80; supt. Okla. Dept. Corrections, Oklahoma City, 1980-86, Healdton (Okla.) Pub. Schs., 1986-90; supr. Crooked Oak Schs., Oklahoma City, 1990—95; supt. Piedmont (Okla.) Pub. Schs., 1995-98, ret., 1998; registered fin. advisor McDonald & Assocs., 1998—. Contbr. articles to profl. publs. Bd. dirs. United Meth. Prism Ministry, Oklahoma City, 1986—, Children's Shelter, Ardmore, Okla., 1989-90; mem. State Vocat. Edn. Coun., Oklahoma City, 1980-85. Recipient citation Okla. State Senate, 1986. Mem. ASCD, Internat. Reading Assn., Am. Assn. Sch. Adminstrs., Okla. Assn. Sch. Adminstrs., Piedmont C. of C. (v.p. 1997—), Phi Delta Kappa, Alpha Chi, Kappa Delta Phi. Democrat. Roman Catholic. Avocations: furniture refinishing, reading, gardening.

ROBERTS, KATRINA M., real estate agent; d. William B. and Cathleen A. Roberts. BS in Bus., Skidmore Coll., Saratoga Springs, NY, 1997. Exec. dir. resources Creative Technologies NY, NYC, 1998—99; stockbroker TD Waterhouse, San Diego, 2000—01; real estate sales staff Coldwell Banker, San Diego, 2001—03; freelance thoroughbred racehorse trainer/rider San Luis Rey Downs, Bonsall, Calif., 2003—04; show hunter trainer, rider Kennedy Farms, St. Louis, 2004—05; real estate equestrian and estate properties F.C. Tucker Co. Inc, Indpls., 2005—06; real estate sales and devel. Grassland Real Estate, Brentwood, Tenn., 2006—. Mem.: Williamson County C. of C., Mensa. Home Phone: 615-84-7227.

ROBERTS, KATY, editor; married. BA politics, U. Calif., Santa Cuz, 1974; MA journalism & Russian studies, Ind. U., 1977. With Hayward Daily Rev., Calif., 1977—79, Minneapolis Star, 1979—82; op-ed editor NY Times, 1995—2000, nat. editor, 2000—02, editor, The Week in Review, 2002—. Recipient Alumni Achievement award, U. Calif., Santa Cruz, 2001. Office: NY Times 229 W 43rd St New York NY 10036 Office Phone: 212-556-1748. Office Fax: 212-556-3738. E-mail: krobe@nytimes.com.

ROBERTS, KENNETH LEWIS, investor, lawyer, foundation administrator; b. Dungannon, Va., Dec. 12, 1932; s. Clarence Eugene and Katherine (Osborne) R.; m. Anne Foster Cook, Sept. 10, 1955 (dec. Dec. 5, 1999); children— Kenneth L., Patrick Hagan Foster; m. Delphine Oman Sloan, July 20, 2002. BA, Vanderbilt U., 1954, LLB, 1959. Bar: Tenn. Assoc. prof. law Vanderbilt U., 1959-60; assoc. Waller, Lansden & Dortch, Nashville, 1960-66; exec. v.p. Commerce Union Bank, Nashville, 1966-71; pres., CEO, dir. Cen. Nat. Bank, Richmond, Va., 1971-76; pres., CEO First Am. Nat. Bank, Nashville, 1976-90; dir. First Am. Corp., Nashville, 1976-90, vice-chmn., 1976-77, pres., CEO, 1977-79, chmn., CEO, 1979-90; pres., exec. dir. FRIST Found., Nashville, 1991—2002, pres. emeritus, 2002—. Past pres. Cen. Nat. Corp. Trustee Vanderbilt U.; bd. dirs. Leadership Nashville, Country Music Found. Lt. Chem. Corps, AUS, 1955-57. Mem. ABA, Tenn. Bar Assn., Nashville Bar Assn., Nashville C. of C., Belle Meade Country Club, Univ. Club, Ponte Vedra (Fla.) Inn & Club. Office: FRIST Found 3100 W End Ave Ste 1200 Nashville TN 37203-6827

ROBERTS, KEVIN, advertising executive; b. Lancaster, Eng., Oct. 20, 1949; s. John and Jean (Lambert) R.; m. Barbara Beckett; 1 child, Nicola Jane; m. Rowena Joan Honeywill, Dec. 31, 1974; children: Ben, Rebecca, Daniel. D (hon.), Waikato U., Hamilton, New Zealand, 1998. With Mary Quant, London, Gillette, Procter & Gamble; CEO Pepsi-Cola Middle East, 1987—89; COO Lion Breweries, New Zealand, 1989—96; worldwide CEO Saatchi & Saatchi, NYC, 1997—. Sr. fellow Waikato Mgmt. Sch., U. Waikato, New Zealand. Co-author: Peak Performance: Business Lessons from the World's Best Sporting Organizations, 2000. Trustee Team New Zealand, Turn Your Life Around Trust, Auckland. Avocations: rugby, tennis, art, travel, music. Office: Saatchi & Saatchi 375 Hudson St New York NY 10014-3520 *

ROBERTS, LARRY SPURGEON, biological science educator, zoologist; b. Texon, Tex., June 30, 1935; s. E. Fowler and Frances Wray (Huggins) R.; m. Maria Elek, Feb. 7, 1962; children: Gregory Lorinc, Bruce Tibor, Teresa Margit, Eric Miklos. BS, So. Meth. U., Dallas, 1956; MS, U. Ill., Urbana, 1958; DSc, Johns Hopkins U., Balt., 1961. Cert. scuba instr. Nat. Assn. Underwater Instrs. From asst. prof. to prof. zoology U. Mass., Amherst, 1963-79; prof. biol. scis. Tex. Tech U., Lubbock, 1979-90, chmn. dept., 1979-84. Adj. prof. biol. scis. U. Miami, 1990-99, Fla. Internat. U., 1990-93, 99—. Author (with others): Foundations of Parasitology, 1977, 7th edit., 2005; author: Integrated Principles of Zoology, 1979, 13th edit., 2006, Biology of Animals, 1982, 7th edit., 1998, The Underwater World of Sport Diving, 1991, Animal Diversity, 3d edit., 2003. Mem. Amherst Dem. Town Com., 1968-79, vice chmn., 1972-76; mem. Amherst Town Meeting, 1966-76; mem. Amherst Zoning Bd. Appeals, 1972-75, vice chmn., 1972-75; recorder West Tex. Dems., 1985-86; mem. Dade County Dem. Exec. Com., 1991—. NIH postdoctoral trainee, 1961-63; NSF fellow, 1958, NIH fellow, 1969-70; recipient Disting. Svc. cert. Mass. Tchrs. Assn., 1979. Mem. AAAS, ACLU (vice chmn. Hampshire County chpt. 1966-68, bd. dirs. Lubbock chpt. 1985-89, vice chmn. 1988-89, bd. dirs. Miami, Fla. chpt. 1991—, 1st v.p. 1998-00, treas. 2000-06, Fla. State bd. dirs., treas. 2006—), Am. Soc. Parasitologists (Henry Baldwin Ward medal 1971, coun. mem. at large 1980-83, v.p. 1984-85, 96-97, pres. 1998-99), Am. Micros. Soc. (v.p. 1974-75, exec. com. 1978-81), Mass. Soc. Profs. (pres. 1977-78), Soc. Protozoologists, Am. Soc. Tropical Medicine and Hygiene, Southwestern Assn. Parasitologists (v.p. 1982, pres. 1983), Southeastern Soc. Parasitologists (pres.-elect 1993, pres. 1994), Internat. Soc. Reef Studies, Crustacean Soc., Am. Acad. Underwater Scis., Sigma Xi. Home: 27700 SW 164th Ave Homestead FL 33031-2846 E-mail: Lroberts1@compuserve.com.

ROBERTS, LAWRENCE GILMAN, telecommunications industry executive; b. Conn., Dec. 21, 1937; s. Elliott John and Elizabeth (Gilman) R.; m. June Ellen Stuller, 1959 (div. 1973); children: Paul, Kenny. BSEE, MIT, 1959, MSEE, 1960, PhD, 1963. Dir. info. proc. Advanced Rsch. Projects Agy. U.S. Dept. Def., Arlington, Va., 1969-73; pres., CEO, GTE Telenet Corp., Vienna, Va., 1973-82; pres. DHL, Redwood City, Calif., 1982-83; chmn., CEO, NetExpress, Inc., Foster City, Calif., 1983-93; pres. ATM Systems, Santa Clara, Calif., 1993-98; founder, chief tech. officer Caspian Networks, San Jose, Calif., 1998—2004; founder, CEO Anagran Inc., Woodside, Calif., 2004—. Recipient L.M. Ericsson award for comms., 1981, Prince of Asturias award, 2002, NEC Computer Comms. award, 2005. Mem.: AAAS, IEEE (W. Wallace McDowell award 1992, Internet award 2000), NAE (Draper award 2001), Assn. Computing Machinery (SIGCOM award 1998), Am. Fedn. Info. Processing, IEEE Computer Soc., Sigma Xi. E-mail: lroberts@packet.cc.

ROBERTS, LEIGH MILTON, psychiatrist; b. Jacksonville, Ill., June 9, 1925; s. Victor Harold and Ruby Harriet (Kelsey) R.; m. Marilyn Edith Kadow, 1946 (dec. 1995); m. Ellen Rabenhorst, 2003; children: David, Carol Troxell, Paul, Nancy Mills. BS, U. Ill., 1945, MD, 1947. Diplomate Am. Bd. Psychiatry and Neurology. Intern St. Francis Hosp., Peoria, Ill., 1947-48; gen. practice medicine Macomb, Ill., 1948-50; resident in psychiatry U. Wis. Hosps., Madison, 1953-56; staff psychiatrist Mendota (Wis.) State Hosp., 1956-58; mem. faculty U. Wis. Med. Sch., Madison, 1959-89, prof. psychiatry, 1971-89, acting chmn. dept., 1972-75. Cons. in psychiatry, 1989-; mem. spl. rev. bd. Wis. Parole Bd. Sex Crimes Law, 1962-88, forensic cons., 1988—; mem. Dane County Devel. Disabilities Bd., 1962-66, Wis. Planning Com. Mental Health, 1963-65, Wis. Planning Com. Health, 1969-71, Wis. Planning Com. Vocat. Rehab., 1966-68, Wis. Planning Com. Health Centers, 1967-71, Wis. Mental Health Adv. Com., 1973-78; bd. dirs. Methodist Hosp., Madison, Dane County Rehab. House, Dane County Assn. Mental Health; cons. in field. Editor: Community Psychiatry, 1966, Comprehensive Mental Health, 1968; contbr. articles profl. jours. Pres. Wis. Coun. Chs., 1976-78; bd. dirs. Madison Campus Ministry, St. Benedict Center; trustee North Central Coll., Naperville, Ill. Served with USNR, 1943-45, 50-53. Decorated Bronze Stars, Purple Heart. Fellow Am. Psychiat. Assn. (trustee 1981-84), Wis. Psychiat. Assn. (pres. 1967) Methodist. Home and Office: 33 S Midvale Blvd Madison WI 53705 *Life is a precious gift whose journey is molded and shaped by cumulative experiences and relationships. Religious belief and practice which provides future-oriented hope, disciplined accountability and living service are balanced by professional psychiatric vistas on the uniqueness and worth of each human person.*

ROBERTS, LORIN WATSON, botanist, educator; b. Clarksdale, Mo., June 28, 1923; s. Lorin Cornelius and Irene (Watson) Roberts; m. Florence Ruth Greathouse, July 10, 1967; children: Michael Hamlin, Daniel Hamlin, Margaret Susan. BA, U. Mo., 1948, MA, 1950; PhD in Botany, U. Mo.-Columbia, 1952. Asst. prof., then assoc. prof. botany Agnes Scott Coll., Decaur, Ga., 1952-57; vis. asst. prof. Emory U., 1952-55; mem. faculty U. Idaho, 1957—, prof. botany, 1967-91, prof. botany emeritus, 1991—; Fulbright research prof. Kyoto (Japan) U., 1967-68; research fellow U. Bari, Italy, 1968; Cabot fellow Harvard, 1974; Fulbright teaching fellow North-Eastern Hill U., Shillong, Meghalaya, India, 1977; Fulbright sr. scholar and fellow Australian Nat. U., Canberra, 1980; sr. researcher U. London, 1984; pres. botany sect. 1st Internat. Congress Histochemistry and Cytochemistry, Paris, 1960; Alexander von Humboldt vis. fellow Australian Nat. U., 1992. Author: Cytodifferentiation in Plants, 1976; author: (with J. H. Dodds) Experiments in Plant Tissue Culture, 1982, 3d edit., 1995; author: (with P. B. Gahan and R. Aloni) Vascular Differentiation and Plant Growth Regulators, 1988; contbr. articles to profl. jours. With USAAF, 1943—46. Decorated chevalier de l'Ordre du Merit Agricole France; Alexander von Humboldt fellow, 1992. Fellow: AAAS; mem.: Idaho Acad. Scis., Am. Inst. Biol. Scis., Internat. Assn. Plant Tissue Culture, Am. Soc. Plant Physiologists, Bot. Soc. Am., N.W. Sci. Assn. (pres. 1970—71), Sigma Xi, Phi Sigma, Phi Kappa Phi. Home (Winter): 920 Mabelle St Moscow ID 83843-3834

ROBERTS, LOUISE NISBET, philosopher, educator; b. Lexington, Ky., Apr. 21, 1919; d. Benjamin and Helen L. Nisbet; m. Warren Roberts, June 14, 1952 (dec.); children: Helen Ward Roberts Hill, Valeria Lamar Roberts Emmett. AB, U. Ky., 1942, MA, 1944; PhD, Columbia U., 1952. Instr. philosophy Fairfax Hall, Waynesboro, Va., 1943—44, Fairmount Casements, Ormond Beach, Fla., 1944—45; mem. faculty Newcomb Coll., Tulane U., 1948—, prof. philosophy, 1969—85, dept. head, prof. emeritus, 1985—. Contbr. articles to profl. jours. Univ. scholar, 1945-46. Mem. AAUW (fellow 1947-48, pres. New Orleans chpt. 1986-88), DAR (vice regent New Orleans chpt. 1987-90, 2002-03), So. Soc. Philosophy and Psychology, Phi Beta Kappa (chpt. pres. 1956-57), Delta Delta Delta (fellow 1946-47). Democrat. Episcopalian. Office: Tulane U Dept Philosophy New Orleans LA 70118

ROBERTS, MARGARET HAROLD, editor, publisher; b. Aug. 18, 1928; AB, U. Chattanooga, Tenn., 1950. Editor, pub. series Award Winning Art, 1960-70, New Woman mag., Palm Beach, Fla., 1971-84; editor, pub. BONKERS mag., 1992—2001. Author: juvenile book series Daddy is a Doctor, 1965.

ROBERTS, MARK SCOTT, lawyer; b. Fullerton, Calif. s. Emil Seidel and Theda (Wymer) R. BA in Theater, Pepperdine U., 1975; JD, Western State U., 1978; cert. civil trial advocacy program, U. Calif., San Francisco, 1985; cert. program of instrn. for lawyers, Harvard U., 1990. Bar: Calif. 1980, U.S. Dist. Ct. (cen. dist.) Calif. 1980, U.S. Supreme Ct. 1989, U.S. Ct. Mil. Appeals 1989, U.S. Tax Ct. 1990. Prin. Law Offices of Mark S. Roberts, APLC, Fullerton, Calif., 1980—. Instr. bus. law Biola U., La Mirada, Calif., 1980-82; judge pro tem Orange County Superior Ct., Santa Ana, 1989—; adj. prof. wills and trusts Trinity Law Sch., Santa Ana, 2000—. Co-author: Legacy-Plan, Protect and Preserve Your Estate, 1996, Generations Planning Your Legacy, 1999. Mem. Calif. State Bar Assn., Orange County Bar Assn. (charter), Nat. Network Estate Planning Attys., Soc. Cert. Sr. Advisors. Office: 1440 N Harbor Blvd Ste 900 Fullerton CA 92835-4122 Office Phone: 714-449-3353. Personal E-mail: mroberts@marksroberts.com.

ROBERTS, MARKLEY, economist, educator; b. Shanghai, Sept. 3, 1930; s. Donald and Frances Charlotte (Markley) Roberts; m. Jeanne Addison, Feb. 19, 1966; children: Addison, Ellen. AB, Princeton U., 1951; MA, Am. U., 1960, PhD, 1970. Reporter Washington Star newspaper, 1952-57; legis. asst. Office of Senator Hubert Humphrey of Minn., Washington, 1957-62; legis. asst., economist AFL-CIO, Washington, 1962-96, asst. dir. econ. rsch. dept., 1989-96. Bd. dirs., vice-chmn. Econ. Edn. Found. Clergy, 1972—80; chmn. labor rsch. adv. coun. Bur. Labor Stats., Dept. Labor, 1972—96; adj. prof. econs. U. Md., 1966—, George Washington U., 1972—96; bd. dirs., chair Inst. Learning Retirement, 2002—. Contbr. articles to profl. jours.; author: monographs in field. Mem. DC Dem. Ctrl. Com., 1964—68; ward III coord. Washington Mayor Walter Washington, 1974—78; bd. dirs. Laymen's Nat. Bible Com. Inc., NYC, 1972—82. Mem.: Newspaper Guild, Nat. Consumers League (bd. dirs. 1991—99), Am. Statis. Assn., Assn. Evolutionary Econs., Nat. Acad. Social Inst., Am. Polit. Sci. Assn., Indsl. Rels. Rsch. Assn. (exec. bd. 1975—77), Am. Econ. Assn., Social Dems. USA, UN Assn. (bd. dirs. labor chair nat. capitol area chpt. 1996—, mem. exec. com. nat. coun. orgns. 2007—), Ams. Dem. Action (exec. bd. 1992—), Cosmos Club. Democrat. Episcopalian. Home: 4931 Albemarle St NW Washington DC 20016-4359

ROBERTS, MEL (MELVIN RICHARD KELLS), retired film editor; b. Toledo, Aug. 26, 1923; s. Paul Mickle and Letha Ellen (Mize) Kells. BA, U. So. Calif., 1950, postgrad., 1951. Film editor Graphic Films, Hollywood, Calif., 1951-52; music editor Salt of the Earth, Ind. Film Co., Hollywood, 1952-53; film editor Ford Found., Columbia Pictures, Hollywood, 1953-62; cinematographer and film editor Wexler Films, Hollywood, 1956-62; still photographer LA, 1962-81; video prodr., dir., 1993-97. Photographer, pub. (books) Mel Roberts Male, Rex, California Boys-Photographs from the 1960s-1970s, 2000, Mel Roberts California Boys-Photographs from the 1960s and 1970s, 2001, Mel Roberts California Boys-The Wild Ones, and others, photographer Uniforms, 1998, Male Bonding 2, 1998; editor: (films) Paul Coates Confidential File, Tim McCoy Show, Rudy Vallee Prodns., (documentaries) City That Disappears, Graphic Films; prodr., dir.: (films, 4 vols.) Classic Males Videos, 1993—97, 2000; editor: (documentary) Segregation and the South, 1957; Exhibited in group shows at David Aden Gallery, 2000—01, Clampart Gallery, NYC, one-man shows include David Aden Gallery, 2000, Jerry Miller Gallery, Palm Springs, Calif., 2001, West Hollywood Gallery, 2003, Erotic Mus., Hollywood, 2005. Sgt. USAF, 1943-45, PTO. Avocations: collecting classic films and film publications, music. Office: 1335 N La Brea Ave Apt 2102 Hollywood CA 90028-7526 E-mail: melrobertsvideo@aol.com.

ROBERTS, MELVILLE PARKER, neurosurgeon; b. Phila., Oct. 15, 1931; s. Melville Parker and Marguerite Louise (Reimann) R.; m. Sigrid Marianne Magnusson, Mar. 27, 1954; children: Melville Parker III, Julia Pell, Erik Emerson. BS, Washington and Lee U., 1953; MD, Yale U., 1957. Diplomate: Am. Bd. Neurol. Surgery. Intern Yale Med. Ctr., 1957, neurosurgical resident, 1958-60, 62-64, Am. Cancer Soc. fellow in neurosurgery, 1962-64, instr., 1964; asst. prof. surgery Sch. Medicine U. Va., Charlottesville, 1965-69; practice medicine specializing in neurol. surgery Hartford, Conn., 1970-1998; mem. staff Hartford Hosp.; asst. prof. surgery Sch. Medicine U. Conn., Farmington, 1970-71, assoc. prof., 1972-75, assoc. prof. neurology, 1974-77, chmn. divsn. neurosurgery, 1971-84, prof. surgery, 1975—, acting chmn. dept. neurology, 1973-77, acting chmn. dept. surgery, 1974-77, William Beecher Scoville prof. neurosurgery, 1976-98, prof. emeritus, 1998—. James Hudson Brown rsch. fellow Yale U., 1957. Author: Atlas of the Human Brain in Section, 1970, 2d edit., 1987, The Brain Atlas, 1998; mem. editl. bd.: Conn. Medicine, 1973-98; contbr. articles to profl. jours. Capt. MC, US Army, 1960-61. Fellow Royal Soc. Medicine London (life); mem. Am. Assn. Neurol. Surgeons, Soc. Neurol. Surgeons, Congress Neurol. Surgeons (bd. dirs. joint spinal sect. with Am. Assn. Neurol. Surgeons, chmn. ann. meeting 1987, sci. program chmn. ann. meeting 1988), Assn. for Rsch. in Nervous and Mental Diseases, New Eng. Neurosurg. Soc. (bd. dirs. 1976-79, pres. 1989-91), Soc. Brit. Neurol. Surgeons, Rsch. Soc. Neurol. Surgeons, Soc. Rsch. into Hydrocephalus and Spina Bifida, Conn. Acad. Arts and Sci., Vereingung Schweizer Neurochirugen, Mory's Assn., Beaumont Med. Club (pres. 1988, New Haven), Yale Club NY, Sloane Club (London).

ROBERTS, MICHAEL G., lawyer; b. 1956; BA with high honors, Mich. State U., 1977; jd cum laude, Am. U., 1982. Bar: DC 1983, Fla. 1984. Law clerk DC Superior Ct., 1983; maritime atty. Washington; from corp. counsel to v.p., govt. rels. Crowley Maritime Corp., 1991—2000; with Thompson Coburn LLP, Washington, 2000—04; ptnr., transp. law Venable LLP, Washington, 2004—. Adj. prof., bus. law Am. Univ. Mem. Navy League US; bd. gov. Propeller Club US, 1994—2003; founding chmn. CoastWise Coalition. Mem.: Maritime Adminstrv. Bar Assn. (pres. 1999—2000), Nat. Def. Transp. Assn. (life). Office: Venable LLP 575 Seventh St NW Washington DC 20004 Office Phone: 202-344-4350. Office Fax: 202-344-8300. Business E-Mail: mgroberts@venable.com.

ROBERTS, MICHAEL JOSEPH, journalist; b. Canton, Ohio, Nov. 22, 1954; s. Francis Joseph and Flora Louise (Taylor) R.; m. Lynn Ellen Lantry Streetman, 1973 (div. 1984); children: Amy Kathleen, Jennifer Anne; m. Tracy Leigh Sorensen, June 2005. BS in Speech and Telecomms., Kent State U., 1979. Cert. master wildlife conservationist, Fla. News dir. Sta. WNYN-FM, Canton, 1979-80, Sta. WTAL-FM, Tallahassee, 1980-82, Sta. WMGT-TV, Macon, Ga., 2006—; broadcast journalist Sta. WCTV-TV, Tallahassee, 1982-90, mng. editor, 1990-95; journalist, cons. Spl. Projects Group, Tallahassee, 1995—; asst. news dir. Sta. WTXL/WBXT-TV, Tallahassee, 1999—2006. Spl. projects cons. Freestyle Prodns., Fla., 1989-90; mem. tng. cadre manhunt exercise U.S. Army Spl. Forces/Blue Ridge Tech. Coll., Hendersonville, N.C., 1989-94. Author screenplay: Diamondback, 1989; prodr. TV documentaries: Common Ground: A Citizen Summit, 1989, Vietnam: Beyond the Battles, 1991; editor, pub. newsletter Threat Level; co-creator spl. ops. Basic Sniper course. Bd. dirs. Big Bend chpt. ARC, Tallahassee, 1990; mem. Tallahassee-Krasnodar Sister City Program; master wildlife conservationist U. Fla.-IFAS, Gainesville. Recipient Nat. Broadcast award UPI, 1989, Outstanding Documentary award UPI, 1989, Best Documentary award AP, 1991, Best Overall Coverage award AP, 1991, 93, 94, Best Newscast award AP, 1991, 92, 94, POW/MIA award Vietnam Vets Am., 1993, FBI Dir.'s Exceptional Svc. citation, 2000. Mem.: Radio-TV News Dirs. Assn., Soc. Profl. Journalists. Avocations: collecting firearms, shooting sports, cooking. Office Phone: 478-745-4141. Business E-Mail: mroberts@wmgt.com.

ROBERTS, MICHAEL T., lawyer, educator; Attended, Drake U., Des Moines; BS, U. Utah, 1986, JD, 1989; LLM, U. Ark. Sch. Law, 2001. Bar: Utah. Judicial clk Utah Ct. of Appeals, 1989—90; atty. Van Cott Bagley Cornwall & McCarthy, Ogden, Utah; rsch. assoc. prof. U. Ark. Sch. Law, 2001—06, dir. Nat. Agrl. Law Ctr., 2003—06; of counsel Venable LLP, Washington, 2006—. Past chmn., Agribusiness Practice Group Lex Mundi. Contbr. articles to law jours. Mem.: ABA, Food Safety Consortium, Inst. of Food Technologists, Food and Drug Law Inst., Am. Law Sch. Assn., Am. Agrl. Law Assn. Office: Venable LLP 575 7th St, NW Washington DC 20004 Office Phone: 202-334-4684. Office Fax: 202-344-8300. E-mail: mtroberts@venable.com.

ROBERTS, MICHELE A., lawyer; b. NYC, Sept. 14, 1956; BA, Wesleyan U., 1977; JD, Boalt Hall Sch. Law, U. Calif., Berkeley, 1980. Bar: Wash. DC 1980. Atty. Pub. Defender Svc., Washington, 1986—92; ptnr. Rochon & Roberts, 1992—2001, Shea & Gardner, 2001—04; ptnr., civil/white collar litig. Akin Gump Strauss Hauer & Feld LLP, Washington, 2004—. Former mem. adj. faculty George Wash. U. Sch. Law; former lectr. Pub. Defender Svc. Tng. Program; past instr. Nat. Inst. Trial Advocacy; mem. adj. faculty Harvard Law Sch.; serves on DC Adv. Commn. on Sentencing. Named First Among Washington's Top 75 Lawyers, Washingtonian mag. survey, 2002; named one of 75 Best Lawyers in Washington, 2004, Am. Top Black Lawyers, Black Enterprise Mag., 2003. Fellow: Am. Coll. Trial Lawyers; mem.: Nat. Assn. Criminal Def. Lawyers, Nat. Bar

Assn., ABA, DC Bar. Office: Akin Gump Strauss Hauer & Feld LLP Robert S Strauss Bldg 1333 New Hampshire Ave NW Washington DC 20036-1564 Office Phone: 202-887-4306. Business E-Mail: mroberts@akingump.com.

ROBERTS, MONTY, horse trainer, writer; b. Calif., 1935; m. Pat, 3 children, 47 foster children. D (hon.), Univ. Zurich. Stuntman, Hollywood; owner, operator, thoroughbred breeding, training facility Flag Is Up Farms, Solvang, Calif.; owner, operator Monty Roberts Equestrian Acad., Join Up Internat. Inc., Solvang, Calif. Creator Join Up method for non-violent equine training. Author: The Man Who Listens to Horses, 1997 (NY Times Bestseller list), Shy Boy: The Horse that Came in from the Wild, 1999 (NY Times Bestseller list), Horse Sense for People, 2001, From My Hands to Yours, 2002, The Horses in My Life, 2005; subject, with Shy Boy, the mustang (PBS/BBC documentary) Monty Roberts: The Real Horse Whisperer. Achievements include being invited by Queen Elizabeth II to teach Join Up method to her equestrian team, London. Home and Office: Flag Is Up Farms 901 E Hwy 246 PO Box 1700 Solvang CA 93464 Office Phone: 805-688-6288. Office Fax: 805-688-2242. Business E-Mail: admin@montyroberts.com.

ROBERTS, NANCY, computer scientist, educator; b. Boston, Jan. 25, 1938; d. Harold and Annette (Zion) Rosenthal; m. Edward B. Roberts, June 14, 1959; children: Valerie Friedman, Mitchell, Andrea. AB, Boston U., 1959, MEd, 1961, EdD, 1975. Elem. tchr. Sharon (Mass.) Pub. Schs., 1959-63; asst. prof. Lesley U., Cambridge, Mass., 1975-79, assoc. prof., 1980-83, prof., 1983—, dir. grad. programs in tech. in edn., 1980—99, dir. Project Bridge, 1987-92, dir. divsn. tchg., learning and leadership, 2001—04; dir. Ctr. for Math., Sci. and Tech. in Edn., Cambridge, Mass., 1990-91. Rsch. assoc. MIT, Cambridge, 1976-79;mem. nat. steering com. Nat. Edn. Computing Conf., Eugene, Oreg., 1979-96, co-chmn. nat. conf., 1989, vice chmn. steering com., 1991-95. Author: Dynamics of Human Service Delivery, 1976, Practical Guide to Computers in Education, 1982, Computers in Teaching Mathematics, 1983, Introduction to Computer Simulation, 1983 (J.W. Forrester award 1983), Integrating Computers into the Elementary and Middle School, 1987, Computers and the Social Studies, 1988, Integrating Telecommunications into Education, 1990, Computer Modeling and Simulation in Science and Mathematics Education, 1999; mem. editl. bd. Jour. Ednl. Computing, 1983—, Jour. Rsch. in Sci. Teaching; editor Computers in Edn. book series, 1984-89. Mem. Computer Policy Com., Boston, 1982-84, mem. adv. bd. Electronic Learning, 1989-91; bd. dirs. Computers for Kids, Cambridge, 1983-85; mem. State Ednl. Tech. Adv. Coun., 1990-93; bd. dirs. Boston Ctr. Adult Edn., 2000—, Citizens Charter Schs., 1997-05; pres. bd. Littleton Mus. Fine Arts, 2003—. Grantee, NSF, 1985—96, DOE, 1994—2003. Mem. System Dynamics Soc. (bd. dirs. policy com. 1987-89). Republican. Jewish. Home: 300 Boylston St Apt 1102 Boston MA 02116-3940 Office: Lesley Univ 29 Everett St Cambridge MA 02138-2702 Office Phone: 617-349-8419. Business E-Mail: nroberts@lesley.edu.

ROBERTS, NORA, writer; b. Silver Spring, Md., Oct. 10, 1950; m. Ronald Aufdem-Brinke, 1970 (div. 1983); children: Dan, Jason; m. Bruce Wilder, 1985. Fmr. legal secy. Author: Promise Me Tomorrow, 1984, Hot Ice, 1987, Sacred Sins, 1987, Brazen Virtue, 1988, Sweet Revenge, 1989, Public Secrets, 1990, Genuine Lies, 1991, Carnal Innocence, 1992, Divine Evil, 1992, Honest Illusions, 1992, reprint, 1993, Private Scandals, 1993, Hidden Riches, 1994, Born in Fire, 1994, Born in Ice, 1995, True Betrayals, 1995, reprint, 1996, Born in Shame, 1996, Daring to Dream, 1996, Montana Sky, 1996, reprint, 1997, Holding the Dream, 1997, Finding the Dream, 1997, Sanctuary, 1997, Rising Tides, 1998, Once Upon a Castle, 1998, Homeport, 1998, Sea Swept, 1998, The Reef, 1998, Inner Harbor, 1999, Jewels of the Sun, 1999, River's End, 1999, Heart of the Sea, 2000, Tears of the Moon, 2000, Carolina Moon, 2001, Heaven and Earth, 2001, The Villa, 2002, Three Fates, 2002, Chesapeake Blue, 2002, Key of Knowledge, 2003, Key of Light, 2003, Once Upon a Midnight, 2003, Birthright, 2003, Blue Dahlia, 2004, Once Upon a Moon, 2004, Northern Lights, 2004, A Little Fate, 2004, Key of Valor, 2004, Black Rose, 2005, Blue Smoke, 2005 (Quill award romance The Quills Literacy Found., 2006); (under pseudonym J.D. Robb) Naked in Death, 1995, Glory in Death, 1995, Immortal in Death, 1996, Rapture in Death, 1996, Ceremony in Death, 1997, Vengeance in Death, 1997, Holiday in Death, 1998, Loyalty in Death, 1999, Conspiracy in Death, 1999, Judgment in Death, 2000, Witness in Death, 2000, Betrayal in Death, 2001, Seduction in Death, 2001, Interlude in Death, 2001, Purity in Death, 2002, Reunion in Death, 2002, Imitation in Death, 2003, Portrait in Death, 2003, Visions in Death, 2004, Survivor in Death, 2005, Origin in Death, 2005, Memory in Death, 2006, Dance of the Gods, 2006, High Noon, 2007, Angles Fall, 2007; author numerous category romances for Silhouette. Recipient Lifetime Achievement award Waldenbooks. Mem. Romance Writers Am. (charter, mem. Washington chpt., inductee Hall of Fame, Centennial award, Lifetime Achievement award 1997), Mystery Writers Am., Sisters in Crime, The Crime League of Am., Novelists, Inc. Achievements include having each of her novels since 1999 reach the New York Times Bestseller list; having 124 of her novels (out of over 150) have ranked on the Times bestseller list, including 29 that debuted in the number-one spot; her books have ranked in the number-one position on the NYT bestseller list for a combined 90 weeks. Office: GP Putnams Sons 375 Hudson St New York NY 10014-3658 *

ROBERTS, (GRANVILLE) ORAL, clergyman; b. nr. Ada, Okla., Jan. 24, 1918; s. Ellis Melvin and Claudius Priscilla (Irwin) R.; m. Evelyn Lutman (dec. 2005), Dec. 25, 1938; children: Rebecca Ann (dec.), Ronald David (dec.), Richard Lee, Roberta Jean. Student, Okla. Bapt. U., 1942-44, Phillips U., 1945-47; LLD (hon.), Centenary Coll., 1975; MDiv, Oral Roberts U., 1981; DD, Internat. Ch. Foursquare, 1988. Ordained to ministry Pentecostal Holiness Ch., 1936, United Meth. Ch., 1968. Evangelist, 1936-41; pastor Fuquay Springs, N.C., 1941, Shawnee, Okla., 1942-45, Toccoa, Ga., 1946, Enid, Okla., 1947; began worldwide evangelistic ministry thru crusades, radio, TV, printed page, 1947; founder Oral Roberts Evangelistic Assn., Inc., Tulsa, 1948, Univ. Village Retirement Center, 1970, City of Faith Med./Research Ctr., 1981, Healing Outreach Ctr., 1986; founder, pub. Miracles Now mag., Your Daily Guide; founder, pres. Oral Roberts U., Tulsa, 1963-93, chancellor, 1993—. Founding chmn. Internat. Charismatic Bible Ministries, 1986. Author over 122 books including: If You Need Healing, Do These Things, 1947, God is a Good God, 1960, If I Were You, 1967, Miracle of Seed-Faith, 1970, The Miracle Book, 1972, A Daily Guide to Miracles, 1975, 3 Most Important Steps to Your Better Health and Miracle Living, 1976, How to Get Through Your Struggles, 1977, Don't Give Up, 1980, Your Road to Recovery, 1986, Attack Your Lack, 1985, How to Resist the Devil and His Demons, 1989, Fear Not!, 1989, A Prayer Cover Over Your Life, 1990, Is God Your Source?, 1992, Unleashing the Power of Praying in the Spirit, 1993, (autobiography) Expect a Miracle, My Life and Ministry, 1995, A Thousand Times More!, 1997, Don't Park Here!, 1997, Keys to Success, 1998, Seed-Faith 2000, 1999, Still Doing the Impossible, 2002; also numerous tracts, brochures, Bible commentaries. Recipient Outstanding Am. Indian of Yr. award Am. Indian Expn., 1963; inducted into Okla. Hall of Fame, 1972; named Oklahoman of Yr., Am. Broadcasters Assn., 197, One of 50 Most Influential Oklahomans, Okla. Today mag., 2000. Mem.: Rotary. Methodist. Office: Oral Roberts U 7777 S Lewis Ave Tulsa OK 74171-0001

ROBERTS, PAMELA J., lawyer; b. Oakland, Calif., Aug. 30, 1955; BA in Econs., U. Calif., Berkeley, 1977; attended, Hastings Coll. Law; JD, Southwestern U., 1980. Bar: Calif. 1981, Ga. 1987, S.C. 1990, U.S. Dist. Ct. S.C., U.S. Dist. Ct. (no. and mid. dists.) Ga., U.S. Dist. Ct. (no. dist.) Calif., U.S. Ct. Appeals (4th, 9th and 11th cirs.), U.S. Supreme Ct., cert.: Supreme Ct. S.C. (mediator) 1997. Ptnr. Nelson, Mullins, Riley & Scarborough LLP, Columbia, SC. Instr. Harvard Law Sch., 1999; mediation instr. U.S. Dept. Justice Advocacy Ctr.; presenter in field. Chair bd. trustees EdVenture Children's Mus.; mem. adv. bd. Trinity Housing Corp.; bd. dirs. YWCA of the Midlands; trustee Claflin Coll. Fellow: S.C. Bar Found., Am. Bar Found.; mem.: ABA (ho. del. 1992—95, 1997—, bd. govs. 2002—05, chair Commn. on Women in the Profession, former mem. Commn. on Opportunities for Minorities in the Profession, chairwoman young lawyers divsn., mem. nominating com., mem. spl. com. on governance), Barristers Club San Francisco, Bar Assn. San Francisco, U.S. Fourth Cir. Jud. Conf., Richland County Bar Assn., S.C. Women Lawyers Assn. (bd. dirs. 1993—2002, pres. 1999—2001), S.C. Bar (ho. dels. 1997—, bd. govs. 2000—04), Nat. Bar Assn., Phi Alpha Delta. Office: Nelson Mullins Riley & Scarborough Meridian Suite 1700, 1320 Main St PO Box 11070 Columbia SC 29211 Office Phone: 803-255-9566.

ROBERTS, PATRICIA LEE, education educator; b. Coffeyville, Kans. d. Philip Lee Brighton and Lois Ethel Wortham; m. James E. Roberts, Oct. 5, 1953; children: James Michael, Jill Frances. BA, Calif. State U., Fresno, 1953, MA, 1964; EdD, U. Pacific, Stockton, Calif., 1975. Lifetime tchg. diploma; sch. adminstrn. cert. Prof. edn. Calif. State U., Sacramento, 1969—. Cons. in field. Author (textbooks): Alphabet: A Handbook of ABC Books and Book Extensions for the Elementary Classroom, 2d edit., 1994, Integrating Language Arts and Social Studies for Kindergarten and Primary Children, 1996, Literature-Based History Activities for Children, Grades 4-8, 1997, Taking Humor Seriously in Children's Literature, 1997, Multicultural Friendship Stories and Activities for Children Ages 5-14, 1997, Language Arts and Environmental Awareness, 1998, Literature-Based History Activities for Children, Grades 1-3, 1998, Family Values Through Children's Literature, Grades K-3, 1999, Family Values Through Children's Literature, Grades 4-6, 2005, A Guide for Developing an Interdisciplinary Thematic Unit, 4th edit., 2008, A Resource Guide for Elementary School Teaching. 6th edit., 2006. Named Disting. Alumnae of Yr., U. Pacific, 1975-76. Mem. Internat. Reading Assn., Nat. Coun. Rsch. on English.

ROBERTS, PATRICIA LEE, small business owner, consultant; b. Tuscaloosa, Ala., Feb. 13, 1942; d. Felton H. and Floy Robin Lee; m. Tom David, July 27, 1993; m. Ralph Myron Roberts (div.); children: Sharon DeeAnne Aizer, Frances Lee Revere. BA in Elem. Edn., U. Ala., Tuscaloosa, 1968; BA in Social Work, U. Western Fla., Pensacola, 1975; MA, Troy State, Mobile, Ala., 1977. Loan officer First Am. Bank, Pensacola, 1970—74; social worker CETA, Pensacola, 1974—78; owner constrn. cleaning co., Pensacola, 1978—2005; ct. appt. receiver Ct. Sys., Pensacola, 1985—91; owner, mgr. golf course, Pensacola, 1989—91; tchr. Returning Women U. West Fla., Pensacola, 1989—91; cons., counselor. Adv. bd. Coun. on Aging, Pensacola, Am. Red Cross, Pensacola, United Way, Pensacola. Com. chmn. Am. Red Cross; com. mem. Jaycess, Lions Club. Recipient Outstanding Svcs., Jaycees, Cancer Soc., numerous awards to contrb. to cmty. and social svc. activities. Mem.: Home Bldg. Assn. NW Fla., Pensacola Beach Yacht Club. Achievements include patents pending in field. Avocations: boating, skiing, golf, walking, beach. Office Phone: 850-932-0087.

ROBERTS, PAUL CRAIG, III, economics professor, writer, columnist; b. Atlanta, Apr. 3, 1939; s. Paul Craig and Ellen Lamar (Dryman) R.; m. Becky B. Bickerstaff, 1959 (div. 1968); m. Linda Jane Fisher, July 3, 1969 (div. 1994); children: Becky Ellen, Stephanie Bradford, Pendaran Struan Sherman. BS, Ga. Inst. Tech., 1961; postgrad., U. Calif., Berkeley, 1962—63, Merton Coll., Oxford U., Eng., 1964—65; PhD, U. Va., 1967. Asst. prof. econs. Va. Poly. Inst., 1965-69; assoc. prof. U. N.Mex., 1969-71; rsch. fellow Hoover Instn., Stanford U., 1971-77, sr. rsch. fellow, 1978—2004; mem. U.S. Congl. Staff, 1975-78; asst. sec. of treasury for econ. policy Dept. Treasury, Washington, 1981-82; William E. Simon prof. polit. economy Georgetown U. Ctr. for Strategic and Internat. Studies, Washington, 1982-93; chmn. Inst. for Polit. Economy, 1985—, John M. Olin fellow, 1994—2004; rsch. fellow Ind. Inst., 1990—. Disting. adj. scholar Ctr. Strategic and Internat. Studies, Washington, 1993-96; adj. scholar Cato Inst., 1987-93, disting. fellow, 1993-96; assoc. editor, columnist Wall St. Jour., N.Y.C., 1978-80; columnist Bus. Week, 1983-98, Fin. Post, Can., 1988-89, Liberation, Paris, 1988-89, Erfolg, Fed. Rep. of Germany, 1988, Washington Times, 1988—, San Diego Union, 1988-92, Le Figaro, Paris, 1992-96, Investors Bus. Daily, 1998-2005; nationally syndicated columnist Scripps Howard News Svc., 1989-97, Creators Syndicate, 1997—; contbr. editor: Nat. Rev., 1993-2003, Reason Mag., 1993-95, World Trade mag., 1997-98; mem. Pres.-elect Reagan's Task Force on Tax Policy, 1980; dir. Value Line Investment Funds, N.Y.C., A. Schulman, Akron, Ohio; cons. Morgan Guaranty Trust Co., Lazard Freres Asset Mgmt., 1983-97; pres. Econ. & Communication Svcs. Inc.; cons. Dept. Commerce, 1983, Dept. Def., 1983-84; mem. adv. bd. Marvin and Palmer, 1986-96, Am. studies program Harding U.; mem. ad. com. Ctr. for the Am. Founding; mem. Wright Investors' Svc. Internat. Bd. Econ. and Invesmtent Advisors; bd. dirs. Com. on Present Danger; trustee Intercollegiate Studies Inst., Com. on Developing Am. Capitalism; mem. selection com. Frank E. Seidman disting. award in Polit. Economy; pres. Inlet Beach Water Co., 2000-06. Author: Alienation and the Soviet Economy, 1971, new edit., 1990, Marx's Theory of Exchange, 1973, new edit., 1983, The Supply-Side Revolution: An Insider's Account of Policymaking in Washington, 1984, The Cost of Corporate Capital in the U.S. and Japan, 1985, Meltdown: Inside the Soviet Economy, 1990, The New Color Line: How Quotas and Privilege Destroy Democracy, 1995; The Capitalist Revolution in Latin America, Oxford U. Press, 1997, The Tyranny of Good Intentions, 2000, Chile: Dos Visiones-la Era Allende-Pinochet, 2000; mem. editl. bd. Modern Age, Intercollegiate Rev.; contbg. editor Harper's Mag. Drafted original Kemp-Roth Bill, 1976. Recipient Meritorious Svc. award Dept. Treasury, 1982, Pub. Svc. award GSA, 1991, Warren Brookes award for Excellence in Journalism, 1992; Am. Philos. Soc. grantee, 1968; named to Chevalier de la Légion d'Honneur, 1987, Gridiron Secret Soc., U. Ga.; Earhart fellow U. Va., 1966-67, Nat. Chamber Found. fellow, 1984-85. Mem. Mont Pelerin Soc., Beethoven Soc., Am. Soc. French Legion of Honor, U.S. C. of C. (taxation com.), Polanyi Soc., Sierra Club, Amnesty Internat. Home and Office: 169 Pompano St Panama City FL 32413-7245

ROBERTS, PAUL DALE, state agency administrator, writer; b. Fresno, Calif., Jan. 17, 1955; s. Paul Marceau and Rosemarie Roberts; divorced; 1 child, Jason Randall Porter. AA, Sacramento City Coll., Calif., 1977; diploma in pvt. investigations, Ctrl. Investigation & Security, 1984. Office asst. I, Dept. Benefit Payments, Sacramento, 1976-77; firefighter Calif. Divsn. Forestry, Colfax, 1977; key data operator Dept. Justice, Sacramento, 1977-78; intelligence analyst, spl. forces instr. US Army Mil. Intelligence, Seoul, Republic of Korea, 1979-84; office asst. 1 Calif. State Lottery Commn., 1987-89; law libr. Employment Devel. Dept., Sacramento, 1989-92; office asst. II, Calif. Dept. Health Svcs., Sacramento, 1992-98, chief cert. support, 1992-93; supervising program technician II Dept. Cmty. Svcs. and Devel., State Calif., Sacramento, 1998-2000; divsn. supr. polit. reform Sec. of State, Sacramento, 2000—07; office mgr. Calif. Dept. Fish and Game, Sacramento, 2007—. Office asst I, Calif. Lottery Commn., 1987-89; disaster courier dept. social svcs. Gov.'s Office of Emergency Svcs., LA, 1994. Author: Organization of D.E.A.T.H. (Destroy Evildoers and Teach Harmony), 1984, The Cosmic Bleeder, 1991, Madam Zara, Vampiress, 1993, People's Comic Book Newsletter, 1996, The Legendary Dark Silhouette, 1997, Vacationing in Dublin, Ireland and Newry, Northern Ireland, 1997, (comic book) The Legendary Dark Silhouette, 1997, Jazma Universe Online!, 1998, Jazma League of Justice, 1999, Jazma Man/Jazma Girl, 2000, My Adventures in Brazil, 2001, My Adventures in Thailand/Burma, 2003, My Adventures in Moscow, Russia, 2004, Nicole Mila Phengaroune Growing Up Years, 2005, My 50th Birthday on Catalina Island, 2005, My Crazy Adventure to Spain, Gibralter, Portugal and Tangiers/Morocco- North Africa, 2005, The Amsterdam/Belgium/Berlin Romp!, 2006, Ghost Hunting with Haunted and Paranormal Investigations, 2007. Sgt. U.S. Army Mil. Police, 1973-76. Republican. Roman Catholic. Avocations: flying, tennis, photography, ballooning, skydiving. Home: 5606 Moonlight Way Elk Grove CA 95758-6837 Office: 1500 11th St Rm 495 Sacramento CA 95814 Office Phone: 916-928-5848. Personal E-mail: jazmapika@cs.com.

ROBERTS, PAUL HARRY, mathematics professor; b. Aberystwyth, Wales, Eng., Sept. 13, 1929; s. Percy Harry and Ethel Frances (Mann) R.; m. Maureen Frances Tabrett, Dec. 16, 1989. BA, Cambridge U., Eng., 1951, MA, PhD, 1954, ScD, 1966. Rsch. assoc. U. Chgo., 1954-55, assoc. prof., 1961-63; scientific officer Atomic Weapons Rsch. Establisment, Aldermaston, U.K., 1955-56; rsch. fellow U. Durham, Newcastle, U.K., 1956-59, lectr., 1959-61; prof. math. U. Newcastle upon Tyne, Eng., 1963-86; prof. math. and geophysical scis. U. Calif., LA, 1986—. Author: (book) An Introduction to Magnetohydrodynamics, 1967; co-editor: (book) Rotating Fluids in Geophysics, 1979; editor: Geophysical and Astrophysical Fluid Dynamics, 1976—. Mem. Royal Astronomical Soc., Royal Soc. London, Am. Geophysical Union (John Adam Fleming medal, 1999. Office: UCLA Inst of Geophysics & Planetary Physics Los Angeles CA 90095-1567

ROBERTS, PETER C., real estate company executive; AB in Economics, magna cum laude, Dartmouth Coll.; MBA, Harvard U. Aerospace and def. contractor group Morgan Guaranty Trust Co., NY; joined Jones Lang LaSalle, 1986, v.p. tenant rep. group, 1993, sr. v.p. tenant rep. group, exec. v.p. tenant rep. group, mng. dir. tenant rep. group, 1996, co-pres. tenant rep. group, 1999, CFO, 2001, COO, 2002, CEO America, 2003, bd. dirs., 2001—04, mem. global exec. com. Bd. dirs. Corus Bankshares Inc. Office: Jones Lang SaLalle Inc 200 E Randolph Dr Chicago IL 60601 *

ROBERTS, PHILIP JOHN, history professor, editor; b. Lusk, Wyo., July 8, 1948; s. Leslie J. and LaVerne Elizabeth (Johns) R. BA, U. Wyo., 1973, JD, 1977; PhD, U. Wash., 1990. Bar: Wyo. 1977. Editor Lake Powell Chronicle, Page, Ariz., 1972-73; pvt. practice in law Carbon and Laramie County, Wyo., 1977-84; historian Wyo. State Hist. Dept., Cheyenne, 1979-84; owner, pub. Capitol Times, Cheyenne, 1982-84; co-editor Wyo. History Jour., 1995-96; editor Annals of Wyo., Cheyenne, 1980—84, 1995—2004; owner, pub. Skyline West Press, Seattle, 1985-90; prof. history U. Wyo., Laramie, 1990—; law liaison ABA-Ctrl. European and Eurasian Law Initiative, Baku, Azerbaijan, 2004—05. Indexer Osborne-McGraw-Hill, Berkeley, 1988-95; guest lectr. media law, Dubai, United Arab Emirates, 1996, Cairo, 2001; mem. editl. bd. Annals of Wyo., 1990-95, 2005—. Author: Wyoming Almanac, 1989 (pub. annually), Buffalo Bones: Stories from Wyoming's Past, 1979, 3d edit., 1984, Readings in Wyoming History, 1994, 5th edit., 2007, Penny for the Governor, A Dollar for Uncle Sam: The Politics of Taxation in Washington, 2002; contbr. articles to profl. jours. Mem. Albany County Hist. Preservation Commn., 2000—06; bd. mem. Laramie Plains Mus., 2000—04; apptd. mem. Wyo. Coin Adv. Commn., 2005; cand. for gov. of Wyo., 1998; chmn. Albany County Dem. Party, 1999—2001, 2003—04; pres. Albany County Hist. Soc., 2000—02. With USMC, 1970—72. Mem. Wyo. State Hist. Soc. (life), Wyo. State Bar, Am. Bar Assn., Pacific N.W. Historians' Guild, 9th Judicial Cir. Hist. Soc., Western History Assn., Am. Hist. Assn., Orgn. of Am. Historians, Albany County Hist. Soc. (pres. 2000-02). Office Phone: 307-766-5311. Personal E-mail: philwyo@yahoo.com. Business E-Mail: philr@uwyo.edu.

ROBERTS, R. MICHAEL, animal scientist, biochemist, educator; b. U.K., 1941; BA in Botany, Oxford U., PhD in Plant Physiology and Biochemistry; doctorate (hon.), U. Liege, Belgium, 1998. Prof. animal scis. and biochemistry U. Mo., Columbia, 1985—, curators' prof., 1996—, dir. Life Scis. Ctr., 2004—. Vice-chmn. Gordon Conf. on Mammalian Genital Tract Plymouth State Coll., 1986; chmn. Gordon Conf. on Reproductive Tract Biology Brewster Acad., 1988; fgn. specialist Nat. Inst. Animal Industry, Japan, 1998; chief scientist Nat. Rsch. Initiative Competitive Grants Program/Coop. State Rsch., Edn., Extension Svc./USDA, 1998—2000. Contbr. articles to profl. jours. Named Disting. Scientist, USDA, 1992; recipient Rsch. award, Soc. for Study of Reproduction, 1990, Merit award, NIH, 1990—2000, Milstein award, Internat. Soc. Interferon and Cytokine Rsch., 1995, Alexander von Humboldt award for agr., 1996, Wolf prize in agr., Wolf Found., Israel, 2003. Mem.: NAS. Office: U Mo Columbia Life Scis Ctr Columbia MO 65211

ROBERTS, RALPH JOEL, telecommunications industry and cable broadcast executive; b. NYC, Mar. 13, 1920; s. Robert and Sara (Wahl) Roberts; m. Suzanne Fleisher, Aug. 23, 1942; children: Catherine, Lisa, Ralph Jr., Brian, Douglas. BS in Econs., U. Pa., 1941; LHD (hon.), Holy Family Coll., 1994; HHD (hon.), Arcadia U., 2004; LLD (hon.), U. Pa., 2005. Account exec. Aitken Kynett Advt., Phila., 1946-48; v.p. Muzak Corp., NYC, 1948-50; pres., chief exec. officer Pioneer Industries, Inc., Darby, Pa., 1950-61; pres. Internat. Equity Corp., Bala Cynwyd, Pa., 1961-83; chmn., chief exec. officer Sural Corp. (merger with Internat. Equity Corp. 1983); chmn. Comcast Corp., Phila., 1997—2002, chmn. exec. com., 2002—. Trustee, chmn. conflict interest com. Albert Einstein Med. Ctr.; bd. dirs. Phila. Electric Co., Phila. Nat. Bank, Corestates, Penn Medicine; bd. trustees U. Pa. Health Sys., 2002. Bd. dirs. regional NCCJ; trustee Brandywine Mus. and Conservancy, charter mem. World Bus. Coun.; past mem. mentor program and Benjamin Franklin assocs. U. Pa.; bd. dirs. Phila. Orch., 1993; past v.p. Family Svc. Phila.; past bd. dirs., mem. budget and fees com. State Coll. and Univ. Dirs.; mem. re-regulation and legis. affairs coms. Nat. Cable TV Assn.; past mem. Gov.'s Rev. of Govt. Mgmt., Inc. Lt. USNR, 1942-45. Reipient Americanism award Anti-Defamation League of B'nai B'rith, Brotherhood award NCCJ, 1989, award for outstanding svc. to cable TV industry Walter Kaitz Found., 1990, Acres of Diamonds Entrepreneurioal Excellence award Entrepreneurial Inst. Temple U., 1991, Disting. Vanguard award for leadership Nat. Cable TV Assn., 1993, Golden Plate award Am. Acad. Achievement, 1994, PAL award Police Athletic League Phila., 1995, Edward Powell award for cmty. svc. City of Phila., 1995, Joseph P. Wharton award U. Pa., 1995, Whitney M. Young Jr. Leadership award Urban League Phila., 1997, Disting. Cmty. Leadership award Operation Understanding, 1997, Cable TV Hall of Fame award, 2000, Mensa Achievement award, 2000, Heroes of Liberty award Liberty Mus., 2000, William Penn award Greater Phila. C. of C., 2002, Am. Horizon award for Visionary Leadership, Media Inst., Washington, 2002, Humanitarian award United Jewish Appeal Fedn. of NY, 2003, Trustee award NATAS, 2003, Excellence in Leadership award Temple U., 2005, Partnership for Drug Free Am. hon., 2005; named to Broadcasting and Cable Hall of Fame, 1993. Avocations: tennis, travel. Home: Sural Farm 505 Fairview Rd East Fallowfield Township PA 19320-4451 Office: Comcast Corp 1500 Market St Philadelphia PA 19102-2148 Office Fax: 215-981-7790. Business E-Mail: rroberts@comcast.com.

ROBERTS, RANDY W., history professor; PhD, La. State U., 1978. Prof. hist. and Am. studies Purdue U., West Lafayette, Ind. Contbr. chapters to books, articles to profl. publs.; author: Jack Dempsey: The Manassa Mauler, 1979, Papa Jack: Jack Johnson and the Era of White Hopes, 1983, "But They Can't Beat Us:" Oscar Robertson and the Crispus Attucks Tigers, 1999; co-author (with James S. Olson): Winning is the Only Thing: Sports in America since 1945, 1989, Where the Domino Fell: America in Vietnam, 1990, John Wayne American, 1995, A Line in the Sand: The Alamo in Blood and Memory, 2000, American Experiences: Readings in American History, 2005; co-author: (with J. Gregory Harrison) Heavy

Justice: The State of Indiana v. Michael G. Tyson, 1994; co-author: (with David Welky) The Steelers Reader, 2001, One for the Thumb: The New Steelers Reader, 2006; co-author: America and Its People: A Mosaic in the Making, 2003; co-author: (with Elliott J. Gorn and Terry D. Bilhartz) Constructing the American Past: A Source Book of a People's History, 2005; co-editor (with James S. Olson): My Lai: A Brief History with Documents, 1998; co-editor: (with David Welky) Charles Lindbergh: The Power and Peril of Celebrity, 1927-1941, 2003; editor: Pittsburgh Sports: Stories from the Steel City, 2000, The Rock, the Curse and the Hub: A Random History of Boston Sports, 2005. Recipient US Prof. of Yr. award, Carnegie Found. for Advancement of Tchg. and Coun. for Advancement and Support of Edn., 2006. Office: Dept Hist Purdue U University Hall 672 Oval Dr West Lafayette IN 47907-2087 Office Phone: 765-494-0040. Office Fax: 765-496-1755. E-mail: rroberts@purdue.edu. *

ROBERTS, RICHARD CHARLTON, III, lawyer; b. Jackson, Miss., Mar. 18, 1951; BA, U. Miss., 1973, JD with distinction, 1976. Bar: Miss. 1976, U.S. Dist. Ct. (no. and so. dists.) Miss. 1976, U.S. Ct. Appeals (5th cir.) 1976, U.S. Ct. Appeals (11th cir.) 1981, U.S. Supreme Ct. 1989. Pvt. practice, Jackson, Miss. Assoc. editor Miss. Law Jour., 1976. Named Middle South Super Lawyers, 2006; named one of Best Lawyers in Am., Outstanding Lawyers Am. Fellow: Nat. Conf. Bar Pres., Miss. Bar Found.; mem.: ABA (sect. on family law, gen. practice, solo and small firm practice), Nat. Lawyer's Assn., Bar Assn. 5th Fed. Cir., Miss. Bar (chmn. solo and small firm practitioner's task force 1993—94, exec. com. family law sect. 1994—95, chmn. 1996, bd. bar commrs. 1996—99, nominating com. 1998—99, bench-bar liaison standing com. 2001—, bd. bar commrs. 2002—05, pres. 2003—04), Hinds County Bar Assn. (bd. dirs. 1990—96, sec.-treas. 1992—93, pres. 1994—95, chmn. long range planning com. 1995—97), Fed. Bar Assn. (pres. Miss. chpt. 1987—88, nat. coun. 1988, jud. liaison for U.S. Dist. Cts.-So. Dist. Miss. 1989), Am. Inss of Ct., Phi Kappa Phi. Office: PO Box 55882 Jackson MS 39296-5882 Office Phone: 601-607-4140.

ROBERTS, RICHARD JOHN, molecular biologist, consultant, research director; b. Derby, Eng., Sept. 6, 1943; came to U.S., 1969; s. John Walter and Edna Wilhelmina (Allsop) R.; m. Elizabeth Dyson, Aug. 21, 1965 (dec.); children: Alison, Andrew; m. Jean E. Tagliabue, Feb. 14, 1986; children: Christopher, Amanda. BS, Sheffield (Eng.) U., 1965, PhD, 1968. Rsch. fellow Harvard U., Cambridge, Mass., 1969-70, rsch. assoc., 1971-72; sr. staff investigator Cold Spring Harbor Lab., N.Y., 1972-87, asst. dir., 1987-92; cons. New Eng. Biolabs, Ipswich, Mass., 1974-92, rsch. dir., 1992—; sci. adv. bd. Genex, Rockville, Md., 1977-85; chief sci. officer Molecular Tool, Balt., 1994—. Contbr. articles to profl. jours. Recipient Nobel prize in physiology or medicine, Nobel Found., 1993. John Simon Guggenheim Found. fellow, 1979. Fellow Royal Soc.; mem. Am. Soc. Microbiology. Office: New Eng Biolabs 240 County Rd Ipswich MA 01938-2723 Office Phone: 978-380-7405. E-mail: roberts@neb.com.

ROBERTS, RICKY ELIAS, linguist, educator; b. Oct. 20, 1961; PhD in Old Testament and New Testament, Christian Bible Coll., 1991; ThD in Greek, Hebrew, Latin and Aramaic. Founder, pres. True Light Ministries, Inc., Jacksonville, Fla., 1997—. Home: 10507 Villanova Rd Jacksonville FL 32218-5124

ROBERTS, ROBERT WINSTON, social worker, educator, dean; b. Balt., July 23, 1932; s. Kelmer Swan Roberts and Lettie Mae (Collins) Johnston; m. Helen Elizabeth Perpich, Mar. 4, 1964 (div. Aug. 1997); life ptnr. Paul Edwards. BA with high honors, San Francisco State U., 1957; MSW, U. Calif., Berkeley, 1959; D in Social Welfare, Columbia U., 1970. Caseworker Edgewood Protestant Orphanage, San Francisco, 1959-62, Jewish Family Service, San Francisco, 1962-63; research assoc. U. Calif., Berkeley, 1963-65; research analyst Family Service Assn. Am., NYC, 1965-69; asst. prof. U. Chgo., 1967-70; prof. U. So. Calif., Los Angeles, 1970-90, dean sch. social work, 1980-88, dean emeritus, prof. emeritus, 1990—. Vis. prof. Western Australia Inst. Tech. (now Curtin U.), Perth, 1976-77, Chinese U. Hong Kong and U. Hong Kong, 1980; cons. Crittenton Services, Los Angeles, 1970-72, James Weldon Johnson Community Ctr., N.Y., 1966-67; bd. dirs. El Centro, Los Angeles. Editor: The Unwed Mother, 1966; co-editor: Theories of Social Casework, 1970, Child Caring: Social Policy and the Institution, 1973, Theories of Social Work with Groups, 1976, Theory and Practice of Community Social Work, 1980; editorial bd. Social Work Jour.; contbr. articles to profl. jours. Staff sgt. USAF, 1950-54; sgt. 1st class USAR, 1956-59. Fellow NIMH, 1957-58, 65-67, Crown Zellerbach Found., 1958-59; recipient Outstanding Educator award Los Amigos de la Humanidad, 1979; named Disting. Assoc., Nat. Acad. Practice in Social Work, 1985; decorated Commendation ribbon USAF, Korean Svc. ribbon USAF, Svc. medal UN, Good Conduct medal USAF, Nat. Def. Svc. medal, Ribbon medal, USAF. Mem. ACLU, NASW (chmn. social action com. 1960-61), Coun. on Social Work Edn. (bd. dirs. 1970-73, del. to assembly 1971-72, commn. minority groups 1972-73). Avocations: cooking, reading, travel, photography. Office: U So Calif Montgomery Ross Fisher Rm 21 Los Angeles CA 90089-0001 Personal E-mail: winstonr@cox.net.

ROBERTS, ROBIN, newscaster; b. Nov. 23, 1960; d. Lawrence Roberts and Lucy Marion. BA in Comms. cum laude, Southeastern La. U., 1983. Sports dir. WHMD/WFPR Radio, Hammond, La., 1980-83; spl. assignment sports reporter KSLU-FM, 1982; sports anchor, reporter WDAM-TV, Hattiesburg, Miss., 1983-84, WLOX-TV, Biloxi, Miss., 1984-86, WSMV-TV, Nashville, 1986-88, WAGA-TV, Atlanta, 1988-89; with WVEE-FM, Atlanta; host. Sunday SportsDay, contbr. NFL Prime Time, reporter, interviewer ESPN, Bristol, Conn., 1990-95, host, anchor SportsCenter, host In the SportsLight, 1995—2005; host Wide World of Sports ABC, 1995—2001; co-anchor Good Morning Am., 2005—. Mem., adv. bd. Fedn. Internat. Football Assn., 1999. Author: From the Heart: Seven Rules to Live By, 2007. Apptd. adv. bd. Women's Sports Found., 1991; spkr. charity, civic functions. Recipient DAR T.V. Award of Merit, 1990, Women at Work Broadcast Journalism award, 1992, Excellence in Sports Journalism award Broadcast Media Northeastern U. Ctr. Study of Sport in Society and Sch. Journalism, 1993, Disting. Achievement award, DiGamma Kappa, U. Ga., 1996, Media award, New England Women's Fund, 1998, Pres. award, Women's Sports Found., 2001; named Journalist of Yr., Ebony mag., 2002 named to Inst. Sport and Edn. Found., Hall of Fame, 1994; named one of Five Most Intriguing People in Coll. Basketball, Basketball Times, 1997 Office: Good Morning America 147 Columbus Ave New York NY 10023 *

ROBERTS, RODNEY R., systems analyst, educator; b. Dover, NJ, May 25, 1956; s. Raymond Gilbert and Luella Gertrude Roberts. BS, Embry-Riddle Aeronautical U., Daytona Beach, Fla, 1982; MS, Stevens Inst. Tech., Hoboken, NJ, 2004. Programmer, analyst Omega Sys., Parsippany, NJ, 1984—88; sr. sys. analyst St.-Gobain Performance Plastics, Wayne, 1989—2001; guest tchr. Carbon Lehigh Intermediate Sch., Schnecksville, Pa., 2006—; adj. faculty Lehigh Carbon CC, Schnecksville, 2006—. Contbr. articles to profl. jours. Mem.: IEEE. Avocations: auto mechanics, electronics, social science. Office Phone: 610-799-1050 3373.

ROBERTS, SAMUEL SMITH, television news executive; b. Port Chester, NY, Feb. 8, 1936; s. Robert M. and Lillian (Smith) R.; m. Harriet Rubin, July 27, 1975; children: Rachel, David; children by previous marriage: Nancy, Pamela. BS, Northwestern U., 1957. With UPI, NYC, 1961, Capital Cities Broadcasting, Providence, 1962, CBS News, 1962-95; sr. prodr. CBS Evening News, NYC, 1978-81, nat. editor, 1982-84, fgn. editor, 1984-87; exec. prodr. CBS News Prodns., 1992-95, 20th Century, 1994-95; pres. Roberts Media Internat., NYC, 1995-96; v.p., gen. mgr. TV programming Electronic Media Co., N.Y. Times, 1996-99; Frances L. Wolfson chair U. Miami, Coral Gables, Fla., 1999—. Served to lt. USN, 1957-61. Office: U Miami Sch Comm PO Box 248127 Coral Gables FL 33124-8127

ROBERTS, SIDNEY, biological chemist; b. Boston, Mar. 11, 1918; s. Samuel Richard and Elizabeth (Gilbert) R.; m. Clara Marian Szego, Sept. 14, 1943. BS, MIT, 1939; postgrad., Harvard U., 1939-41; MS, U. Minn., 1942, PhD, 1943. Instr. physiology U. Minn. Med. Sch., 1943-44, George Washington U. Med. Sch., 1944-45; rsch. assoc. Worcester Found. Exptl. Biology, Shrewsbury, Mass., 1945-47; asst. prof. physiol. chemistry Yale U. Med. Sch., 1947-48; mem. faculty U. Calif. Med. Sch., Los Angeles, 1948—, prof. biol. chemistry, 1957—; chmn. acad. senate UCLA, 1989-90; mem. adv. panel regulatory biology NSF, 1955-57, adv. panel metabolic biology, 1957-59; mem. metabolism study sect. NIH, 1960-63; basic sci. study sect. Los Angeles County Heart Assn., 1958-63. Cons. VA Hosp., Long Beach, Calif., 1951-55, Los Angeles, 1958-62, Pew Fin. Biomed. Scholar Program, 1992-; air conservation tech. adv. com. Los Angeles County Lung Assn., 1972-76 Author articles, revs.; editor med. jours. Served to 2d lt. AUS, 1944-48. MIT Nat. Entrance scholar, 1935; Guggenheim fellow, 1957-58. Fellow AAAS; mem. Am. Physiol. Soc., Endocrine Soc. (v.p. 1968-69, Ciba award 1953), Brit. Biochem. Soc., Soc. Neurosci., Am. Chem. Soc. (exec. com. div. biol. chemistry 1956-59), Am. Soc. Biol. Chemists, Am. Soc. Neurochemistry, Internat. Soc. Neurochemistry, Phi Beta Kappa, Sigma Xi (pres. UCLA chpt. 1959-60). Home: 1371 Marinette Rd Pacific Palisades CA 90272-2627 Office: UCLA Sch Med Dept Biol Chemistry Los Angeles CA 90095-1737 Office Phone: 310-825-6997. Business E-Mail: sr@ucla.edu.

ROBERTS, STANLEY DWAYNE, physician, educator, academic administrator; b. Edmonton, Alta., Can., Sept. 17, 1959; came to U.S., 1994; s. Stan and Margaret Rosslyn (Rye) R.; m. Debra Elizabeth Bell, Aug. 20, 1981; children: Matthew, Brent, Michelle, Jared, Bradley. BSc with honors, U. Alta., Edmonton, 1980, BSc in Psychology with distinction, 1981, MD, 1985; grad., IHC Inst., 1999. Diplomate in family practice and sports medicine Am. Bd. Family Practice; cert. Family Medicine and Emergency Medicine, Coll. Family Physicians of Can. Resident in family medicine U. Alta., 1985-87; resident in physical rehab. and sports medicine McMaster U., Hamilton, Ont., Can., 1987-88, resident in emergency medicine, 1988-89, asst. prof. family and emergency medicine, 1989-94; med. dir., internat. med. cons. Med. Emergency, Inc., Toronto, Ont., Can., 1990-94; chief emergency svcs. Queensway Gen. Hosp., Toronto, Ont., Can., 1992-94; employee health physician, family physician Norman (Okla.) Regional Hosp., 1994-95; family physician Bigstone Cree Indian Reserve, Alberta, 1995—96; pvt. practice Provo, Utah, 1996-97; faculty physician Utah Valley Family Practice Residency, Provo, 1997—2003; emergency physician Utah Valley Regional Med. Ctr., Provo, 1997—; assoc. team physician Brigham Young U., 1999—2002. Med. dir. Redcliff Ascent Wilderness Behavioral Reclamation Program Youth, 2000—; moderator, planner Telemedicine Can./USA Broadcasts, 1990—98; team doctor World Cup Speed Skating, 1999; dir. Utah Valley Sports Medicine Fellowship, 1999—2003; site physician 2002 Winter Olympics and Paralympics/Ice Hockey, Sledge Hockey; developer internat. tng. program for physicians, Nepal, 2000, Western Samoa, 01, Fiji, 01; cons. Global Emergency Medicine Support; cons. devel. plan emergency svcs., Malaysia, 1990—92, Thailand, 1990—92; mem. spkrs. burs. Abbott Labs., Glaxo-Smith-Kline, Burroughs-Wellcome, Pfizer, 1999—; lectr. in field. Contbr. articles to profl. jours.; guest radio talk shows; developer internat. tng. program in emergency medicine: Art in EM = Advanced Resuscitation Training in Emergency Medicine. Chmn. coms. life support Heart and Stroke Found. (Can.) Ont., 1991-93; scoutmaster Boy Scouts Am., Kaysville, Utah, 1995, Orem, Utah, 1998-99. Recipient Achievement award for internat. distinction in music Govt. Alberta, 1976, Disting. Lectr. award Thailand and Asia Coll. Surgeons, 1993. Mem. AMA, Am. Acad. Family Physicians, Utah Med. Assn., Coll. Family Physicians (Can.), Am. Coll. Sports Medicine, Spkrs. Bureau. Mem. Lds Ch. Avocations: mountain biking, photography. Home Phone: 801-423-7958. Personal E-mail: sdwayne.roberts@intermountain.org.

ROBERTS, STEPHEN M., library director; With U. Buffalo, 1972—, assoc. dir. univ. librs., asst. v.p. univ. librs., acting assoc. v.p. univ. librs., 2005—. Founder Buffalo FreeNet, 1993. Office: U Buffalo Librs Directors Office 433 Capen Hall North Campus Buffalo NY 14260-1625 Office Phone: 716-645-2966. Office Fax: 716-645-3844. E-mail: sroberts@buffalo.edu. *

ROBERTS, SUSAN STURGEON, art educator, writer; b. Aurora, Colo., Aug. 15, 1953; d. Thomas James Sturgeon, Lela Selby Nagle; m. Eugene Arden Roberts. BS, Calif. State Poly. U., 1978. Tchr. Redlands Unified Sch. Dist., Calif., 1978—80; needle arts tchr. Grants Pass, Oreg., 1974—. Double knits designer Western Textile MIll., Ontario, Calif., 1978. Author: (book) The Complete Needlepoint Guide 400+ Needlepoint Stitches, 2000; sculpture, Stitchin Suzi and Three Ply, 1998. Mem.: Embroiderer's Guild Am. Inc. (asst. editor 1973—76, program dir. 2001—03, master craftsman, canvas embroidery), Am. Needlepoint Guild Inc. Home Phone: 541-471-0917; Office Phone: 541-471-0917. Fax: 541-471-0917. Business E-Mail: susanroberts15@hotmail.com.

ROBERTS, SUZANNE CATHERINE, artist; b. San Antonio, Oct. 27, 1953; d. Thomas Simons and Marceline Margaret (Conrady) Garrett; m. Ted Blake Roberts, May 22, 1976; 1 child, Elizabeth. BS Radio-TV-Film, U. Tex., 1975, B Journalism, 1977; MA Interdisciplinary Studies, Corpus Christi State U., Tex., 1982; MS Gen. Counseling, Corpus Christi State U., 1989; MA Polit. Sci., S.W. Tex. State U., 1995. News announcer Sta. KIXL Radio, Austin, Tex., 1976, Sta. KSIX Radio, Corpus Christi, 1977—78; news anchor Sta. KZTV-TV, Corpus Christi, 1979, news reporter, 1977—80; news announcer, reporter Sta. KRYS-AM-FM, Corpus Christi, 1983—87; freelance reporter UPI, Austin, 1989—94, Tex. State Network, Austin, 1995—97, Des Moines, 1997—2000; artist, 1998—.

ROBERTS, THOMAS ALBA, lawyer; b. Ft. Wayne, Ind., Sept. 7, 1946; s. Jack and Elizabeth (Wallace) R.; m. Mary Alice Buckley, Aug. 11, 1973; children: Kaitrin M., John A., Kara B. BA, Georgetown U., 1969, JD, 1972. Bar: NY 1973, US Dist. Ct. (So. Dist.) NY 1973, US Ct. Appeals (2nd cir.) 1973, Tex. 1976, US Supreme Ct. 1977, US Dist. Ct. (So. Dist.) Tex. 1978, US Ct. Appeals (5th and 11th cirs.) 1982. Assoc. Winthrop, Stimson, Putnam & Roberts, NYC, 1972-76; ptnr. Moore & Peterson, Dallas, 1976-89, mng. ptnr., 1980-88; ptnr. Johnson & Gibbs, Dallas, 1989-92; sr. ptnr., head corp. dept. Weil, Gotshal & Manges, LLP, NYC, 1992—. Chmn. Internat. Corp. Practice Group, 1997—2001, chmn. corp. dept., 2001—, mem. mgmt. com., 1997—; adj. prof. law So. Meth. U., Dallas, 1977—78; lectr. in field. Mem. Georgetown Law Jour. 1971-72; contbr. to publs. Mem. lawyers com. N.Y. Pub. Libr., 2006—; mem. fin. com. St. Rita Ch., Dallas, 1983—88; mem. Ch. of the Resurrection; mem. fin. com. Our Lady of the Lake, Rockwall, Tex., 1995—98; mem. exec. com., bd. dir. Make-A-Wish Found. Met. N.Y., 1998—; mem. exec. com., bd. dir., chmn. fin. com. Make-A-Wish of Am., 2002—, chmn. elect bd. dirs., 2006—; bd. dir. Memorial Sloan Kettering Cancer Ctr. Prostrate Cancer Rsch. Fund; mem. bd. visitors Georgetown Law Ctr., 2004—. Recipient Dealmakers for the Yr., Am. Lawyer, 2001. Mem. ABA, State Bar Tex., Dallas Bar Assn., Assn. of Bar of City of NY Roman Catholic. Avocations: skiing, golf, literature. Home: 133 Grandview Ave Rye NY 10580-2030 Office: Weil Gotshal & Manges LLP 767 Fifth Ave New York NY 10153 Office Phone: 212-310-8479. Office Fax: 212-310-6717. E-mail: thomas.roberts@weil.com.

ROBERTS, THOMAS ANDREW, II, development executive; b. Jersey City, Sept. 5, 1949; s. Thomas Andrew and Muriel Cecelia (Burt) R.; m. Myrtle Beatrice Mumford, Sept. 15, 1971 (div. May 1991); children: Chantey P., Thomas Andrew III; m. Yvonne Coleta Belefanti, Apr. 3, 1994; children: Andrew Belefanti, Oliver Basilio, Murleve Coleta. BA, Rutgers U., 1973; JD, Seton Hall U., 1977. Bar: N.J. 1984. Cmty. specialist City of Newark, 1970-73; area coord. project Jersey City Redevel. Agy., 1973-75; dir. housing Urban League Essex County, Newark, 1976; dist. supr. Nat. Neighborhood Reinvestment Corp., Washington, 1977-85; lawyer East Orange, NJ, 1985-88; exec. dir. Camden (N.J.) Redevel. Agy., 1988-2000, NOAH Devel. Corp., Belle Glade, Fla., 2000—. Bd. dirs. A Better Camden Corp. Pres. Camden Coun. on Alcohol Abuse, 1990-2000; trustee, vice chmn. CamCare Health Corp., Camden, 1990-2000; trustee South Jersey Mus. Art, Lawnside, 1996-99, Camden Empowerment Zone Corp., 1996-2000; advisor Explorer Post 2044, Camden, 1995-97; fellow Leadership N.J., 1999. Mem. Fencing Acad. South Jersey (instr. 1997-2000). Presbyterian. Avocation: fencing. Home: 168 Park Rd N Royal Palm Beach FL 33411 Office: 601 Covenant Dr Belle Glade FL 33430-5728 E-mail: Troberts@noahark.org.

ROBERTS, THOMAS GEORGE, retired physicist; b. Ft. Smith, Ark., Apr. 27, 1929; s. Thomas Lawrence and Emma Lee (Stanley) R.; m. Alice Anne Harbin, Nov. 14, 1958 (dec. 1994); children: Lawrence Dewey, Regina Anne; foster child, Marcia Roberts Dale; m. Betty Howard McElyea, July 28, 1995. AA, Armstrong Coll., 1953; BS, U. Ga., 1956, MS, 1957; PhD, N.C. State U., 1967. Rsch. physicist U.S. Army Missile Command, Huntsville, Ala., 1958-85; cons. industry and govt. agys., 1970—, SAIC, Huntsville, Ala., 1997-2001; owner Technoco, Huntsville, 1985-96. Contbr. articles to profl. jours.; patentee in field. Sgt. USAF, 1948-52. Fellow Am. Optical Soc.; mem. Am. Phys. Soc., IEEE, Huntsville Optical Soc. Am. (pres. 1980, 92), Toastmaster Internat. (pres. 1963). Episcopalian. Achievements include research in laser physics, optics, particle beams and instrumentation; diagnostic devices and techniques development. Personal E-mail: robertsbetty@bellsouth.net.

ROBERTS, VIRGIL PATRICK, lawyer, judge; b. Ventura, Calif., Jan. 4, 1947; s. Julius and Emma D. (Haley) R.; m. Brenda Cecilia Banks, Nov. 10, 1979; children: Gisele Simone, Hayley Tasha. AA, Ventura Coll., 1966; BA, UCLA, 1968; JD, Harvard U., 1972. Bar: Calif. 1972. Assoc. Pacht, Ross, Warne Bernhardt & Sears, LA, 1972-76; ptnr. Manning, Reynolds & Roberts, LA, 1976-79, Manning & Roberts, 1980-81; mng. ptnr. Bobbitt & Roberts, 1995—; exec. v.p., gen. counsel Solar Records, LA, 1981—; pres. Dick Griffey Prodns., LA, 1982—, Solar Records, 1988—; judge pro tem L.A., Beverly Hills Mcpl. Cts., 1975—. Bd. mem. The Bridgespan Consulting Group, 2004—, Broadway Fed. Bank, 2003—. Past bd. dirs. LA Black Leadership Coalition, LA Mus. African Am. Art, Beverly Hills Bar Assn., LA Legal Aid Found.; bd. dirs. Coro Found., 1984-90, LA Ednl. Alliance Restructuring Now, Cmty. Build; bd. dirs. Calif. Cmty. Found., 1991-99, chmn. bd., 1999-02; past pres. Beverly Hills Bar Scholarship Found.; commr. Calif. Commn. Tchr. Credentialing, 1980-83; chmn. LA Ednl. Partnership, 1989—, v.p. 1983-89; vice-chmn. Nat. Pub. Edn. Fund Network; chmn. bd. dirs. LA Annenberg Met. Project; trustee Com. Econ. Devel., 1991—, Occidental Coll., Marlborough Sch. (trustee 1994-03); mem. bd. councillors UCLA; trustee Claremont Grad. Sch., 2006-. Recipient NAACP Legal Def. Fund Equal Justice award, 1988, Rose award U. So. Calif., 1998. Mem. Recording Industry Assn. Am., Black Entertainment and Sports Lawyers (treas., bd. dirs. 1982—). Lead atty. for NAACP in Crawford vs. Bd. Edn. desegregation case, L.A., 1979-80. Address: 4820 Vista De Oro Ave Los Angeles CA 90043-1611 Office: Bobbitt & Roberts 6100 Center Dr Ste 910 Los Angeles CA 90404 Office Phone: 310-645-4100. Business E-Mail: vroberts@bobroblaw.com.

ROBERTS, WALTER RONALD, retired diplomat; b. Waltendorf, Austria, Aug. 26, 1916; arrived in U.S., 1939, naturalized, 1944; s. Ignatius and Elizabeth (Diamant) R.; m. Gisela K. Schmarak, Aug. 22, 1939; children: William M., Charles E., Lawrence H. MLitt, Cambridge U., Eng., 1940, PhD, 1980. Rsch. asst. Harvard U. Law Sch., 1940-42; writer, editor Voice of Am., 1942-49; press officer U.S. del. to Austrian Treaty talks, 1949, 55; fgn. affairs officer Dept. State, 1950-53; dep. asst. dir. USIA, 1954-60; counselor of embassy for pub. affairs Am. Embassy, Belgrade, Yugoslavia, 1960-66; diplomat-in-residence Brown U., Providence, 1966-67; counselor U.S. Mission to Internat. Orgns., Geneva, 1967-69; dep. assoc. dir. USIA, Washington, 1969-71, assoc. dir., 1971-74; dir. diplomatic studies Ctr. Strategic and Internat. Studies Georgetown U., Washington, 1974-75; exec. dir. Bd. Internat. Broadcasting, Washington, 1975-85; diplomat-in-residence George Washington U., Washington, 1986-96. Author: Tito, Mihailovic and the Allies, 1941-45, 73, paperback, 1987, (with Terry L. Deibel) Culture and Information: Two Foreign Policy Functions, 1976; contbr. articles to profl. pubs. Apptd. mem. U.S. Adv. Commn. on Pub. Diplomacy, 1991-97, sr. advisor, 1998-2003; bd. dirs. Salzburg Seminar, 1993-97, Coun. Sr. Fellows, 1998—, Oxford and Cambridge com., 1975-, Pub. Diplomacy Coun., 1996—, mem. emeritus bd. dirs. 2005—; bd. dirs. Pub. Diplomacy Inst., George Washington U., 2001-2004, sr. advisor 2006—. Recipient Disting. Honor award USIA, 1974. Mem. Washington Inst. Fgn. Affairs, Coun. Fgn. Rels., Oxford-Cambridge Com., USIA Alumni Assn. (bd. dirs. 1995-98), Met. Club. Home: 4449 Sedgwick St NW Washington DC 20016-2713

ROBERTS, WILLIAM B., lawyer; b. Detroit, Aug. 23, 1939; s. Edwin Stuart and Marjorie Jean (Wardle) R.; m. Cathleen Anne Thompson, Sept. 1, 1962; children: Bradford William, Brent William, Katrina Marjorie. BA, Mich. State U., East Lansing, 1961; JD with distinction, U. Mich., Ann Arbor, 1963; China law diploma, U. East Asia, Macau, 1989. Bar: Mo. 1964, Fla. 1983, US Dist. Ct. (ea. dist.) Mo. 1964, US Dist. Ct. (mid. dist.) Fla. 1993. Mem. firm Thompson & Mitchell, St. Louis, 1963-67; atty. Monsanto Co., 1967-70; sr. exec. v.p. adminstrn., sec., gen. counsel Chromalloy Am. Corp. (successor Segua Corp. N.Y.), St. Louis, 1970-78, exec. v.p.-adminstrn., gen. counsel, sec. Clayton, Mo., 1978-82; pvt. practice, 1983-87, St. Louis and Naples, 1989-90, Naples, 1994—, Kansas City, Mo., 1999—; mng. ptnr., corp. bus. counselor and broker Fairborne Group, Ltd., 1986—89; mng. ptnr. Roberts and Nordahl, St. Louis and Naples, Fla., 1988-89, Darrow & Roberts, P.A., Naples, 1992-93. Pres., mng. dir. The Fairborne Group, Ltd., St. Louis and Naples, 1988-91, William B. Roberts & Assocs. Co., Merger and Acquisitions Specialists, 1982—; mem. exam. com. of policyowners Northwestern Mut. Life Ins. Co., Milw., 1978; del. to U.S.-China Joint Session on Trade Investment and Econ. Law, Beijing, 1987; sports rep. Steve Carlton, St. Louis Cardinals, Phila. Phillies baseball clubs, 1987-89; pres., CEO Tropical Tracks, Inc., Naples, 1994—, BBB Arbitration, 2004—; owner Security K.C. Royals, 2000-01; internat. bus. and legal adviser, 1982—. Mem. ABA, Fed. Bar Assn. (Mid. Dist. Fla.), Mo. Bar Assn., St. Louis Bar Assn. (chmn. antitrust sect. 1973, spl. assignments law & counsel corp. and internat.), Fla. Bar Assn., Collier County Bar Assn., Delta Theta Phi. Methodist. Home: 133 Crestview Terr Lake Placid FL 33852 Personal E-mail: billkcmo@swbell.net.

ROBERTS, WILLIAM CLIFFORD, medical association administrator; b. Atlanta, Sept. 11, 1932; s. Stewart Ralph and Ruby (Holbrook) R.; m. Frances Carey Cansler, Aug. 20, 1955 (div. Apr. 1993); children: William Clifford, Charles Stewart, Frances Carey, John David. AB, So. Meth. U., Dallas, 1954; MD, Emory U., Atlanta, 1958. Chief pathology br. Nat. Heart, Lung & Blood Inst., NIH, Bethesda, Md., 1959-93; dir. Baylor Heart and Vascular Inst., Baylor U. Med. Ctr., Dallas, 1993—. Editor-in-chief: The Am. Jour. Cardiology, 1982—, Baylor U. Med. Ctr. Procs., 1994—; contbr. articles to profl. jours. With USPHS, 1959-93. Fellow Am. Coll. Cardiology (trustee, Gifted Tchr. award 1978, Coll. Medalist award 1983),

Am. Heart Assn. (Richard and Linda Rosenthal Found. award Coun. Cardiology 1984); mem. Assn. Univ. Cardiologists (elected mem.), Halsted Soc. (elected mem.). Avocations: reading, travel. Home: 3415 Harvard Ave Dallas TX 75205-3242 Office: Baylor Univ Med Ctr 3500 Gaston Ave Dallas TX 75246-2096 Office Phone: 214-820-7911. Business E-Mail: wc.roberts@baylorhealth.edu.

ROBERTS, WILLIAM EVERETT, lawyer; b. Pierre, SD, May 12, 1926; s. Everett David and Bonnie (Martin) R.; m. Cynthia Cline, July 18, 1953; children: Catherine C. Roberts-Martin, Laura M., Nancy F., David H. BS, U. Minn., 1947; LLB, Yale U., 1950. Bar: Ind. 1950, U.S. Supreme Ct. 1964. Employee, ptnr. Duck and Neighbours, Indpls., 1950-58; ptnr. Cadick, Burns, Duck & Neighbours, Indpls., 1958-60, Roberts, Ryder, Rogers & Scism, Indpls., 1960-85, Barnes & Thornburg, Indpls., 1986-93, of counsel, 1994—. Pres., bd. dirs. Park-Tudor Sch., Indpls., 1982-83; elder Second Presbyn. Ch., Indpls., 1962—; trustee Indpls. Mus. Art, 1978—; pres. New Hope of Ind., Indpls., 1986-87. Fellow Am. Bar Found.; mem. ABA, Ind. Bar Assn., Indpls. Bar Assn., Rotary Club, Meridian Hills Country Club (pres. 1983-84). Republican. Home: 10466 Spring Highland Dr Indianapolis IN 46290-1101 Office: Barnes & Thornburg 11 S Meridian St Ste 1313 Indianapolis IN 46204-3535 Office Phone: 317-231-7520.

ROBERTS, WILLIAM H., lawyer; b. Buffalo, June 14, 1945; s. Esther C. Roberts and William H. Roberts, Jr. JD, U. Pa., Phila., 1970; AB, Harvard Coll., Cambridge, MA, 1967. Bar: Pa. 1970, U.S. Ct. Appeals (3d cir.) 1972, U.S. Supreme Ct. 1974, U.S. Ct. Appeals (11th cir.) 1982, U.S. Claims Ct. 1986, U.S. Ct. Appeals (4th cir.) 1987, U.S. Ct. Appeals (9th cir.) 2000. Ptnr. Blank Rome LLP, Phila., 1977—. Co-author: (book) Com. Free Speech, 1985. Trustee The Curtis Inst. of Music, Phila., 1997—; trustee, pres. Chamber Orch. of Phila., Phila., 1988—; trustee Harvard Rev. of Philosophy, Cambridge, Mass., 1993—, Marlboro Music Sch., 2004—. Named Disting. Honoree, Nat. Assn. of Fundraising Execs., 2002. Mem.: Phila. Bot. Club, Harvard Club NYC. Avocations: violin, botany, salmon fishing.

ROBERTS, WILLIAM S., lawyer; b. Riverside, Calif., June 26, 1946; BA, U. Colo., 1969; MS, U. So. Calif., 1979; JD, U. San Diego, 1989. Bar: Calif. 1989, US Dist. Ct. Ctrl. Dist. Calif. 1989, US Dist. Ct. So. Dist. Calif. 1989, Nev. 2000, US Dist. Ct. Dist. Nev. 2000. Regional mng. ptnr. San Diego office Wilson, Elser, Moskowitz, Edelman & Dicker LLP. Mem.: Am. Soc. Naval Engineers, San Diego Bar Assn. Office: Wilson Elser Moskowitz Edelman & Dicker LLP Emerald Tower Plz Ste 1500 402 W Broadway San Diego CA 92101 Office Phone: 619-595-3181 ext. 3166. Office Fax: 619-595-3183. Business E-Mail: robertsw@wemed.com.

ROBERTS-BROWN, ARLENE MARIA, executive assistant; b. East St. Louis, Ill., May 30, 1939; d. Joe Roberts and Elizabeth Smith; m. Johnny Purchase (div. 1968); children: Johnny Purchase Jr., Francena Purchase-Owens, Darlene Pleas-McLemore, Regenia Pleas-Taylor, Rodney Brown. Student, Jordan Coll., Grand Rapids, Mich., 1987—89. Cert. long-term care facility nurse aid, State of Mich. Dept. Pub. Health, 1990. Nurse aide Raybrook Nursing Home, Grand Rapids, 1990—91; asst. Grand Rapids Pub. Schs., 1994—95; tchg. asst. New Branches Sch., Grand Rapids, 1992—93; exec. asst. Francena Purchase Consulting Svcs., Grand Rapids, 2004—. Mem. Rev. Popov Ministries, Grand Rapids, 1994—. Recipient cert. of recognition, Grand Rapids Pub. Schs., 1994, Francena Purchase Consulting Svcs., 2006. Avocation: reading. Office: Francena Purchase Consulting Svcs PO Box 7421 Grand Rapids MI 49510-7421

ROBERTS-MAMONE, LISA A., lawyer; BA magna cum laude, Grove City Coll., 1985; JD magna cum laude, Case Wester Res. U., 1988. Bar: Ohio 1988. With Jones Day, Cleve., 1988—, ptnr., 2000—. Trustee The Laub Found.; mem. Estate Planning Coun. of Cleve., Estate Planning Discussion Group, Cleve., Case Western Reserve U. Estate Planning Adv. Coun., Hathaway Brown Sch. Profl. Advisors Com.; mem. diamond adv. group U. Hosps. Cleve.; mem. nominating com. Girl Scouts NE Ohio. Mem.: Cleve. Bar Assn. (estate planning, probate and trust law sect.), Ohio State Bar Assn. (estate planning, trust and probate sect.). Office: Jones Day North Point 901 Lakeside Ave Cleveland OH 44114-1190 Office Phone: 216-586-7172.

ROBERTSON, A. HAEWORTH, actuary, foundation executive, benefits consultant; b. Oklahoma City, May 10, 1930; s. Albert Haeworth and Bonnie Tennessee (Duckett) R.; m. Mary Adeline Kissee, Feb. 3, 1952 (div. July 1979); children— Valerie Lynn, Alan Haeworth, Mary Kathryn. BA in Math., U. Okla., Norman, 1951; MA in Actuarial Sci., U. Mich., 1953. Actuary Wyatt Co., Washington and Dallas, 1955-58; actuary Bowles, Andrews & Towne, Dallas, 1958-60; v.p., actuary W. Alfred Hayes & Co., St. Louis, 1960-63; pres. First Am. Security Life Ins. Co. Mo., St. Louis, 1964-68; pvt. practice internat. cons. actuary Barbados and Ghana, 1969-72; sr. actuary ILO, Geneva, 1973-75; chief actuary US Social Security Adminstrn., Balt., 1975-78; mng. dir. William M. Mercer, Inc., Washington, 1978-88; pvt. practice, internat. cons., actuary Washington, Kuwait, Turkey, Guyana, Zimbabwe, China, The Philippines, 1988—. Chmn. Retirement Bd. Actuaries, Dept. Def., 1984-95; mem. Edn. Benefits Bd. Actuaries, 1985-95; pres., founder Retirement Policy Inst. Inc., 1986—. Author: The Coming Revolution in Social Security, 1981, Social Security: What Every Taxpayer Should Know, 1992, The Big Lie: What Every Baby Boomer Should Know About Social Security and Medicare, 1997. Served to 1st lt. USAF, 1953-55 Recipient Commrs. citation, Social Security Adminstrn., Washington, 1976, Arthur J. Altmeyer award, HEW, Washington, 1978, Disting. Alumni award, Ctrl. H.S., Oklahoma City, 1997, Wynn Kent Comm. award, The Actuarial Found., 2007. Fellow Soc. Actuaries (bd. govs. 1979-81, v.p. 1985-87), Conf. Cons. Actuaries; mem. Am. Acad. Actuaries (Robert J. Myers Pub. Svc. award 2004), Internat. Actuarial Assn., Internat. Assn. Cons. Actuaries, U.K. Inst. Actuaries (assoc.), Cosmos Club, Phi Beta Kappa, Phi Eta Sigma, Phi Kappa Sigma. Republican. Methodist. Personal E-mail: haeworth@aol.com.

ROBERTSON, ABEL L., JR., pathologist; b. St. Andrews, Argentina, July 21, 1926; came to U.S., 1952, naturalized, 1957; s. Abel Alfred Lazzarini and Margaret Theresa G. (Anderson) R.; m. Irene Kirmayr Mauch, Dec. 26, 1958; children: Margaret Anne, Abel Martin, Andrew Duncan, Malcolm Alexander. BS, Coll. D.F. Sarmiento, Buenos Aires, Argentina, 1946; MD suma cum laude, U. Buenos Aires, 1951; PhD, Cornell U., 1959. Fellow tissue culture div. Inst. Histology and Embryology, Sch. Medicine Inst. Histology and Embryology, 1947-49; surg. intern Hosp. Ramos Mejia, Buenos Aires, 1948-50; fellow in tissue culture research Ministry of Health, Buenos Aires, 1950-51; resident Hosp. Nacional de Clinicas, Buenos Aires, 1950-51; head blood vessel bank and organ transplants Research Ctr. Ministry of Health, Buenos Aires, 1951-53; fellow dept. surgery and pathology Sch. Medicine Cornell U., NYC, 1953-55; asst. vis. surgery U. Hosp. N.Y., NYC, 1955-60; asst. prof. research surgery Postgrad. Med. Sch. NYU, NYC, 1955-56; asst. vis. surgeon Bellevue Hosp., NYC, 1955-60; assoc. prof. research surgery NYU, 1956-60, assoc. prof. pathology Sch. Medicine and Postgrad Med. Sch., 1960-63; staff mem. div. research Cleve. Clinic Found., 1963-73, prof. research, 1972-73; assoc. clin. prof. pathology Case Western Res. U. Sch. Medicine, Cleve., 1968-72, prof. pathology, 1973-82, dir. interdisciplinary cardiovascular research, 1975-82; exec. head dept. pathology Coll. Medicine, U. Ill., Chgo., 1982-88; prof. pathology Coll. Medicine U. Ill., 1982-93, prof. emeritus, 1993—; vis. prof. emeritus cardiovascular med. Core Analysis Lab., Stanford U. Coll. Medicine, 1995—, cardiac pathologist, 2000—. Rsch. fellow N.Y. Soc. Cardiovasc. Surgery, 1957-58; mem. rsch. study subcom. of heart com. N.E. Ohio Regional Med. Program, 1969—. Mem. internat. editl. bd. Atherosclerosis, Jour. Exptl. and Molecular Pathology, 1964—, Lab. Investigation, 1989—, Acta Pathologica Japonica, 1991—; contbr. articles to profl. jours. Recipient Rsch. Devel. award NIH, 1961-63, Disting. Alumnus award Grad. Sch. Med. Sci. Cornell U., 2003. Fellow AAAS, Am. Coll. Cardiology, Am. Coll. Clin. Pharmacology, Am. Heart Assn. (established investigator 1956-61, nominating com. coun. on arteriosclerosis 1972), Royal Microscopical Soc., Royal Soc. Promotion Health (Gt. Britain), Am. Geriat. Soc., N.Y. Acad. Scis., Cleve. Med. Library Assn.; mem. AMA, AAUP, Am. Soc. for Investigative Pathology, Am. Inst. Biol. Scis., Am. Judicature Soc., Am. Soc. Cell Biology, Am. Soc. Pathologists, Am. Soc. Nephrology, Assn. Am. Physicians and Surgeons, Assn. Computing Machinery, Electron Microscopy Soc. Am., Assn. Pathology Chmn., Internat. Acad. Pathology, Soc. Cardiovasc. Pathology, Internat. Cardiovasc. Soc., Internat. Soc. Cardiology (sci. council on arteriosclerosis and ischemic heart disease), Internat. Fed. on Genetic Engring. and Biotechnology, Internat. Soc. for Heart Rsch., Internat. Soc. Nephrology, Internat. Soc. Stereology, Pan Am. Med. Assn. (life, councillor in angiology 1966), Ill. Registry Anatomical Pathology (treas. 1985-87), Chgo. Pathology Soc., Reticuloendothelial Soc. Leucocyte Biology, Soc. Cryobiology, Tissue Culture Assn., Ohio Soc. Pathologists, Electron Microscopy Soc. Northeastern Ohio (pres., trustee 11966-68), Heart Assn. Northeastern Ohio, N.Y. Soc. Cardiovasc. Surgery, N.Y. Soc. Electron Microscopists, Cuyahoga County Med. Soc., Cleve. Soc. Pathologists, The Oxygen Soc., Sigma Xi. Home: PO Box 3125 340 5th Ave Half Moon Bay CA 94019-3125 Office Phone: 650-712-0357. Office Fax: 650-712-0357. Personal E-mail: abelrobertsonmd@yahoo.com.

ROBERTSON, ANDREW J., advertising executive; b. Zimbabwe; Degree in econ., London U. Joined as media planner Ogilvy & Mather, London, 1982, account mgr., bd. dirs., 1986—89, mgmt. supr., new bus. dir., 1989; group account dir. J. Walter Thompson, London, 1989—90; CEO WCRS, London, 1990—95; mng. dir. Abbott Mead Vickers BBDO, London, 1995—99; CEO, pres. BBDO N. Am., NYC, 2001—04; pres. BBDO Worldwide, NYC, 2002—04, pres., CEO, dir., 2004—. Bd. mem. Special Olympics, Ctr. on Media and Child Health. Mem.: Am. Assn. Advt. Agencies (bd. mem.), Advt. Coun. (bd. mem.). Office: BBDO Worldwide Inc 1285 Ave of the Americas New York NY 10019-6028 *

ROBERTSON, ARMAND JAMES, II, judge; b. San Diego, Sept. 23, 1937; s. Armand James and Muriel H. R.; m. Marion Sperry, Aug. 11, 1962; children: Armand James, Laura Marie. A.M. in Econs, Stanford U., 1960; LL.B., Harvard U., 1965. Bar: Calif. 1966. Law clk. to Charles M. Merrill, U.S. Ct. Appeals (9th cir.), 1965-66; assoc. firm Howard, Prim, Rice, Nemerovski, Canady & Pollak, San Francisco, 1966-71, ptnr., 1971-77; dir. Howard, Rice, Nemerovski, Canady, Robertson & Falk (P.C.), San Francisco, 1977-95; judge of the Superior Ct. City and County of San Francisco, 1995—. Bd. dirs. St. Francis Found., 1996—, chmn., 1999—. Lt. (j.g.) USN, 1960-62. Mem. Am. Law Inst., ABA (antitrust sect.), CPR Inst. for Dispute Resolution, Phi Beta Kappa. Office: San Francisco Superior Ct 400 Mcallister St Rm 210 San Francisco CA 94102-4512

ROBERTSON, BEVERLY CARRUTH, retired steel company executive; b. Texarkana, Ark., May 16, 1922; s. Glenn C. Robertson (dec.); m. Ruth Mulcare, Oct. 31, 1945 (dec. Oct. 1993); children: Glenn J., Beverly R. Dodds, Rebecca A. Robertson Deans; m. Charlotte Doty Lawler, June 2, 1995. In sales Nat. Supply Co., Laurel, Miss., 1941-51; purchasing agt. Kirby Petroleum Co., Houston, 1951-54; exec. v.p. mktg. Lone Star Steel Co., Dallas, 1954-85, exec. v.p., 1985-86; pres., dir., chief exec. officer LSSCO Trading Corp., 1985-86; owner BSEER Enterprises, Dallas, 1986—; ptnr. Clayton Equipment Co., Dallas, 1992-97; ret., 1997. Chmn. Sir Alec Inc., 1985-94; cons. Pipeco, Inc., Houston, 1986-88; exec. v.p. mktg. and procurement Nat. Pipe and Tube Co., Houston, 1988-89; pres., CEO Tex. Am. Pipe & Supply Co., Inc., Dallas, 1989—; cons. Ipsco Steel, Inc., Camanche, Iowa, 1991-92. Served to capt. USAF, 1943-46, ETO. Named Supplier of Yr. Petroleum Industry Buyers group Nat. Assn. Purchasing Mgmt., 1982 Mem.: Dallas Petroleum Club, Dallas Country Club. Republican. Episcopalian. Home: PO Box 12688 Dallas TX 75225-0688 Personal E-mail: bcrobby@sbcglobal.net.

ROBERTSON, CHARLES JAMES, museum director emeritus; b. Houston, Sept. 12, 1934; s. Charles James and Felide Corinne (O'Brien) R. BA, U. Va., Charlottesville, 1956; MA, Harvard U., 1958; student, U. London Courtauld Inst., 1960; JD, George Washington U., 1964. Atty. Dow, Lohnes & Albertson, Washington, 1964-69; adminstr. Richard H. Chamberlain, M.D. & Assoc., Phila., 1969-75; assoc. dir. N.C. Mus. Art, Raleigh, 1975-77; deputy dir. Smithsonian Am. Art Mus., Washington, 1977—2001. Treas. Am. Assn. Mus., Washington, 1982-84, mem. exec. com., 1982-84; mem. adv. com. Octagon House Mus., Washington, 1989-97, chmn. 1993-96; bd. dirs. Victorian Soc. Am., Phila., 1990—, v.p., 1994-2000, 06—; mem. Hist. Preservation Rev. Bd. of DC, 1992-2004; bd. regents Am. Archtl. Found., Washington, 1993-96; trustee Cosmos Club Historic Preservation Found., Washington, 1993—, treas., 1999—2003, sec., 2007-. Author: Temple of Invention: History of a National Landmark, 2006; contbr. articles to profl. jours. Pres. Dupont Circle Conservancy, Washington, 1978-92; v.p., bd. mem., Dupont Circle Citizens Assn. Washington, 1980-83, 86; mem. com. 100 Fed. City Washington, 2005—, trustee, 2006—. Recipient Rumrill fellowship Harvard U., Cambridge, Mass., 1956-57. Mem. Cosmos Club, Phi Beta Kappa, Phi Pi Theta, Delta Theta Phi.

ROBERTSON, CLIFF, actor, writer, director; b. La Jolla, Calif., Sept. 9, 1925; s. Clifford Parker and Audrey (Willingham) R.; m. Cynthia Stone, 1957 (div. 1959); 1 child, Stephanie; m. Dina Merrill, Dec. 22, 1966 (div. 1986); 1 child, Heather. DFA (hon.), Bradford Coll., 1981, MacMurray Coll., 1986, Susquehanna U., 1988. Contbr. articles to various publs.; stage appearances include Late Love, Wisteria Trees, Orpheus Descending; films include Picnic, 1956, Autumn Leaves, 1956, The Naked and the Dead, 1958, The Girl Most Likely, 1958, Gidget, 1959, All in a Nights Work, 1961, The Big Show, 1961, Under-World, U.S.A., 1961, As the Sea Rages, 1961, The Interns, 1962, PT 109, 1963, Sunday in New York, 1964, The Best Man, 1964, 633 Squadron, 1964, Love Has Many Faces, 1965, Masquerade, 1965, Up From the Beach, 1965, The Honey Pot, 1967, The Devil's Brigade, 1968, Charly, 1968, (Academy award for Best Actor 1969), The Great Northfield Minnesota Raid, 1972, Ace Eli and Rodger of the Skies, 1973, Too Late the Hero, 1970, Man on a Swing, 1974, 3 Days of the Condor, 1975, Out of Season, Obsession, 1976, Shoot, 1976, Star 80, 1983, Brainstorm, 1983, Malone, 1987, Wild Hearts Can't Be Broken, 1991, Wind, 1992, The Sunset Boys, 1995, Escape from L.A., 1996, Assignment Berlin, 1997, Family Tree, 1999, (star, co writer) Curse of the 13th Child, 2002, Spider-Man, Spider-Man 2, 2004, Riding the Bullet, 2004, Spider-Man 3, 2007; TV films and miniseries appearances include The Days of Wine and Roses, 1958, The Sunshine Patriot, 1968, The Game, 1968 (Emmy award) The Man Without a Country, 1973, A Tree Grows in Brooklyn, 1974, My Father's House, 1975, Return to Earth, 1976, Washington: Behind Closed Doors, 1977, Overboard, 1978, Two of a Kind, 1982, The Key to Rebecca, 1985, Dreams of Gold, 1986, Ford: The Man and The Machine, 1987, Dead Reckoning, 1990, Dazzle, 1995, Pakten, 1995, Melting Pot, 1997, Assignment Berlin, 1998, "With God on Our Side: the Rise of the Religious Right in America," (T.V. Mini Series), 1996, The Last Best Place, Outer Limits, 1998; appeared in TV series Falcon Crest; writer, dir.: play The V.I.P.'s, 1981; J. W. Coop. Served to lt. (j.g.) USNR. Recipient Wallace award Am. Scottish Found., 1984, Sharples aviation award AOPA, 1983, Theatre World award, 1970, award Advt. Age, 1985, E.A.A. Freedom of Flight award, 1986, USAF Outstanding Supporter award, 1997, Nat. Aviation Henderson award, 1995 World Aviation Conf., India, Nat. Soaring Mus. award Expts. Aviation Assn., 1996, I.C.A.S. Aviation award, 1998; holder of Nev. state distance soaring record, 1996. Mem. SAG (bd. dirs. N.Y. chpt. 1980—), Dirs. Guild, Writers Guild Am., Bath & Tennis Club Palm Beach, Maidstone Club (East Hampton), River Club (N.Y.C.), Brook Club (N.Y.C.), Players (N.Y.C.), River Club, Wings Club. Presbyterian. Avocations: flying, skiing, soaring, tennis. *

ROBERTSON, DAMON D., lawyer; b. Linden, Tex., 1974; 2 children. BA in Psych., Tex. A&M U., 1995; JD, Tex. Tech U. Sch. Law, 1998. Bar: Tex. 1999, US Dist. Ct. (all dists. Tex.) 2000, US Ct. Appeals (5th cir.). Ptnr. Savrick, Schumann, Johnson, McGarr, Kaminski & Shirley, L.L.P., Austin, Tex. Named a Rising Star, Tex. Super Lawyers mag., 2006, 2007. Mem.: Tex. Aggie Bar Assn., Austin Young Lawyers Assn., Austin Bar Assn., Tex. Assn. Def. Counsel. Office: Savrick Schumann Johnson McGarr Kaminski & Shirley LLP The Overlook at Gaines Ranch 4330 S Mopac Ste 150 Austin TX 78735 Office Phone: 512-347-1604. E-mail: damon@ssjmlaw.com.

ROBERTSON, DAVID, neurologist, educator; b. Sylvia, Tenn., May 23, 1947; s. David Herlie and Lucille Luther (Bowen) R.; m. Rose Marie Stevens, Oct. 30, 1976; 1 child, Rose. BA, Vanderbilt U., 1969, MD, 1973. Diplomate Am. Bd. Internal. Medicine, Am. Bd. Clin. Pharmacology. Intern Johns Hopkins U., Balt., 1973-74, asst. resident, 1974-75, asst. chief svc. in medicine, 1977-78; fellow in clin. pharmacology Vanderbilt U., Nashville, 1975-77, asst. prof. medicine and pharmacology, 1978-82, assoc. prof., 1982-86, prof., 1986—, prof. neurology, 1991—, Elton Yates prof. autonomic disorders, 1998—, dir. clin. rsch. ctr., 1987—; dir. Ctr. Space Physiology and Medicine, 1989—, Med. Sci. Tng. Program, 1993—2003; mem. staff Vanderbilt Hosp., Burroughs Wellcome scholar in clin. pharmacology, 1985-91. Author: (with B.M. Greene and G.J. Taylor) Problems in Internal Medicine, 1980, (with C.R. Smith) Manual of Clinical Pharmacology, 1981, (with Italo Biaggioni) Disorders of the Autonomic Nervous System, 1995, (with Italo Biaggioni, Geoffrey Burnstock and Phillip A. Low) Primer on the Autonomic Nervous System, 1996, 2d edit., 2004, (with Gordon H. Williams) Principles of Clinical and Translational Science, 2007; editor-in-chief: Drug Therapy, 1991-94; assoc. editor, Jour. Pharmacol. Exptl. Therapy, 1998—; mem. editl. bd. Am. Jour. Medicine, Autonomic Neuroscience, Clin. Pharm. and Therapeutics, Clin. Autonomic Rsch., Am. Jour. Med. Sci., Current Topics in Pharmacology. Logan Clendening fellow, Reykjavik, Iceland, 1969; Adolph-Morsbach grantee Bonn, Germany, 1968; recipient Rsch. Career Devel. award NIH, 1981, Grant W. Liddle award for leadership in rsch., 1991, Tchg. award Nat. Program Dir.'s Assn., 2003, Rschr. of Yr. award Nat. Dysautomia Rsch. Found., 2001. Fellow Am. Heart Assn. Coun. Hypertension and Circulation, ACP (tchg. and rsch. scholar 1978-81), Am. Autonomic Soc. (pres. 1992-94); mem. Am. Acad. Neurology, Soc. Neurosci., Am. Inst. Aeronautics and Astronautics, U.S. Pharmacopeial Conv., Nat. Bd. Med. Examiners, Aerospace Med. Assn. (space sta. sci. and applications com.), NASA (microgravity human rsch. com.), FDA Consortium Rare Disorders, Rare Disorder Network, Am. Fedn. Med. Rsch., Am. Soc. Clin. Investigation, Assn. Am. Physicians, Assn. Patient-Oriented Rsch. (bd. dirs., pres.), So. Soc. Clin. Investigation, Am. Soc. Clin. Pharmacology and Therapeutics, Phi Beta Kappa, Alpha Omega Alpha (hon., bd. dirs. 1995—. William Darby award 2000). Baptist. Home: 4003 Newman Pl Nashville TN 37204-4308 Office: Vanderbilt U Clin Rsch Ctr 21st Ave S Nashville TN 37232-2195 Office Phone: 615-343-6499. Business E-Mail: david.robertson@vanderbilt.edu.

ROBERTSON, DAVID, conductor, music director; b. Santa Monica, Calif. m. Orli Shaham; 2 children. Student in French horn and composition, Royal Acad. Music. Resident condr. Jerusalem Symphony Orch., 1985—87; music dir. Ensemble Interconteporain, Paris, 1992—2000; musical dir. Orchestre Nat. de Lyon, France, 2000—; artistic dir. Lyon Auditorium, 2000; music dir. St. Louis Symphony Orch., 2005—. Guest condr. Minn. Orch., 2001, Phila. Orch., 2001, Chgo. Symphony, 2001, Boston Symphony, 2001, San Francisco Symphony, 2001, NDR Symphony Orch. Hamburg, Germany, 2001, Royal Concertgebouw Orch., 2001, Orch. del Maggio Musicale Fiorentino, 2001, London Symphony Orch., Halle Orch., Bayerisches Staatorchester, Munich, Berlin Staatskapelle, La Scala Philharm., Boston Symphony, Chgo. Orch., NY Philharm., L.A. Philharm., many others; prin. guest condr. BBC Symphony, 2005—. Active outreach programs Ensemble Intercontemporain, Orchestre Nat. de Lyon, Paris Conservatory, Juilliard Sch., Tanglewood, Aspen Music Festival. Named Condr. of Yr., Musical Am., 2000; recipient Seaver/Nat. Endowment for Arts Condr. award, 1997, Ditson Conductor's award, Columbia U., 2006, ASCAP Morton Gould award, Am. Symphony Orch. League, 2006. Office: 82 rue de Bonnel 69431 Lyon France Office Fax: 33 4 78 60 13 08. *

ROBERTSON, DAVID ALAN, museum director, educator; b. Jefferson City, Mo., Oct. 10, 1950; s. Roy Victor and Mary Jane (Threlkeld) R. BA in English, U. Mo., 1973, MA in Art History, 1976; PhD in Art History, U. Pa., 1983. Museum asst. U. Mo. Museum, Columbia, 1975-76; rsch. asst. Victoria and Albert Museum, London, 1976; curatorial asst. Yale Ctr. for British Art, New Haven, 1977-78; teaching fellow U. Pa., Phila., 1978-81; staff supr. Rosenbach Museum and Library, Phila., 1980-82; dir. Dickinson Coll., Carlisle, Pa., 1982—2002; dir. Mary and Leigh Block Mus Art Northwestern U., Evanston, Ill., 2002—, lectr. Art Hist. Dept., 2003—. Fulbright prof. U. Munich, Germany, 1989-90; mem. selection com. Fulbright Commn., Bonn, Germany, 1989; grant reviewer Inst. Mus. Svcs., Washington, 1989-91. Penfield fellow U. Pa., Vienna, Austria, 1981-82, Kress fellow Kress Found., London, 1976, Vienna, 1980. Mem. Am. Assn. Mus., Coll. Art Assn., Assn. Coll. and U. Mus. and Galleries. Office: Mary and Leigh Block Mus Art Northwestern U 40 Arts Circle Dr Evanston IL 60208 Office Phone: 847-491-2562. Business E-Mail: d-robertson@northwestern.edu.

ROBERTSON, DAVID GOVAN, lawyer; b. Chgo., May 3, 1947; AB with great distinction, Stanford U., 1969; JD, Yale U., 1973. Bar: Calif. 1973, US Dist. Ct. (no., cen., ea. and we. dists.) Calif. 1973, US Supreme Ct. 1988. Law clk. to chief judge US Dist. Ct., 1973-74; assoc. Morrison & Foerster, San Francisco, 1974-79, ptnr., 1979; pvt. practice Sea Ranch, Calif. Adj. prof. legal ethics U. San Francisco Law Sch., 1993-94; vis. prof. theology U. San Francisco, 1995—. Danforth Found. Grad. fellow Yale, 1970-73. Mem. Phi Beta Kappa. Office: PO Box 464 The Sea Ranch CA 95497 Office Phone: 707-494-6908.

ROBERTSON, DAWN H., retail executive; b. Birmingham, Ala. m. Tom Robertson; 2 children. BA in Fashion Merchandising, Auburn U., Ala., 1976. Buyer, exec. trainee Davidson's (divsn. R.H. Macy & Co.), Atlanta, 1977; various positions The May Co., 1983—96; pres., CEO McRae's (divsn. Saks Inc.), Jackson, Miss., 1997—98; exec. v.p. men's/children's/home Fed. Merchandising Group, 1998—2000; pres., chief merchandising officer Federated Stores Direct, NYC, 2000—02; mng. dir. Coles Meyer, Australia, 2002—06; pres. Old Navy Gap Inc., San Francisco, 2006—. Named one of 50 Most Powerful Women, Fortune Mag., 2005. Office: Gap Inc Two Folsom St San Francisco CA 94105 Office Phone: 650-952-4400. *

ROBERTSON, DONNA VIRGINIA, architect, educator, dean; b. Richmond, Va., Feb. 26, 1952; d. Charles Henry and Florence (Givens) R.; m. Robert M. McAnulty, May 24, 1986; 1 child, Robertson. Cert. theater arts studies, Webster Coll., St. Louis, 1972; BA, Stanford U., 1974; MArch, U. Va., 1978. Registered arch., N.Y. Asst. prof. Harvard U., Cambridge, Mass., 1983-84; asst. prof. Barnard Coll. Columbia U., NYC, 1984-92; dean Sch. Arch. Tulane U., New Orleans, 1992-96; dean Coll. Arch., prof. Ill. Inst. Tech., Chgo., 1996—; ptnr. Robertson McAnulty Archs., Chgo., 1986—; owner Donna V. Robertson Archs., NYC, 1982-86; sr. designer Kohn

Pedersen Fox Archs., NYC, 1980-82, Mitchell Giurgola Archs., NYC, 1979-80. Adj. asst. prof. Barnard Coll., Columbia U., N.Y., 1982-83, dir. arch. program, fall 1985-92; vis. critic in design Harvard U., Cambridge, fall 1990, U. Va., Charlottesville, fall 1991; organizer, panelist Arch. and Lit. Symposium, N.Y.C., 1985; jury chair Am. Collegiate Schs. Arch., Boston, 1996; mem. bd. dirs. Nat. Archtl. Accrediting Bd., 2000-03; profl. advisor Ford Calumet Environ. Ctr. Competition, City of Chgo., 2004. Prin. arch. Fishback residence, New Orleans, Sunkel residence, New Orleans, Pisar residence, N.Y.C., Dachs residence, N.Y.C.; pres. Nat. Archtl. Accrediting Bd., 2002-03; profiled in Archtl. Record May 2004. Juror invitational competition Seoul Performing Arts Ctr., Republic of Korea, 2006. Named one of Most Influential Women in Chgo., Crain's Chgo. Bus., 2004; recipient Honor award, Chgo. Landmarks Commn., 2005, Education award, Arch. Constrn. Engring. Mentor Program, Chgo., 2007. Mem. AIA (juror annual design hons. awards 1996, Educators and Practitioners Network, co-chair tchrs. seminar 2006, mem. Chgo. bd.), Coll. Fellow of AIA, Am. Coll. Sch. Arch. (co-chair 2006, Endowed Chair Arch., John and Jeanne Rowe, 2007), Chgo. Network-Internat. Women's Forum, Raven Soc. (U. Va.), Arts Club (Chgo.), Nat. Trust His. Preservation, Phi Beta Kappa. Office: Ill Inst Tech Coll Architecture 3360 S State St Chicago IL 60616 Office Phone: 312-567-3263. E-mail: robertson@iit.edu.

ROBERTSON, EDWIN DAVID, lawyer; b. Roanoke, Va., July 5, 1946; s. Edwin Traylor and Norma Burns (Bowles) R.; m. Anne Littelle Ferratt, Sept. 7, 1968, 1 child, Thomas Therit. BA with honors, U. Va., 1968, LLB, 1971. Bar: N.Y. 1972, U.S. Ct. Appeals (2d cir.) 1972, U.S. Dist. Ct. (ea. and so. dists.) N.Y. 1973, U.S. Supreme Ct. 1975, U.S. Dist. Ct. (ea. dist.) Mich. 1986. Assoc. Cadwalader, Wickersham & Taft, NYC, 1972-80, ptnr., 1980—. Bd. dirs. Early Music Found. N.Y.C., 1983-99, chmn., 1993-99; bd. dirs. Oratorio Soc. of N.Y.C., 1988—2004, sec., 1991—2004; judge Ct. of Rev., Episcopal Ch., 2001-03. 1st lt. USAF, 1971-72. Echols scholar. Mem. ABA (ho. of dels. 2004-07), Nat. Conf. Bar Presidents, Fed. Bar Coun., NY County Lawyers Assn. (chmn. bankruptcy com. 1983-87, chmn. fin. com. 1999, bd. dirs. 1985-88, 95-99, 2000—, investment com. 1992-2007, exec. com. 1996—, treas. 2001-02, v.p. 2002-04, pres.-elect 2005—, pres. 2006-07), NY State Bar Assn. (ho. of dels. 2001-04, 05—, nominatng com. 2002-), Assn. Bar City NY, Soc. Colonial Wars, Jefferson Soc., Sons of Revolution, Order of Coif, Phi Beta Kappa, Phi Kappa Psi. Republican. Episcopalian. Home: 315 E 72nd St New York NY 10021-4625 Office: Cadwalader Wickersham & Taft OneWorld Fin Ctr New York NY 10281 Home Phone: 212-628-5810; Office Phone: 212-504-6000. E-mail: darob@cwt.com.

ROBERTSON, GREGORY B., lawyer; b. Sandusky, Ohio, Apr. 2, 1951; BA, Washington & Lee Univ., 1973; JD, Univ. Richmond, 1976. Bar: Va. 1976. Ptnr., co-chmn. labor, employment practice group Hunton & Williams LLP, Richmond, Va. Mem.: ABA, Va. Bar Assn., Energy and Mineral Law Found. (past pres.), Va. CofC (bd. dir., counsel), Phi Delta Phi, Pi Sigma Alpha. Office: Hunton & Williams LLP Riverfront Plz East Tower 951 E Byrd St Richmond VA 23219-4074 Office Phone: 804-788-8526. Office Fax: 804-788-8218. Business E-Mail: grobertson@hunton.com.

ROBERTSON, HORACE BASCOMB, JR., retired law educator; b. Charlotte, NC, Nov. 13, 1923; s. Horace Bascomb and Ruth (Montgomery) R.; m. Patricia Lavell, Aug. 11, 1947; children— Mark L., James D. BS, U.S. Naval Acad., 1945; JD, Georgetown U., 1953; MS, George Washington U., 1968. Commd. ensign U.S. Navy, 1945, advanced through grades to rear adm., 1972; line officer, 1945-55; law specialist, 1955-68; spl. counsel to sec. Navy, Washington, 1964-67, judge adv., 1968-76; spl. counsel to chief naval ops. Washington, 1970-72; dep. judge adv. gen. Navy Dept., Washington, 1972-75, judge adv. gen., 1975-76; prof. law Duke U., 1976-89, sr. assoc. dean, 1986-89, ret., 1990; Chas H. Stockton chair of internat. law Naval War Coll., Newport, R.I., 1991-92. Decorated D.S.M. Mem. ABA, Am. Soc. Internat. Law. Home: 9 Silver Maple Ct Durham NC 27705-5642 Office: Duke U Sch Law Durham NC 27708 Office Phone: 919-613-7038. Business E-Mail: hbr@law.duke.edu.

ROBERTSON, HUGH (ELIHU F.), lawyer; b. Annapolis, Md., 1953; BA, Yale Univ., 1976; JD, Univ. Va., 1979. Bar: N.Y. 1980. Atty. Milbank Tweed Hadley & McCloy, London, Hong Kong, ptnr. Global Fin. Dept. NYC, 1987—. Mem.: ABA, N.Y. State Bar Assn. Office: Milbank Tweed Hadley & McCloy 1 Chase Manhattan Plz New York NY 10005-1413 Office Phone: 212-530-5187. Office Fax: 212-530-5219. Business E-Mail: erobertson@milbank.com.

ROBERTSON, HUGH DUFF, lawyer; b. Grosse Pointe, Mich., Mar. 14, 1957; BBA in Fin., U. Wis., Whitewater, 1978; JD, Whittier Coll., 1982. Bar: Calif. 1983, U.S. Tax Ct. 1984, U.S. Supreme Court, 1999. Pres., CEO, A. Morgan Maree Jr. & Assocs., Inc., LA, 1979—. Mem. State Calif., L.A. County Bar Assn., Beverly Hills Bar Assn., Acad. TV Arts and Scis., Am. Film Inst., Phi Alpha Delta. Avocation: sports. Office: 1125 Gayley Ave Los Angeles CA 90024-3403

ROBERTSON, JACK CLARK, accounting educator; b. Marlin, Tex., Apr. 27, 1943; s. Rupert Cook and Lois Lucille (Rose) R.; m. Caroline Susan Hughes, Oct. 23, 1965; children: Sara Ellen, Elizabeth Hughes. Student, Rice U., 1961-63; BBA with honors, U. Tex., Austin, 1965, M in Profl. Acctg., 1967; PhD, U. N.C., 1970. CPA, Tex. Tax acct. Humble Oil and Refining Co., Houston, 1964-65; auditor Peat, Marwick, Mitchell & Co., Houston, 1965-66; acct. Wade, Barton, Marsh CPAs, Austin, Tex., 1966-67; from asst. prof. to prof. emeritus U. Tex., Austin, 1970—2003, C.T. Zlatkovich Centennial prof. emeritus, 2003—. Acad. assoc. Coopers & Lybrand, N.Y.C., 1975-76; acad. fellow U.S. Securities and Exchange Commn. Office of the Chief Acct., Washington, 1982-83; Erskine fellow U. Canterbury, Christchurch, New Zealand, 1988; tng. the trainers instr. Vilnius, Lithuania, 1993; lectr. in field. Contbr. articles to profl. jours. Lay reader St. Matthews Episcopal Ch., Austin, 1972-75, mem. vestry, 1973-75, 77-79, 84-86, treas., 1974-75, 77-96, chmn. bldg. fund, 1976-87, chmn. everymen. canvass, 1980, sr. warden, 1986; del. Diocese of Tex. Coun., 1993-95; Trompetista El Grupo Valor Latino, 2000—, lector laico, 2000-03, Miembro comite del obispo Iglesia San Francisco de Asis, 2000-03, treas., 2002-03; dir., treas. Austin Chamber Music Ctr., 2003-07; mem. New Horizons Band; ofcl. U.S.A Track and Field, 1996—; bd. dirs. Episcopal Province VII Ctr. for Hispanic Ministries, 2006—. Mem. AICPA, Am. Acctg. Assn. (sec.-treas. auditing sect. 1976-77, v.p. auditing sect. 1977-78, pres. auditing sect. 1978-79, chmn. auditing stds. com. 1980-81, chmn. SEC liaison com. 1983-84, historian auditing sect. 1999-2001), Tex. Soc. CPAs (vice-chmn., profl. ethics com. 1986-94, 95-97, Presdl. citation 1994), Assn. Cert. Fraud Examiners (regent emeritus, cert.), Phi Kappa Phi, Beta Gamma Sigma, Beta Alpha Psi.

ROBERTSON, JAMES, federal judge; b. Cleve., May 18, 1938; s. Frederick Irving and Doris Mary (Byars) R.; m. Berit Selma Persson, Sept. 19, 1959; children: Stephen Irving, Catherine Anne, Peter Arvid. AB, Princeton U., 1959; LLB, George Washington U., 1965. Bar: D.C. 1966, U.S. Supreme Ct. 1969. Assoc. Wilmer, Cutler & Pickering, Washington, 1965-69, ptnr., 1973-94; judge US Dist. Ct. (D.C. dist.), 1994—, Fgn. Intelligence Adv. Ct., 2002—06. Chief counsel, Lawyers Com. for Civil Rights Under Law, 1969-70, dir., 1970-72, co-chmn., 1982-84; mem. com. on grievances U.S. Dist. Ct., 1988-92, vice chmn., 1989-92; bd. dirs. South Africa Legal Svcs. and Edn. Project, Inc., 1987-01, pres., 1989-94; bd. dirs. D.C. Prisoners Legal Svcs., Inc., 1992-94. Editor in chief George Washington Law Rev., 1964-65. Lt. USN, 1959-64. Fellow Am. Coll. Trial Lawyers, Am. Bar Found.; mem. ABA, D.C. Bar (bd. govs. 1986-93, pres.-elect 1990-92, pres. 1991-92), Am. Law Inst. Home: 3318 N St NW Washington DC 20007-2807 Office: US Courthouse Rm 6315 333 Constitution Ave NW Washington DC 20001-2854

ROBERTSON, JAMES THOMAS, neurosurgeon; b. McComb, Miss., Apr. 5, 1931; s. Clyde Aubrey and Catherine Roberta (Darville) R.; m. Valeria Ann Brower, Nov. 26, 1952; children: James T. Jr., Elizabeth, Catherine, Clay, Roberta, Daniel. BS, Southwestern U., 1951; MD, U. Tenn., 1954. Diplomat Am. Bd. Neurol. Surgeons, 1962. Intern Bapt. Meml. Hosp., Memphis, 1955; resident U. Tenn., Memphis, 1956-59, Peter Bent Brigham & Children's Hosp., Boston, 1959-60; chief neurosurgery Travis AFB, Fairfield, Calif., 1960-63; asst. chief nuerosurgery Lackland AFB, San Antonio, 1963-64; assoc. physician Semmes Murphey Clinic, Memphis, 1964-65; asst. prof. neurosurgery U. Tenn., 1964-69, assoc. prof., 1969-73, prof., chmn. dept. neurosurgery, 1973—98, prof., 1998—. Physician dept. neurosurgery U. Tenn., Memphis, 1973—97; med. dir. Medtronic Sofamarc Dansk, Memphis, 2003. Editor: Subarachnoid Hemorrhage and Cerebrocascular Vasopasm, 1975; contbr. articles to mags. Vice chair Rep. Party, Shelby County, Memphis, 1980, treas., DeSoto County, Miss., 1993; pres. Shelby County chpt. Am. Heart Assn., 1996, chmn. stroke coun., 1992-94. Capt. USNR, 1982-98. Recipient Disting. Alumni award U. Tenn., 1990, Rhodes Coll., 1994. Fellow Am. Coll. Surgeons (bd. govs. 1987-92); mem. Am. Assn. Neurol. Surgeons (pres. 1990-91), Congress Neurol. Surgeons (pres. 1975), Am. Acad. Neurol. Surgery (pres. 1988), Soc. Univ. Neurosrugeons (pres. 1965). Presbyterian. Avocations: gardening, fly fishing. Home: 8570 Jones Rd Olive Branch MS 38654-9001 Office: U Tenn 847 Monroe Ave # 427 Memphis TN 38103-4901 Home Phone: 662-895-6867; Office Phone: 901-448-6375. Business E-Mail: jrober52@aol.com.

ROBERTSON, JAQUELIN TAYLOR, architect, educator; b. Richmond, Va., Mar. 20, 1933; s. Walter Spencer and Mary Dade (Taylor) Robertson; m. Marianne Neese, Sept. 15, 1962. BA cum laude, Yale U., New Haven, 1955, MArch, 1961. Archtl. designer Sir Leslie Martin, Cambridge, England, 1961—62, Edward Barnes Assocs., NYC, 1963—66; lectr. architecture Yale U., 1964—65, Columbia U., NYC, 1965—67; prin. urban designer NYC Planning Commn., 1967—69; dir. Office Midtown Planning and Devel., NYC, 1969—72; lectr. The New Sch., NYC, 1973; city planning commr. NYC, 1973; v.p. Arlen Realty Devel., NYC, 1974—75; mng. dir. Llewelyn-Davies Va Shoraka, Tehran, Iran, 1975—77; chmn. Llewelyn-Davies Assocs., NYC, 1977—78; prin. Jaquelin Taylor Robertson FAIA, NYC, 1978—80, Design Devel. Resources, NYC, 1980—88, Eisenman-Robertson Archs., NYC, 1980—88; dean Sch. Architecture U. Va., Charlottesville, 1980—88, Commonwealth prof. architecture, 1985—90; ptnr. Cooper, Robertson & Ptnrs., NYC, 1988—. Vis. faculty mem. Salzburg Seminar, Austria, 1974; vis. prof. archtl. design RI Sch. Design, Providence, 1979; William Henry Bishop prof. Yale U., 1980, William B. and Charlotte Shepherd Davenport prof., 2004. Contbr. articles to profl. jours., mags.; exhibitions include Mus. Modern Art, NYC, 1967, Archtl. League and Mcpl. Arts Soc., 1969, Inst. Architecture and Urban Studies, NYC, 1975. Chmn. policy panel Design Arts Program Nat. Endowment for Arts, 1979—83; mem. art and architecture rev. coun. State of Va., 1982—88; mem. vis. com. Harvard Grad. Sch. Design, 1983—88; advisor Aga Khan Program for Study of Islamic Art & Architecture Harvard U. and MIT, 1983—90; trustee Inst. Architecture and Urban Studies, NYC, 1984—85, Va. Mus. Fine Arts, 1985—90; founder Jeffersonian Restoratior Adv. Bd. U. Va., 1985; founder Mayor's Inst. City Design, Washington, 1986; mem. Congress for New Urbanism, 1993; bd. dirs. Pks. Coun., NYC, 1971—75, Mcpl. Arts Soc., NYC, 1971—75, Archtl. League NY, 1972—75, 1979—81; bd. dirs. Ctr. for Study of Am. Architecture Columbia U., 1984—87. Recipient Thomas Jefferson Found. Medal in Architecture, 1998, Seaside Inst. prize, 2002, Richard H. Driehaus Prize for Classical Architecture, 2007; Rhodes scholar, U. Oxford, 1955—57. Fellow: AIA, Am. Inst. Cert. Planners; mem.: Am. Planning Assn., Maidstone Club, Easthampton, NY, Pundits, U. Yale, Bullingdon Club, U. Oxford, Knickerbocker Club, NYC (bd. govs. 2004—), St. Anthony Hall, U. Yale, Torch. Hon. Soc., U. Yale. Episcopalian. Office: Cooper Robertson & Ptnrs 311 W 43rd St New York NY 10036 Office Phone: 212-247-1717, 631-329-7387. Office Fax: 212-245-0361.

ROBERTSON, JEAN ELIZABETH, sociology educator; b. Galashiels, Scotland, Sept. 20, 1956; arrived in U.S., 1998; d. Frank Robertson and Jean Isabella Connochie; m. Mohan Narayanasamy; children: Sonja Jean Lowit, Simon David Lowit, Nicholas Ian Lowit. MA, U. Aberdeen, Scotland, 1995. ESOL tchr. Spanish Cath. Ctr., Gaithersburg, Md., 1999—2001; adjuct faculty mem. Strayer U. Online, Newington, Va., 2002—, cons. course development, 2006—. Vol. Montgomery County Dept. Health and Human Svcs., Rockville, Md. Home: 19105 Plummer Dr Germantown MD 20876 Office: Strayer U Online Newington VA Home Phone: 301-524-3385; Office Phone: 301-515-1337. Home Fax: 301-515-1337. Personal E-mail: jerliz56@yahoo.com.

ROBERTSON, JERRY D., lawyer; b. Port Clinton, Ohio, Dec. 16, 1948; s. Edgar N. and Delores E. (Brough) R.; m. Kathryn A. Behlmer, Aug. 1, 1970; children: Matthew, Adam. BS, Bowling Green State U., 1971; JD, U. Toledo, 1974. Bar: Ohio 1974, U.S. Ct. Mil. Appeals 1974, U.S. Dist. Ct. (no. dist.) Ohio 1977, U.S. Supreme Ct. 1980. Pvt. practice, Oak Harbor, Ohio, 1977—. Instr. real estate law Terra tech. Coll., Fremont, Ohio, 1978-82; asst. pros. atty. Ottawa County, Ohio, 1980-84; law dir. Village of Oak Harbor, Ohio, 1982-98; bd. dirs. Luther Home of Mercy, Williston, Ohio; cert. estate planning, trust & probate law specialist, Ohio State Bar Assoc. Capt. U.S. Army, 1974-77. Decorated Meritorious Svc. medal. Mem. ABA, Nat. Network of Estate Planning Attys., Nat. Acad. Elder Law Attys., Ohio Bar Assn., Toledo Estate Planning Coun., Am. Legion. Lutheran. Office: Robertson Law Center 3762 E 127Th Ln Denver CO 80241-3173

ROBERTSON, JOEL THOMAS, railroad executive; b. Milo, Maine, Aug. 30, 1947; s. Paul Russell Robertson and Denice Luella Stevens; m. Bonita Louise Hosford, July 29, 1966 (div. Nov. 1968); m. Patricia Rae Willinski, Mar. 14, 1970 (div. May 1990); children: Jason Thomas, April Dawn Robertson Bishop; m. Marie Paulette Melvin, Dec. 31, 1994; 1 child, Stuart Spencer Stratton. BS, W.Va. State U., 1982; MS, Marshall U., 1986. Cert. safety mgr. World Safety Orgn., 85. Agt. Bangor (Maine) & Aroosook R.R., 1966—70, Can. Pacific Rwy., St. John, NB, 1970—80; hazardous materials inspector Fed. RR Adminstrn., Washington, 1980—2001, hazardous materials specialist, 2001—02; ptnr. Robertson & Assocs., LLC, 2002—; regulatory specialist Am. Honda Co. Inc., 2004—. Transp. cons. Union Carbide Corp., Danbury, Conn., 1989—90; expert witness/accident investigator Collins, Collins & Dinardo, Buffalo, 1989—; bus. devel. cons. Brothers Coal Cons., Charleston, W.Va., 1989—90, TransMar Inc., Spokane, Wash., 1994, Coal Tech. Corp., Bristol, Va., 1989—97; appearance on nat. news program ABC Wide World News Tonight, 1985; interviewed by Tass Soviet News Agy., 89; owner Guest Nat. Soc. of Profl. Engrs., Nat. Press Club, Washington, 1989; founder, devel. dir. Stuart Spencer Stratton Meml. Found., unit of Nat. Heritage Found., 2002—; regional sci. fair judge and scholarship founder for environ. scis. INTEL N.W., 2000—; adj. tech. faculty Marshall U., Transp. Safety Inst., 1987—; adv. U.S. Senate Murray U.S. Dept. State, Volpentest Hammer Tng. Inst., Transportation Safety Security, Richland, Wash.; leader, organizer Multi-Agy. Internat. Transp. Safety-Security Strike Force, 2000; internat. trade and devel. cons. Govt. Cameroon, West Africa; loaned exec. Combined Fed. Campaign, 2001—02; assoc. Oreg. Fed. Bd., 2001—02; mem. exec. potential program USDA Grad. Sch. Leadership, 2002; internat. lectr. and citizen amb. China Assn. of Sci. and Tech., 1989; acting regional adminstr., acting staff dir. U.S. Hazardous Materials, 1994—2002. Contbr. articles to profl. publs. Organizer, master of ceremonies First Joint Chem. Industry/Rwy. Safety Symposium, W.Va., 1985, Celebration of Engring. Career Day, Huntington, W.Va., 1989; sci. advisor Bush White House Space Coun., Washington, 1989. Recipient Commendation, Gov. of W.Va., 1985, Superior Achievement award, U.S. DOT-FRA. Mem.: Am. Soc. Metals, Am. Inst. Hygiene Assn., Soc. Mechanical Engrs., AIChE, Am. Soc. Quality Control, Am. Soc. Safety Engrs., Am. Soc. Profl. Engrs. (exec. affiliate 1983—89), Engrs. Club of Huntington (pres. 1987—88), Kiwanis (pres. West Huntington chpt. 1989—90). Republican. Mem. Lds Ch. Avocations: fund-raising activities, event organizing, photography, travel, writing. Address: 16505 A SE 1st St Ste 285 Vancouver WA 98684 Home: 32154 E Punkin Center Rd Hermiston OR 97838-7510 Office Phone: 360-873-2329. E-mail: joel@safety.specialist.com, cameroon313@aol.com.

ROBERTSON, JOHN ARCHIBALD LAW, nuclear scientist; b. Dundee, Scotland, July 4, 1925; arrived in Can., 1957, naturalized, 1963; s. John Carr and Ellen (Law) R.; m. Betty-Jean Moffatt, June 26, 1954 (dec. Feb. 10, 2007); children: Ean Stuart, Clare Deborah, Fiona Heather. BA, Cambridge U., Eng., 1950, MA, 1953. Sci. officer UK Atomic Energy Authority, Harwell, England, 1950-57; rsch. officer Atomic Energy Can. Ltd., Chalk River, Ont., Canada, 1957-63, head reactor materials br., 1963-70, dir. fuels and materials div., 1970-75, asst. to v.p., 1975-82; dir. program planning Atomic Energy Can. Ltd. (Rsch. Co. Head Office), 1982-85; cons., 1985—. Mem. Atomic Energy Control Bd.'s Adv. Com. on Nuc. Safety, 1988-97. Author: Irradiation Effects in Nuclear Fuels, 1969, Decide the Nuclear Issues for Yourself: Nuclear Need Not Be Unclear, 2000; editor: Jour. Nuclear Materials, 1967-71. Capt. Royal Engrs. Brit. and Indian Armies, 1943—47. Recipient W.B. Lewis medal Can. Nuc. Assn., 1987, W.J. Kroll Zirconium medal W.J. Kroll Inst. for Extractive Metallurgy, 1993, Queen's Golden Jubilee medal, 2004, Edn. and Comm. award Can. Nuc. Assn., 2005. Fellow Royal Soc. Can. Office Phone: 613-584-2765. Personal E-mail: jalrober@magma.ca.

ROBERTSON, JOSEPH E., JR., academic administrator, ophthalmologist, educator; b. Jackson County, Ind., July 24, 1952; s. Joseph E. and Virginia Faye (Baxter) R.; children: Kathryn Faye, Charles Joseph. BS in Neuroscience, cum laude, Yale U., 1974; MD, Ind. U., 1978; MBA, U. Oreg., 1997. Diplomate Am. Bd. Ophthalmology. Intern Bapt. Med. Ctr., Birmingham, Ala., 1978-79; resident Oreg. Health Sci. U., Portland, 1979-82; pvt. practice Vancouver, Wash., 1982-83; fellow Oreg. Health Sci. U./Devers Hosp./Good Samaritan Hosp., Portland, 1983-84; vitreous surgery fellow Steve Charles, M.D., Memphis, 1984-85; asst. prof. Oreg. Health Sci. U., Portland, 1985-92, assoc. prof., 1992-97, prof., chmn. dept. ophthalmology, 1997—, dir. Casey Eye Inst., 1998—2003, interim dean, 2001—02, dean Sch. Medicine, 2003—06, pres., 2006—. Contbr. articles to profl. jours., chpts. to books; editor videotapes. Apptd. mem. Oreg. Commn. for the Blind, 1988-94. Mem. Am. Acad. Ophthalmology (Oreg. rep. to coun. 1992-95, COVE com. 1988-93, skills transfer adv. com. 1994-98, nat. chair and state coord. Diabetes 2000), Oreg. Acad. Ophthalmology (pres. 1990-91), Univ. Med. Group (exec. com. 1997—, v.p. 1998—), Oreg. Med. Assn. Democrat. Presbyterian. Avocations: skiing, windsurfing, snowboarding, hiking, jogging. Office: OHSU Office of Pres 3181 SW Sam Jackson Park Rd Portland OR 97239-3098 also: Casey Eye Inst OHSU 3375 SW Terwilliger Blvd Portland OR 97239 Office Phone: 503-494-3056.

ROBERTSON, JOSEPH EDMOND, grain processing company executive; b. Brownstown, Ind., Feb. 16, 1918; s. Roscoe Melvin and Edith Penina (Shields) R.; m. Virginia Faye Baxter, Nov. 23, 1941; 1 son, Joseph Edmond, Jr. BS, postgrad., Kans. State U., 1940. Cereal chemist Ewing Mill Co., 1940—43, engr. flour milling, 1946—50, feed nutritionist, 1951—59; v.p., sec. Robertson Corp., Brownstown, Ind., 1960—80, pres., 1980—97, chmn., 1997—. Author: On Kilroy's Trail, 1998. Mem. Kans. State U. Varsity Basketball Team, 1937-40; pres. Jackson County (Ind.) Welfare Bd., 1948-52; mem. Ind. Port Commn., 1986-91; mem. Ind. Gov.'s Coun. of Sagamores of the Wabash. Served with USAAF, 1943-45. Named to Hon. Order Ky. Cols.; recipient Brownstown (Ind.) First Lifetime Achievement award, 1999. Mem. Hardwood Plywood Mfrs. Assn. (v.p. affiliate div. 1971-73, 87-88, internat. lectr. forest products industry 1973-97), Am. Assn. Cereal Chemists, Assn. Operative Millers, Am. Legion, Brownstown C. of C. (dir. All Am. city program 1955), Kans. State U. Alumni Assn. (life), Blue Key, Phi Delta Theta, Phi Kappa Phi, Alpha Mu. Clubs: Internat. Travelers Century (L.A.), Circumnavigators Club (N.Y.C.), Elks. Presbyterian. Home: Lake and Forest Club 1268 E Lake Shore Dr PO Box A Brownstown IN 47220 E-mail: robmark@glux.com.

ROBERTSON, KENNETH CARL, music educator; b. Bethany, Mo., Oct. 14, 1963; s. Hal Dean and IRetha Robertson. MusB Edn., Drake U., 1986, MusB Performance, 1986; MusM, Conservatory of Music, Kansas City, Mo., 1988. Cert. Orff- Schulwerk Music Specialist 1999. Organist 1st Christian Ch., Pattonsburg, Mo., 1976—82, Glen Echo Christian Ch., Des Moines, 1982—86, Congl. United Ch. Of Christ, Prairie Village, Kans., 1986—89; organist/choirmaster St. Charles Ch., Gladstone, Mo., 1989—91; organist Pk. Christian Ch., Kansas City, Mo., 1991—99; music tchr. North Kans. City Schs., Kansas City, 1993—. Soloist Drake U. Choir, Des Moines, 1982—86; dance accompanist Alvin Ailey Dance Co., Kansas City, Mo., 1987—87. Singer: (recording) Handel's Messiah, 1983, (radio live performance) Three French Songs - Bernstein, 1984. Recipient Ctrl. Iowa 1st Pl. Music, Yamah Corp. Competition, 1979, 5 #1 music ratings, State of Mo., 1978—82. Mem.: Am. Orff-Schulwerk Assn. Office: Gracemor Elem Sch 5125 N Sycamore Kansas City MO 64119 Office Phone: 816-413-6445. Business E-Mail: krobert1@nkcsd.k12.mo.us.

ROBERTSON, LAVERNE, minister; MS, Nova Southeastern U., 1995; DD, Miracle Theol. Coll. Pastor Mansion Ave. Triumphant Bapt. Ch., Richmond, Va., 2001—04; founder, pres. Va. Triumphant Coll. and Seminary, 2006. Singer: (songs) Freedom Day Has Come. Gospel music writer and performer, Richmond, 1980—99. Named 3rd runner up, Miss Black Richmond Pageant. Office Phone: 804-232-6046. Personal E-mail: laverroberts@aol.com.

ROBERTSON, LEON H., management consultant, educator; b. Atlanta; s. Grady Jospeh and Pearline (Chandler) R. BS in Indsl. Mgmt., Ga. Inst. Tech., 1957, MS, 1959; postgrad., U. Okla.-Norman, 1958, U. Mich., 1961; PhD in Bus. Adminstrn., Ga. State U., 1968. Sr. mgr. mgmt. cons. divsn. Arthur Andersen & Co., Atlanta, 1960-65; prof. bus. adminstrn. Ga. State U., 1965-75; corp. v.p. Tex. Gas Corp., Owensboro, Ky., 1975-78, sr. v.p., 1982-83; chmn., CEO Am. Carriers, Inc., Overland Park, Kans., 1978-88; chmn. bd. dirs. Midwest Coast Transport, Overland Park, 1988-89; prof. mgmt., dir. divsn. bus. adminstrn. U. Mo., Kansas City, 1990-96, prof. Internat. Acad. Programs, 1996-98, dir. Ctr. for Internat. Bus., 1999—. Office: Univ of Mo-Kansas City Henry W Bloch Sch Bus & Pub Admn 5110 Cherry St Kansas City MO 64110-2426 Business E-Mail: robertsonl@umkc.edu.

ROBERTSON, MARIAN ELLA (MARIAN ELLA HALL), small business owner, handwriting analyst; b. Edmonton, Alta., Can., Mar. 3, 1920; d. Orville Arthur and Lucy Hon (Osborn) Hall; m. Howard Chester Robertson, Feb. 7, 1942; children: Elaine, Richard. Student, Willamette U., 1937-39; BS, Western Oreg. State U., 1955. Cert. elem., jr. high. tchr., supt. (life) Oreg.; cert. graphoanalyst. Tchr. pub. schs., Mill City, Albany, Scio and Hillsboro, Oreg., 1940-72; cons. Zaner-Bloser Inc., Columbus, Ohio, 1972-85, assoc. cons., 1985-89; pres. Write-Keys, Scio, 1980-90; owner Lifelines, Jefferson, Oreg., 1991-94. Tchr. Internat. Graphoanalysis Soc., Chgo., 1979; instr. Linn-Benton C.C., 1985-89; del. Oreg. Water Resources Congress at Seaside, 2002; mem. Ptnrs. of the Ams., Costa Rica, 2003.

Master gardener vol. Marion County, Oreg. State U. Extension Svc., 1992; floriculture judge Marion County Fair, 1992; master gardener clinic Oreg. State Fair, 1992; sr. intern 5th Congl. Dist. Oreg., Washington1984, mem. sr. adv. coun.; mem. precinct com. Rep. Ctrl. Com., Linn County, 1986, alt. vice chair, 1986, parliamentarian, 1988—; candidate Oreg. State Legislature, Salem, 1986; del. N.W. Friends Yearly Meeting, Newberg, Oreg., 1990—92; clk. Marion Friends Monthly Meeting, 1992—93. Mem.: Ptnrs. of Ams.-Costa Rica., Port Orford Heritage Soc. (hon.). Republican. Mem. Soc. Of Friends. Avocations: piano, organ, violin, gardening, writing. Home: 2757 Pheasant Ave SE Salem OR 97302-3170 Office Phone: 503-371-5940.

ROBERTSON, MARY AMOS, mathematics educator; b. Fairmont, W.Va., Apr. 10, 1963; d. Robert Newton and Martha Evelyn Amos; m. W Scott Robertson, July 6, 1989. B in Math Edn., Fairmont State U., Fairmont, W.Va., 1984; M in Ednl. Leadership, Nova Southeastern U., Ft. Lauderdale, Fla., 1993. Cert. profl. tchg. Fla., 1986. Tchr. Mononghalia County Sch., Morgantown, W.Va., 1985—86, Sch. Dist. Lee County, Ft. Myers, Fla., 1986—. Mem. Matlacha (Fla.) Hookers, 1998—2006. Named Math Tchr. of Yr., Lee County Sch., 2004—05. Mem.: Lee County Math Coun. (pres. 1996—97), Floridia Coun. Tchrs. Math. (regional dir. 1998—99), Nat. Coun. Tchrs. Math. Methodist. Office: Ft Myers High Sch 2635 Cortez Blvd Fort Myers FL 33901 Home Phone: 239-283-9070; Office Phone: 239-334-2167. Office Fax: 239-334-3095. E-mail: maryar@leeschools.net.

ROBERTSON, MERLE GREENE, art historian, academic administrator; b. Miles City, Mont., Aug. 30, 1913; d. Darrel Irving and Ada Emma (Foote) McCann; m. Wallace McNeill Greene, Dec. 2, 1936 (div. Sept. 1950); children: Barbara Merle Greene Metzler, David Wallace Greene; m. Lawrence William Robertson, Dec. 19, 1966 (dec. May 1981). Student, U. Washington, 1933-35; BA, U. San Francisco, 1952; MFA, U. Guana Guato, Mex., 1963; LHD, Tulane U., 1987. Cert. tchr., Calif. Camp dir. Camp Tapawingo, Sequim, Wash., 1951-53; tchr. San Rafael Mil. Acad., 1952-64; camp dir. Marin County Camp Fire Girls, San Rafael, Calif., 1954-56; expedition dir. Tulane U., New Orleans, 1962—; tchr. Monterey (Calif.) Penninsula Coll., 1974-76, Robert Louis Stevenson Sch., Pebble Beach, Calif., 1967-76; exec. dir. Pre-Columbian Art Rsch. Inst., San Francisco, 1971—. Adj. curator H.M. de Young Meml. Art Mus., San Francisco, 1991—, com. mem. pre-Columbian art, 1990—; rsch. assoc. Middle Am. Rsch. Inst./Tulane U., New Orleans, 1976—, U. Calif. Archaeol. Rsch. Facility, Berkeley, 1982—, Calif. Acad. Scis., San Francisco, 1985—; dir. Archaeol. Recording Maya Art in Mex., Gualemala, Belize, Honduras, 1962—. Author: Sculpture of Palenque, 4 vols., 1983-91, Ancient Maya Relief Sculpture, 1967 (Best Design 1967), (CD-ROMS) Merle Greene Robertson's Rubbings of Maya Sculpture; editor: Palenque Round Table, 10 vols., 1973-95; prin. works include over 4500 rubbings of Maya Sculpture, Merle Greene Robertson Rare Manuscript Archives, Tulane U.; exhbns. including rubbings in most major mus. in US and Europe. Merle Greene Robertson Sch. named in her honor, Chiapas, Mex., 1981; recipient Order of the Aztec Eagle award Mexican Govt., 1994, Orden del Pop award, Guatemala, 2004, Reconocimiento Especial "TOH", Merida, Yue, 2004. Fellow AAAS, The Explorers Club, Soc. for Am. Archaeology; mem. 47th Internat. Cong. Americanists (hon. v.p. 1992), Am. Anthropol. Assn., Assn. de Artistes Mougins. Avocations: travel to exotic countries, painting, hiking. Home and Office: 1100 Sacramento St Apt 1004 San Francisco CA 94108-1918 Personal E-mail: pari-merle@mindspring.com.

ROBERTSON, MICHAEL, Internet company executive; B in Cognitive Sci., U. Calif. San Diego. Founder MR Mac Software, 1994—95, Media Minds, Inc., 1995—96; founder, pres. The Z Co., 1996; founder, CEO, chmn. MP3.com, San Diego, 1998—2001; founder, CEO Linspire, Inc., San Diego, 2001—; CEO SIPphone, 2003—. Cons. San Diego Super Computer Ctr.; cons. in field. Founder Robertson Educational Empowerment Found. (REEF), San Diego, 2002—. Named one of 100 most influential individuals in the music industry BAM Mag. Achievements include established Filez and Websitez. Office: Linspire 9333 Genesee Ave 3rd Fl San Diego CA 92121

ROBERTSON, MICHAEL SWING, minister; b. Boston, July 20, 1935; s. Charles Stuart and Elizabeth (Swing) R.; m. Margaret Filoon, Sept. 17, 1960 (dec. Oct. 1996); children: Michael Swing, Ashlee Whipple, Christopher Filoon, Andrew Stuart; m. Emily Erickson, Feb. 22, 1998. AB, Harvard U., 1957, grad. Advanced Mgmt. Program, 1979. With Robertson Factories, Inc., 1957-80, exec. v.p., 1968-73, pres., 1973-79, chmn. bd., 1979-80; dir. Robertson-Swing Co., 1980—; pres. The Berkley Co. Inc., 1981-90, Reactions Inc., 1985-90; treas. Falmouth Marine Inc., 1981-88; pres., treas. Orchard Computer Inc., 1984-91, chmn., treas., 1991-93; exec. sec. Nat. Assn. Congl. Christian Chs., Oak Creek, Wis., 1991-97; minister Pilgrim Congl. Ch., Taunton, Mass., 2000—02; ch. coord. Cmty. Faith Alliance, Milw., 1997-2000; exec. dir. Cmty. Village, Ltd., 1998-2000, 2003—; pastor Pilgrim Congrl. Ch., Taunton, 2001—02, Urban Ministry Cmty. Bapt. Ch., Milw., 2003, Union Congl. Ch., Braintree, Mass., 2004—06, First Ch. of Squantum, Quincy, Mass., 2006—. V.p. adv. coun. Coll. of Bus. and Industry, Southeastern Mass. U., North Dartmouth, Mass., 1979-91; selectman, Town of Berkley, Mass., 1974-80, chmn. 1979-80; mem. Pres.'s Adv. Com. for Trade Negotiations, 1983-86; bd. dirs. Mass. Easter Seal Soc., 1977-91, pres. 1982-83; bd. dirs. Nat. Easter Seal Soc., 1985-91, Wis. Easter Seal Soc., 1994-95; bd. dirs. Trips for Kids, New Bedford, 2005-, treas., 2007; chmn. Berkley Rep. Town com., 1977-91; Rep. nominee U.S. Senate from Mass., 1976, nominee for Mass. state auditor, 1982; co-chmn. Mass Reagan for Pres. Com., 1980; Bristol County coord. Reagan/Bush campaign; co-chmn. Mass. Dole for Pres. Commn., 1987; chmn. Southeastern Mass. campaign Harvard Coll., 1981; chmn. Friends of Harvard Track, 1986-91; trustee Barnstable County Hosp., 1985-90, chmn., 1988. Mem. Harvard Varsity Club, Falmouth Yacht Club, Harvard Club of Boston, Harvard Bus. Sch. Assn. Boston, Squawtum Yacht Club. Congregationalist. Home: 176 Bellevue Rd Squantum MA 02171 Office: 164 Bellevue Rd Squantum MA 02171 Office Phone: 617-328-6649. Office Fax: 617-328-3391. Personal E-mail: emmyandmike@verizon.net. *Accept responsibility with enthusiasm and gratitude. Our individual freedom is unmatched in history, compelling us to remain true to our heritage and our God.*

ROBERTSON, NED, dentist; b. Rumford, Maine, Mar. 3, 1950; s. Edward Norris and Edith Louise (Kirk) Robertson; m. Susan Elizabeth Valentine, July 24, 2004; 1 child, Olivia; children: Christie Portia, Juliet Melissa(dec.), Jenni Celia, Edward Noah, Jessica Edith. BS in Biology, Antioch Coll., Yellow Springs, Ohio, 1973; MS in Epidemiology, Ohio State U., 1977; DDS, Case Western Res. U., 1983, DMD, 2004. Faculty adv. to med. students Ohio State U., Columbus, 1975-77; rsch. cons. Ohio Dept. Health, Columbus, 1976-77; rsch. assoc. UCLA, 1977; epidemiologic/statis. cons. LA, 1977; medic J & L Steel Corp., Cleve., 1979-84; pvt. practice Cleveland Heights, Ohio, 1983-94, Lyndhurst, Ohio, 1995-2000. Mem. adj. faculty Cuyahoga C.C., Cleve., 1986-88; assoc. prof. Sch. Dentistry Case Western Res. U., 1991-96; asst. prof. Case Western Res. U. Sch. Dentistry, Cleve., 1997-2003; pvt. contractor Indian Health Svc. Dental Clinic, Pine Ridge, S.D., 1999-2000; clin. instr. U. Md. Dental Sch., 1999-00. Pres. Robertson Family Assn. of N.Am., 1986-88. Recipient numerous rsch. grants; named one of Best Dentists in Am., No. Ohio Live mag., 2007. Mem.: ADA, Internat. Congress Oral Implantologists, Am. Acad. Craniofacial Pain, Internat. Assn. for Study of Pain, Greater Cleve. Dental Soc., Ohio Dental Assn., Acad. Gen. Dentistry, Midwest Pain Soc., Acad. Laser Surgery, U.S. Dental Inst., Am. Chronic Pain Assn., Ohio Acad. Gen. Dentistry, Am. Pain Soc., Am. Acad. Pain Mgmt. Avocations: scuba diving, cross country skiing, camping, canoeing, bicycling. Office: 24755 Chagrin Blvd Ste 145 Beachwood OH 44122-5692 Office Phone: 216-468-0041. Business E-Mail: dentalned@aol.com.

ROBERTSON, OSCAR PALMER (BIG O ROBERTSON), chemical company executive, former professional basketball player; b. Charlotte, Tenn., Nov. 24, 1938; BBBA, U. Cin., 1960. Player U.S. Olympic Basketball Team, 1960; basketball player Cin. Royals, 1960-70, Milw. Bucks, 1970-74; founder, pres., CEO, Orchem, Inc., Cin., 1981-1996, Orpack-Stone Corp., Herrin, Ill., 1990—, Orflex Ltd., Cin., 1995—, ORDMS, Marlton, N.J., 1997—. Player NBA Championship Team, 1971. Named Sporting News Coll. Player of Yr., 1958, 59, 60, Sporting News All-Star First Team, 1958, 59, 60, NBA Rookie of Yr., 1961, All NBA First Team, 1961-69; player NBA All Star Games, 1961-72; named MVP, NBA, 1964, MVP in NBA All-Star Games, 1961, 64, 69; named to NBA 35th Anniversary All-Star Team, 1980; elected to Naismith Meml. Basketball Hall of Fame, 1979, Nat. Collegiate Basketball Hall of Fame, 2006. Office: Orchem Corp 4293 Mulhauser Rd Fairfield OH 45014-5450

ROBERTSON, PAT (MARION GORDON ROBERTSON), religious broadcasting executive, university president and chancellor; b. Lexington, Va., Mar. 22, 1930; s. A. Willis and Gladys (Churchill) R.; m. Adelia Elmer; children: Timothy, Elizabeth, Gordon, Ann. BA, Washington and Lee U., 1950; JD, Yale U., 1955; MDiv, N.Y. Theol. Sem., 1959; ThD (hon.), Oral Roberts U., 1983. Ordained minister So. Bapt. Conv., 1961-87. Founder, CEO, chmn. Christian Broadcasting Network, Virginia Beach, Va., 1960—; host 700 Club, 1968—; founder, chancellor, pres. Regent Univ. (formerly CBN Univ.), 1977—; founder, chmn. Operation Blessing Internat. Relief and Devel. Inc., 1978—, Internat. Family Entertainment, Inc., 1990-97, Asia Pacific Media Corp., 1993—; chmn. Starguide Digital Networks, Inc., 1995—, Porchlight Entertainment, Inc., 1995—; founder, pres. The Christian Coalition, 1989—, The Am. Ctr. for Law and Justice, 1990—, also chmn. Bd. dirs. United Va. Bank, Norfolk; mem. Pres. Task Force on Victims of Crime, Washington, 1982. Author: (with Jamie Buckingham) Shout It From the Housetops: The Story of the Founder of the Christian Broadcasting Network, 1972, My Prayer for You, 1977, The Secret Kingdom, 1982, Answers to 200 of Life's Most Probing Questions, 1984, (with William Proctor) Beyond Reason: How Miracles Can Change Your Life, 1984, America's Dates with Destiny, 1986, The Plan, 1989, The New Millennium: 10 Trends that Will Impact Your Family by the Year 2000, 1990, The New World Order, 1991, The Turning Tide: The Fall of Liberalism and the Rise of Common Sense, 1993, The End of the Age, 1995, Six Steps to Spiritual Revival: God's Awesome Power in Your Life, 2002, Bring It On: Tough Questions. Candid Answers, 2002, The Ten Offenses: Reclaim the Blessings of God's Eternal Truth, 2003, Courting Disaster: How the Supreme Court Is Usurping the Power of Congress and the People, 2004, Miracles Can Be Yours Today, 2005 Candidate for Rep. nomination for Pres. U.S., 1988. Served in USMC, 1950—52. Recipient Disting. Merit citation NCCJ, Knesset medallion Israel Pilgrimage Com., Faith and Freedom award Religious Heritage Am., Bronze Halo award So. Calif. Motion Picture Council, Humanitarian award Food for the Hungry, 1982, George Washington Honor medal Freedoms Found. at Valley Forge, 1983, Defender of Israel award Christians Israel Pub. Action Campaign, 1994, John Connor Humanitarian Svc. award Operation Smile Internat., 1994, Cross of Nails award, 2000, The State of Israel Friendship award, Zionist Org. of Am., 2002; named Internat. Clergyman of Yr. Religion in Media, 1981, Man of Yr. Internat. Com. for Goodwill, 1981. Mem. Nat. Religous Broadcasters (bd. dirs. 1973—2006), Kentucky Colonels. Office: The Christian Broadcasting Network 977 Centerville Tpke Virginia Beach VA 23463-7701 also: Regent U 1000 Regent U Dr Virginia Beach VA 23464

ROBERTSON, PAUL FRANCIS, mathematician, educator; b. Galveston, Tex., Aug. 23, 1953; s. Gilfred and Wilda Robertson; m. Ana Cecilia Moreno, May 17, 1988 (div. Nov. 1993); m. Cynthia Arnet Gilford, June 3, 1978 (div. Dec. 1980); children: Chiquita Monique, Paul Alexander, Andrea Celeste. BA in Math., Tex. So. U., Houston, 1975. Cert. tchr. Tex., 1997. Instr. data processing Houston C.C. Sys., 1981; tchr. math., computer literacy Galveston Ind. Sch. Dist., Tex., 1997—99; adj. prof. math. Galveston Coll., Tex., 1999; tchr. math., tech. applications Galveston Cath. Sch., Tex., 1999—2004; adj. prof. math. Galveston Coll., 2004; sub. tchr. Tex. City Ind. Sch. Dist., 2004—05, coord. tech. applications, 2005—. Author (chairperson): (technical writing) Galveston Cath. Sch. Instrnl. Tech. Plan. Recipient Unsung Hero award, Galveston County - The Daily News, 2002, Cert. of Appreciation, Communities in Schs. Galveston, Inc., 2002, Cert. for Outstanding Support, Big Bros. Big Sisters of Gulf Coast, 2002; Four Yr. Acad. Scholarship award, The Moody Found., 1971. Mem.: Nat. Assn. Indsl. Tech., Sheriffs Assn. of Tex., Tex. Libr. Assn. Democrat. Roman Catholic. Avocations: reading, tutoring, volunteering, poetry. Office: 8801 Palmer Hwy 2205 Texas City TX 77591 Office Phone: 409-989-7831. E-mail: tutor_8875@yahoo.com.

ROBERTSON, PAULINE DURRETT, publishing executive; b. Amarillo, Tex., Apr. 17, 1922; d. Walter Lucius and Mary Eddie (Jones) Durrett; m. Roy Lewis Robertson, Dec. 18, 1940; children: Kay Linda Robertson Savage, Kent Lewis, Robyn M. Robertson Turner, Paula Jo Robertson Pierce, Roy Durrett, Laurel Annette Robertson Gibson, Virginia Lee Robertson-Baker, Ellen Robertson Green, Neil Thomas, Carrie Beth. AA, Amarillo Coll., 1969; BA in English Writing, St. Edward's U., Austin, Tex., 1992. Editor project history U.S. Reclamation Bur., Amarillo, 1942-43; editor post newsletter U.S. Army Air Force, Amarillo, 1943-44; freelance writer, 1944-73; writer books of history Staked Plains Press, Canyon, Tex., 1973-77; writer books of history and poetry Paramount Pub. Co., Amarillo, 1977—, pub. house pres., editor, 1977—; tchr. poetry writing and history Amarillo Coll., 1971—2002. Tchr. poetry writing Elderhostel, U. Tex., Austin, 1988-89; writer book revs. Amarillo Globe News, 1968—; editor books, articles, newspapers, 1985-; spkr. in field. Author: (with R.L. Robertson) Panhandle Pilgrimage: Illustrated Tales Tracing History in the Texas Panhandle, 1976, 77, 81, 85, 90, Tascosa: Historic Site in the Texas Panhandle, 1978, 2d edit., 1995, Mystery Woman of Old Tascosa: The Legend of Frenchy McCormick, 1979, 2d edit., 1995, Cowman's Country: Fifty Frontier Ranches in the Texas Panhandle 1876-1887, 1981, 2d edit., 1995, (poetry) Fringe Benefits: Light Verse From Living, 1985, Borrowed Moccasins: Poems From Other Viewpoints, 1986, Field Notes: Poems on Late Light, 1987; editor and designer: Austin Originals: Chats With Colorful Characters by Robyn Turner, 1982, Long Shadows: Indian Leaders Standing in the Path of Manifest Destiny 1600-1900 (by Jack Jackson), 1985; designer, editor: (poetry) Bootsteps: Poems of the West-Then and Now (by Mildred C. Speer), 1978, 83, coauthor, editor: Eve's Version: 150 Women of the Bible, 1983; featured in documentary Story Of A Family on NBC-TV, 1960; mem. writing team Ch. Women United U.S.A., 2001—. Co-founder, sec. Cerebral Palsy Treatment Ctr., Amarillo, 1948-60, Opportunity House, Amarillo, 1970-87; founder, pres. Children's Cottage, Amarillo, 1964-84, Women's Coalition for Change: Focus on Poverty, Amarillo, 1989-95; founder, dir. for underprivileged children Camp Friendship, Ceta Glen, Tex., 1971-74; vol. tutor neighborhood pub. schs., 1992-; chair of elders First Christian Ch., 1979-81; host family Internat. Christian Youth Exch., 1963-64, sending family, 1968, 78; active Potter County Hist. Commn., Tex., 1988-96; pres.-elect Ch. Women United of Tex., 1996-98, pres., 1998-2000; chair Amarillo Mayor's Commn. on Early Childhood Nurture/Neglect, 1997—; nat. del. Christian Ch. Named Amarillo's Family of the Yr., Amarillo Globe-News, 1957, Tex. Merit Mother, Am. Mothers Assn., Boston, 1991, 1995 Woman of the Yr. in Amarillo, Beta Sigma Phi, Amarillo, 1995, Yellow Rose Tex., Gov. Anne Richards, 1991, Mayor's Friend of Young Children, 1999, Tex. Mother of Yr., Am. Mothers Assn., Boston, 2003; named to Amarillo HS Hall Fame, 1998; recipient Tex. Panhandle Disting. Svc. award West Tex. A&M U., Canyon, 1977, Lifetime Career Achievement award Amarillo Women's Network, 1996, Woman of Distinction award Girl Scouts Tex. Plains Coun., 2002. Mem. AAUW, LWV (v.p., Amarillo program chair), Western Writers Am., Acad. Am. Poets, Amarillo Photog. Soc. (publicity com., Salon award 1961—), Panhandle Profl. Writers (pres. 1966—, bd. mem.), Poetry Soc. Tex. (founder. area chpt. 1972, pres. area chpt. 1979-81, Tex. state councilor 1973—), Tex. Tchrs. of Creative Writing, Common Cause (area rep. 1971—). Democrat. Avocations: photography, travel, reading, walking. Home: 124 Wayside Dr Amarillo TX 79106-6425 Office: Paramount Pub Co PO Box 3730 Amarillo TX 79116-3730 E-mail: pdr-rlr@cox.net.

ROBERTSON, PETER JAMES, oil industry executive; b. Edinburgh, Jan. 31, 1947; came to U.S., 1969; s. James Donald and Evelyn Patricia (McNaughton) R.; m. Candace Povey, Dec. 29, 1971; children: James Darrell, Nicole Povey, Emily Jemma. BS in Mech. Engring., Edinburgh U., 1969; MBA, U. Pa., 1971. Refinery engr. Union Oil Co. of Calif., (Chgo.), 1971-72; mcht. banker Noble Grossart Ltd., Edinburgh, 1972-73; fin. analyst Standard Oil Co. of Calif. (Chevron), San Francisco, 1973-78, audit mgr. Europe London, 1978-80; comptr. Chevron Oil Europe, London, 1980-83; asst. comptr. Chevron U.S.A., Inc., San Francisco, 1983-86, comptr., 1987-89, v.p. fin., 1989-91; asst. comptr. Chevron Corp., San Francisco, 1986-87; pres. Warren Petroleum Co., Tulsa, 1991—94; exec. V.P. Chevron U.S.A., 1996—97, pres., 1997—2000; VP Chevron Corp., 1997—2000; pres. Chevron Overseas Petroleum Co., San Ramon, Calif., 2000—02; vice chmn. bd. dir. Chevron/Texaco Corp., 2002—. Bd. dirs. Okla. chpt. The Nature Conservancy, Tulsa area United Way, Indian Nations coun. Boy Scouts Am., Tulsa. Recipient Thouron award Thouron Scholarship Found., U. Pa., 1969-71. Mem. Met. Tulsa C. of C., U.S. Hispanic C. of C. (sr. exec. adv. com. 1990-92), Midcontinent Oil and Gas Assn. Avocations: travel, collecting antique maps, skiing. Office: Chevron/Texaco 6001 Bollinger Canyon Rd San Ramon CA 94583-2324 *

ROBERTSON, RALPH S., secondary school principal; Prin. Richmond Sr. High Sch., Rockingham, N.C. Recipient Blue Ribbon Sch. award U.S. Dept. Edn., 1990-91, Nat. award Dale Parnell Tech. Prep Program of Excellence, 1991; named Prin. of Yr., N.C. Burger King/Nat. Assn. of Secondary Sch. Prin., 1987. Office: US Hwy 1 North PO Box 1748 Rockingham NC 28380-1748 Office Phone: 910-997-9812. E-mail: ralphrobertson@richmond.k12.nc.us.

ROBERTSON, RICHARD EARL, physical chemist, educator; b. Long Beach, Calif., Nov. 12, 1933; s. Earl Austin and A. Isobel (Roberts) R.; m. Joyce W. Conger, Sept. 4, 1955 (div. 1972); children: Christopher, Jill; m. Patricia L. Richmond, Apr. 20, 1974. BA, Occidental Coll., LA, 1955; student, UCLA, 1955-56; PhD, Calif. Inst. Tech., 1960. Phys. chemist rsch. lab. GE, Schenectady, NY, 1960-70; staff scientist Ford Motor Co., Dearborn, Mich., 1970-86; prof. materials sci. and engring. U. Mich., Ann Arbor, 1986—, dir. Macromolecular Sci. and Engring. Ctr., 1995—2000. Contbr. articles to profl. jours. Postdoctoral fellow Washington U., St. Louis, 1959-60. Fellow Am. Phys. Soc.; mem. Am. Chem. Soc., Sigma Xi. Office: U Mich Dept Materials Sci Eng Ann Arbor MI 48109-2136 E-mail: rer@umich.edu.

ROBERTSON, RICHARD L., lawyer; b. Temple, Tex., May 15, 1953; BBA, U. Tex., 1976, JD, 1978. Bar: Tex. 1979. Ptnr. Koons, Fuller, Vanden Eykel & Robertson, P.C. Named one of Best Lawyers in Dallas, D Mag., 2005. Fellow: Tex. Bar Found.; mem.: Dallas Bar Assn., Tex. Bar Assn., Coll. State Bar Tex., Tex. Acad. Family Law Specialists, ABA, Collin County Bar Assn. Office: Koons Fuller Vanden Eykel & Robertson Ste 2200 5700 W Plano Pky Plano TX 75093 Office Phone: 972-769-2727. Office Fax: 972-769-0313. E-mail: Rick@koonsfuller.com. *

ROBERTSON, ROBERT GRAHAM HAMISH, physicist; b. Ottawa, Ont., Can., Oct. 3, 1943; arrived in US, 1971, naturalized, 1993; s. Hugh Douglas and Alice Madeleine (Bell) R.; m. Peggy Lynn Dyer, July 4, 1980; 1 child, Ian. BA, Oxford U., Eng., 1965, MA, 1969; PhD, McMaster U., Can., 1971. Rsch. assoc. Mich. State U., East Lansing, 1971-72, asst. rsch. prof., 1972-73, asst. prof., 1973-78, assoc. prof., 1978-81, prof., 1981-82; mem. staff Los Alamos (N.Mex.) Nat. Lab., 1981—, fellow, 1988—; prof. U. Washington, Seattle, 1994—; sci. dir. Ctr. for Exptl. Nuc. Physics and Astrophysics, 2000—. Rsch. assoc. Princeton U., NJ, 1975—76; vis. scientist Argonne Nat. Lab, Ill., 1979, Chalk River Nuc. Labs., Ont., Canada, 1980; dir. Sudbur Neutrino Obs., 2003. Contbr. over 60 articles to profl. jours. Alfred P. Sloan Found. fellow Mich. State U., 1976; Trevelyan scholar Eng., 1962-65, NRC scholar McMaster U., 1965-69, Oriel Coll. scholar, 1962-65. Fellow Am. Phys. Soc. (chair divsn. nuclear physics 2000, Tom W. Bonner prize 1997), Inst. Physics of Eng., Am. Acad. Arts and Scis.; mem. NAS, Can. Assn. Physicists. Achievements include first observation of nuclear isobaric quintet; development of technique for precise measurement of neutrino mass; determination of Lithium-6 synthesis in early universe; demonstration of neutrino mass, oscillations with Sudbury Neutrino Obs. Home Phone: 425-743-7468. E-mail: rghr@u.washington.eu.

ROBERTSON, ROBIN ALAYNE, headmaster, anthropologist; b. Tex. B, U. Penn.; M in Anthropology, PhD in Anthropology, Harvard U. Former asst. prof. So. Methodist U., former assoc. dean for gen. ed., 1984—90; head of sch. Emma Willard Sch., Troy, NY, 1990—99, Milton Acad., Milton, Mass., 1999—. Trustee-at-large CASE; bd. v.p. Nat. Coalition of Girls' Schools, 1994—; mem. pres. council Sage Colleges, Troy, NY. Mem. Troy Redevelopment Found., 1994—, pres., 1995—96. Office: Milton Acad 170 Centre St Milton MA 02186 E-mail: robin_robertson@milton.edu. *

ROBERTSON, ROSE MARIE, cardiologist, educator; b. Detroit, May 15, 1945; d. Joseph Michael and Rose Marie (Pink) Stevens; m. David Robertson, Oct. 31, 1978; 1 child, Rose Marie. BA, Manhattanville Coll., 1966; MD, Harvard Med. Sch., 1970. Diplomate Nat. Bd. Medicine, 1971, Am. Bd. Internal Medicine, 1974, Cardiovascular Medicine, 1975. Intern in medicine Mass. Gen. Hosp., Boston, 1970-71, resident in medicine, 1970-72; fellow in cardiovasc. medicine Johns Hopkins Med. Sch., Balt., 1973-75, asst. prof. medicine, 1976—77, Vanderbilt U. Med. Ctr., Nashville, 1975-82, assoc. prof. medicine, 1982-89, dir. cardiovasc. tng. program, 1990—2000, assoc. dir. cardiology, 1987—2000, prof. medicine, 1989—. Mem. adv. bd. Robert Wood Johnson Found., 1990-, chair, 2003-; mem. adv. bd. Assn. for Patient-Oriented Rsch.; mem. cardiovasc. study sect. NIH, Bethesda, Md., 1993-97; invited spkr., lectr. Contbr. articles to profl. jours., chpts. to books. Fellow Am. Coll. Cardiology, Am. Heart Assn. (pres. 2000-01, chief sci. officer 2003-), European Soc. Cardiology; mem. Am. Autonomic Soc., Am. Fedn. for Clin. Rsch., Am. Soc. Clin. Investigation, Am. Clin. and Climatol. Assn., Assn. Univ. Cardiologists. Home: 4003 Newman Pl Nashville TN 37204-4308 Office: 7272 Greenville Ave Dallas TX 75240 Office Phone: 214-706-1295. E-mail: rosemarie.robertson@heart.org.

ROBERTSON, SAMUEL LUTHER, JR., psychotherapist, educator; b. Houston, Apr. 28, 1940; s. Sam L. and Portia Louise (Burns) R.; children: Samuel Luther IV, Sean Lee (dec.), Ryan William, Susan Elizabeth (dec.), Henry Philmore. BS, McMurry U., 1969; MA, Hardin-Simmons U., 1973; PhD, U. Tex., 1993. Cert. tchr., adminstr., counselor, Tex.; lic. chem. dependency counselor, Tex., lic. clin. mental health counselor, N. Mex. Instr., coach, athletic dir. Tex. and La. schs., 1969-94; social worker, supr. Children's Protective Svcs., Abilene, Tex., 1978-79; instr., adminstr.

Harlandale Sch. Dist., San Antonio, 1980-84, 87-90; adminstr. night sch. Harlandale Ind. Sch. Dist., San Antonio, 1988-89; instr. Edgewood Ind. Sch. Dist., San Antonio, 1985-87; developer, instr., integrated unit program San Antonio, 1990—; CEO The Educative Inst., San Antonio, 1992—. CEO Educative Therapeutic Processes, 1972—; co-founder, dir. Inst. Orgnl. Personal Devel.; mem. faculty writing program U. Tex., San Antonio, 2000—, founder, dir. Recovery Ctr., 2004-05. Author: (play) The Challenged, 1965, Dream Poems, 1998; (poem) Trains in the Night, 1969; (screenplay) Tom & Jane, 2000; dir. (film) Tom & Jane, 2003. State co-chmn. Youth for Kennedy-Johnson, Tex., 1960; mem. W. Tex. Dem. Steering Com., Abilene, 1962-63; founding dir. Way Off Broadway Cmty. Theater, Eagle Pass, Tex., 1971-72; founding bd. dirs. Battered Women's Shelter, Abilene, 1978-79; v.p. bd. dirs. Mental Health Assn., San Antonio, 1980-83, Palmer Drug Abuse Program, San Antonio, 1985-87; pres., bd. dirs. Alcoholic Rehab. Ctr., 1985-86, 1987-92; bd. mem., v.p. Woman at the Well, 2006—; vice-chmn. Civilian and Mil. Addictive Programs, San Antonio, 1991-92; author, implementer Cmty. Vitalization Program, 1994—; mem. vestry St. George Episc. Ch., mem. day sch. bd., 1999-02; stds. chair com. Tex. Certification Bd. Addiction Profls., chmn. 1999-01. Named Tchr. of Yr. Southside Ind. Sch. Dist., San Antonio, 1970-71, Harlandale Alternative Ctr., San Antonio, 1987-88; Vol. of Yr., Mental Health Assn., San Antonio, 1982, Alcoholic Rehab. Ctr., San Antonio, 1992-93; Businessman of Yr., 2003. Mem. ACA, NEA, Am. Mental Health Counseling Assn., Tex. State Tchrs. Assn., Am. Ednl. Rsch. Assn., Am. Assn. Sch. Adminstrs. (mem. exec. com.), Internat. Consortium Reciprocity Commn. Nat. Alcoholism and Drug Abuse Counselors, N.Mex. Mental Health Counselors Assn., N.Mex. Profl. Counselors Assn., Phi Kappa Phi, Kappa Delta Pi. Episcopalian. Avocations: reading, writing, travel, theater, sports. Office: Educative Therapeutic Processes 339 E Hildebrand Ave San Antonio TX 78212-2412 Office Phone: 210-828-9919. Personal E-mail: samdr9@yahoo.com. *I have participated in my life, my family's life, and my community's life in a responsible fashion through the Grace of God.*

ROBERTSON, STERLING CLIFTON, music educator, musician; b. Tientsin, Tiangjin, China, Jan. 22, 1928; arrived in U.S., 1932; s. Sterling Clifton and Mary Letitia (Grimes) Robertson. Student, Tex. Christian U., Ft. Worth, 1945—47, U. Tex., 1948—50, Julliard Sch. Music, NYC, 1952—53, Columbia U., 1952—53, Royaumont-12th Century Monastery-Libr. and Found. Artists; grad., Ft. Worth Conservatory Music, 1945. Tchr. piano, NYC, 1950—70, San Antonio, 1970—. Staff pianist Four Seasons Hotels, San Antonio, Hyatt Regency, San Antonio, Wyndham-St. Anthony, San Antonio; concert pianist Carnegie Hall, 1961, 63, Royal Danish Ballet, Royal Danish Ballet, Columbia Artist, 1961, Boston Music Ctr. (Music Circus), Ted Shawn's Jacob's Pillow. Grantee for piano study with George Copeland, Fairfield Found. and William Hale Harkness/Rebekah Harkness, 1952—53. Democrat. Avocations: theater, films, art. Mailing: 314 Bryn Mawr Dr San Antonio TX 78209

ROBERTSON, THOMAS SINCLAIR, dean, marketing educator; b. Scotland, Nov. 16, 1942; s. Thomas C. and Ann Gorman (Mundie) R.; m. Diana S. Conway, June 18, 1966; children: Brian, Ashley, Alexandra BA, Wayne State U., Detroit, 1963; MA, PhD, Northwestern U., 1966. Asst. prof. mktg. UCLA, 1966-68, Harvard U., 1968-71; prof. mktg. Wharton Sch., U. Pa., 1971, Pomerantz prof. mktg., chmn. mktg. dept., 1978-84, assoc. dean, 1984—88, dean, 2007—; assoc. dean London Bus. Sch., 1994-98; dean Goizueta Bus. Sch., Emory U., Atlanta, 1998—2004, Asa Griggs Candler prof. mktg.; spl. asst. to pres. for internat. strategy Emory U., Atlanta, 2005, exec. dir. Inst. Devel. Nations. Bd. dirs. Profit Recovery Group. Author: Innovative Behavior and Communication, 1971, Televised Medicine Advertising and Children, 1979, Consumer Behavior, 1984, Handbook of Consumer Behavior, 1991. Grantee NSF NIH. Mem. Am. Mktg. Assn., Assn. Consumer Rsch., Cherokee Town Club, Commerce Club. Republican. Office: Wharton Sch, U Pa Office of Dean 3733 Spruce St Philadelphia PA 19104 *

ROBERTSON, TIMOTHY JOEL, statistician, educator; b. Denver, Oct. 4, 1937; s. Flavel P. and Helen C. (Oliver) Girdner; m. Joan K. Slater, Aug. 18, 1959; children— Kelly, Jana, Doug, Mike BA in Math., U. Mo., 1959, MS in Math., 1961, PhD in Stats., 1966. Asst. prof. Cornell Coll., Mt. Vernon, Iowa, 1961-63; prof. stats. U. Iowa, Iowa City, 1965—2004, prof. emeritus, 2004—. Vis. prof. U. N.C., Chapel Hill, 1974-75, U. Calif.-Davis, 1983-84; Eugene Lukacs Disting. vis. prof. Bowling Green State U., 1991-92; vis. lectr. Com. Pres. Statis. Soc., 1971-74. Author: (with F.T. Wright and R.L. Dykstra) Order Restricted Statistical Inference; assoc. editor Am. Math. Monthly, 1977-81; mem. editl. bd. Comms. in Stats., 1981-92; assoc. editor Jour. Am. Statis. Assn., 1990-96; contbr. numerous articles to profl. jours. Recipient Collegiate Teaching award U. Iowa, 1990. Fellow Am. Statis. Assn. (council 1974-75), Inst. Math. Stats., Internat. Statis. Inst.; mem. Math. Assn. Am., Sigma Xi, Sierra Club Democrat. Avocations: canoeing, camping, bicycling, walking. Home: 673 Garfield Rd West Branch IA 52358-8574 Office: Univ Iowa Dept Stats/Actuarial Sci Iowa City IA 52242 Home Phone: 319-643-3118; Office Phone: 319-335-2019. Personal E-mail: rttincity@aol.com.

ROBERTSON, WILLIAM OSBORNE, physician; b. NYC, Nov. 24, 1925; s. William Osborne and Barbara Konvalinka (Bennett) R.; m. Barbara Foster Simpson, Feb. 23, 1952; children: Kathy, Lynn, Kerry, Douglas, Andrew. BA, U. Rochester, NY, 1946, MD, 1949. Intern Strong Meml. Hosp., Rochester, NY, 1949-51, resident, 1951-52, Grace New Haven Hosp., 1954-56; acting med. dir. Ross Labs., Columbus, Ohio, 1956-59; mem. faculty Ohio State Coll. Medicine, 1956-63, assoc. prof. pediatrics, 1961-63; mem. faculty dept. pediatrics U. Wash., Seattle, 1963—, prof., 1972—, assoc. dean, 1967-72, med. dir., 1963-67, acting chmn. dept. pediatrics, 1972-73, 80-84, head div. ambulatory pediatrics, 1975-77, 78-79; dir. med. edn. div. Children's Orthopedic Hosp., 1971-90, med. dir., poison control ctr., 1971—. Mem. staffs Children's, Harborview, Univ. hosps.; mem. advisory com., chmn. Wash. Alaska Regional Med. Program; bd. dirs. Wash. Med. Edn. and Research Found., 1968-73 Contbr. articles to profl. publs. Served with USNR, 1943-45, 52-54. Mem. Am. Acad. Pediatrics (chmn. edn. com. 1971-73, med. liability com. 1985-90, chmn. task force on quality assurance 1988-92), Am. Clin. Acad. Toxicology, King County Med. Soc. (pres. 1971-72), Wash. State Med. Assn. (pres. 1975-76), Am. Assn. Poison Control Ctrs. (pres. 1988-90), Phi Beta Kappa, Alpha Omega Alpha, Am. Coll. Med. Toxicology. Home: 18724 40th Pl NE Seattle WA 98155-2806 Office: Wash Poison Ctr 155 NE 100th St Seattle WA 98125 Home Phone: 206-364-4544; Office Phone: 206-517-2356. E-mail: mryuk@wapc.org.

ROBERTSON, WILLIAM WITHERS, lawyer; b. Morristown, NJ, Nov. 3, 1941; s. Thomas Withers and Jessie (Swain) R.; m. Elizabeth Jeanne Robertson; children: Barbara Ellen Richmond, William Withers, Jr., Jessie Swain Wilt. BA, Rutgers U., 1964, LL.B., 1967. Bar: N.J. 1968. Law sec. to judge Superior Ct. N.J., 1967-68; asst. U.S. atty., 1972-76; 1st asst. U.S. atty., 1978-80; U.S. atty. Dist. N.J., 1980-81; chief Newark Organized Crime Strike Force, 1976-78; ptnr. Hannoch Weisman, Roseland, NJ, 1981-99, Robertson, Freilich, Bruno & Cohen, LLC, Newark, 1999—. Mng. editor: Rutgers Law Rev., 1966—67. Trustee Rutgers U., 1984-88. Served to capt. JAGC USAR, 1968-72. Mem. Nat. Assn. Former U.S. Attys. (bd. dirs. 1990-93, 2005-, pres. 2002-2003), Rutgers U. Law Sch. Alumni Assn. (pres. 1990-91), Rutgers U. Alumni Fedn. (pres. 1981-83). Office: Robertson Freilich et al 1 Riverfront Plz Newark NJ 07102-5401 Home Phone: 973-538-3156; Office Phone: 973-848-2100. Business E-Mail: wrobertson@rfbclaw.com.

ROBERTSON, WILLIAM WRIGHT, JR., orthopedist, educator; b. Mayfield, Ky., Dec. 26, 1946; m. Karel Virginia Dierks, Jan. 26, 1974. BA, Rhodes Coll., 1968; MD, Vanderbilt U., 1972; MBA, Geo Washington U., 2000. Intern U. Calif., San Diego, 1972-73, resident in orthop. surgery, 1975-76, Vanderbilt U., Nashville, 1976-79; asst. prof. orthop. Tex. Tech U., Lubbock, 1979-86; assoc. prof. U. Pa., Phila., 1986-90; prof. orthop. surgery George Washington U., Washington, 1990-2000; chmn. pediat. orthop. Children's Nat. Med. Ctr., Washington, 1990-99. Field rep. accreditation coun. grad. med. edn. Fellow Am. Acad. Orthop. Surgeons, Am. Orthop. Assn., Pediat. Orthop. Soc. (bd. dirs. 1993-96—). Avocations: gardening, music. Office: Accreditation Coun Grad Med Edn 515 N State St Chicago IL 60610 Home Phone: 301-718-7867. Business E-Mail: wrobertson@acgme.org.

ROBERTSON, WYNDHAM GAY, university official, journalist; b. Salisbury, NC, Sept. 25, 1937; d. Julian Hart and Blanche Williamson (Spencer) R. AB in Econs., Hollins Coll., Roanoke, Va., 1958. Rsch. asst. Standard Oil Co., NYC, 1958-61; rschr. Fortune Mag., NYC, 1961-67, assoc. editor, 1968-74, bd. of editors, 1974-81, asst. mng. editor, 1981-86; bus. editor Time Mag., NYC, 1982-83; v.p. comm. U. N.C., Chapel Hill, 1986-96. Contbr. numerous articles to Fortune Mag. Trustee Thomas S. Kenan Inst. for the Arts, Hollins U. Recipient Gerald M. Loeb Achievement award, U. of Conn., 1972. Mem. Phi Beta Kappa. Episcopalian.

ROBERTS-RAMSBOTHAM, HAZEL RUTH, piano educator; b. Graham, Tex., Apr. 1, 1930; d. John Charles and Daisy Mae (Glosup) Roby; m. Quentin Cyrus Roberts, Sept. 4, 1949 (div. June 1977); children: Roma Ruth, Randall Ray, Ronda Renee, Ronald Roy, Ronelda Ree; m. Elwyn Clare Ramsbotham, Sept. 30, 1990. BA, U. Wyo., 1959; MusM, U. Idaho, 1967. Cert. Music Tchrs. Nat. Assn. Tchr. Las Vegas Pub. Schs., 1955-56, Bosler (Wyo.) Pub. Sch., 1956-57, 58-59, Cowdrey (Colo.) Pub. Sch., 1957-58, Lander (Wyo.) Pub. Sch., 1959-60; pvt. practice piano instr. Roberts Studio, Lander, 1959-80, Aurora, Colo., 1980-90, Roberts Ramsbotham Studio, Aurora, Colo., 1990—. Recipient Cmty. Svc. award Lander Seventh Day Adventist Ch., 1978, Colo. Music Tchr. Yr., Colo. Music Tchrs. Assn., 2006. Mem. Nat. Piano Guild (organizer Lander Ctr., 1962-80, Aurora Ctr., 1981—), Am. Coll. Musicians, Wyo. Music Tchrs. Assn. (from treas. to pres. 1974-80), Lander Music Tchrs. Assn. (pres., others 1967-79), Aurora Music Tchrs. Assn. (pres., others 1980—). Republican. Mem. Ch. of Christ. Avocations: gardening, travel, crocheting, quilting. Home: 377 S Wheeling Way Aurora CO 80012-2448

ROBFOGEL, SUSAN SALITAN, lawyer; b. Rochester, NY, Apr. 4, 1943; d. Victor and Janet (Rosenthal) Salitan; m. Nathan Joshua Robfogel, July 12, 1965; children: Jacob Morris, Samuel Salitan. BA cum laude, Smith Coll., 1964; JD, Cornell U., 1967. Bar: N.Y.1967, U.S. Dist. Ct. (we. dist.) 1968, U.S. Ct. Appeals (2d cir.) 1971, U.S. Supreme Ct. 1971, U.S. Dist. Ct. (no. dist.) 1974, D.C. 1982. From asst. corp. counsel to sr. asst. corp. counsel City of Rochester, NY, 1967-70; assoc. Harris, Beach & Wilcox, Rochester, 1970-75; ptnr. Harris, Beach, Wilcox, Rubin & Levey, Rochester, 1975-85, Nixon, Peabody, LLP, Rochester and NYC, 1985—; chair bd. Office of Compliance, Washington, 1999—. Panel mem., Fed. Svc. Impasses Panel, Washington, 1983-94; mem., past chair Data Protection Rev. Bd., Albany, N.Y., 1984-2007. Recipient Brockport Coll. Found. Community award, 1989. Fellow Am. Bar Found., N.Y. State Bar Found., Coll. Labor and Employment Lawyers; mem. ABA, N.Y. State Bar Assn., Washington D.C. Bar Assn., Monroe County Bar Assn. (Rodenbeck award 1988). Office: 437 Madison Ave New York NY 10022-7001 Office Phone: 212-940-3116. Business E-Mail: srobfogel@nixonpeabody.com.

ROBILLARD, JEAN EUGENE, dean, educator; b. Montreal, 1943; m. Renee Robillard. BA, U. Montreal, 1964, MD, 1968. Pediat. residency Saint Justine Hosp., Montreal, 1969—72; pediat. nephrology fellowship UCLA Med. Ctr., Los Angeles, 1972—73, U. Iowa Med. Ctr., Iowa City, 1973—74; asst. prof., dept. pediat. U. Montreal Coll. Med., 1975—76; asst. prof. Dept. Pediat., Coll. Med., U. Iowa, 1974—75, 1976—78, assoc. prof., 1978—82, dir. nephrology div., 1976—96, prof., 1982—96, vice chmn.; chief pediat. U. Mich., Ann Arbor, 1996—2003; physician-in-chief C.S. Mott Children's Hosp., 1996—2003; dean Roy J. and Lucille A. Carver Coll Medicine, U. Iowa, 2003—. Editl. bd. Jour. Pediat., 2001—; bd. dirs. Am. Bd. Pediat., 2001—, chmn. bd. dirs., 2006—. Author of over 220 sci. papers. Recipient Disting. Alumni Award for Achievement, U. Iowa, 2002. Fellow: Coun. for High Blood Pressure Rsch., Am. Heart Assn., Royal Coll. Physicians & Surgeons; mem.: Assn. Med. Sch. Pediat. Dept. Chairs, Inc., Am. Soc. Transplant Physicians, The Perinatal Rsch. Soc., Soc. for Gynecologic Investigation, Am. Physiol. Soc., Am. Assn. for Advancement Sci. (fellow 1999), Am. Soc. Pediat. Nephrology (pres. 1994—95), Soc. Pediat. Rsch., Am. Heart Assn., Am. Soc. Nephrology, Internat. Soc. Nephrology, Internat. Pediat. Nephrology Assn., Midwest Soc. Pediat. Rsch. (Founder's Award 2002), Am. Acad. Pediat., Am Pediat. Soc. Office: Roy J & Lucille A Carver Coll Med 200 CMAB Iowa City IA 52242

ROBIN, ALAN JAY, lawyer; b. Norwich, Conn., Oct. 8, 1950; s. Louis and Rose (Rutchik) R.; m. Jean D. Wizig, July 15, 1973; children: Jeffrey Scott, Ross Michael. BBA, U. Tex., 1972, JD, 1975. Bar: Tex. 1975, U.S. Dist. Ct. (so. dist.) Tex., U.S. Tax Ct., U.S. Ct. Appeals (5th cir.), U.S. Ct. Claims. Assoc. Vinson & Elkins LLP, Houston, 1975-82, ptnr., 1983—, head Employee Benefits and Exec. Compensation Sect. Mem. Houston Bar Assn., Tex. Soc. CPAs, Order of Coif, Beta Alpha Psi, Beta Gamma Sigma, Phi Kappa Phi. Home: 11635 Arrowwood Cir Houston TX 77063-1401 Office: Vinson & Elkins First City Tower 1001 Fannin St Ste 2300 Houston TX 77002-6706 E-mail: arobin@velaw.com.

ROBIN, CLARA NELL (CLAIRE ROBIN), English language educator; b. Harrisonburg, Va., Feb. 19, 1945; d. Robert Franklin and Marguerite Ausherman (Long) Wampler; m. Phil Camden Branner, June 10, 1967 (div. May 1984); m. John Charles Robin, Nov. 22, 1984 (div. Dec. 1990) BA English, Mary Washington Coll., 1967; MA English, James Madison U., 1974; postgrad., Jesus Coll., Cambridge, Eng., 1982, Princeton U., 1985—86, Auburn U., 1988, U. No. Tex., 1990—91. Cert. tchr. English, French, master cert., Tex. Tchr. 7th grade John C. Myers Intermediate Sch., Broadway, Va., 1967—68; tchr. 10th grade Waynesville H.S., Mo., 1968—70; tchr. 6th, 7th, 8th grades Mary Mount Jr. H.S., Santa Barbara, Calif., 1970—72; tchr. 9th grade Forest Meadow Jr. H.S. Richardson Ind. Sch. Dist., Tex., 1972—78, tchr. 10th grade Lake Highlands H.S., 1972—84; tchr. 11th, 12th grades Burleson H.S. Burleson Ind. Sch. Dist., Tex., 1986—2003; tchr. 9th and 10th grade English Ft. Worth Country Day Sch., 2003—. Instr. composition Hill Coll., 1989-90 Contbg. author: (book revs.) English Jour., 1989-94, (lit. criticism) Eric, 1993 Vol. Dallas Theater Cir., 1990—96; active Kimbell Art Mus., Ft. Worth, 1990—, Modern Art Mus., Ft. Worth, 1992—, KERA Pub. TV, Dallas, 1990—, Amon Carter Mus., Ft. Worth, 2001—. Fellow NEH, 1988, 89, 92, 95, Fulbright-Hays Summer Seminar Abroad, 1991; ind. study grantee Coun. Basic Edn., 1990; recipient Chpt. Achievement award Epsilon Nu Delta Kappa Gamma, 1993, Hon. Mention Tex. Outstanding Tchg. of Humanities award, 1995, Burleson Ind. Sch. Dist., Campus Ednl. Improvement Com., 1997-2000, Dist. Ednl. Improvement Com., 1998-2001 Mem.: Tex. State Reading Assn., Nat. Coun. Tchrs. English (spring conf. presenter 2000, 2002), Epsilon Nu of Delta Kappa Gamma (1st v.p. 1988—94, v.p. 1992—94, profl. affairs com. 1996—98, comms. chair 1998—). Avocations: bicycling, travel, reading, writing, landscaping. Home: 4009 W 6th St Fort Worth TX 76107-1619 Office: Ft Worth County Day Sch 4200 Country Day Ln Fort Worth TX 76109-4299 Office Phone: 817-302-3203 ext. 102. Personal E-mail: crbkrd@aol.com. Business E-Mail: crobin@fwcds.org.

ROBINETT, BETTY WALLACE, linguist, educator; b. Detroit, June 23, 1919; d. Henry Guy and Beulah (Reid) Wallace; m. Ralph F. Robinett, Apr. 10, 1952 (dec. div. 1960); 1 child, Richard Wallace. BA, Wayne State U., 1940; MA, U. Mich., 1941, PhD, 1951. Instr., adminstrv. asst. English Lang. Inst., U. Mich., Ann Arbor, 1945-50; cons. Dept. Edn., San Juan, P.R., 1950-51, 52-57; lectr. English, U. Mich., 1951-52, 55-56; asso. prof. English InterAm. U., San German, P.R., 1957-59; asst. prof. English and linguistics Ball State U., Muncie, Ind., 1959-63, assoc. prof. English and linguistics, 1963-67, prof., 1967-68; prof. dept. linguistics U. Minn., Mpls., 1968-88, dir. program in English as a second lang., 1968-80, acting asst. v.p. acad. affairs, 1979-80, asst. v.p. acad. affairs, 1980-84, assoc. v.p. acad. affairs, 1984-88, prof. emerita, 1988, Morse alumni disting. tchg. prof. emerita, 1996; chmn. Univ. Senate Consultative Com., 1977-78. Vis. prof. Pa. State U., 1994-95; chmn. adv. panel on English tchg. USIA, 1988-93. Author: (with C.H. Prator) Manual of American English Pronunciation, 1972, 4th edit., 1985, Teaching English to Speakers of Other Languages, Substance and Technique, 1978, (with J. Schachter) Second Language Learning: Contrastive Analysis, Error Analysis and Related Aspects, 1983, (with Virginia F. Allen) Easy Latin Crossword Puzzles: Quid Pro Quo, 1999, Easy French Crossword Puzzles: Le mot Juste, 2002; editor Tesol Quar., 1967-72. Internat. Programs travel grantee, 1972, 77; recipient Morse-Amoco award for Excellence in Teaching, 1977 Mem. Tchrs. English to Speakers of Other Langs. (pres. 1974, James Alatis Svc. award 1990), Assn. Tchrs. ESL (chmn. 1976-77), Am. Assn. Applied Linguistics (v.p., pres. 1980-82), Linguistic Soc. Am. (life). Home: 1936 Park Forest Ave State College PA 16803-1329 E-mail: brobin4049@aol.com.

ROBINOV, JEFF, film company executive; Literary agent Internat. Creative Mgmt., 1992—97; with Warner Bros. Pictures, 1997—, exec. v.p. prodn., pres. prodn., 2002—. Exec. prodr.: (films) On Deadly Ground, 1994. Office: Warner Bros Entertainment Inc 4000 Warner Blvd Burbank CA 91522 Office Phone: 818-954-6000.

ROBINOWITZ, CAROLYN BAUER, psychiatrist, educator, director; b. Bklyn., July 15, 1938; d. Milton Leonard and Marcia (Wexler) Bauer; m. Max Robinowitz, June 10, 1962; children: Mark, David AB, Wellesley Coll., 1959; MD, Washington U., 1964. Diplomate Am. Bd. Psychiatry and Neurology. Chief physician tng. NIMH, Bethesda, Md., 1968-70; dir. pediatric liaison U. Miami Sch. Medicine, Fla., 1970-72, dir. child psychiatry tng., 1971-72; dir. edn. George Washington U. Sch. Medicine, Washington, 1972-74; project dir. Psychiatrist as Tchr., Washington, 1973-75; dep. med. dir. Am. Psychiat. Assn., Washington, 1976-86, dir. Office Edn., 1976-87, sr. dep. med. dir., 1986-94, COO, 1986-94, treas., 2004—05, sec.-treas., 2005—06, pres.-elect, 2006—07, pres., 2007—. Assoc. dean Georgetown U. Sch. Medicine, 1995—98, dean, 1998—2000, lectr., 1976—82, professorial lectr., 1982—94, prof., 1995—2000, clin. prof., 2000—; dir. Am. Bd. Psychiatry and Neurology, Evanston, Ill., 1979—86, sec., 1984, v.p., 85, pres., 86; clin. prof. psychiatry and behavioral scis., child health and devel. George Washington U., 1984—98, 2001—; professorial lectr. Uniformed Svcs. U. of Health Scis., 1986—. Editor: Women in Context, 1976; contbr. articles to jours., chpts. to books Admissions com. Wellesley Coll. Club, Washington, 1983-84. Served with USPHS, 1966-69. Recipient NIMH Mental Health Career Devel. award, 1966-70, NIMH grantee, 1974-94. Fellow Am. Psychiat. Assn. (Disting. Svc. award 1991, Vestermark award 1995, Adminstrv. Psychiatry award 1999), Am. Coll. Psychiatrists (bd. dirs. 1993-96, 1st v.p. 1996-97, pres. 1999-00, past pres. 2000-04, sec. gen. 2005—07, Bowis award 1994, Disting. Svc. award 2001); mem. AMA (coun. psychiatry sect. 2000-, coun. on sci. affairs 2001-05, coun. on sci. and pub. health 2005—), Assn. for Acad. Psychiatry (disting. life fellow, pres. 1994-95, dir. 1992-96, 03-06, Lifetime Achievement award 2003), Group for Advancement of Psychiatry (dir. 1982-84, pres. 1989-91), Coun. Med. Splty. Socs. (dir. 1977-82, pres. 1981-82). Office: #514 5225 Connecticut Ave NW Washington DC 20015 Home Phone: 301-229-9252, 202-270-9252; Office Phone: 202-237-1466. E-mail: cbrobinowitzmd@usa.net.

ROBINS, CRAIG, construction executive; b. Miami Beach, Fla., 1963; BA, U. of Michigan, 1984; grad., U. Miami Law Sch., 1987. Pres. Dacra Devel., 1987—; founder Bridge House, 1994. Founder, chmn. Anaphiel Found.; vice-chmn. Wolfsonian-Florida Internat. Univ. Mus. adv. bd.; mem. bd. of trustees Hirshhorn Mus. and Sculpture Garden, Miami Art Mus.; mem. trustee com. Architecture and Design at the Mus. of Modern Art; mem. bd. dir. Colonial Bank; investor Thorium Power, Inc. Recipient Design Patron Award, Smithsonian Inst. Cooper-Hewitt Nat. Design Mus., 2006. Mem.: Yale Sch. of Architecture Dean's Coun., Inaugural Nat. Adv. Coun. of the Mayor of Miami's Inst. on City Design. Office: Dacra Devel 3841 NE 2nd Ave Ste 400 Miami FL 33137 Office Phone: 305-531-8700. E-mail: info@craigrobins.com.

ROBINS, JOEL, import/export company executive; Pres. Robbins Trading Co., Chgo., 1983—. Office: Robbins Trading Co 8700 W Bryn Mawr Ave Ste 760 Chicago IL 60631-3512

ROBINS, LEE NELKEN, medical educator; b. New Orleans, Aug. 29, 1922; d. Abe and Leona (Reiman) Nelken; m. Eli Robins, Feb. 22, 1946 (dec. Dec. 1994); children: Paul, James, Thomas, Nicholas; m. Hugh Chaplin, Aug. 5, 1998. Student, Newcomb Coll., 1938-40; BA, Radcliffe Coll., 1942, MA, 1943; PhD, Harvard U., Cambridge, Mass., 1951. Mem. faculty Washington U., St. Louis, 1954—, prof. sociology in psychiatry, 1968-91, prof. sociology, 1969-91, prof. social sci. and social sci. in psychiatry, 1991-2000, prof. emeritus, 2001—. Past mem. Nat. Adv. Coun. on Drug Abuse; past mem. task panels Pres.'s Commn. on Mental Health; mem. expert adv. panel on mental health WHO; Salmon lectr. NY Acad. Medicine, 1983; Cutter lectr. Harvard U., 1997. Author: Deviant Children Grown Up, 1966; editor 11 books; mem. editl. bd. Psychol. Medicine, Jour. Studies on Alcohol, Social Psychiatry and Psychiatric Epidemiology, Epidemiol. e Psichiat. Sociale; contbr. articles to profl. jours. Recipient Rsch. Scientist award USPHS, 1970-90, Pacesetter Rsch. award Nat. Inst. Drug Abuse, 1978, Radcliffe Coll. Grad. Soc. medal, 1979, Sutherland award Am. Soc. Criminology, 1991, Nathan B. Eddy award Com. on Problems of Drug Dependence, 1993, Spl. Presdl. Commendation Am. Psychiat. Assn., 1999, Am. Acad. Arts and Scis., 1999, Commendation and Appreciation award Harvard Inst. Psychiat. Epidemiology and Genetics, 2000, Disting. Sci. Devel. award Soc. Rsch. in Child Devel., 2003, Peter Raven Lifetime award Acad. Sci. St. Louis, 2006; rsch. grantee NIMH, Nat. Inst. on Drug Abuse, Nat. Inst. on Alcohol Abuse and Alcoholism. Fellow Am. Coll. Epidemiology, Royal Coll. Psychiatrists (hon.), Am. Soc. Psychiatrists (hon.), Soc. Study of Addiction (hon.); mem. APHA (Rema Lapouse award 1979, Lifetime Achievement award sect. on alcohol and drug abuse 1994), Internat. Fedn. Psychiat. Epidemiology (com.1992-2002), World Psychiat. Assn. (sect. com. on epidemiology and cmty. psychiatry, 1985-2002, co-chmn. sect. on rsch. instruments in psychiatry), Soc. Life History Rsch. in Psychopathology, Am. Coll. Neuropsychopharmacology, Inst. Medicine, Am. Psychopath. Assn. (pres. 1987-88, Paul Hoch award 1978), World Innovation Found. (hon. mem. 2004). Office: Washington U Med Sch Dept Psychiatry Saint Louis MO 63110 Business E-Mail: robinsl@psychiatry.wustl.edu.

ROBINS, NORMAN ALAN, management consultant, retired metal products executive; b. Chgo., Nov. 19, 1934; s. Irving and Sylvia (Robbin) Robins; m. Sandra Ross, June 10, 1956; children: Lawrence Richard, Sherry Lynn. BSChemE, MIT, 1955, MSChemE, 1956; PhD in Math., Ill. Inst. Tech., 1972. Asst. mgr. process sys. and controls Inland Steel Co., East Chicago, Ind., 1962—67, assoc. mgr. process sys. and controls, 1967—72, dir. process rsch., 1972—77, v.p. rsch., 1977—84, v.p. technol. assessment,

1984—86, v.p. strategic planning, 1986—91; ret., 1991; ind. cons. in strategic planning, 1991—. Mem. bd. edn. Homewood-Flossmoor HS, Ill., 1974—77. Mem.: AIChE, Assn. Iron and Steel Tech. (Nat. Open Hearth Conf. award 1972).

ROBINS, ROBERT SIDWAR, political science professor, department chairman; b. Spangler, Pa., Apr. 20, 1938; s. Sydney and Katherine (Sidwar) R.; m. Marjorie McGann, Nov. 25, 1959; children: Anthony P., Nicholas A. BA, U. Pitts., 1959; MA, Duke U., 1961, PhD, 1963. Prof. polit. sci. Tulane U., New Orleans, 1965—, chmn. dept. polit. sci., 1979-90, dep. provost, 1991-98. Acad. visitor Inst. Commonwealth Studies, U. London, 1969-70, 78-79, mem. 1987-88; sr. assoc. mem. St. Antony's Coll., Oxford, Eng., 1972-73; vis. scholar Hastings Ctr., 1982; vis. scientist Tavistock Clinic, London, 1987-88. Author: Political Institutionalization and the Integration of Elites, 1976 (Carnegie Commn. report) Legislative Attitudes Toward Higher Education in Louisiana, 1968, Psychopathology and Political Leadership, 1977, Disease and Political Leadership, 1990; co-author: When Illness Strikes the Leader, Political Paranoia; contbr. articles to profl. publs. Vice-chmn. Elections Integrity Commn., State of La., 1981-82; active Conn. Bd. Govs. Higher Edn., Stamford Urban Redevel. Commn., Conn. Recipient Excellence in Tchg. award Tulane U., 1978; Fulbright scholar, 1961-62. Mem. Am. Polit. Sci. Assn., Internat. Soc. Polit. Psychology. Avocations: carpentry, gardening. Home: 64 Pond Rd Stamford CT 06902 Personal E-mail: robins_06902@yahoo.com.

ROBINSON, ADELBERT CARL, lawyer, judge; b. Shawnee, Okla., Dec. 13, 1926; s. William H. and Mayme (Forston) R.; m. Paula Kay Settles, Apr. 16, 1988; children from previous marriage: William, James, Schuyler, Donald, David, Nancy, Lauri. Student, Okla. Bapt. U., 1944-47; JD, Okla. U., 1950. Bar: Okla. 1950. Pvt. practice, Muskogee, Okla., 1956-97; with legal dept. Phillips Petroleum Co., 1950-51; adjuster U.S. Fidelity & Guaranty Co., 1951-54, atty., adjuster-in-charge, 1954-56; ptnr. Fite & Robinson, 1956-62, Fite, Robinson & Summers, 1963-70, Robinson & Summers, 1970-72, Robinson, Summers & Locke, 1972-76, Robinson, Locke & Gage, 1976-80, Robinson, Locke, Gage & Fite, 1980-83, Robinson, Locke, Gage, Fite & Williams, Muskogee, 1983-95, Robinson, Gage, Fite & Williams, Muskogee, 1995-97. Police judge City of Muskogee, 1963—64, mcpl. judge, 1964—70; prin. justice 84Temp. Divsn. 36 Okla. Ct. Appeals, 1981—84, spl. dist. judge, 1997—; pres., dir. Wall St. Bldg. Corp., 1969—78, Three Forks Devel. Corp., 1968—77, Rolo Leasing Inc., 1971—97, Suroya II Inc.1, 1977—99; mng. ptnr. RLG Ritz, 1980—97; ptnr. First City Real Estate Partnership, 1985—94; dir. First City Bank, Tulsa, Okla., 1985—92; del. to U.S./China Jt. Session on Trade, Investment and Econ. Law, Beijing, 1987; dir. First Bankshares of Muskogee, 1980—95, First of Muskogee Corp., 1980—95; adv. dir. First Nat. Bank and Trust Co. of Muskogee, 1978—95. Chmn. Muskogee County (Okla.) Law Day, 1963, Muskogee Area Redevel. Authority, 1963, Muskogee County chpt. Am. Cancer Soc., 1956; pres., bd. dirs. United Way of Muskogee Inc., 1980-88, v.p., 1982, pres., 1983; bd. dirs. Muskogee Cmty. Concert Assn., Muskogee Tourist Info. Bur., 1964-68; bd. dirs., gen. counsel United Cerebral Palsy Eastern Okla., 1964-68; trustee Connors Devel. Found., Connors Coll., 1981-99, chmn., 1987-89; active Muskogee Housing Authority, 1992-95. With inf. AUS, 1945-46. Mem. ABA, Okla. Bar Assn. (chmn. uniform laws com. 1970-72, chmn. profl. coop. com. 1965-69, past regional chmn. grievance com.), Muskogee County Bar Assn. (pres. 1971, mem. exec. coun. 1971-74), Okla. Assn. Def. Counsel (dir. 1970-74), Okla. Assn. Mcpl. Judges (dir. 1968-70), Muskogee c. of C., Delta Theta Phi., Rotary (pres. 1971-72). Methodist. Office: Muskogee County Courthouse PO Box 1350 Muskogee OK 74402-1350 Home: 3405 Park Pl N Muskogee OK 74403-1815

ROBINSON, ALEXANDER JACOB, retired psychologist; b. St. John, Kans., Nov. 7, 1920; s. Oscar Frank and Lydia May (Beitler) R.; m. Elsie Louise Riggs, July 29, 1942; children: Madelyn K., Alicia A., David J., Charles A., Paul S., Marietta J., Stephen N. BA in Psychology, Ft. Hays State U., Kans., 1942, MS in Clin. Psychology, 1942; postgrad., U. Ill., 1942-44. Cert. psychologist, sch. psychologist. Chief psychologist Larned State Hosp., Kans., 1948-53, with employee selection, outpatient services, 1953-55; sch. psychologist County Schs., Modesto, Calif., 1955-61, Pratt Jr. Coll., Kans., 1961-66; fed. grantee, writer assoc. dir. Exemplary Federally Funded Program for Spl. Edn., Pratt, 1966-70; dir. spl. edn., rschr. Stafford County Schs., St. John, 1970-81, ret., 1981. Supr. testing and data Incidence of Exceptional Children in Kansas, Kans. State U., Ft. Hays, 1946; writer, asst. dir. Best Exemplary Federally Funded Program on Spl. Edn., Pratt, 1966-70; fed. grantee, rschr., writer, study dir. Edn. for the High-Performance Child, St. John, 1970—, Psychogenesis of the Sociopathic Personality. Minister, The Ch. of Jesus Christ. Served to 2d lt. U.S. Army, 1944-46, PTO. Mem. NY Acad. Scis., Libr. of Congress. Lodges: Lions (program chmn. St. John 1974-76). Achievements include research in normal children with a learning disability and their specific developmental requirement. Avocations: history, ethnology, anthropology, music, literature. Home and Office: 402 E 1st Saint John KS 67576 Office Phone: 620-549-3373.

ROBINSON, AMINAH BRENDA LYNN, artist, illustrator; b. Columbus, Ohio, Feb. 18, 1940; d. Leroy Edward William and Helen Elizabeth (Zimmerman) R.; m. Clarence Adrian Robinson (div. 1981); 1 child, Sydney Edward (dec. July 17, 1994). Student, Columbus Coll. of Art & Design, 1956-60, Ohio State U., 1960-61, Franklin U., 1961-62, Bliss Coll., 1963. Asst. libr., illustrator, artist Ohio Pub. Libr., Columbus, 1958-64; draftsman Mountain State Telephone Co., Boise, Idaho, 1964-66; illustrator TV Oper. Br. TV, Miss., 1966-67; sr. illustrator N.Am. Rockwell Corp., Columbus, 1971; with City Recreation and Pks. Dept., Columbus, 1972—. Lectr. to numerous orgns., 1971—; spkr. numerous workshops, 1970—. One woman shows include Otterbein Coll., Worthington, Ohio, 1982, 89, 91, Columbus Mus. Art, 1983, 90, 2003, Esther Saks Gallery, Chgo., 1984, Akron Art Mus., 1987, 88, So. Ohio Mus., Portsmouth, 1990, U. Wis., Greenbay, 1990, Museo Nacional de Bellas Artes, Santiago, 2004; exhibited in group shows at Wexner Art Ctr., Columbus, 1992, Nat. Mus. Women in the Arts, Washington, 1990, 91, Memphis Brooks Mus. Art, 1991; represented in permanent collections Cin. Art Mus., Newark Art Mus., Otterbein Coll., Nat. Underground R.R. Freedom Ctr.; numerous others; seried artist: Pages in History, 1981-, Afrikan Pilgrimage: the Extended Family, Sapelo Series, New York Stories, People of the Book, Chilean Suite; author: A Street Called Home; illustrator: Elijah's Angel, 1992, Sophie, 1994, A School for Pompey Walker, 1995, To Be A Drum, 1998. Ohio Arts Coun. fellow 1979-80, 86-87, 88-89, 991-92, Travel-Study fellow Am. Forum for Internat. Study, 1979, PSI Residency fellow, 1989; resident Israel, 1998, Santiago, Chile, 2004; recipient Gov.'s award for the visual arts in Ohio, 1984, Columbus Star of 1980 Achievement award, 1980; named Outstanding Citizen in the Community, Nat. Epicureans, 1974, named a MacArthur Fellow, 2004.

ROBINSON, AMORIE ALEXIA, psychologist, educator; b. Detroit, Oct. 19, 1956; d. David Everett Robinson, II and Jane Marian Robinson; m. Hattie Corine Francis, Oct. 17, 2001. BA in Psychology, Oberlin Coll., Ohio, 1978; MA in Ednl. Psychology, U. Mich., 1979, PhD in Clin. Psychology, 1996. Dir. counseling svcs. Lewis Coll. Bus., Detroit, 1981—84; admissions counselor U. Detroit, 1984—89; forensic psychologist Recorders Ct. Psychiat. Clinic, Detroit, 1996—2002; psychotherapist Counseling Assocs., Farmington Hills, Mich., 1996—; guest lectr. U. Mich., Ann Arbor, 2002—. Adv. bd. Gay Lesbian Straight Edn. Network, Detroit, 2004—; co-founder Com. for Study of Culture, Class and Mental Health, U. Mich., 1990—96; condr. workshops in field; lectr. in field; designer Kofi Kards. Illustrator, cartoonist children's coloring books, 1975—2004; author: There's A Stranger in This House: African American Lesbians and Domestic Violence in Battered Black and Blue: Violence in the Lives of Black Women, 2000, Misunderstood, Misled, & Misfit: The Marginalization Experiences of African American Lesbian Youth, 2000. Co-founder, v.p. bd. dirs. Ruth Ellis Ctr., Detroit, 1999—; co-founder, pres., bd. dirs. Karibu House, Inc., Detroit, 1997—; co-founder, bd. dirs. African-Am. Lesbians Organized to Renew Dignity and Empowerment, Detroit, 1994—, Unity Fellowship Ch., Detroit, 1989—. Recipient Catalyst Activist award, Triangle Found., Detroit, 2001, Lorraine Hansberry award, Affirmations Gay and Lesbian Cmty. Ctr., 1997, Coretta Scott-King Black Achievement award, Alpha Phi Alpha, 1989; fellow half-term fellow, U. Mich., 1994—95, Rackham Minority Merit fellow, 1989—95. Mem.: APA (Sci. Directorate award 1993), Detroit Metro Assn. Black Psychologists (sec. 1997—, Outstanding Svc. award 2002), Assn. for Women in Psychology (suite coord. 1993—95). Avocations: violin, tennis, African drumming. Office: Counseling Associates 33045 Hamilton Ct #W-300 Farmington Hills MI 48334 Business E-Mail: kofi@umich.edu.

ROBINSON, ANDREA J., lawyer; b. 1960; AB magna cum laude, Harvard Univ., 1981; JD, Univ. Va., 1984. Bar: NY 1985, DC 1988, Mass. 1990. Atty. Debevoise & Plimpton, NYC, Washington; ptnr., Litigation dept. Wilmer Cutler Pickering Hale & Dorr, Boston, 1990—, co-vice chmn., Securities dept. Spl. asst. dist. atty. Middlesex County, Mass., 1994. Named a Mass. Super Lawyer, Boston Mag., 2004, Top 50 Female Mass. Super Lawyer, 2004. Mem.: ABA, Boston Bar Assn., Phi Beta Kappa, Order of the Coif. Office: Wilmer Cutler Pickering Hale & Dorr 60 State St Boston MA 02109 Office Phone: 617-526-6360. Office Fax: 617-526-5000. Business E-Mail: andrea.robinson@wilmerhale.com.

ROBINSON, ANTHONY CHRISTOPHER, novelist, educator; b. Biskupitz, Germany, Mar. 10, 1931; came to U.S., 1931; s. Henry Morton and Gertrude (Ludwig) R.; m. Mary Chika, Nov. 16, 1957 (dec. Mar. 1976); children: Jennifer Eve, Henry David; m. Tatiana Padwa, Feb. 14, 1998. BA, Columbia Coll., NYC, 1953; MA cum laude, Columbia U., 1960; grad., Phillips Acad., Andover, Mass., 1949. Prof. English, dir. creative writing SUNY, New Paltz, 1964-2000, prof. English emeritus, 2000—. Vis. prof. U. Paris, 1971-72. Author: A Departure From the Rules, 1960 (Bread Loaf fellow 1960), The Easy Way, 1963, Home Again, Home Again, 1969, The Whole Truth, 1990, The Member-Guest, 1991. Lt. USNR, 1953-56. Mem.: Alpha Delta Phi. Democrat. Roman Catholic. Avocations: golf, fly fishing, golf club making, hiking. Home: 153 Huguenot St New Paltz NY 12561 E-mail: robinsoa@newpaltz.edu.

ROBINSON, BARBARA PAUL, lawyer; b. Oct. 19, 1941; d. Leo and Pauline G. Paul; m. Charles Raskob Robinson, June 11, 1965; children: Charles Paul, Torrance Webster. AB magna cum laude, Bryn Mawr Coll., 1962; LLB, Yale U., 1965, Order of the Coif. Bar: N.Y. 1966, U.S. Dist. Ct. (so. and ea. dists.) N.Y. 1975, U.S. Tax Ct. 1972, U.S. Ct. Appeals (2d cir.) 1974. Assoc. Debevoise & Plimpton LLP, NYC, 1966-75, ptnr., 1976—2006, with Trusts and Estates Dept., of counsel, 2007—. Mem. adv. bd. Practicing Law Inst.; bd. dirs. Am. Arbitration Assn., 1997—2003. Mem. bd. editors: Chase Jour., 1997—2001; contbr. articles to profl. jours. Mem. adv. coun., bd. vis. CUNY Law Sch., Queens, 1984—90; active Coun. on Fgn. Rels.; mem. commn. women's issues Mayor, 2002—; trustee Trinity Sch., 1982—88, pres., 1986—88; bd. dirs. Found. for Child Devel., 1988—2000, 2001—, chmn., 1991—2000; bd. dirs. Catalyst, 1993—2006, treas., 1993—2006; bd. dirs. Fund for Modern Cts., 1994—2003, Wave Hill, 1994—, Garden Conservancy, 1996—2002, Lawyers Com. for Civil Rights Under Law, 1997—2003, William Nelson Cromwell Found., 1993—, Irish Legal Rsch. Found. Inc., 1996—, Citizens Union Found. Inc., 1996—2004, Am. Friends Brit. Mus., 2003—, The Ocean Conservancy, 2004—, Teagle Found., 2005—, The Greenwall Found., 2006—, The John A. Hartford Found., 2006—; trustee Bryn Mawr Coll., 2000—. Recipient Laura Parsons Pratt award, 1996. Fellow Am. Coll. Trust and Estate Counsel, Am. Bar Found., N.Y. Bar Found.; mem. ABA (commn. on women in profession 1999-2002), N.Y. State Bar Assn. (vice chmn. com. on trust adminstrn., trusts and estates law sect. 1977-81, ho. of dels. 1984-87, 90-92, com. ann. award 1993-94), Assn. of Bar of City of N.Y. (chmn. com. on trusts, estates and surrogates cts. 1981-84, judiciary com. 1981-84, coun. on jud. adminstrn. 1982-84, chair nominating com. 1984-85, 99-2000, exec. com. 1986-91, chair 1989-90, v.p. 1990-91, chair com. on honors 1993-94, com. on long-range planning 1991-94, co-chair coun. on childen 1997-98, pres. 1994-96), Assn. of Bar of City of N.Y. Fund Inc. (bd. dirs. 2000-03, pres. 1994-96), Women's Forum, Yale Coun., Yale Law Sch. Assn. N.Y. (devel. bd., exec. com. 1981-85, 93—, pres. 1988-93), The Century Assn., Yale Club, Washington Club. Office: Debevoise & Plimpton LLP 919 Third Ave New York NY 10022 Home Phone: 212-222-4160; Office Phone: 212-909-6325. Business E-Mail: bprobinson@debevoise.com.

ROBINSON, BARRY R., lawyer; b. Dover, Ohio, Dec. 8, 1946; AB, Princeton U., 1969; JD cum laude, Ohio State U., 1972. Bar: Ohio 1972. Ptnr. Baker & Hostetler, Columbus, Ohio. Fellow Am. Coll. Trust and Estate Counsel; mem. ABA, Ohio State Bar Assn., Columbus Bar Assn. Office: Baker & Hostetler Capital Sq 65 E State St Ste 2100 Columbus OH 43215-4260

ROBINSON, BEATRIZ GONZALEZ, academic administrator; b. Havana, Cuba, Mar. 3, 1964; d. Jose V. and Josefina C. Gonzalez; m. John T. Robinson, Oct. 7, 1989; 1 child, Sean T. BA in English, Barry U., Miami, Fla., 1987, MS in Guidance & Couseling, 1991, PhD in Leadership, 1998. Lic. mental health counselor Fla. Dept. Health, 1998. Prof. St. Thomas U., Miami, 1997—, self-study dir., 2000—03, planning & evaluation officer, 2002—05, interim dean undergrad. studies & programs, 2004—05, v.p. planning, chief staff, 2005—. State coord. women higher edn. Am. Coun. Edn., Miami, 2000—; external evaluator commn. So. Assn. Colls. and Schs. Recipient Grad. Student Rsch. award, Nat. Career Devel. Assn., 1999, Outstanding Svc. award, St. Thomas U., 2001, Faculty Scholarship award, 2002; fellow Fellow, Hispanic Serving Insts., 2005; grantee, Am. Coun. Edn., 2004—05. Office: St Thomas Univ 16401 NW 37th Ave Miami Gardens FL 33054 Office Phone: 305-474-6869.

ROBINSON, BROOKS CALBERT, JR., retired professional baseball player, sports commentator, business consultant; b. Little Rock, May 18, 1937; s. Brooks Calbert and Ethel (Denker) R.; m. Constance Louise Butcher, Oct. 8, 1960; children— Brooks David, Christopher Leslie, Michael Patrick, Diana Agnes. Student, U. Little Rock, 1956-57. Profl. baseball player Balt. Orioles, 1955-77; sports commentator for Baltimore Oriole Games Sta. WMAR-TV, Balt., 1978-90; spl. asst. mktg. dept. Crown Central Petroleum Corp., 1979—; v.p. Personal Mgmt. Assocs., 1979—; spl. asst. Crown Ctrl. Petroleum Co. Selected Most Valuable Oriole, 1960, 62, 64, 71; named Am. League's MVP, 1964, MVP in Major League All-Star game at St. Louis, 1966; MVP, 1970 World Series; recipient Hickock Athlete of Yr. award, 1970; Balt. Decade award, 1970; mem. World Series Championship Team, 1965, 70; named to Baseball Hall of Fame, Cooperstown, NY, All-Time Rawlings Gold Glove Team, 2007. Office: Crown Ctrl PO Box 1168 Petroleum Corp/Dept Mktg 1 N Charles St Ste 1168 Baltimore MD 21201-3740

ROBINSON, CARRIE, pastor; b. Balt., Jan. 11, 1945; d. Charles Dingle and Anna Lemmon; m. Bill Robinson, Nov. 26, 1977 (dec. June 2, 2003); children: Michael Stukes, Maurice Johnson, Monica Johnson. Doctorate, Interdenominational Coll.; degree in Christian edn., Theol. Sem. and Coll. Notary pub. With Verizon Tel. Co., 1968—; pastor Prayer and Faith Ministries Bapt. Ch., Balt., 1987—. Sec. United Bapt. Conf., Balt., 1990—, v.p., 2000—. Mem.: Internat. Women Ministerial Alliance (v.p. 2000—), Order of Ea. Star (Helen Benton House # 34). Avocations: singing, reading, computers, drumming. Office: Prayer and Faith Ministries Bapt Ch Inc 1865 N Gay St Baltimore MD 21213 Home: 2705 Hamilton Ave Baltimore MD 21214-1912 Office Phone: 410-675-0047. E-mail: bishopcrobinson3@aol.com.

ROBINSON, CHARLES FURLONGE, lawyer; b. Phila., 1957; married; 1 child. BA, Harvard U., Cambridge, Mass., 1979; JD, Yale Law Sch., New Haven, Conn., 1982. Bar: US Ct. Appeals, 9th Cir., US Dist. Courts, Calif. Law clk. to Hon. William Orrick US Dist. Ct. (no. dist.) Calif., San Francisco, 1982—83; assoc. Heller Ehrman White & McAuliffe, San Francisco, 1983—88, ptnr., 1989—95; divsn. counsel Raychem Corp., Menlo Park, Calif., 1995—99; asst. gen. counsel, dir. litig. Packard Bell NEC, Sacramento, 1999—2000; acting chief adminstrv. officer Calif. Ind. System Operator Corp., Folsom, Calif., 2004—05, v.p. gen. counsel, corp. sec., 2000—06; gen. counsel U. Calif., Oakland, 2006—. Mem.: Nat. Assn. Corp. Lawyers, Energy Bar Assn., ABA, NAACP Legal Def. Fund (NAACP Legal Def. Fund award 1994), Legal Services Trust Fund Commn. (bd. mem., vice chmn. 1994—97), Pub. Interest Clearinghouse (bd. mem., treasurer, pres. 1990—95), Bar Assn. San Francisco (co-chmn., Com. on Minority Employment 1989—95), La Raza Centro Legal (bd. mem., treasurer 1987—90), Calif. Bd. of Legal Specialization (bd. mem. 1985—88). Avocations: running, photography, music, travel, architecture. Office: Office of General Counsel of The Regents University of California 1111 Franklin St Oakland CA 94607 *

ROBINSON, CHARLES PAUL, nuclear energy industry executive, diplomat; b. Detroit, Oct. 9, 1941; s. Edward Leonard and Mary Opal (Edmondson) R.; m. Barbara Thomas Woodard; children by previous marriage: Paula S., Colin C. BS in Physics, Christian Bros. U., 1963; PhD in Physics, Fla. State U., 1967; doctorate (hon.), Christian Brothers U. Mem. nuclear test staff Los Alamos (N.Mex.) Nat. Lab., 1967-69, chief test operator, 1969-70, mem. advanced concepts staff, 1971-72, assoc. div. leader, lasers, 1972-76, div. leader, 1976-79, assoc. dir., 1980-85; sr. v.p., bd. dirs. Ebasco Services Inc. subs. Enserch Corp., NYC, 1985-88; ambass. to nuclear testing talks U.S. Dept. State, Geneva, 1988-90; v.p. Sandia Nat. Labs., Albuquerque, 1990-95, pres., 1995—2005; capture exec. Lockheed Martin Corp., 2005—. Instr. U. N.Mex., Los Alamos, 1974-76; mem. sci. adv. group Def. Nuclear Agy., Washington, 1981-86; mem. nat. security bd. Los Alamos Nat. Lab., 1985-88; chmn. Presdl. Tech. Adv. Bd., 1991; mem. U.S. Strategic Command Adv. Bd.; bd. dirs. Wells Fargo Bank, Tech. Ventures Corp., Fla. State U. Rsch. Found.; trustee Kazakhstan Nonproliferation Inst. Mem. strategic adv. group for comdr. U.S. Strategic Command; chmn. policy panel, tech. adv. group Verification of Warhead Dismantlement and Spl. Nuc. Materials Controls; mem. threat reduction adv. com. Dept. Def., exec. bd. Boy Scouts of N.Mex. Recipient Outstanding Pub. Svc. medal Joint Chiefs of Staff, 1996. Mem. Am. Phys. Soc. (Pake Prize 2003), Am. Nuclear Soc., NAE. Achievements include testifing before Congress more than 80 times. Avocation: choral singing. Office: Lockheed Martin 1155 Univ Blvd SE Albuquerque NM 87106 Home Phone: 505-856-5311, 505-856-5311; Office Phone: 505-843-4153. Business E-Mail: c.p.robinson@lmco.com, c.probinson@lmco.com.

ROBINSON, CHARLOTTE HILL, artist; b. San Antonio, Nov. 28, 1924; d. Lucius Davis and Charlotte (Moore) Hill; m. Floyd I. Robinson, Mar. 1943; children: Floyd I. Jr., Lawrence H., Elizabeth H. Student, Incarnate Word Coll., 1942—45, NYU, 1947-48, Corcoran Sch. Art, 1951-52. Painting instr. Art League No. Va., Alexandria, 1967-75. Condr. Art World Seminar Washington Women's Art Ctr., 1975-80, drawing workshop Smithsonian Instn. Resident Assocs. Program, Washington, 1977; program dir. Nat. Women's Caucus for Art, 1979; project coord., exhbn. curator The Artist and the Quilt, nat. mus. traveling exhbn., 1983-86; vis. artist S.W. Craft Ctr., San Antonio, 1983-85; lectr. WFUV 90 FM, Fordham U., NYC, 1990, San Antonio Art Inst., 1991, Nat. Mus. for Women in Arts, Washington, 1991, Iowa State U., Ames, 1991; panelist Nat. Mus. Women in Arts, 1997, Woman and the Arts, Douglass Coll./ Rutgers U., 1998, Washington Women's Caucus for Art at the Millenium Art Ctr., 2001. Editor: The Artist & The Quilt, 1983; one-person shows include Thames Sic. Ctr., New London, Conn., 1991, Brunner Gallery & Mus., Iowa State U., 1991, 92, San Antonio Art. Inst., 1991, Fordham U., 1991, de Andino Fine Arts, Washington, 1992, Masur Mus. Art, Monroe, La., 1993, 96, 2001, Lee Hansley Art Gallery, Raleigh, NC, 1993, 97, 2001, Sol Del Rio, San Antonio, 1995, 97-98, 1812 Artic Gallery, Virginia Beach, Va., 1995, Savannah Coll. Art and Design, 1997, Duke U. Sch. Law, 1998, No. Va. CC, 1999, McLean Project for the Arts, 2002, Southwest Sch. Art & Craft, San Antonio, 2003; exhibited in group shows at Franklin Square and Watkins Gallery, Washington, 1992, Rutgers U., New Brunswick, NJ, 1992, 96, 98, Brody's Gallery, Washington, 1992, Lee Hansley Art Gallery, Raleigh, 1993, 96, 98-2001, 02, 03, 05, 06, Emerson Gallery, McLean, 1993, 95, 99, No. Va. CC, 1994, 99, Harvard U., 1996, Ceres Gallery, NYC, 1999-2000, Millennium Art Ctr., Washington, 2001, Am. Ctr. Physics, 2003. Trustee Bronx Mus., NY, 1977; bd. dirs. Washington Women's Art Ctr., 1977, New Art Examiner, 1985-86; nat. bd. dirs. Women's Caucus for Art, 1983-84. Recipient Concourse award Corcoran Sch. Art, 1952; Telfair Acad. Art scholar, Savannah, Ga., 1959; Nat. Endowment for Arts grantee, 1977-81; fellow Va. Ctr. for Creative Arts, Sweet Briar, Va., 1985. Address: Lee Hansley Gallery 225 Glenwood Ave Raleigh NC 27603 Home Phone: 703-941-3865; Office Phone: 703-941-3865. E-mail: bjohnb@mchs1.com, chardyrob@cox.net.

ROBINSON, CHERYL JEFFREYS, special education educator; d. William Charles and Dorothy Crawford Jeffreys; m. Norman Norris Robinson, June 21, 1975; children: Nicole Lorraine, Natalie Lavonne. BS summa cum laude, DC Tchrs. Coll., 1976; MA, George Washington U., 1977; EdD, Nova Southeastern U., 2003. Advanced profl. cert. Md. State Dept. Edn., adminstrv. and supervisory cert. Md. State Dept. Edn., 2005. Diagnostic-prescriptive tchr. Prince George's County Md. Pub. Schs., 1977—83, spl. edn. resource tchr., 1984—90, regional spel. edn. specialist, 1990—2005, spl. edn. area office mgr., 2001—02; spl. edn. supr. Montgomery County Pub. Schs., 2005—. Mem. adv. com. rep. Summer Inst. Nova Southeastern U., Ft. Lauderdale, Fla., 1997; planned and facilitated tchr. ADHD tng., 1998—2001; facilitator sch. staff/parent program ADHD students, 2000—01; mem. sch. CEO's faculty support team, 2003—. Mem.: AAUW (Career Devel. grantee 1997—98), Montgomery County Assn. Adminstrv. and Supervisory Personnel, Nat. Educators Assn., Coun. Exceptional Children, Nat. Coun. Negro Women, Kappa Delta Pi, Alpha Kappa Alpha. Democrat. Baptist. Avocations: art, crafts, antiques, theater. Office: Montgomery County Public Schools Carver Ednl Svcs Ctr 850 Hungerford Dr Rm 230 Rockville MD 20855 Office Phone: 301-279-3837. Personal E-mail: robinson@radix.net.

ROBINSON, CHRISTINA ANNE, secondary school educator; d. John Filmore and Catherine Lavona Neese; m. James Howard Jr. Robinson, July 31, 1971; 1 child, James Howard III. BS, Ind. State U., Terre Haute, 1971. Tchr. Ctr. Grove Jr. High, Greenwood, Ind., 1973—75; mgr. Emma Parrish Theatre, Titusville, Fla., 1983—85; tchr. Cocoa HS, Fla., 1992—97, Astronaut HS, Titusville, 1997—. Named Tchr. of Yr., Cocoa HS, 1994, Wal-Mart, Titusville, 2005. Office: Astronaut High Sch 800 War Eagle Blvd Titusville FL 32796

ROBINSON, CRYSTAL LATRESA, professional basketball coach, retired professional basketball player; b. Atoka, Okla., Jan. 22, 1974; d. Billy and Nancy Robinson. Grad. in Health and Phys. Edn., Southeastern Okla. State U., 1996. Forward Am. Basketball League Colo. Xplosion, NY Liberty, NYC, 1999—2005, Washington Mystics, 2006—07, asst. coach,

2007—. Named MVP, US Sports Festival, 1993; named to Nat. Assn. Intercollegiate Athletics Hall of Fame, 2003; recipient ABL Rookie of Yr. award, 1997. Office: Washington Mystics Verizon Ctr 601 F St NW Washington DC 20004 *

ROBINSON, DAVID BRADFORD, writer, poet; b. Richmond, Va., Apr. 14, 1937; s. Albert Lewis and Martha Ellen (Lovern) R. BS, U. Miami, 1959, MS, 1961; JD, Calif. Ctrl. U., 1961, MA, 1994; AA, Miami-Dade C.C., 1970; DSc, Northwestern Coll., 1978, PhD, 1979, MA, 1994. Author: Characteristics of Cesium, 1978, Collected Poems, 1987. Founder Ronald Reagan Rep. Ctr., Washington; exhibitor Statue of Liberty, Port of NY, 1986; mem. Heritage Found., 1989; sustaining sponsor Ronald Reagan Presdl. Found., 1987; charter mem. Ronald Reagan Trust; charter mem. Honor Roll Rep. Presdl. Task Force, 1990, life mem., 1989, Commemorative Honor Roll, 1991; mem. Nat. Rep. Senatorial Com. with Presdl. Commn., 1992; founding sponsor, founding mem. Space Life Sta., 1989; spkrs. citizen task force Inaugural Mem. Cert. of Honor; life mem. Rep. Nat. Com.; expert solver US Chess Fedn., 2005. Recipient 2d pl. Amateur Trophy, Capablanca Chess Club, 1964, Presdl. Sports award bicycling, 1976, Presdl. Achievement award Rep. Nat. Com., 1982, Cert. Good Standing Rep. Presdl. Task Force, 1982-85, Presdl. Merit medal, 1982, Appreciation cert. Sen. Paula Hawkins, 1986, Golden Poet Trophy award World of Poetry, 1987, Silver Anniversary Album, Nat. Geog. Soc., 1990, Pres. Ronald Reagan Appreciation cert., 1988, Pres. Bush Congl. Victory Squadron Recognition cert., 1989, Affidavit of Life Membership, Cert. from Rep. Nat. Com., Bush Inaugural/Freedom medal, 1989, World Time-Capsule cert., 1990, Am. in Space medal, 1990, Cert. of Appreciation, Nat. Rep. Congl. Com., 1990, Pegasus Time Capsule plaque, 1991, Congl. Merit cert. Nat. Rep. Congl. Com., 1992, Battle of Normandy Found. Appreciation award, 1993, Presdl. Legion of Merit medal, 1993, Congl. Order of Liberty award, 1993, Appreciation cert. Sen. Kay Bailey Hutchinson, 1993, Rep. Presdl. award, 1994, Albert Einstein medal Brit. Bur. Degree Promotion, 1994, Cert. of Appreciation, The Golden Heart Club, Mil. Order of Purple Heart Svc. Found., Congl. Order of Freedom, 1995, Cert. of Meritorious Svc. Rep. Party Planning Com., 1996, Cert. Appreciation World War II Meml., 1997, Chmn.'s Honor Roll cert., Rep. Nat. Com., 1997, Eisenhower Commn., 1997, Caesar medal Trinity Broadcasting Network, 1998, Cert. Recognition Rep. Nat. Com., 1999, Jubilee Yr. Blessing Cert. His Holiness John Paul II/Missionary Assn. Mary Immaculate, 1999, US Congl. Medal of His Holiness Pope John Paul II, 2005, Cert. of Appreciation Concerns of Police Survivors, 2000, Cert. of Appreciation Rep. Nat. Com., 2000, 2004, 2005, Cert. Appreciation, Planetary Soc., 2001, Reagan Ranch Mem. cert. recognition Young Am.'s Found., 2005; rated expert solver U.S. Chess Fedn., 2005. Mem. Am. Air Mus. (Brit., founder 1991), Battle of Normandy Meml. Mus. (charter 1988), Sigma Xi, Russian Club, Phi Theta Kappa. Avocation: chess.

ROBINSON, DAVID BROOKS, retired naval officer; b. Alexandria, La., Oct. 26, 1939; s. Donald and Marion (Holloman) R.; m. Gene Kirkpatrick, Aug. 1, 1964; children: Kirk, David. Student, Tex. A&M U., 1958—59; BS, U.S. Naval Acad., 1963; MS in Physics, Naval Postgrad. Sch., Monterey, Calif., 1969. Commd. ensign USN, 1963, advanced through grades to vice adm., 1993; commdg. officer USS Canon and USS Ready, Guam, 1969-71; adminstrv. aide to Chmn. Joint Chiefs Staff, Washington, 1971-74; commdg. officer USS Luce, Mayport, Fla., 1976-78; surface comdr. assignment officer. and dir. fiscal mgmt. and procedural control divsn. Naval Mil. Pers. Command, 1979-81; mem. Fgn. Svc. Inst. Exec. Seminar, Washington, 1982; commdg. officer USS Richmond K. Turner, Charleston, SC, 1983-84; chief of staff, comdr. Naval Surface Force, Atlantic Fleet, Norfolk, Va., 1984; exec. asst. and sr. aide to vice chief Naval Ops., Washington, 1985, dir. Manpower and Tng. divsn., 1986, dir. Surface Warfare divsn., 1987-88; comdr. cruiser destroyer group 8, 1988-89; vice dir. and subsequently dir. operational plans and interoperability directorate Joint Staff, Washington, 1989-91; dep., chief of staff to comdr. U.S. Pacific Fleet, 1991-93, comdr. naval surface force, 1993-96; ret. USN, 1996. Decorated Navy Cross, Def. D.S.M., D.S.M., Legion of Merit with 4 gold stars, Bronze Star, Purple Heart. Mem. Optimists (pres. Oakton, Va. 1986-87). Methodist. Avocations: golf, bicycling, stamp collecting/philately, reading. Home Phone: 972-763-0760; Office Phone: 703-902-5001.

ROBINSON, DAVID ZAV, not-for-profit consultant; b. Montreal, Que., Sept. 29, 1927; s. Benjamin and Antonia (Seiden) R.; m. Nan Senior, Sept. 6, 1954; children: Marc, Eric. AB, Harvard U., 1946, AM, 1947, PhD, 1950. Asst. dir. rsch. Baird-Atomic Inc., Cambridge, Mass., 1949-59, 60-61; sci. liaison officer Office Naval Rsch., London, 1959-60; sci. advisor staff Office of Pres., Washington, 1961-67; v.p. acad. affairs NYU, 1967-70; v.p. Carnegie Corp. NY, NYC, 1970-80, exec. v.p., 1981-85, exec. v.p., treas., 1986-88; exec. dir. Carnegie Commn. on Sci Tech. and Govt., 1988-97; cons., 1997—. Dir. Urban Research Corp., Chgo., 1968-75; cons. Congressional Office of Tech. Assessment, 1975-78; mem. com. women in sci. NRC, 1975-82, chair com. on tchr. testing, 1999-2000; mem. vis. com. dept. chemistry Harvard U., 1977-83; physics dept. Princeton U., 1970-76 Mem. NY Energy Rsch. and Devel. Authority, 1971-77; trustee CUNY, 1976-81, Amideast, 1983-88, Citizen Union Found., 1985-, Inst. Schs. of the Future, 1986-, NC Sch. Sci. and Math., 1989-97, Santa Fe Inst., 1987—, Prep for Prep, 1989-98, Actors Ctr., 1996—, Inst. Current World Affairs, 2005—. Mem. AAAS, Optical Soc. Am., Coun. on Fgn. Rels., Am. Contract Bridge League, Fedn. Am. Scientists, Harvard Club (NYC). Office Phone: 212-675-1277. Personal E-mail: dzrobinson@aol.com.

ROBINSON, DAVIS ROWLAND, lawyer, international arbitrator; b. NYC, July 11, 1940; s. Thomas Porter and Cynthia (Davis) R.; m. Suzanne Walker, June 11, 1966; children: Christopher Champlin II, Gracyn Walker. BA magna cum laude, Yale U., 1961; LLB cum laude, Harvard U., 1967. Bar: N.Y. 1968, D.C. 1971, U.S. Supreme Ct. 1972. Fgn. svc. officer U.S. Dept. State, Washington, 1961-69; assoc. Sullivan & Cromwell, NYC, 1969—71; assoc., then ptnr. Leva, Hawes, Symington, Martin and Oppenheimer, Washington, 1971-81; the legal adviser U.S. Dept. State, Washington, 1981-85; ptnr. Pillsbury, Madison & Sutro, Washington, 1985-88, Le Boeuf, Lamb, Greene & MacRae LLP, Washington, 1988—2002, ret., 2002—; sr. mng. dir. Richard C. Breeden & Co., LLC, 2003—. Dir. Mid. East Policy Coun., Washington, 1999—. Pres. Harvard Legal Aid Bur., 1966-67. Mem. Am. Law Inst. (adviser fgn. rels. law of U.S.), Am. Soc. Internat. Law, Internat. Centre for Settlement of Investment Disputes (U.S. panel, 2002-), Coun. on Fgn. Rels., Phi Beta Kappa. Business E-Mail: drrobins@breedenco.com.

ROBINSON, DENNIS R., sports association executive; Grad., Wesleyan U.; M in Sports Mgmt., U. Mass.; MBA, Harvard. With U. Houston, NFL; asst. commr. S.W. Athletic Conf.; with NJ Sports and Expn. Authority, 1990—98, pres., CEO, 1998—99; sr. v.p. bus. and league ops. NBA, NYC, 1999—. Office: NYC Olympic Tower 645 5th Ave Fl 10 New York NY 10022-5986 *

ROBINSON, DEVETTE LORRAINE, music educator; d. Horace Edward and Cassie Jones; m. Claude Robinson, Oct. 10, 1992; 1 child, Clarisa. MusB, MA, Prairie View A&M U., Tex., 1981. All-level music cert. Tex. Edn. Agy. Choir dir., Houston, 1994—96; band and percussion dir., 1996—2000; choir dir., 2000—03; choir dir., aux. dir., 2000—03; choir dir., 2003—04, Sheldon Ind. Sch. Dist., Houston, 2004—. Singer: (jazz ensemble) Salute to Martin Luther King and Mahalia Jackson. Named Tchr. of Yr., Sch. Campus and Adminstrv. Office, 2000—01. Mem.: Tex. Music Educators Assn., Iota Phi Lambda (assoc.), Delta Sigma Theta (assoc.). Democrat. Baptist. Avocations: travel, walking, Karate. Home Phone: 713-635-2141.

ROBINSON, DOROTHY K., lawyer; b. New Haven, Feb. 18, 1951; children: Julia Robinson Bouwsma, Alexandra Toby Bouwsma. BA in Econs. with honors, Swarthmore Coll., 1972; JD, U. Calif., Berkeley, 1975; MA (hon.), Yale U., 1987. Bar: Calif. 1975, N.Y. 1976, Conn. 1981, U.S. Ct. Appeals (2d cir.) 1975, U.S. Dist. Ct. (so. dist.) N.Y. 1981. Assoc. Hughes Hubbard & Reed, NYC, 1975-78; asst. gen. counsel Yale U., New Haven, 1978-79, assoc. gen. counsel, 1979-84, dep. gen. counsel, 1984-86, gen. counsel, 1986—95, dir. fed. rels., 1986-88, acting sec., 1993, v.p., gen. counsel, 1995—. Mem. Calif. Law Rev., 1973-75. Trustee Hopkins Grammar Day Prospect Hill Sch., New Haven, 1983-88, sec., 1986-88; trustee Wenner-Gren Found. Anthrop. Rsch., 1991-2003, Newark Pub. Radio, Inc., 2006-, Tchrs. Ins. and Annuity Assn. (TIAA-CREF), 2007—; bd. dirs. Cold Spring Sch., New Haven, 1990-95; mem. adv. bd. Conn. Mental Health Ctr., New Haven, 1979-89; bd. dirs. Nat. Assn. Ind. Coll. and Univs., 1995-98; mem. alumni coun. Swarthmore Coll., 1999-2002. Fellow Ezra Stiles Coll. Yale U., Am. Bar Found.; mem. ABA, Nat. Assn. Coll. and Univ. Attys. (bd. dirs. 1987-90), Conn. Bar Assn., Calif. Bar Assn., Assn. Bar City N.Y., Phi Beta Kappa. Office: Yale U Office of VP and Gen Counsel PO Box 208255 New Haven CT 06520-8255 Office Phone: 203-432-4949.

ROBINSON, DOUGLAS, computer company executive; BBA, St. Michael's Coll.; M in Fin., Babson Coll. Acct. exec. Fred S. James & Co.; comml. underwriter Liberty Mutual Ins. Co.; CFO Cullinet Software; from v.p. fin. to sr. v.p. fin. Computer Assoc. Internat., Islandia, NY, 1989—2003, sr. v.p. fin., interim CFO, 2003—04, sr. v.p., corp. controller, 2004—. Office: Computer Assoc Internat One Computer Assoc Plz Islandia NY 11749

ROBINSON, E. GLENN, lawyer; b. Charleston, W.Va., Jan. 1, 1924; s. Elmer George and Eva Elena (Rexrode) Robinson; m. Emma Lou Legg, Dec. 23, 1947; children: Richard G., Martha L., William E., Ann K. BSc, Ohio State U., 1948; JD, W.Va. U., 1950. Bar: W.Va. 1950, U.S. Ct. Appeals (4th cir.) 1953, U.S. Ct. Appeals (3d cir.) 1980, U.S. Supreme Ct. 1982. Ptnr. Shannon & Robinson, Charleston, 1950—52, James, Wise, Robinson, & Magnuson, Charleston, 1952—76, Love, Wise, Robinson & Woodroe, Charleston, 1976—83, Robinson & McElwee, Charleston, 1983—91, of counsel, 1991—. With AUS, 1942—45. Fellow: W.Va. Bar Found., Am. Coll. Trial Lawyers, Am. Bar Found.; mem.: Am. Bd. Trial Advocates, Kanawha County Bar Assn. (pres. 1968—69), W.Va. Bar Assn. (pres. 1982—83), W.Va. State Bar (pres. 1972—73), Rotary. Republican. Home: 507 Superior Ave South Charleston WV 25303-2024 Office: 400 Fifth Third Ctr 700 Virginia St E Charleston WV 25301 Home Phone: 304-744-2812; Office Phone: 304-347-8334. Business E-Mail: egr@ramlaw.com.

ROBINSON, EARL, JR., marketing, transportation executive, educator, retired air force officer; b. St. George, Bermuda, Nov. 5, 1954; s. Willie Earl and Jeanette (Wilson) Robinson; m. Indera Rodgers, Dec. 11, 1999; children: Aiyana Spring, Jasmine Summer, Earl III. BA in Radio and TV, U. Detroit, 1976; MS in Mgmt., Troy State U., 1986; postgrad., Old Dominion U., 1986—; MS in Computer Info. Sys., U. Detroit, 1998; PhD in Legal Letters, Sunbelt Paralegal Inst., 1999. Commd. lt. USAF, 1976, advanced through grades to lt. col., 1992, gen. officer aide, adminstrv. staff officer Sembach, Germany, 1982-85, with tactical air command Hampton, Va., 1986-88, mem. faculty Air Command and Staff Coll. Montgomery, Ala., 1989-92, comdr. recruiting squadron Clinton Twp., Mich., 1992-94, ret., 1994; pres. Power-Base USA, 1994—; chief advisor solar energy co., 1994—; exec. dir. Detroit Tranist Authority, 1994-95, 1995—. Maj. prof. Spring Arbor (Mich.) Coll., 1992—; adj. prof. Faulkner U., Montgomery, 1991—; pres., CEO ERJ Corp. Ltd., Hampton, Va., 1986-88; pres. Paddle King Corp., Zaragoza, Spain, 1980-82; cons. Inst. Def. Analysis. Inventor info. resource mgmt. system. Mem. Nat. Tech. Assn. (publicity chmn. 1984-85), Urban Youth Action (case worker 1984-85), Housing Opportunity, Inc., Hampton Host Lions Club, Tuskegee Airmen (past chpt. pres.). Avocations: computers, reading, table-trennis, team sports, fishing, golf. Home: 1035 Roslyn St Mount Clemens MI 48043-2934 Office Phone: 313-492-0845. Personal E-mail: earlpower1@yahoo.com. Business E-Mail: erobinson@powerbaseusa.us.

ROBINSON, EDWARD LEE, retired physics professor, consultant; b. Clanton, Ala., Nov. 6, 1933; s. Alonzo Lee and Ollie Sarah (Mims) R.; m. Shirley Anne Burnett (div. Sept. 1972); children: Edward Lee Jr., James Allan, Paul David; m. Linda G. Moon, 1990. AB with honors, Samford U., 1954; MS, Purdue U., 1958, PhD, 1962. Dir. Cyclotron Lab. Samford U., Birmingham, Ala., 1961-67, asst. prof. physics, chmn. dept., 1961-62, assoc. prof., chmn. dept., 1962-66, prof., chmn. dept., 1966-67; assoc. prof. U. Ala., Birmingham, 1967-77, co-radiation safety officer, 1967-85, dir. Van de Graaff Accelerator Lab., 1970-91, acting chmn. dept., 1973-74, prof. physics, 1977-91, adj. prof. forensic sci., 1983-91, cons. in applied physics and accident reconstrn., 1991—; prin., owner Robinson & Assocs., LLC, 1998—. Cons. Hayes Internat. Corp., Birmingham, 1963-68, So. Rsch. Inst., Birmingham, 1968-69; rschr. Oak Ridge Nat. Lab., Tenn., 1968, 74-75, 82, U. Md., College Park, 1966, 67; bd. overseers Samford U., 1999—; adv. com. to dean Howard Coll. of Arts and Scis. of Samford U., 2002—. Active Birmingham YMCA; mem. at large nat. coun., chmn. sci. adv. com. for explorer scouting Boy Scouts Am., 1999—2002. Mem. Am. Phys. Soc., Soc. Automotive Engrs., AAAS, Ala. Acad. Sci. (life, v.p. 1964-65), Tex. Assn. Accident Reconstrn. Specialists (bd. dirs. 1999-2003), numerous other nat. and internat. profl. assns. Baptist. Achievements include discovery, co-discovery of six radioisotopes. Home: 233 Oakmont Rd Birmingham AL 35244-3264 Office Phone: 205-995-8330.

ROBINSON, EDWARD NORWOOD, lawyer; b. Roseboro, NC, June 18, 1925; s. Edward Croswell and Lolita (Underwood) R.; m. Pauline L. Gray, Mar. 22, 1952; children: Edward Norwood Jr., James Gray, Michael Lindsay, Mark Alvin. BS in Engring., U.S. Mil. Acad., 1945; JD, Duke U., 1952. Bar: NC 1952. Atty. Robinson & Lawing, L.L.P., Winston-Salem, NC, 1959—. N.C. Civilian Aide to Sec. of Army, 1994-2001; apptd. to 5th Dist. U.S. Acad. Selection Bd.; mem. ethics com. Bowman Gray Sch. Medicine; bd. visitors Duke U. Sch. Law, Wake Forest U. Sch. Law, Duke Divinity Sch.; lectr. in field. Co-editor Duke Law Jour. Past pres. Winston-Salem Rotary Club; past campaign chmn. United Way; past pres. C. of C.; past pres. local chpt. ARC; past dir. Winston-Salem Housing Found.; mem. Centenary United Meth. Ch., Winston-Salem, tchr. Chapel class, chmn. bd. stewards; past chmn. Winston-Salem Dist. United Meth. Ch., Ch. Ext.; past dir., campaign chmn. Triad United Meth. Home. 1st Lt. U.S. Army, 1942-49. Recipient Charles L. Rhyne award Duke U. Law Alumni, 1997; named to Best Lawyers in Am. Fellow Am. Coll. Trial Lawyers; mem. ABA (antitrust and litig. sects.), U.S. 4th Cir. Jud. Conf. (life), N.C. Bar Assn. (past dir.), Forsyth County Bar Assn. (past pres.), Pvt. Adjudication Ctr. Duke U. (past chmn. bd.), U.S. Mil. Acad. Assn. Grads. (bd. trustees emeritus), Order of the Coif, Joseph Branch Inns of Ct., Am. Inns of Ct. Avocations: golf, travel. Office: Robinson and Lawing LLP 101 N Cherry St Ste 720 Winston Salem NC 27101 Home Phone: 336-725-2643. Business E-Mail: nrobinson@robinson-lawing.com.

ROBINSON, ELLEN M., vocalist, educator; b. New Rochelle, NY, July 9, 1949; d. Robert John Robinson and Helen Hughes. MusB, Ithaca Coll., NY, 1971. Tchr. Family Light Music Sch., Sausalito, Calif., 1977—78, Walden Ctr. Sch., Berkeley, Calif., 1978—80, Beacon and High Schs., Oakland, 1988—2002, U. Calif. Berkeley Ext., 2001—02; tchr. master class in solo singing Oakland, 2003—. Pvt. vocal coach, 1971—. Jazz vocalist numerous concert and club performances, 1968—, performer Women's Sonic Collective, 1976—77, Robin Flower Band, 1983—84, Natural Attraction, 1984—85, Spoolie Sisters, 1985—90, Vocolot, 1990—, (CDs) On My Way to You, 2001, Mercy! Ellen Robinson Live, 2006. Mem.: ASCAP, Nat. Assn. Tchrs. of Singing, Nat. Acad. Rec. Artists, Cabaret West, Internat. Assn. Jazz Educators. Avocation: backpacking. Home: 360 Monte Vista Ave # 314 Oakland CA 94611 Office: EMR Music 3542 Fruitvale Ave PMB 143 Oakland CA 94602

ROBINSON, ENDERS ANTHONY, geophysicist, educator, writer; b. Boston, Mar. 18, 1930; s. Edward Arthur and Doris Gertrude (Goodale) Robinson; m. Eva Arborelius, Sept. 9, 1962 (div. 1973); children: Anna, Erik Arthur, Karin; m. Joyce McPeake, Aug. 8, 1992. BS in Math., MIT, 1950, MS in Econs., 1952, PhD in Geophysics, 1954. Dir. geophys. analysis group MIT, Cambridge, Mass., 1952-54, instr. math., 1955-56; geophysicist Gulf Oil Corp., Pitts., 1954-55; petroleum economist Standard Oil Co. NJ, NYC, 1956-57; asst. prof. stats. Mich. State U., East Lansing, 1958; asst. prof. math. U. Wis., Madison, 1958-61, assoc. prof. math. (with tenure), 1961-62; dep. prof. stats. Uppsala (Sweden) U., 1960-64; v.p., dir. Digicon Inc., Houston, 1965-70; pres. Robinson Rsch. Inc., Houston, 1970-82; vis. prof. theoretical and applied mechanics Cornell U., Ithaca, NY, 1981-82; McMan prof. geophysics U. Tulsa, 1983-93; Maurice Ewing and J.L. Worzel prof. geophysics Columbia U., NYC, 1993—2000, prof. emeritus, 2000—. Author: (book) Seismic Inversion and Deconvolution, Dual Sensor Technology, 1999, 31 other books on sci., tech. and history; editor: Internat. Jour. Imaging Sys. & Tech., 1988—; mem. editl. bd.: Multidimensional Sys. and Signal Processing, An Internat. Jour., 1990—. 2d lt. US Army, 1950—51. Recipient Medal award in recognition of outstanding contribr. to the digital processing of seismic data, Soc. Exploration Geophysicists, 1969, Conrad Schlumberger award, European Assn. Exploration Geophysicists, 1969, Donald G. Fink Prize award, IEEE, 1984, Achivement award, Thayer Acad. Alumni, 1997, Alexander von Humboldt Rsch. award for sr. U.S. scientists, 1999, Maurice Ewing Gold medal Lifetime Achievement, 2001, Blaise Pascal medal Earth Scis., European Acad. Scis., 2003. Fellow: European Acad. Scis.; mem.: Nat. Rsch. Coun. (com. undiscovered oil and gas resources), Nat. Acad. Engring. (petroleum and mining sect.), Soc. Exploration Geophysicists (hon. Classic Paper award 1953, 1957, Best Paper award 1964, Reginald Fessenden medal 1969, father of deconvolution 1983, Best Paper award 2001, Maurice Ewing Gold medal 2001), European Assn. Geoscientists and Engrs. (Conrad Schlumberger award 1969), Renaissance Inst. Washington, NY Athletic Club, MIT Club NY. Known as the "Father of Digital Geophysics". Office: 8 Dorothy E Lucey dr Newburyport MA 01950-1781 Office Phone: 978-465-2053. E-mail: endersrobinson@comcast.net.

ROBINSON, EVELYN EDNA, secondary school educator; b. St. John, Maine, Feb. 23, 1911; d. Registe Jalbert and Olive Michaud; m. Carl Robinson, July 19, 1939; children: Robert, James. BA in Math., U. Maine, 1934; MS, U. N.H., 1963; MEd, Hillyer Coll. U., 1960. Tchr. English and math. Ft. Kent (Maine) H.S., 1934; tchr. English and math., coach girls basketball Madewaska (Maine) H.S., 1935-55; tchr. math. Stamford (Conn.) H.S., 1955-56; tchr. math and English, Bristol (Conn.) H.S., 1956-63; prof. math. Worcester (Mass.) State Coll., 1963-77, chmn. dept., 1970-77. Coord. cmty. bus. Worcester State Coll., 1970-77, class advisor, 1968-72, salary equity bd., 1971-73. Vol. libr. Madawaska Pub. Libr., 1936-55; lector Christ the King, Worcester, 1974-2000. Mem. Delta Kappa Gamma. Republican. Roman Catholic. Avocations: decorating, flower arrangements, ceramics, tailoring. Home: 167 N Spencer Rd Spencer MA 01562-1232

ROBINSON, EVELYN ETTA, principal; b. Pocatello, Idaho, Nov. 5, 1946; d. Luther Nelson Robinson and Marian Rose Smith. Tchr. diploma, Bapt. Bible Coll., 1968; BA, U. Ill., Springfield, 1978, MA, 1979; edn. specialist, Idaho State U., Boise, 1988. Cert. elementary tchr., sch. prin., superintendent. 1st grade tchr. Villa Christian Sch., Broadview, Ill., 1968—74, North Jacksonville Elem., Jacksonville, Ill., 1978—79, Bonneville Elem., Pocatello, Idaho, 1979—88; edn. supr. Grace Acad., Springfield, Ill., 1977—78; prin. Westfair Acad., Jacksonville, 1977—84, Lewis & Clark Elem., Pocatello, Idaho, 1988—. Instr. Idaho Sate U. Coll. Edn., Pocatello, 1987—, Dist. 25 Tech. Portfolio, 1997—; curriculum instr. Integration of Tech. into Idaho history, 1999—; in-svc. instr. Dist. 25, Pocatello, 1988—; mentor Dist. 25 Tech. Mentor Program, 1996—; mem. Dist. 25 Curriculum Com., 1996—2000, Leadership for the 21st Century Com., 1997—, Home Page Devel. Com., 1999—, Tchr. Evaluation Com., 2000—01, Sch. Improvement Criteria Com., 2000—01, Enhancement Learning Project Com., 2000—; commr. Idaho State Bd. Edn. Accountability Commn., 2003—; presenter in field. Author: Lewis & Clark School Improvement Profile, 1988—2005. Tchr. children's program Idaho State Mus. Natural History, Pocatello, 1984; mem. Salvation Army Canned Food Drive Com., Pocatello, 1994—, Neighborhood Watch Program, Pocatello, 1994—, Neighborhood Support Group for the Elderly, Pocatello, 1996—, Ross Park Zoological Soc., Pocatello, 2003—; tchr. Sunday Sch. Workshop Nazarene Ch., Pocatello, 1985—; bd. dirs. Pocatello Zoo, 2003—. Nominee Idaho Tchr. of Yr., 1982—83, Outstanding Adminstr., Pocatello Edn. Assn., 1994; named Tchr. of Yr., Bonneville Elem. Parent-Tchr. Assn., 1982—83, Bonneville Elem., 1988—89, Idaho Nat. Disting. Prin., 2005; recipient Outstanding Svc. award, Messiah Baptist Ch., 1972, Outstanding Leadership award, Am. Assn. Sunday Schools, 1977, Sunday Sch. Leadership award, Westfair Baptist Ch., 1979, Dedication to Youth award, Ctr. for Leadership, Edn., and Devel., 1989, 8 Who Make a Difference award, Idaho Channel 8, Pocatello, 1997, Woman of Achievement award, ZONTA Internat., 2005, Excellence in Edn. award, Northwest Regional, 2006, Idaho's Excellence in Edn. award, Alpha Delta Kappa, 2006. Mem.: ASCD, SE Idaho Reading Assn. (bldg. rep. 1983—88, chair newspaper in edn. week 1984—88), Internat. Reading Assn. (chair newspaper in edn. 1986—87, chair Idaho Honors coun. 1987—88), Assn. Elem. Sch. Prins. (v.p. 1989—90, pres. 1990—91, dist. 25, region V), Idaho Assn. Sch. Adminstrs., Idaho Assn. Elem. Sch. Prins. (Idaho Gem award 1990—91, Idaho's Nat. Disting. Prin. award 2005), Nat. Assn. Elem. Sch. Prins., Internat. and Portneuf Valley Audubon Assn., Phi Delta Kappa (chair program com. 1987—88, v.p. program com. 1988—89, v.p. membership 1989—90, pres. 1990—91), Alpha Delta Kappa (sgt. at arms 1982—84, chair altruistic com. 1986—88, chair courtesy com. 1990—92, historian 1992—94, Idahos Excellence in Edn. award 2006). Avocations: gardening, hunting, fishing, birdwatching, hiking. Office: Lewis & Clark Elem 800 Grace Dr Pocatello ID 83201 Business E-Mail: robinsev@d25.k12.id.us.

ROBINSON, FRANK, former professional baseball manager, retired professional baseball player; b. Beaumont, Tex., Aug. 31, 1935; s. Frank and Ruth (Shaw) R.; m. Barbara Ann Cole, Oct. 28, 1961; children: Frank Kevin, Nichelle. Student, Xavier U., Cin. Outfielder Cin. Reds, 1956-65, Balt. Orioles, 1966-71, L.A. Dodgers, 1972, Calif. Angels, 1973-74, Cleve. Indians, 1974-76, mgr., 1975-77; coach Calif. Angels, 1977, Balt. Orioles, 1978-80, 85-87, mgr., 1988-91, asst. to gen. mgr., 1991-95; mgr. San Francisco Giants, 1981-84; batting coach Milw. Brewers, 1984; dir. baseball ops. Arizona Fall League Major League Baseball, 1997—99, v.p. on-field operations, 1999—2002; mgr. Wash. Nationals (formerly Montreal Expos), 2002—06. Author: (with Al Silverman) My Life is Baseball, 1967, (with Barry Steinbach) Extra Innings, 1989, Frank the First Year, 1976. Named Rookie of Yr. Nat. League, 1956, Most Valuable Player, 1961, Am. League, 1966, Am. League Mgr. of Yr., 1982, 89; mem. World Series

Championship Team, 1966, 70, Nat. League All-Star Team, 1956-57, 59, 61-62, 65, Am. League All-Star Team, 1966-67, 69-71, 74; inducted into Baseball Hall of Fame, 1982; recipient Presdl. Medal of Freedom, The White House, 2005.

ROBINSON, FRED COLSON, language educator; b. Birmingham, Ala., Sept. 23, 1930; s. Emmett Colson and Morwenna Hope (Bennett) R.; m. Helen Caroline Wild, June 21, 1959; children: Lisa Karen, Eric Wild. BA, Birmingham So. Coll., 1953; MA, U. N.C., 1954, PhD, 1961; DLitt (hon.), Williams Coll., 1985; MA (hon.), Yale U., 1989. Instr. Stanford (Calif.) U., 1960-61, asst. prof., 1961-65, assoc. prof., 1967-71, prof. English philology, 1971-72; asst. prof. Cornell U., Ithaca, NY, 1965-66, assoc. prof., 1966-67; prof. Yale U., New Haven, 1972-83, Douglas Tracy Smith prof., 1983—2000, prof. emeritus, 2000—, chmn. medieval studies, 1975-78, 80. Vis. prof. Harvard U., Cambridge, Mass., 1983; pub. com. Medieval Acad. Monographs, Cambridge, 1987-90. Author: Old English Literature: Select Bibliography, 1970, Beowulf and the Appositive Style, 1985, The Tomb of Beowulf, 1993, The Editing of Old English, 1994; co-author: A Bibliography...on Old English Literature, 1980, Old English Verse Texts from Many Sources: A Comprehensive Collection, 1991, A Guide to Old English, 7th edit., 2006, Beowulf: An Edition with Relevant Shorter Texts, 1998, rev. edit., 2006; editor Old English Newsletter, 1966-73, Early English MSS in Facsimile, 1971-2002, Jour. English Linguistics, 1971—, Anglo-Saxon England, 1972—, Anglistica, 1981—; contbr. over 100 articles to profl. jours. Trustee Yale Univ. Libr. Assocs., New Haven, 1986-89, 91-95, 97-2000, 03-06. With U.S. Army, 1954-56. Recipient Disting. Vis. Scholar award U. Ala., 1999, William Clyde DeVane medal, 1999; fellow Guggenheim Found., 1974-75, Am. Coun. Learned Socs., 1968-69, Inst. Social and Econ. Rsch., Rhodes U., 1978, Japan Soc. Promotion of Sci., 1989; grantee NEH, 1976, 79, 81, 85, Am. Philos. Soc., 1973, 85; named Professore solo per ricerca Univ. di Roma "La Sapienza", 2000. Fellow AAAS, Medieval Acad. Am. (pres. 1983-84, Haskins medal 1984), Brit. Acad. (corr., Sir Israel Gollancz prize 1997), Meddeleeue-verenigung van Suidelike Afrika (corr.); mem. Finnish Acad. of Sci. and Letters (fgn. mem.), New Eng. Medieval Conf. (pres. 1982-83), Conn. Acad. Arts and Scis. (pres. 1980-85), Internat. Soc. Anglo-Saxonists (elected hon.), Elizabethan Club (bd. govs. 1986-88, v.p. 1989-90, pres. 1990-92), Manuscript Club (v.p. New Haven chpt. 1990-92), Phi Beta Kappa. Episcopalian. Office: Yale Univ Dept English New Haven CT 06520 Business E-Mail: fred.robinson@yale.edu.

ROBINSON, GAIL PATRICIA, retired mental health counselor; b. Medford, Oreg., Dec. 31, 1936; d. Ivan T. and Evelyn H. (Hamilton) Skyrman; m. Douglas L. Smith; children: Shauna J., James D. BS in Edn., Oreg. State U., 1958, PhD in Counseling, 1978; MS in Counseling, Western Oreg. State Coll., 1974. Tchr. Monterey (Calif.) Pub. Schs., 1958-59, Corvallis (Oreg.) Pub. Schs., 1959-62, 69-75, counselor, 1977-81; pvt. practice Corvallis, 1977-95. Vol. therapist Children's Svcs. divsn., Linn and Benton Counties, 1982-83; asst. prof. Western Oreg. State coll., 1977, counselor, 1982-83; mem. grad. faculty Oreg. State U., Corvallis, 1978-95; presenter workshops, lectr. in field. Contbr. articles to profl. jours. Mem. Benton County Mental Health Citizens Adv. Bd., 1979-85, chair, 1982-83; trustee WCTU Children's Farm Home, 1978-84, chair child welfare com., 1982-83, pres., 1984; adv. bd. Old Mill Sch., 1979-85, chair, 1979-81; bd. dirs. Cmty. Outreach, 1979-83; mem. Benton Com. for Prevention of Child Abuse, 1979-85, v.p., 1982; mem. Oreg. Bd. Lic. Profl. Counselors and Therapists, 1989-95, chair, 1989-90, Aurora Colony Historical Soc., vol., 2000-, bd. dirs., 2005-, sec., 2006—. Mem. ACA (govt. rels. com. 1988-91, professionalization com. 1988-92, pres. 1996-97), Am. Mental Health Counselors Assn. (chair consumer and pub. rels. com. 1988-91, bd. dirs. Western region 1989-91, chair strategic planning com. 1994-95, pres. 1992-93), Oreg. Counseling Assn. (chair licensure liaison com. 1985-91, exec. bd. 1985-88, steering com. 1986-87, register editorial com. 1985-86, Disting. Svc. award 1985, 87, Leona Tyler award 1989), Oreg. Mental Health Counselors Assn. Personal E-mail: robinsgp@comcast.net.

ROBINSON, GARRY LEWIN, television news executive; b. Kansas City, Mo., Oct. 26, 1951; s. Calvin Luin and Reba Kathleen (Owen) R.; m. Linda Sue Payton, Oct. 21, 1973 (div. 1982); children: Penny Lynn, Larry Calvin II, Jeff Noel BS, Ark. State U., 1981. Cert. tech. Dynatech Newstar and AP Newscenter Computer Sys. Various positions Sta. KAWW-AM-FM, Heber Springs, Ark., 1969—76, dir. news, ops., 1978; asst. news dir. Sta. KARV-AM, Russellville, Ark., 1976—78; ops. mgr., news dir. Sta. KCON-AM, Conway, Ark., 1978—79; asst. news dir. Sta. KTVE-TV, El Dorado, Ark., 1979—81; mng. prodr. Sta. KAIT-TV, Jonesboro, Ark., 1981—84; newscast prodr. Sta. KOLD-TV, Tucson, 1984—85; newscast prodr., now news ops. mgr. Sta. KSLA-TV, Shreveport, La., 1984—, exec. prodr., 10 PM prodr., newsroom computer sys. mgr., 1985—2005, exec. prodr., computer sys. mgr., news ops. mgr., 1985—2005, info. sys. engr., 2005—. Bd. dirs. North Ark. Fire Dist., Russellville, 1977; bd. advisors City Cable TV Commn., Conway, 1978; chmn. drama divsn. Conway Regional Arts Commn., 1977-78; advisor Explorer Scouts, Shreveport, 1987 Recipient numerous reporter awards Ark. AP, Little Rock, 1969-84, Radio Documentary award Am. Assn. Women in Radio and TV, Little Rock, 1978, various TV news awards La., Tex., Ark., AP Broadcasters Assn., 1985-90 Mem. Radio TV News Dirs. Assn. (Edward R. Murrow award 1987), Sigma Delta Chi (North La. chpt., bd. dirs. 1987), Phi Eta Sigma (pres. 1970-71) Democrat. Baptist. Avocations: reading, writing, guitar, computers, outdoor sports. Home: 5063 Town North Dr Shreveport LA 71107-2843 Office: Sta KSLA-TV 1812 Fairfield Ave Shreveport LA 71101-4431 Office Phone: 318-677-6720. Personal E-mail: garry@garryrobinson.com.

ROBINSON, GENE EZIA, biologist, educator; b. Buffalo, Jan. 9, 1955; s. Jack and Sonja (Rubin) R.; m. Julia O. Robinson, Aug. 29, 1982; children: Aaron, Daniel, Sol. BS in Life Sciences, Cornell U., 1977, MS, 1982, PhD, 1986. Postdoctoral assoc. Ohio State U., Columbus, 1986-89; asst. prof. biology U. Ill., Urbana, 1989-93, assoc. prof. biology, 1993-98, prof. biology, 1998—2003, dir. neuroscience prog., 2001—, G. William Arends prof. of integrative biology, 2003—; team leader Inst. for Genomic Biology, 2004—. Cons. Songbird Genomic Initiative, 2003—. Assoc. editor Ann. Rev. Entomology, 1998—, editl. bd. Jour. Insect Physiology, 1992—, Genes, Brain, and Behavior, 2002—, Jour. Insect Biology, 2002—. Recipient Fulbright Sr. Rsch. Fellowship, Hebrew U., 1995-96, Guggenheim Fellowship, 2003. Fellow AAAS, Am. Acad. Arts & Sciences; mem. Am. Assn. Behavioral Neuroendocrinology, Animal Behavior Soc., Entomol. Soc. Am. (Founders Meml. award, 2003, Recognition award in insect physiology, 2004), Internat. Bee Rsch. Assn., Internat. Soc. Neuroethology, Soc. Neurosci., Internat. Union Study of Social Insects, Internat. Behavioural and Neural Genetics Soc., NAS, Sigma Xi. Achievements include discovery of hormone, neural and genetic factors that regulate behavioral plasticity and division of labor in honeybee colonies. Office: The Robinson Lab--Univ Ill 320 Morrill Hall 505 S Goodwin Ave Urbana IL 61801-3707 E-mail: generobi@uiuc.edu.

ROBINSON, GLENIECE ARMSTRONG, library director; m. Harry Robinson. BS, Ala. State U., 1973; MLS, U. Mich., 1976, PhD in Libr. Sci., 1982. With Libr. Congress, Washington, Dallas Pub. Libr., 1988, asst. dir. pub. svcs.; dir. Ft. Worth Pub. Libr., 1999—. Mem. Tex. Hist. Records Adv. Bd. Ex officio mem. bd. dirs. Ft. Worth Pub. Libr. Found. Recipient Women of Spirit award, Am. Jewish Congress SW Region's Commn. Women's Equality, 1999. Mem.: Tex. Libr. Assn. (mem. exec. bd. 1997, pres.-elect 1998). Office: Ft Worth Pub Libr Adminstrv Offices 500 W 3rd St Fort Worth TX 76102 Office Phone: 817-871-7706. E-mail: gleniece.robinson@fortworthgov.org.

ROBINSON, GLENN, professional basketball player; b. Gary, Ind., Jan. 10, 1973; Student, Purdue U. Basketball player Milw. Bucks, 1994—2002; small forward Atlanta Hawks, 2002, Phila. 76ers, 2003, San Antonio Spurs, 2004—05. Named mem., Ea. Conf. All-Star Team, 2000, 2001. Achievements include member, NBA National Championship Team, 2005. Office: San Antonio Spurs One SBC Ctr San Antonio TX 78219

ROBINSON, GWENDOLYN NIEMA, elementary school educator; d. John Henry and Beatrice Robinson; m. Ronald E. Peterson; children: Wadiya K. Peterson, Zakia N. Peterson, Niemah G. Peterson. BA, Coll. New Rochelle, NY, 1985; MA, CUNY, NYC, 2000; MS, Touro Coll., NYC, 2006—. Tchr. Gates Acad., Bronx, 1988—89, Cmty. elem. Sch. 114X, 1989—90, Macombs Hr. H.S. 82X, 1990—95, CES 64X, 1995—99, Sisulu Children's Acad., NYC, 1999—2000, Kasholu Montefiore Daycare, Bronx, 2000—01, CES124X, 2001—. Tchr., co-chair Sch. Leadership Team, Bronx, 2005—; advisor Bronx Arts Ensemble, 2005—06. Mem.: NAACP, Alumni Assn. City Colls. Baptist. Office: Bd Edn 175 W 166th St Bronx NY 10452

ROBINSON, HARLOW LOOMIS, language educator, historian, writer; b. Bristol, Conn., Sept. 20, 1950; s. Raymond Loomis and Katherine Chaffee Robinson; life ptnr. Robert Frank Holley. BA magna cum laude, Yale U., 1972; MA, PhD, U. Calif., Berkeley, 1980. Prof. Russian SUNY, Albany, 1980—96; prof. modern langs. and history Northeastern U., Boston, 1996—. Presenter in field. Author: (biography) Sergei Prokofiev: A Biography, 1987, 1988, 2002, The Last Impresario: The Life, Times and Legacy of Sol Hurok, 1994 (Albany, NY, Pub. Libr., Author of the Yr., 1994); translator (editor): (translation) Selected Letters of Sergei Prokofiev, 1998; contbr. articles to profl. jours. Editl. bd. Northeastern U. Press, Boston, 2002—03; bd. mem. Citizen Exch. Coun., NYC, 1988—94, Troy (N.Y.) Savs. Bank Music Hall, 1992—95. Fellow Grad. Student Rsch. in Eng. and France, Fulbright-Hayes, 1978—79, Grad. Student rsch. in USSR, IREX/Fulbright, 1979—80; Nat. Def. Fgn. Lang. fellow, 1973—75, Faculty Rsch. fellow, Am. Coun. Learned Socs., 1985, Sr. Scholar Rsch. fellow, Fulbright-Hayes/IREX in USSR, 1991—92, travel fellow for Czech Republic, Whiting Found., 2002, Sr. Rsch. grantee, NEH, 1988, Soviet Scholars Travel grantee, Soros Found., 1991, Short-Term Rsch. grantee, Kennan Inst., 1993. Mem.: MLA, Am. Assn. for the Advancement Slavic Studies, Authors Guild, Am. Assn. Tchrs. Slavic and East European Langs. (assoc.; v.p. 2001—03), Phi Beta Kappa. Avocations: travel, swimming, singing, piano. E-mail: h.robinson@neu.edu.

ROBINSON, HAROLD GILBERT, retired military officer, civilian military employee; b. NYC, Jan. 21, 1935; s. Mark Joseph and Millie Nmi Robinson; m. Renee Joy Robinson, Mar. 5, 1990; children: Ricky Lee, Gay Lee, John Lee, Robin Kiyoshi, Soontorn Nmi Leoni-Robinson, Marc Allan, Jasmine Sangwan. AA, Leeward CC, Pearl City, Hawaii, 1978; BS summa cum laude, Chaminade U., Honolulu, 1980; MA with honors, Ctrl. Mich. U., 1981; PhD, U. Libre de Terapias Psicobionergeticas, Salvador-Bahia, Brazil, 2006; PhD (hon.), U. Manila, 2004, U. Martial Arts, Arak, Iran, 2004, Internat. U. Martial Arts and Scis., 2006. Spl. ops. escape and evasion instr. Dept. of USAF, Randolph AFB, Tex., 1952—76, gen.'s aide for BGEN C.T. Edwinson Bergstrom AFB, Tex., 1962—67, presdl. support: L.B. Johnson Austin, Tex., 1964—67, ret. res., 1976—86; dir., pers. and cmty. activities Dept. of Army, Republic of Korea, 1989—96, chief cmty. recreation divsn. Bamberg, Germany, 1998—2000; dir. cmty. activities Def. Fgn. Lang. Ctr., Monterey, Calif., 1996—98; chief cmty. recreation and bus. ops. HQ 98th Area Support Group, Wuerzburg, Germany, 2000—03; SE Asia exec. liaison McCoskrie/Threshhold Found., Bangkok, 2002—; sr. exec. officer Armed Services Judo, Naval Air Station Pensacola, Fla., 2005—. US rep. degree rev. and adjudication U. of Therapeutic Psychodynamics, Salvador-Bahia, Brazil, 2004—. Entertainer WOR Radio, NYC. Master sgt. USAF, 1952—76. Decorated Dept. of USAF, Royal Thai Air Force, Govts. Vietnam and South Korea; named to Hall of Fame, Elite Grandmaster of Honor, Internat. Hall of Honor/Hall of Champions Assn., 2006, 10th Internat. Black Belt Martial Arts Hall of Fame, World Martial Arts League, 2007, Hall of Fame, Shihan of Yr. award judo, US Universal Martial Arts Hall of Fame, 2002, Hall of Fame, Platinum Pioneer Over 50 Years Tchg., Sang Kim Celebrity Hall of Fame, 2005, Hall of Fame, Am. Pioneer award, Legends of Champion Martial Arts Assn., 2005, Hall of Fame, Elite Man of Honor Close Quarter Combat, US Head of Family Martial Arts Assn., 2005; recipient Platinum Life award, World Organizer of Martial Arts Assns., 2005, Hall of Fame award, Internat. Kempo Assn., 2006, Martial Arts Hall of Honors and Spirit award, Action Martial Arts Mag., 2007, Hall of Fame and Hall of Honor award, Am. Fedn. Martial Arts Assns., 2007, US Presdl. award, 1989. Master: US Martial Arts Assn. (internat. armed services dir. devel. 2001, Golden Life award 2000, Most Disting. Master 2001, Hall of Fame, Founder's Lifetime Achievement award 2006, Disting. Humanitarian of Yr. 2003), US Judo Assn. (master judo rank examiner and certifier 1996—, benefactor), US Ju-jitsu Fedn. (former nat. program dir. US traditional Kodokan judo 2005); mem.: Internat. Kempo Fedn. (grandmaster Kokusai Kempo Tokukai 2003—), SE Asia Martial Arts Internat. Fedn. (commr. 2005—), Martial Arts Internat. Fedn. (founding bd. dirs. 2005—), US Martial Arts Fedn. (charter gold life founder, bd. dirs. 2005—). Republican. Buddhist. Avocations: physical fitness training, Kodokan judo training, fishing, travel. Home: 569 Batten Blvd Pensacola FL 32507 Home Phone: 850-492-9593. Office Fax: 850-492-6382; Home Fax: 850-492-6382. Personal E-mail: robin0305@aol.com.

ROBINSON, HENRY WARD, meteorologist; b. Schoharie, NY, June 30, 1940; s. Frank Locklyn and Esther (Lawyer) R.; m. Muriel Scott, Aug. 15, 1964; children: Katherine, Heather, David. BS, SUNY, Oneonta, 1964; MS, Pa. State U., 1970. Tchg. asst. Pa. State U., State College, 1968-72; instr. Upsala Coll., East Orange, NJ, 1973-75; analyst Computer Sci. Corp., Silver Spring, Md., 1975-78; meteorologist Nat. Weather Svc. NOAA, Silver Spring, 1978—2005; faculty Embry-Riddle Aeronautical U., 2006—. Adj. prof. Montgomery Coll., Germantown, Md., 1983-2005; mentor NASA Goddard Space Flight Ctr. Ea. Region Remote Sensing Applications Ctr.; vis. instr. NSF program Notre Dame U., South Bend, Ind.; data stream instr., adv. Am. Meteorol. Data Stream Project Contbr. numerous articles to profl. jours.; writer, coord., dir., editor tng. videos. Mem. Am. Meteorol. Soc. (bd. sch. and popular meteorol. and oceanographic edn., contbg. editor operational terms Glossary of Meteorology, bd. women and minorities), Am. Geophys. Union. Home: 19622 Enterprise Way Montgomery Village MD 20886 Business E-Mail: henry.robinson@erau.edu.

ROBINSON, HERBERT HENRY, III, psychotherapist, educator; b. Leavenworth, Wash., Mar. 31, 1933; s. Herbert Henry II and Alberta (Sperber) R.; m. Georgia Murial Jones, Nov. 24, 1954 (div. 1974); children: Cheri Dean Asbury, David Keith, Peri Elizabeth Layton, Tanda Rene Graff, Gaila Daire. Grad. of Theology, Bapt. Bible Coll., 1959; BA in Philosophy/Greek, Whitworth Coll., 1968; MA in Coll. Teaching, Ea. Wash. U., 1976; PhD, Gonzaga U., 2002. Cert. psychotherapist, perpetrator treatment program supervision; nat. bd. cert. counselor. Choir dir. Twin City Bapt. Temple, Mishawaka, Ind., 1959-61; min. Inland Empire Bapt. Ch., Spokane, Wash., 1961-73; tchr. philosophy Spokane C.C., 1969-72; dir. Alternatives to Violence, Women in Crisis, Fairbanks, Alaska, 1985-87; tchr. pub. rels. U. Alaska, Fairbanks, 1986-87; dir. Alternatives to Violence Men Inc., Juneau, 1988-89; tchr. leadership mgmt. U. Alaska S.E., Juneau, 1988-89; min. Sci. of Mind Ctr., Sandpoint, Idaho, 1989-92; dir., therapist Tapio Counseling Ctr., Spokane, 1991—; cert. psychotherapist, supr. perpetrator treatment program Wash. Cons. Lilac Blind/Alpha Inc./Marshall Coll., Spokane, 1975-85, Alaska Placer Mining Co., Fairbanks, 1987; tchr. Spokane Falls C.C., Spokane, 1979-85; seminar, presenter Human Resource Devel., Spokane and Seattle, Wash., Pa., 1980; guest trainer United Way/Kellogg Found. Inst. for Volunteerism, Spokane, 1983. 1st trombone San Diego Marine Band, 1953-56, Spokane Symphony, 1961; bd. dirs. Tanani Learning Ctr., Fairbanks, 1987; mem. consensus bldg. team Sci. of Mind Ctr., Sandpoint, 1989-92. Cpl. USMC, 1953-56. Mem. ACA, Assn. for Humanistic Edn. and Devel., Assn. for Religious Values in Counseling, Internat. Assn. Addictions and Offender Counselors, Internat. Assn. Marriage and Family Counselors, Am. Assn. Profl. Hypnotherapists, Masterson Inst. Office: Tapio Counseling 5325 E Sprague Ave Spokane WA 99212-0820 Home Phone: 509-927-9825; Office Phone: 509-534-5028. E-mail: peace@herb-robinson.com.

ROBINSON, HOBART KRUM, management consulting company executive; b. Quincy, Mass., Oct. 8, 1937; s. Hobart Krum and Charlotte Elizabeth (Hall) R.; m. Gerd Ingela Janhede, Oct. 17, 1964; children: Steven Whitney, Karina Jill, Peter Danforth. BA, Williams Coll., 1959; MBA, Columbia U., 1964. Market analyst Mobil Chem. Co., Richmond, Va., 1964-67; mgr. program analysis and control Polaroid Corp., Cambridge, Mass., 1967-69; exec. v.p., dir. Simplex Wire and Cable, Inc., North Berwick, Maine, 1969-73; sr. engagement mgr. McKinsey and Co., Inc., NYC, 1973-76, prin. Copenhagen, 1977-81, NYC, 1985-89, Stockholm, 1989-95, dir. adminstrn. Eastern Europe, 1993-95, dir. adminstrn. NYC, 1995-98; pres., CEO Brink's Inc., Darien, Conn., 1981-84; ret., 1998. Dir. Burlington No. Air Freight, Inc., Newport Beach, Calif., 1982-84. Pres. Am. Club in Copenhagen, 1980-81; dir. Fulbright Commn., Copenhagen, 1980-81; vice chair Williams Coll. Alumni Fund, 1999—2004. Lt. USNR, 1959-62. Mem. Tournament Players Club (Ponte Vedra, Fla.), Taconic Golf Club (Williamstown, Mass.), Marsh Landing Country Club (Ponte Vedra, Fla.), Sawgrass Country Club (Ponte Vedra), Ponte Vedra Golf and Country Club. Republican. Episcopalian. Home (Summer): 94 Ide Rd Williamstown MA 01267-2815 E-mail: bartrobin@aol.com.

ROBINSON, HOWARD ARTHUR, JR., minister; s. Howard Arthur Sr. and Mary Hairston Robinson; children: Dionne Carol, Angela Marie, Howard Arthur III. MDiv, Morehouse Sch. of Religion / Interdenominational Theol. Ctr., 1976. Cert. advanced marriage and family therapy Puget Sound Counseling Ctr., 1979, consecrated as Bishop Full Gospel Bapt. Ch. Fellowship Internat., 2000. Pres. Berean Kingdom Ctr., Renton, Wash., 1995—2002; adj. prof. N.W. Coll. Assemblies God, Kirkland, 1999—2001; provost Sunday sch. curriculum Full Gospel Bapt. Ch. Fellowship, Seattle, 1999—2003, aux. bishop New Orleans, 2000—03, bishop for Wash. and Oreg. states Seattle, 2000—03; pres. Berean Acad. Christian Devel., Renton, 1995—; presiding bishop and chief apostle Agape Christian Fellowship Internat., Seattle, 2002—; pres. Howard A. Robinson, Jr. Ministries, Kent, Wash., 2002—. Pres. Black United Clergy for Action Pacific N.W., Seattle, 1995—2000; moderator Macedonia Dist. Bapt. Assn.; pres. pastors conf. Nat. Bapt. Conv. Am., Inc., v.p. congress of christian workers, Shreveport, La., 1998—99; sec. Gen. Bapt. Conv. N.W., Portland, Oreg. Author: Changing the 21st Century Ch., 2003. Adv. bd. mem. Wells Fargo Bank, Seattle, 1995—96, First Interstate Bank, Seattle. Maj. USAFR, 1967—90. Decorated Am. Spirit Honor Medal U. S. Army, Trainee of the Cycle; M. L. King scholar, Coun. Chs. Seattle Wash., 1974—76. Avocations: swimming, travel, photography. Office: Agape Christian Fellowship International P O Box # 58009 Tukwila WA 98138 Home Phone: 253-859-0031; Office Phone: 425-255-4562.

ROBINSON, HUGH GRANVILLE, consulting management company executive; b. Washington, Aug. 4, 1932; s. James Hill and Wilhelmina (Thomas) R.; 1 stepchild, Mia; children by previous marriage: Hugh Granville, Susan K. Student, Williams Coll., 1949-50; BS, U.S. Mil. Acad., 1954; MS, MIT, 1959; LLD, Williams Coll., 1983. Commd. 2d lt. U.S. Army, 1954, advanced through grades to maj. gen., 1983; platoon leader, co. comdr. Co. B, 185th Engrs. Bn., Korea, 1955; platoon leader, ops. officer 74th Engr. Co., Korea, 1955-56; br. chief Engr. Supply Control Office, St. Louis, 1956-58; chief Catalog and Authorization div. Engr. Supply Control Agy., Orleans, France, 1960-62; co. comdr. 553d Engr. Bn., Orleans, 1962-63; chief combat br. War Plans divsn. Engr. Strategic Studies Group, Washington, 1963-65; Army asst. to armed forces aide to Pres. Washington, 1965-69; comdr. 39th Engr. Bn., Vietnam, 1969-70; br. chief war plans divsn. Office Dep. Chief Staff for Ops., Washington, 1970-71; assigned Nat. War Coll., 1972; comdr. 3rd regt. U.S. Corps Cadets, West Point, NY, 1973-74, U.S. Army Engr. Sch. Brigade, Fort Belvoir, Va., 1974-76; dist. engr. U.S. Army Engr. Dist., LA, 1976-78; dep. dir. civil works office Chief of Engrs., Washington, 1978-80; comdr. Southwestern Divsn., U.S. Army C.E., 1980-83; ret., 1983; v.p. Southland Corp., Dallas, 1983-88; pres. Cityplace Devel. Corp.; sr. v.p. Grigsby Brandford Powell, Inc., 1988-94; chmn., CEO The Tetra Group, Inc., Dallas, 1989—2002; chmn. Granville Cons. and Devel. Co., Inc., 2001—03, Global Bldg. Sys., Dallas, 2004—. Mem. Mississippi River Commn., 1980-83, bd. engrs. for rivers and harbors, 1980-83, Coastal Engring. Rsch. Bd., 1980-83; bd. dirs. Carmax, Inc., Guaranty Bank, Aleris Internat., New Market Tech.; chmn. Dallas Fed. Res. Bd., 1991; adv. bd. TXU; with Tex. Pub. Broadcasting, LBJ Found., 1989—. Mem. nat. bd. dirs. Keep Am. Beautiful, 1981-85; bd. dirs. Dallas Symphony, 1981-85, Dallas United Way, 1984-92, Baylor U. Med. Ctr. Found., 1983-91, Dallas Opera, 1983-90, Dallas Citizens Coun., 1987-91, Greater Dallas C. of C., 1986-91, Vietnam Vets Meml. Fund Tex.; chmn. African Am. Mus., Dallas Youth Svcs. Corp.; trustee Dallas Mus. Fine Arts, 1988-93; mem. adv. coun. U. Tex. Engring. Fedn., 1991—. Mem. Am. Soc. Mil. Engrs. (past sec. Orleans chpt., regional v.p. Tex., pres. Dallas chpt.), Assn. U.S. Army, Dallas Black C. of C., ASCE Methodist. Office Phone: 214-415-4200. Personal E-mail: general2star@aol.com.

ROBINSON, IRWIN JAY, lawyer; b. Bay City, Mich., Oct. 8, 1928; s. Robert R. and Anne (Kaplan) R.; m. Janet Binder, July 7, 1957; children: Elizabeth Binder Schubiner, Jonathan Meyer, Eve Kimberly Wiener. AB, U. Mich., 1950; JD, Columbia U., 1953. Bar: N.Y. 1956. Assoc. Breed Abbott & Morgan, NYC, 1955-58; asst. to ptnrs. Dreyfus & Co., NYC, 1958-59; assoc. Greenbaum Wolff & Ernst, NYC, 1959-65, ptnr., 1966-76; sr. ptnr. Rosenman & Colin, NYC, 1976-90; of counsel Pryor, Cashman, Sherman & Flynn, 1990-92; sr. ptnr. Phillips, Nizer, Benjamin, Krim & Ballon, NYC, 1992-99; pvt. practice NYC, 1999—. Asst. treas. Saarsteel, Inc., Whitestone, N.Y., 1970—. Bd. dirs. Henry St. Settlement, N.Y.C., 1960-85, Jewish Cmty. Ctr. Assn. N.Am., N.Y.C., 1967-94, mem. adv. bd., 1998—; bd. dirs. Heart Rsch. Found., 1989-94, pres., 1991-93. Mem. ABA, Assn. Bar City of NY, Thai-Am. C. of C. (founder, bd. dirs. 1992-95, pres. 1992-95), Vietnam-Am. C. of C. (founder, bd. dirs. 1992-95, pres. 1992-95), Philippine-Am. C. of C. (bd. dirs. 1960-98), Sunningdale Country Club, Desert Mountain Club. Jewish. Home: 290 West End Ave New York NY 10023 Office: care Kramer Levin Naftalis & Frankel 1177 Avenue of The Americas New York NY 10036 Home Phone: 212-496-2841; Office Phone: 212-715-7656. Personal E-mail: ijrjbr@aol.com.

ROBINSON, J. PATRICK, consumer products company executive; B, Wharton Sch. Univ. Pa.; MBA, Loyola Univ. CPA. Acct. KPMG, Balt.; fin. mgmt. positions through v.p. fin. Black & Decker, 1982—2000; CFO AirClic Inc.; v.p., contr. Newell Rubbermaid Inc., Atlanta, 2001—03, exec. v.p., CFO, 2003—. Office: Newell Rubbermaid 10B Glenlake Pky Atlanta GA 30328 *

ROBINSON, JACK ALBERT, retail executive; b. Detroit, Feb. 26, 1930; s. Julius and Fannie (Aizkowitz) Robinson; m. Aviva Freedman, Dec. 21, 1952; children: Shelby, Beth, Abigail. B in Pharmacy, Wayne State U., 1952. Founder, chief exec. officer, chmn. bd. Perry Drug Stores, Inc., Pontiac, Mich., 1957-95; founder, chmn., pres. JAR Group LLC, Bloomfield Hills, Mich., 1996—. Chmn. Wayne State U. Fund, Detroit, 1986,

Concerned Citizens for Arts Mich., 1990, 1991—; chmn. ann. fund Detroit Symphony Orch.; bd. dirs. United Way Pontiac, Mich., 1986, United Found. Detroit, 1986, Pontiac Area Urban League, Cmty. Found., S.E. Mich., Detroit Svc. Group, Save Orch. Hall, Inc., Cranbrook Inst. Sci., Jewish Fedn. Apts., Wetzman Inst. Sci., Holocaust Meml. Ctr., Harper-Grace Hosp., Detroit; past dir. Pontiac Symphony, Boys Club, Detroit Osteo. Hosp.; pres. United Jewish Found. Met. Detroit, 1992—94; co-chmn. Greater Detroit Interfaith Round Table NCCJ, 1986—92, v.p., 1994—95; pres. Jewish Fedn. Met. Detroit, 1992—94. Named Entrepreneur of the Yr., Harvard Bus. Sch., Detroit, 1982; recipient Disting. Alumni award, Wayne State U. Coll. Pharmacy, 1975, Eleanor Roosevelt Humanities award, State of Israel, 1978, Youth Svcs. Am. Tradition award, B'nai B'rith, 1982, Gt. Am. Traditions award, 1991, Disting. Alumni award, Wayne State U., 1985, Corp. Leadership award, 1985, Tree of Life award, Jewish Nat. Fund, 1985, Disting. Citizen award, Pontiac Boy Scouts Am., 1985, Brotherhood award, Booker T. Washington Bus. Assn., 1986, Humanitarian award, March of Dimes, 1987, Variety Club, 1988, award, Weizmann Rsch. Inst., 1987, Fred M. Butzel award, Jewish Fedn. Met. Detroit, 1991, Cmty. Svc. award, Am. Arabic and Jewish Friends, 1995, Outstanding Philanthropic award, Nat. Soc. Fundraising Execs., 1999, Mich. Hall of Fame award in Real Estate and Retailing, Internat. Coun. Shopping Ctrs., 2001, Gov.'s Arts award Spl. Recognition, 2003. Mem.: Econ. Club (bd. dirs. Detroit chpt.), Am. Found. for Pharm. Edn. (bd. dirs.), Am. Pharm. Assn., Nat. Assn. Chain Drug Stores (chmn. 1987, Lifetime Achievement award 1995, Robert B. Begley award 1995). Avocations: skiing, jogging, photography, classical music, glass collecting. Office: JAR Group LLC Ste 3100 4190 Telegraph Rd Bloomfield Hills MI 48302-2082

ROBINSON, JAMES ALFRED, middle school educator; b. Phila., May 13, 1939; s. James Alfred Sr. and Evelyn (Perry) R.; children: James, John, Marce Balais; m. Gladys Acaba, Mar. 9, 1996. BS, Cheyney U., Pa., 1961; postgrad., U. Pa., 1962, Temple U., 1966—68, Goddard Coll., 1989—90, C.C. Phila., 1989. Mid. sch. tchr. Phila. Pub. Sch. Sys., 1962-95. Mem. reading program grades 4-6, TV lang. arts Project Climb, Sch. Dist. Phila., 1974; mem. panel, asst. prodr. video prodn. Skills for New Teachers, Sch. Dist. Phila., 1975; social sci. specialist Samson L. Freedman Sch. Humanities Alternative Middle sch., Dist. Phila., 1977; chmn. J.A. Robinson Assocs. Video Prodn. Cons., Phila., 1988—; instr. ednl. media Temple U., 1988-90; video prodn. cons. In Search of History: The Underground Railroad, History channel, 1999; video documentaries include Linda Creed Concert, Mayoral Race: Phila., 1985, Duality, Bicentennial Celebration. Media arts fellow Mid-Atlantic region Pitts. Filmmakers NEA, Pa. Coun. for Arts, 1993. Mem. HTML Writers Guild. Baptist. Avocations: photography, music, tennis.

ROBINSON, JAMES ARTHUR, political scientist; b. Blackwell, Okla., June 9, 1932; s. William L. and Ethel Bell (Hicks) R.; children: Adelaide, Luke; m. Andrea C. Hatcher, Jan. 20, 2006 AB, George Washington U., 1954, DPS (hon.), 1977; MA, U. Okla., 1955; PhD, Northwestern U., 1957. Congl. fellow Am. Polit. Sci. Assn., 1957-58; Instr. polit. sci. Northwestern U., 1958-59, asst. prof., 1959-62, assoc. prof., 1962-64; prof. polit. sci. Ohio State U., Columbus, 1964-71; dir. Mershon Center, 1967-70, v.p. acad. affairs, provost, 1969-71; pres., prof. polit. sci. Macalester Coll., St. Paul, 1971-74; pres. U. West Fla., Pensacola, 1974-88, pres. emeritus, 1988—, Regents prof., 1988—2002. Author: (with R. C. Snyder) National and International Decision Making, 1961, Congress and Foreign Policy Making, rev. edit, 1967, House Rules Committee, 1963, (with J. Baum) Party Primaries in Taiwan, 1999, (with D. Brown and E. Moon) Appraising Steps in Democratization: Elections in Taiwan, 1986-2000, 2000. Mem.: Cosmos (Washington).

ROBINSON, JAMES D., III, venture capitalist; b. Atlanta, Nov. 19, 1935; m. Bettye Bradley (div.); 2 children; m. Linda Gosden, 1984; 2 children. BS, Ga. Inst. Tech., 1957; MBA, Harvard U., 1961. Officer various depts. Morgan Guaranty Trust Co. of N.Y., NYC, 1961-66, asst. v.p., staff asst. to chmn. bd. and pres., 1967-68; gen. ptnr. White, Weld & Co., 1968-70; exec. v.p. Am. Express Co., NYC, 1970-75, pres., dir., 1975-77, chmn. bd. dirs., CEO, 1977-93. Pres., CEO Am. Express Internat. Banking Corp., 1970-73; chair Am. Express Credit Corp., 1973-75; co-founder, gen. ptnr. RRE Ventures, 1994—; chmn., CEO RRE Investors LLC; bd. dirs. Coca Cola Co., Novell, Inc., First Data Corp.; former co-chair Bus. Roundtable; non-exec. chmn. Bristol-Myers Squibb Co., 2005—. Author: Inflation Overkill, 1994, Full Steam Ahead, 2000. Active Bus. Coun., Coun. on Fgn. Rels., U.S. Japan Bus. Coun., Dean's Adv. Coun. Roberto C. Goizueta Sch. Bus. Emory U., Exec. Adv. Bd., Ivan Allen Coll.; hon. chmn. bd. Meml. Sloan-Kettering Cancer Ctr.; hon. mem. The Brookings Instn.; mem. bd. dirs. Nat. Acad. Found.; mem. Pres.' Cir. The Asia Soc.; bd. dirs., chair emeritus Partnership of N.Y.C.; chair emeritus World Travel & Tourism Coun.; former chair Internat. Trade and Investment Task Force of the Bus. Roundtable, former chair svcs. policy adv. com.; former chmn. adv. com. on trade and policy negotiations United Way of Am.; former mem. Coun. on Competitiveness; former trustee Alfred P. Sloan Found., Coun. on Econ. Devel.; former mem. Dewitt Wallace Found. Lt. USNR, 1957-59. Mem. Econ. Club (N.Y.C.). Office: RRE Ventures 126 E 56th St Fl 22 New York NY 10022-3613 Office Phone: 212-418-5100.

ROBINSON, JAMES G., film production executive; b. Balt., 1935; five children. Former owner automobile distributorship; profl. photographer; founder, chmn., CEO Morgan Creek Prodns. Prodr.: (films) Major League, 1989, Stay Tuned, 1992, The Crush, 1993, Ace Ventura: Pet Detective, 1994, Major League II, 1994, Trial By Jury, 1994, Silent Fall, 1994, Ace Ventura: When Nature Calls, 1995, Two If by Sea, 1996, Big Bully, 1996, Diabolique, 1996, Bad Moon, 1996, Wild America, 1997, Incognito, 1997, Major League: Back to the Minors, 1998, Wrongfully Accused, 1998, Soldier, 1998, The King and I, 1999, Chill Factor, 1999, The In Crowd, 2000, American Outlaws, 2001, Juwanna Man, 2002, I'll Be There, 2003, Exorcist: The Beginning, 2004, Dominion: Prequel to the Exorcist, 2005, Two for the Money, 2005, Man of the Year, 2006; exec. prodr.: The Stone Boy, 1984, Girls Just Want to Have Fun, 1985, Grunt! The Wrestling Movie, 1985, Where the River Runs Black, 1986, Young Guns, 1988, Dead Ringers, 1988, Skin Deep, 1989, Renegades, 1989, Enemies A Love Story, 1989, Nightbreed, 1990, Coupe de Ville, 1990, Young Guns II, 1990, The Exorcist III, 1990, Pacific Heights, 1990, Robin Hood: Prince of Thieves, 1991, Freejack, 1992, White Sands, 1992, The Last of the Mohicans, 1992, True Romance, 1993. Office: Morgan Creek Prodns 4000 Warner Blvd Bldg 76 Burbank CA 91522-0001 *

ROBINSON, JAMES WILLIAM, chemistry professor; b. Kidderminster, Eng., July 12, 1923; arrived in U.S., 1955, naturalized, 1958; s. James William and Eva Robinson; m. Winifred Gladys Nixon, Jan. 8, 1946; children: James William, Linda Juanita, Sandra Jacqueline. BSc with hons., U. Birmingham, England, 1949, PhD, 1952, DSc, 1978. Sr. sci. officer Brit. Civl Svc., Birmingham, England, 1952—55; from rsch. assoc. to prof. emeritus La. State U., Baton Rouge, 1955—93, prof. emeritus, 1993—; sr. chemist Esso Rsch. Labs., Baton Rouge, 1956—63; tech. advisor Ethyl Corp., Baton Rouge, 1963—64. Mem. rsch. grants adv. com. EPA, 1969—75; vis. prof. U. Sydney, 1983; lectr. in field. Author: Atomic Absorption Spectroscopy, 1966, 2d edit., 1975, Undergraduate Instrumental Analysis, 1970, 6th edit., 2005, Atomic Spectroscopy, 1990, 2d edit., 1996; editor: Analytica Chemica Acta, 1956—80, Spectroscopy Letters, 1966—98, Environl. Sci. and Health, 1971—97, Monograph Series Analysis Environ. Control, 1977—85, Applied Spectroscopy Revs., 1977—90, Jour. Applied Spectroscopy, 2003, Handbook of Spectroscopy, Vol. I, 1974, Handbook of Spectroscopy, Vol. II, 1974, Handbook of Spectroscopy, Vol. III, 1981, Practical Handbook of Spectroscopy, 1991; contbr. articles to profl. jours., chapters to books. Recipient Gold medal, N.Y. Soc. Applied Spectroscopy, 2000; fellow, Guggenheim Found., 1975. Fellow: Royal Chem. Soc. Avocations: gardening, travel, snorkeling. Office: Dept Chemistry La Sate Univ Baton Rouge LA 70803 Office Phone: 225-578-3025. Business E-Mail: jwrobi24@lsu.edu.

ROBINSON, JANET L., publishing executive; BA in English cum laude, Salve Regina Coll., Newport, RI, 1972; diploma in Exec. Edn., Dartmouth U., 1996; DBA (hon.), Salve Regina U., Newport, RI, 1998. Tchr., reading specialist, 1972—83; account exec., Tennis Mag. NY Times Co., 1983—85, nat. resort and travel mgr., Golf Digest/Tennis, 1985—87, advt. dir., Tennis Mag., 1987—90, v.p. advt. sales and mktg., The Women's Mag. Group, 1990—92, group sr. v.p., advt. sales and mktg., The Women's Mag. Group, 1992—93, v.p., dir. advt., 1994, sr. v.p. advt., 1995, pres., gen. mgr., N.Y. Times newspaper, 1996—, sr. v.p. newspaper ops., 2001—04, exec. v.p., COO, 2004—, dir., 2004—, pres., CEO, 2005—. Cons. Dept. Edn., Mass., 1977—83; chair. Advertising Council, 2004—. Mem. Literacy Vols. NY; mem. adv. bd. Salve Regina Coll.; trustee Carnegie Corp., 2004—. Named Outstanding Newspaper Exec., Frohlinger's Mktg. Report, 1994; named one of 100 Most Powerful Women in World, Forbes Mag., 2005—06. Mem.: Women in Comm., Advt. Women NY, Advt. Club NY. Office: NY Times 229 W 43rd St New York NY 10036-3959 *

ROBINSON, JAY (THURSTON), artist; b. Detroit, Aug. 1, 1915; s. Carter Boston and Marie Rose (Steger) R.; m. Dorothy June Whipple, Sept. 15, 1937 (dec. 1968); children: Theodore Carter, Thomas Whipple, James Jay; m. Anne Frances Helen Posch, Nov. 5, 1970 (dec. 1999). BA, Yale U., New Haven, Conn., 1937; MFA, Cranbrook Acad. Art, 1943. One-man shows include, Guggenheim Mus. Non-Objective Painting, NYC, 1947, Milch Galleries, NYC, 1948, 51, 53, 54, 55, 56, J.B. Speed Art Mus., Louisville, 1953, Dayton Art Inst., 1953, Phila. Art Alliance, 1957, Monede Gallery, NYC, 1961, 62, Raymond Burr Galleries, Beverly Hills, Calif., 1963, xxth Century West Gallery, NYC, 1968, E. Kuhlik Gallery, NYC, 1971, New Canaan Soc. for Arts, 1983, Broome St. Gallery, NYC, 1994, Ga. Mus. Art, Athens, 2006; group shows include, Guggenheim Mus., 1947, 49, Carnegie Inst., Pitts., 1949, Des Moines Art Center, 1950, Butler Inst., Youngstown, Ohio, 1953, also Audubon Artists, NYC, Corcoran Gallery, Washington, Mich. Artists, Detroit, NAD, NYC, Pa. Acad., Phila., Provincetown Annual, Mass., Va. Biennial, Richmond; represented in permanent collections, including, Detroit Inst. Art, Houston Mus. Fine Art, Witte Meml. Mus., San Antonio, Philbrook Art Center, Tulsa; Berea Coll., Goucher Coll., Fisk U.; represented also in corp. collections, including, IBM; Republic Steel Co., Bristol-Myers Squibb, portrait painter, designer china and textiles; illustrator: Seventeenth Summer (Maureen Daly), 1948, The New York Guide Book, 1964; contbr. illustrations to other books. Served with OSS, 1943; Served with USN, 1943-46. Louis Comfort Tiffany Found. award, 1950; various purchase awards Am. Acad. Arts and Letters, 1951-64; Outstanding Alumnus award Detroit Country Day Sch., 1966 Home: 305 E Landing Williamsburg VA 23185-8254 *I have always been drawn to the theme of Man in His Environment. By extension to our own, I love jazz music, many of whose players I have painted; classic cars; Japanese gardens; good company and active social life. Travel enables me to see what others have done and are doing.*

ROBINSON, JEFFERY P., lawyer; b. Memphis, Aug. 30, 1956; BA cum laude, Marquette U., 1978; JD, Harvard U., 1981. Bar: Wash. 1981, US Dist. Ct. (we. dist. Wash.) 1981, US Ct. Appeals (9th cir.) 1986. Pub. defender state, fed. courts, 1981—88; atty. criminal def. Schroeter, Goldmark & Bender, P.S., Seattle. Instr. trial advocacy prog. U. Wash. Sch. Law, 1988—; faculty Nat. Criminal Def. Coll., Macon, Ga.; mem. trial advocacy workshop Harvard Law Sch., 1990—. Contbr. articles to law jours. Named Lawyer of Yr., King County Bar Assn., 2003; named one of Am. Top Black Lawyers, Black Enterprise Mag., 2003. Fellow: Am. Coll. Trial Lawyers; mem.: Nat. Inst. Trial Advocacy, NACDL (bd. dirs.), Wash. Assn. Criminal Def. Lawyers (past pres.), Wash. State Trial Lawyers Assn., Wash. State Bar Assn. (mem. criminal law exec. com. 1989). Office: Schroeter Goldmark & Bender PS 810 Third Ave Ste 500 Seattle WA 98104 Office Phone: 206-622-8000. Office Fax: 206-682-2305. *

ROBINSON, JENNIFER META, academic administrator, consultant; b. Boston, 1962; d. Samuel Sachs and Catherine Greenacre Robinson; m. J. A. Hartenfeld, 1946; 1 stepchild, Sarah Meghan Hartenfeld. PhD in Am. Lit., Ind. U., 2001. Dir., campus instrnl. cons. Ind. U., Bloomington, 2002—. Coord. scholarship of tchg. and learning Ind. U., 2003—; adj. lectr. Ind. U. Dept. Comm. and Culture, 2006—. Contbr. chapters to books, articles to profl. jours; author: Kate Douglas Wiggin:Bibliography of American Fiction, 1866 to 1918, 1993, A Question of Authority: Dealing With Disruptive Students." In Our Own Voice: Graduate Students Teach Writing, 1999, The Farmers' Market Book: Growing Food, Cultivating Community, 2007, poems. Institutional coord. Carnegie Acad. Advancementof Scholarship of Tchg. and Learning Leadership, 2003—; treas. People and Animal Learning Svcs., Bloomington, Ind., 2000—05; mem. dir. com. Big Ten Tchg. Ctr., 2002—. Recipient Tchg. Excellence Recognition award, Ind. U., 1997, Hesburgh award for a faculty devel. program, TIAA-CREF, 2003, Wagner award, Ind. U., 2005; Noyes fellowship, 1995. Mem.: Internat. Soc. Scholarship of Tchg. and Learning (conf. exec. com. 2004, interim exec. com. 2004—05, v.p. 2005—, founding com. 2003—05, chair, going public com., mem. vision and planning com., conf. and covening com.), Hoosier Folklore Soc. Office: Indiana Univ 601 East Kirwood Ave Bloomington IN 47405 Office Phone: 812-855-9023. Business E-Mail: jenmetar@indiana.edu.

ROBINSON, JERI, museum program director; Grad., Wheelock Coll., 1967—71. With Boston Children's Mus., 1973—, v.p. early childhood programs, 2006—. Founder Boston Cultural Collaborative for Early Learning; co-founder Families First-parenting programs, CountDown to Kindergarten, Boston. Author: Activities for Anyone. Anytime. Anywhere, 1982, Playspace: Creating Family Spaces in Public Spaces, 1984. Named to Centennial Honor Roll, Am. Assn. Museums, 2006. Office: Boston Children's Mus 300 Congress St Boston MA 02210 Office Phone: 617-426-6500 ext. 219. Business E-Mail: earlychild@BostonChildrenMuseum.org. *

ROBINSON, JOANNE ADELE, retired secondary school educator, volunteer; b. Alameda, Calif., May 9, 1936; d. Herbert William and Jeanne Adele (Stoddard) Justin; m. William Grant Robinson, Aug. 26, 1961; children: Deann Adele, Scott William, Paul Justin. BS in Physical Edn./Bio. Sci., San Francisco State U., 1958. Cert. secondary tchr. Calif., 1959. Phys. edn. tchr. San Mateo Union High Dist., Menlo Park, Calif., 1959—64, Alameda Unified Sch. Dist., 1964—66; program dir. Girls Club Am., Alameda, 1975—80, Camp Fire Boys & Girls, Inc., Oakland, Calif., 1980—85; phys. edn. tchr. Alameda Adult Sch., 1990—2004; ret., 2004. Vol. 1st aid/CPR instr. ARC, Alameda, 1960—2007, tech. leadership coord., 1978—2007. Pres., fundraiser bd. mem. Alameda Girls Club, 1967—89; mem. UN Assn. E. Bay Chpt., Alameda, 1968—2007; active summer faire Alameda Welfare Coun., 1981—2007, past pres., bd. mem.; area rep. Youth For Understanding Internat. Exchange, Alameda, 1986—91; vol. coord. food distribution to low-income families SHARE No. Calif., 1988—98; v.p., program coord. Ch. Women United, Alameda, 1985—2007. Recipient Gulick award, Camp FIre Boys & Girls, Inc., 1982, Woman of Yr. award, City of Alameda, 1996. Mem.: Key Women Educators (Zeta Phi chpt.) (past pres., corr. sec.), Philanthropic Ednl. Organ. (corr. sec. 1999—), Womans Nat. Sports Assn. (nat. acquatics judge 1959—67), Calif. Assn. Health, Phys. Edn., Recreation & Dance (life), Delta Kappa Gamma Internat. Avocations: hiking, bicycling, kayaking, drawing. Home: 2857 Lincoln Ave Alameda CA 94501

ROBINSON, JOE SAM, neurosurgeon, educator; b. Atlanta, July 21, 1945; s. Joe Sam and Nell (Mixon) R.; m. Elizabeth Ann Moate, Apr. 3, 1982; children: Joe Sam III, Edward Richard, Thomas McRae. AB cum laude, Harvard Coll., 1967; MD, U. Va., 1971; MS, Northwestern U., 1975. Surg. intern Emory U., 1971-72, resident in surgery, 1972-73; resident in neurosurgery Northwestern U., 1973-78; instr. U. Ill., 1978-79, Yale U., 1979-81; pres. Ga. Neurosurg. Inst. P.A., Macon, 1981—. Prof., chief neurosurgery Mercer U. Sch. Medicine, Macon, 1986; chief surgery Med. Ctr. Ctrl. Ga., Macon, 1989—, vice chmn. surgery, 1991-97, chmn. dept. surgery, 1996—; vis. neurosurgeon China, 1992, Konaus Acad. Neurosurgery Inst., Lithuania, 1992; clin. prof. Med. Coll. Ga., 2002; chmn. Ga. Bd. Physicians Workforce, 2007. Lt. col. USANG, 1972-95. Fellow Internat. Coll. Surgeons (vice regent 1983-93); mem. Am. Assn. Neurol. Surgeons, Congress Neurol. Surgeons, AAAS, Ga. Neurosurg. Soc., Alpha Omega Alpha. Republican. Methodist. Office: Ga Neurosurg Inst PA 840 Pine St Ste 880 Macon GA 31201-7525 E-mail: teriwyn@ganeurosung.org.

ROBINSON, JOHN ALAN, information scientist, educator; b. Halifax, Eng., Mar. 9, 1930; came to U.S., 1952; naturalized citizen, 1990. s. Harry and Clara (Pilkington) R.; m. Gwen Groves, Dec. 18, 1954; children: Alan Groves, Hugh Parke Custis, Gwen Owen. BA in Classics with honours, Corpus Christi Coll., Cambridge U., Eng., 1952; MA, 1955; MA in Philosophy, U. Ore., 1953; MA, Princeton U., 1955, PhD, 1956; D in Applied Sci. honoris causa, U. Leuven, 1988; D in Philosophy honoris causa, U. Uppsala, 1994; D in Informatics honoris causa, U. Politechnica, Madrid, 2003. Operations research analyst E.I. du Pont de Nemours & Co., Inc., 1956-60; post-doctoral research fellow U. Pitts., 1960-61; mem. faculty Rice U., 1961-67, prof. philosophy, 1964-65, prof. computer sci. and philosophy, 1965-66, prof. computer sci., 1966-67; disting. prof. logic and computer sci. Syracuse U., 1967-84, Univ. prof., 1984-92, univ. prof. emeritus, 1993—. Cons. in applied math. divsn. Argonne Nat. Lab., 1961-67, Stanford Linear Acceleration Ctr., 1966-68; vis. rsch. fellow Australian Nat. U., 1989; Fujitsu vis. prof. U. Tokyo, 1991-92. Author: Logic: Form and Function, 1979; founder, editor-in-chief Jour. Logic Programming, 1984-86; contbr. articles to profl. jours. Served with RAF, 1948-49. Recipient Sr. U.S. Scientists prize Humboldt Found., 1995, Herbrand award, 1996; Guggenheim Found. fellow, 1967-68; hon. rsch. fellow U. Edinburgh, 1967—. Fellow Am. Assn. for Artificial Intelligence; mem. Kokusai Bunka Kaikan (Tokyo). Home and Office: PO Box 988 Northampton MA 01601-0988 E-mail: rishworth1941@yahoo.com.

ROBINSON, JOHN BECKWITH, development management consultant; b. Portland, Oreg., May 23, 1922; s. Jewell King and Arvilla Agnes (Beckwith) R.; m. Dilys Walters, Sept. 8, 1945; children— John Gwilym, David Gwyn. BA, U. Oreg., 1944; postgrad., U. Shrivenham, Eng., 1945, U. Oxford, 1946, Am. U., 1947. Staff U.S. Bur. Budget, 1947—48; sr. program and budget officer UNESCO, 1948—51; mem. staff U.S. Bur. Budget, 1951—52; chief personnel policy Mut. Security Agy., Washington, 1952-54, program officer Guatemala, 1954-59, planning officer, later acting asst. dep. dir. for program and planning AID Washington, 1959-61; dep. U.S. rep. devel. assistance com. OECD, 1961-64, asst. dir. devel. policy Pakistan, 1964-68; dep. dir. North Coast Affairs, AID, State Dept., Washington, 1969-71; dep. mission dir. U.S. Econ. Aid Program, Colombia, 1971-73, mission dir. Dominican Republic, 1973-76, mission dir. Honduras, 1976—79; privatization adviser Gov. of Costa Rica, 1986-88; prin. assoc. J.B. Robinson & Assocs. (devel. mgmt. cons.), 1979—. Mem. faculty, fellow Harvard U., 1968-69; cons. NATO, 1951, UN, 1951. Served to 1st lt., inf. AUS, 1943-46, ETO. Named Knight Commdr., Order Morazan, Republic Honduras, 2007. Mem. Oriental Club (London), DACOR BACON House (Washington), Minchinhampton Probus Club (pres. 1983-84). Episcopalian. Address: Anglezarke The Hithe Rodborough Common Stroud GL5 5BN Gloucestershire England also: 2323 SW Park Pl Portland OR 97205 Office Phone: 44-1453-873346. Business E-Mail: jbrdil@ukonline.co.uk. *Summary: always do more than what is asked for the task at hand. The extra effort always leads to unexpected opportunities for career advancement. Helping others to realize their potential has its own rewards and their success helps to realize your own hopes and aspirations, and improve your own quality of life and satisfaction in a life well-spent. Never underestimate the contribution of your wife and family.*

ROBINSON, JOHN HAYES, law educator; b. Providence, Apr. 4, 1943; s. William Philip and Dorothy Frances (Hayes) R.; m. Deborah Ann Deery, Aug. 15, 1981; children: Gena, John. BA, Boston Coll., 1967; MA, Notre Dame U., Ind., 1972, PhD, 1975; JD, U. Calif., Berkeley, 1979. Bar: RI 1980. Asst. prof. U. San Francisco, 1973-76; instr. law U. Miami, Coral Gables, Fla., 1979-80; jud. clk. US Dist. Ct., Hartford, Conn., 1980-81; asst. prof. law and philosophy U. Notre Dame, 1981-96, assoc. prof. law, 1996—, assoc. dean acad. affairs, 2002—04, exec. assoc. dean, 2005—. Office: U Notre Dame Law Sch Box 780 Notre Dame IN 46556 Office Phone: 574-631-6980. Business E-Mail: robinson.1@nd.edu.

ROBINSON, JOHN WILLIAM, IV, lawyer; b. Atlanta, Apr. 29, 1950; s. J. William III and Elizabeth (Smith) R.; m. Ellen Showalter, Dec. 28, 1976; children: William, Anna. BA with honors, Washington & Lee U., 1972; JD, U. Ga., 1975. Bar: Fla., Ga., U.S. Dist. Ct. (no., so. and mid. dists.) Fla., U.S. Ct. Mil. Appeals, U.S. Ct. Appeals (5th and 11th cirs.), U.S. Supreme Ct.; cert. labor & employment law, Nat. Bd. Trial Advocacy, civil trial and bus. litigation lawyer, Fla. Trial atty. Nat. Labor Rels. Bd., New Orleans, 1975—76; trial def. counsel 8th infantry U.S. Army, Mainz, Germany, 1977—78, trial counsel 8th infantry, 1979; law clk., commr. Ct. Mil. Rev., Washington, 1980; atty. Fowler, White, Boggs & Banker, PA, Tampa, Fla., 1980—, head labor and employment law dept., 1993—, dir., 1998—, sec./treas., 2001—. Mem. faculty U. Md., 1977-79; arbitrator U.S. Dist. Ct. (mid. dist.) Fla.; mem. Leadership Fla., 2004— Editor-in-chief: Employment & Labor Relations Law, 1991-95; editor: Developing Labor Law, 1982—, Model Jury Instructions for Employment Litigation, 1994—; editor: Employment Litigation Handbooks, 1998, 2007. Chmn. Tampa Bay Internat. Trade Coun., 1990-91, Rough Riders Dist. Boy Scouts Am., 1990; legal counsel, chair Drug Free Workplace Task Force, 1999-00; legal counsel, chair, gen. counsel, bd. dirs., 1996, 04-, Greater Tampa C. of C., 1996, 05-; trustee U. Tampa, bd. fellows, chair bus. symposia, 2006-. Capt. U.S. Army, 1976-80. Named one of Best Lawyers in Am. for labor and employment law, Top Ten Super Lawyers in Fla., Fla. Legal Elite. Fellow: Am. Bar Found., Coll. Labor and Employment Lawyers (Founding fellow); mem.: ABA (chmn. employment and labor rels. com. 1993—96, divsn. dir. 1996—2000, mem. coun. 2000—03, chmn. com. on multijurisdictional practice 2000—, task force on electronic discovery 2003—04, litigation sect.), Acad. Fla. Mgmt. Attys. (chair-elect 2006—, charter mem.), Leadership Tampa (chmn. 2006), Hillsborough County Bar Assn. Trial Lawyers (bd. dirs. 1996—, chmn. 2003—), Comml. Bar Assn. (hon.), Am. Inn of Ct. (pres., dir. and master barrister, trustee Am. Inns of Ct. Found., exec. com. Am. Inns of Ct. Found.), Washington & Lee U. Bd. (pres. nat. alumni bd. 1990—91, trustee 1995—2005), Fla. Bar Assn. (chmn. labor and employment law sect. 1992—93), Rotary (bd. 1984—, exec. com. 1984—, bd. dirs. Tampa Bay History Ctr. 2006—, past pres. Tampa Bay chpt.). Avocations: tennis, history. Office: Fowler White Boggs Banker PA 501 E Kennedy Blvd Tampa FL 33602-5237

ROBINSON, JOYCE MCPEAKE, academic administrator; b. Newark, July 28, 1941; d. Salvatore and Wilhelmina (Cervetto) Guinta; m. John David McPeake, June 15, 1963 (div. Aug. 1974); children: John Paul, David Samuel; m. Enders Anthony Robinson, Aug. 8, 1992. BA in English, Tufts U., 1962; MA in English, Boston U., 1965, EdD, 1979. Asst. to dean women & dept. adminstrn. Boston U., 1962—63; 1965—67; reading specialist Hingham Pub. Schs., Mass., 1963—64; reading and learning specialist Manter Hall Sch., Cambridge, Mass., 1964—67; reporter Patriot

Ledger, Quincy, Mass., 1967—69; dir. Christ Luth. Sch., Scituate, Mass., 1971—74; prin. and reading specialist Scituate Pub. Schs., 1974—80; chair English, dir. reading programs St. Andrew's Sch., Boca Raton, Fla., 1980—88; chair English, learning specialist Broadwater Acad., Exmore, Va., 1988—89; dir. learning resources, English Fountain Valley Sch., Colorado Springs, Colo., 1989—91; asst. prin. Islamic Saudi Acad., Alexandria, Va., 1991—93; chair English Masters Sch., Dobbs Ferry, NY, 1993—94; head QUEST program Dwight Sch., NYC, 1994—96, head of sch., 1996—2004; dir. reading programs Mass. Pub. Schs., 2004—. Adj. prof. Nova U., Ft. Lauderdale, Fla., 1984-88, St. Thomas U., Miami, Fla., 1987-88; sch. evaluator Fla. Coun. Ind. Schs., 1985-88; cons. in field. Author: Teaching Study Skills, 1987, Wordworks, 1990, Fostering Creativity in Children, K-8: Theory and Practice, 2001; editor: How to Double Your Child's Grades in School, 1997; author numerous poems; contbr. chpts. to books. Coord. Am. Inst. Fgn. Study, Boston, 1987; parent agt. Hamilton Coll. Parents Fund, Clinton, N.Y., 1986—; mem. town adv. com. Scituate Town Com., 1975-80. Mem.: MLA (com. on instn.-wide accreditation 2000—), Nat. Acad. Ednl. Rsch., Assn. for Advancement Ednl. Rsch. (pres. 2006—), Coun. Exceptional Children, Internat. Reading Assn., Ea. Ednl. Rsch. Assn. (membership chair 1993—95), Fla. Coun. Librs., Nat. Assn. Ind. Schs., Am. Acad. Poets, Nat. Coun. Tchrs. English, Hemingway Soc. Home: 8 Dorothy Lucey Dr Newburyport MA 01950 Business E-Mail: joycerobinson@comcast.net.

ROBINSON, JUNE KERSWELL, dermatologist, educator; b. Phila., Jan. 26, 1950; d. George and Helen S. (Kerswell) R.; m. William T. Barker, Jan. 31, 1981. BA cum laude, U. Pa., 1970; MD, U. Md., 1974. Diplomate Am. Bd. Dermatology, Nat. Bd. Med. Examiners, Am. Bd. Mohs Micrographic Surgery and Cutaneous Oncology. Intern Greater Balt. Med. Ctr., Hanover, NH, 1974, resident in medicine, 1974—75; resident in dermatology Dartmouth-Hitchcock Med. Ctr., Hanover, 1975—78, chief resident, clin. instr., 1977—78, instr. in dermatology, 1978; fellow Mohs; chemosurgery and dermatologic surgery NYU Skin and Cancer Clinic, NYC, 1978—79; instr. in dermatology NYU, NYC, 1979; asst. prof. dermatology Northwestern U. Med. Sch., Chgo., 1979, asst. prof. surgery, 1980—85, assoc. prof. dermatology and surgery, 1985—91, prof. dermatology and surgery, 1991—98; prof. medicine and pathology, dir. divsn. dermatology Cardinal Bernardin Cancer Ctr., Loyola U. Med. Ctr., 1998—2004, program leader skin cancer clin. program, 1998—2004; prof. medicine Med. Sch. Dartmouth U., 2004—05, chief Dermatology Sect. Hitchcock Med. Ctr., 2004—05; prof. clin. dermatology Feinberg Sch. Medicine, Northwestern U., Chgo., 2006—. Mem. consensus devel. conf. NIH, 1992; mem. panel on use of sunscreens Internat. Agy. for Rsch. on Cancer, WHO, 2000; lectr. in field. Author: Fundamentals of Skin Biopsy, 1985, also audiovisual materials; editor: (textbooks) Atlas of Cutaneous Surgery, 1996, Cutaneous Medicine and Surgery: An Integrated Program in Dermatology, 1996, Surgery of the Skin, 2005; mem. editl. bd. Archives of Dermatology, 1988-97; sect. editor The Cutting Edge: Challenges in Med. and Surg. Therapeutics, 1989-97, editor, 2004—; contbg. editor Jour. Dermatol. Surgery and Oncology, 1985-88; mem. editl. com. 18th World Congress of Dermatology, 1982; contbr. numerous articles, abstracts to profl. publs., chpts. to books. Bd. dirs. Northwestern Med. Faculty Found., 1982-84, chmn. com. on benefits and leaves, 1984, nominating com. 1988. Grantee Nat. Cancer Inst., 1985-91, 2004—, Am. Cancer Soc., 1986-89, Skin Cancer Found., 1984-85, Dermatology Found., 1981-83, Northwestern U. Biomed. Rsch., 1981, Syntex, 1984. Fellow: Am. Coll. Chemosurgery (chmn. sci. program ann. meeting 1983, chmn. publs. com. 1986—87, chmn. task force on ednl. needs 1989—90, co-editor bull. 1984—87); mem.: Chgo. Dermatol. Soc., Women's Dermatol. Soc. (pres. 1990—92, Wilma Bergeld, MD Visionary and Leadership award 2002), Soc. Investigative Dermatology, Am. Soc. Dermatol. Surgery (pres. 1994—95, Samuel J. Stegman award disting. svc. 2006), Dermatology Found. (trustee 1995—98), Am. Acad. Dermatology (asst. sec.-treas. 1995—98, sec.-treas. 1998—2001, bd. dirs. 1993—95, Stephen Rothman Lectr. award 1992, Presdl. citation 1992, 2000), Am. Dermatol. Assn., Am. Cancer Soc. (pres. Ill. divsn. 1996—98, St. George Disting. Svc. medal 2004). Office: Northwestern U Feinberg Sch Med Dept Dermatology 132 E Delaware Pl #5806 Chicago IL 60611

ROBINSON, KAREN VAJDA, dietician; BS in Home Econs., Montclair State Coll., 1980; MS in Health Scis./Dietetics, James Madison U., 1992. Cert. food svc. sanitation mgr., N.J. 1984. Dietician Roosevelt Hosp., Edison, NJ, 1980-85; asst. mgr. UVA (U. Va.) Dining Svcs., Charlottesville, 1985-86; temp. sales sec., mem. banquet prep. staff Boar's Head Inn, Charlottesville, 1986-88; head diet counselor Diet Ctr., Charlottesville, 1986-90; dietetic intern VA Med. Ctr., Hampton, Va., 1991; pub. health nutritionist Ctrl. Shenandoah Health Dist., Waynesboro Health Dept., Va., 1993-97. Grad. dietetic intern mentor, 1993—97; cons. dietitian Hebrew Hosp. Home, Bronx, NY, 1998; food svc. mgr. Sodexho Marriott Svcs., Morningside House Nursing Home, Bronx, 1998—99; clin. dietitian Yonkers (NY) Gen. Hosp., 1999—2001; cmty. svcs. instr. Westchester C.C., Valhalla, NY, 2001, mentor student dietetics, 06; inpatient/out patient dietitian Park Care Pavilion (formerly Yonkers Gen. Hosp.), 2001—; clin. dietitian St. John's Riverside Hosp., Yonkers, 2002—; outpatient dietitian St. John's Riverside, Valentine Lane Family Practice, Yonkers, 2005, 07. Contbr. articles to local newspapers. Mem. Charlottesville Health Promotion Coalition, 1993-97. Mem.: Westchester Rockland Dietetic Assn. (health fairs chair 1998—2001, pub. rels. co-chair 2000—01, sec. 2001—07, chmn. nominating com. 2003—04, health fairs com. 2005—07, scholarship com. 2000, 2006, grantee 2000), Va. Dietetic Assn. (exec. bd. 1996—97), Blue Ridge Dietetics Assn. (nat. nutrition month coord. 1993—95, editor newsletter 1993—96, mem. exec. bd. 1993—97, pres.-elect 1995—96, scholarship com. 1996, pres. 1996—97), Va. Pub. Health Assn. (sec. 1995, awards chair 1996—97), Dietitians in Nutrition Support, Gerontol. Nutritionists Practice Group, Cons. Dietitians in Health Care Facilities, Am. Dietetic Assn. (registered), Nutrition Entrepreneurs. Home: 10-02 Hunter Ln Ossining NY 10562 Office Phone: 914-964-4216. Personal E-mail: kvrobinson@aol.com.

ROBINSON, KAYNE B., lobbyist, former political organization officer; m. Donna R. Robinson. B, Drake U. With Des Moines Police Dept., 1968—99; dep. Iowa chmn. Dole Presdl. campaign, 1988; Iowa chmn. Gramm Presdl. campaign, 1996; chmn. Iowa Rep. Party, 1999—2001; 1st v.p. NRA, Fairfax, Va., 1997—2003, pres., 2003—. With USMC. Named Police Officer of the Yr. Iowa Assn. Women Police. Office: NRA 11250 Waples Mill Rd Fairfax VA 22030

ROBINSON, KENNETH CHARLES, management educator; b. Macon, Ga. s. Charles William Robinson and Joyce R. Sorrow. BBA, U. Ga., 1984, MBA, 1991, PhD, 1995. Gen. mgr., CFO Shoe Shack, Inc., Macon, 1984-90, controller, buyer, 1990-91, mgmt. advisor, 1991-94; grad. tchg. asst. U. Ga., Athens, 1991-95; lectr. U. Wollongong, NSW, Australia, 1995-96; assoc. prof. strategy & entrepreneurship Kennesaw (Ga.) State U., 1996—. Mem. rels. com. Greater Macon C. of C., 1988—90, vice chmn. small bus. coun., 1989—90. Recipient Heizer Best Doctoral Dissertation award, Entrepreneurship Divsn., Acad. Mgmt., 1996, Mescon/Coles Best Empirical Paper award, Acad. Mgmt., 1999, Best Paper award, Entrepreneurship/Ethics Track, So. Mgmt. Assn., 2001; fellow Kauffman Ctr. Entrepreneurial Leadership, 1994, Comer fellow, U. Ga., 1994. Mem.: Strategic Mgmt. Soc., U.S. Assn. Small Bus. and Entrepreneurship (Runner-Up award 1999), Acad. Mgmt. (mem. exec. com. entrepreneurship divsn. 1996—, chair awards com. 1998—). Presbyterian. Avocations: travel, skiing, scuba diving, hiking. Office: Kennesaw State U Coles Coll Bus 1000 Chastain Rd NW #0404 Kennesaw GA 30144-5591 Home: 2941 Lookout Pl Ne Atlanta GA 30305-3217 Office Phone: 770-423-6446. Office Fax: 770-423-6606. Personal E-mail: kcrobinson@bellsouth.net.

ROBINSON, KENNETH PATRICK, lawyer, electronics executive; b. Hackensack, NJ, Dec. 12, 1933; s. William Casper and Margaret Agnes (McGuire) r.; m. Catherine Esther Lund, Aug. 26, 1961; children: James, Susan. BS in Elec. Engring., Rutgers U., 1955; JD, NYU, 1962. Bar: N.Y. 1962, U.S. Ct. Appeals (fed. cir.) 1990. With Hazeltine Corp., Greenlawn, N.Y., 1955-88, patent counsel, 1966-69, gen. counsel, 1969-88, sec., 1971-88; v.p. Hazeltine Rsch. Inc., Chgo., 1966-88; of counsel Brumbaugh, Graves, Donohue & Raymond, NYC, 1989-92; prin. Kenneth P. Robinson, Huntington, N.Y., 1992—. Dir. Hazeltine Ltd., London, 1973-80; dir. Imlac Corp., Needham, Mass., 1978-83. Served to 1st lt. USAF, 1955-57. Mem. ABA, IEEE, Am. Intellectual Law Assn., Licensing Execs. Soc. Roman Catholic. Home: 137 Darrow Ln Greenlawn NY 11740-2923 Office: PO Box 0328 Greenlawn NY 11740-0328

ROBINSON, KIM STANLEY, science fiction author; b. Waukegan, Ill., Mar. 23, 1952; m. Lisa Howell; 2 children. BS, U. Calif., San Diego, PhD in English and Am. Lit., 1982; MS, Boston U. Author: (book series) Mars (Red Mars 1992, Green Mars 1993, Blue Mars 1995), Orange County (The Wild Shore 1984, The Gold Coast 1988, Pacific Edge 1990), (novels) Icehenge, 1984, The Memory of Whiteness, 1985, Escape from Kathmandu, 1989, A Short, Sharp Shock, 1990, Antarctica, 1998, The Years of Rice & Salt, 2002, Forty Signs of Rain, 2004, (collections) The Planet on the Table, 1986, Escape From Kathmandu, 1990, Remaking History, 1991, The Martians, 1999, (anthologies) Future Primitive: The New Ecotopias, 1994, (non-fiction series) Studies in Speculative Fiction, 1984; author numerous short fiction, essays and articles. Recipient World Fantasy award, 1984, John W. Campbell Meml. award, 1991, Nebula award, 1987, 93, Locus Poll award, 1985, 91, 94, 97, Hugo award, 1994, 97, SF Chronicle award, 1984, 92, Brit. Sci. Fiction award, 1993. Avocations: mountain trekking, swimming. Office: c/o Random House Inc Bantam Books 1540 Broadway New York NY 10036-4039

ROBINSON, LARRY CLARK, professional hockey coach; b. Winchester, Ont., Can., June 2, 1951; m. Jeannette Robinson; children: Jeffery, Rachelle. Defenseman Montreal Canadians, 1971—89, LA Kings, 1989—92; asst. coach NJ Devils, 1993—95, 1999—2000, 2007—, head coach, 2000—02, 2005, spl. assignment coach, 2002—05, 2006—07; head coach LA Kings, 1995—99. Player Team Canada, 1976, 81, 84. Named to NHL All-Star game, 1974, 1976—78, 1980, 1982, 1986, 1988, 1989, 1992; recipient Norris Meml. Trophy, 1977, 1980, Conn Smythe Trophy, 1978. Achievements include being a member of 9 Stanley Cup Championship teams; being inducted into the Hockey Hall of Fame, 1995. Avocations: polo, boating. Office: NJ Devils 33 Fl 744 Broad St Newark NJ 07102 *

ROBINSON, LAWRENCE R., medical educator, vice-dean, director; b. Nov. 10, 1956; m. LeiLei Wang; children: Sarah, Rachael. BA in Chemistry, Brandeis U., Waltham, Mass., 1974—78. Diplomate Baylor Coll. Medicine, 1982. Asst. prof. rehab. medicine U. Pitts. Sch. Medicine, 1986—89; prof. rehab. medicine U. Wash. Sch. Medicine, Seattle, 1989—, chmn. rehab. medicine, 2000—05, vice-dean clin. affairs, 2005—. Dir. electrodiagnostic svcs. Dept. Rehab. Medicine, Harborview Hosp., Seattle, 1989—; dir. post-polio clinic U. Wash. Med. Ctr., 1990—94; physiatrist-in-chief Harborview Med. Ctr., Seattle, 1994—2001. Rsch. grant for somatosensory evoked potentials and cooling in multiple sclerosis, Nat. Multiple Sclerosis Soc., 1983—94, Rsch. grant for peripheral nerve Lesions in burn patients, Grad. Sch. Rsch. Fund, 1991—92, Rsch. grant for study of peripheral lesions in burn patients, NW Burn Found., 1991—92, 1993—94, Rsch. grant for Mgmt. Chronic Pain in Rehab. program project, NIH, 1996—2001. Office: Unive Wash Med Sch 1959 NE Pacific St Box 356380 Seattle WA 98195-6380

ROBINSON, LINDA GOSDEN, communications executive; b. LA, Jan. 10, 1953; d. Freeman Fisher and Jane Elizabeth (Stoneham) Gosden; m. Stephen M. Dart (div. June 1977); m. James Dixon Robinson III, July 1984. Student, UCLA, 1970-72; BA summa cum laude in Psychology, U. So. Calif., 1978. Dep. press sec. Reagan Presdl. Campaign, LA, 1979; press sec., dir. pub. relations Rep. Nat. Com., Washington, 1979-80; dir. pub. affairs US Dept. Transp., Washington, 1981-83; sr. v.p. corp. affairs Warner Amex Cable Communications, NYC, 1983-86; chmn. Robinson Lerer & Montgomery, LLC, NYC, 1986—, CEO, 1986—2002. Bd. dirs. Revlon, Inc., NYC; dir. BlackRock, Inc., NYC. Del. Rep. Nat. Conv., 1985; trustee NYU Sch. Medicine Found. Bd., vice chair; trustee NYU Hosp. Ctr.; bd. dirs. Lustgarten Found. Pancreatic Rsch. Mem.: Phi Beta Kappa. Avocations: tennis, horseback riding.

ROBINSON, LOGAN GILMORE, lawyer; b. Cin., Dec. 26, 1949; s. Landon Graves and Alis (Rule) R.; m. Edrie Baker Sowell, Sept. 22, 1983; children: Leyland G., Landon G., Linden G., Lane G. BA in Econ. and History magna cum laude, Cornell U., 1972; JD, Harvard U., 1976; Cert. Competence in German, Goethe Inst., Freiburg, Germany, 1978. Bar: Ohio 1977, N.Y. 1979, Mich. 1989, U.S. Ct. Internat. Trade 1983. Rsch. faculty Leningrad State U., Russia, 1976-77; rsch. officer U. Leiden, Netherlands, 1977-78; assoc. Wender, Murase & White, NYC, 1978-81, Coudert Bros., NYC, 1981-83; sr. counsel TRW Inc., Cleve., 1983-87; asst. gen. counsel Chrysler Corp., Highland Park, 1987—96; sec., v.p., gen. counsel ITT Automotive, Auburn Hills, Mich., 1996—98; v.p., gen. counsel Delphi Corp., Troy, Mich., 1998—2006; exec. v.p., gen. counsel, govt. rels. Metaldyne Corp., Plymouth, Mich., 2006—. Author: An American in Leningrad, 1982, paperback, 1984, Evil Star, 1986, paperback, 1987. Mem. Assoc. Gen. Counsels, Internat. Bar Assn. (co-chair corp. counsel forum), Mich. State Bar (former chmn. internat. sect., Outstanding Contbn. award), German Am. C. of C. Mich. (bd. dirs.), Coun. US and Italy, Phi Beta Kappa. Office: Metaldyne Corp 47603 Halyard Dr Plymouth MI 48170-2429

ROBINSON, MARGUERITE STERN, anthropologist, educator, consultant; b. NYC, Oct. 11, 1935; d. Philip Van Doren and Lillian (Diamond) Stern; m. Allan Richard Robinson, June 12, 1955; children: Sarah Penelope, Perrine, Laura Ondine. BA, Radcliffe Coll., 1956; PhD, Harvard U., 1965. Assoc. scholar Radcliffe Inst. for Advanced Studies, Cambridge, Mass., 1964-65; asst. prof. anthology Brandeis U., 1965-72, assoc. prof., 1972-78, prof., 1978-85, dean Coll. Arts and Scis., 1973-75; assoc. fellow Inst. Internat. Devel. Harvard U., Cambridge, 1978—79, fellow Inst. Internat. Devel., 1980-85, inst. fellow Inst. Internat. Devel., 1985-2000, inst. fellow emeritus Inst. Internat. Devel., 2000—; dir. Cultural Survival Inc., 1981-99, Am. Inst. Indian Studies, Chgo., 1977—, chmn., 1983-84; faculty mem. Microfinance Tng. Program, Boulder, Colo. and Turin, Italy, 1995—2006. Bd. dirs. MasterCard Found., 2006—, Equity Bank Found., Kenya, 2006—; cons. in field. Author: Political Structure in a Changing Sinhalese Village, 1975, Local Politics: The Law of the Fishes, 1988, Pembiayaan Pertanian Pedesaan, 1993, The Microfinance Revolution, Vol. 1: Sustainable Finance for the Poor, 2001, Vol. 2: Lessons from Indonesia, 2002, Mobilizing Savings from the Public: Basic Principles and Practices, 2005, The Future of the Commercial Microfinance Industry in Asia, 2005, Commercial Microfinance and Employment in Developing Countries, 2005; contbg. author: Cambridge Papers in Social Anthropology 3, 1962, Cambridge Papers in Social Anthropology 5, 1968, Enterprises for the Recycling and Composting of Municipal Solid Waste, 1993, The New World of Microenterprise Finance, 1994, New Perspectives on Financing Small Business in Developing Countries, 1995, Assisting Development in a Changing World, 1997, New World of Microfinance, 1997, Agricultural Development in the Third World, 1998, Strategic Issues in Microfinance, 1998, Microfinance: Conversations with the Experts, 1999, Microbanking: Creating Opportunities for the Poor Through Innovation, 2005, Transforming Microfinance Institutions, 2006; contbr. articles to profl. jours. Mem. internat. coun. advisors Calmeadow Found., 1996-2000; pres. Greatest Gift Corp. Fellow NIH, 1964-65; grantee NSF, 1966-70, Ford Found., 1972-74, 79, Calmeadow Found., 1994; fellow Indo-Am. Fellowship Program-Indo-U.S. Subcommn. on Edn. and Culture, 1976-77, Am. Inst. Indian Studies, 1976-77; grantee Calmeadow Found., 1994. Fellow Am. Anthrop. Assn., Soc. Bunting Inst. Fellows; mem. Assn. Asian Studies, India Internat. Centre. Personal E-mail: MRobinsol@aol.com.

ROBINSON, MARIETTA S., lawyer; b. Platteville, Wis., Dec. 26, 1951; BA, U. Mich., 1973; JD, UCLA, 1978. Bar: Calif. 1978, Mich. 1979, U.S. Dist. Ct. (ea. dist.) Mich. 1979, U.S. Ct. Appeals (6th cir.) 1983, U.S. Supreme Ct. 1989. Data processing mktg. rep. IBM Corp., Flint, Mich., 1973-75; assoc. The Bank of Bermuda Legal Dept., Hamilton, 1978-79; from assoc. to ptnr. Dickinson, Wright, Moon, VanDusen & Freeman, Detroit, 1979-94; ptnr. Sommers, Schwartz, Silver & Schwartz, P.C., Southfield, Mich., 1985-89; pvt. practice Detroit, 1989—. Adj. prof. U. Detroit Sch. of Law, 1982-83, Wayne State U., Detroit, 1983-84; mem. Rep. of State Bar Rep. Assembly, 1984-85; Dem. nominee for Mich. Supreme Ct., 2000; lectr. in field. Contbg. author: Evidence in America, The Federal Rules in the States, 1987, Introducing Evidence, A Practical Guide for Michigan Lawyers, 1988; contbr. articles to profl. jours. Trustee Dalkon Shield Claimants Trust, 1989-97; appointee Gov. James Blanchard, State of Mich. Bldg. Authority, 1985-89, State Bar Mich./Mich. State Med. Soc. Coalition, 1993—; appointee Transition Team of Wayne County Exec. Robert Ficano, 2002; bd. dirs. Mich. Women's Found., 2003—. Named one of ten Mich. Lawyers of Yr., Lawyers Weekly, 2000. Fellow ABA, Internat. Soc. Barristers (bd. govs., officer), Am. Bar Found., Mich. State Bar Found.; mem. State Bar Mich., State Bar Calif., ATLA, Mich. Trial Lawyers Assn., Women Lawyers Mich., Am. Bd. of Trial Advocates, Detroit Bar Assn., Oakland Bar Assn., U.S. Ct. Appeals (6th cir.) Jud. Conf. (life). Democrat. Avocations: running, biking, tennis, boating, skiing, reading, horseback riding. Office: 436 S Broadway St Ste C Lake Orion MI 48362 Office Phone: 248-693-6245. Personal E-mail: msebreerobinson@aol.com.

ROBINSON, MARILYNNE, writer; b. Sandpoint, Idaho, Nov. 26, 1943; d. John J. and Ellen (Harris) Summers; children: James, Joseph. BA, Brown U., 1966; PhD in English lit., U. Wash., 1977. Mem. faculty Writer's Workshop U. Iowa, 1991—. Spkr. in field. Author: (novels) Housekeeping, 1981 (PEN/Hemingway Award, 1981, Richard and Hinda Rosenthal Award, AAAL), Gilead, 2004 (Nat. Book Critics Cir. prize for fiction, 2004, Pulitzer Prize for fiction, 2005, Publishers Weekly Hardcover Bestseller list, 2005), (non-fiction) Mother Country: Britain, the Welfare State and Nuclear Pollution, 1989, (essay collection) The Death of Adam: Essays on Modern Thought, 1998; Has contbd. to Harper's, Paris Rev., The NY Times Book Rev., others. Recipient Mildred and Howard Strauss Living Award, AAAL, 1998; Lila Acheson Wallace Reader's Digest Grant, 1991. Office: Farrar Straus & Giroux 19 Union Sq W New York NY 10003

ROBINSON, MARK LEIGHTON, gas industry executive, petroleum engineer, farmer; b. San Bernardino, Calif., Aug. 4, 1927; s. Ernest Guy and Florence Iola)Lemmon) R.; m. Jean Marie Ries, Feb. 8, 1954; children; Francis Willis, Mark Ries, Paul Leighton. AB cum laude in Geology, Princeton U., 1950; postgrad., Stanford U., 1950-51. Geologist Shell Oil Co., Billings, Mont., Rapid City, S.D., Denver, Midland, Tex., dist. geologist Roswell, N.Mex., 1957-60, divsn. mgr., 1961-63, Jackson, Miss., 1964-65, Bakersfield, Calif., 1967-68, mgr. exploration econs. NYC, 1969; ctrl. office staff BIPM (Royal Dutch Shell Oil Co.), The Hague, The Netherlands, 1966; pres., chmn. bd. dirs. Robinson Resource Devel. Co., Inc., Roswell, 1970—. Chmn., pres. Como Petroleum Corp., Roswell, 1994—. Campaign chmn. Chaves County Rep. Com., Roswell, 1962; mem. alumni schs. com. Princeton U., 1980—; vestry St. Andrew's Episcopal Ch., Roswell, N.Mex., 1999-2002. With USNR, 1945-46. Mem. Assn. Petroleum Geologists, Stanford U. Earth Scientists Assn., Yellowstone Bighorn Rsch. Assn., Am. Horse Show Assn., SAR, Sigma Xi. Episcopalian. Achievements include discovery of Lake Como oil field, Miss., 1971, McNeal oil field, Miss., 1973, North Deer Creek gas field, Mont., 1983, Bloomfield East oil field, Mont., 1986, West Cat Claw Draw gas field, N.Mex., 1997, Southeast Cemetary Gas Field, N.Mex., 2000. Office: Robinson Resource Devel Co Inc PO Box 1227 Roswell NM 88202-1227

ROBINSON, MARLA HOLBROOK, community care nurse; b. Grass Valley, Calif., Sept. 15, 1934; d. Hilmer Harrison and Mable Lucille (Kline) Holbrook; m. Donald Wilson Robinson Jr., June 25, 1961; children: Jeffrey Brian, Jennifer Lee Villa. BSN, PHN, U. Calif. Chico, 1956. RN; cert. audiometer. Nurse U. Calif. San Francisco Hosp., 1956-59; supr. clinic St. Luke's Hosp., San Francisco, 1959-60; sch. nurse, pub. health nurse San Francisco City and County, 1960-62; sch. nurse All Saints Sch., Carmel, Calif., 1969-79; cmty. care nurse, founder Care & Choice Home Health Care, 1994. Mem. Carmel Found., 2003. Mem. AAUW, Quata Internat. Monterey Peninsula (pres. 1993), Jacettes (pres. 1967), Long Term Dir. of Nursing Salinas, Calif., Ea. Star Monterey (50 Yr. mem.). Episcopalian. Avocations: growing orchids, crafts, reading, travel. Office: Community Care 80 Garden Ct Ste 105 Monterey CA 93940 Office Phone: 831-645-1400. Personal E-mail: marlarob@yahoo.com.

ROBINSON, MARTIN (MARTY ROBINSON), television and radio broadcaster, media consultant; b. Chgo., Sept. 7, 1932; s. Edward Emmanuel Robinson and Florence Ruth (Cohen) Mayer; m. Mary Alice Wellingham, May 31, 1959; children: Paul Edward, Jill Marie. Broadcaster, host Stas. WAAF, WGN and WNIB, Chgo., 1956-58, Sta. WFMT, Chgo., 1958-93, Sta. WTTW-TV, Chgo., 1971-99. Speaker, concert narrator; lectr. Lyric Opera Chgo.; media cons. J. Walter Thompson, Hill & Knowlton, Burson Marsteller, Newell & Matthews, 1973—. Host, narrator programs (Peabody award, 15 Emmy awards, 8 Ohio State awards, Chgo. and San Francisco Film Festival Gold medals); prodr., host nationally syndicated opera program The First Fifty Years, 1967-93. Served with USN, 1950-53. Recipient Emmy awards, 1977, 78. Avocations: biking, weight training, the internet. Office: 5 Lynnbrook Dr Prospect Heights IL 60070-1022 E-mail: martyrob@comcast.net.

ROBINSON, MARY ELIZABETH GOFF, retired historian, researcher; b. East Providence, RI, Jan. 3, 1925; d. Newell Darius and Eva Agnes (Crane) Goff; m. Charles Albert Robinson, July 30, 1954; 1 child, Thomas Goff (dec.). BA, Wheaton Coll., Norton, Mass., 1947. Cataloger, fine arts, trustee Chester County Hist. Soc., Pa., 1873—1980. Cataloger artifacts Chester County Hist. Soc., Chadds Ford, Pa., 1973—80. Co-author: (monograph) Ada Clendenin Williamson, 1983, (history) The Ingalls and the Hoyts, The Crane Sawmill, The Ingalls-Crane House, 1995; author: (monograph) The Life of a Young Entrepreneur at the Turn of the Twentieth Century, 1992; editor: A Quiet Man from West Chester (Pa.), 1974. Mem. Jr. League, Providence, 1957-62, Providence Athenaeum, 1955-63, Providence Preservation Soc., 1959-63, Brandywine Conservancy, Del. Symphony Orch., Winterthur Mus.; donor Newell D. Goff Fund Chester County Cmty. Found.; founder Chester County Artists Register, Chester County Art Assn., acting libr., 1994-2000. Donor T. Morris Longstreth Libr. endowment West Chester U., Greater Lewes (DE) Found., Friends of Lewes Pub. Libr. Mem. AAUW, R.I. Hist. Soc. (trustee 1994-99, founder Newell D. Goff Edn. Ctr.), Danville (Vt.) Hist. Soc., Hershey's Mill Country Club, Hope Club (Providence, RI). Avocations: writing, reading, hiking, travel.

ROBINSON, MARY LOU, federal judge; b. Dodge City, Kans., Aug. 25, 1926; d. Gerald J. and Frances Strueber; m. A.J. Robinson, Aug. 28, 1949; 3 children. BA, U. Tex., 1948, LL.B., 1950. Bar: Tex. 1949. Ptnr. Robinson & Robinson, Amarillo, 1950-55; judge County Ct. at Law, Potter County, Tex., 1955-59, (108th Dist. Ct.), Amarillo, 1961-73; assoc. justice Ct. of Civil Appeals for 7th Supreme Jud. Dist. of Tex., Amarillo, 1973-77, chief justice, 1977-79; U.S. dist. judge No. Dist. Tex., Amarillo, 1979—. Named Woman of Year Tex. Fedn. Bus. and Profl. Women, 1973; recipient Sandra Day O'Connor award profl. excellence, 2005. Mem. Nat. Assn. Women Lawyers, ABA, Tex. Bar Assn. (Outstanding 50-Yr. Lawyer award 2002), Tex. Bar Found. (Samuel Pessara Outstanding Judge award), Amarillo Bar Assn., Delta Kappa Gamma. Presbyterian. Office: US Dist Ct Rm 226 205 E 5th Ave # F13248 Amarillo TX 79101-1559 Office Phone: 806-468-3822.

ROBINSON, MAUREEN LORETTA, retired secondary school educator; b. NYC, May 17, 1945; d. Arthur Vincent and Paula (Dillon) R.; m. Derish Michael Wolff, Feb. 13, 1992. BA in English, Wagner Coll., 1967; MS, CUNY, 1970; LHD (hon.), Wagner Coll., 2003. Cert. tchr. secondary sch. English, K-12 reading, N.Y. Tchr. English Curtis H.S., SI, NY, 1968-95, coord. student activities, 1985-94. Vis. lectr. Coll. of S.I., 1982; guest lectr. NYU, 1991, Pace U., N.Y.C., 1993; dir. Soc. de Management de Projets Internat., Paris, 1996—. Class agt. Wagner Coll., 1995—, trustee, 1998—, vice chair bd. trustees, 2001—03; pub chair Bernardsville Garden Club, 1995—97, pres., 1997—99, sec., 1999—2001, pub chair, 2001—03, bd. dirs., 2004—, nominations chair, 2004—07, yearbook chair, 2005—; trustee Somerset Hills Edn. Found., 1996—97; pub. chair Friends of the Bernardsville Libr., 1996—2002, bd. dirs., nominations chair, 2004—07; elected mem. Somerset Hills Bd. Edn., Bernardsville, NJ, 1997—2003; v.p. Somerset County Ednl. Svcs. Commn., Raritan, 2000—02, pres., 2002—03; bd. dirs. Clarence Dillon Pub. Libr., 2002—03; sec. Friends for a Greener Bernardsville Inc., 2003—04, pres., 2005, co-pres., 2006—07, v.p, 2007—. Staff sgt. USAR, 1979—85. Recipient Human Rels. award Greater N.Y. Region of NCCJ, 1994, Army Achievement medal Dept. of Army, 1983, Bernardsville Vol. of Yr. award, 2003, Outstanding Comty. vol. award Borough Coun. and Mayor Bernardsville, 2003. Mem. AAUW, Wagner Coll. Nat. Alumni Assn. (1st v.p. 1999-2001), Friends of the Shelter, Omicron Delta Kappa. Avocations: reading, gardening, skiing, cooking, travel. Home: 160 Jockey Hollow Rd Bernardsville NJ 07924-1312

ROBINSON, MICHAEL HILL, retired zoological park director, biologist; b. Preston, Eng., Jan. 7, 1929; came to U.S. 1984; s. Samuel and Ethel (Hill) R.; m. Barbara Cragg Robinson, May 19, 1955 (divorced). BS, U. Wales, UK, 1963; DPhil, U. Oxford, Eng., 1966; DSc (hon.), U. Westminster, Eng., 2000. Tchr. sci. U.K. Secondary Schs., 1953-60; sr. sci. master Camborne Grammar Sch., 1958-60; biologist Smith. Tropical Research Inst., Panama, 1966-71; vis. lectr. U. Pa., Phila., 1969; reader in biology New U. Ulster, No. Ireland, 1971; biologist Smithsonian Tropical Research Inst., Panama, 1971-84, asst. dir., 1980, acting dir., 1980-81, dep. dir., 1981-84; dir. Nat. Zool. Park, Washington, 1984—2000; sr. scientist emeritus Smithsonian Tropical Rsch. Inst., 1999—. Contbr. articles to profl. jours. Mem.: Soc. for Study of Animal Behavior. Address: 8291 SW Bent Oak Ct Stuart FL 34997 Personal E-mail: michael-robinson@usa.net.

ROBINSON, MICHELLE, curator; b. Tulsa, Dec. 13, 1950; d. Robert Bruce and Elizabeth Faye Maine; 1 child, Melissa Anne. BS in Edn., Geneva Coll., Beaver Falls, Pa., 1972; MA in Art History, U. Kans., Lawrence, 1994, PhD in Art History, 2006. Instr. art history U. Kans., Lawrence, 1994—96; asst. registrar Spencer Mus. Art, Lawrence, 1996—98; curator Figge Art Mus., Davenport, Iowa, 1998—. Cons. Davenport One Art and Culture Task Force, 2000—06; mem. design com. bldg. project Figge Art Mus., 1999—2005. Editor: Edouard Duval-Carrié: Migration of the Spirit, 2005, Accidentally on Purpose: The Aesthetic Management of Irregularities in African Textiles and African-American Quilts, 2006. Active Gen. Svcs. Adminstrn. Fed. Art Project, Davenport, 2001—04; mem. adv. bd. Haitian Art Appraisers Soc., 2004—. Grantee, Mellon Found., 1995, Luce Found., 2006; Pearson fellow, Kans. Bd. Regents, 1996. Mem.: Historians Brit. Art, Coll. Art Assn., Am. Assn. Museums. Home: 1212 E 10th St #4 Davenport IA 52803 Office: Figge Art Museum 225 W 2nd St Davenport IA 52801

ROBINSON, MILDRED WIGFALL, law educator; b. Charleston, SC, Dec. 1, 1944; d. Switzon Samuel and Mildred Gwendolyn (Mance) Wigfall; m. William Hudson Ravenell, Aug. 29, 1969 (div. Apr. 1986); children: William Samuel, Teressa Emlynne; m. Armstead Louis Robinson, June 27, 1987; 1 child, Allison Louise Wigfall. BA, Fisk U., 1965; JD, Howard U., 1968; LLM, Harvard U., 1971. Bar: Mass. 1971. Dir. admissions, asst. dean Boston U., 1971-72; asst. prof. law Fla. State U., Tallahassee, 1972-76, assoc. prof., 1976-84, assoc. dean, 1983-84; vis. assoc. prof. U. Va., Charlottesville, 1984-85, assoc. prof., 1985-88, prof., 1988—, currently Henry L. & Grace Doherty Charitable Found. prof. law. Currently trustee Martha Jefferson Hosp.; bd. dir. Law Access, Inc., 1993—96; mem. exec. com. Assoc. Am. Law Sch., 2000—03; commr. Nat. Conf. of Commn. on Uniform State Laws, 1990—94; bd. visitors J. Reuben Clark Law Sch. Brigham Young U., Provo, Utah, 1993—96. Mem.: ALI, Phi Beta Kappa. Democrat. Episcopalian. Avocations: aerobics, needlecrafts, reading. Office: U Va Sch Law 580 Massie Rd Charlottesville VA 22901 E-mail: mwr@virginia.edu.

ROBINSON, MOLLY JAHNIGE, statistician, educator; b. Cleve., July 8, 1936; d. John White and Mary Tayler (Sullivan) McCaslin; m. Thomas Paul Jahnige (dec.); m. Donald Leonard Robinson, Jan. 1, 1983; children: Katherine Jahnige Mathews, John Samuel, David Wynn, Paul John Jahnige. Student, Swarthmore Coll., Pa., 1954—56; BA, Pomona Coll., Claremont, Calif., 1958; MA, Claremont U., 1962. Tchr. 4th, 7th, and 8th grades Claremont Sch. Dist., 1958—63; instr. stats. Smith Coll., Northampton, Mass., 1973—2004. Leader Girl Scouts US, 1957—; vol. Cmty. Found. We. Mass., 2000—05, Ashfield Youth Commn., 1995—2005; Sunday sch. dir., youth leader St. John's Episcopal Ch., Northampton, 1973—75, 2002—04; coord. Episcopal Relief and Devel. We. Mass., 2005—; mem. sch. bd. Mohawk Region, Ashfield, Mass., 2003—06; edn. chair Wells Trust Fund, Greenfield, Mass., 1996—; chair Town Common Com., Ashfield, 2003—05. Recipient World Friendship medal, Girl Scouts USA. Democrat. Avocations: writing, working with children.

ROBINSON, MURIEL COX, psychiatrist; d. Henry Willard and Veola Garry Cox; m. Julius Ceasar Robinson (div.); children: Julius W., Rosalyn P. Student, Ohio State U., 1945—48; MD, Meharry Med. Coll., 1952. Psychiatry resident Homer Phillips Hosp./Washington U., St. Louis, 1953—56; staff psychiatrist St. Louis Child Guidance Ctr., St. Louis, 1956—57, Napa (Calif.) St. Hosp., 1958, Cmty. Mental Health Centers, Richmond, Calif., 1958—75; pvt. practice psychiatry Calif., 1960—79; staff psychiatrist East Oakland Mental Health Ctr., Calif., 1976—79, Calif. Youth Authority, Sacramento, 1979—92; with Locum Tenens Physicians Group, 1992—94. Mem. mental health adv. com. Contra Costa County, Martinez, Calif., 1960—64. Bd. dirs. North Richmond Neighborhood Ho., Calif., 1961—63. Mem.: AAAS, AMA, NAACP, Am. Psychiat. Assn. (life). Avocations: block flute, keyboards. Home: PO Box 292148 Sacramento CA 95829-2148 E-mail: mcrobinson@webtv.net.

ROBINSON, NATHANIEL DAVID, JR., physician, consultant; b. Kansas City, Mar. 6, 1941; s. Nathaniel David Robinson and Dorothy Mae McLaughlin; m. Joanne Marie Kaleida, July 7, 1979; children: Donelle, Nathaniel David Robinson III. BSEE, U. RI, 1963; MD, U. Bologna, 1975. Cert. bd. cert. ins. medicine. Intern Roger Williams Gen. Hosp. Brown U., Providence, 1975—76; resident St. Francis Hosp. and Med. Ctr. U. Conn., Hartford, 1976—77; resident Hamot Med. Ctr., Erie, Pa., 1977—79, Mt. Sinai Med. Ctr., Miami Beach, Fla., 1981—82; med. officer USPHS Hosp., Seattle, 1979—81, VA, Nashville, 1982—85; med. dir. CNA, Nashville, 1985—95, v.p., med. dir., 1997—2004; asst. med. dir. Am. United Life, Indpls., 1995—97; med. cons. AIG Am. Gen., Nashville, 2005—. Cons. in field. Contbr. articles to profl. jours. Mem.: IEEE, AMA, Fla. Med. Assn., Midwest Med. Dirs. Assn., So. Med. Assn., Providence Engring. Soc., Nashville Acad. Medicine, Tenn. Med. Assn., Am. Acad. Ins. Medicine, Am. Radio Relay League. Avocation: amateur radio. Home: 1304 Choctaw Trail Brentwood TN 37027-7422 Office: AIG Am Gen American General Ctr Nashville TN 37250-0001 Home Phone: 615-373-3024; Office Phone: 615-749-1793. Personal E-mail: djdrobinson@comcast.net. Business E-Mail: k1ant@ieee.org.

ROBINSON, NEIL CIBLEY, JR., lawyer; b. Columbia, SC, Oct. 25, 1942; s. Neil C. and Ernestine (Carns) R.; m. Judith Ann Hunter, Sept. 4, 1971 (div. Nov. 1979); 1 child, Hunter Leigh; m. Vicki Elizabeth Kornahrens, Mar. 2, 1985; children: Neil C. III, Taylor Elizabeth. BS in Indsl. Mgmt., Clemson U., 1966; JD, U. SC, 1973. Bar: SC 1974, US Ct. Appeals (4th cir.) 1974, US Dist. Ct. SC 1976. Asst. to dean U. SC Law Sch., Columbia, 1973-74; law clk. to Hon. Charles E. Jr. Simons Jr. US Dist. Ct. SC, Aiken, 1974-76; assoc. Grimball & Cabaniss, Charleston, SC, 1976-78; ptnr. Grimball, Cabaniss, Vaughan & Robinson, Charleston, 1978-84; ptnr., pres. Robinson, Wall & Hastie, P.A., Charleston, 1984-91; ptnr., exec. com. Nexsen, Pruet, Jacobs, Pollard & Robinson, Charleston, 1991—2003; mem. exec. com. Nexsen Pruet, LLC, 2004—, real estate practice group leader, 2006—. Permanent mem. 4th Cir. Jud. Conf., 1982—; pres. Coastal Properties Inst., Charleston, 1981—. Co-founder, chmn. Charleston Planning Project Pub. Edn., 1996; pres. Clemson Advancement Found., 2003—06; mem. SC Edn. Oversight Com., 2005—; mem. devel. coun. SC Homebuilders Assn.; mem. Gov. Sanford's Quality of Life Task Force, 2003; bd. dirs. SC Tourism Coun., Columbia, 1991—2000, Charleston Maritime Festival, 1993—99; bd. dirs Charleston Edn. Found., Clemson U. Humanities Found., 2000—03, Charleston Edn. Network, chmn. bd. dirs, 2000—03; bd. dirs. Clemson U. Found., 2003—05, bd. visitors, 2007—; bd. dirs. Southeastern Wildlife Expn. Found., 1987—, pres., 2003—; bd. dirs. Clemson Real Estate Devel. Found., 2006—, Parklands Found. of Charleston County, pres., Southeastern Wildlife Expn., 1994—99; edn. adv. bd. Coll. of Charleston; pres. Charleston Maritime Festival, 1994—98. Cpl. USMCR, 1960—66. Recipient Order of Palmetto, Gov. David Beasley, SC, 1996. Mem. Urban Land Inst. (recreational devel. coun.), SC Bar Assn., Fed. Bar Assn., Hibernian Soc. (mgmt. com. 1984—98, sec. 1998-2000, chmn. 2000-02, v.p. 2002-04, pres. 2004-06), Kiawah Club, Haig Point Club, Country Club of Charleston, Carolina Yacht Club, Phi Delta Phi. Presbyterian. Avocations: golf, boating. Home: PO Box 121 Charleston SC 29402-0121 Office: Nexsen Pruet LLC 205 King St Ste 400 Charleston SC 29401 Office Phone: 843-577-9440. Personal E-mail: nrobinson@nexsenprenet.com, nrobinson@npsp.com. Business E-Mail: nrobinson@npjp.com.

ROBINSON, NELL BRYANT, nutrition educator; b. Kopperl, Tex., Oct. 15, 1925; d. Basil Howell and Lelia Abiah (Duke) Bryant; m. Frank Edward Robinson, July 14, 1945 (dec.); 1 child, John Howell. BS, North Tex. State U., 1945; MS, Tex. Woman's U., 1958, PhD, 1967. Registered dietitian, Tex. Tchr. Comanche H.S., Tex., 1945-46, Kopperl H.S., 1946-48; county extensin agt. Agrl. Extension Svc., Tex., 1948-56; prof. nutrition Tex. Christian U., Ft. Worth, 1957—92, chmn. dept. nutrition and dietetics, 1985-91; ret., 1992. Contbr. chpt. to book. Pres., bd. dirs. Sr. Citizens Svcs. Greater Tarrant County, 1990-91. Named Top Prof., Tex. Christian U. Mortar Bd., 1978. Mem. Am. Dietetic Assn. (del. 1983-88, ethics com. 1985-88, coun. edn. 1988-90, chmn. coun. on edn. divsn. edn. accreditation and approval 1989-90, Medallion award 1990), Am. Assn. Family and Consumer Scis., Tex. Dietetic Assn. (pres. 1972-73, Disting. Dietitian awafd 1981), Tex. Assn. Family and Consumer Scis. (pres. 1978-80, Home Economist of Yr. award 1975), Ft. Worth Women's Club, Order Ea. Star. Home: 4459 Kirkland Dr Fort Worth TX 76109-4952

ROBINSON, NICHOLAS ADAMS, law educator, department chairman; b. NYC, Jan. 20, 1945; s. Albert Lewis and Agnes Claflin (Adams) R.; m. Shelley Miner, Jan. 5, 1969; children: Cynthia M., Lucy A. BA cum laude, Brown U., 1967; JD cum laude, Columbia U., 1970. Bar: N.Y. 1971, U.S. Dist. Ct. (so. and ea. dists.) N.Y. 1972, U.S. Supreme Ct. 1974, U.S. Ct. Appeals (2d and 7th cirs.) 1972. Law clk. to U.S. dist. judge So. Dist. Ct., NY, 1970-72; assoc. Marshall, Bratter, Greene, Allison & Tucker, NYC, 1972-78, counsel, 1978-82; assoc. prof. Pace U. Sch. Law, White Plains, NY, 1978-81, prof., 1981-99, Gilbert and Sarah Kerlin Disting. prof. environ. law, 1999—; counsel Winer, Neuburger & Sive, NYC, 1982-83; dep. commr., gen. counsel NY State Dept. Environ. Conservation, Albany, 1983-85; counsel Sive, Paget & Reisel, 1985-92, Sidley & Austin, NY and London, 1992-96; legal advisor Internat. Union Conservation of Nature and Natural Resources, 1996—2004; counsel to Internat. Union Conservation of Nature and Natural Resources Observer Mission to UN, 2002—05, counsel to Asian African Consultative Orgn., 2005—; chair Internat. Union Conservation of Nature Acad. Environ. Law, 2004—. Co-dir. Ctr. Environ. Legal Studies, Pace U., 1982—; mem. environ. adv. coun. European Bank for Reconstron. and Devel., 2005-; del. U.S.A. environ. law meetings with USSR, 1974-92; chmn. Environ. Adv. Bd. to Gov. Mario Cuomo, 1985-94; mem. environ. adv. coun. European Bank Reconstruction and Devel., London, 2004-. Contbr. articles to profl. jours. Nat. bd. dirs. UN Assn. U.S.A., 1966-76, 79-84, U.S. Com. for UNICEF, 1970-80, World Environment Ctr., 1981—, chmn., 1993-96; bd. dirs. Westchester County Soil and Water Conservation Dist., 1976-83; chmn. N.Y. State Freshwater Wetlands Appeals Bd., 1976-83; chmn. planning bd. Village of Sleepy Hollow, N.Y., 1999—; bd. edn. Union Free Sch. Dist., Tarrytown, 1981-83, 85. Recipient NY State Gov.'s Citation for Hist. Preservation, 1983, Eliz Haub prize Free U., Brussels, 1992, Nat. Environ. Quality award Natural Resources Coun. Am., 2002. Fellow Am. Bar Found.; mem. Internat. Coun. Environ. Law (gov. 1993—), Commn. Environ. Law (chmn. 1996-04), Am. Soc. Internat. Law, ABA, ALI, N.Y. State Bar Assn. (chmn. environ. law sect. 1979-80, Environ. Law award 1981), Assn. Am. Law Schs. (chair sect. on postgrad. legal edn. 1999-00, chair sect. environ. law 1987-88), Assn. Bar City N.Y. (chmn. environ. law com. 1977-78, internat. law com. 1985-88, internat. environ. law com. 1990-92, Russian law com. 1992-95), Westchester County Bar Assn., Sierra Club (nat. bd. dirs. 1979-83, hon. v.p. 2004-), Phi Beta Kappa. Democrat. Unitarian Universalist. Home: 258 Kelbourne Ave Sleepy Hollow NY 10591-1322 Office: Pace U Sch Law 78 N Broadway White Plains NY 10603-3710 Office Phone: 914-422-4244. Business E-Mail: nrobinson@law.pace.edu.

ROBINSON, OLA MAE, accountant; b. Worsham Ranch, Tex., Nov. 17, 1903; d. Franklin Earle and Jennie Rachael (Gay) R. B of Acctg., Draughons Bus. Coll., 1935. Tchr. rural schs., Tex., 1924-34; bookkeeper Ins. Cos., Wichita Falls, Tex., 1935-40; acct., bookkeeper U.S. War Dept., Washington, 1941-50; acct. Air Force Acctg. & Fin. Ctr., Denver, 1951-65; bookkeeper 1stMeth. Ch., Denver, 1966-70. Author, editor: Robinson Family, 1995. Recipient Pres. award Denver Rose Soc., 1980. Mem. Nat. Assn. Retired Persons, Nat. Genealogical Soc., Am. Rose Soc. (pres.), Clay County Hist. Soc. Republican. Methodist. Avocations: travel, photography, reading, writing, gardening. Home: 400 W 14th Ave #213B Amarillo TX 79101-4140

ROBINSON, OLIVER DALE, counselor, pastor; b. Mound Bayou, Miss., Dec. 8, 1939; s. Commodore Perry and Ada Mae Robinson; m. Drucilla C. Robinson, May 3, 1964; children: Oliver A. Jr., Andrew L. BTh, Miss. Bapt. Sem., 1968; BMA, St. Leo Coll., Fla., 1978; MA, Northwestern U., Oklahoma City, 1978; PsyD, Neotarian Coll., Kansas City, Mo., 1980; BA in Bus. Adminstrn., Ctr. Distance Learning, 1981; postgrad., La. State U. Pastor Beautiful New Hope Ch., Mound Bayou, 1969—; dir. counseling Urban Life Ctr. Inc., Mound Bayou, 1984—. Scoutmaster sch. troop 302 Boy Scouts Am., Mound Bayou, 1964—66. Recipient Band Booster Club award, Mound Bayou, 1989—2007. Mem.: NAACP, Mound Bayou Alumni Assn. Democrat. Baptist. Mailing: PO Box 205 Mound Bayou MS 38762 Home: 202 Miller St Mound Bayou MS 38762 Personal E-mail: beauthope@nexband.com.

ROBINSON, PATRICK, apparel designer; b. 1967; married; 1 child. Grad., Parsons Sch. Design, NYC. Design dir. Giorgio Armani, Milan, 1990—94; creative dir., sr. v.p. Anne Klein, NYC, 1994—96; designer Patrick Robinson Inc., NYC, 1996—2001; creative dir. Perry Ellis Womenswear, NYC, 2003—04, Paco Rabanne, 2005—07; designer GO Internat. prog., Target, 2007; exec. v.p. design Gap Adult, Gapbody, 2007—. Named one of Vogue's 100 Rising Stars, 1996. Mem.: Coun. Fashion Designers Am. Avocation: boating. Office: Gap Inc 2 Folsom St San Francisco CA 94105 *

ROBINSON, PAUL ARNOLD, historian, educator, writer; b. San Diego, Oct. 1, 1940; s. Joseph Cook and Beryl Marie (Lippincott) R.; m. Ute Brosche, Aug. 3, 1964 (div. Aug. 1967); 1 child, Susan Marie; life ptnr. Stephen Dunatov. BA, Yale U., 1962; postgrad., Free U. Berlin, 1962-63; PhD, Harvard U., 1968. Asst. prof. history Stanford U. (Calif.), 1967-73, assoc. prof., 1973-80, prof. history, 1980—, Richard W. Lyman prof. in the humanities, 1994—. Author: The Freudian Left, 1969, The Modernization of Sex, 1976, Opera and Ideas: From Mozart to Strauss, 1985, Freud and His Critics, 1993, Ludwig van Beethoven: Fidelio, 1996, Gay Lives: Homosexual Autobiography from John Addington Symonds to Paul Monette, 1999, Opera, Sex, and Other Vital Matters, 2002, Queer Wars: The New Gay Right and Its Critics, 2005; editor: Social Thought in America and Europe, 1970; contbg. editor The New Republic, 1979—85. Guggenheim fellow, 1970-71, Stanford Humanities Ctr. fellow, 1984-85, 96-97, Inst. for Advanced Study fellow, 1990-91, Ctr. for Advanced Study in the Behavioral Scis. fellow, 2002-03. Mem. Am. Acad. Arts and Scis., Am. Hist. Assn. Home: 671 Santa Ynez St Stanford CA 94305-8542 Office: Stanford Univ Dept History Stanford CA 94305 Business E-Mail: paulr@stanford.edu.

ROBINSON, PAUL M., lawyer; b. Bklyn., 1958; BA in English cum laude, Williams Coll., 1980; JD, Fordham U., 1983. Bar: NY 1984. Ptnr. Mayer, Katz, Baker, Leibowitz & Roberts, NYC; mem. Legal Dept. Warner Music Group, NYC, 1995, acting gen. counsel, 2006—; sr. v.p., gen. counsel Sony Music Entertainment, NYC. Office: Warner Music Group 75 Rockefeller Plaza New York NY 10019 *

ROBINSON, PETER J., dean, periodontal educator, pathologist; b. St. Louis, May 31, 1941; s. Hamilton Burrows-Greaves and Katherine (Long) R.; m. Letticia Schumacher, July 18, 1964; children: Elizabeth Haskins Vance, Emily Hamilton. BA, Drake U., Des Moines, 1963; DDS, U. Mo., Kansas City, 1966; PhD, U. Pa., Phila., 1972. Dental intern U.S. Army, Washington, 1966-67; asst. prof. U. Pa., Phila., 1973-75; prof., chmn. periodontics Northwestern U., Chgo., 1975-88, chmn. stomatology, 1988-97; dean, prof. periodontology U. Conn. Sch. Dental Medicine, 1997—. Co-author: Transplantation for Dental Specialties, 1980. Pres. Dist. 38 Sch. Bd., Kenilworth, Ill., 1985-87. Capt. U.S. Army, 1966-69. Recipient Procter & Gamble Guest Scientist award Am. Dental Assn. Rsch. Inst., Chgo., 1983, Fogarty award NIH, Washington, 1984. Mem. ADA (sr. scientist Rsch. Inst.), Internat. Assn. Dental Rsch. (pres. periodontal rsch. group 1990-92), Midwest Soc. Periodontology (pres. 1986-87), Ill. Soc. Periodontology (pres. 1985-86). Achievements include patent on Northwestern periodontal probe. Office: U Conn Sch Dental Medicine 263 Farmington Ave Farmington CT 06030

ROBINSON, PETER M., business association executive; BA, U. Del., 1977; MA in Internat. Affairs, Columbia U., 1979. Dir. Inbound Div. Am. Inst. Fgn. Study, 1986—89; mng. Trade and Transport Policy US Coun. for Internat. Bus., v.p. memberships, sr. v.p., COO, pres., 2005—. Bd. dirs. Am. Field Svc.-USA; mem. internat. bd. trustees Am. Field Svc. Intercultural Programs, 1997—2004; bd. dirs. WAND, Inc. Fellow: Fgn. Policy Assn.; mem.: Econ. Club of NY. Office: US Coun for Internat Bus 1212 Ave of Americas New York NY 10036 Office Phone: 212-354-4480. Office Fax: 212-575-0327. E-mail: probinson@uscib.org.

ROBINSON, PREZELL RUSSELL, academic administrator; b. Batesburg, SC, Aug. 25, 1922; s. Clarence and Annie (Folks) R.; m. Lulu Harris, Apr. 9, 1950; 1 dau. AB in Econs. Social Sci., St. Augustine's Coll., 1946; MA in Sociology, Econs., Cornell U., 1951, EdD in Sociology-Ednl. Adminstrn., 1956; degree (hon.), St. Augustine's Coll.; DCL (hon.), U. South, 1970; LHD, degree, Cuttington U. Coll., Monrovia, Liberia; LHD (hon.), Voorhees Coll., 1981, degree (hon.); LHD (hon.), Episcopal Theol. Sem., 1982; LLD (hon.), Bishop Coll., 1979; DCL (hon.), Columbia U., 1980, degree (hon.); DHL (hon.), Kenyon Coll., 1988; degree (hon.), Va. Theology Sem., Alexandria, Barton Coll., Campbell U., NC State U., Shaw U. Tchr. social sci., French Bettis Jr. Coll., Trenton, SC, 1946-48; sucessively registrar, tchr., acting prin. high sch., acting dean jr. coll., instr., dir. adult edn. Voorhees Jr. Coll., Denmark, SC, 1948-56; prof. sociology, dean coll. St. Augustine's Coll., Raleigh, NC, 1956-64, exec. dean, 1964-66, acting pres., 1966-67, pres., 1967-95, pres. emeritus, 1995—. Pres. United Negro Coll. Fund, Inc., 1978-81, Nat. Assn. Equal Opportunity Higher Edn., 1981-84, N.C. Assn. Coll. & U., Cooperating Raleigh Colls., 1981, 86—; bd. dirs. Learning Inst. N.C.; scholar-in-residence Nairobi (Kenya) U., 1973; vis. lectr. Dept. State del. to African nations, 1971, 73, 78; dir. Wachovia Bank & Trust Co.; vice chmn. N.C. State Bd. Edn., mem., 1973-99, vice-chmn., 1994-99. Contbr. articles to profl. publs. Exec. com. N.C. Edn. Com. on Tchr. Edn.; active N.C. Bd. Edn.; chmn. bd. Assn. Episcopal Colls.; mem. Mayor's Community Relations Com.; vice-chmn. Wake County divsn. Occoneechee coun. Boy Scouts Am., 1959-67; chmn. Wake Occoneechee coun., 1963-66, exec. com., 1965—; vice-chmn. Wake County chpt. ARC; chmn. edn. divsn. United Fund of Raleigh, budget com., 1965—; exec. com. Wake County Libraries.; trustee Voorhees Coll. Fulbright fellow to India, 1965; appointed US alt. rep. or public mem. amb. Gen. Assembly UN, by Pres. George Bush, 1992, by Pres. Clinton, 1996. Served with AUS, 1942. Recipient Distinguished Alumni award Voorhees Coll., 1967, Silver Anniversary award N.C. Community System, 1989; decorated Star of Africia Liberia; recipient numerous service awards and citations; named one of the most effective coll. pres.s in U.S. Coun. for Advancement and Support of Edn., Washington, 1986; Univ. fellow Cornell U., 1954, rsch. fellow, 1955-56; Fulbright fellow, 1965. Mem. AAAS, Nat. Assn. Collegiate Deans and Registrars, Am. Acad. Polit. and Social Sci., Am. Sociol. Soc., N.C. Sociol. Soc. (exec. com.), Ctrl. Intercollegiate Athletic Assn. (exec. com.), N.C. Assn. Ind. Colls. and Univs. (dir.), Raleigh C. of C. (A.E. Finley Disting. Svc. award 1989), So. Sociol. Assn., Am. Acad. Polit. Sci., N.C. Lit. and Hist. Soc., N.C. Hist. Soc., Delta Mu Delta, Phi Delta Kappa, Phi Kappa Phi, Alpha Kappa Mu, Phi Beta Lambda. Protestant Episcopalian (lay reader). Home: 821 Glascock St Raleigh NC 27604-2317 Office: St Augustine's Coll 1315 Oakwood Ave Raleigh NC 27610-2247

ROBINSON, RALPH W., lawyer; b. San Francisco, Mar. 26, 1947; BA, U. Calif., Berkeley, 1968; JD, Golden Gate U., 1971. Bar: Calif. 1972, US Supreme Ct., Supreme Ct. Calif. Mng ptnr. San Francisco office Wilson, Elser, Moskowitz, Edelman & Dicker LLP, head San Francisco trial practice area. Mem.: ABA, Alameda County Bar Assn., Bar Assn. San Francisco. Office: Wilson Elser Moskowitz Et Al Sten 1700 525 Market St

San Francisco CA 94105-2725 Office Phone: 415-433-0990 ext. 3001. Office Fax: 415-434-1370. Business E-Mail: robinsonr@wemed.com.

ROBINSON, RAYMOND EDWIN, conductor, music educator, writer; b. San Jose, Calif., Dec. 26, 1932; s. Elam Edwin and Zula Mai (Hatley) R.; m. Ruth Aleen Chamberlain, Mar. 12, 1954; children: Cynthia Rae, Greg Edwin, David L., Brent Steven, Jeffrey Vernon. BA, San Jose State U., 1956; MMus, Ind. U., 1958, D in Mus. Edn., 1969; LHD, Westminster Choir Coll., 1987; postdoctoral study, Jagiellonian U., Poland, 1995, Cambridge U., 1987—89, postdoctoral study, 2002—03. Instr. music Ind. U., Bloomington, 1958-59; music critic Portland Reporter, 1962-63, Balt. Evening Sun, 1964-68, Palm Beach (Fla.) Post, 1991—, Palm Beach Daily News, 2003—04; founder, tchr. seminar for music adminstrs., 1972—; chmn. divsn. fine arts Cascade Coll., Portland, Oreg., 1959-63; dean Peabody Inst., Balt., 1963-69; pres. Westminster Choir Coll., Princeton, NJ, 1969-87; vis. fellow Wolfson Coll. U. Cambridge, England, 1987—89, 2002—03; disting. prof. choral studies, choral condr. Palm Beach Atlantic U., West Palm Beach, Fla., 1989—; pres. Prestige Publs., Inc., 1978—; prof. Sch. Ch. Music Knox Theol. Sem., Ft. Lauderdale, Fla., 1989—; vis. prof. U. Miami, 2001—. Choral condr. Palm Beach CC, Lake Worth, Fla., 1992-93; condr.-in-residence, dir. music First Presbyn. Ch., West Palm Beach, 1989-97; dir. music Coral Ridge Presbyn. Ch., Ft. Lauderdale, Fla., 1997, music dir., conductor Palm Beach Symphony Orch., 2004—; spl. guest choral condr. Palm Beach Opera, 1990—; interim condr. Choral Soc. Palm Beaches, 1992; condr. Ray Robinson Chorale, 1994—, Cambridge (Eng.) U., Cambridge, Eng., 1987-89, 2002-03, Kiev, Ukraine, 1997, Budapest, 1997, Cracow, 2002, Coral Ridge Presbyn. Ch., 1997; vis. prof. U. Miami, Fla., 2001-2002. Author: The Choral Experience, 1976, Choral Music, 1978; Krzysztof Penderecki, A Guide to His Works, 1983, A Study of the Penderecki St. Luke Passion, 1983, John Finley Williamson: A Centennial Appreciation, 1987, Postcards from Cambridge, 2005; co-author: German Diction for the Choral Singer, 1992, A Bach Tribute: Bach Essays in Honor of William H. Scheide, 1993; co-author, editor: Studies in Penderecki, 1998, 2003; editor: Labyrinth of Time: Five Addresses for the End of the Millenium, 1998; The Choral Tradition Series, Hinshaw Music Inc., 1978—. Bd. dirs. Balt. Symphony Orch., 1967-69, Am. Boy Choir Sch., 1970-73, N.Y. Choral Soc., 1972—, Palm Beach Atlantic U. choral series Hinshaw Music Inc., 1990—; bd. dirs. Palm Beach County Coun. Arts, chmn. profl. artists com., mem. task force for master plan, 1990-92; mem. cultural plan com. Palm Beach County Cultural Coun., 1992; mem. task force for edn. Fla. Philharm. Orch., 1994-95; mem. art in pub. places com. West Palm Beach, Fla. 2004—. Recipient Disting. Alumni Merit award Ind. U., 1975, Disting. Alumni award Sch. Music Ind. U., 1973, Disting. Alumni award San Jose State U., 1990. Mem. Coll. Music Soc. (life), Am. Choral Dirs. Assn. (life, chmn. rsch. and publs. com. 1986—), Internat. Heinrich Schütz Soc. (chmn. Am. sect. 1984-87), Univ. Club N.Y., Nassau Club Princeton, Govs. Club West Palm Beach. Presbyterian. Home: 2413 Medina Way West Palm Beach FL 33401-8019 Business E-Mail: ray_robinson@pba.edu.

ROBINSON, REBECCA LYNNE, medical researcher; b. Evansville, Ind., Dec. 9, 1967; d. Sherman Joseph and Joyce Jeane Black; m. Robert Wayne Robinson, Aug. 8, 1992; children: Calder Luke, Mary Helen Ellie. BA, U. So. Ind., 1990; MS, Purdue U., 1995. Tchg. asst. Ind. U.-Purdue U., 1990—92; rsch. asst. Osgood Lab. for Cross-Cultural Rsch., Indpls., 1990—93; rsch. analyst Regenstrief Inst./Bowen Rsch. at Ind. U. Sch. Medicine, Indpls., 1993—98; rsch. scientist St. Vincent Hosp., Indpls., 1996—98; health outcomes rsch. cons. U.S. Med. Divsn., Eli Lilly and Co., Indpls., 1998—. Cons. Osgood Lab. for Cross-Cultural Rsch., 1993—98, Ind. Hand Ctr., Indpls., 1996—98, Ind. State Dept. Health, Indpls., 1996—98; presenter in field. Contbr. articles to profl. jours. Facilitator, team leader, participant Ministry of Moms, Nativity Ch., Indpls., 2001—05. Recipient Outstanding Grad. Student award, Purdue U., 1992, Best Author Presentation award, 17th World Congress on Psychosomatic Medicine, 2003, Rsch. award, Marketscan, 2005; grantee Agy. for Health Care Policy and Rsch., 1990—95. Mem.: DAR. Home Phone: 317-862-8292; Office Phone: 317-433-1323. Office Fax: 317-277-7444. E-mail: rlrobinson@lilly.com.

ROBINSON, REGINALD R., musician; b. Chgo., Oct. 19, 1972; Pianist and composer of classical ragtime music; signed by Delmark Records, 1992. Composer: (albums) The Strongman, 1993, Sounds in Silhouette, 1994, Euphonic Sounds, 1998, Man Out of Time, 2003. Named MacArthur Fellow, John D. and Catherine T. MacArthur Found., 2004. Office: c/o Delmark Records 4121 N Rockwell Chicago IL 60618

ROBINSON, RICHARD, publishing executive; b. Pitts., May 15, 1937; s. Maurice Richard and Florence (Liddell) Robinson; children: John Benham, Maurice. BA in English magna cum laude, Harvard U., 1959; postgrad., St. Catharines Coll., Cambridge U., 1959-60, Columbia U., 1959-61. Tchr. English, Evanston Twp. (Ill.) H.S., 1960-62; asst. editor Lit. Cavalcade, Scholastic Inc., NYC, 1962-63; editor Scholastic lit. units Scholastic Inc., 1963-64; founder, editor Scope mag., 1964, editorial dir. English, 1967-71, pub. sch. divsn., 1971-74; pres. Scholastic Corp., 1974—, CEO, 1975—, chmn. bd., 1982—. Named Corp. Citizen of Yr., Robin Hood Found., 1999, The Creative Coalition, 2000, Publisher of Yr., UJA Fedn., N.Y., 2000; recipient EdPress Hall of Fame award, Assn. Ednl. Publrs., Cleveland E. Dodge medal, Tchrs. Coll. Columbia U., Best Friend award, LA's BEST After Sch. Enrichment Program, For the Love of Reading award, UJA-Fedn., Spotlight award, Creative Coalition, British Am. Bus. award Save the Children, Partners for Children award, 2003. Mem. Nat. Coun. Tchrs. English, Nat. Assn. Bilingual Edn. (Corp. Citizen of Yr. 1996), Assn. Am. Pubs. (bd. dirs. 1989—, exec. com., chmn. 1996-98, LMP Publ. of Yr. 1998), Century Assn., Pubs. Lunch Club, University Club (N.Y.C.), Phi Beta Kappa Office: Scholastic Inc 557 Broadway New York NY 10012-3919 E-mail: drobinson@scholastic.com. *

ROBINSON, RICHARD M., communications executive; b. Bklyn., Nov. 28, 1934; s. Allen and Syd (Bell) R.; m. Rochelle Wolf, Dec. 25, 1967; children: Michelle P., Steven E. BS in Physics, Rensselaer Poly. Inst., 1956, MS in Tech. Comm., 1959. Assoc. engr. Convair-Astronautics, San Diego, 1956—57; tech. writer Raytheon, Andover, Mass., 1957—58; pubs. engr. Hazeltine Electronics, Little Neck, NY, 1959—61; sr. pubs. engr. Sperry Gyroscope, Great Neck, NY, 1961—68; mgr. editl. svcs. Grumman Corp., Bethpage, NY, 1968—94; tech. comm. specialist/cons. Setauket, NY, 1995—. Adj. faculty Suffolk County C.C. Contbr. articles to profl. jours. Mem. IEEE (life sr., conf. chmn. 1989, tech. activities bd. 1992-93, Profl. Com. Soc. adminstrv. com. 1977-97, Profl. Com. Soc. pres. 1992-93, referee papers Trans. on Profl. Comm., Alfred N. Goldsmith award 1983, 3d Millennium medal 2000), Soc. Tech. Comms. (sr. mem.), Miramar Ski Club (pres. 1966-67), Amateur Ski Instrs. Assn. (cert. instr.). Home and Office: 10 Penelope Dr Setauket NY 11733-2010 Personal E-mail: r.robinson@ieee.org.

ROBINSON, ROBERT BLACQUE, foundation administrator; b. Long Beach, Calif., Apr. 24, 1927; s. Joseph LeRoi and Frances Hansel R.; m. Susan Amelia Thomas, Jan. 21, 1960; children: Victoria, Shelly, Blake, Sarah. Student, Oreg. State Coll., 1946; BA, UCLA, 1950; student, U. Hawaii. Partner, Pritchard Assocs. (Mgmt. Cons.), Honolulu, 1956-58; asst. dir. Econ. Planning and Coordination Authority, Hawaii, 1959; dep. dir. dept. econ. devel. State of Hawaii, 1960-63; asst. mgr. Pacific Concrete and Rock Co., Ltd., Honolulu, 1963-66, exec. v.p. and gen. mgr., 1966-68, pres. and gen. mgr., 1968-75, chmn., 1976-77; pres. C. of C. of Hawaii, Honolulu, 1977—. Bd. govs. Hawaii Employers Coun., 1969-74, mem. exec. com., 1969-74, vice chmn., 1973-74; bd. dirs. Pacific Aerospace Mus., 1982-86; mem. Hawaii Tourism Conf., 1977, chmn., 1981-82; bd. dirs. Aloha United Fund, 1970-76, sec., 1972, v.p., 1973-76; bd. dirs. Oahu Devel. Conf., 1970-75; treas., bd. dirs. Crime Stoppers Hawaii, 1981—; mem. Hawaii Joint Coun. on Econ. Edn., 1985—; bd. dirs. Jr. Achievement Hawaii, 1967-73, pres., 1969; bd. dirs. Hawaii Ednl. Coun., 1974-75, Health and Community Services Coun. Hawaii, 1982-84; mem. exec. com. Hawaii Conv. Ctr. Coun., 1984—, Interagency Energy Conservation Coun., State of Hawaii, 1978—; trustee Cen. Union Ch., 1983-86; bd. dirs. Waikiki Improvement Assn. Inc., 1986—; mem. Ctr. for Tropical and Subtropical Aquacultute industry Adv. Coun., 1987—; chmn. Mayor's Adv. Com. on Pacific Nations Ctr., 1988-89. Lt. comdr. USNR, 1945-46, ret. Mem. Japan-Am. Conf. of Mayors and C. of C. Pres. (mem. Am. exec. com. 1974—), Am. Soc. Assn. Execs. (past dir. Hawaii chpt.), Hawaii Execs. Coun. (found., Young Pres. Assn. (past mem.), Aloha Soc. Assn. Execs., C. of C. Hawaii (dir. 1972-75, chmn. 1975), Coun. of Profit Sharing Industries (past dir. Hawaii sect.), Cement and Concrete Products Industry of Hawaii (pres. 1968), Hawaii Mfrs. Assn. (past dir.), Navy League of U.S. (Hawaii council), Engring. Assn. Hawaii, Pacific Club, Rotary, Sigma Chi. Home: 1437 Kalaepohaku St Honolulu HI 96816-1804 Office: C of C Hawaii 735 Bishop St Ste 220 Honolulu HI 96813-4816

ROBINSON, ROBERT L., retired diversified financial services company executive, lawyer; b. Ridgeway, Va., Feb. 22, 1936; s. Gerald L. and Annie (McBride) R.; m. Audrey M. Allen, July 30, 1960; children: Robert, Diane, Kelly. BA, Va. State Coll., 1957; LL.B., Harvard U., 1960; MBA, U. Conn., 1976. Bar: N.Y. 1961, Pa. 1978. Atty. N.Y. Central Ry. Co., NYC, 1960-63; asst. gen. counsel Crane Co., NYC, 1963-71; counsel Xerox Corp., Stamford, Conn., 1971-77; v.p., asst. gen. counsel and sec. INA Corp., Phila., 1977-82; sr. v.p., gen. counsel investment group CIGNA Corp., Bloomfield, Conn., 1982-84, sr. v.p., asst. gen. counsel, corp. sec., 1984-87, sr. v.p., gen. counsel property & casualty group Phila., 1987-88, sr. v.p., chief counsel litigation and ins., 1988-2000; ret., 2000. Dir. Phila. Reinsurance Corp., Am. Arbitration Assn., CPR Inst. for Dispute Resolution. Served to lt. U.S. Army, 1957. Mem. ABA, Pa. Bar Assn., Westchester-Fairfield Corp. Counsel Assn. (founder, bd. dirs. pres. 1976-77), Great Oak Yacht Cub, Harvard Club (N.Y.C.), Merion Cricket Club, Phila. Club., Phila. Cricket Club. Republican. Office: 451 Moreno Rd Wynnewood PA 19096 Office Phone: 610-896-0758. Personal E-mail: rlrobinson@verizon.net.

ROBINSON, ROBIN, newscaster; b. Chgo. m. Terrence Brantley, 1986 (div. 1989). B, San Diego State U., 1980. Reporter KGTV, San Diego, 1979—81; consumer reporter CBS affiliate, Denver, 1981—84; reporter WBBM-TV, Chgo., 1984—87; co-anchor Fox News at 9 WFLD-TV, Chgo., 1987—. Co-recipient Emmy awards. Office: WFLD-TV 205 N Mich Ave Chicago IL 60601

ROBINSON, RONALD ALAN, manufacturing executive; b. Louisville, Mar. 23, 1952; s. J. Kenneth and Juanita M. (Crosier) R.; m. Joan Parker, 1986; children: Rex, Jay. BS, GA Inst. Tech., 1974; MBA, Harvard U., 1978. Staff engr., asst. to exec. v.p. ops. Dual Drilling Co., Wichita Falls, Tex., 1978-80; v.p. Dreco, Inc., Houston, 1980-84, pres., dir. subs. Triflo Industries Internat., Inc.; pres., COO Ramteck Sys., Inc., 1984-87; chmn., CEO Denver Techs. Inc., 1988-95; pres. Svedala Industries, Inc., 1996-99; pres., CEO Alamo Group Inc., Seguin, Tex., 1999—. Recipient Optimist Internat. Citizenship award, 1970; Gardiner Symonds fellow, 1977. Mem. Harvard Alumni Assn. Home: 18 Pourtales Colorado Springs CO 80906 Office: Alamo Group Inc 1502 E Walnut St Seguin TX 78155-5202 Office Phone: 830-372-9615.

ROBINSON, RONALD MICHAEL, financial executive, consultant; b. NYC, May 1, 1942; s. Arthur John and Matilda (Siegel) R.; m. Mary Jane Reemelin, Feb. 25, 1972; children: Scott Edward, Elizabeth Drew. BS, Ohio State U., 1964; MBA, U. Pa., 1966. CPA, Pa. Fin. mgr. Am. Airlines, Inc., NYC, 1969-72; mgmt. cons. Coopers & Lybrand, Phila., 1973-75; pres. Robinson Assocs., Inc., Paoli, Pa., 1975-81; dir. fin. and adminstrn., chief fin. officer Presbyn. Homes, Inc., Camp Hill, Pa., 1982-99. Bd. dirs. Healthamerica, Healthassurance, Mems. First Fed. Credit Union, Continuing Care Rx, Geneva House. Mem. Carlisle (Pa.) Borough Coun., 1988-92. Home: 1214 Georgetown Circle Carlisle PA 17013-3548 Office: PO Box 908 Carlisle PA 11701 Office Phone: 717-379-3275. E-mail: ronaldmrobinson@comcast.net.

ROBINSON, SALLY SHOEMAKER, lay associate; b. NYC, Dec. 31, 1931; d. Samuel M. and Helen Dominick Smith S.; m. James Courtland Robinson, Dec. 31, 1931; children: Samuel Shoemaker, W. Courtland, A. Alexander, Ellen Whitridge Robinson Mihalski. BA cum laude, Bryn Mawr Coll., 1953; postgrad. studies, Yonsei U. Lang. Inst., Korea, 1960-62, Children's Theatre Assn., 1964; MA, Towson State U., 1974. Ordained elder Brown Meml. Presbyn. Ch., 1985. Commd. missionary to Korea United Presbyn. Ch., Republic of Korea, 1959-71; dir. Brown Meml. Tutorial Program, 1974-84; exec. dir. Episcopal Social Ministries Diocese of Md., Balt., 1984-97; canon for social ministry Episcopal Diocese of Md., Balt., 1985-96; chair, global bd. United Bible Societies, 2001. Trustee Am. Bible Society. Met. chmn. 10th Decade Campaign Bryn Mawr Coll., 1974-76, nat. chmn. Centennial Campaign. 1980-85, trustee, 1985—; trustee Am. Bible Soc., 1988—, v.p., 1993—, chmn. bd., 1996-2001; chmn. global bd. United Bible Socs., 2001—; trustee United Bd. for Christian Higher Edn. in Asia, 1990-95; trustee emeritus Bryn Mawr Coll., 1997—. Home: 10522 Burnside Farm Rd Stevenson MD 21153-2024 Office: Brown Meml Ch 1316 Park Ave Baltimore MD 21217-4185

ROBINSON, SALLY WINSTON, artist; b. Detroit, Nov. 2, 1924; d. Harry Lewis and Lydia (Kahn) Winston; m. Eliot F. Robinson, June 28, 1949; children: Peter Eliot, Lydia Winston, Sarah Mitchell, Suzanne Finley. BA, Bennington Coll., 1947; postgrad., Cranbrook Acad. Art, 1949; grad., Sch. Social Work, Wayne U., 1948, MA, 1972; MFA, Wayne State U., 1973. Psychol. tester Detroit Bd. Edn., 1944; psychol. counselor and tester YMCA, NYC, 1946; social caseworker Family Svc., Pontiac, Mich., 1947; instr. printmaking Wayne State U., Detroit, 1973—. Tchr. children's art Detroit Inst. Art, 1949-50, now artistic advisor, bd. dirs. drawing and pring orgn. One-woman shows include, U. Mich., 1973, Wayne State U., 1974, Klein-Vogel Gallery, 1974, Rina Gallery, 1976, Park McCullough House, Vt., 1976, Williams Coll., 1976, Arnold Klein Gallery, 1977, exhibited in group shows, Bennington Coll., Cranbrook Mus., Detroit Inst. Art, Detroit Artists Market, Soc. Women Painters, Soc. Arts and Crafts, Bloomfield Art Assn., Flint Left Bank Gallery, Balough Gallery, Detroit Soc. Woman Painters, U. Mich., U. Ind., U. Wis., U. Pitts., Toledo Mus., Krannert Mus., Represented in permanent collections. Bd. dirs. Planned Parenthood, 1951—, mem. exec. bd., 1963—; bd. dirs. PTA, 1956-60, Roeper City and Country Sch., U. Mich. Mus. Art, 1978; trustee Putnam Hosp. Med. Rsch. Inst., 1978; mem. Gov.'s Commn. Art in State Bldgs., 1978-79; mem. art and devel. coms. So. Vt. Art Ctr., 1987-88; mem. vol. com. Marie Selby Gardens; patron Graphic Art Studio, U. So. Fla., Tampa; patron, benefactor Clark Mus., Williamstown, Mass.; vol. Shelburne Art Ctr., Vt. Fellow: Williams Coll. Mus. Art (mem. visiting com.); mem.: Bloomfield Art Assn. (program co-chmn. 1956), Birmingham Soc. Women Painters (pres. 1974—76), Detroit Soc. Women Painters, Detroit Artists Market (dir. 1956—, hon. bd. mem.), Founders Soc. Detroit Inst. Art, Bennington Coll. Alumnae Assn. (regional co-chmn. 1954), Harvard Club, Williams Club, Cosmopolitan Club (N.Y.C.), Founders Garden Club (Sarasota, Fla.), Garden Club Am. (bd. dirs.), Oaks Club (Fla.), Women's City Club (coord. art shows Detroit 1950), Village Women's Club (Birmingham, Mich.). Unitarian Universalist. Home: 209 Hills Point Rd Charlotte VT 05445-9698 also: 639 Eagle Watch Ln Osprey FL 34229 Personal E-mail: sallyrobinsonflorida@msn.com.

ROBINSON, SHARON BETH, health science association administrator; b. Balt., Sept. 28, 1959; BS, Towson State U., 1981; MS, Johns Hopkins U., 1986. Exec. asst. Congress of Neurol. Surgeons, Balt., 1983-86; office adminstr. Md. Inst. Emergency Med. Svcs., Balt., 1986-87; coord. spl. projects U. Md. Med. Systems, Balt., 1986-88; adminstr. Am. Bd. Med. Genetics, Bethesda, Md., 1988—, Am. Coll. Med. Genetics, Bethesda, 1992-98, Am. Bd. Genetic Counseling, Bethesda, 1993—. Mem. Catonsville Community Coll. Alumni Assn. (bd. dirs. 1984-89, sec. 1986, v.p. 1987, pres. 1988). Office: ABMG/ABGC 9650 Rockville Pike Bethesda MD 20814-3998 E-mail: srobinson@genetics.faseb.org.

ROBINSON, SHARON PORTER, educational association administrator; b. Louisville; B in Edn., English and Psych., U. Ky., 1966, M in Edn., Curriculum and Instrn., 1976, D in Ednl. Adminstrn. and Supervision, 1979; D (hon.), U. Louisville. Tchr., Lexington, Ky., US AFB, Bitburg, Germany; assoc. dir. Jefferson County Edn. Consortium, Ky.; dir. instrn. and profl. devel. NEA, 1980—89, dir. Nat. Ctr. Innovation, 1989—93; asst. sec. edn. Office Ednl. Rsch. and Improvement US Dept. Edn., 1993—96; v.p. tchg. and learning for state and fed. rels. Ednl. Testing Svc., Washington, 1997—98, sr. v.p., COO, 1998, exec. v.p., pres. Ednl. Policy Leadership Inst., 2002—04; interim dep. dir. Progs. and Legis. Office PTA; pres., CEO Am. Assn. Colls. for Tchr. Edn., Washington, 2005—. Cons. Nat. Bd. Profl. Tchg. Stds.; head tchr. edn. initiative Nat. Ctr. Innovation. Bd. trustees Alfred Harcourt Found. Recipient Award of Appreciation, Nat. Head Start Found., Founders award, Nat. Commn. African Am. Edn., Pinnacles of Excellence award, Helping Hands Enrichment & Leadership Found., Tchr. for Am. award, Girl Scouts' Woman of Distinction award. Office: Am Assn Colls for Tchr Edn 1307 New York Ave NW Ste 300 Washington DC 20005-4701 E-mail: srobinson@aacte.org. *

ROBINSON, SMOKEY (WILLIAM ROBINSON), singer, composer; b. Detroit; m. Claudette Rogers, 1959 (div. 1986); children: Berry William, Tamla Claudette; m. Frances (Gladney) Robinson, 2002. V.p. Motown Record Corp., 1961-1988; bd. dirs. Smokey Robinson Foods. Formed group, Smokey Robinson and the Miracles, with Miracles, 1957-72, performed Detroit nightclubs, co-founder, Tamla record label, 1959; numerous singles and album recs. including: Sweet Harmony, 1973, Virgin Man, 1974, Agony and the Ecstasy, 1975, Quiet Storm, 1976, Open, 1976, There will Come a Day (I'm Gonna Happen to You), 1977; appearances at clubs, colls., also network TV shows including Shindig; star own TV spl., 1971; solo albums include Smokey, 1973, A Quiet Storm, 1975, Smokey's Family Robinson, 1976, Deep in My Soul, 1977 Smokin', 1978, Warm Thoughts, 1980, Being with You, 1981, Touch the Sky, 1983, Smoke Signals, 1986, One Heartbeat, 1987, Love Smokey, 1990, Blame It on Love & All the Great Hits, 1990, Double Good Everything, 1992, Motown Legends, 1995, Intimate, 1999, Food for the Spirit, 2004; appeared on Broadway in An Evening with Smokey Robinson, 1985, Chicago, 2006; author: (autobiography with David Ritz) Smokey: Inside My Life, 1989. Inducted Rock 'n Roll Hall of Fame, 1986, Songwriters Hall of Fame, 1986; recipient Grammy award for best male rhythm & blues vocal perfomance, 1987, Founders award ASCAP, 1988, Lifetime Achievement award, Motor City Music Awards, 1992, Kennedy Ctr. Honor, John F. Kennedy Center for Performing Arts, 2006. Office: SFGL Foods Inc #200 100 N Brand Ave Glendale CA 91203 also: SBK Records 1290 Ave of the Americas New York NY 10104

ROBINSON, STEPHEN MICHAEL, mathematician, educator; b. Columbus, Ohio, Apr. 12, 1942; s. Arthur Howard and Mary Elizabeth (Coffin) R.; m. Chong-Suk Han, May 10, 1968; children: Diana Marie Oestreich, James Andrew. BA, U. Wis., 1962, PhD, 1971; MS, NYU, 1963; Diploma, U.S. Army War Coll., 1986; Dr. honoris causa, Univ. Zürich, 1996. Adminstr. U. Wis., Madison, 1969-72, asst. prof., 1972-75, assoc. prof., 1975-79, prof. indsl. and sys. engring. and computer scis., 1979—, chmn. dept. indsl. engring., 1981-84. Cons. to various agys. Dept. Def., 1971—. Author: (with Jagdish Chandra) An Uneasy Alliance: The Mathematics Research Center at the University of Wisconsin, 1956-1987, 2005; editor: Math. of Ops. Rsch., 1981-86, assoc. editor, 1975-80, Jour. Ops. Rsch., 1974-86, Math. Programming, 1986-91; mem. bd. editors Annals Ops. Rsch., 1984-99, Set-Valued Analysis, 1992-99, Jour. Convex Analysis, 1994—2002; adv. editor Math. of Ops. Rsch., 1987—, Ops. Rsch. Letters, 2002-; mem. editl. bd. Springer Series in Ops. Rsch. and Fin. Engring., 1996—; contbr. numerous articles to profl. jours. Trustee Village of Shorewood Hills, Wis., 1974-76, mem. fin. com., 1973-87; bd. on math. scis. and their applications NRC, 2001-07, bd. overseers Simon's Rock Coll., Great Barrington, Mass., 1991-02. Served to capt. US Army, 1963—69, Korea, Vietnam, col. AUS, ret. Decorated Legion of Merit, Bronze star, Air medal, Army Commendation medal with 2 oak leaf clusters; recipient John K. Walker Jr. award, Mil. Ops. Rsch. Soc., 2001. Fellow Inst. Ops. Rsch. and Mgmt. Scis. (mem. Ops. Rsch. Soc. Am. coun. 1991-94, sec. 2000-03, treas. 2007—); mem. Inst. Indsl. Engrs., Soc. Indsl. and Applied Math., Math. Programming Soc. (mem.-at-large of coun. 1991-94, George B. Dantzig prize 1997), Madison Club. Home: 1014 University Bay Dr Madison WI 53705-2251 Office: U Wis Dept Indsl and Sys Engring 1513 University Ave Madison WI 53706-1539 Home Phone: 608-231-3065; Office Phone: 608-263-6862. Business E-Mail: smrobins@wisc.edu.

ROBINSON, STEVE, real estate company executive; b. 1967; BS in Civil Engring., Mich. Technol. U. V.p. Silverman Devel. Co., Bingham Farms, Mich., 1995—99, pres.; regional v.p. Toll Bros. Inc., 1999—2001. Named one of 40 Under 40, Crain's Detroit Bus., 2006. Mem.: Mich. Assn Planning (exec. bd. 2005), Am. Soc. Civil Engineers. Office: Silverman Development Co 32100 Telegraph Rd Ste 220 Bingham Farms MI 48025 Office Phone: 248-540-6400. Office Fax: 248-932-9131.

ROBINSON, SUE L(EWIS), federal judge; b. 1952; BA with highest honors, U. Del., 1974; JD, U. Pa., 1978. Assoc. Potter, Anderson & Corron, Wilmington, Del., 1978-83; asst. U.S. atty. U.S. Attys. Office, 1983-88; U.S. magistrate judge U.S. Dist. Ct. (Del. dist.), 1988-91, dist. judge, 1991—, chief judge. Named to U. Del. Wall of Fame, 1994. Mem.: Del. State Bar Assn. (sec. 1986—87). Office: US Dist Ct J Caleb Boggs Fed Bldg 844 N King St Lockbox 31 Wilmington DE 19801-3519

ROBINSON, THOMAS CHRISTOPHER, health science educator; b. Buffalo, Oct. 16, 1944; s. Christopher Sidney and Eleanor Florence (Martin) R.; m. Rena H. Robinson; children: Diane Dunn, Kristen O'Melia. BA, SUNY, Buffalo, 1966, EdM, 1968, PhD, 1971; grad. mgmt. devel. program, Harvard U., Cambridge, Mass., 1989. Admissions officer, office of admissions and records SUNY, Buffalo, 1966-72, assoc. dean Sch. Health Related Professions, 1975-78; asst. dir. Erie County Lab., Buffalo, 1972-75; assoc. dean Coll. Allied Health Professions, U. Ky., Lexington, 1978-84, dean Coll. Health Scis., 1984—2004, prof., 1984—, dean emeritus, 2005—. Cons. MDS Labs., Hamilton, Ont., Can., 1973-75, Joint US-Arabian Commn. on Econ. Cooperation, 1986-87, West Sussex Inst. Higher Edn., Bogner Regis, U.K., 1987, U. Wis. Sys. Ctrs. of Excellence Program, 1988, Pub. Health Svc. Health Resources Adminstrn., 1983, 90-91; mem. exec. com. Nat. Practitioner Data Bank, 1992-94, cons. 1994-95; hon. mem. faculty Khabarovsk (Russia) Med. Inst., 1996; bd. dirs. Health Ky. Contbr. articles to profl. jours. Mem. Health Sys. Agy. Coun., Buffalo, 1977-78, Western NY Hemophilia Soc. Bd. Buffalo, 1977-78, Lexington-Fayette County Bd. Health, Lexington, 1987-91, program excellence project Ohio Bd. Regents, United Way of Bluegrass Healthcare Devel. Bd., 1991; cons. La. Bd. Regents, 1995, 98, 2001, 04, 06, 07, Univ. Wolverhampton fellow, UK, 1991; bd. dirs. Ky. HealthCare Improvement Authority, 2006—; mem. leadership coun. Am. Diabetes Assn., Lexington, 2007. Sgt. NY Army N.G., 1968-74. Recipient Svc.

award, Jour. Allied Health, 1986; Internat fellow, Hatfield Coll., Un. Durham, Eng., 2005. Mem. Assn. Schs. Allied Health Professions (bd. dirs. 1985-87, Svc. award 1987, Fellow award 1988, pres. 1991-94, past pres. 1994-95, Outstanding Mem. award 1995), Ky. Allied Health Consortium (bd. dirs. 1985-93, chair 1995-96), So. Assn. Allied Health Deans (sec. 1986-88, chmn. 1988-90), Assn. Schs. Allied Health Professions (pres. 1991-94), Ky. Hosp. Assn., Ky. Assn. Healthcare Facilities, So. Assn. Colls. and Schs. (accreditation evaluator), Sigma Phi Epsilon. Avocations: golf, travel, genealogy, gardening. Office: U Ky Coll Health Scis CTW Bldg 900 S Limestone Rm 209H Lexington KY 40536-0200 Home: 121 Gleneagles Way Versailles KY 40383 Office Phone: 859-323-1100 x 80559. Business E-Mail: tcrobi@uky.edu.

ROBINSON, V. GENE (THE RIGHT REVEREND V. GENE ROBINSON), bishop; life ptnr. Mark Andrew; children: Jamee, Ella. BA in Am. Studies and History, U. South, 1969; MDiv, Gen. Theol. Sem., 1973. Curate Christ Ch., Ridgewood, NJ, 1973—75, youth ministries coord. Province 1, 1978—85; exec. sec. Episc. Province New England, 1983—2003; canon to the ordinary Episc. Diocese N.H., 1988—2003, bishop coadjutor, 2003—04, Bishop Diocesan, 2004—. Bd. trustees Gen. Theol. Sem., 2001—; co-owner, dir. Girl's Summer Camp and Horse Farm, 1975—78; founding dir. Sign of the Dove Retreat Ctr., Temple, NH; mem. Nat. Youth Ministries Devel. Team. Founder Concord Outright. Avocations: cooking, gardening, music, running. Office: Episcopal Diocese of NH 63 Green St Concord NH 03301-4243 Office Phone: 603-224-1914.

ROBINSON, VERNA COTTEN, retired librarian, real estate manager; b. Enfield, NC, Oct. 6, 1927; d. Ernest and Ida (Faulcon) Cotten; m. Elbert Crutcher Robinson, Aug. 14, 1953 (dec. Feb. 1992); children: Angela, Elbert Cotten. BS, NC Ctrl. U., Durham, 1948; MS in Libr. Sci., Carnegie Mellon U., Pitts., 1950. Br. libr. Blyden br. Norfolk Pub. Libr., Va., 1950-51; serials libr. Howard U., Washington, 1951-52; sch. libr. Spingarn H.S., Washington, 1952-53, Cardozo H.S., Washington, 1955-60, Roosevelt H.S., Washington, 1960-67, 70-85; ret. DC Pub. Schs., 1985. Pres. Robinson Property Mgmt. Inc., Washington, 1993—; bd. dirs. New Birth Corp., Miami. V.p. DC Assn. Sch. Librs., Washington, 1972-74; vice-chair Diaconate Lincoln Congrl. Temple/United Ch. of Christ, 1999—, chair, 2000-02. Recipient Elder Wise Woman award, Ctrl. Atlantic Conf. of United Ch. of Christ, 2002, Pioneer's Achiever's award United Ch. Christ, 1995; Daisy Scarborough scholar NC Ctrl. U., 1946-48, Carnegie Libr. Alumni scholar Carnegie Libr. Sch. Alumni Assn., 1948-50. Mem. African Am. Women's Assn. (internat. com. 1992-95), Delta Sigma Theta (tuition scholar Grand chpt. 1948-50), Delta Sigma Theta (Washington DC Alumnae chpt. 1970-). Avocations: reading, walking, travel, theater. Home Phone: 202-882-0864; Office Phone: 202-882-1737.

ROBINSON, VIANEI LOPEZ, lawyer; b. Houston, Mar. 6, 1969; d. David Tiburcio and Romelia Gloria (Guerra) Lopez. AB in Psychology cum laude, Princeton U., 1988; JD, U. Tex., 1991. Bar: Tex. 1991; mediator's cert. Assoc. Bracewell & Patterson LLP, Houston, 1991-94, Wagstaff Law Firm, Abilene, Tex., 1994-97; owner Robinson Law Firm, Abilene, 1997—. Contbr. articles to profl. jours., chpts. to School Law in Texas, A Practical Guide, 1996, Texas Employment Law, 1998; weekly wine columnist, Abilene Reporter News, San Angelo Std. Times. Bd. dirs., pres. Historic Paramount Theatre, 2006, bd. dirs. Abilene C. of C., Cmty. Fund Abilene; mem. adv. bd., Day Nursery of Abilene, Noah Project, Ctr. Contemporary Arts. Presdl. scholar, Nat. Merit scholar, Nat. Hispanic scholar, 1985, Vinson & Elkins scholar U. Tex. Sch. Law, Austin, 1988-91. Fellow Tex. Bar Found.; mem. ABA, State Bar Tex. (minority dir. 2000-05, various coms.), Coll. of the State Bar of Tex. (bd. dirs. 2000-01), Tex. Young Lawyers Assn. (bd. dirs. 1994-97), Abilene Bar Assn., Abilene Young Lawyers Assn., Big Country Soc. for Human Resource Mgmt. (pres. 1999). Avocations: theater and dance, fine art, food and wine. Home: 2410 Wyndham Ct Abilene TX 79606-4370 Office: Robinson Law Firm First Nat Bank Tower 400 Pine St Ste 1070 Abilene TX 79601-5173 Office Phone: 325-672-6041. Office Fax: 325-677-6044. Business E-Mail: vlr@robinsonlawfirm.com.

ROBINSON, W. LEE, lawyer; b. Rome, Ga., Sept. 24, 1943; m. Irene Scales, 1966; children: Christine, Jacquelyn. BS, Ga. Inst. Tech.; MBA, JD, Mercer U., 1985. With Robinson Hardware Store, Macon, Ga., 1954-86; mem. Ga. Senate, Atlanta, 1975-83; mayor City of Macon, Macon, 1988-92; pvt. practice Macon, 1985—2004; circuit pub. defender Macon Jud. Circuit, 2005—. Judge mcpl. ct. (part time), Macon. Bd. dirs. Cherry Blossom Festival, 2006—. 2d lt. US Army, col. USAR. Decorated Bronze Star with two oak leaf clusters, Legion of Merit with oak leaf cluster; recipient Justice Robert Benham award for Cmty. Svc., 2007; named to U.S. Army Officer Candidate Sch. Hall of Fame. Mem. Ga. Assn. Criminal Def. Lawyers, Macon C. of C. (former bd. dirs.), Macon Bar Assn, Alzheimer's Assn. (chmn., bd. govs. Ga. chpt. 2005-) Address: 3824 Overlook Ave Macon GA 31204-1325 Office: 201 2nd St Ste 550 Macon GA 31201-8282 also: PO Box 4852 Macon GA 31208-4852 E-mail: wlrmcnlaw@aol.com.

ROBINSON, WALTER J., III, lawyer; b. Seattle, Apr. 24, 1941; BA magna cum laude, Univ. Wash., 1963; JD magna cum laude, Univ. Chgo., 1966. Bar: Calif. 1967, Wash. 1967. Ptnr., chmn. Securities Litigation group Pillsbury Winthrop Shaw Pittman, Palo Alto, Calif. Contbr. articles to profl. jours. Mem.: ABA, San Francisco Bar Assn. Office: Pillsbury Winthrop Shaw Pittman 2475 Hanover St Palo Alto CA 94304-1114 Office Phone: 650-233-4792. Office Fax: 650-233-4545. Business E-Mail: walter.robinson@pillsburylaw.com.

ROBINSON, WILKES COLEMAN, retired federal judge; b. Anniston, Ala., Sept. 30, 1925; s. Walter Wade and Catherine Elizabeth (Coleman) R.; m. Julia Von Poellnitz Rowan, June 24, 1955 (dec.); children: Randolph C., Peyton H., Thomas Wilkes Coleman; m. Dorothy Anne LaVictoire, Jan. 17, 2004. BA with honors, U. Ala., 1948; JD, U. Va., 1951. Bar: Ala. 1951, Va. 1962, Mo. 1966, Kans. 1983; cert. mediator, Fla., Ala. Assoc. Bibb & Hemphill, Anniston, 1951-54; city recorder City of Anniston, 1953-55; judge Juvenile and Domestic Rels. Ct. of Calhoun County, Ala., 1954-56; atty. legal dept. GM&O R.R., Mobile, Ala., 1956-58; commerce counsel, asst. gen. atty. Seaboard Air Line R.R., Richmond, Va., 1958-66; chief commerce counsel Monsanto Co., St. Louis, 1966-70; gen. counsel, v.p. Marion Labs., Inc., Kansas City, Mo., 1970-79; pres. Gulf and Gt. Plains Legal Found., Kansas City, Mo., 1980-85, also bd. dirs.; atty. Howard, Needles, Tammen & Bergendoff, Kansas City, 1985-86, also bd. dirs.; v.p. S.R. Fin. Group, Inc., Overland Park, Kans., 1986-87; judge U.S. Ct. Fed. Claims, Washington, 1987-97, sr. judge, 1997—2003; ret., 2003—; of counsel Morris, Cary, Andrews, Talmadge, Jones & Driggers, Dothan, Ala., 2006—. Bd. govs. Kansas City Philharm. Orch., 1975-77. Served with USNR, 1943-44. Mem. Indian Bayou Golf Club, Destin Athletic Club, Scottish Rite, Phi Beta Kappa (past treas. Kansas City, Mo. chpt.), Phi Eta Sigma, Phi Alpha Theta, Kappa Alpha. Episcopalian. Home: 12 Weekewachee Cir Destin FL 32541-4426 Office Phone: 850-654-9137. E-mail: wilkescrob@cox.net.

ROBINSON, WILLIAM See ROBINSON, SMOKEY

ROBINSON, WILLIAM H., curator, art historian, educator; PhD in Art History, Case We. Res. U., Cleve., 1988; Cert. in Spanish Lang. Studies, U. Barcelona, Spain, 2001; Cert. in Mgmt., Weatherhead Sch. Mgmt., Cleve., 2003. Asst. curator modern art Cleve. Mus. Art, 1991—2000, head dept. European and Am. painting and sculpture, 2003—, curator modern european art, 2003—. Bd. trustees Sculpture Ctr., Cleve.; adj. prof. art history Case We. Res. U., Cleve., 1986—2007; grant reviewer in field. Co-author: Puvis de Chavanne's Summer and the Symbolist Avant-Garde, " in Art History, vol. 2, 1992, Masterpieces from East and West: The Cleveland Museum of Art, 1992, Nineteenth-Century European Paintings in the Cleveland Museum of Art, 1999; contbr. chapters to books;, author catalogues in art; contbr. articles to profl. jours. Recipient Ann. Hon. award, Cleve. Artists Found., 2000, MUSE award, Am. Assn. Museums, 2002; fellow, Cleve. Mus. Art, Case We. Res. U., 1980, 1982, Met. Mus. Art, NY, 1981, Getty Rsch. Inst., 2000—01; grantee, Ohio Arts Coun., 1997, NEH, 1998—99, NEA, 2006—07. Mem.: Painting and Drawing Soc. (mem. governing bd.), Internat. Com. Mus. Modern Art, ICOM, French Regional Am. Mus. Exch., Assn. Art Mus. Curators, Ohio Museums Assn., Coll. Art Assn., Am. Soc. Hispanic Art Hist. Studies. Office: Cleve Mus Art 11150 East Blvd Cleveland OH 44106 Home Phone: 216-932-5273; Office Phone: 216-707-2406. Office Fax: 216-421-9409. Business E-Mail: wrobinson@clevelandart.org.

ROBINSON, WILLIAM I., sociologist; b. NYC, Mar. 28, 1959; s. Howard Sydney and Jo-Ann Phyllis Robinson; m. Gloconda Lucia Robinson, May 10, 1985 (div. Oct. 9, 2000); children: Amaru Alejandro, Tamara Yoconda; m. Marielle Mayorga, Sept. 27, 2003. BA, Friends World Coll., NYC, 1982; M, U. N.Mex., 1992, PhD, 1994. Editor, reporter Agencia Nueva Nicaragua, Managua, 1982-87; Washington bur. chief Agencia Nueva Nicaragua Internat. News Agy., Washington, 1987-90; news analyst, cons. Latin Am. Data Base, Albuquerque, 1990-94; prof. sociology U. N.Mex., Albuquerque, 1994-96, U. Tenn., Knoxville, 1996-98, N.Mex. State U., Las Cruces, 1998-2001; prof. sociology and global studies U. Calif., Santa Barbara, 2001—. Author: David & Goliath, 1987, A Faustian Bargain, 1992, Promoting Polyarchy, 1996, Transnational Conflicts: Central America, Globalization and Social Change, 2003, A Theory of Global Capitalism, 2004, Critical Globalization Studies, 2005. Mem.: Internat. Studies Assn., Latin Am. Studies Assn., Am. Sociol. Assn., Global Studies Assn., Phi Kappa Phi. Avocation: Latin dance. Home Phone: 805-968-2980; Office Phone: 805-893-5607. Business E-Mail: wirobins@soc.ucsb.edu.

ROBINSON, WILLIAM P., academic administrator, consultant, speaker; b. Elmhurst, Ill., Sept. 30, 1949; s. Paul Frederick and Lillian (Horton) R.; m. Bonnie Van Laan, Aug. 10, 1974; children: Brenna Kay, Benjamin Paul, Bailley Kay. Student, Moody Bible Inst., Chgo., 1967-70; AB, U. No. Iowa, 1972; postgrad., Princeton Theol. Sem., NJ, 1972-73; MA, Wheaton Coll., 1975; PhD, U. Pitts., 1979. Assoc. minister First Presbyn. Ch., Pitts., 1975-77; instr. U. Pitts., 1977-79; asst. prof. sch. continuing studies Nat. Coll. Edn., Evanston, Ill., 1979-80, dean sch. continuing studies, 1980-84, sr. v.p., 1984-86; pres. Manchester Coll., North Manchester, Ind., 1986-93, Whitworth Coll., Spokane, Wash., 1993—. Bd. dirs. Coun. Indep. Colls., Ind. Colls. Wash., ING Educators Adv. Bd., Whitworth Coll., Whitworth Found.; founding co-chmn. Higher Edn. Leadership Group of Spokane; cons., speaker for U.S. corps. and svc. orgns. Author: Leading People from the Middle: The Universal Mission of Mind and Heart, 2002. Bd. dirs. Wash. Friends of Higher Edn., Princeton Theol. Sem., Spokane Regional C. of C. (past chmn.), Spokane Symphony; vol. various orgns., especially prion work and hunger projects. Recipient various acad. awards. Mem. Nat. Assn. Ind. Colls. and Univs., Coun. Ind. Colls., Spokane Country Club, Spokane Club. Avocation: sports. Office: Whitworth Coll Office of Pres 300 W Hawthorne Rd Spokane WA 99218-2515 *

ROBINSON, WILLIAM PHILIP, III, state supreme court justice; b. Providence, Jan. 30, 1940; s. William Philip and Dorothy Frances (Hayes) R. BA, U. de Louvain, Belgium, 1962; MA, U. R.I., 1966; PhD, U. Conn., 1971; JD, Boston Coll., 1975. Bar: R.I. 1975, Mass. 1985, U.S. Ct. Appeals (1st cir.) 1977, U.S. Supreme Ct. 1989. Instr. U. Conn., Storrs, 1967-71; law clk. U.S. Ct. Appeals, Boston, 1975-77; assoc. Edwards & Angell, Providence, 1977-81, ptnr., 1981—2004; justice RI Supreme Ct., 2004—. Bd. trustees Providence Country Day Sch., East Providence, 1991-97. Mem. East Greenwich Sch. Com., 1988-96, vice chmn., 1990-94; mem. exec. com. R.I. Assn. of Sch. Coms., 1990-96; mem. East Greenwich Dem. Town Com., 1988-2004; mem. Fed. Bd. Bar Examiners, R.I., 1994-2004; mem. R.I. Jud. Performance Evaulation Com., 1993-2004, R.I. Bd. Govs. for Higher Edn., 2000-03. Mem. Boston Coll. Law Sch. Alumni Assn. (v.p. R.I. chpt. 1990-93, pres. 1993-97, nat. del. 1997—), Order of Coif, Phi Beta Kappa. Avocations: reading, skiing, literary translation. Office: RI Supreme Ct Frank Licht Jud Complex 250 Benefit St Providence RI 02903 E-mail: wrobinson@courts.ri.gov.

ROBINSON, WILLIAM T., III, lawyer; b. Covington, Ky., Jan. 6, 1945; s. William T. Jr. and Hilda C. (Tatermann) R.; m. Joan Mary Wernersbach, Aug. 2, 1969; children: William Taylor IV, Todd Arthur. AB, Thomas More Coll., 1967; JD, U. Ky., 1971. Bar: Ohio 1971, Ky. 1972, Tenn. 1999, U.S. Dist. Ct. (ea. dist.) Ky. 1972, U.S. Dist. Ct. (so. dist.) Ohio 1971, U.S. Dist. Ct. (we. dist.) Ky. 1993, U.S. Dist. Ct. (so. dist.) Ind. 1996, U.S. Ct. Appeals (6th cir.) 1972, U.S. Supreme Ct 1978. Ptnr. Robinson, Arnzen, Parry & Wentz, P.S.C., Covington, Ky., 1971—; mem. in charge, Greater Cincinnati & No. Ky., exec. comm. Greenebaum Doll & McDonald, Covington, Ky. Found. bd. mem. Appellate Judges Edn. Inst., 2003; adj. prof. No. Ky. U., 1977—; lectr. numerous seminars. Bd. of trustees Redwood Sch. and Rehabilitation Ctr., 1971-81, 83—, sec., 1972-73, 1st v.p., 1973-75, pres., 1975-78, bd. of overseers, 1981-83; bd. of trustees, chmn. Dorothy Wood Found., 1980—, bd. mem. emeritus 2003-; bd. dirs. Cin. chpt. ARC, 1979-85; sust. atty. mem. Product Liability Adv. Council 1997-; Coll. Law Univ. Ky. Lafferty Soc. 1981-, mem. visiting comm. 1988- (chmn. 1995 & 1998), commencement speaker 1988, Hall of Fame 2004; bd. mem. Boy Scouts Am. Powder Horn dist. 1994-; bd. mem. Cincinnati Inst. Fine Arts 1999-2004; bd. dir. Cincinnati/No. Ky. Internat. Airport 1998-, vice chmn. 2004-; bd. trustees Cincinnati Symphony 1998-2004; found. bd. mem. Cincy-Tech USA, 2002-; found. bd. mem. Forward Quest 1997-; policy bd. mem. Partnership for Greater Cincinnati 1999-, chmn. 1999-2003; bd. mem. Greater Cincinnati C. of C. 1994-, exec. comm. 1999-2003; bd. mem. Greater Cincinnati Scholrship Assn. 1994-; bd. mem. Kentuckians for Better Transp. 1996-2004; bd. mem. Ky. C. of C. 1987-93, chmn. 1992-92, Dunlevy frontiersman Comm. Svc. award 1991; mem. Legatus Cincinnati chptr. 1996-2004; bd. trustees Mt. St. Joseph Coll. 1997-; bd. mem. Nat. Conf. Community & Justice 1986-97, treas. 1990-97, co-chmn. 1995-97, emeritus bd. 1997-, Disting. Svc. Citation 2004; adv. trustee Nat. Underground Railroad Freedom Ctr. 2001-; found. bd. mem. & sec./treas. Tri-County Econ. Dev. Corp. 1987-; co-found. & charter bd. mem. Tri-County Econ. Devel. Found. 1996-, charter sec./treas. 1996-2000, treas. 2000-; life mem. Univ. Ky. Alum. Assn., fellow 1981-. Recipient Covington award, Friends of Covington, 1998, Judge Learned Hand Human Rels. award, Am. Jewish Comm., 1998, Governor's Econ. Devel. Leadership award, Ky., 1997, Knight of Malta, 1992. Fellow Am. Acad. Appellate Lawyers 1998, Internat. Soc. Barristers 1988; Mem. ABA (bd. gov. 2000-, exec. comm. 2002-03, treas.-elect 2004-2005, treas. 2005-, chmn. fin. comm. 2002-03), Ohio Bar Assn., Fed. Bar Assn. (mem. steering comm. 2002-), Ky. Bar Assn. (Outstanding Lawyer award, 1989), Am. Bar Found. (life fellow, fellows chmn Ky. 2000-2004), Am. Law Inst., Sixth Cir. Jud. Conf. (life mem.), Ky. Bar Found. (pres. 1988-89, charter life fellow 1986-), No. Ky. Bar Assn., Louisville bar Assn., Cincinnati Bar Assn. (Themis award 2003), Kenton County Bar Assn. (mem. exec. com. 1973-75, chmn. legal-med. com. 1978-83, Ann. Merit award 1973), Ky. Def. Counsel Assn., Internat. Assn. Ins. Counsel, Internat. Assn. Def. Counsel, Salmon P. Chase Am. Inn Ct. (co-founder & pres. 1993-94, master 1993-),Acad. Trial Lawyers Am., So. Conf. Bar Pres., Nat. Conf. Bar Pres.s', U. Ky. Alumni Assn. (bd. dirs. 1981—), No. Ky. C. of C. (vice chmn. 1985-86, bd. dirs. 1980—, Profl. of Yr. 1980), Thomas More Coll. Alumni Assn. (bd. dirs. 1972—, pres. 1974-75, chmn. alumni fund drive 1974-75, Disting. Alum. award 1982), Phi Alpha Theta, Alpha Delta Gamma, Phi Delta Phi. Office: Greenebaum Doll & McDonald PO Box 122673 Covington KY 41012-2673 *

ROBINSON, ZELIG, lawyer; b. Balt., July 7, 1934; s. Morton Matthew and Mary (Ackerman) R.; m. Karen Ann Bergstrom (div. Oct. 1987); children: John, Christopher, Kristin; m. Linda Portner Strangmann, Dec. 23, 1987. BA, Johns Hopkins U., 1954; LLB, Harvard U., 1957. Bar: Md. 1958. Legis. analyst Md. Ho. of Dels., Annapolis, 1958; tech. asst. IRS, Washington, 1958-60; pvt. practice Balt., 1960-62; assoc. gen. counsel commerce com. U.S. Ho. of Reps., Washington, 1962-64; assoc. Weinberg & Green, Balt., 1964-66; spl. legal cons. commerce com. U.S. Ho. of Reps., Washington, 1966-68; pvt. practice Balt., 1966—70; mem. Gordon, Feinblatt, Rothman, Hoffberger & Hollander, LLC, 1972—. Mem. Gov.'s Commn. to revise Md. Code, Annapolis, 1968-90, Md. Pub. Broadcasting Commn., 1984—91, chmn. 91—95, Balt. City Minimum Wage Commn., 1974-82. Contbr. articles to profl. jour. Bd. dirs., v.p., sec. Gov.'s Mansion Found., Annapolis, Md.; v.p. bd. dirs. Md. Cmty. and Citizens Fund, Chestertown, Md.; sec. bd. dirs. William Donald Schaefer Civic Fund, 1980-88; bd. dirs. Md. Arts Pl., 1988-94; bd. trustees Md. Art Pl., 2002-03, bd. dirs., v.p.; bd. dirs. Balt. Coalition of Homeowners, 1989—; v.p., bd. dirs. Everyman Theatre, 2002-03, pres., 2004—; mem. Found. for Md. Pub. Broadcasting; sec., trustee Balt. City Hist. Soc.; bd. dirs., pres. Celebration 2000, Inc., 1998—2001; founder, bd. dirs. Balt. Efficiency and Econ. Found., 1999—; chmn. Balt. City Coun. Transition Commn., 2005. With US Army, 1958. Mem. ABA, Md. State Bar Assn. (laws com., internat. law com.), Md. Lawyers for Arts (bd. dirs. 2005—). Democrat. Office: Gordon Feinblatt Rothman Hoffberger & Hollander LLC 233 E Redwood St Baltimore MD 21202-3332 Home Phone: 410-366-7441. Business E-Mail: zrobinson@gfrlaw.com.

ROBINSON PEETE, HOLLY, actress, writer; b. Phila., Sept. 18, 1964; d. Matthew T. and Dolores Robinson; m. Rodney Peete, June 10, 1995; children: Rodney Jackson, Ryan Elizabeth, Robinson James, Roman. BA in French and Psychology, Sarah Lawrence Coll., 1986. Cofounder (with Rodney Peete) HollyRod Found., 1997—. Actress (TV films) Dummy, 1979, Howard the Duck, 1986, Killers in the House, 1998, After All, 1999, Earthquake, 2004, (TV miniseries) The Jacksons: Am American Dream, 1992, (TV series) 21 Jump Street, 1991, Hangin' With Mr. Cooper, 1996, For Your Love, 1998, Like Family, 2003, Love, Inc., 2005, appeared on Sesame Street, 1969, ABC TGIF, 1990, Booker PI, 1990, Gabriel's Fire, 1991, Pacific Blue, 1997, Touch By An Angel, 1997, Strong Medicine, 2001, One on One, 2001—02, Pepsi Smash Superbowl Bash, 2006; author: Get Your Own Damn Beer, I'm Watching the Game!: A Woman's Guide to Loving Pro Football, 2005 (Quills award sport The Quills Literacy Found., 2006). Recipient Women of Conscience award, 1999, Am. Mentor award, Buddy award, Nat. Orgn. Women Legal Def. and Edn. Fund, Cmty. Svc. award, So. Calif. Broadcasters Assn., Gerald R. Ford People Helping People award, 2004, Healthy Babies, Healthy Futures award, March of Dimes, 2004, Woman of Distinction award, U. So. Calif., 2004, Anheuser Busch John E. Jacob Cmty. Svc. award, Disting. Achievement award, Huntington Disease Soc., Mentor award, Girls, Inc., 2004. Avocations: hiking, travel, pilates, football. Mailing: c/o HollyRod Foundation Ste LL15 9250 Wilshire Blvd Beverly Hills CA 90212

ROBISON, BRIAN E., lawyer; b. Aurora, Colo., Mar. 13, 1970; BA with highest distinction, U. Kans., 1991; JD with honors, U. Tex. Sch. Law, 1995. Bar: Tex. 1995. Law clk. to Hon. John Cornyn Supreme Ct. Tex., 1995—96; asst. dist. atty. Dallas County, Tex., 1999—2000; ptnr. Vinson & Elkins, LLP, Dallas. Mem. Pvt. Antitrust Litig. Com. Named a Tex. Rising Star, Tex. Monthly, 2004, 2005, 2006; named one of Best Lawyers in Dallas Under Age of 40, D Mag., 2002, 2004. Mem.: Dallas Bar Assn., ABA. Office: Vinson & Elkins LLP Trammell Crow Ctr 2001 Ross Ave Ste 3700 Dallas TX 75201-2975 Office Phone: 214-220-7770. Office Fax: 214-999-7770. E-mail: brobison@velaw.com. *

ROBISON, BRUCE H., marine biologist; BS in Biol. Scis., Purdue U., 1965; MA in Marine Sci., Coll. William & Mary, Va. Inst. Marine Sci., 1968; PhD in Biol. Oceanography, Stanford U., Hopkins Marine Sta., 1973. Cert. sci. rsch. pilot for ADS submersibles 1982, 2000. Postdoctoral fellow Woods Hole Oceanog. Instn., Mass., 1973, postdoctoral investigator, 1974; asst. rsch. oceanographer U. Calif. Santa Barbara Marine Sci. Inst., 1974—82, assoc. rsch. oceanographer, 1982—88; sr. scientist Monterey Bay Aquarium Rsch. Inst., 1987—. Chair sci. dept. Monterey Bay Aquarium Rsch. Inst., 1991—96; Morris scholar in residence U. Md. Horn Point, 1996. Contbr. articles to profl. jours.; mem. editl. bd.: Marine Tech. Soc. Jour., 1997—2004. Recipient Sci./Rsch. award, Monterey Bay Nat. Marine Sanctuary, 1997, Lockheed-Martin award, Ocean Sci. and Engring., Marine Tech. Soc., 2002. Fellow: Calif. Acad. Scis., AAAS. Office: Monterey Bay Aquarium Rsch Inst 7700 Sandholdt Rd Moss Landing CA 95039 E-mail: robr@mbari.org.

ROBISON, CAROLYN LOVE, retired librarian; b. Orlinda, Tenn., Aug. 9, 1940; d. Fount Love and Martha Desha (Jones) R. BA, Denison U., 1962; MLS, Emory U., 1965; PhD, Ga. State U., 1982. Tchr. Dag Hammarshjold Jr. H.S., Wallingford, Conn., 1962-64; asst. libr., lectr. Architecture Libr., Ga. Inst. Tech., Atlanta, 1965-67; head circulation Ga. State U., Atlanta, 1967-71, asst. prof., then assoc. prof., asst. libr., 1971-75, prof., assoc. libr., 1975-98, prof. emeritus, 1998. Active Friends of Atlanta-Fulton County Pub. Libr., 1981—98. Recipient Woman of Achievement award YWCA, 1989. Mem. ALA, Ga. Libr. Assn., Delta Kappa Gamma, Phi Kappa Phi, Kappa Delta Pi. Presbyterian. Home: 1057 Capital Club Cir NE Atlanta GA 30319-2662 Personal E-mail: clrobison@mindspring.com.

ROBISON, EMILY BURNS, musician; b. Pittsfield, Mass., Aug. 16, 1972; d. Paul and Barbara Burns; m. Charlie Robison, May 1, 1999; children: Charles Augustus, Julianna Tex, Henry Benjamin. Performer Blue Night Express, 1984—89; banjo player, guitarist, vocalist Dixie Chicks, 1989—. Musician: (albums) Thank Heavens for Dale Evans, 1990, LIttle Ol' Cowgirl, 1992, Shouldn't a Told You That, 1993, Wide Open Spaces, 1998 (Maximum Vision Clip of Yr., Billboard, 1998, Best New Country Artist Clip of Yr., Billboard, 1998, Best Country Album, Grammy Awards, 1998, Album of Yr., Acad. Country Music, 1998, Best Selling Album, Can. Country Music Awards, 1999, Song of Yr., WB Radio Music Award, 1999, Album of Yr., ACM, 1999), Fly, 1999 (Best Country Album, Grammy Awards, 1999, Best Selling Album, Can. Country Musc Awards, 2000, Internat. Album, British Country Music Award, 2000, Country Album of Yr., Billboard Awards, 2000, Album of Yr., ACM, 2000, Album of Yr., CMA, 2000), Home, 2002 (Favorite Country Album, Am. Music Awards, 2002, Best Recording Package, Grammy Awards, 2002, Best Country Album, Grammy Awards, 2002), Top of the World Tour: Live, 2003 (Best Country Group Vocal Performance, Grammy Awards, 2005), Taking the Long Way, 2006 (Album of Yr. and Best Country Album, Grammy Awards, 2007), (songs) Not Ready to Make Nice, 2006 (Record of Yr., Song of Yr., Best Performance by a Duo or Group with Vocal, Grammy Awards, 2007); performer: (documentary) Dixie Chicks: Shut Up and Sing, 2006. Named Most Significant New Country Act, Country Monitor, 1998, Top New Country Artist, Billboard, 1998, Top Vocal Group, Acad. Country Music, 1998, Country Artist of Yr., Rolling Stone, 1999, Top Country Artist, Billboard, 1999, Internat. Rising Star, British Country Music Awards, 1999, Artist of Yr. (Country), WB Radio Music Award, 1999, Favorite New Artist (Country), AMA, 1999, Vocal Group of Yr., CMA, 1999, Country Artist of Yr., Billboard, 1999, 2000, Entertainer of Yr., CMA, 2000, ACM, 2000, Vocal Group of Yr., 2001, Entertainer of Yr., 2001, Favorite Musical

Group or Band, People's Choice Award, 2002, Vocal Group of Yr., Country Music Assn., 2002, others; named one of 100 Most Influential People, Time Mag., 2006; recipient Horizon award, CMA, 1998. *

ROBISON, PAULA JUDITH, flutist; b. Nashville, June 8, 1941; d. David Victor and Naomi Florence R.; m. Scott Nickrenz; Dec. 29, 1971; 1 child, Elizabeth Hadley Amadea Nickrenz. Student, U. So. Calif., 1958-60; BS, Juilliard Sch. Music, 1963. Founding artist, player Chamber Music Soc., NYC, 1970-90, NY ChôroBand, 1994; co-dir. chamber music Spoleto Festival, Charleston, SC, 1978-88; Filene artist-in-residence Skidmore Coll., Saratoga Springs, NY, 1988-89; mem. faculty New Eng. Conservatory Music, 1972—76, 1991—, Donna Heiken flute chair 1st occupant, 2005—; co-dir. Gardner Chamber Orch., Boston, 1995—; artist-in-residence Gardner Mus., 2005. Mem. faculty Juilliard Sch., NYC, 1978—82; annual concert series Met. Mus. Art, NYC, 1990—; With Art series PS 1 Art Gallery, NY, 2000, Mass. Mus. Contemporary Art, 2001; dir. Vivaldi in the Courtyard, Gardner Mus., Boston, 2002—; founder Pergola Recs., 2006; collaboration with Sol Le Witt, Variations on a Theme, Gardner Mus., 2005; mem. Robison Lubambo Baptista Trio, 2000—. Soloist with various major orchs., including N.Y. Philharm., London Symphony Orch.; player, presenter Concerti di Mezzogiorno, Spoleto (Italy) Festival, 1970-2003; commd. flute concertos by Leon Kirchner, Toru Takemitsu, Oliver Knussen, Robert Beaser, Kenneth Frazelle; premiered works by Pierre Boulez, Elliott Carter, William Schuman, Thea Musgrave, Carla Bley, John Tavener, Michael Tilson Thomas; premiered Rio Days Rio Nights, Music Theatre Group prodn. in N.Y.C., 1998; participant Marlboro Music Festival, 1999-05; founder Pergola Recs., 2005; author: The Paula Robison Flute Warmups Book, 1989, The Andersen Collection, 1994, Paula Robison Masterclass: Paul Hindemith, 1995, The Sidney Lanier Collection, 1997, Frank Martin: Ballade, 2002, To a Wild Rose, 2003, MasterClass Series, Diller-Quaile Sch. of Music, 2004-; recs. on CBS Masterworks, Music Masters, Vanguard Classics, New World Records, Omega, Arabesque, Sony Classical, King Recs., Mode Recs., Artemis Recs.; two person show Gardner Mus., Boston, 2005; featured in PBS documentary and book: Juilliard; collaborator project with visual artist Jim Schantz and Pucker Gallery of Boston: Places of the Spirit, 2003, Places of the Spirit II-The Holy Land, 2007. Named Musician of Month, Musical Am., 1979, Ho. Musician for Isamu Noguchi Garden Mus., NYC, 1988; recipient Disting. Svc. award, Music Tchrs. Nat. Assn., 1989, Laurence Lesser Presdl. award, 1999, Lifetime Achievement award, Usdan Ctr. for Creative and Perfomring Arts, 2000, Hon. Citizen for Life award, City of Charleston, S.C., 2002, Lifetime Achievement award, Nat. Flute Assn., 2004, 1st prize, Geneva Internat. Competition, 1966, Adelaide Ristori prize, 1987; grantee, Nat. Endowment for Arts, 1978, 1986, Fromm Found., 1980; Martha Baird Rockefeller grantee, 1966, Housewright Eminent scholar, Fla. State U., 1990—91. Mem. Sigma Alpha Iota (hon.).

ROBISON, SHANE V., computer company executive; BS in Computer Sci., MS in Computer Sci., U. Utah. With Apple Computer Co., 1988, v.p., gen. mgr., 1994—95; exec. v.p. rsch. & develop., pres. design productivity grp. Cadence Design Systems; exec. v.p. AT&T, 1995—97, pres. design productivity grp., 1997—99, pres. internet tech. and devel., 1999—2000; sr. v.p., chief tech. officer strategy and tech. Compaq Computer Corp., 2000—02; exec. v.p., chief strategy and tech. officer Hewlett-Packard Co., Palo Alto, Calif., 2002—. Cons. database systems architecture U. Utah. Office: Hewlett-Packard Co 3000 Hanover St Palo Alto CA 94304 *

ROBISON, VICTOR JAMES, JR., retired military officer; b. Youngstown, Ohio, Apr. 29, 1920; s. Victor James Robison and Babe Albert. BS, Case We. Res. U., 1942, MA, 1948; Qualified Comms. Officer, U.S. Naval Acad. Grad. Sch., 1943; student, Sorbonne U., Paris, 1949—50, Columbia U., 1950—51. Commd. ensign USN, 1943, advanced through grades to comdr., comm. officer USS Taylor Pacific PTO, 1943—45, tng. officer U.S. Naval Res. Tng. Ctr. Balt., 1952—55, asst. ops. officer USS Worcester Mediterranean and Pacific, 1955—56; U.S. Naval attaché and U.S. Naval attaché for air U.S. Embassy, Warsaw, 1957—58, Brussels, 1962—65; officer in charge Navy Liaison Group and Chief Plant Engring and Maintenance Divsn. Joint Commns. Ctr., Ft. Ritchie, Md., 1958—61; asst. curator for Navy Dept., Office Chief of Naval Ops. USN, Washington, 1966—69, ret., 1969; tchr. English Corcoran Coll. Art, Washington, 1969—70; pvt. practice appraiser Navy artifacts and memorabilia Washington and Annapolis, Md., 1970—84. Decorated Order of Leopold II, 1966, Navy Unit Commendation, 13 Battle Stars, USN, Asiatic Pacific Campaign medal, others. Mem. VFW, Am. Legion, Fleet Res. Assn., Smithsonian Instn., Beta Theta Pi. Avocations: stamp collecting/philately, jogging, poetry, learning. Home: 423 7th St SE Washington DC 20003-2756

ROBISON, WILLIAM ROBERT, lawyer; b. Memphis, May 5, 1947; s. Andrew Cliffe and Elfrieda Robison. AB, Boston U., 1970; JD, Northeastern U., 1974. Bar: Mass. 1974, D.C. 1975, U.S. Dist. Ct. Mass. 1975, U.S. Ct. Appeals (1st cir.) 1975, U.S. Dist. Ct. Conn. 1977, U.S. Supreme Ct. 1977, Calif. 1978, U.S. Dist. Ct. (cen. dist.) Calif. 1979, U.S. Ct. Appeals (9th cir.) 1979. Assoc. Meyers, Goldstein, et al, Boston, 1975-76, Cooley, Shrair, et al, Springfield, Mass., 1976-78, Hertzberg, et al, Los Angeles, 1978-79, Marcus & Lewi, Santa Monica, Calif., 1980-81; pvt. practice, Santa Monica, 1981—. Lectr. Northeastern U., Boston, 1975-76; judge pro-tem., Mcpl. Ct., Los Angeles, 1984—, Los Angeles Superior Ct., 1987—. Co-author: Commercial Transactions, 1976. Bd. dirs. Boston Legal Asst. Project, 1972-75, Action for Boston Community Devel., Inc., 1971-75. Mem. ABA, Los Angeles County Bar Assn., Santa Monica Bar Assn. (Cert. of Appreciation 1987). Democrat. Unitarian Universalist. Home and Office: 2546 Amherst Ave Los Angeles CA 90064-2712 Office Phone: 310-473-2816. E-mail: billrobison1@netzero.net.

ROBITAILLE, LUC, sports team executive, retired professional hockey player; b. Montreal, Que., Can., Feb. 17, 1966; Left wing Hull Olympiques Major Jr. Hockey League, Que., 1983—84, LA Kings, 1984—94, 1997—2001, 2003—06, Pitts. Penguins, 1994—95, NY Rangers, 1995—97, Detroit Red Wings, 2001—03; owner, pres. Omaha Lancers, US Hockey League, 2006; asst. to gov. and alt. gov. LA Kings, 2006—07, pres. bus. ops., 2007—. Guest appearance (films) D2: The Mighty Ducks, 1994, Sudden Death, 1995, H-E Double Hockey Sticks, 1999. Named NHL Rookie of Yr., 1986—87; named to NHL All-Star Team, 1987, 1988, 1990—91, 1992—93, Quebec Major Junior Hockey League Hall of Fame, 2007; recipient Guy LaFlleur Trophy, 1985—86, Can. Hockey Player of Yr. award, 1985—86, Calder Meml. Trophy. Achievements include scoring the winning goal for the national team of Canada at the 1994 World Hockey Championship; being a member of Stanley Cup Champion Detroit Red Wings, 2002; having his number, 20, retired by LA Kings, 2007. Office: LA Kings Suite 3100 1111 S Figueroa St Los Angeles CA 90015 also: Omaha Lancers Mid-Am Ctr One Arena Way Council Bluffs IA 51501 *

ROBLE, CAROLE MARCIA, accountant; b. Bklyn., Aug. 22, 1938; d. Carl and Edith (Brown) Dusowitz; m. Richard F. Roble, Nov. 30, 1969. MBA with distinction, N.Y. Inst. Tech., 1984. CPA, Calif., N.Y. Compt. various orgns. various orgns., 1956-66; staff acct. ZTBG CPA'S, LA, 1966-67; sr. acct. J.H. Cohn & Co., Newark, 1967-71; prin. Carole M. Roble, CPA, South Hempstead, NY, 1971-90; ptnr. Roble & Libman, CPAs, Baldwin, NY, 1990-93; prin. Carole M. Roble, CPA, Baldwin, NY, 1993—. Spkr., moderator Found. for Acctg. Edn., N.Y., 1971-99; lectr. acctg. various schs. including New Sch., Queens Coll., Empire State Coll., Touro Coll., N.Y. Inst. Tech., N.Y.C., Parsons Sch., 1971-90. Guest various N.Y. radio and TV stas., 2 noted various newspapers. Treas. Builders Devel. Corp. of L.I., Westbury, N.Y., 1985; dir. Women Econ. Devels. of L.I., 1985-87. Recipient Sisterhood citation Nat. Orgn. Women, 1984, 85, cert. of Appreciation Women Life Underwriters, 1988, Women in Sales, 1982, 84; named top Tax Practitioner Money Mag., 1987, one of Top 100 Most Influential People, Acctg. Today, 1999. Mem. AICPA (mem. small firm advocacy com. 1996—), Am. Acct. Assn. (auditing sect.), Am. Soc. Women Accts. (pres. N.Y. chpt. 1980-81), Am. Woman's Soc. CPAs, Nat. Conf. CPA Practitioners (trustee L.I. chpt. 1981-82, sec. 1982-83, treas. 1983-84, v.p. 1984-85, 1st v.p. 1985-86, pres. 1986-87, nat. nominating com. 1983-84, 88-89, nat. continuing profl. edn. chmn. 1988-90, nat. treas. 1991-94, nat. v.p. 1994-96, exec. v.p. 1996-98, first woman nat. pres. 1998-99), Calif. Soc. CPAs, N.Y. State Soc. CPAs (bd. dirs. Nassau chpt. 1981-86, 91-93, bd. dirs. profl. devel., 1982-86, sec., mem. fin. acctg. standards com. 1990-95), Kiwanis (program chmn. County Seat chpt. 1989-90, sec. 1990-91, pres. 1991-92), Baldwin C. of C. (treas. 1990-93). Avocations: golf, gourmet cuisine, water-skiing, music.

ROBLE, RAYMOND GERALD, science administrator; b. Mar. 14, 1935; BS in Engring. Physics, U. Mich., 1957, BS in Engring. Math., 1957, MSME, 1961, PhD in Aeronomy, 1969. Engr. Bendix Rsch. Labs., Southfield, Mich., 1961-64; rsch. sci. Space Physics Rsch. Lab., U. Mich., 1964-69; postdoctoral fellow advanced study program Nat. Ctr. Atmospheric Rsch., 1969-70, scientist lab. for atmospheric scis., 1970-73, scientist atmospheric quality and modification div., 1973-77, project leader thermospheric dynamics and aeronomy project atmosphericchem. and aeronomy div., 1977-81, sr. scientist atmospheric chem. and aeronomy div., 1978-84, sr. scientist high altitude obs., 1984—, head, terrestrial impact of solar output sect. high altitude obs., 1986—2001, dep. dir. high altitude obs., 1993-95, acting dir. high altitude obs., 1995—. Commn. URSI III Working Group 8 Incoherent Scatter, 1975-77; guest investigator OSO-8 Satellite Team Occultation Studes, 1975-79, NASA Atmospheric Explorer Satelite Team, 1975-80; panel mem. USRA Sci. Definition for Atmosphere, Magnetosphere and Plasmas in Space Payload, 1976-78, Upper Atmosphere Geophysics, Geophysics Study com., Geophysical Rsch. bd., NAS, 1976-77, USRA Computer Simulation in Space Physics, 1977-79, NASA Sci. Definition Panel UARS Satellite Program, 1977-78, Sun, Weather and Climate Geophysics Study com., Geophysical Rsch. bd., NAS, 1977-82, Survey on Solar-Terrestrial Rsch. in the 1980's, com. on Solar-Terrstrial Rsch. Geophysical Rsch. bd., NAS program, 1979-81, Mid. Atmosphere Program Panel, NAS, 1981-86; theoretician NASA Dynamics Explorer Satellite Team, 1977—; mem. AGU com. for Pub., 1977-84, Atmospheric and Space Physics Mgmt. Ops. Working Group, NASA Solar-Terrestrial Physics Program, 1978-81, Space Power Sys. Overviewcom. Inst. Telecomms., 1978-82; lecturer Dept. Astrophysical, Planetary and Atmospheric Scis. U. Colo., 1978—; com. Solar and Space Physics, Space Sci. bd. NAS, 1980-83, Geophysics Study com. Geophysical Rsch. bd. NAS, 1980-84, IUGG on Atmospheric Electricity, 1981—, AGU for Pub. Affairs, 1982-84, IUGG com. Solar-Terrestrial film Planet earth, 1984-86; sec. Aeronomy Div. Solar-Planetary Relationships Sect. AGU, 1982-84; mem. Earth Scis. Task Group Study Major Dirs. for Space Scis.: 1995-, Space Sci. bd., 1984-88; chmn. Am. Geophysical Union com. on Atmospheric and Space Electricity, 1984-88; co-investigator, prin. investigator, NASA; mem. Arecibo Observatory vis. com. Cornell U., 1997-2001; mem. rev. bd. Geophys. Inst. U. Alaska, 1984-. Contbr. over 250 articles to profl. jours. With USN, 1957-60. Recipient CEDAR Prize Lecture, 1994; grantee NASA, USAF. Fellow Am. Geophys. Union (chmn. space physics and aeronomy fellows com. 1996-98); mem. NAS (Arctowski medal, 1996), Am. Inst. Aeronautics and Astronautics. Office: Nat Ctr Atmospheric Rsch High Altitude Obs PO Box 3000 Boulder CO 80307-3000 Business E-Mail: roble@ncar.ucar.edu.

ROBLES, CARLOS, hematologist, oncologist; b. Mexico City, Dec. 22, 1968; s. Carlos and Margarita Robles; m. A. Martha Robles, Oct. 8, 1968; children: Carlos, Juan-Pablo, Angelica. MD, U. Anahuac, Mexico City, 1993; degree in Internal Medicine, U. Miami, Fla., 1996, degree in Hematology/Oncology, 2000. Diplomate Am. Bd. Internal Medicine, 1996, bd. cert. med. oncology Am. Bd. Internal Medicine, 2000, recert. internal medicine Am. Bd. Internal Medicine, 2006; cert. instrument rated pvt. pilot. Staff med. oncologist VA Med. Ctr., Miami, 2001—. Named Best Student in Mex., Diario de Mex., 1991, Best Tchg. Physician, U. Miami, 2001—02; recipient Eric Reiss award for best tchg. resident in medicine, U. Miami/Jackson Meml. Hosp., 1996; fellow, Amgen, 1999. Office: VA Medical Ctr 1201 NW 16th St Miami FL 33125 Office Phone: 305-575-3244.

ROBLES, DARLINE P., school system administrator; AA in History, East L.A. Coll., 1968; B in History, Calif. State U., LA, 1972; MEd, Claremont Grad. Sch., 1976; D in Edn. Policy and Adminstrn., U. So. Calif. Cert. tchr., adminstr. Tchr. Montebello Intermediate Sch., Calif., 1973—79; dir. bilingual program Montebellow Unified Sch. Dist., Calif., 1979—81; prin. Washington Elem., Montebello, Calif., 1981—85, Montebello Intermediate, Montebello, Calif., 1985—88; asst. supt. Montebello Unified Sch. Dist., Montebello, Calif., 1988—91, acting supt., 1991—92, supt., 1992—95, Salt Lake City Sch. Dist., 1995—2002; county supt. schs. L.A. County Office of Edn., 2002—. Office: LA County Office of Edn Rm EC 109 9300 Imperial Hwy Rm EC109 Downey CA 90242-2890 Office Phone: 562-922-6127. Business E-Mail: Robles_Darline@lacoe.edu. *

ROBLES, JOSUE, JR., insurance company executive; b. Rio Piedras, PR, Jan. 24, 1946; B in Acctg., Kent State U., Ohio, 1972; MBA, Ind. State U., Terre Haute. CFO, sr. v.p., treas. USAA (United Svcs. Automobile Assn.), San Antonio, 1994, exec. v.p., chief adminstrv. officer, CFO, corp. treas. Mem. Def. Base Closure and Realignment Commn., 1995. Joined US Army, 1966, ret., maj. gen. US Army, 1994. Office: USAA 9800 Fredericksburg Rd San Antonio TX 78288-0002 Office Phone: 210-498-2211. *

ROBLES, MARICELA, architect; b. 1975; Sr. designer D.R. Horton Homes. Mem. Tucson Xicano Mexicano Com. for Self-determination, Access Tucson Cmty. TV, National Chicano Moratorium Com.; co-founder Radio Chicana. Named one of 40 Under 40, Tucson Bus. Edge, 2006. Mem.: Am. Diabetes Assn., La Raza Unida Club (co-founder). Avocations: kickboxing, bikram yoga, mariachi music. Office: D R Horton Homes 5255 E Williams Circle Tucson AZ 85711

ROBLES, ROSALIE MIRANDA, elementary school educator; b. LA, Oct. 30, 1942; d. Richard and Carmen (Garcia) Miranda; m. Ralph Rex Robles, July 12, 1986; children: Gregory, Eric, Karen Cassandra. BA, Calif. State Coll., LA, 1964; postgrad., Northridge State Coll. Playground supr. L.A. City Schs., 1961-64; elem. tchr. Montebello Unified Schs., Calif., 1964—; sch. site rep., faculty club chair, PTA La Merced Elem., 2006—. Rep. Montebello Credit Union, 1973-75, Bilingual Com., 1983-88; mem. Sch. Site Coun., 1989-92, chmn. 1980-83; union rep. Montebello Unified Schs. Chmn. Monterey Park Christmas Food Baskets, 1973-91; boys coord. Am. Youth Soccer, 1993-94, girls coord.; chmn. Boy Scouts Am., 1980-85; exec. bd. PTA, 1978, 80, 85, 87, 92—, pres. 1990-92; sec. St. Paul Parent Group, 1992-93, Palimentarian, 1993—; rep. Cost Containment Com., 1994-96; Eucharistic minister Roman Cath. Ch.; team mother Boys and Girls Club, 2005-06. Recipient Hon. Svc. award PTA, 1979, Hon. Svc. Continuing award, 1982, Golden Oak award, 1995. Mem. AAUW (pres. 2001-2003, v.p. program 2003—, cultural chair), Montebello Tchrs. Assn. (faculyt club chair), Delta Kappa Gamma (sec., recording sec., pres., 2004—). Roman Catholic.

ROBO, JAMES L., utilities executive; BA summa cum laude, Harvard Coll.; MBA, Harvard Bus. Sch. V.p. Strategic Planning Assocs.; various positions including gen. mgr. distbn. ops. GE Lighting, gen. mgr. Six Sigma GE Lighting, pres. and CEO GE Mex. GE, pres., CEO Capital TIP/Modular Space; pres. FPL Energy, 2002—06; v.p. corp. devel. and strategy FPL Group Inc., 2002—06, pres., COO, 2006—. Bd. dirs. J.B. Hunt Transport Svcs., Inc., Lowell, Ark., 2003—. Mem.: Phi Beta Kappa. Office: FPL Group Inc 700 Universe Blvd Juno Beach FL 33408-0420 *

ROBOCK, ALAN, meteorology professor; b. Boston, Sept. 7, 1949; s. Stefan Hyman and Shirley Robock; m. Sherri Robock, May 12, 1990; children: Brian, Daniel. BA, U. Wis., Madison, 1970; SM, MIT, Cambridge, Mass., 1974, PhD, 1977. Vol. Peace Corps, The Philippines, 1970-72; rsch. scientist Lawrence Livermore Lab., Calif., 1973; asst. prof. dept. meteorology U. Md., College Park, 1977-82, assoc. prof., 1982-96, prof., 1996-97; prof. dept. environ. scis. Rutgers U., New Brunswick, NJ, 1998—2003, prof. II, 2003—. Dir. Ctr. Environ. Prediction Rutgers U., 2001-05; snow forecaster Montgomery County Pub. Schs., Md., 1980-81; state climatologist State of Md., 1991-97; vis. rsch. scientist Princeton U., NOAA/Geophys. Fluid Dynamics Lab., 1994-95 Editor: Jour. Climate and Applied Meteorology, 1985—87, Jour. Geophys. Rsch-Atmospheres, 2000—05; assoc. editor Jour. Geophys. Rsch-Atmospheres, 1998—2000, Revs. Geophysics, 1994—2000, 2006—; contbr. articles to profl. jours., chapters to books. Fellow Am. Meteorol. Soc.; mem. AAAS (Congressional sci. fellow 1986-87), Am. Geophys. Union (pres.-elect, atmospheric sci. sect., 2006-). Avocations: tennis, Bob Dylan music, travel, politics. Office: Rutgers U Dept Environ Scis 14 College Farm Rd New Brunswick NJ 08901-8551 E-mail: robock@envsci.rutgers.edu.

ROBOCK, STEFAN HYMAN, retired economics professor; b. Redgranite, Wis., July 31, 1915; s. Samuel and Elizabeth (Kushner) R.; m. Shirley Bernstein, June 17, 1946 (div. Mar. 1980); children: Alan David, Jerry, Lisa (Mrs. Stephen Shaffer); m. Hanne Miree, June 13, 1998. BA, U. Wis., 1938; MA (Adminstrn. fellow), Harvard U., 1941, PhD, 1948; Prof. Honoris Causa, U. Recife, Brazil, 1956; M. Honoris Causa, E.S.T.E., San Sebastian, Spain, 1974. Economist Nat. Resources Planning Bd., Washington, 1940-41; antitrust div. U.S. Dept. Justice, Washington, 1941-42, Boston, 1948-49; chief economist TVA, Knoxville, 1949-54; devel. adviser UN, Brazil, 1954-56, tech. asst. missions India, 1959, Bolivia, 1963; with Midwest Rsch. Inst., 1956-58, Com. Econ. Devel., 1958-60; prof. internat. bus. Ind. U., Bloomington, 1960-67; with World Bank, Philippines, 1961, Ford Found., Pakistan, 1964; R.D. Calkins prof. internat. bus. Columbia U., NYC, 1967-84, prof. emeritus, 1984—. Internat. economist Dept. Commerce, 1975-76; trustee Inst. Current World Affairs, 1981-86; cons. fgn. countries, 1959—; bd. dirs. Econs. Inst., Boulder, Colo., 1984-89; adv. bd. World Trade Inst., 1974-95; mem. bd. sci. and tech. NAS, 1969-72; vis. prof. Beijing Mgmt. Inst., 1985, U. Internat. Bus. and Econ., Beijing, 1989, Internat. Mgmt. Ctr., Budapest, Hungary, 1992. Author: Brazil's Developing Northeast, 1963, Brazil: A Study in Development Progress, 1975, International Business and Multinational Enterprises, 4th edit., 1989; Editorial bd.: Columbia Jour. World Bus, 1975-85. Served with USNR, 1942-46. Mem. Soc. Internat. Devel. (mem. council 1966-69), Am. Econ. Assn., Acad. Internat. Bus. (v.p. 1983-85), Harvard Club NYC, Phi Kappa Phi, Beta Gamma Sigma, Phi Eta Sigma. Clubs: Columbia Tennis. Home: 560 Riverside Dr Apt 21J New York NY 10027-3237

ROBOL, RICHARD THOMAS, lawyer; b. Norfolk, Va., Feb. 8, 1952; s. Harry James and Lucy Henley (Johnson) R. BA, U. Va., 1974; JD, Harvard U., 1978. Bar: Va. 1979, Ohio 1996, U.S. Dist. Ct. (ea. dist.) Va. 1979, U.S. Ct. Appeals (4th cir.) 1979, U.S. Dist. Ct. (we. dist.) Va. 1981, U.S. Supreme Ct. 1982, D.C. 1991, U.S. Ct. Appeals (4th, 6th and 9th cirs.) 1995. Law clk. to presiding justice U.S. Dist. Ct. (ea. dist.) Va., 1978-79; ptnr. Seawell, Dalton, Hughes & Timms, Norfolk, 1979-87, Hunton and Williams, Norfolk, 1987-92; exec. v.p., gen. counsel Columbus Am. Discovery Group, Inc., 1992—. Adj. prof. U. Dayton Law Sch.; asst. prof. mil. sci. Capital U.; pro bono counsel Nat. Commn. for Prevention Child Abuse, Norfolk, 1983, Tidewater Profl. Assn. on Child Abuse, 1983, Parents United Va., 1981-82, Sexual Abuse Help Line, 1983-86; mem. Boyd-Graves Conf. on Civil Procedure in Va., 1981-87. Contbr. articles to law revs.; contbg. editor: International Law for General Practitioners, 1981. Bd. dirs. Va. Opera Assn. Guild, Norfolk, 1983-87, Tidewater br. NCCJ, 1991-92; deacon Ctrl. Bapt. Ch., Norfolk, 1980-83. Maj. USAR, 1992—. Fulbright scholar, 1974. Mem. Va. State Bar Assn. (bd. dirs. internat. law sect. 1984-87, chmn. 1982-83), Va. Young Lawyers Assn. (cir. rep. 1984-88), Va. Assn. Def. Attys., Maritime Law Assn., Norfolk-Portsmouth Bar assn. (chmn. speakers bur. 1987-88), Assn. Def. Trial Attys. (chmn. Va. 1987), Def. Rsch. Inst., 1982-88. Avocations: camping, rowing, scuba diving. Home: 60 Kenyon Brook Dr Worthington OH 43085-3629 Office: Robol Law Office LPA 433 W Sixth Ave Columbus OH 43201 Office Phone: 614-737-3739. Business E-Mail: rrobol@robollaw.com.

ROBOTTOM, DAVID T., lawyer, energy executive; m. Bonnie Robottom; 2 children. B of Commerce with distinction, MBA; LLB, U. Alta., 1979. Bar: Alta. 1980. Nat. mng. ptnr., CEO Fraser Milner Casgrain, LLP; sr. ptnr. Stikeman Elliot, LLP, Calgary, Alta., Canada, 2004—06; grp. v.p. corp. law Enbridge Energy Partners, 2006—. Bd. trustees Enbridge Comml. Trust; dir. Noverco, Inc., Gaz Métro Inc. Office: Enbridge Energy Ptnrs 3000 5th Ave Pl 425 1st St SW Calgary AB T2P 3L8 Canada *

ROBSON, DONALD, physics professor; b. Leeds, Eng., Mar. 19, 1937; came to U.S., 1963; s. Albert and Rose Hannah (Parbutt) Robson; m. Joy Olivia Burkitt Findlay, Aug. 1960 (div. May 1971); children: Donald Peter, David Ian, Karen Joy; m. Martha Breitenlohner, Aug. 26, 1971 (div. Sept. 1999); m. Kimberly G. Kitchen, Dec. 18, 1999; 1 child, Nadirah Berge. BSc, U. Melbourne, Australia, 1959, MSc, 1961, PhD, 1963. Rsch. assoc. Fla. State U., Tallahassee, 1963-64, asst. prof. physics, 1964-65, assoc. prof., 1965-67, prof., 1967—, chmn. dept. physics, 1985-91, Disting. prof., 1990—2003, emeritus prof., 2003—. Editor: (with J.D. Fox) Isobaric Spin in Nuclear Physics, 1966, Nuclear Analogue States, 1976; assoc. editor Nuclear Physics A., 1972-96; contbr. more than 100 articles to profl. jours. Chmn. bd. trustees Southeastern Univ. Rsch. Assn., 1996-98. Fulbright scholar, 1963-64; A.P. Sloan fellow, 1966-67; Alexander Von Humboldt sr. scientist, 1976-77. Fellow Am. Phys. Soc. (co-recipient Tom W. Bonner prize 1972). Avocations: chess, golf, running. Office: Fla State U Dept Physics Tallahassee FL 32306 Office Phone: 850-644-1767. Business E-Mail: robson@csit.fsu.edu.

ROBSON, GLENN R., engineering and design company executive; BS in Econs., U. Pa.; MBA, Harvard U. Various positions to mng. dir. investment banking divsn. Morgan Stanley, 1990—2002; sr. v.p., CFO Aecom Tech., LA, 2002—. Office: Aecom Tech 555 S Flower St Los Angeles CA 90071 Office Phone: 213-593-8000. Office Fax: 213-593-8730. Business E-Mail: info@aecom.com.

ROBSON, LARRY J., physician; b. Almont, Mich., June 27, 1937; s. Charles William and Lucille Fay Robson; m. Sally Kay Klana, Aug. 21, 1960; children: William Charles, Rebecca Lynn. BA, Albion Coll., Mich., 1959; MD, U. Mich., Ann Arbor, 1963. Staff vascular surgeon Blodgett Meml. Med. Ctr., Grand Rapids, 1971—2002, St. Mary's Hosp., Grand Rapids, 1971—2002; cons. Mary Free Bed Hosp., Grand Rapids, 1971—2002; vascular surgeon Grand Rapids Vein Clinic, 2004—05; dir. vascular ultrasound West Mich. Heart Lab., Grand Rapids, 2002—; med. dir. vascular ultrasound tng. Grand Valley State U., Grand Rapids, 2006—. Bd. trustees Albion Coll., 1980; nat. adv. bd. Cardiovasc. Way Ctr., Ann Arbor, 2002—. Trustee Blodgett Meml. Med. Ctr., Grand Rapids, 1980—95; bd. dirs., sec. com. Salvation Army, Grand Rapids, 2004—, Grand Rapids Symphony, 2005—. Lt. comdr. USN, 1968—70. Recipient Tchr. Yr., Blodgett Meml. Med. Ctr. Fellow: Am. Coll. Surgeons; mem.:

Soc. Vascular Surgery. Republican. Congregationalist. Avocations: fishing, golf, music. Home: 2765 Woodcliff Cir SE Grand Rapids MI 49506 Office: W Mich Heart 2900 Bradford NE Grand Rapids MI 49525 Personal E-mail: ljrobsonmd@aol.com.

ROBUCHON, JOËL, restaurateur; b. Poitiers, France, Apr. 7, 1945; s. Henri and Julienne (Douteau) R.; m. Janine Pallix, Apr. 16, 1966; children: Eric, Sophie. Asst. Grand Hotel de Dinard, 1963, Vert Galant, Paris, 1963-64; chef Hotel Cosmos, Contrexéville, France, 1964-65, Clos de Bernardios, 1965-66, Berkeley, Paris, 1966-69, Hotel Alboro á Thiais, Paris, 1969-70, Hotel Frantel, Rungis, France, 1972-73, Hotel Concorde Lafayette, Paris, 1974-78; dir. Hotel Nikko, 1978-81; restaurateur, propr. Jamin, Paris, 1981—, Joël Robuchon, Paris, 1993-94; mgr. Relais du Parc, Paris, 1992—; chef, owner L'Atelier de Joël Robuchon, NYC. Author: Ma cuisine pour vous, 1986, Simply French, 1991, Le Meilleur et le plus simple de Robuchon, 1992. Recipient 3 stars Guide Michelin, 4 stars Guide Bottin Gourmand, 4 hats Guide Gault et Milau, Trophée Nat. de l'Académie Culinaire de France, 1972, Meilleur Ouvrier de France, 1976, Lauréat du Prix Hachette, 1985, Chef de l'Amée, 1987; named Officier du Mérite Agricole, Chevalier des arts et des Lettres, Chevalier, Ordre Nat. du Mérite, Chevalier de la Courtoisie de France, Chef of Yr., 1987, Chef of the Century, 1989, Best New Restaurant for L'Atelier de Joël Robuchon, James Beard Found., 2007 Avocations: rugby, tennis. Office: Restaurant Joel Rëbuchon 59 Ave Raymond Poincaré 75116 Paris France *

ROBUSTO, DINO E., insurance company executive; With Chubb Corp., 1986—, comml. lines underwriter, field ops. officer Chubb Comml. Ins., mng. dir. Multinational Resource Group, sr. v.p., NY brokerage zone officer, exec. v.p., worldwide claims officer Chubb & Son. Office: Chubb Corp 15 Mountain View Rd Warren NJ 07059 Office Phone: 908-903-2000. Office Fax: 908-903-2027. *

ROBY, BRIAN L., bank executive; b. Kansas City, Mo., Apr. 16, 1960; s. F. Alan Roby and Mimi Jean (Halliburton) King; m. M. Elizabeth Santander, June 6, 1987. BSBA, U. Mo., 1982, MBA, 1983. V.p. Commerce Bank of Kansas City, 1983-90; sr. v.p. First Nat. Bank of Olathe, Kans., 1990—98, exec. v.p., 1998—2001, pres., CEO, 2001—. Mem. U. Mo. Bus. and Pub. Adminstrn. Alumni Assn. (v.p. 1989-92), Overland Park C. of C. (dir. 1993—). Republican. Roman Catholic. Avocations: tennis, bicycling. Office: First Nat Bank Olathe PO Box 1500 Olathe KS 66051-1500

ROBY, PAMELA ANN, sociologist, educator; b. Milw., Nov. 17, 1942; d. Clark Dearborn and Marianna (Gillman) Roby; m. James Peter Mulherin, July 15, 1977 (div. 1987). BA, U. Denver, 1963; MA, Syracuse U., NYC, 1966; PhD, NYU, 1971. Instr. ednl. sociology NYU, NYC, 1966; asst. prof. George Washington U., Washington, 1970—71; asst. prof. sociology and social welfare Brandeis U., Waltham, Mass., 1971—73; assoc. prof. U. Calif., Santa Cruz, 1973—77, prof. sociology and women's studies, 1977—2007, chair cmty. studies bd., 1974-76, 79, dir. sociology doctoral program, 1988—91, 2006—, chair sociology dept., 1998—2001, prof. emerita, 2007—. Mem. social sci. rsch. rev. com. NIMH, Washington, 1976—80; vice chair Nat. Commn. Working Women, Washington, 1977—80; cons. James Irvine Found., San Francisco, 1986; mem. sociology program rev. com. Northeastern U., Boston, 1990; mem. anthropology, linguistics and sociology panel NSF, Washington, 1993; assessor Social Scis. and Humanities Rsch. Coun. Can., Toronto, 1993; mem. postdoc. and dissertation fellowship evaluation panel Ford Found., 2005—07; mem. commn. women in higher edn. coun. edn. U. Calif., Santa Cruz, 1973—76. Co-author: The Future of Inequality, 1970; editor: Child Care: Who Cares? Foreign and Domestic Infant and Early Childhood Development Policies, 1973—75, The Poverty Establishment, 1974; author: Women in the Workplace, 1981; adv. editor: Social Quar., 1990—93, Gender and Society, 1986—89, mem. editl. bd.: Contemporary Sociology, 2006—07. Vis. scholar, Indian Coun. Social Sci. Rsch., 1979, U. Wash., Seattle, 1991—92; Andrew W. Mellon Sr. scholar, Wellesley Coll., 1978—79. Mem.: Alpha Kappa Delta, Re-Evaluation Counseling (coll. and univ. faculty reference person 1980—), Eastern Sociol. Assn. (exec. coun. mem.-at-large 1973—74), Pacific Sociol. Assn. (v.p. 1996—97), Internat. Sociol. Assn. (rsch. coun. mem.-at-large 1978—82), Am. Sociol. Assn. (chair sect. sex and gender 1974—78, exec. coun. mem.-at-large 1975—78), Sociologists Women in Soc. (pres. 1978—80), Soc. Study Social Problems (pres. 1996—97), Phi Beta Kappa. Avocations: camping, hiking, painting, swimming, pen and ink drawing. Office: U Calif Dept Sociology C8 Santa Cruz CA 95064

ROBYT, JOHN F., chemistry professor; b. Moline, Ill., Feb. 17, 1935; s. Frank A. and Mary Margret Robyt; m. Lois Tefft Kennedy, Apr. 12, 1958; children: Clare, William John. BS in Chemistry, St. Louis U., 1958; PhD in Biochemistry, Iowa State U., Ames, 1962. Fellow Lister Inst. Preventive Medicine, London, 1963—64; assoc. prof. Iowa State U., Ames, 1967—73, 1974—83, prof., 1984—, dir. lab. carbohydrate chemistry and enzymology, 1984—. Author: (textbook) Biochemical Techniques: Theory and Practice, 1987, Essentials of Carbohydrate Chemistry, 1997; contbr. articles to numerous profl. jours. Recipient Merit award, Japanese Soc. Glycosci., 1994, Alsberg-French-Schoch award for Outstanding Contrbns. to Starch Chemistry, Assn. Cereal Chemists and Corn Refiners Assn., 2001. Mem.: Am. Chem. Soc. (chmn. divsn. carbohydrate chemistry 2001—03, Wolfrom award in Carbohydrate Chemistry, divsn. carbohydrate chem. 1998). Achievements include 11 patents on the chemistry and enzymology of carbohydrates; research in carbohydrate enzymology; enzymology of dextransucrase, x-amylase, and starch synthase. Office: Iowa State Univ 4252 Molecular Biology Bldg Ames IA 50011 Home Phone: 515-232-8490; Office Phone: 515-294-1964. Business E-Mail: jrobyt@iastate.edu.

ROCCA, CHRISTINA B., ambassador, former federal agency administrator; b. Washington, 1957; m. Gordon L. Rocca; 2 children. BA in History, King's Coll., London, 1980. Staff ops. officer, Directorate of Ops. CIA, Washington, 1982—97; fgn. affairs advisor to Senator Sam Brownback US Senate, Washington; asst. sec for South Asian Affairs US Dept. State, Washington, 2001—06; US perm. rep. & amb. UN Conf. on Disarmament, Geneva, 2006—.

ROCCO, NIKKI, film company executive; m. Joseph Rocco. Sales dept. Universal Pictures, 1967, asst. to gen. sales mgr., 1981—84, v.p. distbn., 1984—90, sr. v.p. distbn. and mktg., 1990—95, exec. v.p., distbn., 1995—96, pres., distbn., 1996—. Bd. dirs. Will Rogers Motion Picture Pioneers Found. Named one of 100 Most Powerful Women in Entertainment, Hollywood Reporter, 2004, 2005, 2006; recipient Crystal award, Women in Film, 2000. Office: Universal Pictures 100 Universal City Plaza Universal City CA 91608 *

ROCEK, JAN, retired chemist; b. Prague, Czech Republic, Mar. 24, 1924; came to U.S., 1960, naturalized, 1966; s. Hugo and Frida (Loebl) Robitschek; m. Eva Trojan, June 26, 1947; children: Martin, Thomas. MS, Tech. U., Prague, 1949, PhD, 1953. Scientist Czechoslovak Acad. Sci., Prague, 1953-57, sr. scientist, 1957-60; vis. scientist U. Coll., London, 1958; research fellow Harvard U., 1960-62; asso. prof., then prof. Cath. U. Am., 1962-66; prof. chemistry U. Ill., Chgo., 1966-95, acting head dept., 1980-81, head dept., 1981-93, vice chancellor rsch., dean grad. coll. Chgo., 1993-95, acting dean Grad. Coll., 1969-70, dean Grad. Coll., 1970-79, asso. mem. Ctr. for Advanced Studies, 1968-69; ret., 1995. Vis. scholar Stanford U., 1979-80, Cambridge U., 1980 Contbr. articles to profl. jours. Mem. Am. Chem. Soc., AAAS, Czechoslovak Soc. Arts and Scis. in Am., AAUP, Sigma Xi (pres. chpt. 1976-77, 85-86), Phi Kappa Phi. Home: 4031 Kennett Pike # 24 Greenville DE 19807 Personal E-mail: rocek@uic.edu.

ROCH, LEWIS MARSHALL, II, ophthalmic surgeon, medical entrepreneur; b. Mineola, Tex., Aug. 13, 1934; s. Lewis Marshall and Gladys Irene (Hoover) R.; m. Lois Afton Price; children: Lewis Marshall Roch III, Katrina Ann Seitz. BA, U. Tex., Austin, 1955; MD, U. Tex. Southwestern, Dallas, 1959. Diplomate Am. Bd. Ophthalmology. Intern USPHS Hosp., Boston, 1959-60, resident in ophthalmology New Orleans, 1960-63, dep. chief ophthalmology, 1963-64, chief opthalmology Seattle, 1964-67; attending ophthalmic surgeon Ball Meml. Hosp., Muncie, Ind., 1967—, chmn. dept. surgery, chmn. clin. staff, 1975, chmn. exec. com., 1984—87, bd. dirs., 1984—90, mem. fin. com., 1984—87; founder, CEO, med. dir. The Eye Ctr. Group, Muncie, 1985—, The Surgi Ctr. Group, Muncie, 1985—. Mem. exec. com. Ind. Acad. Ophthalmology, 1978-82; bd. dirs. Cardinal Health Ventures, Paragent, LLC, Cardinal Ethanol, LLC, Cardinal Health Found., Inc., 1999-, Ball Meml. Found., 1998-; clin. asst. prof. Ind. U. Sch. Medicine, 1978—. Chmn. Muncie-Delaware Devel., 2000-03; active Ball State U. Bus. Forecasting Roundtable, 2000—; exec. v.p. Muncie-Delaware Econ. Devel., 2000-02; trustee Minnetrista Cultural Ctr., 2002—; bd. dirs. United Way Delaware County, 2003-06. Fellow ACS, Am. Acad. Ophthalmology; mem. AMA, Ind. State Med. Assn., Muncie Acad. Medicine (pres. 1981-82), Am. Soc. Cataract and Refractive Surgeons, Am. Coll. Physician Execs., Muncie-Delaware C. of C. (bd. dirs. 1999-2003), Rotary. Republican. Achievements include first to work in outpatient ambulatory surgery; innovation in intraocular lens implantation in cataract surgery; integration of physician's practices with hospital health care delivery systems. Home: 2006 E Robinwood Dr Muncie IN 47304-2857 Office: The Eye Ctr Group LLC 200 N Tillotson Ave Muncie IN 47304-3988 Office Phone: 765-289-7073. E-mail: lmroch@comcast.net.

ROCHA, GUY LOUIS, archivist, consultant, historian; b. Long Beach, Calif., Sept. 23, 1951; s. Ernest Louis and Charlotte (Sobus) R. BA in Social Studies and Edn., Syracuse U., 1973; MA in Am. Studies, San Diego State U., 1975; postgrad., U. Nev., 1975—. Cert. archivist Am. Acad. Cert. Archivists. Tchr. Washoe County Sch. Dist., Reno, 1975-76; history instr. Western Nev. C.C., Carson City, 1976; curator manuscripts Nev. Hist. Soc., Reno, 1976-81, interim asst. dir., 1980, interim dir., 1980-81; state adminstr. archives and records Nev. State Libr. and Archives, Carson City, 1981—, interim divsn. adminstr., 2006—. Hist. cons. Janus Assocs., Tempe, Ariz., 1980, Rainshadow Assocs., Carson City, 1983—. Co-author: The Ignoble Conspiracy: Radicalism on Trial in Nevada, 1986, The Earp's Last Frontier: Wyatt and Virgil Earp in Nevada 1902-1905, 1988; contbr. to books and govt. study; host weekly radio talk show Sta. KPTL, Carson City, 1988-2000, KUNR/NPR, Reno, 2001-; hist. cons. to documentary Las Vegas, A&E Network, 1996, documentary Truckee and Carson Rivers, PBS Network, 1997, documentary Hoover Dam, PBS Network, 1999, documentary Lake Tahoe, PBS Network, 2001; dir. documentary Comstock Miners Union, 2003, Goldfield, 2004, They Died to Make the Desert Bloom, 2005, Whose Right to Work?, 2006, Nev. AFL-CIO; mem. editl. bd. Nev. Hist. Soc., 1983-2003. Mem. Washoe Heritage Coun., Reno, 1983—85; ex-officio mem. Nev. Commn. Bicentennial U.S. Constn., 1986—91; mem. Washoe County Dem. Ctrl. Com., Reno, 1984—87. Mem. Conf. Intermountain Archivists (coun. mem. 1979-87, v.p. 1984-85, pres. 1985-86), No. Nev. Pub. Adminstrs. Group (pres. 1986-87), S.W. Labor Studies Assn., State Hist. Records Adv. Bd. (dep. coord. 1984-86, coord. 1986—), Westerners Internat. Nev. Corral (dep. sheriff 1980-81, sheriff 1984-85, mem. state coords. steering com. 1985-87, vice chmn. 1986-87), Soc. Am. Archivists, Western History Assn., Nat. Assn. Govt. Archives and Records Adminstrs., Orgn. Am. Historians. Office: Nev State Libr & Archives 100 N Stewart St Carson City NV 89701-4285 Office Phone: 775-684-3317.

ROCHA, LUIS M., physics professor, director; s. Jose Luis and Micaela Mateus Silva Rocha; m. Deborah S. Stungis; children: Alexandre L., Madalena S. PhD in Sys. Sci. & Computer Sci., SUNY, Binghamton, 1997. Tech. staff mem. Los Alamos Nat. Lab., N.Mex., 1997—2004; assoc. prof. Ind. U., Bloomington, 2004—. Dir. FLAD Computational Biology Collaboratorium, Oeiras, Portugal, 2004—. Office: Ind Univ 1900 E Tenth St Bloomington IN 47406 Office Fax: 812-856-3015. Business E-Mail: rocha@indiana.edu.

ROCHE, CATHY, energy executive; m. Terry Roche; 2 children. BA in Journalism, U. NC, Chapel Hill. Reporter AP, Charlotte News; self-employed pub. rels. cons., 1980—83; dir. publs. Duke Power Co., 1983—89; v.p. pub. and industry comm. Nuc. Energy Inst., Washington, 1989—96; v.p. corp. comm. Entergy Corp., New Orleans, 1996—99; dir. external rels. pub. affairs dept. Duke Energy, Charlotte, NC, 2000—03, v.p. corp. comm., 2003—06, sr. v.p., chief comm. officer, 2006—. Bd. visitors U. NC Sch. Journalism; bd. visitors Carolina Environ. Prog. U. NC, Chapel Hill. Office: Duke Energy 526 S Church St Charlotte NC 28202-1904 Office Phone: 704-594-6200. *

ROCHE, GAIL CONNOR, editor; b. Phila., Aug. 14, 1953; d. Donald Russell Connor; m. Richard Roche, Nov. 21, 1981; children: Alex James, Clare Evelyn. AB cum laude, Franklin & Marshall Coll., Lancaster, Pa., 1975; MA with distinction, Rider U., 1988. Cert. tchr., Pa. Tchr. Pennsbury Schs., Fallsington, Pa., 1975-76, Cen. Bucks Sch., Doylestown, Pa., 1977-79; reporter Trenton Times, NJ, 1979-82; editor Dow Jones & Co., Princeton, NJ, 1982-95; mem. adv. bd. Dow Jones Women's Network, Princeton, 1990-95; tech. editor Bloomberg News, Princeton, 1995-2000; sr. editor, letters editor Bloomberg Markets, 2000—. Contbr. articles to mags. Mem. Phi Beta Kappa. Home: 23 Jericho Run Washington Crossing PA 18977-1027 Office Phone: 609-394-0738. Personal E-mail: groche@bloomberg.net.

ROCHE, GERARD RAYMOND, management consultant; b. Scranton, Pa., July 27, 1931; s. Joseph Arthur and Amelia Jane (Garcia) R.; m. Marie Terotta, Apr. 27, 1957; children: Mary Margaret, Anne Elizabeth, Paul Joseph. BS in Acctg., U. Scranton, 1953; MBA, NYU, 1958. Mgmt. trainee AT&T, Phila., 1955-56; account exec. ABC-TV, NYC, 1956-58; sales and mktg. positions Kordite Corp. subs. Mobil Oil Co., Macedon, NY, 1959-63; assoc. Heidrick & Struggles, Inc., NYC, 1964-68, ptnr., 1968—, mgr. N.Y., 1968-73, mgr. East, 1973-77, pres., chief exec. officer, 1978—81, chmn., 1981-2000, sr. chmn., 2000—. Former trustee Cath. U. Am., U. Scranton; mentor Nat. Mentoring Partnership. Served to lt. USN, 1953-55. Mem.: Cmty. Anti-Drug Coalitions of am. (bd. dirs.), Knights of Malta, Loblolly Pines Country Club, Blind Brook Club, Sleepy Hollow Country Club, Univ. Club, Yale Club, Alpha Sigma Nu (past treas.). Roman Catholic. Office: Heidrick & Struggles Inc 245 Park Ave Fl 43 New York NY 10167-0152 Office Phone: 212-551-0505.

ROCHE, JAMES GERARD, former civilian military employee; m. Diane Lee. BS in Language, Lit. & Philosophy, Illinois Inst. Tech., Chicago, 1960; MS, U.S. Naval Postgrad. Sch., Monterey, Calif., 1966; PhD in Bus. Adminstrn., Harvard U., Cambridge, Mass., 1972; PhD (hon.), Illinois Inst. of Tech., 2002, St. Thomas Aquinas Coll., 2003. Advanced through ranks to capt. USN, 1960-83; with Office Sec. Def., 1975-79; sr. profl. staff mem. Senate Select Com. Intelligence, 1979-81; princ. dep. dir. policy planning staff US Dept. State, 1981-83; Dem. staff dir. U.S. Senate Com. on Armed Svcs., 1983—84; v.p., dir. analysis ctr. Northrop Grumman Corp., Washington, 1984-89, v.p., special asst. to chmn., pres., CEO LA, 1989-91, v.p., adv. devel. planning, 1991—92, chief advanced develop., planning, pub. affairs, 1992—96, corp. v.p., pres. elec. sensors, systems sector Balt., 1996—2001; sec. USAF, Washington, 2001—05. Mem. The Coun. Fgn. Relations, Internat. Institute of Strategic Studies, Fleet Reserve Assn., Mil. Order of the Carabao, Conquistadores Del Cielo. Decorated Def. Superior Svc. medal, Legion of Merit, Navy Commendation medal, Navy Expeditionary medal, Nat. Def. Svc. medal, Vietnam Svc. medal, USN Disting. Pub. Svc. medal; recipient Disting. Civilian Svc. medal, Dept. Army, 2003, Ill. Inst. Tech. Profl. Achievement award, 2003, Air Force Order of the Sword, 2003, Exceptional Civilian Svc. award, 2005.

ROCHE, JOHN EDWARD, college administrator, human resources specialist, educator; b. St. Albans, NY, Nov. 11, 1946; s. John F. and Carolyn C. (Miller) R.; m. Valerie Vastola; children: Christopher B., Danielle, Ryan J., Jennifer M. BA, Marist Coll., 1968, MBA, 1975; MS in Edn., SUNY, New Paltz, 1974; EdD, Nova Southeastern U., 1998. Tchr. Kingston City Schs., NY, 1968-76; employment supr. ACLI Internat. Inc., NYC, 1976-78; dir. pers. Balfour MacLaine Internat., NYC, 1978-80; mgr. employee rels. Harcourt Brace Jovanovich, NYC, 1980-82; nat. dir. pers. Hayt, Hayt & Landau, Great Neck, NY, 1982-86; pres. Pers. Mgmt. Svcs., Great Neck, NY, 1983-86, Martin-Roche Assocs., Inc., Levittown, NY, 1986-94, Human Resources Dept. Inc., Syosset, NY, 1994—2002, LI Bus. Network, Inc., 1994-2000, Martin-Roche Internat. Ltd., Plainview, NY, 1992—94; prof. instrnl. tech. NY Inst. Tech., Old Westbury, 1989-2000, chair Sch. Edn. Manhattan Campus, 1997-2000, acting dir. Ctr. Labor & Indls. Rels., 2000; dean Sch. Continuing Studies LI U., Bklyn., 2000—04; dean Sch. Profl. Devel. Berkeley Coll., NYC, 2004—07, v.p. career svcs., 2006—07; pres. Hesser Coll., Manchester, NH, 2007—. Pres. coun. Berkeley Coll., 2004—07. Exec. dir. Jr. Achievement, Kingston, 1972-76; coach Syosset Baseball Assn., 1993-97, CYO Basketball Assn.; coach CYO Girls Softball Assn., 2004-06, commr., 2007; mem. Syosset Youth Athletic Commn., 2000-04; human resource com. mem. Adults and Children with Learning and Devel. Disabilities, 1990-2000; mem. LI U. Coun. Deans, 2000-04, Middle States Com., 2001-03. Mem. ASTD, Assn. Continuing Higher Edn. (exec. com. region III), WorldatWork (cert. compensation profl.), Soc. for Human Resource Mgmt. (cert. sr. profl. in human resources), KC (grand knight 1967-68). Republican. Roman Catholic. Avocations: astronomy, photography, painting. Home: 17 Meadow Ln Syosset NY 11791-4126 Office: Hesser Coll Manchester NH 03103 Home Phone: 516-650-4970; Office Phone: 603-668-6660. Personal E-mail: jeroche1@verizon.net. Business E-Mail: jroche@hesser.edu.

ROCHE, (EAMONN) KEVIN, architect; b. Dublin, June 14, 1922; came to U.S., 1948, naturalized, 1964; s. Eamon and Alice (Harding) R.; m. Jane Tuohy, June 10, 1963; children: Eamon, Paud, Denis, Anne, Alice. B.Arch., Nat. U. Ireland, 1945; D.Sc. (hon.), Nat. U. Ireland, 1977; postgrad., Ill. Inst. Tech., 1948; D.F.A. (hon.), Wesleyan U., 1981, Yale U., 1995. With Eero Saarinen and Assocs., Bloomfield Hills, Mich., 1950—61; ptnr. Kevin Roche John Dinkeloo and Assocs., Hamden, 1966—. Prin. works include Ford Found. Hdqs., 1967, Oakland (Calif.) Mus, 1968, Met. Mus. Art, N.Y.C., Creative Arts Ctr., Wesleyan U., Middletown, Conn., 1971, Fine Arts Ctr., U. Mass., 1971, Union Carbide Corp. World Hdqs., Conn., Gen. Foods Corp. Hdqs., Rye, N.Y., 1977, 1978, Conoco Inc. Hdqrs., Houston, 1979, Central Pk. Zoo, N.Y.C., 1980, DeWitt Wallace Mus. Fine Arts, Williamsburg, Va., 1980, Bouygues World Hdqrs., Paris, 1983, J.P. Morgan and Co. Hdqrs., N.Y.C., 1983, UNICEF Hdqs., N.Y.C., 1984, Leo Burnett Co. Hdqrs., Chgo., 1985, Cummins Engine Co. Corp. Hdqrs., Columbus, Ind., 1985, Corning (N.Y.) Inc. Hdqs., 1986, Merck & Co. Hdqs., N.J., 1987, Dai Ichi Hdqs./Norinchukin Bank Hdqrs., Tokyo, 1989, Nations Bank Hdqs., Atlanta, 1989, Pontiac Marina Pvt. Ltd., Singapore, 1990, Metropolitano, Madrid, 1990, Borland Internat. Headquarters, Scotts Valley, Calif., 1990, Tanjong & Binariang/Ampang Tower, Kuala Lumpur, Malaysia, 1993, Mus. Jewish Heritage Holocaust Meml., N.Y.C., 1993, Tata Cummins Pvt. Ltd., Jamshedpur, India, 1994, Vis. Ctr., Columbus, Ind., 1994, Cummins Engine Co. APEX Mfg. Facility, 1994, Lucent Techs. Hdqs., Murray Hill, N.J., 1996, Wuxi Newage Cummins, Wuxi, China, 1996, Total Sys. Svcs. Corp. Hdqrs., Columbus, Ga., 1997, Zesiger Sports and Fitness Ctr., MIT, Cambridge, 2000, Lucent Tech. R&D Facilities, various locations including The Netherlands and Germany, 2001, Shiodome City Ctr., Tokyo, 2003, Hdqrs. Santander Ctrl. Hispano, Madrid, 2005, SEC, Washington, 2005, Bouygues SA Holding Co. Hdqrs., Paris, 2005, Nat. Conf. Ctr., Dublin, 2005, 1101 New York Ave., Washington, 2006. Mem. Fine Arts Commn., Washington; trustee Am. Acad. in Rome, 1968-71, Woodrow Wilson Center for Scholars in Smithsonian Instn. Recipient Creative Arts award Brandeis U., 1967; A.S. Bard award City Club N.Y., 1968, 77, 79; award Gov. of Calif., 1968; N.Y. State award Citizens Union N.Y., 1968; total design award Am. Soc. Interior Design; Pritzker Archtl. prize, 1982; Albert S. Bard award, 1990. Fellow AIA (medal of honor N.Y. chpt. 1968, Gold Medal award 1993, 25-yr. award 1995), AAAS; mem. NAD (academician), AAAL (pres. 1994-97), Am. Acad. Arts and Letters (Brunner award 1965, Gold medal 1990), Académie d'Architecture (Grand Gold medal 1977), Mcpl. Art Soc. N.Y. (Brendan Gill prize 1989), Acad. di San Luca. Office: Kevin Roche John Dinkeloo & Assoc PO Box 6127 20 Davis St Hamden CT 06517-0127 Office Phone: 203-777-7251. Business E-Mail: info@krjda.com.

ROCHE, MARK A., lawyer, consumer products company executive; b. 1954; m. Barbara Roche. BA, U. Va.; JD, Cornell U. Bar: NY 1980. Assoc. to counsel Chadbourne & Park, LLP, NYC, 1981-88; group gen. counsel Fortune Brands Inc., Deerfield, Ill., 1988-91, Lincolnshire, Ill., 1991-96, v.p., assoc. gen. counsel, 1996-98, v.p., gen. counsel, 1998-99, sr. v.p., gen. counsel, 1999—2000, sr. v.p., sec., gen. counsel Deerfield, Ill., 2002—. Office: Fortune Brands Inc 520 Lake Cook Rd Deerfield IL 60015-5611 Office Phone: 847-484-4400. *

ROCHE, MICHAEL J., insurance company executive; BS in math., No. Ill. U., MBA. Various info. tech. positions Continental Ill. Nat. Bank, Heller Fin.; v.p. info. tech. Allstate Ins. Co., Northbrook, Ill., 2002—03, group v.p. protection tech., 2003—05, chief info. officer, 2003—05, sr. v.p. protection tech. and adminstrn., 2005—06, sr. v.p. property & casualty claims svc. org., 2006—. Mem. bd. trustees Rosary High Sch., Aurora, Ill.; mem. bd. dir. One Economy. Named one of Premier 100 IT Leaders, Computerworld, 2006. Office: Allstate Corp 2775 Sanders Rd Northbrook IL 60062 Fax: 847-402-2351. *

ROCHE, PAULINE JENNIFER, artist; b. London, Sept. 22, 1961; arrived in U.S., 1995; d. Walter Daniel and Doreen Molly Roche; m. Hany Massarany, Feb. 27, 1986; children: Thomas Daniel, Natalie Jane. BS, Monash U., Melbourne, Australia, 1982. Rsch. physiology dept. physiology Monash U., Melbourne, 1983—86; rsch., policy and planning officer Victorian State Govt. Dept. Edn./Pub. Svc. Bd., Melbourne, 1986—92; artist, 1989—. Exhibitions include Sherbrooke Art Award exhbns., 1991—97, Victorian Artists Soc. Ann. Exhbns., 1992—2001, Alice Bale Ann. Nat. Exhbns., 1993—98, Camberwell Rotary Ann. Juried Art Exhbn., 1992—98, 1993, 2000, Kew Gallery Invitational Exhbn., 1994, Victorian Artists Soc. Artist of Yr. Invitational Exhbn., 1997, Salmagundi Club 20st Ann. Open Exhbn., Salmagundi Club, 1997—98, Catherine Lorillard Wolfe Art Club Exhbn., 1997, Am. Artists Profl. League 69th Grand Nat. Exhbn., 1997, Newbury Fine Arts, Boston, 1998—2007, Newbury Fine Arts Figurative Art Group Exhbn., 2000, Celebrate! Exhbn., Tucson, 2002, Catherine Lorillard Wolfe Art Club 109th Art Exhbn., 2004, El Presidio Gallery, Tucson, 2005—07, Australian Guild of Realist Artists Summer Mem. Exhbn., 2006, Alice Bale Art Award Exhbn., 2006, one-woman shows include Cato Gallery, Victorian Artists Soc. Galleries, Melbourne, 1994, Ventana Med. Sys. Nat. Hdqs., Tucson, 2003. Recipient Gold Medal of Honor, Audubon Artists 55th Ann. Exhn., 1997, Hans Heysen award, Sherbrooke Art Soc., 1992, Award for Oil Painting, Alice Bale Nat. Art Awards, 1994, Mavis Hill Acquisitive Award, Sherbrooke Spring Exhbn., 1995, Gordon Moffat award, Victorian Artists Soc., 1997, Highly Commended, Victorian Artists Soc. Dep. Lord Mayor's Exhbn., 1999, N.J. Chpt. award for artistic excellence, Am. Artists Profl. League, 1997, Pres. award, Salmagundi Club, 1997, Artist Showcase award, Manhattan Arts Internat., 1997, 1998, Leonard J. Meiselman Meml. award, Catherine Lorillard Wolfe Art Club, 1997, Sharon and Danielle Ortlip Meml. award, Salmagundi Club, 1998, Highly Commended award, Australian Guild Realist Artists, 2006. Mem.: Tucson Plein Air Painters Soc., Australian Guild Realist Artists, Portrait Soc. Am., Victorian Artists Soc. (signatory mem., Gordon Moffat award 1997). Office Phone: 520-219-2902. Personal E-mail: paulineroche@comcast.net.

ROCHÉ, ROBERT RICHARD, artist; m. Bettie Fistere, Dec. 6, 1945. Apprenticeship, Studio of Sebastian Cruset, NYC, 1931—32; at, Nat. Acad. Design, NYC, 1933—36, Art Students League, 1936—40, Columbia U., 1941. Artist Roché Studio, NY, Conn., N.H. and Maine, 1941—2004; instr. Roché Tchg. Studio, NY, Conn. and N.H., 1942—79. Curator Mus. Fine Arts, Richmond, Va., 1947—48; art commentator Nat. Antiques Rev., Portland, Maine, 1969—71; critic and art judge; lectr. in field. Represented in permanent collections N.Y. Racing Assn., Aqueduct and Belmont, Wilmington Race Track, Del., prin. works include portraiture, including Pres. Harry S. Truman, Eleanor Roosevelt, Dr. Ralph Bunche, James Farley, Old Saratoga Race Track, 1960, FB-111 Before Take-Off, 1982, Amish Children, 1984, Cat Portfolio, 1984, prin. works and pvt. collections, in publs., Sunny Jim: The life of America's Most Beloved Horseman, 1962, American Racetracks and Contemporary Art, 1966, Birds and Beasts of Mark Twain, 1966, Thoroughbred Record, 1973, 1974, one-man shows include Frank K.M. Gallery, 1949, 1952, Retrospectives, U.S. Air Force Acad., 1988, Nat. Mus. Racing, Saratoga Springs, N.Y., 2000—01. Instr. diagnostic rsch. Northampton State Hosp., Mass., 1946—47; dir. art auction Cerebral Palsy, Conn., 1950. Mem.: Royal Soc. Arts, Am. Watercolor Soc. Avocations: writing, music, antiques, farming and animal husbandry, literature. Home: Windswept Farm PO Box 467 York ME 03909-0467

ROCHELLE, LUGENIA, academic administrator; b. Maple Hill, NC, July 14, 1943; d. John Edward and Ruby Lee (Holmes) R. BA, St. Augustine's Coll., 1965; MS, N.C. A & T State U., 1969; D of Pedagogy, Barbar-Scotia Coll., 1993. Cert. tchr., N.C. Tchr. French, English Butler High Sch., Barnwell, SC, 1965-67; instr. English N.C. A & T State U., Greensboro, 1970-77, St. Augustine's Coll., Raleigh, NC, 1977-86, dir. freshman studies program, 1986-91, dean lower coll., 1991-95, asst. to v.p. acad. affairs, 1991-92; dir. gen. studies, asst. prof. English Voorhees Coll., Denmark, SC, 1996-98, spl. asst. to pres. external affairs, 1999—2002, dir. Hons. Coll., 1999—, dean, Coll. of General Studies, 2002—. Dir. Mellon program St. Augustine's Coll., Raleigh, 1980-83; adv. bd. cooperating Raleigh Colls., 1986—, Off to Coll., Montgomery, Ala., 1993—; mem. profl. practices commn. N.C. Dept. Pub. Instrn., 1994-96; coord. Title III, 1999-00, coord. Bd. Trustees Rels., 1999-02; dir. Ctr. Excellence in Humanities, Vorhees Coll., April 2000-02; Hostess for Radio Talk Show, Views and News from Voorhees Coll., Sept. 2001-03. Author: English Manual of Writing, 1980, (with others) Off to College, 1997, 98, reprinted, 1999, 2000, 01; editor: Can't Nobody Do You Like Jesus, 1998. Judge oratorical contests, Optimist Club, Raleigh, 1985-93; chair pro tem Raleigh Bicentennial Hist. Com., Raleigh, 1991-92; initiated, effected chartering of Phi Eta Sigma St. Augustine's Coll., 1995; bd. dirs. Garner Rd. YMCA, Raleigh, 1994-1996; coord. Honda Campus All-Star Challenge, 1996—; lay min., sec. vestry St. Philip's Episcopal Ch., 1997—; instnl. rep. S.C. Women in Higher Edn., Voorhees Coll., 1998—. Nat. teaching fellow N.C. A & T State U., Greensboro, 1968-70. NCTE Fellow Nat. Coun. Tchrs. English; mem. ASCD (assoc.), Am. Assn. U. Women (pres. Denmark Br.), Cardinal Club. Avocations: reading, collecting antique birds, travel. E-mail: rochelle@voorhees.edu.

ROCHELLE, VICTOR CLEANTHUS, retired lawyer; b. Nov. 4, 1918; s. Floyd Emerson and Goldie Opal (Dunbar) Rochelle; m. Marjorie Armitage, Dec. 20, 1946 (div. 1956); children: Vickie Adrianne, Margo Renee; m. Patricia Ann Leary, Mar. 20, 1964; children: Elizabeth Ann, Linda Raquel. BA, U. Tex., 1940; LLB, Columbia U., 1947. Bar: Tex. 48, U.S. Dist. Ct. Ill. 53. Assoc. Tom Hartley, Atty., Pharr, Tex., 1947—49, Kelly, Looney, McLean & Littleton, Edinburg, Tex., 1949—52; personal injury supr. County Mut. Ins. Co., Chgo., 1952—57, claims mgr., 1957—61, Bloomington, Ill., 1961—69; cons., dir. litigation Country Mut., Country Casualty, Mid-Am., 1969—84; ret., 1984; ins. law cons. pvt. practice, 1984—2006; ret., 2006. Lectr. in field.; arbitrator Mut. Casualty, 1965—70, Lt. comdr. USN, 1941—45. Mem.: ABA, Am. Judicature Soc., Def. Rsch. Inst., Property Loss Bur., Internat. Assn. Ins. Counsel, McLean County Bar Assn., Ill. Bar Assn., Tex. Bar Assn. Reform. Address: 27 Lateer Dr Normal IL 61761-3925 Personal E-mail: vprochelle@aol.com.

ROCHELSON, BURTON L., obstetrician; MD, U. Mich., 1978. Cert. Maternal Fetal Medicine Am. Coll. Ob-Gyn, 1988. Dir. obstetrics and maternal fetal medicine North Shore U. Hosp., Manhasset, NY, 1999—. Contbr. numerous articles to profl. jours. Office: North Shore Univ Hosp 300 Community Dr Manhasset NY 11030 Office Phone: 516-562-2892. E-mail: brochels@nshs.edu.

ROCHESTER, MICHAEL GRANT, geophysics educator; b. Toronto, Ont., Can., 1932; s. Reginald Rochester and Ruth Rochester Konrad; m. Elizabeth Manser, 1958; children: Susan, Fiona, John. BA with honors, U. Toronto, 1954, MA, 1956; PhD, U. Utah, 1959. Aerodynamicist A. V. Roe Can. Ltd., Malton, Ont., 1954-55; lectr. geophysics U. Toronto, 1959-60, asst. prof., 1960-61, U. Waterloo, Ont., 1961-65, assoc. prof., 1965-67, Meml. U. Nfld., St. John's, Canada, 1967-70, prof., 1970-98, univ. research prof., 1986—, prof. emeritus, 1998—. Officer Nat. Spiritual Assembly of Baha'is of Can., 1963—92. Grantee, NRC, Natural Scis. and Engring. Rsch. Coun. Can, 1961—2002. Fellow Royal Soc. Can.; mem. Internat. Union Geodesy and Geophysics (Can. nat. com. 1971-75, 84-88), AAAS, Am. Geophys. Union, Can. Assn. Physicists, Can. Geophys. Union (Tuzo Wilson medal, 1986), Internat. Astron. Union (commn. rotation of the Earth 1973—), Royal Astron. Soc. London, Sigma Xi Avocations: hiking, swimming, history. Office: Meml Univ Nfld Dept Earth Scis Saint John's NL Canada A1B 3X5 Office Phone: 709-737-7565. E-mail: mrochest@mun.ca.

ROCHETTE, LOUIS, water transportation executive; b. Quebec City, Que., Can., Feb. 19, 1923; s. Evariste and Blanche (Gaudry) R.; m. Nicole Barbeau, Oct. 12, 1968; children: Louise (dec.), Anne, Guy. M. Commerce, Laval U., Que., 1948. Chartered acct., Que. Chief auditor Sales Tax Govt. Que., Quebec City, 1952—55; treas. Davie Ltd., Lauzon, Que., 1955—65; chmn., CEO Davie Ltd., Lauzon, Que., 1976—81; exec. v.p. Marine Industries, Ltd., Montreal, 1965—76; pres., CEO Soconav Inc., Quebec, 1976—86; pres. Gesconav Inc., 1986—. Past chmn. Lloyd's Com. for Can. Author: Le Reve Separatiste, 1969. Bd. dirs. Gov. Coun. for Can. Unity; gov. Laval U. Found, Quebec Opera Found. Pilot RCAF, 1943-45, ETO. Fellow Inst. Chartered Accts. Can., Can. Inst. Mgmt. Accts. Home and Office: 2500 Pierre Dupuy 508 Montreal PQ Canada H3C 4L1 *Whatever success I have met with throughout my career was mainly achieved through perseverance in the face of what often looked like insurmountable obstacles.*

ROCHINSKI, STEPHEN JAMES, musician, educator; b. Washington, Jan. 20, 1954; s. Stanley James Rochinski, Jr. and Lorraine Agnes Rochinski, Carol Rochinski (Stepmother); m. Laurie Fox, May 24, 1986; children: Anna F., Alex F. Diploma, Berklee Coll. Music, 1980. Freelance guitarist, Washington, 1972—77; freelance guitarist, arranger Boston, 1977—80; guitarist, arranger, music dir. Anthony Tillman Show with The East Coast Brass, 1980—84; prof. Berklee Coll. Music, 1984—. Writer Hal Leonard Corp., Milw., 1995—; jazz clinician numerous nat. and internat. locations, 1996—. Musician: (recording) Until Further Notice, 1993, A Bird In The Hand, 1999, Otherwise, 2001, Live in Louisville, 2006; author: The Jazz Style of Tal Farlow, 1994, The Motivic Basis for Jazz Guitar Improvisation, 1998, composer numerous jazz compositions and arrangements; Jardis Records, Spiesen-Elversberg, Germany, 1999—; contbg. editor (and author): Berklee Press and Advance Music, 1991—; performances with Tal Farlow, Tim Hagans, Jimmy Raney, Attila Zoller, Pete and Conte Candoli, Chuck Redd, Brad Goode and Joe Lovano. Jazz artist-in-residence Nat. and Internat. locations. Recipient Paul Revere award Graphic Excellence, Music Pubs. Assn., 1995; grantee, NEA, 1992, Berklee Coll. Music, 1989, 1994, 1998, 2001. Mem.: ASCAP (writer, pub. affiliate 2006—), Broadcast Music Inc. (writer, pub. affiliate 1991—2003), Rec. Acad. (voting mem. 2001—03). Roman Catholic. Avocations: reading, political affairs, history. Home: 2 Wellington Terr Brookline MA 02445 Office: Berklee Coll Music Faculty Box #273 1140 Boylston St Boston MA 02215 Home Phone: 617-277-0228; Office Phone: 617-747-8335. Business E-Mail: srochinski@berklee.edu.

ROCHKIND, LOUIS PHILIPP, lawyer; b. Miami, Fla., June 25, 1948; s. Reuben and Sarah R.; m. Rosalind H. Rochkind, July 4, 1971. BA in Psychology cum laude, U. Mich., 1970, JD cum laude, 1974. Bar: Mich. 1974, U.S. Dist. Ct. (ea. dist.) Mich. 1974. Ptnr. Jaffe, Raitt, Heuer & Weiss, Detroit, 1974—. Adj. prof. law Wayne St. U. Law Sch.; lectr. various profl. assns. and orgns. Assoc. editor U. Mich. Law Rev.; contbr. articles to profl. jours. publs. Mem. Am. Coll. Bankruptcy Lawyers, Detroit Bar Assn. (local rules in bankruptcy subcom. creditor-debtor law sect. 1980—), Phi Kappa Phi. Office: Jaffe Raitt Heuer Weiss 27777 Franklin Rd Ste 2500 Southfield MI 48034-8222 E-mail: larrol@jafferaitt.com.

ROCHLIN, PAUL R., lawyer; b. Balt., Dec. 14, 1934; s. Jack and Sara (Levin) Rochlin; m. Lois David, Oct. 25, 1962 (div. 1969); children: Greg, Jennifer; m. Joyce Tretick, July 12, 1973; children: Keith Sopher, Maura Sopher. JD, U. Balt., 1958. Bar: Md. 59, U.S. Dist. Ct. Md. 59. Assoc. Milton Talkin, Balt., 1959—61, Rochlin & Settleman, Balt., 1961—63, ptnr., 1963—78; pres., sr. ptnr. Rochlin Settleman & Dobres, P.A., Balt., 1978—2001, of counsel, 2001—06; pres., sr. ptnr. Rochlin & Goldman, P.A. Bd. dirs. Balt. Jewish Coun., 1979. Mem.: Balt. City Bar Assn., Md. Trial Lawyers Assn. (bd. dirs. 1988—92), Md. State Bar Assn., Suburban Club (pres. 2003—05). Jewish. Office Phone: 410-602-0222.

ROCHON, MARK, lawyer; b. Detroit, Mich. BS, Western Mich. U., 1980; JD, Stanford U., 1983. Bar: DC 1983, Md. 1990. Former chief, trial divsn. Pub. Defender Svc., Washington; ptnr. Rochon & Roberts, Miller & Chevalier Chartered, Washington. Lectr. on trial practice to students and practitioners. USN, 1975—77. Named one of 75 Best Lawyers in Washington, Washingtonian Mag., 2002. Office: Miller & Chevalier Chartered 655 Fifteenth St NW Ste 900 Washington DC 20005-5701 Office Phone: 202-626-5819. Office Fax: 202-628-0858. Business E-Mail: mrochon@milchev.com.

ROCHOWICZ, JOHN ANTHONY, JR., mathematician, mathematics educator, physics educator; b. Reading, Pa., Mar. 20, 1950; s. John Anthony and Sara Jane (Binckley) R. BS in Math., Albright Coll., Reading, Pa., 1972, secondary edn. cert. math., 1975; MS in Math., Lehigh U., Bethlehem, Pa., 1974, EdD in Edn1. Tech., 1993. Cert. secondary tchr. Pa. Tchr. math. Bethlehem Cath. H.S., Pa., 1980—81; instr. math. Pa. State U.-Berks, Reading, 1982—84, Kutztown U., Pa., 1983—84, Lehigh County C.C., Schnecksville, Pa., 1984, Alvernia Coll., Reading, 1984, prof. math., 1984—; instr. math. Reading Area C.C., 1984—86. Contbr. articles to profl. jours. Recipient Alumni Educator award Albright Coll., Reading, 1987. Mem. Math. Assn. Am., Assn. for Advancement Computing in Edn., Assn. for Ednl. Comm. and Tech., Nat. Coun. Tchrs. Math., Beta Kappa Chi. Democrat. Roman Catholic. Avocations: music, computers, calculators, billiards, swimming. Home: 825 Brighton Ave Reading PA 19606-1316 Office: Alvernia College 400 Saint Bernardine St Reading PA 19607-1799 Office Phone: 610-796-8257. Business E-Mail: john.rochowicz@alvernia.edu.

ROCK, ALLAN MICHAEL, ambassador, former Canadian government official; b. Ottawa, Ont., Can., Aug. 30, 1947; s. James Thomas and Anne (Torley) R.; m. Deborah Kathleen, June 24, 1983; children: Jason, Lauren, Andrew, Stephen. BA, U. Ottawa, 1968, LLB, 1971. Certified specialist in civil litigation. Sr. ptnr. Fasken Campbell & Godfrey, Toronto, Ont.; min. of justice, atty. gen. Govt. of Can., 1993-97, min. of health, 1997—2002, min. of industry, 2002—03; permanent Can. rep. UN, New York, 2004—. Treas. Law Soc. Upper Can., 1992-93; bencher Law Soc., 1983, 87, 91; former chmn. discipline and legal edn. coms.; past chmn. litigation dept. Fasken Campbell Godfrey. Fellow Am. Coll. Trial Lawyers. Office: UN One Dag Hamarskjold Plz 885 Second Ave 14th Fl New York NY 10017

ROCK, ARTHUR, venture capitalist; b. Rochester, NY, Aug. 19, 1926; s. Hyman A. and Reva (Cohen) Rock; m. Toni Rembe, July 19, 1975. BS, Syracuse U., 1948; MBA, Harvard U., 1951. Gen. ptnr. Davis & Rock, San Francisco, 1961-68, Arthur Rock & Assocs., San Francisco, 1969-80. Mem. exec. com. Teledyne, Inc., L.A., 1961-94; dir. emeritus, founder, past chmn., chmn. exec. com., lead dir. Intel Corp., Santa Clara, Calif.; bd. dirs. Echelon Corp., San Jose, Calif.; bd. govs. Nasdaq Stock Market, Inc. Trustee Calif. Inst. Tech.; pres. Basic Fund; bd. dirs. San Francisco Opera Assn., 1970-92, San Francisco Mus. Modern Art; mem. vis. com. Harvard U. Bus. Sch., 1982-88. Recipient Medal of Achievement Am. Electronics Assn., 1987, Am. Acad. Achievement, 1989, Lifetime Achievement in Entrepreneurship and Innovation award U. Calif., 1999; named to Jr. Achievement Hall of Fame, 1990, Calif. Bus. Hall of Fame, 1990, Bay Area Bus. Coun. Hall of Fame, 1995, Arents Pioneer medal Syracuse U., 1997, Outstanding Dir., Corp. Am., 1999, SDForum Visionary award, 2001, Bus. Leader of Yr. award Harvard Bus. Sch. Assn. No. Calif., 2002. Fellow Am. Acad. Arts & Scis. Office: 1 Maritime Plz Ste 1220 San Francisco CA 94111-3502 *

ROCK, CHRIS, actor, comedian; b. Bklyn., Feb. 7, 1965; s. Julius and Rose Rock; m. Malaak Compton, Nov. 23, 1996; children: Lola Simone, Zahra Savannah. Actor (films) Beverly Hills Cop II, 1987, I'm Gonna Git You Sucka, 1988, New Jack City, 1991, Boomerang, 1992, Panther, 1995, The Immortals, 1995, Sgt. Bilko, 1996, Beverly Hills Ninja, 1997, (voice) Doctor Dolittle, 1998, Lethal Weapon 4, 1998, Dogma, 1999, Torrance Rises, 1999, Spin Doctor, 1999, Nurse Betty, 2000, (voice) Artificial Intelligence, 2001, Pootie Tang, 2001, (voice) Osmosis Jones, 2001, Jay and Silent Bob Strike Back, 2001, Bad Company, 2002, Paparazzi, 2004, (voice) Madagascar, 2005, The Longest Yard, 2005; (TV series) Saturday Night Live, 1990-93; Def Comedy Jam, 1992, In Living Color, 1993-94, (voice) Happily Ever After: Fairy Tales for Every Child, 1995, Politically Incorrect, 1996, The Remarkable Journey, 2000; actor, writer, dir. (films) I Think I Love My Wife, 2007; actor, writer (films) Comedy's Dirtiest Dozen, 1988, actor, writer, exec. prodr. Down to Earth, 2001; actor, dir., prodr. Head of State, 2003; actor, writer, prodr. (with Nelson George) CB4, 1993; actor, writer, exec. prodr. (TV series) The Chris Rock Show, 1997-2000 (Emmy for Outstanding Writing for a Variety or Music Program, 1998); exec. prodr. The Hughleys, 1998; writer (TV special) Chris Rock: Big Ass Jokes, 1993, Saturday Night Live: The Best of Chris Rock, 1999; writer, exec. prodr. Chris Rock: Bring the Pain, 1996 (Emmy for Outstanding Variety, Music or Comedy Special), Chris Rock: Bigger and Blacker, 1999 (American Comedy award for Funniest Male Performer in a TV Special, 2000), Chris Rock: Never Scared, 2004 (Grammy award, Best Comedy Album, 2006), Everybody Hates Chris, 2005-; writer, prodr. Best of Chris Rock, 1999; (voice) Whatever Happened to Michael Ray?, 2000; TV appearances include Miami Vice, 1987, The Fresh Prince of Bel-Air, 1995, Martin, 1996, Homicide: Life on the Street, 1996, (voice) King of the Hill, 1998, Chappelle's Show, 2003; albums: Born Suspect, 1991, Roll with the New, 1997 (Grammy award for Best Spoken Comedy Album, 1997), Bigger & Blacker, 1999 (Grammy award for Best Spoken Comedy Album, 1999), Never Scared, 2004; Author Rock This!, 1998. Recipient Star, Hollywood Walk of Fame, 2003. *

ROCK, DOUGLAS LAWRENCE, manufacturing executive; b. Glen Cove, NY, Jan. 25, 1947; s. Herb and Beatrice (Vyse) R.; m. Cindy Pegoraro, May 11, 1967 (div. Apr. 1973); 1 child, Jason; m. Mary Sue Bell, Mar. 23, 1991 (div. Jan. 1996). BS in Psychology and Chemistry, Pa. State U., 1968; postgrad., U. Chgo., 1971-73. Rsch. chemist FMC Corp., Princeton, NJ, 1968-69; mfg. system project leader A.O. Smith Corp., Erie, Pa., 1969-71; dir. materials and info. systems Joy Mfg., Michigan City, Ind., 1971-74; dir. info. systems Smith Tool div. Smith Internat. Inc., Irvine, Calif., 1974-75, dir. materials, 1975-77, v.p. mfg., 1977-80, sr. v.p. ops., 1980-82, pres., 1985-87, Drilco div. Smith Internat. Inc., Houston, 1982-85; pres., chief exec. officer Smith Internat. Inc., Houston, 1987—, chmn. bd., 1991—. Bd. dirs. Viad Corp. Named Golden Knight, Nat. Mgmt. Assn., 1983. Mem. Internat. Assn. Drilling Contractors, Am. Petroleum Inst., Petroleum Equipment Suppliers Assn. (bd. dirs. Houston chpt. 1987—, 1st v.p. 1996), Nat. Offshore Industries Assn. (fin. com. 1988, audit com. 1989), Greenspoint Club. Avocations: golf, racquetball, reading. Office: Smith Internat PO Box 60068 16740 Hardy Rd Houston TX 77205 *

ROCK, EDWARD BARON, law educator; b. Phila., June 16, 1956; s. Eli and Florence (Baron) R.; m. Andrea White, Jan. 9, 1983; children: Aaron, Esther. BS cum laude, Yale U., 1977; BA first class honors, Oxford U., Eng., 1980; JD magna cum laude, U. Pa., 1983. Bar: Pa. 1983, U.S. Dist. Ct. (ea. dist.) Pa. 1983, U.S. Ct. Appeals (3rd cir.) 1988. Assoc. Fine, Kaplan & Black, Phila., 1983-87, ptnr., 1988; asst. prof. Univ. Pa. Law Sch., Phila., 1989—93, prof., 1993—2001, Saul A. Fox disting. prof., 2001—; co-dir. Inst. Law & Econ., Univ. Pa., 1998—. Vis. prof. Goethe Universität, Frankfurt am Main, Germany, 1994; vis. prof. & Fulbright scholar Hebrew Univ., Jerusalem, 1995—97; vis. prof. Columbia Univ. Law Sch., NYC, 2000. Contbr. articles to profl. jour.; co-author (with Reinier Kraakman, et. al.): The Anatomy of Corporate Law: A Comparative and Functional Approach, 2004. Home: 620 W Upsal St Philadelphia PA 19119-3626 Office: U Pa Law Sch 3400 Chestnut St Philadelphia PA 19104-6204 Office Phone: 215-898-8631. Business E-Mail: erock@law.upenn.edu. *

ROCK, HAROLD L., lawyer; b. Sioux City, Iowa, Mar. 13, 1932; s. Harold L. and Helen J. (Gormally) R.; m. Marilyn Beth Clark Rock, Dec. 28, 1954; children: Michael, Susan, John, Patrick, Michele, Thomas. BS, Creighton U., 1954, JD, 1959. Bar: Nebr., N.Y., Wyo. Law clk. to judge Woodrough U.S. Ct. Appeals 8th Circuit, Omaha, 1959-60; assoc. law clk. Fitzgerald Hamer Brown & Leahy, Omaha, 1960—65; of counsel Kutak Rock, Omaha, 1965—. Chmn. Nebr. Bd. Bar Examiners, 1989-96; bd. dirs. Mid City Bank, Omaha. Bd. dirs. Douglas County Hist. Soc., 1992-99, Nat. Equal Justice Libr., 1995—, Nebr. Nebr. Humanities Coun., 1996-2002. Served to 1st lt. U.S. Army, 1954-56. Recipient Alumni Achievement award Creighton U., 1995. Mem. ABA (ho. of dels. 1970-96, bd. govs. 1992-95), Nebr. Bar Assn. (ho. of dels., bd. dirs. 1985—, pres. 1988, Nebr. Bar found. bd. dirs., 1982-2003), Omaha Bar Assn. (pres. 1972-73), Omaha Legal Aid Soc. (pres. 1969-72), Nebr. State Bd. Pub. Accts. (bd. dirs. 1981-85). Roman Catholic. Office: Kutak Rock The Omaha Bldg 1650 Farnam St Omaha NE 68102-2186

ROCK, JOHN AUBREY, gynecologist, obstetrician, educator, administrator, retired chancellor; b. Corpus Christi, Tex., Oct. 21, 1946; s. William A. and Burta (Wheeler) R.; children: John Aubrey Jr., Deborah Ellen, Daniel Authur; m. Martha Miller. BS in Zoology, La. State U., Baton Rouge, 1968; MD, La. State U., New Orleans, 1972; MS in Healthcare Mgmt., Harvard U., 2003. From asst. prof. to prof. ob-gyn. Sch. Medicine Johns Hopkins U., Balt., 1978-80, prof. pediatrics Sch. Medicine, 1988-92, dir. reproductive endocrinology Sch. Medicine, 1979-91, dep. dir. Sch. Medicine, 1985-88; chmn. Union Meml. Hosp., Balt., 1991-92; James Robert McCord prof., chmn. dept. ob-gyn. Emory U. Sch. Medicine, Atlanta, 1992—2002; chancellor La. State U. Health Scis. Ctr., New Orleans, 2002—06, chancellor emeritus, prof. ob-gyn., pediat. and pub. health, 2002—07; sr. v.p. health affairs Fla. Internat. U., Miami, 2007—. Cons. Dept. Army, Washington, 1982-93, NASA, Houston, 1988—; chmn. ad hoc com. on in vitro fertilization State of Md., 1985. Author: Reparative and Constructive Surgery of the Female Generative Tract, 1983, Endometriosis, 1988, TeLinde's Operative Gynecology, 1991, 9th edit., 2003, Reproductive Endocrinology, Surgery and Technology, 1995; mem. editl. bd. Fertility and Sterility jour., 1986-94, Gynecology Surgery, 1989—. Fellow ACOG; mem. Am. Gynecol. and Obstet. Soc., Soc. Gynecol. Surgeons (pres. 1998-99), Am. Soc. for Reproductive Medicine (pres. 1996-97), Soc. Gynecologic Investigation, Soc. Reproductive Surgeons (pres. 1986), World Endometriosis Soc. (pres. 2000-02), Rotary, Phi Kappa Phi, Alpha Omega Alpha. Methodist. Office Phone: 305-348-0570. Business E-Mail: rockj@fiu.edu.

ROCK, MARY ANN, artist, educator; b. St. Louis, Mar. 2, 1931; d. Clobert Bernard and Mary Henrietta (Jones) Broussard; m. William Ralph Rock, Mar. 18, 1960 (div. Sept. 1967); 1 child, John Henry C. BS, Bennett Coll., 1952; postgrad., Chgo. Art Inst., 1953—54, So. Ill. U., Carbondale, 1955. Instr. arts and crafts Presidio Hill Sch., San Francisco, 1966; dir. gallery Cannery House Gallery, Friday Harbor, Wash., 1974—76; co-founder Island Artisans, Friday Harbor, 1980—85; gallery asst. Waterworks Gallery, Friday Harbor, 1986—95; with European study tour, 1996; patron sponsored painting sabbatical, 2001—03; prin., owner Dream Keeper Art Card Co., 2002—. Guest instr. Spring St. Sch., Friday Harbor, 2001, Friday Harbor, 02; presenter art workshops Friday Harbor Elem. Sch., 1976, 87, Portland CC, 1989, 90. Author, illustrator: DreamKeeper, 1995; brochures, one-woman shows include Trofeo Gallery, Seattle, 2006, exhibitions include 13th Saloon Internat. del Alpha, Lyon, France, Waterworks Gallery, Friday Harbor, 1986—, 7th Whatcomb County Mus., Bellingham, 1988, Portland CC, 1990, Chetwynn Stapleton Gallery, Portland, 1989—98, San Juan Art League, 2005, 06. Curator African art exhibit NAACP, San Francisco, 1961. Vt. Studio Ctr. fellow, Johnson, 1999. Democrat. Avocations: collecting ethnic artifacts, skiing, rock climbing, travel, reading.

ROCKABOVE, MAGDALENE M., special education educator; d. Walter M. Stewart Sr. and Meto M. Stewart; married; 3 children. AA, Mont. State U., 1996, BS in Elem. Edn., 1997, M in Spl. Edn., 2001; student, Mont. State U., Bozeman, 2006—. Clk. Indian Health Sci., Billings, Mont., 1999—2000, stats. asst., 2000—01; spl. edn. tchr. Lodge Grass (Mont.) H.S., 2001—05. Mentor Mont. Youth Leadership, Dillon, 2004—; mem. World Vision, 2000—. Recipient Partnerships for Diversity award, U. Mont., 2004—05. Mem.: Civil Rights Movement. Democrat. Avocations: jogging, reading, singing. Home: PO Box 176 Pryor MT 59066 Office: Lodge Grass High Sch PO Box 810 Lodge Grass MT 59050

ROCKBURNE, DOROTHEA GRACE, artist; b. Montreal; naturalized; Student, Black Mountain Coll.; PhD (hon.), Coll. of Creative Studies, Detroit, 2002. Milton and Sally Avery Disting. prof. Bard Coll., 1986. Trustee Ind. Curators Inc., N.Y., Art in Gen.; artist in residence Am. Acad. in Rome, 1991; vis. artist Skowhegan Sch. Painting and Sculpture, 1984; Rockefeller Found. resident Bellagio (Italy) Conf. and Study Ctr., 1997.

One-woman shows at Sonnabend Gallery, Paris, 1971, New Gallery, Cleve., 1972, Bykert Gallery, NYC, 1970, 72-73, Galleria Toselli, Milan, Italy, 1972-74, Galleria D'Arte, Bari, Italy, 1972, Lisson Gallery, London, 1973, Daniel Weinberg Gallery, San Francisco, 1973, Galerie Charles Kriwin, Brussels, 1975, Galleria Schema, Florence, Italy, 1973, 75, 92, John Weber Gallery, NYC, 1976, 78, Galleria la Polena, Geona, Italy, 1977, Tex. Gallery, Houston, 1979-81, Xavier Fourcade Gallery, NYC, 1981-83, 85-86, David Bellman, Toronto, 1980-81, Margo Leavin, Calif., 1982, Arts Club Chgo., 1987, André Emmerich Gallery, NYC, 1988-89, 91-92, 94-95, Rose Art Mus., 1989, P. Fong & Spratt Galleries, San Jose, Calif., 1991, Sony Music Hdqs., NYC, 1993, Frederick Spratt Gallery, San Jose, 1994, Guild Hall Mus., Easthampton, N.Y., 1995, Portland Mus. Art, Maine, 1996, Ingrid Raab Gall., Berlin, 1997, Art in Gen., NY, 1999, Greenberg, Van Doren, NYC, 2000, Dieu Donné Papermill, NYC, 2003, Jan Abrams Fine Art, NY, 2003; group exhbns. at Leo Castelli Gallery, NYC, 1966, Whitney Mus. Am. Art, 1970, 73, 77, 79, 82, 05, Mus. Modern Art, NYC, 71, 73, 81, 84, 86, 91, 93-94, 05, Buenos Aires, 1971, Kolner Kunst Market, Cologne, Germany, 1971, Stedelijk Mus., Holland, 1971, Spoleto (Italy) Festival, 1972, Palazzo Taverna, Rome, 1973, Nat. Gallery Victoria, Melbourne, Australia, 1973, Art Gallery NSW, Sydney, 1973, Auckland (New Zealand) City Art Gallery, 1973, Inst. Contemporary Art, London, 1974, Mus. d'Arte de la Ville, Paris, 1975, Galerie Aronowitsch, Stockholm, 1975, Stadtiches Mus., Manchengladbach, Germany, 1975, Galleria D'Arte Moderna, Bologna, Italy, 1975, Art Gallery Ont., Toronto, Can., 1975, Mus. Fine Art, Houston, 1975, Contemporary Arts Ctr., Cin., 1973, 75, 81, Mus. Contemporary Art, Chgo., 1971, 77, 86, Corcoran Gallery of Art, Washington, 1975, 87, Städtisches Mus., Leverkusen, Germany, 1975, Cannaviella Studio d'Arte Rome, 1976, Phila. Coll. Art, 1976, 83, New Mus., NYC, 1977, 80, 84, 83, Renaissance Soc. of U. Chgo., 1976, Lowe Art Mus., U. Miami, Fla., 1976, Inst. Contemporary Art, Boston, 1976, Seibu Mus. Art, Tokyo, 1976, NY State Mus., Albany, 1977, Drawing Ctr., 1977, Kansas City (Mo.) Art Inst., 1977, Smithsonian Inst., Washington, 1977, Kassel, Fed. Republic Germany, 1972, 77, Ackland Art Ctr., Chapel Hill, NC, 1979, 84, Milw. Art Ctr., 1978, 81, Biblioteca Nacional, Madrid, 1980, Gulbenkian Mus., Lisbon, Portugal, 1980, Bklyn. Mus., 1981, 89, Guggenheim Mus., 1982, 88-89, 2004, Albright Knox Art Gallery, Buffalo, 1979-80, 88-89, Kuustforeningen Mus., Copenhagen, 1980, Venice Biennale, 1980, Cranbrook (Mich.) Acad. Art, 1981, Mus. Fine Arts, Boston, 1983, Contemporary Arts Mus., Houston, 1983, Norman Mackenzie Art Gallery, U. Regina, Sask., Can., 1983, Galleriet, Sweden, 1983-84, Seattle Art Mus., 1979-84, Nat. Mus. Art., Osaka, Japan, 1984, Fogg Art Mus., Cambridge, Mass., 1984, Am. Acad. and Inst. Arts and Letters, NYC, 1984, 87, LA County Mus. Art, 1984, 86, Wadsworth Atheneum, Hartford, Conn., 1981, 84, Evehart Mus., Pa., 1984, Grey Art Gallery, NYU, 1977, 84, 87, Avery Ctr. Arts, Bard Coll., N.Y., 1985, 87-88, Stamford (Conn.) Mus., 1985, Aldrich Mus., Conn., 1979, 82, 95, Bronx Mus. Arts, N.Y.C., 1985, High Mus., Atlanta, 1975, 81, Phila. Mus. Art, 1986, Nat. Gallery Art, Washington, 1984, 94, 97, Mus. Art, Ft. Lauderdale, Fla., 1986, Nat. Mus. Women in Art, Washington, 1987, Xavier Fourcade Gallery, 1982, 83, 86-87, LA County Mus. Modern Art, 1986-87, The Hague, The Netherlands, 1986, Carnegie-Mellon Art Gallery, Pitts., 1979, 87, Balt. Mus. Art, 1975-76, 88, Ctr. for Fine Arts, Miami, 1989, Milw. Art Mus., 1989, Cin. Art Mus., 1989, New Orleans Mus., 1989, Denver Art Mus., 1989, Parrish Art Mus., South Hampton, NY, 1990-91, 99, Margo Leavin Gallery, LA, 1991, Guild Hall Mus., East Hampton, NY, 1991, Am. Acad., Rome, 1991, Mus. Contemporary Art, LA, 1991, 99, Hunter Coll., NY, 1991, CentroCultural/Arte Contemporanea, MexicoCity, 1991, Hilton, San Jose, Calif.,1992, Hillwood Art Mus., L.I., NY, 1992, Am. Acad. and Inst. Arts and Letters, 1992, Neuberger Mus., 1992, 00, Kohn-Abrams Gallerie, LA, 1993, Gallery at Bristol Myers Squibb, NJ, 1993-94, Friends of Art and Preservation in Embassies, NYC, 1993, Andre Emmerich Gallery, NYC, 1993, Fred Spratt Gallery, San Jose, Calif., 1994, Raab Galarie, Berlin, 1994, NY Studio Sch., NYC, 1995, 02, Rose Art Mus., Brandeis U., 1996, Addison Gallery Am. Art, Andover, Mass., 1997, 04, Fine Arts Mus. San Francisco, 1997, Wexner Ctr., Columbus, 1997, Dieu Donne Papermill, Inc., NYC, 1998, Pub. Sch. 1, Long Island City, NYC, 1999, Gemini G.E.L., 1998, Am. Acad. Arts and Letters, 1999, 01, Parsons Sch. Design, NYC, 1999, David Dorsky Gallery, NY, 2000, Greenberg Van Doren Fine Art, NYC, 2000, 02, 04, 05, 06, NAD, NYC, 2002, Armory Show, NYC, 2002, Nat. Gallery of Art, 2001, Krannert Art Mus., 2002, Selby Gallery, Fla., 2002, Geffen Contemporary, LA, 2002, Marcus Ritter, NYC, 2002, Bowdoin Coll. Mus. Art, 2002, Reina Sophia Mus., Madrid, 2003, Cleve. Mus. Art, 2003, New Britain (Conn.) Mus. Am. Art, 2003, Mus. New Zealand, 2003, Guggenheim Mus., NYC, 2004, ACA Galleries, NYC, 2004, Bruce Mus., Greenwich, Conn., 2004, MOCA at Calif. Plz., L.A., 2004, Boca Raton Mus. Art, 2005, Betty Cunningham Gallery, 2005, Spanierman Gallery, East Hampton, NY, 2005, Black Mtn. Coll. Mus., Asheville, NC, 2005, Mus. Modern Art, NYC, 2006, Nat. Acad. Design, NYC, 2006, Yellow Bird Gallery, Newburgh, NY, 2005, Pa. Acad. Fine Arts, Phila., 2006, Cleve. Mus. Art, 2006, Weatherspoon Mus., Greensboro, NC, 2006, Morgan Libr., 2006, others; print exhbns. at Nat. Gallery, Washington, 1994, 97, 2001, Kate Ganz, Ltd., NYC, 2000, David Adamson Gallery, Washington, 2000, Fine Arts Mus. San Francisco, 1997, Bklyn. Mus., 1989, Mt. Holyoke Coll. Art Mus., 1987, Harcus Gallery, Boston, 1985, Xavier Fourcade Gallery, NYC, 1982, Mus. Modern Art, NYC, 1981, 91, Yale U. Art Gallery, New Haven, 1981, New Gallery Contemporary Art, Cleve., 1978, Art Gallery Ont., Toronto, 1978, Stadtiches Mus., Monchengladbach, Germany, 1971, Mus. New Zealand Te Papa Tongarewa, Wellington, 2003, Ralls Collection, Washington, 2004, Addison Gallery Am. Art, Mass., 2004, Mus. Fine Arts, Boston, 2003, 04, 05; represented in permanent collections Milw. Art Ctr., Mus. Modern Art NYC, Fogg Mus., Cambridge, Mass., Phila. Mus. Art, High Mus. Art, Atlanta, Houston Mus. Fine Arts, Corcoran Gallery, Washington, Mpls. Art Inst., Mpls. Art Mus., Met. Mus. Art, NYC, Guggenheim Mus., NYC, Nat. Acad. Design, NYC, J. Paul Getty Trust, LA, Ludwig Mus., Aachen, Fed. Republic Germany, Holladay, Washington, Saatchi, London, Bard, Albright-Knox Art Gallery, Buffalo, Whitney Mus. Am. Art, NYC, U. Mich., Ann Arbor, Ohio State U., Columbus, Gilman Paper Co., NY, Auckland (New Zealand) City Art Mus., Portland (Oreg.) Art Mus., Aaken Art Mus., Oberlin, Ohio, Highhold Internat., South Africa, U. Ohio Art Gallery, Columbus, HHK Charitable Found., Milw., Art Gallery Ont., Nat. Mus. Women in Art, Washington, Chase Manhattan Bank, NYC; installations: Hilton Hotel, San Jose, Calif., Sony Music Hdqrs., Aldridge Mus., Conn., Edward T. Gignoux Courthouse, Portland, Maine. Recipient Witowsky prize, Art Inst., Chgo., 1976, Creative Arts award, Brandeis U., 1985, Bard Coll., 1986, Alliance for Young Artists and Writers Inc. award, 1997, Jimmy Ernst Lifetime Achievement award in art, Am. Acad. Arts and Letters, 1999, Pike award, Nat. Acad. of Art and Design, 2002, Adolph and Clara Obrig prize, Nat. Acad. Design, 2002, Pollock Krasner award, 2002, 2004, Omi Internat. Francis J. Greenberger award, 2003; fellow, Guggenheim fellow, 1972; grantee, Nat. Endowment Arts, 1974, Am. Acad. Rome, 1991. Mem.: AAAL. Personal E-mail: drockburne@gmail.com.

ROCKEFELLER, DAVID, banker; b. NYC., June 12, 1915; s. John Davison Jr. and Abby Greene (Aldrich) R.; m. Margaret McGrath, Sept. 7, 1940 (dec. Mar. 1996); children: David, Abby A., Neva, Margaret D., Richard G., Eileen M. BS, Harvard Coll., 1936; student, London Sch. Econs.; PhD, U. Chgo., 1940; LLD (hon.), Columbia U., 1954, Bowdoin Coll., 1958, Jewish Theol. Sem., 1958, Williams Coll., 1966, Wagner Coll., 1967, Harvard U., 1969, Pace Coll., 1970, St. John's U., 1971, Middlebury, 1974, U. Liberia, 1979, Rockefeller U., 1980, Am. U., 1987, U. Miami, 1988; DEng (hon.), Colo. Sch. Mines, 1974, U. Notre Dame, 1987. Sec. to Mayor Fiorello H. La Guardia, 1940-41; asst. regional dir. Office Def., Health and Welfare Services, 1941-42; asst. mgr. for. dept. Chase Nat. Bank, NYC, 1946-47, asst. cashier, 1947-48, 2d v.p., 1948-49, v.p., 1949-51, sr. v.p., 1951-55; exec. v.p. Chase Manhattan Bank (Chase Nat. Bank merged with Bank of Manhattan), 1955-57; vice chmn. bd. Chase Manhattan Bank, 1957-61, pres., chmn. exec. com., 1961-69, chmn., 1969-81, CEO, 1969-80. Chmn. Chase Internat. Adv. Com., 1981-99, Rockefeller Group, Inc., 1981-95, N.Y. Clearing House, 1971-78, Ctr. for Intern-Am. Rels., 1966-70, Overseas Devel. Coun., U.S.-USSR Trade and Econ. Coun. Inc.; chmn. Internat. Exec. Svc. Corps., 1964-68; chmn. Rockfeller Ctr. Properties Trust, Inc., 1996-2000 Author: Unused Resources and Economic Waste, 1940, Creative Management in Banking, 1964. Active Urban Devel. Corp., N.Y. State Bus. Adv. Coun., 1968-72, U.S. Adv. Com. on Reform on Internat. Monetary System, 1973-77, U.S. exec. com. Dartmouth Conf. Bd. Inst. Internat. Econs., Am. Friends of LSE, U.S. Hon. Fellows LSE, Bus. Com. for Arts; founding mem. Commn. on White House Fellows, hon. mem., 1964-65; exec. com., chmn. Downtown Lower Manhattan Assn., 1958-75; trustee Rockefeller U., 1940-95, Carnegie Endowment Internat. Peace, Hist. Hudson Valley, 1981-95; chmn. Rockefeller Bros. Fund, 1981-87, vice-chmn., 1968-80; hon. trustee Rockefeller Family Fund; life trustee U. Chgo.; trustee, chmn. emeritus, Mus. Modern Art, N.Y.C.; bd. overseers Harvard Coll., 1954-60, 62-68; co-founder Trilateral Commn., 1973-91, N.Am. chmn. 1981-92, hon. chmn., 1992; hon. chmn. Internat. House, 1940—, dir., 1940-63; pres. Morningside Heights, Inc., 1947-57, chmn., 1957-65; chmn. Am. Soc., 1981-92, hon. chmn., 1992—, N.Y.C. Partnership, 1979-88. Capt. AUS, 1942-45, NATOUSA, ETO. Decorated Legion of Honor France, Order of Arts and Letters; Order of the Liberator San Martin, Argentina, Order of Valor, Rep. of Cameroun, Order of Boyaca, Colombia, Order of Christopher Columbus, Domincan Republica, Nat. Order of Merit, Ecuador, Knight Comdr.'s Cross of the Order of Merit, Germany, Order of the Republic, Guinea, Gwengha Medal of the Rep. of Korea, Order of the Aztec Eagle, Mexico, Order of the Throne, Morocco, Hilal-i'Quaid-e-Azam, Pakistan, Order of Vasco Nunez de Balboa, Panama, Order of Manuel Amador Guerrero, Panama, Nat. Order of Merit/Grand Cross, Paraguay, Order of Merit, Italy, Order of Southern Cross, Brazil, Order of the White Elephant and Order of Crown, Thailand, Order of the Cedars, Lebanon, Order of the Sun, Peru, Nicholas Copernicus award, Porland, Order of Prince Henry the Navigator, Portugal, Nat. Order of the Lion, Rep. of Senegal, Order of Francisco de Miranda, Venezuela, Order of the Humane African Redemption, Liberia, Order of the Crown, Belgium, Nat. Order of Ivory Coast, Grand Cordon Order of Sacred Treasure, Japan, Order Bernardo O'Higgins, Chile, others; recipient Merit award N.Y. chpt. AIA, 1965, Gold medal Nat. Inst. Social Scis., 1967, AIA medal of Honor for City Planning N.Y.C., 1968, Charles Evans Hughes award NCCJ, 1974, World Brotherhood award Jewish Theol. Sem, 1953, C. Walter Nichols award NYU, 1970, Regional Planning Assn. award, 1971; Hadrian award, World Monuments Fund, 1994, U.S. Presdl. Medal of Freedom, 1998; named one of Top 200 Collectors, ARTnews Mag., 2004, Forbes' Richest Americans, 2006. Mem. Council Fgn. Relations (dir. 1949-51, v.p. 1951-70, chmn. 1970-85), Japan Soc. (hon. chmn.), Internat. House (hon. chmn.), Bilderberg Conf., Harvard Club, Univ. Club, Century Club, The Links, The Knickerbocker. Avocations: sailing, collecting 19th-century Am. art, impressionism and modern art, porcelain. Address: 30 Rockefeller Plz Rm 5600 New York NY 10112-0002

ROCKEFELLER, EDWIN SHAFFER, lawyer; b. Sept. 10, 1927; s. Edwin and Nancy Rhea (McCullough) R.; m. Marilie Gould Wallace, Dec. 22, 1952; children: Ben Wallace, Edwin Palmer. AB, Yale U., 1948, LLB, 1951; M in Internat. Pub. Policy, Johns Hopkins U., 1989. Bar: Conn. 1951, D.C. 1956, U.S. Supreme Ct. 1957. Atty. FTC, 1956—61, asst. to gen. counsel, 1958—59, exec. asst. to chmn., 1960—61; pvt. practice Washington, 1961; chmn. adv. bd. bna.antitrust rept., 1961—. Mem. USIA Inspection Team, Pakistan, 1971; adj. prof. Georgetown U. Law Ctr., Washington, 1987. Author: Antitrust Questions & Answers, 1974, Desk Book of FTC Practice & Procedure, 3d edit., 1979, Antitrust Counseling for the 1980s, 1983. Mem.: ABA (chmn. sect. antitrust law 1976—77, ho. of dels. 1979—82), Met. Club, Chevy Chase Club. Office: Ste 1024 2801 New Mexico Ave NW Washington DC 20007-3940

ROCKEFELLER, JOHN DAVISON, IV, (JAY ROCKEFELLER), senator, retired governor; b. NYC, June 18, 1937; s. John Davison III and Blanchette Ferry (Hooker) R.; m. Sharon Percy, Apr. 1, 1967; children: John, Valerie, Charles, Justin. Student, Japanese lang. Internat. Christian U., Tokyo, 1957-60; BA in Far Eastern Languages and History, Harvard U., 1961, MA, 1954—57; postgrad. in Chinese, Yale U., 1961-62. Apptd. mem. nat. adv. council Peace Corps, 1961, spl. asst. to dir. corps, 1962, ops. officer in charge work in Philippines, until 1963; desk officer for Indonesian affairs Bur. Far Eastern Affairs, U.S. State Dept., 1963; later asst. to asst. sec. state for Far Eastern affairs; cons. Pres.'s Commn. on Juvenile Delinquency and Youth Crime, 1964; field worker Action for Appalachian Youth program, from 1964; mem. W.Va. Ho. of Dels., 1966-68; sec. of state W.Va., 1968-72; pres. W.Va. Wesleyan Coll., Buckhannon, 1973-75; gov. State of W.Va., 1977—85; U.S. senator from W.Va., 1985—. Mem. com. commerce, sci. and transp. US Senate, com. fin., com. veterans affairs, joint com. taxation, vice chmn., select com. intelligence. Contbr. articles to mags. including N.Y. Times Sunday mag. Trustee U. Chgo., 1967—; chmn. White House Conf. Balanced Nat. Growth and Econ. Devel., 1978, Pres.'s Commn. on Coal, 1978-80, White House Adv. Com. on Coal., 1980 Named one of Top 200 Collectors, ARTnews Mag., 2004, 2005, 2006; recipient Excellence in Public Svc. award, Am. Acad. Pediatrics, 1990, Congressional Adv. of Yr. award, Child Welfare League of Am., 1997, Langer Chip award, Sci. Coalition, 1999, Award Excellence in Public Svc., Consortium Sch. Networking, 2002, Wellstone award, United Steelworkers of Am., 2003. Mem.: Nat. Gov. Assn. Democrat. Presbyn. Avocation: collecting 19th-century Am. art and Am. impressionism. Office: US Senate 531 Hart Senate Bldg Washington DC 20510-0001 also: District Office Ste 308 405 Capitol St Charleston WV 25301-1786 Office Phone: 202-224-6472, 304-347-5372. Office Fax: 202-224-7665, 202-228-4656, 304-347-5371. Business E-Mail: senator@rockefeller.senate.gov. *

ROCKEFELLER, SHARON PERCY, broadcast executive; b. Oakland, Calif., Dec. 10, 1944; d. Charles H. and Jeanne (Dickerson) Percy; m. John D. (Jay) Rockefeller IV; children: John, Valerie, Charles, Justin. BA cum laude, Stanford U.; LLD (hon.), U. Charleston, 1977, Beloit Coll., 1978; LHD (hon.), West Liberty State Coll., 1980, Hamilton Coll., 1982, Wheeling Coll., 1984. Founder, chmn. Mountain Artisans, 1968—78; teacher's asst., Head Start Head Start program, Coal Branch Heights, W.Va.; chmn. Corp. Pub. Broadcasting, Washington, 1981—84; bd. dirs. Stas. WETA-TV-FM, Washington, 1987—89, pres., CEO, 1989—. Bd. dirs. Pub. Broadcasting Svc., W.Va. Edn. Broadcasting Authority, PepsiCo, Smithsonian Instn., Nat. Gallery of Art, Nat. Cathedral, Stanford Univ., Chgo. Univ., George Washington Univ., Phillips Collection, Colonial Williamsburg Found.; trustees coun. Nat. Gallery of Art. Mem.-at-large Dem. Nat. Conv., del., 1976, 1980, 1984; trustee Fed. City Coun.; bd. dirs. Rockefeller Bros. Fund; former mem. bd. dir. Sunrise Mus., W.Va.; bd. mem. Sotheby's, NYC, Mus. Modern Art, NYC, Colonial Williamsburg Found; former chmn. Va. Assn. Pub. TV Stas. Named Washingtonian of Yr., Washingtonian Mag., 1994; named one of Top 200 Collectors, ARTnews Mag., 2004, 2005, 2006; recipient Charles Frankel Prize, Nat. Endowment for the Humanities, 1994, Distinguished Broadcaster Award, 1994, Woman of Vision Award, Women in Film & Video, CINE Lifetime Achievement Award. Fellow: Am. Acad. Arts & Sciences, Smithsonian Am. Art Commn. (bd. mem.); mem.: Stanford-in-Washigngton Coun. (former chmn.). Avocation: collecting 19th-century Am. art and Am. impressionism. Office: Sta WETA-FM 2775 S Quincy St Arlington VA 22206-2236

ROCKENSIES, JOHN WILLIAM, mechanical engineer; b. NYC, May 30, 1932; s. John William and Wilma (Mercz) R.; m. Marion Pauline Peachman, Sept. 16, 1956; children: Kenneth John, Karen Martha Rockensies Steinbeck. B of Mech. Engring., CCNY, 1954, M of Mech. Engring., 1960; postgrad., Bklyn. Poly. Inst., 1955, Columbia U., 1956. Registered profl. engr., NY. Jet engine performance and compressor devel. Curtiss Wright Corp., Woodridge, NJ, 1954—56; product devel. engr. Sperry Gyroscope Corp., Lake Success, NY, 1956—60; sr. exptl. test engr. Pratt & Whitney Corp., East Hartford, Conn., 1960—62; project engr. Stratos Corp., Bayshore, NY, 1962; prin. propulsion engr. Republic Aviation Corp., Farmingdale, NY, 1963—64; power plant design engr., group and project leader, project engr., engr. specialist and mgr. Grumman Aerospace Corp., Bethpage, NY, 1964—95; ret., 1995; contract staff engr. Northrop-Grumman Corp., Bethpage, 1996—98. Mem. SAE E-32 Engine Condition Monitoring com., 1983; lt. comdr. Smithtown Bay Power Squadron, instr. navigation. Author tech. papers in field; co-author chpt. in book. Deacon, trustee, elder First Presbyn Ch. Smithtown; docent Cradle of Aviation Mus., Garden City, NY, 2002-. Recipient Apollo Achievement award NASA, Washington, 1970. Assoc. fellow AIAA (mem. air breathing propulsion tech. com. 1996—, mem. coun. LI sect. 2002—, Chmn.'s award 2003, 06, instr. air breathing propulsion design course); mem. NSPE, ASME, US Power Squadrons (sr. navigator). Avocations: sailing, boating, jogging, camping, travel, model aircraft. Home: 65 Parnell Dr Smithtown NY 11787-2428 Personal E-mail: jrock8@optonline.net.

ROCKENSTEIN, WALTER HARRISON, II, lawyer; b. Pittsburgh, SC, Jan. 2, 1943; s. Walter Harrison and Martha Lee (Morris) R.; m. Jodell Lynn Steinke, July 29, 1972; children: Martha Liv, Andrew Harrison. BA cum laude, Coll. of Wooster, 1965; LLB, Yale U., 1968. Bar: Minn. 1968, U.S. Dist. Ct. Minn. 1968, U.S. Ct. Appeals (8th crct.) 1977. Spl. asst. atty. gen., chief antitrust divsn. Office of Minn. Atty. Gen., 1970-72; assoc. Head & Truhn, 1972-73; alderman 11th ward Mpls. City Coun., 1974-83; assoc. Faegre & Benson, Mpls., 1984-85, ptnr., 1986—. Mem. Capital Long-Range Improvements Com., 1974-82, Gov.'s Econ. Roundtable, 1980-82, Hennepin County Waste Disposal & Energy Recovery Adv. Com., 1976-77; chmn. devel. strategies com. League of Minn. Cities, 1979-80, bd. dirs., 1980-83; Mpls. del. Metro. Aircraft Sound Abatement Coun., 1977-90, chmn., 1982-90; mem. aviation subcom. of transp. tech. adv. com. Metro. Coun., 1977-83; mem. airport noise adv. bd. Minn. Pollution Control Agy., bd. dirs. noise com., 1982-85, mem. tech. adv. com., 1990; adv. com. Nat. League of Cities, steering com. Environmental Quality, 1975-79, vice chmn., 1976, chmn., 1978, steering com. Energy, Environment and Natural Resources, 1980-83, Energy Task Force, 1977-79, Nat. Urban Policy Com., 1978; mem. Noise Task Force, Nat. League of Cities/Nat. Assn. of Counties, 1977-80; regional dir. Nat. Org. to Insure a Sound-Controlled Environment, 1976-90, v.p. legal affairs, 1983-90; cons. group nuclear waste mgt., U.S. Dept. Energy, 1978. Elder Westminster Presbyn. Ch., 1975-80, 95-2001; trustee, 1982-87, chair stewardship com., 1989, chair pastor nominating com., 1992-94, co-chair bldg. centennial com.; bd. dirs. Loring Nicollet-Bethlehem Cmty. Ctrs., Inc., 1984—, pres., 1988-92; bd. dirs. U. Minn. Underground Space Ctr. Adv. Bd., 1985-95, chair, 1988-95; bd. dirs. Minn. Ctr. for Book Arts, 1988-93; com. mem. Cub Scout pact 196, Diamond Lake Luth Ch., 1988-91, com. chair, 1990-91; alumni trustee, alumni bd. dirs. The Coll. of Wooster, 1990-96; com. mem. Boy Scout Troop 187, 1994-97; bd. dirs. Minn. Safety Coun., 1997-2002, v.p., 2001-2002, chair, 2003-04, immediate past chair, 2005-06. Served to sgt. USMC, 1968—70. Recipient Cert. of Appreciation, Upper Midwest chpt. Acoustical Soc. Am., 1977, Resolution of Appreciation, City of Mpls., 1983, Citation of Honor, Hennepin County, 1983, Cert. of Recognition, League of Minn. Cities, 1983, Hope of Rotary award City of Lakes Rotary Club, 1989, WCCO Good Neighbor award, 1992; named Best Lawyers in Am., Land Use & Zoning, 2006-. Mem. Minn. State Bar Assn. (coun. mem. environ. and natural resources law sect. 1997-98, 2000-2001), Hennepin County Bar Assn., Delta Sigma Rho-Tau Kappa Alpha, Phi Sigma Alpha. Republican. Presbyterian. Avocations: reading, backpacking, cross country skiing, woodworking. Office: Faegre & Benson LLP 2200 Wells Fargo Ctr 90 S 7th St Minneapolis MN 55402-3901 E-mail: wrockenstein@faegre.com.

ROCKETT, D. JOE, lawyer, director; b. Drumright, Okla., May 3, 1942; s. Gordon Richard and Hazel Peggy (Rigsby) R.; m. Mary Montgomery, Aug. 31, 1963; children: David Montgomery, Ann Morley. BA, U. Okla., 1964, JD, 1967. Bar: Okla. 1967, U.S. Dist. Ct. (we. dist.) Okla. 1968. Assoc. Kerr, Davis, Irvine & Burbage, Oklahoma City, 1967-69, Andrews Davis Legg Bixler Milsten & Price, Oklahoma City, 1969—, mem., 1973—, also bd. dirs., pres., 1986-90, 96-00. Securities law advisor Oil Investment Inst., Washington, 1984-87. Bd. dirs. Myriad Gardens Found., Oklahoma City, 1987—, chmn., 1991-92. Mem. ABA (fed. regulation of securities and partnership coms. of bus. law sect. 1984), Okla. Bar Assn. (securities liaison com. 1983, chmn. bus. assocs. sect. 1985, securities adminstr.'s select com. 1986—). Avocations: sailing, fishing, skiing. Office: Andrews Davis 100 N Broadway Ste 3300 Oklahoma City OK 73102-8812 Business E-Mail: djrockett@andrewsdavis.com.

ROCKHILL, MARSHA, special education educator; AA, Gulf Coast CC, Panama City, Fla., 1976; BA in Music Edn. - Choral, Fla. State U., Tallahassee, 1978; M in Social Sci. Edn., Fla. State U., Panama City, 2002; student, Fla. State U., Tallahassee, 2003—. Cert. art tchr. Fla. Dept. Edn., Tallahassee, 2000. Spl. edn. tchr. Rosenwald Mid. Sch., Panama City, 1988; music/art tchr. St. Andrew Sch. Ctr. for Exceptional Students, Panama City, 1989—; music tchr., physically handicapped Margaret K. Lewis, Panama City, 1993—98. Founder, coord. Very Spl. Art Festival, Bay County, 1990—; charter mem. Fla. League Arts Tchrs., Tallahassee, 1999—; bd. mem. Svc. Learning Coun., Bay County, 2002—; artist in residency Fla. Dept. Very Spl. Arts, Tampa, 2004—; historian St. Andrew Waterfront Project, 1989—; oral history project coord. St. Andrew Sch., 2005—; presenter in field. Recipient Tchr. of Yr. award, St. Andrew Sch., Panama City, 1995, 2006, Golden Spike award, Bay Arts Alliance, Panama City, 2001; grantee scholarship, Bay Edn. Found., 2004, 2005, John David Jones ABCD scholarship, 2005. Mem.: Garnet and Gold Honor Soc., Pi Lambda Theta. Avocations: singing, writing plays. Office: St Andrew Sch 3001 W 15th St Panama City FL 32401

ROCKLAND, LAWRENCE HOWARD, psychiatrist, educator; b. NYC, Apr. 13, 1932; s. Milton and Bess Sherry Rockland; m. Charlotte Francis Roberts, June 29, 1957; children: Nancy, Thomas, Peter. BS, Union Coll., 1952; MD, Albany Med. Ctr., 1956. Diplomate Am. Bd. Psychiatry and Neurology. Rsch. psychiatrist NIMH, Bethesda, Md., 1959—61; pvt. practice Scarsdale, Larchmont, NY, 1961—; instr. psychiatry Georgetown Med. Coll., Washington, 1961—63; asst. prof. psychiatry Albert Einstein Coll. Medicine, NYC, 1967—76; assoc. prof. clin. psychiatry Cornell U. Med. Coll., NYC, 1982—99; assoc. prof. psychiatry emeritus Weill/Cornell Med. Coll., NYC, 1999—; assoc. prof. clin. psychiatry U. Mass. Med. Coll., Worcester, 1999—2002. Cons. Montgomery County Child Clinic, Rockville, Md., 1962—66, US Peace Corps, Washington, 1963—66, Carson Adult Family Clinic, Westfield, Mass., 1999—2002. Contbr. articles to profl. jours., chapters to books; author: Supportive Therapy, 1989, Supportive Therapy for Borderlines, 1992, La Terapia di Sostegno, 1994. Surgeon USPHS, 1959—2005. Fellow: Am. Psychoanalytic Assn. (exec. coun. 1976—79, 1985—2005), Am. Psychiat. Assn. (disting. life fellow); mem.: Group for Advancement Psychiatry, Sigma Xi, Phi Beta Kappa, Alpha Omega Alpha. Avocations: music, hiking, physical exercise, reading. Home and Office: 7 East Drive Larchmont NY 10538 Office Phone: 914-834-7601.

ROCKLEN, KATHY HELLENBRAND, lawyer; b. NYC, June 30, 1951; BA, Barnard Coll., NYC, 1973; JD magna cum laude, New England Sch. Law, 1977. Bar: NY 1978, US Dist. Ct. (so. and ea. dists.) NY 1982, US Dist. Ct. (no. dist.) Calif. 1985. Interpretive counsel NY Stock

Exchange, NYC; 1st v.p. E.F. Hutton & Co. Inc., NYC; v.p., gen. counsel, sec. S.G Warburg (USA) Inc., NYC; mem. Proskauer Rose LLP, NYC. Adj. prof. Fordham Sch. Law. Vice-chair, mem. exec. com. NY lawyers Pub. Interest; mem. exec. com. lawyers divsn. Am. Friends Hebrew U.; mem. lawyers' divsn. exec. com. ADL; mem. adv. bd. NY Women's Bar Found. Mem. NY State Bar Assn., NY Women's Bar Assn., Assn. Bar City NY (v.p., chmn. exec. com., chmn. drugs law com., chmn. fed. legis. com., chmn. libr. com., securities law com., sec. 2d century com., sex law com., young lawyers' com., corp. law com.). Office: Proskauer Rose LLP 1585 Broadway New York NY 10036 Office Phone: 212-969-3755. E-mail: krocklen@proskauer.com.

ROCKMORE, DANIEL NAHUM, mathematician; b. Boston, Dec. 5, 1961; s. Ronald Marshall and Miriam (Miller) R. AB in Math. cum laude, Princeton U., 1984; MA in Math., Harvard U., 1986, PhD in Math., 1989. Rsch. scientist Thinking Machines Corp., 1986; asst. prof. math. Columbia U., NYC, 1989—91; asst. prof., dept. math and computer sci. Dartmouth Coll., Hanover, NH, 1991—96, assoc. prof., dept. math and computer sci., 1996—2000, prof., dept. math., 1999—, vice chmn., dept. math., 1999—, also mem. faculty, Ctr. for Cognitive Neuroscience. Vis. scientist IBM, 1989, mem. Inst. for Advanced Study, 1995-96, 2002; external faculty, Santa Fe Inst., 2000-; bd. mem., Defense Sci. Study Group, Inst. Defense Analyses, 2000-2002; sci. adv. bd., Poindexter Sys.; adv. bd. InSite One; co-dir. fMRI Data Ctr., Dartmouth Coll., 1999-; sr. search chair, dept. math., 2003, search chair, dept. math., 2004, 2005; search chair, Bioinformatics, 2004; vis. positions: dept. math., Harvard U., 1992, dept. computer sci., U. Chgo., 1992, 1993, Nat. Ctr. for Atmospheric Rsch., 1997, 1998, 1999, NYU Courant Inst., 2000, 2001-02; spkr. in field. Author: Stalking the Reimann Hypothesis, 2005; editl. bd. mem. SIAM Review; editor: Spl. Issue on Computer Algebra and Signal Processing, Journal of Symbolic Computation; contbr. articles to profl. journs., documentaries. Fellow Fulbright, 1984, NSF, 1985-87, 1991-93, 1995-2000, IBM, 1988, Phi Beta Kappa; named Sigma XI, Disting. Lectr., 2005-07 Mem. Am. Math. Soc. Office: Math Dept Dartmouth Coll Hanover NH 03755 Home Phone: 603-643-0169; Office Phone: 603-646-3260. Office Fax: 603-646-1672. Business E-Mail: rockmore@cs.dartmouth.edu.

ROCKOFF, HUGH TOUFF, economist, educator; b. Dayton, Ohio, Feb. 8, 1945; s. Joseph Rockoff and Mildred Touff; m. Hope Corman; children: Jessica, Steven. BA, Earlham Coll., 1967; PhD, U. of Chgo., 1971. Prof. of economics Rutgers U., New Brunswick, NJ, 1971—. Author: The Free Banking Era, 1975, Drastic Measures: A History of Wage and Price Controls, 1984, History of the American Economy, 2002. Mem.: Econ. History Assn. (v.p. 2002—03). Office: Rutgers University 75 Hamilton Street New Brunswick NJ 08901 Office Phone: 732-932-7857.

ROCKOFF, MARK ALAN, pediatric anesthesiologist; b. Jersey City, Apr. 13, 1948; s. Aaron and Rose Rockoff; m. Elizabeth Sceery, Aug. 6, 1978; children: Benjamin, Jillian, Michael. BS, MIT, 1969; MD, Johns Hopkins U., 1973. Diplomate Am. Bd. Pediatrics, Am. Bd. Anesthesiology. Pediatric intern and resident Mass. Gen. Hosp., Boston, 1973-75, anesthesia resident, 1975-77, assoc. dir. pediatric ICU, 1979-81; neuroanesthesia fellow U. Calif., San Diego, 1978-79; assoc. dir. ICU Children's Hosp., Boston, 1981-89, assoc. anesthesiologist-in-chief, 1988—; med. dir. operating rm., 1992-99; prof. anaesthesia Harvard Med. Sch., Boston, 1999—. Editor jours. Survey of Anesthesiology, 1984-94, Jour. Neurosurg. Anesthesiology, 1994-98. Fellow: Soc. Critical Care Medicine, Am. Acad. Pediats., Am. Soc. Anesthesiologists; mem.: Soc. Pediat. Anesthesia (pres. 1996—98), Am. Bd. Anesthesiology (dir. 2000—). Office: Children's Hosp 300 Longwood Ave Boston MA 02115-5737

ROCKOFF, S. DAVID, radiologist, physician, educator; b. Utica, NY, July 21, 1931; s. Samuel and Sarah (Rattinger) R.; m. Jacqueline Garsh; children— Lisa E., Todd E., Kevin D. AB, Syracuse U., 1951; MD, Albany Med. Coll., 1955; M.Sc. in Medicine, U. Pa., 1961. Diplomate: Am. Bd. Radiology. Intern U.S. Naval Hosp., Bethesda, Md., 1955-56; resident and fellow in radiology, USPHS trainee dept. radiology p. of U. Pa., Phila., 1958-61; staff radiologist NIH, Bethesda, Md., 1961-65; asst. prof. radiology Yale U. Sch. Medicine, New Haven, 1965-68, assoc. prof., 1968; asst. attending radiologist Yale-New Haven Med. Center, 1965-68; assoc. prof. radiology Washington U. Sch. Medicine, St. Louis, 1968-71; asst. radiologist Barnes and Allied Hosps., St. Louis, 1969-71; cons. radiologist VA Hosp., St. Louis, 1969-71, Homer G. Phillips Hosp., St. Louis, 1968-71; prof. radiology George Washington U. Sch. Medicine, Washington, 1971—, chmn. dept. radiology, 1971-77, head pulmonary radiology, 1978—, interim chmn. dept. radiology, 1989-90, prof. emeritus radiology, 1993—. Cons. NIH, 1972—; vis. prof. Hadassah U., Beersheba U., Rambam Hosp., Israel, 1977; cons. in radiology VA Hosp., Washington, 1972-77, U.S. Naval Med. Center, Bethesda, 1973-77; mem. diagnostic radiology adv. com. NIH, 1973-76; mem. Cancer Research Manpower Rev. Com., NIH, 1978 Editor-in-chief: Investigative Radiology, 1965-76; editor-in-chief emeritus, 1976—; editor Jour. Thoracic Imaging, 1985; reviewer Jour. Computed Tomography, 1997—; contbr. articles to profl. jours. Served with USN, 1955-58; Served with USPHS, 1961-63. Recipient numerous USPHS grants. Fellow Am. Coll. Radiology (pres.-elect DC chpt. 1976), Am. Coll. Chest Physicians; mem. Am. Fedn. Clin. Rsch., DC Med. Soc. (med.-legal com. 1975-78), AMA, Radiol. Soc. N.Am. (roster of disting. sci. advisors Rsch. and Edn. Found. 1999), Assn. Univ. Radiologists, Soc. Thoracic Radiology (pres. 1983-84, exec. dir. 1984-87, Gold medal 2007). Home: PO Box 675650 Rancho Santa Fe CA 92067-5650 E-mail: drockoff@cox.net.

ROCKWELL, ELIZABETH DENNIS, retirement specialist, financial planner; b. Houston, Tex., 1921; d. Robert Richard and Nezzell Alderton (Christie) Dennis. Student, Rice U., 1939—40, U. Houston, 1938—39, student, 1940—42, D (hon.), 1999. Purchasing agt. Standard Oil Co., Houston, 1942—66; v.p. mktg. Heights Savs. Assn., Houston, 1967—82; exec. dir. investments CIBC Oppenheimer Corp., Houston, 1982—2001; exec. prof. U. Houston Coll. Bus., 1992—. Contbr.: articles on retirement planning, tax planning and tax options, monthly article 50 Plus sect. for Houston Chronicle newspaper. V.p. Desk and Derrick Club Am., 1960—61; bd. dirs. ARC, 1985—91, Houston Heights Assn., 1973—77; sr. v.p. Oppenheimer, 1986—; mem. found. bd. Coll. Bus. U., Houston, 1990, mem. million dollar roundtable, 1991—, mem. ct. of the table, 1991—, Top of Table, 1996—; mem. U. Houston Sys. Planned Giving Coun., U. Houston Found., 2000—; mem. coll. bus. adv. bd. U. Houston Coll. Bus., 1992—, mem. alumni bd., 1987—95; apptd. trustee U. Houston Sys. Found., Inc.l, 1992; bd. govs. Houston Forum; active Tex. Leader's Round Table, 1994; pres. U. Houston Coll. Bus. Adminstrn. Found., 1986—2000; mem. Houston C.C. Adv. Bd. for Edn. TV. Named Disting. Alumnae, Coll. Bus. Alum. Assn., U. Houston, 1992, YWCA Outstanding Woman of Yr., 1978; recipient Disting. Alumna, U. Houston Alumni Orgn., 1996, award, Freemons Found., 2004, Jesse H. Jones award for philanthropy, ARC, 2004, Roger Eichhorn Leadership Svc. award, U. Houston Coll. Engring., 2004. Mem.: Houston Heights Assn. (charter, dir. 1973—77), U.S. Savs. and Loan League (com. on deposit acquisitions and adminstrn.), Soc. Savs. Instns., Fin. Mgrs., Inst. Fin. Edn., Savs. Inst. Mktg. Soc. Am. (Key Person award 1974), Am. Savs. and Loan League (chpt. pres. 1971—72, pres. 1972—73, state dir. 1973—76, Leaders award 1972), Greater Houston Women's Found. (charter), U. Houston Alumni Orgn. (life), U. Houston Bus. Women's Assn. (pres. 1985), Rice U. Bus. and Profl. Women, Harris County Heritage Soc., Friends of Bayou Bend, Forum Club, River Oaks Bus. Women's Exch. Club.

ROCKWELL, ELIZABETH GOODE, dance company director, consultant, educator; b. Portland, Oreg., Sept. 10, 1920; d. Henry Walton and Elizabeth (Harmon) Goode; m. William Hearne Rockwell, Feb. 3, 1948; children: Enid, Karen, William. BA, Mills Coll., 1941; MA, NYU, 1946. Instr. dance Monticello Jr. Coll., Alton, Ill., 1941-42; dir. masters program in dance Smith Coll., Northampton, Mass., 1946-48; 1st dir. dance dept. High Sch. of Performing Arts, NYC, 1948-51, 53-54; dir. Elizabeth Rockwell Sch. Dance, Bedford, N.Y., 1956-86, Rondo Dance Theater Internat. Dance Touring Co., Bedford, 1971-93; tchr. continuing dance classes CCAE, 1994—; with Martha Graham, 1944-46; with Hanya Holm, 1946-48; with José Limon, 1949-52. Mem. adv. ednl. com. Calif. Ctr. for Arts, Escondido, Calif., 1993-95, dir. dance classes, 1994—; tchr. master class, choreographer Waitukubuli Dance Theater, Dominica, 1999; dir. prime dance performance Artists Coming of Age, U. San Diego, 1999. Choreographer (suite of dances) Jazz Suite, 1966, (50-minute dances) Catch the Wind, 1969, Genesis, 1972, (narrative modern ballet) The Executioner, 1974, Decathalon, 1982; dir. (subscription series) Dance-Art-Poetry-Jazz, 1978-79, (dance/music 1600-1900) Stages in Ages, 1981, (Am. dance revivals) Masterpieces of American Dance, 1982-84, Dances of the Decades, 1985-90, (revival & new choreography) Dances of Our Times, 1991; dir. dance workshops for Calif. Ctr. Arts, 1994, 95, 96; creator, founder performing group of older dancers Golden Connections Dance Ensemble of Women, CCAE, (touring San Diego area), 1996—. Bd. dirs. Coun. for Arts in Westchester, White Plains, N.Y., 1978-79, affiliate, 1978— Recipient Medal for Performance, Israeli Army, 1966, Award for Excellence in Arts Edn. Alumnae of High Sch. of Performing Arts, 1990, Tommy Dance award of distinction San Diego Area Dance Alliance, 1999; various grants N.Y. State Coun. on Arts, 1971-93, Coun. Arts in Westchester, 1973-92, dance touring program grant Nat. Endowment for Arts, 1975-79. Mem. Am. Dance Guild, Westchester Dance Coun. (program dir. 1965-69), Assn. Am. Dance Cos., San Diego Area Dance Alliance (bd. dirs. 1995—). Avocations: writing, swimming, touring, reading. Home: 205 Tampico Gln Escondido CA 92025-7359

ROCKWELL, JOHN SARGENT, dance critic, writer, former arts administrator; b. Washington, Sept. 16, 1940; s. Alvin John and Anna Sargent (Hayward) Rockwell; m. LInda Mevorach; 1 child, Sasha Eve. BA, Harvard U., 1962; postgrad., U. Munich, 1962-63; MA, U. Calif., Berkeley, 1964, PhD, 1972. Music and dance critic Oakland Tribune, Calif., 1969; asst. music and dance critic LA Times, 1970-72; freelance music critic NY Times, 1972-74, staff music critic, 1974-91, European cultural corr. and prin. classical recordings critic Paris, 1992-94, editor Arts & Leisure sect., 1998—2002, sr. cultural corr., 2002—05, chief dance critic, 2005—; dir., Lincoln Ctr. Festival Lincoln Ctr. Festival, NYC, 1994—98. Lectr. in field. Author: All American Music: Composition in the Late 20th Century, 1983, Sinatra: An American Classic, 1984, The Idiots, 2003, Outsider: John Rockwell on the Arts 1967-2006, 2006. Harvard-German Govt. fellow, 1962—63, Woodrow Wilson fellow, 1963—64. Mem.: Dance Critics Assn., Century Assn., Music Critics Assn., Phi Beta Kappa. Office: NY Times Dance Critic 229 W 43rd St New York NY 10036 Office Phone: 212-556-1418. Office Fax: 212-334-5073. Business E-Mail: rockwell@nytimes.com.

ROCKWELL, THEODORE, nuclear engineer; b. Chgo., June 26, 1922; s. Theodore G. and Paisley (Shane) R.; m. Mary Juanita Compton, Jan. 25, 1947; children: Robert C. (dec.), W. Teed, Lawrence E., Juanita C. BS in Engring, Princeton U., 1943, Chem.E. (MS), 1945; grad. courses, Oak Ridge, 1944-49; D.Sc. (hon.), Tri-State U., 1960. Registered profl. engr., D.C. 1964-1990. Process improvement engr. Manhattan Project, Oak Ridge, 1944-45; head shield engring. group Oak Ridge Nat. Lab., 1945-49; nuclear engr., naval reactors br. AEC, also nuclear propulsion divs. Navy Bur. Ships, 1949-55, tech. dir., 1955-64; founding officer, dir. MPR Assos., Inc., Washington, 1964—; rsch. assoc. Johns Hopkins U. Sch. Advanced Internat. Studies, 1965—66. Chmn. Atomic Indsl. Forum Reactor Safety Task Force, 1966-72; mem. adv. group artificial heart program NIH, 1966; cons. to Joint Congl. Com. on Atomic Energy, 1967; founding officer, dir. Radiation, Sci. and Health, Inc., 1996—; Disting. lectr. World Nuc. U., 2006. Author: The Rickover Effect: How One Man Made a Difference, 1992, Creating the New World, 2003 (First Place award non-fiction JADA Pub. Ann. Book Competition, 2005, Ind. Publishers award, 2005); coauthor: Shippingport Pressurized Water Reactor, 1958, Arms Control Agreements/Designs Verification, 1968; co-founder Princeton Engr.; editor: Reactor Shield Design Manual, 1956; contbg. editor: New Realities, 1988—92; contbr. sci. articles to profl. publs., non-tech. articles to nat. mags. Mem. adv. council dept. chem. engring. Princeton U., 1966-72. Recipient Disting. Civilian Svc. medal USN, 1960, Disting. Svc. medal AEC, 1960, Lifetime Contbn. award Am. Nuclear Soc. (1st, now known as Rockwell award), 1986, Edward Teller award Drs. for Disaster Preparedness, 2006. Fellow Am. Nuclear Soc., Am. Soc. Psychical Rsch. (life); mem. AAAS (rep. of Parapsychol. Assn. to AAAS 1975-87), N.Y. Acad. Scis., Soc. for Sci. Exploration, U.S. Psychotronic Assn. (dir. 1988-91), Nat. Inst. for Discovery Sci. (sci. adv. bd. 1995—), Nat. Acad. Engring. (Sigma Xi disting. lectr. 2003—), Authors Guild, Writers Ctr., Washington Ind. Writers, Philos. Soc. Washington (life), Cosmos Club (Washington), Nat. Press Club. Presbyterian (elder). Achievements include patent applications for neutron-absorbing cermets and plastics; patents in field. Address: 3403 Woolsey Dr Chevy Chase MD 20815-3924 Home Phone: 301-652-9509. E-mail: tedrock@starpower.net.

ROCKWELL, WINTHROP ADAMS, lawyer; b. Pittsfield, Mass., May 7, 1948; s. Landon Gale Rockwell and Ruth (Adams) Lonsdale; m. Barbara Washburn Wood, June 20, 1970; children: Samuel Adams, Madeleine McCord. AB, Dartmouth Coll., 1970; JD, NYU, 1975. Bar: Minn. 1975, U.S. Dist. Ct. Minn. 1975. Asst. newsman fgn. desk N.Y. Times, NYC, 1970-71; asst. to pres. Dartmouth Coll., Hanover, NH, 1971-72; assoc. Faegre & Benson, Mpls., 1975-79; assoc. chief counsel Pres.'s Commn. on Accident at Three Mile Island, Washington, 1979; assoc. Faegre & Benson, Mpls., 1979-82, ptnr., 1983—. Chmn. diversity com. Faegre & Benson, 1990—95, head gen. litig. group, 1995—2004, mem. mgmt. com., 2004—, head internat. ops., 2004—. Bd. dirs., v.p. Children's Theatre, Mpls., 1982-83; bd. dirs. Actors Theatre St. Paul, 1975-79, Trinity Films, Mpls., 1978-82, Minn. Ctr. for Book Arts, 1996-2003; adv. bd. U. Minn. Joint Degree Program in Law, Health and the Life Scis. Brit.-Am. Project fellow, 1987. Mem. ABA, Minn. Bar Assn., Hennepin County Bar Assn., Am. Agrl. Law Assn., Adirondack 46ers, Adirondack Mountain Club. Avocations: writing, tennis, mountain climbing, gardening. Home: 1901 Knox Ave S Minneapolis MN 55403-2840 Office: Faegre & Benson 2200 Wells Fargo Ctr 90 S 7th St Ste 2200 Minneapolis MN 55402-3901 Office Phone: 612-766-6901. E-mail: wrockwell@faegre.com.

ROCKWOOD, FREDERICK WHITNEY, insurance company executive; b. Salt Lake City, Dec. 18, 1947; s. Lewis Frederick and Muriel (Whitney) R.; m. Alyce Jolene Edmunds, Aug. 26, 1970; children: Justin, Melissa, Jennifer, Katherine, Elizabeth, David. Student, U. Utah, 1966-67, Columbia U., NYC, 1970; AB in Anthropology, Stanford U., 1972; JD, Harvard U., 1975. Bar: Mass. Corp. strategy cons. Boston Cons., 1975-77; corp. strategy cons. Bain & Co., Boston, 1977; dir. corp. strategy Hillenbrand Industries, Inc., Batesville, Ind., 1977-78, sr. v.p., 1978-85; pres. The Forethought Group, Batesville, 1985—. Mem. adj. faculty U. Mich. Grad. Sch. Bus., 1980; pres., bd. dirs. Rockwood Furniture, Inc., Salt Lake City, 1985—; chmn. curriculum adv. coun. Ind. State Bd. Edn., 1987-92. Rep. Ch. of Jesus Christ of Latter-day Saints, Hong Kong, 1967-69; unit scouting coord. Dan Beard coun. Boy Scouts Am., Cin., 1982-91; bishop Ch. of Jesus Christ, Batesville, 1986-90. Mem. ABA, Fellow Life Mgmt. Inst. (chartered life underwriter 1990, chartered fin. cons. 1992), Am. Mgmt. Assn., Phi Beta Kappa. Republican. Avocations: philatey, genealogy.

ROCKWOOD, LINDA LEE, lawyer; b. Cedar Rapids, Iowa, July 25, 1950; BA, U. Denver, 1972; JD, U. Tex., 1984. Bar: Colo. 1984, U.S. Dist. Ct. Colo., U.S. Ct. Appeals (10th cir.). Assoc. Holland & Hart, Denver, 1984-88; shareholder, dir. Parcel, Mauro & Spaanstra, Denver, 1988-98, pres., 1996-98; ptnr. Faegre & Benson, Denver, 1998—, exec. ptnr., 2001—. Author: New Mines From Old Environmental Considerations in Remining and Reprocessing of Waste Materials, 1991, The Alcan Decisions: Causation Through the Back Door, 1993, RCRA Demystified: The Professional's Guide to Hazardous Waste Law, 1996, Citizen Suits: Public Interest or Private Advocacy, 2000, Institutional Controls: Brownfields Superweapon or Ultimate Trojan Horse?, 2000, Orange Alert: Developing Responsibilities of Natural Resource Companies for Chemical Security in an Unsafe World, 2005. Bd. dirs. Colo. Hazardous Waste Mgmt. Soc., 1986, 89-91, pres., 1987-88; mem. Mayor's Conv. Ctr. Task Force, 1997-99, Ctrl. Platte Valley Devel. Coun., 1999-03, Downtown Devel. Coun., 2003—, adv. com. Justice Ctr., 2006-. Mem. Colo. Bar Assn. (exec. coun. environ. law sect. 1987-90), Environ. Law Inst., Rocky Mountain Mineral Law Found., Women's Vision Found., Order of Coif, Phi Beta Kappa. Office: Faegre & Benson LLP 3200 Wells Fargo Ctr 1700 Lincoln St Denver CO 80203 Office Phone: 303-607-3500. Business E-Mail: lrockwood@faegre.com.

ROCQUE, VINCENT JOSEPH, lawyer; b. Franklin, NH, Nov. 27, 1945; s. Francis Albert and Mary Helen (O'Grady) R.; m. Emily Adams Arnold, May 31, 1969; children: Amanda Adams, Peter O'Connor, Caroline Quin. BA magna cum laude, Georgetown U., 1967; JD, Columbia U., NYC, 1970. Bar: D.C. 1971, U.S. Supreme Ct., 1973. Assoc. Hogan & Hartson, Washington, 1970-73; counsel, spl. asst. to Commr. Barbara Franklin, U. S. Consumer Product Safety Commn., Washington, 1973-77; asst. dir. bur. trade regulation U.S. Dept. Commerce, Washington, 1977-80; ptnr. Sullivan & Worcester, Washington, 1980-90; pvt. practice law Washington, 1990—. V.p., co-pres. Janney Pub. Elem. Sch. PTA, Washington, 1982-84; vol. coord. homeless shelters Cath. Charities, Washington and Silver Spring, Md., 1984-90. Staff sgt. USAR, 1969-75. Mem. ABA (adminstrv. law and regulatory practice sect. and internat. law and practice sect.), D.C. Bar (internat. law sect. and adminstrv. law and agy. sect.), Mid-Atlantic Literary Edification Soc., Nat. Capital YMCA, Phi Beta Kappa. Catholic. Avocations: reading, travel, American Civil War history. Office: Ste 1000 1155 Connecticut Ave NW Washington DC 20036-4306 Office Phone: 202-429-6659. Personal E-mail: vinrocque@aol.com.

RODALE, ARDATH HARTER, publishing executive; 5 children. B in Art Edn., Kutztown U., LLD (hon.), 1995; LHD (hon.), DeSales U., 1994, Lehigh U., 1994; HHD (hon.), New Coll. of Calif., San Francisco, 2006. Chmn. Prevention Mag., Rodale Press, Inc., 1990—2007; owner, CEO Rodale Press Inc., Emmaus, Pa., 1990—2002, chief inspiration officer, 2007—. Chmn. emeritus on the bd. Rodale Inst. Author: Climbing Toward the Light, 1989, Gifts of the Spirit, 1997, Reflections: Finding, Love, Hope and Joy in Everyday Life, 2002. Mem. internat. adv. com. Harvard AIDS Inst. Named a Disting. Daughter of Pa., Gov. Tom Ridge, 1997; named one of 50 Best Women in Bus. in Pa., Ctrl. Pa. Bus. Jour., 1996, Top 50 Women Bus. Owners in the US, Working Woman mag., 1997, 50 Leading Women Entrepreneurs in the World, Star Group, 1999; recipient Outstanding Alumni award, Kutztown U., 1990, Human Rels. award, Allentown Human Rels. Commn., 1995, Extraordinary Voices award, Mothers' Voices, 1996, Woman of Distinction award, Great Valley Girl Scout Coun., 1998, Friend of Lehigh award, Lehigh U., 2002, Lifetime Cmty. Achievement award, Boys & Girls Club of Allentown, 2002, Shining Star award, St. Luke's Hosp., Allentown, 2003, Life & Breath award, Am. Lung Assn., 2003, Exceptional Woman award, Women in Periodical Pub., 2004, LifePath's Cmty. Svc. award, Pa. Inst. of CPA's, 2004, Cir. of Excellence - Enlightened Media award, Internat. Furnishings & Design Assn., 2005, Lehigh Valley Coalition for Alt. Transp. award, 2006. Office: Rodale Press Inc 33 E Minor St Emmaus PA 18098-0099 *

RODALE, MARIA, publishing executive; b. 1962; d. Ardath and Robert Rodale; 1 child, Maya. BA in Art & Comm., Muhlenberg Coll., 1985. With Rodale Inc., Emmaus, Pa., 1987—96, 1998—, dir. strategy, 1998, dir. Organic Living divsn., vice-chmn., 2001—07, chmn., 2007—. Editor: Organic Gardening, 1999—2001, Organic Style, 2001—05; author: Maria Rodale's Organic Gardening, 1998, Maria Rodale's Organic Gardening Companion, 1999, Betty's Book of Laundry Secrets, 2001; co-author: It's My Pleasure, 2005. Bd. mem. NY Restoration Project. Co-recipient Exceptional Women in Pub. award, Women in Periodical Pub., 2004; recipient Rachel Carson award, Nat. Audubon Soc., 2004, Spl. Citizen award, Arts for Healing & Children's Health Environ. Coalition, 2005. Office: Rodale Inc 33 E Minor St Emmaus PA 18098-0099 Office Phone: 610-967-5171. Office Fax: 610-967-8963. *

RODAY, LEON E., lawyer, finance company executive; BA, U. Calif., Santa Barbara; JD, Brooklyn Law Sch. Assoc. LeBoeuf, Lamb, Greene & MacRae, LLP, 1982—91, ptnr., 1991—96; sr. v.p., gen. counsel, sec. GE Financial, 1996—2004, Genworth Financial, Inc., Richmond, Va., 2004—. Chmn. Ins. Marketplace Standards Assn., 2005. Mem.: NY Bar Assn. Office: Genworth Financial, Inc 6620 W Broad St Richmond VA 23230 Office Fax: 804-281-6000. *

RODBELL, CLYDE ARMAND, retired distribution executive; b. Atlanta, Aug. 16, 1927; s. Joseph Hirsch and Fannie (Turetzky) R.; m. Cecile Rosenson, Mar. 27, 1949 (div.); children: Marsha, Jeffrey, Keith, Kim; m. Robin Graham McKenzie Rodbell, Dec. 15, 1974; 1 child, Lindsey. BBA, Emory U., 1949. Chmn. Apex Supply Co. Inc., Atlanta, 1949—2002. Co-chmn. George Bush Presdl. Fund Raising, Ga., 1988-89; mem. State of Ga. Electoral Coll., 1989, exec. commr. Am. Bicentenial Pres. Inaugural Bus. Adv., 1989, Pres' Commn. on White House Fellowships, 1989-92. With U.S. Army, 1945. Mem. Wholesale Assn. Ga., Southern Wholesalers Assn., Am. Supply Assn., Standard Club, Rotary Club. Republican. Jewish. Avocations: reading, gardening, antiques, politics. Personal E-mail: rrodbell@aol.com.

RODDICK, ANDY STEPHEN, professional tennis player; b. Omaha, Aug. 30, 1982; s. Jerry and Blanche Roddick. Profl. tennis player ATP, 2000—; winner jr. Grand Slam titles Australian Open and US Open, 2000; quarter-finalist Roland Garros, 2000; singles titles, Atlanta, Houston, Washington US Clay Court Championships, 2001, singles titles, Memphis, Houston, 2002; runner up US Open, 2002, winner Grand Slam title, 2003; quarterfinalist Indian Wells TMS, 2003; semifinalist Paris TMS, Basel, Tennis Masters Cup, Wimbledon, Australian Open, Washington, 2003; finalist Houston, Memphis, 2003; winner Raiffeisen Internat. Grand Prix, 2003, Stella Artois Championships, 2003, RCA Championships, 2003, Montreal Masters, 2003, Cin. Masters, 2003, 2006, Artois Championship, London, 2007, Legg Mason Tennis Classic, 2007. Mem. U.S. Olympic Tennis Team, Athens, 2004. Host: Saturday Night Live, 2003. Founder The Andy Roddick Found. Named to President's Coun. of Sports and Fitness, Pres. George W. Bush, 2006; recipient Espy Award for Best Male Tennis Player, 2004, Arthur Ashe Humanitarian award, ATP, 2004. Achievements include finishing the year as the youngest player at 18 years, 3 months in the top 200 and as the No. 1 junior in the world, 2000. Avocations: movies, music, skydiving. *

RODECKER, STEPHEN BAILEY, science specialist, secondary school educator; b. San Bernardino, Calif., July 10, 1953; s. Charles and Merilyn Rodecker; m. Jelen Gonzales, July 24, 1993. BA in German, San Diego State U., 1975, BA in Biology, 1977, MA in German, 1977, MS in Biology, 1987. Cert. tchr. Calif., 1978. Tchr. San San Diego (Calif.) Office Edn., 1983—84; instr. Upward Bound San Diego (Calif.) State U., 1990; tchr. Sweetwater Union H.S. dist., Chula Vista, Calif., 1985—, specialist sci. curriculum, 1999—. Prin., owner Spectrum Pubs., Bonita, Calif., 1990—; bd. dirs. Greater San Diego (Calif.) Sci. and Engring. Fair; cons. in field. Author: Laboratory Experiments and Activity in Physical Science, 1995, Biological Experiments and Activities Integrating Math, 1999. Named Tchr. of Yr., Tandy Tech., 1995, Nat. Sci. Tchr. of Yr., Disney, 1995; grantee, Tapestry, 1995, Gen. Telephone and Electronics, 1996, Dept. of Def., 1996, Calif. Tchr. Appreciation and Advancement Program, 1996, 2000. Master: San Diego (Calif.) Sci. Educators Assn. (pres. 2005—); mem.: Calif. Sci. Tchrs. Assn. (bd. dirs. 1990—91). Avocations: tennis, gardening, collecting porcelain.

RODEFER, JEFFREY ROBERT, lawyer; b. Santa Fe, Mar. 29, 1963; s. Robert Jacob and Joanne D. (Thomas) R. BS, U. Nev., Reno, 1985; JD, Willamette U., Salem, Oreg., 1988, cert. dispute resolution, 1988. Bar: Calif. 1990, Nev. 1990, US Dist. Ct. Nev. 1990, US Dist. Ct. (ea. dist.) Calif. 1990, US Ct. Appeals (9th cir.) 1990, Colo. 1991, Oreg. 1997, US Supreme Ct. 1997; cert. arbitrator, Nev. Legal intern Willamette U. Legal Aid Clinic, Salem, Oreg., 1987-88; legal rschr. transp. divsn. Nev. Atty. Gen. Office, Carson City, 1989-90, dep. atty. gen. taxation divsn., 1990-93, dep. atty. gen. gaming divsn., 1993-99, sr. dep. atty. gen. gaming divsn., 1999-2001, asst. chief dep. atty. gen. gaming divsn., 2001—02; corp. compliance officer, assoc. gen. counsel and asst. sec. Boyd Gaming Corp., Las Vegas, 2002—05, v.p. legal affairs, corp. compliance officer, asst. sec., 2005—07, v.p. legal affairs, asst. gen. counsel and corp. compliance officer, 2007—. Author: Nevada Property Tax Manual, 1993, Nevada Gaming Law Index, 1999; contbr. articles to Nev. Lawyer. Contbg. mem. U. Nev. Coll. Bus. Adminstrn. and Athletic Dept., Reno, 1992, Willamette U. Coll. Law, Ann. Law Fund, Salem, 1992; active Nat. Parks and Recreation Assn., Washington, 1991; mem. First Christian Ch. Mem. Internat. Assn. Gaming Attys., U. Nev. Coll. Bus. Alumni Assn., Am. Inns of Ct. (Bruce R. Thompson chpt.), State Bar Nev., (functional equivalency com. 1993—2002, vice chmn. 2003-, chmn. gaming law sect. 2000—), Phi Delta Phi. Republican. Office: Boyd Gaming Corp 6465 S Rainbow Blvd Las Vegas NV 89119-1150 Office Phone: 702-696-1117. Business E-Mail: jeffreyrodefer@boydgaming.com.

RODEIRO, JOSÉ M., art historian, educator; b. Feb. 5, 1949; BA, U. Tampa, Fla., 1971; MFA, Pratt Inst., Bklyn., 1973; PhD, Ohio U., Athens, 1976. Tchg. asst. Ohio U. Coll. Fine Art, Athens, 1975—75; vis. lectr. art and design NYU, NYC, 1975—77; vis. lectr. art history Pratt Inst. Grad. Sch. Art and Design, Bklyn., 1975—76; adj. prof. art history and criticism U. South Fla., Tampa, 1977—79; asst. prof. art history and art Frostburg State U., Md., 1980—93; prof. art dept., coord. art history NJ City U., Jersey City, 1993—. Presenter in field. Contbr. articles to profl. jours. Named Artist-in-Resident, Md. State Arts Coun., 1992; recipient Best of Show award, Western Md. Ann., Washington County Mus., 1985, Grand prize, Internat. New Talent Competition and Exhbn., Lucia Gallery, 1989; grantee, Inter-Am. Devel. Bank, 1991; Cintas fellow, Oscar B. Cintas Found., 1982—83, Visual Artist fellow, Nat. Endowment for the Arts, 1985—86, Fulbright fellow, C.I.E.S. U. Centroamericano, 1995, Devel. Fund grantee, Jersey City State Coll., 1997, New Tech. Implementation grantee, NJ City U. Sch. Arts and Scis., 2000, Internat. Incentive grantee, NJ City U., 2004. Home: 208 Park Ave Madison NJ 07940 Office: NJ City Univ Dept Art 129 Visual Arts Bldg 100 Culver Ave Jersey City NJ 07305

RODEMEYER, MICHAEL LEONARD, JR., lawyer; b. Balt., May 25, 1950; s. Michael Leonard and Claire Isabel (Gunther) R.; m. Dorrit Carolyn Green, June 7, 1975; children: Justin, Christoffer. AB, Princeton U., 1972; JD, Harvard U., 1975. Bar: Md. 1977, D.C. 1980, U.S. Ct. Appeals (10th cir.) 1980. Atty. Fed. Trade Commn., Washington, 1976-81, atty. advisor, 1981-84; counsel Subcom. on Natural Resources, Agr. Rsch. & Environ., Washington, 1984-88; staff dir., counsel U.S. Ho. of Reps., Washington, 1988-90, house com. on sci., chief dem. counsel, 1990-98; asst. dir. for environment White House Office of Sci. and Tech. Policy, Washington, 1998-99, dem. legis. dir., 1999-2000; exec. dir. Pew Initiative on Food and Biotech., Washington, 2000—. Democrat. Avocations: computing, bicycling. Office: Pew Initiative on Food and Biotech 1331 H St NW Ste 900 Washington DC 20005 Office Phone: 202-347-9044. Business E-Mail: mrodemeyer@pewagbiotech.org.

RODEN, MICHAEL FRANK, geochemist, educator, director; b. Jersey City, Sept. 10, 1950; s. John Michael and Grace (Connors) R.; m. Mary Kathleen Sheehan, June 23, 1973 (div. June 1984); children: Katherine, Christopher; m. Grayce Todd Watkins, Nov. 16, 1993. AB, Hamilton Coll., 1972; MA, U. Tex., 1977; PhD, MIT, 1982. Rsch. assoc. U. Minn., Mpls., 1982-84; asst. prof. U. Ga., Athens, 1984-89, assoc. prof. geochemistry, 1989-98, prof., 1998—, head dept. geology, 2006—. Contbr. chpts. to books, numerous articles to profl. jours. Served with U.S. Army, 1972-75. Mem. Am. Geophys. Union, Geol. Soc. Am., Geochem. Soc. Achievements include contribution to understanding Hawaiin volcanism and mantle geochemistry. Office Phone: 706-542-2416.

RODENBERG, JOHANNA KRISTINE, education educator, consultant; d. Edward Ellis and Francess Irene Rodenberg; m. Andrew Thomas Myers, Sept. 3, 1994; children: Justin Grant, Jeffrey Richard Myers, Jakob Edward Myers. AA in Fine Art, Mesa C.C., 1980; BA in Linguistics, San Diego State U., 1982; MA in Ednl. Psychology, U.S. Internat. U., San Diego, 1987; postgrad., U. San Diego/San Diego State U., 2000—. Cert. Nat. Bd. Profl. Tchg. Stds. English lang. tchr. EF Internat. Sch., San Diego, 1983—90; reading specialist San Diego Unified Sch. Dist., 1996—99, peer coach/staff developer, 1999—2002, peer assistance and support consulting tchr., 2002—. Ednl. cons. Nat. Ctr. on Edn. and the Economy, Washington, 1998—2002; ind. ednl. cons., faculty devel., 2003—; faculty San Diego State U., 2000—; spkr., presenter in field. Rm. mom Holmes Elem. Sch., San Diego, 2003. Mem.: ASCD, Internat. TESOL, Nat. Coun. Tchrs. of English, Internat. Reading Assn. Avocations: cooking, reading, gardening. Office: San Diego Unified Schs/SDSU San Diego CA Home Phone: 858-278-6556; Office Phone: 858-496-1883. Personal E-mail: jkr1007@earthlink.net.

RODENBERGER, CHARLES ALVARD, aerospace engineer, consultant; b. Muskogee, Okla., Sept. 11, 1926; s. Darcy Owen and Kathryn Martha (Percival) R.; m. Molcie Lou Halsell, Sept. 3, 1949; children: Kathryn Sue Wilcox, Charles Mark. Student, U. Ark., 1944—45; BS in Gen. Engring., Okla. State U., 1948; MSM.E., So. Meth. U., 1959; PhD in Aero. Engring., U. Tex.-Austin, 1968. Registered profl. engr., Tex. Petroleum engr. Amoco Oil Co., Levelland, Tex., 1948-51; chief engr. McGregor Bros., Odessa, Tex., 1953; petroleum engr. Gen. Crude Oil Co., Hamlin, Tex., 1954; sr. design engr. Gen. Dynamics, Ft. Worth, 1954-60; aerospace engr. NASA, Houston, summer 1962; prof. aerospace engring. Tex. A&M U., College Station, 1960-82, prof. emeritus, 1982—; chmn. bd. Meiller Research, Inc., College Station, 1967-82; pres. JETS, Inc., NYC, 1977-79; cons. Southwest Research Inst., Gen. Motors Corp., Gen. Dynamics. Patentee hypervelocity gun and orthotic device; newspaper columnist: Livestock Weekly, 1986—; mag. columnist, Santa Gertrudis, Tex., 2002. Bd. dirs. Cross Plains Pub. Libr., 1986—, pres., treas.; meth. Sunday sch. tchr., 1984—. Served with USAAF, 1945, served with USAF, 1951—53. NSF fellow, 1964-65; recipient Disting. Teaching award Tex. A&M U., 1962 Fellow AIAA (assoc.); mem. ASME, NSPE (v.p. 1980-81), Tex. Soc. Profl. Engrs., Am. Soc. for Engring. Edn., Sigma Xi, Kiwanis Club (pres. Cross Plains chpt. 2002-03). Methodist. Home: 8377 FM 2228 Baird TX 79504-4813 Office Phone: 254-725-6816. Personal E-mail: crodenberg@aol.com. Business E-Mail: car926@aol.com.

RODENBURG, CLIFTON GLENN, lawyer; b. Jamestown, ND, Apr. 5, 1949; s. Clarence and Dorothy Irene (Peterman) R.; m. Donna Michele Stockman, Mar. 1, 1980. BS, N.D. State U., 1971; JD, U. N.D., 1974; M.L.I.R., Mich. State U., 1976. Bar: N.D. 1974, U.S. Dist. Ct. N.D. 1974, U.S. Ct. Appeals (8th cir.) 1974, Minn. 1980, U.S. Supreme Ct. 1980, S.D. 1983, Nebr. 1984, U.S. Dist. Ct. Minn. 1984, U.S. Dist. Ct. Nebr. 1984, Wis. 1985, U.S. Dist. Ct. Wis. 1985, Mont. 1986, U.S. Dist. Ct. Mont. 1986, bd. cert. Creditors' Rights Law, Am. Bd. Cert. Ptnr. Johnson, Rodenburg & Lauinger, Fargo, ND, 1976—; pres., gen. counsel Rodenburg Group, Inc., Fargo, 1980—. Contbg. editor: The Developing Labor Law, 1976-80; drafter N.D. garnishment statutes, 1982. Mem. Acad. Comml. and Bankruptcy Law Specialists. Office Phone: 701-235-6411.

RODGERS, BERNARD FRANCIS, JR., literature and language professor; b. Hazleton, Pa., Mar. 21, 1947; s. Bernard F. and Anna V. (Gulla) R.; m. Patricia Hick, Dec. 9, 1969 (div. 1982); m. Jane Powell, Oct. 27, 1984 (dec. Sept. 2002). BS in English and Edn., Mt. St. Mary's Coll., 1969; MA in English, U. Bridgeport, 1972; PhD in English with honors, U. Chgo., 1975. Tchr. Eng., dir. drama Somers Ctrl. High Sch., Lincolndale, NY, 1969-72; instr., asst. prof. lit. and humanities City Colls. Chgo., 1975-82, spl. asst. to chancellor, 1984—85; faculty Eng. Simon's Rock Coll. of Bard, Great Barrington, Mass., 1985—, dean acad. affairs, 1985—87, v.p. and dean, 1987—2004, Emily H. Fisher prof. lit., 2004—. Chair lit. and humanities sect. coll. accreditaiton program Chgo. City-Wide Coll., 1977—78, chair coll. acceleration program, 1977—78, mem. adminstrv. coun., 1980—81; bd. overseers Simon's Rock Coll. of Bard, 1987—2004; mem. planning com. humanists Write On, Chgo., 1982—83; mem. nom. com. Eisenhower Fellowship Am. Embassy, Warsaw, 1980; mem. writing panel artists-in-residence program Chgo. Coun. Fine Arts, 1978; spkr. in field. Author: Philip Roth: A Bibliography, 1974, 2nd edit., 1984, Philip Roth, 1978, Contemporary American Fictoin 1944-79: A Chronology, 1980, Voices and Visions: Selected Essays, 2001; essayist, reviewer in field; contbr. articles; assoc. prodr. TV talk show U. Chgo., 1974—75; prodr.: TV talk show U. Chgo., 1975—76; prodr., host interview program City Colls. Chgo., 1981—82. Bd. dirs. Fairview Hosp., Great Barrington, 1988-94, Mass. Found. for Humanities, chair, 1992-94, vice chair, 1991-92, chair program com., 1990-92, pres., 1992-94, Friends of Chgo. Pub. Libr., 1982; mem. South County chapter Berkshires United Way, 1988, mem. planning com. humanists Read Ill., 1984-85, ad hoc com. excellence Ill. C.C. Trustees Assn., 1984-85. U. Chgo. fellow, 1973, Ford Found. fellow, 1974-75, Fulbright-Hays sr. lectr. to Poland, 1979-80, Chgo. Pub. Libr. assoc. scholar, 1976-78. Mem. So. Berkshire C. of C. (bd. dirs. 1987-90), New Eng. Assn. Schs. and Colls. (evaluation team chair commn. instns. higher edn. 1986—), North Ctrl. Assn. Colls. and Schs. (asst. dir. commn. instns. higher edn 1982-84), Soc. Midland Authors (chair fiction award com. 1985). Home: PO Box 778 Great Barrington MA 01230-0778 Office: Simon's Rock Coll of Bard 84 Alford Rd Great Barrington MA 01230-1559 Office Phone: 413-528-7496. Business E-Mail: brodgers@simons-rock.edu.

RODGERS, BRUCE ALAN, government agency administrator, psychologist; s. Bernice Junior and Louise Andreason Rodgers; m. Angela Lei Lani Wiseman; children: Diana Louise, Sarah Brooke, Daniel Alan, Hartley Elizabeth, Alexus Lei Lani Maldonado. BS, Tex. State U., 1989; PhD, U. Denver, 2000. Undersheriff Park County Sheriff's Office, Fairplay, Colo., 1996—98; dir. Ea. Colo. Plains Drug Task Force, Yuma, 1998—2000; immigration adjudication officer US Dept. Homeland Security, Dallas, 2000—. Author: The Psychological Aspects of Police Work: An Officer's Guide to Street Psychology. Mem.: APA, Soc. Police and Criminal Psychology, Soc. for Theoretical and Philos. Psychology, Sovereign Mil Order of Temple of Jerusalem. Home Phone: 817-306-0733. Personal E-mail: rodgersbruce@sbcglobal.net.

RODGERS, CLIFTON EUGENE, JR., trade association administrator, lobbyist; b. Harrisburg, Pa., Sept. 15, 1954; s. Clifton Eugene and Jean Rodgers; m. Shelley Church Rodgers; children: John Spencer, Henry August. Student, Yale U., 1976—77; BA in History and Lit., Hampshire Coll., 1978. Corp. sales rep. Mellon Bank, NA, Pitts., 1979—81; spl. asst. to exec. v.p.s Fannie Mae, Washington, 1981—83; mgr. secondary mktg. The First Boston Corp., NYC, 1983—85; v.p. Phillips Realty Capital, Bethesda, Md., 1985—91; dir. Office of Bus. Liaison U.S. Dept. Treasury, Washington, 1991—93; asset mgr. Archon Group. L.P., Alexandria, Va., 1993—94; v.p. Legg Mason, Bethesda, 1994—96; sr. v.p. The Real Estate Roundtable, Washington, 1996—; founding dir. The Bank of Georgetown, Washington, 2004—; mem. internat. trade adv. com. U.S. Dept. Commerce. Mid-Atlantic pres. Starlight Children's Found., Washington, 1998—, bd. dirs., 1999; vestry Christ Ch., Georgetown, Washington, 1998—; dir. Starlight Children's Found. Internat., L.A., 1999—. Mem. Urban Land Inst., Mortgage Bankers Assn. of Am. (vice chmn. capital mkts. com. 1999—). Republican. Episcopalian. Avocations: skiing, shooting, fly fishing, mountain biking, tennis. Office: Real Estate Roundtable Market Sq W 801 Pennsylvania Ave NW Ste 720 Washington DC 20004 Home Phone: 703-998-2323; Office Phone: 202-639-8400. Business E-Mail: crodgers@rer.org.

RODGERS, DANIEL TRACY, historian, educator; b. Darby, Pa., Sept. 29, 1942; s. Oliver Eliot and Dorothy (Welch) R.; m. Irene Wylie, 1971; children: Peter Samuel, Dwight Oliver. AB, BS in Engring., Brown U., 1965; PhD in History, Yale U., 1973. Instr. history U. Wis., Madison, 1971-73, asst. prof., 1973-78, assoc. prof., 1978-80; assoc. prof. history Princeton U., NJ, 1980-86, prof., 1986-98, chair, 1988—95, 1997—98, Henry Charles Lea prof. history, 1998—. Fulbright lectr., Frankfurt, Fed. Republic Germany, 1983-84; Pitt prof., Cambridge Univ., 2003-04. Author: The Work Ethic in Industrial America, 1860-1920 (Frederick Jackson Turner award 1978), 1978, Contested Truths: Keywords in American Politics since Independence, 1987, Atlantic Crossings: Social Politics in a Progressive Age, 1998 (Ellis W. Hawley award 1979, George Louis Beer prize 1979). Recipient Chancellor's award U. Wis., Madison, 1978, Am. Coun. Learned Socs. fellow, 1976, NEH fellow, 1987-88, Ctr. for Advanced Study in Behavioral Scis. fellow, 1991-92; Woodrow Wilson Ctr. fellow, 1999-2000; Guggenheim fellowship, 2007-. Office: Princeton U Dept History Princeton NJ 08544-0001 E-mail: drodgers@princeton.edu.

RODGERS, DARYL MARK, language educator; b. Glasgow, Scotland, Oct. 15, 1974; s. David and Jean Rodgers; m. Rebecca Grace Folkerts, June 1, 1996; 1 child, Siena Bridget. BA French & Missions, Harding U., Searcy, Ark., 1996; MA in Italian, Ohio State U., Columbus, 2001; PhD in Italian Linguistics, U. Ill., Urbana, 2002. English lang. instr. Bertrand Russell Lang. Inst., Padova, Italy, 1997—98; grad. tchg. assoc. Ohio State U., Columbus, 1999—2001; grad. tchg. asst. U. Ill., Urbana, 2002—. Contbr. Italian lang. workbook. Fellow, U. Ill., Urbana-Champaign, 2005, 2006; U. Block grant, 2006. Mem.: Am. Assn. Tchrs. Italian, Am. Assn. Applied Linguistics, Alpha Chi Honor Soc. Avocations: tennis, exercise. Office: Univ Ill Ubana-Champaign 4080 FLB 707 S Mathews Ave Urbana IL 61801 Home Phone: 217-355-1135; Office Phone: 217-333-3390. Business E-Mail: dmrodger@uiuc.edu.

RODGERS, FRANK, librarian; b. Darlington, Eng., July 28, 1927; came to U.S., 1956; s. Charles Bede and Frances (Page) R.; m. Sarah Louise Edelson, Dec. 18, 1971; children: Hilda Marie, Norah Frances. BA with honors, King's Coll., U. Durham, 1947; diploma librarianship, London U., 1952. Libr. Poplar Tech. Coll., London, 1951-53, St. Martin's Sch. Art, 1953-56; sr. libr. adult svcs. divsn. Akron (Ohio) Pub. Libr., 1956-59; asst. reference libr. U. Ill., 1959-64; chief reference libr., then asst. dir. pub. svcs. Pa. State U. Librs., 1965-69; dir. Portland (Oreg.) State U. Libr., 1969-79; dir. librs. U. Miami, Fla., 1979-97. Mem. Oreg. adv. coun. librs., 1973-74; bd. dirs. Pacific N.W. Bibliog. Ctr., 1973-77; tech. adv. com. librs. Columbia Regional Assn. Govts., 1976-79; vis. fellow U. Southampton Eng., 1975-76; pres. Oreg. Libr. Assn., 1974-75; mem. nominating com. Southeastern Libr. Network, 1984-85; bd. dirs. S.E. Fla. Libr. Info. Network, 1984-97, pres. 1991-92; mem. exec. coun. Assn. Caribbean U. Rsch. and Instl. Librs., 1985-88; chmn. local organizing com. for 1981 and 1987 confs. in Miami; mem. Fla. Libr. Network Coun., 1985-91; NEH challenge grant rev. panel, 1987, Howard U. ann. inspection team, 1989, Reaffirmation com., Tex. Christian U., 1993. Author, editor various libr. publs., guides. Patron Jerome K. Jerome Soc., 1986—. Sr. fellow Grad. Sch. Libr. and Info. Sci. UCLA, 1983; grantee Coun. Libr. Resources, 1975-76. Fellow Libr. Assn. U.K.; mem. ALA, Assn. Rsch. Librs. (office mgmt. studies adv. com. 1981-83, stats. and measurements com. 1993-96), Assn. Specialized and Coop. Libr. Agys. (membership promotion com. 1994-96, chair 1990 program com.), Assn. Southeastern Rsch. Librs. (chmn. membership com. 1982-97). Address: 7a Avenida Norte #25 Antigua Guatemala E-mail: frodgers@conexion.com.gt.

RODGERS, FREDERIC BARKER, judge; b. Albany, NY, Sept. 29, 1940; s. Prentice Johnson and Jane (Weed) R.; m. Valerie McNaughton, Oct. 8, 1988; 1 child: Gabriel Moore. AB in Polit. Sci., Amherst Coll., Mass., 1963; JD, Union U., Albany, 1966. Bar: NY 1966, US Ct. Mil. Appeals 1968, Colo. 1972, US Supreme Ct. 1974, US Ct. Appeals (10th cir.) 1981, US Ct. Appeals (fed. cir.) 2001. Chief dep. dist. atty., Denver, 1972-73; magistrate Denver Juvenile Ct., 1973—79; mem. Mulligan Reeves Teasley & Joyce, P.C., Denver, 1979-80; pres. Frederic B. Rodgers, P.C., Breckenridge, Colo., 1980-89; ptnr. McNaughton & Rodgers, Central City, Colo., 1989-91; county ct. judge Gilpin County Combined Cts., Colo., 1987—; probate judge Jefferson County Dist. Ct., 2005—07. Presiding mcpl. judge cities of Breckenridge, Blue River, Black Hawk, Central City, Edgewater, Empire, Idaho Springs, Silver Plume and Westminster, Colo., 1978-96; chmn. com. on mcpl. ct. rules of procedure Colo. Supreme Ct., 1984-96; mem. Colo. Supreme Ct. Task Force Probate Protective Procs., 2006—; mem. Colo. Supreme Ct. jud. Conf. Planning Com., 2007—; mem. gen faculty Nat. Jud. Coll. U. Nev., Reno, 1990—, mem. faculty coun., 1993-99, chair 1999, trustee, 2004—, sec., 2007—. Author (with Dilweg, Fretz, Murphy and Wicker): Modern Judicial Ethics, 1992; contbr. articles to profl. jours., chapters to books; author: The Improvement of The Administration of Justice 7th edit., 2001. Mem. Colo. Commn. on Children, 1982-85, Colo. Youth Devel. Coun., 1989-98, Colo. Family Peace Task Force, 1994-96. Served with JAGC, US Army, 1967-72; to maj. USAR, 1972-88. Decorated Bronze Star with oak leaf cluster, 1969, 1970, Air medal, 1969, Army Commendation medal with silver oak leaf cluster, 1969-1972; recipient USAR Achievement Medal, 1986, Am. Spirit Honor medal, 1966, Outstanding County Judge award Colo. 17th Judicial Dist. Victim Adv. Coalition, 1991; Spl. Cmty. Svc. award Colo. Am. Legion, 1979, Lifetime Achievement award Denver Law Club, 2003; USAID grant, 2002-2003. Fellow Am. Bar Found. (life, Colo. state chair 2005—), Colo. Bar. Found. (life); mem. ABA (jud. div. exec. coun. 1989-2000, vice-chair 1996-97, chair-elect 1997, chair 1998-99, mem. House of Dels. 1993-2004, jud. divsn. del. to ABA nominating com. 2000-01, bd. govs. Dist. 11 2001-04, chair traffic ct. program com. 2005-06), Colo. Bar Assn. (bd. govs. 1986-88, 90-92, 93-99, 2002-05, sr. v.p. 2004-05), Continental Divide Bar Assn., Denver Bar Assn. (trustee 1979-82), First Jud. Dist. Bar Assn. (trustee 2000-02), Nat. Conf. Spl. Ct. Judges (chmn. 1989-90), Colo. County Judges Assn. (pres. 1995-96), Colo. Mcpl. Judges Assn. (pres. 1986-87), Colo. Trial Judges Coun. (v.p. 1994-95, sec. 1996-97, 2006—), Denver Law Club (pres. 1981-82), Colo. Women's Bar Assn., Am. Judicature Soc. (bd. dirs. 2003—), Nat. Coun. Juvenile and Family Ct. Judges, Nat. Coll. Probate Judges, Federalist Soc. for Law and Pub. Policy Studies, Judge Advs. Assn., Univ. Club (Denver), Arlberg Club (Winter Park), Marines Meml. Club (San Francisco), Rotary (charter pres. Peak to Peak 2000-01, Paul Harris fellow 1996). Episcopalian. Avocations: bicycling, skiing, hiking, music, writing. Office: First Judicial Dist Courts Gilpin County Justice Ctr 2960 Dory Hill Rd Golden CO 80403-8827 Office Phone: 303-582-5323 ext. 16. Personal E-mail: rodgers@abanet.org. Business E-Mail: frederic.rodgers@judicial.state.co.us.

RODGERS, GRACE ANNE, university official; b. South Bend, Ind., Apr. 19, 1936; d. Morris and Barbara Mae (Hamm) Morrow; m. Eugene M. Rodgers, July 7, 1956; children: Craig Eugene, Kimberly Sue. BS, Ind. State U., 1981; pub. mgmt. cert., Ind. U., South Bend, 1991, MPA, 1993. Dir. spl. programs Ivy Tech. State Coll., South Bend, 1990-94, mktg. cons., 1994; mem. assoc. faculty dept. pub. affairs--non-profit marketing and environ. Ind. U., 1994—, dir. internships-student svcs. Sch. Pub.-Environ. Affairs, 1994—, dir. cmty. links, 1997—. Author: (manuals) Resume and Beyond, 1990, Strategic Marketing Plan, 1994. Mem. Youth Svcs. Bur., South Bend Recipient Indiana U. South Bend Student Gov. Lifetime Achievement award. Mem. Ind. U. Sch. Pub. end Environ. Affairs Alumni Assn. (adv. coun. 1993—), Ind. U.-South Bend Alumni Assn., Ind. State U. Alumni Assn., Phi Theta Kappa (hon., award for outstanding svc. 1993), Pi Alpha Alpha (sec. 1996—). Republican. Methodist. Avocations: travel, reading, classical music. Office: Ind U 1800 Mishawaka Ave South Bend IN 46615-1621 Home: 14394 Shoreline Dr Granger IN 46530-4852 E-mail: profgrac@aol.com.

RODGERS, JAMES FOSTER, insurance research executive, economist; b. Columbus, Ga., Jan. 15, 1951; s. Laban Jackson and Martha (Jackson) R.; m. Cynthia Lynne Bathurst, Aug. 20, 1975. BA, U. Ala., Tuscaloosa, 1973; PhD, U. Iowa, 1980. Fed. intern Office Rsch. and Stats., Social Security Adminstrn., Washington, 1976-77; rsch. assoc. Ctr. Health Policy Rsch., AMA, Chgo., 1979-80, rsch. dir., 1980-82, asst. to dep. exec. v.p. AMA, 1982-85; dir. AMA Ctr. Health Policy Rsch., Chgo., 1985-96, v.p. health policy, 1996—2003; sr. rsch. exec. Blue Cross Blue Shield Assn., Chgo., 2003—. Contbr. articles on health econs. to profl. jours. Pharm. Mfrs. Assn. grantee, 1978; NSF grantee, 1978; Hohenberg fellow, 1969-70 Mem. Am. Econ. Assn., Am. Statis. Assn. Home: 2233 N Orchard St Chicago IL 60614-3713 Office: Blue Cross Blue Shield Assn 225 N Michigan Ave Chicago IL 60601 Office Phone: 312-297-6535.

RODGERS, JOHN HUNTER, lawyer; b. Lubbock, Tex., Jan. 18, 1944; s. James O'Donnell Rodgers and Dorothy (Ulin) Carpenter; m. Anne C. Smith, Nov. 29, 1969; children; Anne Elizabeth, Catherine Hunter. BA, Tex. A&M, 1966; JD, U. Tex., 1969. Bar: Tex. 1969, U.S. Supreme Ct. 1973. Atty. The Southland Corp., Dallas, 1973-79, gen. counsel, 1979-91, sec., 1987-95, sr. v.p., chief adminstrv. officer, 1991-93, exec. v.p., chief adminstrv. officer, 1993-95; pres. Clairemead Corp., Dallas, 1996-2000; sr. v.p., gen. counsel, sec. Am. Pad & Paper Co., Dallas, 1998-2000, pres., 2000—04; prin. J. Hunter & Assocs., Dallas, 2003—. Mem. visual arts com. Tex. A&M U., 1985-94, bd. dirs. student fund enrichment bd., 1986-94; mem. exec. com. Jr. Achievement Dallas, 1988-93; mem. Dallas Citizens Coun., 1992-95; bd. dirs. Boys and Girls Clubs of Greater Dallas, 1998—, vice chmn., 2003-04, chmn., 2005—; nat. chair Tulane U. Parents Coun., 1997-98; trustee Goals for Dallas, 1991-92; bd. trustees The Sci. Pl. Mus., 2004-06, Dallas Mus. Nature and Sci., 2006-; nat. bd. dirs. Boys and Girls Clubs Am., 1993-98; mem. mktg. com. Dallas Mus. Art, 1994-97. Capt. JAGC, US Army, 1969-73, Vietnam. Mem. ABA, Tex. Bar Assn. (coun. mem. corp. counsel sect. 1988), Dallas Bar Assn., Southwestern

Legal Found. (adv. bd. Internat. and Comparative Law Ctr., rsch. fellow 1986-94), Nat. Assn. Convenience Stores (bd. dirs. 1993-95). Roman Catholic. Office: 4655 Insurance Ln Ste 100 Dallas TX 75205 E-mail: Jhunterlp@sbcglobal.net.

RODGERS, JOHN JOSEPH, III, educational administration consultant, educator; b. Jamaica, NY, Oct. 13, 1941; s. John Joseph Rodgers, Edith (McInerney) Rodgers; m. Iris Rodgers; children: Janet, John Joseph IV, Yvette. BS, Fordham U., 1962; Profl. diploma, St. Johns U., 1970, EdD, 1979; postgrad., CUNY, Flushing. Asst. prin. NYC Bd. Edn., 1972—82, project dir., 1985—88; prin. Howard T. Herber Sch., Malverne, N.Y., 1982-85, Norman Thomas H.S., NYC, 1988-96, Matawan Regional H.S., Aberdeen, N.J., 1996-97; cons. on ednl. adminstrn. Valley Stream, NY, 1999—; prof. math. Farleigh Dickinson U., Madison, N.J., 1999-2001; prof. ednl. adminstrn. Coll. New Rochelle, N.Y., 2000-01; dean acad. affairs Five Towns Coll., Dix Hills, NY, 2001—02; acad. dean Bus. Informatics Ctr., The Coll. for Bus., Valley Stream, NY, 2002—05. Mem. ASCD, Am. Assn. Sch. Adminstrs., Math. Assn. Am., Nat. Assn. Secondary Sch. Prins. Home: 1355 W Diamond Shore Loop Hernando FL 34442-6288 E-mail: drjohnrodgers@hotmail.com.

RODGERS, JOHNATHAN, broadcast executive; b. San Antonio, Jan. 18, 1946; s. Marion Alford and Barbara (Merriwether) Rodgers; m. Royal Graves Kennedy, Sept. 27, 1976; children: David, Jamie. BA, U. Calif., Berkeley, 1967; MA, Stanford U., 1972; PhD (hon.), Columbia Coll., Chgo., 1991. Writer-reporter Sports Illustrated, NYC, 1966—68; assoc. editor Newsweek, NYC, 1968—72; prodr. WNBC-TV, NYC, 1972—73; reporter WKYC-TV (NBC), Cleve., 1973—74; sta. mgr., news dir. KCBS-TV, LA, 1978—83; exec. prodr. CBS News, NYC, 1983—86; v.p., gen. mgr. WBBM-TV (CBS), Chgo., 1986—90; former pres. CBS TV Stas., Chgo.; pres. Discovery Networks, US, Bethesda, Md., 1996—2003; pres., CEO TV One, LLC, Silver Spring, Md., 2003—. Bd. dirs. Procter & Gamble. Trustee U. Calif., Berkeley, 2000—. With US Army, 1969—71, Korea. Mem.: Nat. Assn. Black Journalists. Home: 3120 Newark St NW Washington DC 20008-3343 Office: TV One, LLC 1010 Wayne Ave Silver Spring MD 20910

RODGERS, JUDY, chef; Grad., Stanford U., 1978. Lunch chef Chez Panisse; chef Union Hotel, Benicia, Calif.; exec. chef, owner Zuni Café, San Francisco, 1987—. Author: Zuni Café Cookbook, 2002 (KitchenAid Cookbook of Yr. award, James Beard Found., 2003). Named Best Chef: Calif., James Beard Found., 2000, Outstanding Chef, 2004; recipient S.Pellegrino Outstanding Restaurant award, 2003. Office: Zuni Cafe 1658 Market St San Francisco CA 94102 Office Phone: 415-552-2522. *

RODGERS, KATHY, legal association administrator, lawyer; BA, Smith Coll.; JD, Columbia U. Atty. Poletti, Freidin, Prashker, Feldman and Gartner; gen. counsel, v.p. Barnard Coll., acting pres., 1993—94; pres. Legal Momentum (formerly NOW Legal Def. and Edn. Fund), 1995—. Bd. mem. Lawyers Alliance, Nat. Coun. Rsch. on Women, Fair Labor Assn., Nat. Council Women's Orgns. Mem.: Bar Assn. City of NY. Office: Legal Momentum 395 Hudson St New York NY 10014 *

RODGERS, KIRK PROCTER, international environmental consultant; b. Balt., Oct. 15, 1932; s. Samuel Procter and Florence Eugenia (Besley) R.; m. Karen Frances Johnson, Jan. 3, 1959; children: Brian Kirk, Kimberly Paige. BA in Geography, Yale U., 1954, MS in Natural Resource Conservation, 1956. Timber surveyor U.S. Forest Svc., Colo., Calif., 1953-54; land use planner Balt. (Md.) County Planning Commn., 1955; natural resources specialist, dept. econ. affairs Orgn. of Am. States, Washington, 1960-63, chief natural resources unit, dept. econ. affairs, 1963-69, dir. dept. regional devel. and environment, 1970-96, dir. unit of sustainable devel. and environ., 1996—98, ret. cons., 1998—. Mem. strategic policy coun. Yale U. Sch. Forestry and Environ. Studies, 1992-97; permanent sec. Interamerican Travel Congress, Washington, 1986-94; pres. Besley and Rodgers Inc., Woolford, Md., 1988—; mem. U.S. Sci. Com. on Problems of the Environment, Washington, 1990-93; advisor UN Environment Program, 1986; mem. internat. bd. advisors UN Internat. Environ. Tech. Ctr., Osaka, Japan, 1995-98; bd. advisors Jour. Environ. and Devel., 1992-98; bd. govs. World Water Coun., 1997-98; cons. to Orgn. Am. States & NAFTA Commn. Environ. Coop., 1998—. Author: Physical Resource Investigations for Economic Development, 1969, Integrated Regional Development Planning-Guidelines and Case Studies from OAS Experience, 1984, Conservation in the Big Picture-Development Approaches for the Next Decade, 1992, Ecological and Economic Evaluation of Protected Areas, 1995, The Interamerican Water Resources Network: A Tool for Capacity Building, 1996; contbr. The Careless Technology-Ecological Consequences of Internat. Development, 1970, Managing the Environment in Developing Countries, 1992, Governance in the Western Hemisphere, 1982. Mem. nat. bd. dirs. Fla. Mus. Sci. and Tech., 1994-98; pres. Interam. Water Resources Found., 1997-01. Lt. (j.g.) USNR, 1956-59. Recipient Grad. fellowship Conservation Found., Yale U., 1955-56, Population Workshop fellowship Ford Found., Washington, 1956; recipient Disting. Alumnus award Yale U. Sch. Forestry and Environ. Studies, 2004. Mem. Forest Landowners Assn. (chair govtl. affairs 1993-95, pres. 1997-99, exec. com. 1999-), Am. Forest Paper Assn. (mem. pvt. forestry bd. dirs.), Am. Water Resources Assn. (hon. mem. 1996), Md. Forests Assn. (bd. dirs. 2000—, pres. 2002-04, v.p. govtl. affairs 2006-), Assn. Yale Alumni (del. 2001-04), Yale Sch. Forestry and Environ. Studies (exec. coun. Alumni Assn. 2004-), Forest Landowners Tax Coun. (bd. dirs. 2003—), Nat. Network Pvt. Forest Landowners (bd. dirs. 2005-). Avocations: hunting, fishing, skiing. Home: 3508 Stoneybrae Dr Falls Church VA 22044-1229

RODGERS, LANA LORETTA LUSCH, retired elementary school educator; b. Lehighton, Pa., Jan. 26, 1943; d. Charles Norman and Loretta Margaret (Gaumer) Lusch; m. Harold Eugene Rodgers, Aug. 15, 1964; children: Jacqui Rodgers Kirchner, Travis Dustin. BS in Elem. Edn., Kutztown U., Pa., 1964, BS in Blind and Partially Sighted Edn., 1967; M Elem. Edn., Kutztown U., 1968, specialist in reading, 1983. Tchr. Honey Brook Elem. Sch., Twin Valley Sch. Dist., Elverson, Pa., 1964—67, 1986—2000, Berkshire Bldg., Wilson Sch. Dist., Reading, Pa., 1967—68; substitute tchr. Robeson Elem. Sch., Twin Valley Sch. Dist., 1981—83, reading tchr., 1985; ret. Portrait artist; English tchr. Reading Area CC. Sec. Twin Valley Sch. Dist. Tchr.'s Orgn., Elverson, 1966; leader Girl Scouts USA, Wyomissing, Pa., 1966—68; vol. Ct. Apptd. Spl. Advocates, Reading Ct., 2000—; mem. Literacy Coun., 1977—79; Stephen min. West Lawn United Meth. Ch. Recipient CASA Cert. Recognition, Pa. Sen. Michael O'Pake, 2001—07, Cert. Recognition, West Lawn United Meth. Ch., 1998, Tutor award, Reading Area CC, 2004. Mem.: AAUW. Republican. Avocations: piano, painting, surfing, motorcycling, ice skating. Home: 106 Halsey Ave Reading PA 19609-2110

RODGERS, LAWRENCE RODNEY, internist, educator; b. Clovis, N.Mex., Mar. 9, 1920; s. Samuel Frank and Lillian (O'Connor) R.; m. Ivy Lorna Piper, Aug. 6, 1943; children: Lawrence Rodney (dec.), Ivy Elizabeth, George Piper. BS, West Tex. State U., 1940; MD, U. Tex., 1943. Diplomate Am. Bd. Internal Medicine. Intern Phila. Gen. Hosp., 1943-44, resident in medicine, 1946-49; assoc. internist Tumor Inst., U. Tex. M.D. Anderson Hosp., Houston, 1949—; chmn. dept. medicine Hermann Hosp., Houston, 1966-71; assoc. prof. clin. medicine Baylor U., 1949—; prof. clin. medicine U. Tex., 1972—. Editor: Harris County Physician, 1976-80. Bd. dirs. Tex. Med. Found.; trustee Houston Mus. Med. Sci., 1981. Maj. M.C. AUS, 1944-46. Decorated Bronze Star with two oak leaf clusters; recipient Ashbel Smith Disting. Alumnus award U. Tex. Med. Br.-Galveston, 1993, Mastership award Am. Coll. Physicians, 1996. Fellow ACP (gov. for Tex. 1979-83, Laureate Internist Tex. award 1994); mem. AMA (del. 1975-94), Tex. Med. Assn. (elected emeritus), Harris County Med. Soc. (exec. bd. 1978-82, v.p. 1984), Am. Heart Assn., Houston Soc. Internal Medicine (pres. 1974), Houston Acad. Medicine (pres. 1981), Houston Philos. Soc. (pres. 1993-94), Doctor's Club Houston (bd. govs. 1984-88, pres. 1986). Personal E-mail: rod3920@aol.com.

RODGERS, LOIS EVE, secondary school educator; BA, U. So. Miss.; MEd, William Carey Coll.; student, Bread Loaf Sch. English. Tchr. Hattiesburg (Miss.) High Sch. Named Miss. State English Tchr. of Yr., 1993.

RODGERS, MARY COLUMBRO, literature educator, writer, academic administrator; b. Aurora, Ohio, Apr. 17, 1925; d. Nicola and Nancy (DeNicola) Columbro; m. Daniel Richard Rodgers, July 24, 1965; children: Robert, Patricia, Kristine. AB, Notre Dame Coll., 1957; MA, Western Res. U., 1962; PhD, Ohio State U., 1964; postgrad., U. Rome, 1964-65; EdD, Calif. Nat. Open U., 1975, DLitt, 1978. Tchr. English Cleve. elem. schs., 1945-52, Cleve. secondary schs., 1952-62; supr. English student tchrs. Ohio State U., 1962-64; asst. prof. English U. Md., 1965-66; assoc. prof. Trinity Coll., 1967-68; prof. English D.C. Tchrs. Coll. U. D.C., 1968—2000; pres. Md. Nat. U., 1972—2006; founder, chancellor Open U. Am., 1965—; dean Am. Open U. Acad.; ret., 2000; ind. rschr., writer, 2000—. Author: A Short Course in English Composition, 1976, Chapbook of Children's Literature, 1977, Comprehensive Catalogue: The Open University of America System, 1978-80, Open University of America System Source Book, V, VII, VII, 1978, Essays and Poems on Life and Literature, 1979, Modes and Models: Four Lessons for Young Writers, 1981, Open University Structures and Adult Learning, 1982, Papers in Applied English Linguistics, 1982, Twelve Lectures on the American Open University, 1982, English Pedagogy in the American Open University, 1983, Design for Personalized English Graduate Degrees in the Urban University, 1984, Open University English Teaching, 1945-85: Conceptual History and Rationale, 1985, Claims and Counterclaims Regarding Instruction Given in Personalized Degree Residency Programs Completed by Graduates of California National Open University, 1986, The American Open University, 1965 to 1985: History and Sourcebook, 1986, New Design II: English Pedagogy in the American Open University, 1987, The American Open University, 1965 to 1985: A Research Report, 1987, The American Open University and Other Open Universities: A Comparative Study Report, 1988, Poet and Pedagogue in Moscow and Leningrad: A Travel Report, 1989, Foundations of English Scholarship in the American Open University, 1989, Twelve Lectures in Literary Analysis, 1990, Ten Lectures in Literary Production, 1990, Analyzing Fact and Fiction, 1991, Analyzing Poetry and Drama, 1991, Some Successful Literary Research Papers: An Inventory of Titles and Theses, 1991, Catalogue for the Mary Columbro Rodgers Literary Trust, 1992, A Chapbook of Poetry and Drama Analysis, 1992, Convent Poems, 1943-1961, 1992, Catholic Marriage Poems 1962, 1979, 1993, Catholic Widow with Children Poems 1979-1993, 1994, First Access List to the Mary Columbro Rodgers Trust by Year, 1994, Nicola Columbro: A Brief Biography, 3d edit., 1994, Biographical Sourcebook I: Mary Columbro Rodgers 1969-1995, 1995, Catholic Teacher Poems, 1945-1995, 1995, Fables and Farm Stories for Fiction Analysis, 1995, Second Access List to the Mary Columbro Rodgers Literary Trust by Alphabet, 1995, Third Access List to the Mary Columbro Rodgers Literary Trust by Subject, 1996, Fourth Access List to the Mary Columbro Rodgers Literary Trust for K-PhD Open Learning-Open University Methods with Data Batches Delineated, 2002, Journals: Reflections and Resolves 1992-2002, 03, 04, 16 vols., 2002, Fifth and Final Access List to the Mary Columbro Rodgers Literary Trust with Annotations, 2004, Journals: Reflections and Resolves, 2005, Catholic Open University of America System Poems, 1962-2005, 2005; contbr. articles to profl. jours. Fulbright scholar U. Rome, 1964-65. Fellow Cath. Scholars; mem. U.S. Distance Learning Assn., Poetry Soc. Am., Nat. Coun. Tchrs. English, Am. Ednl. Rsch. Assn., Am. Acad. Poets, Pi Lambda Theta. Home and Office: Coll Heights Estates 3916 Commander Dr Hyattsville MD 20782-1027 Home Phone: 301-779-0220; Office Phone: 301-779-0220. Personal E-mail: openuniv@aol.com.

RODGERS, ROBERT AUBREY, physicist; b. Huntsville, Ala., May 10, 1967; s. Aubrey and Peggy H. Rodgers; m. Rocio M. Palacios, Oct. 25, 1997. BS in Optical Sci., U. Ala., Huntsville, 1990, MS in Physics, 1992; MS in Health Physics, Ga. Inst. Tech., 1993; MS in Med. Physics, U. Tex. Health Sci. Ctr., Houston, 2005; diploma, Air Force Squadron Officer Sch., 2001, Air Command, Staff Coll., 2005. Diplomate in med. nuclear physics Am. Bd. Radiology, in diagnostic radiol. physics Am. Bd. Radiology, in therapeutic radiol. physics Am. Bd. Radiology, in nuc. medicine physics and instrumentation Am. Bd. Sci. Nuc. Medicine, in radiation safety and protection Am. Bd. Sci. Nuc. Medicine, Nat. Registry of Radiation Protection Technologist. Commd. 2d lt. USAF, 1995, advanced through grades to maj., staff med. health physicist Lackland AFB, Tex., 1996-97, diagnostic med. physics fellow, 1997-98, chief diagnostic med. physics element, 1998-2000; assoc. chief med. physics Keesler AFB, Miss., 2000—01; grad. rsch. asst. electron rsch. group dept. radiation physics U. Tex./M.D. Anderson Cancer Ctr., Houston, 2001—03; chief med. physics Travis AFB, Calif., 2003—05; diagnostic imaging dep. flight comdr., 2004—05; dep. chief radiation protection divsn. and USAF radioisotope com. secretariat Bolling AFB, DC, 2005—. Decorated Meritorious Svc. medal, Air Force Commendation medal with two oak leaf clusters, Air Force Recognition Ribbon; named Health Physicist of Yr., Air Material Command, 2005, USAF, 2005; scholar, U. Ala., Huntsville, 1986—87; Honor scholar, 1988—89. Mem. Am. Assn. Physicists in Medicine, Health Physics Soc., Air Force Assn. Baptist. Achievements include development of scattering polarimeter and measurement/analysis of diffraction grating polarization and efficiency properties; validation of compton scatter and attenuation correction methods for cardiac SPECT imaging; electron conformal therapy for postmastectomy irradiation.

RODGERS, STEPHEN JOHN, lawyer, physician, consultant; b. Phila., July 10, 1943; s. Harry Edward Rodgers and Antoinette Julia Muckenfuss; m. Roberta Elaine Rhine, Sept. 21, 1974; children: Abigail Elizabeth, Rebecca Elizabeth. MD, Hahnemann U., 1969; JD, Widener U., 1989. Bar: Pa. 1990, N.J. 1990; med. lic., Pa., Del., N.J. Pvt. practice in family practice and emergency medicine Del. Pain Clinic, Wilmington, 1975-89, asst. dir., 1989-92; pvt. practice as medicolegal cons. Wilmington, 1992—. Mem. Med. Assistance and Health Svcs. Adv. Bd., NJ, 1996-98; chair Task Force on Ind. Med. Exam., Dept. Labor and Industry, Commonwealth of Pa., 1996-98. Comdr. USN, 1968-75; capt. USNR, 1975—; surgeon gen. N.J. Naval Militia Joint Command. Fellow Am. Acad. Family Physicians, Am. Acad. Disability Evaluating Physicians, Am. Acad. Emergency Medicine, Am. Coll. Legal Medicine; mem. Aerospace Med. Assn., Pa. Bar Assn. (health care com. 1991—), Del. Acad. Medicine, NJ Acad. Family Physicians (ho. of dels. 1989-91), Vietnam Vets. Am. Republican. Roman Catholic. Avocations: equestrian, pro bono veterans and disability advocate. Home: PO Box 54 Alloway NJ 08001-0054 Office: Ste 14 1701 Augustine Wilmington DE 19803

RODGERS, SUZANNE HOOKER, physiologist, consultant; b. Rochester, NY, Dec. 26, 1939; d. John Ashmead and Priscilla May (Bodman) Rodgers AB, Vassar Coll., 1961; PhD, U. Rochester Med. Ctr., 1967. Postdoctoral fellow USPHS Middlesex Hosp., London, 1966—68; ergonomist Eastman Kodak Co., Rochester, 1968—82; ind. cons. in ergonomics Rochester, 1982—. Author: Working With Backache, 1985; tech. editor, prin. author Ergonomic Design for People at Work, 1983, 86, co-editor, contr. Kodak's Ergonomic Design for People at Work 2d edit., 2003 Bd. dirs., chmn. com., v.p. Rochester Philharm. Orch. Inc., 1969-75; bd. dirs. Opera Theatre Rochester, 1969-75; bd. dirs., chmn. com., pres. Monroe County Bd. Health, Rochester, 1979-88 Mem. Human Factors and Ergonomics Soc., (pres. We. N.Y. chpt. 1971-72), Am. Coll. Sports Medicine Avocations: photography, gardening, reading, silent films. Home and Office: 169 Huntington Hls Rochester NY 14622-1121 Office Phone: 585-544-3587. Personal E-mail: shrodgers@aol.com.

RODGERS, T(HURMAN) J., semiconductor company executive; AB in physics and chemistry, Dartmouth Coll., 1970; MS in electrical engring., Stanford U., 1973, PhD in electrical engring., 1975. Managed MOS memory design group Am. Microsystems Inc., 1975—80; managed static RAM product group Advanced Micro Devices, 1980—82; founder, pres., CEO Cypress Semiconductor Corp., San Jose, Calif., 1982—. Bd. dirs. Silicon Light Machines, Bloom Energy (formerly Ion Am.), SunPower Corp., Cypress MicroSystems, Provina. Bd. trustees Dartmouth Coll., 2004—. Named CEO of the Year, Financial World mag., 1996; named one of 100 People Who Changed Our World, Upside mag., 2001, Top 100 Chief Executives, Chief Executive mag., 2002, 100 Best Corporate Citizens, Business Ethics mag., 2005; recipient Encore award entrepreneurial company of the year, Stanford U. Bus. Sch., 1988, Entrepreneur of the Year award, Ernst & Young, 1991. Mem.: Semiconductor Industry Assn. Achievements include patents in field. Avocations: cooking, movies, collecting wines, jogging. Office: Cypress Semiconductor Corp 198 Champion Ct San Jose CA 95134 *

RODGMAN, ALAN, chemist, consultant; b. Aberdare, Wales, Feb. 7, 1924; came to U.S. from Canada, 1954, naturalized, 1961; s. Arch and Margaret (Llewellyn) R.; m. Doris Curley, June 7, 1947; children: Eric, Paul, Mark. BA in Chemistry, U. Toronto, 1949, MA in Organic Chemistry, 1951, PhD in Organic Chemistry, 1953. Rsch. asst. med. rsch. dept. U. Toronto, 1947-51, rsch. assoc., 1951-54; tchr., courses in organic chemistry, phys. chemistry, math. Chem. Inst. Can., 1951-54; sr. rsch. chemist R.J. Reynolds Tobacco Co., Winston-Salem, N.C., 1954-65, head smoke rsch. sect., 1965-75, mgr. analytical rsch., 1975-76, dir. rsch., 1976-80, dir. fundamental rsch. and devel., 1980-87; cons. in field, 1987—. Mem. editl. bd. Tobacco Sci., 1963-67 (Vol. 31 Tobacco Sci. dedicated in his name 1987), Beitrage zur Tabakforschung Internat., 1978-87. Mem. Tobacco Working Group, Nat. Cancer Inst., 1976-77, Tech. Study Group on Cigarette and Little Cigar Fire Safety, 1984-87, Sci. Commn. Cooperation Ctr. for Sci. Rsch. Relative to Tobacco, 1982-84. With Royal Can. Navy, 1942-45. Recipient Tobacco Sci. Rsch. Conf. Inaugural Lifetime Achievement award, 2005. Mem. Coun. Tobacco Rsch. (industry tech. com. 1956-62), Chem. Inst. Can., Can. Chem. Soc., Am. Chem. Soc. Episcopalian. Home: 2828 Birchwood Dr Winston Salem NC 27103-3410

RODIN, EUGENE, aerospace scientist, researcher, engineering educator; b. Moscow, Feb. 20, 1937; arrived in U.S., 1993; s. Ivan Fedotovich Rodin and Maria Ivanovna Rodina; m. Bella Medvedeva, Jan. 15, 1981; children: Oleg Medvedev, Karmela Medvedeva. MS, Bauman State Tech. U., Moscow, 1960, PhD, 1969. Instr. Bauman State Tech. U., Moscow, 1960—64, asst. prof., 1964—70, assoc. prof., 1970—93; head sci. lab. Suffolk U., Boston, 1995—2005, asst. prof., 2005—. Sci. rschr. Inst. Spl. Mech. Engring., Moscow, 1970—93, Heat Engring. Rsch. inst., Moscow, 1972—93. Author: Heat Exchanges in Cryogenic Engineering, 1988, Heat Calculation of Cryogenic System, 1990; contbr. articles to profl. publs. Recipient Gold medal, Ministry Spl. Engring., Moscow, 1985, Jubilee Gagarin's medal, NASA, Russia, 2001, Jubilee Tereshkova's medal, 2002. Avocations: travel, reading, sailing, skiing.

RODIN, JUDITH SEITZ, foundation administrator, former academic administrator, psychologist, educator; b. Phila., Sept. 9, 1944; d. Morris and Sally R. (Winson) Seitz. m. Paul Verkuil. AB, U. Pa., 1966; PhD, U. Columbia, 1970. Asst. prof. psychology NYU, 1970—72; assoc. prof. Yale U., 1975—79, prof., dir. grad. studies, 1982—89, Philip R. Allen prof. psychology, medicine and psychiatry, 1984—94, chmn. dept. psychology, 1989—91, dean Grad. Sch., 1991—92, provost, 1992—94; pres. U. Pa., Phila., 1994—2004, prof. psychology, medicine and psychiatry, 1994—2004; pres. Rockefeller Found., NYC, 2005—. Chmn. John D. and Catherine T. MacArthur Found. Rsch. Network on Determinants and Consequences of Health-Promoting and Health-Damaging Behavior, 1983-93; vice chair coun. press. U. Rsch. Assn., 1994-95, chair, 1995-96; mem. Ind. Panel to Review Safety Procedures at The White House, 1994-95; chair adv. com. Robert Wood Johnson Found., 1994—; mem. Pres. Clinton's Com. Advisors Sci. and Tech., 1994—; mem. Coun. Competitiveness, 1997—; mem. nominating com. N.Y. Stock Exch., 1998—; bd. dirs. Aetna, Electronic Data Sys., AMR, Citigroup Inc., 2004-. Author: (with S. Schachter) Obese Humans and Rats, 1978, Exploding the Weight Myths, 1982, Body Traps, 1992; chief editor Appetite Jour., 1979-92; contbr. articles to profl. jours. Mem. Pa. Task Force on Higher Edn. Funding, 1994; bd. dirs. Catalyst, N.Y.C., 1994—; trustee Brookings Inst., 1995—; pres. steering com. Am. Reads, 1997—. Recipient Phila. award, 2004, William Penn award; grantee NSF, 1973—82, NIH, 1981—. Fellow AAAS, APA (bd. sci. affairs 1979-82, pres. divsn. 38 health psychology 1982-83, Outstanding Contbn. award 1980, Disting. Sci. award 1977, Lifetime Achievement award 2005), Am. Acad. Arts and Scis., Soc. Behavioral Medicicine; mem. AAU (mem. exec. com. 1996—), Am. Philosophical Soc., Inst. Medicine of NAS, Acad. Behavioral Medicine Rsch., Ea. Psychol. Assn. (exec. bd. 1980-82), Phi Beta Kappa, Sigma Xi (pres. Yale chpt. 1986-87). Achievements include being the first women to be named president of an Ivy League institution, 1993. Office: Rockefeller Found 420 Fifth Ave New York NY 10018 Business E-Mail: president@rockfound.org.

RODIN, RITA ANGELA, lawyer; b. NYC, 1968; BS magna cum laude, Boston Coll., 1990; JD, St. John's U., 1990. Bar: N.J. 1994, N.Y. 1994. Law clk. Hon. Thomas C. Platt U.S. Dist. Ct. (ea. dist.) NY, 1993—94; atty. Skadden, Arps, Slate, Meagher & Flom LLP, NYC, 1994—2001, ptnr. Intellectual Property and Tech. Group, 2001—. Office: Skadden Arps Slate Meagher & Flom LLP Four Times Sq New York NY 10036 Office Phone: 212-735-3774. Business E-Mail: rrodin@skadden.com.

RODINO, VINCENT LOUIS, insurance company executive; b. NYC, June 25, 1929; s. Vincenzo and Sofia (De Toro) R.; m. Marie Green; children: Peter Vincent, Vincent Douglas. BA, NYU, 1957. CLU. With Equitable Fin. Cos., NYC, 1946—, chief mktg. svcs. sector, 1983—84, chief traditional products sector, 1984—86, chmn., CEO Traebco subs., 1984—86, chief sales support sector, 1986—89; dep. pres. northeastern region Equitable Ins. Cos., NYC, 1989—92; bd. dirs. Traebco subs. Equitable. Trustee Life Underwriter Tng. Coun., Washington, 1987. Served as sgt. U.S. Army, 1951-53. Mem. Assn. Advanced Life Underwriting, Nat. Assn. Life Underwriters, N.Y.C. Chpt. CLUs. Business E-Mail: vlrodino@aol.com.

RODITE, ROBERT R.R., research scientist, finance and computer consultant, educator; b. Easton, Pa., Oct. 17, 1942; s. Victor James and Alice Cecilia (Zatovich) R.; m. Patricia Ann Sule, Apr. 8, 1967; children: Colleen P., Robert J. BSEE, Lafayette Coll., 1964; MSEE, Caif. Inst. Tech., 1965. Rsch. engr., mgr. mfg. rsch. lab. IBM, Endicott, N.Y., 1965-70, mfg. engring. mgr. electronic packaging mfg., 1970-72, devel. engring. mgr. electronic packaging engring., 1972-77, program dir. corp. engring., programming & tech. staff Armonk, N.Y., 1977-79, product engring. mgr., sr. engr. multichip module devel. East Fishkill, N.Y., 1979-81, system mgr., sr. tech. staff mem. fin. industry devel. Charlotte, N.C., 1981-92, sr. tech. staff mem. corp. tech. strategy devel. staff Armonk, 1992-93; pres. Rodite Assocs., Inc., Charlotte, 1993—; lectr. math. and bus. Belmont Abbey Coll., 2001—04. Workgroup mem. Am. Nat. Standards Inst. Com. X9B Stds. Com., 1991-97; chmn. IBM Image Processing and Visualization

Interdivisional Tech. Liaison Com., 1992-93. Contbr. articles to profl. jours.; patentee in field. Asst. scoutmaster Boy Scouts Am., Charlotte, 1991, 92; mid. sch. basketball asst. coach, Charlotte, 1991-94; com. mem. Town County Consolidation Com., Endicott, 1970s; mem. Cath. sch. bd. Diocese of Charlotte, 1988-90; pres. Homeowners Assn., Charlotte, 2001-03, bd. dirs., 2000—. Tau Beta Pi fellow, Calif. Inst. Tech., 1964. Mem. IEEE (sr.), Assn. for Info. and Image Mgmt. Internat. (designated Master Info. Tech. 1997, cert. document Image Architech, Laureate of Info. Technologies 1998), Phi Beta Kappa, Tau Beta Pi, Eta Kappa Nu. Avocations: personal computers, travel. Home: 9664 Chaumont Ln Charlotte NC 28277-2140

RODITTI, ESTHER C(LAIRE), lawyer, writer; b. LA, Feb. 7, 1933; d. David and Lucy Roditti; m. Oscar H. Schachter, Aug. 8, 1957 (div. Oct. 1992); children: Charles David, Susan Dayana. BA, UCLA, 1954; JD, Harvard U., 1957. Bar: N.Y. 1959. Assoc. Stickles, Hayden and Kennedy, NYC, 1957-62; asst. dir. Legis. Drafting Fund Columbia U., NYC, 1962-65, cons., 1965-67, N.Y.C. Air Pollution Control Dept., 1965-67; instr. and cons. New Sch. for Social Rsch., NYC, 1968-70; cons. Internat. League for Rights of Man, NYC, 1969, Rand Inst., NYC, 1969, U.S. Soviet Environ. Studies Program, UN Assn., NYC, 1969; sr. rsch. assoc. Ctr. for Policy Rsch. Columbia U., 1970-73; sr. program officer Ford Found., NYC, 1972-78; pres. Esther Roditti Schachter, P.C., NYC, 1978-83; ptnr. Schachter & Froling, NYC, 1983-85, Schachter, Courter, Purcell & Kobert, NYC, 1985-92; pres. Esther C. Roditti, P.C., 1992—. Spkr., lectr., panelist profl. assn. confs., forums, workshops, U.S., Can., Tokyo, London. Author: N.Y.C. Air Pollution Control Code Annotated, 1965, Enforcing Air Pollution Controls, 1979, Financial Support of Women's Programs in the 1970's, 1979, Computer Contracts Reference Directory, 1979-83, Hiring and Firing Knowledge Workers, 1995, Tax and Business Handbook for Consultants and Clients, 1998; co-author: Charities and Charitable Foundations, 1974; author, co-author articles in field; legal editor: Computer Economics, 1983-89; editor Computer Law & Tax Report, 1984-86, pub., editor, 1986-2000; author, editor Computer Contracts-Negotiating Drafting Treatise, 1992—. Nat. governing bd. Common Cause, 1979-82, mem. state governing bd., N.Y., 1982-84; mem. com. on urban environ. Citizens Union, N.Y.C., 1969-73; mem. West Side Dem. Club, 1958-63. Recipeint Outstanding Svc. award Brandeis U., Nat. Women's Com., 1973; grantee Ford Found., 1970, NSF, 1971. Mem. ABA (lectr. 1987), Assn. Bar City NY (founder, chmn. com. on computer law 1980—), NY State Bar Assn., Computer Law Assn. (lectr. 1985, bulletin editor 1998-, bd. dirs. 2000-), Am. Arbitration Assn. (chair com. for computer disputes 1985-), Phi Beta Kappa. Office Phone: 212-879-3322. E-mail: ecroditti@aol.com.

RODKIN, GARY M., food products executive; BA in Econs., Rutgers U., NJ; MBA, Harvard Bus. Sch. Various mktg. and gen. mgmt. positions up to pres. Yoplait-Colombo yogurt unit Gen. Mills; pres. Tropicana N.Am., 1995—98, pres., CEO, 1998—99, PepsiCola N.Am., 1999—2002; pres. PepsiCo, Beverages and Foods N.Am., 2002—03, CEO, 2002—05, chmn., 2003—05; pres., CEO ConAgra Foods, Inc., Omaha, 2005—. Office: ConAgra Foods Inc 1 ConAgra Dr Omaha NE 68102-5001 Office Phone: 402-595-4000. *

RODLEY, CAROL A., federal agency administrator; b. Mass. married; 3 children. Grad., Smith Coll. Dep. chief of mission Am. Embassy, Phnom Pehn, Cambodia, 1997—2000; dep. exec. sec. US Dept. State, Washington, 2001—03, prin. dep. asst. sec. Bur. Internat. Orgn. Affairs, 2003—, acting asst. sec. Bur. Intelligence and Rsch., 2005—. Recipient Christian A. Herter award, Am. Fgn. Svc. Assn., 2000, Sr. Performance award, US Dept. State, Human Rights & Democracy award, James Clement Dunn award for Leadership, Dir. Ctrl. Intelligence Exceptional Humint Collector award, Intelligence Community Seal Medalion. Office: Bur Intelligence and Rsch US Dept State 2201 C St NW Washington DC 20520

RODMAN, ALPINE C., arts and crafts company executive, photographer; b. Roswell, N. Mex., June 23, 1952; s. Robert Elsworth and Verna Mae (Means) R.; m. Sue Arlene Lawson, Dec. 13, 1970; 1 child, Connie Lynn. Student, Colo. State U., 1970—71, U. No. Colo. Ptnr. Pinel Silver Shop, Loveland, Colo., 1965-68, salesman, 1968-71; real estate salesman Loveland, 1971-73; mgr. Traveling Traders, Phoenix, 1974-75; co-owner Deer Track Traders, Loveland, 1975-85; pres. Deer Track Traders, Ltd., Loveland, 1985—. Spkr., lectrs. at seminars in field, 2004—. Author: The Vanishing Indian: Fact or Fiction?, 1985. Mem. Civil Air Patrol, 1965-72, 87-92, dep. comdr. for cadets Greeley, Colo., 1988-90; cadet comdr. Ft. Collins, Colo., 1968, 70, Colo. rep. to youth tng. program, 1969, U.S. youth rep. to Japan, 1970. Mem. We. and English Salesmen's Assn. (bd. dirs. 1990), Indian Arts and Crafts Assn. (bd. dirs. 1988-94, exec. com. 1989-92, v.p. 1990, pres. 1991, market chmn. 1992), Crazy Horse Grass Roots Club. Office: Deer Track Traders Ltd PO Box 448 Loveland CO 80539-0448 *Personal philosophy: I believe that most good and bad in the world comes out of respect or lack of respect for one's self, fellow man, environment and creator.*

RODMAN, LEIBA, mathematician; b. Riga, Latvia, June 9, 1949; arrived in U.S., 1985; s. Zalman and Haya Rodman; m. Ella Levitan, Feb. 2, 1983; children: Daniel, Ruth, Benjamin, Naomi. Diploma in maths., Latvian State U., 1971; MA in Statis., Tel Aviv U., 1976, PhD in Maths., 1978. Instr. Tel Aviv U., 1976-78, sr. lectr., 1981-83, assoc. prof., 1983-85; postdoctoral fellow U. Calgary, Can., 1978-80; from assoc. to full prof. Ariz. State U., Tempe, 1985-87; prof. math. Coll. William and Mary, Williamsburg, Va., 1987—. Author: Introduction to Operator Polynomials, 1989, (with others) Matrix Polynomials, 1982, Matrices and Indefinite Scalar Products, 1983, Invariant Subspaces of Matrices with Applications, 1986, Interpolation of Rational Matrix Functions, 1990, Algebraic Riccati Equations, 1995, Indefinite Linear Algebra and Applications, 2005; co-editor: Contributions to Operator Theory and Its Applications, 1988, Current Trends in Operator Theory and its Applications, 2004. Mem. Am. Math. Soc., Internat. Linear-Algebra Soc., Soc. Indsl. and Applied Math. Office: Coll of William & Mary Dept Math PO Box 8795 Williamsburg VA 23187-8795 Office Phone: 757-221-2027. E-mail: lxrodm@math.wm.edu.

RODMAN, LEONARD C., engineering and construction executive; BS in Civil Engring., Iowa State U., 1971; MS in Environ. Engring., U. Mo., 1978. Joined Black & Veatch, Kansas City, Mo., 1971, various project mgmt. positions environ. divsn., named head N.Am. divsn. infrastructure bus., 1992, CEO, pres., 1998—, also chmn., 2000—. Bd. trustees, cmty./legis. affairs com. U. Mo., Kansas City; bd. advisors U. Kans. - Edward Campus; mem. Iowa State Engring Coll. Indsl. Adv. Consul. Recipient Profl. Achievement Citation in Engring., U. Iowa Coll. Engring., 2003. Mem.: Am. Acad. Environ. Engineers, Water Environment Fedn., Nat. Soc. Profl. Engineers, Mo. Soc. Profl. Engineers, Am. Water Works Assn., Am. Soc. Civil Engineers. Office: Black & Veatch 11401 Lamar Ave Overland Park KS 66211

RODMAN, PETER WARREN, foreign policy specialist; b. Boston, Nov. 24, 1943; s. Sumner and Helen Rhoda (Morris) R.; m. F. Veronique Boulad, Apr. 13, 1980; children: Theodora, Nicholas. BA summa cum laude, Harvard U., 1964, JD, 1969; BA, MA, Oxford U., Eng., 1966. Staff mem. NSC, Washington, 1969-77; fellow in diplomatic studies Ctr. for Strategic and Internat. Studies, Washington, 1977-83; dir. rsch. Kissinger Assocs., Washington, 1982-83; mem. policy planning council US Dept. State, Washington, 1983-84, dir. policy planning staff, 1984-86; dep. asst. to pres. for nat. security affairs (fgn. policy) NSC, Washington, 1986-87, NSC counselor, spl. asst. to pres. for nat. security affairs, 1987-90; fellow Johns Hopkins Fgn. Policy Inst., Washington, 1990-93; dir. Middle East and Eurasian studies Ctr. for Strategic and Internat. Studies, Washington, 1994-95; dir. nat. security programs Nixon Ctr., Washington, 1995-2001; asst. sec. for internat. security affairs US Dept. Def., Washington, 2001—07; sr. fellow Brookings Inst., Washington, 2007—. Author: More Precious Than Peace: The Cold War and the Struggle for the Third World, 1994; sr. editor Nat. Rev., 1991-99; contbr. articles to profl. jours. V.p. World Affairs Coun., Washington, 1996-2001; trustee Freedom House, 1997-2001. Mem. Coun. on Fgn. Rels., Internat. Inst. for Strategic Studies, Atlantic Coun. U.S., Cosmos Club. Office: Brookings Inst 1775 Massachusetts Ave NW Washington DC 20036-2103 Office Phone: 202-797-6046. Business E-Mail: prodman@brookings.edu.

RODMAN, SUE A., wholesale company executive, artist, writer; b. Ft. Collins, Colo., Oct. 1, 1951; d. Marvin F. Lawson and Barbara I. (Miller) Lawson Shue; m. Alpine C. Rodman, Dec. 13, 1970; 1 child, Connie L. Rodman; m. Graham L. Jackson. Student, Woodbury Bus./Arts Coll., Calif., 1969, Colo. State U., 1970—73. Silversmith Pinel Silver Shop, Loveland, Colo., 1970-71; asst. mgr. Traveling Traders, Phoenix, 1974-75; co-owner, co-mgr. Native Am. arts and crafts company Deer Track Traders, Loveland, 1975-85; v.p. Deer Track Traders, Ltd., Loveland, 1985—. Author: The Book of Contemporary Indian Arts and Crafts, 1985, short stories; contbr. articles to popular mags. Mem. U.S. Senatorial Club, 1982-87, Rep. Presdl. Task Force, 1984-90; mem. Civil Air Patrol, 1969-73, 87-90, pers. officer, 1988-90. Mem.: Indian Arts and Crafts Assn., Western and English Sales Assn., Compassion Internat. (sponsor), Nat. Wildlife Fedn., Crazy Horse Grass Roots Club. Mem. Am. Baptist Ch. Avocations: museums, piano, recreation research, fashion design.

RODMAN, SUMNER, insurance company executive; b. Malden, Mass., Aug. 5, 1915; s. Nathan Markel and Sara Ruth (Slater) Rodman; m. Helen Rhoda Morris, July 2, 1942; children: Peter Warren, John Slater. AB cum laude, Harvard U., 1935. CLU. Ins. broker, employee benefits specialist Aetna Life Ins. and Annuity Co., Boston, 1935-98; with Rodman Ins. Agy., Inc., Needham, Mass.; life ins. adviser, 1953—. Pres. Boston Life Ins. and Trust Coun., 1958—59. Bd. dirs. Boston Estate Planning Coun., 1960—85, pres., 1958; mem. Anti-Defamation League B'nai Brith, World Affairs Coun. Boston; chmn. class com. Harvard, 1935; bd. dirs. Jewish Family and Children's Svc., Boston, 1953—85; active Am. Jewish Com.; hon. trustee Temple Israel, Boston; bd. dirs. Youth Tennis Found. New Eng., 1963—85, Simons-Gutman Found., 1965—, Alzheimers Assn. Ea. Mass., 1990—97; hon. trustee Combined Jewish Philanthropies of Greater Boston, 1967—. Served to capt. AUS, 1941—46, ETO. Fellow CLU Inst., 1952, 1961. Mem.: New Eng. Tennis Assn. (bd. dirs. 1966—68, Hall of Fame 1992), Am. Soc. CLUs (pres. 1972—73), Boston Life Underwriters Assn. (pres. 1965—66), Am. Coll. (trustee 1971—74), Million Dollar Round Table (life), Wightman Tennis Ctr. Club (Weston, Mass.), Harvard Varsity Club (Boston), Harvard Club (Boston), Newton Club (Mass.), Squash and Tennis Club, Masons, Golden Key Soc. Jewish. Office: Rodman Ins Agy Inc 145 Rosemary St Needham MA 02494-3238 Home Phone: 617-527-8745; Office Phone: 781-247-7835. Business E-Mail: srodman@rodmanins.com.

RODNING, CHARLES BERNARD, surgeon; b. Pipestone, Minn., Aug. 4, 1943; s. Selmer Bernard and Ida Amanda (Selness) R.; m. Mary Elizabeth Lipke, June 15, 1968; children: Christopher Bernard, Soren Piers, Kai Johannes. BS, Gustavus Adolphus Coll., St. Peter, Minn., 1965; MD, U. Rochester, 1970; PhD, U. Minn., 1979. Diplomate Am. Bd. Med. Examiners, Am. Bd. Surgery. Intern, asst. resident dept. surgery U. Rochester Sch. Medicine and Dentistry, 1970-72; assoc. resident to chief resident, med. fellow dept. surgery U. Minn. Health Scis. Ctr., Mpls., 1972-79; prof. dept cell biology and neurosci. U. South Ala., Mobile, 1981—, prof. dept. surgery, 1981—, vice chmn. dept. surgery, 1981—2006, chmn. dept. surgery, 2006—, dir. gen. surgery, 1996—. Field liaison physician Commn. on Cancer-ACS, Chgo., 1984—; mem. med. adv. bd. Ala. Organ & Tissue Ctr., Birmingham, 1988—; mem. bd. censors Med. Soc. County of Mobile, 2006; mem. Bd. Health County of Mobile, pres., 2007. Author: Elan Vital, 1988, Wode and Ston, 1988, Sorrowful Wheel, 1989, Ponderings, 1990, The Sea Rises in the West, 1991, Stepping Stones, 1991, Snowbound Below the Firn Line, 1991, Love Knot, 1994, Papering Dreams, 1994, Carry Onward, 1996, Swaying Grass, 1998, Tradition of Excellence: Pictorial History of Surgical Education at the Mobile General Hospital and University of South Alabama College of Medicine and Medical Center, 1999; reviewer: Jour. Histochem. Cytochem., 1988—; contbr. (articles) Clin. Anatomy, Surg. Endoscopy, Pharos, Jours. Thoracic Cardiovasc. Surgery, So. Med. Jour., others. Bd. dirs. Mobile Mental Health Ctr., Mental Health Found. of South Ala., Mobile Med. Mus., Christian Med. Ministry of South Ala. Comdr. USN, 1974-81. Recipient Physicians Recognition award AMA, 1980, 85, 88, 91, 95, 99, 02, Bacaner Rsch. award Minn. Med. Found., 1979, Humanism in Medicine award Arnold P. Gold Found., Healthcare Found. N.J., 2002, Howard L. Holley award Med. Assn. State Ala., 2002. Fellow ACS, Internat. Coll. Surgeons (vice regent Ala. chpt. 1989—); mem. Iota Delta Gamma, Alpha Omega Alpha, Phi Kappa Phi. Office: U South Ala Coll Med Allied Health Professions Mobile AL 36617-2293 Office Phone: 251-471-7034. Business E-Mail: crodning@usouthal.edu.

RODNUNSKY, SIDNEY, lawyer, educator; b. Edmonton, Alta., Can., Feb. 3, 1946; s. B. and I. Rodnunsky; m. Teresita Asuncion; children: Naomi, Shawna, Rachel, Tevie, Claire, Donna, Sidney Jr. BEd, U. Alberta, 1966, LLB, 1973; MEd, U. Calgary, 1969, grad. diploma, 1990; BS, U. of State of N.Y., 1988; MBA, Greenwich U., 1990. Served as regional counsel to Her Majesty the Queen in Right of the Dominion of Can.; former gov. Grande Prairie Regional Coll.; now prin. legal counsel Can. Nat. exec., Alta. coord. for gifted children, ombudsman, SIG coord. Mensa Can.; past pres. Grande Prairie and Dist. Bar Assn., Alta Tchrs. Assn., Aspenview. Author: Breathalyzer Casebook; editor: The Children Speak. Decorated knight Grand Cross Sovereign and Royal Order of Piast, knight Grand Cross Order of St. John the Baptist; knight Hospitaller Order St. John of Jerusalem; Prince of Kiev, Prince of Trabzon, Prince and Duke of Rodari, Duke of Chernigov, Count of Riga, Count of St. John of Alexandria; named to Honorable Order of Ky. Colonels; named adm. State of Tex.; recipient Presdl. Legion of Merit. Mem. Law Soc. Alta., Law Soc. Sask., Can. Bar Assn., Inst. Can. Mgmt., Phi Delta Kappa. E-mail: wonderfulschool@hotmail.com.

RODOWSKY, LAWRENCE FRANCIS, retired state judge; b. Balt., Nov. 10, 1930; s. Lawrence Anthony and Frances (Gardner) R.; m. Colby Fossett, Aug. 7, 1954; children: Laura Rodowsky Ramos, Alice Rodowsky-Seegers, Emily Rodowsky Savopoulos, Sarah Jones Rodowsky, Gregory, Katherine Rodowsky O'Connor. AB, Loyola Coll., Balt., 1952; LLB, U. Md., 1956. Bar: Md. 1956. Ct. crier, law clk. U.S. Dist. Ct. Md., 1954-56; asst. atty. gen. Md., 1960-61; assoc., ptnr. firm Frank, Bernstein, Conaway & Goldman, Balt., 1956-79; judge Ct. Appeals Md., Annapolis, 1980-2000, mem. rules com., 1969-80; sr. status judge Ct. of Spl. Appeals Md., Annapolis, 2001—. Lectr., asst. instr. U. Md. Law Sch., 1958-68, 87-91; reporter jud. dept. Md. Constl. Conv. Commn., 1966-67. Chmn. Gov. Md. Commn. Racing Reform, 1979. Fellow Am. Coll. Trial Lawyers; mem. Md. Bar Assn., Balt. Bar Assn. Roman Catholic. Home: 6614 Walnutwood Cir Baltimore MD 21212-1213 Office: 620 CM Mitchell Jr Courthse 100 N Calvert St Baltimore MD 21202 Office Phone: 410-333-4374. Business E-Mail: lawrence.rodowsky@mdcourts.gov.

RODRICKS, DANIEL JOHN, columnist, television commentator; b. Brockton, Mass., Mar. 8, 1954; s. Joseph Allen and Rose Mary (Popolo) Rodricks; m. Lillian M. Donnard, Sept. 6, 1980. BA, U. Bridgeport, 1976. Reporter Patriot Ledger, Quincy, Mass., 1973-75; wire editor Middletown Times Record, NY, 1975; reporter Balt. Evening Sun, 1976-79; columnist Balt. Sun, 1979—; reporter, commentator Sta. WBAL-TV, Balt., 1980-93; host The Dan Rodricks Show Sta. WBAL Radio, 1989-93; host Rodricks For Breakfast Sta. WMAR-TV, Balt., 1995-99. Author: Mencken Doesn't Live Here Anymore, 1989, Balt., Charm City, 1998. Recipient Heywood Broun award Newspaper Guild, 1983, Front Page award, 1983, numerous regional journalism awards, 1990-2000; awards from Sigma Delta Chi, Md.-Del.-D.C. Press Assn., AP, Firefighters Internat., and others. Mem. Sigma Delta Chi Democrat. Roman Catholic. Avocations: cooking, fishing, theater, operetta. Office: Balt Sun 501 N Calvert St PO Box 1377 Baltimore MD 21278 E-mail: TJIDAN@aol.com.

RODRIGUES, MARGARET L., elementary school educator, consultant; BA, San Jose State U., Calif., 1972, M in adminstrn. and leadership, 1990. Cert. K-8th grade life tchr. Tchr. Cupertino Union, Calif., 1973—76, Morgan Hill Unified Sch., Calif., 1976—, prin., 1990—98. Author: (book) Journey to the Melting Pot, 1990; prodr.: (DVD) Two Rivers Run Through It, 2005 (Calif. Multi Media Best Elem. Project). Bd. dirs. Calif. Assn. for Gifted, LA, 1994—98. Named Tchr. Yr., Calif. Assn. for Gifted, 1990; recipient, Santa Clara County Dept. Edn., 2005. Mem.: San Jose Hist. Mus., Young Ladies Inst., Delta Kappa Gamma. Democrat. Roman Catholic. Avocation: reading. Office: Los Paseos Elem Sch 121 Avenida Grande San Jose CA 95139-1107

RODRIGUES-PAVAO, ANTONIO, vocal music teacher; b. Fall River, Mass., Dec. 13, 1943; s. Joseph and Maria Teresa Rodrigues-Pavao; children: Aaron, Stephen; m. Nora Macins, July 7, 1984. BMusic, MMusic, U. Mass., 1970, U. Ill., 1974. Cert. secondary music tchr., Mass., Ill., Wis. Vocal music tchr. William Horlick H.S., Racine, Wis., 1977-2000; voice tchr. Carroll Coll., Waukesha, Wis., 2000—; pvt. studio tchr. Artistic dir. Elizabethan High Renaissance Feaste, Racine, 1977-2000. Composer various choral pieces, pieces for voice and piano; bass-baritone solo profl. performances; dir. numerous profl. and amateur musicals and operas; dir. choirs touring U.K., Denmark, Czech Republic, Austria, Slovakia, Bulgaria, Carnegie Hall, 27 states. Served with USAF, 1961-65. Mem. Nat. Assn. Tchrs. of Singing (chpt. corr. sec. 1992-98, exec. v.p. 1998-2001), Voice Found. Avocations: weightlifting, home design and remodeling. Home: 1239 N Osborne Blvd Racine WI 53405-1719 E-mail: apavao@wi.rr.com.

RODRIGUEZ, ALCIBIADES J., neurologist, educator; s. Alcibiades Rodriguez and Flora Sanchez; m. Mae Cafarella, Apr. 6, 2001. MD, U. Panama, Panama City, 1994. Cert. in internal medicine St. Vincent's Med. Ctr., NY, 2000, in neurology Tufts U. Sch. Medicine, 2003, in clin. neurophysiology EEG/epilepsy Mayo Clinic, Minn., 2004, in sleep medicine Mayo Clinic, Minn., 2005, diplomate Am. Bd. Internal Medicine, Am. Bd. Neurology, Am. Bd. Clin. Neurophysiology, Am. Bd. Sleep Medicine. Asst. prof. neurology Sch. Medicine NYU, NYC, 2005—; med. dir. NY Sleep Inst., NYC, 2006—. Mem.: Am. Acad.Sleep Medicine, Am. Epilepsy Soc., Am. Acad. Neurology. Achievements include research in sleep related disorders and epilepsy research. Office: New York Sleep Inst 724 Second Ave New York NY 10016 Home Phone: 718-392-8581; Office Phone: 212-871-0227. Office Fax: 212-871-1827. Business E-Mail: alcibiades.rodriguez@med.nyu.edu.

RODRIGUEZ, ALEX (ALEXANDER EMMANUEL RODRIGUEZ), professional baseball player; b. NYC, July 27, 1975; s. Victor Rodriguez and Lourdes Navarro; m. Cynthia Scurtis, Nov. 2, 2002; 1 child, Natasha Alexander. Draft pick Seattle Mariners, 1993, profl. baseball player, 1995—2001, Tex. Rangers, 2001—03, NY Yankees, 2004—. Mem. US Team World Baseball Classic, 2006. Co-author (with Greg Brown): (children's book) Hit a Grand Slam, 1998; author: Out of the Ballpark, 2007. Founder Grand Slam for Kids, 1996—, Alex Rodriguez Found., 1998—. Named Maj. League Player of Yr., 1996, 2002, Am. League Batting Champion, 1996, Am. League MVP, 2003, 2005; named to Am. League All-Star Team, 1996—98, 2000—07; recipient Hank Aaron award, 2001—03, Gold Glove award, 2002—03, Silver Slugger award, 1996, 1998—2003, 2005. Achievements include being the third player in major league history with 40 home runs and 40 stolen bases in one season; leading the Am. League in home runs, 2001-03; leading the Am. League in runs scored, 2001, 2003; leading the Am. League in RBI's, 2002; youngest player in MLB history to hit 400 home runs, June 8, 2005; most home runs in a season by right-handed hitter in Yankee History, 2005; youngest player in MLB history to hit 500 home runs, August 4, 2007. Office: c/o NY Yankees E 161st St and River Ave Bronx NY 10452 *

RODRIGUEZ, ANGEL LUIS, electrical engineer; b. Hartford, Conn., June 30, 1976; s. Angel Felipe Rodriguez, Sr. and Marlene Rodriguez; m. Kimberly Rodriguez, Oct. 6, 2001; 1 child, Cassandra Grace. BS in Elec. Engring., U. Conn., Storrs, 1994—98, MS in Elec. Engring., 1998—2001, PhD in Elec. Engring., 2001—06. Rsch. asst. Elec. & Computer Sci. Dept. U. Conn., 1998—2005, calculus/engring. instr. Engring. Diversity Program, 1999—2004, engring. embassador Engring. Dept., 2002—03. Cons. Elec. & Computer Sci. Dept., Micro/Opto Lab. U. Conn., 2006—. Contbr. articles to profl. jours. Grantee Elec. & Computer Engring. Rsch. fellowship, scholarship, Nat. Soc. Hispanic Engrs., 1997. Home Phone: 505-903-0418.

RODRIGUEZ, ANNABELLE, judge, former attorney general; b. Santurce, PR; m. Francisco de Jesus-Schuck; children: Ricardo Enrique Candle, Fernando Manuel Vela. BA in history magna cum laude, U. PR, JD, 1985. From asst. solicitor gen. to solicitor gen. PR Dept. Justice, 1986—93; ptnr. Martino, Odell & Calabria, Hato Rey, PR, 1993—96; judge US Dist Ct. (PR dist.), 1996; sec. justice PR, 2001—04; assoc. judge PR Supreme Ct., 2004—. Democrat. Office: Tribunal Supremo de PR PO Box 2392 San Juan PR 00902 *

RODRIGUEZ, CARLOS A., lawyer; b. 1960; AB, Harvard Coll., 1982; JD, Columbia Law Sch., 1985. Bar: NY 1986. Ptnr., securitization and structured fin. Sidley Austin Brown & Wood LLP, NYC, mem. exec. com. Mem.: Assn. of Bar City of NY (com. to enhance diversity in the profession).

RODRIGUEZ, CARLOS AUGUSTO, lawyer; b. Havana, Cuba, Sept. 1, 1954; came to U.S., 1960; s. Urbano and Estela (Cardenas) R.; m. Valerie Carr, May 27, 1989. BA magna cum laude, Furman U., 1977; JD, U. Fla., 1980. Bar: Fla. 1980, U.S. Ct. Appeals (5th cir.) 1981, U.S. Dist. Ct. (so. dist. and trial bar) Fla. 1984, U.S. Ct. Appeals (11th cir.) 1995; bd. cert. civil trial atty. Asst. pub. defender Broward County Pub. Defender's Office, Ft. Lauderdale, Fla., 1980-83, chief asst. pub. defender, 1983-85; assoc. Fazio, Dawson & DiSalvo, Ft. Lauderdale, Fla., 1985-87; sole practice Ft. Lauderdale, Fla., 1987—. Assoc. prof. U. Miami Sch. Law, Miami, 1983-85; lectr. criminal procedure Nova Law Cen., Ft. Lauderdale, 1983-85, lectr. on law Broward Community Coll., Ft. Lauderdale, 1983-87; mem. Nuisance Abatement Bd., 1989—, chmn., 1996—; vice chmn. Marine ADv. Bd., 1990. Mem. Marine Adv. Bd., Broward, Fla., 1986-96; rep. Primary Rep. Port Everglades Commn., Broward, 1984. Mem. ABA, ATLA, Am. Bd. Trial Advocacy, Acad. Fla. Trial Lawyers, Broward County Bar Assn., Phi Beta Kappa. Republican. Roman Catholic. Avocations: scuba diving, fishing, water and snow skiing. Fax: 954-463-9492.

RODRIGUEZ, CHI CHI (JUAN RODRIGUEZ), professional golfer; b. Bayamon, PR, Oct. 23, 1935; m. Donnette Iwalani, Apr. 6, 1962. Profl. golfer PGA, 1960—; joined Sr. PGA, 1985—. Contbg. columnist golf. mags. Winner Denver Open Invitational, 1963, Lucky Internat. Open, 1964, Western Open, 1964, Tex. Open Invitational, 1967, Sahara Invitational, 1968, Byron Nelson Golf Classic, 1972, Greater Greensboro Open, 1973, Tallahassee Open, 1979, Sr. Tournament Players Championship, 1986, Digital Srs. Classic, 1986-88, United Va. Bank Srs., 1986, Gen. Foods PGA Srs.' Championship, 1987, Vantage at The Dominion, 1987, United Hosps. Sr. Golf Championship, 1987, Silver Pages Classic, 1987, Sr. Players Reunion Pro-Am., 1987, GTE Northwest Classic, 1987, Doug Sanders Kingwood Celebrity Classic, 1988, Crestar Classic, 1989, Las Vegas Sr. Classic, 1990, 91, Vintage Arco Invitational, 1990, 91, Ameritech Sr. Open, 1990, Sunwest/Charley Pride Classic, 1990, GTE West Classic, 1991, Murata Reunion Pro-Am., 1991, KO Olina Sr. Invitational, 1992, Burnet Sr. Classic, 1993; winner with JoAnn Washam Pepsi Mixed Team Championship, 1976, Bahamas Open, 1979, Sr. Skins Games, 1988-89, Vantage Championship Mastercard Charity Team, 1999; named to Ryder Cup Team, 1973; inducted into the World Sports Humanitarian Hall of Fame, 1994; Best Sr. PGA Tour Finish T5 Comfort Classic, 1998. Achievements include being the leading money winner on sr. tour, 1987; representing P.R. in 12 world cups; ranked # 5 on PGA sr. tour, 1992; ranking # 4 among scoring leaders PGA sr. tour, 1992. Office: PGAAmerica PO Box 109601 112 Tpc Blvd Ponte Vedra Beach FL 32082-3077 Address: The Chi Chi Rodriguez Foun 3030 N Mcmullen Booth Rd Clearwater FL 33761-3331 also: care Eddie Elias Enterprises LLC 1720 Merriman Rd 3916 Clock Pointe Trl Ste 101 Stow OH 44224-2932

RODRIGUEZ, CIRO DAVIS, congressman; b. Piedras Negras, Mex., Dec. 9, 1946; m. Carolina Pena; 1 child. BA, St. Mary's U., 1973; MSW, Our Lady of the Lake U., 1978. Mem. Harlandale Ind. Sch. Dist. Bd., 1975-87; faculty assoc., Worden Sch. Social Work Our Lady of the Lake U., 1987-96; mem. Tex. Ho. of Reps., 1987-97, US Congress from 28th Tex. dist., 1997—2005, US Congress from 23rd Tex. dist., 2007—. Mem. Mil. Readiness subcom. House Nat. Security Com., Health subcom. House Vets. Affairs Com.; 2d vice chair and health care task force chair Congrl. Hispanic Caucus, 2004-2005. Democrat. Roman Catholic. Office: US Congress 2458 Ho Rayburn Office Bldg Washington DC 20515 *

RODRIGUEZ, DANIEL, tenor, former protective services official; Police officer NYC Police Dept., 1995—2004, singer ceremonial unit, ret., 2004; tenor, 2004—; known as "the singing policeman". Performances include: 2002 Winter Olympics, PBS Meml. Day concert, Tournament of Roses Parade, Rep. Nat. Convention, 2004, Celebration of Freedom Inauguration concert; singer: (albums) God Bless America, 2001, The Spirit of America, 2002, Be My Love, 2003, From My Heart, 2003, In The Presence, 2005. Office: c/o POW Inc 5657 Wilshire Blvd Ste 280 Los Angeles CA 90036

RODRIGUEZ, DANIEL B., dean, law educator; b. 1962; BA, Calif. State U., Long Beach, 1984; JD, Harvard U., 1987. Law clk. to Hon. Alex Kozinski U.S. Ct. Appeals (9th cir.), Pasadena, Calif., 1987-88; acting prof. U. Calif., Boalt Hall Sch. Law, Berkeley, 1988—94, prof., 1994—98; dean, prof. law U. San Diego Sch. Law, 1998—2005, Warren Disting. prof. law, 2005—. Vis. scholar Hoover Inst., Stanford U.; vis. prof. McGeorge Sch. Law-Govt. Affairs Program, U. So. Calif., U. Tex., Austin, U. Ill.; John M. Olin Fellow in Law and Econs. U. Va.; adj. prof. U. Calif., San Diego Sch. Internat. Rels. and Pacific Studies. Contbr. articles to profl. jours. Mem.: Am. Bar Found., Am. Law Inst. Office: U San Diego Sch Law 5998 Alcalá Park San Diego CA 92110-2492 *

RODRIGUEZ, DOUGLAS, chef; Grad., Johnson & Wales U. Owner, exec. chef Patria, NYC, 1994, Chicama, NYC, Pipa, NYC, Ola, NYC, Miami, Alma de Cuba, Phila.; cons. chef Deseo, Westin Kierland, Scottsdale, Ariz., 2002—, Gaucho Restaurants. Author: Nuevo Latino, Latin Ladles, Latin Flavors on the Grill, The Great Ceviche Book. Nominee Best Chef: NY, James Beard Found., 1999; recipient Chef of Am. award, 1991, Culinary Master on N. Am. and NY award, 1994, Rising Star Chef award, James Beard Found., 1996. Office: Deseo Kierland Westin 6902 E Greenway Pkwy Scottsdale AZ 85254 *

RODRIGUEZ, EDUARDO ROBERTO, lawyer; b. Edinburg, Tex., 1943; BA, George Wash. U., 1965; JD, U. Tex., 1968. Bar: Tex. 1968, U.S. Dist. Ct. (so. dist. Tex.) 1969, U.S. Ct. Appeals (5th Cir.) 1969, U.S. Supreme Ct. 1971. Sr. ptnr. Rodriguez Colvin Chaney & Saenz LLP, Brownsville, Tex. Lectr. in field; v.p. Tex. adv. coun. Nat. Legal Svcs. Corp., 1976—78; mem. bd. disciplinary appeals Supreme Ct. Tex., 1991, mem. task for on discovery, 91; bd. advisors Tex. Jour. Law and Pub. Policy U. Tex. Sch. Law, 2001—02, pres. law alumni com., 2001, mem. dean's roundtable, 1992. Chmn. Greater Brownsville Incentives Corp., 1997—98; bd. dirs. Brownsville Pub. Libr. Found., Inc., 1992; dir. Brownsville Boys' Club, 1973, basketball coach, Brownsville Girls' Club; mem. Downtown Devel. Corp. Brownsville, 1991; dir. Driscoll Found. Children's Hosp. Corpus Christi, 1969—77. Fellow: Tex. Bar Found. (mem. adv. bd. 1994); mem.: ABA (standing com. fed. jud. improvements 1991, ho. of delegates 1991—95, mem. nom. com. 1996—97, presdl. adv. coun. diversity in the profession 2002, chmn. Hispanic-Am. lawyers com., mem. drug and alcohol abuse com. criminal justice sect.), Mex. Am. Assn. Houston, Hispanic Nat. Bar Assn., Tex. Criminal Def. Lawyers Assn. (dir.), State Bar Tex. (dir. 1987—90, exec. com. 1988—90, pres.-elect 2004—), Cameron County Bar Assn. (law day chmn. 1970—71, dir. 1972—74, v.p. 1974—75, pres. 1975), Internat. Assn. Def. Counsel (mem. gen. convention com. 1994—95), Philosophical Soc. Tex., Am. Law Inst., Tex. Assn. Def. Counsel (v.p. 1992—96, mem. political action com. 2000—), Product Liability Advisory Coun., Inc., Kiwanis Club (v.p. 1971—72, pres. 1972—73). Office: Rodriguez Colvin Chaney & Saenz LLP PO Box 2155 1201 E Van Buren Brownsville TX 78522-2155 Office Phone: 956-542-7441. Office Fax: 956-541-2170. E-mail: er.rodriguez@rcclaw.com.

RODRIGUEZ, ELENA GARCIA, retired pension fund administrator; b. Havana, Cuba, Mar. 21, 1944; arrived in US, 1959; d. Eliseo and Elena (Suarez) Garcia; divorced; children: Victor, Yvonne, Daniel. B in Profl. Studies, Barry U., 1983; MS in Mgmt., St. Thomas U., 1985; postgrad., U. Phila., 1989, UCLA, 1990. Pension adminstr. City of Miami, Fla., 1969—95, ret. Fla., 1995. Bd. dirs. Mediation Ethics Adv. Bd. Author: General and Sanitation Pension Benefit Booklet, 1982, Fire and Police Pension Benefit Booklet, 1982, Retirement Planning Booklet, 1985 Mem. Leadership Miami, 1985—; mediator County Ct.; vol. Reading Blind and Dyslexic. Mem.: Nat. Assn. Securities Dealers (arbitrator, mediator), Better Bus. Bur. (former arbitrator, mediator), Assn. South Fla. Mediators (mediator), Fed. Emergency Mgmt. Agency, N.Y. Stock Exch. (arbitrator), Nat. Ctr. Dispute Resolution (arbitrator). Democrat. Roman Catholic. Avocations: growing orchids, stained glass, tile mosaics, painting.

RODRIGUEZ, ENSOR, physician, scientist, writer; b. San Juan, Jan. 11, 1937; s. Ensor A. Rodriguez and Josefina Lopez; m. Aida Lucia Herrera, Sept. 3, 1957; children: Jose E., Mariela, Marisol, David E. MD, U. Salamanca, Spain, 1961; MPH, Harvard U., 1968; PhD, Johns Hopkins U., 1976. Diplomate Am. Bd. Preventive Medicine. Commd. med. officer USAF, 1964, advanced through grades to col., 1976; deputy dir. Aerospace Med. Rsch. Lab., Dayton, Ohio, 1978-80; intern USAF Hosp., Patrick AFB, Fla., 1961—62, resident, 1968—70, med. dir., 1980-82; staff surgeon USAF Sys. Command, Washington, 1982-84; corp. med. dir. Atlantic Richfield Co., LA, 1984-92; intern Dist. Hosp., Arecibo, P.R.; residency Sch. Pub. Health Harvard U.; resident Sch. Aerospace Medicine USAF; cons. PACT, LA, 1993—. Fellow Ctr. Performance Humana. Office: PACT 121 S Hope St Apt 2 Los Angeles CA 90012-5002 E-mail: rodensor@sbcglobal.net.

RODRÍGUEZ, FÉLIX M., oil industry executive; Grad. in Petroleum Engring., U. Oriente, Venezuela; student in Sys. Analysis, Harvard U., Columbia U. With Corporación Venezolana de Petróleo, Exxon Rsch., ELF Aquitaine; v.p. Petróleos de Venezuela, S.A. (CITGO's ultimate parent co.); dep. pres. CITGO Petroleum Corp., 2004—05, pres., CEO, 2005—. Prof. math. and stats. Ctrl. U. of Venezuela Sch. Geography. Office: CITGO Petroleum Corp 1293 Eldridge Pky Houston TX 77077 *

RODRÍGUEZ, FERDINAND, chemical engineer, educator; b. Cleve., July 8, 1928; s. José and Concha (Luís) R.; m. Ethel V. Koster, July 28, 1951; children: Holly Edith, Lida Concha. BS, Case Western Res. U., 1950, MS, 1954; PhD, Cornell U., 1958. Devel. engr. Ferro Corp., Bedford, Ohio, 1950-54; asst. prof. chem. engring. Cornell U., 1958-61, asso. prof., 1961-71, prof., 1971—. On sabbatic leave at Union Carbide Corp., 1964-65, Imperial Chem. Industries, Ltd., 1971, Eastman Kodak Co., 1978-79; cons. to industry. Author: Principles of Polymer Systems, 5th edit., 2003; contbr. articles; songwriter:. Served with U.S. Army, 1954-56. Recipient Excellence in Teaching award Cornell Soc. Engrs., 1966, Edn. Achievement award Hispanic Engr. Mag., 1991. Fellow Am. Inst. Chem. Engrs.; mem. Am. Chem. Soc., Soc. Hispanic Profl. Engrs., Soc. Plastics Engrs. Lutheran. Office: Cornell U 267 Olin Hall Ithaca NY 14853 Business E-Mail: FR13@cornell.edu.

RODRIGUEZ, FRANCISCO JOSE, professional baseball player; b. Caracas, Venezuela, Jan. 7, 1982; Pitcher LA Angels of Anaheim (formerly Anaheim Angels), 2002—. Mem. Venezuelan Nat. Team Pan-Am. Youth Championship, Mexico, 1998. Named to Am. League All-Star Team, 2004, 2007; recipient Am. League Rolaids Relief award, 2006. Achievements include leading the Am. League in saves (45), 2005, and (47), 2006. Mailing: LA Angels of Anaheim 2000 Gene Autry Way Anaheim CA 92806 *

RODRIGUEZ, FREDDY, actor; b. Chgo., Jan. 17, 1975; m. Elsie Rodriguez; 3 children. Actor: (TV series) Oh Grow Up, 1999, Six Feet Under, 2001—05; (films) The Fence, 1994, A Walk in the Clouds, 1995, Dead Presidents, 1995, The Pest, 1997, Can't Hardly Wait, 1998, Shock Television, 1998, Joseph's Gift, 1998, Payback, 1999, Beyond City Limits, 2001, Chasing Papi, 2003, Dallas 362, 2003, Pledge of Allegiance, 2003, Dreamer: Inspired by a True Story, 2005, Poseidon, 2006, Harsh Times, 2006, Lady in the Water, 2006, Bobby, 2006, Grindhouse, 2007; (TV films) Seduced by Madness: The Diane Borchardt Story, 1996, For Love or Country: The Arturo Sandoval Story, 2000. Office: c/o Innovative Artist Talent Agy 7th Fl 235 Park Ave South New York NY 10003 *

RODRIGUEZ, IRMINA BESTARD, science educator; b. Havana, Cuba, Apr. 29, 1945; came to U.S., 1961; d. Gaspar and Ester Antonia (Bas) Bestard; m. Luis Felipe Rodriguez, June 8, 1968; children: Damien Brandon, Leslie Christina. BA in Chemistry, Coll. of New Rochelle, 1967; postgrad., U. Bridgeport, 1969-71, Barry U., Fla. Internat. U. Cert. tchr. Fla. Rsch. technician in pharmacology N.Y. Med. Coll., NYC, 1967-70; rsch. chemist Clairol, Inc., Stamford, Conn., 1970-74; pre-sch. instr. Happi-tymes, Miami, 1981-84; educator St. John Neumann Sch., Miami, 1984-92; sci. educator Carrollton Sch., Miami, 1992—. Coord. sci. dept. Carrollton Sch., 2004—. Contbr. articles to profl. jours. Mem. ways/means chmn. Stamford Women's Rep. Club, 1975-79, v.p. 1979. Mem. AAUW, Nat. Sci. Tchrs. Assn., Fla. Sci. Tchrs. Assn., Dade County Sci. Tchrs. Assn. Republican. Roman Catholic. Avocations: swimming, biking, reading, art collecting, ecology club advisor. Office: Carrollton Sch of the Sacred Heart 3747 Main Hwy Miami FL 33133-5907 Office Phone: 305-446-5673. Business E-Mail: irodriguez@carrollton.org.

RODRIGUEZ, IVAN TORRES, professional baseball player; b. Vega Baja, PR, Nov. 30, 1971; Catcher Tex. Rangers, 1991—2002, Florida Marlins, 2003, Detroit Tigers, 2004—. Named Am. League MVP, 1999, Nat. League Championship Series MVP, 2003; named to Am. League All-Star Team, 1992—2001, 2004—07, Am. League Silver Slugger Team, The Sporting News, 1994—99, 2004; recipient Gold Glove award, 1992—2001, 2004, 2006. Achievements include winning a World Series Championship as a member of the Marlins, 2003. Office: c/o Detroit Tigers 2100 Woodward Ave Detroit MI 48201 *

RODRIGUEZ, JOSEFA NIEVES, special education educator, language educator; b. Mantanzaz, Cuba, Nov. 7, 1942; d. Basilio Gonzalez Santana and Edelmira Margarita Escalona; m. Manuel B. Rodriguez, June 17, 1972; children: Josie, Aimee, Manuel Jr. B in Secretarial Sci., Barry U., Miami Shores, Fla., 1965, BS, 1980, MS, 1992. Profl. educator's cert. Fla., cert. ESOL, Spanish, specific learning disabilities, mentally handicapped, tchr. birth-4 Fla. Dept. Edn., trainer of trainers State of Fla. Child Care CDA Progam. Sales agt. Eastern Airlines, Inc., Miami, Fla., 1965—90; pre-sch. tchr. Archdiocese Miami, 1994—96; ESOL tchr. adult edn. Dade County Pub. Schs., Miami, 1996—, spl. edn. tchr., 2000—, tchr. of students with phys. impairments, 2005—06; trainer of child care trainers State Fla. Dept. Children and Families, Dade County Pub. Schs., 2006—07. Substitute tchr. Dade County Pub. Schs., Miami, 1992—2000; adj. prof. Miami Dade CC, Miami, 1997, ESOL instr., 2000; facilitator U. Miami Reading Inst.; ESOL tutor adult edn. Dade County Pub. Schs., Miami, 2005—06. Mem.: AFT, NEA, Dade Art Educators Assn., Coun. for Exceptional Student Edn., Fla. Edn. Assn., United Tchrs. Dade, Barry U. Alumnae Assn. Republican. Roman Catholic. Avocations: opera, piano, painting, tennis, languages. Office: Dade County Pub Schs 1500 Biscayne Blvd Miami FL 33132 Office Phone: 305-995-1000.

RODRIGUEZ, JUAN ALFONSO, information technology executive; b. Santiago, Cuba, Feb. 10, 1941; came to U.S., 1953; s. Alfonso and Marie Madeleine (Hourcadette) R. BEE, CCNY, 1962; MEE, NYU, 1963. Engr. IBM, Poughkeepsie, NY, 1963-68, Boulder, Colo., 1963—68, engring. mgr., 1968-69; dir. tech. Storage Tech. Corp., Louisville, Colo., 1969-74, v.p. engring., 1974-77, v.p., gen. mgr. disk, 1977-79, v.p., gen. mgr. optical disk Longmont, Colo., 1979-85; pres., CEO Exabyte Corp., Boulder, 1985-87, CEO, 1987-90, chmn., 1987-92; pres. Sweetwater Corp., 1992-93, chmn., 1992-95, also bd. dirs.; prof. elec. and computer engring. and engring. mgmt. U. Colo., 1992—, co-exec. dir. Deming Ctr. Entrepreneurship, 1994-2000; mem. adv. coun., 1994—; chmn. Datasonix, 1992-96, Vixel, 1995-99; chmn., CEO Ecrix Corp., 1996—2001; chief technologist, bd. dirs. Exabyte Corp., 2001—03, interim CEO, pres., 2002, chmn., 2003—06; connectivity ptnr. Appian Ventures, 2002—. Mem. devel. coun. Coll. Engring. U. Colo., 1990-92, mem. tech. transfer office adv. bd., 2000-, adv. bd. Boulder grad. sch., 2007-; Decisionism Corp.; mem. engring. adv. bd. CCNY, bd. dirs. Colo. Advanced Tech. Enterprise, 1994-98; Robert J. Appel Disting. lectr. law and tech. Law Sch. U. Denver, 1990. Patentee in field. Bd. dir. Boulder YMCA, 1982-87, U. Colo. Artist Series, 1988-92; mem. bd. govs. Boulder County United Way, 1989-93, chairperson campaign, 1992; commr. Colo. Advance Tech. Inst., 1988-92. Finalist Entrepreneur of Yr., Arthur Young & Inc Mag., 1989; named Boulder Spirit Entrepreneur of Yr., 1989, Entrepreneur of the Decade, 1994; named one of Top 50 Tech. Innovators, VAR Bus., 2004; recipient Ind. Quality award, Am. Soc. Quality Control (Rocky Mountain sect.), 1990, Gen. Palmer award Outstanding Engr. in Industry, Am. Cons. Engrs. Coun. Colo., 1995, Career Achievement award, Engring. Sch. Alumni CCNY, 2002, Townsend Harris medal, Alumni Assn. CCNY, 2003, Sprit Visionary award, Boulder C. of C., 2004, Hispanic Engr. of Yr., Entrepreneur Hispanic Engr. Nat. Achievement Awards Coun., 1995. Fellow IEEE (life); mem. Computer Soc. of IEEE (mem. steering com. on mass storage 1981-93), Soc. Photo-Optical Instrumentation Engrs., Boulder C. of C. (chmn. entrepreneurs support program 1989), Greater Denver C. of C. (bd. dirs. 1990-91); mem. Beta Gamma Sigma (medallion of Entrepreneurship 2003). Office: Appian Ventures 1512 Larimer St Ste 200 Denver CO 80202 Personal E-mail: jar@ieee.org.

RODRÍGUEZ, LILIANA CRISTINA, mathematics educator; b. Valencia, Carabobo, Venezuela, May 19, 1975; d. Rodolfo Rodríguez and Ana Rosa Sanabria de Rodriguez; m. Harold Enrique Torrence, Dec. 22, 1999; children: Jonathan Enrique Torrence, Susana Andreina Torrence. BS in Math and Learning Disabilities (hon.), U. of Carabobo/Nat. Open U., Valencia, 1999. Cert. 7-12 Mathematics tchr. Minn. Dept. of Edn., 2002. Bilingual Spanish-English tchr. Aurora Charter Sch., Mpls., 2000—03; secondary math tchr. Hazel Pk. Acad. (St. Paul Pub. Sch.), St. Paul, 2003—. Music tchr. Aurora Charter Sch., Mpls., 2000—03. Musician (singer): (music writer) Mensaje de Hermandad. Chorus dir. Holy Rosary Ch., Mpls., 2000—06. Scholar Cum laude scholar, U. of Carabobo -Venezuela, 1999—2003. Mem.: Nat. Coun. of Tchrs. of Math. (assoc.). Achievements include development of Spanish curriculum for children. Avocations: swimming, music, travel, drawing, painting. Home: 6145 Courtly Alcove Unit C Woodbury MN 55125 Office: Saint Paul Public School 360 Colborne St Saint Paul MN 55102 Home Phone: 651-702-2586; Office Phone: 651-767-8100. Personal E-mail: lilianac75@hotmail.com. E-mail: liliana.rodriguez@spps.org.

RODRIGUEZ, MARIA DOLORES, librarian; arrived in US, 1965; d. Leandro and Victorina Perez; m. Hugo Cesar Rodriguez, Dec. 27, 1990; children: Hugo Cesar Jr., Kassandra Marie. BS in Elem. Edn., Pan Am. U., Edinburg, Tex., 1989; MLS, Sam Houston State U., Huntsville, Tex., 2001. Cert. tchr. Tex., 1989. English, lang. arts tchr. Nellie Schunior Mid. Sch., La Joya, Tex., 1989—97; libr. Roosevelt Elem. Sch., McAllen Ind. Sch. Dist., Tex., 1997—2002, Alonzo De Leon Mid. Sch., McAllen Ind. Sch. Dist., 2002—. Sec. Alonzo De Leon PTA, McAllen, 2004—07. Recipient Summertime Active Reading Campus award, McAllen Ind. Sch. Dist., 2001, Family Literacy Expo award, McAllen Edn. Found., 2002; Beatrice Crain scholar, Sam Houston State U., 2001, Tellabrations grantee, McAllen Edn. Found., 2004, Families Reading Together grantee, 2006, Bridging the Gap:Families Reading Together grantee, Best Buy Corp., 2005, Day Lit. Splendor grantee, McAllen Jr. League, 2005, Tell a Story grantee, Tex. Commn. Arts, 2000, Our Melting Pot grantee, 2004, Monterrey and Guadalajara Internat. Book Festival grantee, ALA, 2000, 2003, 2004. Mem.: Tex. Libr. Assn. Roman Catholic. Avocations: travel, reading, shopping. Office: Alonzo De Leon Mid Sch 4201 North 29th Street Mcallen TX 78504 Home Phone: 956-583-6451; Office Phone: 956-632-8450. Office Fax: 956-632-8450. Business E-Mail: mrodriguez@cur.mcallen.isd.tenet.edu.

RODRIGUEZ, MICHELLE (MAYTE MICHELLE RODRIGUEZ), actress; b. Bexar County, Tx, July 12, 1978; Actor: (films) Girlfight, 2000, 3 A.M., 2001, The Fast and the Furious, 2001, Resident Evil, 2002, Blue Crush, 2003, S.W.A.T., 2003, Control, 2004, Sian Ka'an (voice), 2005, BloodRayne, 2005; (TV series) Lost, 2005— (Outstanding Performance by an Ensemble in a Drama Series, Screen Actors Guild award, 2006, Outstanding Supporting Actress in a TV Series, Nat. Coun. La Raza ALMA award (Am. Latin Media Arts), 2006); voice over: (video game) True Crime: Streets of L.A., 2003; Driv3r, 2004; Halo 2, 2004.

RODRIGUEZ, NARCISO, fashion designer; b. NJ, 1961; Studied, Parsons Sch. Design, NY. With Anne Klein, Calvin Klein; design dir. TSE, 1995, Cerruti, Paris, Loewe leather, Madrid, 1997—2001; owner Narciso Rodriguez, NYC, 1997—. Released signature fragrance Musc for Her. Women's ready-to-wear signature collection debuted in 1998 in Milan. Named one of 25 Most Influential Hispanics, Time Mag., 2005; recipient Best New Designer, VH1 Fashion Awards, 1997, Perry Ellis award, Coun. of Fashion Designers Am., 1998, Womenswear Designer of Yr., 2002, 2003, Hispanic Designer of Yr., 1997. Achievements include becoming a household name after designing Carolyn Bessette's wedding dress for her marriage to John F. Kennedy, Jr. Office: PR Consulting 50 Bond St New York NY 10012 also: 9th fl 30 Irving Pl New York NY 10003 Office Phone: 212-677-2989. *

RODRIGUEZ, RAUL PEDRO, plastic surgeon; b. Havana, Cuba, Nov. 4, 1955; MD, U. Tex., Dallas, 1983. Resident gen. surgery Meth. Hosp., Dallas, 1983—85, USAF Keesler Med. Ctr., Biloxi, 1985—88; with HCA Med. Ctr., Plano, Tex., Richardson Med. Ctr., Tex., Rejuvenex Med. Aesthetics Ctr., Dallas. Featured: magazines Modern Luxury Dallas, New York, In Touch Weekly, Us Weekly, US News & World Report, People, W, Harper's Bazaar, Allure, Southern Vanity, Elle. Served in USAF. Achievements include developing Slimjection, a nonsurgical alternative to liposuction that involves injecting small amounts of specific medications and fat-burning hormones directly into fat pockets. Office: Rejuvenex Med Aesthetics Ctr 7839 Park Ln Ste 120 Dallas TX 75225 Office Phone: 214-363-2388. *

RODRIGUEZ, RENÉ F., orthopedic surgeon; MD, Salamanca Univ., Spain; postgrad study, NY Polyclin. Hosp., Queens Hosp. Ctr., Jewish Cronic Diseases Hosp., Health Policy Inst. at George Washington Univ. Cert. Am. Bd. Orthopedic Surg. Chief Veterans Adminstrn. Med. Ctr., Miami; and orthopedic staff Jackson Meml. Med. Ctr., Cedars Med. Ctr., Univ. Miami Sch. Med. Bd. sci. counselors, Nat. Ctr. for Health Statistics CDC, Atlanta, 2003—. Founder, editor-in-chief Medico Interamericano, Medico Familia. Co-founder, co-chmn. Nat. Hispanic Youth Initiative. Recipient Officer of the Cross, Spain, Knight of the Order of Jerusalem, Knight of Malta, Freddie award in recognition of pub. svc. as an Adv. to the underserved in Am., MediMedia USA, 2004. Fellow: Soc. Med. Cons. to Armed Forces, Cuban Orthopaedic Soc. in Exile, Am. Coll. internat. Physicians, Internat. Coll. Surgeons, Am. Fracture Assn., Am. Coll. Surgeons, Am. Trauma Soc. (founding mem.), NY Acad. Medicine.; mem.: Nat. Confederation of Hispanic-Am. Med. Assns. (founder, chmn.), Interamerican Coll. Physicians and Surgeons (pres.). Office: Orthoped Surg Sect VA Med Ctr 1201 NW 16th St Miami FL 33125 E-mail: rrr@icps.org.

RODRIGUEZ, RICH, college football coach; b. Grant Town, W.Va. m. Rita Rodriguez; children: Raquel, Rhett. BS in Phys. Edn., W. Va. Univ., 1986. Secondary coach, spl. teams coord. Salem Coll., 1986, asst. head coach, defensive coord., 1987, head coach, 1988; asst. coach WVU, 1989; head football coach Glenville State Coll., 1990—96; offensive coord. Tulane, 1997—98; head coach WVU, 2000—. Named to Glenville Sports Hall of Fame, 2003; recipient Coach Yr., WVIAC, 1993—94, Nat. Coach Yr., NAIA, 1993, Coll. Coach Yr., W.Va. Sports Writer's Assn., 1993, Big East Coach Yr., 2002, Dist. I Coach Yr., Am. Football Coaches Assn., 2003. Office: WVU Athletics PO Box 0877 Morgantown WV 26507-0877 *

RODRIGUEZ, RICK, executive editor; b. Salinas, Calif., Apr. 5, 1954; m. Emelyn Cruz Lat Rodriguez, July 25, 1998. Grad., Stanford U., 1976, Guadalajara, Mex. Newspaper intern Salinas Californian; reporter Fresno (Calif.) Bee, Sacramento (Calif.) Bee, asst. mng. editor, mng. editor, 1993—98, exec. editor & sr. v.p., 1998—. Mem. Pulitzer Prize juries 1994, 95. Mem. Am. Soc. Newspaper Editors (bd. dirs. 1997-2001, treas. designate 2001-02, treas. 2002-03, sec. 2003-04, v.p. 2004-2005, pres. 2005-06), Calif. Chicano News Media Assn. (co-founder Sacramento chpt., past bd. dirs.). Office: Sacramento Bee PO Box 15779 Sacramento CA 95826 Office Phone: 916-321-1007. E-mail: rrodriguez@sacbee.com. *

RODRIGUEZ, ROBERT, filmmaker; b. San Antonio, June 20, 1968; s. Cecilio and Rebecca Rodriguez; m. Elizabeth Avellan, July 9, 1990 (separated), 5 children. Student, U. Tex. Dir. (films) Bedhead, 1991 El Mariachi, 1992, Desperado, 1995, Four Rooms (segment The Misbehaviors), 1995, From Dusk Till Dawn, 1995, The Faculty, 1998, Spy Kids, 2001, Spy Kids II: Island of Lost Dreams, 2002, Spy Kids 3-D: Game Over, Once Upon A Time in Mexico, 2003, Sin City (co-directed with Frank Miller & Quentin Tarantino), 2005, The Adventures of Shark Boy & Lava Girl in 3-D, 2005, Grindhouse, 2007; TV films: Roadracers (also wrote), 1994; wrote and prod.(films), From Dusk Til Dawn 3: The Hangman's Daughter, 2000, Once Upon A Time in Mexico, 2003; prodr. only (films), From Dusk Til Dawn II: Texas Blood Money, 1999; TV appearances: Nash Bridges, 1997, Deadline, 2000. Named one of 25 Most Influential Hispanics, Time Mag., 2005, 50 Most Powerful People in Hollywood, Premiere mag., 2005.

RODRIGUEZ, ROBERTO MIGUEL, investment company executive; arrived in US, 1977; s. Jose Rodriguez and Onelia R. Diaz; m. Lourdes Maria Rodriguez, Nov. 9, 1968; children: Jose Enrique, Mayra. B in Bus. Adminstrn., The Havana Bus. U., 1961; MBA in Mktg., Acctg. and Fin., U. Minn., 1981, MB, 1992, BA, 1995, MA in Ednl. Policy and Adminstrn., 1995, M in Pub. Health, 1993, MLA, 1997, PhD in Ednl. Policy and Adminstrn., 1998, M in Agrl., 2005; BS in Social Scis. cum laude, Colo. State U., 2001; M in Software Sys., U. St. Thomas, 2002; M in Agrl., Iowa State U., 2002; MS in Econs., Americus U., 2003; M in Liberal Studies, U. State NY, 2003; M in Humanities, Calif. State U., Dominguez Hills, 2004; JD, Northwestern Calif. Sch. Law, 2006; M in Liberal Arts, Tex. Christian U., 2006; MS, Ctr. Mich. U., 2007; D in Laws, Canterburg U., 2007; PhD, Commonwealth U., British Virgin Islands, 2007. Pres. RMR Real Estate Co., Blaine, Minn., 1979—; sr. acct. Palm Beach Beauty Products, 1997—98; fin. analysis Conwed Plastics, Mpls., 1998—2002; pres. AHR Properties, Inc., 2000—, Shoreview Investments LLC, 2002—, Blaine Investments Inc., 2004—, AHR Constrn., Inc., 2004—. Mgr. fin. analysis, forecasting Tennant Co., Golden Valley, Minn., 1977—92; contr. J and M Properties, Inc., Mpls., 1992—97. Sec. Latin Am. affairs Christian Solidarity Internat., Zurich, 1988—98. Mem.: Assn. Trial Lawyers Am., Inst. Mgmt. Accountants, Nat. Ctr. Missing Youth (hon.), Nat. Narcotics Officers Assn. (hon.). Republican. Roman Catholic. Avocations: travel, reading. Home: 11916 Davenport Ct NE Minneapolis MN 55449 Office: AHR Constrn Inc 5840 Hodgson Rd Saint Paul MN 55126 Office Phone: 763-754-2932. Personal E-mail: rbrtrod@earthlink.net.

RODRÍGUEZ, ROCÍO, artist; b. Caibarién, Las Villas, Cuba, 1952; BFA, MFA, U. Ga. One-woman shows include Carl Solway Gallery, Cin., 1982, 1985, Young Harris Coll., Ga., 1986, The Arts Exch., Atlanta, 1989, McIntosh Gallery, 1989, Sandler Hudson Gallery, 1991, 1993, 1995, Studio Exhbn., 1992, Brenau Coll., Gainesville,Ga., 1995, Nexus Contemporary Art Ctr., Atlanta, 1996, Fay Gold Gallery, 1998, Hemphill Fine Arts, Washington, 1999, exhibited in group shows at Birmingham (Ala.) Art Mus., 1989, High Mus. Art, Atlanta, 1990, Nexus Contemporary Arts Ctr., 1991, Galerie Simonne Stern, New Orleans, 1992, Montgomery (Ala.) Mus. Fine Arts, 1994, Michael Solway Gallery, Cin., 1996, Spelman Mus., Atlanta, 1997, New Orleans Mus., 1998, numerous others, Represented in permanent collections; contbr. articles to profl. jours. Recipient So. Regioanl Vis. Artists award, Am. Acad. Rome, 1997; fellow, Ford Found., 1978, Oscar B. Cintas fellow, 1980, Mayor's fellowship in arts, 1990, regional fellow, So. Arts Fedn./NEA, 1990. Office: Fay Gold Gallery 764 Miami Cir Ne Ste 210 Atlanta GA 30324-3026

RODRIGUEZ, SERGIO RAUL, music educator, conductor; b. San Pedro Sula, Cortes, Honduras, Aug. 29, 1961; s. Maria Alicia Mejia and Juan Pablo Rodriguez; m. Silvia Maria Montoya, Dec. 19, 1995; children: Yasmin Elizabeth, Arianna Rocio. MusB, Victoriano Lopez Music Sch., San Pedro Sula, Honduras, 1980, U. Ky., 1993; MusM, Southeastern La. U., 1999. Cert. tchr. Ga. Profl. Standards Com., 1998. Carl Orff music tchr. Exptl. Sch. for Children, Tegucigalpa, Francisco Morazan, Honduras, 1981—95; condr. violin and viola tchr. Nat. Sch. Music, Tegucigalpa, 1994—95, Conservatory of Music Fco. Zelaya, Tegucigalpa, 1994—95; music theory, violin and viola tchr. Honduras Nat. U., Tegucigalpa, 1994—95; violin and viola tchr. String Acad. of Southeastern La. U., Hammond, 1995—96; orch. dir., violin and viola tchr. Acadiana Conservatory of Music, Lafayette, La., 1996—97; orch. tchr. Dougherty County Sch. Sys., Albany, Ga., 1997—; orch. condr. Dougherty County Youth Symphony Orch., Albany, Ga., 1997—. Violinist Vermont Symphony Orch., Ga., 1986—89, Dartmouth Symphony Orch., Hanover, NH, 1987—89, Harvard-Radcliffe Symphony Orch., Cambridge, Mass., 1988—88, Lexington Philharm., Ky., 1989—93, Baton Rouge Symphony Orch., 1995—97, Albany Symphony Orch., Ga., 1997—, Macon Symphony Orch., Ga., 1998—, Valdosta Symphony Orch., Ga., 1998—; educator Radium Springs Magnet Mid. Sch. for the Arts; educator, dir. orchs. North Cobb HS. Composer: (string orch.) A Silvia, Flint River Dusk to Dawn for chamber orch., (on violin and piano) Memories from My Childhood. Founder Nat. Youth Orch., Honduras; founder, conductor Dougherty County Youth Symphony Orch. Recipient 2d pl., Music in the Parks, 2003, 1st pl., 2005; scholar, Longy Sch. of Music, 1987—89; Academic Excellence scholar, U. Ky., 1989, Fellowship Condr., S.C.'s Conducting Inst., 1998. Mem.: Nat. Assn. Music Edn., Music Educators Nat. Conf., Nat. Assn. Music Educators. Office: Dougherty County Youth Symphony Orchestr 1615 Newton Rd Albany GA 31701 Home: 1750 Shiloh Rd 1020 Kennesaw GA 30144 Office: North Cobb HS 3400 Highway 293 N Kennesaw GA 30144 Office Phone: 770-975-6685. Personal E-mail: sergio.rodriguez@gmail.com.

RODRIGUEZ, TIMOTHY ALLEN, language educator; b. Fond Du Lac, Wis., July 11, 1958; s. Donald William and Margaret Ann Rodriguez; m. Kathryn Marie Hébert, July 9, 1988; children: William Joseph, Kathryn Ann, Bryan Allen. BS, Western Ill. U., 1982, MS, 1984; PhD, U. Iowa, 1995. Tchr. bilingual edn. Danville (Ill.) Sch. Dist. 118, 1982-83, Houston Ind. Sch. Dist., 1984-86; ESL tchr. Palm Beach (Fla.) County Sch. Dist., 1986-88, 95-97, Martin County Sch. Dist., Stuart, Fla., 1988-91, 98-99; asst. prof. Western Ill. U., Macomb, 1993-95; adj. prof. Nova Southeastern U., Ft. Lauderdale, Fla., 1996-2000; asst. prof. U. Findlay, Ohio, 2001—03; lectr. Ohio State U., Lima, 2003—. Vis. prof. Fla. Atlantic U., 2000-01, Port St. Lucie; validator Nat. Bd. for Profl. Tchg. Stds.; keynote spkr. Ala.-Miss. TESOL Conf., 2007. Contbr. articles to profl. jours.; presenter Internat. TESOL Conf., 1996. Named Excellence in Edn., Ohio Mag., 2005; recipient Outstanding Tchg. award, Ohio State U., 2005. Mem. Internat. TESOL, Internat. Reading Assn., Nat. Assn. Bilingual Edn., Sunshine State TESOL (bd. dirs. 1998-2001). Home Phone: 419-873-1753; Office Phone: 419-495-8250. Business E-Mail: rodriguez.238@osu.edu.

RODRIGUEZ, VINCENT ANGEL, lawyer, director; b. Cayey, PR, 1921; s. Vicente and Maria (Antongiorgi) R. BS, Harvard U., 1941; LLB, Yale U., 1944. Bar: N.Y. 1947. Assoc. Sullivan & Cromwell, NYC, 1944-56, ptnr., 1956—. Mem. Council Fgn. Relations, ABA, Assn. Bar City N.Y., Am. Soc. Internat. Law Clubs: River (N.Y.C.). Home: 3400 Southwest 27th Ave Apt 902 Coconut Grove FL 33133 Office: Sullivan & Cromwell 125 Broad St Fl 28 New York NY 10004-2489

RODRIGUEZ, VIVIAN N., lawyer, accountant; b. Riverdale, NY, Dec. 16, 1969; d. Felix and Maria Rodriguez. AA in Bus., Miami Dade C.C., Miami, Fla., 1989; B of Acctg., Fla. Internat. U., Miami, 1991, M of Acctg., 1992; JD, U. Miami, 1995, LLM in Taxation, 2001. Bar: Fla.; CPA, Fla. Acct. Norman A. Eliot & Co., Miami, 1991-96; atty., acct. Managed Recovery Svcs. Corp., Miami, 1996-97; sole practitioner Miami, 1997—2001; atty. Office Chief Counsel/IRS/Dept. Treasury, 2001—. Mem. ABA, AICPA, Am. Assn. Atty.-CPAs, Fla. Assn. Atty.-CPAs, Fla. Inst. CPAs, Fla. Bar. Republican. Roman Catholic. Avocation: science fiction.

RODRIGUEZ, WILLIAM JULIO, physician; b. Ponce, PR, June 18, 1941; BS, MD, Georgetown U., Washington, 1967; PhD, Georgetown U., 1976. Intern Univ. Hosp., San Juan, 1967—68, resident in pediat., 1970—72; fellow Children's Hosp., Washington, 1972-75; attending in infectious disease Children's Hosp. Nat. Med. Ctr., Washington, 1975—; pediat. sci. dir. Office of Counterterrorism and Pediatric Drug Devel. Ctr. Drug Evaluation and Rsch. FDA, Rockville, Md., 2000—06; sci. adv. Office of Pediat. Therapeutics/Office of the Commr., 2006—. Assoc. chief infectious disease and microbiology rsch. Children's Hosp. Med. Ctr., 1979—80, chmn. infectious disease dept., microbiology rsch., 1983—2000; cons. staff Hosp. for Sick Children, Washington, 1985—2000, Shady Grove Adventist Hosp., Rockville, Md., 1988—2001, Holy Cross Hosp., Silver Spring, Md., 1988—2001, Columbia Hosp. for Women, 1990—2000; prof. emeritus pediat. George Washington Med. Sch., 2000—. Contbr. articles to profl. jours. With med. corps. USN, 1968—70. MARC fellow, XIII, 1973-76. Fellow Infectious Disease Soc.; mem. AAAS, APS, Am. Acad. Pediat., Soc. Pediat. Rsch., Am. Fedn. Clin. Rsch., Am. Soc. Microbiology, Ctr. Drug Evaluation and Rsch.

RODRIGUEZ-CAMILLONI, HUMBERTO LEONARDO, architect, historian, educator; b. Lima, Peru, May 30, 1945; came to U.S., 1963; s. Alfonso and Elda (Camilloni) R.; m. Mary Ann Alexanderson, July 1, 1972; children: Elizabeth Marie, William Howard. BA magna cum laude, Yale U., 1967, MArch, 1971, MPhil, 1973, PhD, 1981. Rsch. asst. Sch. Architecture Yale U., 1964-70, teaching fellow dept. history art, 1971-72, 74-75; chmn. research dept. Centro de Investigacion y Restauracion de Bienes Monumentales Instituto Nacional de Cultura, Lima, 1973; restoration architect OAS, Washington, 1976—; prof. Sch. Architecture Tulane U., New Orleans, 1975-82; prof., dir. Henry H. Wiss Ctr. Theory and History of Art and Architecture, Coll. Architecture and Urban Studies Va. Poly. Inst. and State U., Blacksburg, 1983—, dir. Ctr. for Preservation and Rehab. Tech., Coll. Architecture, 1986—. Vis. prof. U. Ill., Chgo., 1982-83; reviewer, cons. Choice, 1975—; interim bd. dirs. Ctr. Planning Handbook Latin-Am. Art, 1978-87; cons., adviser Internat. Exhbn. and Symposium Latin-Am. Baroque Art and Architecture, 1980; adv. bd. Mountain Lake Symposium on Art and Architecture Criticism, 1985—, Internat. Symposium Luis Barragan, 1990; coord., advisor exhbn. Tradition and Innovation: Painting, Architecture and Music in Brazil, Mex. and Venezuela between 1950-80, 1991, Internat. Art History Colloquium, 1993, Internat. Congress of Americanists, 1994, 97, 2006, Frank Lloyd Wright: An Architect in America, 1995, Congress Internat. Union Architects, 1996, European Assn. for Archtl. Edn./Archtl. Rsch. Ctrs. Consortium Conf., 2000, The Jesuits, Conf. II: Cultures, Scis. and the Arts, 1540-1773, 2002, Internat. Congress on Constrn. History, 2003, 06, III Internat. Copan Maya Congress, 2007. Author: (with Walter D. Harris) The Growth of Latin American Cities, 1971; (with Charles Seymour, Jr.) Italian Primitives, The Case History of a Collection and its Conservation, 1972, Religious Architecture in Lima of the Seventeenth and Eighteenth Centuries: The Monastic Complex of San Francisco el Grande, 1984; contbg. editor Handbook of Latin American Studies, 1987—, The Retablo Facade as Transparency: A Study of the Frontispiece of San Francisco, Lima, 1991, Tradición e Innovación en la Arquitectura del Virreinato del Perú, Constantino de Vasconcelos y la Invención de la Arquitectura de Quincha en Lima Durante el Siglo XVII, 1994, (with Graziano Gasparini) Arquitectura Iberoamericana, 1997, Manuel de Amat y Junyent y la Navona de Lima: un ejemplo de diseño urbano barroco del siglo XVIII en el virreinato del Perú, 1999, (with Mehdi Setareh) Monticello's Dome: Development of an Integrated Resource for the Study of Thomas Jefferson's Architecture, 2000, Quincha Architecture: The Development of an Antiseismic Structural System in Seventeenth Century Lima, 2003, The Rural Churches of the Jesuit Haciendas in the Southern Peruvian Coast, 2004, The Survival of Gothic Rib Vaulting in the Viceroyalty of Peru, 2006; contbg. editor: The Dictionary of Art, 1991-96, Encyclopedia of Twentieth Century Architecture, 1999. Named Ellen Battell Eldridge fellow, 1970-72, Robert C. Bates Jr. fellow Jonathan Edwards Coll., Yale U., 1970-71, Social Sci. Rsch. Coun. fellow, 1972-74, Yale Concilium Internat. Studies fellow, 1972-73, Giles Whiting fellow, 1974-75, NEH fellow Columbia U., 1983, Hobart and William Smith Colls. fellow, 1987, U. Ill. fellow, 1990, Edilia De Montequin fellow, 1991, NEH fellow U. N.Mex., 1992. Mem.: KC, Preservation Resource Ctr. (past bd. dirs.), Inter-Am. Inst. Advanced Studies in Cultural History (bd. dirs. 1998—), Blacksburg Regional Art Assn., Assn. for Preservation Tech., Save Our Cemeteries (past bd.dirs.), Nat. Trust Hist. Preservation, New River Valley Preservation League (bd. dirs. 1987—), Assn. Preservation Va. Antiquities, Coll. Art Assn. Am., S.E. section Soc. Archtl. Historians, Soc. Archtl. Historians (bd. dirs. 1977—80, past pres., past sec. South Gulf chpt.), Internat.Archive of Women in Architecture (treas. 1999—2002), Assn. Latin Am. Art, S.E. Coll. Art Conf., Latin Am. Studies Assn., Phi Beta Delta, Sigma Delta Pi, Tau Sigma Delta. Roman Catholic. Office: Va Poly Inst and State U Coll Architecture & Urban Studies Blacksburg VA 24061-0205 Home Phone: 540-961-1296; Office Phone: 540-231-5324. E-mail: hcami@vt.edu. *As an educator across the years, I have come to realize that the true art of teaching consists of reaching both the human mind and the human heart.*

RODRIGUEZ-DIAZ, JUAN E., lawyer; b. Ponce, PR, Dec. 27, 1941; s. Juan and Auristela (Diaz-Alvarado) Rodriguez de Jesus; m. Sonia de Hostos-Anca, Aug. 10, 1966; children: Juan Eugenio, Jorge Eduardo, Ingrid Marie Rodriguez. BA, Yale U., 1963; LLB, Harvard U., 1966; LLM in Taxation, NYU, 1969. Bar: N.Y. 1968, P.R. 1970. Assoc. Baker & McKenzie, NYC, 1966-68, McConnell, Valdes, San Juan, P.R.; undersec. Dept. Treasury P.R., 1971-73; mem. Sweeting, Pons, Gonzalez & Rodriguez, 1973-81; pvt. practice San Juan, 1981-94, Totti & Rodriguez-Diaz, 1994—. Bd. dirs. Ochoa Indsl. Sales Corp., G.A. Life Assurance Co. Inc., Industrias Vassallo, Inc., Luis Ayala Colon Sucres., Inc., Triangle Cargo Svcs., Inc., Triple S, Inc., Triple S Mgmt., Inc., G.A. Life Assurance Co. Puerto Rico. Bd. govs. Aqueduct and Sewer Authority P.R., 1979-84; mem. adv. com. collective bargaining negotiation of P.R. elec. Power Authority to Gov. P.R., 1977-78; bd. govs. P.R. coun. Boy Scouts Am., mem. transition com., 1984-85; mem. adminstrv. coun. Ballajá, 1993-00. Mem. N.Y. State Bar Assn., P.R. Bar Assn., AFDA Club, Berwind Country Club, Palmas de Mar Country Club. Office: Ste 1200 416 Ave Ponce De Leon Hato Rey San Juan PR 00918-3418 Office Phone: 787-753-7910. Business E-Mail: JERD@TRDLAW.com.

RODRIGUEZ-VELEZ, ROSA EMILIA, prosecutor; Grad., U. Sacred Heart, 1973; M in Criminal Justice, Interamerican U., PR, JD, 1977. Bar: PR 1977. Asst. dist. atty. PR Dept. Justice, 1979—88, asst. US atty. dist. PR, 1988—94; violent crime coord. dist. PR US Atty.'s Office, 1994—2002, exec. asst., 1994—2992, acting chief civil divsn., 1995—97, first asst. US atty., 2002; US atty., PR US Dept. Justice, 2006—. Coord. High Intensity Drug Trafficking Area, 1994—96, chair, 2006. Recipient Dir. Commendation Letter, FBI, 1987. Office: US Attys Office Torre Chardon Ste 1201 350 Carlos Chardon Ave San Juan PR 00918 *

RODRIGUEZ-WALLING, MATILDE BARCELO, special education educator; b. Santiago, Cuba, Aug. 15, 1950; d. Humberto Jacinto and Matilde Amelia (Cuervo) Barcelo; m. Luis Alfredo Rodriguez-Walling, June 29, 1973; 1 child, Alfredo Luis. BA, U. Miami, Fla., 1972; MS in Diagnostic Tchg., Fla. Internat. U., 1981; EdS, Barry U., 1988. Cert. ednl. specialist computer edn., Fla. Tchr., chair fgn. lang. dept. Notre Dame Acad., Miami, Fla., 1972-80; tchr., coord. English as 2d lang. adult edn. program Dade County Pub. Schs., Miami, elem. sch. tchr., tchr. middle sch. spl. edn. Homestead, Fla., elem. spl. edn. tchr. Miami, 1986—, behavior mgmt. specialist, exceptional edn. dept. chair; tchr. on spl. assignment Fla. Dept. of Edn., 1994—. Mem. spkrs. bur. Nat. Clearinghouse for Professions in Spl. Edn.; sch. adv. chairperson Blueprint 2000; presenter and spkr. at state and nat. profl. confs.; coord. Fla. Spkrs. Bur.; mem. Fla. Edn. Stds. Commn. Commr. Fla. Edn. Stds. Commn.; mem. State Adv. Com.; mem. Commrs. Blue Ribbon Panel Edn. Governance; co-chair Nat Commn. Improve Spl. Edn. Teaching & Learning. Recipient Gran Orden Martiana, Cuban Lyceum, Miami, 1976. Mem. Coun. Exceptional Children (sec. 1989, v.p. 1990, pres. 1991-92, multicultural chair 1992-93, Mainstreaming Tchr. of Yr. 1983, region finalist Dade County Tchr. of Yr. 1991, Fla. Tchr. of Yr.), Fla. Fedn. Coun. for Exceptional Children (pres. 1997-98, past pres. 1998-99), Coun. Children with Behavior Disorders, Nat. Bd. for Profl. Tchg. Stds. (exceptional needs com.), Internat. Coun. for Exceptional Children (Tchr. of Yr. 1994), Delta Kappa Gamma (Epsilon chpt.). Roman Catholic. Avocations: travel, guitar. Office: Miami-Dade County Pub Schs 1500 Biscayne Blvd Ste 409G Miami FL 33132-1400 Home: 12501 SW 78th St Miami FL 33183-3516 E-mail: mrodriguez-walling@dadeschools.net.

RODRIK, DANI, economics and international affairs educator; b. Istanbul, Turkey, Aug. 14, 1957; AB in Govt. and Econs. summa cum laude, Harvard U., 1979; MPA with distinction, Princeton U., 1981, PhD in Econs., 1985. Asst. econ. affairs officer UN Conf. on Trade and Devel., Geneva, 1980, 81-82; asst. prof. pub. policy Kennedy Sch. Govt. Harvard U., Cambridge, Mass., 1985-89, assoc. prof. pub. policy, 1989-92; prof. econs. and internat. affairs Columbia U., NYC, 1992-96; Rafiq Hariri prof. internat. polit. econs. Kennedy Sch. Govt., Harvard U., 1996—, chmn. MPA/ID prog., 2005—. Mem. adv. bd. METU Studies in Devel., New Perspectives on Turkey; Wei Lun vis. prof. Chinese U. of Hong Kong, 1992-93; vis. scholar fiscal affairs dept. Internat. Monetary Fund, 1990, Internat. Fin. div. Bd. Govs. Fed. Reserve System, 1987; advisor Ministry of Fgn. Econ. Rels., Govt. of Poland, 1990; rsch. assoc. Nat. Bur. Econ. Rsch.; rsch. fellow Ctr. Econ. Policy Rsch.; cons. and spkr. in field. Author: Has Globalization Gone Too Far?, 1997, The New Global Economy and Developing Countries: Making Openness Work, 1999; co-author: Eastern Europe and the Soviet Union in the World Economy, 1991, External Debt, Adjustment and Burden Sharing: A Unified Framework, 1992; co-editor: The Political Economy of Turkey: Debt, Adjustment and Sustainability, 1990, The Economics of Middle-East Peace, 1993; editor: Search of Prosperity: Analytic Narratives on Economic Growth, 2003; assoc. editor Jour. Internat. Econs., Jour. Devel. Econs., Econs. & Politics; contbr. articles to profl. publs., chpts. to books. Sr. rsch. fellow Inst. for Policy Reform, vis. fellow Inst. for Internat. Econs., NBER Olin fellow, 1990-91, Robert S. McNamara fellow, 1987-88, Hoover Instn. Nat. fellow, 1991-92, Harbison fellow, 1980-81; recipient Raymond Vernon prize Assn. for Pub. Policy Analysis and Mgmt., 1988. Office: Harvard U Kennedy Sch Govt 79 Jfk St Cambridge MA 02138-5801 *

ROE, BENSON BERTHEAU, surgeon, educator; b. LA, July 7, 1918; s. Hall and Helene Louise (Bertheau) R.; m. Jane Faulkner St. John, Jan. 20, 1945; children: David B., Virginia St. John. AB, U. Calif., Berkeley, 1939; MD cum laude, Harvard U., 1943. Diplomate Am. Bd. Surgery, Am. Bd. Thoracic Surgery (dir. 1971-83, chmn. bd. 1981-83, chmn. exam. com. 1978, chmn. long-range planning com. 1980, chmn. program com. 1977). Intern Mass. Gen. Hosp., Boston, 1943-44, resident, 1946-50; nat. rsch. fellow dept. physiology Med. Sch., Harvard U., Boston, Mass., 1947, instr. surgery, 1950; Moseley Traveling fellow Harvard. U. at U. Edinburgh, Scotland, 1951; asst. clin. prof. surgery U. Calif., San Francisco, 1951-58, chief cardiothoracic surgery, 1958-76, prof. surgery, 1966-89, emeritus prof., 1989—; pvt. practice medicine specializing in cardiothoracic surgery San Francisco, 1952-85. Sr. scientist Cardiovascular Rsch. Inst., 1956-89; cons. thoracic surgery VA Hosp., San Francisco Gen. Hosp., Letterman Army Hosp., St. Lukes Hosp., Blue Shield of Calif., Baxter Labs., Ethicon, Inc.; bd. dirs. Control Laser Corp.; vis. prof. U. Utah, U. Ky., U. Gdansk, Poland, Nat. Heart Hosp., London, U. Ibadan, Nigeria, Sanger Clinic, Charlotte, Rush-Presbyn. Hosp., Chgo., Penrose Hosp., Colorado Springs. Author: Maverick Among the Moguls, 2002; mem. editl. bd. Annals of Thoracic Surgery, 1969-82, Pharos, E-Medicine; editor 2 med. texts; author 21 textbook chpts.; contbr. more than 175 articles to profl. jours. Bd. dirs. United Bay Area Crusade, 1958-70, exec. com., 1964-65; bd. dirs. chmn. exec. com. San Francisco chpt. Am. Cancer Soc., 1955-57; bd. dirs. San Francisco Heart Assn., 1964-72, pres., 1964-65, chmn. rsch. com., 1966-71; com. mem. Am. Heart Assn., 1967-70; pres. Miranda Lux Found., 1982-94; trustee Avery-Fuller-Welch Found.; bd. dirs. Internat. Bioethics Inst., Point Reyes Bird Obs. With M.C., USNR, 1944-46. Named to Rowing Hall of Fame, 1979, Athletic Hall of Fame, U. Calif., 1995. Fellow Am. Coll. Cardiology, ACS (chmn. adv. coun. thoracic surgery, program chmn. thoracic surgery, cardiovascular com.), Polish Surg. Assn. (hon.); mem. Am. Assn. Thoracic Surgery (chmn. membership com. 1974-75), AMA (residency rev. com. for thoracic surgery), Am. Surg. Assn., Pacific Coast Surg. Assn., Calif. Acad. Medicine (pres. 1974), Calif. Med. Assn., Soc. Univ. Surgeons, Soc. Thoracic Surgeons (pres. 1972, chmn. standards and ethics com.), Soc. Vascular Surgery (v.p.). Clubs: Cruising of Am, Pacific Union, St. Francis Yacht, Calif. Tennis. Office: Univ Calif Div Cardiothoracic Surgery 500 Parnassas Ave W Ste 420 San Francisco CA 94143-0118 Personal E-mail: ghotieg@earthlink.net.

ROE, BYRON PAUL, physics professor; b. St. Louis, Apr. 4, 1934; s. Sam S. and Gertrude Harriet (Claris) R.; m. Alice Susan Krauss, Aug. 27, 1961; children: Kenneth David, Diana Carol. BA, Washington U., St. Louis, 1954; PhD, Cornell U., 1959. Instr. physics U. Mich., Ann Arbor, 1959-61, asst. prof., 1961-64, assoc. prof., 1964-69, prof., 1969—. Guest physicist SSC Lab., 1991. Author: Probability and Statistics in Experimental Physics, 1992, 2d edit., 2001, Particle Physics at the New Millennium, 1996 (Libr. Sci. Book Club selection). CERN vis. scientist Geneva, 1967, 89; Brit. Sci. Rsch. Coun. fellow, Oxford, 1979; recipient inventor's prize CDC Worldtech, Edina, Minn., 1982, 83. Fellow Am. Phys. Soc. Home: 3610 Charter Pl Ann Arbor MI 48105-2825 Office: U Mich Physics Dept 500 E University Ave Ann Arbor MI 48109-1040 E-mail: byronroe@umich.edu.

ROE, CHARLES BARNETT, lawyer; b. Tacoma, June 25, 1932; s. Charles Brown and Gladys Luvena (Harding) Roe; m. Marilyn Marie Quam, July 31, 1954; children: Sharon Lynn Roe De Groot, Jeannine Carole Roe Dellwo. AB, U. Puget Sound, 1953; postgrad. Boalt Hall, U. Calif. Law Sch., Berkeley, 1957—58; JD, U. Wash., 1960. Bar: Wash. 1960, U.S. Dist. Ct. (ea. and we. dists.) Wash. 1960, U.S. Ct. Appeals (9th cir. 1963, U.S. Supreme Ct. 1963, U.S. Ct. Appeals (D.C. cir.) 1964, Oreg. 2007. Asst. atty. gen. depts. natural resources, conservation, water resources and pollution control commn. State of Wash., Olympia, 1960—70, asst. dir. dept. water resources, 1967—69, sr. asst. atty. gen., 1970—90; of counsel Perkins Coie, Olympia, 1991—. Chief counsel Dept. Ecology, 1970—85, Nuclear Waste Bd., 1983—90; counsel natural resources com. Wash. Ho. of Reps., Olympia, 1970; supr. sea grant trainees U. Wash. Law Sch., 1970—72; adj. prof. Gonzaga U. Sch. Law, Spokane, 1973—76, U. Puget Sound Law Sch., 1985—90; contr. Nat. Water Commn., Washington, 1970—71; environ. aide Gov. Daniel J. Evans, 1969—77. Spl. asst. atty gen. State of Mont, Helena, 1983; rep. Western States Water Coun., Salt Lake City, 1970—90; sec. Olympia Audubon Soc., 1962—63; chmn. bd. mgrs. United Chs., 1967—68. 1st lt. USAF, 1954—57. Mem.: SAR, ABA (chmn. water resources com. natural resources sect. 1981—83), Oreg. State Bar Assn., Wash. Cts. Hist. Soc. (bd. dirs. 1998—), Wash. State Bar Assn. (chmn. environ. law sect. 1971—72), Rotary, Am. Legion, Masons, Phi

Delta Phi, Kappa Sigma. United Ch. Of Christ. Home: 2400 Wedgewood Dr SE Olympia WA 98501-3841 Office: 111 Market St NE Olympia WA 98501-6965 Office Phone: 360-956-3300. Business E-Mail: croe@perkinscoie.com.

ROE, JOHN H., manufacturing executive; b. 1939; BA, Williams Coll., 1962; MBA, Harvard U., 1964. With Bemis Co. Inc., Mpls., 1964—, plant supt., 1964-67, sales rep., 1967-68, sales mgr., 1968-70, plant mgr., 1970-73, gen. mgr. film div., 1973-76, exec. v.p. ops., 1976-87, pres., chief oper. officer, from 1987, chief exec. officer, 1990—, also bd. dirs., chmn. Office: Bemis Co Inc 222 S 9th St Ste 2300 Minneapolis MN 55402-4099

ROE, KATHRYN JANE, elementary school educator; b. Indpls., July 25, 1958; d. Max Richard and Marthana Jane Kidwell; m. Patrick Allen Dawson, June 14, 1980 (div. Jan. 15, 1996); 1 child, Gregory Scott Dawson; m. William R. Roe, Jr., July 24, 2006. BS, Ball State U., 1987, MA in Edn., 1992. Cert. tchr. NC, Ind. Aide Blue River Valley Schs., Mt. Summit, Ind., 1987—88; grad. asst. Ball State U., Muncie, Ind., 1988—92, adj. faculty, 1992—97; tchr. Muncie Cmty. Schools, 1997, Cumberland County Schs., Fayetteville, NC, 2005—. Article reviewer Ind. Reading Quar., Muncie, 1994—97; presenter in field. Author: (textbook) Academic Survival Skills: Batteries Not Included. Active lit. walk-a-thon Cumberland County Schs., Fayetteville, NC, 2005; active Habitat for Humanity, Ball State U., Muncie, 1994—96; mem. walk-a-thon Longfellow Student Coun., Muncie, 2002—03; mem. neighborhood clean-up Whitely Assn., Muncie, 2004. Named Longfellow Tchr. of Yr., Muncie Cmty. Schools, 2003, Tchr. Vol. of Yr., Longfellow PTA, 2003, Student Body Tchr. of Yr., Longfellow Student Coun., 2003; named one of Outstanding Am. Tchrs., 2006; grantee, Florence Rogers Charitable Trust, 2005, Armed Services Sci. Tchg. award, 2005, Buddy Project, 2003—04, Arts Coun., 2006; Buddy grantee, Buddy Writing Project, 1999—2005. Mem.: Internat. Reading Assn. (assoc.). Independent. Pentecostal. Avocations: travel, reading, writing, choral singing. Office: Cumberland County Schs 3876 Sunnyside School Rd Fayetteville NC Home: 7141 Canary Dr Fayetteville NC 28314 Home Phone: 910-484-4403; Office Phone: 910.483.4319. Office Fax: 910.483.5711. Personal E-mail: kjdawson58@peoplepc.com, kidiewell@yahoo.com, kathy@roesolutions.com. Business E-Mail: kathrynroe@ccs.k12.nc.us.

ROE, LESA B., federal agency administrator; b. 1963; m. Ralph Roe. B. in elec. engring., U. Fla., Gainesville; M. in elec. engring., U. Ctrl. Fla., Orlando. Satellite comm. analyst Hughes Space & Comm., El Segundo, Calif.; with NASA, 1987—, comm. engr. Space Shuttle Engring. Directorate Kennedy Space Ctr., Fla., 1987, payloads office mgr. Internat. Space Sta. (ISS) Program Office, Johnson Space Ctr. Houston; assoc. dir. bus. mgmt. Langley Rsch. Ctr., NASA, Hampton, Va., 2003—04, dep. dir., 2004—05, dir., 2005—. Office: Bldg 1219 Rm 213 Mail Stop 106 Hampton VA 23681-2199 also: Langley Rsch Ctr 100 NASA Rd Hampton VA 23681 Office Phone: 757-864-4111. E-mail: lesa.b.roe@nasa.gov.

ROE, MARK J., law educator; b. NYC, Aug. 8, 1951; m. Helen Hsu, Aug. 12, 1974; children: Andrea Hsu, Jessica Hsu. BA, Columbia U., 1972; JD, Harvard U., 1975. Bar: N.Y. 1976. Atty. Fed. Res. Bank, NYC, 1975-77; assoc. Cahill Gordon & Reindel, NYC, 1977-80; prof. Rutgers U. Law Sch., Newark, 1980-86, U. Pa. Law Sch., 1986-88, Columbia U. Law Sch., NYC, 1988-2001, Harvard Law Sch., Cambridge, Mass., 2001—. Author: (book) Strong Managers, Weak Owners: The Political Roots of American Corporate Finance, 1994, Political Determinants of Corporate Governance, 2003, Bankruptcy and Corporate Reorganization, 2006. Business E-Mail: mroe@law.harvard.edu.

ROE, MARY ANN, retired postmaster; b. Greenwich, Conn., Jan. 10, 1945; d. Frederick Johnston and Doris Irene Capp; m. Robert Andrew Roe, June 17, 1966; children: Jeffrey Brian, Jennifer Yvonne. Student, S.W. Mo. State U., 1969, N.E. Mo. State U., 1970. Clk. U.S. Postal Svc., Brookfield, Mo., 1977-82, supt. postal ops., 1983-93, postmaster, 1993—2007; ret., 2007. Author: Roe's Reference, 1987; contbr. articles to mags. Sec.-treas. Busy Women's Club, Brookfield, 1990—; asst. leader Girl Scouts U.S.A., Brookfield, 1990-99. Recipient Best Column award Show Me Postmaster, 1997. Mem. Nat. Assn. Postmasters U.S. (instr. conv. 1996, 97, 2001,& 2002. Mo. Career Devel. com. 1996-98, state editor 1999-2002). Methodist. Avocations: reading, sewing, travel.

ROE, ROGER ROLLAND, JR., lawyer; b. Mpls., Dec. 31, 1947; s. Roger Rolland Roe Jr.; m. Paula Speltz, 1974; children: Elena, Madeline. BA, Grinnell Coll., 1970; JD, U. Minn., 1973. Bar: Minn. 1973, U.S. Dist. Ct. Minn. 1974, U.S. Ct. Appeals (8th cir.) 1977, U.S. Supreme Ct. 1978, Wis. 1988, U.S. Dist. Ct. Nebr. 1995, U.S. Dist. Ct. (ea. and we. dists.) Wis. Law clk. to Hon. Judge Amdahl Hennepin County Dist. Ct., Mpls., 1973-74; from assoc. to ptnr. Rider, Bennett, Egan & Arundel, Mpls., 1974-91; mng. ptnr. Yaeger, Jungbauer, Barczak, Roe & Vucinovich, PLC, Mpls., 1992-2000; ptnr. Best & Flanagan LLP, Mpls., 2000—. Mem. nat. panel arbitrators Am. Arbitration Assn.; judge trial practice class and moot ct. competitions law sch. U. Minn.; guest lectr. Minn. Continuing Legal Edn. courses. Fellow Internat. Soc. Barristers; mem. ATLA (guest lectr.), Am. Bd. Trial Advs. (diplomat, Minn. chpt. pres. 1996-97), Million Dollar Round Table. Avocations: golf, skiing. Office: Best & Flanagan LLP 225 S 6th St # 4000 Minneapolis MN 55402 Home Phone: 612-377-6964; Office Phone: 612-349-5683. Business E-Mail: rroe@bestlaw.com.

ROE, THOMAS COOMBE, former utility company executive; b. Dover, Del., Sept. 22, 1914; s. John Moore and Elizabeth Lindale (Cooper) R.; m. Emma Lillian Scotton, Oct. 16, 1937 (dec.); children: Thomas C., Margaret Ruth (dec.); m. Carolyn Scotton, May 4, 2002. BS in Elec. Engring, U. Del., Newark, 1935; DHL (hon.), Wesley Coll., Dover, Del., 1987. With Eastern Shore Public Service, 1936-43; with Delmarva Power & Light Co., 1943—; pres. subs. Delmarva Power & Light Co., 1971-76, chmn. bd., 1976-79, dir., 1971-80, ret., 1980. Hon. trustee Peninsula Regional Med. Ctr., Salisbury, Md.; hon. trustee, former chmn. Wesley Coll., Dover, Del.; former trustee Wesley Theol. Sem., Washington. Served with AUS, 1941-45. Mem.: Rotary (past pres.). Republican. Methodist.

ROE, THOMAS F., retired endocrinologist; s. Thomas F. and Mary E. Roe; m. Catherine A. Roe; children: Tracey A. Botero, Stephanie E. Shintani, Michael C., Cynthia Lane, William T. BS, Seattle U., 1957; MD, Marquette U., Milw., 1961. Lic. pediatrician Am. Acad. Ped. Endocrinology, 1968. Intern Milw. County Gen. Hosp., 1961—62; resident Children's Hosp., LA, 1962—64, fellow, 1966—68; pediat. endocrinologist Childrens Hosp., LA, 1970—87, head, endocrine metabolic divsn., 1987—97; ret. Prof. pediat. sch. medicine U. So. Calif., 1968—2000. Bd. mem. Greater Wilshire Neighborhood Coun., LA, 2005—. Capt. USAF, 1964—66, Goose Bay, Labrador. Mem.: Am. Pediat. Soc., We. Soc. Pediat. Rsch., Am. Diabetes Assn., Lawson Wilkins Pediat. Endocrinology Soc., Am. Acad. Pediat. Liberal. Roman Catholic. Avocations: tennis, skiing, travel, reading.

ROE, THOMAS LEROY WILLIS, retired pediatrician; b. Bend, Oreg., Sept. 1, 1936; MD, U. Oregon Health Scis. U., Portland, 1961. Diplomate Am. Bd. Pediatrics. Intern U. Calif., San Francisco, 1961-62, resident, 1962-64; physician Sacred Heart Med. Ctr., Eugene, Oreg.; pvt. practice Peace Health Med. Group, Eugene, 1969—2006; clin prof. pediatrics U. Oreg., Portland, 1985—2006; ret., 2006. Fellow Am. Acad. Pediatricians; mem. AMA, North Pacific Pediatrics Soc. Office: Peace Health Med Clinic 1162 Willamette St Eugene OR 97401-3568 Business E-Mail: troe@peacehealth.org.

ROEBUCK, DEBORAH MAE BRITT, management consultant, educator; b. San Antonio, Tex., Apr. 11, 1952; d. Aubrey Clarence and Marian Lavita Britt; m. Robert Leroy Roebuck; 1 child, Hillary Grace. BSE, Truman State U., Kirksville, 1972—74, MA, 1975; PhD, Ga. State U., Atlanta, 1986—90. Cert. tchr. Mo., Iowa, 1974. Prof. mgmt. Kennesaw State U., Ga., 1992—2001, chair leadership and profl. devel., 2001—05; exec. dir., prof. mgmt. Siegel Inst. Leadership, Ethics and Character, 2006—. Author: (textbook) Improving Business Communication Skills; contbr. articles to profl. jours. Mem.: Orgnl. Behavior Tchg. Soc., Acad. Mgmt. Baptist. Avocations: travel, reading. Office: Kennesaw State U 1000 Chastain Rd House # 55 Kennesaw GA 30144-5591 Office Phone: 770-423-6364.

ROEBUCK, JAMES RANDOLPH, JR., state legislator; b. Phila., Feb. 12, 1945; m. Cheryl Arrington. BA cum laude, Va. Union U., 1966; MA, U. Va., 1969, PhD, 1977. Lectr. Drexel U., 1970—77, asst. prof., 1977—84; legis. asst. Office of Mayor, Phila., 1984—85; mem. Pa. Ho. of Reps., Harrisburg, 1985—. Chmn. Pa. Legis. Black Caucus, 1998-2000; Democratic chmn. Ho. Edn. Com., 2003—; mem. Pa. History and Mus. Commn., 1990-95; bd. dirs. Pa. Higher Ednl. Assistance Agy. Author: The Shaping of William Howard Tafts View of East Asia 1900-1908; co-editor: Biographical Dictionary of Internationalists, 1983. Recipient Young Leadership award Hamilton Watch Co., 1966, Outstanding Svc. award Va. Union U. Alumni Assn., 1973, Legion of Honor award Chapel Four Chaplains, 1980. Mem. Nat. Black Caucus State Legislators, Alpha Phi Alpha. Address: 4800 Baltimore Ave Philadelphia PA 19143-3419 Home Phone: 215-382-1268; Office Phone: 215-724-2227. E-mail: jroebuck@pahouse.net.

ROEDDER, WILLIAM CHAPMAN, JR., lawyer; b. St. Louis, June 21, 1946; s. William Chapman and Dorothy (Reifeiss) R.; m. Gwendolyn Arnold, Sept. 13, 1968; children: William Chapman, Barcley Shane. BS, U. Ala., 1968; JD cum laude, Cumberland U., 1972. Bar: Ala. Law clk. to chief justice Ala. Supreme Ct., Montgomery, 1972; ptnr. McDowell Knight Roedder & Sledge, L.L.C., Mobile, Ala., 1997—. Comments editor Cumberland-Samford Law Rev.; contbr. articles to legal publs. Bd. dirs. Def. Rsch. Inst., 1999—2002; mem. Bd. Lawyers for Civil Justice. Named to Best Lawyers in Am. Mem.: ABA (vice chair com. trial tactics, torts and ins. practice 1995—96), Lawyers for Civil Justice (pres. 2006—07, bd. dirs), Def. Rsch. Inst. (bd. dirs. 1999—2002), Ala. Def. Lawyers Assn., Fedn. Def. and Corp. Counsel (chmn. products liability sect. 1990—93, bd. dirs. 1993—2000, regional v.p. 1994—96, exec. com. 1997—, sec.-treas. 1999—2000, pres.-elect 2000—01, pres. 2001—02, chmn. bd. dirs. 2002—03), Mobile County Bar Assn. (sec., chmn. ethics com. 1988—90, grievance com. 1994—96), Ala. State Bar Assn., Order of Barristers, Curia Honoris, Phi Alpha Delta (pres. 1971—72). Home: 211 Levert Ave Mobile AL 36607-3219 Office: McDowell Knight Roedder & Sledge LLC PO Box 350 Mobile AL 36601-0350 E-mail: broedder@mcdowellknight.com.

ROEDER, JOHN LOUIS, physics educator; b. St. Louis, June 2, 1940; s. George Louis and Alma Christina (Stuckenberg) R.; m. Rae Ann Clauser, July 6, 1968. AB, Washington U., 1962; MA, Princeton U., 1964, PhD, 1966. Officer, intelligence analyst U.S. Army, Washington, 1966-68; asst. prof. of physics Transylvania U., Lexington, Ky., 1968-73; physics and chemistry tchr. The Calhoun Sch., NYC, 1973—. Resource agt. N.Y.Sci., Tech. and Soc. Edn. Project, Albany, 1983-97; team leader for STS Inst., SUNY, Purchase, 1989-93. Editl. bd.: The Physics Tchr., Stony Brook, N.Y., 1976-79; editor: (newsletter) Teachers Clearinghouse for Science and Society Education, 1982—; contbg. author: Active Physics Communications, 1997. Tuba player Mercer County Cmty. Band, West Windsor, N.J., 1981—; environ. commr. West Windsor, 1974-95; mem. Zoning Bd. of Adjustment, West Windsor, 1995—. Recipient Presdl. award L.I. U., Bklyn., 1985, Presdl. award finalist Nat. Sci. Tchrs. Assn., Arlington, Va., 1990, Tandy Technol. scholar Tandy Corp., Ft. Worth, Tex., 1991. Mem. Am. Assn. Physics Tchrs. (Physics Tchg. Resource Agt. 1985-92, 98—, at-large mem. exec. bd. 2005—, Pre-Coll. Physics Tchg. Excellence award, 2003), Nat. Assn. for Sci., Tech. and Soc. (sec. 1996-99), Assn. of Tchrs. in Ind. Schs. (pres. 1989-92), Physics Club N.Y. (sec./treas. 1986—), Chemistry Tchrs. Club N.Y. (Oscar Foster award 2005) Democrat. Baptist. Avocation: music. Home: 194 Washington Rd Princeton NJ 08540-6447 Office: The Calhoun Sch 433 W End Ave New York NY 10024-5799 Office Phone: 212-497-6500. E-mail: JLRoeder@aol.com.

ROEDER, RICHARD KENNETH, business owner, lawyer; b. Phila., Oct. 11, 1948; s. Walter August and Gloria (Miller) R.; 1 child, William Frederick; m. Allison Nunn Roeder, June 12, 1999. AB, Amherst Coll., 1970; JD, U. Calif., Berkeley, 1973, Cambridge U., 1973-74. Assoc. Paul, Hastings, Janofky & Walker, LA, 1974-81, ptnr., 1981-90; founding ptnr. Aurora Capital Group, LA, 1990—. Office: Aurora Capital Group Ste 2100 10877 Wilshire Blvd Los Angeles CA 90024-4341

ROEDER, ROBERT GAYLE, biochemist, molecular biologist, educator; b. Boonville, Ind., June 3, 1942; s. Frederick John and Helene (Bredenkamp) Roeder; m. Suzanne Himsel, July 11, 1964 (div. 1981); children: Kimberly, Michael; m. Cun Jing Hong, June 2, 1990; 1 child, Maxine. BA summa cum laude (Gilbert scholar), Wabash Coll., 1964, DSc (hon.), 1990; MS, U. Ill., 1965; PhD (USPHS fellow), U. Wash., 1969; DSc (hon.), Washington U., 2005. Am. Cancer Soc. fellow dept. embryology Carnegie Instn. Washington, Balt., 1969-71; asst. prof. biol. chemistry Washington U., St. Louis, 1971-75, assoc. prof., 1975-76, prof., 1976-82, prof. genetics, 1978-82, James S. McDonnell prof. biochem. genetics, 1979-82; prof. lab. biochemistry and molecular biology Rockefeller U., NYC, 1982—, Arnold O. and Mabel S. Beckmann prof. molecular biology and biochemistry, 1985—. Cons. USPHS, 1975-79, Am. Cancer Soc., 1983-86. Recipient Dreyfus Tchr.-Scholar award Dreyfus Found., 1976, molecular biology award NAS-U.S. Steel Found., 1986, outstanding investigator award Nat. Cancer Inst., 1986-2002, Dickson prize in medicine, 2001, Albert Lasker Basic Med. Rsch. award 2003; co-recipient Lewis S. Rosenstiel award for disting. work in basic med. scis. Brandeis U., 1995, Passano award Passano Found., Inc., 1995, Alfred P. Sloan prize GM Cancer Rsch. Found., 1999, Louisa Gross Horowitz award Columbia U., 1999, Gairdner Found. Internat. award, 2000, ASBMB-Merck Award, 2002; grantee NIH, 1972-, NSF, 1975-79, Am. Cancer Soc., 1979-85. Fellow AAAS, Am. Acad. Arts and Scis., Am. Acad. Microbiology, NY Acad. Scis.; mem. NAS, Am. Chem. Soc. (Eli Lilly award 1977), Am. Soc. Biol. Chemists, Am. Soc. Microbiologists, Am. Soc. Immunologists, Am. Diabetes Assn., European Molecular Biology Orgn. (assoc.), Harvey Soc. (pres. 1994), Phi Beta Kappa. Office: Rockefeller U 1230 York Ave New York NY 10021-6399 Office Phone: 212-327-7600. Business E-Mail: roeder@rockefeller.edu.

ROEDERER, JUAN GUALTERIO, retired physics professor; b. Trieste, Italy, Sept. 2, 1929; came to U.S., 1967, naturalized, 1972; s. Ludwig Alexander and Anna Rafaela (Lohr) R.; m. Beatriz Susana Cougnet, Dec. 20, 1952; children: Ernesto, Irene, Silvia, Mario. PhD, U. Buenos Aires, 1952. Research scientist Max Planck Inst., Gottingen, W.Ger., 1952-55; group leader Argentine Atomic Energy Commn., Buenos Aires, 1953-59; prof. physics U. Buenos Aires, 1959-66, U. Denver, 1967-77, U. Alaska, Fairbanks, 1977-93, prof. emeritus, 1993—, dir. Geophys. Inst., 1977-86, dean Coll. Environ. Scis., 1978-82. Vis. staff Los Alamos Nat. Lab., 1969-81; chmn. U.S. Arctic Research Com., 1987-91; sr. adviser Internat. Ctr. Theoretical Physics, Trieste, Italy, 1998—2002. Author: Dynamics of Geomagnetically Trapped Radiation, 1970, Physics and Psychophysics of Music, 1973, 3d edit., 1995, Mecanica Elemental, 2002, Information and Its Role in Nature, 2005; contbr. articles to profl. jours Nat. Acad. Sci. NASA sr. rsch. fellow, 1964—66. Fellow AAAS, Am. Geophys. Union (Edward A. Flinn III award, 2000); mem. Assn. Argentina de Geodestas y Geofisicos (hon.), Nat. Acad. Sci. Argentina (corr.), Nat. Acad. Sci. Austria (corr.), Third World Acad. Scis. (assoc.), Internat. Assn. Geomagnetism and Aeronomy (hon.), Sci. Com. on Solar-Terrestrial Physics (hon.). Lutheran. Achievements include research in plasma and energetic particles in earth's and Jupiter's magnetosphere, policy issues for Arctic, perception of music, information theory. Office: Univ Alaska Geophys Inst Fairbanks AK 99775-7320 Business E-Mail: jgr@gi.alaska.edu.

ROEDING, CYRIAC R., broadcast executive; b. Germany, Mar. 26, 1973; M in Engring. and Bus. Adminstrn., Tech. Sch. Karlsruhe, Germany; MBA in Corp. Strategy and Entrepreneurship, U. Ga.; student in Japanese Mgmt., Sophia U., Tokyo. With Roland Berger Strategy Consultants, McKinsey & Co.; co-founder 12snap, 1999—2004; v.p. wireless CBS Corp., 2005—. Co-author: Secrets on Software Success: Management Insights from 100 Software Firms Around the World, 1999. Mem.: Mobile Mktg. Assn. (European chmn. 2001, global bd. mem. 2006). Office: CBS Corp 51 W 52nd St New York NY 10019-6119 *

ROEG, NICOLAS JACK, film director; b. London, Aug. 15, 1928; s. Jack Nicolas and Mabel Getrude (Silk) R.; m. Susan Rennie Stephen, May 12, 1957; children: Joscelin Nicolas, Nicolas Jack, Lucien John, Sholto Jules; m. Theresa Russell, 1985; children: Maximilian Nicolas Sextus, Statten Jack. Student Brit. schs.; LittD honoris causa, Hull U., Eng., 1995; DFA (hon.), CUNY, 2004. Cinematographer films The Caretaker, 1963, Masque of Red Death, 1964, Fahrenheit 451, 1966, A Funny Thing Happened on the Way to the Forum, 1966, Far from the Madding Crowd, 1967, Petulia, 1968; co-dir. film Performance, 1970; dir. films Walkabout, 1970, Don't Look Now, 1973, Glastonbury Fayre, 1973, The Man Who Fell to Earth, 1976, Bad Timing, 1980, Eureka, 1982, Insignificance, 1985, Castaway, 1986, 89, Track 29, 1987, Aria, 1987, The Witches, 1988-89, Cold Heaven, 1990, Heart of Darkness, 1994, Two Deaths, 1994, Hotel Paradise, 1995, Full Body Massage, 1995, Samson & Delilah, 1996, Puffball, 2006; dir. TV films: Sweet Bird of Youth, 1989, Heart of Darkness, 1994; exec. prodr. Without You I'm Nothing, 1989, Young Indy, 1991, The Sound of Claudia Schiffer, 1999-; co-prodr. Rock Concert, 2002; writer (screenplays) Night Train, 2000, Ivanhoe, 2000, History Play, 2004. Decorated comdr. Brit. Empire. Fellow Brit. Film Inst.; mem. Dirs. Guild Am., Dir. Guild Gt. Britain, Acad. Motion Picture Arts and Scis., Assn. Cinematograph, TV and Allied Technicians. Office Phone: 02072578723. Business E-Mail: nicolas@roegmovies.com.

ROEHL, JERRALD J., lawyer; b. Austin, Dec. 6, 1945; s. Joseph E. and Jeanne Foster (Scott) R.; m. Nancy J. Meyers, Jan. 15, 1977; children: Daniel J., Katherine C., J. Ryan, J. Taylor. BA, U. N.Mex., 1968; JD, Washington and Lee U., 1971. Bar: N.Mex. 1972, U.S. Ct. Appeals (10th cir.) 1972, U.S. Supreme Ct. 1977. Practice of law, Albuquerque, 1972—; pres. Roehl Law Firm P.C. and predecessors, Albuquerque, 1976—. Lectr. to profl. groups; real estate developer, Albuquerque. Bd. advs. ABA Jour. 1981-83; bd. editors Washington and Lee Law Rev., 1970-71. Bd. dirs. Rehab. Ctr. of Albuquerque, 1974-78; mem. assocs. Presbyn. Hosp. Ctr., Albuquerque, 1974-82; incorporator, then treas. exec. com. Ctr. City Coun., 1991-98, law coun. Washington & Lee U. Law Sch., 2002—. Recipient award of recognition State Bar N.Mex., 1975-77. Mem. ABA (award of achievement Young Lawyers divsn. 1975, coun. econs. of law practice sect. 1978-80, exec. coun. Young Lawyers divsn. 1979-81, fellow divsn. 1984—, coun. tort and ins. practice sect. 1981-83), N.Mex. Bar Assn. (pres. young lawyers sect. 1975-76), Albuquerque Bar Assn. (bd. dirs. 1976-79), N.Mex. Def. Lawyers Assn. (pres. 1983-84), Albuquerque Country Club, Albuquerque Petroleum Club, Sigma Alpha Epsilon, Sigma Delta Chi, Phi Delta Phi. Roman Catholic. Office: 300 Central Ave SW Ste 2500e Albuquerque NM 87102-2320 Office Phone: 505-242-6900. Business E-Mail: jjr@roehl.com.

ROEHLING, CARL DAVID, architect; b. Detroit, June 25, 1951; m. Barbara K. Jeffries; children: Carl Robert, Kristin Virginia. BS in Architecture, U. Mich., 1973, MArch, 1975. Registered arch., Mich.; cert. Nat. Coun. Archtl. Registration Bds. Arch. Minoru Yamasaki and Assocs., Inc., Troy, Mich., 1976-77, TMP Assocs., 1977-81, Harley Ellington Pierce Yee Assocs., Inc., Southfield, Mich., 1981-83, Giffels/Hoyem Basso Assocs., Troy, 1983-87, Smith, Hinchman & Grylls Assocs., Inc., Detroit, 1987; pres., CEO SmithGroup, Detroit. With Chrysler World Hdqs., 1994. Prin. works include CBS/Fox Video Hdqs., Livonia, Mich. (Honor award Mich. Masonry Inst., 1985), First Ctr. Office Bldg., Southfield, Mich. (Honor award FAIA Mich., 1988), Ind. U. Chemistry Bldg., Bloomington (Honor award AIA Detroit, 1990, AIA Mich., 1990), U. Mich. Aerospace Lab. Bldg., Ann Arbor, 1993, Los Alamos Materials Sci. Lab., N.Mex., 1993, others. Fellow AIA (Mich. chpt. pres. bd. dirs. 1989, mem. nat. com. on environ. 1991, Detroit chpt. pres. 1994, Young Arch. of Yr., AIA Detroit, 1986, AIA Mich., 1991, regional dir. 1996, nat. bd. dirs.); mem. Am. Archtl. Found. (bd. dirs. 1997), Mich. Archtl. Found. (chmn. pres. scholarship program 1990). Office: Smith Group 500 Griswold St Ste 1700 Detroit MI 48226-3802 Office Phone: 313-983-3600. Office Fax: 313-983-3636. *

ROEHM, JULIE A., marketing executive; b. Sept. 1970; m. Michael Roehm; children: Nick, Luke. BS in Civil Engring., Purdue U., 1993; MBA, U. Chgo., 1995. Mktg. comms. mgr. Ford Motor Co., Detroit, 1995—2001; dir. mktg. comms. Chrysler, Jeep and Dodge Daimler-Chrysler, Detroit, 2001—04; dir. mktg. Chrysler Group, Detroit, 2004—06; sr. v.p. mktg. comms. Wal-Mart Stores, Inc., Bentonville, Ark., 2006. Bd. dirs. BIAP Inc., 2007—. Named Automotive Marketer of Yr., Brandweek, 2004; named to Advt. Hall of Achievement, 2004; recipient Advt. Working Mothers of Yr. Award. *

ROEHRIG, C(HARLES) BURNS, internist, consultant; b. Brookline, Mass., Jan. 21, 1923; s. Gilbert Haven and Helen (Burns) R.; m. Patricia Joan Orme, July 22, 1952 (dec. 2002); children: Joan Russell Roehrig Vater, Jennifer Orme Roehrig Munn, Charles Burns, Jr. Student, Amherst Coll., 1941-43, Vanderbilt U., 1943-44; MD, U. Md., 1949; cert. in internal medicine, U. Pa., Phila., 1953. Diplomate Am. Bd. Internal Medicine. Intern Boston City Hosp., 1949-50; resident in internal medicine and diabetes Joslin Clinic, New Eng. Deaconess Hosp., Boston, 1952-54; practice medicine specializing in internal medicine and diabetes Boston, 1954-91; chief of staff, pres. med. adminstrv. bd. New Eng. Deaconess Hosp., Boston, 1972-75; dir., mem. exec. com. Blue Shield of Mass., Inc., Boston, 1977-88; exec. com. Met. Boston Hosp. Coun., 1982-86; physician adv. coun. Mass. Hosp. Assn., Burlington, 1982-86. Editor: Today's Internist, Washington, 1987-99; contbr. articles to profl. jours. Bd. dirs. Camping Svcs. Bd., Greater Boston YMCA, 1966—; mem. physician adv. group Health Care Financing Adminstrn., Washington, 1983-88; mem. adv. panel on physician payment and med. tech. Office of Tech. Assessment, U.S. Congress, Washington, 1984-85; chmn. Federated Coun. for Internal Medicine, Washington, 1985-86; trustee New Eng. Deaconess Hosp. Capt. (flight surgeon) USAF, 1949-52. Master ACP (pres. emeritus); mem. AMA (chmn. coun. on long range planning and devel., Chgo.), New Eng. Diabetes Assn. (pres. 1963-64), Mass. Soc. Internal Medicine (pres. 1971-72), Am. Soc. Internal Medicine (pres. 1984-85), Country Club of Hilton Head, Wellesley (Mass.) Country Club. Republican. Episcopalian. Office: 5 Summer Breeze Ct Hilton Head Island SC 29926-2536 Office Phone: 843-681-7713. Personal E-mail: burnsroehrigmd@aol.com.

ROEHRS, CHRISTOPHER SCOTT, lawyer; b. King of Prussia, Pa., Oct. 20, 1963; s. Anthony Gair and Jean Affleck Asch. BA, U. BC, 1991, LLB, 1994. Bar: BC 1995, NY 1999. Collections field auditor Revenue Can. Taxation, Vancouver, BC, Canada, 1982—86; assoc. atty. Baker and McKenzie, NYC, 1999—2004; asst. gen. counsel Am. Internat. Group,

Inc., NYC. Mem.: Travelers Century Club. Avocation: photography. Office: Am Internat Group Inc 175 Water St 23d Flr New York NY 10038 Office Phone: 212-458-2426. E-mail: csr212@hotmail.com.

ROELANDTS, WILLEM P., data processing executive; b. Jan. 4, 1945; came to U.S., 1982; BEE, Rijks Hogere Technische Sch., Belgium, 1965. Various position including sr. v.p. Hewlett-Packard, 1966—96; CEO, pres. Xilinx Inc., San Jose, 1996—, chmn., 2003—. Spkr. in field. Mem.: Fabless Semiconductor Assn. (pres.), Tech. Network (bd. dirs.), Semiconductor Industry Assn. (bd. dirs.). Office: Xilinx Inc 2100 Logic Dr San Jose CA 95124-3400 *

ROELL, STEPHEN A., manufacturing executive; Mgmt. positions Johnson Controls, Inc., Milw., 1982—91, v.p., CFO, 1991—98, sr. v.p., CFO, 1998—2004, exec. v.p., CFO, 2004—05, bd. dir., 2004—, exec. v.p., vice chmn., 2005—07, CEO, 2007—. Bd. dir. Covenant Healthcare Sys., Inc., Interstate Battery Svc. of Am., Inc. Office: Johnson Controls Inc 5757 W Green Bay Ave Milwaukee WI 53201 *

ROELLER, HERBERT ALFRED, biology professor; b. Magdeburg, Germany, Aug. 2, 1927; came to U.S., 1962; s. Alfred H. and Elfriede (Wartner) R.; m. Manuela R. Buresch, Dec. 20, 1957. Abiturium, Christian Thomasius Schule, Halle/Saale, 1946; PhD, Georg August U., Goettingen, 1962; MD, U. Muenster, 1955. Project assoc. zoology U. Wis., Madison, 1962-65, asst. prof. pharmacology, 1965-66, rsch. assoc. zoology, 1966-67, assoc. prof. zoology, 1967-68; prof. biology Tex. A&M U., 1968-83, prof. biochemistry and biophysics, 1974-83, dir. Inst. Devel. Biology, 1973-83, Disting. prof., 1977—, Alumni prof., 1980-85. V.p. rsch. Zoecon Corp., Palo Alto, Calif., 1968-72, sci. adv., 1972-85, chief scientist, Zoecon Rsch. Inst., Palo Alto, 1985-88; sci. advisor Syntex Rsch., Palo Alto, 1966-68, European Cmty., 1988—, Affymax Rsch. Inst., Palo Alto, 1989-96; corp. advisor Symyx Techs., Sunnyvale, Calif., 1996—; mem. adv. panel regulatory biology, divsn. biol. and med. scis. NSF, 1969-72; mem. Internat. Centre Insect Physiology and Ecology, Nairobi, Kenya, 1970—, dir. rsch., 1970-75. Mem. editl. bd. Jour. Chem. Ecology, 1974—; Contbr. articles to profl. jours. Recipient Disting. Achievement award for research Tex. A&M U., 1976. Fellow Tex. Acad. Sci.; mem. German Acad. Naturforscher Leopoldina, AAAS, Am. Soc. Zoologists, Entomol. Soc. Am., Am. Soc. Devel. Biology, Sigma Xi.

ROELLIG, LEONARD OSCAR, physics professor; b. Detroit, May 17, 1927; s. Oscar Otto and Laura K. (Rutz) R.; m. B. Pauline Cowdin, June 20, 1952; children: Thomas Leonard, Mark Douglas, Paul David. AB, U. Mich., 1950, MS, 1956, PhD, 1959. From asst. prof. to prof. physics Wayne State U., Detroit, 1958-78, dean, 1971-72, asso. provost, 1972-76; pres. Central Solar Energy Research Corp., Detroit, 1977; prof. physics CCNY, 1978-96, prof. emeritus, 1996—; vice chancellor acad. affairs CUNY, 1978-83. Vis. prof. Univ. Coll., London, 1968-69, Tata Inst. Fundamental Rsch., Bombay, India, 1973, Paul Scherrer Inst., Villigen, Switzerland, 1991-92; chmn. bd. advisers Midwest Regional Solar Energy Planning Venture, 1977. Co-author: Positron Annihilation, 1967; contbr. articles to profl. jours. Bd. dirs. Luth. Publicity Bur., 1981-91, v.p., 1984-85, pres., 1985-89; v.p. Grosse Pointe (Mich.) Human Rels. Coun., 1969-70. With USN, 1945-46, U.S. Army, 1950-52. Recipient Wayne State U. Fund Research Recognition award, 1963, Probus Club award for acad. achievement, 1968, Probus Club award for acad. leadership, 1977 Mem. Am. Phys. Soc. Home: 4520 Sioux Dr Boulder CO 80303-3733 Office: U Colo Dept Physics Boulder CO 80302 Office Phone: 303-492-8707. Personal E-mail: loroellig@aol.com.

ROELLIG, MARK D., lawyer; BS in Applied Maths. with highest distinction, U. Mich., 1976; JD, George Washington U., 1979; MBA, U. Washington, 1988. Assoc. Perry & Smity, Seattle, Reed, McClure, Moceri & Thonn, Seattle; litigation and regulator atty. law dept. Pacific Northwest Bell Telephone Co., Seattle, 1983-92, v.p. law and litigation sect. Denver, 1992-95, v.p. law and human resources, asst. sec. corp. sect., 1995, exec. v.p. pub. policy and regulatory law, 1996-97, exec. v.p. pub. policy, human resources, law, gen. counsel, 1997—2000; dir., sec., consultant Bulletin News Network, Inc., 2000—02; v.p., gen. counsel. sec. StorageTek, Louisville, Colo., 2002—05, Fisher Scientific Internat. Inc., Hampton, NH, 2005; exec. v.p., gen. counsel Mass. Mut. Life Ins. Co., Springfield, 2005—. Mem. Beta Gamma Sigma. Office: MassMutual Fin Group 1295 State St Springfield MA 01111-0001 *

ROELOFS, WENDELL LEE, biochemistry professor, consultant; b. Orange City, Iowa, July 26, 1938; s. Edward and Edith (Beyers) Roelofs; m. Joanna Roelofs, Jan. 13, 2005; children: Brenda Jo, Caryn Jean, Jeffrey Lee, Kevin Jon. BS, Central Coll., Pella, Iowa, 1960; PhD, Ind. U., 1964; DSc (hon.) (hon.), Central Coll., Pella, Iowa, 1985, Ind. U., 1986, Hobart and William Smith Colls., 1988; DSc (hon.), U. of Lund, Sweden, 1989, Free U. Brussels, 1989. Predoctoral fellow NIH, 1962—64; NIH postdoctoral fellow MIT, 1964; asst. prof. Dept. Entomology Cornell U., Geneva, NY, 1965—69, assoc. prof. Dept. Entomology, 1969—76, prof., 1976—, Liberty Hyde Bailey prof. insect biochemistry, 1978—, chmn. dept., 1991—. Contbr. articles to sci. jours. Recipient Alexander von Humboldt award in agr., 1977, Outstanding Alumni award, Central Coll., 1978, Wolf prize for agr., Wolf Found., Israel, 1982, Disting. Alumnus award, Ind. U., 1983, Nat. Medal of Sci., 1983, Disting. Svc. award, USDA, 1986, Silver medal, Internat. Soc. Chem. Ecology, 1990. Fellow: Entomol. Soc. Am. (J. Everett Bussart Meml. award 1973, Founder's Meml. award 1980, Disting. Achievement award Ea. br. 1983), AAAS; mem.: Am. Acad. Arts and Sci., Am. Chem. Soc. (Sterling B. Hendricks award 1994, Spencer award 2001), NAS, Sigma Xi. Republican. Presbyterian. Achievements include patents in field. Home: 4 Crescence Dr Geneva NY 14456-1302 Office: Cornell Univ Dept Entomology Barton Lab Geneva NY 14456

ROEMER, CAROL KALUGA, art educator; b. Cleve., Sept. 24, 1941; d. Joseph and Helen (Belavich) Kaluga; m. William Daniel Roemer, Dec. 21, 1974 (dec. Mar. 1998). BA, Calif. State U., Long Beach, 1970, MA, 1972; PhD, Claremont Grad. U., Calif., 1992. Cert. c.c. tchr., Calif. Classroom tchr. Holy Spirit Sch., LA, 1966-67; adj. instr. Cerritos C.C., Norwalk, Calif., 1972-81, Calif. State U., Long Beach, 1973-79, Golden West Coll., Huntington Beach, Calif., 1980-81; replacement instr. (full-time) Pasadena City Coll., 1977-80; prof. art Long Beach City Coll., 1981—2004, prof. emeritus, 2004—. Author: The Bread of Angels: Charles Eliot Norton's Art History, 1992; multi-media author/developer: Looking at Art, 1997-98. Recipient Tchg. Excellence award Nat. Inst. for Staff and Organizational Devel., U. Tex., 1995. Mem. Coll. Art Assn., Mus. Latin Am. Art, Long Beach Mus. Art (guest lectr. 1990-93), L.A. County Mus. Art (guest lectr. 1997), Cairn Terrier Club of So. Calif. (bd. dirs., newsletter editor). Avocations: cairn terrier exhibitor, breeder.

ROEMER, ELIZABETH, retired astronomer, educator; b. Calif., 1929; d. Richard Quirin and Elsie Roemer. BA with honors, U. Calif., Berkeley, 1950, PhD (Lick Obs. fellow), 1955. Tchr. adult class Oakland pub. schs., 1950-52; lab technician U. Calif. at Mt. Hamilton, 1954-55; grad. research astronomer U. Calif. at Berkeley, 1955-56; research asso. Yerkes Obs. U. Chgo., 1956; astronomer US Naval Obs., Flagstaff, Ariz., 1957-66; asso. prof. dept. astronomy, also in lunar and planetary lab. U. Ariz., Tucson, 1966-69, prof., 1969-97; prof. emerita, 1997—; astronomer Steward Obs., 1980-97, astronomer emerita, 1997—. Chmn. working group on orbits and ephemerides of comets commn. 20 Internat. Astron. Union, 1964-79, 85-88, v.p. comm. 20, 1979-82, pres., 1982-85, v.p. commn. 6, 1973-76, 85-88, pres., 1976-79, 88-91; adv. panel Office Naval Rsch., Nat. Acad. Scis.-NRC, NASA. Recipient Dorothea Klumpke Roberts prize U. Calif., Berkeley, 1950, Mademoiselle Merit award, 1959; asteroid (1657) named Roemera, 1965; Benjamin Apthorp Gould prize Nat. Acad. Scis., 1971, NASA Spl. award, 1986. Fellow AAAS (council 1966-69, 72-73), Royal Astron. Soc. (London); mem. Am. Astron. Soc. (program vis. profs. astronomy 1960-75, council 1967-70, chmn. div. dynamical astronomy 1974), Astron. Soc. Pacific (publs. com. 1962-73, Comet medal com. 1968-74, Donohoe lectr. 1962), Internat. Astron. Union, Am. Geophys. Union, Brit. Astron. Assn., Phi Beta Kappa, Sigma Xi. Achievements include research in astrometry and astrophysics of comets and minor planets including 79 recoveries of returning periodic comets, visual and spectroscopic binary stars, computation of orbits of comets and minor planets. Office: U Ariz PO Box 210092 Lunar & Planetary Lab Tucson AZ 85721-0092

ROEMER, JAMES PAUL, data processing executive, writer; b. Cin., June 6, 1947; s. Charles William and Lillian (Vollman) R.; m. Patricia Pipenger: children: Kimberly, Michelle. Student, U. Cin., 1965-68; A.M.P., U. Va., 1978. Systems analyst Union Central Life Ins. Co., Cin., 1965-70; program and systems mgr. Computer Systems, Inc., Florence, Ky., 1970-72; mgr. data processing Mead Products, Dayton, Ohio, 1972-77; dir. ops. Mead Data Central, Dayton, 1977-78, v.p. ops., 1978-80, acting pres., 1980-81, v.p. product devel., 1981-82, sr. v.p. legal, govt., acctg., sr. v.p. with responsibility for lexis, 1982-89; pres. Michie Group, Charlottesville, Va., 1989-91; pres., COO Bell and Howell Publs. Systems Co., 1991-93; pres., CEO Univ. Microfilms Internat., Ann Arbor, 1994-95; chmn., pres., CEO Bell & Howell, Skokie, Ill., 1995—. Active Harvard, 1989. Mem. Info. Industry Assn., Assn. for Info. and Image Mgmt. Republican. Roman Catholic.

ROEMER, JOHN E., economics educator; b. Washington, Feb. 1, 1945; s. Milton I. and Ruth J. (Rosenbaum) R.; m. Carla N. Muldavin, 1968. BA in Math., summa cum laude, Harvard U., 1966; PhD in Economics, U. Calif., Berkeley, 1974. Math. tchr. Lowell HS, San Francisco, 1969—74, Pelton Jr. HS, San Francisco, 1969—74; Ford Found. grad. fellow U. Calif., Berkeley, 1966—68, Nat. Sci. Found. grad. fellow, 1966—68; Social Sci. Rsch. Coun. postdoctoral rsch. fellow Stanford U., 1977; asst. prof. economics U. Calif., Davis, 1974—78, assoc. prof., 1978—81, prof., 1981—2000, acting chair Dept. Economics, 1987—88, dir. Program on Economy, Justice and Society, 1988—2000; Elizabeth S. and A. Varick Stout prof. polit. sci. and economics Yale U., 2000—. Editor Marxian economics Ency. of Economics, 1984—, Fundamentals of Pure and Applied Economics, 1984—; editl. bd. Economics and Philosophy, 1983—, Ethics, 1989—, Social Choice and Welfare, 1990—, Mathematical Social Sciences, 1993—, Jour. Economic Inequality, 2001—; assoc. editor Jour. Economic Perspectives, 1988—96, Economics and Politics, 1988—90, Jour. Economic Literature, 1988—97, Rev. Economic Design, 1992—, Jour. Ethics, 1997—, Jour. Economics, 2004—; vis. prof. Dept. Economics and Dept. Polit. Sci. UCLA, 1987; vis. prof. Université de Cergy-Pontoise, 1995, Ecole Polytechnique, Paris, Université de Paris I, 2006. Author: Analytical Foundations of Marxian Economic Theory, 1981, A General Theory of Exploitation and Class, 1982, Value, Exploitation and Class, 1986, Free To Lose: An Introduction to Marxist Economic Philosophy, 1988, Egalitarian Perspectives: Essays in Philosophical Economics, 1994, A Future for Socialism, 1994, Theories of Distinctive Justice, 1996, Equality of Opportunity, 1998, Political Competition: Theory and Applications, 2001, Democracy, education and equality, 2006; co-author: Sustainable Democracy, 1995. Fellow John Simon Guggenheim Meml., 1980—81, Russell Sage Found., 1998—99. Fellow: Econometic Soc., Am. Acad. Arts and Sciences; mem.: Am. Polit. Sci. Assn., Soc. for Social Choice and Welfare (exec. bd. mem. 1991—), Am. Economic Assn. (exec. bd. mem. 1995—97), The Brit. Acad. (corr. fellow 2005—). Office: Dept Politcal Science Yale Univ PO Box 208302 New Haven CT 06520 Office Phone: 203-432-5249. Office Fax: 203-432-6196. E-mail: john.roemer@yale.edu.

ROEMER, TIMOTHY JOHN, think-tank executive, former congressman; b. South Bend, Ind., Oct. 30, 1956; m. Sarah Lee Johnston, 1989. BA in pol. sci, U. Calif., San Diego, 1979; MA, PhD in internat. rels., U. Notre Dame, 1986. Staff asst. to congressman John Brademas U.S. Congress, def., trade and fgn. policy advisor to senator Dennis DeConcini; mem. U.S. Congress from 3rd Ind. dist., 1991—2003, mem. economic and ednl. opportunity com., mem. sci. com., mem. edn. and the workforce com., mem. permanent select committee on intelligence; ptnr. Johnston & Assocs., Washington, 2003; pres. Ctr. for Nat. Policy, Washington, 2003—. Adj. prof. Am. U.; commr. The Nat. Commn. on Terrorist Attacks Upon the U.S. (The 9-11 Commn.), 2002—04. Mem.: Nat. Commn. Terrorists Attacks U.S. Democrat. Office: Ctr for Nat Policy One Massachusetts Ave NW Ste 333 Washington DC 20001

ROEN, SHELDON R., psychologist, publishing executive; b. NYC; s. Morris Rosenthal and Gussie (Weininger) R.; children: Randa M., Marjorie A., Harris L. BS, City U. N.Y., 1950, MA, 1951; PhD, Columbia U., 1955; postgrad., New Sch. Social Research, 1951-53, Harvard Sch. Pub. Health, 1961-62. Diplomate: Am. Bd. Examiners in Profl. Psychology. Tchr. pub. schs., NYC, 1950-53; chief Clin. Psychology Svc., Ft. Sill, Okla., 1955-58; instr. Cameron Coll., Okla. A. and M. U., 1956-58; asst. prof. U. N.H., 1958-60; asst. chief psychol. services Mass. Mental Health Center, Boston, 1960-63; instr. Harvard, 1961-63; rsch. assoc. Med. Sch., 1960-63; dir. rsch. S. Shore Mental Health Center, Quincy, Mass., 1962-66; assoc. prof. dept. psychology Tchrs. Coll., Columbia, NYC, 1966-72; dir. Psychol. Consultation Center, 1966-72; chmn. bd., pres. human scis. Human Scis. Press, NYC, 1972—90. Lectr. L.I. U., summer 1958, Tufts U., 1961-62; mem. N.H. Gov.'s Com. on Spl. Edn., also Study Com. on Mental Health Reorgn., 1961-62; cons. VISTA program OEO, 1966-67; mem. juvenile problems research rev. com. NIMH, 1968-69; mem. research rev. com. Title III Elementary and Secondary Edn. Act project application Ohio Dept. Edn., 1969-72; mem. mental health coordinating com. local sch. dist. 5, N.Y.C., 1969-72; mem., research dir. work incentive program for welfare recipients Wharton Sch. Pa., U.S. Dept. Labor, 1969-72; mem. mental health and community control com. N.Y. Psychologists for Social Action, 1969-72 Authors, editor books.; Editor: Mass. Psychol. Assn. Newsletter, 1963-65, Community Mental Health Jour; contbr. articles to profl. jours. and chpts. to books. Chmn. bd. trustees Bristol Acres Sch., Taunton, Mass., 1965-67. Fellow Am. Psychol. Assn. (mem. com. pre-coll. behavioral scis. 1968-71, founder div. 27 community psychology div. 1969, chmn. subcom. pre-high sch. behavioral sci. 1969-72), Am. Pub. Health Assn., Am. Orthopsychiat. Assn. (com. on research edn. 1965-67), Am. Sociol. Assn.; mem. New Eng. Psychol. Assn. (steering com. 1965-68), N.H. Psychol. Assn. (legis. chmn. 1961-62) Office: 3205 Beacon St Pompano Beach FL 33062-1207

ROENICK, JEREMY, professional hockey player; b. Boston, Jan. 17, 1970; m. Tracy Roenick; children: Brandi, Brett. Center Chgo. Blackhawks, 1988—96, Phoenix Coyotes, 1996—2001, Pheonix Coyotes, 2006—07, Phila. Flyers, 2001—05, LA Kings, 2005—06, San Jose Sharks, 2007—; hockey analyst TSN, Canada, 2007. Mem. US Olympic Hockey Team, Nagano, Japan, 1998, Salt Lake City, 2002; player NHL All-Star Game, 1991—94, 1999, 2000, 2002—04. Named NHL Rookie of Yr., The Sporting News, 1989—90. Achievements include being a member of silver medal winning USA Hockey Team, Salt Lake City Olympics, 2002. Office: San Jose Sharks 525 W Santa Clara St San Jose CA 95113

ROENIGK, MARTIN ALLEN, insurance company executive; b. Cleve., Sept. 19, 1942; s. Henry Herman and Irene Lena (Rini) Roenigk; m. Elise Feutz, July 5, 1965. BA, Antioch Coll., 1965; MBA, U. Chgo., 1967. CPA Conn. Staff auditor Arthur Andersen & Co., Cleve., 1968; with Travelers Ins. Co., Hartford, Conn., 1970—80, v.p., 1980—. Editor (pub.): MBS News Bull, 1976—. Pres. Greater Middletown Preservation Trust, Conn., 1981, trustee Conn., 1978—; mem. Rep. Town Com., 1981—. With US Army, 1968—70. Mem.: Am. Inst. CPAs, Musical Box Soc. (trustee).

ROENS, STEVEN THOMAS, music educator, associate dean; b. Phila., Mar. 1, 1949; s. Burt Beaudry and Jacqueline Roens; m. Cheryl Anne Clarke, Aug. 18, 1994; stepchildren: David Hart, Sarah Hart, Edward Alexander Hart, Isaac Hart. BA, Swarthmore Coll., Pa., 1971; MFA, Brandeis U., Mass., 1977; DMA, Columbia U., NYC, 1986. Vis. asst. prof. music Wellesley Coll., Mass., 1986—90; assoc. prof. music U. of UT, Salt Lake City, 1990—, assoc. dean, 1998—. Composer: (musical compositions) Time and Again, 1991 (Commn. from Stony Brook Contemporary Chamber Players), (musical composition) Delicate Arch, 1992, In the Night Fields, 1977, Invocation, (piano solo) starry skies, 1978, quartet for clarinet, violin, cello and piano. Mem. League of Composers Internat. Soc. for Contemporary Music, NYC, 1983—86. Fellow, MacDowell Colony, 1987. Mem.: Soc. of Composers. Democrat. Avocations: astronomy, photography, hiking. Office: U of UT Sch of Music 1375 E Presidents Cir Salt Lake City UT 84112 Personal E-mail: steve.roens@music.utah.edu.

ROEPENACK, DWIGHT ELMER, public health service officer; b. Chgo., May 23, 1947; s. Elmer Henry and Hazel Ethel Roepenack; m. Carol Ann Jasica, Oct. 11, 1980. AA, Wilbur Wright Jr. City Coll., Chgo., 1968; BS in Biology, Northland Coll., Ashland, Wis., 1970; postgrad. in Pub. Policy and Adminstrn., Northwestern U., Chgo. Lic. environ. health practitioner, environ. health specialist, cert. scuba diver, lic. amateur radio, cert. emergency preparedness FEMA, 2002, hazardous materials awareness Ill, 2002, emergency repsonse tng. cert. 2004. Quality assurance auditor Wyler Foods, Northbrook, Ill., 1971—72; engrng. product supr. NPC Pronto Foods, Inc., Chgo., 1972—75; dept. head sanitation salerno Megownen Biscuit Co., Niles, Ill., 1976—78; plant sanitarian Revere Sugar Corp., Chgo., 1978—82; health dept. inspector Evanston North Shore Health Dept., Ill., 1983—88; health and lic. officer Village Niles, 1988—. Self employed contract sanitarian pest control, 1982—89. Weather spotter Nat. Weather Svc., 1992—; mem. zoning bd. appeals, planning commr. Villiage Morton Grove, Ill., 1993—; water safety instr. ARC; mem. Morton Grove Traffic Safety Commn., Morton Grove, Ill., 1984—92; theatre adv. bd. Loyola U., 1992—93. Mem.: Nat. Orgn. Am. Radio Relay League, Chgo. Art Inst., Chgo. Field Mus., Interlochen Nat. Music Camp, Nat. Environ. Health Assn., Ill. Environ. Health Assn. Independent. Lutheran. Office: Village Niles 100 Civic Center Dr Niles IL 60714

ROEPER, RICHARD, columnist; b. Chgo., Oct. 17, 1959; s. Robert and Margaret R. BA, Ill. State U., 1982. Freelance writer, 1982-87; syndicated columnist Chgo.-Sun Times, 1987—, NY Times; regular contbr., film crtic WBBM-CBS 2, Chgo., 2002—; and co-host Ebert & Roeper, 2000—. Talk show host Sta. WLS-FM, Chgo.; commentator Fox Thing in the Morning, Sta. WFLD-TV, Fox TV, Chgo.; contbr., film critic WLS-Channel 7. Author: Ten Sure Signs a Movie Character is Doomed and Other Surprising Movie Lists, 2002, Schlock Value: Hollywood at Its Worst, 2005; contbr. monthly essays on film in Esquire. Recipient Outstanding Columnist Ill. Press Assn., 1992, Nat. Headliner award for top columnist Atlantic City Press Club, 1992, Emmy award, 1994. Mem. Am. Fedn. TV & Radio Artists, Chgo. Newspaper Guild. Office: Chicago Sun Times 350 N Orleans St Ste 1270 Chicago IL 60654-2148

ROER, RICKI E., lawyer; b. NYC, May 22, 1956; BA, U. Pa., 1978; JD, Am. U., 1981; LLM in internat. law, Oxford U., 1982. Bar: NY 1982, US Dist. Ct. Ea. Dist. NY, US Dist. Ct. So. Dist. NY, US Ct. Appeals 2nd Cir. Ptnr. Wilson, Elser, Moskowitz, Edelman & Dicker LLP, NYC, head nat. employment litig. team. Mem.: ABA, NY State Women's Bar Assn., Assn. of the Bar of the City of NY. Office: Wilson Elser Moskowitz Edelman & Dicker LLP 23rd Fl 150 E 42nd St New York NY 10017-5639 Office Phone: 212-490-3000 ext. 2375. Office Fax: 212-490-3038. Business E-Mail: roerr@wemed.com.

ROES, NICHOLAS A., writer, artist; b. Jersey City, Dec. 26, 1952; s. Nicholas R. and Mimi (Maresca) R.; m. Nancy Bennett. BS in Edn., U. Bridgeport, 1974, MA in Bus. and Pub. Mgmt., 1983; PhD in Addictions Treatment, Westbrook U., 1997. Credentialed substance abuse counselor NY, credentialed alcohol and substance abuse counselor, credentialed justice counselor, registered addiction specialist. Chmn. bd. Tchr. Update, Inc., Saddle River, NJ, 1976—; pres., cons., author Nicholas A. Roes & Assocs., Saddle River, 1979—; mng. ptnr. Barryville (N.Y.) Investors, 1985—; exec. dir. New Hope Manor, residential substance abuse treatment ctr. for women, Barryville, NY, 1992—. Dir. NAR Prodns., 1987, Idea Group, Inc., 1986—, aodceus.com, 2004—, nartisticreations.com, 2004—; instr. Marist Coll., Poughkeepsie, N.Y., 1989—; curator online gallery NartisticCreations.com. Author: Helping Children Watch TV, 1978, rev., 1992, America's Lowest Cost College, 1977, 10th edit., 1997, Gambling for Fun, 1988, Pick Your Own, 1989, Solutions for The Treatment Resistant Addicted Client, 2002; editor (newsletter) Tchr. U pdate, 1977; columnist The Investment Column, 1980—, Addiction Profl. Mag., 2003—. Exec. dir. New Hope Manor, Barryville, 1992—; chair alcohol and substance abuse subcom. Sullivan County Cmty. Svcs. Bd., 2006-. Recipient Cert. of Recognition, N.Y. State Office Alcohol and Substance Abuse Svcs., 2002. Mem. Internat. Assn. Fin. Planners, Direct Mail Club of N.Y., EDPRESS, C. of C., Mensa, Internat. Platform Assn. Avocation: music. Office: Nicholas A Roes & Assocs PO Box 205 Saddle River NJ 07458-0205 Office Phone: 845-557-8713. Personal E-mail: nickaroes@aol.com.

ROESCH, CLARENCE HENRY, banker; b. Egg Harbor City, NJ, Aug. 22, 1925; s. Joseph Aloysius and Bertha (Heumann) R.; m. Helen Regina Owens, Sept. 25, 1954; children: Kathleen Marie, Helena Patricia, Maryanne Cornelia. BBA, Rutgers U., 1949, postgrad., 1961; cert., Am. Inst. Banking, Atlantic City, 1961; grad. Trust Sch., Bucknell U., Lewisburg, Pa., 1971. Cert. internal auditor, data processing auditor. Bookkeeper, teller, head teller, asst. sec., trust officer, auditor Egg Harbor Bank & Trust Co., 1949-61; bank examiner Phila. Fed. Res. Bank, 1962-65; chief auditor Am. Bank & Trust Co. of Pa. (name changed to Meridian Bancorp Inc. 1985), Reading, 1966-88, v.p. audit dept., 1968-88, ret. officer, 1988; parish sec. St. Benedict Ch., Plowville, 1989-99; sr. staff auditor Nat. Penn Bank, Boyertown, 1990-97. Census enumerator, 2000; mem. faculty Berks County chpt. Am. Inst. Banking, 1966-68; instr. bank auditing Bank Adminstrn. Inst., U. Richmond, 1968; pres., past mems. chpt. Am. Banking Inst., Atlantic County, NJ, 1958-59. Budget com. Berks County chpt. United Way, 1967-73; bd. dirs. Berks Reading Coun. Camp Fire, 1966-93, chmn. fin. com., 1973, 75, treas., 1974-84; instr. 55 Alive Program AARP, 1989-93. Recipient John Johnston award as outstanding banker NJ, 1955; award U.S. Savs. Bond Com., 1961; Luther Halsey Gulick award for vol. services Camp Fire, 1975; John C. Collier award for outstanding bus. and fin. services, 1981, Blue Ribbon award for vol. services Camp Fire, 1984, award for corp. vol. of yr. Meridian Bancorp Inc., 1984, 85, Outstanding Svc. in Fin. Mgmt. award Camp Fire, 1988. Mem. Inst. Internal Auditors (dir. ctrl. Pa. chpt.), Berks County Bankers Assn., Travelers Protective Assn., Berks Reading C. of C., Bank Administration Inst. (past pres., dir. Penn-Jersey chpt.), Spring Lawn Optimist Club (bd. dirs. 1992, Key Mem. award 1992, chmn. fin. and budget com. 1992-94), St. BEnedict Ch. Prime Timers Srs. Home: 433 S Kinzer Ave #212GN New Holland PA 17557

ROESE, NEAL J., psychology professor, consultant; b. Vancouver, Canada, Feb. 13, 1965; s. Joseph and Geraldine Roese; m. Karen Grabowski, June 4, 1994; children: Emma, Anna. PhD, U. Western Ont., London, Can., 1993. Asst. prof. Northwestern U., Evanston, Ill.,

1994—2000; assoc. prof., rsch. chair social psychology Simon Fraser U., Vancouver, Canada, 2000—02; prof. U. Ill., Champaign, 2002—. Cons. Foresight Reconstruction, Inc., Northbrook, Ill., 2006—, Hinshaw & Culbertson LLP, Chgo., 2007—, Seyfarth Shaw, LA, 2007—. Author: If Only, 2005. Grantee, Nat. Inst. Mental Health, 1997—2002, 2004—. Avocation: skiing. Office: U Ill 603 East Daniel St Champaign IL 61820 Office Phone: 217-244-0751.

ROESER, ANDY, professional sports team executive; m. Anne Roeser; 2 children. Grad., Mich. State U., East Lansing. Exec. v.p. LA Clippers, 1986—, NBA alt. gov. Mem. adv. com. Grad. Prog. Sport Mgmt. Calif. State U., Long Beach; bd. dirs. LA Sports Coun. Pres., CEO LA Clippers Found. Office: LA Clippers 1111 S Figueroa St Ste 1100 Los Angeles CA 90015 *

ROESER, RONALD O., lawyer, consultant; b. Berwyn, Ill., May 6, 1950; s. John O. and Mary Jean (Marsden) R.; m. Susan Marie Gill, July 22, 1972; children: Michelle Marie, Michael Franklin. BA, So. Ill. U., 1972; JD, DePaul U., 1975. Bar: Ill. 1975 1975, U.S. Dist. Ct. (no. dist.) Ill. 1975, U.S.Tax. Ct. 1975, U.S. Ct. Appeals (7th cir.) 1975. Assoc. Imming & Faber, Elgin, Ill., 1975-77; ptnr. Imming, Faber & Roeser, Elgin, 1977-81, Imming & Roeser, Elgin, 1981-83, Roeser & Vucha, Elgin, 1983-84, Roeser, Vucha & Carbary, Elgin, 1984—. Mem. Fed. Trial Bar, Ill. Bar Assn., Kane County Bar Assn., Chgo. Bar Assn., Ill. Trial Lawyers Assn., Dundee Jaycees (treas., bd. dirs. 1975—, Outstanding Merit awards 1976, 78, 81), Lions. Republican. Roman Catholic. Avocations: history, reading, contact sports. Home: 34w921 Duchesne Dr Dundee IL 60118-3101 Office: Roeser & Vucha 920 Davis Rd Elgin IL 60123-1390 Office Phone: 847-888-1820. Business E-Mail: ronroeser@roeserlaw.com.

ROESLER, JOHN BRUCE, lawyer; b. Portland, Oreg., Oct. 9, 1943; s. Bruce Emil and Charlotte Amanda (Naess) R.; m. Kathryne Elise Nilsen, Aug. 14, 1965; children: Paul, Mark, Nico. BA, U. Kans., 1966, JD, 1971. Bar: Mo. 1971, N.Mex. 1979, Colo. 1998, U.S. Dist. Ct. (we. dist.) Mo. 1971, U.S. Dist. Ct. N.Mex. 1979, U.S. Dist. Ct. Colo. 1998. U.S. Ct. Appeals (10th cir.) 1979, U.S. Ct. Appeals (5th cir.) 1988, U.S. Ct. Appeals (4th cir.) 1992, U.S. Supreme Ct. 1987. Assoc. The Gage Firm, Kansas City, Mo., 1971—74; civil rights advocate State of N.Mex. Human Rights, Santa Fe, 1977—78; law clk. Hon. Edwin L. Felter N.Mex. Supreme Ct., Santa Fe, 1978—79; asst. dist. atty. Taos Dist. Atty.'s Office, N.Mex., 1979—80; asst. spl. pros. Santa Fe Dist. Atty.'s Office, 1980—82; pvt. practice Santa Fe, 1982—97; of counsel Roth, Van Amberg, Gross, Rogers & Ortiz, 1991—94; spl. asst. atty. gen. Colo. Atty. Gen.'s Office, 1997—99; assoc. Jones & Keller, Denver, 1999—2000; pvt. practice Denver, 2000—. Instr. John Marshall Law Sch., Chgo., 1974; spkr. edn. law and civil rights issues U. Miami Law Sch., 2000, Nat. Com. for Prevention of Child Abuse, Chgo., 1989, Little Rock, 90, Lorman Educators Svcs., 2004. Author: (books) How To Find the Best Lawyers; In Harm's Way: Is Your Child Safe in School, Beyond Special Education and the IDEA; mem. law rev. U. Kans. Sch. Law, 1970-71; contbr. articles to profl. jours. and Am. Jur. treatise. Mem. Colo. Bar Assn., Denver Bar Assn. Democrat. Roman Catholic. Avocations: skiing, hiking, gardening. Home: 2571 S Sherman St Denver CO 80210-5725 Office: 303 E 17th Ave Ste 200 Denver CO 80203 Office Phone: 303-832-1282. E-mail: jroesler@lawyer.com.

ROESLER, ROBERT HARRY, media consultant; b. Hammond, La., Oct. 5, 1927; s. Albert N. and Hilda (Schwartz) R.; m. Cloe Alferez, May 7, 1955; children: Kim, Bob, Toby. Student, Tulane U. Mem. sports staff Times Picayune, New Orleans, 1949-94, sports editor, 1964-80; exec. sports editor Times Picayune and States-Item, 1980-94; sports coord. New Orleans Met. Conv. and Visitors Bur., 1994—99; CEO Roesler Media Cons. Chmn. faculty coun., Student Publs. Bd., U. New Orleans, 1998-2001. Author: Fair Grounds: Big Shots and Long Shots, 1998. Vice-chmn. Navy Recruiting Dist.; mem. assistance coun., New Orleans, 1992-96. With USN, WWII, Korean conflict. Mem. Profl. Football Writers Assn. Am. (pres. 1976-77, PFWA McCAnn Meml. award NFL Hall of Fame, 1997), Nat. Turf Writers Assn., Football Writers Am., Am. Legion, Navy League U.S., New Orleans Press Club (pres. 1959-60, sports writing awards). Home and Office: 1700 Bailey Hill Rd Apt 9 Eugene OR 97402 Home Phone: 541-338-3066; Office Phone: 541-338-3066. Personal E-mail: bobroesler@gmail.com.

ROESNER, LARRY AUGUST, civil engineer; b. Denver, Mar. 14, 1941; s. Walter George and Sarah Jane (Merrick) R.; m. Kathleen Ann Fahrenbruch, Dec. 13, 1964; children: David John, Kevin Walter, Nathan August, Melissa Jane. BS in Civil Engring, Valparaiso U., Ind., 1959—63; MS in Civil Engring, Hydrology, Colo. State U., 1963—65; PhD, U. Wash., Seattle, 1969. Registered profl. engr., Calif., Colo., hydrologist. From assoc. engr. to prin. engr. Water Resources Engrs., Inc., Walnut Creek, Calif., 1968-77; from assoc. to v.p. Camp Dresser & McKee Inc., Annandale, Va., 1977-85, sr. v.p., dir. water resources Maitland, Fla., 1985-92, chief tech. officer, 1992-98; dean Camp Dresser & McKee Corp. U., 1998-99; Harold H. Short prof. urban water infrastructure systems Colo. State U., Ft. Collins, 1999—, interim head dept. civil engring., 2000. Guest lectr., cons. urban hydrology and surface water quality; NRC exec. com. Wastewater Mgmt. in Urban Coastal Areas, 1992; chair Engring. Found. Conf. Stormwater Mgmt.-Sustainable Urban Water Resources in the 21st Century, 1997, NRC study panel Oil in the Sea, 2001; urban wet weather adv. Water Environ. Rsch. Found. Contbr. articles to profl. jours. Recipient Water Resource Planning and Mgmt. Divsn. Svc. to the Profession award 1999. Fellow ASCE (life, chmn. 1995 water resources planning and mgmt. divsn. splty. conf., nat. Walter L. Huber civil engring. rsch. prize 1975); mem. NAE (elected mem. 1990), Am. Acad. Water Resource Engrs. (diplomate), Am. Water Resources Assn., Water Environ. Fedn., Tau Beta Pi (eminent engr.). Democrat. Lutheran. Achievements include development of mathematical models for U.S. government agencies including QUAL-II stream quality model for the EPA; an urban stormwater management model, the dynamic hydraulics model SWMMEXTRAN for storm drainage and sewer systems. Home: 5926 Huntington Hills Dr Fort Collins CO 80525-7118 Office: Colo State U Dept Civil Engring Fort Collins CO 80523-1372 Business E-Mail: larry.roesner@colostate.edu. *An environmental engineer is a caretaker in God's garden, the earth. The challenge for the environmental engineer is to maintain a balance between the needs of people and those of nature so that we may both use and enjoy the garden. It is the responsibility of the environmental engineer to leave the garden a little nicer than he found it.*

ROESNER, PETER LOWELL, manufacturing executive; b. Winchester, Ind., July 3, 1937; s. Lowell LeClair and Martha Christine (Overmyer) R.; children: Peter Lowell II, David Brandon, John Franklin. Student, Durham U., Eng., 1957-58; BA, DePauw U., 1959; JD, U. Mich., 1962; MBA, Harvard U., 1964. Bar: Ind. 1962, N.J. 1992. Asst. to pres. Overmyer Corp., Muncie, Ind., 1964-65, corp. sec., 1965-69, pres., 1969-84, also dir.; pres. Clinitemp Inc., Indpls., 1985-88; pres., owner Middletown (N.J.) Interiors Inc., 1993—. Dir. Mchts. Nat. Bank, 1974-84 Trustee Purdue U., 1978. Mem. Ind. Mfrs. Assn. (dir. 1970-82, pres. 1975, chmn. Phoenix Award com. 1974), Glass Packaging Inst. (trustee 1981-84), ABA Episcopalian.

ROESSER, JEAN WOLBERG, state official; b. Washington, May 8, 1930; d. Solomon Harry Wolberg and Mary Frances Brown; m. Eugene Francis Roesser, Aug. 3, 1957 (dec.); children: Eugene Francis, Jr., Mary Roesser Calderon, Anne. BA, Trinity Coll., Washington, 1951; postgrad. in econs., Cath. U. of Am., 1951-53. Congl. relations asst. U.S. Info. Agy., Washington, 1954-58; news reporter for Montgomery County Coun., Suburban Record, 1983-86; mem. Md. Ho. of Dels., Annapolis, 1986-94, Md. Senate, Annapolis, 1994—2002; mem. fin. com., ethics com. State Senate, Md. Gen. Assembly, Annapolis, 1994—2002, joint com. welfare reform, 1996, joint com. healthcare delivery & financing, 1996—2002, joint budget & audit com., 1997—2002, chair joint com. on welfare reform, 2002; sec. Md. Dept. Aging, 2003—. Former mem. Md. Gov.'s Task Force on Energy; former pres. Montgomery County Fedn. Rep. Women, Potomac Women's Rep. Club; former 3d v.p. Md. Fedn. Rep. Women; founding mem. Montgomery County Arts Coun.; alt. del. Rep. Nat. Conv., 1992, del., 1996. Named one of Md.'s Top 100 Women, Daily Record, 2002; recipient Cmty. Achievement award, Washington Psychiat. Soc., 1994, 1998, Trinity Coll. Leadership award, 1994, Common Cause Md. award, 1993, Md. Underage Drinking Preventio Coalition award, 1994, Legislator of the Yr. award, Montgomery County Med. Soc., 1996, 2000, Best in Class award, Md. C. of C., 1997, Cmty. Svc. award, Washington Psychiatric Soc., 1998, Legislator of Yr. award, Md. State's Atty.'s Assn., 2000. Republican. Roman Catholic. Home: 10830 Fox Hunt Ln Potomac MD 20854-1553 E-mail: jeanroesser@aol.com.

ROESSLER, CAROL ANN, state legislator; b. Madison, Wis., Jan. 16, 1948; m. Paul Roessler. BS, U. Wis., Oshkosh, 1972. Dir. nutrition program for older adults County of Winnebago, Wis., 1973-82; instr. pre-retirement planning Fox Valley Tech. Inst., 1978—81; elected to assembly, 1982—86; mem. Wis. Assembly, Madison, 1983-87; elected to senate in spl. election, 1987; mem. Wis. Senate from 18th dist., Madison, 1987—. Home: 1506 Jackson St Oshkosh WI 54901-2942 Office: PO Box 7882 Madison WI 53707-7882 E-mail: Sen.Roessler@legis.state.wi.us.

ROESSLER, P. DEE, lawyer, educator, mediator, former judge; b. McKinney, Tex., Nov. 4, 1941; d. W.D. and Eunice Marie (Medcalf) Powell; m. George L. Roessler, Jr., Nov. 16, 1963 (div. Dec. 1977); children: Laura Diane, Trey. Student, Austin Coll., 1960-61, 62-64, Wayland Bapt. Coll., 1961-62; BA, U. West Fla., 1968; postgrad., East Tex. State U., 1975, U. Tex.-Dallas, 1977; JD, So. Meth. U., 1982. Bar: Tex. 1982, U.S. Dist. Ct. (ea. dist.) Tex. 1983, U.S. Dist. Ct. (no. dist.) Tex. 1983, U.S. Supreme Ct. 2000. Tchr. Van Alstyne Ind. Sch. Dist., Tex., 1968-69; social worker Dept. Social Svcs., Fayetteville, N.C., 1971-73, Dept. Human Svcs., Sherman and McKinney, 1973-79, 81; assoc. atty. Abernathy & Roeder, McKinney, 1982-85, Ronald W. Uselton, Sherman, 1985-86; program coord. Collin County C.C., McKinney, 1986—99; asst. county atty. Grayson County, Tex., 1999—2000; solo practice, 2000—. Mcpl. judge City of Mckinney Mcpl. Ct., 1986-89; mem. Tex. State Bar Com. on Legal Assts., 1990-94, Tex. State Bar Com. on Child Abuse and Neglect, 1996-2001. Mem. Collin County Shelter for Battered Women, 1984-86, chmn., 1984-85; v.p. Collin County Child Welfare Bd., 1986, pres., 1987-88, 96-97, treas., 1989, mem., 1985-89, 94-98; Rep. jud. candidate Collin County, 1986; chmn. bd. Tri County Consortium Mental Health Mental Retardation, 1984-85; mem. Tex. Area 5 Health System Agy., 1979, Collin County Mental Health Adv. Bd., 1978-79; trustee Willow Park Hosp., HCA, 1987-88; chair Collin County Criminal Justice Sub-com., 1987-88; mem. Collin County Pub. Responsibility Com., 1991-96, chair, 1994-95; bd. dirs. Ct. Apptd. Spl. Advocates, 1991-95. Mem. Collin County Bar Assn. Baptist. Avocations: gardening, reading, writing, travel. Home: 5 Shadybrook Cir Melissa TX 75454-8912 Office: 1600 1st Ave Mc Kinney TX 75069 Office Phone: 972-548-7525.

ROETHE, JAMES NORTON, lawyer; b. Milw., Jan. 27, 1942; s. Arthur Frantz and Bess Irma (Norton) R.; m. Nita May Dorris, July 15, 1967; children: Melissa Dorris, Sarah Rebacca. BBA, U. Wis., Madison, 1964, JD, 1967. Bar: Wis. 1967, Calif. 1968, U.S. Dist. Ct. (we. dist.) Wis. 1967, U.S. Dist. Ct. (no. dist.) Calif. 1972, U.S. Ct. Claims 1975, U.S. Ct. Appeals (9th cir.) 1980, U.S. Dist. Ct. (ea. dist.) Calif. 1982, U.S. Dist. Ct. (ctrl. dist.) Calif. 1986). U.S. Ct. Appeals (4th cir.) 1988, U.S. Ct. Appeals (2d cir.) 1989. Assoc. Pillsbury, Madison & Sutro, San Francisco, 1971-77, ptnr., 1978-92; sr. v.p., dir. litigation Bank of Am., San Francisco, 1992-96, exec. v.p., gen. counsel, 1996-98, dep. gen. counsel, 1998-99; ptnr. Litigation, Corp. & Securities practices Pillsbury Winthrop LLP (now Pillsbury Winthrop Shaw Pittman), San Francisco, 2000—. Staff atty. Commn. on CIA Activities within U.S., Washington, 1975. Editor: Africa, 1967; editor-in-chief Wis. Law Rev., 1966-67. Bd. dirs. Orinda (Calif.) Assn., 1984-85, pres., 1986; active City of Orinda Planning Commn., 1988-94, chmn., 1990, 93; bd. dirs. Calif. Shakespeare Festival, 1993—, pres., 2001-06; bd. vis. U. Wis. Law Sch., 1994-99. Lt. USNR, 1967-71 Fellow Am. Bar Found.; mem. ABA, Wis. Bar Assn., Calif. Bar Assn., Bar Assn. San Francisco, Wis. Law Alumni Assn. (bd. dirs. 2000—), Legal Aid Soc. (bd. dirs.), Orinda Country Club (pres. 2003-04), Order of Coif, Phi Kappa Phi Office: Pillsbury Winthrop Shaw Pittman 50 Fremont St San Francisco CA 94105 Office Phone: 415-983-1414. Office Fax: 415-983-1200. Business E-Mail: james.roethe@pillsburylaw.com.

ROETHENMUND, OTTO EMIL, finance company and bank executive; b. Thun, Switzerland, Sept. 1, 1928; came to U.S., 1951, naturalized, 1957; s. Franz and Berta (Dallenbach) R.; m. Ermina Grassi, May 7, 1955; children— Robert, Denise. MA, U. Neuchatel, 1948. Mgmt. trainee Kantonalbank, Bern, 1948-51; exec. trainee J. Henry Schroeder Banking and Trust Corp., NYC, 1951-56; with Deak-Perera Group, NYC, 1956—, vice chmn., group partner, 1962—; v.p., then sr. v.p. Deak & Co. (holding co.), 1962-74, exec. v.p., 1974-80, pres., chief exec. officer, 1980-86; pres., dir. Inter-Nation Capital Mgmt. Corp., 1986—. Lectr. internat. monetary and investment seminars; emeritus trustee Dickinson Coll., Carisle, Pa.; bd. trustees Mercy Coll., Dobbs Ferry, NY. Served to lt. Swiss Army, 1948-51. Decorated knight Mil. Order Sts. Salvador and Brigitta (Sweden). Mem. Explorers Club, Met. Club (N.Y.C.), Westchester Country Club. Home: 2 Shore Rd Rye NY 10580-1031 Office: Inter-Nation Capital Mgmt Corp 230 Park Ave Rm 1536 New York NY 10169-0699 E-mail: oeratincm@aol.com.

ROETHLISBERGER, BEN, professional football player; b. Findlay, Ohio, Mar. 2, 1982; s. Ken and Brenda Roethlisberger (Stepmother). BA, Miami U. of Ohio, 2004. Quarterback Pitts. Steelers, 2004—. Named Offensive Rookie of the Yr., AP, 2004. Achievements include setting NFL record for wins by a rookie quarterback (15); holding the highest compeletion percentage by a rookie quarterback (66.1%), 2004; being a member of Super Bowl XL Champion Pittsburgh Steelers, 2006; being the youngest starting QB in NFL history to win a Super Bowl, 2006. Office: c/o Pittsburgh Steelers 3400 S Water St Pittsburgh PA 15203

ROETTELER, MARTIN HENRI, computer scientist, researcher; b. Mannheim, Baden-Wuerttemberg, Germany, Jan. 28, 1972; s. Siegfried and Inge Roetteler; m. Simone Marie Holderbach, Aug. 18, 2001; 1 child, Ella Marie. Diploma in Computer Sci., Universität Karlsruhe, Germany, 1997, PhD, 2001. Post-doctoral fellow Universität Karlsruhe, Germany, 2001—02, U. Waterloo, Ontario, Canada, 2003—04; rsch. staff mem. NEC Labs. Am., Inc., Princeton, NJ, 2005—. Scholar Promotionsstipendium, Deutsche Forschungsgemeinschaft, 1998—2001. Mem.: IEEE. Home: 465 Meadow Rd Apt 8203 Princeton NJ 08540 Office: NEC Labs Am Inc 4 Independence Way Ste 200 Princeton NJ 08540 Office Phone: 609-951-2771.

ROFF, ALAN LEE, retired lawyer, consultant; b. Winfield, Kans., July 2, 1936; s. Roy Darlis and Mildred Marie (Goodale) R.; m. Sonyia Ruth Anderson, Feb. 8, 1954; 1 child, Cynthia Lee Roff Edwards; m. Molly Gek Neo Tan, July 21, 1980 BA with honors and distinction, U. Kans., 1964, JD with distinction, 1966. Bar: Okla. 1967. Staff atty. Phillips Petroleum Co., Bartlesville, Okla., 1966—75, sr. atty., 1976—85, sr. counsel, 1986—94; cons. in Asia, 1995—. Mem. editl. bd. Kans. Law Rev., 1965-66. Precinct committeeman Rep. Party, Lawrence, Kans., 1963-64; assoc. justice Kans. U. Chancery Club; mem. Kans. U. Young Reps Elizabeth Reeder scholar U. Kans., 1965-66, Eldon Wallingford award, 1964-66 Mem. ABA, Okla. Bar Assn., Washington County Bar Assn., Phoenix Club Bartlesville (bd. dirs. 1985-86, gen. counsel 1986-91), Order of Coif, Masons, Hon. Order Ky. Cols., Phi Alpha Delta, Pi Sigma Alpha Mem. First Christian Ch Avocation: travel. Home and Office: 2247 Mountain Dr Bartlesville OK 74003-6954 Personal E-mail: amroff@cableone.net.

ROFF, J(OHN) HUGH, JR., energy executive; b. Wewoka, Okla., Oct. 27, 1931; s. Hugh and Louise Roff; m. Ann Green, Dec. 23, 1956; children— John, Charles, Andrew, Elizabeth, Jennifer AB, U. Okla., 1954, LL.B., 1955. Bar: Okla., Mo., N.Y. Law clk. to presiding justice U.S. Ct. Appeals (10th cir.), 1958; atty. Southwestern Bell Telephone Co., St. Louis, 1959-63, AT&T, NYC, 1964-68; v.p., gen. atty. Long Lines, NYC, 1969-73, gen. atty., 1973-74; chmn., pres., chief exec. officer United Energy Resources, Houston, 1974-86; chmn. PetroUnited Terminals Inc., Houston, 1986-98, Roff Resources LLC, Houston, 1998—. Past chmn. Cen. Houston Inc.; mem. adv. bd. Ctr. for Strategic and Internat. Studies, Washington; mem. coun. overseers Jones Sch. Bus. Adminstrn., Rice U.; trustee Baylor Coll. Medicine; past chmn. adv. bd. The Salvation Army, Houston. 1st lt. U.S. Army, 1955-58. Mem. Order of Coif, Phi Beta Kappa, Beta Theta Pi. Clubs: Houston Country, Coronado, Houstonian. Office: 333 Clay St Ste 4300 Houston TX 77002-4103 E-mail: hughroff@roffresources.com.

ROFF, WILLIAM ROBERT, historian, educator, writer; b. Glasgow, Scotland, May 2, 1929; arrived in U.S., 1969; s. Robert Henry William and Isabella (Anderson) R.; m. Susanne Rabbitt, Aug. 2, 1978; children: Sarah, Emily. BA, U. New Zealand, 1957, MA, 1959; PhD, Australian Nat. U., 1965. Lectr. history Monash U., Australia, 1963-66; lectr., sr. lectr. U. Malaya, Malaysia, 1966-69; assoc. prof. Columbia U., NYC, 1969-73, prof., 1973-90, prof. emeritus, 1990—. Vis. prof. Yale U., 1971, L'Ecole des Hautes Etudes en Scis. Sociales, Paris, 1985; vis. fellow Australian Nat. U., 1974; hon. fellow Edinburgh U., Scotland, 1992—. Author: The Origins of Malay Nationalism, 1967, Bibliography of Malay and Arabic Periodicals, 1972, (with others) The Emergence of Modern Southeast Asia, 2004; author, editor: Kelantan: Religion, Society and Politics, 1973; editor: Islam and the Political Economy of Meaning, 1987. Guggenheim Found. fellow 1973; Rockefeller Found. fellow, 1982. Mem. Royal Asiatic Soc. (life), Assn. for Asian Studies, Asian Studies Assn. Australia, Brit. Soc. for Mid. East Studies, Mid. East Studies Assn. Avocation: parenting. Home: 29 Shore St Cellardyke Fife KY10 3BD Scotland Personal E-mail: william.roff@btinternet.com.

ROG, JOSEPH W., engineering company executive; BS, Kent State U. Pres. Corrpro Cos., Inc., Medina, Ohio, 1984—93, chmn., 1993—2004, CEO, 1984—2004, bd. dirs., 2004—. Office: Corrpro Cos Inc 1090 Enterprise Dr Medina OH 44256-1328 Office Phone: 330-723-5082.

ROGACHEFSKY, ARLENE SANDRA, dermatologist; b. Rochester, NY, June 29, 1970; d. Hymen Rogachefsky and Deanna Rogachefsky Luntz; m. David Black, Oct. 27, 2001; children: Mitchell Harris Black, Ellie Rachel Black. BA with honors, Brown U., Providence, 1992; MD magna cum laude, SUNY, Buffalo, 1996. Diplomate Am. Bd. Dermatology, cert. Am. Coll. Mohs Micrographic Surgery and Cutaneous Oncology. Intern in internal medicine Cleve. Clinic Found., 1996—97, resident in dermatology, 1997—2000; fellow Mohs and cosmetic laser surgery Office of Dr. David Goldberg, Westwood, NJ, 2000—01; assoc. Skin Laser and Surgery Specialists NY and NJ, Hackensack and Westwood, NJ, 2001—03, Affiliated Dermatologists and Dermatol. Surgeons, Morristown, NJ, 2005—. Program dir. procedural dermatology fellowship Affiliated Dermatologists and Dermatol. Surgeons, 2006—. Contbr. articles to profl. jours. Home: 160 Myrtle Ave Millburn NJ 07041 Office: Affiliated Dermatologists and Dermatologic Surgeons 182 S St Ste 1 Morristown NJ 07960 Office Phone: 973-267-0300. E-mail: arogachefsky@hotmail.com.

ROGACZEWSKI, SHERRIE REECE, small business owner, singer; b. Greenwood, SC, Nov. 23, 1966; d. George Washington and Hazel Irene Reece; m. Wayne Robert Rogaczewski, Nov. 29, 1986; 1 child, Brett. Grad. high sch., Greenwood, SC. Singer, songwriter Sherreece, New Orleans, 1990—; co-owner World Gym, 2001—. Singer, songwriter: recs. Wild Life, 1997, New Age Dawning, 2000, Holy of Holies, 2004. Mem.: Gospel Music Assn. Avocations: history, archaeology. Office Phone: 504-813-8486. E-mail: sherreece@hotmail.com.

ROGAL, ANDREW L., insurance company executive; b. Pitts., Dec. 13, 1948; s. Alvin and Ann (Lawrence) R.; m. Vicki Loveness, Dec. 30, 1971; children: Erin, Lisa, Samuel. BS in Journalism, Northwestern U., Chgo., 1970; JD, U. Pitts., 1975. Law clk. Hon. Hubert I. Teitelbaum, Fed. Dist. Ct. of We. Dist. Pa., Pitts., 1975-77; jr. ptnr. Titus, Marcus & Shapira, Pitts., 1977-80; pres., chief exec. officer Hilb, Rogal and Hamilton Co. of Pitts., Inc., 1987-91, Hilb, Rogal and Hamilton Internat. Ltd., 1991—; exec. v.p. Hilb, Rogal & Hamilton Co., Glen Allen, Va., 1990—. Mem. bd. trustees Children's Hosp., Pitts., mem. investment com.; bd. dirs. Pitts. Ballet Theatre, Jewish Community Ctr., Pitts., United Jewish Fedn., Pitts., Jewish Healthcare Found., Pitts., mem. investment com., mem. distbn. com.; mem. budget and allocations com. United Jewish Fedn. of Pitts. Avocation: skiing. Office: Hilb Rogal & Hamilton Co 4951 Lake Brook Dr Ste 400 Glen Allen VA 23060-9273

ROGAL, GARY JEFFREY, cardiologist; b. Newark, Nov. 20, 1952; s. David and Bert Shane Rogal; m. Camille Elizabeth Rogal, Oct. 18, 1981; children: David, Jennifer, Sarah. BA, George Washington U., 1974, MD, 1978. Diplomate Am. Bd. Internal Medicine, Am. Bd. Cardiovasc. Disease. Resident in internal medicine L.I. Jewish-Hillside Med. Ctr., 1978-81; resident in cardiology U. Rochester-Strong Meml. Hosp., 1981-84; asst. prof. medicine Albany Med. Coll., NY, 1984-86; chief cardiology St. Barnabas Med. Ctr., Livingston, NJ, 1998—, dir. cardial rehab.; pvt. practice gen. and invasive cardiology, spl. interest complementary medicine and cardiology, 1986—. Fellow Am. Coll. Cardiology; mem. Am. Heart Assn. (bd. dirs.), Hertiage Affiliation (bd. dirs.), Phi Beta Kappa Avocations: photography, skiing, resistance/aerobic training. Office: Diagnostic and Clin Cardiology PA 769 Northfield Ave West Orange NJ 07052-1198 Office Phone: 973-731-9442. E-mail: grogal@sbhcs.com.

ROGALSKI, LOIS ANN, speech and language pathologist; b. Bklyn. d. Louis J. and Filomena Evelyn (Maro) Giordano; m. Stephen James Rogalski, Jun e 27, 1970; children: Keri Anne, Stefan Louis, Christopher James, Rebecca Blair, Gregory Alexander. BA, Bklyn. Coll., 1968; MA, U. Mass., 1969; PhD., NYU, 1975. Lic. speech and lang. pathologist, N.Y.; cert. Nat. Acad. Sports Medicine; cert Powerhouse Pilates; cert. for yoga. Speech, lang. and voice pathologist Rehab. Ctr. of So. Fairfield County, Stamford, Conn., 1969, Sch. Health Program-P.A. 481, Stamford, 1969-72, pvt. practice speech, lang. and voice pathology Scarsdale, NY, 1972—. Cons. Bd. Coop. Ednl. Svcs., 1976-79, Handicapped Program for Preschoolers for Alcott Montessori Sch., Ardsley, N.Y., 1978—; rsch. methodologist Burke Rehab. Ctr., 1977. Mem. profl. adv. bd. Found. for Children with Learning Disabilities, 1978—; bd. dirs. United Way of Scarsdale-Edgemont, 1988-89; instr. religious instr. CCD Immaculate Heart of Mary Ch., Scarsdale, 1991—; bd. dirs. Scarsdale Teen Ctr., Inc., 1998—. Fellow Rehab. Svcs. Adminstrn., 1968-69; N.Y. Med. Coll., 1972-75. Mem. N.Y. Speech & Hearing Assn., Westchester Speech & Hearing Assn., Am. Speech, Hearing & Lang. Assn. (cert. clin. competence), Coun. for Exceptional Children, Assn. on Mental Deficiency, Am.

Acad. Pvt. Practice in Speech Pathology & Audiology (bd. dirs., treas. 1983-87, pres. 1987-89), Internat. Assn. Logopedics & Phoniatrics, Sigma Alpha Eta. Avocations: yoga, pilates.

ROGAN, ELEANOR GROENIGER, oncologist, educator; b. Nov. 25, 1942; d. Louis Martin and Esther (Levinson) G.; m. William John Robert Rogan, June 12, 1965 (div. 1970); 1 child, Elizabeth Rebecca. AB, Mt. Holyoke Coll., 1963; PhD, Johns Hopkins U., 1968. Lectr. Goucher Coll., Towson, Md., 1968-69; rsch. assoc. U. Tenn., Knoxville, 1969-73, U. Nebr. Med. Ctr., Omaha, 1973-76, asst. prof., 1976-80; assoc. prof. Eppley Inst., dept. pharm. scis. U. Nebr., Omaha, 1980-90, prof. dept. pharm. scis. and dept. biochem. & molecular biol, 1990—. Contbr. articles to profl. jours. Predoctoral fellow USPHS, Johns Hopkins U., 1965-68; recipient Linus Pauling Functional Medicine award, 2006. Mem. AAAS, Am. Assn. Cancer Rsch., Soc. Toxicology. Democrat. Roman Catholic. Home: 8210 Bowie Dr Omaha NE 68114-1526 Office: U Nebr Med Ctr Eppley Inst 986805 Nebr Med Ctr Omaha NE 68198-6805 Home Phone: 402-397-7342; Office Phone: 402-559-4095. Business E-Mail: egrogan@unmc.edu.

ROGAN, JAMES EDWARD, former federal agency administrator, former congressman; b. San Francisco, Aug. 21, 1957; s. John and Alice (Kleupfer) Rogan; m. Christine Apffel; children: Dana, Claire. BA in Polit. Sci., U. Calif., Berkeley, 1979; JD, UCLA, 1983. Past atty. Lillick McHose and Charles (now Pillsbury, Madison and Sutro), LA; past dep. dist. atty. L.A. County; judge Glendale (Calif.) Mcpl. Ct., 1990—93, presiding judge, 1993—94; past mem. Calif. Assembly, 1994—96, assembly majority leader, 1996; mem. U.S. Congress from 27th Calif. dist., 1996—2001; mem. house jud. com., mem. commerce com., asst. minority whip; ptnr. Venable, Baetjer, Howard & Civiletti, Washington, 2001; under sec. for intellectual property US Dept. Commerce, Washington, 2001—04; dir. US Patent & Trademark Office, Washington, 2001—04; of counsel Preston Gates Ellis LLP, Irvine, Calif., 2006—. Adj. prof. trial advocacy Sch. Law Southwestern U.; adj. prof. criminal law Coll. Law Glendale U.; past adj. prof. criminal law Glendale C.C.; mem. Selective Svc. Sys. U.S. Govt., 1981—; adj. prof. trial practice Chapman U. Law Sch. Republican. Office: Preston Gates Ellis LLP 1900 Main Ste Ste 600 Irvine CA 92614-7319

ROGAN, MICHAEL P., lawyer; BA, Oberlin Coll., 1970; JD, U. Conn., 1974. Joined Skadden, Arps, Slate, Meagher & Flom LLP, Washington, 1980—, ptnr., 1984—, head, corp. mergers and acquisitions, 1994—, leader, 1998—. Office: Skadden Arps Slate Meagher & Flom LLP 1440 New York Ave NW Washington DC 20005 Office Phone: 202-371-7550. Office Fax: 202-661-8200. Business E-Mail: mrogan@skadden.com.

ROGAN, RICHARD A., lawyer; b. LA, Sept. 6, 1950; AB with honors, Hamilton Coll., 1972; JD, U. Calif., 1975. Bar: Calif. 1975. Ptnr. Broad, Schulz, Larson & Wineberg, 1978-94, chmn., 1991-93; ptnr. Jeffer, Mangels, Butler & Marmaro, San Francisco, 1994—, mng. ptnr., San Francisco office, 2002—. Editorial assoc. Hastings Law Jour., 1974-75. Trustee Bentley Sch., 1989-92. Mem. ABA (mem. corp., banking, and bus. sect.), Bar Assn. of San Francisco (mem. comml. law and bankruptcy sect.), Calif. Receivers Forum (bd. dirs. Bay Area chpt.), Delta Sigma Rho. Office: Jeffer Mangels Butler Marmaro-JMBM 2 Embarcadero Ctr 5th Fl San Francisco CA 94111-3823 Home Phone: 925-258-3505; Office Phone: 415-398-8080. E-mail: rrogan@jmbm.com.

ROGAN, ROBERT, management educator, consultant, osteopath, psychiatrist, lawyer; BA, MBA, SUNY; cert. in data processing, Cornell U.; DO, W.Va. Sch. Osteo. Medicine, 1983; postgrad., Virginia Beach, 1986-88; JD, Regent U., 1990. Bar: Pa. 1992; diplomate Nat. Bd Examiners for Osteo. Medicine and Surgery, Am. Bd. Psychiatry; cert. data processor, data educator. Assoc. prof. bus. West Liberty (W.Va.) State Coll., 1976-79; chief intern Metro Health Ctr., Erie, Pa., 1983-84; asst. prof. computer sci. Gannon U., Erie, Pa., 1984-85; asst. prof. mgmt. Slippery Rock (Pa.) U., 1985-86; practice medicine specializing in osteopathy Harborcreek Family Practice, Erie, Pa., 1985; resident physician Univ. Med. Ctr.-East Carolina U., Greenville, N.C., 1992-96; med. officer M/V Anastasis, 1988—89, M/V Logos II, 2006. Temp. physician Oceana (W.Va.) Med. Ctr., 1992-95; rschr., tchr. law Inst. Fine Mechanics and Optics, St. Petersburg, Russia, 1993, Poland, 1994; part-time radio announcer Sta. WGHB, Farmville, N.C., 1993-96; psychiat. and mgmt. cons., critical incident stress debriefer, 1996—; asst. prof. W.Va. U. Sch. Medicine, 1999—; chmn. ethics com. William R. Sharpe Hosp., 2000— Counselor Contact Crisis Care, Lewisburg, W.Va., 1980—81; constrn. vol. various locations internationally, 1991, Ecuador, 2001; mem. Hist. Preservation Commn., City of Greenville, disaster vol., 2001—; med. vol. various orgns., Jamaica, 1988—, Haiti, 1989; candidate for U.S. Congress Ho. of Rep. Scholar U. Buffalo, N.Y. State Bd. Regents; grantee NSF, Cornell U.; Group for Advancement of Psychiatry fellow, 1995-96. Mem. Am. Osteo. Assn., N.C. Psychiat. Assn. (psychiatry and law rep. 1994-96, mem. econ. affairs com. 1995-96, mem. exec. coun. 1994-96, candidate Raleigh city coun.). Avocations: travel, sports, volunteering. Personal E-mail: nagor36@hotmail.com. Business E-Mail: doulos@di-ve.com.

ROGATZ, PETER, retired physician; b. NYC, Aug. 5, 1926; s. Julian and Sally (Levy) Rogatz; m. Marjorie Plaut, June 10, 1949; children: Peggy Joy, William Peter. BA, Columbia Coll., 1945; MD, Cornell U., 1949; M.P.H., Columbia U., 1956. Cert. Am. Bd. Preventive Medicine 1958. Intern Lenox Hill Hosp., NYC, 1949-50, resident, 1950-51, VA Hosp., Bronx, NY, 1951-52, N.Y. Hosp., NYC, 1952-53; dep. dir. Montefiore Hosp., NYC, 1960-63; dir. L.I. Jewish Med. Center, 1964-68, Univ. Hosp., SUNY, Stony Brook, 1968-71; sr. v.p. Blue Cross/Blue Shield of Greater N.Y., 1971-76; prin., founding ptnr. RMR Health and Hosp. Mgmt. Cons., Inc., Roslyn Heights, NY, 1976-84; v.p. med. affairs Vis. Nurse Service, NY, 1984-91; med. dir. Staff Builders, Inc., 1992-98. Prof. cmty. medicine SUNY, Stony Brook, 1968—94; mem. N.Y.C. Mayor's Commn. on Delivery of Health Svcs., 1967; v.p. Health and Welfare Coun. of Nassau County, 1968—72; bd. dirs. Cmty. Coun. Greater N.Y., 1974—77; mem. Task Force on N.Y.C. Crisis, 1976—81; chmn. bd. dirs. Cmty. Health Program affiliated with L.I. Jewish Med. Ctr., 1989—94; chmn. bd. dirs. Managed Health Inc., 1990—94. Author: Organized Home Medical Care in New York City, 1956; co-author (with Eli Ginzberg): Planning for Better Hospital Care, 1961; mem. editl. bd. Preventive Medicine, 1975—81; contbr. articles to profl. jours. Bd. dirs. Choice in Dying, 1994—2000, Compassion and Choices of N.Y., 1998—. Recipient Dean Conley award, Am. Coll. Hosp. Adminstrs., 1975; fellow, Commonwealth Fund, 1955. Fellow: ACP, Am. Coll. Preventive Medicine, N.Y. Acad. Medicine, APHA; mem.: N.Y. County Med. Soc., N.Y. State Med. Soc., N.Y. Pub. Health Assn., Am. Hosp. Assn., AMA. Home and Office: 299 E Overlook Port Washington NY 11050 Home Phone: 516-767-0189; Office Phone: 516-767-0189. Personal E-mail: rogatz2@aol.com.

ROGEL, STEVEN R., forest products company executive; BS in Chem. Engring., U. Wash., 1965. With St. Regis Paper Co., 1965—70; asst. mgr. St. Anne-Nackawic Pulp and Paper, Nackawic, N.B., Canada, 1970—72; tech. dir. Willamette Industries, Inc., Albany, Oreg., 1972—95, pres., CEO, 1995—97, Weyerhaeuser Co., Tacoma, 1997—, chmn., 1999—. Bd. dirs. Kroger Co. Trustee Pacific U.; bd. dirs. Pacific Harbors coun. Boy Scouts Am. Mem.: Am. Forest and Paper Assn. (bd. dirs.). Office: 33663 Weyerhaeuser Way S Federal Way WA 98003-9620 *

ROGEN, SETH, actor; b. Vancouver, Canada, Apr. 15, 1982; Actor: (films) Donnie Darko, 2001, Anchorman: The Legend of Ron Burgundy, 2004, Wake Up, Ron Burgundy: The Lost Movie, 2004, You, Me and Dupree, 2006; actor, co-prodr. (films) The 40 Year Old Virgin, 2005, actor, exec. prodr. Knocked Up, 2006, actor, exec. prodr., writer Superbad, 2007; actor(voice): (films) Shrek the Third, 2007,: (TV films) North Hollywood, 2001, Early Bird, 2005; (TV series) Freaks and Geeks, 1999—2000, Undeclared, 2001—02, (appearances) Dawson's Creek, 2003, Help Me Help You; staff writer (TV series) Da Ali G Show. *

ROGENESS, MARY SPEER, state legislator; b. Kansas City, Kans., May 18, 1941; d. Frederic A. and Jeannette (Hybskmann) Speer; m. Dean Rogeness, Aug. 31, 1964; children: Emily, James, Paul. BA, Carleton Coll., 1963. Computer analyst Dept. Def., Ft. Meade, Md., 1963-66; freelance writer, editor Longmeadow, Mass., 1982-91; mem. Mass. Ho. of Reps., Boston, 1991—, asst. minority leader, 2003—. Editor: Reflections of Longmeadow, 1983. Active Longmeadow Rep. Town Com., 1983—; bd. dirs. Goodwill Industries Hartford-Springfield, 1996—2004; com. mem. Longmeadow Sch., 1982-88; corp. trustee Trustees of Reservations. Mem. Am. Legis. Exch. Coun., World Affairs Coun. of Western Mass. Office: Mass House of Reps State House Rm 124 Boston MA 02133 Office Phone: 617-722-2100.

ROGER, JANICE LOWENSTEIN, cantor; b. Chgo., July 6, 1951; d. Herbert and Gertrude Tauf Lowenstein; m. Brandon Anthony Roger, Nov. 30, 1980; children: Edwin Sidney, Miles Lawrence. B of sacred music, Hebrew Union Coll.Jewish Inst. of Religion, 1975—79; MusB, Roosevelt U., 1969—73; MusD (hon.), Hebrew Union Coll.-Jewish Inst. of Religion, 2004—04. Cantor Am. Conf. of Cantors, 1979. Cantor Indpls. Hebrew Congregation, 1979—. Cantorial chmn., nat. commn. on cantorial/congl. rels. Union for Reform Judaism, NY, 1995—; chmn., conv. adminstrn. com. Am. Conf. of Cantors, NY, 2004—, v.p., 1991—95, conv. co-chairman 1987, 1993; mem., artist evaluation com. Young Audiences, Indpls., 1991—92; bd. mem. Indpls. Chamber Orch., 1997—99; com. mem. Ind. Arts Coun., 2002. Singer: (concert) Hymns and Anthems, Ronen Chamber Ensemble; collaborating producer (dance performance) Avodah Dance Ensemble. Allocations com. United Way, 1990—91. Creative Renewal, Arts Coun. of Indpls., 1999. Mem.: Coalition on Advancements in Jewish Edn., Music Educators' Nat. Conf., Am. Conf. of Cantors. Avocations: reading, knitting, playing scrabble. Office: Indpls Hebrew Congregation 6501 North Meridian St Indianapolis IN 46260 Home Phone: 317-253-7452; Office Phone: 317-255-6647. Personal E-mail: janicer@ihcindy.org.

ROGER, JERRY LEE, academic administrator; b. Chase, Kans., Mar. 11, 1945; s. LeRoy J. and Lottie E. (Maphet) R.; m. Tucky Saint Roger, 1995. BS, U. Tulsa, 1966, MA, 1969, EdD, 1975. Cert. tchr., supt., Okla. Math. tchr. Kansas City (Mo.) Pub. Schs., 1966-67, Shawnee Mission (Kans.) Pub. Schs., 1967-71; rsch. asst. Tulsa Pub. Schs., 1972-73, rsch. coord., 1973-81, adminstrv. asst., 1981-90, rsch. dir., 1990-95, dir. planning and assessment, 1995-2000; chmn. U. Phoenix Sch. Gen. Studies, Tulsa, 2000; dir. acad. affairs U. Phoenix, Tulsa, 2001—05, doctoral faculty, 2005—. Adj. instr. Tulsa Jr. Coll., 1975-88; adj. asst. prof. U. Tulsa, 1980-85; sr. faculty U. Phoenix, Tulsa campus, 1998-2000. Contbr. book revs. to Tulsa Sunday World, 1990-92. Paul Harris fellow; Rotary benefactor. Mem. NEA, Am. Ednl. Res. Assn., Nat. Book Critics Cir., Nature Conservancy, Nat. Conf. for Cmty. and Justice, Phi Delta Kappa. Home: 3504 N Narcissus Ave Broken Arrow OK 74012 Office: U Phoenix 10810 E 45th St Tulsa OK 74146-3818 E-mail: jerryroger@yahoo.com.

ROGER, KENT M., lawyer; b. San Francisco, May 8, 1955; s. Alberto Vasquez del Mercado and LaVerne Annette (Stadler) Newcombe; m. Margaret Ann Murphy, Aug. 10, 1985; children: Nicole, Lauren. AB, U. Calif., Berkeley, 1977; JD, U. Calif., San Francisco, 1980. Bar: Calif. 1980. Assoc. Brobeck, Phleger & Harrison, San Francisco, 1980-87, ptnr., 1987—2003; ptnr., leader litig. practice group Morgan, Lewis & Bockius LLP, San Francisco. Mem. ABA, Bar Assn. San Francisco, San Francisco Bank Atty. Assn Roman Catholic. Office: Morgan Lewis & Bockius LLP Spear St Tower 1 Market Plz San Francisco CA 94105-1420

ROGERS, ALAN VICTOR, former career officer; b. Hannibal, Mo., Nov. 13, 1942; s. Julian Alan and Gladys Cuneo R.; m. Linda Rae Peterson, May 8, 1966; children: Kimberly Rae, Krista Anne, Peter Alan. BS in Mil. Sci., USAF Acad., 1964; MBA with distinction, Harvard Bus. Sch., 1972; grad. with distinction, Air War Coll., 1980. Commd. 2d lt. USAF, 1964, advanced through grades to maj. gen., 1989, ret., 1993; combat fighter pilot 355th Tactical Fighter Wing, Takhli, Thailand, 1966-67; jet pilot instr. Flying Tng. Wing, Williams AFB, Ariz., 1967-69; student Harvard Bus. Sch., Cambridge, Mass., 1970-72; pers. officer Cols. Group USAF Pentagon, Washington, 1972-75; student Air War Coll., Maxwell AFB, Ariz., 1980; wing comdr. 5th Bomb Wing, Minot AFB, ND, 1982-84, 96th Bomb Wing (1st B-1 Wing), Dyess AFB, Tex., 1984-86; dir. ops. SAC, Offutt AFB, Nebr., 1986-89; asst. chief of staff ops. Supreme HQ Allied Powers Europe NATO, Mons, Belgium, 1989-91; dir. J-7 Joint Staff, Pentagon, Washington, 1991-93; assoc. Burdeshaw Assocs., Ltd., Bethesda, Md., 1993-94; prin. Gemini Consulting, Morristown, NJ, 1994-97; sr. v.p., gen. mgr. Fed. Defense Group, Am. Mgmt. Sys., Inc., Fairfax, Va., 1997—2002; exec. v.p. CACI Internat., 2003—. Mem. Active Angel Investors, Vienna, 2003—; mem. adv. bd. Infodata, Inc., 2003—06; bd. dirs. RGS & Assocs., Inc., 2003—06. Mem., mil. adviser C. of C., Minot, N.D., 1982-84, Abilene, Tex. 1984-86; trustee The Falcon Found., Colorado Springs, 2003—; mem. bd. advisors Our Mil. Kids, 2006—. Decorated Defense Disting. Svc. Medal, Legion of Merit, D.F.C. with two oak leaf clusters, Purple Heart, Def. Superior Svc. medal, Disting. Svc. medal, Def. Disting. Svc. medal; recipient Am. U. Leadership award, 2000. Mem.: Nat. Assn. Corp. Dirs., Nat. Def. Industry Assn. (bd. dirs.), Potomac Officers Club, Daedalians (chpt. pres. 1986), Nat. Eagle Scout Assn., Red River Valley Fighter Pilots Assn., Sabre Soc., USAF Acad. Assn. Grads. (bd. dirs. 1999—2007), Air Force Assn. Republican. Lutheran. Avocations: skiing, travel, antiques. Home: 4600 32nd Rd N Arlington VA 22207-4406 Office Phone: 703-795-3802. E-mail: alanvrogers@aol.com.

ROGERS, ALICE LOUISE, retired bank executive, writer, researcher; b. McLoud, Okla., Feb. 18, 1929; d. John Edmond and Katy McNora (Williams) Stanka; m. Jesse Ray Rogers, Apr. 18, 1948; children: Jimmy Allen Rogers, Bonnie Kay (Rogers) Calhoun. Student, Am. Inst. Banking, 1967-69. Clk. typist loan dept. Security Pacific Nat. Bank, LA, 1960-64; office mgr., adminstrv. asst. to v.p. loan adminstn. divsn. City Nat. Bank, Beverly Hills, 1964-75, credit mgr. Pershing Square branch, 1975-77. Author, editor: Dance Bands and Big Bands Reference Book and Price Guide, 1986, Dance Bands, Big Bands and Swing Reference Book and Price Guide, 1993; contbr. articles to DISCoveries mag., Internat. Assn. of Jazz Record Collectors Jour., Joslin's Jazz Jour., Dancing USA mag., Am.'s Registry of Outstanding Profls. Mem.: Big Band Acad. Am. Republican. Avocations: phonograph record collection, researching jazz and dance information, postcard collection.

ROGERS, BENJAMIN FRANKLIN, retired history professor; b. St. Paul, Minn., Dec. 10, 1917; s. Benjamin Franklin and Ruth De Coster Rogers; m. Peggy Louise Brodrick, Sept. 9, 1972; children: Ruth, Benjamin, Karl, David, Susan, Sara, Clay. AB, Harvard U., 1940, MA, 1941; PhD, U. Minn., 1951. Prof. history Fla. State U., Tallahassee, 1950—60; v.p. Jacksonville U., Fla., 1960—64; dean Coll. Humanities Fla. Atlantic U., Boca Raton, Fla., 1964—66; head Dept. History Parsons Coll., Fairfield, Iowa, 1966—73; prof. history Ottumwa Heights Coll., Iowa, 1973—80, ret., 1980. Lt. USNR, 1942—45. Decorated Air medal Three Stars Presdl. Unit. Mem.: Fla. Hist. Soc. (bd. dirs., mem. editl. bd.), Am. Hist. Assn. Democrat. Episcopalian. Home: PO Box 877 Fairfield IA 52556

ROGERS, BENJAMIN TALBOT, mechanical engineer, consultant; b. Cleve., Oct. 4, 1920; s. Benjamin Talbot and Marie Aline (Miller) Rogers; m. Dale Hays, Sept. 11, 1961 (dec. Nov. 1975); children: Leslie, Phyllis. BSME, U. Wis., 1944. Registered profl. engr., N.Mex, Colo., Ariz., Tex. Mech. engr. Black & Veatch, Kansas City, Mo., 1946-49; staff mem. U. Calif., Los Alamos, N.Mex., 1949-76; cons. engring. Los Alamos, N.Mex., 1949-76, Embudo, N.Mex., 1976-80, 81-2000; ret., 2000. Vis. prof. Ariz. State U., 1980—81, 1984; v.p. Barkmann & Rogers Cons. Engrs., Santa Fe, 1964—70. One-man shows include Millicent Rogers Mus., Taos, N.Mex, 1994, Roller Mill Mus., Cleveland, N.Mex, 1995, Ariz. State U. Coll. Architecture, Tempe, 1996, First State Bank Taos, 1997 (Artist of the Month, 1997), Johnson Gallery, Madrid, N.Mex, 1998—99; contbr. articles to tech. and profl. jours. Commr. Rinconada Cmty. Acequia, Embudo, 1961—70; v.p. adv. bd. Embudo Presbyn. Hosp., 1972; pres. Embudo Valley Health Found., 1974. 1st lt. C.E. US Army, 1942—46. Recipient Solar Design award, HUD, Dept. Energy, Solar Energy Rsch. Inst., 1978, Peter van Dresser award, N.Mex Solar Energy Assn., 1983, Maharishi award, Maharishi Found., 1984; grantee, Graham Found. Advanced Studies Fine Arts, 1992, 1995. Fellow: ASHRAE; mem.: NSPE (life), ASME (life), Nat. Assn. Scholars, Am. Soc. Materials (life), Celtic Confederation (founding sec. 2000—03). Republican. Achievements include patents in field. Home: PO Box 2 Embudo NM 87531

ROGERS, BERNARD WILLIAM, military officer; b. Fairview, Kans., July 16, 1921; s. William Henry and Lora (Haynes) R.; m. Ann Ellen Jones, Dec. 28, 1944; children: Michael W., Diane E., Susan A. Student, Kans. State Coll., 1939-40; BS, U.S. Mil. Acad., 1943; BA (Rhodes scholar), Oxford U., Eng., 1950, MA, 1954, DCL (hon.), 1983; grad., Command and Gen. Staff Coll., 1954-55, Army War Coll., 1959-60; LLD, Akron U., 1978, Boston U., 1981. Commd. lt. US Army, 1943, advanced through grades to gen., 1974; aide to supt. US Mil. Acad., 1945-46, comdr. cadets, 1967-69; aide to high commr. Austria Gen. Mark W. Clark, 1946-47; bn. comdr. Republic of Korea, 1952; exec. to comdr.-in-chief Far East Command, 1953-54; mil. asst. to Chief of Staff, US Army, 1956-59; exec. to chmn. Joint Chiefs of Staff, 1962-66; asst. divsn. comdr. 1st Inf. Divsn., Vietnam, 1966-67; comdg. gen. 5th Inf. Divsn., Ft. Carson, Colo., 1969-70; chief legis. liaison Dept. Army, 1971-72, dep. chief of staff for personnel, 1972-74; comdg. gen. US Army Forces Command, 1974-76; chief of staff US Army, 1976-79; NATO supreme allied comdr., comdr. in chief US European Command, 1979-87; ret. US Army, 1987. Former bd. dirs. Atlantic Coun. US, George C. Marshall Found., Gen. Dynamics Co., Kemper Nat. Ins. Co., Thomas Industries; former sr. cons. The Coca-Cola Co; vol. chmn. USO World Bd. of Govs., 1988-94. Decorated DSC, Def. DSM with oak leaf cluster, DSM of Army, Navy and Air Force, Silver Star, Legion of Merit with 3 oak leaf clusters, D.F.C. with 2 oak leaf clusters, Bronze Star medal with V device; hon. fellow Univ. Coll., Oxford U.; recipient Disting. Svc. Citation U. Kans., 1984, Disting. Grad. award US Mil. Acad., 1995, Assn. US Army George C. Marshall medal, 1999. Mem.: VFW, Mil. Order of World Wars, Ret. Officers Assn., Assn. Am. Rhodes Scholars, Soc. 1st Inf. Divsn., Am. Soc. French Legion of Honor, Assn. US Army (bd. dirs.), Alibi, Alfalfa, Army and Navy Club, Army-Navy Country Club, Phi Delta Theta. Personal E-mail: rogers1467@aol.com.

ROGERS, BETSY, elementary school educator; b. Birmingham, Ala., Mar. 2, 1952; children: Alan, Rick. BA in Elem. Edn., Samford Univ., 1974, MA, 1998, PhD, 2002. Cert. generalist/early childhood Nat. Bd. Profl. Tchg. Standards, 2000. Tchr. Hewitt Elem. Sch., 1974—76; kindergarten tchr. Leeds First Baptist Church, 1982—85; first grade tchr. Leeds Elem. Sch., Ala., 1985—2004; tchr., curriculum coord. Brighton Sch., Ala., 2004—. Chair Governor's Task Force on Tchr. Quality. Named Nat. Tchr. of Yr., 2003. Mem.: Ala. Conf. of Educators (past pres.). Office: Brighton Sch 3300 Brown Cir Birmingham AL 35203 *

ROGERS, BRENDA GAYLE, educational administrator, educator, consultant; b. Atlanta, July 27, 1949; d. Claude Thomas and Louise (Williams) Todd; m. Emanuel Julius Jones Jr., Dec. 17, 1978; children: Lavelle, Brandon, Albre Jede, Briana Adanne. BA, Spelman Coll., Atlanta, 1970; MA, Atlanta U., 1971, EdS, 1972; PhD, Ohio State U., 1975; postgrad., Howard U., DC, 1980, Emory U., Atlanta, 1986. Program devel. specialist HEW, Atlanta, 1972; rsch. assoc. Ohio State U., Columbus, 1973-75; asst. prof. spl. edn. Atlanta U., 1975-78, program adminstr., 1978—, CIT project dir., 1977-91, exec. dir. Impact project, 1992—. Tech. cons. Dept. Edn., Washington, 1978-93, 96, 97-98, cons. Head Start, 1990-91; cons. Princeton Testing Svcs., 1996—; due process regional hearing officer Ga. State Dept. Edn., Atlanta, 1978-84, adv. bd., 1980-84; regional cons. Access project, 1995—; mem. parent adv. coun. APS, 1988—; cons. program devel. Ga. Respite Care, Inc., 1988-89; mem. exec. bd., pres. PTA Stone Mountain elem. Sch., 1989-92; mem. test verification panel Edn. Testing Svcs., Princeton, N.J., 1995-96; cons. So. Assn. Colls. & Univs., 1998. Mem. Ga. Assessment Project com. Atlanta Pub. Schs. Adv. Coun., 1986—; bd. dirs. Mountain Pines Civic Assn., 1988—; mem. Grady Meml. Hosp. Cmty. Action Network, Atlanta, 1982-83; exec. bd. PTA Shadow Rock Elem. Sch., 1992-94. Recipient disting. svc. award Atlanta Bur. Pub. Safety, 1982, Mountain Sch. PTA, 1995, award Atlanta Pub. Sch. Sys., 1980, 82, 83, 89-90, Disting. Svc. award CAU, 1998; fellow Ohio State U., 1972-74, Howard U., 1980. Mem. NAFE, Assn. for Retarded Citizens, Coun. for Exceptional Children, So. Assn. Colls. and Univs. (cons. com. 1998—), Nat. Assn. Learning Disabilites, Phi Delta Kappa, Phi Lambda Theta. Democrat. Roman Catholic. Avocation: gourmet cooking. Office: Clark Atlanta U James P Brawley Atlanta GA 30314-3913 Personal E-mail: drbrendarogers@comcast.net.

ROGERS, BRIAN CHARLES, portfolio manager, investment company executive; b. Beverly, Mass., June 27, 1955; s. Charles E. and Margaret A. (Sweeney) R.; m. Mary Jo Skayhan, Oct. 7, 1979; children: Hilary, Peter, Sydney. AB, Harvard U., 1977, MBA, 1982. Chartered fin. analyst, investment counselor. Asst. treas. Bankers Trust Co., NYC, 1977-80; portfolio mgr. T. Rowe Price Equity Income Fund, Balt., 1985—; mng. dir. T. Rowe Price Assocs., Balt., 1982—2004, chief investment officer, 2004—, chmn., 2007—. Bd. dirs. Balt. County Econ. Devel. Commn., 1988—, Fund for Ednl. Excellence, Batl. 1988-92. Home: 1708 Ruxton Rd Baltimore MD 21204-3505 Office: T Rowe Price Group, Inc 100 E Pratt St Fl 4 Baltimore MD 21202-1090 Office Phone: 410-547-5758. Office Fax: 410-752-3477. *

ROGERS, BRIE S., lawyer; b. Cin., May 26, 1978; BA, Auburn U., 1998; JD, U. Cin., 2002. Bar: Ohio 2002. Assoc. Taft, Stettinius & Hollister LLP, Cin., mem., Intellectual Property Practice Grp., mem., Profl. Women's Resource Grp. Fundraising dir. Give Back Cin., mem., Operational Bd., 2005. Named one of Ohio's Rising Stars, Super Lawyers, 2006. Mem.: Order of Coif. Office: Taft Stettinius & Hollister LLP 425 Walnut St Ste 1800 Cincinnati OH 45202 Office Phone: 513-381-2838. Office Fax: 513-381-0205.

ROGERS, BRYAN L., dean; Chmn. Sch. Art Carnegie Mellon U., 1988—99; Dean Sch. Art & Design U. Mich., 1999—. Office: Office of the Dean U Mich Sch Art & Design 2055 Art & Arch Bldg Ann Arbor MI 48109 Office Phone: 734-763-4093. E-mail: blrogers@umich.edu.

ROGERS, BRYAN LEIGH, dean, artist, art educator; b. Amarillo, Tex., Jan. 7, 1941; s. Bryan Austin and Virginia Leigh (Bull) R.; m. Cynthia Louise Rice; 1 child, Kyle Austin Rogers. BE, Yale U., 1963; MS, U. Calif., Berkeley, 1966, MA, 1969, PhD, 1971. Design engr. Monsanto Co., Texas City, Tex., 1962; research engr. Rocketdyne, Canoga Park, Calif., 1963-64; research scientist Lawrence Livermore (Calif.) Lab., 1966; lectr. U. Calif., Berkeley, 1972-73; fellow Akademie der Bildenden Künste,

Munich, 1974-75; prof. art San Francisco State U., 1975-88; head, prof. sch. art Carnegie Mellon U., Pitts., 1988-99, dir. Studio for Creative Inquiry, 1989-99; dean, prof. Sch. of Art and Design U. Mich., Ann Arbor, 2000—. Fellow Ctr. Advanced Visual Studies MIT, Cambridge, Mass, 1981. Editor Leonardo Jour., San Francisco, 1982-85. One-man shows include: Laguna Beach (Calif.) Mus. Art, 1974, DeSaisset Art Gallery U. Santa Clara, Calif., 1974, San Francisco Mus. Modern Art, 1974, Baxter Art Gallery Calif. Inst. Tech., Pasadena, 1979, Contemporary Crafts gallery, Portland, Oreg., 1987; group exhbns. include: Berkeley (Calif.) Art Ctr., 1969, Hansen-Fuller Gallery, San Francisco, 1970, San Francisco Arts Commn. Gallery, 1984, Clocktower Gallery, N.Y.C., 1984, Otis-Parsons Gallery, L.A., 1985, P.P.O.W. Gallery, N.Y.C., 1985, 18th Internat. Bienal, São Paulo, Brazil, 1985, MIT, Cambridge, 1990, Objects Gallery, Chgo., 1992, ARTEC 93 Internat Biennale, Nagoya, Japan, 1993, Chgo. Cultural Ctr., 1993, Am. Iron and Steel Expo., Pitts., 1993, Pitts. Ctr. for Arts, 1994, Allegheny Coll. Gallery, Meadville, Pa., 1997, Aichi Art Ctr., Nagoya, Japan, 1997. Fellow NEA, Washington, 1981, 82, Deutscher Akademischer Austauschdienst, Fed. Republic of Germany, 1974, NSF, Washington, 1965-69; recipient SECA award San Francisco Mus. Modern Art, 1974. Office: Sch Art & Design Univ Michigan Ann Arbor MI 48109 Office Phone: 734-763-4093. Business E-Mail: blrogers@umich.edu.

ROGERS, CARLETON CARSON, JR., trade show and convention executive; b. Chgo., Nov. 5, 1935; s. Carleton Carson and Eleanor (Lowell) Rogers; m. Loretta Zirkel; children: Kirsten Ann, Mark, Brett. BS in Bus. Adminstrn., Am. U., 1957; postgrad., Northwestern U., 1957, Chgo.-Kent Coll. Law, 1957—58. Mgmt. trainee Ill. Bell Telephone Co., Chgo., 1959-61; sales mgr. Programs Internat., Chgo., 1961-64, pres., 1964-71; show mgr. Indsl. & Sci. Conf. Mgmt., Chgo., 1975-78; pres. Expo Mgmt., Inc., Chgo., 1978-82, Trade Expositions and Assoc. Mgmt. Ltd., Chgo., 1982-92, Expn. Mmgt., Inc., Elgin, 1992-99, National Show Mgmt., Inc., Elgin, 1999—. Adj. prof. Roosevelt U., Chgo. Pres. Kane County, Ill., Young Republican Club, 1962-64; trustee Gail Borden Pub. Libr., Elgin; bd. dirs. Area C Coun. on Aging for Ill., Upper Kane County chpt. Am. Heart Assn., Chgo. Conv. and Tourism Bur.; mem. adminstrv. bd., pres. bd. trustees First United Meth. Ch., Elgin.; sec.-treas. found. pres. Ctr. for Exhbn. Industry Rsch. Mem. Internat. Assn. Exhibit Mgmt. (chmn. bd., recipient Disting. Svc. award), Masons, Shriners, Omicron Delta Kappa, Alpha Tau Omega. Home: 11n937 Almora Ter Elgin IL 60124-4705 Office: Nat Show Mgmt Inc PO Box 6282 Elgin IL 60121-6282 Office Phone: 847-695-5330. Personal E-mail: expomgmt@juno.com.

ROGERS, CARTON (H. CARTON ROGERS III), library director; BA in History, Marietta Coll., Ohio, 1970; MLS, Drexel U., 1973. Joined libraries staff U. Pa., Phila., 1975; head reference & tech. services Biomedical Libr., 1975—79; sr. bus. officer U. Libr., 1979—85; Patricia and Bernard Goldstein Dir. Info. Processing U. Pa. Libraries, 1985—2003, acting dir. collections devel. & mgmt., 2003; interim vice provost & dir. libraries U. Pa., 2003—04, vice provost & dir. libraries, 2004—. Office: Van Pelt-Dietrich Libr Ctr 3420 Walnut St Philadelphia PA 19104-6206 Office Phone: 215-898-7091. Office Fax: 215-898-0559. Business E-Mail: rogers@pobox.upenn.edu. *

ROGERS, CHARLES EDWIN, physical chemistry and polymer science professor; b. Rochester, NY, Dec. 29, 1929; s. Charles Harold and Maybelle (Johnson) R.; m. Barbara June Depuy, June 12, 1954; children: Gregory Newton, Linda Frances, Diana Suzanne. BS in Chemistry, Syracuse U., 1954; PhD in Phys. Chemistry, SUNY at Syracuse U., 1957. Rsch. assoc. dept. chemistry Princeton U., 1957-59, Goodyear fellow, 1957-59; mem. tech. staff Bell Telephone Labs., Murray Hill, NJ, 1959-65; assoc. prof. macromolecular sci. Case Western Res. U., Cleve., 1965-74, prof., 1974-98, prof. emeritus, 1998—. Sr. vis. fellow Imperial Coll., U. London, 1971; assoc. dir. Ctr. for Adhesives Sealants Coatings, Case Western Res. U., 1984-88, dir., 1988-91; co-dir. Edison Polymer Innovation Corp., Ctr. for Adhesives, Sealants and Coatings, 1991-97; cons. to polymer and chem. industries; devel. overseas ednl. instns. Editor: Permselective Membranes, 1971, Structure and Properties of Block Copolymers, 1977; contbr. numerous articles to profl. jours.; patentee in field. Staff sgt. 82nd airborne divsn. US Army, 1946—49, staff sgt. USAR, 1949—53, commd. officer USAR, 1953—63. Mem.: Adhesion Soc., N.Am. Membrane Soc., Am. Phys. Soc., Am. Chem. Soc. Home: 8400 Rockspring Dr Chagrin Falls OH 44023-4645 Office: Case Western Reserve U Dept Macromolecular Sc Cleveland OH 44106-7202 Office Phone: 216-368-6376. Business E-Mail: cer@case.edu.

ROGERS, CHARLES MYERS, lawyer; b. Monticello, Utah, Nov. 21, 1947; s. Milton David and Wanda (Myers) R.; m. Jean Evelyn Rankin, Dec. 12, 1970 (div. June, 1983); m. Christine Theresa Sill, Apr. 14, 1984; children: Christopher Thales, Fiona Eleanor. BA in Philosophy, U. Mo., Kansas City, 1973, JD, 1976. Bar: Mo. 1976, U.S. Dist. Ct. (we. dist.) Mo. 1976, U.S. Ct. Appeals (8th cir.) 1997, U.S. Ct. Appeals (9th cir.) 1999, U.S. Dist. Ct. Kans. 1999., U.S. Dist. Ct. (ea. dist.) Mo. 2001, U.S. Supreme Ct. 1994, U.S. Ct. Appeals (10th cir.) 2004. From asst. pub. defender to 1st asst. pub. defender Jackson County Pub. Defender's Office, Kansas City, Mo., 1976-89; regional defender Mo. State Pub. Defender Sys., Kansas City, 1989-94; staff atty. Mo. Capital Punishment Resource Ctr., Kansas City, 1994-95; shareholder Wyrsch Hobbs & Mirakian, Kansas City, 1995—. Sole practice law, Kansas City, 1982-86. With US Army, 1968—70. Mem.: ABA, Kansas City Metro Bar Assn. (chair criminal law com. 2000), Mo. Assn. Criminal Def. Lawyers (bd. dirs. 1988—2001, v.p. 2002—03, pres. 2003—04), Mo. Bar Assn., Nat. Assn. Criminal Def. Lawyers. Democrat. Avocations: cycling, oenology. Home: 11403 Holly Ct Kansas City MO 64114-1506 Office: Wyrsch Hobbs et al 1000 Walnut St Ste 1600 Kansas City MO 64106-2180 Office Phone: 816-221-0080. E-mail: acquit@whmlaw.net.

ROGERS, CHARLES RAY, minister, religious organization administrator; b. Grapevine, Tex., Nov. 26, 1935; s. Arlin Avery and Bessie Lorene (Deaton) R.; m. Oma Fay Hines, Aug. 21, 1954; children: Sheree Gay Rogers, Charles Denne Ray, Robin Celeste Rogers Eddins. MS in Christian Edn., Faith Bible Coll., 1980, DD in Humanities (hon.), 1981; B of Theology, M of Theology, Ctrl. Am. Theol. Sem., Escuintla, Guatemala, 2000; D of Ministry in Humanities (hon.), Sem. of Theol. Missions, Escuintla, Guatemala, 1992. Pastor various Bapt. chs., Athens, Dallas, Ft. Worth, 1960-64, various interdenominational chs., Houston, Longview, 1965-69; pres. Evangelism in Action, Ft. Worth, 1969—. Bd. dirs. World Ministry Fellowship, Plano, Tex., dir. world missions, 1970—; leader Over 100 Mission, humanitarian trips Evangelism in Action, Ft. Worth, 1976—. Author: Joy, 1979, Handbook for Victorious Living, 1980, How to Develop Christian Love, 1981; vocalist (rec.) Charlie, 1981. Republican. Avocations: golf, tennis, swimming, running, computers. Home: 6417 Rogers Dr Fort Worth TX 76180-4817 Office: Evangelism in Action PO Box 820724 Fort Worth TX 76182-0724 Home Phone: 817-247-6948; Office Phone: 817-498-3589. Personal E-mail: chasrog@swbell.net.

ROGERS, CHASE THEODORA, state supreme court justice; b. Conn., Nov. 12, 1956; d. Richard B. and Nancy Chase Rogers; m. Edward O'Hanlan, Dec. 21, 1985; 2 children. BA, Standord U., 1979; JD, Boston U. Sch. Law, 1983. Atty. Cummings & Lockwood, ptnr., 1991—98; judge Conn. Superior Ct., 1998—2006, presiding judge, juvenile matters Bridgeport, judge, regional child protection session Middletown, judge, complex litig. docket Stamford, 2001—05, presiding judge, civil matters, Stamford-Norwalk dist., 2005—06; judge Conn. Appellate Ct., 2006—07; chief justice Conn. Supreme Ct., 2007—. Office: Conn Supreme Ct 231 Capitol Ave Hartford CT 06106 Office Phone: 860-757-2200. *

ROGERS, CLAYTON RUSH, application developer, small business owner, consultant; b. Springfield, Mo., July 15, 1957; s. Francis Lee and Lora Elaine Rogers; m. Jana Sue Sloan, July 8, 1978. BSEE, U. Mo., Rolla, 1979. Undergraduate rsch. asst. U. Mo., 1979; programmer, analyst Control Data Corp., Mpls., 1980—82; electrical engr. Dayco Products, Inc., Springfield, 1982—89; engring. applications specialist Mark IV Automotive, Springfield, 1989—2001, sr. sys. tech. analyst, 2001—03; owner Springware, Springfield, 2003—. Cons. Springware, Springfield, 1988—2006. Mem.: IEEE. Achievements include invention of offset starter generator drive utilizing a fixed offset dual arm pivoted tensioner; development of dietary nutrient tracking software. Avocations: reading, model building, fishing, camping, golf. Home: 3774 W Woodland St Springfield MO 65807

ROGERS, DALE CRAIG, finance company executive; b. Wichita Falls, Tex., Jan. 21, 1945; s. Moral W. and Opal Davlin Rogers; m. Judy Carole Coburn, Sept. 11, 1965; children: Lori Alyssa Rogers-Williams, Craig Coburn. Cert. pension cons. Am. Soc. Pension Profls. & Actuaries Wash., D.C., 1989. Ins. & securities agt. Penn Mut. Life Ins. Co., Wichita Falls, Tex., 1966—68; divsn. mgr. Jefferson-Pilot Equity Co., Fort Worth, Tex., 1968—73; chmn., CEO Rogers Co., Fort Worth, 1973—, Rogers & Associates- Pension Cons., Fort Worth, 1973—, Rogers Capital Mgmt., Inc., Fort Worth, 1990—. Author: The First Time Investor, How to Build, Protect & Maintain Your 401(k) Plan. Pres., bd. trustees Keller Ind. Sch. Dist., Tex., 1983—89; bd. dirs. Keller Youth Assn., 1980—88. Mem.: Am. Soc. Pension Actuaries & Cons. (licentiate). R-Conservative. Avocations: travel, boating. Home: 6905 Old Homestead Rd Fort Worth TX 76132 Office: Rogers Co 1330 Summit Ave Fort Worth TX 76102 Home Phone: 817-263-6578; Office Phone: 817-334-0351. Business E-Mail: dcrogers@rogersco.com.

ROGERS, DARLA POLLMAN, lawyer; b. 1952; BA, Wheaton Coll.; JD, U. S.D. Bar: S.D. 1979. Ptnr. Meyer & Rogers, Pierre, SD, Riter, Rogers, Wattier & Brown LLP, Pierre, SD, 2003—. Mem. ABA, S.D. Bar Assn. (pres., 1998-99); fellow, Am. Bar Found. Office: Riter Rogers Wattier & Brown PO Box 280 Pierre SD 57501-0280

ROGERS, DAVID, playwright, actor; b. NYC; s. George and Deborah (Samuels) Rosenberg; m. June Lois Walker, Oct. 14, 1962; children: Dulcy Dru, Amanda Brooke. Student, Am. Theatre Wing Sch., 1948-49. Author (N.Y.C. prodns.): Ziegfeld Follies, 1957, Vintage '60, 1960, New Faces of 1962, Fun City, 1967, Charlie and Algernon, 1980 (Tony award nomination); author: (London prodns.) Jubilee Girl, 1956, Young at Heart, 1961, Flowers for Algernon, 1979, Killing Jessica, 1986; pub. plays Tom Jones, 1964, Flowers for Algernon, 1969, Brave New World, 1970, F.L.I.P.P.E.D., 1971, Here and Now, 1973, Soft Soap, 1982, Rehearsal for Murder, 1983, pub. musical Best of Broadway, 1961, Cheaper by the Dozen, 1969, The Hobbit, 1972, The Truth About Cinderella, 1974, The Dream on Royal Street, 1981; author: (TV series) The Hero, 1966, Opera, 1966 (winner Prix d'Italia Concorso Internat. Per Opera Radiofoniche e Televisive), The Carol Burnett Show, 1970, (novels) Oh Eden, 1974, The Bedroom Set, 1976, Somewhere There's Music, 1977, The Great American Alimony Escape, 1979, The In-Laws, 1979; actor: (Broadway plays) Doubles, 1985, George Abbott's Broadway, 1987, A Funny Thing Happened On the Way to the Forum, 1997, (Off Broadway Play) Down the Garden Paths, 2000, Jewtopia, 2006, internat. tour Grand Hotel, 1991, (regional theatre appearances): Players Theatre, 1992,: Birmingham Theatre, 1993, Jupiter Theatre, 1993, Great Lakes Theatre Festival, 1994, Phoenix Theatre, 1995, Denver Ctr. Theatre Co., 1996, Repertory Theatre of St. Louis, 1998, Cin. Playhouse in the Park, 1998, Westport Playhouse, 1998, San Jose Repertory Theatre, 1999 (Dean Goodman Choice award), Va. Stage Co., 2000, Fla. Studio Theatre, 2002, Two Rivers Theatre Co., 2002, Merrimack Repertory Theatre, 2003—07, Rich Forum, 2004, 2005, Conn. Repertory, 2005; writer, performer: (one-man show) Naked on Broadway, 2004; actor: Norton Playhouse, 2006, (TV guest appearances): Law and Order, 2000, Law and Order: Criminal Intent, 2001, 2005, Law and Order: Special Victims Unit, 2003. With US Army, 1951—52, Korea. Mem.: AFTRA, SAG, Actors Equity, Broadcast Music Inc., Writers Guild Am. East, Dramatists Guild, Theatre Artists Workshop Westport (bd. dirs. 1985).

ROGERS, DAVID BOOTH, lawyer; BA with honors and distinction, Stanford Univ., 1980, JD, 1983. Bar: Calif. 1983, DC 2002. With Latham & Watkins, 1983—, chair, fin. dept., 1997—2001, ptnr. LA, 2001—. Exec. com. Latham & Watkins, 2001—. Named one of Top 20 Lawyers in Calif. under age 40, Calif. Law Bus. mag., 1997. Mem.: ABA. Office: Latham & Watkins Ste 4000 633 W Fifth St Los Angeles CA 90071-2007

ROGERS, DAVID FREEMAN, aerospace engineering educator; b. Theresa, NY, Sept. 3, 1937; s. Lewis Freeman and Gladys Marion Zoller; m. Nancy Ann Nuttall, Sept. 5, 1959; children: Stephen David, Karen Nanci, Ransom Robert. B in Aero. Engring., Rensselaer Poly. Inst., 1959, MS in Aero. Engring., 1960, PhD, 1967. From asst. prof. to prof. U.S. Naval Acad., Annapolis, Md., 1964—2003, dir. aeronautics, 1999—2003, prof. emeritus, 2004—. Fujitsu Rsch. prof. Royal Melbourne Inst. Tech.; hon. rsch. scholar U. Coll. London, 1977-78. Author: Mathematical Elements for Computer Graphics, 1976, 2d edit. 1990; Procedural Elements for Computer Graphics, 1985, 2d edit., 1997, Laminar Flow Analysis, 1992, Flying Adventures, Vols. 1-2, 1999, An Introduction to NURBS: with Historical Perspective, 2001; editor Meml. edit. for P. Bezier, CAD Jour., 2001; mem. editl. bd. Visual Computer, CAD, the Computer Aided Design Jour.; contbg. editor World Beechcraft Soc. Mag., 1995—; contbr. articles to profl. jours. David F. Rogers Chair in Aerospace Engineering named in his honor, 2000. Avocations: flying, photography, sailing. Office: US Naval Acad Aerospace Engring Dept Annapolis MD 21402

ROGERS, DAVID HUGHES, banking and financial service professor, dean, real estate company executive; b. Chgo., May 21, 1947; s. Joseph Gordon and Viola Winifred (Hughes) R.; Bonnie Hope Sinai, 1997; children: Kirsten Morgan, Loren Avery, Daniel Jay. BA, U. Mich., 1968; PhD, Columbia U., 1975. Economist Fed. Res. Bank of Cleve., 1974-75; asst. treas. B.F. Goodrich Co., Akron, Ohio, 1975-82; exec. v.p., chief fin. officer First Tex. Savs. Assn., Dallas, 1982-83; sr. exec. v.p., chief operating officer PriMerit Bank, Las Vegas, 1984-87, pres., dir., 1987-91, vice chmn., 1991-92; COO, The Baird Cos., Las Vegas, 1992-99; v.p., chief fin. officer Norall Labs., Las Vegas, 1999—2001; v.p., relationship mgr. Wells Fargo Bank, Las Vegas, Nev., 2001—04; CFO Lloyd Cos., Sioux Falls, SD, 2004—06; prof. banking and fin. svcs., asst. dean external programs No. State U., 2006—. Adj. prof. econs. C.C. So. Nev., 1998-2004. Author: Consumer Banking in New York, 1975; also articles. Bd. dirs. Boulder Dam Area coun. Boy Scouts Am., 1986—2004; bd. dirs. Nev. Sch. Arts, 1988-98; chmn. Las Vegas Bus. Bank, 1995-99. Office: No State U 2205 Career Ave Rm 268 D Sioux Falls SD 57107 Home Phone: 605-271-1103; Office Phone: 605-782-3236. Personal E-mail: dhrogers14@aol.com. Business E-Mail: dhrogers@northern.edu.

ROGERS, DESIREE GLAPION, utilities executive; b. New, June 16, 1959; d. Roy and Joyce Glapion; 1 child, Victoria. B in Polit. Sci., Wellesley Coll., 1981; MBA, Harvard U., 1985. Customer svc. mktg. mgr. AT&T, N.J., 1985-87; dir. devel. Levy Orgn., Chgo., 1987-89; founder, pres. Mus. Ops. Consulting Assocs., Chgo., 1989-91; dir. Ill. State Lottery, Chgo., 1991-97; chief mktg. officer Peoples Energy, Chgo., 1997—; pres. Peoples Gas and North Shore Gas, 2004—. Bd. dirs. Equity Residential, Blue Cross Blue Shield Ill. Bd. dirs. Mus. Sci. and Industry, Ravinia; trustee Lincoln Park Zoo. Named a Woman to Watch, Crain's Chgo. Bus., 2007. Mem. Com. of 200, Young Pres.' Orgn., The Econ. Club, Execs. Club, Comml. Club Chgo. Office: Peoples Energy 130 E Randolph Dr Fl 18 Chicago IL 60601-6207 *

ROGERS, DEWITT RALPH, lawyer; b. Durham, NC, Sept. 26, 1952; s. Ralph P. and Elizabeth (Stutts) R.; m. Claire Hamby, Sept. 25, 1982; children: DeWitt Ralph Jr., Elizabeth Lee, Laura Alice. BA, Emory U., 1974, JD with distinction, 1986; MS in Journalism, Columbia U., 1975. Bar: Ga. 1986. Staff writer The Atlanta Constn., 1975-77, bus. editor, 1977-79, city editor, 1979-82; asst. mng. editor The Atlanta Jour. & Constn., 1982-83; assoc. Troutman Sanders LLP, Atlanta, 1986-93, ptnr., regulatory group, 1994—. Bd. dirs. So. Inst. Bus. and Profl. Ethics, 1998-2006. Editor-in-chief Emory Law Jour. Mem.: Order of Coif. Office: Troutman Sanders LLP 600 Peachtree St NE Ste 5200 Atlanta GA 30308-2216 Office Phone: 404-885-3412. Office Fax: 404-962-6671. Business E-Mail: dewitt.rogers@troutmansanders.com.

ROGERS, DONALD L., music educator, department chairman, animal breeder; b. Bayshore, NY, Jan. 22, 1945; s. Donald Hampton and Laura Rogers; m. Bonnie L. Nieman, June 25, 1967; 1 child, Rebecca L. B.S, SUNY, Fredonia, 1966. Tchg. cert. Bd. of Regents State of NY, 1966. H.s. band dir. Attica (NY) Ctrl. Sch. Dist., 1966—. Music dept. chmn. Attica Ctrl. Sch., 1980—. Dir.: (band performance) Tournament of Roses Parade, 2003. Pres. Western NY Pheasant & Waterfowl Assn., NY, 1985—. Sgt. U.S. Army, 1969—72. Decorated Army Commendation U.S. Army; named Tchr. of Yr., U. Rochester, 1993, Educator of Yr., Phi Delta Kappa, 2001; recipient Service award, Wyoming County Youth Bd., 2001, Lifetime Achievement award, Wyo. County Arts Coun., 2006. Mem.: Music Educators Nat. Conf., NY State Sch. Music Assn., Am. Pheasant & Waterfowl Assn., Western NY Pheasant and Waterfowl Assn. (life; pres. 1985—). Home: 2338 Chick Rd Darien Center NY 14040 Office: Attica Senior High Sch 3338 East Main St Attica NY 14011 Home Phone: 585-591-0862; Office Phone: 585-591-0400 Ext.1433. Personal E-mail: wildwingedhaven2@aol.com.

ROGERS, DOROTHEA MAY, education educator; b. Detroit, Dec. 14, 1951; d. Lawrence Edward Peter Dietrich and Thelma Louise St. Clair; m. Paul Douglas, Sr. Rogers, Apr. 12, 1975; children: Paul Douglas Jr., Matthew Lawrence. AA in Gen. Bus., Schoolcraft Coll., Mich., 1991; BA in Religious Edn., Christian Bible Coll. and Seminary, Independance, Mo., 1996; BA in Family Life Edn. magna cum laude, Spring Arbor U., Mich., 1998; MA in Family and Consumer Sci., Western Mich. U., 2001; D in Ministry Family Studies, Am. Christian Coll. and Seminary, Oklahoma City, 2005. Cert. family life educator, presch. tchr., gerontology, child devel. assoc. Asst. preschool tchr. Children's Care Ctr., Howell, Mich., 1993—95; head preschool tchr. A Helping Hand Preschool, Linden, Mich., 1996—97; sub. tchr. Howell (Mich.) Pub. Schs., 1998—2001; prof. health & human svcs. Baker Coll., Flint, Mich., 1999—2003; social work prevention Kids in New Directions, Lapeer, Mich., 2001—03; prof. Spring Arbor U., 2005—. Adv. bd. Making A Difference For Children Conf., Flint, Mich., 1999—2002; advisor curriculum Baker Coll., Flint, Mich., 1999—2003, sys. meeting cons., 1999—2003. Author: (book) First-Line Supervision, 1990, The Postparental Life Stage in Middle Age Women, 2005; composer, presenter (seminar) Preventing and Treating Job Burnout for Childcare Workers, 2002. Quiz bowl moderator Hartland (Mich.) HS, 1992—96; geriatric advocate Stephen Ministry, Fenton, Mich., 1997—2006; tutor, mentor Family Literacy Ctr., Lapeer, Mich., 2003—06; counselor Pregnancy Resource Ctr. Lapeer, 2006. Mem.: Nat. Assn. Edn. of Young Children, Am. Assn. Christian Counselors, Nat. Counsel on Family Rels., Phi Kappa Phi. Democrat. Presbyterian. Avocations: gardening, hiking, flower arranging.

ROGERS, DOUGLAS L., lawyer; b. White Plains, NY, Oct. 9, 1946; BA, Cornell U., NY, 1968; JD, Yale U., Conn., 1971. Bar: Ohio 1971, DC 1978, US Dist. Ct. (so. dist., no. dist.) Ohio, US Ct. of Appeals (6th cir., 10th cir.) US Dist. Ct. DC. Mem. Vorys, Sater, Seymour & Pease, Columbus, ptnr. Dir. Ohio Legal Rights Svc., 1975-80, Legal Aid Soc. of Columbus, 1980-82; trustee Columbus Coun. on World Affairs, 1987-91. Contbr. Mem.: ABA, Columbus Bar Assn., Ohio State. Office: Vorys Sater Seymour & Pease LLP 52 E Gay S PO Box 1008 Columbus OH 43216-1008 Office Phone: 614-464-5407. Office Fax: 614-719-4928. Business E-Mail: dlrogers@vssp.com.

ROGERS, EARL LESLIE, artist, educator; b. Oakland, Calif., July 8, 1918; s. Robert Ray and Addie Myrtle (Dice) R.; m. Eileen Estelle MacKenzie, Apr. 9, 1945; children: Leslie Eileen, Brian Donald (dec.). Student, L.A. Valley Coll., 1949-52, Northridge State U., 1958-59, UCLA Extension, 1967, Sergei Bongart Sch. Art, 1967-68; AA, Pierce Coll., 1958; MA equivalency, Merced Coll., 1996. Cert. tchr., Calif. Various positions City of L.A., Van Nuys, Calif., 1948-55, Reseda, Calif., 1955-68; pvt. practice Canoga Park, Calif., 1948-68; art tchr. Mariposa (Calif.) County High Sch., 1969-70; art instr. Merced (Calif.) County Coll., 1970—. Instr. Earl Rogers Studio Workshop, Mariposa, Calif., 1969—; art dir. Yosemite Nat. Park, Calif., 1973; instr. art Asilomar Conf. Grounds, Pacific Grove, Calif., 1980; juror various art orgns., 1971-2004; demonstrator Clovis (Calif.) Art Guild, 1971, 89, Sierra Artists, Mariposa, 1972, 81, 82, 84, 91, 2000, Merced Art League, 1976, Yosemite Western Artists, Oakhurst, Calif., 1973, Madera (Calif.) Art Assn., 1978, Chowchilla (Calif.) Art Guild, 1983, 86, 87, 89, 91, Soc. Western Artists, 1981, 89, 93, 97. One-man shows include L.A. City Hall, 1968, Merced Coll., 1969, 1995, Mariposa Title Co. Bldg., 1969, Coffee's Gallery, 1970, Bear Valley Hist. Bon-Ton, Calif., 1999, Sierra Artists Gallery, Mariposa, Calif., 2007, others, exhibited in group shows at West Valley Artists Assn., 1966—68, L.A. City Hall, 1967, Yosemite Nat. Park, 1973, Soc. Western Artists, 1977—78, Cannon Bldg. Rotunda, Washington, 1982, Mother Lode Gallery, Columbia, Calif., 1977—78, Arbor Gallery, Merced, 1988, 1998, 2001, Gold Country Gallery, 1990—91, Merced Coll., 1969—92, 1996, Mariposa County Arts Coun., 1999, at others, Represented in permanent collections John C. Freemont Hosp., Mariposa, Mariposa County Arts Coun., Mariposa Mus. and History Ctr., Capital Hill Br. Pub. Libr., Seattle, Merced Coll., Br. Pub. Libr., San Francisco, Merced Court House Mus., North Mariposa County History Ctr., Coulterville, Calif. Asst. scout master Boy Scouts Am., Canoga Park, Calif., 1956-58; art instr. L.A. Recreation Corps, L.A. Parks and Recreation Dept., 1967. Mem. Soc. Western Artists (Neva Rall Meml. award 1978), Mariposa Mus. and Hist. Ctr. (life). Avocations: piano, reading. Office: 5323 State Hwy 49 N Mariposa CA 95338-9503 Home: 700 Northshore Dr #4 Bellingham WA 98226

ROGERS, EDNA LOVEDAY, elementary school educator; BS, U. Tenn., Knoxville, 1978, MS in Edn., 1985. Tchr. Dixie County HS, Tenn., 1962—63, Sevierville Elem., Tenn., 1963—67; tchr. Pre-K Sevier County Head Start, Tenn., 1971—77; tchr. kindergarten Sevierville Primary Sch., Tenn., 1978—2000. Named to Nat. Tchrs. Hall of Fame, 2007; recipient Joint Resolution Award, Ho. of Reps., 1989, Gov.'s Outstanding Tennessean Award, 1989, Presdl. Award for Excellence in Sci. and Math., 1990, Rotary Disting. Svc. Award, 1992, TASP Outstanding Svc. to Children's Award, 1993, Nat. Coun. Tchrs. of English Literacy Award, 1998, Family and Consumer Svcs. Vision Award, TN Association, 1999, TEA Friend of Edn. Award, 1999. Office: Sevierville Primary Sch 755 Middle Creek Rd Sevierville TN 37862 *

ROGERS, EDWARD SAMUEL, communications company executive; b. Toronto, Can., May 27, 1933; s. Edward Samuel and Velma Melissa (Taylor) R.; m. Loretta Anne Robinson, Sept. 25, 1963; children: Lisa Anne, Edward Samuel, Melinda Mary, Martha Loretta. BA, Trinity Coll.,

U. Toronto, 1956; LLB, Osgoode Hall Law Sch., 1961; DSc (hon.), Clarkson U., 1989; LLD (hon.), U. Victoria, 1990; LLD, York U., 1994; LittD, U. of New Brunswick, 2001; LLD, U. of Toronto, 2002, D of sacred letters, 1997. Bar: Ont., 1962. Founder, prin. Rogers Telecomm. Ltd., Toronto, 1960—; pres., CEO Rogers Comm. Inc., Toronto, 1978—, Rogers Cablesystems, Toronto, 1990—96; vice chmn. Rogers Media Inc., Toronto, 1994, Rogers Cable Inc., Toronto, 1997—; chmn. Rogers Wrieless Comms. Inc., 1991. Bd. dirs. Toronto Blue Jays Baseball Club. Bd. dirs. Jr. Achievement Can. Named one of World's Richest People, Forbes mag., 1999—. Mem. Royal Can. Yacht Club, Albany Club, Granite Club, York Club, Muskoka Golf & Country Club, Rideau Club Ottawa, Lyford Cay Club (gov.), Balboa Bay Club, Sigma Chi (Beta Omega chpt.). Progressive Conservative. Mem. Anglican Ch. Office: Rogers Comm Inc 333 Bloor St E Toronto ON Canada M4W 1G9

ROGERS, ELIZABETH (BETTY) CARLISLE, education educator, consultant; d. Charles Bunyan and Maggie Era (Little) Carlisle; children: Kellie Elizabeth, Sean Lewis. BS, U. Miss., 1972, MS, 1974; PhD, U. Ga., 1997. Chair divsn. sci. and math. Truett-McConnell Coll., Cleveland, Ga., 1974—84; chair dept. math. Lakeview Acad., Gainesville, Ga., 1984—89; prof. math. and edn. Piedmont Coll., Demorest, Ga., 1989—; prin. R&H Analytics, 2004—. Pres. BCR Inc., Gainesville, Ga., 1990—; ptnr. The Ednl. Solutions Task Force, Washington, 2000—. Author: (profl. book) A Study of Curriculum and Pedagogy, 1997; editor (contbg. author): Cooperative Learning In Undergraduate Mathematics, 2001; author: (textbook) Mathematics for Agriculture, 2000. Chair, ceremonies and events Spl. Olympics of Ga., 2001—04. Grantee Faculty Devel. in Ga., State of Ga., 1992—95; scholar Carrier Scholarship, Carrier Found.; Tchg. Fellow, U. of Miss., 1971—73. Mem.: Women in Math., Math. Assn. of Am., Alpha Delta Pi (Dorothy Shaw Leadership award), Alpha Lambda Delta (pres.), Kappa Delta Phi (pres.), Phi Kappa Phi. Achievements include research in advantages of coop. learning for undergraduate math. students; history of math. in Ctrl. and South Am. Home: 4733 Highland Rd Gainesville GA 30506 Office: Piedmont Coll Ctrl Ave Demorest GA 30535 Office Phone: 770-287-4634. Personal E-mail: b.rogers@prodigy.net. E-mail: brogers@piedmont.edu.

ROGERS, ELIZABETH LONDON, retired geriatrics services professional; BA, Mt. Holyoke Coll., Shelley, Mass., 1967; MD, Jefferson Med. Sch., Phila., 1971. Lic. internal medicine, gastroenterology, and geriatrics Am. Bd. of Internal Medicine. Chief of staff Balt. VA Med. Ctr., 1982—93; prof. dept. of medicine U. of Md. Med. Sch., Baltimore, 1990—93; assoc. dean for clin. medicine Duke U. Med. Sch., Durham, NC, 1993—96; acting chief of staff VA Healthcare Sys., New Haven, 1996—2002; chief ambulatory and primary care Yale New Haven VA Med. Ctr., 1996—2002; ret., 2002. Pres. Bradmer Biotech, Miami, 2002—05; dir. Cardiome Pharma, Vancouver, B.C., Canada, 2003—04; assoc. prof. med. sch. Yale U., 1996—2002. Chmn., pres. London Charitable Found., Miami, Fla. Recipient Geriat. scholarship, Hartford Found., 1984—85. Fellow: ACP. Home Phone: 305-674-7072.

ROGERS, ERNEST MABRY, lawyer; b. Demopolis, Ala., Sept. 22, 1947; s. James B. and Ernestine B. (Brewer) R.; m. Jeanne Edwards, Dec. 15, 1979; children: Gilbert B., Katherine B., Mary C. BA, Yale U., New Haven, Conn., 1969; JD, Harvard U., Cambridge, Mass., 1974. Bar: Ala. 1974, US Dist. Ct. (no. dist.) Ala. 1975, US Ct. Appeals (5th cir.) 1976, US Ct. Appeals (11th cir.) 1981, US Supreme Ct. 1981, US Ct. Claims 1983, US Ct. Appeals (6th cir.) 1987. Law clk. to judge U.S. Dist. Ct. (no. dist.) Ala., 1974—75; ptnr. Bradley Arant Rose & White LLP, Birmingham, Ala., 1981—. Contbr. articles to profl. jours. Mem. Jefferson County Bd. of Code Appeals, Ala., 2001—, City of Birmingham Bd. of Code Appeals. Fellow: Am. Coll. Constrn. Lawyers; mem.: Am. Arbitration Assn. (bd. dirs. 2001—05), Kiwanis. Episcopalian. Office: One Federal Pl 1819 5th Ave N Birmingham AL 35203-2104 Office Phone: 205-521-8225. Business E-Mail: mrogers@bradleyarant.com.

ROGERS, EUGENE JACK, retired medical educator; b. Vienna, June 13, 1921; came to U.S., 1937; s. Louis and Malvina (Haller) R.; m. Joyce M. Lighter, Feb. 9, 1952; children: Jay A., Robert J. BS, CCNY; M.B., Chgo. Med. Sch., 1946, MD, 1947. Diplomate Am. Bd. Phys. Medicine and Rehab. Intern Our Lady of Mercy Med. Ctr. and Cabrini Meml. Hosps., NYC, 1946-48; resident Madigan Hosp., Tacoma, 1951, Mayo Clinic, Rochester, Minn., 1951, N.Y. Med. Coll. Met. Med. Ctr., 1953-55; USPHS fellow, 1955-56; ship's surgeon U.S. Lines, Grace Lines, NYC, 1948-49; indsl. physician Abraham & Strauss Stores, Bklyn., 1949-51; practice medicine specializing in phys. medicine and rehab. Bklyn., 1956-73; dir. rehab. service, attending physician N.Y. City Hosp. Dept., 1955-73; prof., chmn. dept. rehab. medicine Chgo. Med. Sch., North Chicago, Ill., 1973—2005, prof. emeritus dept. rehab. medicine, 2005—, Rosalind Franklin U. Medicine & Sci., 2005. Cons. N.Y.C. Mayor's Adv. Com. for Aged, 1957; asst. prof. SUNY Downstate Med. Sch., Bklyn., 1958-73; med. dir. Schwab Rehab. Hosp., Chgo., 1973-75; acting chief rehab. service VA Center, North Chicgo, 1975-77; chmn. Ill. Phys. Therapy Exam. Com., 1977-78; examiner Am. Bd. Phys. Medicine and Rehab., 1983; sec., dir. Microtherapeutics, Inc., 1972 Editor: Total Cancer Care, 1975; contbr. articles to med. jours.; contbg. editor Ill. Med. Jour., 1983-89 Served to capt. US Army, 1951—53. Recipient Bronze medal Am. Congress Rehab. Medicine, 1974 Fellow: ACP, Am. Acad. Phys. Medicine and Rehab. (Cert. Appreciation 1993); mem.: Chgo. Med. Sch. Alumni Assn. (asst. treas. 1983—93, treas. 1993—95, sec. 1995—97, 1st v.p. 1999, pres. 2001—03, exec. com., Disting. Alumnus award 1980, Presdl. plaque Greater N.Y. chpt.), Chgo. Med. Sch. Faculty Assembly (spkr. 1978—80), Ill. Soc. Phys. Medicine and Rehab. (pres. 1983—84), Ill. Med. Soc. (chmn. workmen's compensation com. 1980—83), Odd Fellows (pres. 1961—62), Phi Lambda Kappa (trustee 1980), Alpha Omega Alpha. Home: 1110 N Lake Shore Dr Chicago IL 60611-5248 Personal E-mail: eugenerogers@att.com. *To render good medical care: Prevent disease, evaluate the patient, treat the condition, educate patient and family, restore function, support group referral, on-line medical knowledge maintenance, never neglect or lie to or for patients, never divulging patient med. info. without consent.*

ROGERS, FRED BAKER, medical educator; b. Trenton, NJ, Aug. 25, 1926; s. Lawrence H. and Eliza C. (Thropp) R. AA, Princeton U., 1947; MD, Temple U., 1948; MS in Medicine, U. Pa., 1954; MPH, Columbia U., 1957; spl. student, Johns Hopkins U., 1962. Diplomate: Am. Bd. Preventive Medicine. Intern Temple U. Hosp., Phila., 1948-49, chief resident physician, 1953-54; USPHS fellow Temple U. Sch. Medicine, 1954-55, asst. prof. preventive medicine, 1956-58, assoc. prof., 1958-60, prof., 1960-90, prof. emeritus, 1991—, chmn. dept., 1970-77. Lectr. epidemiology Columbia U. Sch. Pub. Health, 1957-68, Sch. Nursing, U. Pa., 1964-67; cons. USN Hosp., Phila., 1964-73 Author: A Syllabus of Medical History, 1958, Help-Bringers: Versatile Physicians of N.J, 1960, Epidemiology and Communicable Disease Control, 1963, Studies in Epidemiology, 1965, (with A.R. Sayre) The Healing Art, 1966, (with M.E. Cashel) Your Body is Wonderfully Made, 1974; mem. editorial bd. Am. Jour. Pub. Health, 1967-73; contbr. articles to profl. jours. With M.C. USNR, 1950-53, Korea, capt. (ret.) USNR. Recipient Chapel of Four Chaplains award, 1982. Fellow ACP; mem. AMA (past chmn. sect. preventive medicine), Am. Pub. Health Assn., Royal Soc. Medicine of London (hon.), Sigma Xi, Alpha Omega Alpha, Phi Rho Sigma. Clubs: Campus (Princeton); Franklin Inn (Phila.); Charaka (N.Y.C.); Osler (London). Home: 333 W State St Apt 6K Trenton NJ 08618-5722 Office: Temple U Sch Med Philadelphia PA 19140

ROGERS, GARDNER SPENCER, railroad company executive; b. Bryn Mawr, Pa., Sept. 16, 1926; s. Gardner Spencer and Frances (Lloyd) R.; m. Margaret Elizabeth Windsor, July 18, 1954; children: Ann Rogers Wilbanks, Barbara Rogers Coombs. Student, Episc. Acad., 1940-44, MIT, 1944-45; BS, U. Colo., 1951. Registered ret. profl. engr., Calif. With We. Pacific R.R. Co., San Francisco, 1947-70, engr. costs, valuation and stats., 1964-69, asst. to gen. mgr. planning and control, 1969, asst. gen. mgr., 1970; gen. mgr. Civil & Mech. Maintenance Pty. Ltd., Perth, Australia, 1970-77; mgr. We. Australian ops. Fluor Australia Pty. Ltd., 1971-73, gen. mgr. ry. divsn., 1973-77; gen. mgr. Pilbara Industries, 1971-73; dir. budgets and control Consol. Rail Corp., 1978-79, sr. dir. budgets, planning and control, 1980, dir. corp. planning, 1981-87; cons., 1987—2001. Adv. com. on R.R. property ICC, 1966-70; mem. spl. adv. team R.R. Ofcls. to U.S. Govt., 1962. Mng. trustee Daniel B. Gardner Trust, Chgo.; alt. trustee Cathedral Sq. Found., Perth; vestryman Ch. of Eng., 1971-77, mem. synod and provincial synod, 1973-77, mem. diocesan coun., 1974-77, bd. dirs. sch.'s trust, 1975-77; vestryman, chmn. fin. com., sr. warden St. Mary's-by-the-Sea Episc. Ch., Pacific Grove, Calif., 1989-91; vestryman St. Mark's Episc. Ch., Medford, Oreg.,, 1996-98, 2007—, chmn. stewardship com., jr. warden, 1996-98, personnel com., welcoming com. 1998—. Mem. Instn. Engrs. Australia, Am. C. of C. in Australia (bd. dirs., v.p., chmn. We. Australian exec. com. 1976-77), Swanleigh (chmn. exec. com. 1974-77, coun.), Am. Mgmt. Assn., Am. Ry. Engr. Assn. (sec. com. 11 1983-87), Epis. Diocese of El Camino Real (bd. dirs. 1991-93, lay Eucharistic Min. 1991-94), Diocese of Oreg. (lay Eucaristic Min. 1995—, lic. lay reader 1996—), Ry. and Locomotive Hist. Soc., Soc. of Cin., Mil. Order Loyal Legion (vice comdr.), Colo. Alumni Assn. No. Calif. (pres. 1951-52), Rogue Valley Manor (pres. residents coun. 1999-2000), Berkeley Tennis Club, Pacific Ry. Club, Commonwealth Club, Australian-Am. Club, Alpha Tau Omega (high coun. 1964-68, 82-90). Home: Apt 1020 1200 Mira Mar Ave Medford OR 97504 E-mail: grogersRVM@charter.net.

ROGERS, GARTH WINFIELD, lawyer; b. Fort Collins, Colo., Nov. 4, 1938; s. Harlan Winfield and Helen Marie (Orr) R.; m. Joanne Kathleen Rapp, June 16, 1962; children: Todd Winfield, Christopher Jay, Gregory Lynn, Clay Charles. BS, U. Colo., 1958, LLB, 1962. Bar: Colo. 1962, U.S. Dist. Ct. Colo. 1962. Law clk. to presiding justice U.S. Dist. Ct., Denver, 1962-63; assoc. Allen, Stover & Mitchell, Ft. Collins, 1963-68; ptnr. Allen, Rogers & Vahrenwald, Ft. Collins, 1968-97; ret., 1997. Articles editor Rocky Mountain Law Rev., 1961-62. Past bd. dirs. Salvation Army, Ft. Collins, Ft. Collins C. of C., Home Fed. Savings and Loan, United Way of Ft. Collins, Trinity Luth. Ch., Ft. Collins, Poudre Sch. Dist. Bd. Edn., treas. Water and People, others. Mem. ABA, Colo. Bar Assn., Larimer County Bar Assn. Avocations: nicaragua projects, participative sports, amateur writing, reading. Office: 215 W Oak St Ste 777 Fort Collins CO 80521-2734

ROGERS, GARY FRANCIS, plastic surgeon; s. William D. and Lillian D. Rogers; m. Wendy D. Moser, June 5, 1995; children: Sophia E., Brandt M., Chancey K. MD, MBA, MPH, Tulane U., New Orleans, 1991; JD, U. NC, Chapel Hill, 1997. Diplomate orthop. surgery Am. Bd. Orthop. surgery, 2005, plastic surgery Am. Bd. Plastic Surgery, 2006, cert. added qualification hand surgery Am. Bd. Plastic Surgery, 2006. Staff surgeon Childrens Hosp., Boston, 2002—07. Recipient Alpha Omega Alpha, Tulane U., 1991. Fellow: Am. Soc. Plastic Surgeons (assoc.), Am. Acad. Orthop. Surgeons (assoc.), ACS (assoc.). Achievements include patents for plagiocephaly prevention devices. Office: Children's Hosp Harvard Med 300 Longwood Ave Boston MA 02081 Home Phone: 508-668-5423; Office Phone: 617-355-8509.

ROGERS, HAROLD DALLAS (HAL), congressman; b. Barrier, KY, Dec. 31, 1937; BA, U. Ky., 1962, LLB, 1964. Bar: La. 1964. Assoc. Smith & Blackburn, 1964—67; pvt. practice Somerset, Ky., 1967-69; Commonwealth atty. Pulaski and Rockcastle counties, Ky., 1969-80; mem. US Congress from 5th Ky. dist., 1981—, mem. appropriations com., subcom. homeland security, transp., commerce, justice and state. Mem. Congressional Horse Caucus, Tenn. Valley Authority Caucus. Founder So. Ky. Economic Council. With KY and NC Nat. Guard, 1957—64. Mem.: Ky. Commonwealth Atty. Assn. (past pres.). Republican. Office: US Ho Reps 2406 Rayburn Ho Office Bldg Washington DC 20515-1705 *

ROGERS, HOWARD H., retired chemist; b. NYC, Dec. 26, 1926; s. Julian Herbert and Minnie (Jaffa) R.; m. Barbara Kniaz, Mar. 27, 1954 (div. 1978); children: Lynne, Mark David, Susan; m. Maureen Dohn, Dec. 28, 1978. BS in Chemistry, U. Ill., 1949; PhD in Inorganic Chemistry, MIT, 1953. Research group leader Allis-Chalmers Mfg. Co., West Allis, Wis., 1952-61; sr. tech. specialist Rocketdyne div., Rockwell, Canoga Park, Calif., 1961-70; chief research scientist Martek Instruments, Newport Beach, Calif., 1970-73; scientist Boeing Satellite Systems, Torrance, Calif., 1973—2002; ret., 2002. Contbr. sci. papers to profl. publs. in field. Vol. LA County Disaster Comm. Svc., 1998—. With USN, 1944—46. Recipient Lawrence A. Hyland Patent award Hughes Aircraft Co., 1987. Mem. Electrochem. Soc. (chmn. So. Calif./Nev. sect. 1976-78), Am. Chem. Soc. Achievements include development of nickel-hydrogen battery; 27 US patents. Avocation: amateur radio. Home: 18361 Van Ness Ave Torrance CA 90504-5309 Personal E-mail: howard.rogers@alum.mit.edu. *In my 80 plus years of living experience I have found that these two items are vital: focus on what you intend to do, not what you have already done; complete honesty to yourself and to others in interpreting and reporting results is mandatory.*

ROGERS, JACK DAVID, plant pathologist, educator; b. Point Pleasant, W.Va., Sept. 3, 1937; s. Jack and Thelma Grace R.; m. Belle C. Spencer, June 7, 1958. BS in Biology, Davis and Elkins Coll., 1960; MF, Duke U., 1960; PhD, U. Wis., 1963. From asst. prof. to prof. Wash. State U., Pullman, 1963-72, chmn. dept. plant pathology, 1986-99, Regents prof., 2007—. Contbr. articles to profl. jours. Recipient Eminent Faculty award, Wash. State U., 2006. Mem. Mycol. Soc. Am. (pres. 1977-78, William H. Weston Tchg. Excellence award 1992, Disting. Mycologist award 2004), Am. Phytopathol. Soc., Bot. Soc. Am., Brit. Mycol. Soc. Office Phone: 509-335-9541.

ROGERS, JAMES BEELAND, JR., (JIM ROGERS), retired investment company executive; b. Balt., Oct. 19, 1942; s. James Beeland and Ernestine Barbara (Brewer) Rogers; m. Paige Parker; 1 child, Hilton Augusta. BA cum laude, Yale U., 1964; BA with honors, Balliol Coll., Oxford U., Eng., 1966, MA in Politics, Philosophy, Econs. Investment analyst Bache & Co., NYC, 1968-69, R. Gilder & Co., NYC, 1969-70; asst. to chmn. Neuberger & Berman, NYC, 1970-71; with Arnhold and S. Belichroeder, Inc., 1971-73; exec. v.p. Soros Fund Mgmt., NYC, 1973-80; chmn. bd. dirs. Rogers Holdings, 1980—. Adj. prof. Columbia U. Sch. Bus., 1983—85, prof. fin., 1986—90, vis. prof., 1994—96. Host (TV series) The Profit Motive with Jim Rogers, 1989—90, Guinness Record Motorcycle Trip Around World, 1990—92, co-host, commentator various TV shows, 1992—; author: Investment Biker: On the Road with Jim Rogers, 1994, Guiness Record Drive Around the World on Millennium Adventure, 1999—2001, Adventure Capitalist: The Ultimate Road Trip, 2003, Hot Commodities: How Anyone Can Invest Profitably in the World's Best Market, 2004. With US Army, 1966—68. Achievements include being listed 3 times in Guinness Book of World Records for Henley Regatta Race, for 100,000 mile motorcycle trip across six continents in 1990-92, for automobile trip around world, 1999-2001. Home: 352 Riverside Dr New York NY 10025-2731 E-mail: jim@jimrogers.com.

ROGERS, JAMES DEVITT, judge; b. Mpls., May 5, 1929; s. Harold Neil and Dorothy (Devitt) R.; m. Leanna Morrison, Oct. 19, 1968. AB, Dartmouth Coll., 1951; JD, U. Minn., 1954. Bar: Minn. 1954, U.S. Supreme Ct. 1983. Assoc. Johnson & Sands, Mpls., 1956-60; sole practice Mpls., 1960-62; judge Mpls. Municipal and Dist. Ct., 1959-91. Mem. faculty Nat. Judicial Coll. Bd. dirs. Mpls. chpt. Am. Red Cross, chmn. service to mil. families and vets. com.; bd. dirs. Minn. Safety Coun., St. Paul, 1988-91; founding dir., sec. Forest Landowners Tax Coun. Served sgt. U.S. Army, 1954-56. Mem. ABA (chmn. nat. conf. spl. ct. judge, spl. com. housing and urban devel. law, traffic ct. program com., chmn. criminal justice sect., jud. adminstrn. div.), Nat. Jud. Coll. (bd. dirs.), Nat. Christmas Tree Grower's Assn. (pres. 1976-78), Mpls. Athletic Club. Congregationalist. Office: 14110 Prince Pl Minnetonka MN 55345-3027

ROGERS, JAMES EUGENE, energy executive; b. Birmingham, Ala., Sept. 20, 1947; s. James E. and Margaret (Whatley) R.; m. Robyn McGill (div.); children: Chrissi, Kara, Ben; m. Mary Anne Boldrick, Oct. 28, 1977. BBA, U. Ky., 1970, JD, 1974; LLD (hon.), Ind. State U.; DHL (hon.), Queens Univ., Charlotte NC. Reporter Lexington (Ky.) Herald Leader, 1967—70; asst. atty. gen. Commonwealth Ky., Louisville; asst. chief trial atty. Fed. Energy Regulation Commn., Washington, dep. gen. counsel litigation and enforcement; law clk. to presiding justice Supreme Ct Ky., Louisville; ptnr. Akin, Gump, Strauss, Hauer & Feld LLP, Dallas, Akin Gump Strauss Hauer & Feld LLP, Houston, 1985-86; exec. v.p. Enron Gas Pipeline Group, 1986—88; pres., CEO, chmn. PSI Resources, Inc, 1988—94, Cinergy Corp. (formerly PSI Resources, Inc.), Cin., 1994—2006; pres., CEO Duke Energy Corp., Charlotte, NC, 2006—07, chmn., pres., CEO, 2007—. 2nd vice chmn. Edison Electric Inst., 2004—05, vice chmn., 2005—06, chmn., 2006—; bd. dirs. Chesapeake Corp., 1999—2004, Duke Energy Corp., 2006—, Fifth Third Bancorp, Fifth Third Bank, Am. Gas Assn., US C. of C., Bus. Roundtable, Nat. Coal Coun.; bd. dir., mem. exec. com. Nuclear Energy Inst. Trustee Nat. Symphony Orch.; bd. dirs. Cin. Mus. Assn., The Nature Conservancy-Ind. chpt., U. Ky. Bus. Partnership Found. Named to Hall of Fame Gatton Coll. Bus. & Econ., Univ. Ky., Hall of Fame Coll. Law, Univ. Ky.; recipient Disting. Svc. Citation, NCCJ, 2004, Keystone Ctr. in Leadership in Industry award, 2005, Ronald McDonald House Lifetime Achievement award, 2005, Human Rels. award, Am. Jewish Com., 2006, Ellis Island Medal of Honor, Nat. Ethnic Coalition of Org., 2007. Mem. Ky. Bar Assn., D.C. Bar Assn., Meridian Hills Country Club, Crooked Stick Golf Club, Queen City Club, Met. Club. Baptist. Avocations: tennis, bicycling, skiing, golf. Office: Duke Energy Corp 526 S Church St Charlotte NC 28202 also: Edison Electric Inst 701 Pennsylvania Ave NW Washington DC 20004 *

ROGERS, JAMES FREDERICK, banker, management consultant; b. Centerville, Iowa, June 27, 1935; s. John W. and Mildred Holly (Morris) R.; m. Janet L. Marsden, July 27, 1957; children: Jennifer Burke, John William. AB, U. Mo., 1957; postgrad., Rutgers U. Grad. Sch. Banking, 1970-72. With Am. Security and Trust Co., Washington, 1959-85, exec. v.p., 1980-83. Bd. dirs., pres. Am. Security Corp., 1983-85; cons. B.E.I.-Golembe Assocs., 1985-93; chmn. Nat. Bank of No. Va., 1988-89. Commr. Arlington County Planning Commn., 1979-80; asst. treas. Kennedy Ctr. Performing Arts; pres., trustee Leonard Wood Found.; trustee Friends of Nat. Zoo, Greater Washington Rsch. Ctr., Washington Dulles Task Force, Arena Stage, Sch. Commerce U. Va. Officer AUS, 1958-59. Mem. D.C. Bankers Assn. (pres. 1984-85), Davenport Soc., U. Mo., Met. Club (Washington), Chevy Chase Club. Presbyterian. Home: 4201 38th Rd N Arlington VA 22207-4554 Personal E-mail: jroger@comcast.net.

ROGERS, JAMES GORDON, JR., art educator; b. Dec. 16, 1944; AB in English, U. Mo., 1967, MA in Art History and Archaeology, 1983, PhD, 1989. Asst. prof. art history William Woods Coll., Fulton, Mo., 1989-90; prof. art history Savannah Coll. Art & Design, Ga., 1990-92, Fla. So. Coll., Lakeland, Fla., 1992—. Adj. prof. Sch. Arch. and Cmty. Design, U. S. Fla., 1995—2002; cons. Design Ctr., 1977—84, chair dept. art and art history; dir. art & art history program Melvin Art Gallery, 1999—2006; chair divsn. fine, applied and performing arts Fla. So. Coll., 2007—; lectr. in field. Contbr. articles to profl. jours. Active Nat. Holocaust Meml. Mus.; past bd. dirs. Mid-Mo. chpt. Am. Heart Assn.; past bd. dirs. Sta. KBIA Pub. Radio, Columbia, Mo., Columbia Art League, co-chmn. fin. com.; past mem. peer rev. com. Fla. Arts Coun. Mem.: AAUP, Hist. Lakeland Inc. (bd. dirs.), Coll. Art Assn., Soc. Archtl. Historians, Am. Soc. Hispanic Art Hist. Studies. Office: Fla So Coll Lake Hollingsworth Dr Lakeland FL 33803 Home Phone: 863-619-5494; Office Phone: 863-680-4223. E-mail: jrogers@flsouthern.edu.

ROGERS, JOEL EDWARD, law, sociology and political science educator; b. Long Ranch, NJ, Mar. 19, 1952; s. Edward Franklin and Ann (Flemming) Rogers; m. Sarah Siskind, Dec. 2, 1980; children: Helen, Sophia. BA, Yale U., 1972, JD, 1976; MA, Princeton U., 1978, PhD, 1984. Bar: NY, US Ct. Appeals (7th and 8th cirs.). Assoc. prof. law U. Miami, 1986—87; asst. prof. law and sociology U. Wis., Madison, 1987—88, assoc. prof. law and sociology, 1988—90, prof. law and sociology, 1990—; affiliate Inst. for Rsch. on Poverty, Madison, 1988—; assoc. dir. A. Eugene Havens Ctr., Madison, 1988—; co-dir. Disputes Processing Rsch. Program, Madison, 1988—; dir., founder Ctr. on Wis. Strategy, Madison, 1993—; prof. law, polit. sci. and sociology U. Wis., Madison, 1991—. Co-author (book): Right Turn: The Decline of the Democrats and the Future of American Politics, 1986, On Democracy, 1983; co-editor: Works Councils: Consultation, Representation, and Cooperation in Industrial Relations, 1995; author: (book) America's Forgotten MajorityWhy the White Working Class Still Matters, 2000, Working Capital: Using the Power of Labor's Pensions, 2001; contbr. articles to profl. jour., book. Exec. com. chair New Party, NYC, 1992—, Sustainable America, Madison, 1994—; bd. chair Ctr. for a New Democracy, Washington, 1992—. Office: U Wis Law Sch 975 Bascom Mall Madison WI 53706-1399 Office Phone: 608-262-4266. Business E-Mail: jrogers@cows.org.

ROGERS, JOHN L., III, lawyer; b. Balt., Dec. 30, 1948; BA with high distinction, U. Va., 1970; JD magna cum laude, Harvard U., 1973. Bar: Ill. 1974. Law clerk to Judge Warren H. Young Dist. Ct. V.I., 1973-74; ptnr. Hopkins & Sutter, Chgo., Foley & Lardner LLP, Chgo. Recipient Am.'s Leading Bus. Lawyers, Chambers USA. Mem. ABA, Ill. State Bar Assn., Phi Beta Kappa. Office: Foley & Lardner LLP 321 N Clark Ste 2800 Chicago IL 60610 Office Phone: 312-832-4915. Office Fax: 312-832-4700. Business E-Mail: jrogers@foley.com.

ROGERS, JOHN MARSHALL, judge, educator; b. Rochester, NY, June 26, 1948; s. Harry Lovejoy III and Virginia Kathryn (Meyers) R.; m. Ying Juan Xiong, 1990. BA, Stanford U., 1970; JD, U. Mich., 1974. Bar: DC 1975, Ky. 1980, US Ct. Appeals, US Supreme Ct. Commd. USAR, 1970; appellate atty. civil div. US Dept. Justice, Washington, 1974-78; asst. prof. U. Ky., Lexington, 1978-81, assoc. prof., 1981-86, prof., 1986—2002, prof. emeritus, 2002—; cir. judge US Ct. Appeals (6th cir.), 2002—. Vis. prof. Civil Divsn. US Dept. Justice, Washington, 1983-85; Fulbright lectr. Fgn. Affairs Coll., Beijing, 1987-88, Zhongshan U., Guangzhou, People's Republic of China, 1994-95; spl. counsel impeachment com. Ky. Ho. of Reps., 1991. Author: Internat. Law and U.S. Law, 1999; contbr. articles to profl. jours. Mem. Coun. on Fgn. Rels., Am. Law Inst., Order of Coif, Phi Beta Kappa. Office: 532 Potter Stewart US Courthouse 100 E 5th St Cincinnati OH 45202-3988 also: Cmty Truste Bank Bldg 100 E Vine St Ste 1442 Lexington KY 40507 *

ROGERS, JOHN W., JR., investment company executive; s. John W. Sr. and Jewel (Mankarious) R.; m. Sharon Fairley. AB in Econs., Princeton U., NJ, 1980. Broker William Blair & Co.; founder, chmn., CEO Ariel Capital Mgmt., LLC, Chgo., 1983—. Bd. dirs. Aon Corp., Exelon Corp., McDonald's Corp., Ariel Capital Mgmt., LLC, and Ariel Mutual Funds.

Columnist: Forbes mag. Trustee U. Chgo.; dir. Chgo. Urban League; alumnus Leadership Greater Chgo. Named one of 50 for the Future, Time mag., 1994; recipient Disting. Fellow award, Leadership Greater Chgo., 2000, Most Influential Black Americans, Ebony mag., 2005. Office: Ariel Capital Mgmt # 2900 200 E Randolph St Chicago IL 60601-6436

ROGERS, JOSEPH A., mental health association administrator; With Mental Health Assn Southeastern Pa, Phila., 1984—, exec. dir., 1997—; founder Self-Help & Advocacy Resource Exch. (Project SHARE), 1984. Mem. Congl. Task Force on the Rights & Empowerment of Americans with Disabilities; former chmn. Pa Protection & Advocacy Inc. Recipient Heinz award for the Human Condition, 2005. Office: Mental Health Assn Southeastern Pa 1211 Chestnut St Philadelphia PA 19107

ROGERS, JOSEPH SHEPPERD, art educator; s. James Webb and Anna Phillips (Clarke) Rogers. BA, Greensboro Coll., NC, 1967; MA, U. NC, Greensboro, 1969. Dir. Garfinckles, Washington, 1972—74, Fettings, Balt., 1974—75, Torpedo Factory Arts Ctr., 1976—96; tchr. Corcoran Pub. Sch., Washington. Home: PO Box 1268 Landover MD 20785-0268

ROGERS, JUDITH ANN WILSON, federal judge; b. NYC, 1939; AB cum laude, Radcliffe Coll., 1961; LLB, Harvard U., 1964; LLM, U. Va., 1988; LLD (hon.), DC Sch. Law, 1992. Bar: DC 1965. Law clk. Juvenile Ct. DC, 1964-65; asst. U.S. atty. DC, 1965-68; trial atty. San Francisco Neighborhood Legal Assistance Found., 1968-69; atty. assoc. atty. gen.'s office US Dept. Justice, 1969-71, atty. criminal divsn., 1969-71; gen. counsel Congl. Commn. on Organization of D.C. Govt., 1971-72; coordinator legis. program Office of Dep. Mayor DC, 1972-74, spl. asst. to mayor for legis., 1974-79, corp. counsel, 1979-83; assoc. judge DC Ct. Appeals, 1983-88, chief judge, 1988-94; judge US Ct. Appeals (DC cir.), 1994—. Mem. DC Law Revision Commn., 1979-83; mem. grievance com. US Dist. Ct. DC, 1982-83; mem. exec. com. Conf. Chief Justices, 1993-94. Bd. dirs. Wider Opportunities for Women, 1972-74; mem. vis. com. Harvard U. Sch. Law, 1984-90; trustee Radcliffe Coll., 1982-88. Recipient citation for work on DC Self-Govt. Act, 1973, Disting. Pub. Svc. award DC Govt., 1983, award Nat. Bar Assn., 1989; named Woman Lawyer of Yr., Women's Bar Assn. DC, 1990. Fellow ABA; mem. DC Bar, Nat. Assn. Women Judges, Conf. Chief Justices (bd. dirs. 1988-94), Am. Law Inst., Phi Beta Kappa. Office: US Ct Appeals Fed Cir 717 Madison Pl NW Washington DC 20001-2866 also: US Courthouse 333 Constitution Ave NW STE 5800 Washington DC 20001 *

ROGERS, JUSTIN TOWNER, JR., retired utility company executive; b. Sandusky, Ohio, Aug. 4, 1929; s. Justin Towner and Barbara Eloise (Larkin) R. AB cum laude, Princeton U., 1951; JD, U. Mich., 1954. Bar: Ohio 1954. Assoc. Wright, Harlor, Purpus, Morris & Arnold, Columbus, 1956-58; with Ohio Edison Co., Akron, 1958-93, v.p., then exec. v.p., 1970-79, pres., 1980-91, chmn. bd., 1991-93; ret., 1993. Past mem. coal adv. bd. Internat. Energy Agy. Past pres., trustee Akron Cmty. Trusts, Akron Child Guidance Ctr.; past chmn. Akron Assoc. Health Agys., U. Akron Assocs., Ohio Electric Utility Inst.; past chmn., trustee, Akron Gen. Health Sys.; trustee Sisler McFawn Found.; former trustee Stan Hywet Hall & Gardens, VNS-Hospice Found.; past dir. Edison Elec. Inst., Elec. Power Rsch. Inst., Assn. of Edison Illuminating Co.'s. Mem. Portage Country Club, Mayflower Club, Rockwell Springs Trout Club (Castalia, Ohio), Princeton Club (NYC), Columbus Beach Club, Phi Delta Phi, Beta Gamma Sigma.

ROGERS, KATHARINE MUNZER, retired English language educator, writer; b. NYC, June 6, 1932; d. Martin and Jean (Thompson) Munzer; B.A. summa cum laude, Barnard Coll., 1952; Fulbright scholar, Newnham Coll., Cambridge U., 1952-53; Ph.D., Columbia U., 1957; m. Kenneth C. Rogers, Aug. 4, 1956; children: Margaret, Christopher, Thomas. Instr. English, Skidmore Coll., Saratoga Springs, N.Y., 1954-55, Cornell U., 1955-57; lectr. to prof. English, Bklyn. Coll., 1958-88; mem. doctoral faculty CUNY, 1972-88. Author: The Troublesome Helpmate: A History of Misogyny in Literature, 1966; William Wycherley, 1972; Feminism in Eighteenth Century England, 1982; Frances Burney: The World of "Female Difficulties", 1990, The Cat and the Human Imagination, 1998, L. Frank Baum: Creator of Oz: A Biography, 2002, First Friend: A History of Dogs and Humans, 2005, Cat, 2006. Editor anthologies: The Signet Classic Book of 18th and 19th Century British Drama; Selected Writings of Samuel Johnson, 1981, The Meridian Anthology of Early American Women Writers, 1991, The Meridian Anthology of Restoration & Eighteenth Century Plays by Women, 1994; co-editor: (with William McCarthy) The Meridian Anthology of Early Women Writers: British Literary Women from Aphra Behn to Maria Edgeworth, 1987. Contbr. articles to profl. jours.

ROGERS, KENNY (KENNETH SCOTT ROGERS), professional baseball player; b. Savannah, Ga., Nov. 10, 1964; Student, Plant City, Fla. Pitcher Texas Rangers, 1989-95, 2000—02, 2004—05, NY Yankees, 1996—97, Oakland A's, 1998—99, New York Mets, 1999, Toronto Blue Jays, 1999, Minnesota Twins, 2003, Detroit Tigers, 2006—. Named to Am. League All-Star Team, 1995, 2004, 2005; pitched perfect game against Calif. Angels, 1994, recipient Am. League Gold Glove Award, 2000, 2004, 2005, 2006; 200 career wins, 2006. Achievements include joining top five consecutive scoreless innings in playoffs, 2006. Office: Detroit Tigers 2100 Woodward Ave Detroit MI 48201 *

ROGERS, LAURENCE STEVEN, lawyer; b. NYC, Jan. 19, 1950; s. Henry and Frances (Kanarek) R.; m. Iris S. Rosen, July 2, 1977; children: Matthew Benjamin, Heather Aimee. BSEE with distinction, Cornell U., 1972; JD, NYU, 1975. Bar: NY 1976, US Dist. Ct. (ea. and so. dists.) NY 1976, US Ct. Appeals (Fed. cir.) 1983, US Supreme Ct. 1999, US Patent and Trademark Office. Ptnr. Fish & Neave, NYC, 1986-2004, Ropes & Gray, NYC, 2005—. Mem. ABA, NYC Bar Assn., NY Intellectual Propert Law Assn., Fed. Cir. Bar Assn., Phi Kappa Phi, Eta Kappa Nu, Tau Beta Pi. Home: 15 Aspen Rd Scarsdale NY 10583-7346 Office: Ropes & Gray LLP 1251 Avenue Of The Americas Fl 50 New York NY 10020-1105 Office Phone: 212-596-9033. Business E-Mail: laurence.rogers@ropesgray.com.

ROGERS, LEE FRANK, radiologist; b. Colchester, Vt., Sept. 24, 1934; s. Watson Frank and Marguerite Mortimer (Cole) R.; m. Donna Mae Brinker, June 20, 1956; children: Michelle, Cynthia, Christopher, Matthew. BS, Northwestern U., 1956, MD, 1959. Commd. 2d lt. U.S. Army, 1959, advanced through grades to maj., 1967; rotating intern Walter Reed Gen. Hosp., 1959-60; resident radiology Fitzsimons Gen. Hosp., 1960-63; ret., 1967; radiologist Bapt. Meml. Hosp., San Antonio, 1967-68, U. Tex. Med. Sch., San Antonio, 1968-71, dir. residency tng., radiologist Houston, 1972-74; prof., chmn. dept. radiology Northwestern U. Med. Sch., Chgo., 1974-95; editor-in-chief Am. Jour. Roentgenology, Winston-Salem, NC, 1995—2003; prof. radiology U. Ariz. Health Scis. Ctr., 2003—. Fellow Am. Coll. Radiology (past pres.), Am. Roentgen Ray Soc. (past pres.); mem. Assn. Univ. Radiologists (past pres.), Radiol. Soc. N.Am., Am. Bd. Radiology (past pres.), Alpha Omega Alpha. Episcopalian. Home: 8235 N Fairway View Dr Tucson AZ 85742 Office Phone: 520-626-6794. Personal E-mail: lfrogers@comcast.net. *The source of most problems is previous solutions.*

ROGERS, LEONARD DAVID, lawyer; b. Norton, Va., Oct. 13, 1962; s. Jack D. and Marylou (Sturgill) R.; m. Donna Geneva Salyers, Oct. 11, 1991. BA in History, U. Va., Wise, 1985; JD, U. Tenn., 1988. Bar: Va. 1988, U.S. Dist. Ct. (we. dist.) Va. 1989, U.S. Dist. Ct. (we. dist.) Va. 1989, U.S. Ct. Appeals (4th cir.) 1989, U.S. Bankruptcy Ct. 1989. Assoc. Mullins, Thomason & Harris, Norton, 1988-90; ptnr. Cline, Adkins, Cline & Rogers, Norton, 1990-95; pvt. practice, 1996—. Mem. Forward Wise County, 1989. Mem. ABA, Va. Bar Assn., Va. State Bar, Va. Trial Lawyers Assn., Wise County C. of C. Avocations: golf, mountain biking, travel. Office: Leonard D Rogers PC PO Box 1097 Wise VA 24293-1097

ROGERS, MAL DAVID, JR., chemical engineer; b. July 26, 1922; BSChemE, U. Okla., 1948, M of Chem. Engring., 1949; cert. in nuc. engring., Pa. State U. and Argonne Nat. Lab., 1957. Chem. engr. Pure Oil, Wyo., 1949-51, Shell Chem., Deer Park, Tex., 1951-56; sr. chem., nuclear engr. Gen. Dynamics, Ft. Worth, 1956-59; sr. chem. engr., tech. staff Tex. Instruments, Dallas, 1959-90. Lt. USAF, 1942-45. Decorated DFC, Purple Heart; recipient Air medals with 2 oak leaf clusters USAF. Mem. N.Y. Acad. Scis. Home: 5117 Greensboro Dr Sachse TX 75048-3603

ROGERS, MALCOLM AUSTIN, museum director, art historian; b. Scarborough, Yorkshire, Eng., Oct. 3, 1948; s. James Eric and Frances Anne (Elsey) R. BA in English Language & Literature, Oxford U.; MA, Magdalen Coll., U. Oxford, Eng., 1976; DPhil, Christ Ch., Oxford U., 1976. Asst. keeper Nat. Portrait Gallery, London, 1974-83, dep. dir., 1983—85, dep. keeper, 1985—94; Ann and Graham Gund dir. Mus. Fine Arts, Boston, 1994—. Noted authority on 16th, 17th & early 18th century portraits. Author: Blue Guide: Museums and Galleries of London, 1983; contbr. articles to profl. publs. Mem. Harvard overseers' com. Visit the Art Mus.; trustee Found. for the Arts, Nagoya, Japan, Wednesday Evening Club of 1777, Club of Odd Volumes. Comdr. British Empire, 2004. Fellow Soc. Antiquaries; mem. Thursday Evening Club of 1846, Chevalier de L'Ordre des Arts et Lettres, Comml. Club Boston. Avocations: wine and food, travel, opera. Home: 540 Chestnut Hill Ave Brookline MA 02445-4155 Office: Mus Fine Arts 465 Huntington Ave Boston MA 02115-5597 E-mail: mrogers@mfa.org.

ROGERS, MARGARET ELLEN JONSSON, civic worker; b. Dallas, Aug. 7, 1938; d. John Erik and Margaret Elizabeth (Fonde) Jonsson; m. Robert D. Rogers; children: Emily, Erik, Laura. Student, Skidmore Coll., 1956—57, So. Meth. U., 1957—60. Civic worker, Dallas. Dir. Sta. KRLD radio, Dallas, 1970-74; dir. 1st Nat. Bank, Dallas, 1976-85, vice-chmn. dirs. trust com.; trustee Meth. Hosps., 1972-82, mem. exec. com., 1977-82, corp. bd. mem., 1990-94, mem. fin. com., 1990-93; bd. dirs. Lamplighter Sch., 1967—; past mem. vis. com. dept. psychology MIT; mem. vis. com. Stanford U. Librs., 1984-90; bd. dirs. Callier Ctr. Communication Disorders, 1967-90, Winston Sch., 1973-85; bd. dirs., mem. exec. com. Episc. Sch., 1976-83; chmn. Crystal Charity Ball; co-chmn. nat. major gifts com. Stanford Centennial Campaign; bd. dirs. Children's Med. Ctr., Hope Cottage Childrens' Bur., Baylor Dental Sch., Dallas Health and Sci. Mus., Dallas YWCA, Day Nursery Assn.; mem. devel. bd. U. Tex., Dallas, 1988-90; bd. govs. The Dallas Found., 1988-95, chmn. investment com. 1991-92; trustee So. Meth. U., mem. investment com., 1988—, chmn. investment com., 1992-99; mem. vis. com. Dedman Coll., 1989-90; life trustee Dallas Mus. Art, mem. investment com.; mem. collectors com. Nat. Gallery Art; bd. dirs. Dallas Arboretum, 1991-92; trustee, mem. fin. com. Monterey Bay Aquarium, 1995—, chair devel. com., 1995-2000, mem. fin. com., 2000—. Mem. internat. coun. Mus. Modern Art; pres. MJR Fund, Jonsson Found. Margaret Jonsson Charlton Hosp. of Dallas named in her honor, 1973. Mem.: The Lamplighter Sch. (life).

ROGERS, MARK CHARLES, physician, entrepreneur, anesthesiologist, pediatrician, educator; b. NYC, Oct. 25, 1942; m. Elizabeth Rogers. BA, Columbia U., 1964; MD, SUNY, Syracuse, 1969; MBA, U. Pa., 1991; PhD (hon.), U. Ljubljana Slovenia, 1995. Diplomate Am. Bd. Anesthesiology (examiner 1982-96), Am. Bd. Pediatrics. Intern Mass. Gen. Hosp., Boston, 1969-70, resident, 1973-75, Boston Children's Hosp., 1970-71; fellow Duke U. Med. Ctr., Durham, NC, 1971-73; asst. prof. dept. anesthesiology and critical care medicine Johns Hopkins U., Balt., 1977-79, assoc. prof., 1979-80, prof., chmn. dept., 1980-93, assoc. dean Sch. Medicine, 1990-93, dir. pediatric ICU, 1977-93; CEO Duke Hosp. and Health Network, 1993-96; sr. v.p. Perkin Elmer, Wilton, Conn., 1996-98; pres. Paramount Capital, NYC, 1998—2002; chmn. Cardiome Pharma, 2002—, Adherex Pharma, 2002—04, Aptamera, 2004—05, Bradmer Ventures, LLC, 2004—, Bradmer Pharm., 2005—. Pres. Critical Care Found., Balt., 1981-96; cons. WHO, Bangkok, 1982-83. Editor in chief: Yearbook of Critical Care, 1983-96, Textbook of Pediatric Intensive Care, 1987, 91, 96, Principles and Practices of Anesthesiology, 1990; editor: Perioperative Management, 1989, dep. editor in chief Critical Care Medicine Jour., 1990-96. Maj. U.S. Army, 1975-77. Recipient Club of Mainz award, Mainz, Fed. Republic of Germany, 1981, award Assn. Univ. Anesthetists, 1980; Fulbright scholar, Ljubljana, Yugoslavia, 1990. Mem. NAS, Inst. Medicine. E-mail: mrogers@bradmer.com.

ROGERS, MARK NICHOLL, lawyer; b. Rochester, NY, June 21, 1965; s. Howard James and Nancy Ellen (Nicholl) R.; m. Karen Marie Rettig, Mar. 14, 1992. BA, Brown U., 1987; JD, NYU, 1992. Bar: Ariz. 1992, U.S. Dist. Ct. Ariz. 1993. Assoc. Fennemore Craig, P.C., Phoenix, 1992-95, Quarles & Brady, Phoenix, 1996-99; v.p., gen. counsel Excell Global Svcs., Inc., Tempe, Ariz., 1999—2001; gen. counsel Integrated Info. Sys., Inc., Tempe, Ariz., 2001—03; corp. counsel Insight Enterprises Inc., Tempe, Ariz., 2003—. Com. mem. Childrens Cancer Ctr. Card Project, Phoenix, 1993—. Mem. ABA (bus. law sect., fed. regulation of securities com. and corp. practice com.), Ariz. State Bar, Maricopa County Bar Assn., Brown Club of Phoenix, Phi Beta Kappa. Avocations: golf, photography, travel. Office: Insight Enterprises Inc 1305 W Auto Dr Tempe AZ 85284 Office Phone: 480-333-3000. Office Fax: 480-760-9068.

ROGERS, MICHAEL ALAN, writer; b. Santa Monica, Calif., Nov. 29, 1950; s. Don Easterday and Mary Othilda (Gilbertson) R.; m. Donna Rini, Oct. 9, 2000. BA in Creative Writing, Stanford U., Calif., 1972. Assoc. editor Rolling Stone Mag., San Francisco, 1972-76; editor-at-large Outside mag., San Francisco, 1976-78; vis. lectr. fiction U. Calif., Davis, 1980; sr. writer Newsweek mag., San Francisco, 1983—; mng. editor Newsweek InterActive, San Francisco, 1993-97; exec. prodr. broadband divsn. The Washington Post Co., 1995-96; v.p. Washingtonpost.Newsweek Interactive, 1996—2004. Editor, gen. mgr. Newsweek.MSNBC.com, NYC, 1998-2004, columnist, MSNBC.com, 2005—; prin. Practical Futurist, 2005-; futurist-in-residence NY Times Co., 2006-. Author: Mindfogger, 1973, Biohazard, 1977, Do Not Worry About The Bear, 1979, Silicon Valley, 1982, Forbidden Sequence, 1988; contbr. articles to mags., newspapers. Recipient Disting. Sci. Writing award AAAS, 1976, Best Feature Articles award Computer Press Assn., 1987, MIN Mag. Digital Hall of Fame, 2007. Mem. Author Guild, Sierra Club. Achievements include patents for for multimedia storytelling technology. Avocations: travel, hiking. Address: 535 Dean St # 704 Brooklyn NY 11217 Business E-Mail: mr@practicalfuturist.com.

ROGERS, MICHAEL BRUCE, orthodontist; b. Augusta, Ga., Aug. 25, 1945; s. Bruce Latimer and Dorothy (Baird) R.; m. Elizabeth Bennett, Dec. 21, 1968; children: Bruce, Kay, Alison, Lisa. Student, Emory U., 1963-65, DDS, 1969; cert. in orthodontics, Med. Coll. Ga., 1973. Diplomate Am. Bd. Orthodontists. Pvt. practice orthodontia, Augusta, 1973—. Part-time asst. clin. prof. Sch. Dentistry, Med. Coll. Ga., Augusta, 1973—. Capt. Dental Corps U.S. Army, 1971-73. Decorated Army Commendation medal. Fellow: Ga. Acad. Dental Practice, The Internat. Acad. Dentists, Pierre Fauchard Acad., Ga. Dental Assn. (hon.; spkr. ho. of dels. 1999—2004, v.p. 2004—05, pres.-elect 2005—06, pres. 2006), Internat. Acad. Dental Studies, Am. Coll. Dentists; mem.: Ea. Dist. Dental Soc. (pres. 1982—83), Med. Coll. Ga. Orthodontic Alumni Assn. (pres. 1981—83), Ga. Assn. Orthodontists (v.p. 1983—84, pres. 1984—85, exemplary svc. award), So. Assn. Orthodontists (spokesperson, sec.-treas. 1993—95, dir. 1995, pres. 2000, Disting. Svc. award 2001—), Am. Assn. Orthodontists (Ga. del., chmn. mem., ethics and jud. conderns, spkr. of house 1995—97, trustee 2002—), ADA (del.), Omicron Kappa Upsilon, Psi Omega (pres. 1967—68). Roman Catholic. Home: 3214 Candace Dr Augusta GA 30909-3259 Office: 3545 Wheeler Rd Augusta GA 30909-6517

ROGERS, MIKE (MICHAEL J. ROGERS), congressman; b. Livonia, Mich., June 2, 1963; m. Diane Rogers; 1 child. BA in Sociology and Criminal Justice, Adrian Coll., 1985. Spl. agt. FBI, 1989—94; small bus. owner; mem. Mich. Senate from 26th dist., 1995-2000; vice chmn. judiciary com. Mich. Senate, mem. fin. svc., human resources, labor and vet affairs coms., mem. reappropriations com., mem. tech. and energy commn., mem. banking and fin. com.; mem. US Congress from Mich. 8th dist., Washington, 2001—; mem. fin. svcs. and transp. coms.; mem. Com. on Energy and Commerce. Bd. trustees Cleary Coll., Mich. Served as 2nd Lt. rapid deployment US Army, 1985—88. Recipient Nextel Prepared award, Nextel Comm. Inc., 2004, ITS Congl. Champion awrad, Intelligent Transp. Systems Am., 2005, Joseph M. Magliochetti Industry Champion award, Motor and Equipment Manufacturers Assn., 2005. Mem.: Soc. Former Spl. Agents for FBI, Home Builders Assn., Livingston County, Mich., Am. Heart Assn. Republican. Meth. Office: US Congress 133 Cannon HOB Washington DC 20515-2208 also: District Office 1327 E Michigan Ave Lansing MI 48912 Office Phone: 202-225-4872, 517-702-8000. Office Fax: 202-225-5820, 517-702-8642. *

ROGERS, MIKE, congressman; b. Hammond, Ind., July 16, 1958; m. Beth Rogers; children: Emily, Evan, Elliot. BA in Polit. Sci., Jacksonville State U., 1981, MPA, 1985; JD, U. Birmingham, 1991. Dir., dislocated worker's project United Way of Etowah County; community rep., psychiatric counselor Northeast Ala. Regional Med. Ctr.; atty. Bolt, Isom, Jackson and Bailey; assoc. then ptnr. Rogers, Young, Wollstein and Hughes; mem. Ala. Ho. Reps., 1994—2002; congressman 3rd Dist. Ala. U.S. Ho. Reps., 2003—. Mem. Calhoun County Commn., 1987—91; active State Rep. Exec. Com., 1990—. Republican. Baptist. Office: US Ho of Reps 514 Cannon Ho Office Bldg Washington DC 20515-0103 *

ROGERS, MIMI, actress; b. Coral Gables, Fla., Jan. 27, 1956; m. Jim Rogers, 1977 (div. 1980); m. Tom Cruise, May 9, 1987 (div. 1990); m. Chris Ciaffa, Mar. 20, 2003; children: Lucy Julia, Charlie. Appeared in films Blue Skies Again, 1983, Gung Ho, 1985, Someone to Watch over Me, 1987, Street Smart, 1987, Hider in the House, 1989, The Mighty Quinn, 1989, Desperate Hours, 1990, The Palermo Connections, 1990, The Doors, 1991, The Rapture, 1991, Dark Horse, 1992, The Player, 1992, Monkey Trouble, 1994, Far From Home: The Adventures of Yellow Dog, 1995, Lost in Space, 1998, Austin Powers: International Man of Mystery, 1997, Seven Girlfriends, 1999, Ginger Snaps, 2000, The Upgrade, 2000, Dumb and Dumberer: When Harry Met Lloyd, 2003, Seeing Other People, 2004, The Gunman, 2004, The Door in the Floor, 2004, Dancing in Twilight, 2005, others; appeared on TV series The Rousters, 1983-84, Paper Dolls, 1984, The Geena Davis Show, 2000, The Loop, 2006-; appeared on TV spls. and pilots; TV movies include Divorce Wars, 1982, Deadlock, 1991, Fourth Story, 1991, Ladykiller, 1992, A Kiss to Die For, 1993, Tricks, 1997, The Christmas List, 1997, Weapons of Mass Distraction, 1997, Virtual Obsession, 1998, Host, 1998, Devil's Arithmetic, 1999, Manchester Prep, 1999, Common Ground, 2000, My Horrible Year!, 2001, Reel Comedy: Austin Powers in Goldmember, 2002, Charms for the Easy Life, 2002, Cave In, 2003, Stone Cold, 2005, Selling Innocence, 2005. Office: Creative Artists Agy c/o Jane Berliner 9830 Wilshire Blvd Beverly Hills CA 90212-1825

ROGERS, NANCY HARDIN, dean, law educator; b. Lansing, Mich., Sept. 18, 1948; d. Clifford Morris and Martha (Wood) Hardin; m. Douglas Langston Rogers, Jan. 30, 1970; children: Lynne, Jill, Kim. BA with highest distinction, U. Kans., 1969; JD, Yale U., 1972. Bar: D.C. 1975, Ohio 1972, U.S. Ct. Appeals (6th cir.) 1973, U.S. Dist. Ct. (no. dist.) Ohio 1974, U.S. Dist. Ct. (so. dist.) Ohio 1975. Law clk. U.S. Dist. Judge Thomas D. Lambros, Cleve., 1972-74; staff atty. Cleve. Legal Aid Soc., 1974-75; vis. asst. prof. Coll. of Law Ohio State U., Columbus, 1975-76, asst. prof., 1976-78, 83-89, assoc. prof., 1989-92, prof., assoc. dean acad. affairs, 1992-97, prof., 1992—, Joseph S. Platt, Porter, Wright, Morris & Arthur prof. law Columbus, 1995—2001, vice provost acad. adminstrn., 1999—2001, dean, Michael E. Moritz chair in alternative dispute resolution Michael E. Moritz Coll. Law, 2001—. Adj. prof. Ohio State Coll., 1981-83; vis. prof. law Harvard Law Sch., 2000. Author (with Frank E.A. Sander, Sarah R. Cole, Stephen B. Goldberg): (Book) Dispute Resolution: Negotiation, Mediation and Other Processes), 2007; author: (book with Craig A. McEwen and Sarah R. Cole) Mediation: Law, Policy, Practice, 2nd edit., 1994; mem. (adv. bd.) World Arbitration and Mediation Report, 1991—, Alternatives, 1992—, co-chair (editl. bd. with Frank E.A. Sander) Dispute Resolution mag., 1994—2002; contbr. chapters to books, articles to profl. jours. Bd. dirs. Assn. for Developmentally Disabled, Columbus, 1980-85; Legal Svcs. Corp. 1995-2003. Named Outstanding Prof., Ohio State U. Coll. Law Alumni Assn., 1996; recipient Book prize, Ctr. Pub. Resources for A Student's Guide to Mediation and the Law, 1987, Ctr. Pub. Resources for Mediation: Law, Policy, Practice, 1989, Peacemaker of Yr. award, Comty. Mediation Svcs. Ctrl. Ohio, 1990, Disting. Svc. Recognition, Soc. Profls. in Dispute Resolution, 1990, Whitney North Seymour sr. medal, Am. Arbitration Assn., 1990, Svc. Recognition award, Legal Aid Soc. Columbus, 1996, Ritter award, Ohio State Bar Found for outstanding contbns. to adminstrn. of justice, 1998; grantee Exxon Edn. Found., 1986, William and Flora Hewlett Found., 1990, Ohio State U. Interdisciplinary Seed, 1990, Ohio State U. Symposium, 1992, William and Flora Hewlett Found., 1992—96, Nat. Sci. Found., 1993—95, State Justice Instn., 1994, Fund for Improvement Post-Secondary Edn., U. Mo., 1996—97, William and Flora Hewlett Found., 1997—2003. Mem. ABA (chair, standing com. dispute resolution 1988-91, D'Alemberte-Raven award sect. on dispute resolution 2002), Assn. Am. Law Schs. (pres. 2007), Phi Beta Kappa. Office: Ohio State U Coll Law 55 W 12th Ave Columbus OH 43210-1306 Office Phone: 614-292-0574. Business E-Mail: rogers.23@osu.edu.

ROGERS, PATRICIA LOUISE, education educator, consultant, dean; b. St. Paul, Apr. 16, 1956; life ptnr. W. S. Larson. BS, U. Minn., Twin Cities, 1979, MA, 1982, PhD, 1997. Lic. tchr. art and theatre Minn., 1979. Tchr. St. Paul Schs., 1979—82; cancer rschr. U. Minn. Sch. Pub. Health, Mpls., 1984—95; prof. Bemidji State U., Minn., 1996—2006; dean Sch. Edn. and Grad. Studies Valley City State U., ND, 2006—07; dean Coll. Social and Natural Scis., Bemidji State U., Minn., 2007—. Cons. and trainer for online tchg. Minn. State Colls. and Univs., Twin Cities, cons., 1998—; spkr. in field. Editor: (book) Designing Instruction for Technology-Enhanced Learning, Ency. of Distance Learning, Teaching, Technologies and Applications; contbr. articles to profl. jours. Vice chair Minn. Online Coun., 2003—04, chair, 2004—06. Recipient 1st Ann. Pioneer award, Minn. Online Coun.; grantee, Minn. State Colls. and Univs. under a FIPSE Grant, 2001—02; scholar, Fulbright, Coun. for Internat. Exch. Scholars, 2000—01; Dissertation fellow, Getty Ctr. for Arts in Edn., 1996. Mem.: ND Assn. Colls. of Tchr. Edn., Nat. Art Edn. Assn., Assn. Ednl. Comm. and Tech., Rotary Internat. (assoc.). Dfl. Office: Bemidji State Univ Coll Social and Natural Scis 1500 Birchmont Dr NE Bemidji MN 56601 Office Phone: 218-755-2965. Business E-Mail: progers@bemidjistate.edu.

ROGERS, PAULLETO, researcher, writer; b. Washington, Mich., Aug. 22, 1961; s. Paulleto Rogers I and Dorothy L.R. Rogers; children: Alexis R. Roycia July, Ambre L. Majasticaa. Student, Wayne County CC; cert. computer ops., Mother Waddles Sch. Cert. paralegal. Pres. C.C.OA, LA, 1983; gen. operator CBOU, 1983—; regent agent Security MGN, 1984; collector Nat. Credit Corp., LA, 1985; craftman Vinyl Indsl. Products, Chgo., 1986; field insp. Mortgage Svcs. Assoc., Inc., 1995; sales cons.

Swepo, 1996; legal tech. Probone Legal Svcs., 1997; directorate Prousa Internat. Projects 2001, 1998. Substaining member Rep. Platform Commn., 1986; substaining sponsor Ronald Reagan Presdl. Found., Libr., and Ctr. Pub. Affairs, Ventura County, Calif., 1988; sponsor Statue of Liberty Ellis Island Centennial Commn., 1985, Ronald Reagan Congressional-Vicotry Fund, 1987; advisorate Senate Adv. Coun., 1997; co-founder Justice Inst.; vol. Mother Waddles-Petr. Mission Support; del. at large Del. Adv. Coun.; legal adv. Alexis, Ambre, Dorthy-Lewis, Paul, Paulleto, Rogers, Sutton, Profl. Corp., 2001. Creator, founder The Collectionals Survey. At-large-del. Rep. Presdl. Task Force, 1992—, lobbyist, 1994—; activist US Def. Com., 1985; lobbyist Prousa Legal Corpsusa, 1999; del. Wayne County Clk. Office; Mich. state advisor Rep. Senatorial Com.; active GOPAC, congl. VIP, 1984; GOP Victory Fund sponsor NRCC, 1984; supporter Kidsfirst YESMI, 2000; assoc. mem. Ch. Tae Adv., 2000—. Decorated Rogers Coat of Arms, Medieval Knight, Chevron, 2000; recipient Cert. Recognition, NRCC, 1990, Cert. Appreciation, Presdl. Commn. A.A., 1990, Presdl. award Rep. Presdl. Legion of Merit, 1994. Mem. Oahspe (assoc.), World Peace Tonite/Freedom Inst. (assoc.), 2nd Ch. of Tae. Avocations: copyrights, activism, lobbying, community reinvesting. Home: PO Box 27473 Detroit MI 48227-0473 Personal E-mail: rogerspaulleto@yahoo.com.

ROGERS, PETER PHILLIPS, environmental engineer, educator, urban planner; b. Liverpool., England, Apr. 30, 1937; arrived in U.S., 1960, naturalized, 1970; s. Edward Joseph and Ellen (Duggan) R.; m. Suzanne Ogden, Oct. 24, 1998; children: Christopher, Justin. B in Engring., Liverpool U., 1958; MS, Northwestern U., 1961; PhD, Harvard U., 1966. Asst. engr. Sir Alfred McAlpine & Sons Ltd., Cheshire, Eng., 1958-60; mem. faculty Harvard U., 1966—, Gordon McKay prof. environ. engring., 1974—, prof. city planning, 1974—. Mem. Ctr. for Environment Harvard U., 2002—; cons. World Bank, UN, U.S. Agy. for Internat. Devel., Govt. India, Govt. Pakistan, Govt. Bangladesh, Govt. Nepal, Govt. Italy, Govt. Costa Rica, Commonwealth P.R. Co-author: Urbanization and Change, 1970, Land Use and The Pipe: Planning for Sewerage, 1975, Resource Inventory and Baseline Study Methods for Developing Countries, 1983, Systems Analysis for River Basin Management, 1985, Evaluacion de Projectos de Desarrollo, 1990, America's Waters, 1993, Water in the Arab World, 1994, Measuring Environmental Quality in Asia, 1997, Science with a Human Face, 1997, Water Crisis: Myth or Reality, 2006, Introduction to Sustainable Development, 2006. Mem. World Commn. for Water in 21st Century. Gordon McKay tchg. fellow 1961; Radley rsch. student, 1962-64; doctoral dissertation fellow Resources for Future 1964-65; recipient Clemens Herschel prize Harvard U., 1964; Guggenheim fellow, 1973, 20th Century Found. fellowship, 1989, Maass-White fellow U.S. Army C.E., 2003. Mem.: ASCE, Third World Acad. Scis. (corr.), Indian Inst. Agrl. Engring. (life), Cambridge Tennis Club, Cosmos Club (Washington). Home: 20 Berkeley St Cambridge MA 02138 Office: Harvard U 116 Pierce Hall Cambridge MA 02138 Home Phone: 617-547-7473; Office Phone: 617-495-2025. Business E-Mail: rogers@deas.harvard.edu.

ROGERS, RALPH A., JR., insurance company executive; BBA, Tenn. Technol. U., Cookeville. CPA. Sr. v.p. fin. resources UnumProvident Corp.; sr. v.p. fin. svcs. AFLAC Inc., Columbus, Ga., 2000—02, sr. v.p., fin. svcs. acctg. officer, 2002—. Mem.: AICPA, Inst. Mgmt. Accts., Fin. Execs. Internat., Tenn. Soc. CPAs. Office: AFLAC Inc 1932 Wynnton Rd Columbus GA 31999 Office Phone: 706-323-3431. *

ROGERS, RAYMOND JESSE, retired federal railroad associate administrator; b. Eugene, Oreg., Mar. 1, 1941; s. Raymond Everett and Virginia Elaine (Simpkins) R.; m. Joan Katherine Peterson, June 6, 1964 (div. Aug. 1974); 1 child, Virginia Arlene; m. Kim Lien Nguyen, Dec. 26, 1974; children: Kim Lan, Vincent Minh. Student, Santa Rosa Jr. Coll., Calif., 1960-61, U.S. Army Non-commd. Officer Acad., Anchorage, Alaska, 1963, U. Md., 1967-74, Fed. Exec. Inst., Charlottsville, Va., 1981. Lic. real estate agt., Va. Sr. asst. mgr. Household Fin. Corp., Md., 1964-67; contract specialist Dept. Navy, Washington, 1967-71; contract svcs. officer AID, Saigon, Vietnam, 1971-76; contracting officer Dept. Transp., Fed. R.R. Adminstrn., Washington, 1976-80, dir. fin. svcs., 1980-84, assoc. adminstr. for adminstrn., 1984—2002, CFO, CIO, 1994—2002, ret., 2002. Leader local group Boy Scouts Am., Vienna, Va., 1987-92, Izaac Walton League of Am., Am. Legion, Am. Assn. of Retired Persons. Sgt. U.S. Army, 1961-64. Decorated Vietnam Civilian Svc. medal. Mem. U.S. Sr. Exec. Svc., Fed. Exec. Inst. Alumni Assn. Avocations: fishing, hiking, camping, waterskiing. Home: 102 Yvonna Dr SW Vienna VA 22180-6557 Personal E-mail: Rayvin78@aol.com.

ROGERS, RICHARD DEAN, federal judge; b. Oberlin, Kans., Dec. 29, 1921; s. William Clark and Evelyn May (Christian) R.; m. Helen Elizabeth Stewart, June 6, 1947; children— Letitia Ann, Cappi Christian, Richard Kurt. BS, Kans. State U., 1943; JD, Kans. U., 1947. Bar: Kans. 1947. Ptnr. firm Springer and Rogers (Attys.), Manhattan, Kans., 1947-58; instr. bus. law Kans. State U., 1948-52; partner firm Rogers, Stites & Hill, Manhattan, 1959-75; gen. counsel Kans. Farm Bur. & Service Cos., Manhattan, 1960-75; judge U.S. Dist. Ct., Topeka, Kans., 1975—. City commr., Manhattan, 1950-52, 60-64, mayor, 1952, 64, county atty., Riley County, Kans., 1954-58, state rep., 1964-68, state senator, 1968-75; pres. Kans. Senate, 1975. Served with USAAF, 1943-45. Decorated Air medal, Dfc. Mem. Kans., Am. bar assns., Beta Theta Pi. Clubs: Masons. Republican. Presbyterian. Office: US Dist Ct 444 SE Quincy St Topeka KS 66683 Office Phone: 785-295-2735.

ROGERS, RICHARD HILTON, hotel executive; b. Florence, SC, May 26, 1935; s. Leslie Lawton and Bessie (Holloway) R.; m. Evelyn Pasciuto; children: Richard Shannon, Leslie Anne. Student, U. N.C., 1953-55; BA in Bus. Adminstrn. cum laude, Bryant U., 1961; postgrad., Memphis State U., 1964; DHL (hon.), Schiller Internat. U., Dunedin, Fla., 2003. Innkeeper Helmsley Spear, NYC, 1961—62; v.p. Holiday Inns of Am., Memphis, 1963—73; exec. v.p. First Hospitality Corp., Hackensack, NJ, 1974—77; v.p., chief oper. officer Cindy's Inc., Atlanta, 1978—82; v.p. 1982 World's Fair, Knoxville, Tenn.; pres., chief exec. officer Hospitality Internat., Atlanta, 1982—92; dir. franchise devel. Baymont Inns, 1992, 2000. Developer, operator The Warehouse Restaurant, Oxford, Miss., 1973-75, Beauregard's Restaurant, Hattiesburg, Miss., 1975-78. Contbr. to profl. jours. Mem. adv. bd. U. South Fla. With USN, 1954-58, Korea. Mem. Am. Hotel/Motel Assn. (mktg. com. 1986-92, adv. coun. 1987-92, industry adv. bd., chmn.), Economy Lodging Coun. Avocations: sailing, photography. Home and Office: 8525 Hope Vine Roswell GA 30076 Personal E-mail: innkpr@charter.net.

ROGERS, RICHARD MICHAEL, judge; b. Lorain, Ohio, Dec. 8, 1944; s. Paul M. and Lillie (Morris) R.; m. Sophia Lydia Wagner, Dec. 23, 1967; children: L. Danielle, David K., Marisa D., Matthew D. BA, Ohio No. U., 1966, JD, 1972. Bar: Ohio 1972, U.S. Dist. Ct. (no. dist.) Ohio 1973. Assoc. Martin, Hall & Rogers, Marion, Ohio, 1972-76; atty. Rogers & Rogers, Marion, 1976-81; asst. law dir., police prosecutor City of Marion, 1973-74; pub. defender, 1975; asst. county prosecutor Marion County, 1976-81; village solicitor La Rue, Ohio, 1976-81; judge Marion Mcpl. Ct., 1982-88, Common Pleas Ct., 1989—2004, 3d Dist. Ct. Appeals Ohio, Lima, Ohio, 2004—; mem. Traffic Rules Rev. Commn., 1989—2004, Commn. on CLE, 2007—, Ohio Supreme Ct. Judge competition Nat. Bicentennial Competition on Constitution and Bill of Rights, judge state competition, 1988-01, judge nat. competition, 1989, 93, 95; occasional instr. faculty Ohio Jud. Coll. Mem. Marion Active 20/40 Svc. Club, 1973-84, treas., 1976-80, bd. dirs., 1976-84, pres., 1980-81; chmn. bd. dirs., pres., co-founder Marion Area Driver Re-edn. Project, 1974-81; pres. Big Bros./Big Sisters Marion County, 1986-87, bd. dirs., 1984-88; mem. sch. bd. St. Mary's Elem. Sch., 1985-88, v.p., 1986, bd. dirs. Marion Cath. HS Endowment Fund, 1986—, v.p., 1991—; mem. Marion Cath. Jr./Sr. HS Bd., 1988-94, pres., 1990-91; mem. criminal justice steering com. Marion Campus Ohio State U., 1996-00; mem. paralegal adv. com. Marion Tech. Coll., 1994-96; trustee Ohio State Bar Found., 1997-99, 05—. With US Army, 1968-69. Mem. Ohio State Bar Assn. (modern cts. com. 1982-85, jud. adminstrn. and legal reform com. 1982-93, legis. subcom. of jud. adminstrn. and legal reform com. 1989-93, coun. dels. 1991-93, bd. govs. 1996-99, chmn. govt. affairs com. 1998-99, vice-chair criminal justice com. 2001-02, chmn. jury instrn. com. 2002-06), Marion County Bar Assn. (pres. 1985-86), Ohio Jud. Conf. (gen. adminstrn. 1984-85, vice chair family matters video com. 1991-94, chmn. subcom. legal matters video, civil law and procedure com. 1991-95, editl. bd. Ohio Jury Instrn. 1995—), Marion County Law Libr. Assn. (trustee 1982-04, pres. 1991-93), Ohio Cts. Appeal Judges Assn., Delta Theta Phi, Sigma Pi. Republican. Methodist. Avocations: golf, tennis. Home: 310 Edgefield Blvd Marion OH 43302-5802 Office: 3d Dist Ct Appeals Ohio 204 N Main St Lima OH 45801-4462 Office Phone: 419-223-1861. Business E-Mail: rogers@third.courts.state.oh.us. *Notable cases include: Hines vs. Thermal-Gard of Ohio, Inc., 1988, applicability of home solicitation sales acts, Augenstein vs. Augenstein, deeds sufficient to convey, reserve life estate, Scioto Conservancy Dist., establishment of conservancy dist.*

ROGERS, RICHARD RAYMOND, cosmetics company executive; b. Houston, Apr. 15, 1943; s. J. Ben and Mary Kay (Ash) Rogers; children: Terri, Rick, Ryan. BA, North Tex. State U. Co-founder Mary Kay Cosmetics, Inc., Dallas, 1963, gen. mgr., 1963—65, v.p., 1965—68, pres., 1968—87, chmn. bd., dir., 1987—. With USMCR. Named Man of Yr., North Tex. Mktg. Assn., 1968. Republican. Baptist. Office: Mary Kay Cosmetics Inc 16251 Dallas Pkwy Addison TX 75001-6801

ROGERS, ROBERT ERNEST, medical educator; s. Jessie H. and Willie L. (Bahr) Rogers; m. Barbara Ann Hill, May 16, 1950; children: Robert E., Jr., Stephanie Ann Thompson, Cheri Lee Heck. BS in Biology, John B. Stetson U., 1949; MD, U. Miami, 1957. Diplomate Am. Bd. Ob-Gyn. Commd. 1st lt. M.C., U.S. Army, 1952, advanced through grades to col., 1971—74; ret. U.S. Army, 1974; intern Brooke Gen. Hosp., San Antonio, 1957-58, chief resident ob-gyn, 1960-61; resident in ob-gyn Jackson Meml. Hosp., Miami, Fla., 1958-60; fellow gynecology M.D. Anderson Hosp., Houston, 1965-66; asst. chief ob-gyn Tripler Army Med. Ctr., Honolulu, 1966-69; chmn. ob-gyn Walter Reed Med. Ctr., Washington, 1969-70, Madigan Army Med. Ctr., Tacoma, 1970-74; prof. Ind. U. Sch. Medicine, Indpls., 1974—, also chief gynecol. div., 1974—; chief ob-gyn svd. Wishard Meml. Hosp., Indpls., 1983-87. Contbr. articles to profl. jours.; editl. bd. Jour. Am. Coll. Surgeons, 2003—. Bd. dirs. Lake Stonebridge Homeowner's Assn., 2000—03, sec., 2000—03. Recipient Army Commendation medal, 1969, Army Meritorious Service Medal, 1971, Army Legion of Merit, 1974, Army Surgeon General's "A" Prefix for Profl. Excellence, 1974. Mem.: ACS, ACOG (chmn. gynecol. practice com., commr. practice, Sci. Exhibit award Armed Forces dist. 1971, Zimmerman Cons. award Armed Forces dist.), AMA (Certificate Merit for Sci. Exhibit 1971), Felix Rutledge Soc. (pres. 1981, historian), Internat. Soc. Advancement Humanistic Studies Medicine (pres. 1997—98), Soc. Gynecol. Oncologists, Soc. Gynecol. Surgeons (pres. 1983—84). Avocations: gardening, photography. Office: Ind U Sch Medicine 550 University Blvd Indianapolis IN 46202-5149 Home Phone: 317-849-4330; Office Phone: 317-849-4026. Personal E-mail: Bobberogers@hotmail.com. Business E-Mail: reroger@iupui.edu.

ROGERS, ROBERT M., architect; BA, Rice U., Houston, BArch, 1983; M of Design Studies, Harvard U., Cambridge, Mass., 1989. With I.M. Pei & Ptnrs., Archs., NYC, 1981—82, 1983—88; cons. Kallmann, McKinnell & Wood, Archs., Boston, 1988; prin. Robert M. Rogers, Archs., NYC, 1988—91, Rogers Marvel Archs., PLLC, NYC, 1991. Vis. asst. prof. architecture Pratt Inst. Sch. Architecture, 1989—; adj. asst. prof. architecture Columbia U., NYC, 1996—; Cullinan chair prof. Rice U., 2004. Prin. works include Studio Mus. in Harlem (NYC AIA Honor award, 1998), Higgins Hall, Pratt Inst. (Nat. AIA Honor award, 2001, NY State AIA Award of Excellence, 2001), Shapiro Frey Residence (NY State AIA Award of Merit, 2001). Mem.: AIA. Office: Rogers Marvel Archs PLLC 145 Hudson St 3rd Fl New York NY 10013 Office Phone: 212-941-6718. Office Fax: 212-941-7573. *

ROGERS, ROBERT MARK, physician; b. Upper Darby, Pa., June 9, 1933; s. John Francis and Clara (Baumann) R.; m. Sandra Betz, Feb. 14, 1968; children: Janet Marie, Robert Mark, Linda, William Bradford, David Philip. BA cum laude, LaSalle Coll., Phila., 1956; MD, U. Pa., 1960. Intern Hosp. of U. Pa., 1960-61, chief emergency svcs., 1968-69, founder, dir. respiratory ICU, 1968-72, dir. pulmonary disease sect. tng. program, 1970-72; resident Case Western Res. U. Hosps., Cleve., 1961-63; fellow in pulmonary disease VA Hosp., Cleve., 1963-64, U. Pa., 1964-65, postdoctoral trainee in physiology, 1966-68, asst. prof. medicine and assoc. in physiology, 1968-72; prof.medicine, assoc. prof. physiology Okla. Health Scis. Ctr. Coll. Medicine, 1972-80, also chief pulmonary disease sect., dept. medicine, dir. clin. pulmonary physiology lab. hosp. and clinics; dir. Comprehensive Lung Ctr. U. Pitts. Med. Sch., 1990-97, chief pulmonary, allergy and critical care medicine, 1980-96, prof. medicine, 1980—. Editor: Respiratory Intensive Care, 1977; mem. editl. bd. Current Opinion in Pulmonary Medicine and Critical Care; contbr. rsch. articles to profl. publs. Mem. ACP (US rep. to Chinese Med. Assn. 1979, founding editor-in-chief audio cassettes program 1978-80), Am. Thoracic Soc. (founding dir. Learning Resources Ctr. 1971-77, Presdl. commendation 1977, Outstanding Achievement award 2002), Am. Fedn. Clin. Rsch., Am. Coll. Chest Physicians (Presdl. citation 1998), Am. Physiol. Soc., Soc. Critical Care Medicine, Am. Heart Assn., Ctrl. Soc. Clin. Rsch., So. Soc. Clin. Rsch., Pa. Thoracic Soc. (pres. 1985-88), Coll. Physicians Phila. Home: 4116 Bigelow Blvd Pittsburgh PA 15213-1408 Office: U Pitts Sch Medicine 628 NW Montefiore Hosp 3459 Fifth Ave Pittsburgh PA 15213 Office Phone: 412-692-2210. Business E-Mail: rogersrm@upmc.edu.

ROGERS, ROY STEELE, III, dermatologist, educator, dean; b. Hillsboro, Ohio, Mar. 3, 1940; s. Roy S. Jr. and Anna Mary (Murray) R.; m. Susan Camille Hudson, Aug. 22, 1964; children: Roy Steele IV, Katherine Hudson. BA, Denison U., 1962; MD, Ohio State U., 1966; MS, U. Minn., 1974. Cert. dermatologist, dermatopathologist and immunodermatologist. Intern Strong Meml. Hosp., Rochester, NY, 1966—67; resident Duke U. Med. Ctr., Durham, NC, 1969—71, Mayo Clinic, Rochester, Minn., 1972—73, cons., 1973—, prof. dermatology, 1983—, dean Sch. Health Related Scis., 1991—99. Adv. coun. Rochester Community Coll., 1991-2000. Contbr. over 250 sci. articles to publs. Mem. Rochester Planning and Zoning Comm., 1980—88; bd. dir. Casabella Assn., 2006—. Capt., flight surgeon USAF, 1967—69. Recipient Alumni Achievement award Ohio State U. Coll. Medicine, 1991, Alumni citation Denison U., 1993, Faculty Svc. award Mayo Med. Sch., 1993, Gold medal 2d Med. Sch., Charles U., Prague, 2002; named Disting. Educator, Mayo Clinic, 2004, Thomas G. Pearson Meml. Edn. award, 2004, Everett J. Fox Lectureship, 2005, Paul A. O'Leary Lectureship, 2005. Mem. Am. Acad. Dermatology (hon., bd. dirs. 1987-91, v.p. 1999, Everett C. Fox lectureship 2005, Gold Triangle award 2004, Thomas G. Pearson Meml. Edn. award 2005), Am. Soc. Dermatologic Allergy and Immunology (sec.-treas. 1988-2000), Am. Dermatologic Assn. (v.p. 2002-03), Soc. Investigative Dermatology, Assn. Schs. Allied Health Professions, Dermatology Found. (Annenberg Circle 2002). Avocations: travel, reading, walking. Office: Mayo Clinic 200 1st St SW Rochester MN 55905-0002 Home: 10101 N Arabian Tail No 1006 Scottsdale AZ 85258 Home Phone: 480-991-4197; Office Phone: 507-284-2555. Business E-Mail: rogers.roy@mayo.edu.

ROGERS, RUTH FRANCES, retired microbiologist; b. Chgo., Nov. 5, 1925; d. Frank Joseph and Ruth Elizabeth (Abbott) Kucera; m. James Alvin Rogers, June 17, 1950; children: Kenneth James, David Wayne. BS, U. Ill., 1948. Microbiologist No. Rsch. Ctr., Nat. Ctr. for Agrl. Utilization Rsch., Peoria, Ill., 1963—85; ret., 1985. Contbr. articles to profl. jours. Recipient Sustained Superior Performance award USDA, 1984. Methodist.

ROGERS, RUTHERFORD DAVID, librarian; b. Jesup, Iowa, June 22, 1915; s. David Earl and Carrie Zoe (Beckel) R.; m. E. Margaret Stoddard, June 4, 1937; 1 child, Jane Shelley; m. Bernette W. Barton, Feb. 28, 2002. BA, U. No. Iowa, 1936, Litt.D., 1977; MA, Columbia, 1937, BS (Lydia Roberts fellow), 1938; D.Library Adminstrn. (hon.), U. Dayton, 1971. Asst. N.Y. Pub. Library, 1937-38; reference librarian Columbia Coll. Library, Columbia U., 1938- 41, acting librarian, 1941-42, librarian, 1942-45; research analyst Smith, Barney & Co., NYC, 1946-48; dir. Grosvenor Library, Buffalo, 1948-52, Rochester Pub. Library, 1952-54; chief pers. office N.Y. Pub. Libr., 1954-55; chief reference dept., 1955-57; chief asst. librarian of Congress, Washington, 1957-62, dep. librarian of, 1962-64; dir. univ. libraries Stanford U., 1964-69; univ. librarian Yale U., 1969-85, univ. librarian emeritus, 1985—. Founder, chmn. bd. dirs. Rsch. Librs. Group, Inc.; mem. Exam. Com. for Pub. Librarians' Certs., N.Y. State, 1951-54; mem. U.S. Adv. Coun. Coll. Libr. Resources; bd. govs. Yale U. Press; bd. dirs., v.p. H.W. Wilson Found., 1969-98; chmn. program mgmt. com. Internat. Fedn. Libr. Assns. Author: Columbia Coll. Library Handbook, 1941, (with David C. Weber) University Library Administration, 1971; also articles in profl. jours. Served from pvt. to 1st sgt. Air Transp. Command USAAF, 1942-43; from 2d lt. to capt., planning officer, chief, spl. Planning Div., Office Asst. Chief Staff, Plans, Air Transport Command 1943-46. Decorated officier de L'Ordre de la Couronne Belge; recipient U. No. Iowa Alumni Achievement award, 1958, Disting. Alumni award Columbia U. Sch. Libr. Svc., 1992, medal Internat. Fedn. of Libr. Assns., 1977. Fellow Am. Acad. Arts and Scis.; mem. A.L.A. (chmn. com. Intellectual Freedom 1950-51), (1950-60), (2d v.p. 1965-66), (mem. exec. bd. 1961-66), (trustee endowment fund), Assn. Research Libraries (dir., pres. 1967-68), N.Y. Library Assn., AAUP, Bibliog. Soc. Am., Assn. Coll. and Reference Libraries, Blue Key, Kappa Delta Pi, Sigma Tau Delta, Theta Alpha Phi. Clubs: Grolier; N.Y. Library (N.Y.C.), Columbia U. (N.Y.C.), Yale (N.Y.C.); Cosmos (Washington), Kenwood Country (Washington); Roxburghe (San Francisco); Book of Calif. Home (Winter): 1081 Lakemont Ct Winter Park FL 32792-5025

ROGERS, SALLY J., psychologist, educator; d. Calvin Y. and Helen N. Rogers; m. John R. Brown, July 26, 1975; children: Sara V. Brown, Amy E. Brown. PhD, Ohio State U., 1975. Lic. Psychologist Calif., 2003, Colo., 2003. Prof. psychiatry and behavioral scis. U. Calif., Sacramento, 2002—. Author: (textbook) Imitation and the Social Mind. Recipient Lifetime Achievement award, NYU, 2004. Mem.: Internat. Soc. Autism Rsch. (pres. 2005—). Avocations: music, hiking, kayaking, cooking, gardening. Home Phone: 916-703-0264; Office Phone: 916-703-0264.

ROGERS, SAMUEL SHEPARD *See* **SHEPARD, SAM**

ROGERS, SHERRY ANNE, physician; b. Syracuse, NY, Apr. 15, 1943; d. Rodney Wellington and Jayne Hammond; m. Robert Hamilton Rogers, June 30, 1970. BA, Syracuse U., 1969; MD, SUNY, 1969-70. Diplomate Am. Bd. Family Practice, 1973, Am. Bd. Environ. Medicine, 1985. Intern Health Scis. Ctr. Syracuse, 1969-70; pvt. practice pediat., Auburn, NY, 1970-71; emergency physician Cmty. Gen. Hosp., Syracuse, NY, 1971-72; pvt. practice family medicine, Syracuse, 1972-85; pvt. practice environ. medicine, 1978—. Lectr. in field. Author: (books) Total Health, 1989, Tired or Toxic?, 1990, Wellness Against All Odds, 1994, Chemical Sensitivity, 1995, You Are What You Ate, The E.I. Syndrome, 1997, Depression Cured At Last, 1997, Alternative and Complementary Veterinary Medicine, 1998, No More Heartburn, 2000, The Cure is in the Kitchen, The Scientific Basis of Environmental Medicine Techniques, 2000, Pain Free in 6 Weeks, 2001, Detoxify or Die, 2003, The High Blood Pressure Hoax, 2005, Total Wellness, 2006; editor: Internal Medical World Report, 1992—93; contbr. articles to profl. jours., chapters to books Molds & Mycotoxins, Arch. Environ. Health, others. Fellow: Am. Coll. Nutrition, Am. Coll. Asthma, Allergy and Immunology. Office: Northeast Center Environmental Medicine PO Box 2716 Syracuse NY 13220-2716 Home Phone: 941-346-2494; Office Phone: 800-846-6687, 315-488-2856.

ROGERS, STEPHEN HITCHCOCK, retired ambassador; b. Flushing, NY, June 21, 1930; s. Francis Walker and Julia (Wheeler) R.; m. Kent Brain, June 23, 1956; children: Kryston R. Fischer, F. Halsey, Julia L., John H. BA, Princeton U., 1952; MA, Columbia U., 1956; MPA, Harvard U., 1962. Fgn. svc. officer Dept. of State, 1956-93; econ. counselor Am. Embassy, London, 1970-72; counselor U.S. Mission to OECD, Paris, 1972-75; office dir. Bur. Inter.-Am. Affairs Dept. of State, Washington, 1975-78; econ. counselor Am. Embassy, Mexico City, 1978-82; prof. Nat. Def. U., Washington, 1982-85; econ. counselor Am. Embassy, Pretoria, South Africa, 1986-90, amb. Mbabane, Swaziland, 1990-93; ret., 1993. Bd. dirs. Cen. Atlantic Conf., United Ch. of Christ, 2000-03; v.p. Princeton U. Class 1952, 2002-07, pres., 2007—. Lt. (jg) USN, 1952-55. Recipient Outstanding Civilian Svc. award Dept. of Army, 1985. Mem. Am. Fgn. Svc. Assn., Diplomatic and Consular Officers Ret., Nassau Club (Princeton, N.J.). Mem. United Ch. Of Christ. Home: 3803 Ivydale Dr Annandale VA 22003-2006

ROGERS, STEVEN A., energy executive; B in Econs./Acctg., Coll. Holy Cross, Worcester, Mass., 1983. Contr.-treas. Rehab Mgmt. Inc.; with Deloitte & Touche; mgr. internal audit Dominion, Richmond, Va., 1996—97, v.p., contr. OptaCor Fin. Svcs. Co. subs. of Dominion Capital Inc., 1997—98, corp. contr. Dominion Energy Inc., 1998—2000, v.p., contr., 2000—06, sr. v.p., contr., 2006—. Mem. acctg. exec. adv. com. Edison Electric Inst., 2002—, chmn. acctg. exec. adv. com., 2005—06. Bd. mem. Crisis Pregnancy Ctr. Met. Richmond, 2003—, chmn. bd. Office: Dominion PO Box 26532 Richmond VA 23261-6532 *

ROGERS, THEODORE COURTNEY, investment company executive; b. Lorain, Ohio, Aug. 25, 1934; s. William Theodore and Leona Ruth (Gerhart) Rogers; m. Elizabeth B. Barlow, June 28, 1984; children from previous marriage: Pamela Anne Rogers Harmon, Theodore Courtney Jr. BS in Social Sci., Miami U., Oxford, Ohio, 1956, LHD (hon.), 2001; postgrad., Johns Hopkins U., 1957; MBA summa cum laude, Marquette U., 1968; MALA, St. John's Coll., Annapolis, Md., 2004. With Armco Inc., 1958-80; pres. Olympic Fastening Sys., 1970-74; with Bathey Mfg. Co. subs., 1970, group v.p. indsl. products, 1971-74; exec. v.p. Nat. Supply Co. subs., Houston, 1974-76, pres., 1976-80, v.p. parent co., 1976-79, group v.p. parent co., 1979-80; pres., COO NL Industries, Inc., NYC, 1980-82, pres., CEO, 1982-83, chmn., pres., CEO, 1983-87; chmn. Am. Indsl. Ptnrs., NYC, 1987—. Chmn. Bucyrus Internat., Consoltex Inc., Gt. Lakes Carbon Corp., JHT Holdings Inc.; vice chmn. bd. trustees St. John's Coll. Nat. coun. Theatre Comm. Group; bd. dirs. Lincoln Ctr. Peforming Arts, City Ctr. Music and Drama; chmn. bd. dirs. Theatre for New Audience; former chmn. Ctr. Cmty. Interests; emeritus chmn. N.Y.C. Ballet; bd. dirs., trustee Ballet Rev. Qur. Lt. USN, 1956—58. Mem.: Poets and Writers (bd. dirs.), Bus. Roundtable, N.Y. Soc. Libr. (trustee), Grolier Club, Univ. Club (Milw.), Met. Club (Washington), Sky Club, Achilles Track Club (founder, bd. dirs.), Century Assn. (N.Y.), Links Club, Econs. Club (N.Y.), Union Club (Cleve.), Kappa Phi Kappa, Sigma Chi (Significant Sig, Sigma Chi Hall of Fame 2005), Beta Gamma Sigma (bd. dirs.). Office: Am Indsl Ptnr 551 5th Ave Ste 3800 New York NY 10176-0001 Office Phone: 212-983-1399.

ROGERS, THEODORE OTTO, JR., lawyer; b. West Chester, Pa., Nov. 17, 1953; s. Theodore Otto and Gladys (Bond) R.; m. Hope Tyler Scott, Nov. 7, 1981; children: Helen Elliot, Theodore Scott, Robert Montgomery Bond. AB magna cum laude, Harvard U., 1976, JD cum laude, 1979. Bar: NY 1980, US Ct. Appeals (2nd cir.) 1984, US Dist. Ct. (so. and ea. dists.) NY 1980, DC 1981, US Ct. Claims, 1982, US Supreme Ct. 1983, US Ct. Appeals (6th and 10th cirs.) 1983, US Ct. Appeals (1st cir.) 1984, US Ct. Appeals (fed. cir.) 1986. Assoc. Sullivan & Cromwell, NYC, 1979—87, ptnr., 1987—, and coord. labor and employment practice area. Co-author: (books) Employment Litigation in New York, 1996, Employment Law DeskBook for Human Resources Professionals, 2001. Mem. US Presdl. Transition Team, 1980. Named one of Two Leading Labor and Employment Lawyers in NYC, Global Counsel Handbooks 2003-06 guides; named to Best Lawyers in America, 2006, 2007. Fellow Coll. Labor and Employment Lawyers; mem. NY State Bar Assn. (labor and employment law sect.), Assn. Bar City NY (labor and employment law). Republican. Office: Sullivan & Cromwell 125 Broad St Fl 28 New York NY 10004-2489 Office Fax: 212-558-3588. Business E-Mail: rogerst@sullcrom.com.

ROGERS, THOMAS FRANCIS, foundation administrator; b. Providence, Aug. 11, 1923; s. Thomas Francis and H. Ann (Flaharty) R.; m. Estelle E. Hunt, July 6, 1946; children: Clare Hibschman, Judith Reynolds, Hope Grove. BS cum laude, Providence Coll., 1945; MA, Boston U., 1949. Rsch. assoc. Radio Rsch. Lab. Harvard U., Cambridge, Mass., 1944-45; TV engr. Bell and Howell Co., Chgo., 1945-46; electronics scientist AF Cambridge Rsch. Ctr., Cambridge, Mass., 1946-54; assoc. group leader MIT Lincoln Lab., Cambridge, 1951-53; lab. head AF Cambridge Rsch. Ctr., Bedford, Mass., 1954-59; div. head and steering com. mem. MIT Lincoln Lab., Bedford, 1959-64; asst. dir. def. rsch. and engring. Office of Sec. Def., Washington, 1964-65, dep. dir. def. rsch. and engring., 1965-67; dir. rsch. and tech. Office of Sec. HUD, Washington, 1967-69; v.p. The Mitre Corp., Washington, Bedford, 1969-72; chmn. The Sophron Found., McLean, Va., 1980—; dir. U.S. Congress Office of Tech. Assessment Study on Civilian Space Stas. and U.S. Future in Space, Washington, 1982-84; from pres. to chief scientist The Space Transp. Assn., Arlington, Va., 1992—2005. Founding chmn. bd. dirs. External Tanks Corp., Boulder, Colo.; bd. dirs. Internat. Radio Satellite Corp., Washington, Space Destinations Svcs., Inc., 1994-97; chmn. bd. dirs. Luna Corp., Great Falls, Va., 1991-95; dir. Share Space Found., 2000; chmn. POLARIS Command-Comm. Co., USN, 1960-64; mem. Satellite Comm. Panel, Pres.'s Sci. Adv. Com., 1961-63; mem. Dept. Def. NASA Satellite Comm. Com., 1961-64; U.S.A. del. UN Conf. on Applications of Sci. and Tech. by Lesser Developed Nations, Geneva, 1963; mem. Fed. Aeronautics and Astronautics Coordinating Bd., 1965-67; Fed. Coun. on Sci. and Tech., 1967-69; mem. Space Program Adv. Coun., NASA, 1971-73, chmn. applications com., 1972-73; mem. NAS com. on regional emergency med. comm. systems, 1976-78; mem. space applications bd. com. on NASA space comms. 1986-87; mem. com. on antenna, satellite broadcasting and emergency preparedness for Voice of Am., 1986-88; mem. adv. com. study space transp. U.S. Congrl. Office Tech. Assessment, 1994-95. Contbr. articles to jours., chpts. to books. Trustee X-Prize Found., 1995-2000. Recipient Outstanding Performance award CSC, 1957, cert. commendation Sec. Navy, 1961, Meritorious Civilian Svc. award and medal, Sec. Def., Constrn.'s Man of Yr. award Engring. News Record, 1969, Space Pioneer award Nat. Space Soc., 1988, Best Vision of the Future award Space Frontier Found., 1997, NASA Disting. Pub. Svc. award, 1999, Pioneer award Visionary Lifetime Achievement award Space Tourism Soc. Fellow IEEE (mem. transp. and aerospace policy com., chmn. 1991-95, Profl. Achievement award 1995, Citation of Honor 2005); mem. Internat. Acad. Astronautics (Paris), Cosmos Club (Washington). Home and Office: 5400 Vantage Point Rd # 210 Columbia MD 21044 Home Phone: 410-992-1210; Office Phone: 410-992-1210.

ROGERS, THOMAS SYDNEY, communications company executive; b. New Rochelle, NY, Aug. 19, 1954; s. Sydney Michael Rogers Jr. and Alice Steinhardt; m. Sylvia Texon, Oct. 9, 1983; children: Robert, Jessica, Jason. BA, Wesleyan U., 1975; JD, Columbia U., 1979. Bar: N.Y. 1980, U.S. Dist. Ct. (so. and ea. dists.) N.Y. 1980, U.S. Ct. Appeals (D.C. cir.) 1981. Legis. aide to Congressman Richard Ottinger U.S. Ho. Reps., Washington, 1975-76, sr. counsel subcom. telecommunications, 1981-86; assoc. Lord, Day & Lord, NYC, 1979-81; v.p. policy planning and bus. devel. Nat. Broadcasting Co., Inc., NYC, 1987-88; pres. NBC Cable, 1988-89, NBC Cable & Bus. Devel., 1989-99; exec. v.p. NBC, NYC, 1992-99; pres., CEO internat. coun. NATAS, 1994—97, chmn., 1998—99; vice chmn. NBC Internet, NYC, 1999; chmn., CEO Primedia, Inc., NYC, 1999—2003; chmn. TRget Media, NYC, 2003—; sr. oper. exec., media and entertainment exec. Censerus Capital, 2004—05; vice chmn. Tivo, Inc., Alviso, Calif., 2003—05, pres., CEO, 2005—; chmn. Teleglobe, Inc., 2004—06. Named one of Outstanding Young Men in Am., 1985. Mem. N.Y. State Bar Assn., Internat. Radio and TV Soc. Office: TiVo Inc 2160 Gold St PO Box 2160 Alviso CA 95002

ROGERS, THOMASINA VENESE, commissioner; b. 1951; m. Gregory M. Gill; 1 child, Cleo. BS in Journalism, Northwestern U., 1973; JD, Columbia U. Chmn. Adminstrv. Conf. U.S., Washington, 1994-95; presdl. pers. staff The White House, Washington; dep. legal counsel, then legal counsel EEOC, Washington; mem. Occupl. Safety and Health Rev. Commn., Washington, 1998—, chmn., 1999—2002. Bd. dirs. Children's Nat. Med. Ctr. Mem. Am. Arbitration Assn. (bd. dirs.) Office: Occupl Safety and Health Review Commn One Lafayette Ctr 1120 20th St NW Washington DC 20036-3457 *

ROGERS, WANDA FAYE, vocalist; b. Oct. 24, 1929; d. John Riley and Bessie Louise Narmore; m. Weldon Nelson Rogers Sr., Feb. 27, 1959 (div. 1967); 1 child, Weldon Nelson. Student, Modesto Jr. Coll. Lic. radio broadcast. Author: (song book) Wanda Faye Song Book, 2004; singer: (CD) UFO, recorded with Jewel Records, 1958-64, Germanys Bear Import Records, 1998, Columbia Records, 1965, The Sunset Westerners, Sta. KGFL, 1946—53, Sta. WBAP, Ft. Worth, Tex., 1954—57. Named to, Cowgirl Mus. Hall of Fame, 2002, Hall of Fame, Western Swing Soc., Sacramento, 2003. Avocations: music, writing songs.

ROGERS, WAYNE M., actor, investor, investment strategist, consultant; b. Birmingham, Ala., Apr. 7, 1933; m. Mitzi, 1960-79; children Laura, Billy; m. Amy Hirsh, 1988. BA, Princeton U., 1954; student acting, Sanford Meisners Neighborhood Playhouse, Martha Graham. Founder Wayne Rogers & Co. Bd. dirs. Vishay Intertechnology Inc., 2006—. Stage appearances in Misalliance, Bus Stop, Under the Yum-Yum Tree; TV series Housecalls, 1979 (also writer, dir.), Stagecoach West, 1960, M*A*S*H, 1972-75, City of Angels, 1976, High Risk, 1988; film debut Odds Against Tomorrow, 1959; other films include The Glory Guys, 1965, Chamber of Horrors, 1966, Cool Hand Luke, 1967, WUSA, 1970, Pocket Money, 1972, The Hot Touch, 1982, The Gig, 1985, The Goodbye Bird, 1993, Ghost of Mississippi, 1996, Love Lies Bleeding, 1999, Frozen with Fear, 2000, Coo Coo Cafe, 2000, 3 Days of Rain, 2000, Miracle Dogs, 2003, Nobody Knows Anything!, 2003 (also prodr.); TV appearances The Top of the Hill, 1980, The Edge of Night, Attack on Terror: The F.B.I. vs Ku Klux Klan, 1975, The November Plan, 1976, Having Babies II, 1977, It Happened One Christmas, 1977, Thou Shalt Not Commit Adultry, 1978, Once in Paris, 1978, (mini series) Chiefs, 1983, He's Fired, She's Hired, 1984, The Lady from Yesterday, 1985, I Dream of Jeannie: 15 Years Later, 1985, One Terrific Guy, 1986, The Girl Who Spelled Freedom, 1986, American Harvest, 1987, The Killing Time, 1987, Drop-Out Mother, 1988, Bluegrass, 1988, Passion and Paradise, 1989, Miracle Landing, 1990; guest appearances include Gunsmoke, 1959, 1962, 1965, Gomer Pyle, U.S.M.C., 1964, The F.B.I. (6 episodes), 1966-73, Barnaby Jones, 1973, Murder, Memories of M*A*S*H, 1991, She Wrote, 1993, 1994, & 1997, Diagnosis Murder, 1997, M*A*S*H: TV Tales, 2002, M*A*S*H 30th Anniversary Reunion, 2002, TV Land Confidential, 2005, The O'Reilly Factor, 2005 and several others; exec. prodr., writer Dr. Sex, 1964, The Astro-Zombies, 1969; exec. prodr. (TV) Perfect Witness, 1989, Night of the Twisters, 1996, Money Plays, 1997; regular contbr., finances and stocks, Fox News Channel. With USN. Named to Hollywood Walk of Fame, 2005. Avocations: basketball, tennis, reading. Office: Wayne M Rogers & Co 11828 La Grange Ave Los Angeles CA 90025

ROGERS, WILLIAM DILL, lawyer; b. Wilmington, Del., May 12, 1927; m. Suzanne Rochford, Sept. 7, 1926; children: William Rogers, Daniel. BA, Princeton U., 1948; LL.B., Yale U., 1951. Bar: D.C. 1952, U.S. Supreme Ct. 1954. Ptnr. Arnold & Porter, Washington, intermittently 1953—; dep. U.S. coordinator Alliance for Progress, AID, 1962-65; pres. N.Y. Ctr. Inter.-Am. Relations, 1965-72; asst. sec. of state inter-Am. relations Dept. State, 1974-76, undersec. of state for econ. affairs, 1976-77; mem. law faculty Cambridge U., Eng., 1982-83. Sr. counselor Bipartisan Commn. on Central Am., 1983-84; vice chmn. Kissinger Assocs. Inc. Author: The Twilight Struggle: The Alliance for Progress and U.S.-Latin-American Relations, 1967. Co-chmn. U.S.-Mexico Binat. Commn.; bd. dirs. Coun. Fgn. Rels., 1981-90. Mem. Am. Soc. Internat. Law (pres. 1971-73), ABA. Office: Arnold & Porter 555 12th St NW Washington DC 20004-1206 Home Phone: 202-337-7725; Office Phone: 202-942-5915. E-mail: william_rogers@aporter.com.

ROGERS, WILLIAM H., JR., bank executive; Exec. v.p. SunTrust Securities, Inc., Atlanta; sr. v.p. fin. SunTrust Banks, Inc., Atlanta, corp. exec. v.p. wealth and investment mgmt., mortgage, comml. and corp. and investment banking lines of bus. Office: SunTrust Banks Inc PO Box 4418 Atlanta GA 30302-4418 Office Phone: 404-588-7711. Office Fax: 404-827-6173. *

ROGERS, WILLIAM RAYMOND, retired academic administrator, psychologist, educator; b. Oswego, NY, June 20, 1932; s. William Raymond and A. Elizabeth (Hollis) R.; m. Beverley Claire Partington, Aug. 14, 1954; children: John Partington, Susan Elizabeth Apple, Nancy Claire Glassman. BA magna cum laude, Kalamazoo Coll., 1954; BD, U. Chgo. and Chgo. Theol. Sem., 1958; PhD, U. Chgo., 1965; MA (hon.), Harvard U., 1970. Cons., staff counselor Counseling and Psychotherapy Rsch. Ctr., U. Chgo., 1960-62; tchg. fellow, counselor to students Chgo. Theol. Sem., 1961-62; asst. prof. psychology and religion, dir. student counseling Earlham Coll., Richmond, Ind., 1962-68, assoc. prof. psychology and religion, assoc. dean of Coll., 1968-70; vis. lectr. pastoral counseling Harvard U. Div. Sch., Cambridge, Mass., 1969-70, prof. religion and psychology Div. and Edn. Schs., 1970-80, faculty chmn. clin. psychology and pub. practice, 1970-72, chmn. counseling and cons. psychology, 1979-80; prof. psychology and religious studies Guilford Coll., Greensboro, NC, 1980—, pres., 1980-96, pres. emeritus, 1996—. Bd. dirs. Moses Cone Health Sys., 1984-96, Moses Cone-Wesley Long Cmty. Health Found., 1996-2002, chmn. 1996-2002; bd. dirs. BB&T, Kendal Corp., chmn. 2005—. Author: The Alienated Student, 1969, Project Listening, 1974, Nourishing the Humanistic in Medicine, 1979; Contbr. articles to profl. jours. Bd. dirs. Greensboro Symphony Soc.; mem. Cemala Found. Danforth Found. fellow, Blatchford Traveling fellow U. Chgo. and Chgo. Theol. Sem. Mem.: Islesboro Hist. Soc. (pres. 1999—2002), So. Assn. Colls. and Schs., Nat. Assn. Ind. Colls. and Univs., Friends Com. on Nat. Legislation (mem. policy com.), Friends Assn. Higher Edn., Soc. Values in Higher Edn., Tarratine Club of Dark Harbor (bd. govs.), Rotary (past pres.). Mem. Soc. Of Friends. Home: 661 Main Rd Islesboro ME 04848-4201

ROGERS, WILLIAM WARREN, historian, educator, publishing executive, writer; b. Sandy Ridge, Ala., Aug. 18, 1929; s. Harry Ernest Rogers and Mittie Pate Loftin; m. Miriam Arnold Rogers, June 6, 1951; children: Warren, Arnold, Kate, Amy. BS, MS, Auburn U., Ala., 1951; PhD, U. N.C., Chapel Hill, 1959. With U.S. Army Counter Intelligence Corps, Stuttgart, Germany, 1954—56; instr. U. Md., Stuttgart, Germany, 1955—56; dir. Moody AFB program Fla. State U., Valdosta, Ga., 1958—59, prof. history Tallahassee, 1959—96; vis. prof. Fla. A&M, 1990, Auburn U., Ala., 1993, 1996; dir. Sentry Press, Inc., Tallahassee, 1996—. Bd. editors Fla. Historical Quarterly, 1970—2000; bd, dir Southern Studies, Nachitaches, La.; spkr. on politics and history to groups and orgns. Author: Ante-Bellum Thomas County, 1825-1861, 1963, Thomas County During the Civil War, 1964, The One-Gallused Rebellion, 1970 (Am. Assn. State and Local History award of Merit, 1972), Thomas County 1865-1900, 1973, Transition to the Twentieth Century Thomas County, Ga., 1900-1920, 2002, A Historic Sampler of Tallahassee and Leon County, 2005; co-author: Montgomery as the Confederate Capital: A View of a New Nation, 1964, Labor Revolt In Ala.: The Great Strike of 1894, 1965, Stephen S. Renfroe Ala.'s Outlaw Sheriff, 1972, Favored Land: A History of Tallahassee and Leon County, 1972 (Tallahassee/Leon County Historic Preservation Bd. award, 1972), August Reckoning Jack Turner and Racism in Post Civil War Ala., 1973, Convict's, Coal and the Banner Mine Tragedy, 1987, Ala.: The History of a Deep South State, 1994 (James F. Sulzby award, 1995), Fla.'s Clerks of the Circuit Ct. Their History and Experiences, 1996, Fla. Sheriffs: A History 1821-1945, 2001 (James J. Horgan award, 2002), The Croom Faily and Goodwood Plantation, 2001 (Nat. Assn. State and Local History Commendation of Merit, 2002), Ala.'s Response to the Penitentiary Movement, 1829-1865, 2003; editor: Am. Siberia by J.C. Powell, 1976; co-editor: Fla.'s Heritage of Diversity Essays in Honor of Samuel Proctor, 1997; contbr. scholarly articles to profl. jours. Finalist Prof. of Yr., Am. Hist. Assn.; named Outstanding Alumnus, Auburn U.; recipient Coyle Moore award Outstanding Tchg., Fla. State U. Faculty and Student Com., 1972, Lifetime Commitment commendation, Am. Assn. for State and Local History, 1994, Outstanding Tchr. award, Phi Alpha Theta (Fla. State chpt.), 1996; fellow, NEH, 1980; grantee, Am. Philosophical Soc., 1970. Democrat. Avocations: reading, walking, tennis, birdwatching, antique books. Office: Sentry Press Inc 424 E Call St Tallahassee FL 32301 Office Phone: 850-224-7423. Business E-Mail: www.wrogers@fsu.edu.

ROGERS, WINTON (LARRY) LAWRENCE, public information officer; b. Victoria, Tex., Feb. 16, 1944; s. John Ira Rogers and Pauline Inez Greenup; m. Maria Virginia Rosnare-Rogers, Dec. 1, 1970; children: Jennifer, Catherine, Christine, Coleen, John David. Grad. in Pub. Affairs, Def. Info. Sch., Indpls., 1990. Master sgt. US Army, 1964—84; pub. affairs officer Sierra Army Depot, Herlong, Calif., 1988—2003; county vets. svc. officer Lassen County, Susanville, Calif., 2003—. V.p. Lassen County Sr. Housing Coun., Susanville, 2006—. Mem.: DAV, VFW, Elks, Lassen County C. of C. (pres. 1990—95). Office: County Vets Svc Office 1205 Main St Susanville CA 96130

ROGERSON, ANTHONY RICHARD, otolaryngologist; s. John Richard Rogerson and Nancy Kay Rice; m. Angie Marie Dessner, May 9, 1992; children: Rachel, Abigail, Jack. BA, U. No. Iowa, Cedar Falls, 1984; MD, U Iowa, Iowa City, 1989. Diplomate Am. Bd. Otolaryngology. Staff surgeon Monroe Clinic, Wis., 1994—2006; clin. staff U. Wis., Madison, 2000—06. Bd. dirs. Monroe Clinic, 2003—06. Bd. dirs. Green County Golden Gators, Monroe, 2004—06. Fellow: Am. Acad. Otolaryngology Head & Neck Surgery, Am. Coll. Surgeons; mem.: Am. Rhinologic Soc. Republican. Cath. Avocations: guitar, sailing, coaching, skiing. Office: Monroe Clinc ENT Dept 515 22d Ave Monroe WI 53566

ROGERSON, CRAIG ALLAN, manufacturing executive; b. Detroit, July 4, 1956; s. William Durie and Eunice Clara (Richert) R.; m. Carina Joy Ballato, Sept. 11, 1982; children: Scott Allan, Kristen Joy, Colin William. BS in Chem. Engring., Mich. State U., 1979. Tech. rep. Water Mgmt. Chemicals div. Hercules Inc., Charlotte and Wilmington, N.C., 1979-82, sales rep. Fibers div. Atlanta, 1982-85, market devel. supr., 1985-87, product mgr., 1987-88, nat. sales mgr., 1989-90, dir. ops. Oxford, Ga., 1991-92, bus. dir. Wilmington, Del., 1992-94, sales dir. paper tech. divsn., 1995-96, v.p., gen. mgr. fibers divsn., 1996—97; pres., CEO Wacker Silicones Corp., 1997—2000; v.p., Betz Dearborn Div. Hercules Inc., 2000, pres., Betz Dearborn Div., 2000—02, pres., FiberVisions, 2002—03, pres., Pinova, 2002—03, v.p., Global Procurement, 2002—03, acting pres., COO, 2003, pres., CEO, 2003—. Bd. dirs. PRL Corp., First State Innovation. Mem. Del. Bus. Roundtable (bd. dirs.), Am. Chemistry Coun. (bd. dirs.). Republican. Lutheran. Avocations: racquetball, golf, travel. Home: PO Box 702 Gwynedd Valley PA 19437-0702 Office: Hercules Inc 1313 N Market St Wilmington DE 19894 Office Phone: 302-594-6601. *

ROGGE, RENA WOLCOTT, librarian; b. Bklyn., Nov. 3, 1920; d. Ralph Stratton and Mona Florence (Shannon) Wolcott; m. Carl Frederick Rogge Jr., Aug. 4, 1942; 1 son, Carl Frederick Rogge. B.A., Elmira Coll., 1941; M.L.S., Rutgers U., New Brunswick, N.J., 1966; M.A.L.S., New Sch. Social Research, N.Y.C., 1972, D. Info. Services, Nova Univ., 1987. Sec. Sch. Dist. South Orange, Maplewood, N.J., 1958-65; head reference librarian Cranford (N.J.) Pub. Library, 1966-68; readers' advisor Jersey City, 1968-69; reference librarian Newark State Coll., Union, N.J., 1969—; reference coordinator, asst. dir. for info. services Kean Coll. Library, sec. faculty senate, 1978-79, archivist faculty senate, 1979—, chmn. constn. revision, 1982—, grad. research com. 1983—. Recipient Outstanding Pub. Employee award, State of N.J., 1972, merit Award, 1983; online research grantee, Kean Coll. N.J., 1979. Mem. N.J. Library Assn., Am. Soc. Indexers, N.J. State Coll. Librarians' Assn., Kean Coll. Fedn. Tchrs. (exec. com.). Club: Elmira Coll. Home: 27 Bodwell Ter Millburn NJ 07041-1201 Office: Kean Coll Nancy Thompson Library Morris Ave Union NJ 07083-7117

ROGGENSACK, PATIENCE DRAKE, state supreme court justice; b. Joliet, Ill., 1941; BA, Drake U., 1962; JD, U. Wis. Law Sch., 1980. Atty. Dewitt Ross and Stevens, 1980—96; judge Wis. Ct. of Appeals, 1996—2003; justice Wis. Supreme Ct., 2003—. Mem.: ABA, Wis. Bar Assn. Office: Wis Supreme Ct PO Box 1688 Madison WI 53701-1688

ROGIN, GILBERT LESLIE, editor, author; b. NYC, Nov. 14, 1929; s. Robert I. and Lillian Carol (Ruderman) R. Student, State U. Iowa, 1947-49; AB, Columbia, 1951. Editor-at-large Miller Pub., LA, 1955—. Author: The Fencing Master, 1965, What Happens Next?, 1971, Preparations for the Ascent, 1980. Served with AUS, 1952-54. Recipient award for creative work in lit. Am. Acad. Inst. Arts and Letters 1972 Home: 21 W 10th St New York NY 10011

ROGOFF, JEROME HOWARD, psychiatrist, psychoanalyst, forensic expert; b. Detroit, Dec. 21, 1938; s. Abraham Solomon and Sarah Riva (Epstein) R.; (div. 1983); m. Erika Kathleen Keller, Sept. 25, 1983. BA cum laude, Harvard Coll., Cambridge, Mass., 1960; MD, Case Western Res. U., Cleve., 1965. Diplomate Am. Bd. Psychiatry and Neurology. Physician Peace Corps USPHS, Kathmandu, Nepal, 1966-68; clin. fellow psychiatry Harvard Med. Sch., Boston, 1975-79; staff psychiatrist Westwood (Mass.) Lodge Hosp., 1972-74; assoc. clin. prof. psychiatry Tufts Med. Sch., Boston, 1977-86; assoc. chief, psychiatry and dir., inpatient Psychiatry, day hosp. Faulkner Hosp., Boston, 1975-94; pvt. practice psychiatry, psychoanalysis and forensic psychiatry, 1994—. Cons. psychiatrist Mass. Parole Bd. Probate Ct. Plymouth County, Mass., LEAA, Washington, 1971-78; med. psychiat. dir. ct. diversion program Boston TASC-A, 1974-75; treas. Guild for Continuing Edn., Boston, 1981-95; founding dir. Law and Psychiatry Resource Ctr., Boston, 1983-2005; adj. prof. Simmons Sch. Social Work, Boston, 1981-85; lectr. psychiatry Harvard Med. Sch., Boston, 1986-94, 2001-. Chmn. psychiatry team Combined Jewish Philanthropies, Boston, 1978—83, assoc. chmn. med. team, 1984—87, social planning and allocations com., 1991—98, cmty. svcs. com., 1998—2007, chmn. chronic mental illness com., 1999—2000, disabilities com., 2000—04; bd. dirs. Jewish Vocat. Svc., Boston, 1987—91. Fellow: Am. Psychiat. Assn. (life; Disting., pub. affairs rep. 1988—94, budget com. 1996—2002, assembly rep. 2000—07, chmn. corr. com. on confidentiality 2003—07, task force to revise code of ethics 2005—, area dep. rep. 2007—, dep. rep. area coun. 2007—); mem.: APA, AMA, Am. Assn. Pvt. Practice Psychiatrists, Am. Acad. Psychiatry and Law, Mass. Psychiat. Soc. (councillor 1988—94, chair pub. affairs com. 1988—92, 1993—94, chair nominating com. 1990, 2000, pres.-elect 1998—99, pres. 1999—2000, Mass. rep. to Assembly 2000—07). Democrat. Avocations: cabinetry, carpentry, cooking, classical music, languages. Home and Office: 659 Chestnut St Waban MA 02468-2035 Office Phone: 617-964-1805. *Two guiding principles, both from my father: "When in doubt, do the right thing." Sounds trite and naive, but turns out in the event to be profound; one almost always knows deep down what the right thing is. "When you are born, you cry, and everyone around you laughs. So live your life that when you come to leave it, you laugh, and everyone around you cries." On my profession of psychiatry and psychoanalysis: psychotherapy adds insight to injury.*

ROGOFF, KENNETH SAUL, economics professor; b. Rochester, NY, Mar. 22, 1953; s. Stanley Miron and June Beatrice (Goldman) R.; m. Evelyn Jane Brody, Aug. 18, 1979 (div. 1989); m. Natasha Lance, June 25, 1995; children: Gabriel, Juliana. BA/MA in Econs., Yale U., 1975; PhD in Econs., MIT, 1980. Economist Internat. Monetary Fund, Washington, 1983; economist, sect. chief Internat. Fin. divsn., Bd. Govs. of the Fed. Res. Sys., Washington, 1979-84; assoc. prof. econs. U. Wis., Madison, 1985-89; prof. econs. U. Calif., Berkeley, 1989-92; prof. econs. and internat. affairs Princeton U., 1992—, Charles and Marie Robertson prof. of internat. affairs, 1995-98; prof. econs. Harvard U., 1999—, Thomas D. Cabot prof. pub. policy, 2004—, dir. Ctr. Internat. Devel., 2003—04; econ. counselor, dir. rsch. IMF, 2001—03. Vis. scholar San Francisco Fed. Res., 1990-92, World Bank, Washington, 1989, IMF, Washington, 1988-94. Author books and contbr. articles to profl. jours. Alfred P. Sloan Rsch. fellow, 1986-87, Hoover Instn. Nat. fellow, 1986-87, NSF fellow, 1985—, John Simon Guggenheim fellow, 1998. Fellow World Econ. Forum, Econometric Soc., Am. Acad. Arts and Scis., World Econ. Forum; mem. Am. Econ. Assn.(mem. trilateral com., v.p., 2007), Coun. on Fgn. Rels., Internat. Grandmaster Chess. Office: Harvard U Econs Dept Littauer Ctr Cambridge MA 02138-3001 Home Phone: 202-363-4529; Office Phone: 617-495-4022. Business E-Mail: krogoff@harvard.edu.

ROGOFF, PAULA DRIMMER, English and foreign language educator; b. NYC; d. George and Florence (Levine) Drimmer; m. Arnold Stevan Rogoff; children: Jeffrey Scott, Eric Todd, Brian Craig. BA cum laude, Hunter Coll., 1961; MEd summa cum laude, William Paterson Coll., 1979. Cert. elem. tchr., ESL tchr., supr., N.J. Tchr. handicapped Herricks Bd. Edn., Williston Park, NJ, 1965—68; tchr. reading compensatory edn. Oakland Bd. Edn., Oakland, NJ, 1981—84; tchr., coord. gifted-talented program North Haldeon Bd. Edn., NJ, 1984—85; ESL adult tchr., h.s. students Passaic County Tech. Inst., Wayne, NJ, 1989—2004. Presenter Children's Libr. programs. Named Tchr. of Yr., Passaic County Tech. Inst., 1999-2000. Mem. ASCD, NEA, TESOL, Internat. Platform Assn., N.J. Edn. Assn., Phi Beta Kappa, Phi Lambda Theta, Kappa Delta Pi. Home: 11 Furman Dr Wayne NJ 07470-5304 Office: Passaic County Tech Inst 45 Reinhardt Rd Wayne NJ 07470 Office Phone: 973-790-6000.

ROGOSKI, PATRICIA DIANA, corporate financial executive; b. Chgo., Dec. 29, 1939; d. Raymond Michael and Bernice Rose (Konkol) R. BS in Acctg. and Econs., Marquette U., 1961, postgrad., 1965-66, NYU, 1966-68, St. John's U., NYC, 1975-76; cert. mgmt. acct., 1979. Sr. fin. analyst

Blackhawk Mfg. Co., Milw., 1961-66; mgr., sr. analyst Shell Oil Co., NYC, 1966-71; mgr. data processing Bradford Nat./Penn Bradford, Pitts., 1971-75; asst. mgr. fin. controls ITT, NYC, 1975-79; v.p., comptr. ITT Consumer Fin. Corp., Mpls., 1979-80; sr. v.p. fin. ITT Fin. Corp., St. Louis, 1980-84; v.p., exec. asst., group exec. ITT Coins, Secaucus, NJ, 1984-85; pres. Patron S., Ltd., Wilmington, Del., 1986—; CFO, sr. v.p. Guardsmark, Inc., Memphis, 1989-94; sr. v.p. Peoplemark, Inc., Memphis, 1989-94. Bd. dirs. St. Louis Repertory Theater, 1983-84. Named to Acad. Women Achievers, YWCA, N.Y.C., 1980. Mem. Fin. Execs. Internat., Inst. Mgmt. Acctg., Econ. Club, Memphis Symphony Chorus. Avocation: duplicate bridge. Office: Patron S Ltd 2711 Centerville Rd Ste 400 Wilmington DE 19808- Personal E-mail: patron-s@msn.com.

ROGOVIN, JOHN A., lawyer; b. Washington, July 10, 1961; s. Mitchell and Sheila Ann (Ender) R. AB, Columbia U., 1983; JD, U. Va., 1987. Bar: NY 1989, DC 1990. Law clk. Hon. Laurence Silberman U.S. Ct. Appeals (DC Cir.), Washington, 1987—88; assoc. Kramer, Levin et al, NYC, 1988—89, O'Melveny & Myers, Washington, 1990—92, spl. counsel, 1996—97, ptnr., 1997—2001; dep. transition counsel Presdl. Transition, Little Rock, 1992—93; asst. to atty. gen. U.S. Dept. Justice, Washington, 1993, dep. asst. atty. gen. Civil Divsn., 1993—96; dep. gen. counsel FCC, Washington, 2001—02, gen. counsel, 2003—05; ptnr., Comm., E-Commerce and Litig. Dept. Wilmer Culter Pickering Hale & Dorr LLP, Washington, 2005—. Mem. ABA, DC Bar Assn. Office: Wilmer Culter Pickering Hale & Dorr LLP 1875 Pensylvania Ave NW Washington DC 20006 Office Phone: 202-663-6270. Office Fax: 202-663-6363. Business E-Mail: john.rogovin@wilmerhale.com.

ROGOVIN, LAWRENCE H., lawyer; b. NYC, June 10, 1932; s. Abraham and Laura R.; m. Saundra Schwartz, Aug. 11, 1957; children: Jayne Lina, Wendy Renee, Evan Lewis. BS in Econ., U. Pa., 1953; LLB cum laude, NYU Law Sch., 1956. Bar: NY 1956, Fla. 1971. Dep. asst. atty. gen. State of N.Y., 1956-57, asst. atty. gen., 1960-61; assoc. Squadron, Gartenberg, Ellenoff & Plesent and predecessors, NYC, 1962-67, ptnr., 1967-72; pvt. practice Miami, Fla., 1972—74, Lawrence H. Rogovin, P.A., Pa., 1983—98, Miami, 2002—; ptnr. Squadron, Ellenoff, Plesent & Lehrer, NYC, 1974-75, Cohen, Angel & Rogovin, North Miami, Fla., 1978-82, Cohen, Rogovin, Reed & Ivans, Miami, 1982-83; v.p., gen. counsel Rare, Inc., Miami, 1998—2002. 1st lt. JAGC, USAFR, 1957-60. Recipient NYU Founders Day award, 1956. Mem.: ABA, Fla. Bar Assn. Office: Ste 265 South 4000 Hollywood Blvd Hollywood FL 33021 Office Phone: 954-367-0666. Office Fax: 954-272-0225. Business E-Mail: lrogovin@bellsouth.net.

ROGOWSKI, CHERYL, farmer; AS, Orange County CC, 1981; BS, Mount St. Mary Coll., 1984. Farm mgr., 1977—. Founder Warwick Valley Farmer's Market, 1993; mentor New Farmer Devel. Project. Named MacArthur fellow, John D. and Catherine T. MacArthur Found., 2004. Achievements include establishment of the first low-income Cmty. Supported Agrl. program (CSA) in NY; creation of literary programs for migrant farm workers. Mailing: 327-329 Glenwood Rd Pine Island NY 10969 Office Phone: 845-258-4574.

ROGOWSKY, ROBERT ARTHUR, federal official, educator; b. Vancouver, BC, Can., Mar. 12, 1951; s. Michael Randall and Ruth Ann (Wellman) R.; m. Linda Sue George, June 17, 1972; children: Vanessa, Heather, Tara, Nichole, Alexis. BA in Econs., Boston U., 1973; MA in Econs., U. Va., 1975, PhD in Econs., 1982. Asst. prof. dept. econs. George Mason U., Fairfax, Va., 1977-78; rsch. economist Bur. Econs. FTC, Washington, 1979-83; econ. advisor to commrs. Consumer Product Safety Commn., Washington, 1983-84, acting exec. dir., asst. to dir., 1984; pres. Econ. Edn. for Clergy, Inc., Bethesda, Md., 1985-86; exec. asst. to chmn. Internat. Trade Commn., Washington, 1986-87; dep. dir. Bur. Consumer Protection FTC, Washington, 1987-89; dir. office of industries U.S. Internat. Trade Commn., Washington, 1989-92, dir. ops., 1992—; adj. prof. George Mason U., 1997—. Instr. U. Va., 1976-77; econ. rschr. Am. Enterprise Inst., 1976; econ. rsch. analyst Econ. Policy Office, U.S. Dept. Justice, 1974-75; adj. prof. George Mason U., 1997—; presenter in field. Contbr. articles to profl. jours. Mem. Am. Econs. Assn. Lutheran. Home: 9542 Locust Hill Dr Great Falls VA 22066 Office: US International Trade Comm Operations 500 E St NW Washington DC 20436-0003 Business E-Mail: robert.rogowsky@usitc.gov.

ROHACK, JOHN JAMES, cardiologist; b. Rochester, NY, Aug. 22, 1954; s. John Joseph and Margaret Elizabeth (McLaughlin) R.; m. Charlotte McCown, Dec. 7, 1980; 1 child, Elisha Monique Feigle. BS, U. Tex., El Paso, 1976; MD, U. Tex., Galveston, 1980. Diplomate Am. Bd. Internal Medicine. Intern U. Tex. Med. Br. Hosps., Galveston, 1980—81, resident internal medicine, 1981-83, chief resident internal medicine, 1983-84, fellow cardiology, 1984-86; instr. medicine U. Tex. Med. Br., Galveston, 1983-86; asst. prof. medicine to assoc. prof. Tex. A&M Coll. Medicine, College Station, 1986—2002, prof., 2002—, sect. chief cardiology, 1989-97, prof., 2002—. Assoc. med. dir. Scott and White Health Plan Bryan Coll. Sta., 1995-97; assoc. med. dir. for med. ops. Scott and White Health Plan and Clinic, 1997-2000, med. dir. Health Plan, 2000-04, med. dir. sys. improvement, 2004—; dir. S.W. Ctr. Healthcare Policy, 2004—; bd. dirs. Health for All Clinic, v.p., 1994-96; mem. Accreditation Coun. on Continuing Med. Edn., 1995-99, Liaison Com. on Med. Edn., 1999-2001; med. dir. Fitlife Ctr. Tex. A&M U., College Station, 1990-97; mem. bd. commrs. Joint Commn. on Accreditation of Healthcare Orgns., 2002—. Bd. dirs. Am. Heart Assn., Brazos Valley College Station, 1987-97, Tex. affiliate Austin, 1991-98, 1st v.p., 1994-95, pres.-elect, 1995-96, pres., 1996-97. Fellow ACP, Am. Coll. Cardiology (bd. dirs. Tex. chpt. 1992-97); mem. AMA (alt del. ho. of dels. 1984-93, del. 1993-2001, coun. on med. edn. 1995-2001, chair elect 1996-97, chair 1997-98, trustee 2001—, exec. com. 2003-06, chair 2004-05), Tex. Med. Assn. (exec. coun. med. student sect. 1981-82, ho. of dels. 1982—, trustee 1994-2002, pres.-elect 1999-2000, pres. 2000-2001). Avocations: golf, gardening, reading, ranching. Office: Scott and White Clinic 2401 S 31st St Temple TX 76508-0001

ROHAN, KAREN S., insurance company executive; BS, Boston Coll., 1984; MBA, Boston U., 1999. CPA. With CIGNA Corp., 1991—, contr., sr. v.p. underwriting CIGNA HealthCare, v.p., bus. fin. officer CIGNA HealthCare, 2000—02, chief underwriting officer CIGNA HealthCare, 2003—04, pres. CIGNA Specialty Cos., 2004—05, pres. CIGNA Dental & Vision Care, 2004—, pres. CIGNA Group Ins., 2005—. Office: CIGNA Corp Two Liberty Pl 1601 Chestnut St Philadelphia PA 19192-1550 *

ROHATYN, FELIX GEORGE, diversified financial services company executive, former ambassador; b. Vienna, May 29, 1928; came to U.S., 1942, naturalized, 1950; s. Alexander and Edith (Knoll) R.; m. Jeannette Streit, June 9, 1956; children: Pierre, Nicolas, Michael; m. Elizabeth Fly, May 31, 1979. BS, Middlebury Coll., Vt., 1948; LLD (hon.), Adelphi U., Bard Coll., Hofstra U., 1981, L.I. U., 1981, Middlebury Coll., 1982, Fordham U., 1983; LLB (hon.), NYU, 1979, Brandeis U., 1987. With Lazard Freres & Co., LLC, NYC, 1948—97, mng. dir., 1960—97; US amb. to France US Dept. State, Paris, 1997—2001; pres. Rohatyn Assocs., NYC, 2002—06; sr. adv. to chmn. Lehman Brothers Inc., NYC, 2006—. Bd. dirs. Publicis Group, Rothschild, Lagardere Group, LVMH, Inc.; mem. bd. govs. N.Y. Stock Exch., 1968—72. Served with AUS, 1951—53, Korea. Office: Lehman Brothers Inc 745 7th Ave 30th Fl New York NY 10019

ROHDE, JAMES VINCENT, software systems company executive; b. O'Neill, Nebr., Jan. 25, 1939; s. Ambrose Vincent and Loretta Cecillia Rohde; children: Maria, Sonja, Daniele, Olga. B of Comml. Sci., Seattle U., 1962. Chmn. bd. dirs., pres. Applied Telephone Tech., Oakland, Calif., 1974; v.p. sales and mktg. Automation Electronics Corp., Oakland, 1975-82; founder, pres., CEO, chmn. Am. Telecorp, Inc., Redwood City, Calif., 1982-99; founder, vice-chmn., bd. dirs. Ceon Corp., Redwood City, 1999—. Chmn. exec. com., chmn. emeritus Pres.'s Coun. Heritage Coll., Toppenish, Wash., 1985—; chmn. bd. dirs. Calif. chpt. Coun. Growing Cos., 1990—93. Bd. dirs. Ind. Colls. No. Calif., 1991—93. With aux. USCG, 2005—. Named Export Exec. of the Yr. No. Calif., US Dept. Commerce, 1993. Mem.: Am. Electronics Assn. (bd. dirs. 1992—94, vice-chmn. No. Calif. coun. 1992—93, chmn. 1993—94). Republican. Roman Catholic. Office: Ceon Corp 1600 Seaport Blvd Redwood City CA 94063 Home Phone: 415-897-1613. Personal E-mail: jvrohde@aol.com.

ROHDE, JOE (JOSEPH MARTIN ROHDE), theme park executive, designer; b. Sacramento, Calif., Sept. 10, 1955; m. Melody Malmberg; children: Kellan, Brandt. BA in Fine Arts, Occidental Coll., LA. With Walt Disney Imagineering, Walt Disney Co., Lake Buena Vista, Fla., 1980—, exec. designer and v.p. creative; lead designer Disney's Animal Kingdom Lake Buena Vista. Featured (documentaries) Expedition Everest: Journey to Sacred Lands, Travel Channel, 2006. Achievements include principal creative force behind Disney's Animal Kingdom Expedition Everest thrill ride; model designer, scenic painter Epcot's Mexico pavilion; designer on refurbishment of Fantasyland at Disneyland, Captain EO 3-D film attraction, Epcot's Norway pavilion, and Adventurers Club. Avocations: painting, travel, reading.

ROHLF, F. JAMES, biologist, educator; b. Blythe, Calif., Oct. 24, 1936; BS, San Diego State Coll., 1958; PhD in Entomology, U. Kans., 1962. Asst. prof. biology U. Calif., Santa Barbara, 1962-65; assoc. prof. statis. biology U. Kans., 1965-69; assoc. prof. biology SUNY, Stony Brook, 1969-72, prof., 1972—2004, chmn. dept. ecology and evolution, 1975—80, 1990—91, disting. prof., 2004—, grad. program dir., 2005—06. Statis. cons. N.Y. Pub. Svc. Commn., 1975-78, IBM, 1977-81, U.S. EPA, 1978-80; vis. scientist IBM, Yorktown Heights, N.Y., 1976-77, 80-81; vis. prof. U. Rome, 1997, 99; guest prof. U. Vienna, 2004. Fellow: Am. Acad. Arts and Scis., AAAS; mem.: Internat. Fedn. Classification Socs. (coun. 2005—), Classification Soc. N.Am. (pres. 1975—78, editl. bd. 1984—, bd. dirs. 1994—97, fin. com. 2004—06, rep. to coun. 2004—, election com. 2006—, bd. dirs. 2006—), Soc. Systematic Biologists, Biometric Soc. Achievements include research and development of statistical methods and software for geometric morphometrics and applications of multivariate analysis to systematics and population biology. Office: Stony Brook U Dept Ecology And Evolution Stony Brook NY 11794-5245

ROHLFF, GERI, secondary school educator; BA, U. Calif., Davis, 1976; MA in Spl. Edn., San Francisco State U., 1983. Tchr. remedial reading and math Opportunity Sch., Sacramento, 1976—77; tchr. English, spl. edn. Independent Learning Sch., Larkspur; adult edn. tchr. Capuchino HS, San Mateo HS, 1984—89; tchr. English Lakeridge Jr. High, Wash., 1989—90, Auburn HS, Wash., 1990—95, Heritage Inst., Clinton, Wash., 1992—; tchr. language arts Auburn Riverside HS, Wash., 1995—. Named to Nat. Tchrs. Hall of Fame, 2007; recipient Christa McAuliffe Award for Excellence in Edn., 1993, Wal-Mart Wash. State Tchr. of Yr., 2004, Puget Sound Regional Tchr. of Yr., 2005. Office: Auburn Riverside HS 501 Oravetz Rd Auburn WA 98092 *

ROHLFING, FREDERICK WILLIAM, lawyer, retired judge, political scientist; b. Honolulu, Nov. 2, 1928; s. Romayne Raymond and Kathryn (Coe) R.; m. Joan Halford, July 15, 1952 (div. Sept. 1982); children: Frederick W., Karl A., Brad (dec.); m. Patricia Ann Santos, Aug. 23, 1983. BA, Yale U., 1950; JD, George Washington U., 1955. Bar: Hawaii 1955, Am. Samoa 1978. Assoc. Moore, Torkildson & Rice, Honolulu, 1955-60; ptnr. Rohlfing, Nakamura & Low, Honolulu, 1963-68, Hughes, Steiner & Rohlfing, Honolulu, 1968-71, Rohlfing, Smith & Coates, Honolulu, 1981-84; pvt. practice Honolulu, 1960-63, 71-81, Maui County, Hawaii, 1988—; dep. corp. counsel County of Maui, Wailuku, Hawaii, 1984-87, corp. counsel, 1987-88; land and legal counsel Maui Open Space Trust, 1992-97, also bd. dirs. Polit. cons., 1996, 98, 2002; magistrate judge U.S. Dist. Ct. Hawaii, 1991-96. Active Hawaii Ho. Reps., 1959-65, 80-84, Hawaii State Senate, 1966-75; US alt. rep. So. Pacific Commn., Noumea, New Caledonia, 1975-77, 1982-84; mem. adv. coun. State Reapportionment Commn., Maui, Hawaii, 2001, mem. salary commn. Maui (Hawaii) County, 2005—; hon. chmn. Maui coms. George W. Bush for Pres., 2000. Mem. Hawaii Bar Assn., Maui Country Club, Naval Intelligence Profls. Avocations: golf, swimming. Home: 2807 Kekaulike Ave Kula HI 96790

ROHM, ROBERT HERMANN, sculptor, educator; b. Cin., Feb. 6, 1934; s. Hermann George and Anna Katherine (Sager) R.; m. Patricia Jean Cutlip, Dec. 6, 1959 (div. 1978); children: Hans Tobin, Kyle Curtis. B in Indsl. Design, Pratt Inst., 1956; MFA in Sculpture, Cranbrook Acad. Art, 1960. Instr. Columbus (Ohio) Coll. Art and Design, 1956-59, Pratt Inst., Bklyn., 1960-65; prof. art U. R.I., Kingston, 1965-95, pres. emeritus, 1996—. One-man shows include O.K. Harris Gallery, N.Y.C., 1970, 72, 73, 75, 77, 80, 83, 84, 86, 89, 92, 94, 97, 99, 2002, 05, Parker St. 470 Gallery, Boston, 1970, 72, Univ. Rochester, N.Y., 1971, N.S. Coll. Art, Halifax, 1970, Worcester Art Mus. (Mass.), 1978, Univ. R.I., 1981, 88, 94, Nielsen Gallery, Boston, 1985, 86, 92, 93, 2001, Wheaton Coll., Norton, Mass., 2002, La Jolla Mus. Contemporary Art, Calif., 1985, Lenore Gray Gallery, Providence, 1990, 93, 95, Wheeler Gallery, Providence, 1996, R.I. Coll., Providence, 1998, Salve Regina U., Newport, R.I., 2003; group shows include Boston Mus., 1974, Whitney Mus., N.Y.C., 1962, 64, 69, 70, 73, 83, Va. Mus., Richmond, 1970, Fogg Mus., Cambridge, Mass., 1971, Seattle Art Mus., 1969, Vancouver Art Mus., B.C., Can., 1970, N.J. State Mus., Trenton, 1969, R.I. State Coun. on Arts, 1973, 82, Vassar Coll., 1971, Inst. Contemporary Art, Boston, 1975, Miss. Mus. Art, Jackson, 1979-80, Grey Art Gallery, NYU, 1980, Montclair (N.J.) Art Mus., 1978, Aldrich Mus. Contemporary Art, Ridgefield, Conn.,1981, 82, SUNY-Plattsburgh, 1981, Zone Gallery, Springfield, Mass., 1982, Cumberland Gallery, Nashville, 1986, 93, Allan Frumkin Gallery, N.Y.C., 1985, Beitzel Fine Arts Inc., N.Y.C., Addison Gallery Am. Art, Andover, Mass., 1989, Nielsen Gallery, Boston, 1990-91, 99, 2004, Soma Gallery, San Diego, 1993, Palo Alto (Calif.) Cultural Ctr., Centre Coll., Danville, Ky., Harn Mus., U. Fla., Gainesville, 2004, Brevard Mus. Art & Sci., Melbourne, Fla., 2004; represented in permanent collections Columbus Gallery Fine Art, Finch Coll., N.Y.C., Pa. State U., Kunsthalle, Zurich, Va. Mus. Fine Arts, Mus. Modern Art, N.Y.C., U. N.Mex., Albuquerque, Albright-Knox Gallery, Buffalo, Whitney Mus. Am. Art, N.Y.C., Met. Mus. Art, N.Y.C., Rose Art Mus., Brandeis U., Waltham Mass., Mus. Fine Art, Boston, Mus. of Contemporary Art, Chgo., Newport (R.I.) Art Mus., Tucson Mus. of Art, Ariz., Flint Inst. Arts, Mich., Butler Inst. Am. Art, Youngstown, Ohio, Munson-Williams Proctor Arts Inst. Mus. Art, Utica, N.Y., Harn Mus., U. Fla., Gainesville, Amarillo Mus. Art, Tex. Grantee Guggenheim Found., 1964, R.I. State Council on Arts, 1973, 82, 93, NEA, 1974, 86; recipient Cassandra Found. award, 1967, award Boston 200 Bicentennial Commn., 1975. Achievements include subject of numerous articles in jours. and catalogues. Home: PO Box 1679 Charlestown RI 02813-0909 Personal E-mail: robertrohm@netsense.net.

ROHMAN, THOMAS P., lawyer; b. Portsmouth, Va., 1955; BBA in acctg., Notre Dame U., 1977; JD summa cum laude, Mich. State U., 1982; LLM in Taxation, NYU, 1983. CPA Va., 1980; bar: Va. 1983, US Tax Ct. 1986. With KPMG Peat Marwick, 1977—80; ptnr. McGuireWoods LLP, Richmond, Va., 1991—, chmn. firm taxation & employee benefits dept., 1999—2005. Adj. prof. corp. reorganizatiosn Va. Commonwealth U. Grad. Tax Program, 1986—92; adj. prof. partnership taxation & corp. taxation TC Williams Sch. Law, U. Richmond, 1989—; mem. adv. coun. William and Mary Tax Conf., 1994—. Co-author: S Corporations: Federal Taxation, 1989. Mem. adv. bd. Meml. Found. for Children, 1987—. Fellow: Am. Coll. Tax Counsel; mem.: ABA (mem. com. on S corporations, com. on corp. tax, com. on partnerships), Va. Soc. Cert. Pub. Accountants, Am. Inst. Cert. Pub. Accountants. Office: McGuireWoods LLP One James Ctr 901 E Cary St Richmond VA 23219-4030 Office Phone: 804-775-1032. Office Fax: 804-698-2154. Business E-Mail: trohman@mcguirewoods.com.

ROHN, REUBEN DAVID, medical educator, director; b. Israel, Apr. 12, 1945; came to U.S., 1954; s. Aryeh and Rachel (Brenner) R.; m. Judith Semel, Sept. 6, 1971; 1 child, Karen. BA cum laude, Bklyn. Coll., 1967; MD, N.Y. Med. Coll., 1971. Diplomate Am. Bd. Pediat., Am. Bd. Pediatric Endocrinology, Am. Bd. Pediatrics-Adolescent Medicine. Intern in pediat. Montefiore Hosp., Bronx, N.Y., 1971-72, resident in pediat., 1972-74; fellow in adolescent medicine U. Md. Hosp., Balt., 1974-76; preceptor in pediat. Johns Hopkins U. Sch. Health Svcs., Balt., 1975-76; asst. prof. dept. pediat. Ea. Va. Med. Sch., Norfolk, 1976-82; coord. pediat. clerkship Ea. Va. Med. Sch., Children's Hosp. of King's Daus., Norfolk, 1977-90; prof. dept. pediat. Ea. Va. Med. Sch., Norfolk, 1989—; adj. prof. chemistry Old Dominion U., Norfolk, 1984—; dir. adolescent medicine/endocrinology Children's Hosp. of King's Daus., Norfolk, 1976—. Mem. curriculum com. Ea. Va. Med. Sch., 1977-79, clerkship coords. com. 1977-90, genetics com., 1978-80, evaluation com. 1979-91, chmn. selectives com., 1981-82, ad hoc com. on consultation, 1982-83, student progress com., 1983-85, student health com., 1985-87, LCME com. on curriculum, 1990-92; mem. child abuse com. Children's Hosp. of King's Daus., 1976-80, chmn. adolescent adv. com., 1976-80, patient care com. 1980-94, nutrition com. 1980-94, utilization rev. com., 1980-82, med. records com., 1987-89, gen. med./surg. task force com., 1987-88, chmn. dept. promotions com., 1990—; bd. dirs. Pediat. Faculty Assocs., 1994-98, mgmt. com. Children's Specialty Group, 1998-2000; spkr. in field. Reviewer Jour. Adolescent Health Care, 1986—, mem. editl. bd., 1989-92; contbr. articles to profl. jours. Mem. Norfolk Sch. Health Coun., 1977—93, mem. ad hoc com. infant screening program for hypothroidism Commonwealth of Va., 1977-79, cons., 1979—; mem. cmty. adv. bd. Norfolk Adolescent Pregnancy Prevention Svc. Project, 1981-83; bd. dirs. Elizabeth River chpt. Am. Diabetes Assn., 1982-85, South Hampton Roads chpt. 1985-93; mem. adv. com. Norfolk-Virginia Beach Jr. League, 1987-88; judge ann. Health Edn. Fair, Norfolk Pub. schs., 1980-94; pres. VA/Carolines chpt. Soc. Adolescent Medicine, 1998-2000. Recipient grant Bressler Rsch. Fund, 1975-76, Biomed. Rsch. Devel. grant Ea. Va. Med. Sch., 1978, 78-79, 79-80. 81-82, 83-84, Children's Health Found. grant, 1988-89. Fellow: Am. Acad. Pediat. (youth and adolescence com. Va. chpt. 1978—2000); mem.: Lawson Wilkins Pediat. Endocrine Soc., Soc. Adolescent Medicine (abstract reviewer 1984—91), Sigma Xi. Avocations: photography, folk dancing. Home: 4653 Larkwood Dr Virginia Beach VA 23464-5815 Office: Childrens Hosp Kings Daus 601 Childrens Ln Norfolk VA 23507-1910 Office Phone: 757-668-7237. Business E-Mail: rohnrd@chkd.org.

ROHN, WILLIAM R., biotechnology company executive; BA, Mich. U. Mktg. and sales mgmt. positions Abbott Labs., Warren-Teed Pharms., Miles Labs., Mead Johnson Labs.; sr. v.p. sales and mktg. Adria Labs. (Pharmacia Corp.), 1984—93; sr. v.p. comml. and corp. devel. IDEC Pharms., Inc., San Diego, 1993—96, sr. v.p. comml. ops., 1996—98, COO, 1998—2003, pres., 2002—03; COO Biogen Idec, 2003—. Bd. dirs. Pharmacyclics, Cerus Corp., 2002—. Office: Biogen Idec 5200 Research Pl San Diego CA 92122-4616

ROHNER, NICHOLAS K., lawyer; b. Cin., Sept. 14, 1974; BA, Miami U., 1997; JD, U. Cin. Coll. Law, 2001. Bar: Ohio 2001, US Dist. Ct. Southern Dist. Ohio 2001, Ind. 2002, US Dist. Ct. Southern Dist. Ind. 2002, US Dist. Ct. Northern Dist. Ind. 2002. Assoc. Weltman, Weinburg & Reis Co., L.P.A., Cin. Named one of Ohio's Rising Stars, Super Lawyers, 2006. Mem.: Cin. Bar Assn., Ohio State Bar Assn., Ind. State Bar Assn., Alpha Phi Omega. Office: Weltman Weinberg & Reis Co LPA 525 Vine St Ste 800 Cincinnati OH 45202 Office Phone: 513-723-2200. Office Fax: 513-723-2239.

ROHNER, RALPH JOHN, lawyer, educator, dean; b. East Orange, NJ, Aug. 10, 1938; AB, Cath. U. Am., 1960, JD, 1963. Bar: Md. 1964. Teaching fellow Stanford (Calif.) U., 1963-64; atty. pub. health div. HEW, 1964-65; prof. law Cath. U. Am. Sch. Law, Washington, 1965—, acting dean, 1968-69, assoc. dean, 1969-71, dean, 1987-95; staff counsel consumer affairs subcom. U.S. Senate Banking Com., 1975-76; cons. Fed. Res. Bd., 1976-83, chmn. consumer adv. council, 1981; cons. FDIC, 1978-80; spl. counsel Consumer Bankers Assn., 1984—. Cons. U.S. Regulatory Coun., 1979-80. Co-author: Consumer Law: Cases and Materials, 1979, 3d edit., 2007; co-author, editor The Law of Truth in Lending, 1984, republished, 2000. Bd. dirs. Migrant Legal Action Program, Inc., Washington, Automobile Owners Action Coun., Washington, Credit Rsch. Ctr., Georgetown U., Am. Fin. Svcs. Assn. Edn. Found. Conf. on Consumer Fin. Law. Mem. ABA, Am. Law Inst., Coll. of Consumer Fin. Svcs. Lawyers. Home: 10909 Forestgate Pl Glenn Dale MD 20769-2047 Office: Cath U Sch Law 620 Michigan Ave NE Washington DC 20064-0001 Office Phone: 202-319-5140. Business E-Mail: rohner@law.edu. *We learn from those we teach, we are inspired to write by those who read, and we should serve as examples to those who aspire.*

ROHNER, THOMAS JOHN, JR., urologist; b. Trenton, NJ, Jan. 1, 1936; s. Thomas J. and Julia (Kanyo) R.; m. Jessie Rohner; children: Christopher, James. BA, Yale U., 1957; MD, U. Pa., 1961. Diplomate Am. Bd. Urology. Intern Hosp. U. Pa., Phila., 1961-62, resident in gen. surgery, 1962-64, resident in urology, 1964-67; asst. prof. surgery M.S. Hersey Med. Ctr., Pa. State U., Hershey, 1970-71, assoc. prof., 1971-75, prof., 1975—, chief urol. divsn., 1970-2000; assoc. dean for clin. affairs M.S. Hershey Med. Ctr., Pa. State U., Hershey, 1996-99, interim chair dept. surgery, 1998-99, chief of med. staff, 1999-2000. Corp. mem. Pa. Blue Shield, 1991—; bd. dirs. Highmark, Inc., 2003-. Contbr. articles to profl. jours. Served to maj. M.C., U.S. Army, 1967-69. USPHS fellow, 1969-70; grantee HEW, 1971-76, USPHS, 1971-76 Fellow ACS (pres. ctrl. Pa. chpt. 1983-84, bd. govs. 1991-97); mem. AMA, Am. Urol. Assn. (pres. mid-Atlantic sect. 1986-87, bd. dirs. 2006-), Urol. Assn. Pa., Phila. Urol. Soc. (pres. 1980-81), Assn. Acad. Surgeons, Am. Bd. Urology (trustee 1995-2001), Pa. Med. Soc., Dauphin County Med. Soc., Soc. Pediat. Urology, Soc. Univ. Urologists (pres. 1990-91), Nat. Urol. Assn. (bd. dirs. 2006), Societe Internationale d'Urologie, Transamerican Urol. Rschrs., Internat. Continence Soc., Coll. Physicians of Phila. Home: 2907 Mt Gretna Rd Elizabethtown PA 17022-9689 Office: Milton S Hershey Med Ctr Pa State Univ PO Box 850 Hershey PA 17033-0850 Home Phone: 717-367-0404; Office Phone: 717-531-8849. Business E-Mail: trohner@psu.edu.

ROHR, CAROL ANN, composer, pianist, music educator; d. Herbert Samuel and Cecil Leotta Neale; m. Stephen P. Rohr, May 30, 1968. MusM, U. S.D., 1967—71. Composer: (piano composition) Dorian Grey for Piano (Cedar Rapids, Iowa Beethoven Club, 2004), (piano, violin and cello composition) Stream of Consciousness (Iowa Composer's Concert, 1994), (piano composition) Sonata and Postlude (Iowa Composers Forum Ann. Concert at Coe Coll., Cedar Rapids, Iowa, 1980). Chair, orgn. support Cedar Rapids City Music Contest, 1975—2004. Scholar Swensrud scholarship award, Northwood Pub. Sch., 1955—58. Mem.: Nat. Music Tchrs. Assn. (assoc.), Iowa Music Tchrs. Assn. (assoc.; student performance auditions and festivals 1980—), Iowa Composers Forum (assoc.), Beethoven Club of Cedar Rapids, Iowa (assoc.; libr./historian

1995—2005). Home: 4008 Glen Elm Drive NE Cedar Rapids IA 52402-2667 Office: Carol A Rohr Private Piano Instruction 4008 Glen Elm Dr NE Cedar Rapids IA 52402-2667 Home Phone: 319-393-6332.

ROHR, DAVIS CHARLES, aerospace consultant, retired military officer; b. Burlington, Wis., Oct. 29, 1929; s. Charles Davis Rohr and Dorothy Elizabeth (Hahn) Rohr Larson; m. Gayle Lynn White, Aug. 22, 1959; children— Ellen Louise, Jean Elizabeth Student, Northwestern U., 1947-48; B.Sc., U.S. Mil. Acad., 1952; MA, U. Wash., 1960. Commd. 2d lt. USAF, 1952, advanced through grades to maj. gen, 1980, fighter pilot Ohio, Korea, Japan, 1954-58; asst. prof. history USAF Acad., Colo., 1960-64; fighter pilot, squadron ops. officer Idaho and, Fed. Republic Germany, 1965-69; fighter squadron comdr. Vietnam, 1969-70; country dir. S.Am. Office of Sec. of Def., Washington, 1970-73; exec. officer, dep. dir. maintenance Hdqrs. Tactical Air Command, 1973-75; tactical fighter wing comdr. Tex., Utah, 1976-79; chief Office of Mil. Coop., Cairo, 1979—81; dir. plans and policy U.S. European Command, Stuttgart, Fed. Republic Germany, 1981-84; dep. comdr. in chief U.S. Cen. Command, MacDill AFB, Fla., 1984-87, ret.; aerospace cons., 1988—. Adj. prof. history Paradise Valley C.C., 1991-94; real estate broker, 1991—. Decorated Def. D.S.M., 2 Def. Superior Service medals, Legion of Merit with cluster, D.F.C., Meritorious Service medal, Air medal with 14 clusters, Air Force Commendation medal, Purple Heart

ROHR, DONALD GERARD, history professor; b. Toledo, Oct. 10, 1920; s. Lewis Walter and Marie (Pilliod) R.; m. Joan Willis Michener, Sept. 14, 1948; children: Karen, Kristin. BA, U. Toronto, Ont., Can., 1943, MA, 1949; PhD, Harvard U., 1958. Instr., then asst. prof. Williams Coll., 1953—59; mem. faculty Brown U., 1959—, prof. history, 1963—86, prof. history emeritus, 1986—, chmn. dept., 1960—65, 1966—69, 1972—74, sec. faculty, 1969—72, assoc. dean faculty and acad. affairs, 1976—81; adminstrv. dir. Howard Fedn., 1989—92. Author: The Origins of Social Liberalism in Germany, 1963, (with Robert Ergang) Europe Since Waterloo, 1967; editor: The Young John Carter Brown in Europe, 2005. Served with AUS, 1943-46, ETO. Mem. Providence Com. Fgn. Rels. (sec. 1968-81, chmn. 1981-92), Thomas Becket Fedn. (v.p. 1983-84, pres. 1984-86), English Speaking Union (pres. Providence br. 1986-88), U. Club, Faculty Club (Providence, pres. 1981-83). Roman Catholic. Home: 71 Grotto Ave Providence RI 02906 Office Phone: 401-863-2131.

ROHR, DWIGHT MASON, news director, radio marketing consultant; b. Covington, Va., July 18, 1952; s. Edward Mason and Betty (Eppling) R.; m. Betty Erwin, Aug. 1, 1977; children: Christopher Mason, Joseph Michael. AAS in Bus. Mgmt., Dabney S. Lancaster C.C., Clifton Forge, Va., 1997. Cert. radio operator; cert. radio mktg. cons. Audio engr. WJBR, Wilmington, Del., 1971-72; announcer WASA/WHDG, Havre de Grace, Md., 1972-73; news dir. mktg. WKEY Inc., Covington, 1974—2005. Active Stonewall Jackson Area coun. Boy Scouts Am., 1990-99; dir. cmty. rels. ARC, Covington, 1975-98; mem. adv. bd. Salvation Army, Covington, 1995-2001, Alleghany County chpt. March of Dimes, 2001-, Alleghany Heart Unit, Potts Valley Singers; city coucilman, Covington, 1997-98; mountaineer Amateur Radio Emergency Svc; mem. Alleghen Anti-Violence Task Force. Recipient Scouter of Yr. awrd VFW Post 1033, 1994, Dist. award of merit Boy Scouts Am., 1995, Silver Beaver, 1998; named to Outstanding Young Men of Am., 1980. Mem. Soc. Profl. Journalists, Radio TV News Dirs. Assn., Masons, Scottish Rite, Eastern Star, Va. Mountain Amateur Radio Club, Covington Ruritan Club, Highland Toastmasters. Avocations: amateur radio, broadcasting, coin collecting/numismatics. Home: 347 E Gray St Covington VA 24426-2109 Office Phone: 540-962-1133. Personal E-mail: w4spj@aol.com.

ROHR, JAMES EDWARD, diversified financial services company executive; b. Cleve., Oct. 18, 1948; s. Charles E. and Loretta (Kramer) R.; m. Sharon Lynn Chambers, Dec. 29, 1970; children: Julie, James, Kristen. BA, Notre Dame U., 1970; MBA, Ohio State U., 1972. From comml. banking officer to pres. Pitts. Nat. Bank, 1974-89, chmn., CEO, 1989-93, pres., CEO, 1993—; vice-chmn. PNC Bank Corp., 1989-92, pres., 1992—98, pres., COO, 1998—2000; pres., CEO PNC Fin. Svcs. Group, Inc., Pitts., 2000—01, chmn., CEO, 2001—. Bd. dirs. Allegheny Techs. Corp., Equitable Resources, Inc., Rand Corp., Black Rock, Inc., PFPC Worldwide, Inc. Bd. dirs. Greater Pitts. coun. Boy Scouts Am., Carnegie-Mellon U.; chair Cultural Trust. Mem. Am. Bankers Assn., Internat. Monetary Conf., Fin. Svcs. Roundtable, Allegheny Conf., Orgn., Pa. Bus. Roundtable. Roman Catholic. Office: PNC Financial Services Group Inc 249 5th Ave Pittsburgh PA 15222-2709 *

ROHR, MARK C., chemicals executive; Sr. v.p. Occidental Chem. Corp.; exec v.p. ops. Albemarle Corp., Richmond, Va., 1999, pres., COO, 2000—02, pres., CEO, 2002—. Office: Albemarle Corp 330 S 4th St Richmond VA 23219 *

ROHR, RICHARD DAVID, lawyer; b. Toledo, Aug. 31, 1926; s. Lewis Walter and Marie Janet (Pilliod) R.; m. Ann Casey, Aug. 25, 1951; children: Martha, Elizabeth, Matthew, Sarah, Margaret, Thomas. BA magna cum laude, Harvard U., 1950; JD, U. Mich., 1953. Bar: Mich. 1954, U.S. Dist. Ct. (so. dist.) Mich. 1954, U.S. Ct. Appeals (6th cir.) 1960, U.S. Supreme Ct. 1961. Assoc. Bodman, Longley & Dahling, L.L.P., Detroit, 1954-58, ptnr., 1958-75, mng. ptnr., 1975-2000; with Bodman LLP, Detroit, 2000—. Adj. prof. U. Mich., Ann Arbor, 1976-82. With US Army, 1945—46. Mem. ABA, Detroit Bar Assn., Mich. Bar Assn., Detroit Athletic Club, Order of Coif, Phi Beta Kappa. Roman Catholic. Home: 441 Rivard Blvd Grosse Pointe MI 48230-1627 Office: Bodman LLP 6th Fl at Ford Field 1901 St Antoine St Detroit MI 48226 Office Phone: 313-393-7550. Business E-Mail: rrohr@bodmanllp.com.

ROHR, RICHARD EDWARD, physician, administrator; b. New Rochelle, NY, Jan. 18, 1955; s. Robert Lewis and Grace Ann Rohr. BA, Columbia U., 1976; MD, N.Y. Med. Coll., 1980; M of Med. Mgmt., Tulane U., 2003. Diplomate Am. Bd. Internal Medicine. Resident in internal medicine Danbury (Conn.) Hosp., 1980-83; fellow in pulmonary disease U. Conn. Sch. Medicine, Farmington, 1983-85; physician Med. West Cmty. Health Care Plan, Chicopee, Mass., 1985-88, Cmty. Health Care Plan, New Haven, 1988-93; med. dir. Cedar Lane Rehab. and Health Care Ctr., Waterbury, Conn., 1993-96; asst. dir. respiratory and intensive care Milford Hosp., Conn., 1996—2007; v.p. med. affairs Courtland Regional Med. Ctr., NY, 2007—. Acting health dir. City of Milford, 1998-99. Grant reviewer United Way Milford, 1997—. Chmn. bd. dirs. Milford-Orange YMCA, 1993-2001 dir. Milford chpt. ARC, 1998-2001, Ctrl. Conn. Coast YMCA, New Haven, 1999-2001; dir. United Way of Milford, 2005—. Fellow Am. Coll. Chest Physicians, Am. Coll. Physicians; mem. Am. Coll. Physician Execs., Am. Thoracic Soc. Roman Catholic. Avocation: photography. Home: 269 Captain Thomas Blvd West Haven CT 06516-5953 Office: Courtland Regional Med Ctr 134 Homer Ave Cortland NY 13045 Office Phone: 607-756-3500.

ROHRABACHER, DANA, congressman; b. Coronado, Calif., June 21, 1947; s. Donald and Doris Rohrabacher; m. Rhonda Carmont, Aug. 1997. Student, L.A. Harbor Coll., 1965-67; BA in History, Long Beach State Coll., 1969; MA in Am. Studies, U. So. Calif., 1976. Reporter City News Svc./Radio West, LA; editorial writer Orange County Register, 1979-80; asst. press. sec. Reagan for Pres. Campaign, 1976, 80; speechwriter, spl. asst. to Pres. Reagan White House, Washington, 1981-88; mem. U.S. Congress from 46th Calif. dist., Washington, 1989—. U.S. del. Young Polit. Leaders Conf., USSR; disting. lectr. Internat. Terrorism Conf., Paris, 1985; mem. Internat. Rels. com.; chmn. Sci. Subcom. on Space and Aeroratics. Recipient Disting. Alumnus award L.A. Harbor Coll., 1987. Republican. Avocations: surfing, white water rafting. Office: US Ho Reps 2338 Rayburn HOB Washington DC 20515-0546 *

ROHRABACHER, JANET HAMMOND, genealogist, archivist; b. Williamston, Mich., Apr. 24, 1913; d. Herbert Moore and Anna Eugenia (Lane) Hammond; m. Albert Hazen Rohrabacher (dec.); children: Ardenne Anna Brigham, Jeffrey. Tchg. cert., We. Mich. U., Kalamazoo, 1936; degree in practical nursing, McPherson Nursing Sch., Howell, Mich., 1965; student, Mich. State U., East Lansing, 1940. Cert. Geneologist, LPN. Nurse Mich. State Sanatorium, Howell, 1939-41, Ingham County Chest Hosp., Lansing, 1940, Ea. Mich. Sanatorium, Ypsilanty, 1941, McPherson Hosp., Howell, 1942-66; archivist Howell Carnegie Libr., Howell, 1977-2001. Author: Livingston County Courthouse, 2006; writer Bicentennial History of Howell. Chmn. Livingston County Civil War Obs. Com., 1963; active Bicentennial Com. Howell, 1973-77, Mich. State Sesquicentennial Com., 1985-89, The Livingston County Courthouse: An Historic Site, 2005; sec. Howell Archives Bd., 1977—. Recipient award, Mich. Geneal. Coun., 1997. Mem. DAR (award 1976), Livingston County Historical Soc. (charter, founder), Livingston County Genealogical Soc. (founder, 1982), Ancient and Honorable Artillery Soc. Mass, Descendents of Early Quakers, Palatines Am., Detroit Soc. Geneol. Rsch., Descendents of the Latin Kingdom of Jersulam (crusader). Methodist. Avocations: antiques, dance, genealogy. Home: 1320 Ashebury Ln # 356 Howell MI 48843

ROHRBACH, HEIDI A., lawyer; b. Buffalo, Jan. 25, 1953; d. William R. and A.T. R.; m. Leonard Lance, Aug. 9, 1996; 1 child, Peter R. Frank. BA, Northwestern U., 1974; JD, Vanderbilt U., 1977. Bar: NY, 1978. V.p., asst. gen. counsel J.P. Morgan Chase & Co., NYC, 1985—2004. Home Phone: 908-236-7502.

ROHRBAUGH, LISA ANNE, librarian; b. Girard, Ohio, Sept. 17, 1956; d. John Michael and Josephine Antoinette (Oliva) Sultan; m. Paul Hugh Rohrbaugh Jr., July 28, 1979. BA, Youngstown State U., 1978; MLS, Kent State U., 1979. Libr. readers assistance dept. Youngstown (Ohio) Pub. Libr., 1979-86; libr., researcher Ajax Magnethermic Corp., Warren, Ohio, 1986-90; asst. reference libr. Youngstown State U., 1990-93; dir. East Palestine (Ohio) Meml. Pub. Libr., 1993—. Translator articles dealing with electronics and induction heating/melting tech. from Spanish, German and French into English; mem. Ohio Regional Libr. Sys. Reviewer for Libr. Jour. Recipient Quest '91 Creative Scholarship award Youngstown State U., 1991. Named one of, Internat. 500 Notable Women; recipient People Who Made a Difference award, Vindicator Pub. Co., 2003. Mem. Ohio Libr. Coun., Rotary (pres. East Palestine, Ohio, 1999-2000, 2003-2004, Paul Harris fellow 2007), Oxford Round Table Avocations: reading, cooking, baseball. Office: East Palestine Meml Pub Libr 309 N Market St East Palestine OH 44413-2153

ROHRER, KATHERINE TINLEY, academic administrator; d. Robert H. and Gere Jenkins Rohrer; m. John A. Sully; 1 child, Julian Clare Sully. MusB with highest honors, Emory U., Atlanta, 1974; PhD in Musicology, Princeton U., NJ, 1980. Instr. dept. music, Princeton U., 1979—80, asst. prof., 1980—82, dept. music, Columbia U., NYC, 1982—88; dir. studies, Wilson Coll. Princeton U., 1988—93, assoc. faculty dean, 1993—2001, asst. coll. dean, 1993, assoc. faculty dean, 1993—2001, vice-provost academic programs, 2001—. Mem. emory alumni bd. Emory U., Atlanta, 2005—; trustee Morristown-Beard Sch., NJ, 2005—. Vestry mem. Trinity Ch., Princeton; trustee William Alexander Procter Found., Diocese NJ. Mem.: Am. Musicological Soc., Phi Beta Kappa. Episcopalian. Home: 84 Coppermine Rd Princeton NJ 08540-8601 Office: Princeton Univ 321 Nassau Hall Princeton NJ 08544 Office Fax: 609-258-7788. Business E-Mail: krohrer@princeton.edu.

ROHRER, RICHARD JEFFREY, surgeon, educator; b. Columbus, Mar. 14, 1950; s. James William and Nancy Lenore (Acheson) R.; m. Jill Ellen Stein, Nov. 29, 1981; children: Benjamin, Noah. BS, Yale U., 1973; MD, Columbia U., 1977. Surgeon New Eng. Deaconess and Harvard Med. Sch., Boston, 1984—87; surgeon, chief transplantation New Eng. Med. Ctr., Boston, 1988—; vice chmn. dept. surgery Tufts-New Eng. Med. Ctr., Boston, 2004—; prof. surgery Tufts U. Sch. Medicine, Boston, 2004—. Trustee New Eng. Organ Bank, Boston, 1988—, chmn. bd. dirs., 1999—2002; councillor United Network for Organ Sharing, 1966—2000, sec., 2000—02. Fellow ACS; mem. Am. Soc. Transplant Surgeons, Transplantation Soc., Physicians for Social Responsibility, Assn. for Acad. Surgery, Assn. for Surg. Edn., Soc. Critical Care Medicine. Office: New England Med Ctr Box 40 750 Washington St Boston MA 02111-1526 Office Phone: 617-636-5592.

ROHRER, SUSAN EARLEY, film producer, film director, scriptwriter; b. Richmond, Va., Mar. 24; d. Charles Marion Jr. and Gloria Jean (Ripley) Earley; m. Mark Brooks Rohrer. BA in Art cum laude, James Madison U. Prodr., dir., co-story writer (tv shows) Never Say Goodbye, 1988 (Emmy award, Humanitas Prize finalist), Terrible Things My Mother Told Me, 1988 (Emmy nomination, Gold award Nat. Ednl. Film Festival); prodr., dir. (TV movies) For Jenny With Love (TV Movie award), Mother's Day, 1989 (3 Image award nominations), prodr., dir., writer (TV show) The Emancipation of Lizzie Stern, 1991 (Angel award, Bronze award Nat. Ednl. Film Festival, Emmy nomination, Monitor award finalist, TV Movie award), If I Die Before I Wake, 1993 (Emmy nomination, Humanitas Prize finalist, Cine Golden Eagle, TV Movie award); dir. (TV show) Sweet Valley High, 1996; dir. TV pilot Dojo Kids, 1996; prodr., dir., co-writer About Sarah, TV movie, 1998 (award of excellence Film Adv. Bd., Best of Festival award Breckenridge Film Festival, The Christopher award, Angel award, N.Y. Festivals finalist); writer (TV movies) Another Pretty Face, 2002, Book of Days, 2003. Recipient Resolution of Recognition Virginia Beach City Coun., 1988. Mem. ATAS, SAG, Writers Guild Am., Dirs. Guild Am. Office: Josh Schechter IPG 9200 Sunset Blvd Ste 820 Los Angeles CA 90069

ROHRICH, ROD(NEY) JAMES, plastic surgeon, educator; b. Eureka, SD, Aug. 5, 1953; s. Claude and Katie (Schumacher) R.; m. Diane Louise Gibby, July 3, 1990; children: Taylor Rodney, Rachel Nicole. BA summa cum laude, ND State U., 1975; MD with honors, Baylor Coll., 1979; LittD (hon.), U. ND, 2006. Diplomate Am. Bd. Plastic Surgery, Nat. Bd. Med. Examiners. Instr. surgery Harvard Med. Sch. Mass. Gen. Hosp., Boston, 1985-86; asst. prof. U. Tex. Southwestern Med. Ctr., Dallas, 1986-89, assoc. prof., 1989-91, prof., chmn. dept. plastic surgery, 1991—, Betty and Warren Woodward chair in plastic surgery, 1999; chief plastic surgery Parkland/Zale Univ. Med. Ctr., Dallas, 1989-99. Pres., faculty senate U. Tex., crystal charity ball disting. chair in plastic surgery. Mem. editl. bd. Selected Readings in Plastic Surgery, The Cleft Palate and Craniofacial Jour.; editor Plastic and Reconstructive Surgery, 2005—; contbr. articles to med. jours. Bd. dirs. Save-the-Children Found., Dallas, March of Dimes, Dallas, Dallas for Children; class mem. Leadership Dallas, 1989-90; mem. Adopt-A-Sch., Dallas Summer Mus. Guild, Dallas Mus. Art, Dallas Symphony Assn., Tex. Health Found., Youth Leadership Dallas. Grantee Urban Rsch. Fund, 1982, United Kingdom Ltd. Ednl. Rsch. Fund, 1983, Oxford Cleft Palate Found., 1983, Am. Assn. Plastic Surgeons, 1985, Plastic Surgery Ednl. Found., 1985, 89, 90, U. Tex. Health Sci. Ctr. Dept. Surgery, 1986, Howmedica, 1989, ConvaTec-Squibb, 1989, 91, ConvaTec, 1991; recipient Disting Svc. award Plastic Surg. Ednl. Found., 1997, Alumni Achievement award, N.D. State U., 1997. Mem. AAAS, AMA (Thomas Cronin award 1988, 90, Clifford C. Snyder award 1990), fellow, ACS, Am. Assn. Hand Surgery, Am. Burn Assn., Am. Cleft Palate Assn., Am. Soc. Law and Medicine, Am. Soc. Maxillofacial Surgeons, Am. Soc. for Surgery the Hand, Am. Soc. Plastic and Reconstructive Surgeons, Am. Trauma Soc., British Med. Assn., Nat. Vascular Malformations Found. Inc. (med. and sci. adv. bd.) Tex. Med. Assn., Tex. Soc. Plastic Surgeons, Mass. Gen. Hosp. Hand Club, Dallas County Med. Soc., Assn. Acad. Chmn. Plastic Surgery, Dallas Soc. Plastic Surgeons, Harvard Med. Sch. Alumni Assn., Inst. for Study of Profl. Risk, Plastic Surgery Rsch. Coun., Reed O. Dingman Soc. Plastic Surgeons, So. Med. Assn., Am. Soc. Plastic Surgeons (pres. 2004). Republican. Roman Catholic. Office: U Tex Southwestern Med Ctr Dept Plastic Surgery 5323 Harry Hines Blvd Dallas TX 75390-9132 Office Phone: 214-645-3119. Business E-Mail: rod.rohrich@utsouthwestern.edu.

ROHR-KIRCHGRABER, THERESA M.B., adolescent medicine; BA, Cornell U., 1984, MD, 1988. Cert. Internal Medicine, Adolescent Medicine. Intern U. Hosp. Cleveland, 1988—89, resident, 1989—91; hosp. appointment Meridia Huron Hosp., Cleve., 1991—94, Crouse-Irving Meml. Hosp., Syracuse, 1994—2003, Grady Hosp., Atlanta, 2004, SUNY Health Sci. Ctr., Syracuse, 1994—2003, academic appointment, 1994—2003, Case Western U., Cleve., 1991—94, Morehouse Sch. Medicine, Atlanta, 2004; asst. prof. Emory U. Sch. Medicine, Atlanta, 2005—. Fellow: Am. Coll. Physicians-Am. Soc. Internal Medicine; mem.: Soc. for Adolescent Medicine. Office: Emory U Sch Medicine 1440 Clifton Rd NE Atlanta GA 30322 Office Phone: 404-778-2700.

ROHRMAN, DOUGLASS FREDERICK, lawyer; b. Chgo., Aug. 10, 1941; s. Frederick Alvin and Velma Elizabeth (Birdwell) R.; m. Susan Vitullo; children: Kathryn Anne, Elizabeth Clelia, Alessandra Claire AB, Duke U., 1963; JD, Northwestern U., 1966. Bar: Ill. 1966. Legal coord. Nat. Communicable Disease Ctr., Atlanta, 1966—68; assoc. Keck, Mahin & Cate, Chgo., 1968—73, ptnr., 1973—97, Lord, Bissell and Brook, Chgo., 1997—. Exec. v.p., dir. Kerogen Oil Co., 1967—; mem. bd. visitors Nicholas Sch. Environment Duke U., 1991-2005, emeritus, 2005—, chmn., 1993-2001; mem. Fin. Aid Initiative com. Duke U., 2005— Co-author: Commercial Liability Risk Management and Insurance, 2 vols., 1978, 86, Lenders Guide to Environmental Law: Risk and Liability, 1993; mem. editl. bd., columnist Ecol. Soc. Am., 2001—; contbr. articles on law to profl. jours Vice chmn., commr. Ill. Food and Drug Commn., 1970-72. Lt. USPHS, 1966-68 Fellow: Am. Numismatic Soc. (life; chmn. adv. com. 2001—03, trustee 2004—), Wigmore Club; mem.: ABA, William Preston Few Assn. (pres. coun.), Duke U. Alumni Assn., James B. Duke Soc., Selden Soc., Am. Soc. Law and Medicine, Environ. Law Inst., 7th Cir. Bar Assn., Chgo. Bar Assn. (chmn. com. food and drug law 1972—73), Am. Numismatic Assn. (life), Mich. Shores Club, Legal Club. Democrat. Epsicopalian. Home: 520 Brier St Kenilworth IL 60043-1064 Office: Lord Bissell & Brook 115 S La Salle St Ste 3200 Chicago IL 60603-3902 Home Phone: 847-256-3875; Office Phone: 312-443-0531. Personal E-mail: drohrman@lordbissell.com.

ROHSENOW, WARREN MAX, retired mechanical engineer, educator; b. Chgo., Feb. 12, 1921; s. Fred and Selma (Gorss) R.; m. Katharine Towneley Smith, Sept. 20, 1946; children— John, Brian, Damaris, Sandra, Anne. BS, Northwestern U., 1941; M.Eng., Yale, 1943, D.Eng., 1944. Teaching asst., instr. mech. engring. Yale, 1941-44; mem. faculty Mass. Inst. Tech., 1946-85, prof. mech. engring., 1955-85, dir. heat transfer lab., 1954-85, prof. emeritus, 1985. Co-founder, chmn. bd. dirs. Dynatech Corp., Thermal Process System. Author: (with Choi) Heat Mass and Momentum Transfer, 1961; Editor: Developments in Heat Transfer, 1964, (with Hartnett) Handbook of Heat Transfer, 1973, 3d edit., 1998. Served as lt. (j.g.) USNR, 1944-46; lt. comdr. USNR, ret. 1956. Recipient Pi Tau Sigma gold medal ASME, 1951; award for advancement sci. Yale Engring. Assn., 1952; merit award Northwestern Alumni, 1955; named hon. alumnus MIT, 2004. Fellow Am. Acad. Arts and Scis., Nat. Acad. Engring., ASME (hon. mem., Heat Transfer Meml. award 1967, Max Jakob Meml. award 1970, ASME medal 2001, Classic Paper award 2003); mem. Sigma Xi, Tau Beta Pi, Pi Tau Sigma. Home: 32 Carroll St Falmouth ME 04105-1908

ROITMAN, JUDITH, mathematician, educator; b. NYC, Nov. 12, 1945; d. Leo and Ethel (Gottesman) R.; m. Stanley Lombardo, Sept. 26, 1978; 1 child, Ben Lombardo. BA in English, Sarah Lawrence Coll., 1966; MA in Math., U. Calif., Berkeley, 1971, PhD in Math., 1974. Asst. prof. math. Wellesley (Mass.) Coll., 1974-77; from asst. prof. to prof. math. U. Kans., Lawrence, 1977—. Author: Introduction to Modern Set Theory, 1990; contbr. articles to profl. jours. Grantee, NSF, 1975—87, 1992—95. Mem. Assn. Symbolic Logic, Am. Math. Soc., Assn. Women in Math. (pres. 1979-81, Louise Hay award 1996), Kans. Assn. Tchrs. Math., Nat. Assn. Tchrs. Math. Avocation: poetry. Business E-Mail: roitman@math.ku.edu.

ROIZEN, MICHAEL F., anesthesiologist, medical educator, writer; b. NY, Jan. 7, 1946; m. Nancy J. Roizen; children: Jeffery, Jennifer. AB in Chemistry with honors, Williams Coll., Williamstown, Mass., 1967; MD, U. Calif. Sch. Medicine, San Francisco, 1971. Cert. Am. Bd. Internal Medicine, Am. Bd. Anesthesiology. Intern, medicine Beth Israel Hosp., Boston, 1971—72, resident, medicine, 1972—73; rsch. assoc. in pharmacology NIH, Bethesda, Md., 1973-75; resident, anesthesia U. Calif., San Francisco, 1975—77, asst. prof., 1977-81, assoc. prof., 1981-85; prof. internal medicine U. Chgo., 1985, prof. and chair dept. anesthesia and critical care, 1985; prof., anesthesiology SUNY Upstate Med. Ctr. and Univ., Syracuse, NY; chmn., divsn. anesthiology, critical care medicine and comprehensive pain mgmt. Cleve. Clinic. Panel mem. FDA, past chmn. adv. com.; co-founder RealAge,Inc., chmn. scientific adv. bd; invited lectr. in field. Author: Essence of Anesthesia Practice, 1997, RealAge: Are You As Young as You Can Be?, 1999(NY Times #1 Best-Seller, Best Wellness Book, Books for a Better Life awards, 1999); co-author (with John La Puma) The RealAge Diet: Make Yourself Younger with What You Eat (NY Times Best-Seller, 2001), RealAge Way, The RealAge Makeover, 2004, (with Tracy Hafen) The RealAge Workout, (with Mehmet C. Oz) YOU: The Owner's Manual: An Insider's Guide to the Body That Will Make You Healthier and Younger (#1 Publishers Weekly Hardcover Bestseller list, NY Times Bestseller List), 2005, YOU: The Smart Patient: An Insider's Handbook for Getting the Best Treatment, 2006, YOU: On a Diet-The Owner's Manual for Waist Management, 2006, (compact disc) YOU: On a Walk, 2007; former editor of several med. jours.; reviewer numerous anesthesia and med. jours.; contbr. of articles to peer-reviewed jours., chpt. to books, med. books; guest appearances on Oprah Winfrey Show, Today Show, 20/20, CBN, CNN, CBS, Good Morning America, Montel Williams Show and PBS; featured in magazines including Fortune, Glamourm Cosmopolitan, Good Housekeeping, Ladies' Home Journal, Reader's Digest, Men's Health and Prevention. Named an Best Doctors in Am., 1989—. Mem. Am. Bd. Anesthesiology (assoc.), Am. Bd. Internal Medicine (assoc.), Am. Soc. Anesthesiologists, Soc. of Cardiovascular Anesthesiologists (pres. 1995-97), U.S. Squash Racquets Assn., Alpha Omega Alpha, Phi Beta Kappa. 12 US patents and several fgn. patents. Office: RealAge Inc 10675 Sorrento Valley Rd Ste 200 San Diego CA 92121 also: RealAge Inc 555 Fifth Ave 14th Fl New York NY 10017 Office Phone: 858-812-3800. Office Fax: 858-812-3801. Business E-Mail: roizenm@upstate.edu. E-mail: mrzz@airway2.bsd.uchicago.edu. *

ROIZEN, NANCY J., physician, educator; b. Hartford, Conn. m. Michael F. Roizen; children: Jeffrey, Jennifer. BS, Tufts U., 1968, MD, 1972. Diplomate Am. Bd. Pediats. Staff physician Oakland (Calif.) Children's Hosp., 1976-84; asst. prof. clin. pediats. Johns Hopkins Hosp., Balt., 1984-85; assoc. prof. pediat. and psychiatry U. Chgo., 1985—. Fellow Am. Acad. Pediats.; mem. Soc. for Devel. Pediats. (pres. 1996-98). Office: U Chgo Hosps MC 900 5841 S Maryland Ave Chicago IL 60637-1463

ROIZMAN, BERNARD, virologist, educator; b. Chisinau, Rumania, Apr. 17, 1929; arrived in US, 1947, naturalized, 1954; s. Abram and Liudmilla (Seinberg) Roizman; m. Betty Cohen, Aug. 26, 1950; children: Arthur, Niels. BA, Temple U., Phila., 1952, MS, 1954; ScD in Microbiology, Johns Hopkins U., Balt., 1956; DHL (hon.), Gov.'s State U., 1984; MD (hon.), U. Ferrara, Italy, 1991; DSc (hon.), U. Paris, 1997, U. Valladolid, Spain, 2001. From instr. microbiology to asst. prof. Johns Hopkins Med. Sch., 1956—65; from mem. faculty Divsn. Biol. Scis. to prof. U. Chgo., 1965—69, prof., 1969—, chmn. dept. molecular genetics and cell biology, 1985—88, Joseph Regoustein Disting. Svc. prof., 1984—. Co-founder Aviron, Inc., 1992; convener herpes virus workshop, Cold Spring Harbor, NY, 72; lectr. Am. Found. for Microbiology, 1974—75; mem. spl. virus cancer program devel. rsch. working group Nat. Cancer Inst., 1967—71; mem. steering com. human cell biology program NSF, 1971—74; mem. adv. com. cell biology and virology Am. Cancer Soc., 1970—74; chmn. herpes virus study group Internat. Commn. Taxonomy of Viruses, 1971—73; mem. Internat. Microbiol. Genetics Commn. Internat. Assn. Microbiol. Scis., 1974—81; mem. sci. adv. coun. NY Cancer Inst., 1971—88; mem. adv. bd. Leukemia Rsch. Found., 1972—77; mem. herpes-virus working team WHO/FDA, 1978—81; mem. bd. sci. cons. Sloan Kettering Inst., NYC, 1975—81; mem. study sect. exptl. virology NIH, 1976—80; mem. task force on virology Nat. Inst. Allergy and Infectious Disease, 1976—77; mem. com. to establish vaccine priorities Nat. Inst. Medicine, 1983—85; chmn. sci. adv. bd. Tampa Bay Rsch. Inst., 1983—, chmn. bd. trustees, 1991—97; cons. in field. Editor: (book) Herpes Viruses, Vol. 1, 1982, Herpes Viruses, Vol. 2, 1983, Herpes Viruses, Vols. 3 and 4, 1985, The Human Herpesviruses, 1993, Infectious Diseases in an Age of Change, 1995; editor-in-chief: Jour. Infectious Agts. and Disease, 1992—96, mem. editl. bd.: Infectious Diseases, 1965—69, Jour. Virology, 1970—, Jour. Intervirology, 1972—85, Archives of Virology, 1975—81, Virology, 1976—78, Microbiologica, 1978—, Cell, 1979—80, Virology, 1983—, Jour. Hygiene, 1985—91, Gene Therapy, 1994, Wiley Encyclopedia of Molecular Medicine, 2002; contbr. scientific papers, chapters to books. Trustee Goodwin Inst. Cancer Rsch., 1977—. Named hon. prof., Shandong Acad. Med. Scis., China, 1985; recipient Lederle Med. Faculty award, 1960—61, Career Devel. award, USPHS, 1963—65, Pasteur award, Ill. Soc. Microbiology, 1972, Esther Langer award for Achievement in Cancer Rsch., 1974, Outstanding Alumnus in Pub. Health award, Johns Hopkins U., 1984, ICN Internat. prize in Virology, 1988, J. Allyn Taylor Internat. prize in Medicine, 1997, Bristol-Myers Squibb award for Disting. Infectious Disease Rsch., 1998; fellow Travelling, Internat. Agy. Rsch. Against Cancer, Karolinska Inst., Stockholm, 1970; grantee Facutly Rsch. Assoc., Am. Cancer Soc., 1966—71, USPHS/NIH, 1958—, Am. Cancer Soc., 1962—90, NSF, 1962—79; scholar Am. Cancer Soc., Pasteur Inst. Paris, 1961—62. Fellow: AAAS, Japanese Soc. for Promotion of Sci., Am. Acad. Arts and Scis.; mem.: NAS, Johns Hopkins U. Soc. Scholars, Chinese Acad. Engring. (fgn.), Hungarian Acad. Scis. (fgn.), Brit. Soc. Gen. Microbiology, Am. Soc. Molecular Biology and Biochemistry, Am. Soc. Virology, Am. Soc. Microbiology, Am. Assn. Immunologists, Am. Acad. Microbiology, Inst. Medicine, Quadrangle Club (Chgo.). Home: 5555 S Everett Ave Chicago IL 60637-1968 Office: U Chgo MB Kovler Viral Oncology Labs 910 E 58th St Chicago IL 60637-1432 Office Phone: 773-702-1898. Business E-Mail: bernard.roizman@bsd.uchicago.edu.

ROJANY, LISA ADRIENNE, publishing company executive, writer; b. LA, Feb. 14, 1964; d. Aviezer Rojany and Mary Marks; m. Kristian Buccieri. B of Comms. magna cum laude, UCLA; cert. in translation, Sorbonne U., Paris; M English and Am. Lit., Brown U. Newspaper journalist UCLA Daily Bruin, Together Newsmag., LA, 1985-86; English tutor Paris, 1986-87; writer, reviewer TV Guide, LA, 1987-88; sr. editor Intervisual Books, Santa Monica, Calif., 1991-93; editl. dir. Price Stern Sloan divsn. Penguin Putnam Pub., LA, 1993-97, Gateway Learning Corp., 1997; west coast publ. dir. Golden Books Family Entertainment, LA, 1998-2000; editl. dir. bus. devel. MyPotential.com, 2000-01; editor/writer, pres. Editl. Svcs. of LA, 1988—; v.p., pub. Americhip Books, 2002—06. Proofreader MIT U. Press, Cambridge, Mass., 1990, Fidelity, Inc., Boston, 1990, Heinle & Heinle Pubs., Inc., Boston, 1990; correlator, proofreader Houghton Mifflin Co., Boston, 1990; v.p., pub. Americhip Books, 2002—06; spkr. in field. Author: (childrens books) The Hands-on Book of Big Machines, 1992, Exploring the Human Body, 1992 (10 Best New Parenting Books, Child Mag., 1993), King Arthur's Camelot, 1993 (Book of the Month Club selection, 1993), The Story of Hanukkah, 1993, Where's That Pig?, 1993, Santa's New Suit, 1993, Jake and Jenny on the Town, 1993, 1996, Andrews & McMeel Mini Pop-Up Quote Books, 1993, Alice in Wonderland, 1994, Token of Love and Spring Gardens, 1994, Mickey Mouse: Where's the Picnic, 1994, Winnie the Pooh: The Suprise Party, 1994, Make Your Own Valentines, 1994, Make Your Own Valentines, 3d edit., 1996 (Pub.'s Weekly Bestseller list, 1994, 1995), Melvin Martian, Dumbo's Circus Train, 1995, Cinderella's Coach, 1995, The Magic Feather, 1995 (Parents Choice Silver Honor award, 1995), Pandora's Box (CD ROM), 1995, Over in the Meadow (CD ROM), 1995, Tell Me About When I Was a Baby, 1996, Gold Diggers: The Novelization, 1996, Hanukkah Candles, 1995, Dragonheart: The Jr. Novelization, 1996, Giant Animal Fold-Outs: Big Trucks & Bigger Diggers, 1996, Giant Giants & Magic Mermaids, 1996, Hippo & Pals, 1996 (Am. Booksellers Pick of the List, 1995), Kangaroo & Company, 1996 (Am. Booksellers Pick of the List, 1995), Dena Dinosaur, Morty Monster, Wanda Witch, 1996, Code Blue: In the Emergency Room, 1996, Code Blue: Making the Grade, 1996, Leave It to Beaver: The Novelization, 1997, Love You Because...Love, Barbie, 1999, Make Your Own Valentine Cards, 2000, (children's books) At the Airport, 2006, At the Ballpark, 2006, Around the House, 2006, (children's books series) Let's Make Noise; co-author: (books) Fund Your Future, 2001 (NY Times Bus. Hardcover Bestseller list #10, 2002, NY Times hardover bus. bestseller, 2001), Writing Children's Books for Dummies, 2005, Let's Make Noise series, 2005; ghostwriter: childrens books Dinotopia Pop-Up Book, 1993, Sliding Surprise Books, 1993—97, The Facts of Life, 1994, All Mixed Up, 1994, Little Merlin's Book of Magic Pets, 1994, Claverie Fairytale Theater, 1994, Bumpty & Boo Visit The Eye Doctor: Guess Who Needs Glasses, 2006. Spkr. UCLA Extension, 1993-98, SCBWI Ventura, 2005; mem. comms. bd., fin. com. UCLA, 2002-04. Recipient one of 10 Best New Parenting Books award Child Mag., 1993. Mem. PEN Ctr. U.S.A. West (editor-in-chief 1992-95), Soc. Children's Book Writers and Illustrators (manuscript reviewer 1995-2003), Internat. Women's Writing Guild, Author's Guild, Brown Alumni Assn. (interviewer 1995-98), UCLA Alumni Assn. (bd. dirs., comms., fin. com. 2002-2004), Phi Beta Kappa Avocations: reading, moderating writing workshops, rollerblading. Office Phone: 818-707-1042. Business E-Mail: gnored@roadrunner.com.

ROJAS, CARLOS, literature and language educator; b. Barcelona, Aug. 12, 1928; s. Carlos and Luisa (Vila) R.; m. Eunice Anne Mitcham, Mar. 19, 1966; children: Carlos, Eunice Anne. MA, U. Barcelona, 1951; PhD, U. Cen., Madrid, 1955; PhD (hon.), U. Simón Bólivar, Barranquilla, Colombia, 1985. Teaching asst. U. Barcelona, 1951-52; fgn. asst. U. Glasgow, Scotland, 1952-54; asst. prof. Rollins Coll., Winter Park, Fla., 1957-60, Emory U., Atlanta, 1960-63, assoc. prof., 1963-68, prof., 1968-80, Charles Howard Candler prof. Spanish lit., 1980-96, Charles Howard Candler prof. emeritus, 1996. Author: Auto de fe, 1968 (Premio Nacional de Literatura 1968), Azana, 1973 (Planeta award 1973), El Igenioso Hidalgo y Poeta F.G. asciende a los infiernos, 1980 (Nadal award 1980), El Sueno de Sarajevo, 1982, El Jardin de las Hespèrides, 1988, El Jardin de Atocha, 1990, Yo, Goya, 1990, Proceso A Godoy, 1992, Salvador Dali, or the Art of Spitting on Your Mother's Portrait, 1993, Alfonso de Borbón Habla Con El Demonio, 1995, !Muera La Inteligencia! !Viva La Muerte! Salamanca, 1995, The Garden of Janus, 1996, Crónica de la Guerra Civil Española, 1996; co-author, contbg. editor Spanish Civil War documents, Momentos estelares de la guerra de España, 1996, La Vida y la Época de Carlos IV, 1997, Los Borbones Destronados, 1997, El bastardo del Rey, 1999, The Garden of the Hesperides, 1999, Puneta La Espaneta, 2000, Despiada Memoria: Memorias, 2002, Diez Crisis del Franquismo, 2003, Por Que Perdimos la Guerra, 2006. Recipient Premio Espejo de España award, Madrid, 1984, Encomienda al Mérito Civil, King of Spain, 1986, Univ. Scholar/Tchr. award Emory U., 1987, Arts and Scis. award of Distinction, Emory U., 2001; honoree of yr. Philol. Assn. of Carolinas, 1987, Llave de Barcelona, 2003. Mem. MLA, Am. Assn. Tchrs. Spanish and Portuguese (Premio a la Lealtad Republicana Madrid 2004), Assn. Doctores y Licenciados Españoles en los Estados Unidos (bd. dirs.), South Atlantic MLA (hon.). Avocation: painting. Home: 1378 Harvard Rd NE Atlanta GA 30306-2413 Business E-Mail: crojas@emory.edu.

ROJAS, EDDY M., engineering educator; b. San Jose, Costa Rica, Feb. 26, 1969; came to U.S., 1993; s. Jorge L. Rojas and Hannia Molina; m. Denise Murillo, Aug. 10, 1991. MSCE, U. Colo., 1995, MA in Econs., 1997, PhD in Civil Engring., 1997. Registered civil engr., Costa Rica. Rschr. Earthquake Engring. Lab. U. Costa Rica, San Jose, 1991, instr., 1991-93; asst. prof. U. Buffalo, 1997—2001, U. Wash., 2001—04, assoc. prof., 2004—. Contbr. papers to profl. jours. Recipient Making Virtual Teams Work award, Constrn. Industry Inst., 2000, Tech. Transfer for Mex. Electrical Contracting Firms award, Electrical Contracting Found., 2000, Automating N.Y. State Dept. Transp. Data Collection, 1998, Millennium Generation award, Electrical Contracting Found., 2001. Mem. ASCE (mem. constrn. rsch. coun. 1997—, computing in constrn. com. 1997—). Roman Catholic. Office: U Washington 116 Architecture Box 351610 Seattle WA 98195-1610 Office Phone: 206-616-1917. E-mail: er@u.washington.edu.

ROJAS, JESUS JON, health products executive, researcher; b. Havana, Cuba, Oct. 29, 1970; s. Bienvenido Amado Rojas and Edelmira Nena Caballero; 1 child, Jonathan Richard-Alexander. Clin. rsch. coord. SFBC Internat., Miami, Fla., 1996—97, dir. pharmacy, 1997—99, assoc. dir. clin. ops., 1999—2004, dir. clin. ops., 2004—06; v.p. project mgmt. OmniComm Sys., Inc., Ft. Lauderdale, Fla., 2006—. Clin. rsch. cons., Miami, 1998—. Dir. activities abused children Cath. Ch., Miami, 1994—2006. Named Best New Artist, 1994. Mem.: Project Mgr. Inst. (licentiate; mem. 1996), Assn. Clin. Rsch. Profls. (assoc. cert. clin. rsch. coord.). Avocations: martial arts, surfing, reading, running. Office: OmniCom Sys Inc 2101 W Commercial Blvd Fort Lauderdale FL 33309 Home Phone: 305-218-6677; Office Phone: 954-473-1254. Office Fax: 954-473-1256; Home Fax: 954-473-1254. Personal E-mail: rojasjonn@aol.com, rijasjonn@aol.com. Business E-Mail: jrojas@omnicomm.com.

ROJAS, VICTOR HUGO MACEDO, retired vocational education educator; b. Mollendo, Peru, Jan. 11, 1923; came to U.S., 1944; s. Mariano A. and Maria Santos (Macedo) R.; m. Mary Emily Bush, Apr. 28, 1945 (dec. 1984). AA, Miami-Dade CC, 1982; BS in Vocat. Edn., Fla. Internat. U., 1986. Cert. tchr., Fla.; personal computer repair tech., Penn Foster Career Sch., 2006. Engine tech. Nat. Sch., 1943; automotive mechanic various Ford dealerships, Miami, Fla., 1945-60; automotive technician East Tenn. Motors, Knoxville, 1960-63; car and truck salesman Ford Mktg. Inst., 1963; automotive technician Tally-Embry Ford, Inc., Miami, 1964-66, shop foreman, then mgr., 1966-75, master technician, automotive instr., 1973-75; instr. automotive tech. Dade County Pub. Schs., Miami, 1975-91; bus. exec. Internat. Correspondence, 1976; ret., 1991. Adviser, sponsor Vocat.-Indsl. Clubs Am., Miami, 1988-91. Contbr. articles to newspapers. With Armada Peruana, 1940-44, USN, 1945. Recipient Cert. of Achievement Motor Age mag., 1961, 62, St. Mary's Cathedral, Miami, 1988, Automotive Svc. Excellence award Nat. Inst. Automotive Svc., 1975, Hon. award Prefect of Arequipa, Peru, 2005. Mem. Am. Legion (historian 1989), Elks. Democrat. Roman Catholic. Avocations: music, ballroom dancing, reading, writing, photography. Personal E-mail: vicbullfighter@aol.com.

ROJO, RUTH M., nutritionist, consultant, director; b. San Antonio, Oct. 23, 1938; d. Fernando and Margie Macias Rojo; 1 child, Amina Ruth. Dr. Naturopathy, Clayton Coll. Natural Health, Birmingham, Ala., 1996, U.S. Sch. Naturopathy, Atlanta, 1999; PhD in Nutrition, Am. Holistic Coll. Nutrition, Birmingham, 1996; Dr. Naturopathic Medicine, Colo. U. Naturopathic Medicine, Denver, 1999. Board Certified Naturopath Am. Naturopathic Med. Certification and Accreditation Bd. Pres. / founder Tex. State Naturopathic Med. Assn., San Antonio, 1998—; Tex. rep. Am. Naturopathic Med. Assn., Las Vegas, Nev., 1998—, bd. dirs., 2000—; cons. in complimentary and alternative medicine. Author: Priority 1--A Guide to Natural Health. Named Businesswoman of Yr., Nat. Rep. Congrl. Com., 2006; recipient Congl. medal distinction, 2006. Avocations: painting, walking, cross stitch, sports. Office: PO Box 1583 Helotes TX 78023 Office Phone: 210-979-0802. Personal E-mail: rrojo@drrojo.com. Business E-Mail: drrojo@togetwell.com.

ROKER, AL, newscaster; b. Queens, NY, Aug. 20, 1954; m. Alice Bell, Dec. 22, 1984 (div. 1994); m. Deborah Roberts, Sept. 16, 1995; 3 children. Grad., SUNY, Oswego. Weathercaster, graphic artist WTVH-TV, Syracuse, N.Y., 1974-76; weathercaster WTTG-TV, Washington, 1976-78, WKYC-TV, Cleve., 1978-83, WNBC-TV, NYC, 1983—; weatherman NBC News Today Show, NYC, 1995—; founder Al Roker Entertainment, Inc., 1994—. Exec. prodr.: (TV series) Roker on the Road, 2003; actor: (TV films) Broadway on Broadway, 2000, (voice): (films) Wholey Moses, 2003, Robots, 2005; author (non-fiction): Don't Make Me Stop this Car: Adventures in Fatherhood, 2000, Big Shoes: In Celebration of Dads and Fatherhood, 2005; author: (cookbooks) Al Roker's Big Bad Book of Barbecue: 100 Easy Recipes for Backyard Barbecue, 2002, Al Roker's Hassle-Free Holiday Cookbook, 2003. Named Best Weatherman, N.Y. mag., 1985. Mem. Am. Meteorol. Soc. (recipient Seal of Approval). Office: NBC News 30 Rockefeller Plz Rm 1420 New York NY 10112-0002 *

ROKER, CHRISTOPHER A., microbiologist, photographer; arrived in US, 1986; s. John A. T. and LueElla Roker; m. Elizabeth Moxey, Apr. 14, 1984; children: Krislar, Kwame, Kofi. BS in Med. Tech., LI U., 1996, post graduate, 2003—; student, NY Inst. Photography, 1975—78; student in Commercial Photography, Germain Sch. Photography, 1980—82. Cert. clin. lab. scientist Nat. Certify Agy. Lab. Profls. Profl. photographer, studio owner Esquire Photography Studio, Nassau, The Bahamas, 1983—88; photographic retoucher Color Wheel Inc., NYC, 1986—95; microbiologist Shield Med. Lab., Bklyn., 1995—99, Sherman-Abrams Med. Lab, Bklyn., 1999—2006, Analytical Diagnostic Labs Inc., Bklyn., 1999—. Photographer (exhibitions), NYC, Nassau, Bahamas, Down by the Sea, Body Works, New York After Dark. Mem.: Am. Soc. Clin. Lab. Sci., Am. Soc. Microbiology (mem. sub-com. 2002—). Avocations: sports, poetry, writing, jazz. Office: Analytical Diagnostic Labs Inc 2115 Ave X Brooklyn NY 11235 Home and Studio: 6119 Braidwood Lane NW Acworth GA 30101 Office Phone: 718-646-6000. Office Fax: 718-646-0820. Business E-Mail: carokers@msn.com.

ROKHLENKO, ALEXANDER, research scientist, educator; b. Kiev, Ukraine, June 13, 1935; arrived in US, 1989; s. Victor Nathan Rokhlenko and Rosa Sakhnovskaya; m. Tatyana Kukavskaya, Aug. 13, 1964; 1 child, Vadim. Physicist, tchr. (hon.), Kiev State U., 1958; PhD in Physics, Inst. Physics, Kiev, 1966. Electronic engr. mil. radio plant, Kiev, 1958—60; engr.-rschr. Inst. of Hydromechanics, Kiev, 1960—63; rsch. scientist Inst. of Material Sci., Kiev, 1963—89; rsch. assoc. Rutgers U., Piscataway, NJ, 1990—. Adj. prof. Drexel U., Phila., 1990—92; cons. Am. Inst. of Physics, Melville, NY, 1991—. Achievements include research in Spectral properties of Schroedinger operator; Plasma in external fields; first to Beams of charged particles; Atomic ionization in external fields; research in Mathematical modelling of corrosion protection; first to Recombination of atoms on solids. Avocations: electronic construction, mechanical devices, swimming, social study, world literature. Home: 26 Greenbriar Row Princeton NJ 08540 Office: Rutgers Univ 110 Frelinghuysen Rd Piscataway NJ 08854 Home Phone: 609-921-3723; Office Phone: 732-445-3989. E-mail: rokhlenk@math.rutgers.edu.

ROKHVARGER, ANATOLY EFIM, materials science and ceramic technology scientist; b. Moscow, July 24, 1937; came to U.S., 1991; s. Efim Laser and Avgustina Naum (Leschiner) R.; m. Zina Gregory Mikhelson, Feb. 17, 1965; 1 child, Avgustina. MS, Mendeleev Chem.-Tech. U., Moscow, 1959, PhD, 1967; cert., Moscow U., 1965; DSc, Tech. U., Leningrad, USSR, 1986. Engr. Electronic Industry Design Inst., Moscow, 1959-63; rschr. Bldg. Materials Inst., 1964-68; project leader, head dept. Ceramic Industry Analytical Ctr., 1969-91; rsch. prof. Poly. U., Bklyn., 1992—2005; v.p. R&D Nucon Sys., Inc., NYC, 1996-2000. Vis. scientist Rutgers U. Ctr. Ceramic Rsch., Piscataway, NJ, 1998-99; CEO HTS Nano-Ceramics, Ltd., NY, 2005—. Author 5 books, 1 textbook in field; contbr. over 175 articles to profl. jours. Named one of 100 Greatest Innovators of 20th Century Am. Ceramic Soc. Achievements include development of nine advanced technological systems and six ceramic products; discovery of 3-D honeycomb-like superconductor nano-architecture of sintered granular ceramics; invention of cost-effective nanotechnology of gas impenetrable and thick-walled ceramics; ultimate safe and durable ceramic containers for permanent storage of solid nuclear and hazardous waste, including techniques for container mass production and seamless covering using microwave; industrial 3-D nanofabrication of 3-G high temperature superconductor continuous wire (3-GHTS wire); other shaped and sintered superconducting ceramic leads with superconductive nano-architecture for electrical/electronic needs using YBCO raw powder, silicone polymer additive and silver powder dope; patents in field. Personal E-mail: aerokhv@aol.com.

ROKITA, TODD, state official; b. Chgo., Feb. 9, 1970; m. Kathy Rokita. BA in Polit. Sci., Wabash Coll., 1992; JD, Ind. U. Sch. Law, 1995. Atty.; gen. counsel to sec. state State of Ind., Indpls., 1997, dep. sec. state, 1997—2003, sec. state, 2003—. Mem.: Indiana Coun. for Economic Edn. (Director's Circle), St. Thomas More Parish, Indiana State Bar Association's Aviation Law Com. (past chair). Republican. Catholic. Office: Office Sec of State 201 State House Indianapolis IN 46204 Office Phone: 317-232-6531, 317-232-6536. Office Fax: 317-233-3283. Business E-Mail: aa@sos.state.in.us. *

ROKKE, ERVIN JEROME, military officer, academic administrator; b. Warren, Minn., Dec. 12, 1939; s. Edwin K. and Joan (Ivery) R.; m. Pamela Mae Patterson, June 6, 1962; children: Lisa Mae, Eric Scott. Student, St. Olaf Coll., 1957-58; BS, USAF Acad., 1962; MPA, Harvard U., 1964, PhD in Polit. Sci., 1970. Commd. 2d lt. USAF, 1962, advanced through grades to lt. gen., 1994; intelligence officer Pacific Air Forces, Hawaii, Japan, 1965-68; assoc. prof. dept. polit. sci. USAF Acad., Colorado Springs, Colo., 1968-73, permanent prof., 1976-80, dean of faculty, 1982-86, chmn. characterand leadership devel., 2007—; plans officer NATO Hdqrs., Brussels, 1973-76; air attache Am. Embassy, London, 1980-82, def. attache Moscow, 1987-89; sr. staff Nat. Security Agy., Ft. Meade, Md., 1989-91; dir. intelligence Hdqrs. European Command, Stuttgart, Fed. Republic Germany, 1991-93; assigned to Hdqs. USAF, Washington, 1993-94; pres. Nat. Def. U., Ft. Lesley J. McNair, DC, 1994-97, Moravian Coll. and Moravian Theol. Sem., 1997—2006; pres. emeritus Moravian Coll., Bethlehem, Pa., 2007—. Cons. Dept. State, 1969. Editor: American Defense Policy, 1973. Decorated Def. Disting. Svc. medal, Disting. Svc. medal, Def. Superior Svc. medal, Legion of Merit. Mem. Coun. on Fgn. Rels., Falcon Found. Lutheran. Avocations: reading, skiing, squash. Home: 810 Dolan Dr Monument CO 80132-2219 Office Phone: 719-333-4510. Personal E-mail: chaos01@comcast.net.

ROKNALDIN, FARZAM, mechanical engineer, educator; b. Tehran, Iran, Jan. 17, 1965; arrived in US, 1991, naturalized, 2003; s. Hassan Roknaldin and Alye Tohidi; m. Maria Valera; 1 child, Aleyeh. PhD in Mechanical Engring., Stanford U., Calif., 2001. Sr. thermal analyst Applied Thermal Technologies, Santa Clara, Calif., 2000—. Faculty San Jose State U., Calif., 2002—, graduate degree advisor, 2004—. Mem.: ASME (assoc. Recognition award 2001), Planetary Soc. (assoc.), Pars FC Soccer Club (co-founder). Democrat. Achievements include development of over 150 different thermal designs for electronic devices ranging from routers, switches, servers, high-definition mediums to notebook computers and hand-held devices. Avocations: soccer, snowboarding, guitar, cars. Office: Applied Thermal Technologies 3255 Kifer Road Santa Clara CA 95051 Home Phone: 408-739-1091; Office Phone: 408-522-8730. Office Fax: 408-522-8729; Home Fax: 408-522-8729. Business E-Mail: roknaldi@athermal.com.

ROLAND, ANNE, registrar Supreme Court of Canada; m. Alphonse Morisette; 1 child, Julien BA Philosophy, Caen, France, 1965; diploma, Inst. Supérieur d'interprétation et de traduction, 1969; lic. in law, Paris, 1969; LLB, U. Ottawa, 1979. Bar: Quebec 1980. Legal trans., revisor, Can., 1971-75; chief trans. svcs. customs and excise Sec. of State, Can., 1975-76; spl. asst. to chief justice Can., 1976-81; chief law editor Supreme Ct. Can., 1981-88, dep. registrar, 1988-90, registrar, 1990. Mem. Can. Bar Assn., Assn. Can. Ct. Adminstrs., Assn. Francophone Jurists, Can. Inst. Adminstrn. Justice, Assn. Reporters Jud. Decisions. Office: Supreme Ct Can Office Reg 301 Wellington St Ottawa ON Canada K1A 0J1 Home Phone: 613-233-0322; Office Phone: 613-996-9277. E-mail: rolanda@scc-csc.gc.ca.

ROLAND, BILLY RAY, electronics company executive; b. Grandview, Tex., June 12, 1926; s. Marvin Wesley and Minnie Mae (Martin) R.; m. Ruth Ranell Sheets, Mar. 9, 1950 (div. 1982); children: Carl Ray and Darla Kay (twins); m. Linda Sue Leslie, Feb. 21, 1986 (div. Nov. 1991); m. Martha Kay Redford, May 17, 1993. BS, Tex. Christian U., 1954. CPA, Tex. Ticket and baggage agt. Southwestern Greyhound Co., Ft. Worth, 1943-44, 46-51; supr. acctg. dept. Tandy Leather Co., 1954-60; controller, asst. sec., treas. Tandy Corp., 1960-75; v.p., 1978-85; ret.; controller, asst. sec., treas. Tandy Crafts, Inc., 1975-78. V.p., treas. David L. Tandy Found., 1966-2003, dir. emeritus, 2004—; mng. trustee James L. and Eunice West Charitable Trust, 1980-91; treas. Benjamin F. Johnston Found., 1984—. Served with U.S. Army, 1944-46. Mem. AICPA, Tex. Soc. CPAs, Colonial Country Club, Petroleum Club. Republican. Methodist. Home: 8937 Random Rd Fort Worth TX 76179-2739

ROLAND, CHARLES GORDON, physician, medical educator, historian; b. Winnipeg, Man., Can., Jan. 25, 1933; s. John Sanford and Leona (McLaughlin) R.; m. Marjorie Ethel Kyles, 1953 (div. 1973); children: John Kenneth, Christopher Franklin, David Charles, Kathleen Siobhan; m. Connie Rankin, 1979; step-children: Gregory Irvine, Christopher Irvine, Randi Irvine. Student, U. Toronto, Ont., Can., 1952—54; MD, BSc, U. Man., 1958, DSc (hon.), 1997. Intern St. Boniface Hosp., Man., 1958—59; pvt. practice medicine specializing in family medicine Tillsonburg, Ont., 1959—60, Grimsby, Ont., 1960—64; sr. editor Jour. Am. Med. Assn., Chgo., 1964—69; head sect. publs. Mayo Clinic, 1969—70, chmn. dept. biomed. communications, 1970—77; prof. history medicine, prof. biomed. comm., coord. family practice track, chmn. adminstrv. com. dept. family medicine Mayo Med. Sch., 1971—77; mem. admissions, edn. and curriculum coordinators coms., hon. mem. med. staff West Lincoln Meml. Hosp., Grimsby; mem. grants com. Hannah Inst. History of Medicine, Toronto, 1974—77, 1987—91, mem. publs. com., 1991—95; Jason A. Hannah prof. history of medicine McMaster U., Hamilton, Ont., Canada, 1977—99,

Hannah prof. emeritus, 1999—, assoc. mem. dept. history, 1978—96, chmn. archives com. Faculty of Health Scis., 1983—98; chmn. spl. grants com. Hannah Inst. for History of Medicine, 1981—85; Sid W. Richardson vis. prof. Inst. Med. Humanities U. Tex. Med. Br., Galveston, 1984. Devel. adv. com. Assoc. Med. Svcs., 1999-2003; inaugural Osler-McGovern lectr. Green Coll., Oxford U., Eng., 2001. Author: (with L.S. King) Scientific Writing, 1968, (with J.P. McGovern) William Osler, The Continuing Education, 1969, Good Scientific Writing, 1971, William Osler's The Master Word in Medicine: A Study in Rhetoric, 1972, (with L.S. Baker) You and Leukemia: A Day at a Time, 1976, (with P. Potter) An Annotated Bibliography of Canadian Medical Periodicals, 1826-1975, 1979, Clarence Meredith Hincks 1885-1964: Mental Health Crusader, 1990, Courage Under Siege: Starvation, Disease and Death in the Warsaw Ghetto, 1992, Harold Nathan Segall: Pioneer Canadian Cardiologist, 1995, Long Night's Journey Into Day: Prisoners of War in the Far East, 1941-45, 2001; editor: (E.P. Scarlett) In Sickness and In Health, 1972; co-editor: An Annotated Checklist of Osleriana, 1976, vol. 2, 2000, Sir William Osler 1849-1919: A Selection for Medical Students, 1982, Health Disease and Medicine: Essays in Canadian History, 1984, Sir William Osler 1849-1919: petite anthologie à l'intention des étudiants in médecine, 1987, Bibliography of Secondary Sources in Canadian Medical History, 1985, 2nd edition, 2000, (with J. Bernier) The Collected Essays of Sir William Osler (3 vols.), 1985, (with Henry Friedlander and Benno Muller-Hill) Medical Science without Compassion: Past and Present, 1992; editor, author introduction: Medical Topography of Upper Canada, 1985; (with Richard Golden) Sir William Osler: An Annotated Bibiography with Illustrations, 1987; co-editor: The Persisting Osler, 1984, The Persisting Osler II, 1994, The Persisting Osler III, 2001, Biography of Archibald Malloch, 2007; editor-in-chief Can. Bulletin of Med. History, 1987-90; mem. editl. adv. bd. Can. Family Physician, 1964-72, Chest, 1966-95, Med. Comm., 1971-75, Postgrad. Med. Jour., London, 1967-72; exec. editor Mayo Clinic Procs., 1969-77, Bioscis. Comm., 1975-80, Ont. Med. Rev., 1979-84, HSTC Jour., 1980-87, Can. Bull. Med. History, 1983-90, Med. History (London), 1982-87, Jour. History of Medicine and Allied Scis., 1991-94, 96—. Mem. bd. curators Osler Libr., McGill U., Montreal, 1981—. Recipient Jason A. Hannah medal Royal Soc. Can., 1994. Fellow AAAS (coun. 1969-74), Am. Med. Writers Assn. (pres. 1969-70); mem. Can. Med. Assn., Am. Assn. History Medicine (sec.-treas. 1976-80, publs. com. 1979-85, 2002—, Garrison lectr. com. 2005—), Acad. Medicine Toronto (Grogan lecture com. 1978-83, chmn. sect. med. history 1979-80, mus. com. 1983-84), Am. Mil. Inst., Internat. Inst. Prisoners of War, Soc. Internat. d'Histoire de la Medicine (internat. del. for Can. 1983-86), Can. Soc. for History Medicine (v.p. 1982-87, pres. 1993-95), Soc. Med. History Chgo. (sec.-treas. 1966-69), Can. Ctr. for Studies in Hist. Horticulture (exec. com. 1982-89), Coun. Biology Editors, Med. Hist. Club Toronto (pres. 1977-78), Ont. Hist. Soc., Can. Hist. Assn., Bibliog. Soc. Can., Am. Osler Soc. (sec.-treas. 1975-85, v.p. 1985-86, pres. 1986-87, historian, 1999-), Japan Osler Soc. (hon.), Royal Soc. Medicine (London), Royal Can. Mil. Inst., Champlain Soc. (Toronto), History of Second World War (Can. com.), Soc. Army Hist. Rsch., Univ. Club (Rochester); Osler Club (London), Alpine Club Can., Lit. Club (Chgo.), Sigma Xi. Office: McMaster U 3N10-HSC Med Ctr 1200 Main St W Hamilton ON Canada L8N 3Z5 Business E-Mail: croland@cogeco.ca.

ROLAND, DONALD EDWARD, advertising executive; b. Dalhart, Tex., Nov. 14, 1942; s. Vernon O. Roland and Doris M. (Cox) Roland Hutson; m. Kathleen Marie Bennett, Feb. 1, 1964; children; Aileen, Donald E., Jenny. BS, Calif. State U., LA, 1964; MA, U. Calif., Riverside, 1967; cert. exec. mgmt., UCLA. Dir. computer graphics Times Mirror Press, LA, 1966-78, plant mgr., 1978-81, v.p. prodn., 1981-83; group v.p. ops. Treasure Chest Advt., Glendora, Calif., 1983-84, sr. v.p. ops., 1984-93, exec. v.p., 1993-94, pres., CEO, 1995-2000, Vertis Inc., Balt., 2000—, chmn., 2001—. Republican. E-mail: droland@vertisinc.com.

ROLAND, RAYMOND WILLIAM, lawyer, mediator; b. Ocala, Fla., Jan. 3, 1947; s. Raymond W. and Hazel (Dunn) R.; m. Jane Allen, Dec. 28, 1968; children: John Allen, Jason William. BA, Fla. State U., Tallahassee, 1969, JD, 1972. Bar: Fla. 1972, US Dist. Ct. (no. dist.) Fla. 1973, US Dist. Ct. (mid. dist.) Fla. 1985, US Ct. Appeals (5th cir.) 1974, US Ct. Appeals (11th cir.) 1983, US Supreme Ct. 1985; cert. cir. ct. mediator. Assoc. Keen, O'Kelley & Spitz, Tallahassee, 1972-74, ptnr., 1974-77; ptnr., v.p. McConnaughhay, Roland, Maida & Cherr, P.A., Tallahassee, 1978-97; owner Roland Mediation Svcs., Tallahassee, 1997—2002; cir. mediator U.S. Ct. Appeals 11th Cir., 2002—. Adj. prof. Bapt. Coll. Fla.; diplomate mem. Fla. Acad. of Profl. Mediators, Inc. Bd. visitors Bapt. Coll. Fla.; bd. dirs. So. Scholarship Found., Tallahassee, 1985—89, 1998—99, v.p., 1989. Capt. USAFR, 1969—78. Mem.: Fla. Kiwanis Found. (life fellow), Capital City Kiwanis Club (pres. 1979, Kiwanian of Yr. 1978), Kiwanis (life; lt. gov. 1984—85). Baptist. Avocations: reading, hiking, camping, golf. Home: 800 Freedom Ln Roswell GA 30075 Office Phone: 404-335-6272. Personal E-mail: BRoland487@aol.com.

ROLDAN, KENNETH ARROYO, executive recruiter, lawyer; married; 2 children. BA, Cornell U., 1986; JD, Touro Law Ctr. Atty. No. Manhattan Coalition for Immigrant Rights, NYC; asst. atty. gen. Civil Rights Bur. State of NY, Albany, 1995—98; gen. counsel Wesley, Brown & Bartle Co., Inc., NYC, 1998—2003, CEO, 2003—07; ptnr., head diversity practice Battalia Winston Internat., 2007—. Mem.: Cornell Latino Alumni Assn. (former pres.). Avocation: gardening. Office: Battalia Winston Internat 19th Fl 555 Madison Ave New York NY 10022

ROLEN, SCOTT BRUCE, professional baseball player; b. Jasper, Ind., Apr. 4, 1975; m. Niki Warner, Feb. 2, 2002. 3d base Phila. Phillies, 1993—2002, St. Louis Cardinals, 2002—. Named Nat. League Rookie Player of Yr., The Sporting News, 1997, Baseball Writers Assn. of Am., 1997; named to Nat. League All-Star Team, 2002—04; recipient Nat. League Gold Glove Award, 1997—2004, 2006. Office: c/o St Louis Cardinals 250 Stadium Plaza Saint Louis MO 63102 *

ROLETT, ELLIS LAWRENCE, cardiologist, educator; b. NYC, July 10, 1930; s. Daniel Meyer and Mary Elaine (Warshaw) R.; m. Virginia Ann Vladimir, Mar. 25, 1956; children: Roderic Lawrence, Barry Vladimir, Daniel Alfred. BS, Yale U., 1952; MD cum laude, Harvard U., 1955. Diplomate: Am. Bd. Internal Medicine, Am. Bd. Cardiovas. Disease. Intern, resident in medicine Mass. Gen. Hosp., Boston, 1955-56, 59-61; asst. resident N.Y. Hosp.-Cornell U. Med. Ctr., NYC, 1956-57; Am. Heart Assn. research fellow Peter Bent Brigham Hosp., Boston, 1961-63; mem. faculty U. N.C., Chapel Hill, 1963-74, then prof., 1971-74; prof. UCLA, 1974-77; chief cardiology VA Wadsworth Hosp., LA, 1974-77, Dartmouth-Hitchcock Med. Ctr., Hanover, NH, 1977—87; prof. Dartmouth Med. Sch., Hanover, 1977-97, prof. medicine active emeritus, 1997—. Vis. scientist August Krogh Inst., Copenhagen, 1984; mem. merit rev. bd. Cardiovasc. studies VA, 1976-79, chmn., 1978-79; mem. regional rsch. rev. com. New Eng. Am. Heart Assn., 1978-83; mem. sci. bd. Stanley J. Sarnoff Endowment for Cardiovasc. Sci., 1992-97, chmn., 1994-95, bd. dirs., 1997-2000; mem. lit. sect. rev. com. Nat. Libr. Medicine, 1995-99, chmn., 1998-99; dir. Vt.-Karelia (Russia) Med. Project, St. Petersburg Univ. Global Fund. Bd. dirs. N.H. affiliate Am. Heart Assn., 1978-85; pres. N.H. affiliate Am. Heart Assn., 1983-85. Served to capt. M.C. USAF, 1957-59. Recipient Lederle Med. Faculty award, 1965-68, USPHS Career Devel. award, 1967-72, grantee USPHS/NIH, 1964-76, VA Merit Rev. Rsch. Program, 1975-77, Mathers Found., 1984-86, 93-96, Am. Heart Assn., 1989-91. Mem. AAAS, Am. Physiol. Soc., Internat. Soc. Heart Rsch., Phi Beta Kappa, Alpha Omega Alpha Home: 4 Balch Hill Ln Hanover NH 03755-1622 Office: Dartmouth Med Sch Hanover NH 03755 Office Phone: 603-650-1360. Business E-Mail: ellis.rolett@dartmouth.edu.

ROLF, HOWARD LEROY, mathematician, educator; b. Laverne, Okla., Nov. 25, 1928; s. James Walter and Edith (Yoho) R.; m. Anita Jane Ward, June 24, 1961; children: James Scott, Jennifer Jane, Stephanie Kaye, Rhonda Mary. BS, Okla. Baptist U., 1951; MA, Vanderbilt U., 1953, PhD, 1956. Instr. math. Vanderbilt U., 1954-56, asst. prof., dir. computer ctr., 1959-64; asst. prof. Baylor U., 1956-57, prof., 1964-98, dir. acad. computing, 1968-70, chmn. dept. math., 1971-97. Assoc. prof. Georgetown Coll., Ky., 1957—59. Author: (with William C. Brown) Mathematics, 1982, Finite Mathematics, 1988, 91, 94, 99, 02, 05, (with Brooks-Cole) Mathematics for Management, Social and Life Sciences, 1991. Mem. Math. Assn. Am. (chmn. Tex. sect. 1977), Sigma Xi, Pi Mu Epsilon, Golden Key. Baptist. Home: 4096 Speegleville Rd Waco TX 76712-4033

ROLFE, CHRISTOPHER C., energy executive; BS in Mech. Engring., NC State U. Registered profl. engr., NC, SC. Engring. asst. design engring. dept. Duke Energy (formerly Duke Power Co.), 1972, v.p. corp. performance, 1992—97, v.p. corp. human resources, 1997—2000, v.p. human resources, 2000, group exec., chief human resources officer, group exec., chief adminstrv. officer, 2006—. Chmn. NC Commn. Workforce Devel. Recipient Jack Callahan Cornerstone award, Goodwill Industries of So. Piedmont of NC, 2007. Office: Duke Energy 526 S Church St Charlotte NC 28202-1904 Office Phone: 704-594-6200. *

ROLFE, ELLEN MARY, retired music educator; b. South Bend, Ind. d. John Philip and Edna Deveraux Gallagher; m. George Obediah Rolfe, Oct. 24, 1964; children: John Joseph, Katherine Elizabeth. MusB, Eastern Mich. U., 1960. Tchr. Lapeer St. Home Tng., Mich., 1960—63; music/spl. edn. tchr. Seaside Regional Ctr., Waterford, Conn., 1963—64; spl. edn. tchr. Valley Regional H.S., Deep River, Conn., 1964—67; music tchr. Torrington Pub. Schools, 1972—2006, ret., 2006. Mentor/tchr. Conn. Bd. Edn. Bd. dirs. Girl Scouts Northest; mem., past pres. Litchfield County Choral Union, 1972—; v.p. Girl Scouts Northest. Recipient Thanks pin, Nat. Coun. Girl Scouts Am., 2006. Mem.: Conn. Music Educators Assn. (Mid. Sch. Educator of the Yr. 1997), Am. String Teachers Assn., Music Educators Nat. Assn., Torrington Symphony Orch. (bd. dirs.). Episcopalian. Home: 172 Wedgewood Dr Torrington CT 06790

ROLFE, HAROLD E., lawyer; b. Dec. 4, 1957; m. Carol Rolfe. BA summa cum laude, Yale U.; JD magna cum laude, Harvard U. Assoc. Cravath, Swaine & Moore, NYC; v.p., gen. counsel Corp. Property Investors, NYC, 1991—98; sr. v.p., gen. counsel Hertz Corp., 1998—, sec., 1999—; gen. counsel, sec. Hertz Global Holdings Inc., Park Ridge, NJ, 2005—, sr. v.p., 2006—. Office: Hertz Global Holdings, Inc 225 Brae Blvd Park Ridge NJ 07656 Office Phone: 201-307-2000. *

ROLFE, ROBERT MARTIN, lawyer; b. Richmond, Va., May 16, 1951; s. Norman and Bertha (Cohen) R.; m. Catherine Dennis Stone, July 14, 1973; children: P. Alexander, Asher B., Joel A., Zachary A. BA, U. Va., 1973, JD, 1976. Bar: Va. 1976, NY 1985, US Dist. Ct. (ea. and we. dists.) Va. 1976, US Ct. Appeals (4th cir.) 1976, US Ct. Appeals (2d cir.) 1979, US Dist. Ct. (ea. dist.) Mich. 1985, US Ct. Appeals (DC cir.) 1985, US Dist. Ct. (so. and ea. dists.) NY 1985, US Ct. Appeals (7th cir.) 1995, US Ct. Fed. Claims, 1997, US Supreme Ct. 1979. Assoc. Hunton & Williams, Richmond, 1976—83, ptnr., 1983—, co-head litig., intellectual property and antitrust team, 1995—2007, gen. counsel, 1995—, exec. com., 1998—2004. Editorial bd. Va. Law Rev., 1976; contbr. articles to profl. jours. Trustee, pres. bd. trustees Jewish Family Supporting Found., chmn. of bd. trustees, 2005-; bd. dirs. Jewish Family Svcs., Richmond, pres., 1993-95; bd. mgrs., 2d v.p. Congregation Beth Ahabah, 1995-97, 1st v.p., 1997-99. Fellow Am. Bar Found.; mem. ABA (litig. sect.), Va. Bar Assn., Va. State Bar, Richmond Bar Assn., Order of Coif (Alumni award for acad. excellence U. Va. 1976). Home: 18 Greenway Ln Richmond VA 23226-1630 Office: Hunton & Williams Riverfront Plz East Tower PO Box 1535 Richmond VA 23218-1535 also: 200 Park Ave New York NY 10166-0005 Office Phone: 804-788-8466. Office Fax: 804-343-4568. Business E-Mail: rrolfe@hunton.com.

ROLFE, RONALD STUART, lawyer; b. NYC, Sept. 5, 1945; s. Nat and Florence I. (Roth) R.; m. Yvonne Quinn, Sept. 1, 1979 (div. Apr. 2002); m. Sara Darehshori; children; Andrew, Dare. AB, Harvard U., 1966; JD, Columbia U., 1969. Bar: N.Y. 1969, U.S. Ct. Appeals (2d cir.) 1970, U.S. Dist. Ct. (so. and ea. dists.) N.Y. 1971, U.S. Supreme Ct. 1973, U.S. Dist. Ct. (no. dist.) Calif. 1982, U.S. Ct. Appeals (6th and 5th cirs.) 1982, U.S. Ct. Appeals (9th cir.) 1983, U.S. Dist. Ct. (ea. dist.) Ky. 1984, U.S. Ct. Appeals (7th and 10th cirs.) 1989, U.S. Ct. Appeals (fed. cir.) 1991, U.S. Ct. Appeals (3d cir.) 1992, U.S. Ct. Appeals (4th cir.) 1991. Law clk. to judge US Dist. Ct. (so. dist.) NY, 1969-70; assoc. Cravath, Swaine & Moore LLP, 1970-77, ptnr., litig., 1977—. Trustee Allen-Stevenson Sch., 1980—, pres., 1992—; trustee Lawrenceville Sch., 1987—, v.p., 2001—05; bd. visitors Law Sch. Columbia U., emeritus bd. adv. Ctr. Corp. Governance, dean's coun. Law Sch. Trustee DeLaSalle Acad., 2002—. Fellow: NY Bar Found., Am. Bar Found.; mem.: ABA, Am. Law Inst., Fed. Bar Coun. (trustee 1989—94), Assn. Bar City NY, NY State Bar Assn., Century Assn., The Bridge (Noyac, NY), Stanwich Club, Univ. Club, Union Club. Office: Cravath Swaine & Moore LLP Worldwide Plz 825 8th Ave 40th Fl New York NY 10019-7475 Office Phone: 212-474-1714. Office Fax: 212-474-3700. Business E-Mail: rrolfe@cravath.com.

ROLFF, JAMES ROBERT, retired locomotive engineer, writer; b. Chgo., May 26, 1939; s. Herman Robert Rolff and Ruth Edna Price; m. Sandra Marie Strong, June 20, 1959; children: Brian, Viktoria. Student, Mt. Carmel Coll., Niagara Falls, Ont., Can., 1955, US Armed Forces Inst., Madison, Wis., 1957. Locomotive engr. Can. Nat. RR, Battle Creek, Mich., 1966—2001. Author: Strong Family of Virginia and Other Southern States, 1982, 1983, Pinehurst, 1988. With USN, 1956—58. Mem.: Brotherhood Locomotive Engrs. (sec.-treas. 1975—80), Mensa. Republican. Roman Catholic. Avocations: genealogy, gardening, travel, sports. Home: 7197 Windy Peak Ct Las Vegas NV 89113

ROLIN, DANIEL WAYNE, JR., military officer; b. San Antonio, Aug. 9, 1981; s. Dan Rolin, Sr. and Diane Higginbotham; m. Judy Galvan; 1 child, Alexis Renee. Grad. H.S., La Vernia, Tex., 2000. Special Reaction Team Phase 1 Entry Team: US Army Mil. Police Sch. 2004, Special Reaction Team Phase 2 Marksman/Observer: US Army Mil. Police Sch. 2004, Multiport Distraction Device Course: Def. Tech. 2005, User/Instructor Certification Course: Taser Internat./ Ga. 2005, Basic/Advanced Sniper Course: Wackenhut Security Services/South Carolina 2005, SWAT Marksman/Observer Course: SC. Tactical Officers Assn./South Carolina 2005, Tactical Team Operations: Team One Network / Fla. 2005, Advanced Close Quarters Shooting: Team One Network/ Fla. 2005, Officers Survival Course: Team One Network/ Fla. 2005, SWAT Level 1 Course: Richmond County Sheriffs Dept./ Ga. 2005, Traffic Accident Investigator Level 1-2 Course: Richmond County Sheriffs Dept./ Ga. 2005, Police Cyclist Course: Richmond County Sheriffs Dept./ Ga. 2005. Sgt. US Army, 2002—, spl. reaction team entry team mem. 35th Mil. Police Detachment Ft. Gordon, Ga., 2003—04, traffic accident investigator 35th Mil. Police Detachment, 2003—05, spl. reaction team marksman/teamleader 35th Mil. Police Detachment, 2004—05, mil. police 204th Mil. Police Co. Ft. Polk, La., 2005—. Decorated Army Achievement medal US Army, Iraqi Campaign Svc. medal, Combat Action Badge, Army Commendation medal; recipient Honor award, Assn. US Army, 2003. Mem.: VFW. Home: 15209B Cooley Pl Fort Polk LA 71459 Home Phone: 210-296-7524.

ROLL, JOHN MCCARTHY, judge; s. Paul Herbert and Esther Marie (McCarthy) Roll; m. Maureen O'Connor; 3 children. BA, U. Ariz., 1969, JD, 1972; LLM, U. Va., 1990. Bar: Ariz. 1972, U.S. Dist. Ct. Ariz. 1974, U.S. Ct. Appeals (9th cir.) 1980, U.S. Supreme Ct. 1977. Asst. pros. atty. City of Tucson, 1973; dep. county atty. Pima County (Ariz.), 1973-80; asst. U.S. Atty. U.S. Attys. Office, Tucson, 1980-87; judge Ariz. Ct. Appeals, 1987-91, U.S. Dist. Ct. Ariz., 1991—2006, chief judge, 2006—. Mem. criminal justice mental health standards project ABA, 1980—83, mem. com. model jury instrns. 9th circ., 1994—2001, chair com. model jury instrns. 9th circ., 1998—2001; mem. panel workshop criminal law CEELI Program, Moscow, 1997; mem. U.S. Jud. Conf. Adv. Com. Criminal Rules, 1997—2003. Contbr. Merit Selection: the Arizona Experience, Ariz. State Law Jour., 1991, The Rules Have Changed: Amendments ot the Rules of Civil procedure, Defense Law Jour., 1994, Ninth Cir. Judges' Benchbook on Pretrial Proceedings, 1998, 00, 02, 04. Recipient Disting. Faculty award Nat. Coll. Dist. Attys., U. Houston, 1979, Outstanding Alumnus award U. Ariz. Coll. Law, 1992. Mem. Fed. Judges Assn., KC (adv. coun. 1991). Republican. Office: US Dist Ct 405 W Congress Tucson AZ 85701

ROLL, RENÉE F., retired psychologist, publishing executive; d. Leo and Helen Feldman; children: Stewart Daniel, Jeri Ann. BA, U. Calif., 1965, MS, 1967. Lic. psychologist Bd. Med. Examiners, Calif., 1973, marriage and family therapist Bd. Behavioral Scis. Calif., 1968, cert. diplomate psychologist Am. Psychotherapy Assn., 1998, therapist Nat. Bd. Cognitive Behavioral Therapists, 1999. Tchr. Manesquan Sch. Dist., NJ, 1959—60, Montebello Unified Sch. Dist., Calif., 1961—70, psychologist, 1961—70; pvt. practice counselor Glendale, Calif., 1970—73; pvt. practice psychologist Chico, Calif., 1974; ret., 1974; cons. Dr. J.P. Haddock, Chico, 1975—82. Author: The Seeds of Growth, A History for the Future, 2002 (appears in the Libr. of Congress, DC), A Crooked Christmas Tree, 2004, A Tale of Two Boys and Wolf Pups, 2006. Vol. fireman Calif. Dept. Forestry, Butte Meadows, Calif., 1983. Recipient Outstanding Achievement award, Internat. Soc. Poets, 2003, Poet of Merit award, 2003, Outstanding Achievement in Poetry award, 2006. Mem.: AAUW, Nat. Assn. Female Execs., Natural Wildlife Assn., Writing Group Stockton, Purse Club. Avocations: piano, poetry, flowers, writing. Home: 4089 Five Mile Dr Stockton CA 95219 Office Phone: 209-481-0273. Personal E-mail: reneeroll@comcast.net.

ROLLAND, KATHY ANN, elementary school educator; b. Pottsville, Pa., May 10, 1963; d. Kenneth Warren Rolland, Sr. and Lilla Catherine Telepchak. BS in Early Childhood Edn., Pa. State U., 1985; MEd in Sch. Leadership and Instrn., Wilmington Coll., 1998. Cert. generalist, early childhood Nat. Bd. Profl. Tchg. Stds. Tchr. Colonial Sch. Dist., New Castle, Del., 1990—. Mem. Investigations Math. Adv. Bd., New Castle, 2002—, Bridges Learning Sys. Dist., New Castle, 2002—. Vol. Freedom Outreach, Wilmington, 1999—. Excellence in Edn. grantee, MBNA Found., 2002. Mem.: NEA, Del. Coun. Tchrs. Math., Del. State Edn. Assn., Phi Lambda Theta. Avocations: travel, guitar, volunteering. Office: So Elem Sch 795 Cox Neck Rd New Castle DE 19720 Office Phone: 302-323-2828.

ROLLAND, LUCIEN GILBERT, paper company executive, director; b. St. Jerome, Que., Can., Dec. 21, 1916; s. Olivier and Aline (Dorion) R.; m. Marie de Lorimier, May 30, 1942; children: Nicolas, Natalie, Stanislas, Dominique, Christine, Etienne, David. Student, Coll. Jean de Brebeuf, Montreal, U. Montreal, BA, BASc., C.E., also D.C.Sc. (hon.), 1960. Registered profl. engr. With Rolland Paper Co. Ltd. (name changed to Rolland inc. 1979), 1942—, v.p., gen. mgr., 1952, pres., gen. mgr., 1952-78, pres., CEO, 1978—, chmn., pres., CEO, 1984, chmn., CEO, 1985, chmn., 1991. Cons. in field, 1995; chmn. bd. Tarascon, Inc. Bd. govs. Notre-Dame Hosp., Montreal Children's Hosp., Montreal Gen. Hosp., Hôpital Marie Enfant. Decorated Knight Comdr. Order St. Gregory, officer Order of Can. Mem. Can. Pulp and Paper Assn. (hon.), Corp. Profl. Engrs., Montreal Bd. Trade, Province of Que., C of C, Montreal C. of C., Engring. Inst. Can. Home: Apt B-60 1321 Sherbrooke St W Montreal PQ Canada H3G 1J4 Office: Tarascon Inc 1200 McGill College #1100 Montreal PQ Canada H3B 4G7 Office Phone: 514-393-9928.

ROLLAND, PETER GEORGE, landscape architect; b. Frankfurt, Germany, July 2, 1930; came to U.S., 1936; s. Curt Henry and Lise (Kahn) R.; m. Wendy Diana Altschul, Dec. 26, 1955; children: David, Seth, Janna. B.Sc., Delaware Valley Coll., 1952; M.L.A., Harvard U., 1955. Registered landscape architect, N.Y., Conn., Coun. Landscape Archtl. Rev. Bds. Chief site planner Perkins & Will Architects, White Plains, NY, 1955-60; project landscape architect Lawrence Halprin & Assocs., San Francisco, 1960-63; prin. Peter G. Rolland & Assocs., Rye, NY, 1963—81, Canberra, Australia, 1963—81; ptnr. Rolland/Towers, Rye, New Haven, 1981—97. Andrew Mellon vis. prof. Yale U. Sch. Forestry, 1979; faculty Sch. Architecture, Yale U., 1973-94; vis. prof. Harvard Grad. Sch. Design, 1990; mem. Office Bldg. Ops., architecture adv. bd., US Dept. State, 2000-05; disting. prof. landscape architecture, Sch. Architecture, CCNY, 2004. Prin. landscape architect, New Parliament House, Canberra, Australia, 1980, SUNY, Coll. at Purchase, 1964-75. Mem., chmn. N.Y. State Bd. Landscape Architects, 1972-82; mem. N.Y. State Coun. on Arts, 1979-82, Rye Archtl. Bd. Rev., 1973-78; trustee Delaware Valley Coll., 1991-2003; mem. grad. coun. Grad. Sch. Design, Harvard U., Cambridge, Mass., 1978-88; trustee Am. Acad. in Rome, 1992-96, pres. Soc. Fellows, 1992-96. Served with U.S. Army, 1956-58. Recipient Arthur Brown award Del. Valley Coll., 1978, Pres.'s award, 2003; Design award AIA, 1975, 78, 85, 90, 92, 94, Inst. Honors award, 1990; Tucker award for IBM Conf. Ctr., 1982; Sir Zelman Cowens award Royal Australian Inst. Archs., 1989; Tucker award for New Parliament Ho., Canberra, Australia, 1990; Rome Prize fellow Am. Acad. in Rome, 1978, Pierson Coll. fellow Yale U., 1982-92. Fellow Am. Soc. Landscape Architects (ann. design awards 1972-85, 92, award of Excellence, 1991); mem. NAD (Academician), Australian Inst. Landscape Architects (Landmarks award for New Parliament House, Canberra, 1988). Office: 731 Milton Rd Rye NY 10580

ROLLANS, JAMES O., service company executive; b. Glendale, Calif., July 7, 1942; s. Henry Leo and Geraldine Ada (Berg) R.; children: Jodie Helene, Thomas James, Daniel Joseph. BS, Calif. State U., Northridge, 1967. Vice pres., dir. Chase Manhattan Bank, 1976-78; v.p. corp. communications Dart Industries, Los Angeles, 1978-80; v.p. bus. analysis and investor relations Dart & Kraft, Chgo., 1980-82; sr. v.p., CFO Fluor Corp., Irvine, Calif., 1982-99, also bd. dirs., 1998—; pres., group exec. Bus. Svcs., Aliso Viego, Calif., 1999. Bd. dirs. Cupertino Elec.; mem. Flowserve Corp. Bd. dirs. Irvine Med. Ctr. Episcopalian. Avocations: boating, skiing, fishing, hunting. Home: 1 Saint Remy Ct Newport Coast CA 92657-1626

ROLLE, ANDREW, historian, writer; b. Providence, Apr. 12, 1922; m. Frances Squires, Dec. 1945 (div.); children: John Warren, Alexander Frederick, Julia Elisabeth.; m. Myra Moss, Nov. 1983. BA, Occidental Coll., 1943; MA, UCLA, 1949, PhD, 1953; grad., So. Calif. Psychoanalytic Inst., 1976. Am. vice consul, Genoa, Italy, 1945-48; editorial asso. Pacific Hist. Rev., 1952-53; from asst. prof. to Cleland prof. history Occidental Coll., 1953-88; rsch. scholar Huntington Libr., San Marino, Calif., 1988—. Author: Riviera Path, 1946, An American in California, 1956, reprinted, 1982, The Road to Virginia City, 1960, reprinted, 1989, Lincoln: A Contemporary Portrait, 1961, (with Allan Nevins, Irving Stone) California: A History, 1963, rev. edits., 1963, 69, 78, 87, 98, 2002, 07, Occidental College: The First Seventy-Five Years, 1963, The Lost Cause: Confederate Exiles in Mexico, 1965, 1992, The Golden State, 1967, rev. edit., 1978, 1989, 2000, California, A Student Guide, 1965, Los Angeles, A Student Guide, 1965; Editor: A Century of Dishonor (Helen Hunt Jackson), 1964, Life in California (Alfred Robinson), 1971, Voyage to California (Jour. of Lucy Herrick), 1998; The Immigrant Upraised, 1968, The American

Italians: Their History and Culture, 1972, Gli Emigrati Vittoriosi, 1973, reprinted, 2003; (with George Knoles others) Essays and Assays, 1973, (with others) Studies in Italian American Social History, 1975, (with others) Los Angeles: The Biography of a City, 1976, 2d edit., 1991; (with Allan Weinstein and others) Crisis in America, 1977, The Italian Americans: Troubled Roots, 1980, 2d edit. 1985, Los Angeles: From Pueblo to Tomorrow's City, 1981, 2nd edit., 1995, Occidental College: A Centennial History, 1986, John Charles Frémont: Character as Destiny, 1991, Henry Mayo Newhall and His Times, 1992, Westward the Immigrants, 1999, The Victorious Immigrants, 2005. Served to 1st lt. M.I. AUS, 1943-45, 51-52. Decorated Cavaliere Ordine Merito Italy; recipient silver medal Italian Ministry Fgn. Affairs; Commonwealth award for non-fiction; Huntington Libr.-Rockefeller Found. fellow; resident scholar Rockefeller Found. Ctr., Bellagio, Italy. Fellow Calif. Hist. Soc.; mem. Phi Beta Kappa. Office: Huntington Libr Rsch Div San Marino CA 91108 Office Phone: 626-405-2100 ext 2321.

ROLLE, MYRA MOSS See MOSS, MYRA

ROLLER, CHAD B., research and development company executive; PhD, Rice U., Houston, 2003—05. V.p. rsch. Ekips Technologies, Inc., Norman, Okla., 2005—. Vol. Leadership Okla. City, 2006—. Finalist Young Investigator award, AAMI, 2004. Mem.: Okla. Venture Forum (assoc.). Independent. Office: Ekips Technologies Inc 710 Asp Ave Ste 500 Norman OK 73069 Office Fax: 405-307-8807. Business E-Mail: ckroller@cox.net.

ROLLER, DAVID ISAAC, financial services company executive; b. Bklyn., Jan. 13, 1949; s. Morton and Helen (Deligtisch) R.; m. Susan Firtle, June 3, 1973; children: Aviva Natanya, Yael Elisheva. BA, L.I. U., 1971; MA, NYU, 1980, PhD, 1983, Cleo Soc., Oakland, Mich., 1991; DD, N.W. Ecumenical Inst., Petaluma, Calif., 1992. Ordained rabbi, 1980; cert. religious counselor. Rabbi North Rockland Jewish Cmty. Ctr., Pomona, N.Y., 1980-81; educator, asst. rabbi Old Westbury (N.Y.) Hebrew Congregation, 1982-83; rabbi Beth Emek Congregation, Livermore, Calif., 1983-85; pres., founder Roller Fin. Assocs., Gilbert, Ariz., 1985—. Guest rabbi High Holidays, East Bay Chavuarah, Danville, Calif., 1990-93; chaplain Masonic Home for Adults, Union City, 1992—; mem. Sys Op AOL-Jew Comm Bd., 1995-2005. Mem. Internat. Assn. Fin. Planners, Am. Assn. Rabbis, No. Calif. Bd. Rabbis, Masons (chaplain 1985-86), Mensa, Rotary. Republican. Jewish. Avocations: photography, reading. E-mail: davetarot@aol.com.

ROLLER, PAMELA JO, elementary school educator; b. Logansport, Ind., Mar. 22, 1952; d. Glen B. Roller and Clara Evelyn Sizemore. BS, Ind. U., Kokomo, 1974; MS, Ind. U./Purdue U. Indpls., 1976. Cert. CFG Coach for Nat. Sch. Reform Faculty 2004. Tchr. 5th and 6th grade Southeastern Sch. Corp., Logansport, 1974—76, tchr. 1st grade, 1976—79, tchr. 2d grade, 1979—82, tchr. 1st grade, 1982—88, readiness tchr. 1st grade, 1988—94, tchr. 2d grade, 1994—. Founder/coord., mentoring program K-12 Tender Loving Care, 1989—; coord. Young Astronauts, 1988—; founder/coord. Sch. on Sat., Galveston, Ind., 1994—; third grade tchr., Bolivia, 2004; mem. faculty Challenger Learning Ctr., 1996; workshop presenter Ind. Dept. Edn., 1989—91, Nature's Classroom. Flight dir. Mission Possible, Galveston, 1996—; pres. Southeastern Edn. Assn., 1981—82; dist. lay spkr. United Meth., Logansport, Ind., 1992—. Named Jaycee's Outstanding Young Educator, 1981, Tchr. of Yr., Cass County Soil and Water Dist. Conservation, 1997; recipient NASA/NSTA Newest award, 1993, Good Neighbor award, 2001, Disney's Am. Tchr. Awards Honoree, Calif., 2003, Make a Difference Day honoree award, USA Weekend Mag., 2006, 2007; scholar, Japan Fulbright Meml. Fund, 2005. Mem.: NSTA, Profl. Assn. in Edn., Hoosier Assn. Sci. Tchrs. (workshop presenter 1994—), Pi Lambda Theta. Democrat. Methodist. Achievements include classroom business called chocolate lollipops, Inc. has earned over 5,000 dollars, and given to numerous charities. Office Phone: 574-699-6687. Personal E-mail: proller1@msn.com.

ROLLE-RISSETTO, SILVIA, foreign languages educator, writer, artist; b. Rosario, Argentina, Apr. 19, 1967; d. Dante and Gladys Rolle. BA in Spanish, Calif. State U., Long Beach, 1987, BA in French and Italian, 1987, MA in Spanish, 1990; PhD in Spanish, U. Calif., Riverside, 1996. Assoc. prof. Spanish, grad. coord. and fgn. lang. assessor of Spanish and Italian, dept. world langs. and lit. Calif. State U., San Marcos, 1996—, chair, world lang. & hispanic lit., 2000—. Participant numerous confs. Author: La Obra de Ana Maria Fagundo: Una Poetica Femenino-Feminista, 1997, Plazas: un lugar de encuentro para la hispanidad (lab manual); contbr. articles to profl. jours.; translator. Recipient Patrons of Italian scholarship U. degli Studi di Siena, 1987. Mem. MLA, Nat. Hispanic Soc., Asociacion de Literatura Femenina Hispanica, Hispanic Assn. of the Humanties, Letra Femeninas, Mairena, Assn. Internat. Hispanistas. Democrat. Office: Calif State U San Marcos World Langs & Hispanic Lit 333 S Twin Oaks Valley Rd San Marcos CA 92096-0001 Business E-Mail: srolle@csusm.edu.

ROLLETT, REBECCA A., musician, director; b. Salisbury, NC, Dec. 2, 1953; d. Richard H. and Mary Frances Naffziger; m. Anthony D. Rollett, Apr. 29, 1978; children: Edmund P., Adrian C., Cecily A., Sarah C. MusB, Oral Roberts U., Tulsa, 1978; MusM, Carnegie Mellon U., Pitts., 1998. Dir. music Ch. of the Holy Faith, Santa Fe, 1981—95; prin. keyboard Santa Fe Symphony, 1984—95, chorus dir., 1989—93; artistic dir. Coro de Camara, Los Alamos, 1988—95, The Pitts. Camerata, 1998—. Adj. faculty Duquesne U., Pitts., 2003—. Mem.: Am. Guild Organists, Pi Kappa Lambda. Office: Duquesne Univ 600 Forbes Ave Pittsburgh PA 15282 Home Phone: 412-421-2562. Personal E-mail: rrollett@rollett.org.

ROLLIN, BETTY, writer, television journalist; b. NYC, Jan. 3, 1936; d. Leon and Ida R.; m. Harold M. Edwards, Jan. 21, 1979. BA, Sarah Lawrence Coll., 1957. Assoc. features editor Vogue mag., 1964; sr. editor Look mag., 1965-71; network corr. NBC News, NYC, 1971-80, contbg. corr., 1985—2003; network corr. ABC News Nightline, 1982-84. Contbr. corr. Religion and Ethics Newsweekly PBS; lectr. in field. Profl. actress: on stage and TV, 1958—64; author: I Thee Wed, 1962, Mothers Are Funnier Than Children, 1964, The Non-Drinkers' Drink Book, 1966, First, You Cry, 1976, reissue, 2000, Am I Getting Paid for This?, 1982, Last Wish, 1985, reissue, 1998; columnist: Hers, N.Y. Times; contbr. articles to popular mags. Bd. mem. Death With Dignity Nat. Ctr., 1997—. Office: Care NS Bienstock Inc 1740 Broadway New York NY 10019-4315 Office Phone: 212-664-7171.

ROLLIN, MICHAEL FREDRICK, history professor; b. Laredo, Tex., Apr. 25, 1975; s. Michael William and Maria Farias Rollin. BA in Polit. Sci., St. Mary's U., San Antonio, 1996; MA, U. Tex., San Antonio, 2000—02. Adj. instr., history St. Philip's Coll., San Antonio, 2003—05; lectr. U. Tex., San Antonio, 2004—. Mem.: Am. Hist. Assn., The Sons of the Republic of Tex. Republican. Roman Catholic. Home: 13122 Brook Garden Ln San Antonio TX 78232-5155 Office: Univ Texas 6900 N Loop 1604 W San Antonio TX 78249-0652 Home Phone: 210-402-5413. Home Fax: 210-402-5413. E-mail: michael.rollin@utsa.edu.

ROLLINGS, DALE LINN, lawyer; b. St. Louis, June 23, 1940; s. Jake Floyd and Ruby Ann Rollings; divorced; children: Mark, Matthew. BA, Washington U., St. Louis, 1962, JD, 1964. Bar: Mo. 1964, US Cir. Ct. (8th cir.) 1970, US Supreme Ct. 1970. Atty. Lincoln Haseltine Keet Forehand & Springer, Springfield, Mo., 1964—68; asst. pros. atty. Green County, Mo., Springfield, 1968—69; asst. atty. gen. Mo. Atty. Gen.'s Office, Jefferson City, 1969—71; pres. Rollings, Shaw & Assocs. (and predecessors), St. Charles, Mo., 1971—. Owner Yellow Farmhouse Vineyard, Defiance, Mo.; dir. New Frontier Bank, St. Charles, 1999—. Author: (book) Exit Laughing, 1999. Bd. dirs. Lindenwood U., St. Charles, 1989—, mem. exec. com., 1989—; mem. gen. counsel, 1989—; chmn. Daniel Boone Home Governing Bd., 2005—. Office: Rollings Shaw & Assocs PC 1000 Fairgrounds Rd Ste 200 Saint Charles MO 63301

ROLLINGS, MICHAEL THOMAS, insurance company executive; Grad. in Fin., Georgetown U., Washington; grad., Northwestern U. Kellogg Sch. Mgmt. Head capital markets divsn. MassMutual Fin. Group, Springfield, Mass., 2001, sr. v.p., dep. CFO, interim CFO, 2006, exec. v.p., CFO, 2006—. Bd. mem. Bus. Friends of the Arts, Springfield. Office: MassMutual Fin Group 1295 State St Springfield MA 01111-0001 Office Phone: 800-767-1000. *

ROLLINS, ALBERT WILLIAMSON, civil engineer, consultant; b. Dallas, July 31, 1930; s. Andrew Peach and Mary (Williamson) R.; m. Martha Ann James, Dec. 28, 1954; children: Elizabeth Ann, Mark Martin. BS in Civil Engring., Tex. A&M U., 1951, MS in Civil Engring., 1956, disting. grad. in Civil Engring., 2005. Registered profl. engr., Tex., La., Okla. Engring. asst. Tex. Hwy. Dept., Dallas, 1953-55; dir. pub. works City of Arlington, Tex., 1956-63, city mgr., 1963-67; ptnr. Schrickel, Rollins & Assocs., Land Planners-Engrs., Arlington, 1967—. Contbr. articles to profl. jours. Mem. Gov.'s Energy Adv. Coun.; chmn. Tex. Mass Transp. Commn.; bd. dirs. Tex. Turnpike Authority. Served as 1st lt. AUS, 1951-53. Mem. ASCE (Award of Honor Tex. sect. 2002), NSPE, Internat. City Mgmt. Assn., Am. Water Works Assn., Water Pollution Control Fedn., Sigma Xi, Phi Eta Sigma, Tau Beta Pi, Phi Kappa Phi, Chi Epsilon. Home: 3004 Yellowstone Dr Arlington TX 76013-1166 Office: Suite 200 1161 Corporate Dr W Ste 200 Arlington TX 76006-6819

ROLLINS, ALFRED BROOKS, JR., historian, educator; b. Presque Isle, Maine, May 28, 1921; s. Alfred Brooks and Clarissa (Jack) R.; m. Ernestine Emma McMullin, Nov. 6, 1942 (dec. Aug. 28, 1972); children: John Douglas, Nancy Jane, James Scott; m. Faith Kenyon, June 16, 1973 (dec. Mar. 8, 1979); m. Helen Anrod Jones, Feb. 28, 1981. BA, Wesleyan U., Middletown, Conn., 1942, MA, 1946; PhD, Harvard U., 1953. From instr. to prof. history State U., N.Y. at New Paltz, 1948-63; prof., chmn. dept. history State U. N.Y. at Binghamton, 1964-67; dean U. Vt., Burlington, 1967-70, v.p. acad. affairs, 1970-76; pres. Old Dominion U., Norfolk, Va., 1976-85, prof. history, 1976-91, pres. emeritus, prof. emeritus, 1991—. Cons. oral history project John F. Kennedy Library, 1965 Author: Roosevelt and Howe, 1962; Editor narrative: Franklin D. Roosevelt and the Age of Action, 1960, Woodrow Wilson and the New America, 1965; Contbr. articles to profl. jours. Served to 1st lt. USAAF, 1943-46. Decorated D.F.C., Air medal with four clusters. Mem. Am. Hist. Assn., Orgn. Am. Historians, Phi Beta Kappa, Chi Psi.

ROLLINS, CAROLE ANN, writer, artist; b. Stockton, Calif., Feb. 3, 1948; d. Jack Elmer and Gladys Ester (Bartholomew) Rollins. BS in Conservation of Natural Resources, U. Calif., Berkeley, 1971, AB in Arch., 1971, MA, 1974, postgrad., 1975; postgrad. in environ. studies, U. Nev., Las Vegas, 2000—. Coord., initiator IDS 120 course U. Calif., Berkeley, 1970-74; ptnr., initiator Ca Song Records, NYC, 1976-86; trustee, founder Environ. Celebration Found., Las Vegas, 1994—. Co-owner Nature Tech. Internat., 2004—. Author, illustrator: Me and My Friends, 1992, The Ecology Book, 1996; co-author: Adding Biology, 2006; singer writer Nostalgia Goes Country, 1986; author of essays, poetry. Nat. Wildlife Fedn. fellow, 1973-74; NEA grantee, 1974-75. Avocations: singing, dance, poetry, plants. Home Phone: 415-898-5895; Office Phone: 415-898-5895.

ROLLINS, DIANN ELIZABETH, occupational health nurse, educator, primary school educator; b. Newark, Dec. 13, 1943; d. Lewis Paul and Letitia Lavinia Rollins. RN, Meth. Hosp. Sch. Nursing, Phila., 1964; postgrad., Howard U., 1966, Milton Coll., 1969—72, West Chester State Coll., 1972—79; cert. bldg. maintenance, John F. Kennedy Vocat. Tech., 1992; BSN, Thomas Jefferson U., 2000. RN Pa., N.J.; lic. religious sci. practioner United Ch. Religious Sci., 2003. Nurse Meth. Hosp., Phila., 1964—66, 1967—69, Mercy Hosp., Janesville, Wis., 1969—72, Chester County Hosp., West Chester, Pa., 1972—74, Cheyney U., Pa., 1974—75, Embreeville State Hosp., coatesville, 1976—78; agy. nurse Norristown, Phila., 1978—86, Medox, Olsten, Kimberly, Phila., 1985-86; RN supr. New Ralston House, Phila., 1986-87, 88-89; agy. nurse Kimberly, Quality Care, Olsten, Medox, others, Phila., 1987-89; info. and referral specialist Nat. Mental Health Consumer Self Help Clearing House, Phila., 1992-93; intern ACT NOW Southeastern Mental Health Program, Phila., 1993-94; nursery sch. tchr. Bambino Gesu Child Devel. Ctr., Phila., 1994-99; primary instr. nursing assts. ARC, 2000—01, Clin. Pathways Educators Ins., 2001—02; supplemental staff nurse Breslin Learning Ctr., 2002—, LPN instr., 2003—; staff nurse Bayada Nurses, 2002—; postal nurse (occupl. health nurse) US Post Office, 2003—07. Spkr. in field. Vol. instr. program Franklin Inst., Phila., 1973-74; vol. multimedia first aide instr. ARC, Wilmington, Del., 1975-83; vol. plan II nurse blood mobiles ARC, S.E. Pa., 1982-85. Recipient Stella M. Mummert maternal/child care award, Meth. Hosp., 1964. Mem. Alumnae Meth. Hosp. Sch. Nursing, Four Chaplains Legion of Honor. Avocations: reading, writing, walking, singing. Office Phone: 215-829-1609. Personal E-mail: dynamyte19107@yahoo.com.

ROLLINS, FAYE LORRAINE, medical transcriptionist; b. Hallock, Minn., Dec. 12, 1940; d. Helmer Stenquist and Grace Evelyn Brown; children: John Wilkinson, Dean Wilkinson. Medical transcriptionist Eureka Family Practice, Calif., 1985—91, Faye's Secretarial Svc., Eureka, 1989—95, Humboldt Occpl. & Environ. Medicine, Eureka, 1991—95, Rollins Transcription Svc., Redding, Calif., 1995—. Mem.: Am. Assn. Medical Transcription. Avocation: piano.

ROLLINS, JAMES (JIM CZAJKOWSKI, JAMES CLEMENS), writer, veterinarian; b. Chgo., 1961; DVM, Univ. Mo., 1985. Author: (novels) Subterranean, 1999, Excavation, 2000, Deep Fathom, 2001, Amazonia, 2002, Ice Hunt, 2003, Sandstorm, 2004 (named one of best Mystery/Thrillers by Readers Read, 2004, Publishers Weekly paperback bestseller, 2005), Map of Bones, 2005; author: (as James Clemens) (fantasy) Wit'ch Fire, 1999, Wit'ch Storm, 2000, Wit'ch War, 2000, Wit'ch Gate, 2001, Wit'ch Star, 2002, Shadowfall, 2005, The Black Order, 2007. Avocations: scuba diving, spelunking. Mailing: c/o Author Mail William Morrow/HarperCollins 10 E 53d St New York NY 10022 E-mail: jpcdvm@aol.com. *

ROLLINS, JAMES CALVIN (JIMMY ROLLINS), professional baseball player; b. Oakland, Calif., Nov. 27, 1978; Grad., Encinal HS, 1996. Profl. baseball player Phila. Phillies, 2000—. Co-recipient NL Cool Papa Bell award, Negro League Hall of Fame; named 5th Best Rookie in Major Leagues, Baseball Am., 3d Best in Nat. League; named to Topps Major League Rookie All-Star team, MLB mgrs., NL All-Star Team, 2001—02, 2005. Achievements include eighth longest hitting-streak in MLB history (38 games), 2005-2006. Avocation: recreational activities. Office: Citizens Bank Park 1 Citizens Bank Way Philadelphia PA 19148 *

ROLLINS, JOHN MAXWELL, mathematics professor, disc jockey; b. Blakely, Ga., Jan. 2, 1959; s. Hursteen West and Miriam Christine Rollins; m. Donna Jean McDaniel, Apr. 20, 1991; children: Rebecca, Robert. BS in Math., Coll. Charleston, 1988; MA in Edn. Math., Citadel, 1990; MBA, Charleston So. U., 1995. Owner, disc jockey Jay Maxwell's Music by Request, Summerville, SC, 1982—; disc jockey Sta. WXLY, Charleston, SC, 1990—93; math. prof. Charleston Southern U., 1993—2007, bus. prof., 2007—. Weddiing cons. Jay Maxwell's Music by Request, Summerville, 1983—; chair admissions com. Charleston So. U., 2004—, chair faculty senate, 1999—2000; mem. edn. com. Low Country Wedding Profls., Charleston, 1997—2000, pres., 2000—02, mem., 2002—04, edn. chair, 2007—. Author: (book) Play Something We Can Dance To, 1997; contbr. articles to Mobile Beat mag. With USN, 1977—83. Recipient Excellence in Tchg. award, Charleston So. U., 1999, Faculty of Yr. award, 1998. Republican. Baptist. Avocation: music. Home: 422 Eastover Cir Summerville SC 29483 Office: Charleston So U 9200 University Blvd Charleston SC 29423 E-mail: jay@jaymaxwell.com.

ROLLINS, KEVIN B., former computer company executive; b. 1952; m. Debra S. Rollins; children: Marisa, Stephanie, Lauren, Alex. BS, Brigham Young U., 1983, MBA, 1984. Ptnr. Bain & Co., 1984—96; cons. Dell Inc., 1993—96, sr. v.p., corp. strategy, 1996—97, vice-chmn., 1997—2001; pres. Dell Americas, 1997—2001; pres., COO Dell Inc., 2001—04, pres., CEO, 2004—07; sr. adv. TPG Capital L.P., Ft. Worth, 2007—. Bd. dirs. Dell Inc., 2004—07; mem. Am. Enterprise Inst.; pres. leadership council Brigham Young U., Marriot Sch. Nat. Advisory Council, founder, mem. exec. com., Kevin & Debra Rollins Ctr. for eBusiness, 2000—; mem. Presdl. Adv. Com. Trade Policy and Negotiation. High tech chmn. Juvenile Diabetes Rsch. Found.; trustee Arts Center Stage; bd. dir. Austin Symphony, KLRU. Office: TPG Capital LP 301 Commerce St Ste 3300 Fort Worth TX 76102 *

ROLLINS, SONNY (THEODORE ROLLINS), composer, musician; b. NYC, Sept. 7, 1930; s. Walter and Valborg (Solomon) R.; m. Dawn Finney, 1956 (div.); m. Lucille Pearson, Sept. 7, 1959 (dec. Nov. 2004). ArtsD, Bard Coll., 1992, Long Island U., 1998, Wesleyan U., 1998, Duke U., 1999; D of Music, New Eng. Conservatory of Music, 2002; MusD (hon.), Berklee Coll. Music, 2003. Tenor saxophonist, 1946—59, 1961—68, 1971—; mem. Max Roach-Clifford Brown Quintet, 1955—57, leader, 1956—57; co-founder Doxy Records, NYC, 2005—. Ann.concert tours in Europe and Asia; composer (songs) Airegin, Alfie's Theme, Blessing in Disguise, Blue 7, Doxy, East Broadway Run Down, He's Younger Than You Are, Movin' Out, Oleo, On Impulse, Pent-Up House, Sonnymoon for Two, St. Thomas, Tenor Madness, The Bridge, Freedom Suite, Way Out West; performer (albums) Sonny Rollins Quartet, 1951, Sonny & the Stars, 1951, Mambo Jazz, 1951, Movin' Out, 1954, Sonny Rollins Quintet, 1954, Taking Care of Business, 1955, Work Time, 1955, Saxophone Colossus, 1956, Sonny Rollins Plus Four, 1956, Three Giants, 1956, Tenor Madness, 1956, Sonny Boy, 1956, Tour de Force, 1956, Way Out West, 1957, Sounds of Sonny, 1957, Newk's Time, 1957, A Night at the Village Vanguard, 1957, Freedom Suite, 1958, Shadow Waltz, 1958, The Bridge, 1962, What's New?, 1962, Our Man in Jazz, 1962, Sonny Meets Hawk!, 1963, All the Things You Are, 1963, Now's the Time, 1964, There Will Never Be Another You, 1965, Alfie, 1966, East Broadway Run Down, 1966, Next Album, 1972, Horn Culture, 1973, Cutting Edge, 1974, Nucleus, 1975, The Way I Feel, 1976, Easy Living, 1977, Don't Stop the Carnival, 1978, Green Dolphin Street, 1978, Don't Ask, 1979, Love at First Sight, 1980, No Problem, 1981, Reel Life, 1982, Sunny Days, Stary Nights, 1984, Solo Album, 1985, G-Man, 1986, Dancing in the Dark, 1987, Falling in Love with Jazz, 1989, Here's to the People, 1991, Old Flames, 1993, The Meeting, 1994, Without a Song, 1995, Sonny Rollins Plus Three, 1996, Global Warming, 1998, Dearly Beloved, 1998, This is What I Do, 2000 (Grammy award for Best Instrumental Jazz Performance, 2001), Scoops, 2002, Solid, 2002, Without a Song: The 9/11 Concert, 2005 (Grammy award for Best Jazz Instrumental Solo: Why Was I Born?, 2006), Sonny Please, 2006, Soneymoon, 2007. Named to Big Band & Jazz Hall of Fame, 1999; recipient Lifetime Achievement award, Nat. Acad. Recording Arts and Scis., 2004, Polar Music prize, Sweden, 2007, Golden Plate award, Acad. Achievement, 2006, numerous others; Guggenheim fellow, 1972. Office: Doxy Records Parkwest Fin Sta PO Box 21063 New York NY 10025 *

ROLLINS, TONY JAMES, organizational consultant; b. Wichita, Kans., July 24, 1946; s. James Benjamin Rollins and Muriel Maxine Gunn; m. Billie Kay Woods, Mar. 29, 1969. BA, U. Mo., Columbia, 1968; MA, U. Kans., Lawrence, 1971, PhD, 1973. Cert. tchr. Mo., 1973. Exec. dir. Miss. Assn. Educators, Jackson, Miss., 1981—84, Colo. Edn. Assn., Denver, 1984—94; asst. exec. dir. NEA, Washington, 1994—2001; dir. Knowledge-Gate, LLC, Tucson, 2001—. Presenter in field. Contbr. articles to profl. jours. Co-chmn. conf. bd. Bus./Edn. Coun., NYC, 1999—2001; mem. Colo. Commn. Sch. Fin., Denver, 1993—94, Am. Inst. Pub. Svc., Wilmington, Del., 1998—2001; founding mem. Learning First Alliance, Washington, 1996—2001. Capt. US Army, 1968—76. Mem.: Soc. Orgnl. Learning (mem. coun. 2006—), Pi Mu Epsilon. Achievements include research in use of applications in teaching secondary school mathematics. Avocations: golf, flying. Home: PO Box 2526 Silverthorne CO 80498 Office: KnowledgeGate LLC 5350 N Fairway Heights Dr Tucson AZ 85749 Home Phone: 970-513-6697; Office Phone: 240-605-1031.

ROLLINS, TREE (WAYNE MONTE ROLLINS), professional basketball coach, former professional basketball player; b. Winter Haven, Fla., June 16, 1955; 3 children. Student, Clemson U., SC. Ctr. NBA Atlanta Hawks, 1977—88, NBA Cleve. Cavaliers, 1988—90, NBA Detroit Pistons, 1990—91, NBA Houston Rockets, 1991—93; ctr., coach NBA Orlando Magic, Fla., 1993—95, asst. coach, 1996, NBA Washington Wizards, 1999—2000, Ind. Pacers, 2000—02, WNBA Washington Mystics, 2006—07, head coach, 2007—. NBA Devel. League Greenville Groove, 2002. Named to NBA All-Def. First Team, 1984. Avocations: deep sea fishing, movies. Office: Washington Mystics Verizon Ctr 601 F St NW Washington DC 20004 *

ROLLO, F. DAVID, healthcare company executive, cardiologist; b. Endicott, NY, Apr. 15, 1939; s. Frank C. and Augustine L. (Dumont) R.; m. Linda Wood, June 1, 1991; children: Mindee, Alex. BA, Harpur Coll., 1959; MS, U. Miami, 1965; PhD, Johns Hopkins U., 1968; MD, Upstate Med. Ctr., Syracuse, NY, 1972. Diplomate Am. Bd. Nuc. Medicine. Asst. chief nuc. medicine svcs. VA Hosp., San Francisco, 1974-77, chief nuc. medicine Nashville, 1977-79; sr. v.p. med. affairs Humana Inc., Louisville, 1980-92; dir. nuc. medicine div. Vanderbilt U. Med. Ctr., Nashville, 1977-81; prof. radiology Vanderbilt U., Nashville, 1979—; pres., CEO Metricor Inc., Louisville, 1992-95; sr. v.p. med. affairs HCIA, Louisville, 1995-96; sr. v.p. med. affairs, med. dir. Raytel Med. Corp., San Mateo, Calif., 1996-99; chief med. officer ADAC Labs., Milpitas, Calif., 1999—2002; internat. chief med. officer Philips Med. Sys., 2003—. Mem. med. adv. com. IBT, Washington, 1984—; mem. pvt. sector liaison panel Inst. of Medicine, Washington, 1983—; bd. dirs. ADAC Labs. Editor: Nuclear Medicine Physics, Instruments and Agents, 1977; co-editor: Physical Basis of Medical Imaging, 1980, Digital Radiology: Focus on Clinical Utility, 1982, Nuclear Medicine Resonance Imaging, 1983; mem. editorial adv. bd. ECRI, 1981—. Pres. bd. dirs. Youth Performing Arts Coun., Louisville, 1984-85; bd. dirs. Louisville-Jefferson County Youth Orch., 1983-85; sr. v.p., exec. com. USA Internat. Harp Competition, 1992-, chmn., 1994-. Fellow Am. Coll. Cardiology, Am. Coll. Nuc. Physicians (profl. Am. Coll. Radiology com. 1982-84, chmn. 1984); mem. AMA, Soc. Nuc. Medicine (trustee 1979-83, 84—, Cassen Meml. lectr. western region 1980, 84), Radiol. Soc. N.Am., NEMA (chmn. nuc. medicine sect., 2002-, bd. mem., 2002-, testimony medicine expert, 2003-), Am. Coll. Radiology, Ky. Sci. Tech. Coun. (exec. bd. 1987—), Advancement Med. Instrumentation (bd. dirs. 1986—), Louisville C. of C. (chmn. MIC com. 1987—). Avocations: racquetball, squash, golf. Home: 15735 Peach Hill Rd Saratoga CA 95070-6447

ROLSTON, HOLMES, III, theology studies educator, philosopher; b. Staunton, Va., Nov. 19, 1932; s. Holmes and Mary Winifred (Long) R.; m. Jane Irving Wilson, June 1, 1956; children: Shonny Hunter, Giles Campbell. BS, Davidson Coll., 1953; BD, Union Theol. Sem., Richmond, Va., 1956; MA in Philosophy of Sci., U. Pitts., 1968; PhD in Theology, U. Edinburgh, Scotland, 1958. Ordained ministry Presbyn. Ch. (USA), 1956. Asst. prof. philosophy Colo. State U., Ft. Collins, 1968-71, assoc. prof., 1971-76, prof., 1976—. Vis. scholar Ctr. Study World Religions, Harvard U., 1974-75; ofcl. observer UN Conf. on Environ. and Devel., Rio de Janiero, 1992; vis. prof. bioethics Yale U., 2005-06. Author: Religious Inquiry: Participation and Detachment, 1985, Philosophy Gone Wild, 1986, Science and Religion: A Critical Survey, 1987, Environmental Ethics, 1988, Conserving Natural Value, 1994, Genes, Genesis and God, 1999; assoc. editor Environ. Ethics, 1979—; mem. editl. bd. Zygon: Jour. of Religion and Sci.; contbr. chpts. to books, articles to profl. jours. Recipient Univ. Disting. Prof., 1992; Disting. Russell fellow Grad. Theol. Union, 1991, Disting. Lectr., Chinese Acad. of Social Scis., 1991, Disting. Lectr., Nobel Conf. XXVII, Gifford Lectr., U. Edinburgh, 1997; featured in Fifty Key Thinkers on the Environment, 2001, Templeton Prize in Religion, 2003, Gregor Mendel medal, Villanova Univ., 2005 Mem. AAAS, Am. Acad. Religion, Soc. Bibl. Lit. (pres. Rocky Mountain-Gt. Plains region), Am. Philos. Assn., Internat. Soc. Environ. Ethics (pres. 1989-94), Phi Beta Kappa. Avocation: bryology. Home: 1712 Concord Dr Fort Collins CO 80526-1602 Office: Colo State U Dept Philosophy Fort Collins CO 80523-0001 Home Phone: 970-484-5883; Office Phone: 970-491-6315. Business E-Mail: rolston@lamar.colostate.edu.

ROMA, AIDA CLARA, artist; b. Phila., July 17, 1924; d. Carlo and Giustina S. R.; widowed; 4 children. Student, Camden County Coll., 1990-99. Dental Dr. Martin Apother, Runnemede, N.J., 1956-66; owner Rogers Auto Sales, Runnemede, N.J., 1966-90; tchr. St. Joseph's Sch., Camden, N.J., 1955-56. Author of poems, Jealousy, 1999, My 2 Best Friends, 2001, "Pal" My Pal, 2004. Art tutor, Haddenfield, N.J.; v.p. Girl Scouts Am., Runnemede, 1964; sec. Boy Scouts Am., 1960; mem. St. Teresa's Choir, 1993—, Atlantic City Choirs. Recipient Internat. Poet award, Artistic Artistry award, England, 2004. Mem. Sons of Italy. Republican. Achievements include invention of Rack on the Back auto addition. Avocation: singing. Home: PO Box 2076 Laurel Springs NJ 08021

ROMAINE, GRANT HIRSCH, protective services official; s. Hirschl Edward and Louise M. Romaine; m. Laura L. Harris, Sept. 17, 1990 (div. Apr. 1, 1993); 1 child, Diane V.L. AS in Electronics Tech., Gavilan Coll., Gilroy, Calif., 1981; student, U. Wash., Tacoma, 1992. Cert.: Wash. State Criminal Justice Tng. Commn. (Law Enforcement Officer) 1989, Wash. State Criminal Justice Tng. Commn. (Instr. Devel.) 2000, (crime scene analyst) 2007; Electronics Instr. USN, 1982. Electronics technician first class submarines USN, Pearl Harbor, Hawaii, 1975—88; electronics/computer technician Kachemak Gear Shed, Homer, Alaska, 1989; police detective Poulsbo Police Dept., Wash., 1989—. Bd. mem. Spl. Assault Investigation & Victim Svcs., Port Orchard, Wash., 2000—. Vol. Hilder Pearson Elem. Sch., Poulsbo, 1996—2001; bd. mem. United Way Kitsap County, Bremerton, Wash., 1991—92, Big Bros. & Big Sisters Kitsap County, Bremerton, Wash., 1992—95. With USN, 1975—88. Decorated Lifesaving Letter Commendation award USN; recipient Superior DUI Enforcement award, MADD, 1993, Lifesaving Letter Commendation award, Poulsbo Fire Dept., 1996. Master: Masons; mem.: Internat. Assn. for Identification, Am. Legion, MENSA. Jewish. Avocations: computer repair, motorcycling, camping, fishing. Home: PO Box 1992 Poulsbo WA 98370 Office: Poulsbo Police Dept 367 NE Hostmark St/PO Box 98 Poulsbo WA 98370 Home Phone: 360-697-1496; Office Phone: 360-779-3113. Personal E-mail: gromaine@msn.com. Business E-Mail: gromaine@poulsbopoa.org.

ROMAINE, HENRY SIMMONS, retired investment company executive, consultant; b. NYC, May 30, 1933; s. Theodore Cole and Cornelia (Simmons) R.; m. Susan Donaldson; children: Henry, Hilary, Kathryn. BA, Harvard U., 1954. Asst. security analyst Mutual Life Ins. Co., NYC, 1958-60, investment analyst, 1960-61, investment specialist, 1961-64, asst. dir. investments, 1964, dir. investments, 1964-66, asst. v.p. for securities investment, 1966-68, 2d v.p. for securities investment, 1969-71, v.p. for securities investment, 1971-72, sr. v.p., 1972-78, sr. v.p., chief investment officer, 1976-78, exec. v.p., 1978-81, pres., 1981-86; vice chmn., chief investment officer Am. Gen. Corp., Houston, 1986-93. Dir. MONY Life Ins. Co. of Can.; chmn. bd. MONY Real Estate Investors, 1978-86; mem. adv. bd. Chem. Bank, 1974-83. Served with USN, 1954-57. Mem.: Harvard Club. Home: 7 Conquest Ave Sullivans Island SC 29482-9779

ROMAN, ALFRED VICTOR, science education educator; b. Yonkers, NY, Feb. 26, 1940; s. Alfred Ignatius and Helen Marie (Danin) R.; m. Patricia Jeanne Gardinier, Oct. 25, 1946; 1 child, Caroline Elizabeth. BA, Montclair State Coll., NJ, 1961; MA, NYU, 1963, D Edn, 1967. Speed reading specialist N.Y. Speed Reading Inst., NYC, 1965-67; teaching fellow NYU, NYC, 1965-67, instr., 1967; asst. prof. N.Y.C. Community Coll., Bklyn., 1965-67; dir. rsch. and devel. and ednl. adminstrn. Universal Edn. and Visual Arts, div. Universal City Studios, Calif., 1967-71; dir. div. media arts and tech. Potsdam Coll. SUNY, 1971-87, asst. prof. ednl. communications, 1988—, prof. sci. edn., 1987—. Film cons., N.Y.C., 1967—. Contbr. articles to profl. jours. Bd. mem. Ch. of the Nazarene, Potsdam, 1988-89; v.p. Potsdam Interfaith Community Svc. Coun., 1989, Nixa Area Arts Coun., 2002-06; supr. info. svcs. Olympic Village XIII Olympic Winter Games, Lake Placid, N.Y., 1980; adv. bd. Nixa Cmty. Found., 2004-06; Life Group leader The Bridge Ch., 2004-06. Recipient Pres. award Potsdam Coll., 1981; award NEH, 1980. Mem. Alexandria Bay Flotilla, U.S. Coast Guard Aux., Rotary, Masons, Shriners, Sigma Xi, Sigma Pi Sigma, Tau Epsilon Pi, Phi Delta Kappa, Kappa Delta Pi. Republican. Nazarene. Avocations: music, decorating, films. Personal E-mail: alpatroman@earthlink.net.

ROMAN, EDIBERTO, law educator; b. Oct. 5, 1963; 4 children. BA in Bus. Mgmt. and Econs. magna cum laude, CUNY, 1985; JD, U. Wis., 1988. Assoc. Lord Day and Lord, Barrett Smith, NYC, 1988—94, Haythe and Curley, NYC, 1994—95; assoc. prof. St. Thomas U. Sch. Law, Miami, 1995—2001, prof. law, 2001—02, Fla. Internat. U. Coll. Law, Miami, 2002—, assoc. dean acad. affairs, 2005. Adj. prof. CUNY Lehman Coll., NYC, 1993—94; faculty advisor human rights and environ. law student assn. Fla. Internat. U., Miami, 2002—04, faculty advisor Hispanic law student assn., 2002, mem. law moot ct. com., 2002—04, mem. coll. law acad. stds. com., 2002—04, co-chair acad. support com., 2002—04, mem. honors coll. admissions com., 2004, chair. law appt. com., 2004—05, chair coll. law admissions com., 2004, mem. coll. law acad. support com., 04, faculty hooding com., 05, chair. law appt. com., 2006—; organizer habitat humanity working group St. Thomas U. Sch. Law, Miami, 1998—2001, mem. law sch. admissions com., 1995—2002, chair sub-com., 1995—96, dir. vol. st. law. clin. program, 1996—99, faculty advisor, 1997—2001, honor coun. faculty advisor, 1997—98, mem. Mayor Alex Penela's Mosaic Initiative, 2000—01, chair law sch. curriculum com., 2001—02, mem. Broward County steering com. Al Gore's presdl. eletion, 2001—02, vis. prof., 2003—04, tchg. fellow, 2003—04; lectr. and presenter in field. Contbr. articles to profl. jours., chapters to books. Recipient Prof. of Yr., St. Thomas U. Sch. Law, 1996—97, 1999—2000, Execellence Tchg. and Scholarship award, St. Thomas U., Barry U., 2001, Enmea Tarafa Legal Excellence award, Fla. Internat. U. Law Student Assn., 2007. Mem.: Hispanic Nat. Bar Assn., Am. Law Inst. Office: Fla Internat Univ Coll Law 11200 SW 8th St Miami FL 33199

ROMAN, ELOY, oncologist; b. Miami, Fla., Dec. 15, 1974; s. Anolan and Eloy Severo Roman. MD, U. Ctrl. del Este, Dominican Republic, 1999. Diplomate Am. Bd. Internal Medicine, 2004. Resident Mt. Sinai Med. Ctr., Miami Beach, Fla., 2002—04; hematology and oncology fellow U. Miami, Fla., 2004—. Contbr. articles to profl. jours. Fellow, U. MIami, 2004—07. Mem.: Oncology Nursing Soc. (med. contbr. 2005—06), Am. Soc. Clin. Oncology (assoc.). Roman Catholic. Achievements include research in methods of reirradiation for squamous cell carcinoma; chemotherapy with concurrent radiation for lung cancer; chemotherapy for pancreas cancer. Avocations: diving, boating. Office: Advanced Med Specialties 7100 W 20th Ave Ste 201 Hialeah FL 33016 Office Phone: 305-231-3150. Office Fax: 305-231-5020. Business E-Mail: eroman@oncologyradiation.com.

ROMAN, JOSÉ LUIS, nursing administrator; b. Bronx, NY, Nov. 17, 1960; s. José Luis and Elba Luz (Curbelo) Roman; m. Pamela Tarrant, Apr. 25, 1987 (div.); children: Joseph Aaron, Timothy Jude, Cara Mia, Tiffany Rafaelle. LPN, Norwalk State Tech. Coll., Conn., 1990; AS, U. State N.Y., 1991; ASN, 1993. Cert. CMC Am. Inst. Outcomes Case Mgmt., BCLS, oper. rm. tech., nurse asst., med. case mgr.; RN. Rehab. aide Orange Grove Neuro Rehab. Facility, Garden Grove, Calif., 1984-86; nurses asst. Fairview Oddfellows Home, Groton, Conn., 1986-90; oper. rm. tech. USAR 340th Gen. Hosp., New Haven, 1987-90; LPN, ICU U.S. Army 31st Combat Support Hosp., Hafal Al Batin, Saudi Arabia, 1990-91; LPN cardiac care nurse Lawrence Meml. Hosp., New London, Conn., 1990-91, 1991-92, extended care placements case mgr., 1992-94, cardialpulmonary/med. svcs. RN casemanager, 1994-96, emergency dept. case mgr., 1996—2002; RN critical care, open heart surgery unit Brooks Army Med. Ctr., Tex., 1999—. Spkr. Task Force Briefing Com. USAR, West Hartford, Conn., 1992—95, rep. Practical Nurse Recruitment Task Force, 1992—96; weekend nurse Baylor evening nurse mgr. Mariner Health Care at Bridebrook, Niantic, Conn., 1994—; mem. skilled nursing facility comm. task force Lawrence Meml. Hosp., 1996—, mem. skilled nursing facility to emergency dept. utilization sub-com., 1996—2001. Contbr. articles to profl. jours. Mem. Conn. Bd. Examiners Nursing, 1992—96. 1st lt. USAR, 1996—2001. Decorated Army Achievement medal,, Army Commendation medal, Army Res. Component Achievement medal; recipient plaque of honorable recognition, Puertorican Ho. Reps. Mem.: Conn. LPN Assn., Gen. Dynamics Mgmt. Assn., Am. Assembly Men Nursing, Nat. Assn. Practical Nurse Edn. and Svc., Nat. Assn. Hispanic Nurses, Nurses Christian Fellowship (assoc.), Internat. Platform Assn., U.S. Army Med. Dept., Am. Legion. Presbyterian. Avocations: travel, watching drum corps competitions, hiking, bicycling. Office: Mariner Health Care Bridebrook 23 Liberty Way Niantic CT 06355 Home: 96 Leha Ave Griswold CT 06351-1531 E-mail: poozlelelu@aol.com.

ROMAN, NANCY GRACE, astronomer, consultant; b. Nashville, May 16, 1925; d. Irwin and Georgia Frances (Smith) R. BA (Joshua Lippincott Meml. fellow), Swarthmore Coll., 1946; PhD, U. Chgo., 1949; D.Sc., Russell Sage Coll., 1966, Hood Coll., 1969, Bates Coll., 1971, Swarthmore Coll., 1976. Asst. Sproul Obs., Swarthmore Coll., 1943-46; asst. Yerkes Obs., U. Chgo., at Williams Bay, Wis., 1946-48, research asso., 1949-52, instr. stellar astronomy, 1952-55, asst. prof., 1955; research asso. Warner and Swasey Obs., Case Inst. Tech., Cleve., summer 1949; physicist radio astronomy br. U.S. Naval Research Lab., Washington, 1955-56, astronomer, head microwave spectroscopy sect., 1956-58, astronomer cons., 1958-59; head observational astronomy program Office Space Flight Devel., NASA, Washington, 1959-60, chief astronomy and solar physics, geophysics and astronomy programs, 1960—79, chief astronomy and relativity programs, 1965—80, program scientist for space telescope, 1979-80; astronomy cons., 1980-89; prin. scientist Astronomical Data Ctr., NASA, 1981—97. With McDonnell Douglas Space Systems, 1988-94. Contbr. articles to sci. periodicals. Trustee Russell Sage Coll., 1973-78; bd. mgrs. Swarthmore Coll., 1979-83. Recipient Fed. Woman's award., 1962; citation for pub. service Colo. Woman's Coll., 1966; 90th Anniversary award Women's Ednl. and Indsl. Union, 1967; NASA Exceptional Sci. Achievement award, 1969; NASA Outstanding Leadership medal, 1978 Fellow AAAS, Am. Astronautical Soc. (William Randolf Lovelace II award 1980); mem. AAUW, Am. Astron. Soc., Internat. Astron. Union (editor symposia 1956-58), Astron. Soc. Pacific. Acheivements include rsch. on stellar clusters, high velocity stars, radio astronomy; 1st noted correlation of metallic lines in stars with their space velocity; asteroid named Roman, 1989. *This guiding principle sounds old fashioned but I have found it useful: "Forget that you are a woman but never forget that you are a lady."*

ROMAN, RAY, communications executive; BS finance, U. of Ill., Chicago; MBA finance and marketing, U. of Chicago. Gen. mgr., sales and service Ameritech Small Business Services; corp. controller, v.p. of financial planning and analysis Alliant Foodservice, pres. N.E. div.; v.p. sales AT&T Wireless, 2001—03; corp v.p., gen. mgr. of No. Am., mobile devices Motorola Inc. 2003—03, sr. v.p. worldwide sales, mobile devices, 2005—. Coach youth soccer team, youth basketball team. Named one of the best 40 under 40 in business, Crain's Chicago Business, 2005. Office: c/o Motorola Inc 1303 E Algonquin Rd Schaumburg IL 60196

ROMAN, STANFORD AUGUSTUS, JR., medical educator, dean; b. NYC; s. Stanford Augustas and Ivy L. (White) D.; m. Norma Dabney Roman; children: Mawiyah Lythcott, Jane E. Roman-Brown. AB, Dartmouth Coll., 1964, MA (hon.), 1992; MD, Columbia U., 1968; MPH, U. Mich., 1975. Diplomate Nat. Bd. of Med. Examiners. Intern Columbia U.-Harlem Hosp. Ctr., NYC, 1966—69, resident in medicine, 1969—71, chief resident in medicine, 1971—73; 1972assoc. dir. ambulatory care Columbia U. Harlem Hosp., 1972—73; instr. medicine Columbia U., NYC, 1972—73; asst. physician Presbyn. Hosp., 1972—73; clin. dir. Healthco, Inc., Soul City, NC, 1973—74; dir. ambulatory care, asst. prof. medicine/sociomed. scis. Boston City Hosp., Boston, 1974—78; asst. prof. medicine U. N.C., Chapel Hill, 1973—74; asst. dean Boston U. Sch. Medicine, 1974—78; med. dir. D.C. Gen. Hosp., Washington, 1978—81; from assoc. dean acad. affairs to dep. dean Dartmouth Med. Sch., Hanover, NH, 1981—87, assoc. prof., 1981—87, dep. dean, 1986—87; dean, v.p., prof. medicine Morehouse Sch. Med., Atlanta, 1987—89; sr. v.p., med. and profl. affairs Health and Hosps. Corp., NYC, 1989—90; dean med. sch., prof. cmty. health and social medicine Sophie Davis Sch. Biomed. Edn., 1990—; interim pres. CCNY, 1999—2001. Dir. Boston Comprehensive Sickle Cell Ctr., 1975—78; bd. dirs. Winifred Masterson Burke Rehab. Hosp., White Plains, NY, 1993—94; mem. Dartmouth Hitchcock Med. Ctr. Bd. of Medicine, NY, 1993—2002; mem. bd. trustees Dartmouth Coll., Hanover, NH, 1992—2002. Contbr. to book chpts. and profl. jours. and editls. Fellow N.Y. Acad. Medicine; mem. AMA, APHA, Nat. Med. Assn., N.Y. State Coun. Grad. Med. Edn., N.Y. State Dept. Edn. Bd. Medicine. Democrat. Episcopalian. Avocations: photography, travel, music.

ROMANCE, MARY C., library director; b. Rabat, Morocco, June 20, 1957; d. Francis Joseph and Ann (Pickert) Romance. BA in Orgnl. Comms. and Mgmt., U. Mich., 1979; MLS, Rutgers U., 1992. Libr. coord. Bernardsville (N.J.) Pub. Libr., 1991-93; libr. dir. Rockaway (N.J.) Borough Pub. Libr., 1993-94, Lincoln Park (N.J.) Pub. Libr., 1994-97, Roxbury Twp. Pub. Libr., Succasunna, N.J., 1997—. Pres. Morris Automated Info. Network Inc. Mem.: Roxbury Area C. of C. (bd. dirs.). Office: Roxbury Public Library 103 Main St Succasunna NJ 07876-1417

ROMANI, JOHN HENRY, health science association administrator, educator; b. Milan, Mar. 6, 1925; s. Henry Arthur and Hazel (Pettengill) R.; m. Barbara A. Anderson; children: David John, Paul Nichols, Theresa A. Anderson. BA, MA, U. N.H., 1949; PhD, U. Mich., 1955. Instr. U. N.H., 1950-51; instr. U. Mich., Ann Arbor, 1954-55, assoc. prof., asst. to assoc. dean Sch. Pub. Health, 1961-69, assoc. v.p., 1971-75, chmn. health planning and adminstrn., 1975-80, prof., 1971-93, prof. emeritus pub. health adminstrn., 1993—, faculty assoc. program on the environment, 2004—; interim chair Pub. Health Policy and Adminstrn., 1991-92. Asst. prof. We. Mich. U., 1956-57; assoc. dir. Cleve. Met. Svcs. Commn., 1957-59; assoc. prof. U. Pitts., 1959-61; vice chancellor, prof. U. Wis.-Milw., 1969-71; rsch. fellow Brookings Instn., 1955-56; mem. task force Nat. Commn. on Orgn. Cmty. Health Svcs., 1963-66; dir. staff Sec.'s Com. on Orgn. Health Activities, HEW, 1965-66; dir. Govtl. Affairs Inst., 1969-75, chmn., 1970-72; trustee Pub. Adminstrn. Svc., 1969-75, chmn., 1973-75; mem. Delta Dental Plan Mich., 1972-78, bd. dirs. 1972-78, chmn. consumers' adv. coun., 1975-77; bd. dirs. Ctr. for Population Activities, 1975-81, chmn., 1975-81; lifetime vis. prof. Capital U. Economics and Bus., Beijing, 1996—; vis. rschr. Human Scis. Rsch. Coun., Pretoria, South Africa, 1999—. Author: The Philippine Presidency, 1956; editor: Changing Dimensions in Public Administration, 1962; contbr. articles to profl. jours. Mem. Citizens League, Cleve., 1957-59; mem. Ann Arbor Citizens Coun., 1965-69; bd. dirs. Southeastern Mich. Family Planning Project, 1975-77; trustee Congregational Summer Assembly, 1982-85; commr. Accrediting Commn. on Edn. for Health Svcs. Adminstrn., 1989-95. Served with AUS, 1943-46, ETO. Fellow Am. Pub. Health Assn. (chmn. program devel. bd. 1975-77, exec. bd. 1975-80, governing coun. 1975—, pres. 1979, chmn. publs. bd. 1984-88), Royal Soc. Health (hon.), Am. Polit. Sci. Assn. (life); mem. ASPA (past mem. coun.), Population Assn. Am., Phi Kappa Phi, Pi Sigma Alpha, Pi Gamma Mu, Delta Omega. Home and Office: 2125 Nature Cove Apt 108 Ann Arbor MI 48104

ROMANO, CARMEN J., lawyer; b. Phila., 1955; BS, U. Pa., 1977; JD, Columbia U., 1980. Note editor Columbia U. Law Review, 1979—80; law clk. to Hon. Dolores K. Sloviter US Ct. Appeals (3rd cir.), 1980—81; ptnr. Dechert LLP, Phila., chmn. bus. dept. Office: Dechert LLP Cira Ctr 2929 Arch St Philadelphia PA 19104 Office Phone: 215-994-2971. E-mail: carmen.romano@dechert.com.

ROMANO, FERNANDA (FEFA ROMANO), advertising executive; b. São Paulo, Brazil, 1972; BA Bus. Mgmt., Pub. Adminstrn., Fundação Getúlio Vargas. Worked for Carillo, Pastore EURO RSCG, São Paulo, Parlo.com, Starmedia, Tantofaz.net (Loquesea Inc.), iBest; dir. interactive comm. DM9DDB, 2002—04, dir. other medias and spl. projects, 2004—05; exec. creative dir. Lowe NY, 2005—. Teacher Interactive Creative Concepts, Miami Ad Sch., Interactive Comm., MBA in Comm. program at ESPM São Paulo; jury mem. CCSP-Brazil, 2003, 05, London Internat. Awards, 2004, One Show Interactive and London Advt. Awards, 2005. Contbr. articles BlueBus.com.br; TV column (TV series) Qual é a Boa?, radio column (Radio Bandeirantes FM), Sao Paulo. Named a Woman to Watch, Advt. Age, 2007; recipient three Cannes CyberLions awards, 2004, seven Cannes CyberLions, 2005, Cannes CyberLions Grand Prix, 2005, Two Pencils, One Show Interactive, 2006, Merits in the One Show Interactive, 2005. Office: Lowe NY 150 E 42nd St New York NY 10017 Office Phone: 212-605-8000. Office Fax: 212-605-8100. *

ROMANO, GAETANO, research scientist, educator; b. Milan, Italy, May 11, 1959; s. Antonio Romano and Gemma Matilde Santangelo. PhD, State U. Milan, 1985. Assoc. prof. biology and medicine Temple U., Phila., 2006—. Editor, co-author Cell Cycle Control and Dysregulation Protocols: Cyclins, Cyclin-dependent Kinases and Other Factors, 2004, review editor Jour. Exptl. & Clin. Cancer Rsch., 2004—; contbr. articles to profl. jours. Grantee Pilot Rsch. award, Thomas Jefferson U., 2004. Mem.: Internat. Soc. Stem Cell Rsch. (assoc.). Achievements include research in engineering of an inducible system based on a retroviral-encoded Drosophila HSP70 promoter to deliver a proapoptotic factor into cancer cells; development of retroviral and lentiviral vector systems; research in characterization of the biology of the receptor of the insulin-like growth factor 1 (IGF-1R) in cancer research; retroviral-mediated gene transfer of the retinoblastoma-related gene Rb2/p130 to suppress lung tumor growth; characterization of the tissue-specific gene expression of the human tyrosine hydroxylase promoter; stem cell transplantation in animal models for Parkinson's disease. Personal E-mail: gromano@temple.edu.

ROMANO, JOHN FRANCIS, dermatologist; b. SI, NY, July 4, 1948; BS, St. Peter's Coll., 1969; MD, Cornell U., 1973. Diplomate Am. Bd. Dermatology. Intern Einstein Hosps., NYC, 1973—74; resident in medicine St. Vincent's Hosp., NYC, 1974—76; resident in dermatology N.Y. Hosp., NYC, 1976—78; pvt. practice dermatology NYC, 1979—; attending physician St. Vincent's Hosp., NYC, 1979—; clin. asst. prof. dermatology Weill Hosp. Cornell U., 1979—; also asst. attending dermatologist N.Y. Presbyterian Hosp. Mem.: N.Y. State Dermatologic Soc., Am. Soc. for Laser Medicine and Surgery, Am. Soc. for Dermatologic Surgery, Am. Acad. Dermatology. Avocation: sailing. Office: 36 7th Ave New York NY 10011-6609 Office Phone: 212-242-5815. Business E-Mail: info@romanodermatology.com.

ROMANO, JOSEPH ANTHONY, healthcare education and marketing consultant; b. Bklyn., Sept. 5, 1946; s. Anthony Wilbur and Anne R.; m. Linda Rose Giacalone, Sept. 23, 1972; children: Nicholas Joseph, Christine Dianne. Student, Villanova U., 1964-66; BS Pharm. Sci., Columbia U., 1970, D Pharmacy, 1972. Clin. resident Lenox Hill Hosp., NYC, 1970-72; asst. dean, asst. prof. Columbia U., NYC, 1972-76, SUNY, Buffalo, 1976-78; assoc. dean, assoc. prof. U. Wash., Seattle, 1978-83; assoc. dir. medicine Pfizer Labs., NYC, 1983-85, product mgr., 1985, asst. to pres., 1985-87; sr. v.p., group dir. Hill & Knowlton, Inc., NYC, 1987-88; exec. dir. external affairs Sandoz (Novartis), NYC, 1988-89; pres., COO, Visual Med. Mktg., NYC, 1989-92; vice chair Nelson Communications, Inc. Worldwide (divsn. Publicis), NYC, 1992-2001; chmn., CEO, SCIENS Worldwide Healthcare Comms., 1996-2001; co-chmn. Nelson Profl. Sales, 1998-2000. Mem. U.S. Nat. Adv. Com. Health Profls., Washington, 1980-86. Co-author: Clinical Pharmacology, 1980, Pharmacy State Board Reviews, 1976, 78, 85, The Vitamin Book, 1985, 2000; contbr. articles to profl. jours. Fellow Royal Soc. Health London; mem. Am. Pharm. Assn., Am. Soc. Healthcare Pharmacists, Am. Assoc. Study Headaches, U.S. Golf Assn., Rho Chi. Avocations: photography, stamp collecting/philately, golf, music, cooking. Home Phone: 908-874-3302. Personal E-mail: josepharomano@earthlink.net.

ROMANO, LOUIS GEORGE, education educator; b. Milw., Jan. 1, 1921; s. Liborio and Maria (Pelligrino) R.; m. Shirely Mae Romano; children: Jill, Pamella Ann. BS, Milw. State Tchrs. Coll., 1943; MS, U. Wis., 1948, PhD, 1955. Asst. supt. Shorewood (Wis.) Pub. Schs.; supt. schs. Wilmette, Ill.; exec. dir. Mich. Assn. Middle Sch. Educators, East Lansing, Mich.; prof. dept. ednl. adminstrn. Mich. State U., East Lansing. Co-author: Focus on Parent-Teacher Conferences, 1984, The Effective Middle School, 1986, A Guide to Classroom Skills, 1978, A Guide to Study Skills, 1978. Mem. ASCD, NEA, Nat. Soc. Study Edn., Nat. Mid. Sch. Assn., Phi Delta Kappa.

ROMANO, RAY, actor, comedian; b. Forest Hills, NY, Dec. 21, 1957; m. Anna Scarpula; 4 children. Stand-up comedian; sitcom actor. Actor: (TV series) Everybody Loves Raymond, 1996—2005 (Best Actor, Quality Comedy, Viewers for Quality TV, 1998, TV Critics Assn. award for outstanding ind. achievement in comedy, 1999, nominee Emmy award outstanding lead actor in comedy series, 1999, nominee Golden Globe award best performance by actor in comedy, People's Choice award favorite male TV performer, 2002, nominee Screen Actors Guild award outstanding performance by a male actor in comedy series, 2002, TV Guide award Favorite Actor in a Comedy, Funniest Male Lead in a TV Series at 14th Ann. Am. Comedy Awards), (voice): (films) Ice Age, 2002, Welcome to Mooseport, 2004, Eulogy, 2004, Grilled, 2005, (voice) Ice Age: The Meltdown, 2006; TV guest appearances in Dr. Katz Professional Therapist, 1995, The King of Queens, 1998, Hollywood Squares, 1998—2004, Becker, 1998, Who Wants to Be a Millionaire, 1999; author: Everything and a Kite, 1999; co-author (with Richard & Robert Romano): (children's book) Raymie, Dickie & the Bean: Why I Love and Hate My Brothers, 2005; performer: (CD) Ray Romano: Live at Carnegie Hall, 1999; appeared in (TV films) Ray Romano & Kevin James: Making the Cut (HBO), 2005; prodr.: 95 Miles to Go, 2004. Recipient People's Choice award, favorite male TV star, 2006.

ROMANO, ROBERTA, law educator; b. Bklyn., Jan. 27, 1952; AB with highest honors, U. Rochester, 1973; MA, U. Chgo., 1975; JD, Yale U., 1980. Law clk. U.S. Ct. Appeals (2d cir.), Hartford, Conn., 1980-81; asst. prof. Stanford (Calif.) U., 1981-84, assoc. prof., 1984-85; prof. of law Yale U., New Haven, 1985—, Allen Duffy prof. of law, 1991; Oscar M. Ruebhausen prof. of law and dir. Yale Law Sch., New Haven. Co-editor Jour. Law, Econs., and Orgn., 1988—, author The Advantage of Competitive Federalism for Securities Regulation, The Genius of American Corporate Law. Mem. Assn. Am. Law Schs. (exec. coun., bus. assns. sect. 1987-90, chmn. 1990), Phi Beta Kappa, fellow Am. Acad. of Arts and Sci., past pres. Am. Law and Econ. Assn. Office: Yale Law Sch 127 Wall St PO Box 208215 New Haven CT 06511 Office Phone: 203-432-4992.

ROMANOFF, MARJORIE REINWALD, retired education educator; b. Chgo., Sept. 29, 1923; d. David Edward and Gertrude (Rosenfield) Reinwald; m. Milford M. Romanoff, Nov. 6, 1945; children: Bennett Sanford, Lawrence Michael, Janet Beth (dec.). Student, Northwestern U., 1941-42, 43-45, Chgo. Coll. Jewish Studies, 1942-43; BEd, U. Toledo, 1947, MEd, 1968, EdD, 1976. Tchr. Old Orchard Elem. Sch., Toledo, 1946-47, McKinley Sch., Toledo, 1964-65; substitute tchr. Toledo, 1964-68; instr. Mary Manse Coll., Toledo, 1974; instr. children's lit. Sylvania (Ohio) Bd. Edn., 1977; supr. student tchrs. U. Toledo, 1968—73, 1985—2001, instr. advanced comms., 1977, rschr., 1973-74; instr. Am. Lang. Inst., 1978—2002. Asst. prof. elem. edn. Bowling Green (Ohio) State U., 1978—88; chair rsch. com. Am. Lang. Inst., U. Toledo, 1985—94, asst. prof. elem. edn. in lang. arts, 1985—87, asst. prof. elem. edn., ESL specialist, 1978—2002; condr. workshop Internat. Conf./Teaching Langs., U. Cin., 1996; presenter in field. Author: Language and Study Skills: For Learners of English, Prentice Hall Regents, 1991. Trustee Children's Svcs. Bd., 1974-76; pres. bd. Cummings Treatment Ctr. for Adolescents, 1978-80; mem. Crosby Gardens Adv. Bd., 1976-82, Cmty. Planning Coun., 1980-84, Citizens Rev. Bd. of Juv. Ct., 1979—; allocations com. Mental Health and Retardation Bd., 1980-81; active Bd. Jewish Edn., 1976—, pres., 1982-84; active Jewish Family Svc., 1978-85, v.p., 1980-85; allocations com. Jewish Welfare Fedn., 1980, 89-91; bd. dirs. Family Life Edn. Coun., 1984-90, sec., 1988-90; budget and allocations com. Jewish Fedn., 1989-93; bd. dirs. Friends Toledo-Lucas County Librs., 1991—, bd. pres., 1991-93; program chair U. Toledo Women's Commn., 1991-93; bd. dirs. Ohio Friends of Pub. Librs., 1992-94. Named One of Ten Women of Yr., St. Vincent's Hosp., Guild, 1984, Outstanding Instructional Staff Woman, U. Toledo, 1990, Excellence award Citizen's Rev. Bd., 2003. Mem. Tchrs. English to Speakers Other Langs., Toledo Libr. Legacy Found., Orgn. Rehab. and Tng. (named Outstanding Woman in Cmty. Svc. 1987), Hadassah (chpt. pres. regional bd. 1961-64), Northwestern U. Alumni Assn., Phi Kappa Phi, Phi Delta Kappa, Kappa Delta Pi (pres., faculty adv. 1971-75, Point of Excellence award 1992), Pi Lambda Theta (chpt. pres. 1978-80, nat. com. 1979-84). Home: Stratford in the Hills 4343 W Bancroft St Apt 4B Toledo OH 43615

ROMANOFF, MILFORD MARTIN, retired building contractor; b. Cleve., Aug. 21, 1921; s. Barney Sanford and Edythe Stolpher (Bort) R.; m. Marjorie Reinwald, Nov. 6, 1945; children: Bennett S., Lawrence M., Janet Beth (dec.). Student, U. Mich. Coll. Arch., 1939-42; BBA, U. Toledo, 1943. Pres. Glass City Constrn. Co., Toledo, 1951-55, Milford Romanoff, Inc., Toledo, 1956—2003. Co-founder Neighborhood Improvement Found. Toledo, 1960; active Lucas County Econ. Devel. Com., 1979—, Childrens Svcs. Bd. Lucas County, 1981—97, Arthritis Bd. Dirs., Crosby Gardens Bd. Advisors, 1983—96, Toledo Met. Area Govt. Exec. Com., 1996—; citizens adv. bd. Recreation Commn. Toledo, 1973—86; campus adv. com. Med. Coll. Ohio, 1980—; trustee Cummings Treatment Ctr. for Adolescents, 1981—; pres. Toledo B'nai Brith Lodge, 1958—59, Cherry Hill Nursing Home, 1964—85; bd. dirs. Anti-Defamation League, 1955—60, Ohio Hillel Orgns., Lucas County Dept. Human Svcs., Arthritis Assn., 1995—, Comprehensive Addiction Svc. Sys., 1998, Kidney Found. Northwestern Ohio, 1986—, sec., 1989; chmn. Comprehensive Addiction Svc. Sys., 1999, Toledo Amateur Baseball and Softball Com., 1979—81; cons. U.S. Care Corp., 1985—; bd. govs. Toledo Housing for Elderly, 1982—84, sec., 1989, pres. bd. govs., 1990—, pres., 1991—; bd. adv. Ret. Sr. Vol. Program, 1987—89, chmn., 1988—90, 1993—, sec. adv. bd., 1990—, bd. dirs., 2000—; vice chmn. adv. bd. Salvation Army, 1986—87, chmn. adv. bd., 1988—90, ct. apptd. spl. advocate adv., bd. treas., 1988—; chmn. Mental Health Adv. Bd., 1983—84, sec., 1989; bd. dirs. Toledo Urban Forestry Commn., 1991—, pres., 1993, 1995, Lucas County Dept. Human Svcs. Bd.; adv. coun. Renaissance Sr. Apts., 1997, chmn. adv. coun., 1999; adv. bd. Lucas Co. Correctional Facility, 1999—; chmn. Compass Bd., 2002—; bd. dirs. Area Office on Aging of Northwest Ohio, 2001, Lucas County Mental Health, 2001; chair Compass Corp. for Recovery Svcs., 2002—; mem. Lucas County Mental Health Bd., 2002, Juvenile Correction Bd. Lucas County, 2004—; bd. dirs. Mental Health Lucas Co.; mem. Juvenile Correction Bd. Lucas County, 2003—; mem. adv. bd. ACLU, 2005—, 2005—; active Dem. Precinct Com., 1975—78; trustee Temple Brotherhood, 1956—58, bd. dirs., 1981—; pres. Ohio B'nai Brith, 1959—60; bd. mem. ACLU, 2005—. Mem.: Friends Libr. Bd., Mental Health Bd. of Lucas County, U. Mich. Alumni Assn., Juvenile Justice (adv. bd.), Toledo Zool. Soc., Econ. Opportunity Planning Assn. Greater Toledo (adv. bd.), Nat. Coun. on Alcoholism & Drug Dependence, Toledo Mus. Art (assoc.), U. Toledo Alumni Assn., Am. Legion, Hadassah (assoc. Toledo chpt.), Masons (Outstanding Cmty. Svc. award of Lucas County 2001), Zeta Beta Tau. Home: Stratford in the Hills 4343 W Bancroft St Apt 4B Toledo OH 43615-3956

ROMANOS, JOHN, JR., (JACK ROMANOS), publisher; b. Stamford, Conn., Nov. 1, 1942; s. John and Grace (Frano) R.; m. Mary Jane Veach, Jan. 29, 1972; 1 child, Cary Lynne. BS, U. Conn., 1965. Sales mgr. Fawcett Publs., Inc., Greenwich, Conn., 1966-73, Bantam Books, Inc., NYC, 1973-76, dep. to pres., 1976-78, v.p., dir. sales planning, 1978-79, dir. mktg., 1979-81, pub., 1981-85; pres. Simon and Schuster Trade Pub. Group, 1985-87, pres. Mass Market Pub., 1987-91; pres., chief exec. officer Simon & Schuster Consumer Pub. Group, NYC, 1991-93; pres., COO Simon & Schuster, NYC; pres., CEO Simon & Schuster (Viacom Entertainment Group), NYC, 2002—; pres., chief exec. officer Paramount Pub. Consumer Group, NYC, 1993—. Bd. dirs. Periodicals Inst., N.Y.C., 1980-81 With Army N.G., 1967. Mem. Assn. Am. Pubs. (mem. heads of houses com.), Internat. Periodical Distbrs. Assn. (bd. dirs.), Country Club of Darien (Conn.), exec. com. The Quills. Republican. Greek Orthodox. Office: Simon and Schuster Inc Ste 383 1230 Avenue Of The Americas Fl Concl New York NY 10020-1586 Office Phone: 212-698-7000. Office Fax: 212-698-7099.

ROMANOV, VOLODYMYR ALEXEEVICH, computer science educator, researcher; b. Kamynino, Kursk, Russia, Jan. 23, 1960; s. Alexey Filippovich and Olga Sergeevna Romanov; children: Olga Volodymyrivna, Volodymyr Volodymyrovych. MD, Nat. U., Kharkov, Ukraine, 1983, PhD, 1987. Cert. computer scis. and nuc. physics. Rschr. Nuc. Phys. Lab., Kharkiv, Ukraine, 1983-88; prof. State Tech. Univ. Agr., Kharkiv, 1988—2000, head Info. Tech. Ctr., 1996—2000; prof. Newton Coll., Montreal, Canada, 2000—05; sr. rsch. assoc. 3D Digital Corp., Newtown, Conn., 2005—06; rsch. assoc. Concordia U., Montreal, 2006—. Vice-head Coun. Young Rschrs., Kharkiv, 1984-91; editor Regional TV, Kharkiv, 1985-87 Author: (with S. Troubnikov) Nuclear Forces, 1992, (with I. Furman) Programmed Microcontrollers, 2000; contbr. articles to profl. jours. Mem. Can. Info. Processing Soc. Russian Orthodox. Avocations: russian literature, history, music. Office: 1455 De Maisonneuve Blvd W Montreal PQ H3G 1M8 Canada Home Phone: 617-501-0809; Office Phone: 203-304-2443. Personal E-mail: volodymyr_romanov@yahoo.com.

ROMANOVICH, PATRICIA M., parochial school educator; b. Akron, Ohio, Dec. 11, 1937; d. Joseph and Mary (Dorosz) Siwik; m. Paul Romanovich, Sept. 13, 1958; children: Paula Marie, Gregory Joseph, Jeffrey John, Martin Paul. BS in Edn., St. John Coll., Cleve., 1971; M.Curriculum and Instrn., Cleve. State U., 1988. Tchr. St. Josaphat Sch., Parma, Ohio, 1964—87, tchr., tech. coord., 1998—2004, tech. advisor, 2004—; tchr. St. Columbkille Sch., Parma, 1987—90; tchr., computer coord. St. Anthony Sch., Parma, 1990—93, Greenbriar Jr. H.S., Parma Heights, Ohio, 1993—98. Tech. adv. bd. chair St. Josaphat Sch., 1998—2004, curriculum chair, 1998—2004, drama club dir., 1998—; creator, rschr. flip chart Sch. Crisis Mgmt. Plan, 1999—2003. Named one of Outstanding Elem. Tchrs. of Am., 1974; recipient Excellence in Tchg. award, Diocese of Cleve., 2001; grantee Tech. grantee, Sch. Net, Columbus, 2001. Mem.: Korean War Vets. Assn. Ukrainian Catholic. Avocations: reading, travel, country walks. Home: 5400 Sandy Hook Dr Parma OH 44134 Home Phone: 440-885-5101; Office Phone: 440-884-1812. Personal E-mail: sandyvalley@sbcglobal.net.

ROMANOVSKI, MIKHAIL REM, mathematician; b. Samara, Russia, June 22, 1952; s. Rem Vladimir and Lubov Mikhail (Volgina) R.; m. Elena Vladimir Kurtashina, Aug. 27, 1983 (div.); children: Victoria, Valeria. MS, Moscow Tech. U., 1975; PhD, Heat and Mass Transfer Inst., Kiev, Ukraine, 1982. Engr. Ctrl. Constrn. Bur., Moscow, 1975-78; head dept. math. Kriogenmash, Balashikha, Russia, 1978-93; head dept. CAD/CAE Point Ltd., Moscow, 1992—. Tcrh. math. modeling Chem. Industry Inst., Moscow, 1982-93. Contbr. articles to profl. jours. Mem. NY Acad. Sci. Avocations: sports, skiing. Home: Schelkovskoe Ave 79-1-334 107497 Moscow Russia Office: Point Ltd Lomonosovskiy pr 43/2 Moscow Russia Office Phone: 7(985)7683489. E-mail: mromanovski@netscape.net.

ROMANOVSKY, VLADIMIR EVGENI, physics professor; s. Evgeni and Inessa Romanovsky; m. Noel Ember Balough, Aug. 14, 1994; children: Michael, Derek, Ivan. MS in Geophysics with honors, Moscow State U., 1970—75, MS in Math. with honors, 1982—85, PhD in Geology, 1976—82; PhD in Geophysics, U. Alaska, Fairbanks, 1992—96. Sci. rschr. Moscow State U., 1975—85, assoc. prof. geophysics, 1985—92; rsch. asst., assoc. U. Alaska, 1992—98, rsch. assoc. prof., 1998—99, assoc. prof. geophysics, 1999—2006, prof. geophysics, 2006—. Recipient Constrn. of Baikal-Amur RR award, Govt. Russian Fedn., 1981. Mem.: US Permafrost Assn. (pres. 2004—06), Am. Geophys. Union. Office: Geophysical Inst UAF 903 Koyukuk Dr Fairbanks AK 99775-7320 Office Fax: 907-474-7290. Business E-Mail: ffver@uaf.edu.

ROMANOW, JOSH, lawyer; b. 1964; BA, Brandeis U.; JD, Tulane U., 1991. Bar: Pa. 1992, DC 1993. Ptnr. Aviation practice, chmn. Travel Leisure & Hospitality practice Pillsbury Winthrop Shaw Pittman, Washington. Contbr. articles to profl. jours & newspapers; commentator (NPR, CNBC), mem. editl. bd. Gaming Law Rev. Office Phone: 202-775-9864. Office Fax: 202-833-8491. Business E-Mail: romanow@pillsburylaw.com.

ROMANOWICZ, BARBARA, geology and geophysics professor; married; 2 children. Maîtrise de Mathématiques Pures, Université Paris 6, 1972; MS in Applied Physics, Harvard U., 1975; Doctorat in Astronomy, Université Paris 6, 1975; Doctorat d'Etat, Université Paris 7, 1979. Postdoctoral assoc. MIT, Cambridge, Mass., 1979—81; attachée de recherches Nat. Coun. Sci. Rsch. Institut de Physique du Globe, Paris, 1978—79, chargée de recherches, 1981—86, directeur de recherches, 1986—90, dir. Geoscope program; prof. geophysics U. Calif., Berkeley, 1991—, chair Dept. Earth and Planetary Sci., 2002—; dir. Berkeley Seismological Lab. Recipient A. Wegener medal, European Union of Geosciences, 1999, Gutenberg medal, European Geophysical Soc., 2003. Fellow: Am. Acad. Arts & Sci., Am. Geophysical Union; mem.: NAS. Office: Univ Calif Berkeley 209 McCone Hall Berkeley CA 94720-4767 Office Phone: 510-642-1844, 510-643-5811. E-mail: barbara@seismo.berkeley.edu.

ROMANOWITZ, BYRON FOSTER, architect, engineer; b. Covington, Ky., Nov. 14, 1929; s. Harry Alex and Mildred (Foster) R.; m. Mildred Elaine Gize, June 15, 1957; children: Laura Ann, Mark Walter, Cynthia Ellen. BS in Civil Engring, U. Ky., 1951; M.F.A. in Architecture, Princeton, 1953. Instr. sch. architecture Princeton U., 1954; architect Brock & Johnson, Lexington, 1958-59, Johnson & Romanowitz, Architects, Lexington and Louisville, 1960-2000; ret., 2000. Pres. Ky. Bd. examiners and Registration of Archs., 1975-91; instr. U. Ky. Sch. Architecture, 1996, 2000; mem. Ky. Archtl. Svcs. Selection Com., 2006, 07. Prin. works include U. Ky. campus bldgs., 1959-96, Ea. Ky. U. campus bldgs., 1959-77, Centre Coll., Danville, Ky., campus bldgs., 1967-89, Georgetown (Ky.) Coll. campus bldgs., 1964-84, Asbury Coll., Wilmore, Ky., 1972-78, Asbury Theol. Sem., 1978-93, Berea Coll. bldgs., 1978-91, Transylvania U. bldgs., 1974-98, U. Louisville, 1990-98, 11 downtown Lexington office bldgs.; leader Men of Note Orch., 1986—, Jazzberry Jam Combo, 1993—; author: Jazz in Lexington, A Personal View, 2006. Mem. Lexington Urban Renewal Commn., 1963-69; chmn. adv. bd. Salvation Army, 1971-72; trustee Midway (Ky.) Coll., 1986-95; appt. architect svcs. sel. com. Commonwealth Ky., 20050172. With USNR, 1955-58; lt. comdr. Res. Recipient award of merit nat. archtl. competition AIA/Ednl. Facilities Lab., 1966 Fellow AIA (1st honor awards Ky. archtl. competition 1959, 61, 68, 70, 73, 78, 80, 81, pres. East Ky. chpt. 1965); mem. Ky. Soc. Architects (pres. 1966), Masons, Rotary, Lexington Club, Navy League, Tau Beta Pi, Phi Mu Alpha, Phi Sigma Kappa. Home: 2057 Lakeside Dr Lexington KY 40502-3016

ROMANOWSKI, THOMAS ANDREW, physicist, educator; b. Warsaw, Apr. 17, 1925; came to U.S., 1946, naturalized, 1949; s. Bohdan and Alina (Sumowski) R.; m. Carmen des Rochers, Nov. 15, 1952; children: Alina, Dominique. BS, MIT, Boston, 1952; MS, Case Inst. Tech., Cleve., 1956, PhD, 1957. Rsch. assoc. physics Carnegie Inst. Tech., 1956-60; asst. physicist high energy physics Argonne Nat. Lab., Ill., 1960-63, assoc. physicist, 1963-72, physicist, 1972-78; prof. physics Ohio State U., Columbus, 1964-92, prof. emeritus, 1992-98; sr. scientist Argonne Nat. Lab., 1992; physicist U.S. Dept. Energy, Washington, 1992-98; cons. in pvt. practice, 1998—. Contbr. articles to profl. jours. With high energy program U.S. Dept. Energy, 1993-98. Served with C.E. AUS, 1946-47. Fellow Am. Phys. Soc., AAAS; mem. Lambda Chi Alpha. Achievements include research in nuclear and high energy physics. Personal E-mail: romanowski@santafe-newmexico.com, romanowski@cyberview.com.

ROMANS, DONALD BISHOP, manufacturing executive; b. Louisville, Apr. 22, 1931; s. Albert D. and Moneta (Bishop) R.; m. Marilyn Yvonne Neff, June 13, 1953 (dec. Aug. 2000); children: Rebecca Ann, Jennifer. BS, U. Louisville, 1953; MBA, Harvard U., 1958. Mgr. internal auditing and data processing, mem. contr. staff Container Corp. Am., Chgo., 1958-62; successively asst. to pres., asst. treas., treas., v.p. fin., sr. v.p. fin., exec. v.p. Trans Union Corp., Chgo., 1962-81; exec. v.p., chief fin. officer Sunbeam Corp., Chgo., 1981-82, Bally Mfg. Corp., Chgo., 1982-87; fin. cons. Chgo., 1987; pres. Romans and Co., Chgo., 1987-93. Bd. dirs. Burnham Investment Trust, NYC; life trustee St. Mary of Nazareth Hosp. Capt. USMCR, 1953-56. Republican. Avocations: tennis, boating. Home: 39 S Sheridan Rd Lake Forest IL 60045-3269 Office Phone: 847-615-2537. Personal E-mail: dbromans@yahoo.com.

ROMANS, JAY, waste management executive; BS, Kent State U., Ohio; MS, Tex. A&M U., College Station. Corp. orgn. devel. specialist Firestone Tire & Rubber Co., 1974; mgr. orgnl. devel. Clark Equipment, 1979—81; mgr. tng. and devel. Union Pacific/Champlin Petroleum Co., 1981—88; supr. orgnl. devel. Amoco Pipeline Co., 1988—89; dir. orgn. devel. and staffing Ecolab/Chemlawn Svc. Corp.; mgr. tng. and devel. to dir. employee and orgn. devel. Amoco Oil Co., 1990—93; sr. ptnr. STS Internat., 1993—95; dir. orgn. effectiveness and learning to worldwide v.p. human resources for pre-analytical solutions bus. Becton Dickinson; founder, pres. Romans & Assocs.; sr. v.p. Std. Register Co., Dayton, Ohio, 2001—04; sr. v.p. human resources Hughes Supply, 2004; with St. Joe Co.; sr. v.p. people Waste Mgmt., Inc. Office: Waste Mgmt Inc 1001 Fannin Ste 4000 Houston TX 77002 Office Phone: 713-512-6200. *

ROMANS, JOHN NIEBRUGGE, lawyer; b. Bklyn., May 23, 1942; s. John McDowell and Helen Pond (Niebrugge) R.; m. Caroline Ward; children: John A., Andrew C. BA, Williams Coll., 1964; LLB, Columbia U., 1967. Bar: N.Y. 1967, U.S. Dist. Ct. (so. and ea. dists.) N.Y. 1971, U.S. Ct. Appeals (2d cir.) 1971, U.S. Supreme Ct. 1971, U.S. Ct. Appeals (3rd cir.) 1976, U.S. Ct. Appeals (4th and 7th cirs.) 1987, U.S. Ct. Appeals (9th cir.) 1992, U.S. Ct. Appeals (11th cir.) 1996, U.S. Ct. Appeals (D.C. cir.), 2004. Ptnr. Curtis, Mallet-Prevost, Colt & Mosle, NYC, 1980—90, Katten Muchin & Zavis, NYC, 1990—98, Rosen Weinhaus, LLP, NYC, 1998—. Lectr. on air law topics at various seminars. Contbr. articles to profl. jours. Trustee Summit (N.J.) Unitarian-Universalist Ch., 1978, Mamaroneck Pub. Libr. Dist., 1990-99; mem. budget com. Village of Mamaroneck, 2001-05, chmn., 2002-2005; dir. The Univ. Glee Club NYC, 1993-. Lt. USNR, 1968-71. Mem. Assn. Bar City N.Y. (aero. com. 1983-85, 2004-, chmn. 1986-89, 92-94, 2000, products liability com. 1989-91), Larchmont (N.Y.) Yacht Club. Avocation: sailing. Office: Rosen Greenberg LLP 40 Wall St 32d Fl New York NY 10005-1304 Office Phone: 212-530-4827.

ROMANUCCI-ROSS, LOLA, anthropologist, educator; b. Hershey, Pa., June 13, 1928; d. Ignazio and Josephine (Giovannozzi) R.; m. John Ross Jr., Aug. 26, 1972; children: Deborah Lee, Adan Anthony. BA, Ohio U., 1948; MA, U. Minn., 1953; postgrad., Ecole des Hautes Etudes, Paris, 1961-63; PhD in Anthropology, Ind. U., 1963. Rsch. assoc. Am. Mus. Natural History, NYC, 1963-67; assoc. prof. U. Hawaii, Honolulu, 1967-68; from asst. prof. to prof. family and preventive medicine and anthropology Sch. Medicine U. Calif., San Diego, 1969—. Mem. study sect. HEW Maternal and Child Health, Bethesda, Md., 1973-75; cons. NSF, 1988—. Author: Conflict, Violence and Morality in a Mexican Village, 1973, 2d edit., 1986, Mead's Other Manus: Phenomenology of the Encounter, 1985, One Hundred Towers; an Italian Odyssey of Cultural Survival, 1991, When Law and Medicine Meet: A Cultural View, 2004; editor: Ethnic Identity, 1975, 4th edit., 2006, The Anthropology of Medicine, 1982, 3d edit., 1997; mem. editl. bd.: Anthropology and Humanism Quarterly, Interdisciplinary Jour. Study of Health, Illness and Medicine, 1997—, contbr. articles to profl. jours., book chpts. Grantee Wenner-Gren Found. for Anthropol. Rsch., 1974-75. Fellow Am. Anthropol. Soc.; mem. Soc. Med. Anthropology, Soc. Psychol. Anthropology, Soc. Anthropology of Europe, Soc. Cultural Anthropology, Soc. Health and Human Values. Achievements include field research in New Guinea, South Pacific, Italy and Mexico. Avocations: music, hiking, literature, writing.

ROME, ELLEN S., physician; d. Leonard P. and Nancy Rome; m. Frederick S. Asbeck, Jr., July 29, 1995; children: Andrew Asbeck, Katherine Asbeck. BA, Yale U., 1984; MD, Case We. Res. U., 1988; MPH, Harvard Sch. Pub. Health, 1994. Cert. Am. Bd. Pediat., 1991, in adolescent medicine 1994. Head, sect. adolescent medicine Cleve. Clinic, 1994—, assoc. chief staff, 2006—; resident pediat. Johns Hopkins Hosp., 1988—91; fellowship adolescent medicine Children's Hosp., Boston, 1991—94. Faculty mem. Ctr. for Adolescent Health, Case We. Res. U., Cleve., 1994—; mem. sci. com. U.S. Tennis Assn., Cleve., 2004—; assoc. prof. Cleve. Clinic Lerner Coll. Medicine Case We. Res. U., 2005—. Contbr. articles to profl. jours. Fellow: Am. Acad. Pediat. (com. on adolescence 1996—2002, chair AM PREP planning com. 2005—07); mem.: N.Am. Soc. for Pediatric and Adolescent Gynecology (trustee 2006—), Acad. of Eating Disorders (com. pub. affairs 2003—, chmn. media com. 2004—07), Soc. for Adolescent Medicine (chair membership com. 1996—2002, nominations com. 2002—04). Avocation: skiing. Office: Cleve Clinic Children's Hosp 9500 Euclid Ave A120 Cleveland OH 44195 Office Phone: 216-444-3566. Business E-Mail: romee@ccf.org.

ROMEO, JOANNE JOSEFA MARINO, mathematics educator, department chairman; b. Youngstown, Ohio, Nov. 21, 1943; d. Joseph James and Ann Marie (Bonamase) Marino; m. John Homer Romeo, Aug. 14, 1965; children: Christopher, Chrisanne, Jonathan; m. Harwood D. Schaffer, Apr. 25, 2003. BS, Ohio State U., 1965; postgrad., Youngstown State U., 1969-70; MS, Purdue U., 1974; postgrad. in computer sci., U. Tenn., Knoxville, 1982-91. Substitute tchr., Columbus, Ohio, 1964-65; tchr. geometry, math. and French Hamilton Sch. Dist., Columbus, Ohio, 1965-66; tchr. gifted children Bluegrass Elem. Sch., Knoxville, Tenn., 1976-77; tchr. math. and sci. Webb Sch., Knoxville, 1977-85, also developer computer sci. program, 1977-85; headmistress Greenbrier Acad., Sevierville, Tenn., 1985-86; instr. math. Pellissippi State Tech. Community Coll., Knoxville, 1986—; dir. religious edn. Sacred Heart Parish, Knoxville, 1987—2001; tchr. advanced math. Knox County Sch., Knoxville, 2000—02; math. dept. chair Washburn HS Grainger County Schs., Tenn., 2005—. Delegate to go to Russia and Lithuania Ministries of Edn., NCEA. Vol dir. religious edn. Sacred Heart Parish, Knoxville, 1979-87, lay pastoral minister, 1988-2004. Mem. Nat. Council Tchrs. Math., Nat. Cath. Edn. Assn., Nat. Council Parish and Religious Coordinators and Dirs., Nat. Sci. Tchrs. Assn., Nat. Assn. Exec. Females, Ohio State U. Alumni Assn., Tenn. Assn. Dirs. Religious Edn., Purdue U. Alumni Assn., Alpha Gamma Delta. Independent. Home: 1708 Capistrano Dr Knoxville TN 37922-6302 Office: Grainger County Schs Washburn HS 1725 Hwy 131 Washburn TN 37888 Personal E-mail: joannejmr@yahoo.com.

ROMEO, PETER JOHN, lawyer; b. Darby, Pa., Aug. 1, 1942; s. Joseph Paul and Rose Marie (Beckett) R.; m. Nancy Virginia Schmidt, July 15, 1972; children: Christopher, Jeffrey, Michael. BSBA, Georgetown U., 1964; JD, George Washington U., 1967, LLM, 1969. Bar: Va. 1968, U.S. Dist. Ct. D.C. 1969, U.S. Supreme Ct. 1972; CPA, D.C. Acct. Schumaker & Yates, Washington, 1964-69; atty. U.S. Securities and Exch. Com., Washington, 1969-72, spl. counsel, 1972-79, chief counsel divsn. corp. fin., 1980-84; ptnr. Hogan & Hartson LLP, Washington, 1984—. Author: The Registration Process (updated triannually) 7th edit., 2007; co-author: Section 16 Reporting Guide, 1989, Section 16 Forms and Filing Handbook, 1991, 8th edit., 2005, Section 16 Treatise and Reporting Guide, 1994, 2d edit., 2004, Section 16 Deskbook (updated annually), 2007; contbr. articles to profl. jours. Mem. ABA (mem. fed. regulation securities com.), D.C. Bar, Va. State Bar. Roman Catholic. Office: Hogan & Hartson LLP 555 13th St NW Washington DC 20004-1161 Home Phone: 703-715-8320; Office Phone: 202-637-5805. Business E-Mail: pjromeo@hhlaw.com.

ROMER, DANIEL, university official, psychologist, educator; b. Caracas, Venezuela, Apr. 19, 1947; arrived in U.S., 1948; s. Adolf and Eleanor (Rittermann) R.; m. Lauren B. Alloy, Jan. 4, 1985; 1 child, Adrienne. AB,

Dartmouth Coll., 1969; PhD, U. Ill., Chgo., 1974. Rsch. fellow Dept Mental Health, Chgo., 1976-79; vis. asst. prof. Northwestern U., Evanston, Ill., 1979-81; adj. assoc. prof. U. Ill., 1981-89; assoc. rsch. dir. Leo Burnett Co., Chgo., 1982-89; sr. rschr. Annenberg Sch. for Comm., U. Pa., Phila., 1990—2000, sr. fellow Ctr. for Cmty. Partnerships, 1996—, rsch. dir. Inst. for Adolescent Risk Comm., 2001—. Mem. nat. expert panel on adolescent STD prevention Ctr. for Disease Control and Prevention, Atlanta, 2000-01; mem. rev. panels NIH, Washington, 1994-97, 98—. Mem. editl. bd. Jour. Exptl. Social Psychology, 1988-91, Youth and Society, 2001—; contbr. over 60 articles to psychol. and pub. health jours., chpts. to books. Grantee NIMH, 1992—, Ford Found., 1994. Mem. APA, APHA. Office: Annenberg Pub Policy Ctr 3535 Market St Ste 550 Philadelphia PA 19104 E-mail: dromer@asc.upenn.edu.

ROMER, DAVID, economics professor; AB, Princeton U., 1980; PhD, MIT, 1985. Jr. staff economist Coun. Economic Advisors, 1980—81; asst. prof. Princeton U., 1985—88; acting assoc. prof. U. Calif., Berkeley, 1988—90, assoc. prof., 1990—93, prof., 1993—2000, Herman Royer prof. polit. economy, 2000—. Vis. asst. prof. MIT, 1988; vis. assoc. prof. Stanford U., 1993, vis. prof., 95; vis. scholar Nat. Bur. Economic Rsch., 1987—88, faculty rsch. fellow, 1986—93, rsch. assoc., 1993—, mem. bus. cycle dating com., 2003—, co-dir. Monetary Economics program, 2003—; co-editor B.E. Journals in Macroeconomics, 2000—; adv. editor Economic Letters, 1992—2003; assoc. editor Jour. Money, Credit, and Banking, 1992—, Quarterly Jour. Economics, 1990—98; bd. editors Am. Economic Rev., 1996—2002. Author: Advanced Macroeconomics, 1996; co-editor (with N. Gregory Mankiw): New Keynesian Economics, 1991; co-editor: (with Christina D. Romer) Reducing Inflation, 1997; contbr. articles to profl. journals. Fellow: Am. Acad. Arts and Sciences. Office: Dept Economics Univ Calif Berkeley 549 Evans Hall #3880 Berkeley CA 94720-3880 Office Phone: 510-642-1785. E-mail: dromer@econ.berkeley.edu.

ROMER, DENISE PATRICE, lawyer; b. Tulsa, Jan. 11, 1975; d. Franz Karl and Trudy Maria Romer. BS in Sociology, Okla. State U., 1997; M in Alternative Dispute Resolution, Pepperdine U., 2000, JD, 2000. Bar: Calif. 2001, Wis. 2002, Okla. 2004. Clk. Tulsa Early Settlement - Divsn. Tulsa County Ct. Sys., 1999—99, Tulsa County Office Dist. Atty., 1998—98; asst. to counsel Nat. Assn. Securities Dealers, LA, 1999—99; legal clk. Calif. Lawyers for Arts, Santa Monica, 2000—00; assoc. atty. Korenberg, Abramowitz & Feldun, Sherman Oaks, Calif., 2001—02; criminal def. atty. Boyle, Boyle & Paulus, S.C., Milw., 2002—03; litig. and employment support GE Med. Sys., Waukesha, Wis., 2003—; assoc. atty. Gibbs, Armstrong, Borochoff, Hillican & Hart, 2003—. Apprentice KFAQ Talk Radio, Tulsa, Okla., 2004. Author poetry. Rep. internet team leader Rep. Nat. Com., Tulsa, Okla., 2003—; supporter/ mem. So. Poverty Law Ctr.-Nat. Campaign for Tolerance, LA, 2001—. Mem.: ABA (assoc.), State Bar Okla. (assoc.), State Bar Calif. (assoc.), State Bar Wis. (assoc.), L.A. County Bar Assn. (assoc.), The Smithsonian Instn. (assoc.), Pepperdine U. Alumni Assn. (life). Conservative. Roman Catholic. Avocations: writing, yoga, travel. Personal E-mail: romer33@hotmail.com.

ROMER, ROY R., retired school system administrator, former governor; b. Garden City, Kans., Oct. 31, 1928; s. Irving Rudolph and Margaret Elizabeth (Snyder) R.; m. Beatrice Miller, June 10, 1952; children: Paul, Mark, Mary, Christopher, Timothy, Thomas, Elizabeth BS in Agrl. Econs., Colo. State U., 1950; LLB, U. Colo., 1952; postgrad., Yale U. Bar: Colo. 1952. Engaged in farming in Colo., 1942-52; ind. practice law Denver, 1955-66; mem. Colo. Ho. of Reps., 1958-62, Colo. Senate, 1962-66; owner, operator Arapahoe Aviation Co., Colo. Flying Acad., Geneva Basin Ski Area; engaged in home site devel.; owner chain farm implement and indsl. equipment stores Colo.; commr. agr. State of Colo., 1975, chief staff, exec. asst. to gov., 1975-77, 83-84, state treas., 1977-86, gov., 1987-98; chmn. Dem. Nat. Com., 1997—2000; supt. LA Unified Sch. Dist., 2000—06. Chmn. Gov. Colo. Blue Ribbon Panel, Gov. Colo. Small Bus. Council; mem. agrl. adv. com. Colo. Bd. Agr. Bd. editors Colo. U. Law Rev., 1960-62. Past trustee Iliff Sch. Theology, Denver; mem., past chmn. Nat. Edn. Goals Panel; co-chmn. Nat. Coun. on Standards and Testing; mem. adv. bd. Ad Coun.; former chair Dem. Nat. Com., now chair Dem. Nat. Conv. Com. With USAF, 1952-53. Mem. Dem. Gov.'s Assn. (chmn.), Nat. Gov.'s Assn. (former chmn.), Colo. Bar Assn., Order of the Coif. Democrat. Presbyterian.

ROMERO, ANTHONY D., legal association administrator; b. NYC, July 9, 1965; s. Demetrio and Coralie Romero. BA, Princeton U., NJ, 1987; JD, Stanford U., Calif., 1990. With Rockefeller Found., 1990—92; prog. officer for civil rights and racial justice Ford Found., 1992—96, prog. dir. for human rights and internat. cooperation, 1996—2001; exec. dir. ACLU, NYC, 2001—. Co-author (with Dine Temple-Raston): In Defense of Our America: The Fight for Civil Liberties in the Age of Terror, 2007. Named Stanford Pub. Interest Lawyer of Yr., Stanford U., 2003; named one of 25 Most Influential Hispanics, Time mag., 2005; Cane scholar, Princeton U., Nat. Hispanic scholar, Dinkelspiel scholar, Stanford U., Nat. Hispanic scholar. Mem.: Coun. Fgn. Rels., NY State Bar Assn. Office: ACLU 18th Fl 125 Broad St New York NY 10004 *

ROMERO, RICARDO VICENTE, gastroenterologist; b. Ponce, PR, Mar. 5, 1972; s. Vicente Romero and Ana Rosa Soler; m. Susana Lauraelena Dipp, June 23, 2001; 1 child, Sofia Gabriela. MD, Ponce Sch. of Medicine, Ponce, PR, 1999. Diplomate Am. Bd. Internal Medicine, 2002, Am. Bd. Internal Medicine Gastroenterology, 2005. Gastroenterology staff, clin. educator Baystate Med. Ctr., Springfield, Mass., 2005—; asst. prof. medicine Tufts U. Md. Sch. Dir. endoscopy Baystate Med. Ctr., 2005—. Recipient Samuel Floch award, Norwalk Hosp. Affiliated with Yale U., 2002. Mem.: ACP, Am. Soc. for Gastrointestinal Endoscopy, Am. Coll. Gastroenterology. Roman Catholic. Avocations: travel, painting, music. Office: Baystate Med Ctr 759 Chestnut St Springfield MA 01199 Home Phone: 508-405-0064; Office Phone: 413-794-3570. E-mail: ricardo.romero@bhs.org.

ROMERO, TONY, information technology executive; Mgr. tech. svc. Western Airlines; tech. support specialist Mitsubishi Motors No. Am., Cypress, Calif., 1982, chief info. officer, 2001—, and sr. v.p. info. tech., 2003—. Named one of the Premier 100 IT Leaders, Computerworld mag., 2004. Office: SVP & CIO Mitsubishi Motors No Am 6400 Katella Ave Cypress CA 90630-0064

ROMETTY, GINNY (VIRGINIA M. ROMETTY), information technology executive; b. 1957; BS in Computer Sci., Elec. Engring. with high hon., Northwestern U. Applications, sys. devel. GM Corp.; bus., IT cons. IBM, 1985—91, supr. ops. ins. rsch., gen. mgr. strategy mktg., sales ops., gen. mgr. global services Am., mng. ptnr. bus. cons. services, 2002—05, sr. v.p., global bus. services, 2005—. Mem. bd. IBM Worldwide Mgmt. Coun., Sr. Leadership Team; bd. dirs. Am. Internat. Group (AIG), 2006—. Named a Global Bus. Influential, Time Mag., 2002; named one of 50 Most Powerful Women in Bus., Fortune mag., 2006, Next 20 Female CEOs, Pink Mag. & Forté Found., 2006. Office: IBM Corp 1133 Westchester Ave White Plains NY 10604 *

ROMEY, BARBARA SASSMANN, gifted and talented educator; b. NYC, Sept. 29, 1948; d. William Paul and Rita McGinley Sassmann; m. James Brooke Romey, July 8, 1976; 1 child, Elizabeth. BA, Wittenberg U., Springfield, Ohio, 1970; MA, Drew U., Madison, NJ, 1972; EdS, U. Ala., Tuscaloosa, 1999. Instr. Defiance Coll., Ohio, 1983—85; tchr. Greensburg Cath. Mid. Sch., Pa., 1985—90, Edwardsville C.C., Ill., 1990—95; tchr., gifted coord. Phenix City Schs., Ala., 1995—; instr. Columbus State U., Ga., 2001—06. Contbr. articles to profl. jours. Mem. ACLU, 2000—; regional dir. Ala. History Day, Montgomery, 2000—07; chair policy com. Future Problem Solving Program, Melbourne, Fla., 1998—2004, affiliate dir., 1997—. Named Outstanding History Educator, History Channel, 2007. Mem.: Coun. Exceptional Children, Nat. Coun. Social Studies, Nat. Assn. Gifted Children. Roman Catholic. Avocations: theater, bridge, reading, travel. Home: 6317 Milgren Rd #1 Columbus GA 31907 Office: Phenix City Schs 2400 Dobbs Dr Phenix City AL 36870

ROMEY, WILLIAM DOWDEN, geologist, educator; b. Richmond, Ind., Oct. 26, 1930; s. William Minter and Grace Warring (Dowden) R.; m. Lucretia Alice Leonard, July 16, 1955; children: Catherine Louise Keener, Gretchen Elizabeth Tanzer, William Leonard. AB with highest honors, Ind. U., 1952; student, U. Paris, 1950—51, student, 1952—53; PhD, U. Calif., Berkeley, 1962. Asst. prof. geology and sci. edn. Syracuse (NY) U., 1962-66, assoc. prof., 1966-69; exec. dir. earth sci. ednl. program Am. Geol. Inst., 1969-72; prof., chmn. dept. geology and geography St. Lawrence U., Canton, NY, 1971-76, prof., 1976—93, prof., chmn. dept. geography, 1983-93, prof. emeritus, 1993—. Ednl. cons., 1962—; NAS visitor USSR Acad. Sci., 1967; vis. geoscientist Am. Geol. Inst., 1964-66, 71; earth sci. cons. Compton's Ency., 1970-71; adj. prof. Union Grad. Sch., 1974-2000; bd. rsch. advisors and readers Walden U., 1981-2000; prof. Grad. Sch. Am., 1993-99; travel writer and cruise ship lectr., 1990—. Author: (with others) Investigating the Earth, 1967, (with J. Kramer, E. Muller, J. Lewis) Investigations in Geology, 1967, Inquiry Techniques for Teaching Science, 1968, Risk-Trust-Love, 1972, Consciousness and Creativity, 1975, Confluent Education in Science, 1976, Plus Ça Change..., 1996, Illustrated Guide to the Geology of commonly visited sites on the Antarctic Peninsula, South Georgia, and the Falkland Islands, 2004, Norway Through a Geologist's Eyes, 2006, The Norman Conquest: How Normandy Conquered Us, 2007; co-editor: Geochemical Prospecting for Petroleum, 1959; assoc. editor: Jour. Coll. Sci. Tchg., 1972-74, Geol. Soc. Am. Bull., 1979-84, Jour. Geol. Edn., 1980—2003; editor-in-chief: Ash Lad Press, 1975—; contbr. articles to profl. jours. Bd. dirs. Onondaga Nature Ctrs., Inc., 1966—69. Served to lt. j.g. USNR, 1953—57, lt. comdr. res., 1957—66. Woodrow Wilson Found. fellow, 1959-60, 61-62; NSF sci. faculty fellow U. Oslo, 1967-68. Fellow AAAS, Geol. Soc. Am., Explorers Club; mem. Nat. Assn. Geology Tchrs. (v.p. 1971-72, Neil Miner award, 2006), NY Acad. Scis., Nat. Assn. Geology Tchrs. (pres. 1972-73), Assn. Am. Geographers, Am. Geophys. Union, Geol. Soc. Norway, Can. Assn. Geographers, Assn. for Can. Studies in US, Internat. Assn. Volcanology and Chemistry Earth's Interior, Phi Beta Kappa, Sigma Xi, Phi Delta Kappa. Home and Office: PO Box 294 East Orleans MA 02643-0294 Home Phone: 508-255-2590; Office Phone: 508-255-2301. Personal E-mail: romeywd@comcast.net.

ROMIG, THOMAS J., judge, career military officer; b. Manhattan, Kans., Dec. 27, 1948; married; 2 children. Grad., Nat. War Coll., Armed Forces Staff Coll.; BS, Kans. State U., 1970; JD with honors, Santa Clara U., 1980. Commd. U.S. Army, 1971, advanced through grades to maj. gen., mil. intelligence officer Ft. Bragg, NC, Ft. Huachuca, Ariz.; trial counsel, sr. trial counsel, chief of legal assistance and chief criminal law 2d Armored Divsn., Ft. Hood, Tex., 1980—83; instr. internat. and operational law Judge Advocate Gen.'s Sch., Charlottesville, Va., 1984—87, plans officer, pers., plans and tng. office, 1988—90; staff judge advocate 32d Army Air Def. Command, Darmstadt, Germany, 1990—93, chief pers./asst. chief pers., plans and tng. office, 1993—95; staff judge advocate V Corps, Heidelberg, Germany and Taszar, Hungary, 1996—98; asst. JAG for mil. law and ops. Office of the JAG, Rosslyn, Va., 1998—2001, JAG Washington, 2001—. Decorated Legion of Merit, Meritorious Svc. medal with 4 oak leaf clusters, Army Commendation medal, Army Achievement medal, Nat. Def. Svc. medal with 1 bronze service star, Armed Forces Svc. medal, NATO medal, Army Svc. Ribbon, Army Overseas Svc. Ribbonn (2d award), Parachutist Badge, Army Staff Identification Badge.

ROMIJN, REBECCA, actress, model; b. Berkeley, Calif., Nov. 6, 1972; m. John Stamos, Sept. 19, 1998 (div. Mar. 1, 2005); children: Jaap Romihn Stamos, Elizabeth Kuizenga Stamos; m. Jerry O'Connell, July 14, 2007. Attended, U. Calif., Santa Cruz. Model Sports Illustrated, Christian Dior, Victoria's Secret, Biotherm, Clarins, Dillards, Escada, Furla, Got Milk?, J.Crew, La Senza, Liz Claiborne, Matrix Essentials, Maybelline, Pantene Pro V, Tommy Hilfiger, various others. Actor: (films) Dirty Work, 1998, X-Men, 2000, Rollerball, 2002, Femme Fatale, 2002, X2, 2003, The Punisher, 2004, Godsend, 2004, The Alibi, 2006, Man About Town, 2006, X-Men: The Last Stand, 2006; (TV films) Hefner: Unauthorized, 1999; (TV series) Just Shoot Me, 1999—2000, Pepper Dennis, 2006, Ugly Betty, 2007—, (TV appearances) Friends, 1997, Jack & Jill, 2000. Office: Bragman Nyman Cafarelli 8687 Melrose Ave West Hollywood CA 90069-5701 *

ROMITA, MAURO CHARLES, plastic surgeon; b. NYC, Jan. 16, 1947; MD, U. Miami, 1973. Diplomate Am. Bd. Surgery, Am. Bd. Plastic Surgery. Resident, fellow NYU Med. Ctr., 1974—81; pvt. practice plastic surgery NYC, 1999—. Attending physician St. Vincent Hosp. Med. Ctr., NYC; asst. clin. prof. surgery N.Y. Med. Coll. Contbr. articles to numerous profl. jours. Mem. Boys Town of Italy; bd. govs. Sound Shore Med. Ctr. Mem.: Am. Bd. Plastic Surgery (diplomate), Am. Soc. Plastic Surgeons. Office: 853 5th Ave New York NY 10021-5802

ROMJUE, JOHN LAWSON, historian, writer; b. Washington, Oct. 4, 1936; s. Lawson Rodney Romjue, Joanne Romjue; m. Ingeborg Gertrud Schaefer, Mar. 25, 1961; children: Martin John, Kristin Elisabeth. BA in History and Polit. Sci., U. Mo., 1962, MA in Modern European History and German Lit., 1963. Staff historian USN Facilities Engring. Command, Port Hueneme, Calif., 1966—69; command historian US Army Combat Devel. Experimentation, Fort Ord, Calif., 1969—74; staff historian, dep. staff historian field programs Mil. Hist. Office US Army Tng. and Doctrine Command, Fort Monroe, Va., 1974—85, chief hist. studies and publs. Mil. Hist. Office, 1985—98. Author: From Active Defense to Airland Battle, 1984, The Army of Excellence, 1993, American Army Doctrine for the Post-Cold War, 1996, Out of the Riven Century, 2001, Merry Town, Missouri, 1945-1948, A Novel, 2005, The Black Box: Darwin, Marx, Nietzsche, Freud-Stories, 2006; co-author: Prepare the Army for War, 1993. Specialist 5 US Army, 1957—61. Grantee Fulbright Commn., 1963—64. Mem.: Va. Writers Club (1st v.p. 1995—96, bd. govs. 1997—2001). Republican. Lutheran. Home: 105 Lochmere Ct Yorktown VA 23693 Personal E-mail: johnlromjue@cox.net.

ROMM, DANIEL F., writer, retired computer technician; b. LA, Dec. 2, 1940; s. Abe and Katherine Romm; children: Gary, Janelle. BS, Calif. Inst. Tech., 1962; MA, UCLA, 1967; JD, U. Ill., 1997. Computer programmer Blue Cross, LA, 1978—80; info. sys. mgr. ARCO (formerly Atlantic Richfield Co.), 1981—94; ret., 1994. Author: (books) A Grain of Salt: Why You Must Make Your Own Decisions, 2004, Things Your Bridge Teacher Won't Tell You, 2006. Mem.: Am. Math. Assn. Avocations: duplicate bridge, physics, philosophy, travel. Home: 1221 1st Ave #25F Seattle WA 98101

ROMMEL, A. ROSS, JR., lawyer; b. Houston, 1947; BA, U. Va., 1969; JD, U. Houston, 1973. Bar: Tex. 1973, admitted to practice: US Dist. Ct. (No. Dist.) Tex., US Dist. Ct. (So. Dist.) Tex., US Dist. Ct. (Ea. Dist.) Tex., US Dist. Ct. (We. Dist.) Tex., US Ct. Appeals (5th Cir.), US Ct. Appeals (11th Cir.). Asst. dist. atty. Harris County, Tex., 1973-81; mcpl. judge West Univ. Place, Tex., 1984-87; gen. counsel Andrews & Kurth LLP, Houston. Lectr. - investigation of fraud in fin. inst. FBI Nat. Acad.; instr. U. Houston Law Ctr. (Trial Advocacy Inst.). Commr. Harris County Civil Svc. Commn., 1990—98; pres. bd. dir. AA White Dispute Resolution Inst., 1996—97; bd. arbitrators Nat. Assn. Securities Dealers. USMC. Mem.: Houston Bar Assn., State Bar Tex., ABA, Order of Barons, Phi Delta Phi. Office: Andrews Kurth LLP 600 Travis St Ste 4200 Houston TX 77002-3090 Office Phone: 713-238-3830. Office Fax: 713-238-7227. Business E-Mail: rrommel@andrewskurth.com.

ROMNEY, CARL F., seismologist; b. Salt Lake City, June 5, 1924; m. Barbara Doughty; children: Carolyn Ann, Kim. BS in Meteorology, Calif. Inst. Tech., 1945; PhD, U. Calif., Berkeley, 1956. Seismologist U.S. Dept. Air Force, 1955-58; asst. tech. dir. Air Force Tech. Applications Center, 1958-73; dep. dir. Nuclear Monitoring Research Office, Def. Advanced Research Projects Agy., 1973-75, dir., 1975-79; dep. dir. Def. Advanced Research Projects Agy., 1979-83; dir. Ctr. Seismic Studies, 1983-91; v.p. Sci. Applications Internat. Corp., 1987—2001. Tech. adviser U.S. reps. in negotiations Test Ban Treaty; mem. U.S. del. Geneva Conf. Experts, 1958, Conf. on Discontinuance Nuclear Weapons Tests, 1959, 60; negotiations on threshold Test Ban Treaty, Moscow, 1974; mem. U.S. del. Peaceful Nuclear Explosions Treaty, Moscow, 1974-75 Contbr. articles to tech. jours. Recipient Exceptional Civilian Service awards Air Force, 1959, Exceptional Civilian Service awards Dept. Def., 1964, 79; Pres.'s award for Distinguished Fed. Civilian Service, for outstanding contbns. to devel. of control system for underground nuclear tests, 1967; Presdl. Rank of Meritorious Exec., 1980; inducted in Hall of Honor, Air Intelligence Agy., 1996. Achievements include research on earthquake mechanism, seismic noise; generation, propagation, detection seismic waves from underground explosions. Home: 4105 Sulgrave Dr Alexandria VA 22309-2629 E-mail: cromney@earthlink.net.

ROMNEY, (WILLARD) MITT, former governor; b. Detroit, Mar. 12, 1947; s. George W. and Lenore (Lafount) R.; m. Ann Davies, Mar. 21, 1969; children: Taggart, Matthew, Joshua, Benjamin, Craig. BA, Brigham Young U., 1971; JD, MBA, Harvard U., 1975. Cons. Boston Consulting Group, 1975-77, Bain & Co., Boston, 1977-78, v.p., 1978-84, chmn., CEO, 1991—2001; mng. ptnr., CEO Bain Capital, Inc., Boston, 1984—2001; pres., CEO Salt Lake Organizing Com. (Winter Olympics), Utah, 1999—2002; gov. Commonwealth of Mass., 2003—07. Bd. dirs. Marriott Corp., Bethesda, Md., Staples Inc., Framingham, Mass., Babbages Inc., Dallas, Tex., Damon Corp., Needham, Mass. Author: Turnaround: Crisis, Leadership, and the Olympic Games, 2004. Pres. Boston Stake LDS Ch., 1986-1994; adv. bd. Brigham Young U. Sch. Bus., Provo, Utah, 1990—; vis. com. Harvard Bus. Sch., Cambridge, Mass; mem. nat. exec. bd. Boy Scouts Am.; trustee Belmont (Mass.) Hill Sch., 1989—. Baker scholar Harvard Bus. Sch., Cambridge, Mass., 1975. Mem. Belmont Hill Club. Republican. Lds Ch. Office: Romney for President, Inc PO Box 55899 Boston MA 02205-5899 Office Phone: 857-288-5899. *

ROMNEY, RICHARD BRUCE, lawyer; b. Kingston, Jamaica, Dec. 29, 1942; arrived in U.S., 1945, naturalized, 1956; s. Frank Oswald and Mary Ellen (Burton) Romney; m. Beverly Cochran, Sept. 11, 1965 (dec. 1984); children: Richard Bruce Jr., Stephanie Cochran; m. Lynthia H. Walker, Aug. 14, 1988; children: Alisa Dawn, Kristen Elizabeth. BA, U. Pa., 1964; JD, U. Va., 1972. Bar: N.Y. 1973, U.S. Ct. Appeals (2d cir.) 1975. Assoc. Dewey, Ballantine, Bushby, Palmer & Wood, NYC, 1972—80, ptnr., 1981—2004, of counsel, 2004—05. Mem. editl. bd. U. Va. Law Rev., 1970—72. Served to lt. USN, 1964—68. Fellow: ABA; mem.: Westchester County Bar Assn., Assn. Bar City of NY, NY State Bar Assn., Order of Coif. Home and Office: 35 Deerfield Rd Chappaqua NY 10514-1604 Home Phone: 914-238-2145; Office Phone: 914-238-3222. Personal E-mail: rromney@aol.com.

ROMNEY-MANOOKIN, ELAINE CLIVE, retired music educator, composer; b. Salt Lake City, July 11, 1922; d. Joseph Campbell Clive and Katie Winifred Gilroy; m. Eldon Brigham Romney, May 5, 1941 (dec. May 1998); children: Ruth Romney Powell, Frederic Clive Romney, Clive Jay Romney, Stanley Clive Romney, Eldon Clive Romney, Roslyn Kay Romney Reynolds, Rae Lynne Romney Johnson, Vincent Clive Romney; m. Stuart Midgley Manookin. Studied piano, violin and cello, Clive Music Studios, Salt Lake City, 1938; cert., U. Utah, 1941; studied organ, U. S.C., 1954; studied piano with Frederic Dixon, McCune Sch., 1938—42; studied paino with Alton O'Steen, Juilliard, 1936. Musician: Assembly Hall with McCune Symphony, 1941, author organ book for beginning organists; composer: (sch. song) South H.S., 1939, Skyline H.S., 1962, Wasatch Jr. H.S., 1964; organist Grandview Second Ward, 2001—; organist: Columbia (S.C.) Stake Ctr., 1953—54, East Millcreek Stake, 1956—, Monument Pk. Stake, 1955—56. Bd. dirs. Utah Hemophlia Found., Salt Lake City, 1965—99; vol. specialist Welfare Employment; vice chmn. dist. Rep. Party, Salt Lake City, 1970—90. Recipient Dedicated Svc. award, Hemophilia Found., 1991. Mem.: Alpha Dorian Fine Arts Soc. (past pres.), AXO Luncheon Club (pres.), Agalia Mu (past pres.). Avocations: travel, writing, volunteering. Address: 2987 Hartford St Salt Lake City UT 84106-3468

ROMO, RANDULFO, physiologist, educator; b. Aug. 28, 1954; MD, Nat. Autonomous U. Mexcio, 1978; DSc in Neuroscience, U. Paris, France, 1985. Postdoctoral rsch. U. Fribourg, Switzerland, John Hopkins U.; prof. neuroscience, Inst. Cellular Physiology Nat. Autonomous U. Mexico, Mexico City, 1991—, Howard Hughes Med. investigator, 1996—. Recipient Demuth prize in neuroscience, Demuth Found., Nat. prize sciences and arts, Govt. Mexico, Prize in Basic Med. Sciences, Acad. Sciences for Developing World. Mem.: Mexican Acad. Sciences, NAS (fgn. assoc.).

ROMO, THOMAS, III, plastic surgeon; m. Diane Romo. BA, Trinity U., 1974; MD, Baylor Coll. Medicine, 1979. Cert. Am. Bd. Otolaryngology, Am. Bd. Facial Plastic & Reconstructive Surgery, lic. Fla., Tex., NY. Intern gen. surgery Baylor Affiliated Hospitals, 1979—82; resident otolaryngology NY Eye & Ear Infirmary, 1982—84; dir emeritus, facial plastic and reconstructive surgery NY and Ear Infirmary; fellow facial plastic surgery Tampa Gen. Hosp., 1985; dir. facial plastic and reconstructive surgery NY Eye & Ear Infirmary, Lenox Hill Hosp. Spkr. in field. Author: Aesthetic Facial Plastic Surgery: A Multidisciplinary Approach, 2000, Silver Book Edition on Endoscopic Brow Lifting. Chmn. med. adv. bd. Little Baby Face Found., pres. bd. dir. Named one of Best Doctors, NY Mag., 2005. Fellow: Am. Coll. Surgeons; mem.: NY Facial Plastic Surgery Soc. (past pres.), Am. Acad. Facial Plastic and Reconstructive Surgery (ea. regional dir. 1999—2004, Disting. Edn. award), Am. Acad. of Otolaryngology-Head and Neck Surgery. Achievements include patents in field. Office: Lenox Hill Hosp Dept Otolaryngology 100 East 77th St New York NY 10021 E-mail: docromo@aol.com. *

ROMO, TONY (ANTONIO RAMIRO ROMO), professional football player; b. San Diego, Apr. 21, 1980; BBA, Ea. Ill. U., Charlston, 2003. Quarterback Dallas Cowboys, 2003—. Co-host (radio show) Inside the Huddle, 2006. Named to All-Ohio Valley Conf. 1st team, All-Am. 3rd team, AP; recipient Player of Yr., Ohio Valley Conf., Walter Payton award, 2002. Mem.: Sigma Pi. Avocation: golf. Office: Dallas Cowboys 1 Cowboys Pky Irving TX 75063-4999

ROMOFF, JEFFREY ALAN, healthcare executive; b. NYC, Nov. 30, 1945; s. Richard Warren and Evelyn (Alter) Romoff; m. Vivian Irene Goodman, Aug. 25, 1966 (dec. June 1983); children: Jennifer Ann, Rebecca Lynn; m. Stefania Ferrarese, Dec. 2002. BS magna cum laude in Social Scis., CCNY, 1967; M.Phil. in Polit. Scis., Yale U., 1971; Doctor Pub. Svc. (hon.), Chatham Coll., 2005. Teaching fellow Yale U., 1969-70, teaching assoc., 1970-71; exec. dir. Central Naugatuck Valley Mental

Health Council, Waterbury, Conn., 1971-73; regional programing dir. Western Psychiat. Inst. and Clinic (U. Pitts.), 1973-74, assoc. dir. div. edn. and research, 1974-75; assoc. dir. Western Psychiat. Inst. and Clinic, 1975—86; adj. asst. prof. pub. health U. Pitts., 1981—, instr. psychiatry, 1982—, assoc. v.p. health scis., 1984-86, vice chancellor health scis., 1986-92, sr. vice chancellor for Health Adminstrn., 1992—96; exec. v.p. U. Pitts. Med. Ctr., 1986-92, pres., 1992—. N.Y.C. Regents scholar CCNY, 1963-67 Mem. Am. Hosp. Assn. (governing coun. sect. for mental health and psychiat. scvs. 1986-89), Am. Psychiat. Assn. (chmn. joint com. with Am. Hosp. Assn. 1983-84), Hosp. Assn. Pa., Coun. Psychiat. Svc. Providers (exec. com. 1981-84) Jewish. Home: 3208 Fox Run Rd Allison Park PA 15101-1506 Office: U Pitts Med Ctr Forbes Tower 200 Lothrop St Ste 11045 Pittsburgh PA 15213-2546

ROMOSER, GEORGE KENNETH, political and social science educator; b. Kingston, NY, Sept. 14, 1929; s. Carl August and Alva (Becker) R.; m. Mechthild von Tresckow, Apr. 30, 1967; children: Alexandra Ada, Valerie Anna. AB, Rutgers U., 1951; A.M., U. Chgo., 1954, PhD, 1958. Research asst. Nat. Opinion Research Center, 1953; fellow Social Sci. Rsch. Coun., 1953-54; lectr. Indiana Univ., 1954—55; asst. Freiburg (Germany) U., 1955-56; instr. Ohio State U., 1957-61; from asst. prof. to assoc. prof. Conn. Coll., 1963-67; assoc. prof., prof. polit. sci. U. N.H., Durham, 1961-62, 67-96, chmn. dept., 1968-71, prof. internat. affairs, 1986-93, course dir. Internat. Perspective Ctr., 1986-88, dir. program on tech., society and values, 1996-2000. Fulbright prof. Faculty of Law, Mainz U., Fed. Republic Germany, 1962-63; dir. Émigré Meml. German Internship Programs, 1965-2005; vis. prof. Free U., Berlin, 1964, Mannheim U., 1968, 82-83, Johns Hopkins, Bologna, Italy, 1969, Munich U., 1973-74, U. Pa., 1986, Kobe U., Japan, 1988-89, Bowdoin Coll., 1990, Freiburg U., Germany, 1993-94, Fulbright Sr. Prof.; adj. prof. Mannheim U., Fed. Republic Germany, 1983—; Fulbright sr. rsch. fellow Munich U., 1974; Rockefeller fellow Aspen Inst. for Humanistic Studies, 1978-79; rsch. fellow Inst. on Far Ea. Studies, Kyungnam U., Republic of Korea, 1997; cons. Com. on Internat. Exchange of Persons, 1965-66; NEH fellow Yale U., 1993; co-founder Conf. Group on German Politics, 1968—, chmn., 1968-84, regional dir., 1984-87; founder, dir. New Eng. Workshops on German Affairs, 1980—; co-founder Pacific Coast Workshops on German Affairs, 1983-93; commuting fellow Ctr. European Studies Harvard U., 1983—; founder The Japanese Circle, 1989-2000; coord. German programs in rsch. and pub. affairs, 2004-. Co-author: West German Politics in the Mid-Eighties, 1985, Germany's New Politics, 1995; contbr. articles to profl. jours., books. Chmn. com. on govtl. reorgn. Democratic party N.H., 1962; chair Eliot (Maine) Planning Bd., 1969—72; chmn. Eliot Conservation Commn., 1984—88; vice chair Eliot Bd. Appeals, Eliot, Maine, 1977—82. Decorated Civilian Knight's Cross Fed. Republic of Germany, 1972. Mem. Am. Coun. on Germany, Internat. Polit. Sci. Assn., Am. Polit. Sci. Assn., New England Circle, Phi Delta Theta, Pi Sigma Alpha, Delta Phi Alpha, Phi Alpha Theta. Home: Shipmast Farm 86 Worster Rd Eliot ME 03903-1113 Office: Univ NH Huddlerrun Hall Durham NH 03824 Business E-Mail: gkr@unh.edu.

ROMPALA, RICHARD M., chemical company executive; B in Liberal Arts and Chem. Engring., Columbia U.; MBA, Harvard U. Bus. mgr. Olin Corp.; sr. v.p. ops. Mueller Brass Co.; joined PPG Industries, 1985, v.p. corp. devel., group v.p. chems., group v.p. coatings and resins; pres. Valspar Corp., Mpls., 1994, CEO, 1995—, chmn., 1998. Office: The Valspar Corp 1101 Third St S Minneapolis MN 55415

RONALD, PETER, utilities executive; b. Duluth, Minn., Aug. 26, 1926; s. George W. and Florence (Jones) R.; m. Mary Locke Boyd, Nov. 25, 1950 (dec. 2003); children: Peter Webb, Pauline Morton, Samuel Herschel; m. Anne H. Moore, Dec. 28, 2005. BA, U. Va., 1950. With Louisville Gas & Electric Co., 1950-88, treas., 1962—, v.p., 1969-82, sr. v.p., 1982-88, dir., 1979-89. Bd. dirs., mem. exec. com. Bus. Devel. Corp. Ky., 1967-75, pres., 1971-72; bd. dirs. Louisville Community Chest, 1967-72, v.p., 1969-72; bd. dirs., v.p. Louisville Rehab. Ctr., 1964-82, pres., 1970-71; bd. overseers Louisville Country Day Sch., 1967-70; trustee Children's Hosp. Found., 1978-81, sec.-treas., 1978-81; bd. govs. Captiva (Fla.) Civic Assn., 1990-94, v.p., 1992; commr. Captiva, Fla. Erosion Prevention Dist., 1996-98. With USNR, 1945-46. Mem. Louisville Country Club, Captiva Yacht Club, Zeta Psi. Home: 4710 Indian Hills Green Louisville KY 40207-1366 also: PO Box 877 Captiva FL 33924

RONALDINHO, (RONALDO DE ASSIS MOREIRA), professional soccer player; b. Porto Alegre, Brazil, Mar. 21, 1980; Player Gremio FC, Brazil, 1998—2001, Paris Saint Germain, France, 2001—03, FC Barcelona, Spain, 2003—. Mem. Brazil Nat. Team, 1999—, World Cup Champion, Brazil, 2002; mem. & capt. Confederations Cup Champion, Brazil, 2005. Named FIFA World Player of the Yr., 2004, FIFPro World Player of the Year, 2005; named to FIFA 100, 2004, FIFPro World XI, 2005; recipient Best Soccer Player, ESPY award, 2006. Mailing: FC Barcelona Av Aristedes Maillol 08028 Barcelona Spain

RONALTER, CHELSEA MARIA, artist, graphic designer; b. Manchester, NH, Jan. 30, 1974; d. Donald Edward and Lynn Elise Ronalter. AA in Comml. Design and Illustration, Manchester Cmty. Tech. Coll., NH, 1997; AA in Interior Design summa cum laude, Hesser Coll., Manchester, 2001; postgrad., Notre Dame Coll., Manchester, 2001—02, Rivier Coll., Nashua, 2005—. Graphic designer Notre Dame Coll., Manchester, NH, 1998—2002; instl. advancement So. NH U., Manchester, 2002—03; freelance designer, 2003—04; with broker rels. New England BCE, Derry, NH, 2004—. Mem.: Phi Theta Kappa. Roman Catholic. Avocations: art, literature, history.

RONAN, CLIFFORD JOHN, literature and language professor; b. Boston, July 22, 1935; s. J(ohn) Clifford and Frances Goodwin Ronan; m. Denise Shual, Dec. 2, 1960; children: David Goodwin, Michelle Ronan Noteboom. AB, Amherst Coll., Mass., 1957; PhD in English Lit., U. Calif., Berkeley, 1971. Asst. prof. English U. Tex., Austin, 1965—72; prof. English Tex. State U., San Marcos, 1972—. Reader in Advanced Placement in English Ednl. Testing Svc., 1976—79; exec. sec.-treas. South-Central Renaissance Conf., 1978—80; core faculty Nat. Endowment for Humanities, 1987—93; sr. Fulbright lectr. in Am. Lit. U. Silesia, Poland, 1995—96; cons., presenter, lectr. in field. Author: Antike Roman: Power Symbology and the Roman Play in Early Modern England 1585-1635, 1995; contbr. articles to profl. jours., chapters to books. Mem. Voluntary Action Ctr., Caldwell County, Lockhart, Tex., 1973—75, sec., 1973—75; adv. bd. mem. Catholic Student Ctrs., U Tex., Austin, 1970—72, Catholic Student Ctrs., Tex. State U., 1989—. Sgt. US Army, 1957—58. Recipient Presdl. Seminar award, SW Tex. State U., 1997. Democrat. Roman Catholic. Home: 211 Harvard St San Marcos TX 78666 Office: Tex State Univ Dept English San Marcos TX 78666 Home Phone: 512-392-0399; Office Phone: 512-245-2163. Office Fax: 512-245-8546. Business E-Mail: cr06@txstate.edu.

RONAN, JOHN, architect; BS with honors in Architecture, U. Mich., Ann Arbor, 1985; MArch with distinction, Harvard U., Cambridge, Mass., 1991. With Lohan Archs., Tigerman Fugman, McCurry Archs. (now Tigerman McCurry Archs.), Kruek and Sexton Archs.; prin. John Ronan Arch., Chgo., 1997—. Prin. works include Caspe Residence, Chgo., 1999, Perry Residence, 2000, Cath. Ext. Chapel, 2000, House on the Edge of a Forest, 2002, Concrete Townhouse, 2005, Akiba-Schechter Jewish Day Sch., 2005, Gary Comer Youth Ctr., Chgo., 2006 (Richard H. Driehaus Found. Award for Archtl. Excellence in Cmty. Design, Chgo. Neighborhood Devel. Awards, 2007). Office: John Ronan Arch 320 W Ohio St 4e Chicago IL 60610 Office Phone: 312-951-6600. E-mail: ronan@jrarch.com. *

RONAN, MARK A., mathematician, writer; s. Colin Alistair and Kathleen Mary Ronan; children: Piers Jan Tonder, Tamsin Jana Katherine. BSc, London U., 1968; PhD, U. Oreg., Eugene, 1977, U. Oxford, Eng., 1978. Wissenschaftlicher mitarbeiter Tech. U. Braunschweig, Germany, 1980; asst. prof. Free U. Berlin, 1981—82; vis. reader Queen Mary Coll. London, 1986—87; Mason prof. math. U. Birmingham, 1989—92; vis. prof. U. Coll. London, 1999—; prof. U. Ill., Chgo., 1989—. Author: (textbook) Lectures on Buildings, (book) Symmetry and the Monster; actor: (operas) Lyric Opera of Chicago; dancer (ballet) Nutcracker; contbr. numerous rsch. papers on math. to profl. jours. Mem.: Cliffdwellers Club, Savile Club. Avocations: opera, ballet, theater, languages, history.

RONAN, WILLIAM JOHN, management consultant; b. Buffalo, Nov. 8, 1912; s. William and Charlotte (Ramp) R.; m. Elena Vinadé, May 29, 1939; children: Monica, Diana Quasha. AB, Syracuse U., 1934; PhD, NYU, 1940, LLD, 1969; certificate, Geneva Sch. Internat. Studies, 1933. Mus. asst. Buffalo Mus. Sci., 1928-30; with Niagara-Hudson Power Co., 1931; transfer dept. NYC R.R., 1932; Penfield fellow internat. law, diplomacy and belles lettres, 1935; Univ. fellow, 1936; editor Fed. Bank Service, Prentice-Hall, Inc., 1937; instr. govt. NYU, 1938, exec. sec. grad. div. for tng. in pub. services, 1938, asst. dir., 1940, asst. prof. govt., dir. grad. div. for tng. pub. service, 1940, assoc. prof. govt., 1946-47, prof., 1947, dean, grad. sch. pub. adminstrn. and social service, 1953-58; Cons. NYC Civil Service Commn., 1938; prin. rev. officer, negotiations officer US Civil Service Commn., 1942; prin. div. asst. US Dept. State, 1943; cons. Dept. State, 1948, Dept. Def., 1954; dir. studies NY State Coordination Commn., 1951-58; project mgr. NYU-U. Ankara project, 1954-59; cons. ICA, 1955, NY State Welfare Conf.; adminstrv. co-dir. Albany Grad. Program in Pub. Adminstrn.; 1st dep. city adminstr. NYC, 1956-57; exec. dir. NY State Temporary Commn. Constl. Conv., 1956-58; sec. to Gov. NY, 1959-66; chmn. interdept. com. traffic safety, commr. Port Authority NY and NJ, 1967-90, vice chmn., 1972-74, chmn., 1974-77; with UTDC Corp., West Palm Beach, Fla. Trustee Crosslands Savs. Bank; chmn. bd. LI R.R., 1966-74; chmn. Tri-State Transp. Com., NY, NJ, Conn., 1961-67; chmn. interstate com. New Haven R.R., 1960-63; chmn. NY Com. on LI R.R., 1964-65; mem. NY State Commn. Interstate Coop., 1961, NY State Com. Fgn. Ofcl. Visitors, 1961, NY State Coordination Commn., 1960; mem. NY Civil Svc. Commn., Temporary State Commn. on Constl. Conv., 1966-67; chmn. NY State Met. Commuter Transp. Authority, 1965-68, Met. Transp. Authority, 1968-74, Tri-Borough Bridge and Tunnel Authority, 1968-74; NYC Transit Authority, 1968-74, Manhattan and Bronx Surface Transit Operating Authority, 1968-74; chmn. bd., pres. 3d Century Corp., 1974-94; mem. Commn. Critical Choices for Am., 1973—, acting chmn., 1975—; mem. urban transp. adv. com. US Dept. Transp.; sr. adviser Rockefeller family, 1974-80; pres. Nelson Rockefeller Collection, Inc., 1977-80; trustee Power Authority of State of NY, 1974-77; cons. to trustees Penn Ctrl. Transp. Co.; vice chmn. bd. CCX, Inc.; sec.-treas. Sarabam Corp. N.V.; chmn., dir. UTDC (USA) Inc., 1987-88; chmn. UTDC Corp., 1989-94, Transit Svcs. Corp., 1989-94; cons. Herzog Transit Svcs., 1995-99, Dime Savs. Bank, Metal Powder Products Inc., Flomet Inc., 1997—, Teckna Seal, LLC, 2002--; Internat. Mining and Metals Inc., Quadrant Mgmt. Inc., 1990—, Ohio Highspeed Rail Authority, 1991-93; chmn. NY and NJ Inland Rail Rate Com.; dir. Nat. Mgmt. Coun., 1951. Author: Money Power of States in International Law, 1940, The Board of Regents and the Commissioner, 1948, Our War Economy, 1943, (with others), articles in profl. jours.; adviser: Jour. Inst. Socio-Econ. Studies. Mem. US FOA, Am. Public Health Assn.; staff relations officer NYC Bd. Edn.; Mem. Nat. Conf. Social Work, Nat. Conf. on Met. Areas, Citizens Com. on Corrections, Council on Social Work Edn.; bd. dirs. World Trade Club; adv. bd. World Trade Inst.; mem. 42d St. Redevel. Corp., chmn., 1980-94; mem. Assn. for a Better NY; bd. advisers Inst. for Socioecon. Studies, 1977—; dir. Nat. Health Council, 1980-86; dep. dir. policy Nelson Rockefeller campaign for Republican presdl. nomination, 1964; mem. NY State Gov.'s Com. on Shoreham Nuclear Plant, 1983-85, Nassau County Indsl. Devel. Authority, 1982-90, US Dept. Transp. Com. on Washington and Capital Dist. Airports, 1985-86; bd. dirs. Ctr. Study Presidency, 1986-90, Alcoholism Council of NY, 1986—; trustee NY Coll. Osteopathic Medicine, 1986-91; v.p. Am. Cancer Soc., Palm Beach. Served as lt. USNR, 1943-46. Mem. ASPA, NEA, Am. Polit. Sci. Assn., Am. Acad. Pub. Adminstrn., Civil Svc. Assembly of US and Can., Internat. Assn. Met. Rsch. and Devel., Nat. Mcpl. League, Mcpl. Pers. Soc., Citizens Union of NY, Nat. Civil Svc. League, Am. Acad. Polit. and Social Sci., LI Assn. Commerce and Industry (dir.), Internat. Inst. Adminstrv. Scis., Am. Fgn. Law Assn., Internat. Union Pub. Transport (mgmt. com., v.p.), Am. Pub. Transit Assn. (chmn. 1974-76), Nat. Def. Transp. Assn. (v.p. for Mass transit), English Speaking Union (bd. dirs. Palm Beach), Met. Opera Club, Maidstone Club, Devon Yacht Club, Knickerbocker Club, Hemisphere Club, Harvard Club, Creek Club, Wings Club, Traffic Club, Univ. Club, Am. Club Riviera, Beach Club (Palm Beach), Everglades Club. Home: 525 S Flagler Dr West Palm Beach FL 33401-5922 Address: Villa La Pointe Du Cap 29 Ave de La Corniche 06230 Saint Jean Cap Ferrat France Personal E-mail: w.j.ramp@aol.com.

RONAYNE, MICHAEL RICHARD, JR., academic dean; b. Boston, Apr. 29, 1937; s. Michael Richard and Margaret (Fahey) R.; m. Joanne Maria, Aug. 7, 1971; 1 child, Michelle Eileen. BS, Boston Coll., 1958; PhD, U. Notre Dame, 1962. Instr. chemistry Providence Coll., 1962-63, asst. prof. chemistry, 1963-64; rsch. chemist Panametrics, Inc., Waltham, Mass., 1964-66; asst. prof. chemistry Suffolk U., Boston, 1966-67, assoc. prof., 1967-70, prof., chmn. dept. chemistry, 1970-72, dean Coll. Arts and Sci., 1972—. Reaccreditation vis. team mem. New Eng. Assn. Schs. and Colls., Winchester, Mass., 1974-80, Mass. Dept. Edn., Boston, 1975; mem. acad. adv. com. Mass. Bd. Higher Edn., Boston, 1977. Contbr. articles to sci. jours., profl. publs. Mem. Winchester Sch. Com., 1983-92, chmn., 1984-85, 86-87; mem. Winchester Town Meeting, 1983-98, mem. town capital planning com., 1983-84, town coun. on youth, 1987-88, 89-90; mem. exec. com., bd. dirs. Mass. Bay Marine Studies Consortium, 1985-87; project dir. U.S. Dept. of Edn. Title III Grants. Shell Oil Corp. fellow, 1958-59, AEC fellow 1959-62; recipient Contbns. in Sci. and Edn. citation New Eng. Sch. Art and Design, Boston, 1991; named to Matignon High Sch. Alumni Achievement Hall of Fame, 1997. Mem. AAAS, Am. Chem. Soc., Am. Conf. Acad. Deans, Coun. for Liberal Learning, Am. Assn. for Higher Edn., Sigma Xi, Phi Alpha Theta, Phi Gamma Mu, Sigma Tau Delta, Omicron Delta Epsilon, Sigma Zeta, Pi Sigma Alpha. Office: Suffolk U Beacon Hill Boston MA 02114 E-mail: mronayne@suffolk.edu.

RONCAL, ROGELIO, psychiatrist; b. Bataan, Philippines, 1939; MD magna cum laude, Manila Ctrl. U., 1962. Diplomate Am. Bd. Psychiatry and Neurology, Am. Bd. Forensic Medicine, Am. Acad. Integrative Medicine. Intern French Hosp., NYC, 1963; resident in psychiatry Middletown PC-NY Psychiat. Inst., NYC, 1965-67; physician Horton Meml. Hosp., Middletown, NY; founding dir. Middletown Alcohol Treatment Ctr. (now R. Ward Addictions Treatment Ctr.), 1974—; pvt. practice., 1974-89; clin. dir. Middletown Psychiat. Ctr., NY; attending psychiatrist Mid Hudson Psychiat. Ctr., New Hampton, NY, 1984-95; med. dir. chemical dependency program Pius XII Youth and Family Svcs., 1995—. Instr. clin. psychiat. Columbia U.; psychiatrist N.Am. Province Order Carmelites, 1975-95; med. cons. NY State Divsn. Alcoholism and Alcohol Abuse, 1981-84; pychiat. cons. McQuade Found. for Children, 1974-81; attending psychiatrist NY State Dept. Corrections, 1992-95. Maj. MC, USAR, 1983. Recipient Life Achievement award Alcoholism and Drug Abuse Coun. Orange County, N.Y., 2001, medal of honor MCU Coll. Medicine, 2000, MCU Alumni in Am. Eagle award, 2004, MCU Centennial Medallion, 2004; donor M. Roncal achievement award for acad. excellence given to delinquent youth in group homes served by Pius XII Youth and Family Svcs., 1990-95; named to First Alumni Hall of Fame, Manila Ctrl. U., 2001. Fellow: APA (disting. life), Am. Assn. Integrative Medicine (life; cert.), Am. Psychiat. Assn. (life); mem.: Caloocan H.S. Alumni Assn., Acad. Internat. Med. Study, Manila Ctrl U. Med. Alumni Assn. (pres. N.E. chpt. 1998, pres. found. in Am. 1999, pres. 2000—), West Hudson Psychiat. Soc. (sec. 1979, pres. 1981), NY State Med. Soc. (task force on smoking cessation 1997—), Am. Soc. Addiction Medicine, Am. Acad. Psyciat. Adminstrn., Am. Coll. Forensic Examiners, Orange County Med. Soc., Am. Coll. Physician Execs., Am. Med. Dirs. Assn., Med. Staff Orgn. Middletown Psychiat. Ctr., Med. Staff Orgn. Mid-Hudson Forensic Psychiat. Ctr. (pres. 1995), Filipino Psychiatrists in Am. (life). Fax: 914-294-1402.

RONDE, JOHN HERMAN, writer, translator; b. Lonneker, Overyssel, The Netherlands, July 12, 1929; arrived in US, 1961; s. Johannes Maria Ronde and Lamberdina Hulsschreuder. BA in Econs., Columbia U., NYC, 1973, MA in Social Studies, 1974, MPhil in Geography, 1983. With Irving Trust Co., NYC, Loeb, Rhoades & Co., NYC, Bache & Co., NYC, Import-Export Industries, NYC, Winter-Wolff Internat. Corp., NYC; substitute tchr. NYC HS, 1985-86, 92-93; asst. geographer US Census Bur., NYC, 1988-91. Author: Migration, Social Infrastructure and Urban Devel. in Selected German Cities, and Housing Policy and Supply in the Fed. German Republic (1970-85), 1996, Urban Devel. and Migration in Kiel with Reference to City Ctr. and Fringe Area Devel. Initiatives, 1971-84, Philosophical Interpretations of Modern Science, The Developing New World View of Man and His Activities for The Fulfillment of His Needs, An Introd. To and A Discussion of A Model of The Location of Man and His Activities, or: Geography as a Theory of Man. Aide, advisor to Sen. George McGovern, 1972; advisor Dem. Party. Mem.: AAAS, Baron Johannes Hermanus Ronde Inst. Urban Geography and Locational Studies (founder), Am. Chem. Soc. (nat. affil.), NY Acad. Sci. Democrat. Avocations: bibliophile in history, philosophy of science, music, Bandonion player. Home: 75 E 3rd St C-3 New York NY 10003-9015

RONDEAU, CLEMENT ROBERT, petroleum geologist; b. Ironwood, Mich., July 6, 1928; BS, Tulane U., 1955. Geol. supr. Texaco, Inc., New Orleans, 1955-63; area mgr. Pubco Petroleum Corp., New Orleans, 1963-69; cons. petroleum geologist Harahan, La., 1969—; owner Natural Gas Exploration Co., Harahan, 1977—. Mem. AAAS, Am. Assn. Petroleum Geologists, Soc. Exploration Geophysicists, New Orleans Geol. Soc., N.Y. Acad. Sci., The Explorers Club, Phi Beta Kappa, Sigma Gamma Epsilon. Democrat. Roman Catholic. Home and Office: 119 W Southland Ave Ironwood MI 49938 Personal E-mail: gasfinder@aol.com.

RONDEAU, GEORGE CHARLES, JR., lawyer; b. Phila., May 2, 1946; BSEE, Drexel U., Phila., 1969; MBA, U. So. Calif., LA, 1972; JD, UCLA, 1976. Assoc. atty. Fulwider, Patton, Lee & Utecht, LA, 1976—82; ptnr., atty. Seed Intellectual Property Law Group PLLC, Seattle, 1983—2002, Davis Wright Tremaine, LLP, Seattle, 2002—. Mem.: ABA, Licensing Execs. Soc. (chmn. seattle chpt. 1995—99), Wash. State Patent Law Assn., Wash. State Bar Assn. (chmn. 1990—91, intellectual property sect.). Office: Davis Wright Tremaine LLP 1201 Third Ave Ste 2200 Seattle WA 98101-3045 Office Phone: 206-757-8133. Office Fax: 206-757-7133. Business E-Mail: georgerondeau@dwt.com.

RONDEAU, JAMES EDWARD, curator; b. Holyoke, Mass., Sept. 10, 1969; s. John Patrick and Norine Patricia Shevlin Rondeau. BA, Middlebury Coll., Vt., 1991; MA in History of Art, Williams Coll., Williamstown, Mass., 1994. Asst./assoc. curator Wadsworth Atheneum, Hartford, Conn., 1994—98; assoc. curator contemporary art Art Inst. Chgo., Chgo., 1998—2004, Frances and Thomas Dittmer chmn. dept. of contemporary art, 2004—. Author: (exhibition catalogue) Gaylen Gerber, Musee d'Art Moderne Grand-Duc Jean, Luxembourg, Alighiero Boetti: an introduction to his work, Interview: a conversation between James Rondeau and Paul McCarthy, Event Horizons: new work by Iñigo Manglano-Ovalle, The Mobility of the Real: Olafur Eliasson is Now, (exhibition brochure) Mark Manders, Steve McQueen, 2002, Maureen Gallace, 2002, (exhibition catalogue) Rineke Dijkstra, 2001, Excavation: Robert Gober's New Work in Venice, The Manhole Cover Project: A Gun Legacy Wadsworth Atheneum, Charles LeDray: Handmade Thoughts, (exhibition brochure) Yoshihiro Suda, Pipilotti Rist/ MATRIX 136 Wadsworth Atheneum, Gaylen Gerber with Stephen Prina, Art Institute of Chicago, 2001, Lee Lozano/ MATRIX 135 Wadsworth Atheneum, 1998, Spencer Finch/ MATRIX 133, 1997, Marlene Dumas, 2003, Cecilia Edefalk, Magnus von Plessen, Art Institute of Chicago, Anri Sala, Roni Horn, Margherita Manzelli. Writing fellow, Lannan Found., 2003. Office: Art Inst Chgo 111 S Michigan Ave Chicago IL 60603 Home Phone: 773-334-4942; Office Phone: 312-443-3678. Office Fax: 312-443-0195. Business E-Mail: jronde@artic.edu.

RONDEAU, PATRICK JOHN, lawyer; b. South Hadley, Mass., July 13, 1959; s. John Patrick and Norine Patricia (Shevlin) R.; m. Valerie Anne Cameron, May 4, 1991. BA summa cum laude, Williams Coll., 1981; JD cum laude, Harvard U., 1984. Bar: Mass. 1985. Assoc. Hale and Dorr, Boston, 1984-89, jr. ptnr., 1989—92, sr. ptnr., 1994—2004; ptnr., vice chmn. Corp dept., co-chmn. Venture Capital group Wilmer Cutler Pickering Hale & Dorr, Boston, 2004—. Lectr. MIT Sloan Sch. Mgmt. Named a Mass. Super Lawyer, Boston Mag., 2004. Mem. ABA, Mass. Bar Assn., Boston Bar Assn. (past co-chmn. securities law com.), Phi Beta Kappa. Roman Catholic. Avocation: sports. Office: Wilmer Cutler Pickering Hale & Dorr 60 State St Boston MA 02109-1816 Office Phone: 617-526-6670. Office Fax: 617-526-5000. Business E-Mail: patrick.rondeau@wilmerhale.com.

RONDEPIERRE, EDMOND FRANCOIS, insurance executive, lawyer; b. NYC, Jan. 15, 1930; s. Jules Gilbert and Margaret Murray R.; m. M. Anne Lerch, July 5, 1952; children: Aimee S., Stephen C., Peter E., Anne W. BS, U.S. Mcht. Marine Acad., 1952; JD, Temple U., 1959. Bar: D.C. 1959, Conn. 1988, U.S. Supreme Ct. 1992. Third mate Nat. Bulk Carriers, 1952-53; field rep. Ins. Co. N.Am., Phila., 1955-59, br. mgr., 1959-61, asst. sec. underwriting, 1965-67, asst. gen. counsel, 1967-70, sr. v.p., gen. counsel, 1970-76; v.p., dep. chief legal affairs INA Corp., Phila., 1976-77; v.p., gen. counsel Gen. Reins. Corp., Stamford, Conn., 1977-79, sr. v.p., corp. sec., gen. counsel, 1979-94, sr. v.p., 1994-95; pres., dir. ARIAS-US, 1994—99, dir. emeritus, 1999—. Bd. dirs. Arias-US. Lt. USN, 1953-55. Mem. ABA, Conn. Bar Assn., D.C. Bar Assn., Soc. CPCU, Internat. Assn. Def. Counsel (past bd. dirs.), AIDA Reins. and Ins. Arbitration Soc. (dir., pres.), Stamford Yacht Club, Wee Burn Country Club. Roman Catholic. Office Phone: 203-662-0059.

RONDINELLI, DENNIS A(UGUST), business administration educator, researcher; b. Trenton, NJ, Mar. 30, 1943; s. August P. and Vincentia Rondinelli; m. Soonyoung Chang, Dec. 19, 1976; children: Linda, Lisa. BA, Rutgers U., 1965; PhD, Cornell U., 1969. Asst. prof. urban affairs U. Wis., Milw., 1971-73; assoc. prof. grad. sch. of mgmt. Vanderbilt U., Nashville, 1973-76; assoc. prof. planning Maxwell Sch. of Citizenship and Pub. Affairs Syracuse U., NY, 1976-79, prof. social scis. NY, 1979-86; prin. scientist and sr. policy analyst Office for Internat. Programs, Research Triangle Inst., Research Triangle Park, NC, 1986-90; Glaxo Disting. Internat. Prof. Mgmt. emeritus Kenan-Flagler Bus. Sch., 2005—, emeritus, 2005—; sr. rsch. scholar Duke Ctr. Internat. Devel., 2005—; dir. Pacific Basin Rsch. Ctr., Soka U. Am., 2005—. Cons. World Bank, U.S. Dept.

State, UN Devel. Program, Govts. of Colombia, South Korea, Can., Indonesia, Philippines, China, India, mem. com. of experts on pub. adminstrn. UN Econ. and Social Coun., 2002—. Author: Decentralization and Development: Policy Implementation in Developing Countries, 1983, Applied Methods of Regional Analysis: The Spatial Dimensions of Development Policy, 1985, Development Administration and U.S. Foreign Aid Policy, 1987, Urban Services in Developing Countries: Public and Private Roles in Urban Development, 1988, Planning Education Reforms in Developing Countries, 1990, Development Projects as Policy Experiments, 1993, Privatization and Economic Reform in Central Europe, 1994, Expanding Sino-American Business and Trade: China's Economic Transition, 1994, Great Policies: Strategic Innovations in Asia and the Pacific, 1995, Policies and Institutions for Managing Privatization, 1996, Market Reform in Vietnam, 1999, Reinventing Government for the 21st Century, 2003, Beyond Reconstruction in Afghanistan, 2004, Globalizataion and Change in Asia, 2007, Decentralizing Governance, 2007; mem. editl. bd. Leadership Rev., Jour. Internat. Bus. Edn., Jour. Internat. Devel. Planning; contbr. articles to profl. jours. Mem. expert com. pub. admin. econ. and social coun. UN, 2002—. Capt. US Army, 1965—72. Decorated Julio Lieras Order of Merit (Colombia), 1988; recipient Rural Devel. medal Republic of Vietnam, 1971, Ethnic Minorities Devel. medal, 1971, W. Bloomberg award for excellence in futures studies, 1997, Weatherspoon Disting. Rsch. award, 1997; East-West Ctr. sr. fellow, 1975-76, Pacific Basin Rsch. Ctr./Soka U. of Am./Harvard U. rsch. fellow, 1991-92. Avocations: gardening, writing nonfiction. Office: Duke Univ Duke Ctr Internat Devel Box 90237 Durham NC 27708 E-mail: rondined@duke.edu.

RONDON, EDANIA CECILIA, lawyer; b. Santiago, Cuba, Oct. 22, 1960; came to U.S., 1965; d. Edalio Marcelino and Ylia Nayda (Jacas) R.; m. Antonio Omar Maldonado, Sept. 5, 1987. BA, Syracuse U., 1982; JD, Boston U., 1985. Bar: N.J. 1985, U.S. Ct. Appeals (3d cir.) 1985. Assoc. Thomas A. Declemente, P.C., Union City, N.J., 1985-88; pub. defender City of Union City, 1985—; assoc. ins. def. James D. Butler, P.A., Jersey City, 1988-93; assoc. Edania C. Rondon, P.A., Union City, 1993—. Mem. ABA, Hudson County Bar Assn. Democrat. Roman Catholic. Home: 630 Slocum Ave Ridgefield NJ 07657-1837 Office: Edania C Rondon PA 3700 Bergenline Ave Ste 201 Union City NJ 07087-4847 Office Phone: 201-866-0157.

RONE, JAMES STEPHEN, performing arts association administrator; b. Bristol, Eng., Dec. 28, 1978; arrived in US, 1989; s. Stanley Dean and Julie Gay (Wall) Rone. BA in Theater and Polit. Sci., U. Mo., Columbia, 2001. Actor Rocky Mountain Repertory, Grand Lake, Colo., 2000, Minn. Repertory, Duluth, 2001; actor, educator Climb Theatre, Inver Grove Heights, Minn., 2001—02, resident playwright, arts adminstr., 2002—05, tchg. co. dir., 2005—. Lead singer, guitarist, songwriter The Seagraves & Robinson Caruso. Mem.: Am. Alliance Theatre and Edn. (Minn. state rep. 2006—), The Playwright's Ctr. Office: Climb Theatre 6415 Carmen Ave E Inver Grove Heights MN 55076 Office Phone: 651-453-9275 ext 20. Business E-Mail: james@climb.org.

RONEY, CARLEY, wedding company executive, writer; m. David Liu; 2 children. BFA, NYU Tisch Sch. Arts, Inst. Film & TV; MA Cultural Studies, NYU. Creative dir., editor Nat. Mus. Am. History, McGraw-Hill Co., Simon & Schuster, 1988—94; cofounder RunTime Inc., 1994, pres., 1994—96; cofounder The Knot, 1996, v.p. creative devel., 1996—99, editor in chief, 1996—; syndicated columnist Scripps Howard News Svc., 2003—. Author: The Knot's Complete Guide to Weddings, 1998, The Knot Ultimate Wedding Planner, 1999, The Knot Book of Wedding Vows & Traditions, 2000, The Knot Book of Wedding Gowns, 2001, The Knot Book of Wedding Flowers, 2002, The Knot Complete Guide to Weddings in the Real World, 2003, The Knot Guide for the Groom, 2005, The Knot Guide for the Mother of the Bride, 2005; author: (foreword) Forever & a Day, 1999; author: (syndicated column) Ask Carley, 2003—; contbr.: NY Times, Wall St. Jour., USA Today, Glamour, Vogue, Elle, Self, Naples Daily News; appearances on Oprah, The View, ABC, Today Show, NBC, The Early Show, CBS. Achievements include The Knot named Best Wedding Hub 4 years in a row by Yahoo! Internet Life. Office: The Knot 6th Fl 462 Broadway New York NY 10013 Office Phone: 212-219-0724. Office Fax: 212-219-1929.

RONEY, JOHN M., lawyer; b. Sept. 21, 1939; m. Barbara Kennedy; children: Christopher, Carley, Kristina. BA, Providence Coll.; JD, Cath. U. Am.; degree (hon.), Katherine Gibbs Sch., 2002. Senator R.I. State Senate, 1994—2002; sr. staff atty. R.I. Legal Svcs., 1970—75; assoc. Winograd Shine & Zacks, PC, 1975—78; ptnr. Mann & Roney, 1978—83, Roney & Labinger LLP, Providence, 1983—. Dep. majority leader, vice chair fin., health, edn. welfare RI State Senate, parliamentarian, 2005—; commr. Uniform Law Commn., 2006—. Mem. Leadership R.I.; pres. RI Coun. on Alcoholism, 1990—93, Narragansett Bay Commn., 1996—2003; bd. dirs. Sophia Acad., 2003—, Katherine Gibbs Sch., 2002—04, RI Philharmonic, 1996—2001, Family Svc., Inc., 1973—90, pres., 1987—89; mem. neighborhood coun. Mayor, 2003—; mem. R.I. Commn. Women, 2000—03, R.I. Retirement Bd., 1998—2003. Recipient Dorothy Lohmann Cmty. Svc. award, 1995, Unsung Hero award, R.I. Assn. Developmentally Disabled Children, 1999, Bronze Key award, Nat. Coun. Alcoholism, 1999, Disting. Alumni award, Cath. U. Am., 2004. Mem.: R.I. Bar Assn. (v.p. 1999—2002, sec. 2000—01, pres.-elect 2002—03, pres. 2003—04, exec. com.), Fox Point Citizens Assn. (mem. bd. 1988—, pres. 2002—). Democrat. Office: Roney & Labinger LLP 344 Wickenden St Providence RI 02903 Office Phone: 401-421-9794.

RONEY, ROBERT KENNETH, retired aerospace transportation executive; b. Newton, Iowa, Aug. 5, 1922; s. Louie Earl and Hazel Iona (Cure) R.; m. Alice Lorraine Mann, Oct. 6, 1951; children: Stephen P., Karen Margaret Dahl. BSEE, U. Mo., 1944; MSEE, Calif. Inst. Tech., 1947, PhD, 1950. Engr. rsch. Jet Propulsion Lab. Calif. Inst. Tech., Pasadena, 1948-50, Hughes Aircraft Co., Culver City, Calif., 1950-54, mgr. sys. analysis, 1955-59, dir. tech. R&D, 1960, assoc. mgr. space sys. divsn., 1961-68, mgr. space sys. divsn., 1968-70, v.p. asst. group exec., 1970-85, sr. v.p. corp. tech., 1986-88, ret., 1988. Mem. adv. bd. Dept. Transp. Comml. Space Transp., 1984-87, Engring. Sch. U. Kans., 1988-91. Lt. (j.g.) USNR, 1944-46, PTO. Recipient Honor award for Disting. Svc. in Engring. U. Mo.-Columbia, 1979. Fellow IEEE; mem. NAE, Caltech Assocs. Home: 1105 Georgina Ave Santa Monica CA 90402-2027

RONSHAUSEN, NINA LORRAINE, retired mathematics professor, genealogist; b. LaCrofte, Ohio, Apr. 17, 1941; d. Elbert Jay Ronshausen and Helen Lorain Nichols. BS in Edn., Kent State U., Ohio, 1963; MS, Miami U., Oxford, Ohio, 1969; D of Edn., Ind. U., Bloomington, 1971. Provisional tchg. cert. Ohio, 1963. Project dir. math. tutorial project Ind. U., Bloomington, 1971—75; assoc. prof. Tex. Tech U., Lubbock, 1975—96, assoc. prof. emeritus; vis. prof. Wayland Bapt. U., Lubbock, 1985—92. Genealogist, Salem, Ohio, 1975—. Contbr. articles to profl. jours.; editor: (yearbook) Facilitating Evaluation: The Role of the Mathematics Supervisor. Grantee, NSF. Mem.: DAR, NEA, Nat. Coun. Suprs. Math. (chair nominations com., chmn. publs. com.), Nat. Coun. Tchrs. Math., First Families of Ohio, New Matamoras Hist. Soc. (life), Ohio Geneal. Soc., Alpha Lambda Delta, Kappa Delta Pi, Alpha Gamma Delta (life). Unitarian. Home: 12757 Lisbon Rd Salem OH 44460-9281 Home Phone: 330-533-4798.

RONSTADT, LINDA MARIE, singer; b. Tucson, July 15, 1946; d. Gilbert and Ruthmary (Copeman) R. Rec. artist numerous albums including Evergreen 1967, Evergreen Vol. 2, 1967, Linda Ronstadt, The Stone Poneys and Friends, Vol. 3, 1968, Hand Sown, Home Grown, 1969, Silk Purse, 1970, Linda Ronstadt, 1972, Don't Cry Now, 1973, Heart Like a Wheel, 1974, Different Drum, 1974, Prisoner In Disguise, 1975, Hasten Down the Wind, 1976, Greatest Hits, 1976, Simple Dreams, Blue Bayou, 1977, Living in the U.S.A., 1978, Mad Love, Greatest Hits Vol. II, 1980, Get Closer, 1982, What's New, 1983, Lush Life, 1984, For Sentimental Reasons, 1986, Trio (with Dolly Parton, Emmylou Harris), 1986, 'Round Midnight, 1987, Canciones de Mi Padre, 1987, Cry Like a Rainstorm-Howl Like the Wind, 1989, Mas Canciones, 1991, Frenesi, 1992, Winter Light, 1993, Feels Like Home, 1995, Dedicated to the One I Love, 1996, We Ran, 1998, Trio 2, 1999 (with Emmylou Harris & Dolly Parton), Western Wall: The Tucson Sessions (with Emmylou Harris), A Merry Little Christmas, 2000, Hummin' to Myself, 2004, Adieu False Heart, 2006; starred in Broadway prodn. of Pirates of Penzance, 1981, also in film, 1983, off Broadway as Mimi in La Boheme, 1984. Recipient Am. Music awards, 1978, 1979, Grammy awards, 1975, 1976, 1987 (with Emmylou Harris and Dolly Parton), 1988, 1989 (with Aaron Neville), 1990, 1991, (with Aaron Neville), 1992 (2), 1996, 2000, Acad. Country Music award, 1987, 1988; named one of 100 Greatest Women of Rock 'n' Roll, VH1, 1999. Office: Electra Records 75 Rockefeller Plz New York NY 10019-6908

ROOBOL, NORMAN RICHARD, chemistry professor, consultant; b. Grand Rapids, Mich., Aug. 19, 1934; s. Pleune and Henrietta (Sietsema) Roobol; m. Joan Lois Ezinga, Aug. 15, 1957; children: Kerri Linda, Michael Eric, Victoria May, Sara Elizabeth Angelique. BS, Calvin Coll., Grand Rapids, Mich., 1958; PhD in Organic Chemistry, Mich. State U., East Lansing, 1962. Rsch. chemist Shell Oil Co., Emeryville, Calif., 1962-65; asst. prof. chemistry GMI Engring. Inst., Flint, Mich., 1965-68, assoc. prof., asst. head dept. math., sci., 1968-72, prof., 1972-89; pres. NR Painting Cons. Co., Peachtree City, Ga., 1989—. Rhodes prof., Russelsheim, Germany, 1980—81; tchr. short courses paint; cons. coatings application processes; spkr. indsl. painting methods; painting advisor, instr. Outboard Marine Corp., 1986—2001, Bombardier Can., 1988—, Compaq-Asia, Singapore, 1991—, Harley-Davidson, 1992—, Metagal Comercie e Industri, San Paulo, Brazil, 1996—, Decometal S.A., Panama City, Panama, 1997—2001, J. R. McDermott Corp., Jebel Ali, 2000—; adj. prof. Kent State U., 1986—94, Okla. State U., 1994—98, U. Wis., 1992—2001; chmn. Peruvian Decorative & Protective Finishes Coun., 2005—. Author: (book) Painting Problems Solved, 1987, Industrial Paint and Powder Coating Principles and Practices, 3d edit., 2003; monthly columnist, tech. editor: Finishing Today Jour.; contbr. articles to profl. jours. Treas. Piedmont-Fayette Cmty. Hosp., Ga., bd. dirs. With Signal Corps US Army, 1954—56. Fellow Johnson, 1957—58, NSF, 1960—62, Dow, 1961—62. Fellow: Am. Inst. Chemists; mem.: AAUP, Assn. Finishings Proc. (v.p. profl. devel. coun.), Soc. Mfg. Engrs. (bd. dirs.), Am. Sci. Affiliation, Atlanta Oenophilic Soc., Pi Tau Sigma (chpt. sr. adviser 1979—86), Alpha Tau Omega, Sigma Xi. Achievements include patents in field. Home and Office: Powder Coating & Painting Cons 507 Haddington Ln Peachtree City GA 30269-3340 Personal E-mail: drpaint@consultant.com.

ROOD, CYNTHIA HOOPER, landscape architect, consultant; b. Columbus, Miss., Jan. 22, 1944; d. James Fullerton and Virginia Fite Hooper; children: Virginia Rood Pates, Amelia Gordon. BS in Landscape Architecture, U. Ga., Athens, 1966. Registered landscape arch. Miss., 1974, landscape designer, horticultural supr. Ala., 2005. Landscape arch., assoc. Olmsted Assocs., Landscape Archs., Brookline, Mass., 1966—67; budget and design US Naval Air Systems Command, Adak, Alaska, 1968—69; landscape arch. C. H. Rood, Landscape Arch., Columbus, Miss., 1969—. Pres. AMD, Inc., Columbus, 1990—; pres. Miss. chpt. Am. Soc. Landscape Archs., Jackson, 1991—92, dep. chmn. residential design com., Washington, 2002—03. Author: (articles) Miss. Dental Assn. Jour. Dir. Nat. Assn. Jr. Auxs., Greenville, Miss., 1983—86, 2007—, pres., 1984—85; mem. Nat. Assn. Colonial Dames Am., Washington, 1970—, Golden Triangle Regional Med. Ctr. Found., Columbus, 1986—90. Finalist, Nat. Merit Scholarship Found., 1962; recipient E. C. Martin scholarship award, U. Ga., 1962—66, Award of Excellence, Nat. Coun. Tchrs. English, 1962, Scholarship award, Alpha Zeta chpt. U. Ga., 1963, Queen of Pilgrimage Ball, Columbus Jr. Aux., 1966, Award of Merit, Miss. chpt. Am. Soc. Landscape Archs., 1989, Merit award, Associated Builders and Contractors, 1994, Award of Merit, Main St. Columbus, Inc., 1996. Mem.: Magowah Country Club (life), Chi Omega (life; state pres. 1985—86, Outstanding Chi Omega in Miss. 1985). Office: C H Rood Landscape Architect 800 Eighth St N Columbus MS 39701 Home Phone: 662-328-1816; Office Phone: 662-327-6498. E-mail: abraco@aol.com, chr@amddesign.com.

ROOD, DAVID S., linguistics educator; b. Albany, NY, Sept. 14, 1940; s. J. Henry and Pearl B. (Stanley) R.; m. Juliette A. Victor; 1 child, Jennifer. AB, Cornell U., 1963; MA, U. Calif., Berkeley, 1965; PhD, U. Calif., 1969. Instr. U. Colo., Boulder, 1967-69, asst. prof., 1969-77, assoc. prof., 1977-82, prof., 1982—; vis. prof. U. Köln, Germany, 1998-99. Author: Wichita Grammar, 1975, Siouan Languages Archive, 1982; (with others) Beginning Lakhota, 1976; editor Internat. Jour. of Am. Linguistics, 1981-2002, (with others) Linguistic Diversity and Language Theories, 2005; contbr. articles to profl. jours. Grantee, NSF, 1972—96, 2006—, NEH, 1972—96, Volkswagen Stiftung, 2000—05. Mem.: Tchrs. English to Speakers Other Langs., Soc. for Study Indigenous Langs. Am. (pres. 2004), Linguistic Soc. Am. Office: U Colo Dept Linguistics 295 UCB Boulder CO 80309-0295 Home Phone: 303-494-0558; Office Phone: 303-492-2747. Business E-Mail: rood@colorado.edu.

ROOD, JOHN C., federal agency administrator; b. 1968; BS in Economics, Ariz. State U., 1990. Analyst CIA, nonproliferation briefer; sr. policy adv. to Senator Jon Kyl US Senate, Ariz., 1997—2001; dir., Proliferation Strategy, Counterproliferation, and Homeland Def. NSC, 2001—03, spl. asst. to pres., sr. dir., Counterproliferation Strategy, 2005—06; dep. asst. sec. for forces policy US Def. Dept., 2003—05; asst. sec. for internat. security & nonproliferation US Dept. State, 2006—. Office: US Dept State 2201 C St NW Washington DC 20520

ROODMAN, DAVID A., lawyer; b. St. Louis, Apr. 17, 1962; BSME, U. Mo., 1984, JD, 1990. Bar: Mo., Ill., U.S. Dist. Ct. (ea. dist.) Mo., U.S. Patent and Trademark Office, U.s. Ct. Appeals (fed. cir.), U.S. Dist. Ct. (so. dist.) Ill. Mech. design engr. Unidynamics Corp., St. Louis, 1985; sales engr. Reliance Elec. Co., Kansas City, Mo., 1985-87; assoc. Bryan Cave LLP, St. Louis, 1990, ptnr., group co-leader Intellectual Property. Assoc. editor-in-chief Mo. Law Rev. Mem. ABA (intellectual property law sect., patent legislation com., litigation sect.), Mo. Bar Assn. (civil practice and procedure com., tech. and computer law com., patent, trademark and copyright law com.), Order of Coif, Order of Barristers. Office: Bryan Cave One Metropolitan Sq 211 N Broadway Saint Louis MO 63102-2733 Office Phone: 314-259-2000. Business E-Mail: daroodman@bryancave.com.

ROOF, JOSEPH A., educational association administrator; b. Kenton, Ohio, Sept. 30, 1950; s. Warren Thomas and Suzanne (Steiner) R.; m. Marilyn Roof, Jan. 19, 1974 (div.); 1 child, Brian. BA, Ohio No. U., 1972; MBA, U. So. Fla., 1982. Supr. admissions/records Edison CC, Ft. Myers, Fla., 1973—75, asst. dir. admissions/records, 1975—81, dir. admissions/records, 1981—84, Seminole CC, Sanford, Fla., 1984—87, dean admissions/records, 1987—2002; assoc. v.p. enrollment and student svcs. Daytona Beach CC, 2002—07; regional dir. Nat. Student Clearinghouse, Herndon, Va., 2007—. Mem. Goals 2000, Orlando C. of C., 1988-89; mem. edn. task force Seminole County Pub. Schs., Sanford, 1990—. Mem. So. Assn. Collegiate Registrars and Admissions Officers (v.p. registration 1989-91, treas. 1991—), Fla. Assn. Collegiate Registrars and Admissions Officers (pres. 1983-84), Fla. CC Registrars and Admissions Officers (chmn. 1989-90), Am. Assn. Collegiate Registrars and Admissions Officers (pres. 2005). Democrat. Methodist. Office: Nat Student Clearinghouse 13454 Sunrise Valley Dr Ste 300 Herndon VA 20171 *

ROOF, MICHAEL KITCHING, demographer, researcher; b. Lexington County, SC, Dec. 18, 1921; s. Michael Lowman and Eunice Ernestine (Kitching) R.; m. June Elizabeth Witmyer, July 24, 1949 (div. Sept. 1970); children: Michael Kitching Jr., Melanie June Roof Brown, Brian Eugene; m. Kristina Marietta Medrano, Dec. 18, 1976. Student, Am. U., Washington, DC, 1954—57; BA, George Washington U., Washington, DC, 1956; postgrad., US Dept. Agr. Grad. Sch., 1979—83. Manpower specialist Office of Prodn. Mgmt. and War Prodn. Bd., Washington, 1941—46; labor editor Bur. Nat. Affairs, Inc., Washington, 1947—48; demographer rsch. divsn. ref. svc. Libr. Congress, Washington, 1949—64; sr. demographer fgn. manpower rsch. office U.S. Bur. Census, Suitland, Md., 1958—59, expert demographic cons. fgn. manpower rsch. office, 1960—61, demographer, statistician Ctr. Internat. Studies, 1977—89; ret., 1989; cons. on demography to various orgns., 1965—76. Author: (monograph) Demography and Family Planning in Iran, 1971-72: Final Report to the U.N., (mongraph) Angelenos on the Move: 1960-74, 1975, (mongraph) Detailed Statistics on the Population of Israel, 1950-84, with Projections to 2010, 1984, (monograph) Jordan Population and Manpower Estimates and Projections: 1979 to 2010, 1987; co-author: (monograph) Detailed Statistics on the Population of Turkey, 1950-82, with Projections to 2000, 1982, (monograph) Palestinian Population: 1950-84, 1985, The Roof (Rueff, Ruff) Family and Kinfolk of Central South Carolina: 1748-1999, 1999, The Roof-Ruff Family of South Carolina: 1748-, 2002; contbr. numerous articles to profl. jours., chpts. to books. Mem. Population Assn. Am., Internat. Union Scientific Study of Population. Democrat. Lutheran. Avocations: genealogy, aerobics, swimming, softball. Home: 306 E Custis Ave Alexandria VA 22301-1202 Personal E-mail: michaelroof@comcast.net.

ROOF, ROBERT L., broadcast executive, sales executive; b. Circleville, Ohio, Apr. 15, 1946; s. Roger D. and Doris (Kraft) R.; m. Linda Anderson, Nov. 28, 1969; children: Jennifer, Leslie. BA, Franklin U. Sales, disc jockey Sta. WPKO Radio, Waverly, Ohio, 1969-72, Sta. WSCR Radio, Scranton, Pa., 1972-75; sales Sta. WSPD Radio, Toledo, Ohio, 1975-78, Sta. WTVN Radio, Columbus, Ohio, 1978-81, local sales mgr., 1981-83, gen. sales mgr., 1984-87; v.p., gen. mgr. Sta. WDVE Radio, Pitts., 1987-93, pres., gen. mgr., 1993—. Bd. dirs. Southwest PA Jr. Achievement, Pitts., 1994—. Recipient Bronze Leadership award Jr. Achievement, Pitts., 1994. Mem. Columbus Sales Club (pres. 1982), Pitts. Sales Club (pres. 1989), Pitts. Radio Orgn. (pres. 1994). Methodist. Avocations: golf, hunting, history. Office: Sta WDVE-FM 200 Fleet St Pittsburgh PA 15220-2908

ROOF, SALLY JEAN-MARIE, library and information scientist, educator; b. Cleve., Dec. 29, 1947; d. James William and Marie Monreal Roof; m. Christian John Hoffmann III, Sept. 22, 1973; children: Christian Graham Hoffmann, Joscelyn Nicole Hoffmann, Gavin Leigh Hoffmann. BA in English Lit., Dunbarton Coll. of Holy Cross, DC, 1969; MS in Libr. and Info. Sci., Cath. U. of Am., 1972; degree in Profl. Mgmt. (hon.), Miami U., 1976; MA in Elem. Edn., No. Ariz. U., 2001. Cert. tchr. in libr. media ctr. adminstrn. Nat. Bd. of Cert. Tchrs., 2004. Asst. libr. U.S. Postal Svc. Libr., Washington, 1971—72; head of acquisitions George Wash. U. Libr., Washington, 1972—74; libr. adminstr. and mgr. Calgon Corp. Libr. Merck Inc., Pitts., 1974—77; libr. info. specialist U. of Phoenix, 1979—81; reference libr. Grand Canyon U., Phoenix, 1990—91; reference libr. West Campus Libr. Ariz. State U., Phoenix, 1994—95; libr. tchr. info. specialist Madison Meadows Sch., Phoenix, 1998—. Libr. cons. U. of Phoenix, 1981—82; presenter Ariz. Libr. Assn., Scottsdale, 2003; mem., presenter People to People Amb. Program Children's Lit. Del., Spokane, Wash., 2004; participant rep., 04; cons. in field. Editor: Serial Titles in the Washington, D. C. University Consortium Libraries, No School Left Behind at Your Library. Librarians Meet Arizona Legislators, 2004; author: (pamphlet) Madison Meadows Library Media Center; designer (school website) Madison Meadows Sch. website. Chmn. grade level patroness Nat. Charity League, Phoenix, 1994—99; pres. Phoenix (Ariz.) Mus. of History, 1991—94. Mem.: ALA (assoc.), Ariz. Libr. Assn. (assoc.), Phi Kappa Phi, Beta Phi Mu, Jr. League of Phoenix. Democrat-Npl. Roman Catholic. Avocations: yoga, fast walking, reading, bicycling. Office: Madison Meadows School 225 W Ocotillo Rd Phoenix AZ 85013 Office Phone: 602-664-7640. Personal E-mail: sroofhoff@cox.net. E-mail: sroof@msd38.org.

ROOK, JUDITH RAWIE, television producer, writer; d. Wilmer Ernest and Margaret Jane (Towle) Rawie; m. Dr. John Holland, 1964 (div. 1978); children: Daryn Simons, Dawn Reinard; m. Tim Rook, 1993. BA, Loyola-Marymount Univ., 1964; postgrad., U. Calif., San Diego, 1978. Syndicated columnist Environ. Forum, 1971-74; dir. video IABC, San Francisco, 1982; dir. programming Westinghouse Cable, 1983-85; dir. devel. Embassy/Nelson Home Entertainment, 1985-87; ptnr. Real Magic, 1987-89; prodr., writer, ptnr. BrantHol Prodns., 1990-93; co-sponsorship Beetle Juice, The Last Emperor, 1987—89; founder, pres. R2 Group, 1990—. Assoc. dir.: (off-broadway play) Arms and the Man, 1967; The Man Who Came to Dinner, 1981; exec. prodr.: Neighborhood Without Bars (Emmy award, 1986); prodr., writer: PBS series Focus, 1980; Achieving, 1982 (Emmy award, ACE nominee, PBS nominee); NBC pilot Christmas Comes to Silverton, 1990—93; CNN pilot Clever Encounters, 1991; prodr.: One Creative Moment, 1992, Close up: The 60s, 1995—97; assoc. prodr.: Fox Latin Am. Billboard Music Awards, 1998—2000; (TV pilot) Fempresario, 2005; assoc. prodr. (documentaries) Rising Revisited, 2005, (films) Somewhere in Between, 2005; playwright: Theatre 40 Writer's Workshop Anniversary for Three, 2003; assoc. prodr.: (films) Highway 101, 2005—. Mem. adv. bd. U. Calif. Irvine Screenwriting/Film Prodn., 1996-2000; mem. adv. bd. Univ. Art Mus., 1996-97, co-pres. contemporary coun., 1996-97; mem. exec. bd. Long Beach Mus. Art, 1995-96; bd. dirs. Counseling 4 Kids, 1998-2005, bd. sec., 2001-2005; editor, bd. LWV, Santa Monica, 2004-05, Getty Mus., 2005-. Mem. Am. Film Inst., Women in Film (dir. seminars on women in film), IFP West. Democrat. Episcopalian. Office Phone: 310-633-3292. Personal E-mail: tirook@earthlink.net.

ROOK, VICKI LYNN, safety specialist; b. Denton, Tex., Oct. 14, 1954; d. Lonzo Lester and Myrtle Jodelle Roberts; m. Rickey Hugh Rook, Jan. 27, 1979; children: Brandon Nicholas, Katy Lynn Student, Richland Jr. Coll., Dallas, 1974-75. Safety supr. United Parcel Svc., Dallas, 1975-81; pers., safety adminstr. Boeing Airport Equipment, Carrollton, Tex., 1981-83; safety rep. Loral Vought Sys. Corp., Grand Prairie, Tex., 1983-95; sr. safety specialist Fed. Express Corp., Dallas, 1995—. Mem. workers comp claims mgmt. various cos., Dallas, 1975—; mgr. union contract negotiation Boeing Airport Equipment, Dallas, 1983; com. mem. mgmt. safety program tng. Fed. Express, Memphis, 1997-2001 Tchr. Sunday sch. Walnut Ridge Bapt. Ch., Mansfield, Tex., 1997-2001, 1st Bapt. Ch., Grand Prairie, 1980-82, counselor ch. camp, 1980-82; vol. ednl. TV Loral Vought Sys., Dallas, 1993. Named Safety Specialist of Yr. Fed. Express, 1997. Mem. Am. Soc. Safety Engineers, Nat. Safety Coun. Republican. Office Phone: 469-524-4623. Business E-Mail: vlrook@fedex.com.

ROOKLIDGE, WILLIAM CHARLES, lawyer; b. Portland, Oreg., Aug. 10, 1957; s. Chester Herbert and Barbara Kathryn (Dodson) R.; m. Kathryn Elaine Roosa, Aug. 20, 1983; children: Elizabeth Jill, Matthew Joseph. BS, U. Portland, 1979; JD, Lewis & Clark, 1984; LLM, George Washington U., 1985. Bar: Oreg. 1985, U.S. Patent Office 1985, U.S. Ct. Appeals (fed. cir.) 1985, Calif. 1988, U.S. Ct. Appeals (9th cir.) 1988, U.S. Supreme Ct. 1993. Engr. Tube Forgings Am., Inc., Portland, 1978-82; jud. clk. U.S. Ct.

Appeals (fed. cir.), Washington, 1985-87; assoc. Knobbe, Martens, Olson & Bear, Newport Beach, Calif., 1987-89, ptnr., 1990-94; dir. Howard, Rice, Nemerovski, Canady, Falk & Rabkin, Newport Beach, Calif., 1995—2000. Contbr. articles to profl. jours. Recipient Joseph Rossman Meml. award Patent & Trademark Office Soc., 1988, Gerald Rose Meml. award John Marshall Law Sch., 1993. Mem. ABA (sect. intellectual property law, com. chair 1992-96), Am. Intellectual Property Law Assn. (com. chair 1988-93, dir. 1995-98, pres. 2005, Robert C. Watson award 1987), Orange County Patent Law Assn. (bd. dirs. 1990-93, pres. 1994). Republican. Presbyterian. Office: Howrey LLP 2020 Main St Ste 1000 Irvine CA 92614-8224 Office Phone: 949-759-3904. Office Fax: 949-721-6910. Business E-Mail: rooklidgew@howrey.com.

ROOKS, CHARLES S., foundation administrator; b. Whiteville, NC, June 29, 1937; BA in English, Wake Forest Coll., 1959; Rockefeller Brothers fellow, Harvard U., 1959-60; MA in Polit. Sci., Duke U., 1964, PhD in Polit. Sci., 1968. Rsch. assoc. Voter Edn. Project, Atlanta, 1969-70, dir. tech. assistance programs, 1970-71, dep. dir., 1971-72; exec. dir. Southeastern Coun. of Founds., Atlanta, 1972-78; dir. mem. svcs. Coun. on Founds., Washington, 1979-80, v.p., 1981-82, acting CEO, 1981-82; exec. dir. Meyer Meml. Trust, Portland, Oreg., 1982—2002, Miller Found., 2007. Instr. polit. sci. Duke U., Durham, N.C., 1963, 65-67; asst. prof. of govt. Lake Forest Coll., Ill., 1967-69; asst. prof. polit. sci. Clark Coll., Atlanta, 1969-71; bd. dirs. Pacific Northwest Grantmakers Forum, Forum of Regional Assns. of Grantmakers; mem. adv. bd. Neighborhood Partnership Fund (Oreg. Cmty. Found.); mem., adv. bd. Giving in Oreg. Coun.; co-chair Northwest Giving Project; bd. mem. Oreg. Coll. Art and Craft; spl. advisor Oreg. Cultural Trust. Contbr. articles to profl. jours. Home: 2706 SW English Ct Portland OR 97201-1622 Personal E-mail: charlesrookspdx@hotmail.com.

ROOKS, GEORGE MALCOLM, writer, educator, small business owner; b. Anderson, SC, Mar. 5, 1951; s. George and Miriam (Bailey) R.; divorced, 1983; children: George, Brendan; m. Hila Zizov, Feb. 1, 1983; children; Kanon, Maayan. BA in English, U. Ga., 1973; MA in English, U. Calif., Davis, 1975. Mem. faculty U. Calif., Davis., 1976—; owner, CEO Teletext Corp., 1989—. Author: The Book of Losers, 1980, The Nonstop Discussion Workbook!, 1980, 2d edit., 1988, Can't Stop Talking, 1981, 2d edit., 1988, Share Your Paragraph, 1988, 2d edit., 1995, Paragraph Power, 1988, Beat the TOEFL: A Video-Workbook-Computer Series, 1990, videotape, 2006, Let's Start Talking, 1990, Power TOEFL Deluxe CD Rom and Workbook, 1998, Power 3000 Grammar Review CD rom, 2001, TOEIC Test Master CD Rom, 2001, Power TOEFL Listening CD Rom with Listening Scripts, 2001, The Ttext Word Frequency CD Rom Dictionary for the TOEIC Test, 2003, (DVD) Understanding the New TOEFL Test, 2005; (with others) Conversar Sin Parar, 1981, Conversations San Fin, 1982, Was Sagen Sie Dazu?, 1983, Japanese Listening and Grammar Exercises for TOEFL, 1996; editor: Vocabulary Enrichment for ESL Students (15 disks), 1994, Grammar Enrichment for ESL Students (9 disks), 1994; contbr. articles to profl. jours. Mem. Calif. Tchrs. ESL, Zionist Orgn. Am. Avocations: tennis, travel. Address: 10 Sara Emanu Tet Vav 77724 Ashdod Israel Office: 710 Valencia Ave Davis CA 95616-0153 Office Phone: 866-862-6420.

ROOKS, JOHN NEWTON, lawyer; b. Evanston, Ill., Jan. 7, 1948; s. R. Newton and Ruth Dunlop (Darling) R.; m. Mary Preston Noell, Sept. 15, 1973; children: John Newton, Thomas N. BA, DePauw U., 1970; JD, Washington U., 1973. Bar: Ill. 1973, U.S. Dist. Ct. (no. dist.) Ill. 1973. Corp. atty. No. Trust Co., Chgo., 1973—76; ptnr. Hynds, Rooks, Yohnka & Bzdill, Morris, Ill., 1976—. Chmn. bd. dirs. ARC, Morris, 1980-82, adv. com., 1996-97; adminstrv. coun. 1st United Meth. Ch., Morris, 1985-86; trustee, 1982-84; citizens adv. com. Morris Cmty. H.S., 1984-87; bd. dirs. Morris Elem. Sch. Dist. 54, 1987-91, 95; bd. dirs. Morris Downtown Devel. Partnership, Inc., 1996—, v.p., 1996-2000, pres., 2000-03; sec.-treas. Morris Progress, LLC, 1997-2004. Mem. ABA, Ill. Bar Assn., Chgo. Bar Assn., Grundy County Bar Assn. (pres. 1983-84), Grundy County C. of C. (chmn. bd. 1982). Republican. Methodist. Office: Hynds Rooks Yohnka & Bzdill PO Box 685 Morris IL 60450-0685 Home: 1064 Forest View Dr Morris IL 60450 Office Phone: 815-942-0049. Business E-Mail: jnr@hrymb.com.

ROOKS, LINDA, writer; d. Harold John and Marianna Wieck; m. Marvin Edward Rooks, Dec. 19, 1967; children: Juliana Wolf, Laura Katherine Voorhees. BA, San Francisco State U., 1965. Tchr. Seminole Jr. H.S., Fla., 1970—72; pro-life liaison for Paula Hawkins senatorial campaign Nat. Right to Life, Winter Park, Fla., 1986; asst. editor Ctr. Stage Mag., Maitland, Fla., 1987—89; office coord., newsletter editor Adoption by Shepherd Care, Orlando, Fla., 1994—2000; freelance writer Maitland, 2000—. Author: Broken Heart on Hold, 2006, (devotional) Tapestry; scriptwriter: radio and tv Testimony of An Unborn Child (Cammeo Award for Best of Show, 1987); contbr. articles to profl. jours., chapters to books. Pres. Ctrl. Fla. Right to Life, 1984—85, 1990—96; staff position state coord. for families Bob Dole Presdl. Campaign, Fla., 1995—96; pub. rels. co-chmn. Nat. Right to Life Conv., Orlando, 1983. Mem.: Word Weavers Writers Group (sec. steering com. 2002—). Republican. Avocation: travel. Office: PO Box 241 Winter Park FL 32790-0241 Personal E-mail: linda@brokenheartonhold.com.

ROONEY, ANDREW AITKEN, writer, journalist; b. Albany, NY, Jan. 14, 1919; s. Walter S. and Ellinor (Reynolds) R.; m. Marguerite Howard, Mar. 21, 1942; children: Ellen, Martha, Emily, Brian. Student, Colgate U., 1942. Writer-producer CBS-TV News, 1959—; newspaper columnist Tribune Co. Syndicate, 1979—. Author: (with O.C. Hutton) Air Gunner, 1944, The Story of Stars and Stripes, 1946, Conquerors' Peace, 1947, The Fortunes of War, 1962, A Few Minutes with Andy Rooney, 1981, And More By Andy Rooney, 1982, Pieces of My Mind, 1984, Word for Word, 1986, Not That You Asked, 1989, Sweet and Sour, 1992, My War, 1995, Sincerely, Andy Rooney, 1999, Common Nonsense, 2002, Years of Minutes, 2003; TV programs include An Essay on War, Mr. Rooney Goes to Washington, Mr. Rooney Goes to Dinner; regular commentator-essayist: 60 Minutes, 1978—. Served with AUS, 1941-45. Decorated Air Medal, Bronze Star.; recipient awards for best written TV documentary Writers Guild Am., 1966, 68, 71, 75, 76, Emmy awards, 1968, 78, 81, 82

ROONEY, DANIEL M., professional sports team executive; b. Pitts., July 20, 1932; s. Arthur Joseph and Kathleen (McNulty) Rooney; m. Patricia Rooney; 9 children. BA in Acctg., Duquesne U., Pitts., 1955. Salesman advt., editor, other positions Pitts. Steelers Program, 1955—75; pres. to chmn. Pitts. Steelers, 1975—; mem. exec. coms. NFL. Bd. dir. United Way of Am., Am. Ireland Fund, Am. Diabetes Assn., Presbyn. U. Hosp., Pitts. History and Landmarks Found., Duquesne U. Recipient Reds Bagnell award for Outstanding Contbns. to the Game of Football, Maxwell Football Club, 1999. Achievements include presented with Vince Lombardi Trophy for the winning team, Pittsburgh Steelers at Super Bowl XL in 2006. Office: Pitts Steelers Three Rivers Stadium 3400 S Water St Pittsburgh PA 15203-2349 Office Phone: 412-323-1200. *

ROONEY, FRANCIS, ambassador; married; 3 children. AB, Georgetown U., 1975, JD, 1978. Bar: DC, Tex.; 100-Ton Master's Lic. U.S. Coast Guard. CEO Rooney Holdings, Inc., Naples, Fla.; US amb. to Holy See US Dept. State, Vatican City, 2005—. Vice-chmn. Okla. Turnpike Authority; dir. Okla. Capital Investment Bd.; dir. 20/20 com., Wash. adv. coun. Ctr. Strategic and Internat. Studies, Washington; officer Tex. Bus. Hall of Fame, Houston; dir. Inst. Nautical Archaeology, College Station, Tex., Young President's Orgn., 1992—98, internat. pres., 1997—98. Bd. dirs., chmn. strategic planning com. St. Francis Health Sys., Okla.; chmn. bd. Cascia Hall Preparatory Sch., Tulsa; mem. sch. of architecture coun. U. Notre Dame; mem. Fla. Coun. 100. Mem.: Sovereign Mil. Order of Malta. Office: Am Embassy 5660 Vatican City Pl Washington DC 20521

ROONEY, JOE DON, country musician; b. Baxter Springs, Kans., Sept. 13, 1975; s. Windell and Jo Rooney. Student, A&M Jr. Coll. (Northwestern Okla. A&M). Performer Printers Alley, Nashville, Chely Wright Band; guitarist Rascal Flatts, 2000—. Musician: (albums) East to West, 1993, Rascal Flatts, 2000, Melt, 2002, Feels Like Today, 2004 (Group/Duo Video of Yr., Country Music Television Music awards, 2005), Me and My Gang, 2006; performer: (songs) "Walk the Llama Llama", Emperor's New Grove (Original Soundtrack), 2000. Recipient Vocal Group Yr., Country Music Assn., 2002, 2004—06, Song Yr. for "I'm Movin On", Acad. Country Music Awards, 2002, Top Vocal Group, 2003, 2005—07, Country Song Yr. for Bless the Broken Road, Radio Music Awards, 2005, Best Country Song, Grammy Awards, 2006, Group/Duo Video of Yr. for Skin (Sarabeth), Country Music TV Awards, 2006, Group Video of Yr. for What Hurts the Most, 2007, Favorite Country Band, Am. Music Awards, 2006, Favorite Song from a movie & Favorite Remake-Life is a Highway, People's Choice Awards, 2007. Office: Lyric Street Records 1100 Demonbreun St Nashville TN 37203-3108 Office Phone: 615-963-4848. *

ROONEY, JOHN EDWARD, communications company executive; b. Evergreen Park, Ill., Apr. 24, 1942; s. John Edward and Margaret Wilma (Stolte) R.; m. Germaine Rose Dettloff, June 26, 1965; children: Kathleen, John, Colleen. BS, John Carroll U., 1964; MBA, Loyola U., 1969. Credit analyst Fed. Res. Bank, Chgo., 1964-69, adminstrv. asst., 1969-70; asst. treas. Pullman Inc., 1970-73, asst. contr., 1973-78; v.p. fin. Pullman Standard, 1978-79; sr. v.p. fin. Trailmobile, Chgo., 1979-81; treas. Firestone Tire & Rubber Co., Akron, Ohio, 1981-87, v.p. retail fin. services, 1987-88, sr. v.p. MasterCare Svc. Ctrs., 1988-90; v.p., treas. Ameritech, Chgo., 1990-92; pres. Ameritech Cellular Svcs., Chgo., 1992—. Instr. fin. Ill. Benedictine Coll., 1975-80 Mem. Ohio Mfrs. Assn. (trustee 1983-87), Ohio Pub. Expenditure Coun. (trustee 1986-87), Glen Oak Country Club (Glen Ellyn, Ill.), Boulders Club (Carefree, Ariz.), The Tavern Club (Chgo.). Home: 2S 311 Davis Ct Wheaton IL 60187 Office: Ameritech # 3H 70 2000 W Ameritech Center Dr Hoffman Estates IL 60196-1025

ROONEY, JOHN PHILIP, law educator; b. Evanston, Ill., May 1, 1932; s. John McCaffery and Bernadette Marie (O'Brien) R.; m. Jean Marie Kliss, Feb. 16, 1974 (div. Oct. 1988); 1 child, Caitlin Mairin. BA, U. Ill, 1953; JD, Harvard U., 1958. Bar: Ill. 1958, Calif. 1961, Mich. 1975, U.S. Tax Ct. 1973. Assoc. lawyer Chapman & Cutler, Chgo., 1958-60, Wilson, Morton, San Mateo, Calif., 1961-63; pvt. practice San Francisco, 1963-74; prof. law Cooley Law Sch., Lansing, Mich., 1975—. Author: Selected Cases (Property), 1985; contbr. articles to profl. jours. Pres. San Francisco coun. Dem. Clubs, 1970. 1st lt. U.S. Army, 1953-55. Recipient Beattie Teaching award Cooley Law Sch. Grads., 1979, 90, 92. Fellow Mich. Bar Found.; mem. ABA (real estate fed. tax problems com., title ins. com.), Ingham County Bar Assn., Univ. Club. Democrat. Unitarian Universalist. Office: Cooley Law Sch 300 S Capitol Ave Lansing MI 48933-1586 Office Phone: 517-371-5140. Business E-Mail: rooneyj@cooley.edu.

ROONEY, KEVIN DAVITT, federal agency administrator; b. Springfield, Mass., June 23, 1944; s. Davitt Michael and Elizabeth Isabel (Wlodyka) R.; m. Annette Eloise Benevento, Nov. 11, 1972; children: Kathryn Denise, Mary Elizabeth. BA, St. Marys Coll., 1966; JD, George Washington U., 1975. Bar: Va. 1975, D.C. 1977. Computer systems analyst VA, Washington, 1967-68, 70-73; chief legal programs & budget US Dept. Justice, Washington, 1973-77, exec. asst. to assoc. atty. gen., 1977, asst. atty. gen. for adminstrn., 1977-84; prin. Rooney & Assocs, Washington, 1984-87, 90-94, Rooney & Barry, Washington, 1987-89; assoc. dir. Exec. Office for Immigration Rev. US Dept. Justice, Falls Church, Va., 1995-97, asst. dir. Fed. Bur. Prisons Washington, 1997-99, dir. Exec. Office for Immigration Rev. Falls Church, Va., 1999—, acting commr. Immigration and Naturalization Svc., 2001. Bd. dirs., v.p. Joint Action in Cmty. Svcs., Inc., Washington, 1988-94. With U.S. Army, 1968-70. Mem. ASPA, Fed. Bar Assn., Va. Bar Assn., D.C. Bar Assn. Office: Executive Office for Immigration Review 5107 Leesburg Pike Falls Church VA 22041

ROONEY, LAURENCE FRANCIS, III, ambassador to the Vatican, construction executive; b. Dec. 4, 1953; m. Kathleen Rooney; 3 children. AB, Georgetown U., 1975, JD, 1978. CEO Rooney Bros., Tulsa, Okla.; CEO, chmn. Rooney Holdings, Naples, Fla.; US ambassador to The Holy See, 2005—. Bd. dirs. BOL Fin. Corp., NASDAQ, Helmerich and Payne, Inc., NY Stock Exch., Cimarex Energy Co.; vice chmn. Okla. Turnpike Authority; dir. Okla. Capital Investment Bd., 20/20 com., Wash. Advisory Coun. Ctr. for Strategic and Internat. Studies; transition team for gov. elect Brad Henry State of Okla.; bd. advisors Panama Canal Authority Republic of Panama. Mem. Sch. of Architecture Coun. U. of Notre Dame; mem. Sovereign Military Order of Malta (Fed. Assn.). Mem.: Young President's Org. (dir. 1992—98, internat. pres. 1997—98). Republican. Roman Catholic. Office: Rooney Bros 111 W 5th St Ste 1000 Tulsa OK 74103-4264 also: Am Embassy to the Holy See via delle Terme Deciane 26 00153 Rome Italy Office Phone: (39) 06-4674-3428. Office Fax: (39) 06-575-8346.

ROONEY, MARIA DEWING, photographer; b. NYC, July 25; d. Madeleine L'Engle Franklin; m. John Bryan Rooney, Jan. 21, 1984; children: Bryson, Alexander. BFA, Phila. Coll. Art. Tchr. photography Bishop Bright Grammar Sch., Leamington Spa, Eng., Mid-Warwickshire Sch. of Further Edn., Leamington Spa, 1976-80; photographer, owner The Studios, Shipston-on-Stour, Eng., 1977-80; photographer Gary Studios & Comini Studios, Dallas, 1980-83; pvt. practice Mystic, Conn., 1990—. One-woman shows include Emporium Gallery, 2004, exhibitions include Warwick (Eng.) Gallery, Derby (Eng.) Coll. Art Gallery, Bath (Eng.) Pl. Cmty. Ctr., Midland Group Galley, Nottingham, Eng., Wimbledon Sch. Art, London, Warwich U. Arts Ctr., Birmingham, Eng., Essex Art Assn., 1998, R. J. Julia, Madison, Conn., 1998, State Capitol Hartford, Conn., 1999, Emporium Gallery, 2003, Brick Gallery, Essex, Conn., 2003, 2004, Emporium Gallery, 2004, Mystic Art Ctr., 2005; contbr. photographs Anytime Prayers, 1994, Mothers and Daughters, 1997, Mothers and Sons, 1999, photographs published in Co-Optic Publs., London, 1976—80; prodr.: series greeting cards with personal photography. Mem. Child and Family Svcs. Mem.: AAUW, Mystic Art Assn., Essex Art Assn. (photography award 1997, 2002, 2003). Avocations: sailing, writing. Home and Office: 77 High St Mystic CT 06355 Office Phone: 860-884-7582. E-mail: vlad0121@aol.com.

ROONEY, MATTHEW A., lawyer; b. Jersey City, May 19, 1949; s. Charles John and Eileen (Dunphy) R.; m. Jean M. Alletag, June 20, 1973 (div. Dec. 1979); 1 child, Jessica Margaret; m. Diane S. Kaplan, July 6, 1981; children: Kathryn Olivia, S. Benjamin. AB magna cum laude, Georgetown U., 1971; JD with honors, U. Chgo., 1974. Bar: Ill. 1975, U.S. Dist. Ct. (no. dist.) Ill. 1975, U.S. Ct. Appeals (7th cir.). 1990. Law clk. to cir. judge US Ct. Appeals (7th cir.), Chgo., 1974-75; assoc. Mayer, Brown, Rowe & Maw LLP, Chgo., 1975-80, ptnr., 1981—. Assoc. editor U. Chgo. Law Rev., 1973. Fellow Am. Coll. Trial Lawyers; mem. ABA, 7th Cir. Bar Assn., Order of Coif, Phi Beta Kappa. Democrat. Roman Catholic. Avocations: jogging, golf. Home: 2718 Sheridan Rd Evanston IL 60201-1754 Office: Mayer Brown Rowe & Maw LLP 71 S Wacker Dr Chicago IL 60606-4637 Office Phone: 312-702-7279. Business E-Mail: mrooney@mayerbrownrowe.com.

ROONEY, MICKEY (JOE YULE JR.), actor; b. Bklyn., Sept. 23, 1920; s. Joe and Nell (Carter) Yule; m. Ava Gardner, Jan. 10, 1942 (div. May 1943); m. Betty Jane Rase, Sept. 30, 1944 (div. 1949); children: Mickey Jr., Timothy (dec. 2006); m. Martha Vickers, June 3, 1949 (div.); m. Elaine Mahnken (div. 1958); m. Barbara Thomason, Dec. 1958; children: Kerry, Kyle, Kelly Ann, Kimmy Sue; m. Margie Lang, Sept. 1966 (div. 1967); m. Carolyn Hockett, (div.); 1 adopted child, Jimmy, 1 child, Jonell; m. Jan Chamberlin, July 28, 1978; stepchildren: Chris Aber, Mark Aber. Student, Pacific Mil. Acad. First appeared in vaudeville with parents; then appeared with Sid Gould, numerous TV programs; appeared in motion pictures Judge Hardy's Children, Hold That Kiss, Lord Jeff, Love Finds Andy Hardy, Boys Town, Stablemates, Out West With the Hardys, Huckleberry Finn, Andy Hardy Gets Spring Fever, Babes in Arms, Young Tom Edison, Judge Hardy and Son, Andy Hardy Meets Debutante, Strike Up the Band, Andy Hardy's Private Secretary, Men of Boystown, Life Begins for Andy Hardy, Babes on Broadway, A Yank at Eton, The Human Comedy, Andy Hardy's Blonde Trouble, Girl Crazy, Thousands Cheer, National Velvet, Ziegfeld Follies, The Strip, Sound Off, Off Limits, All Ashore, Light Case of Larceny, Drive A Crooked Road, Bridges at Toko-Ri, The Bold and Brave, Eddie, Private Lives of Adam and Eve, Comedian, The Grabbers, St. Joseph Plays the Horses, Breakfast at Tiffany's, Somebody's Waiting, Requiem For A Heavyweight, Richard, Pulp, It's a Mad, Mad, Mad, Mad World, Everything's Ducky, The Secret Invasion, The Extraordinary Seaman, The Comic, The Cockeyed Cowboys of Calico County, Skidoo, B.J. Presents, That's Entertainment, The Domino Principle, Pete's Dragon, The Magic of Lassie, Black Stallion, Arabian Adventure, Erik the Viking, My Heroes Have Always Been Cowboys, 1991, (voice) Little Nimo: Adventures in Slumberland, 1992, Long Road Home, 1996, Kings of the Court, 1997, Animals, 1997, Babe: Pig in the City, 1998, Internet Love, 1998, The First of May, 1999, (voice) Lady and the Tramp II: Scamps Adventure, 2001, Topa Topa Bluffs, 2002; starred in TV prodns. Pinocchio, 1957, Leave 'Em Laughing, 1981, Bill, 1981 (Emmy, Golden Globe), Senior Trip!, 1981, Bill on His Own, 1983, Little Spies (Acad. Hon. award 1982), It Came upon the Midnight Clear, 1984, Bluegrass, 1988, Legend of Wolf Mountain, 1992, That's Entertainment! III, 1994, Revente of the Red Baron, 1994, Radio Star-die AFN-Story, 1994, The Legend of O.B. Taggart, 1995; appeared on stage in Sugar Babies, 1979, The Will Rogers Follies, 1993; appeared in TV series A Year at the Top, The Mickey Rooney Show; author: I.E. An Autobiography, 1965, Life Is Too Short, 1991, Search for Sonny Skies, 1994, Brother's Destiny (T.V.), 1995, Michael Kael in Katango, 1997, Boys Will be Boys, 1997, Sinbad: The Battle of the Dark Knights, 1998, The First of May, 1998, The Face on the Barroom Floor, 1998, Babe: Pig in the City, 1998; fgn. films: Midsummer Nights Dream, 1937, Words and Music, 1946, Rachels, 1973, To Hong Kong with Love, 1975, Oddessy of the Pacific, 1979. With AUS, WWII. Recipient Spl. Acad. Award, 1940, Tony award for best mus. actor, 1980; named One of Top 10 Money-Making Stars, Herald-Fame Poll, 1938-43 Office: PO Box 3186 Thousand Oaks CA 91359-0186

ROONEY, PAUL C., JR., retired lawyer; b. Winnetka, Ill., Oct. 23, 1943; s. Paul C. and Mary K. (Brennan) R.; m. Maria Elena Del Canto, Sept. 6, 1980. BA, Harvard U., 1963, LLB, 1966. Bar: Mass. 1968, N.Y. 1972, Fla. 1980, U.S. Dist. Ct. (ea. and so. dists.) N.Y., U.S. Ct. Appeals (2d cir.). Ptnr. White & Case, NYC, 1983-98, ret., 1998. Served to lt. USNR, 1966-69. Mem. Fla. Bar Assn., Univ. Club (N.Y.C.), Mashomack Preserve (N.Y.), Sharon Country Club (Conn.). Home: 11 Lilac Ln PO Box 271 Sharon CT 06069-0271 Office: White & Case 1155 Avenue Of The Americas New York NY 10036-2787 Office Phone: 212-819-8200.

ROONEY, PAUL GEORGE, mathematics professor; b. NYC, July 14, 1925; s. Geoffrey Daniel and Doris Elizabeth (Babcock) R.; m. Mary Elizabeth Carlisle, June 20, 1950; children: Francis Timothy, Elizabeth Anne, Kathleen Doris, John Edward, James Carlisle. B.Sc., U. Alta., 1949; PhD, Calif. Inst. Tech., 1952. Asst. prof. math. U. Alta., 1952-55; asst. prof. U. Toronto, 1955-60, assoc. prof., 1960-62, prof., 1962-91, prof. emeritus, 1991—. Dir. Commonwealth Petroleum Co., Calgary, 1946-59 Editor in chief Can. Jour. Math. 1971-75; contbr. articles to profl. jours. Bd. dirs. Francis F. Reeve Found., 1954-85. Served with Can. Army, 1943-45. Fellow Royal Soc. Can.; Mem. Can. Math. Soc. (councillor 1960-64, 66-70, 76-78, v.p. 1979-81, pres. 1981-83), Am. Math. Soc., Math. Assn. Am. Office: U Toronto Dept Math 40 St George St Toronto ON Canada M5S 2E4 Home Phone: 416-966-3792. Business E-Mail: rooney@math.toronto.edu.

ROONEY, PHILLIP BERNARD, service company executive; b. Chgo., July 8, 1944; BA magna cum laude, St. Bernard Coll., 1966. With Waste Mgmt., 1969-97, Service Master Co., Downers Grove, Ill., 1997—2003; chmn. Claddaugh Investments LLC, 2004—. Trustee U. Notre Dame. Capt. USMC, 1966—69. Decorated Bronze Star USMC, 1966-69; recipient Semper Fidelis award Marine Corps Scholarship Found., El Valor's Corp. Visionary award, Man of Yr. award Ill. Viet Nam Vets. Mem.: Econ. Club Chgo. (past chmn.). Roman Catholic. Office: 1301 W 35th St Chicago IL 60609 Office Phone: 773-579-2474. Personal E-mail: pbrooney78@aol.com.

ROOP, JAMES JOHN, public relations executive; b. Parkersburg, W.Va., Oct. 29, 1949; s. J. Vaun and Mary Louise (McGinnis) R.; m. Margaret Mary Kuneck (div. 1982); m. Susan Lynn Hoell (div. 1989); m. Daisy P. Billue, 1990 (div. 1999); m. Constance E. West, 2005. BS in Journalism, W. Va. U., 1971. Various account mgmt. postions Ketchum Pub. Rels., Pitts., 1972-77, v.p., 1977-79, Burson-Marsteller, Chgo., 1979-81; sr. v.p. Hesselbart & Mitten/Watt, Cleve., 1981-84, exec. v.p., 1984-86, pres., 1986-87, Watt, Roop & Co. (formerly Hesselbart & Mitten/Watt), Cleve., 1987-96; chmn., pres., CEO Roop & Co., Cleve., 1996—. Contbr. articles to profl. jours. Mem. Leadership Clevel.; bd. dirs. Malachi House, Home Repair Resource Ctr., Animal Protective League. Fellow Pub. Rels. Soc. Am. (chmn. investor rels. sect. 1984-85, chmn. honors and awards com. 1995); mem. Nat. Investor Rels. Inst. (pres. Cleve./Akron/Pitts. chpt., sr. investor rels. roundtable), Cleve. Skating Club, Mayfield Country Club, Hermit Club. Republican. Home: 2697 Scarborough Rd Cleveland Heights OH 44106-3241 Office: Roop & Co 650 Huntington Bldg 925 Euclid Ave Cleveland OH 44115-1408

ROOP, JOSEPH MCLEOD, economist; b. Montgomery, Ala., Sept. 29, 1941; s. Joseph Ezra and Mae Elizabeth (McLeod) R.; m. Betty Jane Reed, Sept. 4, 1965; 1 dau., Elizabeth Rachael. BS, Ctrl. Mo. State U., Warrensburg, 1963; PhD, Wash. State U., Pullman, 1973. Economist Econ. Rsch. Svc., USDA, Washington, 1975-79; sr. economist Evans Econs., Inc., Washington, 1979-81; staff scientist Battelle Pacific N.W. Nat. Lab., Richland, Wash., 1981—. Adj. prof. dept. econs. Wash. State U., 1999—; with Internat. Energy Agy., Paris, 1990-91. Contbr. articles to profl. jours. With US Army, 1966—68. Grantee Rsch. grant, Dept. Agr. Coop. State Rsch. Svc., 1971—73. Mem. Am. Econ. Assn., Econometric Soc., Internat. Assn. Energy Econs., Am. Statis. Assn. Home: 715 S Taft St Kennewick WA 99336-9587 Office: PO Box 999 MSIN K6-05 Richland WA 99352-0999 Office Phone: 509-372-4245. Business E-Mail: joe.roop@pnl.gov.

ROOP, OPHELIA GEORGIEV, library director; b. Kyustendil, Bulgaria; came to US, 1961; d. Boris Vangev and Raina Georgiev; m. Edward Donald Roop, May 8, 1973; 1 child, Zachary Andrei. BA in Russian and Slavic Studies, Ind. U., 1969, M Libr. and Info. Sci., 1982. Reference libr. arts divsn. Indpls.-Marion County Pub. Libr., 1970-81, asst. mgr. adult svcs., 1982-91; libr. dir. Herron Sch. Art Ind.-Purdue U., Indpls., 1992-96; libr. dir. San Bernardino Pub. Libr., Calif., 1997—. Contbr. book revs. to profl. publs., chpt. to book, entries to Ency. of Indpls. Mem. ALA, Calif. Libr. Assn. (mgmt. svcs. sect. 1998—, pres.-elect, pres.). Avocations:

skiing, travel, writing, reading, foreign films. Office: San Bernardino Pub Libr 555 W 6th St San Bernardino CA 92410-3094 Office Phone: 909-381-8215. E-mail: oroop@sbpl.org.

ROORDA, JOHN FRANCIS, JR., manufacturing executive, consultant; b. Evanston, Ill., Jan. 16, 1923; s. John Francis and Sadie M. (Daley) R.; m. Elizabeth Mulcahy, July 2, 1949; children: Elizabeth Roorda Barker, John F., Ann Roorda Hollis. BSChemE, Purdue U., 1943, PhD, 1949. With Shell Oil Co., 1949-83; gen. mgr. combined oil products/chem. econs. dept., 1973-74; v.p. planning and econs., 1974-77; v.p. Shell Devel. Co., Houston, 1977-78; v.p. corp. planning Shell Oil Co., 1978-83; pres. John Roorda, 1983—. Coordinator Exec. Service Corps, Houston, 1985—. Served to lt. (j.g.) USNR, 1943-46. Recipient Disting. Engring. Alumnus award Purdue U., 1976, Outstanding Chem. Engr. award Purdue U., 1993. Mem. Sigma Xi. Roman Catholic. Personal E-mail: graycell@houston.rr.com, tyro@houston.rr.com.

ROOS, CASPER, actor; b. NYC, Mar. 21, 1925; s. Jacob and Sabina (Uhlenbusch) R.; m. Shirley Anne Nicholson, June 27, 1953; 1 child, Pieter Nicholson. Student, N.Y. Coll. Music. Treas. Actors Equity Found., N.Y.C., 1982-88; co-chmn. research subcom. Nat. Theater Com., N.Y.C., 1983—; chair supv. com. Actors Fed. Credit Union, 1990-2001, 2003—. Prin. actor Shenandoah, N.Y.C., 1975-78, Brigadoon, N.Y.C., 1979-80, My One and Only, N.Y.C., 1982-85, Into the Light, 1986, Man of La Mancha, Zurich, 1988, (Broadway prodn.) Shenandoah Revival, 1989; numerous regional theater prodns. Served with U.S. Mcht. Marines, 1943-46. Mem. Actors Equity (treas. 1982-88, councilor 1964-79, 88-93). Home: 3 Cozzens Ct Newport RI 02840 *Don Quixote wanted to 'add a little grace to the world.' I, too, would like to add a 'little' to this world, whether it be grace or laughter or tears to an audience or service to my colleagues. If, like Don Quixote, I look a little foolish, so be it. I prefer a life of striving for the ultimate to the easier smug acceptance of the status quo.*

ROOS, DANIEL, engineering educator; b. Bklyn., Apr. 12, 1939; s. Sigmund and Anita (Sperling) R.; m. Eva Bonis, June 1, 1969; children—Richard Joseph, Linda Suzanne. BS in Civil Engring, MIT, Cambridge, Mass., 1961, MS, 1963, PhD, 1966. Mem. faculty MIT, 1963—, assoc. prof. civil engring., 1970—76, prof., 1976—, head transp. systems div., 1977—78, dir. Ctr. for Transp. Studies, 1978—85, dir. Ctr. Tech., Policy and Indsl. Devel., 1985—97, Japan Steel Industry prof., 1985—, mem. Commn. on Indsl. Productivity, 1987—89, assoc. dean engring. systems, 1997—, spl. asst. provost and chancellor, 1996—2003, co-dir. Ford Indsl. Ptnrships, dir. engring. sys. divsn., 1998—2004, dir. Portugal program, 2005—. Founder, dir. Multisystems Inc., Cambridge, 1965—85; chmn. com. to assess advanced vehicle and hwy techs. NRC, 1990—91, mem. com. on fuel economy, 1991—92; dir. Internat. Motor Vehicle Program, 1980—99; co-dir. Lean Aircraft Initiative, 1992—97; mem. coun. indsl. relationships MIT, 1996—97. Author: ICES System Design, 1964; The Future of the Automobile, 1984, Auto Futures, 1990; co-author: Made in America, 1989, The Machine That Changed the World, 1990; contbr. articles to profl. jours. Mem. U.S. Task Force on Transp., 1969. Recipient Shingo Prize for Excellence in Mfg. Rsch., 1994. Mem. ASCE (Frank M. Masters Transp. Engring. award 1989), Assn. Computing Machinery, Ops. Research Soc. (treas. transp. sci. sect. 1970-71), Transp. Research Bd. (chmn. para-transit com. 1974-80, group coun. 1980-84), Coun. Univ. Transp. Ctrs. (pres. 1983), Coun. Engring. Sys. Univs. (founding pres. 1990—). Achievements include developing Dial-A-Ride transp. concept, 1965; dir. Internat. Motor Vehicle. Home: 44 Summit Rd Belmont MA 02478 Office: MIT Engring Sys Divsn 77 Massachusetts Ave Cambridge MA 02139-4307 Office Phone: 617-253-1661. E-mail: roos@mit.edu.

ROOS, JOHN VICTOR, lawyer; b. San Francisco, Feb. 14, 1955; AB, Stanford U., 1977, JD, 1980. Bar: Calif. 1980. Ptnr. Wilson, Sonsini Goodrich & Rosati, San Francisco, 1988—, mng. dir. profl. services, CEO, 2005—, mem. exec. mgmt. com. & policy com. Mem.: Calif. Bar Assn., Order of the Coif. Office: Wilson Sonsini Goodrich & Rosati 650 Page Mill Rd Palo Alto CA 94304 Office Phone: 650-493-9300. Office Fax: 650-493-6811. E-mail: jroos@wsgr.com. *

ROOS, RAYMOND PHILIP, medical educator; Bd. cert. Am. Bd. Psychiatry and Neurology, 1976. Marjorie and Robert E. Straus prof. in neurol. sci. U. Chgo., 1986—. Recipient Matthew T. Moore award, Am. Assn. Neuropathologists, 1971, Career Devel. award, Schweppe Found., 1978—81, Sr. Fellowship award, Nat. MS Soc., 1988—89, Donald W. Mulder award, ALS Assn., 2004, Nat. Rsch. Svc. award, NIH. Fellow: AAAS, Am. Acad. Neurology (mem. sci. com.); mem.: Nat. MS Soc. (chmn. 2007—, rsch. program adv. com.), Am. Soc. Virology, Am. Neurol. Assn. (assoc.), Soc. Neuroscience, Johns Hopkins Soc. Scholars. Achievements include research in Neurovirology. Office: U Chgo Dept Neurology MC2030 5841 S Maryland Ave Chicago IL 60637 Office Phone: 773-702-5659.

ROOS, SYBIL FRIEDENTHAL, retired elementary school educator; b. LA, Jan. 29, 1924; d. Charles G. and Besse (Weixel) Friedenthal; m. Henry Kahn Roos, May 8, 1949 (dec. Dec. 1989); children: Catherine Alane Cook, Elizabeth Anne Garlinger, Virginia Ann Bertrand. BA in Music, Centenary Coll., 1948; MEd, Northwestern State U., 1973. Cert. elem. edn. tchr., spl. edn. tchr. Tchr. Caddo Parish Schs., Shreveport, 1968-75, Spring Branch Ind. Schs., Houston, 1975-85; vol. Houston Grand Opera/Guild, 1979—, Houston Mus. of Fine Arts/Guild, 1990—, Houston Symphony Soc./Guild, 1997—. Pres. Nat. Coun. Jewish Women, Shreveport, 1958; life mem. Mus. Fine Arts; area coord. Spl. Olympics, Shreveport, 1974-75; bd. dirs. U. Houston Moore Sch. Music. With USN, 1944-46. Mem. AAUW (pres. Spring Valley Houston chpt. 1985-87), Houston Grand Opera Guild (pres. 1989-91), Houston Symphony League, Houston Ballet Guild, Am. Needlepoint Guild, Delta Kappa Gamma (bd. dirs., treas. 1987-89), Phi Mu. Republican. Avocations: music, tennis, needlepoint, volunteering. Home: 10220 Memorial Dr Apt 78 Houston TX 77024-3227 Personal E-mail: s.roos@worldnet.att.net.

ROOSA, JAN BERTOROTTA, psychologist, writer; b. Champaign, Ill., Apr. 19, 1927; s. Walter Laidlaw and Giannina (Bertorotta) Roosa; m. Joan Herr. BS, U. Ill., 1950; MA, U. Denver, 1951, PhD, 1957. Coord., clin. psychologist Child Rsch. Coun., Kansas City, Mo., 1954-57, dir. neighborhood rsch. project, 1957; supr., psychologist State Hosp., Fulton, Mo., 1957-59; chief of psychotherapy VA Hosp., Kansas City, 1959-63; pvt. practice clin. psychologist Kansas City, 1963—. Dir., co-founder Learning Resource Ctr., Kansas City, 1969—79; dir. Gestalt, Social Competence Inst., Kansas City, 1969—89, Competence and Coop. Group, 1992—. Author: Situation-Options-Consequences-Simulation: A Technique for Teaching Social Skills, 1973, Psychological and Social Competence Model and Skills, 1975, 1992, Pet Peeves of a Psychologist and Other Flights into Reality, 2005, Brainspire.com: Psychological Tools for a New Way of Life, 2006; creator SOCCSS and SOCCSS: A Decision Making Process, 1973, 1996, The Competence and Cooperation Based Program, 1995. With USN, 1945—47, with USN, 1951—52. Mem.: APA, Nat. Register Health Providers Psychology, Mental Health Profls., Kans. Assn. Profl. Psychologists, Mo. Psychol. Assn., Greater Kansas City Psychol. Assn. Office: 9229 Ward Pkwy Ste 365 Kansas City MO 64114-3334 Office Phone: 816-444-3366. E-mail: jbroosa@planetkc.com.

ROOSA, MARK S., dean, librarian; m. Alexandra Roosa; 1 child, Bronwen. BA in Music, U. Minn.; MLIS, U. Calif., Berkeley. Preservation officer U. Del. Libr.; Lloyd E. Cotsen chief preservation officer Huntington Libr., Art Collections, and Botanical Gardens, San Marino, Calif.; chief conservation div. Libr. of Congress, 1998—2000, dir. preservation, 2000—04; dean librs. Pepperdine U., Malibu, Calif., 2004—. Faculty mem. Calif. Rare Book Sch., LA. Contbr. articles to profl. jours. UCLA Sr. Fellow, 2006. Office: Pepperdine U Payson Libr 24255 Pacific Coast Highway Malibu CA 90263 Office Phone: 310-506-4252. E-mail: Mark.Roosa@pepperdine.edu. *

ROOSEVELT, JAMES, JR., insurance company executive, lawyer; b. LA, Nov. 9, 1945; s. James and Romelle (Schneider) R.; m. Ann M. Conlon, June 15, 1968; children: Kathy, Tracy, Maura. AB, Harvard U., 1968, JD, 1971. Bar. Mass. 1971, DC 1973, US Ct. Appeals (DC cir.) 1973, US Ct. Appeals (1st cir.) 1976, US Supreme Ct. 1975. Assoc. Winthrop, Stimson, Putnam & Roberts, NYC, 1971, Herrick & Smith, Boston, 1975-80, ptnr., 1981-86, Nutter, McClennen & Fish, Boston, 1986-88, Choate, Hall & Stewart, Boston, 1988-98; assoc. commr. for retirement policy Social Security Adminstrn., Washington, 1998-99; sr. v.p., gen. counsel Tufts Health Plan, Waltham, Mass., 1999—2005, pres., 2005—, CEO, 2005—. Mem. Dem. Nat. Com., Washington, 1980—, Dem. State Com., Boston, 1980—; trustee Emmanuel Coll., Boston, 1982-92, 95—; trustee Care Group, Inc., Boston, 1996-00, Mt. Auburn Hosp., Cambridge, Mass., 1984-2000, chmn., 1988-92, chmn. bd. overseers, 2000—06. Lt. JAGC, USN, 1972-75. Mem. ABA, Boston Bar Assn., Mass. Bar Assn., Am. Health Lawyers Assn. (pres. 2002-03), Mass. Hosp. Assn. (trustee 1987-99, chmn. 1996-97), Harvard Club. Roman Catholic. Avocation: public policy. Office: Tufts Health Plan 333 Wyman St Waltham MA 02451-1282 Office Phone: 781-466-8564. Business E-Mail: james_roosevelt@tufts-health.com.

ROOSEVELT, THEODORE, IV, investment banker; b. Jacksonville, Fla., Nov. 27, 1942; s. Theodore III and Anne Mason (Babcock) Roosevelt; m. Constance Lane Rogers, Aug. 1, 1970; 1 child, Theodore V. AB, Harvard U., 1965, MBA, 1972. Fgn. svc. officer U.S. Dept. of State, 1967—70; assoc. Lehman Bros., NYC, 1972-76; corp. v.p. Lehman Bros. Kuhn Loeb, NYC, 1976-82; sr. v.p. Lehman Comml. Paper Inc., NYC, 1982-85; mng. dir. Lehman Brothers, NYC, 1985—. Chmn., bd. dirs. Lehman Bros. Fin. Products, Inc. Mem., commr. N.Y. State Pk. Recreation and Hist. Preservation Commn. City of N.Y.; commr. Hudson River Pk. Conservancy; mem. Cultural Inst. Retirement Sys.; chmn. Pew Ctr. Global Change; vice chmn. Allicance for Climate Protection; trustee World Resources Inst. With underwater demolition team USN, 1965—67. Mem.: Fgn. Policy Assn. (gov.), Coun. Fgn. Rels., Trout Unlimited, Wilderness Soc., Somerset Club (Boston), Clove Valley Rod and Gun Club, Econ. Club N.Y., Harvard Club (N.Y.C.), Explorers Club, Heights Casino Club (Bklyn.), Edgartown Yacht Club, Links (N.Y.C.). Republican. Home: 1 Pierrepont St Brooklyn NY 11201-3302 Office: Lehman Bros 745 7th Ave 20th Fl New York NY 10019 Home Phone: 718-237-9172; Office Phone: 212-526-8363. E-mail: troosere@lehman.com.

ROOT, ALAN CHARLES, diversified manufacturing company executive; b. Essex, Eng., Apr. 11, 1925; arrived in U.S., 1951, naturalized, 1959; s. Charles Stanley and Lillian (Collins) Root. BA, Oxford U., 1943; MA, Cambridge U., 1951; MBA, Stanford U., 1953. Rsch. analyst Dow Chem. Co., Midland, Mich., 1954—55; mgr. mktg. rsch. GE Co., 1955—61; v.p. bus. planning Mosler Safe Co., Hamilton, Ohio, 1961—70; v.p. corp. planning Am. Standard Inc., NYC, 1970—76, sr. v.p. ops. svcs., 1976—86, sr. v.p., 1986—88, sr. advisor, 1989. Trustee 1995 Trust Fund; sr. advisor Unit Ice, 1995—; bd. dirs. Am.-Standard Energy Inc., Amstan Trucking Inc., 1976-86. Trustee, treas. N.J. Chamber Music Soc., 1988—95; mem. Sheriff's Jury, N.Y. Cty., 1971—79; bd. dirs., chmn. Brit. Schs. and Univs. Found., 1970—2002, hon. dir., 2002—. Capt. Brit. Army, 1944—48. Admission to Order of St. John of Jerusalem sanctioned by Her Majesty Queen Elizabeth II, 1986, comdr., 1994. Mem. AIChE (assoc. producer TV series Midland sect. 1955), Pilgrims U.S., Newcomen Soc. N.Am., Univ. Club (N.Y.C.). Home: PO Box 2626 Rancho Santa Fe CA 92067-2626 Fax: 702-227-8885. *Good luck meant that my industrial career drew on the education I enjoyed as a young man. Professional advancement came by building on prior experience at each step and through long-term, managerial continuity.*

ROOT, ALLEN WILLIAM, pediatrician, educator; b. Phila., Sept. 24, 1933; s. Morris Jacob and Priscilla R.; m. Janet Greenberg, June 15, 1958; children: Jonathan, Jennifer, Michael. AB, Dartmouth Coll., 1955, postgrad. Med. Sch., 1954-56; MD, Harvard U., 1958. Diplomate Am. Bd. Pediatrics (mem. bd. 1985—), Am. Bd. Pediatric Endocrinology (mem. bd. 1985-90, chmn. 1990). Intern Strong Meml. Hosp., Rochester, NY, 1958-60; resident in pediatrics Hosp. U. Pa., Phila., 1960-62; fellow in pediatric endocrinology Children's Hosp. of Phila., 1962-65; assoc. physician in pediatrics U. Pa. Sch. Medicine, 1964-66, asst. prof. pediatrics, 1966-69; assoc. prof. pediatrics Temple U. Sch. Medicine, Phila., 1969-73, prof., 1973; asst. physician in endocrinology Children's Hosp. Phila., 1965-69; chmn. divsn. pediatrics Albert Einstein Med. Center., Phila., 1969-73; prof. pediatrics U. South Fla. Coll. Medicine, Tampa, 1973—, prof. biochemistry, 1987—, assoc. chmn. dept. pediatrics, 1974-99, dir. sect. pediatric endocrinology, 1973-96. Dir. univ. tchg. svcs. All Children's Hosp., St. Petersburg, 1973-89; mem. Fla. Infant Screening Adv. Coun., 1979-06, chmn., 1994-06; mem. Hillsborough County Thyroid Adv. Com., 1980; mem. med. adv. com. Nat. Pituitary Agy., 1974-78, mem. growth hormone subcom., 1972-79, 81-85; chmn. Fla. Legis. Infant Screening Task Force, 2002. Author: Human Pituitary Growth Hormone, 1972; co-editor: (with C. La Cauza) Problems in Pediatric Endocrinology, 1980; mem. editl. bd. Jour. Pediats., 1973-81, Jour. Adolescent Health Care, 1979-95, Jour. Pediat. Endocrinology and Metabolism, 1985—, Jour. Clin. Endocrinology and Metabolism, 1993-96, 2001-04, Growth, Genetics and Hormones, 1993—, Pediat. in Rev., 1995-2001; assoc. editor Adolescent and Pediat. Gynecology, 1992-95, Current Opinion in Pediats., sect. editor, Endocrine and Metabolism, 1993-, mem. editl. bd. 2006-. USPHS grantee; Birth Defects Found. grantee. Mem. AAAS, Am. Pediatric Soc., Soc. Pediatric Rsch., Lawson Wilkins Pediatric Endocrine Soc. (treas. 1979-88, pres. 1988-89), Endocrine Soc., Am. Acad. Pediatrics, Am. Fedn. Clin. Rsch., Soc. Exptl. Biology and Medicine, Soc. Nuclear Medicine, N.Y. Acad. Sci., Phila. Coll. Physicians, Phila. Endocrine Soc. (bd. dirs. 1971-72, treas. 1973), Dartmouth Coll. Alumni Coun., Dartmouth Club. Office: 801 6th St S Saint Petersburg FL 33701-4816 Business E-Mail: roota@allkids.org.

ROOT, EDWARD LAKIN, education educator, academic administrator; b. Cumberland, Md., Dec. 5, 1940; s. Lakin and Edna Grace (Adams) Root. BS, Frostburg State U., Md., 1962, MEd, 1966; EdD, U. Md., 1970. Cert. tchr. Md. Tchr. Allegany County Bd. of Edn., Cumberland, Md., 1962—66; grad. fellow U. Md., College Park, 1966-67, fellow, 1967—69; with Frostburg State U., 1969—99, prof., head edn. dept., 1980—87, dean, 1987—95, prof., head EdM adminstrn., 1995—99; gubernatorial appointee Md. State Bd. Edn., 1999—2007, pres., 2003—07. Mem. Profl. Stds. Bd. Md., Balt., 1980—87, Balt., 1995—99, Cert. Rev. Bd. Md., Balt., 1987—90, Md. Task Force Adminstrn., Balt., 1985—88, Md. Task Force: Prisoners Time and Response, task force tchr. assessment, 1995—97, Md. Task Force Tchr. Quality, 2002—03, Md. Task Force Disadvantaged but Capable Students, 2000—02; chmn. Md. Tchr. Quality Task Group, 2002—03. Mem. Allegany County (Md.) Planning and Zoning Bd. Appeals, 1995—96. Named Md. Ednl. Leader of Yr., 2003. Mem.: Mensa, Masons, Shriners, Phi Delta Kappa. Democrat. Methodist. Avocations: photography, travel. Home: 100 Pennsylvania Ave Cumberland MD 21502-4236 Office: Frostburg State U College Ave Frostburg MD 21532-1724

ROOT, GEORGE LINCOLN, JR., lawyer; b. 1947; BA, Syracuse U.; JD cum laude, U. San Diego. Ptnr. Procopio, Cory, Hargreaves & Savitch LLP, San Diego, 2007—. Guest lectr. U. Calif., San Diego Nat. U.; adj. prof. San Diego State U. Mem. San Diego County Bar Assn. (chmn. mental health com. 1983, task force on children at risk 1995), Calif. Soc. Healthcare Attys., Healthcare Fin. Mgmt. Assn., Healthy San Diego (past vice-chmn. provider adv. com.). Office: Procopio Cory Hargreaves & Savitch LLP 530 B St Ste 2100 San Diego CA 92101-4469 Office Phone: 619-238-1900. Business E-Mail: jr@procopio.com.

ROOT, GERALD EDWARD, legal administrator; b. Gridley, Calif., May 5, 1948; s. Loris Leo Root and Mary Helen (Wheeler) Murrell; m. Tricia Ann Caywood, Feb. 13, 1982 (dec.); children: Jason Alexander, Melinda Ann. AA in Bus., Yuba C.C., Marysville, Calif., 1968; BA in Psychology, Calif. State U., Sonoma, 1974; MA in Social Sci., Calif. State U., Chico, 1977; postgrad., U. San Francisco, 1994—99. Gen. mgr. Do-It Leisure Therapeutic Recreation, Chico, Calif., 1977-79; CETA projects coord. City of Chico, 1980-81; exec. dir. Voluntary Action Ctr., Inc., South Lake Tahoe, 1981-83; devel. dir. Work Tng. Ctr., Inc., Chico, 1983—91; exec. dir. North Valley Rehab. Found., 1986-92; spl. projects adminstrn. officer Superior Ct. of Calif., County of Sacramento, 1992—. Project mgr. Juvenile Detention Alternatives Initiative, 1992-98, Feather River Industries Vocat. Tng., 1991, Creative Learning Ctr. Constrn., 1988-89, Correctional Options-Drug Ct., 1994, Violence Prevention Resource Ctr., 1995-96, Communities That Care-Juvenile Delinquency Prevention Initiative, 1995, Securing the Health and Safety of Urban Children Initiative, 1995-97, Joint Cabinets Youth Work Group/Child Welfare League Am., 1996-97, Task Force on Fairness-The Juvenile Justice Initiative, 1994-97, SacraMentor, Inc., Calif. Wellness Found., 1994-95, Violent Injury Prevention Coalition/Calif. Dept. Health and Human Svcs., 1995-2000, Domestic Violence Coord. Coun., Sacramento County, 1995-98, Family Violence Summit, 1997, Ptnrs. in Protection Conf. 1997 Child Abuse Prevention Coun., The Drug Store, Calif. N.G. drug demand reduction program, 1996-97, disporportionate minority confinement rsch. com. Criminal Justice Cabinet, 1997-99, dir. planning and operational support, 1998-2000, Court Cmty.-Focused Strategic Plan, 1998-2001, Sunrise Recreation and Park Dist. 10 Yr. Master Plan, 1999-2000, virtual courthouse tour-distance learning, 2001-2002, lang. brochures program, 2002-03, self-represented litigants action plan initiative, 2000-03, jud. and ct. staff tng. videos, 2003-2005, ct. forms stds., 2003-04, ct. pub. info. officer, 2000-04, ct. interpreters recruitment, 2004-05, Ct. Records Retention and Mgmt. Study, 2004-06, Visual Arts Pub. Edn. Display, 1850-2005, Justice in Sacramento County, 2004-05, Sacramento County Presiding Judges, 2006—, Biennial Report Photography, 2003-05, Grand Jury Outreach Video, 2006—, Alternative Dispute Resolution Project, 2006—, Cmty. Based Orgn. Tng., 2006—, Disaster Recovery Bus. Resumption Plan, 2006—, Jury Orientation and Courtroom Advisement videos, 2006—; Temporary Judge Training, 2006-, CSU Sacramento, Judicial Coun.; graduate Judicial Administration Program, 2006; steering com. Multicultural Family Violence Prevention Conf., 1996-2001; legis. coord., 2003-04; presenter in field. Bd. dirs. Cmty. Action Agy., Butte County, Calif., 1990-92, ARC, Butte County, 1989-90, Sunrise Recreation and Park Dist., 1996-2001; adv. bd. Butte C.C. Dist., 1978-82, Cmty. Svcs. Planning Coun., 1994-96; blue ribbon task force for strategic plan Calif. Found. for Parks and Recreation, 2000. Grantee Annie E. Casey Found., USDA, U.S. Dept. Justice, Robert Wood Johnson Found., Calif. Office Criminal Justice Planning, U.S. Dept. Labor, Office Juvenile Justice and Delinquency Prevention, Sacramento Criminal Justice Cabinet, Calif. Wellness Found., Calif. Endowment, Adminstrv. Office of the Cts., 1998-2006; recipient Ralph N. Kleps award Calif. Jud. Coun., 2000. Office: Superior Ct Calif County of Sacramento 720 9th St Sacramento CA 95814-1302 Business E-Mail: rootg@saccourt.com.

ROOT, JAMES BENJAMIN, landscape architect; b. Detroit, Jan. 26, 1934; s. William Jehial and Helen Elizabeth (English) R. BBA, Memphis State U., 1960; B Landscape Architecture, U. Ga., 1966. Registered landscape architect; lic. real estate agt., Va. Asst. prof. W.Va. U., Morgantown, 1973-75, 93; pvt. practice Charlottesville, Va., 1976-85, 91—; site planner LBA, PH&R, Charles P. Johnson & Assocs., Fairfax, Va., 1986-90. Pvt. practice as golf course architect, Charlottesville, 1976—; instr. Parkersburg C.C., 1975, Piedmont Va. C.C., 1981. Author: Fundamentals of Landscaping and Site Planning, 1985, From Stardust to Insanity: The Moral Demise of a Troubled Nation, 2007; contbr. articles to profl. jours., also poetry. Mem. Planning Commn., Marietta, Ohio, 1972. Mem. Nat. Golf Found., Golf Course Builders Assn. Am. (assoc.), Va. Writers Club. Avocations: piano, drums. Office: PO Box 7017 Charlottesville VA 22906-7017 Office Phone: 434-971-4000. E-mail: jamesbroot@aol.com.

ROOT, NINA J., librarian, writer; b. 1934; d. Jacob J. and Fannie (Slivinsky) R. BA, Hunter Coll.; MSLS, Pratt Inst.; postgrad., USDA Grad. Sch., 1964-65, CUNY, 1970-75. Reference and serials libr. Albert Einstein Coll. Medicine Libr., Bronx, NY, 1958-59; asst. chief libr. Am. Cancer Soc., NYC, 1959-62; chief libr. Am. Inst. Aeros. and Astronautics, NYC, 1962-64; head ref. and libr. svcs. sci. and tech. divsn. Libr. Congress, Washington, 1964-66; mgmt. cons. Nelson Assocs., Inc., NYC, 1966-70; dir. libr. svcs. Am. Mus. Natural History, NYC, 1970—98; freelance mgmt. cons. and libr. planning, 1970-99. Trustee Barnard Found., 1984-91; mem. libr. adv. coun. N.Y. State Bd. Regents, 1984-89, trustee Metro, 1987-92; bd. dirs. Hampden/Booth Libr. Players, 1990-97, Sutton Area Cmty., 1997-2001; trustee Mercantile Libr. N.Y., 1993-95; dir. emerita Libr. AMNH, 1998—. Recipient Meritorious Svc. award Libr. of Congress, 1965, Founders medal SHNH, 1997. Mem. ALA (preservation com. 1977-79, chmn. libr./binders com. 1978-80, chmn. preservation sect. 1980-81, mem. coun. 1983-86), Spl. Librs. Assn. (sec. documentation group N.Y. chpt. 1972-73, 2d v.p. N.Y. 1975-76, treas. sci. and tech. group N.Y. 1975-76, mus. arts and humanities divsn. program planning chairperson-conf. 1977), Archons of Colophon (convener 1978-79), Soc. for Hist. of Natural History (N.Am. rep. 1977-85), N.Y. Acad. Scis. (mem. publs. com. 1975-80, 89-91, archives com. 1976-78, search. com. 1976), Explorers Club. Home: 400 E 59th St New York NY 10022-2342

ROOT, STUART DOWLING, lawyer, retired government agency administrator, banker; b. Chagrin Falls, Ohio, Oct. 14, 1932; s. Elton Albert and Virginia Saxton (Dowling) R.; m. Jean D. Youse, Dec. 28, 1957 (div. Jan. 1972); children: Bryan, Kathleen, Timothy, Todd; m. Patricia Stoneman Graff, Apr. 24, 1976. BA, Ohio Wesleyan U., 1955; JD, Columbia U., 1960. Bar: N.Y. 1960. Assoc. Cadwalader Wickersham and Taft, NYC, 1960-68, ptnr., 1969-81, 84-87; pres. Bowery Savs. Bank, NYC, 1981-82, vice chmn., 1982-83; exec. dir. Office Fed Savs. and Loan Ins. Corp., Washington, 1988-89; chmn. bd. Fin. Instn. Svcs. Corp., Washington, 1989. Lectr. ABA, Practicing Law Inst., Infocast, Am. Law Inst.; bd. dirs Bowest Corp., 1969-81. Contbr. articles to profl. jours. Chmn. bd. dirs. Harlem Sch. Arts, N.Y.C., 1974-83, trustee emeritus, 1984—; bd. dirs. Open Space Inst., 1976-80, 84-87, 89—, Nat. Choral Soc. N.Y.C., 1981-86, Canterbury Choral Soc., N.Y.C.; trustee N.Y. Geneal. and Biographical Soc., 1981-85; pub. interest dir. Fed. Home Loan Bank N.Y., N.Y.C., 1985-87. With U.S. Army, 1955-57. Mem. Century Assn. (N.Y.C.). Republican. Episcopalian. Avocations: liturgical music, fly fishing, golf. Home and Office: Beaverkill/Campsite Rd PO Box 417 Livingston Manor NY 12758-0417 Office Phone: 845-439-4255. E-mail: rootlaw32@aol.com.

ROOT-BERNSTEIN, ROBERT SCOTT, biologist, educator; b. Washington, Aug. 7, 1953; s. Morton Ira and Maurine (Berkstresser) Bernstein; m. Michèle Marie Root-Bernstein, Sept. 2, 1978; children: Meredith Marie, Brian Robert. AB, Princeton U., 1975, PhD, 1980. Postdoctoral fellow Salk

Inst. for Biol. Studies, La Jolla, Calif., 1981-82, rsch. assoc., 1983-84; from asst. to assoc. prof. Mich. State U., East Lansing, 1987-96, prof., 1996—. Cons. Parke-Davis Pharm. Rsch. Divsn., Ann Arbor, 1990-96, Chiron Corp., 1992-96; mem. adv. bd. Soc. for Advancement Gifted Edn., Chgo., 1987-92; Sigma Xi nat. lectr., 1994-96. Author: Discovering, 1989, Rethinking AIDS, 1993, Honey, Mud, Maggots and Other Medical Marvels, 1997, Sparks of Genius, 1999; columnist The Scis. mag., 1989-92, The Leonardo mag., 2004—; contbr. numerous articles to profl. jours. MacArthur Found. fellow, 1981-86; recipient D.J. Ingle Meml. Writing prize, 1988. Mem. Phi Beta Kappa (hon.), Sigma Xi. Avocations: painting, photography, cello, drawing, model building. Office: Mich State U Dept Physiology Biomed & Phys Scis Bldg East Lansing MI 48824 Office Phone: 517-355-6475 ext. 1101. Business E-Mail: rootbern@msu.edu.

ROOTH, SIGNE ALICE, editor, consultant; b. NYC, Aug. 14, 1924; d. Gerhard Teodor and Florence Elizabeth (Miner) Rooth. BA summa cum laude, U. Miami, 1944; MA, U. So. Calif., 1945; PhD, U. Chgo., 1953. Translator IMF, Washington, 1954—56, UN Secretariat, NYC, 1956—58, editor Official Records Editing sect., 1958—69; translator/interpreter UN Mission to Congo, Leopoldville, 1962—63; editor/sr. editor divsn. Gen. Assembly Affairs UN Secretariat, NYC, 1969—84, cons. editor UN Devel. Programme, 1985—92, cons. editor trusteeship dept., dept. pub. info., dept. gen. assembly and conf. mgmt., 1993—. Editor Econ. and Social Commn. for Asia and the Pacific, Bangkok, 1999; bd. mem. Assn. Culturelle Francophone, UN Secretariat. Author: Seeress of the Northland: Fredrika Bremer's American Journey, 1849-1851, 1955; editor: Procs. of UN Congress on Pub. Internat. Law: International Law as a Language for International Relations, 1995; contbr. articles and essays to jours. Recipient Am. Swedish Woman of Yr., Woman's Auxiliary of Am. Swedish Hist. Mus., Phila., 1984. Mem.: French Inst./Alliance Francaise, Swedish Women's Ednl. Assn., Am. Scandinavian Soc., Am.-Scandinavian Found., Am. Swedish Hist. Found. (life), Southampton Hist. Mus., Rogers Meml. Libr., Parrish Art Mus., Paris Am. Club. Avocations: reading, travel, art, music, collecting F. Bremer autographs.

ROPER, HARRY JOSEPH, lawyer; b. Bridgeport, Conn., Apr. 15, 1940; BEE, Rensselaer Poly. Inst., 1962; LLB, NYU, 1966. Assoc. Neuman, Williams, Anderson & Olson, 1966-70, ptnr., 1970-90, Roper & Quigg, 1990—2004, Jenner & Block, 2004—. Home: 611 W Fullerton Pky Chicago IL 60614-2613 Office: Jenner & Block 330 N Wabash Ave Chicago IL 60611-7603 Home Phone: 773-472-0983; Office Phone: 312-923-8303. Business E-Mail: hroper@jenner.com.

ROPER, RICHARD B., III, prosecutor; BA, U. Tex., Arlington; JD, Tex. Tech. U. Asst. dist. atty. Tarrant County, Tex., 1982—87; asst. US atty. (no. dist.) Tex. US Dept. Justice, Dallas, 1987—2004, interim US atty. (no. dist.) Tex., 2004, US atty. (no. dist.) Tex, 2004—. Office: US Attys Office Third Fl 1100 Commerce St Dallas TX 75242-1699 Office Phone: 214-659-8600. *

ROPER, SALLY ANN, health facility administrator; b. Hazelton, Pa., Aug. 24, 1950; d. Robert H. and Margaret F. (Baskin) Walk; children: Julia Kane, Laurie Kane. Diploma in Nursing, Kings County Hosp., 1972; cert. Health Adminstrn., Kings Coll., 1995, MS in Healthcare Adminstrn., 1996; student, Bklyn. Coll., Luzerne County C.C.; BA in Mgmt. Health Svcs., Ottawa U., Kans., 1992. RN Pa., cert. ACLS instr., BLS instr., HIV instr. Nurse Kings Highway Hosp., Bklyn.; staff nurse ICU, CCU Kings County Hosp., Bklyn.; staff nurse program care Nesbitt Meml. Hosp., Kingston, Pa., 1982—89, coord. quality improvement, 1989—2001; coord. performance improvement Wyoming Valley Health Care Sys.; dir. quality mgmt. N.E. Health and Hospice Care, Inc., 2002—03; dir. total quality mgmt., human resources New Life Home Care, Inc., 2003—. Mem.: Pa. Assn. Healthcare Quality, Am. Coll. Healthcare Execs., Nat. Assn. Healthcare Quality. Office Phone: 570-602-3093. Business E-Mail: sallyr@newlifehomecare.com.

ROPER, SCOTT CHRISTOPHER, geographer, researcher; b. Quincy, Mass., Oct. 24, 1969; s. James Henry and Lynne Patricia (Dunlop) Roper; m. Stephanie Abbot, Aug. 3, 1991. BA, Clark U., Mass., 1991; MA, U. ND, 1993; PhD, U. Kans., 1997. Grad. tchg. asst. U. of ND, Grand Forks, ND, 1991—93, U. of Kans., Lawrence, 1993—96; adj. prof. Rivier Coll., Nashua, NH, 1999—2002; asst. prof. of geography West Tex. A&M U., Canyon, Tex., 2002—05, Castleton (Vt.) State Coll., 2005—. Co-president Lyndeborough Hist. Soc., NH, 1998—2001; book rev. editor Material Culture, Springfield, Ohio, 2003—07; rsch. cons., Lyndeborough, NH, 1997—2002. Co-author (nonfiction book) Citizen Soldiers: New Hampshire's Lafayette Artillery Company, 1804-2004; author: (nonfiction book) The Peterborough Savings Bank, 1847-1997, (monograph) Citizens' Hall: A History of Lyndeborough's 'Other' Town Hall, 1888-2000; co-editor (monograph) A Soldier's Life: Reminiscences of the Civil War; contbr. articles to profl. jours. Chmn. Lyndeborough Conservation Commn., 2006—; selectman Lyndeborough, NH, 1999—2002; chmn. bd. selectmen, 2001—02. Recipient Govs. Citation, Gov. of the State of NH., 2000, Award for Excellence in Geography, Assn. of Am. Geographers and Nat. Coun. for Geog. Edn., 1991, Ellen Churchill Semple Geography award, Clark U., 1991, Paul P. Vouras Social Scis. award, 1991; Summer scholar, ND State Bd. of Higher Edn., 1992. Mem.: Assn. for Gravestone Studies, Soc. for Am. Baseball Rsch., Assn. Am. Geographers, Pioneer Am. Soc. (life; editor Pioneer Am. Soc. Transactions 2006—), Phi Kappa Phi, Phi Beta Kappa, Gamma Theta Upsilon (chpt. pres. pro tem 1991). Home: 157 Pettingill Hill Rd Lyndeborough NH 03082 Office: Castleton State Coll Dept History, Geography, Econs and Polit Castleton VT 05735 Office Phone: 802-468-1270.

ROPER, STEPHANIE ABBOT, history professor, writer; b. Manchester, NH, June 19, 1966; d. Edward M. Abbot, Jr. and Stella Mary (Cernota) Abbot; m. Scott Christopher Roper, Aug. 3, 1991. AB, Smith Coll., Northampton, Mass., 1988; MA, U. ND, Grand Forks, 1993; PhD, U. Kans., Lawrence, 1998. Grad. tchg. asst. U. ND, Grand Forks, 1991—93, U. Kans., Lawrence, 1993—96; instr. Mondanock Tng. Coun., Amherst, NH, 1998—2002; instr. history West Tex. A&M U., Canyon, Tex., 2003—05; instr. So. NH U., Hooksett, NH, 2006—. Preservation cons. renovation com. Citizens' Hall, Lyndeborough, NH, 1998—2000; adj. prof. history Rivier Coll., Nashua, NH, 1999—2002, adj. prof. of history and geography, 2005—, NH. Cmty. Tech. Coll., Nashua, 2005—; adj. prof. humanities Daniel Webster Coll., Nashua, 2006—. Author: (nonfiction book) Citizen Soldiers: New Hampshire's Lafayette Artillery Company, 1804-2004, A Soldier's Life: Reminiscences of the Civil War by Azro Cram; editor: A Soldiers Life. Mem. budget com. Lyndeborough, 1998—2002, mem. conservation commn., 2006—, chmn. supr. checklist, 2006—. Recipient Walter W. Ristow prize, Wash. Map Soc., 1995, Student Paper Competition First prize, East Lakes and West Lakes Divsn. Assn. Am. Geographers, 1996, Andrew Hill Clark award, Hist. Geography Splty. Group, Assn. Am. Geographers, 1997, Gov.'s Citation Cmty. Svc., State of NH, 2000; fellow, Newberry Libr., 1996; Jeannette D. Black Meml. fellowship, John Carter Brown Libr., 1997. Mem.: Lyndeborough Hist. Soc. (bd. dirs. 1998—, co-pres. 1998—2002), Soc. Am. Baseball Rsch., Assn. Gravestone Studies, Gamma Theta Upsilon, Phi Alpha Theta. Home: 157 Pettingill Hill Rd Lyndeborough NH 03082 Home Phone: 603-654-9663.

ROPER, WILLIAM ALFORD, JR., Internet company executive; b. Birmingham, Ala., Mar. 14, 1946; BA in Math., U. Miss., 1968; grad., Southwestern Grad. Sch. So. Meth. U., 1974; grad. fin. mgmt. program, Stanford U., 1986. Owner, gen. mgr. real estate devel. and wholesale distbn. cos.; loan officer, br. mgr. Deposit Guaranty Nt. Bank, until 1981; various positions, including corp. v.p., treas. Bell & Howell Co., 1981-87; exec. v.p., CFO, Intelogic Trace, Inc., 1987-90; sr. v.p., CFO, Sci. Applications Internat. Corp., San Diego, 1990-2000, exec. v.p. strategic investments, 2000—07; lead independent dir. VeriSign, Inc., Mountain View, Calif., 2003—, pres., CEO, 2007—. Mem. adv. bd. Allendale Mut. Ins. Co., Johnston, R.I.; mng. dir. Carlisle Enterprises, LLC, La Jolla, Calif.; bd. dirs. Factory Mutual Ins. Co., Regents Bank, N.A., SkinMedica, Inc., Cush Automotive Group, San Diego, Network Solutions, Inc., Herndon, Va., Holiday Bowl, San Diego, San Diego Regional Econ. Develop. Corp. Chmn. bd. ACCION San Diego; bd. dirs. Alvarado Hosp. Med. Ctr., San Diego; vice chmn. bd. San Diego Conv. Ctr. Corp. Mem. CEO Roundtable, Calif. C. of C. (bd. dir.), Greater San Diego C. of C. (bd. dirs., exec. com., chmn. fin. com.). Office: VeriSign Inc 487 E Middlefield Rd Mountain View CA 94043

ROPER, WILLIAM LEE, dean, preventive medicine physician, administrator; b. Birmingham, Ala., July 6, 1948; s. Richard Barnard and Jean (Fyfe) R.; m. Maryann Roper, Jan. 14, 1978 AA, Fla. Coll., 1968; BS, U. Ala, 1970, MD, 1974, M.P.H., 1981. Diplomate Am. Bd. Pediatrics, Am. Bd. Preventive Medicine. Intern, resident in pediatrics U. Colo. Med. Ctr., Denver, 1974-77; health officer Jefferson County Dept. Health, Birmingham, 1977-82, 83; White House fellow Washington, 1982-83; spl. asst. to Pres. for health policy, 1983-86; adminstr., Health Care Finance Adminstrn. HHS, Washington, 1986-89; dep. asst. to pres. for domestic policy The White House, Washington, 1989-90; adminstr. Agy. for Toxic Substances and Disease Registry and dir. Ctrs. for Disease Control and Prevention, Atlanta, 1990-93; sr. v.p. Prudential Health Care, Roseland, NJ, 1994-97; pres. Prudential Ctr. for Health Care Rsch., Atlanta, 1993-95; dean, sch. pub. health, prof. medicine and health policy U. NC, Chapel Hill, 1997—2004, dean sch. medicine, 2004—, vice chancellor med. affairs, 2004—, CEO U. NC Health Care, 2004—. Mem. Inst. Medicine, Phi Beta Kappa, Alpha Omega Alpha Republican. Office: Office of Dean U NC Med School 125 MacNider Bldg CB #7000 Chapel Hill NC 27599 Office Phone: 919-966-4161.

ROPPEL, MARK, lawyer; b. Calgary, Can., Aug. 29, 1963; arrived in U.S., 1989; s. Howard Ross and Karen Elaine Roppel. Student, U. Alta., Edmonton, Can., 1981—84; LLB, BCL, McGill U., Montreal, 1988; LLM, Columbia U., NYC, 1990. Bar: NY. With LeBoeuf, Lamb, Greene & MacRae, NYC, 1990—94, Shearman & Sterling, NYC, 1994—2000, ptnr., 2000—05, Cadwalader, Wickersham & Taft, NYC, 2005—; mng. ptnr. Beijing office, 2006—. Author: Practical Law Handbook, 2005—06, Corporate Governance & Client Strategies, 2007; contbr. articles to profl. jours. Mem.: ABA, Bar Assn City NY. Office: Cadwalader Wickersham & Taft One World Financial Ctr New York NY 10281 Office Phone: 212-504-5674, 8610-6599-7288. Business E-Mail: mark.roppel@cwt.com.

ROPPLE, LISA M., lawyer; b. June 25, 1962; BA summa cum laude, Holy Cross Coll., 1984; JD magna cum laude, Boston Coll., 1989. Bar: Mass. 1989, US Ct. Appeals (1st cir.). Ptnr., co-chair litigation dept. Ropes & Gray, Boston, 1989—. Editor (articles): Boston Coll. Law Rev. Office: Ropes & Gray 1 International Pl Boston MA 02110-2624 Office Phone: 617-951-7554. Office Fax: 617-951-7050. Business E-Mail: lisa.ropple@ropesgray.com.

ROPSKI, GARY MELCHIOR, lawyer; b. Erie, Pa., Apr. 19, 1952; s. Joseph Albert and Irene Stefania (Mszanowski) R.; m. Barbara Mary Schleck, May 15, 1982. BS in Physics, Carnegie-Mellon U., 1972; JD cum laude, Northwestern U. Sch. Law, 1976. Bar: Ill. 1976, U.S. Patent and Trademark Office 1976, U.S. Dist. Ct. (no. dist.) Ill. 1976, U.S. Ct. Appeals (7th cir.) 1977, U.S. Dist. Ct. (ea. dist.) Wis. 1977, U.S. Ct. Appeals (3d cir.) 1981, Pa. 1982, U.S. Ct. Claims 1982, U.S. Ct. Appeals (fed. cir.) 1982, U.S. Supreme Ct. 1982, U.S. Dist. Ct. (ea. dist.) Mich. 1984, U.S. Dist. Ct. (no. dist.) Calif. 1986. Assoc. Brinks Hofer Gilson & Lione, Chgo., 1976-81, shareholder, 1981—, pres., 2006—. Adj. prof. patents and copyrights Northwestern U. Sch. Law, Chgo., 1982-97. Contbr. numerous articles to profl. jours. Mem. ABA, Internat. Bar Assn., Internat. Trademark Assn., Am. Intellectual Property Law Assn., Ill. Bar Assn., Intellectual Property Law Assn. Chgo., Chgo. Bar Assn., Univ. Club, Chgo. Yacht Club. Roman Catholic. Office: Brinks Hofer Gilson & Lione Ste 3600 455 N Cityfront Plaza Dr Chicago IL 60611-5599 Office Phone: 312-321-4216. E-mail: gropski@brinkshofer.com.

ROREM, NED, composer, writer; b. Richmond, Ind., Oct. 23, 1923; s. Clarence Rufus and Gladys (Miller) R. Student, Northwestern U., 1940-42, Curtis Inst., Phila., 1943; BA, Juilliard Sch. Music, 1946, MA, 1948; D.F.A. (hon.), Northwestern U., 1977, Curtis Inst., 1982. Slee prof., composer-in-residence Buffalo U., 1959-61; prof. composition U. Utah, 1965-67, Curtis Inst., 1980—2004, Yale U., New Haven, 1998—, Manhattan Sch. of Music, 1995—2000. Guest composer New Music New Haven Series Sch. Music Yale U., 1998, vis. prof., 1998-99; composer-in-residence Great Lakes Chamber Music Festival, 1999. Composer: symphonies No. 1, premiere Vienna, Austria, 1951, No. 2, premiere La Jolla, Calif., 1956, No. 3, premiere with Leonard Bernstein and N.Y. Philharmonic, 1959, Three Piano Sonatas, 1949, 50, 54, Lento for Strings, 1950, Design for Orch., 1954, The Robbers, 1956, Pilgrims for Strings, 1958, Eagles for Orch., 1958, Last Day, 1959, Lions, 1964, Ideas for Easy Orch. 1961, Piano Concerto No. 2, 1951, 3d Piano Concerto, 1970, Eleven Studies for Eleven Players, 1959, Water Music, 1966, Sun; for voice and orch., commd. by N.Y. Philharmonic, 1966, Air Music for Orch, 1974 (Pulitzer prize 1976), Assembly and Fall, 1975, Sunday Morning for Orch., 1977, Remembering Tommy, 1981; numerous chorus works, latest being Letters from Paris, 1965; for chorus and orch., commd. by Koussevitzky Found. in Library of Congress, Little Prayers, 1972, Whitman Cantata, 1982, An American Oratorio, 1983, Homer, 1986, Seven Motets, 1986, Te Deum, 1986, What is Pink?, 1987, The Death of Moses, 1987, Goodbye My Fancy, 1988; operas A Childhood Miracle, 1952, Three Sisters Who Are Not Sisters, 1969, Fables, 1970, Bertha, 1968, Miss Julie, 1964 (Ford Found. grantee), Hearing, 1976, Cycles: War Scenes, 1969, Six Songs for High Voice and Orchestra, 1954, Six Irish Poems, 1951, Poems of Love and the Rain, 1964, Ariel for Voice, clarinet and piano, 1971, Last Poems of Wallace Stevens for voice, cello and piano, 1971, Serenade for voice, violin, viola and piano, Women's Voices, 1975, The Nantucket Songs, 1979, Three Calamus Poems, 1982, The Schuyler Songs, 1987, Day Music and Night Music for Violin, 1972-73, Etudes for Piano, 1975, Book of Hours for flute and harp, A Quaker Reader for Organ, 1976, The Santa Fe Songs, 1980, Remembering Tommy, 1980, Views From the Oldest House for organ, 1981, Winter Pages, 1981, Picnic on the Marne for saxophone and piano, 1982, Dances for Cello, 1983, Violin Concerto, 1984, Organ Concerto, 1985, String Symphony, 1985, Septet: Scenes from Childhood, 1985, Trio: End of Summer, 1985, Quintet: Bright Music, 1988, Diversions for Brass Quintet, 1989, Trio (Spring Music), 1990, Three Organbooks; The Auden Poems, Trio for Violin, Cello, Piano, 1990, Swords and Plowshares (for 4 solo voices and orch.), 1991, Third Quartet, 1991, Fourth Concerto for Piano (left hand) and Orch., 1991, Present Laughter for mixed chorus, piano and brass, 1993, Fourth Quartet, 1994, Songs of Sadness for quartet of baritone, guitar, clarinet and cello, 1994, More Than a Day for countertenor and orch., 1995, Six Variations for Two Pianos, 1995. Evidence of Things Not Seen, 1997; Autumn Music for Violin and Piano, 1997, Six Organ Pieces, 1998, Double Concerto for Violin, Cello and Orchestra, 1998, An Oboe Book, 1999, Another Sleep., Cello Concerto, 2001 Aftermath, 2002, Pas de Trois (oboe, violin, piano), 2002, Fifth String Quartet, 2002, Flute Concerto, 2002, Mallet Concerto, 2003, Our Town, an opera, 2005; commns. for U.S. Bicentennial include compositions for, Cin. Symphony, N.C. Symphony, Nat. Endowment of the Arts, Am. Harp Soc.; author: The Paris Diary of Ned Rorem, 1966, Music from Inside Out, 1967, The New York Diary, 1967, Music and People, 1968, Critical Affairs, 1970, Pure Contraption, 1973, The Later Diaries, 1974, An Absolute Gift, 1978, Setting the Tone, 1983, Paul's Blues, 1985, The Nantucket Diary, 1987, Settling the Score, 1988, Knowing When To Stop, 1994, Other Entertainment, 1996, Dear Paul, Dear Ned, 1997 (letters between Paul Bowles and Ned Rorem), Lies: A Diary (1986-1999), 2000 A Ned Rorem Reader, 2002, Wings of Friendship, 2005, Facing the Night, 2006; also articles newspapers, mags., Recs. for, Columbia, Decca, Odyssey, Desto, Phillips, Premier, C.R.I., Westminster, Orion, New World Records. Recipient Music Libraries Assn. award for song Lordly Hudson 1948, Gershwin Meml. award 1949, Lili Boulanger award 1950, Nat. Inst. Arts and Letters award 1968, Pulitzer prize in music 1976, Grammy award for Best Orchestral Rec., 1989; Fulbright fellow Paris, 1951-52; Guggenheim fellow, 1957-58, 77-78 Mem.: AAAL (pres. 2000—), ASCAP, PEN, Am. Acad. Arts & Letters (pres. 2000—03), Soc. Friends. Mem. Soc. Of Friends. Address: PO Box 764 Nantucket MA 02554-0764

RORER, JOHN WHITELEY, publisher, consultant; b. Phila., Aug. 4, 1930; s. Ronald Erle and Hazel (Whiteley) R.; m. Beverly Case, June 6, 1953. BS, U. Pa., 1952; MBA, Drexel U., 1956. Credit analyst Phila. Nat. Bank, 1954-56; with Curtis Pub. Co., Phila., 1956-68; dir. purchasing Chilton Pub. Co., Phila., 1968-70; founding pres. Focus Bus. Weekly, Bus. News, Inc., Phila., 1968—, pres., pub., 1974—; owner Pubs. Systems Assocs., Upper Darby, Pa., 1979—. Mem. Phila. World Affairs Council, 1979—. Served to capt. U.S. Army, 1952-54. Mem. Nat. Assn. Bus. Publs. (co-founder, bd. dirs. 1978-81), Nat. Assn. Indsl. Advt., Mktg. and Communications Execs. Assn., Union League Club, Engrs. Club (Phila.), Downtown Club. Republican. Episcopalian. Avocation: economics research. Office: 1015 Chestnut St Philadelphia PA 19107-4316

RORICK, WILLIAM CALVIN, retired librarian, portrait artist; b. Elyria, Ohio, June 23, 1941; s. Harold R. and Edythe E. (Harris) R.; m. Anne L. Sherbondy, Aug. 21, 1971. BA in Econs. and Bus. Adminstrn., Ohio Wesleyan U., 1963; MusB in Music History and Lit., U. Utah, 1968; MusM in Music History and Lit., Northwestern U., 1970; MLS, Pratt Inst., 1974; MA in Musicology, NYU, 1982; studied portraiture, various art schs., workshops. Curator orchestral-choral libr., reference asst., office mgr. Manhattan Sch. Music Libr., NYC, 1970-74; music reference libr. CUNY Queens Coll. Music Libr., Flushing, 1974-96, instr., 1974-79, asst. prof., 1979-96, asst. prof. emeritus, 1996—, mem. senate nominating com., del.-at-large arts divsn., 1984-86. Portrait painting demonstrator, show juror various art orgns. Corp., instnl., pub. and pvt. portrait commns.; contbr. articles and revs. to profl. jours. Bd. deacons South Britain (Conn.) Congl. Ch., 1998—2001, historian, 2002. With US Army, 1964—66. Grantee Rsch. Found. CUNY, 1981-84; recipient regional and nat. art awards including Best in Show Conn. Classic Arts Assn. Mem.: Kent Art Assn. (bd. dirs. 2003—07, elected artist, mem. exhbn. com.), Acad. Artists Assn. (artist mem.), N.Y. Soc. Portrait Artists (mem. leadership team 2001—02), Conn. Soc. Portrait Artists, Portrait Soc. Atlanta, Portrait Soc. of Am., Inc., Soc. Creative Artists of Newtown (corr. sec. 1999—2002), Conn. Classic Arts, Inc. (publicity chmn. 1996—99), Sonneck Soc., Am. Soc. Portrait Artists, Music Libr. Assn. (program chmn. Greater N.Y. chpt. 1977—79, mem. nat. subcom. on basic music collection 1977—79, sec.-treas. 1979—81, chmn. nat. membership com. 1979—82, chpt. chmn. 1983—85, mem. Music Pub. Assn. joint com. 1986—88), Libr. Assn. CUNY (chmn. grants com. 1978—80, mem. publ. com. 1979—81, editor Directory 1980—81, del. 1983—85), Internat. Assn. Music Libr., Assn. for Recorded Sound Collections, Am. Printing History Assn., Am. Musicological Soc., Portrait Clubs Am. (cert. leader-instr. 2003—, Greater Southbury chpt.), Beta Phi Mu, Phi Mu Alpha Sinfonia. Home and Studio: 63 Beacon Hill Dr Southbury CT 06488-1914 Office Phone: 203-264-4380. Personal E-mail: williamrorick@aol.com.

RORIE, CONRAD JONATHAN, research scientist, retired military officer; b. Henning, Tenn., Oct. 28, 1930; s. Elvy and Lena (Jenkins) R.; m. Patricia Paris Cunliffe, Feb. 7, 1952; children: Michael Stephen, Catherine Jean, Patrick Jonathan. BS, Union U., Jackson, Tenn., 1952; MSEE, US Naval Postgrad. Sch., 1961; PhD in Elect. Engring., Vanderbilt U., Nashville, 1970. Enlisted USN, 1952, advanced through grades to adm., 1971; comdg. officer various ships, 1957—72; comdr. US Naval Surface Weapons Ctr., Dahlgren, Va., 1974—77; dep. comdr. for surface combatants and weapons sys. engr. Naval Sea Sys. Command, Washington, 1977—81; comdr. Naval Surface Forces Mid. Pacific & Naval Base Pearl Harbor, Hawaii, 1981—84. Planning dir. Johns Hopkins U., Applied Physics Lab., 1984—; mem. numerous naval bd. for officer career devel., chmn. Weapons Systems Mgr./Ordnance Adv. Bd. to Naval Postgrad. Sch. President Hawaii Navy Relief Soc. and Red Cross, 1980; chmn. Combined Fed. Campaign Charity Dr., 1981; bd. dirs. Govs. for Navy Charity Retail Store, 1981; commissioning chmn. USS Antietam, 1987, USS Arleigh Burke, 1991; mem. panel Navy/Civilian U. Lab., 1988; mem. curricula rev. com. Naval Postgrad. Sch., 1977-81; bd. dirs. Historic USS Constellation, 1996; mem. warfare sys. adv. panel for 21st century aircraft carriers. Decorated Legion of Merit (4), Meritorious Svc. medal with gold star; recipient Ann. Disting. Alumnus award Union U., 1975, Am. Spirit of Honor medal, APL Disting. Svc. award Johns Hopkins U., 1998; named Tenn. Number One State Future Farmer, 1948; C.J. Rorie annual award for Excellence established in his honor, 1987, Navy Surface Warfare Ctr. established in his honor. Mem. Naval Inst., Am. Soc. Naval Engrs., Nat. Security Indsl. Assn., AIAA, Am. Astronaut. Soc., US Navy League, Armed Forces Communications and Electronics Assn., Mil. Order of Carabao, Masons, Bapt. Club, Sigma Xi, Eta Kappa Nu, Alpha Tau Omega. Conservative. Baptist. Office: Johns Hopkins U Applied Physics Lab Johns Hopkins Rd Laurel MD 20707 Home: 2124 McDonough Lane San Diego CA 92106 Personal E-mail: conradrorie@aol.com.

RORIG, KURT JOACHIM, chemist, science association director, educator; b. Bremerhaven, Germany, Dec. 1, 1920; came to U.S., 1924, naturalized, 1929; s. Robert Herman and Martha (Grundke) R.; m. Helen Yonan, Mar. 20, 1949; children: James, Elizabeth, Miriam. BS, U. Chgo., 1942; MA, Carleton Coll., 1944; PhD, U. Wis., 1947. Lectr. Loyola U., Chgo., 1950-62; chemist to dir. Chem. Research G.D. Searle & Co., Chgo., 1947-87; pres. Chemo-Delphic Cons. Ltd., Chgo., 1987—. Adj. prof. chemistry U. Ill., Chgo., 1989—. Patentee in field. Mem. Sch. Bd., Wilmette, Ill., 1969-71. Mem. Am. Chem. Soc. (dir. Chgo. sect.), Am. Soc. Pharm. and Exptl. Therapeutics, N.Y. Acad. Scis., AAAS, Chgo. Chemists Club (past pres.) Presbyterian. Home and Office: 337 Hager Ln Glenview IL 60025-3329 Home Phone: 847-724-2808; Office Phone: 847-724-2808.

RORKE-ADAMS, LUCY BALIAN, pathologist, educator; b. St. Paul, June 22, 1929; d. Aram Haji and Karzouhy (Ousdigian) Balian; m. Robert Radcliffe Rorke, June 4, 1960 (dec. Mar. 31, 2002); m. Boyce M. Adams, Apr. 16, 2004 (dec. June 21, 2006). AB, U. Minn., Mpls., 1951, MA, 1952, BS, 1955, MD, 1957. Diplomate Am. Bd. Pathology. Intern Phila. Gen. Hosp., 1957-58, resident anat. pathology and neuropathology, 1958-62, asst. neuropathologist, 1963-67, chief pediat. pathologist, 1967-68, chief neuropathologist, 1968-69, chmn. dept. anat. pathology and chief neuropathologist, 1969-73, chmn. dept. pathology, 1973-77, pres. med. staff, 1973-75; neuropathologist Children's Hosp., Phila., 1965—, pres. med. staff, 1986-88, acting pathologist-in-chief, 1995-2000. Cons. neuropathologist Wyeth Rsch. Labs., Radnor, Pa., 1961—87, Wistar Inst. Anatomy and Biology, Phila., 1967—93; assoc. prof. pathology U. Pa. Sch. Medicine, Phila., 1970—, prof. pathology, 1973—, clin. prof. neurology, 1979—, clin. prof. pediat., 1997—; forensic neuropathologist Office Med. Examiner, Phila., 1977—2004. Author: Myelinization of the Brain in the Newborn, 1969, Pathology of Perinatal Brain Injury, 1982; mem. editl. bd.

Jours. Neuropathology Exptl. Neurology, 1980—85, 1993—98, Pediat. Neurosurgery, 1984—2002, Child's Nervous Sys., 1984—88, Brain Pathology, 1990—95; contbr. articles to profl. jours. Recipient Provost's award for excellence in tchg., U. Pa., 2003; NIH fellow, 1961—62, NIH grantee, 1963—68. Fellow: Coll. Am. Pathologists; mem.: AMA, Phila. Coll. Physicians (trustee 2002—04, treas. 2004—), Burlington County Med. Soc., Am. Neurol. Soc., Am. Soc. Neuroradiology (hon.), Am. Assn. Neuropathologists (exec. coun. 1976—85, v.p. 1979—80, pres. 1981—82, Meritorious Svc. award 1999), Phila. Neurol. Soc. (v.p. 1971—72, editor transactions 1973, pres. 1975—76). Office: Childrens Hosp Phila 324 S 34th St Philadelphia PA 19104-4399 Home: 316 E Maple Ave Moorestown NJ 08057-2014 Business E-Mail: Rorke@email.chop.edu.

RORSCHACH, RICHARD GORDON, lawyer; b. Tulsa, Aug. 9, 1928; s. Harold Emil and Margaret (Hermes) R.; m. Martha Kay King, Dec. 23, 1979; children by previous marriage: Richard Helm, Reagan Cartwright, Andrew Maxwell. BS, MIT, 1950; MS, U. Okla., 1952; JD, U. Houston, 1961. Bar: Tex. 1961; lic. prof. engr., Tex. Cons. civil engr. Freese & Nichols, Ft. Worth, 1955; cons. engr. Freese, Nichols & Turner, Houston, 1955-56; petroleum engr. Marathon Oil Co., Bay City, Tex., 1956-57, Houston, 1957-61, atty., 1961-64; ptnr. Broady, Kells & Rorschsch, Houston, 1964-68, Ragan, Russell & Rorschach, Houston, 1968-80, R.G. Rorschach & Assocs., Kilgore, Tex., 1980—. Mem. exec. com. Colonial Royalties Co., Tulsa, 1970-77; officer Little River Oil & Gas Co., 1980-88; mng. ptnr. Pentagon Oil Co., 1988—; pres. Nat. Assn. Royalty Owners-Tex., 1993-96, trustee, 2004-05; chmn. Nat. Assn. Royalty Owners, Inc., 1996-99, bd. dirs., 1999-2000, adv. bd. dirs., 2004-05; mem. exec. com. Nat. Assn. Royalty Owners, Inc.; owner, breeder, exhibitor Arabian Horses Shadowbrook Farm, Kilgore, Tex., 1980—. Author: How to Protect Your Royalty Interests: Texas Perspectives, Vols. 1 & 2, 2002, The Ultimate Royalty Owner's Guide: A Manual of Procedure and Operation. 1st lt. CE US Army, 1952—54, Korea. Mem. ASME, ASCE, Tex. Bar Assn., Rotary Club (pres. Kilgore chpt. 1984-85), Sigma Xi, Sigma Alpha Epsilon. Republican. Presbyterian. Avocations: fly fishing, fly tying, golf, tennis. Home: 1893 CR 186 East Kilgore TX 75662-9023 Office: 1100 Stone Rd PO Box 1934 Kilgore TX 75663-1934

ROSA, JOHN WILLIAM, academic administrator, career military officer; m. Donna Kangeter; children: Jonathan, Brad. BA in Bus. Adminstrn., The Citadel, 1973; M in Pub. Adminstrn., Golden Gate U., 1985. Commd. 2d. lt. USAF, 1973, advanced through grades to lt. gen., 2003; A-7D pilot, scheduler, weapons officer 353rd Tactical Fighter Fighter Squadron, Myrtle Beach AFB, SC, 1975-77; A-10 pilot 356th Tactical Fighter Squadron, Myrtle Beach AFB, 1977—78; weapons officer 353rd Tactical Figher Squadron, Myrtle Beach AFB, 1979—80; pilot Hunter and Jaguar Aircraft, RAF Lossiemouth, Scotland, 1980-81; weapons instr. RAF Lossiemouth, 1981-83; instr. pilot, weapons officer, flight comdr. 61st Tactical Fighter Tng. Squadron, MacDill AFB, Fla., 1983-86; programmer, dir. of programs and resources Hdqrs. USAF, Washington, 1987-90; comdr. 35th Tactical Fighter Squadron, Kunsan AB, Korea, 1991-92, 366th Ops. Support Squadron, Mountain Home AFB, Idaho, 1992, dep. comdr., 1992-93; dep. comdr. to comdr. 49th Ops. Group, Holloman AFB, N.Mex., 1994-95; comdr. 20th Fighter Wing, Shaw AFB, SC, 1995-97; inspector gen. Hdqrs. Pacific Air Forces, Hickman AFB, Hawaii, 1997-98; comdt. Air Command and State Coll., Air U., Maxwell AFB, Ala., 1998—2000; comdr. 347th Wing, Moody AFB, Ga., 2000—01, 347th Rescue Wing, Moody AFB, 2001; dep. dir. ops. Ops. Directorate, the Joint Staff, Washington, DC, 2001—03; supt. USAF Acad., Colorado Springs, 2003—05; pres. The Citadel, Charleston, SC, 2005—. Decorated Def. Superior Svc. award, Meritorious Svc. medal with four oak leaf clusters, Air Force Commendation medal, Legion of Merit with oak leaf cluster, Combat Readiness medal with two oak clusters. Office: The Citadel Office of Pres 171 Moultrie St Charleston SC 29409 Office Phone: 843-225-3294. *

ROSA, RAYMOND ULRIC, retired banker; b. New Britain, Conn., Jan. 30, 1927; s. Kenneth E. and Regina (Chenette) R.; m. Irene M. Asselin, Feb. 5, 1949; children: R. James, David M., Cathryn P., Michael F., Nancy A., Kenneth E. AS, Hillyer Coll., 1949. CPA, Conn. Pvt. practice pub. accounting, Manchester, Conn., 1949-52; auditor Auditors of Pub. Accounts, State of Conn., Hartford, 1952-65; dir. Fed.-State Relations Dept. Finance and Control, Conn., 1965-69; dep. commr. Finance and Control, Conn., 1969-71; sr. v.p., auditor Soc. Savings, Hartford, 1971-90, ret., 1990. Mem. Windsor Locks (Conn.) Bd. Fin., 1973—81; pres. Savs. Bank Forum, 1981—82; trustee, sec.-treas. Mease Manor, Inc., Dunedin, Fla., 1995—2001, vice chmn., 2001—03, chmn., 2003—05. Treas. Mental Health Assn. Conn., 1974-77, v.p., 1977-80, pres., 1980-83; bd. dirs. Nat. Assn. Mental Health, 1977-85, v.p. region 1, 1982-83; bd. dirs. Combined Health Appeal of Greater Hartford, 1982-90. Served with USNR, 1944-46. Mem. AICPA, Conn. Soc. CPAs, Conn. Soc. Govtl. Accts., KC, Dunedin Country Club (bd. dirs. 1997-2000, v.p. 1998-99, pres. 1999-00), Suffield Country Club (bd. govs. 1984-91). Home: 2060 Golf View Dr Dunedin FL 34698-2330 E-mail: rrosa1@tampabay.rr.com.

ROSA, RICHARD ANGELO, orthopedist, surgeon, educator; b. Camden, NJ, 1951; BS in Biology, Seton Hall U., 1973; MD, Coll. Medicine & Dentistry of NJ-MJ Med. Sch., 1978. Diplomate Am. Bd. Orthopaedic Surgery, Am. Acad. Neurological and Orthopaedic Surgeons, Nat. Bd. Medical Examiners. Intern orthopaedics U. Medicine and Dentistry of NJ-NJ Med. Sch., Newark, 1978—79, resident orthopaedic surgery, 1979—83, adminstrv. chief resident, 1981—83, asst. prof. surgery, 1985; fellowship, comprehensive arthritis program, total joint replacementand adult reconstructive Hosp. for Special Surgery, NYC, 1983—84; attending St. Barnabas Med. Ctr., Livingston, NJ, 1997—; private practice Advanced Orthopaedic and Joint Replacement Ctr., West Orange, NJ. Spkr. in field. Contbr. articles to med. jours. Named one of NJ Top Doctors, 2006; recipient Best Doctors in Am., 2006. Fellow: Am. Coll. Surgeons, Am. Acad. Orthopaedic Surgeons; mem.: AMA, Am. Soc. Legal and Industrial Medicine, Eastern Orthopaedic Assn., Am. Acad. Neurological and Orthopaedic Surgeons, Acad. Medicine of NJ, NJ Rheumatism Assn., NJ Orthopaedic Soc., Am. Assn. Arthritic Hip and Knee Surgeons. Office: Advanced Orthopaedic and Joint Replacement Ctr Ste 200 741 Northfield Ave West Orange NJ 07052 Office Phone: 973-736-9980. Office Fax: 973-736-9981. *

ROSADO, JOSE ELIAS, religious organization administrator, priest; b. Cayer, PR, July 20, 1947; arrived in US, 1960; s. Francisco and Margarita (Ortiz) Rosado; m. Abigail Fontanez (dec.); m. Magdalena Cruz, Feb. 26, 1994; 1 child, Kathleen Charis. BA in Theology, Albert Prince Regional Tech. Sch., 1975; MA in Theology, Emmanuel Bible Inst., 1976; ThM, Carolina U. Theology, 1998, ThD, 2000, D of Christian Edn., 2002, D of Counseling Psychology, 2004. Machinist Spencer Turbine Co., 1970—78; chaplin prison ministry Dept. Correction, Windsor, Conn., 1970—79; mold and tool maker maintenance mechanic Wheaton Plastics, Cayer, PR, 1979—80; prof. theology Assembly of God Theol. Coll., Cayey, 1982; sr. pastor, pres. Mahanain Christian Ch., Cidra, PR, 1982—. Prof. theology Defensores de la fe Theol. Coll., Cidra, 2000—02; quality control insp., tech. support I.S. Tech. Corp., Cayey, 1980—. Adv. for blind people Cmty. Renual Team, Hartford, Conn.; 1970—75. Republican. Achievements include design of vertical and horizontal glass lathe. Home: 56 Padre Martinez Cayey PR Office: Pentecostal Christian Ch PO Box 255 Barceloneta PR 00617 Office Phone: 787-846-6989. Fax: 787-263-3947.

ROSADO, RODOLFO JOSE, psychologist, educator; b. NYC, Jan. 9, 1959; s. Rodolfo Jose and Maria (Gonzalez) R.; m. Ruth Laura Morrison, June 11, 1982; children: Emily Hope, Adam Philip. BS in Psychology, Fordham U., Bronx, NY, 1979, MA in Clin. Psychology, 1986, PhD in Clin. Psychology, 1992. Diplomate in clin. psychology and child psychology Am. Bd. Psychol. Specialties; lic. psychologist, N.Y., Conn. Psychology tng. fellow N.Y. Med. Coll., Valhalla, 1979-81; clin. psychology intern Hall-Brooke Hosp., Westport, Conn., 1982-83; therapist Child Guidance Ctr., Bridgeport, Conn., 1983-85, office coord., 1985-90, program dir., 1990-93; asst. prof. Fairfield (Conn.) U., 1993-97, program dir. coll. access, 1995-96; pvt. practice specializing in psychol. evaluations Norwalk, Conn., 1993—. Initial Rev. Group profl. reviewer USPHS, Rockville, Md., 1990-95; regional adv. com. Dept. Children & Families, Bridgeport, 1995—; oversight collaborative Bridgeport Futures, 1994-95; faculty co-sponsor SALSA Hispanic Students Assn., Fairfield U., 1995-97; bd. dirs., clin. cons. R.E.A.C.H. Program, Riverside, Conn.; bd. dirs. Side by Side Charter Sch., Norwalk, Conn., 2002--. Author, moderator TV show Conversation in Edn., 1994; co-author proposal Empowerment Zone Grant, 1994; author proposal Comprehensive Child & Adolescent Svc., 1993. Mem. Youth Svc. Bur., City of Bridgeport, 1991-93; family preservation initiative Conn. Dept. Children & Families, Bridgeport, 1995-2000; coach Little League Baseball, 2000-02; asst. coach Biddy Basketball Youth Program, Norwalk, 2001-02; vice chmn. bd. dirs. Side by Side Charter Sch., Norwalk, Conn., 2002—. Recipient N.Y. Regents scholarship, 1975-79, scholarship Fordham U., Bronx, 1975-79, Appreciation award for collaborative support State of Conn. Dept. Children & Families, 1995, Outstanding Contbns. to Latino Cmty. Recognition award Puerto Rican/Latino employees of Human Resources Adminstrn. and Affiliated Agys., Dept. Homeless Svcs. and Adminstrn. for Children's Svcs., 1999. Mem. APA, Am. Coll. Forensic Examiners, Hispanic Assn. Mental Health and Allied Professions (exec. com., treas. 1988-92), Conn. Coalition for Children of Alcoholics (steering com. 1986-87), Sigma Xi. Avocations: racquetball, hiking. Office: 71 East Ave Ste U Norwalk CT 06851

ROSALDO, RENATO IGNACIO, JR., cultural anthropology educator; b. Champaign, Ill., Apr. 15, 1941; s. Renato Ignacio and Mary Elizabeth (Potter) R.; m. Michelle Sharon Zimbalist, June 12, 1966 (dec. Oct. 1981); children: Samuel Mario, Manuel Zimbalist; m. Mary Louise Pratt, Nov. 26, 1983; 1 child, Olivia Emilia Rosaldo-Pratt. AB, Harvard U., 1963, PhD, 1971. Asst. prof. cultural anthropology Stanford (Calif.) U., 1970-76, assoc. prof., 1976-85, prof., 1985—2003, Mellon prof. interdisciplinary studies, 1987-90, dir. Ctr. for Chicano Rsch., 1985-90, chair anthropology, 1994-96, Lucie Stern prof. social scis., 1993—. Author: Ilongot Headhunting 1883-1974, 1980, Culture and Truth, 1989, Prayer to Spider Woman/Rezo a la mujer araña, 2003. Recipient Harry Benda prize Assn. for Asian Studies, 1983 Am. Book award, 2004; Guggenheim fellow, 1993. Fellow Am. Acad. Arts and Scis. Avocations: poetry, swimming, drawing, dance. Home: 120 W 15th St Apt 7H New York NY 10011-6792 Office: NYU Dept Anthropology 25 Waverly Pl New York NY 10003-6790 Business E-Mail: rr86@nyu.edu.

ROSALES, JENNIFER, professional golfer; b. Manila, Philippines, Sept. 17, 1978; Attened, U. So. Calif. Winner Philippine Ladies Amateur Open, 1994—98, Chick Fil-A Charity Championship, 2004. NCCC individual champion, 1998; winner Golf World Invitational, 1998. Achievements include being tied for lead after three rounds of the 2004 US Open. Avocations: shopping, movies, pets. Office: c/o LPGA 100 International Golf Dr Daytona Beach FL 32124-1092

ROSALES, SUZANNE MARIE, hospital coordinator; b. Merced, Calif., July 23, 1946; d. Walter Marshall and Ellen Marie (Earl) Potter; children: Anita Carol, Michelle Suzanne. AA, City Coll., San Francisco, 1966. Diplomate Am. Coll. Utilization Review Physicians. Utilization review coord. San Francisco Gen. Hosp., 1967-74; mgr. utilization review/discharge planning UCLA Hosp. and Clinics, 1974-79; nurse III Hawaii State Hosp., Kaneohe, 1979-80; review coord. Pacific Profl. Std. Review Orgn., Honolulu, 1980-81; coord. admission and utilization re-viewq The Rehab. Hosp. of the Pacific, Honolulu, 1981-85; coord. Pacific Med. Referral Project, Honolulu, 1985-87; dir. profl. svcs. The Queen's Healthcare Plan, Honolulu, 1987-88; utilization mgmt. coord. Vista Psychiat. Physician Assocs., San Diego, 1989; admission coord. utilization review San Francisco Gen. Hosp., 1989-91, quality improvement coordinator, 1991—. Cons. Am. Med. Records Assn. Contbr. articles to profl. jours. Mem. Nat. Assn. Utilization Review Profls. Office: San Francisco Gen Hosp 1001 Potrero Ave San Francisco CA 94110-3594

ROSALES, VERONICA, language educator; b. Cuernavaca, Morelos, Mex., Apr. 13, 1969; arrived in US, 1992; d. Jose Francisco Rosales and Hermelinda Hernandez; m. Glenn D. Gonzalez (div.). AA, Moraine Valley CC, Palos Hills, Ill., 2002; BA, Northeastern Ill. U., Chgo., 2005; degree, U. Ill., Chgo., 2007. ESL tutor Chgo. Commons, 1994—97, ESL tchr., coord., 2000—; vocat. ESL instr. Summer Consulting, Chgo., 1997—99, Inst. Latino Progress, Chgo., 1999—2000. Avocations: reading, bicycling, swimming, jogging, chess. Home: 2100 N Lamon Chicago IL 60639 Office: Chicago Commons 3645 W Chicago Ave Chicago IL 60651 Office Phone: 973-772-5935.

ROSALES HERRERA, RAÚL JOAQUIN, language educator; b. NYC, June 29, 1978; s. Jose Joaquin and Paula Rosales. BA, Drew U., 1999; MA, Columbia U., 2000, MPhil, 2001, PhD, 2007. Tchg. fellow Spanish Columbia U., NYC, 2000—05; asst. prof. Spanish Drew U., Madison, NJ, 2004—. Adj. instr. Spanish New Sch. U., NYC, 2003—05; mem. Columbia U., Lang. Program Com., Dept. Spanish, 2003—. Summer Rsch. fellowship, Columbia U., 2002—05. Mem.: Popular Culture Assn., Am. Assn. Tchrs. Spanish and Portugese, Rocky Mt. Modern Lang. Assn., Modern Lang. Assn. Office: Drew U Dept Spanish 36 Madison Ave Madison NJ 07940 Home: 42 F Loantaka Way Madison NJ 07940 Office Phone: 973-408-3751. Personal E-mail: raulrh29@gmail.com.

ROSALSKY, BARBARA ELLEN, artist, community health nurse; b. NYC, Nov. 16, 1948; d. Ellis M. Rosalsky and Claire (Schwartz) Rosalsky Shapiro; m. Dennis Robinson (div.). BA, SUNY, Plattsburgh, 1970. Sales girl Cambridge Artist mag., Mass., 1970—71; artist Pillar of Fire mag., Zarephath, NJ, 1977; home health aide CMR, Bound Brook, NJ, 1978—; designer New Brunswick Tomorrow, NJ, 1980—93; art therapist Middlesex Hosp., New Brunswick, 1981—83; vol. office Robert Wood Johnson Hosp., 1995—2006. One-woman shows include The Bird and Me, 1980, Highland Pk. Libr., N.J., 2003, The City, 2003, exhibited in group shows at Other Artists Other Art, Robeson Newark Gallery, N.J., 1983. Mem. Cultural Arts Commn., Piscataway, N.J., 1993-2007; mem. Ams. for the Arts Action Fund, 2006-07. SUNY Plattsburgh scholar, 1970. Mem.: Women's Caucus Art, Quality Inn Swim Club. Democrat. Avocations: piano, swimming, dance, print making. Home: 114 Woodland Rd Piscataway NJ 08854-4222

ROSAND, DAVID, art historian, educator; b. Bklyn., Sept. 6, 1938; s. Johan Herbert and Frieda (Grotenstein) R.; m. Ellen Fineman, June 18, 1961; children: Jonathan, Eric. AB, Columbia Coll., 1959; MA, Columbia U., 1962, PhD, 1965. Instr. art history Columbia U., NYC, 1964-67, asst. prof., 1967-69, assoc. prof., 1969-73, prof., 1973-95, chmn. Soc. of Fellows in the Humanities, 1979-83, Meyer Schapiro prof. art history, 1995—. Co-author (with Michelangelo Muraro): Titian and the Venetian Woodcut, 1976, Titian, 1978; author: Painting in Cinquecento Venice: Titian, Veronese Tintoretto, 1982, rev. edit., 1997; author: (with others) Places of Delight: The Pastoral Landscape, 1988; author: The Meaning of the Mark: Leonardo and Titian, 1988, Painting in Sixteenth-Century Venice, rev. edit., 1997, Robert Motherwell on Paper, 1997, Myths of Venice: The Figuration of a State, 2001, Drawing Acts: Studies in Graphic Expression and Representation, 2002, The Invention of Painting in America, 2004; editor: Titian: His World and His Legacy, 1982; editor: (with Robert W. Hanning) Castiglione: The Ideal and the Real in Renaissance Culture, 1983; editor: Interpretazioni Veneziane, 1984. Mem. bd. advisors CASVA Nat. Gallery Art., 1990-94. Fulbright Commn. fellow, 1962-63; NEH fellow, 1971-72, 85-86, 91-92; John S. Guggenheim Meml. Found. fellow, 1974-75. Mem.: Am. Acad. Arts and Scis., Renaissance Soc. Am. (mem. exec. bd. 1981—), Coll. Art Assn. Am., Istituto Veneto di Scienze, Lettere ed Arti (fgn.), Ateneo Veneto (fgn.), Save Venice, Inc. (bd. dirs.). Home: 560 Riverside Dr New York NY 10027-3212 Office: Columbia U Dept Art History & Archaeology 826 Schermerhorn Hall Mail Code 5517 New York NY 10027 Home Phone: 212-222-9915; Office Phone: 212-854-4502. Business E-Mail: dr17@columbia.edu.

ROSANIO, SALVATORE, cardiologist, educator; b. Benevento, Italy, Nov. 23, 1962; 1 child, Ginevra Victoria. Prof. medicine in cardiology U. Tex. Med. Br., Galveston, Tex., 2003—. Fellow: Am. Coll. Cardiology, European Cardiologists. Achievements include research in cardiac pacing and primary prevention of sudden death. Office: The University of Texas Medical Branch 301 University boulevard Galveston TX 77553-0553 Office Phone: 409-772-1533. Office Fax: 409-772-4982. E-mail: sarosani@utmb.edu.

ROSASCHI, JIM, librarian; b. Alma, Mich., Apr. 4, 1949; s. Mary Henry and True Rosaschi; m. Gaylene Reynolds, Aug. 22, 1975; children: Nicole, Daniel, Michelle, Emma. MLS, Brigham Young U., 1979. Cert. K-12 tchrg. Calif., 1982. Dir. Nampa Pub. Libr., Idaho, 1979—82; mgr. Petaluma br. libr. Sonoma County Libr., Sana Rosa, Calif., 1982—95, mgr. ext. svcs. Santa Rosa, 1985—89, mgr. tech. svcs., 1989—2006, mgr. info. tech. divsn., 2007—. Pres. Customers of Dynix, Inc., Salt Lake City, 2003; libr. tech. presentations, Melbourne, Australia, 03, Edinburgh, 04. Adult sunday sch. tchr. Ch. of Jesus Christ of Latter-Day Saints, Santa Rosa, 1998—2002. With US Army, 1969—72. Mem.: Calif. Libr. Assn., ALA, Mormon History Assn. Home: 925 Hyland Dr Santa Rosa CA 95407 Office: Sonoma County Libr 3rd and E St Santa Rosa CA 95404 Office Phone: 707-545-0831.

ROSATI, DIANE CLAIRE, epidemiologist, educator, artist; d. Samual J. Castonguay and Edna Tomasulo; m. Vincent Rosati; children: Elissa, Alexander. Diploma, Bklyn. Hosp. Sch. Nursing, 1962; BS cum laude, Wagner Coll., 1976; MPH, Columbia U., 1980. One-woman shows include Mooring Gallery, Mahone Bay, 1995, Open Ho. Gallery, Anapolis, 1995, McKay Libr., 1996, Herman Hines Mus. Photography & Art Gallery, 1998, Shelburne County Mus., 1999, others, exhibitions include Nat. Art Club, 1997, Art Lab, Snug Harbor, 1997, St. Francis Xavier U., 1997, Krasedale Art Gallery, 1998, Pastel Soc. Can., 2000, Acadia U. Art Gallery, 2001, 2003, others, Represented in permanent collections Housatonic Mus. Art. Recipient Solo Show awards, Pen & Brush, 15 various awards for pastel, graphics, mixed media, 1992—2000, Philip Isenburg award for graphics, Salmagundi Club, Dorothy Koatz Meyer award for innovative work, Augie Napoli Mem. award, Gerald Mennin award for graphics, Nat. Art Club, Silver medal award, Audubon Artist Show, 56th Annual. Mem.: Nat. League Am. Pen Women, Pastel Soc. Can., Visual Arts Nova Scotia, Soc. Am. Graphic Artists, Nat. Assn. Women Artists, Nova Scotia Print Makers Assn., Pen & Brush Soc. (bd.dirs., pastel chair), Print Club Albany, Nat. Art Club. Avocations: beekeeping, sailing.

ROSATO, ANTHONY DOMINICK, mechanical engineer, educator; b. Bklyn., Aug. 28, 1953; s. Michael Joseph and Betty (Rispoli) R. BME, Pratt Inst., 1975; MS in Theoretical and Applied Mechanics, Northwestern U., 1979; MS in Applied Maths., Carnegie Mellon U., 1981, PhD in Mech. Engring., 1985. Devel. engr. Green Fan Co., Beacon, NY, 1975—77; rsch. asst. dept. civil engring. Northwestern U., Evanston, Ill., 1977—79; tchg. asst. mech. engring. and maths. Carnegie Mellon U., Pitts., 1979—82, rsch. asst., 1981—84, rsch. assoc. dept. mech. engring., 1985—86; adj. faculty dept. exact scis. Carlow Coll., Pitts., 1986; asst. prof. mech. engring. NJ Inst. Tech., Newark, 1987—93, assoc. prof. mech. engring., 1993—2002, prof. mech. engring., 2002—, dir. Particle Tech. Ctr., 1995—99, coord. undergrad. rsch. in mech. engring., 2000—02, dir. Granular Sci. Lab., 2000—; vice chair faculty coun. NJIT, 2006—07, chair, 2007—. Faculty Gov.'s Sch. in Scis., Drew U., Madison, N.J., 1988; vis. faculty fellow, physicist dept. earth scis. Lawrence Livermore (Calif.) Nat. Lab., 1989, 90; Joliot professorship Ecole Superieure de Physique et de Chimie Industrielles, Laboratoire H.M.P., Paris, 1994; mem. nat. materials adv. bd. NRC, 1995; vis. scientist The Lovelace Insts., Albuquerque, 1995-96; vis. assoc. prof. mech. engring. Worcester Poly. Inst., 1995; assoc. chmn. mech. engring. grad. studies, N.J. Inst. Tech., 2001-2003; vice chair faculty coun. NJIT, 2006-07; vis. scholar Stanford U., 2003 Co-editor-in-chief Mechanics Rsch. Comms.; mem. editl. bd. Internat. Jour. Nonlinear Sci. and Numerical Simulation. Chair sci. com. IUTAM Symposium, Cape May, N.J., 1999. Vis. scholar mech. engring, Stanford U., 2003. Fellow ASME; mem. Am. Soc. Engring. Edn. (program chair elect grad. studes divsn. 1995), Am. Acad. Mechanics, N.J. Inst. Tech. Ctr. for Applied Maths., Sigma Xi, Tau Beta Pi, Pi Tau Sigma. Roman Catholic. Office: NJ Inst Tech Mech Engring Dept University Heights Newark NJ 07102 Office Phone: 973-596-5829. Business E-Mail: rosato@njit.edu.

ROSBOTTOM, RONALD CARLISLE, language and humanities educator; b. New Orleans, July 15, 1942; s. Albert Carlisle and Marjorie Catherine (Chavez) R.; m. Betty Elane Griffin, Sept. 5, 1964; 1 child, Michael K. BA, Tulane U., 1964; MA, Princeton U., 1966, PhD, 1969; MA (hon.), Amherst Coll., 1990. Instr. U. Pa., Phila., 1967-69, asst. prof., 1969-73; assoc. prof. Ohio State U., Columbus, 1973-78, prof. French lit., 1978-89, chmn. Romance langs., 1982-88; dean of faculty Amherst (Mass.) Coll., 1989-95, prof. French lit. and European studies, 1989—, Winifred L. Arms prof. arts and humanities, 1996—, chair European studies program, 1996—2005, acting chmn. dept. Spanish, 2004—06. Author: Marivaux's Novels, 1974, Choderlos de Laclos, 1979 (Havens prize 1980); editor: Studies in 18th Century Culture, 1975, 76, Essays in the French Enlightenment, 1991 Decorated Ordre des Palmes Académiques; Woodrow Wilson Found. fellow, 1964-65, 66-67; Am. Council Learned Socs. summer fellow, 1970 Mem. Am. Soc. 18th Century Studies (exec. sec. 1978-83, 2d v.p. 1992-93, 1st v.p. 1993-94, pres. 1994-95), Am. Assn. Tchrs. French, Phi Beta Kappa Democrat. Home: 326 Shays St Amherst MA 01002-2943 Office: Amherst Coll PO Box 2255 Amherst MA 01002-2255 Business E-Mail: rcrosbottom@amherst.edu.

ROSCH, JOHN THOMAS (TOM), commissioner, lawyer; b. Council Bluffs, Iowa, Oct. 4, 1939; s. H.P. and Phebe Florence (Jamison) Rosch; m. Carolyn Lee, Aug. 18, 1961; children: Thomas Lee, Laura Lee. BA, Harvard U., 1961, LLB, 1965. Bar: Calif. 1966, US Dist. Ct. No. Dist. Calif. 1966, US Dist. Ct. Ea. Dist. Calif. 1967, US Ct. Appeals 9th cir. 1966. Assoc. McCutchen, Doyle, Brown & Enersen, San Francisco, 1965-72, ptnr., 1972-73, 75-93; dir. Bur. Consumer Protection FTC, Washington, 1973—75; ptnr. Latham & Watkins, San Francisco, 1994—2006, office mng. ptnr., 1994—99; commr. FTC, Washington, 2006—. Adv. bd. Antitrust and Trade Regulation Report, Bur. Nat. Affairs, 1976—2006, Practising Law Inst., NYC; bd. dirs. Eisenhower Inst., Washington, 2003—06. Contbr. articles to profl. jours. Knox Fellow, Cambridge U., 1962. Fellow Am. Bar Found., Am. Coll. Trial Lawyers; mem. ABA (chmn. antitrust sect. 1990), Calif. State Bar Assn. (past chair Antitrust and Unfair Competition Sect., Antitrust Lawyer of Yr. 2003) San Francisco Bar Assn. Republican. Episcopalian. Office: FTC 600 Pennsylvania Ave NW Rm 540 Washington DC 20580 Business E-Mail: trosch@ftc.gov.

ROSCH, PAUL JOHN, internist, educator; b. Yonkers, NY, June 30, 1927; s. Samuel Joseph and Mary (Gang) R.; m. Lorraine Marie Hunt, June 27, 1951; children: David Carl, Jonathan Hunt, Jane Ellen, Michael Edward, Richard Joseph, Donna Marie; m. Marguerite Delamater, Sept. 12, 1972. AB, Brown U., NYU, 1948, MA, 1950; MD, Albany Med. Coll., 1954. Diplomate Am. Bd. Internal Medicine. Fellow Inst. Exptl. Medicine and Surgery, U. Montreal, Que., Canada, 1951-52; intern, asst. resident in medicine Johns Hopkins Hosp., 1954-56; resident in medicine, then chief dept. metabolism Walter Reed Med. Ctr., 1956-58; physician-in-charge nuclear medicine St. John's Riverside Hosp., Yonkers, 1959-67, dir. endocrine clinic, sr. attending physician, 1959-96, vice chief of staff, 1977; chief endocrine clinic St. Joseph's Hosp., 1959, sr. cons. in medicine, 1980—; pres. Am. Inst. Stress, Yonkers, 1978—, sr. cons. in medicine, 1980—; clin. prof. medicine and psychiatry N.Y. Med. Coll., 1980—. Asst. clin. prof. medicine Mt. Sinai Hosp. Sch. Medicine, 1963-67; former adj. prof. medicine in psychiatry U. Md. Sch. Medicine. From asst. to assoc. editor Health Comm. and Informatics; editor-in-chief Stress Medicine, 1990—; mem. editorial bd. AMA Archives Internal Medicine, Folia Clinica Internat, Jour. Human Stress, Internat. Jour. Psychosomatics, Am. Jour. Health Promotion, Cardiovascular Revs. & Reports, Internat. Jour. Stress Mgmt., Comprehensive Therapy, Jour. Human Behavior; contbg. editor Creative Living; contbr. articles to profl. jours. Bd. govs. Jewish Community Ctr.; bd. dirs. Family Svc. Soc., Mensana Clinic, 1980—; chmn. bd. Internat. Found. Biosocial Devel. and Human Health, 1980—; mem. adv. bd. Image Inst., 1980—. Capt. AUS, 1956-58. Fellow ACP, Internat. Stress Mgmt. Assn. (hon. v.p. 1991—), Am. Coll. Cardiology, Internat. Acad. Medicine, Am. Coll. Angiology, NY Diabetes Assn.; mem. Westchester Diabetes Assn. (pres. 1968), Internat. Law Enforcement Stress Assn. (adv. bd. 1980—), Yonkers Acad. Medicine (bd. govs., pres. 1971), NY Cardiology Soc., Acad. Psychosomatic Medicine, Soc. Behavioral Medicine, NY Acad. Scis., Endocrine Soc., Am. Diabetes Assn., Westchester Soc. Internat. Medicine (past pres.), Stress Mgmt. Assn. (hon. v.p.), NY State Soc. Internal Medicine (pres. 1974), Soc. Nuclear Medicine (bd. dirs.), Am. Fedn. Clin. Rsch., Am. Soc. Internal Medicine, Am. Geriatrics Soc., Elmwood Country Club, Atlantis Golf Club, Breakers Golf Club, St. Andrews Golf Club. Home: 10 Old Jackson Ave Hastings On Hudson NY 10706-3203 Office Phone: 914-963-1200. Personal E-mail: stress124@optonline.net.

ROSCHER, DAVID K., lawyer; b. Denville, NJ, July 19, 1956; s. Rudolph P. and Joan P. Roscher; m. Hope K. Raitt (div. 2000); children: Joshua S. Rovner, Matthew P., Sarah E. AB, Franklin and Marshall Coll., Lancaster, Pa., 1978; JD, Villanova U., Pa., 1981. Bar: Pa. 1981, NJ 1983. Assoc. counsel Kravco Co., King of Prussia, Pa., 1982—86; pvt. practice Phila., 1986—96; of counsel Ballard Spahr Andrews & Ingersoll, LLP, Phila., 1996—2003; gen. counsel EBL&S Property Mgmt., Inc., Phila., 2004—. Mem.: ICSC. Avocation: accordion. Office: EBL&S Property Mgmt Inc 230 S Broad St Mezzanine Philadelphia PA 19102 Home Phone: 215-884-0714; Office Phone: 215-790-4728. Office Fax: 215-735-2371. Business E-Mail: droscher@ebl-s.com.

ROSCOE, MICHAEL SHANNON, physician assistant, educator; b. Murphysboro, Ill., Feb. 25, 1972; s. Phillip Thadius and Candace Nellie Roscoe; m. Michelle Christine Hack, June 18, 1994; children: Mahayla Christine, Rachel Kathryn, Kolbe Michael, Abigail Rae. BS, Butler U., Indpls., 1994, B of Health Sci., 1999; MS, Purdue U., Indpls., 1996; M of Physician Asst. Studies, U. Nebr., Omaha, 2001; PhD, Touro U. Internat., Cypress, Calif., 2004. Cert. physicians assistant Ind., 1999, paramedic Ind., 1997. Physician asst. Cmty. Hosp. Anderson, Ind., 1999—; asst. prof. Butler U., Indpls., 2005—. Contbr. articles to profl. jours. Physicians asst. comdr. co. C med. 113th spt bn. US N.G., 2005—, Noblesville, Ind. Decorated Bronze Star US Army; recipient Outstanding Clin. Faculty award, Butler U., 2004, PA Yr. award, Ind. Acad. Physician Assts., 2005. Fellow: Am. Acad. of Physician Assts. Conservative. Roman Catholic. Home: 308 West 46th St Indianapolis IN 46208 Office: Butler Univ 4600 Sunset Ave Indianapolis IN 46208 Home Phone: 317-402-6908; Office Phone: 317-940-6026. Business E-Mail: mroscoe@butler.edu.

ROSCOE, STANLEY NELSON, psychologist, aeronautical engineer; b. Eureka, Calif., Nov. 4, 1920; s. Stanley Boughton and Martha Emma (Beer) R.; m. Margaret Hazel Brookins, Dec. 21, 1948 (dec.); children: Lee Marin Roscoe Bragg, Jack; m. Elizabeth Frances Lage, Mar. 12, 1977 (dec.); 1 child, Catherine Marie; m. Gayle Buchanan Karshner, Mar. 15, 1990. AB in Speech and English, Humboldt State U., 1943; postgrad., U. Calif., Berkeley, 1942-46; MA in Psychology, U. Ill., 1947, PhD in Psychology, 1950. Cert. psychologist, Calif. Research asst. U. Ill., Urbana-Champaign, 1946-50, research assoc., 1950-51, asst. prof., 1951-52; assoc. dir. Inst. Aviation, head aviation rsch. lab., Savoy, 1969—75, prof. aviation, psychology, aero. and astronautical engring., 1969—79, prof. emeritus, 1979—; prof. psychology N.Mex. State U., Las Cruces, 1979-86, prof. emeritus, 1986—; with Hughes Aircraft Co., Culver City, Calif., 1952-69, 75-77, dept. mgr., 1962-69, sr. scientist, 1975-77; tech. adviser, cons. in field. Pres. Illiana Aviation Scis. Ltd., Las Cruces, N.Mex., 1976—; v.p. Aero Innovation, Inc., Montreal. Author: Aviation Psychology, 1980, Flightdeck Performance: The Human Factor, 1990, Heydays in Mattole, 1996, Predicting Human Performance, 1997, Keeping the Picture: The Measurement of Flow Control, 1999; editor: Aviation Research Monographs, 1971-72, Heydays in Humboldt, 1991, From Humboldt to Kodiak, 1992; assoc. cons. editor: Human Factors Jour., 1982—, Internat. Jour. Aviation Psychology, 1991—; contbr. more than 200 articles to profl. jours.; patentee, inventor in field. 1st lt. AC, U.S. Army, 1943-46. Fellow APA (divsn. of applied and engring. psychology, Franklin V. Taylor award 1976), Human Factors and Ergonomics Soc. (pres. 1960-61, Jerome H. Ely award 1968, 73, 89, 91, Alexander C. Williams award 1973, Paul M. Fitts award 1974, Pres.'s award 1990), Royal Aero Soc. (Eng.); mem. IEEE, AIAA, Inst. Navigation, Assn. Aviation Psychologists (ann. career award 1978), Aerospace Human Factors Assn. (Paul T. Hansen award 1994), Sigma Xi, Phi Kappa Phi, Phi Sigma, Chi Sigma Epsilon. Home: 2750 Sunnygrove Ave Mckinleyville CA 95519-7912 Office: PO Box 4498 Las Cruces NM 88003-4498

ROSCOPF, CHARLES BUFORD, lawyer; b. Marvell, Ark., Apr. 21, 1928; s. Emmett Lee and Sally Virginia (King) R.; m. Mary Anne Maddox, Aug. 22, 1954; children— Charles David; Ann Karen. Student, Hendrix Coll., 1948-50; JD, U. Ark., 1954. Bar: Ark. bar 1954, U.S. Dist. Cts 1955, 64, U.S. Supreme Ct. bar 1965. Pvt. practice, Helena, Ark., 1954—; assoc. firm Burke, Moore & Burke, 1954-58; ptnr. firm Burke & Roscopf, 1958-64; sr. ptnr. Roscopf and Roscopf, P.A., 1964—. Mem. Ark. Ho. of Reps., 1953-58; del. Ark. Constl. Conv., 1968; mem. Ark. Probate Drafting Com.; mem. Ark. State Bd. Law Examiners, 1973-79; spl. justice Ark. Supreme Ct. Served with USN, 1946-48; served with USAFR, 1962-68. Fellow Am. Bar Found., Ark. Bar Found. (pres. 1995-96); mem. ABA, Ark. Bar Assn. (pres. 1990-91), Am. Law Inst., Rotary (Paul Harris fellow), Masons, Shriners, Kappa Sigma. Methodist. Home: 117 Avalon Pl Helena AR 72342-1715 Office: Helena Nat Bank Bldg PO Box 610 Helena AR 72342-0610 Office Phone: 870-338-3438.

ROSE, ALBERT SCHOENBURG, lawyer, educator; b. Nov. 9, 1945; s. Albert Schoenberg Sr. and Karleen (Klein) Rose; m. Nancy K. Rose; children: Claudia, Micah Daniel. BSBA, U. Ala., 1967; JD, Washington U., St. Louis, 1970; LLM in Taxation, George Washington U., 1974. Bar: Mo. 1970, U.S. Dist. Ct. (ea. dist.) Mo. 1970, U.S. Tax Ct. 1970, U.S. Ct. Mil. Appeals 1970, U.S. Supreme Ct. 1970. Ptnr. Lewis Rice & Fingersh, St. Louis, 2001—. Adj. prof. law Washington U., 1979-98, Fontbonne Coll., 1993-96. Co-author: Missouri Taxation Law and Practice, 1986, supplement, 1989. Capt. U.S. Army, 1970-74, Korea. Mem.: Civic Entrepreneurs Orgn. (Bd. dirs., sec.), Tax Lawyers Club, Mid.Am. Tax Conf. (chmn.). Office: Lewis Rice & Fingersh 500 North Broadway Ste 2000 Saint Louis MO 63102 Office Phone: 314-444-1300. E-mail: arose@lewisrice.com.

ROSE, ARON D., ophthalmologist, educator; b. Norwalk, Conn., Sept. 23, 1958; s. Gilbert and Anne Rose; m. Stacey L. Miller; children: Jenna, Lauren, Hannah. BA (hon.), Brown U., Providence, 1980; MD, NY Med. Coll., Valhalla, 1985; degree in ophthalmology, Mt. Sinai Sch. of Medicine, NYC, 1989. Fellow Am. Bd. Ophthalmology, 1989. Assoc. clin. prof. Yale U. Sch. Medicine, New Haven, 1989—, Yale U. Sch. Nursing, New Haven, 1996—. Dir., residency tng. Yale U. Dept. Ophthalmology and Visual Scis., New Haven, 1992—94; cons. Advanced Med. Optics, Santa Ana, Calif., 2003—; sect. editor Techniques in Ophthalmology, 2004—. Composer: Quartet for Clarinet & Strings, 1980; contbr. articles various profl. jours. Advisor JusticeWorks Med. Humanitarian Assn., Newtown, Pa., 1994—99; bd. mem. New Haven Med. Assn., 1995—2004; strategic oversight New Haven Hunger & Relief, 1997—2006; invited faculty Project Orbis Internat., NYC, 1992—2006; advisor Yale China Health Adv. Com. Recipient Brand Music Premium for Excellence in Musical Composition, Brown U., 1980, Departmental Honors, 1980. Fellow: Am. Acad. Ophthalmology (life); mem.: European Soc. Cataract and Refractive Surgeons, Conn. Soc. Eye Physicians, Conn. Glaucoma Soc., New Eng. Ophthal. Soc., Conn. State Med. Soc., Am. Soc. Cataract and Refractive Surgeons. Office: Eye Care Group PC 40 Temple St 5B New Haven CT 06405 Home Phone: 203-483-5996; Office Phone: 203-789-2020.

ROSE, ARTHUR ROYAL, financial planner, tax consultant; b. Red Bank, NJ, July 22, 1955; s. Melvin S. and Margaret L. R. BS in Bus. summa cum laude, Monmouth U., 1986, BA in Psychology summa cum laude, 1986, MBA, 1990. CFP; Accredited tax preparer; registered investment advisor, N.J.; enrolled agt. IRS. CFO, Interphase Industries Inc., Red Bank, 1986-91; pres. World-View Inc., Red Bank, 1991—.

ROSE, BEATRICE SCHROEDER, harpist, educator; b. Ridgewood, NJ, Nov. 15, 1922; d. Henry William and Ida (LeHovey) Schroeder; m. William Harrison Rose, Apr. 10, 1954; 1 child, Daniel. Student, Inst. Musical Art, 1940—41, Mannes Coll. Music, 1942—44; studies with, Lucile Lawrence and Carlos Salzedo. Concert and radio debut NY World's Fair, NYC, 1939; soloist Damrosch Music Appreciation Hour broadcast, 1940, Duke of Windsor's Save the Children Fund, Nassau, The Bahamas, 1941; assoc. harpist Radio City Music Hall Orch., NYC, 1944-50; various radio and solo performances NY area, 1944-51; concert artist Italy, US and Can., 1952; prin. harpist Houston Symphony, 1953-84; prof. harp Moores Sch. Music, U. Houston, 1953—98. Soloist Contemporary Music Soc., 1959, 60, Houston Chamber Orch., 1969; dir. Christmas Festival of Harps, Houston Harp Ensemble, PBS, 1978, Harps of Gold, 1983; staff harpist Heritage Club, 1987-95, High Tea Ritz Carlton, 1996-97, St. Regis, 1998-2003. Author: The Harp in the Orchestra: A Reference Book for Harpists, Teachers, Composers and Conductors, 2003; composer works include Enchanted Harp, rev. edit., 1995; recs. for Houston Symphony, Stokowski, Everest, Capitol, Comissiona, Vanguard Records. Recipient 1st prize Federated Music Clubs Contest, 1936; NY Hour of Music award, 1945. Mem. Am. Harp Soc., Tex. Music Educators Assn. (adjudicator All-State competitions), Nat. Fedn. Music Clubs (harp adviser 1991), Phi Beta. Home: 1315 Friarcreek Ln Houston TX 77055-6714 Office: U Houston Sch Music Houston TX 77004

ROSE, CAROL ANN, retired air transportation executive; b. Toledo; d. Donald Lucien and Dorothy Josephine (Maus) Edmunds; m. Saul Rose, Feb. 3, 1971 (div. 1976). life partner Bill Carman. BA, Kent State U., 1963. Entertainer, restaurant supr. S.S. Aquarama Cruiseship, Cleve., 1961-63; airline reservation agt. United Airlines, Cleve., 1963-68, internat. passenger svc. rep. Miami, Fla., 1969-70, V.I.P. customer svc. receptionist-expediter Phila., 1971-79, account exec., 1980-84, spl. events mgr. Chgo., 1984-87, red carpet club coord., 1987-88, corp. meeting planner, 1988-90, comml. aircraft weight and balance planner Seattle, 1991-96, comms. coord., 1996-98, mktg. and promotion coord., 1998-99, coord. workers compensation-comm./return to work Chgo., 1999—2001; ret., 2001; vol. editor Spiceline cmty. newsletter. Speaker Am. Mktg. Assn., Chgo., 1989. Author: Red Carpet Club Procedure Manual-O'Hare, 1987, Corporate Meeting Planners Manual, 1989, United Airlines Foundation Community Connection Report; Editor: Sky Lines Seattle Station Newsletter, 1992, United Airlines Workers' Compensation Newsletter, 1999; editor, marketer (newsletter) Crescent Moon Coffee and Tea. Vol. Relay for Life Am. Cancer Soc. Recipient Oustanding Svc. award Airline Passengers Assn., Phila., 1981, Outstanding Contbn. award Muscular Dystrophy Assn.-Jerry Lewis Telethon, Las Vegas, 1985, 86, 89, Leadership award United Way Campaign, Chgo., 1988. Mem. Meeting Planners Assn., Mgmt. Club (v.p. 1983, pres. 1984), Women United (exec. bd. 1982-83), Spicer Estates Homeowners Assn. (pres. 2004-06), Delta Zeta. Avocations: reading, walking, writing, dance. Home: 468 Woodruff Trl Mullica Hill NJ 08062-2026

ROSE, CAROL MARGUERITE, law educator; b. Washington, Apr. 12, 1940; d. J. Hugh and Marie (Meenehan) R. BA, Antioch Coll., 1962; MA, U. Chgo., 1963, JD, 1977; PhD, Cornell U., 1970. Bar: Ill. 1977, Calif. 1978, D.C. 1978. Instr. history Ohio St. U., Columbus, 1969-73; assoc. dir. So. Govtl. Monitor Project, Atlanta, 1975-76; law clk. to judge U.S. Ct. Appeals (5th cir.), Austin, Tex., 1977-78; asst. prof. law Stanford U., 1978-80; acting prof. law U. Calif., Berkeley, 1980-82; prof. law Northwestern U., Chgo., 1982-88, Yale U., 1989—90, Fred A. Johnston prof. New Haven, 1990—94, Gordon Bradford Tweedy prof. of law and orgn., 1994—2005; emerita, 2005—06; Lohse prof. water and natural resource law U. Ariz., 2006—. Bd. editors Found. Press, Mineola, N.Y., 1986—. Mem. Am. Assn. Law Schs., Am. Acad. Arts and Scis., Order of Coif. Office: U Ariz Coll of Law PO Box 210176 Tucson AZ 85721-0176 Office Phone: 520-621-5544. E-mail: carol.rose@yale.edu.

ROSE, CHARLES ALEXANDER, lawyer; b. Louisville, June 14, 1932; s. Hector Edward and Mary (Shepard) R.; m. Moncie Watson; children: Marc, Craig, Lorna, Gordon, Alex, Sara. BA, U. Louisville, 1954, JD, 1960. Bar: Ky. 1960, U.S. Ct. Appeals (6th cir.) 1970, Ind. 1978, U.S. Supreme Ct. 1978. Pvt. practice, Louisville, 1960-63; assoc. Jones, Ewen & McKenzie, Louisville, 1963-65; ptnr. Curtis & Rose, Louisville, 1965-81, Weber & Rose, Louisville, 1981—. Organist Scottish Rite Temple, Louisville. Lt. USAF, 1954-56. Mem. ABA, Ky. Bar Assn., Ind. Bar Assn., Louisville Bar Assn., Am. Soc. Hosp. Attys., Am. Bd. Trial Advocates, Brandeis Soc., Fedn. Ins. Counsel, River Road Country Club, Pendennis Club (Louisville), Jefferson Club. Republican. Episcopalian. Office: 400 W Market St Ste 2700 Louisville KY 40202-3358

ROSE, CHARLIE (CHARLES PEETE ROSE JR.), television journalist; b. Henderson, NC, Jan. 5, 1942; s. Charles Rose Sr. and Margaret Rose; m. Mary King (div. 1980). B in History, Duke U., JD; Ph.D (hon.), C.W. Post Coll., U.NC-Pembroke. Interviewer Sta. WPIX-TV, NYC, 1972; mng. editor Bill Moyers Internat. Report, 1974—75; exec. producer Bill Moyers Jour., 1975—76; corr. U.S.A.: People in Politics, PBS, 1976; polit. corr. NBC News, 1976-77; co-host A.M. Chgo., 1978; host The Charlie Rose Show Sta. KXAS-TV, Dallas, Ft. Worth, 1979-81, Sta. WRC-TV, Washington, 1981-83; host, interviewer CBS News Nightwatch, Washington, 1984—90; exec. prodr., exec. editor and host The Charlies Rose Show, 1991—; corr. Sixty Minutes II, 1999—. Producer: (TV program) A Conversation with Jimmy Carter (George Peabody Broadcasting award). Recipient News and Documentary Emmy award for Conversation with Roger Payne, 1992, Cable ACE award, 1992, Futrell award, 2005. Office: 499 Park Ave New York NY 10022-1240

ROSE, DALE A.J., performing arts educator; b. Detroit, Sept. 5, 1946; s. Ora Henry Rose and Vida Blanche Birkett. BA, Mich. State U., 1966, MA, 1968. Performing arts coord. Mich. State Arts Coun. for the Arts, 1968—69; asst. prof. U. South Fla., Tampa, 1973—77; asst. prof. divsn. theatre So. Meth. U., Dallas, 1977—81, adj. prof., 1984—85, assoc. prof., 1985—88, Mo. Repertory Theatre/U. Mo., Kansas City, 1988—97, prof., 1997—2004; dir. Sch. Theatre and Dance U. South Fla., Tampa, 2004—05; dir. performance studies U. Conn., Storrs, 2005—; master tchr. acting The Actors Ctr., NYC, 2005—; assoc. artistic dir. Conn. Repertory Theatre, Storrs, 2005—. Artistic dir. Shakespeare Festival of Dallas, 1986—90, The Plaza Theatre, Dallas, 1983—84; acting tchr. George Morrison Studio and Warren Robertson Theatre Workshop, NYC, 1981—83; co-founder, dir. Stage #1, Dallas, 1979—85; artistic dir., founder The Alice People Theatre Co., Tampa, 1974—77; host, commentator The Bergman Films-WUSF-TV, 1975; co-host, theatre/film critic Variety, WTOG-TV, St. Petersburg, Fla., 1973—76; actor, NYC, 1970—73. Dir.: (plays) The Boys Next Door, 1991, Hydrophobia, 1993, The First Family of Africa, 1993, The Very First Family, 1994, The Belle of Amherst, 1996, Babes in Arms, 1996, Les Liaisons Dangereuses, 1998, Charley's Aunt, 2000; author: (plays) The Pearl, 1994; screenwriter Eye for Eye, 1996—98; dir.: (plays) numerous plays, As You Like It, 2006. Office: University of Connecticut 802 Bolton Rd Unit 1127 Storrs Mansfield CT 06269

ROSE, DANIEL, real estate company executive, consultant; b. NYC, Oct. 31, 1929; s. Samuel B. and Belle (Bernstein) R.; m. Joanna Semel, Sept. 16, 1956; children: David Semel, Joseph Benedict, Emily, Gideon Gregory. Student, Yale U., 1947-50; cert. of proficiency in Russian lang., U.S. Air Force Program, 1951; BA, Syracuse U., 1952; postgrad., U. Paris. With Dwelling Mgrs., Inc., NYC, 1954—, pres., 1960—; vice-chmn., sec.-treas. Baltic-Am. Enterprise Fund, 1994—; dir. Dreyfus Tax Exempt Bond Fund Inc., 1976-82, Dreyfus Money Market Fund, Inc., 1980-82; pres., CEO Rose Assocs., Inc., NYC, 1980-99, chmn., 1999—, 22 Dreyfus Funds, 1992—. Assoc. fellow Pierson Coll. Yale U., 1974—; bd. govs., hon. life mem. Technion-Israel Inst. Tech.; bd. dirs., grants com. Realty Found. N.Y.; vice-chmn. Lionel Trilling seminars Columbia U., 1977—; trustee, mem. exec. and compensation and benefits coms. U.S. Trust Co. of N.Y., 1982-92; trustee, vice-chmn. mixed use devel. coun. Urban Land Inst., 1986-93; exec. com. Urban Land Found., 1989—, gov., 1993—; designated Cert. Property Mgr. Inst. for Real Estate Mgmt.; chmn. Forum for Urban Design. Expert adv. to sec. HUD, 1972; expert/cons. to commr. edn. HEW, 1974; cons. HUD panel on urban devel., 1984-86; dir. N.Y. Coun. Humanities, 1980-86, N.Y. Conv. Ctr. Devel. Corp., 1980-90, Get Ahead Found., 1989-98, Fifth Ave. Assn., 1989-98; mem. Governor's Task Force on Housing, 1975, Task Force on Taxation, Mcpl. Assistance Corp., 1976-77, Planning Commn. Theatre Adv. Group, coun. of fellows, vis. com. to grad. faculty, bd. overseers Ctr. for Study of N.Y.C. affairs New Sch. for Social Rsch.; overseers com. to visit Ctr. Internat. Affairs Harvard U., 1992-98; Mcpl. Broadcasting System, 1977-78, MIT Ctr. for Real Estate Devel.; donor Daniel Rose chair urban econs., trustee NYU N.Y. Inst. for Humanistic Studies, Mus. of City of N.Y., 1984-90; chmn. bd. trustees, Horace Mann-Barnard Sch., 1971-74, trustee, 1962-89, hon. trustee, 1989—; v.p., assoc. treas., bd. dirs. Police Athletic League of N.Y., vice chmn. Cen. Harlem Facility; founder and pres. Harlem Ednl. Activities Fund Inc., YM & YWHA of the Bronx, 1963-67; v.p. N.Y. Landmarks Conservancy, bd. dirs. 1977-90; bd. dirs. Jewish Cmty. Ctrs. Assn., 1970—, pres. 1974-78, hon. pres. 1978—; v.p. World Confedn. of Jewish Cmty. Ctrs., 1977-83; former trustee and exec. com. mem. Fedn. of Jewish Philanthropies of N.Y., chmn. standing functional com. on cmty. ctrs., 1969-73; ptnr. N.Y.C. Partnership, 1990—; treas., bd. dirs. Citizens Housing and Planning Coun. of N.Y., 1972—; chmn. Dem. platform adv. com., 1984 Nat. Conv.; bd. advisors Dem. Leadership Coun., 1992—, Progressive Policy Inst.; trustee Dem. Nat. Com., 1988; chmn. Del. Svcs. Host Com., N.Y.C.; bd. trustees MBA of N.Y. Scholarship Found., Inc., 1996—. Served with USAF, 1951-54. Mem. Internat. Inst. Strategic Studies (dir. Am. com. for IISS 1987—), Coun. on Fgn. Rels., Fgn. Policy Assn. (bd. dirs. 1971—, chmn. fgn. policy assocs. 1972-75), East-West Inst. (bd. dirs. 1982—, treas. 1988—, co-chmn. fin. com. 1990—, chmn. exec. com. 2000—), Am. Soc. Real Estate Counselors (mem. publs.-rsch. com.), Real Estate Bd. of N.Y. Inc. (chmn. housing com. 1975—, mem. bd. govs. 1977-80, 90—, mem. REBNY Found.), Assn. of Yale Alumni (del.-at-large 1978-81, class of 1951 del. 1986-89), Century Assn. (N.Y.C.), Coffee House, Yale, Union League Club, Cosmos (Washington), Quaker Ridge Country Club, Noyac Country Club, Econ. Club N.Y. Office: Rose Associates Inc 200 Madison Ave Fl 5 New York NY 10016-3912 E-mail: drose@rosenyc.com.

ROSE, DAVID L., lawyer; b. Ft. Monmouth, NJ, Feb. 18, 1955; s. Llewellyn Paterson and Bebe (Faulk) R.; m. Karen M. Rose; children from previous marriage: Allison Michelle, Jessica Morgan, Ashley Elizabeth. BA in Comm., U. Colo., 1980; JD, Ariz. State U., 1991. Bar: Ariz. 1991, U.S. Dist. Ct. Ariz. 1991, U.S. Ct. Appeals (9th cir.) 1993, U.S. Supreme Ct. 1997, cert.specialist in family law, 2004. Law clk. Bonn & Anderson, Phoenix, 1988-91, Maricopa County Superior Ct., Phoenix, 1990-91; atty. Anderson, Brody, Levinson, Weiser & Horwitz, Phoenix, 1991-92, Brandes, Lane & Joffe, Phoenix, 1992-93, Rose & Hildebrand, P.C., 1997—2006; pvt. practice Phoenix, 1993—2006, 2006—. Judge pro-tem Maricopa County Superior Ct., Maricopa County Justice Ct. Editor: Missive, 1992. Bd. dirs. Maricopa County Family Support Adv. Com., Phoenix; adv. coun. Washington Sch. Dist., Phoenix; mem. Ariz. State Legis., Domestic Rels. Reform Com., Phoenix. Mem. Maricopa County Bar Assn. (adv. family law com.), ABA (adv. family law sect.), Nat. Congress for Men (pres.), Father's for Equal Rights of Colo. (pres.). Avocations: aviation, computer systems. Office: 1440 E Washington St Phoenix AZ 85034-1109 Office Phone: 602-340-8400.

ROSE, DEBRA FIELDS See FIELDS, DEBBI

ROSE, DONALD MCGREGOR, retired lawyer; b. Cin., Feb. 6, 1933; s. John Kreimer and Helen (Morris) R.; m. Constance Ruth Lanner, Nov. 29, 1958; children: Barbara Rose Burgess, Ann Rose Weston. AB in Econs., U. Cin., 1955; JD, Harvard U., Cambridge, Mass., 1958. Bar: Ohio 1958, U.S. Supreme Ct. 1962. Asst. legal officer USNR, Subic Bay, The Philippines, 1959-62, with Office of JAG The Pentagon, Va., 1962-63; assoc. Frost & Jacobs, LLP, Cin., 1963-70, ptnr., 1970-93, sr. ptnr., 1993-97, ret. ptnr., 1997. Co-chmn. 6th Cir. Appellate Practice Inst., Cin., 1983, 90, 6th Cir. adv. com., 1990-98, chmn. subcom. on rules, 1990-94, chmn., 1994-96. Trustee Friends of Cin. Pks., Inc., 1980-89, 93-98, pres. 1980-86; trustee Am. Music Scholarship Assn., Cin., 1985-88; pres. Social Health Assn. Greater Cin. Area Inc., 1969-72; co-chmn. Harvard Law Sch. Fund for So. Ohio, Cin., 1985-87; pres. Meth. Union, Cin., 1983-85; chmn. trustees Hyde Pk. Cmty. United Meth. Ch., Cin., 1974-76, chmn. coun. on ministries, 1979-81, chmn. adminstrv. bd., 1982-84, chmn. mem. canvass, 1985, chmn. staff parish rels. com., 1988-90, chmn. commn. missions, 1993-95; trustee Meth. Theol. Sch. Ohio, vice chmn. devel. com., 1990-94, sec. 1992-94, chmn. devel. com., 1994-98, vice chmn., 1998, chmn., 1999—2004; loaned exec. United Way, Cin., 1999. Lt. USNR, 1959-63. Mem.: 6th Cir. Judicial Conf. (sr.), Boothbay Country Club, Boothbay Harbor Yacht Club (bd. dirs. 2005—), Cin. Country Club. Republican. Avocations: sailing, golf. Home: 8 Walsh Ln Cincinnati OH 45208-3435 also: 11 Blackstone Rd Boothbay Harbor ME 04538-1943 Business E-Mail: dmrose@fbtlaw.com.

ROSE, DWIGHT DEAN, music educator; b. Omaha, Nebr., Apr. 6, 1970; s. Marvin Alan Rose (Deceased) and Betty Jane Rose. BA, Midland Luth. Coll., Fremont, NE, 1993; MA Music Ed., Univ. Nebr., Omaha, NE, 2002. Music educator Laurel-Concord Schools, Laurel, Nebr., 1993—97, Lyons-

Decatur Schools, Lyons, 1997—2003. Recipient Snider Young Band Dir., Nebr. State Bandmasters Assn., 1998. Mem.: Nebr. Choral Dirs. Assn., Am. Choral Dirs. Assn., Music Educators Nat. Conf., Nebr. Music Educators Assn., Nebr. State Bandmasters Assn. Office: Lyons-Decatur Public Schools PO Box 526 Lyons NE 68038 Office Phone: 402-687-2363. E-mail: drose@esu2.org.

ROSE, ELIHU, real estate executive; b. NYC, Mar. 30, 1933; s. Samuel B. and Belle (Bernstein) R.; m. Susan Wechsler, Feb. 6, 1965; children: Amy, Isabel, Abigail. BS, Yale U., 1954; MA, NYU, 1969, PhD, 1978. Vice chmn. Rose Assocs., NYC, 1956—. Contbr. articles to profl. mil. jours. Former chmn. bd. dirs. Internat. Ctr. Photography; bd. dirs. Sta. WNET (PBS), Lincoln Ctr. Theater, 1992—, Nat. Mus. Am. History, Smithsonian Instn. Fellow Am. Acad. Arts and Scis.; mem. Internat. Inst. Strategic Studies, Coun. Fgn. Rels., Century Assn., Union League Club, Yale Club of N.Y., Army and Navy Club (Washington). Office: Rose Assocs 200 Madison Ave New York NY 10016-3903

ROSE, ELIHU ISAAC, lawyer; b. Bklyn., Nov. 27, 1941; s. Aaron Henry and Frances (Klinger) R.; m. Gail Roberta Cohen, Aug. 22, 1964; children: Melissa Kaye, Heidi Jill. AB, Columbia U., 1963, MBA, 1965; JD, St. John's U., Bklyn., 1968. Bar: N.Y.; CPA, N.Y. Sr. tax acct. Price Waterhouse & Co., NYC, 1967-71; dir. taxes Exec. Monetary Mgmt., Inc., NYC, 1971-79; pres. Elihu I. Rose, P.C., Lake Success, NY, 1979—; of counsel Sahn Ward & Baker, PLLC, Uniondale, NY, 2003—. Mem. AICPA, N.Y. State Bar Assn., N.Y. State Soc. CPAs, Bar Assn. Nassau County, Estate Planning Coun. L.I. E-mail: roselaw@sprintmail.com.

ROSE, GEORGE ANDREW, application developer, information systems specialist; b. Mt. Clemens, Mich., Dec. 17, 1950; s. George Hubert and Geraldine Marie (Benoit) R. BA, BSW in Psychology and Biology, Ea. Mich. U., Ypsilanti, 1975; MBA in Internat. Fin., George Wash. U., Washington, DC, 1987. Inpatient substance abuse therapist St. Joseph's Hosp., Mt. Clemens, 1974—77; dep. twp. clk. Twp. of Clinton, Mich., 1977—79; social worker Bur. Rehab, Washington, 1979—84; sr. social worker Comprehensive Alcohol and Drug Abuse Ctr., Washington, 1984—88; contract mgmt. UMWA Health and Retirement Funds, Washington, 1988—91; dir. software devel., info. svcs. United Seniors Health Coop., Washington, 1993—98; pres., CEO Portsmouth Group, Inc., Washington, 1997—. Home: 2929 Connecticut Ave NW Ste 306 Washington DC 20008-1435 Office: The Portsmouth Group Inc Ste 605 1522 K St Washington DC 20005 Business E-Mail: georgerose@portsmouthgroup.net.

ROSE, HUGH, management consultant; b. Evanston, Ill., Sept. 10, 1926; s. Howard Gray and Catherine (Wilcox) R.; m. Mary Moore Austin, Oct. 25, 1952; children: Susan, Nancy, Gregory, Matthew, Mary. BS in Physics, U. Mich., 1951, MS in Geology, 1952; MBA with highest distinction, Pepperdine U., 1982. Mgr. Caterpillar, Inc., Peoria, Ill., 1952-66; v.p., mktg. mgr. Cummins Engine Co., Columbus, Ind., 1966-69; pres., CEO Cummins Northeastern, Inc., Boston, 1969-77; pres. Power Sys. Assocs., LA, 1980—83, C.D. High Tech., Inc., Austin, Tex., 1984-87; mgmt. cons. Rose and Assocs., Tucson, 1984, 87—; molecular cell biology rschr. U. Ariz. Cardio-Thoracic Lab., Tucson, 2004—. Polit. cartoonist. Contbr. articles to profl. jours. Bd. dirs. Raymond Alf Mus., Claremont, Calif., 1975—, Comstock Found., Tucson, 1988, Environ. Edn. Exch., 1991, Heart Ctr. U. Ariz., Tucson, 1992. With USAAF, WWII. Fellow AAAS; mem. Acacia, Soc. Vertebrate Paleontology, Beacon Soc. Boston (pres. 1979-80), Algonquin Club Boston (v.p., bd. dirs. 1974-80), Duxbury Yacht Club, Longwood Cricket Club, Skyline Country Club, Phi Beta Kappa (founding pres. greater Tucson assn.), Delta Mu Delta, Sigma Gamma Epsilon, Sigma Pi Sigma, Beta Beta Beta, Sigma Xi, Beta Gamma Sigma. Republican. Presbyterian. Office: Rose & Assocs 5320 N Camino Sumo Tucson AZ 85718-5132

ROSE, I. NELSON, lawyer, educator; b. LA, May 23, 1950; s. Bernard and Helen Mae (Nelson) Rose. BA, UCLA, 1973; JD, Harvard U., 1979. Bar: Hawaii 79, U.S. Dist. Ct. Hawaii 79, Calif. 80, U.S. Supreme Ct. 91. Pvt. practice, Honolulu, 1979—82; asst. prof. law Whittier Coll., LA, 1982—85, assoc. prof., 1985—89, tenured prof. law, 1989—. Cons. legal gaming; vis. scholar Inst. for Study of Gambling and Comml. Gaming, U. Nev., Reno. Author: Gambling and the Law, 1986; author: (with Robert A. Loeb) Blackjack and the Law, 1998; co-author (with Robert M. Jarvis, J. Wesley Cochran. Ronald J. Rychlak): Gaming Law: Cases and Materials, 2003; co-author: (with Martin D. Owens) Internet Gaming Law, 2005; contbr. articles profl. jour. and books. Founder, counsel Hawaii Lions Eye Bank, Honolulu; founder, v.p., counsel Calif. Coun. on Compulsive Gambling; mem. Calif. Gambling Policy Adv. Com., 2002—04. Mem.: ABA, Internat. Assn. Gaming Attys., Hawaii Bar Assn., Calif. State Bar Assn. Democrat. Jewish. Home: 17031 Encino Hills Dr Encino CA 91436-4009 Office: Whittier Law Sch 3333 Harbor Blvd Costa Mesa CA 92626-1501 Office Phone: 818-788-8509.

ROSE, IRWIN A. (ERNIE ROSE), biochemist, educator; b. NYC, July 16, 1926; BS, U. Chgo., 1948, PhD in biochemistry, 1952. Specialist, Dept. Physiology and Biophysics, Sch. Med. U. Calif., Irvine, Calif. Contbr. articles to profl. jour. Co-recipient Nobel Prize in Chemistry, 2004. Mem.: NAS. Achievements include discovery of ubiquitin-mediated protein degradation. Office: U Calif Dept Physiology and Biophysics Coll Medicine Irvine CA 92697

ROSE, ISRAEL HAROLD, mathematics professor; b. New Britain, Conn., May 17, 1917; s. Abraham and Dora (Dubrow) R.; m. Pearl Nitzberg, Jan. 24, 1942 (div. Feb. 1956); 1 son, Steven Philip; m. Susan Ann Lazarus, Mar. 26, 1961; children: Dora, Eric. Student, CCNY, 1934-36; AB, Bklyn. Coll., 1938, A.M., 1941; PhD, Harvard, 1951. Tutor, instr. Bklyn. Coll., 1938-41; instr. Pa. State Coll., 1942-46; asst. prof. U. Mass., 1948-54, assoc. prof., 1954-60; faculty Hunter Coll., 1960-68, prof. math., 1965-68, chmn. dept., 1966-68; prof. math. Lehman Coll., CUNY, 1968-82, prof. emeritus, 1983—, chmn. dept., 1968-72, 80-82, resident prof., 1983—. Vis. asst. prof. Mt. Holyoke Coll., 1951-52, vis. assoc. prof., 1954-55, 58-59; sci. cons. AID, India, summer 1965 Author: A Modern Introduction to College Mathematics, 1959, Algebra: An Introduction to Finite Mathematics, 1963, Vectors and Analytic Geometry, 1968, Elementary Functions: A Precalculus Primer, 1973, (with Esther R. Phillips) Elementary Functions, 1978. NRC predoctoral fellow Harvard, 1946-48; fellow Fund Advancement Edn., 1952-53 Mem. Am. Math. Soc., Math. Assn. Am. (chmn. Met. N.Y. sect. 1973-75), Nat. Council Tchrs. Math., Assn. Tchrs. Math. New Eng. (pres. Conn. Valley sect. 1956-57), Sigma Xi (pres. Hunter Coll. chpt. 1966-67) Home: 18 Floral Dr Hastings On Hudson NY 10706-1202 Office: Lehman Coll Bedford Park Blvd W Bronx NY 10468

ROSE, JALEN, professional basketball player; b. Detroit, Jan. 30, 1973; s. Jeanne R. Student, U. Mich. Guard Denver Nuggets, 1994-96, Ind. Pacers, 1996—2002, Chicago Bulls, 2002—04, Toronto Raptors, 2004—06, NY Knicks, 2006, Phoenix Suns, 2006—. Named Honorable Mention All-Am., AP, 1991; set Michigan freshman scoring record, 1991; selected as All-Am., Parade Magazine, Third-Team All-Am., USA Today; set Nuggets' rookie record for assists, 1994-95 season; named to All-Rookie Second Team, NBA, 1995 Office: Phoenix Suns 201 E Jefferson St Phoenix AZ 85004

ROSE, JAMES TURNER, aerospace engineer, consultant; b. Louisburg, NC, Sept. 21, 1935; s. Frank Rogers and Mary Burt (Turner) R.; m. Daniele Raymond, Sept. 15, 1984. BS with high honors, N.C. State U., 1957. Aero. rsch. engr. NASA, Langley Field, Va., 1957-59; project engr. NASA (Mercury and Gemini), Langley Field, Va. and Houston, 1959-64; program sys. mgr. McDonnell Douglas Astronautics Co (MDAC), St. Louis, 1964-69; mgr. shuttle ops. and implementation (MDAC) McDonnell Douglas Astronautics Co., St. Louis, 1969-72, mgr. shuttle support (MDAC), 1972-74, mgr. space processing programs, 1976-83; dir. electrophoresis ops. in space McDonnell Douglas Astronautics Co (MDAC), St. Louis, 1983-86; dir. space shuttle engrng. NASA, Washington, 1974-76, asst. adminstr. comml. programs, 1987-91; aerospace cons., 1992—. Chmn. Fla. Space Bus. Roundtable, 1995-98. Recipient Lindberg award for mgmt. leadership AIAA, 1983, Presdl. Meritorious Rank award, 1989, NASA Exceptional Svc. medal, 1990, Laurels award Aviation Week, 1990, Aerospace Contribution to Soc. award AIAA, 1993. Mem. Phi Kappa Phi. Episcopalian. Personal E-mail: jrose935@aol.com.

ROSE, JANE A., financial planner; b. Phila., Sept. 30, 1940; d. Maurice and Miriam (Blank) Auritt; divorced; children: Lynne C., Wendy J., Debora J. Rose-Stewart. Student, Pa. State U., 1958; BA, Rutgers U., 1975; MBA, Temple U., 1978, postgrad., 1978-80. CPA, N.J.; CFP; cert. mgmt. acct., personal fin. specialist. Asst. v.p. Data Control Ctr., Cherry Hill, N.J., 1966-70; statistician, sr. staff asst. I.U. Internat. Corp., Phila., 1970-72; ops. mgr. Bus. Data Ctr., Cherry Hill, N.J., 1972-75; instr. acctg. and mgmt. Rutgers U., Camden, N.J., 1975-80; cost acctg. supr., acctg. mgr. Phila. Nat. Bank, 1980-82; asst. dir. fiscal planning N.J. Dept. Higher Edn., Trenton, 1982-85; contr., CFO Essex County Coll., Newark, 1985-87; v.p. fin. Horizon House, Inc., Phila., 1987-89; v.p. RTD Fin. Advisors Inc., Phila., 1989—. Instr., advisor Cen. Mich. U., McGuire AFB, N.J., 1978-80; instr. MBA Program, Widener U., Chester, Pa., 1980-82; rsch. asst. Temple U. Sch. Bus., Phila., 1975-76. Trustee Contact Cmty. Helpline, Cherry Hill, N.J., 1987-97, v.p., 1988-89, pres., 1989-94, mem. fin. com., 1995—; chair planned giving com. Women's Way, 2001—. Fellow Temple U. Sch. Bus., Phila., 1976-78. Fellow N.J. Soc. CPAs (chair subcom. 1985-89); mem. AICPA (grader CPA exam. 1987), Am. Woman's Soc. CPAs, Inst. Mgmt. Accts. (sec. South Jersey chpt. 1971-73, v.p. 1982-84, bd. dirs. 1971-75, 84-85, 91-93; grader, cons. CMA exam. 1986-99), Fin. Planning Assn., Am. Soc. Women Accts. (sec. Phila. chpt. 1972-74, bd. dirs. 1970-75), Choral Arts Soc. Phila. (singer, 2003—). Office: RTD Fin Advisors Inc 30 S 17th St Ste 1720 Philadelphia PA 19103-1752 Home Phone: 856-795-4235; Office Phone: 215-557-3800. E-mail: jrose@rtdfinancial.com.

ROSE, JEFFREY RAYMOND, retired economist, public servant, trade unionist; b. Toronto, Ont., Can., 1946; s. Albert and Thelma R.; m. Sandra Black; 1 child, Adam. BA with honors, U. Toronto, 1968, M.Indsl. Relations, 1983; postgrad., London Sch. Econs., 1968-69. Planner planning dept. City of Toronto, 1976-80; pres. local 79 Can. Union Pub. Employees, Toronto, 1980-83, nat. pres. Ottawa, Ont., 1983—91, nat. pres. emeritus, 1991—; dep. min. intergovtl. affairs Govt. of Ont., Toronto, 1991-95; sr. fellow Harrowston program in conflict mgmt.-negotiation U. Toronto, 1995—2002. Gen. v.p. Can. Labour Congress, 1983—91. Exec. mem. Ont. New Dem. Party, 1982-91; bd. dirs. Inst. for Rsch. on Pub. Policy, 1988-91; mem. fed. coun. New Dem. Party, 1988-91; co-chmn. Ont.-Que. Commn. for Cooperation, 1991-95. Home: 55 Sunnydene Crescent Toronto ON Canada M4N 3J5

ROSE, JESSICA LEE, actress; b. Salisbury, Md., Apr. 26, 1987; Student, Mount Maunganui Coll., New Zealand, 2000—01; student makeup, Acad.Film and TV, Auckland, New Zealand, 2004; graduate acting for film program, NY Film Acad., Universal City, Calif., 2005—06. Actor: (films) Dearly Beloved, I Know Who Killed Me, (internet video series) The Children of Anchor Cove (as lonelygirl15) (Best Actress film and video cat., Webby Awards, 2007); (TV series) Greek. Named to ad campaign to promote antipoverty cause, United Nations, 2006; named one of Top 25 Web Celebs, Forbes mag., 2007. Mailing: care of United Talent Agy 9560 Wilshire Blvd Ste 500 Beverly Hills CA 90212-2401 *

ROSE, JOANNA SEMEL, volunteer; b. Orange, NJ, Nov. 22, 1930; d. Philip Ephraim and Lillian (Mindlin) Semel; m. Daniel Rose, Sept. 16, 1956; children: David S., Joseph B., Emily, Gideon G. Cert., Shakespeare Inst., UK, 1951; BA summa cum laude, Bryn Mawr Coll., Pa., 1952; postgrad., St. Hilda's Coll., Oxford U., 1953. Mem. exec. com. Am. Friends St. Hilda's Coll., former chmn.; bd. dir., former pres. Paper Bag Players, NYC; former bd. dir., current mem. adv. coun. Poets and Writers, Inc., NYC; former chmn. adv. bd. Partisan Rev., NYC; mem. adv. coun. Nat. Dance Inst., NYC; bd. mem. NY Coun. for Humanities. Bd. dir. Bay St. Theatre, Sag Harbor; adv. coun. Am. Friends Jewish Mus. Greece; assoc. fellow Berkeley Coll. Yale U.; mem. NY Inst. for Humanities; bd. dirs. Ctr. for Humanities CUNY Grad. Ctr. Former bd. dirs. Eldridge St. Project, NYC. Hon. fellow, St. Hilda's Coll. Oxford. Mem. Cosmopolitan Club, Bryn Mawr Club of NY, LVIS East Hampton. Home: 895 Park Ave New York NY 10021-0327 also: 1 Lily Pond Ln East Hampton NY 11937

ROSE, JOANNE W., rating service executive; BA in Polit. Sci. and History magna cum laude, U. Rochester; JD, Columbia U. Assoc. White & Case, NYC; sr. mng. dir., gen. counsel Standard & Poor's Rating Svcs. divsn. McGraw Hill, NYC, 1989—99, chair rating policy bd.; exec. mng. dir., structured fin. ratings Standard & Poor's, NYC, 1999—. Office: Standard & Poors 55 Water St New York NY 10041-0003

ROSE, JOEL ALAN, legal consultant; b. Bklyn., Dec. 26, 1936; s. Edward Isadore and Adele R. Rose; m. Isadora Fenig, Apr. 12, 1964; children: Susan, Terri Angstriech. BS in Econs., NYU, 1958; MBA, Wharton Grad. Sch., U. Pa., 1960. Asst. purchasing agt. Maidenform Inc., NYC, 1960-62; personnel dir. E.J. Korvette Inc., NYC, 1962-66; mgmt. cons. Daniel J. Cantor & Co. Inc., Phila., 1966—, sr. v.p., 1987—; mgmt. cons. to legal profession. Coord. Ann. Conf. on Law Firm Mgmt. and Econs. Author: Managing the Law Office; mem. adv. bd. Law Office Economics and Management, 1987; contbg. columnist N.Y. Law Jour., 1984—, Nat. Law Jour. Extra, 1996—, Phila. Legal Intelligencer, 1995—, L.A. Daily Times, 1999—, Legal Times of Washington, 1998—, N.J. Law Jour., 2000-, The Barrister, 1995-, Pa. Lawyer's Weekly; contbr. articles to profl. jours.; bd. editors Acctg. for Law Firms, Law Firm Partnership and Benefits Report, 2001—; editl. adv. bd. Corp. Counsel's Guide to Law Dept. Mgmt. With U.S. Army, 1960, Res., 1960-66. Fellow Coll. of Law Practice Mgmt.; mem. ABA (chmn. acquisition and mergers com., practice mgmt. sect., large law firm interest group), Inst. Mgmt. Cons., Am. Arbitration Assn. (nat. panel), Adminstrv. Mgmt. Soc. (past chpt. pres.), Am. Mgmt. Assn., Assn. Legal Adminstrs., NY State Bar Assn. (com. law practic mgmt., com. continuing legal edn., spl. com. age discrimination in professions). Office: Joel A Rose & Assoc Inc PO Box 162 Cherry Hill NJ 08003-0162 Office Phone: 856-427-0050. E-mail: jrose63827@aol.com.

ROSE, JOHN CHARLES, internist, educator; b. NYC, Dec. 13, 1924; s. Hugh Stanley and Marie-Louise (Delury) R.; m. Dorothy Anne Donnelly, June 26, 1948; children— Nancy, Ellen, John Charles, Richard, Christopher. BS, Fordham U., 1946; MD magna cum laude, Georgetown U., 1950, D.Sc. (hon.), 1973; D.C.L. (hon.), Mt. St. Mary's Coll., 1973. Diplomate: Am. Bd. Internal Medicine, Am. Bd. Family Practice. Intern Walter Reed Army Hosp., 1950-51; resident, research fellow Georgetown U., VA hosps., Washington, 1950-54; established investigator Am. Heart Assn., 1954-57; instr., asst. prof. medicine Georgetown U., 1954-57, coord. med. edn., 1957-58, assoc. prof. physiology and biophysics, 1958-60, prof., 1960-91, chmn. dept. physiology and biophysics, 1958-63, dean Sch. Medicine, 1963-73, 78-79, prof. medicine, 1973-91, prof. emeritus, 1991—, vice chancellor Med. Ctr., 1984-87. Assoc. editor Am. Family Physician, 1955-62, chief med. editor, 1962-88; assoc. editor Acad. Medicine, 1992-95; contbr. articles to sci. publs. Trustee Charles E. Culpeper Found., 1986-96. Served to 2d lt. USAAF, 1943-45. Decorated Air medal. Master ACP; mem. Am. Physiol. Soc., Soc. Exptl. Biology and Medicine (nat. councillor 1962-63), Am. Heart Assn. (fellow sect. circulation). Clubs: Cosmos (Washington). Home: 5710 Surrey St Chevy Chase MD 20815-5520 E-mail: jrosemd@earthlink.net.

ROSE, JOHN THOMAS, finance educator; b. Ft. Worth, Aug. 20, 1943; s. Paul Pittman and Francis Nan (White) R.; m. Sandra Kaye Rolen, Sept. 5, 1969; children: Melanie Ann, Leah Nan, Lynnelle Renee. BA with honors, Tex. A&M U., 1965; MA, Washington U., St. Louis, 1968, PhD, 1976. Economist Bd. Govs. of FRS, Washington, 1972-82, sr. economist, 1982-84; prof. fin., Harriette L. & Walter G. Lacy, Jr. chair banking Baylor U., Waco, Tex., 1984—, acting chmn. dept. fin. ins. and real estate, 1996-97, chmn. dept., 1997—2006. Contbr. articles to profl. jours. Bd. visitors Abilene Christian U., Tex., 1989-92. Capt. US Army, 1969—71. Decorated Bronze Star; recipient Disting. Bus. Prof. award Baylor U., 1988, Alpha Kappa Psi Favorite Prof. award Hankamer Sch. Bus. Baylor U., 2004; Econ. Devel. Adminstrn. US Dept. Commerce fellow, 1968-69; Ernst & Young Found. Rsch. grantee, 1991. Mem. So. Fin. Assn., Southwestern Fin. Assn., Fin. Mgmt. Assn., Omicron Delta Epsilon, Beta Gamma Sigma. Mem. Ch. of Christ. Office: Baylor U Hankamer Sch of Bus Dept Fin Ins and Real Estate One Bear Pl # 98004 Waco TX 76798-8004 Home Phone: 254-776-6038. Business E-Mail: jt_rose@baylor.edu.

ROSE, JONATHAN CHAPMAN, lawyer; b. Cleve., June 8, 1941; s. Horace Chapman and Katherine Virginia (Cast) R.; m. Susan Anne Porter, Jan. 26, 1980; 1 son, Benjamin Chapman. AB, Yale U., 1963; LL.B. cum laude, Harvard U., 1967. Bar: Mass. 1968, D.C. 1972, U.S. Supreme Ct. 1976, Circuit Ct. Appeals 1977, Ohio 1978. Law clk. Justice R. Ammi Cutter, Mass. Supreme Jud. Ct., 1967-68; spl. asst. to U.S. pres., 1971-73; gen. counsel Coun. on Internat. Econ. Policy, 1973-74, The White House; assoc. dept. atty. gen. U.S. Dept. Justice, 1974-75; dept. asst. atty. gen. U.S. Dept. Justice (Antitrust Div.), 1975-77, asst. atty. gen. Office of Legal Policy, 1981-84; ptnr. firm Jones Day, Washington, 1977-81, 84—. Prin. Ctr. for Excellence in Govt.; pres. Yale Daily News Found.; bd. govs. Yale Alumni Assn., 1996-99. 1st lt. U.S. Army, 1969-71. Mem. ABA, D.C. Bar Assn., Mass. Bar Assn., Ohio Bar Assn., Fed. Bar Assn., Am. Law Inst. Clubs: Met, Chevy Chase, Union, Yale, Harvard. Republican. Episcopalian. Office: Jones Day 51 Louisiana Ave NW Washington DC 20001-2113 Office Phone: 202-879-3888. Business E-Mail: jcrose@jonesday.com.

ROSE, KIM MATTHEW, lawyer, educator; b. Gallipolis, Ohio, Mar. 21, 1956; s. Dave and Lois Ann R.; m. Pamela Carol Sims, Aug. 11, 1990. Student, USMA, 1974—76; BBA, Ohio U., 1977; JD, Capital U. Law, 1981; MBA, Ashland Coll., 1988. Bar: Ohio 1981, U.S. Dist. Ct. (so. dist.) Ohio 1981, U.S. Ct. Appeals (6th cir.) 1987, U.S. Supreme Ct. 1988. Asst. prosecutor Knox County Prosecutor, Mt. Vernon, Ohio, 1982-90; with Critchfield, Critchfield & Johnston, Mt. Vernon, 1982—. Adj. prof. Mt. Vernon Nazarene Coll., 1982-2002. Mem. adv. bd. Salvation Army, Mt. Vernon, 1991—; bd. dirs. Knox Cmty. Hosp., Mt. Vernon, Ohio, 2000-. Maj. USAR, 1974-95. Mem. Ohio State Bar Assn., Knox County Bar Assn. (past pres.), Mt. Vernon Nazarene Coll. Found. (rec. sec. bd. 1995—), Masons. Avocations: flying, skiing, fishing, golf, biking. Home: 1413 Greenbrier Dr Mount Vernon OH 43050-9101 Office: Critchfield Critchfield & Johnston 10 S Gay St Mount Vernon OH 43050-3546 Home Phone: 740-397-3822; Office Phone: 740-397-4040. Business E-Mail: kimr@ccj.com.

ROSE, L. STEVEN See JASHEL, LARRY

ROSE, LYNN (M. LYNN ROSE), history professor; BA in Hist., U. Minn., Mpls., 1985, PhD in Hist., 1995. Asst. prof. hist. Truman State U., Kirksville, Mo., 1995—2000, assoc. prof., 2000—. Guest lectr. Institut für Klassische Altertumswissenschaften Martin Luther Universität Halle-Wittenberg, 2003—04. Contbr. articles to profl. publs., chapters to books; author: The Staff of Oedipus: Transforming Disability in Ancient Greece, 2003. Named Outstanding Tchr. of Yr., Mo. Coun. Pub. Higher Edn., 2006; recipient US Prof. of Yr. award, Carnegie Found. for Advancement of Tchg. and Coun. for Advancement and Support of Edn., 2006. Mem.: Women's Classical Caucus, Soc. Disability Studies, Internat. Assn. for Sci. Study of Intellectual Disabilities, Classical Assn. of Midwest and South, Am. Classical League, Assn. Ancient Historians. Office: Divsn Social Sci Truman State U Kirksville MO 63501 E-mail: lynnrose@truman.edu. *

ROSE, MARGARETE JOYCE, musician, interpreter; d. David G. and Dorothy M. Rose; m. Martin L. Lee, Dec. 21, 2003; children: Berta R. Medina, Monica M. Lorren. BS in Elem. Edn., So. Adventist U., Collegedale, Tenn., 1966; M in Organ Performance, Real Conservatorio Superior de Madrid, 1980. Cert. ct. interpreter Tenn. Adminstrv. Office Cts., 2006. Prof. music, prin., head of music theory dept. Boadilla Sch. Music, Madrid, 1988—2004; prof. music Chattanooga State Coll., 2003—04; organist, choirmaster Thankful Meml. Episcopal Ch., Chattanooga, 2005—. Choirmaster Coral Albor, Madrid, 1993—2003; founder, mem. classical baroque trio, Madrid, 1997—2004. Composer, arranger: various choral pieces. Founder, dir. Confraternitas, Madrid, 2000—03; mem. union com. Seventh Day Adventist Ch., Madrid, 1980—85. Mem.: Am. Guild Organists. Home Phone: 423-893-8960; Office Phone: 423-823-3131.

ROSE, MARIAN HENRIETTA, physics researcher; b. Brussels; (parents Am. citizens); m. Simon Rose, Oct. 20, 1948 (dec. Jan. 1981); children: Ann, James, David, Simon. BA, Barnard Coll., 1942; MA, Columbia U., 1944; PhD, Harvard U., 1947. Teaching fellow Harvard U., Cambridge, Mass., 1945-46; adj. asst. prof. Courant Inst., NYC, 1947-48, rsch. assoc., 1951-65, sr. rsch. scientist, 1965-75; vis. fellow Yale U., New Haven, Conn., 1981-93. Bd. dirs. Minna-James-Heineman Stiftung, Essen, Fed. Republic of Germany. Contbr. articles to profl. jours. Bd. dirs. Jay Heritage Ctr., Rye, N.Y.; mem. Wetlands Control Commn., Bedford, N.Y., 1992-99, Conservation Bd., Bedford, 1989-93; pres. Croton Watershed Clean Water Coalition, 1997-2006, pres. emeritus, 2006—. Mem.: Sierra Club (conservation chair Atlantic chpt. 1992—95, del. at large to Westchester County Environ. Mgmt. Coun. 1994—, chair N.E. regional conservation com. 1995—98, conservation chair Atlantic chpt. 1998—2000, steering com. Atlantic chpt. 2000—02, del. at large N.E. regional conservation com., del. at large Atlantic chpt., exec. com. Atlantic chpt.), Sigma Xi, Phi Beta Kappa. Avocations: skiing, hiking. Personal E-mail: marianr451@aol.com.

ROSE, MARK ALLEN, humanities educator; b. NYC, Aug. 4, 1939; s. Sydney Aaron and Rose (Shapiro) R.; m. Ann (Bermingham); 1 son, Edward Gordon. AB (hon.), Princeton U., NJ, 1961; LittB, Merton Coll., Oxford, Eng., 1963; PhD, Harvard U., Cambridge, Mass., 1967. Instr. to assoc. prof. in English Yale U., 1967-74; prof. English U. Ill., 1974-77; prof. U. Calif., Santa Barbara, 1977—, chmn. dept. English, 1987-89; dir. U. Calif., Humanities Rsch. Inst., Santa Barbara, 1989-94, chmn. dept. English, 1997—2001, assoc. vice chancellor, 2002—06. Author: Heroic Love, 1968; (fiction) Golding's Tale, 1972; Shakespearean Design, 1972; Spenser's Art, 1975; Alien Encounters, 1981; Authors and Owners, 1993; editor: Twentieth Century Views of Science Fiction, 1976; Twentieth Century Interpretations of Antony and Cleopatra, 1977, (with Slusser and Guffey); Bridges to Science Fiction, 1980; Shakespeare's Early Tragedies, 1994; (CD-ROM) Norton Shakespeare Workshops. Woodrow Wilson

Fellow, 1961; Henry Fellow, 1961-62; Dexter Fellow, 1966; Morse Fellow, 1970-71; NEH Fellow, 1979-80, 90-91. Mem. MLA, Renaissance Soc. Am., Shakespeare Soc. Am., Phi Beta Kappa. Office: U Calif English Dept Santa Barbara CA 93106 Business E-Mail: mrose@english.ucsb.edu.

ROSE, MARK E., real estate company executive; BA, City U. NY. CPA. Chmn., CEO US Real Estate Investment Trust British Coal Corp. Pension Funds; founder Metropolitan Realty Advisors, 1993; broker Jones Lang LaSalle, Washington, chief innovation officer, 2000—02, CEO Americas, 2002—05, COO Americas, 2003—05; CEO Grubb & Ellis Co., 2005—, bd. dirs. Adv. bd. RealComm; mem. CoreNet, Internat. Coun. Shopping Centers. Bd. dirs. Chgo. Shakespeare Theatre, SiteStuff Inc., Chgo. Ctrl. Area Com. Office: Grubb and Ellis 500 W Monroe St Ste 2800 Chicago IL 60661 *

ROSE, MARY MABEL, retired elementary school educator; b. Monticello, Iowa, Dec. 16, 1940; d. Ralph Richard and Flora Birdena (Hawkins) Ganfield; m. Paul Roger Rose, Dec. 30, 1961 (dec. Oct. 1979); children: Lynn Marie, Carol Ann. BA, Upper Iowa U., Fayette, 1962; postgrad., U. No. Iowa, Cedar Falls, 1990—93. Cert. tchr. Iowa. Elem. tchr. North Fayette County Cmty. Schs., West Union, Iowa, 1962-67, Marion Ind. Schs., Iowa, 1963—64; instr. adult edn. West Central Sch. Dist., Iowa, 1967; substitute tchr. Bremer County Schs., Waverly, Iowa, 1974-84; tchr. Waverly-Shell Rock Schs., Iowa, 1984—2006, early childhood adv. bd., 1990—91; ret., 2006. Mem. edn. com. Waverly Trinity Meth. Ch., 1979-84, trustee, 1984-86, mem. fin. com., 1989-92, staff parish relationship com., 1999-2001, mem. mission commn., 2005—; vol. Waverly Hosp. Aux., 1984-86 Mem. ASCD, Nat. Assn. for Edn. Young Children, Shell Rock Music Assn. (bd. dirs. 1995-98), Waverly Lions. Avocations: reading, sewing, gardening, walking, golf. Home: 107 S Ridge Dr Waverly IA 50677-3908

ROSE, MARY MCNALLY, federal official; b. Apr. 10, 1946; d. Hugh B. and Margaret (Brady) McNally; m. Philip David Rose, Sept. 12, 1970; children: Sarina Josephine, Aimee Elizabeth, Michael Roddy, Maureen Erin. RN, Bon Secours Sch. Nursing, 1967. Spl. asst. to dir. Fed. Exec. Inst., Washington; asst. dir. office exec. personnel The White House, Washington, 1983-85, asst. office personnel mgmt., 1985, dir. personnel, 1985-86; dep. under sec. for mgmt. U.S. Dept. Edn., Washington; vice chmn. Fed. Salary Coun.; mem. US Merit Systems Protection Bd, Washington, 2005—. Office: US Merit Systems Protection Bd 1615 M St NW Rm 680 Washington DC 20419

ROSE, MARYA MERNITZ, lawyer; b. Sept. 1962; m. Anthony J Rose. BA, Williams College, Williamstown, Mass.; JD, Ind. U. Corp. counsel Cummins Inc, 1997—98, corp. counsel & dir. public relations, 1998—99, corp. counsel & dir. public relations & comm. strategy, 1999—2000, v.p., gen. counsel, 2001—, also corp. sec. Office: Cummins Inc 500 Jackson St Columbus IN 47202

ROSE, MATTHEW K., rail transportation executive; BS in Mktg., U. Mo. With Mo. Pacific RR; various positions Schneider Nat., Internat. Utilities; v.p. transp. Triple Crown Svcs. (Norfolk So. RR subs.); various v.p. positions Burlington No. Santa Fe Corp., 1993—96, sr. v.p. mdse. bus. unit, 1996—97, sr. v.p., COO, 1997—99, pres., COO, 1999—2000, pres., CEO, 2000—, chmn., 2002—. Bd. dirs. AMR Corp., Ctr. Energy & Econ. Devel., Centex Corp., Dallas, 2006—; mem. Tex. Gov.'s Bus. Coun., Bus. Roundtable. Trustee Tex. Christian U.; mem. exec. bd. Boy Scouts of Am. Mem.: Assn. Am. RRs (bd. dirs.). Office: Burlington No Santa Fe Corp PO Box 961056 Fort Worth TX 76161-0056 Office Phone: 817-867-6100. *

ROSE, MICHAEL DEAN, retired lawyer, educator; b. Johnstown, Pa., Oct. 22, 1937; BA, Ohio Wesleyan U., 1959; JD, Case Western Res. U., 1963; LLM, Columbia U., 1967. Bar: Ohio 1963. Assoc. firm Porter, Stanley, Treffinger & Platt, Columbus, Ohio, 1963-66; asst. prof. law Ohio State U., Columbus, 1967-69, assoc. prof., 1969-72, prof., 1972-99, Lawrence D. Stanley prof. law, 1987-99, prof. emeritus, 1999—. Staff asst. to chief counsel IRS, Washington, 1970-71. Author: (with Leo J. Raskind) Advanced Federal Income Taxation: Corporate Transactions, 1978, (with Joseph S. Platt) A Federal Taxation Primer, 1973, Hornbook on Federal Income Taxation, 3d edit., 1988; editor Selected Federal Taxation Statutes and Regulations, 1973-99, Ohio Will Manual, 1986-2002. Mem.: Am. Law Inst. Home: 1327 Friar Ln Columbus OH 43221-1527 Office: Ohio State U 55 W 12th Ave Columbus OH 43210-1338 Business E-Mail: rose.4@osu.edu.

ROSE, MICHAEL ELVIN, oil and gas exploration company executive; b. Beaumont, Tex., Mar. 8, 1947; s. Harold Elvin and Onita (Buckelew) R.; m. Patricia Jan Howell, Aug. 21, 1971; children: Jaime Erin, Dana Lyn. BBA, Lamar U., 1970. CPA, Tex. Various positions Atlantic Richfield Co., Dallas, Midland, Tex., L.A., 1971-77; chief acct. Anadarko Prodn. Co., Houston, 1978-79, asst. contr., 1979-80, contr., 1980-81, v.p., contr., 1981-85, Anadarko Petroleum Corp., Houston, 1985-86, exec. v.p. fin., chief fin. officer, 1986—2003. Mem. Fin. Execs. Inst., AICPA, Tex. Soc. CPAs. Avocations: golf, hunting, sailing.

ROSE, MICHAEL IAN, plastic surgeon; b. NYC, Sept. 29, 1968; MD, NY Sch. Med., 1994. Cert. Am. Bd. Plastic Surgery, Am. Bd. Surgery. Intern, plastic surgery NYU/Bellevue Med. Ctr., NYC, 1994—95, resident, 1995—2000; fellow, plastic and reconstructive surgery Emory U., Atlanta, 2000—02; clin. instructor NYU Sch. Medicine, NYC, 1999—2000; private practice The Plastic Surgery Ctr. (NJ/NY); bus. ptnr. Smoothmed, NYC, 2007—. Contbr. articles to profl. jours.; featured on WPIX News, Good Morning America, ABC News, CBS News, Discovery Channel, News 12 NJ and Asbury Park Press. Fellow: Am. Coll. Surgeons. Office: The Plastic Surgery Ctr 535 Sycamore Ave Shrewsbury NJ 07702 Address: The Plastic Surgery Ctr 308 E 79th St New York NY 10021 Office Phone: 732-741-0970, 212-421-6725. Office Fax: 732-747-2606. *

ROSE, MICHAEL LEONARD, film, television and video producer; b. St. Paul, Aug. 9, 1952; s. Robert L. and Beverly Bain (McKee) R.; m. Carol L. King, 1991. BA, UCLA, 1978, MFA, 1990. Media dir. Com. to Bridge the Gap, LA, 1980-82; producer KPFK Pacifica, LA, 1982-83, GM, Detroit, 1983-92, Network USA, Inc., Rockville, Md., 1993-96; producer 30-part documentary series Automobiles, 1995—; prodr., writer, dir. Michael Rose Prodns., Marina del Rey, Calif., 1996—. Prodr. (film) Character, 1984 (Cine award 1984, 96), (videotape) A New Me, 1985 (U.S. Industry award 1985), Safety Belts for Dummies and People, 1986 (ITVA award, U.S. Industry award, Nat. Com. Films for Safety award), (TV series) Wheels of Survival, History Channel, Dream Machines, Ultimate Autos, History Channel, Great Cars, Wealth TV and PBS, Great Drives, Pvt. Jets, (video) ZZ Top; prodr. (for Travel Channel), Private Jets Revealed, Hot Rod TV; prodr., dir. MI PBS Passing the Touch; prodr., writer (videotape) I Need the Earth and the Earth Needs Me, 1990 (Cine Golden Eagle award, Nat. Edn. Film and Video award 1991), (film) A Tale of Two Cities, 1990 (Expo of Short Film and Video Award, Outstanding Student Documentaty Bklyn. Arts Coun. 1991); dir. pub. svc. announcement Eye Exam, 1988 (ITVA award 1988); prodr. The Game of Your Life, 1989 (Am. Film and Video award, ITVA award), Precious Cargo, (TV series) Wheels of Survival, Dream Machines, Ultimate Autos. Active, prodr. Mahaffey for Coun. campaign, Detroit, 1989; prodr. radio comml. Friends of the Nuclear Freeze, L.A., 1982. Recipient E.P. Ingersoll award Soc. Automotive Historians, 1998, Nat. Ednl. Media Network award, 1998; scriptwriting grantee Calif. Coun. for Humanities, 1999. Mem.: Nat. Acad. Television Arts & Scis., Writers Guild Am., Dirs. Guild Am., Internat. Documentary Assn. (bd. dirs.). Office Phone: 310-821-0800.

ROSE, MICHAEL ROBERTSON, evolutionary biology educator, consultant; b. Iserlohn, Germany; s. James Barry and Charlotte Julia Rose; children: Darius, Caitlin, Liam, Muireann. BS, Queen's U., Kingston, Ont., Can., 1975, MS, 1976; PhD, U. Sussex, Eng., 1979. NATO sci. fellow U. Wis., Madison, 1979-81; asst. prof. Dalhousie U., Halifax, N.S., Canada, 1981-85, assoc. prof., 1985-87; assoc. prof. evolutionary biology U. Calif., Irvine, 1987-90, prof., 1990—, dir. Intercampus Rsch. Program Exptl. Evolution, 2004—05, dir. Network Exptl. Rsch. Evolution, 2006—. Author: Evolutionary Biology of Aging, 1991, Adaptation, 1996, Darwin's Spectre, 1998, Methuselah Flies, 2004, The Long Tomorrow, 2005, Evolution and Ecology of the Organism, 2006. Recipient President's prize Am. Soc. Naturalists, 1992, Busse award World Congress Gerontology, Adelaide, Australia, 1997. Mem. Soc. for Study Evolution. Avocation: music. Office Phone: 949-824-8121. E-mail: mrrose@uci.edu.

ROSE, NOEL RICHARD, immunologist, microbiologist, educator; b. Stamford, Conn., Dec. 3, 1927; s. Samuel Allison and Helen (Richard) R.; m. Deborah S. Harber, June 14, 1951; children: Alison, David, Bethany, Jonathan. BS, Yale U., 1948; MA, U. Pa., 1949, PhD, 1951; MD, SUNY, Buffalo, 1964; MD (hon.), U. Cagliari, Italy, 1990; ScD (hon.), U. Sassari, Italy, 1992; Order of the First Class (hon.), Ctrl. U. Venezuela, 1997. From instr. to prof. microbiology SUNY Sch. Medicine, Buffalo, 1951-73, dir. Center for Immunology, 1970-73, dir. Erie County Labs., 1964-70; dir. WHO Collaborating Center for Autoimmune Disorders, 1968—; prof. immunology and microbiology, chmn. dept. immunology and microbiology Wayne State U. Sch. Medicine, 1973— 82; prof., chmn. dept. immunology and infectious diseases Johns Hopkins U. Sch. Hygiene and Pub. Health, Balt., 1982-93, prof. medicine and environ. health scis., 1982—, prof. molecular microbiology and immunology, 1993—; prof. pathology Johns Hopkins U. Sch. Medicine, 1994—; dir. Johns Hopkins Autoimmune Disease Rsch. Ctr., 1998. Cons. in field. Editor: (with others) International Convocation on Immunology, 1969, Methods in Immunodiagnosis, 1973, 3d rev. edit., 1986, The Autoimmune Diseases, 1986, 2d edit., 1992, 3d edit., 1998, Microbiology, Basic Principles and Clinical Applications, 1983 Principles of Immunology, 1973, 2d rev. edit., 1979, Specific Receptors of Antibodies, Antigens and Cells, 1973, Manual of Clinical Laboratory Immunology, 1976, 6th edit., 2002, Genetic Control of Autoimmune Disease, 1978, Recent Advances in Clinical Immunology, 1983, Clinical Immunotoxicology, 1992, Manual of Human Immunology, 1997; editor in chief Clin. Immunology and Immunopathology, 1988-98; contbr. articles to profl. jours. Recipient award Sigma Xi, 1952, award Alpha Omega Alpha, 1976, Lamp award, 1975, Faculty Recognition award Wayne State U. Bd. Govs., 1979, Pres.'s award for excellence in teaching, 1979, Disting. Service award Wayne State U. Sch. Medicine, 1982, U. Pisa medal, 1986, U. Venezuela medal, 1998; named to Acad. Scholars Wayne State U., 1981; Josiah Macy fellow, 1979 Fellow AAAS (coun. 2004—), APHA, Am. Acad. Allergy and Immunology, Am. Acad. Microbiology, Assn. Med. Lab Immunologists; mem. Acad. Clin. Lab. Physicians and Scientists, Am. Assn. Immunologists, Am. Soc. Investigative Pathology, Am. Soc. Clin. Pathologists, Am. Soc. Microbiology (hon.; Abbott Lab. Clin. and Diagnostic Immunology award 1993, Profl. Achievement award 2003), Brit. Soc. Immunology, Coll. Am. Pathologists, Sociètè Française d'Immunologie, Can. Soc. Immunology, Soc. Exptl. Biology and Medicine Coun., Clin. Immunology Soc. (sec., treas., pres. 1993), Austrian Immunology Soc. (hon. mem.), Sigma Xi (pres. Johns Hopkins U. chpt. 1988), Alpha Omega Alpha, Delta Omega. Office: Johns Hopkins U 615 N Wolfe St Baltimore MD 21205-2103

ROSE, NORMA LOUISE, retired human services manager; d. Elzie Mars and Hattie Mae Rose. MBA, Chapman U., Orange County, Calif., 1979. With Hewlett-Packard Co., San Diego, 1959—98, prodn. worker, 1959—78, order processing clk., prodn. supr., pers. rep., coll. recruiting mgr., human resources mgr.; ret., 1998. Mem. Smithsonian Inst. Mem.: Hewlett Packard Retiree Club, Sierra Club. Home: 24218 Via Llano Murrieta CA 92562-5581 Personal E-mail: normar@murrieta.net.

ROSE, NORMAN, retired lawyer, accountant; b. NYC, July 7, 1923; s. Edward J. and Frances (Ludwig) R.; div.; children: Ellen, Michael; m. Judith Rose; stepchildren: Dwight, Audrey, Jason. BBA, CCNY, 1947; JD, N.Y. Law Sch., 1953. Bar: NY 1954, US Dist. Ct. (ea. dist.) NY 1956, US Tax Ct. 1956, US Dist. Ct. (so. dist.) NY 1960, US Supreme Ct. 1961, US Ct. Appeals (2d cir.) 1967, Fla. 1979. Pvt. practice, NYC, 1954-69, Ft. Lauderdale, Fla., 1979-91; ptnr. Dean, Falanga & Rose, Carle Pl., NY, 1979-81. Referee Small Claims Ct., NYC, 1959-69; arbitrator Accident Claims Tribunal, Am. Arbitration Assn., 1960-65; lectr. in field. Author law note Liability of Golfer to Person Struck by Ball, 1959 (Hon. Mention 1960). Pres. Nassau South Shore Little League, Lawrence, NY, 1966-68; treas. 5 Towns Dem. Club, Woodmere, NY, 1966-67; chmn. United Fund, Village of Lawrence, 1967; citizens observer patrolman Palm Beach County Sheriff's Dept., Ret. Srs. Vol. Program. Capt. USAF, 1943-45, ETO. Decorated DFC, Air medal with 5 oak leaf clusters, Silver Star, Purple Heart. Mem. ATLA (sustaining), Acad. Fla. Trial Lawyers (sustaining), NY State Assn. Plaintiffs Trial Lawyers, NY State Bar Assn., Fla. Bar, Nassau County Bar Assn. (chmn. med-legal com. 1975-77), Air Force Assn., Vets. Fgn. Wars, Lawyer/Pilots Bar Assn., Pompano Beach Power Squadron (safety officer), Masons, Shriners, Bellaggio Men's Club (chmn. gambling com.). Home: 6508 Via Primo St Lake Worth FL 33467 Personal E-mail: normierose@adelphia.net.

ROSE, PAUL EDWARD, systems administrator, educator; b. Denver, Oct. 14, 1978; s. Robert Ferguson and Kathleen Marie Rose; life ptnr. Shontience Nicole Morris; 1 child, Imani Brianna-Lee. Cert. A+ CompTia, Network+ CompTia, Security+ CompTia, Server+ CompTia, i-Net+ CompTia, CIW cert. instr. ProSoft, cert. master CIW adminstr. ProSoft, CIW assoc. ProSoft, CIW profl. ProSoft, master CIW site designer ProSoft, CIW security analyst ProSoft, ITCAP designated instr., MCP Microsoft, MCSA Windows 2000 Microsoft, MCDST Windows XP Microsoft, MCSA Windows 2003 Microsoft, MCSE Microsoft, Security Microsoft, Microsoft cert. trainer Microsoft. Migration cons. Oxford Global Resources, Mountain View, Calif., 2000; owner RoseNet Solutions, Oakland, Calif., 2000—; sr. instr. TechSkills, San Francisco, 2003—; chief tech. officer Computer Svcs. Group, San Jose, Calif., 2004—. Cons. Young Cmty. Developers, San Francisco, 2005—. Bd. dirs. African-American.com, San Jose, 2003—06. With USMC, 1996—99. Decorated Good Conduct medal USMC, Meritorious Mast. Master: Masons (3d degree). Democrat. Avocations: travel, baseball, football, softball. Home Phone: 510-535-9107; Office Phone: 415-442-0150. Personal E-mail: paul@paulrose.net. Business E-Mail: prose@techskills.com.

ROSE, PETER ISAAC, sociologist, writer, editor; b. Rochester, NY, Sept. 5, 1933; s. Aaron E. and Lillian (Feld) R.; m. Hedwig Hella Cohen, Mar. 25, 1956; children: Elisabeth Anne, Daniel Eric. AB, Syracuse U., 1954; MA, Cornell U., 1957, PhD, 1959. Mem. faculty Smith Coll., Northampton, Mass., 1960—2003, sr. fellow Kahn Inst., 2000—, Sophia Smith prof. emeritus, 2003—; mem. grad. faculty U. Mass., 1961—. Fulbright prof. U. Leicester, Eng., 1964-65, Kyoto (Japan) Am. Studies Inst., Flinders U., Australia, 1970, U. Vienna, 2004, Roosevelt Acad. Utrecht U., Netherlands, 2007; vis. prof. Wesleyan U., Middletown, Conn., 1966-67, U. Colo., 1968, Yale U., 1970, Clark U., 1970-71, Doshisha U., Kyoto, Japan, fall 1999, Göteborgs U., Sweden, 2007; vis. scholar Harvard U., 1983, 84-85, vis. prof., spring 1984; vis. scholar Chinese Acad. Social Sci., Beijing, 1986; resident scholar Rockefeller Study Ctr., Bellagio, Italy, summer 1987; vis. fellow St. Catherine's Coll., Oxford, spring, 1995, Stanford U., 1996, 2005, 2007, Liguria Study Ctr., Bogliasco, Italy, spring 1998, fall 2001. Author: They and We, 1964, 6th edit., 2006, The Subject is Race, 1968, Strangers in Their Midst, 1977, Mainstream and Margins, 1983, Tempest-Tost, 1997, Guest Appearances and Other Travels in Time and Space, 2003; co-author: Sociology, 1977, 2d edit., 1982, Understanding Society, 1978, 3d edit., 1986; editor: The Study of Society, 1967, 4th edit., 1977, The Ghetto and Beyond, 1969, Americans From Africa, 1970, Nation of Nations, 1972, reissued, 1981, Seeing Ourselves, 1972, rev. edit., 1975, Through Different Eyes, 1973, Socialization and the Life Cycle, 1979, Working With Refugees, 1986, Interminority Relations in the U.S., 1993, Professorial Passions, 1998, The Dispossessed, 2005, SoGoNow.com Travel Mag., 2007—. Mem. Am. Sociol. Assn. (mem. coun. 1974-77), Mass. Sociol. Assn. (pres. 1967-68), Soc. Study of Social Problems (v.p. 1968-69), Ea. Sociol. Soc. (v.p. 1970-71, pres. 1991-92). Home: 96 Round Hill Rd Northampton MA 01060-2907 Office Phone: 413-585-3515. Business E-Mail: prose@smith.edu.

ROSE, PETER J., delivery service executive; V.p. air divsn. The Harper Group, San Francisco, 1969-81; exec. v.p. Expeditors Internat. Wash. Inc., Seattle, 1981-88, pres., CEO, 1988—, chmn., 1996—. Office: Expeditors Internat Wash Inc 1015 3rd Ave Seattle WA 98104 *

ROSE, RICHARD LOOMIS, lawyer; b. Long Branch, NJ, Oct. 21, 1936; s. Charles Frederick Perrott and Jane Mary (Crotta) R.; m. Marian Frances Irons, Apr. 1, 1960; children: Linda, Cynthia, Bonnie. BA, Cornell U., 1958; JD, Washington and Lee U., 1963. Bar: N.Y. 1963, Conn. 1966, U.S. Dist. Ct. (so. dist.) N.Y. 1964, U.S. Dist. Ct. Conn. 1966, U.S. Ct. Appeals (2d cir.) 1965, U.S. Supreme Ct. 1970. Ptnr. Cummings & Lockwood, Stamford, Conn., 1965-71, 1971-91, Kleban & Samor, P.C., Southport, 1991-93; counsel Whitman Breed Abbott & Morgan, Greenwich, Conn., 1993—95; prin. Roberts, Rose & Bates, P.C., Stamford, Conn., 1995—2005, Murtha Cullina LLP, 2005—. Mem. adv. com. Conn. Banking Commr. on Conn. Securities Laws, 1982—; bd. dirs. Conn. World Trade Assn. Editor: Washington and Lee Law Rev. Chmn. Fgn. Trade Zone Com. to Mayor of City of Bridgeport, Conn., 1988-90; mem. fgn. trade awareness com. S.W. Area Industry and Commerce Assn., Task Force, 1987-88; bd. dirs. German Sch. of Conn., Inc., 1992—, New Canaan Preservation Alliance, Inc.; commr. New Canaan (Conn.) Hist. Dist. Commn., 1995—. 1st lt. U.S. Army, 1958-60, Korea. Mem. ABA, Conn. Bar Assn. (exec. com. corp. sect.), Internat. Bar Assn., New Canaan Country Club, Gridiron Club New Canaan, Phi Delta Phi, Omicron Delta Kappa, Phi Delta Theta. Republican. Office: Murtha Cullina LLP 177 Broad St Stamford CT 06901

ROSE, ROBERT EDGAR, retired state supreme court justice; b. Orange, NJ, Oct. 7, 1939; BA, Juniata Coll., Huntingdon, Pa., 1961; LL.B., NYU, 1964. Bar: Nev. 1965. Dist. atty. Washoe County, 1971-75; lt. gov. State of Nev., 1975-79; judge Nev. Dist. Ct., 8th Jud. Dist., Las Vegas, 1986-88; justice Nev. Supreme Ct., Carson City, 1989—2006, chief justice, 1993-94, 1999—2000, 2006, sr. justice, 2007—. Office Phone: 775-684-1540.

ROSE, ROBERT GORDON, lawyer; b. Newark, June 25, 1943; s. Harry and Ann Shirley (Gordon) R.; m. Ellen Nadley Berkowitz, July 2, 1966; children: Lisa Pauline, Michael Allan. BA, SUNY, Buffalo, 1965; MA, Columbia U., 1969; JD, Seton Hall U., 1974. Bar: NJ 1974, US Dist. Ct. NJ 1974, US Ct. Appeals (3rd cir.) 1974, US Ct. Appeals (2nd cir.) 1975. Law clk. to Hon. John J. Gibbons US Ct. Appeals (3rd cir.), Newark, 1974-75; assoc. Day Pitney LLP, Morristown, NJ, 1975-80, ptnr., 1980—. Mem. com. on unauthorized practice of law NJ Supreme Ct., 1989-2001, apptd. com. chair, 2000-2001; apptd. lawyers adv. com. US Dist. Ct., Dist. NJ, 2002—; trustee Legal Svcs. NJ, 2001—. Contbr. articles to profl. jours. Recipient Disting. Grad. award Seton Hall U. Law Sch., 2000. Mem. ABA, NJ Bar Assn., Morris County Bar Assn. (trustee 1989-90). Avocations: travel, stamp collecting/philately. Office: Day Pitney LLP PO Box 1945 Morristown NJ 07962-1945 Office Phone: 973-966-8070. Business E-Mail: rrose@daypitney.com.

ROSE, ROBERT MICHAEL, materials engineering educator; b. NYC, Apr. 15, 1937; s. Lawrence Lapidus and Lillian (Rosen) R.; m. Martha Gibbs, Oct. 15, 1961; children: Cynthia J., James L., Joshua S. BS, MIT, 1958, DSc, 1961. Registered profl. engr., Mass. Asst. prof. materials sci. and engring MIT, Cambridge, 1961-66, assoc. prof., 1966-72, prof., 1972—2003, prof. emeritus, 2003—, dir. MIT Concourse program, 1988—; prof. health scis. and tech. Harvard Med. Sch.- MIT, 1978-90; dir. Cryoelectro Assocs., Wenham, Mass., 1978-90. Author: Structure and Properties of Materials, 1964, Practical Biomechanics for the Orthopedic Surgeon, 1979, 92, The Chicken From Minsk, 1995. Recipient Kappa Delta prize Am. Acad. Orthop. Surgeons, 1973. Mem. Am. Soc. Metals (vice chmn. 1971-72, Bradley Stoughton prize, chmn. 1972-73), Metal Soc. AIME, Boston Yacht Club. Jewish. Home: 18 Morgan St Wenham MA 01984-1114 Office: Room 4-132 MIT 77 Massachusetts Ave Cambridge MA 02139-4301 Business E-Mail: rose@mit.edu. *I would share my thoughts with you if I were satisfied with what I am. But I submit to you that anyone who is truly satisfied with his personal success doesn't understand the nature of his own achievement.*

ROSE, ROBERT NEAL, investment banker; b. Chgo., Feb. 27, 1951; s. James Allan Rose and Hazel (Gordon) Kaufman; m. Anna Yvette Trujillo, Aug. 23, 1981; children: David James, Michelle Elizabeth, Daniel Jonathan. BS, Georgetown U., 1973; MPA, Harvard U., 1995. Trader Salomon Bros., NYC, 1974-75; regional coord. Latin Am. Merrill Lynch Govt. Securities, NYC, 1975-76; dir. fed. govt. affairs Pub. Svc. of N.Mex., Albuquerque, 1977-78; exec. dir. Gov. Jerry Apodaca, Washington, 1979-80; expert cons. U.S. Dept. Commerce, Washington, 1980-81; asst. treas. Am. Express Internat. Bank, NYC, 1981-82; sr. v.p. Refco, Inc., NYC, 1982-84; v.p., mgr. Thomson McKinnon Securities, NYC, 1984-88; sr. v.p. Lehman Bros., NYC, 1988-92; mng. dir. Credit Agricole Futures Inc., NYC, 1992-95; sr. mng. dir. Bear Stearns, NYC, 1995—. Cons. BDM Corp., McLean, Va., 1981-88; Presdl. appointee J. William Fulbright Fgn. Scholarship Bd., 1993-97; bd. adv. Shenandoah U. Sch. Bus., 2001—. Exec. com. Conn. Yankee Coun. Boy Scouts Am., 2000—, v.p. exec. com., 2003—; mem. arrangements com. Dem. Nat. Conv., San Francisco, 1984, mem. site selection com., 1989—90, alt. del. Boston, 2004, mem.rules com. LA, 2000; chmn. nat. fin. coun. Dem. Nat. Com., 1998—2005; fin. chmn. Conn. Dem. State Ctrl. Com., 1993, 2003—05; trustee Conservative Synagogue of Westport, 2000—02. Wexner Heritage Found. fellow, 1992-94; recipient Disting. Citizen award Conn. Yankee Coun. Boy Scouts Am., 2004. Jewish. Avocation: skiing. Home: 326 Bayberry Ln Westport CT 06880-1315 Office: 383 Madison Ave New York NY 10179 Office Phone: 212-272-2822. E-mail: robrose@att.net.

ROSE, SARAH ELIZABETH, genealogist, writer, counselor, web site designer; d. H. S. Agsanian and B. M. Phillips; children: Julie, Tory, Mary, Alexa, Vincent, Sasha, Zachary. Grad. with honors, U.S. Army Signal Sch., 1975; grad. with distinction, Non-Commd. Officer's Leadership Acad. U.S. Army, 1976; BA in Social Sci., San Jose State U., 1980; MA in History with honors, Hawking Inst., 2004. Prof. genealogist. Author: Many Branches, One Tree, 1997, World Wide Roots, 2001, Poetry: A Tribute to Life, 2003, (novel) Extraordinary Journey: Daughter of Destiny, 2005, numerous poems. Army specialist US Army, 1974—77. Decorated Good Conduct medal, Nat. Def. Svc. medal, weapons medal M-16 U.S. Army; recipient Cold War Recognition Cert., U.S. Dept. Def. Mem.: Daus. of 1812, Nat. Fedn. Poetry Socs., Iowa Pioneers, Internat. Soc. Daus. Utah Pioneers, Pioneers of Kans., Ill. Prairie Pioneers, Am. First Families, Nat. Soc. DAR, The Winthrop Soc. (assoc.), Nat. Soc. Daus. of the Am.

Colonists, Nat. Soc. Colonial Dames XVII Century, Pioneer Families Nebr., Women in Mil. Svc. for Am. (charter), Oreg. Poetry Soc., Am. Legion. Avocation: collecting Egyptian, African, Native American objects. Personal E-mail: genealogical2002@yahoo.com.

ROSE, SCOTT A., lawyer; b. Flint, Mich., Feb. 10, 1953; BS with distinction, Ariz. State U., 1975, JD cum laude, 1979. Bar: Ariz. 1979. Chmn. bd. The Cavanagh Law Firm, Phoenix, Ariz. Articles editor Ariz. State Law Jour., 1978-79. Ariz. Govt. Affairs chmn. Internat. Coun. Shopping Ctrs. Mem. ABA, State Bar Ariz., Maricopa County Bar Assn., Downtown Phoenix Rotary Club 100 (bd. dirs.). Office: The Cavanagh Law Firm 1850 N Central Ave Ste 2400 Phoenix AZ 85004

ROSE, SELWYN H., chemicals executive; b. NYC, May 1, 1933; s. Rubin and Ruth Rosenthal; m. Helen Diana De Mov, July 25, 1957; children: Michelle, Wendy, Suzanne. BS, CCNY, 1954; MS, Ohio State U., 1958, PhD, 1961; MBA with honors, U. Chgo., 1979; CFP, Coll. Fin. Planning, 1994. Sr. rsch. chemist Pennwalk Corp., King of Prussia, Pa., 1961-65; dept. mgr. Horizons Inc., Beachwood, Ohio, 1965-72, dir. rsch., 1972-74; mgr. long range rsch. De Soto Inc., Des Plaines, Ill., 1974-79; dir. rsch., cen. rsch. lab. Borg-Warner Chems., Des Plaines, 1979-85; v.p. tech. Parker Chem. Co., Madison Heights, Mich., 1985-88; gen. mgr. rsch. and devel. Himont Inc., Wilmington, Del., 1988-91, v.p. product devel., 1991-93; pres. SHR Fin. Advisors, Wilmington, 1993—. Contbr. articles to profl. jours.; patentee in field. 1st lt. U.S. Army, 1954-56. Recipient IR 100 award Indsl. Rsch. mag., 1971, award Roon Found., 1979. Mem. Am. Chem. soc., Nat. Assn. Personal Fin. Advisors, Fin. Planners Assn. Achievements include development of polyphosphazene polymers. Home: 1503 Evergreen Ln Wilmington DE 19810-4431

ROSE, SHIRLEY KELLY, retired language educator; b. Marianna, Fla., Jan. 22, 1939; d. James William and Alice Elizabeth Kelly; children: William Timothy Livingston, Kelly Livingston Carlton. BA, Fla. State U., Tallahassee, 1960; MS in Adult Edn., Troy State U., Montgomery, Ala., 1979, MS in English, 1990. English tchr. Bay County HS, Panama City, Fla., 1960—62, St. James HS, Montgomery, 1972—73, Patterson State Tech Coll., Montgomery, 1973—2000, chmn. gen. edn., 1990—2000; ret., 2000. Tech. coll. rep. State Policy Adv. Comm., Montgomery, 1986—99, Postsecondary Exec. Com., Montgomery, 1985—99. Coord. edn. divsn. United Way, Montgomery; organizer, pres. Jr. Woman's Club, Mobile, Ala., 1965—67; co-chmn. mother's march March of Dimes, Montgomery and Mobile, 1965—68; bd. dirs. Cystic Fibrosis, Montgomery. Named Disting. Young Woman, Montgomery Jaycettes, 1969, Outstanding Clubwoman, Montgomery Jr. Woman's Club, 1969, Outstanding Tech Coll. Faculty Mem., Ala. Coll. Sys., 1992; recipient Davenport Meml. award, Nat. Coun. Higher Edn., 1996. Mem.: Ala. Edn. Assn. (pres. postsecondary divsn. 1986—87, Outstanding Postsecondary Mem. 1995). Methodist. Avocations: travel, reading, bridge, exercise. Home: 8620 Lillian Pl Montgomery AL 36117 Home Phone: 334-215-3430.

ROSE, STEPHEN F., columnist; b. Kansas City, Mo., Nov. 5, 1947; s. Stanley J. and Shirley Rose; m. Carol S. Brady, May 31, 1970; children: Joshua Scott, Melissa Rose Faulkner, Rebecca Kathryn. BJ, U. Mo., Columbia, 1966—70. Chmn. Sun Publs., Overland Park, Kans., 1977—. Vice-chmn. Greater Kans. City C. of C., Kansas City, 1995—2003; chmn. U. Kans. Sch. Nursing, Kansas City, 1997—99, UMB Scout Mut. Funds, 1990—2005, dir., 1990—2005; pres. Suburban Newspapers Am., Chgo., 1998—99; dir. Metcalf Bank, Overland Park, Kans., 1986—99; roundtable panelist Sta. KCPT-TV, Kansas City, 1995—2003, weekly Sta. PBS-TV program host. Specialist 4th class/corr. US Army, 1968—69, Vietnam. Recipient Johnson Countian of Yr., Johnson County CC Found., 1999. Achievements include co-chairing the first bi-state cultural initiative in America. Home: 2110 Stratford Rd Mission Hills KS 66208 Home Phone: 913-908-5353. Home Fax: 913-722-5353. Personal E-mail: srose@kc.rr.com.

ROSE, SUSAN PORTER, management and governmental affairs consultant; b. Cin., Sept. 20, 1941; d. Elmer Johnson and Dorothy (Wurst) Porter; m. Jonathan Chapman Rose, Jan. 26, 1980; 1 child, Benjamin Chapman. BA, Earlham Coll., 1963; MS, Ind. State U., 1970; HDL (hon.), Rose-Hulman Inst. Tech., 2002. Staff asst. Congressman Richard L. Roudebush, Washington, 1963-64; asst. dean George Sch., Bucks County, Pa., 1964-66; asst. dir. admissions Mt. Holyoke Coll., South Hadley, Mass., 1966-71; asst. dir. correspondence First Lady Pat Nixon The White House, 1971-72, dir. of scheduling to First Lady Pat Nixon, 1972-74, to First Lady Betty Ford, 1974-77; spl. asst. to asst. atty. gen. Office Improvements in Adminstrn. Justice, Washington, 1977-79; spl. asst. to dep. asst. atty. gen. Justice Mgmt. divsn. U.S. Dept. Justice, Washington, 1978-81; chief of staff to Barbara Bush, asst. to U.S. v.p. Washington, 1981—89; chief of staff to First Lady Barbara Bush, dept. asst. pres. of U.S. The White House, 1989—93; commr. U.S. Commn. Fine Arts, 1993-98. Bd. dirs. Barbara Bush Found. for Family Literacy, 1993—2002; trustee Bush Presdl. Libr.; mem. alumni coun. Earlham Coll., 1977—78, pres. alumni assn., 1978—81. Recipient Disting. Alumni award, Earlham Coll., 1992, Ind. State U., 1991. Mem.: Ind. Acad. Home: 5955 Ranleigh Manor Dr Mc Lean VA 22101-2428

ROSE, THOMAS ALBERT, artist, educator; b. Washington, Oct. 15, 1942; s. Francis John and Ann Elizabeth (Voelkel) R.; m. Mary Melinda Moyer, Aug. 21, 1965; children: Sarah, Jessica. BFA, U. Ill., 1965; MA, U. Calif., Berkeley, 1967; postgrad., Lund U., Sweden, 1967-68. Instr. U. Calif., Berkeley, 1968-69, N.Mex. State U., Las Cruces, 1969-72; faculty mem. U. Minn., Mpls., 1972—, prof. art, 1983—, Fesler-Lampert chair in humanities, 2001—. Author: Winter Book, 1995, Where Do We Start?, 2003, 1018 W. Scott St., 2005; one-man shows include Clock Tower, N.Y.C., 1977, Truman Gallery, N.Y.C., 1977-78, Rosa Esman Gallery, N.Y.C., 1979, 81, 82, Marianne Deson Gallery, Chgo., 1984-86, Robert Thomson Gallery, Mpls., 1986, 91, 92, 95, Deson Saunders Gallery, Chgo., 1989, Mpls. Inst. Art, 1992, Weisman Art Mus., Mpls., 1994, Tweed Mus., Duluth, Minn., 1995, Steinbaum/Krauss Gallery, N.Y.C., 1996, 99, Brevard Mus. Art, Melbourne, Fla., 1997, Gensler Arch., Washington, 1999, 2004, Flanders Gallery, Mpls., 2000, 05, Bernice Steinbaum Gallery, Miami, Fla., 2001, 03, 05, Intermedia Arts, Mpls., 2003, Flanders Gallery, Mpls., 2005, Kent Mueller Gallery, Milw., 2005; exhibited in group shows at Walker Art Ctr., Mpls., 1974, 76, 77, Whitney Mus. Downtown, N.Y.C., P.S. #1, N.Y.C., 1978, Wave Hill, Bronx, N.Y., 1981, Hirshhorne Mus., Washington, 1981, Am. Ctr. in Paris, 1982, Harvard U. Sch. Architecture, 1983, Cultural Ctr., Chgo., 1983, Hal Bromm Gallery, N.Y.C., Sheldon Mus., Lincoln, Nebr., 1989, Tampa (Fla.) Mus., 1988, MCAD, Mpls., 1996, Minn. Mus. Art, 1996, Socrates Sculpture Park, N.Y.C., Fla. Internat. U., Miami, 1997, Gallerie Lipanjepuntin, Trieste, Italy, 2006, Luxan Acad. Art, Shenyang, China, 2006, Beijing Film Acad., 2006; represented in permanent collections Whitney Mus., N.Y.C., Getty Inst. L.A., Walker Art Ctr., Joslyn Mus., Omaha, Park St. Lofts, Springfield, Mass., U. Minn., Mpls., Am. Lung Assn. Target Ctr., Mpls., St. Lukes Episcopal Ch., Mpls., Wonkwang U., Republic of Korea, Mpls. Inst. Art, Weisman Mus. Art, Mpls., Stanford U. Libr., Sch. of the Art Inst., Chgo., Milw. Pub. Libr.; set designer: Fool for Love, Cricket Theater, Mpls., 1985, Circus, Theater de Jeune Lune, 1986; project dir. Works of Art in Pub. Places for Humphrey Inst. Pub. Affairs, Mpls., 1988; prin. works include Minn. Zoo, Marine Edn. Ctr., Sacred Heart U., Fairfield, Conn., Berniece Steinbaum Gallery, Miami, 1999, Steinbaum residence, 2002, Bennett Meml., Mpls., 2002. Named Rockefeller resident, Bellagio, Italy, 1993; recipient McKnight Artist fellow, 1995, travel fellow, Dayton-Hudson/Jerome, 1990, 1995, Jerome Found. Arts, 1993—94, Mellon Found., 1993, Fesler-Lampert Chair in Humanities, 2002; fellow, Nat. Endowment for Arts, 1977, 1981, Bush Found., 1979, Minn. State Arts Bd., 1979, 1984, McKnight Found., 1981, McKnight Found. Rsch., 1993—96, McKnight Photography, 2002; grantee, Arts Bd. Opportunities, 1993. Home: 91 Nicollet St Minneapolis MN 55401-1513 Office: Univ Minn 208 Studio Arts 23D S Avenue Minneapolis MN 55425 Office Phone: 612-889-9871. Personal E-mail: rosex001@umn.edu.

ROSE, VICTORIA LASDON, publishing executive; Pub. YM/Young & Modern mag., NYC, Mademoiselle mag., style365.com, US Weekly mag., NYC, 2000—. Named Pub. the Yr., Delaney Report, 2004. Office: US Weekly 1290 Avenue of the Americas New York NY 10104-0298

ROSE, WALTER DEANE, retired engineering educator; b. Liberty, Ind., Jan. 10, 1920; s. Joseph Sims Rose., Sr and Dorothy Gray Rose; m. Edith Magdalena Dora Schroeder, May 11, 1959; m. Dorris Evelyn Dailey, Mar. 20, 1939 (dec. Feb. 2, 1945); m. Zoe Fern Wilcox, July 14, 1945 (div. Oct. 31, 1952); children: Dixie Rachel Rose-Phillips, Walter Deane Jr., John Gregory, Bonnie Zoe, Deane Michael, Edith Elisabeth. BS, U. of Chgo., 1944. Registered profl. engr., Colo. Rsch. chemist Affils. of Std. Oil of N.J., NYC, 1944—48; rsch. physicist Gulf R&D Co., Physics Divsn., Pitts. and Harmarville, Pa., 1948—50; lectr. in petroleum engring., asst. dir. Tex. petroleum rsch. com. U. Tex. and State of Tex. RR Commn., Austin, 1950—52; editor Gulf Coast dist. Oil and Gas Jour., Houston, 1952—53; group leader oil recovery processes Continental Oil Co. Rsch. Ctr., Ponca City, Okla., 1954—56; fossil energy recovery specialist Petroleum Rsch. Corp., Denver, 1954—55; prof. of petroleum engring. U. of Ill., Champaign, 1955—68; scholar French Petroleum Inst., Rueil Malmaison, France, 1962—63; Albert Albermann vis. prof. of civil engring. TECHNION, Israel Inst. of Tech., Haifa, 1968—69; vis. prof. of freshman engring. Purdue U., West Lafayette, Ind., 1970—71; dean of sci. and prof. of engring. Abadan (Iran) Inst. of Tech., 1971—72; editor, ghost writer Authors and Spkrs. Svcs., Chicago and Champaign, Ill., 1975—2001. Vis. prof. developing grad. student programs Mid. East Tech. U., Ankara, Turkey, 1969—70; rsch. lab. innovator Amdel Spl. Core Labs., Adelaide and Brisbane, Australia, 1991—92; tech. cons. Petronas Rsch. Inst., Kuala Lumpur, Malaysia, 1992—94; cons. on petroleum reservoir engring. matters Mex. Petroleum Inst., Mexico City, 2000—06; reservoir engring. cons. Woodside Peroleum, Perth, Australia, 2000; cons. Mex. Inst. of Petroleum, Mexico City, 2004—05, U. of NSW, Sydney, 1991, Chevron, Brisbane, Australia, 1991, Santos, Adelaide, Australia, 1991; vis. scientist Brit. Nat. Oil Co., London, 1976; vis. prof. U. Ibadan, Nigeria, 1971—74; dir. of rsch. and v.p. EG&G Continental Labs., Denver, 1984—86; vis. prof. UNESCO, Dacca, East Pakistan, 1970—71; vis. prof., head of dept. N.Mex. Inst. of Mining and Tech., Socorro, 1974—76; vis. prof., departmental head U. of Wyo., Laramie, 1976—77; vis. specialist on prodn. of coal bed methane Sci. Applications Internat. Assigned to DOE Funded Natural Gas Recovery Rsch. Projects, Morgantown, W.Va., 1978—79; assoc. dir. U.S. Dept. Fossil Energy Rsch. Projects Inst. of Gas Tech., Chgo., 1980—82; vis. sci. rsch. instigator Commonwealth Sci. Indsl. Rsch. Orgn., Canberra, Australia, 1987—89; vis. scientist Chinese Inst. of Porous Flow, Lang Feng, China, 1988. Contbr. articles to profl. jours. and books (travel and rsch. grants various insts. and univs.). Advocate 'natural law party concept. Recipient Cert. of Appreciation award, CEO of the Alta. Rsch. Coun. in Edmonton, 1998. Mem.: Soc. Petroleum Engring. (sr. Legion of Honor), Chgo. Press Club, Houston Press Club. Achievements include patents for Research Lab and Field Equipment Designs; Developing Mathematical Modeling Ideas; patents for dealing with design and utilization of laboratory and field equipment facilities, also mathematical modeling schemes; research in so-called APTPA applications (Additional Prospective Transport Process Algorithms). Home: POBox 2424 409 E Springfield Ave Champaign IL 61820 Office Phone: 217-355-6510. Business E-Mail: wdrose@uiuc.edu.

ROSE-ACKERMAN, SUSAN, law and political economy educator; b. Mineola, NY, Apr. 23, 1942; d. R. William and Rosalie Rose; m. Bruce A. Ackerman, May 29, 1967; children: Sybil, John. BA, Wellesley Coll., 1964; PhD, Yale U., 1970. Asst. prof. U. Pa., Phila, 1970-74; lectr. Yale U., New Haven, 1974-75, asst. prof., 1975-78, assoc. prof., 1978-82; prof. law and polit. economy Columbia U., NYC, 1982-87; Ely prof. of law and polit. econ. Yale U., New Haven, 1987-92, co-dir. Ctr. Law, Econ. and Pub. Policy, 1988—, Henry R. Luce prof. jurisprudence law and polit. sci., 1992—. Vis. rsch. fellow World Bank, 1995-96. Author: (with Ackerman, Sawyer and Henderson) Uncertain Search for Environmental Quality, 1974 (Henderson prize 1982); Corruption: A Study in Political Economy, 1978, (with E. James) The Nonprofit Enterprise in Market Economies, 1986; editor: The Economics of Nonprofit Institutions, 1986, (with J. Coffee and L. Lowenstein) Knights, Raiders, and Targets: The Impact of the Hostile Takeover, 1988, Rethinking the Progressive Agenda: The Reform of the American Regulatory State, 1992, Controlling Environmental Policy: The Limits of Public Law in Germany and the United States, 1995, Corruption and Government: Causes, Consequences and Reform, 1999 (Levine Prize 2000), (with János Kornai) Building a Trustworthy State in Post-Socialist Transition, 2004, (with Kornai and B. Rothstein) Creating Social Trust in Post-Socialist Transition, 2004, From Elections to Democracy: Building Accountable Government in Hungary and Poland, 2005, International Handbook on the Economics of Corruption, 2006; contbr. articles to profl. jours.; mem. editl. bd. Jour. Law, Econs. and Orgn., 1984—, Internat. Rev. Law and Econs., 1986—, Polit. Sci. Quar., 1988—. Guggenheim fellow 1991-92, Fulbright fellow, Free U. Berlin, 1991-92; fellow Ctr. for Advanced Study in the Behavioral Scis., Stanford, Calif., 2002, Collegium Budapest, 2002. Mem. Am. Law and Econs. Assn. (bd. dirs. 1993-96, 2002-04), Am. Econ. Assn. (mem. exec. com. 1990-93), Am. Polit. Sci. Assn., Assn. Am. Law Schs., Assn. Pub. Policy and Mgmt. (policy coun. 1984-88, treas. 1998-2000). Democrat. Office: Yale U Law Sch PO Box 208215 New Haven CT 06520-8215 Office Phone: 203-432-4891. Business E-Mail: susan.rose-ackerman@yale.edu.

ROSEANNE, (ROSEANNE BARR), actress, comedienne, television producer, writer; b. Salt Lake City, Nov. 3, 1952; d. Jerry and Helen Barr; m. Bill Pentland, 1974 (div. 1989); children: Jessica, Jennifer, Brandi, Buck, Jake; m. Tom Arnold, 1990 (div. 1994); m. Ben Thomas, 1994. Former window dresser, cocktail waitress; prin. Full Moon & High Tide Prodns., Inc. As comic, worked in bars, church coffeehouse, Denver; produced showcase for women performers Take Back the Mike, U. Boulder (Colo.); performer The Comedy Store, L.A.; showcased on TV special Funny, 1986, also The Tonight Show; featured in HBO-TV spl. On Location: The Roseanne Barr Show, 1987 (Am. comedy award Funniest Female Performer in TV spl., 1987, Ace award Funniest Female in Comedy, 1987, Ace award Best Comedy Spl. 1987); writer, dir., star of TV series Roseanne ABC, 1988-97 (U.S. Mag. 2nd Ann. Readers Poll Best Actress in Comedy Series, 1989, Golden Globe nomination Outstanding Lead Actress in Comedy Series 1988, Emmy award Outstanding Lead Actress in Comedy Series, 1993), The Real Roseanne Show, 2003; actress: (motion pictures) She-Devil, 1989, Look Who's Talking Too (voice), 1990, Freddy's Dead, 1991, Even Cowgirls Get the Blues, 1994, Blue in the Face, 1995, Unzipped, 1995, Meet Wally Sparks, 1997, Home on the Range (voice), 2004; TV movies: Backfield in Motion, The Woman Who Loved Elvis, 1993; appeared in TV spl. Sinatra: 80 Years My Way, 1995; exec. prodr. Saturday Night Spl., Fox-TV; author: Roseanne: My Life as a Woman, 1989, My Lives, 1994; (host) Roseanne Show, 1998-2000, I am Your Child, 1997 (TV), Get Bruce, 1999. Active various child advocate orgns. Recipient Peabody award, People's Choice award (4), Golden Globe award (2), Am. Comedy award, Humanitas award, Nickelodeon Kids Choice award, 1990, Eleanor Roosevelt award for Outstanding Am. Women, Emmy award, 1993.

ROSEBERRY, EDWIN SOUTHALL, retired state agency administrator; b. Roanoke, Va., July 4, 1925; s. Edwin Alexander and Gladys Edmonia (Southall) R.; m. Mary Louise Sprengel, Sept. 2, 1949 (dec. 1978); children: Edwin Jr., David, Kevin; m. Alice Proffit Boger, Dec. 27, 1980; 1 stepdaughter, Elizabeth Leigh Boger. BS in Commerce, U. Va., 1949. Registered sanitarian, Hawaii, Va. Store mgr. Allied Arts, Charlottesville, Va., 1949-51; retail credit sales mgr. B.F. Goodrich Co., Charlottesville, 1951-53; environ. health specialist Dept. of Health, Charlottesville, 1953-84, Dept. of Labor, Honolulu, 1987-2000; ret., 1999. Freelance photographer, Charlottesville, 1949-85, Honolulu, 1985—. Contbr. photographs: The Inward Eye, 1986. Election ofcl. State of Hawaii, Honolulu, 1988—. With USN, 1944-46. Recipient Nat. awards Eastman Kodak Co., nat. newspapers, and photography mags., 1951-69. Mem. VFW (life), Am. Indsl. Hygiene Assn., Austrian Hawaiian Club (v.p., bd. dirs. 1985), Antique Auto Assn. (pres. Piedmont region 1964), Hawaii Photo Soc. (v.p. 1989), Elks (tiler and inner guard 1985, officer Honolulu chpt. 1985-2001), Am. Legion (dept. historian, VFW jr. vice commdr.), Mason (32 degree), Shriners (sojourners, heroes of '76, eastern star), Pi Delta Epsilon. Episcopalian. Avocations: photography, stamp collecting/philately, antique automobiles, figure skating. Home: Carriage Hill Apts #302 820 Beverly Dr Charlottesville VA 22911 Personal E-mail: uvaflashed@adelphia.net.

ROSEBROUGH, CAROL BELVILLE, cable television company executive; b. Ironton, Ohio, June 5, 1940; d. Lindsey and Bessie (Reed) Belville; m. John R. Rosebrough, Mar. 4, 1960 (dec. Nov. 1974); children: G. Suzanne, John R., Rebecca J. Student, Columbia Coll., Mo., 1958-59; BSBA, Franklin U., 1985. Cons. CBR and Assocs., Columbus, 1978-82; dir. adminstrn. United Cerebral Palsy Columbus and Franklin County, 1972-82; bus. mgr. Times Mirror, Newark, Ohio, 1982-83, ops. mgr., 1983-85, gen. mgr. Logan/Waverly/Greenfield, Ohio, 1985-86, Times Mirror doing bus. as Dimension Cable Svcs., Marion, Ohio, 1986-88; v.p., gen. mgr. Cable TV div. Comcast of S.E. Pa. (formerly Susquehanna Comms., Times Mirror and Cox Comms.), Williamsport, Pa., 1988—. Bd. dirs United Way, Marion County, 1987-88, Lycoming County, 1989-2000, 2001-, Williamsport/Lycoming C. of C.; personal and bus. coach Coach U., 2002. Named one of Pa.'s Best 50 Women in Bus., 1997, One of Top 100 Bus. Persons in the State of Pa., 1997-99; fellow Betsy Magness Leadership Inst. 1999-2000, Pa. Economy League 2003—. Mem. Ohio Cable TV Assn. (bd. dirs. 1986-88), Pa. Cable TV Assn. (bd. dirs. 1990-96), Pa. Edn. Comms. Sys. (bd. dirs.), Pa. Rural Devel. Coun. (exec. com. telecomms. task force 1992-95), Mid-Ohio Regional Planning Commn. (transp. com. 1980-82), Internat. Women's Writers Guild, Internat. Assn. Counselors and Therapists. Avocations: writing, reading, music, arts/therapies. Office: Susquehanna Comms 330 Basin St Williamsport PA 17701-5216 Personal E-mail: carolrosebrough@suscom.net. Business E-Mail: carol_rosebrough@cable.comcast.com.

ROSEBUSH, JAMES SCOTT, growth strategy executive, former government official; b. Flint, Mich., June 1, 1949; s. Kenneth F. and Jacqueline (Porter) R.; m. Nancy Paull, May 18, 1974; children: Claire Haisley, Lauren Culver. BA, The Principia, Elsah, Ill., 1971; MA, Boston U., 1973. Cons., Boston, 1972-76; v.p. Nat. Chamber Found., Washington, 1976-79; assoc. dir. corp. contbn. Std. Oil Co., Cleve., 1979-81; dir. Office Bus. Liaison, U.S. Dept. Commerce, Washington, 1981, spl. asst. to pres. for pvt. sector initiatives, Washington, 1981-82; dept. asst. to Pres., chief staff for First Lady The White House, Washington, 1982-86; pres. James Rosebush & Co., 1986—; CEO Growth Strategy, Inc., OurfamilyManager-.com. Lectr. Georgetown U., Washington, 1977-79, George Washington U., Washington, 1977-79; presdl. appointee Nat. Mus. Svcs. Bd. Author: First Lady, Public Wife, 1987; contbr. articles to profl. jours. Mem. rev. com. United Way, Cleve., 1979; mem. cmty. rels. com. Cleve. Orch., 1979; bd. dirs. Phillips Collection Mus., SDC, Inc.; art adv. panel Fed. Res. Bd.; mem. adv. bd. Boston U. Recipient Internat. award Rotary Internat., 1970 Republican. Avocations: tennis, skiing, reading, travel. Office: 1250 24th St NW Ste 350 Washington DC 20037-1124 Office Phone: 202-835-1695. Personal E-mail: jsrosebush@aol.com.

ROSEDALE, PHILIP E., computer software company executive; b. San Diego, 1968; m. Yvette Rosedale. BS in Physics, U. Calif., San Diego. V.p., chief tech. officer RealNetworks; entrepreneur-in-residence Accel Partners, San Francisco, 1999; founder, CEO Linden Lab, San Francisco, 1999—. Named one of The World's Most Influential People, TIME mag., 2007, 50 Who Matter Now, Business 2.0, 2007; recipient Rave award (Business), Wired mag., 2006. Achievements include development of Second Life computer game software. Office: Linden Lab 1100 Sansome St San Francisco CA 94111 *

ROSE-DEAL, MARY FRANCES, language educator; d. Robert and Margaret Angeline Rose; m. Fred William Deal, Oct. 21, 2000; 1 child, Heather Madison Rose Deal. BS in Edn., Slippery Rock U., Pa., 1994; MEd, Gannon U., Erie, Pa., 2002. Cert. Spanish K-12 instrucional II Pa. Dept. Edn., 2001. Tchr. Spanish Pleasant Valley Mid. Sch., Brodheadsville, Pa., 1995—96, Harmony Area Sch. Dist., Westover, Pa., 1996—99, Paul Blazer H.S., Ashland, Ky., 1999—2000; tchr. Spanish, French, reading AJ McMullen Mid. Sch., Farmington, Pa., 2001—02; tchr. Spanish Somerset Area H.S., Pa., 2002—. Mem.: Pennsylvania Appalachian Regional Lang. Educators Orgn., Am. Coun. Tchg. of Fgn. Langs., Am. Assn. Tchrs. Spanish and Portuguese (state dir. Sociedad Honoraria Hispánica 2004—). Office: Somerset Area HS 645 S Columbia Ave Somerset PA 15501 Home Phone: 814-395-5783; Office Phone: 814-443-2831.

ROSEFSKY, JONATHAN BENENSOHN, pediatrician; b. Johnson City, NY, June 28, 1939; s. I. J. and Elsie S. Rosefsky; m. Sue Perel, 1964 (div. 2005); children: Katherine, Douglas, Matthew. AB, Cornell U., 1960; B in Med. Sci., Dartmouth U., 1962; MD, Harvard U., 1964. Diplomate Am. Bd. Pediat., lic. Pa., Va. Intern in surgery Vanderbilt Univ. Hosp., Nashville, 1964-65; resident in pediatrics Children's Hosp. Med. Ctr., Boston, 1965-67; pediatrician USAF Med. Corps, Langley AFB, Va., 1967-69; dir. neonatal ICU United Health Svcs. Hosp., Johnson City, NY, 1969-74; pvt. practice Binghamton, NY, 1969-86; pres. Notation Systems, Inc., Binghamton, 1981-89; asst. dir. clin. devel. McNeil Consumer Products Co., Ft. Washington, Pa., 1986-89; dir. med. svcs., sr. dir. med. affairs Wyeth-Ayerst Labs., St. David's, Pa., 1989—99; pres. Fluidmotive, Inc., Haverford, Pa., 2000—, Simulatrix, Inc., Wynnewood, Pa., 2004—, HydroCoil Power, Inc., Wynnewood, Pa., 2006—. Cons. pediat. N.Y. State Dept. Social Svcs., Albany, 1976—86; FDA adv. com. Gen. Hosp. and Personal Use Devices, Rockville, Md., 1986; industry rep. FDA Adv. Com. on Immunology Devices, Rockville, 1987—93; asst. prof. Pediat. Jefferson Med. Sch., Phila., 1987—; chmn. com. on ethics in clin. trials, pharm. sponsored conf., 1998; cons. Pharm. Device R.P.S., 2004—. Contbr. articles to profl. jours. Chmn. Citizen's Adv. Com. to Mayor of Binghamton, NY, 1971. Capt. USAF, 1967—69. Recipient Physician's Recognition award, AMA, 2004. Fellow: Am. Coll. Nutrition, Am. Acad. Pediat.; mem.: Mainline YMCA (bd. dirs. 2005—), Harvard Club NYC. Achievements include invention of back wedge, mole marker, DecTRR electronic camouflage, ribbon drive; propulsion, pump, low head hydroelectric turbine. Avocations: skiing, swimming, photography, languages, travel. Home: 1359 Arbordale Rd Wynnewood PA 19096 Office Phone: 877-790-7972. Business E-Mail: fluidmotive.inc@att.net.

ROSEGARTEN, RORY, personal manager, television producer, theater producer, film producer; b. NYC, Feb. 12, 1962; s. Robert Joel and Rita Honey (Mandel) Rosegarten; m. Wendy Jill Korn, May 4, 1991; children: Danielle Sydney, Ryan Harris. Student, Ariz. State U., 1980-81. Pres. The Conversation Co., Ltd., Great Neck, NY, 1983—. Prodr.: (Broadway plays) Late Nite Comic, 1987; exec. prodr.: (albums) Robert Klein: Let's Not

Make Love, 1990, Brian Regan: Live, 1997; exec. prodr.: (DVD) Brian Regan: I Walked on the Moon, 2004; exec. prodr.: (albums) Ray Romano: Live at Carnegie Hall, 2002, (TV spl.) A Pair of Jokers: Brian Regan and Dennis Regan, 1991, Something's Wrong with the Regan Boy, 1992, Robert Klein: It All Started Here, 1996, Sketch Pad, 2001, Sketch Pad 2, 2003; exec. prodr.: (TV spl.) Making The Cut, 2005, Robert Klein: Child in His 50's, 2000, Brian Regan: Standing Up, 2007; exec. prodr.: (TV series) Everybody Loves Raymond, 1996—2005, New Joke City, 2000—01, The John Henson Project, 2004; exec. prodr.: (TV series) The Lance Krall Show, 2005; exec. prodr.: (TV spl., DVD) Clint Holmes: A Night to Remember, 2001, (TV spl.) Robert Klein: The Amorous Busboy of Decature Ave, 2005; exec. prodr.: (films) Welcome to Mooseport, 2004, Eulogy, 2004; prodr.: Grilled, 2004; exec. prodr.(and creator): (TV series) Free Radio, 2007—. Assoc. trustee North Shore L.I. Jewish Health Sys. Found., 2004—; assoc. bd. dir. Parker Jewish Geriat. Inst., New Hyde Park, NY, 1995—98; bd. gov. Comic Relief, 1999—2002. Recipient Primetime Emmy award for Outstanding Comedy Series: Everybody Loves Raymond, 2002—03, 2004—05. Mem.: SAG, NATAS, Friars Club. Avocation: autograph and memorabilia collecting. Office: The Conversation Co Ltd 1044 No Blvd Ste 304 Roslyn NY 11576

ROSEIG, ESTHER MARIAN See **FOGEL, ESTHER**

ROSELIEB, CRAIG ALAN, band director; b. Dekalb, Ill., Sept. 3, 1961; s. Alan David and Beverly Joan Roselieb; m. Joy Belt, July 4, 2004; children: Jousha Elijah Belt, Abigail Margaret. MusB, No. Ill. U., 1984; MusM, Northwestern U., Evanston, Ill., 1988. Cert. tchr. Ill., 1984. Band dir. Glenbrook North H.S., Northbrook, Ill., 1984—87, Wheaton Ctrl. H.S., Wheaton, Ill., 1988—90, Downers Grove South H.S., Downers Grove, Ill., 1990—. Recipient Citation of Excellence, Nat. Band Assn., 1997. Mem.: Ill. Music Educators Assn. (pres. dist. I 1999—2006), Am. Sch. Band Directors Assn. Democrat. Methodist. Avocations: running, bicycling, baseball. Office: Downers Grove South High School 1436 Norfolk Downers Grove IL 60516 Office Phone: 630-795-8693. Office Fax: 630-795-8599. Business E-Mail: croselieb@csd99.org.

ROSELL, KURT F., lawyer; b. Ithaca, NY, May 12, 1960; BS magna cum laude, Wake Forest U., NC, 1982; JD, Columbia Law Sch., 1985; LLM in Taxation, NYU, 1993. Bar: NY 1986. Atty. Cravath, Swaine & Moore, NYC; hiring ptnr., recruiting com. Schulte Roth & Zapel LLP, NYC. Spkr. in field, sr. editor Columbia Law Rev., 1983—85; contbr. articles to profl. jour. Harlan Fiske Stone Scholar. Mem.: Assn. Bar City NY, Phi Beta Kappa. Office: Schulte Roth & Zapel LLP 919 Third Ave New York NY 10022 Office Phone: 212-756-2099. Office Fax: 212-593-5955. Business E-Mail: kurt.rosell@srz.com.

ROSELL, SHARON LYNN, physics and chemistry professor; b. Wichita, Kans., Jan. 6, 1948; d. John E. and Mildred C. (Binder) Rosell. BA, Loretto Heights Coll., 1970; postgrad., Marshall U., 1973; MS in Edn., Ind. U., 1977; MS, U. Wash., 1988. Cert. profl. educator, Wash. Assoc. instr. Ind. U., Bloomington, 1973-74; instr. Pierce Coll. (name formerly Ft. Steilacoom CC), Wash., 1976-79, 82, Olympic Coll., Bremerton, Wash., 1977-78; instr. physics, math. and chemistry Tacoma CC, Wash., 1979—89; instr. physics and chemistry Green River CC, Auburn, Wash., 1983—86; rschr. Nuc. Physics Lab., U. Wash., Seattle, 1986-88; asst. prof. physics Cen. Wash. U., Ellensburg, 1989—. Faculty senate Ctrl. Washington U., 1992-98. Lector and dir. Rite of Christian Initiation of Adults, St. Andrew's Ch., Ellensburg, Wash., 1993—, mem. parish coun., 1995-2000. Mem.: Soc. Physics Students (councilor zone 17 1998—2004, com. judging Nat. Outreach and Rsch. awards 2000—01, 2003—05, nat. nominating com. 2005—), Pacific NW Assn. Coll. Physics (bd. dirs. 1997—99, 2001—, treas. 2002—), Internat. Union Pure and Applied Chemistry (affiliate), Am. Chem. Soc., Am. Assn. Physics Tchrs. (rep. com. on physics for 2-yr. colls. Wash. chpt. 1986—87, v.p. 1987—88, pres. 1988—89, v.p. 1994—95, pres. 1995—96, past pres. 1996—97), Am. Phys. Soc. Democrat. Roman Catholic. Avocations: leading scripture discussion groups, reading, poetry, needlecrafts. Home: 1100 N B St Apt 2 Ellensburg WA 98926-2570 Office: Ctrl Wash U Physics Dept Ellensburg WA 98926 Office Phone: 509-963-2757. Business E-Mail: rosells@cwu.edu. *Personal philosophy: Every human being is born with a unique set of talents and gifts with which to serve the Lord and other people; the greater the gift, the greater the obligation to serve.*

ROSELLA, JOHN DANIEL, clinical psychologist, educator; b. Phila., Sept. 12, 1938; s. Orazio and Angela Theresa (Cardone) Rosella; m. Rose Mary Theresa Malloy, Nov. 14, 1964; children: Anne-Marie, John Daniel Jr. BS in Psychology, Villanova U., 1961; MEd Temple U., 1966, postgrad. Temple U., 1969—72, PhD Walden U., 1981. Diplomate Am. Bd. Forensic Examiners, Am. Bd. Psychol. Spltys., Profl. Acad. Custody Evaluators, cert. hypnotherapist, lic. psychologist, Pa.; cert. in edn. St. Joseph's U., 1963. Tchr., counselor Father Judge H.S., Phila., 1962—67; counselor Bristol Twp. Sch. Dist., Bucks County, Pa., 1967—69; prof. dept. social and behavioral scis. Bucks County C.C., 1994—2005, prof. emeritus, 2005—, subject area coord., 2004, Newtown, Pa., 1968—, adj. prof., 2005, founder coll. reading and study skills program Newtown, Pa., 1968—70, founding chmn. dept. basic studies, 1970—76; dir. psychol. svcs. Fairless Hills (Pa.) Med. Ctr., 1978—89, dir. clin. svcs., 1989—96; asst. clin. prof. Widener U., 1990—. Cons. Office of Vocat. Rehab., 1977—; psychol. cons. Eugenia Hosp.19890, 1980—, Bur. Disability Determination, 1982—, Human Growth Ctr., Inc., 1982—2003, Crestview North Nursing Home and Rehab. Ctr., 1990—2003; cons. staff psychologist Attleboro Nursing Home and Rehab. Ctr., 1993—2001, Pickering Manor Nursing Home, 1997—2001; clin. assoc. prof., Dept. Mental Health Scis. Hahnemann U., 1982—94; cons. Bucks County (Pa.) Family Ct., 1985—2004; grad. clin. supr. Coll. of N.J., 1985—86; grad. counseling intern supr. Rider Coll., 1988—95; participant 1st Internat. Colloquium on Family Health, Sri Lanka, 1983, Australia, 88; ednl. profl. travel Italy and Switzerland, 1991; clin. supr. doctor of psychology program, 2005—06; lectr. in field. Author: Reading and Study Skills: A Counseling Approach, 1970, Effects of the Basic Studies Program on the Academic Achievement of High Risk Students, 1973—74, The Professor and the Law, 1975, Research in Hypnosis for Students, 1976, Marriage and Family Therapy: Its Evolution from Revolution, 1980, others; author: (audiotapes) Developing Successful Study Skills, Guided Imagery Exercises; author: articles. Active Right to Read Task Force, 1972—73; project dir. Fairless Hills Psychiat. Hosp. bldg. program, 1982—83; pres. bd. trustees Friends of the Libr. Found., Bucks County C.C., 1984—; co-founder Newtown Twp. Dem. Party, 1978, 1st vice chmn., 1979—80, Dem. committeeman, 1989—92; mem. 8th Congressional Dist. Adv. Coun. on Health Care, 1981—83; bd. dirs. Valley Day Sch., 1978—81; Bucks County Cmty. Ctrs., 1980—85. Recipient Man of Yr. award, Assn. to Advance Ethical Hypnosis, 1976, Disting. Tchg. recognition, Phi Theta Kappa, 1981, 1983, Faculty Svc. award, 1989, Profl. AChievement award, Bucks County C.C. Alumni Assn., 1991. Fellow: Pa. Psychol. Assn., Internat. Coun. for Sex Edn. and Parenthood of Am. U.; mem.: APA, Profl. Acad. Custody Evaluators, Pa. Assn. Marriage and Family Therapy, Am. Assn. Marriage and Family Therapy, Am. Coll. Forensic Examiners, Sons of Italy, KC, Am. Legion. Office: Offices at Oxford Crossing Ste 202 333 N Oxford Valley Rd Fairless Hills PA 19030-2626 E-mail: fairrlesspsychassoc@comcast.net.

ROSELLE, DAVID PAUL, retired academic administrator, mathematician, educator; b. Vandergrift, Pa., May 30, 1939; s. William John and Esther Suzanne (Clever) R.; m. Louise Helen Dowling, June 19, 1967; children— Arthur Charles, Cynthia Dowling BS, West Chester State Coll., 1961; PhD, Duke U., 1965; LLD (hon.), West Chester U., 1994; degree (hon.), Westchester U., Soka U., Japan. Asst. prof. math. U. Md., College Park, 1965-68; assoc. prof. math. La. State U., Baton Rouge, 1968-73, prof., 1973-74, Va. Poly. Inst. and State U., Blacksburg, 1974-87, dean grad. sch., 1979-81, dean research and grad. studies, 1981-83, provost, 1983-87, chmn. Commn. on Rsch., 1981-83, chmn. Commn. on Grad. Studies, 1983-87; prof. U. Ky., 1987-90, pres., 1987-90; pres., prof. math. U. Del., 1990—2007. Pres. COMAP, Inc., Lexington, Mass., 1986-95; bd. dirs. Wilmington Trust Corp., VTLS, Inc. Editor: Proc. of the First Louisiana Conf. on Combinatorics, Graph Theory and Computing, 1970, Proc. of the Second Louisiana Conf. on Combinatorics, Graph Theory and Computing, 1971; mem. editorial bd. The Bicentennial Tribute to American Mathematics, 1977; contbr. numerous research articles to profl. jours. Mem. Del. Roundtable, 1990—, Bus.and Pub. Edn. Coun., 1990—; trustee Winterthur Mus., 1991—; bd. dirs. Del. Acad. Medicine, 1991—, Med. Ctr. Del., 1991—, OCLC, Inc., 2004-; mem. USAID adv. com. vol. fgn. aid, 2000-04. Named Outstanding Alumnus West Chester State Coll., 1979; Westinghouse Coop. scholar, 1957; NSF grantee, 1965-75; Teaching Excellence Cert., 1978; Digital Equipment grant, 1984; Nat. Coun. Tchrs. Math. Cert. of Appreciation, 1984; founding fellow of Inst. for Combinatorics and Its Applications, 1990; numerous invited addresses at univs. and profl. soc. meetings. Mem. Am. Math. Soc., Math. Assn. Am. (sec., fin. com., exec. com., com. on publs. 1975-84; com. on spl. funds 1985—; chmn. com. on accreditation 1985; numerous other coms.). Home: 47 Kent Way Newark DE 19711-5201 Business E-Mail: roselle@udel.edu.

ROSELLE, WILLIAM CHARLES, librarian; b. Vandergrift, Pa., June 30, 1936; s. William John and Suzanne Esther (Clever) R.; m. Marsha Louise Lucas, Aug. 2, 1959; 1 child, Paul Lucas. BA, Thiel Coll., 1958; MLS, U. Pitts., 1963. Lic. profl. guide State of Mont., 1978. Mem. faculty Milton Hershey (Pa.) Sch., 1960-62; trainee Pa. State Library, 1962-63; asst. catalog librarian Pa. State U., 1963-65; engring., math. librarian U. Iowa, 1965-66, library adminstrv. asst., 1966-69, asst. dir. libraries, 1969-71; prof., dir. library U. Wis.-Milw., 1971-89; dir. univ. library system U. Pitts., 1989-90; pvt. cons. Thiensville, Wis., 1991—. Chmn. Morris Fromkin Meml. Lectr. Com., 1972-89; chmn. planning task force on computing U. Wis. System, 1973-74, mem. library planning study com., 1978-79, co-chmn. library automation task force, 1983-85; chmn. computing mgmt. rev. team U. Wis.-Stout, 1976; chmn. Council for U. Wis. Libraries, 1981-82; library cons. Grambling (La.) State U., Viterbo Coll., LaCrosse, Wis., N.C. A&T U., Greensboro, Mt. Mary Coll., Milw., U. Ill. at Chgo., Milw. Sch. Engring., Bklyn. Coll., U. South Ala., Concordia Coll., Milw., Metrics Rsch. Corp., Cardinal Stritch Coll., Milw., N.Y. Inst. Tech., Indiana U. of Pa., Med. Coll. Wis., Wis. Luth. Coll., Milw.; participant Library Adminstrs. Devel. Program, U. Md., 1973, micrographics seminar Nat. Microfilm Assn., 1973, Mgmt. Skills Inst., Assn. Rsch. Libraries, Kansas City, Mo., 1977, Meadowbrook Symposium Midwest Library Network, 1976; mem. sect. geography and map libraries Internat. Fedn. Library Assns. and Instns., 1978-83; mem. bldg. com. Ctr. for Rsch. Libraries, 1980-82. Editorial cons. The Quest for Social Justice, 1983, Current Geographical Publications, 1978-89; contbr. articles to profl. jours. Pres. Thiensville (Wis.) Village Bd., 1987; bd. dirs. Charles Allis Art Mus., 1979-84. Served with AUS, 1958-60. Named Disting. Alumnus, Thiel Coll., 1985 Hon. fellow Am. Geog. Soc.; mem. Spl. Libraries Assn. (spl. citation 1979), ALA (life), Iowa Library Assn. (chmn. audit com. 1968-70, chmn. intellectual freedom com. 1969-70), Wis. Library Assn., Midwest Acad. Librarians Conf. (chmn. 1969-71), AAUP (treas. U. Iowa chpt. 1969-70), Coun. Wis. Libraries (chmn. 1973-74), Soc. Tympanuchus Cupido Pinnatus, Internat. CBX Owners Assn., Milw. Civil War Round Table, Ozaukee Corvette Club, Beta Beta Beta, Beta Phi Mu, Phi Alpha Theta, Phi Kappa Phi, Phi Delta Kappa. Lutheran. Home: 324 Sunny Ln Thiensville WI 53092-1334

ROSELLI, RICHARD JOSEPH, lawyer; b. Chgo., Mar. 2, 1954; s. H. Joseph and Dolores Roselli; m. Lisa McNelis; children: Nicholas Joseph, Christiana Elise, Alexandra Grace, Michaela Luciana, Anthony Santino. BA, Tulane U., 1976, JD, 1980. Bar: Fla. 1981, U.S. Dist. Ct. (so. dist.) Fla. 1981, U.S. Ct. Appeals (5th and 11th cirs.); bd. cert. civil trial lawyer. Ptnr. Krupnick, Campbell, Malone, Roselli et al, Ft. Lauderdale, 1981—2002, Roselli & Roselli Trial Lawyers, Boca Raton, Fla., 2002—05, Roselli & McNelis, PA, Boca Raton, Fla., 2006—. Adj. asst. prof., mem. bd. advisors physician asst. program Nova Southeastern U. Trustee Fla. Dem. Party. Mem. ATLA (pres.' coun. 1996-97), Am. Bd. Trial Advocates, Am. Soc. Law and Medicine, So. Trial Lawyers Assn. (founder), Acad. Fla. Trial Lawyers (bd. dirs. 1987—, exec. com. 1990-97, sec. 1993, treas. 1994, pres. elect. 1995, pres. 1996, chmn. Fla. lawyers action group-PAC 1996, Golden Eagle award, 1989, 1996, 98, Silver Eagle award, 1990, Crystal Eagle award 1995), Broward County Trial Lawyers (bd. dirs.), Trial Lawyers for Pub. Justice, Lawyer Pilots Bar Assn., Am. Assn. for Justice, Fla. Justice Assn., Palm Beach Trial Lawyers Assn. Democrat. Roman Catholic. Office: 4800 N Federal Hwy Ste 202E Boca Raton FL 33431 Office Phone: 561-826-0826. Business E-Mail: rroselli@rosellimcnelis.com.

ROSELLON, JUAN, economist, researcher; arrived in U.S., 2002; BA in Econs., Nat. U. Mexico, 1985, BSc in Math., 1986, MSc in Math., 1988; MA in Econs., Rice U., 1992, PhD in Econs., 1993. Dir. gen. econ. policy Energy Regulatory Commn. of Mex., Mexico City, 1995—97; prof. econs. Centro de Investigacion y Docencia Economicas, Mexico City, D.F., 1997—; sr. fellow J. F. Kennedy Sch. of Govt. Harvard U., Cambridge, Mass., 2002—. Faculty mem. Program on Privatization, Regulatory Reform and Corp. Governance Harvard U., Cambridge, Mass., 1997—2000, Princeton (N.J.) U., 2001. Editor: Economia Mexicana, 2000—02; contbr. articles to profl. jours. Recipient Gabino Barreda medal, Nat. U. of Mex., 1986, Nat. Econs. award, Pres. of Mex., 1994; fellow, Rice U., 1988—92, Ora N. Arnold fellowship, 1992—93, Conacyt, Mex., 1992—93, Conacyt, 1999—2003, Fulbright Found., 2002—03, Repsol-YPF-Harvard JFK fellowship, Harvard U., 2003—04; grantee, Energy Regulatory Commn. of Mex., 1997—2004, Tinker Found., 2000—01; scholar, Scholarship Fundacion Mex.-Harvard, 2002—04. Mem.: Internat. Assn. Energy Econs.

ROSEMAN, CHARLES SANFORD, lawyer; b. Jersey City, Feb. 26, 1945; s. Leon and Edith (Neidorf) R.; children: Rochelle Lynn, Loren Scott. BA, Calif. State U., Northridge, 1968; JD, U. San Diego, 1971. Bar: Calif. 1972, U.S. Dist. Ct. (so. dist.) Calif. 1972, U.S. Dist. Ct. (cen. dist.) Calif. 1975, U.S. Supreme Ct. 1980, U.S. Claim Ct. 1990. Assoc. Greer, Popko, Nickoloff & Miller, San Diego, 1972-73; ptnr. Roseman & Roseman, San Diego, 1973-78, Roseman & Small, San Diego, 1978-82, Frank, Roseman, Freedus & Mann, San Diego, 1982-86, Roseman and Mann, 1986-92; pvt. practice San Diego, 1992—; judge pro tem San Diego County Superior Ct., 1975—; also arbitrator, mediator, 1977—; founding ptnr. i2i Resolutions, 2001. Bd. dirs. Glenn Aire Cmty. Devel. Assn., San Diego, 1972-73, Big Bros. San Diego County, 1973-81,; bd. dirs. San Diego County Anti-Defamation League, 1985—; chmn. exec. com. 1984-85, assoc. nat. commr., 1995—; bd. dirs. San Diego County Legal Aid Soc., 1988-89, Tifereth Israel Synagogue, pres. 1982-84, Homeys Youth Found., 2002-. Mem. ABA, Am. Assn. for Justice, Fed. Bar Assn., Consumer Attys. of Calif. (Recognition of Experience award 1985), Calif. Bar Assn., Am. Arbitration Assn. (arbitrator, panel 1985-86), San Diego Bar Assn., Consumer Attys. of San Diego (bd. dirs. 1982-84), U. San Diego Sch. Law Alumni Assn. (bd. dirs. 1972-73), B'nai B'rith (pres. 1978). Democrat. Office: Law Offices Charles S Roseman & Assocs 1761 Hotel Cir S Ste 250 San Diego CA 92108 Office Phone: 619-544-1500. Business E-Mail: csroseman@rosemanlaw.com.

ROSEMAN, JACK, computer services company executive; b. Lynn, Mass., June 13, 1931; s. Abraham and Bessie (Guz) Roseman; m. Judith Ann Rosenthal, Feb. 21, 1960; children: Laura, Alan, Shari. BA, Boston U., 1954; MS, U. Mass., 1955. Instr. U. Mass., 1958—60; dir. info. processing CEIR, Inc., Washington, 1960—66; v.p. KMS Tech. Ctr., Washington, 1966—70; pres., bd. dirs. On-Line Systems, Inc., Pitts., 1970—79; pres., chmn. United Computing Internat. subs. of SPRINT, 1979—80; pres., bd. dirs., later chmn. Actronics, 1981—85; pvt. investor, ptnr. J.R. Assocs., Pitts., 1988—92; chmn. of bd. dirs. Omega Systems, 1994—96; CEO/dir. Roseman Inst., 2001—. Disting. adj. prof. Donald H. Jones Ctr. Entrepreneurship, 1992—2000, assoc. dir., 1992—2001; John Thorne prof. entrepreneurship Carnegie Mellon U., 2000—01; dir. emeritus Pitts. High Tech. Coun.; chmn. Cerebellum, Inc., 1997—2000; bd. dirs. Roseman Inst., Collaborate, Inc., 2001—05, MIT Forum; advisor Donald H. Jones Ctr. for Entrepreneurship, Carnegie Mellon U., Echo Internat. Co-author: Outrageous Optimism: Wisdom for the Entrepreneural Journey. Adv. Kobold Found.; chmn. Nat. Found. Tchg. Extrepreneurships. Recipient Judges' award, Ernst & Young, and Merrill Lynch Inc. mags., 1991. Office Phone: 412-369-5306. Business E-Mail: rosemanj@rosemaninstitute.com.

ROSEMAN, SAUL, biochemist, educator; b. Bklyn., Mar. 9, 1921; s. Emil and Rose (Markowitz) R.; m. Martha Ozrowitz, Sept. 9, 1941; children: Mark Alan, Dorinda Ann, Cynthia Bernice. BS, CCNY, 1941; MS, U. Wis., 1944, PhD, 1947; MD (hon.), U. Lund, Sweden, 1984. From instr. to asst. prof. U. Chgo., 1948-53; from asst. prof. to prof. biol. chemistry, also Rackham Arthritis Research Unit, U. Mich., 1953-65; Ralph S. O'Connor prof. biology Johns Hopkins U., Balt., 1965—, chmn. dept., 1969-73; dir. McCollum-Pratt Inst., 1969-73, chmn. dept. biology, dir., 1988-90. Cons. NIH, NSF, Am. Cancer Soc., Hosp. for Sick Children, Toronto; sci. counselor Nat. Cancer Inst.; Lynch lectr. U. Notre Dame, 1989; Van Niel lectr. Stanford U., 1992. Author articles on metabolism of complex molecules containing carbohydrates and on solute transport.; former mem. editorial bd.: Biochemistry, Jour. Biol. Chemistry. Served with AUS, 1944-46. Recipient Sesquicentennial award U. Mich., 1967, T. Duckett Jones Meml. award Helen Hay Whitney Found., 1973, Rosenstiehl award Brandeis U., 1974, Internat. award Gairdner Found. award, 1981, Townsend Harris award CUNY, 1987, Spl. award 11th Internat. Symposium on Glycoconjugates, 1991, Karl Meyer award Soc. Glycobiology, 1993. Fellow Am. Acad. Microbiology; mem. Am. Soc. Biol. Chemists, Am. Soc. Cell Biology, Am. Acad. Arts and Scis., Nat. Acad. Scis., Am. Chem. Soc., Am. Soc. Microbiologists, Biochem. Soc. Japan (hon.). Office: Johns Hopkins U 34th Charles St Baltimore MD 21218 Office Phone: 410-516-7333.

ROSEMARIN, CAREY STEPHEN, lawyer; b. Englewood, NJ, Aug. 19, 1950; s. Jack L. and Muriel Ruth (Gordon) R.; m. Joan Maxine Lafer, June 17, 1973; children: Benjamin Joseph, Meryl Ruth. BS, U. Mich., 1972; MS, Pa. State U., 1974; JD, U. Tenn., 1978. Bar: Tenn. 1978, Ill. 1982, U.S. Dist. Ct. (ea. dist.) Tenn. 1978, U.S. Dist. Ct. (no. dist.) Ill. 1982. Rsch. assoc. Union Carbide Corp., Oak Ridge Nat. Lab., 1974-80; asst. regional counsel U.S. EPA, Chgo., 1980-86; ptnr. Katten, Muchin, & Zavis, Chgo., 1986-90, Jenner & Block, Chgo., 1990-99; prin. Law Offices of Carey S. Rosemarin, P.C., Northbrook, Ill., 1999—. Mem. ABA, Tenn. Bar Assn., Chgo. Bar Assn. (chmn. environ. law com. 1985-86), Environ. Law Inst. (assoc.), North Suburban Bar Assn. (v.p.). Jewish. Avocations: licensed glider pilot, bicycling. Office: Law Offices of Carey S Rosemarin PC 500 Skokie Blvd Ste 510 Northbrook IL 60062-2893 Office Phone: 847-897-8000. Fax: 312-896-5786. Business E-Mail: csr@rosemarinlaw.com.

ROSEN, ADAM B., lawyer; b. Queens, NY, May 4, 1967; BA in History, LI U., 1989; JD cum laude, Touro Coll., 1993. Bar: NJ 1993, US Dist. Ct. Dist. NJ 1993, NY 1994, US Dist. Ct. Ea. Dist. NY 1995, US Dist. Ct. So. Dist. NY 1995. Ptnr. Wilson, Elser, Moskowitz, Edelman & Dicker LLP, NY. Recipient: Moot Ct. bd. award 1992, Nassau/Suffolk Trial Lawyers Assn. award, Exemplary Contributions to the Quality of Student Life award, First Place Moot Ct. Competition Nassau Acad. Law 1992. Mem.: NY State Bar Assn., Nassau County Bar Assn., Assn. of the Bar of the City of NY. Mem. Touro Jour. of Transnational Law 1991-1992. Office: Wilson Elser Moskowitz Edelman & Dicker LLP 23rd Fl 150 E 42nd St New York NY 10017-5639 Office Phone: 212-490-3000. Office Fax: 212-490-3038. Business E-Mail: adam.rosen@wilsonelser.com. *

ROSEN, ALLEN DAVID, plastic surgeon; b. Bklyn., Mar. 5, 1957; MD, SUNY-Buffalo, 1983. Diplomate Am. Bd. Plastic Surgery with subspecialty in hand surgery. Intern Columbia-Presbyn. Med. Ctr., NYC, 1983—84, resident in surgery, 1984—86, resident in plastic surgery, 1986—88, fellow in hand surgery, 1987; pvt. practice plastic surgery, 1987—; founding ptnr., med. dir. The Plastic Surgery Group, Montclair, NJ, 1995—. Attending plastic surgeon Passaic Gen. Hosp., NJ, Mountainside Hosp., NJ, St. Barnabas Med. Ctr.; clin. asst. prof. U. Medicine and Dentistry N.J.; spokesperson Am. Soc. Plastic and Reconstructive Surgery, 1990—. Fellow: ACS; mem.: N.J. Soc. Plastic and Reconstructive Surgery, Am. Cancer Soc. (past pres.). Office: 37 N Fullerton Ave Montclair NJ 07042

ROSEN, ARTHUR MARVIN, advertising executive; b. NYC, Dec. 28, 1930; s. Joseph and Cornelia (Grob) R.; m. Maureen Elizabeth Reilly; children: Ellen Jessica, Deborah Lynn, Daniel Joshua. BA, CUNY, 1952; MA, Yale U., 1953; postgrad., Columbia U., 1955-57. Analyst research Dancer-Fitzgerald-Sample, NYC, 1955-56; supr. research Benton and Bowles, NYC, 1956-61; account exec. Young and Rubicam, NYC, 1961-66; v.p. account supr. Grey Advt., NYC, 1966-69; pres. Met. Diagnostic, NYC, 1969-73; v.p. group mgmt. Grey Advt., NYC, 1973-81; exec. v.p. Sudler and Hennessey, NYC, 1981-94; mktg. cons. Himmel Nutrition, Inc., 1994-95, Martin Himmel, Inc., 1994-95. Spkr. in field. Contbr. articles to profl. jours. Pres. Temple Beth Or, Washington Twp., N.J., 1973-74; chmn. Soc. Families, Colgate U., 1983-84; chmn. curriculum com., mem. exec. coun., study leader ILEAD, 2004-05, Dartmouth Coll.; v.p. Adventures in Learning, Colby-Sawyer Coll.; pres. Country Squires of New London, NH; mem. bd. dirs. Lake Sunapee Protective Assn.; mem. Jewish-Christian Interfaith Partnership. Cpl. U.S. Army, 1953-55. Republican. Jewish. E-mail: ponderosen@tds.net.

ROSEN, ARYE, microwave, optoelectronics and medical researcher; b. June 26, 1937; BSEE cum laude, Howard U., 1963; MScE, Johns Hopkins U., 1965; MSc in Physiology, Thomas Jefferson U., 1975; PhD in Elec. Engring., Drexel U., 1993. Registered profl. engr., B.C., Can. Assoc. in medicine Jefferson Med. Coll., Phila., 1977—; rsch. prof. Sch. of Biomed. Engring. Sci. and Health Sys. Drexel U., Phila., adj. prof. elec. and computer engring., 1981—2003, acad. prof. biomed. engring. and elec. engring., 2003—. Mem. com. on sci. and the arts The Franklin Inst., 2003—. Co-editor: High-Power Optically Activated Solid-State Switches, 1993, New Frontiers in Medical Device Technology, 1995; co-author: RF/microwave Interaction with Biological Tissues, 2006; contbr. more than 150 articles to profl. jours. Mem. adv. com. John Scott award Phila. Bd. Dirs. City Trusts, 2004—. Recipient Microwave prize 16th European Microwave Conf., 1986, Disting. Alumni award Drexel U. Coll. Engring., Elec. and Computer Engring. Dept., 1997, IEEE MTT-S Microwave Application award, 2000, IEEE Third Millenium medal, 2000, IEEE Reg. I award, 1989. Mem.: NAE, IEEE (mem. MMT-S tech. com. for light-wave tech. 1979—, mem. MTT-S tech. program com., chmn. MTT-S tech. com. on biol. effects and med. applications, mem. editl. bd., assoc. editor IEEE Jour. Light-Wave Tech., editl. bd. Transactions on Microwave Theory and Techniques, editl. bd. Microwave and Optical Tech. Letters, mem. tech. com. IEEE Internat. Conf. Microwaves in Medicine 1991, ednl. activities bd., mem.-at-large health care engring. policy com., Disting. Microwave lectr. 1997—2001). Achievements include 55 patents in the fields of engineering and medicine, including Percutaneous Transluminal Microwave Catheter Angioplasty, Method and Apparatus for High Frequency Catheter Ablation, Catheter with Distally Located Integrated Circuit Radiation Generator, Electrical Phase Shifter Controlled by Light, Direct DC to RF Conversion by Impulse Excitation, Light Controlled Antennas, High Power Optical Switch, Radiation Protection Circuit for Protection Against Gamma Ray and Neutron Radiation. Office: Drexel Univ Sch Biomed Engring Sci and Health Sys 3141 Chestnut St Philadelphia PA 19104-2875 Office Phone: 215-895-1913.

ROSEN, BARRY S., lawyer; BS magna cum laude, U. Ill., 1974; JD, Harvard U., 1977. Bar: Mass. 1977, Ill. 1978. Asst. atty. gen. Antitrust Divsn. Commonwealth of Mass., 1977—79; ptnr. Sachnoff & Weaver, Chgo., 1979—2007, Reed Smith LLP, Chgo., 2007—. Named Charles Merriam Scholar, U. Ill.; recipient Bronze Tablet. Mem.: Phi Beta Kappa. Office: Reed Smith LLP 40th Fl 10 S Wacker Dr Chicago IL 60606 Office Phone: 312-207-6483. Business E-Mail: brosen@areedsmith.com.

ROSEN, BENSON, business administration educator; b. Detroit, Oct. 9, 1942; s. David and Laura R.; m. Brenda M. Leibroder, Dec. 17, 1966; children: Gregory Scott, David Loren. BS, Wayne State U., 1964, MA, 1968, PhD, 1969. Asst. prof. U. N.C., Chapel Hill, 1969-74, assoc. prof., 1974-80, prof. bus. adminstrn., 1980—, Hanes prof. mgmt., 1992—, sr. assoc. dean acad. affairs, 1995-98. Vis. prof. U. Minn., 1981; cons. to bus., industry, govt.; cons. EEOC. Author: Becoming Aware, 1976; Older Employees: New Roles for Valued Resources, 1985; mem. editorial rev. bd. Acad. Mgmt. Jour., 1978-84; contbr. articles to profl. jours. Bd. dirs. SHRM Found., 1994-2001. Recipient Young Scholars award Spencer Found., 1976, 78, Disting. Rsch. award, 1993, PhD Teaching award, 1994; NSF grantee, 1973-75; Adminstrn. on Aging grantee, 1978-80. Fellow APA; mem. Acad. Mgmt., Soc. Human Resource Mgmt. Office: U NC CB 3490 Kenan Flagler Bus Sch Chapel Hill NC 27599-3490 Office Phone: 919-962-3166. E-mail: Ben_Rosen@unc.edu.

ROSEN, CAROL MENDES, artist; b. NYC, Jan. 15, 1933; d. Bram de Sola and Mildred (Bertuch) Mendes; m. Elliot A. Rosen, June 30, 1957. BA, Hunter Coll., 1954; MA, CUNY, 1962. Tchr. art West Orange (N.J.) Pub. Schs., 1959—85. Co-curator exhibit Printmaking Coun. N.J., Somerville, 1981; exhibit curator 14 Sculptors Gallery, NYC, 1988; collection: Nat. Collection of Fine Arts, Smithsonian Instn., Newark Mus., N.J. State Mus., Bristol-Myers Squibb, AT&T, Noyes Mus., N.Y. Pub. Libr., Zimmerli Art Mus., Mus. of Modern Art, Whitney Mus., Libr. Collection Bklyn. Mus., Victoria & Albert Mus., Nat. Art Gallery, London, Mus. of Tolerance, LA, Hunterdon Mus. Art, Nat. Mus. Women in Arts, Tel Aviv U. and The Jewish Nat. & U. Libr., Jerusalem, Houghton Libr., Harvard U., Yale U., Clark Art Inst., Skidmore, Williams Coll. Mus. Art, Oberlin Coll., William Paterson U., Stanford U., Smith Coll., Wellesley Coll., Tate Britain, Kreitman Rsch. Ctr., Ackland Art Mus., U. NC. Contbr. articles to arts mags. Recipient Hudson River Mus. award, Yonkers, 1983; fellow, N.J. State Coun. Arts, 1980, 1983. Jewish. Avocations: gardening, reading. Home: 10 Beavers Rd Califon NJ 07830-3433 Personal E-mail: earosen@earthlink.net.

ROSEN, CHARLES, II, retired lawyer; b. New Orleans, Jan. 29, 1925; s. Louis Leucht and Nita (Silverstein) R.; m. Mary Alice Waldauer (div. 1976); children: Charles III, Virginia, Jane, James Louis; m. Sandra Reed (div. 1995); m. Emily Hart, 1995. BA, Tulane U., 1948, LLB, 1951. Bar: La. 1951. Assoc. Rosen, Kammer, Wolff, Hopkins & Burke, New Orleans, 1951-55, Jones, Walker, Waechter, Poitevent, Carrere & Denegre, New Orleans, 1955-58, ptnr., 1958-90; spl. counsel Locke, Purnell, Rain, Harrell (now Locke Liddell & Sapp), New Orleans, 1990-97; of counsel Sullivan Stolier & Resor, New Orleans, 1997—2005; ret. Past chmn. and mem. exec. com. Golf & Sports Attractions, Inc., ret. mem. fore kids Found. Past trustee Touro Synagogue; hon. trustee Touro Infirmary; chmn. lawyers div. Jewish Fedn. Greater New Orleans, 1969; past chmn. lawyers div. United Fund. 1st lt. U.S. Army, 1944-46, PTO. Mem. ABA, La. Bar Assn., New Orleans Bar Assn., Am. Coll. Real Estate Attys., Anglo Am. Real Property Inst., So. Golf Assn. (past bd. dirs.), New Orleans Golf Assn. (past pres., past bd. dirs.), Tulane Green Wave Club (past bd. dirs.), Lakewood Country Club (past pres., bd. dirs.). Republican. Avocation: golf. Home: 126 Brokenbraugh Ct Metairie LA 70005 also: 126 Brockenbraugh Ct Metairie LA 70005 Office Phone: 504-561-1044. Business E-Mail: atty@ssrlawfirm.com.

ROSEN, CHARLES ARTHUR, lawyer; b. NYC, May 28, 1940; s. David H. and Mildred R.; m. Suzanne M. Diamond, Aug. 17, 1963; children—Laurence, Caroline. BS, Cornell U., 1962; JD, NYU, 1965. Bar: NY 1966, NJ 1967. Labor relations specialist NJ Mfrs. Assn., Newark, 1965-71; counsel NJ Dept. Labor and Industry, Trenton, 1971-73; ptnr., shareholder Irwin, Post & Rosen, Roseland, NJ, 1973—87, ptnr. Law Office of Charles A. Rosen, NJ, 1987-, also NYC Mem. cons. com. Inst. Mgmt. and Labor Relations, Rutgers U., 1965-71; mem. State Bd. Cert. Shorthand Reporters, 1973-73; mem. NJ Vocat. Edn. Adv. Council, 1970-80, chmn., 1977-79. Mem. ABA, NJ State Bar Assn., NY State Bar Assn., Atty. Roseland NJ Planning Bd., 1987-, Essex County Bar Assn. Republican. Jewish. Clubs: Roseland Rep. (pres.), Masons. Contbr. articles to legal pubs. Office: 5 Becker Farm Rd Roseland NJ 07068-1741 Office Phone: 973-535-2800.

ROSEN, ERIC S., state supreme court justice; b. Topeka, May 25, 1953; BA, MA, U. Kansas; JD, Washburn U., 1984. Former social worker Topeka Public Sch.; former ptnr. Hein, Ebert and Rosen; former asst. dist. atty. & asst. public defender Shawnee County; judge domestic div. U.S. Dist. Ct., Third Dist., Shawnee County, Kans., 1993—95, judge Kans., 1993—2005; justice Kansas Supreme Ct., 2005—. Former assoc. gen. counsel Kans. Securities Commn.; former adjunct prof. Washburn U. Sch. of Law; mem. Koch Crime Commn., 1994; lecturer Menninger Sch. of Law and Psychiatry; mem. Kans. Sentencing Commn., 2004—. Recipient Atty. General's Victim's Svc. award, 2000, Martin Luther King Living the Dream Humanitarian award, 2002. Mem.: ABA, Kans. Bar Assn., Kans. Dist. Judges Assn., Am. Judicature Soc., Am. Judges Assn. Office: Kans Supreme Ct 301 W 10th Topeka KS 66612 Office Phone: 785-233-8200 ext. 4303. Office Fax: 785-296-1028. *

ROSEN, EVAN MARK, executive communication advisor, journalist; b. NYC; s. Gerald Robert and Lois Ann Rosen; m. Katherine Hirzel. BA, U. Mich., 1983. Reporter Our Town, NYC, 1977—78; copy clk., reporter The N.Y. Post, 1979—80; intern ABC News, NYC, 1980; news dir. WCBN-FM, Ann Arbor, Mich., 1980—81; desk asst. WABC-TV, 1981—82; writer, prodn. asst. WXYZ-TV, Detroit, 1982—83; reporter KODE-TV, Joplin, Mo., 1983—85; reporter, anchor WTOL-TV, Toledo, 1985—93, KICU-TV, San Jose, Calif., 1993—94; chief strategist, mng. ptnr. Impact Video Comm. Inc., San Francisco, 1994—. Lectr. Stanford U. Ctr. for Profl. Devel., Palo Alto, Calif.; on-air contbr. CNN, Atlanta, 1985—90, CBS News Newspath, NYC, 1985—93; consulting mem. Personal Conferencing Work Group, Santa Clara, Calif., 1993—95. Author: (books) Personal Videoconferencing, 1996, The Culture of Collaboration: Maximizing Time Talent and Tools to Create Value in the Global Economy, 2007; columnist Telemedicine Today mag.; contbg. editor: Network World Mag., Information Week Mag.; contbr. articles to profl. jours., mags. Intern Office of U.S. Rep. Ed Koch, Washington, 1977; press aide Ed Koch for Mayor of N.Y. campaign, 1977, Office of The Mayor of N.Y., 1978. Nominee Emmy award, NATAS, 1991; recipient 2d pl. award best spot news coverage-large market, Ohio AP, 1988, Crystal award of excellence, Women In Comm., 1990. Office: Impact Video Comm Inc 1750 Montgomery St San Francisco CA 94111 E-mail: erosen@impactvid.com.

ROSEN, FREDERICK SEMENOV, otolaryngologist; b. Torrance, Calif., June 15, 1972; s. Sherwin Zola and Debora Semenov Rosen; m. Rosa Sanchez, May 18, 2002; 1 child, Samuel. BS, U. Calif., Berkeley, 1994; MD, U. So. Calif., L.A., 1999. Diplomate Am. Bd. Otolaryngology. Fellow in pediat. otolaryngology Stanford U., Palo Alto, Calif., 2004—06; attending Children's Hosp., Oakland, Calif., 2006—. Sports editor: Daily Californian, 1993. Mem.: Am. Acad. Otolaryngology. Office: Children's Hosp Oakland ENT Dept 744 52d St Oakland CA 94609

ROSEN, GEORGE, economist, educator; b. St. Petersburg, Russia, Feb. 7, 1920; s. Leon and Rebecca (Rosenoer) Rosen; m. Sylvia Vatuk; 1 child, Mark. BA, Bklyn. Coll., 1940; MA, Princeton U., NJ, 1942, PhD, 1949. Prof. econs. Bard Coll., Annandale-on-Hudson, NY, 1946-50; economist Dept. State, Washington, 1951-54, Council Econ. Indsl. Research, Washington, 1954-55, MIT, CENIS, Cambridge, 1955-59, UN, NYC, 1959-60, Ford Found., NYC, Nepal and India, 1960-62, Rand Corp., Santa Monica, Calif., 1962-67; chief economist Asian Devel. Bank, Manila, Philippines, 1967-71; prof. econs. U. Ill.-Chgo., 1972-85, prof. econs. emeritus, 1985—, head dept., 1972-77; fellow Woodrow Wilson Internat. Ctr., Washington, 1989-90. Adj. prof. Johns Hopkins U.-Nanjing U. Ctr. Chinese-Am. Studies, 1986—87; cons. USAID, Egypt, 1994; treas. Am. Com. Asian Econ. Studies, 1990—2000; Golden Jubilee spkr. dept. commerce Osmania U., Hyderabad, India, 1999; disting. spkr. Ctr. Advanced Study Internat. Devel., Mich. State U., East Lansing, 1999. Author: Industrial Change in India, 1958, Some Aspects of Industrial Finance in India, 1962, Democracy and Economic Change in India, 1966, 1967, Peasant Society in a Changing Economy, 1975, Decision-Making Chicago-Style, 1980, Western Economists and Eastern Societies, 1985, Industrial Change in India 1970-2000, 1988, Contrasting Styles of Industrial Reform: China and India in the 1980s, 1992, Economic Development in Asia, 1996; co-author: The India Handbook, 1997, Globalization and Some of Its Contents: The Autobiography of a Russian Immigrant, 2005; book rev. editor: Econ. Devel. and Cultural Change, 1988—2004. Grantee, U. Ill., 1977—78, Social Sci. Rsch. Coun. and Am. Inst. Indian Studies, 1980—81, Am. Inst. Indian Studies, 1983—84, 1987—88, Rockefeller Found. Bellagio Study Ctr., 1984; Ford Found. fellow, NYU, 1971—72. Office: U Ill Dept Econs M/C 144 601 S Morgan St Chicago IL 60607-7121 Home: 5830 S Stony Island Ave Apt 11a Chicago IL 60637-2024

ROSEN, GERALD ELLIS, federal judge; b. Chandler, Ariz., Oct. 26, 1951; s. Stanley Rosen and Marjorie (Sherman) Cahn; m. Laurie DeMond; 1 child, Jacob DeMond. BA, Kalamazoo Coll., 1973; JD, George Washington U., 1979. Researchist Swedish Inst., Stockholm, 1973; legis. asst. U.S. Senator Robert P. Griffin, Washington, 1974-79; law clk. Seyfarth, Shaw, Fairweather & Gerardson, Wash., 1979; from assoc. to sr. ptnr. Miller, Canfield, Paddock and Stone, Detroit, 1979-90; judge U.S. Dist Ct. (ea. dist.) Mich., Detroit, 1990—. Mem. Jud. Evaluation Com., Detroit, co-chmn. 1983-88; adj. prof. law Wayne State U., 1992—, U. Detroit Law Sch., 1994-98, Cooley Law Sch., 2005-; mem. U.S. Jud. Conf. Com. on Criminal Law; lectr. CLE confs., 1996-05, others. Co-author: Federal Civil Trials and Evidence, 1999, Michigan Civil Trials and Evidence, 2001, Federal Employment Litigation, 2006; contbr. articles to profl. jours. Rep. candidate for U.S. Congress, Mich., 1982; chmn. 17th Congl. Dist. Rep. Com., 1983-85; mem. Mich. Criminal Justice Commn., 1985-87; mem. Birmingham Athletic Club; bd. visitors George Washington U. Law Sch., 2000—; bd. dirs. Focus Hope, 2000—. Fellow Kalamazoo Coll. (sr. 1972); recipient Career Achievement award Rolex/Intercollegiate Tennis Assn. Mem. Fed. Judges Assn. (bd. dirs.). Jewish. Office: US Courthouse 231 W Lafayette Blvd Rm 730 Detroit MI 48226-2707 Office Phone: 313-234-5135.

ROSEN, GERALD HARRIS, physicist, consultant, educator; b. Mount Vernon, NY, Aug. 10, 1933; s. David A. and Shirley (Schapiro) R.; m. Sarah Louise Sweet, June 8, 1963; children: Lawrence A., Karlyn Rosen Aires. BSE, Princeton U., 1955, MA, 1956, PhD, 1958. Rsch. assoc. dept. aero. engring. Princeton U., 1958-59, NSF predoctoral fellow, 1956, Inst. Theoretical Physics, Utrecht, Netherlands, 1957-58, NSF postdoctoral fellow Stockholm, 1959-60; tech. cons. weapon sys. evaluation divsn. The Pentagon, 1960; prin. scientist Martin-Marietta Aerospace divsn., Balt., 1960-63; cons. to a tech. v.p. Southwest Rsch. Inst., 1963-66; prof. physics Drexel U., Phila., 1966-73, M.R. Wehr prof. physics, 1973-98, prof. emeritus, 1998—. Cons. fin., indsl. and govt. agys., 1966—. Author: Formulations of Classical and Quantum Dynamical Theory, 1969, A New Science of Stock Market Investing, 1990; assoc. editor Bull. Math. Biology, 1982-98; contbr. over 300 articles to profl. jours.; patentee in field. Sponsor San Antonio Chamber Music Soc., 1963-66; mem. Franklin Inst., 1967—; mem. publ. bd. Soc. Math. Biol., 1983—. Guggenheim Jet Propulsion scholar, Princeton U., 1955, Whiton Engring.-Physics scholar, 1955. Fellow Am. Phys. Soc., AAAS; mem. Am. Math. Soc. Home and Office: 415 Charles Ln Wynnewood PA 19096-1604 Office Phone: 610-896-8727. Personal E-mail: gr@geraldrosen.com. *The meaning of life has transcended human understanding up to the present time, but there are reasons to believe that future discoveries in science will illuminate the significance of life in nature. We must break completely free of non-rational dogma and illusion, and attempt to solve this mystery with factual clues revealed by scientific progress.*

ROSEN, GERALD ROBERT, editor; b. NYC, Nov. 17, 1930; s. Sol and Essie (Shapiro) R.; m. Lois Lehrman, May 9, 1958; 1 son, Evan Mark. BS, Ind. U., 1951, MA, 1953. Intelligence analyst Dept. Def., NYC, 1955-58; assoc. editor Challenge: The Mag. of Econ. Affairs, NYC, 1959-61, mng. editor, 1961-64, 65-66; sr. editor Dun's Rev., NYC, 1964-65, nat. affairs editor, 1967—; exec. editor Dun's Rev. (now Bus. Month), 1978-90; editor IMF survey Washington, 1990-93; mng. dir. Global Insights Svcs., Washington, 1993—. Fin. corr. Westinghouse Broadcasting Co. Served with CIC U.S. Army, 1953-55. Mem. Soc. Am. Bus. and Econ. Writers, N.Y. Fin. Writers Assn., White House Corrs. Assn. Clubs: Nat. Press. Home: 1625 31st St NW Washington DC 20007-3628 Office Phone: 202-337-7748. Personal E-mail: gerry308@aol.com.

ROSEN, HARVEY SHELDON, economics professor, former federal official; b. Chgo., Mar. 29, 1949; s. Edward and Eleanor (Altman) R.; m. Marsha E. Novick, June 20, 1976; children: Lynne, Jonathan. AB, U. Mich., 1970; AM, Harvard U., 1972, PhD, 1974. Dep. asst. sec., tax analysis US Dept. Treasury, Washington, 1989-91; asst. prof. econs. Princeton (N.J.) U., 1974-80, assoc. prof., 1980-84, prof., 1984—, chmn. dept. econs., 1993—96, John L. Weinberg prof. economics. & bus. policy, 1995—, co-dir. Ctr. for Econ. Policy Studies, 1991—; mem. Coun. Econ. Advisers The White House, Washington, 2003—05, chmn., 2005. Vis. fellow Inst. Advanced Studies, Hebrew U., Jerusalem, 1978; vis. scholar Hoover Intsn., Stanford, Calif., 1981. Author: Public Finance, 1985; co-author (with (Michael Katz): Microeconomics, 1991; editor: Studies in State and Local Public Finance, 1986, Fiscal Federalism: Quantitative Studies, 1988. Recipient Pres. award for Disting. Teaching, Princeton U., 2003. Fellow Econometric Soc.; mem. Phi Beta Kappa Office: Princeton U Dept Econs Princeton NJ 08544-0001

ROSEN, HOWARD B., biopharmaceutical company executive; BS, MBA, Stanford U.; MS in Chem. Engring., MIT. Dir. corp. devel. GenPharm International, Inc.; cons. McKinsey & Co., San Francisco; head west coast strategy practice Analysis Group, Inc.; pres. ALZA Corp., Mountain View, Calif.; v.p. comml. strategy Gilead Scis., Inc., Foster City, Calif. Lectr. Stanford U., Dept. Chem. Engring.; mem. bd. dirs. Pharsight Corp., CoTherix, Inc., 2005—. Mem. Stanford U. Adv. Couns. on Interdisciplinary Biosciences and Sch. Engring. Mem.: NAE. Office: Gilead Scis, Inc 333 Lakeside Dr Foster City CA 94404 Office Fax: 650-574-3000, 650-578-9264.

ROSEN, JACQUELINE L., musician, educator; b. Los Angeles, Sept. 28, 1952; d. Samuel Morris and Blanche (Seigel) R.; m. James Andrew Meckel, July 14, 1979; children: Sean Aaron, Eric Rosen. Student, Music Acad. of the West, Santa Barbara, Calif., 1973-74; BS in Music, UCLA, 1974; studies with Julius Baker, James Galway, Jean-Pierre Rampal, 1974-80. Freelance musician, Los Angeles, San Francisco and Monterey, Calif., 1974—; mem. Laurel Wind Quintet, 1977-80, Allegra Trio, 1980—, Farrell/Rosen Duo, Carmel, Calif., 1978-87, Terrence Farrell Consort, Carmel, 1980—. Instr. flute pvt. studio, Monterey, 1976—, Monterey Peninsula Coll., 1981-85; instr. Hidden Valley music seminars, Cazadero Music Camp; prin. flutist Hidden Valley Opera, Carmel Valley, Calif., 1976—; condr. master classes numerous Calif. colls., 1982—; music specialist Salinas City Sch. Dist. Premiere performance (flute-guitar duo) Sonatine for Flute and Guitar, 1981; rec. artist (with Terrence Farrell) Alla Romanza, Merry Christmas; appearances with San Francisco Spring Opera, 1979, Cabrillo Music Festival, 1978-84, Carmel Bach Festival, 1996, 98, 99, Camerata Singers; flutist Monterey Harp Trio; editor CTB/Macmillan-McGraw-Hill; radio broadcasts, 1977—. Recipient Southwestern Music Conf. award, 1972; Leonard Bernstein fellow, Tanglewood, 1977. Mem.: Calif. Music Educators Assn., Music Educators Nat. Conf. Avocations: playing jazz, gourmet cooking. Home: 15 Paseo Primero Salinas CA 93908-9110 Personal E-mail: jjmeckel@pacbell.net.

ROSEN, JEFFREY ADAM, lawyer; b. Boston, Apr. 2, 1958; m. Kathleen Nichols, May 29, 1982. BA in Econs., Northwestern U., 1979; JD magna cum laude, Harvard U., 1982. Bar: D.C. 1982, U.S. Ct. Appeals (fed. cir.) 1983, U.D. Dist. Ct. D.C. 1983, U.S. Supreme Ct. 1986, U.S. Ct. Appeals (11th cir.) 1988, U.S. Ct. Appeals (6th cir.) 1990, U.S. Ct. Appeals (3rd cir.) 1996, U.S. Ct. Appeals (4th cir.), U.S. Dist. Ct. (ea. dist.) Mich., U.S. Dist. Ct. (no. dist.) Ill. Assoc. Kirkland & Ellis, Washington, 1982-88, ptnr., 1988—2003; gen. counsel US Dept. Transp., Washington, 2003—06; gen. counsel & sr. policy adv., Office Mgmt. & Budget Exec. Office of the Pres., Washington, 2006—. Adj. prof. Georgetown U. Law Ctr., 1996—2003; mem. Arlington County Hist. Affairs and Landmark Rev. Bd., 1991—93. Mem.: Va. Hist. Soc., U.S. Supreme Ct. Hist. Soc., Am. Law Inst. Office: Office Mgmt & Budget 725 17th St NW Washington DC 20503

ROSEN, JEFFREY J., lawyer; b. NYC, May 13, 1949; s. Fred and Jane (Krieger) R. BA, Harvard U., 1971, JD, 1978. Bar: D.C. 1980. Reporter, columnist Rocky Mountain News, Denver, 1971-75; law clk. to presiding justice U.S. Ct. Appeals, Washington, 1978-79; law clk. to justice William J. Brennan U.S. Supreme Ct., Washington, 1979-80; spl. asst. to sec. US Dept. Treasury, Washington, 1980-81; assoc. Paul, Weiss et al, Washington, 1981—84, O'Melveny & Myers, Washington, 1985-87, ptnr., 1987—2001, Debevoise & Plimpton, 2001—. Supreme Ct. editor Harvard Law Rev. Named a Dealmaker of the Yr., The Am. Lawyer mag., 2004, 2007. Mem. ABA (tax sect.), D.C. Bar Assn. Home: PO Box 273 Clinton Corners NY 12514-0273 Office: Devevoise & Plimpton 919 3rd Ave New York NY 10022 E-mail: jrosen@debevoise.com.

ROSEN, JEFFREY MATTHEW, law educator, journalist; b. NYC, Feb. 13, 1964; s. Sidney and Estelle Rosen. AB summa cum laude, Harvard U., 1986; BA, Oxford U., Eng., 1988; JD, Yale U., 1991. Bar: Pa. 1992, D.C. 1992. Law clk. to Hon. Abner J. Mikva US Ct. Appeals (DC Cir.), Washington, 1991-92; legal affairs editor The New Republic, Washington, 1993—; staff writer The New Yorker, Washington, 1997-99; assoc. prof. George Washington U. Law Sch., 1997—2003, prof., 2004—. Guest commentator NPR, Washington, 1998—. Author: The Unwanted Gaze: The Destruction of Privacy in America, 2000, The Naked Crowd: Reclaiming Security and Freedom in an Anxious Age, 2004, The Most Democratic Branch: How the Courts Serve America, 2006, The Supreme Court: The Personalities and Rivalries That Defined America, 2007. Marshall scholar Balliol Coll., Oxford, 1986-88. Mem. Harvard Club, Cosmos Club, Phi Beta Kappa. Office: George Washington U Law Sch 2000 H St NW Washington DC 20052-0001 E-mail: jrosen@law.gwu.edu.

ROSEN, JON HOWARD, lawyer; b. Bklyn., May 20, 1943; s. Eli and Vera Horowitz Rosen; m. Patricia R. Marshall; children: Jason Marc, Hope Terry. BA, Hobart Coll., 1965; JD, St. John's U., 1968; postgrad. in bus., CCNY, 1969—71. Bar: N.Y. 1969, Calif. 1975, Wash. 1977. Atty. FAA, NYC, 1968-71; regional atty., contract adminstr. Air Line Pilots Assn., NYC, Chgo., L.A., San Francisco, 1971-77; pvt. practice Seattle, 1977-80; ptnr. Frank and Rosen, Seattle, 1981-98, Frank Rosen Freed Roberts LLP, Seattle, 1999—2002, The Rosen Law Firm, 2002—. Instr. labor studies Shoreline C.C., 1978-90; bd. dirs. Music of Remembrance. Chair Ward Springs Pk. Steering Com.; active African-Am./Jewish Coalition for Justice, Interfaith Alliance; trustee Temple DeHirsch Sinai, 1991—98, v.p., 1998—2000, pres.-elect, 2000—01, pres., 2001—03; active mem. Union Reform Judaism Commn. Outreach. Fellow: Am. Bar Found., Coll. Labor and Employment Lawyers; mem.: ABA (union co-chmn. com. on employee rights and responsibilities 1992—96, union co-chmn. regional programs subcom. 1998—2000, union co-chmn. nat. programs. subcom. 2000—02, union co-chmn. ADR in labor and employment law com. 2002—05, co-regional EEOC liaison), Wash. State Trial Lawyers Assn. (past chair employment law com.), Nat. Employment Lawyers Assn. (state steering com. 1990—95, founding state chair), King County Bar Assn. (past chmn. aviation and space law sect., past chmn. Pacific Coast Labor and Employment Law Conf., past chmn. labor law sect.). Office: Rosen Law Firm 705 2nd Ave Ste 1200 Seattle WA 98104-1729 Office Phone: 206-652-1464. Business E-Mail: jhr@jonrosenlaw.com.

ROSEN, JOSHUA NATHAN, lawyer; b. Chicago Heights, Ill., Aug. 9, 1966; s. Stanley and Margit (Kir-Stimon) R.; m. Wen-Ying Rosen. BA, U. Ill., 1988; JD, So. Ill. U., 1993. Bar: Ill. 1993, Calif. 1999, U.S. Dist. Ct. (so. dist.) Ill. 1994, U.S. Dist. Ct. (no. dist.) Calif. 1999, U.S. Ct. Appeals (9th cir.) 1999. Assoc. Craig & Craig, Mt. Vernon, Ill., 1994—98, Hayes & Assocs., 1999—2001; trial atty. Law Offices of Larry Kloenhamer, 2001—04, Law Offices of Dennis Issac, 2004—07; sr. assoc. Bledsoe, Cathcart, Diestel & Pedersen, LLP, San Francisco, 2007—. Mem. State Bar Calif., Bar Assn. San Francisco (Outstanding Barrister award 2004), Barristers Club (litig. sec. 1999-, chmn. judges reception com. 2003-04), So. Ill. Am. Inn of Ct. (barrister). Office: Bledsoe Cathcart Diestel & Pedersen LLP 601 California St 16th Fl San Francisco CA 94108

ROSEN, J(OSHUA) PHILIP, lawyer; b. NYC, Aug. 24, 1956; s. Irving and Tauba (Krieger) Rosen. BA, Yeshiva U., 1978; JD, Georgetown U., 1981. Bar: NY 1982. Law clk. to Hon. David N. Edelstein U.S. Dist. Ct. (So. Dist.) NY, NYC, 1981-82; corp. ptnr., co-head real estate transactions and fin. dept. Weil, Gotshal & Manges LLP, NYC, co-head, Middle East practice. Appt. to Lower Manhattan Develop. Corp. Profl. Firms Adv. Coun., 2002; spkr. in field; spkr. and chaired at seminars on doing bus. in Israel and the Middle East; assoc. mem. Real Estate Bd. NY, 1990—; mem. Nat. Assn. Real Estate Investment Trusts, Urban Land Inst.; bd. advisors NY Real Estate Law Reporter, NYC, 1987. Editor: Jour. Law and Policy Internat. Bus., Georgetown Internat. Law Review, author numerous articles and books on opportunity fund representation, real estate mergers & acquisitions, real estate investment trusts, fin., loan restructuring, workouts and turnarounds, leasing, developing and securitization. Vice-chmn. bd. dirs. Yeshiva Coll. of Yeshiva U., NY; mem. Conf. of Presidents of Major Jewish Am. Orgns., Internat. Council of Shopping Ctrs.; vice-chmn. Republican Jewish Coalition; legal counsel, spkr. on real estate topics NY

Holocaust Meml. Commn., NYC, 1983. Named "40 Under 40 People to Watch in the 1990's", Crain's NY Bus., 1990; named one of Leading Power Brokers in NY Real Estate, GRID Mag. Fellow: Wexner Heritage Found. (Wexner Heritage Scholar); mem.: Am. Coll. Real Estate Lawyers. Jewish. Avocation: tennis. Home: 431 Mistletoe Way Lawrence NY 11559-2716 Office: Weil Gotshal & Manges LLP 767 Fifth Ave New York NY 10153 Office Phone: 212-310-8604. Office Fax: 212-735-4857.

ROSEN, JUDAH BEN, computer scientist; b. Phila., May 5, 1922; s. Benjamin and Susan (Hurwich) R.; children— Susan Beth, Lynn Ruth. BSEE, Johns Hopkins U., 1943; PhD in Applied Math., Columbia U., 1952. Rschr. Manhattan (N.Y.) Project, 1944—46, Brookhaven (N.Y.) Nat. Lab., 1946—48; rsch. assoc. Princeton (N.J.) U., 1952-54; head applied math. dept. Shell Devel. Co., 1954-62; vis. prof. computer sci. dept. Stanford (Calif.) U., 1962-64; prof. dept. computer sci. and math. rsch. ctr. U. Wis., Madison, 1964-71; prof., head dept. computer sci. U. Minn., Mpls., 1971-92, fellow Supercomputer Inst., 1985—2007; sr. fellow Supercomputer Ctr., San Diego, 1993—2007; adj. rsch. prof. dept. computer sci. and engrin. U. Calif. San Diego, La Jolla, 1992—2007, bioinformatics grad. program faculty, 2001—07; ret. Fulbright prof. Technion, Israel, 1968-69, Davis vis. prof. 1980; invited lectr. Chinese Acad. Sci., Peking, 1980, Guilin, 1996, Samos, Greece, 2000; lectr., cons. Argonne (Ill.) Nat. Lab.; mem. Nat. Computer Sci. Bd. Author: Topics in Parallel Computing, 1992; editor: Nonlinear Programming, 1970, Supercomputers and Large-Scale Optimization, 1988; assoc. editor Global Optimization, 1990—, Annals of Ops. Rsch., 1984—; contbr. articles to profl. jours. and procs. Grantee, NSF, 1995—, ARPA/NIST, 1994—97. Mem. Assn. Computing Machinery, Soc. Indsl. and Applied Math., Math. Programming Soc., European Acad. Scis. Achievements include research in supercomputers and parallel algorithms for optimization, computation of molecular structure and drug design by energy minimization and homology models, algorithms for structured approximation in signal processing. Business E-Mail: jbenr55@yahoo.com.

ROSEN, LOUIS, physicist; b. NYC, June 10, 1918; s. Jacob and Rose (Lipionski) R.; m. Mary Terry, Sept. 4, 1941; 1 son, Terry Leon. BA, U. Ala., 1939, MS, 1941; PhD, Pa. State U., 1944; DSc (hon.), U. N.Mex., 1979, U. Colo., 1987. Instr. physics U. Ala., 1940-41, Pa. State U., 1943-44; mem. staff Los Alamos Sci. Lab., 1944-90, group leader nuclear plate lab., 1949-65, alt. div. leader exptl. physics div., 1962-65, dir. meson physics facility, 1965-85, div. leader medium energy physics div., 1965-86, sr. lab. fellow, 1985-90, sr. fellow emeritus, 1990—; Sesquicentennial hon. prof. U. Ala., 1981. Panel on future of nuclear sci., chmn. subpanel on accelerators NRC of NAS, 1976, panel on instnl. arrangements for orbiting space telescope, 1976; mem. U.S.A.-USSR Coordinating Com. on Fundamental Properties of Matter, 1971-90 Mem. editl. bd. Applications of Nuclear Physics; co-editor Climate Change and Energy Policy, 1992; contbr. articles to profl. jours. Mem. Los Alamos Town Planning Bd., 1962-64; mem. Gov.'s Com. on Tech. Excellence in N.Mex.; mem. N.Mex. Cancer Control Bd., 1976-80, v.p., 1979-81; co-chmn. Los Alamos Vols. for Stevenson, 1956; Dem. candidate for county commr., 1962; bd. dirs. Los Alamos Med. Ctr., 1977-83, chmn., 1983; bd. govs. Tel Aviv U., 1986; bd. dirs. Sombillo Nursing and Rehab. Facility, 2004. Recipient E.O. Lawrence award AEC, 1963, Golden Plate award Am. Acad. Achievement, 1964, N.Mex. Disting. Pub. Svc. award, 1978; named Citizen of Yr., N.Mex. Realtors Assn., 1973; Guggenheim fellow, 1959-60; alumni fellow Pa. State U., 1978; Louis Rosen prize established in his honor by bd. dirs. Meson Facility Users Group, 1984; Louis Rosen Auditorium dedicated, 1995; recipient Los Alamos Nat. Lab. medal, 2002. Fellow AAAS (coun. 1989), Am. Phys. Soc. (coun. 1975-78, chmn. panel on pub. affairs 1980, div. nuclear physics 1985, mem. subcom. on internat. sci. affairs 1988). Achievements include research in nuc. sci. and applications of particle accelerators. Home: 1170 41st St Los Alamos NM 87544-1913 Office: Los Alamos Sci Lab PO Box 1663 Los Alamos NM 87544-0600 Office Phone: 505-667-4361. *I have come to believe that only after one has learned to manage and set worthy goals for himself should he attempt to do so for others.*

ROSEN, MATTHEW A., lawyer; b. Phila., 1952; BA, Swarthmore Coll., 1973; JD cum laude, Boston U., 1976; LLM, NYU, 1979. Bar: Pa. 1976, N.Y. 1979. Sr. ptnr. Skadden, Arps, Slate, Meagher & Flom LLP, NYC, co-head, tax law group. Spkr. in the field. Contbr. articles to profl. publs. Named one of 45 Lawyers in the Country under the age of 45 who "are making their mark now and will lead the profession tomorrow", Am. Lawyer Mag. Mem.: NY State Bar Assn. (co-chair, subcommittee on net operating losses 1985—87, co-chair, subcommittee on bankrupty 1988—89, exec. com. mem., tax sect. 1985—89). Office: Skadden Arps Slate Meagher & Flom LLP 4 Times Sq New York NY 10036 Office Phone: 212-735-2230. Office Fax: 917-777-2230. Business E-Mail: mrosen@skadden.com.

ROSEN, MATTHEW STEPHEN, retired botanist; b. NYC, Oct. 7, 1943; s. Norman and Lucille (Cass) R.; m. Deborah Louise Mackay, June 16, 1974 (div. Feb. 1983); children: Gabriel Mackay, Rebecca Mackay; m. Kay Eloise Williams, July 11, 1987. MFSc, Yale U., New Haven, Conn., 1972; BS, Cornell U., Ithaca, NY, 1967. Instr. ornamental horticulture SUNY-Farmingdale, 1968-69; landscape designer Manhattan Gardener, NYC, 1969-70; instr. ornamental horticulture McHenry County Coll., Crystal Lake, Ill., 1972-74; coord. agrl. studies, asst. prof. biology, chemistry Mercer County Community Coll., West Windsor, NJ, 1974-79; adminstr. Des Moines Botanical Ctr., 1979—96; horticulture divsn. mgr. City of DeMoines, 1996—2007; ret., 2007. Cons. dir. West Mich. Hort. Soc., 1993; nat. judge Communities in Bloom, 2001-07, Winter Lights, 2002-04, Am. in Bloom, 2002, sr. nat. judge, 2005; cons. in field. Contbr. articles to profl. jours. Com. chmn. United Way Cen. Iowa, 1982, divsn. chmn. 1983-86, 88-89, 91, 2000, group chmn. 1987, chmn. arts adv. com. 1985-86, pres. 1986, bd. dirs. Arts and Recreation Coun., 1985-86, com. chmn., 1992; career vocat. com. Des Moines Indsl. Sch. Dist., 1986, co-chmn., 1987, ptnrs. for progress com., 1988-90, sci. monitoring program, 1991-92; chmn. Two Rivers Festival, 1987-88; active Des Moines Sister City Program, Kofu, Japan, 1984, delegation, 1989, Naucalpan, Mexico, 1986, 87, Shijiazhuang, China, 1986, 90, 92, 95, 97; vice-chmn. Greater Des Moines Sister City Commn., 2004-05, chmn., 2005—; mem. edn. com. Am. Assn. Bot. Gardens and Arboretum, membership com., conservation com., bd. dirs., 1997—. Mem. Am. Assn. Bot. Gardens and Arboreta (edn. com.), Greater Des Moines C. of C. (team leader 1984—, chmn. new mem. sales, chmn. 8 O'clock new, Pres. Cabinet award 1983-85, bd. dirs., exec. com. 1995—, Achievement award C. of C. Fedn. 1986, exec. com. 1995-97), East Des Moines C. of C. (bd. dirs. 1992—, v.p., sec. 1993—, pres.-elect 1994, pres. 1995-96, sister cities commn. 1994, china chair 1995—, treas. 1995—, vice chair 2003, 04, chair 2005—), Greater Des Moines Conv. and Visitors Bur. (chmn. new mem. sales com. 1988-89), Iowa Advt. Rev. Coun., Affiliate Pres.'s Coun. of Chambers (chair 1995, 97), bd. dirs. DM Gen. Hosp., 1994-97, Bd. Coun. Internat. Trade, Latinos Unidos (bd. dirs. 1996-97), Rotary, Phi Kappa Phi, Pi Alpha Xi. Democrat. Jewish. Avocations: photography, reading, model trains, collecting old books, writing. Home: 1042 22nd St West Des Moines IA 50265-2219 E-mail: m.rosen@mchsi.com.

ROSEN, MEYER ROBERT, chemical engineer; b. Bklyn., Mar. 9, 1943; s. Philip and Jeanne (Rosenzweig) R.; children: Carrie, David; m. Selma Schwartz Mirman. BS, Poly. Inst. Bklyn., 1964, MS, 1966. Diplomate, Am. Bd. Forensic Engring. and Tech., cert. forensic examiner, profl. chemist, profl. chem. engr.; fire and explosion investigator Nat. Cert. Bd., Nat. Assn. Fire Investigators. Rsch. engr. Union Carbide Corp., Tonawanda, NY, 1966-73, project scientist, 1973-79, devel. scientist Tarrytown and Bound-brook, NJ, 1979-92; dir. chemistry and fire investigation Inter-City Testing and Cons. Corp., Mineola, NY, 1993—2003; pres. Interactive Cons. Inc., 1993—. Cons. Brookfield Engring. Labs., Stoughton, Mass., 1979-81; cons. to chem. industry; course dir. Ctr. for Profl. Advancement, East Brunswick, N.J., 1994; adj. prof. chemistry Westchester C.C., 1970-84; exec. advisor Am. Bd. Forensic Engring. and Tech.; Vaaler Awards judge Chem. Processing Mag., 2003; chief sci. advisor HBA Global Expo Tech. Confs.; forensic litigation expert in field; spkr. in field. Co-author: Rheology Modifier Handbook: Practical Use & Application, 2000; editor: Delivery System Handbook for Personal Care and Cosmetic Products Technology, Applications, Formulations, 2005; series editor Breakthroughs in Personal Care and Cosmetic Technology; contbr. articles to profl. jours. Fellow Am. Coll. Forensic Examiners, Royal Soc. Chemistry London (chartered chemist), Am. Inst. Chemists (dir., exec. bd. dirs.); mem. ASTM (mem. various subcoms.), Am. Inst. Chem. Engrs., Am. Chem. Soc. (divsn. colloid and surface chemistry, mem. noise com., organizer, session leader nat. mtgs. 2002—, chmn. and organizer first and second health beauty Am. regulatory summit 2006, cheif scientific advisor health & beauty expo), Am. Indsl. Hygiene Assn. (cons. spl. interest group), Am. Soc. Safety Engrs. (v.p.), Assn. Cons. Chemists and Chem. Engrs., Am. Assn. Colorists and Textile Chemists, Am. Med. Writers Assn., Nat. Assn. Sci. Writers, Soc. de Chimie Industrielle (Am. sect.), Nat. Fire Protection Assn., Soc. Indsl. Chemistry (Am. sect.), Am. Assn. Acupuncture and Oriental Medicine, Acupuncture Soc. Pa., Nat. Dental Acupuncture Soc. (exec. bd.), Nat. Alliance Acupuncture and Oriental Medicine (bd. cert. in pain mgmt.), Nat. Hearing Conservation Assn. Achievements include 21 patents for process for fire fighting foams, antifoams; flocculation of phosphatic slimes, high molecular weight water soluble polymers and flocculating method, process for producing polymer water-in-oil emulsion, process for agglomerating ore concentrate utilizing clay and dispersions of polymer binders or dry powder binders, removal of residual ethylene oxide from poly(ethylene oxide); development of treatment of previously incurable ear disorder, seminar leader in Reflex-Correspondence Training. Publications include Polyox R Water Soluble Resin Worldwide Technical Literature; Rheology of Non-Newtonian Fluids; Energy Medicine; Auriculotherapy; Korean Hand Therapy. Office: Interactive Cons Inc PO Box 66 East Norwich NY 11732-0066 Office Phone: 516-922-2167. Office Fax: 516-922-3830. Business E-Mail: meyer.rosen@chemicalconsult.com.

ROSEN, MICHAEL N., lawyer; AB, Princeton U., 1962; LLB, Harvard U., 1965. Bar: NY 1966, US Dist. Ct., So. Dist NY 1974. Chmn. Robinson Silverman Pearce Aronsohn & Berman LLP, NYC; ptnr., mem. exec. com. Bryan Cave LLP, NYC. Sec., dir., counsel GameStop Corp., 2000—; bd. dirs. Barnes & Noble & Barnes & Noble.com. Office: Bryan Cave LLP 1290 Ave of the Americas New York NY 10104 Office Phone: 212-541-2200. E-mail: mnrosen@bryancave.com. *

ROSEN, MICHEL, retired prosthodontist; b. Mulhouse, France, Jan. 25, 1936; came to U.S., 1970; s. Jean-James and Suzanne (Mulstein) R.; m. Naomi Schultz, May 20, 1965; 1 child, Robert. DDS, U. Louis Pasteur, Stasbourg, France, 1962; MSc in Dentistry, Boston U., 1973, DSc in Biology, 1974. Lic. dentist, Mass. Hosp. prin. French Air Force, Dakar, Senegal, 1963—64; pvt. practice Belfort and Antibes, France, 1964—70, various, Mass., 1974—91, Switzerland, 1991—92; ret., 1992; consul gen. Senegal, West Africa, Boston, 1994—2004. Asst. clin. prof., asst. dir. overseas affairs Boston U., 1971-74; asst. clin. prof. Tufts U., Boston, 1980-81; instr. Harvard U., Boston, 1990-91; internat. cons. West Africa. Contbr. articles to profl. jours. Lt. French Air Force, 1985-94; maj. Mass. Mil. Res. Recipient Gold medal City of Nice, France, 1981, Bronze Eagle award City of Nice, France, 1982, Officier de l'ordre du merite award Rep. of Senegal, 1998, Comdr. de l'ordre du Lion Senegal, 2000. Mem. Assn. Mil. Surgeons of U.S., Rabboni Lodge AF and AM, Nat. Sojourners, Assn. of First Corps. of Cadets, Ancient and Hon. Artillery Co. Avocations: diplomacy, travel, reading. Home and Office: 630 Bridgeway Ln Naples FL 34108-2777 Home Fax: 239-596-5925. Personal E-mail: naomi.michel@comcast.net.

ROSEN, MYOR, harpist, educator; b. NYC, May 28, 1917; s. Caesar and Rose (Seidenberg) R.; m. Esther Rosen, May 25, 1941; children: Linda, David. Diploma, Juilliard Sch. Music, 1940. Faculty Juilliard Sch. Music, 1947-69. Prin. harpist, Mexico Symphony Orch., 1941-42, Indpls. Symphony Orch., 1941-42, Mpls. Symphony Orch., 1943-44, staff harpist, CBS, Columbia Records and free lanced, 1945-60, prin. harpist, N.Y. Philharm., 1960-87; Composer incidental music for; NBC series Arts and the Gods, 1946, CBS Camera Three, 1947, Solomon, The King, 1948. Served with U.S. Army, 1945. Mem. Am. Fedn. Musicians, Bohemians. Office Phone: 561-624-5531. Personal E-mail: myorrosen@bellsouth.net. *Having been the fortunate recipient of a 7-year scholarship through the New York Philharmonic Symphony Society and the Juilliard School of Music when I began my career as a harpist, I can think of no greater honor than my privilege in having been accepted as principal harpist with the same organization which trained me. I now bend my efforts to train future harpists to excel in like manner. In my opinion, the most important function of a teacher is to teach his students how to teach themselves; self-development.*

ROSEN, NATHANIEL KENT, cellist; b. Altadena, Calif., June 9, 1948; s. David Leon and Frances Jean (Kaufman) R.; m. Jennifer Langham, Aug. 27, 1976 (div. 1986); m. Margo Shohl, May 21, 1989 (div. 2001); children: Samuel Gregory, Stella Rosalie. Student, Pasadena City Coll., Calif., 1965-67; MusB, U. So. Calif., 1971. Teaching asst. U. So. Calif., 1968-75, mem. faculty 7th ann. Gregor Piatigorsky Seminar Sch. Music, 1984; asst. prof. Calif. State U. at Northridge, 1970-76; mem. faculty Manhattan Sch. Music, NYC, 1981—, U. Ill., Urbana, 1988-94; artist-in-residence So. Meth. U., Dallas, 2002—05. Prin. cellist, Los Angeles Chamber Orch., 1970-76, Pitts. Symphony, 1977-79, concert cellist worldwide; recordings include Orientale: Romantic Music for the Cello. Recipient 1st prize Naumburg Competition, 1977, 1st prize Moscow Tchaikovsky Competition, 1978; Ford Found. grantee, 1970-71; Rockefeller Found. grantee, 1973-74 Mem. Violoncello Soc. N.Y., Century Assn. N.Y. Office: John Gingrich Mgmt Inc PO Box 1515 New York NY 10023-9462 Home Phone: 719-796-4125; Office Phone: 212-799-5080. E-mail: NRosen8794@aol.com.

ROSEN, PAUL PETER, pathologist; b. Bklyn., Aug. 16, 1938; s. George and Beate (Caspari) R.; m. Mary Sue, Aug. 7, 1994; children: Susan Deborah, Jonathan Daniel. BS, Swarthmore Coll., 1960; MD, Columbia U., 1964. Asst. attending pathologist Meml. Hosp., NYC, 1970-73; asst. prof. pathology Cornell U. Med. Sch., NYC, 1972-78; assoc. attending pathologist Meml. Hosp., NYC, 1973-78, attending pathologist, 1978-98; assoc. prof. pathology Cornell U. Med. Sch., NYC, 1978-84, prof. pathology, 1984—; assoc. mem. Sloan Kettering Inst., NYC, 1980-84; mem. tenure ttile Meml. Sloan-Kettering Cancer Ctr., NYC, 1984-98; sr. cons. pathologist Dickstein Cancer Treatment Ctr., White Plains, NY, 1998-99; attending pathologist, chief of breast pathology N.Y. Presbyn. Hosp., NYC, 1999—. Adj. prof. pathology N.Y. Med. Coll., Valhalla, N.Y., 1996-99. Author: Rosen's Breast Pathology, 1996, 2d edit., 2001, Breast Pathology: Diagnosis by Needle Core Biopsy, 1999; co-author: 2d edit., 2005; co-author: Tumors of the Mammary Gland, 1993; co-editor Pathology Annual, 1977—95, Revs. Pathology, 1996—98; contbr. more than 300 articles to profl. jours. Mem. Internat. Acad. Pathology, Am. Soc. Clin. Pathologists, Soc. Surg. Pathologists, N.Y. Acad. Medicine.

ROSEN, RAYMOND, health facility executive; b. Louisville, Feb. 5, 1950; s. Sam and Olga Rosen; m. Deborah Joy Rubinow, June 25, 1972; children: Lisa, Jessica. BS, Pa. State U., 1972; MA, George Washington U., 1974. Adminstrv. resident York (Pa.) Hosp., 1973-74, asst. to pres., 1974-75, asst. adminstr.-adminstrn., 1975-77, asst. adminstr.-med. affairs, 1977-79, adminstr.-med. affairs, 1979-87, v.p. opers., 1987—. Pres. Young Adminstrs. Group Ctrl. Pa., 1980-82, Rabbit Transit, Inc., 1992—, vice chmn., 1989-92, chmn., 1992—; bd. dirs. Fedn. South Ctrl. Pa. Emergency Health Svcs., 1978-92, mem. adv. com., 1992-93, York County Emergency Health Svcs. Coun., 1978-92, Jewish Cmty. Ctr., 1986-91; divsn. chmn. United Way York County, 1988, York County Transp. Auth., 1995—; bd. mem. York County Econ. Devel. Corp., 2005—. Fellow: Am. Coll. Healthcare Execs. (regent south ctrl. Pa. 1991—95); mem.: Hosp. Assn. Pa. (planning com. 1992—), Am. Hosp. Assn. Office: York Hosp 1001 S George St York PA 17403-3676 Office Phone: 717-851-2122.

ROSEN, RICHARD DAVID, lawyer; b. Pitts., June 24, 1940; s. Benjamin H. and Bertha B. (Broff) R.; m. Ellaine H. Heller, June 23, 1963; children: Deborah H. Fidel, Jaime M. Cohen. BA, Yale U., 1962; JD, Harvard U., 1965. Bar: Pa. 1966, Fla. 1979. Mgr. Bachrach, Sanderbeck & Co., Pitts., 1965-70; ptnr. Grant Thornton, Pitts., 1970—75, mng. ptnr., 1975—76; chmn. tax dept. Baskin & Sears, Pitts., 1977-78; pres. Gas Transmission, Inc., Pitts., 1979—2000; dir., shareholder Cohen & Grigsby, Pitts., 1989—. Dir. UPMC Presbyn./UPMC Shadyside Hosps., 2003—. Contbr. articles to profl. jours. Trustee Jewish Healthcare Found., 1995—, chmn. investment com., 2001—. Fellow: Am. Coll. Trust and Estate Counsel; mem.: ABA, Pa. Bar Assn. (mem. estate planning com. 1996—, com.chmn. 1998—2000), Westmoreland Country Club, United Jewish Fedn. Greater Pitts. (chmn. profl. adv. com. 1997—2001). Avocations: golf, tennis. Home: 1198 Beechwood Ct Pittsburgh PA 15206-4522 Office: Cohen & Grigsby PC 11 Stanwix St 15 Fl Pittsburgh PA 15222-1312 Home Phone: 412-362-6921; Office Phone: 412-297-4927. Business E-Mail: rrosen@cohenlaw.com.

ROSEN, RICHARD LEWIS, lawyer, real estate developer; b. NYC, Mar. 6, 1943; s. Morris and Lorraine (Levy) R.; m. Doris Ellen Bloom, Aug. 28, 1983. BA, Cornell U., 1965; JD, N.Y. Law Sch., 1968; cert., NYU Real Estate Inst., 1980. Bar: NY 1968, US Dist. Ct. (so. and ea. dists.) NY 1972; lic. real estate broker. Pvt. practice, NYC, 1971-73; ptnr. Rosen, Wise, Felzen & Salomon, NYC, 1973-79, Rosen & Felzen, NYC, 1979-84, Rosen, Rudd, Kera, Graubard & Hollender, NYC, 1985-88, Bell, Kalnick, Klee and Green, NYC, 1989-90; shareholder Rosen, Einbinder & Dunn, P.C., NYC, 1990—2005; pvt. practice The Richard L. Rosen Law Firm, PLLC, NYC, 2005—. Contbg. author: Franchising 101, The Complete Guide to Evaluating, Buying and Growing Your Franchise Business; author: Renewal of Your Franchise: Some Solutions, Franchise Times. Named Ea. States Lightweight Weightlifting Champion, 1968; named one of America's 100 Best Franchise Lawyers, Franchise Times; named to Best Lawyers in Am., Super Lawyers, Best of US; NY State Regents scholar. Mem. ABA (mem. Forum Com. on Franchising), Am. Assn. Franchises and Dealers (former chmn. legal steering com., chmn. fair franchising stds. com., chmn. alternate dispute resolution com., bd. dirs.), Franchise Lawyers Assn., Am. Franchise Assn., NY State Bar Assn. (founding mem. franchise law com., chmn. mission statement com. of franchise law com., exec. com. bus. law sect.), Nat. Franchise Mediation Program (mem. steering com., disting. panel neutrals), Assn. Bar City NY (panel mem. com. on franchising, panel mem. com. on corp. law), Red Key Hon. Soc., Cornell U., Sphinx Head Hon. Soc., Cornell U., Spiked Shoe Soc., Cornell U., Ea. Intercollegiate Athletic Assn. (named Lightweight Football All Ea. Selection 1963, 64). Avocations: guitar, reading, coaching youth soccer and track, masters track competition. Home: 1 Old Jericho Tpke Jericho NY 11753-1205 Office: Richard L Rosen Law Firm PLLC 110 E 59th St 23rd FL New York NY 10022 Home Phone: 516-931-0771; Office Phone: 212-644-6644. Business E-Mail: rlr@rosenlawpllc.com.

ROSEN, ROBERT ARNOLD, management consultant, real estate owner, manager, developer, investor, farmer; b. NYC, June 19, 1936; s. Louis and Helen (Weiss) R.; m. Florence Cohen, Oct. 23, 1960; children: David S., Kenneth A., Mark A., Emily B. BBA, CUNY, 1957, MBA, 1960; postgrad. (Ford Found. scholar), NYU, 1961; grad., Indsl. Coll. Armed Forces, Air War Coll., 1960, U.S. Air Force U.; various courses, Naval Edn. and Tng. Command. Sales promotion mgr. Leipzig & Lippe, Inc., 1956-58; advt. and sales promotion mgr. Zenith Radio, 1957-62; chmn., pres., founder Am. Bus. Resources Corp., 1963-64; v.p., dir. Royal Bus. Funds Corp., 1964-68; chmn., CEO Rosen Assocs. Mgmt. Corp., Jericho, NY, 1983—. V.p. corp. finance div., dir. Brand Grumet & Siegel, Inc., 1969-70; pres. Brand Grumet & Siegel Equities, Inc., 1970; former pres., chief oper. officer Bell TV, Inc., N.Y.C.; pres., former chmn. bd. Holmes Protection, Inc.; former chmn. bd., pres. Union Small Bus. Investment Co., 1968-77, Skyway-Laguardia Corp.; dir. past chmn. bd. Okuraya Davos Internat., Inc.; chmn. bd., pres., chief exec. officer, treas. Suburban Broadcasting Corp., 1970-80; chmn., pres. Affiliated Comms. Corp.; vice chmn., pres. Comm. Svcs. Corp.; pres. Wescom Corp.; pres. Androse Corp., 1983—; cons. Asian Devel. Bank, Albert Einstein Coll. Medicine, Nat. Housing Bank of Brazil, 1972-76; mem. U.S. Senatorial Bus. Adv. Bd.; lectr. Baruch Coll. Grad. Sch. Bus., CUNY, 1960-63; adj. prof. Fairleigh Dickinson U. Grad. Sch. Bus., 1968-75; ret. pres., ret. dean Internat. Inst. Real Estate Studies Ltd.; dir. Ctr. for Real Estate Studies, Adelphi U.; adj. prof. mgmt. NYU; mem. faculty New Sch. for Social Rsch.; guest lectr., mem. bd. advs. Fordham U.; prin. owner, developer shopping ctrs., comml. real estate throughout, U.S.; chmn. UN Trade and Tech. Adv. Mission to Israel, 1972, Econ. Devel. Com./UJA Fedn.; active Nat. Builder Mktg. Bd.; owner, investor seat on N.Y. Stock Exch. Chmn. Borough Pres.'s of Manhattan Com. on Narcotics Addiction Control, 1970—75; NY mem. adv. coun. USAF Acad.; mem. editl. policy com. Internat. Property Investment Jour. of Hofstra U. Law Sch.; mem. Navy Recruiting Dist., NY Assistance Coun., NY State Gov.'s Bus. Adv. Coun.; chmn. Navy Task Force to Study Navy Budgeting, Acquisition and Procurement; former mem. Pres.'s Pvt. Sector Survey on Cost Control (Grace Commn.); former trustee Zachary and Elizabeth M. Fisher Found.; trustee North Shore-LI Jewish Health Sys.; chmn. econ. devel. com., former bd. dirs. United Jewish Appeal/Fedn.; former mem. corp. adv. bd. Queens Coll.; mem. adv. bd. Roundabout Theatre; advisor Disaster Preparedness Commn.; sr. advisor NY State Senate for Homeland Security, Vets. Affairs and the Mil.; advisor to adjutant gen. State of NY Divsn. Mil. and Naval Affairs for Homeland Security; bd. dirs. The Film Forum, 1979—86, NYC Housing Partnership, Housing Partnership Devel. Corp., Fed. Law Enforcement Found.; bd. dirs., trustee Intrepid Sea, Air, Space Mus. With USAFR and USNR, 1959—90, ret. as capt. USNR, 1990, rear adm. upper half NY Naval Militia, former comdr. Divsn. Mil. and Naval Affairs, naval aide to the Gov. Mem. Soc. Internat. Devel., Internat. Inst. Valuers (SCV designation), NRA, Nat. Def. Exec. Res., Chief Execs. Orgn., Nat. lPres.'s Orgn., Young Pres.'s Orgn. (past chmn. Met. chpt.), Real Estate Bd. N.Y., Assn. for Better N.Y., Internat. Coun. Shopping Ctrs., Property Cons. Soc., Nat. Assn. Rev. Appraisers (cert. rev. appraiser), Air Force Assn., Res. Officers Assn., Nat. Guard Assn. (life), Naval Res. Assn. (life), U.S. Naval Inst., Navy League U.S., Naval War Coll. Found. (assoc.), Am. Legion, Naval Militia Assn. (chmn.), Jewish War Vets. U.S., Wine Inst. Group Stony Brook State U. N.Y., Militia Assn. N.Y., U.S. Navy Pub. Affairs Assn., Alpha Delta Sigma, Phi Sigma Delta, Sigma Alpha. Home: 60 Apple Lake Ln PO Box 8 Rhinebeck NY 12572 Office: Rosen Associates Mgmnt Corp 33 South Service Rd Jericho NY 11753-1006 Office Phone: 516-333-2000. Business E-Mail: rar@rosenmgmt.com.

ROSEN, SANFORD JAY, lawyer; b. NYC, Dec. 19, 1937; s. Alexander Charles and Viola S. (Grad) R.; m. Catherine Picard, June 22, 1958; children: Caren E. Andrews, R. Durelle Schacter, Ian D., Melissa S. AB, Cornell U., 1959; LLB, Yale U., 1962. Bar: Conn. 1962, Calif. 1974, U.S. Supreme Ct. 1966. Law clk. to Hon. Simon E. Sobeloff U.S. Ct. Appeals, Balt., 1962-63; prof. sch. law U. Md., Balt., 1963-71; assoc. dir. Coun. on

Legal Edn. Opportunity, Atlanta, 1969-70; vis. prof. law U. Tex., Austin, 1970-71; asst. legal dir. Nat. ACLU, NYC, 1971-73; legal dir. Mex.-Am. Legal Def. Fund, San Francisco, 1973-75; ptnr. Rosen, Remcho & Henderson, San Francisco, 1976-80, Rosen & Remcho, San Francisco, 1980-82; prin. Law Offices of Sanford Jay Rosen, San Francisco, 1982-86; sr. ptnr. Rosen & Phillips, San Francisco, 1986-89; prin. Rosen & Assocs., San Francisco, 1990; sr. ptnr. Rosen, Bien & Asaro, San Francisco, 1991—2006, Rosen, Bien & Galvan LLP, San Francisco, 2006—. Mem. Balt. Cmty. Rels. Commn., 1966-69; mem. com. Patuxent Instn., Md., 1967-69; ad hoc adminstrv. law judge Calif. Agrl. Labor Rels. Bd., San Francisco, 1975-80; interim monitor U.S. Dist. Ct. for no. dist. Calif., San Francisco, 1989, early neutral evaluator, 1987—, mediator, 1993—; mediator Calif. Ct. Appeal 1st dist., 2004—; permanent atty. del. Jud. Conf. U.S. Ct. Appeal for 4th Cir.; atty. del. Jud. Conf. U.S. Ct. Appeals 9th cir., 1996-98. Contbr. articles to profl. jours. Mem. Com. on Adminstrn. of Criminal Justice, Balt., 1968; mem. adv. com. HEW, Washington, 1974-75. Mem. ABA, Assn. Trial Lawyers Am. (chair civil rights sect. 1993-94), Calif. Bar Assn., Bar Assn. San Francisco. Avocations: reading, travel, movies. Office: Rosen Bien & Galvan LLP 315 Montgomery St 10th Fl San Francisco CA 94104 Home Phone: 415-563-5707; Office Phone: 415-433-6830. Business E-Mail: srosen@rbg-law.com.

ROSEN, SAUL WOOLF, research scientist, health facility administrator; b. Boston, July 29, 1928; s. David Tsvi and Ida (Hannah) Sadwin; m. Mary Jean Westfall, June 14, 1959 (div. 1986); children: Craig, Laura, David; m. Deborah Susan Kieffer, Nov. 3, 1989. BA cum laude, Harvard U., 1947, MD, 1956; PhD, Northwestern U., 1955. Intern U. Calif. Med. Ctr., San Francisco, 1956-57, resident, 1957-58, sr. res., 1960-61; clin. assoc. Nat. Inst. Arthritis and Metabolic Diseases, Bethesda, Md., 1958-60, sr. investigator NIH, 1961-84; dep. dir. Clin. Ctr. NIH, Bethesda, Md., 1984-90, acting dir. Clin. Ctr., 1990—94. Vis. scientist Nat. Inst. Med. Rsch., London, 1975-76. Contbr. articles to profl. jours. U.S. Rubber Co. fellow, Northwestern U., 1950. Fellow ACP; mem. Assn. Am. Physicians, Endocrine Soc. Avocations: opera, lexicography, weightlifting. Home: 11801 Rockville Pike Apt 1204 Rockville MD 20852-2728 Personal E-mail: saulrosen@earthlink.net.

ROSEN, STANLEY HOWARD, humanities educator; b. Warren, Ohio, July 29, 1929; s. Nathan A. and Celia (Narotsky) R.; m. Francoise Harlepp, Sept. 5, 1955; children: Nicholas David, Paul Mark, Valerie. BA, U. Chgo., 1949, PhD, 1955; postgrad., Am. Sch. Classical Studies, Athens, Greece, 1955-56; D honoris causa, New U. Lisbon, 1997. Mem. faculty Pa. State U., 1956-94, prof. philosophy, 1966-94; Fulbright research prof. U. Paris, 1960-61; research fellow Humanities Research Inst., U. Wis., 1963-64; Inst. Arts and Humanities research sr. fellow Pa. State U., 1972—, Evan Pugh prof. philosophy, 1985-94; Bowne prof. philosophy Boston U., 1994—, univ. prof., 2000—. Vis. prof. U. Calif., San Diego, 1978, U. Nice, 1981, Scuola Superiore Pisa, 1989; vis. lectr. U. Barcelona, Spain, 1992; Priestly lectr. U. Toronto, 1997; Cardinal Mercier lectr. Louvain U., 1998; Gilson lectr. Institut Catholique, Paris, 2003. Author: Plato's Symposium, 1968, Nihilism, 1969, G.W.F. Hegel, 1974, The Limits of Analysis, 1980, Plato's Sophist: The Drama of Original and Image, 1983, Hermeneutics as Politics, 1987, The Quarrel Between Philosophy and Poetry, 1988, The Ancients and the Moderns, 1989, The Question of Being, 1993, Plato's Statesman: The Web of Politics, 1995, The Mask of Enlightenment, 1995, Metaphysics in Ordinary Language, 1999; editor: The Examined Life: A Treasury of Western Philosophy, 2000, The Elusiveness of the Ordinary, 2002, La Production Platonicienne, 2005, Plato's Republic, 2005 Rsch. grantee Am. Philos. Soc., 1961, Earhart Found., 1971, 73, 81, 2000. Mem. Metaphys. Soc. Am (pres. 1990-91). Home: 117 Brook St Wellesley MA 02482-6632 Office: 745 Commonwealth Ave Boston MA 02215-1401 E-mail: srosen@bu.edu.

ROSEN, STEVEN O., lawyer; b. NYC, Jan. 11, 1949; s. Albert I. and Yvette (Sterenbuch) R. BS Aerospace Engring., SUNY, 1970; MS System and Control Engring., Case Western Reserve, 1975; JD, Lewis & Clark Coll., 1977. Bar: Ill. 1977, Oreg. 1978, Wash. 2004. Assoc. Lord, Bissell & Brook, Chgo., 1977-79, Miller, Nash, Wiener, Hager & Carlsen, Portland, Oreg., 1979-84, ptnr., 1984-97; pvt. practice Rosen Law Firm, 1997—. Disting. adj. prof. Lewis & Clark Law Sch., 1986. Mem. ABA (dir. divsns. sect. of litigation 1996-97, chmn. aviation litigation com. 1990-93), Am. Bd. Trial Advocates, Oreg. State Bar Assn. (exec. com. aviation sect. 1984-2001, chmn. 1994-95), Washington State Bar Assn. Avocations: skiing, bicycling. Address: The Rosen Law Firm 620 SW Main St Ste 702 Portland OR 97205-3030 Office Phone: 503-525-2525. Business E-Mail: rosen@rosenlawfirm.com.

ROSEN, STEVEN TERRY, oncologist, hematologist; b. Bklyn., Feb. 18, 1952; married, 1976; 4 children. MB, Northwestern U., Evanston, Ill., 1972, MD, 1976. Genevieve Teuton prof., med. sch. Northwestern U., 1989—, dir. Robert H. Lurie Comprehensive Cancer Ctr., 1989—. Dir. clin. programs Northwestern Meml. Hosp., 1989—. Editor-in-chief Jour. Northwestern U. Cancer Center, 1989—, Contemporary Oncology, 1990-95, Cancer Treatment and Rsch., 1995—, In Touch, 1998-02. Mem. AAAS, ACP, AMA, Am. Soc. Hematology, Am. Soc. Clin. Oncology, Ctrl. Soc. Clin. Rsch. Achievements include research in hematologic malignancies, lung cancer, breast cancer, biologic and hormonal therapies. Office: Northwestern U Lurie 3-125 303 E Chicago Ave Chicago IL 60611-3093 Office Phone: 312-908-5250. Business E-Mail: s-rosen@northwestern.edu.

ROSEN, WILLIAM WARREN, lawyer; b. New Orleans, July 22, 1936; s. Warren Leucht and Erma (Stich) R.; m. Eddy Kahn, Nov. 26, 1965; children: Elizabeth K., Victoria A. BA, Tulane U., 1958, JD, 1964. Bar: La. 1964, US Dist. Ct. (ea. dist.) La. 1965, US Ct. Appeals (5th cir.) 1965, US Supreme Ct. 1984, US Dist. Ct. (mid. dist.) La. 1985, Colo. 1989. Assoc. Dodge & Friend, New Orleans, 1965-68, Law Office of J.R. Martzell, New Orleans, 1968-70; pvt. practice New Orleans, 1970-79, 89-90; ptnr. Lucas & Rosen (and predecessor firm), New Orleans, 1979-87, Herman, Herman, Katz & Cotlar, New Orleans, 1987-88, Rosen and Samuel, New Orleans, 1990-95; of counsel Rittenberg & Samuel, New Orleans, 1996-99; founder & dir. Litigation Consultation Svcs., New Orleans, 1996—; ptnr. Rosen & Lundeen, LLP, New Orleans, 1999—2002; pvt. practice New Orleans, 2002—05, Franklin, Tenn., 2005—. Adj. prof. trial advocacy Law Sch. Tulane U., 1988-2006, mem. adv. com. paralegal studies program, 1977-86, instr. bus. orgns., 1978, instr. legal interviewing, 1980-81; mem. adv. com. Paralegal Inst. U. New Orleans, 1990—, instr. legal interviewing and investigations, 1986-87; lectr. legal and paralegal fields; lectr. real and demonstrative evidence Nat. Edn. Network, 1993; lectr. new judges seminar La. Jud. Coll., 2000, 01, 02, 03. Author: (with others) Trial Techniques publ. La. Trial Lawyers Assn., 1981; columnist Briefly Speaking publ. New Orleans Bar Assn., 1993-2000. Mem. budget and planning com. Jewish Welfare Fedn., 1970-73; mem. adv. coun. on drug edn. La. Dept. Edn., 1973; mem. profl. adv. com. Jewish Endowment Found., 1982—2006; mem. exec. com. US Olympic Com., La., 1982-84; bd. dirs. Planned Parenthood La., 1994-2001, Hillel Found. New Orleans, 2003-05, Dad's Club, Isidore Newman Sch., 1984-85, Uptown Flood Assn., 1982-85; bd. dirs. Jewish Children's Home Svc., 1973-76, Met. Crime Commn. New Orleans, 1976-82. Spl. agt. Office Spl. Investigations USAF, 1958—61. Fellow, Inst. of Politics. Loyola U. Mem. ABA, ATLA (keyperson com. 1986-89, vice chmn. paralegal com. 1986-89, mem. family law adv. com. 1989-90, sec. family law sect. 1990-91, lectr. legal edn. 1979, 81, 83, 86, 88); mem. La. Bar Assn. (vice chmn. pub. rels. com. 1970-73, 88-89, past chmn. state youth drug abuse edn. program, vol. lawyers for arts 1986-96, chmn. sr. counsel com. 1995-96), Am. Arbitration Assn., Nat. Fedn. Paralegal Assn. (adv. coun. 1989-1998), Assn. Atty. Mediators (pres. La. chpt. 1995), Nat. Choice in Dying (legal adv. com. 1992-96), Nat. Edn. Network (lectr. legal edn. 1993), New Orleans Bar Assn. (CLE com. 1990-91, chmn. 1991-92, mem. alternative dispute resolution com. 1996-2000, panel moderator 1997), Inn of Ct. (master 1992-2004), Tenn. Trial Lawyer Assn., Rotary Club New Orleans (bd. dirs. 1996-98, 2003-05, chmn. legal com. 1996—2005), Franklin Rotary Club, Audubon Park Tennis Club (pres. 2004-06), Audubon Pub. Tennis Assn., Inc. (v.p. 2006-). Avocation: photography. Office: 704 Wild Timber Ct Franklin TN 37064 Office Phone: 615-649-8192. Office Fax: 615-646-8192. Personal E-mail: lcsno@aol.com.

ROSENAU, JAMES NATHAN, political scientist, educator, writer; b. Phila., Nov. 25, 1924; s. Walter Nathan and Fanny Fox (Baum) R.; m. Norah McCarthy, Aug. 5, 1955 (dec. July 1974); 1 child, Heidi Margaret; m. Pauline Vaillancourt, June 14, 1987 (div. 1993); m. Hongying Wang, Dec. 11, 1993; children: Fan Elizabeth, Patrick Rosenau (adopted). AB, Bard Coll., 1948; AM, Johns Hopkins U., 1949; PhD, Princeton U., 1957. From instr. to prof. Rutgers U., New Brunswick, NJ, 1949-70; prof. Ohio State U., Columbus, 1970-73; prof. polit. sci. U. So. Calif., LA, 1973-92; prof. internat. affairs George Washington U., 1992—. Rsch. asst. Inst. Advanced Study, Princeton, NJ, 1953-54; rsch. assoc. Princeton U., NJ, 1960-70; dir. Sch. Internat. Rels. U. So. Calif., LA, 1976-79; dir. Inst. for Transnat. Studies, U. Southern Calif., LA, 1973-92. Author: Public Opinion and Foreign Policy, 1961, National Leadership and Foreign Policy, 1963, The Dramas of Politics, 1973, Citizenship between Elections, 1974, The Scientific Study of Foreign Policy, 1980, Turbulence in World Politics, 1990, The United Nations in a Turbulent World, 1992, Along the Domestic-Foreign Frontier, 1997, Distant Proximities, 2003, The Study of World Politics: Vol. 1, Theoretical and Methodological Challenges, Vol. 2, Globalization and Governance, 2005; (play) Kwangju: An Escalatory Spree, 1991; co-author: American Leadership in World Affairs, 1984, Global Voices, 1993, Thinking Theory Thoroughly, 1995, 2nd edit., 2000, International Political Economy, 1995, Understanding Globalization, 1998, On the Cutting Edge of Globalization, 2005; co-editor: Journeys through World Politics, 1989, Global Changes and Theoretical Challenges, 1989, Governance without Government, 1992, Strange Power, 2000, Information Technologies and Global Politics, 2002, Globalization, Security and the Nation State, 2005, Governance and Sustainability, 2005. Trustee Bard Coll., Annandale-on-Hudson, 1968-70, Odyssey Theater Ensemble, LA, 1987-88. With US Army, 1942-46. Ford Found. fellow, 1958-59, Guggenheim fellow, 1987-88; Rsch. grantee NSF, 1970, 73, 78-79, 83, 88, 92, 96, NEH grantee, 1976. Fellow World Acad. Art and Sci.; mem. Internat. Studies Assn. (pres. 1984-85), Am. Polit. Sci. Assn. (exec. coun. 1975-77). Democrat. Office: 2130 H St NW Washington DC 20052-2521 Business E-Mail: jnr@gwu.edu.

ROSENBAUM, ALLAN, public administration educator, academic administrator, international governance advisor; b. NYC, Oct. 5, 1940; s. Frances Lawrence; m. Judith M. Rosenbaum, June 16, 1963; children: Michelle, Amy. BA, U. Miami, 1962; MS in Edn., So. Ill. U., Carbondale, 1964; MA, U. Calif., Berkeley, 1967; PhD, U. Chgo., 1976. Adminstrv. asst. to lt. gov. State of Ill., Chgo., Springfield, 1968-69; dir. Woodlawn manpower planning survey Ctr. Urban Studies, U. Chgo., 1970-71; asst. prof. polit. sci. U. Wis., Madison, 1971-74, U. Conn., Storrs, 1974-77; sr. assoc., study dir. Nat. Inst. Edn., HEW, Washington, 1977-80; chief cons. appropriations subcom. on edn.-human resources Md. Gen. Assembly, Annapolis, 1981, dir. jobs initiative task force, 1982-83; assoc. prof., dir. Md. Inst. Policy Analysis and Rsch. U. Md. Grad. Sch., Balt., 1981-89, dir. Thomas M. Bradley Ctr. Employment and Tng. Edn.-Rsch., 1985-88; prof. pub. adminstrn., dean Sch. Pub. Affairs and Svcs., Fla. Internat. U., Miami, 1988-94, dir. Inst. for Pub. Mgmt., 1995—, coord. PhD program, 2005—06, dir. Sch. Pub. Adminstrn., 2005—06. Advisor, cons. UN Devel. Program, govts. Argentina, Costa Rica, Panama, Paraguay, Peru, Poland, Ukraine, Sierra Leone, Sweden, US AID, OAS, UN Dept. Econ. and Social Affairs, Asian Devel. Bank, others; organizer, speaker State Treas.'s Conf. on Capital Debt Affordability in Md., 1987; mem. policy coun. Fla. Inst. Govt., 1988-89; chmn. 1991 ann. conf. program Policy Studies Orgn., 1990-91; co-prin. Consortium for Legis. Devel. in Latin Am., 1990-95; numerous presentations in field; co-chmn. UN Expert Group on Improving Govt. Leadership, chmn. selection com. 1st UN Pub. Svc. Awards, 2003, chmn. taskforce. Co-author: Policside, 1976, repub., 1989, Local Governence, 1997, Responding to Citizens Needs, 2001, State Modernization and Decentralization - Implications for Education and Training in Public Administration, 2003, Healthcare Delivery Systems: Opportunities for Public Management Education in Central and Eastern Europe; editor-in-chief Policy Studies Rev., 1993-97; contbr. articles to profl. jours., chpts. to books and proc. Pres. Reston (Va.) Community Assn., 1987-88; chmn. sci. adv. com. Greater Miami Coalition for Drug Free Community, 1989-96, bd. dirs., 1990-97; mem. govt. rels. com. United Way Dade County, Miami, 1989-94. Fellow Ford Found., 1966-67, Nat. Inst. Mental Health, Pub. Policy fellow U Chgo.,, 1967-70, U. Conn., 1975, Inst. for Ednl. Leadership, 1976-77; numerous govt. and found. grants. Mem. Nat. Assn. Schs. Pub. Affairs and Adminstrn. (exec. coun.), Am. Soc. for Pub. Adminstrn., Assn. for Pub. Policy Analysis and Mgmt., Am. Polit. Sci. Assn., Greater Miami C. of C. (task force on homelessness in South Fla. 1989-92, pub. affairs and state affairs coms. 1989-96), Internat. Inst. Adminstrv. Scis. (founding mem. working group on environ. mgmt. 1990-93, exec. coun. 2001-04), Internat. Assn. Schs. and Insts. Adminstrn. (task force on women in pub. mgmt. 1990-93, v.p., bd. mgmt., chair ann. conf. 1995, 2000, pres. 2001-04), Cosmos Club. Democrat. Jewish. Home: 5000 Riviera Dr Miami FL 33146-1741 Office: Fla Internat U Sch Pub Policy and Mgmt Univ Park Campus Miami FL 33199 Home Phone: 305-665-1409; Office Phone: 305-348-1271. Business E-Mail: rosenbau@fiu.edu.

ROSENBAUM, DAVID MARK, engineering executive, consultant, educator; b. Boston, Feb. 11, 1935; s. Frederick and Elizabeth (Gelman) R.; m. Karen Jeanne Smith, Dec. 27, 1964; children: Benjamin Micah, Shoshana Elizabeth. BSc, Brown U., 1956; MS, Renessaler Poly. Inst., 1958; PhD, Brandeis U., 1964. Asst. rsch. prof. Boston U., 1964-65; assoc. prof. Poly. U., Bklyn., 1969-70; pres. Network Analysis Corp., Glen Cove, NY, 1970-72; asst. dir. Office of Nat. Narcotics Intelligence, Washington, 1973-74; cons. to comptr. gen. GAO, Washington, 1975-78; dir. Office of Radiation Programs EPA, Washington, 1978-81; pres. Tech. Analysis Corp., McLean, Va., 1981—. Cons. Dir. of Licensing, AEC, Washington, 1972-73. Author: Super Hilbert Space and the Quantum Time Operator, 1969, Liquefield Energy Gases Safety, 1978, A Statistical Procedure for Testing Pacemakers, 1978, Health Effects of Low-Level Radiation, 1981, A Statistical Procedure for Cluster Recognition with Application to Atlanta Leukemia Data, 1983. Mem. IEEE (sr.), Am. Phys. Soc. Office: Tech Analysts Corp # 202 6723 Whittier Ave Mc Lean VA 22101-4533 Personal E-mail: dmrose@radix.net.

ROSENBAUM, GREG ALAN, merchant banker, consultant; b. Toledo, Aug. 7, 1952; s. Marvin and Ida Edith (Millman) R.; m. Martha Jane Radlo, Sept. 3, 1978; children: Eli Samuel, Eve Hannah, Elliott Jacob. AB, Harvard U., 1974, M in Pub. Policy, 1978, JD, 1978. Bar: Ohio 1978, Ill. 1980, US Supreme Ct. 2006. Summer assoc. Jones, Day, Reavis & Pogue, Cleve., 1977; tchg. fellow in govt. and social scis. Harvard U., Cambridge, Mass., 1976-78; cons. Boston Consulting Group, Boston and Chgo., 1978-82; v.p. Dyson-Kissner-Moran Corp., NYC, 1982-87; mng. dir. Carlyle Group, Washington, 1987-88; pres. Palisades Assocs., Inc., Bethesda, Md., 1988—. Debating coach Harvard U., 1976-79; dir. Varlen Corp., Naperville, Ill., 1985-99, Richey Electronics, Inc., Garden Grove, Calif., 1993-99, McLaren/Hart Inc., Rancho Cordova, Calif., 1995-2000, Expressions Furniture, Inc., Anaheim, Calif., 1992-97, AMCO Corp., Chgo., 1993-97, The Whaler on Kaanapali Beach, 1999-2005, PlayCore Holdings, Inc., 2000-07, Nations Rent, Ft. Lauderdale, Fla., 2003-06, TVC Commns., Annaville, Pa., 2003-, Empire Kosner Poultry, Mifflintown, Pa., 2003-. Co-author: The Crime of Poverty, 1973, Beyond Politics, 1974, World Without Plenty, 1975. Dir. Lifeline, A Mental Retardation Partnership, Washington, 1993-98; baseball coach Potomac (Md.) Boys' Club, 1992-96; co-chair Harvard Debate Centennial, 1991—; mem. Harvard Law Sch. 30th Reunion gift com., 2006-07, Harvard Coll. 30th Reunion gift com., 2003-04; chair Dean's Alumni Leadership Coun., Kennedy Sch., Harvard, mem.; mem. com. on univ. resources, Harvard U., 2003-. Winner Ames Moot Ct. competition Harvard Law Sch., 1976. Mem. ABA, Am. Forensic Assn. (nat. intercollegiate debate champion 1974, coach nat. intercollegiate debate champion 1979), Am. Acad. Polit. and Social Scis., Ctr. for Study of Presidency, Toledo Bar Assn., Chgo. Bar Assn., Phi Beta Kappa. Democrat. Jewish. Avocations: major league baseball, golf, computers, sports memorabilia. Office: Palisades Assocs Inc 9140 Vendome Dr Bethesda MD 20817-4021 Business E-Mail: greg@palisadesassociates.com.

ROSENBAUM, HERBERT EDWIN, neurology educator; b. Los Angeles, Dec. 11, 1924; s. Samuel P. and Rebecca (Goldberg) R.; m. Dorothy Goldner, Nov. 2, 1944 (div. Aug. 1972); children: Robert, Barbara, Nancy; m. Velma Rosenbaum, Nov. 5, 1988. BS, U. Oreg., 1947, MD, 1949. Prof. neurology Washington U. Sch. Medicine, St. Louis, 1978—. Served to 1st lt. USAF, 1952-53. Fellow Am. Acad. Neurology (counselor 1970-74); mem. Am. Psychiat. Assn. (life mem., pres. Mo. chpt. 1964-65), Soc. Clin. Neurologists (pres. 1974-75). Avocation: golf. Office: Wash U Sch Medicine Campus Box 8111 660 S Euclid Ave Saint Louis MO 63110-1010 Home: 13 Sackston Woods Ln Creve Coeur MO 63141-8228 Office Phone: 314-747-5355.

ROSENBAUM, JACOB I., retired lawyer; b. Cleve., Oct. 4, 1927; s. Lionel C. and Dora (Heldman) R.; m. Marjorie Jean Arnold, Apr. 20, 1952; children: Laura Rosenbaum, Alexander, Judith Bartell. JD, U. N.Mex., 1951. Bar: N.Mex. 1951, Ohio 1952. Pres. Ohio Savs. Bank., Cleve., 1955—60, sr. v.p., 1960—92, also dir., 1995—; ptnr. Burke, Haber & Berick, 1955-79, Arter & Hadden, 1979-94, of counsel, 1994—2003, Tucker Ellis & West, 2003—05; ret., 2005. Active Judson Retirement Cmty., Cleve. Heights, Ohio, 1990—, trustee, 1994—2003, 2006—, pres., 1992, Cleve. Nat. Air Show, 1987—90, 1994—, pres. Found., 1995—2003, trustee, 1981—, Cleve. Zool. Soc., 1983—, Golden Age Ctrs. of Cleve., 1996—, RSVP, Inc., 2006—; pres. Temple Emanu El, University Heights, Ohio, 1965—67, 1995—. Mem.: Cleve. Execs. Assn. (pres. 1989, chmn. 1990, pres. 2003), Greater Cleve. Bar Assn., Ohio Bar Assn. (chmn. aviation law com. 1981—84), Lawyer-Pilots Bar Assn. (pres. 1981—82, editor jour. 1982—97), Kiwanis Club of Cleve. (pres. 1970—71, pres. found. 1999—). Democrat. Jewish. Home: 28050 N Woodland Rd Cleveland OH 44124-4521 Office: Tucker Ellis & West 1150 Huntington Bldg 925 Euclid Ave Cleveland OH 44115-1475 Office Phone: 216-696-2480. Business E-Mail: jrosenbaum@tuckerellis.com.

ROSENBAUM, JAMES MICHAEL, federal judge; b. Ft. Snelling, Minn., Oct. 12, 1944; s. Sam H. and Ilene D. (Bernstein) Rosenbaum; m. Marilyn Brown, July 30, 1972. BA, U. Minn., 1966, JD, 1969. Bar: (Minn) 1969, (Ill.) 1970, (U.S. Supreme Ct.) 1979. Atty. VISTA, 1969—70, staff atty., leadership coun. met. open communities Chgo., 1970—72; assoc. Katz, Taube, Lange & Frommelt, Mpls., 1972-77; ptnr. Rosenbaum & Rosenbaum, Mpls., 1977-79, Gainsley, Squier & Korsh, Mpls., 1979-81; US dist. atty. US Dept. Justice, Mpls., 1981-85; judge US Dist. Ct., Minn., 1985—, chief judge Minn., 2001—. 8th cir. rep. Jud. Conf. U.S., 1997—2005, mem. exec. com., 1999—2001. Author: (booklet) Guide to Practice Civil Rights Housing, 1972; co-author: U.S. Courts Design Guide, 1991—96; contbr. In Defense of the Hard Drive. Campaign chmn. People for Boschwitz, Minn., 1978; bd. vis. U. Minn. Law Sch. (pres. 1996-97). Mem.: FBA (bd. dirs.). Jewish. Office: US Courthouse 300 S 4th St Minneapolis MN 55415-1320

ROSENBAUM, JAY D., lawyer; b. Chgo., 1971; BA magna cum laude, Boston U., 1995; JD cum laude, Boston U. Sch. Law, 1995. Bar: Mass. 1995. Ptnr. Edwards, Angell, Palmer & Dodge, L.L.P., Boston. Named a Super Lawyer, Mass. Super Lawyers mag., 2006. Mem.: ABA (real property, probate and trust law, taxation and bus. law sects.), Boston Bar Assn. (trusts and estates sect.). Office: Edwards Angell Palmer & Dodge LLP 111 Huntington Ave Boston MA 02199-7613 Office Phone: 617-239-0382. Office Fax: 617-316-8265. E-mail: jrosenbaum@eapdlaw.com. *

ROSENBAUM, JOAN HANNAH, museum director; b. Hartford, Conn. d. Charles Leon and Lillian (Sharasheff) Grossman; m. Peter S. Rosenbaum, July 1962 (div. 1970). AA, Hartford Coll. for Women, 1962; BA, Boston U., 1964; student, Hunter Coll. Grad Sch., 1970-73; cert., Columbia U. Bus. Sch. Inst. Non Profit Mgmt., 1978; DHL (hon.), Jewish Theol. Sem., 1993. Curatorial asst. Mus. Modern Art, NYC, 1966-72; dir. mus. program N.Y. Council on Arts, NYC, 1972-79; cons. Michal Washburn & Assocs., NYC, 1979-80; dir. Jewish Mus., NYC, 1980—. Mem. adv. bd. Pub. Ctr., N.Y.C.; bd. dirs. Creative Time. Bd. dirs. Artists Space, 1980-93; mem. coun. Am. Jewish Mus., 1981-90; mem. policy panel Nat. Endowment Arts, 1982-83. Created knight (Denmark); recipient Disting. Alumni award Boston U. Coll. Libera Arts, 1994, Woman of Distinction award Hadassah, 1997, diploma Chevalier of Order of Arts and Letters (France), 1999; European travel grantee Internat. Coun. Mus., 1972. Mem. Am. Assn. Mus. (cons. 1979—), Assn. Art Mus. Dirs. (com. chair), N.Y. State Assn. Mus. (mem. coun. 1981-90), Art Table. Office: Jewish Mus 1109 5th Ave New York NY 10128-0118

ROSENBAUM, MARK E., health products executive; BBA, Univ. Tenn. Sales & mgmt. positions Am. Hosp. Supply, Baxter Healthcare, 1981—89; v.p., gen. mgr. Amsco Internat., 1989—96; regional v.p. Cardinal Health, Dublin, Ohio, 1996—98, exec. v.p. health sys. sales & mktg., 1998—2002, exec. v.p. corp. sales & mktg., 2002—05, pres. integrated provider solutions, 2005—. Office: Cardinal Health 7000 Cardinal Pl Dublin OH 43017 *

ROSENBAUM, RICHARD A., lawyer; b. Bklyn., Sept. 21, 1954; BA, SUNY, Stony Brook, 1975; JD, St. John's Univ., 1982. Bar: NY 1983, Fla. 1985. Joined Greenberg Traurig, 1985, now nat. operating shareholder, shareholder-in-charge No. Ea. Region, mem. exec. com. NYC. Mem.: Fla. Bar Assn., NY State Bar Assn. Office: Greenberg Traurig LLP MetLife Bldg 200 Park Ave New York NY 10166 Office Phone: 212-801-9320. Office Fax: 212-801-6400. Business E-Mail: rosenbaumr@gtlaw.com.

ROSENBAUM, ROBERT A., lawyer; s. Irwin L. and Marilyn E. Rosenbaum; m. Maggie A. Gilbert, May 1, 1994; m. Peggy A. Daly, Nov. 1982 (div. May 1991); children: Jacob A., Samuel A., Benjamin P. BA, Princeton U., 1978; JD, Harvard Law Sch., 1981. Bar: Calif. 1982, Minn. 1987. Assoc. atty. Latham & Watkins, LA, 1982—87; law clk. to chief justice Minn. Supreme Ct., St. Paul, 1981—82; ptnr., corp. securities law, corp. governance and compliance, and mergers and acquisitions groups Dorsey & Whitney LLP, Mpls., 1987—, and group head, corp., mem., mgmt. com. Mem., bd. dirs. Guthrie Theatre, Mpls., 2001—04. Named Am.'s Leading Bus. Lawyers, Chambers USA, 2003-2004, Minn. Super-lawyer in M&A, Minn. Law and Politics, 1998-2004. Mem.: ABA, Minn. State Bar Assn. (ch. 302a subcommittee), Calif. Bar Assn., Hennepin Bar Assn., Mpls. Club. Office: Dorsey & Whitney LLP 50 South Sixth St Minneapolis MN 55402-1553 Office Phone: 612-340-5681. Office Fax: 612-340-2868. E-mail: rosenbaum.robert@dorsey.com.

ROSENBERG, ALAN, actors guild executive; b. Passaic, NJ, Oct. 4, 1950; m. Robin Bartlett (div.); m. Marg Helgenberger, Sept. 9, 1989; 1 child. Actor: (Broadway plays) Lost in Yonkers; (films) The Wanderers, 1979, Happy Birthday, Gemini, 1980, Not for Publication, 1984, Stewardess School, 1986, White of the Eye, 1987, The Last Temptation of Christ, 1988, Miracle Mile, 1988, After Midnight, 1989, Impulse, 1990, The Bum, 2002, (voice) Robots, 2005,: (TV films) Kojak: The Belarus File, 1985, Promise, 1986, The King of Love, 1987, The Revenge of Al Capone, 1989, The Preppie Murder, 1989, Parker Kane, 1990, The Boys, 1991, Partners, 1993, On Hope, 1994, Witch Hunt, 1994, Freaky Friday, 1995, On Seventh Avenue, 1996, Undue Influence, 1996, Breaking Through, 1996, Cloned, 1997, Bronx County, 1998, Giving Up the Ghost, 1998, The Temptations, 1998, A Touch of Hope, 1999, A Mother's Fight for Justice, 2001, On the Edge, 2001; (TV series) Civil Wars, 1991—93, L.A. Law, 1993—94, Cybill, 1995—98, The Guardian, 2001—04, (guest appearances) Barnaby Jones, 1978, The Days and Nights of Molly Dodd, 1987, Coach, 1989, Empty Nest, 1989, ER, 1994, Murphy Brown, 1998, Touched by an Angel, 1999, Chicago Hope, 1999, 2000, NYPD Blue, 2005, CSI, 2005, Numb3rs, 2005. Mem.: SAG (pres. 2005—). Office: SAG 5757 Wilshire Blvd Los Angeles CA 90036

ROSENBERG, ALAN DAVID, accountant; b. Mt. Vernon, NY, Apr. 11, 1946; s. Benjamin Bernard and Miriam (Nierenberg) R.; m. Wendy Patricia Cutler, May 25, 1975; children: Kerri L., Joshua Z., Brian S. BS in Acctg., NYU, 1967; MBA in Taxation, Baruch Coll., 1970. CPA NY. Sr. acct. Ernst & Ernst, NYC, 1967-70; dir. acctg., CFO various firms, NYC, 1970-75; pres. Alan D. Rosenberg, CPA, P.C., NYC, New Rochelle, N.Y., 1975—. Mem. AICPA (mem. tax practice mgmt. com. 1992—), N.Y. State Soc. CPAs, Inst. Mgmt. Accts., Nat. Conf. CPA Practitioners, Alliance of Practicing CPAs, Estate Planning Coun. Westchester County, Tax Soc. NYU. Jewish. Avocations: sports, reading, family activities. Office: 2 W 45th St Ste 1208 New York NY 10036-4212

ROSENBERG, ALAN GENE, editor; b. Chgo., Sept. 14, 1957; s. Earl David and Lorraine Faith (Blum) R.; m. Avis Beth Gunther-Rosenberg, Apr. 8, 1984; children: Ethan Elijah, Rebecca Greer, Jacob Sigmund. BS in Journalism, Northwestern U., 1978. From state staff reporter to South County regional editor Providence Jour., 1978—. Tchr. Temple Beth-El Religious Sch., Providence, 1998—. Recipient Goldberg Tchr. Creativity award, Bur. Jewish Edn., 2003, Jenny Klein Religious Tchr. of Yr. award, 2006. Office: Providence Jour 32 Old Tower Hill Rd Wakefield RI 02879 Home Phone: 401-885-0768; Office Phone: 401-277-7409. Business E-Mail: alan_rosenberg@projo.com.

ROSENBERG, ALAN STEWART, lawyer; b. NYC, Mar. 29, 1930; s. Louis and Sadye (Knobler) R.; m. Ilse Rosenberg/Klein, Aug. 15, 1963; children: Gary, Robert. BA, Stanford U., 1949; LLB, Columbia U., 1952; LLM, NYU, 1960. Bar: N.Y. 1955. Assoc. Wolf Haldenstein Adler & Freeman, NYC, 1955-56; ptnr., chmn. tax dept. Proskauer Rose LLP, NYC, 1957—92. Contbr. articles to profl. jours. Mem. exec. com., bd. visitors Stanford (Calif.) U. Law Sch., 1982-85, Jewish studies program, 1986—; chmn. bd. NY Alliance for the Pub. Sch., 1988-91; mem. adv. com. on pub. issues Advt. Coun., 1991-94; bd. dirs., sec. Univ.-Urban Schs. Nat. Task Force Inc., 1981-96; mem. bd. visitors Columbia U. Law Sch., 1991-96; trustee Ctr. Ednl. Innovation Pub. Edn. Assn., 2000—; mem. bd advisors Spl. Music Sch Am., 1999—; bd. dirs., treas. Justice Resource Ctr., 1994-97; bd. dirs., The Abraham Fund, 2000—; chmn. bd. dirs. Richalan Found., 1996-2003. Lt. (j.g.) USN, 1952-55. Lt (jr. grade) USNR, 1952—55. Jewish. Avocations: singing, tennis. Home: 115 Central Park W New York NY 10023-4153 Personal E-mail: aandi98@aol.com.

ROSENBERG, ALEX JACOB, art appraiser, educator, art dealer; b. NYC, May 25, 1919; s. Israel and Lena (Zar) R. Student, Albright Coll., 1935-37, Sch. Phila. Mus. Art, 1937-40; BS, Phila. U., 1948; DHL (hon.), Hofstra U., 1989; DSc in Art, Inst. Superior Art, Havana, Cuba, 2003. completed Personal Property courses, levels I, II, III and IV, Am. Soc. Appraisers, Uniform Standards of Profl. Appraisal Practice, 1994, 2000, 06. Pres. Anserphone, 1959-66; sec., dir. Gen. Cablevision Tex., 1968-72; v.p., dir. Communicable, Inc., Fla., 1967-71, Gen. Cablevision Palatka, Fla., 1967-71, Beacon Cable Corp., 1966-71; pres., dir. Modern Cable Corp., 1966-71, B.F.C.-C.A.T.V. Corp., 1966-71; v.p., dir. Starfax Corp. Real Estate, 1968-70; gen. ptnr. Lakewood Plaza Assocs., NJ, 1973-92, Rostin Assocs., Austin, Tex., 1970-83; pres. Transworld Art Inc., Alex Rosenberg Gallery and Alba Edits., NYC, 1968-89, Rostin Mgmt. Corp., 1986-89, The Abbot Group, 1987-89, Ardmore Affiliates Ltd., Alex Rosenberg Fine Art, 1985—, Neikrug-Rosenberg Assocs., 1989-97. Lectr. Parsons Sch. Design, NYC, 1979—88; instr. appraising modern art NYU, 1992—95, adj. asst. prof. appraising, 1995—; vis. prof. fine art Inst. Superior Art, Havana, Cuba, 1993—; organizer Henry Moore exhbn. Mus. Budapest, Bratislava and Prague, Hungary, 1993; co-curator Leonoid Sokov, Albright Coll., Reading, Pa., 2002; guest lectr. CUNY, NYC, 2000—03; organizer Henry Moore Exhbn., Havana, 1998; chmn. Salvadore Dali Rsch. Ctr., 2006. Curator An American Portrait, 1976—78, Mus. Fine Art, Havana, 1992—93, co-curator Romare Bearden as Printmaker, 1992—97, Henry Moore Mother and Child Exhbn., 1987—88, assoc. editor exhbn. catalogue. Trustee Alice Baber Art Fund, 1991-93, Phila. Coll. Textiles and Sci., 1992-95; mem. internat. bd. dirs. Tel Aviv Mus. Art, 1999—, bd. dirs., 2000-06; bd. dirs. Artists' Rights Today, 1974-80; mus. adv. bd. Hofstra Mus., Hempstead, N.Y., 1987-92; mem. collection and exhbn. com. Parrish Art Mus., Southhampton, N.Y., 1989-95; mem. adv. com. Pollock-Krasner House and Study Ctr., 2000—; trustee Guttman Inst., 1979-92; mem. exec. bd. Nat. Emergency Civil Liberties Com., 1970-98, treas., 1981-98; trustee Nat. Emergency Civil Liberties Found., 1964-98, chmn., 1992-98; nat. bd. dirs. and bd. dirs. local coun. SANE, 1974-83, bd. trustees Ctr. for Constitutional Rights, 1998—, v.p. 2003—; trustee, treas. New Lincoln Sch., 1968-71; trustee Givat Haviva Ednl. Found., N.Y.C., 1969—, chmn. exec. com., 1992-99, v.p., 1998—; trustee Stephen Wise Free synagogue, 1967-70, 73-76, 99-2000, Mus. Borough Bklyn., 1986-89; del. 28th World Zionist Congress, Jerusalem, 1972; mem. Cmty. Planning Bd. # 7, 1965-67, 70-72; mem. Lower West Side Anti-Poverty Bd., 1965-66, Lincoln Ctr. Cmty. Coun., 1968-74, Com. for Ind. Civilian Police Rev. Bd., 1967; mem. steering com. Com. Pub. Edn. and Religious Liberty; chmn. Am. Israel Civil Liberties Coalition, 1988-89; Dem. dist. leader, 1964-74, state committeeman, 1970-73, mem. county exec. com., 1964-74; del. Dem. Nat. Convs., 1968, 72; bd. dirs. Raoul Wallenberg Commn. of U.S., 1986-90, chmn., 1990-92; mem. print and drawing coun. Israel Mus., 1980-85; assoc. dir. Snug Harbor Cultural Ctr., S.I., 1982-88; mem. AAA del. to Pres. Coun. of Appraisal Orgns., 1995-96; bd. mem. Ludwig Found. of Cuba, 1995—, Am. Friends Ludwig Found. Cuba, 2000—; mem. Assn. Governing Bds. of Univs. and Colls., 1994-96, Nat. Registry of Forensic Examiners, 1994-96; hon. fellow Tel. Aviv Mus. Art, 2002. Recipient Spl. prize Grenschen Triennial, Switzerland, 1976, Cuban Order of Culture, 1995, Cert. of Commendation, Am. Soc. Appraisers, 1993, Cert. for Disting. Svc., Appraisers Assn. of Am., 1993, Graham J. Littlewood III award for profl. excellence Phila. Coll. of Textiles and Sci., 1996, Alex and Carole Rosenberg Collection, Savannah Coll. of Art and Design, 1999, Alex Rosenberg Gallery Hofstra U., 1996—, Alex and Carole Rosenberg Collection Albright Coll., Reading, Pa.; named to Silver Cir., Pres.'s Coun., Albright Coll., 2007, Diploma for Service, Nat. Mus. of Fine Art, Havana, Cuba, 2003. Mem. Am. Soc. Appraisers (sr., bd. examiners 1987-95, personal property com. 1987-89), Appraisers Assn. Am. (cert. mem., bd. dirs. 1990-96, v.p. 1992-94, 1st v.p. 1994, pres. 1994-96, Pres.' award 2005), Fine Art Pubs. Assn. (v.p., bd. dirs. 1981-83, pres. 1983-86, treas. 1986-89), Nat. Arts Club (Lifetime Achievement Gold medal 2004). Home and Office: 3 E 69th St New York NY 10021-4943 Office Phone: 212-628-0606. Fax: 212-628-4969.

ROSENBERG, ALISON P., public policy officer; b. Miami, Fla., Sept. 5, 1945; d. Mortimer I. and Gail (Sklar) Podell; m. Jeffrey Alan Rosenberg, May 4, 1969; 1 child, Robert Aaron. BS in Econs., Smith Coll., 1967. Mng. officer Citibank, NYC, 1967-69; legis. aide Senator Charles Percy, Washington, 1969-80; profl. staff mem. Senate Fgn. Rels. Com., Washington, 1981-85; assoc. asst. adminstr. Agy. for Internat. Devel., Washington, 1985-87; dir. African affairs Nat. Security Coun., Washington, 1987-88; dep. asst. sec. for Africa State Dept., Washington, 1988-92; asst. admnstr. for Africa Agy. for Internat. Devel., Washington, 1992-93; lead partnerships specialist (Africa) The World Bank, Washington, 1993—2007, partnership cons. (Africa), 2007—. E-mail: arosenberg@worldbank.org.

ROSENBERG, BRIAN C, academic administrator; BA in English, Cornell U.; MA in English, PhD in English, Columbia U. Tchg. asst. Columbia U., NYC, 1979—80; English instr. Queens Coll., NY, 1980—82; asst. prof. The Cooper Union, NYC, 1982—83; asst. prof. to assoc. prof. to prof. to chmn., dept. of English Allegheny Coll., Meadville, Pa., 1983—98; chief acad. officer to dean of faculty and prof. English Lawrence U., Appleton, Wis., 1998—2003; pres. Macalester Coll., 2003—. Pres. fellowship Columbia U., 1977—78, 1980—81; bd. trustees The Dickens Soc., 2000—. Author: (book) Mary Lee Settle's Beulah Quintet: The Price of Freedom, 1991, Little Dorrit's Shadow's: Character and Contradiction in Dickens, 1996. Mem.: Phi Beta Kappa. Office: Office of the Pres, Macalester Coll 208 Weyerhaeuser Hall 62 Macalester St Saint Paul MN 55105 Office Phone: 651-696-6207. *

ROSENBERG, CHARLES ERNEST, historian, educator; b. NYC, Nov. 11, 1936; s. Bernard and Marion (Roberts) R.; m. Carroll Ann Smith, June 22, 1961 (div. 1977); 1 child, Leah; m. Drew Gilpin Faust, June 7, 1980; 1 child, Jessica. BA, U. Wis., 1956, DHL, 1997; MA, Columbia U., 1957, PhD, 1961. Fellow Johns Hopkins U., Balt., 1960-61; asst. prof. U. Wis., 1961-63; assoc. prof. U. Pa., Phila., 1965-68, prof. history, 1968—, chmn. dept., 1974—75, 1979—83, 1991—95; prof. history of sci. Harvard U., 2001—, chmn. dept. history of sci., 2003—04. Author: The Cholera Years: The United States in 1832, 1849 and 1866, 1962, The Trial of the Assassin Guiteau: Psychiatry and Law in the Gilded Age, 1968, No Other Gods: On Science and Social Thought in America, 1976, The Care of Strangers: The Rise of America's Hospital System, 1987, Explaining Epidemics and Other Studies in the History of Medicine, 1992, Our Present Complaint: American Medicine Then and Now, 2007; editor Isis, 1986-89. Bd. dirs. Mental Health Assn. Southea. Pa., 1973—76, Libr. Co. of Phila., 1980—, Ctr. Advanced Study Behavioral Scis., 1999—2005. Nat. Inst. Health Research grantee, 1964-70; Guggenheim Found. fellow, 1965-66, 89-90; Nat. Endowment Humanities fellow, 1972-73; Rockefeller Found. humanities fellow, 1975-76; fellow Inst. Advanced Study, 1979-80, Ctr. Advanced Study in Behavioral Scis., 1982-83. Fellow: Am. Philos. Soc. (coun. 2006—), Am. Acad. Arts and Scis.; mem.: Orgn. Am. Historians (exec. bd. 1985—88), Soc. Social History of Medicine (pres. 1981), History of Sci. Soc. (coun. 1972—75, George Sarton medal 1995), Am. Assn. History of Medicine (coun. 1974—76, pres. 1992—94, William H. Welch medal 1969), Inst. Medicine of NAS. Office: Harvard U Dept History of Sci Cambridge MA 02138 Home: 33 Elmwood Cambridge MA 02138 Office Phone: 617-495-9953. Business E-Mail: rosenb3@fas.harvard.edu.

ROSENBERG, CHUCK (CHARLES P.), prosecutor; b. 1960; BA, Tufts U., 1982; MA in Pub. Policy, Harvard U.; JD, U. Va. Atty. Hunton & Williams LLP, McLean, Va., 2000—02; legal analyst NBC TV; asst. US atty. (ea. dist.) Va US Dept. Justice, chief of staff to dep. atty. gen. Washington, counselor to atty. gen. John Ashcroft, counselor to FBI Dir. Robert S. Mueller III, interim US atty. (so. dist.) Tex. Houston, 2005—06, interim US atty (ea. dist.) Va. Alexandria, 2006, US atty. (ea. dist.) Va., 2006—. Office: US Atty's Office 2100 Jamieson Ave Alexandria VA 22314 *

ROSENBERG, DAN YALE, retired plant pathologist; b. Stockton, Calif., Jan. 8, 1922; s. Meyer and Bertha (Naliboff) R.; m. Marilyn Kohn, Dec. 5, 1954; 1 son, Morton Karl. AA, Stockton Jr. Coll., 1942; AB, Coll. of the Pacific, 1949; MS, U. Calif., Davis, 1952. Jr. plant pathologist State of Calif. Dept. Agr., Riverside, 1952-55, asst. plant pathologist Sacramento, 1955-59, assoc. plant pathologist, 1959-60, pathologist IV, 1960—63, program supr. Riverside, 1963-71, chief exclusion and detectin, divsn. plant industry, 1971-76, chief nursery and seed svcs. divsn. plant industry, 1976-82, spl. asst. divsn. plant industry, 1982-87; pres. Health Inc., 1972-73. Agrl. cons., 1988—; mem. Citrus Rsch. Adm. Com., U. Calif., Riverside, 1992—; mem. Gov.'s Interagy. Task Force on Biotech., 1986—; agrl. cons. Calif. Avocado Commn., 1994—. Contbr. articles to profl. jours. Served with AUS, 1942-46, ETO. Mem. Am. Phytopath. Soc. (fgn. and regulatory com. 1975—, chmn. 1978, grape diseases and pests 1977-98), Calif. State Employees Assn. (pres. 1967-69), Sacto. Met. C. of C. (internat. trade com. 1993-97), N.Am. Plant Protection Orgn. (industry adv. group), Plant Patents Fruit Trees and Ornamental Trees, Olive Trees and Grapevines Achievements include research in grape genetics; new olive varieties. Home and Office: 2328 Swarthmore Dr Sacramento CA 95825-6867 Office Phone: 916-929-4620.

ROSENBERG, DAVID ALAN, military historian, strategic analyst; b. NYC, Aug. 30, 1948; s. Sidney and Fay (Breitman) R.; m. Deborah Lee Haines, July 1, 1973; 1 child, Rebecca Haines. BA in History, Am. U., 1970; MA in History, U. Chgo., 1971, PhD in History, 1983. Asst. historian, cons. Lulejian & Assocs., Inc., Falls Church, Va., 1974-75; instr. history U. Wis., Milw., 1976-78; pvt. practice cons., rschr. Chgo., Washington, 1978-82; asst. prof. history U. Houston, University Park, 1982-83; sr. fellow Strategic Concepts Devel. Ctr., Nat. Def. U., Washington, 1983-85; prof. strategy and ops. U.S. Naval War Coll., Newport, RI, 1985-90; assoc. prof. history Temple U., Phila., 1990-2000, professorial lectr., 2001—; Adm. Harry W. Hill prof. maritime strategy Nat. War Coll., Washington, 1996—2003; sr. prof. U.S. Naval War Coll., 1998—2006, asst. to vice chief naval ops., 1996—2004; dir. Task Force History for chief naval ops. Operation Iraqi Freedom, Global War on Terror, 2003—04; rsch. staff mem. intelligence studies Inst. for Defense Analyses, 2006—. US exec. com. four Nation Nuc. History Program, project dir. Berlin Crisis, 1989-95; cons. Office of Sec. Def., 1991-93, Office Chief of Naval Ops., 1991-2005, Office Sec. of Navy, 1992-2003; chair Sec. Navy's Adv. Subcom. Naval History, 1995-2005 Co-author: The Admiral's Advantage U.S. Navy Operational Intelligence in World War II and the Cold War, 2005; co-editor: (15 vol.) U.S. Plans for War, 1945-1950, 1990; contbr. articles to profl. jours., chpts. to books. With USNR, 1982—. Recipient Meritorious Pub. Svc. award Dept. of Navy, 1995, Superior Civilian Svc. medal, 2000; Advanced rsch. scholar U.S. Naval War Coll., 1974-79; Ford Found grantee, 1985-86, MacArthur rsch. grantee 1987-88; MacArthur fellow 1988-93. Mem. Orgn. Am. Historians (Binkley-Stephenson article prize), Soc. for Historians of Am. Fgn. Rels. (Bernath article prize), Soc. for Mil. History, U.S. Naval Inst., Internat. Inst. for Strategic Studies. Jewish.

ROSENBERG, DEBORAH A., special education educator; d. Samuel and Ethelle Wells Luque; married, June 6, 1970; children: Aimee, Corey. BSc in Bus. Adminstrn. Pers. Mgmt., SUNY, Albany, 1971; MSc in Spl. Edn., LI U., 1987; profl. diploma in Adminstrn. and Supervision, St. Johns U., 2003. Cert. Sch. Dist. Adminstr. U. of State of NY Edn. Dept., Provisional Cert. in Sch. Adminstrn. and Supervision. Prodn., sales office mgr. Electronic Essentials, Inc., Woodside, NY, 1974—85; reading, English tchr. NYC Bd. Edn., Bushwich, NY, 1985—88, tchr. Rikers Island, NY, 1988—89, spl. edn. tchr. Jamaica, NY, 1989—92, edn. evaluator Hollis, NY, 1992—2003; spl. edn. math. tchr. NYC Dept. Edn., Flushing, NY, 2003—. Pvt. tutor, NYC, 1985—; adult edn. tchr. Phoenix House, LI, NY, 1987—93; reading tchr. Jamaica Learning Ctr., NYC, 1993—2002. Mem.: Assn. of Tchrs. of Math. NYC, Phi Delta Kappa (UFT chpt. leader JHS189 2006—). Democrat. Avocations: reading, crossword puzzles, role playing games. Office: JHS189Q Dist 25 Region 3 144 80 Barclay Ave Flushing NY 11355 Office Phone: 718-359-6676. Personal E-mail: debrose49@aol.com.

ROSENBERG, DONALD JAY, lawyer, computer company executive; b. Feb. 19, 1951; BS in Math., SUNY, Stony Brook, 1972; JD, St. John's U. Sch. Law, 1975. Bar: NY 1976. Atty. CHQ IBM Corp., 1976—80, lab counsel data systems divsn., 1981—83, sr. atty., 1983—85, sr. counsel, 1985—86, divsn. counsel DSD, 1986—92, assoc. gen. counsel CHQ/L, 1992—97, asst. gen. counsel, 1997—98, v.p., asst. gen. counsel litig., 1998—2006, sr. v.p., gen. counsel, 2006; sr. v.p., gen. counsel, sec. Apple Inc. (formerly Apple Computer Inc.), Cupertino, Calif., 2006—. Adj. prof. law Pace U. Sch. Law, NY. Contbr. chapters to books; editor: St. John's Law Rev. Chmn. bd. visitors Pace U. Sch. Law. Office: Apple Inc 1 Infinite Loop Cupertino CA 95014 *

ROSENBERG, EDWIN HAROLD, systems analyst; b. Balt., June 17, 1949; s. Mervin and Helen Rosenberg. BS, Towson U., 1976, MS, 1984. Rsch. psychologist Gerontology Rsch. Ctr., Nat. Inst. on Aging NIH, Balt., 1983—92; programmer analyst Johns Hopkins Health Sys., Balt., 1993—. Contbr. articles to profl. jours. Avocations: writing, computers, bridge, crossword puzzles. Home: 4501-A Dunton Terr Perry Hall MD 21128 Office: Johns Hopkins Health System 5300 Alpha Commons Suite 200 Baltimore MD 21224 Personal E-mail: erosenb@comcast.net.

ROSENBERG, GERALD ALAN, lawyer; b. NYC, Aug. 5, 1944; s. Irwin H. and Doris (Lowinger) R.; m. Rosalind Navin, Aug. 13, 1971; children: Clifford D., Nicholas D. BA cum laude, Yale U., 1966; JD, Harvard U., 1969. Bar: N.Y. 1970, U.S. Dist. Ct. (so. dist.) N.Y. 1971, U.S. Ct. Appeals (2d cir.) 1974, U.S. Dist. Ct. (we. dist.) N.Y. 1977, U.S. Dist. Ct. (cen. dist.) Calif. 1978, U.S. Supreme Ct. 1979, U.S. Dist. Ct. (ea. dist.) N.Y. 1981, U.S. Tax Ct. 1984. Atty. Legal Aid Soc. San Mateo/VISTA, Redwood, Calif., 1969-70; asst. atty. U.S. Dept. Justice, NYC, 1971-75; assoc. Rosenman & Colin, NYC, 1975-77, ptnr., 1978—2002, mem. mgmt. com., 1991—94; counsel KMZ Rosenman, NYC, 2002—04; chief charities bur. Office of the Atty. Gen., NYC, 2005—. Arbitrator U.S. Dist. Ct. (ea. dist.) NY; faculty Ctr. Internat. Legal Studies, Salzburg, Austria, 1999-2004. Bd. dirs. Non Profit Coord. Com. Inc., NYC, 1983-2004, NY Lawyers for the Pub. Interest Inc., 1988-2004, Parks Coun., 1988—, pres., 1991-95; trustee Central Park Conservancy, 1995-2004. Mem. Am. Law Inst. Office: Office of the Atty Gen 120 Broadway New York NY 10271 Office Phone: 212-416-8490. Business E-Mail: gerald.rosenberg@oag.state.ny.us.

ROSENBERG, HAROLD NMI, preventive medicine physician, consultant; b. NYC, Nov. 23, 1921; s. Jacob and Rose Rosenberg; m. Sharon Rosenberg, June 6, 1962; children: Marla Holben, Victor. BA, Drake U.; DO, Phila. Coll. Of Osteo. Medicine, 1951; MS, Columbia Coll. Physicians and Surgeons, 1999. Physician Health Awareness/lifesustainer, NYC, 1999—; cons./advisor LIFESUSTAINER, NYC, 1999—. Pres. Internat. Acad. Of Preventive Medicine, Houston. Author (sr. editor): Book Of Vitamin Therapy/web Site:lifesustainer. With US Army, 1944—46, ETO. Decorated Purple Heart, Bronze Star medal. Mem.: Internat. Acad. Preventive Medicine (pres. 1970—75), Mil. Order Of The Purple Heart (life; sr. vice comdr./N.Y. Dept. 2002—04). Independent-Republican. Hebrew. Avocations: swimming, hiking, painting landscape, portrates. Home: Po Box 678 New York NY 10023 Office: Lifesustainer 37 West 72nd St New York NY 10023 Home Phone: 917-441-5906. E-mail: hr89@columbia.edu.

ROSENBERG, HENRY A., JR., petroleum executive; b. Pitts., Nov. 7, 1929; s. Henry A. and Ruth (Blaustein) R.; children: Henry A. III, Edward Lee, Frank Blaustein; m. Dorothy Lucibello, June 30, 1984. BA in Econs., Hobart Coll., 1952. With Crown Cen. Petroleum Corp., Balt., 1952—, pres., 1966-75, chmn. exec. com., 1966—, chmn. bd., 1975—, also CEO. Dir. Am. Trading & Prodn. Corp., USF&G Corp., Signet Banking Corp. Bd. dirs. Johns Hopkins Hosp., Goucher Coll., McDonogh Sch., Nat. Flag Day Found., YMCA Greater Balt., United Way Ctrl. Med., Crohn's and Colitis Found. Md., Nat. Aquarium Balt.; mem. nat. exec. bd., mem. N.E. regional bd., v.p. program group nat. coun., past pres., exec. bd., adv. coun. Balt. Area coun. Boy Scouts Am.; past chmn., mem. adv. bd. William Donald Schaefer Ctr. for Pub. Policy; past chmn. bd. dirs. Balt. Area Conv. and Visitors Assn.; trustee Hobart and William Smith Colls. and Loyola Coll. Med. Mem. Nat. Petroleum Refiners Assn. (chmn., bd. dirs., exec. com.), Nat. Petroleum Coun., 25 Yr. Club Petroleum Industry, Nat. Assn. Mfrs. (bd. dirs.). Office: Crown Cen Petroleum Corp 1 N Charles St PO Box 1168 Baltimore MD 21203-1168

ROSENBERG, HOWELL K., lawyer; b. Phila., June 3, 1950; s. Martin and Thelma Rosenberg; m. Sondra Kramer, Dec. 25, 1971; children: Sydney, Carrie, Jake. BA in Polit. Sci., Pa. State U., 1971; JD cum laude, Villanova U., 1974. Bar: Pa. 1974, U.S. Dist. Ct. (ea. dist.) Pa. 1976, U.S. Ct. Appeals (4th cir.) 1993, U.S. Ct. Appeals (3d cir.) 1994, U.S. Surpeme Ct. 1997. Asst. dist. atty. Phila. Dist. Attys. Office, 1974—80, asst. dist. atty. chief spl. investigations, 1980—82; assoc. Shein & Brookman, 1982—84; founding ptnr. Brookman, Rosenberg, Brown & Sandler, 1984—. Clin. prof. law Widener Law Sch., Del., 1985—91. Assoc. editor: Villanova U. Law Rev., 1973—74. Bd. dirs. Libr. Co. of Phila. Named Pa. Super Lawyer, Pa. Mag. Law and Politics, 2004, 2005, 2006. Fellow: Am. Coll. Trial Lawyers; mem.: ATLA, Phila. Trial Lawyers Assn. (bd. dirs. 2001—), Order of Coif. Office: Brookman Rosenberg Brown & Sandler 305 15th St 17th Fl Philadelphia PA 19102 Office Phone: 215-569-4000. Business E-Mail: hrosenberg@brbs.com.

ROSENBERG, JEROME DAVID, physicist; s. Hyman D. and Hilda (Cantor) R.; m. Shirley Sirota, 1947; children: Jonathan, Hindy. BS in Physics, CCNY, 1948; postgrad., Nat. Bur. Standards Grad. Sch., 1949-52, George Washington U., 1952, U. Md., 1951-53, Cath. U. Am., 1953-54. Engr. officer USCG Acad., 1942, APA-34, 1943-45; dir. microphonics Nat. Bur. Stds., 1949—52; project mgr., mgr. Triga test nuclear reactor Harry Diamond Labs., Washington, 1952-62; ops. mgr. tech. utilization NASA, Washington, 1962-64, program and project mgr. Nat. Geodetic Satellite Program, Satellites Pageos, GEOS 1 and 2, 1964—72, dep. dir. comm. divsn., 1972-74, dir. tech. applications divsn., 1974-77, dir. office energy programs divsn. bus. mgmt., 1977-78; spl. assignment to solar applications & conservation, barriers and incentive br. Dept. Energy, 1978-79; leader solar energy group Mitre Corp., McLean, Va., 1979-80; prin. cons. energy and environ. divsn. Booz, Allen & Hamilton, Washington, 1980-82; sr. staff officer Bd. Telecomm. and Computer Applications, NRC-NAS, Washington, 1982-85. Exec. dir. NASA Alumni League, Washington, 1986—; mem. Outlook for Space Study Group, NASA planning group to develop U.S. space programs, 1975. Lt. (j.g.) USCG, 1943—45. Recipient NASA Exceptional Svc. medal, 1973. Mem.: Fed. Exec. Inst., Sigma Pi Sigma. Office: NASA Alumni League 750 1st St NE Washington DC 20002-4241 Office Phone: 202-336-6136. Personal E-mail: jerry@ssrinc.com.

ROSENBERG, JEROME IRA, lawyer; b. Passaic, NJ, June 9, 1931; s. Emanuel and Sylvia S. (Schwartz) R.; m. Dorothy Elaine Teninbaum, Aug. 21, 1955; children: Peter, Michael BA, NYU, 1953; LLB, Harvard U., Cambridge, Mass., 1956. Bar: NY 1966, DC 1957, US Supreme Ct. 1961. Tax law specialist IRS, Washington, 1960-63; ptnr. Hughes Hubbard & Reed LLP, NYC, 1968—2000, counsel, 2000—. Exec. dir. NYU Tax Inst.; pres. Close Encounters with Music; trustee The Austen Riggs Hosp. Ctr.

Contbr. articles to Jour. of Taxation. Lt. USAF, 1957-60. Mem. Phi Beta Kappa. Office: Hughes Hubbard & Reed LLP One Battery Park Plz New York NY 10004-1466 Office Phone: 212-837-6788. Business E-Mail: rosenber@hugheshubbard.com.

ROSENBERG, JEROME LAIB, chemist, educator; b. Harrisburg, Pa., June 20, 1921; s. Robert and Mary (Katzman) R.; m. Shoshana Gabriel, Sept. 15, 1946; children— Jonathan, Judith. AB, Dickinson Coll., 1941; MA, Columbia U., 1944, PhD, 1948. Rsch. chemist S.A.M. Labs., 1944-46; Instr. chemistry Columbia U., 1946-48; rsch. assoc. (asst. prof.) inst. Radiobiology and Biophysics, U. Chgo., 1950-53; mem. faculty U. Pitts., 1953-91, chmn. dept. biophysics and microbiology, 1969-71, prof. biol. scis., 1976-91, dean faculty arts and scis., 1970-86, vice provost, 1978-89, chmn. biol. scis., 1989-90, interim chmn. communication, 1991, assoc. dean faculty arts and scis., 1991-92, rsch. integrity officer, 1992—, prof. emeritus biol. scis., 1991—, dir. Jewish studies program, 1991-99. Author: Photosynthesis, 1965; editor, reviser: Outline Theory and Problems of College Chemistry (Schaum), 1949, 58, 66, 80, 90, 97; contbr. articles to profl. jours. NSF sr. fellow Technion Israel Inst. Tech., 1962-63, AEC fellow U. Chgo., 1948-50; recipient Pitts. award Am. Chem. Soc., 1987. Mem. AAUP (nat. coun. 1968-69, pres. Pa. div. 1968-69). Home: 1029 S Negley Ave Pittsburgh PA 15217-1045 Office Phone: 412-624-3007. Business E-Mail: jrosenb@pitt.edu.

ROSENBERG, JOEL BARRY, economist; b. Bronx, Aug. 14, 1942; s. Benjamin and Miriam Dorothy (Yellin) Rosenberg; m. Judith Lynne Jackler, Aug. 26, 1965; children: Jeffrey Alan, Marc David. BA, Queens Coll., 1964, MA, 1966; PhD, Brown U., 1972. Accredited valuation appraiser 2002. Cons. Commonwealth Svcs., Washington, 1970—71; asst. prof. econs. SUNY, Geneseo, 1971—75, Case Western Res. U., Cleve., 1975—76; mgr., industry economist IRS, Washington, 1976—. NDEA fellow Brown U., 1966—69. Contbr. articles to profl. jours. Mem.: Am. Statis. Assn., Nat. Assn. Bus. Economists, Am. Econ. Assn. Home: 16 Flameleaf Ct Gaithersburg MD 20878-5216 Office: IRS 500 N Capitol St NW Washington DC 20221-0003

ROSENBERG, JOHN DAVID, language educator, critic; b. NYC, Apr. 17, 1929; s. David and Dorothy Lilian (Shatz) R.; m. Barbara E. Hatch, 1952 (div. 1969); m. Maurine Ann Hellner, June 11, 1972; 1 child, Matthew John. BA, Columbia U., 1950, MA, 1951, PhD, 1960; BA, Clare Coll., Cambridge U., 1953, MA, 1958. Editor-in-chief Columbia Rev., 1949-50; lectr. English Columbia U., NYC, 1953-54, asst. prof., 1962-65, assoc. prof., 1966-67, prof. English, 1967—, William Peterfield Trent prof., 1994—; instr. CCNY, 1954-62; chmn. Columbia Coll. humanities program, 1970-73, dir. grad. studies in English, 1986-89. Vis. prof. English Harvard U., 1968, U. B.C., 1970, Princeton U., 1978; vis. fellow Clare Hall Cambridge U., England, 1969; guest lectr. U.S. Mil. Acad., Cambridge U., Lancaster U. Author: The Darkening Glass: A Portrait of Ruskin's Genius, 1961, The Fall of Camelot: A Study of Tennyson's Idylls of the King, 1973, Carlyle and the Burden of History, 1985, Elegy for an Age: The Presence of the Past in Victorian Literature, 2005; editor: The Genius of John Ruskin, 1963, 2nd edit., 98, Mayhew, 1968, Swinburne: Selected Poetry and Prose, 1968, The Poems of Alfred, Lord Tennyson, 1975; contbr. essays and reviews on English lit. to N.Y. Times Book Rev., N.Y. Rev. Books, Harper's mag., Hudson Rev. and profl. jours. Recipient Clarke F. Ansley award Columbia U., 1960, Disting. Svc. award Columbian Coll. Core Curriculum, 1997; Coun. for Rsch. in Humanities grant-in-aid, 1965; Euretta J. Kellett fellow Cambridge U., 1951-53, Edward Coe fellow, 1956-57, Samuel S. Fels fellow, 1959-60, Am. Coun. Learned Soc. fellow, 1965-66, 70, Lawrence H. Chamberlain fellow, 1965-66, Guggenheim fellow, 1968-69, NEH fellow, 1982-83. Mem. MLA (life), Tennyson Soc., Ruskin Assn., Camp Rising Sun Alumni Assn., Columbia Coll. Alumni Assn. (dir. 1980-82, Alexander Hamilton medal 1994), Phi Beta Kappa. Office: Columbia U Dept English 1150 Amsterdam Ave New York NY 10027-7051 Office Phone: 212-854-6407. Business E-Mail: jdr6@columbia.edu.

ROSENBERG, JONATHAN, information technology executive; BA in Econ. (hon.), Claremont McKenna Coll.; MBA, U. Chgo. Former mgr. eWorld product line Apple Computer Inc.; former dir. product mktg. Knight-Ridder Info. Svcs., Palo Alto, Calif.; former sr. v.p. online products and svcs. Excite@Home, Redwood City, Calif.; founder @Home Product Group, Redwood City; v.p. product mgmt. Google Inc., Mountain View, Calif., 2002—. Office: Google Inc 1600 Amphitheatre Pky Mountain View CA 94043 Office Phone: 650-623-4000. Office Fax: 650-618-1499.

ROSENBERG, LAWRENCE, lawyer; b. NYC; BBA with spl. honors & distinction, George Washington U., 1974, JD with honors, 1978; LLM Taxation, NYU Sch. Law, 1980. Bar: Pa. 1978, NY 1982, US Tax Ct. Law clk. to Judge Sheldon V. Ekman US Tax Ct., 1980—81, law clk. to Judge Theofore Tannenwald, 1981—82; ptnr., taxation Chadbourne & Parke LLP, NYC, mem. mgmt. com. Contbr. articles to profl. jour. Mem.: ABA (Taxation Sect.), NY State Bar Assn. (Tax Sect.). Office: Chadbourne & Parke LLLP 30 Rockefeller Plaza New York NY 10112 Office Phone: 212-408-5274. Office Fax: 212-541-5369. Business E-Mail: lrosenberg@chadbourne.com.

ROSENBERG, LEE, lawyer; m. Jennifer Rosenberg, 2004. BA, SUNY, Stony Brook, 1983; JD, Touro Coll., NY, 1986. Ptnr. Saltzman Chetkof McLoughlin & Robinson, Garden City, NY, 1995—96, Saltzman Chetkof & Rosenberg LLP, Garden City, 1996—. Arbitrator-attorney client fee dispute panel State of NY Unified Ct. Sys., Mineola, 1993—. Editor: NY Family/Matrimonial Practice Insights, 2005—; mem. editl. bd.: NY Family Law Monthly, 2005—. Fellow: Am. Acad. Matrimonial Lawyers; mem.: ABA (family law sect.), Suffolk County Bar Assn. (matrimonial law com.), NY Family Law Am. Inn of Ct., Nassau County Bar Assn. (mem. exec. com. 2006—07, matrimonial com. 2006—), NY State Bar Assn. (family law sect., asst. editor family law rev. 2005—). Office: Saltzman Chetkof & Rosenberg LLP 300 Garden City Plaza Garden City NY 11530 Office Phone: 516-873-7200.

ROSENBERG, LEE EVAN, financial planner; b. Bklyn., Nov. 6, 1952; s. Daniel and Rita (Blanket) R.; m. Saralee Hymen, Aug. 27, 1977; children: Zachary Martin, Alexandra Lynn, Taryn Jessica. BA, Bklyn. Coll., 1974. Cert. fin. planner. Underwriter Fin. Life Ins. Co., NYC, 1974-75, Mony, NYC, 1975-80; pres. Lee Rosenberg Assoc., NYC, 1980-83; co-founder, sr. ptnr. ARS Fin. Svcs. Inc., Valley Stream, NY, 1983—2003, Jericho, NY, 2003—. Co-host radio show Moneytalk WBAB, L.I., 1991; guest Nat. CNBC TV show Money Club, 1995, 96; cons. fin. sections New Choices Mag., 1995-2002; mem. adv. bd. Forum for Investor Advice, 2000-02. Author (with Saralee Rosenberg): Destination Fla.: Guide to a Successful Relocation, 1989, 50 Fabulous Places to Retire in Am., 1991, 50 Fabulous Places to Raise Your Family, 1993, Retirement Ready or Not! How to Get Financially Prepared in a Hurry, 1993; guest CNBC Power Lunch, 1997—2005, contbr. CNBC.com, 2000—06; contbr. chapters to books, articles to profl. jours. Named one of Best 200 Fin. Advisors in USA, Worth Mag., 1996, 97, 98. Mem. Internat. Assn. Fin. Planners, Internat. Assn. Registered Fin. Planners, Internat. Soc. Preretirement Planners, L.I. Inst. Cert. Fin. Planners (bd. dirs., pres. 1988-90), Nat. Speakers Assn. (bd. dirs. N.Y. chpt.). Home: 5 Cobblers Ln Dix Hills NY 11746-5001 also: 500 N Broadway Jericho NY 11753-2127 Office: Boca Corp Plaza 1801 Clint Moore Rd Ste 109 Boca Raton FL 33487 Home Phone: 631-462-8334; Office Phone: 561-997-0300. Business E-Mail: jericho@arsfinancial.com.

ROSENBERG, LEON JOSEPH, marketing educator; b. Atlanta, Oct. 9, 1918; s. Harry Manville and Gertrude Dora (Hassenbusch) R.; m. Phylis Jane Israel, Feb. 6, 1943 (dec. Mar. 1976); children: Joanne Rosenberg Larson, Paul Harvey; m. Louise Nachman Mayer, Oct. 15, 1977. BS in Indsl. Mgmt, Ga. Inst. Tech., 1939; MS, Columbia U., 1940; PhD, NYU, 1967. Mem. staff Nat. Retail Mchts. Assn., NYC, 1947-49; sr. rsch. analyst Federated Dept. Stores, Inc., Cin., 1949-52; rsch. dir. Sanger Harris Dept. Store, Dallas, 1952-56, gen. supt., 1956-67; assoc. prof. Coll. Bus. Adminstrn., U. Ark., Fayetteville, 1967-74; prof. mktg. and transp. Sam M. Walton Coll. Bus. Adminstrn., U. Ark., 1975-89; dept. head mktg. and transp. U. Ark., 1986-88, prof. emeritus, 1989—; mktg. cons., sales assoc. Lindsey & Assocs. Inc., Fayetteville, 1990—. Disting. vis. prof. Calif. State U., San Bernardino, 1990. Contbr. articles to profl. jours. Pres. Jewish Family Svc., Dallas, 1960-62, Temple Shalom, Fayetteville, 1992-96; mem. exec. com. Dallas Jewish Fedn., 1963-67; bd. dirs. New Orleans Jewish Children's Regional Svc., 1962-73, 75-2003, Jewish Fedn. Ark., 1992-96; pres. N.W. Ark. unit B'nai B'rith, 1992-2001; bd. dirs. Washington County (Ark.) chpt. Am. Cancer Soc., 1979-86, pres., 1982-83. Capt. USAAF, 1940-46. Mem. Am. Mktg. Assn., So. Mktg. Assn., Nat. Bd. Realtors, Ark. Bd. Realtors, Econs. and Bus. History Soc. (trustee 1986-89), Alpha Phi Omega (Svc. award 1971), Beta Gamma Sigma, Delta Nu Alpha. Home: 1923 E Joyce Blvd # 168 Fayetteville AR 72703 Office: Lindsey & Assocs Inc 3900 Front St Fayetteville AR 72703

ROSENBERG, MARC STEVEN, lawyer; b. NYC, June 15, 1958; s. Marvin and Bette Rosenberg; m. Tina Rosenberg; children: Brett, James, Katherine. AB, Princeton U., 1980; JD, Harvard U., 1983. Bar: NY 1984. Assoc. Cravath Swaine & Moore LLP, NYC, 1985-90, ptnr., corp., 1990—. Named one of Best Lawyers in Am., Securities Law, 2007. Mem.: Assn. of the Bar in the City of New York. Office: Cravath Swaine & Moore LLP 825 8th Ave Fl 47 New York NY 10019-7475 Office Fax: 212-474-3700. Business E-Mail: mrosenberg@cravath.com.

ROSENBERG, MARILYN ROSENTHAL, artist, poet; b. Phila., Oct. 11, 1934; m. Robert Rosenberg, June 12, 1955; 2 children. B in Profl. Studies in Studio Arts, SUNY, Empire State Coll., 1978; MA in Liberal Studies, NYU, 1993. Represented in permanent collections Avant Writing Collection, The Ohio State U. Librs., Whitney Mus. Libr., N.Y.C., Tate Gallery Libr., London, Mus. Modern Art Libr., NYC, Bklyn. Mus. Lib., Bibliotheque Nat., Paris, Fogg Arts Lib., Harvard U., Everson Mus., Syracuse, NY, Chappaqua Libr. Gallery, NY, one-woman shows include Westchester CC, Valhalla, N.Y., 2002, Chappaqua Libr. Gallery, NY, 2007, exhibited in group shows at Fla. Atlantic U., Boca Raton, Fla., 2000, U. Ctrl. Ark., Conway, 2000, Ocean Grove Libr., Victoria, Australia, 2000, City Gallery, Székesfehervár, Hungary, 2000, 2006, The Temple Judea, Elkins Park, Pa., 2001, Art Acad. Cin., 2002, Ohio State U. Librs., Columbus, 2002, Cuesta Coll. Art Gallery, San Luis Obispo, Calif., 2002, Pensacola (Fla.) Mus. Art, 2002, U. Indpls. (Ind.) Gallery, 2002, Lowenstein Gallery, Miami, Fla., 2003, Starr Gallery, Newton Ctr., Mass., 2003, Wexford (Ireland) Arts Centre, 2003, The Buddy Holly Ctr., Lubbock, Tex., 2003, Peck Arts Ctr. Gallery, Ctrl. Wyo. Coll., Riverton, 2003, Purdue U. Galleries, Lafayette, Ind., 2003, Ellipse Art Ctr., Arlington, Va., 2003, The Ctr. for Book Arts, NYC, 2003, 2005, Durango Art Ctr., Colo., 2004, Neopolis Gallery, Cleve., 2004, Ceres Gallery, NYC, 2004, 2005, 2006, Westchester Gallery/Westchester Art Workshop, 2004, 2006, 2007, Futernic Gallery, Alper Jewish Cmty. Ctr., Miami, Fla., 2005, Art Ctr. Hasselt Belgium, 2005, Gallery Durban Segnini, Miami, Fla., 2005, Rutgers U., Camden, N.J., 2005, Gallery 308, Mpls., 2005, Pelham Art Ctr., NY, 2006, Osók István Gallery Székes feshérvár, Hungary, 2006, Kyoto Art U. Gallery, Japan, 2006, Prateus Gowanus Gallery, Bklyn., 2006, Budapest Mus. Fine Arts, Hungary, 2007, Bklyn. Coll. Libr., 2007, Fuller Craft Mus., Brockton, Mass., 2007, Rutgers U. Libr., New Brunswick, NJ, 2007, works in exhib. catalogs, reviews, ref. books, anthologies and websites. Home and Studio: 67 Lakeview Ave W Cortlandt Manor NY 10567-6415

ROSENBERG, MARK B., academic administrator; b. Athens, Ohio, Aug. 15, 1949; married; 2 children. BA, Miami U., Oxford, Ohio, 1971; PhD in Polit. Sci., U. Pitts., 1976. Prof. polit. sci. Fla. Internat. U., Miami, 1976—, chmn. Caribbean L.Am. studies coun., 1977-79, founding dir. L.Am. and Caribbean Ctr., 1979—, founding/acting dean Coll. Urban and Pub. Affairs, 1994-97, vice provost for internat. studies, 1996-98, provost, acting pres., 1998—, acting pres., 1999-2000, provost, exec. v.p. acad. affairs, 2000—05; chancellor State Univ. Sys. of Fla., Tallahassee, 2005—. Mem. exec. com. OLAM; mem. articulation coordination com. Fla. Bd. Edn.; mem. Coun. of Fgn. Relations, Pacific Coun. on Internat. Realtions. Author, editor, co-editor 6 books; former bd. editors Fla. Trend, Latin Trade; contbr. articles to profl. jours. Presdl. appointee U.S. Customs Dist. Export Coun.; mem. exec. com. OLAM, the Jewish Leadership Inst./Jewish Fedn. Miami; mem. statewide articulation coordination com. Fla. Bd. Edn. Mem. Greater Miami C. of C. (vice chair exec. com. for internat. econ. devel. 1992-94), Coun. Fgn. Rels., Pacific Coun. in Internat. Rels. Office: State Univ Sys of Fla 325 W Gaines St, Ste 1614 Tallahassee FL 32399 Office Phone: 850-245-0466. Office Fax: 850-245-9685. E-mail: Chancellor@flbog.org. *

ROSENBERG, MARK L., health facility administrator; b. Newark, July 30, 1945; m. Jill Alison Dimond; children: Julie, Ben. BA in Biology magna cum laude, Harvard Coll., 1967, MD cum laude, 1972, M of Pub. Policy, 1972. Diplomate Am. Bd. Internal Medicine, Am. Bd. Psychiatry and Neurology. Intern Mass. Gen. Hosp., Boston, 1972—73, resident in medicine, 1973—74; resident in preventive medicine Ctrs. for Disease Control, Atlanta, 1975—76; resident in psychiatry Beth Israel Hosp., Boston, 1980—83; clin. prof. dept. cmty. medicine and family practice Morehouse Sch. Medicine, Atlanta, 1984—93; clin. prof. psychiatry Emory U. Sch. Medicine, Atlanta, 1994—99; exec. dir. Task Force for Child Survival and Devel., 1999—; dir. sci. devel., dir. programs Ctr. for Child Well-being, 1999—. Dir. Nat. Ctr. for Injury Prevention and Control, Atlanta, 1994—99, acting assoc. dir. for pub. health practice, 1992—93; dir. divsn. injury control Ctr. for Environ. Health and Injury Control, 1989—92; spl. asst. for behavioral sci., office of dep. dir. CDC, Atlanta, 1989, advisor to dep. dir., 88, asst. dir. for sci. divsn. injury epidemiology and control, 1986—88, liaison officer office program planning and evaluation, 1979—80; assoc. dir. office extramural health programs Harvard Sch. Pub. Health, Boston, 1979—80; clin. fellow in psychiatry Harvard Med. Sch., Boston, 1980—83; vis. prof. dept. cmty. health Emory U. Sch. Medicine, Atlanta, 1984—91, clin. asst. prof. psychiatry, 1985—87, clin. assoc. prof., 1988—93; adj. prof. Emory U. Sch. Pub. Health, Atlanta, 1991—; clin. prof. dept. cmty. health and preventive medicine Morehouse Sch. Medicine, Atlanta, 1993—; staff physician Women's Med. Clinic, Atlanta, 1974—76, Harvard St. Neighborhood Health Ctr., Boston, 1976—77, Winchester (Mass.) Hosp., 1978—83; emergency rm. physician Burbank Hosp., Fitchburg, Mass., 1976—77, Harrington Hosp., Southbridge, Mass., 1976—77; vis. physician dept. psychiatry Grady Meml. Hosp., Atlanta, 1985—; lectr. and cons. in field. Author: Patients: The Experience of Illness, 1980, Violence in America: A Public Health Approach, 1990; mem. editl. bd. Violence and Victims, 1985—88, Violence, Aggression and Terrorism, 1986—; contbr. articles to profl. jours. Active Calif. Wellness Found., 1993—; bd. dirs. southeastern divsn., sci. adv. coun. Am. Suicide Found., 1990—. Recipient Coulter Lecture award, Am. ongress Rehab. Medicine, 1991, William S. one award, Am. Trauma Soc., 1991, Outstanding Achievement award, 1994, World Health Day award, Am. Assn. for World Health, 1993, Disting. Svc. award, Ga. Assn. Family and Marital Therapists, 1994, Disting. Achievement award, Disability Wellness Assn., 1998, Outstanding Svc. medal, USPHS, 2000, Meritorious Svc. medal, 2000, DSM, 2000; fellow, Mass. Gen. Hosp., 1977—78, Mead-Johnson, 1982; scholar, John Harvard, 1964. Mem.: Alpha Omega Alpha, Inst. of Medicine of NAS, Phi Beta Kappa. Avocation: photography. Home: 972 Oakdale Rd NE Atlanta GA 30307-1272 Office: 750 Commerce Dr Ste 400 Decatur GA 30030

ROSENBERG, MARK LOUIS, lawyer; b. Lexington, Ky., Sept. 21, 1947; s. Edward George and Shirley Lee (Berkin) R.; m. Betty Adler, May 16, 1982; stepchildren: Aaron, Sarah Claxton; children: Eli, Daniel. BA, U. Mich., 1969; JD, harvard U., 1973; LLM in Taxation, Georgetown U., 1985. Bar: D.C. 1973, Md. 1991, U.S. Dist. Ct. D.C. 1973, U.S. Ct. Appeals (D.C. cir.) 1973. Asst. to v.p. George Washington U., 1973-75; counsel U.S. Ho. of Reps., Washington, 1975-77; sr. atty. FTC, Washington, 1977-85; ptnr. Gordon, Feinblatt et al, Washington, 1989-91; prin. Law Offices of Mark L. Rosenberg, 1991—; of counsel The Jacobovitz Law Firm, 1994-97, Spirer & Goldberg, PC, Bethesda, Md. Mem. Fed. Bar Assn. (dep. sect. coord., Disting. Svc. award 1982, 83, 87). Democrat. Jewish. Home: 6101 Shady Oak Ln Bethesda MD 20817-6027 Office: Spirer & Goldberg PC 7101 Wisconsin Ave Ste 1201 Bethesda MD 20814 Office Phone: 301-913-0077. Personal E-mail: marklro@aol.com.

ROSENBERG, MATTHEW WILLIAM, plastic surgeon; b. Chgo. s. Thomas Louis and Florence Gilberg Rosenberg; m. Amy Katherine Matthews; children: Sedona Felicia, Summit Arthur. MD, U. Ill., Chgo., 1984. Diplomate Am. Bd. Plastic Surgery, 1995. Med. dir. So. Nev. Cleft Palate and Craniofacial Team, Las Vegas, Nev., 1992—2001; physician and cleft and craniofacial team dir. The Wichita (Kans.) Clinic, 2001—03; clin. assoc. prof. Ohio State U. Med. Ctr., Columbus, 2004; with Wichita Clin. PA, Wichita, Kans. Pres. Las Vegas Inst. Plastic Surgery, 1992—2001. Office: Wichita Clin PA 3311 E Murdock St Wichita KS 67208-3079 Office Phone: 614-293-9885. *

ROSENBERG, MICHAEL, lawyer; b. NYC, Oct. 13, 1937; s. Walter and Eva (Bernstein) Rosenberg; m. Jacqueline Raymonde Combe, Apr. 29, 1966; children: Andrew James, Suzanne Jennifer. AB in Econs. with honors, Ind. U., 1959; LLB, Columbia U., 1962. Bar: NY 1963, US Ct Appeals (2d cir) 1975, US Dist Ct (ea dist so div) Mich 1989. From. dep. asst. atty. gen. to asst. atty. gen. N.Y. State Dept. Law, NYC, 1963-66; assoc. Hellerstein, Rosier & Rembar, NYC, 1966-73; assoc. gen. counsel Gen. Instrument Corp., NYC, 1973-78; from assoc. gen. counsel to dep. gen. counsel U.S. Filter Corp., NYC, 1978-82; v.p., gen. counsel, sec. Alfa-Laval Inc., Ft. Lee, NJ, 1982-88; counsel Becker Ross Stone De Stefano & Klein, NYC, 1988-89; ptnr. Rosenberg & Rich, White Plains, NY, 1989-95, Quinn, Marantis & Rosenberg, LLP, White Plains, NY, 1995-97, Marantis, Rosenberg & van Nes, LLP, 1997-2001; atty. Law Offices of Michael Rosenberg, Armonk, 2001—. Mem Zoning Bd. Appeals Town of North Castle, NY, 1995—2006. Mem.: ABA, Westchester County Bar Assn., NY State Bar Assn. Office: Law Offices of Michael Rosenberg 3 Spruce Hollow Armonk NY 10504

ROSENBERG, NORMAN JACK, agricultural meteorologist, educator; b. Bklyn., Feb. 22, 1930; s. Jacob and Rae (Dombrowitz) R.; m. Sarah Zacher, Dec. 30, 1950; children: Daniel Jonathon, Alyssa Yael. BS, Mich. State U., East Lansing, 1951; MS, Okla. State U., 1958; PhD, Rutgers U., 1961. Soil scientist Israel Soil Conservation Service, Haifa, 1953-55, Israel Water Authority, Haifa, 1955-57; asst. prof. agrl. meteorology U. Nebr., Lincoln, 1961-64, assoc. prof., 1964-67, prof. agrl. meteorology, 1967—, prof. agrl. engring., 1975—, prof. agronomy, 1976—, George Holmes prof. agrl. meteorology, 1981-87, prof. emeritus, 1987—, leader sect. agrl. meteorology, 1975-79, acting asst. vice chancellor for rsch., 1983-85; sr. fellow, dir. climate resources program Resources for the Future, Washington, 1987-92; chief scientist integrated earth studies energy sci. divsn. Battelle Pacific N.W. Nat. Lab., Washington, 1992—2003, lab. fellow emeritus, 2003—; scientist Joint Global Change Rsch. Inst., Pacific N.W. Nat. Lab. and U. Md., 2001—; affiliate mem. Washington Adv. Group, 2003—. Cons. Dept. State AID, NOAA Oak Ridge Assoc. Univs., 1986—87; cons. Elec. Power Rsch. Inst., 1989—92, Sandia Nat. Labs., 1990; mem. numerous ad hoc coms. and mem. standing com. on atmospheric sci. NAS/NRC, 1975—78, mem. bd. atmospheric sci. and climate, 1982—85; mem. US com. Internat. Geosphere-Biosphere Program, 1984—86; mem. panel on policy implications of climate change, 1990—91; mem. bd. coun. Agrl. Sci. and Tech.; vis. prof. agrl. meteorology Israel Inst. Tech., Haifa, 1968; trustee Nat. Inst. Global Environ. Change, 1992, vice-chmn., 1992—95, chmn., 1996—2000; adj. prof. dept. geography U. Md., College Park, adj. prof. Sch. Natural Resources Sci., 2003; bd. dirs. Ctr. for Rsch. on the Changing Earth Sys., Columbia, Md., 2002. Author: Microclimate: The Biological Environment, 1974, 2d edit., 1983, Chinese transl., 1983, Malay transl., 1987, A Biomass Future for the North American Great Plains, 2007; editor: North American Droughts, 1978, Drought in the Great Plains: Research on Impacts and Strategies, 1980, Greenhouse Warming: Abatement and Adaptation, 1989, Toward an Integrated Impact Assessment of Climate Change: The MINK Study, 1993, Carbon Sequestration in Soils: New Science, Monitoring and Beyond, 1999; editor: (with V.C. Cole and K. Paustian) Mitigation of Greenhouse Gas Emissions by the Agricultural Sector, Spl. issue of Climate Change, 1998; editor: (with R.C. Izaurralde) Storing Carbon in Agricultural Soils: A multipurpose environmental strategy, Spl. issue of Climatic Change, 2001; editor: (with J.A. Edmonds) Climate Change Impacts for the Conterminous USA: An Integrated Assessment, 2005; tech. editor: Agronomy Jour., 1974—79, cons. editor: Agrl. and Forest Meteorology, Climatic Change; contbr. articles to profl. jours. Mem. Intergovernmental Panel on Climate Change, 1993—. Recipient Centennial medal Nat. Weather Svc., 1970; sr. fellow in sci., NATO, 1968, rsch. fellow U. Nebr., 1968, Lady Davis fellow Hebrew U., Jerusalem, 1977, nat. resources fellow Resources for Future, 1986; grantee State of Nebr., 1970-73, NSF, 1971-87, 96, US Dept. Commerce, 1972-74, 80-82, 83-85, 88-89, NASA, 1972-73, 85-86, US Dept. Interior, 1974-75, 77-79, 88—, USDA, 1979-82, 88-89, U. Nebr. Found., 1982, Nat. Ctr. Atmospheric Rsch., 1984-85, US Dept. Energy, 1989-92, G. Gunnar Vetleson Found., 1987-92, UN Environ. Program, 1989, EPA, 1988-89, 98, NASA, 1995-97, 98, NOAA, 1996, 2005-. Fellow AAAS (com. climate 1984-89, com. global change 1992-96, adv. panel Earth Explorer ency. 1992-95), Am. Soc. Agronomy, Am. Meteorol. Soc. (Outstanding Achievement in Bioclimatology award 1978, councillor 1981-84), Am. Water Resources Assn. (Boggess award, 2004); mem. Am. Assn. State Climatologists (Nebr. rep. 1979-81), Arid Zone Soc. India, Sigma Xi, Alpha Zeta, Gamma Sigma Rho. Clubs: Cosmos (Washington). Jewish. Office: Joint Global Change Rsch Inst 8400 Baltimore Ave College Park MD 20740-2496 Office Phone: 301-314-6753. Business E-Mail: nj.rosenberg@pnl.gov.

ROSENBERG, PAMELA, opera director, conductor; b. LA, 1945; m. Wolf Rosenberg (dec. 1996); 2 children. Diploma, London Opera Ctr.; B, U. Calif. at Berkely, 1966; M in Russian hist., Ohio State U. Various positions Frankfurt Opera, 1974—87; dir. of ops. Deutscher Schauspielhaus, Hamburg, Germany, 1987—88; mgr., artistic affairs Netherlands Opera, 1988—90; co-gen. dir. Stuggart Opera, 1990—2000; gen. dir. San Francisco Opera, 2001—06, exec. adv., 2006. Office: San Francisco Opera 301 VanNess Ave San Francisco CA 94102

ROSENBERG, PAUL I., lawyer; b. Newark, Feb. 26, 1937; BS in Econs., U. Pa. Wharton Sch., 1959; MBA, NYU, 1964, JD, 1970, LLM, 1975. Bar: NJ 1970, US Dist. Ct. NJ 1970, NY 1982, US Dist. Ct. (3rd dist.) NY 1982, US Tax Ct. 1983, US Supreme Ct. Ptnr. Fox and Fox LLP, Livingston, 1974—2006, Bressler, Amery & Ross, PC, 2006—. Mem. Essex Co. Probate Early Settlement panel. Fellow Am. Coll. Trust and Estate Counsel (nat. employee benefits in estate-planning, estate and gift tax com.); mem.

ABA, Essex County Bar Assn., NJ State Bar Assn. Home: One Belgrade Terr West Orange NJ 07052 Office: Bressler Amery & Ross 325 Columbia Tpke Florham Park NJ 07932 Office Phone: 973-514-1200. Business E-Mail: prosenberg@bressler.com.

ROSENBERG, PETER N., lawyer; b. Aug. 29, 1958; BA, Dartmouth Coll., 1980; JD, Boston Univ., 1984. Bar: Mass. 1985. Assoc. to ptnr. Ropes & Gray, Boston, 1984—, head employee benefits practice group. Editor: Boston Univ. Law Rev. Office: Ropes & Gray 1 International Pl Boston MA 02110-2624 Office Phone: 617-951-7273. Office Fax: 617-951-7050. Business E-Mail: peter.rosenberg@ropesgray.com.

ROSENBERG, RAND L., utilities executive; B, Whitman Coll., Walla Walla, Wash.; MBA, U. Chgo. Engagement mgr. Marakon Assocs.; head corp. devel. Pacific Telesis Group; ptnr., founder media and telecom. group Montgomery Securities; sr. positions Goldman Sachs & Co.; mng. dir., head global telecom. investment banking Salomon Bros.; exec. v.p., CFO Infospace; sr. v.p. corp. strategy and devel. PG&E Corp., San Francisco. Office: PG&E Corp One Market Spear Tower Ste 2400 San Francisco CA 94105-1126 Office Phone: 415-267-7070. Office Fax: 415-267-7268. *

ROSENBERG, RAYMOND DAVID, special education educator, consultant; b. Jersey City, Apr. 25, 1951; s. Fabulous Sam and Arlene (White) R.; m. JoAnn Gabriella Simchera, June 10, 1984; 1 child, Anna Teresa. BA, Boston U., 1974; MEd in Spl. Edn., William Paterson Coll., 1978, MEd in Ednl. Adminstrn. and Supervision, 1994. Cert. tchr., N.J.; profl. recognized spl. educator in ednl. diagnosis, PRSE, 2005. Tchr. reading Passaic County Tech. Vocat. High Sch., Wayne, NJ, 1980-82; specialist learning disabilities North Jersey Devel. Ctr., Totowa, 1983-84; ednl. specialist Div. Devel. Disabilities, Totowa, NJ, 1984-85, North Jersey Devel. Ctr., Totowa, NJ, 1986—93; learning disabilities tchr., cons. Office of Edn., NJ, 1993-96; learning cons. child study team North Bergen HS, NJ, 1996-98; learning disabilities tchr., cons., 1997—2002; mem. child study team West NY Early Childhood Sch., 2002—03; staff Office of the Child Study Team, Garfield, NJ, 2003—05; learning disabilities tchr. cons., supr. child study team Morris Plains Elem. Sch. Dist., 2005—06; mem. bd. edn. child study team, learning disabilities tchr., cons. Bryant Hawthorne Elem. Schs., 2006—; learning disabilities tchr. cons., mem. child study team Teaneck, 2006—. Pres. Ednl. Assessment Svcs., Inc. With ABA discrete trial learning with PDD autistic students, 2002—. Mem. Nat. Eagle Scout Assn., Pi Lambda Theta (Beta Chi chpt.). Episcopal. Lodge: Order of Arrow. Office Phone: 201-862-2338, 201-833-5547 ext. 3. Personal E-mail: cstadvocate@nj.rr.com. Business E-Mail: rrosenberg@teaneckschools.org.

ROSENBERG, RICHARD F., physician, radiologist; b. NYC, June 13, 1942; s. Henry J. and Sylvia (Harris) R.; m. Judith Wolf, May 5, 1985; 1 child, Glen. BA, Colgate U., 1964; MD, N.Y. Med. Coll., 1968. Diplomate Am. Bd. Radiology. Intern Met. Hosp., NYC, 1968-69; resident Montefiore Hosp. and Med. Ctr., Bronx, NY, 1969-70, 72-74, chief resident, 1974; radiologist Lipsay & Rosenberg, Great Neck, NY, 1974-78; dir. gastrointestinal radiology North Shore U. Hosp., Manhasset, NY, 1978-82; radiologist, owner Great Neck Radiologists, 1982—. Mem. adv. bd. Bank of Great Neck, 1990-94. Contbr. articles to profl. jours. Lt. comdr. USN, 1970-72. Fellow Am. Coll. Gastroenterology; mem. Am. Coll. Radiology, Alpha Omega Alpha. Republican. Office: Great Neck Radiologists 935 Northern Blvd Great Neck NY 11021-5309 Office Phone: 516-829-4414.

ROSENBERG, ROBERT BRINKMANN, information technology executive; b. Chgo., Mar. 19, 1937; s. Sidney and Gertrude (Brinkmann) Rosenberg; m. Patricia Margaret Kane, Aug. 1, 1959 (dec. Feb. 1988); children: John Richard, Debra Ann; m. Maryann Bartoli Manrot, June 25, 1989. BSChemE with distinction, Ill. Inst. Tech., 1958, MS in Gas Tech, 1961, PhD in Gas Tech, 1964. Registered profl. engr., Ill. Adj. asst. prof. Ill. Inst. Tech., 1965-69; mem. staff Inst. Gas Tech., Chgo., 1962-77, v.p. engring. rsch., 1973-77; v.p. R & D Gas Rsch. Inst., Chgo., 1977-78, exec. v.p., sr. v.p., 1978-84, v.p., 1984-96; pres. RBR Vision, Burr Ridge, Ill., 1996—; bd. dirs. IEA Internat. Ctr. Gas Tech. Info. Tech. program dir. World Energy Congress, 1996—98. Pres. Triangle Frat. Edn. Found., 1974—96, bd. dirs., 1996—2001, dir. emeritus; bd. dirs. Hinsdale Arts Coun., 1977—85, dir. emeritus, 1985—95; mem. adv. coun. U. Tex. Coll. Natural Scis. Found., 1990—95; mem. giving com. Morton Arboretum, 2004—; mem. Hinsdale Home Rule Ad Hoc Com., Ill., 1975—77; mem. vis. com. dept. chemistry U. Tex.; bd. advisors Chgo. 502, 2004—07; pres. Lake Ridge Club Homeowners Assn., 2001—. Recipient Gas Industry Rsch. award, 1985, Energy Exec. of the Yr. award, 1987, Profl. Achievement award, Ill. Inst. Tech. Alumni Assn., 1991. Mem.: AIChE, Triangle (Svc. Key and Outstanding Alumnus award 1987), Air Pollution Control Assn. (past sect. com. residential pollution sources), Gas Appliance Engrs. Soc. (past trustee), Internat. Gas Union, Atlantic Gas Rsch. Exch., Combustion Inst. (past treas. bd. dirs. ctrl. states sect.), Inst. Gas Engrs., Am. Gas Assn. (oper. sect. award of merit 1989). Achievements include patents for 13 patents in field. Avocations: cooking, gardening, travel. Home: 28 Lake Ridge Club Dr Burr Ridge IL 60527-7937 Office: RBR @ Vision 28 Lake Ridge Club Dr Burr Ridge IL 60527-7937 Office Phone: 630-654-3213. Personal E-mail: RBR3@comcast.net.

ROSENBERG, ROBERT CHARLES, housing corporation executive; b. Bronx, NY, Oct. 21, 1934; s. Bernard L. and Flora (Popiel) R.; m. Diane Stricof, Jan. 29, 1962 (dec.); children: Andrew, Scott; m. Frances Kaufman, Sept. 11, 1976; stepchildren: Michael Kaufman, Benjamin Kaufman. BS, NYU, 1955, JD (hon.), 1995; LLB, Columbia U., 1958. Bar: N.Y. 1959. Adminstrv. asst. N.Y. State Dept. Law, NYC, 1957-58; assoc. firm Barron Rice & Rochmore, NYC, 1959-62, Carro Spanbock & Londin, NYC, 1962-68; 1st dep. commr. for devel. dept. N.Y.C. Housing and Devel. Adminstrn., 1968-73; 1st sr. v.p., dir. Starrett Corp., NYC, 1973-97; gen. mgr. Starrett City; pres., chmn. bd. Grenadier Realty Corp., 1976-97; pres. Rosenberg Housing Group, 1997—. Lectr. Practicing Law Inst., Real Estate Bd. N.Y.C., Harvard U. Kennedy Sch. of Govt., Beijing Inst. of Design, U. Nancy (France), Columbia U., NYU, others; fed. receiver Chester (Pa.) Housing Authority, 1994—; adj. prof. dept. urban affairs Hunter Coll., N.Y.C., 1998—. Author N.Y. acts for residential constrn., rent. Candidate for N.Y. State Assembly, 1958, 65; sec. N.Y. State Assn. Young Rep. Clubs, 1959-61; bd. dirs., chmn. emeritus Bklyn. Philharm.; bd. dirs. Bklyn. Acad. Music, 1978-99; v.p. Citizens Housing and Planning Coun.; dir. Nat. Housing Conf. Served with USAF, 1958. Mem. ABA, N.Y. State Bar Assn., N.Y. County Lawyers Assn., Nat. Assn. Housing and Renewal Ofcls., Urban Land Inst., N.Y.C. Assn. Builders and Owners (v.p.). Home: 201 E 79th St New York NY 10021-0830 Office: 419 Park Ave S New York NY 10016-8410 E-mail: bob@rhgcommunities.com.

ROSENBERG, ROBERT D., radiologist, researcher; s. Martin and Miriam Rosenberg; m. Jane Wishner; children: Zachary, Leah. MD, Washington U., St. Louis, 1979. Asst. prof. radiology U. Wis., Madison, 1984—86; prof. radiology U. N.Mex HSC, Albuquerque, 1986—. Fellow: Soc. Breast Imaging (life Fellowship 2003), Am. Coll. Radiology (life Fellowship 1999). Democrat. Jewish. Office: University of New Mexico HSC MSC10 5530 1 University of New Mexico Albuquerque NM 87131 Home Phone: 505-856-6719; Office Phone: 505-272-0011. Office Fax: 505-272-5821.

ROSENBERG, ROBERT JAY, lawyer; b. Providence, Jan. 7, 1947; s. Elias B. and Ida (Weinberg) R.; m. Pamela Conrad, 1990; 1 child, Lauren. BA, Columbia U., 1967; JD, Harvard U., 1970. Bar: N.Y. 1971, U.S. Dist. Ct. (so. and ea. dists.) N.Y. 1972, U.S. Ct. Appeals (2d cir.) 1973, U.S. Supreme Ct. 1973. Assoc. Weil, Gotshal & Manges, NYC, 1970-73; asst. prof. Ohio State U. Coll. Law, Columbus, 1973-75; from assoc. to ptnr. Cole & Deitz, NYC, 1975-80; ptnr. Moses & Singer, NYC, 1980-85, Latham & Watkins, NYC, 1985—. Adj. prof. Rutgers U. Law Sch., Newark, 1975-77, NYU Law Sch., 1977-86. Author: (with others) Collier Lending Institutions and the Bankruptcy Code, 1986, Collier Bankruptcy Practice Guide, 1988; contbr. articles to profl. jours. Pres. New Grp. Recipient Outstanding Bankruptcy Lawyers, Turnaround and Workouts, 2001, 2005, Top 10 leading Practitioners, Global Counsel, World's 20 leading Insolvency lawyers, Euromoney's. Fellow Am. Coll. Bankruptcy; mem. ABA (chmn. com. on uniform fraudulent transfer act) 1983-86, Assn. Bar NYC (bankruptcy com.), Am. Bankruptcy Inst. (bd. dirs. 1985-89), Turnaround Mgmt. Assn., Internat. Insolvency Inst., Century Assn. Office: Latham & Watkins 885 3rd Ave Fl 9 New York NY 10022-4834 Office Phone: 212-906-1370. Office Fax: 212-751-4864. Business E-Mail: robert.rosenberg@lw.com.

ROSENBERG, ROGER NEWMAN, neurologist, educator, department chair; b. Milw., Mar. 3, 1939; s. Sol J. and Cora D. (Newman) R.; m. Adrienne Turick, June 24, 1962; children— Jennifer, Lara Student, Tufts U., 1957-60; BS, Northwestern U., 1961, MD with distinction, 1964. Diplomate Am. Bd. Psychiatry and Neurology. Intern Harvard Med. Service, Beth Israel Hosp., Boston, 1964-65; resident in neurology Neurol. Inst., Columbia U., NYC, 1965-67, instr. neurology, 1967-68; research assoc. Lab. of Biochem. Genetics, NIH, Bethesda, Md., 1968-70; clin. instr. Howard U. Med. Sch., Washington, 1969-70; asst. prof. neuroscis. Sch. Medicine, U. Calif.-San Diego, 1970-71; assoc. prof. neuroscis. and pediatrics, attending neurologist Univ. Hosp., U. Calif.-La Jolla, 1971-74; prof., chmn. dept. neurology U. Tex. Southwestern Med. Ctr., Dallas, 1973-91, prof. physiology, 1976—, Zale Disting. chair, prof. neurology, 1990—, dir. Alzheimer's Disease Rsch. Ctr., 1989—. Attending neurologist Parkland Meml. Hosp. and Children's Med. Ctr., Dallas, 1974—, Zale Lipshy Univ. Hosp., 1990—; mem. staff Presbyn. Hosp., Dallas, 1974—, St. Paul's Hosp., Dallas, 1974—; cons. staff VA Hosp., Dallas, 1974—; mem. nat. med. adv. bd. Nat. Ataxia Found., Mpls., 1971—, Myasthenia Gravis Found., 1973; chmn. med. adv. bd., dir. med. sci. research Internat. Joseph Diseases Found., Livermore, Calif., 1977—; lectr. Japanese Soc. Neurology, 1987, 94, Chinese Neurol. Soc., 1987, Spanish Neurol. Soc., 1992; chmn. bd. sci. councilors NINDS/NIH, 1984-86; pres. (hon.), Intl. French Soc. of Neurology Charcot Centenary Symposium, 1993. Editor Jour. Neurogenetics; mem. editl. bd. Neurology, 1977-82, 91-97, Trends in Neurosci., 1980-86, Current Opinion in Neurology & Neurosurgery, 1990—, Jour. of AMA, 1997—; chief editor Archives of Neurology, 1997—; contbr. articles to profl. jours. Bd. dirs. Winston Sch., Dallas, 1974-80; trustee World Fedn. Neurology, 2005. 1st Woody Guthrie scholar, 1971; USPHS grantee; recipient Disting. Alumnus award Neurol. Inst., N.Y., 1994, Nancy R. McCune Alzheimer's Rsch. award Alzheimer's Ass., 2005, Lifetime Achievement award Tex. Neurol. Soc., 2005. Fellow AAAS; mem. Am. Neurol. Assn. (hon.), Am. Acad. Neurology (chmn. sci. program com. nat. meetings 1979-84, elected councillor exec. bd. 1984-89, pres. 1991-93), Am. Neurochem. Soc., Tissue Culture Soc., Soc. Neurosci., Am. Fedn. Clin. Rsch., Soc. Pediat. Rsch., Internat. Child Neurology Assn., Am. Neurol. Assn. (hon., 1st v.p. 1987), Ctrl. Soc. Neurol. Rsch., Can. Congress Neurol. Scis. (hon.), Spanish Neurol. Soc. (hon.), Sigma Xi, Alpha Omega Alpha (Merit award Northwestern U. Alumni Assn. 1986). Home: 4425 Wildwood Rd Dallas TX 75209-2801 Office: U Tex Southwestern Med Ctr Dallas TX 75235 Business E-Mail: rogerrosenberg@utsouthwestern.edu.

ROSENBERG, RUDY, chemical company executive; b. Feb. 26, 1930; came to U.S., 1949, naturalized, 1954; s. Hilaire and Frieda Rosenberg; m. Rose H. Wauters, Nov. 7, 1953; 1 child, Rudy. Student in classical studies, Atheneum Leon Lepage, Brussels, 1946. Buyer Lever Bros., Brussels, 1946-49; head biochem. divsn. Mann Rsch. Labs., NYC, 1954-61, Gallard-Schlesinger, Carle Place, NY, 1961-75; pres. Accurate Chem. & Sci. Corp., Westbury, NY, 1975—. Prin., v.p., Leeches U.S.A. Ltd. Served with U.S. Army, 1951-53. Mem. Reticuloendothelial Soc. Internat. Clubs: Antique Automobile, Rolls Royce, Puppetry Guild Greater N.Y. Democrat.

ROSENBERG, SAMUEL NATHAN, French and Italian language educator; b. NYC, Jan. 19, 1936; s. Israel and Etta (Friedland) R. AB, Columbia U., 1957; PhD, Johns Hopkins U., 1965. Instr. Columbia U., NYC, 1960-61; lectr. Ind. U., Bloomington, Ind., 1962-65, asst. prof., 1965-69, assoc. prof., 1969-81, prof. dept. French and Italian, 1981-99, prof. emeritus, 2000—. Chmn. dept. French and Italian Ind. U., Bloomington, 1977—84; editor ENCOMIA jour. of internat. Courtly Lit. Soc., 2005—. Author: Modern French CE, 1970, (with others) Harper's Grammar of French, 1983, (with W. Apel) French Secular Compositions of the 14th Century, 3 vols., 1970-72, (with H. Tischler) Chanter m'estuet: Songs of the Trouveres, 1981; translator: (with S. Danon) Ami and Amile, 1981, rev. edit., 1996, Lyrics and Melodies of Gace Brulé, 1985; (with H. Tischler) The Monophonic Songs in the Roman de Fauvel, 1991, Lancelot-Grail Cycle, vol. 2, 1993, Chansons des trouvères, 1995, Songs of the Troubadours and Trouvères, 1997; (with others) Early French Tristan Poems, 2 vols., 1998; (with C. Callahan) Les Chansons de Colin Muset, 2005, (with E. Doss-Quinby) The Old French Ballette, 2006; (with Patricia Terry) Lancelot and the Lord of the Distant Isles, 2007. Pres. Mid-Am. Festival of the Arts, Inc., Bloomington, Ind., 1984-85. Woodrow Wilson Found. fellow, 1959-60; Fulbright fellow, 1960-61; Lilly Faculty fellow, 1986-87. Mem MLA, Am. Assn. Tchrs. French; mem. Medieval Acad. Am., Internat. Courtly Lit. Soc. (editor Encomia 2005—), Am. Lit. Translators Assn. (bd. dirs. 2002-06), Romance Philology Adv. Bd., Phi Beta Kappa. Home: PO Box 1164 Bloomington IN 47402-1164 Business E-Mail: srosenbe@indiana.edu.

ROSENBERG, SARAH ZACHER, retired cultural organization administrator; b. Kelem, Lithuania, Jan. 10, 1931; came to U.S., 1938; d. David Meir Zacher and Rachel Korbman; m. Norman J. Rosenberg, Dec. 30, 1950; children: Daniel, Alyssa. BA in History, U. Nebr., 1970, MA in Am. History, 1973. Rsch. historian U. Mid-Am., Lincoln, Nebr., 1974-78, program developer dept. humanities, 1978-79, asst. dir. div. acad. planning, 1980-81, dir. program devel., 1981-82; exec. dir. Nebr. Humanities Coun., Lincoln, 1982-87, Nebr. Found. for Humanities, Lincoln, 1984-87, Am. Inst. for Conservation Hist. and Artistic Works, Washington, 1987-97, exec. dir. found., 1991-97; program officer, spl. cons. mus. div. NEH, Washington, 1987, external reviewer, 1981, 89; pvt. practice Potomac, Md., 1997—2004; ret., 2004. Lay participant long-range planning conf. Nebr. Bar Assn., Hastings, 1986. Co-editor: The Great Plains Experience: Readings in the History of a Region, 1978; contbr. articles to profl. jours. Action mem. Hadassah, Lincoln, 1961—87, Tifereth Israel Synagogue, Lincoln, 1961—87, Beth El Congregation, Besthesda, Md., 1988—2001, Kol Shalom Congregation, 2001—; bd. dirs. Sta. KUCV, affiliate Nat. Pub. Radio, Lincoln, 1986—87, Lincoln Cmty. Playhouse, Lincoln, 1986—87. NEH grantee, 1981, 86, merit awards, 1983, 87; Humanities Resource Ctr. grantee, Peter Kiewit Found., 1984. Mem. Am. Hist. Assn., Western Hist. Assn., Alpha Theta. Democrat. Home: 8102 Appalachian Ter Potomac MD 20854-4050 Personal E-mail: srosenb435@aol.com.

ROSENBERG, SAUL ALLEN, oncologist, educator; b. Cleve., Aug. 2, 1927; BS, Western Res. U., 1948, MD, 1953. Diplomate Am. Bd. Internal Medicine, Am. Bd. Oncology. Intern Univ. Hosp., Cleve., 1953—54; resident in internal medicine Peter Bent Brigham Hosp., Boston, 1954—61; research asst. toxicology AEC Med. Research Project, Western Res. U., 1948—53; asst. prof. medicine and radiology Stanford (Calif.) U., 1961—65, assoc. prof., 1965—79, chief divsn. oncology, 1965—93, prof., 1970—95; prof. emeritus, 1995—; Am. Cancer Soc. prof. Stanford (Calif.) U., 1983—89, assoc. dean, 1989—92. Chmn. bd. No. Calif. Cancer Program, 1974—80. Contbr. articles to profl. jours. Served to lt. M.C. USNR, 1954—56. Master: ACP; fellow: Am. Coll. Radiology (hon.); mem.: Western Assn. Physicians, Western Soc. Clin. Rsch., Radiation Rsch. Soc., Calif. Acad. Medicine, Assn. Am. Physicians, Am. Soc. Clin. Oncology (pres. 1982—83), Inst. Medicine NAS, Am. Assn. Cancer Rsch., Am. Soc. Therapeutic Radiotherapy Oncology (hon.). Office: Stanford U Sch Medicine Div Oncology 269 Campus Dr Stanford CA 94305

ROSENBERG, SEYMOUR, psychologist, educator; b. Newark, Sept. 7, 1926; s. Morris and Celia (Weiss) R.; children: Harold Stanley, Michael Seth. BS, The Citadel, 1948; MA, Ind. U., 1951, PhD, 1952. Rsch. psychologist USAF, San Antonio, 1952-58, U. Kans., Lawrence, 1958-59, Bell Tel. Labs., Murray Hill, NJ, 1959-65; vis. prof. psychology Columbia U., NYC, 1965-66; prof. psychology Rutgers U., New Brunswick, NJ, 1966—2000, chmn. dept. psychology, 1981-83, 94-95, prof. emeritus psychology, 2001—. Adj. prof. Rutgers U. Med. Sch., 1974—2000; vis. scholar U. Leuven, Belgium, 1983, Belgium, 92, Univ. de Provence, France, 1990; panel mem. NSF, 1970—72. Cons. editor Jours. Personality Social Psychology, 1968-69; assoc. editor, 1970-73; contbr. articles to profl. jours. With USN, 1945—46. Grantee, NSF, 1965—90, NIMH, 1966—68; Rsch. scientist grantee, 1968—73, Social Sci. Rsch. Coun. fellow, 1973—74. Fellow APA; mem. Soc. Exptl. Social Psychology, Psychometric Soc., Classification Soc., NY Acad. Sci., Ea. Psychol. Assn. Home: 689 Canal Rd Somerset NJ 08873-7327 Office: Rutgers U Dept Psychology ED Livingston Campus New Brunswick NJ 08903 Business E-Mail: srpsych@rci.rutgers.edu.

ROSENBERG, SHELI ZYSMAN, retired finance company executive; b. NYC, Feb. 2, 1942; d. Stephen B. and Charlotte (Laufer) Zysman; m. Burton X. Rosenberg, Aug. 30, 1964; children: Leonard, Marcy. BA, Tufts U., 1963; JD, Northwestern U., 1966. Bar: Ill. 1966. Ptnr. Schiff, Hardin & Waite, Chgo., 1973-80; exec. v.p., gen. counsel Equity Fin. Mgmt., Chgo., 1980-90, Equity Group Investments, Inc., Chgo., 1988-94, pres., CEO, 1994—99, Equity Group Investments, LLC, Chgo., 1999—2000, vice chmn., 2000—03; prin. Rosenberg & Liebentritt, P.C., Chgo., 1980—97. Adj. prof. Northwestern U., 2000—03, J.L. Kellogg Grad. Sch. Bus., 2003—; bd. dirs. CVS/Caremark Corp., Capital Trust, Cendant Corp., Manufactured Home Communities, Inc., Equity Residential Properties Trust, Equity Office Properties Trust, Ventas, Inc.; adv. bd. J.L. Kellogg Grad. Sch. Bus. N.W. Univ.; trustee Equity Residential, 1993—, lead trustee, 2002—. Trustee Rush Presbyn. St. Luke's Med. Ctr., exec. com.; co-founder, pres. Ctr. for Exec. Women, J.L. Kellogg Grad. Sch. Bus., 2001—.

ROSENBERG, STANLEY DAVID, psychologist, educator; b. NYC, Mar. 30, 1944; s. Milton I. and Miriam Rosenberg; m. Harriet Jane Rosenthal, June 5, 1966; children: Karen Beth Marks, Eric William. BS, cornell U., 1965; PhD, Yale U., 1968. Lic. psychologist NH, Vt. Assoc. prof. Dartmouth Med. Sch., Hanover, NH, 1975—81, prof. psychiatry, 1981—. Cons. in field. Author: The Cold Fire, 1976, Men at Midlife, 1981, The Mid-Life Transition, 1981; contbr. articles to profl. jours., chapters to books. Recipient Margaret Riggs award for Disting. Contbn., NH. Psychol. Orgn., 1992; grantee, Ittleson and van Amerigen Founds., 1972—74, 1985—88, NIH, 1983—88, Mellon Found., 1984, 1986—89, Rockefeller Ctr., 1989—90, NIMH, 1990—, UCLA, 1999—2000, Schering-Plough, 2001—04, Substance Abuse and Mental Health Svcs. Adminstrn., 2005—, Nat. Health Endowment for Health, 2006—07. Fellow: Soc. for Personality Assessment; mem.: Phi Kappa Phi. Home: 139 River Rd Lyme NH 03768 Office: DMS Dept Psychiatry 1 Medical Center Dr Lebanon NH 03756 Home Phone: 606-795-4002; Office Phone: 603-653-0740. Personal E-mail: stan.rosenberg@dartmouth.edu.

ROSENBERG, STEVEN JOEL, urologist; b. LA, Aug. 14, 1957; s. Harlan Kenneth and Audrey Krantz Rosenberg; m. Tracy Ann Fridley, Oct. 2, 1999; children: Robert Casey Lister, Chelsea Ann Lister, Andrew Samuel. BA, U. Iowa, Iowa City, 1979, MD, 1982. Cert. Am. Bd. Urology. Intern U. Iowa Hosps., 1982—83, resident, 1983—87; urologist Iowa Clinic, PC, Des Moines, 1987—. Fellow: ACS; mem.: AMA, Am. Urol. Assn. Office: Iowa Clinic PC 1215 Pleasant St Ste 520 Des Moines IA 50309 Home Phone: 515-279-7050; Office Phone: 515-244-8000.

ROSENBERG, THEODORE ROY, finance company executive; b. Nyack, NY, Aug. 6, 1933; s. Rebecca Sheer Rosenberg; m. Eleanor Schmalsteig, Feb. 19, 1956 (div.); children: Bradley Scott, Martha Ann; m. Mary Frances McVay, Sept. 21, 1991. BS, U. Conn., 1955; MBA, U. Pa., 1964. Commd. 2nd lt. U.S. Army, 1955, advanced through grades to col., 1976, retired, 1982; portfolio mgr. Burney Co., Falls Church, Va., 1979—, v.p. mktg., 1982-94, v.p., 1994-95, pres., 1995—2003, CEO, 2003—. Bd. dirs. Army Transp. Mus., U. Conn. Found., 1995—2001; supr. bd. dirs. Bay Creek Cmty. Dist. Decorated Legion of Merit, Bronze Star, Vietnam medal of Honor Govt. of Vietnam; named to Alumni Hall of Fame, U. Conn. Sch. Bus. Adminstrn., 1994. Mem.: U. Pa. Mid-Atlantic Regional Adv. Bd., Bonita Spring Men's Club (pres. 2006—), Wharton Club Washington (Man of the Yr. 1995). Avocations: scuba diving, snorkeling, golf. Office: The Burney Co 121 Rowell Ct Falls Church VA 22046-3114 Home Phone: 703-798-6269; Office Phone: 703-531-0400. E-mail: ted@burney.com.

ROSENBERG, THOMAS D., orthopedic surgeon; b. Ogden, Utah, Oct. 31, 1946; s. Mont and Winnie R.; former marriage: Christine Lake; children: Amie, Meggan, Andrew; m. Kelene Clark, May 1993; 1 child, Chandler McKenzie. Undergrad. degree, Weber State Coll., 1968; MD, U. Utah Med. Sch., 1973. Diplomate Am. Bd. Orthopedic Surgeons, 1979. Fellow U. Wis., Madison, 1977-78; attending The Orthopedic Specialty Hosp., Salt Lake City, 1991—, Park City (Utah) Knee & Orthopedic Clin., Salt Lake City, 1991—; asst. clin. prof. orthop. Univ. Utah Sch. Medicine, Salt Lake City; ptnr. Rosenberg, Cooley, Metcalf Clin., Park City, Utah. Med. cons., Nutriex, Salt Lake City, dir., Pro-Health Lab, Park City, physician, US Ski Team, US Speed Skating Team, US Snowboarding Team. Mem. Am. Acad. Orthop. Surg., Am. Orthop. Soc. Sports Medicine, Arthroscopic Assn. N. Am., European Soc. Knee Surgery & Arthroscopy, Herodicus Soc., Internat. Arthroscopy Assn., Internat. Soc. of Knee. Office: Ortho Specialty Clinic 5848 S 300 E Salt Lake City UT 84107-6121 also: Rosenberg Cooley Metcalf Clin Prospector Square 1820 Sidewinder Dr Ste 100 Park City UT 84060 Office Phone: 435-655-6600. *

ROSENBERG, TINA, reporter; b. Bklyn., 1958; BS, Northwestern U., 1981, MS, 1982. Fgn. policy editl. writer The New York Times, freelance writer New York Times mag., 1983-96, fgn. policy editl. writer, 1996—, mem. editl. bd.; adj. prof. internat. rels. Columbia U., NYC. Vis. fellow Nat. Security Archive; former sr. fellow World Policy Inst., New Sch. U. Author: Children of Cain: Violence and the Violent in Latin America, The Haunted Land: Facing Europe's Ghosts After Communism (Pulitzer prize for general nonfiction, Nat. Book award, 1996); contbr. articles to publs. Recipient MacArthur Fellowship "genius" award. Office: NY Times Editl Bd 229 W 43rd St New York NY 10036

ROSENBERG, WILLIAM MARK, chef, restaurant owner; b. North Miami, Fla., Sept. 30, 1967; s. Herman and Norma Rosenberg; m. Gina Marie Faranda, Oct. 2, 1994; children: Hannah Mae, Joseph Samson, Joshua Elijah. A in Culinary Arts, Culinary Inst. Am., Hyde Park, NY, 1991. Exec. chef Dome Restaurant, Greenwich, Conn., 1999—2001; owner, exec. chef F.i.s.h. Restaurant, Port Chester, NY, 2001—. With USAF, 1986—88. Home: 21 Irenhyl Ave Port Chester NY 10573 Office:

Fish Restaurant 102 Fox Island Rd Port Chester NY 10573 Home Phone: 914-939-7522; Office Phone: 914-939-4227. Office Fax: 914-939-1594. Personal E-mail: wrosen7922@aol.com. Business E-Mail: fishies2@optonline.net.

ROSENBERGER, BRYAN DAVID, lawyer; b. Johnstown, Pa., Oct. 8, 1950; s. Clarence Haines and Ida Rae (Neiderheiser) Rosenberger; m. Barbara Leah Byer, July 4, 1977; children: Laura Michelle, Lisa Renee. BS, Juniata Coll., 1971; JD, Coll. of William and Mary, 1974. Bar: Pa 1974. Assoc. Eckert Seamans Cherin & Mellott, Pitts., 1974-82, ptnr., 1983—, chmn. corp. and bus. dept., 1992-98, mem. exec. com., 1994-98, also bd. dirs., chmn. bus. div., 2001—04. Active new leadership bd Pitts. Symphony Soc, 1990—98. Mem.: Allegheny County Bar Assn. Home: 1358 Oakledge Ct Upper Saint Clair PA 15241-3540 Office: Eckert Seamans Cherin & Mellott 600 Grant St Ste 4400 Pittsburgh PA 15219-2702 Home Phone: 412-221-1529; Office Phone: 412-566-6123. Business E-Mail: brosenberger@eckertseamans.com.

ROSENBERGER, MARGARET ADALINE, retired elementary school educator, writer; b. Micanopy, Fla., Oct. 30; d. Eugene David and Lillian Adeline (Bauknight) Rosenberger. Student, Stetson U., 1946—48; BA in Edn., U. Fla., 1949, MEd, 1952. Drama sec. Nat. Youth Adminstrn., Gainesville, Fla., 1939—40; civil svc. clk. U.S. Army, Camp Blanding, Fla., 1940—46; tchr. J.J. Finley, Gainesville, 1949—52; prin., tchr. Micanopy Jr. H.S., 1952—55; gen. supr. Alachua County Schs., Gainesville, 1955—57, elem. supr., 1958—59; tchr. U.S. Army Dependents' Sch., Heidelberg, Germany, 1957—58; prin. Littlewood Elem. Sch., Gainesville, 1959—73, Prairie View Elem. Sch., Gainesville, 1973—82, ret., 1982; owner Rose Hill Publs. Mem. sch. adv. com. Prairie View Elem. Sch., 1975—82. Author: My God of Love, Mercy, Miracles and Angels, 1996, Secrets and Songs of Payne's Prairie, 1998, vol. 2, 2004—, A Teacher's Odyssey, 2001, My Pets and I, 1999, Poems for Children, 2001, My Angels and I, 2001, Spiritual Interpretations of God's Truths, 2002, The Birth and Growth of the Village, 2003, The Other Side Where Love Knows No Color, 2005, numerous poems; co-author: Reflections of Light, 1995; co-author: (with Frances B. Head) A Lifetime of Humor, 2005; author, composer: St. Augustine Song; contbr. articles to local newspapers. Pres. Govs. Children's Commn., Gainesville, 1956—57; dir. Village Chorus, Gainesville, 1987—; active Gainesville Schs. PTA, 1959—82, PTA Micanopy, 1952—55; dir. emeritus North Fla. Retirement Village, Fla., 2007—; Dem. candidate Fla. House Rep., 1974; pianist, organist Village Vespers on Sunday Evenings, 1990—; bd. dir. Foster Grandparents, Gainesville, 1974—76; v.p. bd. dir. No. Fla. Retirement Village, Inc., 1981, chmn. bd. dir., 1982—86, rep. bd. dirs., 1986—2006, chmn. bd. dir., historian, 1988—, emeritus bd. mem., 2007. Named Woman of Distinction Alachua and Bradford Counties, 2005; recipient Disting. Alumna award, U. Fla., P.K. Yonge Devel. Rsch. Sch., 2006. Mem.: ASCAP, Altrusa Internat. Club of Gainesville Fla. (emeritus mem. 2007—), Internat. Soc. Poets, Micanopy Hist. Soc., Order of Eastern Star, Delta Kappa Gamma. Democrat. Baptist. Avocations: stamp collecting/philately, coin collecting/numismatics, book collecting, post card collecting, creative writing. Home: 410 SW Wacahoota Rd Micanopy FL 32667 Mailing: 8015 NW 28th Pl B 105 Gainesville FL 32606

ROSENBERRY, WILLIAM KENNETH, lawyer, educator; b. St. Louis, Aug. 14, 1946; s. William Hugh and Shirley Anne (Love) Rosenberry; m. Linda Lou Lang, Aug. 24, 1968 (div. Jan. 1985); children: Ashlie Anne, Allison Renee; m. Donna L. Pruitt; stepchildren: Corey David Pruitt, Lindsey Lee Pruitt. BBA, U. Tex., Arlington, 1967; JD, Baylor U., 1970. Bar: Tex. 1970, Colo. 1991, U.S. Dist. Ct. (no. dist.) Tex. 1971, cert.: Coll. State Bar Tex. (specialist in comml. real estate law) 03, Tex. (residential real estate law). Assoc. Hinds & Chambers, Arlington, 1970-71; ptnr. Duke, Rosenberry, Duke & Jelinek, Arlington, 1971-76; pvt. practice, Arlington, 1976—. Mem. faculty U. Tex., 1991—; bd. dirs. Equitable Bank, NA, Arlington, Equitable Bankshares, Dallas; gen. mgr. Triple R. Properties; escrow officer Am. Title Co., 1984—; assoc. bd. dirs. Southwest Securities Bank, Arlington. Assoc. editor Baylor Law Rev., 1969. Pres. Pantego Christian Acad. Boosters, Arlington, 1990—92; active Arlington City Zoning Bd., 1989—92; bd. dirs. Baylor Bear Found. Baylor U., Ft. Worth Charities, Inc., Children's Charities, Ft. Worth, v.p., 1999—; bd. dirs. Arlington Margarita Soc., Arlington Children's Toys, Inc., 2004—. Named, Outstanding Young Men in Am., 1980; recipient Outstanding Part-Time Faculty Tchg. award, U. Tex. Dept. Real Estate and Fin., 1992. Mem.: Arlington Bar Assn. (bd. dirs. 1987), Arlington Rep. Club, Arlington Sportsmans Club. Mem. Pantego Bible Ch. Avocation: Avocations: fishing, hunting, jogging. Office: 3010 W Park Row Dr Arlington TX 76013-2048 Office Phone: 817-461-6601.

ROSENBLATT, ALBERT MARTIN, retired state appeals court judge; b. NYC, Jan. 17, 1936; s. Isaac and Fannie (Dachs) R.; m. Julia Carlson, Aug. 23, 1970; 1 child, Elizabeth. BA, U. Pa., 1957; JD, Harvard U., 1960. Bar: NY 1961. Dist. atty. Dutchess County, NY, 1969-75, county judge NY, 1976-81; supreme ct. justice NY State Supreme Ct., 1982-89, chief adminstrv. judge, 1987—89, assoc. justice, appellate divsn., second dept., 1989-98; assoc. judge NY State Ct. Appeals, Poughkeepsie, NY, 1998—2006. Instr. judge NY State, 1987-89; vis. prof., victorian studies dept., Vassar Coll., 1992-94; moderator NY State Fair Trial Free Press Conf., 2000-07; instr. newly elected state supreme ct. judges and county judges; asst. dist. attys., 1974, 75; instr. law tng. NY State Police Acad., 1997; lectr. Nat. Dist. Attys. Assn., 1968-74; tchg. team mem. trial advocacy workshop Harvard Law Sch., 1998, 99; chmn. State-Fed. Jud. Coun., 2005-06; jud. fellow NYU Law Sch., 2007. Mem. bd. editors NY State Bar Jour., 1992-99; former editor, Baker Street Jour.; contbr. articles on law to profl. jours. and popular mags. Bd. dirs. United Way Cmty. Chest, 1970; bd. dirs. Bardavon 1869 Opera House, Dutchess County Hist. Soc.; mem. adv. bd. Jewish Cmty. Ctr., 1987—; pres. Hist. Soc. Cts. of State of N.Y., 2002—; mem. State-Fed. Jud. Coun., 2003—, chmn., 2005—; mem. U.S. Master's Maccabiah Team, 1997; With USAR, 1960-66. Mem. NY State Bar Assn. (named Outstanding Prosecutor 1974, Outstanding Jud. Svcs. award 1994), NY State Dist. Attys. Assn. (pres. 1974, Frank S. Hogan award 1987, Jud. Svcs. award 1994), Profl. Ski Instrs. Am. (cert. 1984—), Baker St. Irregulars Club (former assoc. editor Baker St. Jour.). Republican. Jewish. Avocations: cert. profl. assoc. ski instructor, squash. Home: 300 Freedom Rd Pleasant Valley NY 12569-5431 Office: 10 Market St Poughkeepsie NY 12601-3228 Office Phone: 845-486-6444.

ROSENBLATT, ALICE F., healthcare insurance company executive; With The New Eng., William M. Mercer, Inc., Mut. of NY; chief actuary, sr. v.p. HMO and grp. svcs. Blue Cross of Calif., 1987—89; sr. v.p., chief actuary Blue Cross/Blue Shield Mass., 1989—93; prin. health and welfare grp. Coopers & Lybrand, Boston; positions through chief actuary, exec. v.p. integration planning and implementation Wellpoint Health Networks, Inc., 1996—2004; exec. v.p. integration planning/implementation, chief actuary WellPoint, Inc., Indpls., 2004—07, exec. v.p., integration & info. mgmt. officer, chief actuary, 2007—. Commr. Medicare Payment Adv. Commn. Fellow: Soc. Actuaries (bd. dirs.); mem.: Am. Acad. Actuaries (bd. dirs.). Office: WellPoint Inc 120 Monument Cir Indianapolis IN 46204 *

ROSENBLATT, BRIAN A., lawyer; b. Rochester, NY, Nov. 5, 1969; s. Gary Bruce and Elaine Ruth Rosenblatt; m. Robin M. Stone, Oct. 25, 1997; children: Madeline Ashley, Zachary Michael. BA, Washington U., St. Louis, 1991; jd, Ill. Inst. Tech., Chgo., 1997. Bar: Ill. 1997. Atty. Allstate Ins., Chgo., 1997—2000; ptnr. SmithAmundsen LLC, Chgo., 2000—. Author: (legal text) Chapter 14-IICLE Commercial and Business Litigation- Mediation. Named one of Top 40 Attorneys Under the Age of 40 in Ill., Chgo. Pub., 2006. Mem.: ABA, Nat. Acad. Rec. Arts and Scis. Office: SmithAmundsen LLC 150 N Michigan Ave Ste 3300 Chicago IL 60601 Home Phone: 847-831-3696; Office Phone: 312-894-3358. Office Fax: 312-894-3210. Business E-Mail: brosenblatt@salawus.com.

ROSENBLATT, CYNTHIA SCHAFFER, lawyer; b. Alexandria, Minn., June 18, 1947; m. Fredric T. Rosenblatt, Dec. 27, 1970 (dec. Sept. 22, 1993); 1 child Hart L. Rosenblatt; m. Burton G. Ross, Mar. 4, 1995 (dec. May 1, 2003). Student, U. Wis., 1965-66; BA magna cum laude, U. Minn., 1969, MA, 1971, JD cum laude, 1976. Bar: US Dist. Ct. Minn. 1976, US Tax Ct. 1977, US Ct. Appeals (11th cir.) 1985, US Supreme Ct. 1991. Mng. editor law rev. vol. 60 U. Minn., 1975—76; assoc. atty. Doherty, Rumble & Butler, P.A., St. Paul, 1976-81, ptnr., 1981-84; founder, v.p. Ross, Rosenblatt, Ltd., Mpls., 1984—2002; of counsel Lindquist & Vennum, P.L.L.P., Mpls., 2002—. Chmn. bd. of visitors U. Minn. Law Sch., Mpls., 1984-93; bd. dirs. Children's Hosps. and Clinics, Mpls., St. Paul. Bd. of advisors U. Minn. Art Mus., Mpls., 1989-95. Mem. ABA (taxation sect., generation-skipping bd. 1995). Office: Ste 4200 80 S 8th St Minneapolis MN 55402-2223 Office Phone: 612-371-3211. Business E-Mail: crosenblatt@lindquist.com.

ROSENBLATT, JASON PHILIP, literature and language professor; b. Balt., July 3, 1941; s. Morris D. and Esther (Friedlander) R.; m. Zipporah Marton, June 2, 1964; children: Noah David, Raphael Mark. BA, Yeshiva U., 1963; MA, Brown U., 1966, PhD, 1969. Asst. prof. English U. Pa., Phila., 1968-74, Georgetown U., Washington, 1974-76, assoc. prof., 1976-83, prof. English, 1983—. Vis. lectr. English lit. Swarthmore (Pa.) Coll., 1972-73; cen. exec. com. Folger Inst./Folger Shakespeare Libr., Washington, 1976-88. Author: Torah and Law in "Paradise Lost", 1994, Renaissance England's Chief Rabbi: John Selden, 2006; co-editor: Not in Heaven: Coherence and Complexity in Biblical Narrative, 1991; mem. editl. bd. Milton Studies, 1992—; contbr. articles to scholarly publs. Recipient Virginia Graham Healey award, 1998-99; Guggenheim Found. fellow, 1977-78, NEH fellow, 1990-91, Folger Shakespeare Libr./NEH fellow, 1999-2000. Mem. MLA (del. assembly 1989-91, exec. com. div. religion and lit. 1982-86, exec. com. 17th century Eng. lit. 2002—), Milton Soc. Am. (exec. com. 1977-80, James Holly Hanford award 1989, v.p. 1998, pres. 1999), Milton Seminar, Phi Beta Kappa. Democrat. Jewish. Avocations: talmud study, music, swimming. Office: Dept English Georgetown Univ Box 571131 Washington DC 20057-1131 Office Phone: 202-687-7577. E-mail: rosenblj@georgetown.edu.

ROSENBLATT, JOAN RAUP, mathematical statistician; b. NYC, Apr. 15, 1926; d. Robert Bruce and Clara (Eliot) Raup; m. David Rosenblatt, June 10, 1950. AB, Barnard Coll., 1946; PhD, U. N.C., 1956. Intern Nat. Inst. Pub. Affairs, Washington, 1946-47; statis. analyst U.S. Bur. of Budget, 1947-48; rsch. asst. U. N.C., 1953-54; mathematician Nat. Inst. Standards and Tech. (formerly Nat. Bur. Standards), Washington, 1955—, asst. chief statis. engring., 1963-68, chief statis. engring. lab., 1969-78, dep. dir. Ctr. for Applied Math., 1978-88; dep. dir. Computing and Applied Math. Lab., Gaithersburg, 1988-93, dir., 1993-95, guest rschr. Statis. Engring. Divsn., 1996—. Mem. com. on indsl. rels. Dept. Stats. Ohio State U., 1981-90; mem. adv. com. in math. and stats. USDA Grad. Sch., 1971—; mem. Com. Applied and Theoretical Stats., Nat. Rsch. Coun., 1985-88. Mem. editorial bd. Communications in Stats., 1971-79, Jour. Soc. for Indsl. and Applied Math., 1965-75, Nat. Inst. Stds. and Tech. Jour. Rsch., 1991-93; contbr. articles to profl. jours. Chmn. Com. on Women in Sci., Joint Bd. on Sci. Edn., 1963—64. Rice fellow, 1946, Gen. Edn. Bd. fellow, 1948-50; recipient Fed. Woman's award, 1971, Gold medal Dept. Commerce, 1976, Presdl. Meritorious Exec. Rank award, 1982. Fellow AAAS (chmn. stats. sect. 1982, sec. 1987-91), Inst. Math. Stats. (coun. 1975-77), Am. Statis. Assn. (v.p. 1981-83, dir. 1979-80, Founders award 1991), Washington Acad. Scis. (achievement award math. 1965); mem. AAUW, Royal Statis. Soc. London, Philos. Soc. Washington, Internat. Statis. Inst., Caucus Women Stats. (pres. 1976), Assn. Women Math., Exec. Women Govt., Phi Beta Kappa, Sigma Xi (treas. Nat. Bur. Standards chpt. 1982-84). Home: 2939 Van Ness St NW Apt 702 Washington DC 20008-4628 Office: Nat Inst Stds and Tech 100 Bureau Dr Stop 8980 Gaithersburg MD 20899-8980 Business E-Mail: jrr@nist.gov.

ROSENBLATT, LIEF D., investment company executive; s. Franklin D. and Florence Rosenblatt; m. Melinda Lande, Feb. 4, 1990. BA summa cum laude, Harvard U., JD; MA in Philosophy, Politics and Economics, Rhodes Scholar, Oxford U. Sr. v.p. Risk Arbitrage Dept. Lehman Brothers; gen. ptnr. Plaza Securities Co.; mng. dir. and head Arbitrage, High Yield and Distressed Securities Dept. Soros Fund Mgmt. LLC; sr. mng. mem. Satellite Asset Mgmt. LP, 1999—. Waynflete fellow Magdalen Coll., Oxford. Trustee Am. Hosp. in Paris Found., AVI CHAI Found.; chmn. Nat. Yiddish Book Ctr., Amherst, Mass.; bd. dirs. Cancer Rsch. Inst., 2001—. Mem.: Phi Beta Kappa. Office: Satellite Asset Mgmt 623 5th Ave New York NY 10022-6842 Office Phone: 212-209-2000.

ROSENBLATT, MICHAEL, internist, academic administrator, educator, researcher; b. Lund, Sweden, Nov. 27, 1947; s. Arthur Rosenblatt and Jean (Strosberg) Bialer; m. Patricia Ellen Regenbogen, Aug. 23, 1969; children: Anna Miriam, Adam Richard. AB summa cum laude, Columbia U., NYC, 1969; MD magna cum laude, Harvard U., Cambridge, Mass., 1973. Diplomate Am. Bd. Internal Medicine. Intern to resident Mass. Gen. Hosp., Boston, 1973-75, clin. rsch. fellow endocrinology and metabolism, 1975-77, chief endocrine unit, 1981-84; instr. medicine Harvard U., Boston, 1976-78, asst. prof. medicine, 1978-82, assoc. prof. medicine, 1982-85; v.p. for biol. rsch. Merck Sharp & Dohme Rsch. Labs., 1984-87, v.p. for biol. rsch. and molecular biology, 1987-89, sr. v.p. rsch., 1989-92; dir. divsn. health sci. and tech. Harvard-MIT, 1992-98; Ebert prof. molecular medicine Harvard Med. Sch., Boston, 1992-98; chief divsn. bone and mineral metabolism Beth Israel Hosp., Boston, 1992—2000, 2002—03; dean, prof. physiology and medicine Tufts U. Sch. Medicine, 2003—. Faculty dean acad. programs Beth Israel Deaconess Med. Ctr., Harvard Med., 1996—2000, George R. Minot prof. med., 1996—2003; exec. dir. Carl J. Shapiro Inst. Edn. and Rsch. at Harvard Med. Sch. and Beth Israel Deaconess Med. Ctr., 1996—2000, pres., 1999—2001. Editor: Atrial Natriuretic Factor Endocrinology and Metabolism Clinics of N.Am., 1987; contbr. numerous sci. articles on parathyroid hormone and calcium metabolism to leading sci. jours. Recipient Vincent du Vigneaud award Gordon Confs., Kingston, R.I., 1986, Fuller Albright award Am. Soc. for Bone and Mineral Rsch., 1986, citation Japan Endocrine Soc., Tokyo, Taiwanese Osteoporosis Soc., Tainan. Fellow AAAS, Am. Coll. Physicians; mem. The Endocrine Soc., Am. Soc. for Biochemistry and Molecular Biology, Am. Soc. for Clin. Investigation, Am. Soc. Bone and Mineral Rsch. (pres. 1997-98), Assn. Am. Physicians, Inter-Urban Clin. Club (pres. 1997-98). Office: Tufts U Sch Medicine 136 Harrison Ave Boston MA 02111-1800

ROSENBLATT, PETER RONALD, lawyer, former ambassador; b. NYC, Sept. 4, 1933; s. William and Therese (Steinhardt) Rosenblatt; m. Naomi Henriette Harris; children: Therese Sarah Sonenshine, Daniel Harris, David Steinhardt. BA, Yale U., 1954, LLB, 1957. Bar: NY 1959, DC 1969. Tchg. asst. history Yale U., New Haven, 1954—55; asst. dist. atty. NY County, 1959—62; assoc. Stroock & Stroock & Lavan, NYC, 1962—66; dep. asst. gen. counsel AID, Washington, 1966; mem. White House staff, Washington, 1966—68; jud. officer, chmn. bd. contract appeals US Post Office Dept., Washington, 1968—69; v.p., dir. EDP Technology, Inc., Washington, 1969—71; chmn. bd. Internat. Devel. Svcs., Washington, 1969—71; spl. cons. to Senator Edmund S. Muskie, 1970—72; practice law Washington, 1972—77, 1981—91; founding ptnr. Heller & Rosenblatt, Washington, 1991—. Personal rep. of Pres. with rank amb. to conduct negotiations on future polit. status of Trust Ter. of Pacific Islands, Washington, 1977-81; mem. Mid. East study group Dem. Adv. Coun. Elected Ofcls., 1974-76; bd. dirs. MediSense, Inc., 1983-96. Sec., chmn. exec. com. Coalition for a Dem. Majority, 1973-77, pres., 1983-93; bd. dirs. Com. on Present Danger, 1976-77, 82-93, 04-; mem. US Nat. Com. Pacific Econ. Cooperation, 1986, sec., 1987-03; bd. govs. Haifa U., Israel, 1990-94, 98—; sec.-treas. Fund for Democracy and Devel., 1991-94, pres., 1994—; mem. adv. coun. Nixon Ctr., 1994—; mem. task force on fgn. policy Dem. Policy Commn., 1986; bd. govs. Am. Jewish Com., 1998—, v.p. 2005-, pres. DC chpt. 2003-05, bd. dirs. UN Watch, 2000—, chmn., bd. govs. Koppelman Inst. on Am. Jewish-Israeli Rels., 1999-02, chmn. strategic policy group, 2007-; bd. advisors Jewish Inst. Nat. Security Affairs, 2000—; mem. Nat. Security Initiative, 2001—. 2nd lt. USAR, 1957—58, 1st lt. USAR, 1958—65. Recipient Superior Honor award, Dept. of State, 1981; postgrad. fellow, Tel-Aviv U., 1971. Mem. ABA, NY, DC Bar, Coun. Fgn. Rels. Jewish. Office: Heller & Rosenblatt 1101 15th St NW Ste 205 Washington DC 20005-5002 Office Phone: 202-466-4700. Personal E-mail: ffddprosenblatt@erols.com.

ROSENBLATT, RANDALL LEE, internist; b. Evansville, Ind., Dec. 9, 1948; s. Bernard B. and Anne Mae Rosenblatt; m. Barbara B. Glazer, Sept. 13, 1986; children: Anna Glazer, Molly Glazer. BA, U. Evansville, 1969; MD, Ind. U., Indpls., 1973. Assoc. dir. internal medicine St. Paul U. Hosp., Dallas, 1999—2006; med. dir. lung transport program U. Tex., Southwestern Med. Sch., Dallas, 2006—. Prof. U. Tex., Dallas; com. mem. Cystic Fibrosis Found. Ctr., Bethesa, Md., 2001—; bd. dirs. Cystic Fibrosis Found. Chmn. dinner Am. Lung Assn., Dallas; chmn. legends fundraising dinner St. Paul Med. Found.; bd. dirs. Dallas Holocaust Mus. Fellow: ACP (bd. dirs.), Am. Coll. Chest Physicians; mem.: Dallas County Med. Soc. (bd. dirs.). Office: Univ Tex Southwestern Med Sch 5323 Harry Hines Blvd Dallas TX 75390-8550

ROSENBLATT, ROGER, writer; b. NYC, Sept. 13, 1940; m. Virginia Rosenblatt; children: Carl, Amy, John. PhD in English and Am. Lit., Harvard U.; doctorate (hon.), U. Md., Claremont Grad. Sch., U. Utah, Pace U., Brigham Young U. Briggs-Copeland prof. creative writing Harvard U., 1968-73; dir. edn. NEH, 1973-75; lit. editor The New Republic, 1975-78; columnist Washington Post, mem. editorial bd., 1976-79; essayist, sr. writer Time, 1980-88; essayist MacNeil/Lehrer News Hour, PBS, 1983—; columnist, editor-at-large Life mag., 1989-92; editor-at-large Time, Inc., 1999—2001. Prof. English and writing Stony Brook U. Author: Black Fiction, 1974, Children of War, 1983 (Robert F. Kennedy Book prize), Witness: The World Since Hiroshima, 1985, Life Itself: Abortion in the American Mind, 1992 (Melcher award), The Man in the Water, 1994, Coming Apart, 1997, Consuming Desires, 1999, Rules for Aging, 2000, Where We Stand, 2002, Anything Can Happen, 2003, (novels) Lapham Rising, 2006, Beet, 2007, (plays) Free Speech in America, 1991, And, 1992, Bibliomania, 1993, Ashley Montana Goes Ashore in the Caicos, 2005. Fulbright scholar, Dublin, Ireland, 1965; recipient numerous honors including two George Polk awards, George Foster Peabody award, Emmy award.

ROSENBLATT, STEPHEN PAUL, marketing and sales promotion company executive; b. NYC, Feb. 13, 1935; s. Jack Aaron and Ruth (Kloth) R.; m. Dorothy Freedman, Apr. 7, 1962; children: Gregg, Amy, Robert. BEd, NYU, 1957. Tchr. art N.Y.C. Schs., 1957-58; art dir. Morse Internat., NYC, 1958-65; v.p. L.C. Gumbinner Advt., NYC, 1966-71; group mktg. dir. Norcliff Thayer, Tarrytown, NY, 1971-75; pres. BMS Mktg. Services, Inc., NYC, 1975-89, The Promotion Group Inc. subs. Doctus PLC, NYC, 1989-91, SPQR Inc., Yorktown Heights, NY, 1991-93, ret., 1993. Home: 50 Watkins Dr Sandy Hook CT 06482

ROSENBLOOM, BERT, marketing educator, consultant, writer; b. Phila., Feb. 2, 1944; s. Max and Dora (Cohen) R.; m. Pearl Friedman, Aug. 18, 1968; children: Jack Alan, Robyn. BS, Temple U., 1966, MBA, 1968, PhD, 1974. Instr. mktg. Rider Coll., Trenton, NJ, 1968-72, asst. prof., 1972-74; asst. prof. mktg. Baruch Coll. CUNY, 1974-76; assoc. prof. Drexel U., Phila., 1976-80, prof., 1980-85, G. Behrens Ulrich prof. mktg., 1985-98, assoc. dean grad. programs, 1994-97, Rauth chair electronic commerce mgmt., 1999—2005, Rauth prof. mktg. mgmt., 2005—. Vis. scholar Higher Sch. Commerce Paris, 1993; cons. editor mktg. Random House, N.Y.C., 1977—; exec. dir. Safe Guard Sci. E-Commerce Mgmt. Ctr., 1999-2000, sr. rsch. fellow, 2000—; cons. in field; bd. dirs. Reality Landscaping Corp., McKee Real Estate Devel. Corp., RESHARE Corp.; vis. disting. prof. Hannon U., Japan, 2000; vis. disting. scholar U. St. Gallen, 2000; Disting. vis. fellow Sogang U., Korea, 2001; bd. dirs. Reshare Corp., 2004—; mem. adv. bd. Duttweiler Inst. Mktg. and Retailing. Author: Marketing Channels, 1978, 3d edit., 2003, Market Functions and the Wholesaler Distribution, 1987, Marketing Channels: A Management View, 5th edit., 1997, 6th edit., 1999, 7th edit., 2003, Retail Marketing, 1981, Direct Selling Channels, 1993, Wholesale Mktg. Channels, 1994; editor Jour. Mktg. Channels, 1989—, Jour. Consumer Mktg., Jour. Global Mktg., Jour. Acad. Mktg. Sci.; contbr. articles to profl. jours. Mem. E-Commerce Commn., Mayor Phila., 1999—. Named Disting. Erskine fellow U. Canterbury, New Zealand, 1986; recipient Outstanding Educator award Chapel of Four Chaplains, 1984, Nomura Fund Collaborative rsch. award U. Rykus, Japan, 1998; rsch. award Distbn. Rsch. and Edn. Found., 1986, rsch. award Direct Selling Found., 1986, 91, 96, Literati Club award for excellence, 2002; Nat. Assn. Wholesaler Distbrs. grantee, 1991; honored as disting. prof. Retail Mktg. Inst. of Australia, 1985. Fellow Acad. Mktg. Sci. (bd. govs. 1978-89); mem. Internat. Mgmt. Devel. Assn. (pres. 1992-94), Am. Mktg. Assn. (v.p. Phila. chpt. 1978-79), Beta Gamma Sigma. Office: Drexel U Sch Bus 32d and Market Sts Philadelphia PA 19104 Home Phone: 856-722-0142. Business E-Mail: rosenblb@drexel.edu.

ROSENBLOOM, DANIEL, investment advisor, lawyer; b. NYC, Feb. 11, 1930; s. Sol and Florence (Vogel) R. BA, U. Va., 1951, JD, 1954; LLM, NYU, 1960. Bar: Va. 1954, N.Y. 1956. Atty. Paskus, Gordon, and Hyman, NYC, 1956—61; v.p., sec., gen. counsel Phila. and Reading Corp., NYC, 1962—67; ptnr. First Manhattan Co., NYC, 1968—2002, sr. mng. dir., 2002—. Trustee Nat. Found. for Facial Reconstruction, N.Y. Univ. Med. Ctr., Univ. Va. Law Sch. Found. 1st lt. AUS, 1954—56. Mem. Sunningdale Country Club, Farmington Country Club, Harmonie Club, Atlantic Golf Club, River Club, Phi Alpha Delta, Phi Epsilon Pi. Office: First Manhattan Co 437 Madison Ave New York NY 10022-7001

ROSENBLOOM, DAVID HARRY, political science and law educator; b. NYC, Aug. 27, 1943; s. Jerome and Rita R. BA, Marietta Coll., 1964, LLD (hon.), 1994; MA, U. Chgo., 1966, PhD in Polit. Sci., 1969. Asst. prof. U. Kans., Lawrence, 1969-71; fellow Am. Soc. Pub. Adminstrn. U.S. Civil Svc. Commn., Washington, 1970-71; vis. sr. lectr. Tel Aviv (Israel) U., 1971-73; asst. prof. U. Vt., Burlington, 1973-75, assoc. prof., 1975-78; vis. assoc. prof. Syracuse (N.Y.) U., 1978-79, prof., 1979—88, disting. prof., 1988-90, Am. U., Washington, 1990—. Bd. trustees Marietta Coll., 2003—; guest prof. pub. adminstrn. People's U., Beijing, 2003—, Northwest U., Xi'an, China, 2005—. Author: (Books) Federal Service and Constitution, 1971, Public Administration, 2004, 6th edit., Public Administration and Law, 1997, Building a Legislative-Centered Public Administration, 2000, Administrative Law for Public Managers, 2003. Mem. Clinton-Gore Transition Team, U.S. Office Pers. Mgmt., Washington, 1992; chair Am. U. Faculty Senate, 2004—05; acting chair Am. U. Dept. Pub. Adminstrn. and Policy, 2005—06. Recipient Charles Levine Meml. award for excellence and Disting. Rsch. award Am. Soc. for Pub. Adminstrn. and Nat. Assn. Schs. of Pub. Affairs and Administration, Washington, 1992, 93, Thomas Dye award for outstanding svc. Policy Studies Orgn., 1996, Dwight Waldo award for outstanding contbns. to lit. and leadership of Pub. Adminstrn., Am. Soc. Pub. Adminstrn., Washington, 1999, Louis Brownlow Book award Nat. Acad. Pub. Adminstrn., 2001, John Gaus award for exemplary scholarship in joint tradition polit. sci. and pub. adminstrn. Am. Polit. Sci. Assn., 2001. Fellow Nat. Acad. Pub. Adminstrn. Recipient John Gaus award for exemplary scholarship in joint tradition polit. sci. and pub. adminstrn. Am. Polit. Sci. Assn., 2001. Avocations: bicycling, motorcycling. Office: American U 4400 Massachusetts Ave NW Washington DC 20016-8070 Office Phone: 202-885-2361. Business E-Mail: rbloom@american.edu.

ROSENBLOOM, H(ARRY) DAVID, lawyer; b. NYC, May 26, 1941; s. Milton M. and Rose (Gold) Rosenbloom; m. Carla L. Peterson, June 23, 1968; children: Sarah Alix, Julia Micol. AB, Princeton U., 1962; postgrad. (Fulbright scholar), U. Florence, Italy, 1962-63; JD, Harvard U., 1966. Bar: N.Y. 1967, DC 1968. Spl. asst. to Arthur J. Goldberg U.S. amb. UN, 1966-67; law clk. to Abe Fortas U.S. Supreme Ct., 1967-68; assoc. Caplin & Drysdale, Washington, 1968-72, ptnr., 1972-77, 81—. Spl. asst. to dep. asst. sec. for tax policy Dept. Treasury, Washington, 1977, internat. tax counsel, 1978—81; lectr. Harvard U. Law Sch., 1984—87, 1990—93, 1995—96, 1999, Pub. Fin. Tng. Inst., Taipei, 1985—86, 1989, Stanford U. Law Sch., 1988, Inst. Tecnologico Autonomo d' Mex., 1993, 95, 97, Columbia U. Law Sch., 1997, U. Pa. Law Sch., 1998, U. Luigi Bocconi, Milan, 2001, 04, 05, So. African Tax Inst., U. Pretoria, 2002, Petrobras U., Rio de Janeiro, 2006, NYU Law Sch., 2000—, dir. internat. tax program, 2002—; faculty law U. Sydney, 2001, 03, 2005—07. Home: 2948 Garfield Ter NW Washington DC 20008-3507 Office: 1 Thomas Cir NW Washington DC 20005-5802 Home Phone: 202-797-1215; Office Phone: 202-862-5037. Business E-Mail: hdr@capdale.com.

ROSENBLOOM, LEWIS STANLEY, lawyer; b. Fort Riley, Kans., Feb. 28, 1953; s. Donald and Sally Ann (Warsawsky) R.; children: Micah, Shaina. BA, Lake Forest Coll., 1974; JD with high honors, DePaul U., 1977. Bar: Ill. 1977, US Dist. Ct. (no. dist.) Ill, 1977, US Ct. Appeals (7th cir.) 1979, US Supreme Ct. 1983, US Ct. Appeals (9th cir.) 1987, US Ct. Appeals (3rd cir.) 1993. Sr. acct. Gale, Takahasi & Channon (now Ernst & Young), Chgo., 1973-74; law clk. to Hon. Robert L. Eisen U.S. Bankruptcy Ct. (no. dist.) Ill., Chgo., 1976; assoc. Nachman, Munitz & Sweig, Ltd., Chgo., 1976-82, prin., 1982-87; ptnr., co-chmn. involvency, bankruptcy & bus. reorgn. dept. Winston & Strawn, Chgo., 1987-93; ptnr., sr. corp. reorgn. counsel, practice group head McDermott, Will & Emery, Chgo., 1993—2006; ptnr., chmn. dept. bankruptcy and reorganization LeBoeuf, Lamb, Green & MacRae, LLP, Chgo., 2006—. Mem. bd. advisors to bankruptcy, comml. law advisor Bus. Laws, Inc., 1988—; lectr. in field. Contbr. articles to profl. jours. Mem. adv. com. and fin. subcom. Ill. Bd. Higher Edn., Springfield; mem. state edn. and legal aid subcom. Ill. Coun. on Children and Youth Welfare. Coll. Scholar Lake Forest Coll., 1973-74. Fellow Am. Coll. Bankruptcy (dir.); mem. ABA (bus. bankruptcy com. 1982—, chmn. new and pending bankruptcy legis. com. 1982-85, chmn. transp. reorganizations com. 1985-88), Chgo. Bar Assn. (bankrupcy reorganization com., co-chmn. subcom. on retention and fees 1987-88). Office: LeBoeuf Lamb Greene & MacRae LLP Two Prudential Plaza 180 N Stetson Ste 3700 Chicago IL 60601 Home Phone: 847-630-6943; Office Phone: 312-794-8090. Business E-Mail: lrosenbloom@llgm.com.

ROSENBLOOM, MOREY STEPHEN, lawyer; b. Phila., Aug. 26, 1944; s. Howard and Esther (Medvene) R.; m. Marsha Riffkin, May 26, 1968; children: Brett, Eric. BS in Acctg., Temple U., 1966, JD, 1969. Bar: Pa. 1970, US Tax Ct., 1975, US Supreme Ct., 1980, NY, 2001. Law asst. to chief justice Pa. Supreme Ct., 1969-70; ptnr. Blank Rome Comisly & McCauley, Phila., 1970—90; prin. CMS Co., 1990—95; ptnr. Blank Rome LLP, Phila., 1995—, chair, tax and fiduciary dept., 1996—2001, chmn., bus. dept., 2001—06. Adj. prof. law Temple U. Sch. Law, Phila., 1977-2000, Villanova Law Sch., 1999-2004; lectr., prof. Am. Coll., Bryn Mawr, Pa., 1978-90. Co-author: Tools and Techniques of Estate Planning, 13th edit., 1990, Funding Corporate Buy-Sell Agreements with Life Insurance, 1980, The Wait and See Buy Sell, 1978. Bd. visitors Temple U. Sch. of Law; bd. mem. Am. Friends of Hebrew U., Elwyn Jerusalem, Thomas Jefferson U. Cardiology Rsch. Found. Fellow Am. Coll. Trust and Estate Coun.; mem. ABA, Pa. Bar Assn. (past chmn. real property probate and trust law sect.), Phila. Bar Assn., Phila. Estate planning Coun. Office: Blank Rome LLP One Logan Sq Philadelphia PA 19103-6998 Office Phone: 215-569-5599. Office Fax: 215-832-5599. Business E-Mail: rosenbloom@BlankRome.com.

ROSENBLUM, BRUCE ROBERT, neurosurgeon; b. Bklyn., Dec. 5, 1959; s. Norman Saul and Pauline Barbara Rosenblum; m. Nancy Elise Herman, June 12, 1984; children: Jared, Brandon. BS, CCNY, 1980; MD, Mt. Sinai, NYC, 1982. Cert. Am. Assn. Neurosurgeons, 1991. Chmn. neurosurgery Riverview, Red Bank, NJ, 1992—. Office: 160 Ave At The Commans Shrewsbury NJ 07702

ROSENBLUM, CONSTANCE, newspaper editor; Culture editor Phila. Inquirer; John Rockwell arts and leisure sect. editor NY Times, NYC, 1998, city sect. editor. Author: Gold Digger: The Outrageous Life and Times of Peggy Hopkins Joyce, 2000; contbg. editor: The Best of the City Section of the NY Times, 2005. Office: NY Times City Section 229 West 43rd St New York NY 10036-3959

ROSENBLUM, EDWARD G., lawyer; b. Union City, NJ, Aug. 2, 1944; s. Milton and Frances (Nardi) R.; m. Charis Ann Schlatter, Dec. 1, 1971; children: Deborah, Michelle. BA, Rutgers U., 1966, JD, 1969. Bar: N.J. 1969. Ptnr. Rosenblum & Rosenblum, P.A., Jersey City, 1971-79, Secaucus, N.J., 1979-93, Rosenblum Wolf & Lloyd, P.A., Secaucus, 1994—, Teaneck, 1998—. Lectr. in field. Author: N.J. Lawyer, 1980, N.J. Municipalities, 1987. Active Table to Table, Englewood, N.J. Mem. N.J. State Bar Assn. (vice chmn. tax ct. rules com. taxation sect. 1984—, chmn. real property tax com. 1984—, vice chmn. taxation sect. 1987—, chmn.-elect 1987, chmn. 1988-89, Supreme Ct. com. on tax ct. 1982-92). Office: 115 W Allendale Ave Allendale NJ 07401 Office Phone: 201-327-0222.

ROSENBLUM, ELLEN F., judge; b. 1951; m. Richard Meeker. BS, Sociol., U. Oreg., 1971, JD, 1975. Bar: Oreg. 1975. Atty. priv. practice, Eugene, Oreg., 1975—80; asst. U.S. atty. Eugene, Oreg., 1981—89; circuit ct. judge Multnomah County Ct., Portland, Oreg., 1989—. Trustee Nat. Jud. Coll.; past chmn., Jud. Conduct Comm. Oreg. Jud. Conf.; chmn. Gov. Adv. Comm. Corrections, Oreg. Citizens Just. Conf., 2000. Chmn. Oreg. Citizen's Justice Conf. Recipient Pres. Public Svc. award, Oreg. State Bar, Andrea Swanner Redding Mentoring award, Lewis & Clark Law Sch., Honorary Alumna award, Merit. Svc. award, Univ. Oreg. Law Sch.; Alumni Fellow, Univ. Oreg. Coll. Arts & Sci., 1990. Fellow: Am. Bar Found. (life); mem.: U.S. Dist. Ct. Oreg. Hist. Soc. (past pres.), Owen M. Panner Am. Inn of Ct. (past pres.), Oreg. Women Lawyers (founding bd. mem. 1989, Justice Betty Roberts award 2000), ABA (bd. govs., sec. 2002—06, mem. Comm. Racial & Ethnic Diversity). Office: Multnomah County Courthouse Rm 512 1021 SW 4th Ave Portland OR 97204

ROSENBLUM, ESTELLE H., retired dean, nursing educator; b. Davenport, Iowa, Feb. 8, 1933; d. Dan and Cecil (Spiewak) Masters; m. Sidney Rosenblum, Aug. 30, 1953 (dec. 1988); children: Jay Douglas, Gail Rae, Paul Mitchell; m. Jack Grevey, Mar. 31, 1996; stepdaughter: Eileen Grevey Hillson. Student, U. Iowa, 1950—53; BSN, Wayne State U., Detroit, 1956; MA in Audiology, U. N.Mex., 1971, PhD, 1979; MSN, U. Tex., El Paso, 1981. Head nurse Northville (Mich.) State Hosp., 1956; head nurse, supr. Sister Kenny Polio/Rehab. Hosp., 1957-60; pub. health nurse Englewood County Health Dept., 1961-62; nursing supr. Bernalillo County Indian Hosp., Albuquerque, 1962-63, asst. dir. nursing, 1963-64; clin. tchr. U. N.Mex. Coll. Nursing, Albuquerque, 1964-65, inst. to prof., 1972-86, dean and prof. nursing, 1986-93, dean and prof. emerita, 1993—; sch. nurse West Mesa H.S., Albuquerque, 1967-69. Internat. nursing cons.; dir. ANA Approved CE program, Profl. Seminar Cons., 1979-89; spkr. Hong Kong Nurse Educators Soc., 1985; founder convenio U. N.Mex. and U. Mex., 1990, first nurse practitioner program at grad. level, 1987. Author: Fundamentals of Hearing for Health Professionals, 1981; contbr. articles to profl. jours., chpts. to books. Bd. dirs. U. N.Mex. Found., 1996—, bd. sec. 2000-04, Nancy Floyd Haworth Breast Cancer Found., 1995—; docent City of Albuquerque, 1996—; chair recognition com. Jewish Cmty. Ctr., 1998—; chair opening events N.Mex. Holocause Mus., 2006—. USPHS grantee, 1989; Albuquerque Rotary Charitable Found. Clinton P. Anderson fellow; recipient Centennial Disting. Alumni award, U. N.Mex., 1989, Helene Fuld award to Coll. Nursing, U. N.Mex., 1987, Sigma Delta Tau Nat. Disting. Alumni award, 1988, State N.Mex. Gov.'s Disting. Svc. award, 1993, Estelle H. Rosenblum Thesis award U. N.Mex. Coll. Nursing, 1995, Nurse of the Yr. Awards "Legend of Nursing" award March of Dimes, 2002, Myrtle K. Aydelotte Dean's award U. Iowa Coll. Nursing, 2004; Rosenblum-Weiss Ctr. for Nursing Excellence in women and children's health care established at U. N.Mex., 2000. Univ. Iowa Coll. of Nursing Alumni award, 2004. Fellow Am. Acad. Nursing; mem. Am. Assn. Colls. of Nursing (emeritus, exec. devel. series 1988-92), Am. Colls. Nursing (bd. dirs. 1990-92), N.Mex. Nurses Assn. (pres. 1975), N.Mex. Health Resources (bd. dirs. 1986-88), The Rotary Club of Albuquerque (Harvest ball fundraiser 1994—), Sigma Theta Tau (founder, pres. Gamma Sigma chpt. 1974-76, Mentor award), Phi Kappa Phi.

ROSENBLUM, FRANK MICHAEL, civil engineer, consultant, surveyor; b. Calif., Nov. 12, 1961; s. Jerald and Lois Rosenblum; 1 child, Jane. BCE, Calif. Poly. State, San Luis Obispo, 1983. Profl. civil engr., Calif., 1987, profl.land surveyor, Calif., 1990. Prin. engr. and pres. Underwood & Rosenblum, Inc., San Jose, Calif., 1993—. Facility planning cons. Calif. Pub. Schs., Calif.; vol. profl. svcs. Calif. State Parks and U.S. Nat. Parks, Calif., 1999—2006. Mem.: ASCE (assoc.), Calif. Assn. Sch. Bus. Ofcls. (assoc.), Calif. Land Surveyors Assn. (assoc.), Am. Pub. Works Assn. (assoc.), Coalition for Adequate Sch. Housing (assoc.). Achievements include development of 9-step sch. traffic safety planning sys; digital mapping and planning system. Office: Underwood & Rosenblum Inc Ste A114 1630 Oakland Road San Jose CA 95131 Home Phone: 510-651-4066; Office Phone: 408-453-1222. Home Fax: 408-453-1207.

ROSENBLUM, JAY ALAN, neurologist; b. Newark, June 12, 1933; s. Irving and Peggy (Carpenter) R.; m. Judith Grandes, Sept. 1958 (div. 1965); children: Melissa, Shepherd, Todd; m. Sue Goldman Rosenblum, June 13, 1971; 1 child, Steven. AB with honors, U. Pa., 1954; MD, Wake Forest Med., 1958; GM, U. Pa., 1965. DIplomate Am. Acad. of Pain Mgmt., Am. Bd. Forensic Medicine; cert. neurorehabilitation physician. Dir. neurology Madison Ave Hosp., NYC, 1980, N.Y. Infirmary Hosp., NYC, 1980; clin. cons. in neurology N.Y. State Dept of Health, NYC, 1985; instr. in neurology N.Y. Med. Coll., 1985; clin. asst. prof. neurology NYU Med. Sch., 1965, 1970—. Asst. vis. neurologist Bellevue Hosp., NYC; bd. dirs. Am. Bd. Forensic Medicine, Spingifield, Mo., bd. adv. for profl. standing; dir. indsl. medicine seminar Coll. of Ins., NYC, 1988-89; moderator diagnosis and treatment back disorders Acad. of Medicine, NYC, 1991; lectr. in field; pres. med. bd. NY Infirmary-Beekman Downtown Hosp., 1982; mem. NY State Bd. for Profl. Med. Conduct, 2004. Contbr. articles to profl. publs. Task force of handicap vehicles Dept. Health, City of N.Y., 1985; impartial specialist-neurology U.S. Dept. Labor, 1985. Capt. U.S. Army, 1959-62. Fellow Am. Soc. Indsl. Medicine (pres. 1993), Am. Acad. of Infared Imaging (pres. 1995); mem. Am. Back Soc. (dir. neurothemograhy workshop 1989), NY County Med. Soc. (bd. dirs., chmn. bd. censors 2002). Office: 175 E 79th St New York NY 10021-0432 Office Phone: 212-249-7867. Personal E-mail: ps206@aol.com.

ROSENBLUM, JEFFREY IRA, consulting economist; b. NYC, Mar. 12, 1956; s. Charles and Sylvia Lilian (Silverstein) R.; m. Monica Rosales, Sept. 15, 2000. BS, SUNY Brockport, 1983; PhD, U. Tex., 1992. Analyst Pub. Utility Commn. Tex., Austin, 1986—91, asst. mgr., 1991—94; mgr. KPMG Peat Marwick LLP, NYC, 1994—96, sr. mgr. Dallas, 1996—99, KMPG LLP (formerly KPMG Peat Marwick), Short Hills, NJ, 1999—2001, Arthur Andersen LLP, Roseland, NJ, 2001—02; pres. Monrosen, Inc., 2002—05; sr. mgr. Deloitte Tax LLP, Seattle, 2005—. Mem. Am. Econ. Assn., Law and Econs. Assn. Home: 11917 SE 198th Ct Renton WA 98058 Office: 925 4th Ave Ste 3300 Seattle WA 98104 Home Phone: 253-859-5481; Office Phone: 206-716-7158. Business E-Mail: jrosenblum@deloitte.com. E-mail: jeffr3@comcast.net.

ROSENBLUM, MARTIN JEROME, ophthalmologist; b. NYC, Apr. 7, 1948; s. Philip and Rita (Steppel) R.; m. Zina Zarin, May 31, 1975; children: Steven David, Richard James. BS, Bklyn. Coll., 1968; MD, U. Ariz., 1973; postgrad., Columbia U., 1977. Diplomate Am. Bd. Ophthalmology, Nat. Bd. Med. Examiners. Intern Cornell U., NYC, 1973-74; resident N.Y. Med. Coll., 1975-78, instr., 1978-79; practice medicine specializing in eye surgery St. Petersburg, Fla., 1979—. Chief ophthalmology Edward White Hosp.; asst. clin. prof. ophthalmology, U. So. Fla.; attending surgeon St. Anthony's Bayfront Med. Ctr., Am. Soc. for Cataract and Refractive Surgery, Ctr. Spl. Surgery; med. dir. Suncoast Eye Clinic, Pa. Fellow ACS, Am. Acad. Ophthalmology; mem. AMA, Am. Soc. Ophthalmic Plastic and Reconstructive Surgery, Fla. Med. Assn., Fla. Soc. Ophthalmology, Pinellas County Med. Soc., Bayou Country Club. Republican. Jewish. Avocations: tennis, golf, travel, skiing. Office: 2200 16th St N Saint Petersburg FL 33704-3106 Home: 7676 Hunter Lane Pinellas Park FL 33782 Office Phone: 727-822-4729. E-mail: mjreye@aol.com.

ROSENBLUM, MINDY FLEISCHER, pediatrician; b. Bronxville, NY, June 5, 1951; d. Herman and Muriel (Gold) Fleischer; m. Jay S. Rosenblum, June 22, 1971; children: Meira, Tamar, Rafi, Rachel. BA, Yeshiva U., 1972; MD, Albert Einstein Coll., 1976. Diplomate Am. Bd. Pediat., Am. Bd. Pediatric Endocrinology. Intern in pediat. Bronx Mcpl. Hosp. Ctr., 1976-77, residency in pediat., 1977-79; fellow in pediatric endocrinology Children's Hosp. of Phila., 1981; asst. prof. U. Pa., Phila., 1981—95; attending physician Bryn Mawr (Pa.) Hosp., 1981—, Lankenau Hosp., Wynnewood, Pa., 1983—; clin. assoc. Children's Hosp. of Phila., 1995—. Fellow Am. Acad. Pediat.; mem. Phila. Pediat. Soc. (bd. dirs. 1988-92), Am. Diabetes Assn., Lawson Wilkins Pediatric Endocrine Soc. Office Phone: 610-642-9200. Personal E-mail: jmr101@comcast.net.

ROSENBLUM, NANCY LIPTON, political science professor; BA with high honors, Radcliffe Coll., 1969; PhD, Harvard Univ., 1973; LHD (hon.), Kalamazoo Coll., 1993. Asst. prof. Harvard Univ., 1973—77, assoc. prof., 1977—80; prof. Brown Univ., 1980—97; vis. prof. Harvard Univ., 1985; chair, Polit. Sci. dept. Brown Univ., 1989—95, Henry Merritt Wriston prof., 1997—2001, founder & dir., Stephen Robert Inst. for Study of Values, 1998—2000; Sen. Joseph Clark prof. of ethics in politics & govt. Harvard Univ., 2001—. Mem. exec. com. Conf. for Study of Polit. Thought, 1988—; rev. editor Political Theory, 1989—93, mem. editl. bd., 1993—97; council mem. Am. Polit. Sci. Assn., 1991—93, Tocqueville Soc., 2001—; mem. vis. com. dept. Polit. Sci. Brandeis Univ., 1986, Univ. Mich., Ann Arbor, 1993, Queens Coll., 1993, Stanford Univ., 1994, Univ. Alta., Canada, 1995; mem. vis. com. Dept. Polit., Princeton Univ., 2002. Author: Membership & Morals: The Personal Uses of Pluralism in America, 1998, Another Liberalism: Romanticism and the Reconstruction of Liberal Thought, 1987, Bentham's Theory of the Modern State, 1978; editor: Obligations of Citizenship and Demands of Faith, 2000, Liberalism and the Moral Life, 1993; co-editor: Breaking the Cycles of Hatred, 2002, Civil Society and Government, 2002; contbr. articles to profl. jour., chapters to books. Bd. dir. Civil Liberties Union Mass., Fine Arts Work Ctr., Provincetown, Mass. Recipient David Easton award, APSA, 2002; Bunting Inst. Fellow, Radcliffe Coll., 1988—89. Fellow: Am. Acad. Arts & Sci. Office: Harvard University Littauer 318 Cambridge MA 02138 Office Phone: 617-384-5851. Business E-Mail: nrosenblum@latte.harvard.edu.

ROSENBLUM, PETER M., lawyer; b. NYC, June 26, 1949; m. Peggy R. Rosenblum; 1 child, Travel. BA summa cum laude, Amherst Coll., 1970; MA, Yale U., 1972; JD cum laude, Harvard U., 1974. Bar: Mass. 1974, US dist. Ct. dist. Mass. Law clk. to Hon. G. Joseph Tauro Supreme Judicial Ct. Mass., 1974-75; mem. Foley, Hoag & Eliot, Boston; ptnr. Foley Hoag LLP, Boston. Co-author: Venture Capital Manual, 1990, Massachusetts Business Lawyering, 1991; contbr. articles to profl. jours. Recipient Worlds Leading Private Equity Lawyers, 2005, Best Lawyers Am., 1999—2007, Mass. Super Lawyers, 2006, Best VC Lawyers, 2001. Mem.: ABA, Boston Bar Assns., Mass. Bar Assns., Mass. Continuing Legal Edn., Inc. (Bus. and Comml. Law Curriculum Com.), Boston Bar Assn. (chmn. Corp. Law Com. 1995—97, chmn. Business Law Sect. 1997—99), Boston Lawyers Grp. (chmn.). Avocation: hist. and sci. fiction. Office: Foley Hoag LLP 155 Seaport Blvd Boston MA 02210-2600 Office Phone: 617-832-1151. Office Fax: 617-832-7000. Business E-Mail: pmr@foleyhoag.com.

ROSENBLUM, RICHARD MARK, utilities executive; b. NYC, Apr. 28, 1950; s. Victor Sigmund and Julia K. R.; m. Michele E. Cartier, Aug. 30, 1979; children: Gialisa, Jeremy Scott. BS, MS, Rensselaer Poly. Inst., 1973. Startup engr. Combustion Engring., Inc., Windsor, Conn., 1973-76; engr. So. Calif. Edison Co., Rosemead, 1976-82; project mgr. San Onofre Nuclear Generating Sta., 1982-83, tech. mgr., 1983-84, nuclear safety mgr., 1984-86, mgr. quality assurance, 1986-89, mgr. nuclear regulatory affairs, 1989-93, v.p. engring. and tech. svcs., 1993-95, v.p. distbn., 1996-98, sr. v.p. T&D, 1998—2005; sr. v.p. generation, chief nuc. officer Generation Bus. Unit, 2005—. N.Y. State Regents scholar, 1968-73. Office: 2244 Walnut Grove Ave Rosemead CA 91770-3714 Business E-Mail: richard.rosenblum@sce.com.

ROSENBLUM, WILLIAM F., JR., lawyer; b. NYC, May 11, 1935; AB cum laude, Princeton U., 1957; JD, Columbia U., 1960. Bar: N.Y. 1961, U.S. Dist. Ct. (so. dist.) N.Y. 1965. Gen. atty. Stanley Warner Corp., 1964-66; assoc. Leon, Weill & Mahony, 1967-70, Finley, Kumble, Wagner & Heine, 1970-74; pvt. practice, 1975; v.p. legal affairs Rep. Nat. Bank N.Y., 1976-82; sr. v.p., dep. gen. counsel, corp. sec. Rep. N.Y. Corp., 1987—2001; sr. v.p., dep. gen. counsel HSBC USA Inc., 2000—01; mng. dir., gen. counsel NuVerse Advisors LLC, NYC, 2001—. Mem.: ABA (mem. bus. law sect., mem. futures and derivatives regulation and pvt. investment cos. coms.), Assn. Bar City N.Y. (fgn. and comparative law UN com. 2000—04, investment mgmt. regulation com., banking law com., investment funds com.), N.Y. State Bar Assn. (mem. sect. internat. law, bus. law, futures and derivatives regulation 1990—). Office: Nuverse Advisors LLC 645 Fifth Ave New York NY 10022 Business E-Mail: wrosenblum@nuverse.com.

ROSENBLUM, ZINA MICHELLE ZARIN, psychology professor, marketing professional, researcher; b. NYC, Mar. 4, 1949; d. Harry and Miriam (Bachrach) Zarin; m. Martin Jerome Rosenblum, May 31, 1975; children: Steven David, Richard James. BA magna cum laude, Queens Coll., 1971; MEd, Columbia U., 1973, MEd Counseling Psychology, 1973. Prof. psychology Marymount Manhattan Coll., NYC, 1971—73; addictions counselor Manhattan Vets. Hosp., NYC, 1971—73; project dir. BBD&O Advt., NYC, 1973—74, Grey Advt., NYC, 1974—75; supr. market rsch. Doyle Dane & Bernbach, NYC, 1975—77, SSC& B, NYC, 1977—78; dir. rsch. Hershey Co., Pa., 1978—79; adminstr. Suncoast Eye Clinic, St. Petersburg, Fla., 1979—97; prof. psychology St. Petersburg Coll., Seminole, Fla., 1997—. Sec. Nat. Coun. Jewish Women, Fla., 1980—81; docent Fla. Holocaust Mus., 2005—. Scholar, Columbia U., 1971; Nat. Merit acholar, Coll. Bd., 1970. Mem.: APA, Phi Beta Kappa. Office: Suncoast Eye Clinic Martin Rosenblum 2200 16th St North Saint Petersburg FL 33704 Home Phone: 727-547-4818; Office Phone: 727-822-4729. Personal E-mail: zcurl@aol.com.

ROSENBLUTH, FRANCES MCCALL, political scientist, educator; b. Osaka, Japan, Oct. 22, 1958; d. Robert Donnell McCall and Virginia Lancaster Montgomery; m. James Edward Rosenbluth, Oct. 5, 1985; children: Benjamin Lee, John Gabriel, William Lancaster. BA, U. Va., 1980; MIA, Colubia U., 1983, PhD, 1988. Asst. prof. U. Va., Charlottesville, 1988-89, U. Calif., San Diego, 1989-92, UCLA, 1992, prof., 1993, Yale U., New Haven, 1994—. Mem. editl. bd. Am. Polit. Sci. Rev., Washington, 1996-2000, Internat. Orgn., MIT Press, 1996-2000, Am. Asian Rev., 2000--. Author: Financial Policies in Japan, 1989; co-author: Japan's Political Marketplace, 1993, The Politics of Oligarchy, 1995 (Luebbert award 1997). Fellow Fulbright Found., 1985-86, Social Sci. Rsch. Coun., 1987-88, Coun. on Fgn. Rels., 1999-2000; NSF rschr., 1991; ABE fellow, 2000-02. Fellow Am. Acad. Arts & Scis.; mem. Am. Polit. Sci. Assn. Democrat. Presbyterian. Avocations: reading, hiking. Office: Yale U Dept Polit Sci New Haven CT 06520-8301 E-mail: frances.rosenbluth@yale.edu. *

ROSENBLUTH, MORTON, periodontist, educator; b. NYC, Sept. 28, 1924; s. Jacob and Eva (Bigeleissen) R.; m. Sylvia Fradin, July 2, 1946; children: Cheryl Bonnie, Hal Glen. BA, NYU, 1943, grad. program in periodontia, oral medicine, 1946, DDS, 1946. Diplomate Am. Bd. Periodontology. Intern Bellevue Hosp., NYC, 1946-47, resident, 1947; individual practice dentistry NYC, 1947-59; individual practice periodontia North Miami Beach, Fla., 1960—; individual practice periodontia, TMJ, implantology Bay Harbor Islands, Fla., 1995—. Periodontist Mt. Sinai Hosp., N.Y., Polyclinic Hosp. and Med. Sch. N.Y., Mt. Sinai Hosp., Miami Beach, Fla., Parkway Gen. Hosp.; chief dental dept. North Miami Gen. Hosp.; chmn. periodontia sect. Dade County Rsch. Ctr.; clin. assoc. prof. divsn. oral and maxillofacial surgery U. Miami Sch. Medicine; assoc. clin. prof. Southeastern U. Health Scis.; assoc. prof. Nova Southeastern U. Coll. Dental Medicine; lectr. throughout U.S.A., Israel, Mexico, Rome, Teheran, Bangkok, Hong Kong, Tokyo, Honolulu, Jamaica, Paris, London, Sicily, Budapest, Berlin, Luxembourg, South Africa and others; vis. lectr. U. Tenn. Dental Coll., NYU Dental Coll.; cons. VA Hosp., Miami. Contbr. articles to profl. jours. Mem. adv. bd. U. Fla. Coll. Dentistry; mem. profl. adv. bd. North Dade Children's Ctr., Hope Sch. Mentally Retarded Children; mem. sci. adv. com. United Health Found.; chmn. Dental divsn. United Fund of Dade County, Combined Jewish Appeal; nat. chmn. Hebrew U. Sch. Dental Medicine; bd. dirs. Health Planning Coun. South Fla.; pres. Condominium Assn.; bd. dirs. and bd. overseers Am. Friends of Hebrew U.; mem. med. adv. bd. Dade-Broward Lupus Found.; trustee Jewish Congregation, 1961-64. With AUS, 1943-44, as capt. USAF, 1951-52. Recipient Maimonides award State of Israel, 1979. Fellow Am. Coll. Dentists, Internat. Coll. Dentists; mem. ADA, Am. Acad. Periodontology, Am. Assn. Hosp. Dental Chiefs, Am. Acad. Dental Medicine, Am. Soc. Advancement Gen. Anesthesia in Dentistry, Am. Soc. Periodontists, Fla. Soc. Periodontists, Northeastern Soc. Periodontists, Fla. Dental Soc. (chmn. coun. on legislation), Miami Dental Soc., Miami Beach Dental Soc., East Coast Dental Soc. (sec.-treas. 1968, pres. 1971-72), North Dade Dental Soc. (pres. 1963-64), Fedn. Dentaire Internat., Fla. Acad. Dental Practice Adminstrn., Alpha Omega (pres. 1978-78, internat. regent 1973-75, internat. editor 1975-77, internat. pres.-elect 1977-78, internat. pres. 1979, chmn. bd. Alpha Omega Found. 1985-90), Am. Dental Interfrat. Coun. (pres. 1981-82), Nocoma Club (pres. 1958-60), NYU Century Club (local chmn.), Jockey Club (bd. govs.), KP, Masons, Kiwanis (bd. dirs. 1965), Chaine Des

Rotisseurs (Miami Beach charge de missions). Home: 20281 E Country Club Dr Apt # 1001 Aventura FL 33180 Office: 1048 Kane Concourse Bay Harbor Islands FL 33154-2000 Office Phone: 305-867-0005. Personal E-mail: periomort@aol.com.

ROSENDHAL, JEFFREY DAVID, federal agency administrator, educator, astronomer, consultant; b. Bklyn., June 21, 1941; s. Louis and Beulah (Goldsmith) R.; m. Sharon E. Katzman, Dec. 27, 1964 (div. Jan. 25, 1989); children: Martin Andrew, Rachel Lynn; m. Ellen R. Anderson, Feb. 14, 1992. BA, Williams Coll., 1962; MS, U. Ill., 1963; PhD, Yale U., 1968. Vis. asst. prof. astronomy U. Wash., Seattle, 1968-69; asst. prof. U. Wis., Madison, 1969-71, U. Ariz., Tucson, 1971-74; with NASA, Washington, 1974—2004, mgr. advanced programs and tech., astrophysics divsn., 1978-80, asst. assoc. adminstr. advanced planning Office Space Sci., 1980-81, asst. assoc. adminstr. sci. Office Space Sci., Applications, 1981-87, spl. asst. to assoc. adminstr. for space sci. and applications, 1987-89, 92-93, spl. asst. for policy Office Exploration, 1989-90, asst. dir. exploration (internat.) Office Aeronautics, Exploration and Tech., 1990-91, asst. dir. strategic planning Astrophysics Divsn. Office of Space Sci., 1993-96, asst. assoc. adminstr./edn. and outreach Office Space Sci., 1996-2001, edn. and pub. outreach dir. Office of Space Sci., 2001—04, asst. assoc. adminstr. for edn. programs Office of Edn., 2004. Vis. prof. internat. rels. George Washington U., 1988-89; mem. staff energy subcom. House Sci. Space and Tech. Com., 1992; vis. sr. scholar Nat. Air and Space Mus., 2005-06; cons., Jet Propulsion Lab., NASA, 2005—, NRC, TERC, Boston Mus. Sci., 2007—; dep. dir. U. Space Rsch. Assn. Nat. Ctr. Earth and Space Sci. Edn., 2006. Mem. editl. bd.: Jour. Brit. Interplanetary Soc., 1988—; contbr. articles to profl. jours. Recipient Team Achievement award European Space Agy., 1983, 85, 86, Presdl. award of Meritorious Exec. in Sr. Exec. Svc., 1987, 2001, Outstanding Leadership medal, NASA, 1984, 2003, Group Achievement award, (2)1986, 1995, 1996; NSF grantee, 1971, 72-73; NASA fellow Yale U., 1966-68; hon. Woodrow Wilson fellow, 1962. Fellow: AIAA (assoc.); mem.: Sr. Execs. Assn., Internat. Astron. Union, Internat. Acad. Astronautics, Am. Astron. Soc. (divsn. planetary scis., hist. astronomy divsn.), Astron. Soc. Pacific (adv. com. 2006—, Klumpke-Roberts award 2006), Cosmos Club, Phi Beta Kappa. Achievements include discovery of the variability of the microturbulence in early-type high luminosity stars; direction of the selection of flight experiments for every major NASA scientific mission 1980-1988; development of strategic and implementation plans for incorporating education and the public understanding of science into space science research programs and missions; establishment of a national support network for space science education; creation of the largest single program in astronomy and space science education ever undertaken, an effort that, at it's peak, reached tens of millions of people every year. Home: 11446 Links Dr Reston VA 20190-4813 Home Phone: 703-437-6363. E-mail: jeffrosendhal@comcast.net.

ROSENE, PAUL EARL, music educator; b. Chgo., Ill., Mar. 26, 1930; s. Earl Nile and Dorothy Mae Rosene; m. Doris J. Mehrkens, Nov. 18, 1951; children: Richard, Cindy Mann. MusD Edn., U. of Ill., Champaign-Urbana, Illinois, 1968—76; Master degree in Edn. -Psychology and Music, Ill. State U., Normal, IL, 1955—57; BS in Music Edn., Ill. State Normal U., Normal, Illinois, 1947. Cert. master tchr. Ill., supr. student tchg. in music Ill., master tchr. Music Educators Nat. Conf. Dir. music edn. Saybrook Pub. Sch., Ill., 1951—52; supr. music, dir. bands Chenoa Pub. Schs., Ill., 1952—53; instructor band sch. USAF, Geneva, NY, 1953—54, bandsman French horn Dayton, Ohio, 1954—55, dir. men's glee club, 1954—55; dir. instrumental music Avon Pub. Schs., Ill., 1955—57; supr. music and dir. HS bands Pittsfield Pub. Schs., Ill., 1957—67; prof. music edn., supr. student tchg. music Ill. State U., Normal, 1967—90; music cons. handbells and choirchimes Malmark, Inc., Lady Lake, Fla., 1990—. USA pers. dir. Sch. Band/Chorus of Am., Bloomington, 1967—79. Author: (music book) Making Music With Choirchimes Instruments, 1982; author: (composer) (music techniques book) Making Music with Choirchimes Instruments - Advanced Method, 1986; composer (music for choirchimes): (music publ.) Pontifest, 1988; author: (techniques book) Special Effects for Choirchimes, 2003. Dir. of handbells Bethany Luth. Ch., Leesburg, Fla., 1990—; dir. Ctrl. Ill. Cmty. Band, Bloomington-Normal, 1979—90; dir. and founder Ill. State U. Handbells and Choirchime Ensembles, Normal, 1974—90. Staff sgt. band dir., instr. band sch. USAF, 1953—55. Mem.: Pittsfield Tchrs. Assn. (pres. 1960—67), Ill. Music Edn. Assn. (v.p. 1972—80, pres. dist. III 1972—84, Disting. Svc. Award 1991), Fla. Music Educators Assn., Nat. Assn. for Music Therapy (editor Gt. Lakes newsletter 1967—90), Music Educators Nat. Conf. (univ. contact Gt. Lakes divsn. 1979—84), Fla. Band Assn. (adjudicator 1994—). Republican. Lutheran. Avocations: Bible study, walking, reading, attending concerts, computer technology. Home: 822 Pinar Dr Orlando FL 32825-7822 Office: Music Edn Cons 822 Pinar Dr Orlando FL 32825-7822 Personal E-mail: rosenebell@aol.com.

ROSENFELD, ALBERT HYMAN, science and medical writer; b. Phila., May 31, 1920; s. Samuel and Annie (Zeiffert) R.; m. Lillian Elizabeth Snow, Aug. 24, 1948; children: Robert, Shana. BA in History and Social Scis., N.Mex. State U., 1950, DLett (hon.), 1971. Freelance mag. writer, corr., Santa Fe, 1950-56; sci. editor Life mag., NYC, 1956-69; mng. editor Family Health mag., NYC, 1969-71; writer, prodr. Time-Life Video, NYC, 1971-72; sci. editor, columnist Saturday Rev., NYC, 1973-79; cons. on future programs March of Dimes Birth Defects Found., White Plains, NY, 1973—2005; adj. asst. prof. U. Tex. Med. Br., Galveston, 1973-98. Author: The Quintessence of Irving Langmuir, 1962, The Second Genesis, 1969, Prolongevity II, 1985; co-author: Responsible Parenthood, 1980; contbr. articles to profl. publs. Sgt. U.S. Army, 1942-45, ETO. Recipient award for leadership in med. journalism Lasker Found., 1967, Nat. Mag. award Columbia U., 1975, James P. Grady medal Am. Chem. Soc., 1981. Mem. World Future Soc., Nat. Assn. Sci. Writers, Authors Guild, Smithsonian Assocs., Hastings Ctr. Democrat. Jewish. Avocations: music, sketching, tennis, baseball, hiking. E-mail: alrosenf@westnet.com.

ROSENFELD, ARTHUR F., federal official, lawyer; b. Allentown, Pa., 1944; m. Carla Toledo. BA, Muhlenberg Coll., 1970; MBA, Lehigh U., 1974; JD, Villanova U., 1979. Bar: D.C. 1979, U.S. Supreme Ct., U.S. Ct. Appeals (4th, 5th and D.C. cirs.). Labor atty. U.S. C. of C., Washington, 1979—84; atty. Hansell & Post, 1984—86; numerous positions including counsel for regulations divsn. employee benefits, spl. asst. to solicitor of labor, assoc. dep. sec. U.S. Dept. Labor, 1986—97; sr. labor advisor to chmn. James M. Jeffords Senate Com. Health, Edn., Labor and Pensions, 1997—2001; gen. counsel NLRB, 2001—05, acting gen. counsel, 2005—06; dir. Fed Mediation & Concilation Svc., Washington, 2006—. Fellow: The Coll. of Labor and Employment Lawyers. Office: Fed Mediation & Concillation Svc 2100 K St NW Rm 900 Washington DC 20427

ROSENFELD, ARTHUR H., physics professor, researcher; b. Birmingham, Ala., June 22, 1926; BS in Physics, Va. Poly. Inst., 1944; PhD in Physics, U. Chgo., 1954; DSc (hon.), U. Durham, Eng., 1983. Rsch. assoc. Inst. Nuclear Studies U. Chgo., 1954-55; rsch. assoc. Lawrence Berkeley Lab. U. Calif., Berkeley, 1955-57; asst. prof. to assoc. prof. U. Chgo., 1957-63; prof. physics U. Calif., Berkeley, 1963-94, dir. particle data group Lawrence Berkeley Lab., 1964-75, acting chmn. dept. computer sci., 1967-68, leader rsch. group A Lawrence Berkeley Lab., 1971-73, leader energy-efficient bldgs. rsch program Lawrence Berkeley Lab., 1975-83, vice chmn. energy and resources grad. program, 1986-94, dir. Ctr. Bldg. Sci. Lawrence Berkeley Lab., 1986-94, founder, acting dir. Calif. Inst. for Energy Efficiency, 1988-90, prof. emeritus, 1994—; sr. advisor to asst. sec. energy efficiency U.S. Dept. Energy, Washington, 1994-99; commr. Calif. Energy Commn., Sacramento, Calif., 2000—. Vis. prof. Coll. de France, Paris, 1978; co-founder Am. Coun. Energy-Efficient Econ., 1979, chmn., 1981-83, pres., 1984-90, bd. dirs., 1990-94; mem. steering com. advanced customer tech. test maximum energy efficiency Pacific Gas & Electric Co., 1989-98; mem. tech. adv. panel joint com. on energy regulation and environ. State of Calif., 1990-91; mem. Nat. Sci. and Tech. Coun., 1994—, civilian indsl. tech. com, 1994—, co-chmn. subcom. constrn. and bldg., 1994—. Author: (with E. Fermi and others) Nuclear Physics, 1949, Experimental Meson Spectroscopy, 1968, 3d edit., 1972, Supplying Energy Through Greater Efficiency: The Potential for Conservation in California's Residential Sector, 1983, A New Prosperity: The SERI Solar/Conservation Study, 1991, Scenarios of U.S. Carbon Reductions, Interlaboratory Working Group, 1997; contbr. articles, seminars to profl. jours., confs.; assoc. editor Jour. Computational Physics, 1964-73, Energy and Bldgs., 1979—, Energy, the Internat. Jour., 1985-91; editl. cons. Ency. of Applied Physics, 1988—. Mem. governing bd. Am. Inst. Physics, 1974-77; co-founder Am. Coun. for an Energy Efficient Economy, 1979, Ctr. for Energy and Climate Solution, Washington, DC; chmn. 1981-83, pres. 1984—, mem. adv. com. Calif. Legis. Joint Com. on Energy Regulation and Environ., 1990-91. Recipient Leo Szilard award for Physics in Pub. Interest, 1986, Sadi Carnot award for Energy Efficiency, US Dept. Energy, 1993, Star Energy Efficiency for outstanding contbn. in promoting energy efficiency Alliance to Save Energy, 1995, 2005 Enrico Fermi award, US Dept. Energy. Fellow Am. Physical Soc. (sec., treas. divsn. particles and fields 1967-71, Leo Szilard award for physics in the pub. interest 1986); mem. NAS (panel on policy implications of greenhouse warm 1990—), Fedn. Am. Sci. (coun. 1964-72, 77-81, 83-87, 94-98, 2004—), Am. Inst. Physics (mem. governing bd. 1974-77). Achievements include co-developement of Ultra-Violet Water Works to purify water in villages and slums, 1996; studied under Enrico Fermi at U. Chgo. Office: Calif Energy Commn 1516 9th St Sacramento CA 95814 Office Phone: 916-654-4930. Business E-Mail: AHRosenfeld@LBL.gov.

ROSENFELD, GERALD, investment company executive, financial analyst; b. NYC, Dec. 29, 1946; s. Jack and Shirley (Otter) R.; m. Nancy P. Henenfeld, Jan. 18, 1970 (div. Dec. 1984); 1 child, Erica; m. Judith Ellen Zarin, May 26, 1985; 1 child, Jack. BCE, CCNY, 1968; M in Engring. Sci., CUNY, 1970; PhD, NYU, 1973. Instr. NYU, NYC, 1970-73; asst. prof. U. Md., Catonsville, 1973-76; mgr. analytical services McKinsey & Co., NYC, 1976-79; assoc. Salomon Bros., Inc., NYC, 1979-80, v.p., 1980-85, mng. dir., 1985-87, chief fin. officer, 1987-88; mng. dir. Bankers Trust Co., NYC, 1988—92, Lazard Freres & Co., 1992—98; sr. mng. dir. Nations-Banc Montgomery Securities, 1998; mng. mem. G. Rosenfeld & Co., 1998—2000; CEO Rothschild North America, 2000—. Bd. dir. Resources Connection, ContiGroup Companies, Case Corp.; mem. adv. bd. Corpedia Edn. Mem. bd. overseers Stern Sch. Bus., N.Y. Univ., bd. dir., Jewish Theol. Sem.; mem. bd. adv. Lerner Sch. Bus., Univ. Del. Fellow: Am. Acad. Arts & Sci. Office: Rothschild North America 51st Fl 1251 Ave of the Americas New York NY 10020

ROSENFELD, HARRY MORRIS, editor; b. Berlin, Aug. 12, 1929; arrived in US, 1939, naturalized; s. Sam and Esther Rosenfeld; m. Anne Hahn, Feb. 28, 1953; children: Susan, Amy, Stefanie. BA, Syracuse U., 1952; postgrad., NYU, 1954, Columbia U., 1955-59. With N.Y. Herald Tribune, 1954-66, fgn. editor, 1962-66; mng. editor Herald Tribune News Svc., 1959-62; with Washington Post, 1966-78, fgn. editor, 1969; asst. mng. editor Met. News, 1970-74, Nat. News, 1974-76, Outlook/Book World, 1976-78; editor Times Union and Knickerbocker News, Albany, NY, 1978-88, L.A. Herald Examiner, 1985, The Times Union and Sunday Times Union, 1978-96; editor-at-large, columnist L.C. Times Union, Albany, NY, 1996—. Dir. daily Watergate coverage Washington Post; pres. NYS Assn. Assoc. Press, 1983; vice-chmn. NY Fair Trial Free Press Conf., 1985—98, vice chmn. emeritus, 1998—; co-chmn. NY State Reporters Com. Freedom Press; mem. adv. com. Harvard Journalism Fellowship Advanced Studies Pub. Health; Pulitzer juror, 1987—88, 1996, 97; mem. 3 commns. Cameras in Cts. Commr. NY State Regents Commn. Libr. Svcs.; chmn. Elder Network Capital Region. Recipient newspaper award Pulitzer Gold medal for pub. svc., Black United Front award, 1973, First Amendment award, Anti-Defamation League-B'nai B'rith, Oustanding Alumni award, Syracuse U. Coll. Arts and Scis., 1993, Media Responsibility award, NY State Martin Luther King Jr. Inst. Non-Violence, 1993, Dr. Morton Berger Meml. award, Malmonides Day Sch., 2005. Office: Times Union PO Box 15000 Albany NY 12212-5000 Office Phone: 518-454-5450. Business E-Mail: hrosenfeld@timesunion.com.

ROSENFELD, HOWARD H., lawyer; b. Chgo., Nov. 6, 1938; s. Edward M. and Eve R. (Lenetzky) R.; m. Honey B. Jordan, Apr. 14, 1962; children: Julie, Lisa. LLB, DePaul U., 1962. Bar: Ill. 1962, U.S. Dist. Ct. (no. dist.) Ill. 1962. Assoc. Gillen, Owens & Willens, Chgo., 1963-67; ptnr. Rosenfeld, Hafron & Shapiro, Chgo., 1967-81, Rosenfeld Hafron Shapiro & Farmer (formerly Rosenfeld, Rotenberg, Schwartzman, Hafron & Shapiro), Chgo., 1981—. Adj. prof. family law DePaul U. Served with U.S. Army, 1962-63. Fellow Am. Acad. Matrimonial Lawyers, Am. Trial Lawyers Assn.; mem. Ill. State Bar Assn., Chgo. Bar Assn. Office: Rosenfeld Hafron Shapiro & Farmer 221 N La Salle St Ste 1763 Chicago IL 60601-1422 *

ROSENFELD, IRENE B., food products company executive; b. Bklyn., 1953; BA in Psychology, Cornell U, 1975, MS in Bus., 1977, PhD in Mktg. & Statistics, 1980. With Dancer, Fitzgerald Sample Advertising (now Saatchi and Saatchi), 1979—81, Kraft Foods Inc., 1981—2004, exec. v.p., gen. mgr., beverages divsn., 1991—94, exec. v.p., gen. mgr. desserts & snacks divsn., 1994—96; pres. Kraft Foods Canada, 1996—2004; group v.p. Kraft Foods Inc., 2000—04; pres. Kraft Food N. Am., 2003—04; chmn., CEO Frito-Lay Inc. (divsn. of PepsiCo Inc.), Plano, Tex., 2004—06; CEO Kraft Foods Inc., Northfield, Ill., 2006—07, chmn., CEO, 2007—. Bd. dirs. AutoNation, Inc. Mem. YWCA Acad. Women Achievers; bd. trustees Cornell U. Named one of Most Powerful Women, Forbes mag., 2006, 50 Most Powerful Women in Bus., Fortune mag., 2006, 50 Women to Watch, Wall St. Jour., 2006, Next 20 Female CEOs, Pink Mag. & Forté Found., 2006; recipient The Masters in Excellence award, Jewish Student Cmty. at Cornell Univ., 2005. Office: Kraft Foods Inc 3 Lakes Dr Northfield IL 60093 *

ROSENFELD, ISADORE, cardiologist, educator; b. Sept. 7, 1926; arrived in U.S., 1958; s. Morris and Vera (Friedman) Rosenfeld; m. Camilla Master, Aug. 19, 1956; children: Arthur, Stephen, Hildi, Herbert. BS, McGill U., 1947, M.D.C.M., 1951, diploma in internal medicine, 1956, DSc (hon.), 1999; PhD (hon.), Tel Aviv U. Intern Royal Victoria Hosp., Montreal; resident Balt. City Hosp.; clin. asst. prof. medicine NY Hosp. Weil Cornell Med. Ctr., NYC, 1964—71, clin. assoc. prof., 1971—79, clin. prof., 1979—. Now hon. fellow; attending physician NY Hosp., NYC, 1989—, Meml. Sloan Kettering Cancer Ctr.; juror Lasker Sci. Awards, 1974—90; dir. Rsch. Am., 1990; Rossi Disting prof. clin. medicine NY Hosp. Weil Cornell Med. Ctr., 1993—; vis. prof. Baylor U. Coll. Medicine, 1982; mem. practicing physicians adv. coun. to U.S. Sec Health and Human Svcs., practicing physician, 1992—96; bd. overseers Cornell U. Med. Coll., 1980—; bd. vistors U. Calif. Sch. Medicine, Davis, 1983—; cons. NIH; invited lectr. Am. Coll. Physicians; lectr. in field; TV commentator in field. Author: EKG and X-Ray in Diseases of the Heart, 1963, The Complete Medical Exam, 1978, Second Opinion, 1981, Modern Prevention, 1986, Symptoms, 1988, The Best Treatment, 1991, Doctor, What Should I EAT?, 1995, Dr. Rosenfeld's Guide to Alternative Medicine, 1997, Love Now-Age Later, 1999, Power to the Patient: The Treatment to Insist on When You're Sick, 2002, Dr. Isadore Rosenfeld's Breakthrough Medicine, 2004, Healing Breakthroughs, 2004, Dr. Isadore Rosenfeld's Breakthrough Health, 2005; med. cons.: Vogue mag., 1993—97, FOX News Channel, 1996—; contbg. editor: Parade mag., 1997—; health editor:, 1998—. Pres. Rosenfeld Heart Found., NYC, 1974—; bd. dirs. N.Y. Heart Assn., 1979—82; mem. nat. adv. com. Harriman Inst. Advanced Study of Soviet Union, 1982—; mem. nat. adv. comm. increasing physical activity program Robert Wood Johnson Found. Recipient Vera award, The Voice Found., 1981, Inaugural award, N.Y. Heart Assn., Silver award for patient edn. and info., Nat. Health Info. Rsch. Chr., 1996, Citizen of the World award, U.N., 1999, Siver award, Nat. Health Info., 1999, Gold Triangle award, Am. Acad. Dermatology, Silver award, Nat. Mature Media awards, Dist. Med. Svc. award, Am. Physicians Fellowship, Merit award, Consumer Health Pub. Assn., Am. Consumer Publ. Assn. and Am. Consumer Publ. Corp, 2000, Advocacy award for impact on pub. opinion through the Media, Rsch. Am., 2001, Lifetime Achievement award, Found. Biomed. Rsch. Fellow: Am. Physician's Fellowship for Israel (hon. nat. pres. 1975—), N.Y. County Med. Soc. (bd. censors 1979—83, v.p. 1983—84, pres. 1984—85, bd. trustees 1985—), Royal Coll. Physicians Can., Am. Coll. Chest Physicians, ACP, Cornell Alumni Assn. (hon.). Jewish. Achievements include research in hypertension; angina pectoris; sudden cardiac death; arteriosclerosis. Office: 125 E 72nd St New York NY 10021-4250 Home Phone: 914-251-0091. Personal E-mail: irmd@earthlink.net. E-mail: irmd@mac.com.

ROSENFELD, JOHN LANG, geology educator; b. Portland, Oreg., July 14, 1920; s. James Wendel and Gladys (Lang) R.; m. Juanita Baker, Oct. 22, 1943 (dec. Feb. 2004); children: Susan Jane, John Lang. AB, Dartmouth Coll., Hanover, NH, 1942; AM, Harvard U., Cambridge, Mass., 1949, PhD, 1954. Asst. prof. geology Mo. Sch. Mines, U. Mo., Rolla, 1949—55; vis. asst. prof. geology Wesleyan U., Middletown, Conn., 1955—57; from asst. prof. to prof. geology UCLA, 1957—91, prof. geology emeritus, 1991—. Commr. Geol. and Natural History Survey, State of Conn., 1955-57. Contbr. articles to profl. jours. Guggenheim fellow, 1963—64. Fellow Mineral. Soc. Am., Geol. Soc. Am.; mem. AAAS, Am. Geophys. Union, Nature Conservancy (life), Union Concerned Scientists. Office: UCLA Dept Earth And Space Scis Los Angeles CA 90095 Office Phone: 310-825-1505. Business E-Mail: rosenfel@ucla.edu.

ROSENFELD, JONATHAN D., lawyer; b. 1961; AB, Brandeis Univ., 1983; JD, Boston Univ., 1986. Bar: Calif. 1986, Conn. 1989, Mass. 1990. Ptnr., chmn. Labor dept. Wilmer Cutler Pickering Hale & Dorr, Boston. Office: Wilmer Cutler Pickering Hale & Dorr 60 State St Boston MA 02109 Office Phone: 617-526-6941. Office Fax: 617-526-5000. Business E-Mail: jonathan.rosenfeld@wilmerhale.com.

ROSENFELD, LAWRENCE J. (LARRY), lawyer; b. Bronx, NY, Aug. 25, 1950; BA magna cum laude, Queens Coll., CUNY, 1972; JD, Yale, 1975. Bar: Ariz. 1976, US Supreme Ct. 1981. Named one of Leading Lawyers, Ariz. Bus. Jour., 2006; named to Best Lawyers in Am., 2003—06, Chambers USA (Labor and Employment Law), 2005—06. Mem.: ABA, Maricopa County Bar Assn., Ariz. State Bar Assn. Office: Greenberg Traurig LLP Ste 700 2375 E Camelback Rd Phoenix AZ 85016-9000 Office Phone: 602-445-8502. Office Fax: 602-445-8100. Business E-Mail: rosenfeldl@gtlaw.com.

ROSENFELD, NACHMAN, plastic surgeon; b. Tel Aviv, Feb. 16, 1943; s. Pinhas and Sara Rosenfeld; m. Hennia Finkelstein; children: Dror, Iris. MD, Hebrew U., 1968. Board Certified Am. Bd. Plastic Surgery, 1978. Resident Albert Einstein Coll. Medicine, NYC, 1977, asst. clin. instr.; pvt. practice, 1977—. Fellow: Am. Coll. Surgeons; mem.: Am. Soc. for Asthetic Plastic Surgery, Am. Soc. Plastic Surgeons.

ROSENFELD, ROBERT A., lawyer; BA in Pub. Affairs with highest distinction, George Washington U., 1971; BA with first class honors, Oxford U., 1973; JD cum laude, Harvard U., 1976. Bar: Calif., US Ct. Appeals (7th and 9th cirs.), US Ct. Fed. Claims, US Supreme Ct. Law clerk for Honorable Marvin Frankel, 1976—77, Honorable Warren E. Burger, US Supreme Ct., 1977—78; atty., shareholder Heller, Erhman, White, & McAuliffe LLP, San Francisco, 1979—. Bd. dirs. Calif. Pacific Med. Ctr. Rhodes scholar, 1973. Office: Heller Ehrman 333 Bush St San Francisco CA 94104 Office Phone: 415-772-6609. Office Fax: 415-772-6268. Business E-Mail: bob.rosenfeld@hellerehrman.com.

ROSENFELD, RONALD ALLEN, federal agency administrator; b. 1939; married; 3 children. Grad., Wharton Sch. Bus., Harvard Law Sch. Dep. asst. sec. for single family housing US Dept. Housing & Urban Devel., Washington, 1989—91, gen. dep. asst. sec. housing, FHA commr.; dep. asst. sec. corp. fin. US Dept. Treasury, Washington, 1992—93; sec. commerce State of Okla., Oklahoma City, 1995—98; pres. Govt. Nat. Mortgage Assn. (Ginnie Mae) US Dept. Housing & Urban Devel., Washington, 2001—04; chmn. Fed. Housing Fin. Bd., Washington, 2004—. Office: Fed Housing Fin Bd 1625 Eye St NW Washington DC 20006

ROSENFELD, STEVEN B., lawyer; b. NYC, Apr. 12, 1943; s. Eugene David and Laura (Sipin) R.; m. Naomi Eve Winkler, Aug. 21, 1965 (dec. Apr. 2006); children: Kathryn Anne, Elizabeth Jane; m. Joan Rappoport, June 3, 2007. BA, Columbia Coll., 1964; LLB, Columbia U., 1967. Bar: NY 1967, DC 1984, US Dist. Ct. (so. dist.) NY 1969, US Dist. Ct. (ea. dist.) NY 1970, US Ct. Appeals (2d cir.) 1971, US Ct. Appeals (3d cir.) 1974, US Ct. Appeals (Fed. cir.) 1978, DC 1979, US Supreme Ct. 1979, US Ct. Appeals (5th cir.) 1982, US Ct. Appeals (6th and DC cirs.) 1984, US Ct. Appeals (4th and 9th cirs.) 1987, US Ct. Appeals (1st cir.) 1989, US Ct. Appeals (10th cir.) 1991. Law clk. to Hon. Charles M. Metzner U.S. Dist. Ct. (so. dist.) NY, 1967-68; assoc. Rosenman & Colin, NYC, 1968-71; dep. gen. counsel NY State Commn. on Attica, NYC, Batavia, NY, 1971-72; assoc. Paul, Weiss, Rifkind, Wharton & Garrison, NYC, 1972-75, ptnr., 1976—. Lectr. Columbia U. Sch. Law, 1995—2002; chmn. Conflicts of Interest Bd. N.Y.C., 2002—. Contbr. articles to profl. jours. Bd. dirs. NY Assn. New Ams., NYC, 1973-95; trustee Dalton Sch., NYC, 1988-94; trustee Putney Sch. Putney, Vt., 1995-01, NY Theatre Workshop, 1996—; chair bd. visitors CUNY Law Sch., 2003—. Mem. NY State Bar Assn. (ho. of dels. 1996-98), Assn. Bar City NY (exec. com. 1992-96, v.p. 1998-99, past mem. various coms.), Legal Aid Soc. (pres. 1989-91, bd. dirs., exec. com. 1978-95). Democrat. Jewish. Avocations: opera music, chamber music, theater, tennis. Office: Paul Weiss Rifkind Et Al 1285 Ave of Americas New York NY 10019-6028

ROSENFELD, STEVEN IRA, ophthalmologist; b. NYC, Nov. 18, 1954; s. Frederick and Pearl (Stern) R.; m. Lisa Allyson Klar, June 24, 1978; children: Michael, Julie. BA, Johns Hopkins U., 1976; MD, Yale U., 1980. Diplomate Am. Bd. Ophthalmology, Nat. Bd. Med. Examiners. Intern Yale-New Haven Hosp., 1980-81; resident Barnes Hosp., St. Louis, 1981-84; fellow Bascom Palmer Eye Inst., Miami, Fla., 1984-85; ptnr. in pvt. practice Delray Eye Assocs., Delray Beach, Fla., 1985—. Clin. instr. Bascom Palmer Eye Inst., 1985-90, asst. clin. prof., 1990-96, assoc. clin. prof., 1996—; assoc. examiner Am. Bd. Ophthalmology, Phila., 1993—. Author: The Eye in Systemic Disease, 1990, Lens and Cataract, 1996; contbr. articles to profl. jours. Recipient Harry Rosenbaum Rsch. award Washington U. Sch. Medicine, 1984; named one of Best Doctors in Am., 1996—; Heed Ophthalmic Found. fellow, 1984. Fellow ACS, Am. Acad. Ophthalmology (chmn. B.C.S.C. section Lens and Cataract Surgery 2002—), Soc. Heed Fellows; mem. Castroviejo Corneal Soc., Eye Bank Assn. Am., Fla. Med. Assn., Fla. Soc. Ophthalmology, Assn. for Rsch. in Vision and Ophthalmology, Ocular Microbiology and Immunology Group, Phi Beta Kappa, Alpha Omega Alpha. Avocations: tennis, golf, fly fishing, lacrosse. Office: Delray Eye Assocs 16201 South Military Trail Delray Beach FL 33484-6503 Office Phone: 561-498-8100.

ROSENFELD, WALTER DAVID, JR., architect, writer; b. NYC, May 30, 1930; s. Walter David and Florence (Romann) R.; m. Marilyn Smith, Oct. 15, 1954; children: John W., Sarah E., Susannah, Elizabeth A. AB, U. Pa., 1952; postgrad., Ind. U., 1953-54, Yale U., 1954-55, 57-60. Registered architect, Mass., N.H.; cert. constrn. specifier. Draftsman, specifier Perry Dean Stewart, Boston, 1960-67; architect, specifier, v.p., prin. The Architects Collaborative, Cambridge, Mass., 1967-86, also dir., 1980-84; cons. architect Walter Rosenfeld CSI, Newton, Mass., 1986—. Author: The Practical Specifier, 1985; contbg. editor Progressive Architecture mag., 1980-94; contbr. articles to profl. jours. Pres. Friends of Newton Free Libr., Mass., 1970-72; chmn. Newton Ward 1 Dem. Com., 1974-80; vice chmn. designer sel. com. City of Newton, 1976-86; bd. dirs. Mass. Audubon Soc., 1987-99, Mass. Audubon Coun., 01—. Mem. AIA, Constrn. Spcifications Inst. (bd. dirs. Boston chpt. 1980-86, pres. Boston chpt. 1987-88), Boston Soc. Architects. Office: Walter Rosenfeld CSI PO Box 568 Edgartown MA 02539-0568 Personal E-mail: walros@rcn.com.

ROSENFIELD, ALLAN, medical educator, dean, obstetrician, gynecologist; b. Cambridge, Mass., Apr. 28, 1933; s. Harold Hermann and Beatrice (Garber) Rosenfield; m. Clare Stein, July 31, 1966; children: Paul Allan, Jill Emilie. BA cum laude, Harvard U., 1955; MD, Columbia U., 1959. Diplomate Am. B. Ob-Gyn. Intern, surgical resident Beth Israel Hosp., Boston, 1959—61; resident in ob-gyn Boston Hosp. for Women (now Brigham and Woman's Hosp.), Boston, 1963—66; rep., med. advisor The Population Council and Ministry Pub. Health, Bangkok, 1967—73; asst. dir. tech. assistance div. Population Coun., NYC, 1973—75; prof. ob-gyn Columbia U., NYC, 1975—88, prof. pub. health, 1975—86, DeLamar Prof. pub. health, 1986—, dir. ctr. for population and family health, 1975—88, acting chmn. dept. ob-gyn., 1984—86, dean Joseph Mailman Sch. Pub. Health, 1986—. Bd. mem. Am. Found. for AIDS Rsch.; chair NY State AIDS Adv. Coun. Contbr. articles to profl. jours. Bd. dirs. Kaiser Family Found., David and Lucile Packard Found. Capt. USAF, 1961—63. Fellow: ACOG, Am. Acad. Arts & Scis.; mem.: APHA, Inst. Medicine of NAS (several coms. and bds.). Jewish. Avocations: tennis, skiing, music. Office: Columbia U Joseph Mailman Sch Pub Hlth 600 W 168th St New York NY 10032-3722 Office Phone: 212-305-3929. *

ROSENFIELD, ANDREW M., lawyer, educator; b. Chgo., Sept. 20, 1951; s. Maurice and Lois (Fried) R.; m. Betsy Bergman, Sept. 10, 1978; children: Zachary William, Edwin Alexander, Betty Alana, Jake Leonard. BA with honors, Kenyon Coll., 1973; MA, Harvard U., 1978; JD cum laude, U. Chgo., 1978. Bar: Ill. 1978. Pres., founder Lexecon Inc., Chgo., 1977; adj. prof. Northwestern U. Law Sch., Chgo., 1985-86; lectr. in law U. Chgo., 1986—; founder, chmn UNext, 2000—; mng. ptnr. Gleacher & Co. LLC. Lectr. numerous law and bus. seminars. Mem. bd. trustees U. Chgo., 1996—; vice chmn. bd. trustees Art Inst. Chgo. Mem. Order of Coif. Clubs: Chicago, Standard (bd. dirs.1985—). Jewish. Home: 10 W Deerpath Rd Lake Forest IL 60045-2111 Office: U Chgo Law Sch 1111 E 60th St Chicago IL 60637 also: UNext Ste 455 111 N Canal St Chicago IL 60606 Office Phone: 773-702-9597. E-mail: rosenfield@unext.com.

ROSENFIELD, JAMES HAROLD, SR., communications executive; b. Boston, July 18, 1929; s. Harold and Beatrice (Garber) R.; m. Nancy Lee Stenbuck, Oct. 19, 1952; 2 children. BA, Dartmouth Coll., 1952; D of Comml. Sci. (hon.), St. John's U., 1981. TV network sales exec. NBC, NYC, 1954-57; advt. mgr. Polaroid Corp., Boston, 1956-59; v.p. mktg. Airequipt, Inc., New Rochelle, NY, 1959-65; TV account exec. CBS, Inc., NYC, 1965-67, dir. daytime sales, 1967-70, v.p. Ea. sales, 1970-75, v.p. network sales adminstrn., 1975-77, v.p., nat. sales mgr., 1977, pres. TV Network Div., 1977-81; exec. v.p. CBS/Broadcast Group, NYC, 1981-83, sr. exec. v.p., 1983-85; chmn., CEO John Blair Communications, Inc., NYC, 1987-93; pres. JHR Assocs., Consulting, NYC, 1993; mng. dir. Veronis, Suhler & Assocs., NYC, 1994-98; pres. JHR & Assocs., 1998—. Bd. dirs. Salon Interactive, Inc.; mem. adv. bd. Columbia U. Sch. Pub. Health; bd. chmn. Entertainment Media Works, LLC, 2004—. Emeritus nat. bd. dirs. Jr. Achievement, Inc.; past alumni trustee Roxbury (Mass.) Latin Sch.; bd. dirs., former chmn. Adv. Coun. With Signal Corps, AUS, 1950-53. Fellow: Internat. Acad. TV Arts (life); mem.: Internat. Radio TV Soc. (past pres.). Business E-Mail: jimr@jhrandassociates.com.

ROSENGART, TODD KENNETH, cardiothoracic surgeon, researcher, neurosurgeon, consultant; b. Bklyn., Jan. 24, 1960; s. Martin Rosengart and Barbara Kodish; m. Debra Helen Rosengart, June 15, 1989; children: Michael, Eric. BS with distinction, Northwestern U., Evanston, Ill., 1981; MD with distinction, Northwestern U., Chgo., 1983. Diplomate Am. Bd. Surgery, Am. Bd. Thoracic Surgery. Intern in gen. surgery NYU Med. Ctr., NYC, 1983-84, resident in gen. surgery, 1984-85, resident and chief resident in gen. surgery, 1987-89; med. staff fellow NIH, Bethesda, Md., 1985-87; asst. thoracic surgeon N.Y. Hosp., 1989-90, thoracic surgeon, 1990-91; instr. Cornell U. Med. Coll., NYC, 1989-90, asst. prof. surgery, 1991-93, asst. prof. cardiothoracic surgery, 1993-97, assoc. prof. cardiothoracic surgeery, 1997—; assoc. prof. cardiothoracic surgery Weill Med. Coll. Cornell U., NYC, 1998—; assoc. attending cardiothoracic surgeon N.Y. Presbyn. Hosp., NYC, 1997-99; chief cardiothoracic surg. Evanston (Ill.) Hosp., 1999—; prof. surgery Northwestern U. Med. Sch., 1999—2006; head CT surgery Stony Brook U., SUNY, Stony Brook, NY, 2007—. Sr. registrar Hosp. for Sick Children, London, 1991; asst. Harley St. Clinic, London, 1991; tchg. asst. NYU Med. Ctr., 1988-89; asst. attending surgeon Jamaica Hosp., 1993-96; United Hosp. Med. Ctr., 1994—; attending physician N.Y. Hosp. Med. Ctr. of Queens, 1995—; mem. Ctr. for Vascular Biology, 1996—; assoc. attending cardiothoracic surgeon N.Y. Hosp., 1997, N.Y. Presbyn. Hosp., 1998—; vis. assoc. prof. surgery Columbia U., 1997—; vis. assoc. attending surgeon Presbyn. Hosp., 1997—; manuscript reviewer, presenter, cons. in field. Editl. bd. Cardiac and Vascular Regeneration: Angiogenesis and Myogenesis, Basic th Therapeutic, 1999—; contbr. numerous articles to profl. publs., chpts. to books; patentee gene transfer therapy delivery devide and method, perfusion and occlusion device and method. Nat. Merit scholar, 1977; recipient rsch. award A.G. Morrow Soc., 1987, 97; grantee miles Labs., 1992—, N.Y. Heart Assn., 1994-97, Datascope Corp., 1995—, AccuLase, Inc., 1995—, St. Jude Med., 1996—, Picower Found., 1996—, U.S. Surg. Corp., 1996—, Thoracic Surgery Found. Rsch. and Edn. 1997-99, OrthoBiotech, 1997—, Baxter Healthcare Corp., 1998—, NIH, 1998—. Fellow ACS, Am. Coll. Cardiology (Ill. chpt. alternate councilor 2002—), Am. Coll. Chest Physicians; mem. AAAS, Am. Fedn. Clin. Rsch., Am. Heart Assn. (sci. coun. on cardiothoracic and vascular surgery, met. Chgo. bd. dirs. 2002—, coun. cardiovascular surgery and anesthesia exec. com. 2002—, coun. cardiovascular surgery and anesthesia chmn. memership and comm. com. 2003—, coun. cardiovascular surgery and anesthesia program 2003—, mem., mktg. and comm. com. 2004—), Am. Soc. Gene Therapy (cardiovascular scientific com. 2003—), Nat. Assn. for Bloodless Medicine and Surgery (bd. dirs. 1997—), Andrew Morrow Soc. Cardiac Surgeons, N.Y. Soc. Thoracic Surgery (membership com. 1994-97, chmn. membership com. 1998—, program com. 1994—, chmn. program com. 1997-99), Soc. Thoracic Surgeons, Soc. Univ. Surgeons, N.Y. Acad. Scis., 21st Century Cardiac Surg. Soc. (pres. 1998-2000, membership chmn. 1995-96, v.p. 1996-98), N.Y. Soc. Thoracic Surgery (chmn., membership com. 2001-2002, workforse health policy, reform and advocacy 20003—), Chgo. Cardiac Surgery Soc. (chmn. orgn. com. 2002, pres. 2003-2004), Spencer Soc. Surgeons, Alpha Omega Alpha, Phi Rho Sigma. Office: Stony Brook Univ Med Ctr T19-030 Stony Brook NY 11794

ROSENGARTEN, FRANK, retired language educator, retired literature educator, writer; b. NYC, June 13, 1927; s. Herbert and Clae Rosengarten; m. Lucille Vera Lindner, Mar. 4, 1979; m. Lillian Lebrecht Rosengarten, Apr. 27, 1959 (div. 1977); children: Philip, Daniel, Lydia. BA in English, Adelphi Coll., 1950; MA in English, Columbia U., 1951, PhD in Italian, 1962; MA in French, CUNY, 1998, PhD in French, 2000. Instr. Queens Coll., Flushing, NY, 1957—59, assoc. prof. Italian and Comparative Lit., 1967—92; instr. Adelphi U, Garden City, NY, 1957—59; instr. Italian Columbia U., NYC, 1959—60; asst. prof. Case Western Res. U, Cleve., 1962—63, assoc. prof., 1964—67; prof. Italian and Comparative Lit. CUNY, NYC, 1980—92; ret., 1992. Co-founder Rsch. Group on Socialism and Democracy, NYC, 1983. Author: Vasco Pratolini:The Devel. of a Social Novelist, 1965, The Italian Antifascist Press, 1968, Silvio Trentin: Dall'interventismo alla Resistenza, 1980, The Writings of the Young Marcel Proust, 2001; editor: (publication) Rsch. Group on Socialism and Democracy, 1984—2001; co-editor: New Studies in the Politics and Culture of US Communism, 1993; editor: Antonio Gramsci: Letters from Prison, 1994; contbr. articles, essays in English and Italian. Seaman second class USN, 1945—46, Norfolk Va. Fellow NEH, 1967; grantee APS, 1965. Mem.: Adv. bd./The Brecht Forum, Columbia U Seminar on Modern Italian Hist., Modern Lang. Assoc. Achievements include research in co-founder of the Group on Socialism and Democracy. Home: 160 E 84th St Apt 7D New York NY 10028-2016 Personal E-mail: frosengart@aol.com.

ROSENGREN, CHRISTOPHER PAUL, lawyer; b. 1968; BS, SUNY, 1995; JD, U. Minn. Law Sch., 1998. Bar: Minn. 1998, US Dist. Ct. (dist. Minn.), US Ct. Appeals (8th cir.). Pros. atty.; assoc. Gislason & Hunter, L.L.P., Mankato, Minn. Paratrooper, Russian translator US Army. Named a Rising Star, Minn. Super Lawyers mag., 2006; recipient Pro Bono Atty. of Yr. award, 5th Jud. Dist., 2004. Office: Gislason & Hunter LLP Landkamer Bldg Ste 200 124 E Walnut St Mankato MN 56001 Office Phone: 507-382-6529. E-mail: crosengren@gislason.com. *

ROSENGREN, ERIC S., bank executive; b. Ridgewood, NJ, June 3, 1957; BA, Colby Coll., 1979; MS, U. of Wis., 1984, PhD., 1986. Rsch. fellow Thomas Watson Found., Melbourne, Australia, 1979—80; teaching asst. U. Wis., 1981—84; dissertation fellowship gen acctg. officer, Washington DC, 1984—85; economist, rsch. dept. Fed. Res. Bank Boston, 1985—89, asst. v.p., economist, rsch. dept., 1989—91, v.p., economist, rsch. dept., 1991—2000, sr. v.p., supervision and regulation dept., 2000—02, sr. v.p., supervision & regulation dept., chief discount officer, 2003—05, exec. sr. v.p., supervision & regulation dept., chief discount officer, 2005—07, pres., CEO, 2007—. Contbr. articles to profl. jours. Office: Fed Res Bank Boston 600 Atlantic Ave Boston MA 02210 Office Phone: 617-973-3090. E-mail: Eric.Rosengren@bos.frb.org. *

ROSENHAUER, JAMES JOSEPH (JIM ROSENHAUER), lawyer; b. Chgo., May 25, 1942; s. Norbert E. and Eleanor E. (Berg) R.; m. Vivian M. Garcia, June 11, 1966; 1 child, Christine. AB, Cath. U. Am., 1966; JD, Yale U., 1967. Bar: D.C. 1968. Assoc. Hogan & Hartson, Washington, 1967-74, ptnr., 1975—, head bus., fin. and tax group. Mem. ABA, DC Bar Assn., DC Bar, Internat. Bar Asssn., Inter-Am. Bar Assn., TriBar Legal Opinion Com. Office: Hogan & Hartson Columbia Square 555 13th St NW Washington DC 20004-1161 Office Phone: 202-637-5641. Office Fax: 202-637-5910. E-mail: jjrosenhauer@hhlaw.com.

ROSENHAUS, DREW, professional sports agent; b. 1966; BA, U. Miami, 1987; JD, Duke U., 1990. CEO Rosenhaus Sports Representation, Miami Beach, Fla. Co-author (with Don Yaeger): A Shark Never Sleeps: Wheeling and Dealing with the NFL's Most Ruthless Agent, 1988; film appearances include Jerry Maguire, 1996, Any Given Sunday, 1999. Office: Rosenhaus Sports Representation 6400 Allison Rd Miami Beach FL 33141 Office Phone: 305-936-1093. Fax: 305-864-3731. *

ROSENHEIM, DANIEL EDWARD, journalist, television news director; b. Chgo., Aug. 12, 1949; s. Edward W. and Margaret Morton (Keeney) R.; m. Christina J. Adachi, May 10, 1974 (div. 1979); m. Cindy Catherine Salans, June 20, 1980; children: Joseph Michael, James Salans, Nicholas Edward. BA, Wesleyan U., 1971. Factory worker, Pitts. and Chgo., 1972-77; reporter Sun-Jour., Lansing, Ill., 1977; bus./labor editor Hammond (Ind.) Times, 1977-80; bus. writer Chgo. Sun Times, 1980-82, spl. writer, 1982-84; bus. writer Chgo. Tribune, 1984-85; econs. editor San Francisco Chronicle, 1985-87, city editor, 1987-94, mng. editor, 1994-96; news dir. KRON-TV, San Francisco, 1996-2000; dir. KPIX-TV, San Francisco, 2000—05, v.p. news, 2005—. Mem. adv. bd. News Lab, Project for Excellence in Journalism. Recipient Peabody award, 1997, James Batten award, 1997, RTNDA Regional award for Overall News Excellence, 2003. Mem. Soc. Profl. Journalists, Radio and TV News Dirs. Assn., San Francisco Tennis Club. Avocations: tennis, golf, book collecting. Office: KPIX-TV 855 Battery St San Francisco CA 94127 Office Phone: 415-765-8618. Personal E-mail: drosen7777@hotmail.com. Business E-Mail: rosenheim@kpix.cbs.com.

ROSENHEIM, DONALD EDWIN, electrical engineer; b. NYC, Mar. 23, 1926; s. Seymour Lawrence and Leah Rebecca (Rosenberg) R.; m. Judith Comfort Hyman, June 22, 1958; children— Micah Robert, Jay Aaron. BSEE magna cum laude, Poly. Inst. Bklyn., 1949; MS, Columbia U., 1957. Devel. engr. Servo Corp. Am., 1949-51; mem. rsch. staff IBM., 1951—, asst. dir. rsch. divsn., 1972-73. Dir. San Jose (Calif.) Rsch. Lab., 1973-83, dir. tech. coordination, 1983-84; asst. dir. Almaden Rsch. Ctr., San Jose, 1984-92 With USN, 1944—46. Fellow IEEE; mem. Sigma Xi, Tau Beta Pi, Eta Kappa Nu. Republican. Jewish. Home: 128 Smith Creek Dr Los Gatos CA 95030-2139 Personal E-mail: jdrosenheim@msn.com. E-mail: rosenheimjudydon@yahoo.com.

ROSENHOUSE, HOWARD, retired lawyer; b. Bklyn., Oct. 15, 1939; s. Barnet and Sonia Rosenhouse. BA, Bklyn. Coll., 1960, MA, 1969; JD, Bklyn. Law Sch., 1963, LLM, 1965; MS, Pace U., 1975. Bar: N.Y. 1963, N.J. 1985, U.S. Dist. Ct. (so. and ea. dists.) N.Y. 1985, U.S. Dist. Ct. N.J. 1985, U.S. Supreme Ct. 1980. Tchr. social studies, guidance counselor, acting asst. prin. N.Y.C. Bd. Edn., 1963-79, counsel to bd. examiners, 1979-90, atty. at bd. edn., 1991-94. Mem. N.Y. State Bar Assn., Bklyn. Law Sch. Alumni Assn. Jewish.

ROSENHOUSE, MICHAEL ALLAN, lawyer, editor, consultant, columnist; b. Chgo., Nov. 8, 1946; s. Seymour Samuel and Jeanne Mozette (Rosenthal) R. BA, Yale U., 1968; JD, U. Chgo., 1974. Bar: Ill. 1974, N.Y. 1982. Atty. pvt. practice, Rochester, NY. Mng. editor: Am. Jurisprudence, 2d edit., 1991—93, Am. Law Reports (Fed.), 1991—93; editor: (newsletter) Bank Employment Law Report, 1998—99; author: Recent Court. of Appeals Decisions Reflect Strict Interpretation of Procedure Requirements, 2003, Employment Law (Syracuse Law Rev.), 1998; columnist: The Daily Record, 2001—03. Bd. trustees Urban Choice Charter Sch., Rochester, NY, 2005. Mem.: ABA, N.Y. State Bar Assn., Monroe County Bar Assn. (co-chair Disability Labor and Employment Law Commn. 1998—99), U. Chgo. Club of Rochester (bd. dirs. 1999—2001), Yale Alumni Assn. (schs. com. 1997—), U. Chgo. Law Sch. Alumni Assn. (bd. dirs. 1977—80). Avocations: squash, tennis, golf. Office: 16 W Main St Rochester NY 14614 Office Phone: 585-232-8500.

ROSENKER, MARK VICTOR, federal agency administrator; b. Balt., Dec. 8, 1946; s. Stanley and Irene (Moss) R.; m. Heather Beldon. BA in Communications, U. Md., 1969, postgrad., 1970-71; grad., USAF Air Command and Staff Coll., 1990, USAF Air War Coll., 1996. Asst. to events producer, relief engr. ABC-TV News, Washington, 1968-69; dep. dir. radio and TV Com. Reelect Pres., Washington, 1972; staff asst. to sec. U.S. Dept. Interior, Washington, 1972-73; account exec. Daniel Edelman Pub. Relations, Inc., Washington, 1973-75; dir. comm. Am. Moped/Motorized Bicycle Assn., Washington, 1975; dep. press sec. Pres. Ford Com., Washington, 1976; v.p. Electronic Industries Alliance, Washington, 1977—99; asst. exec. dir. for external affairs United Network for Organ Sharing, 1999—2001; dep. asst. to Pres. The White House, Washington, 2001—02, dir. Mil. Office, 2001—02; mem. Nat. Transp. Safety Bd. (NTSB), Washington, 2003—, vice chmn., 2003—06, acting chmn., 2005—06, chmn., 2006—. Mem. bd. visitors Cmty. Coll. USAF, Maxwell, Ala., 1981-86; commr. Am. Battle Monument Commn., 1990-94 Active Campaign to Elect Reagan/Bush, Washington, 1980, 84, Campaign to Elect Bush/Quayle, 1988, 92—; sr. advisor Dole/Kemp Campaign, 1995-96, Bush/Cheney Campaign, 2000-01. 1st lt. USAF, 1969-72, maj. gen. USAFR, 1972-2006, ret. 2006. Decorated Air Force Disting. Svc. medal with oak leaf cluster, USAF, Legion of Merit, Meritorious Svc. medal with oak leaf cluster, Air Force Commendation medal, Joint Svc. Achievement medal, Air Force Achievement medal with oak leaf cluster, Confluence award Am. Safe Boating Coun., 2005; recipient Chuck Docekal Meml. award, 1987, Am. Battle Monuments Commn. Meritious Svc. medal, 1994. Mem. Am. Soc. Assn. Execs., Greater Washington Soc. Assn. Execs., Res. Officers Assn. Club, Capitol Hill Club, Army Navy Club. Avocations: sailing, tennis, skiing, golf. Office: Nat Transp Safety Bd 490 L'Enfant Plaza SW Washington DC 20594

ROSENKILDE, CARL EDWARD, retired physicist; b. Yakima, Wash., Mar. 16, 1937; s. Elmer Edward and Doris Edith R.; m. Bernadine Doris Blumenstine, June 22, 1963 (div. Apr. 1991); children: Karen Louise, Paul Eric; m. Wendy Maureen Ellison, May 24, 1992. BS in Physics, Wash. State Coll., 1959; MS in Physics, U. Chgo., 1960, PhD in Physics, 1966. Fellow Argonne (Ill.) Nat. Lab., 1966-68; asst. prof. math. NYU, 1968-70; asst. prof. physics Kans. State U., Manhattan, 1970-76, assoc. prof., 1976-79; physicist Lawrence Livermore (Calif.) Nat. Lab., 1979-93, lab. assoc., 1994-95, participating guest, 1995-97; chief scientist C.R. Sci., 1993-98; ret. Cons. Lawrence Livermore Nat. Lab., 1974-79; astronomy instr. Los Positas Coll., 1997; part-time instr. physics Bellarmine Coll. Prep., 1999-2000; full-time instr., 2000-04, Tchg. Opportunities Ptnrs. Sci., 2004—. Contbr. articles to profl. jours. Woodrow Wilson fellow, 1959-60. Mem.: NSTA, Math. Assn. Am., Accoustical Soc. Am., Am. Geophys. Union, Soc. Indsl. and Applied Math., Am. Astron. Soc., Calif. Math. Coun. C.C., Am. Assn. Physics Tchrs., Am. Phys. Soc., Sigma Xi, Phi Eta Sigma, Phi Kappa Phi, Phi Beta Kappa. Republican. Presbyterian. Achievements include research in nonlinear wave propagation in complex media, theoretical physics, fluid dynamics. Personal E-mail: carlrosenkilde@comcast.net.

ROSENKRANTZ, BARBARA GUTMANN, science and medicine historian; b. NYC, Jan. 11, 1923; d. James and Jeanette (Mack) G.; m. David P. Bennett, Sept. 5, 1942 (div.); 1 child, Louise; m. Paul Rosenkrantz, Apr. 19, 1950 (dec. 1986); children: Judith, Deborah; m. J. Nathaniel Marshall, 1988. AB, Radcliffe Coll., 1944; PhD, Clark U., 1970. Rsch. assoc. Harvard U., Cambridge, Mass., 1970-71, lectr., 1971-73, assoc. prof. history of sci., 1973-75, prof., 1975-93, prof. emeritus, 1993—, chmn. history of sci. dept., 1984-89, master Currier House, 1974-79, faculty adminstr. Author: Public Health and the State, 1972, (with William A. Koelsch) American Habitat, 1973; editor for history Am. Jour. Pub. Health, 1985-89. NIH research grantee, 1970-72; Rockefeller Found. fellow, 1979-80; Ctr. for Advanced Study in Behavioral Scis. fellow Stanford U., 1984, Inst. Medicine fellow; Sherman Fairchild Disting. Scholar, Calif. Inst. Tech., 1989. Fellow: Am. Acad. Arts and Scis., Mass. Hist. Soc.; mem.: Am. Hist. Assn., History of Sci. Soc., Am. Assn. for History of Medicine. Jewish. Office: Harvard U Dept History Sci Ctr 371 Cambridge MA 02138 Office Phone: 617-496-2239. Fax: 617-495-3344.

ROSENKRANTZ, DANIEL J., computer science educator; b. Bklyn., Mar. 5, 1943; s. Harry and Ruth (Sirota) R.; m. Carole Jaffee, Aug. 2, 1969; children: Holly, Sherry, Jody, Andrew. BS, Columbia U., 1963, MS, 1964, PhD, 1967. With Bell Telephone Labs., Murray Hill, N.J., 1966-67; info. scientist GE Co. R & D Ctr., Schenectady, N.Y., 1967-77; prof. dept. computer sci. U. Albany-SUNY, 1977—2005, prof. emeritus, 2005—, dept. chair, 1993-99; prin. computer scientist Phoenix Data Systems, Albany, 1983-85. Author: (with P.M. Lewis II and R.E. Stearns) Compiler Design Theory, 1976. Fellow ACM (editor-in-chief jour. 1986-91, area editor for formal langs. and models of computation 1981-86, mem. spl. interest group on mgmt. of data, mem. numerous conf. coms., Sigmod Contbns. award 2001); mem. IEEE Computer Soc., ACM Spl. Interest Group on Automata and Computability Theory (sec. 1977-79). Office: U at Albany SUNY Dept Computer Sci Albany NY 12222-0001 Home: 6882 Milani St Lake Worth FL 33467-5902 Office Phone: 518-442-4274. Business E-Mail: djr@cs.albany.edu.

ROSENKRANTZ, STEVEN JAY, lawyer; b. NYC, Feb. 4, 1965; s. Michael and Rhona Sue (Dasheff) R. BA, Rutgers U., 1987, JD, 1991. Bar: Pa. 1994, DC 1996. Rsch. assoc. Fedn. Am. Scientists, Washington, 1993-94; rsch. asst. U.S. Dept. Justice, Washington, 1994-95; fgn. affairs specialist U.S. Arms Control & Disarmament Agy., Washington, 1995-99; spl. asst. office of undersec. state arms control U.S. Dept. State, Washington, 1998-2001, fgn. affairs officer Office of Missile Def. and Space Policy, 2001—. Mem.: Mid. East Inst., Phi Beta Kappa. Avocations: history, classical music, fencing, reading, chess. Office: US Dept State Office Missile Def and Spa Washington DC 20520 Home: 1220 Blair Mill Rd Apt 1009 Silver Spring MD 20910 Office Phone: 202-647-8140. Business E-Mail: rosenkrantzsj@state.gov.

ROSENKRANZ, E. JOSHUA, lawyer; b. NYC, Dec. 3, 1961; s. Herbert S. and Deanna (Green) R.; m. Sydney Martin, June 6, 1997. Student, Columbia U., 1979-81; BA, Case Western Res. U., 1983; JD, Georgetown U., 1986. Bar: NY 1986, U.S. Dist. Ct. (so. dist.) N.Y. 1991, U.S. Ct. Appeals (2d cir.) 1991. Law clk. to Hon. Antonin Scalia and Hon. Stephen F. Williams U.S. Ct. Appeals (D.C. cir.), Washington, 1986-87; law clk. to Hon. William J. Brennan Jr. U.S. Supreme Ct., Washington, 1987-88; founding atty.-in-charge, v.p. Office of the Appellate Defender, NYC, 1988-92, pres., CEO, founding atty.-in-charge, 1992-96; founding pres., exec. dir. Brennan Ctr. for Justice at NYU Sch. Law, NYC, 1994—2003; shareholder Heller Ehrman Attys., NYC, 2003—. Mem. Standing Com. on Criminal Law, 1993-97. Author: Buckley Stops Here, 1998; editor: Reason and Passion, 1997, If Buckley Fell, 1999; contbr. articles to profl. jours., chapters to books. Recipient Best Brief award Am. Soc. Creative Writers, 1993, Outstanding Contbn. to Criminal Def. award N.Y. State Bar Assn., 1995; named among 45 Top Pub. Interest Lawyers Under 45, The Am. Lawyer, 1997; named one of Litigation's Rising Stars, The Am. Lawyer, 2007. Office Phone: 212-847-8748. Office Fax: 212-763-7600. E-mail: jrosenkranz@hewm.com. *

ROSENKRANZ, RICHARD IRWIN, lawyer; b. Bklyn., July 7, 1933; s. William and Betty Gersman Rosenkranz; m. Susan Kahn Rosenkranz, Feb. 1, 1981. BS, LI U., Bklyn., 1959; LLB, Bklyn. Law Sch., 1962. Bar: NY 1962, US Dist. Ct. (ea. dist.) NY 1963, US Supreme Ct. 1972. Atty. Legal Aid Soc., NYC, 1962—64, Fed. Defender Ea. Dist., Bklyn., 1964—68, pvt. practice, Bklyn., 1968—. With USN, 1952—56. Mem.: Kings County Criminal Bar Assn. (Lifetime Achievement award 2003), Bklyn. Bar Assn., NY State Assn. Criminal Def. Avocations: tennis, backgammon, chess. Office: 32 Court St Brooklyn NY 11201

ROSENKRANZ, ROBERT BERNARD, military officer; b. Paterson, NJ, Sept. 26, 1939; s. Irving Morton and Lucille (Kane) R.; m. Barbara Jean Larson, May 17, 1970; children: Stephen Robert, Deborah Anne, Diana Rebecca, Susan Leslie. BS, U.S. Mil. Acad., 1961; MA, U. Pa., 1969. Commd. 2d. lt. U.S. Army, 1961, advanced through grades to maj. gen.,

1992, officer Fed. Republic of Germany, 1962-65, bn. exec. officer Republic of Korea, 1973-74, battery comdr. Vietnam, 1966-67, bn. and brigade comdr. Germany, 1977-79, 83-85; assoc. prof. U.S. Mil. Acad., West Point, NY, 1969-72; dir. soviet studies U.S. Army War Coll., Carlisle, Pa., 1981-83; sr. mil. asst. under sec. of def. Pentagon, Washington, 1986-88; dep. dir. Army Ops., Readiness and Mobilization U.S. Army Pentagon, Washington, 1988-89, dir. force programs, 1989-92; comdr. U.S. Army Optec, Washington, 1992-95; sr. v.p. range and logistics svcs. Dyncorp, Reston, Va., also Ft. Worth, 1995-2001; v.p. force mgmt. and logistics MPRI, Alexandria, Va., 2001—04; sr. v.p., gen. mgr. BeamHit, Columbia, Md., 2004—05; v.p. bus. devel. KEI Pearson Inc., Arlington, Va., 2005; pres. GS, Dyncorp Internat., Falls Church, Va., 2005—. Decorated Bronze Star, Air medal; recipient Superior Svc. medal U.S. Dept. Def., 1988, D.S.M., 1992, 95. Mem.: Nat. Def. Indsl. Assn., Internat. Test and Evaluation Assn., Assn. of the U.S. Army, Internat. Inst. Strategic Studies. Republican. Jewish. Avocations: jogging, reading, woodworking, golf, racquetball. Home: 3222 Wynford Dr Fairfax VA 22031-2828 Office Phone: 571-722-0238. E-mail: bob.rosenkranz@dyn-intl.com, rrosen007@aol.com.

ROSENMAN, KENNETH D., medical educator; b. NYC, Feb. 25, 1951; AB, Cornell U., 1972; MD, NY Med. Coll., 1975. Bd. cert. internal medicine; bd. cert. occupational and preventive medicine. Asst. prof. U. Mass., Amherst, 1979-81; dir. occupational and environ. health N.J. Dept. Health, Trenton, 1981-86; pvt. practice Plainsboro, NJ, 1986-88; assoc. prof. Mich. State U., East Lansing, 1988-93, prof., 1993—. Office: Mich State U 117 W Fee Hall East Lansing MI 48824-1316 Office Phone: 517-353-1846. E-mail: rosenman@msu.edu.

ROSENN, HAROLD, lawyer; b. Plains, Pa., Nov. 4, 1917; s. Joseph and Jennie (Wohl) R.; m. Sallyanne Frank, Sept. 19, 1948; 1 child, Frank Scott. BA, U. Mich., Ann Arbor, 1939, JD, 1941; LLD, Coll. Misericordia, Dallas, Pa., 1991. Bar: Pa. 1942, U.S. Supreme Ct. 1957. Ptnr. Rosenn & Rosenn, Wilkes Barre, Pa., 1948-54, Rosenn, Jenkins & Greenwald, Wilkes Barre, 1954-87, of counsel, 1988—. Mem. Pa. State Bd. Law Examiners, 1983-93, Pa. Gov.'s Justice Commn., 1968-73, Pa. Crime Commn., 1968-73, Fed. Jud. Nominating Com., Pa., 1977-79, Appellate Ct. Nominating Com., Pa., 1979-81; asst. dist. atty. Luzerne County, Pa., 1952-54. Chmn. United Jewish Appeal Campaign of Wyo. Valley, 1956, 1984, 2003, ARC, Wilkes-Barre, 1959, chair, 1963—65, life bd. dirs., 1991—; pres. Pa. Coun. on Crime and Delinquency, Harrisburg, 1969—71; chmn. United Way Campaign of Wyo. Valley, 1975, chmn. of bd., 1978—80; hon. mem., bd. dirs. N.E. Pa. Philharmonic, 2005; pres. Temple Israel of Wilkes Barre, 1972—74, chmn. bd., 1974—84, life bd. dir.; bd. dir. Coll. Misericordia, Dallas, Pa., 1976—86, emeritus, 1986—; bd. dir. Hoyt Libr., Kingston, Pa., 1971—78, Nat. Coun. on Crime and Delinquency, NYC, 1969—71, Jewish Cmty. Ctr., Wilkes-Barre, 1964—66, Keystone State Games, Jewish Fedn. Bd. of Greater Wilkes-Barre, St. Vincent de Paul Soup Kitchen, 1987—2000; trustee Wilkes-Barre and Wyoming Valley Vets. Hosp. Fund, 2003; comdr. Post 395 Am. Legion, Kingston, 1948. Capt. USAAF, 1942—45, ETO. Decorated medal with 6 bronze stars, European combatant cross French Govt.; named Golden Key Vol. of Yr., United Way of Pa., 1989; recipient Erasmus medal, Dutch Govt., Disting. Svc. award in Trusteeship, Assn. Governing Bds., Univs. and Colls., 1990, Disting. Cmty. Svc. award, Greater Wilkes-Barre Soc. Fellows Anti-Defamation League, 1991, Clara Barton honor award, Wyo. Valley chpt. ARC, 1992, Lifetime Achievement award, United Way of Wyo. Valley, 1992, Outstanding Vol. Fundraiser award, Greater Pocono chpt. Nat. Soc. of Fundraising Execs., 1995, honoree, Wyo. Valley Interfaith Coun., 1986, Ethics Inst. N.E. Pa., 2001, 11 Gallon Blood Donor award, ARC, inductee, Jr. Achievement Hall of Fame for N.E. Pa., 1997, President's award, Luzerne County Bar, 2003. Mem. ABA, Pa. Bar Assn., Am. Judicature Soc., The Pa. Soc., B'nai B'rith (pres. Wilkes Barre 1952-53, Cmty. Svc. award 1976), U. Mich. Club N.E. Pa. (pres. 1946-76), Westmoreland Club (Wilkes-Barre). Republican. Jewish. Office Phone: 570-826-5602.

ROSENNE, MEIR, lawyer, federal agency administrator; b. Iasi, Romania, Feb. 19, 1931; arrived in Israel, 1944; s. Jacob and Mina Rosenhaupt; m. Vera Ayai, June 9, 1959; children: Mihal, Dafna. MA in Polit. Sci., Inst. Polit. Sci., Paris, 1953; LLB, Sorbonne, U. Paris, 1955, PhD in Internat. Law with honors, 1957; grad., Inst. Internat. Studies, Paris, 1953. In govt. service, Israel, 1953—; consul Israel Consulate, NYC, 1967-69; sr. lectr. in polit. sci. U. Haifa, Israel, 1969-71; coordinator Atomic Energy Commn. Israel, 1969-71; chief legal adviser Fgn. Office Israel, Jerusalem, 1971-79; Israeli amb. to France, Paris, 1979-83; Israeli amb. to U.S. Washington, 1983-87; pres. State of Israel Bonds, NYC, 1989-93; ptnr. Balter, Guth, Aloni & Co., Jerusalem, 1994—. Chmn. overseas com. Jerusalem Bank; bd. dirs. Israel Discount Bank Holding, Ltd. Contbr. articles to newspapers. Chmn. internat. bd. govs. Share-Zedek Hosp., Jerusalem, 1989—94. Sgt. Israeli Air Force, 1948—50. Named comdr., Nat. Order French Legion of Honor; recipient Harold Weil medal, NYU Sch. Law, Elie Wiesel award. Mem.: French Assn. Internat. Law, Am. Soc. Internat. Law, Israeli Bar Assn., Soc. Internat. Law, Internat. Law Soc. France, Internat. Club Washington. Avocations: volleyball, swimming. Office: Balter Guth Aloni 96 Yigal Alou Str 69395 Tel Aviv Israel Business E-Mail: mrosenne@bgalaw.co.il.

ROSENOW, EDWARD CARL, III, medical educator; b. Columbus, Ohio, Nov. 2, 1934; s. Oscar Ferdinand and Mildred Irene (Eichelberger) R.; m. Constance Donna Grahame, Sept. 7, 1957; children: Sheryl Lynn, Scott Edward. BS, Ohio State U., 1955, MD, 1959; MS in Medicine, U. Minn., 1969. Diplomate Am. Bd. Internal Medicine, Am. Bd. Pulmonary Diseases. Intern Riverside Meth. Hosp., Columbus, Ohio, 1959-60; resident in internal medicine Mayo Grad. Sch. Medicine, Rochester, Minn., 1960-65, clin. fellow in thoracic diseases, 1965-66; cons. in internal medicine (pulmonary diseases) Mayo Clinic, Rochester, 1966; instr. in medicine Mayo Grad. Sch. Medicine, Rochester, 1969-73; asst. prof. medicine Mayo Med. Sch., Rochester, 1973-77, assoc. prof. medicine, 1977-80, prof. medicine, 1980; chmn. divsn. pulmonary and critical care medicine, 1987-94; assoc. dir. internal medicine residency program Mayo Clinic, Rochester, 1977-79, program dir. internal medicine residency program, 1979-84, sec. Mayo staff, 1979; pres. Mayo staff, 1986; Arthur M. and Gladys D. Gray prof. medicine Mayo Clinic, Rochester, 1987-96, prof. emeritus, 1996—. Cons. NASA, Houston. Capt. M.C., U.S. Army, 1962-64. Recipient Alumni Achievement award Coll. Medicine Ohio State U., 1989, Disting. Mayo Clinician award, 1994, Henry S. Plummer Disting. Internist award, 1994, Karis award Mayo Clinic, 1996, Disting. Alumnus award Mayo Found., 1998; Edward W. and Betty Knight Scripps Professorship named in his honor Mayo Med. Sch., 1994, Edward C. Rosenow, III, Outstanding Subsplty. fellow award established in his honor; inductee Sigma Chi Hall of Fame, 2005 Fellow ACP (gov. Minn. chpt. 1987-91, Ralph S. Claypoole Sr. award for Lifetime Dedication to Patient Care 1995, Minn. chpt. Laureate award 1994, Disting. Lectr. award 1996), Am. Coll. Chest Physicians (master fellow, editl. bd. CHEST 1973-78, editor spl. case reports 1975-90, com. on postgrad. med. edn. 1978-84, sci. program com. 1982, com. on undergrad. med. edn. 1981-82, co-chmn. sci. program com. Internat. Coll. Chest Physicians meeting, Sydney, Australia, 1985, regent 1984-88, pres. elect 1988-89, pres. 1989-90, pres. Chest Found. 1998—, Endowed Hon. Lectr. in name 2004—); mem. AMA, So. Minn. Med. Assn., Minn. Thoracic Soc., Am. Thoracic Soc., Sigma Xi. Office: Mayo Clinic Div Pulmonary Diseases 200 1st St SW Rochester MN 55905-0002 Office Phone: 507-284-2511. Business E-Mail: rosenow.edward@mayo.edu.

ROSENOW, JOHN EDWARD, foundation executive; b. Lincoln, Nebr., Sept. 15, 1949; s. Lester Edward and Lucille Louise (Koehler) R.; m. Nancy Kay Hadley; children: Matthew, Stacy. BS in Agrl. Engring., U. Nebr., 1971. Dir. of tourism Nebr. Dept. Econ. Devel., Lincoln, 1971-79, interim dept. dir., 1985; founder Nat. Arbor Day Found., 1972, exec. dir. million-mem. Lincoln and Nebraska City, 1979-94, pres., 1994—. Co-author: (book) Tourism: the good, the bad, and the ugly, 1979. Democrat. Mem. United Ch. of Christ. Office: Nat Arbor Day Found 211 N 12th St Lincoln NE 68508-1422 Office Phone: 888-448-7337.

ROSENOW, MITCHELL PAUL, sound recording engineer, studio owner, musician, music producer; s. Richard Vernon and Norma Mae Rosenow; m. Ronette Shaleen Dizmang, Nov. 25, 1983; 1 child, Francis (Frank) Vernon. GED, Manhattan Vocat. Tech. Sch., Kans., 1971. Sound sys. design engr. Silvertrain Sound, Lawrence, Kans., 1974—76; self-employed audio engr. Interlace Video, Sunflower Cablevision, HBO, Cinemax, NBC, ABC, CBS, ESPN, Fox, Raycom, Time Warner Cable, various Fortune 500 teleconfs. nationwide, Lee's Summit, Mo., 1975—; sound engr. various local bands Kansas City area, Kans., 1975—80; monitor engr. Amazing Rhythm Aces, Memphis, 1976; audio engr., music show prodr. Columbine Cablevision, Ft. Collins, Colo., 1980—81; rec. engr. Little Apple Studio, Manhattan, Kans., 1981—83; chief audio engr. Interlace Video, Lenexa, Kans., 1987—89. Cons. in rec. and live sound nationwide, 1987—; cons. in audio design TV remote facilities nationwide, 1987—. *A lifelong musician, began playing live and touring at age 12. By age 19, co-designed, built and toured with what became a much sought-after sound system used by famous music acts of the 1970s. The keen ear developed in music, along with in-depth understanding of the science and technology of audio, have served well in the broadcast arena, where many techniques for wiring, miking, and mixing sound have been picked up and incorporated by engineers across the country. Today, combines music and engineering to produce various projects.* Rec. engr. (TV series) Bring It All Back Home (Cable Ace award, 1978); engineer: (DVD) Motivating Moves for People with Parkinson's (U. Continuing Edn. Assn. Nat. Outstanding Program award, 2004). Mem.: Internat. Brotherhood Elec. Workers Local 53 radio and TV divsn., Audio Engring. Soc. Office Phone: 816-554-3782. Business E-Mail: kcmixman@aol.com.

ROSENQUIST, JAMES ALBERT, artist; b. Grand Forks, ND, Nov. 29, 1933; s. Louis A. and Ruth C. (Hendrickson) R.; m. Mary Lou Adams, June 5, 1960; 1 child, John Adams; m. Melinda Thompson, Apr. 18, 1987; 1 child, Lily McLean. Attended, U. Minn., Art Students League, NYC, 1954-55; DFA (hon.), U. So. Fla., 1981, Bard Coll., 1997. Billboard painter A.H. Villepigue, Inc., NYC, 1957—59, Artkraft Strauss Sign Corp., NYC, 1957—59; lectr. Yale Sch. Art, 1964; artist in residence Aspen Inst. Humanist Studies, 1965. One-man shows include Green Gallery, N.Y.C., 1962, 64, Mus. Modern Art, 1963, Sperone Gallery, Turin, Italy, 1964, Sonnabend Gallery, Paris, 1964, 67, 68, Dwan Gallery, Los Angeles, 1964, Moderna Museet, Stockholm, 1965, 66, Castelli Gallery, N.Y.C., 1965, 66, 68, 69, 70, 73, 74, 78, 85, 88, 91, Mus. Modern Art, Turin, 1965, Nat. Gallery Can., Ottawa, Ont., 1968, Met. Mus. Art, N.Y.C., 1968, Max Protech, Washington, 1974, Nat. Gallery, Victoria, Australia, 1978, Sable-Castelli Gallery, Toronto, 1978, Colo. State U., Ft. Collins, 1982, Castelli/Fergen/Corcoran, N.Y.C., 1982, Mayer Gallery, London, 1982, Mus. Contemporary Art, Houston, 1982, Whitney Mus. Am. Art, N.Y.C., 1982, Mus. Fine Arts, Houston, 1983, 88, U. South Fla., 1984, Butler Inst. Am. Art, 1988, Wetterling Gallery, Stockholm, 1989, Mus. Modern Art, Austin, Tex., 1990, Cen. Hall of Artists, Moscow, 1991, IVAM Centre Julio Gonzales, Valencia, Spain, 1991, Gagosian Gallery, N.Y.C., 1992, Leo Castelli Gallery, N.Y.C., 1993, Wetterling Teo Gallery, Singapore, 1994, Seattle Art Museum, 1995, Galerie Thaddaeus Ropac, Paris, 1997, Baldwin Gallery, Aspen, 1999, Salvador Dali Museum, Fla., 2000, Gagosian Gallery, N.Y.C., 2001, numerous others; exhibited in numerous group shows U.S. and, Europe, including 16 Ams. at, Mus. Modern Art, 1963, Artist and Object at, Guggenheim Mus., 1963, São Paulo, Brazil, 1967, Mus. Modern Art, Tokyo, 1967, Musée des Arts Decoratives, Palais Louvre, 1967, Haywood Gallery, London, 1969, Albright-Knox Gallery, Buffalo, 1971, Mus. Contemporary Art, Chgo., 1972, Met. Mus. Art, N.Y.C., 1969-70, Whitney Mus. Am. Art, N.Y.C., 1974, biennial, Whitney Mus. Am. Art, N.Y.C., 1981, including 16 Ams. at, Mayer Gallery, London, 1978, U. Mich. Mus., 1978, Fitzwilliam Mus., Cambridge, Eng., 1978, Bklyn. Mus., 1981, Va. Mus., Richmond, 1981, Haus der Kunst, 1982, Nat. Gallery, Victoria, B.C., Can., 1982; represented in permanent collections Pasadena Mus.; Modern Museet, Stockholm, Stadtlicht, Amsterdam, Holland, Whitney Mus., Albright-Knox Gallery, Mus. Modern Art, N.Y.C., Met. Mus. Art, N.Y.C., Nat. Gallery Can., Wallraf-Richartz Mus., Cologne, Germany, others; Biennial Exhbn. Prints, Nat. Mus. Modern Art, Tokyo 1968, 7th Internat Expn. Graphics, Moderna Gallery, Ljubliana, Yugoslavia 1967); painting of bomber F-111. Bd. dirs. Nat. Endowment for Arts. Recipient Norman Waite Harris award Chgo. Art Inst. 1963, Prix di Tella, Argentina 1965, Friend of Japan award, 1970, World Print award, 1983, Fla. Amb. of the Arts award, 1987, Golden Plate award Am. Acad. Achievement, 1988, Fla. prize, 1991, Skowhegan medal in painting, 1994, FCG Art award, 2002. Mem. Municipal Art Soc., N.Y.

ROSENSAFT, LESTER JAY, management consultant, lawyer; b. Leominster, Mass., Jan. 11, 1958; s. Melvin and Beatrice (Golombek) Rosensaft; m. Elizabeth Amanda Lahti, July 29, 1992 (div. 2004); 1 child, Mia Elisabeth. BS in Econs., Wharton Sch., U. Pa., 1978; JD, MBA, Case Western Res. U., 1981; LLM in Corp. Law with high honors, NYU, 1983. Bar: Ohio 1981, U.S. Dist. Ct. (no. dist.) Ohio 1982, U.S. Dist. Ct. (all dists.) N.Y. 1982, Mass. 1992. With Cons. to Mgmt., Inc., Cleve., NYC, Boston, Hong Kong, 1977—, v.p., 1977—80, pres., 1980—83, chmn., 1983—85; pvt. practice specializing in corp. and comml. law Ohio, 1981—. Mem. Hall, Rosensaft & Yen, Cleve., Singapore, 1981—90; reorganization law fed. cts., Ohio, 1982—, NY, 1982—; pres., CEO Eljay Devel. Corp., 1985—86; chmn., CEO Logistix Ltd., 1987—90; ptnr. Sanctuary Assocs., Boston, 1988—89; pres., CEO Union Meat Co., East Hartford, Conn., 1989—90, also bd. dirs.; pres. Golub Enterprises II, Inc., 1989—90, also bd. dirs.; COO CCC Fin. Orgn., Cleve., 1992—95, also bd. dirs.; pres., CEO ASA Comm., Inc., NYC, 1995—, also bd. dirs.; pres., CEO ASA Adminstrn., Inc., Chgo., 1999—, Greensboro, NC, 1999—, Toronto, 1999—, also bd. dirs.; mem. fin. and strategic planning com. ASA Acquisition Corp., also bd. dirs.; mem. ASA Mgmt. and Exec. Com., 1995—, ASA Investment Com., 1996—98; v.p. corp. devel. Paramount Sys. Design Group, Inc., NYC, also vice chmn. bd. dirs.; v.p., CFO Chipurnoi Inc., Long Island City, NY, also bd. dirs.; v.p., CFO Kinnerton Industries, NYC, London, 1983—85; vice chmn., gen. counsel GIOIA Couture, Inc., Akron, Ohio, 1984—86, also bd. dirs.; chmn., CEO Invictus Ventures, Boston, 2005—; mem., bd. dirs. Artcraft Co., 2005—, Insight Edn., 2005—; mem. exec. com. bd. dirs. The Soffer Orgn., Pitts., 2007—. Co-author: Industrial Development Survey for City of Leominster, 1978; contbr. articles to profl. jours. Active Combined Jewish Philanthropies; participant 40th Anniversary II Pres.'s Mission, 1987; chmn. Region V Outreach Mission, 1988; vice chmn. Regional Campaign Leadership Mission, 1991; mem. Russian Resettlement Com., 1988—91, Maj. Gifts Gala Com., 1989, Leadership Mission to Ukraine, 2006; ednl. cons., advisor indsl. devel. and strategic urbanism; cons. federally funded biomed rsch. projects; mem. exec. adv. coun. Keene State Coll., 1984—88; assoc. alumni trustee U. Pa., 1991—95, active secondary com. ctrl. Mass., bd. govs. Cleve., 1992—95; bd. overseers, mem. pres.'s soc. Beth Israel Deaconess Hosp., Boston, 2003—, mem. adv. bd. Transplant Ctr., mem. fin. and devel. com., bd. dirs., 2004—, mem. bd. overseers; mem. exec. and leadership com., bd. dirs. Horizon for Homeless Children, Boston, 2007—. Recipient Grand award, APEX, 1999, Best of Show award, ESMA, 1999, numerous ACE awards, Silver and Gold Quill awards, 1996—99, Cronite Cup award. Mem.: ABA, Coll. Firm Prins., Coun. Cons. Orgns., Inst. Mgmt. Cons. (cert.), Soc. Profl. Mgmt. Cons., Internat. Soc. Strategic Planning Cons., N.Y.C. Reorganization Roundtable, Bankruptcy Lawyers Bar Assn., Assn. Bar City of N.Y., Ohio State Bar Assn., Greater Cleve. Bar Assn., Turnaround Mgmt. Assn., Assn. Corp. Growth, North Ctrl. Mass. C. of C. (indsl. devel. com. 1984—86), Belmont Country Club, Boca Pointe Golf and Racquet Club, Phi Alpha Delta (vice justice).

ROSENSAFT, MENACHEM ZWI, lawyer, writer, foundation administrator; b. Bergen-Belsen, Germany, May 1, 1948; arrived in U.S., 1958, naturalized, 1962; s. Josef and Hadassah (Bimko) Rosensaft; m. Jean Bloch, Jan. 13, 1974; 1 child, Joana Deborah (Jodi). BA, MA, Johns Hopkins U., 1971, Columbia U., 1975, JD, 1979. Bar: NY 1980. Adj. lectr. dept. Jewish studies CCNY, 1972-74, professorial fellow, 1974-75; rsch. fellow Am. Law Inst., 1977-78; law clk. to judge US Dist. Ct. (so. dist.) NY, NYC, 1979-81; assoc. Proskauer, Rose, Goetz & Mendelsohn, NYC, 1981-82, Kaye, Scholer, Fierman, Hays & Handler, NYC, 1982-89; v.p., sr. assoc. counsel Chase Manhattan Bank, NYC, 1989-93; spl. counsel Hahn & Hessen, NYC, 1994-95; sr. internat. counsel Ronald S. Lauder Found., NYC, 1995-97; exec. v.p. Jewish Renaissance Found., Inc., NYC, 1996-2000; ptnr. Ross & Hardies, NYC, 2000—03, McGuire Woods LLP, NYC, 2003; spl. counsel Van Der Moolen Specialists USA, LLC, NYC, 2004, sr. legal counsel, 2004—05, gen. counsel, 2005—07. Author: Moshe Sharett Statesman of Israel, 1966, Not Backward to Belligerency, 1969, (poetry) Fragments, Past and Future, 1968; editor: Bergen Belsen Youth Mag., 1965, Life Reborn, Jewish Displaced Persons 1945-1951, 2001; book review editor Columbia Jour. Transnational Law, 1978—79; co-editor (with Yehuda Bauer): (book) Antisemitism: Threat to Western Civilization, 1988; contbg. editor: Reform Judaism, 1993—2002; contbr. articles to newspapers and profl. jours.; chmn. editl. bd.: Holocaust Survivors' Memoirs Project, 2000—. Chmn. Internat. Network Children Jewish Holocaust Survivors, 1981—84, founding chmn., 1984—; nat. pres. Labor Zionist Alliance, 1988—91; v.p. Am. Gathering of Jewish Holocaust Survivors and Their Descendants, 2007—; chmn. commn. human rights World Jewish Congress, 1986—, chmn. exec. com. Am. sect., 1986—90; mem. Gen. Coun. World Zionist Orgn., 1987—92; mem. U.S. Holocaust Meml. Coun., 1994—2004, chmn. content com., 1994—2000, chmn. collections and acquisitions com., 1996—2000, chmn. task force on procs. for com. on conscience, 1996, mem. exec. com., 1996—2003, chmn. governance com., 2001—02; bd. dirs., exec. com. Nat. Com. for Labor Israel, 1988—91, 1995—2001; mem. Am. Zionist Tribunal, 1988—90, chmn., 1990; sec. Am. Zionist Fedn., 1990—93; bd. dirs. Am. Jewish Joint Distbn. Com., 1988—91; mem. exec. com. Nat. Jewish Cmty. Rels. Adv. Coun., 1994—97; organizer, leader demonstration in Germany against Pres. Reagan's visit to Bitburg Cemetery and Bergen-Belsen concentration camp, 1985; del. meeting on recognition of Israel between five Am. Jews and leaders of Palestine Liberation Orgn. Stockholm, 1988; mem. NYC Holocaust Meml. Commn., 1982—96, chmn. collections com., 1987—89; mem. NY County Dem. Com., 1981—85; mem. nat. adv. bd. United Synagogue Conservative Judaism, 1995—2002, also chmn. United Synagogue del. to Nat. Jewish Cmty. Rels. Adv. Coun., 1994—97; pres. Park Ave. Synagogue, 2003—, sec., 1988—2003, trustee, 1994—; chmn. Sherr Inst. Adult Jewish Studies, 1993—2002. Recipient Parker Sch. recognition of achievement with honors in internat. and fgn. law, 1979, Abraham Joshua Heschel Peace award, 1989, 400th Anniversary medal, City of Warsaw, 1999, commendation Jewish Heritage Week, Comptr. NYC, 1999, Elie Wiesel Holocaust Remembrance award, Israel Bonds, 2003, Simon Rockower award for excellence in feature writing, 2006; Harlan Fiske Stone scholar, Columbia U. Law Sch., 1977—79. Mem.: ABA, Phi Beta Kappa. Jewish. Home: 179 E 70th St New York NY 10021-5109 Personal E-mail: mzrosensaft@yahoo.com.

ROSENSHINE, ALLEN GILBERT, retired advertising agency executive; b. NYC, Mar. 14, 1939; s. Aaron and Anna (Zuckerman) R.; m. Suzan Weston-Webb, Aug. 31, 1979; children: Andrew, Jonathan. AB, Columbia Coll., 1960. Copywriter J.B. Rundle, NYC, 1962-65, Batten, Barton, Durstine & Osborn, NYC, 1965, copy supr., 1967, v.p., 1968, asso. creative dir., 1970, sr. v.p., creative dir., 1975-77, exec. v.p., 1977-80, pres., 1980-82, CEO, 1981-86, chmn., 1983-86, also dir., mem. exec. com.; pres., CEO BBDO Internat., NYC, 1984-86, also bd. dirs.; pres., CEO Omnicom Group, NYC, 1986-88; chmn., CEO BBDO Worldwide, NYC, 1989—2004, chmn., 2004—07, chmn. emeritus, 2007—. Lectr. gen. studies Bklyn. Coll., 1961-65 Office: BBDO Worldwide Inc 1285 Avenue Of The Americas New York NY 10019-6028 *

ROSENSTEEL, GEORGE THOMAS, physics professor, nuclear physicist; b. Balt., Sept. 30, 1947; s. Walter St. George and Marie Emily (White) R.; m. Tsetsa Dankova. BSc, U. Toronto, Ont., Can., 1973, PhD, 1975. Can. fellow NRC, 1976-78; prof. physics Tulane U., New Orleans, 1978—, chmn. dept., 1985-91. Vis. fellow Brit. Sci. and Engring. Coun., U. Sussex, Eng., 1986; vis. prof. Nat. Inst. Nuclear Theory, U. Washington, 1992, Inst. Theoretical Physics U. Gent, Belgium, 1999. Contbr. numerous articles to profl. jours. Delivered grad. sch. commencement address Tulane U., 1987; recipient 7 grants NSF, 1979—. Mem. Am. Phys. Soc., Am. Math. Soc., Sigma Xi (young scientist award 1987). Office: Tulane U Dept of Physics New Orleans LA 70118 Home Phone: 504-738-0160; Office Phone: 504-862-3174. Business E-Mail: george.rosensteel@tulane.edu.

ROSENSTEIN, BARRY, investment company executive; s. Herbert Rosenstein; m. Lizanne Teitelbaum, Dec. 20, 1986. BA, Lehigh U., 1981; MBA, U. Pa., 1984. CPA. Investment banker mergers and acquisitions Merrill Lynch, NY; prin. corp. takeovers Asher Edelman's Plaza Securities Corp.; mng. ptnr. Reatta Partners; founder, head investment and banking group Genesis Merchant Group; founder and mng. ptnr. Sagaponack Partners, JANA Partners LLC. Mem.: Phi Beta Kappa. Office: JANA Partners Ste 1000 201 Post St San Francisco CA 94108

ROSENSTEIN, NEIL, surgeon, genealogist, researcher; b. Cape Town, South Africa, Oct. 31, 1944; came to US, 1969; s. Emanuel Boruchovich and Annie (Marine) R.; m. Mavis Joyce Naumann, Jan. 14, 1968; children: Joel, Ari, Moshe Baruch, Rafael Samuel, Jonathan Simcha. MD, U. Cape Town Med. Sch., 1967. Intern Tel Hashomer Hosp., Tel Aviv, 1968-69; surg. resident Mt. Sinai Hosp., Cleve., 1970—73, NYC, 1973—75; mem. surg. staff Trinitas, Elizabeth, NJ, 1975—, The Union Hosp., NJ, 2001—. Author: These Are the Generations, 1969, The Unbroken Chain, 1976, 90, The Margolis Family, 1984, The Gaon of Vilna and his Cousinhood, 1997, The Lurie Legacy: The House of Davidic Royal Descent, 2004, The Grandees of New Jersey: Naar, Baiz, Peixotto, Pretto and Seixas Families, 2006, Saul Wahl: Polish King for a Night or Lithuanian Knight for a Lifetime, 2006; co-author: From King David to Baron David—A Rothschild Saga, 1989, Avnei Zikaron, 1999; editor: Latter Day Leaders, Sages and Scholars, 1982, The Feast and the Fast, 1984, Illustrated History of Union County, 2005; contrbr. to various publications. Founder, pres. Jewish Geneal. Soc., NYC, 1977-79; bd. dirs. YMHA, Union, NJ, 1990-2001; mem. adv. bd. Auschwitz Jewish Center Found., NYC, 1999—; founder, dir. Computer Ctr. for Jewish Genealogy; rep. to genealogy com. Ctr. for Jewish History bd. dirs. Yeshiva U., NY, 2001—; co-pres. synagogue Elmora Hills Minyan, 1994-2004, pres., 2005-06; spkr. in field. Mem. Med. Soc. NJ, Union County Med. Soc. NJ, AmeriGroup NJ, Inc. (med. adv. com.). Republican. Jewish. Home: 185 Shelley Ave Elizabeth NJ 07208-1061 Personal E-mail: neil@tali.com.

ROSENSTEIN, ROBERT ALAN, scientific consultant; b. Chgo., July 12, 1938; s. Milton W. and Gayle (Blacher) R.; 1 child, Daniel Jeremy. BS, U. Ill., 1961; PhD, Northwestern U., 1970. Aerospace technologist NASA Lewis Rsch. Ctr., Cleve., 1961-64; rsch. assoc. Inst. Theoretical Chem.

Tech. U., Munich, 1970-72; cons. Chgo., 1972-76; sr. rsch. chemist Armak Rsch. Lab. (now Akzo Chemie USA), McCook, Ill., 1977-79; coatings engr. Fansteel/VR Wesson, Waukegan, Ill., 1979-80; application programmer Nuclear Data, Schaumburg, Ill., 1981; sci. cons., Glenview, Ill., 1982—. Cons. Internat. Union Pure and Applied Chemistry, Commn. on Solubility Data, 1978-87. Active Project Upward Bound, Northwestern U., 1968-69, Jewish Vocational Service Prof. Mgr. Tech. Program, Chgo., 1975-98. NIH predoctoral fellow, 1967. Mem. Am. Phys. Soc., U. Ill. Alumni Assn., Chgo. Pub. Sch. Alumni Assn. (founding mem.), Northwestern Alumni Assn., Chgo. Chemists Club (pres. 1986-87). Avocations: history, sightseeing, current events, Wagnerian opera. Office Phone: 773-381-7166. E-mail: elucidates@gmail.com.

ROSENSTEIN, ROD J., prosecutor; b. Phila., Jan. 13, 1965; s. Robert Jacob and Gerry M. (Stoloff) R. BS in Econ., U. Pa., Phila., 1986; JD, Harvard U., 1989. Bar: Pa. 1989, DC 1992, Md. 2002, US Ct. Appeals (DC cir.) 1990, US Ct. Appeals (5th cir.) 1991, US Ct. Appeals (9th cir.) 1992, US Ct. Appeals (4th cir.) 1998, US Ct. Appeals (8th cir.) 2003, US U.S. Tax Ct. 2003, US Ct. Appeals (1st, 2d, 10th and 11th cirs.) 2004, US Supreme Ct. 2002. Law clk. to Hon. Douglas H. Ginsburg US Ct. Appeals (DC cir.), Washington, 1989-90; trial atty. Pub. Integrity Sect., Washington, 1990-93; counsel to dep. atty. gen. US Dept. Justice, Washington, 1993-94, spl. asst. crminal divsn., 1994-95, asst. US atty. dist. MD, 1997—2001, dep. asst. atty. gen. criminal matters, 2001—02, prin. dep. asst. atty. gen. tax divsn., 2002—05, US atty. dist. Md. Baltimore, Md., 2005—; assoc. counsel Office Ind. Counsel, Washington, 1995—97. Office: US Attys Office 36 S Charles St 4th Fl Baltimore MD 21201 *

ROSENSTOCK, ARTHUR RICHARD, plastic surgeon, educator; b. NYC, Feb. 4, 1947; MD, U. Libre de Bruxelles, 1976. Intern, gen. surgery Metro Hosp.-NY Med. Coll., NY, 1976—77; resident, plastic reconstructive surgery NY Med. Coll., Valhalla, NY, 1977—81; fellow Med. Coll. Va., Richmond, Va., 1981—83; hosp. appointment, surgery, admitting privileges Stamford Cmty. Hosp., 1983—; clin. instr. Columbia Presbyn. Coll. Physicians and Surgeons, NYC, 2005—; private practice Stamford, Conn., 1983—. Mem.: Am. Soc. Plastic Surgeons, Am. Soc. for Aesthetic Plastic Surgery. Avocations: painting, photography, architectural design, exhibiting quality flies. Office: 1290 Summer St Ste 3100 Stamford CT 06905 Office Phone: 203-359-1959. Office Fax: 203-359-9344. E-mail: arosenstockmd@aol.com, arr52@columbia.edu. *

ROSENSTOCK, LINDA, dean, medical educator; b. NYC, Dec. 20, 1950; m. Lee Bailey; children: Adam Lee, Matthew Lynn. AB in Psychology, Brandeis U., 1971; student, U. B.C., Vancouver, Can., 1971-72; MD, MPH, Johns Hopkins U., 1977. Diplomate Am. Bd. Internal Medicine, Am. Bd. Preventive Medicine; lic. physician and surgeon, Wash. Med. resident then chief resident U. Wash., Seattle, 1977-80, resident in preventive medicine, instr. medicine, 1980-82, asst. prof., 1982-83, 83-87, lectr. environ. health, 1982-83, adj. asst. prof., 1983-86, mem. grad. sch. faculty, 1985—, assoc. prof., 1987-93, prof. medicine and environ. health, 1993—94, also dir. programs, 1994; dir. Nat. Inst. Occupational Safety and Health, Washington, 1994—2000; dean UCLA Sch. of Pub. Health, 2000—, prof. environ. health sciences, 2000—; prof. medicine UCLA Sch. Medicine, 2000—. Dir. Harborview Med. Ctr., Seattle, 1981-87, acting sect. head, 1992-94; dir. Nat. Inst. Occupational Safety and Health, Washington, 1994—. Assoc. editor Internat. Jour. Occupational Medicine and Toxicology, 1991—; mem. editorial bd. Am. Jour. Indsl. Medicine, 1985-94, Jour. Gen. Internal Medicine, 1987-90, Environ. Rsch., 1987—, Western Jour. Medicine, 1990—; contbr. numerous articles to profl. jours. Mem. exec. bd. Physicians for Human Rights, 1990—; mem. occupl. health adv. bd. United Auto Workers GM, 1990-94, chair, 1993-94; mem. task force on pneumoconioses Am. Coll. Radiology, 1991-94; mem. external adv. panel Agrl. Health and Safety Ctr., 1992-93; mem. adv. com. Ctrs. for Disease Control, 1992-94; mem. com. to survey health effects of mustard gas and lewisite Inst. Medicine, 1992, mem. bd. health promotion and disease prevention, 1993-94; mem. bd. sci. counselors HHS, 1993-94, mem. exec. com. nat. toxicology program, 1994—; mem. med. adv. bd. Teamsters Internat., 1993-94. Recipient Upjohn Achievement award Harborview Med. Ctr., 1978, Jean Spencer Felton MD award Western Occupational Med. Assn., 1988, Environ. and Occupational Medicine award Nat. Inst. Environ. Health Scis., 1991-94; Robert Wood Johnson scholar, 1980-82, Henry J. Kaiser scholar, 1984-89. Fellow ACP (health promotion subcom. 1989-90, clin. practice subcom. 1990-91), Collegium Ramazzini; mem. APHA (chair membership com. 1983-85, chairperson occupational helath and safety sect. 1985-86, gov. coun. 1986-88), Am. Coll. Occupational Medicine (mem. jud. com. 1989-94), Am. Thoracic Soc. (com. health care policy and clin. practice 1990-93), Internat. Commn. Occupational Health (sci. com. epidemiology in occupational health 1989—), Soc. Gen. Internal Medicine (program planning com. 1987, Glaser award com. 1993-94), Western Assn. Physicians, Pacific Interurban Clin. Club. Office: UCLA Sch Pub Health 16-035 Ctr for Health Sciences Box 951772 Los Angeles CA 90095

ROSENSTOCK, SUSAN LYNN, orchestra administrator; b. Bklyn., Nov. 2, 1947; BS, SUNY, Cortland, 1969; MBA, So. Meth. U., 1977, MFA, 1978. Asst. mgr. Columbus (Ohio) Symphony Orch., 1978-82; grants program dir., info. officer Greater Columbus Arts Coun., 1982-83, asst. dir. grants and adminstrn., 1983-84; dir. ann. giving and spl. events Columbus Symphony Orch., 1984-86, dir. devel., 1986-90, orch. mgr., 1990-98, gen. mgr., 1998—. Panelist Ohio Arts Coun. Music Panel, 1986, 87, NEA, 2002, Challenge Grants Panel, 1991, J.C. Penney Gold Rule Award Judges Panel, 1993, 94. Mem. Am. Symphony Orch. League (devel. dirs. steering com. nat. conf. 1987, 88), Nat. Soc. Fund Raising Execs. (program com. Ctrl. Ohio chpt. 1988-94, chmn. program com. 1993, 94, bd. dirs. 1993-95, treas. 1995). Office: Columbus Symphony Orch 55 E State St Columbus OH 43215-4203 E-mail: susanr@columbussymphony.com.

ROSENSTREICH, DAVID LEON, medical educator, immunologist, allergist; b. NYC, Nov. 16, 1942; s. Joseph S. and Gertrude (Tankenbaum) R.; m. Victoria Abokrek, June 13, 1965; children: Jonathan, Peter, Rebecca. BS in Chemistry, CCNY, 1963; MD, NYU, 1967. Intern, resident Bronx (N.Y.) Mcpl. Hosp. Ctr., 1967-69; clin. assoc. NIAID, NIH, Bethesda, Md., 1969-72; sr. investigator NIDR, NIH, Bethesda, 1972-78; vis. assoc. prof. Rockefeller U., NYC, 1978-80; prof. medicine Albert Einstein Coll. Medicine, NYC, 1980—, dir. div. allergy and immunology, 1980—. Dir. Bronx Asthma Project. Editor: Mitogens in Immunobiology, 1975, Cellular Functions in Immunity and Inflamation, 1980; assoc. editor Clin. Revs. in Allergy, 1987—, Annals of Allergy, 1994—. Comdr. USPHS, 1969-78. Fellow Am. Soc. Clin. Investigation, Am. Acad. Allergy and Immunology, Am. Coll. Allergy, Am. Assn. Physicians. Avocation: winemaking. Office: Albert Einstein Coll Med 1635a Poplar St Bronx NY 10461-1926 Home Phone: 914-834-5163; Office Phone: 718-405-8075. Business E-Mail: rosenstr@aecom.yu.edu.

ROSENSWEIG, DANIEL L., Internet company executive; b. 1961; BA in Polit. Sci., Hobart Coll., NY. Assoc. pub. PC Mag., 1992—94, v.p., pub. NYC, 1994—96; pres. Ziff-Davis Internet Pub. Group, 1996-97; pres., CEO ZDNet, Inc., NYC, 1997—2000; pres. CNET Networks, 2000—02; COO Yahoo!, Inc., Calif., 2002—. Mem. adv. bd. DonorsChoose.org. Office: Yahoo! Inc 701 First Ave Sunnyvale CA 94089 *

ROSENSWEIG, RONALD ELLIS, chemical engineer, consultant; b. Hamilton, Ohio, Nov. 8, 1932; s. Herman and Deana (Meisel) Rosensweig; m. Ruth Evelyn Cohen, Sept. 5, 1954; children: Scott Elliot, Beth Ellen, Perry Ethan. BSChemE, U. Cin., 1955; SM, MIT, 1956, ScD, 1959. Asst. prof. dept. chem. engring. MIT, Cambridge, 1959-62; prin. scientist Avco Corp., Wilmington, Mass., 1962-69; pres., tech. dir., co-founder Ferrofluidics Corp., Burlington, Mass., 1969-73, also dir., 1969-85; rsch. assoc. Exxon Corp., Annandale, NJ, 1973-78, sr. rsch. assoc., 1978-85, sci. advisor, 1985-95; internat. rsch. chair Blaise Pascal, Paris, 1996-98; rsch. affiliate MIT, 2004—. Vis. prof. U. Minn., Mpls., 1980, U. Chgo., 1990, Weizmann Inst. Sci., Israel, 1997, HEIG, Yverdon-les-Bains, Switzerland, 2007. Author: Ferrohydrodynamics, 1985; contbr. articles to profl. jours. Named Young Engr. of the Yr., Avco Corp., 1966, Disting. Engring. Alumnus, U. Cin., 1986; recipient IR-100 award, Indsl. Rsch. Pubs., 1968, 1969, 1971; fellow, NSF, MIT, 1955—56. Mem.: AIChE (Alpha Chi Sigma award for Rsch. 1985), Internat. Steering Com. (chmn. 1977—92), Magnetic Fluids Conf., Am. Phys. Soc., Nat. Acad. Engring. Jewish. Achievements include patents in field. Home: 34 Gloucester Rd Summit NJ 07901-3023 E-mail: rerosen@comcast.net.

ROSENTHAL, ALAN SAYRE, government official, lawyer; b. NYC, Sept. 30, 1926; s. Morris S. and Elizabeth (Ralph) R.; m. Helen Miller, Sept. 8, 1951; children: Edward S., Susan L., Richard M., James M. AB, U. Pa., 1948; LL.B., Yale U., 1951. Bar: N.Y. 1952. Asst. in instrn. Yale U. Law Sch., 1950-51; law clk. to U.S. Circuit Judge Henry W. Edgerton, Washington, 1951-52; atty. appellate sect., civil div. Justice Dept., 1952-72, asst. chief, 1958-72; admnstrv. judge atomic safety and licensing appeal panel AEC (now Nuclear Regulatory Commn.), Washington, 1972-91, chmn., 1972-88; adminstrv. judge pers. appeals bd. GAO, Washington, 1991-96, chmn., 1992-94; adminstrv. judge atomic safety and licensing bd. panel Nuclear Regulatory Commn., Washington, 1999—. Mem. ethics panel Montgomery County Bd. Edn., 1987-93; lectr. law U. Pa., 1981-83, Am. U., 1991-92. Pres. Kensington Elem. Sch. PTA, 1966-67; pres. North Chevy Chase Swimming Pool Assn., 1974-76; chmn. trustees Cedar Ln. Unitarian Universalist Ch., 1970-71; bd. dirs. Montgomery chpt. ACLU, 1967-69. Served with USAAF, 1944-46. Recipient John Marshall award Justice Dept., 1969, Disting. Svc. award Nuclear Regulatory Commn., 1988. Mem. Order of Coif, Phi Beta Kappa, Pi Gamma Mu, Delta Sigma Rho Home: 3203 Kent St Kensington MD 20895-3210 Personal E-mail: rsnthl@comcast.net.

ROSENTHAL, ALBERT JAY, advertising executive; b. Chgo., Sept. 30, 1928; s. Harry and Jennie (Comm) R.; m. Rhoda R. Rosenstein, June 18, 1950; children: Jayne, Michael, James, Nancy. BA, U. Ill., 1950. Reporter Transradio Press., Chgo., 1950-51; columnist Lerner Newspapers, Chgo., 1951-53; creative dir. Elliot, Jaynes & Baruch, Chgo., 1953-61; chmn. Albert Jay Rosenthal & Co., Chgo. and NYC, 1961-85; chmn. Midwest div. HBM/Creamer-Albert Jay Rosenthal, Chgo., 1985-88, Della Femina, McNamee WCRS, Inc., Chgo., 1988-93; chmn. DFM/Tatham, Chgo., 1993; founder, pres. Franchising & Licensing World Ctr., Chgo., 1994-98; v.p. mktg., chief mktg. officer Terry Farms Inc., Wayzata, Minn., 1998—. Weekly columnist Franchising and You, Chgo. Sun-Times. Bd. dirs. Ill. Arts Alliance Found., Ill. Arts Alliance, Court Theatre U. Chgo.; mem. sustaining fund com. Ravinia Festival Assn.; mem. mktg. com. World Bus. Coun., Washington; vice chmn. Chgo. Internat. Film Festival; v.p. Gastro-Intestinal Rsch. Found. U. Chgo. Named one of Chgo. Ten Outstanding Young Men, Chgo. Jr. Assn. of Commerce, 1962, Advt. Man of Yr., Alpha Delta Sigma, 1978, Communicator of Yr., Jewish United Fund, 1988 Jewish. Home: 1110 N Lake Shore Dr Apt 32N Chicago IL 60611-1022

ROSENTHAL, ALBERT LESTER, dermatologist, educator; b. New Bedford, Mass., July 25, 1926; s. Myer and Ruth Naomi (Gourse) R.; m. Carol Ash, July 30, 1969; children: Robert, Jill, Bruce. BA magna cum laude, Tufts U., 1946, MD, 1951. Diplomate Am. Bd. Dermatology. Intern RI Hosp., Providence, 1951-52, asst. resident surgery, 1952-53; asst. resident dermatology Mass. Gen. Hosp., Boston, 1955-56; asst. in dermatology NYU, 1958-60; practice medicine specializing in dermatology Trenton, NJ, 1958—; attending dermatologist Mercer Hosp., 1958—, chief dermatologist, 1958-93; chief dermatology Helene Euld Hosp., 1973-85; assoc. in dermatology U. Pa., Phila., 1969-73; assoc. prof. dermatology Hahnemann Med. Coll., Phila., 1973-87, clin. prof. dermatology, 1987—; mem. staff Grad. Hosp. Pa., 1969-73, Hamilton Hosp., chief dermatologist, 1972-76. Contbr. articles to profl. jours. Trustee Friend of the NJ State Mus., 1972—, chmn. bd. trustees, 1980-82, v.p. fine arts, 1978-80; gov. appointee adv. coun. NJ State Mus., 1994-2000, exec. com., 2001-; adv. bd. Princeton Sr. Resource Ctr., 1997—, exec. com.; adv. bd. Am. Art Newark Mus., 1998-2002; mem. Mercer County Cultural and Heritage Commn., 1982-2000, chmn., 1984-2000; mem. Mercer County Open Space Preservation Commn., 1992-2000; founding mem. Leader's Soc. Dermatology Found., 1988; gov. appointee Bd. Trustees NJ State Mus., 2000—, exec. com. sec. 2002—. Served to capt., M.C., USAF, 1953-55. Mem. Am. Acad. Dermatology, Pa. Acad. Dermatology, Noah Worcester Dermatology Soc., Phila. Dermatology Soc. (pres. 1984-85), NJ Dermatology Soc., NJ Med. Soc., Mercer Med. Soc., AMA. Jewish. Office: 74 Franklin Corner Rd Lawrenceville NJ 08648-2102 E-mail: carosentha@aol.com.

ROSENTHAL, AMNON, pediatric cardiologist; b. Gedera, Israel, July 14, 1934; came to U.S., 1949, naturalized, 1959; s. Joseph and Rivka Rosenthal; m. Prudence Lloyd, July 22, 1962; children: Jonathan, Eben, Nathaniel. MD, Albany Med. Coll., 1959. Intern Buffalo Children's Hosp., 1959-60; resident in pediatrics Children's Hosp. Med. Center, Boston, 1960-62, resident in pediatric cardiology, 1965-68; asso. prof. pediatrics Children's Hosp. Med. Center and Harvard U. Med. Sch., Boston, 1975-77; prof. pediatrics C.S. Mott Children's Hosp., U. Mich., Ann Arbor, 1977—2006, assoc. dir. dept. pediatrics, 1989-92, dir. pediatric cardiology, 1977-97, prof. emeritus pediatrics, 2006—. Served to capt. M.C. USAF, 1962-65. Recipient Founders award, Am. Acad. Pediat., 2003, Disting. Svc. award, U. Mich., 2003; Amnon Rosenthal endowed professorship, 1994. Mem. Am. Acad. Pediatrics, Soc. for Pediatric Rsch., Am. Pediatric Soc., Am. Heart Assn., Am. Coll. Cardiology, Am. Bd. Pediatrics, Am. Bd. Pediatric Cardiology (chmn. 1987-88). Office: CS Mott Children's Hosp Ann Arbor MI 48109-0204 Office Phone: 734-936-6703. Business E-Mail: amnonr@umich.edu.

ROSENTHAL, ANDREW MARK, newspaper editor; b. 1956; s. Abraham Michael and Ann Marie (Burke) Rosenthal; m. Mary Beth Bierut, Jan. 15, 1994. BA in Am. History, U. Denver, 1978. Police reporter The Rocky Mountain News, Denver; Moscow bur. chief AP; Washington correspondent The NY Times, 1987—92, Washington bur. editor, 1992—97, fgn. editor, 1997—2000, nat. editor, 2000—01, asst. mng. editor, 2001—03, dep. editl. page editor, 2003—07, editl. page editor, 2007—. Office: The NY Times 229 W 43rd St New York NY 10036-3959 *

ROSENTHAL, DOUGLAS EURICO, lawyer; b. NYC, Feb. 12, 1940; s. Jacob and Edna Louise (Muir) R.; m. Erica Switzen Kremen, Nov. 12, 1967; children: Benjamin Muir, Rachel Elizabeth. BA summa cum laude, Yale U., 1961, LLB, 1966, PhD in Polit. Sci, 1970; postgrad., Oxford U., Eng., 1962; MA, Columbia U., 1963. Bar: NY 1968, DC 1980, US Dist. Ct. DC, US Dist. Ct. (so. and ea. dists.) NY, US Ct. Appeals (D.C. cir.), US Ct. Appeals (2d cir.), US Supreme Ct. 1976. Project dir. Russell Sage Found., NYC, 1968-70; assoc. Fried, Frank, Harris, Shriver & Jacobson, NYC, 1970-74; asst. chief fgn. commerce sect., antitrust divsn. Dept. Justice, Washington, 1974-77, chief, 1977-80; prtnr. Sutherland, Asbill & Brennan, Washington, 1980-88, Coudert Bros., 1989-94, Sonnenschein, Nath & Rosenthal, LLP, Washington, 1994—2005, Constantine/Cannon LLP, Washington, 2005—. Adj. prof. Tokyo U. Law Sch., 1992; spkr. USIA, Australia, France, England, Canada, Germany, Japan, Portugal. Author: Lawyer and Client: Who's in Charge?, 1972, 2d rev. edit.; co-author: (with Donald I. Baker) US Dept. Justice Antitrust Guide for International Operations, 1977, (with William Knighton) National Law and International Commerce: The Problem of Extraterritoriality, 1982; co-editor (with Carl J. Green) Competition Regulation in the Pacific Rim, 1996. mem. bd. advisors Antitrust and Trade Regulation Report, 1989-, George Washington Jour. Internat. Law and Econ.; mem. editl. bd. CCH Merger Notification and Clearance in Can.; contbr. articles to profl. publs. Mem. Sedona Conf. Working Group on econs. and antitrust Inst. for Consumer Antitrust Studies, Loyola U., Chgo.; committeeman Nassau County (N.Y.) Dem. Party, 1963—65; lifetime mem. corp. Culinary Inst. Am.; mem. Brookings Roundtable on Trade and Investment; mem. trade and competition com. Internat. C. of C. Recipient Edward S. Corwin Nat. Award Am. Polit. Sci. Assn., 1971; Henry Fellow Balliol Coll., Oxford U., 1962, Nobel Internat. and Woodrow Wilson Fellow Columbia U., 1963. Mem. ABA (antitrust sect.), Coun. Fgn. Rels., Am. Law Inst. (life, adv. com. law governing lawyers), Confrerie des Chevaliers du Tastevin, Mory's Assn., Phi Beta Kappa. Jewish. Achievements include being lead attorney in 19 major international antitrust litigations. Office: 1627 Eye St NW Washington DC 20006 Office Phone: 202-204-3510. Business E-Mail: drosenthal@constantinecannon.com.

ROSENTHAL, EARL EDGAR, art history educator; b. Milw., Aug. 26, 1921; s. Edgar Ernst and Reneé (Wyler) R. BS, U. Wis. at, Milw., 1943; PhD, NYU, 1953; Doctor honoris causa, U. Granada, 1994. Asst. dir. Milw. Art Inst., also Layton Art Gallery, Milw., 1952-53; vis. lectr., dept. art history U. Chgo., from 1953, prof., 1968-91, prof. emeritus, 1991—. Author: The Cathedral of Granada, 1961; The Palace of Charles V in Granada, 1985, translated to Spanish 1988, Arquitectura imperial, 1988. Contbr. articles to profl. publs. Served to lt. (j.g.) USNR, 1943-46, PTO. Recipient Gold medal in Fine Arts King of Spain, 1989, medal of honor Fundación Rodríguez Acosta (Granada), 1989; Spanish govt. grantee, 1948-49; Fulbright grantee Italy, 1949-50; Fulbright grantee Spain, 1963-64; Guggenheim grantee Italy, 1963-64 Mem. Hispanic Soc. Am., Coll. Art Assn., Soc. Archtl. Historians (dir. 1957-58, 66-69), Academia de San Fernando (Madrid) (corr.), Academia de Bellas Artes (Granada) (corr.). Home: 203 Hutchcock Way Apt 214 Santa Barbara CA 93105

ROSENTHAL, EDWARD LEONARD, secondary school educator; b. Chgo., June 15, 1948; s. Irving H. and Nina (Kritchevsky) R.; m. Hilary Rosenberg, June 29, 1969; children: Rachel, Rebecca. BS in Sci. and Letters, U. Ill., 1969; MEd in Earth Sci., Northern Ill. U., 1972. Tchr. St. Joseph Sch., Dyer, Ind., 1969-70; tchr., golf coach Joliet Cath. HS, Ill., 1970-77; tchr., girls golf coach Naperville N. HS, Ill., 1977—. Chmn. United Multi Family Homeowners, Bolingbrook, Ill., 1974-75; v.p. Ill. Jr. Miss Program, Bolingbrook, 1985-87; trustee Village of Bolingbrook, 1975-81, mayor, 1981-85; bd. dirs. West Suburban Temple Har Zion, 1988-92. Named one of Outstanding Young Men Am., 1975, 82, Ill. Girls' Golf Coach Yr., 1988-89; elected to Ill. Golf Coaches Hall Fame, 1995; recipient Disting. Svc. award, 1974. Mem. NEA, (bd. dirs. 1999-2005, resolutions com. 2006-), Ill. Edn. Assn. (bd. dirs., 1992-98, 99-2005, exec. com. 1994-98, 2001-05, chmn. legis. com. 1987-90), Ill. Earth Sci. Assn., Nat. Sci. Tchrs. Assn., Ill. Girls' Golf Coaches Assn. (pres. 1985-88), Naperville Unit Edn. Assn. (1st v.p. 1990-95), Cmty. Assn. Inst. Ill. (bd. dirs. 1980-83), Ill. Jr. Golf Assn. (bd. dirs. 2001-06). Jewish. Avocation: golf. Home: 508 Clover Ln Bolingbrook IL 60440-1416 Office: Naperville N High Sch 899 N Mill St Naperville IL 60563-2909 E-mail: edrosenthal@hotmail.com.

ROSENTHAL, GABRIEL, lawyer; b. Pomona, Calif., May 13, 1972; BA magna cum laude, Claremont McKenna Coll., 1994; JD, Univ. Wash., 1997. Bar: Wash. 1997. Prin. atty., corp. law Hillis Clark Martin & Peterson, Seattle. Contbr. articles to numerous profl. jours. Named Wash. Rising Star, SuperLawyer Mag., 2006. Office: Hillis Clark Martin & Peterson Ste 500 1221 Second Ave Seattle WA 98101

ROSENTHAL, GARY L., lawyer; b. Tulsa, July 19, 1949; s. Charles Orkin and Sylvia (Falk) R.; m. Lee Hyman, Mar. 30, 1982; 1 child, Rebecca Falk. AB, Harvard U., 1971, JD, 1975. Law clk. to presiding justice U.S. Ct. Appeals (5th cir.), Dallas, 1975-76; pres. Heaney Rosenthal; chmn. of bd. HydroChem; ceo AXIA, Wheatley TXT Corp., chmn. of bd.; sr. v.p. Cain Chemical; ptnr. Vinson & Elkins, Houston, 1976—; prin. Sterling Grp., Houston, 1989—90, 2005. Office: Sterling Grp 8th Greenway Plaza Ste 702 Houston TX 77046 Office Phone: 713-877-8257. Office Fax: 713-877-1824. Business E-Mail: grosenthal@sterling-group.com.

ROSENTHAL, HERBERT SEYMOUR, orthopedist, surgeon; b. Detroit, July 28, 1925; s. Samuel and Mary Rosenthal; m. Florence Rosen, Jan. 10, 1951; children: Jane, Barbara. BS, U. Mich., Ann Arbor, 1946, MD, 1950. Diplomate Am. Bd. Orthopedic Surgeons. Orthop. resident Harper Hosp., Mich., 1950—52, NYC, 1954—57; pvt. practice Wayne, NJ, 1958—. Lt. (s.g.) USN, 1952—54. Fellow: ACS. Avocations: photography, golf, fitness, hiking. Home: 339 Pompton Ave Pompton Lakes NJ 07442 Office: 1777 Hamburg Turnpike # 204 Wayne NJ 07470 Office Phone: 973-831-0337.

ROSENTHAL, HOWARD LEWIS, political science professor; b. Wilkinsburg, Pa., Mar. 4, 1939; s. Arnold Sidney R. and Elinor (Kaufman) (Rosenthal) Lewis; m. Annie Regine Lunel, June 30, 1960 (div. Nov., 1967); children: Illia Rebecca, Jean Laurent; m. Margherita Guastoni Spampinato, Feb. 6, 1968; 1 son, Gil Guastoni. BS, MIT, 1960, PhD, 1964. Asst. prof. polit. sci. U. Calif.-Irvine, 1965-66; asst. prof. and assoc. prof. polit. sci. Carnegie-Mellon U., Pitts., 1966-71, prof., 1971-93; Roger Williams Straus prof. social scis. Princeton U, NJ, 1993—2005; prof. polit. sci. NYU, 2005—; prof. emeritus Princeton U., 2005—. Vis. prof. Hebrew U., Jerusalem, 1968-69, U. Calif., San Diego, 1976-77, MIT, Cambridge, 1989-90, U. Paris I, 1990; Walras-Pareto lectr. U. Lausanne, Switzerland, 1996; vis. grad. lectr. Fondation Nat. des Scis. Politiques, Paris, 1972-73; disting. vis. prof. Brown U., 2003—05. Author: Prediction Analysis of Cross Classifications, 1977, Analysis of Ordinal Data, 1977, Partisan Politics, Divided Government and the Economy, 1995, Flexible Integration: Towards a More Effective and Democratic Europe, 1995, The Realignment of National Politics and Income Redistribution, 1997, Congress: A Political-Economic History of Roll Call Voting, 1997, Credit Markets for the Poor, 2005, Polarized America: The Dance of Ideology and Unequal Riches, 2006, Ideology and Congress, 2007; mem. editl. bd. Economics of Governance. Fellow NSF, 1969-92, 98-2003, 2006-, Ford Found., 1972-73, Social Sci. Rsch. Coun., 1964-65, nat. fellow Hoover Instn., Stanford U., 1979-80; Sherman Fairchild disting. scholar Calif. Inst. Tech., 1982-83; fellow Internat. Ctr. for Econ. Rsch., Turin, Italy, 1991-93, Ctr. for Advanced Study in Behavioral Scis., 1991-92, 98-99, ECARE U. Libre de Brussels, 1995, Russell Sage Found., 2002-03, 2005-, John Simon Guggenheim Meml. Found., 2002-03, 05-06. Fellow Am. Acad. Arts and Scis.; mem. Pub. Choice Soc. (Duncan Black award 1979), Am. Polit. Sci. Assn. (CQ Press award 1985). Office: NYU Politics Dept New York NY 10003 E-mail: hr31@nyu.edu.

ROSENTHAL, J. THOMAS, hospital administrator, medical educator; b. Richmond, 1949; BA, Johns Hopkins U.; MD, Duke U., 1974. Intern Johns Hopkins U., Balt., 1970; resident U. Va. Hosp., Charlottesville, Va., 1976, Lahey Clinic Found., Boston, 1980; exec. vice chmn. dept. surgery UCLA Sch. Medicine, 1991, prof. surgery/urology, 1993—, assoc. vice chancellor, 2003—; dir., vice provost UCLA Med. Group, 1996—; chief med. officer UCLA Health Sys., 1999—; vice provost UCLA Med. Group Affairs. Office: UCLA Urology/David Geffen Sch Medicine Box 951731 14-214R CHS Los Angeles CA 90095-1731 Office Phone: 310-825-4686.

ROSENTHAL, JACOB (JACK ROSENTHAL), foundation executive; b. Tel-Aviv, June 30, 1935; came to U.S., 1938, naturalized, 1943; s. Manfred and Rachel (Kaplan) R.; m. Holly Russell, Dec. 21, 1985; children by previous marriage: John, Ann; stepchildren: Christopher Russell, Andrew Russell. AB, Harvard U., 1956. Reporter, editor Portland Oregonian, Reporter, 1950-61; asst. dir., dir. public info. U.S. Dept. Justice, Washington, 1961-66; exec. asst. to Undersec. of State, 1966-67; Kennedy fellow Harvard Inst. Politics, 1967-68; nat. urban corr. Life Mag., NYC, 1968-69; urban corr. N.Y. Times, Washington, 1969-73, asst. Sun. editor, mag. editor NYC, 1973-77, dep. editor editl. page, 1977-86, editor editl. page, 1986-93; editor-in-chief N.Y. Times Mag., NYC, 1993-99; pres. N.Y. Times Co. Found., NYC, 2000—; chmn. ReServe, Inc., 2005—. Editor: Kerner Commn. Report on Urban Riots, 1968. Mem. Harvard Crimson Grad. Coun. Recipient Best Editl. award Internat. Labor Press Assn., 1961, Loeb award, 1973, Pulitzer prize for editls., 1982, Charles Loring Brace medal, 2002. Office: NY Times Co 229 W 43d St New York NY 10036-3959 E-mail: rosebud@nytimes.com.

ROSENTHAL, JAMES D., retired federal official, retired ambassador; b. San Francisco, Jan. 15, 1932; BA, Stanford U., 1954; student, Fgn. Svc. Inst., 1960—61, Nat. War Coll., 1974—75. With U.S. Fgn. Svc., 1956—90, adminstrv. officer Port of Spain, Trinidad and Tobago, 1958—60; polit. officer Saigon, Vietnam, 1961—65; mem. faculty U.S. Mil. Acad., 1965—67; internat. rels. officer Vietnam affairs Dept. State, 1967—70, dir. Vietnam, Laos and Cambodia affairs, 1975—77, dep. dir. mgmt. ops. Washington, 1986—90; mem. U.S. del. to Vietnam Peace Talks Paris, 1970—72; dep. chief of mission Bangui, 1972—74, Kuala Lumpur, Malaysia, 1977—79, Manila, Philippines, 1979—83; amb. to Guinea Conakry, 1983—86; exec. dir. Commonwealth Club of Calif., 1990—96. Personal E-mail: jrosent333@aol.com.

ROSENTHAL, JANE, film company executive; b. Providence, 1957; d. Martin and Ina; m. Craig Hatkoff; children: Juliana, Isabella. Student, Brown U.; BA, NYU, 1977. Rsch. staff CBS Sports, NY; editor program practices CBS Entertainment, 1977, program exec. miniseries LA, 1978, assoc. dir. motion pictures for TV, 1979; v.p. feature prodn. Universal Studios, 1984—85; v.p. in charge of motion pictures and TV Walt Disney, 1985—87; v.p. in charge of movies and miniseries Warner Bros. TV, 1987—88; co-founder (with Robert DeNiro), ptnr. Tribeca Film Ctr., NYC, 1989—; co-founder Tribeca Film Festival, NYC, 2002. Prodr.: (films) Thunderheart, 1992, Night and the City, 1992, A Bronx Tale, 1993, Faithful, 1996, Marvin's Room, 1996, Wag the Dog, 1997, Analyze This, 1999, Entropy, 1999, Flawless, 1999, The Adventures of Rocky & Bullwinkle, 2000, Meet the Parents, 2000, Prison Song, 2001, Showtime, 2002, About a Boy, 2002, Analyze That, 2002, House of D, 2004, Stage Beauty, 2004, Meet the Fockers, 2004, Rent, 2005, The Good Shepherd, 2006; (TV series) Tribeca, 1993; exec. prodr.: (films) Nine, 1996, The Repair Shop, 1998; (TV films) Witness to the Mob, 1998, Holiday Heart, 2000. Named one of 100 Most Powerful Women in Entertainment, Hollywood Reporter, 2006. Office: Tribeca Prodns 6th Fl 375 Greenwich St New York NY 10013 *

ROSENTHAL, JEFFREY M., lawyer; b. Poughkeepsie, NY, Aug. 14, 1951; BA in Econ., English, U. Pitts., 1973, MBA, 1974; JD, Rutgers U., Camden, 1982. Bar: NJ 1982, DC 1984, NY 2004. Shareholder, co-chair nat. fin. inst. practice group Greenberg Traurig LLP, Florham Park, NJ. Mem.: ABA (bus. law sect.), NJ State Bar Assn. (bd. dir.). Office: Greenberg Traurig LLP 200 Campus Dr PO Box 677 Florham Park NJ 07932 Office Phone: 973-360-7900. Office Fax: 973-301-8410. Business E-Mail: rosenthalj@gtlaw.com.

ROSENTHAL, JOEL, manufacturing executive; b. Ft. Worth, Oct. 25, 1946; s. Melvin and Jane (Hertzman) R.; m. Susan Ellman, Nov. 15, 1970; children: Jackie Ilene, Harold Joseph. BBA, No. Tex. State U., 1969. V.p. First Street Corp., Ft. Worth, 1969-72; mgr. Edison Jewelers & Distbrs., Ft. Worth, 1972-73; v.p. Yankton Sioux Industries, Wagner, S.D., 1973-81, pres., 1981-85; cons., Canton, S.D., 1985—; pres. Ctrl. Plains Tractor Parts, Sioux Falls, S.D., 1986—. Cons. econ. devel. State of S.D., Pierre, 1985-86; guest lectr. U. S.D., 2003. Chmn. S.D. Rep. Com., 1995-2003; mem. Electoral Coll., 1996, 2000; pres. City Coun., Wagner, 1978-83; trustee Carnegie Libr., Wagner, 1978-83; active Rep. Nat. Com., Washington, 1985-2003, S.D. Jud. Qualifications Commn., 1983-86, Pvt. Industry Coun., Pierre, 1985-86, SD Coun. of Econ. Advs., 2003. Named S.D. Vol. of Yr. Office of Gov., 1983. Republican. Jewish. Home: 6001 S Tomar Rd Sioux Falls SD 57013 Office: PO Box 1818 Sioux Falls SD 57101-1818 Office Phone: 605-334-0021.

ROSENTHAL, JOEL, chemist, researcher; b. NYC, Dec. 5, 1979; s. Peter Rosenthal and Christine (Giglio) Nanni. BS in Chemistry with honors, NYU, NYC, 2001; PhD, MIT, Cambridge, Mass., 2006. Undergraduate rsch. fellow NYU, NYC, 1998—2001; Fannie and John Hertz rsch. fellow MIT, Cambridge, 2001—06, postdoctoral NIH rsch. fellow, 2006—; rsch. asst. Cornell Med. Coll., NYC, 1995—98. Chemistry tchg. fellow NYU, NYC, 1999—2001. Editor: John W. Draper Chem. Soc.'s Ann. Jour.; contbr. articles to profl. jours. Recipient award for Sci. Achievement, NY Acad. Scis., 1997, Sustainable Chemistry award, MIT, 2006, Am. Inst. Chemists prize, 2001, Outstanding Tchg. award, NYU Coll. Arts and Sci., 2000—01, Harold Seidenstein award, 2000, Allison Huang Rsch. Conf. award, 2001, Dean's award for Scholarship, 2001; Trustee scholar, 1997-2001, Founders Day scholar, 2001, Nat. Def. Sci. and Engrng. Grad. fellow, Dept. of Def., 2001, Myron Kove Rsch. grantee, NYU, 1999, Pfizer Summer Undergraduate Rsch. grantee, Pfizer Ctrl. Rsch., 2000. Mem.: Am. Chem. Soc. (assoc.), Phi Beta Kappa, Phi Lambda Upsilon. Achievements include research in role of the human gene CD36 in the development of aerteriosclerosis; photocycloaddition of cyclic enones to C60 and C70. Synthesized extended fullerine-triazine hybrids for the generation of long-lived photoinduced charge separated states; mechanistic role of Proton-Coupled Electron Transfer in small molecule activation and water splitting. Business E-Mail: jr330@mit.edu.

ROSENTHAL, LARRY W., cosmetic dentist; b. NYC, Feb. 14, 1948; m. Sandy Rosenthal; 1 child, Eric. DDS, U. Pa. Sch. Dental Medicine, 1974. Dir. aesthetic continuum Baylor Coll. Dentistry, Dallas, Advanced Program, NYU, U. Ky. Coll. Dentistry; dir. Aesthetic Advantage Inc., Rosenthal Group Aesthetic Dentistry, NY. Spkr. in field. Named one of Top Cosmetic Dentists in NY, NY Mag., 2004; recipient Internat. Five-Star Diamond award, Am. Acad. Hospitality Sci. Mem.: Am. Acad. Cosmetic Dentistry (asst. editor, AACD Jour.). Achievements include print features in Vogue Mag., Elle, Glamour, Town & Country, New York Times, and Wall Street Jour; TV appearances on Weekend Today, The View, Access Hollywood. Office: Rosenthal Group Aesthetic Dentistry 30 E 76th St Ste 5B New York NY 10021 Office Phone: 212-794-9600. Office Fax: 212-794-3644.

ROSENTHAL, LEE H., federal judge; b. Nov. 30, 1952; m. Gary L. Rosenthal; children: Rebecca, Hannah, Jessica, Rachel. BA in Philosophy with honors, U. Chgo., 1974, JD with honors, 1977. Bar: Tex. 1979. Law clk. to Hon. John R. Brown U.S. Ct. Appeals (5th cir.), 1977-78; assoc. Baker & Botts, 1978-86, ptnr., 1986-92; judge U.S. Dist. Ct. (so. dist.) Tex., 1992—. Mem. Fed. Jud. Conf. Adv. Com. for Fed. Rules of Civil Procedure, 1996-2003, chair 2003-; chair 1999 Fifth Cir. Jud. Conf.; mem. Am. Law Inst., cons. group on transactional rules of civil procedure, adviser aggregate litigation project. Mem. bd. editors Manual for Complex Litigation, 1999—. Mem. vis. com. Law Sch. U. Chgo., 1983-86, 94-97, 99-2001; pres. Epilepsy Assn. Houston/Gulf Coast, 1989-91; trustee Briarwood Sch. Endowment Found., 1991-92; bd. dirs. Epilepsy Found. Am., 1993-98, DePelchin Children's Ctr., 2000-; bd. trustees Kinkaid Sch. Fellow Tex. Bar Found.; Mem. ABA, Texas Bar Assn., Houston Bar Assn. Office: US Dist Ct US Courthouse Rm 11535 515 Rusk St Houston TX 77002-2600

ROSENTHAL, LUCY GABRIELLE, writer, editor, educator; b. NYC; d. Henry Moses and Rachel (Tchernowitz) Rosenthal. AB, U. Mich., 1954; MS in Journalism, Columbia U., 1955; MFA, Yale Sch. Drama, 1961; postgrad. Writers Workshop, U. Iowa, 1965—68. Asst. editor Radiology mag., Detroit, 1955—57; free-lance editl. cons. various pub. houses, lit. agts. NYC, 1957—73; mem. admissions staff Writers Workshop U. Iowa, Iowa City, 1965—68; editor Book-of-the-Month Club, NYC, 1973—74, mem. editl. bd. judges, 1974—79, sr. editl. advisor, 1979—87. Mem. biography jury Pulitzer Prize, 1980; mem. bd. Am. Book Awards, 1981-82; adj. prof. English, NYU, 1986-2004; mem. guest faculty in writing Sarah Lawrence Coll., 1988-96, regular faculty writing, 1996—; lectr., adj. asst. prof. writing program Columbia U., 1990-96, Humanities faculty, 92nd St. YM/YWCA, 1987; fiction workshop The Writer's Voice, West Side YMCA, summer 1991; adj. prof. NYU Sch. Continuing Edn., 1988; mem. faculty Sarah Lawrence Ctr. for Continuing Edn., 1989, 90; instr. fiction writing course Art Workshop Internat., Assisi, Italy, summer 1993. Plays produced at Eugene O'Neill Meml. Theater Ctr., 1966, 1967; author: The Ticket Out, 1983; editor: Great American Love Stories, 1988, The World Treasury of Love Stories, 1995, The Eloquent Short Story: Varieties of Narration, 2004; contbr. to Global City Rev., 1995, articles and revs. to mags. and periodicals. Pulitzer fellow critical writing, 1968. Mem. Authors Guild, Authors League, Nat. Book Critics Circle, Women's Media Group (bd. mem. 1979-81), PEN, Phi Beta Kappa, Phi Kappa Phi. Office: Sarah Lawrence Coll Bronxville NY 10708 Business E-Mail: lrosenth@slc.edu.

ROSENTHAL, MARK DAVID, screenwriter; b. Phila., Jan. 15, 1950; s. Sidney and Tillie (Block) R.; m. Kim Helen Gross, June 26, 1993; children: Hayley Samm, Harry Arthur. BA, Temple U., 1971; MA, U. Vt., 1974; ArtsD, U. of the Pacific, 1978. Screenwriter: (films) The Jewel of the Nile, 1985, Superman IV: The Quest for Peace, 1987, Desperate Hours, 1990, Star Trek VI: The Undiscovered Country, 1991, For Love or Money, 1993, The Beverly Hillbillies, 1993, Mercury Rising, 1998, Mighty Joe Young, 1998, Planet of the Apes, 2001, Mona Lisa Smile, 2003, Flicka, 2006, Eragon, 2006; dir. The In Crowd, 1988; screenwriter, co-prodr.: Legend of Billie Jean, 1985. Democrat. Jewish. Avocations: horses, mountain climbing, painting, theater, dance. Office: Creative Artists Agy 9830 Wilshire Blvd Beverly Hills CA 90212-1804

ROSENTHAL, MEYER LOUIS, lawyer; b. Wilkes-Barre, Pa., May 27, 1944; s. Samuel J. and Lottie G. (Goncher) R.; m. Susan M., Aug. 19, 1967; children: Norman, Bonnie. BA, Rutgers U., 1966, JD, 1969. Bar: N.J. 1969, U.S. Dist. Ct. N.J. 1969, Calif. 1975, U.S. Dist. Ct. (cen. dist.) Calif. 1981, U.S. Dist. Ct. (ea. dist.) N.Y. 1980, U.S. Dist. Ct. (so. dist.) N.Y. 1981, U.S. Ct. Appeals (9th cir.) 1981. Law sec. Hon. Leon Milmed N.J. Superior Ct., Newark, 1969-70; assoc. Kaufman & Kaufman, Elizabeth, N.J., 1970-76; ptnr. Trueger & Rosenthal, Morristown, N.J., 1976-82; atty. pvt. practice, Morristown, N.J., 1982—. Editor Rutgers Law Rev. Cub scout leader Morris Area Boy Scouts Am., Randolph, NJ, 1980; chmn. Morris City Human Rels. Commn., Morristown, NJ, 1992—95, chmn. emeritus, 1999; trustee United Jewish Cmtys. of Metrowest NJ, 2002—; mem. cmty. adv. com. County Coll. of Morris, 2002—06. Recipient Cmty. Hero award Morris County Orgn. Hispanic Affairs, 1996. Mem.: NJ Bar Assn., Calif. Bar Assn., Comml. Law League Am., Anti-Defamation League (regional adv. com. 1979—, exec. bd NJ 1982—, nat. commn. 1992—), B'nai B'rith (bd. govs. 1975—92, pres. Dist. 3 1988—89, Young Leadership award 1982, Internat. Founders award 1985). Office: 161 Washington St Morristown NJ 07960-3753 Home Phone: 973-361-2048; Office Phone: 973-898-0500. E-mail: meyer@therosenthals.net.

ROSENTHAL, MICHAEL ROSS, academic administrator, consultant; b. Youngstown, Ohio, Dec. 2, 1939; s. Samuel Herman and Frances Vance (Schlesinger) R.; m. Linda Gabler, Sept. 6, 1963; children: Heidi, Erika, Nicolas Gabler. AB, Case Western Res. U., 1961; MS, U. Ill., 1963, PhD, 1965. Asst. prof. chemistry Bard Coll., Annandale, NY, 1965-68, assoc. prof. chemistry, 1968-73, prof. chemistry, 1973-84, assoc. dean acad. affairs, 1980-84; v.p. acad. affairs St. Mary's Coll. of Md., St. Mary's City, 1984-89; provost, dean faculty, prof. chemistry Southwestern U., Georgetown, Tex., 1989-96; dep. sec. Md. Higher Edn. Commn., Annapolis, 1996—99; spl. asst. to provost McDaniel Coll., Westminster, Md., 1999—2007, vis. prof., chair dept. chemistry, 2005—07; cons., 2007—. Contbr. articles to profl. jours. Chmn. Environ. Mgmt. Coun., Dutchess County, N.Y., 1978-84; founding chmn. Heritage Task Force for Hudson River Valley, 1980-84; pres., bd. dirs. Hudson River Heritage, N.Y., 1978-84; bd. dirs. Hudson River Rsch. Coun., 1976-84; teaching assoc. Danforth Found., 1980. Recipient Outstanding Cmty. Svc. award Dutchess County (NY) Legislature, 1980 Mem. Am. Chem. Soc., The Royal Society (Chemistry, London), Hudson River Environ. Soc., Sigma Xi, Phi Beta Kappa, Phi Lambda Upsilon Democrat. Achievements include research in inorganic chemistry and chem. edn. Personal E-mail: chesdog@erols.com. *Those of us who spend our professional lives as educators are subject to many pressures and influences - financial influences, political influences, intellectual influences. I try to remember that in the usually chaotic world of education the only really important thing is the welfare of the student.*

ROSENTHAL, RICHARD JAY, psychiatrist; b. NYC, Jan. 12, 1939; s. Sam and Yvette Loraine (Kapelov) Rosenthal; m. Strawn Rosenthal, Nov. 10, 1984. BA, Cornell U., 1960; MD, Albert Einstein Coll. of Medicine, 1964. Diplomate Nat. Bd. Med. Examiners, Am. Bd. Psychiatry and Neurology. Resident in psychiatry Mt. Sinai Hosp., NYC, 1968; clin. assoc. L.A. Psychoanalytic Inst., 1980; pvt. practice Los Angeles, 1970—; asst. clin. prof. psychiatry UCLA, 1971—2005; faculty L.A. Psychoanalytic Inst., 1984—; dir. inpatient gambling treatment program Westwood Hosp., 1990—93; chief of psychiatry CPC Westwood Hosp., LA, 1992—93; supr. attending Cedars Sinai Med. Ctr., LA, 1982—; co-dir. UCLA Gambling Studies Program, 2003—. Founder/pres. Calif. Coun. on Problem Gambling, 1986—99; com. on impulse disorders APA Task Force on DSM IV, 1988—93; com. on social and econ. impact of path. gambling Nat. Acad. Sci., 1998—99; vis. prof. psychiatry UCLA, 2005—. Contbr. chapters to books, articles to jours. Beit T'Shuvah Residential Treatment Ctr. L.A., 1992—94; adv. com. Little Hoover Commn. on Gambling in Calif., 1997; trustee Mus. Photog. Arts, San Diego. Lt. comdr. USN, 1968—70. Recipient Rsch. award, Nat. Coun. on Problem Gambling, 1993, Herman Goldman award, 1995, Robert Custer award, 2004. Fellow: Am. Psychiat. Assn. (life disting.); mem.: Internat. Dostoevsky Soc., So. Calif. Psychiat. Soc. (ethics com. 1992—), Inst. for the Study of Gambling and Comml. Gaming (adv. bd. 1993—), Am. Acad. Psychiatrists in Alcoholism and Addictions. Achievements include first controlled study of repetitive self mutilation(demonstrated progression and role of dissociation); author of current diagnostic criteria for pathological gambling; co-investigator on first genetic study of pathological gambling (demonstrating physiological predisposition); research establishing the legitimacy of the disorder; founding of California council on problem gaming, started first inpatient treatment program on the west coast, began UCLA gambling studies program, mentored researchers and clinicans. Avocations: photography, fly fishing. Office: 435 N Roxbury Dr Beverly Hills CA 90210 Office Phone: 310-278-3746.

ROSENTHAL, ROBERT, psychology professor; b. Giessen, Germany, Mar. 2, 1933; came to U.S., 1940, naturalized, 1946. s. Julius and Hermine (Kahn) R.; m. Mary Lu Clayton, Apr. 20, 1951; children: Roberta, David C., Virginia. AB, UCLA, 1953, PhD, 1956; PhD (hon.), U. Giessen, 2003. Diplomate clin. psychology Am. Bd. Examiners Profl. Psychology. Clin. psychology trainee Los Angeles Area VA, 1954-57; lectr. U. So. Calif., 1956-57; acting instr. UCLA, 1957; from asst. to assoc. prof., coordinator clin. tng. U. N.D., 1957-62; vis. assoc. prof. Ohio State U., 1960-61; lectr. Boston U., 1965-66; lectr. clin. psychology Harvard U., Cambridge, Mass., 1962-67, prof. social psychology, 1967-95, chmn. dept. psychology, 1992-95, Edgar Pierce prof. psychology, 1995-99, Edgar Pierce prof. emeritus, 1999—; disting. prof. U. Calif., Riverside, 1999—. Author: Experimenter Effects in Behavioral Research, 1966, enlarged edit., 1976; (with Lenore Jacobson) Pygmalion in the Classroom, 1968, expanded edit., 1992, Meta-analytic Procedures for Social Research, 1984, rev. edit., 1991, Judgment Studies, 1987; (with others) New Directions in Psychology 4, 1970, Sensitivity to Nonverbal Communication: The Pons Test, 1979; (with Ralph L. Rosnow) The Volunteer Subject, 1975, Primer of Methods for the Behavioral Sciences, 1975, Essentials of Behavioral Research, 1984, 3d edit., 2008, Understanding Behavioral Science, 1984, Contrast Analysis, 1985, Beginning Behavioral Research, 1993, 6th edit., 2008, People Studying People: Artifact and Ethics in Behavioral Research, 1997, (with Ralph L. Rosnow and Donald B. Rubin) Contrasts and Effect Sizes in Behavioral Research: A Correlational Approach, 2000; (with Brian Mullen) BASIC Meta-analysis, 1985; editor: (with Ralph L. Rosnow) Artifact in Behavioral Research, 1969, Skill in Nonverbal Communication, 1979, Quantitative Assessment of Research Domains, 1980, (with Thomas A. Sebeok) The Clever Hans Phenomenon: Communication With Horses, Whales, Apes and People, 1981, (with Blanck and Buck) Nonverbal Communication in the Clinical Context, 1986, (with Gheorghiu, Netter and Eysenck) Suggestion and Suggestibility: Theory and Research, 1989, (with Harrigan and Scherer) The New Handbook of Methods in Nonverbal Behavior Research, 2005 Recipient Donald Campbell award Soc. for Personality and Social Psychology, 1988, James McKeen Cattell Sabbatical award, 1995-96; co-recipient Golden Anniversary Monograph award Speech Comm. Assn., 1996; named Watson lectr. U. N.H., Lanzetta Meml. lectr. Dartmouth Coll., Bayer lectr. Yale Sch. Medicine, Foa lectr. Temple U., Disting. Alumni lectr. UCLA, Marschak lectr. UCLA; Guggenheim fellow, 1973-74, fellow Ctr. for Advanced Study in Behavioral Scis., 1988-89; sr. Fulbright scholar, 1972; recipient Gold Medal for Life Achievement in Sci. of Psychology Am. Psychol. Found., 2003. Fellow AAAS (co-recipient Sociopsychol. prize 1960, co-recipient Behavioral Sci. Rsch. prize 1993), APA (divsn. evaluation, measurement, and stats., co-recipient Cattell Fund award 1967, co-chmn. Task Force on Statis. Inference, Disting. Sci. award for applications of psychology, 2002, Disting. Sci. Contbns. award, 2002, divsn. evaluation, measurement and stats., others), Am. Psychol. Soc. (charter, James McKeen Cattell award 2001); mem. Soc. Exptl. Social Psychology (Disting. Scientist award 1996), Ea. Psychol. Assn. (Disting. lectr. 1989), Mid-we. Psychol. Assn., Mass. Psychol. Assn. (Disting. Career Contbn. award 1979), Soc. Projective Techniques (past treas.), Phi Beta Kappa, Sigma Xi. Office: U Calif Olmsted Hall Riverside CA 92521-0001 Office Phone: 951-827-4503.

ROSENTHAL, ROBERT JON, newspaper editor, journalist; b. NYC, Aug. 5, 1948; s. Irving and Ruth (Moss) R.; m. Inez Katherina von Sternenfels, Nov. 22, 1985; children: Adam, Benjamin, Ariella. BA, U. Vt., 1970. News asst. N.Y. Times, NYC, 1970-73; reporter Boston Globe, 1974-79, Phila. Inquirer, 1979-82, Africa corr., Nairobi, Kenya, 1982-86, fgn. editor, Phila., 1986-91, city editor, 1991-93, asst. mng. editor, daily, 1993-94, assoc. mng. editor, 1994-96, exec. editor, 1996-98, editor, exec. v.p., 1998—2001; mng. editor, v.p. San Francisco (Calif.) Chronicle, 2002—. Recipient Third World Reporting award Nat. Assn. Black Journalists, 1983, Mag. award Overseas Press Club, 1985, Disting. Fgn. Corr. award Sigma Delta Chi, 1985, Mag. Writing award World Population Inst., 1986. Avocations: ice hockey, gardening, fishing, cooking. Office: 1 Stevens Ct Belvedere Tiburon CA 94920-1549

ROSENTHAL, SETH A., lawyer; b. Cleve., Oct. 30, 1966; s. Jeremy S. Rosenthal and Rosenthal K. Sandra; m. Stephanie A. Robinson, Nov. 8, 1997; children: Aaron Robinson, Rosenthal Robinson Simon. AB, Dartmouth Coll., 1989; JD, Harvard U., 1993. Bar: D.C. 2003, Ga. 1993, U.S. Ct. Appeals (4th cir.) 2002. Skadden pub. interest fellow So. Ctr. for Human Rights, Atlanta, 1993—95; trial atty. Civil Rights Divsn., Housing and Civil Enforcement sect. US Dept. Justice, Washington, 1995—2000, atty. Atty. Gen.'s Task Force on the Assassination of Dr. Martin Luther King, Jr., 1999—2001, trial atty. Civil Rights divsn. Criminal Sect., 2000—05; legal dir. Alliance for Justice, Washington, 2005—07; ptnr. Venable LLP, Washington, 2007—. Adj. prof. Georgetown U. Law Ctr., George Washington U. Law Sch. V.p. Anne Frank Ho., Washington, 2000; tutor/mentor Friends of Tyler Sch., Washington, 1996; mem. Wash. Rugby Football Club, Washington, 1995. Mem.: ABA, D.C. Bar Assn. Office: Venable LLP 575 7th St NW Washington DC 20004 Home Phone: 202-966-7407. E-mail: sarosenthal@venable.com.

ROSENTHAL, SHIRLEY LORD, cosmetics magazine executive, novelist; b. London, Aug. 28; came to U.S., 1971; d. Francis J. and Mabel Florence (Williamson) Stringer; m. James Hussey; m. Cyril Lord; m. David Anderson; m. A. M. Rosenthal, June 10, 1987; children: Mark, Richard. Student, S.W. Essex Coll., London, 1948—50. Reporter London Daily Mirror; fiction editor Woman's Own, 1950-53; features editor Good Taste mag., 1953-56; features, fiction editor Woman and Beauty, 1956-59; women's editor Star Evening newspaper, 1959-60, London Evening Standard, 1960-63, London Evening News, 1963-68; beauty editor Harper's Bazaar, London, 1963-71, NYC, 1971-73; beauty, health editor Vogue mag., Condé Nast Publs., NYC, 1973-75; v.p. corp. rels. Colgate, Helena Rubinstein, NYC, 1975-80; beauty dir. Vogue mag., 1980—95, contbg. editor, 1995—. Chairwoman media coun. The Am. Acad. Dermatology, 1995—; corp. v.p. content iBeauty.com, 1999—2002; enrichment advisor Silverson Cruises, 2004—. Syndicated Field columnist on beauty, health; author 3 beauty books; also novels: Golden Hill, 1982; One of My Very Best Friends, (Lit. Guild Selection), 1985; Faces, 1989; My Sister's Keeper, 1993, The Crasher, 1998. City commr. Craigavon City, No. Ireland, 1963-68. Address: 131 E 66th St New York NY 10021-6129 E-mail: Shirlord3@aol.com.

ROSENTHAL, SOL, lawyer; b. Balt., Oct. 17, 1934; s. Louis and Hattie (Getz) R.; m. Diane Myra Sackler, June 11, 1961; children: Karen Abby, Pamela Margaret, Robert Joel. AB, Princeton U., 1956; JD, Harvard U., 1959. Bar: Md. 1959, Calif. 1961. Law clk. to chief judge U.S. Ct. Appeals, 4th cir., Balt., 1959-60; assoc. Kaplan, Livingston, Goodwin, Berkowitz & Selvin, Beverly Hills, Calif., 1960-66, ptnr., 1966-74, Buchalter Nemer, LA, 1974—96; of counsel Blanc, Williams, Johnston & Kronstadt, LA, 1996-2000, Arnold & Porter, 2000—. Bd. dirs. Playboy Enterprises, Inc., Chgo.; arbitrator Dirs. Guild Am., L.A., 1976—, Writers Guild Am., L.A., 1976—, Ind. Film and TV Alliance, 1989—, SAG, L.A., 1992—; negotiator Writers Guild-Assn. Talent Agts., L.A., 1978—; mem. entertainment and large complex case panels Am. Arbitration Assn., 1997—. Founder Camp Ronald McDonald for Good Times, L.A., 1985; charter founder Mus. Contemporary Art, L.A., 1988. Fellow: Coll. Comml. Arbitrators, Am. Bar Found.; mem.: ABA, Beverly Hills Bar Assn. (pres. 1982—83), Acad. TV Arts and Scis. (bd. govs. 1990—92), L.A. Copyright Soc. (pres. 1973—74), Los Angeles County Bar Assn. (trustee 1981—82), Calif. Bar Assn., Phi Beta Kappa. Office: Arnold & Porter 777 S Figueroa St Ste 4400 Los Angeles CA 90017-5844 Home Phone: 310-472-8473; Office Phone: 213-243-4000. Business E-Mail: sol_rosenthal@aporter.com.

ROSENTHAL, STEVEN SIEGMUND, lawyer; b. Cleve., May 22, 1949; s. Fred Siegel and Natalie Josephine Rosenthal; m. Ilene Edwina Goldstein, Oct. 1, 1983; children: Alexandra M., Eliana D. AB, Dartmouth Coll., 1971; JD, Harvard U., 1974. Bar: Fla. 1974, D.C. 1975, U.S. Supreme Ct.

1978, Calif. 1983. Law clk. judge Malcolm R. Wilkey U.S. Ct. Appeals (D.C. cir.), 1974-75; assoc. Covington & Burling, Washington, 1975-80, Morrison & Foerster, Washington, 1980-81, ptnr., 1981-97, Cooper, Carvin & Rosenthal, PLLC, Washington, 1998-2001, Holland & Knight LLP, Washington, 2001—02, Kaye Scholer LLP, Washington, 2002—, exec. com., 2005—. Lawyer rep. Jud. Conf. D.C. Cir., 1981-83, 2004—; mem. adv. com. on procedures U.S. Ct. Appeals D.C. Cir., 2003—. Pres. Family and Child Svcs. Washington, 1986-88, trustee, 1978—. Mem. Am. Law Inst., Phi Beta Kappa. Republican. Office: Kaye Scholer LLP 901 Fifteenth St NW Ste 1100 Washington DC 20005-2327

ROSENTHAL, SUSAN BARBARA, retired librarian; b. Elberon Park, NJ, Apr. 7, 1946; d. Joseph and Anna (Warar) Rosenthal. BA, Montclair State Coll., NJ, 1967; MEd in Libr. Sci., U. Miami, 1973. Cert. media specialist, tchr., Fla., NJ. Tchr. Manasquan Bd. Edn., NJ, 1967-71; tech. svcs. libr. Oakland Park Libr., Fla., 1978-92, asst. dir. Fla., 1992-93, acting dir. Fla., 1993, ret. Fla. Author: (mag.) Galumph, 1965-67; contbr. A Micro Handbook for Small Libraries and Media Centers, 1983, 2d edit., 1986, 3d edit., 1991. Mem. Humane Soc., Broward County, Fla., 1981, WPBT-TV PBS sta., 1975-2000, So. Mus. Flight, 1997—, Friends of the Oakland Park Libr., 1998—, mem. luncheon com., 1999, mem. planning com., 1999; charter mem. Mus. of Discovery and Sci., 1989-96, US Holocaust Meml. Mus., 1994—; donor Miami Book Fair Internat., 1990—, Cats Exclusive, Boca Raton Mus. Art, Fla., So. Poverty Law Ctr. Wall of Tolerance, Survivors of the Shoah Visual History Found., Martin Luther King Jr. Meml. Found., Poverello Ctr., thehungersite.com, Friends of the Oakland Park Libr., Sierra Club, WPBT-TV PBS Sta., Am. Coming Together, Abandoned Pet Rescue, Becca's Closet, Black Box Voting, Broward House, Coconut Grove Arts Festival, Defenders of Wildlife, Delray Affair, others. Recipient St. Cloud Tchg. award Société d'Enseignement, St. Cloud, France, 1966, 2 awards Libr. Pub. Rels. Coun., winner, 1983, hon. mention, 1985, cert. appreciation U.S. Holocaust Meml. Mus., 1996, 2000. Mem. ALA, AARP, Nat. Alliance for Mentally Ill, Fla. Libr. Assn., Fla. Pub. Libr. Assn., Broward County Libr. Assn. (treas. 1981-83, continuing edn. com. 1980), Apple Libr. Users Group, Apple Computer Enjoyment Soc. (chpt. sec. 1984-87, corp. sec. 1985-89), Consumers Union, NFO Rsch., Wilderness Soc., World Wildlife Fund, Environ. Def. Fund, People for Ethical Treatment of Animals, Nat. Resources Def. Coun., Nature Conservancy, Nat. Wildlife Fedn., Mensa, actforchange.org, moveon.org, Procrastinators Club Am., Pi Delta Phi.

ROSENTHAL, TAMARA, apparel executive; b. 1973; married. Undergrad., Cornell U., 1994; MBA, Columbia U., 2000. V.p. mktg. Lacoste USA Inc., NYC, 2004—. Named one of America's Top Women in Bus.-Game Changers, Pink mag. & Forté Found., 2007. Avocations: marathon running, hiking. Office: Lacoste USA Inc 551 Madison Ave New York NY 10022-3212 Office Phone: 212-822-6982. Business E-Mail: trosenthal@lacoste-usa.com.

ROSENTHAL, TONY (BERNARD), sculptor; b. Highland Park, Ill., Aug. 9, 1914; s. Nathan H. and Bessie (Baumgarden) R.; m. Halina Kotlowicz, Apr. 2, 1946 (dec. 1991); m. Cynthia Dillon, 1995. AB, U. Mich., 1936; student, Art Inst. Chgo., Cranbrook Acad. Arts; doctorate (hon.), Hofstra U., 1989. Exhbns. include Art Inst. Chgo., Met. Mus. Art, Mus. Modern Art, N.Y., Whitney Mus. Am. Art, N.Y.C., Pa. Acad. Fine Arts, Archtl. League, N.Y., Yale U., U. Ill., U. Nebr., 100 Biennale Exhbn., Sao Paulo, Brazil, Brussel's Fair, 1958, others; one man shows include San Francisco Mus, Western Mus. Assn. Travel Exhbn., Santa Barbara (Calif.) Mus., Long Beach (Calif.) Mus., Catherine Viviano Gallery N.Y., Kootz Gallery, N.Y.C., M. Knoedler & Co., Denise Rene Gallery, Paris, 1988, others; archtl. commn. include Temple Emanuel, Beverly Hills, Calif., 1955, IBM Bldg., 1958, Southland Ctr., Dallas, IBM Western Hdqrs., Los Angeles, Police Plaza, N.Y.C., Fullerton (Calif.) State Coll., Fin. Ctr. Pacific, Honolulu, Holocaust Meml., Buffalo, Metro-Rail Sta., Miami, S.E. Nat. Bank, Miami, Grove Isle, Miami, Met. Hosp., Phila., 1010 Lamar, Houston, Crantsrook Acad. Art, Bloomfield Hills, Mich., Steelpark, 400 E. 80th St, N.Y.C., Alamo, Astor Pl., N.Y.C., Rondo, 111 E. 59th St., N.Y.C., U. Ind., Hofstra U., N.Y., others; works in permanent collections Milw. Art Ctr., Ill. State U., Los Angeles County Mus., Long Beach, Lincoln (Mass.) Mus., Ariz. State Coll., Mus. Modern Art, Whitney Mus. Art, Albright Knox Art Gallery, Buffalo, U. Ill., NYU, Yale U., Middelheim Mus., Antwerp, Belgium, Guggenheim Mus., N.Y.C., Hofstra U. Fashion Inst. Art, N.Y.C., others; pvt. collections. Served with AUS, 1942-46. Recipient awards, prizes San Francisco Mus., 1950, Los Angeles City Exhbn., 1951, 52, Audubon Artists, N.Y., 1953, Pa. Acad. Fine Arts, 1953, Los Angeles County Mus., 1950, 57, Santa Barbara Mus. Art, 1959, Art in Steel award Iron and Steel Inst., 1974-75, Disting. Alumni award U. Mich., 1977, Sculpture award Inst. Arts and Letters, N.Y.C., 1985. Mem. NAD, 1992-(Academician, 1994-)

ROSENTHAL, WILLIAM J., lawyer; b. Balt., Nov. 4, 1920; s. Justin J. and Ray Marian (Stern) Rosenthal; m. Margaret Irwin Parker, July 4, 1956; children: Adriane Leigh, Jacqueline Rae, John Justin. AB, Johns Hopkins U., Balt., 1941; LL.B., U. Balt., 1950. Bar: Md. 1950. Adminstrv. asst. Office Price Adminstrn., Washington, 1941-42; assoc. Earle K. Shawe, Balt., 1951-67; ptnr. Shawe & Rosenthal (formerly Earle K. Shawe), Balt., 1967—. Lectr. U. Balt., 1952—56; mem. regional adv. coun. NLRB; vets. rep. Md. Constrn. Adv. Coun., 1946—49; lectr. NYU Conf. Labor Rels., 1981, Boston U. Labor Law Seminar, 1985; expert witness on labor law, legis. and congl. coms. Author: D-Day Through V-E Day, WWII Veterans Archives, US Library of Congress, 2005; co-author: The Developing Labor Law; contbr. articles to profl. jours. Served to lt. USNR, 1942—46, ETO. Mem.: ABA, Balt. Bar Assn., Md. Bar Assn., Johns Hopkins Club, Suburban Club (bd. govs., pres.), Spiked Shoe Soc., Pi Delta Epsilon, Omicron Delta Kappa. Home: 8207 Cranwood Ct Baltimore MD 21208-1823 Office: Shawe & Rosenthal 20 S Charles St Baltimore MD 21201 Office Phone: 410-752-1040. Business E-Mail: rosenthal@shawe.com.

ROSENWASSER, MIKE, lawyer; b. Texarkana, Ark., 1946; BBA, U. Tex., 1968, JD, 1971. Bar: Tex. 1971, NY 1992. Ptnr., co-head Corp. Fin. & Securities Vinson & Elkins LLP, NYC. Office: Vinson & Elkins LLP 26th Fl 666 Fifth Avenue New York NY 10103 Office Phone: 212-237-0019. E-mail: mrosenwasser@velaw.com.

ROSENZWEIG, CHARLES LEONARD, lawyer; b. NYC, Apr. 12, 1952; s. William and Frieda (Dechner) R.; m. Rya R. Mehler, June 14, 1975; children: Jessica Sara Newshel, Erica Danielle. AB cum laude, Princeton U., 1974; JD, NYU, 1977. Bar: NY 1978, US Dist. Ct. (ea. and so. dists.) NY 1978, US Ct. Appeals (7th cir.) 1980, US Ct. Internat. Trade 1981, US Ct. Appeals (2d cir.) 1985. Assoc. Graubard, Moskovitz et al, NYC, 1977-85; ptnr. Rand Rosenzweig Radley & Gordon LLP, NYC, 1987—. Mem. panel of neutrals comml. divsn. Supreme Ct. State NY. Editor NYU Jour. Internat. Law. and Politics. Chmn. bd. Jewish Cmty. Ctr., Harrison, 1998-2000. Mem. ABA (internat. law sect.), NY State Bar Assn. (co-chair internat. litig. com. 1995-98, mem. exec. com. comml. and fed. litig. sect. 1995-2005), Westchester County Bar Assn. (mem. ethics com.), NYU Alumni Assn. (chmn. jour. internat. law and politics alumni 1985-87), Assn. Comml. Fin. Attys. Avocations: skiing, bicycling, scuba diving, languages. Home: 9 Hadley Rd Armonk NY 10504-2417 Office: Rand Rosenzweig et al 800 3rd Ave New York NY 10022 also: 50 Main St 12th Fl White Plains NY 10606 Home Phone: 914-730-3132; Office Phone: 212-687-7070. Business E-Mail: crosenzweig@randrose.com.

ROSENZWEIG, MARK RICHARD, psychologist, neuroscientist, educator; b. Rochester, NY, Sept. 12, 1922; s. Jacob and Pearl (Grossman) R.; m. Janine S.A. Chappat, Aug. 1, 1947; children: Anne Janine, Suzanne Jacqueline, Philip Mark. BA, U. Rochester, 1943, MA, 1944; PhD, Harvard U., 1949; doctorate (hon.), U. René Descartes, Sorbonne, 1980, U. Louis Pasteur, Strasbourg, France, 1998, U. Montreal, Can., 2006. Postdoctoral rsch. fellow Harvard U., 1949-51; asst. prof. U. Calif., Berkeley, 1951-56, assoc. prof., 1956-60, prof. psychology, 1960-91, assoc. rsch. prof., 1958-59, rsch. prof., 1965-66, prof. emeritus, 1991—, prof. grad. studies, 1994—. Vis. prof. biology U. Sorbonne, Paris, 1973-74; mem. U.S.`nat. com. for Internat. Union Psychol. Sci., NRC and NAS, 1984-96. Author: Biologie de la Mémoire, 1976, (with A.L. Leiman) Physiological Psychology, 1982, 2nd edit., 1989, (with M.J. Renner) Enriched and Impoverished Environments: Effects on Brain and Behavior, 1987, (with D. Sinha) La Recherche en Psychologie Scientifique, 1988, (with W.H. Holtzman, M. Sabourin and D. Bélanger) History of the International Union of Psychological Science, 2000; editor: (with P. Mussen) Psychology: An Introduction, 1973, 2nd edit., 1977, International Psychological Science: Progress, Problems, and Prospects, 1992, (with A.L. Leiman and S.M. Breedlove) Biological Psychology, 1996, 3d edit., 2002, (with S.M. Breedlove and N.V. Watson) 5th edit., 2007; co-editor: (with E.L. Bennett) Neural Mechanisms of Learning and Memory, 1976, (with L. Porter) Ann. Rev. of Psychology, 1968-94, (with K. Pawlik) International Handbook of Psychology, 2000; contbr. articles to profl. jours. Served with USN, 1944-46. Recipient Disting. Alumnus award U. Rochester; Fulbright Rsch. fellow; faculty Rsch. fellow Social Sci. Rsch. Coun., 1960-61; Rsch. grant NSF, USPHS, Easter Seal Found., Nat. Inst. Drug Abuse. Fellow AAAS, APA (Disting. Sci. Contbn. award 1982, Disting. Contbn. award for Internat. Advancement of Psychology 1997), Am. Psychol. Soc.; mem. NAS, NAACP (life), Am. Physiol. Soc., Internat. Union Psychol. Sci. (hon. life, mem. exec. com. 1996—, v.p. 1980-84, pres. 1988-92, past pres. 1992-96), Internat. Brain Rsch. Orgn., Soc. Exptl. Psychologists, Soc. for Neurosci., Société Française de Psychologie, Sierra Club (life), Common Cause, Fulbright Assn. (life), Phi Beta Kappa, Sigma Xi. Office: U Calif Dept Psychology 3210 Tolman Hall Berkeley CA 94720-1650 Office Phone: 510-642-5292. Business E-Mail: memory@socrates.berkeley.edu.

ROSENZWEIG, RICHARD STUART, publishing company executive; b. Appleton, Wis., Aug. 8, 1935; s. Walter J. and Rose (Bahcall) R. BS, Northwestern U., 1957; Advanced Mgmt. Program, Harvard U., 1975. Credit rep. Dun & Bradstreet, Inc., 1958; with Playboy Enterprises, Inc., 1958—, exec. asst. to pres., 1963-73, sr. v.p., dir., 1973-82, dir. mktg., 1974-82, exec. v.p. publs. group, 1975-77, exec. v.p., head West Coast ops., 1977-80, exec. v.p. corp. affairs Los Angeles, 1980-82, exec. v.p., chmn. emeritus, 1982—; pres. Playboy Jazz Festivals, 1989—. Dir. I. Bahcall Industries, Appleton; exec. v.p. (dir. 1973—) Playboy Enterprises; chmn. Alta Loma Entertainment, 2000—. Trustee L.A. Film Expn.; mem. 2d decade coun. Am. Film Inst.; bd. dirs. Mus. Contemporary Art, Chgo., Periodical and Book Assn. Am., Internat. Inst. Kidney Diseases of UCLA, Children of Night, Maple Ctr. Beverly Hills; mem., chmn. bd. UCLA Legis. Network, Town Hall of Calif.; adv. bd. West Hollywood Mktg. Corp., 1985—; bd. dirs. So. Calif. ACLU, 1985—; mem. Los Angeles County Mus.; apptd. to blue ribbon com. project West Coast Gateway. With AUS, 1957; chmn. Modern and Contemporary Art Coun. L.A. County Mus. of Art.; pres. Beverly Hills Cultural Ctr.; exec. com. Henry Mancini Inst.; v.p. Fraternity of Friends music Ctr.; dir. Variety Club So. Calif., West Hollywood C. of C; mem. UCLA Chancellor's Assocs., UCLA Royce 270; offcl. amb. Govt. Beverly Hills. Recipient Do-ers award, 1988, Beverly Hills medal Beverly Hills City Coun., 1993. Mem. Am. Mktg. Aslsn., L.A. Pub. Affairs Officers Assn., Pres.'s Cir., Beverly Hills C. of C. (bd. dirs., visitors' bur., v.p.), Beverly Hills Fine Art Commn. (chmn.), Beverly Hills Econ. Devel. Coun., Founders Circle of Music Ctr., Pub. Affairs Coun., Craft and Folk Art Mus., Pres.' Coun. and Contemporary Arts Coun. L.A. Mus. Contemporary Art, The Am. Cinematheque (groundbreaker), Beverly Hills Rotary Club, Acad. TV Arts and Scis. Office: Playboy Enterprises Inc 2706 Media Center Dr Los Angeles CA 90065-1733

ROSES, ALLEN DAVID, neurologist, educator; b. Paterson, NJ, Feb. 21, 1943; BS in Chemistry summa cum laude, U. Pitts., 1963; MD, U. Pa., 1967. Diplomate Am. Bd. Psychiatry and Neurology. Intern Hosp. of the U. Pa., Phila., 1967—68; resident in neurology N.Y. Neurol. Inst., Columbia U., NYC, 1968—70; chief resident divsn. neurology Duke U. Med. Ctr., 1970—71, assoc. in medicine divsn. neurology, 1970—73, asst. prof. medicine divsn. neurology, 1973—76, assoc. prof. medicine divsn. neurology, 1976—79, asst. prof. biochemistry, 1977—89, prof. neurology dept. medicine, 1979—97, prof. neurobiology, 1989—97, Jefferson-Pilot Corp. prof. neurobiology and neurology, 1990—97, chief divsn. neurology dept. medicine, 1977—97; v.p., worldwide dir. genetics Glaxo Wellcome R&D, Research Triangle Park, NC, 1997—. Fellow Nat. Multiple Sclerosis Soc., Lab. Neurochemistry, Divsn. Neurology, Duke U. Med. Ctr., Lab. Virology, Divsn. Pediat. Neurology, Duke U. Med. Ctr., 1971-73, dir. Duke Neuromuscular Rsch. Clinic, 1974—, dir. neurosciences study program Sch. Medicine, 1975-85, investigator Howard Hughes Med. Inst., 1977-81, dir. Duke Muscular Dystrophy Assn. Clinic, 1979—, Joseph and Kathleen Bryan Alzheimer's Disease Rsch. Ctr., 1985—; cons. neurologist N.C. State Hosp. Sys., Cherry Hosp., Goldsboro, 1973-76, N.C. State Hosp. Sys., Lenox Baker Hosp., Durham, 1974—; chmn. internat. sci. adv. com. Australian Neuromuscular Rsch. Inst., 1989-92; sci. adv. Cyprus Isnt. Neurology and Genetics. Assoc. editor Molecular and Cellular Neuroscis., 1989-94; mem. editl. bd. Amyloidosis Jour., 1993-96, Neurobiology of Disease, 1993—, Fondation Ipsen, Rsch. and Perspectives in Neuroscis., 1994—, Alzheimer's Rsch., 1995—, Contemporary Neurology, 1995—, Alezheimer's Disease Rev., 1995—; contbr. articles to profl. jours. Capt. USAFR, 1967-72. Recipient Rsch. Career Devel. award Nat. Inst. Neurol. and Communicative Disorders and Stroke, 1976, Best in the Triangle-Aerobics Instr. award Spectator Mag., 1986, Leadership in Excellence in Alzheimer's Disease award Nat. Inst. Aging, 1988, Met.-Life Found. prize for outstanding med. rsch., 1994, Potamkin prize for Alzheimer's Disease Rsch., 1994, Internat. Alzheimer's Disease award Parke-Davis, 1996, award for muscular dystrophy rsch. Svc. Merchandise, 1997; Basil O'Connor Starter Rsch. grantee Nat. Found. March of Dimes. Fellow Am. Acad. Neurology; mem. Am. Soc. for Clin. Investigation, Am. Soc. for Clin. Rsch., Am. Neurol. Assn. (trustee 1982-84, 96—), Assn. Univ. Profs. Neurology, Assn. Brit. Neurologists (hon. fgn. mem.), Muscular Dystrophy Assn. (genetics task force and rev. com. 1989—, med. adv. com. 1990—, nat. v.p. 1994—), Alzheimer's Assn. (med. sci. adv. com. 1989—, chair 1996—, Sigma Tau award 1990, Rita Hayward Gala award 1994), Phi Beta Kappa. Office: Glaxo Wellcome 5 Moore Dr Research Triangle Park NC 27709

ROSETT, ARTHUR IRWIN, lawyer, educator; b. NYC, July 5, 1934; s. Milton B. and Bertha (Werner) R.; m. Rhonda K. Lawrence; children: David Benjamin, Martha Jean, Daniel Joseph. AB, Columbia U., 1955, LL.B., 1959. Bar: Calif. 1968, N.Y. State 1960, U.S. Supreme Ct. 1963. Law clk. U.S. Supreme Ct., 1959-60; asst. U.S. atty. So. Dist. N.Y., 1960-63; practice law NYC, 1963-65; assoc. dir. Pres.'s Commn. on Law Enforcement and Adminstrn. Justice, 1965-67; acting prof. law UCLA, 1967-70, prof., 1970—. Author: Contract Law and Its Application, 1971, 6th edit. (with D.J. Bussell), 1999, (with D. Cressey) Justice by Consent, 1976, (with E. Dorff) A Living Tree, 1987. Served with USN, 1956-58. Mem. Am. Law Inst. Home: 641 S Saltair Ave Los Angeles CA 90049-4134 Office: UCLA Law Sch 405 Hilgard Ave Los Angeles CA 90095-1476 Business E-Mail: rosett@law.ucla.edu.

ROSETT, DANIEL J., film company executive; b. 1962; BS in bus. and econ., U. Calif., Santa Barbara, 1984. CPA. Mgr. KPMG Peat Marwick; with Walt Disney Co., exec. dir. studio ops.; v.p., corp. controller MGM Studios, 1994—95, sr. v.p. fin. ops., 1995—98, exec. v.p. studio fin. and ops., 1998—2001, exec. v.p. mktg. and distribution, 2001—04; pres. United Artists Corp., 2004—05; COO Overture Films, 2006—. Exec. prodr.: (films) Capote, 2005. *

ROSEVEAR, CORA, curator; b. NYC; d. Kenneth White and Leslie Ferguson Rosevear. BA, Skidmore Coll., Saratoga Springs, NY; grad., Courtauld Inst. Art, London. Assoc. curator painting and sculpture Mus. Modern Art, NYC, 1988—. Mem.: Am. Assn. Mus. Curators, Internat. Coun. Museums, Am. Assn. Museums. Office: Mus Modern Art 11 W 53 St New York NY 10019 Office Phone: 212-708-9648. Business E-Mail: cora_rosevear@moma.org.

ROSHA, UZI, lawyer; b. Tel Aviv, Dec. 11, 1968; arrived in U.S., 1999; s. Rachel and Yossi Rosha. JD, Tel Aviv U., 1998; LLM, Columbia U., 2000. Bar: N.Y. 2004, Israel 1998. Clk. Supreme Ct., Chief Justice, Jerusalem, 1998—99, Ministry of Justice, Jerusalem, 1998; compliance officer Bear Stearns & Co., NYC, 2001—04; compliance mgr. Lehman Bros., NYC, 2004—05; chief compliance officer Fulcrum Global Ptnrs., NYC, 2005—, CarVal Investors. Chmn. Orgn. for Democracy and Equality, Tel Aviv, 1996—99; mem. moot trial assoc. prof. sociology Columbia U. Law Sch.; bd. dirs. ISEF, NYC, 2005. Lt. Israeli Paratroopers, 1987—91. Scholar, Columbia U., Sch. of Law, 1999, Tel Aviv U., 1994, 1995, 1996, 1997. Mem.: Israeli Bar Assn. (assoc.), N.Y. State Bar Assn. (assoc.).

ROSHAN, DANIEL, obstetrician, gynecologist; arrived in U.S., 1987; s. Mordechai Cohen and Mom Lea Roshan; m. Elana Roshan, Mar. 21, 1998; children: Jacqueline, Rebecca, Joshua, Ariel. BS, Pahlavi U., 1987; MD, Sackler U., Tel Aviv, Israel, 1992; grad., Johns Hopkins U. Diplomate Maternal Fetal Medicine Am. Bd. of Ob-gyn., 2001, cert. Am. Bd. of Ob-gyn, 1999. Asst. prof. NYU Sch. of Medicine, NYC, 2000—; dir. perinatology svcs. NYU Med. Ctr./Tisch Hosp., 2000—. Sec. Iranian-Am. Jewish Med. Assn., NYC, 2003. Recipient America's Top Ob-gyn, SLD Industries, 2004. Fellow: ACOG. Home Phone: 516-487-6088; Office Phone: 212-263-3234. Office Fax: 212-263-0616. Business E-Mail: roshad01@med.nyu.edu.

ROSHEL, JOHN ALBERT, JR., orthodontist; b. Terre Haute, Ind., Apr. 7, 1941; s. John Albert and Mary M. (Griglione) R.; m. Kathy Roshel; children: John Albert III, James Livingston, Angela Kay. BS, Ind. State U., 1963; DDS, Ind. U., 1966; MS, U. Mich., 1968. Individual practice dentistry specializing in orthodontics, Terre Haute, 1968—. Mem. ADA, Am. Assn. Orthodontists, Terre Haute C. of C., Terre Haute Country Club, Lions, Elks, K.C., Lambda Chi Alpha, Delta Sigma Delta, Omicron Kappa Upsilon. Roman Catholic. Home: 15 E Wedgeway Dr Terre Haute IN 47802-4983 Office: 4241 S 7th St Terre Haute IN 47802-4367 Office Phone: 812-238-2451. Personal E-mail: drjrosh@aol.com.

ROSHKO, ANATOL, aeronautical engineer; b. Bellevue, Alta., Can., July 15, 1923; arrived in U.S., 1950, arrived in U.S., 1950; married, 1957; 2 children. BSc, U. Alta, 1945; MS, Calif. Inst. Tech., 1947, PhD in Aero. Engring., 1952. Instr. math. U. Alta., 1945—46, lectr. engring., 1949—50; rsch. fellow Calif. Inst. Tech., Pasadena, 1952—55, asst. prof. to prof., 1955—85; acting. dir. Grad Aero. Labs, Pasadena, 1985—87; Theodore Von Karman prof. aeronautics Calif. Inst. Tech., Pasadena, 1985—, prof. emeritus, 1994—. Sci. liaison officer Office Naval Rsch., London, 1961-62; cons. McDonnell Douglas Corp., 1954-90, Rocketdyne Corp. Divsn., Rockwell Internat., 1984-90; founding dir. Wind Engring. Rsch. Inc., 1970; mem. Aero. & Space Engring. Bd., 1988-93. Recipient Timoshenko medal ASME, 1999; named to U. Alta. Alumni Wall of Recognition, 1998. Fellow AAAS, AIAA (Dryden Rsch. lectr. 1976, Fluid Dynamics award 1998), Am. Phys. Soc. (Fluid Dynamics prize 1987), Indian Acad. Scis. (hon.), Can. Aeronautics and Space Inst.; mem. NAS, ASME, NAE. Office: Calif Inst Tech Mail Sta 105-50 1201 E California Blvd Pasadena CA 91125-0001 Office Phone: 626-395-4484. E-mail: roshko@caltech.edu.

ROSHOLT, ROBERT A., diversified financial services company executive, insurance company executive; b. Mar. 24, 1950; BA, St. Olaf Coll.; MBA, U. Rochester. Asst. v.p. Profit Planning Group First Chicago NBD Corp., Chgo., 1974-82, mem. Treasury Dept., 1982-87, head Treasury Dept., sr. v.p., 1987; former CFO First Chgo. NBD Corp., Chgo.; exec. v.p. First Nat. Bank of Chgo.; exec. v.p., head of ops. AON Corp., Chgo., 2000—02; exec. v.p. fin. and investments Nationwide Fin. Svc., 2002—03, exec. v.p., chief fin. and investment officer, 2003—. Office: 1 Nationwide Pl Columbus OH 43215 *

ROSHONG, DEE ANN DANIELS, dean, educator, counselor; b. Kansas City, Mo., Nov. 22, 1936; adopted d. Vernon Edmund and Doradell (Kellogg) Daniels, d. Ken Garner and Lucille Cronin Davidson; m. Richard Lee Roshong, Aug. 27, 1960 (div.). BMusEd., U. Kans., Lawrence, 1958; MA in Counseling and Guidance, Stanford U., Calif., 1960; postgrad., Fresno State U., U. Calif., Berkeley; EdD, U. San Francisco, 1980. Cert. in spiritual direction Claritas Inst., 2007. Counselor, psychometrist Fresno City Coll., 1961-65; counselor, instr. psychology Chabot Coll., Hayward, Calif., 1965-75, coord. counseling svcs. Livermore, Calif., 1975-81, asst. dir. student pers. svcs., 1981-89, Las Positas Coll., Livermore, Calif., 1989-91, assoc. dean student svcs., 1991-94, dean student svcs., 1991—2003, life coach, 2000—; counselor Experience Unltd., Pleasant Hill, Calif., 2004—; symposium organizer Calif. State U., East Bay, 2004—. Writer, coord. I, A Woman Symposium, 1974, Feeling Free to Be You and Me symposium, 1975, All for the Family Symposium, 1976, I Celebrate Myself Symposium, 1978, Person to Person in Love and Work Symposium, 1978, The Healthy Person in Mind and Spirit Symposium, 1980, Change Symposium, 1981, Sources of Strength Symposium, 1982, Love and Friendship Symposium, 1983, Self Esteem Symposium, 1984, Trust Symposium, 1985, Prime Time: Making the Most of This Time in Your Life Symposium, 1986, Symposium in Healing, 1987, How to Live in the World and Still Be Happy Symposium, 1988, Student Success is a Team Effort, Sound Mind, Sound Body Symposium, 1989, Creating Life's Best Symposium, 1990, Choices Symposium, 1991, Minding the Body, Mending the Mind Symposium, 1992, Healing through Love and Laughter Symposium, 1993, Healing Ourselves Changing the World Symposium, 1994, Finding Your Path Symposium, 1995, Build the Life You Want Symposium, 1996, Making Peace With Yourself and Your Relationships Symposium, 1997, Everyday Sacred Symposium, 1998, Wisdom of the Heart Symposium, 1999, Inner Wisdom Symposium, 2000, Second Half of Life Symposium, 2001, A Celebration of Life Symposium, 2003, Viewing Mental Health and Mental Illness From a Multi-Cultural Perspective Symposium, 2004, Promoting Mental Health in Multi-Cultural Settings Symposium, 2005, Building Bridges to Hope and Recovery: Healing Ourselves, Transforming the System Symposium, 2006; mem. cast TV prodns. Eve and Co., Best of Our Times, Cowboy; chmn. Falling Awake Symposium, 2002, Calif. C.C. Chancellor's Task Force on Counseling, Statewide Regional Counseling Facilitators, 1993-95, Statewide Conf. Emotionally Disturbed Students in Calif. C.C.s, 1982—, Conf. on the Under Represented Student in Calif. C.C.s, 1986, Conf. on High Risk Students, 1989; spiritual dir. Claritas Inst., 2005-07, Calif. State U., East Bay, 2007—. Author: Counseling Needs of Comunity College Students, 1980. Bd. dirs. Teleios Sinetar Ctr., Ctr. Cmty. Dispute Resolution, 1998—, Pleasanton Youth Collaborative Bd., 1997-2002, Pleasanton Youth Master Plan Bd., 1998—; choir dir., 1996-99; pres. bd. Tri-Valley Unity Ch., 1998-2005, v.p. 2005, lay minister 2005, Tri-Valley Haven bd., 2000—, Calif. State U. East Bay Inst. Mental Illness and Wellness Edn. bd., 2000—, Ellis Life Coach Tng., 1999—, Interspiritual Mentor Tng. Program, 2005; title III activity dir. Las Positas Coll., 1995-99, dir. pace program,

1999-2003, dir. quest program, 2000-03. Mem.: Calif C.C. Counselors Assn. (svc. award 1986—87, award for Outstanding and Disting. Svc. 1986—87, Pleasanton Mayor's award 2000—01, 2002), Calif. Assn. C. C. (chmn. commn. on students svcs. 1979—84), Assn. Counseling and Devel., Nat. Assn. Women Deans and Counselors, Western Psychol. Assn., Assn. Humanistic Psychologists. Home and Office: 1856 Harvest Rd Pleasanton CA 94566-5456 Personal E-mail: deeroshong@comcast.net.

ROSHWALD, AVIEL ISAIAH, history professor; b. Mpls., Mar. 19, 1962; s. Miriam Mindla Roshwald; m. Alene Moyer, Oct. 17, 1999. BA, U. Minn., 1980; PhD, Harvard U., 1987. Prof. history Georgetown U., Washington, 1991—. Author: Estranged Bedfellows: Britain and France in the Middle East during the Second World War, 1990, Ethnic Nationalism and the Fall of Empires: Central Europe, Russia & the Middle East, 1914-1923, 2001, The Endurance of Nationalism: Ancient Roots and Modern Dilemmas, 2006; co-editor (with Richard Stites): European Culture during the Great War: The Arts, Entertainment, and Propaganda, 1914-1918, 1999. Jewish. Office: Georgetown U Dept History 37th and O Sts NW Washington DC 20057-1035 Office Phone: 202-687-6089.

ROSICA, GABRIEL ADAM, retired manufacturing executive, electrical engineer; b. NYC, Jan. 9, 1940; s. Gabriel J. and Elma (P.) R.; m. Bettina R. Nardozzi, Sept. 8, 1962; children: Gregory A., Julie Ann, Mark A. BA in Math. and Physics, Columbia U., 1962, BSEE, 1963; MSEE, Rensselaer Poly. Inst., 1966; MBA, Boston U., 1971. Registered profl. engr., Mass. Rsch. engr. United Aircraft Research Labs., East Hartford, Conn., 1963-67; mgr. electronic devel. The Foxboro (Mass.) Co., 1967-75, gen. mgr. U.S. div., 1975-77, v.p., 1977-80; pres., COO Modular Computer Sys., Inc., Ft. Lauderdale, Fla., 1980-82, pres., chmn., CEO, 1982-88; pvt. practice bus. cons. Boca Raton, Fla., 1988-91; sr. v.p. Elsag Bailey Corp., Pepper Pike, Ohio, 1991-92; exec. v.p. Bailey Controls Co., Wickliffe, Ohio, 1993-94; COO Bailey Control Co., Wickliffe, Ohio, 1994-96; sr. v.p. Keithley Instruments, Solon, Ohio, 1996-2001, exec. v.p., 2001—05, ret., 2005—. Chmn. engring. adv. coun. U. Fla., Gainesville, 1987-90; chmn. hi tech adv. coun. Coll. Boca Raton, Fla., 1987-90. Mem. Pres.'s Coun. Fla. Atlantic U., Boca Raton, 1987-91; trustee Nova U., Ft. Lauderdale, Fla., 1987-94. Recipient Boston U. Chair, 1971, Outstanding Young Engr. of Year award Mass. Soc. Profl. Engrs., 1974. Mem. IEEE (sr. mem.), Am. Electronics Assn. (bd. dirs. 1987, chmn Fla. bd. dirs. 1987-88), Fla. High Tech. and Industry Coun. Home: 35640 Spicebush Ln Solon OH 44139-5063 E-mail: gabe.rosica@att.net.

ROSIER, DAVID LEWIS, retired investment banker; b. Sioux City, Iowa, Mar. 22, 1937; s. Orel Lewis and Jewell May (Palmer) R.; m. Jackie Dodd, July 1965 (div. 1973); 1 child, Michele, m. Carol Mary Byre, Nov. 25, 1982 (dec. Sept. 1997); m. Rosemarie Dimino, Sept. 9, 1999 (div. Jan. 2004). BSBA, U. Denver, 1960. Registered rep. NASD; registered investment assoc. V.p., mgr. mktg. Hertz Internat., Ltd., NYC, 1970-71; regional v.p. Amtrak, NYC, 1971-73; mng. ptnr. Rosier & Assocs., Ltd., San Diego, 1969—; sr. v.p. for strategic mktg. Am. Prins. Holdings, Inc., San Diego, 1979-84; v.p., registered prin. Am. Diversified Equity Corp., Costa Mesa, Calif., 1984-85; pres. Glen Eagle, Inc., 1986-87; sr. v.p. Western Region Cozad Investment Svcs. Inc., San Diego, 1987-88; dir. corp. fin. Brookstreet Securities Corp., Irvine, Calif., 1993—2005; ret.; dir. fixed asset group U.S. Euro Securities, Inc. Global Investment Bank, 2005. Spkr. in field. Bd. dirs. Nautical Heritage Soc. (Hamburg award 1988). Mem. Oceanside Rotary (Paul Harris fellow, benefactor, pres., founder Rotary Club of Oceanside Found.), Kona Kai Internat. Yacht Club (commodore 1987), Internat. Order of the Blue Gavel (founder, past chmn. bd. trustees Humanities Found.), Phone Charities Internat. (founder, mng. mem. 1996-98), Nat. Investment Banking Assn. (bd. dirs. 2001-04), Golf Club of Calif. (bd. gov. 2005-). Home: 16840 Hoffman Ln Sandy OR 97055 Office Phone: 760-310-2030. E-mail: daverosier@verizon.net.

ROSINEK, JEFFREY, judge; b. NYC, Sept. 13, 1941; s. Isidore and Etta (Kramer) R.; m. Sandra Gwen Rosen, Aug. 7, 1977; 1 child, Ian David. BA in History, U. Miami, 1963; postgrad. in polit. sci., JD, 1974. Bar: Fla. 1974. Tchr. Coral Gables (Fla.) High Sch., 1963-78; pvt. practice Miami, 1974-76; assoc. Tendrich and Todd, Miami, 1976-77; ptnr. Todd, Rosinek & Blake, Miami, 1984-86; judge Dade County Ct., Miami, 1986-89, 11th Jud. Cir., Fla., 1990—, assoc. administr. appeal divsn. Miami, Fla., 1999—; judge Miami Dade County Drug Ct., 1999—. Instr. Boston U., 1975; mem. faculty Fla. Coll. Advanced Jud. Studies, 1992—, Nat. Jud. Coll., 2000—; mem. task force on substance abuse Fla. Supreme Ct., 2002—; lectr., presenter in field of juvenile justice and substance abuse. Contbr. articles to profl. jours. Chmn. Miami Environ. Rsch. Adv. Com., 1969-73; mem. Miami Beach Tranportation commn., Nat. Bicentennial Competition on the Constn. and Bill of Rights com., Dade County Youth Adv. Bd., 1973-75; bd. dirs. U. Miami Law Sch., treas., 1973-75; bd. dirs. U. Miami Law Sch., treas. alumni, jud. dir.; past pres. Dade County Young Dems.; mem. Congl. Civilian Rev. Bd., 1975-90, chmn., 1976-78; bd. dirs., treas. fla. Congl. Com., Legal Svcs. Greater Miami; chmn., 1976-78; chmn. Dade County adv. Coun. Close-Up Found.; Fla. chmn. Project Concern Internat.; internat. state chmn. Fla. Walk for Mankind, Project Concern, legal adv. com., Kiwanis, 1982-86; v.p. Beth David Congregation, 1982-86; trustee Haven Ctr.; bd. dirs., treas., organizer South Miami-Kendall pro bono project Legal Svc. of Greater Miami, 1983-86; traffic rev. com. Dade County, 1987-92; bd. dirs. Fla. Law Related Edn., 1988—, Adv. Program, 1988—; mem. Miami-Dade County task force for homeless, 1992-94; active Dade Coalition for the Homeless, 1992-04, Dade County Homeless Trust, 1993-01, 03-, chmn. criminal justice com.; chmn. Beck Mus. Judaica, 1988-00; mem. Miami Coalition for the Homeless, 2003—, treas., 2005; edn1. dir. Temple Judea; jud. cir. rep. Dept. corrections Boot Camp program, 1994-98; 11th jud. cir. organizer, rep. Homeless Alt. Rehab. Tracking Program, 1994—, rep. Comprehensive Homeless Integration Program (CHIP), 1992-94, chair Fla. 1st Annual Edn. Seminar/Retreat, 1995, Eugent P. Spellman Am. Inn of Ct., 1996—, bd. dirs., 2002—, sec., 2003-04, South Fla. Super Bowl XXXIII Host Com.; 1st v.p. Coral Gables High Sch. Parent-Tchr.-Students Assn., 1995-96, pres., 1996-98; adv. bd. Coconut Grove Art Festival, 2002-06, bd. dirs. 2006—; subatance abuse task force Fla. Supreme Ct., 2006—. Recipient award Jewish Theol. Sem., 1978, Outstanding Law Student Merit award Profl. Law Enforcement Assn., Appreciation award Liberty City Christian Assn., Svc. award Dade County Chief of Police, 2001, Cmty. Svc. award Mellon United, 2005. Mem.: ABA (task force reduction litig. cost and delay 1995—2000), Supreme Ct. Task Force on Treatment Based Drug Cts., Fla. Assn. Criminal Def. Lawyers (Justice Kegan Jud. Distinction award 2005), Fla. Assn. Drug Ct. Profls. (inaugural chair 2003—05, bd. mem. 2005—), Nat. Ct. Reporters Assn. (strategic com. 1993—2000), Am. Judges Assn. (bd. govs. 1988—92, domestic violence com. 1990—96, chair 32d Ann. Edn. Conf., Miami Beach 1992, sec. 1992—93, 2d v.p. 1993—94, 1st v.p. 1994—95, chair fed.-state rels. com. 1994—96, pres. 1996—97, exec. com. 1997, chair nominations com. 1997, coord. Close-UP Found. project 1997—, chair 38th Ann. Edn. Conf., Orlando 1998, edn. com. 1998—, exec. com. 2000—01, Image of Judiciary com.), Bar and Gavel Soc., Wig and Robe (chancellor 1973—74), Fla. Conf. Cir. Ct. Judges (criminal justice com. 1995—), Cuban Am. Bar Assn., Miami Beach Bar Assn. (bd. dirs.), Fla. Bar Assn. (rules com. family law sect. 1984—87, jud. nominating procedures com.), Coral Gables Bar Assn., South Miami-Kendall Bar Assn. (past pres.), Dade County Bar Assn. (criminal cts. com. 1994—), Friends of Drug Ct. (Hon. chair 2003—), Chabad of Dade (bd. dirs. 1999—), Greater Miami C. of C. (v.p. permanent housing 1996—98, pres. 1999—2000, Carrefour Housing Corp. for homeless), U. Miami Law Sch. Alumni Assn. (sec.-treas. 1985—87, jud. dir. 1987—), Dade Ptnrs., Miami-Dade Lions Club (charter), Key Internat. (pres. 1980—81, 1994—95, sec. 1995—, counselor Fla. dist., Key of Honor 1979, honoree 1984), Biscayne Bay Kiwanis (pres. 1994—, disting. past pres., Major Emphasis chmn., lt. gov. Fla. Dist., Kiwanian of Yr. 1983—84), Kiwanis Internat. (life). Home: 535 Bird Rd Coral Gables FL 33146-1307 Office: 1351 NW 12th St Miami FL 33125-1644 Office Phone: 305-548-5703. Personal E-mail: jefaroz@aol.com. Business E-Mail: jrosinek@jud11.flcourts.org.

ROSINSKI, EDWIN FRANCIS, medical educator; b. Buffalo, June 25, 1928; s. Theodore Joseph and Josephine M. (Wolski) R.; m. Jeanne C. Hueniger, Oct. 27, 1951; children: John T., Mary E., Sarah J. BS, SUNY, Buffalo, 1950; EdM, U. Buffalo, 1957, EdD, 1959. Prof. health scis. Med. Coll. Va., Richmond, 1959-66; dep. asst. sec. HEW, Washington, 1966-68; exec. vice chancellor U. Calif., San Francisco, 1968-72, prof., 1972-94; prof. emeritus medicine & pharmacy, 1994—. Adv. Rockefeller Found., N.Y.C., 1962-67, WHO, Geneva, 1962-78, Imperial Com. Health, Tehran, Iran, 1974-77; cons. Stanford Research Inst., Menlo Park, Calif., 1975-79. Author: The Assistant Medical Officer, 1965; contbr. over 100 articles to profl. jours. Served with USAF, 1950-54. Recipient spl. citation HEW, 1968, Merrell Flair award, 1991; named disting. prof. Australian Vice Chancellors Office, 1974, disting. vis. prof. Tulane U., New Orleans, 1983, Alumni of Yr. SUNY, Buffalo, 2006. Fellow AAAS; mem. Assn. Am. Med. Colls. (Merrel Flair award), Am. Ednl. Research Assn., Soc. Health and Human Values (founding mem.), Calif. Pharmacists Assn. (hon.), Phi Delta Kappa. Roman Catholic. Avocation: physical fitness. Home: 80 Sotelo Ave San Francisco CA 94116-1423

ROSKAM, CATHERINE S., bishop; b. May 30, 1943; m. Philip K. Roskam, Sept. 3, 1966; 1 child, Gemma. BA in theatre, Middlebury Coll., 1965; MDiv, Gen. Theol. Sem., NYC, 1984. Worked in theatre as an actress and prodr., NYC; ordained deacon, 1984, priest, 1984; asst. rector Holy Apostles Ch., NYC; priest-in-charge Holy Innocents' mission congregation, San Francisco; interim rector Ch. of Our Savior, Mill Valley, Calif.; diocesan missioner Episcopal Diocese of Calif., 1991—95; consecrated bishop, 1996; suffragen bishop Episcopal Diocese of NY, 1996—. Mem. exec. coun. Episcopal Ch. in the USA, 2000—; mem. Anglican Consultative Coun., 2001—; mem. bd. trustees Gen. Theol. Sem., NYC, vice chair, 2001—02. Named one of New York's Influentials, New York Mag., 2006. Office: Episcopal Diocese of NY 1047 Amsterdam Ave New York NY 10025 Office Phone: 212-316-7400. Office Fax: 212-316-7405. *

ROSKAM, JAN, aerospace engineer; b. The Hague, The Netherlands, Feb. 22, 1930; arrived in U.S., 1957; s. Kommer Jan and Agatha (Bosman) Roskam; m. Janice Louise Thomas-Barron, Dec. 21, 1994. MA in Aerospace Engring., Tech. U. Delft, 1954; PhD in Aeros. and Astronautics, U. Wash., 1965. Asst. chief designer Aviolanda Aircraft Co., Netherlands, 1954-57; sr. aerodynamics engr. Cessna Aircraft Co., Wichita, Kans., 1957-59; sr. group engr. Boeing Co., Wichita and Seattle, 1959-67; prof. emeritus aerospace engring. U. Kans., Lawrence, 1967—; cons. Design, Analysis and Rsch. Corp., 1991—. Cons. to govt. and industry. Author: Airplane Flight Dynamics and Automatic Flight Controls, 2 vols., 1979; co-author: Airplane Aerodynamics and Performance, 1981, Airplane Design, Part I-VIII, 1986, Roskam's Airplane War Stories, 2002. Served to 1st lt. Royal Netherlands Air Force, 1954—56. Fellow: AIAA, Soc. Automotive Engrs.; mem.: Exptl. Aircraft Assn., U.S. Chess Fedn., Koninklijk Instituut van Ingenieurs, Royal Aero. Soc., Air Force Assn., Aircraft Owners and Pilots Assn., Omicron Delta Kappa, Sigma Gamma Tau, Tau Beta Pi, Sigma Xi. Office: U Kans 2004 Lea Hl Lawrence KS 66045-0001 Personal E-mail: roskam@sunflower.com. Business E-Mail: roskam@darcorp.com.

ROSKAM, PETER JAMES, congressman, former state legislator, lawyer; b. Hinsdale, Ill., Sept. 13, 1961; s. Verlyn Ronald and Martha (Jacobsen) R.; m. Elizabeth Andrea Gracey, June 18, 1988; children: Gracey, James (dec.), Frances, Stephen, Alec. BA, U. Ill., 1983; JD, Ill. Inst. Tech., 1989. Bar: Ill. 1989. Tchr. All Saints H.S., St. Thomas, VI, 1984-85; legis. asst. to Rep. Tom Delay US Congress, Washington, 1985-86, legal asst. to Rep. Henry Hyde, 1986-87; exec. dir. Ednl. Assistance Ltd., Glen Ellyn, Ill., 1987-93; ptnr. Salvi & Roskam, Wheaton, Ill., 1994—2006; mem. Ill. Gen. Assembly from Dist. 40, Springfield, 1993—99, Ill. State Senate from Dist. 20, 2000—06, US Congress from 6th Ill. dist., 2007—, mem. fin. svcs. com. Legis. chmn. Ill. State Crime Commn. Named Hero of the Taxpayer, Americans for Tax Reform, 2005. Republican. Mem. Evangelical Covenant Ch. Presbyterian. Office: 150 S Bloomingdale Rd Bloomingdale IL 60108 also: 507 House Office Bldg Washington DC 20515 *

ROSKENS, RONALD WILLIAM, management consultant, retired academic administrator; b. Spencer, Iowa, Dec. 11, 1932; s. William E. and Delores A.L. (Beving) R.; m. Lois Grace Lister, Aug. 22, 1954; children: Elizabeth, Barbara, Brenda, William. BA, U. No. Iowa, 1953, MA, 1955, LHD (hon.), 1985; PhD, U. Iowa, 1958; LLD (hon.), Creighton U., 1978, Huston-Tillotson Coll., 1981, Midland Luth. Coll., 1984, Hastings Coll., 1981; LittD (hon.), Nebr. Wesleyan U., 1981; PhD (hon.), Ataturk U., Turkey, 1987; DSc (hon.), Jayewardenepura U., Sri Lanka, 1991; LHD (hon.), U. Akron, 1987, Am. Coll. Greece, Athens, 1994, Kent State U., 2005. Lic. min. United Ch. of Christ (Congl. and E&R). Tchr. Minburn (Iowa) High Sch., 1954, Woodward (Iowa) State Hosp., summer 1954; asst. counselor to men State U. Iowa, 1956-59; dean of men, asst. prof. spl. edn. Kent (Ohio) State U., 1959-63, assoc. prof., then prof., 1963-72, asst. to pres., 1963-66, dean for adminstrn., 1968-71, exec. v.p., prof. ednl. adminstrn., 1971-72; chancellor, prof. ednl. adminstrn. U. Nebr., Omaha, 1972-76; pres. U. Nebr. System, 1977-89, pres. emeritus, 1989; hon. prof. East China Normal U., Shanghai, 1985; adminstr. USAID, Washington, 1990-92; pres. Action Internat., Inc., Omaha, 1993-96, Global Connections, Inc., Omaha, 1996—. Interim exec. officer Omaha Pub. Libr., 1996-98; mem. Bus.-Higher Edn. Forum, 1979-89, exec. com., 1984-87; mem. govtl. relations com. Am. Council Edn., 1979-83, bd. dirs., 1981-86, vice chair, 1983-84, chair, 1984-85; chmn. com. on financing higher edn. Nat. Assn. State Univs. and Land Grant Colls., 1978-83, vice chmn. com. on financing higher edn., 1983-84, chmn. com. on fed. student fin. assistance, 1981-87; mem. nat. adv. com. on accreditation and instl. eligibility U.S. Dept. Edn., 1983-86, chmn., bd. dirs., 1986; exec. bd. North Cen. Assn., 1979-84, chmn. exec. bd., 1982-84, pres., 1989-90; active Environ. Ams. Bd., 1991-92, Strategic Command Consultation Commn., 1993-96, Nat. Exec. Res. Corps, Fed. Office Emergency Preparedness, 1968-88; chmn. Omaha/Douglas Pub. Bldg. Commn., 1996—. Co-editor: Paradox, Process and Progress, 1968; contbr. articles profl. jours. Mem. Kent City Planning Commn., 1962-66; bd. dirs. United Ch. of Christ Bd. Homeland Ministries, 1968-74, Met. YMCA, Omaha, 1973-77, Mid-Am. council Boy Scouts Am., 1973-77, Midlands United Community Services, 1972-77, NCCJ, 1974-77, Omaha Rotary Club, 1974-77, 93—, Found. Study Presdl. and Congl. Terms, 1977-89, First Plymouth Congl. Ch., 1989-90, Midland Luth. Coll., 1993-2000, Coun. Aid to Edn., 1985-89, ConAgra Foods, Inc., 1993—, Russian Farm Cmty. Project, Capitol Fed. Found., Topeka, Kans., 1999—, The Silverstone Group, 2004—; trustee Huston Tillotson Coll., Austin, Tex., 1968-81, chmn., 1976-78, Joslyn Art Mus., 1973-77, Nebr. Meth. Hosp., 1974-77, 1st Ctrl. Congregational Ch., Brownell-Talbott Sch., 1974-77, Harry S. Truman Inst., 1977-89, Willa Cather Pioneer Meml. and Ednl. Found., 1979-87; pres. Kent Area C. of C., 1966; mem. Met. Commn. Coll. Found., 1993-96; min.-in-residence Countryside Cmty. United Ch. Christ, Omaha, 2003—. Decorated comdr.'s cross Order of Merit (Germany); recipient Disting. Svc. award Kent, Ohio, 1967, Brotherhood award NCCJ, 1977, Americanism citation B'nai B'rith, 1978, Legion of Honor, Order of DeMolay, 1980, gold medal Nat. Interfrat. Coun., 1987, Agr. award Triumph Agr. Expn., Omaha, 1989, Disting. Alumni Achievement award U. Iowa, 2004; named Nat. 4-H Alumnus, 1967, Outstanding Alumnus, U. No. Iowa, 1974, Midlander of Yr., Omaha World Herald, 1977, King Ak-Sar-Ben LXXXVI, 1980; named to DeMolay Hall of Fame, 1993; named Hon. Consul Gen. of Japan, 1999. Mem. AAAS, APA, AAUP, Am. Coll. Pers. Assn., Assn. Urban Univs. (pres. 1976-77), Am. Ednl. Rsch. Assn., Coun. on Fgn. Rels., Chief Execs. Orgn., Young Pres. Orgn., Scottish Rite (bd. dirs. Omaha coun. 1999-), Lincoln C. of C. (bd. dirs. 1989-90), Masons (33 deg.), Rotary (bd. dirs. Omaha 1974-77, pres. Kent, Ohio chpt., 1970-71), Phi Delta Kappa, Phi Eta Sigma, Sigma Tau Gamma (pres. grand coun. 1968-70, Disting. Achievement award 1980, Disting. scholar 1981), Omicron Delta Kappa (nat. pres. 1986-90, Found. pres. 1986-96). Home: 10849 N 58th Plz Omaha NE 68152 Office Phone: 402-399-0928.

ROSKI, EDWARD P., JR., real estate developer, professional sports team executive; s. Edward P. Roski, III; m. Gayle Roski. BS in Fin. and Real Estate, U. So. Calif., 1962. Joined Majestic Realty Co., 1966, chmn., CEO; part owner Staples Ctr., LA Kings, LA Lakers; owner Silverton Hotel & Casino, Las Vegas, Nev. Bd. dirs. Comerica Bank, Calif., LA Sports & Entertainment Commn. Dir. Big Bros. of Greater L.A.; bd. govs. Natural History Mus. of L.A. County, Bowers Museum of Cultural Art; bd. trustees Loyola Marymount U., U. So. Calif.; bd. regents Loyola High School; founder Majestic Realty Found., 2002-. Served USMC, 1962—66. Named a Champions of Industry, Calif. Bus. Properties Assn., 2004; named one of Forbes' Richest Americans, 2006; recipient Partners with Youth award, Big Sisters of Greater Los Angeles and the Inland Empire, 2004, Woodrow Wilson award for Public Service, 2006. Mem. Explorers Club, Soc. Indsl. Realtors. Avocations: bicycling, mountain climbing. Office: Majestic Realty 13191 Crossroads Pkwy N 6th Fl City Of Industry CA 91746-3497 Office Phone: 562-948-4301. Business E-Mail: eroski@majesticrealty.com.

ROSKIN, WILLIAM A., communications executive; BBA, City Coll. of NY, 1963; LLB, St. John's U. Sch. of Law, 1966; LLM, NY U. Grad. Sch. of Law, 1968. Staff, law dept. RCA Global Comm., Inc.; gen. counsel City NY Dept. Pers., City Svc. Commn., NYC, 1971—76; v.p., labor rels. Warner Comm., 1976—86; sr. v.p., human resources Coleco Industries, Inc., 1986—88; v.p. human resources, admin. Viacom, Inc., NYC, 1988—92, sr. v.p., human resources, admin., 1992—2004, exec. v.p., 2004—06, sr. advisor, 2006—. Office: Viacom Inc 1633 Broadway 8th Fl New York NY 10019 Office Phone: 212-258-6230. E-mail: bill.roskin@viacom.com.

ROSKO, MARYANN A., nurse; b. McKeesport, Pa., Sept. 22, 1930; d. George Rosko and Anna Makar. Grad. in Nursing, Homestead Hosp., Pa., 1951; postgrad. in Nursing, Chgo. Lying In, Ill., 1952—53. RN Pa. RN staff Homestead Hosp., Pa., 1951—55; RN supr. McKeesport Hosp., Pa., 1959—62, RN staff devel., 1963—68; RN insvc. edn. Magee Women's, Pitts., 1968—85. 1st lt. U.S. Army Nurse Corp, 1955—58. Home: 2605 Sunset Dr West Mifflin PA 15122-3564

ROSKOSKI, JOHN, religious studies educator, coach; b. Rahway, NJ, May 23, 1960; s. Charles Clement and Elaine Magdelene Roskoski; m. Tracy Ann Abrego, Apr. 23, 1995; children: Nicholas Thaddeus, Samuel John. BA in Religious studies, Seton Hall U., 1981, MA in Jewish-Christian studies, 1990; MA in Theology, New Brunswick Theol. Sem., 1986; MPhil in Theology, Fordham U., 2004; PhD in Bibl. Studies, Omega Bible Inst. and Sem., 2006. Cert. strength trng. instr. YMCA, catechist cert. Archdiocese Newark, 1986. Tchr. religion St. Michael's HS, Jersey City, 1982—83; instr. logic Middlesex CC, Edison, NJ, 1986; strength coach Bishop Ahr HS, Edison, 1984—89; tchr. religion Marist HS, Bayone, NJ, 1989—91; adj. prof. theol. St. Peter's Coll., Jersey City, 1992—. Adj. faculty theology Omega Bible Inst. Seminary. Contbr. articles to profl. jours. Recipient Pres. award, Theology Omega Bible Inst. Seminary. Mem.: Assn. Bibl. Rsch., Nat. Honor Soc., Theol. Honor Soc. Roman Catholic. Avocations: chess, walking sticks, coin collecting/numismatics, powerlifting. Home: 23 Morse Ave Edison NJ 08817 Personal E-mail: sampson95@optonline.net.

ROSKOSKI, ROBERT, JR., biochemist, educator, author; b. Elyria, Ohio, Dec. 10, 1939; s. Robert and Mary R.; m. Laura Martinsek, Aug. 27, 1974. BS, Bowling Green State U., 1961; MD, U. Chgo., 1964, PhD, 1968. Asst. prof. U. Iowa, Iowa City, 1972-75, assoc. prof., 1975-79, vis. prof. Iowa City, 1993; prof. dept. biochemistry and molecular biology Health Scis. Ctr., La. State U., New Orleans, 1979—2006; Fred G. Brazda prof. Med. Ctr., La. State U., New Orleans, 1991—2006; founder, sci. dir. Blue Ridge Inst. for Med. Rsch., 2006—. Sr. investigator USAF Sch. Aerospace Medicine, 1967-69; assoc. dir. Med. Sci. Tng. Program, 1978-79; cons. biochemistry test com. Nat. Bd. Med. Examiners, 1981-84, 2003-06, Assn. Internat. Cancer Rsch., Royal Soc. New Zealand; mem. merit rev. bd. for basic scis. VA, 1992-95; mem. rev. com. biol. scis. U. South Fla., 1992-, biochemistry St. George's U. Sch. Medicine, 1997, Kuwait U. Health Scis. Ctr., 2002. With USAF, 1966—69. NIH postdoctoral fellow U. Chgo., 1964-66; NIH spl. fellow Rockefeller U., 1969-71 Mem. Am. Chem. Soc., Am. Soc. Neurochemistry, Soc. for Neurosci., Am. Soc. Biol. Chemists, Am. Soc. Pharmacology and Exptl. Therapeutics, Internat. Soc. Neurochemistry, Assn. Med. and Grad. Depts. Biochemistry (sec. 1994-96, pres. 1997), Am. Assn. Med. Colleges (coun. Acad. socs., 1998-01), Greater New Orleans Soc. for Neurosci. (pres. 1982-83), Am. Med. Writers Assn. Achievements include research in signal transduction and cancer therapy. Home: 221 Haywood Knolls Dr Hendersonville NC 28791-8717 Office: 3754 Brevard Rd Ste 116A Box 19 Horse Shoe NC 28742-8814 Office Phone: 828-891-5637. Office Fax: 828-890-8130. Personal E-mail: rrj@brimr.org.

ROSKY, BURTON SEYMOUR, lawyer; b. Chgo., May 28, 1927; s. David T. and Mary W. (Zelkin) R.; m. Leatrice J. Darrow, June 16, 1951; children: David Scott, Bruce Alan. Student, Ill. Inst. Tech., 1944-45; BS, UCLA, 1948; JD, Loyola U., LA, 1953. Bar: Calif. 1954, U.S. Supreme Ct 1964, U.S. Tax Ct 1964; C.P.A., Calif. Auditor City of L.A., 1948- 51; with Beidner, Temkin & Ziskin (C.P.A.s), LA, 1951-52; supervising auditor Army Audit Agy., 1952-53; practiced law L.A., Beverly Hills, 1954—; ptnr. Duskin & Rosky, 1972-82, Rosky, Landau & Fox, 1982-93, Rosky, Landau & Stahl, Beverly Hills, 1993-99; pvt. practice Beverly Hills, 1999—. Lectr. on tax and bus. problems; judge pro tem Beverly Hills Mcpl. Ct., L.A. Superior Ct.; mem. L.A. Mayor's Community Adv. Council. Contbr. profl. publs. Charter supporting mem. Los Angeles County Mus. Arts; contbg. mem. Assocs. of Smithsonian Instn.; charter mem. Air and Space Mus; mem. Am. Mus. Natural History, L.A. Zoo; supporting mem. L.A. Mus. Natural History; mem. exec. bd. So. Calif. coun. Nat. Fedn. Temple Brotherhoods, mem. nat. exec. bd.; mem. bd. govs. Loyola Sch. Law, L.A.; regent Coll. Am. Assn. Atty.-CPAs. With USNR, 1945-46. Walter Henry Cook fellow Loyola Law Sch. Bd. Govs. Fellow Jewish Chautauqua Soc. (life mem.); mem. Am. Arbitration Assn. (nat. panel arbitrators), Am. Assn. Attys.-CPAs (charter mem. pres. 1968), Calif. Assn. Attys.-CPAs (charter mem., pres. 1963), Calif. Soc. CPAs, Calif., Beverly Hills, Century City, Los Angeles County bar assns., Am. Judicature Soc., Chancellors Assocs. UCLA, B'nai B'rith, Tau Delta Phi, Phi Alpha Delta. Jewish (mem. exec. bd., pres. temple, pres. brotherhood). Club: Mason. Office Phone: 323-655-9757.

ROSKY, THEODORE SAMUEL, insurance company executive; b. Chgo., Apr. 14, 1937; s. Theodore and Lora Marie (O'Connell) R.; m. Jacqueline Reed, Apr. 19, 1958; 1 child, Laura Marie. BA, State U. Iowa, 1959. Various actuarial positions Conn. Gen. Life Ins. Co., Hartford, 1959-66, assoc. actuary, 1967-70, controller, 1970-73, 2d v.p., actuary, 1973, v.p., 1973-78; exec. v.p. Capital Holding Corp., 1978-84, exec. v.p.,

CFO, 1984-91, exec. v.p., 1991-92; bd. dirs. Legend Funds, 1993-98, SBM Mut. Funds, 1995-97, SBM Certificate Co., 1996-98; fin. svcs. Dory L.P., 1998-99. Instr. State U. Iowa, 1958-59, U. Hartford, 1964-66, U. Conn., 1967-68. Active Mayor's Adv. Com. on Pub. Art, 1990—2005; mem. bd. pensions Evang. Luth. Ch. Am., 1974—82, 1984—87, 1989—95; bd. dirs. Hartford Coll. for Women, 1974—78, Macauley Theater, 1983—85, Louisville Fund for the Arts, 1980—97, Louisville Luth. Home, 1983—97, Louisville Orch., 1982—88, 1989—95, Ky. Opera, 1992—2001, Lincoln Found., 1992—2002, Actors Theatre of Louisville, 1995—, New Performing Arts, 1996—98, Oak and Acorn, 1995—2001, Glassworks Found., 2002—03, Pub. Radio Partnership, 2003—04, YMCA Safe Place, 2003—, Sch. Choice Scholarships, 2004—05. Recipient award Soc. Actuaries, 1958 Fellow Soc. Actuaries; mem. Am. Acad. Actuaries, Southeastern Actuaries Club. Republican. Lutheran. Home and Office: 2304 Speed Ave Louisville KY 40205-1642

ROS-LEHTINEN, ILEANA CARMEN, congresswoman; b. Havana, Cuba, July 15, 1952; arrived in US, 1959; d. Enrique Emilio and Amanda (Adato) Ros; m. Dexter Lehtinen; 2 children, 2 stepchildren. AA, Miami-Dade Community Coll., Fla., 1972; BA, Fla. Internat. U., 1975, MS, 1987. Prin. Ea. Acad., from 1978; mem. Fla. Ho. of Reps., Tallahassee, 1983—86, Fla. Senate, 1986—89, U.S. Congress from 18th Fla. dist., 1989—; mem. govt. reform com., internat. rels. com. Recipient Nat. Legis. award LULACH, 1999, Official of the Year, Youth Crime watch of Am., 2001. Republican. Episcopalian. Office: US Ho of Reps 2160 Rayburn Ho Office Bldg Washington DC 20515-0918 also: Dist Office Ste 100 9210 Sunset Dr Miami FL 33173 *

ROSMAN, HOWARD S., cardiologist, educator; b. Detroit, Aug. 29, 1947; s. Carl and Mae S. Rosman; m. Sarine John-Rosman, Aug. 21, 1999; m. Nancy R Rosenhaus, Aug. 4, 1974 (div. Apr. 17, 1997); 1 stepchild, Akash D. Patel children: Sarah Z., Benjamin J., David A., John M. BA, Harvard Coll., Cambridge, Mass., 1969; MD, U. Mich., Ann Arbor, 1975. Resident in internal medicine Emory U., Ga., 1978; vis. fellow cardiology Royal Postgraduate Med. Sch., London, 1979; fellowship in cardiovascular disease Emory U., Ga., 1981; sr. staff physican Henry Ford Health Sys., Detroit, 1982—99; sr. staff physician St John Hosp. and Med. Ctr., Detroit, 1999—. Clin. asst. prof. of medicine U. of Mich., Ann Arbor, Mich., 1983—88; assoc. chief divsn. of cardiology Henry Ford Health Sys., Detroit, 1987—99; clin. assoc. prof. of medicine U. of Mich., Ann Arbor, Mich., 1989—94; program dir. cardiology fellowship Henry Ford Hosp., Detroit, 1987—99, dir. of undergraduate med. edn., 1992—99; prof. of internal medicine Case Western Res. U., Cleveland, Ohio, 1995—99; mem. bd. of governors Henry Ford Health Sys., Detroit, 1997—99; councilor Am. Coll. of Cardology, Mich. Chpt., Mich., 1999—2005; cardiology program dir. St John Hosp. and Med. Ctr., Detroit, 1999—; prof. of medicine Wayne State U., Detroit, 1999—. Pres. Am. Heart Assn., Metro Detroit, 2004—06. Recipient Outstanding Faculty Tchr., U. Mich. Med. Students, 1982 - 1994 (11 awards), Henry Ford Hosp. Residents, 1983 - 1999 (6 awards), Instr. of the Yr., St John Hosp. Cardiology Fellows, 1999 - 2005 (3 awards), Dept. of Internal Medicine Tchg. award, Wayne State U. Med. Sch., Medicine Faculty, 2003. Fellow: Am. Heart Assn., Am. Coll. Cardiology (pres. Mich. chpt. 2007). Office: St John Hosp and Med Ctr 22151 Moross #126 Detroit MI 48202 Office Phone: 313-343-4612. E-mail: howard.rosman@stjohn.org.

ROSMAN, MICHAEL E., lawyer; BA in Polit. Sci. and Econs. summa cum laude, U. Rochester, 1981; JD, Yale Law School, 1984. Assoc. Rosenman & Colin, New York City, 1984—93; gen. counsel Ctr. for Individual Rights, 1994—. Guest lecturer Washington Semester, American U. Office: Center for Individual Rights 1233 20th Street NW Suite 300 Washington DC 20036

ROSMUS, ANNA ELISABETH, writer; b. Passau, Germany, Mar. 29, 1960; d. Georg Rudolf and Anna Johanna (Friedberger) R.; divorced; children: Dolores Nadine, Beatrice Salome Kassandra M Sociology, German Lit. and Fine Arts, U. Passau, 1994; PhD (hon.), U. S.C., 2000. Spkr. and organizer in field. Author: Resistance and Persecution, 1983 (Geschwister Scholl prize, 1984), Exodus in the Shadow of Mercy, 1988, Robert Klein A German Jew Looks Back, 1991, Wintergreen Suppressed Murders, 1993 (Conscience in Media award, 1994), Pocking End and Renewal, 1995, What I Think, 1995, Out of Passau, 1999, Against the Stream, 2002, Leaving a City Hitler Called Home, 2004; guest talk shows, including documentaries and features in Germany, Austria, Gt. Britain, Denmark, Holland, France, Italy, Sweden, Poland, Can., U.S., S.Am., Australia, 1983-. Fundraiser Anne Frank Found., Jewish Cmty. Ctrs., Holocaust Ctrs., others, 1992—. Recipient Immigrant Achievement award Am. Immigration Lawyers Assn., 1998; named Best German Writer, European essay Competition, 1980; Sarnat award Anti Defamation League, 1994; Anna Rosmus Day, City of Santa Cruz, 1994. Mem. PEN Internat. Avocations: environment protection, multicultural projects, minority programs. Personal E-mail: passau11@yahoo.com.

ROSNER, ANN See SEAMAN, BARBARA

ROSNER, JONATHAN LINCOLN, physicist, researcher; b. NYC, July 23, 1941; s. Albert Aaron and Elsie Augustine (Lincoln) R.; m. Joy Elaine Fox, June 13, 1965; children: Hannah, Benjamin. BA, Swarthmore Coll., 1962; MA, Princeton U., 1963, PhD, 1965. Research asst. prof. U. Wash., Seattle, 1965-67; vis. lectr. Tel Aviv U., Ramat Aviv, Israel, 1967-69; asst. prof. physics U. Minn., Mpls., 1969-71, assoc. prof., 1971-75, prof., 1975-82, U. Chgo., 1982—. Contbr. numerous articles to profl. and scholarly jours. Alfred P. Sloan fellow, 1971-73, Guggenheim fellow, 2002. Fellow Am. Phys. Soc. Democrat. Jewish. Avocations: fishing, hiking, skiing, amateur radio. Office: U Chgo Enrico Fermi Inst 5640 S Ellis Ave Chicago IL 60637-1433 Business E-Mail: rosner@hep.uchicago.edu.

ROSNER, LEONARD ALLEN, lawyer; b. NYC, Apr. 13, 1967; s. Arnold and Betty (Zimmerman) R.; m. Rachel Stein, Nov. 19, 1994; children: Andrew N., Leah Rose. AB in Polit. Sci. Pub. Rels., Syracuse U., 1989, JD cum laude, 1992. Bar: NY State Bar 1993, Dist. of Columbia Bar 1995, US Dist. Ct. (we. dist.), NY 1995. With Gallo & Iacovangelo LLP, Rochester, NY. Fin. editor Syracuse Jour. Internat. Law and Commerce, 1991—92. Bd. mem. Temple B rith Kodesh, Rochester, NY; bd. mem. legal counsel Rochester Children's Theater; com. mem. J C C. Campership Golf Tournament. Mem.: Syracuse U. Alumni Club of Rochester, Monroe County Bar Assn. (mem., real estate com., mem., prof. performance com.), N.Y. Bar Assn. Avocations: golf, reading, television sports, nautilus, travel. Office: Gallo & Iacovangelo LLP Ste 700 39 State St Rochester NY 14614 Business E-Mail: leonardrosner@gallolaw.com.

ROSNER, LOUIS JOSEPH, medical educator; b. Shreveport, La., Dec. 14, 1929; s. Marcus and Mae Florence Rosner; m. Janet Berg (div.); 1 child, Jon Van Caneghem; m. Rosner Larraine Rosner, Nov. 23, 1974. BA, Tex. Christian U., Ft. Worth; MD, Baylor U., Houston. Clin. prof. neurology UCLA, 1970—. Author: Multiple Sclerosis: New Hope and Practical Advice for People With MS and Their Families, 1987, 2d edit., 2007. Fellow: Am. Acad. Neurology. Avocation: coin collecting/numismatics. Home: 15500 High Knoll Rd Encino CA 91436

ROSNER, ROBERT, astrophysicist, educator; b. Garmisch-Partenkirchen, Bavaria, Germany, June 26, 1947; came to U.S., 1959; s. Heinz and Faina (Brodsky) R.; m. Marsha Ellen Rich, Sept. 5, 1971; children: Daniela Karin, Nicole Elise. BA, Brandeis U., 1969; PhD, Harvard U., 1976. Asst. prof. Harvard U., Cambridge, Mass., 1978-83, assoc. prof., 1983-86; astrophysicist Smithsonian Astrophys. Observatory, Cambridge, 1986-87; prof. U. Chgo., 1987—, William E. Wrather prof., 1998—; chief scientist Argonne Nat. Lab., 2002—05, dir., 2005—; pres. UChicago/Argonne LLC, 2006—. Trustee Adler Planetarium, Chgo., 1989-98, chmn. dept. astronomy and astrophysics, 1991-97. Contbr. more than 190 articles to profl. jours. Woodrow Wilson fellow, 1969. Fellow Am. Phys. Soc., Am. Acad. Arts and Scis. (elected); mem. Am. Astron. Soc., Soc. Indsl. and Applied Math., Am. Geophys. Union, Norwegian Acad. Sci. and Letters (fgn. mem.). Home: 4950 S Greenwood Ave Chicago IL 60615-2816 Office: U Chicago Astrophysics 5640 S Ellis Ave Chicago IL 60637-1433 Business E-Mail: r-rosner@uchicago.edu.

ROSNER, SETH, lawyer, educator; b. NYC, Jan. 6, 1931; s. Oscar S. and Miriam (Reinhardt) R.; m. Sara Jane Sheldon, Dec. 4, 1970 (div. Mar. 1978); m. Ann E. Del Toro, June 23, 1983; 1 child, Rachel Ferrer. AB, Wesleyan U., Middletown, Conn., 1952; JD, Columbia U., 1955; LLM in Comparative Law, NYU, 1960; postgrad., U. Paris, 1960-61. Bar: N.Y. 1955, U.S. Dist. Ct. (so. and ea. dists.) N.Y. 1956, U.S. Supreme Ct. 1967. Ptnr. Rosner & Rosner, NYC, 1955-80; sr. ptnr. Marchi Jaffe Cohen Crystal Rosner & Katz, NYC, 1981-88; pvt. practice NYC, 1989-97, 2001—; counsel Jacobs Persinger & Parker, NYC, 1997-2001. Adj. prof. NYU Sch. of Law, 1961—89. Trustee, v.p. exec. com. Fedn. Jewish Philanthropies, N.Y.C., 1977-86; trustee Jewish Home and Hosp. for Aged, N.Y.C., 1970-95, pres., 1978-82, chmn., 1982-86; bd. trustees Wesleyan U. Middletown, Conn., 1982-86; bd. govs. Josephson Inst. of Ethics, Marina Del Rey, Calif., 1986-99, 00-06, chmn. bd., 2000-03; bd. dirs. Saratoga Automobile Mus., Saratoga Springs, N.Y., 1999—, N.Y. State Judicial Inst. on Professionalism in the Law, 01-. Lt. USN, 1956-59. Fellow Am. Bar Found. (life); mem. ABA (chmn. gen. practice sect. 1980-81, ethics and profl. responsibility com. 1983-89, chmn. professionalism com. 1992-95, chmn. com. on scope, chmn. com. on lawyer competence 1995-97, bd. govs. 1997-00, chmn. coordinating coun. Ctr. Profl. Responsibility 2002-), Assn. Profl. Responsibility Lawyers (bd. dirs. 1990-96, pres.-elect 1993-94, pres. 1994-95), Assn. of Bar of City of N.Y. (ethics com. 1970-73), N.Y. State Bar Assn. (chmn. gen. practice sect. 1982-83), Leica Hist. Soc. (bd. dirs., v.p. 2001-04, pres. 2004-06). Avocations: writing, photography, Ferrari automobiles. Personal E-mail: sethrosner@nycap.rr.com.

ROSNOW, RALPH LEON, psychologist, educator; b. Balt., Jan. 10, 1936; s. Irvin and Rebecca (Faber) R.; m. Mimi Quin Medinger, Aug. 12, 1963. BS, U. Md., 1957; MA, George Washington U., 1958; PhD, Am. U., 1962. Asst. prof. Boston U., 1963-67; assoc. prof. Temple U., Phila., 1967-70, full prof., 1970-2001; vis. prof. London Sch. Econs., 1973, Harvard U., Cambridge, Mass., 1978, 1988-89; Thaddeus Bolton prof. Temple U., 1982—2001, Thaddeus Bolton prof. emeritus, 2002—, dir. social and orgnl. psychology divsn. psychology, 1988-2000. Cons. editor jours. and encys. in psychology and comm.; cons. on rsch. methods and data analysis, 1976—. Author: Paradigms in Transition, 1981; author: (with Robert Rosenthal) The Volunteer Subject, 1975, Essentials of Behavioral Research, 2d edit., 1991, Contrast Analysis, 1985; author: Beginning Behavioral Research, 5th edit., 2005, People Studying People, 1997, Contrasts and Effect Sizes in Behavioral Research, 2000; author: (with Gary Fine) Rumor and Gossip, 1976; author: (with Mimi Rosnow) Writing Papers in Psychology, 7th edit., 2006; editor (with Robert Rosenthal): Artifact in Behavioral Research, 1969; editor: (with Marianthi Georgoudi) Contextualism and Understanding in Behavioral Science. Recipient George A. Miller award Soc. Gen. Psychology, 1999. Fellow: APA, AAAS, Am. Psychol. Soc.; mem.: Soc. Exptl. Social Psychology. Home: 177 Biddulph Rd Radnor PA 19087-4506

ROSOFF, WILLIAM A., lawyer; b. Phila., June 21, 1943; s. Herbert and Estelle (Finkel) R.; m. Beverly Rae Rifkin, Feb. 7, 1970; children: Catherine D., Andrew M. BS with honors, Temple U., 1964; LLB magna cum laude, U. Pa., 1967. Bar: Pa. 1968, U.S. Dist. Ct. (ea. dist.) Pa. 1968. Law clk. to Hon. Abraham L. Freedman. U.S. Ct. Appeals (3d cir.), 1967-68; instr. U. Pa. Law Sch., Phila., 1968-69; assoc. Wolf, Block, Schorr & Solis-Cohen, Phila., 1969-75, ptnr., 1975-96, chmn. exec. com., 1987-88; also vice chmn. bd. dirs. Advanta Corp., Spring House, Pa., 1996—, pres., 1999—. Trustee RPS Realty Trust, 1990-96, Atlantic Realty Trust, 1996—; guest lectr. confs. and seminars on tax law; mem. tax adv. bd. Commerce Clearing House, 1983-94; mem. legal activities policy bd. Tax Analysts, 1978-95; mem. Little, Brown Tax Adv. Bd., 1994-96; chmn. bd. dirs. RMH Telesvcs., Inc., 1997-99. Editor U. Pa. Law Rev., 1965-67; mem. editl. bd. Jour. Partnership Taxation, 1983-2000; contbr. articles to profl. jours. Past mem. com. on law and social action Phila. coun. Am. Jewish Congress; bd. visitors Temple Fox Sch. Bus., 2005-. Fellow Am. Coll. Tax Counsel; mem. Am. Law Inst. (cons. taxation of partnerships 1976-78, assoc. reporter taxation of partnerships, 1978-82, mem. adv. group on fed. income tax project 1982-, cons. taxation of pass-through entities 1995-2000), Order of Coif, Beta Gamma Sigma, Beta Alpha Psi. Office: PO Box 918 Spring House PA 19477-0918 Business E-Mail: wrosoff@advanta.com.

ROSOFF, WILLIAM L., lawyer; b. NYC, May 23, 1946; BA, Columbia U., 1968; MA, U. Calif., Berkeley, 1969, PhD, 1975; JD, Harvard U., 1978. Bar: NY 1979. From assoc. to ptnr. Davis Polk & Wardwell, NYC, 1978-98; sr. v.p., gen. counsel RJR Nabisco Holdings Corp., NYC, 1998, Marsh & McLennan Co.; ptnr. O'Melveny & Myers LLP, NYC. Bd. dirs. Deltic Timber Corp, Murphy Oil Co. Mem. ABA. Office: OMelveny & Myers LLP Times Sq Tower 7 Times Square New York NY 10036 Office Phone: 212-326-2210. Office Fax: 212-326-2061. Business E-Mail: wrosoff@omm.com.

ROSOVSKY, HENRY, economist, educator; b. Danzig, Sept. 1, 1927; came to U.S., 1940, naturalized, 1949; s. Selig S. and Sophie (Rosovsky) R.; m. Nitza Brown, June 17, 1956; children— Leah, Judith, Michael. AB, Coll. William and Mary, 1949, LL.D., 1976; A.M. (John E. Thayer scholar), Harvard U., 1953, PhD, 1959; L.H.D. (hon.), Yeshiva U., 1977, Hebrew Union Coll., 1978, Colgate U., 1979, Brandeis U., 1984; PhD (hon.), Hebrew U. of Jerusalem, 1982; LL.D. (hon.), Queen's U., Ont., 1984, U. Hartford, 1984, CUNY, 1986, U. Mass., 1986, Harvard U., 1998; DHL (hon.), Hebrew Coll., Brookline, Mass., 1987, NYU, 1993; DL, St. Mary's Coll. Md., 1989, Jewish Theol. Sem., 1995. From asst. prof. to prof. econs. and history U. Calif.-, Berkeley, 1958-65; chmn. Center Japanese and Korean Studies, 1962-65; prof. econs. Harvard U., 1965—, Walter S. Barker prof. econs., 1975-84, Geyser univ. prof., 1984-96, Geyser univ. prof. emeritus, 1996—, chmn. dept., 1969-72, dean Faculty Arts and Scis., 1973-84; assoc. dir. East Asia Research Center, 1967-69. Mem. Harvard U. Corp., 1985-97; vis. prof. Hitotsubashi U., Tokyo, 1957, Tokyo U., 1962, Hebrew U., Jerusalem, 1965; hon. dir. Japan Fund.; dir. emeritus Corning, Inc.; hon. prof. Centro U. Francisco, De Vitoria, Madrid, 1996. Author: Capital Formation in Japan, 1868-1940, 1961, Quantitative Japanese Economic History, 1961, (with K. Ohkawa) Japanese Economic Growth, 1973, The University: An Owner's Manual, 1990; editor: Explorations in Entrepreneurial History, 1954-56, Industrialization in Two Systems, 1966, Discord in the Pacific, 1972, (with H. Patrick) Asia's New Giant, 1976, (with P. Higonnet, D. Landes) Favorites of Fortune, 1991, (with S. Kumon) The Political Economy of Japan, Vol. 3: Cultural and Social Dynamics, 1992. Chmn. bd. trustees Am. Jewish Congress, 1975-88. Served to lst lt. AUS, 1946-47, 50-52. Jr. fellow Soc. Fellows, 1954-57; recipient Schumpeter prize Harvard, 1963, Clark Kerr medal U. Calif., Berkeley, 1992. Fellow Am. Acad. Arts and Scis., Am. Philos. Soc.; mem. Am. Econ. Assn., Econ. History Assn., Assn. Asian Studies, Chevalier, Legion of Honor, Order of Sacred Treasure, Star (Japan). Office: Harvard Univ Loeb House 17 Quincy St Cambridge MA 02138-3805 Home: 130 Mount Auburn St Apt 506 Cambridge MA 02138 Office Phone: 617-495-4151. E-mail: hrosovsky@harvard.edu.

ROSOW, STUART L., lawyer; b. NYC, Mar. 28, 1950; s. Bernard and Lillian (Bonime) R.; m. Amy Berk Kuhn. AB cum laude, Yale U., 1972; JD cum laude, Harvard U., 1975. Law clk. to presiding justice U.S. Ct. Appeals (7th cir.), Chgo., 1975-76; assoc. Paul, Weiss et al, NYC, 1976-79, Kaye, Scholer, Fierman, Hays & Handler, NYC, 1979-84, ptnr., 1984-97, Proskauer Rose LLP, NYC, 1997—. Adj. prof. Columbia Law Sch., N.Y.C., 1998—. Mem. ABA, N.Y. State Bar Assn., Assn. of Bar of City of N.Y. Office: Proskauer Rose LLP 1585 Broadway Fl 27 New York NY 10036-8299 Home Phone: 212-439-6157; Office Phone: 212-969-3150. Business E-Mail: srosow@proskauer.com.

ROSPUT REYNOLDS, PAULA GAIL (PAULA ROSPUT REYNOLDS), energy executive; b. Newport, RI, Oct. 2, 1956; m. Stephen P. Reynolds, Oct. 2004. BA with highest honors, Wellesley Coll., 1978. Economist consulting firm, Boston; sr. v.p. Pacific Gas Transmission Co.; pres. CEO Duke Energy N.Am., Houston; pres., COO AGL Resources, Atlanta, pres., CEO, 2000—05, chmn., 2002—05; pres., CEO Safeco Corp., Seattle, 2006—. Bd. dir. AGL Resources, Coca Cola Enterprises, Delta Air Lines, Inc.; ind. bd. dir. Anadarko Petroleum Corp., 2007—. Bd. dir. United Way Met. Atlanta, Ga. Rsch. Alliance, Ga. C. of C., Commerce Club, Atlanta. Named one of 100 Most Powerful Women, Forbes Mag., 2006, 50 Most Powerful Women in Business, Fortune mag., 2006; named to Ga. State Univ. Bus. Hall Fame, 2004. Mem.: Am. Gas Assn. (bd. dir.). Office: Safeco Corp 1191 2nd Ave Seattle WA 98101 Office Phone: 404-584-4000. *

ROSS, AMI L., insurance company executive, finance company executive; m. William Hyde. BS in Econs., U. Colo., Boulder. CLU long term care Calif., 2006. Fin. planner Prudential Fin., San Diego, 2003—06; pres. Ross Ins. & Fin. Svcs., LA, 2007—. Fin. cons., chairperson Tiny Stars - Charity, Malibu, Calif. Mem.: Nat. Assn. Ins. and Fin. Advisors, Mensa Internat. Office: Ross Insurance & Financial Services 10940 Wilshire Blvd Ste 950 Los Angeles CA 90024 Home Phone: 310-428-9936; Office Phone: 310-428-9936. Office Fax: 866-449-5357; Home Fax: 866-449-5357. Business E-Mail: ami@ross-financial.com.

ROSS, ANNETTE LEE, educational consultant; b. Detroit, May 15, 1940; d. Jesse O. and Sylvia Irene Ross. BS Edn., Ctrl. Mich. U., Mt. Pleasant, 1963; M Edn., Wayne State U., Detroit, 1971. Cert. tchr. Mich. Tchr. Marian H.S., Bloomington, Mich., 1963—64, Macomb K-8 Sch., Mt. Clemens, Mich., 1964—71, Seminole K-8 Sch., Mt. Clemens, 1972—88; ednl. cons. Susan Kovalik & Assocs., Federal Way, Wash., 1988—2006, reflexologist Ctr. Integrative Therapy Spring Lake, Mich., 2006—. Girls basketball coach Seminole Middle Sch., 1978—88, girls volleyball coach, 1978—88, boys golf coach, 1978—88; varsity volleyball coach Mt. Clemens H.S., 1981—88; ptnr. Ctr. Reflexology Therapy, Spring Lake, 2005—. Author: The Way We Were The Way We Can Be, 1989, 2002. Recipient Slovak Republic award, Susan Kovalik & Assocs., 1997. Mem.: LWV. Home: 5970 Avalon Dr #211 Muskegon MI 49444

ROSS, ANTHONY DEWAYNE, engineering educator; PhD in Bus. Adminstrn., Ind. U., Bloomington, 1989—95. Semiconductor test engr. Advanced Micor Devices, San Antonio, 1984—88; sr. software engr. ASK Computer Sys., Mountain View, Calif., 1988—89; asst. prof. Tex. A&M U., College Station, 1995—2000; assoc. prof. Mich. State U., E.Lansing, 2000—. Study abroad Africa co-dir. Mich. State U. & Intl. Inst. Pub. Policy, 2005—06; study abroad Japan faculty dir. Mich. State U. Intl. Studies Ctr. & CIBER, 2005—. Chairperson Union Missionary Bapt. Ch., Lansing, 2005—06. Mem.: Coun. Supply Chain Mgt. Profls. (com. chair 2005—). Office: Mich State Univ Eli Broad College of Business N370 East Lansing MI 48824-1122 Home Phone: 517-353-6381. Office Fax: 517-432-1112. Business E-Mail: rossant@msu.edu.

ROSS, ANTHONY ROBERT, retired drafting engineer; b. Olean, NY, July 30, 1921; s. Guy and Florence Irene Ross; m. Marilyn Faith Teachman, Sept. 5, 1987; m. Rita Mae Russell (dec.); children: Gary Lee, Linda Marie. Student, Clemson U., SC, 1946—46. Aircraft worker Curtiss-Wright Corp., Buffalo, 1941—42; drafting engr. Clark Bros. Co., Olean, NY, 1948—86; drafting engr. cons. Olean, 1986—88; ret. Prodn. supr. Dresser Industries, Olean, 1970—86. Active Boy Scouts Am., Radio-Controlled Model Airplanes Club. Capt. USAF, 1942—59. Decorated various medals and citations USAF. Mem.: VFW, ASME, 47th Bombardment Squadron Assn., Am. Legion. Home: 314 S 4th St Olean NY 14760-3517

ROSS, BARRY C., lawyer; BS, SUNY, Albany, 1971; JD magna cum laude, Brooklyn Law Sch. Bar: NY 1975. Ptnr., group co-leader Bryan Cave LLP, NYC. Office: Bryan Cave LLP 1290 Ave of the Americas New York NY 10104 Office Phone: 212-541-2255. E-mail: bcross@bryancave.com.

ROSS, BOBBY (ROBERT JOSEPH ROSS), retired college football coach; b. Richmond, Va., Dec. 23, 1935; s. Leonard Aloysius and Martha Isabelle (MMiller) R.; m. Alice Louise Bucker, June 13, 1959; children: Chris, Mary Catherine, Teresa, Kevin, Robbie. BA, Va. Mil. Inst., 1959. Tchr., head football coach Benedictine High Sch., Richmond, 1959-60; tchr., coach Colonial Heights (Va.) High Sch., 1962-65; asst. football coach Va. Mil. Inst., Lexington, 1965-67, Coll. William & Mary, Williamsburg, Va., 1967-71, Rice U., Houston, 1971-72, U. Md., College Park, 1972-73; head football coach The Citadel, Charleston, SC, 1973-77, U. Md., College Park, 1982-87, Ga. Tech., Atlanta, 1987-91; asst. coach Kansas City Chiefs, 1978-82; head coach San Diego Chargers, 1992-96, Detroit Lions, 1997-2001, U.S. Mil. Acad., West Point, NY, 2003—07. 1st lt. U.S. Army, 1960-62. Named Coach of Yr., Washington Touchdown Club, 1982, Kodak Coach of Yr., 1990, Bobby Dodd Coach of Yr., 1990, Bear Bryant Coach of Yr., 1990, Scripps-Howard Coach of Yr., 1990, Nat. Coach of Yr., CBS Sports, 1990, Coach of Yr., Walter Camp Football Found., 1990, NFL Coach of Yr. UPI, 1992, Pro Football Weekly, 1992, Pro Football Writers' Assn., 1992, Football News, 1992, Football Digest, 1992, Maxwell Football Club, 1992, AFC Coach of Yr. Kansas City 101 Banquet. Mem. Am. Football Coaches Assn., Coll. Football Assn. (coaching com. 1988-92). Roman Catholic.

ROSS, BRIAN ELLIOTT, chief investigative correspondent; b. Chgo., Oct. 23, 1948; s. Kenneth Earl and Shirley Louise (Johnston) R. BA, U. Iowa, 1971. Corr. KWWL-TV, Waterloo, Iowa, 1971, WCKT-TV, Miami, Fla., 1972-74; news corr. NBC News, Cleve. and NYC, 1974—94; chief investigative corr. ABC News, NYC, 1994—. Named to U. Iowa Journalism Sch. Hall of Fame, 1998; recipient Peabody award, 1974, 1991, 1999, 2001, DuPont-Columbia U. award, 1975, 1985, 1986, 2002, 2004, Sigma Delta Chi award, 1976, Nat. Headliner award, 1976—78, 1987, 2004, 2005, Emmy award, 1980, 1985, 1988, 1992, 2004, 2006, Overseas Press Club award, 1988, 1990, 1992, 1994, 1998, George M. Polk award, 1989, 1993, 1997, 1998, 2005, Sidney Hillman award, 1993, Outstanding Internat. Investigative Reporting award, Ctr. Pub. Integrity, 2005, Disting. Alumni award, U. Iowa, 2005. Office: ABC News 147 Columbia Ave New York NY 10023 Office Phone: 212-456-7612.

ROSS, BRUCE SHIELDS, lawyer; b. LA, Feb. 1, 1947; s. Floyd and Mary Louise (Shields) R.; m. Janet G. Ross, Jan 27, 1968 (div. Jan. 1977); 1 child, Stephanie; m. Carol Burlingame, Apr. 2, 1977; children: Andrew, Tiffany. AB cum laude, Oberlin Coll., 1968; JD, U. Calif., Berkeley, 1971. Bar: Calif. 1971, US Tax Ct. 1973, US Dist. Ct. (ctrl. dist. Calif.) 1977; cert. specialist in estate planning, trust, probate law, Calif. Assoc. Nossman & Krueger, LA, 1971-73; assoc. to ptnr. Poindexter & Doutre, LA, 1973-78; assoc. Alschuler & Grossman, LA, 1978, ptnr., 1979-84, Morrison & Foerster, LA, 1984—90, Ross, Sacks & Glazier, LA, 1991—2001; exec. ptnr. Holland & Knight, LLP, LA and Rancho Santa Fe, Calif., 2001—06; ptnr.-in-charge Luce, Forward, Hamilton & Scripps, LLP, LA, 2006—. Participant Temp. Judge Prog. LA Mcpl. Ct., 1989—95; mem. adv. bd. Philip E. Heckerling Inst. Estate Planning U. Miami, 2000—, adj. prof. law grad. prog. in estate planning, 2000—03; academician Internat. Acad. Estate and Trust Law; mem. panels, lectr. in field. Mem. U. Calif. Law Rev., 1969-71, note and comment editor 1970-71; author: Calif. Practice Guide: Probate, 1986-2004 (updated annually); co-editor Guidebook to the Calif. Rules of Profl. Conduct for Estate Planning, Trust and Probate Counsel, 1997; contbr. articles to profl. jours. Trustee Pacific Asia Mus., Pasadena, Calif., 1983-1991, pres., 1988-1991; fin. chmn. Boy Scouts Am., Glendale, Calif., 1984-85; gov. The Webb Schs. of Calif., Claremont, 1987—. Named one of Top 100 Attys., Worth mag., 2006. Fellow Am. Coll. Trust and Estate Counsel (sec., treas., v.p. and pres.-elect 2001-05, pres, 2005, mem. bd. regents 1995-2001, 02, mem. bd. exec. com. 2000-01, 02-).Mem. ABA (chair task force on state and local regulation, com. on exempt orgns., sect. taxation 1984-88, chair estate and trust litig. com. 1991-93, group chair litig. and controversy com. 1996-, mem. supervisory coun. 1997-2003, co-chair multijurisdictional practice com. 2000-02, sect. liasion to ethics 2000 commn. 1998-2000, real property, probate and trust law sect.), LA County Bar Assn. (exec. com. tax. sect. 1984-85, exec. com. estates and trusts sect. 1994-97, exec. com. alternative dispute resolution sect. 1996-97), State Bar Calif. (mem. 1987-89, vice-chair 1989-90, chair 1990-91, adv. 1991-1994. Democrat. Unitarian Universalist. Avocations: music, opera, swimming, stamp collecting/philately. Office: Luce Forward Hamilton & Scripps 601 S Figueroa Ste 3900 Los Angeles CA 90017 Office Phone: 213-896-2400, 213-892-4962. Office Fax: 213-452-8042. Business E-Mail: bruce.ross@hklaw.com. E-mail: bruce@luce.com. *

ROSS, CAROL, retired women's college basketball coach; b. Oakland, Miss. BA in Edn., U. Miss., 1982. Volunteer asst. Bellhaven Coll., Jackson, Miss., 1982—83; asst. coach Auburn U., 1984—90; women's basketball head coach U. Fla., 1991—2002, U. Miss., 2002—07. Head coach US Select Team, 1998. Named Coach of Yr., SEC Conf., 1994, 2001, co-Coach of Yr., 2003, Dist. 9 Coach of Yr., Women's College Basketball Assn., 1994, 1997, 2001; named one of The Top 50 Bus. Women in Miss., Miss. Bus. Jour.; named to U. Miss. Athletic Hall of Fame, 2001; recipient Coaches vs Cancer Champion award, 2000, Regional Coach Yr. award, Women's College Basketball Assn., 2001. Achievements include playing on US Women's Olympic Basketball Team, 2000. *

ROSS, CHARLES, artist; b. Phila., Dec. 17, 1937; s. Fred H. and Gertrude (Hill) R.; m. Elizabeth Ginsberg, 1977; m. Jill O'Bryan, 2007. AB in Math, U. Calif., Berkeley, 1960, MA in Sculpture, 1962. Adj. prof. dept. art Coll. Santa Fe. Exhibited in one-man shows: Dilexi Gallery, San Francisco, 1961, 65, 66, 68, Dwan Gallery, NYC, 1968, 69, 71, Daytons Gallery 12, Mpls., 1968, John Weber Gallery, NYC, 1972, 77, 79, 81, The Clocktower, NYC, 1974, Utah Mus. Fine Arts, Salt Lake City, 1975, Mus. Contemporary Art, La Jolla, Calif., 1976, Chgo., 1976, Inst. Contemporary Art, Phila., 1977, Susan Caldwell Gallery, NYC, 1977, MIT, 1977, Portland Center for Visual Arts, 1981, Sena Gallery, Santa Fe, 1991, Johnson Gallery U. N.Mex., 1992, Humphrey Gallery, NYC, 1995, Mus. de Arte y Diseno Contemporaneo, San Jose, Costa Rica, 1996, Braunstein/Quay Gallery, San Francisco, 2007; exhibited in group shows: Archtl. League of NY, 1967, Albright Knox Art Gallery, Buffalo, 1967, Finch Coll., NYC, 1967, Aldrich Mus., Ridgefield, Conn., 1967, Nelson Atkins Mus., Kansas City, 1968, Milw. Art Ctr., 1968, Whitney Mus., NYC, 1969, Art Inst. Chgo., 1969, Art Gallery of Ont., Toronto, 1969, Galeries-pilotes, Lausanne, Switzerland, 1970, Mus. Fine Arts, Boston, 1971, Indpls. Mus. Art, 1974, Neuberger Mus., SUNY, Purchase, 1975, Stadtisches Mus., Leverkusen, Germany, 1975, Phila. Coll. Art, 1977, Hirshhorn Mus., Washington, 1977, Old Customs House, NYC, 1977, Mus. Natural History, NYC, 1977, Leo Castelli Gallery, NYC, 1978, Yale U. Art Gallery, 1978, Dartmouth Coll. Gallery, 1978, Aspen Ctr. for Visual Arts, Colo., 1980, Centre Georges Pompidou, Paris, 1980, Renwick Gallery, Smithsonian Instn., Washington, 1980, Mus. Contemporary Art, Chgo., 1981, MIT, Cambridge, 1981, Bard Coll., 1984, Light Gallery, NYC, 1985, Venice Biennale, 1986, Differentes Natures la Defense, Paris, 1992, Anchorage Mus. History and Art, 1994, Richard Humphrey Gallery, NYC, 1995, Kunsthallen Brandts Klaedefabrik, Odense, Denmark, 1996, SITE Santa Fe, 1996, Ctr. Pompidou, Paris, 1997, NIT Intercomm. Ctr., Tokyo, 1997, Biennale de Lyon, France, 2000, Chiaroseuro Gallery, Santa Fe, 2004, Harwood Mus., Taos, N.Mex., 2005, Artempo, Palazzo, Fortuny, Venice, Italy, 2007; commns. include: prism/solar spectrum skylight sculpture for Fed. Bldg, Lincoln, Nebr., 1976, U. Pa., 1977, Dietrich Found., Phila., 1979, Spectrum Bldg, Denver, 1980, Grand Rapids Art Mus., Mich., 1982, Towson State U., Md., 1983, Cumberland Rapid Transit Sta., Chgo., 1983, Linay Corp., Kansas City, Mo., 1985, Plaza of the Americas, Dallas, 1985, Wells Fargo Bldg., San Diego, 1986, San Francisco Internat. Airport, 1987, Anchorage Internat. Airport, 1987, Naugatuck Higher Edn. Ctr., Conn., 1990, Harvard Bus. Sc. Chapel, 1992, French Ministry of Culture Chateau d'Oiron, 1993, Cook Inst., Grand Rapids, Mich., 1996, Dwan Light Sanctuary, United World Coll., Montezuma, N.Mex., 1996, US Fed. Courthouse, Tampa, 1998, Saitama U., 1999, Japan, Kauffman Found., Kansas City, 2001, Nat. Mus. of the Am. Indian, Smithsonian Inst., Washington, DC, 2004, Meiji U., Tokyo, 2004, Albuquerque Conv. Ctr., 2004, Highlands U., Las Vegas, 2005; represented in permanent collections Nelson Atkins Mus., Whitney Mus. Am. Art, Berkeley Art Mus., Indpls. Mus. Art, Butler Inst. Am. Art, Herbert F. Johnson Mus. Art Cornell U., GSA Art and Architecture Program, U. Pa., Dietrich Found., Grand Rapids Art Mus., Gen. Elec. Corp., City Chgo., Towson State U., Becton Dickinson Corp., Security Pacific Bank, Found. Ctr., N.Y.C., Wynne Jackson Inc., Albuquerque Mus., Linclay Corp., Witco Chem. Corp., City of San Diego, Walker Art Ctr., City of San Francisco, State of Alaska, Koll Co., Los Angeles County Mus. Art, Mus.de Arte y Diseno Contemporaneo, San Jose, Kunsthallen Brandts Klaedefabrik, Odense, Des Moines Art Ctr., French Ministry of Culture, Frederick A. Weisman Mus., Mpls., Harvard Bus. Sch., Mus. Fine Arts, Santa Fe, United World Coll., N.Mex., Saitama U., Japan, Kauffman Found., Kansas City, Meiji U., Tokyo, Nat. Mus. Am. Indian, Washington (Wash. Bldg. Congress award, 2005), Kramarsky Found.; works in progress include: Star Axis, architectonic earthwork/naked eye observatory atop a mesa in N.Mex. Author: Sunlight Convergence Solar Burn (Am. Inst. Graphic Arts award 1976); films Sunlight Dispersion, 1972, Solar Eclipse, 1972. Recipient Art and Architecture Collaborations award Boston Soc. Architects, 1993, Interfaith Forum on Religion, Art and Arch. Design award Harvard Bus. Sch. Chapel, 1993, award for distinction for artistic achievement Nat. Coun. Art Adminstrs., 1997. Office: Loïc Malle 167 Blvd Haussmann 75008 Paris France Business E-Mail: malle.loic@wanadoo.fr. E-mail: info@staraxis.org. *My work deals with the nature of light, time, and planetary motion.*

ROSS, CHRISTOPHER WADE STELYAN, diplomat; b. Quito, Ecuador, Mar. 3, 1943; parents Am. citizens; s. Claude G. Anthony and Antigone Andrea R.; m. Carol Geraldine Canning, Nov. 30, 1968 (div.); 1 child, Anthony Gordon. AB summa cum laude, Princeton U., 1965; cert., Mid. East Ctr. Arab Studies, 1964; MA, Johns Hopkins U., 1967. Editl. asst. Mid. East Jour., Washington, 1965-68; instr. Arabic lang. Columbia U., NYC, 1966, Princeton (N.J.) U., 1967; pub. affairs trainee USIA, 1968-69; jr. officer trainee Am. Embassy, Tripoli, Libya, 1969-70; dir. Am. Cultural Ctr., Fez, Morocco, 1970-73; press attache Am. Embassy, Beirut, 1973-76, pub. affairs officer Algiers, 1976-79, dep. chief mission and charge d'affaires, 1979-81; pub. affairs advisor Bur. Nr. East & South Asian Affairs Dept. of State, Washington, 1981-82, spl. asst. to presdl. emissaries to Lebanon & Mid. East, 1982-84, dir. regional affairs Bur. Nr. East & South Asian Affairs, 1984-85; exec. asst. to Under Sec. State for Polit. Affairs Washington, 1985-88; amb. Algeria, 1988-91, Syria, 1991-98; coord. counterterrorism Dept. State, Washington, 1998; spl. coord. pub. diplomacy, 2001—03; sr. adv. Bureau Internat. Info. Programs, 2003—04; spl. adv. Iraq polit. affairs Bur. N.E. Affairs, 2005—; exec. dir. Search for Common Ground in Mid. East, 1999—2001; sr. advisor polit. affairs Coalition Provisional Auth., Baghdad, 2004; sr. adv. US delegation UN Gen. Assembly, 2006. Chmn. bd. trustees Am. Sch. Algiers, 1978-80; hon. chmn., bd. trustees Damascus Cmty. Sch., 1991-98. Contbr. articles to profl. jour. Recipient Superior Honor award USIA, 1976, 83, Superior Honor award Dept. of State, 1988, Presdl. Meritorious Svc. award, 1983, 85, 89, 93, Disting. Honor award Dept. of State, 1997, Disting. Pub. Svc. medal Dept. Def., 2005. Mem. Coun. Fgn. Rels., Am. Fgn. Svc. Assn., Assn. Diplomatic Studies and Tng., Mid. East Inst., Mid East Studies Assn. N.Am., Royal Soc. Asian Affairs, Am. Inst. Maghrib Studies, Princeton Club. Greek Orthodox. Avocations: classic cars, bicycling. Personal E-mail: cwsross@starpower.net.

ROSS, CLARK GRANT, economics professor; b. Gloucester, Mass., June 24, 1950; s. Norman C. and Helen (Blecher) Ross. BA, U. Pa., 1971; PhD, Boston Coll., 1975. Asst. prof. Dept. Economics Coll. William and Mary, 1975—76; research scientist U. Mich., 1976—79; asst. prof. economics Davidson Coll., NC, 1979—83, assoc. prof., 1983, chmn. Dept. Economics, 1983. Cons. in field. Contbr. articles to profl. jour. Mem.: Southern Economics Assn., Am. Economics Assn. Roman Catholic. Office: Dept Economics Davidson College PO Box 7147 Davidson NC 28035-7147 Office Phone: 704-894-2204. Office Fax: 704-894-2105. *

ROSS, COLEMAN DEVANE, accountant, insurance company executive; b. Greensboro, NC, Mar. 18, 1943; s. Guy Matthews and Nancy McConnell (Coleman) R.; m. Carol Louise Morde, Aug. 26, 1965; children: Coleman, Jonathan, Andrew. BSBA, U. NC, Chapel Hill, 1965; MA in Econs., Trinity Coll., Hartford, Conn., 2006; MS in Fin. Svcs., Am. Coll., Bryn Mawr, Pa., 2007. CPA, CPCU, CLU. With Price Waterhouse, Tampa, Fla., Toronto, Can., Hartford, Conn., NYC, 1965—99, ptnr., 1977—99; chmn., mng. ptnr. Nat. Ins. Svcs. Group, 1988-94; exec. v.p., CFO Trenwick Group Ltd., Hamilton, Bermuda, 2000—02, Phoenix Cos., Inc., Hartford, Conn., 2002—03. Bd. dirs. NCCI Holdings, Inc., Boca Raton, Fla., 2004—, Pan-Am. Life Ins. Co., New Orleans, 2006—, Security Capital Assurance Ltd., Hamilton, Bermuda, 2006—. Exec. bd. Conn. Rivers coun. Boy Scouts Am., 1978—, pres., 1985-88, bd. dirs. N.E. Region, 1988—, v.p., 1993-96, 2002—, pres. New England area, 1988-91, bd. dirs. Greater NY coun., 1994-2004; participant Leadership Greater Hartford, 1977; bd. visitors U. NC, 2001-05. Recipient Silver Beaver award Boy Scouts Am., 1987, Silver Antelope award, 1991. Mem. AICPA (reins. auditing and acctg. task force 1979-85, rels. with actuaries com. 1982-85, ins. cos. com. 1985-88, acctg. stds. exec. com. 2002-05, property and liability ins. co. task force 2005—), NC Assn. CPAs, Nat. Assn. Corp. Dirs., CFA Inst., Soc. Fin. Svc. Profls., CPCU Soc., Chartered Ins. Inst., Fin. Exec. Internat., Internat. Ins. Soc., NY Soc. Security Analysts (com. improved corp. reporting 1999-2001, 05—), Inst. Mgmt. Accountants, Inst. Internal Auditors, Polytechnic Club, Carolina Club, Williams Club. Avocation: running. Home: 318 W Univ Dr Chapel Hill NC 27516 Personal E-mail: coleman@colemanross.com.

ROSS, CURTIS BENNETT, lawyer; b. Carbondale, Ill., June 7, 1955; s. Bernard Harris and Marian Frager Ross. BS in Acctg., U. Ill., 1977, JD, 1980. Bar: Ill., 1984. Tax staff Arthur Andersen & Co., Chgo., 1980-82; lawyer Jerome H. Torshen, Ltd., Chgo., 1983, Curtis Bennett Ross, Chgo., 1984—. Attorney We Are Concerned, Chgo., 1995-99. Mem. Chgo. Bar Assn., CBA Matrimonial Com., Decalogue Soc. Office: 19 S La Salle St #13 Chicago IL 60603-1401

ROSS, DANIEL J.J., publishing executive; b. Albany, NY, June 2, 1943; AB, Hamilton Coll., 1966; MA, U. Fla., 1969. Prodn. mgr. U. Fla. Press, 1976-80; mktg. mgr. U. Ala. Press, 1980-85; asst. dir. Duke U. Press, 1985-89; editor-in-chief U. Nebr. Press, Lincoln, 1989-95, dir., 1995—2001; dir. editor-in-chief Univ. Ala. Press, 2001—. Office: 20 Rsch Dr Tuscaloosa AL 35487-0380 Office Phone: 205-348-5180. Business E-Mail: danross@uapress.ua.edu.

ROSS, DANIEL R., lawyer; b. Stamford, Conn., Oct. 20, 1941; s. Adrian E. and Ruth (Hill) R.; m. Faye Zerwekh, Aug. 15, 1965; children: Kevin S., Eric D., David W. SB, MIT, 1963; LLB, U. Pa., 1966. Atty. adviser to Hon. Theodore Tannenwald, Jr. U.S. Tax Ct., Washington, 1966-68; assoc. Drinker, Biddle & Reath, Phila., 1970-77, ptnr., 1977-98, Commons & Commons, Phila., 1998—2005, Ross & McCrea, 2005—. Presenter in field. Pres. bd. trustees First United Meth. Ch. Germantown, 1984-2004; bd dirs Smith Playground and Playhouses, Inc, 2003—. Capt. U.S. Army, 1968-70, Vietnam. Mem. ABA (chair com. on income of estates and trusts 1985-87, com. on govt. subcoms. 1988-91, taxation sect.). Avocations: bicycling, skiing, tennis, computers. Office: 7169 Germantown Ave 2d Fl Philadelphia PA 19119 Home Phone: 215-247-8059; Office Phone: 215-247-3550. Personal E-mail: danrross@aol.com. Business E-Mail: dross@rossmccrea.com.

ROSS, DAVID EDMOND, church official; b. Lewiston, Maine, Oct. 1, 1950; s. Rev. and Mrs. Lorne Arla Collins R.; m. Shirley Evelyn Godin, Aug. 19, 1972. BA in Theology cum laude, Berkshire Coll., 1973; MPA, U. Maine, 1989. Ordained to ministry Advent Christian Ch., 1975. Pastor State Road Advent Christian Ch., Presque Isle, Maine, 1973-91; exec. dir. Advent Christian Ch. Gen. Conf., Charlotte, NC, 1991—2003; sr. pastor Fellowship Advent Christian ch., Bethlehem, NC, 2003—. V.p. Maine State Conf. Advent Christian Chs., 1975-76, pres., 1976-81, 86-91; mem. exec. coun. Advent Christian Ch., 1981-90, long range strategy com., 1986—; seminar leader Am. Festival of Evangelism, Kansas City, 1981; dir. Northern Lights Youth Choir, 1974-90. Exec. dir., CEO Advent Christian Gen. Conf., 1991—2003. Office: Fellowship Advent Christian Church 885 Icard Ridge Rd Taylorsville NC 28681 Office Phone: 828-495-8086. Personal E-mail: bethlehemshepherd@hotmail.com.

ROSS, DEBRA BENITA, marketing executive, jewelry designer; b. Carbondale, Ill., May 1, 1956; d. Bernard Harris and Marian (Frager) R. BS, U. Ill., 1978; MS, U. Wis., 1979. Dir. mktg. Ambion Devel., Inc., Northbrook, Ill., 1983-89, Fitness Horizons, Inc., Northbrook, 1989-91, v.p. mktg., 1991-97; owner Benita Ross Designs, Northbrook, 1992—. Home: 1853 Mission Hills Ln Northbrook IL 60062-5760

ROSS, DENNIS B., former diplomat; b. San Francisco, Nov. 26, 1948; married; 3 children. Grad, UCLA, 1970; PhD (hon.), Amherst Coll., Jewish Theological Seminary, Syracuse U. Dep. dir. Office of Net assessment The Pentagon, 1982—84; exec. dir. Berkeley-Stanford program on Soviet internat. behavior, 1984—86; dir. Near East and South Asian affairs NSC; dep. dir. office net assessment The Pentagon, Washington; dir. policy planning office US Dept. State, Washington, 1988—92, spl. Middle East coord., 1997—2001; counselor and Ziegler disting. fellow Washington Inst. for Near East Policy, Washington. Spkr. in field; fgn. affairs analyst Fox News Channel; commentator Washington Post, NY Times, LA Times; chmn. Inst. Jewish People Policy Planning. Author: (book) The Missing Peace: The Inside Story of the Fight for Middle East Peace, 2004; contbr. articles to profl. jours. Recipient Presdl. Medal for Disting. Fed. Civilian Svc. Achievements include facilitation of Israeli-Jordan peace treaty; assisting the Israelis and Palestinians in reaching 1995 Interim Agreement; brokered Hebron Accord, 1997. Office: Washington Inst Near East Policy 1828 L St NW Ste 1050 Washington DC 20036

ROSS, DENNIS E., retired automotive executive, lawyer; b. 1951; Bachelors, Law Degree, U. Mich. Tax legis. counsel, dep. asst. sec. Office Tax Policy U.S. Treasury Dept., 1986—89; tax ptnr. Davis Polk and Wardwell, NY, 1989—95; chief tax officer Ford Motor Co., Dearborn, Mich., 1995—2000, v.p., gen. counsel, 2000—05, ret., 2005. *

ROSS, DIANA (DIANA ERNESTINE EARLE ROSS), singer, actress, entertainer, fashion designer; b. Detroit, Mar. 26, 1944; d. Fred and Ernestine R.; m. Robert Ellis Silberstein, Jan. 1971 (div. 1976); children: Rhonda, Tracee, Chudney; m. Arne Naess, Oct. 23, 1985 (div. 2000, dec. 2004); children: Ross Arne, Evan Olaf. Pres. Diana Ross Enterprises, Inc., Anaid Film Prodns., Inc., RTC Mgmt. Corp., Chondee Inc., Rosstown, Rossville, music pub. Started in Detroit as mem. the Primettes; lead singer until 1969, Diana Ross and the Supremes; solo artist, 1969—; albums include Diana Ross, 1970, 76, Everything Is Everything, 1971, I'm Still Waiting, 1971, Lady Sings The Blues, 1972, Touch Me In The Morning, 1973, Original Soundtrack of Mahogany, 1975, Baby It's Me, 1977, The Wiz, 1978, Ross, 1978, 83, The Boss, 1979, Diana, 1981, To Love Again, 1981, Why Do Fools Fall In Love?, 1981, Silk Electric, 1982, Endless Love, 1982, Swept Away, 1984, Eaten Alive, 1985, Chain Reaction, 1986, Diana's Duets, 1987, Workin' Overtime, 1989, Red Hot Rhythm and Blues, 1987, Surrender, 1989, Ain't No Mountain High Enough, 1989, The Force Behind the Power, 1991, Stolen Moment: The Lady Sings... Jazz & Blues, 1993, Musical Memories Forever, 1993, The Remixes, 1994, A Very Special Season, 1994, Making Spirits Bright, 1994, Take Me Higher, 1995, Voice of Love, 1996, Gift of Love, 1996, The Greatest, 1998, The Real Thing, 1998, Every Day is a New Day, 1999, Love From...Diana Ross, 2001, The #1's, 2004, Complete Symphony, 2004, The Blue Album, 2006, I Love You, 2007; films include Lady Sings the Blues, 1972, Mahogany, 1975, The Wiz, 1978; NBC-TV spl., An Evening With Diana Ross, 1977, Diana, 1981, numerous others; TV movie Out of Darkness, 1994; author: Secrets of a Sparrow, 1993, Diana Ross: Going Back, 2002, Upside Down: Wrong Turns, Right Turns and the Road Ahead. Recipient citation V.P. Humphrey for efforts on behalf Pres. Johnson's Youth Opportunity Program, citation Mrs. Martin Luther King and Rev. Abernathy for contbn. to SCLC cause, awards Billboard, Cash Box and Record World as worlds outstanding singer, Grammy award, 1970, Female Entertainer Yr. NAACP, 1970, Cue award as Entertainer Yr., 1972, Golden Apple award, 1972, Gold medal award Photoplay, 1972, Antoinette Perry award, 1977, nominee as Best Actress Yr. Lady Sings the Blues Motion Picture Acad. Arts and Scis., 1972, Golden Globe award, 1972, BET (Black Entertainment Television) Walk Fame award, 1999, Heroes award, NARAS, NY Chpt., 2000; named to Rock and Roll Hall Fame, 1988. Office: c/o Motown Records 825 8th Ave New York NY 10019

ROSS, DONALD, JR., language educator, academic administrator; b. NYC, Oct. 18, 1941; s. Donald and Lea (Meyer) R.; m. Sylvia Berger (div.); 1 child, Jessica; m. 2d, Diane Redfern, Aug. 27, 1971; children—Owen, Gillian BA, Lehigh U., 1963, MA, 1964; PhD, U. Mich., 1967. Asst. prof. English U. Pa., Phila., 1967—70; prof. English U. Minn., Mpls., 1970—, dir. composition program, 1982—86, 2002—03, dir. Univ. Coll., 1984—89. Author: American History and Culture from the Explorers to Cable TV, 2000; co-author: Word Processor and Writing Process, 1984, Revising Mythologies: The Composition of Thoreau's Major Works, 1988; co-editor, contbr.: American Travel Writers, 1776-1865, 1997, American Travel Writers, 1850-1915, 1998; contbr. articles to profl. jours. Grantee Am. Coun. Learned Socs., 1976, 90, NSF, 1974, Fund for Improvement of Postsecondary Edn., 1982-85; recipient Disting. Teaching award U. Minn., 1992. Mem. MLA, Assn. for Computers and Humanities (exec. sec. 1978-88), Internat. Soc. for Travel Writing (exec. sec. 2001—). Office: U Minn Dept English 207 Lind Hall 207 Church St SE Minneapolis MN 55455-0152 Business E-Mail: rossj001@umn.edu.

ROSS, DONALD EDWARD, former academic administrator; b. Mineola, NY, June 29, 1939; s. Alexander Walker and Florence M. (Carville) R.; m. Helen Landgren, July 23, 1966; children: Ellen Ross Sarafian, Kevin McAndrew. BFA, NY Inst. Tech., 1962, LLD (hon.), 1978; MS, Hofstra U., 1970. Dean of students NY Inst. Tech., Old Westbury, 1962-68; co-founder, pres. Wilmington Coll., Del., 1967—77; pres., CEO Lynn U. (formerly Coll. of Boca Raton), Fla., 1971—2006. Chmn. adv. com. U.S. Army Command and Gen. Staff Coll. Bd. dirs. Fla. Endowment Fund, 1989—; trustee Boca Raton Community Hosp., 1990—; mem. governing bd. Philharmonic Orch. Fla., 1990—; mem. U.S. Mil. Screening Com. Named Industrialist of Yr., Greater Boca Raton C. of C., 1992, Man of the Yr., City of Hope; recipient Boy Scouts Am. Leadership Svc. award, Boca Raton award, 1991, LEAH Bridge Builder of the Year, 1999. Mem. Assn. Univ. Pres., Econ. Coun. of Palm Beach County, Royal Palm Yacht and Country, Loggerhead Club, Adirondack League Club, Old Forge Club, City (Boca Raton). Avocations: snowskiing, tennis, reading, travel, golf. Home: 7411 Floranada Addison Res Delray Beach FL 33484 Office Phone: 561-237-7782. E-mail: president@lynn.edu.

ROSS, DONALD K., lobbyist, environmental organization administrator, lawyer; Grad., Fordham Coll., NYU. Dir. Citizens Action Group; founding dir. NY Pub. Interest Rsch. Group; ptnr. Malkin & Ross, Albany, NY; CEO M&R Strategic Svcs.; chair Greenpeace Inc., Washington, DC, 2004—. Office: Greenpeace 702 H St, NW Washington DC 20001 also: M&R 2120 L St, NW Ste 400 Washington DC 20037 also: Malkin & Ross 100 State St, Ste 400 Albany NY 12207 E-mail: dkross@mrss.com.

ROSS, DONALD ROE, federal judge; b. Orleans, Nebr., June 8, 1922; s. Roe M. and Leila H. (Reed) Ross; m. Janice S. Cook, Aug. 29, 1943; children: Susan Jane, Sharon Kay, Rebecca Lynn, Joan Christine, Donald Dean. JD, U. Nebr., 1948, LLD (hon.), 1990. Bar: Nebr. 1948. Practice law, Lexington, Nebr., 1948—53; mayor City of Lexington, 1953; ptnr. Swarr, May, Royce, Smith, Andersen & Ross, 1956—70; U.S. atty. Dist. Nebr. US Dept. Justice, 1953—56; gen. counsel Rep. Nat. Com., 1956—58; mem. Rep. Exec. Com. for Nebr., 1952—53; com. mem. Rep. Nat. Com., 1958—70, vice-chmn., 1965—70; judge US Ct. Appeals (8th cir.), 1970—87, sr. judge, 1987—. Office: 5815 N 148th Plaza Omaha NE 68116 Office Phone: 402-493-2129. *

ROSS, DOUGLAS, lawyer; b. LA, July 12, 1948; s. Mathew and Brenda Butler (Boynton) R.; m. Lynne Rose Maidman, June 14, 1970. AB cum laude, Tufts U., 1970; JD with honors, George Washington U., 1973. Bar: Ohio 1973, D.C. 1980, U.S. Supreme Ct. 1976. Asst. atty. gen., antitrust sect. Office of Ohio Atty. Gen., Columbus, 1973-74; spl. asst. U.S. atty. Ea. Dist. Va., Alexandria, 1977; trial atty. antitrust divsn. U.S. Dept. Justice, Washington, 1975-82; atty. advisor Office of Legis. Affairs, 1984-86, Office of Legal Policy, 1987-89, Office Policy Devel., 1989-92; Supreme Ct. counsel Nat. Assn. Attys. Gen., 1982-91. Ran advocacy project for states to enhance their effectiveness before Supreme Ct., 1982—91; operated clearinghouse on state constl. law, 1987—91; civil divsn. Appellate Staff U.S. Dept. Justice, Washington, 1992—94, Office of Consumer Litigation, 1994—2000, spl. counsel for agr. antitrust divsn., 2000—. Recipient Meritorious award Dept. Justice, 1979, Spl. Achievement award, 1984, 96, 97. Mem. Supreme Ct. Hist. Soc., D.C. Bar Assn., Supreme Ct. Opinion

Network (bd. dirs. 1989-91), Arlington County Sports Commn. (chair aquatics com. 2004—), North Tract Master Plan Oversight Com. (chair indoor subcom. 2004—). Jewish. Home: 3153 19th St N Arlington VA 22201-5103 Office: US Dept Justice 950 Pennsylvania Ave NW Washington DC 20530-0001 Home Phone: 703-528-6386; Office Phone: 202-514-1874.

ROSS, EDWARD, cardiologist; b. Fairfield, Ala., Oct. 10, 1937; s. Horace and Carrie Lee (Griggs) R.; m. Catherine I. Webster, Jan. 19, 1974; children: Edward, Ronald, Cheryl, Anthony. BS, Clark Coll., 1959; MD, Ind. U., 1963. Diplomate Am. Bd. Internal Medicine; cert. specialist in clin. hypertension Am. Soc. Hypertension. Intern Marion County Gen. Hosp., Indpls., 1963; resident in internal medicine Ind. U., 1964-66, 68, cardiology rsch. fellow, 1968-70, clin. asst. prof. medicine, 1970; cardiologist Capitol Med. Assn., Indpls., 1970-74; pvt. practice medicine, specializing in cardiology Indpls., 1974—. Staff cardiologist Winona Meml. Hosp., Indpls., chief cardiovascular disease, 2000-04, med. dir. cardiovascular svcs., 2000—, med. dir. cardiac cath lab, 2000—, chief interventional cardiology, 2000-04; staff Meth. Hosp., Indpls., chmn. cardiovasc. sect., 1989-96; chmn. cardiovasc. sect., dir. cardiovasc. ctr. Meth. Hosp., 1990-92; bd. dirs. Meth. Hosp. Heart-Lung Ctr., med. dir. cardiovasc. svcs., 1991-98; med. dir. cardiovascular svcs. Methodist Hosp., Indpls., Ind., 2000—, cardiac catheterization lab., 2000—, cardiovascular programs, Clarian Health Indpls., 2000—, cardiovascular svcs., Cardicac Cath. Lab., cardiovascular programs, Clarian Health Ptnrs., 2000-. Assoc. editor Angiology, Jour. Vascular Disease; sr. editor Jour. Vascular Medicine, 1983—. Mem. Ctrl. Ind. Health Planning Coun., 1972-73; bd. dirs. Ind. chpt. Am. Heart Assn., 1973-74, multiphasic screening East Side Clinic, Flanner Ho. of Indpls., 1968-71; med. dir. Nat. Ctr. for Health Svc. R&D, HEW, 1970; consumer rep. radiologic device panel health FDA, 1988-92; dir. hypertensive screening State of Ind., 1974; J.B. Johnson Cardiovasc. lectr. Nat. Med. Assn., 1991. Capt. MC, USAF, 1966-68. Recipient Lifetime Achievement award, Ctr. Leadership Devel., 2003, Leadership award, Indpls. Police Dept., 2005; scholar, Nat. Found. Health, 1955, Gorges Found., 1956; Woodrow Wilson fellow, 1959. Fellow Royal Soc. Promotion of Health (Eng.), Am. Coll. Angiology (v.p. fgn. affairs, sec. 1993—), Internat. Coll. Angiology, Am. Soc. of Angiology, Am. Coll. Cardiology, Assn. Black Cardiologists (mem. bd. dirs. 1990-94); mem. NAACP, AMA, Am. Soc. Contemporary Medicine and Surgery, Nat. Med. Assn. (coun. sci. assembly 1985-89), Ind. Med. Soc., Marion County Med. Soc., Am. Coll. Physicians, Am. Heart Assn., Ind. Soc. Internal Medicine (pres. 1987-89), Ind. State Med. Assn. (chmn. internal medicine sect. 1987-89), Ind. Med. Soc., Aesculapean Med. Soc., Hoosier State Med. Assn. (pres. 1980-84, 90-95), Urban League, Alpha Omega Alpha, Alpha Kappa Mu, Beta Kappa Chi, Omega Psi Phi. Methodist. Office: 1801 N Senate Blvd #310 Indianapolis IN 46202 Home Phone: 317-966-4848; Office Phone: 317-962-2500. Business E-Mail: eross@clarian.org.

ROSS, EDWARD JOSEPH, architect; b. Dec. 13, 1934; s. Miriam Ross; children: Linda Joy, Melissa Carol. Student, Boston Archtl. Ctr., 1952-55, 61-62, USAF Surveying Sch., 1955-56, Boston Soc. Civil Engrs., 1956-57, Carl Bolivar Structural Engr., 1962-63. Registered arch., Mass., Calif., NY, Fla., NH, Vt., cert. Nat. Coun. Archtl. Registration Bds.; lic. constrn. supr. Mass., expert witness constrn. law. Draftsman, assoc. William W. Drummey, Architect, Boston, 1952-59; job capt., designer Drummey-Rosane-Anderson, Boston, 1959-64; projects arch. Maginnis & Walsh & Kennedy, Boston, 1964-69; v.p. William Nelson Jacobs Assocs., Inc., Boston, 1969-73; staff arch. Robert Charles Assocs., Inc. Archs., Boston, 1973-74; office mgr. Charles F. Jacobs Assocs., Inc., Cambridge, Mass., 1974-76; cons. arch. Linenthal, Eisenberg & Anderson, Boston, 1976-77; staff arch. Eisenberg Haven Assocs., Inc., Boston, 1977-78; chief arch., chief insp. Boston Housing Authority, 1978-83; prin. Edward J. Ross, AIA/FARA, Randolph, Mass., 1983-84; arch., sr. assoc., dir. constrn. adminstrn. Stull and Lee, Inc., Boston, 1984-91; pvt. practice Randolph, Stoughton, Mass., West Palm Beach, Fla., 1963—2000; consulting arch., contrn. adminstr., expert witness, 2000—06. Mem. FCC Tech Plus. Mem. exec. bd. and ops. com. United Civic Orgn.; bd. dir. Linderhof Property Owners Assn., Knollsbrook Condominium Complex. Staff sgt. USAF, maj. Mass. Mil. Res. Fellow: Soc. Am. Registered Archs.; mem.: USO (New Eng. coun.), AIA, Boston Soc. Archs. (mem. housing com. 1982—86), Constrn. Specifications Inst., Mass. State Assn. Archs., Am. Arbitration Assn. (nat. panel 1965—2005), United Civic Orgn. (mem. exec. bd. and ops. com.), Assn. First Corps Cadets, Am. Assn. Ret. Persons, Air Force Assn. (pres. Boston chpt.), Mass. Air N.G. Hist. Assn., Mil. Hist. Soc. Mass., Oxford 100 Condominium Assn. (pres.), Linderhof Golf Course Site One Assn. (pres. 1980—86), Ancient and Hon. Arty. Co. Mass., Oxford Colony Club Century Village (v.p.), Ten of Us Club, Am. Legion, KP, Elks. Address: 201 Oxford 100 West Palm Beach FL 33417-1412 Office Phone: 561-615-6680. Office Fax: 561-686-6345.

ROSS, E(DWIN) CLARKE, association executive, educator; b. Balt., Sept. 21, 1948; s. Harry Edwin and Margaret Frances (Turner) R.; m. Elizabeth Christine Shannon, Mar. 26, 1988; 1 child, Andrew Clarke. BA, U. Md., 1970, MA, 1974; D of Pub. Adminstrn., George Washington U., 1981. Vol. VISTA, Washington, 1970-71; legis. asst. Nat. Assn. State Mental Health Program Dirs., Washington, 1971-72; from asst. dir. to dir. Govt. Rels. United Cerebral Palsy Assns., Washington, 1972-84; asst. prof. European region Troy State U., Weisbaden, Germany, 1984-86; asst. exec. dir. for fed. rels. Nat. Assn. State Mental Health Dirs., Washington, 1986-93, dep. exec. dir., 1993-95; exec. dir. Am. Managed Behavioral Healthcare Assn., Washington, 1995-98; dep. exec. dir. pub. policy Nat. Alliance for the Mentally Ill., Arlington, Va., 1998-2000; CEO Children and Adults with Attention Deficit/Hyperactivity Disorder, Landover, Md., 2000—. Adj. grad. faculty, Cen. Mich. U., Washington, 1983-84, 87-93, 99—; adj. assoc. prof. U. Md., College Park, 1992-95. Author: Managed Behavioral Health Care Handbook, 2001; contbr. articles to profl. jours. and chpts. to books; author: Endurance as a Virtue: Army of Northern Virginia Civil War Experiences. Vol. Com. for Legal Svcs., Washington, 1970-71; mem. U.S. Olympic Com. on Winter Sports for Disabled, Colo. Springs, Colo., 1983-84; mem. program com. Dem. Club, Annapolis, Md., 1984. Recipient Maternal and Child Health scholarship to Johns Hopkins U., State of Md., 1975. Mem. SAR, Am. Coll. Mental Health Adminstrn., Am. Soc. Pub. Adminstrn., Am. Polit. Sci. Assn., St. Andrew's Soc., Sovereign Mil. Order of Temple of Jerusalem, Beta Gamma Sigma (life). Presbyterian. Avocations: Scottish country dance, skiing, Scottish and U.S. history. Home and Office: 1718 Reynolds St Crofton MD 21114-2635 E-mail: clarke_ross@chadd.org.

ROSS, EDWIN WILLIAM, rubber company executive; b. Phila., May 28, 1938; s. Edwin Morrison and Frances Louise (Ort) R.; m. Dorothy Anne Reilly, Sept. 24, 1966; children: E. William Jr., Catherine Ross Conlin, James David. BS, Lehigh U., 1960. Chmn. bd., CEO Key Chems., Inc., Phila., 1965-87; pres., CEO Pelmor Labs., Inc., Newtown, Pa., 1989—; chmn. Pelseal Techs., LLC, Newtown, Pa., 1998—2005; shareholder Pelmor Thailand Co., Ltd., 2006—. Mem. adv. bd. Prime Bank, Ft. Washington, Pa., 1995—98. Deacon Bryn Mawr (Pa.) Presbyn. Ch., 1977-81, elder, 1985-91, trustee, 1997-2003, pres. bd. trustees, 2001-2003; bd. dirs. Main Line Adult Day Care Ctr., 1999. With US Coast Guard Reserve 1961-69. Recipient Alumni award Lehigh U. Alumni Assn., 1985. Mem. SAR, MidAtlantic Employers Assn. (chmn. 1995-96), Metal Finishing Suppliers Assn. (pres. 1986-88, 89-90, Munning award 1992), N.E. Phila. C. of C. (chmn. 1983), Lehigh U. Alumni Assn. (bd. dirs. 1997-2000), Swedish Colonial Soc., Sons. of the Revolution Soc., St. Andrew's Soc., Colonial Soc., Exch. Club (pres. Frankford-Phila. 1972), Phila. Country Club (pres. 1986-89). Republican. Avocations: downhill skiing, hunting, travel, golf. Office: Pelmor Labs Inc 401 Lafayette St Newtown PA 18940-0309 Office Phone: 215-968-3334. Personal E-mail: ewmross@hotmail.com.

ROSS, ELEANOR, retired medical association administrator; M.Nursing, U. Toronto, Ont., Can. RN Ont., Can. Chief nursing practice Women's Coll. Hosp., Toronto, Ont.; asst. prof. U. Toronto Sch. Nursing; dir. Internat. Coun. Nurses, Geneva, 1997—2005; ret. Mem.: Can. Nurses Respiratory Assn. (pres. 1984—85), Registered Nurses Assn. of Ont. (pres. 1987—89), Can. Nurses Assn. (pres. 1994—96). Office: Internat Council Nurses 3 Pl Jean Marteau 1201 Geneva Switzerland Home: 858 Metler Rd Fenwick ON L0S 1C0 Canada Office Phone: 41-22-908-01-00.

ROSS, ELIZABETH, marketing executive; BS, Mich. State U. Bus. devel., account mgmt. J. Walter Thompson, Chgo., NYC; head bus. devel. group Modem Media, San Francisco, Norwalk, Conn.; joined Tribal DDB, 2004, gen. mgr. San Francisco, pres. west Dallas, LA, 2006—07. Named a Woman to Watch, Advt. Age, 2007. Office: Tribal DDB West Ste 500 555 Market St San Francisco CA 94105 *

ROSS, EUNICE LATSHAW, retired judge; b. Bellevue, Pa., Oct. 13, 1923; d. Richard Kelly and Eunice (Weidner) Latshaw; m. John Anthony Ross, May 29, 1943 (dec. Jan. 1978); 1 child, Geraldine Ross Coleman. BS, U. Pitts., 1945, LLB, 1951. Bar: Pa. 1952. Atty. Pub. Health Law Rsch. Project, Pitts., 1951-52; atty. jud. asst., law clk. Ct. Common Pleas Allegheny County, Pitts., 1952-70, dir. family divsn., 1970-72, judge, 1972-96, Commonwealth Ct. Pa., 1997—2004. Adj. law prof. U. Pitts., 1967-73; mem. Bd. Jud. Inquiry and Rev., Commonwealth of Pa., 1984-89, Gov's Justice Commn., 1972-78; mem. orphan's ct. rules com. Supreme Ct. Pa., 1998—2005. Author: (with others) Survey of Pa. Public Health Laws, 1952, Justice, 1995, Lötschers of Latterbach, Mennonite Heritage Mag., 2003; co-author: Will Contests, 1992; contbr. articles to law publs. Mem. exec. com. bd. trustees U. Pitts., 1980—86, bd. visitors Law Sch., 1985—, bd. visitors Sch. Health, 1986—98; mem. adv. bd. Animal Friends, Pitts., 1973—98; committeewoman for 14th ward, vice chmn. Pitts. Dem. com., 1972; bd. dirs. The Program, Pitts., 1983—87, Pitts. History and Landmarks Found., West Pa. Hist. Soc., West Pa. Conservancy. Named Girls Scouts Woman of Yr., Pitts. coun. Girl Scouts U.S.A., 1975, Alumni of Yr., U. Pitts. Law Sch., 2001; recipient Disting. Alumna award, U. Pitts., 1973, Medal of Recognition, 1987, Alumni award, U. Pitts. Sch. of Law, 2001, Susan B. Anthony award, Women's Bar Assn. Western Pa., 1993, Probate and Trusts award, 1994, cert. of achievement, Pa. Fedn. Women's Clubs, 1975, 1977. Mem.: ABA, Allegheny County Bar Assn. (vice chmn., exec. com. young lawyers sect. 1958—59), Scribes, Order of Coif. Home: 1204 Denniston Ave Pittsburgh PA 15217-1329 Personal E-mail: rossdent@comcast.net.

ROSS, FRANK HOWARD, III, management consultant; b. Charlotte, NC, Aug. 28, 1946; s. Frank Howard Jr. (dec.) and Alma (Richardson) R. (dec.); m. Beverly Hazel Ross, June 30, 1973 (dec.); children: Martha McCausland, Frank Howard IV; m. Barbara Rydz-Roth, July 9, 2005; children: Ingrid Rydz, Veronica Anne, Karl Vincent. BS in Engring., NC State U., Raleigh, 1968. Cons. Fails & Assocs., Inc., Raleigh, NC, 1968-73; ptnr. Ross-Payne & Assocs., Inc., Barrington, Ill., 1973—. Bd. dirs. Gilldorn Savs., Chgo., 1982-85, Brickman Industries, Inc., Chgo., 1980-90; CFO WRT, Inc., Chgo., 1993-95; pres., chmn. bd. dirs. Emerald Capital Investments, Inc., Barrington, 1993-97; adviser, spkr. on constrn. and fin.; bd. dirs. Sherman Plumbing, 1975-95. Author: More $ Through $ Management, 1975, MIS and You, 1978, Planning and Budgeting, 1979, Profit by Design, 1981, Pricing for Profit, 1983, Wealthbuilding, 1984, Equipment Cost Analysis, 1988, Survivial in a Tight Economy, 1988, Associated Landscape Contractors of America Operating Cost Survey, 1989, 91, Cash Flow, 1989, Dealing with the Competition of the 90's, 1990, Designing Your Accounting System, 1991, Bidding in a Tight Market, 1992, Industry's Wage and Benefit Study, 1992, Financing Your Business, 1993, Pricing, 1994, 2d edit., 1997, How Low Can You Go?, 1995, Valuing Your Business, 1998, Posturing for Growth and Prosperity, 1999, My Executive Dashboard, 2004, If You Can't Track It, You Can't Control It!, 2007. Active Presbyn. Ch. Barrington. Named to Anla Contractors Hall of Fame. Mem. Inst. Mgmt. Cons., Barrington Hills Country Club, Haig Point Country Club, Sigma Alpha Epsilon. Home and Office: Ross Payne Assocs Inc 190 Kimberly Rd Barrington IL 60010-2017 Office Phone: 847-381-8939.

ROSS, GARY EARL, writing educator; b. Buffalo, Aug. 12, 1951; s. Earl Ross and Marlene (Edwards) Anderson; m. Katharyn Ellen Ketter, Dec. 23, 1970 (div. 1993); children: Colleen, Timothy, David; m. Patrice Lynette Cox, Aug. 14, 1999; children: Cody, Madelynne. BA in English, SUNY, Buffalo, 1973, MA in Humanities, 1975. Cert. English tchr., N.Y. Secondary English tchr. Buffalo Pub. Schs., 1973-76, Canisius High Sch., Buffalo, 1976-77; writing instr. Ednl. Opportunity Ctr. SUNY, Buffalo, 1977—94, assoc. prof., 1994—2003, prof., 2003—. Writing instr. Upward Bound SUNY, Buffalo, summers 1980—, acting dir., summer 1984; presenter in field, U.S., Can., Europe, 1975—; reader various profl. fiction readings, 1985-; bd. dirs. Just Buffalo Literacy Ctr. Contbr. articles, short stories, poems, essays to profl. publs.; videographer Writers on Video, Buffalo Pub. Libr., 1989; author (book) Wheel of Desire, 2000, Dots, 2002, Shimmerville, 2002, (plays) Sleepwalker, 2002, Matter of Intent, 2005 (Edgar Allan Poe award, Mystery Writers Am., 2006), The Best Woman, 2007, Picture Perfect, 2007. Bd. dirs. Ujima Theatre Co., 2005—07. Local Incentive Funding Test fellow for fiction Buffalo Arts Coun., 1989; recipient Excellence award N.Y. State/United Univ. Professions, 1990, Artist of Yr. Arts Coun., 2003. Mem. Niagara Erie Writers (chmn. bd. dirs. 1987-89), Just Buffalo, Inc. (fiction resident 1987, 92, bd. dirs. 2003-), Mid-Atlantic Popular/Am. Culture Assn. (bd. mem., pres. 2006-07), United Univ. Professions, Assn. Tchg. Artists (bd. dirs. 2003-06). Avocations: computing, games, film history, contemporary literature. Office: SUNY EOC Buffalo 465 Washington St Buffalo NY 14203-1707 Office Phone: 716-849-6727 ext. 119. E-mail: geross@buffalo.edu.

ROSS, GERALD FRED, electrical engineering executive, researcher; b. NYC, Dec. 14, 1930; s. Samuel Henry and Jenny (Saltzman) Rozansky; m. Vivian Ida Turkish, Dec. 24, 1953; children: Jayne T. Ross Kaufman, Steven A., Helene B. Ross Joseph. BEE, CCNY, 1952; MEE, Poly. U., 1955, PhD, 1963; MBA, Harvard Bus. Sch., Boston, 1979. Registered profl. engr., N.Y., Mass., Fla. Rsch. asst. U. Mich., Ann Arbor, 1952-53; sr. engr. W.L. Maxson Corp., NYC, 1954-58; rsch. sect. head Sperry Gyroscope Co., Great Neck, L.I., NY, 1958-65; dept. mgr. Sperry Rsch. Ctr., Sudbury, Mass., 1965-81; chmn. Geospatial Sys. Inc. (formerlyANRO Engring.), Sarasota, Fla., 1981—, Ana Lux Corp., 2002—. Pres., v.p., treas. Adams Pool Corp., Lexington, Mass., 1968-81. Capt. USAFR, 1953—. Contbg. author 3 books, 1986, 90, 93; contbr. numerous articles to profl. jours.; patentee in field. Fellow Polytechnic U. Fellow IEEE (life; K.C. Black Nerem Best paper award 1974, Pioneer award 2004), Nat. Acad. Engring. (life); mem. Electromagnetics Acad., Lexington Golf Club, Longboat Key Club, Laurel Oak Country Club, Sigma Xi (sr.), Tau Beta Pi, Eta Kappa Nu. Republican. Jewish. Avocations: golf, bridge. Personal E-mail: drgfr@aol.com.

ROSS, GERALD HARVEY, family practice and environmental medicine physician; s. Henry Warburton and Norine Hazel (Bishop) Ross; m. Heather M. Pollett, Aug. 15, 1970; children: Graham D.P., Andrew W.J. BSc, Dalhousie U., 1969, MD, 1974. Diplomate Internat. Bd. Environ. Medicine, Am. Bd. Environ. Medicine. Med. dir. N.S. Environ. Medicine Clinic, Halifax, Canada, 1970—74; family medicine practice New Minas, Nova Scotia, Canada, 1974—87; med. fellow Environ. Health Ctr., Dallas, 1987—89, med. staff, 1989—99; rschr. Gerald H. Ross, M.D., P.L.L.C., Bountiful, Utah, 1999—2004. Mem. adv. com. Environ. Hypersensitivites Ont. Dept. Health, Toronto, 1989—94; rsch. fellow Breakspeare Hosp. for Environ. Medicine, Kings Langley, Hertfordhsire, England, 1988—89. Co-author reports to Ont. Ministry of Health; contbr. chapters to books, articles to profl. jours., scientific papers; mem. editl. bd. Internat. Jour. Hygiene and Environ. Health, 2001—03, Environ. Epidemiology and Toxicology, 1998—2001, mem. East Coast adv. com. The Med. Post, Toronto, 1978—94. Many leadership positions Ch. LDS, Dallas, 1988—99. Internat. fellow in environ. medicine, N.S. Dept. Health, 1987—89, Innovations in Edn. Utah grantee, 2003. Fellow: Royal Soc. Medicine UK, Am. Acad. Environ. Medicine (pres. 1995—97, chair rsch. com. 1991—94, bd. dirs. 1993—98, Award of appreciation for serving as Pres. 1997, Carlton Lee award for excellence in tchg. the principles of environ. medicine 2005); mem.: AMA, Assn. Am. Physicians and Surgeons, Am. Coll. Nutrition, Am. Coll. Occupl. and Environ. Medicine, Can. Soc. Environ. Medicine, Coll. Family Physicians Can., Am. Bd. Environ. Medicine (bd. govs. 1993—2004), Chem. Sensitivity Found. (bd. dirs.), Can. Med. Assn., Tex. Med. Assn. Mem. Lds Ch. Avocations: reading, movies. Office: Gerald H Ross MD PLLC PO Box 115 Bountiful UT 84011

ROSS, HAROLD ANTHONY, lawyer; b. Kent, Ohio, June 2, 1931; s. Jules and Helen Assumpta (Ferrara) R.; m. Elaine Louise Hunt, July 1, 1961; children: Leslie Ann, Gregory Edward, Jonathan Harold. BA magna cum laude, Case Western Res. U., Cleve., 1953; JD, Harvard U., Cambridge, Mass., 1956. Bar: Ohio 1956. Assoc. Marshman, Hornbeck, Hollington, Steadman & McLaughlin, Cleve., 1961—64; pres. Ross & Kraushaar Co., Cleve., 1964—2005. Gen. counsel Brotherhood of Locomotive Engrs., Cleve., 1966-2005; adv. bd. mem. Ctr. for Advanced Study of Law and Dispute Resolution Procedures, George Mason U. Sch. Law, 2000—. Trustee Citizens League Greater Cleve., 1969-75, 76-82, pres., 1981-82; active Charter Rev. Com. North Olmsted, 1970, 75. With AUS, 1956-58. Fellow Coll. Labor and Employment Lawyers; mem. ABA (co-chair rwy. and airline labor law sect. 1976-78), Ohio State Bar Assn., Cleve. Bar Assn., Phi Beta Kappa, Delta Sigma Rho, Omicron Delta Kappa. Roman Catholic. Business E-Mail: haross@ble-t.org.

ROSS, HOWARD PHILIP, lawyer; b. May 10, 1939; s. Bernard and Estelle (Maremont) Ross; m. Loretta Teresa Benquil, 1962 (div.); children: Glen Joseph, Cynthia Ann, Ryan Reeve; m. Jennifer Kay Shirley, 1984. BS, U. Ill., 1961; JD, Stetson Coll. Law, 1964. Bar: Fla. 1964, U.S. Ct. Appeals (5th cir.) 1965, U.S. Supreme Ct. 1969, U.S. Ct. Appeals (11th cir.) 1981, cert.: civil trial lawyer, bus. litigator. Assoc. Parker & Battaglia and predecessor firm, St. Petersburg, Fla., 1964-67; ptnr. Battaglia, Ross, Dicus & Wein, P.A., St. Petersburg, 1967—, pres., CEO, 1992-99, chmn. bd. dirs., 2000—. Lectr. Stetson Coll. Law, St. Petersburg, 1971—72, adj. prof., 1987. Author: Florida Corporations, 1979; co-author: Managing Discovery in Commercial and Business Litigation, 1993; contbr. articles to profl. jours. Hon. chair St. Petersburg br. Awards Banquet NAACP, 1995; bd. dirs. St. Petersburg Neighborhood Housing Svcs., Inc., 1997, legal counsel, 1997—, pres., 2000—02; bd. dirs. Cmty. Alliance, 1997—2002; chmn. subcom. Citizen Rev. Com. City of St. Petersburg, 1992—94, co-chair, 1994—97. Named to Fla. Super Lawyers, Law & Politics, 2006—07; recipient Fla. Bar Merit citation, 1974, Woman's Svc. League Best Groomed award, 1979, Cmty. Svc. award, NAACP, 1998, Humanitarian award, YMCA of Tampa Bay, 1999, C.W. Bill Young Pinellas Pinnacle award, 2002, Disting. Alumni award, Stetson Lawyers Assn., 2006. Mem.: ABA, Am. Arbitration Assn. (roster of neutrals, large complex cases and comml. 2003—), St. Petersburg Bar Assn., Fla. Bar Assn. (chmn. civil trial certification com. 1993—94), St. Petersburg Area C. of C. (bd. govs. 1990—95, v.p. pub. affairs 1992—93, exec. com. 1992—95, v.p. membership 1993—94, counsel 1994—95, dean entrepreneurial acad. 1996—, treas. 2000—02, bd. govs. 2000—05, chmn.-elect 2002—03, chmn. 2003—04, Mem. of Yr. 1993—94). Republican. Jewish. Office: Battaglia Ross Dicus & Wein PA PO Box 41100 980 Tyrone Blvd N Saint Petersburg FL 33710-6382 Home Phone: 727-345-7442; Office Phone: 727-381-2300. Business E-Mail: hross@brdwlaw.com.

ROSS, HUGH COURTNEY, electrical engineer; b. Dec. 31, 1923; s. Clare W. and Jeanne F. Ross; m. Sarah A. Gordon (dec.); m. Patricia A. Malloy; children: John C., James G., Robert W. Student, Calif. Inst. Tech., 1942, San Jose State U., 1946-47; BSEE, Stanford U., 1950, postgrad., 1954. Registered profl. elec. engr., Calif. Instr. San Benito (Calif.) High Sch. and Jr. Coll., 1950-51; chief engr. vacuum power switches Jennings Radio Mfg. Corp., San Jose, Calif., 1951-62; chief engr. ITT Jennings, San Jose, Calif., 1962-64; pres. Ross Engring. Corp., Campbell, Calif., 1964—. Contbr. articles to profl. jours. Fellow IEEE (life) (chmn. Santa Clara Valley subsect. 1960-61); mem. Am. Vacuum Soc., Am. Soc. Metals. Achievements include patents in field. Avocations: electronics, electric autos, camping, ranching, solar power. Office: 540 Westchester Dr Campbell CA 95008-5012 Office Phone: 408-377-4621.

ROSS, IVY E., apparel executive, artist; b. 1955; Completed programs in indsl. design, Syracuse U. Sch. Design; completed programs in jewelry design, Fashion Inst. Tech.; profl. mgmt. development program, Harvard Bus. Sch. Positions with Coach, Liz Claiborne, Calvin Klein, Swatch Watch, Victoria's Secret, Bausch & Lomb; sr. v.p., design Mattel, Inc.; exec. v.p., product design & devel., Old Navy Brand Gap, Inc., 2004—07; sr. v.p., chief creative officer Disney Store N Am., 2007—. Lectr. and workshops on a variety of topics RI Sch. Design, Phila. Coll. Art, Fashion Inst. Tech., Cooper-Hewitt Mus. and the Montreal Visual Arts Ctr. Artist, metal work in jewelry (permanent collections) Smithsonian Inst., Victoria and Albert Mus. London, Cooper-Hewitt Mus. NY; contbr. chapters to books. Named one of 25 Masters of Innovation, BusinessWeek; recipient Women in Design award, Diamond Internat. award; Nat. Endowment for the Arts grant. *

ROSS, JAMES OWEN, education educator, researcher; b. Morganton, NC, Sept. 27, 1948; s. Owen and Vivian Chapman Ross; life ptnr. Charles Anthony Staley; 1 child, Juliana Adele. BFA, U. of NC at Greensboro, Greensboro, North Carolina, 1971; AM, Brown U., 1986, PhD, 2003. Prof. Ringling Sch. of Art and Design, Sarasota, Fla., 1974—75, Ctrl. Piedmont C.C., Charlotte, ND, 1976—80, Appalachian State U., Boone, NC, 1983—84, RISD, Providence, 1985—86, U. of Okla., 1987—88, Wentworth Inst. of Tech., Boston, 1990—91; tchg. fellow Brown U., 1990—92; prof. ND State U., 1991—92, Western Carolina U., 1992, U. of Memphis, 1995—96, East Tenn. State U., 1997—98. Building, Preliminary Design Windsor Locks Rapids Exhbn. Ctr. (Interior Design Educators Coun. Internat. Exhbn., Nashville, Tenn., 1995), building interior, Hynes Residence Libr. (Interior Design Educators Coun. Internat. Exhibit, Denver, Colo., 1996). Dem. nominee in NC state senate, 27th dist. NC Dem. Party, NC, 1996; vestry mem. St. Peter's Episcopal Ch., Charlotte, NC, 1981—82; represented bus. in hist. dist. Friends of Fourth Ward Hist. Dist., Charlotte, NC, 1979—82. Tchg. fellow, Brown U., 1990—91. Mem.: Internat. Interior Design Assn. (Presdl. Commendation 1999), AIA (assoc.), Soc. of Archtl. Historians (life). Democrat-Npl. Soc. Of Friends. Achievements include research in impact of nineteenth-century public health movement upon American architecture: Theories of Disease, Ventilation, and Sunlight, 1840-1944. Avocations: travel, back packing, swimming, gardening, cooking. Home: 132 Malbon's Mills Rd Skowhegan ME 04976 Personal E-mail: james.ross.g86@alumni.brown.edu.

ROSS, JEFFREY S., lawyer; b. NYC, Mar. 7, 1951; AB with highest honors, U. Mich., 1972; JD, Stanford U., 1975. Bar: Calif. 1975, US Dist. Ct. (no. Calif. dist.), US Ct. Appeals (9th cir.), US Supreme Ct. Atty., pres. Friedman Ross & Hersh PC; ptnr. Pillsbury Winthrop Shaw Pittman, San

Francisco. Mem.: San Francisco Barrister Club (bd. dirs. 1981—83, pres. 1983), Nat. Assn. Bar Presidents, Bar Assn. San Francisco (bd. dirs. 1986—88, pres. 1997, Award of Merit 1990, 1998), Phi Beta Kappa, Phi Eta Sigma. Office: Pillsbury Winthrop Shaw Pittman 50 Fremont St San Francisco CA 94105 Office Phone: 415-983-1730. Office Fax: 415-983-1200. Business E-Mail: jeff.ross@pillsburylaw.com.

ROSS, JERROLD, music educator; b. NYC, Feb. 8, 1935; s. James Murray and Alice (Gubernick) R. BS, NYU, 1955, PhD, 1963; MS, Queens Coll., 1959; HHD, Emerson Coll., 1997. Music tchr., Syosset, N.Y., 1956-58, Great Neck, N.Y., 1958-61; instr. music edn. NYU, 1961-63; chmn. tchr. edn. dept. N.Y. Coll. Music, 1963-65, pres., 1965-67; head divsn. music edn. NYU, 1967-74, head divsn. arts and arts edn., 1974-82, assoc. dean, 1982-95, acting vice dean, 1979, mem. senate, 1977-80, chmn. faculty coun., 1979-80, dir. Nat. Ctr. for Rsch. in Arts Edn., 1987-95; dean Sch. Edn. St. John's U., NY, 1995—. Dir. Town Hall of NYU, 1971-74; bd. dirs. Town Hall Found., 1973-75; asst. bd. examiners N.Y.C. Pub. Schs.; mem. Tchr. Edn. Certification and Practice Bd., State of N.Y., 1987-93; mem. charter bd. Tchr. Edn. Accreditation Coun., Coun. Ind. Colls., 1998-05; cons. to and mem. music com. N.Y. State Edn. Dept. Coll. Proficiency Exam. Program; mem. adv. coun. on arts in edn.; mem. NY State Commr.'s Adv. Com. on Tchr. Edn., chair, Coun. U. Deans; mem. participant various confs.Nat. Endowment for Arts, U.S. Office Edn., Am. Assn. Colls. Tchr. Edn., Getty Ctr. for Edn. in Arts; bd. dirs. various projects N.Y. State Edn. Dept., Nat. Found on Arts and Humanities, N.Y. State Council on Arts, Andrew W. Mellon Found., Rockefeller Found., Reimann Found., Henry and Lucy Moses Found., Pinkerton Found., Rubin Scholars Program in Israel. Author: Interpreting Music Through Movement, 1963. V.p. Concert Artists Guild N.Y., 1964-69; bd. dirs. Usdan Ctr. Arts, chmn. bd. dirs., 1972-80, 85-02; founding mem. Arts Edn. Group NY, 1998-; bd. dirs. Broadway Assn., Village Nursing Home, 1984-86; bd. dirs. Am. Assn. Music Therapists, pres., 1978-80; mem. citizens adv. bd. Sta. WNCN AM-FM, 1976-94; bd. dirs. Alumni LaGuardia Sch. Music and Arts, NYC, 1990—; mem. adv. bd. arts edn. NYC Dept. Edn., 2006-. Mem. Music Educators Nat. Conf., Coll. Music Soc. (mem. coun. 1975-78), Nat. Assn. Schs. Music (mem. govtl. rels. com., mem. grad. commn. 1979-84), Lotos Club NY, Phi Delta Kappa, Phi Mu Alpha Sinfonia (province gov. 1964-70). Home: 175 E 62nd St Apt 11C New York NY 10021-7626 Office Phone: 718-990-1305. Business E-Mail: rossj@stjohns.edu.

ROSS, JERRY L., astronaut; b. Crown Point, Ind., Jan. 20, 1948; s. Donald J. and Phyllis E. Ross; m. Karen S. Pearson; 2 children. BS in Mech. Engring., Purdue U., West Lafayette, Ind., 1970; MS in Mech. Engring., Purdue U.; Grad. Test Flight Engr., USAF Test Pilot Sch., 1976; DSc (hon.), Purdue U. Commd. 2d lt. USAF, 1970, ret., 2000; rschr. ramjet engring divsn. Air Force Aeropropulsion Lan, Wright-Patterso AFB, Ohio, 1972—74; lab. exec. officer, chief mgmt. ops. office Wright Patterson AFB Labs., Dayton, Ohio, 1974—75; flight test engr., supr. crew mem. 6510th; Flight Test Engring. USAF, Edwards AFB, Calif., 1976—79; payload officer, flight controller Lyndon Johnson Space Center, Houston, 1979—80, chief vehicle integration test office; astronaut NASA, Houston, 1980—; chief astronaut NASA Engring. and Safety Ctr. Named a Disting. Grad. of the USAF Test Pilot Sch.; recipient 13 NASA medals, Victor A. Prather award, Am. Astron. Soc., 1985, 1990, 1999, Defense Superior Svc. Medal with one Oak Leaf, Air Force Legion of Merit, Defense Meritorious Svc. Medal with 3 Oak leaf Clusters, Air Force Meritious Svc. Medal with one Oak Leaf, Outstanding Flight Test Eng. Award Class 75B. Mem.: Internat. Acad. Astronautics (corr.), Purdue Alumni Assn. (life), Assn. of Space Explorers (life). Achievements include seven space flights; over 1133 hours in space, including 58 hours, 18 minutes on nine space walks. Avocations: genealogy, stained glass, racquetball, woodworking, photography. Office: Astronaut Ctr NASA Johnson Space Ctr Houston TX 77058

ROSS, JIMMY DOUGLAS, retired military officer; b. Hosston, La., May 23, 1936; s. Horace Eugene and Lucile Marie (Pontious) R.; m. Patricia L. Cox., Dec. 18, 1955; children: Sabra, DiAnna, Tony. BS, Henderson State U., 1958; MA in Bus. Mgmt., Central Mich. U., 1975. Commd. 2d lt. U.S. Army, 1958, advanced through grades to 4 Star Gen., 1994, served comdr. co., bn., brigade levels, comdg. gen. 2d Support Command (Corps) VII Corps Nellingen, Germany, 1980-82; dir. transp., energy and troop support Office Dep. Chief of Staff for Logistics, U.S. Army, Washington, 1982-84; chief staff U.S. Army Materiel Command, Alexandria, Va., 1984-86; comdr. U.S. Army Depot System Command, Chambersburg, Pa., 1986-87; dep. chief of staff for logistics U.S. Army, Washington, 1987-92; commdg. gen. U.S. Army Materiel Command, Alexandria, Va., 1992-94; retired, 1994. Bd. dirs. VSE Engring. Co., Stanley Assoc., Inc., Armed Forces Svcs. Corp., Integrated Data Corp., Am. Ecology Corp.; chmn. Def. Industry Conf. Bd.; pres. bd. dirs. Indsl. Coll. of Armed Forces Assn.; pres., COO Cypress Internat., 2000-03; sr. logistics officer Cypress Internat., Inc., 2004. Dist. commr. Alpine dist. Boy Scouts Am., 1980-82; sr. v.p., COO Biomed. Svcs., ARC Nat. Hdqrs., 1994-99; chmn. Army Sci. Bd.; pres. Buffalo Soldiers Meml. Fund Found., 2001; bd. dirs. Buffalo Soldiers Found., 2001. Decorated D.S.M. with oak leaf cluster, Legion of Merit, Bronze Star, Air medal. Fellow Assn. U.S. Army (sr.); mem. Am. Def. Indsl. Assn., Nat. Def. Transp. Assn., Armed Forces Benefit Assn. (bd. dirs.). Methodist. Home: 4981 Maple Glen Pl Lake Forest FL 32771 Office Phone: 703-549-5880. E-mail: jross27@cfl.rr.com.

ROSS, JO ANN, media buyer; b. Bklyn., June 8, 1953; d. James Patrick and Rita Marie (McDonnell) R.; m. Michael Edward Zelman, Nov. 3, 1984. BA in Govt. and Pub. Adminstrn., Am. U., Washington, 1975. Negotiator Boxell & Jacobs, NYC, 1980-84; supr. Young & Rubicam, NYC, 1984; sr. negotiator Bozell, Jacobs, Kenyon & Eckhardt, NYC, 1984-85, v.p., 1985-88; sr. v.p. Bozell, Inc., NYC, 1988-89; account exec. ABC TV Network, NYC, 1989; v.p. Olympic sales CBS, 1992—2002, pres. network sales, 2002—. Named one of 100 Most Powerful Women in Entertainment, Hollywood Reporter, 2005, 2006; recipient Woman of Yr. award, Women in Sports and Events, 2005. Mem. Am. Assn. Advt. Agencies (broadcast and program com. 1988—). Avocations: ballet, exercise. Office: CBS 51 West 52nd St New York NY 10019 *

ROSS, JOHN, physical chemist, educator; b. Vienna, Oct. 2, 1926; arrived in U.S., 1940; s. Mark and Anna (Krcmar) Ross; m. Virginia Franklin (div.); children: Elizabeth A., Robert K.; m. Eva Madarasz. BS, Queens Coll., 1948; PhD, MIT, 1951; D (hon.), Weizmann Inst. Sci., Rehovot, Israel, 1984, Queens Coll., SUNY, 1987, U. Bordeaux, France, 1987. Prof. chemistry Brown U., Providence, 1953—66, MIT, Cambridge, 1966—80, chmn. dept., 1966—71, chmn. faculty of Inst., 1975—77; prof. Stanford (Calif.) U., 1980—2001, chmn. dept., 1983—89, prof. emeritus, 2001—. Cons. to industries; mem. emeritus bd. govs. Weizmann Inst., 1971—. Author: Physical Chemistry, 1980, 2d edit., 2000, Determination of Complex Reaction Mechanisms, 2006; editor: Molecular Beams, 1966; contbr. articles to profl. jours. 2nd lt. US Army, 1944—46. Recipient medal, Coll. de France, Paris, Presdl. Nat. Medal of Sci., 1999, Austrian Cross of Honor for Sci. and Art, 1st class, 2002. Fellow: AAAS, Am. Phys. Soc.; mem.: NAS, Am. Chem. Soc. (Irving Langmuir Chem. Physics prize 1992, Peter Debye award in phys. chemistry 2001, Theodore William Richards medal 2004), Am. Acad. Arts and Sci. Office: Stanford U Dept Chemistry Stanford CA 94305-5080 Home Phone: 650-858-2203; Office Phone: 650-723-9203. Business E-Mail: john.ross@stanford.edu.

ROSS, JOHN, JR., cardiologist, educator; b. NYC, Dec. 1, 1928; s. John and Janet (Moulder) R.; children: Sydnie, John, Duncan; m. Lola Romanucci, Aug. 26, 1972; children: Adan, Deborah Lee. AB, Dartmouth Coll., 1951; MD, Cornell U., 1955. Intern Johns Hopkins Hosp., 1955—56; resident Columbia-Presbyn. Med. Center, NYC, 1960—61, NY. Hosp.-Cornell U. Med. center, 1961—62; chief sect. cardiovascular diagnosis cardiology br. Nat. Heart Inst., Bethesda, Md., 1962—68; prof. medicine U. Calif., San Diego, 1968—2000, also dir. cardiovascular div., 1968—91, rsch. prof. medicine, 2000—, disting. prof. medicine, 2003—; prof. cardiovascular research Am. Heart Assn. Western States Affiliate, 1984—99. Mem. cardiology adv. com. Nat. Heart, Lung and Blood Inst., 1975-78, task force on arteriosclerosis, 1978-80, adv. council, 1980-84; bd. dirs. San Diego Heart Assn.; vis. prof. Brit. Heart Assn., 1990. Author: Mechanisms of Contraction of the Normal and Failing Heart, 1968, 76, Understanding the Heart and Its Diseases, 1976; mem. editorial bd. Circulation, 1967-75, 80-88, editor in chief 1988-93, Circulation Research, 1971-75, Am. Jour. Physiology, 1968-73, Annals of Internal Medicine, 1974-78, Am. Jour. Cardiology, 1974-79, 83-88, Jour. Clin. Investigation, 1992-97, Italian Heart Jour., 1998-99, Jour. Cardiac Failure, 2000-05, Circulation Jour. Japan, 2000—; cons. editor Circulation, 1993-03; contbr. chpts. to books, sci. articles to profl. jours. Served as surgeon USPHS, 1956—63. Decorated grande ufficiale Order of Merit of Republic of Italy, 1998; recipient Ing. Enzo Ferrari prize for Enzo Ferrari, Modena, Italy, 1989, James B. Herrick award Coun. Clin. Cardiology Am. Heart Assn., 1990, Academic Mentorship award Am. Heart Assn., 2004. Master Am. Coll. Cardiology (v.p. trustee, pres. 1986-87, Disting. Scientist award 1990); fellow ACP; mem. Am. Soc. Clin. Investigation (councillor), Am. Physiol. Soc., Assn. Am. Physicians, Cardiac Muscle Soc., Assn. Univ. Cardiologists, Assn. West. Physicians (councillor), Japanese Circulation Soc. (hon.). Achievements include development of and application of transseptal left heart catherization for the diagnosis of heart disease; conceptualized "afterload mismatch" in the left ventricle of the heart and its application in the diagnosis and treatment of valvular heart disease and heart failure; demonstrated experimentally that reperfusion of a coronary artery after prolonged occlusion salvages heart muscle and partially restores heart function. Home: 8599 Prestwick Dr La Jolla CA 92037 Office: U Calif Dept Med M # 0613B San Diego CA 92093

ROSS, JOHN T., artist, educator; b. NYC, Sept. 25, 1921; s. Ferdinand Joseph and Mary Agnes (Higgins) R.; m. Clare Romano; children: Christopher, Timothy. Student, Cooper Union Art Sch., 1939-48, BFA, 1975. Art dir. Pageant Mag., NYC, 1946-48; mem. faculty New Sch. for Social Rsch., NYC, 1957—; prof., chmn. dept. art Manhattanville Coll., Purchase, NY, 1964-86. Adj. prof. Yale U., New Haven, 1982; adj. faculty Columbia U., N.Y.C., 1983-85; art dir. Aquarius Press, N.Y.C., 1968-72; chmn. bd. Ctr. for Book Arts, N.Y.C., 1995-99; bd. dirs. Art Ctr. No. N.J., Englewood, 1966-67; fgn. svc. staff officer USIA, Romania and Yugoslavia, 1964-66. Writer-illustrator: (with Clare Romano) Complete Printmaker, 1972 (rev. 90), John Ross and Clare Romano: The Artists and the Book, 2001; exhibited works in 70 one-man shows at various galleries, 1950—; pub. artists books, 1971—; printmaker, artist-designer, 1950—; dir. High Tide Press, N.Y.C., 1991—. Chmn. adv. panel Cooper Union Art Sch., N.Y.C., 1967-69. Sgt. U.S. Army, 1943-46, Italy. Recipient Citation for profl. achievement Cooper Union Art Sch., 1966, Benjamin Clinedinst medal Artists Fellowship, 1992, others; Tiffany Found. grantee, 1954, McDowell Colony fellow, 1978, 82, 87. Mem. NAD, Century Assn. N.Y.C., Soc. Am. Graphic Artists (pres.), Ctr. for Book Arts N.Y.C., Typophiles N.Y.C., Grolier Club. Avocation: swimming. Home Phone: 212-533-5109. Personal E-mail: rossromano@earthlink.net.

ROSS, JOSEPH COMER, pulmonologist, educator, academic administrator; b. Tompkinsville, Ky., June 16, 1927; s. Joseph M. and Annie (Pinckley) R.; m. Isabelle Nevins, June 15, 1952; children: Laura Ann, Sharon Lynn, Jennifer Jo, Mary Martha, Jefferson Arthur. BS, U. Ky., 1950; MD, Vanderbilt U., 1954. Diplomate Am. Bd. Internal Medicine (bd. govs. 1975-81), with added qualifications in pulmonary disease. Intern Vanderbilt U. Hosp., Nashville, 1954-55; resident Duke U. Hosp., Durham, NC, 1955-57, rsch. fellow, 1957-58; from instr. medicine to prof. Ind. U. Sch. Medicine, Indpls., 1958-70; prof., chmn. dept. medicine Med. U. of S.C., Charleston, 1970-80; vis. prof. Vanderbilt U. Sch. Medicine, Nashville, 1979-80, prof. medicine, 1981-99, prof. medicine emeritus, 1999—, assoc. vice chancellor for health affairs, 1982-99, assoc. vice chancellor for health affairs emeritus, 1999—. Mem. cardiovascular study sect. NIH, 1966-70, program project com., 1971-75; mem. adv. coun. Nat. Heart, Lung and Blood Inst., 1982-86; mem. ad hoc coms. NAS, 1966, 67; mem. Pres.'s Nat. Adv. Panel on Heart Disease, 1972; mem. merit rev. bd. in respiration VA Rsch. Svc., 1972-76, chmn., 1974-76. Mem. editorial bd. Jour. Lab. and Clin. Medicine, 1964-70, Chest, 1968-73, Jour. Applied Physiology,1968-73, Archives of Internal Medicine, 1976-82, Heart and Lung, 1977-86; contbr. articles to profl. jours. Bd. dirs. Nashville Ronald McDonald Ho., past pres.; bd. dirs. Agape, Leadership Nashville, v.p.; mem. adv. com. Davidson County Cmty. Health Agy.; active Tenn. Lung Assn.; elder Ch. of Christ. With US Army, 1945—47. Fellow: ACP, Am. Coll. Cardiology, Am. Coll. Chest Physicians (gov. S.C. 1970—76, chmn. sci. program com. 1973, vice chmn. bd. govs. 1974—75, exec. coun. 1974—80, chmn. bd. govs. 1975—76, pres.-elect 1976—77, pres. 1977—78, chmn. by-laws com. 2002—04, bd. regents 2002—04); mem.: AMA (sect. on med. schs.), Am. Soc. Internal Medicine, So. Soc. Clin. Rsch., Am. Thoracic Soc. (nat. councillor 1972—76), S.C. Med. Soc., Ctr. Social Clin. Rsch., Assn. Profs. Medicine, Assn. Am. Physicians, Am. Soc. Clin. Investigatrion, Am. Physiol. Soc., Am. Fedn. Clin. Rsch. (chmn. Midwest sect.), S.C. Lung Assn. (v.p. 1974—75), Phi Beta Kappa, Alpha Omega Alpha. Office: Vanderbilt U Med Ctr Oxford House Ste 212 Nashville TN 37232-0001 Personal E-mail: joseph.ross@comcast.net.

ROSS, JUNE ROSA PITT, biologist, educator; b. Taree, NSW, Australia, May 2, 1931; came to U.S., 1957; d. Bernard and Adeline Phillips; m. Charles Alexander, June 27, 1959. BSc with honors, U. Sydney, New S. Wales, Australia, 1953, PhD, 1959, DSc, 1974. Rsch. assoc. Yale U., New Haven, 1959—60, U. Ill., Urbana, 1960—65, Western Wash. U., Bellingham, 1965—67, assoc. prof., 1967—70, prof. biology, 1970—2003, prof. emeritus, 2004—, chair dept. biology, 1989—90. Pres. Western Wash. U. Faculty Senate, Bellingham, 1984-85; conf. host Internat. Bryozoology Assn., 1986. Author (with others): A Textbook of Entomology, 1982, Geology of Coal, 1984; editor (assoc.): Palaios, 1985—89; contbr. 155 articles to profl. jours. Recipient J. Wolfensohn Award of Excellence Sydney U. Grad. Union of N.Am., 1995, P. and R. Olscamp Outstanding Rsch. award Western Wash. U., 1986; NSF grantee. Mem.: Internat. Bryozoology Assn. (pres. 1992—95), The Paleontol. Soc. (councillor 1984—86, treas. 1987—93), Australian Marine Scis. Assn., U.K. Marine Biol. Assn. (life). Avocations: hiking, classical music. Office: Western Wash U Dept Biology Bellingham WA 98225-9160 Office Phone: 360-650-3634. E-mail: ross@fire.biol.wwu.edu.

ROSS, KATHLEEN ANNE, academic administrator; b. Palo Alto, Calif., July 1, 1941; d. William Andrew and Mary Alberta (Wilburn) Ross. BA, Ft. Wright Coll., 1964; MA, Georgetown U., 1971; PhD, Claremont Grad. U., 1979; LLD (hon.), Alverno Coll. Milw., 1990, Dartmouth Coll., 1991, Seattle U., 1992, Pomona Coll., 1993, U. Notre Dame, 1999, Gonzaga U., 1999; LHD (hon.), Whitworth Coll., 1992, Coll. New Rochelle, 1998, Carroll Coll., 2003, Pacific Luth. U., 2004, U. Portland, Oreg., 2006. Cert. tchr. Wash. Secondary tchr. Holy Names Acad., Spokane, Wash., 1964-70; dir. rsch. and planning Province Holy Names, Wash. State, 1972-73; v.p. acads. Ft. Wright Coll., Spokane, 1973-81; rsch. asst. to dean Claremont Grad. Sch., Calif., 1977-78; assoc. faculty mem. Harvard U., Cambridge, Mass., 1981; pres. Heritage U., Toppenish, Wash., 1981—. Cons. Wash. State Holy Names Schs., 1971-73; coll. accrediting assn. evaluator N.W. Assn. Schs. and Colls., Seattle, 1975—; dir. Holy Names Coll., Oakland, Calif., 1979—; cons. Yakama Indian Nation, Toppenish, 1975—; speaker, cons. in field. Author: (with others) Multicultural Pre-School Curriculum, 1977, A Crucial Agenda: Improving Minority Student Success, 1989; Cultural Factors in Success of American Indian Students in Higher Education, 1978. Chmn. Internat. 5-Yr. Convocation of Sisters of Holy Names, Montreal, 1981, 96; TV Talk show host Spokane Coun. of Chs., 1974-76; mem. Nat. Congl. Adv. Com. on Student Fin. Assistance, 2002-06. Named Yakima Herald Rep. Person of Yr., 1987, MacArthur fellow, 1997; recipient E.K. and Lillian F. Bishop Founds. Youth Leader of Yr. award, 1986, Disting. Citizenship Alumna award, Claremont Grad. Sch., 1986, Golden Aztec award, Wash. Human Devel., 1989, Harold W. McGraw Edn. prize, 1989, John Carroll awrd, Georgetown U., 1991, Holy Names medal, Ft. Wright Coll., 1981, Pres.'s medal, Estern Wash. U., 1994, First Ann. Leadership award, Region VIII Coun. Advancement and Support Edn., 1993, Wash. State Medal of Merit, 1995, Lifetime Achievement award, Yakima YWCA, 2001, numerous grants for projects in multicultural higher edn., 1974—. Mem. Nat. Assn. Ind. Colls. and Univs., Soc. Intercultural Edn., Tng. and Rsch., Sisters of Holy Names of Jesus and Mary-SNJM. Roman Catholic. Office: Heritage U Office of Pres 3240 Fort Rd Toppenish WA 98948-9562 Office Phone: 509-865-8600.

ROSS, KEVIN MCANDREW, academic administrator; m. Kristen Carr Ross; children: Ainsley, Graham. AB, Colgate U., 1994; MA in Liberal Arts, St. John's Coll., 1997; PhD in Higher Edn. Leadership and Policy, Vanderbilt U. Admissions officer, assoc. dir. admissions The Hill Sch., Pottstown, Pa., Avon Old Farms Sch., Conn.; asst. to pres. Wilmington Coll., Del.; assoc. dean Eugene M. and Christine E. Lynn Coll. Internat. Comm. Lynn U., Boca Raton, Fla., 1999, COO, 2004—06, pres., 2006—. Bd. dirs. Palm Beach Literacy Coalition. Office: Lynn U Office of Pres 3601 N Military Trail Boca Raton FL 33431 E-mail: kross@lynn.edu.

ROSS, LEONARD LESTER, retired academic administrator; b. NYC, Sept. 11, 1927; s. Aaron Theodore and Shirley (Smolen) R.; m. Marcella Gamel, June 23, 1951 (dec. Aug. 1995); children: Jane, Jill; m. Frances Robb, Nov. 12, 1998; 1 chld, Jennifer. AB, NYU, 1946, PhD, 1954. Asst. prof. U. Ala. Med. Coll., 1954-57; assoc. prof. Cornell U. Med. Coll., 1957-69, prof., 1969-73; vis. prof. Cambridge U., 1967-68; prof., chmn. dept. anatomy Med. Coll. Pa., Phila., 1973-89, exec. v.p., Annenberg dean, 1989-93, pres. and Annenberg dean, 1993-94, provost and Annenberg dean Phila., 1993-96; provost Allegheny U., Phila., 1996-98. Exec. v.p. Allegheny Health, Edn. and Rsch. Found. Assoc. editor: Anat. Record, 1976. Served with M.C., U.S. Army, 1946-47. Recipient Lindback award for teaching, 1976; NIH sr. research fellow, 1967-68 Mem. Am. Assn. Anatomists (exec. com. 1984-88), Soc. Neurosci., Soc. Cell Biology, N.Y. Soc. Electron Microscopists (pres. 1975-76), Assn. Anatomy Chairmen (pres. 1983-84), AAUP (nat. council 1974-77), Sigma Xi.

ROSS, LESA MOORE, quality assurance professional; b. New Orleans, Jan. 25, 1959; d. William Frank and Carolyn West Moore; m. Mark Neal Ross, Nov. 30, 1985; children: Sarah Ann, Jacquelyne Caroline. BS in Engring., U. N.C., Charlotte, 1981; MBA in Quality and Reliability Mgmt., U. North Tex., 1991; MS in Reliability Engring., U. Md., 2004. Seismic qualification engr. Duke Power Co., Charlotte, N.C., 1981-82; quality assurance engr. Tex. Instruments Inc., Lewisville, Tex., 1982-91; compliance mgr. Am. Med. Electronics, Inc., 1992-93; owner Ross Quality Cons., 1993-95; customer quality assurance sect. mgr. Hitachi Semiconductor (Am.) Inc., 1995-96; v.p. quality Ross Networking Cons. Inc., Flower Mound, Tex., 1996—. Bd. dirs. Greater Lewisville YMCA, 2000—03. Recipient Nat. Sci. Found. Rsch. Grant, U. N.C., Charlotte, 1980. Mem. Am. Soc. Quality Control (cert. quality engr., quality auditor, reliability engr., cert. quality technician, cert. quality mgr., sec. Dallas sect. 1994-95, chair-elect Dallas sect. 1995-96, chair 1996-97), Zeta Tau Alpha (pres. 1984-85). Avocations: crafts, cross-stitching, reading, travel. Home and Office: 4925 Wolf Creek Trl Flower Mound TX 75028-1955 E-mail: Lross@rnc-inc.com.

ROSS, LEVI ANDRE, public health educator; b. Phila., Oct. 5, 1968; s. Yvonne Diane Ross; 1 child, Cassandra. BA, U. West Fla., Pensacola, 1997; MPH, U. Ala., Birmingham, 2000, PhD, 2004. Cert. health edn. specialist Nat. Commn. Health Edn. Credentialing, 2004. Cryptographer USN, 1986—93; sci. data mgr. TRW, Atlanta, 2000—01; instr. U. Ala. Birmingham, Sch. Edn., 2003—04; asst. prof. Fla. A&M U., Inst. Pub. Health, Tallahassee, 2006—. Cryptographer U.S. Navy, 1986—93; manuscript reviewer Health Edn. and Behavior, Ann Arbor, Mich. Contbr. articles to profl. jours. Behavioral and social sci. vol. APA, Washington; faculty advisor Future Pub. Health Profls., Tallahassee. Talented Undergrad. Women and Minority Rsch. fellow, U. Tenn., Knoxville, 1993, Ronald McNair Summer Rsch. fellow, 1997, Comprehensive Minority Faculty Devel. Grad. fellow, U. Ala. Birmingham, 1997—2000, Predoctoral Cancer Prevention and Control Tng. fellow, Nat. Cancer Inst., 2001—04, Prevention Rsch. Ednl. Postdoctoral (PREP) Tng. Program fellow, 2004—05, Cancer Info. Svc. grantee, 2007—, Rsch. Devel. grantee, Nat. Cancer Inst./Deep South Network Cancer Control, 2002—03, Genetic Health Edn. Curriculum Devel. grantee, APA, 2006—07, Faculty Devel. grantee, Ctr. for Healthy Options and Innovative Cmty. Empowerment, 2006—07. Mem.: APHA, Soc. Pub. Health Edn., Am. Assn. Cancer Edn. (R. Davilene Carter Presdl. prize 2005, 2006), Soc. Behavioral Medicine, Phi Theta Kappa, Golden Key. Home: 2712 Keator St Tallahassee FL 32310-5110 Office: Florida A&M U 203-B FSH Sci Rsch Ctr Tallahassee FL 32307 Home Phone: 850-575-9889; Office Phone: 850-412-5494. Office Fax: 850-599-8830; Home Fax: 850-599-8830. E-mail: levi.ross@famu.edu.

ROSS, LORI A., lawyer; b. Cin., Apr. 14, 1975; BA in Psych., Miami U., 1997, BA in Sociology, 1997; JD, U. Cin., 2000. Bar: Ohio 2000, US Dist. Ct. Southern Dist. Ohio 2000, Ky. 2001. Assoc. Strauss & Troy, Cin. Named one of Ohio's Rising Stars, Super Lawyers, 2006. Mem.: Ohio State Bar Assn., Ky. Bar Assn., Cin. Bar Assn., Order of Coif, Phi Beta Kappa, Phi Kappa Phi. Office: Strauss & Troy Federal Reserve Bldg 150 E Fourth St Cincinnati OH 45202-4018 Office Phone: 513-621-2120. Office Fax: 513-241-8259.

ROSS, MADELYN ANN, academic administrator, newspaper editor; b. Pitts., June 26, 1949; d. Mario Charles and Rose Marie (Mangieri) R. BA, Indiana U. of Pa., 1971; MA, SUNY-Albany, 1972. Reporter Pitts. Press, 1972-78, asst. city editor, 1978-82, spl. assignment editor, 1982-83, mng. editor, 1983-93, Pitts. Post-Gazette, 1993—2005; assoc. vice chancellor U. Pitts., 2005—. Bd. dirs. PG Pub. Co.; instr. Community Coll. Allegheny County, 1974-81; Pulitzer Prize juror, 1989, 90. Mem. Task Force Leadership Pitts., 1985-92; v.p. Old Newsboys Charity Fund; bd. dirs. Dapper Dan Charity. Mem. Am. Soc. Newspaper Editors, Press Club of Western Pa. (pres.), Internat. Women's Forum. Democrat. Roman Catholic. Avocations: tennis, piano, organ. Office: U Pitts 424 Craig Hall Craig St Pittsburgh PA 15260

ROSS, MALCOLM, minerals consultant; b. Washington, Aug. 22, 1929; s. Clarence Samuel and Helen Hall (Frederick) R.; m. Daphne Dee Virginia Riska, Sept. 1, 1956; children: Christopher A., Alexander MacC. BS in Zoology, Utah State U., 1951; MS in Chemistry, U. Md., 1959; PhD in Geology, Harvard U., 1962. Rsch. mineralogist U.S. Geol. Survey, Washington, 1954-5, 61-74, Reston, Va., 1974-95, scientist emeritus, 1996—; minerals and health cons., 1999—. Prin. investigator lunar sci. program NASA, 1969—74. Author: Asbestos and Other Fibrous Minerals, 1988; contbr. over 100 articles to profl. jours. First lt. US Army, 1952—54. Recipient Disting. Svc. award, U.S. Dept. Interior, 1986; grantee Fulbright Commn., Cyprus, 2000. Fellow Mineral. Soc. Am., Geol. Soc. Am., AAAS; mem. Am. Geophys. Union, Clay Minerals Soc., Can. Mineral Assn., Mineral Soc. Am. (bd. dirs. treas. 1976-80, v.p. 1990, pres. 1991, Pub. Svc. award, 1990). Republican. Congregationalist. Achievements include research in on asbestos and asbestos-related disease. Avocations: long distance bicycling, photography. Home: 1608 44th St NW Washington DC 20007-2025 Home Phone: 202-338-6572; Office Phone: 202-338-6572. E-mail: mrdrr@earthlink.net.

ROSS, MARILYN J., language and communications educator; BA in Am. Studies, U. Miami, Fla., 1969, MA in Am. Studies, 1971, PhD in Higher Edn. Leadership, 1995. Asst. prof. English Fla. Meml. Coll., 1971-84, assoc. prof. English and mass comm. arts, 1985-94, prof. higher edn., 1995—. Founder mass comm. arts program Fla. Meml. Coll., 1980, coord. modern langs., 1999—; presenter Round Table Oxford U., Eng., 2005, others. Author: Success Factors of Young African American Males at a Historically Black College, 1998, Success Factors of Young African American Women at a Historically Black College, 2002; prodr. over 100 hrs. African Am., Caribbean and Hispanic programming, WLRN-TV. Recipient Outstanding Svc. award Vets. Club, 1979, Outstanding and Dedicated Svc. in Behalf of FMC award Miami Cable Access Corp., 1987, award Fla. Meml. Coll./Black Archives History and Rsch. Found. of South Fla., Inc., 1999. Mem. MLA, AAUW, Assn. Ednl. Leadership, Nat. Coun. Tchrs. English, Nat. Assn. African Am. Studies, Am. Studies Aassn., Epsilon Tau Lambda, Kappa Delta Pi, Phi Lambda Pi, Delta Theta Mu, Phi Kappa Phi, Phi Alpha Theta. Address: Unit F-602 1121 Crandon Blvd Apt F602 Key Biscayne FL 33149-2781 E-mail: ross1848@bellsouth.net.

ROSS, MARION, actress; b. Albert Lea, Minn. children: Jim, Ellen. Grad., San Diego State U. Performed with Globe Theatre, San Diego, LaJolla Summer Theatre; Broadway debut in Edwin Booth; starred in touring prodns. of Never Too Late, Barefoot in the Park, The Glass Menagerie, Long Days Journey Into Night, Love Letter, Steel Magnolias, Over The River and Through The Woods, Barefoot in the Park, film debut in Forever Female, 1953; on woman show A Lovely Light, 1988—; TV series include Life with Father, 1953-55, Paradise Bay, 1965-66, Happy Days, 1974-84, Love Boat, 1985-86 (2 Emmy nominations), Bklyn. Bridge, 1991-93 (Emmy nomination for lead actress in a comedy 1992, 93), Hidden in Silence, 1995, Evening Star, 1996, The Great War, 1996, The Third Twin, 1997, About Search, 1998, The Lake, 1998, Drew Carey Show, 1998, That 70's Show, 1998, Touched By an Angel, 1999 (Emmy nomination 1999), The Ladies and the Champ, 2001, The Gilmore Girls, A Family of Strangers, Brothers & Sisters; voice of Sponge Bob's grandmother. Office: Dale Olson & Assocs 7420 Mulholland Dr Los Angeles CA 90046-1306 Office Phone: 323-876-9331.

ROSS, MARK SAMUEL, lawyer, educator, funeral director, writer; b. Newark, June 6, 1957; s. Herbert and Selma Ruth (Feldman) R.; m. Robin Liebman, May 19, 1984; children: Adam Micah, Danielle Leah. BA with honors, Rutgers U., 1979; JD, Benjamin Cardozo Law Sch., 1982; diploma, McAllister Inst. Funeral Svc., 1983. Bar: NJ 1983, US Dist. Ct. NJ 1983, NY 1989. V.p. Art/Craft Monuments-Shalom Memls., Union, NJ, 1980—2005; sec., treas., counsel Menorah Chapels at Millburn, Union, NJ, 1983—, funeral dir., 1983; atty. pvt. practice, Union, NJ, 1983—. Counsel Com. for Consumer Protection, Union, 1985—; adj. prof. law Am. Acad.-McAllister Inst., NYC, 1984-85; instr. Jewish law Emanu-El Religious Sch., Westfield, NJ, 1985. Author: (newspaper column) Through My Father's Eyes, 1995—. V.p. Temple Beth Am, Springfield, NJ, 1986-92, pres., 1992-94; counsel Found. Jewish Arts and Heritage, Inc., Union, 1986—; sec. United Synagogue of Conservative Judaism, NJ Region, 2007-. Named Man of Yr., Springfield B'nai B'rith, 1995, Temple Beth Ahm, Springfield, 2001; recipient Internat. Cmty. Svc. award, B'nai B'rith Internat., 1995. Mem. NJ Bar Assn., Union County Bar Assn., B'nai B'rith (pres. 1980-83, Nat. Founders award 1982). Avocations: art, music, photography, golf. Office: 2950 Vauxhall Rd Vauxhall NJ 07088-1246 also: PO Box 641 Millburn NJ 07041-0641 Office Phone: 908-686-4844. Business E-Mail: RØsslaw@cs.com.

ROSS, MATHEW, medical educator; b. Boston, July 29, 1917; s. Abraham and Frances (Lampke) R.; m. Brenda Boynton, Dec. 24, 1946; children: Douglas Ross, Gail Ross, Craig Ross, Bruce Ross. BS, Tufts U., Medford, Mass., 1938, MD, 1942. Diplomate Am. Bd. Psychiatry and Neurology. Intern Kings County Hosp., NYC, 1942-43; resident VA Med. Ctr., LA, 1946-48, L.A. Psychoanalytic Inst., 1949-53; prof. Sch. Medicine UCLA, 1953-58, George Washington U., Washington, 1958-73; psychiat. adminstrn. U. Chgo., 1959; prof. Sch. Medicine Harvard U., Boston, 1963-73, Brown U., Providence, 1964-65, R.I. U., Providence, 1964-65, U. Calif., Irvine, 1974—; fellow Sch. Alcoholism U. Utah, 1977. Fulbright prof., rsch. scholar U. Gronigen and U. Amsterdam, The Netherlands, 1962-63; med. dir. Am. Psychiat. Assn., Washington, 1958-62. Editor: Newsletter Am. Psychiat. Assn., 1958-62, Mental Hosp. & Community Psychiatry, 1958-62, PDE Scientific Journal, 1975-90. Sr. legislator State of Calif., 1985-86, sr. senator, 2002-2004; mem. Newport Beach (Calif.) Arts Commn., 1989-95; pres. Med. Soc. of Leisure World, 2000—. Maj. U.S. Army, 1943-46, ETO. Fellow ACP (life), Am. Psychiat. Assn. (life), Am. Assn. Psychoanalysts, Am. Pub. Health Assn., So. Calif. Psychiat. Soc. (founding pres. 1953-60); hon. fellow Australia-New Zealand Royal Coll. Psychiatrists; mem. Soc. Med. Cons. to Armed Svcs. Home: Unit 1162 24055 Paseo Del Lago Laguna Woods CA 92637-2675 Office Phone: 949-462-0232. E-mail: matross@att.net.

ROSS, MATHEW P., lawyer; b. NYC, Aug. 2, 1964; BA, Syracuse U., 1986; JD, We. New England Coll., 1990. Bar: NY 1991, US Ct. Mil. Appeals 1991, US Dist. Ct. So. Dist. NY 1995, US Dist. Ct. Ea. Dist. NY 1995, US Dist. Ct. No. Dist. NY 2004. Ptnr. Wilson, Elser, Moskowitz, Edelman & Dicker LLP, NYC. Capt. Judge Adv. Gen.'s Corps, 1991—94, Fort Eustis, Va. Mem.: Xavier Bar Assn., NY State Bar Assn. Office: Wilson Elser Moskowitz Edelman & Dicker LLP 23rd Fl 150 E 42nd St New York NY 10017-5639 Office Phone: 212-490-3000 ext. 2287. Office Fax: 212-490-3038. Business E-Mail: rossm@wemed.com.

ROSS, MATTHEW, lawyer; b. NYC, Dec. 28, 1953; s. Harvey and Cecile (Shelsky) R.; m. Susan Ruth Goldfarb, Apr. 20, 1986; children: Melissa Danielle, Henry Max, Thomas Frank. BS in Econs., U. Pa., Phila., 1975; JD, U. Va., Charlottesville, 1978. Bar: NY 1979, US Dist. Ct. (so. dist.) NY 1979. Assoc. Cravath, Swaine & Moore, NYC, 1978-84; prin., assoc. gen. counsel KPMG LLP, NYC, 1984-90; prin., deputy gen. counsel Deloitte & Touche USA LLP, NYC, 1990—. Mem. ABA (corp. law sect.), NY State Bar Assn. (corp. banking and bus. law sect.), Assn. Bar of City of NY (corp. law com.), Beta Gamma Sigma. Avocations: basketball, golf, tennis, skiing. Home: 5 Barker Ln Scarsdale NY 10583-7507 Office: Deloitte & Touche USA LLP 1633 Broadway New York NY 10019-6708 Office Phone: 212-492-3898. Business E-Mail: mross@deloitte.com.

ROSS, MATTHEW ALAN, real estate company executive; AB, Harvard U., 1984, JD, MBA, 1989. Ptnr. Hall Properties, Inc., Boston, 1989-98; pres. ValueRealty, Inc., Cambridge, 1998—. Office: Ste 200N 124 Mt Auburn St Cambridge MA 02138-5787

ROSS, MICHAEL AARON, lawyer; b. Newark, Sept. 15, 1941; s. Alexander Ash and Matilda (Blumenthal) R.; m. Leslie Gordon, June 26, 1976; children: Christopher Gordon, Alan Gordon. BA, Franklin and Marshall Coll., 1963; JD, Columbia U., 1966; MS in Internat. Law, U. London, 1967. Bar: N.Y. 1968. Assoc., then ptnr. Shearman & Sterling, NYC, 1967-93; dep. gen. counsel Citigroup, NYC, 1993—2001; gen. counsel Citibank, NYC, 1998—2003, Citigroup Internat., 2002—03; counsel Wilmer Cutler Pickering Hale and Dorr LLP, NYC, 2004—05; with Blaqwell Legal Consulting, NYC, 2006—. Mem. ABA, N.Y. State Bar Assn., Am. Law Inst., New York County Lawyers Assn., Assn. Bar City of N.Y., Univ. Club. Home Phone: 212-724-3839; Office Phone: 646-746-8083. Personal E-mail: mikeaross262@yahoo.com. Business E-Mail: michael.ross@blaqwell.com.

ROSS, MICHAEL WALLIS, public health educator; b. Palmerston North, New Zealand, Nov. 17, 1951; arrived in U.S., 1993; s. Wallis Malcolm and Lois Verrell (Stewart) R. BA with honors, Massey U., New Zealand, 1974; BS in Sociology, SUNY, 1976; MA in Social-Clin. Psychology, Victoria U. Wellington, New Zealand, 1975; diploma in Tertiary Edn., U. New Eng., Australia, 1984; PhD, U. Melbourne, Australia, 1980; MPH, U. Adelaide, Australia, 1989; M in Health Pers. Edn., U. NSW, Australia, 1991; diploma in STDs, Prince of Songkla U., Thailand, 1992, diploma in Applied Criminology, 2003; MSt in Criminology, U. Cambridge, 2004; DrMedSc, U. Malmö, Sweden, 2006. Mem. Secular Franciscan Order. Postdoctoral fellow U. Helsinki, Finland, 1979; sr. demonstrator psychiatry Flinders U., Adelaide, 1979-85; dir. STD/HIV Epidemiology and Rsch. South Australian Health Commn., Adelaide, 1985-89; assoc. prof. Sch. Cmty. Medicine U. NSW, Sydney, 1989-93; prof. Sch. Pub. Health, U. Tex., Houston, 1993—. Bd. dirs. Kolbe House, Houston, 1994-2005; chmn. bd. Saving Lives Through Alternate Options, Houston, 2000-. Author: The Married Homosexual Man: A Psychological Study, 1983, Psychovenereology: Personality and Lifestyle Factors in Sexually Transmitted Diseases in Homosexual Men, 1986; (with L.C. Channon-Little) Discussing Sexuality: A Guide for Health Practitioners, 1991; (with L.A. Lewis) A Select Body: The Gay Dance Party Subculture and the HIV/AIDS Pandemic, 1995; (with L. Nilsson Schönnesson) Coping With HIV Infection: Psychological and Existential Responses in Gay Men, 1999; (with L.C. Channon-Little and B.R.S. Rosser) Sexual Health Concerns: Interviewing and History Taking for Health Practitioners, 1999; editor: Homosexuality and Social Sex Roles, 1983, Homosexuality, Masculinity and Femininity, 1985, The Treatment of Homosexuals with Mental Health Disorders, 1988, Psychopathology and Psychotherapy in Homosexuality, HIV/AIDS and Sexuality, 1995; (with W.A.W. Walters) Transsexualism and Sex Reassignment, 1986; (with L. Bennett and D. Miller) Health Workers and AIDS: Rsch., Intervention and Current Issues in Burnout and Response, 1995; co-sci. editor: Surgeon-General's Call to Action on Sexual Health and Responsible Sexual Behavior, 2001; contbr. articles to profl. jour. Recipient U.S. Surgeon Gen.'s Exemplary Svc. award, 2002, Kinsey award, 2003. Fellow APA, Brit. Psychol. Soc., Royal Soc. Health, Royal Inst. Pub. Health and Hygiene, Royal Soc. Arts, New Zealand Psychol. Soc., Soc. for the Sci. Study of Sexuality (pres. 2000-01, Disting. Sci. Achievement award 2005), Soc. Antiquaries Scotland. Roman Catholic. Avocations: aerobatic flying, reading. Home: 401 Anita St Apt 34 Houston TX 77006-3434 Office: Sch Pub Health U Tex PO Box 20036 Houston TX 77225-0186 Office Phone: 713-500-9652. Business E-Mail: michael.w.ross@uth.tmc.edu.

ROSS, MIKE, congressman; b. Texarkana, Ark., Aug. 2, 1961; m. Holly Ross; children: Sydney, Alex. BA in Political Sci., U. Ark., 1987. Owner Holly's Health Mart and Home Med. Epuipment; area mgr. Fox Meyer Drug Co.; chief of staff to Lt Gov. of Ark., 1985—89; mem. Ark. Senate, 1990-2001, chair children and youth com.; mem. US Congress from 4th Ark. dist., Washington, 2001—; mem. com. on Energy and Commerce US Ho. Reps. Democrat. Methodist. Office: US Ho Reps 314 Cannon Ho Office Bldg Washington DC 20515-0404 *

ROSS, MOLLY OWINGS, small business owner, sculptor; b. Ft. Worth, Feb. 5, 1954; d. James Robertson and Lucy (Owings) R. BFA, Colo. State U., 1976; postgrad., U. Denver, 1978-79. Graphic designer Amber Sky Illustrators and Sta. KCNC TV, Denver, 1977—79; art dir. Mercy Med. Ctr., Denver, 1979-83, Molly Ross Design, Denver, 1983-84; co-owner Deltex Royalty Co., Inc., Castle Rock, Colo., 1981—, pres., 2007—; co-owner LMA Royalties, Ltd., Castle Rock, 1993—2007; pres. LMA Royalties Ltd., 2007—; art dir., account mgr. Schwing/Walsh Advt., Mktg. and Pub. Rels., Denver, 1984-87, prodn. mgr., 1987-88; jewelry designer Molly O. Ross, Gold and Silversmith, Denver, 1988—2002. Coun. mem. feminization of poverty critical needs area coun. Jr. League Denver, 1989—90, chmn. children in crisis/edn. critical needs area, 1990—91, chmn. project devel., 1991—92, co-chmn. Done in a Day Cmty. Project 75th Anniversary Celebration, 1991—93, bd. dirs., 1993—94, co-chmn. project IMPACT, 1994—95, exec. v.p. external affairs, 1995—96, co-chmn. cmty. coalitions com., 1996—98; mem. steering com. Denver Urban Resources Partnership, 1995—2002, steering com. chmn., 1996—99; pres.-elect Jr. League Denver, 1989—99, pres., 1999—2000; steering com. Internat. Conf. on Vol. Adminstrn., 2001—02; bd. dirs. Environ. Def. Regional Adv. Bd., 2003—06; nat. adv. bd. Am. Farmland Trust, 2005—; mem. Rachel's Network, 2005—; bd. trustees Am. Solar Energy Soc., 2006—; bd. dirs. ArtReach, 2001—; pres. Four Mile Hist. Pk. Vol. Bd., 1985—86; bd. dirs. Four Mile Hist. Pk. Assn., 1985—86, Hist. Denver, Inc., 1986—87, Denver Emergency Housing Coalition, 1989—90; co-founder, bd. dirs. Ctr. Ethics and Social Responsibility/PREP, 1994—2001, pres. bd. dirs., 1997—99, treas. bd. dirs., 1999—2000; bd. dirs. Jr. League Denver Found., 1998—2002, Friends of Warren Village, 2000—01, Excelsior Youth Ctr. Found., 2001—, Excelsior Youth Ctr., 2006—. Named Vol. of Month (March), Jr. League Denver, 1990, Vol. of Yr., Four Mile Hist. Pk., 1988; recipient Gold Peak Mktg. award-team design Am. Mktg. Assn., 1986, Silver Peak Mktg. award-team design Am. Mktg. Assn., 1986, Gold Pick award-art dir. Pub. Rels. Soc. Am., 1980-81, cert. Appreciation USDA, 1999, 2001. Mem. Natural Resources Def. Coun., Physicians for Social Responsibility, Am. Farmland Trust, Nat. Trust for Hist. Preservation, Environ. Def., Rachel's Network. Avocations: horseback riding, bicycling, hiking, backpacking, pastel drawing.

ROSS, MONTE, electrical engineer, researcher; b. Chgo., May 26, 1932; s. Jacob Henry and Mildred Amelia (Feller) R.; m. Harriet Jean Katz, Feb. 10, 1957; children— Karyn, Dianne, Ethan BS in Elec. Engring., U. Ill., 1953; MS, Northwestern U., 1962. Devel. engr. Chance Vought, Dallas, 1953-54; sr. electronics engr. Motorola, Chgo., 1955-56, project engr., 1957-59, assoc. dir. rsch., 1960-63; dir. rsch. Hallicrafters Co., Chgo., 1964-65; mgr. laser tech. McDonnell Douglas Astronautics Co., St. Louis, 1966-70, dir. laser comms.; program mgr. Laser Space Comms., 1971-87; pres. Ultradata Sys., Inc. (formerly Laser Data Tech.), St. Louis, 1987—2001, CEO, 2001—07; cons., 2007—. Mem. alumni bd. dept. elec. and computer engring. U. Ill., 1985-90; guest lectr. various univs.; cons. NSF. Author: Laser Receivers, 1966; tech. editor Laser Applications Series, vol. 1, 1971, vol. 2, 1974, vol. 3, 1977, vol. 4, 1980; patentee in field. Chmn. Laser Mus. and Space Signal Obs., 1997—. Recipient St. Louis High Tech. Entrepreneur of Yr. award, 1995; McDonnell Douglas Corp. fellow, 1985. Fellow IEEE; mem. Internat. Laser Comms. Soc. (pres. 1988-89), Sigma Xi. Home: 19 Beaver Dr Saint Louis MO 63141-7901 Business E-Mail: mross@ultradatasystems.com.

ROSS, MURRAY LOUIS, lawyer; b. Rochester, NY, Apr. 26, 1947; s. Charles Allen and Florence L. (Falk) R.; m. Linda Marie Wabschall, Dec. 26, 1970. AB in History, Lycoming Coll., 1969; JD, U. Toledo, 1972. Bar: Pa. 1976. Asst. to exec. v.p. Falk Machinery Inc., Rochester, 1972-74; asst. v.p. Phila. (Pa.) Stock Exch., 1975-78, dir. securities dept., 1978-79, dir. market surveillance, 1979-82, v.p., corp. sec., 1982—; exec. v.p. Shiffrin Selections, Ltd., 1994—. Corp. sec. Phila. (Pa.) Bd. Trade Inc., 1984—, Phila. (Pa.) Depository Trust Co., 1986—, Stock Clearing Corp. Phila., 1986—. Mem. ABA, Phila. Bar Assn., Securities Assn. of Phila. Avocations: wine, golf, ice hockey. Home: 1126 Woodstock Ln West Chester PA 19382-7244 Office: Phila Stock Exchange Inc 1900 Market St Lbby 4 Philadelphia PA 19103-3584

ROSS, NELSON G., lawyer; b. Jan. 4, 1938; BA, Boston Univ., 1960; LLM, Boston Coll., 1964. Bar: Mass. 1964. Assoc. Ropes & Gray, Boston, 1967—76, ptnr., 1976—, head labor & employment dept. Contbg. editor: The Developing Labor Law. Pres. bd. trustees South Shore Conservancy; trustee Hingham Pub. Libr.; mem. Hingham Personnel Bd. Recipient Cushin-Gavin award, Boston Labor Guild, 2001. Mem.: ABA, Mass. Bar Assn., Boston Bar Assn. Office: Ropes & Gray 1 International Pl Boston MA 02110-2624 Office Phone: 617-951-7450. Office Fax: 617-951-7050. Business E-Mail: nelson.ross@ropesgray.com.

ROSS, NORMAN ALAN, publisher; b. Bklyn., Nov. 1, 1942; s. Robert E. and Bertha (Cohen) Ross; m. Leslie Ann Sandler, Oct. 10, 1969; children: Caroline Beth, Juliet Michelle. BBA, CCNY, 1964, postgrad., 1967-74. Prodn. mgr. Thomas Pub. Co., 1964-67; sys. analyst Reuben H. Donnelley Corp., 1968-70; project mgr. Holt Rinehart & Winston, 1971-73; pres. Clearwater Pub. Co., Inc., NYC, 1973-88, Video Strategies USA, Inc., NYC, 1981-84, Broadside Ltd. pub. Broadside Mag., 1983-87, Norman Ross Pub. Inc., 1987—2002, Acad. Microforms Inc., 1999—2003; exec. dir. Norman Ross Pub., subs. Proquest, 2003—; pres. Ross Pub., Inc., 2003—. Author: (book) Index to the Decisions of the Indian Claims Commission, 1973, Index to the Expert Testimony Before the Indian Claims Commission, 1973, Guide to Yiddish Children's Books from the Yivo Institute, 1989. Home: 392 Central Park W Apt 20-c New York NY 10025-5878 Office: Ross Pub Inc 250 W 57th St New York NY 10107 Office Phone: 212-765-8200. Business E-Mail: norman@rosspub.com.

ROSS, PATTI JAYNE, obstetrics and gynecology educator; b. Nov. 17, 1946; d. James J. and Mary N. Ross; m. Allan Robert Katz, May 23, 1976. BS, DePauw U., 1968; MD, Tulane U., 1972. Diplomate Am. Bd. Ob-Gyn. Asst. prof. U. Tex. Med. Sch., Houston, 1976—82, assoc. prof., 1982—98, prof., 1998—2004, dir. adolescent ob-gyn., 1976—, dir. student edn., dir. devel. dept. ob-gyn. Cons. in field; spkr. in field; appeared on Lifetime TV network. Contbr. articles to profl. jours. Mem. Rape Coun.; vol. Children's Miracle Network/Hermann's Children's Hosp.; Olympic torch relay carrier, 1996; founder Women's Med. Rsch. Fund, U. Tex. Med. Sch., Houston; bd. dirs. Am. Diabetes Assn., 1982—, Susan Komen Found. Recipient Patti Jayne Ross Professorship, 2004. Mem.: Profl. Women Execs., Orgn. Women in Sci., Am. Women's Med. Assn., AAAS, Soc. Adolescent Medicine, Assn. Profs. Ob-Gyn., Houston Ob-Gyn. Soc., Harris County Med. Soc., Tex. Med. Assn., River Oak Breakfast Club, Sigma Xi. Roman Catholic. Office: 6431 Fannin St 3278 Houston TX 77030-1501 Office Phone: 713-500-6431. Business E-Mail: patti.j.ross@mth.tmc.edu.

ROSS, PHILIP ROWLAND, retired library director; b. Indiana, Pa., Apr. 7, 1940; s. David Biddle and Miriam Elizabeth (Hill) R.; m. Elaine Lucille George, July 17, 1965; children: Mary Elizabeth, David Bruce. BA, Pa. State U., 1962; MSLS, U. Md., 1969. Postal fin. officer USAF, Tachikawa AFB Tokyo, 1963-65; chief data control and quality control Hdqrs. Air Force Systems Command, Andrews AFB, Md., 1965-68; asst. libr. acquisitions West Liberty (W.Va.) State Coll., 1969-86; dist. mgr. Wheeling (W.Va.) office First Investors Corp., 1986-89, divs. mgr. State of Ark. Little Rock, 1989-92; dir. Lonoke (Ark.) Prairie County Regional Libr. System, 1992-2000; ret., 2000. Founder, treas.-mgr. West Liberty (W.Va.) State Coll. Fed. Credit Union, 1977-82, chmn. bd., 1984-85; co-founder, bd. dirs., Lonoke County Mus., sec., 2005-07; mem. Ark. On Line Network Adv. Com., Little Rock, 1993-96, Libr. Devel. Dist. State Coun., Little Rock, 1993-2000, vice chmn., 1996. Capt. USAF, 1962—68, maj. Res. USAF, 1968—84. Decorated various USAF medals and decorations. Mem.: AARP (chpt. v.p. 2003, pres. 2004—06), ALA, S.E. Libr. Assn., Ark. Libr. Assn. (membership com. 1994—95, conv. com. 1996, 1997), Assn. Ark. Pub. Librs. (treas.-sec. 1993, 1994, v.p., pres.-elect 1995, pres. 1996), Lonoke C. of C., Lions (pres. 2003—05), Am. Legion (life). Republican. Methodist. Avocations: reading, gardening, refinishing antique furniture. Home: 691 Wayne Elmore Rd Lonoke AR 72086-9126

ROSS, R. DALE, medical products executive; Sales mgmt. positions Am. McGaw Laboratories; founder, pres., CEO HMSS Inc., 1982—90; chmn., CEO Am. Oncology Resources, Houston, 1992—99, US Oncology, Houston, 1999—. Served USAF. Office: US Oncology 16825 Northchase Dr Houston TX 77060 *

ROSS, RANDOLPH ERNEST, investor; b. NYC, Mar. 17, 1955; s. David Harvey and Pearl (Frandsen) R.; m. Joan Frances Healey, Apr. 2, 1982. AB in History, Brown U., 1977; MBA in Fin., Columbia U., 1981. CFA; comml. pilot FAA. Nat. editor Sta. WEAN Radio, Providence, 1977-79; rsch. analyst, asst. v.p. Kidder, Peabody & Co., Inc., NYC, 1981-85; rsch. analyst First Manhattan Co., NYC, 1985-86; portfolio mgr. Brundage, Story and Rose, NYC, 1986-92; sr. portfolio mgr., v.p. Bankers Trust Co., NYC, 1992-93; investment strategist, sr. v.p. Kidder, Peabody & Co. Inc., NYC, 1993-94; pvt. investor Bklyn., 1994-96; mng. dir. Morgan Hill Corp., NYC, 1996—2004; pvt. investor, 2004—. Mem. CFA Inst., N.Y. Soc. Security Analysts. Republican. Avocations: commercial pilot, sailing, trap and skeet shooting, architectural and urban history, fiction. Home: 111 Hicks St Ste 4A Brooklyn NY 11201-1638

ROSS, RICH, broadcast executive; b. NYC, Oct. 7, 1961; BA in internat. rels. and English, U. Pa., 1983; JD, Fordham U., 1986. Mgr. talent rels. Nickelodeon, 1986—90, v.p. talent rels., 1990—92, v.p. program enterprises, 1992—93; sr. v.p. devel. and prodn. FX Networks, 1993—96; sr. v.p. programming and prodn. Disney Channel, 1996—99, exec. v.p., gen. mgr. programming and prodn., 1999—2002, pres., 2002—04, Disney Channel Worldwide, 2004—. Bd. dirs. Cable in the Classroom. Office: Disney Channel 500 S Buena Vista St Burbank CA 91521

ROSS, RICHARD FRANCIS, veterinarian, educator, dean, microbiologist; b. Washington, Iowa, Apr. 30, 1935; s. Milton Edward and Olive Marie (Berggren) R.; m. Karen Mae Paulsen, Sept. 1, 1957; children: Scott, Susan D.V.M., Iowa State U., 1959, MS, 1961, PhD, 1965. Rsch. assoc. Iowa State U., Ames, 1959—61, asst. prof., 1962—65, assoc. prof., 1966—72, prof., 1972—, assoc. dir., assoc. dean Coll. Vet. Medicine, 1990—92, interim dean, 1992—93, dean Coll. Vet. Medicine, 1993—2000, interim dean, dean Coll. Agr., dir. Agrl. Expt. Sta., 2000—02, prof. emeritus, 2004; oper. mgr. Vet. Lab. Inc., Remsen, Iowa, 1961—62; postdoctoral fellow NIAID, Hamilton, Mont., 1965—66. Sr. U.S. scientist Alexander von Humboldt Found., Bonn, Fed. Republic Germany, 1975-76; chmn. Internat. Rsch. Program on Comparative Mycoplasmology, 1982-86; pres. Iowa State U. Rsch. Found., Ames, 1984-86; Howard Dunne meml. lectr. Am. Assn. Swine Practitioners, 1984; mem. adv. bd. Sec. Agr., 1996-99; mem. strategic planning task force USDA, 1997-99, mem. safeguarding task force, 2001-02, mem. implementation team, 2003-04; bd. govs. ISU Found., 2004—. Contbr. numerous articles to profl. publs., 1963— Vol. Union Sta. Homeless Shelter, Pasadena, Calif., 2007—. Named Disting. Prof., Iowa State U., 1982, Hon. Master Pork Producer, Iowa Pork Producers Assn., 1985; recipient faculty citation Iowa State U. Alumni Assn., 1984, Beecham award for rsch. excellence, 1985, Howard Dunne Meml. award Am. Assn. Swine Practitioners, 1988, Am. Feed Mfg. award for rsch., 1995, Sec. of Agr. award for personal and profl. accomplishment, 1996, Gamma Sigma Delta Merit award for disting. achievement in agr. 2002. Mem. Am. Coll. Vet. Microbiologists (diplomate, vice chmn. 1974-75, sec.-treas. 1977-83), Am. Soc. Microbiology (chmn. div. 1985-86), Internat. Orgn. Mycoplasmology (chair 1990-92, Bd. Dirs. award 2002), AVMA, AAAS, Osborn Research Club, Conf. Rsch. Workers in Animal Diseases (coun. mem., pres. 1992), Assn. Am. Vet.

Med. Colls. (pres. 1997-98), Rotary Club. Republican. Lutheran. Avocations: fishing, gardening, walking, reading, history. Home: 4022 Stone Brooke Rd Ames IA 50010-2900 Personal E-mail: rfross@iastate.edu.

ROSS, RICHARD FREDERICK, lawyer; b. Coral Gables, Fla., May 12, 1952; s. Norman and Jeanne (Gustafson) Ross; m. Carolyn Ross, June 30, 1985. BA magna cum laude, Mich. State U., 1974; JD, U. Detroit, 1977. Bar: Ariz. 1977; cert. real estate specialist Ariz. Bd. Legal Specialization. Atty. Cunningham, Goodson & Tiffany, Phoenix, 1977-81; founding ptnr. Storey & Ross, Phoenix, 1981-89; ptnr. Squire, Sanders & Dempsey LLP, Phoenix, 1989—, co-chmn., Real Estate & Hospitality Practice Group. Former bd. dirs. dean's coun. of 100 Ariz. State U. Coll. Bus., Tempe; former bd. dirs. Ctrl. Ariz. chpt. Am. Heart Assn., Phoenix; former bd. dirs. Phoenix Symphony, HomeBase Cmty. Youth Shelter, Phoenix, Terraco Properties (subs. Phoenix Meml. Hosp.), Phoenix. Mem. ABA (mem. hospitality com., mem. real property, probate and trust law), Internat. Soc. Hospitality Cons., Am. Hotel and Motel Assn., Urban Land Inst., Internat. Coun. Shopping Ctr., Valley Partnership. Office: Squire Sanders & Dempsey LLP Two Renaissance Sq 40 N Central Ave Ste 2700 Phoenix AZ 85004-4424 Office Phone: 602-528-4018. Office Fax: 216-479-8780. Business E-Mail: rross@ssd.com.

ROSS, RICHARD STARR, retired medical school dean, cardiologist, educator; b. Richmond, Ind., Jan. 18, 1924; s. Louis Francisco and Margaret (Starr) Ross; m. Elizabeth McCracken, July 1, 1950; children: Deborah Starr, Margaret Casad, Richard McCracken. Student, Harvard U., 1942—44, MD cum laude, 1947; ScD (hon.), Ind. U., 1981; LHD (hon.), Johns Hopkins U., 1994. Diplomate Nat. Bd. Med. Examiners, Am. Bd. Internal Medicine (subsplty. bd. cardiovasc. disease). Successively intern, asst. resident, chief resident Osler Med. Service, Johns Hopkins Hosp., 1947—54; research fellow physiology Harvard Med. Sch., 1952—53; instr. medicine Johns Hopkins Med. Sch., 1954—56, asst. prof. medicine, 1956—59, assoc. prof., 1959—65, assoc. prof. radiology, 1960—71, prof. medicine, 1965—. Clayton prof. cardiovascular disease, 1969—75; dir. Wellcome Research Lab., Johns Hopkins; physician Johns Hopkins Hosp.; dir. cardiovascular div. dept. medicine, adult cardiac clinic Johns Hopkins Sch. Medicine and Hosp., dir. myocardial infarction research unit, 1967—75; dean med. faculty, v.p. medicine Johns Hopkins U., 1975—90, dean emeritus, 1990—. Sir Thomas Lewis lectr. Brit. Cardiac Soc., 1969; John Kent Lewis lectr. Stanford U., 1972; bd. dirs. emeritus Johns Hopkins Hosp., Francis Scott Key Med. Ctr.; mem. cardiovasc. study sect. Nat. Heart and Lung Inst., 1965—69, chmn. cardiovasc. study sect., 1966—69, mem. tng. grant com., 1971—73, chmn. heart panel, 1972—73, adv. coun., 1974—78; mem. Inst. Medicine, 1976—; chmn. vis. com. Harvard Med. and Dental Sch., 1979—86; bd. overseers Harvard U., 1980—86. Editor: Modern Concepts Cardiovascular Disease, 1961—65, The Principles and Practice of Medicine, 17th-22nd edits., 1968—88; mem. editl. bd.: Circulation, 1968—74, mem. editl. com.: Jour. Clin. Investigation, 1969—73; contbr. numerous articles to profl. jours. Capt. M.C. US Army, 1949—51. Named hon. fellow, UMDS, Guy's and St. Thomas's Hosps., London, 1996; recipient Flexner award, Assn. Am. Med. Coll., 1994, Pres.'s medal, Johns Hopkins U., 2005. Master: ACP; fellow: Am. Coll. Cardiology (Convocation medal 1990); mem.: Heart Assn. Md. (pres. 1967—68), Am. Heart Assn. (chmn. sci. sessions program com. 1965—67, chmn. publs. com. 1970—73, pres. 1973—74, dir. 1974—77, Gold Heart award 1976, Connor lectr. 1979, James B. Herrick award 1982), Assn. Univ. Cardiologists (councillor 1972—75), Am. Clin. and Climatol. Assn. (pres. 1978—79, councillor 1979—83, Metzger lecture 1986), Am. Soc. Clin. Investigation (councillor 1967—69), Sociedad Peruana de Cardiologie (corr.), Brit. Cardiac Soc. (corr.), Cardiac Soc. Australia and New Zealand (corr.), Assn. Am. Physicians, Am. Physiol. Soc., Am. Fedn. Clin. Rsch., Boylston Med. Soc., Elkridge Club, Interurban Club (pres. 1978), Peripatetic Club, Alpha Omega Alpha, Sigma Xi. Home: 830 W 40th St # 851 Baltimore MD 21211-2181 Office: Johns Hopkins U 1830 E Monument St Baltimore MD 21287 E-mail: rross@jhmi.edu.

ROSS, ROBERT DONALD, library director; b. NYC, Mar. 28, 1931; s. William and Ceceile (Cross) Rosenfeld. BA, CCNY, 1954; postgrad., NYU, 1960—64, Columbia U., NYC, 1968; MLS, Rutgers U., New Brunswick, 1966. m. Madeleine Ladner, May 28, 1961; children: Jeffrey Laurence, Jodie Dianne. Ref. libr. Bklyn. Pub. Libr., 1965; reader svcs. libr., asst. prof. Suffolk County (N.Y.) C.C., 1966-69; dir. South Brunswick (N.J.) Pub. Libr., 1969-73, Ridgewood (N.J.) Pub. Libr., 1973-95. Adj. prof. Middlesex County C.C., NJ, 1973—76. Mem. exec. bd. South Brunswick Cmty. Coun., 1970-73, Human Rels. Coord. Coun., Ridgewood, 1988-94; mem. adv. com. Nat. Project Ctr. for Films and Humanities, N.Y.C., 1971-75; treas. Bergen-Passaic Regional Libr. Coop., 1987-88, mem. exec. bd., 1986-89; mem. Ridgewood Bicentennial Commn., 1975-76; treas. Temple Emanu-El, Reno, 1998-2000, bd. dirs., 2002-2003; bd. dirs. For the Love of Jazz, Reno, 1998-2000; docent Nev. Mus. Art, 2004—. Mem. ALA (chmn. discussion group com. fundraising and fin. devel. sect. libr. adminstrn. and mgmt. divsn. 1984-85), N.J. Libr. Assn. (libr. devel. com. 1977-93, chmn. edn. for librarianship com. 1982-83, govt. rels. com. 1982, 100th ann. com. 1988-91), Librs. South Middlesex (chmn. 1970-73), North Bergen Fedn. Librs. (chmn. dirs. coun. 1975), Bergen County Coop. Libr. Sys. (pres., treas. 1982-83, 86-87, exec. bd. computer consortium 1987-89, budget com. 1989-94), Ridgewood C. of C. (bd. dirs. 1983-93, treas. 1988-93), Soc. Valley Hosp. Ridgewood, Ridgewood Kiwanis (pres. 1982-83, treas. 1987-88, Disting. Club. Pres. award 1983). Home: 4910 Deer Pass Dr Reno NV 89509-0577

ROSS, ROBERT EVAN, bank executive; b. Alliance, Ohio, Sept. 22, 1947; s. James Jacob Ross and Eva Mae (Forsha) Bodo; m. Susan Margaret Burd, June 20, 1970; children: Margaret Mae, James William. BBA, Kent State U., 1970; MBA, U. Chgo., 1977. Advisor to fraternities, dean of men's office Kent (Ohio) State U., 1970-71; trainee, supr. of trainees Northern Trust Co., Chgo., 1971-73, jr. analyst, 1973-74, trust rep., 1974-77, trust officer, 1977-81, v.p., div. head for personal fin. planning, 1981-85; portfolio mgr., investment rep. Morgan Stanley, Chgo., 1985-89; pres. Northern Trust Bank in Winnetka, Ill., 1989-92; exec. v.p. Northern Trust Bank/Lake Forest, Ill., 1992-95, vice chmn., 1995-97, pres., CEO, 1997—2001; pres., CEO Northern Trust Bank-Ohio, 2001—04; sr. v.p. wealth strategies group No. Trust Co., 2004—06; mng. dir. pvt. banking Harris Bank, Chgo., 2006—. Bd. dirs. No. Trust Bank, Lake Forest, O'Hare, Ill., DuPage, Ill. Bd. dirs. The Camerata Singers of Lake Forest, Lake Forest Symphony, 1992-2001, Ragdale Found., 1999-2000, Cleve. Zool. Soc., 2003; bd. govs. Ill. St. Andrew Soc., 1998-2001; suburban chair United Way North Region, 1993—; mem. centennial commn. on identity, values and comm. Kent State U., 1998; trustee DePaul U., Chgo., Barat Coll. Edn. Found., Kent State U. Found., 2003. Avocations: sports, reading, stock market, painting. Office: No Trust Bank Lake Forest Deerpath And Bank Ln Lake Forest IL 60045

ROSS, ROBIN S., investment company executive; b. 1950; BA Mktg., U. of Ark., Little Rock. Bond sales Atlantic Nat. Bank of Fl., 1978—80, bond trader, 1980—82; Chgo. Mercantile Exch. (CME) fl. mgr. Credit Suisse First Boston Corp., 1991—95; CME fl. sales mgr. J.P. Morgan Futures', 1995—2001; sales cons., rep, v.p. JPMorgan Chase Futures, 2001—03; mng. dir. Chgo. Futures Divsn. for Cantor Fitzgerald & Co., 2004; mng. dir., interest rates Chgo. Mercantile Exch., 2004—; joined, bond trader GNP Commodities Inc., 1982. Head Swapstream. Spkr. in field. Named a Women to Watch, Crain's Chgo. Bus., 2007. Office: Chgo Mercantile Exch 20 S Wacker Chicago IL 60606 Office Phone: 312-930-1000. *

ROSS, ROBINETTE DAVIS, publisher; b. London, May 16, 1952; d. Raymond Lawrence and Pearl A. (Robinette) Davis; m. William Bradford Ross, III, Mar. 16, 1979; children: Nellie Tayloe, William Bradford IV. Student, Am. U., 1977-78. Asst. to editor The Chronicle of Higher Edn., Washington, 1978, advt. mgr., 1978-82, advt. dir., 1983-88, assoc. pub., 1988-94, The Chronicle of Philanthropy, 1988-94; publ. The Chronicle of Higher Edn., Washington, 1994—; pub. The Chronicle of Philanthropy, Washington, 1994—. Mem. Am. News Women's Club, City Tavern Club, Mt. Vernon Club. Episcopalian. Office: The Chronicle of Higher Edn 1255 23rd St NW Ste 700 Washington DC 20037-1146

ROSS, RODERIC HENRY, retired insurance company executive; b. Jamestown, NY, July 14, 1930; s. Edwin A. and Mary (Dornberger) R.; m. Patricia Johnson, Aug. 6, 1955; children: Timothy, Amy, Jane, Christopher. BA, Hobart Coll., 1952, LLD (hon.), 1979. CLU, ChFC. Gen. agt. Phila. Life Ins. Co., 1957-70, sr. v.p. mktg., 1972-73, pres., 1973-83, vice chmn., 1983-84; chmn., CEO Keystone State Life Ins. Co., Phila., 1985-2000; ret., 2001. Bd. dirs. PMA Capital Corp., Phila.; past chmn. Ins. Fedn. Pa.; dir. Intergroup Svcs. Corp., Malvern, Pa. Rector's warden St. David's Ch., Radnor, Pa., 1989-90; hon. trustee Hobart-William Smith Colls., Geneva, N.Y., 1972—, chmn. bd., 1983-88. Sgt. U.S. Army, 1952-54. Mem. Am. Soc. CLUs, Nat. Assn. Nat. Assn. Life Underwriters, Million Dollar Round Table (life), Union League (former dir.), Orpheus Club, St. David's Golf Club (Wayne, Pa.), Penna Soc., Pine Valley Golf Club (Clementon, N.J.). Republican. Episcopalian. Avocations: golf, tennis. Home (Summer): PO Box 332 Bemus Point NY 14712-0332 Home: 770 Buck Rd Wayne PA 19087 Home Phone: 610-688-2763. E-mail: rodnpatross@verizon.net.

ROSS, STANFORD G., lawyer, government official; b. St. Louis, Oct. 9, 1931; m. Dorothy Rabin, June 9, 1958; children: John, Ellen. AB with honors, Washington U., 1953; JD magna cum laude, Harvard U., 1956. Bar: D.C. 1969, Calif. 1956, N.Y. 1959. Assoc. Irell & Manella, LA, 1956-57; tchg. fellow, rsch. asst. Harvard Law Sch., 1957-58; assoc. Dewey, Ballantine, Bushby, Palmer & Wood, NYC, 1958-61; asst. tax legis. counsel U.S. Dept. Treasury, 1961-63; prof. law N.Y. U., 1963-67; White House staff asst. to Pres. Johnson, 1967-68; gen. counsel U.S. Dept. Transp., 1968-69; ptnr. Caplin & Drysdale, Washington, 1969-78; commr. Social Security Adminstrn., Washington, 1978-79; ptnr. Califano, Ross & Heineman, Washington, 1980-82, Arnold & Porter, Washington, 1983—2002. Pub. trustee Social Security Trust Funds, Washington, 1990-95; chmn. Social Security Adv. Bd., 1997-2002. Editor: Harvard Law Rev, 1954-56. Mem. ABA, Fed. Bar Assn., Internat. Fiscal Assn., Nat. Acad. Social Ins. Office: Arnold & Porter 555 12th St NW Washington DC 20004-1206

ROSS, STEPHEN M., real estate company executive; BS, U. Mich., 1962; JD, Wayne State U.; LLM in Taxation, NYU. Dir. Insignia Fin. Group, Inc.; founder, dir. Charter Mcpl. Mortgage Acceptance Co.; founder, chmn., CEO The Related Cos. LP, NYC. Dir. Juvenile Diabetes Found.; bd. trustees Solomon R. Guggenheim Mus.; trustee Jackie Robinson Found., Jewish Assn. for Svcs. for Aged. Named one of Forbes' Richest Americans, 2006. Mem.: Real Estate Board of NY (dir.). Office: The Related Cos LP 60 Columbus Cir New York NY 10023 Office Phone: 212-421-5333.

ROSS, STEVE J., publishing executive; Grad., Cleve. State U., Hunter Coll., NYU. Editor John Wiley & Sons, NYC; sr. editor Putnam, NYC; exec. editor Delacorte Press, NYC; with Crown Pubs. Random House, NYC, 1996—2007, editl. dir. Crown and Crown Bus., sr. v.p., pub. Crown Pubs., Crown Bus., Crown Forum and Three Rivers Press; pres., pub. Collins US HarperCollins Pubs., NYC, 2007—. Avocation: tennis. Office: HarperCollins Pubs 10 E 53rd St New York NY 10022 *

ROSS, STEVEN ELLIOT, surgeon; b. Wilmington, Del., Sept. 12, 1951; s. Morris H. and Anita Selma (Luterman) R.; m. Carolyn Gross, June 13, 1981; children: Leah Jane, Asher Joshua, Tovah Jennifer. BA, U. Del., 1972; MD, Jefferson Med. Coll., Phila., Pa., 1976. Diplomate Am. Bd. Surgery, Am. Bd. Surg. Critical Care. Resident, general surgery York Hosp., York, Pa., 1976-81; fellow trauma and surgical critical care medicine Univ. Kansas Med. Ctr., Kansas City, 1981-82; attending surgeon Cooper Hosp., Camden, NJ, 1984—, head, divsn. trauma and emergency surgical services, vice chief, dept. surgery, residency dir., general surgery; prof. surgery Univ. Medicine Dentistry NJ/Robert Wood Johnson Med. Sch., Camden, NJ, 1984—. Contbr. several sci. articles to profl. jours. Chmn. NJ State Trauma Ctr. Coun., 1991-93, 97; mem. Governors Med. Disaster Planning MEDPREP Com. Fellow Am. Coll. Surgeons (chmn. com. trauma NJ chpt. 1991-96, mem.), Am. Assn. Surgery Trauma, Assn. Advancement Automotive Medicine (chair membership com. 1994-95), Soc. Critical Care Medicine, Western Trauma Assocs. (bd. dirs. 1993-95), Alpha Omega Alpha (faculty mem.) Jewish. Office: Cooper Hosp Dept Surgery 3 Cooper Plz Rm 411 Camden NJ 08103 Address: 1 Cooper Plz Camden NJ 08103 Office Phone: 856-342-3014, 856-342-2657. Office Fax: 856-342-2817, 856-968-8306.

ROSS, SUE HOISINGTON, music educator; b. Silver Creek, NY, Sept. 30, 1951; d. Richard Leroy and Jeanne Marie Hoisington; 1 child, Michael Parrish Wilkerson. MusB in Edn., Shenandoah Conservatory Music, 1973; MusM with hons. in Edn., SUNY, Fredonia, NY, 1987. Cert. tchr. Va., NY. Tchr. elem. vocal music Loudoun County Pub. Schs., Leesburg, Va., 1973—76; tchr. vocal music Loudoun Country Day Sch., Leesburg, 1976—79; tchr. elem. vocal music Lakeshore Ctrl. Schs., Angola, NY, 1980—. Supr. student tchrs. Lake Shore Ctrl. Schs., 1980—; lectr. in field. Active MADD; mem. beautification program Lake Erie; vol. Erie County Rep. Com., Fornham, NY, 1983—85. Mem.: Nat. Assn. Music Educators, NY State Sch. Music Assn. Republican. Office: Lake Shore Central Schools Beach Rd Angola NY 14006 Home: 2203 Pleasant Ave Lake View NY 14085 Office Phone: 716-549-2300. Personal E-mail: sucross51@aol.com.

ROSS, TERENCE P., lawyer; b. 1958; BA with honors, Stanford U., 1980; JD, U. Va. Sch. Law, 1983. Bar: Commonwealth Va., DC, NY, US Supreme Ct., US Ct. Appeals Fed. Circuit. Law clk. to Judge Roger Robb, US Ct. Appeals Dist. Columbia Circuit; assoc. Gibson, Dunn & Crutcher LLP, Washington, 1984—91, ptnr., 1991—. Adj. prof. George Mason U. Law Sch.; writer and spkr. in field on intellectual property topics; rsch. editor, mem. mng. bd. Va. Law Review. Author: Intellectual Property Law: Damages and Remedies, 2000. Mem. bd. visitors U. Va. Named to Magnificent Seven: IP's Best Young Trial Lawyers, IP Worldwide, 2002. Mem.: ABA (mem. steering com., mem. intellectual property lit. com.), DC Bar Assn. (chair annual develop. in intellectual property law forum). Office: Gibson Dunn & Crutcher LLP 1050 Conn Ave NW Washington DC 20036 Office Phone: 202-955-8664. Business E-Mail: tross@gibsondunn.com.

ROSS, TERRY D., lawyer; b. Glendale, Calif., Aug. 12, 1943; BA, U. Calif., Santa Barbara, 1965; JD, U. Calif. Hastings Coll. Law, 1968. Bar: Calif. 1969, U.S. Dist. Ct. (so. dist.) Calif. 1969, U.S. Dist. Ct. (ctrl. dist.) Calif. 1992, U.S. Dist. Ct. (no. dist.) Calif. 1999, U.S. Ct. Appeals (9th cir.) 1977, U.S. Supreme Ct. 1983. Ptnr. DLA Piper US LLP, San Diego. Mem. panel arbitrators Am. Arbitration Assn. Note and comment editor Hastings Law Jour., 1967-68. Bd. dirs., mem. exec. bd., 1st v.p. E. San Diego Co. YMCA. Mem. ABA (sect. litig.), State Bar Calif., San Diego County Bar Assn. (mem. arbitration panel, superior ct. com., client rels. com.), S.D. Marlin Club, SDMB Boat and Ski Club, Phi Delta Phi. Office: DLA Piper US LLP Ste 1700 401 B St San Diego CA 92101-4297 Office Phone: 619-699-2749. E-mail: Terry.Ross@dlapiper.com.

ROSS, THOMAS J., JR., personal financial adviser; b. NYC, Aug. 25, 1954; s. Thomas J. Sr. and Margaret (Byrne) R.; m. Elise Mary Bishop, Sept. 20, 1980; children: Kaitlyn Ann, John Patrick, Brendan Christopher. BA in English magna cum laude, Boston Coll., 1976; MBA in Fin., U. Pa., 1980. Cons. Wharton Applied Rsch. Ctr., Phila., 1978-80; part owner, v.p. Asset Mgmt. Group, Parsippany, NJ, 1980-86; dir. Coopers & Lybrand, Parsippany, 1986-89, ptnr., 1989-92, regional ptnr. personal fin. svcs. group, NY Metro Area, 1992—97; pres. Wealth Mgmt. Cons. LLC, Morristown, NJ, 1998—. Mem. nat. PFS steering com. Coopers & Lybrand, NYC, 1987-98; mem. investment policy com. Coopers & Lybrand Fin. Advs. LLC, 1996-97. Editor newsletter Growing Your Wealth, 1992-97; contbr. numerous tax and fin. articles to Chief Exec. Mag., Bottom Line Fin., NJ Law Jour. Mem. Boston Coll. Alumni Admissions Coun., Chestnut Hill, Mass., 1976—, Kickoff Classic Tix Com., Ind. Coll. Fund of NJ, Summit, 1990-98; bd. trustees Tri-County Scholarship Fund, 2001-, Mayo Ctr. for Performing Arts; mem. exec. com. Boston Coll. Wall St. Coun., 1996—; soccer, baseball and basketball coach Mountain Lakes Youth Leagues, 1989—; mem. pre-cana team, Parish Fin. Coun., Parish Coun., St. Catherine of Siena. Recipient scholarships Boston Coll., Imaculate Heart Guild, others, 1972-76; named Fin. Coun. of Yr., Asset Mgmt. Group, 1983-85, one of Top 250 Fin. Advisors in Am., Worth Mag., 1997-99, one of Top 100 Advisors in Am., Worth Mag., 2004. Mem. AICPA, Callan Assn. Ind. Adv. Group, NJ Soc. CPAs (PFP com. mem. 1990-92), Wharton Bus. Club of NY, Rockaway River CC, Park Ave. Club, Boston Coll. Clubs of NJ and NYC, Wharton Club of NY, Buck Hill Golf Club. Avocations: golf, youth coaching, reading, running. Home: 140 Kenilworth Rd Mountain Lakes NJ 07046-1156 Office: Wealth Mgmt Cons The Abbey 355 Madison Ave Morristown NJ 07980 Office Phone: 973-401-1500. Business E-Mail: tross@wmcnj.com.

ROSS, TRACEE ELLIS (TRACEE JOY SILBERSTEIN), actress, model, fashion editor; b. LA, Calif., Oct. 29, 1972; d. Diana Ross. BA, Brown U.; ed., William Esper Acting Studio. Fashion editor Mirabella, NY Mag.; contbg. editor Distinction Mag. Actress (TV series) The Dish, 1997, The Lyricist Lounge Show, 2000, Girlfriends, 2000— (BET Comedy award outstanding lead actress in a comedy series, 2000, NAACP Image award best actress in a comedy series, 2007), (TV films) Race Against Fear: A Moment of Truth, 1998, Life Support, 2007, (films) Sue, 1997, A Fare to Remember, 1998, Hanging Up, 2000, In the Weeds, 2000, I-See-You.com, 2006, Daddy's Little Girls, 2007, (plays) Blackout, The Vagina Monologues. Named Vol. of Yr., LA Urban League, 2004. Mailing: c/o ICM 8942 Wilshire Blvd Beverly Hills CA 90211 *

ROSS, TRACEY, actress; b. Bklyn., Feb. 27, 1959; 1 child, Bryce. Actress (TV series) Ryan's Hope, All My Children, Passions, NBC, 1999— (Outstanding Actess in Daytime Drama Series, NAACP Image Awards, 2007), guest appearances The Cosby Show, 1989, Doctor, Doctor, 1991, ROC, 1991, Baywatch Nights, 1996, Gregory Hines Show, actress (TV films) Mayflower Madam, 1987, Valley of the Dolls, (films) Unconditional Love, 1999. Achievements include winning Miss NJ Pageant, 1975; first $100,100 Star Search spokesmodel champion, 1984. *

ROSS, VIOLET BICA, retired elementary school educator, retired psychologist; d. Ellie A. and Anna (Muresan) Bica; m. L. Clayton Ross, Oct. 23, 1976 (dec.). BS, Mount Union Coll., 1944; MA, Kent State U., 1952. Tchr. Alliance Bd. Edn., 1945—53; psychologist Maple Heights Bd. Edn., Ohio, 1954—56, Cleveland Heights Bd. Edn., 1956—61, Shaker Heights Bd. Edn., Ohio, 1961—76; ret., 1976. Psychologist chair Kent Area Sch., 1959—60, Cleve. Area Sch., 1962—63; editl. bd. Sch. Counselor Journal, 1962—64; del. nat. conventions. Named Dormitory at Mt. Union Coll. Bica-Ross Hall, 1999, Dormitory at Wash. Jefferson Coll. Bica-Ross Hall, 2004. Mem.: Kappa Delta, Kappa Delta Pi, Delta Kappa Gamma. Achievements include donations of scholarships to Mount Union College, Washington and Jefferson College. Avocations: reading, travel, golf. Home: 112 Royal Oak Dr Aurora OH 44202

ROSS, WALTER BEGHTOL, music educator, composer; b. Lincoln, Nebr., Oct. 3, 1936; s. Robert Thurber and Barbara Adeline (Ellis) R.; m. Marion Helen Wright, July 22, 1960; 1 child, Douglas Campbell. BA, U. Nebr., 1960, MusM, 1962; student, Inst. Torcuato Di Tella, Buenos Aires, 1965-66; D of Mus. Arts, Cornell U., 1966. Asst. prof. music CUNY, Cortland, 1966-67; prof. U. Va., Charlottesville, 1967—. Mem. judging panel symphonic awards ASCAP, 1978, Internat. Biennial Composition Contest, P.R., 1981, Va. chpt. Coll. Band Dir.'s Nat. Assn. Nat. Band Composition Contest, 1982, 88; bass Blue Ridge Chamber Orch., Charlottesville, 1992—. Composer over 100 works, including compositions for symphony orch., symphonic band, brass, chamber music, piano, voice, opera, theatre, and film; recs. include Clarinet Concerto for Piano and Orch., Wind Quintet, Nos. 2 and 3, Harlequinade for piano and wind quintet, Escher's Sketches, Concerto for Wind Quintet and String Orch., Piano Concerto, also others. Nominee Pulitzer Prize, 1973; recipient ASCAP award, 1974—, 1st prize Internat. Trombone Assn., 1982; grantee Am. Music Ctr., 1983; fellow Presser Found., 1958, 59, Orgn. Am. States, 1965, NEA, 1975. Democrat. Avocations: chess, cooking, amateur astronomy. Office: U Va Dept Music Charlottesville VA 22903 E-mail: wbr@virginia.edu.

ROSS, WAYNE ANTHONY, lawyer; b. Milw., Feb. 25, 1943; s. Ray E. and Lillian (Steiner) R.; m. Barbara L. Ross, June 22, 1968; children: Gregory, Brian, Timothy, Amy. BA, Marquette U., 1965, JD, 1968. Bar: Wis. 1968, Alaska 1969. Asst. atty. gen. State Alaska, 1968-69; trustee, standing master Superior Ct. Alaska, 1969-73; assoc. Edward J. Reasor & Assocs., Anchorage, 1973-77; prin. Wayne Anthony Ross & Assocs., Anchorage, 1977-83; ptnr. Ross, Gingras & Frenz, Anchorage and Cordova, Alaska, 1983-84, Ross & Gingras, Anchorage and Cordova, 1985; pres. Ross, Gingras and Miner, P.C., Anchorage, 1986-93, Ross and Miner, P.C., Anchorage, 1993—. Col. area def. counsel Alaska State Def. Force; pres. Tyone Mountain Syndicate, Inc. Alaska Rep. Nat. Committeeman, 1992-98; Republican candidate for Gov. of Alaska, 1998, 2002. Decorated knight comdr. Order of Polonia Restituta (Poland), knight Equestrian Order of the Holy Sepulchure of Jerusalem (Vatican). Mem.: NRA (bd. dirs. 1980—92, 1994—, benefactor), Anchorage Bar Assn., Alaska Bar Assn. (Stanley award), Alaska Peace Officers Assn., Mil. Vehicle Preservation Assn. (v.p. 1994—96), Alaska Territorial Cavalry (sec. 1991—97, 2001—05), 49th Territorial Guard Regiment (pres. 1987—94, 1995—96, v.p. 2007), Smith and Wesson Collectors Assn., Ohio Gun Collectors Assn. (hon. life), Alaska Gun Collectors Assn. (pres.). Roman Catholic. Home: PO Box 101522 Anchorage AK 99510-1522 Office: Ross & Miner 327 E Fireweed Ln Ste 201 Anchorage AK 99503-2110 Home Phone: 907-346-2697; Office Phone: 907-276-5307. Personal E-mail: waralaska@alaska.com.

ROSS, WILBUR LOUIS, JR., investment banker; b. Weehawken, NJ, Nov. 28, 1937; s. Wilbur Louis and Agnes (O'Neill) R.; m. Judith Nodine, May 26, 1961 (div. 1995); children: Jessica, Amanda; m. Hilary Geary, Oct. 9, 2004. AB, Yale U., 1959; MBA with distinction, Harvard U., 1961. Assoc. Wood, Struthers and Winthrop, NYC, 1963-64; pres. Faulkner, Dawkins and Sullivan Securities Corp., NYC, 1964-76; sr. mng. dir. Rothschild, Inc., NYC, 1976-2000; CEO News Comms., Inc., NYC, 1996-98; chmn., chief investment officer Rothschild Recovery Fund, NYC, 1997-2000; chmn., CEO WL Ross & Co. LLC, NYC, 2000—. Bd. dirs. Biocraft Labs Inc., Rutherford, NJ, FurVault Inc., NYC, Investors Ins. Co., Lawrence Harbor, NJ, Revere Copper and Brass Co., Stamford, Syms Corp., Secaucus, NJ, Am. Bankruptcy Inst., Washington, Allis Chalmers Corp., Milw., KTI Inc., RH Cement Co., Seoul, Korea, Tong Yang Life Ins. Co., Seoul, Kansai Sawayaka Bank, Osaka, Fresca Credit Card Co., Osaka;

fin. advisor equity holders com. Texaco Co., A.H. Robins Co., Pub. Service NH; hon. econ. amb. from Korea to APEC Investment, Mont., 1999; chmn. Asia Recovery Fund L.P., WL Recovery Fund LP, Asia Co. Investment Ptnrs. L.P., Clarent Hosp. Corp., Compaigne Europeanee Wagan, Internat. Auto Computer Group, Internat. Steel Group, Inc., Cleve., 2002—, Ohizumi Mfg. Co., Japan, 2003-, Burlington Industries, 2003-, Marquis Who's Who LLC, 2003-06, Marquis Who's Who Inc., 2004-06, Internat. Coal Group, 2004-, Internat. Textile Group, 2005—; dir. Nikko Elec. Co., Japan, Miltal Steel Co., Nev., Internat. Steel Group, Japan Soc., Montpelier ReHoldings, Arcelor Mittal Steel Co., Wagon, PLC, Plascar Participacoes. Treas. NY State Dem. Com., 1980-83, Am. Fedn. Arts, 1993—, The New Mus., 1993—; vice chmn. Bklyn. Mus., 1981—; chmn. univ. coun. com. on art Yale U., 1983-88; chmn. NAD, NYC, 1985—, Am. Art Forum, Smithsonian Instn., 1987—; trustee, vice chmn. Nat. Mus. Am. Art, Washington, 1986-91, chmn., 1991—; trustee, Mus. Am. Fin. History, Gustave Hyde Ctr. Nat. Mus. Am. Indian, 2001—, Nat. Mus. Am. Fin. History, Whitney Mus. Am. Art, Preservation Found. of Palm Beach; trustee Sarah Lawrence Coll., 1986—, chmn. art gallery, 1984—; pres. Parrish Art Mus., 1991-95; chmn. NY Hist. Soc., 1993-94; bd. dirs. Smithsonian Inst. Nat. Bd., 1994—, chmn. bd. 1995; nat. chmn. Smithsonian Bicentennial Celebration, 1996; bd. dirs. Turnaround Mgmt. Assn., 2001—; chmn. Absolute Recovery Hedge Fund, Ltd., Hamilton, Bermuda, Taiyo Fund, 2003-, Japan Real Estate Recovery Fund, 2003-; dir. Palm Beach Civic Assn., Yale U. Sch. Mgmt.; mem. com. on univ. rels., com. on capital markets regulation Harvard U.; mem. US India Bus. Coun., chmn. circle. With US Army, 1961—63. Named one of Forbes' Richest Americans, 2006; recipient Legend in Leadership award, Yale Sch. Mgmt., 2005. Fellow Jonathan Edward Coll. of Yale U., Met. Mus. Art; mem. Fin. Analysts Fedn. (chartered), Century Assn., The Bus. Round Table, Bath and Tennis Club, Everglades Club, Harvard Bus. Sch. Club NY (bd. dirs.), Beach Club. Avocation: collecting art. Office: WL Ross and Co LLC 600 Lexington Ave New York NY 10022 Office Phone: 212-826-2111. Business E-Mail: wlross@wlross.com.

ROSS, WILLIAM JARBOE, lawyer; b. Oklahoma City, May 9, 1930; s. Walter John and Bertha (Jarboe) R.; m. Mary Lillian Ryan, May 19, 1962; children: Rebecca Anne Roten, Robert Joseph, Molly Kathleen Fritch. BBA, U. Okla., 1952, LLB, 1954; LHD (hon.), Oklahoma City U., 2005. Bar: Okla. 1954. Since practiced in, Oklahoma City; asst. mcpl. counselor, 1955-60; mem. firm Rainey, Ross, Rice & Binns, 1960—, ptnr., 1965-99, of counsel, 2000—; chmn. bd. Ethics and Excellence in Journalism Found., Inasmuch Found. Mem. bd. visitors U. Okla. Coll. Law; bd. dirs. Ethics and Excellence in Journalism Found., Inasmuch Found. Mem. Okla. Bar Assn., Okla. Heritage Assn., Newcomen Soc., Okla. City Golf and Country Club, Econ. Club, Fortune Club, Rotary, Phi Alpha Delta, Beta Theta Pi, KC Home: 6923 Avondale Ct Oklahoma City OK 73116-5008

ROSSAVIK, IVAR KRISTIAN, obstetrician, gynecologist; b. Stavanger, Rogaland, Norway, Nov. 3, 1936; came to U.S., 1982; s. Andreas and Bergit (Berge) R.; divorced; children: Line, Anne Britt, Kirsten, Solveig; m. Claudia Lagos, May 23, 1987; children: Claudia Kristina, Eevar Benjamin. MD, U. Oslo, 1962, PhD, 1982. Pvt. practice, medicine, Stavanger, 1974; asst. chief, acting chmn. U. Tromsoe, Norway, 1974-76; clin. fellow Nat. Hosp. of Norway, Oslo, 1976-81, Norwegian Radium Hosp./U. Oslo, 1981-82; pvt. practice Oslo, 1977-82; rsch. asst. prof. Baylor Coll. Medicine, Houston, 1983-86; assoc. prof. U. Okla., Oklahoma City, 1987-93, prof., 1993—2001; owner, cons. Clinica Guadalupana, 2001—. Inventor Rossavik Growth Equation, 1980; author: (textbook) Practical Obstetrical Ultrasound: With and Without A Computer, 1991 (Italian translation 1998). Lt. Royal Norwegian Navy, 1964-65. Lutheran. Avocation: computers. Office: Clinica Guadalupana 801 NW 23d St Oklahoma City OK 73106 Personal E-mail: iros@ionef.net.

ROSSBACHER, LISA ANN, academic administrator; b. Fredericksburg, Va., Oct. 10, 1952; d. Richard Irwin and Jean Mary (Dearing) R.; m. Dallas D. Rhodes, Aug. 4, 1978. BS, Dickinson Coll., 1975; MA, SUNY, Binghamton, 1978, Princeton U., 1979, PhD, 1983. Cons. Republic Geothermal, Santa Fe Springs, Calif., 1979-81; asst. prof. geology Whittier (Calif.) Coll., 1982-84, Calif. State Poly. U., Pomona, 1984-86, assoc. prof. geol. sci., 1986-91, assoc. v.p. acad. affairs, 1987-93, prof. geol. sci., 1991-93; v.p. acad. affairs, dean faculty Whittier (Calif.) Coll., 1993-95; dean of coll., prof. geology Dickinson Coll., Carlisle, Pa., 1995-98; pres. So. Poly. State U., Marietta, Ga., 1998—. Vis. rschr. U. Uppsala, Sweden, 1984. Author: Career Opportunities in Geology and the Earth Sciences, 1983, Recent Revolutions in Geology, 1986; (with Rex Buchanan) Geomedia, 1988; columnist Geotimes, 1988—; contbr. articles to profl. jours. Recipient scholarship Ministry Edn. of Finland, Helsinki, 1984; grantee Sigma Xi, 1976, NASA, 1983-94. Fellow AAAS (geol. nominating com. 1984-87, chair-elect geology and geography sect. 1997-98, chair 1998-99, past chair 1999-00); mem. Geol. Soc. Am., Ga. Assn. Colls. (pres. 2005-06). Office: So Poly State U 1100 S Marietta Pkwy SE Marietta GA 30060-2855

ROSSBY, HANS THOMAS, oceanographer, educator; BS, Royal Inst. Tech., 1962; PhD in Oceanography, MIT, 1966. Prof. oceanography Grad. Sch. Oceanography, U. RI. Contbr. articles to profl. jours. Mem.: NAE. Office: U RI URI Bay Campus Box 52 South Ferry Road Narragansett RI 02882 Business E-Mail: trossby@gso.uri.edu.

ROSSEAU, GAIL L., neurosurgeon, educator; b. Nov. 30, 1956; m. Rick Rosseau; children: Natalie, Brendan. BS, U. Iowa, 1978; MD, George Washington Med. Sch., Washington, DC, 1981. Cert. Neurosurgery. Intern, gen. surgery George Washington U., Washington, 1985—86, resident, neurol. surgery, 1986—91; cranial base surgery fellow H.I.A. du Val-de-Grace Hosp., Paris, 1990; cranial base surgery and microvascular surgery fellow U. Pitts. Presbyn.-U. Hosp., Pa., 1991—92; staff mem., neurol. surgery Gottlieb Meml. Hosp., 1992—99, Columbus Hosp., 1992—2001, Ingalls Hosp., 1998—2000, Elmhurst Meml. Hosp., 1999, Ravenswood Hosp., 2001—02, Neurologic & Orthopedic Inst. Chgo., 2003—; mem. Chgo. Inst. Neurosurgery and Neuroresearch (CINN), Neurologic & Orthopedic Inst. Chgo., 1992—, dir., cranial base surgery, 2003—; staff mem., neurol. surgery Rush Med. Coll., Rush U. Med. Ctr., Ill., 1998, asst. prof., neurol. surgery Ill., 1998—. Lectr. in field. Contbr. articles to profl. jours., chapters to books. Recipient Harry B. Zehner, Jr. Meml Traveling Fellowship award, ACS, Chgo. Women of Yr. Mentor award. Mem.: Congress Neurol., Am. Assn. Neurol. Surgeons. Achievements include pioneering the use of endoscopic techniques in treating pituitary tumors. Office: Chgo Inst Neurosurgery and Neuroresearch Neurologic & Orthopedic Inst Chgo 4501 N Winchester Ave 2nd Fl Chicago IL 60640 Address: Chgo Inst Neurosurgery and Neuroreseach Med Group 1200 S York Rd Elmhurst IL 60126 *

ROSSELLINI, ISABELLA, actress, model; b. Rome, June 18, 1952; d. Roberto Rossellini and Ingrid Bergman; m. Martin Scorsese, Sept. 1979 (div. Nov. 1982); m. Jonathan Wiedemann (div.); 1 child, Elettra Ingrid. Student, Finch Coll., 1972, New Sch. for Social Research, NYC. Model for Lancôme cosmetics, 1982—95. Actor (films) A Matter of Time, 1976, Il Pap'occhio, 1980, The Meadow, 1982, White Nights, 1985, Blue Velvet, 1986, Siesta, 1987, Red Riding Hood, 1987, Tough Guys Don't Dance, 1987, Zelly and Me, 1988, Cousins, 1989, Wild at Heart, 1990, Les Dames Galantes, 1990, Death Becomes Her, 1992, The Pickle, 1992, Fearless, 1993, Wyatt Earp, 1994, Immortal Beloved, 1994, The Innocent, 1995, The Funeral, Crime of the Century, 1996, Big Night, 1996, The Real Blonde, 1998, Empire, 2002, Roger Dodger, 2002, The Tulse Luper Suitcases: The Moab Story, 2003, The Saddest Music in the World, 2003, The Tulse Luper Suitcases, Part 2: Vaux to the Sea, 2004, King of the Corner, 2004, Heights, 2004, The Feast of the Goat, 2005, The Architect, 2006; (TV films) The Last Elephant, 1990, Lies of the Twins, 1991, Don Quixote, 2000, Monte Walsh, 2003, Earthsea, 2004; (TV miniseries) The Odyssey, 1997, Merlin, 1998, The Impostors, 1998, Left Luggage, 1998; (TV series) Napoléon, 2002; (TV appearances) Friends, 1996, Chicago Hope, 1997, The Simpsons, 1999, Alias, 2004, 2005; writer (films) My Dad is 100 Years Old, 2005; Author: Some of Me, 1997, In the Name of the Father, the Daughter and the Holy Spirits: Remembering Roberto Rossellini, 2006 Office: United Talent Agy 9560 Wilshire Blvd Ste 500 Beverly Hills CA 90212

ROSSELLO, PEDRO JUAN, legislator, former governor; b. San Juan, Apr. 5, 1944; m. Maga Nevares, Aug. 9, 1969; children: Juan Oscar, Luis Roberto, Ricardo Antonio. BS, U. Notre Dame, 1966; MD, Yale U., 1970; MPH, U. P.R., 1981; LLD (hon.), U. Notre Dame, 1995, U. Mass., 1995. Intern straight surgery Beth Israel Hosp., Boston, 1970-71, resident gen. surgery, 1971-74; resident cardiac and burns Mass. Gen. Hosp., Boston, 1972; resident trauma San Francisco Gen. Hosp., 1973; sr. resident pediat. surgery Children's Hosp., Boston, 1974-75, chief resident, pediat. surgery-urology, 1975-76; instr. surgery Harvard Med. Sch., 1975-76; pvt. practice San Juan, 1976-92; asst. prof. surgery U. P.R., 1978-82, assoc. prof. surgery, 1982-92; dir. Dept. Health City of San Juan, 1985-87; chief surgery San Jorge Hosp., San Juan, 1989-92, med. dir., 1990; gov. P.R., San Juan, 1993-2001; senator P.R. Legis., San Juan, 2005—. Lead gov. So. Regional Project Infant Mortality, 1993-95; chair So. States Energy Bd., 1995-96; chmn. So. Growth Policies Bd., 1999-2000; chair So. Tech. Coun., 1998-99, So. Internat. Trade Coun., 1998-99; mem. intergovtl. policy adv. com. U.S. Trade Rep., 1994-2001; pres. Coun. State Govts., 1998; mem. adv. coun. Welfare to Work Partnership; mem. Dem. Nat. Com.; bd. dirs. U.S.-Spain Coun.; mem. nat. adv. bd. Initiative and Referendum Inst. Contbr. articles to profl. jours. Mem. P.R. Olympic Com., 1982-84, 87-88; v.p. New Progressive Party, 1988-91, pres., 1991-99; mem. exec. com. Edn. Commn. States, 1995-2000; bd. visitors emeritus Georgetown U. Law Ctr., Washington; del. Dm. Nat. Conv., Chgo., 1996, 2000. Capt. USNG, 1970-76. Recipient Pres.'s award U.S. Hispanic C. of C., 1996, Pres.'s award League of United Latin Am. Citizens, 1998, Rolex Achievement award, 1999. Mem. Nat. Govs. Assn. (host 1996 ann. meeting), So. Govs. Assn. (chair 1997-98), Dem. Govs. Assn. (chair 1998), P.R. Tennis Assn. (pres. 1982-84), Caribbean Tennis Assn. (pres. 1983-84), Alpha Omega Alpha. Avocations: jogging, tennis, ocean kayaking. Office: PR Legis PO Box 9023431 San Juan PR 00902 *

ROSSEN, JORDAN, lawyer; b. Detroit, June 13, 1934; s. Nathan Paul and Rebecca (Rizy) R.; m. Susan Friebert, Mar. 24, 1963 (div. June 1972); 1 child, Rebecca; m. M. Elizabeth Bunn, Jan. 3, 1981; children— N. Paul, Jordan David. BA, U. Mich., 1956; JD, Harvard U., 1959. Bar: Mich. 1960, N.Y. 1998, U.S. Dist. Ct. (ea. dist.) Mich. 1960, U.S. Dist. Ct. (ea. and so. dists.) N.Y. 1999, U.S. Ct. Appeals (6th cir.) 1966, U.S. Ct. Appeals (7th cir.) 1974, U.S. Ct. Appeals (D.C. cir.) 1984, U.S. Ct. Appeals (3rd cir.) 1987, U.S. Ct. Appeals (2d cir.) 2004, U.S. Supreme Ct. 1966. Assoc. Sullivan, Elmer, Eames & Moody, Detroit, 1960-62; assoc. Sugar & Schwartz, Detroit, 1962-64; asst. gen. counsel UAW, Detroit, 1964-74, assoc. gen. counsel, 1974-83, gen. counsel, 1983-98; of counsel Meyer, Suozzi, English and Klein, NYC, 1998—; prof. labor studies Wayne State U., 2000—04. Vice pres. N.P. Rossen Agy., Inc., Detroit, 1960-83; gen. counsel Mich. Health & Social Security Research Inst., Inc., Detroit, 1965-83; dir. UAW Job Devel. & Tng. Corp., Detroit, 1984-90; mem. 6th Cir. Jud. Conf. Editor: Mich. Bar Labor Section Publication, 1961-64. Contbr. articles to profl. jours. Pres. Young Democrats, Mich., 1963-65; chmn. Americans for Democratic Action, Mich., 1966-68; chmn. Voter Registration Dem. Party, Mich., 1967. Recipient Human Rights award, City of Detroit, 1978. Mem.: Nat. Assn. Adminstrv. Law Judges, Coll. Labor and Employment Lawyers, Fed. Bar Assn., N.Y. Bar Assn., Mich. Bar Assn. Jewish. Office: 1350 Broadway Ste 501 New York NY 10018-7705 Home Phone: 646-742-1220; Office Phone: 212-763-7034. Business E-Mail: jrossen@msek.com.

ROSSER, ALVIN RAYMON, artist; b. Port Clinton, Ohio, July 5, 1928; s. Samuel Webster and Reba Della Rosser; m. Barbara Emma Roth, June 10, 1953; children: Rachelle Karen, Jill Allyn. BFA, Ohio U., 1950, MFA, 1953; postgrad., Hans Hofmann Sch. of Art, NYC, 1953—54. Comml. artist Mutual Broadcasting System, NYC, 1954; art tchr. Chagrin Falls H.S., Ohio, 1955; instr. Lehigh U., Bethlehem, Pa., 1956—58; artists' rep. Gerard Agy., NYC, 1958—60; art dir. Topper Toy Co., Elizabeth, NJ, 1961—62; scenic designer Harnick-Adams Prodns., NYC, 1963—66; art tchr. Sparta Bd. of Edn., NJ, 1966—89. Exhibited in group shows at Ward Eggleston Gallery, N.Y.C., 1953, Roko Gallery, 1953, Koltnow Gallery, 1953—57, Cleve. Mus. Art, 1954, N.Y.C. Ctr., 1954, 1955, 1956, 1957, Jersey City Mus., 1959, Montclair Mus., 1967; artist (one-man shows) Ohio U., 1953, Lehigh U., 1955, Paper Mill Playhouse, N.J., 1960, featured artist N.J. State Fair, 2000, Artery Gallery, Milford, Pa., 2000—02; author: (short stories) A Lesson in Love, I Thought My Father was God, 2002. Trustee, v.p. Sussex County Arts Coun., Newton, NJ, 1970—76. Cpl. US Army, 1950—52. Recipient Emerson Poetry award 1st prize, Ohio U., 1954, Skylands Best in Show award, Sussex County Arts Coun., 1989, Skylands Select Best in Show award, 2001, Patrick-Claus award, 2003. Avocations: fishing, gardening, beekeeping, pool, ventriloquy. Mailing: PO Box 76 Sparta NJ 07871-0076

ROSSER, ANNETTA HAMILTON, composer; b. Jasper, Fla., Aug. 28, 1913; d. Carlos Calvin and Jermai Reuben (Gilbert) Hamilton; m. John Barkley Rosser, Sept. 7, 1935 (dec. Sept. 1989); children: Edwenna Merryday, John Barkley Jr. BM, Fla. State U., 1932. Cert. tchr. Fla. Tchr. music Kirby-Smith Jr. High Sch., Jacksonville, Fla., 1932-35; 1st violinist Santa Monica (Calif.) Symphony, 1949-50; concertmaster Ithaca (N.Y.) Chamber Orch., 1948-56, Cornell Univ. Orch., Ithaca, 1948-56, soloist, 1957; 1st violinist Princeton (N.J.) Symphony, 1959-61; concertmaster Madison (Wis.) Symphony Orch., 1963-66, 1st violinist, 1967-82. Composer of over 100 vocal and instrumental compositions including Meditations on Cross, song cycle for 2 voices, flute and piano, 1976, An Offering of Song, book of 48 songs, 1977, Songs of a Nomad Flute, song cycle for soprano, flute and piano, 1978, Six Songs of the T'ang Dynasty for soprano and violin, 1983, Nocturne for violin and piano, 1989, Trio for flute, violin and piano, 1991, Scherzo for flute ensemble, 1991, (book of 21 songs) Another Offering of Song, 1998. Bd. dirs. Madison Opera Guild, 1972-86, Madison Civic Music Assn., 1983-85; past pres. Madison Symphony Orch. League, Ithaca Federated Music Club, Ithaca Composers Club; bd. dirs. Madison Art Ctr., 1979-83, Madison Woman of Distinction, 1980, Madison Civics Club, 1976-79, pres., 1977-78; pres. Art League Madison Art Ctr., 1980-82, Univ. League Scholarship Benefit Concert of Rosser Compositions, U. Wis., MMadison, 2003. Recipient Sr. Svc. award Rotary Club, 1994; original music manuscripts and programs were added to archives of U. Wis.-Madison Music Libr., 1996. Mem. AAUW, Wis. Acad. Scis., Arts, and Letters, Univ. League, Univ. League Bird Study Group, Madison Club, Wis. Acad. Scis., Arts, and Letters, PEO, Phi Kappa Phi, Pi Kappa Lambda, Sigma Alpha Iota. Republican. Presbyterian. Avocations: Chinese snuff bottles, English brass rubbings, birding. Home: 4209 Manitou Way Madison WI 53711-3703

ROSSER, EDWIN MICHAEL, mortgage company executive; b. Denver, Oct. 11, 1940; s. Edwin Michael and Ann (Ratliff) R.; m. Keren Call, July 17, 1969; children: Kevin, William. BS, Colo. State U., 1964; MA, U. No. Colo., 1974. Cert. mortgage banker. Mktg. officer United Bank Mortgage, Denver, 1968-74; dir. nat. accounts PMI Mortgage Ins. Co., Denver, 1974-85; v.p. Moore Mortgage Co., Denver, 1985-87, Pacific First Mortgage Corp., Englewood, Colo., 1987-89; 1st v.p. 1st Nat. Bank, San Francisco, 1990-93; v.p. nat. accounts United Guaranty Corp., 1993—. Bd. dirs. Rocky Mtn. Women's Inst. Photographer represented in Denver Art Mus., The Buffalo in Winter, (1st place award 1981). Steering com. Blueprint for Colo., Govs. Unified Housing Task Force; mem. Colo. Housing Coun. (chmn. 1986-87); bd. dirs. Colo. State U. Found.; mem. adv. bd. Arapahoe County Open Space and Trails, 1999-; mem. Colo. Land Use Commn., 1999, Colo. State Housing Bd., 2003; bd. dirs. The Conservation Campaign, 2004. Fellow Soc. Mortgage Bankers; mem. Am. Planning Assn., Soc. of Cert. Mortgage Bankers (chmn.), Mortgage Bankers Assn. Am. (cert., bd. govs. 1986-90, state and local achievement award 1986, Ernest P. Schumacher award 1988, disting. svc. award 2003, Burton Wood Legis. Svc. award), Colo. Mortgage Bankers Assn. (bd. dirs. 1979-88, pres. 1986, adv. bd. trust for pub. land, E.C. Spelman award 1978, Lifetime Achievement award 1998), Colo. Assn. Commerce and Industry, Denver Nat. Soc. Real Estate Fin., Mus. Natural History, Denver C. of C., Rocky Mtn. Mutual Housing Assn. (bd. dirs.), Ctr. of Fin. Real Estate (bd. dirs.), Colo. State U. Alumni Assn. (nat. pres. 1985, bd. dirs. 1979-87, mem. found. bd. 1987-91, 93-2000, Honor Alumnus 1984, ha Sasso award Dept. Athletics 1993), Univ. Club, City Club Denver, Nat. Soc. for Real Estate Fin. (CRF designation 1997), Colo. State U. Henry Alumni (Svc. award 2000), Univ. Club, Alpha Sigma Gamma Republican. Roman Catholic. Avocations: photography, fly fishing. Home: 12478 E Amherst Cir Aurora CO 80014-3306 Office: United Guaranty Residential Ins Co 6312 S Fiddlers Green Cir Englewood CO 80111-4943 Personal E-mail: emrcmb@aol.com.

ROSSER, ESSIE, minister, counselor, marketing professional; b. Dawson, Ga., Apr. 15, 1939; d. James Andrews and Essie Louise Kimbrough; children: Evelyn Ellington, Augustus Reid, Anthony Reid, Lassels Reid. Student, Corp. Coll., 1968—69; AA, Onondaga C.C., Syracuse, NY, 1972; BA, Oswego State Coll., 1974; JD, Atlanta Law Sch., 1982; ThD, 1998; DD, Abotra Bible Inst. and Sem. Trained nursing technician Syracuse Meml. Hosp., NY, 1957—62; employment counselor, dir. People's Employment Agy., Syracuse, 1962—64, CEO, dir. job readiness/placement clients, writer manual Decatur, Ga.; cons. families/food plan Family Food Svs., Fulton, NY, 1964—68; sales dir., CEO Dependable Janitorial Svs., North Syracuse, NY, 1969—73; rsch. supr. Math., Inc., Dayton, Ohio, 1975—77; adminstrv. asst. psychology dept. Clark Coll., Atlanta, 1977—82; min., counselor drug deliverance/prevention counselor ch. Worldwide Word Ministries., Inc., Atlanta. Achievements include development of faith based deliverance programs; drug prevention currciulums beginning with pre-k child, extending through high school presently being established in faith based organizations engaging their help with the drug problem. Avocations: antiques, music, writing, travel.

ROSSET, BARNET LEE, JR., publishing executive; b. Chgo., May 28, 1922; s. Barnet Lee and Mary (Tansey) R.; m. Joan Mitchell, 1950 (div. 1952)); m. Hannelore Eckert, Aug. 1953 (div. 1957); 1 child, Peter; m. Cristine Agnini, Mar. 11, 1965 (div. 1979); children: Tansey, Beckett; m. Elisabeth Krug, 1980 (div. 1991; 1 child, Chantal; m. Astrid Myers, June 11, 2007. Ph.B., U. Chgo., 1947; BA New Sch. Social Research, NYC, 1952. Pub., editor Grove Press, Inc., 1951-86, Evergreen Rev., 1957-73, Blue Moon Books, Inc., NYC, 1987-98, Evergreen Rev. Inc., 1998—, Foxrock, Inc., 1995—. Served to 1st lt. Signal Corps AUS, 1942-46. Recipient Ninth Pub. citation PEN Am. Ctr., 1988, Poor Richard's award Small Press Ctr., 1999, Commandeur De L'Ordre Des Arts et Des Lettres, French Govt., 1999, Nat. Book Critics Cir. Lifetime Achievement award, 2001, Curtis Benjamin award Assn. Am. Pubs., 2001, 1st Ann. Hadada award Paris Rev., 2003. Mem. PEN, Overseas Press Club. Office: 61 4th Ave New York NY 10003-5204 Home Phone: 212-777-2480; Office Phone: 212-505-6880. Personal E-mail: evergreen@nyc.rr.com.

ROSSI, ANTHONY GERALD, lawyer; b. Warren, Ohio, July 20, 1935; s. Anthony Gerald and Lena (Guarnieri) R.; m. Marilyn J. Fuller, June 22, 1957; children: Diana L., Maribeth, Anthony Gerald III. BS, John Carroll U., 1957; JD, Cath. U. Am., 1961. Bar: Ohio 1961. Ptnr. Guarnieri & Secrest, Warren, 1961—; former acting judge Warren Municipal Ct. Mem. Mahoning-Shenango Estate Planning Coun., 1968—, past sec.; past pres. Warren Olympic Club; past bd. govs. Cath. U. Am. Law Sch. Coun.; past trustee Trumbull Art Guild, Warren Civic Music Assn. Capt. Transp. Corps, AUS, 1957-65. Mem. ABA, Ohio Bar Assn., Trumbull County Bar Assn. (exec. com. 1975—, pres. 1976-77), Am. Arbitration Assn., Ohio State Bar Found., Ohio Motorist Assn. (corp. mem., trustee 1980-86, 92-98), Wolf's Club, KC, Elks, Ohio Acad. of Trial Lawyers. Home: 2500 Hidden Lakes Dr NE Warren OH 44484-4159 Office: 151 E Market St Warren OH 44481-1102 Home Phone: 330-856-3774; Office Phone: 330-393-1584. E-mail: ganslaw@netdotcom.com.

ROSSI, DINO J., former state legislator; b. Seattle, Oct. 15, 1959; s. John and Eve Rossi; m. Terry Rossi, 1987; children: Juliauna, Jake, Joseph, Jillian. BA in Bus. Mgmtr., Seattle U., 1982. Mem. Wash. Senate, Dist. 5, Olympia, 1996—2003; mem. energy, tech., and telecom. com. Wash. Senate; mem. natural resources, parks and recreation com.; mem. ways and means com.; chmn., 2003; mem. capital budget subcom.; mem. joint com. on pension policy. Vol. Sr. Ctr.; co-founder Operation Homefront; past bd. dirs. Boys and Girls Club, Mountains to Sound Greenway Bd. Mem. Rotary (Issaquah). Republican.

ROSSI, ENNIO C., internist, educator; b. Madison, Wis., Apr. 3, 1931; s. Joseph and Esther (D'Amelio) R.; m. Anna Maria Bianchi, June 22, 1957; children: Roberta, Marco. BA, U. Wis., 1951, MD, 1954. Diplomate Am. Bd. Internal Medicine. Intern Ohio State U. Hosps., 1954-55; resident medicine U. Wis. Hosps., 1958-61, fellow, 1961-63; instr. medicine Marquette U., Milw., 1963-64, asst. prof. medicine, 1964-66; assoc. prof. medicine Northwestern U., Chgo., 1966-72, prof. medicine, 1972-96, prof. emeritus, 1996—, chief hematology, 1967-84, chief transfusion medicine, 1984-96. V.p. med. affairs Life Source Blood Ctr., Glenview, Ill., 1988-93; vis. scientist Mario Negri Inst., Milan, 1977. Co-editor: Haemostasis and the Kidney, 1989; sr. editor: Principles of Transfusion Medicine, 1991, 2d edit., 1996. Capt. U.S. Army, 1956-58. Fulbright scholar, U.S. Dept. State, U. Rome, 1955; Nat. Heart, Lung Blood Inst. Transfusion Medicine Acad. awardee, 1983; WHO travelling fellow, 1985. Fellow ACP; mem. Am. Soc. Hematology, Am. Soc. Pharmacology and Exptl. Therapeutics, Am. Assn. Blood Banks (chmn. acad. transfusion medicine com. 1988-93), Internat. Soc. Blood Transfusion. Home: 812 Oak St Apt 302 Winnetka IL 60093-2560

ROSSI, GUIDO A(NTONIO), mathematics professor, researcher; b. Moretta, Cuneo, Italy, Jan. 17, 1944; s. Giulio Cesare and Anna Maria (Ferraris di Celle) R.; m. Maria Emilia Zucchi, Mar. 27, 1978. Dr. in Math., U. Torino, Italy, 1967. Asst. U. Torino, 1969-82; asst. prof. Facoltà di Economia e Commercio, 1969-82, assoc. prof. math., 1982-86, prof. math. social scis. and econs., 1986, full prof., 1986—, prof. math. for fin., 1996. Dir. Inst. Math Finanziaria, 1974-81, 83-85, 1992-94, dir. dept. stats. and applied math. human scis., 1995-2003, coord. rsch. projects, 1986—; pres. Sch. U. Mgmt. d'Impresa, 2002—, pres.bd. tchrs. acturial scis., 2005-; prof. Scuola di Applicazione Italian Army, 1992—; mem. sci. bd. 3d A.F.I.R. Colloquium, 1993; mem. Internat. Sci. Com.; organizer FUR X conf.; bd. tchrs. doctorate program in math. for fin. markets joint Univs. Brescia, Milano, Torino, Pavia, 1991-2003, decision scis. U. Torino, 2003—. Contbr. articles to profl. and sci. jours. Served to lt. Italian Army, 1967-68, diplomated Sommelier, 1986. Decorated Knight of the Order of Civil Merit of Savoy, 1990, comdr., 1996, Knight of the Order of the S.S. Maurice and Lazarus, 2005. Mem. Unione Matematica Italiana, Assn. per la Matematica Applicata alle Scienze Economiche Sociali (auditor 1977-89, 2002—, adminstr. 1990—2001), Assn. Italiana di Ricerca Operativa (auditor 1990—), Italian Order of Actuaries, Assn. Italiana Sommeliers,

Assn. Museo Ferroviario Piemontese (pres. 1986-2005, bd. mem. 2005—), Am. Math. Soc., European Math. Soc., Inst. Vienna Cir., Istituto Italiano dei Castelli-Internat. Burgen Institut, Fondo per l'Ambiente Italiano, Italian Fedn. Ferrovie Turistiche and Museali (co-founder, first pres. 1997-99), European Fedn. Mus. Tourist Railways (co-founder, bd. mem., 2003-); Clubs: I Neoteri (pres. 1990-92). Roman Catholic. Achievements include contributions to the foundations of probability, decision theory and financial decisions. Office: Dept Statistica & Matematica Applicata Piazza Arbarello 8 I-10122 Turin Italy E-mail: guido.rossi@unito.it.

ROSSI, JEROME R., retail executive; b. Boston, Aug. 12, 1943; m. Geraldine R.; children: Joseph, Jeffrey. Grad., Bentley Coll., 1966, Northeastern U., Boston, 1970. Sr. fin. analyst IT&T, 1966-68; supervising auditor Arthur Young & Co., 1968-72; v.p., contr. Dayton-Hudson Co., 1972-80; sr. v.p., CFO KDT Industries, 1980-82; sr. v.p. fin. G. Fox Co., 1982-85, chmn., 1985-89, Foley's, Houston, 1989; pres., COO Marshalls, 1990—96; exec. v.p. Marmaxx Group TJX Cos., Inc., 1996—2000, pres. HomeGoods, 2000—05, sr. exec. v.p., COO Marmaxx Group, 2005—07, sr. exec. v.p., group pres., 2007—. Office: TJX Cos Inc 770 Cochituate Rd Framingham MA 01701 Office Phone: 508-390-1000. Office Fax: 508-390-2091. *

ROSSI, JOSEPH ANTHONY, film and television make-up artist, educator; b. Providence, July 10, 1955; s. Michael Thomas and Jennie (Paolucci) R.; m. Christina Elliott; children: Michael Elliott, Sofia Rose. BS, R.I. Coll., 1977. Tchr. film and TV R.I. Coll., Providence, 1983-86, Salve Regina Coll., Newport, R.I., 1983—; owner, prin. Joe Rossi Makeup, Providence, 1977—, 1001 Faces, Providence, 1979—. Dept. head Underdog and Showtimes' Brotherhood. Make-up artist Pres. William Clinton and Hillary Rodham Clinton, v.p. Albert Gore, make-up artist on feature films War of the Worlds, Fever Pitch, The Last Shot, Stuck on You, Little Black Book, Moonlight Mile, Mona Lisa Smile, Goodbye, Hello, Shallow Hal, Osmosis Jones, Passionada, Prozac Nation, Me, Myself and Irene, Bye, Bye, America, David Mamet's State and Main, Thirteen Days, Lift, The Human Stain, Pink Floyd, Zoom, Crimestoppers 800, First Person, Saturday Night Live, Rivera Live, Wide World Sports, Nat. Geog. Lost Subs K-19, 2004, make-up artist Evening, The Great Debaters, The War That Made America, Face the Nation, 60 Minutes, 1995 Skating Finals ABC-TV, Unsolved Mysteries, Providence, Face the Nation, 2004, Peter Jennings, Outside Providence, Universal feature Meet Joe Black, Session 9, Lift, Percy Julian: Forgotten Genius, Nova, Slave Catchers, The History Channel, The American Experience, PBS, Lizzie Borden: Case Reopened, original design Philip Glass Opera, The Fall of the House of Usher and Genet's The Balcony, at the Bolshoi Theatre, Russia; contbr. chapters to books. Bd. dirs. R.I. State Coun. on Arts, 1996-2003. Home and Office: 137 Abbott Run Valley Rd Cumberland RI 02864-3249 Office Phone: 401-334-3436. E-mail: joe@rossimakeup.com.

ROSSI, RONALD ALDO, sports association administrator, Olympic athlete; b. Bronx, NY, Dec. 2, 1956; s. Aldo D. and Jeanette (Morretta) R.; m. Susan Veltman, Mar. 26, 1983; children: Scott, Lauren. BEE, Manhattan Coll., 1978. Registered profl. engr., N.Y. Mem. computer ops. staff John Blair and Co., NYC, 1978-83, communications engr., 1984; sports program dir. U.S. Luge Assn., Lake Placid, NY, 1984-85, exec. dir., 1985—. Com. mem. U.S. Luge Assn., 1978—, athlete's rep., 1980-83; com. mem. U.S. Olympic Com., Colorado Springs, Colo., 1989-90, 93-96. Mem. U.S. Olympic Luge Team, Sarajevo, Yugoslavia, 1984; mem. Olympic team staff, Calgary, Can., 1988, Albertville, France, 1992, Lillehammer, Norway, 1994, Nagano, Japan, 1998, Salt Lake City, 2002, Torino, Italy, 2006. Avocations: luge, golf, softball, movies, computers. Address: US Luge Association 57 Church St Lake Placid NY 12946-1805

ROSSI, RUTH HARRIS, special education educator; d. Everett Tomlinson Harris and Clora Ethel Stanley; m. Raymond Anthony Rossi, Feb. 26, 1977; children: Hillary Niles, Tess Virginia, Anthony John. BA, U. R.I., 1967, postgrad., 1973; EdM, Seattle U., 1975. Spl. edn. tchr. Lakota Mid. Sch., Federal Way, Wash., 1989—, spl. edn. dept. chair, 2002—. Mem. post-secondary transition adv. com. Federal Way Sch. Dist., 1999—2004. Treas. PTA, Woodmont East Sch., Federal Way, 1982, 1996, 1997; leader, membership facilitator CampFire, Kent, Wash., 1982—86; mem. customer adv. com. Puget Sound Power, Renton, Wash., 1983, 1984. Grantee, Federal Way Edn. Found., 2003. Mem.: ASCD, ACLU, Audubon Soc. Avocations: reading, walking, gardening, cooking, needlepoint. Office: Lakota Mid Sch 1415 SW 314th St Federal Way WA 98023

ROSSI, WILLIAM MATTHEW, lawyer; b. Coldwater, Ohio, June 11, 1954; s. Hugh Dominic and Patricia Jean (Putts) R.; m. Constance Sue Streacker, July 21, 1973; children: Bryan Thomas, Lauren Michelle, Alexandria Marie. BA cum laude, Miami U., Oxford, Ohio, 1977; JD magna cum laude, U. Dayton, 1981. Bar: Ohio 1981 (inactive), US Dist. Ct. (so. dist.) Ohio 1982, US Supreme Ct. 1986, US Ct. Appeals (6th cir.) 1987, Fla. 1991, US Dist. Ct. (so. and mid. dists.) Fla. 1992, US Ct. Appeals (11th cir.) 1992. Assoc. Milliken & Fitton, Hamilton, Ohio, 1981-83; dep. law dir., chief city negotiator City of Middletown, 1984—89; pvt. practice, 1989-92; assoc. Jackson, Lewis, Schnitzler and Krupman, Orlando, Fla., 1992-93; dep. county atty. Sarasota County, Fla., 1993—2005; chief deputy city atty. City of Miami, 2005—. Bd. dirs. Columbia Inst. Bus., Middletown, 1977-78; lectr. Sawyer Coll., Dayton, 1982-83; mcpl. ct. magistrate, 1984-92. Asst. coach Knothole Baseball, Middletown, 1981; bd. dir. Butler County Mental Health Ctr., Hamilton, 1983-85, Summer Youth Theatre, Middletown, 1985-86; mem. bd. rev. Troop 20 Boy Scouts Am., 1986-87; mem. Sch. Adv. Coun., 1996-2002; mem. nat. adv. bd. St. Joseph's Coll.; chmn. allocations panel United Way, Sarasota, Fla., 2001-2005; mem. impact coun. United Way, Miami, Sarasota, 2007—. Recipient Am. Jurisprudence award Lawyers Coop. Pub. Co., 1979, 81, Internat. Youth Achievement award Internat. Biog. Ctr. and Am. Biog. Inst., 1982. Mem. ABA, Fla. Bar Assn. (co-chmn. labor rels. com. 2002), Nat. Pub. Employer Labor Rels. Assn., Phi Beta Kappa, Phi Delta Phi (bd. dirs., historian 1979-80). Republican. Roman Catholic. Avocations: golf, travel, writing. Office: City of Miami 444 SW 2nd Ave Miami FL 33130 Home: Apt 1702 1111 Brickell Bay Dr Miami FL 33131-2957 Office Phone: 305-416-1800. Business E-Mail: wmrossi@ci.miami.fl.us.

ROSSIDES, EUGENE TELEMACHUS, lawyer, writer; b. NYC, Oct. 23, 1927; s. Telemachus and Anna (Maravel) R.; m. Elinor Burcham (div.); 1 child, Gale; m. Aphrodite Macotsin, Dec. 30, 1961; children: Michael, Alexander, Eleni. AB, Columbia U., 1949, JD, 1952. Criminal law investigator Office of Dist. Atty., NYC, 1952; assoc. Rogers & Wells, NYC, 1954-56, 61-66, ptnr., 1966-69, 73-92, sr. counsel, 1993—; asst. atty. gen. State of N.Y., NYC, 1956-58; asst. to undersec. Dept. Treasury, Washington, 1958-61, asst. sec., 1969-73. Bd. dirs. Sterling Nat. Bank, N.Y.C. Author: U.S. Import Trade Regulation, 2d edit., 1986, Foreign Unfair Competition, 3d edit., 1991, United States Import Trade Law, 1992, also articles; chief import editor Internat. Trade Reporter, Bur. Nat. Affairs, 1980—; editor: The Truman Doctrine of Aid to Greece: A Fifty-Year Retrospective, 1998, Doing Business in Greece, 1996, U.S. Rels. with Greece and Cyprus, 1990—. Mem. Grace Commn., Washington, 1981-82; chmn. nationalities div. Reagan Bush Com., Washington, 1980; campaign mgr. N.Y.C. Nixon for Pres. Com., 1968, Keating for Senator Com., N.Y. State, 1964; bd. dirs. Eisenhower World Affairs Inst., Washington, Am. Hellenic Inst. Inc. Capt. USAF, 1952-60. Recipient Medal for Excellence, Columbia U., 1972, Young Lawyer's award Columbia Law Sch. Alumni Assn., 1972, Silver Anniversary award NCAA, 1974, John Jay award Columbia Coll. Alumni Assn., 1994. Mem. ABA, N.Y. State Bar Assn., Fed. Bar Assn. Republican. Greek Orthodox. Avocations: tennis, photography. Home: 3666 Upton St NW Washington DC 20008-3125 Office: Clifford Chance Rogers & Wells LLP 2001 K St NW Washington DC 20006-1037

ROSSIN, LAWRENCE GEORGE, ambassador; b. NJ, Nov. 3, 1952; m. Debra J. McGowan; children: Claire, Alec. BA in Economics, Claremont Men's Coll., Calif., 1975; student, NATO Def. Coll., Rome, 1988—89. Former dir. Office of South Cen. European Affairs, Dept. of State; US chief of mission in Kosovo US Embassy, Pristina, 1999—2000; US amb. to Croatia US Dept. State, Zagreb, 2001—03; spl. asst. to Pres., sr. dir. for strategic planning & S.W. Asia NSC, Washington, 2003—04; prin. dep. spl. rep. of sec. gen. for UN Adminstrv. Mission in Kosovo UN, Pristina, 2004—06, prin. dep. spl. rep. of sec. gen. for UN Stabilization Mission in Haiti Port-au-Prince, 2006—. Recipient Presdl. Disting. Svc. award, 2001, Award for Valour, US Dept. State, Superior Honor award (4), Meritorious Honor award, Order of Duke Branimir, Croatian Govt.

ROSSINGTON, GARY, musician; b. Jacksonville, Fla., Dec. 4, 1951; m. Dale Krantz, 1982; 2 children. Founding mem., guitarist Lynyrd Skynyrd, 1964—77, 1987—; co-founder The Rossington-Collins Band, 1980—82. Musician: (albums) (with Lynyrd Skynyrd) Pronounced Leh-Nerd Skin-Nerd, 1973, Smokes, 1973, Second Helping, 1974, Nuthin' Fancy, 1975, Gimme Back My Bullets, 1976, One More from the Road, 1976, Street Survivors, 1977, Southern by the Grace of God, 1988, Lynyrd Skynyrd 1991, The Last Rebel, 1993, Endangered Species, 1994, Freebird: The Movie, 1996, Southern Knights, 1996, Twenty, 1997, Lyve, 1998, Edge of Forever, 1999, Universal Masters Collection, 1999, Christmas Time Again, 2000, Vicious Cycle, 2003, (with The Rossington-Collins Band) Anytime, Anyplace, Anywhere, 1980, This is the Way, 1982. Named to Rock and Roll Hall of Fame, 2006. Office: Vector Mgmt PO Box 120479 Nashville TN 37212 also: Sanctuary Records 5226 Greens Dairy Rd Raleigh NC 27616-4612

ROSSINI, JOSEPH, contracting and development corporate executive; b. New Rochelle, NY, Nov. 25, 1939; m. Antonia Rossini; children: Katherine, Anthony, Andrew. *Wife, Antonia Rossini, is a nationally recognized American wildlife artist, known for the 1995 Florida State Duck Stamp; she has received numerous awards. She received a BA from Stonybrook State University and an MA from New York University. She is a member of the New Rochelle Council on the Arts. Great-great Uncle Gioachino Rossini was the composer of the "William Tell Overture" and the "Barber of Seville", among other works. Father, Carmelo, was a contractor-builder in the United States and Canada. Brother, Frank, was a deep sea diver and soldier of fortune; he was one of the last Americans to leave Saigon at the end of the war.* Student, Fordham U., 1965—66, Iona Coll., 1972. Pres. Rossini Contracting Corp., Mt. Vernon, NY, 1963—; prin. Rossini Devel. Co., Monticello, NY, 1965—. Bd. dirs. Circuit Realty Corp., New Rochelle, 1970-71. Mem. planning bd. City of New Rochelle, 1986-92, mem. bldg. dept. adv. com., 1985; vol. instr. N.Y. State Dept. Environ. Conservation, Albany, 1968-95; vice chmn. New Rochelle Conservative Party, 1984-2001, chmn., 2001—; county committeeman Westchester County Conservative Party; pres., bd. trustees Beechwoods Cemetery, New Rochelle; dir. New Rochelle Neighborhood Revitalization Corp., 1993-96. With USN, 1959-61. Mem. NRA (benefactor life patron), Gen. Contractors Assn. N.Y., Constrn. Industry Coun. Westchester and Hudson Valley, Bldg. Trades Employers Assn., Soc. Explosives Engrs., Deep Founds. Inst., Young Ams. for Freedom, Am. Lauretana Assn., Mensa, Assoc. Gen. Contractors Am., Caths. in Constrn., Tin Can Sailors, Westchester County Firearm Owners Assn., N.Y. State Rifle and Pistol Assn., ASCE Constrn. Inst., Cath. League. Roman Catholic. Office: Rossini Contracting Corp 113 Edison Ave Mount Vernon NY 10550-5005 Office Phone: 914-664-4300. Personal E-mail: joe@rossinicontracting.com.

ROSSITER, ALEXANDER, JR., publishing executive, editor; b. Elmira, NY, Mar. 2, 1936; s. Alexander H. and Eleanor (Howell) R.; m. Sylvia Lee Vanlandingham, June 11, 1960; children: Alexander H. III, Jill Jarrell. BA, Rutgers U., 1958; postgrad., Emory U., 1959. With UPI, 1959-92; newsman Atlanta, 1959-61, Richmond, Va., 1961-63; bur. mgr. Cape Canaveral, Fla., 1963-73; sci. editor Washington, 1973-87; exec. editor, 1987-88; exec. editor, sr. v.p., 1988-91; editor, exec. v.p., 1991-92; asst. v.p., dir. news svc. Duke U., Durham, NC, 1992—2001, dir. com. Pratt Sch. Engrs., 2001—02, assoc. dean pub. affairs, 2003—. Mem. nat. adv. bd. Knight Ctr. for Specialized Journalism, Colleg Pk., Md., 1988-92; mem. adv. bd. Med. Journalism Program, U. N.C., Chapel Hill, 2000-04. Recipient Grady-Stack medal Am. Chem. Soc., 1987, other journalism awards. Mem. Nat. Assn. Sci. Writers, Edn. Writers Assn. Office: Duke U 305 Teer Bldg Box 90271 Durham NC 27708 *Enthusiasm is the key to success. Take on your education, your family responsibilities and your work with enthusiasm and good things will result.*

ROSSITER, BRYANT WILLIAM, chemistry consultant; b. Ogden, Utah, Mar. 10, 1931; s. Bryant B. and Christine (Peterson) R.; m. Betty Jean Anderson, Apr. 16, 1951; children: Bryant, Mark, Diane, Steven, Linda, Karen, Matthew, Gregory. BA, U. Utah, 1954, PhD, 1957. Researcher Eastman-Kodak Co., Rochester, NY, 1957-63, head color phys. chem. lab., 1963-70, dir. chemistry div., 1970-84, dir. sci., tech. devel., 1984-86; pres. Viratek Inc., Costa Mesa, Calif., 1986-89; sr. v.p. ICN Pharms., Costa Mesa, 1989-90; ret., 1990; pres., CEO WRECON, Inc., Laguna Hills, Calif., 1991-96, ret., 1996. Sr. editor John Wiley & Sons, N.Y.C., 1970—; chmn. bd. Nucleic Acid Rsch. Inst., Costa Mesa, 1987-88; trustee Eastman Dental Ctr., Rochester, 1973-93 (bd. pres. 1982-85); bd. dirs. Verax & Corp. Editor: (chem. treatises) Physical Methods of Chemistry (11 vols.), 1970-76, Physical Methods, (12 vols.), 1986—, Chemical Experimentation Under Extreme Conditions, 1979. Mem. rsch. adv. com. U.S. Agy. for Internat. Devel., Washington, chmn. rsch. adv. com., 1989-92; mem. panel on biosci. Pres.' Coun. Advisors on Sci. and Tech., 1991; mem. adv com. Cornell Internat. Inst. for Food, Agr. and Devel., 1991; presiding officer Ch. Jesus Christ Latter Day Saints, Ea. U.S. and Can., 1959-86, dir. cmty. rels. Orange County, 2004—; counselor presidency San Diego temple, 1998-2002, dir. cmty. rels. Orange county pub. affairs coun., 2005—. 1st lt. USAFR, 1951-58. Named Hon. Alumni Brigham Young U., Provo, Utah, 1982. Fellow AAAS, Am. Inst. Chemists (lectr., Fellows award 1988, Will Judy award Juanita Coll. 1978); mem. Internat. Union Pure and Applied Chemistry (chmn. U.S. nat. com., orignator, chmn. Chemical Rsch. Applied to World Needs com. 1975-87, chmn. Chemical Rsch. Applied to World Needs II The Internat. Conf. on Chemistry and World Food Supplies, 1982), Am. Chem. Soc. (chmn. internat. activities). Avocations: horseback riding, reading, fishing. Home and Office: 25662 Dillon Rd Laguna Hills CA 92653-5800 E-mail: bwr@ni.net.

ROSSITER, PETER L., lawyer; b. Evanston, Ill., July 22, 1948; AB, Princeton U., 1970; JD, Yale U., 1973. Bar: Ill. 1973. Law clk. to Hon. Alvin B. Rubin U.S. Dist. Ct. (ea. dist.), La., 1973-75; law clk. to Hon. Warren E. Burger U.S. Supreme Ct., 1975-76; mem. Schiff., Hardin & Waite, Chgo., 1976—92; gen. counsel Northern Trust Corp., 1992—2000, exec. v.p., 2000—04; ptnr. Schiff Hardin LLP, 2004—. Lectr. Tulane U. Law Sch. 1975, U. Chgo. Law Sch. 1978-80, chaired Northwestern Corp. Counsel Inst. Mem. ABA, Chgo. Bar Assn., Ill. State Bar Assn. Bd. editors Yale Law Journal 1972-73. Office: Schiff Hardin LLP 6600 Sears Tower Chicago IL 60606-6473 Office Phone: 312-258-5579. Office Fax: 312-258-5600. Business E-Mail: prossiter@schiffhardin.com.

ROSSITER, ROBERT E., manufacturing executive; b. Detroit, 1946; BBA, Northwood U. With Lear Siegler Inc., 1971-87, pres. seating divsn.; pres. Lear Corp., 1984—2002, COO, 1988—97, 1998—2000, bd. dirs. Southfield, Mich., 1988—, COO internat. ops., 1997—98, CEO Southfield, Mich., 2000—, chmn., 2003—. Bd. dirs. Detroit Renaissance, Focus: HOPE, Detroit. Office: Lear Seating Corp 21557 Telegraph Rd Southfield MI 48034 *

ROSSITER, STEPHEN J., surgeon; b. Lafayette, Ind., Apr. 6, 1946; m. Cheryl Lynn Carlson, Apr. 29, 1978; children: Kimberly Lynn, Michael James. MD, U. Mich., Ann Arbor, 1971. Diplomate Am. Bd. Thoracic Surgery, 1998, Am. Bd. Surgery, 1978. Resident Stanford U. Med. Ctr., Calif., 1971—78; asst. prof. cardiovasc. surgery Stanford U. Med. Sch., 1978—79; cardiac surgeon Good Samaritan Hosp., Los Gatos, Calif., 1979—83, Mercy Gen. Hosp., Sacramento, 1983—. Contbr. articles to profl. jours. Fellow: ACS (life; diplomate), Am. Coll. Chest Physicians (life), Am. Coll. Cardiology (life). Office: Cardiac Surgery West 3941 J St Suite 270 Sacramento CA 95819 Home Phone: 916-733-6850.

ROSSKY, PETER JACOB, chemistry professor, chemical engineer, researcher; BA, Cornell U., 1971; MA, Harvard U., 1972, PhD in Chemical Physics, 1978. Postdoctoral rschr. SUNY, Stony Brook, 1978—79; prof. then George W. Watt Centennial prof. chemistry U. Tex., Austin, 1979—, Collie Welch Regents Chair in chemistry, 2002. Dir. Ctr. for Computational Molecular Sci.; dir. Inst. for Theoretical Chemistry U. Tex. Mem. editl. bd.: Theoretical Chemistry Accts., Understanding Chem. Reactivity, Jour. Chem. Theory and Computation. Fellow: AAAS, Am. Phys. Soc., Am. Acad. Arts & Sciences. Office: U Tex Dept Chemistry & Biochemistry 1 University Station A5300 Austin TX 78712

ROSS-LEE, BARBARA, dean, educator; BS Biology and Chemistry, Wayne State U., M Tchr. Spl. Populations; grad., Mich. State U., 1973; DSc (hon.), N.Y. Coll. Osteo. Medicine; degree (hon.), Wilmington Coll., 2001. Legis. asst. Senator Bill Bradley; chmn. dept. family medicine, assoc. dean health policy Mich. State U. Coll. Medicine; dean Ohio U. Coll. Osteo. Medicine, 1993—2001; dean, v.p. health scis. and med. affairs N.Y. Coll. Osteo. Medicine, 2001—. Lectr. in field; dir. Osteo. Heritage Health Policy Fellowship Program; exec. dir. Inst. Nat. Health Policy and Rsch., NOMA (the osteo. affiliate NMA); mem. bd. dirs. Assn. Acad. Health Ctrs., Nat. Fund Med. Edn., Nat. Health Svs. Corps' Assn. Clinicians Underserved; trustee Found. Appalachian Ohio; participant confs. Contbr. more than 30 scholarly articles med. and health-care issues. Named to Ohio Women's Hall of Fame, 1998; recipient Magnificent 7 award, Bus. and Profl. Women/USA, 1993, Women's Health award, Blackboard African-Am. Nat. Bestsellers, Disting. Pub. Svc. award, Okla. State U. Coll. Osteo. Medicine, Walter F. Patenge medal pub. svc., Mich. State U. Coll. Osteo. Medicine, 2001. Fellow: Am. Osteo. Bd. Family Physicians; mem.: NIH (adv. com. rsch. on women's health), Future Primary Care (Inst. Medicine's com.), U.S. Dept. Health and Human Svs. (nat. adv. com. rural health), Appalachian Health Policy (Appalachian regional commn.'s adv. coun.), AACOM Bd. Govs. (chair-elect exec. coun.), AOA Bur. Profl. Edn., Trilateral Internat. Med. Workforce Group. Achievements include first to be an osteopathic physician to participate in the prestigious Robert Wood Johnson Health Policy Fellowship. Office: NY Coll of Osteopathic Med Old Westbury No Blvd Rockefeller Bldg Rm 107 Westbury NY 11568-8000 Office Phone: 516-686-3747. E-mail: brosslee@nyit.edu.

ROSSMAN, STUART T., lawyer; b. Bklyn., Jan. 7, 1954; s. Marvin Warren and Phyllis (Berenbaum) R.; m. Rochelle S. Sorkin, May 18, 1975; children: Jessie Joanne, Rachel Joy. BA, U. Mich., 1975; JD, Harvard U., 1978. Bar: Mass. 1978, U.S. Dist. Ct. Mass. 1979, U.S. Ct. Appeals (1st cir.) 1979, U.S. Claims Ct. 1984, U.S. Supreme Ct. 1984. Assoc. Gaston & Snow, Boston, 1978-87, ptnr., 1987-91; asst. atty. gen. Mass. Atty. Gen's. Office, Mass., 1991, chief of trial divsn., 1992-95, chief bus. and labor protection bur., 1995—; pvt. practice; staff atty. Nat. Consumer Law Ctr., Boston. Adj. prof. Northeastern U. Sch. Law, 1993. Editor: (handbook) Homeless Not Helpless, 1988, Social Change, 1986, Boston Bar Jour. Mem. United Jewish Appeal Young Leadership Cabinet, NYC, 1983-92, nat. chmn., 1991-92, Coun. Jewish Fedns. Leadership Devel. Com., NYC, 1986-92; mem. exec. bd. Combined Jewish Philanthropies, Boston, 1994—, chmn., 1994—; dir. Vol. Lawyers Project, Boston, 1983—; HRD CJP chmn., 1994—; bd. dirs. Bur. Jewish Edn., 1993—, v.p. 1994, mem. Jewish Cmty. Rels. Coun., 1992—, v.p. 1994—, founder & chaired Atty. Gen's. Abandoned Housing Task Force, former chmn. Volunteer Lawyers Project. Recipient 10 Outstanding Young Leaders award Boston Jaycees, 1995; Wexner Heritage Found. fellow, 1991-93. Mem. Mass. Bar Assn., Boston Bar Assn. (chmn. young lawyers sect. 1983-86). Democrat. Office: Nat Consumer Law Ctr 77 Summer St 10th Fl Boston MA 02110 Office Phone: 617-542-8010. Office Fax: 617-542-8028.

ROSSMANN, JACK EUGENE, psychologist, educator; b. Walnut, Iowa, Dec. 4, 1936; s. Wilbert C. Rossmann and Claire L. (Mickel) Walter; m. Marilyn Martin, June 14, 1958; children: Ann, Charles, Sarah. BS, Iowa State U., 1958, MS, 1960; PhD, U. Minn., 1963; MA (hon.), Macalester Coll., St. Paul, 2007. Lic. psychologist Minn. Asst. prof. Macalester Coll., St. Paul, 1964-68, assoc. prof., 1968-73, prof., 1973—, v.p. acad. affairs, 1978-86, chair dept. psychology, 1990-2000. Cons.-evaluator North Ctrl. Assn., 1975—; cons. Pers. Decisions Internat., Mpls., 1989—2000, Bush Found., 1993—; sr. advisor Spencer Found., 2004—. Author: (with others) Open Admissions at CUNY, 1975; contbr. articles to profl. jours. Bd. dirs. Twin City Inst. for Talented Youth, St. Paul, 1978-91; trustee United Theol. Sem., New Brighton, Minn., 1984-96; pres. Minn. Intercollegiate Athletic Conf., 2003-06. 2d lt. US Army, 1959. Recipient Thomas Jefferson award, Macalester Coll., 1990, Outstanding Svc. award, Minn. Intercollegiate Athletic Conf., 2007; Admintrv. fellow, Am. Coun. on Edn., 1977—78. Mem.: AAUP (pres. Minn. conf. 1993—95, Robert Sloan award, Minn. Conf. 2003), APA, Minn. Psychol. Assn. (treas. 2001, pres. 2003), Assn. Instl. Rsch., Am. Psychol. Soc., Phi Kappa Phi, Phi Beta Kappa (hon.). Home: 99 Cambridge St Saint Paul MN 55105-1947 Office: Macalester Coll 1600 Grand Ave Saint Paul MN 55105-1801 Home Phone: 651-690-4370; Office Phone: 651-696-6110. Business E-Mail: rossmann@macalester.edu.

ROSSMANN, MICHAEL GEORGE, biochemist, educator; b. Frankfurt, Germany, July 30, 1930; s. Alexander and Nelly (Schwabacher) R.; m. Audrey Pearson, July 24, 1954; children: Martin, Alice, Heather. BSc with honors, Polytechnic, London, 1951, MSc in Physics, 1953; PhD in Chemistry, U. Glasgow, 1956; PhD (hon.), U. Uppsala, Sweden, 1983, U. Strasbourg, France, 1984, Vrije U., Brussels, 1990, U. Glasgow, 1993, U. York, Eng., 1994, U. Quebec, 1998. Fulbright scholar U. Minn., 1956-58; research scientist MRC Lab. Molecular Biology, Cambridge, Eng., 1958-64; assoc. prof. biol. scis. Purdue U., West Lafayette, Ind., 1964-67, prof., 1967-78, Hanley Disting. prof. biol. scis., 1978—, prof. biochemistry, 1975—. Editor: The Molecular Replacement Method, 1972; contbr. more than 400 articles to profl. jours. Grantee NIH, NSF, HFSP; recipient Fankuchen award Am. Crystallographic Assn., 1986, Horwitz prize Columbia U., 1990, Gregori Arminoff prize Royal Swedish Acad. Sci., 1994, Stein & Moore award Protein Soc., 1994, Ewald prize Internat. Union Crystallography, 1996, Cole award Biophys. Soc., 1998, Elion award Internat. Soc. for Antiviral Rsch., 2000, Ehrlich and Darmstaedter prize Paul Erhlich-Fedn., 2001. Mem. Am. Soc. Biol. Chemists, Am. Chem. Soc., Biophys. Soc. (Cole award 1998), Am. Crystallographic Assn. (Fankuchen award 1986), Brit. Biophys. Soc., Inst. Physics., Chem. Soc. (U.K.), AAAS, NAS, Indian Nat. Sci. Acad., Royal Soc., Nat. Sci. Bd., Lafayette Sailing Club. Democrat. Home: 1208 Wiley Dr West Lafayette IN 47906-2434 Office: Purdue U Dept Biol Scis 915 W State St West Lafayette IN 47907-2054 Office Phone: 765-494-4911. Business E-Mail: mr@purdue.edu.

ROSSO, JEAN-PIERRE, electronics executive; b. Aix-les Bains, Savoie, France, July 11, 1940; Diploma in civil engring., Ecole Polytechnique, Lausanne, Switzerland, 1964; MBA, U. Pa., 1967. Mgr. fin. and adminstrn. Honeywell, Paris, 1969—70, dir. African divsn., 1970—71, sales dir., 1971—75; pres., CEO Rossignol Ski, Burlington, Vt., 1975—81; dir. gen. Rossignol SA, Voiron, France, 1980—81; v.p. bus. devel. Honeywell Europe SA, Brussels, 1981—83, pres., 1981—94; v.p., gen. mgr. Honeywell Med. Electronics, NYC, 1983—85; group v.p. Honeywell Info. Systems, Mpls., 1985—87; pres., CEO Case Corp., Racine, Wis., 1994—99, chmn., 1996—99; former chmn., CEO CNH Global, 1999—. Mem. adv. com. Trade Policy and Negotiations, 2002—02; bd. overseers Wharton Sch.; bd. dirs. ADC Telecoms., Inc., Medtronic, Inc. Mem.: Bus. Roundtable. Avocations: golf, skiing. Office: Case Corp 700 State St Racine WI 53404-3392

ROSSOLIMO, ALEXANDER NICHOLAS, management consultant, corporate director; b. Paris, June 8, 1939; came to U.S., 1952; naturalized, 1958; s. Nicholas S. and Vera A. (Boudakovitch) R.; m. Meryl Louise Stowbridge, Sept. 10, 1977; children: Gregory, Katherine, Elizabeth. Student, Lycée Français of N.Y., 1955—57; BEE with honors, CUNY, 1962; MA in Applied Math., Harvard U., Cambridge, Mass., 1963, PhD in Applied Physics, 1973; MBA, MIT, Cambridge, 1973. Cert. in bus. French. Tchg. fellow Harvard U., 1963-65, rsch. asst., 1966-71; fin. analyst Péchiney, Paris, 1972; brand/advt. mgmt. The Clorox Co., Oakland, Calif., 1973-74; project leader The Boston Consulting Group, 1974-77; dir. planning and fin. analysis United Brands, Boston, 1977-80; sr. dir. Digital Equipment Corp., Maynard, Mass., 1980-92; pres. Strategy Assocs. Internat., Newton, Mass., 1992-94, pres., chief exec. officer, 1994—; co-founder, acting CEO, vp. bus. strategy and corp. devel. IntellectExchange Inc., 1999—2001; regional dir. F2 Intelligence Group LLC, Mpls., 2004—. Vis. fellow Harvard U., Cambridge, Mass., 1991-93; bd. dirs. ACG Internat., Chgo.; founding dir. Forum 128, 1996—; bd. dirs. Ctr. for Security and Social Progress, Inc., chmn., 1998—; dir. Law Enforcement Assistance Found., 1999—; mem. bd. advisors Radia Techs. Corp., 2004-05. Contbr. numerous articles to bus. and internat. newspapers. Mem. search com. Ecole Bilingue, Internat. Sch. of Boston, 1991-93; fund raiser Milton (Mass.) Acad., 1994-97, Phillips Exeter Acad., 1997—, Phillips Andover Acad., 2000—. Recipient award in elec. engring. Blonder-Tongue Co., N.Y.C., 1961, Belden prize, gold medal in math., 1960; NSF postgrad. fellow, 1962-63; ACG Dealmaker Challenge winner, 1995. Mem. IEEE, Nat. Assn. Corp. Dirs., Bus. Execs. for Nat. Security, Boston Security Analysts Soc., Royal United Svcs. Inst. for Def. Studies (London), French Am. C. of C., Japan Soc. Boston, World Affairs Coun., Internat. Assn. of Macro-Engring. Socs. (mem. commn. on macro-engring.), Assn. for Corp. Growth Boston (chmn. 1995-96), Harvard Club Boston, Harvard Faculty Club, Toastmasters Internat. (pres.), Tau Beta Pi, Eta Kappa Nu. Avocations: jogging, tennis, foreign languages, professional organizations, theater. Office: Strategy Assocs Internat PO Box 207 Waban MA 02468-0002 Business E-Mail: arossolimo@yahoo.com.

ROSSON, GLENN RICHARD, building products and furniture company executive; b. Galveston, Tex., Aug. 17, 1937; s. John Raymond and Elsie Lee R.; m. Edwina Lucille Hart, June 2, 1956; children— Darrell Richard, Alex Mark. BBA, Tex. Tech U., 1959. C.P.A., Tex. Supr., accountant Axelson div. U.S. Industries Inc., Longview, Tex., 1960-67, controller, 1968, group financial v.p. Dallas, 1969, group chmn., 1969-72, v.p., 1973-74, sr. v.p., 1974, exec. v.p., 1974-80, also dir.; pres. Rosson Investment Co., 1980—; chmn. bd. Yorktowne Inc., 1988—. Chmn. bd. dirs. Quality Product Finishing, Inc., 1998—. Mem. Am. Inst. C.P.A.s, Tex. Soc. C.P.A.s, Nat. Assn. Accts. (past nat. dir., past pres. E. Tex. chpt.), Assn. for Corp. Growth (past pres.). Clubs: Dallas Athletic, TBARM Raquet. Home: 11367 Drummond Dr Dallas TX 75228-1946 Office: 6060 N Central Expy # 560 Dallas TX 75206-5142 Office Phone: 214-891-6357. E-mail: rosson@gte.net.

ROSSOUW, JACQUES E., preventive medicine physician, researcher; b. S. Africa, 1943; Former acting dir. Women's Health Initiative, NIH, Bethesda, Md.; lead project officer, Women's Health Initiative, Nat. Heart, Lung, and Blood Inst. NIH, Bethesda, Md. Named one of 100 Most Influential People, Time Mag., 2006. Achievements include performing studies concerning women's health in areas of menopause, estrogen replacement, calcium and vitamin D supplements, and high-fat diet, others. Office: Women's Health Init NHLBI-NIH PO Box 30105 Bethesda MD 20824-0105 Office Phone: 301-592-8573. *

ROSS-PARSONS, DONNA MICHELLE, counselor, small business owner; b. Redwood City, Calif., Aug. 29, 1962; d. Fayne David Ross and Norma G. Moore, Francis Allen Moore (Stepfather); m. Eugene William Parsons, Nov. 4, 2000. MA, Sam Houston State U., Huntsville, Tex., 1995. Lic. profl. counselor Tex. State Bd. Examiners Profl. Counselors, 1998. Milieu activity therapist Ming Quong Children's Home, Los Gatos, Calif., 1988—90; mental health worker Sandstone Ctr., College Station, Tex., 1990—91; child protective services worker Tex. Dept. Protective & Regulatory Svcs., Centerville, 1992—94; social worker Gulf Coast Trade Ctr., New Waverly, 1995—96; therapist Ctrl. Plains Ctr. Mental Health, Mental Retardation & Substance Abuse, Plainview, 1996—99; clin. dir. Mesa Lake Residential Ctr., Zephyr, 1999—99; pvt. practice Donna M. Ross, LPC-S, Early, 1999—; therapist New Horizions Ranch & Ctr., Goldthwaite, 2001—02. Vol. ARC, Brownwood, Tex., 1996—98. Mem.: Tex. Counseling Assn., Am. Counseling Assn. Office: Donna M Ross LPC S Ste K 104 E Industrial Dr Early TX 76802 Home Phone: 325-643-2895; Office Phone: 325-649-9313. Office Fax: 325-643-4647; Home Fax: 325-643-2895. Personal E-mail: dparsons@bwoodtx.com.

ROSSUM, RALPH ARTHUR, political science professor; b. Alexandria, Minn., Dec. 17, 1946; s. Floyd Arthur and June Marion (Carlson) R.; m. Constance Mary Brazina, Aug. 19, 1972; children: Kristin, Brent, Pierce. BA summa cum laude, Concordia Coll., 1968; MA, U. Chgo., 1971, PhD, 1973. Instr. Grinnell (Iowa) Coll., 1972-73; asst. prof. Memphis State U., 1973-77, assoc. prof., 1977-80, Loyola U., Chgo., 1980-83, assoc. dean grad. sch., 1981-82; dep. dir. bur. justice stats. U.S. Dept. Justice, Washington, 1983-84; Alice Tweed Tuohy prof. govt. Claremont (Calif.) McKenna Coll., 1984-88, v.p. and dean of faculty, 1988-91; pres. Hampden-Sydney (Va.) Coll., 1991-92; Salvatori Vis. prof. Claremont (Calif.) McKenna Coll., 1992-93, Salvatori prof. Am. Constitutionalism, 1994—; Fletcher Jones Prof. of Am. Politics U. Redlands, Redlands, Calif., 1993-94. Mem. adv. bd. Nat. Inst. Corrections, U.S. Dept. Justice, 1988-91; mem. Robert Presley Inst. Corrections Rsch. and Tng., State of Calif., 1988-91; dir. Rose Inst. of State and Local Govt., 2000—; mem. nat. bd. dirs. FIPSE, U.S. Dept. Edn., 2002—. Author: Federalism, the Supreme Court and the Seventeenth Amendment, 2001, others, Antonin Scalia's Jurisprudence: Text and Tradition, 2006; co-author: The American Founding, 1981, American Constitutional Law, 1983, 1987, 1991, 1995, 1999, 2003—, others; editor (sr.): Benchmark, 1983—86; book rev. editor:, 1986—91; contbr. 65 articles to profl. jours., chapters to books. Trustee Episcopal Theol. Sch., Claremont, 1987-91. Ford Found. fellow, 1968—72. Mem.: Am. Polit. Sci. Assn. Episcopalian. Office: Claremont McKenna Coll Dept Govt 850 Columbia Ave Claremont CA 91711-3901 Home Phone: 909-625-3802; Office Phone: 909-607-3392. Business E-Mail: ralph.rossum@claremontmckenna.edu.

ROST, PETER, pharmaceutical company executive; b. Bollebygd, Sweden, May 31, 1959; came to U.S., 1987; s. Siegfrid and Kathie (Zerne) Rost; m. Tina Forssten, Apr. 21, 1984; children: Maximilian Forssten, Sebastian Forssten. MD, U. Gothenburg, Sweden, 1984. Intern anesthesiology dept. Ea. Hosp., Gothenburg, 1984, practice medicine specializing in anesthesiology, 1984; pres., CEO Bus. Lit. Inc., Gothenburg, 1985-87; account supr., copywriter Grey Gothenburg, Gothenburg, 1985-87; med. dir., account supr. Maher Kaump & Clark, Inc., LA, 1987-92; assoc. dir. med. edn. Lederle Labs. divsn. Am. Cyanamid Co., Wayne, NJ, 1992, dir. med. edn., 1993; product mgr. Lederle Labs. divsn. Am. Cyanimid Co., Wayne, NJ, 1993-94; mkt. planning mgr. Wyeth-Ayerst Internat., St. Davids, Pa., 1995, dir. mktg internal medicine products, 1995-96, dir. comml. ops. Europe, 1996-98; gen. mgr. Wyeth-Ayerst Global Pharma., Sweden, 1999—2001; v.p. endocrine care, global prescription bus. Pfizer, Peapack, NJ, 2001—. Chmn., chief exec. officer W. Swedish Model Group, Gothenburg, 1985. Author: Emergency Surgery, 1985, The Art of Driving a Car Free, 1985. Mem. AMA, Am. Coll. Physician Execs., Pharm. Advt. Coun. Office: Pfizer 100 Rte 206 N Peapack NJ 07977-8616 Home: 29 Great Hills Rd Short Hills NJ 07078 Personal E-mail: Rostpeter@hotmail.com.

ROST, THOMAS LOWELL, retired botany educator; b. St. Paul, Dec. 28, 1941; m. Ann Marie Ruhland, Aug. 31, 1963. BS, St. John's U., Collegeville, Minn., 1963; MA, Minn. State U., 1965; PhD, Iowa State U., 1971. Postdoctoral fellow Brookhaven Nat. Lab., Upton, NY, 1970-72; asst. to full prof. dept. botany U. Calif., Davis, 1972-82, faculty asst. to chancellor, 1982-83, prof., chmn. plant biology sect., 1994-96, assoc. dean divsn. biol. sci., 1996—2003, exec. assoc. dean, 2003—05, prof. emeritus, 2006—. Cons. faculty of agronomy U. Uruguay, 1979, 89, 2005; vis. fellow Rsch. Soc. Biol. Sci., Canberra, Australia, 1979-80; vis. prof. U. Wroclaw, Poland, 1987, U. Exeter, Eng., 1993, Copenhagen U., 2003, Aristotle U., Thessalaniki, Greece, 2005. Co-author: Botany: A Brief Introduction to Plant Biology, 1979, Botany: An Introduction on Plant Biology, 1982; co-editor: Mechanisms and Control of Cell Division, 1977, Plant Biology, 1998, 2d edit., 2005; contbr. articles to profl. jours. Internat. pres. Gamma Sigma Delta, 2004—06. Served to capt. US Army, 1965—67. Fellow Japan Soc. Promotion of Sci.; mem. Bot. Soc. Am., Soc. Exptl. Biology, Am. Inst. Biol. Sci. Democrat. Roman Catholic. Avocation: community theatre. Office: U Calif Sect Plant Biology Davis CA 95616-8537 Business E-Mail: tlrost@ucdavis.edu.

ROST, WILLIAM JOSEPH, chemist; b. Fargo, ND, Dec. 8, 1926; s. William Melvin and Christine Ruth (Hamerlik) R.; m. Rita Cincoski, Sept. 15, 1951; children— Kathryn, Patricia, Carol. BS, U. Minn., 1948, PhD, 1952. From asst. prof. to prof. pharm. chemistry Sch. Pharmacy U. Kansas City, Mo., 1952-63; prof. pharm. chemistry Sch. Pharmacy U. Mo., Kansas City, 1963—. Co-author: Principles of Medicinal Chemistry, 1974, 3d rev. edit., 1988; contbr. articles profl. jours. Mem. Am. Pharm. Assn., Am. Chem. Soc., Sigma Xi, Kappa Psi, Rho Chi, Phi Lambda Upsilon. Office: U Mo Sch of Pharmacy Kansas City MO 64110 Home: 709 W 100th Ct Kansas City MO 64114

ROSTER, MICHAEL, lawyer; b. Chgo., May 7, 1945; AB, Stanford U., 1967, JD, 1973. Bar: Calif. 1973, DC 1980. Ptnr. McKenna, Conner & Cuneo, LA, Washington, 1973—87, Morrison & Foerster, LA, Washington, 1987—93; gen. counsel Stanford (Calif.) U., 1993—2000; exec. v.p., gen. counsel Golden West Fin. Corp., Oakland, Calif., 2000—07. Bd. dirs. Silicon Valley Bancshares, vice chmn., 1995—98; chmn. Encirq, 1998—2000, Insert Therapeutics, 2000—04; vice chmn. Fed. Home Loan Bank, San Francisco, 2005—07. Contbr. articles to profl. jours. Bd. dirs. Pasadena Heritage, 1986—87. Lt. (j.g.) USN, 1969—71. Mem.: ABA (fin. svcs. com. 1981—, chmn. com. savs. instns. 1985—89, banking com. 1989—, vice chmn. 2005—), Calif. Bankers Assn., Am. Corp. Counsel Assn. (chmn. 2000—01), Calif. Bar Assn. (chmn. banking com. 1978—79), Stanford U. Alumni Assn. (chmn. 1992), LA Athletic Club.

ROSTKER, BERNARD, civilian military employee; m. Louise Cowen; children: David, Michael. BS in Econs. and Edn., NYU, 1964; M in Econs., Syracuse U., 1967, PhD in Econs., 1970. Economist Manpower Requirements Directorate Office of the Asst. Sec. of Def. for Sys. Analysis, 1968-70; rsch. economist RAND Corp., 1970-72, program dir. manpower per. and tng. program, 1972-77; prin. dep. asst. sec. for manpower and res. affairs USN, 1977-79, dir. Selective Svc., 1979-81, dir. navy mgmt. program Ctr. for Naval Analyses, 1981-83; dir. sys. mgmt. divsn. Sys. Rsch. and Applications Corp., 1983-84; program dir. force devel. and employment program RAND Corp.-The Arroyo Ctr., 1984-90, assoc. dir., 1984-90; dir. Def. Manpower Rsch. Ctr. RAND Nat. Def. Rsch. Ctr., 1990-94; asst. sec. for manpower and res. affairs USN, 1994—98, spl. asst. to dep. sec. def. for Gulf War illnesses, 1996—; under sec. of the Army, 1998—2000; under sec. for pers. and readiness, 2000—. Office: Spl Asst Gulf War Illnesses Suite 901 Four Skyline Place 5113 Leesburg Pike Falls Church VA 22041

ROSTOW, CHARLES NICHOLAS, lawyer, educator; b. Geneva, Mar. 3, 1950; s. Eugene Victor and Edna (Greenberg) R.; m. Heyden White, Oct. 31, 1987; children: Theodore Isaac, Celia A.M. BA, Yale U., 1972, PhD, 1979, JD, 1982. Assoc. Shearman & Sterling, NYC, 1982-85; spl. asst. to legal adviser Dept. State, Washington, 1985-87; dep. legal adviser NSC, Washington, 1987, legal adviser, 1987—93; spl. asst. to Pres. Ronald Reagan, George H. W. Bush, 1987—93; assoc. prof. Coll. of Law U. Tulsa, 1993—95, disting. rsch. prof. Coll. of Law, 1995—98; exec. dir. Mass. Office Internat. Trade and Investment, 1995-98; counsel and dep. staff dir. House Select Comm. on Nat. Security & Mil./Comm. Concerns with the PRC, 1998; staff dir. Senate Select Com. on Intelligence, 1999-2000; Charles H. Stockton prof. internat. law U.S. Naval War Coll., Newport, RI, 2001; gen. coun. U.S. Mission UN, NYC, 2001—05; sr. counsel Rsch Found. of SUNY, 2005—06; univ. counsel, vice chancellor for legal affairs, univ. fellow, full prof. SUNY, 2006—. Author: Anglo-French Relations 1934-36, 1984; editor: Akten zur deutschen auswaertigen Politik: 1918-1945, vols. XIV-XXI, 1980-83; contbr. articles to prof. jours. Hon. dir. John Goodwin Tower Ctr. Polit. Studies, So. Meth. U.; nat. adv. bd. Am. Jewish Com.; dir. Toreador Resources, Am. Jewish Internat. Rels. Inst.; trustee Internat. House. Mem. Assn. Bar City of N.Y., Coun. Fgn. Rels., Phi Beta Kappa, Cosmos Club, Yale Club (N.Y.C.), Elizabethan Club (New Haven). Jewish. Office: SUNY State Univ Plz Albany NY 12246 Office Phone: 518-443-5400. Business E-Mail: nicholas.rostow@suny.edu.

ROSTOW, ELSPETH DAVIES, political science professor; b. NYC; d. Milton Judson and Harriet Elspeth (Vaughan) Davies; m. Walt Whitman Rostow, June 26, 1947 (dec. Feb. 2003); children: Peter Vaughan, Ann Larner. AB, Barnard Coll., 1938; AM, Radcliffe Coll., 1939; MA, Cambridge U., Eng., 1949; LHD (hon.), Lebanon Valley Coll.; LLD (hon.), Austin Coll., 1982, Southwestern U., 1988; LHD (hon.), Wheaton Coll., 2006. Mem. faculty various instns. Barnard Coll., N.Y.C. and MIT, Cambridge, 1939-69; mem. faculty U. Tex., Austin, 1969—, dean div. gen. and comparative studies, 1975-77, prof. govt., 1976—, dean Lyndon B. Johnson Sch. Pub. Affairs, 1977-83, Stiles prof. Am. studies, 1985-88, Stiles prof. emerita, 1988—. Mem. Pres.'s Adv. Com. for Trade Negotiations, 1978-82, Pres.'s Commn. for a Nat. Agenda for the Eighties, 1979-81; rsch. assoc. OSS, Washington, 1943-45; Geneva corr. London Economist, 1947-49; lectr. Air War Coll., 1963-81, Army War Coll., 1965, 68, 69, 78, 79, 81, Nat. War Coll., 1962, 68, 74, 75, Indsl. Coll. Armed Forces, 1961-65, Naval War Coll., 1971, Fgn. Svc. Inst., 1974-77, Dept. of State, Europe, 1973; bd. dirs. U.S. Inst. of Peace, vice chmn., 1991, chmn. 1991-92; co-founder The Austin Project, 1991; mem. Gov.'s Task Force on Revenue, Tex., 1991. Author: Europe's Economy After the War, 1948, (with others) American Now, 1968, The Coattailless Landslide, 1974; editor (with Barbara Jordan) The Great Society: A Twenty-Year Critique, 1986; columnist Austin Am. Statesman, 1985-92; contbr. articles to revs., poems to scholarly jours., newspapers, and mags. Trustee Nat. Acad. Pub. Adminstrn., 1989—95, Sarah Lawrence Coll., 1952—59, So. Ctr. for Internat. Studies, 1990—; bd. visitors and govs. St. Johns Coll., 1986—89; bd. dirs. Barnard Coll., 1962—66, Lyndon Baines Johnson Found., 1977—83, Salzburg Seminar, 1981—89, co-chair sr. fellows, 1997—2001; vis. scholar Phi Beta Kappa, 1984—85; bd. adv. to pres. Naval War Coll., Newport, RI, 1995—99; nat. advisor Commn. on Deliberative Polling, 1999—2001. Decorated Order of St. Joan D'Arc; named Fulbright lectr.; recipient Top Hand award, U. Tex. Ex-Students Assn., 1996, Presdl. citation, U. Tex., 1998, Disting. Alumna award, Barnard Coll., 1998, Dist. Svc. award, Tex. Exec., 2005, Disting. Svc. award, U. Tex., 2005, Civilian Svc. award, US Army, 2006; grantee, USIA, 1983—84, 1990. Mem.: Tex. Philos. Soc. (trustee 1989—95, 1997—2001), Headliners Found. (vice-chmn. 1996—2002), Phi Beta Kappa, Omicron Delta Kappa, Mortar Bd. (hon.), Phi Nu Epsilon (hon.). Home: 1 Wildwind Pt Austin TX 78746-2434 Office: U Tex PO Box Y University Station Austin TX 78713 Office Phone: 512-471-8909. Business E-Mail: elspeth.rostow@mail.utexas.edu.

ROSZKOWSKI, JOSEPH JOHN, lawyer; b. Pawtucket, RI, Aug. 11, 1938; s. Joseph J. and Anna T. Roszkowski; m. Geraldine J. Szpila, July 2, 1966. BA, Alliance Coll., 1960; JD, Marquette U., 1964. Bar: Wis. 1964, U.S. Dist. Ct. (ea. dist.) Wis. 1964, R.I. 1965. Ptnr. Zimmerman, Roszkowski & Brenner, Woonsocket, R.I., 1965—. Corporator Fogarty Hosp., North Smithfield, RI, 1976—88; counsel Landmark Med. Ctr., 1989—90; mem. R.I. Bd. Bar Examiners, 1994—2001; R.I. probate judge, 1996—2000, 2005—. Mem. Nat. Ski Patrol, RI, 1974—83; legal counsel R.I. Tuna Tournament, 1975—; bd. dirs. R.I. Legal Svcs., Providence, 1974—87, Legal Aid Soc., Providence, 1985—; chair Town of Cumberland, 2000. Mem. ABA (ho. of dels. 1996-2003, state del. 2000-2001, 2003—, bd. govs. 2001, 2002, commr. Interest on Lawyers' Trust Accounts 1986-90, 2002—), R.I. Bar Found. (pres. 1990-95), R.I. Bar Assn. (pres. 1985-86), Am. Law Inst., Am. Judicature Soc., Fed. Tax Inst. New England (adv. com. 1985-86), R.I. Med. Examiners, U.S. Jaycees (nat. dir. 1968), Am. Acad. Hosp. Attys. Lodges: Rotary (pres. Cumberland, R.I. 1987). Avocations: skiing, sailing, gardening, tennis. Home: 1o Little St Cumberland RI 02864-1101 Office: Zimmerman Roszkowski & Brenner 1625 Diamond Hill Rd Woonsocket RI 02895-1541 E-mail: jroskow@aol.com.

ROSZKOWSKI, STANLEY JULIAN, retired federal judge; b. Boonville, NY, Jan. 27, 1923; s. Joseph and Anna (Christkowski) R.; m. Catherine Mary Claeys, June 19, 1948; children: Mark, Gregory, Dan, John. BS, U. Ill., 1949, JD, 1954. Bar: Ill. 1954. Sales mgr. Warren Petroleum Co., Rockford, Ill., 1954; ptnr. Roszkowski, Paddock, McGreevy & Johnson, Rockford, 1955-77; judge U.S. Dist. Ct. (we. dist.), Rockford, Ill., 1977-98; pres. First State Bank, Rockford, 1963-75, chmn. bd., 1977—; mediator-arbitrator JAMS/ENDISPUTE, Chgo., 1998—. Chmn. Fire and Police Commn., Rockford, 1967-74, commr., 1974—; chmn. Paul Simon Com., 1972; active Adlai Stevenson III campaign, 1968-71, Winnebago County Citizens for John F. Kennedy, 1962, Winnebago County Dem. Cen. Com., 1962-64; bd. dirs. Sch. of Hope, 1960—; mem. Ill. Capital Devel. Bd., 1974—. With USAAF, 1943-45. Decorated Air medal with 2 oak leaf clusters.; recipient Pulaski Nat. Heritage award Polish Am. Congress, Chgo., 1982 Mem. ABA, Ill. Bar Assn., Fla. Bar Assn., Winnebago County Bar Assn., Am. Coll. Trial Lawyers, Am. Judicature Soc., Assn. Trial Lawyers Am., Ill. Trial Lawyers Assns., Am. Arbitration Assn. (arbitrator), Fed. Judges Assn. (bd. dirs. 1988—). Business E-Mail: sjrassoc@aol.com.

ROTBERG, EUGENE HARVEY, investment banker, lawyer; b. Phila., Jan. 19, 1930; s. Irving Bernard and Blanche Grace (Levick) R.; m. Iris Sybil Comens; children— Diana Golda, Pamela Lynn. BS, Temple U., 1951; LL.B., U. Pa., 1954; PhD (hon.), Salem-Teikyo U., 1992. Chief counsel Office Policy Research Securities and Exchange Commn., Washington, 1963-66; v.p., treas. World Bank, Washington, 1969-87; exec. v.p. Merrill Lynch & Co., NYC, 1987-90. Served with U.S. Army. Decorated King Leopold II medal (Belgium); recipient Disting. Svc. award Securities and Exch. Commn., 1968; named Alumnus of Yr., Temple U. Home: 7211 Brickyard Rd Potomac MD 20854-4808 Office: 1250 24th St NW Ste 350 Washington DC 20037-1124 Office Phone: 202-944-3810. E-mail: genebanker@aol.com.

ROTBERG, IRIS COMENS, social scientist; b. Phila., Dec. 16, 1932; d. Samuel Nathaniel and Golda (Shuman) Comens; m. Eugene H. Rotberg, Aug. 29, 1954; children: Diana Golda, Pamela Lynn. BA, U. Pa., 1954, MA, 1955; PhD, Johns Hopkins U., Balt., 1958. Research psychologist Pres.'s Commn. on Income Maintenance Programs, Washington, 1968-69, Office Planning, Research and Evaluation, Office Econ. Opportunity, Washington, 1970-73; dep. dir. compensatory edn. study Nat. Inst. Edn., Washington, 1974-77, dir. Office Planning and Program Devel., 1978-82; program dir. NSF, Arlington, Va., 1985-87, 89-91, 1993-96; tech. policy fellow Com. on Sci., Space and Tech., U.S. Ho. of Reps., Washington, 1987-89; sr. social scientist RAND, Washington, 1991-93; rsch. prof. edn. policy Grad. Sch. Edn. and Human Devel. George Washington U., Washington, 1996—. NSF fellow, 1956-58. Home: 7211 Brickyard Rd Potomac MD 20854-4808 Home Phone: 301-983-0965; Office Phone: 202-994-2735. Business E-Mail: irotberg@gwu.edu.

ROTBERG, ROBERT IRWIN, historian, political scientist, educator, academic administrator; b. Newark, Apr. 11, 1935; s. Louis and Mildred S. R.; m. Joanna H. Henshaw, June 17, 1961; children: Rebecca T.H., Nicola S.D., Fiona J.Y. AB, Oberlin Coll., 1955; MPA, Princeton U., 1957; DPhil, U. Oxford, 1960. Asst. prof. history, rsch. assoc. Ctr. for Internat. Affairs Harvard U., 1961-68, rsch. assoc. Ctr. for Internat. Affairs, 1968-95; rsch. dir. Twentieth Century Fund, 1968-71; prof. polit. sci. and history MIT, 1968-87; acad. v.p. for Arts, Scis. and Tech. Tufts U., Medford, Mass., 1987-90; pres. Lafayette Coll., Easton, Pa., 1990-93, World Peace Found., Cambridge, 1993—; coord. Inst. for Internat. Devel. Harvard U., 1993-99, dir. program on intrastate conflict Kennedy Sch., 1999—. Adj. prof. Kennedy Sch. Govt., Harvard U., 1993—; mem. coun. NEH, 1993-99; cons. Dept. State, 1968-78, Commrs. of Middlesex County, Mass., 1976-77. Author: A Political History of Tropical Africa, 1965, The Rise of Nationalism in Central Africa, 1965, Protest and Power in Black Africa, 1970, Joseph Thomson and the Exploration of Africa, 1971, Haiti: The Politics of Squalor, 1971, Africa and Its Explorers, 1971, The Black Homelands of South Africa, 1977, Black Heart: Gore-Browne and the Politics of Multiracial Zambia, 1978, Conflict and Compromise in South Africa, 1980, Suffer the Future: Policy Choices in Southern Africa, 1980, Imperialism, Colonialism and Hunger, 1982, Namibia: Economic and Political Prospects, 1983, South Africa and its Neighbors, 1985, The Founder: Cecil Rhodes and the Pursuit of Power, 1988, rev. edit. 2002, Africa in the 1990s and Beyond: Policy Opportunities and Choices, 1988, From Massacres to Genocide: The Media, Public Policy, and Humanitarian Crises, 1996, Vigilance and Vengeance: NGOs Preventing Ethnic Conflict in Divided Societies, 1996, Haiti Renewed: Political and Economic Prospects, 1997, Burma: Prospects for a Democratic Future, 1998, War and Peace in Southern Africa, 1998, Creating Peace in Sri Lanka, 1999, Peacekeeping and Peace Enforcement in Africa, 2000, Truth v. Justice, 2000, Patterns of Social Capital, 2001, Ending Autocracy, Enabling Democracy, 2002, State Failure and State Weakness in a Time of Terror, 2003, When States Fail: Causes and Consequences, 2004, Crafting the New Nigeria, 2004, Battling Terrorism in the Horn of Africa, 2005; Building a New Afghanistan, 2007, A Leadership for Peace: How Edwin Ginn Tried to Change the World, 2007; editor Jour. Interdisciplinary History, 1970—. Chmn. Middlesex County Govtl. Rev. Task Force, 1972; v.p. Cambridge Civic Assn., 1969-72; mem. Lexington Town Meeting, 1973-90, 94—, Lexington Sch. Com., 1974-77; mem. Ciskel Commn., 1979-80; trustee World Peace Found., 1980—, Oberlin Coll., 1983—, Coun. Internat. Exch. Scholars, 1991-95, Sec. of State, Africa's Policy Panel, 2003-04. Rhodes scholar U. Oxford, 1960; Guggenheim fellow, 1970-71; Hazen Found. fellow, 1976-77. Fellow Royal Geog. Soc., Am. Acad. Arts and Scis.; mem. Am. Hist. Assn., African Studies Assn., Coun. on Fgn. Rels., Oberlin Coll. Alumni Assn. (pres. 1981-82). Office: World Peace Found Belfer Ctr 79 John F Kennedy St Cambridge MA 02138-5758 Office Phone: 617-496-2258.

ROTCH, JAMES E., lawyer; b. Auburn, Ala., Mar. 26, 1945; s. Elroy B. and Martha (Ellison) R.; m. Darlene Edwards, June 26, 1999; children: Jamison B., Susannah R., Amie L. Vaughn. BS, Auburn U., 1967, postgrad., 1967-68; JD, U. Va., 1971. Bar: Ala. 1971, U.S. Dist. Ct. (no. dist.) Ala. 1973. Rsch. asst. Office Instl. Rsch. Auburn (Ala.) U., 1967-68; clk. U.S. Judiciary System, Birmingham, Ala., 1971-72; assoc. Bradley Arant Rose & White LLP, Birmingham, 1971-76; ptnr. Bradley, Arant, Rose & White LLP, Birmingham, 1976—, administrv. ptnr., 1990-93; chmn. bd. dirs. Kaleidoscope Prodns., Inc. Mem. adv. com. Bioelastics Rsch. Ltd., Birmingham, 1992—, Gov.'s Task Force on Biotechnology, Ala., 1993. Author: The Birmingham Pledge. Pres. adv. com. Birmingham Mus. Art, 1989-92; bd. dirs. Operation New Birmingham, 1990-91, 95—, co-chmn. cmty. affairs com., mem. exec. com.; Coalition for Better Edn., Birmingham, 1990—; active Boy Scouts Am.; bd. dirs. Birmingham Com. for Olympic Soccer, 1994-96, Ala. Sports Found., 1994-98, Entrepreneurial Ctr. Inc., 1996—, chmn., 2002; mem. adminstrv. bd. Canterbury United Meth. Ch., 1991-93; chmn. Birmingham Pledge Found., 2000—; chmn. Birmingham Area Tech. Leadership Alliance. Capt. USAR, 1972-78. Named Communicator of Yr., Birmingham Bus. Jour., 2001; recipient Outstanding Achievement award, Operation New Birmingham, 1994, Liberty and Justice award, 2000, Key to Unlocking Door to Adversity award, Mercedes-Benz U.S. Internat., 2002. Mem. ALA, Auburn U. Bar Assn., Birmingham Bar Assn. (L. Burton Barnes Cmty. Svc. award 2006), Internat. Bar Assn., Ala. State Bar Assn. (Merit award 1999-2000), Leadership Birmingham, Leadership Ala. (bd. dirs. 1998—),, Auburn Coll. Liberal Arts (adv. coun.), U. Va. Alumni Assn., Newcomen Soc., Birmingham Regional C. of C. (bd. dirs. 2001, vice chmn. for tech. devel. 2002, chmn.-elect 2003, chmn 2004, chmn. exec. com. 2005), Auburn U. Alumni Assn., Birmingham Venture Club (bd. dirs. 2001), Country Club of Birmingham, Jockey Club, Summit Club (charter), Kiwanis (sec. 1998-99). Methodist. Avocations: horses, bird hunting, cattle farming, golf. Office: Bradley Arant Rose & White LLP One Federal Pl 1819 5th Ave N Birmingham AL 35203 Home Phone: 205-967-3444; Office Phone: 205-521-8000. E-mail: jrotch@bradleyavant.com.

ROTE, NELLE FAIRCHILD HEFTY, management consultant; b. Watsontown, Pa., May 23, 1930; d. Edwin Dunkel and Phebe Hill (Fisher) Fairchild; m. John Austin Hefty, Mar. 20, 1948 (div. June 1970); children: Harry E. Hefty, John B. Hefty, Susan E. Hefty DeBartolo; m. Keith Maynard Rote, Dec. 16, 1983 (dec. Aug. 1985). Student, Bucknell U., 1961, Williamsport Sch. Commerce, 1968—69, Pa. State U., 1971—72, student, 1983, Susquehanna U., 1986. Typesetter, page designer Colonial Printing House, Inc., Lewisburg, Pa., 1970-76; account exec. Sta. WTGC Radio, Lewisburg, 1976-78; co-owner Colonial Printing Co., Lewisburg, 1978-83; temp. HATS-Temps, Lewisburg, 1986-89; artist, editor Create-A-Book, Inc., Milton, Fla., 1980-92; census crew leader, spl. svc. Dept. Commerce, Washington, 1990; cons. Create-A-Book, Inc., Gulf Breeze, Fla., 1991—99. Children's Playmate Mag., 1942; author: McGruff and Me, 1999, My Christmas Wish, 1999, School Fun Book, 1999, My Fishing Adventure, 1999, Nurse Helen Fairchild,World War I, 1917-1918, 2006; contbr., articles to profl. jours.; exhibitions include Union County Libr., Lewisburg, 2003. Charter mem. Women's Art Mus., Washington; charter sponsor Women in Mil. Svc. Meml., Arlington, Va., 1991; founder, donor Nelle Fairchild Rote Book Fund, Union County Libr.; editor, poet Holiday Newspaper Bus. Assn., Lewisburg, 1987. Recipient Humanitarian recognition, Tri-County Fedn. Women's Clubs, Pa., 1965, Grand prize in Cooking, Milton Std., 1966, Most Profl. Photo award, Lewisburg Festival Arts, 1980, Hon. Mention award, Women in Arts, Harrisburg, Pa., 1981, Photo Contest award, Congressman Allen Ertel, 1981, 2d pl. Photo award, Union County Fair, 1981, 3d pl. Photo award, 1981, Hon. Mention Photo award, Susquehanna Art Soc., 1981, Silver award for Poetry, World of Poetry, 1990. Mem.: DAR (nat. def. reporter Shikelimo chpt. 1989—95, sec. 1992—95, regent 1995—2001, vice chmn. Pa. State Soc. DAR women vets com. 1998—2001, vice-regent 2001—04, Prize for safety poster 1942), Soc. Profl. Journalists, Warrior Run Heritage Soc., Western Front Assn., Marine Corps League Aux. (life), Civic Club Lewisburg (v.p. 1994—97), Am. Legion Aux. Achievements include Initiator for renaming bridge in Watsontown, Pa. to "Nurse Helen Fairchild Meml. Bridge" (a WWI Reserve Army Nurse relative), 2002. Home: 1015 St Paul St Lewisburg PA 17837-1213 Office Phone: 570-523-3741. Personal E-mail: elle12@ptd.net.

ROTELLA, STEPHEN J., bank executive; BA, SUNY, Stony Brook, 1975; MBA, SUNY, Albany, 1978. Dir. mortgage products Shearson Lehman Bros.; with JP Morgan Chase, 1987—2005, COO Chase Home Fin., 1998—2001, exec. v.p., mem. exec. com., CEO Chase Home Fin., 2001—04; pres., COO Washington Mutual Inc., Seattle, 2005—. Mem. exec. com. Housing Policy Council Fin. Services Roundtable; bd. dir., mem. residential bd. gov. Mortgage Bankers Assn. Bd. dir. St. Barnabas Med. Ctr., NJ. Office: Washington Mutual Inc Washington Mutual Tower 1201 Third Ave Seattle WA 98101 *

ROTELLINI, FELECIA A., state agency administrator; b. Sheridan, Wyo., 1957; Grad. magna cum laude in Hist. and Polit. Sci., Rocky Mountain Coll., Billings, Mont., 1981; grad., Notre Dame Law Sch., 1986. Bar: Ariz. 1986, Wyo. Pvt. practice atty., Ariz., 1986—92; asst. atty. gen. State of Ariz., 1992—2005; asst. supt. Ariz. Dept. Fin. Instns., 2005—06, supt., 2006—. Trustee Boys and Girls Clubs Met. Phoenix Found., 1990—2002. Mem.: Wyo. State Bar, Ariz. State Bar (mem. adminstrv. law sect.). Office: Ariz Dept Fin Instns 2910 N 44th St Ste 310 Phoenix AZ 85018 Office Phone: 602-255-4421. Office Fax: 602-381-1225. E-mail: frotellini@azdfi.gov.

ROTENBERG, MANUEL, physics professor; b. Toronto, Ont., Can., Mar. 12, 1930; came to U.S., 1946; s. Peter and Rose (Plonzker) R.; m. Paula Weissbrod, June 22, 1952; children: Joel, Victor. BS, MIT, 1952, PhD, 1956. Staff Los Alamos (N.Mex.) Nat. Lab., 1955-58; instr. physics Princeton (N.J.) U., 1958-59; asst. prof. U. Chgo., 1959-61; prof. applied physics U. Calif., San Diego, 1961-93, dean grad. studies and research, 1975-84, chmn. dept. elec. engring. and computer sci., 1988-93, rsch. prof., 1993—. Author: The 3-j and 6-j Symbols, 1959; founding editor: Methods of Computational Physics, 1963, Jour. of Computational Physics, 1962; editor: Biomathematics and Cell Kinetics, 1981. Fellow Am. Phys. Soc.; mem. AAAS, Sigma Xi. Office: U Calif San Diego La Jolla CA 92093-0407 Home Phone: 858-552-0415; Office Phone: 858-534-2726. Business E-Mail: rote@ucsd.edu.

ROTENBERG, MARC STEVEN, advocate, lawyer; b. Boston, Apr. 20, 1960; s. Michael and Karen (Sethur) R.; m. Anna Markopoulos; children: Chaz, Chloe. AB, Harvard Coll., 1982; JD, Stanford U., 1987; student, Georgetown U., 1994—. Bar: Mass. 1987, D.C. 1990. Teaching fellow Harvard U., Cambridge, Mass., 1980-82; exec. dir. Pub. Interest Computer Assn., Washington, 1983-84; instr. Stanford (Calif.) U., 1986-87; counsel Senate Jud. Com., Washington, 1987-88; dir. Washington office Computer Profls. for Social Responsibility, 1988-94; pres. Electronic Privacy Info. Ctr., Washington, 1994—. Adj. prof. law Georgetown Law Ctr., 1991—, Washington Coll. Law, 1997—; chmn. pub. interest registry, Privacy Internat., 2004-05; mem. adv. panels NSF, ABA, AAAS, ALA, Orgn. for Econ. Coop. and Devel., Paris, Austrian Inst. on Law and Policy, Salzburg. Author: Information Privacy Law, 2005; co-author: Intomation Privacy Law, 2003; editor: Technology and Privacy: The New Frontier, 1998; bd. editors Electronic Info. Law Reporter, Govt. Info. Quar., Computer Law and Security Report, Ency. Computer Sci.; contbr. articles to profl. jours. Ford Found. fellow internat. law, 1994; recipient 3rd Pl. U.S. Amateur Chess Championship, 1993, Law award World Tech. Network, 2002. Mem. ABA (Cyberspace Law Excellence award 2005), Assn. Computing Machines. Avocations: chess, basketball, german expressionism, record producing.

ROTERMUND, DONALD O., musician, minister; b. St. Louis, June 14, 1932; s. Erich William Otto and Adelia Ida (Pott) Rotermund; m. Doris Ann Doehrman, July 21, 1956; children: Deborah Ruth, David Erich. BS in Edn., Concordia Tchrs.' Coll., River Forest, Ill., 1955; MA in Music, North Tex. State U., Denton, 1958; LittD (hon.), Concordia U., River Forest, 1987. Tchr., musician St. Paul Luth. Ch., Rockford, Ill., 1953—54; min. music, tchr. Zion Luth. Ch., Dallas, 1955—99, min. music emeritus, 1999—. Mem. music ednl. adv. com. Concordia Pub. Ho., St. Louis, 1973—97; lectr. in field. Author: We Praise You Alleluia, 1978; co-author, editor: Children Sing His Praise, 1985; author: Off the Page, 2007, composer more than 125 pieces for choir, organ, instruments. Pres. Richland Meadows Neighborhood Assn., Richardson, Tex., 2002—05, bd. dirs., 2005—. Recipient Te Deum Laudamus award, Haritage Series, Zion Luth. Ch., 1996. Mem.: Assn. Luth. Ch. Musicians (dir. ednl. concerns 1993—97), Am. Guild Organists (dean, sub dean Dallas chpt. 1971—75), Dallas Bach Soc. (bd. dirs. 2005—). Avocations: woodworking, travel, concerts, reading.

ROTH, CLIFFORD JOEL, lawyer, consultant; b. NYC, June 28, 1935; s. Herman Noah Roth and Ethel Ann Lederman; children: Toni Wells-Roth, David Wells-Roth. BA, Hunter Coll., NYC, 1951; JD, Bklyn. Law Sch., NYC, 1962. Bar: NY 1962, Ohio 1967. Dep. counsel Dept. Army, NYC, 1963—65; asst. gen. counsel Maritime Adminstrn., NYC, 1965—68; gen. counsel Litton Industries, Cleve., 1968—70, Am. Ship Bldg., Cleve., 1970—76; dep. prodr. Sea-Land Svc., Edison, NJ, 1976—83; gen. counsel Prudential, NYC, 1983—86; with Dept. Navy, Washington, 1987—97; cons., security Wells Roth Bloud, Washington, 1997—. Mem. bd. advisors Universal Guarddian, Newport Beach, 2006—, S2 Global Sys., LA, 2006—. Mem.: Am. Soc. Indsl. Security. Avocations: reading, swimming. Home: 10769 Gloxinia Dr Rockville MD 20852

ROTH, DALE DAVIS, music educator, religious organization administrator; b. Williamston, SC, June 1, 1960; d. Carl Hampton and Marion Garrett Davis; m. Ronald D. Roth, June 11, 1988; children: Elizabeth, Garrett. MusB, Columbia Coll., 1982; MEd, Southern Wesleyan U., 2003. Tchr. cert. Columbia Coll., SC, 1982—, team evaluator SC, 1998; tchr. cert. Converse Coll., Spartanburg, SC, 1991. Piano, voice tchr. pvt. practice, 1982—; jv and varsity cheerleader coach Clinton H.S., 1982—, prom advisor, 1986—, spring musical music dir., 1990—. Bible sch. dir. First Baptist Ch., Joanna, SC, 2001—. Mem.: SC Music Educators (region chair coord. 1999—), Music Educators Nat. Conf. Baptist. Avocations: knitting, baking. Home: 707 E Ferguson St Clinton SC 29325 Office: Clinton HS 800 N Adair St Clinton SC 29325 Business E-Mail: ddroth@laurens56.k12.sc.us.

ROTH, DANIEL BENJAMIN, lawyer, company executive; b. Youngstown, Ohio, Sept. 17, 1929; s. Benjamin F. and Marion (Benjamin) R.; m. Joann M. Roth; children: William M., Jennifer A., Rochelle. BS in Fin., Miami U., Oxford, Ohio, 1951; JD, Case-Western Res. U., 1956. Bar: Ohio 1956, U.S. Supreme Ct. 1960, D.C. 1983. Chmn. Roth, Blair, Roberts, Strasfeld & Lodge, LPA, Youngstown, 1969—; co-founder, vice chmn. Nat. Data Processing Corp., Cin., 1961-69; chmn., pres., CEO Torent, Inc., Youngstown, 1971—; chmn. McDonald Steel Corp., 1980—; vice chmn. Torent Oil & Gas Co., 1979—2002, Vaughn Indsl. Car & Equipment Co., 1988—2002. Bd. dirs. Gasser Chair Co. Profl. singer: appearances including Steve Allen Show, 1952. Bd. dirs. Youngstown Symphony, Stambaugh Auditorium; bd. dirs. Youngstown Playhouse, v.p., 1991-93; pres. Rodef Sholom Temple, Youngstown, 1982-84. 1st lt. USAF, 1951-53, lt. col. Res., ret. Recipient Mgr. of Yr. award Mahoning Valley Mgmt. Assn., 1989, Man of Yr. award Youngstown YWCA, 1995. Mem. ABA, D.C. Bar Assn., Ohio Bar Assn., Mahoning County Bar Assn., Lawyer-Pilots Bar Assn., Soc. Benchers of Case Western Res. U. Law Sch., Youngstown Club, Pelican Marsh Club (Naples, Fla.), Zeta Beta Tau (nat. v.p. 1964-66), Omicron Delta Kappa, Phi Eta Sigma, Tau Epsilon Rho. Jewish. Office: Roth Blair Roberts Strasfeld & Lodge 600 City Centre One Youngstown OH 44503-1514 Office Phone: 330-744-5211.

ROTH, DAVID LEE, singer; b. Bloomington, Ind., Oct. 10, 1954; s. Nathan J. and Sybil Roth. Lead singer Van Halen, 1974—85; solo career, 1985—. Singer: (albums) Crazy from the Heat, 1985, Eat 'Em and Smile, 1986, Skyscraper, 1988, A Little Ain't Enough, 1991, Your Filthy Little Mouth, 1994, Best of David Lee Roth, 1997, DLR Band, 1998, Diamond Dave, 2003, (with Van Halen) Van Halen, 1978, Van Halen II, 1979, Women and Children First, 1980, Fair Warning, 1981, Diver Down, 1982, 1984, 1983, Best of Van Halen, 1996, (songs) Jump (MTV Video Music award, Best Stage Performance, 1984); author: Crazy from the Heat, 1997; host The David Lee Roth Show, Sirius Radio, 2006. Named one of 100 Sexiest Artists, VH1, 2002; named to Rock & Roll Hall of Fame, with Van Halen, 2007. Avocation: mountain climbing. Office: c/o Eddie Anderson Diamond Dave Enterprises 11288 Ventura Blvd Ste 430 North Hollywood CA 91606 *

ROTH, ERIC, screenwriter; b. NYC, Mar. 22, 1945; 6 children. Student, Columbia U., UCLA. Screenplays include: The Stranger in 7A, 1972, The Nickel Ride, 1975, The Concorde - Airport '79, 1979, Suspect, 1987, Memories of Me, 1988 (with Billy Crystal), Mr. Jones, 1993, Forrest Gump, 1994 (Acad. award Best Adapted Screenplay), the Postman, 1997, The Horse Whisperer, 1998, The Insider (nominated for Acad., Golden Globe 1999), Munich, 2005, The Good Shepherd, 2006, Lucky You, 2007; co-writer: (with Michael Mann) Ali, 2001. Office: care Creative Artists Agy 9830 Wilshire Blvd Beverly Hills CA 90212-1804 *

ROTH, ERIC M., lawyer; b. Bklyn., Jan. 16, 1954; BA with distinction in all subjects, Cornell U., 1974; JD, NYU, 1977. Bar: N.Y. 1978; U.S. Dist. Ct. (so., ea. dists.) N.Y. 1978, D.C. 1980; U.S. Supreme Ct. 1981; U.S. Ct. Appeals (2nd. cir.) 1984, (4th, 5th cirs.) 1985, (8th cir.) 1989, (11th cir.) 1995, (9th cir.) 1997. Law clk. to Hon. Lee P. Gagliardi U.S. Dist. Ct., 1977-79; atty. Wachtell, Lipton, Rosen & Katz, NYC. Bd. dirs., former chmn. MFY Legal Svcs., Inc. Note and comment editor: NYU Law Review, 1976-77. Trustee NYU Sch. Law Found. Mem. ABA, N.Y. State Bar Assn., The D.C. Bar, Fed. Bar Coun., NYU Law Alumni Assn. Inc. (former mem. bd. dirs). Office: Wachtell Lipton Rosen & Katz 51 W 52nd St Fl 29 New York NY 10019-6150

ROTH, EUGENE, lawyer; b. Wilkes-Barre, Pa., June 28, 1935; s. Max and Rae (Klein) R.; m. Constance D. Smulyan, June 16, 1957; children: Joan Roth Kleinman, Steven P., Jeffrey H., Lawrence W.(dec.). BS, Wilkes U., 1957; LLB, Pa. State U., 1960. Bar: Pa. 1960, U.S. Dist. Ct. (mid. dist.) Pa. 1961. Assoc. Rosenn, Jenkins & Greenwald LLP, Walkes-Barre, 1960—64, ptnr., 1964—. Chmn. Greater Wilkes-Barre Partnership, Inc., 1991-93; chmn. Wyoming Valley Retirement Cmty., Inc., 2004-07; dir. Joint Urban Studies Ctr., 2006-. Trustee Wilkes U., 1979—, chmn. 1993-98; chmn. United Way Wyoming Valley, 1983, annual campaign Osterhout Free Libr. Campaign, 1999; chmn. Eastern Pa. regional bd. dirs. Geiseinger-Wyoming Valley Hosp., City of Wilkes-Barre Transition Team, 2004. Recipient Disting. Pennsylvanian award Phila. C. of C., 1980, Cmty. Svc. award B'nai B'rith, 1994, Disting. Citizen award N.E. Pa. Boy Scouts Am., 1998, Shofar award United Hebrew Inst., 2001; named Outstanding Vol. Fund Raiser Nat. Soc. Fund Raising Exec., 1993, Pa. Super Lawyer, 2006. Mem. ABA, Pa. Bar Assn., Luzerne County Law and Libr. Assn., Wilkes-Barre C. of C. (chmn. 1980, vice com. for econ. growth), Wyo. Valley United Jewish Campaign (chmn. 1978 and 1993), B'nai B'rith. Republican. Jewish. Avocations: reading, community svc. Office: Rosenn Jenkins & Greenwald LLP 15 S Franklin St Wilkes Barre PA 18711-0076 Home Phone: 570-825-4830; Office Phone: 570-826-5636. Business E-Mail: eroth@rjglaw.com.

ROTH, GEORGE STANLEY, biochemist, physiologist, researcher; b. Honolulu, Aug. 5, 1946; s. George Frederick and Laura Ann (Zembrzuski) Roth; m. Mary Jane Fletcher, Mar. 11, 1972; children: Susan Marie, George William. BS, Villanova U., 1968; PhD, Temple U., 1971. Fellow Fels Rsch. Inst., Phila., 1971-72; staff fellow Gerontology Rsch. Ctr. NIH, Balt., 1972-76, rsch. chemist, 1976—, chief molecular physiology and genetics sect., 1984-99, sr. guest scientist, 2000—04; CEO GeroScience, Inc. (formerly Gerotech Inc.), 2000—; exec. dir. Am. Aging Assn., 2002—03. Vis. prof. Mehary Med. Coll., Nashville, 1983; Alpha Omega Alpha prof. U. P.R. Med. Sch., San Juan, 1986; chmn. Gordon Rsch. Conf. Biology of Aging, Oxnard, Calif., 1985; rsch. cons. George Washington U., 1977—82; Ben Cohen Meml. lectr. U. Mich., 1998; lectr. Med. Sci. Ctr. Student Sci. program, 1980; Sandoz lectr. gerontology, Basel, Switzerland, 84, Basel, 86, Basel, 94. Contbr. articles to profl. jours.; editor: Exptl. Gerontology, Exptl. Aging Rsch., Proc. Soc.Exptl. Biology and Medicine; co-editor: Chem. Rubber Co. Press Series in Aging, 1981—; mem. editl. bd. Ency. of Aging, 1987—. Co-dir. Ea. Harford County Civic Assn., Bel Air, 1981—88; v.p. Cmty. Coalition Harford County, Bel Air, Md., 1988—90, bd. dirs., 1990—92. Recipient Rsch. award, Am. Aging Assn., 1981, prize for gerontol. rsch., Sandoz Ltd., 1989, Third Age award, Internat. Assn. Gerontology, 1989, Spl. award, Balt. Longitudinal Study Aging, 1991, Equal Opportunity award, NIH, 1995, Merit award, 1996; Sigma Chi scholar, Miami U., Oxford, Ohio, 1989. Fellow: Gerontol. Soc. Am. (chair biol. scis. sect. 1975—76, chair rsch. com. 1978—79, chmn. fellowship com. 1986—87); mem.: Soc. Exptl. Biology and Medicine. Republican. Roman Catholic. Avocations: basketball, fishing, hiking, canoeing. Office: GeroSci Inc 1124 Ridge Rd Pylesville MD 21132

ROTH, GREGORY EDWARD, social studies educator; b. Canton, Ohio, May 1, 1949; s. Edward and Rosemary Roth; m. Connie May Roth, Sept. 1, 1973; children: William Martin, Jonathan Edward. BA, Malone Coll., Canton, 1972; postgrad., Bowling Green State U., Ohio, 1972—74; MA, U. Akron, Ohio, 1977. Cert. permanent secondary edn. Ohio. Social studies tchr. Jackson Jr. High, Massillon, Ohio, 1976—77; tchr. Cuyahoga Falls H.S., Ohio, 1977—. Active First Friends Ch., Canton. Mem.: NEA, Ohio Edn. Assn., Cuyahoga Falls Edn. Assn. (exec. bd. mem. 1978—, v.p. 1994—96, pres. 1986—88, Lifetime Achievement award 2002). Republican. Mem. Evangelical Friend Ch. Home: 2826 Midvale Rd NW Canton OH 44708-1751 Office: Cuyahoga Falls HS 2300 Fourth St Cuyahoga Falls OH 44221 Personal E-mail: groth@neo.rr.com.

ROTH, HADDEN WING, lawyer, mediator, arbitrator; b. Oakland, Calif., Feb. 10, 1930; s. Mark and Jane (Haley) R.; m. Alice Becker, Aug., 1987; 1 child, Elizabeth Wing. AA, Coll. Marin, 1949; BA, U. Calif., Berkeley, 1951; JD, U. Calif., San Francisco, 1957. Bar: Calif. 1958, U.S. Dist. Ct. (no. dist.) Calif. 1958, U.S. Ct. Appeals (9th cir.) 1958, U.S. Supreme Ct. 1966. Atty. Calif. and fed. courts, 1957—; judge Municipal Ct., Marin County, Calif., 1966—70, Superior Ct. pro tem, Marin County, Calif., 1966—70; instr. Golden Gate Coll. Law, Calif., 1971—73; counsel Corte Madera Sanitary Dist., 1971, Marin Muni Water Dist., 1972—87, Town of San Anselmo, 1973—2006, Ross Valley Fire Svc., 1982—2006, Town of Ross, 1984—, San Rafael Sch. Dist., 1984, Bolinas Pub. Utility Dist., 1991—2005; hearing officer Mendocino Coast Hosp., Petaluma Valley Hosp., Redbud Cmty. Hosp., 1981—92; arbitrator, mediator, spl. master, 1990—. Chmn. Marin County prison task force, 1973; bd. dirs. Marin Gen. Hosp., 1964-66. Named Outstanding Citizen of Yr., Coll. Marin, 1972. Mem. ABA, Calif. Bar Assn., Marin County Bar Assn., Mediation Soc. San Francisco, Am. Assn. Ind. Investors, Nat. Assn. Securities Dealers, Nat. Arbitration Forum. Democrat. Avocations: running, weightlifting, reading. Office: Law Offices of Hadden Roth 343 Fairhills Dr San Rafael CA 94901 Office Phone: 415-479-5623. Business E-Mail: hwroth@pacbell.net.

ROTH, HAROLD, architect; b. St. Louis, June 30, 1934; s. Samuel and Dorothy (Yawitz) R.; m. Dvora Feigon, Dec. 6, 1959; children: Elizabeth, David. AB, Washington U., 1956; MArch, Yale U., 1957. Designer Warner Burns Toan & Lunde, NYC, 1957; sr. designer Eero Saarinen & Assocs., Roche Dinkeloo & Assocs., Hamden, Conn., 1959-65; ptnr. Harold Roth—Edward Saad, Hamden, Conn., 1965-72; sr. ptnr. Roth & Moore Architects, New Haven, 1973—; critic archtl. design Yale U. Sch. Architecture, New Haven, 1964-98. Pres., trustee Perspecta, Yale Archtl. Jour. Trustee Long Wharf Theatre, New Haven, 1972-98, Conn. Trust for Hist. Preservation, 1983-90; pres. bd. trustees Conn. Architecture Found., 1990-93; bd. govs. Bldg. Stone Inst., 1999-2003; bd. regents Am. Arch. Found., 1999-2001; profl. advisor Western European Architecture Found., 2000—. Officer U.S. Army, 1957-59, Korea. Recipient Design award Nat. Coun. Religious Arch., 1970, 96, Design award New Haven Preservation Trust, 1978, 88, Tucker award Bldg. Stone Inst., 1983, 88, Honor award Concrete Reinforcing Steel Inst., 1983, Design award Portland Cement Assn., 1984, Design award Archtl. Record, 1970, 80, Design award AIA/ALA, 1983, Faculty Design award Assn. Collegiate Schs. of Arch., 1988, Healthcare Facilities Design award Boston Soc. Archs., 1992; fellow Pierson Coll., Yale U., 1978—. Fellow: AIA (chmn. nat. com. on design 1990, bd. dirs. 1992—94, sec. Coll. of Fellows 1998—99, vice-chancellor 2000, chancellor 2001, Design award Conn. 1974, 1978, 1983, 1986, 1988, 1990, 1993, 1997, 1998, Design award New Eng. 1968, 1984, 1992, 2001, N.Y. State Design award of merit 2000). Home: 37 Autumn St New Haven CT 06511-2220 Office: Roth and Moore Architects 65 Audubon St New Haven CT 06510-1205 Office Phone: 203-787-1166. Business E-Mail: hroth@rothandmoore.com.

ROTH, HARVEY PAUL, retired publishing executive; b. NYC, Feb. 20, 1933; s. Lewis Theodore and Harriet (Wallow) R.; m. Tanya Cohen; children by previous marriage: Andrea Warriner, Matthew Jay; stepchildren: Laura Meryl Becker, Matthew Robert Turetzky. AB, Bklyn. Coll., 1954; LL.B., N.Y. U., 1957. Bar: N.Y. bar 1959. Editor West Pub. Co., NYC, 1959-61; pres. BFL Communications, Inc., Plainview, NY, 1961-76, Roth Pub., Inc., Great Neck, NY, 1976—2005, ret., 2005. Chmn. Alcove Press, London, 1970—75, Nash Pub. Corp., LA, 1971—75. With US Army, 1957—58. Personal E-mail: rothharvey@hotmail.com.

ROTH, JAMES FRANK, chemicals executive, chemist; b. Rahway, NJ, Dec. 7, 1925; s. Louis and Eleanor R.; m. Sharon E. Mattes, June 20, 1969; children by previous marriage: Lawrence, Edward, Sandra. BA in Chemistry, U. W.Va., 1947; PhD in Phys. Chemistry, U. Md., 1951. Research chemist Franklin Inst., Phila., 1951-53, mgr. chemistry lab., 1958-60; chief chemist Lehigh Paints & Chems. Co., Allentown, Pa., 1953-55; research chemist GAF Corp., Easton, Pa., 1955-58; with Monsanto Co., St. Louis, 1960-80, dir. catalysis research, 1973-77, dir. process sci. research, 1977-80; corp. chief scientist Air Products and Chems., Inc., Allentown, 1980-91; indsl. cons., 1991—. Contbr. articles to profl. jours.; mem. editl. bd. Jour. Catalysis, 1976-85, Catalysis Revs., 1973-93, Applied Catalysis, 1981-85; editor for Ams., 1985-88, assoc. editor, 1988-95. With USN, 1943-46. Recipient Richard J. Kokes award Johns Hopkins U., 1977, Chem. Pioneer award Am. Inst. Chemists, 1986, Perkin medal Soc. Chem.

Industry, 1988. Mem. NAE, Am. Chem. Soc. (St. Louis sect. St. Louis award 1975, E.V. Murphree nat. award 1976, Indsl. Chemistry award 1991), Catalysis Soc. N.Am. (E.J. Houdry award 1991), Catalysis Club of Phila. (award 1981). Inventor process biodegradable detergents, for acetic acid; U.S., fgn. patents in field. Home: 8040 Frankford Rd Apt 432 Dallas TX 75252

ROTH, JANE RICHARDS, federal judge; b. Phila., June 16, 1935; d. Robert Henry Jr. and Harriett (Kellond) Richards; m. William V. Roth Jr., Oct. 9, 1965; children: William V. III, Katharine K. BA, Smith Coll., 1956; LLB, Harvard U., 1965; LLD (hon.), Widener U., 1986, U. Del., 1994. Bar: Del. 1965, US Dist. Ct. Del. 1966, US Ct. Appeals (3d cir.) 1974. Adminstrv. asst. various fgn. service posts US Dept. State, 1956-62; assoc. Richards, Layton & Finger, Wilmington, Del., 1965-73, ptnr., 1973-85; judge US Dist. Ct. Del., Wilmington, Del., 1985-91, US Ct. Appeals (3d cir.), Wilmington, Del., 1991—2006, sr. judge, 2006—. Adj. faculty Villanova U. Sch. Law. Hon. chmn. Del. chpt. Arthritis Found., Wilmington; bd. overseers Widener U. Sch. Law; bd. consultors Villanova U. Sch. Law; trustee Hist. Soc. Del. Recipient Nat. Vol. Service citiation Athritis Found., 1982. Fellow Am. Bar Found.; mem. ABA, Del. State Bar Assn. Republican. Episcopalian. Office: US Court of Appeals 3rd Cirt Lock Box 12 5100 Fed Bldg 844 King St Wilmington DE 19801-1790 *

ROTH, JOE, motion picture company executive; b. NYC, June 13, 1948; m. Donna Roth. BA, Boston U. Prodn. assistant various commls. and feature films, San Francisco; also lighting dir. Pitchel Players, San Francisco, then producer LA; co-founder Morgan Creek Prodns., LA, 1987-89; chmn. 20th Century Fox Film Corp., LA, 1989-92; founder Caravan Pictures, LA, 1992-94; chmn. Walt Disney Motion Pictures Group, Burbank, 1994—96, Walt Disney Studios, Burbank, 1996—2000; founder Revolution Pictures, 2000—. Bd. dirs. Pixar Studios, 2000—. Prodr. (films) Tunnel Vision, 1976, Our Winning Season, 1978, Americathon, 1979, Ladies and Gentlemen, the Fabulous Stains, 1981, Final Terror, 1983, The Stone Boy, 1984, Moving Violations, 1985, Off Beat, 1986, Where the River Runs Black, 1986, Streets of Gold, 1986, P.K. and the Kid, 1987, Young Guns, 1988, Skin Deep, 1989, Major League, 1989, Nightbreed, 1990, The Three Musketeers, 1993, Angels in the Outfield, 1994, Low Down Dirty Shame, 1994, Houseguest, 1995, The Jerky Boys, 1995, Heavyweights, 1995, Tall Tale, 1995, While You Were Sleeping, 1995, The Forgotten, 2004; exec. prodr. (films) Cracking Up, 1977, Bachelor Party, 1984, Revenge of the Nerds II: Nerds in Paradise, 1987, Dead Ringers, 1988, Renegades, 1989, Enemies: A Love Story, 1989, The Exorcist III, 1990, Pacific Heights, 1990, Angie, 1994, Before and After, 1996, Tears of the Sun, 2003, Daddy Day Care, 2003, Hollywood Homicide, 2003, Mona Lisa Smile, 2003, An Unfinished Life, 2005; dir. Streets of Gold, 1986, Coupe de Ville, 1990, America's Sweethearts, 2001, Christmas with the Kranks, 2004, Freedomland, 2006. Named one of 50 Most Powerful People in Hollywood, Premiere mag., 2002—05. Office: Pixar 1200 Park Ave Emeryville CA 94608

ROTH, JOHN REECE, electrical engineer, educator, researcher, inventor; b. Washington, Pa., Sept. 19, 1937; s. John Meyer and Ruth Evangeline (Iams) R.; m. Helen Marie DeCrane, Jan. 14, 1972; children: Nancy Ann, John Alexander. BS in Physics, MIT, 1959; PhD, Cornell U., 1963. Engring. aide Aerojet-Gen. Corp., Azusa, Calif., 1957, 1958; aerospace engr. N.Am. Aviation, Canoga Park, Calif., 1959; prin. investigator NASA Lewis Rsch. Ctr., Cleve., 1963—78; prof. U. Tenn., Knoxville, 1978—2004, prof. emeritus, 2004—; hon. prof. U. Electronic Sci. and Tech. China, Chengdu, 1992—; prin. investigator Office Naval Rsch., Washington, 1980—89, Air Force Office Sci. Rsch., Washington, 1981—95, 2001—03, Army Rsch. Office, 1988—93, NASA Langley Rsch. Ctr., Hampton, Va., 1995—98, 2001—03, March Instruments, Inc., Concord, Calif., 1996—98, NSF, 2002—03. Cons. TVA, Chattanooga, 1982-84, BDM Corp., 1987-88, Tenn. Eastman, 1989-90, March Instruments, 1995-98, Procter & Gamble, 1996, 2000, Internat. Eco Scis., 1997-98, Environ. Elements Corp., 1997-00, Tetra Pak Suisse, 1998-00, Atmospheric Glow Techs., Inc., 1999-05, YTC-Am., Inc., 2005, Harrick Plasma, 2006; mem. NAS-NRC Com. on Aneutronic Fusion, 1986-87; hon. guest prof. Tsinghua U., Shenzhen campus, 2006-; spkr. at profl. meetings Author: Industrial Plasma Engineering, Introduction to Fusion Energy; contbr. articles to profl. jours. Sloan scholar, 1955-59; Ford fellow, 1961-62; recipient B. Otto and Katherine Wheeley award for Excellence in Tech. Transfer, 1999, NASA Inventor's award, 2004, Gonzalez Family Lifetime Achievement award, 2006. Fellow IEEE, AIAA (assoc.); mem. Am. Phys. Soc., Am. Chem. Soc., Am. Nuc. Soc. (exec. com. No. Ohio sect. 1975-78), Nuc. and Plasma Scis. Soc., Am. Soc. Engring. Edn., Knoxville Mus. Art, East Tenn. Soc. Archaeol. Inst. Am., Sigma Xi (pres. U. Tenn. Knoxville chpt. 1985-86). Achievements include 11 US patents. Home: 12359 N Fox Den Dr Knoxville TN 37934-3755 Office: U Tenn Dept Elec Computer Engring 409 Ferris Hall Knoxville TN 37996-2100 Office Phone: 865-974-4446. Business E-Mail: jrr@utk.edu.

ROTH, JOHN ROGER, geneticist, biology educator; b. Winona, Minn., Mar. 14, 1939; s. Frederick Daniel and Louise Mae (Wirt) R.; m. Uta Goetz (div.); children: Katherine Louise, Frederick Phillip; m. Sherylynne Harris, Jan. 4, 1986. BA, Harvard U., 1961; PhD, John Hopkins U., 1965. From asst. prof. molecular biology to prof. molecular biology U. Calif., Berkeley, 1967-76; prof. biology U. Utah, Salt Lake City, 1976—2002; prof. sect. microbiology U. Calif., Davis, 2002—, chair sect. microbiology, 2003—. Recipient Disting. Prof. award, 1990, Rosenblatt award, 1990. Mem. NAS, Am. Soc. for Microbiology, Genetics Soc. Am. Office: Univ Calif Microbiology 314 Briggs Hall One Shields Ave Davis CA 95616

ROTH, KENNETH, human rights advocate; b. Elmhurst, Ill., Sept. 23, 1955; s. Walter and Muriel (Teitell) R.; m. Nina Brodsky, May 29, 1983; children: Lisa, Emma. BA magna cum laude, Brown U., 1977; JD, Yale U., 1980. Bar: N.Y. 1981. Law clk. to Judge Edward Weinfeld U.S. Dist. Ct. for So. Dist. N.Y., NYC, 1980-81; assoc. Paul, Weiss, Rifkind, Wharton & Garrison, NYC, 1981-83; from asst. U.S. atty. to chief appellate atty. criminal div. U.S. Atty.'s Office for So. Dist. N.Y., NYC, 1983-87; assoc. counsel Office Ind. Counsel for Iran/Contra, Washington, 1987; dep. dir. Human Rights Watch, NYC, 1987-93, exec. dir., 1993—. Editor, author numerous reports on human rights worldwide; contbr. articles to newspapers and mags. Mem. Assn. Bar City N.Y., Coun. Fgn. Rels. Office: Human Rights Watch Floor 34 350 Fifth Ave New York NY 10118-3499 *

ROTH, LANE, communications educator; b. NYC, Apr. 10; BA with nat. honors in German, NYU; MA, Fla. State U., 1974, PhD in Mass Comm., 1976. Camera operator Sta. WFSU-TV, Tallahassee, 1973-74; broadcast engr., producer-creator, writer, performer Sta. WFSU-FM, Tallahassee, 1974-76; co-host Sta. WNIN-TV, Evansville, Ind., 1976-77; asst. prof. radio-TV-film U. Evansville, 1976-78; asst. prof. comm. Lamar U., Beaumont, Tex., 1978-82, assoc. prof., 1982—. Bd. dirs. Mental Health Assn. of Jefferson County, pres., 1997, 98; writer, performer fund-raising promos, Sta. KVLU-FM, Beaumont, 1995—. Author: Film Semiotics, Metz, and Leone's Trilogy, 1983; contbr. articles to profl. mags., jours.; contbr. to acad. books. Bd. dirs. Mental Health Assoc. of Jefferson Co., 1993—. Recipient Regents Merit award for excellence in tchg., 1980, Mental Health Assn. award for dedicated leadership, 1999. Mem. Popular Culture Assn. Roman Catholic. Avocations: Jungian psychology, analysis of popular film and tv, singer-impressionist-songwriter. Office: Lamar U Dept Communications Beaumont TX 77710 Office Phone: 409-880-8152.

ROTH, LAWRENCE MAX, pathologist, educator; b. McAlester, Okla., June 25, 1936; s. Herman Moe and Blanche (Brown) R.; m. Anna Berit Katarina Sundstrom, Apr. 3, 1965; children: Karen Roth Hart, David Josef. BA, Vanderbilt U., 1957; MD, Harvard U., 1960. Diplomate Am. Bd. Pathology. Rotating intern U. Ill. Research and Ednl. Hosps., Chgo., 1960—61; resident in anat. pathology Washington U. Sch. Medicine, St. Louis, 1961—64; resident in clin. pathology U. Calif. Med. Ctr., San Francisco, 1967—68; asst. prof. pathology Tulane U. Sch. Medicine, New Orleans, 1968—71; assoc. prof. pathology Ind. U. Sch. Medicine, Indpls., 1971—75, dir. divsn. surg. pathology, 1971—2001, prof., 1975—2001, prof. emeritus pathology, 2001—. Series editor: Contemporary Issues in Surgical Pathology; mem. editl. bd. Am. Jour. Surg. Pathology, Human Pathology, Seminars in Diagnostic Pathology, Internat. Jour. Gynecol. Pathology, Endocrine Pathology; contbr. articles to med. jours. Served to capt. US Army, 1965—67. Recipient James Harshman award, Ind. Assn. Pathologists, 1989. Mem. Am. Assn. Investigative Pathologists, U.S. and Can. Acad. Pathology, Am. Soc. Clin. Pathologists, Coll. Am. Pathologists, Internat. Soc. Gynecol. Pathologists, Arthur Purdy Stout Soc. Surg. Pathologists, Assn. Dirs. Anatomic and Surg. Pathology. Home: 7898 Ridge Rd Indianapolis IN 46240-2538 Office: 635 Barnhill Dr Indianapolis IN 46202-5120 Business E-Mail: lroth@iupui.edu.

ROTH, LOREN H., psychiatrist; b. May 9, 1939; m. Ellen A. Roth; children: Jonathan, Alexandra, Elizabeth. BA in Philosophy, Cornell U., 1961; MD cum laude, Harvard U., 1966, MPH, 1972; postgrad., Am. U., 1972-73. Diplomate Am. Bd. Psychiatry and Neurology; lic. physician, Conn., Md., Mass., Pa. Med. intern Univ. Hosps., Western Res. U., Cleve., 1966-67; resident psychiatry Yale U., New Haven, 1969-70, Mass. Gen. Hosp., Boston, 1970-72; staff psychiatrist Ctr. for Studies Crime and Delinquency, NIMH, Rockville, Md., 1972-74; co-dir., dir. law and psychiatry program Western Psychiat. Inst. and Clinic/U. Pitts., 1974—, chief adult clin. svcs., 1983-87, 88-89, chief clin. svcs., 1989-95, co-dir., dir. law and psychiatry program, 1974-94; vice-chmn. dept. psychiatry U. Pitts., 1988-97, asst. prof., 1974-78, assoc. prof., 1978-82, prof., 1982—; v.p. for managed care U. Pitts. Med. Ctr., 1993-97; assoc. vice chancellor for edn., health scis. U. Pitts. Sch. Medicine, 1995-97, assoc. sr. vice chancellor Health Scis., 1997—; sr. v.p., quality care U. Pitts. Med. Ctr. Health Sys., 2003—, chief med. officer, 1997—. Med. staff Presbyn.-Univ. Hosp., Pitts., 1983—; gen. med. officer Fed. Penitentiary, Lewisburg, Pa., 1967-69; William E. Schumacher disting. lectr. Maine Dept. Mental Health and Mental Retardation, Portland, 1982; mem. commn. on mentally disabled ABA, Washington, 1987; cons. law and psychiatry Dept. Welfare, Commonwealth Pa., 1974; cons. reviewer, site visitor crime and delinquency sect. NIMH, 1977; examiner Am. Bd. Psychiatry and Neurology, 1985. Author: (with others) Informed Consent: A Study of Decisionmaking in Psychiatry, 1984; editor: (with others) Psychiatry, Social, Epidemiologic and Legal Psychiatry, Vol. 5, 1986; contbr. articles to profl. jours., chpts. to books; editorial bd. Criminology, 1974-78, Law and Human Behavior, 1980-85, Internat. Jour. Law and Psychiatry, 1980-88, Behavioral Scis. and the Law, 1987-95; assoc. editor Am. Jour. Psychiatry, 1982-90; cons. editor Criminal Justice and Behavior, 1982-85. Lt. comrd. USPHS Res., 1967—. Recipient Steve Allen award United Mental Health, Inc., 1990, Sr. Vice Chancellor's Extraordinary Svc. award, U. Pitts. Med. Ctr.; grantee NIMH, 1979, 80-81, 89, Founds. Fund for Rsch. in Psychiatry, 1980-82. Fellow Am. Psychiat. Assn. (Isaac Ray award 1988), Am. Coll. Utilization Rev. Physicians, Am. Coll. Psychiatrists; mem. AMA, Am. Acad. Psychiatry and Law (pres. 1983-84), Group for Advancement Psychiatry (com. on psychiatry and law 1979-80, chmn. 1981-84), Am. Soc. Criminology, Am. Soc. Law and Medicine (bd. dirs. 1982-85), Internat. Acad. Law and Mental Health (bd. dirs.), Am. Psychopath. Assn., Phi Beta Kappa, Phi Kappa Phi. Home: 6820 Edgerton Ave Pittsburgh PA 15208-2803 Office: U Pitts Med Ctr Forbes TWR 200 Lothrop St Ste 11016 Pittsburgh PA 15213-2546 Office Phone: 412-647-4860.

ROTH, MARJORY JOAN JARBOE, special education educator; b. Ranger, Tex., May 24, 1934; d. James Aloysius and Dorothy Knight (Taggart) Jarboe; m. Thomas Mosser Roth, Jr., Dec. 22, 1959; children: Thomas Mosser III, James Jarboe. BA in English, Rice U., 1957; MEd in Ednl. Adminstrn., U. N.C., Greensboro, 1981. Cert. tchr.-specific learning disabilities, middle grades lang. arts and social studies, intermediate grades, adminstr.-prin., N.C. Tchr. 4th grade Houston Ind. Sch. Dist., 1957-60; specific lang. disabilities instr. Forsyth Tech. C.C., Winston-Salem, N.C., 1976-77; specific learning disabilities tchr. Forsyth Country Day Sch., Winston-Salem, 1977-80; tchr. 5th grade Winston-Salem/Forsyth County Schs., 1982-83, specific learning disabilities tchr. Mt. Tabor High Sch., 1983-86; part time instr. English and Learning Disabilities Forsyth Tech. C.C., 1986-90; founding pres., prin. Greenhills Sch., Winston-Salem, 1990—. Co-author, co-editor booklets. Sunday Sch. dir., tchr. Galloway Meml. Episcopal Ch., 1960-70, pres., treas., sec. Churchwomen, 1963-74; treas. Elkin Jr. Woman's Club, 1962; chmn. Elkin Heart Fund Drive, 1968; bd. dirs. Hugh Chatham Hosp. Auxillary, 1968, Friends of the Elkin Pub. Libr., 1968-74, chmn., 1970-72, chmn., exhibits chmn. summer reading program; pres. South Surry Heart Assn., 1969; mem. Churchwomen of St. Paul's Episcopal Ch., Winston-Salem, 1982—, Fiddle and Bow Folk Music Soc., Winston-Salem, 1992—. Recipient June Lyday Orton award for outstanding svc. in the field of dyslexia, 1997; Forsyth fellow NEH, 1985; grantee in field. Fellow Acad. Orton-Gillingham Practitioners and Educators; mem. ASCD, Children with Attention Deficit Disorder (profl. adv. bd. N.C. Triad chpt. 1990-96), Learning Disability Assn. N.C. (sec., bd. dirs. 1981-86), Internat. Dyslexia Assn. (sec., bd. dirs. Carolinas br. 1981-85, founding pres. N.C. br. 1987-91, bd. dirs. 1987-96, nat. nominating com. 1992-94), Internat. Multisensory Structured Lang. Edn. Coun., Inc. (bd. dirs. 2000-03, 05—, mem. coun. 1995—). Republican. Avocations: tennis, hiking, folk music. Home: 940 Fox Hall Dr Winston Salem NC 27106-4431 Office: Greenhills Sch 1360 Lyndale Dr Winston Salem NC 27106-9739 Office Phone: 336-924-4908.

ROTH, MICHAEL, lawyer; b. NYC, July 22, 1931; s. Philip Arthur and Mollie (Breitenbach) R.; m. Jeanny Macoir, Nov. 24, 1957; 3 children BA, Yale Coll., 1953; JD, Columbia U., 1956, M. Internat. Affairs, 1964. Bar: NY 1956. Law assoc. Stroock & Stroock & Lavan, NYC, 1956-63; ptnr. Roth, Carlson, Kwit & Spengler, NYC, 1964-74; chmn. N.Y. State Liquor Authority, NYC, 1974-77; ptnr. Shea & Gould, NYC, 1979-89; of counsel Katten, Muchin, Rosenman, NYC, 1989—. Mem. U.S. del. to UN Population Commn., 1969; Rep.-Conservative candidate for N.Y. State atty. gen., 1978; mem. Pres.' Task Force on Internat. Pvt. Enterprise, 1983-84, Pres.' Commn. on Mgmt. AID Programs, 1991-92. Mem. Sunningdale Country Club (Scarsdale, N.Y.). Republican.

ROTH, MICHAEL I., communications executive, lawyer; b. Bklyn., Nov. 22, 1945; s. Harry A. and Sally (Kutin) R.; m. Carole A. Snofsky, Aug. 10, 1968; children— Barrie, Marc, Andrew BS, CCNY, 1967; JD, Boston U., 1971; LL.M., NYU, 1973. Bar: N.Y. 1971. CPA: N.Y. 1973, Conn. 1973. With Coopers & Lybrand, NYC, 1969-76; ptnr. Stamford, Conn., 1976-82; exec. v.p. corp. fin., tax and adminstrn. Primerica Corp. (formerly Am. Can Co.), Greenwich, Conn., 1982-87, exec. v.p., 1987, chief fin. officer, 1987-88; exec. v.p., chief fin. officer MONY Fin. Svcs., NYC, 1989-91; pres., COO, MONY-Mut. Ins. Co., NYC, 1991-94, chmn. bd. dirs., CEO, 1994—2004; bd. dir. Interpublic Group, NYC, 2002—, chmn., 2004—, CEO, 2005—. Bd. dirs. Pitney Bowes Corp., Gaylord Entertainment Mem. leadership com. Lincoln Ctr. for Performing Arts; bd. dirs. Child Guidance Ctr., Stamford, 1984-85, Baruch Coll. Fund, Enterprise Found., Partnership for NYC; trustee Temple BethEl, Stamford, 1984-85 Mem. Am. Inst. CPA's, Conn. Soc. CPA's, Stamford Tax Assn. (pres. 1981-82) Office: Interpublic Group 1114 Ave of the Americas New York NY 10036 *

ROTH, MICHAEL S., academic administrator, art educator; b. Bklyn. m. Kari Weil; 1 child, Sophie Weil-Roth. BA, Wesleyan U.; MA, Princeton U., Phd in history. H.B. Alexander Prof. Humanities & Cultural Studies Claremont Grad. Sch., Calif.; prof. humanities, founder Humanities Ctr. Scripps Coll., Claremont; assoc. dir. Getty Rsch. Inst., chmn. Rsch. & Edn. Dept.; pres. Calif. Coll. Arts, San Francisco, 2000—07, Wesleyan U., Middletown, Conn., 2007—. Author: Freud: Conflict & Culture, 1998; curator (exhibitions) Sigmund Freud: Conflict & Culture, Libr. Congress, 1998; author: Looking for L.A.: Architecture, Film, Photography & Urban Landscape, 2001, Disturbing Remains: Memory, History, & Crisis in Twentieth Century, 2001. Office: Wesleyan U Office of Pres Wesleyan Station Middletown CT 06459 *

ROTH, PAUL BARRY, dean, educator, emergency medicine physician; b. Glen Ridge, NJ, Oct. 7, 1947; s. Jerome M. and Selma (Leitner) R. BS, Fairleigh Dickinson U., 1969, MS, 1972; MD, George Washington U., 1976; postgrad., U. N.Mex., Albuquerque, 1976-79. Resident in family practice U. N.Mex. Sch. Medicine, Albuquerque, 1976—79; owner, pres. EMS of N.Mex., Albuquerque, 1978-82; owner, mem. of bd. Heights Urgent Care Ctr., Albuquerque, 1980-82; dir. divsn. emergency medicine dept. family, cmty. and emergency medicine U. N.Mex. Sch. Medicine, Albuquerque, 1982-91, prof. emerg. med., 1991—, chair dept. emergency medicine, 1991-93, interim chief med. officer, 1992—93, interim dean, 1994—95, dean, 1994—; interim dir. U. N.Mex. Med. Ctr., Albuquerque, 1994—95; med. dir. disaster medicine Nat. Disaster Med. Sys.; exec. v.p. U. N.Mex. Health Sci. Ctr., 2005—. Chair disaster com. U. N.Mex. Med. Ctr. Contbr. articles to Annals of EM, Current Practice of EM-Disaster Medicine, Jour. of AMA. Recipient Outstanding Individual Svc. award Nat. Disaster Med. Sys., 1986. Fellow Am. Coll. Emergency Physicians (chair sect. on disaster medicine, 1991-92), Am. Acad. Family Practice; mem. AMA, Soc. for Acad. Emergency Medicine, Am. Coll. Physician Execs., Am. Acad. Family Physicians.

ROTH, PHILIP MILTON, writer; b. Newark, Mar. 19, 1933; s. Herman and Bess (Finkel) R.; m. Margaret Martinson, Feb. 22, 1959 (dec. 1968); m. Claire Bloom, Apr. 29, 1990 (div. June 1994). Student, Rutgers U., 1950-51; AB, Bucknell U., 1954; MA, U. Chgo., 1955. Tchr. English U. Chgo., 1956-58; faculty Iowa Writers Workshop, 1960-62; writer in residence Princeton U., 1962-64; adj. prof. U. Pa., 1967-77; disting. prof. Hunter Coll. CUNY, 1989-92. Author: Goodbye, Columbus, 1959 (Nat. Book award for Fiction, 1960), Letting Go, 1962, When She Was Good, 1967, Portnoy's Complaint, 1969, Our Gang, 1971, The Breast, 1972, The Great American Novel, 1973, My Life as a Man, 1974, Reading Myself and Others, 1975, The Professor of Desire, 1977, The Ghost Writer, 1979, A Philip Roth Reader, 1980, Zuckerman Unbound, 1981, The Anatomy Lesson, 1983, The Prague Orgy, 1985, Zuckerman Bound, 1985, The Counterlife, 1987 (Nat. Book Critics Circle award for fiction, 1988), The Facts: A Novelists's Autobiography, 1988, Deception, 1990, Patrimony, 1991 (Nat. Book Critics Circle award for biography/autobiography 1992), Operation Shylock: A Confession, 1993 (PEN-Faulkner award for fiction, 1993), The Conversation of the Jews, 1993, Sabbath's Theater, 1995 (Nat. Book award for fiction, 1995), American Pastoral, 1997 (Pulitzer prize for fiction, 1998), I Married A Communist, 1998 (Amb. Book award of English-Speaking Union), The Human Stain, 2000 (PEN-Faulkner award for fiction, 2000, Prix Medicis Etranger, 2000), The Dying Animal, 2001, Shop Talk: A Writer and His Colleagues and Their Work, 2002, The Plot Against America, 2004 (Book Sense Honor Book for adult fiction, 2005), Everyman, 2006 (PEN-Faulkner award for fiction, 2006); works pub. in Harper's, New Yorker, Epoch, Commentary, others; reprints in Best Am. Short Stories of 1956, 59, 60, O'Henry Prize Stories of 1960 Recipient prize for fiction Paris Rev., 1958, Nat. Inst. Arts and Letters award, 1960, Daroff award Jewish Book Coun. Am., 1960, Medal of Honor for Lit., Nat. Arts Club, 1991, Karel Capek prize Czech Republic, 1994, PEN/Saul Bellow award for Achievement in Am. Fiction, 2007; Guggenheim fellow, 1959-60, Rockefeller fellow, 1966. *

ROTH, RICHARD, news correspondent; b. NYC, Apr. 27, 1949; married; 1 child. BA with honors, Union Coll., Schenectady, NY, 1970; MA, Columbia U., 1972. With CBS News, 1972—, bur. chief, corr. Moscow, 1974—76, fed. corr. Washington, 1976—81, corr. Rome, 1981—86, NYC, 1986—90, LA, 1990—94, London, 1998—, NBC News, London, 1994—98. Reporter, substitute anchor (TV series) CBS Evening News, corr. 48 Hours, corr. (documentaries) 48 Hours on Crack Street, 1986. Co-recipient Edward R. Murrow award, Radio-TV News Dirs. Assn. & Found., George Foster Peabody award, 2 Emmy awards; recipient David Kaplan award, Overseas Press Club, 2006.

ROTH, ROBERT, lawyer, journalist; s. Andrew and Sarah Roth. BA cum laude, Bklyn. Coll., 1974; JD, Ind. U., 1977. Bar: NY 1980. V.p., gen. counsel Andrew Roth and Sons, Inc., Bklyn., 1980—; corr., contbg. photographer UPI, NYC, 1980—96; aviation analyst Fox News Channel, 1999—2000. Chair NY County Lawyers Assn. Continuing Legal Edn. Program. Photojournalist (news photograph) Statue of Liberty Centennial (UPI Pictures of the Yr., 1989), lead correspondent, Fox News Channel (series of television news reports on) Crash of Egyptair Flight 990. Mem. young fellows The Frick Collection, NYC, 2003. Recipient Sam Castan Meml. award Excellence Journalism, Bklyn. Coll., 1974. Mem.: ABA, NY County Lawyers Assn. Avocation: travel. Office: Andrew Roth and Sons Inc PO Box 190293 Brooklyn NY 11219-3736 Home Phone: 718-851-1416; Office Phone: 718-851-1416.

ROTH, ROBERT A., newspaper executive; b. Upper Darby, Pa., Mar. 19, 1947; s. Robert Raymond and Ruth Lorrayne (Jonas) R. BA magna cum laude, Carleton Coll., 1969; postgrad., U. Chgo., 1969-71. Co-founder Chgo. Reader, 1971, pub., 1971—94, editor, 1975-90; pres. Chgo. Reader, Inc., 1975—, Washington Free Weekly, Inc., 1982—. Dir. Inst. for Alternative Journalism, San Francisco, 1983-89, Raw Vision, Ltd., London, 1991—, Stonington (Maine) Sea Products, Inc., 2002—. Co-founder Intuit: The Ctr. for Intuitive and Outsider Art, Chgo., 1991, pres., 1991-96, bd. dirs., 1991—; trustee Carleton Coll., Northfield, Minn., 1994-98. Recipient Alumni Disting. Achievement award Carleton Coll., 1989, Donald J. Cowling Cup, 2002; named to Esquire Register, Esquire mag., 1984; named among Who's Who in Chgo. Bus., Crain's Chgo. Bus., 1990, 91, 92, 93, 94, 95, 96. Mem. Assn. Alternative Newsweeklies (pres. 1983-87). Avocations: folk and outsider art, architecture. Office: Chgo Reader 11 E Illinois St Chicago IL 60611-5652 Business E-Mail: broth@chicagoreader.com.

ROTH, ROBERT CHARLES, lawyer; b. Racine, Wis., Feb. 6, 1945; s. Robert Charles and Lucille (Holy) R.; m. Karen Trombley, May 18, 1974; children: David, Michael BBA, St. Norbert Coll., 1967; JD, Marquette U., 1970; postgrad. course in law, George Washington U., 1972. Bar: Wis. 1970, U.S. Dist. Ct. (ea. dist.) Wis. 1970, U.S. Ct. Mil. Appeals 1970, U.S. Army Ct. Mil Rev. 1971, Colo. 1974, U.S. Dist. Ct. Colo. 1974, U.S. Ct. Appeals (10th cir.) 1974, U.S. Ct. Appeals (5th cir.) 1979, U.S. Ct. Claims 1980. Atty. Shaw & Coghill, Denver, 1974—76; ptnr. Shaw, Spangler & Roth, Denver, 1976—96, Kutak Rock, Denver, 1996—. Pub. arbitrator Nat. Assn. Securities Dealers Capt. U.S. Army, 1970-74 Mem. ABA, Colo. Bar Assn., Denver Bar Assn., Wis. Bar Assn Avocations: basketball, golf. Office: Kutak Rock LLP 1801 California St Denver CO 80202 Office Phone: 303-297-2400. Business E-Mail: robert.roth@kutakrock.com.

ROTH, ROBERT EARL, ecologist, educator; b. Wauseon, Ohio, Mar. 30, 1937; s. Earl Jonas and Florence Lena (Mahler) R.; m. Carol Sue Yackee, Aug. 8, 1959; children: Robin Earl, Bruce Robert. BS, Ohio State U., 1959, BS in Secondary Sci. Edn., 1960, MS in Conservation Edn., 1960; PhD in Environ. Edn., U. Wis., 1969. Supr. conservation edn. Ethical Culture Schs., NYC, 1961-63; naturalist, sci. tchr. Lakeside Sch., Spring Valley, NY, 1963-65; instr. No. Ill. U., Oregon, 1965-67; asst. prof. Ohio State U.,

Columbus, 1969-73, assoc. prof., 1973-78, prof. environ. edn. and sci. edn., 1978-2001, prof. emeritus, 2001—, chmn. divsn., 1973-84, coord. office internat. affairs, 1985-89, asst. dir., sch. sec. Sch. Natural Resources, 1989-93, acting dir. Sch. Natural Resources, 1993-94, assoc. dir., 1994-2001, state extension specialist Environ. Edn., 1993-2001. Rsch. & devel. assoc. Mosely & Assocs., Columbus, 1986-89; project cons. NARMA project, U.S. Agy. internat. Devel., Santo Domingo, Dominican Rep., 1982-87; cons. Richard Trott & Assocs., 1988-90, Kinzelman & Kline, 1990-2001, Midwest consortium Internat. Activity, 1995; evaluator Montclair State U., N.J. Sch. Conservation, 1999; workshop leader Carribean Conservation Assn., Bridgetown, Barbados, 1981-83; vis. scholar Indonesian Second U. Devel. project, Jakarta, 1988; AID lectr., Thesolonika, Greece, 1992; bd. supr. Franklin Soil & Water Conservation Dist., 2003-05. Exec. editor Jour. Environ. Edn., 1974-91 (Pub.'s prize 1970); contbr. articles to profl. jours. Committeeman Boy Scouts Am., 1983-86; adv. coun. McKeever Environ. Learning Ctr., Pa., 1977-83. Named vis. scholar, Uganda Makerere U., 1989, Pacific Cultural Found., Taipei, Taiwan, 1989, 1999, 2001; recipient Pomerene Tchg. Enhancement award, Ohio State U., 1986, 1995, Environ. Edn. award, Ohio Alliance for the Enrivon., 1992, Outstanding Advising award, Coll. Food Agrl. and Environ. Scis., 1996. Mem.: Sch. Nat. Resource Alumni Assn. (inducted hon. 100), Nat. Sci. Tchrs. Assn. (life), N.Am. Assn. Environ. Edn. (life; bd. dirs. 1972—82, pres. 1977—78, Walt Jeske award 1988, Outstanding Contbns. to Rsch. award 2000). Avocations: swimming, canoeing, camping, fishing, travel. Home: 570 Morning St Columbus OH 43085-3775 E-mail: roth.3@osu.edu.

ROTH, RONALD LEE, engineering educator; b. Oakland, Calif., May 20, 1947; s. Howard Benjamin and Lillian Roth; m. Alma Hayes, July 7, 1984; children: Owen Howard, Adam Ronald. BS in Engring., Harvey Mudd Coll., Claremont, Calif., 1969; MS in Mech. Engring., Stanford U., Calif., 1971, PhD, 1976; MD, St. Georges U., Grenada, 1986. Engr. Westinghouse Corp., LA, 1969—70; lectr. Calif. State U., Fresno, Calif., 1975—76, U. Calif., Berkeley, 1977, 1979; vis. prof. U. Auckland, New Zealand, 1992—93, lectr., 1980—82, San Jose State U., Calif., 1979; postdoctoral rsch. affiliate Stanford U., 1976—77, lectr., 1973, 1980; assoc. prof. Calif. State U., Chico, 1986—90, prof., 1990—. Dept. chair Calif. State U., Chico, 2001—04, Chico, 2007—. Contbr. articles to profl. jours. Recipient Profl. Promise award, Calif. State U., 1987; John F O'Connell fellow, 1998—2000, NSF Traineeship fellow, Stanford U., 1970—74. Mem.: Am. Soc. Engring. Edn., Tau Beta Pi. Office: Calif State Univ Mech Engring and Mfg Tech Dept Chico CA 95929-0789 Home Phone: 530-342-6210; Office Phone: 530-898-4960. Office Fax: 530-898-4070.

ROTH, SANFORD IRWIN, pathologist, educator; b. McAlester, Okla., Oct. 14, 1932; s. Herman Moe and Blanche (Brown) R.; m. Kathryn Ann Corliss, Sept. 3, 1961; children: Jeffrey Franklin, Elisabeth Francyne, Gregory James, Suzannah Joan. Student, Vanderbilt U., 1949-52; MD, Harvard U., 1956. Intern Mass. Gen. Hosp., Boston, 1956-57, resident in pathology, 1957-60, pathologist, 1962-75, Armed Forces Inst. Pathology, 1960-62; asst. prof. Med. Sch. Harvard U., 1962-69, assoc. prof. Med. Sch., 1969-75; pathologist, prof., chmn. dept. Coll. Medicine U. Ark., Little Rock, 1975-81; prof. Med. Sch. Northwestern U., Chgo., 1981—2000, asst. dean admissions, 1998-2000, prof. emeritus, 2000—; chief lab. svc. VA Lakeside Med. Ctr., Chgo., 1981-86. Attending pathologist Northwestern U. Hosp., 1981-2002; vis. prof. pathology Harvard Med. Sch., 2001-06, lectr., 2007—; cons. in pathology Mass. Gen. Hosp., 2001—. With M.C. U.S. Army, 1960-62. Mem. AMA, AAAS, Coll. Am. Pathology, U.S.-Can. Acad. Pathology, Soc. for Investigative Dermatology, Mass. Med. Soc. Home: 169 Tisquantum Rd Chatham MA 02633-2578 Office: Fruit St Boston MA 02114 Office Phone: 508-945-2995. Personal E-mail: siroth@northwestern.edu. Business E-Mail: sroth@partners.org.

ROTH, SOL, rabbi; b. Rzeszow, Poland, Mar. 8, 1927; came to U.S., 1934, naturalized, 1939; s. Joseph and Miriam (Lamm) R.; m. Debra H. Stitskin, Nov. 26, 1957; children: Steven, Michael (dec.), Sharon. BA, Yeshiva U., 1948; MA, Columbia U., 1953, PhD, 1966; D in Divinity (hon.), Yeshiva U., 1977. Rabbi Yeshiva U. Theol. Sem., 1950. Ordained rabbi Orthodox Jewish Congregations, 1950; pres. Rabbinical Council Am., 1980-82, N.Y. Bd. Rabbis, 1976-79; chmn. Israel Commn. Rabbinical Council Am., 1976-78; dean Chaplaincy Sch., N.Y. Bd. Rabbis, 1976-79; Samson R. Hirsch prof. dept. philosophy Yeshiva U., NYC. Rabbi Jewish Ctr. Atlantic Beach, N.Y., 1956-86; rabbi Fifth Ave Synagogue, 1986-2003, rabbi emeritus, 2003—; pres. Rabbinical Coun. Am., 1980-82, Religious Zionists Am., 1991-94 Author: Science and Religion, 1967, The Jewish Idea of Community, 1977, Halakhah and Politics: The Jewish Idea of a State, 1988 (Samuel Belkin Meml. Lit. award 1989), The Jewish Idea of Culture, 1997, The Jewish Idea of Ethics and Morality, 2007; editor: Morasha. Recipient award Synagogue Adv. Council United Jewish Appeal, 1975; named Rabbi Dr. Sol Roth Chair in Talmud and Contemporary Halakha established at Yeshiva U., 1989. Jewish. Home: 201 E 62nd St New York NY 10021-8026 Office: Yeshiva U Dept Philosophy 500 W 185th St Dept New York NY 10033-3299 Home Phone: 212-421-0066. Personal E-mail: rothsol@aol.com.

ROTH, STEVEN, real estate company executive; AB, Dartmouth Coll., 1962, MBA with highest distinction, 1963. With Kenilworth Assoc., NJ, 1975—79; co-founder, mng. gen. ptnr. Interstate Properties, 1979—; CEO, chmn. bd. Vornado Realty Trust, NYC, 1989—; CEO Alexander's Inc., 1995—, chmn., 2004—. Bd. dir. Amos Tuck Sch., Dartmouth Coll., 1981—87; trustee Whitney Mus. Am. Art, NYC, Intrepid Mus. Found., NYC; bd. dir. Jewish Theol. Seminary Am., NYU Sch. Med. Found. With USAR. Named one of Forbes' Richest Americans, 2006. Office: Vornado Realty Trust 888 Seventh Ave New York NY 10019 also: Alexander's Inc 210 Rte 4 E Paramus NJ 07652 Office Phone: 212-894-7000. *

ROTH, TIM, actor; b. London, May 14, 1961; m. Nikki Butler, 1993; children: Timothy, Cormac. With Glasgow Citizen's Theatre, The Oval House, The Royal Ct. Appeared in play Metamorphosis; films include The Hit, 1985, A World Apart, 1988, The Cook, the Thief, His Wife and Her Lover, 1990, Vincent and Theo, 1990, Rosencrantz and Guildenstern Are Dead, 1991, Jumpin' at the Boneyard, 1992, Reservoir Dogs, 1992, Bodies, Rest and Motion, 1993, Pulp Fiction, 1994, Rob Roy, 1995 (Acad. award nominee for best supporting actor 1996), Little Odessa, 1995, Four Rooms, 1995, No Way Home, 1996, Everyone Says I Love You, 1996, Hoodlum, 1997, Gridlock'd, 1997, Animals, 1997, Deceiver, 1998, The Legend of the Pianist on the Ocean, 1998, Vatel, 1999, Leggenda del pianista sull'oceano, 1998, The Million Dollar Hotel, 2000, Lucky Numbers, 2000, Planet of the Apes, 2001, Invincible, 2001, The Musketeer, 2001, Emmett's Mark, 2002, Whatever We Do, 2003, To Kill a King, 2003, With It, 2004, Silver City, 2004, New France, 2004, The Beautiful Country, 2004, Dark Water, 2005, Jumpshot, 2005, The Last Sign, 2005, Don't Come Knocking, 2005, Even Money, 2006; TV movies include Meantime, Made in Britain, Metamorphosis, Murder in the Heartland, 1993; dir.: The War Zone, 1998; TV guest appearance Tales From the Crypt, 1989. Office: Ilene Feldman Agy 8730 W Sunset Blvd Ste 490 Los Angeles CA 90069-2248

ROTH, WILLIAM MCKINLEY, psychologist; b. Phila., Jan. 24, 1945; s. William M. and Ethel M. Roth; m. Ledjie Baird Roth (div.); m. Gretchen O. Roth. BA in journalism, Penn. State U., 1966, Ba in psychology, 1966; MA in psychology, Temple U., 1969. Lic. profl. psychologist Pa., 1977, cert. sch. psychologist and pupil svcs. suprv. Dir. employment and tng. Southco Inc., Concordville, Pa., 1969—72; supr. of pupil svcs. Del. County Intermediate Unit, Morton, Pa., 1973—2003. Prvt. practice, Exton, Pa., 1977—; crisis coord. Del. County Sch., Media, Pa., 1985—2003. Contbr. articles various profl. jours. Pres. Pa. Psychology Assn. Sch. Divsn., Harrisburg, Pa., 1980—81; reader, narrator Pa. Assn. For the Blind, Phila., 1970—75. Mem.: Pa. Psychological Assn. (pres., sch. disvsn. 1980—81). Avocation: film study. Home: 608 Pancoast Ln Downingtown PA 19335 Office: William M Roth Psychologist 300 N Pottstown Pike Exton PA 19341 Office Phone: 610-518-6970. Office Fax: 610-518-6970. E-mail: broth124@comcast.net.

ROTH, WILLIAM STANLEY, hospital foundation executive; b. NYC, Jan. 12, 1929; s. Sam Irving and Louise Caroline (Martin) Roth; m. Hazel Adcock, May 6, 1963; children: R. Charles, W. Stanley Roth'. AA, Asheville-Biltmore Jr. Coll., NC, 1948; BS, U. NC, Chapel Hill, 1950. Dep. regional exec. Nat. coun. Boy Scouts Am., 1953-65; exec. v.p. Am. Humanics Found., 1965-67; dir. devel. Bethany Med. Ctr., Kansas City, Kans., 1967-74; exec. v.p. Geisinger Med. Ctr. Found., Danville, Pa., 1974-78; found. pres. Bapt. Med Ctrs., Birmingham, Ala., 1978—. Sec. Western Med. Systems, Cherokee Cmty. Homes, Cullman Sr. Housing, Dekalb Sr. Housing, Limestone Sr. Housing, Oxford Sr. Housing. Editor: Torch and Trefoil, 1960—61. Mem.-at-large Nat. coun. Boy Scouts Am., 1972-86; chmn. NAHD Ednl. Fund, 1980-82; ruling elder John Knox Kirk, Kansas City, Mo., Grove Presbyn. Ch., Danville, Pa. Recipient Silver award United Meth. Ch., 1970, Mid-West Health Congress, 1971; Seymour award for outstanding hosp. devel. officer, 1983, 60 Yr. Vet. award Boy Scouts Am., 2001. Fellow Assn. for Healthcare Philanthropy (life; nat. pres. 1975-76); mem. Nat. Soc. Fund Raising Execs. (pres. Ala. chpt. 1980-82, nat. dir. 1980-84, mem. ethics bd. 1993-98, advanced cert fund raising exec., Outstanding Fund Raising Exec., Ala. chpt. 1983), Mid-Am. Hosp. Devel. Assn. (pres. 1973-74), Mid-West Health Congress (devel. chmn. 1972-74), Am. Soc. for Healthcare Mktg. and Pub. Rels., Ala. Soc. for Sleep Disorders, Ala. Heart Inst., Ala. Assn. Healthcare Philanthropy (pres. 1991-93, chmn. bd. 1993-94), Ala. Planned Giving Coun. (bd. dirs. 1991-2000, pres. 1994-95), Alpha Phi Omega (nat. pres. 1958-62, dir. 1950—, Nat. Disting. Scv. award 1962), Delta Upsilon (pres. NC Alumni 1963-65), Rotary (pres. club 1976-77), Relay House, Summit Club, Green Valley Club (bd. govs.), Elks, Order of the Arrow (Nat. Disting. Svc. award 1958), Order of Holy Grail, Order of Golden Fleece. Home: 341 Laredo Dr Birmingham AL 35226-2325 Office: 3500 Blue Lake Dr Ste 101 Birmingham AL 35243-1908 Office Phone: 205-979-8285. Personal E-mail: billroth1@aol.com.

ROTHBERG, ABRAHAM, writer; b. NYC, Jan. 14, 1922; s. Louis and Lottie (Drimmer) R.; m. Esther Conwell, Sept. 30, 1945; 1 son, Lewis Josiah. AB, Bklyn. Coll., 1942; MA, U. Iowa, 1947; PhD, Columbia U., 1952. Chmn. editorial bd. Stateside (mag.), NYC, 1947-49; instr. English, creative writing Columbia U., NYC, 1948; instr. English, humanities Hofstra Coll., Hempstead, NY, 1947-51; prof. English St. John Fisher Coll., 1973-83, chmn. dept. English, 1981-82; disting. writer-in-residence, vis. prof. Wichita State U., 1985. Editor-in-chief Free Europe Press, NYC, 1952—59, East Europe Mag., 1952—59; mng. editor George Braziller, Inc., NYC, 1959, New Leader mag., NYC, 1960—61; cons. editor New Jewish Ency., 1960—62; writer, editl. con.; European corr. Nat. Observer, Washington, Manchester (Eng.) Guardian, 1962—63; sr. editor Bantam Books, Inc., NYC, 1966—67; cons. editor The New Union Prayer Book, NYC, 1975. Author: Abraham, Eyewitness History of World War II, 1962, The Thousand Doors, 1965, The Heirs of Cain, 1966, The Song of David Freed, 1968, The Other Man's Shoes, 1969, The Boy and the Dolphin, 1969, The Sword of the Golem, 1971, Aleksandr Solzhenitsyn: The Major Novels, 1971, The Heirs of Stalin: Dissidence and the Soviet Regime, 1953-1970, 1972, The Stalking Horse, 1972, The Great Waltz, 1978, The Four Corners of the House, 1981, The Holy Warriors, 2005, A Beast in View, 2005, Pinocchio's Sister: A Feminist Fable, 2005, The Torii Gate, 2005, The Former People, 2006, Coming to Terms, 2006, numerous short stories, essays and poems; editor: U.S. Stories, 1949, Flashes in the Night, 1958, Anatomy of a Moral, 1959, A Bar-Mitzvah Companion, 1959, Great Adventure Stories of Jack London, 1967; contbr. articles to profl. jours. Served with AUS, 1943-45. Recipient John H. McGinnis Meml. award for short story, 1970, John H. McGinnis Meml. award for essay, 1973—74, Lit. award, Friends of Rochester Libr., 1980; Ford Found. fellow, N.Y.C., 1951—52. Home: 340 Pelham Rd Rochester NY 14610-3355

ROTHBERG, GERALD, editor, publishing executive; b. Bklyn., Oct. 29, 1937; s. Abraham and Pauline Rothberg; m. Glenda Fay Morris, June 18, 1970 (div. 1988); children: Laura, Abigail. BA, Bklyn. Coll., 1960; postgrad., Dickinson Law Sch., 1962. Spl. projects editor Esquire, 1963-66; owner, editor, pub., founder Circus, NYC, 1966—; owner, founder, editor Sci. and Living Tomorrow, 1980—, Who's In, 1981; founder, editor Sports Mirror mag., 1983—, MGF mag., 1985—, Country Mirror mag., 1994—. Author: (novels) Composition 36, 1993, The Six Hour Song, 1994, Redeeming Esau, 1995, The Esau Swindle, 2004, (novels) Saturday Books, 2006, The Golem Code, 2007. Mem.: Periodical and Book Assn. Am. (pres.). Office: Ste 455 527 Third Ave New York NY 10016 Office Phone: 212-242-4902.

ROTHBERG, GLENDA FAY MORRIS, lawyer; b. Rome, Ga., Aug. 7, 1946; d. Glenn Howell and Fay (Givens) Morris; m. Gerald Rothberg, June 18, 1970 (div. Jan. 1989); children: Laura, Abigail. AB, Randolph-Macon Woman's Coll., 1968; JD, Benjamin Cardozo Law Sch., 1985. Bar: N.Y. 1986, U.S. Dist. Ct. (so. and ea. dists.) N.Y. 1987, U.S. Supreme Ct. 1990. Law guardian juvenile rights divsn. Legal Aid Soc., NYC, 1988-91; pvt. practice NYC, 1992—. Faculty dir. Inst. for not-for-profit Mgmt. Columbia Bus. Sch., N.Y.C., 1994-98. Vol. Manhattan Mediation Ctr., N.Y.C., 1996-99; chair legal com. N.Y.C. Comptr. Task Force on Open Adoption, 1999-2001 Fellow Am. Bar Found.; mem. ABA, Assn. of Bar of City of N.Y. (com. chair 1996-99, mem. coun. on children 1999-2002). Office: Ste 400 363 Seventh Ave New York NY 10001 E-mail: gmrlaw@aol.com.

ROTHBERG, JONATHAN M., medical products executive, researcher; b. New Haven, Conn., 1963; BSChemE, Carnegie Mellon U.; MS, MPhil, Yale U., PhD in Biology. Postdoctoral fellow Boyer Ctr. for Molecular Medicine, Howard Hughes Med. Inst.; founder Clarifi Corp., CuraGen Corp., Branford, Conn., 1991, CEO, pres., chmn., 1991—2005, bd. dirs.; founder 454 Life Sciences, Conn., 1999, chmn., 2005. Co-founder, chmn., bd. dir. RainDance Technologies, Inc.; founder Rothberg Inst. for Childhood Diseases; invited tech. pioneer World Econ. Forum, Davos, Switzerland; spkr. in field. Bd. trustee Carnegie Mellon U. Named Ernst and Young Entrepreneur of Yr.; recipient Irvington Institute's Corporate Leadership award in Sci., Gold Winner, Wall Street Jour. Tech. Innovation award, 2005, Biotech-Med. Winner, 2005. Mem.: NAE, Conn. Acad. Sci. and Engring. Achievements include invention of new way to sequence DNA on a chip, called 454 sequencing; development of a series of new medicines, now in over 14 human clinical trials, for the treatment of a wide range of cancers; being the first person to sequence an individual human genome (that of James D. Watson) and initiated the Neanderthal Genome project; initiated the age of the personal genomics. Office: 454 Life Scis 20 Commercial St Branford CT 06405 Office Phone: 203-871-2300. *

ROTHBERG, JUDITH, elementary school educator, researcher; b. NYC, Mar. 4, 1934; d. Louis and Esther (Charloff) Jablowsky; m. Lawrence Rothberg, Apr. 13, 1957; children: Richard, Loretta. BA, Bklyn. Coll., 1955, MS, 1960; cert. in guidance, L.I. U., 1969; cert. in adminstrn., Columbia U., 1988, PhD in Ednl. and Family Counseling, 1997. Tchr. grades 2 to 6, supr. Lindenhurst (N.Y.) Sch. System, 1955—. Pvt. practice ednl. counseling, Glen Cove, N.Y., 1990-92. Author: Meet Me in West Africa, 1992, Meet the Russian Historic Rivers Then and Now, 1992; co-host (cable program) Innersight; prodr. (cable program) Exploring Your Emotions. Mem., lectr. Bnai Zion, Glen Cove Chpt., 1989-93; bd. dirs. Innersight-Assn. for the Blind. Mem. Tchrs. Assn. Lindenhurst. Avocations: drama club, aerobics, writing, traveling to africa and asia, lecturing. Home: 1 Cedar Ln Glen Cove NY 11542-1320 Office Phone: 516-759-1779.

ROTHBERG, MOREY DAVID, historian, editor; b. Phila., Apr. 5, 1951; s. Herman Jacob and Dorothy Slotkin Rothberg. BA, U. Md., 1973; MA, PhD, Brown U., 1982. Pers. mgmt. specialist U.S. Office Pers. Mgmt., Washington, 1982—86; dir. John Franklin Jameson papers project Am. Hist. Assn., Washington, 1984—94; editor Comptr. Currency, Washington, 1999—. Editor: (documentary edit.) John Franklin Jameson and the Development of Humanistic Scholarship in America (3 vols.). Founding pres. Wash. Guitar Soc., Silver Spring, Md., 1992—94. J. Franklin Jameson fellow, Am. Hist. Assn. and Libr. of Congress, 1983—84. Mem.: Orgn. Am. Historians (assoc.), Am. Hist. Assn. (assoc.), Phi Beta Kappa. Home: Unit A 10801 Amherst Ave Silver Spring MD 20902 Home Phone: 301-649-9615; Office Phone: 202-874-6211.

ROTHBERG, PAUL G., medical geneticist, educator; b. Bklyn., Sept. 14, 1955; m. Marcia B. Rothberg. PhD, SUNY, Stony Brook, 1981. Diplomate Am. Bd. Med. Genetics. Cancer rsch. scientist Roswell Pk. Cancer Inst., Buffalo, 1985—88; lab. dir. Children's Mercy Hosp., Kansas City, Mo., 1988—2001; prof. U. Rochester Med. Ctr., NY, 2001—. Mem. sci. adv. bd. Bio-Reference Labs., Newark, 2003—. Office: U Rochester Med Ctr 601 Elmwood Ave Rochester NY 14642 Office Phone: 15852732229. Office Fax: 15852736120. Business E-Mail: paul_rothberg@urmc.rochester.edu.

ROTHBERG, ROBERT, lawyer; b. 1949; BS, Cornell U., 1970, ME, 1971; JD cum laude (hon.), Harvard U., 1974. Bar: Ga. 1974, Mass. 1976. Mem. Choate, Hall & Stewart, Boston, of counsel. Lectr. Boston U. Sch. of mgmt., 2001—02; dir. Gifford Sch. Mem.: Boston Bar Assn. Office: Choate Hall & Stewart LLP 2 International Place Boston MA 02110 Office Phone: 617-248-5021. Business E-Mail: rrothberg@choate.com.

ROTHBERG-BLACKMAN, JUNE SIMMONDS, retired nursing educator, psychotherapist; b. Phila., Sept. 4, 1923; d. David and Rose (Protzel) Simmonds; m. Jacob Rothberg, Sept. 7, 1952 (dec. Feb. 2001); children: Robert Rothberg, Alan Rothberg; m. Stanley F Blackman, May 27, 2002 (dec. July 2005). Diploma in nursing, Lenox Hill Hosp., 1944; BS, N.Y. U., 1950, MA, 1959, PhD (NIH fellow), 1965; Diploma in Psychotherapy and Psychoanalysis, Adelphi U., Inst. for Advanced Psychol. Studies, 1987. USPHS traineeship N.Y. U., 1957-59; sr. public health nurse Bklyn. Vis. Nurse Assn., 1951-53; prin. investigator in nursing, homestead study project Goldwater Hosp. and N.Y. U., 1959-61; instr. N.Y. U., 1964-65, asst. prof., 1965-68, assoc. prof., 1968-69, project dir. grad. program rehab. nursing, 1964-69, prof., 1969-87, prof. emeritus, 1987—; dean Adelphi U., Garden City, NY, 1969-85, v.p. acad. adminstrn., 1985-86; pvt. practice West Hempstead, NY, 1993-97. Pres. David Simmonds Co. Inc., Med. Supply Co., 1982-89; dir., chmn. compensation com. Quality Care, Inc.; cons. region 2 Bur. Health Resources Devel., HHS.; audit com. Ipco Corp. (formerly Sterling Optical Corp.), 1991; cons., spkr. in field. Contbr. articles to profl. jours. Mem. pres's coun. N.Y. U. Sch. Edn., 1973-75; treas. Nurses for Polit. Action, 1971-73; trustee Nurses Coalition for Action in Politics, 1974-76; bd. visitors Duke Med. Ctr., 1970-74; mem. governing bd. Nassau-Suffolk Health Systems Agy., 1976-79; leader People-to-People Internat. med. rehab. del. to People's Republic of China, 1981; mem. com. for the study pain disability and chronic illness behavior Inst. Medicine, 1985-86, com. on ethics in rehab. Hastings Ctr., 1985-87; trustee Paget's Disease Found., 1987-89. Recipient Disting. Alumna award NYU, 1974, recognition award Am. Assn. Colls. Nursing, 1976, Achievers award Ctr. for Bus. and Profl. Women, 1980 Fellow Am. Acad. Nursing (governing coun. 1980-82); mem. Nat. League Nursing (exec. com. coun. of baccalaureate and higher degree programs 1969-73), Am. Nurses Assn. (joint liaison com. 1970-72), Commn. Accreditation of Rehab. Facilities, Am. Congress Rehab. Medicine (pres. 1977-78, chmn. continuing edn. com. 1979-86, 34th Ann. John Stanley Coulter Meml. lectr. 1984, Gold Key award 1984, Edward W. Lowman award 1990), Am. Assn. Colls. Nursing (pres. 1974-76), L.I. Women's Network (pres. 1980-81), Kappa Delta Pi, Sigma Theta Tau, Pi Lambda Theta. Achievements include having June S. Rothberg collection in Nursing Archives, Mugar Meml. Library, Boston U. Home and Office: 3941 Redondo Way Boca Raton FL 33487 Personal E-mail: stanleyb2@aol.com.

ROTHBLATT, DONALD NOAH, urban and regional planner, educator; b. NYC, Apr. 28, 1935; s. Harry and Sophie (Chernofsky) Rothblatt; m. Ann S. Vogel, June 16, 1957; children: Joel Michael, Steven Saul. BCE, CUNY, 1957; MS in Urban Planning, Columbia U., 1963; diploma in comprehensive planning, Inst. Social Studies, The Hague, 1964; PhD in City and Regional Planning, Harvard U., 1969. Cert. Am. Inst. Cert. Planners; registered prof. engr., NY. Planner NYC Planning Commn., 1960-62, NY Housing and Redevel. Bd., 1963-66; research fellow Ctr. for Environ. Design Studies, Harvard U., Cambridge, Mass., 1965-71; tchg. fellow, instr., then asst. prof. city and regional planning Harvard U., 1967-71; prof. urban and regional planning, chmn. dept. San Jose (Calif.) State U., 1971—. Lady Davis vis. prof. urban and regional planning Hebrew U., Jerusalem, 1978, Tel-Aviv U., 1978; vis. scholar Indian Inst. Architects, 1979, Shandong Province, China, 1996, U. Lodz, Poland, 2000, Paris Transp. Authority, 2002, Greater London Authority, 2003, Sydney Regional Orgn. Councils, 2004, Toronto Urban Devel. Svcs., 2005, NY Met. Transp. Coun., 2006, Phila., Del. Valley Regional Planning Commn., 2007; cons. to pvt. industry and govt. agys. Author: Human Needs and Public Housing, 1964, Thailand's Northeast, 1967, Regional Planning: The Appalachian Experience, 1971, Allocation of Resources for Regional Planning, 1972, The Suburban Environment and Women, 1979, Regional-Local Development Policy Making, 1981, Planning the Metropolis: The Multiple Advocacy Approach, 1982, Comparative Suburban Data, 1983, Suburbia: An International Assessment, 1986, Metropolitan Dispute Resolution in Silicon Valley, 1989, Good Practices for the Congestion Management Program, 1994, Activity-Based Travel Survey and Analysis of Responses to Increased Congestion, 1995, An Experiment in Sub-Regional Planning: California's Congestion Management Policy, 1995, Estimating the Origins and Destinations of Transit Passengers from On/Off Counts, 1995, Changes in Property Values Induced by Light Transit, 1996, Comparative Study of Statewide Transportation Planning Under ISTEA, 1997, North American Metropolitan Planning Reexamined, 1999; actor: Government Performance Measures Linking Urban Mass Transportation with Land Use and Accessibility Factors, 2000, Best Practices in Developing Regional Transportation Plans, 2001, Comparative Study of U.S. Metropolitan Transportation Planning, 2004; editor: National Policy for Urban and Regional Development, 1974, Regional Advocacy Planning: Expanding Air Transport Facilities for the San Jose Metropolitan Area, 1975, Metropolitan-wide Advocacy Planning: Dispersion of Low and Moderate Cost Housing the San Jose Metropolitan Area, 1976, Multiple Advocacy Planning: Public Surface Transportation in the San Jose Metropolitan Area, 1977, A Multiple Advocacy Approach to Regional Planning: Open Space and Recreational Facilities for the San Jose Metropolitan Area, 1979, Regional Transportation Planning for the San Jose Metropolitan Area, 1981, Planning for Open Space and Recreational Facilities in the San Jose Metropolitan Area, 1982, Regional Economic Development Planning for the San Jose Metropolitan Area, 1984, Planning for Surface Transportation in the San Jose Metropolitan Area, 1986, Expansion for Air Transportation Facilities in the San Jose Metropolitan Area, 1987, Provision of Economic Development in the San Jose Metropolitan Area, 1989, Metropolitan Governance: American/Canadian Intergovernmental Perspectives, 1993, Metropolitan Governance Revisited, 1998; contbr. articles to profl. jours.; dir.: (TV series) Sta. KTEH, 1976. Mem. adv. coun. Bay Area

Met. Transp. Commn., 1995—. Served to 1st lt. C.E. US Army Corps of Engrs., 1957—59. Co-recipient Best of West award, Western Ednl. Soc. Telecom., 1976; recipient Innovative Tchg. award, Calif. State U. and Coll., 1975—79, award, Internat. Festival Films Architecture and Planning, 1983, Meritorious Performance award, San Jose State U., 1986, 1988, 1990, 1996—2001; grantee, Nat. Inst. Dispute Resolution, 1987—88, Can. Studies Enrichment Program, 1992—93; Rsch. fellow, Harvard U., 1967—69, William F. Milton Rsch. fellow, 1970—71, Faculty Rsch. grantee, NSF, 1972—82, Calif. State U., 1977—78, Univ. Rsch. and Tng. Program grantee, Calif. Dept. Transp., 1993—97. Fellow: Am. Inst. Cert. Planners; mem.: AAUP, Architecture and Urban and Regional Planning (chmn. 1973—75), Calif. Edn. Com. Architecture and Landscape, Internat. Fedn. Housing and Planning, Planners Equal Opportunity, Am. Planning Assn., Assn. Collegiate Schs. Planning (pres. 1975—76). Office: San Jose State U Dept Urban & Regional Planning San Jose CA 95192-0185 *My basic view is that we should try to develop ourselves fully and help others do the same, so that we will be able to live in harmony with, and contribute to, our world community.*

ROTHENBERG, ALAN DAVID, lawyer; b. Newark, Nov. 30, 1947; s. John F. and Ruth (Parent) R.; m. Karen Lynn (Jacobson) R.; m. May 17, 1970; children: Scott Michael, Kelli Brooke. BA, Franklin and Marshall Coll., 1970; JD, U. Md., 1975. Bar: D.C. 1976, Md. 1975, U.S. Dist. Ct. Md. 1976. Atty. I.C.C., Washington, 1975-96; pvt. practice Rockville, Md., 1975—. Bd. dirs. U.S. Premier Fed. Credit Union, Washington. Author: Landlord Tenant Handbook, 1974. With U.S. Army N.G., 1970-72. Mem. Md. Bar Assn., Md. Trial Lawyers Assn., Montgomery County Bar Assn. Jewish. Avocations: skiing, tropical fish. Home: 1721 Sunrise Dr Potomac MD 20854-2667 Office: 401 N Washington St Ste 500 Rockville MD 20850-2225 Office Phone: 301-424-7224. E-mail: adrothenberg@hotmail.com.

ROTHENBERG, ALAN I., lawyer, professional sports association executive; b. Detroit, Apr. 10, 1939; m. Georgina Rothenberg; 3 children. BA, U. Mich., 1960, JD, 1963. Bar: Calif. 1964. Assoc. O'Melveny & Myers, LA, 1963—66; ptnr. Manatt Phelps Rothenberg & Phillips, LA, 1968—90, Latham & Watkins, LA, 1990—2000; instr. sports law U. So. Calif., 1969, 1976, 1984, Whittier Coll. Law, 1980, 1984; pres., gen. counsel LA Lakers and LA Kings, 1967—79, LA Clippers Basketball Team, 1982—89; pres. U.S. Soccer Fedn., Chgo., 1990—98; founder, past chmn., trustee Maj. League Soccer, 1993—; chmn. Premier Partnerships, 1st Century Bank, LA, 2002—. Bd. dir. Calif. Pizza Kitchen Inc., 2006—, Arden Realty Inc., Zenith Nat. Corp.; mem. exec. com. CONCACAF. Bd. dirs., pres. Constl. Rights Found., 1987—90; soccer commr. 1984 Olympic Games; chmn., pres., CEO 1994 World Cup Organizing Com., 1990—94. Named to U.S. Nat. Soccer Hall of Fame, 2007. Mem.: NBA (bd. govs. 1971—79, 1982—89), ABA, N.Am. Soccer League (bd. govs. 1977—80, Major League Soccer mgmt. com. 1994—), LA Bar Assn., LA County Bar Assn., State Bar Calif. (pres. 1989—90), Order of Coif. Office: 1st Century Bank Ste 1400 1875 Century Park E Los Angeles CA 90067

ROTHENBERG, ALBERT, psychiatrist, educator; b. NYC, June 2, 1930; s. Gabriel and Rose (Goldberg) R.; m. Julia C. Johnson, June 28, 1970; children: Michael, Mora, Rina. AB, Harvard U., 1952; MD, Tufts U., 1956. Diplomate Am. Bd. Psychiatry and Neurology. Intern Pa. Hosp., Phila., 1956-57; resident in psychiatry Yale U., West Haven (Conn.) VA Hosp., 1957-58, Grace-New Haven Hosp., 1958-59, Yale Psychiat. Inst., New Haven, 1959-60, chief resident, 1960-61; practice medicine specializing in psychiatry New Haven, 1960-61, 1963-75; chief neuropsychiatry Rodriguez U.S. Army Hosp., San Juan, P.R., 1961-63; practice medicine specializing in psychiatry Farmington, Conn., 1975-79, Stockbridge, Mass., 1979-94, Chatham, NY, 1994—2006, Canaan, NY, 2006—, Great Barrington, Mass., 1994-98; dir. rsch. Austen Riggs Center, Stockbridge, Mass., 1979-94. Asst. dir. Yale Psychiat. Inst., 1963-64, sr. staff mem., 1964-83; mem. staff Yale-New Haven Med. Ctr., West Haven VA Hosp., U. Conn. Health Ctr., Farmington; cons., mem. editorial bd. various jours. in psychiatry and psychology; instr. dept. psychiatry Yale U. Sch. Medicine, 1960-61, 63-64, asst. prof., 1964-68, assoc. prof., 1968-74, clin. prof., 1974-84; prof. psychiatry U. Conn. Sch. Medicine, Farmington, 1975-79, dir. residency tng., 1976-78, dir. clin. svcs., 1975-78; prin. investigator Studies in the Creative Process, 1964—; vis. prof. Pa. State U., 1971, adj. prof., 1971-78; vis. prof. dept. Am. studies Yale U., 1974-76, U. Capetown Med. Sch., South Africa, 1999, Saltpêtrière Hosp., Paris, 1999; lectr. dept. psychiatry Harvard U. Med. Sch., 1982-86, clin. prof., 1986—; researcher in psychotherapy. Author: (with B. Greenberg) Index of Scientific Writings on Creativity: Creative Men and Women, 1974, Index of Scientific Writings on Creativity: General 1566-1974, 1976; (with C.R. Hausman) The Creativity Question, 1976; The Emerging Goddess: The Creative Process in Art, Science and Other Fields, 1979; The Creative Process of Psychotherapy, 1988; Adolescence: Psychopathology, Normality, and Creativity, 1990; Creativity and Madness: New Findings and Old Stereotypes, 1990, Living Color, 2001; contbr. articles to profl. jours. Researcher on creativity in the arts, sci. and tech. Served with M.C. U.S. Army, 1961-63. Recipient Tufts Med. Alumni award 1956, Rsch. Scientist Career Devel. award NIMH 1964, 69, Golestan Found. award 1991, 92, Kovler award MESAB, 1999; Guggenheim Meml. fellow 1974-75, Ctr. Adv. Study in Behavioral Studies fellow 1986-87, Netherlands Inst. for Adv. Study in Humanities and Social Scis. fellow, 1992-93. Fellow Am. Psychiat. Assn. (disting. life), Am. Coll. Psychoanalysts; mem. AAAS, Mass. Psychiat. Soc., Am. Soc. Aesthetics, Rapaport-Klein Group, Sigma Xi. Democrat. Achievements include research in the creative process, schizophrenia, anorexia nervosa, and psychotherapy. Business E-Mail: albert_rothenberg@hms.harvard.edu.

ROTHENBERG, ELEANORE, psychotherapist; d. Max and Dora (Kaplan) Dubin; children: David, Michael, Seth. BA cum laude, Bklyn. Coll., 1955; MPA, N.Y. U., NYC, 1969, PhD, 1975; MSW, Yeshiva U., NYC, 1992. Cert. group psychotherapist Am. Group Psychotherapy Assn.; LCSW Office of Professions N.Y. State Edn. Dept. Exec. dir. N.Y.C. Profl. Standards Rev. Orgn., 1974—80; dir. stds. and evaluation N.Y.C. HHC, 1981—83; social worker Cmty. Living Corp., Mt. Kisco, 1992—94; founder, exec. dir. and group leader Sibling Ctr. Sisters and Brothers of People with Disabilities, NYC, 1994—. Chair bd. dir. Sibling Ctr., NYC; adj. asst. prof. Columbia U. Sch. Pub. Health, 1980—2001; lectr. New Sch. U., 1984—86; preceptor King's Fund Coll., London, 1980; pro bono psychotherapist N.Y. Disaster Counseling Coalition, 2001—; conducted psychotherapy group with 9/11 survivors, NYC, 2002; conducted 9/11 commemorative art exhibit Am. Group Psychotherapy Assn./N.Y. Times/9/11 Fund, NYC, 2002—04; presenter to workshops and confs.; book reviewer. Contbr. scientific papers, articles to profl. jours. Vol. Physicians Social Responsibility, 1980. Fellow, NIH, 1965—75; grantee, W.T. Grant Found., 2002—03, Pettus Found., 2004. Mem.: Ea. Group Psychotherapy Soc. (co-chair mentoring com. 2002—), Am. Group Psychotherapy Assn., NYU Alumni Assn., Bklyn. Coll. Alumni Assn. Democrat. Jewish. Avocations: drawing, skiing, kayaking, cooking, dancing. Office: Sibling Ctr 525 E 89th St #4C New York NY 10128 also: 180 E 79th St Ste 1C New York NY 10021 Office Phone: 212-831-5586.

ROTHENBERG, ELLIOT CALVIN, lawyer, writer; b. Mpls., Nov. 12, 1939; s. Sam S. and Claire Sylvia (Feller) R.; m. Sally Smalying; children: Sarah, Rebecca, Sam. BA summa cum laude, U. Minn., 1961; JD, Harvard U., Cambridge, 1964. Bar: Minn. 1966, U.S. Dist. Ct. Minn. 1966, D.C. 1968, U.S. Supreme Ct. 1972, N.Y. 1974, U.S. Ct. Appeals (2d cir.) 1974, U.S. Ct. Appeals (8th cir.) 1975. Assoc. project dir. Brookings Inst., Washington, 1966-67; fgn. svc. officer, legal advisor U.S. Dept. State, Washington, 1968-73; Am. Embassy, Saigon; U.S. Mission to the UN; nat. law dir. Anti-Defamation League, NYC, 1973-74; legal dir. Minn. Pub. Interest Rsch. Group, Mpls., 1974-77; pvt. practice law Mpls., 1977—. Adj. prof. William Mitchell Coll. Law, St. Paul, 1983—; faculty mem. several nat. comm. law and First Amendment seminars. Author: (with Zelman Cowen) Sir John Latham and Other Papers, 1965, The Taming of the Press: Cohen v. Cowles Media Co., 1999, The Taming of the Press, 1999; co-author: Defending the First, 2005, Whose First Amendment?, 2005; contbr. articles to profl. and scholarly jours. and books, newspapers, popular mags. State bd. dirs. YMCA Youth in Govt. Program, 1981-84; v.p. Twin Cities chpt. Am. Jewish Com., 1980-84; mem. Minn. Ho. of Reps., 1978-82, asst. floor leader (whip), 1981-82; pres., dir. North Star Legal Found., 1983—; legal affairs editor Pub. Rsch. Syndicated, 1986—; briefs and oral arguments published in full Landmark Briefs and Arguments of the Supreme Ct. of the U.S., Vol. 200, 1992; mem. citizens adv. com. Voyageurs Nat. Pk., 1979-81. Recipient Legis. Evaluation Assembly Legis. Excellence award, 1980, Vietnam Civilian Svc. medal U.S. Dept. State, 1970, North Star award U. Minn., 1961; Fulbright fellow, 1964-65. Mem. ABA, Minn. Bar Assn., Harvard Law Sch. Assn., Am. Legion, Mensa, Phi Beta Kappa. Jewish. Office: 2751 Hennepin Ave S Ste 231 Minneapolis MN 55408-2614 Personal E-mail: srothenbe@aol.com.

ROTHENBERG, JEROME, writer, literature educator; b. NYC, Dec. 11, 1931; s. Morris and Estelle (Lichtenstein) R.; m. Diane Brodatz, Dec. 25, 1952; 1 son, Matthew. BA, CCNY, 1952; MA, U. Mich., 1953; LittD (hon.), SUNY, Oneonta, 1997. With Mannes Coll. Music, NYC, 1961—70. Vis. prof. U. Calif., San Diego, 1971, 77-84, U. Wis.-Milw., 1974-75, San Diego State U., 1976-77, U. Calif., Riverside, 1980, U. Okla., Norman, 1984; vis. Aerol Arnold prof. English U. So. Calif., 1983; vis. writer in residence SUNY, Albany, 1986, prof. English SUNY, Binghamton, 1986-88; prof. visual arts and lit. U. Calif., San Diego, 1989—, chmn. visual arts, 1990-93; head, creative writing, 1994-95. Poet, freelance writer, 1956—; author: numerous books of poetry and prose including Between, 1967, Technicians of the Sacred, 1968, Poems for the Game of Silence, 1971, Shaking the Pumpkin, 1972, America a Prophecy, 1973, Revolution of the Word, 1974, Poland/1931, 1974, A Big Jewish Book, 1978, A Seneca Journal, 1978, Vienna Blood, 1980, Pre-Faces, 1981, Symposium of the Whole, 1983, That Dada Strain, 1983, New Selected Poems, 1986, Khurbn, 1989, Exiled in the Word, 1989, The Lorca Variations I-VIII, 1990, Apres le jeu de silence, 1991, The Lorca Variations (complete), 1993, Gematria, 1994, An Oracle for Delfi, 1995, Poems for The Millennium, vol. 1, 1995, Seedings, 1996, The Book, Spiritual Instrument, 1996, Poems for the Millennium, Vol. 2, 1998, A Paradise of Poets, 1999, A Book of The Book, 2000, The Case for Memory, 2001, Livre de Temoignage, 2002, A Book of Witness, 2003, María Sabina, 2003, Writing Through: Translations and Variations, 2004, A Book of Concealments, 2004, 25 Caprichos after Goya, 2004, The Burning Babe, 2005, China Notes & The Treasures of Dunhuang, 2006, Triptych, 2007; editor, pub. Hawk's Well Press., N.Y.C., 1958-65, Some/Thing mag., 1966-69, Alcheringa: Ethnopoetics, 1970-76, New Wilderness Letter, 1976-86. Served with AUS, 1953-55. Recipient award in poetry Longview Found., 1960, Am. Book award, 1982, PEN Ctr. USA West award, 1994, 02, PEN Oakland Josephine Miles award, 1994, 96, Alfonso el Sabio award for translation San Diego State U., 2004, Poetry in Transl. award PEN Am. Ctr., 2004, Lifetime Achievement award San Diego Authors, 2007; Wenner-Gren Found. grantee-in-aide for rsch. in Am. Indian poetry, 1968; Guggenheim fellow in creative writing, 1974; NEA poetry grantee, 1976. Mem. PEN Am. Ctr., New Wilderness Found., World Poetry Acad. Office: care New Directions 80 8th Ave New York NY 10011-5126 Office Phone: 760-436-9923. Personal E-mail: jrothenberg@cox.net. Business E-Mail: jrothenb@ucsd.edu.

ROTHENBERG, KAREN H., dean, law educator; BA magna cum laude, Princeton U., 1973, MPA, 1974; JD, U. Va., 1979. Faculty mem. U. Md. Sch. Law, 1983—, founding dir. Law & Health Care Prog., Marjorie Cook Prof. Law, interim dean, 1999—2001, dean, 2001—. Assoc. Covington and Burling, Washington, DC; pres. Am. Soc. Law, Medicine and Ethics; spl. asst. to dir. Office Rsch. on Women's Health, NIH, 1995—96. Co-editor-in-chief Jour. Law, Medicine, and Ethics; co-editor: Women and Prenatal Testing: Facing the Challenges of Genetic Technology; contbr. articles to profl. jours. Named one of Md. Top Women, Daily Record; recipient Joseph Healey Health Law Tchr.'s award, Am. Soc. Law, Medicine and Ethics, 1996, Md. Leadership in Law Award, 2003. Fellow: Md. Bar Found., Am. Bar Found.; mem.: ABA (coordinating group on bioethics and the law), NIH (sect. on prenatal care, recruitment & ret. of women in clin studies, sect. on ethical, legal and social implications of genetics), Am. Law Deans Assn. (bd. dirs.), Nat. Inst. Child & Human Develop. (adv. coun.), Nat. Action Plan Breast Cancer, Ethics in Reproduction (nat. adv. bd.), Inst. Medicine's Com. (sect. legal and ethical issues for inclusion of women in clin. stud.). Office: U Md Law Sch Dean's Office 500 W Baltimore St Baltimore MD 21201 Office Phone: 410-706-2041. Fax: 410-706-4045. Business E-Mail: krothenberg@law.umaryland.edu. *

ROTHENBERG, LARAINE S., lawyer; b. Bklyn., Feb. 20, 1947; BA, U. Pa., 1967; JD, Columbia U., 1971. Bar: N.Y. 1972. Atty. Proskauer Rose LLP, 1974—90; ptnr. McDermott, Will & Emery, NYC, 1990—94, Fried Frank Harris Shriver & Jacobson LLP, NYC, 1994—. Contbr. articles to profl. jour. Bd. dir. Wallace Found., Pig Iron Theatre Co.; mem. bd. vis. Columbia Law Sch. Recipient Tax Mmgt. Disting. Author award, 1997, Women of Power and Influence award, NOW-NYC, 2002, DSM, Columbia U. Alumni Fedn., 2003, award for outstanding pro bono svc., Legal Aid Soc., 2005. Mem. N.Y. State Bar Assn. (mem. exec. com. 1981-89, co-chmn. continuing legal edn. 1988-89, problems of the profession 1987-88, chmn. employee benefits com. 1985-86, co-chmn. 1984-85, chmn. exempt orgns. com. 1982-84, mem.-at-large exec. com. 1981-82), Assn. Bar City N.Y. (mem. taxation of corporations com. 1990—, chmn. spl. com. on employee benefits 1987-88, mem. taxation com. 1979-82), Internat. Bar Assn., Internat. Fiscal Assn.; founding mem. Alumnae Columbia Law Sch. Office: Fried Frank Harris Shriver & Jacobson LLP 1 New York Plz New York NY 10004 Business E-Mail: rothela@friedfrank.com.

ROTHENBERG, LINDA ANN, science educator; b. NYC, May 11, 1956; d. John and Muriel Angus; m. Thomas Charles Rothenberg, Apr. 23, 1977; children: Mark, Jason. BA in Elem. Edn., Queens Coll., 1978, MS in Spl. Edn., 1982. Cert. early childhood edn. tchr. Fla. Bd. Edn., elem. edn. tchr. Fla. Bd. Edn. Sci. tchr. Hernando County Sch. Bd., Spring Hill, Fla., 2004—, elem. tchr., 1988—, dist. sci. fair dir., 1995—2004, tchr. trainer ESL, 1993—98, exceptional student educator, 1988—93; adj. instr. St. Leo's Coll., Dade City, Fla., 1994; elem. tchr. NYC Bd. Edn., 1978—88. Chmn. Pine Grove Sch. Adv. Bd., Brooksville, Fla., 1990—92. V.p. Springstead H.S. Band Boosters, Spring Hill, Fla., 2001—03; chmn. of charity events Nature Coast Corvettes, Spring Hill, 2003; support group leader Internat. Waldenstrom's Macroglobulin Anemia Found., 2004—. Grant, Hernando County Edn. Found., 2004. Mem.: Nat. Sci. Teachers Assn. Achievements include established Hands On Sci. Mus. for Children at Pine Grove Elem. Sch; established first science lab for Westside Elementary School. Avocations: painting, music, swimming. Office: Westside Elem Sch 2400 Applegate Dr Spring Hill FL 34609

ROTHENBERG, MACE L(AWRENCE), physician, medical educator; b. NYC, Nov. 9, 1956; s. William Harry and Corinne (Kaufman) R.; m. Joyce Elaine Fryburg, June 12, 1988; children: Stephanie, Bryce. BA, U. Pa., 1978; MD, NYU Sch. Medicine, 1982. Diplomate Am. Bd. Internal Medicine, Am. Bd. Internal Medicine (Oncology). Intern to resident, internal medicine Vanderbilt U., Nashville, 1982—85; fellow med. oncology Nat. Cancer Inst., Bethesda, Md., 1985-88, sr. staff mem., 1988-91, spl. asst. to dir. div. cancer treatment, 1988-91; asst. prof. medicine U. Tex. Health Sci. Ctr., San Antonio, 1991-95, assoc. prof. medicine, 1995-98; exec. officer S.W. Oncology Group, San Antonio, 1991-98; assoc. prof. Vanderbilt U. Med. Ctr., Nashville, 1998—2002, prof. medicine, 2002—; Ingram prof. cancer rsch. Vanderbilt-Ingram Cancer Ctr., Nashville, 2002—. Chmn. devel. therapeutics com., co-chmn. gynecologic cancer com. S.W. Oncology Group, 1991-98; dir. Phase I Drug Devel. Program, Vanderbilt Cancer Ctr., Nashville, 1998—. Editor: Gynecologic Oncology - Controversies and Developments, 1994; assoc. editor (jour.) Investigational New Drugs, 1991—; mem. editl. bd., Clinical Cancer Research, Clinical Colorectal Cancer and Investigational New Drugs, Journal of New Anticancer Agents; contbr. articles to profl. jours. Grantee Nat. Cancer Inst., 1993-. Fellow Am. Coll. Physicians; mem. Am. Soc. Clin. Oncology, Am. Assn. Cancer Rsch. Democrat. Jewish. Avocations: tennis, jazz, bicycling, travel. Home: 524 Sandpiper Cir Nashville TN 37221-4396 Office: Divsn Med Oncology Vanderbilt U Med Ctr 1903 The Vanderbilt Clinic Nashville TN 37232-5536 also: Divsn Med Oncology Vanderbilt U Med Ctr 777 Preston Rsch Bldg Nashville TN 37232-6307 Office Phone: 615-936-1796. Business E-Mail: mace.rothenberg@vanderbilt.edu. *

ROTHENBERG, PAMELA V., lawyer; b. Ft. Knox, Ky., Dec. 11, 1958; BA in History summa cum laude, Tufts U., 1981; JD, Northwestern U., 1984. Bar: Ill. 1984, DC 1985. Assoc. Rudnick & Wolfe, Chgo., 1984—85, Lane & Edson PC, Washington, 1985—86; assoc & prin. David, Hagner, Kuney & Davison, Washington, 1986—98; mem. Womble Carlyle Sandridge & Rice PLLC, Washington, 1998—, co-mng. mem. Washington, DC office, 2004—. Mem.: ABA, Women's Bar Assn. of DC, Phi Beta Kappa. Office: Womble Carlyle Sandridge & Rice PLLC 7th Fl 1401 Eye St NW Washington DC 20005 Office Phone: 202-857-4422. Office Fax: 202-261-0022. Business E-Mail: prothenberg@wcsr.com.

ROTHENBERG, PETER JAY, lawyer; b. NYC, Apr. 3, 1941; s. Max and Judith (Berkowitz) R.; m. Laraine H. Silver, Aug. 29, 1970; children: Daniel, Jason. AB, Harvard U., 1961, LLB, 1964. Bar: N.Y. 1965, U.S. Tax Ct. 1969. Dep. counsel judiciary sub. com. on jud. machinery U.S. Senate Com., Washington, 1965-66; assoc. Paul, Weiss, Rifkind, Wharton & Garrison, NYC, 1969-73, ptnr., 1974—, coordinator, tax dept. Served to capt. U.S. Army, 1966-69. Mem. N.Y. State Bar Assn. (exec. com. tax sect. 1979-87), Assn. Bar City N.Y. (tax com. 1977-79, com. on taxation of internat. transactions 1990-93), Internat. Fiscal Assn. Democrat. Jewish. Home: 895 Park Ave New York NY 10021-0327 Office: Paul Weiss Rifkind Wharton & Garrison Ste 417 1285 Avenue Of The Americas Fl 21 New York NY 10019-6028 Fax: 212-373-2004. E-mail: prothenberg@paulweiss.com.

ROTHENBERG, RANDALL, advertising executive; Sr. cons. editor Bloomberg Bus. News; sr. writer, columnist, editorial dir. Esquire mag.; politics editor Sunday mag. NY Times, tech. editor; daily adv. columnist NY Times, media and mktg. reporter; editor-in-chief Strategy+Bus., strategy-business.com; editor-at-large Adv. Age. mag.; sir. dir. intellectual capital Booz Allen Hamilton Inc.; pres., CEO Interactive Adv. Bur., 2006—. Office: Interactive Adv Bur 116 E 27th St 7th Fl New York NY 10016 Office Phone: 212-380-4700. *

ROTHENBERG, ROBERT PHILIP, public relations counselor; b. NYC, June 5, 1936; s. Robert Edward and Lillian Babette (Lustig) R. BA, Cornell U., 1956; MS, Boston U., 1958. With publicity dept. Columbia Pictures Corp., NYC, 1959-60; asst. to pres., pub. rels. dir. Harry N. Abrams Pub. Co., NYC, 1960-62; press sec. to gubernatorial candidate William R. Anderson Tenn., 1962; with Rowland Co., NYC, 1963-70, v.p., 1965-67, sr. v.p., 1967-70; ptnr., exec. v.p. Robert Marston and Assocs., NYC, 1970-88, sr. exec. v.p., 1978-88, also bd. dirs.; ptnr., pres. Marston and Rothenberg Pub. Affairs, Inc., NYC and Washington, 1977-88; chmn., pres. Rothenberg Pub. Rels. Comms. Counsel, NYC, 1988—; v.p. Medbook Publs., Inc., 1995—2004; dir. pub. rels. BigChange Networks, LLC, Washington and NYC, 1998—2004. Sr. cons. The Lund Group, Inc. Trustee Mus. of Holography, N.Y.C.; bd. dir. Found. to Save African Endangered Wildlife, World Rehab. Fund, N.Y.C., 1982-98, Amas Musical Theatre, Inc., 2002-03; assoc. Nat. Park Found.; counselor Am. Bus. Cancer Rsch. Found., Southport, Conn.; fellow Met. Mus. Art, 1990—; pres., chmn., bd. trustees St. Bartholomew's Preservation Found., 1992-95; mem. Blue Hill Troupe, Ltd. With USAFR, 1959-65. Mem. Internat. Soc. Poets, Pride and Alarm Soc., Harriman Soc. of ARC, English-Speaking Union, Anchor Soc. Morgan Libr. and Mus., DeWitt Clinton Soc. Mus. of City of NY, Players Club. Unitarian Universalist. Home and Office: 400 E 54th St Apt 29B New York NY 10022-5169

ROTHER, JOHN, association executive, lawyer; b. Springfield, Mo., Apr. 18, 1947; s. Charles C. and Eleanor J. (Morrison) R. BA with honors, Oberlin Coll., 1969; JD with honors, U. Pa., 1975. Bar: Pa. 1975, D.C. 1977. Appellate litigator NLRB, Washington, 1975-77; counsel Senator Jacob Javits U.S. Senate labor & human resources commn., Washington, 1977-81; staff dir., chief counsel spl. commn. on aging U.S. Senate, Washington, 1981-84; policy and strategy dir. AARP, Washington, 1984—. Chair Generations United; vice chair Nat. Quality Forum; founding mem. Nat. Acad. Social Ins., Corp. for Nat. Service. Named One of 150 Who Make A Difference, Nat. Jour., Washington, 1986. Mem. D.C. Bar, Gerontol. Soc. Am. Office: AARP 601 E St NW Washington DC 20049-0001 E-mail: jrother@aarp.org.

ROTHERT, MARILYN L., dean, nursing educator; b. June 4, 1939; married; 3 children. BSN cum laude, Ohio State U., 1961; MA in Ednl. Psychol., Mich. State U., 1979, PhD in Ednl. Psychol., 1980. RN, Mich. Staff nurse Univ. Hosp., Columbus, Ohio, 1961; instr. sch. nursing Hurley Hosp., Flint, Mich., 1961-66; asst. instr. sch. nursing Mich. State U., East Lansing, 1967-77, grad. asst. dept. community health sci., 1977-80, asst. prof. Coll. Human Medicine, 1980-82, asst. prof., dir. lifelong edn. Coll. Nursing, 1982-84, asst. prof. Coll. Human Medicine, 1982-84, assoc. prof., dir. lifelong edn. Coll. Nursing, 1984-88, assoc. prof. Coll. Human Medicine, 1984-86, prof., dir. lifelong edn. Coll. Nursing, 1988-92, prof., assoc. dean outreach and profl. devel., 1992-96, prof., dean Coll. Nursing, 1996—. Cons. No. Ill. U., Ohio State U., Mich. State Dept. Natural Resources, Can. Nurses Assn., Mich. Judicial Inst., Med. Coll. Va., U. Wash., Kirtland Coll., Anderson Coll. Contbr. articles to profl. jours. Co-chmn. Capitol Health Event, 1987-88; mem. worksite health subcom. Mich. Dept. Pub. Health; mem. State 4-H Health Com. Coop. Extension Svc., 1972-75, 82—; mem. med. adv. com. Mich. Civil Svc. Health Screening Unit, 1984. Mem. ANA (mem. coun. continuing edn., nurse researchers), Mich. Nurses Assn. (chmn. continuing edn. adv. com. 1989), Soc. for Med. Decision Making, The Brunswik Soc., Soc. for Judgment and Decision Making, Soc. for Rsch. in Nursing Edn., Midwest Nursing Rsch. Soc., Am. Pub. Health Assn., Nat. Ctr. for Health Edn., Nat. League for Nursing, Mich. State U. Faculty/Profl. Women's Assn. (bd. dirs. 1989—), Capitol Area Dist. Nurses Assn. (mem. nom. com. 1984-86, continuing edn. com. 1984), Phi Kappa Phi. Office: Mich State U Coll Nursing A-230 Life Sci Bldg East Lansing MI 48824

ROTHFELD, MICHAEL B., theatrical producer, investor; b. NYC, May 19, 1947; m. Ella M. Foshay, May 22, 1970; 2 children. BA, Columbia U., 1969, MS, MBA, Columbia U., 1971, cert. internatl fellows program, 1971. With Time, Inc., 1971-76, assoc. editor Fortune NYC, 1971-74; asst. to chmn. bd. dirs., CEO Time Inc., NYC, 1974-76; with Salomon Bros., NYC, 1976-83, v.p., 1979-83, The First Boston Corp., NYC, 1983-84, mng. dir., 1985-89; gen. ptnr. Bessemer Ptnrs. and Bessemer Holdings, 1989-97, ltd. ptnr., 1997-98. Chmn. bd. dirs. Graphic Controls Corp., 1995-98; bd. vis. Columbia Coll., 1998—, vice chmn. 2002-05, chair, 2005—, bd. adv. Knight-Bagheot program in fin. journalism Grad. Sch.

Journalism, 1998—, trustee, 2005—; chmn. Redfields, LLC, Eagle Prodns., LLC, N.Y.C. Prodr. Gore Vidal's The Best Man, 2000 (winner Drama Desk award, Outer Critics Circle award, Tony nomination). Office: Eagle Productions LLC 200 E 69th St New York NY 10021

ROTHFIELD, LAWRENCE I., microbiology educator; b. NYC, Dec. 30, 1927; s. Joseph and Henrietta (Brown) R.; m. Naomi Fox, Sept. 18, 1953; children: Susan Anne, Lawrence, Jane, John. BA, Cornell U., 1947; MD, NYU, 1951. Intern, then resident Bellevue, Presbyn. hosps., NYC, 1951-53, 55-57; successively instr., clin. asst. prof., asst. prof. NYU Sch. Medicine, 1957-64; from asst. prof. to assoc. prof. Albert Einstein Coll. Medicine, NYC, 1964-68; prof. U. Conn. Sch. Medicine, Farmington, 1968—, chmn. dept. microbiology, 1968-80. Mem. molecular biology rev. panel NIH, 1970-75, microbiology and immunology adv. com. Pres.'s Biomed. Rsch. Panel, 1975, molecular biology rev. panel NSF, 1979-83; mem. microbial physiology and genetics rev. panel NIH, 1990-94, chairperson, 1991-93. Author: Structure and Function of Biological Membranes, 1972; mem. editorial bd. Jour. Membrane Biology, 1969-83, Jour. Biol. Chemistry, 1974-80. With M.C. U.S. Army, 1953-55. Mem. Am. Soc. Biol. Chemists, Am. Soc. Microbiology (chmn. microbial physiology div. 1975). Home: 540 Deercliff Rd Avon CT 06001-2859 Office: U Conn Health Center Farmington CT 06032 Office Phone: 860-679-3581. Business E-Mail: lroth@neuron.uchc.edu.

ROTHFIELD, NAOMI FOX, physician; b. Bklyn., Apr. 5, 1929; d. Morris and Violet (Bloomgarden) Fox; m. Lawrence Rothfield, Sept. 18, 1954; children: Susan, Lawrence, John, Jane. BA, Bard Coll., 1950; MD, NYU, 1955. Intern Lenox Hill Hosp., NYC, 1955-56; instr. NYU Sch. Medicine, 1956-62, asst. prof., 1962-68; assoc. prof. U. Conn. Sch. Medicine, Farmington, 1968-72, prof., 1972—, chief divsn. rheumatic diseases, 1972—99. Contbr. chpts. to books, articles to med. jours. Bd. dirs. Conn. Choral Artists, 1999—. Mem. Am. Soc. Clin. Investigation, Am. Rheumatism Assn., Assn. Am. Physics. Jewish. Home: 540 Deercliff Rd Avon CT 06001-2859 Office: U Conn Sch Medicine Divsn Rheumatic Diseases Farmington CT 06030-0001 Home Phone: 860-677-4781; Office Phone: 860-679-3604. E-mail: rothfield@nso.uchc.edu.

ROTHKOPF, ARTHUR J., association executive; b. NYC, May 24, 1935; s. Abraham and Sarah (Mehlman) Rothkopf; m. Barbara Sarnoff, Dec. 25, 1958; children: Jennifer, Katherine. AB, Lafayette Coll., 1955; JD, Harvard U., 1958. Bar: N.Y. 1959, D.C. 1967. Atty. U.S. Dept. Treasury, NYC, 1958—60, SEC, Washington, 1960—63; assoc. tax legis. counsel U.S. Dept. Treasury, Washington, 1963—66; ptnr. Hogan & Hartson, Washington, 1967—91; gen. counsel U.S. Dept. Transp., Washington, 1991—92, dep. sec., 1992—93; pres. Lafayette Coll., Easton, Pa., 1993—2005, pres. emeritus, 2005—; sr. v.p. U.S. C. of C., 2005—. Bd. dirs. Ins. Svcs. Office, Inc., Jersey City, Bristol West Holdings; sr. v.p. U.S. C. of C.; mem. Sec. of Edn.'s Commn. on Future of Edn., 2005. Trustee Fed. City Coun., Washington, 1983—91, The Am. U.; past chair bd. dirs. Coun. Higher Edn. Accreditation; bd. dirs., past chmn. Assn. Ind. Colls. and Univs. Pa. Mem.: The Pa. Soc. (pres.), Univ. Club (N.Y.C.), Harvard Club of NYC, Chevy Chase Club, Met. Club of Washington. Jewish. Office: 1615 H St NW Washington DC 20062 Home Phone: 202-667-1373; Office Phone: 202-463-5359. Business E-Mail: ajrothkopf@uschamber.com.

ROTHLISBERGER, RODNEY JOHN, music educator; b. Bottineau, ND, May 13, 1940; s. Forrest John and Ellen Rothlisberger; m. Gay Elaine Mohr, Dec. 20, 1975 (div.). BA, St. Olaf Coll., Northfield, Minn., 1962; MA, Eastman Sch. Music, Rochester, NY, 1967; DMusA, U. Colo., Boulde, 1978. Anacortes Washington Pub. Schs., 1962-64; organist, choirmaster U.S. Mil. Acad., West Point, NY, 1965-67; instr., prof. Bowdoin Coll., Brunswick, Maine, 1967-70; instr. Melbourne (Australia) HS, 1973-75; prof. Berea (Ky.) Coll., 1976-77; instr. Concordia Coll., Moorhead, Minn., 1979-81, Moorhead Pub. Schs., 1989-95; prof. Minn. State U., Moorhead, 1995—, chmn. music dept., 2002—05. Active Civic Opera Bd., 1996—2002; bd. dir. Fargo-Moorhead Symphony, 2004—05; bd. dirs. Luth. Brotherhood, Moorhead, 1988—2002, Red River Boy Choir, Moorhead, 1984—2000, Arts Coun. Fargo-Moorhead, 1985—89. With US Army, 1965—67. Recipient Achievement award, Lake Agassiz Arts Coun., 1987. Mem.: Am. Guild Organists (dean Red River Valley chpt. 1985—87, Minn. state chmn. 1995—2002, chmn. nat. com. membership 1994—2000), Music Educators Nat. Conf., Am. Choral Dirs. Assn., Nat. Assn. Tchrs. Singing. Presbyterian. Avocation: reading. Home: 1021 River Dr Moorhead MN 56560-3369 Office: Minn State U Moorhead 1104 7th Ave S Moorhead MN 56563-0002 Office Phone: 218-477-2966. Business E-Mail: rothlisb@mnstate.edu.

ROTHMALER, PETER ANTELL, mathematician, educator; b. Bklyn., July 9, 1939; s. Oswald Rothmaler and Fanny Dorothea Antell; m. Ann Vellaire, June 25, 1966. BA in Math. with honors, Hamilton Coll., 1961; MA, U. Mich., 1962. Math. instr. Coll. DuPage, Glen Ellyn, Ill., 1979—. Mem.: Assn. Christians in Math. Scis., Math. Assn. Am. Messianic Jewish. Avocations: chess, astronomy, baseball, nature. Home: 69 Wilcox Ave Elgin IL 60123 Office: Coll DuPage 425 Fawell Blvd Glen Ellyn IL 60137

ROTHMAN, BARBARA KATZ, sociology educator; b. NYC, June 21, 1948; d. Marcia Katz Berken; m. Herschel M. Rothman; children: Daniel Colb, Leah Colb, Victoria Colb. BA, Bklyn. Coll., 1969, MA, 1972; PhD, NYU, 1979. Prof. sociology CUNY, 1979—. Author: Recreating Motherhood, 1989, The Tentative Pregnancy, 1986, In Labor: Women and Power in the Birthplace, 1982, Of Maps and Imaginations: Genetic Thinking and The Meaning of Life, 1998, The Book of Life, 2000, Weaving a Family: Untangling Race and Adoption, 2005; editor: Ency. of Childbearing, 1993. Mem. Soc. for Study of Social Problems (pres. 1993-94). Office: CUNY Sociology Dept 55 Lexington Ave New York NY 10010-5518 Office Phone: 646-387-4470. Business E-Mail: bkatzrothman@gc.cuny.edu.

ROTHMAN, BERNARD, lawyer; b. NYC, Aug. 11, 1932; s. Harry and Rebecca (Fritz) R.; m. Barbara Joan Schaeffer, Aug. 1953; children: Brian, Adam, Helene. BA cum laude, CCNY, 1953; JD, NYU, 1959. Bar: NY 1959, US Dist. Ct. (ea. and so. dists.) NY 1962, US Ct. Appeals (2d cir.) 1965, US Supreme Ct. 1966, US Tax Ct. 1971. Assoc. Held, Telchin & Held, 1961-62; asst. US atty. Dept. Justice, 1962-66; assoc. Edward Gettinger & Peter Gettinger, 1966-68; ptnr. Schwartz, Rothman & Abrams, P.C., 1968-78, Ferster, Bruckman, Wohl, Most & Rothman, LLP, NYC, 1978-98, Law Offices of Bernard Rothman, NYC, 1999—2004; coun. Sankel, Skurman & McCartin, LLP, 2004—. Acting judge Village of Larchmont, 1982-88, dep. Village atty., 1974-81, former arbitrator Civil Ct., N.Y.C., family disputes panel Am. Arbitration Assn.; guest lectr. domestic rels. and family law on radio and TV, also numerous legal and mental health orgns. Author: Loving and Leaving-Winning at the Business of Divorce, 1998; co-author: Family Law Syracuse Law Rev. of NY Law, 1992, Leaving Home, Family Law Review, 1987, Put Your Kids First, Am. Bar Assn. Family Adv. Quar., 2000; contbr. articles to profl. jours. Mem. exec. bd., past v.p. Westchester Putnam coun. Boy Scouts Am., 1975—; past mem. nat. coun., 1977-81; mem. adv. com. NY State PEACE, 1994—; pres. Congregation B'nai Israel, 1961-63, B'nai Brith, Larchmont chpt., 1981-83. Recipient Silver Beaver award Boy Scouts Am., Wood Badge award. Fellow Am. Acad. Matrimonial Lawyers (bd. govs. NY chpt. 1986-87, 91-93), Interdisciplinary Forum on Mental Health and Family Law (co-chair 1986-97); mem. ABA (family law sect., contbr. Family Advocate Quar.), NY State Bar Assn. (exec. com. family law sect. 1982—, co-chmn. com. on mediation and arbitration 1982-88, 93-99, chair com. on parent edn. 2004—, com. on legis. 1978-88, com. on child custody 1985-88, com. alt. dispute resolution 1982-88), NY State Magistrate Assn., Limousine 6 Track Club. Democrat. Office: 750 3rd Ave New York NY 10017 Home Phone: 917-612-1361; Office Phone: 212-682-2288. E-mail: divorcelawyer@att.net.

ROTHMAN, DAVID BILL, lawyer; b. NYC, Apr. 25, 1952; s. Julius and Lillian (Halpern) R.; m. Jeanne Marie Hickey, July 7, 1974; children: Jessica Suzanne, Gregory Kozak. BA, U. Fla., 1974, JD, 1977. Bar: Fla. 1977, U.S. Dist. Ct. (so. dist.) Fla. 1980, U.S. Ct. Appeals (5th cir.) 1980, U.S. Supreme Ct. 1981, U.S. Ct. Appeals (11th cir.) 1982, U.S. Dist. Ct. (ea. dist.) Ky. 1985, U.S. Dist. Ct. (mid. dist.) Fla. 1986, cert.: Fla. Bar, Nat. Bd. Trial Advocacy (criminal trial law). Asst. state atty. Dade County State Atty.'s Office, Miami, Fla., 1977-80; ptnr. Thornton Rothman, P.A., Miami, 1980—. Adj. prof. U. Miami Sch. Law, 1995—; com. mem. Fla. Rules Criminal Procedures, 1990-93, metro Dade Ind. Rev. Panel, 1989-97, co-chmn., 1990-91, chmn., 1991-92, 95-97; panel mem. fee arbitration 11th Cir. Ct., 1994-96, co-chair, 1995-96. Mem. ABA, Fla. Bar Assn. (bd. govs. 1999—, exec. com. 2004-05, 2005-06, 2006-07, 07—), Dade County Bar Assn. (criminal ct. com. 1984—, chmn. 1987-90, bd. dirs. 1990-93, treas. 1993-94, sec. 1994-95, v.p. 1995-96, pres. 1997-98, chmn. pro bono com. 2007—), Nat. Assn. Criminal Def. Lawyers, Fla. Assn. Criminal Def. Lawyers (bd. dirs. Miami chpt. 1991—, pres. Miami chpt. 1993-94, statewide sec. 1996-97, treas. 1997-98, v.p. 1998-99, pres.-elect 1999-2000, pres. 2001), Eugene Spellman Inns of Ct. Democrat. Jewish. Avocations: running, weightlifting, reading. Home: 9951 SW 127th Ter Miami FL 33176-4833 Office: Thornton & Rothman PA 200 S Biscayne Blvd Ste 2770 Miami FL 33131-5331 Home Phone: 305-253-4045; Office Phone: 305-358-9000. Business E-Mail: dbr@thorntonrothmanlaw.com.

ROTHMAN, DAVID J., historian, educator; b. NYC, Apr. 30, 1937; s. Murray and Anne (Beier) R.; m. Sheila Miller, June 26, 1960; children: Matthew, Micol. BA, Columbia U., 1958; MA, Harvard U., 1959, PhD, 1964. Asst. prof. history Columbia U., NYC, 1964-67, assoc. prof., 1967-71, prof., 1971—, Bernard Schoenberg prof. social medicine, dir. Ctr. for Study of Society and Medicine. Fulbright-Hayes prof. Hebrew U., Jerusalem, 1968-69, India, 1982; vis. Pinkerton Prof. Sch. Criminal Justice, State U. N.Y., at Albany, 1973-74; Samuel Paley lectr. Hebrew U., Jerusalem, 1977; Mem. Com. for Study of Incarceration, 1971-74; co-dir. Project on Community Alternatives, 1978-82; chmn. adv. bd. on criminal justice Clark Found., 1978-82; mem. bd. advisors The Project on Death in Am., Open Soc. Inst., 1995-2000, trustee; mem. bd. trustees Open Soc. Inst., 1996—, pres. Inst. on Medicine as a Profession, 2003—. Author: Politics and Power, 1966, The Discovery of the Asylum, 1971; co-author: Doing Good, 1978, Conscience and Convenience: The Asylum and its Alternatives in Progressive America, 1980; (with Sheila M. Rothman) The Willowbrook Wars, 1984; Strangers at the Bedside, 1991, Beginings Count: The Technological Imperative in American Health Care, 1997; editor: The World of the Adams Chronicles, 1976, (with Sheila M. Rothman) On Their Own: The Poor in Modern America, 1972, The Sources of American Social Tradition, 1975, (with Stanton Wheeler) Social History and Social Policy, 1981, (with Norval Morris) The Oxford History of the Prison, 1995, (with Steven Marcus and Stephanie Kiceluk) Medicine and Western Civilization, 1995, (with Sheila M. Rothman) The Pursuit of Perfection, 2003, (with Sheila M. Rothman) Trust is Not Enough. Recipient Albert J. Beveridge prize Am. Hist. Assn., 1971. Mem. Am. Hist. Assn., N.Y. Acad. Medicine, Phi Beta Kappa. Office: Columbia U Coll Physicians and Surgeons Ctr Study Soc and Medicine 630 W 168th St New York NY 10032-3702

ROTHMAN, ESTHER POMERANZ, social agency executive, psychologist; b. NYC, Nov. 25, 1919; d. Max and Anne (Reiner) Pomeranz; m. Arthur M. Rothman, Apr. 13, 1946; 1 dau., Amy. BA, Hunter Coll., 1942; MA, Columbia U., NYC, 1944; MA, CCNY, 1946; PhD, NYU, 1958. Cert. psychologist, NY Tchr., NYC Bd. Edn., 1944-57, prin., 1957-80; exec. dir. Glie Youth Program, NYC, 1980-85; exec. dir. Correctional Edn. Consortium, 1985—91; pres. Correctional Edn. Consortium, 1991—; research psychologist Tchrs. Hot Line, NYC, 1972-74. Author: Angel Inside Went Sour, 1972; Troubled Teachers, 1974; co-author: Disturbed Child, 1967. Mem. Citizens Com. for Children, NYC, 1972—. Recipient Valley Forge Freedom award, 1976; named to Hall of Fame Hunter Coll., 1972. Fellow Am. Assn. Orthopsychiatry (sec. 1976-79); mem. Am. Psychol. Assn. Home and Office: 200 E 16th St New York NY 10003-3707 Office: Correctional Edn Consortium 500 8 Ave New York NY 10018 Office Phone: 212-674-1973. Personal E-mail: esther.art@verizon.net.

ROTHMAN, HENRY ISAAC, lawyer; b. Rochester, NY, Mar. 29, 1943; s. Maurice M. and Golde (Nusbaum) R.; m. Golda R. Shatz, July 3, 1966; children: Alan, Miriam, Cheryl, Suri. BA, Yeshiva U., 1964; JD, Cornell U., 1967. Bar: NY 1967. Trial atty. SEC, NYC, 1967-69; ptnr. Booth, Lipton & Lipton, NYC, 1969-87, Parker, Chapin, Flattau & Klimpl, NYC, 1987-2000, Jenkens & Gilchrist Parker Chapin LLP, NYC, 2001—05, Troutman Sanders LLP, NYC, 2005—. Bd. dir. Camp Morasha, Lake Como, Pa., 1982-06, vice chmn., 1992-00; bd. dir. Assn. Jewish Sponsored Camps, Inc., 1986-00; bd. dir. Yeshiva U. High Schs., NYC, 1984-99, vice chmn. bd., 1990-91, chmn. bd., 1992-95; v.p. Manhattan Day Sch., NYC, 1985-96, bd. dir.; assoc. v.p. Orthodox Union, NYC, 1990-00, v.p., 2001-06, sr. v.p., 2006-; vice chmn. bd. dir. Azrieli Grad. Sch. Jewish Edn. and Adminstrn., 2000—. Mem.: ABA (com. on fed. regulation of securities), Yeshiva U. Alumni Assn. (pres. 1986—88, hon. pres. 1988—90). Office: Troutman Sanders LLP The Chrysler Bldg 405 Lexington Ave New York NY 10174-0002 Office Phone: 212-704-6000. Business E-Mail: henry.rothman@troutmansanders.com.

ROTHMAN, HOWARD JOEL, lawyer; b. NYC, July 10, 1945; BA, CCNY, 1967; JD, Bklyn. Law Sch., 1971; LLM, NYU, 1972. Bar: N.Y. 1972. From assoc. to ptnr. Marshall, Bratter, Greene, Allison & Tucker, NYC, 1972—82; ptnr. Rosenman & Colin LLP, NYC, 1982—97, Kramer, Levin, Naftalis & Frankel LLP, NYC, 1997—. Mem. adv. panel Commr. Fin. of City of N.Y., 1981-83. Author profl. books and articles. Mem. ABA (corp. tax. com. 1977-87, income from real property com. 1980—), Internat. Bar Assn., NY State Bar Assn. (exec. com. tax sect. 1999-2000, corp. tax com. 1979-, partnerships com. 1979—, NYC tax matters com. 1977—, income from real property com. 1987—), Bur. Nat. Affairs (real estate jour. 1984—, tax mgmt. adv. bd. 1979—), Alliance for Young Artists and Writers (bd. dirs.), Poetry Soc. Am. (bd. dirs.), NY Found. for Arts (bd. dirs.).

ROTHMAN, JAMES EDWARD, cell biologist, educator; b. Haverhill, Mass., Nov. 3, 1950; BA summa cum laude, Yale U., 1971; PhD in Biochemistry, Harvard U., 1976; D h.c., U. Regensburg, 1995, U. Geneva, 1997. Fellow MIT, Cambridge, 1976-78; asst. prof., dept. biochemistry Stanford (Calif.) U., 1978—81, assoc. prof., 1981—84, prof., 1984—88; E.R. Squibb prof. molecular biology Princeton (N.J.) U., 1988—91; Paul Marks chair Sloan-Kettering Inst., NYC, 1991—2003, chmn. program in cellular biochemistry and biophysics, 1991—2003, vice chmn., 1994—2003; prof. physiology, head ctr. chem. biol. Columbia U., 2003—. Editl. bd. Molecular and Cellulat Biology, 1982—84; chmn. Gordon Conf. on Molecular Membrane Biology, 1983; bd. editors Science, 1984—89; editl. com. Ann. Review Biochemistry, 1985—90, assoc. editor, 2003; editl. bd. Cell, 1984—94; study sect., Molecular Cytology NIH, 1990—94, coun., Nat. Inst. Digestive and Kidney Diseases, 1997—99; Devel. Therapeutics Review Group Nat. Cancer Inst., 1997—98; bd. sr. editors Jour. Clin. Investigation, 2002—. Recipient Eli Lily award for Fundamental Rsch. in Biol. Chemistry, 1986, Passano Young Scientist award, 1986, Alexander Von Humboldt award, 1989, Heinrich Wieland prize, 1990, Rosenstiel award in Biomedical Sciences, 1994, V.D. Mattia award, 1994, Fritz Lipmann award, 1995, Mayor's award for Excellence in Sci. and Tech., 1995, Gairdner Found. Internat. award Gairdner Found., 1996, King Faisal Internat. prize in Sci., 1996, Harden medal, 1997, Feodor Lynen award, 1997, Jacobaeus prize, 1999, Heineken prize, 2000, Otto-Warburg medal, 2001, Albert Lasker award for Basic Medical Rsch., Lasker Found., 2002, Louisa Gross Horwitz prize of Columbia U., 2002; Fellow Andrew W. Mellon, 1979-1982; scholar Dreyfus Found. Teacher, 1981-86; commd. as a Kentucky Col., by Gov. State of Kentucky, 1997. Fellow: Am. Acad. of Arts and Sciences, NAS (Richard Lounsbery award 1997); mem.: European Molecular Biology Orgn. (foreign assoc. 1995), Inst. Medicine, NAS. Office: Columbia U Russ Berrie Med Sci Pavilion 1150 St Nicholas Ave Rm 520 New York NY 10032 Office Phone: 212-851-5565. Business E-Mail: jr2269@columbia.edu.

ROTHMAN, MELVIN L., retired judge; b. Montreal, Que., Can., Apr. 6, 1930; s. Charles and Nellie (Rosen) R.; m. Joan Elizabeth Presant, Aug. 4, 1954; children: Ann Elizabeth, Claire Presant, Margot Sneyd. BA, McGill U., 1951, B.C.L., 1954. Bar: Que. 1954. Practice law, Montreal, 1954-71; mem. Phillips, Vineberg, Goodman, Phillips & Rothman; judge Superior Ct., Dist. of Montreal, 1971-83, Ct. Appeal of Que., 1983—2005; dep. judge Supreme Ct. N.W. Territories, 1977—2005. Named Queen's Counsel. Mem. Jr. Bar of Montreal (pres. 1963-64), Bar of Montreal (council 1964-65), Institut Philippe Pinel (sec., dir. 1965-70). Home: 487 Argyle Ave Westmount PQ Canada H3Y 3B3 E-mail: melvin.rothman@sympatico.ca.

ROTHMAN, PAUL ALAN, publishing executive; b. Bklyn., June 26, 1940; s. Fred B. and Dorothy (Regosin) R.; m. Mary Ann Dalson, July 28, 1966 (div. 1992); m. Carol Ann Liske, Sept. 17, 1999; children: Deborah, Diana. BA, Swarthmore Coll., 1962; JD, U. Mich., 1965; LLM in Taxation, NYU, 1967. Bar: NY 1965. Assoc. Dewey, Ballentine, Busby, Palmer & Wood, NYC, 1965-67; v.p. Fred B. Rothman & Co., Littleton, Colo., 1967-85, pres., 1985-2000; chmn. bd. Colo. Plasticard, Littleton, 1983-95; owner LoDo Law Books, Denver, 1998—. Editor: Mich. Law Rev., 1963—65. Home: 1801 Wynkoop St Apt 708 Denver CO 80202-1196 Office: LoDo Law Books 1701 Wynkoop St Union Sta # 300 Denver CO 80202 Office Phone: 720-904-5145. E-mail: parothman@yahoo.com.

ROTHMAN, STEVEN R., congressman; b. Englewood, NJ, Oct. 14, 1952; div.; 2 children. BA in Polit. Philos., Syracuse U., NY, 1974; JD, Washington U. Sch. Law, St. Louis, 1977. Bar: NJ 1977, NY 1984. Atty. Miller, Hochman, Meyerson and Schaeffer, Esquires, 1978—80, Steven R. Rothman, Esquire, Englewood, NJ, 1980—93; mayor Englewood, NJ, 1983—89; judge Bergen County Surrogate Ct., NJ, 1993-96; mem. US Congress from 9th NJ dist., 1997—, mem. appropriations com. Gen. counsel NJ Young Dems., 1981-82; treas. Bergen County Dem. Party, 1982; Dem. nominee for Bergen County Freeholder, 1989; bd. dirs. Jewish Cmty. Ctr. on the Palisades, 1990-92, United Jewish Cmty. of Bergen and North Hudson. Recipient Humane Legislator of Yr., Am. Humane Assn., 2000, Legislator of Yr., Nat. Orgn. to Insure Sound-Controlled Environment, 2001, David Bodian Meml. award, Internat. Post-Polio Task Force, 2002, Human award, Am. Jewish Com. Mem.: NJ Trial Lawyers Assn., Assn. Trial Lawyers Am., Bergen County Bar Assn., NJ Bar Assn., ABA. Democrat. Jewish. Office: US House Reps 2303 Rayburn House Office Bldg Washington DC 20515 Office Phone: 202-225-5061. Office Fax: 202-225-5851. *

ROTHMEIER, STEVEN GEORGE, investment company executive; b. Mankato, Minn., Oct. 4, 1946; s. Edwin George and Alice Joan (Johnson) R. BBA, U. Notre Dame, 1968; MBA, U. Chgo., 1972. Corp. fin. analyst Northwest Airlines, Inc., St. Paul, 1973, mgr. econ. analysis, 1973-78, dir. econ. planning, 1978, v.p. fin., treas., 1978-82, exec. v.p., treas., dir., 1982-83, exec. v.p. fin. and adminstrn., treas., dir., 1983, pres., chief operating officer, 1984, pres., chief exec. officer, 1985-86, chmn., chief exec. officer, 1986-89, also bd. dirs.; pres. IAI Capital Group, Mpls., 1989-93; chmn., CEO Great No. Capital, St. Paul, 1993—. Bd. dirs. Arvin Meriter Inc., Precision Castparts, Waste Mgmt., Inc. Chmn. St. Agnes Found. Decorated Bronze Star. Mem. Mpls. Club, Chgo. Club. Republican. Roman Catholic. Office: Great Northern Capital 332 Minnesota St Ste W2900 Saint Paul MN 55101-1377 *Success is not an accident; it is a habit. Success is the result of desire, dedication, sacrifice, mental toughness, hard work— and prayer. And you are not successful until you can share your success with others.*

ROTHROCK, CARSON, music educator; b. Tyrone, Pa., Jan. 25, 1935; s. Frances Raquepau and Jack Rothrock; m. Mary Ann Pfeiffer, June 22, 1959; children: Rosalind Sue Carrillo, Randall Allen, Roshelle Ann Klek. MEd, Pa. State U., University Park, 1962. Tchr. Sch. Dist., Lancaster, Pa., 1956—60, Ewing Twp. Bd. Ed., Trenton, NJ, 1960—94. Author: (book) Training the High School Orchestra; composer: (orchestral composition) Vertigo, (ballet) For Johnny Would a Soldier Be; musician: (arranging and orchestration) Band, Orchestra, Ensemble Publications. Mem.: ASCAP (life), Am. String Tchrs. Assn. (pres. NJ chpt.). Home: 9632 Cherry Canyon Ave Las Vegas NV 89129 Home Phone: 702-368-0304. Personal E-mail: cr8914@aol.com.

ROTHROCK, LINDSEY NICHOLE, lawyer; b. Richmond, Ind., Nov. 19, 1978; d. Dale Ray Croley and Robin Lynn Lotich, Scott D. Lotich (Stepfather); m. Michael David Rothrock, July 16, 2005. BA in Psychology (hon.), Ind. U., Bloomington, 2001; JD, DePaul U. Coll. Law, Chgo., 2004. Law clk. Goldstein, Fishman, Bender & Romanoff, Chgo., 2002—04; atty. Burns, Figa & Will, PC, Greenwood Village, Colo., 2004—. Sr. law student DePaul Tech., Intellectual Property Clinic, Chgo., 2003—04; legal writing and analysis tchr. asst. DePaul U. Coll. Law, 2002—03. Project site mgr. Chgo. Cares, 2002—03; vol. judge U. Denver Sturm Coll. Law, 2005—; vol. coach Colo. HS Mock Trial Program, 2006—. Recipient Ctr. for Computer-Assisted Legal Instrn. Legal Writing and Analysis award, DePaul U. Coll. Law, 2002. Mem.: ABA, Moot Court Soc., Douglas Elbert County Bar Assn., Colo. Bar Assn., Blue Key Hon. Frat., Golden Key Nat. Honor Soc., Nat. Honors Soc., Alpha Lambda Delta, Phi Eta Sigma, Order of Omega Greek Honor Frat. (life), Phi Beta Kappa (life), Alpha Xi Delta (life; pres. 1999—99). Office: Burns Figa & Will PC 6400 S Fiddler's Green Cir Ste 1000 Greenwood Village CO 80111 Home Phone: 303-814-8550; Office Phone: 303-796-2626. E-mail: lrothrock@bfw-law.com.

ROTHROCK, ROGER LEE, corporate financial executive, retired military officer; b. Oakland City, Ind., Feb. 22, 1924; s. George Riley Rothrock and Lula Bell Pearson. BA, Ind. U., Bloomington, 1949; MA, George Washington U., DC, 1952; postgrad., Am. U., Washington, 1956—58; LLD (hon.), Ricker Coll., Houlton, Maine, 1974. Chmn., asst. Mediq Fin. Svcs., La Quinta, Calif., 1972—90; chmn. Amb. Care, La Quinta, 2000—. Mem.: SAR. Republican. Episcopalian. Office: 50855 Washington St #212 La Quinta CA 92253

ROTHSCHILD, AMALIE RANDOLPH, filmmaker, film producer, film director, photographer; b. Balt., June 3, 1945; d. Randolph Schamberg and Amalie Getta (Rosenfeld) R. BFA, R.I. Sch. Design, 1967; MFA in Motion Picture Prodn., NYU, 1969. Spl. effects staff in film and photography Joshua Light Show, Fillmore E. Theatre, NYC, 1969-71; artist-photographer represented by Staley-Wise Gallery NYC, 2004. Still photographer TWA Airlines Pub. Rels. Dept., Village Voice newspaper, Rolling Stone mag., Newsweek mag., After Dark, N.Y. Daily News, others, 1968-72; co-founder, ptnr. New Day Films, distbn. coop., 1971—; owner operator Anomaly Films Co., NYC, 1971—; mem., co-founder Assn. Ind. Video and Filmmakers, Inc., N.Y.C., 1974; bd. dirs., 1974-78; instr. in film and TV, NYU Inst. of Film and TV, 1976-78; cons. in field to various organizations including Youthgrant Program of Nat. Endowment for Humanities, Washington, 1973-76. Exhibitions include Soho Triad Fine Arts Gallery, 1997, 2000, 02, Gomez Gallery, 1998, 2000, VH-1 Mus. First Gallery, 1999, Govinda Gallery, 2001, Snap Galleries, Birmingham, Eng., 2005, SACI, Florence, Italy, 2005, Tate Gallery, Liverpool, England, 2005, Holden Luntz Gallery, 2005, Redferns Music Picture Gallery, London, 2006, Tremaine Gallery, Conn., 2007, Staley Wise Gallery, NYC, 2007, Whitney Mus., NYC, 2007, Musee d'Arte Contemporaneo, Bologna, Italy, 2007, David Gallery, LA, 2007, Arts Co. Gallery, Nashville 2007; (film): Woo Who? May Wilson, 1969, It Happens to Us, 1972, Nana, Mom and Me, 1974, Radioimmunoassay of Renin, Radioimmunoassay of Aldosterone, 1973, Conversations with Willard Van Dyke, 1981, Richard Haas: Work in Progress, 1984, Painting the Town: The Illusionistic Murals of Richard Haas, 1990 (Emily award Am. Film and Video Festival 1990); editor: Doing It Yourself, Handbook on Independent Film Distribution, 1977; author: Live at the Fillmore East: A Photographic Memoir, 1999; licensed photograph collections include Corbis/Bettmann Archive, 1994—, Star File Photo Agy., 1997-. Mem. Cmty. Planning Bd. 1, Borough of Manhattan, N.Y.C., 1974-86. Recipient spl. achievement award Mademoiselle mag., 1972; Ind. filmmaker grant Am. Film Inst. 1973; film grantee N.Y. State Coun. on the Arts, 1977, 85, 87, Nat. Endowment Arts, 1978, 85, 87, Md. Arts Coun., 1977, Ohio Arts and Humanities Couns., 1985. Mem.: AIVF, Ind. Documentary Assn., NY Women in Film, Univ. Film and Video Assn. Democrat. Address: 135 Hudson St New York NY 10013-2102 also: Via Carrand 22 Florence 50133 Italy E-mail: a.rothschild@agora.it.

ROTHSCHILD, DONALD PHILLIP, retired lawyer, arbitrator; b. Mar. 31, 1927; s. Leo and Anne (Office) R.; m. Ruth Eckstein, July 7, 1950; children: Nancy Lee, Judy Lynn Hoffman, James Alex. AB, U. Mich., 1950; JD summa cum laude, U. Toledo, 1965; LLM, Harvard U., Cambridge, Mass., 1966. Bar: Ohio 1966, DC 1970, US Supreme Ct. 1975, RI 1989. Tchg. fellow Harvard U. Law Sch., Cambridge, Mass., 1965—66; instr. solicitor's office U.S. Dept. Labor, Washington, 1966—67; prof. law George Washington U. Nat. Law Ctr., Washington, 1966—89, prof. emeritus, 1989; prof. law NY Law Sch., 1989—96; ret., 1996. Vis. prof. U. Mich. Law Sch., Ann Arbor, 1976; dir. Consumer Protection Ctr., 1971—, Inst. Law and Aging, Washington, 1973—89, Ctr. for Cmty. Justice, Washington, 1974—78, Nat. Consumers League, Washington, 1981—87; v.p. Regulatory Alternatives Devel. Corp., Washington, 1982—; cons. Washington Met. Coun. Govt., 1979—82; counsel Tillinghast, Collins & Graham, Providence, 1989—95, chair human resource group. Author: From the Cockpit of the Rubaiyat, 2002, Kiosks Keep the Devils Away: A Novel About Mental Health, 2006; co-author: Consumer Protection Text and Materials, 1973, Collective Bargaining and Labor Arbitration, 1979, Fundamentals of Administrative Practice and Procedure, 1981; contbr. articles to profl. jours. Chmn. bd. dirs. D.C. Citizens Complaint Ctr., Washington, 1980; mayoral appointee Adv. Com. on Consumer Protection, Washington, 1979—80. Recipient Cmty. Svc. award, Television Acad., Washington, 1981. Mem.: ABA, D.C. Bar Assn., Am. Arbitration Assn., Fed. Mediation and Conciliation Svc., Nat. Acad. Arbitrators, Nat. Assn. Coll. and Univ. Attys. (Brown U.), Fed. Trade Commn. Adv. Coun., Phi Kappa Phi. Jewish. Office: Donald P Rothchild Esq Captain's Walk Unit C8 601 Periwinkle Way Sanibel FL 33957 Office Phone: 239-395-3711. Personal E-mail: dpchild@earthlink.net.

ROTHSCHILD, GIDEON, lawyer; b. Tel Aviv, Mar. 17, 1950; s. Joseph and Henny (Weissberger) R.; m. Jeryl Pine, Nov. 21, 1982; 1 child, Marissa. BBA, Baruch Coll., CUNY, NYC, 1973; JD with honors, NYU, 1980. Bar: NY 1981, US Tax Ct. 1982, US Dist. Ct. (so. dist. NY) 1991; CPA. Tax supr. Larenthol & Horwath, NYC, 1975-78; ptnr. Rothschild & Landau, NYC, 1979-89; pvt. practice NYC, 1989; atty. Moses & Singer, LLP, NYC. Bd. advs. Practical Acct. Mag., NYC, 1992—, Asset Protection Strategies, 1994—; adj. prof. U. Miami Sch. Law, NY Law Sch. Grad. Progs. Contbr. articles to profl. jours. Bd. dirs. Anti-Defamation League, NYC, 1993—. Recipient Prof. Joseph Arenson Award for Excellence in Decedent's Estates, NY Law Sch., 1980; named one of Top 100 Attys., Worth mag., 2005-06. Mem. ABA (mem. supervisory coun. 2003-, mem. real property, probate and trust sect.), NY State Bar Assn. (mem. estate tax sect.), Assn. of Bar of the City of NY (mem. estate and gift tax com.), Am. Assn. Atty.-CPAs, Offshore Inst., Estate Planning Coun. NYC, Soc. Trust and Estate Practitioners (vice-chair NY chpt.). Office: Moses & Singer LLP The Chrysler Bldg 405 Lexington Ave New York NY 10174-1299 Office Phone: 212-554-7806. Office Fax: 917-206-4306. E-mail: grothschild@mosessinger.com. *

ROTHSCHILD, GITA F., lawyer; b. 1950; BA, George Washington U., 1971; MS, Boston U., 1972; JD cum laude, Temple U. Sch. of Law, 1977. Bar: NJ 1977, NY 1984, US Ct. of Appeals, Second & Third Circuits, US Supreme Ct. Ptnr., insurance group McCarter & English, Newark. Chmn., dist. V fee arbitration com. NJ Supreme Ct., 1984—88; mem. Am. Law Inst., Defense Rsch. Inst.; faculty mem. Defense Trial Academy, 1996; ed. bd. mem. NJ Lawyer, 1996—99. Mem.: ABA, Internat. Assn. of Defense Counsel, Essex County Bar Assn., NJ State Bar Assn. Office: McCarter & English Four Gateway Ctr 100 Mulberry St Newark NJ 07102 Office Phone: 973-639-5959. Office Fax: 973-624-7070. Business E-Mail: grothschild@mccarter.com.

ROTHSCHILD, MARY ANN, music educator; b. June 10, 1952; Student, U. N.W. Fla.; AA, Okallosa Walton, 1979; student, conservatory, Canberra, Australia, 1980—82; BA, U. N.Mex., 1985. Cert. (hon.) Calif. Music Tchrs. Assn. Music tchr. Composer Daughter of Zion I, 1990, Daughter of Zion II, 1994, La Chayim, 1997. Pres. Right to Life, Albuquerque, 1987-89. Mem. Music Tchrs. Nat. Assn. (sec. local chpt. Montgomery, Ala., 1981-88, Redlands, Calif., 1988-90, Palm Beach County, Fla., 1994-96, v.p. 1996-98, pres. 1998-99), Women's Algow (v.p. 1985-87, pres. 1987-89). Republican. Home: 1433 SE Cambridge Dr Port Saint Lucie FL 34952-5410 Home Phone: 772-398-6808; Office Phone: 561-398-6808. Personal E-mail: csom@bellsouth.net.

ROTHSCHILD, NATHANIEL PHILIP (VICTOR JAMES), investment company executive; b. July 12, 1971; s. Jacob Rothschild and Serena Mary Dunn. MA, Oxford U. Co-chmn. Atticus Capital LLC; dir. RIT Capil Ptnrs. plc, The Rothschild Found.; chmn. JNR Ltd., Trigranit, 2006—. Mem. Belfer Ctr. Internat. Coun., John F. Kennedy Sch. Govt., Harvard U., internal adv. coun., Brookings Inst., internal adv. bd., Barrick Gold Corp. Nominee Young Global Leader, World Econ. Forum, 2005; named, 2004. Office: Atticus Capital LLC 152 W 57th St 45th Fl New York NY 10019

ROTHSCHILD, RICK, entertainment company executive; b. Santa Monica, Calif., Sept. 26, 1950; s. Wilfred A. and Janet W. Rothschild; m. Adrienne Rothstein, July 11, 1999; children: Elijah Aden, Mason Adler, Arin Isabel. BA in Theater Arts, Lawrence U., Appleton, Wis., 1971. Exec. show dir., sr. v.p. Walt Disney Imagineering, Glendale, Calif., 1978—. Dir.: (theme park attraction) Disney's Am. Adventure - EPCOT, Stitch's Great Escape!, Soarin' Over Calif.-Disney's Calif. Adventure (THEA award for outstanding acheivement, 2002), It's Tough to be a Bug!-Disney's Animal Kingdom (THEA award for outstanding acheivement, 1999), Honey, I Shrunk the Audience - EPCOT (THEA award for outstanding acheivement, 1996). Recipient Theodore F. Cloak award, Lawrence U., 1971. Home Phone: 818-544-6770; Office Phone: 818-544-6770.

ROTHSTEIN, BARBARA JACOBS, federal judge; b. Bklyn., Feb. 3, 1939; d. Solomon and Pauline Jacobs; m. Ted L. Rothstein, Dec. 28, 1968; 1 child, Daniel BA, Cornell U., 1960; LL.B., Harvard U., 1966. Bar: Mass. 1966, Wash. 1969, U.S. Ct. Appeals (9th cir.) 1977, U.S. Dist. Ct. (we. dist.) Wash. 1971, U.S. Supreme Ct. 1975. Pvt. practice law, Boston, 1966-68; asst. atty. gen. State of Wash., 1968-77; judge Superior Ct., Seattle, 1977-80, Fed. Dist. Ct. Western Wash., Seattle, 1980—, chief judge, 1987-94, dir. Fed. Jud. Ctr., 2003—. Faculty Law Sch. U. Wash., 1975-77, Hastings Inst. Trial Advocacy, 1977, N.W. Inst. Trial Advocacy, 1979—; mem. state-fed. com. U.S. Jud. Conf., chair subcom. on health reform; dir. Fed. Jud. Ctr.; bd. dirs. Inst. Jud. Adminstrn., NYU Sch. Law. Recipient Matrix Table Women of Yr. award Women in Communication, Judge of the Yr. award Fed. Bar Assn., 1989; King County Wash. Women Lawyers Vanguard Honor, 1995 Mem. Am. Judicature Soc. (mem. commn.), Nat. Assn. Women Judges, Fellows of the Am. Bar, Am. Law Inst. (bd. dirs.), Wash. State Bar Assn., Am. Law Inst., Phi Beta Kappa, Phi Kappa Phi. Office: Fed Jud Ctr 1 Columbus Cir NE Washington DC 20002-8003

ROTHSTEIN, FRED C., health facility administrator; b. Cleve. m. Jackie Rothstein; 2 children. BA, Miami U., Oxford, Ohio; MD, Chgo. Med. Sch. U. Health Scis., 1976. Bd. cert. pediatrics and pedatric gastroenterology. Pediat. intern Cleve. Metro Gen. Hosp., Ohio, 1976—77, Rainbow Babies & Children's Hosp., Ohio, 1976—77, pediat. resident Ohio, 1977—79, pediat. gastroenterology fellow Ohio, 1979—81, chief divsn. pediat. gastroenterology Ohio, practicing physician, pediat. gastroenterologist Ohio, pres., CEO; dir. dept. pediatrics, sr. v.p. med. affairs Mt. Sinai Med. Ctr., Cleve., 1989; sr. v.p. clin. integration U. Hosps. Health System, Cleve., 1990—96, acting pres., CEO, 2002—03; pres., CEO U. Hosps. Cleve., 2003—. Asst. prof. pediatrics Case Western Reserve U., Cleve., 1981—86; prof. pediatrics Case Western Res. U., Cleve., 2004—; bd. trustees Ctr. Health Affairs (CHA), 2004, Geauga Regional Hosp., Chardon, Ohio, 1997; bd. dirs. BioEnterprise. Contbr. more than 60 peer-reviewed abstracts, articles, and book chapters on issues concerning pediatric gastroenterology. Mem.: N.Am. Soc. Pediat. Gastroenterology and Nutrition, Am. Gastroenterological Assn., Am. Acad. Pediatrics, Am. Coll. Gastroenterology. Office: Univ Hosps Cleve 11100 Euclid Ave Cleveland OH 44106 Office Phone: 216-844-6217.

ROTHSTEIN, GERALD ALAN, investment consultant; b. Bklyn., Oct. 18, 1941; s. Manuel and Gertrude (Buxbaum) R.; m. Cynthia Bea Pincus, June 11, 1967; children: Michael Neil, Lori Pamela, Meryl Patricia. BBA, City Coll. N.Y., 1962; MBA, U. Pa., 1965. 1st v.p. Shearson Hammill & Co., NYC, 1966-74, Shearson Hayden Stone, NYC, 1974-75; v.p. William D. Witter, Inc., NYC, 1975-76; from v.p. to internat. investment banker Oppenheimer & Co., NYC, 1976—95, internat. investment banker, 1995—2004; mng. dir. internat. money mgmt. CIBC World Markets, NYC, 1998—2004; cons. Marshepaug Advisors, 2004—; mem. Progressive Capital, LLC, 2006—. Trustee Ctr. Social and Emotional Edn., NYC. Mem. N.Y. Soc. Security Analysts, CFA Inst. Home Phone: 212-369-5828; Office Phone: 212-426-6002. Personal E-mail: gerald.rothstein@verizon.net.

ROTHSTEIN, LAURA, dean, law educator; BA, U. Kans., 1971; JD, Georgetown U. Law Ctr., 1974. Asst. prof. law Ohio No. U., 1976—79, dir. admissions, 1978—79; assoc. prof. law W.Va U., 1980—84, prof. law, 1984—86, U. Houston, 1985—96, assoc. dean Student Affairs, 1988—93, Law Found. prof., 1996—2000, assoc. dean Grad. Studies and Spl. Progs., 1999—2000; prof. law Brandeis Sch. Law, U. Louisville, 2000—, dean, 2000—. Vis. asst. prof. law U. Pitts., 1979—80; staff atty. Dept. Justice, Antitrust Div., Washington, DC, 1974—75, Ohio State Atty. Gen., Antitrust Sec., 1975—76, Devel. Disabilities Law Project, U. Pitts. Sch. Law, 1979—80; affiliated Appalachian Rsch. & Defense Fund, Inc., Charleston, W.Va., 1980—85; assoc. dir. devel. Health Law and Policy Inst., U. Houston, 1997—2000. Editor: Health Law News, 1993—98; contbr. articles to law jours. Bd. mem. Urban Montessori Sch., Louisville, 2001—; adv. bd. mem. Children's Organ Transplant Assn., 2000—. Mem.: ABA (mem. Diversity Com. 2002—), Soc. Am. Law Tchrs., Brandeis Inns Ct., Ky. Bar Assn., Ky. Bar Found., Louisville Bar Assn., River Oaks Women's Breakfast Club. Office: Louis D Brandeis Sch Law U Louisville Wilson W Wyatt Hall 2301 S Third St Louisville KY 40292 Office Phone: 502-852-6879. Office Fax: 502-852-0862. E-mail: laura.rothstein@louisville.edu.

ROTHSTEIN, PAUL FREDERICK, lawyer, educator; b. Chgo., June 6, 1938; BS, Northwestern U., 1958, LLB, 1961. Bar: Ill. 1962, D.C. 1967, U.S. Supreme Ct. 1975. Instr. U. Mich. Law Sch., 1963; assoc. prof. law U. Tex., 1964-67; mem. Surrey, Karasik, Gould & Greene, Washington, 1967-70; prof. Georgetown U. Law Ctr., Washington, 1970—; spl. counsel U.S. Senate Jud. Com. Subcom. on Criminal Laws and Procedures, 1975-77; spl. counsel U.S. Ho. of Reps. Jud. Com. Subcom. on Criminal Law, 1980. Cons. Treasury, 1967-74, HEW, 1970, Commrs. on Uniform State Laws, 1969-75, Nat. Acad. Scis., 1976-77, 95-96, D.C. Law Revision Commn., 1976-78; spkr., coord. numerous legal edn. seminars for judges and lawyers, 1970—. Author: Evidence in a Nutshell, 1970, 2d edit., 1981, 3d edit., 1997, Understanding the New Federal Rules of Evidence, 1973, 74, 75, Federal Rules of Evidence with Practice Comments and Annotations, 1978, 2d edit., 1981, 3d edit., 2001, Cases, Materials and Problems in Evidence, 1986, 2d edit., 1998; contbr. articles on various legal matters to profl. jours.; editor-in-chief Northwestern U. Law Rev., 1960-61. Recipient U. Iowa Legal Edn. award 1974, Disting. Pub. Svc. award Crime Victims Compensation Bd., 1978; other civic and profl. awards; Fulbright scholar, Oxford, Eng., 1962-63. Mem. Fed. Bar Assn. (chmn. fed. rules of evidence com. 1974-77, Disting. Svc. award 1975, nat. coun. 1976-80, chmn. continuing legal edn. com. 1980), D.C. Bar (continuing legal edn. bd. 1980—), ABA (chmn. rules of evidence and criminal procedure com., criminal justice sect. 1984-88), Assn. Am. Law Schs. (sec. evidence sect. 1976, chmn. 1977), Nat. Assn. Criminal Injuries Compensations Bds. (sec. 1977-80), Internat. Assn. Criminal Injuries Compensation Bds. Office: Georgetown U Law Ctr 600 New Jersey Ave NW Washington DC 20001-2022

ROTHSTEIN, RONALD, professional basketball coach; b. Bronxville, NY, Dec. 27, 1942; m. Olivia Pierorazio; children: David, Dana. Grad., U. RI, 1964; M, CCNY. Asst. coach Upsala Coll., 1974-75; HS coach, 1976-79; northeastern regional scout Atlanta Hawks, 1979-82; scout NY Knicks, 1982-83; asst. coach Atlanta Hawks, 1983-86, Detroit Pistons, 1986-88; head coach Miami Heat, 1988-91, Detroit Pistons, 1992-93; asst. coach Cleveland Cavaliers, 1993-99; head coach Miami Sol (WNBA), Miami, 1999—2002; asst. coach Ind. Pacers, 2003—04, Miami Heat, 2005—, interim head coach, 2007—. Office: The HEAT Group AmericanAirlines Arena 601 Biscayne Blvd Miami FL 33132 *

ROTHSTEIN, SAMUEL, librarian, educator; b. Moscow, Jan. 12, 1921; arrived in Can., 1922, naturalized, 1929; s. Louis Israel and Rose Rothstein; m. Miriam Ruth Teitelbaum, Aug. 26, 1951; children: Linda Rose, Sharon Lee. BA, U. B.C., 1939, MA, 1940, LLD, 2004; grad. student, U. Calif., Berkeley, 1941-42, grad. student, 1946-47, BLS, 1947; postgrad., U. Wash., 1942—43; PhD (Carnegie Corp. fellow 1951-54), U. Ill., 1954; DLitt, York U., 1971. Teaching fellow U. Wash., 1942-43; prin. libr. asst. U. Calif., Berkeley, 1947; mem. staff U. B.C. Libr., Vancouver, 1947-51, 54-62; acting univ. libr. U. B.C., Vancouver, 1961-62, prof. libr. sci., 1961—86, prof. emeritus, 1986—, dir. Sch. Librarianship, 1961-70. Vis. prof. U. Hawaii, 1969, U. Toronto, 1970, 79, Hebrew U., Jerusalem, 1973; mem. Commn. Nat. Plan Libr. Edn., 1963—; mem. assoc. com. sci. info. Nat. Rsch. Coun. Can., 1962-69; councillor B.C. Med. Libr. Svc., 1971; mem. exec. com. Pacific divsn. Can. Jewish Congress, 1962-69, Internat. House Assn. B.C., 1959-60; mem. Can. Adv. Bd. Sci. and Tech. Info.; mem. cabinet Combined Jewish Appeal of Greater Vancouver, 1992-95; pres. Vancouver Pub. Libr. Trust, 1987-88. Author: The Development of Reference Services, 1955, (with others) Training Professional Librarians for Western Canada, 1957, The University-The Library, 1972, Rothstein on Reference..., 1989; also articles.; co-editor: As We Remember It, 1970. Life mem. bd. dirs. Jewish Cmty. Ctr. of Greater Vancouver, 1977-, pres., 1972-74, 1997-98; bd. dirs. Jewish Fedn. of Greater Vancouver, 1993-2000. Recipient ALISE award Assn. Library Info. Sci. Edn., 1987, Beta Phi Mu award ALA, 1988. Mem. Can. Libr. Assn. (hon. life), Assn. Am. Libr. Schs. (pres. 1968-69), Can. Assn. Libr. Schs. (hon. life, pres. 1982-84), ALA (coun. 1963-69, Beta Phi Mu award 1988), B.C. Libr. Assn. (hon. life, pres. 1959-60, Helen Gordon Stewart award 1970), Pacific N.W. Libr. Assn. (pres. 1963-64, hon. life), Can. Libr. Assn. (hon. life, coun. 1958-60, Outstanding Svc. to Librarianship award 1986), Bibliog. Soc. Can. (coun. 1959-63), Can. Assn. Univ. Tchrs. Home: 1416 W 40th Ave Vancouver BC Canada Personal E-mail: sammir@shaw.ca. Business E-Mail: samuelr@interchange.ubc.ca.

ROTHWELL, ELAINE B., artist; b. Mpls., May 8, 1926; d. Frederick Roscoe and Stella Frances (LaVallee) Bartholomew; m. William Stanley Rothwell, May 10, 1946; children: Suzanne, Amy Verrett, Wendy Rothwell-Lopez, Bart. BFA, San Jose State U., 1966; pvt. study, Woodbury Graphic Studio, Los Altos, Calif., 1975-76, Amaranth Intaglio Workshop, Los Altos, 1985. *Rothwell was first known for her series of 14 etchings using chess imagery and chess positions. This series was featured in a cover story in Chess Life Magazine in March 1979. Her 1983 Spiritus Loci series of eight etchings forms a cartographical puzzle. Her later series, Art History Mysteries, 1994, Mad Meg Amok, 1997, Inklings, 1999, Seasons of Romance, 2006 and Moons, 2005, are online at www.artbyrothwell.com. By means of figure ground ambiguities and enigmatic images, Rothwell's etchings baffle the viewers' eyes with games of visual discovery.* One-woman shows include Triton Mus. Art, Santa Clara, Calif., 1976, Palo Alto Civic Ctr., Calif., 1977, Stanford Art Spaces, Stanford U., Calif., 1985, 1988, 1989, West Valley Art Mus., Surprise, Ariz., 1996, 2007, Roseville Arts Ctr., Calif., 2003, exhibited in group shows at Carnegie Art Ctr., North Tonawanda, N.Y., 1995, 1996, N.J. Ctr. Visual Arts Internat., Summit, 1997, 1998, Brand Libr. and Art Ctr., Glendale, Calif., 1996, Internat. Exhbn. Art League Manatee County, Fla., 1996, Printwork '98, Barrett Ho., Poughkeepsie, N.Y., 1998, 73d Ann. Internat. Print Competition/Print Ctr., Phila., 1999, Manhattan Arts Internat., 1999, Chautauqua Nat. Exhbn. Am. Art, 1999, No. Colo. Ann. Nat. Exhbns., 1999, 2000, Stage Gallery, Merrick, N.Y., 2000, Pacific Prints, Palo Alto, Calif., 2006, Allied Artists Am., NYC, 2006, Gallery West, Alexandria, Va., 2007, Ctr. for Visual Arts, Wausau, Wis., 2007, 20th Parkside Nat. Small Print Exhbn., Kenosha, Wis., 2007, Red River Valley Mus. Internat., Vernon, Tex., 2007, Conn. Acad. Fine Arts 96th Exhbn., Mystic, 2007, Represented in permanent collections Newberry Libr., Chgo., Triton Mus. Art, Santa Clara, West Valley Art Mus., Brand Libr. Art Ctr., Glendale. Mem.: Am. Color Print Soc., Nat. Mus. Women in Arts (charter), Crocker Art Mus., Auburn Old Town Gallery, Triton Mus. Art. Home and Office: 3030 Eagles Nest Auburn CA 95603-5918

ROTHWELL, TIMOTHY, pharmaceutical executive; b. London, Jan. 8, 1951; came to us., 1966; s. Kenneth Gordon Rothwell and Jean Mary (Stedman) Davey; m. Joanne Claire Fleming; children: Tiffany, Heather. BA, Drew U., 1972; JD, Seton Hall U., 1976; LLM, NYU, 1979, exec. MBA, 1983. With Sandoz Pharms., East Hanover, NJ, 1972—, patent atty., 1974-77, patent and trademark counsel, 1980-82, mng. ops. planning and adminstrn., 1982-84, dir. mktg. ops., 1984-85, exec. dir. field ops., 1985-86, v.p. field ops., 1986-87, pres. profl. bus. ops., 1987-88, corp. v.p., chief oper. officer, 1989—91; sr. v.p. sales and mktg. Squibb, Princeton, NJ, 1991; v.p. global mktg. and sales Burroughs-Wellcome, 1992; pres., CEO Sandoz Pharm. Corp., 1995; pres. pharm. op. Rhone-Poulenc Rorer Inc., 1996, pres., bd. dirs., 1996-97; exec. v.p., pres. pharm. ops. Pharmacia Corp., NJ, 1998—2003; pres., CEO Sanofi-Synthelabo N.Am., 2003—, Sanofi-Aventis U.S., 2004—, chmn., 2007. Bd. dirs. PhRMA; trustee Somerset Med. Ctr., Healthcare Inst. NJ; found. bd. dirs. U. Medicine and Dentistry of NJ. Mem. NJ State Bar Assn., NY State Bar Assn., Am. Soc. Pharmacy Law, Nat. Health Care Quality Coun., Am. Found. Pharm. Exec. (bd. dirs.), NJ Patent Law Assn. (pres. 1986), Health Inst. NJ. Avocations: stamp collecting/philately, soccer.

ROTHWELL, WENDY, biology educator; b. Milw., Aug. 9, 1957; d. William and Elaine Rothwell; m. Alberto Lopez, June 24, 2000. BA in Music (emphasis on Composition), San Jose State U., Calif., 1988, BS in Molecular Biology, 1992; PhD in Molecular, Cell & Devel. Biology, U. Calif., Santa Cruz, 1992—98. Sheet metal mechanic Hewlett Packard, Palo Alto, Calif., 1980—91; post-doctoral rschr. U. Calif., Santa Cruz, 1998—2000, lectr. molecular, cell and devel. biology, 1998—2004, lectr. biomolecular engring., 2005—; instr. exptl. methods U. Calif. Ext., Cupertino, 2005; biology instr. Foothill Coll., Los Altos, 2006—07. Lectr. in field. Composer: Schlieman Breathing, 1986, War Fever, 1987, The Shop, 1988, Sonata for a Clarinet and Piano, 1988. Recipient Excellence in Tchg. award, Ctr. for Tchg. Excellence, U. Calif., Santa Cruz, 2001—02. Avocations: playing the saxophone, writing. Office: Univ Calif 210 Engring 2 Santa Cruz CA 95064

ROTI, THOMAS DAVID, judge; s. Sam N. and Theresa S. (Salerno) R.; m. Donna Sumichrast, 1972; children: Thomas S., Kyle D., Rebecca D., Gregory J BS, Loyola U., Chgo., 1967, JD cum laude, 1970. Bar: Ill. 1970, U.S. Dist. Ct. (no. dist.) Ill. 1971, U.S. Ct. Appeals (7th cir.) 1971. Sr. law clk. to Judge Frank McGarr, U.S. Dist. Ct. No. Dist. Ill., 1971-72; assoc. Arnstein, Gluck & Lehr, Chgo., 1972-73, Boodell, Sears et al, Chgo., 1973-75; asst. gen. counsel Dominick's Finer Foods, Inc., Northlake, Ill., 1975-77, v.p., gen. counsel, 1977-97; judge Cir. Ct. Cook County, 2000—. Mem. nat. conf. lawyers and econs. com. Food Mktg. Inst., Washington, 1987—97; trustee Nat. Conf. Cmty. and Justice, 1995—2000; legis. com. Ill. Retail Mchts. Assn., Chgo., 1987—97. Trustee Joint Civic Com. Italian Ams., Chgo., 1986-95; mem. Chgo. Coun. EDU-CARE Scholarship Program, 1988; dir. Chgo. Clean Streak, 1990-97. Maj., Qartermaster Corps, USAR, 1967-83 Recipient Am. Jurisprudence award, 1970, Alumni Assn. award Loyola U., 1970. Mem. ABA, Ill. Bar Assn., Ill. Judges Assn. (bd. dirs. 2005-), Chgo. Bar Assn., N.W. Suburban Bar Assn. (bd. govs. 2006-, co-chair civil practice com.), Justinian Soc. Lawyers, Cath. Lawyers Guild Chgo. (bd. govs., dir. 2004—), Phi Alpha Delta, Alpha Signa Nu. Roman Catholic. Office: 2121 Euclid Ave Rolling Meadows IL 60008 Business E-Mail: tdroti@cookcountygov.com.

ROTONDI, NICHOLAS JOHN, automotive executive; b. Hackensack, NJ, Aug. 15, 1976; s. Salvatore and Geraldine Rotondi. BA, Rutgers U., New Brunswick, NJ, 1998; MS, London Sch. Econs., 2001. Fin. asst. Ferrari N.Am., Englewood Cliffs, NJ, 1998—2000; distbn. specialist Nissan Divsn., Nissan N.Am., Inc., Somerset, NJ, 2002—06, sales ops. specialist, 2003—04; dist. parts and svc. mgr. Infiniti Divsn., Nissan N.Am., Inc., Somerset, NJ, 2004—06, regional tng. mgr., 2006—06; svc. dir. Pk. Ave. Infiniti, Englewood, 2006—. Mem.: Rutgers U. Alumni Assn., London Sch. Econs. Alumni Assn., Nat. Honor Soc., Mensa, Zeta Psi Frat. (life). Independent. Avocations: photography, poetry, guitar, golf, motorcycling. Home: 4843 Bloomingdale Dr Hillsborough NJ 08844 Office: Park Ave Infiniti 227 N Dean St Englewood NJ 07631 Home Phone: 908-428-7276; Office Phone: 201-568-1200. Home Fax: 201-568-1840. Personal E-mail: nrotondi@yahoo.com.

ROTTA, ALEXANDRE TELLECHEA, pediatrician, educator; b. Porto Alegre, Rio Grande do Sul, Brazil, May 13, 1967; m. Andrea Zomer, Oct. 14, 2000. MD, U. Fed. do Rio Grande do Sul, Porto Alegre, 1989. Diplomate Am. Bd. Pediat., 1994, pediat. critical care Am. Bd. Pediat., 2000. Clin. instr. pediat. Wayne State U., Detroit, 1994—95; asst. prof. pediat. and emergency medicine SUNY, Buffalo, 1998—2004; assoc. prof. anesthesiology U. Tex. Med. Br., Corpus Christi, 2004—. Assoc. dir. Pedia.

ICU Driscoll Children's Hosp., Corpus Christi, 2004—; lectr. in field. Contbr. chapters to books, articles to profl. jours. Recipient Excellence in Tchg. as a Faculty Attending award, Children's Hosp. Buffalo, 2000, Young Investigator award, World Fedn. Pediat. Intensive and Critical Care Socs., 2000, 2003. Fellow: Am. Acad. Pediat. (Outstanding Sci. Paper in Basic Sci. Rsch. award 1998, Best in Tng. Rsch. award 2005); mem.: Soc. Critical Care Medicine (Ednl. Rsch. scholar for excellence in critical care rsch. 1997). Achievements include patents for method for reducing free-radical injury; research in partial liquid ventilation; lung protective strategies; aspiration pneumonia; high frequency oscillatory ventilation. Avocation: long distance running. Office: Dept Anesthesiology 3533 South Alameda Corpus Christi TX 78411 Office Phone: 361-695-5445.

ROTTENSTEIN, JESSICA BROOKE, biology educator, earth science educator, researcher; b. Suffern, NY, Aug. 26, 1981; d. Michael and Arlene Rottenstein. BS in Anthropology magna cum laude, Binghamton U., NY, 2003; MA in Anthropology, Human Skeletal Biology Track, NYU, NYC, 2006. Tchg. asst. U. N.Mex. Ann. Bioarchaeological Field Sch., Kampsville, Ill., 2002—03; anthrop. collections mgr. and lab rschr. NYU, NYC, 2005—06; anthropology cons. NYU Coll. Dentistry, NYC, 2006; biology and earth sci. tchr. Mt. St. Michael Acad., Bronx, NY, 2006—. Departmental fellow, NYU, 2004—05, Undergraduate Rsch. grantee, Binghamton U., 2002. Mem.: Golden Key, Phi Beta Kappa. Home Phone: 845-641-4619.

ROTTER, ANDREW JON, history educator; b. Madison, Wis., June 13, 1953; m. Padma A. Kaimal, June 24, 1984; children: Sophie, Phoebe. BA in History, Cornell U., 1975; MA in History, Stanford U., 1976, PhD in History, 1981. Instr. Stanford U., Palo Alto, 1979; vis. asst. prof. Calif. State U., Chico, 1980-81; asst. prof. St. Mary's Coll. Calif., 1981-84, 85-86; vis. asst. prof. Colgate U., 1986-87, asst. prof., 1988-90, assoc. prof., 1990—98, prof., 1998—; asst. prof. Vanderbilt U., 1987-88. Author: The Path to Vietnam: Origins of the American Commitment to Southeast Asia, 1987, Comrades at Odds: The United States and India, 1947-1964, 2000; editor: Light at the End of the Tunnel: A Vietnam War Anthology, 1999; contbr. articles, rev. essays, book revs. to profl. jours. James Birdsall Weter fellow Stanford U., 1979-80, Stanford U. Ctr. for Rsch. Internat. Studies fellowship, 1980, Gandhi Peace Found. fellowship, 1984-85, Sr. Rsch. fellowship Am. Coun. Learned Socs., 1990-91, Picker Rsch. fellowship Colgate U., 1990-91; Albert J. Beveridge Rsch. grantee Am. Hist. Assn., 1984, Rsch. grantee Harry S. Truman Libr. Inst., 1987; recipient David M. Potter award Stanford U. Dept. History, 1978-79. Mem. Am. Hist. Assn., Orgn. Am. Historians, Soc. for Historians of Am. Fgn. Rels. Home: 9 W Pleasant St Hamilton NY 13346-1203 Office: Colgate U Dept History 13 Oak Dr Dept History Hamilton NY 13346-1383

ROTTER, PAUL TALBOTT, retired insurance executive; b. Parsons, Kans., Feb. 21, 1918; s. J. and LaNora (Talbott) R.; m. Virginia Sutherlin Barksdale, July 17, 1943; children: Carolyn Sutherlin, Diane Talbott. BS summa cum laude, Harvard U., 1937. Asst. mathematician Prudential Ins. Co. of Am., Newark, 1938-46; with Mut. Benefit Life Ins. Co., Newark, 1946—, successively asst. mathematician, asso. mathematician, mathematician, 1946-59, from v.p. to exec. v.p., 1959-80, ret., 1980. Mem. Madison Bd. Edn., 1958-64, pres., 1959-64; Trustee, mem. budget com. United Campaign of Madison, 1951-55; mem. bd., chmn. advancement com. Robert Treat council Boy Scouts Am., 1959-64. Fellow Soc. Actuaries (bd. govs. 1965-68, gen. chmn. edn. and exam. com. 1963-66, chmn. adv. com. edn. and exam. 1969-72), Phi Beta Kappa Soc.; mem. Brit. Inst. Actuaries (assoc.), Am. Acad. Actuaries (v.p. 1968-70, bd. dirs., chmn. edn. and exam. com. 1965-66, chmn. rev. and evaluation com. 1968-74), Assn. Harvard Alumni (regional dir. 1965-69), Actuaries Club NY (pres. 1967-68), Harvard Alumni Assn. (v.p. 1964-66), Am. Lawn Bowls Assn. (pres. SW divsn.), Harvard Club NJ (pres. 1956-57); Harvard Club (NYC), Morris County Golf Club (Convent, NJ), Joslyn-Lake Hodges Lawn Bowling Club (pres. 1989-90). Home: 18278 Canfield Pl San Diego CA 92128-1002

ROTTLER, JUERGEN, computer software company executive; Grad. in Computer Sci. and Bus. Adminstrn., Fachhochschule Furtwangen, Germany; MBA, Bentley Coll., Waltham, Mass. Mng. dir. Delphi Consulting Group; various positions up to sr. v.p. pub. sector, healthcare and edn. customer segment Hewlett-Packard, 1986—2004; exec. v.p. Oracle customer svcs. Oracle Corp., Redwood City, Calif., 2004. Office: Oracle Corp 500 Oracle Pky Redwood City CA 94065 Office Phone: 650-506-0024. *

ROTUNDA, ADAM MICHAEL, dermatologist; b. Mineola, NY, Aug. 2, 1974; s. Robert and Josephine Rotunda; m. Thuy Nguyen, July 20, 1997; 1 child, Tia Linh. BS in Nutritional Scis. summa cum laude with honors, Cornell U., Ithaca, NY, 1996; MD valedictorian, SUNY Downstate Med. Sch., Bklyn., 2001. Bd. Cert. Am. Bd. Dermatology, 2005. Intern St. Vincent's Hosp., NYC, 2001—02; resident, dermatology divsn. UCLA Sch. Medicine, LA, 2002—05, clin. prof., dermatology divsn., 2006—; mohs micrographic surgery and cutaneous oncology fellowship Bennett Surgery Ctr., Santa Monica, 2005—06; med. dir. dermatology r&d Allergan, Inc., 2006—. Contbr. articles to profl. jours. Named Review Article Incentive Program Competition winner, Dermatologic Surgery, 2006; recipient Alumni Svc. award, SUNY Downstate Health Sci. Ctr., 2001, Lifetime Membership award, Downstate Student Ctr., 2001. Mem.: L.A. Met. Dermatologic Soc., Calif. Soc. Dermatology and Dermatologic Surgery, Pacific Dermatologic Assn., Am. Soc. Dermatologic Surgery, Am. Coll. of Mohs Micrographic Surgery and Cutaneous Oncology, Am. Acad. Dermatology. Achievements include invention of Methods and related compositions for non-invasive reduction of fat and skin tightening. Personal E-mail: arotunda@hotmail.com. Business E-Mail: rotunda_adam@allergan.com.

ROTUNDA, DONALD THEODORE, public relations consultant; b. Blue Island, Ill., Feb. 14, 1945; s. Nicholas and Frances (Manna) R. BA, Georgetown U., 1967; MA, London Sch. Econs., 1968, PhD, 1972. Analyst NASA, Washington, 1972; lectr. in econs. U. DC, 1973; legis. asst. Ho. of Reps., Washington, 1974-76, economist budget com., 1977; mgmt. analyst Office Mgmt. and Budget, Washington, 1977-81; cons., 1981-82; mgr. editorial svcs. United Technologies Corp., Hartford, Conn., 1982-87, Pepsico, Inc., Purchase, NY, 1987-89, Union Carbide Corp., Danbury, Conn., 1989-90; dir. editorial svcs. Martin Marietta, Bethesda, Md., 1990-92; cons. pub. rels., 1992—. Contbr. numerous articles to Washington Post, New Republic, Saturday Rev. Roman Catholic. Home: 4431 Klingle St NW Washington DC 20016-3578 Office Phone: 202-966-4855. Personal E-mail: donaldrotunda@verizon.net.

ROTUNDA, RONALD DANIEL, law educator, consultant; b. Blue Island, Ill., Feb. 14, 1945; s. Nicholas and Frances (Manna) R.; children: Nora, Mark. AB magna cum laude, Harvard U., 1967, JD magna cum laude, 1970. Bar: N.Y. 1971, U.S. Ct. Appeals (2d cir.) 1971, U.S. Ct. Appeals (D.C. cir.) 1971, U.S. Ct. Appeals (7th cir.) 1990, U.S. Supreme Ct. 1974, Ill. 1975. Law clk. U.S. Ct. Appeals (2d cir.), 1970-71; assoc. Wilmer, Cutler & Pickering, Washington, 1971-73; asst. majority counsel Watergate Com., U.S. Senate, Washington, 1973-74; spl. cons. Office of Ind. Counsel, Washington, 1997-99; asst. prof. U. Ill. Coll. Law, Champaign, 1974-77, assoc. prof., 1977-80, prof., 1980-93, Albert E. Jenner, Jr. prof. of law, 1993—2002; found. prof. law George Mason U., Arlington, Va., 2002—06, prof. law, 2006—; spl. counsel Dept. Def., 2004—05. Vis. prof. law European U. Inst., Florence, Italy, 1981, U. Ala., 1999; mem. profl. responsibility exam. com. Nat. Conf. Bar Examiners, 1980-87; constl. advisor Supreme Nat. Coun. Cambodia, 1993; cons. Supreme Ct. Moldova, 1996; vis. sr. fellow in constnl. studies Cato Inst., 2000. Author: (with Morgan) Problems and Materials of Professional Responsibility, 1976, 9th edit., 2006; (with Nowak and Young) Constitutional Law, 1978, (with Nowak) 2d edit., 1983, 7th edit., 2004, Modern Constitutional Law: Cases and Materials, 1981, 8th edit., 2007, (with Nowak) Treatise on Constitutional Law, 1992, 4th edit., 2007, Legal Ethics, 2002, 5th edit., 2007. Fulbright research scholar, Italy, 1981, Venezuela, 1986. Fellow Am. Bar Found. (life), Ill. Bar Found. (life); mem. Am. Law Inst. Roman Catholic. Office: George Mason Univ Law Sch 3301 Fairfax Dr Arlington VA 22201 Business E-Mail: rrotunda@gmu.edu.

ROUB, BRYAN R(OGER), electronics executive; b. Berea, Ohio, May 1, 1941; s. Bernard Augustus and Pearl Irene (Koeblitz) R.; m. Judith Elaine Penman, June 19, 1965; children: Paul, Bradley, Michael. Student, Ohio Wesleyan U., 1959-62; BS, Ohio State U., 1966; MBA, U. Pa., 1978. Mem. audit staff Ernst & Ernst, Cleve., 1966-70; asst. contr. Midland-Ross, Cleve., 1970-73, contr., 1973-81, v.p., 1977-81, sr. v.p., 1981-82, exec. v.p. fin., 1982-84; sr. v.p. fin. Harris Corp., Melbourne, Fla., 1984-93, sr. v.p., CFO, 1993—2006. Bd. dirs. Fairchild Semicondr., 2004-; mem. fin. coun. II Machinery and Allied Products Inst., Washington, 1978-84, coun. I, 1984—2004, vice chmn., 1994-95, chmn., 1996-98; mem. conf. bd. coun. CFOs, 1993-96. Mem. adv. coun. Coll. Adminstrv. Scis., Ohio State U., 1978-81; mem. citizen's adv. coun. Westlake (Ohio) Schs., 1981-83; trustee Alcoholism Svcs. Cleve., 1982-84; mem. devel. bd. St. John's Hosp., 1983-84; pres. Westridge Homeowners' Assn., 1977; dir., treas. Tortoise Island Homeowners' Assn., 1988-90; bd. dirs. Easter Seal Soc. of Brevard County, 1993-98. Mem. AICPA, Ohio Soc. CPAs, Fin. Execs. Inst. (treas. N.E. Ohio chpt. 1976-78, bd. dirs. 1980-81, 83-84, v.p. 1981-82, pres. 1982-83, bd. dirs. Orlando chpt. 1984—, v.p. 1985-86, pres. 1986-87, nat. bd. dirs. 1987-90, area v.p. 1990-91, chmn. budget and fin. com. 1988-89, chmn. planning com. 1995-97, v.p. at large 1997-99, vice-chmn. 1999-2000, chmn. 2000-01, office of chmn. 1997-2002), Fin. Execs. Rsch. Found. (trustee 1994-97, 1999-2000), Westwood Country Club, Eau Gallie Yacht Club (bd. govs., treas. 1990-92), Suntree Country Club. Address: 10280 S Tropical Trail Merritt Island FL 32952-6919 Personal E-mail: bryan@roub.net.

ROUBIN, GARY SIDNEY SAMUEL, interventional cardiologist, educator, researcher; b. Brisbane, Qld., Australia, Apr. 25, 1948; came to U.S., 1984; s. Victor Joseph and Ruth Rachel (Rosebery) R.; m. Peta; 4 children. MD, U. Queensland, 1975, Post Doctorate in medicine for basic and clin. rsch. in develop. coronary stenting, 1985; PhD in Cardiovascular Physiology, Sydney U., 1983. Diplomate Am. Bd. Internal Medicine, Am. Bd. Cardiology. Resident, internal medicine and cardiology Royal Prince Alfred Hosp.; fellow Hallstrom Inst. Cardiology, Sydney; rsch. dir. Andreas Gruentzig Cardiovasc. Ctr. Emory U., Atlanta, 1985-89; prof. medicine and radiology U. Ala. Hosp., Birmingham, 1989—97, dir. cardiac catheterization lab. and interventional cardiology, 1989—97; dir. endovascular theraphy Lenox Hill Hosp., NY, 1997—2003, chmn., dept. interventional cardiology NY, 2004—; clin. prof. medicine NYU Sch. Medicine. Co-principal investigator NIH-funded Carotid Revascularization vs. Stenting Trial (CREST); lectr. in field. Author: Interventional Cardiovascular Medicine, 1993; contbr. articles to profl. jours.; edited and contbr. to textbooks. Recipient award Internat. Andreas Gruentzig Soc., 1995. Fellow Am. Coll. Cardiology, Coun. Clin. Cardiology Am. Heart Assn., Soc. for Cardiac Angiography and Intervention, Soc. Vascular Medicine and Biology, Internat. Soc. Endovascular Specialists, Soc. Interventional Radiology, Internat. Soc. for Vascular Surgery; mem. Royal Australasian Coll. Physicians. Achievements include being internationally recognized as pioneer in development of stents for blocked arteries. Avocations: polo, scuba diving, windsurfing, skiing. Office: Lenox Hill Hosp Dept Interventional Cardiology 100 E 77th St New York NY 10021 *

ROUBINI, NOURIEL, economics professor; b. Istanbul, Turkey; BA, Universita'L. Bocconi, 1982; MA, Harvard U., 1988. Asst. prof. Yale U., New Haven, 1988—93, assoc. prof., 1993—95, NYU, 1995—. Vis. scholar Internat. Monetary Fund, Washington, 1987, 1993—94, 2001—03; adv. Office Under Sec. for Internat. Affairs US Dept. Treasury, 2000; bd. govs. Fed. Reserve Sys., 1995; vis. economist Bank of Israel, Jerusalem, 1996; sr. economist for internat. affairs White House Coun. of Econ. Advisors, 1998—99; dir. office policy devel. and rev., 1999—2000; rsch. fellow Ctr. Econ. Policy Rsch., London, 1991—, Nat. Bur. Econ. Rsch., Cambridge, Mass., 1998—. Author: (books) Political Cycles and the Macroeconomy, 1997, Bailouts or Bail-ins? Responding to Financial Crisis in Emerging Economics, 2004. Office: Stern Sch Bus NYU 44 W 4th St New York NY 10012 Office Phone: 212-998-0886. Office Fax: 212-995-4218. E-mail: nroubini@stern.nyu.edu. *

ROUDA, HARLEY, JR., real estate company executive; m. Kaira Rouda; children: Trace, Avery, Shea, Dylan. Atty. Porter, Wright, Morris and Arthur; pres. HER Realtors, 1996—99, gen. counsel Columbus, Ohio, 1997—2002, CEO, 1999—2002; CEO and gen. counsel Real Living Inc., Columbus, Ohio, 2002—. Bd. dirs. Rocky Shoe and Boots, 2003, The Realty Alliance, Real Living Mortgage; spkr. in field. Mem. Columbus Theatrical Assn., Upper Arlington Cultural Arts Commn., March of Dimes, Prevent Blindness, Mid-Ohio Foodbank, Columbus Area Leadership Program, Ballet Met, St. John's Church, Upper Arlington Civic Assn., Southern Theatre Restoration, Ctr. Sci. and Industry, World of Children, The Fisher Coll., Ohio State U., Capital U. Law Sch., Greater Columbus C. of C. Named Entrepreneur of Yr., Ernst & Young, 2002; named one of Real Estate's 25 Most Influential Thought Leaders, Realtor Mag., 2006. Office: Real Living Inc 77 East Nationwide Blvd Columbus OH 43215 Office Phone: 614-273-6004. Office Fax: 614-442-2907. E-mail: hjr@realliving.com. *

ROUDEBUSH, JAMES GORDON, career military officer; B in Medicine, U. Nebr., 1971, MD, 1975; M in Pub. Health, U. Tex., San Antonio, 1983; attended, Aerospace Medicine Primary Course, Brooks AFB, Tex., 1980, Tri-Service Combat Casualty Care Course, Fort Sam Houston, 1981; attended by seminar, Air War Coll., 1988; attended, Inst. for Fed. Health Care Executives, George Washington U., Washington, DC, 1989, Nat. War Coll., Fort Lesley J. McNair, Washington, DC, 1991—92, Exec. Mgmt. Course, Def. Sys. Mgmt. Coll., Fort Belvoir, Va., 1993. Commd. 2d lt. USAF, 1972, advanced through grades to lt. gen., 2006; resident in family practice Wright-Patterson USAF Med. Ctr., Wright-Patterson AFB, Ohio, 1975-78; physician in family practice, flight surgeon USAF Hosp., Francis E. Warren AFB, Wyo., 1978-82; resident in aerospace medicine USAF Sch. of Aerospace Medicine, Brooks AFB, Tex., 1982—84; chief of aerospace medicine 81st Tactical Fighter Wing, RAF Bentwaters, England, 1984-86, comdr., 1986-88, 36th Tactial Fighter Wing Hosp., Bitburg AB, Germany, 1988-91; vice comdr. Human Systems Ctr., Brooks AFB, Tex., 1992—94; command surgeon U.S. Ctrl. Command, MacDill AFB, Fla., 1994-97, Pacific Air Forces, Hickam AFB, Hawaii, 1997-98; comdr. 89th Med. Group, Andrews AFB, 1998-2000; command surgeon U.S. Transp. Command and Hdqs. Air Mobility Command, Scotts AFB, Ill., 2000—01; dep. surgeon gen. USAF, Bolling AFB, Washington, DC, 2001—06, surgeon gen., 2006—. Decorated Legion of Merit with oak leaf cluster, Def. Superior Svc. Mmdal with oak leaf cluster, Meritorious Svc. medal with two oak leaf clusters, Air Force Commendation medal, Joint Meritorious Unit award, Air Force Outstanding Unit award with oak leaf cluster, Nat. Def. Svc. Medal with bronze star, Southwest Asia Svc. medal with bronze star, Air Force Overseas Long Tour Ribbon with oak leaf cluster, Air Force Longevity Svc. award Ribbon with silver oak leaf cluster, Small Arms Expert Markmanship Ribbon, Air Force Training Ribbon, Chief Physician Badge, Chief Flight Surgeon Badge. Mem. Soc. of USAF Flight Surgeons, Aerospace Med. Assn., Internat. Assn. of Mil. Flight Surgeons Pilots, Assn. of Mil. Surgeons of the U.S., Air Force Assn., Am. Coll. of Preventive Medicine, Am. Coll. of Physician Execs., AMA.

ROUECHE, JOHN EDWARD, II, education educator, director; b. Sept. 3, 1938; s. John Edward and Mary (Harris) R.; m. Suanne Davis; 1 stepchild, Robin Sue Maca; children by previous marriage: Michelle Renee, John Edward II. BA, Lenoir Rhyne Coll., Hickory, NC, 1960, LittD, 2001; LHD, Lenoir Rhyne Coll., 2001; MA, Appalachian Coll., Boone, NC, 1961; PhD, Fla. State U., 1964. Dean Gaston Coll., Gastonia, NC, 1964-67; assoc. rsch. educator UCLA, 1967-69; dir. jr. coll. divsn. Nat. Lab. Higher Edn., 1968-71; assoc. prof. edn. Duke U.; prof. edn., dir. c.c. leadership program U. Tex., Austin, 1971—, Sid W. Richardson regents chair, 1987—. Chancellor's coun. U. Tex. Sys., 1990—, U. Tex. Littlefield Soc., 1992—; lectr. Earl Pullias lectr. U. So. Calif., 1992, Coll. Bd. Disting. Lectr. NYC, 1993, Frances Crain Cook Disting. Lectr. U. Tex., 1994; chmn. nat. ednl. adv. bd. Gt. Am. Res. Ins. Co., 1988-94; co-chair Nat. Adv. Bd. for C.C.s, Invest Learning Corp., 1993-96; chair nat. adv. com. Kaplan Ednl. Partnerships, 1995-98; La Platica Disting. lectr. Ariz. State U., 1999; chmn. nat. adv. bd. 3-D Internat., 2000-. C.C. editor Jossey-Bass Publs., 1971-82; editor Creative Teaching Series, Media Systems Corp., 1980-85; mem. editl. bd. C.C. Times, C.C. Jour., 1990-94, others; author 35 books, including Profiles of Excellence in America's Schools, 1986, Access with Excellence, 1987, Shared Vision, 1989, Teaching as Leading, 1990, Under-representation: A Question of Diversity, 1991, Between a Rock and a Hard Place, 1993, The Company We Keep, 1995, Strangers in Their Own Land: Part Time Faculty, 1995, Embracing the Tiger: The Effectiveness Debate and the Community College, 1997, High Stakes, High Performance: Making Remedial Education Work, 1999, In Pursuit of Excellence: The Community College of Denver, 2001, Practical Magic: On the Front Lines of Teaching Excellence, 2003, Opting for Opportunity: Entrepreneurship in the Community College, 2005; contbr. articles to profl. jours. Pres. Doss Sch. PTA, 1974-75; chmn. bd. N.W. Hills United Meth. Ch., 1973-76. Recipient Disting. Svc. award Nat. Coun. Univs. and Colls., 1984, Disting. Rsch. Publ. award, 1990, 93, 95, 97, Outstanding Alumnus award Appalachian State U., 1979, Disting. Grad. award Fla. State U., 1981, Tchg. Excellence award U. Tex., 1982, Outstanding Rschr. award, 1985, Excellence award for outstanding learned article U.S. Edn. Press Assn., 1983, Disting. Rsch. award Nat. Assn. Devel. Edn., 1984-86, Disting. Rsch. Publ. award Nat. Coun. Student Devel., 1987, Disting. Rsch. award Nat. Coun. Staff, Program, and Orgn. Devel., B. Lamar Johnson Nat. Leadership award League for Innovation in the Cmty. Coll., 1988, Disting. Svc. & Leadership award CCP, INC., 1993, Disting. Faculty award U. Tex., 1994, Disting. Rsch. award Interassn. Student Devel. Orgns., 1995, Chancellor's Leadership award State of Ala., 1995, Career Rsch. Excellence award U. Tex., 1998, Disting. Grad. award Lenoir-Rhyne Coll., 2000; named lifetime amb. for N.C., 1978; Kellogg fellow, 1962-64, Disting. Internat. Leadership award Govt. of South Africa, 2000, 01, Disting. Nat. Svc. award Nat. Coun. Instrnl. Adminstrs., 2001, Disting. Leadership award Tex. Assn. Cmty. Colls., 2003 Star Leadership award Nat. Hispanic Border Inst., 2005, Mirabeau Lamar award Assn. Tex. Colls. and Univs., 2005. Mem. Am. Assn. Cmty. and Jr. Colls. (bd. dirs. 1989-94, Nat. Leadership award 1986, Disting. Rsch. award coun. colls. and univs. 1990, 94, 96, dist. rsch. sr. scholar award 1994, 96, nat. student devel. inter-assn. rsch. award 1995-96), Am. Assn. Higher Edn., Coun. Univs. and Colls. (past pres., bd. dirs.), Phi Beta Kappa, Phi Delta Kappa. Home: 4700 Lookout Mountain Cv Austin TX 78731-3654 Office: U Tex Austin One University Sta D5600 Austin TX 78712-0378 Office Phone: 512-471-7545. Business E-Mail: roueche@mail.utexas.edu.

ROUGHEAD, GARY, career military officer; b. 1951; Grad., U.S. Naval Acad., 1973. Advanced through ranks to adm. USN, 2005; formerly with weapons dept. USS Josephus Daniels; former exec. officer USS Douglas & USS Tacoma; former commissioning chief engnr. USS O'Bannon, USS Spruance; former flag lt. to comdr. Naval Surface Force, US Atlantic Fleet; former surface warfare analyst, Office Program Appraisal USN, former adminstrv. aide to sec.; former exec. asst. to comdr.-in-chief US Pacific Command; former comdt. US Naval Acad.; chief legis. affairs USN; dep. comdr. US Pacific Command, Honolulu, 2004—05; comdr. US Pacific Fleet, Honolulu, 2005—07, US Fleet Forces Command, Norfolk, Va., 2007—. Decorated Defense Disting. Svc. Medal, Navy Disting. Svc. medal, Def. Superior Svc. medal, Navy Commendation medal, Legion of Merit; recipient Navy Achievement medal, Meritorious Svc. medal. Office: US Fleet Forces Command Fleet Public Affairs 1562 Mitscher Ave Ste 250 Norfolk VA 23551 *

ROUGHGARDEN, JOAN E., biology professor; b. Paterson, NJ, Mar. 13, 1946; BS in Biology, U. Rochester, NY, 1968, AB with highest honors in Philosophy, 1968; MS/PhD in Biology, Harvard U., Cambridge, Mass., 1971. Asst. prof., instr. biology U. Mass., 1970—72; prof. biol. scis. and geophysics Stanford U., Calif., 1972—. Dir., founder Stanford U. Earth Systems Prog., 1992—99; vis. rsch. fellow Merton Coll., U. Oxford, 1994; mem. sci. adv. bd. Pacific Ocean Conservation Network, Calif., 1997—99, Channel Islands Nat. Marine Sanctuary, Santa Barbara, Calif., 1999—2001; ctr. fellow Nat. Ctr. Ecol. Synthesis and Analysis U. Calif., Santa Barbara, 1998. Contbr. articles to profl. jours.; mem. editl. bd.: Theoretical Population Biology, 1975—86, Oecologia, 1979—82, Am. Naturalist, 1984—89; author: Theory of Population Genetics and Evolutionary Ecology: An Intro., 1979, Anolis Lizards of the Caribbean: Ecology, Evolution and Plate Tectonics, 1995, Primer of Ecol. Theory, 1998, Evolution's Rainbow: Diversity, Gender and Sexuality in Nature and People, 2004 (Stonewall prize for nonfiction, Am. Libr. Assn., 2005); co-author: Sci. of Ecology, 1987; co-editor: Perspectives in Ecol. Theory, 1989. Grantee Guggenheim Found. fellowship, 1985. Fellow: Am. Acad. Arts & Scis. Office: Dept Biol Scis Stanford U Stanford CA 94305-5020 E-mail: joan.roughgarden@stanford.edu.

ROUHANI, SHAHROKH, civil engineering environmental educator, consultant; b. Tehran, Iran, Mar. 28, 1956; came to U.S., 1974; s. Aboutorab and Parirokh (Garakani) R.; m. Firouzeh Yekta, Aug. 18, 1983; children: Nina, Shiva. BSCE, U. Calif., Berkeley, 1978, BA in Econs., 1978; SM in Engring., Harvard U., 1980, PhD in Environ. Scis., 1983. Registered profl. engr., Ga. Asst. prof. Ga. Inst. Tech., Atlanta, 1983-90, assoc. prof. civil engring., 1990-96; sr. cons. Dames & Moore, Atlanta, 1990-95; pres. New Fields, Inc., Atlanta, 1995—. NSF vis. scientist Ctr. Geostats., Paris Sch. of Mines, 1987-88; expert mem. ASTM, EPA, U.S. Geol. Survey, Dept. Def. Geostats. Standardization Com., 1991-96. Co-author: Ground Water, 1991; contbr. articles to profl. publs., chpts. to books., also numerous reports, papers in field. Mem. ASCE (award 1991, chmn. nat. ground water hydrology 1991, chmn. task com. on geostatis. techniques in geohydrology 1987-89, sec. water resources com. Ga. sect. 1988, spl. session organizer 1989, 90, contact mem. task com. 1988-90, symposium organizer 1991), Am. Geophys. Union (assoc. editor Water Resources Rsch. 1989-94), Internat. Water Resources Assn., Am. Water Resources Assn., N.Am. Coun. on Geostats., Internat. Geostatis. Assn., Phi Beta Kappa, Tau Beta Pi, Chi Epsilon, Sigma Chi. Office: Newfields Inc 1349 W Peachtree St NW Ste 2000 Atlanta GA 30309-2926 Office Phone: 404-347-9050. Business E-Mail: srouhani@newfields.com.

ROUKEMA, MARGARET SCAFATI, congresswoman; b. West Orange, NJ, Sept. 19, 1929; d. Claude Thomas and Margaret (D'Alessio) Scafati; m. Richard W. Roukema, Aug. 23, 1951; children: Margaret, Todd (dec.), Gregory. BA with honors in History and Polit. Sci, Montclair State Coll., 1951, postgrad. in history and guidance, 1951-53; postgrad. program in city and regional planning, Rutgers U., 1975. Tchr. history, govt., public schs., Livingston and Ridgewood, N.J., 1951-55; mem. U.S. Congress from 7th

N.J. dist., Washington, 1981—83, U.S. Congress from 5th N.J. dist., Washington, 1983—2003; vice chair fin. svcs. com., chair housing and community opportunity subcom.; mem. banking com., edn. and the workforce com. Vice pres. Ridgewood Bd. Edn., 1970-73; bd. dirs., co-founder Ridgewood Sr. Citizens Housing Corp.; chairwoman Fin. Inst. and Consumer Credit Sub. Com. U.S. Congress; sponcer Family Med. Leave U.S. Congress; lectr. Rutgers Univ. Trustee Spring House, Paramus, N.J.; trustee Leukemia Soc. No. N.J., Family Counseling Service for Ridgewood and Vicinity; mem. Bergen County (N.J.) Republican Com.; NW Bergen County campaign mgr. for gubernatorial candidate Tom Kean, 1977; bd. mem. Children's Aid and Family Svcs., The Red Cross, Ramapo Coll. Mem. Bus. and Profl. Women's Orgn. Clubs: Coll. of Ridgewood, Ridgewood Rep. Republican. *I have served in several roles in my life. Wife, mother, teacher, public servant. All are personally rewarding; each affords the opportunity to help others in need and to enrich the lives of those around you. As a member of Congress, I find the most rewards are in the knowledge that I can truly make a difference and improve the lives of thousands of people. The challenges are frequently insurmountable, but the rewards are incalculable.*

ROULAC, STEPHEN E., real estate consultant; b. San Francisco, Aug. 15, 1945; s. Phil Williams and Elizabeth (Young) R.; children: Arthur, Fiona. BA, Pomona Coll., 1967; MBA with distinction, Harvard Grad. Sch. Bus. Administrn., 1970; JD, U. Calif., Berkeley, 1976; PhD, Stanford U., 1978. CPA, Hawaii. Asst. constrn. supt., foreman, adminstr. Roulac Constrn. Co., Pasadena, Calif., 1963-66; rsch. asst. Econs. Rsch. Assocs., LA, 1966-67; assoc. economist Urbanomics Rsch. Assocs., Claremont, Calif., 1967; acquisition auditor Litton Industries Inc., Chgo., Beverly Hills, 1967-68; tax cons. Lybrand, Ross Bros. and Montgomery, LA, 1968; cons. to constrn. group and corp. planning dept. Owens-Corning Fiberglas Corp., Toledo, 1969-70; CEO Questor Assocs., San Francisco, 1972-83; chmn. nat. mgmt. adv. svcs. Kenneth Leventhal & Co., 1983-84; pres. Stephen E. Roulac & Co., 1985-86; mng. ptnr. Roulac Group of Deloitte Haskins & Sells (Deloitte & Touche), 1987-91; CEO The Roulac Group, Larkspur, Calif., 1992—. Strategic fin. econ. and transactions cons. Roulac Capitol Mkt. Strategies, Roulac Capitol Flows; expert witness, preparer econ. analyses for legal matters including civil trial of Irvine Co., Jewell et. al. vs. Bank of Am., Tchrs. vs. Olympia & York, Calif. Legis., Calif. Corps. Dept., Midwest Securities Commrs. Assn., Nat. Assn. Securities Dealers, SEC, Dept. of Labor, HUD; advisor to investment arm of Asian country, Calif. Pub. Employees Retirement System, U.S. Dept. Labor, numerous others; adj. prof. Tex. A&M U., 1986, U. Chgo., 1985, UCLA, 1983-84, Stanford Grad. Sch. Bus., 1970-79, Pacific Coast Banking Sch., 1978, Hastings Coll. Law, 1977-78, U. Calif., Berkeley, 1972-77, Calif. State U., 1970-71, Northeastern U., 1969-70; keynote speaker, instr. continuing edn. sessions, program chmn., corps., orgns. Author: Real Estate Syndications Digest: Principles and Applications, 1972, Case Studies in Property Development, 1973, Syndication Landmarks, 1974, Tax Shelter Sale-Leaseback Financing: The Economic Realities, 1976, Modern Real Estate Investment: An Institutional Approach, 1976, (with Sherman Maisel) Real Estate Investment and Finance, 1976 (1976 Bus. Book of Yr. The Libr. Jour.); editor-in-chief, pub. Calif. Bicyclist, 1988-95, Tex. Bicyclist, 1989-94, Roulac's Strategic Real Estate, 1979-89; columnist Forbes, 1983, 84, 87, 92, 93, Intuition Network, Ctr Real Estate Rsch. Nortwestern U., Nat. Bureau Real Estate Rsch., New Leaders, World 2000, NACORE/ARES Corp. Rsch. Found., Mystery Sch.; mem. editorial adv. bd. Am. Real Estate and Urban Econs. Assn. Jour., 1977-81, Housing Devel. Reporter, 1978-80, Fin. Edn. Jour., 1976-70, Jour. Housing Rsch., 1996—, Jour. Real Estated Edn. and Practice, 1996—, Jour. Real Estate Lit., 1996—, Jour. Property Valuation and Investment, 1992—, Real Estate Workouts and Asset Mgmt., 1992—; assoc. editor Real Estate Rev., 1993—; editor Jour. Real Estate Rsch., 1992—; contbg. editor Real Estate Law Jour., 1973-78, Real Estate Rev., 1973-75; spl. issue editor Calif. Mgmt. Rev., 1976; editor: Real Estate Syndication Digest, 1971-72, Notable Syndications Sourcebook, 1972, Real Estate Securities and Syndication: A Workbook, 1973, Due Diligence in Real Estate Transactions, 1974, Real Estate Venture Analysis, 1974, Real Estate Securities Regulation Sourcebook, 1975, Questor Real Estate Investment Manager Profiles, 1982, Questor Real Estate Securities Yearbook, 1980-85, Retail Giants and Real Estate, 1986, Roulac's Top Real Estate Brokers, 1984-88, (monograph) Ethics in Real Estate; contbr. articles to profl. jours., newspapers; cassettes; frequent appearer on TV shows including MacNeil/Lehrer Newshour, 1986, Cable News Network, 1987, ABC TV, 1987, KCBS Radio, 1986, WABC Radio, Dallas, 1986. Mem. real estate adv. com. to Calif. Commr. Corps., 1973, Calif. Corp. Commr.'s Blue Ribbon Com. on Projections and Track Records, 1973-74; mem. adv. bd. Nat. Bicycle Month, League of Am. Wheelmen, Ctr. for Real Estate Rsch. Kellogg Grad. Sch. Mgmt., Northwestern U. Named Highest Instr. Student Teaching Evaluations, Schs. Bus. Adminstrn., U. Calif., Berkeley, 1975-76; named to Pomona Coll. Athletic Hall of Fame, 1981; W.T. Grant fellow Harvard U., 1969-70,; George F. Baker scholar Harvard Grad. Sch. Bus. Adminstrn., 1970; Stanford U. Grad. Sch. Bus. fellow, 1970-71. Mem. Strategic Mgmt. Soc., Am. Acad. Mgmt., Am. Fin. Assn., Am. Planning Assn, European Real Estate Soc., Internat. Real Estate Soc., Inst. Mgmt. Cons., ISSSEEM, Soc. Sci. Exploration, Am. Real Estate and Urban Econs. Assn., Intuition Network (bd. dirs.), World Future Soc. (exec. com. and adv. bd. World 2000), Am. Econ. Assn., Am. Real Estate Soc. (pres. 1995-96, award for best paper presented in ann. meeting, 1995, 96), Noetic Soc., Nat. Bur. Real Estate Rsch. (founder, bd. dirs.), Harvard Club N.Y., L.A. Adventures Club. Avocations: art, antiquarian books, reading, bicycling. Office: The Roulac Group 709 5th Ave San Rafael CA 94901-3202

ROULEAU, R. MICHAEL, retail executive; Co-founder, pres. Office Warehouse; exec. v.p. store ops. Lowe's, 1992-95, pres. contractor yard divsn., 1995-96; CEO Michaels Stores, Inc., Irving, Tex., 1996—, pres., 1997—. Office: Michaels Stores Inc 8000 Bent Branch Dr Irving TX 75063

ROULY, ELLIE ARCENEAUX, dancer, educator; b. New Iberia, La., Sept. 18, 1977; d. James and Paula Arceneaux; m. Karl Anthony Rouly, June 1, 2002; 1 child, Karrigan Elizabeth Andrea'. BA in Elem. Edn., U. La., Lafayette, 2001. Presch. tchr. ABC 123's Presch. Daycare, New Iberia, La., 1995—2001; dir., choreographer Dance Connection, 1998—; tchr. VB Glencoe Charter Sch., Franklin, 2001—. Lt. Mystic Krewe de Fou of Iberia, 1998. Scholar, Ladies Aux. Club, 1995. Office: VB Glencoe Charter School 4491 La 83 Franklin LA 70538 Home Phone: 337-924-8003; Office Phone: 337-923-6900.

ROUMAIN, DANIEL BERNARD, composer, violinist; b. 1974; Music dir. Bill T. Jones/Arnie Zane Dance. Co., NYC; asst. composer-in-residence Orch. St. Luke's, NYC; artist-in-residence Seattle Theatre Group; band leader DBR & The Mission, 2003—. Composer: Voodoo Violin Concerto No. 1, 2002, A Civil Rights Reader, 24 Bits: Hip Hop Studies & Etudes, Call Them All: Fantasy Projections for Violin, Laptop & Orch., 2006, Seen & Heard: Philip Glass & DBR Together on Stage, Screen & in Sound, Sonata for Violin & Turntables, 2006, One Loss Plus. Named one of 40 Under 40, Crain's NY Bus., 2007. Office: DBR Music Prodns LLC 14th Fl 220 W 42nd St New York NY 10036 Office Phone: 917-421-5552. E-mail: music@dbrmusic.com. *

ROUMAN, JAMES CHRIST, anesthesiologist; b. Tomahawk, Wis., May 15, 1927; s. Christ John Rouman and Soteria Dendes. BS, Northwestern U., Evanston, Ill., 1949; MD, Northwestern U., Chgo., 1953. Diplomate An. Bd. Anesthesiology. Intern Meml. Hermann-Tex. Med. Ctr., Houston, 1953—54; resident Hartford Hosp./McGill U., Conn., 1956—59; attending staff Hartford Hosp., 1959—92; asst. prof. U. Conn., Sch. Medicine, Farmington, 1978—92. Author: (novels) Underwater Deaths, 2006. With USN, 1945—47. Greek Orthodox.

ROUMAN, JOHN CHRIST, classics educator; b. Tomahawk, Wis., May 1, 1926; s. Christ and Soteria (Dedes) R. BA in Greek, Carleton Coll., 1950; MA in Greek, Columbia U., 1951; student, Rutgers U., 1951-53, U. Kiel, Germany, 1956-57, U. Minn., Mpls., 1959-60; PhD in Classics, U. Wis., 1965. German tchr. Seton Hall Preparatory Sch., South Orange, NJ, 1954-56; ancient history tchr. Malverne (N.Y.) High Sch., 1957-59; tchg. asst. in ancient history U. Wis., Madison, 1960-61, rsch. asst. in ancient history, 1961-65; rsch. asst. in Greek epigraphy Inst. Advanced Study, Princeton, NJ, 1962-63; asst. prof. classics U. N.H., Durham, 1965-71, assoc. prof., 1971-91, prof., 1991—, prof. classics emeritus, 1999, co-chmn. Spanish and classics depts., mem. adv. bd. Prof. John C. Rouman classical lectr. series, 1997—. Examiner N.H. State Bd. Edn. in Latin and Greek, 1979-80; judge Warren H. Held Jr. Exam-Contests in Latin and Mythology, 1988—; cons. Nat. Classical Greek Examination, 1980; presenter, lectr. in field; mem. adv. bd. Christos and Mary Papoutsy Disting. Endowed Chair in Bus. Ethics, N.H. Coll./So. N.H. U., 2000—03; exec. bd. Hellenic Soc. PAIDEIA, NH, 2001. Active Colovos Rd. Com., 1981-82. With USN, 1944-46. Fulbright scholar U. Kiel, 1956-57; recipient Disting. Tchg. award U. N.H. Alumni Assn., 1985, Pericles award Am. Hellenic Ednl. Progressive Assn. and Daus. of Penelope, 1993, Profile of Svc. award U. N.H. Aumni Assn., 2000; Prof. John C. Rouman Classical Lecture Series named in his honor. Mem. Am. Classical League (rep. to TCNE at ann. meeting 1978, mem. fin. com. 1981-82, treas. 1982-83, contbg. editor newsletter, 2005—), Am. Philol. Assn. (Nat. Excellence in Tchg. Classics award, 1991), Archaeol. Inst. Am., Classical Assn. Can., Classical Assn. New Eng. (mem. exec. com. at-large 1981-84, mem. nominating com. 1983-84, 86-87, pres. 1987-88, Barlow-Beach award 1991, mem. ad hoc com. on elections and appointments), Medieval Acad. Am., Modern Greek Studies Assn., Nat. Assn. Advisors Health Professions, NH Classical Assn. (mem. exec. com. 1965—, chair nominating com. 1986—), Strafford County Greco-Roman Found. (pres. 1978—), Vergilian Soc. Am., Carleton Coll. Alumni Assn. (Alumni award for Dist. Achievement 2000), Phi Kappa Theta (faculty advisor, 1982—, chmn. nat. bd., 1993-94, nat. found. 1993—, Man of Achievement award 2000, Chpt. Advisor award 2002). Independent. Greek Orthodox. Personal E-mail: Jrouman@comcast.net.

ROUMANI-DENN, VIVIENNE RACHEL, library and information scientist, consultant; d. Josef and Elisa Tammam Roumani; m. Morton M. Denn; children: Aryeh B. Bourkoff, Dania T. Matheos, Natan D. Bourkoff. BA, Simmons Coll., Boston, 1971; MLS, U. Md., College Park, 1984; M in Adminstrv. Sci., Johns Hopkins U., Balt., 1990. Head interlibrary loan Libr. of Congress, Washington, 1989—90; head interlibrary loan and document delivery svcs. U. Calif., Berkeley, 1990—93, earth scis. and maps libr., 1993—97, Judaica libr., 1997—99; founding dir. libr. and archives Am. Sephardi Fedn., NYC, 1999—2000, exec. dir., 2000—03; pres. VR Consulting, NYC, 2003—. Author: (online publication) The Last Jews of Libya, 1999, (documentary film), 2006; contbr. chapters to books, articles to profl. jours. Exec. bd. Oakland (Calif.) Hebrew Day Sch., 1996—99, U. Calif. Berkeley Hillel, 1996—99, Ctr. for Jewish Living and Learning, Berkeley, 1996—99, Jewish Inst. Pitigliano, Italy, Washington, 2000, Friends of Gerona, Spain, NYC, 2000—00. Office: VR Consulting 140 Riverside Dr New York NY 10024 Office Phone: 917-957-4132. Business E-Mail: vroumani@nyc.rr.com.

ROUNDS, MIKE (MARION MICHAEL ROUNDS), governor; b. Huron, SD, Oct. 24, 1954; m. Jean Vedvei, 1978; children: Christopher, Lindsay, Brian, Carrie, John. BS in Polit. Sci., SD State U., Brookings, 1977. Ptnr. Fischer, Rounds & Assocs., Inc.; mem. SD State Senate from Dist. 24, 1991—2002, minority whip, 1993—94, majority leader, 1995—2002; gov. State of S.D., Pierre, 2003—. Bd. pres. Oahe YMCA; v.p. Home and Sch. Assn. St. Joseph Sch.; pres. Pierre-Ft. Pierre Exch. Club. Mem.: Ducks Unlimited, Knights of Columbus, Pierre Elks Lodge. Republican. Roman Catholic. Avocations: racquetball, hunting, boating, camping. Office: Office of Gov 500 E Capitol Ave Pierre SD 57501 Office Phone: 605-773-3212. Office Fax: 605-773-5844. *

ROUNICK, JACK A., lawyer, clothing retail executive; b. Phila., June 5, 1935; s. Philip and Nettie (Brownstein) Rounick; m. Noreen A. Garrigan, Sept. 4, 1970; children: Ellen, Eric, Amy, Michelle. BBA, U. Mich., Ann Arbor, 1956; JD, U. Pa., Phila., 1959. Bar: Pa. 1960, US Dist. Ct. (ea. dist. Pa.) 1960. Ptnr. Israelit & Rounick, 1960-67, Moss & Rounick, 1968-69, Moss, Rounick & Hurowitz, Norristown, Pa., 1969-72, Moss & Rounick, Norristown, 1972-73, Pechner, Dorfman, Wolffe, Rounick and Cabot, Norristown, 1973-87; spl. asst. atty. gen., 1963-71; v.p., gen. counsel Martin Lawrence Ltd. Edits., Inc., 1987-93, dir., 1984—95; asst. sec., dir. Deb Shops, Inc., 1974—; counsel to firm Wolf Block, Schorr & Solis-Cohen LLP, 1997—2006; of counsel Flamm, Boroff & Bacine, P.C., Blue Bell, Pa., 2006—. Author: Pa. Matrimonial Practice, 6 vols., 1982; editor: Pa. Family Lawyer, 1980—87; bd. editors Family Adv. Fin. chmn. Pa. Young Reps., 1964—66, treas., 1966—68, chmn., 1968—70. Named one of Top 100 Attys., Worth mag., 2005; recipient Boss of Yr. award, Montgomery County Legal Secs. Assn., 1970, cert. of appreciation, Pa. Bar Inst., 1980. Fellow: Am. Acad. Matrimonial Lawyers (pres. Pa. chpt. 1982—84, gov. 1983—85, v.p. 1985—87, chmn. bd. rev. 1997—98), Internat. Acad. Matrimonial Lawyers; mem.: FLS, ABA (coun. family law sect. 1982—87, coun. 2000—03), Am. Coll. Family Trial Lawyers (diplomate), Scope and Correlation Com. (chmn. 2005—06), Family Adv. (bd. editors), Montgomery Bar Assn., Pa. Bar Assn. (past chmn. family law sect. 1978—80, Spl. Achievement award 1979—80), Friends of Hebrew U. (bd. dirs. 1987—93, nat. coun. trustees 1987—93, bd. trustees 1987—2006, pres. Phila. chpt. 1988—91, v.p. 1990—91). Republican. Jewish. Office: Flamm Boroff & Bacine PC 794 Penllyn Pike Blue Bell PA 19422-1669 Office Phone: 267-419-1504. Office Fax: 267-419-1560. Business E-Mail: jarounick@flammlaw.com.

ROUNSAVILLE, KEITH EUGENE, lawyer; b. Ancon, Panama, Aug. 6, 1945; s. William Russell Rounsaville and Dorothy Naletta Chambers; m. Linda Ann White, Feb. 14, 1976 (div. Oct. 1, 1994); m. Karla Rae Spaulding, May 24, 2000; children: Keith Chambers, David William. BA with honors, Yale U., 1967; JD cum laude, Columbia U., 1970. Cert.: Fla. Bar (in antitrust and trade regulation), bar: Calif. 1971, DC 1972, Fla. 1974. Assoc. O'Melveny & Myers LLP, LA, 1970; shareholder Trenam, Kemker, Scharf, Barkin, Frye, O'Neill & Mullis, P.A., Tampa, Fla., 1974—2000, Stearns Weaver Miller Alhadeff & Sitterson, P.A., Tampa, 2000—02, Litchford & Christopher, P.A., Orlando, 2007—; shareholder, chmn. antitrust dept. Akerman Senterfitt, Orlando and Tampa, Fla., 2002—06. Chmn. Rough Riders dist., Gulf Ridge coun. Boy Scouts Am., Tampa, 1991—92, dist. commr., 1990—91; pres. Rotary Club of Tampa Bay, Tampa, 1994—95, sec., 1993—94. Capt. JAGC USMC, 1971—73, Vietnam. Named Rotarian of the Yr., Rotary Club of Tampa Bay, 1992; named one of America's Leading Lawyers Bus., Antitrust Law, Chambers USA, 2003—07, The Best Lawyers in Am. Antitrust Law, Fla., 2006, 2007, Fla. Super Lawyers Antitrust Law, 2006, 2007; recipient Dist. award of Merit, Boy Scouts Am., 1991; Harlan Fiske Stone scholar, Columbia U. Sch. of Law. Mem.: ABA (mem. Sherman Act com. sect. antitrust law 1974), Fla. Bar (chmn. and vice chmn. antitrust com. 1984—92, exec. coun., bus. law sect. 1984—92, chair antitrust law and trade cert. com. 2006—), Am. Law Inst. Avocations: hiking, international travel. Office: Litchford & Christopher PA 390 N Orange Ave Ste 2200 Orlando FL 32801 Office Phone: 407-422-6600. Office Fax: 407-841-0325. Business E-Mail: krounsaville@litchfordchristopher.com.

ROUNTREE, ASA, lawyer; b. Birmingham, Ala., Aug. 9, 1927; s. John Asa and Cherokee Jemison (Van de Graaff) Rountree; m. Elizabeth Rhodes Blue, Aug. 11, 1951 (dec.); m. Helen Hill Updike, Oct. 10, 1998. AB, U. Ala., 1949; LLB, Harvard U., 1954. Bar: Ala. 1954, U.S. Dist. Ct. (no. dist.) Ala. 1954, U.S. Ct. Appeals (5th cir.) 1955, N.Y. 1962, U.S. Dist. Ct. (so. dist.) N.Y. 1963, U.S. Ct. Appeals (2d cir.) 1963, U.S. Supreme Ct. 1972. Assoc. Cabaniss & Johnston, Birmingham, Ala., 1954-60, ptnr., 1960-62; assoc. Debevoise & Plimpton, NYC, 1962-63, ptnr., 1963-91; spl. counsel Maynard, Cooper, & Gale, P.C., Birmingham, 1991—2006. Bd. dirs. U. Ala. Law Sch. Found. With US Army, 1945—46, lt. US Army, 1951—53. Mem.: ABA (chmn. litig. sect. 1980—81), Am. Coll. Trial Lawyers, Am. Law Inst., Assn. Bar City of N.Y., N.Y. State Bar Assn., Ala. Bar Assn., Am. Bar Found., Mountain Brook Club (Birmingham), River Club (N.Y.C.). Episcopalian. Home: 8 Cross Creek Dr Birmingham AL 35213

ROUPE, JAMES PAUL, accountant; b. Havre de Grace, Md., Apr. 20, 1957; s. Paul Clyde and Shirley Louise (Trivette) R. AA, Harford C.C., Bel Air, Md., 1977; BS, Towson State U., 1979. CPA, Md. Mgmt. asst. Loyola Fed. Savings and Loan, Balt., 1979—81; asst. treas. Legum Chevrolet-Nissan, Balt., 1983—89; contr. Bob Bell Chevrolet/Nissan, Inc., Balt., 1989—92, corp. sec.-treas., 1992—, Bob Bell Chevrolet of Bel Air Inc., 1992—, Bob Bell of Upper Marlboro, LLC, 1992—95, Robel, LLC, 2007—. Recipient Bus. Mgmt. Excellence award Nissan Motor Corp., 1990-2006. Mem. AICPA, Md. Assn. CPAs, Chevrolet Coun. Bus. Acctg. Mgrs. Republican. Baptist. Office: Bob Bell Chevrolet Nissan 7900 Eastern Blvd Baltimore MD 21224-2125

ROURKE, DIANE MCLAUGHLIN, librarian; d. Frank and Mary McLaughlin; m. Otto Porter Ream IV; children: Sunny Ream Spillane, Sarah Ream Gable. BA in English, U. Miami, Coral Gables, Fla., 1966; MS in Libr. Sci., Fla. State U., Tallahassee, 1968. Children's libr., br. libr. Miami Dade Pub. Libr., 1968—69; children's libr. Surfside Libr., Miami Beach, 1972; med. libr., mgr. libr. svcs. Bapt. Hosp., Miami, 1976—95; dir. libr. svcs. Bapt. Health, 1995—. Founding chair Miami Health Sci. Libr. Consortium, 1978—79; cons. and presenter in field. Mem.: Med. Libr. Assn. Democrat. Episcopalian. Avocations: reading, singing, classical music, gardening. Home: 9641 SW 77 Ave 204D Miami FL 33156 Office: South Miami Hospital Medical Library 6200 SW 73 St Miami FL 33143

ROURKE, MICKEY (PHILIP ANDRE ROURKE JR.), actor; b. Schenectady, NY, Sept. 16, 1956; m. Debra Feuer, 1981 (div. 1989); m. Carre Otis, June 26, 1992 (div. Dec. 1998). Profl. boxer, 1991—95; gym owner Shapiro, West Hollywood. Actor (films) including 1941, 1979, Heaven's Gate, 1980, Fade to Black, 1980, Body Heat, 1981, Diner, 1982 (Nat. Soc. of Film Critics award best supporting actor 1982), Rumblefish, 1983, The Pope of Greenwich Village, 1984, Year of the Dragon, 1985, Eureka, 1985, 9 1/2 Weeks, 1985, Angel Heart, 1987, A Prayer for the Dying, 1987, Barfly, 1987, Homeboy (also screenwriter), 1988, Johnny Handsome, 1989, Wild Orchid, 1990, The Desperate Hours, 1990, Harley Davidson and the Marlboro Man, 1991, White Sands, 1992, F.T.W., 1994, Fall Time, 1995, Exit in Red, 1996, Bullets, 1996, The Rainmaker, 1997, Love in Paris, 1997, Double Team, 1997, Buffalo '66, 1997, Thursday, 1998, Shergar, 1999, Shades, 1999, Out in Fifty, 1999, The Animal Factory, 2000, Get Carter, 2000, The Pledge, 2001, Spun, 2002, Masked and Anonymous, 2003, Once Upon a Time in Mexico, 2003, Man on Fire, 2004, Sin City, 2005, Domino, 2005; (TV movies) Act of Love, 1980, City in Fear, 1980, Rape and Marriage: The Rideout Case, 1980, Thicker Than Blood, 1998. Avocation: motorcycling.

ROUS, STEPHEN NORMAN, urologist, educator; b. NYC, Nov. 1, 1931; s. David H. and Luba (Margulies) R.; m. Margot Woolfolk, Nov. 12, 1966; children: Benjamin, David. AB, Amherst Coll., 1952; MD, N.Y. Med. Coll., 1956; MS, U. Minn., 1963. Diplomate: Am. Bd. Urology. Intern Phila. Gen. Hosp., 1956-57, resident, 1959-60, Flower-Fifth Ave. and Met. Hosp., NYC, 1957-59, Mayo Clinic, Rochester, Minn., 1960-63; practice medicine specializing in urology San Francisco, 1963-68; assoc. prof. urology N.Y. Med. Coll., NYC, 1968-72, assoc. dean, 1970-72; prof. surgery, chief div. urology Mich. State U., East Lansing, 1972-75; prof., chmn. dept. urology Med. U. S.C., Charleston, 1975-88; urologist-in-chief Med. U. S.C. and County hosps., Charleston, 1975-88; editorial dir. Norton Med. Books div. W.W. Norton and Co., 1988-94, editorial cons., 1994—; clin. prof. surgery Uniformed Svcs. U. of Health Scis., Bethesda, Md., 1992-2001; clin. prof. surgery urology Brown U. Med. Sch., 2006—. Adj. prof. urology Med. U. S.C., 1988-99, prof. emeritus, 1999—; adj. prof. surgery Dartmouth Med. Sch., 1988-91, prof. surgery (urology), 1991-2001, prof. surgery emeritus, 2001—; staff urologist Dartmouth-Hitchcock Med. Ctr., 1991-99; cons. urologist Saginaw VA Hosp., 1971-75, Charleston VA Hosp., 1975-88; hon. cons. St. Peter's Hosp., London, 1981-82; sr. vis. fellow Inst. Urology, London, 1981-82; mil. cons. in urology USAF Surgeon Gen., 1982-85; chmn. alumni devel. com. Mayo Clinic, 1979-82; hon. staff The Exeter Hosp., N.H., 1988—; nat. bd. visitors N.Y. Med. Coll., 1988-97; chief urology VA Med. Ctr., White River Junction, Vt., 1991-2001; mem. reparative justice bd. Vt. Dept. Corrections, 2004; urologist VA Med. Ctr., Providence, 2005— Author: Understanding Urology, 1973, Urology in Primary Care, 1976, Spanish edit., 1978, Russian edit., 1979, Urology: A Core Textbook, 1985, 2d edit., 1996, The Prostate Book, 1988, latest rev. edit., 2001, (with Judge Hiller B. Zobel) Doctors and the Law: Defendants and Expert Witnesses, 1993, (with Dr. Pamela Ellsworth) The Little Black Book of Urology, 2001; editor Urology Ann., 1987-97, Stone Disease: Diagnosis and Management, 1987; mem. editl. bd. Mil. Medicine, 1984-94; contbr. articles to med. jours. Mem. East Lansing (Mich.) Planning Commn., 1974-75; vestryman, jr. warden All Saints Episcopal Ch., East Lansing, 1973-75, lay reader, mem. diocesan com. on continuing edn., 1975-86; vestryman St. Michael's Episc. Ch., 1979-82, Charleston, S.C., chmn. every mem. canvas, 1979-80, chmn. lay readers, 1983-86; mem. fin. com., lay reader Christ Episc. Ch., Exeter, N.H., 1989-91; lector St. Thomas Episc. Ch., Hanover, N.H., 1991-96, vestryman, 1992-96, stewardship chmn., 1992-94; jr. warden 1994-96; chalicist, lector, del. to diocesan conv. Trinity Ch., Newport, R.I, 2006—; mem. selectman's alt. Hampton Falls Planning Bd., 1989-91; alt. mem. Zoning Bd. Adjustment, Hanover, 1997-2000; bd. trustees, Nat. Hypertension Assn., N.Y.C., 20010¼; bd. dirs. Med. Sci. Techs. Inc., Newport News, Va., 2001—. Col. USAFR, 1981-85, col. USAR, 1985-2000, col. AUS, ret., 2001—. Recipient "A" designator in urology, U.S. Army Surgeon Gen., 1986. Fellow ACS, Am. Acad. Pediatrics; mem. AMA, Soc. Univ. Urologists, Internat. Soc. Urology, Am. Urol. Assn., Nat. Urologic Forum, Soc. Pediatric Urology, Brit. Assn. Urol. Surgeons, German Urol. Assn. (hon.), English Speaking Union (v.p. Newport County br. 2006—), Mayo Alumni Assn. (v.p. 1979-81, pres. 1983-85), Army and Navy Club (Washington), Lotos Club (N.Y.C.), Dartmouth Club of N.Y.C., Brown U. Faculty Club (bd. mgrs. 2006—), Sigma Xi, Alpha Omega Alpha. Home: 421 Bellevue Ave #2A Newport RI 02840 Personal E-mail: stephen.n.rous@dartmouth.edu.

ROUSE, CHRISTOPHER CHAPMAN, III, composer, educator; b. Balt., Feb. 15, 1949; s. Christopher Chapman Jr. and Margery (Harper) Rouse; m. Ann Jensen, Aug. 28, 1983; children: Jillian, Alexandra, Adrian 1 stepchild, Angela. MusB, Oberlin Conservatory, 1971; MFA, DMA, Cornell U., 1977; DMus (hon.), Oberlin Coll., 1996, SUNY, Geneseo, 2000. Asst. prof. composition U. Mich., Ann Arbor, 1978—81, Eastman Sch. Music, Rochester, NY, 1981—85, assoc. prof. composition,

1985—91, prof. composition, 1991—2002; mem. faculty Juilliard Sch., 1997—. Composer-in-residence Balt. Symphony Orch., 1986—89, Schleswig Holstein Festival, 1989, Helsinki Bienniale, 1997, Tanglewood Music Ctr., 1997, Pacific Music Festival, 1998, Aspen Music Festival, 1999—; writer numerous musical subjects; historian rock music. Composer for numerous renowned soloists and ensembles, including Yo-Yo Ma, Evelyn Glennie, Emanuel Ax, Dawn Upshaw, Cho-Liang Lin, Charles Castleman, James VanDemark, Jan de Gaetani, Leslie Guinn, Sharon Isbin, Carol Wincenc, William Albright, Soc. New Music, Blackearth Percussion Group, Boston Pops, Boston Musica Viva, Aspen Music Festival, Chamber Music Soc. Lincoln Ctr., N.Y. Internat. Festival of Arts, Chamber Music Am., New Eng. Conservatory Music, Nonesuch Records, orchestral works programmed by Berlin, Helsinki, Stockholm, NYC, Israel, Netherlands, Buffalo, L.A., Rochester Philharms., Orch. Nat. de France, Orch. de Paris, Residentie, Concertgebouw, Vienna & Zurich Tonhalle, New Zealand, Philharmonia, also Vienna, BBC, Berlin, Montreal, Chgo., Boston, St. Louis, Detroit, Balt., Nat., Pitts., Houston, Denver, Milw., Cleve., Minn., Phila., Oakland, Cin., Atlanta, N.J., Utah, Indpls., Memphis, San Francisco, Dallas, Göteboro U., Bournemouth symphony orchs, also The Netherlands, Finnish, Frankfurt, Moscow, Austrian, Flemish, BBC and NHK Tokyo Radio Orchs., commd. composer Atlanta Symphony, Phila. Orch., N.Y. Philharm., L.A. Philharm., Balt. Symphony, Houston Symphony, Minn. Orch., London Symphony, Cleve. Orch., Detroit Symphony, St. Louis Symphony, Boston Pops, Rochester Philharm., Cleve. Quartet, NYC Ballet. Recipient awards, Guggenheim Found., League Composers/ISCM, NEA, Rockefeller Found., Am. Music Ctr., Warner Bros. Record Co., Koussevitzky Found., BMI and Pitney Bowes, Friedheim 1st prize, Kennedy Ctr., 1988, Pulitzer prize for music, 1993, Grammy award, 2002. Mem.: Am. Acad. Arts and Letters (Acad. award 1993). Office: Juilliard Sch 60 Lincoln Center Plz New York NY 10023

ROUSE, DORIS JANE, physiologist, research scientist; b. Greensboro, NC, Oct. 3, 1948; d. Welby Corbett and Nadia Elizabeth (Grainger) R.; m. Blake Shaw Wilson, Jan. 6, 1974; children: Nadia Jacqueline, Blair Elizabeth. BA in Chemistry, Duke U., Durham, NC, 1970, PhD in Physiology and Pharmacology, 1980. Tchr. sci. Peace Corps, Tugbake, Liberia, 1970-71; rsch scientist Burroughs Wellcome Co., Rsch. Triangle Park, NC, 1971-76; sr. physiologist Rsch. Triangle Inst., Durham, 1976-83, ctr. dir., 1980-2000, also dir. NASA tech. application team, 1980-2000, dir. TB Tech. Transfer Program, 1999—, dir. Global Health, 2001—; portfolio project mgr. Global Alliance for Tb Drug Devel., 2002—. Adminstr. ANSI Tech. Adv. Group for Wheelchairs, NYC, 1982-86; adj. asst. prof. U. NC Sch. Medicine, 1983-92; chair Instl. Rev. Bd., Profl. Devel. Award com., chair salary com. Rsch. Triangle Inst.; mem. adv. bd. Assistive Tech. Rsch. Ctr., 1994-96; mem. global health adv. com., U. NC, Chapel Hill, 2007-, mem. bd. dirs. ImaGYN, 2007-. Mem. adv. bd. Assn. Retarded Citizens, Arlington, Tex., 1981—88, Western Gerontology Soc., San Francisco, 1982—85; bd. dirs. Simon Found., Chgo., 1983—95; mem. spl. rev. com. small bus. applications Nat. Forum on Tech. and Aging; mem. fund steering com. Academy Venture, 2000—04. Recipient Group Achievement award NASA, 1979, 2000, President's award, RTI, 2003, 05, 06. Mem.: Am. Soc. Microbiology, Assn. Fed. Tech. Transfer Execs., Licensing Execs. Soc., Rehab. Engring. Soc. N.Am. (chmn. wheelchair com. 1981—86). Home: 2410 Wrightwood Ave Durham NC 27705-5802 Office: Research Triangle Inst PO Box 12194 Durham NC 27709-2194 Office Phone: 919-541-6980. Personal E-mail: drouse@nc.rr.com. Business E-Mail: rouse@rti.org.

ROUSE, LEO E., dean, dental educator; Grad., Howard U. Coll. Dentistry, 1973; postgrad. studies in comprehensive dentistry, Watson Army Hosp., 1976—78. Assoc. dean clinical affairs Coll. Dentistry, Howard U., chmn. dept. clinical dentistry, interim dean, 2003—04, dean, 2004—. Examiner cons. and mem. exam. devel. com. N.E. Regional Bd. Dental Examiners. With US Army, 1972—97, comdr. and COO US Army, 1995—97, US Army Dental Command, ret. col., 1997—. Recipient Alumni Achievement award, Howard U. Coll. Dentistry, 1997. Fellow: Am. Coll. Dentists; mem.: ADA, Am. Assn. Dental Examiners, Am. Dental Edn. Assn., Nat. Dental Assn., Omicron Kappa Upsilon. Office: Howard Univ Coll Dentistry 600 W St NW Washington DC 20059 Office Phone: 202-806-0440. Business E-Mail: lrouse@howard.edu.

ROUSE, RICHARD HUNTER, historian, educator; b. Boston, Aug. 14, 1933; s. Hunter and Dorothee (Hüsmert) R.; m. Mary L. Ames, Sept. 7, 1959; children: Thomas, Andrew, Jonathan. BA, State U. Iowa, 1955; MA, U. Chgo., 1957; PhD, Cornell U., 1963. Mem. faculty UCLA, 1963—, prof. history, 1975—. Assoc. dir. Ctr. Medieval and Renaissance Studies, 1966-67, acting dir., 1967-68; dir. Summer Inst. in Paleography, 1978, chair grad. coun., 1989-90; adv. bd. Hill Monastic Microfilm Libr., St. John's U., Collegeville, Minn., Ambrosiana Microfilm Library, Notre Dame (Ind.) U., Corpus of Brit. Medieval Libr. Catalogues, Brit. Acad. Author: Serial Bibliographies for Medieval Studies, 1969, (with M.A. Rouse) Preachers, Florilegia and Sermons: Studies on the Manipulus Florum of Thomas of Ireland, 1979; (with others) Texts and Transmission, 1983; (with C.W. Dutschke) Medieval and Renaissance Manuscripts in the Claremont Libraries, 1986; (with M.A. Rouse) Cartolai, Illuminators and Printers in Fifteenth-Century Italy, 1988; (with L. Bataillon and B. Guyot) La Production du livre universitaire au moyen age, exemplar et pecia, 1988; (with others) Guide to Medieval and Renaissance Manuscripts in the Huntington Library, 1989; (with M. Ferrari) Medieval and Renaissance Manuscripts at the University of California, Los Angeles, 1991; (with M.A. Rouse and R.A.B. Mynors) Registrum de libris doctorum et auctorum veterum, 1991; (with M.A. Rouse) Authentic Witnesses: Approaches to Medieval Texts and Manuscripts, 1991; (with M.A. Rouse) Manuscripts and Their Makers: Commercial Book Producers in Medieval Paris 1200-1500, 2 vols., 2000, (with M.A. Rouse) Henry of Kirkestede, Catalogus de libris autenticis et apocrifis, 2004; co-editor: Viator: Medieval and Renaissance Studies, 1970-; mem. editorial bd. Medieval and renaissance manuscripts in Calif. libraries, Medieval Texts, Toronto; Medieval Texts, Binghamton, Library Quar., 1984-88, Speculum, 1981-85, Revue d'histoire des Textes, 1986-, Cambridge Studies in Paleography and Codicology, 1990-96, Catalogue of Medieval and Renaissance Manuscripts in the Beinecke Rare Book and Manuscript Library Yale University, 1984-, Filologia MedioLatina, 1994-, Manuscripta, 2000—, Utrecht Studies in Medieval Literacy, 2000—, Litterae Caelestes, 2005— Am. Coun. Learned Socs. fellow, 1972-73, vis. fellow All Souls Coll., Oxford, 1978-79, Guggenheim fellow, 1975-76, Rosenbach fellow in bibliography U. Pa., 1976, NEH fellow, 1981-82, 84-85, 94-96, Inst. for Advanced Studies fellow Jerusalem, 1991; J.R. Lyell reader in bibliogrpahy U. Oxford, 1991-92; vis. fellow Pembroke Coll., U. Oxford, 1992, Pembroke Coll., U. Cambridge, 2000-01. Fellow Royal Hist. Soc., Medieval Acad. Am.; mem. Medieval Assn. Pacific (councillor 1965-68, pres. 1968-70), Medieval Acad. Am. (councillor 1977-80), Comité international de paléographie (treas. 1985-90), Comité international du vocabulaire des institutions et de la communication intellectuelles au moyen age, 1987—, Societa internazionale per lo studio del medioevo latino, 1988—. Home: 11444 Berwick St Los Angeles CA 90049-3416 Office: Dept History U Calif Los Angeles CA 90024 Office Phone: 310-472-2314, 310-825-4168. Business E-Mail: rouse@history.ucla.edu.

ROUSE, ROBERT KELLY, JR., judge; b. Lexington, Ky. s. Robert Kelly and Luane (Adams) R.; m. Donna R. Walker, Dec. 21, 1969; children: Kelly B., Erin E. Smith. AA, Daytona Beach CC, Fla., 1966; BS, Fla. State U., 1968; JD, U. Fla., 1974. Bar: Fla. 1975. Ptnr. Regency Talent, Daytona Beach, Fla., 1968-69; supr. food divsn. Walt Disney Co., Anaheim, Calif., 1969-70; mgr. restaurants Walt Disney World Co., Orlando, Fla., 1970-71; from assoc. to ptnr. Smalbein, Eubank, Johnson, Rosier & Bussey, P.A., Daytona Beach, 1974-81; ptnr. Smith, Schoder, Rouse & Bouck, P.A., Daytona Beach, 1981-95; circuit judge Volusia County Courthouse, Daytona Beach, 1995—; chief judge Seventh Jud. Cir., Daytona Beach, 1999—2003. With USAR, 1969—75. Mem.: Am. Inns. of Ct. (founding mem. Dunn-Blount chpt. 2001—, pres. Dunn-Blount chpt. 2006—), Am. Bd. Trial Advs., Volusia County Bar Assn. (pres. 1989—90), Volusia Civil Trial Attys. Assn. (pres. 1993—95). Office: Volusia County Courthouse 101 N Alabama Ave Deland FL 32724 Office Phone: 386-626-6590.

ROUSE, ROSCOE, JR., retired librarian, educator; b. Valdosta, Ga., Nov. 26, 1919; s. Roscoe and Minnie Estelle (Corbett) R.; m. Charlie Lou Miller, June 23, 1945; children: Charles Richard, Robin Rouse Wells. BA, U. Okla., 1948, MA, 1952; student (Grolier Soc. scholar), Rutgers U., 1956; AMLS, U. Mich., 1958, PhD, 1962. Bookkeeper C & S Nat. Bank, Valdosta, Ga., 1937-41; draftsman R.K. Rouse Co. (heating engrs.), Greenville, SC, 1941-42; student asst. U. Okla. and Rice U., 1947-48; asst. librarian Northeastern State Coll., Tahlequah, Okla., 1948-49, acting librarian, instr. library sci., 1949-51; circulation librarian Baylor U., 1952-53, acting univ. librarian, 1953-54, univ. librarian, prof., 1954-63, chmn. dept. library sci., 1956-63; dir. libraries State U. N.Y. at Stony Brook, LI, 1963-67; dean libr. svcs., prof. Okla. State U., Stillwater, 1967-87, univ. libr. historian, 1987-92, chmn. dept. libr. edn., 1967-74; ret., 1987. Grolier Soc. scholar, Rutgers U., 1956; vis. prof. U. Okla. Sch. Library Sci., summer 1962, N. Tex. State U., summer 1965; acad. library cons.; pub. dir. Seretean Wellness Ctr., Okla. State U., 2002—; mem. AIA-Am. Library Assn. Library Bldg. Awards Jury, 1976; bd. dirs. Fellowship Christian Libr. and Info. Specialists; in retirement, volunteers writing and photography for local newspaper. Author: A History of the Baylor University Library, 1845-1919, 1962; editor: Okla. Librarian, 1951-52; co-author: Organization Charts of Selected Libraries, 1973; A History of the Okla. State U. Library, 1992; contbr. articles, book revs., chpts. to publs. in field. Bd. dirs. Okla. Dept. Librs., 1989-92, chmn., 1990-92. 1st lt. USAAF, 1942-45. Decorated Air medal with 4 oak leaf clusters; recipient citation Okla. State Senate, 1987, Rotary Outstanding Achievement award, 1996; named in 150 Prominent Individuals in Baylor's History. Mem. ALA (life, mem. coun. 1971-72, 76-80, 83-84, 84-88, chmn. libr. orgn. and mgmt. sect. 1973-75, planning and budget assembly 1978-79, coun. com. on coms. 1979-80, bldgs. and equipment sect. exec. bd. 1979-80, chmn. bldgs. for coll. and univ. librs. com. 1983-85, chmn. nominating com. libr. history roundtable 1993-94), AARP, (sec. local chpt. 1998-2000), Okla. Libr. Assn. (life, pres. 1971-72, ALA coun. rep. 1976-80, 83-84, OLA Disting. Svc. award 1979, Spl. Merit award 1987), S.W. Libr. Assn. (chmn. coll. and univ. div. 1958-60, chmn. scholarship com. 1968-70), Internat. Fedn. Libr. Assns. (standing com. on libr. bldgs. and equipment 1976-88), Assn. Coll. and Rsch. Librs. (chmn. univ. librs. sect. 1969-70, mem. exec. bd. and rep. to ALA Coun., 1971-72), U. Mich. Sch. Libr. Sci. Alumni Soc. (pres. 1979-80, Alumni Recognition award 1988), mem. Alumni Found. Com., 1992-94, Payne County Ret. Educators Assn. (v.p., pres. elect 1991-92, pres. 1992-93), Okla. State U. Emeriti Assn. (pres. 2000-01), Okla. Hist. Soc. (com. on Okla. Higher Edn. mus. 1985—, pub. dir. 2002—), Stillwater Rotary Club (pres. 1980-81, Rotarian of Yr. 1999, editor Rotary Weekly bulletin, various coms., pub. dir. 1998—), Beta Phi Mu, Archons of Colophon. Baptist (chmn. bd. deacons 1973). Personal E-mail: rouse74074@aol.com. *It is sometimes a hidden influence in our lives which drives us toward a set goal. We ourselves may not recognize the real source of that urge to fulfill a dream. Only after many years was I able to look back and discern the factors in my youth that pushed me toward my goal of attaining a good education. They grew out of the influence that the Great Depression had on my early life. Because of that experience the preparation for a career became my first goal in life, yet the ways and means for achieving it were virtually nonexistent. It was to be, however, and I was fortunate to realize that goal. It causes me to think now that perhaps the degree of determination and endurance one possesses is paced more by adverse condition than by times of comfort and ease.*

ROUSE, TERRIE SUZITTE, museum director; b. Youngstown, Ohio, Dec. 2, 1952; d. Eurad and Florence (Wilcox) Rouse; 1 child, Malcom Adam Rouse-West. BA, Trinity Coll., 1974; MS in Profl. Studies, Cornell U., 1977; cert. in internat. affairs, Columbia U., 1979, MA, 1979. Mgr., curator Adam Clayton Powell St. Office Bldg., NYC, 1979-81; sr. curator Studio Mus. Harlem, NYC, 1981-86; dir. mus. N.Y. Transit Mus., Bklyn., 1986—91; dir. Calif. Afro-Am. Mus., 1991—93; artistic exec. dir. Atlanta Ballet, 2002—03; exec. arts mgr., mus. dir. Union Sta., Kansas City, 2005—. Advisor Bellevue Hosp. Art Bd., 1981—. Contbr. articles to profl. jours. Mem. Conf. Mil. Transp. Ofcls. Named Outstanding Young Women Am., 1981—83. Mem.: Am. Assn. Mus. (assessor 1981—). Avocations: sewing, reading, doll collecting. Personal E-mail: trouse3008@aol.com.

ROUSH, GLENN A., state senator; m. Ardith Roush. Served in Mont. Ho. of Reps., 1981—84, State Senate, 1999—; ret. Mont. Power Co.; Dem. senator dist. 8 Mont. State Senate, 1998—, mem. bus. and industry com., mem. energy and telecom. com., legis. com. and mem. coms. on coms. com., chmn. natural resources com. With US Army. Democrat. Home: PO Box 185 Cut Bank MT 59427-0185

ROUSH, JOHN A., academic administrator; b. Wis. m. Susie Miller Roush; children: Luke, Mark. B in English, Ohio U.; M, M, D, Miami U., Ohio. Grad. asst. football coach to exec. asst. to pres. Miami U., Ohio; exec. asst. to pres. U. of Richmond, 1982—90, v.p. planning, 1990—98; pres. Centre Coll., Danville, Ky., 1998—. Mem. Coun. of Pres., Assn. of Gov. Bds., Nat. Assn. Independent Coll. & Univ.; treas. Assn. Presbyn. Coll. & Univ., 2002—03. Contbr. articles to profl. jours. Capt. US Army. Office: Centre Coll 600 W Walnut St Danville KY 40422 Office Phone: 859-238-5200. E-mail: jroush@centre.edu. *

ROUSH, NADINE MARIE, elementary school educator; b. Elmhurst, Ill., Sept. 25, 1957; d. Donald Raymond and Roberta Helen (Foulis) Stoike; m. Jan Alan Roush, Dec. 17, 1977. BA, Purdue U., West Lafayette, Ind., 1982; MS, Purdue U., 1986. Facilitator gifted K-12 Ft. Larned Unified Sch. Dist. #495, Larned, Kans., 1982—84; tchr. grade 4 Avon Upper Elem., Ind., 1984—85; facilitator gifted K-12 Lafayette Sch. Corp., Ind., 1985—86; tchr. grades 4/5 Vinton Elem. Sch., Lafayette, 1986—90, tchr. 4/5, 1992—95; tchr. grade 5 Edgelea Elem. Sch., Lafayette, 1991—92, Earhart Elem. Sch., Lafayette, 1995—. Mem. adv. bd. Grad. Profl. Devel. Purdue U. Coll. Edn., West Lafayette, 2002—06. Author: Get Moving! The Transportation Activity Book, 1984; contbg. author: Preparing a Professional Portfolio, 2005. Mem. Feast of Hunters Moon Ops. com. Tippecanoe County Hist. Assn., Lafayette, 1995—2002. Recipient Crystal Apple for Outstanding Tchg. award, Purdue U., 1996, Golden Apple for Tchg. award, Greater Lafayette C. of C., 1989; Democratic Citizenship fellow, James F. Ackerman Ctr. Mem.: Ind. Coun. Social Studies (bd. dirs. 1997—2001, named Disting. Educator of Yr. 2004), Internat. Reading Assn., Nat. Coun. Social Studies, Delta Kappa Gamma. Home: 2356 N 600 W Frankfort IN 46041 Office: Earhart Elem Sch 3280 S 9th St Lafayette IN 47909

ROUSSAKIS, PETER ELLWOOD, minister, publisher; b. Bridgeport, Conn., Oct. 16, 1946; s. Charles and Dorothy Roussakis; m. Phyllis Ann Berkshire, Oct. 31, 1970; children: Alex, Aaron. BSc, So. Conn. State U., 1968, MSc, 1973; M in Ch. Music, So. Bapt. Theol. Sem., 1973; D in Ministry, Austin Presbyn. Theol. Sem., 1986; MST, Boston U., 1991; PhD, Grad. Theol. Found., 1998. Elem. sch. tchr. Trumbull Pub. Schs., Conn., 1968—71; min. music and edn. Brethren Ch., New Lebanon, Ohio, 1973—75; assoc. pastor First United Meth. Ch., Shelby, Ohio, 1977—80; asst. prof. ch. music Southwestern U., Georgetown, Tex., 1980—86; pastor First Bapt. Ch., Hampton, NH, 1986—89; pastor, min. of music Cmty. Ch. Alton, NH, 1989—98; pastor First Brethren Ch., Burlington, Ind., 2000—. Editor Meetinghouse Press, Burlington. Author: (religion text) Classic Worship: With Brethren in Mind, 2005, Confessing the Compendium: Praying the Lord's Prayer as Confessing Faith, 2005. Mem.: Nat. Assn. Brethren Ch. Elders, Hymn Soc. of US and Can. Mem. The Brethren Church. Avocation: collecting antique records. Home and Office: PO Box 246 Burlington IN 46915 Home Phone: 765-566-3274; Office Phone: 765-566-3265. E-mail: jsbaklava@sbcglobal.net, meetinghousepress@sbcglobal.net.

ROUSSEAU, CHRISTINA JEANNIE, elementary school educator; b. Gardner, Mass., Jan. 18, 1951; d. Edward Patrick and Marjorie Forbes (Arey) O'Connor; m. Douglas Edward Rousseau, Aug. 11, 1973; children: Justin Douglas, Amanda Leigh. BSc, We. Conn. State U., Danbury, 1973, MSc, 1975; postgrad., L.I. U., Bklyn., 1986—88. Cert. tchr. Conn., 1973, N.Y., 1975. Tchr. Beacon City Sch. Dist., NY, 1973—. Sci. coord. Beacon Sch. Dist., 1987—88. Den mother Boy Scouts Am., Hopewell Junction, NY, 1984—85; participant holiday meal delivery Trinity Ch., Fishkill, NY. Named Sci. Tchr. of Yr., Ctrl. Hudson Corp., Poughkeepsie, N.Y., 1989; grantee, Area Fund Dutchess County, N.Y., 1990. Mem.: NEA, NSTA. Episcopalian. Achievements include selected for National Science Foundation program for exemplary teachers. Avocations: travel, exercise, reading, cooking, theater. Office: Beacon City Sch Dist Education Dr Beacon NY 12508 Personal E-mail: crousse44@optonline.net.

ROUSSEAU, EUGENE ELLSWORTH, musician, music educator, consultant; b. Blue Island, Ill., Aug. 23, 1932; s. Joseph E. and Laura M. (Schindler) R.; m. Norma J. Rigel, Aug. 15, 1959; children: Lisa-Marie, Joseph. B of Mus Edn., Chgo. Mus. Coll., 1953; MusM, Northwestern U., 1954; student, Paris Conservatory of Music, 1960-61; PhD in Music Lit. and Performance, U. Iowa, 1962. Instr. Luther Coll., 1956-59; asst. prof. Cen. Mo. State Coll., 1962-64; prof. music Ind. U., Bloomington, 1964-88, disting. prof. music, 1988—; prof. U. Minn., 2000—. Guest prof. U. Iowa, 1964, Hochschule fur Musik, Vienna, Austria, 1981-82, Ariz. State U., 1984, Prague Conservatory Music, 1985, Showa Coll. Music, 1996, 98, Tokyo Coll. Music, 1997, Paris Conservatory, 1997, Munshino Acad. Music, Tokyo, 2000; tchr. U. Wis.-Ext., 1969—; R&D of saxophone mouthpieces; music arranger; svc. on numerous acad. coms.; tchr. 1st course in saxophone Mozarteum in Salzburg, Austria, 1991—; mem. jury Munich Internat. competitions, 1987, 90, 2001, pres. of juries, 1991-92; first solo saxophonist to perform on Prague Spring Festival, 1993; mem. jury Can. Nat. Music competition, 1994; juror Japan Wind and Percussion Competition, 1997; v.p. jury Adolphe Sax Internat. Competition, Belgium, 1998; guest artist prof. Villa Musica, Mainz, 1998, 2000; faculty saxophone Ticino Music, Lugano, 2001, 02, 03; chief cons. saxophone R&D Yamaha corp., 1972-92; soloist Hamamatsu Wind Instrument Festival; faculty ann. master class Vancouver C.C.; host World Saxophone Congress XIII, U. Minn., Mpls., 2003; recorded for Deutsche Grammophon, 1971; guest faculty Am. Band Coll., 2000, 03, 06; adjudicator Thailand Internat. Composition Competition, 2006; artist-in-residence U. Ga., 2007. Worldwide concert saxophonist; Carnegie Hall debut, 1965; author: Marcel Mule: His Life and the Saxophone, 1982, Saxophone High Tones, 1978, revised 2d edit., 2003, Method for Saxophone (2 vols.), 1975; performer 1st solo saxophone recitals, several European cities, 1st Am. solo saxophone performance in Japan, 1984; 1st to record concert saxophone on compact disc (Delos); radio broadcasts in Berlin, Bremen, London, Montreal, Ostrava, Paris, Prague, Toronto, Vienna; saxophone recs. for Deutsche Gramophon, Golden Crest, Coronet, Delos, Liscio, ALM, McGill, RIAX, and Jeanné; CD rec. with Belgian RAF Band; numerous world premieres of composition written for him. Instr., asst. band leader 25th Infantry Div. U.S. Army, 1954-56. Named Hon. Prof. Music, Prague Conservatory, 1993, Braga Inst., Italy, 2001; recipient Edwin Franko Goldman award, Am. Bandmasters Assn., 1995, Disting. Alumni award, U. Iowa, 1996; grantee, Fulbright Found., 1960—61, Rsch. and Exchange Bd., 1985, NEA, 1986. Mem. N.Am. Saxophone Alliance (pres. 1978-80), Comite Internat. de Saxophone (pres. 1982-85), Coll. Music Soc., Clarinet and Saxophone Soc. (U.K.), Music Tchrs. Nat. Assn. (Tchr. of Yr. award for Ind. 1993), Fulbright Assn. (life), World Saxophone Congress (co-founder 1969, pres. organizing com. 2000--). Home Phone: 812-332-3284; Office Phone: 612-624-3875. E-mail: rouss007@umn.edu.

ROUSSEAU, IRENE VICTORIA, artist; children: Douglas, Scott. BA, Hunter Coll., NYC; MFA, Claremont Grad. U., Calif., 1969; PhD, N.Y. U., 1977. Tenured prof. William Paterson Coll., Wayne, NJ, 1970-74. Invited spkr. and exhibiting artist Lehman Lecture, Morristown Beard Sch., NJ, 2007; spkr. in field. Exhbns. include Betty Parsons Gallery, N.Y.C., Claremont Colls., State Mus. Sci. and Industry, L.A., Morris Mus. Arts and Scis., Morristown, N.J., The Bronx Mus. of Art, Galleri Sci. Agnes, Copenhagen/Roskilde, Denmark, Sculptors 5, Madison, N.J., Edmund Sci. Co., Barrington, N.J., AT&T World Hdqrs., Basking Ridge, N.J., N.J. Ctr. for Visual Arts, The Brotherhood Synagogue Holocaust Meml. Gramercy Pk. (mosaic), N.Y.C., 1986, 1st Internat. Art Biennale, Malta, 1995, U. Lausanne (Switzerland), 1997, Internat. Biennale Malta, 1997 (awards), Am. Inst. Archs., N.Y., 1998, Southwestern Coll., Kans., 1999, Lausanne, Switzerland, 2001, BRIDGES, Internat. Joint Conf., 2003, Math. Soc. France and Ministry of Culture Exhbn., 2004-05, Internat. Interdisciplinary Conf., Athens, Greece, 2005, Renaissance Banff, Alb., Can., 2005, traveling exhibit, Soc. Math. France and The Min. Culture, 2005, Yellow Bird Gallery, Newburg, N.Y., 2005; artist in residence Program Greece, 2000, Internat. Conf. Internat. Soc. Art, Math., Architecture, Freiburg, Germany, 2002, Internat. Conf. Connections in Math., Music, Art, Sci., and Arch., Granada, Spain, 2003, Internat. Soc. Arts, Math., and Arch. and BRIDGES (Math. Connections in Art, Music, and Sci.) Internat. Joint Conf., Granada, Spain, Inst. Math. Scis. Banff Ctr., Can. Math.Soc., Banff Internat. Rsch. Sta.; one woman shows Weston Gallery Sch. Arch., Newark, 2003, N.J. Inst. Tech. Sch. Arch., 2003, Weston Art Gallery Sch. Arch. NJIT, Newark, 2004; traveling exhibit Math. Soc., 2005; contbr. articles and works of art to jours., books and catalogues. Recipient seven 1st prize awards for creative work in N.J., ER Squibb and Sons Sculpture award, AIA N.J. Presentation Design award, 1995, Internat. Art Biennale Malta Installatin award, 1997, Traveling Exhibit throughout Europe and Middle East and Africa of Winners of the 1997 Biennale in Malta, 1997-99. Mem. AIA (profl. affiliate N.J., N.Y., chmn. architecture dialogue com. Presentation award 1995), Internat. Sculptors Assn., Am. Abstract Artists (exhbn. chmn. 1978-79, pres. 1979-82), Fine Arts Fedn. (bd. dirs.), Coll. Art Assn., Women's Caucus on Art (conf. spkr.), Phi Delta Kappa. Home: 41 Sunset Dr Summit NJ 07901-2322 Personal E-mail: mosaicartforms@comcast.net.

ROUSSEL, LEE DENNISON, economist; b. NYC, May 15, 1944; d. Ethan Allen and Frances Isabel (Ferry) Dennison; m. Andre Homo Roussel, Sept. 6, 1980; children: Cecilia Frances, Stephanie Anne. AB, Wellesley Coll., 1966; MA, Northeastern U., 1974. Mgmt. intern U.S. Dept. HEW, 1966-68; with Planning Office Commonwealth of Mass., 1968-70; exec. dir. Gov.'s Commn. Citizen Participation, Boston, 1973; with Boston area office U.S. Dept. HUD, 1970-78; fgn. svc. officer USAID, 1978-99, with housing and urban devel. office Washington and Tunis, 1978-82, chief housing and urban devel. office for C.Am. Honduras, 1982-87, asst. dir. office housing and urban programs Washington, 1987-91, country rep. for Czech and Slovak Fed. Rep., 1991-92, country rep. for Czech Rep., 1993-94; min. counselor, U.S. rep. to devel. assistance com. OECD, Paris, 1994-99; sr. advisor USAID, Panama, 1999—2002, chief, exec. mgmt. human resources, 2004—05, mgmt. advisor Office of Econ. growth, 2006—. Episcopalian. Home: 2333 N Oak St Falls Church VA 22046 Office Phone: 202-712-0718. Personal E-mail: leeroussel@hotmail.com.

ROUSSELOT, PETER FRESE, lawyer, consultant; b. NYC, Jan. 7, 1942; s. Louis Marcel and Evelyn Valdez (Hastrup) R.; m. Mary Dumesnil, Cobb, Nov. 22, 1975; children: Laura Rodman, Richard Frese, Anne Stewart, Louise Dierks. BA summa cum laude, Yale U., 1963; LLB, Harvard U., 1966. Bar: US Dist. Ct. DC 1967, US Ct. Appeals (DC cir.) 1967, US Ct. Appeals (3d cir.) 1993, US Supreme Ct. 1970. Assoc. Hogan & Hartson, Washington, 1966-74, ptnr., 1975-94, mem. exec. com., 1986-88; mng. dir. corp. affairs So. Pacific Rail Corp., Washington, 1994-97; ind. internat. railroad cons., 1997—. Asst. to nat. co-chmn. Citizens for Robert F. Kennedy, Washington, 1968; del. Dem. Nat. Conv., 2004; chair Arlington County Dem. Com., Va., 2006-. Mem. Yale Club Washington, Phi Beta Kappa. Democrat. Episcopalian. Avocations: hiking, photography. Office: 3182 Key Blvd Arlington VA 22201-5065 Home Phone: 703-276-0341; Office Phone: 703-276-1584. E-mail: pfrou@aol.com.

ROUSSOS, CHRISTOPHER WAYNE, dental association administrator; b. Dec. 23, 1964; BS in Mgmt. and Mktg., Clarkson U., Potsdam, NY, 1986; MBA, U. Phoenix. Mgmt. position Newell Rubbermaid, Inc.; market mgr. Pepsico, Inc.; gen. mgr. Fleetwood Enterprises, Inc.; divsn. gen. mgr. Am. Homestar Corp.; pres., Matrix Outpatient Rehabilitation and Theraphysics Beverly Enterprises, Inc., pres., Ceres Purchasing Solutions, sr. v.p., Supply Chain Ops.; pres. AseraCare, Inc., 2004—07; CEO OCA, Inc., Metairie, La., 2007—. Cap. US Army, 1985—90. Office: OCA Inc 3850 N Causeway Blvd Ste 800 Metairie LA 70002 *

ROUSUCK, J. WYNN, theater critic; b. Cleve., Mar. 19, 1951; d. Morton I. and Irene Zelda (Winograd) R. BA summa cum laude, Wellesley Coll., 1972; MS, Columbia U., 1974. Assoc. editor, program guide, Sta. WCLV-FM, Cleve., 1972-73; theater and film reviewer Cleve. Press, 1973; gen. assignment arts reporter Balt. Sun, 1974-84, theater critic, 1984—. Instr. English Goucher Coll., Towson, Md., 1981; master critic O'Neill Critics Inst., Waterford, Conn., 1990—; theater critic Md. Pub. TV., 1986; faculty Nat. Endowment for Arts Journalism Inst. in Theater U. So. Calif., 2005; spkr. in field. Recipient Dog Writers Assn. Am. awards 1977, 79, Md. chpt. 1st Place Arts Reporting award Soc. Profl. Journalists, 1993, Front Page award, Disting. Criticism Washington-Balt. Newspaper Guild, 1997, 99, 2002, Bill Pryor Meml. grand prize for writing, 1999, Bernie Harrison Meml. award for commentary, 2002; NEH journalism fellow U. Mich., 1979-80, fellow O'Neill Critics Inst., 1982. Mem. Balt. Bibliophiles (bd. dirs. 1982-83), Octavo Plus, Walters Art Gallery, Balt. Wellesley Club (pres. 1978-79). Jewish. Avocations: rare books, art. Office: The Baltimore Sun 501 N Calvert St Baltimore MD 21278-0001

ROUT, BIBHUDUTTA, research scientist; s. Uttam Kumar and Kanak Manjari Rout; m. Sujata Khuntia, Apr. 17, 2002; 1 child, Reina. PhD, Utkal U., Bhubaneswar, 2000. Doctoral fellow Inst. Physics, Bhubaneswar, 1994—2000; postdoctoral fellow U. Melbourne, Australia, 2001—03; rsch. assoc. La. Accelerator, U. La., Lafayette, 2003—. Recipient Young Scientist award, Orissa State Sci. Acad., 1999. Mem.: Internat. Soc. Optical Engring. (corr.). Office: La Accelerator Ctr 320 Cajundome Blvd Lafayette LA 70506

ROUTE, CANDACE, elementary school educator; d. Hubert Lee and Julianne Jackson; m. Leslie Ray Route, Dec. 28, 1974; 1 child, Brian. EdB, Tex. Tech U., Lubbock, 1972; Med, East Tex. State U., Commerce, 1985. Cert. kindergarten tchr. Tex., 1972. Kindergarten tchr. Hale Ctr. ISD, Tex., 1972—73, Dallas ISD, 1973—74, Gibert ISD, Ariz., 1978—81, North Lamar ISD, Paris, 1981—85, Kerrville ISD, Tex., 1993—97, Harlandale ISD, San Antonio, 1997—2001, reading tchr., 2001—03, reading coach, 2003—; ednl. cons. Region VIII Edn. Svc. Ctr., Mt. Pleasant, Tex., 1985—89, Region XII Edn. Svc. Ctr., Waco, Tex., 1989—90; adminstrv. asst. Ingram ISD, Tex., 1991—92; reading coach Harlandale Ind. Sch. Dist., San Antonio, 2003—. Early childhood cons. Tex. Dept. Human Resources, Paris, 1974—78; owner/ednl. cons. A Child's Garden of Learning, Kerrville, Tex., 1992—93. Recipient Ednl. Achievements award, Notable Women Tex., 1985. Mem.: Tex. Fedn. Tchrs., Kappa Delta Pi. Independent. Avocations: architecture, antiques. Home: 610 Mello Oak San Antonio TX 78258 Home Phone: 210-402-1288; Office Phone: 210-977-1580.

ROUTH, BRANDON, actor; b. Des Moines, Iowa, Oct. 9, 1979; s. Katie and Ron Routh. Student, U. of Iowa. Actor: (TV series) Odd Man Out, 1999, Undressed, 2000, One Life to Live, 2001—02, (guest appearance) Gilmore Girls, Cold Case, Will & Grace, Oliver Beene,: (films) Superman Returns, 2006. Office: PMK/HBH Public Relations c/o Simon Halls & Kacey Spies 700 San Vicente Blvd Ste G910 West Hollywood CA 90069 *

ROUTH, DONALD K(ENT), psychologist, educator; b. Oklahoma City, Mar. 3, 1937; s. Ross Holland and Fay (Campbell) R.; m. Marion Starbird Wendler, Sept. 10, 1960; children: Rebecca Ann (dec.), Laura Diane. BA, U. Okla., 1962; PhD, U. Pitts., 1967; BA in History, Fla. Gulf Coast U., 2006. Diplomate Am. Bd. Profl. Psychology. Asst. prof. psychology and pediatrics U. Iowa, Iowa City, 1967-70, prof., 1977-85; assoc. prof. psychology Bowling Green State U., Ohio, 1970-71; assoc. prof. U. N.C., Chapel Hill, 1971-77; prof. psychology and pediat. U. Miami, Coral Gables, Fla., 1985—2002, prof. emeritus, 2002—. Chmn. behavioral medicine study sect. NIH, 1983-85 Editor Jour. Pediatric Psychology, 1976-82, Jour. Clin. Child Psychology, 1987-91, Jour. of Abnormal Child Psychology, 1992-98, Am. Jour. on Mental Retardation, 1998-2002, Internat. Clin. Psychologist, 2001—04; contbr. numerous articles to profl. jours., books Pres. Eno River Unitarian Universalist Fellowship, 1976-77; vol. faculty Fla. Gulf Coast U., 2002—05. Recipient award for disting. contbn. Soc. Pediatric Psychology, 1981, Presdl. award, 1988; Rsch. Psychologist of Yr. award Fla. Psychol. Assn., 1987, Reconocimiento, El Colegio Nacional de Psicologis de Mex., 1999, Disting. Alumni award Okla. Mil. Acad., 2004. Mem. APA (pres. div. child, youth and family svcs., 1984, pres. div. on mental retardation 1987, pres. divsn. clin. psychol. 1998), Internat. Soc. Clin. Psychology (founder, pres. 1998-99), Disting. Profl. Contbns. to Clin. Psychology (sect. on clin. child psychology 1989, div. clin. psychology, 1992, Nicholas Hobbs award div. child youth and family svcs., 1996, Edgar A. Doll award divsn. mental retardation and devel. disabiities 2001), Assn. Southwest Fla. (founder, 2003),Phi Beta Kappa. Democrat. Home: 20131 Seagrove St #402 Estero FL 33928 Personal E-mail: donaldrouth@mac.com.

ROUTH, JOHN WILLIAM, lawyer; b. Knoxville, Tenn., Dec. 3, 1957; s. John C. and Mary (Parker) R.; m. Martha Carol Carter, Aug. 6, 1983; children: John Carter, Carol Ann. BA, U. Tenn., 1979, JD, 1983. Bar: Tenn. 1983, U.S. Dist. Ct. (ea. dist.) Tenn. 1983. Assoc. Francis W. Headman, Knoxville, 1983-87, Wm. R. Banks and Assocs., Knoxville, 1987-97; judicial commr. Knox County Gen. Sessions Ct., Knoxville, 1992-94; sole practice law Knoxville, 1997—. Bd. dirs. Cerebral Palsy Ctr. for Handicapped Adults, Knoxville, 1985-88; chmn. adminstv. bd. Emerald Ave. United Meth. Ch., Knoxville, 1988-90, 1998-2000. Mem. Tenn. Bar Assn., Knoxville Bar Assn., Tenn. Assn. Criminal Def. Lawyers, City Salesman Club (v.p. 1988, sec. 1987, pres. 1998), Gideons Internat., Fountain City Bus. and Profl. Assn. (sec. 2004, v.p. 2005-06, pres. 2007). Methodist. Office: 3214 Tazewell Pike Ste 105 Knoxville TN 37918 Home Phone: 865-689-7460; Office Phone: 865-687-0021. Personal E-mail: routhbill@yahoo.com.

ROUVAS, SAKAS, singer, gymnast; b. Island of Corfou, Greece, Jan. 5, 1974; Signed by Polygram, 1991. Represented Greece in pole vault Hellenic Nat. Team; rep. Greece Eurovision Song Contest, 2004. Performer: Thessaloniki Song Festival, (TV) Athen 2004-Die Gala, 2004, singer 6 albums, 4 single albums; notable guest appearences Fort Boyard, 2002, 20h10 pétantes, 2003, Hallo Deutschland, 2004, Leute heute, 2004, Bettina S., 2004. Recipient Best New Singer, Best Song, and Best Stage Performance, Hellenic Music Awards (four years in a row), 3rd Place for song "Shake it", Eurovision Song Contest, 2004. He played a role in reconciliation efforts with Turkey. In 1997, he performed on stage with Turkish singer Barat Kud in a concert in UN-controlled territory on Cyprus. For this he was awarded the International Ipeksi prize for understanding and cooperation. Mailing: Polygram Records Inc 185 Miles Ave Akron OH 44306-1606 E-mail: sakis@sakisrouvas.com.

ROUVELAS, EMANUEL LARRY, lawyer; b. Seattle, Sept. 10, 1944; s. Larry E. and Mary (Derezes) R.; m. Marilyn S. Edmunds, Jan. 23, 1967; children: Eleftherios, Mary. BA, U. Wash., 1965; JD, Harvard U., 1968, AMP, 1996. Bar: Ill. 1968, D.C. 1973. Assoc. Kirkland & Ellis, Chgo., 1968-69; counsel U.S. Senate Com. on Commerce, Washington, 1969-73; chief counsel U.S. Senate Mcht. Marine and Fgn. Commerce Subcoms., Washington, 1969-73; chmn., ptnr. Preston, Gates, Ellis & Rouvelas Meeds, Washington, 1974—. Advisor to two Presdl. transitions and bi-partisan congl. caucus; bd. dirs. Am. Comml. Lines, 2005-, chmn. nominating governance com., 2005-. Regent Am. Architectural Found., 2005—. Office: Preston Gates Ellis Et Al 1735 New York Ave NW Washington DC 20006-5209 Office Phone: 202-628-1700.

ROUXEL, OLIVIER, geochemist, research scientist; s. J. C. and N. Rouxel; m. Ouafae Rafie; 1 child, Ryan. PhD, INPL, Vandoeuvre, France, 2002. Registered engr. geology, ENSG-INPL, 1999. Rsch. assoc. U. Cambridge, England, 2002—03; asst. scientist Woods Hole Oceanog. Instn., Mass., 2003—. Contbr. articles to profl. jours.

ROUZE, JEFFREY ALAN, real estate executive; b. Rockford, Ill., Feb. 5, 1952; s. Robert Lloyd and Ellen Erma (Korpi) R. BBA in Real Estate Fin., U. Wis., 1974, MS in Bus. and Real Estate, 1977. Lic. real estate broker, Wis.; notary pub., Wis. Exec. mgmt. trainee Grootemaat Corp., Milw., 1977-79; real estate cons. CUNA Mut. Ins. Soc., Madison, Wis., 1979-84, real property and mortgage mgr., 1984-93, sr. asset mgr., 1994—2001; pres. Hollywood Econ. Alliance, 2002—; ptnr. Hollywood Devel. LLC, LA, 2001—. Treas. Strollers Theatre, Ltd., Madison, 1985-89; bd. dirs. Hollywood Entertainment Dist., Calif., 1998-99, 2005—, Hollywood Historic Trust, 2000—; treas. St. Paul's Luth. Ch., Santa Monica, Calif., 2002—; bd. dirs. Hollywood Neighborhood Coun., 2003—, Hollywood Heritage, 2003—; pres. Landmark Communities LLC, 2005—. Named Real Estate Pioneer, LA Bus. Jour., 2005. Mem. Nat. Assn. Corp. Real Estate Execs. (master corp. real estate), Inst. Real Estate Mgmt. (cert. property mgr.), Mortgage Bankers Assn. Am., Urban Land Inst., Coml. Investment Real Estate Inst., Hollywood C. of C. (treas. 2002—). Address: 530 S Barington Ave No 307 Los Angeles CA 90049 Home Phone: 310-440-3462; Office Phone: 310-451-6719. E-mail: jarouze@earthlink.net.

ROVAK, STEPHEN H., lawyer; b. St. Louis, Feb. 18, 1948; AB cum laude, Washington U., 1969; MS in Forensic, George Wash. U., 1975; JD, Harvard U., 1972; Fellow in Forensic Medicine, Armed Forces Inst. Pathology Walter Reed Med. Ctr., Wash., 1974—75; Grad., Nat. Def. U. Def. Mgmt. Course. Bar: Mo. 1972, DC 1972, Ill. Fellow legal medicine AFIP Walter Reed Med. Ctr., 1974-75; atty. Peper, Martin, Jensen, Maichel and Hetlage, St. Louis; ptnr. Sonnenschein Nath & Rosenthal LLP. Legal adv. Air Mobility Command; with litig. divsn. Office Army Judge Adv. Gen.; sr. reserve Air Warfare Ctr., Nev. Colonel USAF. Recipient Reginald C. Harmon award outstanding Reserve Judge Adv., US Air Force, 1990, Legion of Merit, 2000. Mem. ABA (chmn. franchise law com., gen. practice sect. 1985-86), DC Bar, Mo. Bar, Bar Assn. Met. St. Louis, Phi Beta Kappa, Fellow Am. Coll. Trial Lawyers, Fellow Internat. Acad. Trial Lawyers. mem. North Am. Overseas Com. Comml. Bar Assn. London. Office: Sonnenschein Nath & Rosenthal LLP 1 Metropolitan Sq Ste 3000 Saint Louis MO 63102 Office Phone: 314-259-5886. Office Fax: 314-259-5959. Business E-Mail: srovak@sonnenschein.com.

ROVE, KARL CHRISTIAN, former federal official; b. Denver, Dec. 25, 1950; s. Louis C. (Jr.) and Reba Louise (Wood) Rove; m. Valerie Wainright Rove, July 10, 1976 (div. Jan. 1980); m. Darby Tara Hickson, Jan. 25, 1986; 1 child, Andrew Madison. Student, U. Utah, 1969—71, U. Md., 1972, George Mason U., 1973—75, U. Tex., 1977. Exec. dir. Coll. Rep. Nat. Com., Washington, 1971—73; spl. asst. to chmn. George Bush Nat. Com., Washington, 1973—75, exec. asst. to co-chmn. Richard Obenshain, 1975, also mem. RC exec. com., 1971—75; fin. dir. Va. Rep. Com., Richmond, 1976; dir. Fund for Ltd. Govt., Houston, 1977—79; dep. dir. Gov. William P. Clements Jr. Com., Houston, 1979—80; dir. Tex. Victory Com., Austin, 1980; spl. asst. for adminstrn., dep. exec. asst. to Gov. State of Tex., Austin, 1980—81; pres. Karl Rove & Co., Austin, 1981—99; polit. adv. & chief strategist George W. Bush gubernatorial and presdl. campaigns, 1993—2001; sr. adv. to Pres. The White House, Washington, 2001—07, asst. to Pres., dep. chief of staff for policy, 2005—06. Pres. U.S. Youth Coun., Washington, 1975—77, chmn., 1973—77, selection panel, 1973—77; regent Tex. Woman's U., Denton, 1981—83, East Tex. State U., 1990—91; treas. Tex. Women's Employment and Edn. Program, Austin, 1981—83; mem. regional selection panel White House Fellows Commn., 1987—90. Mem. spl. com. on governance Tex. Higher Edn. Coord. Bd., 1989—91; bd. dirs. Tex. Bus. Hall of Fame, 1987—88; mem. Bd. for Internat. Broadcasting, 1991—; bd. visitors McDonald Obs., 1993—. Named one of 100 Most Influential People in the World, Time mag., 2005. Mem.: Barton Creek Country Club (Austin). *

ROVELSTAD, GORDON H., dentist, researcher; b. Elgin, Ill., May 19, 1921; s. Henry Randolph and Margot Helen (Greenhill) R.; m. Barbara Jean Johnson, Apr. 8, 1945; children: Craig Gordon, Martha Kay, Andrew Todd. Student, St. Olaf Coll., 1939-41; DDS, Northwestern U., Chgo., 1944, MSD, 1948, PhD, 1960; DSc (hon.), Georgetown U., 1970. Diplomate Am. Bd. Pediatric Dentistry. Asst. prof. pediatric dentistry Northwestern U., Chgo., 1946-53; head dental dept. Children's Meml. Hosp., Chgo., 1948-53; ensign USNR, 1943, advanced through grades to capt. Camp Peary, Va., 1945-46; with USNTC, Bainbridge, Md., 1954-59; dir. rsch. US Naval Dental Sch., Bethesda, Md., 1960-65; officer in charge US Naval Dental Rsch. Inst., Gt. Lakes, Ill., 1965-69; dir. rsch. USN Dental Corp., Washington, 1969-74; ret., 1974; asst. dean, prof. U. Miss. Sch. Dentist, Jackson, 1974-80; exec. dir. Am. Coll. Dentists, Gaithersburg, Md., 1981-94, exec. dir. emeritus, 1994—; pres. William J. Gies Found., 1982-98, pres. emeritus, 1998—. Hon. bd. dirs. William J. Gies Found. for Advancement of Dentistry, Am. Dental Edn. Assn., 2003—. Contbr. articles to profl. jours. Fellow Am. Coll. Dentists (pres., v.p.), Internat. Coll. Dentists, N.Y. Acad. Sci., N.Y. Acad. Dentists; mem. ADA, Am. Acad. Pediatric Dentistry (pres., v.p.), Internat. Assn. Dental Rsch. (pres., v.p., sec.), Rotary Internat., Sigma Xi. Avocations: miniatures, music, golf, fishing. Home: 5400 Vantage Point Rd Apt 706 Columbia MD 21044-2663

ROVELSTAD, MATHILDE V(ERNER), retired library and information scientist, educator; b. Germany, 1920; came to U.S., 1951. m. Howard Rovelstad, 1970. PhD, U. Tubingen, 1953; MLS, Cath. U. Am., Washington, DC, 1960. Prof. libr. sci. Cath. U. Am., 1960-90, prof. emeritus, 1990—; ret., 1990. Vis. prof. U. Montreal, 1969 Author: Bibliotheken in den Vereinigten Staaten, 1974; translator Bibliographia, an Inquiry into its Definition and Designations (R. Blum), 1980, Bibliotheken in den Vereinigten Staaten von Amerika und in Kanada, 1988; contbr. articles to profl. jours. Research grantee German Acad. Exch. Svc., 1969, Herzog August Bibliothek Wolfenbüttel, Germany, 1995. Mem. Internat. Fedn. Libr. Assns. and Instns. (standing adv. com. on libr. schs. 1975-81), Assn. for Libr. and Info. Sci. Edn. Office: Cath U Am Sch Libr & Info Sci Washington DC 20064-0001 Mailing: c/o Lisa Swei 6836 26th Ave NE Seattle WA 98115

ROVEN, ALFRED NATHAN, surgeon; came to the U.S., 1949. BA in Psychology, Calif. State U., Northridge, 1969; MD, U. So. Calif., 1977. Diplomate Am. Bd. Plastic and Reconstructive Surgery, Am. Bd. Otolaryngology. Resident in otolaryngology U. So. Calif., 1977-82; clin. chief plastic surgery Cedars Sinai Med. Ctr., LA, 1989-91; resident in plastic and reconstructive surgery U. N.C., 1982-84; clin. chief burns Cedars Sinai Med. Ctr., LA, 1990-92, clin. chief hands, 1990-92. Qualified med. examiner State of Calif., 1985. Contbr. articles to jours. Avocation: reading. Office: 5757 Wishire Blvd 6 Los Angeles CA 90036 Office Phone: 323-937-7733.

ROVER, EDWARD FRANK, foundation administrator, lawyer; b. Oct. 4, 1938; s. Frederick James and Wanda (Charkowski); m. Maureen Wyer, June 15, 1968; children: Elizabeth, Emily, William. AB, Fordham U., 1961; JD, Harvard U., 1964. Bar: N.Y. 1964, U.S. Tax Ct. 1968, U.S. Dist. Ct. (so. dist.) N.Y. 1975, U.S. Supreme Ct. 1994. Assoc. White & Case, NYC, 1964-71, ptnr., 1972—2004, of counsel, 2004—; pres. Dana Found., NYC, 2004—. Bd. dirs. Markel Found., NYC, Cranshaw Corp., Harvard-Mahoney Neurosci. Inst., Boston, Rumsey-Cartier Found., Geneva, Charles A. Dana Found., NYC, pres. Bd. dirs. Waterford Sch., Sandy, Utah, Dana-Farber, Boston, Norton Simon Art Mus., L.A.; sec. Solomon R. Guggenheim Found., NY. Mem.: Century Assn., Assn. Bar City NY, Univ. Club, Harvard Club, Scarsdale Golf Club. Home: 1111 Park Ave New York NY 10128-1234 Office: Dana Found 745 Fifth Ave Ste 900 New York NY 10151 Home Phone: 212-876-8377; Office Phone: 212-223-4040. Business E-Mail: erover@dana.org.

ROVINE, ARTHUR WILLIAM, international arbitrator; b. Phila., Apr. 29, 1937; s. George Isaac and Rosanna (Lipsitz) R.; m. Phyllis Ellen Hamburger, Apr. 7, 1963; children: Joshua, Deborah. AB, U. Pa., 1958; LLB, Harvard U., 1961; PhD, Columbia U., 1966. Bar: D.C. 1964, N.Y. 1984. Assoc. Curtis, Mallet-Prevost, Colt & Mosle, NYC, 1964—66; asst. prof. Cornell U., Ithaca, NY, 1966—72; editor Digest of U.S. Practice in International Law U.S. Dept. State, Washington, 1972—75, asst. legal adviser, 1975—81, first agt. of U.S. Govt. to Iran-U.S. Claims Tribunal The Hague, Netherlands, 1981—83; of counsel Baker & McKenzie, NYC, 1983—85, ptnr., 1985—2005. Adj. prof. law Georgetown U., Washington, 1977-81; vis. lectr. law Yale U., 1998; adj. prof. law Fordham U., 2005—; dir. internat. arbitration confs. Fordham Law Sch.; arbitrator in internat. and other matters. Author: The First Fifty Years: The Secretary-General in World Politics, 1920-1970, 1970; editor: Digest of U.S. Practice in International Law, 1973, 74; co-editor: The Case Law of the International Court of Justice, 1968, 1972, 1974, 1976; bd. editors Am. Jour. Internat. Law, 1977-87; also articles on internat. law and arbitration. Mem. panel on settlement of transnat. bus. disputes, N.Y. panel Ctr. for Pub. Resources; chmn. law subcom. of internat. adv. coun. on profl. edn. Coun. on Internat. Ednl. Exch.; mem. Coun. on Fgn. Rels. Mem. ABA (chmn. internat. law sect. 1985-86, del. to Ho. of Dels. 1988-90), Am. Soc. Internat. Law (cert. of merit 1974, exec. coun. 1975-77, v.p. 1998-99, pres. 2000-02), U.S. Coun. for Internat. Bus. (arbitration com.), Am. Arbitration Assn., Internat. Ctr. for Dispute Resolution (panel of arbitrators), Assn. Bar City N.Y. (arbitration com.), London Ct. Internat. Arbitration. Home: 215 East 68th St New York NY 10021 Office Phone: 212-891-3550. E-mail: arthur.w.rovine@bakernet.com.

ROVINSKY, JOSEPH JUDAH, obstetrician, gynecologist; b. Phila., Sept. 4, 1927; s. Israel and Sarah (Blackman) R.; m. Judith S. Levin, June 24, 1964; children: Audrey, John, Jill, Michael, Paul, David. BA, U. Pa., 1948, MD, 1952. Diplomate Am. Bd. Ob-Gyn. Intern U. Pa. Hosp., Phila., 1952-53; resident in ob-gyn Mt. Sinai Hosp., NYC, 1953-58; practice medicine specializing in ob-gyn, 1958—; chmn. dept. ob-gyn City Hosp. Center, Elmhurst, NY, 1964-74; prof. ob-gyn Mt. Sinai Sch. Medicine, NYC, 1969-74; prof., chmn. dept. ob-gyn Sch. Medicine Health Scis. Center, SUNY, Stony Brook, 1975-79, prof., 1975-89; chmn. dept. ob-gyn L.I. Jewish Med. Center, 1973-92; prof. ob-gyn. Albert Einstein Coll. Medicine, 1989-94; dir. dept. ob/gyn. Sound Shore Med. Ctr. of Westchester, New Rochelle, 1992—. Mem. obstetric adv. com. N.Y.C. Dept. Health, 1964-92. Author: Medical, Surgical and Gynecological Complications of Pregnancy, 1961, 2d edit., 1965; editor: Davis' Gynecology and Obstetrics, 1968-73. Served to capt., M.C. USAF, 1964-66. Mem. ACS, Am. Coll. Obstetricians and Gynecologists, Am. Soc. Reproductive Medicine, Am. Uro-Gynecologic Soc., N.Y. Acad. Medicine, N.Y. Obstetrical Soc., N.Y. Gynecol. Assn., Med. Soc. State N.Y. Jewish. Office: Sound Shore Med Ctr Westchester 16 Guion Pl New Rochelle NY 10801-5500

ROVIRA, LUIS DARIO, state supreme court justice; b. San Juan, Sept. 8, 1923; s. Peter S. and Mae (Morris) R.; m. Lois Ann Thau, June 25, 1966; children: Douglas, Merilyn. BA, U. Colo., 1948, LL.B., 1950. Bar: Colo. 1950. Justice Colo. Supreme Ct., Denver, 1979-95, chief justice, 1990-95, ret., 1995. Mem. Pres.'s Com. on Mental Retardation, 1970-71; chmn. State Health Facilities Council, 1967-76; arbiter and mediator Jud. Arbiter Group, Denver. Trustee Temple Buell Found. With AUS, 1943-46. Mem. ABA, Colo. Bar Assn., Denver Bar Assn. (pres. 1970-71), Colo. Assn. Retarded Children (pres. 1968-70), Alpha Tau Omega, Phi Alpha Delta. Clubs: Athletic (Denver), Country (Denver). Home: 4810 E 6th Ave Denver CO 80220-5137 Office: Judicial Arbiter Group 1601 Blake St Denver CO 80202 Office Phone: 303-572-1919.

ROVIT, RICHARD LEE, neurosurgeon; b. Boston, Apr. 3, 1924; s. Samuel and Frances (Ehrenberg) R.; m. Barbara Sayre Margolis, Mar. 29, 1953; children: Sandra Amy Golze, Adam John, Hugh Russel. Grad., U. Mich., 1944; MD, Jefferson Med. Coll., 1950; MSc, McGill U., 1961. Diplomate Am. Bd. Neurol. Surgery (dir. vice chmn. 1986-92). Intern in surgery Beth Israel Hosp., Boston, 1950-51; resident, then chief resident Mass. Gen. Hosp., Boston, 1951-58; USPH fellow in neurology The Nat. Hosp., London, 1956; sr. fellow in neurosurgery Lahey Clinic, Boston, 1957; fellow in neurophysiology and EEG Montreal (Can.) Neurol. Inst., 1958-59; prof. clin. neurosurgery NYU, 1967—; chmn. neurosurgery St. Vincent's Hosp. and Med. Ctr., NYC, 1967-92; prof. neurosurgery N.Y. Med. Coll., Valhalla, 1990—. Editor, author: Trigeminal Neuralgia, 1991; contbr. articles to profl. jours. Trustee Sarah Neuman divsn. Jewish Home and Hosps., N.Y.C., 2004-. Lt. USN, 1952-54. Fellow ACS (v.p. 1994-95), Am. Assn. Neurol. Surgeons (v.p. 1980-81); mem. N.Y. Soc. Neurosurgeons (pres. 1974-76, 79-80), Soc. Neurol. Surgeons, Fairview Country Club (Greenwich, Conn.), Harvard Club of N.Y. Avocations: golf, running. Home: 42 Brite Ave Scarsdale NY 10583-2309 Office: Manhattan Neurosurg 153 W 11th St New York NY 10011-8305 Home Phone: 914-723-5936; Office Phone: 212-604-7767.

ROVIT, SAM BRIAN, food products executive; b. Louisville, Jan. 24, 1958; s. Earl Herbert and Honey Weisenfeld Rovit; m. Abigail Caitlin Mackenzie, Feb. 2, 1985; children: Nathaniel, Emma, Eli. BA, Duke U., 1979; MA in Law and Diplomacy, Tufts U., 1987; MBA, Harvard U., 1989. Editor McGraw-Hill, Washington, 1981-82; pub. Dawon-Butwick, Washington, 1982-85; assoc. Bain & Co., Chgo., 1988—95, ptnr., 1995—2005; pres., CEO Swift & Co., Greeley, Colo., 2005—. Author: Mastering the

Merger, 2005; contbr. articles to profl. jours. Mem. pres's coun. Mus. Sci. & Industry, Chgo., 1998—. Mem. Chgo. Club. Office: Swift & Co 1770 Promontory Circle Greeley CO 80634 *

ROVNER, ILANA KARA DIAMOND, federal judge; b. Riga, Latvia, 1938; arrived in U.S., 1939; d. Stanley and Ronny (Medalje) Diamond. AB, Bryn Mawr Coll., 1960; postgrad., U. London King's Coll., 1961, Georgetown U., 1961—63; JD, Ill. Inst. Tech., 1966; LittD (hon.), Rosary Coll., 1989, Mundelein Coll., 1989; DHL (hon.), Spertus Coll. of Judaica, 1992. Bar: Ill. 1972, US Dist. (no. dist.) Ill. 1972, US Ct. Appeals (7th cir.) 1977, US Supreme Ct. 1981, Fed. Trial Bar (no. dist.) Ill. 1982. Jud. clk. US Dist. Ct. (no. dist.) Ill., Chgo., 1972—73; asst. US atty. US Atty.'s Office, Chgo., 1973—77, dep. chief of pub. protection, 1975—76, chief pub. protection, 1976—77; dep. gov., legal counsel Gov. James R. Thompson, Chgo., 1977—84; dist. judge US Dist. Ct. (no. dist.) Ill., Chgo., 1984—92; cir. judge US Ct. Appeals (7th cir.), Chgo., 1992—. Mem. Gannon-Proctor Commn. on the Status of Women in Ill., 1982—84; mem. civil justice reform act adv. com. 7th Cir. Ct., Chgo., 1991—95, mem. race and gender fairness com., 1993—; mem. fairness com. US Ct. Appeals (7th cir.), 1996—, mem. gender study task force, 1995—96; mem. jud. conf. US Com. Ct. Adminstrn. Case Mgmt., 2000—. Ctrl. and East European law initiative vol. ABA, 1997—; trustee Bryn Mawr Coll., Pa., 1983—89; mem. bd. overseers Ill. Inst. Tech./Kent Coll. Law, 1983—; trustee Ill. Inst. Tech., 1989—; mem. adv. coun. Rush Ctr. for Sports Medicine, Chgo., 1991—96; bd. dirs. Rehab. Inst. Chgo., 1998—; bd. visitors No. Ill. U. Coll. Law, 1992—94; vis. com. Northwestern U. Sch. Law, 1993—98, U. Chgo. Law Sch., 1993—96, 2000—03; chair Ill. state selection com. Rhodes Scholarship Trust, 1998—2000. Named Today's Chgo. Woman of the Yr., 1985, Woman of Achievement, Chgo. Women's Club, 1986; named one of 15 Chgo. Women of the Century, Chgo. Sun Times, 1999; named to Today's Chgo. Women Hall of Fame, 2002; recipient Spl. Commendation award, US Dept. Justice, 1975, Spl. Achievement award, 1976, Ann. Nat. Law and Social Justice Leadership award, League to Improve the Cmty., 1975, Ann. Guardian Police award, 1977, Profl. Achievement award, Ill. Inst. Tech., 1986, ORT Women's Am. Cmty. Svc. award, 1987—88, commendation def. of prisoners com., Chgo. Bar Assn., 1987, Svc. award, Spertus Coll. of Judaica, 1987, Ann. award, Chgo. Found. for Women, 1990, Louis Dembitz Brandeis medal for Disting. Legal Svc., Brandeis U., 1993, 1st Woman award, Valparaiso U. Sch. Law, 1993, Hebrew Immigrant Aid Soc. Chgo. 85th Anniversary honoree, 1996, Arabella Babb Mansfield award, Nat. Assn. Women Lawyers, 1998, award, Chgo. Attys. Coun. of Hadassah, 1999, First Woman award, Chgo. Bar Assn. Alliance for Women and Women's Bar Assn. Ill., 2000, Georgetown U. Law Ctr., 2001, Chgo. Hist. Soc. Trailblazers Award, 2003, Lifetime Achievement award, Decalogue Soc. Lawyers, 2004, Vanguard award, Chgo. Bar Assn. and Lesbian and Gay Bar Assn. Chgo., 2004, Thurgood Marshall Career Achievement award, Assn. Corp. Counsel Chgo. chpt., 2005, Hero of Liberty award, Nat. Liberty Mus., 2005, Inaugural Judge Abraham Lincoln Marovitz Mentoring award, Chgo. Bar Assn. and Found. Lend-a-Hand Program, 2005. Mem.: Chgo. Bar Assn. (Justice John Paul Stevens award 2005), Jewish Judges Assn. Ill. (Lifetime Achievement award 2004), Decalogue Soc. of Lawyers (citation of honor 1991, Merit award 1997), Chgo. Coun. Lawyers, Women's Bar Assn. Ill. (ann. award 1989, 1st Myra Bradwell Woman of Achievement award 1994, 1st Woman Award (in conjunction with Chicago Bar Assn. Alliance for Women) 2000), Fed. Judges Assn., Fed. Bar Assn. (mem. selection com. Chgo. chpt. 1977—80, treas. 1978—79, sec. 1979—80, 2d v.p. 1980—81, 1st v.p. 1981—82, pres. 1982—83, 2d v.p. 7th cir. 1983—84, v.p. 7th cir. 1984—85), Kappa Beta Pi, Phi Alpha Delta (hon.). Office: 219 S Dearborn St Ste 2774 Chicago IL 60604-1803 *

ROWAN, HERMAN T., art educator, artist; b. NYC, July 20, 1923; s. Charles and Hannah Rosen; m. Helen June Rowan (div.); m. Terri Deane Rowan, Sept. 15, 1968; children: Nathaniel, Samuel. BS, Kans. State U., 1950; MFA, State u. Iowa, 1952. Prof. U. Minn., Mpls., 1963—. Author: (retrospective exhbn.) U. Minn., 1992; exhibitions include Joan of Art Gallery, Mpls., 2006. Sgt. Air Corps US Army, 1941—45, ETO. Home: 1915 19th Ave NE Minneapolis MN 55418

ROWAN, RICHARD G., former academic administrator; BS, Furman U.; MEd, EdS, Ga. State U.; D of Design (hon.), Nottingham Trent U., Eng. Pres., co-founder Savannah Coll. Art and Design, Ga., 1978—2000, chancellor Ga., 2000—01. Mem. Savannah adv. bd. Bank of Am. Recipient Oglethorpe award, Freedom award NAACP; named to Hon. Order Ky. Cols. Mem. Savannah C. of C. (pres., bd. dirs.). Office: Savannah Coll Art & Design Office of the Chancellor PO Box 3146 Savannah GA 31402-3146

ROWAN, RICHARD LAMAR, business management educator; b. Guntersville, Ala., July 10, 1931; s. Leon Virgle and Mae (Williamson) R.; m. Marilyn Walker, Aug. 3, 1963; children: John Richard, Jennifer Walker. AB, Birmingham-So. Coll., 1953; postgrad., Auburn U., 1956-57; PhD, U. N.C., 1961. Instr. Auburn (Ala.) U., 1956-57, U. N.C., Chapel Hill, 1958-59, 60-61; lectr. U. Pa., Phila., 1961-62, asst. prof., 1962-66, asso. prof. industry, 1966-73, prof. industry, 1973—. Dir. indsl. research unit, 1989-91; co-dir. Ctr. for Human Resources, 1991—; visitor to Faculty Econs. and Politics Cambridge (Eng.) U., 1972; pvt. sector advisor U.S. State Dept. Com. on Internat. Investment and Multinational Enterprises, OECD, 1982-89; chmn. Labor Relations Council, 1985—. Author: (with H.R. Northrup) The Negro and Employment Opportunity, 1965, Readings in Labor Economics and Labor Relations, 5th edit., 1984, The Negro in the Steel Industry, 1969, The Negro in the Textile Industry, 1970, (with others) Studies of Negro Employment, 1970, Educating the Employed Disadvantaged for Upgrading, 1972, Collective Bargaining: Survival in the 1970's, 1972, Opening the Skilled Construction Trades to Blacks, 1972, The Impact of Government Manpower Programs, 1975, International Enforcement of Union Standards in Ocean Transport, 1977, The Impact of OSHA, 1978, Multinational Bargaining Attempts: The Record, the Cases, and the Prospects, 1980; (with H.R. Northrup) Employee Relations and Regulations in the 80s, 1982; (with others) Multinational Union Organizations in the Manufacturing Industries, (with D.C. Campbell) The Multinational Enterprises and the OECD Industrial Relations Guidelines, 1984, Trade Union Clout Erodes, But For How Long?, 1985, Employee Relations Trends and Practices in the Textile Industry, 1986; contbr. articles to profl. jours. Mem. personnel com. Del. Valley Settlement Alliance, 1966-68. Served with Transp. Corps U.S. Army, 1953-56. Recipient Disting. Alumni award, Birmingham-So. Coll., 2000. Mem. Indsl. Rels. Rsch. Assn. (sec. Phila. 1964-65), Acad. Internat. Bus. Democrat. Episcopalian. Home: 113 Blackthorn Rd Wallingford PA 19086-6046 Office: U Pa Wharton Sch 3733 Spruce St Philadelphia PA 19104-6301 Office Phone: 610-565-0409.

ROWAN, STEVEN WILLIAM, history professor; b. Bremerton, Wash., Apr. 4, 1943; s. James Harvey and Dorothy Virginia Rowan; m. Marilyn Anne Schuster, July 6, 1966; children: Jonna Diane Rowan Needle, Austin Günther James. BA, U. Wash., Seattle, 1965; PhD, Harvard U., Cambridge, Mass., 1970. Prof. history U. Mo., St. Louis, 1970—. Vis. sr. lectr. King's Coll., London, 1975—76; rsch. fellow Alexander-von-Humboldt-Stiftung, Freiburg, Germany, 1979—80; Fulbright disting. chmn. Karl-Franzens-U., Graz, Austria, 2007; mem. Sch. Hist. Studies, Inst. Advanced Study, Princeton, NJ, 1989—90. Author: Ulrich Zasius: Jurist in German Renaissance, 1987; editor, translator: L. von Reizenstein, Mysteries of New Orleans, pub.: 16 books. Recipient Outstanding Achievement award, Soc. German-Am. Studies, Balt., 2003; fellow, NEH, 1971; rsch. fellow, Newberry Libr., Chgo., 1978—79. Fellow: Sixteenth Century Studies Conf. Lutheran. Avocations: travel, reading. Office: U Mo History Dept 1 University Blvd Saint Louis MO 63121

ROWAND, AARON RYAN, professional baseball player; b. Portland, Oreg., Aug. 29, 1977; m. Marianne Griffen, Nov. 27, 1999; children: Tatum, McKay. Student, Calif. State U., Fullerton. Draft pick Chgo. White Sox, 1998, outfielder, 2001—05, Phila. Phillies, 2005—. Named to Nat. League All-Star Team, Maj. League Baseball, 2007; recipient Roberto Clemente award, 2005. Achievements include winning a World Series Championship with the White Sox, 2005. Avocations: hunting, golf. Office: Phila Phillies Citizens Bank Park One Citizens Bank Way Philadelphia PA 19148 *

ROWARK, MAUREEN, fine arts photographer; b. Edinburgh, Midlothian, Scotland, Feb. 28, 1933; came to U.S., 1960, naturalized, 1970; d. Alexander Pennycook and Margaret (Gorman) Prezdpelski; m. Robert Rowark, May 3, 1952 (div. July 1965). 1 child, Mark Steven. Student, Warmington Bus. Coll., Royal Leamington Spa, Eng., 1950-51, Royal Leamington Spa Art Sch.; diploma, Speedwriting Inst., NYC, 1961; AS in Edn., St. Clair County C.C., Port Huron, Mich., 1977, AA, 1978. Supr. proof reading Nevin D. Hirst Advt., Ltd., Leeds, England, 1952-55; publicity asst. Alvis Aero Engines, Ltd., Coventry, England, 1955-57; adminstrv. asst. Port Huron Motor Inn, 1964-66; adminstrv. asst. pub. rels. dept. Geophysics and Computer Svcs., Inc., New Orleans, 1966-68; sales mgr. Holiday Inn, Port Huron, 1968-70; adminstrv. asst. Howard Corp., Port Huron, 1971-73; sales and systems coord. Am. Wood Products, Ann Arbor, Mich., 1973-74; systems coord. Daniels & Zermack Architects, Ann Arbor, 1974; systems coord., cataloger fine arts dept. St. Clair County Community Coll., Port Huron, 1976-79; freelance fine arts photographer Port Huron, 1978—. Photographer Patterns mag. front cover, 1978, Erie Sq. Gazette, 1979, Bluewater Area Tourism Bur. brochure, 1989, 92, 95, 97, 2000, 01, Corits Castle, Lexington, 2002, Port Huron, Can. Legion, Wyo., Ont. Br., 1987, 88—, Grace Episcopal Ch. Mariner's Day, Port Huron, 1987, 92-2001, Homes mag., 1989. Photographer (one-woman shows) Grace Episcopal Ch., 1995, Port Huron Mus., 1995, St. Clair River Remedial Action Plan, 1995 (Best in Landscape Category), Mich. Waterways Coun. Girl Scouts Exhibit, 1996; Exhibited in group shows at Ea. Mich. Internat. Juried Exhbn., 2000, 1981—98 (Award of Excellence, 1982, 1983, Best Photography award, 1995, 1996, 1997), Our Town Juried Exhbn., 1997, St. Clair County C.C., 1983, 1986 (Award of Excellence, 1986), Gallery Lambton, Sarnia, Ont., Can., 1983—92 (Best Photography, 1988), 1994, 1996—97, 2000, Bluewater Bridge, 1988, Kaskilaaksontie, Finland, 1991 (Par Excellence award), Swann Gallery, Detroit, 1996, St. Clair (Mich.) Art Gallery, Genesis Gallery, Lexington, Mich., others, Represented in permanent collections Royal Can. Legion, Wyo. Br. Centaph, Capac State Bank, Grace Episcopal Ch., Thomas Edison Inn, Port Huron Hosp., Front Cover Good Health News; costume design, manufacture and modelling Bluewater Art Assn., 2000—01, photographer Bluewater Percussion Brochure, 2001;, author short stories. Cons., buyer interior decor Grace Episcopal Ch., 1994; active Port Huron Mus., 1978; founder Bluewater les Chapeaux Rouge chpt. Red Hat Soc., 2000—; prodr., dir. calendar We Can Still Make Waves, 2005, Waiting for Our Ship to Come In, 2007; prodr., designer parade float Rotary Internat., 2005 (1st pl. award). Recipient hon. mention Gallery Lambton, Sarnia, 1981, 2d pl. memoir writing women's history month St. Clair County C.C., 1999; winner 2d and 3d place awards Times Herald Newspaper, 1988, 1st place juried photography award Port Huron Art Festival, 1997, 1st place St. Patrick's Day Parade Float, 2006, 1st place Rotary Internat. Day Parade Float, 2005. Mem. St. Clair County C.C. Alumni Assn., Phi Theta Kappa, Lambda Mu. Democrat. Episcopalian. Avocations: costumes, interior design and parade floats, travel, theater, memoir writing. Home and Office: 3512 Walnut St Port Huron MI 48060 E-mail: ha-penerth-oftar@prodigy.net.

ROWDEN, MARCUS AUBREY, lawyer, retired government agency administrator; b. Detroit, Mar. 13, 1928; s. Louis and Gertrude (Lifsitz) Rosenzweig; m. Justine Leslie Bessman, July 21, 1950; children: Gwen, Stephanie. BA in Econs, U. Mich., Ann Arbor, 1950, JD with distinction, 1953. Bar: Mich. 1953, D.C. 1978. Trial atty. Dept. Justice, 1953-58; legal advisor U.S. Mission to European Communities, 1959-62; solicitor, assoc. gen. counsel, gen. counsel AEC, 1965-74; commr., chmn. U.S. NRC, Washington, 1975-77; ptnr. Fried, Frank, Harris, Shriver and Jacobson, Washington, 1977—. With US Army, 1946—47. Decorated officer Order Legion of Honor Republic of France; Recipient Disting. Service award AEC, 1972 Mem. ABA, Fed. Bar Assn., Mich. Bar Assn., DC Bar Assn., Internat. Nuc. Law Assn., Order of Coif. Home: 7937 Deepwell Dr Bethesda MD 20817-1927 Office: Fried Frank Harris Shriver and Jacobson 1001 Pennsylvania Ave NW Washington DC 20004-2505 Office Phone: 202-639-7070.

ROWE, AUDREY, paralegal; b. Albuquerque, June 26, 1958; d. James Franklin Ringold and Geneva Doris (Jennings) Robinson. A in Specialized Bus. in Acctg., ICS Ctr. for Degrees, Scranton, Pa., 1988, A in Specialized Bus. in Fin., 1989; BSBA, Century U., 1991, MBA, 1995, cert. paralegal studies, 1996, A in Specialized Bus. in Paralegal Studies, 1999. Svc. rep. Mountain and Southwestern Bell Telephone Co., Albuquerque, Houston, 1978-83; clk., carrier U.S. Postal Svc. PS05, Bellaire, Sugar Land, Tex., 1983-86; supr. mails U.S. Postal Svc. EAS15, Sugar Land, 1986-87; officer-in-charge U.S. Postal Svc. EAS 18, Rosharon, Tex., 1987; from supr. mails EAS 15 to gen. supr. mails EAS 17 U.S. Postal Svc., Houston, 1987-89; relief tour supt. U.S. Postal Svc. EAS 21 (Detail Assignment), Houston, 1989; mgr. gen. mail facility U.S. Postal Svc. EAS22 (Detail Assignment), Capitol Heights, Md., 1989-90; mgr. mail processing U.S. Postal Svc. EAS21, Charlottesville, Va., 1990-91; MSC dir. city ops. U.S. Postal Svc. EAS23 (Detail Assignment), Roanoke, Va., 1991; mgr. gen. mail facility U.S. Postal Svc. EAS24, Washington, 1991-96; plant mgr. U.S. Postal Svc. EAS25, Dulles, Va., 1992; pvt. contractor, paralegal, 1996-98; paralegal Lenox, Biddinger & Conrad, P.C., Woodbridge, Va., 1997-99, Wilson Strickland & Benson P.C., Atlanta, 1999-2000, Chamberlain, Hrdlicka, White, Williams & Martin, 2000—03, Holland & Knight, LLP, 2003—. Mem. Nat. Fedn. Paralegal Assn., Nat. Assn. Legal Assts. Avocations: piano, violin, reading. Office Phone: 404-817-8500. Personal E-mail: audrey_rowe@comcast.net.

ROWE, BONNIE GORDON, music company executive; b. Buford, Ga, May 3, 1922; s. Bonnie Gordon and Alma (Poole) R.; m. Mary Wilburta Shidler; 1 child, Sharon Lynn; m. Gloria Lucille Fairfax, Feb. 17, 1962 (div.); 1 child, Susan Rebecca. Student, Ga. Evening Coll., 1939-41, U. Wichita, 1948-49, Ga. State Coll., 1949-52. Traffic mgr. Bonanza Air Lines, Las Vegas, 1946-48, music tchr., 1948-52; owner Rowe Accordion Distbg. Co., Rowe Accordion Ctr., Atlanta, 1952-56, Atlanta Music Pub. Co., 1956—, B. Rowe Music Co., Atlanta, 1957—. Pres.-treas. B. Rowe Enterprises, Inc., 1973—. Bd. dir. Sandtown Found., Atlanta. Lt. col. USAAF, World War II, ETO. Decorated Air medals with three oak leaf clusters. Mem.: Nat. Assn. Music Mchts., Atlanta Fedn. Musicians (life), The Mil. Order of the World Wars (past comdr. Atlanta chpt.), Internat. Platform Assn., Sandtown Civitan Club (pres., past pres. Met. Atlanta Coun., lt. gov.), Air Force Assn., Res. Officers Assn., Travelers Protective Assn., 781st Bomb Squadron Assn. (465th bomb group WWII), Atlanta C. of C., Mil. Officers Assn. Am., Southea. Accordion Assn. (past pres.), Dobbins AFB Officers Club, Elks (exalted ruler 1987, 1988, 1989, past pres. past exalted rulers assn., past state organist Ga. Elks Assn., trustee Union City), Am. Legion, Gamma Delta Phi. Home: 5085 Erin Rd SW Atlanta GA 30331-7810 Office: 6102 Mableton Pkwy Mableton GA 30126-4302 Office Phone: 770-948-8403. Personal E-mail: brga30331@aol.com.

ROWE, CHARLES ALFRED, artist, graphics designer, educator; b. Great Falls, Mont., Feb. 7, 1934; s. Alfred Lewis and Alice Lillian (Ledbetter) R.; m. Eugenia Dean, July 5, 1958; children: Allison Rene, Jon Garner, Dorian Leigh. Student, Mont. State U., 1952—53, So. Meth. U., 1956—57, U. Chgo., 1959—60; BFA, Sch. Art Inst., Chgo., 1960; MFA, Tyler Sch. Art, 1968. Prin. Charles Rowe Advt., Chgo., 1957-60; graphic designer Am. Can Co., Bellwood, Ill., 1960-62, Abrams-Bannister Engraving, Inc., Greenville, SC, 1962-64; prof. art U. Del., Newark, 1964-97, emeritus prof., 1997—. One-man shows include Tyler Sch. Art, Phila., 1968, Mickelson Gallery, Washington, 1970, 1974, C.M. Russell Mus., Great Falls, 1972—73, 1981, 1992, Pleiades Gallery, NYC, 1977, 1981, Vision of La Herradura, Almuñecar, Spain, 1988, USAF exhbn. Soc. Illustrators, NYC, 1991, 2004, West Chester U., Pa., 1992, Soc. Illustrators, NYC, 1993, 2004, exhibited in group shows at C.M. Russell Mus., 1974, 1976, 1978, 1980, 1982—83, 1986—91, Am. Painters in Paris, 1976, Monac-Western Art Exhibit, Spokane, Wash., 1977—78, Easton Waterfowl Festival, Md., 1981—82, USAF Nat. Collection, 1987, 1989, 1991, USAF exhbn. Soc. Illustrators, NYC, 1989, Our Own Show, Soc. Illustrators, 1990, 1991—96, 1998—2007, Atrium Gallery, 1995, 1996, One Small Step, NASA, U. Del., Newark, 1995, Art and Antiques, Wilmington, Del., 2005, LDAR Gala Exhbn., 2003—07, over 220 other exhbns., Represented in permanent collections U. Del., Mont. State Collection, Mont. State U., Del. State Collection, Libr. Congress, Washington, Great Falls Pub. Schs., Michael Landon Prodns., Calif., Meredith Corp., Des Moines, Collection Knissel, Austria, Star Showers Found., Graveson-en-Provence, France, Archives Victoria and Albert Mus., London, artists USAF Nat. Collection, Washington, Jacqueline Pierson, Nice, France, artists USAF Nat. Collection, Washington, Banco de Granada, Spain, NASA Space Mus., Hauptman and Greenwood Collections, NYC, Vera Haas, Dallas, Jerry Pinkney, Croton-On-Hudson, Baker, Palm Springs, Calif., David Duncan, Spokane, Wash.; fabric designer Galleon Fabrics, Inc., NYC, Jones of NY, Saks Fifth Ave., Bush Collection, Swampscott, Mass., Steele Collection, Big Fork, MT, Jordan Baker, Kevin Kilner, Hollywood, Calif., 1987, Kevin Costner Collection, 1997, designer graphics Mont. State Arts Coun., Del. state duck stamp, 1981. With inf. U.S. Army, 1954-56. Ctr. for Advanced Study fellow, 1981-82; grantee U. Del., 1964-79, Nat. Endowment for Arts and Humanities, 1972-73, U. Del. Bicentennial, 1976. Mem. Soc. of Illustrators (N.Y.C.). Home: Chapel Hill 133 Aronimink Dr Newark DE 19711-3802 Office Phone: 302-584-2925. Business E-Mail: CharlesRoweStudio@comcast.net. *In my paintings and other artforms I strive for perfection, uniqueness, and a special inner beauty, but more than that, I try to create art that has a universal quality. This universality makes an artform communicate beyond a specific locale, continent or a limited time reference. All great works of art have this special element regardless of when they were created.*

ROWE, DAVID LEE, financial advisor; b. Colorado Springs, Colo., Jan. 30, 1954; s. Prentiss Eldon and Jo Ann (Osborn) R.; m. Elizabeth Webb, June 21, 1986; children: Schuyler Jourdan, Thomas Prentiss. BA, U. Colo., Boulder, 1976; M, Johns Hopkins U., Washington and Bologna, Italy, 1979; MBA, NYU, 1995. Asst. to undersec. U.S. Dept. Commerce, Washington, 1979—80; analyst Commodities Rsch. Inst., NYC, 1980—81; fin. advisor Merrill Lynch, NYC, 1981—83, Prudential Wachovia Securities, NYC, 1983—, sr. v.p., asst. br. mgr., 1997—. Bd. dirs. 133 E. 80th St. Corp., 1999—; adv. bd. Health Advs. Older People, 2003—; 2nd v.p. Health Advocates for Older People, 2005-; bd. dirs. Quogue Jr. Theatre Troupe, 2006-; mem. cmty. ministry coun. St. Bartholomew's Ch., N.Y.C., 1987-96, mem. vestry, 1997-2005, treas., 2000-05; mem. vestry St. George's Ch., 2006—; pres. Quogue Jr. Theatre Troupe, 2007-. Home: 133 E 80th St New York NY 10021-0317 Office: Wachovia Securities 650 Madison Ave New York NY 10022-1801 Personal E-mail: cujhunyu@yahoo.com. Business E-Mail: david.l.rowe@wachoviasec.com.

ROWE, DAVID WINFIELD, lawyer; b. Chgo., Nov. 7, 1954; s. Bernard John and Gertrude Katherine (Johnson) R.; m. Martha Lynn Plott, June 12, 1977; children: Daniel, Peter. BA in Psychology with honors, cum laude, Davidson Coll., NC, 1976; PhD in Psychology, U. Tenn., Knoxville, 1981; JD, U. Mich., Ann Arbor, 1987. Bar: Colo. 1987, Nebr. 1989, U.S. Dist. Ct. Colo. 1987, U.S. Dist. Ct. Nebr. 1989, U.S. Ct. Appeals (10th cir.) 1987, U.S. Ct. Appeals (8th cir.) 2004, U.S. Supreme Ct. 2006. Post doctoral fellowship in law and psychology U. Nebr., Lincoln, 1989—91; vis. asst. prof. Davidson Coll., NC, 1981—82; mental health worker Peninsula Psychiat. Hosp., Louisville, Tenn., 1982-84; instr. dept. psychology U. Tenn., Knoxville, 1982-84; assoc. Gorsuch, Kirgis, Campbell, Walker & Grover, Denver, 1987-89; assoc. and ptnr. Kinsey, Ridenour, Becker & Kistler, Lincoln, Nebr., 1991—2005; ptnr. Kinsey, Rowe, Becker & Kistler, LLP, 2006, Kinsey Morris Becker Kistler Titus & Rowe, LLP, 2006—. Mem. interim study group on foster care Health and Human Svcs. com. Nebr. State Legislature, 1990-91; adj. prof. psychology U. Nebr., Lincoln, 1992-94; bd. dirs., past treas. Lincoln Attention Ctr. for Youth; mem. The Mediation Ctr., Detention Ctr. Adv. Bd., 2003-. Author: (with others) Dimensions of Child Advocacy: Advocating for the Child in Protection Proceedings, 1990, Children Under Three in Foster Care, 1991. Exec. com. Lancaster County Rep. Com., 1991-97, chmn., 1993-95; bd. dirs. Lincoln-Lancaster Mental Health Found., 1993-, v.p., 1995-96, pres., 1996-97; mem. Ctrl. Com. Nebr. Rep. Com., 1993-97; bd. dirs. The Arc of Lincoln Lancaster County, 2003-; deacon Westminster Prebyn. Ch., 1996-99. Mem. ABA, Nebr. Bar Assn. (alternative dispute resolution com. 1990—2000), Cornhusker Kiwanis (pres. Lincoln 1997-98). Avocations: bicycle touring, bicycle racing. Office: Morris Becker Kistler Titus & Rowe LLP 121 S 13th St#601 PO Box 85778 Lincoln NE 68501-5778 Home Phone: 402-488-3870; Office Phone: 402-438-1313. Business E-Mail: drowe@kinseymorris.com.

ROWE, ERNEST RAS, education educator, academic administrator; b. Hot Springs, Ark., July 19, 1933; s. Stephen Paul and Emma Leathia (Martin) R.; m. Carla True Dirk, May 27, 1995. BS with distinction, Ariz. State U., 1955, MEd, 1962, EdD, 1965; postgrad., Gonzaga U., 1975, Dublin City U., Ireland, 1989. Tchr. Madison Sch. Dist., Phoenix, 1960-61, Garden Grove (Calif.) Unified Sch. Dist., 1964-66; cons. spl. edn. Ariz. Dept. Pub. Instrn., Phoenix, 1966-67; asst. prof. Idaho State U., Pocatello, 1967-70, assoc. prof., 1970-74, prof. edn., 1974-95, interim chmn. dept. edn., summer 1992; adminstrv. intern Cen. Adminstrn., 1982-83, 94-95. Vis. prof. edn. Calif. State U., Long Beach, summer 1965; adv. mem. Idaho Task Force on Higher Edn., 1982-83; gov. apptd. Idaho commr. to Edn. Commn. of the States, 1979-93, rep. to steering com., 1989-93; elected chmn. Idaho State U. Faculty Senate, 1970, 71-72, 86-87. Contbr. articles to profl. jours. Bd. dirs. Bannock Meml. Hosp., 1975-78; mem. Idaho Bd. Medicine pre-litigation panel for malpractice hearings, 1980-95. 1st lt. U.S. Army, 1955-57. Mem.: AAUP, Am. Inst. Parliamentarians (gov. N.W. region 1992—94, univ. parliamentarian), Nat. Soc. Study Edn., Kyrene Corridor Club, Rotary (pres. Pocatello, Idaho club 1981—82, asst. dist. gov. 1998—99, Ariz. pres. Chandler chpt. 2002—03), Masons, Phi Kappa Phi (pres. 1972—73, 1987—88). Episcopalian. Avocations: exercise, music, travel, photography. *Initiative and responsibility are cornerstones of a meaningful personal and professional life. Sadly they are missing in much of contemporary society. Apathy, the absence of civility and self-indulgence appear most prominently at the turn of the century and thus far in the 21st century.*

ROWE, G. STEVEN, state attorney general; m. Amanda Rowe; 4 children. BS, US Mil. Acad.; MBA, U. Utah; JD, U. Maine. Mem. Dist. 30 Maine Ho. Reps., 1993-95, mem. Dist. 35, 1995—2001; litig. counsel UNUMProvident; atty. gen. State of Maine, 2001—. Bd. mem. Pine Tree

Legal Assistance, Inc. With US Army, with USAR. Mem.: NE Legis. Assn. on Prescription Drug Prices, Maine Econ. Growth Coun. Democrat. Office: Office of Atty General State House Station 6 Augusta ME 04333 Office Phone: 207-626-8800.

ROWE, HARRISON EDWARD, electrical engineer; b. Chgo., Jan. 29, 1927; s. Edward and Joan (Golden) R.; m. Alicia Jane Steeves, Feb. 10, 1951; children: Amy Rogers, Elizabeth Joanne, Edward Steeves, Alison Pickard. BS in Elec. Engring, Mass. Inst. Tech., 1948, MS, 1950, Sc.D., 1952; M of Engring. (hon.), Stevens Inst. Tech., 1988. Mem. tech. staff Radio Research Lab., Bell Labs., Holmdel, NJ, 1952-84; Anson Wood Burchard prof. elec. engring. Stevens Inst. Tech., Hoboken, NJ, 1984-93, prof. emeritus, 1993—. Vis. lectr. U. Calif., Berkeley, 1963, Imperial Coll., U. London, 1968; mem. Def. Sci. Bd. Task Force, 1972-74 Author: Signals and Noise in Communication Systems, 1965, Electromagnetic Propagation in Multi-Mode Random Media, 1999; assoc. editor: IEEE Trans. on Communication, 1974-76; contbr. articles to profl. jours.; patentee in field. Served with USN, 1945-46. Co-recipient Microwave prize, 1972, David Sarnoff award, 1977. Fellow IEEE; mem. Monmouth Symphony Soc., Navesink Country Club, Sigma Xi, Tau Beta Pi, Eta Kappa Nu. Clubs: Shrewsbury Sailing and Yacht, Appalachian Mountain. Unitarian Universalist. Home: 9 Buttonwood Ln Rumson NJ 07760-1045 Office Phone: 732-747-0356. Business E-Mail: harrisonrowe@comcast.net.

ROWE, HERBERT JOSEPH, retired trade association executive; b. Granite City, Ill., Mar. 25, 1924; s. Herbert Bernard and Maude (Klein) R.; m. Ann Muter, Dec. 2, 1950; children: Douglas H., Stephen F., James D., Edith L., Allen. Student, U. Tex., 1942—43, Purdue U., 1943—44; BS in Mktg., U. Ill., 1948; LittD (hon.), London Inst. for Applied Rsch., 1975. With Edward Valves, Inc. (subs. Rockwell Mfg. Co.), 1948—50, Muter Co., Chgo., 1952—71, v.p., 1957—64, pres., 1964—71, treas., 1964—67, chmn. bd., 1965—71, also dir., 1957—71; pres., treas., dir. Wescoil Co., 1964—66, Tri-Axial Corp., 1966—67; v.p., treas. Gen. Magnetic Corp., 1965—67, chmn. bd., dir., 1967—70, Pemcor, Inc., Westchester, Ill., 1971—75; assoc. adminstr. external affairs NASA, 1975—78; sr. v.p. Electronic Industries Assn., 1978—89; chmn. Famro Corp., 1989—90; pres. Internat. Electronics Fedn., 1989—90. Sec.-treas. Englewood Elec. Supply Wis., Inc., 1972-75, Rahr's Inc., 1972-75; pres. Enclave of Naples, Inc., 1992-94, treas., 1994-96; pres. Rowe Corp., 1994-97; treas. Quality wholesale Foods of S.W. Fla., 1994-96. Pres. Pokagon Trails coun. Boy Scouts Am., 1964-66, pres. Calumet coun., 1966-68, region 7 exec. com., 1966-72, vice chmn., 1971-72, bd. dirs. East Ctrl. region, 1972-75, nat. program com., 1970-78, 90-94, nat. Cub Scout com., 1970-80, chmn., 1990-94, S.E. regional exec. com., 1975-78, So. regional exec. bd., 1993—, bd. dirs. Nat. Capital Area coun., 1978-90, adv. bd., 1990-94, exec. bd. S.W. Fla. coun., 1992—, nat. exec. com., exec. bd., 1990-95, nat. adv. bd., 1995—; membership chmn. Nat. Eagle Scouts Assn., 1976-80; corp. campaign chmn. Chgo. Met. Crusade Mercy, 1964-68; chmn. bd. Edn. Caucus, Flossmoor, Ill., 1962; bd. dirs. Flossmoor United Party, 1963-68; mem. U. Ill. Found., 1967—; adv. com. U. Ill. Coll. Commerce and Bus. Adminstrn., 1968-78, 97-2002; bd. dirs. Electronic Industries Found., 1974-94; adv. bd. Air and Space Mus., Smithsonian Inst., 1975-78; active Moorings Presbyn. Ch., Naples, Fla. With USMCR, 1942-46, 50-52. Recipient Silver Beaver award Boy Scouts Am., 1966, Silver Antelope award, 1969, Silver Buffalo award, 1994; NASA team award Bicentennial Expo on Sci. and Tech., Exceptional Svc. medal, 1978, Baden-Powell fellow World Scout Found., 1992. Mem. AIAA, AAAS, Electronic Industries Assn. (hon., bd. dirs. 1967-69, bd. govs. 1969-75, exec. com. parts divsn. 1966-75, vice chmn. parts divsn. 1970-74, chmn. 74-75, bd. dirs. consumer electronics divsn. 1972-75, chmn. world trade com. 1968-70, vice-chmn. 1970-73, chmn. membership and scope com. 1972-74, Disting. Svc. award 1989), Am. Loudspeaker Mfrs. Assn. (v.p., dir. 1967-68, pres., bd. dirs. 1968-70), Assn. Electronic Mfrs. (bd. dirs. 1970-73), Nat. Space Club, Nat. Space Inst., Am. Acad. Polit. Social Sci., Am. Soc. Assn. Execs. (vice chmn. internat. sect. 1986-87, chmn. 1987-88), US Naval Inst., Field Mus. Natural History, European Soc. Assn. Execs., Greater Washington Soc. Assn. Execs., Naples Coun. World Affairs (bd. dirs. 2003-05), Explorers Club, Chgo. Art Inst., Am. Legion, Chaine des Rôtisseurs, L'Ordre Mondial, Internat. Wine and Food Soc. (pres. Naples br. 2001-07), English-Speaking Union (pres. Naples chpt. 1996—2007, nat. dir. 1997—, regional vice chmn. 2000-03, chmn. 2003-), Conservancy, S.W. Fla., Forum Club S.W. Fla. (bd. dirs. 2000-03), Naples Press Club (bd. dirs. 1998-2000), Royal Poinciana Golf Club, Naples Yacht Club, Circumnavigators Club, Beta Gamma Sigma, Alpha Phi Omega, Sigma Chi (dir. Kappa Kappa corp. 1954-75, sec. 1971-73, pres. 1973-75, Charles J. Kiler award 1975, Grand Consul's citation 1976, Significant SIG award 2006). Home: 4601 Gulf Shore Blvd N Apt 12 Naples FL 34103-2214 Personal E-mail: hrowe13@comcast.net.

ROWE, JOHN WALLIS (JACK ROWE), retired insurance company executive, education educator; b. Jersey City, June 20, 1944; s. Albert Wallis and Elizabeth (Lynch) R.; m. Valerie Ann DelTufo, Aug. 10, 1968; children: Meredith, Abigail, Rebecca. BS with honors, Canisius Coll., 1966; MD with distinction, U. Rochester, 1970. Diplomate Am. Bd. Internal Medicine, Am. Bd. Nephrology. Resident in internal medicine Harvard Med. Sch., Beth Israel Hosp., Boston, 1970-72; clin. assoc. Nat. Inst. Child Health and Human Devel., Balt., 1972-74; rsch., clin. fellow Harvard Med. Sch., Mass. Gen. Hosp., Boston, 1974-75; from instr. to prof. Harvard Med. Sch., Boston, 1976-88; pres. Mt. Sinai Sch. Medicine, NYC, 1988-99, Mt. Sinai Hosp., NYC, 1988-98; prof. geriatrics & medicine Mt. Sinai Sch. Medicine and Mt. Sinai Hosp., NYC, 1988—; CEO Mt. Sinai-NYU Med. Ctr. and Health Sys., NYC, 1998-2000; pres. Aetna Inc., Hartford, Conn., 2000—02, CEO, 2000—06, chmn., 2001—06; prof. health policy Columbia U., NYC, 2006—. Chmn. bd. trustees U. Conn., 2003—; mem. Medicare Payment Adv. Com., 1997-2004; trustee ROckefeller Found., 2007-; trustee Ctr. for Advancement of Health. Editor: Health and Disease in Old Age, 1982, Geriatric Medicine, 1988, Handbook of the Biology of Aging, 1990, Geriatric Neurology, 1991; author: Successful Aging, 1998; contbr. articles to jours. in field. Lt. comdr. USPHS, 1972-74. MacArthur Found. grantee, 1985-98, 2007. Mem. NAS Inst. Med., Am. Acad. Arts & Scis., Gerontol. Soc. Am. (pres. 1988), Am. Fedn. for Aging Rsch. (pres. 1988), N.Y. Yacht Club, Century Assn. Roman Catholic. Avocation: sailing. Office Phone: 860-273-4455. Business E-Mail: jwr2108@columbia.edu.

ROWE, JOHN WILLIAM, utilities executive; b. Dodgeville, Wis., May 18, 1945; s. William J. and Lola R. (Rule) Rowe; m. Jeanne M. Rowe; 1 child, William John. BS, U. Wis., 1967, JD, 1970; D (hon.), DePaul U., Ill. Inst. Tech., Drexel U., U. Mass., Dartmouth, Bryant Coll. Bar: Wis. 1970, Ill. 1970, US Supreme Ct. 1979, Pa. 1982. Assoc. Isham, Lincoln & Beale, Chgo., 1970-77, ptnr., 1978-80; counsel to trustee Chgo. Milw. St. Paul & Pacific RR, Chgo., 1979-80; v.p. law Consol. Rail Corp., Phila., 1980-82, sr. v.p. law, 1982-84; pres., CEO Ctrl. Maine Power Co., Augusta, 1984-89, New Eng. Elecric Sys., Westboro, Mass., 1989-98, bd. dirs.; chmn., pres., CEO Unicom Corp. & Commonwealth Edison Co., 1998-2000; pres., co-CEO Exelon Corp., Chgo., 2000—03, chmn., pres., CEO, 2003—. Vice-chmn. Nuc. Energy Inst., 2006—07, chmn., 2007—; bd. dirs. Sunoco, No. Trust Co. Former pres. USS Constn. Mus., 1993—95; former chmn. Edison Electric Inst.; pres. Field Mus. Natural History; trustee Mechanics Hall, Pioneer Inst.; bd. trustees Art Inst. Chgo., Chgo. Hist. Soc., Wis. Alumni Rsch. Found., Am. Enterprise Inst.; bd. trustees Ill. chpt. Nature Conservancy; nat. trustee Northwestern U. Recipient World of Difference award, Anti-Defamation League, 2000, Citizen of Yr. award, City Club of Chgo., 2002, Corp. Leadership award, Spanish Coalition for Jobs, 2002, Civic Leadership award, Am. Jewish Com., 2004, Founder's award for Bus. Leadership, Union League Phila., 2005. Mem.: Comml. Club Chgo., Econ. Club Chgo., Order of the Coif, Phi Beta Kappa. Office: Exelon Corp 10 S Dearborn St 37th Fl PO Box 805398 Chicago IL 60680-5398 Office Phone: 800-483-3220. *

ROWE, LARRY JORDAN, lawyer; b. Boston, May 24, 1958; s. Benson and Marcia Rowe; m. Nancy Ellen Cardinal; children; Jonathan B., Elizabeth J., David C. AB, Dartmouth Coll., 1980; MPP, JD, Harvard U., 1984. Bar: Mass. 1985, U.S. Dist. Ct. Mass. Assoc. Ropes & Gray, Boston, 1984-93, ptnr. corp. dept., 1993—, co-head pvt. equity practice group, 2001—06. Editor: Harvard Internat. Law Jour. Mem. Sudbury Fin. Com., Mass., 1998-2007; pres. Hillel Found. New Eng., 1991-94, bd. dirs., 1986-05; counsel Physicians for Human Rights. Mem. ABA, Mass. Bar Assn., Boston Bar Assn. Home: 10 Spiller Cir Sudbury MA 01776-2681 Office: Ropes & Gray 1 International Pl Fl 4 Boston MA 02110-2624 Office Phone: 617-951-7407. Office Fax: 617-951-7050. Business E-Mail: larry.rowe@ropesgray.com.

ROWE, LARRY LINWELL, lawyer, former state senator; b. Bluefield, W.Va. m. Julia Beury; 3 children. BA, W.Va. U., 1970, MPA, JD, W.Va. U., 1976. Bar: W.Va. 1976, U.S. Dist. Ct. (so. dist.) W.Va. 1976, U.S. Ct. Appeals (4th cir.) 1978, U.S. Supreme Ct. 1992. Staff counsel W.Va. Housing Devel. Fund, Charleston, 1976-77; sr. law clk. to Hon. K. K. Hall U.S. 4th Cir. Ct. Appeals, Charleston, 1978-79; pvt. practice Charleston, 1980—. Adj. prof. law U. Charleston, 1980—81. Bd. dirs. W.Va. Artists & Craftsmen's Guild, Charleston, 1980—84, Cedar Lakes' Mountain State Arts & Crafts Fair, Ripley, 1981—82; chmn., mem. Legal Aid Soc. Charleston, 1981—84; pres. W.Va. Dance Theatre, Charleston, 1981—82; hearing examiner W.Va. Bd. Regents, Charleston, 1985—89, W.Va. Bd. Medicine, Charleston, 1987—88; mem. W.Va. Ho. of Del., 1997—2000, W.Va. Senate, 2001—05. W.Va. Bd. Regents scholar, W.Va. U. Coll. Law, 1974—76, Cato scholar, 1974—76. Mem.: Phi Beta Kappa, Order of Coif. Democrat. Office: 4200A Malden Dr Charleston WV 25306-6442 Home Phone: 304-925-9382; Office Phone: 304-925-1333. Business E-Mail: larrylrowe@larrylrowe.com.

ROWE, MARY P., organizational ombudsman, management educator; b. Chgo., Feb. 18, 1936; married; children: Katherine, Susannah, Timothy. BA in History, Swarthmore Coll., 1957; PhD in Econs., Columbia U., 1971; LLD (hon.), Regis Coll., 1975. With World Council of Chs./Office of UN High Commr. for Refugees, Salzburg and Vienna, Austria, 1957-58; research asst. Nat. Bur. Econ. Research, NYC, 1961; economist planning bd. Office of Gov., V.I., 1962-63; free-lance cons. Nigeria, 1963-66, Boston, 1967-69; cons., sr. economist with Ctr. for Ednl. Policy Research, Harvard U. Harvard U., Cambridge, Mass., 1970, cons., sr. economist with Abt Assocs., 1970, tech. dir. early edn. project, 1971-72, cons. economist with Abt Assocs., 1971; dir. Carnegie Corp. Grant Radcliffe Inst., Cambridge, 1972; spl. asst. to pres., ombudsperson MIT, Cambridge, 1973—, adj. prof. Sloan Sch. Mgmt., 1985—. Mem. steering com., program on negotiations Harvard U., 1995—. Mem. editorial bd. Negotiation Jour., 1985—, Alternative Dispute Resolution Report, 1987-90; contbr. articles to profl. jours. Trustee Cambridge Friends Sch., 1969-75; mem. bd. advisors Brookline Children's Ctr., 1971-76; mem. Cambridge Friends Meeting and Com. on Clearness, 1971-78, New Eng. Concerns Com., 1973—, Mass. Policy Adv. Com. on Child Abuse/Neglect, 1977-79, Mass. State Youth Council, 1978-83; mem. Mass. State Employment and Tng. Council, 1975-83, chair, 1980-83; mem. nat. adv. Com. Black Women's Ednl. Policy and Research Network Project/Wellesley Coll. Ctr. for Research on Women, 1980-83; bd. dirs. Bay State Skills Commn., 1980-81, Wellesley Women's Research Ctr., 1984-87; sec. bd. dirs. Bay State Skills Corp., 1981-90; mem. panel on employment disputes Ctr. for Pub. Resources, 1986—. Recipient Meritorious Civilian Svc. award Dept. of Navy, 1993. Mem. Soc. Profls. in Dispute Resolution (chair com. on ombudspersons 1982-92), Calif. Caucus, Univ. and Coll. Ombudsman Assn., Ombudsman Assn. (co-founder, 1982, pres. 1985-87, program on negotiation steering com. 1995—, Disting. Neutral Ctr. for Pub. Resources 1990—). Office: MIT 10-213 77 Massachusetts Ave Cambridge MA 02139

ROWE, MARY R., lawyer; AD, Blinn Jr. Coll., 1994; BS in Agribusiness, Tex. A&M U., 1996; JD, U. Mo.-Kansas City Sch. Law, 1999. Bar: Tex. 2000. Shareholder bus. sect. Cotton, Bledsoe, Tighe & Dawson, P.C., Midland, Tex. Named a Rising Star, Tex. Super Lawyers mag., 2006. Office: Cotton Bledsoe Tighe & Dawson PC 500 W Illinois Ste 300 PO Box 2776 Midland TX 79701 Office Phone: 432-684-3136. E-mail: mrowe@cbtd.com. *

ROWE, MELINDA GRACE, public health service officer; b. Decatur, Ala., Aug. 18, 1953; m. Dana Calvin Craig Jr., Jan. 1, 1994. MD, U. Ala., 1978, MPH, 1985, MBA, 1987. Bd. cert. Am. Bd. Pediatrics, Am. Bd. Preventive Medicine. Pediatrics intern U. Ky., Lexington, 1978-79; pediatrics resident Lloyd Nolan Hosp., Fairfield, Ala., 1979-81; physician Columbus (Miss.) Children's Clinic, 1981, pvt. practice, Winfield, Ala., 1982-84; preventive medicine resident U. Ala., Birmingham, 1984-85; asst. state health officer Pub. Health Area III, Pelham, Ala., 1985-95; dir. health Jefferson County Health Dept., Louisville, 1995—2001; dist. health officer Savannah (Ga.) East Health, 2001—03; commr. of health Lexington Fayette County Health Dept., Lexington, Ky., 2003—. Asst. prof. U. Ala., Birmingham, 1988—, U. Louisville, 1995—. Bd. dirs. Cahaba River Soc., Birmingham, 1988—95, U. Ala.-Birmingham Nat. Alumni Soc., 1988—93, Health Ky., Goodwill Industries; bd. dirs. Wilderness Road coun. Girl Scouts U.S., Lexington, 2006—. Mem.: Lexington Med. Soc., Ga. Med. Assn., Ky. Health Depts. Assn. (v.p.), Louisville/Jefferson County Primary Care Assn. (bd. dirs.), Jefferson County Med. Soc., Ky. Pediat. Soc., Ky. Pub. Health Assn. (pres.-elect), Ky. Med. Assn., Rotary of Lexington. Methodist. Avocations: reading, walking, travel, music. Office Phone: 859-288-2300. Business E-Mail: melindag.rowe@ky.gov.

ROWE, MICHAEL DUANE, artist; b. Lykens, Pa., Nov. 5, 1947; m. Kathryn Jean Branoff. Student, Art Inst. Pitts., 1971-72. Exhibited in shows at Art Assn. Harrisburg, Pa., 1985, 86, 87, State Mus. Pa., 1986, 87, 2007, Doshi Gallery, Harrisburg, 1987, Cheltenham (Pa.) Art Ctr., 1989, 92, Delaplaine Art Ctr., Frederick, Md., 1989 (1st prize 1989), 90, 91, Immaculata (Pa.) Coll., 1990, U. of the Arts, Phil., 1990, Butler Inst. of Am. Art, Youngstown, Ohio, 1990, 92, Phila. Art Alliance, 1990, Altenative Mus., N.Y.C., 1990, 91, 95, Spaces, Cleve., 1991, Alexandria (La.) Art Mus., 1991, Pa. State U., 1992, Allentown (Pa.) Mus. Art, 1992, Muhlenberg Coll., Allentown, 1992 (award 1992), Michael Stone Gallery, Washington, 1992, Ea. N.Mex. U., 1992, Del. Ctr. for Contemporary Arts, Wilmington, 1993, Laguna Gloria Art Mus., Austin, Tex., 1993, Silvermine Art Guild Exhibit, New Cannan, Conn., 1993, Pa. State U., Univ. Park, 1993, East Tenn. U., Johnson City, 1994, Chrysler Mus., Norfolk, Va., 1994, Davidson (N.C.) Coll. Visual Arts Ctr., 1995, Southern Alleghenies Mus. of Art, 1995, Loretto, Pa., 1996, 97, 99, Susquehanna Art Mus., Harrisburg, Pa., 1998. Whitaker Ctr., Harrisburg, 1999, 2000; represented in permanent collection So. Alleghenies Mus., Loretto, Pa. Grantee Art Matters, Inc., 1988; Pa. Coun. of the Arts fellow, 1993. Episcopalian. Avocations: running, travel, reading. Home: 814 Meadow Ln Camp Hill PA 17011-1545 Business E-Mail: krowe@state.pa.us.

ROWE, MIKE, television personality; b. Balt., Md., Mar. 18, 1962; Grad., Towson U., Md. Singer: Baltimore Opera; writer (TV series) The Jamie Kennedy Experiment, 2002, announcer American Chopper: The Series, 2003—07, Ghost Hunters, 2004, Kevin and Drew Unleashed, 2004, Deadliest Catch: Crab Fishing in Alaska, 2005—, former host QVC, host (TV series) Worst Case Scenario, On-Air TV, The Most, No Relation, New York Expeditions, Your New Home, Evening Magazine, 2001—05, Egypt Week Live!, 2004, Dirty Jobs, 2005—; co-prodr.: (TV series) You Spoof Discovery, 2007. Office: Discovery Holding Co 12300 Liberty Blvd Englewood CO 80112 *

ROWE, NANCIE E., director, minister; b. New Castle, Pa., Nov. 4, 1943; d. John Francis and Ellen Mae Gwin; m. Ronald Allen Rowe, June 10, 2001; m. Edward Dwight Sickels, Oct. 24, 1958 (div.); children: Teddy Edward Sickels, Terrie Ellen Wells. BA in Bus., M in Psychology, Dallas Bapt. Coll.; PhD, Salt Lake Bapt. U., Dallas, 2001. Sch. adminstr. Calvary Christian Acad., Desoto, Tex., 1991—99; CEO, sch. adminstr., pastor Cmty. Christian Acad., Glenn Heights, 1999—. Assoc. pastor Victory Bapt. Ch., Desoto, 1997—2005; pastor Soulspiration Outreach Ch., Dallas, 1997—. Dir.(writer, editor, actor, singer): over 30 drama/mus. prodns. for children. Chairwoman ways & means Desoto BiCenntennial, 1973—76; prayer ptnr., support troops Presedential Prayer Team, 2000—06. Fellow Assoc. Christian Sch. Internat., Am. Salesmasters, 1970—76. Mem.: Assn. Christian Sch. Adminstrs. (assoc.). Liberal. Achievements include design of Commercial/Residential Design Firm; 1976 -1990; development of Hands on Teaching program for at risk students; Counseling program for troubled or at risk youth. Avocation: interior decorating. Office: Cmty Christian Acad PO Box 762 1931 S Hampton Rd Glenn Heights TX 75154 Home Phone: 214-923-3733; Office Phone: 972-274-0015. Office Fax: 972-274-0078. Personal E-mail: ccaacademy137@sbcglobal.net.

ROWE, PETER A., columnist; b. Walnut Creek, Calif., Sept. 7, 1955; s. Raymond Alan and Marion (Green) R.; m. Lynn Hanson, Aug. 13, 1977; children: Kyle, Reid, Alec. BA in History, U. Calif., Berkeley, 1977, BA in Journalism, 1977; MSJ, Northwestern U., 1981. Reporter Argus, Fremont, Calif., 1977-80, Va.-Pilot, Norfolk, 1981-84, San Diego Union, 1984-87, asst. features editor, 1987-88, features editor, 1988-92; columnist San Diego Union-Tribune, 1992—. Gannett fellow Northwestern U., 1980-81, Jefferson fellow, 2006; Fulbright scholar, 2003. Mem.: Nat. Soc. Newspaper Columnists (pres. 2000—02). Roman Catholic. Office: San Diego Union Tribune PO Box 120191 San Diego CA 92112-0191 Office Phone: 619-293-1227. Business E-Mail: peter.rowe@uniontrib.com.

ROWE, RACHAEL A., lawyer; b. Cin., July 7, 1971; BA, Miami U., 1993; JD, U. Cin. Coll. Law, 1996. Bar: Ohio 1996, Ky. 1997, US Dist. Ct. Southern Dist. Ohio, US Dist. Ct. Eastern Dist. Ky., US Dist. Ct. Western Dist. Ky., US Ct. of Appeals Sixth Cir., US Dist. Ct. Eastern Dist. Mich. 2006. Ptnr. Keating Muething & Klekamp PLL, Cin. Juvenile ct. magistrate Hamilton County, Ohio; mem., Bd. Trustees Cin. Classic Hammer Soccer Club; bd. mem. Dress for Success. Named one of Ohio's Rising Stars, Super Lawyers, 2005, 2006. Mem.: Cin. Acad. Leadership for Lawyers (mem., Class VI), Ohio State Bar Assn., Ky. Bar Assn., Cin. Bar Assn. (mem., Adminstrn. & Fin. Com., mem., Jud. Endorsement Com.), ABA. Office: Keating Muething & Kleklamp PLL One E Fourth St Ste 1400 Cincinnati OH 45202 Office Phone: 513-579-6400. Office Fax: 513-579-6457.

ROWE, RICHARD HOLMES, lawyer; b. Waltham, Mass., Jan. 2, 1937; s. Robert C. Rowe and Roberta (Holmes) Hayes; m. Sylvia C. Barrow, Aug. 23, 1963; children: Elizabeth C., Dorothy H., Christopher H. AB, Bates Coll., 1957; JD, Harvard U., 1964. Bar: DC 1965, NY 1980. Atty., exec. SEC, Washington, 1964-69, 70-79; v.p. Shareholders Mgmt. Co., LA, 1969-70; ptnr. Proskauer Rose Goetz & Mendelsohn, Washington, 1979—. 1st lt. USMCR, 1957-60. Mem. ABA, FBA, DC Bar Assn., Assn. Bar City of NY Democrat. Office: Proskauer Rose LLP 1001 Pennsylvania Ave NW Ste 400 Washington DC 20004-2537 Office Phone: 202-416-6820. Personal E-mail: rrowe@proskavor.com.

ROWE, ROBERT C., bank executive; B in Econs., Boston Coll.; MBA, Ind. U., Bloomington. Corp. assoc. Nat. City Corp., Cleve., 1990, head equity sponsor group, 1999, chief credit officer Capital Markets Group, sr. v.p., chief credit officer, chmn. corp. credit com. Bd. dirs., treas. Positive Edn. Program, Cleve. Office: Nat City Corp Nat City Ctr 1900 E Ninth St Cleveland OH 44114-3484 Office Phone: 216-222-2000. *

ROWE, SANDRA MIMS, editor; b. Charlotte, NC, May 26, 1948; d. David Lathan and Shirley (Stovall) Mims; m. Gerard Paul Rowe, June 5, 1971; children: Mims Elizabeth, Sarah Stovall. BA, East Carolina U., Greenville, NC, 1970; postgrad., Harvard U., 1991. Reporter to asst. mng. editor The Ledger-Star, Norfolk, Va., 1971-80, mng. editor, 1980-82, The Virginian-Pilot and The Ledger Star, Norfolk, Va., 1982-84, exec. editor, 1984-86, v.p., exec. editor, 1986-93; editor The Oregonian, Portland, 1993—. Mem. Pulitzer Prize Bd., 1994-2003, chair, 2003. Bd. visitors James Madison U., Harrisonburg, VA., 1991-95; chair journalism adv. bd. Knight Found.; mem. adv. bd. The Poynter Inst., Medill Sch. Journalism, Northwestern U.; chair bd. visitors Knight Fellowships, Stanford U. Recipient George Beveridge Editor of Yr. award Nat. Press Found., 2003; named Woman of Yr. Outstanding Profl. Women of Hampton Rds., 1987; inducted into Va. Journalism Hall of Fame, 2000. Mem. Am. Soc. Newspaper Editors (pres., bd. dirs. 1992-99), Va. Press Assn. (bd. dirs. 1985-93). Episcopalian. Office: The Oregonian 1320 SW Broadway Portland OR 97201-3499 Office Phone: 503-221-8400. Office Fax: 503-294-4175. E-mail: srowe@news.oregonian.com. *

ROWE, THOMAS DUDLEY, JR., law educator; b. Richmond, Va., Feb. 26, 1942; s. Thomas Dudley and Georgia Rosamond (Stripp) R.; m. Susan Fletcher French, Jan. 5, 2001. BA, Yale U., 1964; MPhil, Oxford U., Eng., 1967; JD, Harvard U., 1970. Bar: D.C. 1971, N.C. 1976. Law clk. to assoc. justice Potter Stewart U.S. Supreme Ct., Washington, 1970-71; asst. counsel adminstrv. practice subcom. U.S. Senate, Washington, 1971-73; assoc. Miller, Cassidy, Larroca & Lewin, Washington, 1973-75; assoc. prof. Duke U. Sch. Law, Durham, NC, 1975-79, prof., 1979-96, Elvin R. Latty prof., 1996—, assoc. dean for rsch., 1981-84, sr. assoc. dean acad. affairs, 1995-96. Vis. prof. Georgetown U. Law Ctr., Washington, 1979—80, U. Mich. Law Sch., Ann Arbor, 1985, U. Va. Law Sch., Charlottesville, 1991, UCLA Law Sch., 2002, 04; Straus Disting. vis. prof. Pepperdine U. Sch. Law, 2006; atty. Munger, Tolles & Olson, LA, 1991; adv. com. on rules of civil procedure U.S. Jud. Conf., 1993—99. Co-author: Constitutional Theory: Arguments and Perspectives, 1993, 2000, 2007, Federal Courts in the 21st Century: Cases and Materials, 1996, 2002, 2007, Civil Procedure, 2004; contbr. articles to profl. jours. Fellow U.S. Dept. Justice, Washington, 1980-81; Rhodes scholar, 1964-67; recipient Disting. Teaching award Duke Bar Assn., 1985. Mem.: ABA, Am. Law Inst. (life). Democrat. Office: Duke U Sch Law Durham NC 27708-0360 Office Phone: 919-613-7099. Business E-Mail: trowe@law.duke.edu.

ROWE, WILLIAM DAVIS, finance company executive; b. Hibbing, Minn., June 5, 1937; s. Richard Lawrence and Alicia (Davis) R.; m. Bobbie Grace Childress, Apr. 20, 1963; children— Lisa, William BA in Psychology, U. Minn, 1959, postgrad. in indsl. relations and bus. adminstrn., 1960; grad. exec. devel. program, Northeastern U., 1975; grad. Advanced Mgmt. Program, Harvard U., 1980. Dir. personnel, adminstrn. EDP Control Data Corp., Mpls., 1964-70; with Comml. Credit Co. subs. Control Data Corp, 1971-84, 85—; sr. v.p. consumer group Balt., 1975-81; sr. v.p. consumer realty services, 1981-83; sr. v.p. consumer banking services, 1983-84; v.p. market devel. Computer Service Co., Control Data Corp., Mpls., 1984; sr. v.p., chief adminstrv. officer Comml. Credit Co., Balt., 1985-87; pres. Enterprise Bank Network Bank Svcs. Co., Atlanta, 1988-91; exec. mng. dir., vice chmn. Foster Ptnrs. Inc., Peat Marwick Alliance Co., 1991—; pres., COO Foster Ptnrs., 2001—. Bd. dirs. Fla. Corp.; co-owner Spirit of West Land Co., Glenwood Springs, Colo., 2001—; lectr. in field Mem. Mayor's Vol. Council of Equal Opportunity, Balt.; trustee St. Paul's Sch.

for Girls, Brooklandville, Md., 1981—; bd. dirs. Boy Scouts Am., Take Stock in Children, 1996—. Served to capt. USMC, 1960-63. Mem. Am. Fin. Services Assn. (bd. dirs. and mem. exec. com. 1980-84, consumer banking adv. com. 1983-84), Am. Mgmt. Assn. (pres.'s roundtable 1976) Republican. Avocations: hunting, skiing, cattle ranching. E-mail: browe@spiritwestland.com.

ROWE, WILLIAM JOSEPH, internist; b. Cin., Oct. 31, 1927; s. Alvin Harold and Ida Claire (Omansky) R.; m. Mary Elaine Kenkel, Apr. 16, 1955. BS, U. Cin., 1950, MD, 1954. Diplomate Am. Bd. Internal Medicine. Asst. clin. prof. medicine Med. U. Ohio, Toledo, 1962—93; chmn. dept. medicine St. Vincent's Hosp., Toledo, 1979-83; chief adv. com. cardiac rehab. N.W. Ohio Heart Assn., Toledo, 1981-83. Del. citizen amb. program to China People to People, 1988. Contbr. articles to profl. jours., including Acta Astronautica, Lancet, Circulation. Capt. USAF, 1955-57. Fellow Brit. Interplanetary Soc.; mem. Nat. Space Soc. Republican. Achievements include research in describing only the second space syndrome, the Apollo 15 Space Syndrome; first to describe mechanisms for endothelial injuries of cardiovascular systems complicating extraordinary unremitting endurance exercise on earth or secondary to too little exercise and microgravity; show how inhalation of moon dust in the lunar module can cause severe hypertension. Avocations: tennis, running, writing, travel. Home: 1485 Bremerton Ln Keswick VA 22947 Personal E-mail: rowerun@aol.com.

ROWE, WILLIAM L. S., lawyer; b. Martinsville, Va., Mar. 31, 1948; s. Mason Cole Rowe and Catherine (Thomas) Showalter; m. Carol Lawhorne, June 6, 1970 (div. 1991); children: William L. S. Rowe, Jr., Benjamin C., Susannah B.; m. Pamela-Jean Love, Feb. 29, 1992. BA, Washington & Lee Univ., Va., 1970; JD, Univ. Va., 1973. Bar: Va. 1973, U.S. Dist. Ct. E.D. Va., U.S. Ct. Appeals (4th cir.), U.S. Claims Ct., U.S. Tax Ct. Assoc. Hunton & Williams, Richmond, Va., 1973-1980, ptnr., 1980—. Special tax counsel, Va. Mfg. Assn.; general counsel Greater Richmond Community Found. 1990—; speaker in the field. Contbr. articles to profl. jours. Bd. gov., trustee, Greater Richmond Community Found., 1979-91, bd. dirs. REB Found., Massey Found., 1980-89. Fellow Am. Coll. of Tax Counsel; mem. ABA, Va. State Bar (bd. trustees sect. on taxation 1988-90), Va. Bar Assn. (chmn. com. on taxation 1985-87), Richmond Bar Assn., Va. State C. of C. (chmn. tax com. 1994—). Avocations: fly fishing, wild flowers, gardening. Office: Hunton & Williams Riverfront Plz East Tower PO Box 1535 Richmond VA 23218-1535

ROWE, ZANE CONRAD, air transportation executive; BSBA, Embry-Riddle Aero U., Daytona Beach, Fla., 1991; MBA in Fin., San Diego State U. With Continental Airlines, Inc., Houston, 1993—, mng. dir. fin. analysis, staff v.p. fin. planning & analysis, 2001, v.p. network strategy, sr. v.p. network strategy. Bd. dirs. ARINC. Mem. indsl. adv. coun. Embry-Riddle Aero. U. Office: Continental Airlines Inc PO Box 4607 Houston TX 77210 Office Phone: 713-324-5000. Office Fax: 713-324-2637. *

ROWELL, BARBARA CABALLERO, retired academic administrator; b. New Orleans, Sept. 5, 1922; d. Albert Henry Wischnewske (stepfather) and Antoinette (Angelo) Caballero; m. J.C. Rowell, Dec. 17, 1941; children: Jerrie Carlene, Kerry Gene, Ricky Ray. AA in Bus. Adminstrn., Okaloosa Walton Coll., 1972; BA in Social Sci., U. West Fla., 1987. Exec. sec. Bishop Enterprises, Ft. Walton Beach; office mgr. and real estate property mgr. Fred Cooke Real Estate, Ft. Walton Beach, Fla.; adminstrv. sec. to v.p. Okaloosa Walton Coll., Niceville, Fla. Leader brownie scouts Girl Scouts U.S., Cub Scouts; bd. dirs. U. West Fla. Ctr. for Life Long Learning; chair univ svc. com., pres., began Writing Lab; originator, implementor U. West Fla. Tutor Program, Career Fair, started scholarship program, Proctor Program; curriculum com. U. West Fla.Ctr. for Lifelong Learning, presenter S.E. Conf. Insts. of Learning in Retirement, Charleston, S.C.; gov.'s campaign vol.; state legislature campaign vol.; active Ctr. for Life Long Learning, U. West Fla. Mem. AAUW, DAV Aux., Order of Ea. Star (past matron). Avocations: travel, reading, gardening, dance.

ROWELL, EDWARD MORGAN, retired foreign service officer, educator; b. Oakland, Calif., Oct. 13, 1931; s. Edward Joseph and Mary Helen (Mohler) Rowell; m. Lenora Mary Wood, Aug. 23, 1957; children: Edward Oliver, Karen Elizabeth Schuler, Christopher Douglas. BA in Internat. Relations, Yale U., 1953; postgrad., Stanford U., 1964-65, Stanford Bus. Sch., 1970-71. Fgn. service insp. U.S. Dept. State, Washington, 1971-74; dep. dir., econ. officer Office Iberian Affairs, Washington, 1974-75; dep. dir. Office West European Affairs, Washington, 1975-76, dir., 1977-78; minister-counselor U.S. Embassy, Lisbon, Portugal, 1978-83; dep. asst. sec. Bur. Consular Affairs, Washington, 1983-85; U.S. amb. to Bolivia La Paz, 1985-88; U.S. amb. to Portugal Lisbon, 1988-90; U.S. amb. to Luxemburg, 1990-94; sr. assoc. Global Bus. Access, Ltd., 1994—. Mem. adv. bd. Portuguese-Am. Leadership Coun. U.S.; mem. Cleveland Park Congregational Ch, Washington, 1956—; trustee Cleveland Park Ch., 2000—03; bd. dirs. Luso-Am Develop Found., 1988—90. With US Army, 1953—55. Decorated grand cross Bolivian Condor of the Andes, grand cross Luxembourg Oaken Crown; recipient State Dept. Superior Honor award, 1983, 1991, Presdl. Honor Award, 1988; grantee, Una Chapman Cox Found., 1984; Yale U. scholar, 1949—52, U. Calif. fellow, 1953. Mem.: Diplomatic & Consular Officers Ret. (gov. 2001—, treas. 2005—07, v.p. 2007—), Arena Stage Assocs., Yale Univ. Alumni Assn., Stanford Univ. Alumni Assn., Wash. Inst. Foreign Affairs (membership com. 1999—2007), Assn. Diplomatic Studies & Training (pres. 1997—2001, treas. 2005—), Am. Foreign Svc. Assn. (v.p. 1995—97), Am Acad. Diplomacy (bd. dirs. 2002—, chmn. audit com. 2006—), Cosmos Club. Avocations: photography, tennis, music. Home: 5414 Newington Rd Bethesda MD 20816-3316 Personal E-mail: edmrowell@aol.com.

ROWELL, LESTER JOHN, JR., retired insurance company executive; b. Cleve., Apr. 2, 1932; s. Lester John and Francis Laureen (Corbett) R.; m. Patricia Ann Loesch, Jan. 16, 1953 (div. Sept. 1970); children: Deborah, Cynthia, Gregory, Maureen, Diane; m. Carol Ann Jankowski, Sept. 26, 1970. BS, Pa. State U., 1955; grad. Advanced Mgmt. Program, Harvard U. Bus. Sch., 1971. CLU. Second v.p., field mgmt. Mut. Life Ins. Co. N.Y., NYC, 1969-70, v.p. agys., 1970-72, v.p. sales, 1972-78, sr. v.p., 1978-80; exec. v.p. Provident Mut. Life Ins. Co., Phila., 1980-84, pres., 1984-86, pres., chief oper. officer, 1987, pres., chief exec. officer, 1991-93, chmn., pres., chief exec. officer, 1993-96; ret. Bd. dirs. Pa. State U., The PMA Group. Capt. USMC, 1953-62. Recipient Alumni award Pa. State U., 1972, Disting. Alumni award Pa. State U., 1988; Alumni Fellow Pa. State U., 1987. Republican. Personal E-mail: budrowell@aol.com.

ROWELL, ROBERT, professional sports team executive; B in Broadcast Journalism, Calif. Poly. State U., San Luis Obispo, 1989, M in Bus. Adminstrn., 1993. Bus. mgr. intercollegiate athletics dept. Calif. Poly. State U., 1989—91, asst. athletics dir., 1992—94, assoc. athletics dir., 1994—95; asst. contr. Golden State Warriors, 1995—96, dir. fin., contr., 1996—98, v.p. bus. ops., 1998—2001, NBA chief mktg. officer, COO, 2001—03, pres., 2003—. Golden State Warriors rep. NBA Bd. Govs. Recipient Forty Under 40 award, St. & Smith's Sports Bus. Jour., 2001. Office: Golden State Warriors 1011 Broadway Oakland CA 94607 *

ROWELL, VICTORIA, actress; b. Portland, Maine, May 10, 1960; m. Tom Fahey, 1989 (div. 1990); 2 children. Attended, Sch. Am. Ballet. Dancer Am. Ballet Theatre, Dance Theatre Harlem, Am. Ballet Theatre II. Actor: (TV series) The Young and the Restless, 1990—98, 2000, 2002—(Outstanding actress in daytime drama series, NAACP Image award, 2006), As the World Turns, 1988, The Cosby Show, 1989—90, The Fresh Prince of Bel-Air, 1990, Herman's Head, 1991, 1993, Deadly Games, 1995, Diagnosis Murder, 1993—2001, Family Law, 2001; (TV films) Full Eclipse, 1993, Secret Sins of the Father, 1994, Feast of All Saints, 2001, Without Warning, 2002, A Town Without Pity, 2002, Polly and Marie, 2007; (films) Leonard Part 6, 1987, The Distinguished Gentleman, 1992, Dumb and Dumber, 1994, One Red Rose, 1995, Barb Wire, 1996, Eve's Bayou, 1997, Dr. Hugo, 1998, Secrets, 1998, A Wake in Providence, 1999, Fraternity Boys, 1999, Black Listed, 2003, Motives, 2004, Midnight Clear, 2005, A Perfect Fit, 2005, Home of the Brave, 2006. Founder Rowell Foster Children's Positive Plan Fine Arts Scholarship Fund. Mem.: Sigma Gamma Rho. Mailing: c/o CBS Television City 7800 Beverly Blvd Los Angeles CA 90036 *

ROWEN, ANDREW S., lawyer; b. Seattle, 1954; AB, U. Calif., Berkeley, 1976; JD, Harvard U., 1979. Bar: NY 1980. Assoc. Sullivan & Cromwell, NYC, now ptnr. fin. institutions and coord. insurance practice area. Mem.: ABA, NYC Bar Assn. (com. on insurance law). Office: Sullivan & Cromwell 125 Broad St Fl 28 New York NY 10004-2489 Office Phone: 212-558-3896. Office Fax: 212-558-3588. Business E-Mail: rowenas@sullcrom.com.

ROWEN, HARVEY ALLEN, investment company executive; b. Chgo., Sept. 21, 1943; BS in Acctg., UCLA, 1964; JD, U. Calif., Berkeley, 1967; MBA in Mktg. & Fin., NYU, 1981. Bar: Calif., D.C., N.Y. Pvt. practice, Beverly Hills, Calif., 1967-68; counsel Securities & Exch. Commn., Washington, 1968-71, Com. Energy & Commerce, U.S. Congress, Washington, 1971-75; sr. cons. SRI Internat. (formerly Stanford Rsch. Inst.), Palo Alto, 1975-77; asst. to pres. Merrill Lynch, Pierce, Fenner & Smith, Inc., NYC, 1977-80, v.p. corp. planning, 1980-81, Merrill Lynch & Co., Inc., NYC, 1981-83, v.p. banking devel., banking divsn., 1983-84; exec. v.p. Merrill Lynch Bank & Trust Co., NYC, 1984-85, pres., 1985-88; chmn. trust com. Merrill Lynch Trust Co., NYC, 1987-90; prin. Harvey Rowen & Assocs., Newport Beach, Calif., 1990-91; pres., CEO The Charles Schwab Trust Co., S.F., 1992—; sr. v.p. Schwab Instl. Svcs. to Corps. Charles Schwab & Co., Inc., 1992—. Mem. dean's adv. bd. Haas Sch. Bus., U. Calif., Berkeley; lectr. in field. Author: The Securities Acts Amendments of 1975, 1975, The Securities Acts Amendments of 1975: A Legislative History, 1976, The Emerging Financial Services Industry, 1983; author: (with others) The Deregulation of the Banking and Securities Industries 305, 1979; mem. editorial adv. bd. Banking Expansion Reporter. Mem. ABA (bus. sect., banking com., fed. regulation securities com., chmn. product and svc. devels. subcom. of com. devels. in investment svcs. 1985-87), Am. Bankers Assn., Calif. Bankers Assn., Calif. Bar Assn. Office: The Charles Schwab Trust Co 1 Montgomery St Fl 7 San Francisco CA 94104-4505

ROWEN, HENRY STANISLAUS, retired economist, former federal agency administrator; b. Boston, Mass., Oct. 11, 1925; s. Henry S. and Margaret ISabelle (Maher) Rowen; m. Beverly Camille Griffiths, Apr. 18, 1951; children: Hilary, Michael, Michael, Christopher, Sheila Jennifer, Diana Louise, Nicholas. BS, MIT, 1949; M in Philosophy, Oxford U., Eng., 1955. Economist Rand Corp., Santa Monica, Calif., 1950—61, pres., 1967—72; dep. asst. sec. internat. security affairs US Dept. Def., Washington, 1961—64; asst. dir. Bur. Budget, 1965—66; prof. pub. policy Stanford (Calif.) U., 1972—95, prof. emeritus, 1995—, dir. pub. policy program, 1972—75; sr. fellow Hoover Inst., Stanford, Calif., 1983—; Edwin B. Rust prof. pub. policy Stanford (Calif.) U., 1986—95, dir. Asia/Pacific Rsch. Ctr., 1997—2001; asst. sec. internat. security affairs US Dept. Def., Washington, 1989—91. Chmn. nat. intelligence coun. CIA, Washington, 1981—83; chmn. US Dept. Energy Task Force on the Future of Sci. Programs, 2002—03; mem. Commn. on the Intelligence Capabilities of the US Regarding Weapons of Mass Destruction, 2004. Co-author (with R. Imai): Nuclear Energy and Nuclear Proliferation, 1980; co-author: (with C. Wolf Jr.) The Future of the Soviet Empire, 1987; editor: Options for U.S. Energy Policy, 1977, Behind East Asian Growth, 1998; co-editor (with C. Wolf Jr.): The Impoverished Superpower, 1990; co-editor: (with C. Lee, W. Miller, M. Hancock) The Silicon Valley Edge, 2001; contbr. articles to profl. jours. Chmn. chief naval ops. exec. panel USN, Washington, 1972—81, mem. exec. panel, 1983—89, 1991—93; mem. Def. Sci. Bd. US Dept. Def., 1983—89; chmn. Def. Policy Bd., 1991—94. With USN, 1943—46, PTO. Mem.: Internat. Inst. Strategic Studies. Republican. Roman Catholic.

ROWEN, HOWARD, financial consultant; s. Harvey Rowen; m. Karee Rowen; 2 children. BA in Econs., U. So. Calif., LA. With Shearson Lehman; positions up to mng. dir. Deutsche Bank Alex. Brown (formerly Alex. Brown), LA, 1993—. Named an Best 100 Brokers, Barron's, 2005—06. Office: Deutsche Bank Alex Brown 300 S Grand Ave 40th Fl Los Angeles CA 90071 Office Phone: 213-437-2570. *

ROWEN, MARSHALL, radiologist; b. Chgo. s. Harry and Dorothy (Kasnow) R.; m. Helen Lee Friedman, Apr. 5, 1952; children: Eric, Scott, Mark. AB in Chemistry with highest honors, U. Ill., Urbana, 1951; MD with honors, U. Ill., Chgo., 1954, MS in Internal Medicine, 1954. Diplomate Am. Bd. Radiology. Intern Long Beach (Calif.) VA Hosp., 1955; resident in radiology Los Angeles VA Hosp., 1955-58; practice medicine specializing in radiology Orange, Calif., 1960—. Chmn. bd. dirs. Moran, Rowen and Dorsey, Inc., Radiologists, 1969—2002; asst. radiologist L.A. Children's Hosp., 1958; assoc. radiologist Valley Presbyn. Hosp., Van Nuys, Calif., 1960; dir. dept. radiology St. Joseph Hosp., Orange, 1961—2004, v.p. staff, 1972; dir. dept. radiology Children's Hosp. Orange County, 1964—2002, chief staff, 1977—78, v.p., 1978—83, v.p., trustee, 1990—91, 1993—98, 2000—06; asst. clin. prof. radiology U. Calif., Irvine, 1967—70, assoc. clin. prof., 1979—82, clin. prof. radiology and pediat., 1976—2007, pres. clin. faculty assn., 1980—81; trustee Choc. Padrinos; sec. Choco Health Svcs., 1987—89, v.p., 1990—93, trustee, 1995—, Found. Med. Care Orange County, 1972—76, Calif. Commn. Adminstrn. Svcs. Hosp., 1975—79, Profl. Practice Systems, 1990—92, Med. Splty. Mgrs., 1990—2004, St. Joseph Med. Corp., 1993—98; v.p. Found. Med. Care Children's Hosp., 1988—89; v.p., sr. v.p. St. Joseph Med. Corp. IPA, 1995—98; sr. v.p. Orange Coast Managed Care Svcs., 1995—98, Paragon Med. Imaging, 1993—2003, Calif. Managed Imaging, 1994—2007, Alliance Premier Hosps., 1995—96; chmn. bd. dirs. Children's Healthcare Calif., 1995—2002, hon. chmn., bd. dirs., 2003—07; corp. mem. Blue Shield Calif., 1995—2002; mem. physician's rev. com. Blue Cross Calif., 1996—2007, mem. Blue Shield coun. advisors, 2001—07; trustee Children's Hosp. at Mission, 2004—07. Mem. editl. bd. Western Jour. Medicine; contbr. articles to med. jours. Founder Orange County Performing Arts Ctr., mem. Laguna Art Mus., Laguna Festival of Arts, Opera Pacific, South Coast Reportory, Am. Ballet Theater, World Affairs Coun. Served to capt. M.C., U.S. Army, 1958-60. Recipient Rea sr. med. prize U. Ill, 1953; William Cook scholar U. Ill., 1951, Friend of Children award Children's Hosp. Guild, 1995, Charley award Children's Hosp., 1996. Fellow Am. Coll. Radiology; mem. AMA, Am. Heart Assn., Soc. Nuclear Medicine (trustee 1961-62), Orange County Radiol. Soc. (pres. 1968-69), Calif. Radiol. Soc. (pres. 1978-79), Radiol. Soc. So. Calif. (pres. 1976), Pacific Coast Pediatric Radiologists Assn. (pres. 1971), Soc. Pediatric Radiology, Calif. Med. Assn. (chmn. sect. on radiology 1978-79), Orange County Med. Assn. (chmn. UCI liaison com. 1976-78), Cardioradiology Soc. So. Calif., Radiol. Soc. N.Am., Am. Roentgen Ray Soc., Am. Coll. Physician Execs., Soc. Chmn. Radiologists Children Hosp., Center Club, Sports Club (Irvine), Phi Beta Kappa, Phi Eta Sigma, Omega Beta Phi, Alpha Omega Alpha. Office: 1201 W La Veta Ave Orange CA 92868-4213 Home Phone: 714-349-8667; Office Phone: 714-771-8171. Personal E-mail: romarsh@aol.com.

ROWEN, RUTH HALLE, musicologist, educator; b. NYC, Apr. 5, 1918; d. Louis and Ethel (Fried) Halle; m. Seymour M. Rowen, Oct. 13, 1940; children: Mary Helen Rowen, Louis Halle Rowen. BA, Barnard Coll., 1939; MA, Columbia U., 1941, PhD, 1948. Mgmt. ednl. dept. Carl Fischer, Inc., NYC, 1954-63; assoc. prof. musicology CUNY, 1967-72, prof., from 1972, mem. doctoral faculty in musicology, from 1967. Author: Early Chamber Music, 1948, reprinted, 1974; (with Adele T. Katz) Hearing-Gateway to Music, 1959, (with William Simon) Jolly Come Sing and Play, 1956, Music Through Sources and Documents, 1979, (with Mary Rowen) Instant Piano, 1979, 80, 83, Symphonic and Chamber Music Score and Parts Bank, 1996; contbr. articles to profl. jours. Mem. ASCAP, Am. Musicol. Soc., Music Library Assn., Coll. Music Soc., Nat. Fedn. Music Clubs (nat. musicianship chmn. 1962-74, nat. young artist auditions com. 1964-74, NY state chmn. Young Artist Auditions 1981, dist. coord. 1983, nat. bd. dirs. 1989-2000, rep. UN 1991-2000), NY Fedn. Music Clubs (pres.), Phi Beta Kappa Home: New York, NY. *Opportunity grows with each constructive thought.* Deceased.

ROWLAND, ALLEN R., former retail executive; b. June 1944; With Albertson's, Boise, 1971, various positions to sr. v.p. various cities, 1971-96; pres., COO Smith's Food & Drug Ctrs., 1996-97; pres., CEO, dir. Winn-Dixie Stores, Inc., Jacksonville, Fla., 1999—2003; owner Sun Chase Air Charter Svc., Rowland Interest.

ROWLAND, ARTHUR RAY, librarian; b. Hampton, Ga., Jan. 6, 1930; s. Arthur and Jennie (Goodman) R.; m. Jane Thomas, July 1, 1955; children: Dell Ruth, Anna Jane. AB, Mercer U., Macon, Ga., 1951; M. Librarianship, Emory U., 1952; postgrad., Oxford U., 1989. Circulation asst. Ga. State Coll. Library, 1952, circulation librarian, 1952-53; librarian Armstrong Coll., Savannah, Ga., 1954-56; head circulation dept. Auburn U. Library, 1956-58; librarian, assoc. prof. library sci. Jacksonville U., 1958-61, Augusta Coll., 1961-76, prof., libr., 1976-91, libr. emeritus, 1991—. Lectr. libr. edn. U. Ga., 1962-66; trustee Augusta-Richmond County Pub. Libr., 1980-93, pres. bd. trustees, 1983-85, v.p. bd., 1988-91; trustee Augusta Regional Libr., chmn., 1984-85; trustee East Cen. Ga. Regional Libr., 1987-93, chmn., 1988-91; chmn. Gov.'s Conf. on Ga. Librs. and Info. Svcs., 1977; del. White House Conf. on Librs. and Info. Sci., 1979; cons. on libr. mgmt. to Govt. of Indonesia, 1986. Author: Bibliography of the Writings of Georgia History, 1966, A Guide to the Study of Augusta and Richmond County, Georgia, 1967, (with Helen Callahan) Yesterday's Augusta, 1976, (with James E. Dorsey) A Bibliography of the Writings on Georgia History 1900-1970, rev. edit., 1978, (with Marguerite F. Fogleman) Reese Library Genealogical Resources, 1988, supplement, 1990, Goodman Cousins, 1988, Rowland Cousins, 1990, New Guide to the Study of Augusta, 1990, Index to City Directory of Augusta, Georgia, 1841-1879, 1991, More Goodman Cousins, 1993, My Fair Grandmother, 1994, Distant Cousins, The Huguenots Connecting Rowland, Bulloch, de Bourdeaux, DeVeaux and Roosevelt Families of S.C., N.C. and Ga., 1995, The Bessent Family of Georgia, 1995, Reeves Family of Georgia, 1996, Descendants of Wiley Reeves, 1996, Rowland-Huckaby Connections, 1996, Georgia Almanacs, 1996, Rowland Family of Virginia, North Carolina and Georgia and Beyond, 1998, Atkinson Family in Virginia, 1998, Ancestors of David Jackson, 1998, Ancestors of Rachael Hines Lewis, 1998, Ancestors of Elizabeth Proctor in Virginia and England, 1998, Ancestors of Martha Whitehead, 1998, Wiley Reeves, His Descendants and Ancestors, 1999, John Rowland, Immigrant, 2000, Reeves Family in England, Virginia, North Carolina, Georgia and Beyond, 2000, The Mississippi Branch of the Rowland Family, 2000, Ancestors and Connections of Dunbar Rowland, 2000, Printing in Louisville, 2000, Confederate Printing in Augusta, Ga., 2000, Goodman Family of N.C., Ga. and Beyond Their Cherokee Indian Heritage, 2000, Hillhouse Family of Wash., Ga., 2000, Printing in Wash., Ga., 2000, Jacob Martin Hugenot of Charleston, S.C., 2000, John Gensel of Charleston, S.C., 2000, Bessent Family, 2000, Rowland Family in Ga., 2000, Printers of Augusta, Georgia, 1786-1900, 2003, Printing in Milledgeville, Georgia, 2003, Preliminary Checklist of Penfield, Georgia Imprints, 2003, A Preliminary Checklist of Georgia Imprints, 1763-1860, 2003, Civil War Marriages Richmond County, Georgia, 2004, Grocers, Butchers, Baker and Others, 2004, 1890 Census of Augusta and Richmond County Georgia, 2004, 2d edit., 2006, Citizens of Augusta and Richmond County, Georgia During the Civil War, 2005, 2d edit., 2006, Confederate Soldiers From Augusta and Richmond County, Georgia, 2005, Name Index to Augusta Georgia City Directories 1880-1891, 2006, Business Directory of Augusta Georgia 1841-1901, 2006, Brides and Grooms: Marriage Licesnes and Certificates of Richmond County Georgia 1785-1890, 2006, China and Immigrants to Augusta and Richmond County Georgia, 2006, Citizens of North Augusta in Aiken County South Carolina, 2006, Black or Mulatto in Richmond County Georgia, 2006, Women in Business in Augusta Georgia 1841-1901, 2006, Ecclesiastical Index to Augusta Georgia 1736-1901, 2006, Foreign Born Citizens in Augusta and Richmond County Georgia 1850 and 1860, 2006, Hephzibah Georgia in Richmond County Georgia, 2006, Village of Summerville 1880-1910, 2006, Names Changed Legally in Georgia 1800-1856, 2007, List of Prisoners in Penitentiary, Convict Camps, Chain Gangs and Jails in Georgia, 2007, McPherson Barracks, 2007, others; editor: Reference Services, 1964, Historical Markers of Richmond County, Georgia, rev. edit., 1971, The Catalog and Cataloging, 1969, The Librarian and Reference Service, 1977, Reminiscences of Augusta Marines, 1985; supervising editor (with Heard Robertson) Jour. Archibald Campbell, 1981; contbr. to profl. jours. V.p. Ga. Libr. Assn. Trustees and Friends, 1989-91. With USN, 1948-49. Recipient Nix-Jones award for disting. service Ga. Library Assn., 1981, Town and Gown award Augusta Coll. Alumni Assn., 1985. Mem. ALA, Am. Assn. State and Local History, Bibliog. Soc. Am., Southeastern Libr. Assn. (hon. life, exec. bd. 1971-72), Ga. Libr. Assn. (hon. life, 2d v.p. 1965-67, 71-73, 1st v.p., pres.-elect 1973-75, pres. 1975-77, chmn. budget com. 1977-79, adv. to pres. 1979-83, 85-92), Ctrl. Savannah River Area Libr. Assn. (past pres., editor union list of serials 1967), Duval County Libr. Assn. (past v.p.), Nat. Geneal. Soc., Ga. Geneal. Soc., N.C. Geneal. Soc., Va. Geneal. Soc., Augusta Geneal. Soc., Richmond County Hist. Soc. (curator 1964-91, pres. 1967-69, founder, editor Richmond County History), Huguenot Soc. S.C., Ga. Hist. Soc. (curator emeritus), Ga. Bapt. Hist. Soc., Nat., Young Men's Libr. Assn. (v.p. 1988-91), Ga. Trusts for Hist. Preservation, Hist. Augusta (trustee emeritus), Soc. Ga. Archivists, Kappa Phi Kappa. Baptist. Address: 172 Adamsville Spring Rd North Augusta SC 29860-7748

ROWLAND, DAVID JACK, retired academic administrator; b. Columbus, Ohio, June 17, 1921; s. David Henry and Ethel (Ryan) R.; m. Mary Ellen Stinson, Apr. 8, 1944; children: David Allen, Ryan Stinson, Sue Ellen Rowland Summers. BS, Ohio U., 1949; MA, U. Ala., 1951; LittD (hon.), Athens State Coll., 1967; LLD (hon.), Jacksonville State U., 1969. Pres. Walker Coll., Jasper, Ala., 1956-88, chancellor, 1988-95; interim pres. U. Ala./Walker Coll., 1995-96; ret., 1996. Bd. dirs. First Nat. Bank, Jasper, first Comml. Bancshares, Birmingham, Ala.; chmn. Ala. ACT Bd., Tuscaloosa, 1968—; real estate developer. Wildlife columnist and illustrator. Chmn. Jasper Indsl. Bd., 1987—; commr. Ala. Mining commn., Jasper, 1976—; mem. Ala. Employer Guard Res. commn., Birmingham, 1988—; trustee Walker Coll.; chmn. adv. bd. Jasper Salvation Army; vice chmn. Walker County Human Resource Coun. Col. U.S. Army, 1942-46, ATO. Decorated Legion of Merit; recipient Silver Beaver award Boy Scouts Am., 1972; named to Ala. Sr. Citizen Hall of Fame. Mem. Res. Officers Assn. (pres. Jasper chpt.), Summit Club, Met. Dinner Club, Rotary (pres. Jasper 1967-68, Paul Harris fellow), Masons, Ala. Silver Hair Legislature. Avocations: tree farmer, growing christmas trees, wildfowl carver. Home: 1000 Valley Rd Jasper AL 35501-4925

ROWLAND, DIANE, health facility administrator, researcher; b. Bridgeport, Conn., Oct. 14, 1948; m. Brian L. Biles, Sept. 17, 1977. BA, Wellesley Coll., 1970; MPA, U. Calif., LA, 1973; SCD, Johns Hopkins U., 1987. Mem. staff U.S. House Rep., Washington, 1983—91; assoc. dir. Commonwealth Fund Commn. on Elderly People Living Alone, Balt., 1985—91; assoc. prof. Johns Hopkins U., Balt., 1987—93; exec. v.p. Kaiser Family Found., Washington, 1993—. Exec. dir. Kaiser Commn. on Future of Medicaid, Washington, 1991—98, Kaiser Commn. on Medicaid & the Uninsured, Washington, 1998—; pres. Assn. Health Svc. Rsch., Washington, 2000; mem. Sec. Task Force on Infant Mortality, Washington, 2000—. Contbr. articles to profl. jours. Fellow Brookdale Nat. fellow, Brookdale Found., 1987. Mem.: Inst. Medicine, 2004. Greek Orthodox. Avocations: travel, reading, sailing. Office: Henry J Kaiser Family Found 1330 G Street NW Washington DC 20005

ROWLAND, ESTHER E(DELMAN), retired dean; b. NYC, Apr. 12, 1926; d. Abraham Simon and Ida Sarah (Shifrin) Edelman; m. Lewis P. Rowland, Aug. 31, 1952; children: Andrew, Steven, Joy Rosenthal. BA, U. Wis., 1946; MA, Columbia U., 1948, MPhil, 1984; cert. in bioethics, Columbia U./Albert Einstein, 1996. Instr. in polit. sci. CCNY, 1947-51, Mt. Holyoke Coll., South Hadley, Mass., 1948-49; dir. health professions adv. bd. U. Pa., Phila., 1971-73; adviser to pre-profl. students Barnard Coll., NYC, 1974-79, dean for pre-profl. students, 1980-93, assoc. dean studies, 1989-95; ret., 1995—. Proofreader Monthly Review, N.Y.C., 1997-2003. Mem. exec. com. Nat. Emergency Civil Liberties Com., N.Y.C., 1975-90; mem. exec. com. Women's Counseling Project, 1981-86. Mem. N.E. Assn. Health Professions Advisers (exec. com. 1973-74), N.E. Assn. Pre Law Advisors (exec. com. 1981-83, 85-86), Neurol. Inst. Aux., N.Y.C. Found. Sr. Citizens (ombudsman 1997-99), Aux. Am. Acad. Neurologists (exec. bd. 1999-2001). Home: 404 Riverside Dr New York NY 10025-1861 E-mail: eerowland@gmail.com.

ROWLAND, FRANK SHERWOOD, chemistry professor; b. Del., Ohio, June 28, 1927; m. Joan Lundberg, 1952; children: Ingrid Drake, Jeffrey Sherwood. AB, Ohio Wesleyan U., 1948; MS, U. Chgo., 1951, PhD, 1952, DSc (hon.), 1989, Duke U., 1989, Whittier Coll., 1989, Princeton U., 1990, Haverford Coll., 1992, Clark U., 1996, U. East Anglia, 1996; LLD (hon.), Ohio Wesleyan U., 1989, Simon Fraser U., 1991, U. Calgary, 1997; laurea honoris causa, U. Urbino, Italy, 1998; DSc, Carleton Coll., 1998, Gustavus Adolphus Coll., 1997, Occidental Coll., 1998, Kanagawa U., Japan, 1999, LaTrobe U., Australia, 2000, U. Waterloo, Can., 2001, Ohio State U., 2002. Instr. chemistry Princeton (N.J.) U., 1952—56; asst. prof. chemistry U. Kans., 1956—58, assoc. prof. chemistry, 1958—63, prof. chemistry, 1963—64, U. Calif., Irvine, 1964—, dept. chmn., 1964—70, Aldrich prof. chemistry, 1985—89, Bren prof. chemistry, 1989—94, Donald Bren rsch. prof., chemistry, 1994—. Humboldt sr. scientist Fed. Republic Germany, 1981; chmn. Dahlem (Germany) Conf. on Changing Atmosphere, 1987; vis. scientist Japan Soc. for Promotion Sci., 1980; co-dir. western region Nat. Inst. Global Environ. Change, 1989—93; del. Internat. Coun. Sci. Unions, 1993—98; fgn. sec. NAS, 1994—2002; lectr., cons. in field; mem. ozone commn. Internat. Assn. Meteorology and Atmospheric Physics, 1980—88, hon. life mem., 1996, mem. commn. on atmospheric chemistry and global pollution, 1979—91; mem. acid rain peer rev. panel U.S. Office of Sci. and Tech., Exec. Office of White House, 1982—84; mem. vis. com. Max Planck Inst., Heidelberg and Mainz, Germany, 1982—96; ozone trends panel mem. NASA, 1986—88; chmn. Gordon Conf. Environ. Scis.-Air, 1987; mem. Calif. Coun. Sci. Tech., 1989—95; mem. exec. com. Tyler Prize, 1992—. Contbr. articles to profl. jours. Named to, GTE Acad. All-Am. Hall of Fame, 2000; recipient numerous awards including, John Wiley Jones award, Rochester Inst. Tech., 1975, Disting. Faculty Rsch. award, U. Calif., Irvine, 1976, Profl. Achievement award, U. Chgo., 1977, Billard award, N.Y. Acad. Sci., 1977, Tyler World Prize in Environ. Achievement, 1983, Global 500 Roll of Honor for Environ. Achievement, UN Environment Program, 1988, Dana award for Pioneering Achievements in Health, 1987, Silver medal, Royal Inst. Chemistry U.K., 1989, Wadsworth award, N.Y. State Dept. Health, 1989, medal, U. Calif. Irvine, 1989, Japan prize in Environ. Sci., 1989, Dickson prize, Carnegie-Mellon U., 1991, Albert Einstein prize, World Cultural Coun., 1994, Nobel Prize in chemistry, 1995, Alumni medal, U. Chgo., 1997, Nevada medal, 1997, Gold medal, Acad. Athens, 2003; fellow Guggenheim Found., 1962, 1974. Fellow: AAAS (pres.-elect 1991, pres. 1992, chmn. bd. dirs. 1993), Am. Geophys. Union (Roger Revelle medal 1994), Am. Phys. Soc. (Leo Szilard award for physics in pub. interest 1979); mem.: NAS (co-DATA com. 1977—82, com. atmospheric scis., solar-terrestial com. 1979—83, sci. com. on problems environment 1986—89, bd. environ. studies and toxicology 1986—91, com. on atmospheric chemistry 1987—89, Infinite Voyage film com. 1988—92, Robertson Meml. lectr. 1993, chmn. com. on internat. orgns. and programs 1993—2002, chmn. office of internat. affairs 1994—2002, coun. 1994—2002, co-chmn. interacad. panel 1995—2000, mem. exec. com. 2000—02, chair bd. atmospheric scis. and climate 2007—), Royal Soc. U.K. (fgn.), Academia Bibliotheca Alexandrinae, Inst. Medicine, Am. Philos. Soc., Am. Meteorol. Soc. (hon.), Korean Acad. Sci. Tech. (fgn. sec.), European Acad. Arts, Scis. and Humanities, Am. Chem. Soc. (chmn. divsn. nuclear sci. and tech. 1973—74, chmn. divsn. phys. chemistry 1974—75, E.F. Smith lectureship 1980, Orange County award 1975, Tolman medal 1976, Zimmerman award 1980, Environ. Sci. and Tech. award 1983, Esselen award 1987, Peter Debye Phys. Chem. award 1993), Am. Acad. Arts and Scis., Sigma Xi, Phi Beta Kappa. Office: Dept Chemistry U Calif Irvine 571 Rowland Hall Irvine CA 92697-2025 E-mail: rowland@uci.edu.

ROWLAND, HOWARD RAY, mass communications educator; b. Eddy County, N.Mex., Sept. 9, 1929; s. Lewis Marion and Ursula Lorene (Hunt) R.; m. Meredith June Lee, Apr. 19, 1951; children: Runay Ilene Olson, Rhonda Lee Fisher. B in Journalism, U. Mo., 1950; MS in Journalism, So. Ill. U., 1959; PhD, Mich. State U., 1969. Feature writer Springfield (Mo.) Newspapers, Inc., 1954; newspaper editor Monett (Mo.) Times, 1954-55; editl. writer So. Ill. U., Carbondale, 1955-59; pub. rels. dir. St. Cloud (Minn.) State U., 1959-86, asst. dean, 1986-87, 88-90; dir. Ctr. for British Studies, Alnwick, Eng., 1987-88, 90-91. Emeritus prof. St. Cloud State U., 1991—; cons. Conf. of Campus Ombudsmen, Berkeley, 1971; recorder Seminar on Fund Raising, Washington, 1985; bibliographer Higher Edn. Bibliography Yearbook, 1987. Author: American Students in Alnwick Castle, 1990, St. Cloud State University—125 Years, 1994, Big War, Small Town, 2003; editor: Effective Community Relations, 1980; sect. editor: Handbook of Institutional Advancement, 1986; author book revs. Chair All-Am. City Com., St. Cloud, 1973-74. With U.S. Army, 1951-53. NDEA doctoral fellow Mich. State U., 1967-69; recipient Appreciation award Mayor of St. Cloud, 1974, Disting Svc. award Coun. for Advancement and Support Edn., 1985. Mem. Soc. of Profl. Journalists (Minn. chpt. pres. 1963-64, dep. dir. 1965-67), Coun. for Advancement and Support of Edn. (dist. 5 chair 1977-79, Leadership award 1979), Phi Delta Kappa (Mich. State U. chpt. pres. 1968-69, St. Cloud State Univ. chpt. pres. 1978-79). Presbyterian. Avocations: writing, fishing, travel, photography, antiques. Home: 29467 Kraemer Lake Rd Saint Joseph MN 56374-9646 *Striving to achieve is more rewarding than striving for acclaim. Achievement brings personal satisfaction more fulfilling than recognition.*

ROWLAND, JAMES RICHARD, electrical engineering educator; b. Muldrow, Okla., Jan. 24, 1940; s. Richard Cleveland and Imogene Beatrice (Angel) R.; m. Jonell Condren, Aug. 24, 1963 (dec. May 1991); children: Jennifer Lynn, Angela Janel; m. Mary Anderson, Jan. 2, 1995. BSEE, Okla. State U., 1962; MSEE, Purdue U., 1964, PhD in Elec. Engring., 1966. Registered profl. engr., Okla. Instr. Purdue U., West Lafayette, Ind., 1964-65; from asst. to assoc. prof. Ga. Inst. Tech., Atlanta, 1966-71; from assoc. to full prof. Okla. State U., Stillwater, 1971-85; prof., chmn. dept. elec. and computer engring. U. Kans., Lawrence, 1985-89, prof., 1985—. Cons. Lockheed-Ga. Co., Marietta, 1966-71, U.S. Army Missile Command, Huntsville, Ala., 1969-79, Sandia Nat. Labs., Albuquerque, 1979, Puritan-Bennett, Lenexa, Kans., 1992. Author: Linear Control Systems, 1986; mem. editorial adv. bd. Computer and Elec. Engring., 1971-98; co-contbr. 60 articles to profl. jours. Fellow IEEE (edn. soc. pres. 1982-83, Centennial medal 1984, edn. soc. Achievement award 1986, edn. conf. award 1988, Region 5 Oustanding Educator award 1995, Svc. award 2002), Am. Soc. Engring. Edn. (dir. grad. div. 1987-89, Midwest sec. chair 2001-02), Eta Kappa Nu (dir. 1989-91), Kiwanis. Republican. Baptist. Avocations: golf, gardening. Home: 2424 Free State Ct Lawrence KS 66047-2831 Office: U Kans Dept Elec Engring & Computer Sci 2001 Eaton Hall Lawrence KS 66045 Home Phone: 785-842-5959; Office Phone: 785-864-8822. E-mail: jrowland@eecs.ku.edu.

ROWLAND, JOHN ARTHUR, lawyer; b. Joliet, Ill., Mar. 6, 1943; s. John Fornof and Grace Ada (Baskerville) R.; children: Sean B., Keira L. BA, U. Notre Dame, 1965; JD, U. San Francisco, 1968. Bar: Calif. 1969, US Dist. Ct. (no. dist.) Calif. 1982, US Dist. Ct. (ctrl. dist.) Calif. 1998, US Dist. Ct. (so. dist.) Calif. 2006. Asst. dist. atty. San Francisco Dist. Atty.'s Office, 1971-81; assoc. Ropers, Majeski, Kohn and Bentley, San Francisco, 1982—, ptnr., 1985—. Pres., South of Market Boys, San Francisco, 1981. Served to capt. U.S. Army, 1969-70, Korea. Recipient Commendation San Francisco Bd. Suprs., 1981, Merit award Mayor of San Francisco, 1982. Mem.: Am. Bd. Trial Advocates. Roman Catholic. Office: Ropers Majeski Kohn and Bentley 201 Spear St Ste 1000 San Francisco CA 94105 Home Phone: 415-359-1204; Office Phone: 415-972-6311. Business E-Mail: jrowland@ropers.com.

ROWLAND, KELLY (KELENDRIA TRENE ROWLAND), singer; b. Atlanta, Ga., Feb. 11, 1981; With Destiny's Child, 1992—2005; solo career, 2005—. Singer (with Destiny's Child): (albums) Destiny's Child, 1998, The Writing's on the Wall, 1999, Survivor, 2001 (Am. Music award for Favorite Pop Album, 2002), 8 Days of Christmas, 2001, Destiny Fulfilled, 2004 (Am. Music award for Favorite R&B Album, 2005), (songs) No, No, No, 1997, Say My Name, 1999 (2 Grammy awards, 2001, MTV Video Music award for Best R&B Video, 2000), Get on the Bus, 1999, Bills Bills Bills, 1999, Bug-A-Boo, 1999, Jumpin' Jumpin', 2000, Independent Woman, 2000, Survivor, 2001 (Grammy award, Best R&B Performance, 2002, MTV Video Music award for Best R&B Video, 2001), Bootylicious, 2001, Emotion, 2001, Lose My Breath, 2004, Soldier, 2005; singer: (solo career) (albums) Simply Deep, 2002, Ms. Kelly, 2007, (songs) Stole, 2002, Can't Nobody, 2003, Train on a Track, 2003; singer: (with Nelly) Dilemma, 2002 (Grammy award for Best Rap/Sung Collaboration, 2003); actor: (films) Freddy vs. Jason, 2003. Recipient Favorite R&B Group, Am. Music Awards, 2001, 2002, 2005, BET award for Best Female Group, 2001, NAACP Image award for Outstanding Duo or Group, 2001, 2005, 2006, Choice Pop Group, Teen Choice Awards, 2001, Brit award for Best Internat. Group, 2002, World's Best-Selling Group, World Music Awards, 2002, World's Best-Selling Pop Group, 2002, 2006, World's Best-Selling R&B Group, 2002, 2006, Best-Selling Female Group of All Time, 2006. Address: 1505 Hadley Houston TX 77002 Office Phone: 713-772-5175.

ROWLAND, LANDON HILL, diversified holding company executive; b. Fuquay Springs, NC, May 20, 1937; s. Walter Elton and Elizabeth Carr (Williams) R.; m. Sarah Fidler, Dec. 29, 1959; children: Sarah Elizabeth, Matthew Hill, Joshua Carr. BA, Dartmouth Coll., 1959; LL.B., Harvard U., 1962. Bar: Mo. Assoc. Watson, Ess, Marshall & Enggas, Kansas City, Mo., 1962-70, ptnr., 1970-80; v.p. Kansas City So. Industries, Inc., 1980-83, pres., chief oper. officer, 1983-86, pres., CEO, 1987—2000, also bd. dirs.; pres., CEO Kansas City So. Ry. Co., 1990—91, chmn., 1990—2000. Lectr. antitrust law U. Mo. Kansas City; chmn. DST Sys., 1983-95. Co-author West's Mo. Practice Series. Trustee Midwest Rsch. Inst., Kansas City, Mo.; chmn. bd. dirs. Swope Ridge Health Care Ctr.; bd. dirs. Lyric Opera of Kansas City, Am. Royal, Jacob L. & Ella C. Loose Found.; chmn. Met. Performing Arts Fund. Mem. ABA, Mo. Bar Assn., Phi Beta Kappa. Clubs: Kansas City Country, Kansas City, River. Home: Ever Glades Farm 12717 NE Mt Olivet Rd Kansas City MO 64166-1236 Office: Ever Glades Fin 920 Main St #204 Kansas City MO 64105-2008

ROWLAND, LEWIS PHILLIP, neurology educator, editor, clinical investigator; b. Bklyn., Aug. 3, 1925; s. Henry Alexander and Cecile (Coles) Rowland; m. Esther Edelman Rowland, Aug. 31, 1952; children: Andrew Simon, Steven Samuel, Joy Rosenthal. BS, Yale U., 1945, MD, 1948; PhD (hon.), U. Aix-Marseilles, France, 1986, U. Padua, 1996. Diplomate Am. Bd. Psychiatry and Neurology. Intern New Haven Hosp., 1949-50; asst. resident NY Neurol. Inst., 1950-52, fellow, 1953; clin. assoc. NIH, Bethesda, Md., 1953-54; practice rsch. medicine, specializing in neurology NYC, 1954-67, Phila., 1967-73, NYC, 1973—; asst. neurologist Montefiore Hosp., NYC, 1954-57; vis. fellow Nat. Inst. Med. Rsch., London, 1956; from asst. prof. to prof. neurology Columbia Coll. Physicians and Surgeons, 1957-67, prof. dept. neurology, 1973—, chmn. dept. neurology, 1973-98; prof., chmn. dept. neurology U. Pa. Med. Sch., 1967-73; from asst. neurologist to attending neurologist Presbyn. Hosp., 1957-67; co-dir. Neurol. Clin. Rsch. Ctr., 1961-67, dir. neurology svc., 1973-98, attending neurologist, 1973—, pres. med. bd., 1991-94. Cons. Harlem Hosp., 1973—; mem. med. adv. bd. Myasthenia Gravis Found., pres., 1971-73; med. adv. bd. Muscular Dystrophy Assocs., Nat. Multiple Sclerosis Soc., NYC Multiple Sclerosis Soc., 1977-92, Com. to Combat Huntington's Disease; chmn. med. adv. bd. NYC Multiple Sclerosis Soc. 1977-92; pres. Parkinson's Disease Found., 1979-; mem. tng. grants com. Nat. Inst. Neurol. Disorders and Stroke, NIH, 1971-73, bd. sci. counselors, 1978-83, chmn., 1981-83, mem. nat. adv. coun., 1986-90, cons. to dir., 2000-01; hon. dir. Motor Neuron Rsch. Ctr., Columbia U., 2005-. Mem. editl. bd. Archives of Neurology, 1968-76, Advances in Neurology, 1969—, Italian Jour. Neurol. Sci., 1979—99, Handbook of Clin. Neurology, 1982—, New Eng. Jour. Medicine, 1990-2000, Med. Letter, 1990-97, Jour. Neurol. Sci., 1991—, Jour. Neuromuscular Disorders, 1991-97, Clin. Neurosci., 1995-98; editor-in-chief Neurology, 1977-87, Neurology Today, 2001—; assoc. editor Medlink, 1995—; editor Merritt's Neurology Textbook, 1995, 11th edit. 2005; author NINDS at 50: An Incomplete History Celebrating the Fiftieth Anniversary of the National Institute of Neurological Disorders and Stroke, 2001. With USNR, 1942—44, with USPHS, 1953—54. Forbes Norris award, 2001, Internat. Alliance of ALS/MND Assns.; Jerry Lewis award, Muscular Dystrophy Assn., 1993; named disting. tchr., Columbia P&S Class of 1975. Mem. Am. Neurol. Assn. (hon. mem. 1959—, pres. 1980; Soriano Lecture, 1991, Geroge W. Jacoby Award 1995), Inst. Medicine, Nat. Acad. Sci. (elected 1999), Am. Acad. Neurology (pres.-elect 1987-89, pres. 1989-91, hon. mem. 1997—), Phila. Neurol. Soc. (pres. 1972), Assn. Rsch. Nervous Mental Disease (pres. 1969, trustee 1976—, v.p. 1980, chmn bd. trustees 1992-98), Assn. Univ. Profs. Neurology (sec. 1971-74, pres. 1978), Am. Acad. Neurol. Found. (pres. 1996, chair bd. trustees 1997-99, trustee 1999—), Am. Acad. Neurol. (Sheil Essey rsch. award 1998) Ea. Pa. Multiple Sclerosis Soc. (chmn. med. adv. bd. 1969-73); hon. mem. Neurol. Socs. France, Poland, Can., Europe, Italy, Gt. Britain, Spain, Japan. Home: 404 Riverside Dr New York NY 10025-1861 Office: Columbia U Med Ctr Neurological Inst 710 W 168th St New York NY 10032-2603 Office Phone: 212-305-8551. Business E-Mail: lpr1@columbia.edu.

ROWLAND, RALPH THOMAS, retired architect; b. Elizabeth, NJ, Oct. 10, 1920; s. Thomas Aloysius and Anna Frances (McQuaid) R.; m. Bernice Barbara Cannizzo, Sept. 7, 1946; children: Glenn Thomas, Mark Louis, Roy Joseph, Lisa Rowland Majewski. Student, Manhattan Coll., 1937-38, Columbia U., 1945-49. Archtl. field supr., specifier Voorhees Walker Foley & Smith, NYC, 1945-50; specifier, project mgr. Sargent Webster Crenshaw & Folley, Watertown, N.Y., 1951-53; pvt. practice Hamden, Conn., 1958-65; field supr. Fletcher Thompson, Inc., Bridgeport, Conn., 1954-56, project mgr., 1957, 65-73, asso., 1969-73, v.p., 1973-81, dir. archtl. research, 1981-85, adv. coun., 1994-98. Chmn. Conn. Bldg. Code Standards Com., 1978-82; vice chmn. Conn. State Codes and Standards Com., 1982-86; cons. in field. Editorial chmn.: Conn. Architect Mag., 1966-74; project mgr. design, St. Vincents Med. Center, Bridgeport. Mem. Cheshire Planning Commn., 1966-72, chmn., 1967-68; pres. Hamden C. of C., 1964, New Eng. Bldg. Code Assn., 1989; mem. Cen. Naugatuck Valley Regional Planning Agy., 1966-74, chmn., 1969; mem. Cheshire Democratic Town Com., 1960-70, treas., 1963-69; mem. Conn. Archtl. Sch. Task Force, 1987-88. With USN, 1942-45. Fellow AIA; mem. AIA Conn. (past pres.), AARP (pres. Cheshire chpt. 1995-97), Conn. Bldg. Ofcls. Assn., Cheshire C. of C. Roman Catholic. Home: 201 N Rolling Acres Rd Cheshire CT 06410-2119

ROWLAND, ROBERT ALEXANDER, III, lawyer; b. McAllen, Tex., Apr. 27, 1943; s. Robert Alexander Jr and Marguerite (Gerry) Rowland; m. Victoria Nalle, Apr. 2, 1977; children: Julia Marie, Emily Nalle. BS, Tex. A&M U., 1966; JD, George Washington U., 1972. Bar: Tex. 1972, U.S. Dist. Ct. (so. dist.) Tex. 1973, U.S. Ct. Appeals (5th cir.) 1973, U.S. Supreme Ct. 1976, U.S. Dist. Ct. (no. dist.) Tex. 1979, U.S. Dist. Ct. (we. dist.) Tex. 1982, U.S. Dist. Ct. (ea. dist.) Tex. 1983. Law clk. U.S. Ct. Appeals (5th cir.), Houston, 1973-74; assoc. Vinson & Elkins, Houston, 1975-81; ptnr. Susman, Godfrey & McGowan, Houston, 1982—88; mng. dir. Johnson and Gibbs, Houston, 1988-91; ptnr. Hutcheson & Grundy, LLP, Houston, 1992-94; chmn., CEO Associated Counsel of Am., 1995—; ptnr. Roach & Rowland, Houston, 2003—. Bd. dirs. Vol. Ctr., Houston, 1975—84, pres., 1982—83; founding mem., bd. dirs. Tex. Accts. and Lawyers for Arts, 1979—92, pres., 1989—91; devel. coun. Sch. Liberal Arts Tex. A&M U., 1992—, steering com., 1995—, devel. coun. George Bush Sch. Govt. and Pub. Svc., 2004—; trustee Houston Pks. Bd. Endowment Fund, 2002—; chmn. endowment com. Houston Audubon Soc., 2006—; endowment com. The Beacon; co-chmn. Mayor's Transition Com. for Parks, City of Houston, 1992—94; candidate for State Rep., Tex. Legis. Dist. 134, Rep. Primary, 2002; fin. com. Harris County Rep. Party, 2003—07, chmn., 2005—07; bd. dirs. United Reps. of Harris County, 2002—; Rep. precinct chmn. Harris County Precinct, 2003—05; mission outreach coun. Christ Ch. Cathedral, 2002—05, chmn., 2004—05, co-chmn., grants subcom., 2005—06, chmn. grants subcom., 2006—07; bd. dirs. Houston Pks. Bd., 1993—2005, chmn., 2003—05; bd. dirs. Contemporary Art Mus. Houston, 1974—80, 1991—94; bd. dirs. Sarah Campbell Blaffer Gallery of Art U. Houston, 1989—94; bd. dirs. Tex. Opera Theater, 1988—89; bd. trustees Nat. Recreation and Pk. Assn., 1992—95; bd. dirs. Cultural Arts Coun., Houston, 1981—86, Pk. People Inc., 1979—2001, pres., 1991—92, endowment com. chmn., 1994—2004; bd. dirs. Compass, 2006—; co-chair parks and open spaces com. Greater Houston Partnership, 2006—, quality of life adv. com., 2006—; bd. dirs. Bot. Garden Houston, 2007—. Capt. US Army, 1966—69, Vietnam. Fellow: Tex. Bar Found., Houston Bar Found.; mem.: Houston Young Lawyers Assn. (bd. dirs. 1975—79, pres. 1978—79), State Bar Tex., Houston Bar Assn. (dir. 1979—88, sec., chmn. law and art com. 1984—85, 2d v.p. 1985—86), C Club (program chmn. 2005, exec. com. 2005—, membership chmn. 2006, treas. 2007—), Coronado Club, River Oaks Country Club, Phi Delta Phi. Episcopalian. Home: 2010 Chilton Rd Houston TX 77019-1502 Office: Associated Counsel Am Inc Ste 125 4605 Post Oak Pl Houston TX 77027-9744 Office Phone: 713-840-7100 Ext. 234. Personal E-mail: rob@robrowland.com.

ROWLAND, THEODORE JUSTIN, physicist, researcher; b. Cleve., May 15, 1927; s. Thurston Justin and Lillian (Nesser) R.; m. Janet Claire Millar, June 28, 1952 (div. 1967); children: Theodore Justin, Dawson Ann, Claire Millar; m. Patsy Marie Beard, Aug. 21, 1968 (div. 2007). BS, Western Res. U., 1948; MA, Harvard U., 1949, PhD, 1954. Rsch. physicist Union Carbide Metals Co., Niagara Falls, NY, 1954-61; prof. phys. metallurgy U. Ill., 1961-92, asst. dean Coll. Engring., acting assoc. dean Grad. Coll., 1990-91, prof. emeritus, 1992—; pres., dir. Materials Cons., Inc. Cons. physicist, 1961—; cons. metallurgist, 1976—. Editor 2 books; author monograph; contbr. articles to profl. jours. Fellow Am. Phys. Soc.; mem. AIME, AAAS, AAUP, Phi Beta Kappa, Sigma Xi. Achievements include initial verification of charge density waves in dilute alloys; original contributions to theory and experiment in nuclear magnetic resonance in metals. Home: 805 Park Lane Dr Champaign IL 61820-7613 Office: U Ill Dept Materials Sci and Engring 1304 W Green St Urbana IL 61801-2920 Business E-Mail: trowland@uiuc.edu.

ROWLANDS, DAVID THOMAS, pathology educator; b. Wilkes-Barre, Pa., Mar. 22, 1930; s. David Thomas and Anna Jule (Morgan) R.; m. Gwendolyn Marie York, Mar. 1, 1958; children: Julie Marie, Carolyn Jane. MD, U. Pa., 1955. Diplomate: Am. Bd. Pathology, Am. Bd. Allergy and Immunology. Intern Pa. Hosp., Phila., 1955-56; resident Cin. Gen. Hosp., 1956-60; asst. prof. U. Colo., 1962-64, Rockefeller U., 1964-66; assoc. prof. Duke U., Durham, NC, 1966-70; prof. pathology U. Pa., Phila., 1970-82, chmn. dept. pathology, 1973-78, prof. medicine, 1979-82; prof., chmn. dept. pathology U. So. Fla., Tampa, 1982-91, assoc. dean, 1983-84, prof. pediatrics, 1986-91; med. dir. Lifelink Tissue Bank, 1991-93. Mem. editorial bd.: Am. Jour. Pathology, 1971-81, Developmental and Comparative Immunology, 1977-79. Served with USNR, 1960-62. Recipient Lederle Med. Faculty award U. Colo., 1964, Jacob Ehrenzeller award Pa. Hosp., 1976 Mem. Am. Assn. Pathologists, Internat. Acad. Pathology, Am. Soc. Clin. Pathology, Am. Assn. Immunologists, Coll. Am. Pathologist, Arthur Purdy Stout Soc. Presbyterian. Home: 13804 Cypress Village Cir Tampa FL 33618-8406 E-mail: drowl30@gte.net.

ROWLANDS, GENA, actress; b. Madison, Wis., June 19, 1936; d. Edwin Merwin and Mary Allen (Neal) R.; m. John Cassavetes, Apr. 9, 1954 (dec. Feb. 3 1989); 4 children. Student, U. Wis., Am. Acad. Dramatic Art, NYC. Theatrical appearance include The Middle of the Night, 1956; Actress: (films) including The High Cost of Loving, 1958, Lonely Are The Brave, 1962, A Child is Waiting, 1962, Spiral Road, 1962, Faces, 1968, At Any Price, 1970, Minnie and Moscowitz, 1971, A Woman Under the Influence, 1974 (Golden Globe award for Best Motion Picture Actress in a Drama, 1975), Two Minute Warning, 1976, Opening Night, 1977, The Brinks Job, 1978, One Summer Night, 1979, Gloria, 1980, Tempest, 1982, Love Streams, 1983, Light of Day, 1987, Another Woman, 1988, Once Around, 1990, Ted and Venus, 1991, Night on Earth, 1992, Silent Cries, 1993, Parallel Lives, 1994, Anything for John, 1995, Something to Talk About, 1995, The Neon Bible, 1995, Enfants de Salaud, 1996, Unhook the Stars, 1996, Hope Floats, 1997, She's so Lovely, 1997, The Mighty, 1997, Paulie, 1998, The Weekend, 1999, Taking Lives, 2004, The Notebook, 2004, The Skeleton Key, 2005, Broken English, 2007; (TV movies) A Question of Love, 1978, Strangers, 1979, Thurday's Child, 1983, Early Frost, 1986, The Betty Ford Story, 1987 (Emmy award for Outstanding Lead Actress in a Miniseries or Special, 1987, Golden Globe award for Best Performance by an Actress in a TV Film, 1988), Montana, Face of a Stranger, 1991 (Emmy award, Leading Actress in a Mini-Series or Special, 1992), Parallel Lives, 1994, Best of Friends for Life, 1996, Ljuset häller mig sällskap, 2000, Color of Love: Jacey's Story, 2000, Wild Iris, 2001, Hysterical Blindness, 2002, (Emmy award best supporting actress in TV movie, 2003), Charms for the Easy Life, 2002, The Incredible Mrs. Ritchie, 2003 (Daytime Emmy award for Outstanding Performer in a Family Special, 2004); numerous other TV appearances. Mem. Actors Equity Assn., Screen Actors Guild, AFTRA, Am. Guild Variety Artists. *

ROWLANDS, KATHLEEN DUDDEN, education educator; b. South Weymouth, Mass., Jan. 11, 1945; d. Arthur Power Dudden and Millicent Ruth (Hancock) Dillon; m. Dennis Earl Rowlands, July 5, 1997; children: Christopher J. Andrasick, Gregory O. Andrasick, Christopher, Jeffrey, Satia T-A. Wang, Jocelyn Vo, Jacquie Vo. AB in English, Conn. Coll., New London, 1966; MA in English, U. Hawaii, Honolulu, 1988; PhD in Composition, Indiana U. Pa., 2004. English tchr. Tottenville HS, NY, 1967—68, Weeks Jr. HS, Newton, Mass., 1969—71, St. Andrews Priory Sch., Honolulu, 1978—81; English tchr., chmn. dept. Iolani Sch., Honolulu, 1981—92; instr. Montgomery CC, Conroe, Tex., 1998, Sam Houston State U., Huntsville, Tex., 1999—2000; asst. prof. Calif. State U., Northridge, 2004—. Co-dir Hawaii Writing Project, Honolulu, 1982—96, dir. literature inst., 1992, Honolulu, 1997—2003; dir. Reading Inst. Acadm. Preparation, Northridge, 2004—. Author: (as Kathleen D. Andrasick) Opening Texts: Using Writing to Teach Literature, 1990; contbr. articles to profl. publs. Named Master Tchr., Iolani Sch., 1990; recipient Excellence in Tchg. English award, English Speaking Union, 1989, award for ednl. contbns. to state of Hawaii, Hawaii State Senate, 1992. Mem.: Nat. Coun. Tchrs. English, Phi Kappa Phi. Avocations: reading, cooking, golf, tennis. Office: Calif State Univ Dept Secondary Edn 18111 Nordhoff St Northridge CA 91330-8265 Office Phone: 818-677-2556. Business E-Mail: krowlands@csun.edu.

ROWLES, MICHAEL G., lawyer; b. Evanston, Ill. m. Maureen Rowles; children: Meagan, Caitlin, Camryn. JD, U. Ill. With Burke, Bosselman & Weaver, Chgo., Jenner & Block, 1993—95, Paige Polin Busch & Boatwright, San Diego, 1995—96, Zevnik Horton Guibord McGovern Palmer & Fognani, 1996; gen. counsel, sr. v.p., sec. Entravision, 2000—06; exec. v.p., gen. counsel Live Nation, Inc., 2006—. Office: Live Nation Inc 9348 Civic Ctr Dr Beverly Hills CA 90210 Home Phone: 310-471-5338; Office Phone: 310-867-7179. Business E-Mail: michaelrowles@livenation.com.

ROWLETT, RALPH MORGAN, archaeologist, educator; b. Richmond, Ky., Sept. 11, 1934; s. Robert Kenny and Daisy (Mullikin) R.; m. Elsebet Sander-Jorgensen, Aug. 25, 1963 (div. Jan. 1986); children: Rolf R. Arvid, Erik Kenneth; m. Elizabeth Helen Dinan, Apr. 21, 1989 (div. Oct. 1995); 1 child, Helen Holly; m. Magda Mircea, 2005. Student, U. Ky., 1952-53; BA summa cum laude, Marshall U., 1956; postgrad., U. London, 1962-63; PhD, Harvard U., 1968. Instr. anthropology U. Mo., Columbia, 1965-67, asst. prof., 1967-69, assoc. prof., 1969-75, prof., 1975—. Postdoctoral fellow Ghent U., 1969; vis. prof. Bucuresti U., 2005. Co-author: Neolithic Levels on the Titelberg, Luxembourg, 1981, Meeting Anthropology Phase to Phase, 2000; anthropology editor Random House Unabridged Dictionary of English, 1980—; editor: Horizons and Styles, 1993, Horizons and Styles in West Eurasiatic Archaeology; developer thermoluminescence dating of flint, 1972; co-developer electron spin resonance dating of flint, 1981. 1st lt. arty., U.S. Army, 1956-58. Decorated officer Legion de Merit (Luxembourg); named Ky. col., 1976; grantee NSF, 1973-75, 76-79, 82-83, Earthwatch, 1985-88, Svc. Archeologique de Neuchatel, 1989, British Coun., 1993, Acad. of Romania, 1996, Internat. Rsch. and Exch. Bd., 1997. Fellow Am. Anthrop. Assn.; mem. AAAS, Archaeol. Inst. Am., Soc. Am. Archaeology, Societe Prehistorique de Luxembourg, Societe Archeologique Champenoise, English Heritage, Palomino Horse Breeders Assn., Sigma Xi. Green Party. Mem. Christian Ch. (Disciples Of Christ). Home: Hollywell Hill 1197 State Road Ww Fulton MO 65251-5106 Office: Univ Mo Dept Anthropology Columbia MO 65211-0001 Office Phone: 573-882-4731. Business E-Mail: rowlettR@missouri.edu.

ROWLETTE, HENRY ALLEN, JR., social worker, counseling psychologist; b. Phila., July 8, 1947; s. Henry Allen Sr. and Ophelia Alberta (Kilson) R.; m. Geraldine Lee Stevens, Mar. 1972 (div. Mar. 1986); children: Cessandra N., Deaeon D., Christiene A.; m. Carolyn Rowlette; 1 child, Janetta M.; m. Ann Laura Rowe, Mar. 19, 1989. BA, Cheyney State Coll., 1970; MEd, Boston U., 1981; MSW, Temple U., 1988; PhD, Suffield Coll. and U., 2003. Cert. sch. social worker, NJ; lic. clin. social worker; diplomate Am. Psychotherapy Assn., Nat. Bd. Cognitive Behavioral Therapists; ordained minister Bapt. Ch. Cardiac monitor technician Bapt. Med. Ctr., Little Rock, 1982-83; mental health technician The Horsham Clinic, Ambler, Pa., 1984; psychiat. technician The Lower Bucks Hosp., Bristol, Pa., 1984-90; mental health technician The Helene Fuld Med. Ctr., Trenton, NJ, 1988-90, psychiat. social worker, 1988-92; profl. sch. social worker The Willingboro Sch. Dist., NJ, 1990—96. Dist. crisis intervention team Willingboro Sch. Dist., 1994-96; therapist The NJ State Prison, Trenton, 1996-98, The Southwoods State Prison, Bridgeton, NJ; clinician Kennedy Meml. Health Ctr., Cherry Hill, NJ, 1998—, The Lumberton Schs./Sch. Social Worker, Lumberton, NJ, 1998; behavioral cons. Founds. Behavioral Health, Willow Grove, Pa., 1999; mental health technician The Children's Hosp. Phila., 1999-2000. Clin. social worker Phila. Prison System, 2000; mem. NAACP, Trenton, 1990. With US Army, 1971-79. Mem. NASW, Am. Assn. Christian Counselors, Omega Psi Phi (Delta Upsilon chpt.), Phi Delta Kappa (Trenton chpt.), Am. Psychotherapy Assn., Nat. Bd. Cognitive Behavioral Therapists, Nat. Bd. Addiction Examiners, Nat. Assn. Forensic Counselors. Democrat. Baptist. Avocations: fishing, reading, computer technology/games. Home: 18 Foxchase Dr Burlington NJ 08016-3044 Office Phone: 609-953-5608. Personal E-mail: drhrowlettejr@comcast.net.

ROWLEY, BEVERLEY DAVIES, sociologist; b. Antioch, Calif., July 28, 1941; d. George M. and Eloise Davies; m. Richard B. Rowley, Apr. 1, 1966 (div. 1983). BS, Colo. State U., 1963; MA, U. Nev., 1975; PhD, Union Inst., 1983. Social worker Nev. Dept. Pub. Welfare, Reno, 1963—65, Santa Clara County Dept. Welfare, San Jose, Calif., 1965—66; field dir. Sierra Sage coun. Camp Fire Girls, Sparks, Nev., 1966—70; program coord. divsn. health scis. Sch. Medicine U. Nev., 1976—78, program coord., health analyst office rural health, 1978—84, acting dir. office rural health, 1982—84; exec. asst. to pres. Med. Coll. of Hampton Rds., Norfolk, Va., 1984—87; rsch. mgr. Office Med. Edn. Info. AMA, Chgo., 1987—88, dir. dept. data systems, 1988-91; dir. med. edn. Maricopa Med. Ctr., Phoenix, 1991—99; pres. Med. Edn. and Rsch. Assocs., Inc., Phoenix, Chgo., 1999—, Med. Edn. & Rsch. Assocs., Tempe, Ariz., 1999—; vis. prof. Ariz. State U. East, Mesa, 1999—2000, profl. and personal coach, 2004—; pres., exec. dir. Maricopa Med. Found., Phoenix, 2004—. Various positions as adj. prof. and lectr. in health scis. U. Nev. Sch. of Medicine, 1972-75; lectr. dept. family and cmty. medicine U. Nev., 1978-84, asst. dir., evaluator Health Careers for Am. Indians Programs, 1978-84; cons. Nev. Statewide Health Survey, 1979-84; interim dir. Health Max, 1985-86; asst. prof. dept. family and cmty. medicine Med. Coll. of Hampton Rds., Norfolk, Va., 1985-87. Editor of five books; contbr. numerous articles to profl. jours. Mem. Am. Sociol. Assn., Nat. Rural Health Assn. (bd. dirs. 1986-88), Assn. Behavioral Sci. and Med. Edn. (pres. 1986), Assn. Am. Med. Colls. (exec. coun. 1993-95), Coun. Acad. Scis. (adminstrv. bd. 1992-97), Assn. Hosp. Med. Edn. (bd. dirs. 1997—), Delta Delta Delta. Achievements include development of three computer systems including AMA-FREIDA; four internet-based educational programs for physicians. Avocations: hiking, skiing, gardening, sewing, ceramics. Office: MERA Inc 1903 E Sarah Ln Tempe AZ 85284-3430 E-mail: BDR@MERAInc.com.

ROWLEY, CYNTHIA, apparel designer; b. Barrington, Ill. m. Bill Powers. Grad., Art Inst. of Chicago. Designer Cynthia Rowley, Inc., 1983—; owner, designer Cynthia Rowley Boutiques, NYC, Chicago, Los Angeles and Japan, Swellco (subsidiary of Cynthia Rowley, Inc.). Work featured in Vogue, Elle, W, Harper's Bazaar, Glamour, New York Times, In Style, Elle Décor, French Vogue. Co-author: Swell: A Girl's Guide to the Good Life, 1999, Home Swell Home, 2002, Swell Holiday, 2003, The Swell Dressed Party, 2005; author: Slim: A Fantasy Memoir, 2007. Recipient New Fashion Talent award, Council of Fashion Designers of Am., 1994. Office: Cynthia Rowley Inc 376 Bleecker St New York NY 10014 *

ROWLEY, GEOFFREY HERBERT, management consultant; b. Harrow, Middlesex, Eng., Nov. 10, 1935; came to U.S., 1962; s. Herbert and Muriel Jessie (Nicolls) R. BA, Bristol U., Eng., 1958; cert. indsl. adminstrn., Glasgow U., Scotland, 1962; MBA, Harvard U., 1964. Purchasing officer Pirelli Ltd., London, 1958-61; rsch. assoc. Assn. for Internat. Rsch., Inc., Cambridge, Mass., 1964-68, v.p., 1968—2002, cons. in expatriate compensation, 1964—. Lectr. in field; dir. U. Bristol Found., Inc. Contbr. articles to profl. jours. Served with Royal Navy, 1953-55. Mem. Am. Compensation Assn., Inst. for Human Resources, Brit. Ins. Mgmt., Harvard Club. Home: 11 Berkeley Pl Cambridge MA 02138-3411 Office Phone: 617-251-3023. Personal E-mail: GHRowley@comcast.net, GHRowley@aol.com.

ROWLEY, GLENN HARRY, lawyer; b. Hyannis, Mass., May 16, 1948; s. Harold Frederick and Olive Nellie (Jones) R.; 1 child, Brewster Westgate. BBA, U. Mass., 1970; JD with cum laude, Western New Eng. Coll., 1980. Bar: Mass. 1980, U.S. Dist. Ct. Mass. 1980, U.S. Tax Ct. 1981, cert.: Nat. Elder Law Found./ABA (elder law atty.). Staff mem. Cape Cod Planning and Econ. Devel. Commn., Barnstable, Mass., 1975-76; staff, estate planning tax dept. Coopers and Lybrand, Springfield, Mass., 1980-81; legal assoc. Roberts and Farrell, West Chatham, Mass., 1982-84; ptnr. Roberts, Farrell & Rowley, West Chatham, 1984-97; pvt. practice Chatham, Mass., 1997—. Cons. Local Citizen Scholarship Trusts, Harwich and Chatham, Mass., 1985—. Contbr. (weekly news column) The Enterprise, others; contbr. articles to profl. jours. Founding mem. Brewster (Mass.) Conservation Trust, 1984; elected mem. Brewster Hist. Dist. Com., 1975; adv. bd. The May Inst., The Cape Cod Writers Ctr., Inc. With USN, 1971-74, Iceland. Recipient Am. Jurisprudence awards Lawyers Co-op. Pub. Co., 1978, 79. Mem. Mass. Bar Assn., Ocean Edge Exec. Club, Profl. Writers of Cape Cod, Cape Cod Estate Planning Coun., Nat. Acad. Elder Law Attys., Phi Delta Phi. Avocations: travel, writing. Home: Annaniases Knoll/Sheep Pond Brewster MA 02631 Office: The Marketplace PO Box 1489 26 George Ryder Rd S West Chatham MA 02669 Office Phone: 508-945-1000. E-mail: glennh.rowley@verizon.net.

ROWLEY, JANET DAVISON, physician; b. NYC, Apr. 5, 1925; d. Hurford Henry and Ethel Mary (Ballantyne) Davison; m. Donald A. Rowley, Dec. 18, 1948; children: Donald, David, Robert, Roger. PhB, U. Chgo., 1944, BS, 1946, MD, 1948; DSc (hon.), U. Ariz., 1989, U. Pa., 1989, Knox Coll., 1991, U. So. Calif., 1992, St. Louis U., 1997, St. Xavier U., 1999, Oxford U., Eng., 2000, Lund U., Sweden, 2003, Dartmouth U., 2004. Diplomate Am. Bd. Med. Genetics. Rsch. asst. U. Chgo., 1949—50; intern Marine Hosp., USPHS, Chgo., 1950—51; attending physician Infant Welfare and Prenatal Clinics Dept. Pub. Health, Montgomery County, Md., 1953—54; rsch. fellow Levinson Found., Cook County Hosp., Chgo., 1955—61; clin. instr. neurology U. Ill., Chgo., 1957—61; USPHS spl. trainee Radiobiology Lab. The Churchill Hosp., Oxford, England, 1961—62; rsch. assoc. dept. medicine and Argonne Cancer Rsch. Hosp. U. Chgo., 1962—69, assoc. prof. dept. medicine and Argonne Cancer Rsch. Hosp., 1969—77, prof. dept. medicine and Franklin McLean Meml. Rsch. Inst., 1977—84, Blum-Riese Disting. Svc. prof., dept. medicine and dept. molecular genetics and cell biology, 1984—, Blum-Riese Disting. Svc. prof. dept. human genetics, 1997—, interim dep. dean for sci. biol. scis. divsn., 2001—02. Bd. sci. counsellors Nat. Inst. Dental Rsch., NIH, 1972—76, chmn., 1974—76; mem. Nat. Cancer Adv. Bd., Nat. Cancer Inst., 1979—84, Nat. Adv. Coun. for Human Genome Rsch. Inst., 1999—2004; adv. com. Frederick Cancer Rsch. Facility, 1983—84; bd. sci. counsellors Nat. Human Genome Rsch. Inst., NIH, 1994—99, chmn., 1994—97; adv. bd. Howard Hughes Med. Inst., 1989—94, MD Anderson Cancer Ctr., 1998—2005; vis. com. dept. applied biol. scis. MIT Corp., 1983—86; bd. sci. cons. Meml. Sloan-Kettering Cancer Ctr., 1988—90; adv. com. Ency. Britannica U. Chgo., 1988—96; W. Jack Stuckey Jr. lectr. Tulane Career Ctr., 1996; Presdl. Symposium Am. Soc. Pediatric Hematology/Oncology, 1995; chmn. sci. adv. com. Translational Genomics Rsch. Inst., Phoenix., 2004—; med. adv. bd. Calif. Inst. Regenerative Medicine, 2005—; mem. sci. adv. coun. Children's Hosp., Boston, 2005—. Co-founder, co-editor: Genes, Chromosomes and Cancer, mem. editl. bd.: Oncology Rsch., Cancer Genetics and Cytogenetics, Internat. Jour. Hematology, Genomics, Leukemia; past mem. editl. bd. Internat. Jour. Cancer, Blood, Cancer Rsch., Hematol. Oncology, Leukemia Rsch.; contbr. chapters to books, articles to profl. jours. Adv. com. for career awards in biomed. scis. Burroughs Wellcome Fund, 1994—98; selection panel for Clin. Sci. award Doris Duke Charitable Found., 2000—02, 2006; mem. Pres.'s Adv. Coun. on Bioethics, 2001—; mem. med. rsch. material command leukemia program U.S. Army, 2002—04; mem. selection com. Rosalind Franklin young investigator award, 2004, 2007; nat. adv. com. McDonnell Found. Program for Molecular Medicine in Cancer Rsch., 1988—98; adv. bd. Leukemia Soc. Am., 1979—84; selection com. scholar award in biomed. sci. Lucille P. Markey Charitable Trust, 1984—87; trustee Adler Planetarium, Chgo., 1978—; med. adv. bd. G&P Charitable Found., 1999—. Co-recipient King Faisal Internat. prize in medicine, 1988, Charles Mott prize, GM Cancer Rsch. Found., 1989; named Chicagoan of Yr., Chgo. mag., 1998; recipient Esther Langer award, Ann Langer Cancer Rsch. Found., 1983, First Kuwait Cancer prize, 1984, A. Cressy Morrison award in natural scis., NY Acad. Scis., 1985, Past State Pres. award, Tex. Fedn. Bus. and Profl. Women's Clubs, 1986, Karnofsky award and lecture, Am. Soc. Clin. Oncology, 1987, Antoine Lacassagne Lique prize, Nat. Francaise Contre le Cancer prize, 1987, Katherine Berkan Judd award, Meml. Sloan-Kettering Cancer Ctr., 1989, Steven C. Beering award, U. Ind. Med. Sch, 1992, Robert de Villiers award, Leukemia Soc. Am., 1993, Kaplan Family prize for cancer rsch. excellence, Oncology Soc. Dayton, 1995, Cotlove award and lecture, Acad. Clin. Lab. Physicians and Scientists, 1995, Nilsson-Ehle lecture, Mendelian Soc. and Royal Physiographic Soc., 1995, Gairdner Found. award, 1996, medal of honor, Basic Sci. Am. Cancer Soc., 1996, Nat. Medal of Sci., 1998, Lasker award for clin. scis., 1998, Woman Extraordinaire award, Internat. Women's Assocs., 1999, Golden Plate award, Am. Acad. Achievement, 1999, Women Achieving Excellence award, YWCA of Met. Chgo., 2000, Philip Levine award, Am. Soc. Clin. Pathology, 2001, Emile M Chamot award, State Microscopy Soc. Ill., 2001, Mendel medal, Villanova U., 2003, Benjamin Franklin medal, Am. Philos. Soc., 2003, Dist. Alumni Award, U. Chgo., 2003. Fellow: AAAS (nominating com. 1998); mem.: NAS (chmn. sect. 41 1995—99, mem. com. 2004), Chgo. Network, Inst. Medicine (coun. 1988—90), Cancer Rsch. (lectr. 2003, G.H.A. Clowes Meml. award 1989, Charlotte Friend award 2003, Dorothy P. Landon award 2005), Am. Soc. Hematology (lectr. Millenium Symposium 1999, Presdl. Symposium 1982, Dameshek prize 1982, Ham-Wasserman award 1995, Henry M. Stratton medal 2003), Genetical Soc., Am. Soc. Human Genetics (pres.-elect 1992, pres. 1993, Allen award and lectr. 1991, Disting. Sci. lectr. 2003), Am. Philos. Soc., Am. Acad. Arts and Scis. (nominating com. 1998), Phi Beta Kappa (hon.), Alpha Omega Alpha, Sigma Xi (William Proctor prize for sci. achievement 1989). Episcopalian. Home: 5310 S University Ave Chicago IL 60615-5106 Office: U Chgo 5841 S Maryland Ave MC 2115 Chicago IL 60637-1463 Office Phone: 773-702-6117. Business E-Mail: jrowley@medicine.bsd.uchicago.edu.

ROWLEY, MAXINE LEWIS, education educator, retired academic administrator; b. Provo, Utah, Sept. 23, 1938; d. Max Thomas Lewis and Illa Lewis Sanford; m. Arthur William Rowley, Sept. 23, 1960; children: Anne, Jenefer. BA (Ford Found. scholar), Brigham Young U., 1960, PhD in Edn. Adminstrn., 1989; BS, U. Utah, 1974; MA, Utah State U., 1980. Promotion writer Sta. ABC KCPX-TV, 1960; extension home economist USDA, 1961; mgmt. trainee Deseret Book Co., Salt Lake City, 1969; dept. chair Patricia Stevens Career Coll., Salt Lake City, 1970; chair consumer and homemaking dept. Sand Ridge Jr. H.S. Weber Sch. Dist., Roy, Utah, 1975, learning experience designer, 1976-78; consumer and home econs. faculty Utah State U., Logan, 1978-79; spl. appointee to Utah State U. by the Utah State Bd. Edn., 1978-86; intern Gladys Chalkley Brannegan Am. Home Econ. Assn., 1993; chair dept. family life and home econs. Brigham Young U., 1988, 1999—2002, tchr., 2007—. Instrumental writer Utah State U. Found., 1979; mem. faculty Brigham Young U., 1979; women's legis. coun. State of Utah, 1992—; cons. Utah State Office Edn., 2005—. Author: NCFR Public Policy Handbook, 1997; (filmstrips, texts and tchrs. guide) CHECS, 1979; (curriculum guide) Operation: Free Enterprise, 1982, Curriculum of Food Sci., Nutrition, vol. I, 1990, vol. II, 1992, vol. III, 1993; co-author: Legacy, vol. I, 1998. Active ward, stake and region positions Ch. of Jesus Christ of Latter-day Saints; leader 4-H Club, coun. mem., adv. bd.; leader Girl Scouts U.S.A., Young Homemakers; active State Text Book Evaluation Com., 1978-86, U. Utah Evaluation Com., 1979; edn. and rsch. com. Am. Cancer Soc., State of Utah, 1993-94. Named Outstanding Leader Am. Edn., 1976, Nat. Tchr. of Yr., 1977, Outstanding Tchr. in Dept., Brigham Young U., 1984-94, Outstanding Vocat. Edn. Leader, State of Utah, 1996, Nat. Honor Roll in vocat. edn. Nat. Assn. Vocat. Family and Consumer Scis., 1999. Mem.: NAFE, NEA, Internat. Fed. Home Econ. (nat. officer), Am. Edn. Rsch. Assn. (Nat. chair, HERSIG 2001—03), Utah Assn. Family and Consumer Scis. (disting. svc. award 2003), Worldwide Orgn. Women (women's legis. coun. State of Utah 1998—2004, internat. bd. dirs. 1999—2003), Vocat. Home Econs. Tchrs. (nat. chmn. public rels. and legis. coms. 1978), Home Econs. Edn. Assn., Am. Edn. Rsch. Assn. (nat.chair Home Econs. Related Spl. Interest Group 2000—03, marriage, family & human devel. dept. 2002—), County Welfare Com., Utah Edn. Assn. (Womens Awareness Task Force Project award 1976), Utah Nutrition Coun. (chair 1995), Utah Coun. for Improvement Edn., Utah Vocat. Assn., Utah Home Econs. Assn., Am. Vocat. Assn., Am. Assn. Family and Consumer Scis. (nat. v.p., bd. dirs., chair ann. meeting, bd. liaison publs. 1995—97, nat. com. publs. 1999—, nat. treas. internat. fedn. home econ. 2007—), Am. Home Econs. Assn. (contbr., author yearbook 1984, Nat. Leadership award 1993), Nat. Assn. Vocat. Home Econs. Tchrs., Ellen H. Richards Cir., Spurs, White Key (pres. 1960), Alpha Delta Kappa, Gamma Phi Omicron, Phi Kappa Phi, Kappa Omicron Nu (advisor 1980—2005, nat. endowment honoree 1989, Nat. award of excellence 1999, nat. leadership endowment 2001).

ROWLING, J.K. (JOANNE KATHLEEN ROWLING), writer; b. Gloucestershire, England, July 31, 1965; d. Peter and Anne Rowling; m. Jorge Arantes, Oct. 16, 1992 (div. Nov. 30, 1993); 1 child, Jessica; m. Neil Murray, Dec. 26, 2001; children: David, Mackenzie. BA in French & Classics, Exeter U., 1986; LittD (hon.), Napier U., 2000, Dartmouth Coll., 2000, U. Exeter, 2000; degree (hon.), U. St. Andrews, 2000, U. Edinburgh, 2004; LLD (hon.), Aberdeen U., 2006. Former rschr. Amnesty International; teacher Scotland, 1990—94. Author: (novels) Harry Potter and the Philosopher's Stone, 1997 (Children's Book of the Year, British Book Awards, 1998, Gold Winner, Smarties Book Prize, 1997, Birmingham Cable Children's Book Award, Young Telegraph Paperback of the Year, Sheffield Children's Book Award, Sorcieres Prix, 1999, Premio Cento per la Letteratura Infantile, 1998), Harry Potter and the Sorcerer's Stone (U.S. title), 1998 (Anne Spencer Lindbergh Prize in Children's Literature, 1998, ABBY Award, American Booksellers Assoc., 1999), Harry Potter and the Chamber of Secrets, 1998 (Gold Winner, Smarties Book Prize, 1998), Harry Potter and the Prisoner of Azkaban, 1999, Harry Potter and the Goblet of Fire, 2000, Quidditch Through the Ages, 2001, Fantastic Beasts & Where to Find Them, 2001, Harry Potter and the Order of the Phoenix, 2003, Harry Potter and the Half-Blood Prince, 2005 (Quills award for Book of Yr., 2005, Brit. Book of Yr. award, 2006), Harry Potter and the Deathly Hallows, 2007. Named Officer of the Most Excellent Order of the British Empire (O.B.E.) by Charles, Prince of Wales, No. 2 on the list, "British Top 50 Movers and Shakers", BBC 3, Amazon.com's No. 1 of Top 10 authors, 1995—2005; named one of Most Powerful Women, Forbes mag., 2005; recipient Rave award for Bus., WIRED Mag., 2007. Five novels from her Harry Potter series have been made into highly successful motion pictures. Office: Christopher Little Literary Agency 10 Eel Brook Studios 125 Moore Park Rd London SW6 4PS England *

ROWLINGSON, JOHN CLYDE, anesthesiologist, physician, educator; b. Syracuse, NY, Aug. 3, 1948; s. John Winthrop and Genevieve Estelle (Mahan) R.; m. Rosemary Colette Laney, Oct. 26, 1974 (div. 1992); children: Kristen, Andrew; m. Karen Wheeler, Aug. 4, 2001; stepchild, Isaac. BS, Allegheny Coll., 1970; MD, SUNY, Buffalo, 1974. Intern Millard Fillmore Hosp., Buffalo, 1974-75; resident in anesthesiology U. Va., Charlottesville, 1975-77; fellow in anesthesia pain mgmt. U. Va. Med. Ctr., 1977-78; asst. prof. anesthesiology U. Va. Sch. Medicine, Charlottesville, 1978-82, assoc. prof., 1982-86, prof., 1986—, Cosmo A. DiFazio prof. anesthesiology, 2005. Assoc. dir. Pain Mgmt. Ctr., U. Va. Health Sci. Ctr., 1978-79, dir., 1980-98, dir. acute pain svc., 1987—. Author: Regional Anesthesia, 1984; co-editor: Handbook of Critical Care Pain Management, 1993. Recipient Nils Lofgren award ASTRA, 1999; Nat. Inst. Handicapped Rsch. fellow, 1983-87, Pain fellow 1977-78. Fellow Am. Coll. Anesthesiology; mem. Am. Soc. Anesthesiologists, Am. Soc. Regional Anesthesia (rsch. grantee 1977, pres. 1996-97, recipient Disting. Svc. award 2007), Am. Pain Soc., Internat. Assn. Study of Pain, Am. Acad. Pain Medicine (editl. bd. Anesthesia Analg 1996—, Reg. Anesthesia and Pain Medicine, 1997—), Va. Soc. Anesthesiology (sec, treas. 2005-07, pres. elect 2007—). Methodist. Avocations: running, tennis, skiing, biking. Home: 5006 Lake Tree Ln Crozet VA 22932 Office: U Va Hlth Sys Health Sci Ctr Anesthesiology PO Box 800710 Charlottesville VA 22908-0710 Home Phone: 434-823-9626; Office Phone: 434-924-2283. Business E-Mail: jcr3t@virginia.edu.

ROWSON, SEBASTIAN, engineering executive; s. Norman William and Josette Eva Rowson. MS in Fundamental Physics, U. Paris Sud Orsay, 1995, MS in Elecs., Sensors, and Integrated Circuits, 1996, PhD in Physics, 2000. Rsch. engr. UCLA, 2000—00; sr. engr. Ethertronics, San Diego, 2000—02, dir. tech. transfer, 2002—04, dir. R & D, 2004—. Contbr. articles to profl. jours. Mem.: IEEE (assoc.). Achievements include patents for antenna technology. Office: Ethertronics Inc 9605 Scranton Rd Ste 300 San Diego CA 92121 Home Phone: 858-349-3005; Office Phone: 858-550-3826.

ROY, ABHRA, plasma engineer, researcher; b. Calcutta, India, Sept. 21, 1966; m. Kuhu Banerjee, Aug. 4, 1972. PhD in Mech. Engring., Indian Inst. Tech., Kharagpur, India, 1998. Post doctoral rsch. scientist SUNY, Stony Brook, NY, 1998—2000; rsch. engr. CFD Rsch. Corp., Sunnyvale, Calif., 2000—. Reviewer Jour. Heat Transfer; contbr. articles to profl. jours. Recipient Univ. Gold medal, Jadavpur U., Calcutta, India, 1994. Mem.: Sigma Xi (life). Achievements include help in designing world's largest diameter silicon tube growth system. Office: 2880 Lakeside DR STE 226 Santa Clara CA 95054-2821 Home: 1485 De Rose Way Unit 227 San Jose CA 95126 Personal E-mail: abhra_roy@yahoo.com. Business E-Mail: aro@cri-cfd-na.com.

ROY, BRANDON DAWAYNE, professional basketball player; b. Seattle, July 23, 1984; Student in Am. Ethnic Studies, U. Wash., 2002—06. Guard Portland Trail Blazers, Oreg., 2006—. Named Pacific-10 Conf. Player of Yr., 2006, NBA Rookie of Yr., 2007; named to All-Pacific-10 First Team, 2006, All-Am. First Team, 2006, NBA All-Rookie First Team, 2007. Office: Portland Trail Blazers Rose Quarter One Center Court Portland OR 97227 *

ROY, DAVID TOD, literature educator; b. Nanking, China, Apr. 5, 1933; s. Andrew Tod and Margaret (Crutchfield) R.; m. Barbara Jean Chew, Feb. 4, 1967. AB, Harvard U., 1958, AM, 1960, PhD, 1965. Asst. prof. Princeton U., 1963-67; assoc. prof. U. Chgo., 1967-73, prof., 1973—99, prof. emeritus, 1999—, chmn. com. on Far Eastern Studies, 1968-70, chmn. dept. Far Eastern Langs. and Civilizations, 1972-75. Author: Kuo Mo-jo: The Early Years, 1971; contbr.: How to Read the Chinese Novel, 1990, Minds and Mentalities in Traditional Chinese Literature, 1999; co-editor: Ancient China: Studies in Early Civilization, 1978; translator: The Plum in the Golden Vase or Chin P'ing Mei, vol. 1, 1993, vol. 2, 2001, vol. 3, 2006. Served with U.S. Army, 1954-56. Ford Found. fellow, 1958-60, Jr. fellow Harvard Soc. Fellows, 1960-63, fellow Fulbright-Hays Commn., 1967, Chgo. Humanities Inst. fellow, 1994-95; grantee Am. Coun. Learned Socs., 1976-77, NEH, 1983-86, 95-96. Mem. Am. Oriental Soc., Assn. for Asian Studies. Clubs: Quadrangle (Chgo.). Democrat. Office: U Chgo 1050 E 59th St Chicago IL 60637-1559 Home: 5443 S Cornell Ave Chicago IL 60615-5603 Business E-Mail: davidroy@uchicago.edu.

ROY, DELLA MARTIN, materials science educator, researcher; b. Merrill, Oreg., Nov. 3, 1926; d. Harry L. and Anna (Cacka) Martin; m. Rustum Roy, June 8, 1948; children: Neill R., Ronnen A., Jeremy R. BS, U. Oreg., 1947; MS, Pa. State U., 1949, PhD, 1952. Various rsch. positions Pa. State Univ., Univ. Park, 1952—60, sr. rsch. assoc. geochemistry, 1960—62, sr. rsch. assoc. materials sci. engring., 1962—69, assoc. prof. materials sci. engring., 1969—75, prof. materials sci. engring., 1975—92, prof. emeritus materials sci., 1992—; rsch. prof. Ariz. State U., 2005—. Cons. in field; chmn. status of cement, concrete materials adv. bd., Washington, 1977—80; spl. adv. concrete durability NRC, 1985—. Editor: Instructional Modules in Cement Science, 1985, Jour. Cement & Concrete Rsch., 1971—; contbr. articles to profl. jours. Fellow: AAAS, Am. Concrete Inst. (Keynote address 1980, Can. Ctr. Mineral and Energy Tech. award 1989), Mineral. Soc. Am., Inst. Concrete Tech. (hon.), Am. Ceramic Soc. (trustee 1990—, Jeppson Medal award 1982, Copeland award 1987, Bleininger award 2004); mem.: NAS (exec. com., transp. rsch. bd. 1991—), Internat. Acad. Ceramics, Nat. Acad. Engring. (acad. adv. bd. 1989—, membership policy com. 2001—), Coun. Materials Rsch. Soc. (chmn. cement symposia 1980—81, 1986—88, trustee 1988—90), Friends of Health (mem. bd.). Democrat. Office: Pa State U Hastings Rd 110 Materials Rsch Lab University Park PA 16802 Business E-Mail: dellaroy@psu.edu.

ROY, ELMON HAROLD, minister; b. Russell Springs, Ky., Dec. 17, 1924; s. Leslie C. and Olza (Gosser) R.; m. Retha Adkins; children: Joel, Michael. BA in Theology, So. Missionary Coll., 1953; MA, Belin U., 1958, Spalding U., 1970; PhD in Theology, Pacific We. U., 1966; postgrad., Andrews Theol. Seminary, 1974; LLD, Coll. St. Thomas, 1982. Ordained to ministry, 1959. Assoc. pastor, Bucyrus, Ohio, 1955-56, Akron, Ohio, 1956-57; pastor East Liverpool, Ohio, 1957-60, Coudersport, Pa., 1960-64, Huntsville, Ala., 1964-65, Louisville, 1965-71; chaplain Pleasant Grove Hosp., Louisville, 1971—75; pastor Springfield, Ohio, 1975-85, Wooster, Ohio, 1985-88; chaplain Louisville, 1989—. Cons. religious liberty, 1983-88; chaplain Jefferson County Ct. Author: In Remembrance of Redemption, 1996, Courage for Hospital Days 1973, Earth's Coming Events, 1968, Israel's Early Leaders, 1984, Moments of Meditation, 1975, The Word for These Times, 1988, Morning is Coming, 1989, Something to Live By, 1958, Prescription for Personal Peace, 1995, Decisions Determine Destiny, 1994, Ships, Submarines and Kamikazes, 2000, Poems From a Pastor's Pen, 2003; contbr. numerous articles to mags. Pres. South Oldham Ch. Coun., 1971-72; mem. Ohio conf. bd. edn., 1985-88. With USN, 1943-46. Recipient Outstanding Cmty. Svc. award Pleasant Grove Hosp., 1974, Commrs. Commendation award Wayne County, 1987, Ohio Senate Commendation award, 1988, Gov.'s Outstanding Kentuckian award, 1985; decorated six battle stars, knight Sovereign Order of St. John of Jerusalem, Knights of Malta, Hospitallers, comdr. Star of Peace Fedn. des Combattants En Europe, Tenn. Col., Ky. Adm., Croix De Guerre, Croix du Combattant Volontaire, Cross of Valor, Royal Afghanistan Order of Crown of Amanullah, Order of Polonia Restituta, Orderu Virtuti Militari, Philippine Presdl. citation, Philipine Liberation medal, Order of Lafayette, Naval Order of US; named hon. citizen of Tenn., hon. sheriff Clark County, Ohio, hon. Ky. Sec. of State, Ky. Amb.; named to Order Ky. Cols. Fellow Philos. Soc. Gt. Britain, Huguenot Soc., Royal Soc. Arts; mem. SAR (chaplain Louisville-Thruston chpt. 1974-75), Am. Acad. Religion, Ky. Hist. Soc., Order Founders and Patriots of Am., East Liverpool Ministerial Assn. (sec., treas. 1960), Coudersport Ministerial Assn. (v.p. 1971-72), Soc. Ky. Pioneers, Mil. Order Fgn. Wars. Address: 2417 W Highway 22 Crestwood KY 40014-9481 Home Phone: 502-241-1939; Office Phone: 502-241-1939.

ROY, JAMES PARKERSON, lawyer; b. Lafayette, La., Aug. 27, 1951; Children: John, James Jr., Christopher; m. Virginia R. Roy, 1990. BS, La. State U., 1973, JD, 1976; LLM, Georgetown U., 1977. Bar: La. 1976. Civil trial atty. Domengeaux, Wright, Roy & Edwards, Lafayette, 1976—. Fellow Acad. Trail Lawyers; mem. ABA, Assn. Trial Lawyers Am., La. Trial Lawyers Assn. (pres. 1990-91), La. Bar Assn. Democrat. Episcopal. Avocations: hunting, boating, reading, travel. Office: Domengeaux Wright Roy & Edwards 556 Jefferson St Ste 500 Lafayette LA 70501-6979 Office Phone: 800-375-6186. Business E-Mail: jimr@wrightroy.com.

ROY, KEVIN, newscaster; b. Chgo. BA in Broadcast Journalism summa cum laude, U. Mo., Columbia, 1990. Anchor and reporter KCRG-TV, Cedar Rapids, Iowa, 1990—92; weekend anchor and reporter WHAS-TV, Louisville, 1992—93; Washington corr. Belo Broadcasting Bur., 1993—95; weekend anchor and investigative reporter KGW-TV, Portland, Oreg., 1995—98; reporter WLS-TV, Chgo., 1998—, co-anchor Weekend Morning News, 2002—. TV journalist Son of Suicide, 2001 (Best News Series Emmy, 2001, Silver Dome award Best Series, 2001, nat. media award of Mental Health Assn. of Mentally Ill in Ill., 2001, Gold Bell Media award, Mental Health Assn. of Ill., 2001), AIDS in Africa: The Lost Generation, 2002 (Best Hard News Feature Emmy, 2002), (news segment) Frank Lloyd Wright, 2001 (AP Ill. honors, 2001). Vol. Loving Outreach to Survivors of Suicide Cath. Charities, Chgo.; bd. mem. Mental Health Assn. of Ill. Recipient Best Reporter Individual Excellence on Camera Emmy, NATAS, 2001, Individual Excellence in News Writing Emmy, 2002. Mem.: AFTRA, NATAS. Office: WLS-TV 190 N State St Chicago IL 60601 Home Phone: 847-869-2070; Office Phone: 312-750-7577. E-mail: krroy@sbcglobal.net.

ROY, LAURA GODFREY, history educator, artist; b. Norfolk, Va., Apr. 23, 1961; m. Gregory Allen Roy, Mar. 16, 2001; 1 child, Allen J.; m. Leslie Madison Fisher III (dec.). BS in History, Longwood U., Farmville, Va., 1984. Tchr. F.W. Cox H.S., Va. Beach, 1984—; reader Edn. Testing Svcs., Lincoln, Nebr., 2003—05, Ft, Collins, Colo., 2007—. Christian edn. com. Wycliffe Presbyn. Ch., Virginia Beach, 2006—. Mem.: DAR (History Tchr. of Yr. 2005). Avocations: painting, travel, gardening. Office: FW Cox HS 2425 Shorehaven Dr Virginia Beach VA 23454

ROY, LORIENE, library association executive, library and information scientist; Student, Coll. St. Benedict, St. Joseph, Minn., 1972; AS, BT, Oreg. Inst. Tech., Klamath Falls, 1977; MLS, U. Ariz., Tucson, 1980; student, Ariz. Western Coll., Yuma, 1979—81; PhD, U. Ill., Urbana-Champaign, 1987. Oral history coord. Century House Mus., Yuma, Ariz., 1981—82; reference libr. Yuma City-County Libr., 1981—82; instr. U. Ill. Grad. Sch. Libr. & Info. Sci., Urbana, 1985; rsch. assoc. U. Ill. Libr. Rsch. Ctr., Urbana, 1984—86; instr. U. Tex. at Austin Grad. Sch. Libr. & Info. Sci., 1987, asst. prof., 1987—93, assoc. prof., 1993—99, dir. If I Can Read,I Can Do Anything nat. reading club for native children, 1999—; prof. U. Tex at Austin Sch. Info., 1999—, U. Tex at Austin Ctr. for Women's & Gender Studies, 2002—; rsch. assoc. Four Directions, Pueblo of Laguna Dept. Edn., N.Mex., 1997—2001. Mem. steering com. U. Ariz. Sch. Info. Resources & Libr. Sci., 2001—05; adv. bd. Sequoya Rsch. Ctr., 2001—; adv. bd. for Peep & the Big Wide World & We Shall Remain WBGH-Boston, 2006—. Co-editor: Library & Information Studies Education in the United States, 1998, Getting Libraries the Credit They Deserve: A Festschrift in Honor of Marvin H. Scilken, 2002; manuscript reviewer Am. Indian Culture & Rsch. Jour., 1988, Jour. Edn. for Libr. & Info. Sci., 1998, Can. Jour. Native Studies, 2000, asst. editor Native Am. studies Counterpoise, 1996—98, bd. mem. reviews sect. Libr. Acquisitions: Practice & Theory, 1997—, mem. editl. bd. Librs. & Culture, 1987—97, editl. adv. bd. New Advocate: For Those Involved with Young People & Their Literature, 2000—, Electronic Libr., 2002—; contbr. articles, chapters to books. Adv. com. Internat. Children's Digital Libr., 2002—, El dia de los ninos, 2004—05, El dia de los libros, 2005—06, WebJunction.org, 2002—, Online Computer Libr. Ctr. (OCLC), 2002—, Bill & Melinda Gates Found., 2002—, Pub. Access Computing Portal, 2002—; mem. Freedom to Read Found., 1998—, trustee, 2006—. Named a Mover & Shaker, Libr. Jour., 2005; named an Hon. Tex. Citizen, 1990; recipient Squibb award, Oreg. Inst. Tech., 1975, Tex. Excellence in Teaching award, U. Tex. at Austin Grad. Sch. Libr. & Info. Sci., 1988, 1991, James W. Vick Tex. Excellence award, 1992, Joe & Bettie Branson Ward Excellence award, 2001, Outstanding Alumna award, U. Ariz. Sch. Info. Resources & Libr. Sci., 2002, Texas Exes Teaching award, U. Tex. at Austin, 2005. Mem.: ALA (pub. libr. assn. 1987—, libr. rsch. roundtable 1995—, social responsibilities roundtable 1996—, internat. rels. roundtable 2001—, ethnic & multicultural info. exch. roundtable 2001—, pres. elect 2006—07, ALISE liason 2006—, Am. Indian Libr. Assn. liason 2006—, pres. 2007—08, Equality award 2006), Reference & User Svcs. Assn., Am. Indian Libr. Assn. (v.p./pres. elect 1996—97, exec. bd. 1996—99, pres. 1997—98), Assn. Libr. & Info. Sci. Edn., Libr. Leadership Network, Oral History Assn., Reforma, Tex. Libr. Assn., Wordcraft Cir. Native Writers & Storytellers, Beta Phi Mu, Phi Kappa Phi. Office: Sch Info U Tex at Austin 1 University Sta D7000 Austin TX 78712-0390 Office Phone: 512-471-0390. Office Fax: 512-471-3971. E-mail: loriene@ischool.utexas.edu. *

ROY, MICHELLE E., musician, information technology consultant; b. Lewiston, Maine, Dec. 15, 1969; d. Leonard A. and Joyce B. Roy; m. Andrew Jocuns, Aug. 15, 1997 (div. Mar. 8, 2007). BA, Swarthmore Coll., Pa., 1992; MusM, Ind. U., 1994. Data warehouse support analyst MIT, Cambridge, 1996—2000; tech. lead cons. Buchanan & Edwards, Inc., Alexandria, Va., 2000—06; lead network sys. and distributed sys. engr. MITRE Corp., 2006—. Musician (harpsichord soloist): J.S. Bach Brandenburg Concerto V, 2005; musician: (deuce, harpsichordist) The Bach Project, 2006; musician: (tresorino, harpsichordist) Il Voce d'Amor, 2006; musician: (harpsichord soloist) (CD) G.F. Handel Alexander's Feast, 2006. Active Planned Parenthood. Mem.: Chamber Music Am. (assoc.), Early Music Am. (assoc.). Democrat. Home Phone: 240-461-6341. Personal E-mail: meroyinc@yahoo.com.

ROY, PATRICK, professional sports team executive, coach, retired professional hockey player; b. Quebec City, Que., Can., Oct. 5, 1965; m. Michèle Piuze (div.); children: Jonathan, Frederick, Jana. Goaltender Montreal Canadiens, 1984—95, Colo. Avalanche, 1995—2003; v.p. hockey operations Quebec Remparts, QMJHL, 2003—, owner, gen. mgr., head coach, 2005—. Named to All-Rookie Team, NHL, 1986, Second All-Star Team, 1988, 1991, First All-Star Team, 1989, 1990, 1992, Sporting News All-Star Team, 1989, 1990, 1992, Colo. Sports Hall of Fame, 2004; recipient Conn Smythe Trophy as Playoff MVP, 1986, 1993, 2001, William M. Jennings Trophy, 1987—89, 1992, 2002, Vezina Trophy, 1989, 1990, 1992, Trico Goaltender award, 1989, 1990. Achievements include being a member of Stanley Cup Champion Montreal Canadiens, 1986, 1993, Colo. Avalanche, 1996, 2001; setting the record for most NHL wins by a goaltender with 551; setting the record for most NHL playoff wins by a goaltender with 151; being inducted into the Hockey Hall of Fame, 2006. Office: Quebec Remparts Colisée Pepsi 250 boulevard Wilfrid-Hamel Quebec City PQ G1L 5A7 Canada

ROY, PAUL EMILE, JR., county official; b. Sumter, SC, Dec. 18, 1942; s. Paul Emile and Harriette Orvilla (Sorensen) R.; m. Patricia Jane Stariha, July 2, 1977; children: Lisa Anne, Jennifer Jo AA, Grand Rapids Jr. Coll., 1963; student, Universidad de las Americas, Mexico City, 1963—64, Instituto Mexicano-Norteamericano de Relaciones Culturales, 1964—65; BA, Aquinas Coll., Grand Rapids, 1967; MA, U. Americas Escuela de Graduados, Mexico City, 1968; postgrad., U. Mich., 1977—79; MBA, Calif. Coast U., 1994. Asst. prin., instr. Spanish Muskegon Cath. Ctrl. H.S., Mich., 1971—75; dir. employment and tng. Muskegon/Oceana Consortium County of Muskegon, 1975—87, dir. employment and tng., 1988—95, dir. employment and tng. and facilities mgmt., 1995—2003, dir. pub. facilities, 2003—. Mem. Mich. Com. for Devel. of Romance Lang. Performance Objectives; adult edn. adv. com. Muskegon Pub. Schs.; appointee Mich. Youth Employment Coun.; v.p. regional adv. coun. U.S. Dept. Labor, 1981; mem. City of Muskegon Local Devel. Funding Authority, 1988—, Downtown Devel. Authority, 1988—, City of Whitehall (Mich.) Local Devel. Funding Authority, 1988—, Muskegon Econ. Growth Alliance Edn. Com.; bd. dirs. United Way, 1998-2004, campaign chmn., 1986-88, Pacesetter award, 1987; bd. dirs. YMCA, 1999-2001; cons. U.S. Dept. Labor, Washington, Mich. Dept. Labor, Lansing, Gov.'s Office Manpower, Ind.; U. Mich., Ann Arbor, various pvt. cos., non-profit orgns Mem. Am. Assn. Tchrs. Spanish and Portuguese, Mich. Assn. Tchrs. ESL, Mich. Assn. Employment and Tng. Dirs. (pres. 1980-81), Mich. Employment and Tng. Inst. (founding bd. dirs. 1980-81), Nat. Assn. Counties (employment steering com.), Nat. Assn. County Employment and Tng. Adminstrs. (nat. bd. dirs. 1979-80, nat. chmn. orgnl. resources com. 1981) Avocations: golf, travel, reading, theater. Office: Muskegon Cty Dept Employment & Tng 1611 Oak Ave Muskegon MI 49442-2405 Home Phone: 231-744-8773.

ROY, PRABIR KUMAR, physicist; arrived in US, 2002, permanent resident, 2004; s. Narayan Chandra and Khuku (Datta) R.; m. Chandana, Apr. 22, 1996. BS in Physics with honors, Chittagong U., Bangladesh, 1986, MS in Physics, 1987; PhD, Osaka U., Japan, 1998. Rsch. fellow Inst. Laser Engring., Osaka, Suita, Japan, 1994—98; rsch. scientist Omachron Sci. Inc, Hampton, Ont., Canada, 1998—2001; postdoctoral rschr. La. Tech U., Ruston, La., 2001—02; postdoctoral physicist Lawrence Berkeley Nat. Lab. U. Calif., 2002—03, physicist scientist, 2003—06, sr. sci. assoc., 2006—. Organizing sec. Chittagong Sci. Coun., 1986-92; presenter in field. Exec. editor Shandhan sci. jour., 1984-87, mem. editl. bd., 1990-91; contbr. over 100 sci. articles to profl. publs. Monbusho scholar Japanese Govt., 1995—; rsch. fellow Ministry of Sci. and Tech., Dhaka, Bangladesh, 1994. Mem. IEEE, Canadian Inst. Synchrotron Radiation, Am. Phys. Soc. Office: Lawrence Berkeley Nat Lab 1 Cyclotron Rd MS #47R-0112 Berkeley CA 94720 Office Phone: 510-495-2616. Business E-Mail: pkroy@lbl.gov.

ROY, RACHEL, fashion designer; b. Seaside, Calif., 1974; m. Damon Dash, July 15, 2005; 1 child, Ava; 1 stepchild, Damon Dash Jr. Degree in Comm., Columbia Union Coll., Takoma Park, Md. Stylist intern Rocawear, NYC, 1998, creative dir., children and women divsn.; founder, designer Rachel Roy collection, 2004—. Recipient Bollywood award for Outstanding Contribution to American Fashion, 2006. Achievements include having collections featured in various top fashion magazines and NY Fashion Week, 2007. *

ROY, ROB J., biomedical engineer, anesthesiologist, educator; b. Bklyn., Jan. 2, 1933; m. Carole Ann Apmann, Aug. 1, 1959 (div.); children: Robert Bruce, David John, Bruce Glenn; m. Judith Anne Webb, Oct. 6, 1996. BSEE, Cooper Union, NYC, 1954; MSEE, Columbia U., 1956; DEngSc, Rensselaer Poly. Inst., 1962; MD, Albany Med. Coll., NY, 1976. Profl. engr., N.Y.; diplomate Am. Bd. Anesthesiology. Prof. elec. engrin. dept. Rensselaer Poly. Inst., Troy, N.Y., 1962, prof. elec. engring. dept., 1980—, head biomed. engring. dept., 1985-94; prof. anesthesiology Albany (N.Y.) Med. Ctr., 1979—. Author: State Variables for Engineers, 1965, 2d edit., 1998; author over 200 papers in field. Mem.: IEEE (life), Am. Soc. Anesthesiologists, Sigma Xi. Office: Albany Med Ctr Dept Anesthesiology 47 New Scotland Ave Albany NY 12208-3412 E-mail: royr@rpi.edu, robjroy@att.net.

ROY, ROBERT RUSSELL, toxicologist; b. Mpls., Sept. 14, 1957; s. Rudolph Russell and Arlene Charlotte (Miller) R.; m. Barbara Jane Richie, Oct. 10, 1987; children: Andrew, Katherine. BA cum laude, Augsburg Coll., 1980; MS, U. Minn., 1986, PhD, 1989. Bd. cert. in toxicology. Toxicologist, project mgr. Pace Labs., Inc., Mpls., 1989-90; toxicologist Minn. Dept. Health, Mpls., 1990-93, Minn. Regional Poison Ctr., St. Paul, 1990-97; team leader, toxicology specialist 3M, St. Paul, 1997—, sr. toxicology specialist, 2000—. Lectr. U. Minn., Mpls., 1986-90, Midwest Ctr. Occupl. Health and Safety, St. Paul, 1990—, instr., 1989; adj. assoc. prof. U. Minn., 1993—; grad. faculty toxicology and pub. health U. Minn.; adj. asst. prof. emergency medicine Oreg. Health Sci. U., Portland. Active Mt. Carmel Luth. Ch. Coun., Mpls., 1983-85. Mem. Soc. Toxicology, Am. Indsl. Hygiene Assn., Delta Omega. Home: 6301 Oxbow Bend Chanhassen MN 55317-9110 Office: Corp Toxicology 3 M Ctr Bldg 220-6E-03 Saint Paul MN 55144-1000 Business E-Mail: rroy@mmm.com.

ROY, ROBERT WILLIAM, artist, educator; b. Worcester, Mass., Oct. 7, 1945; s. Vincent Charles and Rita Marie R.; m. Laurie Jean Zephir, Aug. 1, 1981; children: Patrick Zephir, Roy. BFA magna cum laude, U. Mass. Amherst, 1969; MFA, Yale U., New Haven, Conn., 1971. Instr. Sch. of the Worcester Art Mus., 1972-81; prof., chair painting dept. Montserrat Coll. of Art, Beverly, Mass., 1988—. Adj. instr. Mount Wachusett C.C., Gardner, Mass., 1982-98, mem. adv. bd., 1997—; vis. lectr. U. Lowell, Mass., 1982-83, Worcester State Coll., 1986-87; vis. critic Smith Coll., Northampton, Mass., 1983, vis. artist, U. Southern Maine, 2002, Artist-in-residence, Burren Coll. Art, Ireland, 2004. Exhibited in group shows at most recently Montserrat Coll. Art, 2000, Danforth Mus. Art, 2001, European Biennial Contemporary Art, Frankfurt, Germany, 2002, Ben Shahn Galleries, William Paterson U., Wayne, NJ, 2002, The Liverpool Biennial, Eng., 2002, U. Galleries, Ill. State U., Normal, Ill., 2003, River Gallery, Ipswich, Mass., 2003, Schitkamp Gallery, Clark U., Worcester, Mass., 2003, Art Gallery, U. NH, Durham, 2004, Art Complex Mus., Duxbury, Mass., 2004, U. Alta., Edmonton, Can., 2004, U. West Ga., Carrolton, 2004, Ont. Coll. Art, Toronto, Can., 2004, Print Gallery, U. of the Arts, Phila., 2004, HallSpace, Boston, 2005, Boston U., 2005, Art Gallery, Gordon Coll., Wenham, Mass., 2006, Danforth Mus. Art, 2006, one-man shows include Montserrat Coll. Art, 2000, U. So. Maine, 2002, HallSpace, Boston, 2005, Housatonic Mus. Art, Bridgeport, Conn., 2005, Danforth Mus. Art, 2006, Represented in permanent collections Mus. Modern Art, NYC, Danforth Mus. Art, Trenton State Coll., Art Complex Mus., Duxbury, Mass., Housatonic Mus. Art, Bridgeport, Conn. Recipient Ture Bengtz Meml. prize, 2005, Luz Dorrien Faculty award, 2006; fellow Yale U., Norfolk, Conn., 1968, Mass. Artists Found., Boston, 1977; Ford Found. Faculty grantee, 1976, 78, 80, Cornelia Faculty Fellow, 2003. Mem. LA Printmaking Soc., Coll. Art Assn. NYC, Boston Printmakers, Southern Graphics Coun. Home: 55 Olde Tavern Rd Leominster MA 01453 Office: Montserrat Coll Art 23 Essex St Beverly MA 01915-4508 Business E-Mail: rroy@montserrat.edu.

ROY, RUSTUM, citizen scientist; b. Ranchi, India, July 3, 1924; came to U.S., 1945, naturalized, 1961; s. Narendra Kumar and Rajkumari (Mukherjee) R.; m. Della M. Martin, June 8, 1948; children: Neill, Ronnen, Jeremy. BSc with honors, Patna U., India, 1942, MSc, 1944; PhD, Pa. State U., 1948; DSc (hon.), Tokyo Inst. Tech., 1987, Alfred U, 1993. Research asst. Pa. State U., 1948-49, mem. faculty, 1950—, prof. geochemistry, 1957—, prof. solid state, 1968—, chmn. solid state tech. program, 1960-67, chmn. sci. tech. and soc. program, 1977-84, dir., 1984-89, dir. materials research lab., 1962-85, Evan Pugh prof., 1981—, Evan Pugh prof. solid state emeritus, 1999—; sr. sci. officer Nat. Ceramic Lab., India, 1950; mem. com. mineral sci. tech. Nat. Acad. Scis., 1967-69, com. survey materials sci. tech., 1970-74; exec. com. chem. div. NRC, 1967-70, nat. materials adv. bd., 1970-77, mem. com. radioactive waste mgmt., 1974-80, chmn. panel waste solidification, 1976-80, chmn. com. USSR and Eastern Europe, 1976-81. Mem. com. material sci. and engring. NRC, 1986-89; mem. Pa. Gov.'s Sci. Adv. Com.; chmn. materials adv. panel Gov.'s Sci. Adv. Com., 1965-80; mem. adv. com. on engring. NSF, 1968-72, adv. com. to ethical and human value implications sci. and tech., 1974-76, adv. com. div. materials rsch., 1974-77; Hibbert lectr. tech. and religion U. London, 1979; cons. to industry; mem. adv. com. Coll. Engring., Stanford U., 1984-86; internat. sci. lectr. NRC, 1991-92; rsch. prof. materials Ariz. State U., 1999—; vis. prof. medicine U. Ariz., 1999—. Author: Honest Sex, 1968, Crystal Chemistry of Non-metallic Materials, 1974, Experimenting with Truth, 1981, Radioactive Waste Disposal, Vol. 1, the Waste Package, 1983, Lost at the Frontier, 1985; founding editor-in-chief: Materials Rsch. Bull., 1966—, Jour. Materials Edn., 1980-2000, Bull. Sci. Tech. and Soc, 1981-2000, Materials Rsch. Innovations, 1997—; contbr. over 1000 articles to profl. jours., 25 patents in field. Chmn. bd. Dag Hammarskjold Coll., 1973-75; chmn. ad hoc com. sci., tech. and ch. Nat. Coun. Chs., 1966-68; bd. dirs. Kirkridge Retreat, 1958-80, chmn., 1978-80; founder, chmn. bd. Friends of Health; chmn. bd. Campaign for Better Health. Sci. policy fellow Brookings Instn., 1982-83; recipient Ellis Island medal of hon., 1996; named to Order of the Rising Sun with Gold Rays status in Japanese Emperor's birthday honors list, 2002. Fellow: AAAS (chmn. chemistry sect. 1985), Mineral. Soc. Am. (award 1957), Am. Phys. Soc., Indian Acad. Scis. (hon.), Am. Ceramic Soc. (Sosman lectr. 1975, Orton lectr. 1984, disting. life, Educator of Yr. 1993); mem.: U.S. Nat. Acad. Engring., Materials Rsch. Soc. (pres. 1976, founder), Am. Soc. Engring. Educators (Centennial medal 1993, Hall of Fame 1993), Am. Chem. Soc. (Petroleum Rsch. Fund award 1960, Dupont award for Chem. of Materials 1993), Fine Ceramics Assn. Japan (Internat. award), Ceramic Soc.Japan (hon. Centennial award 1991), Mineral Soc. Am., Fedn. Materials Socs. (Nat. Materials Advancement award 1991), Russian Acad. Scis. (elected fgn.), Engring. Acad. Japan (elected fgn.), Indian Nat. Sci. Acad. (elected fgn.), Royal Swedish Acad. Engring. Scis. (elected fgn.). Home: 500 E Marylyn Ave Apt 124 State College PA 16801-5312 Office: 102 Materials Research Lab University Park PA 16802-4800 Office Phone: 814-865-3421. Business E-Mail: rroy@psu.edu. *My major responsibility to the increasingly unified world culture, as a scientist supported largely by the public, is to integrate into its emerging technology-shaped culture, a radically pluralist yet globally unifying Religion, the insights from Science and the impact of Technology on the human condition. As a Christian Radical Pluralist, I am committed to presenting to my fellow humans, scientists, and non-scientists, from Presidents and CEOs to the person in the street—an accurate picture of the whole truth about all scientific "advances" and their limited and ambivalent nature and their relatively minor position in the sum total of human concerns.*

ROY, SITESH RANEN, pediatrician, allergist, immunologist, educator; s. Ranen Bimoloananda and Sumita Ranen Roy; m. Hemangi Sitesh Roy, May 0, 1997. Grad., D.G. Ruparel Coll., Mumbai, India, 1990; MBBS, Seth G. S. Med. Coll., Bombay, India, 1990—96. Cert. Am. Bd. Pediat., 2000, Am. Bd. Allergy & Immunology, Am. Bd. Med. Specialities, 2003.

Pediat. residency U. Ill., Chgo., 1997—2000; fellowship pediat. allergy and immunology Nat. Jewish Med. and Rsch. Ctr., U. Colo., Denver, 2000—02; asst. prof., pediat. & medicine U. Miss. Med. Ctr., Jackson, 2002—. Dir., pediatric allergy & immunology clinic Jackson Med. Mall. Contbr. papers to profl. jours. and pubs. Named one of Best Doctors in Am., 2005—06. Fellow: Am. Acad. Pediat., Am. Acad. Allergy Asthma and Immunology; mem.: Am. Coll. Allergy, Asthma and Immunology. Achievements include research in in field of allergy and immunology. Avocations: hiking, travel, bicycling. Office: Univ Miss Med Ctr 2500 N State St Jackson MS 39216-4505 Home Phone: 601-750-4382; Office Phone: 601-984-5249.

ROY, SUDIPTA D., education educator; b. Bolani, Orissa, India, Aug. 28, 1970; d. Sabita Ranjan and Sati Dutta Roy. MS, Calcutta U., India, 1991; PhD, Indira Gandhi Inst. Devel. Rsch., Mumbai, India, 2000; MBA, Gov.'s State U., Univ. Pk., Ill., 2004. Economist Indsl. Devel. Bank India, Mumbai, 1996—2000; cons. Asian Devel. Bank, Philippines, 2001, Nat. Stock Exch., Mumbai, 2000—03; instr. Gov.'s State U., 2005—; asst. prof. Kankakee CC, Ill., 2006—. Contbr. papers to profl. jours. and pubs. Avocations: reading, badminton. Office: Kankakee CC 100 College Dr Kankakee IL 60901

ROYAL, BRENDA CAMPBELL, biology educator; b. Cookeville, Tenn., Aug. 21, 1957; d. Lloyd W. and Myrtle Owen Campbell; children: Julie Michelle, Emily Ruth. BS, Mid. Tenn. State U., Murfreesboro, 1980, MS, 1982. Instr. biology LaVergne H.S., Tenn., 1988—94; tchr. advanced placement biology Hume-Fogg Acad. Magnet H.S., Nashville, 1994—. Curriculum cons. Ctr. Sci. Outreach, Vanderbilt U., Nashville, 2004—06; instr. biology Freewill Bapt. Bible Coll., 2002—04; cons. advanced placement biology Coll. Bd., 2004—. Author: AP Biology Professional Development Workshop Materials. Tchr. sr. adult women's class First Bapt. Ch., Smyrna, Tenn., 2004—06. Recipient Outstanding Biology Tchr. Yr., Nat. Assn. Biology Tchrs., 2005, Siemens award advanced placement sci., 2006, Outstanding Secondary Sci. Tchr., 2007; grantee, PENCIL Found., 1995, 2002. Mem.: Nat. Sci. Tchrs. Assn., Nat. Assn. Biology Tchrs. Baptist. Achievements include Siemens Advanced Placement Instructor for TN, 2006. Avocations: running, writing, baking, travel. Home: 400 E Gresham Drive Smyrna TN 37167 Office: Hume-Fogg Academic Magnet High School 700 Broadway Nashville TN 37203 Home Phone: 615-223-6600; Office Phone: 615-291-6300. Personal E-mail: brendafcr@aol.com. E-mail: brenda.royal@mnps.org.

ROYAL, DARRELL K., university official, retired football coach; b. Hollis, Okla., July 6, 1924; s. Burley Ray and Katy Elizabeth (Harmon) R.; m. Edith Marie Thomason, July 26, 1944; children: Marian (Mrs. Abraham Kazen III) (dec.), Mack, David (dec.). BS in Bus, U. Okla., 1950. Former head football coach, then dir. athletics U. Tex., now asst. to univ. pres. Author: Darrell Royal Talks Football, 1963. Recipient Horatio Alger award, 1996, Contbns. to Coll. Football award Nat. Coll. Football Award Assn., 2002, Disting. Svc. award U. Tex., 2007; named Coach of Yr., Football Coaches Assn., 1963, 70, Tex. Sports Writers, 1961, 63, 69-70, Southwesterner of Yr., 1961-63, Coach of Decade for 1960's, ABC; named to U. Tex. Longhorn Hall of Fame, 1976, Tex. Sports Hall of Fame, 1976, Jim Thorpe Okla. Hall of Fame, 1977, Nat. Football Hall of Fame, 1983, Southwestern Bell Cotton Bowl Hall of Fame, 1998, Okla. Heritage Soc. Hall of Fame, 2000; Darrell K. Royal Meml. Football Stadium U. Tex. named in his honor, 1996; Hollis HS Football Field named in his honor, 2003. Mem.: Delta Upsilon. Presbyterian. Office: U Tex SRH2 101 D1100 Austin TX 78712

ROYAL, HENRY DUVAL, nuclear medicine physician, educator, director; b. Norwich, Conn., May 14, 1948; BS, Providence Coll., 1970; MD, St. Louis U., 1974. Diplomate Am. Bd. Internal Medicine; Am. Bd. Nuclear Medicine. Intern R.I. Hosp., Providence, 1974, resident in internal medicine, 1975-76; resident in nuclear medicine Harvard Med. Sch., Boston, 1977-79; from assoc. to staff physician Barnes Hosp., St. Louis, 1987—; from assoc. to cons. staff physician Children's Hosp., St. Louis, 1987—; prof. nuclear medicine Washington U., St. Louis, 1993—; exec. dir. Am. Bd. Nuc. Medicine, St. Louis, 2004—. Co-team leader health effects sect. Internat. Atomic Energy Agy. Internat. Chernobyl Project, 1990; mem. com. on assessment of CDC radiation studies NRC/NAS, 1993-98; mem. sci. com. 1 and 4 Nat. Coun. on Radiation Protection and Measurements, 1993—; mem. coun. Nat. Coun. on Radiation Protection, 1996—, bd. dirs., 2000-05; adv. com. environ. hazards Vets., 1997—; bd. dirs. Am. Bd. Med. Specialties, 2005—. Contbr. articles to profl. jours. Mem.: Soc. Nuc. Medicine (v.p. 2002, pres. 2003), Alpha Omega Alpha. Office: W Pavilion B Rm 961 Box 8223 Washington Univ 660 S Euclid Ave Saint Louis MO 63110 Home Phone: 314-454-1312; Office Phone: 314-362-2809. Business E-Mail: royalh@mir.wustl.edu.

ROYAL, WILLIAM HENRY, retired real estate developer, architect; b. Jackson, Tenn., Dec. 16, 1924; s. Joe Henry and Millie Earline (Anderson) R.; m. Odell Peebles, June 16, 1943; children: William H. Jr., Frederick E., Diana, Carolyn M., Wanda H. Diploma, Chicago Tech. Coll., 1959; student, MIT, 1969, '73, U. Neb., 1971-76, U. Minn., 1974-76. Reg. architect, Ill., Mo. Architect, engr. U.S. Army Engr. Dist., Detroit, 1957-61, gen. architect St. Paul, 1959-62, supr. architect Chgo., 1962-70, gen. architect Omaha, Neb., 1970-73; architect, job captain Ellerbe & Co., St Paul, 1962; cons. FREBO, U.S. Postal Svc., St. Paul, 1973-77; constr. mgr. H.Q. U.S. Postal Svc., Washington, 1977-80; pres. William H. Royal & Assoc., Inc., Lake St. Louis, Mo., 1987—2002, Chgo., 1995-97, St. Louis Airport Devel. Corp., 1988-89; v.p. Steelgrade Corp., Clayton, Mo., 1991-93; sec.-treas. Am. Community Telecomms. System, Inc., Ferguson, Mo., 1992-97; pres. Royal King Constrn. Co., St. John, Mo., 1995-97. Author: (tng. manual) Architect Engineer Contracts, 1970; editor: Master Planning, Kinloch Redevelopment, 1987. Steward, United Meth. Ch., Omaha, 1970-73; urban cons. United Meth. Ministries, Omaha, 1970-73, Youth Coord., United Meth. Ch., Omaha, 1971-73; mem. Douglas County Parole Bd., Omaha, 1971-72. Recipient Commendation U.S. Postal Svc., Washington, 1976, Svc. award, 1980, letter of Appreciation, 1982; nominee Rockefeller Pub. Svc. award, U.S. Postal Svc., St. Paul, 1976. Avocations: computer programming, fishing, travel. Home: 1 Berry Ct Lake Saint Louis MO 63367-1921 Office: William H Royal & Assocs 1 Berry Ct Lake Saint Louis MO 63367-1921 Office Phone: 636-561-2735.

ROYALL, MARY-JULIA C., church organist, historian; b. Donalds, SC, Dec. 30, 1925; d. John McCants Campbell and Cordelia Bearden; m. Jervey DuPré Royall, Sept. 18, 1949; children: Julia C., Anne DuPré. BA, Erskine Coll., 1945; MA, U. S.C., 1948, performers cert. in organ, 1953. With Salem Coll. Organ Acad.; mem. staff Brevard Music Camp, 1946; music tchr. Montreat HS and Coll., NC, 1946—47; pvt. piano tchr., 1953—66; dir. glee club Moultrie HS, Mt. Pleasant, SC, 1960—62, Coll. Prep. Sch., Charleston, 1972—74; organist St. Mary's Cath. Ch., Charleston, 1979—. Author: Mt. Pleasant, SC: The Victorian Village, 1997, Mt. Pleasant, SC: The Friendly Town, 2001; musician: (concerts) Huguenot Ch., St. Lukes Chapel. Historian Town of Mt. Pleasant, 1996—; mem. com. Charleston County SC Nat. Heritage Corridor, 1995—98; mem. Mt. Pleasant Presbyn. Ch., 1950—; pres. Confederate Meml. Assn., Mt. Pleasant, 1984—. Christ Ch. Parish Preservation Soc., Mt. Pleasant, 1994—. Named Tree Farmer of Yr., S.C., 1982—83; named to Order of the Gavel, Town of Mt. Pleasant, 1996; recipient Robert N. Pryor Svc. award, Confederation of Local Hist. Socs., S.C., 1997, Outstanding So. Citizen award, Sons of Confederate Vets., 2003. Mem.: SC Fedn. Mus., Charleston Preservation Soc., Poetry Soc. SC, SC Hist. Soc., SC Forestry Assn., Organ Hist. Soc. (editor newsletter S.C. chpt. 1979—84), Am. Guild Organists (S.C. state chmn., mem. Charleston chpt.). Home: 349 Bay View Acres Mount Pleasant SC 29464

ROYBAL, JAMES R., artist; b. Santa Fe, Aug. 23, 1952; Student, Highlands U., Las Vegas, N.Mex., 1971—72, N.Mex. State U., Las Vegas, 1973—75; studies with Albert Handel, 1994—95. Tchr. Valdes Art Workshops, Sante Fe, 2005—07. Exhibitions include N.Mex. State Fair, Albeqerque, 1971 (1st place & Purchase award, 1978), 1978—81, 1986, 1988, Santa Fe Festival of Arts, 1979—80, Taos Arts Assn., Stables Art Ctr., N.Mex., 1986, Albequerque Mus. Miniature Show Invitational, 1991—95, Life Size Geronimo, Santa Fe, 2003, Represented in permanent collections, Govs. Gallery, Santa Fe, pub. collections, Ella Corothers Dunegan Gallery Fine Art, Bolivar, Mo.; contbr. articles to profl. jours. Home and Studio: 25 Lone Pine Spur Santa Fe NM 87505

ROYBAL-ALLARD, LUCILLE, congresswoman; b. Boyle Heights, Calif., June 12, 1941; d. Edward Roybal; m. Edward T. Allard; 4 children. BA in Speech, Calif. State U., LA, 1965. Former mem. Calif. State Assembly, 1987—93; mem. U.S. Congress from 34th Calif. dist., 1993—; mem. appropriations com.; mem. Ho. Com. on Standards of Official Conduct. Recipient Madre y Mujer award, Kimberly-Clark, 2006. Democrat. Office: Ho of Reps 2330 Rayburn Bldg Washington DC 20515-0534 also: 225 E Temple St Ste 1860 Los Angeles CA 90012

ROYCE, BARRIE SAUNDERS HART, physicist, researcher; b. Eng., Jan. 10, 1933; came to U.S., 1957, naturalized, 1978; s. Vincent Pateman Hart and Kathlene (Saunders) R.; m. Dominique J.M. Vallee, May 7, 1964; children: Vincent Rene Hart, Marc Edward Hart. BSc in Physics, King's Coll., U. London, 1954, PhD, 1957. Rsch. assoc. Carnegie Inst. Tech., 1957-60, Princeton U., 1960-61, mem. faculty, 1961—2003, prof. applied physics and materials scis., 1978—2003, prof. emeritus, 2003—, acting dean grad. affairs Sch. Engring. and Applied Sci., 2003—04; master of Dean Mathey Coll., 1986-94. Mem. editl. adv. bd. Jour. Photoacoustics, to 1984. Mem. Princeton Borough Zoning Bd. Adjustment, 1980-93, chair, 1993—. Grantee NSF, Air Force Office Sci. and Rsch., Army Rsch. Office. Mem. Am. Phys. Soc., Sigma Xi. Office: Princeton U J224 Engring Quadrangle Princeton NJ 08544-0001 E-mail: bshroyce@princeton.edu.

ROYCE, ED (EDWARD RANDALL ROYCE), congressman; b. LA, Oct. 12, 1951; m. Marie Porter. BA, Calif. State U., Fullerton. Tax mgr. Southwestern Portland Cement Co.; mem. Calif. Senate, 1983-93, U.S. Congress from 40th Calif. dist. (formerly 39th), 1993—; mem. banking and fin. svcs. com., internat. rels. com. Vice chmn. Public Employment and Retirement Com.; mem. Bus. and Profs. com., Indsl. Rels. com.; legis. author, campaign co-chmn. Proposition 15 Crime Victims/Speedy Trial Initiative; author nation's 1st felony stalking law, bill creating Foster Family Home Ins. Fund, legis. creating foster parent recruitment and tng. program; mem. Banking and Fin. Svcs. Com., Internat. Rels. Com. Named Legis. of Yr. Orange County Rep. Com., 1986, Child Adv. of Yr. Calif. Assn. Svc. for Children, 1987. Mem. Anaheim C. of C. Republican. Office: US Ho Reps 2202 Rayburn Ho Office Bldg Washington DC 20515 *

ROYCE, PAUL CHADWICK, healthcare administrator; b. Mpls., July 2, 1928; BA, U. Minn., 1948, MD, 1952; PhD, We. Res. U., 1959. Diplomate Am. Bd. Internal Medicine. Intern U. Chgo. Clinics, 1952-53; fellow We. Res. U., Cleve., 1953—59; resident internal medicine Bronx Mcpl. Hosp., NYC, 1959-61; asst. prof. of medicine Albert Einstein Coll. of Med., NYC, 1961-69; sr. staff endocrinologist Guthrie Clinic, Sayre, Pa., 1970-81; assoc. prof. of medicine Hahnemann Med. Sch., Phila., 1973-81; emeritus prof. medicine Med. Coll. Pa./Hahnemann U., 1996—; dean and prof. clin. sci. and physiology Sch. Medicine U. Minn., Duluth, 1981-87; sr. v.p., clin. dir. Monmouth Med. Ctr., Long Branch, NJ, 1987-94; med. dir. The Segal Co. N.Y., 1995-98; prin. Royce Assocs., 1995—; tutor Writing Ctr., Monmouth U., NJ, 2001—05. Producer, host TV prgram Doctors on Call, 1983-87 (Nat. Friends of Pub. Broadcasting Hill award 1987). Lt. USNR, 1954-56. Fellow, NSF, 1953—58, Upjohn Found., 1958—59. Mem. Am. Physiol. Soc., Fedn. Am. Scientists, Physicians for Social Responsibility, Sigma Xi, Alpha Omega Alpha. Avocations: skiing, bicycling, canoeing. Home Phone: 732-471-6068.

ROYCE, STANTON, motivational speaker, consultant, marketing professional, sales executive; b. Steubenville, Ohio, June 1, 1950; m. Melanie Espinosa, 1984. Student, Franciscan U., Steubenville, 1973; AS in Elec. Engring., Jefferson C.C., Steubenville, 1983; BS in Psychology, U. Cin., 1991; MBA, U. Phoenix, 1994. Night club entertainer, hypnotist, Wintersville, Ohio, 1970-73; mgr. Liberty Fin. Corp., Columbus, Ohio, 1973-76, Bally Mfg., Steubenville, 1976-79; pres. Cmty. Interfaith Svcs., Steubenville, 1979-83; dir. engring. May Co., Youngstown, Ohio, 1983-84; dir. ops. LaSalle Ptnrs., Chgo., 1984-93; mgr. Core Resources, Inc., Cin., 1993-94; pres. Royce Personal Devel., Hamden, Conn., 1994—97; CEO Extreme Achievers Inc., 1997—. Author: Million Dollar Persuasion, 1994, Encyclopedia of Sales Techniques, 1995, Billion Dollar Success Secrets, 1996, Billion Dollar Power Persuasion, 1997, Rejectionproof Selling, 1999, Recessionproof Selling, 2001, Overcoming Rejection, 2002, Failure Isn't a Four Letter Word, 2003, Billion Dollar Rejection Response, 2007. Founder, 1st pres. Alternatives to Living in Violent Environments, Jefferson County, 1980-81; victims asst. counselor Jefferson County Cmty. Mental Health Ctr., Steubenville, 1977-79; mem. disaster comms. ARC, Jefferson County, 1965-77. Mem., officer Nat. Spkrs. Assn., Alpha Sigma Kappa Honor Soc. Avocations: motorcycling, mountain biking, travel. Office: Achievers Tower 7605 Via de Calma NE Albuquerque NM 87113-1306

ROYCROFT, HOWARD FRANCIS, lawyer; b. Balt., Sept. 9, 1930; s. Howard F. and Bessie (Weaver) R.; m. Barbara Lee Seal, Mar. 20, 1954; children: Suzanne Carol Roycroft Soderberg, Nancy Lee Roycroft Branigan. BA, U. Md., 1953; LLB, Georgetown U., 1958. Bar: D.C. 1958. Mem. firm Hogan & Hartson, Washington, 1958, ptnr., 1965-87, exec. com., 1970-73, counsel, 1987—. Dir. United TV, Inc., 1982—2001, U TV San Francisco, Inc., 1983—2001; mng. ptnr., dir. WIJY, Inc., Hilton Head, SC, 1989—97; lectr. Howard U. Sch. Law, 1973—74; guest lectr. U. Tex., 1980; mem. Met. Washington Bd. Trade. Bd. dirs. YMCA Met. Washington, 1974-76. 1st lt. USMC, 1953-55. Mem. ABA, Va. Bar Assn., Fed. Comm. Bar Assn., Bar Assn. D.C., Nat. Broadcasters Club, Barristers, Aircraft Owners and Pilots Assn., Nat. Acad. TV Arts & Scis., Broadcast Pioneers, Alexandria Rotary Club, Bryce Mountain Ski and Country Club (dir., pres. 1974-87), Mt. Vernon Country Club, Old Dominion Boat Club, Washington Tennis Patrons Club, Army-Navy Club, Chaine des Rotisseurs Gastronome Club, Oysterville Yacht Club, Skull Creek Yacht Club, Kappa Alpha, Beta Kappa, Delta Theta Phi. Republican. Office: Hogan & Hartson 555 13th St NW Ste 800E Washington DC 20004-1161 Home Phone: 703-360-4981. E-mail: HRoycroft@netscape.com.

ROYE, CAROL, nursing educator; d. Jack and Esther Levine; m. David Roye, Aug. 18, 1967; children: Benjamin, Kathryn Gipstein, Seth, Erin Simpson, Emily, Elena. BA, NYU, NYC, 1967; MEd, U. Okla., Norman, 1969; MS, Pace U., Pleasantville, NY, 1984, Columbia U., NYC, 1986; EdD, Columbia U., 1994. Lic. NY State Bd. Regents, 1984, pediatric nurse practitioner, NAPNAP, 1986. Assoc. prof. nursing Columbia U. Sch. Nursing, 1991—97; prof. nursing Hunter Coll., NYC, 1997—; pnp Pediat. 2000, NYC. Editor: (textbook) Adolescent Sexual Development and Sexuality: Assessment and Interventions; contbr. articles to profl. jours., chapter to book. Pres., mem. bd. edn. Pleasantville Union Free Sch. Dist., NY. Recipient Dorothy H. & Thomas L. O'Neil Disting. award, Columbia U. Sch. Nursing, 1993, Outstanding Rsch. Presentation award, Am. Acad. Nurse Practitioners, 1997, Rose & George Doval award for excellence in nursing edn., NYU, 2002, Alumni award, Columbia U. Sch. Nursing, 2002; grantee Rsch. grant, NIH. Mem.: APHA, Soc. Adolescent Medicine, Nat. Assn. Pediatric Nurse Practitioners and Assocs., Nat. Assn. Pediatric Nurse Assocs. and Practitioners, Nat. Nursing Honor Soc., Sigma Theta Tau. Office: Hunter Coll 425 E 25th St New York NY 10570 Business E-Mail: croye@hunter.cuny.edu.

ROYER, KATHLEEN ROSE, pilot; b. Pitts., Nov. 4, 1949; d. Victor Cedric and Lisetta Emma (Smith) Salway; m. Michael Lee Royer, June 6, 1971 (div. Aug. 1975). Student, Newbold Coll., 1968-69; BS, Columbia Union Coll., 1971; MEd, Shippensburg U., 1974; student, Lehigh U., 1974-75. Cert. tchr. Pa. Music. Music tchr. Harrisburg (Pa.) Sch. Dist., 1971-77; flight instr. Penn-Air, Inc., Altoona, Pa., 1977; capt., asst. chief pilot Air Atlantic Airlines, Centre Hall, Pa., 1977-80; capt., chief pilot Lycoming Air Svc., Williamsport, Pa., 1980-81; govs. pilot Commonwealth of Pa., Harrisburg, 1981-87; flight engr. Pan-Am, NYC, 1987-91; pilot, 1st officer B737 United Airlines, Chgo., 1992-96, 1st officer B767 NYC, until 1996, Washington, 1996-99; flight officer B747-400 JFK Internat. Airport, Jamaica, NY, 1999—2001, capt. Airbus 320, 2001—, airbus line check airman, 2005—. Frist woman pilot/engr. crew mem. on 747 Pan Am. Airlines, 1989—91, chief pilot, cons. Mem.: UAL-Airline Pilot Assn. (coord. critical incident stress program 1994—96), Flight Engrs. Internat. Assn. (scheduling rep. 1989, scheduling dir. 1990, 1st vice chmn., mem. bd. adjustments 1989, v.p. dir. scheduling 1991—92), Internat. Soc. Women Airline Pilots, Whirley Girls (Washington), 99's (local chair Ctrl. Pa. chpt. 1987—92). Republican. Avocations: owner/flying 1965 Cessna 180, golf, music, reading. Home: 34 Lazy Eight Dr Daytona Beach FL 32128 Office: San Francisco Intl Airport San Francisco CA Personal E-mail: royer17@bellsouth.net.

ROYER, TOM A., entomologist, educator; b. Cherokee, Iowa; s. Don and Dorothy Royer; m. Joleen Royer; children: Kelly, Kevin. BS, Iowa State U., Ames, 1973—78; MS, S.D. State U., Brookings, 1980—83; PhD, Tex. A&M U., College Station, 1987—90. Ext. specialist U. Ill. Coop. Ext. Svc., Edwardsville, 1991—92, ext. educator, 1992—97; asst. prof. Okla. State U., Stillwater, 1997—2003, assoc. prof., 2003—. Contbr. chapters to books. Mem.: Soc. Southwestern Entomologists (pres. 2005—), Entomol. Soc. Am. (chair, sect. E 2002—03, program co-chair 2006), Gamma Sigma Delta, Sigma Xi, Phi Kappa Phi. Office: Okla State Univ 127 NRC Stillwater OK 74078 Office Phone: 405-744-5531. E-mail: tom.royer@okstate.edu.

ROYHAB, RONALD, journalist, editor; b. Lorain, Ohio, Oct. 6, 1942; s. Halim Farah and Elizabeth Della (Naiser) R.; m. Roberta Lee Libb, Apr. 20, 1969; children: David Libb, Aaron Nicholas. Reporter Lorain Jour., 1966—69; reporter spl. assignment Scripps Howard Cin. Post, 1971—72; investigative reporter Scripps Howard Cleve. Press, 1972—75; chief bur. Scripps Howard Ohio Bur., Columbus, 1975—78; asst. mng. editor Scripps Howard News Svc., Washington, 1978—81; mng. editor Scripps Howard El Paso Herald Post, 1981—83; asst. mng. editor Scripps Howard Pitts. Press, 1983—92; assoc. editor Pitts. Post Gazette, 1992—93; mng. editor Toledo Blade, 1993—97, exec. editor, 1997—; v.p. Toledo Blade Co., 2004—. Bd. dirs. Toledo Blade Co. With USAR, 1964-70. Decorated Knight Order St. Ignatius of Antioch; recipient 7 awards for Excellence Cleve. Newspaper Guild, 1972-75, Spl. Sect. awards Pa. Newspaper Pubs. Assn., 1985, 86, 88, Benjamin C. Bradlee Editor of the Yr. award Nat. Press Found. 2005; named to DeMolay Legion of Honor, 1997; Am. Polit. Sci. Assn. fellow, 1970-71. Mem. Am. Soc. Newspaper Editors, AP Soc. Ohio (pres. 2000-01), Ohio Newspaper Assn., Toledo Press Club (pres. 2002-03). Eastern Orthodox. Home: 27262 Fort Meigs Rd Perrysburg OH 43551-1230 Office: Toledo Blade 541 N Superior St Toledo OH 43660-0002 Home Phone: 419-874-3142; Office Phone: 419-724-6161. Personal E-mail: royhab@theblade.com.

ROYLE, DAVID BRIAN LAYTON, television producer, journalist; arrived in U.S., 1974; s. J. H. L. and J. M. D. Royle; m. Cornelia Boardman Service; children: William Brian Layton, Richard John Boardman. BA cum laude, U. NC, 1978; MA, U. Minn., 1985. Journalist Northcliffe Newspapers, Stoke-on-Trent, England, 1979-82; news producer Ctrl. Ind. TV, Birmingham, England, 1982-83; producer Inside Story, NYC, 1984-86; prodr. New Atlantic Prodns., NYC, 1986-89; pres. David Royle Prodns., NYC, 1989—. Dir. Russian Archive, 1992—97; prodr. Wall St. Jour. TV, 1995; sr. prodr. Nat. Geog. TV, Washington, 1996—98, exec, prodr., 1998—2005, sr. v.p. prodn., 2000—04, exec. v.p. prodn., 2004—05; exec. v.p. programming and prodn. Smithsonian Networks, 2006—. Prodr.: (TV films) Rupert Murdoch: Press Baron Who Would Be King, PBS, 1985 (Emmy nomination), Assignment Africa, PBS, 1986 (Emmy nomination), Senator Sam, PBS, 1988 (Ohio State award, Cine Golden Eagle), Inside Gorbachev's USSR, PBS, 1989 (George Polk award, DuPont-Columbia U. Gold Baton); prodr.: (TV films) American Detective in Russia, ABC, 1992; prodr.: (TV films) The Eagle and The Bear, ABC/A&E, 1993 (Cine Golden Eagle), Dr. Frank, PBS, 1994 (Cine Golden Eagle, Regional Emmy award), TV Nation, NBC/BBC, 1994 (Prime Time Emmy award), Emerging Powers: Brazil, PBS/NHK Japan, 1996, Inside Base Camp, Nat. Geog. Channel, 2001 (Emmy award), Liberia, America Dream?, 2004 (Edward R. Murrow award, duPont-Columbia U. Silver Baton); (TV series) Target: Mafia, 1993, Trauma: Life and Death in the E.R., TLC, 1996, Nat. Geographic Explorer, TBS, 1999— (6 Emmy awards, Emmy nominations), Taboo, 2002—04, National Geographic's Most Amazing Moments, 2004—05. Gov. Clifton Coll., Bristol, England, 1997—. Named Hon. Citizen, Mpls., 1983; recipient Excellence award, U. Minn. Sch. Journalism & Mass Comm., 2000; scholar, Rotary Internat., 1983; Morehead scholar, 1974—78, NJ Arts fellow, 1995. Mem.: NATAS, Writers Guild, Soc. Profl. Journalists, U. NC Alumni Assn. (bd. dirs. 2005—). Avocations: running, sailing, photography, reading. Office: Smithsonian Networks Washington DC

ROYSTER, LYNN CHRISTINE, academic administrator, educator; b. Balt., Md., Aug. 23, 1947; d. Kenneth Frederick and Dorothy Charlotte Umpleby; m. Michael James Royster, Aug. 10, 2002; children: Patrick Bart Holaday, Brett Christine Holaday. BA, U. Mich., Ann Arbor, 1969; MA, Prescott Coll., Ariz., 1993; JD, George Wash. U., Washington, 1975; PhD, Union Inst. and U., Vt., 1999. Bar: Washington 1976, Tex. 1979, N.J. 1986, Ill. 1987. Dir. chronic illness initiative DePaul U., Sch. for New Learning, Chgo., 2003—. Atty. Lorance and Thompson, Houston, 1978—83; adj. faculty Prescott Coll., 1993—96; vis. faculty DePaul U. Sch. for New Learning, 1997—. Contbr. articles to profl. jours. and books. Dir. Lake Forest (Ill.) Lake Bluff Parent Coun., 1988—89; vice chair CFIDS Assn. of Am., Charlotte, NC, 2004—06; bd. sec. Chronic Fatigue Syndrome, Fibromyalgia, and Chem. Sensitivity Coalition of Chgo., 2003—06; trustee Prescott Coll., 1995—96; bd. sec. Touchstone Theatre, Lake Forest, Ill., 1987—89. Mem.: Chi Omega. Avocations: mediation, writing, weightlifting, ballroom dancing. Office: DePaul Univ Sch for New Learning 25 E Jackson Blvd Chicago IL 60611 Home Phone: 312-321-9664. Business E-Mail: lroyster@depaul.edu.

ROZANSKI, MORDECHAI, academic administrator; b. Lodz, Poland, July 4, 1946; came to U.S., 1968; s. Louis and Bertha R.; m. Bonnie Gail Asher, May 30, 1970; 1 child, Daniel K. BA, McGill U., 1968; postgrad. Columbia U., 1970, New Asia Coll., 1971-72; PhD, U. Pa., 1974. Instr. history U. Pa., Phila., 1969-71; assoc. prof. Asian history Berry Coll., Rome, Ga., 1974-76; asst. prof. Asian history, dir. Office of Internat. Edn. and fgn. area studies program Pacific Luth. U., Tacoma, 1976-82; assoc. dean for internat. studies Adelphi U., Garden City, N.Y., 1982-84, assoc.

provost, 1984-86; dean Coll. Liberal Arts, Fairleigh Dickinson U., Teaneck, N.J., 1986-89, v.p. for acad. affairs, 1989-1991, provost, Wagner Coll., Staten Island, 1991-1993, pres. U. Guelph, Ontario, 1993-2003, pres., Rider U., Lawrenceville, 2003-; dir. programs Nat. Council on Fgn. Langs. and Internat. Studies, 1983-86. Trustee, World Affairs Council, Seattle, 1978-81; vice chmn. Nat. Com. on Internat. Studies and Program Adminstrs., 1979-80; chmn. Pacific N.W. Internat./Intercultural Edn. Consortium, 1979-82. Que. Province fellow, 1967; Wilson Meml. scholar, 1968; U. Pa. fellow, 1968-71; Am. Hist. Assn. Am.-East Asian Relations fellow, Columbia U., 1970; Can. Council doctoral fellow, 1971-73; U.S. Office of Edn. research grantee, 1977; Lilly Found. fellow Stanford U., summer 1978. Author: Manual of World History, 1975; Guide to U.S. State Papers on China, 1979; editor-in-chief Am.-East Asian Relations Newsletter, 1980-83; contbr. articles to profl. publs. Office: Rider Univ 2083 Lawrence Rd Lawrenceville NJ 08648-3099

ROZANSKI, STANLEY HOWARD, lawyer; b. NYC, July 19, 1952; s. Israel and Frida (Huber) R.; 1 child, Justin. BA, Hunter Coll., 1974; JD, San Fernando Coll. Law, 1977. Bar: Calif. 1978, U.S. Dist. Ct. (cen. dist.) Calif. 1978, U.S. Ct. Appeals (9th cir.) 1982. Ptnr. Rozanski & Friedland, LA, 1980—, San Jose, Calif., 1983—, L.A., San Jose. Judge pro tem L.A. County Cts., 1985—. Recipient Outstanding Contributions award State Bar Calif., 1985. Mem. Calif. Bar Assn., Assn. Trial Lawyers Am., Calif. Trial Lawyers Assn., L.A. Trial Lawyers Assn., ABA, L.A. County Bar Assn., Beverly Hills Bar Assn. Jewish. Avocations: skiing, swimming, golf. Office: Ste 650 12400 Wilshire Blvd Los Angeles CA 90025-1055

ROZANTINE, GAYLE STUBBS, psychologist; b. Atlanta, Dec. 1, 1944; d. William L. and Louise (Cash) Stubbs; children: Kathryn Patricia, Webb Black III, Gregory William, Benjamin Stubbs, John Paul; m. Barry Rozantine. BA in Psychology, Agnes Scott Coll., 1965; MA in Tchg., Emory U., 1966; MA in Clin. Psychology, Western Carolina U., 1990; PhD, U. Tenn., 1995. Lic. psychologist, Ga.; diplomate Am. Acad. Experts in Traumatic Stress; bd. cert. stress mgmt. Tchr. Fulton Co. Bd. Edn., Ga., 1967-68; psychology resident Med. Coll. of Ga., Augusta, 1994-95, clin. fellow, 1995-96; rsch. psychologist Pain Evaluation and Intervention Program Dept. of VA Med. Ctr., Augusta, 1995-98; staff psychologist Compass Health Systems, Miami Beach, Fla., 1998, Charter Savannah Bevioral Health System, Ga., 1999-2000; CEO Ctr. Health and Well-Being, 2000—. Mem. critical incident stress debriefing team Med. Coll. Ga.; disaster mental health response team ARC; presenter in field. Mem. APA, Coastal Area Psychologists, Ga. Psychol. Assn., Ga. Breast Cancer Coalition and Fund, Nat. Assn. Forensic Counselors, Nat. Register Health Svc. Providers in Psychology. Office: The Ctr for Health and Well-Being PC 400 Commercial Ct Savannah GA 31406 Office Phone: 912-352-9500 ext. 105. Personal E-mail: gaylerozantine@yahoo.com. Business E-Mail: gaylerozantine@quietawakening.com.

ROZBRUCH, S. ROBERT, orthopedist, researcher; b. Bklyn., Sept. 2, 1965; s. Max and Frieda Rozbuch; m. Yonina Jacobs, July 2, 1989; children: Jason, Elizabeth. BA magna cum laude, U. Pa., 1985; MD in Rsch. with honors, Cornell U. Weill Med. Coll., 1990. Resident orthop. Hosp. Spl. Surgery, NYC, 1990—95; fellow Internat. Ctr. Limb Lengthening, Balt., 1998—99; pres. S. Robert Rozbruch MD, PC, NYC, 1999—; now chief limb lengthening svc. Hosp. Spl. Surgery, NYC, dir. Inst. Limb Lengthening and Reconstruction, 2002—; asst. prof. orthop. surgery Weill Med. Sch. Cornell U., 2002—. Treas. Limb Lengthening and Reconstruction Soc., 2002—, bd. dir., 2002; founder Limb Lengthening and Reconstruction Program Hosp. Spl. Surgery, NYC. Author: Fractures of the Knee in Clin. Orthop., 2000, Orthop. Knowledge Update-Trauma 3, 2003; contbr. articles to profl. jours. Bd. trustees Temple Israel Ctr., White Plains, NY, 2002—. Recipient Neer award, Am. Shoulder and Elbow Surgeons, 1991. Fellow: Am. Acad. Orthop. Surgeons; mem.: Orthop. Trauma Assn. Avocations: gardening, exercise. Office: Hosp Spl Surgery 535 E 70th St New York NY 10021 Office Phone: 212-606-1415. Business E-Mail: rozbruchsr@hss.edu.

ROZELL, WILLIAM BARCLAY, lawyer; b. Ossining, NY, Mar. 30, 1943; s. William M. and Doris M. (Mittenmaier) R.; m. Susan Kai Wylie, Oct. 4, 1969; m. Susan Marie Walker, Dec. 5, 1975; children: Rebecca, Mariah. BSc in Engring., Brown U., 1965; JD, Cornell U., 1968. Bar: Ohio 1969, N.Y. 1969, U.S. Dist. Ct. (so. dist.) N.Y. 1970, U.S. Dist. Ct. (ea. dist.) N.Y. 1971, Alaska 1972, U.S. Dist. Ct. Alaska 1972, U.S. Supreme Ct. 1976, U.S. Ct. Appeals (9th cir.) 1977. VISTA atty. Office Econ. Opportunity, Chgo. and Columbus, Ohio, 1968—69; assoc. White & Case, NYC, 1969—72, Faulkner, Banfield, Doogan & Holmes, Juneau, Alaska, 1972—74, ptnr., 1975—81, mem. firm, 1981—98; pvt. practice Juneau, 1998—. Bd. dirs. Alaska Legal Services Corp., 1974-77. Fellow Am. Bar Found.; mem. ABA, Alaska Bar Assn. (gov. 1976-82, pres. 1980-81), Alaska Bar Found. (trustee 1984-2001), Juneau Bar Assn., Order of Coif. Office: PO Box 20730 Juneau AK 99802-0730 Office Phone: 907-586-0142.

ROZEN, JEROME GEORGE, JR., entomologist, curator, researcher; b. Evanston, Ill., Mar. 19, 1928; s. Jerome George and Della (Kretchmar) R.; m. Barbara L. Lindner, Dec. 18, 1948; children: Steven George, Kenneth Charles, James Robert. Student, U. Pa., Phila., 1946-48; BA, U. Kans., Lawrence, 1950; PhD, U. Calif.-Berkeley, 1955. Entomologist in taxonomy U.S. Dept. Agr., 1956-58; asst. prof. entomology Ohio State U., 1958-60; assoc. curator dept. entomology Am. Mus. Natural History, NYC, 1960-65, curator hymenoptera, 1965—, chmn. dept. entomology, 1960-71, dep. dir. research, 1972-86. Field expdns. in U.S., Europe, Mex., Trinidad, Argentina, Chile, Brazil, Peru, Venezuela, Morocco, Pakistan, Republic of South Africa, Namibia, Israel, Egypt, Kyrgzstan, Turkey, Belize; adj. prof. CUNY, 1968—; mus. assoc. Univ. Kans. Nat. History Mus. and Biodiversity Rsch. Ctr., 2004—. Contbr. articles to profl. jours. Fellow AAAS; mem. Am. Inst. Biol. Scis., Entomol. Soc. Am. (editor misc. publs. 1959-60), Soc. Study of Evolution, Soc. Systematic Biology, N.Y. Entomol Soc. (pres. 1964-65), Washington Entomol. Soc., Pacific Coast Entomol. Soc., Kans. Entomol. Soc., Orgn. Biol. Field Stas. (pres. 1990), Internat. Soc. Hymenopterists (co-organizer, Bee Course, 1999-). Achievements include research in bees (Apoidea) and beetles (Coleoptera). Home: 55 Haring St Closter NJ 07624-1709 Office: Am Mus Natural History Central Park West New York NY 10024-5192 Office Phone: 212-769-5466. Business E-Mail: rozen@amnh.org.

ROZENBERG, LANA, cosmetic dentist; b. 1968; DDS, U. Pacific Sch. Dentistry, 1994. Dir. Dental Day Spa, NY. Named one of NY Top Cosmetic Dentists, NY Mag., 2002, 2004. Avocations: boating, golf, skiing, tennis, financial investments. Office: Dental Day Spa 45 W 54th St - Ste 1B New York NY 10019 Office Phone: 212-265-7724. Business E-Mail: office@rozenbergdds.com.

ROZETT, ROBERT BERNARD, library director, historian; b. Summit, NJ, Apr. 21, 1956; s. George Robert and Thelma Frumkin Rozett; m. Shoshana Cohen, May 29, 1985; children: Tamar, Naomi, Hadas, Michael. B, Rutgers U., 1978; M, Hebrew U., Jerusalem, Israel, 1981, PhD, 1987. Lectr. Yad Vashem, Jerusalem, 1981—87, co-curator hist. exhibit, 1990—92, libr. dir., 1993—. Author: Approaching the Holocaust, Texts and Contexts, 2005; editor: Facts on File Encyclopedia of the Holocaust, 2000, The Holocaust, Frequently Asked Questions, 2005; editor: (assoc. editor) Encyclopedia of the Holocaust, 1988—91; contbr. articles numerous articles about the Holocaust, Bibliographical Essay The Holocaust Encyclopedia, 2001, chapters to books. Recipient Phi Beta Kappa, Rutgers U., 1978, Phi Alpha Theta, 1978. Mem.: Israel Hist. Soc. Office: Yad Vashem Mount of Remembrance Jerusalem 91034 Israel Home Phone: 972-2-6783531; Office Phone: 972-2-6443531. Office Fax: 972-2-6443443. Business E-Mail: robert.rozett@yadvashem.org.il.

ROZMAN, ALEXANDER, lawyer, consultant; BA, U. Ill., Urbana, 1996; JD, Chicago-Kent Coll. of Law, Ill., 1999. Bar: NY, Ill. 1999. Gen. counsel, chief compliance officer Capital Market Services, LLC, New York, NY, 2004—06; assoc. dir. Navigant Consulting, Inc., New York, NY, 2006—; in-house counsel Bear Stearns & Co., New York, NY, 2006—. Recipient Found. award, Ill. Bar, 1999. Mem.: Assn. Cert. Anti-Money Laundering Specialists, Assn. Corp. Counsel, Nat. Soc. Compliance Professionals. Office: Navigant Consulting Inc 666 3rd Ave 27th Fl New York NY 10017 Office Phone: 646-227-4332.

ROZMAN, GILBERT FRIEDELL, sociologist, educator; b. Mpls., Feb. 18, 1943; s. David and Celia (Friedell) R.; m. Masha Dwosh, Jan. 25, 1945; children: Thea Dwosh, Noah Dwosh. BA, Carleton Coll., Northfield, Minn., 1965; PhD (Woodrow Wilson fellow 1965-66), Princeton U., 1971. Mem. faculty Princeton U., 1970—, prof. sociology, 1979—, Musgrave prof. sociology, 1992—. Mem. com. studies Chinese civilization Am. Council Learned Socs., 1975-80; mem. U.S.-USSR Bi-Nat. Commn. Humanities and Social Scis., 1978-86, IREX Univ. Coun., 1998-2001. Author: Urban Networks in Ch'ing China and Tokugawa Japan, 1973, Urban Networks in Russia, 1750-1800, and Premodern Periodization, 1976, Population and Marketing Settlements in Ch'ing China, 1982, A Mirror for Socialism: Soviet Criticisms of China, 1985, The Chinese Debate About Soviet Socialism 1978-85, 1987, Japan's Response to the Gorbachev Era, 1985-1991: A Rising Superpower Views a Declining One, 1992, Northeast Asia's Stunted Regionalism: Bilateral Distrust in the Shadow of Globalization, 2004, Strategic Thinking about the Korean Nuclear Crisis: Four Parties Caught between North Korea and the United States, 2007; co-author: The Modernization of Japan and Russia, 1975; editor: The Modernization of China, 1981, Soviet Studies of Premodern China: Assessments of Recent Scholarship, 1984, Japan in Transition: From Tokugawa to Meiji, 1986, The East Asian Region: Confucian Heritage and Its Modern Adaptation, 1991, Dismantling Communism: Common Causes and Regional Variations, 1992, Russia and East Asia: The 21st Century Security Environment, 1999, Japan and Russia: The Tortuous Path to Normalization, 1949-1999, 2000, Korea at the Center: Dynamics of Regionalism in Northeast Asia, 2006, Russian Strategic Thought Toward Asia, 2006, Japanese Strategic Thought Toward Asia, 2007. Guggenheim fellow, 1979-80; grantee NSF, NEH, Social Sci. Rsch. Coun., Nat. Coun. for Soviet and E. European Studies, U.S. Inst. Peace, Woodrow Wilson Internat. Ctr. Mem. Assn. Asian Studies, Am. Sociol. Assn., Am. Assn. Advancement Slavic Studies. Home: 20 Springwood Dr Trenton NJ 08648-1048 Office: Princeton U 149 Wallace Hall Princeton NJ 08544-0001 Home Phone: 609-896-1975. E-mail: grozman@princeton.edu.

ROZOF, PHYLLIS CLAIRE, lawyer; b. Flint, Mich., Aug. 3, 1948; d. Eugene Robert and Loveta Lucille Greenwood; m. Robert James Rozof, July 17, 1970 (dec. Oct. 1995); children: Nathan, Zachary. AB with high distinction, U. Mich., 1970, JD magna cum laude, 1977. Bar: Mich. 1977, Fla. 1978. Assoc. Honigman Miller Schwartz and Cohn, Detroit, 1977-81, ptnr., 1982—. Mem. Comml. Real Estate Women Detroit (pres. 1992-93). Office: Honigman Miller Schwartz & Cohn LLP 2290 1st National Bldg Detroit MI 48226 Office Phone: 313-465-7532. Business E-Mail: prozof@honigman.com.

ROZUMNYJ, JAROSLAV, literature educator; b. Honcharivka, Ukraine, Sept. 6, 1925; s. Hryhory and Anna (Parubocha) R.; m. Oksana Olha Hrycenko, Mar. 10, 1938; children: Larysa, Roman, Istan, Ruslan. BA with honors, Theol. Sem., Culemborg, Netherlands, 1950; MA, U. Ottawa, Ont., Can., 1958, PhD, 1968. Lectr. Laurentian U., Sudbury, Ont., 1960-63; asst. prof. Western Mich. U., Kalamazoo, 1963-64, U. Man., Winnipeg, Can., 1964-71, head dept., 1976-89, prof. lit., 1989—, sr. scholar, 1997. Vis. prof. U. Ottawa, 1972, Ukrainian Cath. U., Rome, 1987; dean Faculty of Philosophy, Ukrainian Free U., Munich, Germany, 1995-96; vis. rsch. scholar Macquarie U., Sydney, 1989; mem. internat. adv. bd. U. Kiev-Mohyla Acad., 1992—, hon. prof., 1996. Editor: New Soil--Old Roots: The Ukrainian Experience in Canada, 1983, I Was Nineteen... KM Academia, 2001; editor & co-author: Yesterday, Today, Tomorrow: The Ukrainian Community in Canada, 2004; co-editor: Jubilee Collection of the Ukrainian Academy of Arts and Sciences, 1976; lit. editor: Anthology of Musical Compositions on the Poems of M. Shashkewych, 1992; editor Can. vol. Ency. of Ukrainian Diaspora, 7 vols.; editor-in-chief: Collection of Scholarly Papers, 1996; mem. editl. bd. Suchasnist, 1984-91. Pres. Ukrainian Cultural and Ednl. Ctr., Winnipeg, 1970-73; pres. Can. Friends of Rukh in Ukraine, Winnipeg, 1990-92; Can. rep. U. Kiev-Mohyla-Acad., 1992—; bd. govs. Man. Mus. Man and Nature, Winnipeg, 1976-80; pres. Markian Shashkevych Inst., Winnipeg, 1999—. Recipient Outreach Activities award U. Man., 1986, Order of the Eternal Flame in Silver World Conf. Ukranian Scouts, 1994, Taras Shevchenko medal Ukrainian Can. Congress, 1995, Petro Mohyla Silver medal Nat. U. Kyiv Mohyla Acad., 2003; honored Festschrift, Can. Inst. Ukranian Studies, 2000. Mem. Ukrainian Acad. Arts and Scis. in Can. (pres. 1977-80, v.p. 1995-01), Schevchenko Sci. Soc. US, Am. Assn. Ukrainian Studies, Ukrainian Am. Assn. U. Profs. Home: 801 Cambridge St Winnipeg MB R3M 3G3 Canada Office Phone: 204-474-9370. Personal E-mail: rozumnyj@cc.umanitoba.ca.

ROZWAT, CHARLES, computer software company executive; B in Fin. and Info. Systems, Marquette U., Milw. Mgmt. staff mem. Digital Equipment Corp.; with Oracle Corp., 1994—, v.p. New Eng. Devel. Ctr., exec. v.p. server techs. divsn. Redwood City, Calif. Office: Oracle Corp 500 Oracle Pky Redwood City CA 94085 Office Phone: 650-506-7000. Office Fax: 650-506-7200. *

ROZZELL, SCOTT ELLIS, lawyer, energy executive; b. Texarkana, Tex., Apr. 12, 1949; s. George M. and Dora Mae (Boyett) Rozzell; m. Karen Brandstrader Rozzell (dec.); children: Stacey Rozzell Murphree, Kimberly Marie. BA, So. Meth. U., 1971; JD, U. Tex., 1975. Bar: Tex. 1975, U.S. Dist. Ct. Tex. (so. dist), 1975, U.S. Dist. Ct. Tex. (no. dist.), 1977, U.S. Ct. Appeals (1st, 3d, 9th cirs.) 1977, U.S. Ct. Appeals (5th and D.C. cirs.) 1976. Assoc. BakerBotts, LLP, Houston, 1975-82, ptnr., 1983-94, sr. ptnr., 1995-2000; exec. v.p., gen. counsel, corp. sec. CenterPoint Energy, Inc., Houston, 2001—; exec. v.p., gen. counsel, corp. sec., bd. dir. Tex. Genco Holdings Inc., 2003—04. Mem. devel. bd. Sci. Ctr. Houston, 1992-03, 2006-, State of Tex. Aircraft Pooling Bd., 1997-02; mem. Tex. Commn. Lawyer Discipline, 2001-03, chair 2002-03; bd. advisors Houston CC Found., 2004-. Bd. dirs. Manned Space Flight Edn. Found., Inc., 1997—, vice chair 2000-06, Tex. Aviation Hall of Fame, 2001-2007; vice-chmn., 2006—, Cancer Counseling Inc., Houston, 1991-92; mem. so. regional adv. bd. Inst. Internat. Edn., 2002—; chmn. Assn. Electric Cos. Tex., 2006-. Fellow Tex. Bar Found. (sustaining life, bd. dirs. 2007—), Houston Bar Found. (sustaining life, bd. dirs. 1991-93, chair 1993), Am. Bar Found. (life); mem. ABA, State Bar Tex. (bd. dirs. 1997-2000), Houston Bar Assn. (bd. dirs. 1991-95, pres. 1996-97), Fed. Energy Bar Assn., Houston Young Lawyers Assn. (bd. dirs. 1978-82, pres. 1983-84), Coronado Club, Houstonian. Republican. Presbyterian. Avocation: flying vintage military aircraft. Office: CenterPoint Energy Inc 1111 Louisiana 47th Floor PO Box 4567 Houston TX 77210-4567 Home: 8 N West Oak Dr Houston TX 77056 Office Phone: 713-207-1502. Office Fax: 713-207-0894. Business E-Mail: scott.rozzell@centerpointenergy.com.

RUAN, JIENING, literature and language professor, director, director, writer; d. W. Ruan; m. D. Sun, 1965. BA in English, Xiamen U., China, 1989; MEd in Elem. Edn., Indiana U. Pa., 1995, MEd in Reading Edn., 1996; PhD, Purdue U., West Lafayette, Ind., 2000. Asst. prof. U. Okla., Norman, 2000—06, assoc. prof., 2006—, dir. reading cert. program, 2005—, dir. Reading Clinic, 2001—. Prin. Purdue Chinese Sch., West Lafayette, Ind., 1998—2000; affiliate US-China Issues Inst. Okla. U., Norman, 2006—. Translator: World Literature Today for Kids; guest editl. rev. bd. Reading Tchr., 2002—05, mem. editl. bd., 2006—, mem. editl. rev. bd. World Lit. Today Kids, 2003—, editl. cons. Jour. Actionin Tchr. Edn., 2003—; contbr. articles to profl. jours. Recipient Jr. Faculty award, U. Okla., 2004; Purdue Rsch. Found. grantee, Purdue U., 1999, Jr. Faculty Rsch. grantee, U. Okla., 2003, Summer Rsch. grantee, 2005. Mem.: Assn. Tchr. Educators, Internat. Reading Assn., Nat. Reading Conf.

RUAN, LIAN JIN, library director; arrived in U.S., 1986; d. Yong-dong Jin and Jin-xiu Dai; m. Zhong-jin Ruan, June 24, 1987; children: Gordon J., George J. BA in World History, Peking U., 1984; MA in African History, UCLA, 1988; MLS, U. Ill., 1990. Rsch. info. specialist Ill. Fire Svc. Inst., Champaign, 1990—99, dir., head libr., 1999—. Newspaper cataloger Ill. State Hist. Libr., Springfield, 1990, manuscript cataloger, 90; libr. cons. Champaign Fire Dept., 1990—. Contbr. articles to profl. jours. Recipient Chancellor's Academic Profl. Excellence award, U. Ill. Mem.: ALA (mem. Illinet network adv. coun. 2003—), Spl. Libr. Assn. (downstate bd. dirs. Ill. chpt. 2002—04, Diversity Leadership Develop. award 2003), Chinese Heritage Assn. (vice prin. chinese sch. 1998—99, prin. chinese sch. 1999—2000, bd. dirs. 2000—03), Internat. Fire Libr. Consortium (adv. com. 1997—2001). Office: Ill Fire Svc Inst Univ Ill 11 Gerty Dr Champaign IL 61820 Office Phone: 217-265-6107. Business E-Mail: lruan@fsi.uiuc.edu.

RUANE, JAMES EDWARD, JR., engineering executive; b. Malden, Mass., July 22, 1954; s. James Edward and Marie Alice Ruane; m. Thelma Cahinde Ruane, Dec. 1, 1990; children: James Edward III, Katheryn Virginia. BSc in Physics, U. Mass., 1981. Test dir. Raytheon, Bedford, Mass., 1983—96; engring. mgr. Equimeter, Dubois, Pa., 1996—98; v.p. ops. Star Track, Morris Plains, NJ, 1998—99; program mgr. Com Tech Sys., Orlando, Fla., 1999—2001, Eaton Vorad, San Diego, 2001—03; dir. datalink applications Cubic Def. Applications, San Diego, 2003—. Platinum sponsor San Diego Telecom Coun., 2004—. Mem.: IEEE, Assn. UN Mannod Vehicle Sys. Internat., Air Force Assn. Avocation: Karate (black belt). Home: 12082 Fairhope Rd San Diego CA 92128 Office: Cubic Defense Applications 9333 Balboa Ave San Diego CA 92123

RUB, TIMOTHY F., museum director; b. NYC, Mar. 9, 1952; s. Louis Rub and Marguerite (Gustafson); m. Sally Rub; children: Peter, Katharine. BA in Art History, Middlebury Coll., 1974; MA in Art History, NYU, 1979; MBA, Yale U., 1987; postgrad., Harvard U., 1998. Curatorial intern Met. Mus. Art, 1983; lectr. art and archtl. history Cooper-Hewitt Mus./Parsons Sch. Design, Stevens Inst. Tech., 1979-84; guest curator Bronx Mus. Arts, NY, 1985-86; curator Cooper-Hewitt Mus., NYC, 1983-87; assoc. dir. Hood Mus. Dartmouth Coll., Hanover, NH, 1987-91, dir., COO, 1991-2000; dir. Cin. Art Mus., 2000—06; dir., CEO, Cleve. Mus. Art, 2006—. Avocation: gardening. Office: Cleveland Mus Art 11150 East Blvd Cleveland OH 44106

RUBARDT, PETER CRAIG, conductor, educator; b. Oakland, Calif., Aug. 7, 1958; s. Kenneth and Betty (Maspero) R.; m. Hedi Salanki; children, Daniel, Vivienna. BA, U. Calif., Berkeley, 1981; M of Music, SUNY, Stony Brook, 1984; student, Hochschule fur Musik, Vienna, 1984-86; D Mus. Arts, Julliard Sch., 1989. Prof., conductor SUNY, Purchase, 1989-90, Rutgers U., New Brunswick, NJ, 1991-96; resident conductor N.J. Symphony, Newark, 1990-93; assoc. conductor Syracuse (N.Y.) Symphony, 1993-97; music dir., condr. Greater Pensacola (Fla.) Symphony Orch., 1997—. Guest conductor various orchs. Condr. rec. Bach Concerti, 1988. Fullbright fellow USIA, 1984-86; Bruno Walter scholar, Julliard Sch., 1986-88. Mem. Am. Symphony Orch. League, Condrs. Guild. Democrat. Home: 8774 Thunderbird Dr Pensacola FL 32514 Office: Pensacola Symphony Orch PO Box 1752 Pensacola FL 32598-1752 Office Phone: 850-435-2533.

RUBBERT, PAUL EDWARD, retired engineering executive; b. Mpls., Feb. 18, 1937; s. Adolf Christian and Esther Ruth Rubbert; m. Mary Parpart, Oct. 6, 1958 (div. 1985); children: Mark, David, Stephen. BS with high distinction, U. Minn., 1958, MS in Aero. Engring., 1960; PhD in Aerodyn., MIT, 1965. Rsch. engr. The Boeing Co., Seattle, 1960-62, 65-72, unit chief aerodyns rsch., comml. airplane group, 1972—, tech. fellow, 1989; ret. Cons. NASA, 1989—, aeronautics adv. com., aerospace rsch. and tech. subcoms.; corp. vis. com. MIT, 1990—; served on various coms. Nat. Rsch. Coun. Panel; aerodyns. cons. GM; speaker in field. Contbr. articles to profl. jours. Recipient Arch T. Colwell Merit award Soc. Automotive Engrs., 1968, Wright Brothers Lectureship in Aeronautics Am. Inst. of Aeronautics and Astronautics, 1994 Fellow AIAA (Outstanding Tech. Mgmt. award Pacific Northwest sect., disting. lectr., assoc. editor jour., past mem. fellow selection com., dir., chmn. various workshops and coms.), Royal Aero. Soc.; mem. NAE. Achievements include three patents in field.

RUBEL, ERIC A., lawyer; b. Hempstead, NY, July 12, 1960; s. Ralph and Josephine Rubel; m. Susan Rubel, Jan. 20, 1991; children: Alexander, Molly. BA cum laude, Middlebury Coll., 1982; JD with highest honors, George Washington U., 1985. Bar: D.C., Pa. Law clk. to Hon. Jane Restani U.S. Ct. Internat. Trade, NYC, 1985-86; assoc. Arnold & Porter, Washington, 1986—92, ptnr., 1993—94; gen. counsel U.S. Consumer Product Safety Commn., Washington, 1994-97; ptnr., Consumer Product Safety Group Arnold & Porter, Washington, 1997—. Mem. ABA (vice chair sect. adminstrv. law and regulatory practice 1997-98), Order of Coif. Office: Arnold and Porter 555 12th St NW Washington DC 20004-1206 Office Phone: 202-942-5749. Office Fax: 202-942-5999. Business E-Mail: eric.rubel@aporter.com.

RUBEL, MATTHEW EVAN, retail executive; b. Ft. Lauderdale, Fla., Nov. 29, 1957; s. Stanley Bernard and Isabell Rubel. BS in Journalism, Ohio U., 1979; MBA, U. Miami, 1980. Pres. splty. store div. Revlon Inc., NYC, 1988; pres., CEO Pepe Jeans USA; exec. v.p. J. Crew Group, 1994—99, CEO Popular Club Plan, 1994—99; chmn., CEO Cole Haan, 1999—2005; pres., CEO Payless ShoeSource, Inc., 2005—. Bd. dirs. Furniture Brands Internat., Inc., 2006—. Trustee Ballet Theatre Found., Inc./Am. Ballet Theatre. Avocations: tennis, boating. Office: Payless ShoeSource Inc 3231 SE 6th Ave Topeka KS 66607 *

RUBELL, DONALD, gynecologist, hotel executive, art collector; m. Mera Rubell; children: Jason, Jennifer. Named one of Top 200 Collectors, ARTnews Mag., 2004, 2005, 2006. Avocation: collector of contemporary art. Mailing: The Rubell Art Collection 95 NW 29th St Miami FL 33127

RUBELL, JENNIFER, writer, hotelier; d. Donald and Mera Rubell; life ptnr. Daniel Phillip Kim; 1 child, Stevie Kim-Rubell. BA in Art History, Harvard U., 1993. Concierge Royalton Hotel, NYC; cofounder Greenview Hotel, South Beach, Fla., 1994, Albion Hotel, South Beach, Fla., 1994, Beach House, Bal Harbour, Fla., 1994; food and entertaining editor, Home & Design mag. Miami Herald, Fla., 2002—, columnist Fla., sr. editor, Style & Entertaining mag. Fla.; contbg. food editor Domino mag., columnist, The Dish. Regular columnist LA Times Syndicate; contbr. Vogue, Harper's Bazaar, W mag., Better Homes and Gardens, Elle, NY Times, Every Day with Rachael Ray, Ocean Drive mag., Food and Wine mag. Creator (vis. artist series) Pillow Talk, 2001; author: Real Life Entertaining, 2006. Vol. Rubell Family Collection, NYC; chair cultural tourism com. Greater

Miami Convention and Visitor's Bur., Fla.; vol. South Beach Wine & Food Festival, Fla. Mailing: Domino Magazine Conde Nast 4 Times Square New York NY 10036 Office Phone: 212-286-2860.

RUBELLO, DAVID JEROME, artist; b. Detroit, Sept. 3, 1935; s. Ludovico and Girolama (Trupiano) R.; m. Mary Anne Keithan, Oct. 14, 1978. BFA, Am. Acad. Art, Rome, 1961; MFA, U. Mich., 1972; cert., Acad. Fine Art, Copenhagen, 1966. Lect. art U. Mich., Ann Arbor, 1973—74; asst. prof. art Pa. State U., University Park, 1974-80; assoc. prof. art Towson (Md.) State U., 1980-81; assoc. prof. U. Mich., Ann Arbor, 1988-90. One man shows include Cade Gallery, Royal Oak, Mich., 1987, GM Design Ctr., Warren, Mich., 2007; exhibited in group shows at Detroit Inst. Art, 1987, GMB Gallery Internat., Bloomfield Hills, Mich., 1991, Kresge Art Inst., 1989, Kalamazoo Art Inst., 1990, 91, Photo Nat. 2, Ella Sharp Mus., Jackson, Mich., BBAA, Birmingham, Mich., Arts Coun., Traverse City, Mich., 1995-96, Patrimonio Invitational Wayne State U., Detroit, 1996, Ann. Celebrate Mich. Artists P.C. Art Ctr., Rochester, 1994, 95, 96, Art Ctr., Mt. Clemens, Mich., 1997, Crative Art Ctr., Pontiac, Mich., 1997, Paint Creek Art Ctr., Rochester, Mich., 2007; exhibited Null Dimension, Fulda, Germany, 1988, Systematica Constructive Art, Madrid, 1989, B4 Pub. Invitational, London, 1990, Archive 90s, Amsterdam and London, Konkrete Miniatures Invitational, Amsterdam, 1991, Planet Art Gallery, Capetown, South Africa, 1999, Detroit Focus, 2000; author: REflectio and Form, 1984, My Sicilian Gardens, Poetry & Photographs, 2004, Moment to Moment, Away at Home Story Poems & Photographs, 2007; contbr. articles to profl. jours. including The Structurist, 1999, 2002, 2005-06. Recipient awards for art work; featured professional artist profile B&W Fine Art Photography Mag., June 2001.

RUBEN, ALAN MILES, law educator; b. Phila., May 13, 1931; s. Maurice Robert and Ruth (Blatt) R.; m. Betty Jane Willis, May 23, 1965. AB, U. Pa., 1953, MA, JD, U. Pa., 1956. Bar: Pa. 1957, Ohio 1972. Law clk. Supreme Ct. Pa., 1956-58; pvt. practice Phila., 1958-65; assoc. counsel Aetna Life & Casualty Co., Hartford, Conn., 1965-69; corp. counsel Lubrizol Corp., Cleve., 1969-70; prof. Cleve.-Marshall Coll. Law, Cleve. State U., 1970—2003, prof. emeritus, 2003—; adv. prof. law Fudan U., Shanghai, People's Republic of China, 1993—; dep. to city solicitor Phila., 1958-61; dep. atty. gen. State of Pa., 1961-65; spl. counsel to U.S. Senate Subcom. on Nat. Stockpile, 1962; commentator Higher Edn. Issues Sta. WCLV-FM, Cleve., 1975-87. Mem. nat. panel labor arbitrators Nat. Acad. Arbitrators, Fed. Mediation and Conciliation Svc. and Am. Arbitration Assn., Ohio State Employment Rels. Bd.; lectr. law U. Conn. Law Sch., 1968; vis. prof. law FuDan U., Shanghai, Peoples Republic of China, 1988-89; cons. Shanghai Law Office for Fgn. Economy and Trade, Peoples Republic of China, 1991-94. Author: The Constitutionality of Basic Protection for the Automobile Accident Victim, 1968, Unauthorized Insurance: The Regulation of the Unregulated, 1968, Arbitration in Public Employee Labor Disputes: Myth, Shibboleth and Reality, 1971, Illicit Sex of Campus: Federal Remedies for Employment Discrimination, 1971, Model Public Employees Labor Relations Act, 1972, Sentencing the Corporate Criminal, 1972, Modern Corporation Law, supp. edit., 1978, An American Lawyer's Observations on the Inauguration of the Shanghai Stock Exchange, 1989, Ohio Limited Partnership Law, 1992-2002, Practice Guides, Ohio Limited Liability Company, Law, 1995; co-editor: How Arbitration Works, 1997, editor-in-chief 6th edit., 2003; contbr.: With an Eye to Tomorrow: The Future Outlook of the Life Insurance Industry, 1968, The Urban Transportation Crisis: The Philadelphia Plan, 1961, Philadelphia's Union Shop Contract, 1961, The Administrative Agency Law: Reform of Adjudicative Procedure and the Revised Model Act, 1963, The Computer in Court: Computer Simulation and the robinson Patman Act, 1964. Bd. dirs. U.S. Olympic Com., 1968-73; chmn. U.S. Olympic Fencing Sport Com., 1969-73; pres. U.S. Fencing Assn., 1968-73; capt. U.S. Pan-Am. Fencing Team, 1971, U.S. Olympic Fencing Team, 1972; bd. dirs. Legal Aid Soc. Cleve., 1973-77; trustee Cleve.-San Jose Ballet, 1999-2001. Winner Internat. Inst. Edn. Internat. Debate Championship, 1953; recipient Harrison Tweed Bowl and Am. Law Inst. prizes Nat. Moot Ct. Competition, 1955; named Guggenheim scholar, 1949-53, Fulbright scholar FuDan U., Shanghai, 1993-94. Fellow Coll. Labor and Enployment Lawyers, Inc.; mem. ABA, Ohio Bar Assn. (corp. law and profl. responsibility com.), Cleve. Bar Assn. (Securities Law Inst. 1995-2002), Assn. Am. Law Schs. (chmn. sect. law and edn. 1976-78), Internat. Indsl. Rels. Rsch. Assn., Internat. Soc. Labor Law, Internat. Bar Assn., Union Internat. Des Avocats, Internat. Law Assn., AAUP (pres. Ohio conf. 1974-75), Rowfant Club, Phi Beta Kappa, Pi Gamma Mu. Home: 9925 Lake Shore Blvd Bratenahl OH 44108-1052 Office: Cleveland Marshall Coll Law Cleve State U 1801 Euclid Ave Cleveland OH 44115 Office Phone: 216-687-2310. Business E-Mail: alan.ruben@law.csuohio.edu.

RUBEN, GARY A., marketing and communications consultant; b. Cochem, Germany, Jan. 1, 1924; came to U.S., 1939, naturalized, 1943; s. Jules and Erna (Hirsch) R.; m. Irene Jehle, Aug. 12, 1962; 1 child, Monique L. Student, Acad. Comml. Art, Indpls., 1940-41. With advt. dept. Indpls. News, 1940-41; advt. mgr. Greater Indpls. Amusement Corp., 1941-42; pres. Ruben Advt. Agy., Indpls., 1948-68; chmn. bd. Ruben, Montgomery & Assos., 1968-76; pres. Prestige Program Sales Inc., 1973-76, Gary A. Ruben Inc. (advt. and mktg. cons.), Indpls., 1976—. Past lectr. advt. and bd. fellows Northwood Inst.; past pres. Nat. Fedn. Advt. Agys., 1971. Hon. trustee Indpls. Children's Mus. With Combat Engrs. AUS, 1943-46. Paul Harris fellow Rotary Internat. Mem.: Ind. Broadcast Pioneers. Office: 7370-D Lions Head Dr Indianapolis IN 46260 *It was years ago, in the late 30's in Vienna, that the cry "Lebensraum" echoed across yet another land. And, a family, judged comfortable by most standards, scattered to the four winds, leaving behind all things material, but salvaging the will to survive and to commence once again in a new land. To a boy in his teens and still dressed in European-style short pants upon arrival in this country, the emotion, the sights, the sounds, and the smells were overwhelming and exciting to say the least...so began another chapter in my life. In the ensuing years, I learned the true meaning of individual freedom. And while the echoes of Vienna have become dim, that dim sound will continue to remind me that all worthwhile things in life are earned—not given, and even in adversity, there is opportunity.*

RUBEN, IDA GASS, state senator; b. Washington, Jan. 07; d. Sol and Sonia E. (Darman) Gass; m. L. Leonard Ruben, Aug. 29, 1948; children: Garry, Michael, Scott, Stephen. Del. Md. Ho. of Dels., Annapolis, 1974-86; mem. Md. Senate, Annapolis, 1986—, majority whip, 1995-99, pres. pro-tem, 2000—. Chair Montgomery County House Delegation, 1981-86, Montgomery County Senate Delegation, 1987—; mem. house econ. matters com., 1974-85, house ways and means com., 1985-86, legis. policy com., 1991—, vice-chair senate budget and taxation com., 1997-99, joint budget and audit com., 1991—, exec. nominations com., 1991—, joint protocol com., 1991—, chair, senate budget and tax., subcom. on pub. safety, transp., econ. devel. and natural resources, 1995-99, mem. joint com. on spending affordability, 1995—, mem. capital budget subcom., 1995—; mem. Gov.'s Motor Carrier Task Force, 1989—; conv. chair Nat. Order Women Legislators, 1980. Chair Women Legislators Caucus Md., 1982-84; trustee Adventist Health Care Mid-Atlantic, Takoma Park, Md.; bd. dirs. Ctrs. for Handicapped, Silver Spring, Md.; former internat. v.p. B'nai Brith Women. Recipient Cert. Appreciation Ctrs. for Handicapped, 1987, Meritorious Svc. award Safety and Survival, 1989, Cover Those Trucks award AAA Potomac, 1989, Leadership Laurel award Safety First Club Md., 1989, Woman of Valor award B'nai B'rith Women, 1991, Pub. Affairs award Planned Parenthood Md., 1992, ESOL support recognition Montgomery County Pub. Schs., 1992, Appreciation award Fraternal Order Police, 1992, John Dewey award Montgomery County Fedn. Tchrs., 1992, ARC of Md., 1992, Safety Leader award Advocates for Hwy. and Auto Safety, 1993, Disting. Svc. award Gov.'s Commn. Employment of People with Disabilities, 1993, award Faculty Guild U. Md. for support of faculty and univ., 1993, Sincere Appreciation award for commitment to Md.'s youth Md. Underage Drinking Prevention Coalition, 1994, Faithful Svc. to citizens Montgomery County award Montgomery County Assn. of Realtors, 1994; named Most Effective Pub. Ofcl. by residents of Silver Spring, 1990, one of 100 Most Powerful Women in Washington Metro Area by Washingtonian Mag., 1994, 97, Legislator of Yr. award Nat. Commn. Against Drunk Driving, 1995, Legislator of Yr. award Montgomery County Med. Soc., 1995, Carmen S. Turner Achievement in Cmty. Svc. award Montgomery County Dept. Transp., 1995, Safety Leader award Advocates for Hwy. and Auto Safety, 1996, Legislator of Yr. award AAA, Potomac, Md., 1997, Vince and Larry award Md. Com. for Safety Belt Use, 1997, Legislative Leadership award Montgomery County, 1998, Leadership award Olney Theater Ctr., 1998, Legislator of Yr. award Greater Montgomery County C. of C., 1999, Hwy. Safety Herd award Advocates for Hwy. and Auto Safety, 1999, One of Md.'s Top 100 Women, The Daily Record, 1994, 97, 2001, 03, Am. Lung Assn. Appreciation award in protecting youth from tobacco industry, 2000, Olney Theater honoree contbns. Olney Theatre and arts in Md., 2000, Pub. Policy Leadership award Am. Cancer Soc., 2002; M.A.D.D. Award of Exellence, 2002, Disting. Pub. Svc. award Am. Lung Assn. of Md., 2003, Disting. Legislator award Md. Impaired Driver Coalition, 2003, S. Robert Cohen award Jewish Found. Group Homes, 2004, Arts Stars award Montgomery Coll., 2004, others; named to Washington, Md., Del., Pa. Svc. Sta. Assn. Hall of Fame, 1994, Suburban Md. Transp. Priorities outstanding leadership in transp. pub. policy adminstrn., 2000; Md. Coll. Art and Design honoree, 2000. Mem. Coun. State Govts. (com. on suggested legislation), Hadassah. Democrat. Jewish. Home: 11 Schindler Ct Silver Spring MD 20903-1329 Office: Md State Senate 422 Miller Senate Office Bldg 11 Bladen St Annapolis MD 21401-8012 Home Phone: 301-439-2332; Office Phone: 301-858-3634. Business E-Mail: ida_ruben@senate.state.md.us.

RUBEN, JEFFREY M., finance company executive, lawyer; b. 1963; BS, Pa. State U.; JD, Temple U. Bar: Pa. 1990. Assoc. Klehr, Harrison, Harvey, Brantzburg & Ellers; joined Am. Bus. Fin. Svcs., Bala Cynwyd, Pa., 1992; sr. v.p.; exec. v.p., gen. counsel, 1998—. Mem. ABA.

RUBEN, LAWRENCE, real estate developer and company executive, lawyer; b. Bklyn., Sept. 28, 1926; s. Irving and Minnie (Sruelif) R.; m. Selma Belfer, Dec. 20, 1952 (dec. 2002); children: Richard Gordon, Lenore Denise, Rochelle Gail Ruben Kivell; m. Jan Gottlieb, Dec. 5, 2004. BA, NYU, 1949; LLB, Bklyn. Law Sch., 1951. Bar: N.Y. 1952. Gen. practice law, NYC, 1952-53; pres. Ru-Min Constrn. Co., NYC, 1953-54; exec. v.p. Belco Petroleum Corp., NYC, 1954-64, dir., 1954-85; v.p. Fundamental Bldg. Corp., 1952—; pres. Randall Devel. Co., Aragon Devel. Corp., Lawrence Ruben Co., Inc.; ptnr. Lexington Madison Co., Tower Plaza Assocs., Devonshire Assocs., Boylston Ptnrs., Devonshire Constrn. Co. Inc., Lawrence Assocs., Granite Ptnrs., Inc., Harper-Lawrence; pres. Washington Mgmt. Corp. Mem. adv. bd. NYU Real Estate Inst.; mem. Rockefeller U. Coun.; med. ctr. adv. bd. NY UJA; bd. Govs. Am. Jewish Com. Patron Albert Einstein Coll. Medicine; sponsor Grad. Sch. Sci.; bd. dirs. Cardoza Sch. Law at Yeshiva U.; chmn. United Jewish Appeal, Scarsdale, N.Y., 1974-75; mem. pres.'s coun. Meml. Sloan Kettering Cancer Ctr. With AUS, 1945-46. Mem. ABA, Fenway Golf Club, Boca Rio Golf Club, Harmonie Club. Office: 600 Madison Ave New York NY 10022-1615

RUBEN, RICHARD S., lawyer; b. Bklyn., Jan. 21, 1950; BS magna cum laude, U. So. Calif., 1972; JD, UCLA, 1975. Bar: Calif. 1975. Ptnr. Pillsbury Winthrop Shaw Pittman LLP, Costa Mesa, Calif., mem. mng. bd., 1999—2003, ptnr. Litigation practice, sr. So. Calif. trial atty., 2005—. Adj. prof. Whittier Coll. Law Sch. Mem.: Order of the Coif. Office: Pillsbury Winthrop Shaw Pittman 7th Fl 650 Town Center Dr Costa Mesa CA 92626 Office Phone: 714-436-6800. Office Fax: 714-436-2800. Business E-Mail: richard.ruben@pillsburylaw.com.

RUBEN, ROBERT JOEL, pediatric otorhinolaryngologist, educator; b. NYC, Aug. 2, 1933; s. Julian Carl and Sadie (Weiss) R.; children: Ann, Emily, Karin, Arthur. AB, Princeton U., 1955; MD, Johns Hopkins U., 1959. Intern Johns Hopkins Hosp., Balt., 1959-60, resident, 1960-64, dir. neurophysiology lab., div. otolaryngology, 1958-64; practice specializing in pediatric otorhinolaryngology NYC, 1964—; asst. prof. otorhinolaryngology N.Y. U. Sch. Medicine, 1966-68; mem. staff hosps. Montefiore Med. Ctr., Bronx Med. Hosp. Ctr., N. Cen. Bronx Hosp., Montefiore Med., Jacobi Hosp., Bronx, NY, Children's Hosp. at Montefiore; prof., chmn. Montefiore Med. Ctr., Bronx Mcpl. Hosp. Ctr., N. Cen. Bronx, Bronx, 1979-99, prof., 1999—; prof. pediatrics Albert Einstein Coll. Medicine, Bronx, 1983—, assoc. prof. otorhinolaryngology NYC, 1968-70, prof., chmn. dept. otolaryngology, 1970-98, prof. dept. otolaryngology, 1970—, chmn. emeritus dept. otolaryngology, 1998—, disting. univ. prof., 1998—; prof. pediatrics Albert Einstein Coll. Medicine and Montefiore Med. Ctr., 1983—. Chmn. Nat. Com. for Rsch. and Neurol. and Communicative Disorders, pres., 1982-84; bd. dirs. Am. Bd. Otolaryngology-Head and Neck Surgery, 1989—; chmn. ENT devices com. FDA, 1993-96. Editor-in-chief: Internat. Jour. Pediatric Otorhinolaryngology, 1979—. Bd. dirs. N.Y. League Hard of Hearing, 1969-75, 76-85, Ctr. for Book Arts, 2006—, Ctr. for Book Arts, 2006—; bd. dirs. Friends of Princeton U. Libr., chair, 2001-05; chairperson Friends of Princeton U. Libr., 2002-06. Served to surgeon USPHS, 1964-66. Recipient Rsch. award Am. Acad. Ophthalmology and Otolaryngology, 1962, Edmund Prince Fowler award Am. Rhinological-Laryngological-Otological Assn., 1973, Gold medal Best Didactic Film, IX World Congress Otorhinolaryngology, 1977, Pres.'s award Am. Acad. Otolaryngology-Head and Neck Surgery, 1992, Johns Hopkins U. Soc. of Scholars, 1993, George E. Schambaugh Otology prize, 1996, Merit award Am. Otological, 2004, Sylvian Tchg. award, Senta, 2005, Presdl. citation Trio, 2005. Fellow ACS, N.Y. Acad. Medicine; mem. AMA, Am. Assn. Anatomists, Audiology Study Group N.Y. (pres. 1964-66), Acoustical Soc. Am., Am. Acad. Ophthalmology and Otolaryngology, Soc. Univ. Otolaryngologists, Am. Otol. Soc. (sec.-treas. rsch. fund 1979—, award of merit 2004), Soc. for Ear, Nose and Throat Advances in Children (pres. 1973), Assn. for Rsch. in Otolaryngology (pres. 1985-86), Am. Acad. Pediat. (chmn. otol. bronchoesphology 1983-85), Am. Soc. Pediat. Otolaryngology (historian 1986-95), Am. Soc. Pediat. Otolaryngologists (historian 1986-93, pres.-elect 1993-94, pres. 1994-95), Internat. Fedn. Otolaryngic Socs. (chmn. com. on pediat. otolaryngology 2004-), Nat. Inst. Deafness and Other Comm. Disorders (adv. coun. 1989-93), Am. Laryngol. Soc., Grolier Club (mem. coun. 2005-). Home: 1025 5th Ave Apt 12C S New York NY 10028-0134 Office: Montefiore Med Ctr 111 E 210th St Bronx NY 10467-2401 Home Phone: 212-734-5368. E-mail: ruben@aecom.yu.edu.

RUBEN, ROBERT JOSEPH, lawyer; b. NYC, Apr. 9, 1923; m. Audrey H. Zweig, Nov. 20, 1949; children: Pamela, James. BS, Columbia U., 1943; MA, Harvard U., 1948; LL.B., Fordham U., 1953. Bar: N.Y. 1954. Exec. trainee Chase Nat. Bank, NYC, 1948-49; economist, 1949-53; assoc. Milbank, Tweed, Hope & Hadley, NYC, 1953-55; assoc., then ptnr. Shea & Gould, NYC, 1955-90; sec. Gen. Battery Corp., Reading, Pa., 1963-73, Fiat Metal Mfg. Co., Inc., Plainview, N.Y., 1961-64, Filtors, Inc., East Northport, N.Y., 1961-64, Trans-Industries, Inc., 1969-2001, dir., 2001—06; asst. sec. Elgin Nat. Industries, 1975-88. Asst. Judge City Ct., Rye, N.Y., 1977-90; arbitrator Nat. Assn. Securities Dealers, 1990—, Pacific Stock Exch., 1992—, Am. Arbitration Assn., 1990—, N.Y. Stock Exch., 1994—. Trustee Rye Hist. Soc.; bd. dirs. Carver Center, Port Chester, N.Y., 1972-90. Served with AUS, 1943-46. Decorated Combat Inf. medal. Mem. ABA, N.Y. State Bar Assn., Assn. Bar of City of N.Y., Harvard Club (N.Y.C.), Harvard-Radcliffe Club So. Calif., Columbia U. Club So. Calif., Beta Gamma Sigma, Zeta Beta Tau. Home: 21285 Amora Mission Viejo CA 92692-4930

RUBENFELD, STANLEY IRWIN, lawyer, director, mediator, arbitrator; b. NYC, Dec. 7, 1930; s. George and Mildred (Rose) R.; children: Lise Susan, Kenneth Michael, Andrew James, Victoria Louise, Alexandria Elizabeth; m. Madeleine Conway, Nov. 5, 2000. BA, Columbia U., 1952, JD, 1956. Bar: N.Y. 1956. Practice law, NYC, 1956—2002, 1965-68; assoc. Shearman & Sterling, 1956-65, ptnr. Paris, 1965-68, NYC, 1968-93, of counsel, 1994—2002. Arbitrator and mediator NASD; mediator U.S. Fed. Ct., IRS Panel, CPR Panel; arbitrator NYSE, Internat. C. of C.; South Shore Music, Inc. Editor-in-chief Columbia Law Rev., 1955-56; contbr. articles to profl. jours. Past pres. Port Washington (N.Y.) Cmty. Chest; former bd. dirs. Residents for a More Beautiful Port Washington. Lt. (j.g.) USNR, 1952-54. Stone scholar, 1951-52, 54-55, 55-56; Rockefeller Found. grantee, 1955 Mem. ABA, N.Y. State Bar Assn. (tax sec., past chmn. fgn. activities com., reorgn. corp.), Assn. Bar City N.Y. (past chmn. com. on recruitment lawyers), Nat. Assn. Law Placement (past bd. dirs., exec. com.), Columbia U. Law Sch. Alumni Assn. (bd. visitors, adviser, past bd. dirs.), Columbia Coll. Alumni Assn., Tax Club (past chmn.), Phi Delta Phi, Tau Epsilon Phi (past pres.). Office Phone: 203-253-1056. Personal E-mail: srubenfeld@optonline.net.

RUBENS, SIDNEY MICHEL, physicist, consultant; b. Spokane, Wash., Mar. 21, 1910; s. Max Zvoln and Jennie Golda (Rubinovich) R.; m. Julienne Rose Fridner, May 11, 1944; 1 child, Deborah Janet. BS, U. Wash., 1934, PhD, 1939. Instr. U. So. Calif., LA, 1939—40; rsch. assoc. UCLA, 1940—41; physicist Naval Ordnance Lab., Washington, 1941—46, Engring. Rsch. Assocs., St. Paul, 1946—52; mgr. physics Univac divsn. Sperry Rand, St. Paul, 1958—61, dir. rsch., 1961-66, staff scientist, 1969—71, dir. spl. projects, 1971—75, cons., 1975—81; tech. advisor Vertimag Sys. Corp., 1981—, Advanced Rsch. Corp., Mpls., 1986—. Lectr. U. Pa., 1960-61; mem. adv. subcom. on instrumentation and data processing NASA, 1967-69; mem. panel on computer tech. NAS, 1969. Author: Amplifier and Memory Devices, 1965; contbg. author: Magnetic Recording—The First Hundred Years, 1999. Hon. fellow U. Minn., 1977—. Fellow IEEE (Magnetic Soc. info. storage award 1987, Millennium medal 2000); mem. AAAS, N.Y. Acad. Scis., Am. Phys. Soc., Am. Geophys. Union, Acad. Applied Sci., Minn. Acad. Sci., Am. Optical Soc., Phi Beta Kappa, Sigma Xi, Pi Mu Esilon. Achievements include patents in magnetic material and devices. Office: Advanced Research Corporation 4459 White Bear Pkwy Saint Paul MN 55110-7626

RUBENSKY, MITCHELL, band director; b. Bronx, Mar. 12, 1954; s. Herman H. and Norma Rubensky. MusB in Percussion, Manhattan Sch. Music, 1978; MusM, Herbert H. Lehman Coll., Bronx, 1984. Dir. music Frank D. Whalen Jr. HS, Bronx, 1982—2001; band dir. Bronx HS of Sci., 2001—. Chmn. student and tchr. programming Frank D. Whalen Jr. HS, 1995—2001. Recipient Prins. Pride of Music award, NYC Bd. Edn., Dist. 11, 1987, Ednl. Svc. award, Assn. Jewish Profls., 2001, Ednl. Leadership award, Jewish Tchrs. Cmty. Chest, 2004. Avocation: antique stereos. Office: Bronx HS Science 75 W 205th St Bronx NY 10468 Office Phone: 718-817-7700 ext. 517. E-mail: mir312@aol.com.

RUBENSTEIN, ALLEN IRA, lawyer; b. NYC, Apr. 1, 1942; BS in Physics, CCNY, 1962; PhD in Physics, MIT, 1967; JD, Boston U., 1974. Bar: N.Y., U.S. Dist. Ct. (so. and ea. dists.) N.Y. 1975, U.S. Ct. Appeals (2d cir.) 1975, U.S. Ct. Appeals (1st and fed. cirs.) 1982, U.S. Supreme Ct. 2000. Physicist Stanford (Calif.) U., 1967-69; fellow Weizmann Inst., Rehovoth, Israel, 1969-71; assoc. Kenyon & Kenyon, NYC, 1974-82; ptnr. Gottlieb, Rackman & Reisman, P.C., NYC, 1982—. Trustee Beth Israel Anshei Emet, Bklyn. 1981—. Recipient Ward medal CCNY, 1962. Mem. ABA, Am. Phys. Soc., Phi Beta Kappa. Office Phone: 212-684-3900. E-mail: arubenstein@grr.com, AllenR@alum.mit.edu.

RUBENSTEIN, ARTHUR HAROLD, academic administrator, dean, internist, educator; b. Johannesburg, Dec. 28, 1937; arrived in U.S., 1967; s. Montague and Isabel (Nathanson) R.; m. Denise Hack, Aug. 19, 1962; children: Jeffrey Lawrence, Errol Charles. MB BCh, U. Witwatersrand, 1960, DSc (hon.) in Medicine, 2002. Diplomate Am. Bd. Internal Medicine. Intern, then resident Johannesburg Gen. Hosp., 1961, 63-65, 66-67; fellow in endocrinology Postgrad. Med. Sch., London, 1965-66; fellow in medicine U. Chgo., 1967-68, from asst. prof. to assoc. prof., 1968-74, prof., 1974-97, Lowell T. Coggeshall prof. med. sci., 1981-97, assoc. chmn. dept. medicine, 1975-81, chmn., 1981-97; attending physician Mitchell Hosp., U. Chgo., 1968-97; dean, Gustave L. Levy disting. prof. Mt. Sinai Sch. Medicine, NYC, 1997—2001; exec. v.p. U. Pa. Health Sys., Phila., 2001—; dean Sch. Medicine U. Pa., Phila., 2001—. Mem. study sect. NIH, 1973-77, Hadassah Med. Adv. Bd., 1986-95, adv. coun. Nat. Inst. Arthritis, Metabolism and Digestive Diseases, 1978-80; chmn. Nat. Diabetes Adv. Bd., 1982, mem., 1981-83. Mem. editl. bd. Diabetes, 1973-77, Endocrinology, 1973-77, Jour. Clin. Investigation, 1976-81, Am. Jour. Medicine, 1978-81, Diabetologia, 1982-86, Diabetes Medicine, 1987-91, Annals of Internal Medicine, 1991-96, Medicine, 1992—; contbr. articles to profl. jours. Mem. Gov.'s Sci. Adv. Coun. State of Ill., 1989-96. Recipient David Rumbough Meml. award Juvenile Diabetes Found., 1978. Master: ACP (John Phillips Meml. award 1995); fellow: NY Acad. Medicine, Royal Coll. Physicians (London), South African Coll. Physicians; mem.: AAAS, Am. Clin. Climatology Assn., Assn. Acad. Health Ctrs. (bd. dirs. 2005—), Assn. Am. Med. Colls. (mem. coun. of deans adminstrv. bd. 2002—), Assn. Profs. Medicine (councillor 1991—94, v.p. 1994—95, pres. 1995—96, Robert Williams award 1997), Inst. Medicine (coun. 1991—96), Residency Rev. Com., Am. Bd. Internal Medicine (bd. govs. 1985—93, exec. com. 1990—93, chmn. 1992—93), Assn. Am. Physicians (treas. 1984—89, councillor 1989—94, v.p. 1994—95, pres. 1995—96), Ctrl. Soc. Clin. Rsch. (v.p. 1988, pres. 1989), Am. Fedn. Clin. Rsch., Endocrine Soc., Brit. Diabetes Assn. (Banting lectr. 1987), Am. Diabetes Assn. (Solomon Berson Meml. lectr. 1985, Eli Lilly award 1973, Banting medal 1983), Am. Soc. for Clin. Investigation. Office: U Penn School Med 295 John Morgan Bldg 3620 Hamilton Walk Philadelphia PA 19104 Business E-Mail: ahrdean@mail.med.upenn.edu.

RUBENSTEIN, ATOOSA BEHNEGAR, former editor-in-chief; b. Tehran, Iran, Jan. 13, 1972; arrived in U.S., 1978; d. Mansoor Behnegar; m. Ari Rubenstein, 1998. BA in Polit. Sci., Barnard Coll., 1993. Fashion asst., assoc. fashion editor, fashion edit to sr. fashion editor Cosmopolitan Mag., 1993—95; founding editor-in-chief CosmoGirl! mag., 1998—2003; editor-in-chief Seventeen Mag., 2003—06.

RUBENSTEIN, BERNARD, orchestra conductor; b. Springfield, Mo., Oct. 30, 1937; s. Milton and Evelyn Marion (Friedman) R.; m. Ann Warren Little, Aug. 28, 1961; children: Tanya, Stefan Alexei. B.Mus. with distinction, Eastman Sch. Music, U. Rochester, 1958; M.Mus., Yale U., 1961. Assoc. prof. conducting, dir. orch. orgns. Northwestern U., Evanston, Ill., 1968-80; music dir. San Juan Symphony, Durango, Colo., 1997—2001, Farmington, N.Mex., 1997—2001, Fargo-Moorhead Symphony, 2003—. Asst. condr. R.I. Philharm. Orch., 1961-62; condr. music dir. Santa Fe Symphony Orch., 1962-64; condr. Greenwood Chamber Orch., Cummington, Mass., 1968-79; asst. condr. Stuttgart Opera, 1966-68; condr., music dir. Music for Youth, Milw., 1970-80; assoc. condr. Cin. Symphony Orch., 1980-86; music dir. Tulsa Philharm., 1984-96, condr. laureate, 1996—; music dir. San Juan Symphony, 1997-2001; guest condr. numerous orchs. including Milw. Symphony Orch., St. Paul Chamber Orch., Guadalajara Symphony Orch., Berlin Radio Orch., Frankfurt Radio Orch., Grant Park

Orch., Chgo., die reihe, Vienna, Austrian Radio Orch., Eastman Philharm., Halle Symphony Orch., E. Ger., Warsaw Philharm., St. Louis Little Symphony, W. German Radio Orch., Palazzo Pitti Orch. Florence, Italy, Frankfurt Opera, Tonkuenstler Orch., Vienna, S.W. German Radio Orch., Baden-Baden, Jerusalem Symphony, Anchorage, Hamilton, Ont., Hartford Conn., L.A. Chamber Orch., Austin (Tex.) Symphony, Am. Composers Orch. N.Y.C., Nat. Opera of Mongolia, Cuban Nat. Symphony, Havana, Orquesta de Oriente, Santiago de Cuba. Winner internat. conducting competition Serate Musicale Fiorentine, 1965; Fulbright scholar, 1964-66; recipient Charles Ditson award Yale U., 1961, Martha Baird Rockefeller award, 1966-68 Mem. Am. Symphony Orch. League, Condrs. Guild. Office: 1070 Governor Dempsey Dr Santa Fe NM 87501-1078 E-mail: baton@ix.netcom.com.

RUBENSTEIN, DAVID AARON, military officer, healthcare administrator; b. Rockville Centre, NY, Nov. 23, 1954; s. Robert R. and Mona Sydney (Feder) R.; m. Patricia Barrier, Mar. 18, 1978; children: Sarah Elizabeth, William Robert. BS in Health Edn., Tex. A & M U., 1977; MHA, Baylor U., 1989; M of Mil. Arts and Sci., Command and Gen. Staff Coll., 1990. Commd. 2d lt. U.S. Army, 1977, advanced through grades to brig. gen., 2006, med. platoon leader 3d inf. div. Germany, 1977—79, ops. officer 3d med. battalion, 1979—80, pers. officer 307th med. battalion Ft. Bragg, NC, 1981—82, co. comdr., 1982—83, mil. instr. Acad. of Health Scis. Ft. Sam Houston, Tex., 1984—87, grad. student, 1987—88, adminstrv. resident William Beaumont Army Med. Ctr. Ft. Bliss, Tex., 1988—89, grad. student Command and Gen. Staff Coll. Ft. Leavenworth, Kans., 1989—90; adminstrv. asst. Office of the Army Surgeon Gen. Army Med. Svc. Corps, Washington, 1990—92; chief coordinated care Army Hosp., Ft. Belvoir, Va., 1992—93; hosp. comdr. 18th Mobile Army Surg. Hosp., Ft. Lewis, Wash., 1994—96; grad. student Army War Coll., Carlisle Barracks, Pa., 1996—97; dep. comdr. Eisenhower Army Med. Ctr., Ft. Gordon, Ga., 1997—99; hosp. comdr. 21st Combat Support Hosp., Ft. Hood, Tex., 1999—2001, Bosnia-Herzegovina, 1999—2000; cmdr. Landstuhl Regional Med. Ctr., Germany, 2001—03; chief of staff Europe Regional Med. Commd., 2003—04; cmdr. 30th Med. Brigade, 2004; asst. surgeon gen., 2005—06; commanding gen. Europe Med. Commd. Pres. Health Orgn. Network, El Paso, Tex., 1989, asst. surgeon gen. force sustainment, 2005; pres. Healthcare Execs. Ctrl. Savannah River Area, 1998-99; participant U.S. Army seminar Baylor U., Ft. Sam Houston, 1989. Author leadership seminar; reviewer books Lehigh U. Press, 1990, Mil. Rev. Jour., Mil. Medicine; contbr. articles to profl. jours. Religious lay leader Office of the Jewish Chapel, Ft. Bragg, 1982-83, Ft. Bliss, 1988-89, Ft. Leavenworth, 1989-90, Bosnia-Herzegovina, 1999-2000; fund drive coord. United Fund, Ft. Leavenworth, 1989; vol. Muscular Dystrophy Assn., Washington, 1990-91. Decorated Legion of Merit; recipient Fed. Healthcare Leadership award, 2003. Fellow: Am. Coll. Healthcare Execs. (Regent's award 1993, regent 2000—02, gov. 2002—, chmn. elect 2007, Fed. Excellence in Healthcare Leadership award, Regent's Healthcare Exec. award); mem.: VFW, Assn. of U.S. Army, Am. Hosp. Assn., Assn. Mil. Surgeons of U.S. (Ray E. Brown 2006). Republican. Jewish. Avocations: flying, running, history, reading. Home Phone: 210-222-1498. Business E-Mail: david.rubenstein@us.army.mil.

RUBENSTEIN, DAVID M., investment company executive; b. Balt., 1949; m. Alice Rogoff; 3 children. BA, Duke U., 1970; JD, U. Chgo., 1973. With Paul, Weiss, Rifkind, Wharton & Garrison, NYC, 1973—75; chief counsel judiciary com. subcom. on constl. amendments U.S. Senate, Washington, 1975—76; dep. asst. to Pres. for domestic policy The White House, 1977—81; with Shaw, Pittman, Potts & Trowbridge (now Pillsbury, Winthrop, Shaw Pittman); co-founder, mng. dir. The Carlyle Group, 1987—. Mem. adv. bd. Stanford Inst. Econ. Policy Rsch.; mem. bus. coun. World Econ. Forum; mem. nat. adv. com. J.P. Morgan Chase. Vice chmn. Lincoln Ctr. Performing Arts; mem. bd. trustees Duke U., John Hopkins U., Meml. Sloan Kettering Cancer Ctr.; mem. vis. com. Kennedy Sch. Govt. Harvard U.; mem. bd. overseers Hoover Instn.; mem. trustees' coun. Nat. Gallery Art; mem. Madison Coun. Libr. Congress, Coun. Nat. Trust for Historic Preservation; mem. dean's coun. Woodrow Wilson Sch. Princeton. Recipient Golden Plate award, Acad. Achievement, 2006. Office: The Carlyle Group 1001 Pennsylvania Ave NW Washington DC 20004-2505 Office Phone: 202-729-5626. Office Fax: 202-347-1818. *

RUBENSTEIN, DONALD P., lawyer; b. New Rochelle, NY, Apr. 6, 1958; BA magna cum laude, U. Pa., 1980; JD, Cornell U., 1985. Bar: Calif. 1985. Assoc. Bronson, Bronson & McKinnon, San Francisco, 1985—92, non-equity ptnr., 1992—93, equity ptnr., 1993—98; ptnr. Crosby Heafey Roach & May (combined with Reed Smith in 2003), San Francisco, 1998—2003, Reed Smith LLP, San Francisco, 2003—, No. Calif. practice group leader litig. group. Mem.: ABA, Bar Assn. San Francisco, State Bar Calif. Office: Reed Smith LLP Two Embarcadero Ctr Ste 2000 San Francisco CA 94111 Office Phone: 415-659-5946. Office Fax: 415-391-8269. Business E-Mail: drubenstein@reedsmith.com.

RUBENSTEIN, EDWARD, physician, educator; b. Cin., Dec. 5, 1924; s. Louis and Nettie Rubenstein; m. Nancy Ellen Millman, June 20, 1954; children: John, William, James. MD, U. Cin., 1947. House staff Cin. Gen. Hosp., 1947—50; fellow May Inst., Cin., 1950; sr. asst. resident Ward Med. Svc., Barnes Hosp., St. Louis, 1953—54; chief of medicine San Mateo County Hosp., Calif., 1960—70; assoc. dean postgrad. med. edn., prof. medicine Stanford (Calif.) U., 1971—, emeritus, active. Faculty Stanford Photon Rsch. Lab.; affiliated faculty Stanford Synchrotron Radiation Lab., 1971—; maj. materials facilities com. NRC, 1984—85, Nat. Steering Com. 6 GeV Electron Storage Ring, 1986—. Author (textbook): Intensive Medical Care; editor: Synchrotron Radiation Handbook, 1988, vol. 4, 1991, Synchrotron Radiation in the Biosciences, Molecular Medicine; mem. editorial bd.: Sci. Am., Inc., 1991—94; editor (textbook): Sci. Am. Medicine, 1978—94; editor: (series) Molecular Cardiovascular Disease, 1995, Molecular Oncology, 1996, Molecular Neuroscience, 1998. With USAF, 1950—52. Named Disting. Scientist, SvrroMed, Inc., 2003; recipient Kaiser award for outstanding and innovative contbns. to med. edn., 1989, Albion Walter Hewlett award, 1993. Master: ACP (Laureate 2002); fellow: AAAS, Royal Soc. Medicine; mem.: Am. Clin. and Climatol. Assn., Soc. Photo-Optical Engrs., Western Assn. Physicians, Calif. Acad. Medicine, Inst. Medicine, APS, Alpha Omega Alpha. Achievements include research in mechanisms of autoimmunity, dysfunction of the choroid plexus and cerebrospinal fluid circulatory system, synchrotron radiation, nonprotein amino acids, autoimmunity, and molecular chirality. Office: Stanford Med Ctr Dept Medicine Stanford CA 94305

RUBENSTEIN, HOWARD JOSEPH, public relations executive; b. NYC, Feb. 3, 1932; s. Samuel and Ada (Sall) R.; m. Amy Forman, Dec. 17, 1959; children: Roni, Richard, Steven. AB, U. Pa., 1953; student law, Harvard, 1953; LL.B. (Dean's scholar), St. Johns Sch. Law, 1959, LLD (hon.), 1990. Bar: NY 1960. Pres. Rubenstein Assocs., Inc. pub. rels. cons., NYC, 1954—; asst. counsel judiciary com. U.S. Ho. of Reps., 1960; cons. U.S. Fgn. Claims Commn., 1961-62; cons. joint legis. com. child care needs NY, 1965-66; adviser SBA, 1965-66. Mem. Gov.'s Com. on Sale of World Trade Ctr., 1981, Mayor's Com. on Holocaust Commemoration, 1981—, NY State Task Force on Energy Conservation, Dept. Housing, 1981-83, Mayor's Coun. Econ. Bus. Advisors, 1991-93; co-chmn. Holocaust Commn., 1993—; v.p. Jewish Cmty. Rels. Coun., 1988-94, advisor, 1995—; past dir. Brownsville Boys Club; bd. dirs. Provide Addict Care Today, Police Athletic League, NY chpt. March of Dimes; active U.S. Internat. Coun., 1977-81, Commn. on Status of Women, 1982-89, NYC Commn. Operation Welcom Home, 1991; mem. Mayor's Bus. Adv. Coun., 1996—; advisor NY Commn. on Status of Women, 1995—; comm. advisor Gov.'s Com. Jerusalem 3000, 1996-01; bd. dirs. Albert Einstein Coll. Medicine, 1997—; bd. govs. Jewish Cmty. Rels. Coun., 1999—; exec. com. Real Estate Bd. NY, 1985—, NYC & Co., 2001—, Partnership for NYC, 2004—. Mem. Assn. Better N.Y. (mem. exec. com. 1972—), Phi Beta Kappa, Beta Sigma Rho. Jewish (dir. congregation). Home: 993 5th Ave New York NY 10028-0105 Office: Rubenstein Assoc Inc 1345 Avenue Of The Americas New York NY 10105-0302 Home Phone: 212-744-6333; Office Phone: 212-843-8080.

RUBENSTEIN, HOWARD S., physician, writer; b. Chgo., June 14, 1931; s. Sidney Howard and Selma Moldofsky Rubenstein; m. Judith Ann Selig, May 26, 1968; children: Emily Rubenstein Engel, Adam Selig, Jennifer Rubenstein Zigun, John Stephen. BA, Carleton Coll., Northfield, Minn., 1953; MD, Harvard U., Boston, 1957. Intern and resident Los Angeles County Gen. Hosp., LA, 1957—60; rsch. fellow Harvard Med. Sch., Boston, 1960—64, rsch. assoc., 1964—68; physician, chief of allergy Harvard U. Health Svcs., Cambridge, Mass., 1968—89; med. cons. State of Calif., Dept. Social Svcs., Disability Program, San Diego, 1989—2000. Physician Albert Schweitzer Hosp., Deschapelles, Haiti, 1964. Author: (epic in free verse) Maccabee, 2004, (plays) Brothers All, 2006, The Golem, Man of Earth, 2007; translator: Agamemnon: A Play by Aeschylus with Reconstructed Stage Directions, 1998, 2003, The Trojan Women: A Play by Euripides, 2002; contbr. articles to profl. jours. Fellow, US Pub. Health Svc., 1960—62; Harold C. Ernst fellow, Harvard Med. Sch., 1962—64. Mem.: Sigma Xi, Phi Beta Kappa (life). Jewish. Home: 8677 Villa La Jolla Dr # 1114 La Jolla CA 92037 Office Phone: 619-804-5926. Home Fax: 858-546-0406. Personal E-mail: hsrubenstein@yahoo.com.

RUBENSTEIN, JEROME MAX, lawyer; b. St. Louis, Feb. 16, 1927; s. Jacob J. and Anne (Frankel) R.; m. Judith Hope Grand, July 31, 1954; children— Edward J., Emily Rubenstein Muslin, Daniel H. AB, Harvard U., 1950, LLB, 1955. Bar: Mo. 1956, U.S. Dist. Ct. (ea. dist.) Mo. 1956, U.S. Ct. Appeals (8th cir.) 1956. Mem. English lit. faculty U. So. Philippines, Cebu, 1950-51; law clk U.S. Dist. Ct., St. Louis, 1955-56; assoc. Lewis, Rice, Tucker, Allen & Chubb, St. Louis, 1956-64, Grand, Peper & Martin, St. Louis, 1964-65, ptnr., 1965-66; jr. ptnr. Bryan Cave, St. Louis, 1966-67, ptnr., 1968-97, of counsel, 1998—. Dir. Commerce Bank, N.A. Bd. dirs. Independence Ctr., St. Louis, 1985-88, The Arts and Edn. Coun. Greater St. Louis, 1991-99. Served with USN, 1945-46. Bd. dirs. Independence Ctr., St. Louis, 1985. Served with USN, 1945-46 Mem. ABA, Mo. Bar Assn., St. Louis Bar Assn., Mo. Athletic Club, Harvard Club of St. Louis (pres. 1982-83, bd. dirs. 1983-90). Jewish. Avocations: jogging, tennis. Home: 7394 Westmoreland Dr Saint Louis MO 63130-4240 Office: Bryan Cave 1 Metropolitan Sq Ste 3600 Saint Louis MO 63102-2750

RUBENSTEIN, JOSHUA SETH, lawyer; b. Bklyn., Aug. 5, 1954; s. Seth and Elaine (Freedman) Rubenstein; children: Mary-Jane, Kenan, Rebecca, Marlena, Isaac. BA magna cum laude, Columbia U., 1976, JD, 1979. Bar: NY 1980, NJ 1980, US Dist. Ct. (ea. and so. dist.) NY 1980, US Dist. Ct. NJ 1980, US Tax Ct. 1986. Assoc. Fried, Frank, Harris, Shriver & Jacobson, NYC, 1979—82, KMZ Rosenman LLP, 1982—88; ptnr. KMZ Rosenman LLP (now Katten, Muchin Rosenman, LLP), 1989—, mem. mgmt. com., 1994—98, chmn., 1998—2002, chmn. trusts and estates dept., 1995—; mng. ptnr. Katten Muchin Rosenman LLP, NYC, 2002—, Charlotte, NC, 2002. Mem. adv. com. surrogate's ct. Office Ct. Adminstrn., 1997—; mem. adv. coun. Law Sch. Trusts, Wills and Estate Planning Columbia U., 1997—; lectr. in field. Author: Answer Guide New York Surrogate's Court, 2004; contbr. articles to legal publ. Dir., sec. Irvington Inst. Med. Rsch., 1991, treas., 1991—92, sec., 1992—93, co-pres., 1993—94, pres., 1994—2000, vice-chmn., 2000—; mem. legis. com., mem. devel. com., mem. bd. governance com., mem. Madeleine Borg com., chmn., mem. exec. com., 1994—; mem. profl. adv. com. Lincoln Ctr., NY Philharm., Mus. Modern Art, Met. Mus. Art, Columbia U., Columbia U. Law Sch., Mus. Art and Design; chmn. estates and trust splty. group, chmn. splty. group task force, mem. exec. com. lawyers divsn. United Jewish Appeal-Fedn., 1989—99; trustee Jewish Bd. Family and Children's Svc., 1991, v.p., 1998—. Named Best Lawyers in NY, NY Mag.; named one of Top 100 Attys., Worth mag., 2005; recipient James H. Fogelson award, Lawyer's divsn. United Jewish Appeal Fedn., 1993, Trusts and Estate Lawyers award, 2001. Fellow: NY State Bar Found. (regent), Am. Coll. Trusts and Estate Counsel (mem. state laws com.); mem.: ABA, Soc. Trust and Estate Practitioners, Internat. Acad. Estate and Trust Law (academician 1997—), Assn. Bar City of NY, NJ Bar Assn. (real property and probate sect., mem. adv. com. rels. legis. and exec. brs.), NY State Bar Assn. (vice chmn. legis. com. 1988, chmn. 1988—91, co-chmn. ad hoc com. rev. proposals EPTL adv. com. N.Y. State 1991—, mem.-at-large exec. com. 1992—95, liaison to legis. policy com. 1995—, treas. 1997—98, sec. 1998—99, chair elect 1999—, chair 2000—01, trust and estate law sect., Pres.'s Pro Bono Svc. award 1991, Exec. Com. award 1992, 1995, 1996), Practising Law Inst. (mem. estate adv. com., lectr. 1984—, Hadassah estate planning seminar faculty and adv. bd. 1993—), Phi Beta Kappa. Democrat. Jewish. Office: Katten Muchin Rosenman LLP 575 Madison Ave New York NY 10022-2511 Office Phone: 212-940-7150. Business E-Mail: joshua.rubenstein@kattenlaw.com.

RUBENSTEIN, LAURIE R., lawyer; b. Bklyn. BA, Cornell U.; JD, Yale U. Chief counsel, Com. Homeland Security and Govtl. Affairs Com. US Senate. Office: Committee on Homeland Security and Govt Affairs 340 Dirksen Senate Office Bldg Washington DC 20510

RUBENSTEIN, LEONARD, engineering company executive; b. NYC, June 18, 1931; s. William and Sylvia (Jaffe) R.; m. Reva Scharf, Jan. 1951 (div. 1960); m. Geraldine Marilyn Porper, Aug. 14, 1965 (dec. Sept. 2000); children: Alan, Elaine, Philip, Ruth, Jennie. BS in Physics, Poly. Inst. N.Y., 1964. Registered profl. engr. NY, NJ, Del., Ga. Equipment engr. We. Elec., NYC, 1957-66; elec. engr. Gibbs & Hill, NYC, 1966-69; chief engr. Kiegl Lighting, NYC, 1969-72; project mgr. Stone & Webster, NYC, 1972-87; pres., prin. Rubenstein Engring. PC, NYC, 1975—; v.p. engring. Laramore Douglas & Popham, NYC, 1988-90; v.p., dir. engring. Gibbs & Hill, NYC, 1990-92; pres., prin. David Internat., 1990—; markter NPS, Florham Pk., NJ, 1992-95. Devel., pipeline project, Costanza, Romania, Trieste, Italy. Contbr. articles to profl. publs. Chmn. Walt Whitman Ind. Dems., Bklyn., 1966-68, chmn. West Bklyn. Ind. Dems., 1964-66; bd. dir. NY Gilbert & Sullivan Players, NYC, 1993—; chmn., bd. dirs. 450 West End Corp, 1984-88; mem. bd. mgr. McBurney YMCA, 1988-97. With US Army, 1951-53. Mem. IEEE (sr., chmn. NY sect. 1995-96, asst. editor Today's Engr. 1997-98, Region I award 1985, 94, 96), NSPE, Soc. Mfg. Engr. (charter mem. Vision Soc., sr. mem. Robotics Internat.), Power Engring. Soc. (chmn. NY/LI chpt. 1984-85). Achievements include development, construction and installation of first large scale waterless power plant; design of first commercial power plant using air stored in salt mines. Avocations: handball, music. Home and Office: 8 W 65th St New York NY 10023 E-mail: repl@nyc.rr.com.

RUBENSTEIN, PAMELA SILVER, manufacturing executive; b. Lansing, Mich., May 12, 1953; d. Neil M. and Leah Rebecca (Coffman) Silver; m. Alec Robert Rubenstein. BA in Linguistics, U. Mich., 1974; MA in teaching English to spkrs. of other langs., Columbia U. Tchrs. Coll., 1976; MA in Linguistics, U. Ill., 1978, doctoral studies in linguistics, 1978-80. Instr. Columbia U. Tchrs. Coll., NYC, 1976, U. Ill., Urbana, 1978, libr. Linguistic Dept., 1978-79; asst. libr. Ill. State Geol. Survey, 1979-80; tchr. Congregation Temple Israel, Springfield, Ill., 1980-81; adminstr., tchr. Springfield Bd. Jewish Edn., 1981-82; instr. Comm. Divsn. Lincoln Land C.C., Springfield, 1981-82; tchr. Cmty. Hebrew Sch., Charleston, SC, 1982-83; instr. The Citadel and Coll. of Charleston, 1983; legal sec. Gibbs & Holmes, Charleston, 1984, May, Oberfell & Lorber, South Bend, Ind., 1984-88; instr. U. Notre Dame, Ind., 1987; tchr. Triton Sch. Corp., Bourbon, Ind., 1988-89; v.p., asst. treas. Allied Splty. Precision, Inc., Mishawaka, Ind., 1989—2005, CEO, owner, 2005—. Contbr. articles to profl. jours. Mem. Temple Beth-El Sisterhood, South Bend, Ind., 1987—. Mem.: Nat. Tooling and Machining Assn. (mem. edn. team, audit team 2005—, bd. mem., Mich. chpt. 2004—), Hadassah (life). Office: Allied Splty Precision Inc 815 E Lowell Ave Mishawaka IN 46545-6480 Office Phone: 574-255-4718. Business E-Mail: pam.rubenstein@aspi-nc.com.

RUBENSTEIN, PAUL D., lawyer; b. LA, Apr. 7, 1946; BA, UCLA, 1967; JD, Harvard U., 1970. Bar: Calif. 1971. Mem. Proskauer, Rose, Goetz & Mendelsohn; pvt. practice Santa Monica, Calif. Office: 1620 26th St Ste 2068N Santa Monica CA 90404 Office Phone: 310-586-3209. Office Fax: 310-586-3233.

RUBENSTEIN, SANFORD MARVIN, English professor, poet; b. Bklyn., Dec. 5, 1945; s. David Rubenstein and Estelle Blumstein; m. Marcia Kornbrodt Rubenstein, Dec. 22, 1968; 1 child, Paul. BA in English, Long Island U., Southampton, 1969. English tchr. Westhampton Beach HS, NY, 1970—72; office/sales mgr. Redtree Housewares Corp., NYC, 1974—85; nat. sales mgr. LaVie, Internat., NYC, 1985—90; office mgr. C&M Direct Mail Systems, Staten Island, NY, 1990—2000; instr. gen. edn. Drake Bus. Sch., Staten Island, 1996—2004; adj. prof. English Katharine Gibbs Sch., NYC, 2004—. Author: (poetry) Reining Words, 2005, Unleashed Letters, 2006. Asst. scout master Boy Scouts Am., 1980—85. Mem.: Nat. Trust Hist. Preservation, Nat. Pks. Conservation Assn. Avocations: reading, cooking, travel, fishing. Office: Katharine Gibbs Sch 232 W 40th St New York NY 10018 Personal E-mail: srubenstein1@verizon.net.

RUBENSTEIN, STEVEN PAUL, newspaper columnist; b. LA, Oct. 31, 1951; s. Victor Gerald and Florence (Fox) R.; m. Caroline Moira Grannan, Jan. 1, 1989; children: William Laurence, Anna Katherine. BA, U. Calif., Berkeley, 1977. Reporter L.A. Herald Examiner, 1974-76, San Francisco Chronicle, 1976-81, columnist, 1981—. Office: San Francisco Chronicle 901 Mission St San Francisco CA 94103-2905

RUBENSTEIN, WILLIAM S., lawyer; b. NYC, 1955; BA, Fairleigh Dickinson U., 1978; JD cum laude, Benjamin N. Cardozo Sch. Law, 1981. Bar: NY 1981. Co-head, banking/savings and loans mergers and aquisitions Skadden, Arps, Slate, Meagher & Flom LLP, NYC. Notes and comment editor: Cardozo Law Rev., 1981. Office: Skadden Arps Slate Meagher & Flom LLP 4 Times Sq New York NY 10036 Office Phone: 212-735-2642. Office Fax: 212-735-2000. Business E-Mail: wrubenst@skadden.com.

RUBERG, ROBERT LIONEL, surgery educator; b. Phila., July 22, 1941; s. Norman and Yetta (Wolfman) R.; m. Cynthia Lief, June 26, 1966; children: Frederick, Mark, Joshua. BA, Haverford Coll., Pa., 1963; MD, Harvard U., 1967. Diplomate Am. Bd. Surgery, Am. Bd. Plastic Surgery. Instr. surgery U. Pa., Phila., 1972-75; asst. prof. Ohio State U., Columbus, 1975-81, assoc. prof., 1981-88, prof., 1988—. Bd. dirs. Am. Bd. Plastic Surgery, 1991-97, vice-chair, 1996-97; chmn. curriculum com. Coll. Medicine, Ohio State U., 1984-97; chief plastic surgery Ohio State U. Hosps., 1985—. Plastic Surgery Ednl. Found. research grantee, 1976, 78. Fellow ACS; mem. Am. Assn. Plastic Surgeons, Assn. Acad. Chairmen of Plastic Surgery (pres. 1994-95), Plastic Surgery Edn. Found. (pres. 2000-01). Avocation: bicycling. Home: 100 Walnut Woods Ct Gahanna OH 43230-6200 Office: N325-B Means Hall 1654 Upham Dr Columbus OH 43210

RUBILLO, JAMES M., educational association administrator; BS, West Chester U.; M, Villanova U.; DSc (hon.), West Chester U., 2004. HS tchr., dept. chair; positions including prof. math., assoc. dean info. systems and svcs. and exec. asst. to pres. for planning assessment and rsch. Bucks County CC, Newtown, Pa.; interim exec. dir. Nat. Coun. Tchrs. Math., Reston, Va., 1997—98, exec. dir., 2001—. Adj. faculty mem. DeSales U. Grad. Sch., Widener U. Grad. Sch. Office: Nat Assn Tchrs Math 1906 Association Dr Reston VA 20191-1502 Office Phone: 703-620-9840. Office Fax: 703-476-2970. E-mail: jrubillo@nctm.org. *

RUBIN, ALAN A., pharmaceutical and biotechnology consultant; b. NYC, July 10, 1926; s. Harry and Gertrude R.; m. Helen M. Feinstein; children: Jeffrey, Ronald, Howard. BS, NYU, 1950, MS, 1953, PhD, 1959. Pharmacologist Schering Corp., Bloomfield, N.J., 1954-64; dir. pharmacology Endo Labs., Garden City, N.Y., 1964-70, v.p. rsch., 1970-74; dir. rsch. DuPont Pharms., Wilmington, Del., 1974-82, dir. sci. info. and tech., 1982-87; dir. licensing tech. DuPont Merck Pharms., Wilmington, Del., 1987-91; pres. ARA Assoc., Rockland, Del., 1991—. Bd. dirs. Redox Pharms., Greenvale, N.Y. Editor: Search for New Drugs, 1972, New Drugs: Discovery and Development, 1978; contbr. articles to profl. jours. With U.S. Army, 1944-46. Mem. AAAS, Am. Soc. Pharmacology and Exptl. Therapeutics, Soc. Exptl. and Biol. Medicine, N.Y. Acad. Sci. Home: 207 Hitching Post Dr Wilmington DE 19803-1914 Office: ARA Assoc PO Box 244 Rockland DE 19732-0244 Personal E-mail: alannar@msn.com.

RUBIN, ALBERT LOUIS, internist, nephrologist, educator; b. Memphis, May 9, 1927; s. Malcolm M. and Sarah Anne (Bryan) R.; m. Carolyn M. Diehl, Sept. 28, 1953; 1 child, Marc. Student, Williams College, 1944-45, MIT, 1945-46; MD, Cornell U., 1950. Diplomate Am. Bd. Internal Medicine. Intern Bellevue Hosp., NYC, 1950-51, resident internal medicine, 1951-54, fellow nephrology, 1954-55, physician-in-charge, 1953-61; established investigator Am. Heart Assn., NYC, 1958-63; dir. Rogosin Labs., Cornell U. Med. Coll., NYC, 1963—, The Rogosin Kidney Ctr., NYC, 1971—, The Rogosin Inst., NYC, 1983—; prof. biochemistry, surgery, medicine Cornell U. Med. Coll., NYC, 1969—; surgeon The N.Y. Hosp., NYC, 1969—. Com. on sci. and tech. aspects of processing materials in space NRC, NYC; dir. affiliations and patient referrals N.Y. Hosp.-Cornell Med. Ctr., 1977-80; bd. dirs., bd. incorporators neuroscis. rsch. program MIT. Author: Physical Diagnosis: A Textbook and Workbook in Methods of Clinical Examination, 1972, Humoral Aspects of Transplantation, 1976, Manual of Clinical Nephrology, 1980; cons. editor Am. Jour. Medicine, Time mag., 1959-94. With USN, 1944-45. Recipient Hoeing award Nat. Kidney Found., 1982. Mem. ACP, AAAS, Am. Soc. for Artificial Internal Organs, Transplantation Soc., Sigma Xi. Home: 220 Allison Ct Englewood NJ 07631-4301 Office: The Rogosin Inst 505 E 70th St 2d Fl Rm 230 New York NY 10021-9809 Business E-Mail: rubina@mail.rockefeller.edu.

RUBIN, ARKADY, biostatistics and data management researcher, executive; b. St. Petersburg, Russia, Jan. 29, 1955; s. Mikhail Rubin and Mikhalina Rubina. BS in econ., Inst. of Nat. Economy, 1972—76, PhD, 1983—86. Prin. biostatistician Johnson & Johnson, Raritan, NJ, 1991—98; assoc. dir., biostatistics Pfizer, NYC, 1998—2003; exec. dir., biostatistics and data mgmt. NovaDel Pharma, Flemington, NJ, 2003—. Contbr. articles to profl. jours. Recipient Corp. award for the design of the low dose contraceptive clin. program, Johnson & Johnson, 1997. Mem.: Am. Statis. Assn. Achievements include design of clinical program for the contraceptive patch currently marketed as Evra; clinical program Norvasc/Lipitor combination pill (trade name Caduet); clinical program for the low-dose oral contraceptive currently marketed as Ortho Tri-Cyclen Lo; patents for Ortho Tri-Cyclen Lo. Office: NovaDel Pharma 25 Minneakoning Rd Flemington NJ 08822 Home: 964 Concord Way Branchburg NJ 08853-4173 E-mail: arubin@novadel.com.

RUBIN, ARTHUR HERMAN, retired academic administrator; b. NYC, Aug. 14, 1927; s. Samuel and Bessie (Moritt) R.; m. Janice Levy, Apr. 9, 1950 (div. 1965); children: Renee Ellen, Linda Joy; m. Audrey M. Schmidt, July 1, 1973. BS, NYU, 1950, MA, 1951. Adminstrv. asst. to asst. dean Sch. Edn. NYU, 1947-54, lab. asst. bus. edn. dept., 1950-54, instr., 1954-56, program dir. grad. students orgn., 1954-63, dir. tours, 1955-58, coord. summer sessions activities, 1959-64, dir. Bur. Pub. Occasions, 1963-74, asst. v.p. pub. occasions, 1974-75, dir. extramural affairs Coll. Dentistry, 1976, assoc. dean adminstrn., 1976-80, adj. asst. prof. behavioral scis. and cmty. health, 1976-80, dir. alumni rels. Sch. of Med., 1980-95, dir. spl. events med. ctr., 1988-95; cons. to Office Alumni Rels. NYU Sch. Medicine, 1995-2000; cons. to Office Spl. Events, NYU Med. Ctr., 1995-2000, ret., 2000. Tchr. Patrick Henry Jr. High Sch., N.Y.C., 1949-58; acting asst. prin. Robert F. Wagner Jr. High Sch., N.Y.C., 1958-63; cons. in field. Trustee Agnew Found., 1967—; mem. Great Valley coun. Girl Scouts U.S., 2005—07; mem. exec. bd., sec. Harris York Condominium Assn., 1998—99, mem. exec. bd., treas., chmn. coms., 2001—. Recipient NYU Presdl. citation, 1971, GSO award, 1980, Ernest O. Melby award Sch. Edn. Alumni Assn., 1976, citation Bus. Edn. Assn. Met. N.Y., 1976, Sesquicentennial award NYU Alumni Fedn., 1982, Meritorious Svc. award, 1985, dir. Emeritus citation, 1992. Mem. Ea. Bus. Tchrs. Assn. (chmn. exhibits 1953-74, exec. bd. 1969-71, pres. 1972-73, award 1974), Bus. Edn. Assn. Met. N.Y. (exec. bd. 1962-83), Nat. Bus. Edn. Assn. (exec. bd. 1972-74, conv. mgr. 1974-92, Disting. Svc. award 1992, Cert. of Appreciation 1992), N.Y. Acad. Pub. Edn. (bd. dirs. 1979-98, pres. 1992-94), NYU Edn. Alumni Assn. (v.p. 1961-62, 64-67), NYU Club (bd. govs. 1972-78, 79-89, v.p. 1983-86, chmn. bd. 1986-87), Delta Pi Epsilon Rsch. Found. Inc. (bd. dirs. 1990-92), Delta Pi Epsilon (Svc. awards Alpha chpt. 1971, 81). Home: 2605 Houghton Lean Macungie PA 18062-9506

RUBIN, ARTHUR LEONARD, systems engineer, mathematician; s. Herman and Jean Estelle Rubin; m. Ronni Petitt, July 10, 1987. PhD, Calif. Inst. of Tech., 1978. Programmer Purdue U. Computer Ctr., West Lafayette, Ind., 1971—72; sr. engr. Jet Propulsion Lab., Pasadena, Calif., 1973—82; sr. mem. tech. staff Aerojet ElectroSystems, Azusa, Calif., 1982—86; programmer cons. Fin. News Network, Los Angeles, 1987—90; contract programmer IdealSoft, Alhambra, Calif., 1987—89; engring. specialist - software Beckman Instruments, Brea, Calif., 1990—95; rsch. engr., sr. staff Lockheed Martin, Goodyear, Ariz., 1996—2000; prin. sys. engr. Raytheon, Fullerton, Calif., 2000—. Contbr. scientific papers. Recipient 4th Pl., USA H.S. Math. Olympiad, 1972; Putnam fellow, 1970—73. Mem.: IEEE, Math. Assn. of Am., Mensa (life; area sec. 1976—78). Libertarian. Jewish. Achievements include patents for methods and apparatus for evaluating operational integrity of a data processing system using moment bounding. Avocation: filksinging (science fiction folksinging). Office: Raytheon 1801 Hughes Dr Fullerton CA 92833 Home Phone: 714-672-0064; Office Phone: 714-446-4218. Personal E-mail: ronnirubin@sprintmail.com.

RUBIN, AVIEL DAVID, computer science educator, writer; b. Manhattan, Kans., Nov. 8, 1967; BS in Computer Sci. (hon.), U. Mich., Ann Arbor, 1989, MSE in Computer Sci., Engring., 1991, PhD in Computer Sci., Engring., 1994. Tchg. asst. U. Mich., 1988—93; programmer, Meyers Corners Lab IBM, Poughkeepsie, NY, 1989; programmer Great Lakes Software Co., Howell, Mich., 1989; mem., cryptography and network security rsch. group Bellcore, 1990; adj. prof. NYU, 1995—99; mem., secure systems rsch. dept. AT&T Labs-Rsch., 1997—2002; assoc. prof., dept. computer sci. John Hopkins U., 2003—04, prof., dept. computer sci., 2004—; tech. dir. John Hopkins U. Info. Security Inst., 2003—. Vis. prof. École Normale Supérieure, Paris, 1999; bd. dir. USENIX Orgn., 2000—04; mem. AT&T Internet Intellectual Property Review, 1999—2001, Govt. Infosec Sci. and Tech. Study Group on Malicious Code, 1999—2000, DARPA Info. Sci. and Tech. Study Group, 2003—06, Security Peer Review Group of the Fed. Voting Assistance Program's Secure Electronic Registration and Voting Experiment Project, 2003—04; mem. steering group ISOC Symposium on Network and Distributed System Security, 2001—04; mem. adv. bd. Info. Security and Cryptography Book Series, 2001—06; mem. exec. com. DIMACS workshop series with spl. focus on network security, 2002—04; mem. technical adv. boards, including Tablus, Site Advisor, Neopath Networks, Hx Technologies, Fortify Software, Bodymedia, Authentica and Arbor Networks; invited spkr. in field; panelist in field. Author: (books) White-hat Security Arsenal, 2001, Brave New Ballot: The Battle to Safeguard Democracy in the Age of Electronic Voting, 2006; co-author: Web Security Sourcebook, 1997, Peer-to-Peer, 2001, Firewalls and Internet Security: Repelling the Wily Hacker, 2nd edit., 2003; contbr. chapters to books, articles to profl. jours.; refereed conf. and jour. publs., mem. editl. bd. Bellcore Security Update Newsletter, 1995—96, Jour. of Privacy Tech., 2004—06, co-editor Electronic Newletter of the IEEE Technical Com. on Security & Privacy, 1998, assoc. editor Electronic Commerce Rsch. Jour., 1999—2002, Assn. for Computing Machinery Transactions on Internet Tech., 2002—05, IEEE Security & Privacy Mag., 2003—, IEEE Transactions on Software Engring., 2005—06, guest editor Communications of the Assn. for Computing Machinery, Spl. Issue on Wireless Networking Security, 2003, guest co-editor IEEE Security & Privacy Mag., Spl. Issue on Electronic Voting Security, 2004, IEEE Computer, Securing the High-Speed Internet, 2004, mem. editl. and adv. bds. Internat. Jour. Info. and Computer Security, 2004—06. Election judge, Baltimore County; dir. ACCURATE, A Ctr. for Correct, Usable, Reliable, Auditable and Transparent Elections, funded by Nat. Sci. Found. Co-recipient Co-author of Best Student Paper, Building Systems that Flexibly Control Downloaded Executable Content, 6th USENIX UNIX Security Symposium, 1996, Best Paper award & Best Student Paper award, The Design and Analysis of Graphical Passwords, 8th USENIX Security Symposium, 1999, Best Paper award, A Robust, Tamper-Evident and Censorship-Resistant Web Publishing System, 9th USENIX Security Symposium, 2000, Best Student Paper award, Security Analysis of a Cryptographically-Enabled RFID Device, 14th USENIX Security Symposium, 2005; named Baltimorean of Yr., Baltimore Mag., 2004; recipient Index on Censorship Freedom of Expression award for the Best Circumvention of Censorship for the Publius project, 2001, Pioneer award, Electronic Frontiers Found., 2004. Achievements include patents in field. Avocations: pool, golf, tennis, soccer, piano. Office: John Hopkins U Whiting Sch Enging Dept Computer Sci Office NEB 224 3400 N Charles St Baltimore MD 21218-2681 Office Phone: 410-516-8177. Office Fax: 443-264-2406. Business E-Mail: rubin@jhu.edu.

RUBIN, BENJAMIN ARNOLD, microbiologist, immunologist, medical educator, researcher; b. NYC, Sept. 27, 1917; s. Eli and Helen Sarah (Arenoff) R.; m. Mae Koenig, Aug. 31, 1951. BS, CCNY, 1937; MS, Va. Polytech. Inst. & State U., 1938; PhD, Yale U., 1947. Asst. dir. Circle Analytical Lab., NYC, 1938-40; chief lab. and radiology U.S. Army C.E., Nfld., also Cen. Am., 1940-44; asst. chief microbiologist Scherly Rsch. Lab., Lawrenceburg, Ind., 1944; rsch. asst. Yale U., New Haven, 1944-47; chief microbiologist Broockhaven Nat. Lab., LI, 1947-52, Syntex, Mexico City, 1952-54; prof. pub. health and preventitive medicine Coll. of Medicine Baylor U., Houston, 1954-60; mgr. biol. rsch. Wyeth, Radnar, Pa., 1960-84; rsch. prof. Phila. Coll. Osteo. Medicine, 1984-95; ret. Cons. GE, Valley Forge, Pa., 1972-80, U.S. Congressional com. energy and commerce, 1976-80, biological applications of space. Contbr. over 150 articles to sci. jours. Named to Inventors Hall of Fame, 1992; recipient John Scott award and medal, 1982, Proctor medal Phila. Drug Exchange, 1993; named Inventor of Yr., 1985. Achievements include invention of bifurcated needle in Smallpox eradication program. Home: 50 Belmont Ave Apt 601 Bala Cynwyd PA 19004-2428 Office: Phila Coll Osteo Medicine 4150 City Ave Philadelphia PA 19131-1610

RUBIN, BRUCE JOEL, screenwriter, director, producer; b. Detroit, Mar. 10, 1943; s. Jim and Sondra R.; m. Blanche Mallins; children: Joshua, Ari. Student, Wayne State U., 1960-62; grad. film sch., NYU, 1965; MA, Ind. U., 1980. Former asst. film editor NBC News; mem. film dept. Whitney Mus., assoc. curator; screenwrtier Sanford-Gross, LA. Screenwriter: (with Robert Statzel and Phillip Frank Messina) Brainstorm, 1983, Deadly Friend, 1986, Ghost, 1990 (Academy award best original screenplay 1990), Jacob's Ladder, 1990, Deceived, 1991, Stewart Little, 2002, The Last Mimzy, 2007; writer, dir., prodr. My Life, 1993; filmmaker (with Brian de Palma and Robert Fiore) Dionysus in '69, 1970; screenwriter (with Michael Tolkin) Deep Impact, 1998.

RUBIN, CATHY ANN, secondary school educator; b. Denver, July 17, 1948; d. Harry Phillip and Charlotte Ruth (Brinig) R. BA, Colo. State U., 1970; MA, U. No. Colo., 1971. Cert. tchr. Colo. Tchr. Adams County Dist. 50 Schs., Westminster, Colo., 1971-72; tchr. educationally handicapped Jefferson County Pub. Schs., Golden, Colo., 1972-98. Typist, bookkeeper Kenmark-Shaw's Jewelers, Denver, 1966—. Sec.-treas. Hillel Found., Denver, 1979-81; fundraiser Women's Am. Orgn. for Rehab. through Tng., Denver, 1979—; bookkeeper Religious Coalition for Abortion Rights, Denver, 1982-90; vol. TV PBS sta., Denver, 1978, Muscular Dystrophy Assn., Colo. AIDS Project; vol. usher DCTC, 1999—; vol. for the blind and dyslexic, 2005-2007. Democrat. Jewish. Avocations: music, reading, sailing, knitting, needlepoint. Home: 3500 S Ivanhoe St Denver CO 80237-1123

RUBIN, CHARLES ALEXIS, writer; b. LA, Dec. 4, 1953; s. Herbert Bernard and Jacqueline (Bashor) R.; m. Doris Sara Villalobos, July, 23, 1978; 1 child, Daniel Charles. BA in English magna cum laude, San Francisco State U., 1978, MA in English, 1980. Communications supr. Am. Protective Services, Oakland, Calif., 1982-83; assoc. editor Personal Computing mag., San Jose, 1983-84; free-lance writer Oakland, 1984—; sr. assoc. Waterside Assocs., Fremont, Calif., 1986-87; sr. analyst Internet Rsch. Group, Los Altos, Calif., 1999-2000; sr. strategist Gallagher Pub. Rels., Alameda, Calif., 2000—02; ptnr. Gallagher Group Pub. Rels., Alameda, Calif., 2002—04, Story Pub. Rels., San Francisco, 2004—. Editorial cons. Televisual Market Strategies, Saratoga, 1985-86. Author: The Endless Apple, 1984, Thinking Small: The Buyer's Guide to Portable Computers, 1984, Appleworks: Boosting Your Business with Integrated Software, 1985, Command Performance: Appleworks, 1986, Microsoft Works, 1986, Macintosh Hard Disk Management, 1988, Running Microsoft Works, 1990, The Macintosh Bible (What Do I Do Now?), 1990, The Macintosh Bible Guide to System 7, 1991, The Macintosh Bible Guide to File Maker Pro, 1991, The Macintosh Bible Guide to Clarisworks, 1993, The Little Book of Computer Wisdom, 1994, Guerrilla Marketing Online Weapons, 1996, Guerrilla Marketing Online, 1997, Managing Your Business with Quickbooks, 1998, Running Microsoft Word 2000, 1999. Democrat. Jewish. Home: 1053 Tahiti Ln Alameda CA 94502-6911 Business E-Mail: charlie@storypr.com.

RUBIN, CHUCK (CARL RUBIN), consumer products company executive; BA, Brandeis U., Waltham, Mass. Positions in merchandising and store mgmt. Federated Dept. Stores; ptnr. Accenture; exec. v.p., chief merchandising/mktg. officer Office Depot, Inc.; Delray Beach, Fla., 2004—06, pres. North Am. retail, 2006—. Office: Office Depot Inc 2200 Old Germantown Rd Delray Beach FL 33445 *

RUBIN, DAVID LEE, humanities educator, critic, editor; b. Indpls., Sept. 30, 1939; s. Ira Bertram and Jeanne Iva (Gamso) R.; m. Carolyn Dettman, June 12, 1965; 1 child, Timothy Craig. BA, U. Tenn., 1962; cert., U. Paris, 1963; MA, U. Ill., 1964, PhD, 1967. Instr. French U. Ill., Urbana, 1966-67; asst. prof. U. Chgo., 1967-69, U. Va., Charlottesville, 1969-74, assoc. prof., 1974-82, prof. French, 1982-2001, mem. Fulbright selection com., 1996—, mem. com. on comparative lit., 1997-2001, prof. emeritus, assoc. univ. seminar program, 2001—; seminar dir. Folger Inst., 1989. Chair poetry bd. Va. Quar. Rev., 2003—, Great Books discussion leader Jefferson Inst. Lifelong Learning, U. Va., 2001-; assoc. ctr. advanced studies U. Va., 1979, 80-81, 87, 93, 99-2000; pub., editor-in-chief Rookwood Press, 1992—; cons. PMLA Can. Coun., Etudes littéraires françaises, NEH, numerous univ. presses; lectr., spkr. in field. Author: Higher Hidden Order, 1972, The Knot of Artifice, 1981, A Pact with Silence, 1991; editor: The Selected Poetry and Prose of John T. Napier, 1972, La poésie française du premier 17e siècle, 1986, 2d edit., 2006, Sun King, 1991; co-editor: La Cohérence Intérieure, 1977, Convergences, 1989, The Ladder of High Designs, 1991, The Fulbright Difference, 1993; founding editor Continuum, 1989-93, EMF: Studies in Early Modern France, 1994-2002, EMF Critiques, 1994-2002, Rookwood Texts, 1997—, Rookwood Reprints, 2002—; mem. editl. bd. Purdue Studies in Romance Literatures, 1975-2001, Oeuvres et Critiques, 1976-2001, French Rev., 1986-94; Am. corr. Cahiers Maynard, 1973-2001, Cahiers Tristan L'Hermite, 1989-2001; contbr. articles to profl. jours., chpts. to books. U.S. State Dept. Fulbright fellow, 1963—64, fellow, Woodrow Wilson Found., 1963—64, Guggenheim Found., 1980—81, Hewlett fellow, summer, 1997, The Shape of Change: Studies in Honor of David Lee Rubin, 2002. Mem. MLA, ACLU, Phi Beta Kappa. Avocations: reading, exercise. Home: 520 Rookwood Pl Charlottesville VA 22903-4734 Personal E-mail: dlr93039@yahoo.com.

RUBIN, DONALD BRUCE, statistician, educator, research and development company executive; b. Washinton, Dec. 22, 1943; s. Allan A. and Harriet Rubin. AB magna cum laude, Princeton U., 1965; MS, Harvard U., 1966, PhD, 1970. Rsch. statistician Ednl. Testing Svc., Princeton, NJ, 1971-75, chmn. stats., 1975-79, sr. statis. advisor, 1979-81; pres. Datametrics Rsch. Inc., Waban, Mass., 1981—; prof. U. Chgo., 1982-84, Harvard U., Cambridge, Mass., 1984—, chmn. stats., 1985-94, 2000—, John L. Loeb Prof. Stats., 2002—. Author: Handling Nonresponse in Sample Surveys by Multiple Imputation, 1980, Multiple Imputation for Nonresponse in Surveys, 1987, classic edit., 2004; author: (with others) Incomplete Data in Sample Surveys (Vol. 2): Theory and Bibliography, 1983; co-author: (with R.J.A. Little) Statistical Analysis With Missing Data, 1987, 2d edit., 2002, (with A. Gelman, J. Carlin. H. Stern) Bayasian Data Analysis, 1995, 2d edit., 2003, (with R. Rosenthal and R. Rosnow) Contrasts and Effect Sites in Behavioral Research: A Correlational Approach, 2000, Matched Sampling for Causal Effects, 2006; co-editor: (with P.W. Holland) Test Equating, 1982; contbr. over 300 articles to profl. jours. Recipient Parzen prize for statis. innovation, 1996; Woodrow Wilson Grad. fellow, 1965; NSF Grad. fellow, 1965, 68, John Simon Guggenheim fellow, 1977-78. Fellow AAAS (chmn. stats. 1992), Am. Statis. Assn. (editor jour. 1980-82, dir. 1980-82, statistician of yr. Boston chpt. 1995, Chgo. chpt. 2000, S.S. Wilks medal 1995), Inst. Math. Stats. (coun. mem. 1990-92, 99-2001, Fisher lectr. 2004); mem. NAS (com. on nat. stats. 1989-92, mem. panel on confidentiality data 1989-92, panel on bilingual edn. 1990-92, working group on statis. analysis of com. on basic rsch. in behavioral and social scis. 1985-86, panel statis. in 21st century 1995, other coms.), AAAS, Am. Acad. Arts and Sci., Biometric Soc., Internat. Assn. Survey Statisticians, Internat. Statis. Inst., Psychometric Soc., Royal Statis. Soc. Office: Harvard U Dept Statistics Cambridge MA 02138 Business E-Mail: rubin@stat.harvard.edu.

RUBIN, EDWARD, dean, law educator; AB, Princeton U., 1969; JD, Yale U., 1979. Curriculum planner NYC Bd. Edn., 1970—76; law clk. to Hon. Jon O. Newman US Ct. Appeals (2nd cir.), 1979—80; assoc. Paul, Weiss, Rifkind, Wharton & Garrison, NYC; acting prof. U. Calif. Sch. Law, 1982—87, assoc. dean, 1989—92, prof., 1987—96, Richard W. Jennings Professor, 1996—98; prof. U. Pa. Law Sch., Phila., 1998—2005, Theodore K. Warner, Jr. prof. law, 2003—05; dean & John Wade-Kent Syverud prof. law Vanderbilt U. Law Sch., Nashville, 2005—. Contbr. articles to law jours.; author: Beyond Camelot: Rethinking Politics and Law for the Modern State, 2005; co-author (with Malcolm Feeley): Federalism: A Theoretical Inquiry, 2005. Mem.: ABA, Am. Assn. Law Sch. Office: U Vanderbilt Law Sch Office of the Dean 131 21st Ave South Rm 290 A Nashville TN 37203-1181 Office Phone: 615-322-9800. Office Fax: 215-573-2025, 615-322-5151. E-mail: ed.rubin@vanderbilt.edu.

RUBIN, ELLEN, education/access consultant; d. Jack and Mary Elizabeth Rubin; m. Rami Gertler, Oct. 4, 1979 (div.). MS in Spl. Edn., Bank St. Coll. Edn., NYC, 1976. Cert. spl. edn. N-6 NY, 1977. Asst. tchr. Helen Keller Services for the Blind (formerly Indsl. Home for the Blind), NYC, 1966—68; rehab. tchr. Lighthouse for the Blind, Haifa, Israel, 1969—70; ednl. program coord. George Simmons Rehab. Ctr. for the Blind, Ministry Welfare, Beersheva, Israel, 1970—79; ednl. counselor Ben Gurion U. of the Negev, Beersheva, 1979—80; ednl. programming counselor Assn. for the Advancement of the Blind and Retarded, Inc., Jamaica, NY, 1981—82; spl. educator Early Intervention Programs, Guild for Exceptional Children, Bklyn., 1982—83; instr., cons., advisor Computer Ctr. for Visually Impaired People, Baruch Coll., NYC, 1983—2004; coord. disability programs Ednl. Equity Concepts, Inc., NYC, 1983—2004; part-time coord. internat. exch. programs Mobility Internat. USA, Eugene, Oreg., 1996—. Lectr. Sch. Occupl. Therapy, U. Hosp., Hadassah Med. Ctr., Jerusalem, 1974—79; team lectr. Haifa U., Natanya, Israel, 1977—78; lectr. Ministry Welfare, Beersheva, 1978—80; adv. panel mem. Commrs. Adv. Panel for the Office Spl. Edn. Svcs., NY State Edn. Dept., Albany, 1982—97; adv. com. mem. Quality Improvement Ctr. for Diabilities, NYU, NYC, 1984—2001; adv. coun. mem. Interagency Coordinating Coun., NY State Health Dept., Albany, NY, 1988—92; bd. dirs. Creative Adaptations for Learning, Great Neck, NY, 1990—; cons./adv. com. mem. Programs and Svcs. for People With Disabilities, Lincoln Ctr. for the Performing Arts, NYC, 1993—; testing coord. Touch Graphics, Inc., NYC, 1996—; trainer in accessibility features Assn. Sci. and Tech. Ctrs., Washington, 1998—2004; cons. Smithsonian Instn., Washington, 1999—2000; guest lectr. mus. edn. Bank St. Coll. Edn., NYC, 2001—; Ams. with Disabilities Act cons. Wildlife Conservation Soc., NY Aquarium, Bklyn., 2002—03. Contbr. articles to profl. jours. Advisor disability adv. com. Taxi and Limousine Commn., NYC, 1996—; cmty. liaison Beth Israel Methadone Clinic, NYC, 2000—04. Recipient Cmty. Svc. award, Jewish Guild for the Blind, 1993, Access Builder award, Baruch Coll., CUNY, 2003. Home Phone: 212-662-8110. Personal E-mail: ellenr5@verizon.net.

RUBIN, ERIC HOWARD, oncologist, researcher; b. Seattle, Wash., Mar. 27, 1959; m. Kimberly A. Rubin; children: Sara, Jacob. BA in Math. and Biology, Tulane U., 1981; MD, U. South Fla. Coll. Medicine, 1985. Cert. Am. Bd. Internal Medicine, Am. Bd. Internal Medicine, Med. Oncology. Intern, internal medicine Yale-New Haven Hosp., Conn., resident, hematologic oncology Conn., 1985—88, hosp. appointment Conn.; fellow Dana Farber Cancer Inst., Harvard Med. Sch., Boston, 1989; asst. prof. Harvard Med. Sch., 1995; assoc. dir., clin. scis. Cancer Inst. NJ, New Brunswick, NJ, dir., investigational therapeutics; prof. medicine & pharmacology U. Medicine and Dentistry NJ-Robert Wood Johnson Med. Sch., New Brunswick, NJ. Contbr. articles to profl. jours.; dep. editor Journal Clin. Cancer Rsch. Achievements include holding a patent for TOPORS, discovery of a new gene that is involved in the development of cancer. Office: U Medicine Dentistry NJ-Robert Wood Johnson Med Sch Dept Pharmacology Cancer Inst NJ 195 Little Albany St New Brunswick NJ 08901 Office Phone: 732-235-6777. Office Fax: 732-235-7735. Business E-Mail: ehrubin@umdnj.edu. *

RUBIN, E(RWIN) LEONARD, lawyer; b. Chgo., Jan. 11, 1933; s. Samuel and Frances Birdie (Rabin) R.; m. Stephanie Siegel, Mar. 4, 1961 (div. Dec. 1981); children: Matthew, Suzanne; m. Audrey Gay Holzer, May 8, 1983; children: Margot, Bette. Student, U. Ill., Urbana, 1948-51; AB, U. Miami, 1956, JD, 1959. s. N.Y. 1960, Ill. 1962, U.S. Dist. Ct. (no. dist.) Ill. 1962, U.S. Ct. Appeals (7th cir.) 1990, U.S. Ct. Appeals (5th cir.) 1998, U.S. Supreme Ct. 2004. Assoc. Hays, St. John A&H, NYC, 1960—62, Devoe, Shadur, Mikva, Chgo., 1962—65; gen. counsel Playboy Enterprises, Inc., Chgo., 1965—78; ptnr. E. Leonard Rubin Law Offices, Chgo., 1978—81, Epton, Mullin & Druth Ltd., Chgo., 1981—86, Brinks, Hofer, Gilson & Lione, Chgo., 1986—96, Gordon & Glickson, LLC, Chgo., 1996—2002, Reed Smith Sachnoff & Weaver, Chgo., 2002—. Adj. prof. U. Ill., Northwestern U. Law Sch., Loyola U. Sch. Law, John Marshall Law Sch. Pres. Lawyers for Creative Arts, Chgo., 1983-85; bd. dirs. Wisdom Bridge Theatre, Chgo., 1983-85; mem., bd. dirs. Appletree Theater of Highland Park. Cpl. U.S. Army, 1953-5, ETO. Mem. ABA, Ill. Bar Assn., Chgo. Bar Assn. (bd. mgrs. 1983-85, chmn. various coms., dir. Christmas Spirits Satire Show 1965-99), Union Internat. Des Avocats (pres. intellectual property commn. 1997-2000), Copyright Soc. Am. (trustee, past pres. midwest chpt.). Jewish. Home: 270 Sunset Dr Northfield IL 60093-1047 Office: Reed Smith Sachnoff & Weaver 10 S Wacker Dr 40th Fl Chicago IL 60606 Home Phone: 847-446-2211; Office Phone: 312-207-1000. Business E-Mail: elrubin@reedsmith.com.

RUBIN, GARY ANDREW, entrepreneur, computer engineer; s. Budd Email and Joanne Lee Rubin. BA in Math., U. Calif., Berkeley, 1978; MS in Computer Sci. & Engring., Stanford U., Palo Alto, Calif., 1982. Cert. instr. Cisco Sys., 1993, network assoc. Cisco Sys., 1996. Software engr., fed. sys. divsn. IBM, Houston, 1978—80, software engr., comm. products divsn. Palo Alto, Calif., 1982—86; software engr., network engr., competitive analyst ROLM Comm., Santa Clara, Calif., 1986—91; pres., founder Advanced Network Info., Inc., Santa Clara, 1992—. Mem. Inst. Nautical Archaeology, ROLMan Forum Toastmasters (forum v.p. 1990—91, Competent Toastmaster award 1992), Young Entrepreneurs' Orgn. (chpt. mentorship chair, forum moderator 2005—07), Mensa. Achievements include development of the digital auto-pilot for the NASA space shuttle; design of General Motors' manufacturing automation protocol, common application service elements. Avocations: travel, archaeology, scuba diving. Home: 3567 Benton St #248 Santa Clara CA 95051 Office: Advanced Network Info Inc 530 Lakeside Dr Ste 200 Sunnyvale CA 94085 Business E-Mail: grubin@ani-training.com.

RUBIN, GERALD MAYER, biochemistry researcher, educator; b. Boston, Mar. 31, 1950; s. Benjamin H. and Edith (Weisberg) R.; m. Lynn S. Mastalir, May 7, 1978; 1 child, Alan F. BS, MIT, 1971; PhD in Molecular Biology, Cambridge U., Eng., 1974, ScD, 2002. Helen Hay Whitney Found. fellow Stanford U. Sch. Medicine, Calif., 1974-76; asst. prof. biol. chemistry Sidney Farber Cancer Inst.-Harvard U. Med. Sch., Boston, 1977-80; instructor, embryology Marine Biol. Lab., Woods Hole, Mass.; staff mem., dept. embryology Carnegie Instn. of Washington, Balt., 1980-83; John D. MacArthur prof. genetics, dept. molecular & cell biology U. Calif., Berkeley, 1983—2000, head, divsn. genetics, dept. molecular and cellular biology, 1987—95, HHMI investigator, 1987—2000, dir. Drosophila Genome Ctr., 2000—02; v.p. biomedical rsch. Howard Hughes Med. Inst., Chevy Chase, Md., 2000—01, v.p., dir. planning Janelia Farm Rsch. Campus, 2002—03, v.p., dir. Janelia Farm Rsch. Campus, 2003—. Adj. prof. dept. biochemistry and biophysics U. Calif. Sch. Medicine, San Francisco, 1987-; assoc. faculty mem., cell and molecular biology divsn. Lawrence Berkeley Nat. Lab., Calif.; mem. sci. adv. bd. Athena Neurosci., Inc., Tularik, Inc.; co-founder, chair sci. adv. bd. Exelixis Pharm., Inc. Predoctoral fello, NSF, Helen Hay Whitney Found. Fellow; Recipient Young Scientist award Passano Found., 1983, Eli Lilly award in biol. chemistry, Am. Chem. Soc., 1985; co-recipient Newcomb Cleveland prize, AAAS, 2000, George W. Beadle Medal, Genetics Soc. Am., 2003; named Scientist of Yr., R&D Mag., 2006. Mem. AAAS, NAS (US Steel Found. award in molecular biology, 1985), Inst. Medicine, Genetics Soc. Am. Med., Phi Beta Kappa, Phi Lambda Epsilon, Royal Soc. UK (fgn.); Fellow

Am. Acad. Arts & Sciences, Am. Acad. Microbiology. Office: Janelia Farm Rsch Campus Howard Hughes Med Inst 19700 Helix Dr Ashburn VA 20147-2408 Business E-Mail: rubing@janelia.hhmi.org. *

RUBIN, GERROLD ROBERT, advertising executive; b. Evanston, Ill., Mar. 31, 1940; s. Bennie George and Anita (Perich) R.; m. Barbara Ann Nieman, Sept. 5, 1962; children: John, Ann. BS in Radio, TV, Film, Northwestern U., 1962. Account exec. Leo Burnett Advt., Chgo., 1962-67, account supr. Toronto, Ont., 1967-68, Needham, Harper Steers, Chgo., 1968-73, account dir. Los Angeles, 1973-78; mgmt. rep. Needham, Harper & Steers, Chgo., 1978-81, pres., CEO Los Angeles, 1981-86, Rubin, Postaer & Assocs., Santa Monica, Calif., 1986—. Bd. dirs. Country Music Assn., Nashville, 1983—. Presbyterian. Office: Rubin Postaer & Assocs 2525 Colorado Ave Santa Monica CA 90404

RUBIN, HARRY MEYER, software industry executive; b. NYC, Dec. 21, 1952; s. Martin J. and Helene Rubin; m. Cathy Hemery, May 26, 1990; children: Gabriella, James. BA, Stanford U., 1974; MBA, Harvard U., 1976. Investment banker Wertheim & Co., Inc., NYC, 1976-77; fin. mgr. Am. Airlines, Inc., NYC, 1977-79; dir. fin. planning-entertainment, electronics groups RCA Corp., NYC, 1979-81; CFO RCA Videodiscs, RCA Home Video, RCA Cable RCA Entertainment Group, NYC; v.p. strategic planning RCA Corp., NYC, group v.p. fin. and bus. affairs RCA entertainment ops., 1981-86; gen. mgr. Home Video Gen. Electric Co., 1986-87; v.p., gen. mgr. home video div. NBC, Inc., 1988-93; exec. v.p. GT Interactive Software Corp., 1994-98; pres. GT Interactive Internat., 1998-2000; pres. internat. Infogrames, Inc., 2000-01; sr. exec. v.p. and chmn. of worldwide pub. Atari Inc., 2001—05, COO, 2004—05; chmn. Henmead Enterprises, Inc., 2005—06. Dir. Image-Metrics PLC, Synthesis Energy Sys., Inc.; dir., co-head exec. com. RCA/Columbia Pictures Worldwide Video; founding ptnr. Samuel Adams Beer; founding dir. Arts and Entertainment Network. Mem.: 22 Club, Phi Beta Kappa. Avocations: travel, foreign languages. Home: 784 Park Ave New York NY 10021-3553 Personal E-mail: harry.rubin@gmail.com.

RUBIN, HERBERT, lawyer; b. Lisbon, Conn., June 4, 1918; s. Simon and Rose (Berko) R.; m. Rose Luttan, July 6, 1941; children: Barbara, Caroline, Donald. AB, CCNY, 1938; JD, NYU, 1942. Bar: N.Y. 1942, U.S. Dist. Ct. (so. and ea. dists.) N.Y. 1951, U.S. Supreme Ct. 1956, U.S. Ct. Appeals (2d, 3d, 4th, 6th, 9th, 10th, 11th and D.C. cirs.). Assoc. Newman & Bisco, 1942; faculty NYU Law Sch., 1946-50, 57-62; prof. creditors' rights Rutgers U. Law Sch., 1949-57; pvt. practice, 1946-56; ptnr. Sereni, Herzfeld & Rubin, and successor Herzfeld & Rubin, NYC, 1956—, sr. ptnr., 1968—. Instr. mil. law U.S. Army, 1944-46; prof. constl. law L.I. U., 1963-68; trustee North Shore L.I. Jewish Hosp. Editor-in-chief NYU Law Rev., 1940-41; bd. editors N.Y. Law Jour., 1971—; contbr. articles to profl. jours. Mem. N.Y. State Banking Bd., 1975-85, N.Y. State Jud. Selection Com., 1975-83, Sen. Moynihan's Jud. Selection Com., 1982-2000, Sen. Schumer's Jud. Selection Com., 1999—, City Charter Revision Commn., 1998-2001; trustee Am. Assn. Jewish Lawyers and Jurists. 1st lt. Signal Corps, AUS, 1942-46. Recipient award, NCCJ, 1967, United Jewish Appeal, 1968, 1997, Israel Bonds, 1973, NYU Law Assn. award, 1987, Judge Weinfeld award, NYU, 1992, Vanderbilt award, 1999. Fellow Am. Bar Found.; mem. ABA (mem. coun. N.Y. state), N.Y. State Bar Assn., Queens County Bar Assn. (pres. 1970), Assn. Bar City Of N.Y., Fed. Bar Coun., Jewish Lawyers Guild (award 2001). Office: Herzfeld & Rubin 40 Wall St Fl 54 New York NY 10005-2301 Office Phone: 212-471-8500. Office Fax: 212-232-6610. Business E-Mail: hrubin@herzfeldrubin.com.

RUBIN, IRIS KEDAR, dermatologist; b. Silver Springs, Md., Aug. 27, 1974; d. Raphael and Tamar Kedar; m. Michael P. Rubin, July 2, 2005; 1 child, Jonathan Alexander. BA, Stanford U., Palo Alto, Calif.; MD, Harvard U., Boston. Diplomate Am. Acad. Dermatology, 2007. Intern NIH, Bethesda, Md., 1992—94; co-creator jour. Nature Am., Inc., Washington, 1995—96; from intern internal medicine to fellow med. sch. Harvard U., 2000—06, laser fellow dermatology med. sch., 2006—; assoc. McKinsey & Co., Inc., Atlanta, 2001—02; resident dermatology U. of Chgo., 2003—05. Contbr. articles to profl. jours. Rschr., writer The Family Van, Boston, 2000. Recipient Cmty. Svc. award, Harvard U. Med. Sch.; fellow, Am. Telemedicine Assn. Mem.: AMA (assoc. Foundation Leadership award), New Eng. Med. Soc. (assoc.), Am. Acad. Dermatology (assoc.). Office: 50 Staniford St Boston MA 02114 Home Phone: 617-383-5770.

RUBIN, JEFFREY WAYNE, lawyer; b. Syracuse, NY, Oct. 10, 1950; s. Harold and Ida Rubin. BA, SUNY, Binghamton, 1971; JD, Syracuse U., 1977. Bar: N.Y. 1978, U.S. Dist. Ct. (so. and ea. dists.) N.Y. 1978, U.S. Supreme Ct. 1991. Assoc. Guggenheimer & Untermyer, NYC, 1978-82, Squadron, Ellenoff, Plesent & Sheinfeld, NYC, 1982-85, ptnr., 1985—2002, Hogan & Hartson LLP, 2002—. Mem. ABA (bus. law sect.), N.Y. State Bar Assn., Assn. of Bar of City of N.Y. Office: Hogan & Hartson L L P 875 3rd Ave New York NY 10022 Office Phone: 212-918-8224. Business E-Mail: jwrubin@hhlaw.com.

RUBIN, JOEL EDWARD, manufacturing executive; b. Cleve., Sept. 5, 1928; s. Morris and Pearl (Jacobs) R.; m. Lucille Schutmaat, Dec. 18, 1953; children: Brian G., Jennifer L., Rebecca R. BS, Case Inst. of Tech., 1949; MFA, Yale U., 1951; PhD, Stanford U., 1960. Exec. v.p. Kliegl Bros. Lighting, NYC, 1954-85; prin. cons. Joel E. Rubin & Assocs., NYC, 1985-93; prin. cons. theater planning Artec Cons. Inc., NYC, 1993—2005; prin. cons. Joel E. Rubin & Assoc., NYC, 2005—. Co-author: Theatrical Lighting Practice 1954; author: Technological Development of Stage Lighting 1960. Member Coll. of Fellows of Am. Theatre, John F. Kennedy Ctr. for the Performing Arts, Washington. Recipient Golden Triaga, Prague Quadrennial, 1987, Zlatou medal, 1991, 1st time award Bus. Com. for the Arts, Forbes Mag., 1987; recipient Founders' award US Inst. for Theatre Tech., 1972, 79, Nat. award, 1990, Lifetime hon. membership award, 1996, Spl. citation, 1996; Dr. Joel E. Rubin Founder's award named in his honor US Inst. Theatre Tchrs., 2000; Internat. Student Rsch. grants established in his honor US Inst. Theatre Tchrs., 2000; nominee Entertainment Design Lifetime Achievement in Lighting, 2005 Fellow Am. Theatre Assn. (v.p. 1961-63), US Inst. of Theatre Technology (pres. 1963-64); mem. Am. Nat. Theatre Acad. (bd. dirs. 1971-75), Internat. Theatre Inst. of the US (bd. dirs. 1975-79), Nat. Coun. of Arts and Govt. (bd. dirs. 1975-79), Internat. Orgn. Theatre Architects and Scenographers (US chmn., rep. 1968-98, pres. 1971-79, Gold medal award 1996), Illuminating Engring. Soc. Avocations: collecting books, stage design, lincolniana. Home: 24 Edgewood Ave Hastings On Hudson NY 10706-2024 Office: Joel E Rubin and Assoc 119 W 57th St Ste 820 New York NY 10019 Office Phone: 212-757-5646. Personal E-mail: booksjoel@aol.com.

RUBIN, KARL COOPER, mathematics educator; b. Urbana, Ill., Jan. 27, 1956; s. Robert J. and Vera (Cooper) R. AB, Princeton U., 1976; MA, Harvard U., 1977, PhD, 1981. Instr. Princeton (N.J.) U., 1982-83; mem. Inst. Advanced Study, Princeton, 1983-84; prof. Columbia U., NYC, 1988-89; asst. prof. math. Ohio State U., Columbus, 1984-87, prof., 1987-97; prof. math. Stanford (Calif.) U., 1997—. Contbr. articles to Inventiones Math. Recipient Presdl. Young Investigator award NSF, 1988; NSF postdoctoral fellow, 1981, Sloan fellow, 1985, Guggenheim fellow, 1994. Mem. Am. Math. Soc. (recipient Cole Prize, 1992), Phi Beta Kappa. Achievements include rsch. on elliptic curves, Tate-Shafarevich groups, Birch and Swinnerton-Dyer conjecture, Iwasawa theory and p-adic L-functions. Office: Stanford U Dept Math Stanford CA 94305-2125

RUBIN, KENNETH ALLEN, lawyer; b. Rockville Centre, NY, Nov. 24, 1947; s. Albert Alton and Marion (Osterweis) R.; m. Susan Kurman, Sept. 14, 1980; children: Jennifer, Kelly. BS, Cornell U., 1969, MS, 1971, JD, 1973. Bar: D.C. 1974, N.Y. 1974, U.S. Ct. Appeals (D.C. crct.) 1974, U.S. Ct. Appeals (5th crct. 1975, U.S. Ct. Appeals (4th, 9th and 10th crct.) 1976, U.S. Ct. Appeals (3d, 8th and 11th crcts.) 1986, U.S. Supreme Ct. 1992. Trial atty. Dept. Justice, Washington, 1973-74; sr. ptnr. Morgan, Lewis & Bockius LLP, Washington, 1974—. Adj. prof. USDA Grad. Sch., Washington, 1977-85, U. Ala., Huntsville, 1978-91, Antioch U., Washington, 1978; lectr. Cornell U., Ithaca, N.Y., 1979—. Author: What the Business Executive Needs To Know about U.S. Environmental Laws and Liabilities, 2006, (manual) A Tidal Wave of Lawsuits and Regulations Flood the Once-Placid Waters of Drinking Water Utilities, 2000, Oil Spill Reporting Manual, 2006. Mem. adv. com. Cornell Ctr. for Environment. Mem. ABA, Am. Water Works Assn., Swiss Club Washington, Cornell Club Washington. Office: Morgan Lewis & Bockius LLP 1111 Pennsylvania Ave NW Washington DC 20004 E-mail: karwaterlawyer@aol.com.

RUBIN, LAWRENCE GILBERT, physicist, science administrator; b. Bklyn., Sept. 17, 1925; s. Harry E. and Ruth (Feirberg) R.; m. Florence Ruth Kagan, Feb. 11, 1951; children: Michael G., Richard D., Jeffrey N. Student, Cooper Union, NYC, 1943, 46-47; BS in Physics, U. Chgo., 1949; MA in Physics, Columbia U., 1950. Staff mem., physicist research div. Raytheon Co., Waltham, Mass., 1950-64; group leader Nat. Magnet Lab., MIT, Cambridge, Mass., 1964-78, divsn. head high magnetic field facility, 1978-93; advisor to high magnetic field facility, 1994-95; vis. scientist MIT, 1996—. Mem. NAS adv. panel Nat. Bur. Standards, 1976-82, 85-90; bd. dirs. Lake Shore Cryotronics, Inc., Columbus, Ohio; gen. chmn. 6th Internat. Temperature Symposium, Washington, 1982, 7th Internat. Temperature Symposium, Toronto, 1992, 8th Internat. Temperature Symposium, Chgo., 2002; chmn. adv. com. Physics Today Buyers' Guide; contbg. editor Physics Today; organizer, mgr. Am. Phys. Soc. Tutorial program, 1993-2003. Mem. editl. bd. Rev. Sci. Instruments, 1968-70, 79-81; contbr. articles to physics jours. With U.S. Army, 1943-46, ETO. Fellow IEEE (life, chmn. Keithley award com. 2002-04), Am. Phys. Soc. (organizer and 1st chmn. instrument and measurement sci. group 1985). Jewish. Home: 1504 Centre St Newton Center MA 02459-2447 Office: MIT Bldg NW14 1209 170 Albany St Cambridge MA 02139-4208 Office Phone: 617-253-5517. Business E-Mail: lrubin@mit.edu.

RUBIN, LEWIS J., physician, researcher; b. New York, NY, Aug. 5, 1950; s. Theodore and Erna Rubin; m. Juanita Rose Brooks; children: Lauren, Rose Sheelah, Jai Sheelah. BA, Yeshiva U., NYC, 1972; diploma in Hebraic studies, Yeshiva U., NYC, 1972; MD, Albert Einstein Coll. of Medicine, 1972—75. Am. Bd. Internal Medicine ABIM/ Wash., DC, 1978, diplomate Nat. Bd. Med. Examiners. Assoc. in medicine Duke U., Durham, NC, 1978—79; assoc. prof. medicine U. Tex. Health Sci. Ctr., Dallas, 1980—84, 1984—85, U. Md., Balt., 1985—89, prof. medicine, 1989—98, dir. divsn. pulmonary medicine, 1995—98; prof. medicine U. Calif. San Diego, 1999—. Cons. in field. Contbr. more than 200 articles to sci. publs.;, editor 6 textbooks. Fellow: ACP, Am. Coll. Chest Physicians (bd. govs. 1997), Am. Heart Assn., Royal Coll. Physicians UK; mem.: Am. Soc. Clin. Investigation. Achievements include basic and clinical research in cardiopulmonary diseases, leading to drug developments and new treatments. Avocations: classical music, opera, travel. Home: 6404 Avenida Wilfredo La Jolla CA 92037 Office: U Calif San Diego Med Ctr 9300 Campus Point Drive #7381 La Jolla CA 92037-7381 Office Phone: 858-657-8700. Business E-Mail: ljrubin@ucsd.edu.

RUBIN, LOUIS DECIMUS, JR., retired language educator, writer, publishing executive; b. Charleston, SC, Nov. 19, 1923; s. Louis Decimus and Janet (Weinstein) R.; m. Eva M. Redfield, June 2, 1951; children: Robert Alden, William Louis. Student, Coll. of Charleston, 1940-42, LittD (hon.), 1989; AB, U. Richmond, 1946, LittD (hon.), 1972; MA, Johns Hopkins U., 1949, PhD, 1954; LittD (hon.), Clemson U., 1986, U. of the South, 1991, U. N.C. at Asheville, 1993, U. N.C., Chapel Hill, 1995. Instr. Johns Hopkins U.; editor Hopkins Rev., 1950-54; fellow criticism Sewanee Rev., 1953-54; exec. sec. Am. Studies Assn., asst. prof. Am. civilization U. Pa., 1954-56; assoc. editor Richmond (Va.) News Leader, 1956-57; assoc. prof. English Hollins Coll., 1957-60, prof., chmn. dept., 1960-67; prof. English U. N.C., 1967-73, Univ. Disting. prof., 1973-89, prof. emeritus, 1989—. Editor Hollins Critic, 1963-68; vis. prof. history La. State U., 1957; Fulbright lectr. U. Aix-Marseille, 1960; lectr. Breadloaf Writer's Conf., 1961; vis. prof. U. N.C., 1965, Harvard U., 1969; lectr. Am. studies seminars Kyoto (Japan) U., 1979; founder, pub., editl. dir. Algonquin Books Chapel Hill, 1982-91. Author: Thomas Wolfe: The Weather of His Youth, 1955, No Place on Earth, 1959, The Golden Weather, 1961, The Faraway Country, 1963, The Teller in the Tale, 1967, The Curious Death of the Novel, 1967, George W. Cable, 1969, The Writer in the South, 1972, William Elliott Shoots A Bear, 1975, Virginia: A History, 1977, The Wary Fugitives, 1978, Surfaces of a Diamond, 1981, A Gallery of Southerners, 1982, The Even-Tempered Angler, 1983, The Edge of the Swamp, 1989, The Algonquin Literary Quiz Book, 1990, The Mockingbird in the Gum Tree, 1991, Small Craft Advisory, 1991, The Heat of the Sun, 1995, Babe Ruth's Ghost, 1996, Seaports of the South, 1998, A Memory of Trains, 2000, An Honorable Estate, 2001, My Father's People, 2002, Where The Southern Cross the Yellow Dog: On Writers and Writing, 2005; editor: Southern Renascence, 1953, The Lasting South, 1957, Teach the Freeman: R.B. Hayes and the Slater Fund for Negro Education, 1959, The Idea of an American Novel, 1961, South: Modern Southern Literature in Its Cultural Setting, 1961, Bibliographical Guide to the Study of Southern Literature, 1969, The Comic Imagination in American Literature, 1973, The Literary South, 1978, The American South, 1980, The History of Southern Literature, 1985, An Apple for My Teacher, 1987, A Writer's Companion, 1995, The Quotable Baseball Fanatic, 2000; co-editor: So. Lit. Jour., 1968-89; contbr. articles to periodicals. Served with AUS, 1943-46. Guggenheim fellow, 1958-59, fellow Am. Coun. Learned Socs., 1964, Fulbright fellow, Oliver Max Gardner award, Mayflower award, Disting. Virginian award, NC award for Lit., 1992, R. Hunt Parker Meml. award for lifetime contributions to NC lit. heritage, Academy award in Lit., Am. Acad. of Arts and Letters, 2004, Ivan Sandrof Lifetime Achievement award, Nat. Book Critics Cir., 2005, John Tyler Caldwell award for the Humanities, 2005. Fellow So. Writers (chancellor 1991-93); mem. Soc. Study So. Lit. (pres. 1975-76), Phi Beta Kappa.

RUBIN, MARTIN N., meeting planner, consultant; b. NYC, Aug. 9, 1928; s. Max and Esther (Chernow) R.; m. Shirley Anne Rubin, Aug. 22, 1954 (div. Aug. 1964); m. Karen Anne O'Brien, Sept. 21, 1981. AB, U. Mich.; AM, Miami U., Oxford, Ohio; PhD., Sussex U., Eng. Lic. psychologist. With Dayton (Ohio) Sch. System, 1951-60, West Alexandria (Ohio) Sch. System, 1961-63; instr. Wright State U., Dayton, 1961—63; with Devereux Found., Pa., N.Y. Dept. Corrections, Bklyn., 1971—73, Council for Retarded Children, Albany, NY, 1973—75; prin. M. Rubin & Co., Inc., Mount Vernon, NY, 1975—. Author: Developmentally Disabled, 1965. Candidate Dem. State Legis., 1982; adv. bd. Mt. Vernon Mental Health Bd., 1985. Master's degree scholar Miami U., 1958; Guidance Inst. grantee Miami U., 1959. Fellow Am. Assn. Mental Deficiency (pres. 1967); mem. Soc. Assn. Execs. (bd. dirs. 1985—), Masons (sr. warden 1983). Avocations: dance, singing. Office Phone: 914-664-4120. Personal E-mail: lockob@aol.com.

RUBIN, MELVIN LYNNE, ophthalmologist, educator; b. San Francisco, May 10, 1932; s. Morris and May (Gelman) R.; m. Lorna Isen, June 21, 1953; children: Gabrielle, Daniel, Michael. AA, U. Calif., Berkeley, 1951, BS, 1953; MD, U. Calif., San Francisco, 1957; MS, Iowa State U., Ames, 1961. Diplomate Am. Bd. Ophthalmology (bd. dirs. 1977-83, chmn. 1984). Intern U. Calif. Hosp., San Francisco, 1957-58; resident in ophthalmology State U. Iowa, 1958-61; attending surgeon Georgetown U., Washington, 1961-63; asst. prof. surgery U. Fla. Med. Sch., Gainesville, 1963-66, assoc. prof. ophthalmology, 1966-67, prof. ophthalmology, 1967—97, prof. emeritus, 1997—, chmn. dept. ophthalmology, 1978-95, eminent scholar, 1989-97, eminent scholar emeritus, 1997. Author: Studies in Physiological Optics, 1965, Fundamentals of Visual Science, 1969, Optics for Clinicians, 1971, 2d edit., 1974, 25th ann. edit., 1995, The Fine Art of Prescribing Glasses, 1978, 3d edit., 2004; editor: Dictionary of Eye Terminology, 1984, 5th edit., 2006, Eye Care Notes, 1989, revised edit., 2001, Taking Care of Your Eyes, 2003; cons. editl. bd. Survey Ophthalmology; contbr. more than 100 articles to profl. jours. Co-founder Citizens for Pub. Schs., Inc., 1965, ProArteMusica Gainesville, Inc., 1969, pres., 1971-73; mem. Thomas Ctr. Adv. Bd. for the Arts, 1978-84, nat. sci. adv. bd. Helen Keller Eye Rsch. Found., 1989-96; bd. dirs. Hippodrome State Theater, 1981-87, Friends of Photography Ansel Adams Ctr., 1991-97, U. Fla. Found., 2005-; trustee U. Fla. Performing Arts Ctr., 1995—2004; chmn. nat. art coun. U. Fla. Harn Mus. Art, 2005—; bd. dirs. Opko Corp., 2007-. With USPHS, 1961-63. Recipient Best Med. Book for 1978 award Am. Med. Writers Assn., 1979, Shaler Richardson award for svc. to medicine Fla. Soc. Ophthalmology, 1995; M.L. Rubin Ann. Lectureship established in his honor by Fla. Soc. of Ophthalmology, 1993. Fellow ACS, Am. Acad. Ophthalmology (sec., dir. 1978-92, pres. 1988, Sr. Honor award 1987. Guest of Honor 1992), Found. Am. Acad. Ophthalmology (bd. trustees, 1988-95, chmn., 1992-94), Joint Commn. on Allied Health Pers. in Ophthalmology (Statesman of Yr. award 1987); mem. Assn. Rsch. in Vision and Ophthalmology (trustee 1973-78, pres. 1979), Retina Soc., Macula Soc., Club Jules Gonin, NY Acad. Sci., Fla. Soc. Ophthalmology, Am. Ophthal. Soc. (coun. 1998-2002), Pan Am. Soc. Ophthalmology, Ophthalmic Photographers Soc., Alachua County Med. Soc., Fla. Med. Assn., AMA (editorial bd. Archives of Ophthalmology 1975-85), Sigma Xi, Alpha Omega Alpha., Phi Kappa Phi. Office: U Fla Med Ctr PO Box 100284 Gainesville FL 32610-0284 Office Phone: 352-846-2132. Business E-Mail: melrubin@eye.ufl.edu.

RUBIN, MICHAEL, lawyer; b. Boston, July 19, 1952; m. Andrea L. Peterson, May 29, 1983; children: Peter, Eric, Emily. AB, Brandeis U., 1973; JD, Georgetown U., 1977. Bar: Calif. 1978, U.S. Dist. Ct. (no. dist.) Calif. 1978, U.S. Ct. Appeals (9th cir.) 1978, U.S. Ct. Appeals (5th, 7th, 10th cirs.) 1982, U.S. Supreme Ct. 1984, U.S. Ct. Appeals (D.C. cir.) 1984, U.S. Ct. Appeals (11th cir.) 1987. Teaching fellow Law Sch. Stanford (Calif.) U., 1977-78; law clerk to Hon. Charles B. Renfrew U.S. Dist. Ct. (no. dist.) Calif., San Francisco, 1978-79; law clerk to Hon. James R. Browning U.S. Ct. Appeals (9th cir.), San Francisco, 1979-80; law clerk to Hon. William J. Brennan, Jr. U.S. Supreme Ct., Washington, 1980-81; assoc. Altshuler & Berzon, San Francisco, 1981-85, ptnr., 1985-89, Altshuler, Berzon, Nussbaum, Berzon & Rubin, 1989-2000, Altshuler, Berzon, Nussbaum, Rubin & Demain, 2000—06, Altshuler Berzon LLP, 2007—. Office: Altshuler Berzon LLP 177 Post St Ste 300 San Francisco CA 94108-4700 Office Phone: 415-421-7151. E-mail: mrubin@altshulerberzon.com.

RUBIN, MICHAEL G., sports internet company executive; Student, Villanova U. Founder KPR Sports Internat. (changed name to Global Sports Inc. in 1997), 1991; chmn., pres., CEO GSI Commerce (changed name in 2002 from Global Sports Inc.), King of Prussia, Pa., 1995—; co-pres. GSI Commerce, 2004—05. Featured in The Wall St. Jour., USA Today, People Mag., CNBC, CNN. Named Entrepreneur of Yr., Ernst and Young, Entrepreneur of Yr., Inc. Mag. Office: GSI Commerce 935 1st Ave King Of Prussia PA 19406-1342 Fax: 610-265-2866.

RUBIN, MICHAEL HARRY, lawyer, educator; BA with honors, Amherst Coll., 1972; JD, La. State U., 1975. Bar: La., 1975; U.S. Ct. Appeals (5th Cir.) 1975; U.S. Dist. Ct. (Mid., Ea. and We. Dists.) La., 1976; U.S. Supreme Ct., 1982. Ptnr. McGlinchey and Stafford, Baton Rouge, 1993—. Adj. prof. La. State U. Law Sch., 1976—, Tulane Law Sch., 1976—. Co-author and author 12 books, numerous law rev. articles. Recipient Gold medal award, Atlanta Found. for the Improvement of Justice, Burton award, Libr. of Congress, 2003. Address: 301 Main St Baton Rouge LA 70825

RUBIN, MICHAEL P., surgeon, researcher; b. LA, July 22, 1975; s. Izhak and Nira Rubin; m. Iris Kedar, Aug. 27, 1974; 1 child, Jonathan Alexander. BS, UCLA, 1998; MD, U. Chgo., 2002. Vitreoretinal surgery fellow Harvard Med. Sch./MEEI, Boston, 2006—; computer programmer, elec. engr. IRI Computer Comm. Corp., LA, 1993—98; intern Harvard Med. Sch., Mt. Auburn Hosp., Cambridge, Mass., 2002—03; resident U. Chgo., 2003—06; rschr. molecular genetics Harvard Med. Sch., MEEI, Boston, 2006—. Cons. med. sch. application InQuarta Corp., LA, 1997—98; med. sch. admissions com. U. Chgo., 1998—2002; instr. med. clin. skills course Harvard Med. Sch., Boston, 2002—03; elected mem. Grad. Med. Edn. Com., Chgo., 2005—06. Contbr. articles to profl. jours., chapters to books. Vol. Habitat Humanity, Chgo., 2001—02; free tutor UCLA, 1998—2002; anti-drugs edn. U. Chgo. Elem. Schs., 1998—2002. Recipient Harvard Med. Sch. Outstanding Tchg. Resident award, Harvard Med. Sch., 2003, Albert Potts award Excellence Rsch., U. Chgo., 2006, Beem-Fisher award, Chgo. Ophthalmology Soc., 2006; scholar, Litton Industries, 1996—98. Mem.: ACS, IEEE, AMA, Mass. Med. Soc., Assn. Rsch. Vision and Ophthalmology, Am. Acad. Ophthalmology, UCLA Alumni Assn. (life), Tau Beta Pi, Eta Kappa Nu. Jewish. Avocations: running, reading, travel, piano, theater. Home Phone: 617-383-5770; Office Phone: 617-573-3288. Personal E-mail: michaelrubinmd@gmail.com. E-mail: michael_rubin@meei.harvard.edu.

RUBIN, PHYLLIS GETZ, health association executive; b. NYC, Aug. 6, 1937; d. Joseph and Sylvia (Rosenberg) Getz; m. James Milton Rubin, Oct. 28, 1961; children: Felicia Sue, Andrea Faith. BA, Syracuse U., 1959; MA, Columbia U., 1961, Adelphi U., 1975. Physical edn. tchr. Hicksville (N.Y.) Pub. Schs., 1959-93; bd. dirs., pres. Assoc. Am. Acad. Allergy, Asthma and Immunology; owner JP Med Fit, 1997—, Phyllis Rubin, Ltd., A Med. Exercise Tng. Co., 1998—. Producer: (video) Aerobic Dancercise for Children, 1987. Bd. dir. COPAY, Great Neck, N.Y., 1986-91; v.p., sec. Pierpont Condominium Bd., 1986-90. Recipient Founder's Day award PTA, 1986. Mem.: N.Y. State Alliance for Health, Phys. Edn., REcreation and Dance (program spkr. 1984, 85, 93, v.p. Nassau zone 1987—2000, Zone Svc. award 1993). Avocations: tennis, reading, meditation, golf. Office Phone: 516-972-2342. E-mail: jpmedfit@aol.com.

RUBIN, RHEA JOYCE, library consultant; b. Chgo., June 14, 1950; d. Harold and Edith (Botkin) B.; m. Lawrence Berman, June 7, 1975; 1 child, Hannah Rubin Berman. BA, U. Wis., 1972, MA, 1973. Dir. Oreg. Regional Library for The Blind and Handicapped, Salem, 1976—78; libr. Nat. Coun. Aging, Inc., Washington, 1978—80; cons. Rubin Cons., Oakland, Calif., 1980—. Author: Using Bibliotherapy, 1978, Bibliotherapy Sourcebook, 1978; (with others) Challenge of Aging, 1983, (with others) Let's Talk About It: A Planners Manual, 1984, Working With Older Adults, 1987, 2d edit., 1988, 3d edit., 1990, Of a Certain Age: A Guide to Contemporary Fiction Featuring Older Adults, 1990, Intergenerational Library Programs: A How to Do It Manual, 1993, (with others) Libraries Inside: A Practical Guide for Prison Librarians, 1995, Humanities Programming: A How to Do It Manual, 1997, Defusing the Angry Patron: A How to Do It Manual, 2000, Planning Library Services for People with Disabilities, 2001, Demonstrating Results: Using Outcome Measurement, 2006; book reviewer Libr. Jour.; contbr. articles to profl. jours. Recipient Shaw award, 1980, Monroe award, 1992, Exceptional Svc. award, Assn. Specialized and

Coop. Libr. Agys., 1993, 2006. Mem. ALA (chair numerous coms. 1972). Office: 5860 Heron Dr Oakland CA 94618-2628 Office Phone: 510-339-1274. E-mail: rhea@rheajoycerubin.org.

RUBIN, RICHARD ALLAN, lawyer; b. NYC, June 19, 1942; s. Louis Max and Ruth Ann (Goldman) R.; m. Susan Deborah Levitt, June 18, 1966; children: Karen, Jill. BS, Queens Coll., 1964; JD, Bklyn. Law Sch., 1967; LLM, NYU, 1968. Bar: N.Y. 1967. Assoc. Schwartz and Frank, NYC, 1968—69, Javits and Javits, NYC, 1969—71; ptnr. Wolf Haldenstein Adler Freeman Herz & Frank, NYC, 1972—76, Parker Chapin LLP, NYC, 1977—2000, Jenkens & Gilchrist, Parker Chapin LLP, NYC, 2001—05, Troutman Sanders LLP, 2005—. Lectr. Am. Mgmt. Assn., N.Y. State Bar Assn., N.Y.C. Bar Assn. Mem. ABA. Office Phone: 212-704-6130. Business E-Mail: rrubin@troutmansanders.com.

RUBIN, RICK (FREDERICK JAY RUBIN), record producer; b. Long Beach, NY, Mar. 10, 1963; s. Mickey and Linda (Tomberg) Rubin. BFA, NYU, 1985. Owner, founding pres. Def Jam Recordings, NYC, 1984—88, Am. Recordings (formerly Def Am. Recordings), LA, 1988—. Composer: (songs) I Need a Beat, 1985, Rock the Bells, 1985, I Can't Live Without My Radio, 1985, Can You Rock It Like This, 1985, Fight for Your Right, 1986, Brass Monkey, 1986, It's Tricky, 1986, My Adidas, 1986, New Style, 1986, No Sleep Till Brooklyn, 1986, She's On It, 1986, Bite the Bullet, 1986, Raising Hell, 1986, You & Me, 1987, Goin' Back to Cali, 1987, That's a Lie, 1988, Cold Chillin' in the Spot, 1989, Jack the Ripper, 1989, Hemp Rally, 1993, Kaught in da Ak, 1993, It's a New Style, 1996, 4,3,2,1, 1997, State to State, 1997, Nowhere to Run, 1998, Squirrels, 1999, Super Dee Jay, 1999, 99 Problems, 2004, Busted in the Hood, 2004, Chavas, 2004; prodr.: (albums) Beavis & Butthead Experience, 1993, Working Class Hero: A Tribute to John Lennon, 1995, Chef & Friends: The Songs of South Park, 1998, Chef Aid: The South Park Album, 1998, Mr. Hankey's Christmas Classics, 1999, Essential Roy Orbison, 2006, (Slayer) Hell Awaits, 1985, Reign in Blood, 1986, South of Heaven, 1988, Seasons in the Abyss, 1990, Decade of Aggression, 1991, Divine Intervention, 1994, Serenity in Murder, 1995, Undisputed Attitude, 1996, Diabolus in Musica, 1998, God Hates Us All, 2001, Soundtrack to the Apocalypse, 2003, (Run-D.M.C.) King of Rock, 1985, Raising Hell, 1986, Tougher Than Leather, 1998, Together Forever, 1991, Greatest Hits, 2002, (LL Cool J) Radio, 1985, Walking with a Panther, 1989, All World, 1996, (Beastie Boys) Licensed to Ill, 1986, Sounds of Science, 1999, Solid Gold Hits, 2005, (The Cult) Electric, 1987, Electric Mixes, 1989, Wildflower, 1990, Pure Cult, 1993, Love Removal Machine, 1994, High Octane Cult, 1996, Rare Cult, 2000, (Danzig) Danzig, 1988, Danzig II: Lucifuge, 1990, Danzig III: How the Gods Kill, 1992, Dirty Black Summer, 1992, Thrall: Demonsweatlive, 1993, Danzig 4, 1994, (Andrew Dice Clay) Andrew Dice Clay, 1990, Day the Laughter Died, 1990, Dice Rules, 1990, 40 Too Long, 1993, (Red Hot Chili Peppers) Blood Sugar Sex Magik, 1991, Give It Away, 1991, What Hits!?, 1992, Plasma, 1994, One Hot Minute, 1995, Under the Covers, 1998, Californication, 1999, Live Rare Remix Box, 1999, One Hot Minute, 1999, Road Trippin', 2001, By the Way, 2002, Greatest Hits, 2003, Phenomenon, 2006, Stadium Arcadium, 2006, (Mick Jagger) Wandering Spirit, 1993, (Tom Petty & the Heartbreakers) Greatest Hits, 1993, Playback, 1995, Songs & Music from She's the One, 1996, Anthology, 2000, (Tom Petty) Wildflowers, 1994, You Don't Know How it Feels, 1994, (Joan Jett & the Blackhearts) Flashback, 1994, (Johnny Cash) American Recordings, 1994, Unchained, 1996, American III: Solitary Man, 2000, Love, 2000, Murder, 2000, American IV: The Man Comes Around, 2002, Unearthed, 2003, My Mother's Hymn Book, 2004, Legend of Johnny Cash, 2005, American V: A Hundred Highways, 2006, (Johnny Cash & Willie Nelson) VH1 Storytellers, 1998, (Nine Inch Nails) Further Down the Spiral, 1995, Downward Spiral, 2004, (Donovan) Sutras, 1996, Try for the Sun, 2005, (Sheryl Crow) Globe Sessions, 1998, Sweet Child O'Mine, 1999, (System of a Down) System of a Down, 1998, Sugar, 1999, Chop Suey, 2001, Toxicity, 2001, Steal This Album!, 2002, Hypnotize, 2005, Mezmerize, 2005, (Rage Against the Machine) Renegades, 2000, Live at the Grand Olympic Auditorium, 2003, (Paloalto) Paloalto, 2000, Sonny, 2000, Heroes & Villains, 2003, (Aerosmith) Young Lust, 2001, O, Yeah!, 2002, Gold, 2005, (Krishna Das) Breath of the Heart, 2001, Door of Faith, 2003, (Audioslave) Audioslave, 2002, Doesn't Remind Me, 2005, Out of Exile, 2005, (Jay-Z) Black Album, 2003, (Jay-Z & Linkin Park) Collision Course, 2004, (Limp Bizkit) Eat You Alive, 2003, Results May Vary, 2003, Greatest Hitz, 2005, (The Mars Volta) De-Loused in the Comatorium, 2003, Intertiatic ESP, 2004, Televators, 2004, (Neil Diamond) 12 Songs, 2005, (Ozzy Osbourne) Prince of Darkness, 2005, (Dixie Chicks) Taking the Long Way, 2006 (Record of Yr. for Not Ready to Make Nice, Album of Yr., Grammy awards, 2007); exec. prodr. (Public Enemy) Yo! Bum Rush the Show, 1987, It Takes a Nation of Millions to Hold Us Back, 1988, Power to the People & the Beats, 2005, (Shakira) Don't Bother, 2005, Fijación Oral, Vol. 1, 2005, Oral Fixation, Vol. 2, 2005, (Sir Mix-A-Lot) Mack Daddy, 1992, Chief Boot Knocka, 1994, Jump On It, 1996, Return of the Bumpasaurus, 1996; prodr.: (soundtracks) Krush Groove, 1985, Less Than Zero, 1987, Marked for Death, 1990, Cool World, 1992, Wayne's World, 1992, Coneheads, 1993, Judgment Night, 1993, Last Action Hero, 1993, Party Girl, 1995, Mortal Kombat, 1996, Twister, 1996, I Know What You Did Last Summer, 1997, Jackie Brown, 1997, Private Parts, 1997, Can't Hardly Wait, 1998, Small Soldiers, 1998, Big Daddy, 1998, Human Traffic, 1999, Blair Witch 2, 2000, Heavy Metal 2000, 2000, Little Nicky, 2000, Scream 3, 2000, Jackass, 2001, Shallow Hal, 2001, Scorpion King, 2002, Spider-Man, 2002, Osbourne Family Album, 2002, Collateral, 2004, Kill Bill Vol. 2, 2004, Resident Evil: Apocalypse, 2004, Spider-Man 2, 2004, One Tree Hill, Vol. 2, 2006, Underworld: Evolution, 2006; actor: (films) Krush Groove, 1985, Men Don't Leave, 1990; writer, dir., actor (films) Tougher Than Leather, 1988. Named Hot Prodr. of Yr., Rolling Stone Mag., 1988; named one of The World's Most Influential People, TIME mag., 2007; recipient Joel Weber award, New Music Seminar, 1990, Best Visionary award, Esquire Esky Music Awards, 2006, Grammy award for Non-Classical Prodr. of Yr., 2007. Office: American Recording 22301 Mulholland Hwy Calabasas CA 91302 Office Phone: 818-223-8030.

RUBIN, ROBERT EDWARD, diversified financial services company executive, former secretary of the treasury; b. NYC, Aug. 29, 1938; s. Alexander and Sylvia (Seiderman) R.; m. Judith Leah Oxenberg, Mar. 27, 1963; children: James Samuel, Philip Matthew. AB in Econ. (summa cum laude), Harvard U., 1960; postgrad., London Sch. Econs., 1960-61; LLB, Yale U., 1964; DHL (hon.), Yeshiva U., 1996. Bar: N.Y. 1965. Assoc. Cleary, Gottlieb, Steen & Hamilton, NYC, 1964-66, Goldman, Sachs & Co., NYC, 1966-70, ptnr., 1971, mem. mgmt. com., 1980, vice chmn., co-COO, 1987-90, co-sr. ptnr., co-chmn., 1990-92; asst. to Pres. for econ. policy The White House, Washington, 1993-95; dir. The Nat. Econ. Coun., Washington, 1993—95; sec. US Dept. Treasury, Washington, 1995-99; dir., chmn. exec. com. Citigroup Inc., NYC, 1999—; vice chmn. Coun. Fgn. Relations, Washington, 2003—. Mem. Pres.'s Adv. Com. for Trade Negotiations, Washington, 1980-82, mem. adv. com. on tender offers SEC, Washington, 1983, Gov.'s Commn. on Trade Competitiveness, 1987, regulatory adv. com. N.Y. Stock Exch., 1988-90, adv. com. internat. capital markets Fed. Res. Bank N.Y., 1989-93, Securities and Exch. Commn. Market Oversight and Fin. Svcs. Adv. Com., 1991-93, Gov.'s Adv. Panel on Fin. Svcs., 1988-89; ptnr., bd. dirs. N.Y.C. Partnership Inc., 1991-93; bd. dirs. Ctr. for Nat. Policy, 1982-93, vice chmn., 1984; bd. dirs. N.Y. Futures Exch., N.Y.C., 1979-85, Chgo. Bd. Options Exch. Inc., 1972-76, Ford Motor Co., 2000-06; bd. trustees Mt. Sinai Hosp., 1977, vice chmn., 1986; trustee Sta. WNET-TV, 1985-93, Carnegie Corp. of N.Y., 1990-93; mem. Mayor's Coun. Econ. Advisors, 1990, Gov.'s Coun. on Fiscal and Econ. Priorities, 1990-92; mem. advisory bd., Insight Venrure Partners, 2000-. Author (with Jacob Weisberg): In an Uncertain World: Tough Choices from Wall Street to Washington, 2003 (named one of Ten Best Bus. Books, Bus. Week, 2003). Trustee Am. Ballet Theatre Found., Inc., N.Y.C., 1969-93, trustee Collegiate Sch., 1978-84; mem. bd. overseers' com. to visit econs. dept. Harvard U., 1981-87, com. on univ. resources, 1987-92; mem. fin. com. N.Y. campaign Mondale for Pres., 1983-84; mem. investment adv. coun. N.Y.C. Pension Fund, 1980-89; chmn. Dem. Congl. Dinner, Washington, 1982; Dems. for the 80s, 1985-89, Dems. for the 90s, 1989-90; chmn. N.Y.C. host com. 1992 Dem. Conv., 1989-92; mem. Commn. Nat. Elections. Recipient award Nat. Assn. Christians and Jews, N.Y.C., 1977, Disting. Leadership in Govt. award Columbia Bus. Sch., 1996, Euromoney Mag. award Fin. Min. Yr., 1996, Medal for High Civic Svc. award Citizens' Budget Com., 1997, Fgn. Policy Assn. medal, 1998, "Chmn." award Washington Greater Boys/Girls Clubs, 1998, Intrepid Sea Air Space Mus. award, 1998, Jefferson award Am. Inst. Pub. Svc., 1998, Award of Merit Yale U., 1998, Global Leadership award UN Assn., 1998, Paul Tsongas award, 1998. Mem. Phi Beta Kappa, Harvard Club (N.Y.C.), Century Country Club (Purchase, N.Y.). Democrat. Jewish. Office: Citigroup Inc 399 Park Ave 3d Fl New York NY 10043-0001 *

RUBIN, ROBERT JAY, colon and rectal surgeon; b. Bklyn., July 26, 1928; s. Louis and Etta B. (Siegel) Rubin; m. Sandra P. Glass (div.); m. Lillian G. Garschovsky, Sept. 1975; children: Lisa Nan, Mark Gordon. BA, Gettysburg Coll., Pa., 1948; MD, Jefferson Med. Coll., Phila., 1953. Diplomate Am. Bd. Colon and Rectal Surgery. Clin. prof. surgery Robert Wood Johnson Med. Sch., New Brunswick, NJ, 1995—2001. Contbr. articles to profl. jours., surg. texts. Lt. USN, 1955—57. Fellow: ACS; mem.: NY Soc. Colon and Rectal Surgery, Soc. Surgeons of Alimentary Tract, Am. Soc. Gastroenterology, Pa. Soc. Colon and Rectal Surgery (v.p.), NJ Soc. Colon and Rectal Surgery (pres.), Am. Soc. Colon and Rectal Surgery (v.p.). Jewish. Avocations: fishing, travel, music. Home: 257 Wooded Rd Watchung NJ 07069

RUBIN, ROBERT JOSEPH, internist, nephrologist, consultant; b. Bklyn., Feb. 7, 1946; s. B. Norman and Suzanne (Fried) R.; m. Fran Auerbach, June 14, 1970; children: Elyse Beth, David Jon. AB, Williams Coll., 1966; MD, Cornell U., 1970. Diplomate Am. Bd. Internal Medicine, Nephrology. Intern New England Med. Ctr. Hosps., Boston, 1970-71, resident, 1971-72, 74-76; epidemic intelligence officer, respiratory disease and spl. pathogens, divsn. viral diseases Ctr. for Disease Control, 1972-74; asst. dean govt. affairs Tufts U., 1979-84, assoc. prof. medicine, 1981-84. Chief renal divsn. Lemuel Shattuck Hosp., Boston, 1979-81; asst. sec. planning and evaluation U.S. HHS, Washington, 1981-84; clin. assoc. prof. Georgetown U., Washington, 1984-95, clin. prof., 1995—; exec. v.p. ICF, Inc., 1984-88; pres. Health and Scis. Internat., 1988-92, Lewin ICF Inc., 1992, Lewin-VHI, Inc., 1992-96, Lewin Group, 1996-99, CEO, 1999-2001. Contbr. articles to profl. jours. With USPHS, 1972-74, asst. surgeon gen., 1981-84. Robert Wood Johnson Health Policy fellow, 1977 Mem. ACP, AMA, Am. Soc. Nephrology, Internat. Soc. Nephrology, Mass. Med. Soc., Kenwood Club, Potomac Club, Williams Club, Phi Beta Kappa. Republican. Jewish.

RUBIN, ROBERT SAMUEL, investment banker; b. Boston, Sept. 22, 1931; s. Jesse Abraham and Rose (Solomon) R.; m. Martha Lucy Adams, Dec. 15, 1956; children: Rebecca, David, James, Nathaniel. BA, Yale U., 1953; MBA, Harvard Coll., 1955. With Lehman Bros., 1958-70, ptnr., 1967-70; mng. dir., bd. dirs. Lehman Bros. Kuhn Loeb, Inc., NYC, 1970-84; mng. dir. Salomon Smith Barney, Inc., NYC, 1989—2001; sr. v.p. Bank One (now J.P. Morgan Chase), 2002—. Trustee Bklyn. Mus. 2d lt. US Army, 1955—58. Home: 218 Columbia Hts Brooklyn NY 11201-2105 Office: JP Morgan Chase 320 Park Ave New York NY 10022

RUBIN, ROBERT TERRY, psychiatrist, researcher, educator; b. LA, Aug. 26, 1936; s. Joseph Salem and Lorraine Grace (Baum) R.; m. Lynne Esther Mathews, Mar. 10, 1962 (div. Dec. 1980); children: Deborah, Sharon, Rachel; m. Ada Joan Mickas, Jan. 18, 1985. AB in premedical studies, UCLA, 1957; MD, U. Calif., San Francisco, 1961; PhD in physiology, U. So. Calif., 1977. Diplomate Am. Bd. Psychiatry and Neurology. Intern Phila. Gen. Hosp., 1961-62; resident in psychiatry Sch. Medicine UCLA, 1962-65, asst. prof. psychiatry, 1965-71, prof. psychiatry, 1972; prof. Pa. State U., Hershey, 1972-93; prof. neuroscis. Coll. Medicine Drexel U., Pitts., 1992—2006, prof. psychiatry, dir. Ctr. Neurosci. Rsch. Allegheny Campus, 1992—2005; prof. psychiatry UCLA Sch. Medicine, 2005—; chief dept. psychiatry & mental health VA Greater LA Healthcare System, 2005—. Cons. Naval Health Rsch. Ctr., San Diego, 1969-70; mem. Brain Rsch. Inst. UCLA, 1969—89; assoc. dir. Pitts. Tissue Engring. Initiative, 1994-2004; trustee Kinsey Inst. Sex Rsch., Ind. U., 1986-90. Contbr. articles to profl. jours. With USNR, 1967—69. Recipient Rsch. Sci. Devel. awards NIMH, 1972-77, Rsch. Scientist award, 1982, 87, 93. Fellow: AAAS, Am. Coll. Psychiatrists, Am. Psychiat. Assn.; mem.: Internat. Soc. Psychoneuroendocrinology (pres. 1984—87). Avocations: swimming, bagpiping. Office: VA Greater LA Healthcare System Dept of Psychiatry 116A 11301 Wilshire Blvd Los Angeles CA 90073 Home Phone: 310-231-0380; Office Phone: 310-268-3319. Business E-Mail: robert.rubin@va.gov.

RUBIN, ROBERTA GAIL, retired pathologist; b. Bklyn., Apr. 2, 1934; d. Victor and Pearl Berger Rubin; m. Walter D'Ull; children: Leon Jesse, Victoria Roslyn. MD, SUNY, Bklyn., 1958. Pathologist Chilton Meml. Hosp., Pompton Plains, N.J., 1968-98; dir. lab. Livingston (N.J.) Cmty. Hosp., 1987-88; assoc. pathologist Bronx Lebanon Hosp. Ctr., 1967-68; staff pathologist Maimonides-Coney Island Med. Ctr., Bklyn., 1964-67; dir. MDS Lab., Wayne, NJ, 1973—89; ret., 1989. Clin. instr. pathology SUNY, Bklyn., 1964-67, Albert Einstein Sch. Medicine, Bronx, 1967-68. Sec., treas. bd. Morris Area Cmty. Fedn., Whippany, N.J., 1989—. Fellow: Coll. Am. Pathologists; mem.: N.J. Soc. Pathologists (bd. dirs. 1989—2001), Found. Am. Med. Women's Assn. (treas. 2001—), Nat. Coun. Women's Health (pres. 1999—2001), Am. Women's Hosp. Assn. (chmn. 1993—), Am. Med. Women's Assn. (v.p. fin. 1993, Camille Mermod award 1995). Avocations: doll art collector, cosmology, reading. Home: 10 Woodland Ave Glen Ridge NJ 07028

RUBIN, SAMUEL HAROLD, internist, consultant; b. NYC, July 24, 1916; s. Joseph and Esther (Goldfarb) R.; m. Audrey Arndt, Nov. 20, 1943; children: James E., David A. AB, Brown U., 1938; MD, St. Louis U., 1943; MS, U. Chgo., 1957; DSc (hon.), N.Y. Med. Coll., 1997. Diplomate: Am. Bd. Internal Medicine. Intern Jewish Hosp., St. Louis, 1943-44; resident St. Louis U. Group Hosp., 1944-45, St. Mary's Hosp., Kansas City, Mo., 1945-46; practice medicine Asbury Park, NJ, 1948-61; vol. faculty mem. N.Y. Med. Coll., 1948-61, assoc. prof. dept. medicine, 1962-65, prof., 1965—, dir. Inst. Human Values in Med. Ethics, 1984-86; chief med. service N.Y. Med. Coll.-Met. Hosp. Center, 1966-71, assoc. dean, 1971-72, exec. dean, 1972-74, dean, v.p. acad. affairs, 1975, provost, dean, 1977-83, provost, dean emeritus, 1983—, cons., 1983—. Mem. bd. trustees St. Clares' Hosp., N.Y.C., 1985-2000, N.Y. Med. Coll., 1988-94. Contbr. articles to med. jours. With M.C. AUS, 1946-48. NIH program dir. grantee, 1966-71 Fellow A.C.P.; mem. N.Y. Acad. Sci. Home: 425E Heritage Hills Dr Somers NY 10589-1912

RUBIN, SANDRA MENDELSOHN, artist; b. Santa Monica, Calif., Nov. 7, 1947; d. Murry and Freda (Atliss) Mendelsohn; m. Stephen Edward Rubin, Aug. 6, 1966. BA, UCLA, 1976, MFA, 1979. Instr. Art Ctr. Coll. Design, Pasadena, Calif., 1980, UCLA, 1981. One-woman exhbns. include LA Louver Gallery, 1982, 92, 2003, 07, LA County Mus. Art, 1985, Fischer Fine Arts, London, 1985, Claude Bernard Gallery, NYC, 1987; group exhbns. include LA County Mus. Art, 1977, 82, 83, LA Mcpl. Art Gallery, 1977, 83, 93, LA Contemporary Exhbns., 1978, LA Inst. Contemporary Arts, 1978, Newport Harbor Art Mus., Newport Beach, Calif., 1981, Odyssia Gallery, NYC, 1981, Nagoya City Mus., Japan, 1982, Long Beach Mus. Art, Calif., 1982, Brooke Alexander Gallery, NYC, 1982, Laguna Beach Mus. Art, Calif., 1982, Jan Baum Gallery, LA, 1984, San Francisco Mus. Art, 1986, Claude Bernard Gallery, NYC, 1986, Struve Gallery, Chgo., 1987, Boise Mus., Idaho, 1988, Judy Youen's Gallery, London, 1988, Tatistscheff Gallery, Inc., Santa Monica, Calif., 1989, Tortue Gallery, Santa Monica, 1990, Contemporary Arts Forum, Santa Barbara, Calif., 1990, San Diego Mus. Art, 1991, Fresno Met. Mus., Calif., 1992, Jack Rutberg Fine Arts, LA, 1993, San Jose Mus. Art, 2003, Pasadena Mus. Calif. Art, 2004, LA Louver at Art 38, Basel, Switzerland, 2007. Recipient Young Talent Purchase award LA County Mus. Art, 1980; Artist's Fellowship grant NEA, 1981, 91. Avocations: gardening, exercise, reading, singing. E-mail: smr@pacific.net.

RUBIN, SETH ISAIAH, psychologist; b. Alexandria, La., Mar. 6, 1945; BA, Northwestern U., 1966, MA, 1968, PhD in Psychology, 1971. Diplomate in psychoanalysis and analytical psychology; cert. profl. qualification in psychology; lic. psychologist, Pa., Calif., Ariz., Mass. Outpatient psychology fellow Hosp. U. Pa., 1978-80; tng. candidate, diploma candidate C.G. Jung Inst., Zurich, 1982-87; instr. dept. psychology Northwestern U., 1969-70; asst. prof. dept. psychology U. Ill. at Chgo. Circle, 1970-72; asst. rsch. prof. dept. psychiatry Med. Coll. Pa., 1974-75; asst. prof. dept. cmty. medicine U. Pa., 1975-76, asst. prof. dept. rsch. medicine, 1976-77, asst. prof. dept. ob-gyn., 1976-83, clin. assoc. dpet. psychiatry, 1987-88, clin. asst. prof./clin. assoc prof. psychology in psychiatry, 1987-92; allied health profl. Phila. Psychiat. Ctr., 1988-92; allied health affiliate, clin. psychologist Calif. Pacific Med. Ctr., 1994—2004. Adj. prof. Union Grad. Sch., 1989-96, Calif. Sch. Profl. Psychology, Berkeley/Alameda, 1992—; vis. prof. psychology Saybrook Inst., 1994-95; lectr. in field; dir. James Goodrich Whitney Clinic, C.G. Jung Inst. San Francisco, 2004. Contbr. articles to profl. jours. Fellow Am. Coll. Advanced Practice Psychologists, Internat. Coll. Prescribing Psychologists; mem. APA, Internat. Assn. for Analytical Psychology, Am. Soc. Clin. Psychopharmacology, Assn. Grad. Analytical Psychologists of the C.G. Jung Inst., San Francisco Jung Inst. (dir., James Goodrich Whitney Clin.), Soc. for Psychotherapy Rsch., othrs. Office: 2019 A Webster St San Francisco CA 94115-2329 Office Phone: 415-771-5115. E-mail: sirseth@well.com.

RUBIN, STANLEY CREAMER, television producer, film producer; b. NYC, Oct. 8, 1917; s. Michael Isaac and Anne (Creamer) R.; m. Elizabeth Margaret von Gerkan (actress Kathleen Hughes), July 25, 1954; children: John, Chris, Angela, Michael. Student, UCLA, 1933-37, BA, 2006. Writer Universal Studios, Universal City, Calif., 1940-42, Columbia Pictures, Los Angeles, 1946-47; writer, producer NBC-TV, Burbank, Calif., 1948-49; theatrical film producer various studios, 1949-55, Rastar Prodns., Columbia Pictures, 1988-91; TV producer CBS-TV, Los Angeles, 1956-59, Universal Studios, Universal City, 1960-63, 20th Century-Fox, Los Angeles, 1967-71, MGM Studios, Culver City, Calif., 1972-77; pres. TBA Prodns., Los Angeles, 1978—. Producer theatrical films including The Narrow Margin, 1950, My Pal Gus, 1950, Destination Gobi, 1951, River of No Return, 1952, Promise Her Anything, 1966, The President's Analyst, 1967, Revenge, 1989; co-producer White Hunter, Black Heart, 1990; TV prodns. include G.E. Theatre, 1959-63, Ghost and Mrs. Muir, 1968-69, Bracken's World, 1969-71; writer, producer TV film The Diamond Necklace, 1948 (Emmy award 1949); producer TV films including Babe, 1975 (Hollywood Fgn. Press Golden Globe award, Christopher medal), And Your Name is Jonah, 1978 (Christopher medal 1979), The Story of Satchel Paige, 1980 (Image award 1981); exec. producer TV prodn. Escape from Iran: The Canadian Caper, 1981. Producer spl. programming Dem. Nat. Conv., San Francisco, 1984, Columbia Pictures and Rastar Prodns., 1988-91. 1st lt. USAAF, 1942-46. Mem. Writers Guild Am. (dir. 1941-42), Producers Guild Am. (bd. dirs. 1968-74, pres. 1974-79, v.p. 1987-94, bd. dirs. 1994-2000), Acad. Motion Picture Arts and Scis., Acad. TV Arts and Scis. (bd. govs. 1971, 73), Phi Beta Kappa. Home and Office: 8818 Rising Glen Pl Los Angeles CA 90069-1222 E-mail: tbaprez@aol.com. *I'm still too young to sum up my life, but here's a thought in progress: Stay curious.*

RUBIN, STEPHEN CURTIS, gynecologic oncologist, educator; b. Phila., May 24, 1951; s. Alan and Helen (Metz) R.; m. Anne Loughran, May 30, 1985; children: Michael, Elisabeth. BS, Franklin & Marshall U., 1972; MD, U. Pa., 1976. Diplomate Am. Bd. Ob-gyn. (dir. divsn. gynecol. oncology 2005—), Nat. Bd. Med. Examiners. Intern in ob-gyn. U. Pa. Hosp., Phila., 1976—77, residency in ob-gyn., 1977—80, fellow in gynecologic oncology, 1980—92; asst. prof. ob-gyn. Med. Coll. Pa., Phila., 1982-85, dir. surg. gynecology, 1982-85, chief gynecol. oncology, 1984-85; asst. mem. gynecol. staff Meml. Sloan-Kettering Hosp., NYC, 1985—90, assoc. mem., 1990—93; asst. prof. ob-gyn Cornell U. Med. Coll., 1985—90, assoc. prof., 1990—93; prof. ob-gyn., chief gynecologic oncology U. Pa., Phila., 1993—, Franklin Payne prof., gyn. oncology, 2003—. Editor: Ovarian Cancer, Cervical Cancer, Chemotherapy of Gynecologic Cancer, Uterine Cancer; contbr. over 250 articles to profl. publs. Recipient Career Devel. award Am. Cancer Soc., 1987, Boyer award Meml. Sloan-Kettering; grantee Nat. Cancer Inst., 1991, 96, 98, 99. Mem. ACS, ACOG, Am. Soc. Clin. Oncology, Soc. Gynecol. Oncologists (Pres.'s award 1993), Am. Gynecol. and Obstet. Soc., Soc. Gynecologic Investigation, Soc. Pelvic Surgeons, Gynecol. Cancer Found. (Karin Smith award 1996). Office: U Pa Med Ctr 3400 Spruce St Philadelphia PA 19104-4206 Office Phone: 215-662-3326.

RUBIN, STEPHEN EDWARD, publishing executive, editor, journalist; b. NYC, Nov. 10, 1941; s. Irving and Evelyn (Halprin) R. BA, NYU, 1965; MS, Boston U., 1966. Editor UPI, NYC, 1966-69; freelance writer NYC, 1969-82; founder, dir. Writers Bloc, NYC, 1976-82; editor Vanity Fair Mag., NYC, 1982-83; exec. editor Bantam Books, NYC, 1984-85, v.p., editorial dir., 1985-88, sr. v.p., editor-in-chief adult fiction and non-fiction, 1987-88, sr. v.p., pub., editor-in-chief adult fiction and non-fiction, 1988-90; pres., pub. Doubleday divsn. Bantam Doubleday Dell Pub. Group, NYC, 1990-95; chmn., CEO Bantam Doubleday Dell Internat. Divsn., London, 1995-98; pres., pub. Doubleday Divsn. Bantam Doubleday Dell Pub. Group (now Doubleday Broadway Group), NYC, 1998—. Author: The New Met in Profile, 1974 Recipient Annual Prize, UJA-Fedn. NY pub. divsn., 2005. Avocations: listening to musical performances, collecting records, tapes and cds, reading, exercising. Office: Random House Inc 1745 Broadway New York NY 10019

RUBIN, STEVEN D., lawyer; b. June 1, 1960; BA in Econs., Tulane U., 1982; JD with honors, U. Fla., 1986. Bar: Fla. 1986. Assoc. Stearns, Weaver, Miller, Weissler, Alhadeff & Sitterson, 1986—91, shareholder, 1991—2000, dir., 1998—2000; sr. v.p., gen. counsel Telergy, Inc., 2000—01, Ivax Corp., Miami, 2001—. Office: Ivax Corp 4400 Biscayne Blvd Miami FL 33137 Office Phone: 305-575-6000. Office Fax: 305-575-6055. E-mail: steven_rubin@ivax.com.

RUBIN, THEODORE ISAAC, psychiatrist, writer; b. Bklyn., Apr. 11, 1923; s. Nathan and Esther (Marcus) R.; m. Eleanor Katz, June 16, 1946; children: Jeffrey, Trudy, Eugene. BA, Bklyn. Coll., 1946; MD, U. Lausanne, Switzerland, 1951; grad., Am. Inst. Psychoanalysis, 1964. Resident psychiatrist Los Angeles VA Hosp., 1953, Rockland State Hosp., NY, 1954, Bklyn. State Hosp., 1955, Kings County Hosp., NY, 1956; chief psychiatrist Women's House of Detention, NYC, 1957; mem. faculty Downstate Med. Sch., NY State U., 1957-59; pvt. practice NYC, 1956—. Tng. and supervising psychoanalyst Am. Inst. for Psychoanalysis of Karen Horney Clinic and Ctr.; mem. faculty Am. Inst. Psychoanalysis, 1962—; pres. emeritus bd. trustees Am. Inst. Psychoanalysis. Author: Jordi, 1960, Lisa and David, 1961, Sweet Daddy, 1963, In The Life, 1964, Platzo and the Mexican Pony Rider, 1965, The Thin Book by a Formerly Fat Psychiatrist,

1966, The 29th Summer, 1966, Cat, 1966, Coming Out, 1967, The Winner's Note Book, 1967, The Angry Book, 1969, Forever Thin, 1970, Emergency Room Diary, 1972, Doctor Rubin Please Make Me Happy, 1974, Shrink, 1974, Compassion and Self-Hate, An Alternative to Despair, 1975, Love Me, Love My Fool, 1976, Reflections in a Goldfish Tank, 1977, Alive and Fat and Thinning in America, 1978, Reconciliations, 1980, Through My Own Eyes, 1982, One to One, Understanding Personal Relationships, 1983, Not to Worry, The American Family Book of Mental Health, 1984, Overcoming Indecisiveness, 1985, Lisa and David, The Story Continues, 1986, Miracle at Bellevue, 1986, Real Love, 1990, Child Potential, 1990, Anti-Semitism: A Disease of the Mind, 1990, Little Ralphie and The Creature, 1998; mem. editl. bd. Am. Jour. Psychoanalysis; also articles, columns.; co-writer (TV movie) Lisa and David, 1998. Served as officer USNR, World War II. Recipient Adolf Meyer award, Assn. Improvement Mental Health, 1963. Fellow Am. Acad. Psychoanalysis; mem. NY County Med. Soc., Am. Psychiat. Assn., Assn. Advancement Psychoanalysis, Authors Guild, Contemporary Authors, Writers Guild East. Office: 141 E 55th St Ste 9B New York NY 10022 Home Phone: 212-838-0758; Office Phone: 917-301-4889.

RUBIN, VERA COOPER, astronomer, researcher; b. Phila., July 23, 1928; d. Philip and Rose (Applebaum) Cooper; m. Robert J. Rubin, June 25, 1948; children: David M., Judith S. Young, Karl C., Allan. BA in Astronomy, Vassar Coll., 1948; MA, Cornell U., 1951; PhD, Georgetown U., 1954, DHL (hon.), 1997; DSc (hon.), Creighton U., 1978, Harvard U., 1988, Yale U., 1990, Williams Coll., 1993, U. Mich., 1996, Ohio State U., 1998, Smith Coll., 2001, Grinnell Coll., 2002, Ohio-Wesleyan U., 2004, Princeton U., 2005. From rsch. assoc. to asst. prof. Georgetown U., Washington, 1955-65; physicist U. Calif., LaJolla, 1963-64; astronomer Carnegie Inst., Washington, 1965—2001, sr. fellow, dept. terrestrial magnetism, 2001—. Chancellor's Disting. prof. U. Calif., Berkeley, 1981; vis. com. Harvard Coll. Obs., Cambridge, Mass., 1976—82, 1992—2002, Space Telescope Sci. Ins., 1990—92; Beatrice Tinsley vis. prof. U. Tex., 1988; Commonwealth lectr. U. Mass., 1991; Yunker lectr. Oreg. State U., 1991; Bernhard vis. fellow Williams Coll., 1993; Oort vis. prof. U. Leiden, The Netherlands, 1995; lectr. in field, Chile, Russia, China, Armenia, India, Japan, Europe; trustee Assoc. Univs., Inc., 1993—96; mem. Pres. Commn. to Select U.S. Nat. Medal Sci. Awardees, 1995—98, chair, 1997—98; Pres.'s disting. visitor Vassar Coll., 1987; Halley lctr. Oxford Univ., 1997; bd. dir. Sci. Service, 2002—; adv. bd. Lowell Observatory. Assoc. editor: Astrophys. Jour. Letters, 1977—82, mem. editl. bd.: Sci. Mag., 1979—87, mem. sr. editl. bd.:, 2001—, co-author several peer reviewed research papers. Named to Nat. Sci. Bd., 1996—2002; recipient U.S. Nat. Medal of Sci., 1993, Jansky Lectureship, Nat. Radio Astronomy Observatory, 1994, Gold medal, Royal. Astorn. Soc. London, 1996, Weizmann Women and Sci. award, 1996, Helen Hogg prize, Can. Astron. Soc., 1997, John Scott Award, City of Phila., 2001, Peter Gruber Internat. prize in cosmology, 2002, Bruce medal, Astron. Soc. of Pacific, 2003. Mem.: NAS (space sci. bd. 1974—77, chair sect. on astronomy 1992—95, James Craig Watson medal 2004), AAAS, Am. Philos. Soc., Assn. Univ. Rsch. in Astronomy (trustee 1973—76, 1994—96), Pontifical Acad. Scis. (Gold medal), Internat. Astron. Union (pres. commn. on galaxies 1982—85, chair U.S. nat. commn. 1999—2001), Am. Astron. Soc. (coun. 1977—80, Henry Norris Russell prize lectr. 1994), Phi Beta Kappa (scholar 1982—83). Democrat. Jewish. Achievements include being the first women permitted to observe at Palomar Observatory in California in 1965; being the first women since 1828 to receive the Gold Medal of the Royal Astronomical Society in London. *As an observational astronomer, it is my aim to obtain data of highest quality in order to answer questions concerning the universe in which we live. In spite of our enormous ignorance, each day offers exciting opportunities to learn a little more. This is the real joy of doing science.*

RUBIN, ZICK, lawyer, writer, psychology professor; b. NYC, Apr. 29, 1944; s. Eli and Adena Rubin; m. Carol Moses, June 21, 1969; children: Elihu James, Noam Moses BA, Yale U., 1965; PhD, U. Mich., 1969; JD, Harvard U., 1988. Bar: Mass., 1988. Asst. to assoc. prof. Harvard U., Cambridge, Mass., 1969—76; Louis and Frances Salvage prof. social psychology Brandeis U., Waltham, Mass., 1976—89; law clk. chief judge U.S. Ct. Appeals (1st cir.), 1988—89; assoc. Palmer & Dodge, Boston, 1990—93, counsel, 1994—2001; of counsel Hill & Barlow, Boston, 2001—03; prin. Law Office of Zick Rubin, Boston, 2003—. Chmn. com. behavioral scis. Yale U. Coun., New Haven, 1981-86. Author: Liking and Loving, 1973, Children's Friendships, 1980; co-author: Psychology, 1993; editor: Doing Unto Others, 1974, Relationships and Development, 1986; contbg. editor: Psychology Today, 1980-85; mem. editl. bd. Harvard Law Rev., 1986-88. Recipient Socio-Psychol. prize AAAS, 1969, Nat. Media award Am. Psychol. Found., 1980; grantee NSF, NIMH, Ford Found., Social Sci. Research Council, Found. Child Devel.; named one of Boston's top lawyers, Boston Mag. 2002. Mem. ABA, Nat. Assn. Coll. and Univ. Lawyers, Copyright Soc. USA, Boston Bar Assn., Soc. Exptl. Social Psychology, Soc. Personality and Social Psychology, Authors Guild, Mass. Hist. Soc. (mem. Adams Papers adminstrv. com. 2001-06, mem. pubs. com. 2007—), Phi Beta Kappa. Clubs: Elihu (New Haven). Jewish. Office Phone: 617-965-9425. Business E-Mail: zrubin@zickrubin.com.

RUBINE, ROBERT SAMUEL, lawyer; b. Rockaway, NY, Feb. 28, 1947; s. George and Beatrice (Simon) R.; m. Marilyn Goldberg Rubine, Aug. 15, 1970; children: Seth B., Marisa H. BA, Queens Coll., 1968; JD, Syracuse U., 1971. Bar: N.Y. 1972, Fla. 1975; U.S. Dist. Ct. (ea. and so. dists.) N.Y., 1976; U.S. Supreme Ct. 1976. Trial atty. Legal Aid Soc. Nassau County, Mineola, N.Y., 1971-77; atty. Reifman and Rubine, Jericho, N.Y., 1977-79; ptnr. Stein, Rubine and Stein, Mineola, 1979-94, Rubine and Rubine, Mineola, 1995—. Adj. prof. C.W. Post Coll., Greenvale, N.Y., 1979-82. Author: (chpt.) Criminal and Civil Investigation Handbook, 1981. Dir. Legal Aid Soc. Nassau County, 1989—, pres., 1994-95, treas., 1996—. Mem. N.Y. State Bar Assn., N.Y. State Assn. Criminal Def. Lawyers, N.Y. State Defenders Assn., Nassau County Bar Assn. Avocation: golf. Home: 5 Woodland Rd Oyster Bay NY 11771-3910 Office: Rubine and Rubine PLLC 114 Old Country Rd Mineola NY 11501-4400 Office Phone: 516-739-0003. Business E-Mail: rubinelaw@aol.com.

RUBINFIEN, LEO H., photographer, writer; b. Chgo., Aug. 16, 1953; Student, Reed Coll.; BFA, Calif. Inst. Arts, 1974; MFA, Yale U., 1976. Instr. in photography Swarthmore Coll., 1977, Sch. Visual Arts, NYC, 1978-87; assoc. prof. art Fordham U., 1981-87; represented by Robert Mann Gallery, NYC; mem. faculty Gallatin Sch., NYU, 2001—. Mem. grad. faculty Sch. of Visual Arts, NYU, 2002—; vis. lectr. Cooper Union, 1982; vis. prof. Musashino Fine Arts U., Tokyo, 2002. One man shows include Castelli Gallery, N.Y., 1981, Fraenkel Gallery, San Francisco, 1982, 86, Robert Mann Gallery, N.Y.C., 1994, 2001, Met. Mus. Art, N.Y.C., 1992, Seibu Art Forum, Tokyo, 1993, Cleve. Mus. Art, 1994, Seattle Art Mus., 1994, Robert Mann Gallery, N.Y.C.; exhibited in group shows at Internat. Ctr. Photography, N.Y., 1981, Inst. Contemporary Arts, London, 1981, San Francisco Mus. Modern Art, 1981, George Eastman House, Rochester, N.Y., 1981, Corcoran Gallery, Washington, 1981, Mus. Modern Art, N.Y., 1984, Met. Mus. Art, 2001, Tokyo Met. Mus. Photography, 2002; dir., co-author (film) The Money Juggler, 1988, My Bed in the Leaves, 1990; author: (books) A Map of the East, 1992, 10 Takeoffs 5 Landings, 1994, Shomei Tomatsu: Skin of the Nation, 2004, (essays) The Man in the Crowd, 1977, Love-Hate Relations, 1978, Investigations of a Dog, 1999, Guesses About the Work of Wu Yiming, 1999, The Poetry of Plain Seeing, 2000, Perfect Uncertainty, 2001, The Mask Behind the Face, 2004, Where Diane Arbus Went, 2005, Doomed Alleys, 2006. Fellow Guggenheim Found., 1982-83, Asian Cult Coun., 1984, Internat. Ctr. Advanced Studies, 1998—, Japan Found., 2002, Asian Cult. Coun., 2002 Home: 145 Nassau St Apt 11c New York NY 10038-1514 Personal E-mail: oscawana@earthlink.net.

RUBINGH, JONATHAN PATRICK, environmental health specialist; s. Gary E. and Rebecca A. Rubingh. BSc in Biol. Scis., Grand Valley State U., Allendale, Mich., 2001. Quality control technician Perrigo, Allendale, Mich., 2002—03; lab. support analyst Cordis, LLC, Mayaguez, PR, 2003—06; environ. health specialist Fresno County, Calif., 2006—. Mem.: APHA (assoc.), Nat. Environ. Health Assn., Amnesty Internat. Non-Partisan. Avocations: travel, running, kayaking, music. Home: 365 E Barstow Ave Apt# 2101 Fresno CA 93710 Office: Fresno County Dept Cmty Health 1221 Fulton Mall Fresno CA 93721 Office Fax: 559-445-3379; Home Fax: 559-570-0181. Personal E-mail: rubinghj@msn.com.

RUBIN-KATZ, BARBARA, sculptor, human services manager; b. Springfield, Mass., May 3, 1931; d. Samuel and Jane (Freeman) Kurn; m. Emanuel Rubin, Mar. 27, 1955 (div. Dec. 1984); children: Raphael, Jonathan, Daniel, Rebecca; m. Robert Nathan Katz, June 15, 1986. BA, U. Ariz., 1952; MSW, Simmons Coll., 1955; MPH, Columbia U., 1977; postgrad. in Sculpture Studies, Phila. Coll. Art, 1981-85. Rschr. Bellevue Hosp., NYC, 1970-75; health svcs. coord. Fedn. Jewish Agencies, NYC, 1977-79, assoc. dir. planning Phila., 1979-84; sculptor Brookline, Mass., 1985—. Prin. works include sculpture at Mass. Gen. Hosp., Villa Campana, Tucson, Worcester Poly. Inst., Regency Park, Brookline, Mass, Temple Emanuel, Tucson, St. Elizabeth's Hosp., Brighton, Mass.; exhibited in group shows at Copley Soc. Boston shows, 1990—, New Eng. Sculptors Assn. shows, 1987—, The Roxbury Latin Sch., 1991, Jr. League Boston Decorator's Showhouse, Walpole, Mass., 1994, Faneuil Hall, Boston, 1994, Prestige Gallery, Danvers, Mass., 1995, Michael Allen Gallery, Brookline, Mass., 1996, Festival Arts, Newton, 1997, Curtis Gallery, Lenox, Mass., 1997, 98, Worcester Poly. Inst., 1997-98, Bradford (Mass.) Coll., 1999; contbr. articles to profl. jours. Mem. Copley Soc. Boston (Copley Artist award 1992), New Eng. Sculptors Assn. (bd. dirs. 1993), Brookline Coun. for Arts and Humanities. Home: 1731 Beacon St Apt 1403 Brookline MA 02445-5329 Office Phone: 617-738-4723. Personal E-mail: katz@wpi.edu.

RUBINO, FRANK A., lawyer; b. 1945; BS in Bus. Adminstrn., Seton Hall U., 1967; JD, U. Miami Sch. Law, Coral Gables, 1975. Bar: US Ct. Appeals (1st Cir.) 1988, US Ct. Appeals (2nd Cir.) 1991, US Ct. Appeals (11th Cir.) 1981, US Ct. Appeals (9th Cir.) 1983, US Ct. Appeals (4th Cir.) 1984, US Ct. Appeals (5th Cir.) 1984, US Supreme Ct. 1985. Atty. Frank A. Rubino, Esq., P.A., Miami. Lectr., guest spkr. in field. Mem.: Assn. Trial Lawyers NJ, La. Criminal Def. Lawyers Assn., Tx. Criminal Def. Lawyers Assn., Ga. Criminal Def. Lawyers Assn., Wash. State Bar Assn., Fl. Bar Assn., The Acad. Fla. Trial Lawyers, ABA, The Assn. Trial Lawyers Am., Nat. Assn. Criminal Def. Lawyer, Fl. Assn. Criminal Def. Lawyers. Office: Frank A Rubino Esq PA 801 Brickell Ave Ste 910 Miami FL 33131 Office Phone: 305-858-5300. Office Fax: 305-350-2001. E-mail: frank@frankrubino.com. *

RUBINO, JOHN ANTHONY, management and human resources consultant; b. Port Chester, NY, Nov. 22, 1956; s. Angelo J. and Ann (Posillipo) R.; m. Cynthia C. Corica, Nov. 9, 1980; 1 child, Sean Anthony. BA in Psychology magna cum laude, Wagner Coll., 1978; MBA with distinction, Pace U., 1985. Cert. compensation profl. Convention svc. mgr. Waldorf-Astoria Hotel, NYC, 1978-80; compensation analyst County of Westchester, White Plains, N.Y., 1980-82; sr. compensation analyst Anaconda-Ericsson, Inc., Greenwich, Conn., 1982-83; compensation mgr. ASEA, Inc., White Plains, N.Y., 1983-84, Sterling Drug, Inc., NYC, 1984-87; dir. exec. compensation The Equitable Life Insur. Co., NYC, 1987-93; sr. mgr. human resources cons. Ernst & Young, NYC, 1993-96; pres. Rubino Cons. Svcs., Pound Ridge, N.Y., 1996—. Author: Developing Compensation Programs, 1990, Communicating Compensation Programs, 2004; contbr. articles to profl. jours. Recipient Lifetime Achievement award, World At Work, 2003. Mem. WorldatWork (course developer, instr., course leader, guest speaker 1988—), Am. Mgmt. Assn. (course developer, instr., course leader, guest speaker 1988—), Soc. for Human Resource Mgmt. (guest spkr. 1999—). Avocations: performing renaissance music, poetry, golf, guitar, lute. Home and Office: Rubino Cons Svcs 29 Conant Valley Rd Pound Ridge NY 10576-1815 Office Phone: 914-533-5310. Personal E-mail: rubinocs@aol.com.

RUBINO, STEPHEN JOHN, secondary school educator; b. Bad Kreuznach, Federal Republic Germany, Nov. 26, 1955; came to U.S., 1956; s. James Vincent and Carolyn Jean (Harper) R.; m. Melane Lea Gray, Sept. 30, 1986. BA in Polit. Sci., Miami U., Oxford, Ohio, 1977; postgrad., Mercer U., 1988-89, U. Ga., 1989-91, Oglethorpe U., 1992. Cert. secondary social scis., polit. sci., history tchr., K-12 gifted tchr., Ga., econs. Sole prop. Furniture Remedies, Chamblee, Ga., 1987-89; tchr. history and polit. sci. DeKalb County Schs., Decatur, Ga., 1989—. Cons. in curriculum revision and textbook adoption, Decatur, 1990-93; judge Odyssey of the Mind, Atlanta, 1991. Author: (poems) First Effort, 1978. Mem. ASCD, Nat. Coun. for Social Studies, Profl. Assn. Ga. Educators (bldg. rep. 1989-93), Phi Kappa Phi. Avocations: military science, strategic and tactical games, reading, golf.

RUBINO, VICTOR JOSEPH, academic administrator, lawyer; b. NYC, Dec. 25, 1940; s. Joseph V. and Olympia (Gayda) R.; 1 child, Victor Gayda. BA in Govt., Cornell U., 1962, LLB, 1965. Bar: N.Y. 1965, U.S. Dist. Ct. (so. dist.) N.Y. 1969. Staff atty. Westchester Legal Svcs., White Plains, NY, 1968-71; assoc. Squadron Ellenoff Plesent & Lehrer, NYC, 1971; treas., program officer Council on Legal Edn., NYC, 1971-79; assoc. dir. Practising Law Inst., NYC, 1979-83, exec. dir., 1983—. Democratic candidate for N.Y. State Assembly, 1970; chmn. Rye (N.Y.) Human Rights Commn., 1975-76. Served to capt. U.S. Army, 1966-68. Mem. ABA, Assn. Bar City N.Y. Office: Practising Law Inst 810 7th Ave Fl 26 New York NY 10019-5818 Office Phone: 212-824-5701. Business E-Mail: vrubino@pli.edu.

RUBINSON, HOWARD ALAN, physician; b. Bklyn., Aug. 24, 1949; s. Samuel and Hilda (Cohen) R.; m. Carol Berman, May 16, 1976; children: Roger, Abby. AB, Cornell U., Ithaca, NY, 1971; MD, Hahnemann Med. Coll., Phila., 1975. Diplomate Am. Bd. Radiology. Radiology instr. Sch. Medicine U. Miami, Fla., 1979-81, asst. prof. radiology Fla., 1981-84; mem. attending staff North Beach Hosp., Ft. Lauderdale, Fla., 1984-89, North Ridge Med. Ctr., Ft. Lauderdale, Fla., 1989—2006, Hollywood Med. Ctr., Fla., 1998—2006, Parkway Regional Med. Ctr., 2001—05; attending staff Holy Cross Hosp., Ft. Lauderdale, Fla., 2004—, Mercy Hosp., Miami, Fla., 2005—. Contbr. articles to profl. jours. Mem. Am. Coll. Radiology, Am. Soc. Emergency Radiology, Soc. Breast Imaging, Radiol. Soc. N.Am., Am. Roentgen Ray Soc., Soc. Thoracic Radiology, South Fla. Radiol. Soc. (pres. 1996-97), Fla. Radiol. Soc., Fla. Med. Assn., Broward County Med. Assn. Office: 2929 E Commercial Blvd Ste 600 Fort Lauderdale FL 33308 Personal E-mail: hrubinson@comcast.net.

RUBINSTEIN, AARON, lawyer; b. NYC, Nov. 15, 1950; s. Jacob and Golda Rubinstein; m. Carri Sue Zogan, Mar. 3, 1974; children: David Michael, Jennifer Lauren. BA magna cum laude, Cornell U., 1972; JD, NYU, 1975. Bar: NY 1976, US Dist. Ct. (so. and ea. dists.) 1976, US Supreme Ct. 1986. Assoc. Kaye, Scholer LLP, NYC, 1975-84, ptnr., 1985—, chair Litig. Dept. and Securities and Derivatives Litig. Mem. ABA, NY State Bar Assn., Assn. of Bar of City of NY, Order of Coif. Office: Kaye Scholer LLP 425 Park Ave New York NY 10022-3506 Office Phone: 212-836-8412.

RUBINSTEIN, ERNEST, librarian, educator; b. Queens, NY, July 11, 1952; s. Jack and Jeanne Rubinstein; life ptnr. Paul Glassman. BA, Brandeis U., 1974; AMLS, U. Mich., 1977; MTS, Harvard U., 1979; MA, Hebrew Union Coll., 1985; PhD, Northwestern U., Evanston, Ill., 1995. Indexer H.W. Wilson Co., Bronx, NY, 1984—88; editor Am. Theological Libr. Assn., Chgo., 1988—90; reference libr. North Park Coll., Chgo., 1990—94; libr. Interchurch Ctr., NYC, 1994—2005; libr. theol. Drew U., Madison, NJ, 2005—. Asst. adj. prof. humanities NYU, NYC, 1995—; adj. faculty New Sch., NYC, 2001—; book reviewer Publs. Weekly, NYC, 1999—2001. Author: (non-fiction) Episode of Jewish Romanticism, 1999; contbr. articles to mags. Vol. peer counselor Horizons, Chgo., 1992—94, Aids Pastoral Care Network, Chgo., 1992—94. Mem.: Am. Acad. Religion. Jewish. Office: Drew Univ Libr Madison NJ 07940 Personal E-mail: ehr3@nyu.edu.

RUBINSTEIN, EVA (ANNA), photographer; b. Buenos Aires, 1933; d. Arthur and Aniela (Mlynarska) R.; m. William Sloane Coffin Jr., 1956 (div. 1968); children: Amy, Alexander (dec.), David. Ballet tng., Paris, NYC, Calif., 1938-53; student, Scripps Coll., Claremont, Calif., 1950-51, UCLA, 1952-53; student in photography, Lisette Model, 1969, Jim Hughes, 1971, Ken Heyman, 1970, Diane Arbus, 1971. Lectr. numerous workshops, seminars, confs.; instr. photo seminars Lodz Film Sch., Poland, 1986, 87. Dancer, actress: off-Broadway and Broadway, including original prodn. The Diary of Anne Frank, 1955-56; European dance tour, 1955; one-person shows of photographs include Underground Gallery, NYC, 1972, Dayton Art Inst., Ohio, 1973, Arles Festival, France, 1975, Canon Photo Gallery, Amsterdam, 1975, Neikrug Gallery, NYC, 1975, 79, 81, 82, 85, La Photogalerie, Paris, 1975, Friends of Photography, Carmel, Calif., 1975, Galerie 5.6, Ghent, Belgium, 1976, Gallery Trochenpresse, Berlin, 1977, Frumkin Gallery, Chgo., 1977, Galeria Sinisca, Rome, 1979, Hermitage Found. Mus., Norfolk, Va., 1982, Photographers Gallery, London, 1983, Galerie Forum Labo, Arles, France, 1983, Galerie Nicephore, Lyon, France, 1983, Image Gallery, Madrid, 1984, Muzeum Sztuki, Lodz, Poland, 1984, Il Diaframma/Canon Gallery, Milan, 1984, A.R.P.A. Gallery, Bordeaux, 1984, Chateau d'Eau, Toulouse, France, 1985, Galerie Demi-Teinte, Paris, 1985, Associated Artist Photographers galleries in Warsaw, Krakow, Lodz, Katowice and Gdansk, Poland, 1985-86, Foto/Medium/Art Gallery, Wroclaw, Poland, 1986, Visions Gallery, San Francisco, 1986, Canon Galerie, Paris, 1986, Salone Internat. SICOF, Milan, 1987, St. Krzysztof Gallery, Lodz, 1987, L'Image Fixe, Lyon, 1988, Artotheque, Grenoble, 1988, Neikrug Photographica, NYC, 1989, Heuser Art Ctr. Gallery, Bradley U., Peoria, Ill., 1989, 3-os Encontros da Imagem, Braga, Portugal, 1989, Bibliotheque Nat. Galerie Colbert, Paris, 1989, Galerie Picto-Bastille, Paris, 1989-90, Portfolio Gallery, London, 1990, Vaison-La-Romaine, France, 1990, Hist. Mus. of City of Lodz, 1990, Galerie Artem, Quimper, France, 1993, Galerie F.N.A.C. Etoile, Paris, 1994, other F.N.A.C. galleries (France, Belgium, Spain), 1994-97, Galerie Augustus, Berlin, 1995, L'Imagerie, Lannion, France, 1995, Zacheta Gallery, Warsaw, 1996, Salon of Modern Art B.W.A., Bydgoszcz, Poland, 1997, Galleries of Polish Insts., Sofia, Bulgaria, Berlin, Moscow, Bratislava, Slovakia, I. Beszkova Gallery, Plewen, Bulgaria, 1997, Hungarian Mus. Photographic Art, Budapest, 1997, LTF Gallery, Lodz, Poland, 1998, Konfrontacje Fotograficzne, Gorzow Wielopolski, Poland, 1998, Centrum Kultury Zamek, Poznan, Poland, 1998, Mus. Regionalny, Wrzesnia, Poland, 1998, Galeria Korytarz, Jelenia Gora, Poland, 1998, Galeria Foto-Medium-Art, Wroclaw, Poland, 1998, Galeria Pusta, Centrum Kultury, Katowice, Poland, 1998, Teatr Wielki, Lodz, Poland, 2000, Gallery Europa Club, NY, 2003, Château de la Petite, Malmaison, France, 2004, Alliance Française, NYC, 2006; numerous group shows since 1971 including most recently Zacheta Gallery, Warsaw, 2002, Lodz Photographic Soc., 2002, Polish/Am.Photographers, Polish Consulate, NY, 2003, Gutman Libr., Harvard, 2003, Floating Found. Photography, NY, 2004, XL, La Collection Photographique du Musée d'Arles, 2005, Lisette Model and her Descendants, Aperture, NY, 2007; represented: in permanent collections Library of Congress, Washington, Met. Mus. Art, NYC, Bibliotheque Nationale, Paris, Musee Reattu, Arles, France, Kalamazoo Inst. Arts, Israel Mus., Jerusalem, Fotografiska Museet, Stockholm, Muzeum Sztuki, Lodz, Poland, Histo Mus. of City of Lodz, others; author: Eva Rubinstein, 1974, Eva Rubinstein, I Grandi Fotografi, 1983, 2 ltd. edit. portfolios with introductions by John Vachon andAndré Kertész, Lodz: Brief Encounters, 1998, Eva Rubinstein: Fotografie 1967-1990, 2003; contbr. photographs in various books, mags., profl. jours. *Making photographs is my way of exploring the questions that keep me alive by ever leading to further questions.*

RUBINSTEIN, FREDERIC ARMAND, lawyer; b. Antwerp, Belgium, Apr. 20, 1931; came to U.S., 1942; s. Samuel N. and Steffa (Warenreich) R.; m. Susan August, Dec. 24, 1968; 1 child, Nicolas Eric August Rubinstein. BA, Cornell U., 1953, JD, 1955. Bar: N.Y. 1955. Assoc. Law Offices of I. Robert Feinberg, NYC, 1955-60, Guggenheimer & Untermyer, NYC, 1960-65, ptnr., 1965-85, Kelley Drye & Warren LLP, NYC, 1985—. Vice chmn. zoning & planning com. Local Community Bd. # 6, N.Y.C., 1980-86. Mem. ABA (bus. law sect., emerging growth ventures subcom., chmn. 1988-96). Office: Kelley Drye & Warren LLP 101 Park Ave New York NY 10178-0002 Business E-Mail: frubinstein@kelleydrye.com.

RUBINSTEIN, JAVIER H., lawyer; b. Buenos Aires, 1963; m. Lisa Rubinstein; children: Stefanie, Jason. BA magna cum laude in Polit. Sci & Econs., U. Mich., 1984; MS in Pub. Policy, Harvard U., 1986; JD cum laude, Georgetown U., 1989. Bar: Ill. 1989, US Dist. Ct. (no. dist. Ill.) 1989, US Dist. Ct. (ea. dist. Wis.) 1992, US Dist. Ct. (dist. Ariz.) 1997, US Ct. Appeals (5th cir.) 1997, US Ct. Appeals (7th cir.) 1991, US Ct. Appeals (9th cir.) 1996, US Supreme Ct. 1993. Atty. Mayer, Brown, Rowe & Maw, Chgo., 1989—98, ptnr., 1998—2006; global gen. counsel Pricewaterhouse-Coopers Internat. Ltd., NYC, 2006—. Lectr. law U. Chgo Law Sch., 1996—. Contbr. articles in prof. law jours. Midwest Comm. Arbitration US Coun. Internat. Bus. Named one of 40 Ill. Attys. Under 40 to Watch, Chgo. Lawyer Mag., 2001, World's Leading Experts in Comml. Arbitration, Euromoney mag., 2006. Mem.: ABA (Midwest co-chmn. Bus. Torts Litig. com.), London Ct. Internat. Arbitration. Office: PricewaterhouseCoopers Internat Ltd 1177 Avenue of the Americas New York NY 10036 *

RUBINSTEIN, JONATHAN J., computer company executive; BSEE, Cornell U., 1978, MSEE, 1979; MS in Computer Sci., Colo. State U. Arch. HP 9000 series, mem. design team HP 9836 workstation Hewlett-Packard; mgr. processor devel. Titan graphics supercomputer family Stardent Computer, designer, arch. 3000 and 2000 computer sys.; v.p., gen. mgr. hardware, v.p. hardware engring. NeXT Computer; exec. v.p., COO FirePower Sys.; sr. v.p. hardware engring. Apple Computer, Inc., Cupertino, Calif., 1997—2004, sr. v.p. iPod divsn., 2004—06, cons., 2006—. Owner, cons. J.R. Ruby Consulting Corp. Patentee in field; contbr. articles to profl. jours. Mem. IEEE, NAE, Assn. for Computing Machinery.

RUBINSTEIN, MOSHE FAJWEL, engineering educator; b. Miechow, Poland, Aug. 13, 1930; came to US, 1950, naturalized, 1965; s. Shlomo and Sarah (Rosen) Rubinstein; m. Zafrira Gorstein, Feb. 3, 1953; children: Iris, Dorit. BS, UCLA, 1954, MS, 1957, PhD, 1961. Designer Murray Erick Assos. (engrs. and archs.), LA, 1954-56; structural designer Victor Gruen Assos., LA, 1956-61; asst. prof. UCLA, 1961-64, assoc. prof. dept. engring., 1964-69, prof., 1969—, chmn. engring. sys. dept., 1970-75, program dir. modern engring. for execs. program, 1965-70. Cons. Pacific

Power & Light Co., Portland, Oreg., Northrop Corp., US Army, NASA Rsch. Ctr., Langley, Tex. Instruments Co., Hughes Space System Divsn., US Army Sci. Adv. Com., Kaiser Aluminum and Chem. Corp., IBM Corp., TRW. Author: (with W.C. Hurty) Dynamics of Structures, 1964 (Yugoslavian transl. 1973), Matrix Computer Analysis of Structures, 1966 (Japanese transl. 1974), Structural Systems, Statics Dynamics and Stability, 1970 (Japanese transl. 1975), Patterns of Problem Solving, 1975, (with K. Pfeiffer) Concepts in Problem Solving, 1980, Tools for Thinking and Problem Solving, 1986; IEEE Press Videotapes; Models for People Driven Quality, 1991, Quality through Innovation, 1991, Creativity for Ongoing Total Quality, 1993, Relentless Improvement, 1993, (with I.R. Firstenberg) Patterns of Problem Solving, 2d edit., 1995, (with I.R. Firstenberg) The Minding Organization, 1999 (Portuguese/Japanese transl. 2000, Spanish/Chinese/Russian transls. 2001). Recipient Disting. Tchr. award UCLA Acad. Senate, 1964, Western Electric Fund award Am. Soc. Engring. Edn., 1965, Disting. Tchr. trophy Engring. Student Soc., UCLA, 1966; Sussman prof. for disting. visitor Technion-Israel Inst. Tech., 1967-68; named Outstanding Faculty Mem., UCLA Engring. Alumni award, 1979, Outstanding UCLA Civil Engring. Alumni award, 1990, Outstanding Faculty Mem., State of Calif. Command Coll., 1987-89, 94-95; Fulbright-Hays fellow, Yugoslavia and Eng., 1975-76; named one of UCLA's Top 20 Profs. of the Century. Mem. ASCE, Am. Soc. Engring. Edn., Seismol. Soc. Am., Sigma Xi, Tau Beta Phi. Achievements include research in use of computers in structural systems, analysis and synthesis; problem solving and decision theory; creativity and innovation in the orgn. Home: 10488 Charing Cross Rd Los Angeles CA 90024-2646 Office: UCLA Sch Engring and Applied Sci Los Angeles CA 90024 Office Phone: 310-825-7731. Business E-Mail: mrubinst@ucla.edu.

RUBINSTEIN, PETER J., rabbi; BA, Amherst Coll.; MHL, Hebrew Union Coll. - Jewish Inst. Religion. Ordained Rabbi Hebrew Union Coll.-Jewish Inst. Religion. Former rabbi Peninsula Temple Beth El, San Mateo, Calif., Woodlands Community Temple, White Plains, NY; sr. rabbi Ctrl. Synagogue Manhattan, NYC, 1991—. Vis. lectr. Manhattanville Coll., Colgate U. Author: Our Rabbis Taught, 1990, How Can I Find a God?, 1997. Rabbinic chmn. Commission on Rabbinic-Congregational Relations; chmn. bd. dir. Auburn Theological Seminary; mem. bd. UJA-Federation of New York, The Partnership of Faith, Plaza Jewish Community Chapel. Named one of The Top 50 Rabbis in America, Newsweek Mag., 2007. Office: Ctrl Synagogue 123 East 55th Street New York NY 10022-3566 Office Phone: 212-838-5122. *

RUBIN-VEGA, DAPHNE, actress; b. Panama City, Panama, Nov. 18, 1969; m. Tommy Costanzo, 2002; 1 child. LHD (hon.), Kean U., 2005. Mem. Pajama Party (pop trio), DRV (rock band). Actress (films) The Occultist, 1987, I Like It Like That, 1994, Lotto Land, 1995, Wild Things, 1998 (Blockbuster award best supporting actress in a suspense thriller), Flawless, 1999, Skeleton Woman, 2000 (Best Actress in a feature film, NY Independent Film and Video Festival), Justice, 2003, Virgin, 2003, Alchemy, 2005, Life on the Ledge, 2005, (TV series) NY Undercover, 1996, Hey Joel, 2003, (Broadway plays) Rent, 1996—97 (Theatre World award best actress in musical, Tony award nomination best actress in a musical, Drama Desk award nomination), (plays) Rocky Horror Picture Show, 2001, Anna in the Tropics, 2004 (Tony award nomination best featured actress in a play), Two Sisters and a Piano, Gum, Between Us (Outstanding Female Performance Rutgers U.), The House of Bernarda Alba, 2006, Everything's Turning into Beautiful, 2006, Jack Goes Boating, 2007. Mailing: c/o Cathexis Inc ATTN Juan Azize PO Box 778 New York NY 10013 E-mail: daphnespeaks@att.net. *

RUBLE, AMANDA L., elementary school educator; b. Sandusky, Ohio, 1973; d. Daniel and Cynthia Matter; m. Eric Ruble; 1 child, Lauryn. BS in Edn., Bowling Green U., Ohio, 1997, MEd in Gifted and Talented, 2001. Nat. bd. cert. adolescent social studies. Tchr. Gibsonburg (Ohio) Exempted Village Schs., 1998—2000, Stamm Elem. - Fremont (Ohio) City Schs., 2000—. Office: Stamm Elem Sch 1038 Miller St Fremont OH 43420

RUBLE, BERNARD ROY, minister, educator, human resources specialist, labor relations consultant; b. Greensburg, Ind., Apr. 4, 1923; s. Jesse Emery and Marietta (Ward) Ruble; m. Mary Helen Rullman, Dec. 22, 1946; children: Barry Reece, Blane Rodney. BS, Ind. U., Bloomington, 1949; postgrad. transactional analysis, Midwest Inst. Human Understanding, 1972—75. Asst. mgr. Morris 5 and 10 Stores, Greensburg, Ind., 1941; store keeper Public Svc. Co., Ind., Greensburg, 1941—43; asst. mgr. pers. Kroger Co., Cin., 1949—51, mgr. pers. Madison, Wis., 1951—56, Ft. Wayne, Ind., 1956—58, Cleve., 1958—73, mgr. labor rels. Erie mktg. area Solon, Ohio, 1973—84; faculty Kroger Edn. Ctr., Cin., 1978—84. Educator Cleve. State U.; trustee Meat Cutters Health and Welfare Fund, 1971—79, Retail Clks. Union Health and Welfare Fund, Akron, 1970—88, No. Ohio Hospice Coun., 1981—84. Active United Appeal Greater Cleve., Cmty. Chest Greater Cleve., Met. Health Planning Corp., Ohio; adv. com. Home Health Care, Washington, 1977—78; hosp. vol. Vis. Nurses Assn., Ohio, Hospice Western Reserve; v.p. trustee Urban League Greater Cleve., 1968—75; trustee Cmty. Health Found., Ohio, Greater Cleve. Interchurch Coun., 1993—99; bd. dirs. N.E. Ohio Hosp. Coun.; team rep. B.R. Ruble Racing, Burton, Ohio. Mem.: Chesterland Ministerial Assn., Indsl. Rels. Rsch. Assn. (pres.), Cleve. Pers. Assn., Am. Soc. Pers. Adminstrn. (charter), Soc. Advancement Mgmt. (trustee Madison chpt. 1952—55), Photog. Soc. Am., Sertoma (trustee Madison 1952—56, Ft. Wayne 1957—58, charter), Masons, Alpha Kappa Psi. Home and Office: 8644 Ranch Dr Chesterland OH 44026-3132 Home Phone: 440-729-4691; Office Phone: 440-729-4691. E-mail: brr3x@sbcglobol.net.

RUBLE, JOHN, architect; BS in Architecture, U. Va., Charlottesville, 1969; grad., UCLA Sch. Architecture and Urban Planning. Arch., planner Peace Corps, Tunisia; founding ptnr. Moore Rubell Yudell Archs. & Planners, Santa Monica, Calif., 1977—. Tchr. grad. design studio UCLA, Cornell U., Ithaca, NY. Fellow: AIA. Office: Moore Ruble Yudell Archs & Planners 933 Pico Blvd Santa Monica CA 90405 Office Phone: 310-450-1400. Office Fax: 310-450-1403. *

RUBLEY, CAROLE A., state legislator; b. Bethel, Conn., Jan. 18, 1939; d. George B. and Evelyn M. (Maloney) Drumm; m. C. Ronald Rubley, Aug. 25, 1962; children: Lauren M. Rubley Simpson, Stephen R., Kristin Rubley Vaughan. BA in Biology, Albertus Magnus Coll., 1960; MS in Environ. Health, West Chester U., 1988. Tchr. biology Danbury (Conn.) High Sch., 1960-62, Waltham (Mass.) High Sch., 1962-63; real estate salesperson Henderson-Dewey, Wayne, Pa., 1976-81; solid waste coord. Chester County Health Dept., West Chester, Pa., 1981-88; environ. cons. Environ. Resources Mgmt., Exton, Pa., 1988-92; mem. Pa. Ho. Reps., Valley Forge, 1992—. Mem. environ. resources, energy, consumer affairs, fin. and children and youth com. House of Reps.; mem. Pa. 21st Century Environ. Commn.; former chair energy and elec. utilities com. NCSL, task force on protecting Democracy. Author: (with others) Leading Pennsylvania into 21st Century, 1990. Chmn. Ea. Chester County Regional Planning Commn., 1976-85; vice chmn. planning commn. Tredyffrin Twp., Berwyn, Pa., 1976-86, mem. bd. suprs., 1987-92; bd. dirs. Pa. Resources Coun., exec. v.p., 1988-92. Recipient Outstanding Legislator award, Pa. Planning Assn., 2004. Mem. LWV (pres. Upper Main Line chpt. 1976-78, Involved Voter of Yr. award 1993), Pa. Environ. Coun., Green Valleys Assn., Open Land Conservancy. Republican. Roman Catholic. Avocations: aerobics, tennis, hiking, reading, travel. Home: 621 Vassar Rd Wayne PA 19087-5312 Home Phone: 610-687-1176; Office Phone: 610-640-2356. Business E-Mail: carole.rubley@verizon.net.

RUBNITZ, MYRON ETHAN, pathologist, educator; b. Omaha, Mar. 2, 1924; s. Abraham Srol and Esther Molly (Jonich) R.; m. Susan Belle Block, Feb. 9, 1952; children: Mary Lu Rubnitz Roffe, Peter, Thomas (dec.), Robert. BSc, U. Nebr., 1945; MD, U. Nebr., Omaha, 1947. Diplomate Am. Bd. Pathology. Intern Mt. Sinai Hosp., Cleve., 1947-48, fellow NYC, 1948-49; resident in pathology Michael Reese Hosp., Chgo., 1949-51; pathologist VA Hosp., Hines, Ill., 1953-56, chief labs., 1956-93, cons., 1993—; assoc. prof. pathology Loyola U. Med. Sch., Maywood, Ill., 1963-70, prof., 1970-99; med. dir. Myron & Rubnitz, MD, Sch. Med. Tech., Hines, Ill., 1973—; prof. emeritus Loyola U. Med. Sch., Maywood, 1999—. Med. dir. Myron E. Rubnitz, MD Sch. Med. Tech. Hines, Ill., 1973-; adj. prof. Ill. State U., Normal, 1979-96, 2003—, U. St. Francis, Joliet, Ill., 1989—, Ea. Ill. U. Charleston, 1991—, Western Ill. U., Macomb, 1991—; clin. instr. Augustana Coll., Rock Island, Ill., 1991—. Chmn. candidates com. Village Caucus, Winnteka, Ill., l969-70; bd. dirs. Chgo. Commons Assn., l968—, North Shore Sr. Ctr., 1998—; mem. New Trier High Sch. Caucus, Winnetka, l972-74. With AUS, l943-46, PTO; lst lt. M.C., U.S. Army, l95l-53. Fellow Am. Soc. Clin. Pathologists, Coll. Am. Pathologists; mem. Internat. Acad. Pathology, Assn. VA Pathologists (pres. 1982-84), Chgo. Pathology Soc., Lake Shore Country Club (Glencoe, Ill.), Mich. Shores Club (Wilmette, Ill.). Avocations: electronics, tennis, travel. Home: 979 Sheridan Rd Winnetka IL 60093 Personal E-mail: northfielddoc@juno.com.

RUBOTTOM, GEORGE MILTON, foundation administrator, chemist; b. London, Mar. 19, 1940; s. Alphonso Milton and Lorna Annie Rubottom. AB, Middlebury Coll., 1962; PhD, MIT, 1967. Lectr. Bucknell U., Lewisburg, Pa., 1968—70; asst. prof. U. PR, Rio Piedras, 1970—75; assoc. and full prof. U. Idaho, Moscow, 1975—84; sr. program dir. in chemistry NSF, Arlington, Va., 1984—. Exec. sec. edn., human resources com. Nat. Sci. Bd., Washington, 1987—2000; mem. dir.'s rev. bd. NSF, Arlington, 1987—2000. Author: (book) Academic Excellence: The Sourcebook, 2001; reviewer: jour. Jour. Org. Chem., Tetrahedron, Tetrahedron Letters. Scuba instr. YMCA, Washington, 1994—. Grantee, NIH, 1973—78, Petroleum Rsch. Fund, 1971—72, 1979—81; Postdoctoral fellow, NIH, 1967—68. Mem.: Am. Chem. Soc., Sigma Xi, Phi Kappa Phi, Phi Beta Kappa. Achievements include research in new methods for the oxidation of C-C double bonds; new methods for the preparation and cleavage of cyclopropanols. Business E-Mail: grubotto@gmail.com.

RUBRIGHT, JAMES ALFRED, paperboard and packaging company executive; b. Phila., Dec. 17, 1946; s. James Alfred and Helen Lucille (Evans) R. (deceased); m. Mary Elizabeth Angelich, Dec. 30, 1987; children: Noah Michael, Benjamin James, Jami Anne, Nathaniel Drew, James McCurdy, William Angelich. BA, Yale U., 1969; JD, U. Va., 1972. Bar: Ga. 1972. Ptnr. King & Spalding, Atlanta, 1972-94; sr. v.p., gen. counsel Sonat Inc., Birmingham, 1994-97; pres. So. Natural Gas Co. subs. Sonat Inc., Birmingham, 1997-98; exec. v.p. Sonat Inc., Birmingham, 1998-99; chmn., CEO Rock-Tenn Co., Norcross, Ga., 1999—. Office: Rock-Tenn Co 504 Thrasher St Norcross GA 30071-1914 *

RUBY, KATHRYN GRACE, education educator; b. Aug. 24, 1957; AA, AS, St. Clair County C.C., Port Huron, Mich., 1991; BS in Student Planned Curriculum, Western Mich. U., Kalamazoo, 1993; MA in Child Devel., Mich. State U., East Lansing, 1995. Instr., prof. early childhood edn., human svcs. and psychology St. Clair County C.C., 1999—, early childhood edn. discipline coord., 2000—. Mem. Port Huron Mus., 1995—, St. Clair County CAN Coun., 1994—. Scholar, Mich. State U., 1995; Mildred B. Erickson fellow, Mich. State U., Kellogg Ctr. Continuing Edn., 1994—95. Mem.: Blue Water Assn. Edn. Young Children, Mich. Assn. Edn. Young Children, Nat. Assn. Edn. Young Children, Coun. Tchrs. Undergrad. Psychology, Assn. Childhood Edn. Internat., Western Mich. U. Alumni Assn., Mich. State U. Alumni Assn., Phi Theta Kappa. Office: St Clair County C C 323 Erie St PO Box 5015 Port Huron MI 48061-5015 Office Phone: 810-989-5692. Business E-Mail: kruby@sc4.edu.

RUCCHIN, STEVE, professional hockey player; b. Thunder Bay, Ont., Can., July 4, 1971; BS, U. Western Ontario. Center Mighty Ducks of Anaheim, 1994—2005, NY Rangers, 2005—06, Atlanta Thrashers, 2006—. Office: Atlanta Thrashers Centennial Tower 101 Marietta St NW Ste 1900 Atlanta GA 30303

RUCK, ROSEMARIE ULISSA, retired social worker, freelance/self-employed writer; b. Buffalo, Aug. 24, 1939; d. Stanley Joseph Ren and Bertha Sosnowski; m. Donald Neal Ruck, Nov. 8, 1958; children: Theresa Dorene Ruck Novak, Donna Rose Ruck Seyler, Michael Donald. AS, Genesee C.C., 1970—72; BS, SUNY Brockport Coll., 1972—75. Chemical Dependency Counselor Pk. Ridge Unity Health Sys. & Brockport Coll., NY, 1999, Basic Reading and ESL Tutor Literacy Volunteers of Am., Inc., NY, 1984. Sr. caseworker/counselor Assn. for Retarded Citizens, Batavia, NY, 1975—79; dir. Literacy Volunteers of Am. - Genesee County Chpt., Batavia, NY, 1983—89. Exec. dir. Literacy Volunteers of Am. - Orleans County Chpt., Albion, NY, 1989—98; chem. dependency counselor Pk. Ridge- Unity Health Sys., Rochester, NY, 1998—99; social worker Lakeside Beikirch Care Ctr., Brockport, NY, 1999—2002; writer Freelance -, Holley, NY, 2002—. Mem. of Genesee c.c. steering com. Genesee County Legislature, Batavia, NY, 1967—68; mem. of com. responsible for devel. of Genesee county registry Genesee County Inter-Agy. Coun., Batavia, NY, 1975—77; grant writer & mem. of program com. for domestic violence program YWCA, Batavia, NY, 1980—81; mem. of steering com. for regional action phone Genesee County Inter-agency Coun., Batavia, NY, 1985—86; mem. of steering com. for vol. connection registry United Way of Genesee County, Batavia, NY, 1983—84; program chair person YWCA, Batavia, NY, 1980—82; voluneer leadership chairperson Young Women's Christian Associaiton, Batavia, NY, 1983—84; strategic planning com. chairperson United Way of Ea. Orleans County, Albion, NY, 1999—2001. Recipient Friends of Edn., Albion Ctrl. Sch. Bd. of Edn., 1991, Recognition of Outstanding Leadership, Literacy Volunteers of Am. - Genesee County Chpt., 1989, Literacy Volunteers of Am. - Orleans County Chpt., 1992, 1993, 1994, 1995, 1996, 1997, 1998, Genesee County Chpt. of Assn. for Retarded Citizens, 1979, Quality Recognition award, Lakeside Beikirch Care Ctr., 2001. Mem.: Literacy Volunteers of Am., Holley's Writers Club. Catholic. Achievements include Revived rural literacy organization and became number one in national organizations from over 450 affiliates; development of first workplace literacy program in Western NY state. Avocations: reading, writing, travel, art, exercise. Home: 5314 Upper Holley Rd Holley NY 14470 Personal E-mail: ruruck@juno.com.

RUCKDESCHEL, JOHN CHARLES, health facility administrator; b. Newport, RI, Jan. 5, 1946; s. John Adam and Rita Frances (Riley) R.; m. Angela Stone, June 15, 2002; children: Daniel, Emily, Darby, Haley. BSc, Rensselaer Poly. Inst., Troy, NY, 1967; MD, Albany Med. Coll., NY, 1971; Found. for Advanced Edn. in the Scis., NIH, 1973, Found. for Advanced Edn. in the Scis., NIH, 1983—84. Lic. NY, Fla., Mich., cert. Am. Bd. Internal Medicine, Med. Oncology. Straight med. intern Johns Hopkins U., Balt., 1971-72; staff assoc. Nat. Cancer Inst., Balt. Cancer Rsch. Ctr., Balt., 1972-75; sr. asst. resident, medicine Beth Israel Hosp., Boston, 1975-76; asst. prof. medicine Albany Med. Coll., NY, 1976-79, assoc. prof. medicine NY, 1979-85, prof. medicine NY, 1985-91, head div. med. oncology NY, 1987-91, dir. joint ctr. for cancer and blood disorders NY, 1999—2001; dir., CEO H. Lee Moffitt Cancer Ctr., Tampa, 1991—2002; pres. H. Lee Moffitt Cancer Hosp., 1991—2002, Moffitt Cancer Found., 1994—2002, Lifetime Cancer Screening, Inc., 1994—2002; prof. oncology and medicine U. South Fla. Coll. Medicine, 1991—2002; pres., CEO Barbara Ann Karmanos Cancer Inst., Detroit, 2002—, Barbara Ann Karmanos Cancer Found., Detroit, 2002—; Case Reserve Prof. U. Tampa Coll. Bus., 1996—2002; prof. medicine & oncology Wayne State U. Sch. Medicine, Detroit, 2002—, assoc. dean, cancer affairs, 2002—, interim chair, radiation oncology, 2002—03; sr. v.p., cancer Detroit Med. Ctr., 2002—; pres. The Cancer Hosp., 2002—. Vis. scientist Nat. Cancer Inst.-Navy Med. Oncology Branch, Bethesda, Md., 1983—84; vis. prof. Found. for Promotion of Cancer Rsch., Nat. Cancer Ctr., Tokyo, 1990; lung cancer steering com. Eastern Cooperative Oncology Group, 1977—2002, lung cancer steering com. chmn., 1982—84, chmn., toxicity com., 1987—89, prin. investigator, Albany Med. Coll., 1989—91, prin. investigator, H. Lee Moffitt Cancer Ctr. & Rsch. Inst., 1991—94, chmn., cancer prevention com., 1993—99, bd. advisor, 2000—02; mem. Lung Cancer Study Group, 1982—90, exec. officer, 1986—90; co-chair Nat. Cancer Inst., Lung Cancer Progress Review Group, 2001; bd. dir. Mich. Cancer Consortium, 2002—, Nat. Comprehensive Cancer Network, 1998—2002, exec. com., 2000—02; Ctr. and Inst. adv. com. Wayne State U. Divsn. Rsch., 2004—; mem. adv. bd. Batelle Pulmonary Therapeutics, 2000—, Internat. Early Lung Cancer Action Project, 2000—, Cancer Control Rsch. Adv. Coun. State of Fla., 1992—2002, chmn., 1994—96; site visitor, ad hoc reviewer Nat. Cancer Inst., 1978—2003; external advisor, reviewer for several organizations and programs, 1986—; bd. dir., physicians group U. Southern Fla., 1992—2002, mem. Dean's exec. coun., 1992—2002, bd. dir., rsch. found., 1992—2002, mem. presdl. search com., 1993, 99, bd. dir., Health Scis. Ctr. Self-Insurance Programs Coun., 1994—2002, leadership coun., 1994—2002, mem. Inst. on Aging, 1996—2002, mem. adv. bd., PhD program in applied physicis, 1999—2002, mem. steering com., Ctr. for Entrepreneurship and Global Mgmt. Tech., 2000—02. Co-editor: (textbook) Thoracic Oncology, 1989, 95; Lung and Mediastinum. sect. editor Current Opinion in Oncology, 1996-99; lead author (lung cancer chpt.) Clinical Oncology, 3rd edit., 2004; editor-in-chief Evidence-Based Oncology 1999-2002; mem. editl. bd. Current Treatment Options in Oncology, Oncology Spectrums, Medical Oncology, Social Marketing Quarterly, Journal Cancer Education, Cancer Control: Journal Moffitt Cancer Ctr.; reviewer Annals Internal Medicine, Annals Oncology, Cancer Chemotherapy and Pharmacology, Cancer Research, Chest, Journal Clinical Oncology, Journal Nat. Cancer Inst., Journal Neuro-Oncology, Investigational New Drugs, Preventative Medicine, Proceedings for NAS; contbr. articles to med. jours. Gen. chair capital campaign Sacred Heart Ch., 1998; staff physician People's Free Med. Clinic, Balt., 1972—75; pres., bd. dir. United Urban Ministry Troy, NY, 1976—80; mem. Sand Lake Ambulance, NY, 1984—91, bd. dir. NY, 1984—85, line officer NY, 1985—87, bd. pres. NY, 1989—91; pres. West Sand Lake Vol. Fire Dept., NY, 1981—83, line officer NY, 1982—83, NY, 1985—86; bd. trustee, Suncoast Chpt. Leukemia Soc. Am., 1995—98; bd. dir. Jesuit HS Found., 1998—2000; chair, health/bio-med. com. Tampa C. of C., 1999, mem. steering com., Com. of 100, 2001—02; bd. trustee Jesuit HS, 2000—02; bd. dir., trust com. bd. Sun Trust Bank, 2000—02; mem. cmty. adv. bd. Jr. League Tampa, 2002. US Pub. Health Srv., 1972—75. Named Brooks Brothers Man of Yr., 1994; named one of Best Doctors in Am., Americas Top Doctors, 1993—, The Med. Bus. Top 25: The Most Influential Physicians in Tampa Bay, 1998, Tampa Bay Mag. Doctors Chosen by Doctors, 2001; recipient Physicians Recognition award, AMA, 1974—, Excel award for Excellence in Comm. Leadership, 1994, Rensselaer Alumni Assn. Fellows award-Biology, 1996, Bellwether award for Lifetime Achievement, 1997, Town and Gown Cmty. Svc. award, 1999, 11th Ann. Fla. Med. Bus. Healthcare Physician Bus. Leadership award, 2000, Exemplary Alumni award, Albany Med. Coll., NY, 2000, Disting. Southern Oncologist award, 2001. Fellow ACP, Am. Coll. Chest Physicians; mem. AMA, Am. Assn. Cancer Insts. (bd. dir. 1997-99, legis. com. 2001-), Am. Cancer Soc. (jr. faculty clin. fellow, 1977-80, nat. adv. com. on psychosocial and behavioral rsch. 1986-89, chair, 1989, bd. dir. Greater Tampa, 1992-97, chair, rsch. com. fla. divsn., 1999-2000, bd. dir. Fla. divsn. 1997-2002, exec. com. Fla. divsn. 1998-2002, med. v.p., Fla. divsn. 1999-2000, pres. Fla. divsn., 2001-2002), Am. Assn. for Cancer Rsch. (mem. fin. com. 2001-), Am. Assn. for Cancer Edn., Am. Soc. Clin. Oncology (AJCC rep. 2000-), Am. Coll. Physician Execs., Am. Fedn. for Clin. Rsch. (coun., eastern sect. 1981-86), Internat. Assn. for the Study of Lung Cancer, Am. Assn. Med. Colls.(Coun. Tchg. Hosps. 1997-), Nat. Coalition for Cancer Rsch. (bd. dir. 1998-2002), US Nat. Com. for the Internat. Union Against Cancer Am. Joint Com. on Cancer, 2000-, Alpha Omega Alpha, Sigma Xi; hon. mem. U. South Fla. Golden Key Internat. Honour Soc. Office: Barbara Ann Karmanos Cancer Inst 4100 John R Detroit MI 48201 Office Phone: 313-576-8670, 313-993-7770. Business E-Mail: ruckdeschel@karmanos.org. *

RUCKELSHAUS, WILLIAM DOYLE, investment company executive, former federal agency administrator; b. Indpls., July 24, 1932; s. John K. and Marion (Doyle) R.; m. Jill Elizabeth Strickland, May 11, 1962; children: Catherine Kiley, Mary Hughes, Jennifer Lea, William Justice, Robin Elizabeth. BA cum laude, Princeton U., 1957; LL.B., Harvard U., 1960. Bar: Ind. 1960. Atty. Ruckelshaus, Bobbitt & O'Connor, Indpls., 1960-68; dep. atty. gen. State of Ind., 1960-65, chief counsel Office of Atty. Gen., 1963-65; minority atty. Ind. Senate, 1965-67; mem. Ind. Ho. of Reps., 1967-69, majority leader, 1967-69; asst. atty. gen. civil divsn. US Dept. Justice, Washington, 1969-70; adminstr. EPA, Washington, 1970-73, 1983-85; acting dir. FBI, Washington, 1973; dep. atty. gen. US Dept. Justice, Washington, 1973; mem. firm Ruckelshaus, Beveridge, Fairbanks & Diamond, Washington, 1974-76; sr. v.p. law and corp. affairs Weyerhaeuser Co., Tacoma, 1976-83; pres. William D. Ruckelshaus Assocs., 1985-88; mem. firm Perkins Coie, Seattle, 1985-88; chmn. bd., CEO Browning-Ferris Industries, Inc., Houston, 1988-95, chmn., 1995—99; founder, prin., also bd. dirs. Madrona Investment Group, LLC, 1996—; strategic dir. Madrona Venture Group, Seattle, 1999—; chmn. World Resources Inst., Washington D.C., 1999—. Bd. dirs. Cummins Engine Co., Nordstrom, Inc., Weyerhaeuser Co., Inc., Vykor, Inc. Rep. nominee for U.S. Senate, Ind., 1968; apptd. by Pres. Clinton to serve as U.S. envoy to Pacific Salmon Treaty with Can., 1997-98; mem., Pres. Council on Sustainable Devel., 1993-97; commr. Commn. on Ocean Policy, 2001-; chmn. Salmon Recovery Funding Bd., Wash. Mem. World Resource Inst. (chmn. 1998—), Fed. Bar Assn., Ind. Bar Assn., D.C. Bar Assn., Indpls. Bar Assn. Office: Madrona Investment Group LLC 1000 2nd Ave Ste 3700 Seattle WA 98104-1053 Office Phone: 206-674-3008. E-mail: bill@madrona.com.

RUCKENSTEIN, ELI, chemical engineering professor; b. Botosani, Romania, Aug. 13, 1925; arrived in U.S., 1969; m. Velina Rothstein, May 15, 1948; children: Andrei, Lelia. BSChemE, Poly. Inst., Bucharest, Romania, 1949, PhD, 1967; PhD (hon.), Tech. U., Bucharest, 1993. Prof. Poly. Inst., Bucharest, 1949—69; vis. prof. U. London, 1969; NSF sr. scientist Clarkson Coll. Tech., Potsdam, NY, 1969—70; prof. U. Del., Newark, 1970—73, SUNY, Buffalo, 1973—81, disting. prof., 1981—. Vis. Humbolt prof. Bayreuth U., Germany, 1986; Gulf vis. prof. Carnegie Mellon U., Pitts., 1988—89; disting. lectr. U. Waterloo, 1985, U. Mo., 1983; Fair Meml. lectr. U. Okla., 1987; Colburn Symposium lectr. U. Del., 1988, Robert L. Pigford meml. lectr., 99; Van Winkle lectr. U. Tex., 1989; Berkeley lectr., 97; Robert A. Welch Found. lectr., 97; Barnett F. Dodge disting. lectr. Yale U., 1998. Contbr. articles to profl. jours. Named Merk Disting. lectr., Rutgers U., 1992; recipient Nat. award, Romanian Dept. Edn., 1958, 1964, Tchg. award, 1961, George Spacu award, Romanian Acad. Sci., 1963, Sr. Humbolt award, Alexander von Humbolt Found., 1985, Creativity award, NSF, 1985, Nat. Medal of Sci., 1998. Mem.: AIChE (Alpha Chi Sigma award 1977, Walker award 1988, Founders award 2002), NAE (Founders award 2004), Am. Chem. Soc. (Kendall award 1986, Jacob F. Schoellkopf medal 1986, Langmuir Disting. Lectr. award 1994, E.V. Murphree award 1996). Office: SUNY Dept Chem Engring 303 Furnas Hall Buffalo NY 14260-4200 Home Phone: 716-834-0711. Business E-Mail: feaeliru@buffalo.edu.

RUCKER, DARIUS, musician; b. Charleston, SC, May 13, 1966; m. Beth Leonard, 2000; 1 child. Albums with Hootie & the Blowfish include: Cracked Rear View, 1994 (two Grammy awards 1995), Fairweather Johnson, 1996, Musical Chairs, 1998, Take 2, 2000, Hootie & the Blowfish, 2003, Looking for Lucky, 2005, Live in Charleston, 2006; solo albums include: Back to Then, 2002. Home: 2519 Devine St Columbia SC 29205-2407

RUCKER, DOUGLAS PENDLETON, JR., lawyer; b. Richmond, Va., Dec. 26, 1945; s. Douglas Pendleton and Margaret (Williams) R.; m. Marian F. Copeland; 1 child, Louise Meredith. BA, Hampden-Sydney Coll., 1968; JD, U. Va., 1972. Bar: Va. 1972, D.C. 1986, U.S. Dist. Ct. (ea. and we. dists.) Va. 1972, U.S. Ct. Appeals (4th cir.) 1982, U.S. Supreme Ct. 1982, U.S. Ct. Claims 1995. Assoc. Sands, Anderson, Marks & Miller, Richmond, Va., 1972-76, mem., 1977—. Mem. adv. com. Venture Richmond; active St. John's Episcopal Ch., mem. vestry, 1994—98, 2005—06, register, 1996, jr. warden, 1997—2006, sr. warden, 1998; bd. dirs., vice chmn. James River Devel. Corp. With Va. Army N.G., 1968—74. Fellow: Am. Bar Found., Twenty-Three Hundred Club; mem.: ABA, Met. Richmond C. of C., Bar Assn. D.C., Soc. Colonial Wars in the State of Va., Richmond Bar Assn. (real estate sect., bd. dirs. 1994—97), Va. Bar Assn. (constrn. law chmn. 1992, real estate and bus. law sects., exec. com. 1992—97, pres. 1996), Va. Law Found. (bd. dirs. 1998—2004), Commonwealth Club. Office: Sands Anderson Marks & Miller PO Box 1998 Richmond VA 23218-1998 Home Phone: 804-644-6210; Office Phone: 804-783-7230. Business E-Mail: DRucker@sandsanderson.com.

RUCKER, FANON A., lawyer; b. Gary, Ind., Oct. 19, 1971; BA, Hampton U., 1993; JD, U. Cin., 1996. Bar: Ohio 1996, US Dist. Ct. Southern Dist. Ohio 2000, US Ct. of Appeals Sixth Cir., US Dist. Ct. Northern Dist. Ohio 2006. Assoc. Santen & Hughes, Cin. Named one of Ohio's Rising Stars, Super Lawyers, 2006. Mem.: Ohio Mcpl. Attorney's Assn., Ohio Assn. Trial Attorneys, Black Lawyers Assn. Cin. (pres. 2001—03, trustee 2003—), Nat. Bar Assn., ABA, Ohio State Bar Assn., Cin. Bar Assn. (trustee 2002—), Lawyers Club. Office: Santen & Huges Ste 3100 312 Walnut St Cincinnati OH 45202 Office Phone: 513-721-4450. Office Fax: 513-721-0109.

RUCKER, GABRIEL, chef; b. 1981; Sous chef Paley's Place, Gotham Building Tavern; owner, exec. chef Le Pigeon, Portland, Oreg., 2006—. Named Chef of Yr., Portland Mag., 2006; named one of Best New Chefs, Food and Wine Mag., 2007. Office: Le Pigeon 738 E Burnside St Portland OR 97214 Office Phone: 503-546-8796. *

RUCKER, ROBERT D., state supreme court justice; b. Canton, Ga. married; 3 children. BA, Ind. U., 1974; JD, Valparaiso Sch. of Law, 1976; LLM, U. Va., 1998. Dep. prosecuting atty., Lake County, Ind.; city atty. City of Gary, Ind.; pvt. practice East Chicago; judge Ind. Ct. of Appeals, 1991—99; justice Ind. Supreme Ct., Indpls., 1999—. Former vice chmn. Ind. Commn. for Continuing Legal Edn. Bd. dirs. Legal Svcs. of N.W. Ind. Decorated Vietnam Vet. Fellow: Indianapolis Bar Foundation; mem.: ABA, Nat. Bar Assn. (exec. com. mem. Judicial Council), Ind. Judges Assn., Am. Judicature Soc. Office: Ind Supreme Ct State House Rm 312 200 W Washington St Indianapolis IN 46204-2798 *

RUCKMAN, ROGER NORRIS, pediatric cardiologist; b. Washington, Dec. 15, 1944; s. Norris Elliott and Eugenia (Campbell) R.; m. Kathleen Anne Smith; children: Robert, Karen, Stephen, Jonathan. BA in Chemistry, Williams Coll., Williamstown, Mass., 1966; MD, U. Va., 1970. Cert. in Pediat. 1976, in Pediatric Cardiology 1979. Intern Peter Bent Brigham Hosp., 1970-71; resident Med. Ctr. Hosp. of Vermont, 1973-75; fellow in cardiology Children's Hosp., Boston, 1975-77; asst. prof. pediatrics U. Nebr., Omaha, 1977-79, George Washington U., Washington, 1980-82, assoc. prof. pediatrics, 1982-90, prof. pediatrics, 1990—; pediatric cardiologist Children's Hosp. Nat. Med. Ctr., Washington, 1980—, chmn. cardiology, 1986-89. Contbr. articles to profl. jours. Served to capt. U.S. Army, 1971-73. Recipient Disting. Service award, Am.-Korea Found., 1972; NIH grantee, 1982—. Fellow Am. Acad. Pediatrics, Am. Coll. Cardiology; mem. Am. Heart Assn., Teratology Soc., Soc. Pediatric Research, Columbia Country Club (Chevy Chase, Md.). Republican. Presbyterian. Avocations: tennis, golf. Office: CNMC Dept Cardiology 111 Michigan Ave NW Washington DC 20010-2916 Home Phone: 301-951-8432; Office Phone: 202-884-2020. Business E-Mail: rruckman@cnmc.org.

RUD, ANTHONY GORDON, JR., education educator; b. Pittsfield, Mass., Jan. 10, 1953; s. Anthony Gordon and Marianne (Ellis) R.; m. Rita Marian Long, Aug. 6, 1983; 1 child, Rachel Anne Elizabeth. AB, Dartmouth Coll., 1976; MA, Northwestern U., 1979, PhD, 1982. Asst. dir. admissions Dartmouth Coll., Hanover, N.H., 1982-86; fellow, sr. fellow N.C. Ctr. for Advancement of Teaching, Cullowhee, 1986-94; assoc. dean Purdue U., West Lafayette, Ind., 1994—2001, prof., 2001—. Editor, author: A Place for Teacher Renewal, 1992, The Educational Conversation, 1995. Office: Purdue U EDST BRNG 100 N University St West Lafayette IN 47907-2098 E-mail: rud@purdue.edu.

RUDA, HOWARD, lawyer, finance company executive; b. NYC, Sept. 7, 1932; s. Menahem and Lucy (Gillenson) R.; m. Leah E. Zeliger, Sept. 22, 1963; 1 child, Amy. BA, CCNY, 1954; JD, Columbia U., 1959. Bar: NY 1959, US Dist. Ct. (so. and ea. dists.) NY 1959. Assoc., then ptnr. Laporte & Meyers, NYC, 1959-63; staff atty., then gen. counsel Meinhard Comml. Corp., NYC, 1963-68; with C.I.T. Group Holdings, Inc., NYC, 1968-87, asst. gen. counsel, 1968—; gen. counsel, v.p., dir. C.I.T. Corp., C.I.T. Leasing Corp., NYC, 1973-84; counsel Hahn & Hessen, NYC, 1987—. Lectr. Practicing Law Inst., Banking Law Inst.; dir. Am. Bankruptcy Inst., 1982-91; arbitrator Am. Arbitration Assn. Editor: Asset Based Financing, Jour. of Bankruptcy Law and Practice. Served with US Army, 1954-56. Fellow Am. Bar Found., Am. Coll. Comml. Fin. Lawyers (regent 1992-95); mem. ABA (chmn. equipment financing com. 1982-85, chmn. ad hoc bulk sales com. 1987-90), Am. Law Inst., Phi Beta Kappa. Jewish. Home: 8 Mirrielees Rd Great Neck NY 11021-2928 Office: Hahn & Hessen 488 Madison Ave New York NY 10022 Office Phone: 212-478-7265. Business E-Mail: hruda@hahnhessen.com.

RUDACILLE, SHARON VICTORIA, medical technician; b. Ranson, W.Va., Sept. 11, 1950; d. Albert William and Roberta Mae (Anderson) Rudacille. BS cum laude, Shepherd Coll., 1972. Med. technologist VA Ctr., Martinsburg, W.Va., 1972—. Instr. Sch. Med. Tech., 1972—76, assoc. coord. edn., 1976—77, edn. coord., 1977—78, quality assurance officer clin. chemistry, 1978—80, lab. svc. quality assurance and edn. officer, 1980—84, clin. chemistry sect. leader, 1984—86, staff med. technologist, 1986—94, supervisory med. technologist, 1994—95, sr. med. technologist, 1995—; adj. faculty mem. Shippensburg (Pa.) State Coll., 1977—78, Shepherd Coll., 1977—78. Mem.: Shepherd Coll. Alumni Assn., W.Va. Soc. Med. Technologists, Am. Soc. Clin. Pathologists, Am. Soc. Med. Tech., Sigma Pi Epsilon. Bapt. Home: PO Box 14 Ranson WV 25438-0014

RUDAVSKY, DAHLIA C., lawyer; b. NYC, Sept. 9, 1951; d. Benjamin Zev and Malka B. (Liben) R.; m. Robert R. Jampol, Oct. 31, 1971; children: Malka, Noah. BA magna cum laude, Yale U., 1972; JD, U. Calif., Berkeley, 1978. Bar: Calif. 1979, Mass. 1980, U.S. Dist. Ct. (no. dist.) Calif. 1979, U.S. Dist. Ct. Mass. 1981, U.S. Ct. Appeals (1st cir.) 1984, U.S. Supreme Ct. 1990. Assoc. Angoff, Goldman, Manning, Pyle, Wanger & Hiatt, Boston, 1980-84, Avery & Friedman, Boston, 1984-86, McDonald Noonan & Kaplan, Newton, Mass., 1986-88; ptnr. Shilepsky, Messing & Rudavsky, P.C., Boston, 1988-93, Messing and Rudavsky, P.C., Boston, 1993—, Messing, Rudavsky & Weliky PC, Boston. Cons. in field; lectr. law Harvard Law Sch., 2006—07, 2007—08. Named one of top Boston lawyers, Boston Mag., 2004; recipient Georgina Smith Award, AAUP, Washington, 1990. Mem. AFL-CIO (lawyers coordinating com., nat. adv. bd. 1983-84), Nat. Employment Lawyers Assn., Mass. Bar Assn. Fluent in french & Hebrew. Office: Messing Rudavsky & Weliky PC 50 Congress St Boston MA 02109 E-mail: drudavsky@mrwemploymentlaw.com.

RUDAVSKY, OREN, film producer, cinematographer, film director; b. 1957; m. Judy Katz, June 12, 1994; 1 child, Eli Katz. BA, Oberlin Coll., 1979; grad., NYU Film Sch. Prodr., dir. (documentaries) Dreams So Real: Three Men's Stories (first place, New Eng. Film Festival, 1981), (films) Spark Among the Ashes: A Bar Mitzvah in Poland, 1986, At the Crossroads: Jews in Eastern Europe Today, 1991, Saying Kaddish, 1991, Hiding and Seeking: Faith and Tolerance After the Holocaust, 2004 (Grand prize, Warsaw Internat. Jewish Film Festival, Best Film, North Am. Interfaith film festival, 2004); cinematographer: (films) The Amish: Not to Be Modern, 1986, Voices from the Attic, 1988, An Empty Bed, 1990, The Last Klezmer: Leopold Kozlowski, His life and Music, 1994 (Berlin Film Festival award), Arguing the World, 1998; prodr., dir., cinematographer (films) A Life Apart: Hasidism in Am., 1997, And Baby Makes 2, 1999, writer, prodr., dir. The Treatment, 2006 (Best Film Made in NY, Tribeca Film Festival, 2006, First prize, Gene Siskel Film Ctr., Christopher Wetzel Ind. Narrative Comedy award). Office: 820 West End Ave #14F New York NY 10025 Office Phone: 212-579-4294. Office Fax: 212-579-4295. E-mail: Orudavsky@aol.com. *

RUDCZYNSKI, ANDREW B., academic administrator, medical researcher; b. Nottingham, England, Sept. 7, 1947; came to U.S., 1951; s. Richard B. and Krystyna Z. R.; m. Andrea Skalny, Oct. 16, 1976 (div. Oct. 1990); children: Christina, Thomas. BSc in Biology/Biochemistry, McGill U., 1969; PhD in Immunology, Syracuse U., 1974; MBA in Adminstrn., So. Ill. U., 1984. Prin. investigator scrub typhus project divsn. Rickettsiology U.S. Army Med. Rsch. Infectious Diseases, Ft. Detrick, Md., 1974—76; rsch. assoc. dept. biology Mich. Cancer Found., Detroit, 1976-77, rsch. scientist dept. immunology, unit chef immunology unit Breast Cancer Prognostic Study, 1977-80; asst. dir. Office Rsch. and Grants U. Md. Eastern Shore, Princess Anne, 1980-83; extramural assoc. Office Extramural Rsch. and Tng., Office of Dir. NIH, 1981-82; asst. dir. Office Rsch. & Sponsored Programs Rutgers U., Piscataway, NJ, 1983-84, dir., 1984-99, asst. v.p. rsch. adminstrn., 1985-93, assoc. v.p. rsch. policy and adminstrn., 1993-99; assoc. v.p. fin., exec. dir. rsch. svcs. U. Pa., Phila., 1999—. Field reader strengthening devel. instns. program U.S. Dept. Edn., 1990; mem. Chancellor's task force instrn. and rsch. infrastructure support N.J. Dept. Higher Edn., 1992. Contbr. articles, abstracts to profl. jours. Capt. U.S. Army Med. Svc. Corps, 1974-76. Recipient traineeship award NSF, 1969-71; predoctoral fellow NIH, 1973-74. Mem. AAAS, Nat. Coun. Univ. Rsch. Adminstrs. (profl. devel. com. 1988-90, region II program com. 1989-90, chmn. region II 1990-92, nat. program com. 1994-95), Coun. Govtl. Rels. (fed. mgmt. devel. com. 1989-90, bd. dirs. 1998-2003, tech. transfer and ethics com. 1998-99, chair rsch. compliance and adminstrn. com. 1999-2003), Beta Gamma Sigma, Sigma Xi. Roman Catholic. Home: 2033 Rodman St Philadelphia PA 19146-1359 Office: Univ Pa Office Rsch Svcs 3451 Walnut St Ste P-221 Philadelphia PA 19104-6205 Office Phone: 215-573-9249. Business E-Mail: abrude@pobox.upenn.edu.

RUDD, D(ALE) F(REDERICK), chemical engineering professor; b. Mpls., Mar. 2, 1935; m. Sandra C. Coryell, 1964; children: Karen, David. BS, U. Minn., 1956, PhD in Chem. Engring., 1960. Asst. prof. chem. engring. U. Mich., Ann Arbor, 1960-61; from asst. prof. to prof. U. Wis., Madison, 1961-94, Schlicter emeritus prof. chem. engring., 1994—. Co-author: Strategy of Process Enging., 1968, Process Synthesis, 1973, Strategy of Pollution Control, 1977, Petrochemical Tech. Assessment, 1981, Microkinetics of Heterogeneous Catalysis, 1993. Named J.S. Guggenheim fellow, 1970; recipient Allan P. Colburn award, 1971. Mem. Nat. Acad. Engring., 1978. Achievements include contributions to the knowlege of process engineering. Personal E-mail: daleandsandy@yahoo.com.

RUDD, DAVID WILLIAM, management consultant, chemical engineer, consultant; b. Floral Park, NY, Dec. 31, 1931; s. Edward Lynn and Joanna (McSorley) Rudd; m. Harriet Fay Sart, Aug. 8, 1953; children: Rebecca, Rachel. BA in Chemistry, Colby Coll., 1953; MS in Phys. Chemistry, Northeastern U., 1962. Rsch. chemist Monsanto Chem. Co., Everett, Mass., 1956-58, Kendall Co., Walpole, Mass., 1958-60, Metal Hydrides, Beverly, Mass., 1960-62; sr. staff engr. Western Electric Co., North Andover, Mass., 1969-78; mem. rsch. staff Engring. Rsch. Ctr., Princeton, NJ, 1978-80; co-founder, dir. David W. Rudd Assocs., mfg. cons., 1985-. Iso-9000 auditor, 1993; co-owner cert. tree farm, Sumner, Maine. Vol. tutor program Mass. Pub. Sch., Lawrence, 1991. With 7th Cav. US Army, 1953—55. Co-recipient Malcolm Baldrige Nat. Quality award, with AT&T's Transmission Divsn., 1992; recipient Engring. Excellence award, Western Electric Co., 1969, C. B. Sawyer Meml. award, 1974, Vol. Tutoring Program award, AT&T, 1991, Lucent Tech. Patent award, 1999. Mem.: We. Electric Engring. Excellence Soc. (pres. 1977—83), Svc. Corp Ret. Execs., Tel. Pioneers Am. (life), Western Foothills Heritage Trust, McLaughlin Found., Sumner Hist. Soc. (bd. dirs. 1996—). Achievements include research in surface chemistry, permeability of metals to hydrogen, rocket propellant synthesis infrared method of Q evaluation synthetic quartz, crystal growth, printed circuit tech., metal joining; computer-integrated mfg. techniques, statis. quality control, soldering tech., environ. modifications of mfg. processes, ISO 9,000 auditor; patents for for growth of synthetic quartz; research in infra red analysis of quartz; computer control of symthetic quartz crystal growth process. Home: 489 Valley Rd Sumner ME 04292-3402 Home Phone: 207-388-2362; Office Phone: 207-388-2362. Personal E-mail: davhar@megalink.net.

RUDD, NICHOLAS, investor, consultant; b. NYC, Mar. 18, 1943; s. Emmanuel and Lucie Lia Rudd; m. Judith Carol Anderson, 1995; children: Alexis Henry, Kenneth Charles. BA, Columbia U., 1964, MBA, 1967. Mem. staff Ford Motor Co., NYC, 1964-65, Young & Rubicam Inc., NYC, 1968-99, sr. v.p. mgmt. svcs., 1980-90, chief info. officer, 1990-95; chief knowledge officer Wunderman Cato Johnson, NYC, 1996-99; prin. Venture Mgmt. Svcs., Inc., 1999—2003, Anderson Rudd Co., 2003—; mktg. chair Stamford Symphony Orch., 2003—. Dir. emeritus Nat. Choral Coun., chmn., 1993-95; bd. dirs. Columbia U. Club NY, A Better Chance of Westport; mem. com. TEAM Westport. Mem. Beta Gamma Sigma. Office: 20 Sea Spray Rd Westport CT 06880

RUDD, PAUL, actor; b. Passaic, NJ, Apr. 6, 1969; m. Julie Yaeger, Feb. 23, 2003; 1 child. BA, U. Kans.; Grad., Am. Acad. Dramatic Arts, Los Angeles. Actor: (films) A Question of Ethics, 1992, Clueless, 1995, Halloween: The Curse of Michael Myers, 1995, The Size of Watermelons, 1996, Romeo + Juliet, 1996, The Locusts, 1997, Overnight Delivery, 1998, The Object of My Affection, 1998, 200 Cigarettes, 1999, The Cider House Rules, 1999, Wet Hot American Summer, 2001, The Château, 2001, Reaching Normal, 2001, The Shapes of Things, 2003, Two Days, 2003, House Hunting, 2003, Anchorman: The Legend of Ron Burgundy, 2004, P.S., 2004, Tennis, Anyone...?, 2005, The Baxter, 2005, The 40 Year Old Virgin, 2005, The OH in Ohio, 2006, Diggers, 2006, Night at the Museum, 2006, The Ex, 2007, Reno 911!: Miami, 2007, Knocked Up, 2007, I Could Never Be Your Woman, 2007; actor, prodr. (films) The Ten, 2007; actor: (TV films) The Fire Next Time, 1993, Moment of Truth: Stalking Back, 1993, Runaway Daughters, 1994, Twelfth Night, or What You Will, 1998, The Great Gatsby, 2000; (TV series) Wild Oats, 1994, Sisters, 1993—95, Friends, 2002—04, Reno 911, 2006—07, (TV appearances) Deadline, 2000, Strangers with Candy, 2000, Cheap Seats: Without Ron Parker, 2004, Stella, 2005, Robot Chicken, 2006, The Naked Trucker and T-Bones Show, 2007, Veronica Mars, 2007. Office: United Talent Agy 9560 Wilshire Blvd Ste 500 Beverly Hills CA 90212-2401 *

RUDD, PEGGY D., library director; b. Tex. B, Stephen F. Austin U.; MLS, U. Tex., Austin, 1975. With N.E. Tex. Libr. Sys., Ctrl. Tex. Libr. Sys.; asst. dir. planning, evaluation & rsch. Libr. Va., Richmond, 1988—94; chief bur. libr. devel. State Libr. Fla., Tallahassee, 1994—99; dir. & libr. Tex. State Libr. & Archives Commn., Austin, 1999—. Mem.: Chief Officers State Libr. Agencies. Office: Tex State Libr & Archives Commn PO Box 12927 Austin TX 78711-2927 Office Phone: 512-463-5460. E-mail: dir.lib@tsl.state.tx.us. *

RUDDY, FRANK, lawyer, retired ambassador; b. NYC, Sept. 15, 1937; s. Francis Stephen and Teresa (O'Neil) Ruddy; children: Neil, David, Stephen. AB, Holy Cross Coll., 1959; MA, NYU, 1962, LLM, 1967; LLB, Loyola U., New Orleans, 1965; PhD, Cambridge U., Eng., 1969. Bar: D.C., N.Y., Tex., U.S. Supreme Ct. Faculty Cambridge U., 1967-69; asst. gen. counsel USIA, Washington, 1969-72, dep. gen. counsel, 1973-74; sr. atty. Office of Telecomm. Policy, White House, Washington, 1972-73; counsel Exxon Corp., Houston, 1974-81; asst. adminstr. AID (with rank asst. sec. state) Dept. State, Washington, 1981-84; U.S. ambassador to Equatorial Guinea, 1984-88; gen. counsel U.S. Dept. Energy, Washington, 1988-89; v.p. Sierra Blanca Devel. Corp., Washington, 1989-92; ptnr. Ruddy & Muir, Washington, 1998—2004, Sale & Quinn, Washington, 2004—. Vis. scholar Johns Hopkins Sch. Advanced Internat. Studies, 1990—94; dep. chmn. UN Referendum for Western Sahara, 1994. Author: International Law in the Enlightenment, 1975; editor: American International Law Cases (series); editor in chief Internat. Lawyer; contbr. articles to legal jours. Bd. dirs. African Devel. Found., Washington, 1983-84, Human Life Internat., 1999—; mem. Coun. of Am. Ambs., Washington, 1988—. Served with USMCR, 1956-61 Mem.: ABA (chmn. treaty compliance sect. 1991—93), Hague Acad. Internat. Law Alumni Assn., Internat. Law Assn., Am. Soc. Internat. Law, Dacor House, Cosmos Club (Washington), Knights of Malta. Republican. Roman Catholic. Office: Sale & Quinn Fifth Fl 910 16th St NW Washington DC 20006 Home Phone: 301-340-6325; Office Phone: 202-872-4712. Personal E-mail: fruddy@hotmail.com. Business E-Mail: globalltd@earthlink.net.

RUDDY, KATHY AAKRE, paralegal; d. Elmer Lawrence and Madge L. Aakre; m. Allen Clifford Ruddy, June 25, 1997. Assoc. Applied Scis. in Exec. Secretarial, Miles CC, Miles City, Mont., 1989, AAS in Legal Sec., 1989; cert. paralegal, Paralegal Inst. Phoenix, 1991. Enlisted US Army, 1992, advanced through ranks to sgt., 1992—2007; criminal law mil. paralegal HHC, 7-158 Aviation Rgt., Fort Hood, Tex., 1992—. Decorated Army Acheivement medals US Army, Army Accomodation medals, Army Good Conduct medals, Mil. Overseas ribbons, Army Svc. ribbon, Operation Iraqi Freedom medal, Global War on Terrorism medal. Mem.: VFW. Republican. Roman Catholic. Avocations: body building, yoga, pilates, reading, cooking. Personal E-mail: kathyruddy@hot.rr.com.

RUDE, BRIAN DAVID, utilities executive; b. Viroqua, Wis., Aug. 25, 1955; s. Raymond and Conelee (Johnson) R.; m. Karen Thulin; children: Erik, Nels. BA magna cum laude, Luther Coll., 1977; MA, U. Wis., Madison, 1994. Mem. Wis. Assembly, Madison, 1982-84, Wis. Senate, Madison, 1984-2000; pres. Wis. State Sen., 1993-96, 98. With corp. comms. Trane Co., La Crosse, Wis., 1981-85; dir. external rels. Dairyland Power Coop.; bd. dirs. Fortress Bank of Westby, Riverfront, Inc. Mem. Lions, Sons of Norway, Norwegian-Am. Hist. Assn. (vice-chmn.), WWTC Found., Rotary. Republican. Lutheran. Avocations: reading, gardening, travel, fishing. Home: 307 Babcock St PO Box 367 Coon Valley WI 54623-0367 Office: 3200 East Ave S PO Box 817 La Crosse WI 54602 Office Phone: 608-788-4000. Personal E-mail: bdr@dairynet.com.

RUDEBECK, CAROL A., school system administrator; d. Bernard Arthur and Cecilia Lucille Andrastek; children: Jaclyn Kate Semple, Megan Beth. BS in Communicative Disorders, U. Wis., Oshkosh, 1971; MS in Edn., U. Wis., Whitewater, 1977; cert. in elem. edn., Cardinal Stritch U., Milw., 1990. Tchr. Wis., 1971. Speech therapist Waukesha County Spl. Edn. Dist., Wis., 1971—73, Manitowoc County Handicapped Children's Edn. Bd., Wis., 1973—74; early childhood exceptional edn. needs tchr. Door County Regional Learning Ctr., Sturgeon Bay, Wis., 1974—76; tchr. trainer U. Wis., Whitewater, 1979—81; early chidlhood exceptional edn. needs tchr. Germantown Sch. Dist., Wis., 1985—90, 2d grade tchr., 1990—2000, instrnl. resource specialist, 2000—; early childhood exceptional edn. needs tchr., speech therapist Wauwatosa Sch. Dist., Wis. Grad. fellow, WI Dept. Pub. Instrn., 1976—77. Mem.: Wis. ASCD, ASCD, Wis. Assn. Tchrs. English, Nat. Coun. Tchrs. English, Nat. Assn. Gifted Children, Wis. Assn. Talented and Gifted. Conservative. Avocations: travel, reading, home decorating, scrapbooks. Office: Germantown Sch Dist W159 N9939 Butternut Rd Germantown WI 53022 Home Phone: 262-251-3308; Office Phone: 262-253-3465. Office Fax: 262-253-3491. Business E-Mail: crudebeck@germantown.k12.wi.us.

RUDEBUSCH, ALICE ANN, lawyer; b. Milw., July 9, 1966; d. Leroy George and Maryann Grace (Carlson) Rudebusch; m. Todd William Nejedlo, May 25, 1991 (div. 1999). BA, Northwestern U., 1988; JD, U. Wis., 1991; Certificat De Langue, Université De Paris, 1986. Bar: Wis. 1991, U.S. Dist. Ct. (we. dist.) Wis. 1991, U.S. Dist. Ct. (ea. dist.) Wis. 1995, U.S. Dist. Ct. (no. dist.) Ill. 1995. Assoc. Hanson Gasiorkiewicz & Weber, S.C., Racine, Wis., 1991-96; ptnr. Hanson & Gasiorkiewicz, S.C., Racine, Wis., 1997—2004; ct. commr. Racine County Cir. Ct., Wis., 2005—. Mcpl. judge City of Oak Creek, Oak Creek, Wis. Alderperson City of Oak Creek Common Coun.; bd. dirs. YWCA, Racine, 1995—2001, sec., 1996—98, pres., 1999—2001. Mem. State Bar Wis., Wis. Acad. Trial Lawyers, Racine County Bar Assn. Office: Hanson & Gasiorkiewicz SC 2932 Northwestern Ave Racine WI 53404-2249 E-mail: info@lawracine.com.

RUDEE, MERVYN LEA, engineering educator, researcher; s. Mervyn C. and Hannah Rudee; m. Elizabeth Eager, 1958; children: Elizabeth Diane, David Benjamin. BS, Stanford U., 1958, MS, 1962, PhD, 1965. Asst. prof. materials sci. Rice U., Houston, 1964-68, assoc. prof., 1968-72, prof. materials sci., 1972-74; prof. U. Calif. San Diego, La Jolla, 1974—, founding provost Warren Coll., 1974-82, founding dean Sch. Engring., 1982-93, coord. grad. program on materials sci., 1994-99, faculty athletic rep., 1999—2007; interim dean engring. U. Calif., Riverside, 1995-97. Vis. scholar Corpus Christi Coll., Cambridge, Eng., 1971-72; vis. scientist IBM Thomas J. Watson Rsch. Ctr., Yorktown Heights, N.Y., 1987; dir. fellows program Calif. Coun. on Sci. and Tech., 1999-2000. Pres., bd. trustees Mus. Photographic Art, San Diego, 1995-96; trustee The Burnham Inst., 1998—2004, The Glen Canyon Inst., 1999—, The San Diego River Park Found., 2003-. Lt. (j.g.) USN, 1958-61. Guggenheim fellow, 1971-72. Fellow AAAS; mem. Microscopy Soc. Am., Materials Rsch. Soc., Tex. Soc. Electron Microscopy (hon., pres. 1966), Sigma Xi, Tau Beta Pi. Office: U Calif San Diego Dept Elec & Computer Engring La Jolla CA 92093-0407 Office Phone: 858-534-8998. Business E-Mail: rudee@ucsd.edu.

RUDEL, BARBARA ELIZABETH, elementary school educator; b. Chgo., Mar. 15, 1964; d. Alfred and Elizabeth Kocialkowski; m. Richard Rudel, Dec. 21, 1986; children: Anna, Cecylia. BA, Concordia U., River Forest, Ill., 1986. Cert. Standard Tchg. Ill. Primary tchr. Union Ridge Sch.,

Harwood Heights, Ill., 1986—. Mentor tchr. Union Ridge Sch., 2003—05, cooperating tchr., 1986—, yearly com. cons., 1986—. Tchr. rep. PTA, Sch. Dist. 86, 1987. Mem.: NEA (union treas. 1989), Nat. Coun. Tchrs. Math., Internat. Reading Assn., Phi Delta Kappa. Avocations: travel, reading, landscape design. Office: Union Ridge Sch 4600 Oak Pk Ave Harwood Heights IL 60706

RUDEL, JULIUS, conductor; b. Vienna, Mar. 6, 1921; came to U.S., 1938, naturalized, 1944; s. Jakob and Josephine (Sonnenblum) R.; m. Rita Gillis, June 24, 1942 (dec. May 1984); children: Joan, Madeleine, Anthony Jason. Student, Acad. Music, Vienna; diploma in conducting, Mannes Coll. Music, 1942; diploma hon. doctorates, U. Vt., 1961, U. Mich., 1971; doctorates hon. causa, Pace Coll., Manhattan Coll., 1994, Mannes Coll. Music, 1994, Manhattanville Coll., 1994, Manhattan Sch. Music, 1996. With N.Y. City Opera, 1943-79, 2004, debut, 1944, gen. dir., 1957-79, 3rd St. Music Sch. Settlement, 1945-52, mus. dir. Chautauqua Opera Assn., 1958-59, Caramoor Festival, Katonah, N.Y., 1964-76, Cin. May Festival, 1971-72, Kennedy Ctr. Performing Arts, 1971-75; music advisor Wolf Trap Farm Pk., 1971, Phila. Opera, 1978-81; condr. Spoleto (Italy) Festival, 1962-63; music dir. Buffalo Philarm. Orch., 1979-85, debut as condr. Met. Opera, 1978, San Franciso Opera, 1979, Vienna State Opera, 1976, Royal Opera, Covent Garden, 1984, Rome Opera, 1987, Opera de la Bastille, 1992, Teatro Colon, Buenos Aires, 1992, Royal Danish Opera, Copenhagen, 1993, L.A. Opera, 1995; condr. Am. premiere of Braunfels's Die Vogel at Spoleto Festival USA, 2005; condr. Cosi fan Tutte, NYC Opera, 2006; dir. prodn.: Kiss Me Kate, Vienna Volksoper Opera, 1956; prin. guest condr. Palm Beach Opera, 2003; guest condr. Chgo. Symphony, Phila. Orch., N.Y. Philharm., Boston Symphony, Detroit Symphony, Israel Philharm., Paris Opera, Munich Opera, Hamburg State Opera, Vienna State Opera, other symphonic, operatic orgns. in U.S. and Europe. Decorated Croix du Chevalier in arts and letters France; recipient gold medal Nat. Arts Club, 1958, citation Nat. Assn. Am. Composers and Conductors, 1958, citation Nat. Fedn. Music Clubs, 1959, Ditson award Columbia, 1959, Page One award in music Newspaper Guild, 1959, hon. insignia for arts and sci. Govt. of Austria, 1961, Handel medallion for music City N.Y., 1965, citation Nat. Assn. Negro Musicians, 1965, citation Nat. Opera Assn., 1971, comdr.'s Cross German Order Merit, 1967, hon. lt. Israeli Army, 1969, Julius Rudel award for young condrs., Pan Am./Pan African award for humanism, 1981, Peabody award, 1985, Disting. Achievement award Kurt Weill Found., 2000. Office: c/o Shuman Assocs 120 W 58th St Apt 8D New York NY 10019-2126 Office Phone: 212-315-1300.

RUDELIUS, WILLIAM, marketing educator; b. Rockford, Ill., Sept. 2, 1931; s. Carl William and Clarissa Euclid (Davis) R.; m. Jacqueline Urch Dunham, July 3, 1954; children: Robert, Jeanne, Katherine, Kristi. BS in Mech. Engring., U. Wis., 1953; MBA, U. Pa., 1959, PhD in Econs., 1964. Program engr., missile and space vehicle dept. Gen. Electric Co., Phila., 1956-57, 59-61; sr. research economist North Star Research Inst., Mpls., 1964-66; lectr. U. Minn., Mpls., 1961-64, asst. prof. mktg. Coll. Bus. Adminstrn., 1964, assoc. prof., 1966-72, prof., 1972—. Co-author: (with W. Bruce Erickson) An Introduction to Contemporary Business, 1973, rev. 4th edit., 1985; (with Eric N. Berkowitz, Roger A. Kerin and Steven W. Hartley) Marketing, 1986, rev. 8th edit., 2006; (with Roger A. Kerin and Steven W. Hartley) Marketing: The Core, 2004, rev. 2d edit., 2007; (with Krzysztof Przybytowski, Roger A. Kerin and Steven W. Hartley) Marketing na Przykładach, 1998; (with others) Mapketkht, 1st Russian edit., 2001; contbr. articles to profl. jours. Served USAF, 1954—55. Home: 1425 Alpine Pass Minneapolis MN 55416-3560 Business E-Mail: rudelius@umn.edu.

RUDENSTINE, DAVID, dean, law educator; BA, Yale U., 1963, MAT, 1965; JD, NY U., 1969. Staff atty. NY City Legal Services Program; dir. Citizen's Inquiry on Parole and Criminal Justice, Inc.; project dir., assoc. dir., acting exec. dir. NY Civil Liberties Union; adminstr. Benjamin N. Cardozo Sch. Law, Yeshiva U., NY, NY, 1979—, assoc. dean academic affairs, 1994—96, interim dean, 1996—97, Dr. Herman George and Kate Kaiser Prof. of Constitutional Law, dean, 2001—. Inaugural fellow Program in Law and Public Affairs, Princeton U., 2000—01. Author: (book) The Day the Presses Stopped: A History of the Pentagon Papers Case. Vol. Peace Corps, Uganda, 1965—66. Office: Yeshiva U Benjamin N Cardozo Sch Law Brookdale Ctr 55 Fifth Ave (at 12th St) New York NY 10003

RUDENSTINE, NEIL LEON, former academic administrator, educator; b. Ossining, NY, Jan. 21, 1935; s. Harry and Mae (Esperito) R.; m. Angelica Zander, Aug. 27, 1960; children: Antonia Margaret, Nicholas David, Sonya. BA, Princeton U., 1956; BA (Rhodes Scholar), Oxford U., 1959, MA, 1963; PhD, Harvard U., 1964. Instr. dept. English Harvard U., Cambridge, Mass., 1964-66, asst. prof., 1966-68; assoc. prof. English Princeton (N.J.) U., 1968-73, prof. English, 1973-88, dean of students, 1968-72, dean of Coll., 1972-77, provost, 1977-88, provost emeritus, 1988—; exec. v.p. Andrew W. Mellon Found., NYC, 1988-91; pres. Harvard U., Cambridge, Mass., 1991-2001, prof. English, 1991-2001, pres. emeritus, 2001—. Chair bd. ArtStor, 2001—. Author: Sidney's Poetic Development, 1967, Pointing Our Thoughts, 2001; (with George Rousseau) English Poetic Satire, 1972; (with William Bowen) In Pursuit of the PhD, 1992. Trustee Princeton U., 2002—06, N.Y. Pub. Libr., Courtauld Inst. Art, London, Goldman Sachs Found., The Barnes Found., Am. Acad. in Berlin, J. Paul Getty Trust, 2007—. 1st lt. arty. US Army, 1959—60. Hon. fellow New Coll./Oxford U., Emmanuel Coll./Cambridge U., 1991. Fellow Am. Acad. Arts and Scis.; mem. Am. Philos. Soc., Coun. on Fgn. Rels., Com. for Econ. Devel. Office: ARTstor 151 E 61st St New York NY 10065 Office Phone: 212-500-2419. Business E-Mail: nlr@artstor.org.

RUDER, DAVID STURTEVANT, government official, lawyer, educator; b. Wausau, Wis., May 25, 1929; s. George Louis and Josephine (Sturtevant) R.; m. Susan M. Small; children: Victoria Chesley, Julia Larson, David Sturtevant II, John Coulter; stepchildren: Elizabeth Frankel, Rebecca Wilkinson. BA cum laude, Williams Coll., 1951; JD with honors, U. Wis., 1957, LLD, 2002. Bar: Wis. 1957, Ill. 1962. Of counsel Schiff Hardin & Waite, Chgo., 1971—76; assoc. Quarles & Brady, Milw., 1957—61; asst. prof. law Northwestern U., Chgo., 1961—63, assoc. prof., 1963—65, prof., 1965—2005, William W. Gurley meml. prof. of law, 1994—2005; emeritus, 2005—; assoc. dean Law Sch. Northwestern U., Chgo., 1965—66, dean Law Sch., 1977—85; chmn. Securities and Exch. Commn., Washington, 1987—89; ptnr. Baker & McKenzie, Chgo., 1990—94, sr. counsel, 1994—99. Cons. Am. Law Inst. Fed. Securities Code; planning dir. Corp. Counsel Inst., 1962-66, 76-77, com. mem., 1962-87, 90—; adv. bd. Ray Garrett Jr. Corp. and Securities Law Inst., 1980-87, 90—; vis. lectr. U. de Liege, 1967; vis. prof. law U. Pa., Phila., 1971; faculty Salzburg Seminar, 1976; mem. legal adv. com. bd. dirs. N.Y. Stock Exch., 1978-82; mem. com. profl. responsibility Ill. Supreme Ct., 1978-87; adv. bd. Securities Regulation Inst., 1978—, chmn., 1994-97; bd. govs. Nat. Assn. Securities Dealers, 1990-93, chmn. Legal Adv. Bd., 1993-96, Arbitration Policy Task Force, 1994-97; trustee Fin. Acctg. Found., 1996-2002, Internat. Acctg. Stds. Com. Found., 2000-05; mem. Internat. Acctg. Stds. Com. Strategy Working Party, 1997-99; chmn. Securities and Exch. Commn. Hist. Soc., 1999-04; chmn. Mut. Fund Dirs. Forum, 1999—. Editor-in-chief: Williams Coll. Record, 1950-51, U. Wis. Law Rev, 1957; editor: Proc. Corp. Counsel Inst, 1962-66; contbr. articles to legal periodicals. Dir. Glen View Club Scholarship Found., 2000-07. 1st lt. US Army, 1951-54. Recipient William O. Douglass award, Assn. Securities and Exchange Comm. Alumni, 2007. Fellow Am. Bar Found.; ABA (sec. bus. law 1970—, coun. 1970-94, com. chmn., mem. various coms.), Chgo. Bar Assn., Wis. Bar Assn., Am. Law Inst., Order of Coif, Comml. Club of Chgo., Lawyers Club Chgo., Gargoyle Soc., Phi Beta Kappa, Phi Delta Phi, Zeta Psi. Home: 325 Orchard Ln Highland Park IL 60035-1939 Office: Northwestern U Sch Law 357 E Chicago Ave Chicago IL 60611 Office Phone: 312-503-8444.

RUDER, JOHN REGAN, physician; b. Colorado Springs, Colo., Oct. 23, 1947; s. Ralph Emerson and Rosemary Pierron (Regan) R.; m. Sheri Dee Rigby, July 6, 1985; children: Elizabeth, Lindsey, John. BA, Dartmouth Coll., 1969, MD, 1977. Intern in surgery U. N.Mex. & Affiliated Hosps., 1977-78; med. dir. Navajo Reservation, 1977-78; resident in surgery Dartmouth-Hitchcock Med. Ctr., 1978-81; resident in plastic and reconstructive surgery U. Utah, 1981-83, asst. clin. prof. plastic & reconstructive surgery Salt Lake City, 1986-90; chief plastic & reconstructive surgery VA Hosp., Salt Lake City, 1986-90; clin. instr. hand & upper extremity surgery Loma Linda (Calif.) U., 1990-91; v.p. Hand Surgery Assocs., Arlington Heights, Ill., 1991—. Co-author: (chpts.) Injuries and Rehabilitation of the Upper Extremity, 1998, Upper Extremity Compressive Neuropathies, 1998. Mem. ACS, Am. Soc. for Surgery of the Hand, Am. Soc. of Plastic and Reconstructive Surgery, Am. Assn. Hand Surgery, Alpha Omega Alpha. Office: Hand Surgery Assocs 515 W Algonquin Rd Ste 120 Arlington Heights IL 60005-4440

RUDER, TIA L., music educator; d. Judy K and Duane F Ruder. MusB cum laude in Edn., Wichita State U., 1992, MusB cum laude in Performance, 1992, BA cum laude, 1993, MusM in Edn., 1999. K-12 vocal and instrumental music Kans., 1992. Instrumental music tchr. Wichita Pub. Schs., Kans., 1992—, asst. dir. all-city band, 1993—2006, tchr. summer sch., 2000—04, summer instrument cleaner, repairer, 2000—05, dir. All-City Band, 2007. Summer sch. tchr. Oakley Pub. Schs., Kans., 1992—97; soprano soloist and instrumental music dir. Mt. Vernon Presbyn. Ch., Wichita, Kans., 1992—2001; pvt. music tchr., Wichita, 1992—2003. State forensics championships adjudicator Kans. State H.S. Activities Assn., Wichita, 1992—2005. Recipient Honors Program Grad., Wichita State U., 1992, Mortar Bd. Scholar, 1991; U. Leader Scholar, 1992—96. Mem.: NEA, Kans. Bandmasters Assn., Fedn. of Teachers, Kans. Music Educators Assn., Music Educators Nat. Conf. Avocations: cooking, home improvement, science fiction, theater. Home Phone: 316-269-6965. Personal E-mail: tia.ruder@cox.net.

RUDER, WILLIAM, public relations executive; b. NYC, Oct. 17, 1921; s. Jacob L. and Rose (Rosenberg) R.; m. Betty Cott, May 23, 1980; children: Robin Ann, Abby, Brian, Michal Ellen, Eric. BSS., City Coll., NYC, 1942. With Samuel Goldwyn Prodns., 1946-48; pres. Ruder & Finn, Inc., NYC, 1948-80, William Ruder Inc., 1981—. Asst. sec. commerce, 1961-62; Tobe lectr. Harvard Grad. Sch. Bus., 1962; mem. grad. adv. bd. City Coll. N.Y., Baruch Sch. Bus., N.Y.C.; cons. State Dept.; bd. dirs. W.P. Carey & Co., Inc.; trustee Continuum Health Ptnrs., Inc. Author: The Businessman's Guide to Washington. Bd. dirs. Bus. Com. for Arts, Jewish Bd. Guardians, Chamber Music Soc. Lincoln Ctr., Fund for Peace, Project Return Found.; exec. com. United Way Am.; trustee, chmn. Manhattanville Coll., Purchase, N.Y., 1974-75; trustee Com. for Econ. Devel., St. Lukes/ Roosevelt Hosp.; bd. overseers Wharton Sch. U. Pa.; mem. pres.'s coun. Meml. Sloan-Kettering Cancer Ctr.; chmn. bd. ACCESS. Capt. USAAF, 1941-45. Mem. UN Assn. U.S.A. (nat. policy panel dir., trustee com. for econ. devel.). Home: PO Box 230 East Hampton NY 11937 Office: Ruder Finn Inc 301 E 57th St New York NY 10022-2900

RUDIGER, LANCE WADE, secondary school educator; b. Bklyn., Mar. 27, 1948; s. H.F. and Muriel Marie (Staudermann) R.; 1 child, Heidi. BS in Chemistry, SUNY, Albany, 1976; MEd, St. Lawrence U., 1982. Cert. tchr., N.Y. Tchr. chemistry Potsdam H.S., 1982—, chmn. dept. sci., 1992—. Adj. prof. Canton (N.Y.) Coll. Tech., Mater Dei Coll., Ogdensburg, N.Y., Empire Coll., Albany, 1986—; tchr. Inst. Chem. Edn.-Sci. demonstration; bd. dirs., treas. St. Lawrence Valley Tchrs. Learning Ctr., Canton; sci. coord. Upward Bound St. Lawrence U.; program com., bd. dirs. N.Y. Assn. State Computers & Tech. in Edn.; writer for N.Y. State Regents chemistry core curriculum; mem. N.Y. State Part D Performance Regents Test Devel. Com.; reviewer chemistry tchr. cert. exam NY State; mem. SED Regents Benchmark Commn.; item writer NYS Chem. Regents; mem. NYSED-McGraw Hill Chemistry Regents Anchor Com.; mem. h.s. chemistry exam com. Am. Chem. Soc., 2005 Co-author: Chemistry Environment, 1990; editor, reviewer Activ Chemistry. Bd. dirs. March of Dimes N.Y. State, Syracuse, N.Y. State chemistry regional and state coord. mentor; mem. environ. mgmt. bd. St. Lawrence County, 1997-, edn. com. chair, 1999-, vice chair, 2003-; mem. bd. examiners Nat. Coun. Accreditation Tchr. Edn., 2001—. Recipient Newmast award NASA, 1987, Dreyfus Master Tchr. award, 1989, Fulbright Symposium award Australia, 2002; grantee NSTA-FDA, 2003, Am. Chem Soc., Woodrow Wilson Found., Binghamtom U. Step Program, St. Lawrence Valley Tchrs. Ctr., 1991-98, Sweetwater Found., Miami U. (Ohio), 1995, Johns Hopkins Space Grant Consortium, Wright Ctr. for Aerospace and Space Engring., Reynolds Metals Excellence in Edn., 1990-94, Cornell U. Sci. Workshop, IRIS; named solar sys. amb. Jet Propulsion Lab., NASA. Mem. Nat. Sci. Tchrs. Assn. (local leader, manuscript review adv. panel The Sci. Tchr., sci. safety com. 2000, webwatchers 2001, Exxon BaP key leader and North Country liaison, mem. reports com.), Nat. Radio Astronomy Obs. (assoc., mentor astronomy workshop), Am. Astron. Soc. (tchr. resource agent 1996-98, Leadership Workshop award 1998), Sci. Tchrs. Assn. N.Y. State (bd. dirs. 1990—, chmn. sect. 1992—, fin. com. 2000—, grant com. chair, presenter at convs. 1988—, hospitality chair ann. conf. NYSC & TE 1996, 98, 2000, bd. dirs.), North Country Conservation Edn. Assn. (life), USCG Acad. Nat. Parents Assn. (bd. dirs. 1997-98), N.Y. State Tchr. Cert. Exam Adv. Com., Canton Club, Lions (past pres. Waddington, N.Y., Pres.'s award, bd. dirs. Canton, pres. 1997-98, treas. 1998-99, dir. 1999-2003), Potsdam Kiwanis (charter, bd. dirs. 1989-91), Phi Delta Kappa (rsch. dir., v.p. program 1999, v.p. membership, pres. 2001—, Phi Delta Kappan 2004, Gerald Read travel scholar 2004). Home: 54 Court St Canton NY 13617-1159 Office: Potsdam High School Leroy St Potsdam NY 13676-1798 E-mail: lrudiger@aol.com.

RUDIN, ANNE, retired mayor, nursing educator; b. Passaic, NJ, Jan. 27, 1924; m. Edward Rudin, June 6, 1948; 4 children. BS in Edn., Temple U., 1945, RN, 1946; MPA, U. So. Calif., 1983; LLD (hon.), Golden Gate U., 1990. RN, Calif. Mem. faculty Temple U. Sch. Nursing, Phila., 1946-48; mem. nursing faculty Mt. Zion Hosp., San Francisco, 1948-49; mem. Sacramento City Council, 1971-83; mayor City of Sacramento, 1983-92; ind. pub. policy cons. Pres. LWV, Riverside, 1957, Sacramento, 1961, Calif., 1969-71, Calif. Elected Women's Assn., 1973—; trustee Golden Gate U., 1993-96; mem. adv. bd. U. So. Calif., Army Depot Reuse Commn., 1992-94; bd. dirs. Sacramento Theatre Co., 1992-99, Japan Soc. No. Calif., Sacramento Symphony, 1993-96, Calif. Common Cause, 1993 -96, Sacramento Edn. Found., 1993-2006; v.p. Sacramento Traditional Jazz Soc. Found.; pres. bd. dirs. Natomas Basin Conservancy; foreman Sacramento County Grand Jury, 2000-01. Recipient Women in Govt. award U.S. Jaycee Women, 1984, Woman of Distinction award Sacramento Area Soroptimist Clubs, 1985, Civic Contbn. award LWV Sacramento, 1989, Woman of Courage award Sacramento History Ctr., 1989, Peacemaker of Yr. award Sacramento Mediation Ctr., 1992, Regional Pride award Sacramento Mag., 1993, Humanitarian award Japanese Am. Citizen's League, 1993, Outstanding Pub. Svc. award Am. Soc. Pub. Adminstrn., 1994, Cmty. Svc. Recognition award, Japanese Am. Citizens League, 1999, Contbr. to Pub. Art award Am. Soc. for Pub. Admin., 2004, Robert T. Malsui award Pub. Svc., Town & Country Dem. Club, 2005; named Girl Scouts Am. Role model, 1989; named to Sacramento Traditional Jazz Soc. Hall of Fame, 2000. Mem.: Calif. Med. Alliance (Mem. of Yr. 2005).

RUDIN, SCOTT, film and theatre producer; b. NYC, July 14, 1958; Prodn. asst., asst. to theatre prodrs. Kermit Bloomgarden and Robert Whitehead; casting dir. motion pictures and theatre, prodr. with Edgar Scherick, exec. v.p. prodn. 20th Century Fox, 1984-86, pres. prodn., 1986-87; founder Scott Rudin Prodns., 1990—. Prodr. (films) Mrs. Soffel, 1984, Pacific Heights, 1990, Regarding Henry, 1991, Little Man Tate, 1991, The Addams Family, 1991, Life With Mikey, 1993, The Firm, 1993, Searching for Bobby Fischer, 1993, Sister Act 2, 1993, Addams Family Values, 1993, I.Q., 1994, Nobody's Fool, 1994, Sabrina, 1995, Clueless, 1995, Up Close and Personal, 1996, Ransom, 1996, Marvin's Room, 1996, The First Wives Club, 1996, In and Out, 1997, Twilight, 1998, The Truman Show, 1998, A Civil Action, 1998. Wonder Boys, 1999, Rules of Engagement, 1999, Brokeback Mountain, 1999, Angela's Ashes, 1999, Bringing Out the Dead, 1999, Sleepy Hollow, 1999, Rules of Engagement, 2000, Zoolander, 2001, The Royal Tenenbaums, Changing Lanes, 2002, The Hours, 2002, The Stepford Wives, 2004, The Manchurian Candidate, 2004, The Village, 2004, I Heart Huckabees, 2004, Life Acquatic with Steve Zissou, 2004, Closer, 2004, Freedomland, 2006, Failure to Launch, 2006; exec. prodr. (films) Flatliners, 1990, Sister Act, 1992, Jennifer Eight, 1992, South Park: Bigger, Longer and Uncut, 1999, Team America: World Police, 2004, Lemony Snicket's A Series of Unfortuante Events, 2004, Wild Tigers I Have Known, 2006, The Queen, 2006; (TV movies) Revenge of the Stepford Wives, 1980, He Makes Me Feel Like Dancing, 1983 (Outstanding Children's Program Emmy award 1982, Feature Documentary Acad. award 1984); (theatre) Passion, 1994 (Best Musical Tony award 1994), Indiscretions, 1995, Hamlet, 1995, Seven Guitars, 1995, Skylight, 1997, A Funny Thing Happened on the Way to the Forum, 1996, On the Town (with the N.Y. Shakespeare Festival), 1997, The Chairs, 1998, The Judas Kiss, 1998, (London) Closer, 1998, The Blue Room, 1998, Closer, 1999, Amy's View, 1999, Wide Guys, 1999, Copenhagen, 1999 (Tony Award); (off broadway) Stupid Kids, 1998, The Most Fabulous Story Ever Told, 1999, Shaft, 2000. Named one of 50 Most Powerful People in Hollywood, Premiere mag., 2002—06. Office: Scott Rudin Prodns c/o Starr & Co 350 Park Ave 9th Fl New York NY 10022 also: Scott Rudin Prodns Inc c/o Star & Co LLC 850 Third Ave 15th Fl New York NY 10022

RUDKIN, GEORGE HENRY, plastic surgeon; b. Wilmington, Del., July 29, 1964; s. George Osborne and Helene Rita (De Sanctis) R. BA in Natural Sciences, Johns Hopkins U., 1986; MD, Columbia U. Coll. Physicians and Surgeons, 1990. Diplomate Am. Bd. Surgery, 1997, Am. Bd. Plastic Surgery, 1999. Intern, gen. surgery UCLA Med. Ctr., 1990—91, resident, gen. surgery, 1991—96, resident, plastic surgery, 1996-98, hosp. appt., asst. prof., divsn. plastic & reconstructive surgery, 1999—2006; chief, plastic surgery W. LA VA Med. Ctr. Co-investigator for VA merit review grant: molecular mechanism of bone regeneration: role of BMP-2, 2002—06; co-investigator for VA Merit Review Grant: stimulations of osteogenesis in a 3D scoffoid, 2006—. Author several textbook chapters; contbr. numerous publications in peer-reviewed plastic surgery literature. Recipient VA Career Develop. award, 1998—2001. Fellow, Am. Coll. Surgeons; mem. Am. Soc. Plastic & Reconstructive Surgeons, Plastic Surgery Rsch. Coun., Calif. Soc. Plastic Surgeons, Alpha Omega Alpha, Phi Beta Kappa. Office: 421 N Rodeo Dr S Terr Level Beverly Hills CA 90210 Office Phone: 310-410-4599. Office Fax: 310-550-6363.

RUDLOFF, UDO, surgeon, researcher; b. Schweinfurt, Bavaria, Germany, Apr. 16, 1969; arrived in US, 2002; s. Herbert and Helga (Gall) Rudloff. PhD, German Cancer Rsch. Ctr., Heidelberg, 1994; MD, Ruprecht Karls U., Heidelberg, Germany, 1997. Rsch. fellow German Cancer Rsch. Ctr., Heidelberg, 1991—94, European Molecular Biology Labs., Heidelberg, 1993; ho. officer dept. surgery and orthop. Zomba Ctrl. Hosp., Malawi, 1997—98; ho. officer U. Hosp. Aintree, Liverpool, England, 1999, Leicester Gen. Hosp., England, 1999—2000, Hinchingbrooke Hosp., Huntington, England, 2000, Dewsbury Dist. Hosp., England, 2000—01; registrar Guy's and St. Thomas' Hosp., London, 2001—02; house officer North Shore - LI Jewish Health Sys., Manhasset, NY, 2002—05, NYU Sch. Medicine, NYC, 2005—07; fellow surg. oncology Meml. Sloan Kettering Cancer Ctr., NY, 2007—. Contbr. Archives Gynecology and Obstetrics, Basel, Switzerland, 2002—07. Contbr. articles to numerous profl. jours. Recipient Academic Exch. Travel award, German Rsch. Found., 1991, Young Talent award, Soc. Advancements Rsch. in Molecular Biology, Heidelberg, Germany, 1995; scholar, German Acad. Scholarship Found., 1994—97, Scholarship Found. Roman Cath. Ch., 1994. Mem.: Royal Coll. Obstetricians and Gynecologists. Achievements include characterization of a new class of polymerase I-specific transcription factors named TAFs; research in DNA binding properties. Office: Memorial Sloat-Kettering Cancer Ctr MSKCC Howard Bldg 1206/12 410 E 68th St New York NY 10021 Home Phone: 917-346-6381; Office Phone: 212-639-7537. Personal E-mail: udo_rudloff@hotmail.com. Business E-Mail: rudloffu@mskcc.org.

RUDMAN, JEFFREY B., lawyer; b. Cambridge, Mass., May 1, 1948; s. Stanley H. and Dorothy (Braidy) R.; m. Susan Victoria Fried, Aug. 25, 1986; children: Samuel Newland, Nicholas Braidy. AB, Columbia U., 1970; BA, Oxford U., Eng., 1972; JD, Harvard U., 1975. Bar: Mass. 1975, U.S. Dist. Ct. Mass. 1975, U.S. Ct. Appeals (1st cir.) 1977. Assoc. Hale and Dorr, Boston, 1975-80, jr. ptnr., 1980-83, sr. ptnr., 1983—2004; ptnr., co-chmn. Securities dept., mem. Litigation dept. Wilmer Cutler Pickering Hale and Dorr, Boston, 2004—. Trustee Boston Mus. Project; chmn. bd. trustees Boston Pub. Libr.; sec. New Eng. & N.J. Rhodes Scholarship Selection Coms., 1985-; former mem. cmty. adv. bd. WGBH. Rhodes scholar, 1970-72. Mem. Mass. Bar Assn., Boston Bar Assn., Phi Beta Kappa, St. Botolph Club Home: 1 Adams St Charlestown MA 02129-3433 Office: Wilmer Cutler Pickering Hale and Dorr 60 State St Boston MA 02109-1816 Office Phone: 617-526-6912. Office Fax: 617-526-5000. Business E-Mail: jeffrey.rudman@wilmerhale.com.

RUDMAN, MARA E., government official; b. San Antonio, Aug. 23, 1962; AB summa cum laude with high honors, Dartmouth Coll., 1984; JD cum laude, Harvard U., 1990. Bar: Mass. 1991, Fla. 1992, D.C. 1992. Legis. asst. to Rep. Gerry E. Studds of Mass., U.S. Ho. of Reps., Washington, 1984-87; law clk. to Judge Stanley Marcus, U.S. Dist. Ct. for So. Dist. Fla., 1990-91; assoc. Hogan and Hartson, 1991-93; dem. legal counsel Ho. Com. on Internat. Rels. (formerly Com. on Fgn. Affairs), 1993-97; spl. asst. to pres. and sr. dir. for legis. affairs NSC, Wash., 1997-99; dep. asst. to pres. Nat. Security Affairs, Wash., DC, 1999; chief staff NSC, Wash., DC, 1999—. Editor-in-chief Harvard Human Rights Jour., 1989-90. Mem. Casque and Gauntlet, Phi Beta Kappa. Office: NSC White House 1600 Pennsylvania Ave NW Washington DC 20500 Office Phone: 202-456-1414. Office Fax: 202-456-2461.

RUDMAN, PAUL LEWIS, lawyer, former state supreme court justice; b. Bangor, Maine, Mar. 26, 1935; s. Abraham Moses and Irene (Epstein) R.; m. Inez Lee Kolonel, Oct. 8, 1961; Andrew Isaac, Carole Sue. AB, Yale Coll., 1957; JD, George Washington U. Sch. Law, 1960. Bar: Maine 1960, D.C. 1960; U.S. Dist. Ct. Maine, 1961. Ptnr. Rudman & Winchell, Bangor, 1960-92; justice Maine Supreme Jud. Ct., Bangor, 1992—2005; atty. Rudman & Winchell LLC, Bangor, 2005—. Ct. liaison Bd. Overseers of Bar, Media & Courts Com.; chair Jud. Education Com., Sentence Review Panel; mem. Jud. Advisory Bd., AEI-Brookings Jud. Education Program. Capt. Maine Air NG, 1960-66. Office: Rudman & Winchell LLC PO Box 1401 84 Harlow St Bangor ME 04402

RUDMAN, SOLOMON KAL, magazine publisher; b. Phila., Mar. 6, 1930; s. Benjamin and Lena (Holtzman) R.; m. Lucille Steinhauer, June 29, 1958; 1 child, Mitchell. BS in Edn., U. Pa., Phila., 1951; MS in Edn., Temple U., Phila., 1957; LHD (hon.), Holy Family U., Phila., 2002, U. Arts, 2003, LHD (hon.), 2005, PhD (hon.), 2006; HHD honoris causa (hon.), Drexel U., Phila., 1970. Chmn. dept. spl. edn. Franklin D. Roosevelt Sch., Bristol Twp., Pa., 1960-68; pub. premier record/ radio trade Fri. Morning Quarterback, Cherry Hill, Pa., 1968—. Bd. dirs. Variety Club, NARAS, Crime Commn., Pa., NJ, Del.; co-host Merv Griffin TV Show, 1981-82; music expert Today Show, 1981-82, Tomorrow Show, 1981-82, Tom Snyder TV Show; host Phila. Franklin Inst. Sci. and Fels Planetarium mobile sci. programs, entertainment shows to Phila.-NJ Sr. Citizens' homes, children's and vets. hosps.; co-host, talent booker Easter Seals Telethon; creator h.s. jazz piano competition U. the Arts, Phila.; created Kal and Lucille Rudman Inst. Drexel U. Pub.: (mag.) MQB (Modern QB); prodr. CD's of advance hits; launched music trade mag. Pro QB, launched Q-Beatl; created 50 billboards for Mothers In Charge. Bd. dirs. Phila. Broadcast Pioneers; sponsor carillon bells Ave. of Arts, Phila., TV cameras Temple U. Sch. Comm., alert systems Phila. police dog cars, Franklin Inst. Travelling Sci. Show to Phila. elem. schs., Citizens' Crime Commn., 1st ann. classical piano HS competition, Chestnut Hill Coll., 100th Anniversary Jewish Fedn. Phila., Franklin Inst. Time Capsule, Phila., Jewish Fedn. Atrium, Phila.; co-sponsor purchase and distbn. of dictionaries to Phila. Elem. Sch. pupils, Robotics Competition Phila. HS, NJ United Cerebral palsy Marathon Dance, Rutgers U.; co-sponsor Succeeding By Reading Program; active Phila. Mid. Schs., Jewish Book week, Phila. Ave. of Arts., Newspapers In Edn., others; founder Kal and Lucille Rudman Inst. for Entertainment Studies, Drexel Hill U. Coll. Media Arts and Design, Phila., 1974; grad. FBI Cmty. Outreach. Recipient Lifetime Achievement award Phila. Music Conf., Lifetime Music Achievement award Delaware Valley Music Poll., Presdl. Citation, Citizens Crime Com., Plaque on Walk of Fame, Ave. of the Arts, Enforcement award Nat. Marines, Radio Milestone award to Phila. Radio Legends, March of Dimes, T. Seddon Duke award; Top Civilian award, Phila Fire Dept., T.Seddon Duke award, Marshall award Phila. Crime Commn.; Top Civilian award Phila./Del. Valley Crime Commn., Top award Citizen's Crime Commn., Phila.; named Penndelphia Humanitarian of Yr., Humanitarian of Yr. Nat. Sunshine Fedn., Hon. Dep. Police Commr., Phila., Hon. Fire Commr., Person of Yr. Phila./Del/ Valley Broadcast Pioneers, 1970; named to Broadcast Pioneers Hall of Fame Phila., Hon. Dep. Police Commr., Phila.; scholar Drexel U., Hahnemann Med. Sch., Phila. Mem. Phila. Music Alliance (bd. dirs.), Nat. Arthritis Found. (bd. dirs.), NARAS (bd. dirs.), Masons (cmty. svc. award, Grand Master), Phila. Police Commrs. Club (named hon. dep. police commr.). Achievements include helping to create Music Theater Dept. at U. Arts, Phila; creating the 1st Police Athletic League, Abington, Pa. Office: Friday Morning Quarterback 1930 Marlton Pike E Cherry Hill NJ 08003-2150

RUDNER, SARA, dancer; b. Bklyn., Feb. 16, 1944; d. Henry Nathaniel and Jeannette (Smolensky) R.; 1 child, Edward Eli Rudner Marschner. AB in Russian Studies, Barnard Coll., 1964; MFA in Choreography, Bennington Coll., 1999. Dancer Sansardo Dance Co., NYC, 1964-65, Am. Dance Co. at Lincoln Ctr., NYC, 1965, Shakespeare Festival Touring Children's Show, NYC, 1966; featured dancer Twyla Tharp Dance Found., NYC, 1966-85; artistic dir., dancer Sara Rudner Performance Ensemble, NYC, 1977—; guest dancer Joffrey Ballet, NYC, 1973, Pilobolus Dance Theatre, NYC, 1975, Lar Lubovitch Dance Co., NYC, 1975-76; guest lectr., choreographer grad. dance dept. UCLA, 1975. Dir. dance Sarah Lawrence Coll.; tchr. master workshop NYU Theater Program, 1988-90; pres., artistic dir. Heart Dance, Inc. Choreographer: Palm Trees and Flamingoes, 1980, Dancing for an Hour or So, 1981, Minute by Minute, 1982, Eight Solos, 1991, Heartbeats, Inside Out, 1993; (with Jennifer Tipton and Dana Reitz) Necessary Weather, 1994; (with Rona Pondick, Robert Feintuch and Jennifer Tipton) Mine, 1996, Alley Theater-The Greeks part I and II, 1997, Heartbeat/mb with Christopher Janney and Mikhail Barysnikov, 1998. Choreographer Dancing-on-View St. Mark's Ch., N.Y.C., 1999, Santa Fe Opera. Grantee Creative Artists Pub. Svc. Program, N.Y., 1975-76, N.Y. State Coun. on Arts, 1975-78, Nat. Endowment for Arts, 1979-81, 91-92, 94-97; Guggenheim fellow, 1981-82; recipient N.Y. Dance and Performance award, 1984. Business E-Mail: srudner@slc.edu.

RUDNICK, ABRAHAM, psychiatrist, philosopher; b. Haifa, Israel, Jan. 13, 1964; s. Samuel and Ruth (Laufer) R.; children: Or, Niv, Lee. MD, Hebrew U., 1990; M in Psychiatry, Tel-Aviv U., 1999, PhD in Philosophy, 1999. Med. officer Israel Def. Forces, 1990—94; resident psychiatry Tel-Aviv Cmty. Mental Health Ctr., 1994—99; fellow psychiatry U. Toronto, 1999—2001; rehab. psychiatrist Abarbanel Mental Health Ctr., 2002, Beer Sheva Mental Health Ctr., Israel, 2003—04; assoc. prof. psychiatry and philosophy U. We. Ont., Canada, 2004—; physician-leader schizophrenia program Regional Mental Health Care, London, Canada, 2004—. Lectr. in behavioral scis. and med. humanities Tel-Aviv U., 1998—2004. Contbr. articles to profl. jour. including Jour. Medicine and Philosophy, Internat. Jour. Law and Psychiatry, Biol. Psychiatry, Psychosomatics. Avocation: music. Office: Regional Mental Healthcare 850 Highbury Ave London ON N6A4H1 Canada Home Phone: 519-6795375. Personal E-mail: harudnick@hotmail.com.

RUDNICK, IRENE KRUGMAN, lawyer, educator, former state legislator; b. Columbia, SC, Dec. 27, 1929; d. Jack and Jean (Getter) Krugman; m. Harold Rudnick, Nov. 7, 1954 (dec.); children: Morris, Helen Gail. AB cum laude, U. S.C., 1949, JD, 1952. Bar: (S.C.) 1952. Individual practice law, Aiken, SC, 1952—; now ptnr. Rudnick & Rudnick; instr. bus. law U. S.C., Aiken, 1962—; tchr. Warrenville Elem. Sch., 1965-70; supt. edn. Aiken County, 1970-72; mem. S.C. Ho. of Reps., 1972—78, 1980—84, 1986—94. Pres. Adath Yeshurun Synagogue; active Aiken County Dem. Party, S.C. Dem. Party; hon. mem. Aiken Able-Disabled. Recipient Citizen of Yr. award, 1976-77, Bus. and Profl. Women's Career Woman of Yr., 1978, 94, Aiken County Friend of Edn. award, 1985, 93, Outstanding Legis. award Disabled Vets., 1991, Citizen of Yr. award Planned Parenthood, 1994, Sertoma Svc. to Mankind award, 1996, Pickens Salley So. Woman of Distinction award, 2005; named Aiken County C. of C. Woman of Yr., 2005. Mem. AAUW, Aiken Able-Disabled (hon.), Aiken Hist. Soc., Hist. Aiken Found., Alpha Delta Kappa, Order Eastern Star, Hadassah Sisterhood, Am. Legion Aux. Office: PO Box 544 135 Pendleton St NW Aiken SC 29801-3859

RUDNICK, JAMIE, geneticist, research scientist; d. James and Jackie Rudnick. BS in Biology, U. Nebr., Lincoln, 2001; PhD in Wildlife Genetics, Purdue U., West Lafayette, Ind., 2006. Zookeeper Folsom Children's Zoo, Lincoln, 1997—2001; conservation assoc. Brookfield Zoo, Ill., 2006—. Author and co-author sci. papers in field. Recipient All Am. Scholar award, 1999, Lynn Fellowship award, Purdue U., 2001. Mem.: Am. Genetic Assn., Am. Zoo and Aquarium Assn., Am. Ornithologists' Union. Office: Chgo Zoological Soc Brookfield Zoo 3300 Golf Rd Brookfield IL 60513 Business E-Mail: jarudnic@brookfieldzoo.org.

RUDNICK, LEWIS G., lawyer; b. May 31, 1935; AB with honors, Univ. Ill., Urbana-Champaign, 1957; MBA, Columbia Univ., 1960; JD, Northwestern Univ., 1964. Bar: Ill. 1964, US Dist. Ct. (no. dist. Ill.) 1964. Ptnr., Franchise & Distribution practice group DLA Piper Rudnick Gray Cary, Chgo. Gen. counsel Internat. Franchise Assn. Edn. Found.; mem. Ill. Franchise Adv. Bd.; mem. gov. com. ABA Forum on Franchising, 1977—84, chmn., 1981—83. Editor: Jour. of Internat. Franchising & Distribution Law; contbr. articles to profl. jours. Mem.: ABA, Internat. Franchise Assn. (counsel). Office: DLA Piper Rudnick Gray Cary Suite 1900 203 N LaSalle St Chicago IL 60601-1293 Office Phone: 312-368-4055. Office Fax: 312-630-7312. Business E-Mail: lewis.rudnick@dlapiper.com.

RUDNICK, PAUL DAVID, lawyer; b. Chgo., May 15, 1940; s. Harry Louis and Cele (Gordon) R.; m. Hope Korshak, June 13, 1963; children: William A., Carolyn. BS, Tulane U., 1962; JD cum laude, Northwestern U., 1965. Bar: Ill. 1965, Colo. 1994, U.S. Dist. Ct. (no. dist.) Ill. Assoc. Schiff, Hardin & Waite, Chgo., 1965-66; ptnr. Piper Rudnick, Chgo., 1966-99, sr. counsel, 2000—04; sr. counsel, Real Estate practice DLA Piper Rudnick Gray Cary, Chgo., 2005—. Editor Northwestern U. Law Rev., 1964-65; co-editor, author: Illinois Real Estate Forms, 1989. Mem. Pitkin County Colo. Planning and Zoning Commn. Mem. Am. Coll. Real Estate Lawyers, Internat. Found. for Employee Benefit Plans, Order of Coif. Office: DLA Piper Rudnick Gray Cary Suite 1900 203 N La Salle St Chicago IL 60601-1293 Office Phone: 312-368-4060. Office Fax: 312-630-7353. Business E-Mail: paul.rudnick@dlapiper.com.

RUDO, MILTON, retired manufacturing executive; b. Balt., Jan. 17, 1919; s. Saul E. and Bertha (Berkowitz) R.; m. Roslind Mandel, Mar. 27, 1943; children: Stephanie Ellen, Neil Dennis. BA, Johns Hopkins U., 1940; AMP, Harvard U., 1964. Various positions Brunswick Corp., Skokie, Ill., 1940-66, corp. v.p., pres. Bowling divsn. Chgo., 1966-74, group v.p. recreation bus., 1974-84, ret., 1984, cons. to the CEO, 1984-87; dir., cons. to the CEO Donlen Leasing Corp., Skokie, 1986-90. Pres. Nat. Bowling Hall of Fame and Mus., 1979. Capt. AUS, 1942-45, ETO. Recipient ann. award N.Y. Mktg. Club, 1960, Industry Svc. award, 1973; named to Bowling Hall of Fame, 1984. Mem. Nat. Bowling Coun. (pres. 1972), Briarwood Country Club (Deerfield, Ill.), Hamlet Country Club (Delray Beach Fla.). Home (Summer): 1755 Lake Cook Rd Highland Park IL 60035 Home (Winter): 712 Pine Lake Delray Beach FL 33445

RUDOFF, SHELDON, lawyer; b. Bklyn., May 29, 1933; s. Raphael and Goldie (Gorelick) R.; m. Hedda Muller, Nov. 22, 1964; children: Shaindy, Sara, Simone. BA cum laude, Yeshiva Coll., 1954; JSD cum laude, NYU, 1958; ordination, RIETS, 1957. Bar: N.Y. 1958, U.S. Dist. Ct. (so. and ea. dists.) N.Y. 1958, U.S. Supreme Ct. 1978. Ptnr. Shatzkin, Cooper & Rudoff, NYC, 1970-84, Labaton Sucharow & Rudoff, NYC, 1984—; pres. Union Orthodox Jewish Congregation Am., 1990-94, hon. pres., 1994—; pres. Beth Din Am., 1996—2003, hon. pres., 2003—. V.p. Yeshiva Coll. Alumni, N.Y.C., 1962-64; pres. Young Israel West Side, N.Y.C., 1969-72; sec. Orthodox Union, 1972-76, v.p., 1976-78, sr. v.p., 1978-84, chmn. bd., 1984-90, pres. 1990-94; trustee Fedn. Jewish Philanthropies, 1980-91, United Jewish Cmtys. Recipient Pres.'s award Orthodox Union, N.Y.C., 1972, Nat. Leadership award Nat. Conf. Synagogue Youth, N.Y.C., 1974, Kesser Shem Tov award Ortohdox Union, 1995. Mem. ABA, N.Y. State Bar Assn., Assn. Bar City N.Y. (transp. com. 1976—). Office: Labaton Sucharow & Rudoff 100 Park Ave New York NY 10017-5516 Office Phone: 212-907-0700. E-mail: srudoff@labaton.com.

RUDOLPH, ABRAHAM MORRIS, pediatrician, educator; b. Johannesburg, Republic of South Africa, Feb. 3, 1924; s. Chone and Sarah (Feinstein) Rudolph; m. Rhona Sax, Nov. 2, 1949; children: Linda, Colin, Jeffrey. MBBCh summa cum laude, U. Witwatersrand, Johannesburg, 1946, MD, 1951; MD (hon.), U. Witwatersrand, Johannesburg, S. Africa, 2006; D (hon.), Rene Descartes U., Paris, 1996. Instr. Harvard Med. Sch., 1955—57, assoc. pediat., 1957—60; assoc. cardiologist in charge cardiopulmonary lab. Children's Hosp., Boston, 1955—60; dir. pediatric cardiology Albert Einstein Coll. Medicine, 1960—66, prof. pediat., assoc. prof. physiology NYC, 1962—66; vis. pediatrician Bronx Mcpl. Hosp. Ctr., NYC, 1960—66; prof. pediat. U. Calif., San Francisco, 1966—94, prof. physiology, 1974—88, Neider prof. pediatric cardiology, prof. ob-gyn and reproductive scis., 1974—94, chmn. dept. pediat., 1987—91, prof. pediatr. emeritus, 1994—; practice medicine, specializing in pediatric cardiology San Francisco. Mem. cardiovasc. study sect. NIH, 1961—65; mem. nat. adv. heart coun., 1968—72; established investigator Am. Heart Assn., 1958—62; career scientist Health Rsch. Coun., NYC, 1962—66; Harvey lectr. Oxford (Eng.) U., 1984; inaugural lectr. 1st Nat. Congress Italian Soc. Perinatal Medicine, 1985. Editl. bd. Pediat., 1964—70, Circulation, 1966—74, 1983—88, assoc. editor Circulation Rsch., 1970, Pediatric Rsch., 1970—77; editor: Rudolph's Pediatrics, Congenital Diseases of the Heart: Clinical-Physiological Considerations, 2001, Rudolph's Fundamentals of Pediatrics; contbr. articles to profl. jours. Recipient Merit award, Nat. Heart, Lung and Blood Inst., 1986, Arvo Yllpo medal, Helsinki (Finland) U., 1987, Jonxis medal, Children's Hosp. Groningen, 1993, Nils Rosen von Rosenstein award, Swedish Pediat. Soc., 1999, Pollin prize for pediat. rsch., N.Y. Presbyn. Hosp., Columbia U. Coll. Physicians and Surgeons, 2005. Fellow: AAAS, Am. Assn. Adv. Sci., Royal Coll. Physicians (London), Royal Coll. Physicians (Edinburgh); mem.: Am. Heart Assn. (Rsch. Achievement award 1991, Founding Disting. Scientist award 2003), Am. Pediatric Soc. (coun. 1985—92, v.p. 1992—93, pres. 1993—94, Howland award 1999), Soc. for Pediatric Rsch. (coun. 1961—64), Soc. for Clin. Investigation, Am. Phys. Soc., Am. Acad. Pediat. (past chmn. sect. on cardiology, E. Mead Johnson award for rsch. in pediat. 1964, Borden award 1979, Lifetime Med. Edn. award 1992, Joseph St. Geme leadership award Pediat. 1993, Founder award, cardiology sect. 2001, Pollin Pediatric Rsch. prize 2005), NAS Inst. Medicine. Office: U Calif Cardiovascular Rsch Inst Calif Rm HSE 1424 Box 0544 San Francisco CA 94143-0544 Home Phone: 415-665-6841. Business E-Mail: abraham.rudolph@ucsf.edu.

RUDOLPH, ANDREW HENRY, dermatologist, educator; b. Detroit, Jan. 30, 1943; s. John J. and Mary M. Rudolph; children: Kristen Ann, Kevin Andrew. MD cum laude, U. Mich., 1966. Diplomate Am. Bd. Dermatology. Intern Univ. Hosp., U. Mich. Med. Ctr., Ann Arbor, 1966-67, resident dept. dermatology, 1967-70; pvt. practice medicine specializing in dermatology, 1972—. Asst. prof. dermatology Baylor Coll. Medicine, Houston, 1972-75, assoc. prof., 1975-83, clin. prof., 1983—; chief dermatology svc. VA Hosp., Houston, 1977-82; mem. staff Meth. Hosp., Tex. Children's Hosp., St. Luke's Episcopal Hosp. Mem. editl. bd. Jour. Sexually Transmitted Diseases, 1977-85; contbr. to med. publs. Served as surgeon USPHS, 1970-72. Regent's scholar U. Mich., 1966. Fellow Am. Acad. Dermatology; mem. AMA, Am. Dermatol. Assn., Tex. Med. Assn., Harris County Med. Soc., Houston Dermatol. Soc. (past pres.), Tex. Dermatol. Soc., Skin Cancre Found., Am. Venereal Disease Assn. (past pres.), Mich. Alumni Assn. (life), Alpha Omega Alpha, Phi Kappa Phi, Phi Rho Sigma, Theta Xi. Office: 6560 Fannin St Ste 724 Houston TX 77030-2768

RUDOLPH, FREDERICK, history professor; b. Balt., June 19, 1920; s. Charles Frederick and Jennie Hill (Swope) R.; m. Dorothy Dannenbaum, June 18, 1949; children: Marta R. MacDonald, Lisa R. Cushman. BA, Williams Coll., 1942, Litt.D., 1985; MA, Yale U., 1949, PhD, 1953; LHD, U. Rochester, 1994, Wilkes U., 1998. Instr. history Williams Coll., 1946-47; asst. instr. Yale, 1949-50; mem. faculty Williams Coll., 1951—, prof., 1961—, Mark Hopkins prof. history, 1964-82, emeritus, 1982—, chmn. Am. civilization program, 1971-80. Williams Coll. marshal, 1978-87; vis. lectr. history and edn. Harvard U., 1960, 61; vis. prof. Sch. Edn., U. Calif.-Berkeley, 1983; mem. commn. plans and objectives Am. Council on Edn., 1963-66; mem. study group on postsecondary edn. Nat. Inst. Edn., 1980-83; mem. com. on baccalaureate degrees Assn. Am. Colls., 1981-85; vis. assoc. Ctr. Studies in Higher Edn., U. Calif.-Berkeley, 1983 Author: Mark Hopkins and the Log, 1956, rev. edit. 1996, The American College and University: A History, 1962, rev. edit., 1990 (Japanese translation, 2003), Curriculum: A History of the American Undergraduate Course of Study Since 1636, 1977, rev. edit., 1993; editor: Essays on Education in the Early Republic, 1965, Perspectives: A Williams Anthology, 1983; exec. editor: Change, 1980-84, cons. editor, 1985-92. Founding mem. Berkshire County Hist. Soc., 1962, v.p., 1962-66, pres., 1966-68, bd. dirs., 1974-76; trustee Hancock-Shaker Cmty. Inc., 1974-91, Wyoming Sem., 1976-79, Bennington Mus., 1985-95; bd. dirs. Armand Hammer United World Coll. Am. West, 1993-2005. Capt. AUS, 1942-46. Guggenheim fellow, 1958-59, 68-69; recipient Frederic W. Ness award Assn. Am. Colls., 1980, Rogerson cup Williams Coll., 1982, Disting. Svc. award Wyo. Seminary, 1986; Frederick Rudolph Professorship of Am. Culture established in his honor, Williams Coll., 2007. Mem. AAUP, Nat. Acad. Edn., Mass. Hist. Soc. (fellow), Am. Hist. Assn., Am. Studies Assn., Phi Beta Kappa. Democrat. Home: PO Box 515 Williamstown MA 01267-2800

RUDOLPH, GILBERT LAWRENCE, lawyer; b. LA, Aug. 23, 1946; s. Martin and Marion R.; Susan Ilene Fellenbaum, Sept. 18, 1983. BA, Ariz. State U., 1967; postgrad., Am. U., Washington, 1967-69; JD, U. Cin., 1973. Bar: D.C. 1973, U.S. Dist. Ct. D.C. 1974, U.S. Ct. Appeals (D.C. cir.) 1974, Ariz. 1975, U.S. Dist. Ct. Ariz. 1975, Calif. 1979. Assoc. Streich, Lang, Weeks & Cardon, P.A., Phoenix, 1975-78; ptnr. Gilbert L. Rudolph, P.C., Phoenix, 1978-87; sr. mem. O'Connor, Cavanagh, Anderson, Killingsworth & Beshears, P.A., Phoenix, 1987-99; shareholder, co-chair fin. instn. practice group Greenberg Traurig LLP, Phoenix, 1999—. Lectr. on lending issues. Bd. dirs. Temple Chai, 2002—, Make-A-Wish Found. of Am., 1984—89, Aid to Adoption of Spl. Kids, Ariz., 1995—2003. Fellow Am. Coll. Consumer Fin. Svcs. Lawyers; mem. ABA (com. on consumer fin. svcs. bus. law sect. 1981—, com. on comml. fin. svcs. 1989—, mem. com. on uniform comml. code 1992—), Conf. on Consumer Fin. Law (governing com. 1986—). Republican. Jewish. Office: Greenberg Traurig LLP Ste 700 2375 E Camelback Rd Phoenix AZ 85016 Office Phone: 602-445-8206. E-mail: rudolphg@gtlaw.com.

RUDOLPH, JAMES LEONARD, lawyer; b. Beverly, Mass., Sept. 26, 1950; s. Robert P. and Joyce B. (Yoffa) R.; m. Susan B. Gouchberg, Oct. 31, 1981. B.A., U. Denver, 1972; J.D., Boston Coll., 1975. Bar: Mass. 1975, U.S. Dist. Ct. Mass. 1976, U.S. Ct. Appeals (1st cir.) 1978, U.S. Supreme Ct. 1984. Ptnr. Gargill, Sassoon & Rudolph, Boston, from 1976; now ptnr. Rudolph Friedmann LLP, Boston; trustee Eastern Bank. Chmn. Swampscott Zoning Bd. Appeals (Mass.), 1984—89, mem., 1983—89; pres. Jewish Rehab. Ctr., Swampscott, 1984-89, Camp Kingswood, Bridgton, Maine, 1987—89; chmn. North Shore; adv. group, chair New Eng. region bd. Anti-Defamation League; trustee Govs. Acad.; past pres. JRC Charitable Found. Mem. ATLA, ABA, Boston Bar Assn., Mass. Bar Assn., Mass. Conveyancers Assn., Mass. Assoc. Builders and Contractors (gen. counsel, past pres.), Belmont Country Club, Boston Yacht (Marblehead, Mass.), Mt. Scopus Lodge (Malden, Mass.). Office: Rudolph Friedmann LLP 92 State St Boston MA 02109-2004 Business E-Mail: jrudolph@rflawyers.com.

RUDOLPH, JAMES ROBERT, psychologist; b. Albuquerque, Mar. 1, 1957; s. Anita Jean and Robert John Rudolph; life ptnr. John Chester Gonsiorek. BA in Psychology, Sociology, U. N. Mex, 1980, MA in Spl. Edn., 1981; PhD in Counseling Psychology, Lehigh U., 1988. Lic. psychologist Minn. Bd. of Psychology, 1990, registered Nat. Register of Health Svc. Providers in Psychology, 1999, Diplomate Am. Bd. of Profl. Psychology, 2000, cert. profl. qualification in psychology Assn. of State and Provincial Psychology Bds., 2001. Spl. edn. tchr. Albuquerque Pub. Schs., 1982—83; psychiat. crisis counselor Mt. Tom Inst. for Human Svcs., Holyoke, Mass., 1988; psychotherapist Constance Bultman Wilson Ctr. for Adolescent Psychiatry, Faribault, Minn., 1988—90, physician's assoc., 1990; adj. asst. prof. St. Mary's Coll. Grad. Ctr., Mpls., 1990—93; pvt. practice Mpls., 1992—2002; clin. dir., dir. of profl. tng. Carver County Mental Health Program, Waconia, Minn., 1991—; adj. faculty Capella U., Mpls., 2004. Clin. adj. faculty Minn. Sch. of Profl. Psychology, Mpls., 1992—2000; practice sample reviewer. oral exam mentor, examiner counseling psychology Am. Bd. of Profl. Psychology, Mpls., 2001—. Contbr. articles to profl. jours., chapters to books. Recipient Certificates of Excellence in Clin. Supervision, Minn. Sch. of Profl. Psychology, 1990's. Mem.: APA, Chi Sigma Iota. Personal E-mail: jamesrrudolph@comcast.net.

RUDOLPH, LAVERE CHRISTIAN, library director; b. Jasper, Ind., Dec. 24, 1921; s. Joseph Frank and Rose (Stradtner) R. AB, DePauw U., 1948; B.D., Louisville Presbyn. Sem., 1951; PhD, Yale, 1958; student, U. Zurich, Switzerland, 1960; M.L.S., Ind. U., 1968. Ordained to Ministry Presbyn. Ch., 1950; pastor in Ind. and Conn., 1950-54; mem. faculty Louisville Presbyn. Sem., 1954-69, prof. ch. history, 1960-69; lectr. history U. Louisville, 1965-69; rare books bibliographer Van Pelt Library U. Pa.; head tech. services Lilly Library, Ind. U., 1970-78, curator of books, 1978-86, librarian emeritus, 1987—. Author: Hoosier Zion, 1963 (Thomas Kuch award Ind. U. Writers Conf. 1964), Story of the Church, 1966, Francis Asbury, 1966, Indiana Letters, 1979, Religion in Indiana, 1986, Hoosier Faiths, 1995. Served to capt. USAAF, 1940-46. Mem.: Am. Soc. Ch. History, Phi Beta Kappa. Democrat. Home: 2455 Tamarack Trail apt 101 Bloomington IN 47408 Office: Ind U Library Bloomington IN 47405

RUDOLPH, LAWRENCE, lawyer; BA in English, Adelphi U., 1973; JD, Georgetown U. Law Ctr., 1976. Bar: DC, Pa., admitted to: DC Dist. Ct., Cir. Ct. Appeals. Staff atty. US Interstate Commerce Commn. Office of Preceedings, 1976—78; assoc. Verner, Liipfert, Bernhard, McPherson and Hand, Washington, 1978—82; sr. atty. then dep. asst. dir. Office of Hearings and Appeals, US Dept. Energy, 1982—88; asst. gen. counsel NSF, Arlington, Va., 1988, dep. gen. counsel, 1988, gen. counsel, 1995—. Bd. trustee Adelphi U. Recipient Presdl. Rank award of Meritious Exec., 1997. Mem.: ABA, Pa. Bar Assn., DC Bar Assn. Office: NSF Rm 1265S 4201 Wilson Blvd Arlington VA 22230-0001 Office Phone: 703-292-8060. Office Fax: 703-292-9041. Business E-Mail: lrudolph@nsf.gov.

RUDOLPH, PETER, chef; Grad., Calif. Culinary Acad., 1995. Pastry cook Brasserie Savoy, San Francisco; chef The Dining Room, Ritz-Carlton, Atlanta; sous chef Jer-ne, Ritz-Carlton, Marina del Rey, Calif., 2000; exec. chef Navio, Ritz-Carlton, Half Moon Bay, Calif., Campton Place, San Francisco, 2006—. Named one of San Francisco's Rising Stars, StarChefs.com, 2007. Office: Campton Place 340 Stockton St San Francisco CA 94108 Office Phone: 415-955-5555. *

RUDOLPH, RICHARD L., medical products executive, physician; b. Jersey City, Mar. 28, 1949; BS in Biology, Georgetown U., Washington, 1972; MD, U. Medicine and Dentistry, Newark, NJ, 1976. Diplomate Am. Bd. Internal Medicine, 1979. Assoc. Guthrie Clinic, Sayre, Pa., 1979—85; sr. dir. Wyeth-Ayerst Rsch., Radnor, Pa., 1985—2001; v.p. Cyberonics, Inc, Houston, Tex., 2001—. Contbr. scientific papers. Mem.: ACP, AMA, Phi Beta Kappa. Achievements include research in antidepressant treatments; patents for uses of Venlafaxine. Office: Cyberonics 100 Cyberonics Blvd Houston TX 77058 Office Phone: 281-228-7200.

RUDOLPH, RONALD ALVIN, human resources specialist; b. Berwyn, Ill., May 12, 1949; s. Alvin J. and Gloria S. (Nicoletti) Rudolph. BA, U. Calif., Santa Cruz, 1971; D in Psychology, Calif. Coast U., 2003. Sr. cons. De Anza Assocs., San Jose, Calif., 1971-73; pers. adminstr. McDonnell Douglas Corp., Cupertino, Calif., 1974-75; employment rep. Fairchild Semiconductor, Mountain View, Calif., 1973-74, 75; compensation analyst Sperry Univac, Santa Clara, Calif., 1975-78; mgr. exempt compensation div. Intel Corp., Santa Clara, 1978-79, compensation mgr., 1979-82, dir. corp. compensation, 1982-85; v.p. human resources UNISYS Corp., San Jose, 1985-91, ASK Group Inc., Mountain View, 1991-94, 3 Com Corp., Santa Clara, 1994-98; v.p. adminstrn. Wyse Tech. Inc., San Jose, 1999—2000; with Infogrames Inc., 2000—01, Netmanage Inc., 2003—. Cons. Rudolph Assocs., Cupertino, 1982—; bd. dirs. Dynamic Temp. Svcs., Sunnyvale, Calif. Mem. spl. com. parolee employment, Sacramento, 1973—75; bd. dirs. Jr. Achievement, San Jose, 1978—88. Mem.: No. Calif. Human Resources Coun., Am. Compensation Assn., Am. Soc. Pers. Adminstrs. Avocations: sailing, reading, running, camping. Office: 3 Com Corp Santa Clara CA 95050 Office Phone: 408-342-7674.

RUDOLPH, SCOTT, pharmaceutical executive; b. 1958; s. Arthur Rudolph. Dir., chmn. of bd., CEO NBTY, Inc., Bohemia, NY, 1986—. Past chmn. of bd. dirs. Dowling Coll., Long Island, NY, 1997—2000; vice chmn. Dowling Coll. Bd., 2004—. Office: NBTY PO Box 9001 Bohemia NY 11716-9001 *

RUDOLPH, WALLACE MORTON, law educator; b. Chgo., Sept. 11, 1930; s. Norman Charles and Bertha (Margolin) R.; m. Janet L. Gordon, Feb. 14, 1964 (div. Jan. 1998); children: Alexey, Rebecca, Sarah; m. Mimi Longworth, Mar. 22, 1998; children: Haille, Bryon. BA, U. Chgo., 1950, JD, 1953. Bar: Ill. 1953, U.S. Ct. Mil. Appeals 1954, U.S. Supreme Ct. 1954, Nebr. 1962, Wash. 1978. Rsch. assoc. Ford Found., 1953-54, Ford Found. (Project in Law and Behavior Sci.), 1954-55; instr. U. Chgo. Law Sch., 1959; assoc. Antonow & Fink, Chgo., 1960-61; asst. prof. law U. Nebr., Lincoln, 1961-63, assoc. prof., 1963-64, prof., 1965-76, U. Puget Sound Sch. Law, 1976-94, dean, 1976-80; prof. Seattle U. Sch. Law, 1994—; prof. law Fla. A&M U. Law Sch., 2006. Vis. prof. law U. Wis., 1980-81, U. Ill., 1984; chair excellence in law Memphis State U. Law Sch., 1991; mem. Commrs. Uniform State Law, 1973-77; judge Ct. Indsl. Rels., Nebr., 1975-77; mem. Wash. Jud. Coun. and Com. II, 1976-80, Pub. Employment Rels. Commn., Wash., 1977-97; dean U. Orlando, 1997-98; dir. acad. support and bar preparation Fla. State U. Law Sch. Author: Handbook for Correctional Law; contbr. articles to profl. jours.; author: Model Criminal Procedure Code, 1975, Model Sentencing and Corrections Act, 1978, Amicus Curiae Brief, Wash. State Supreme Ct, 1979. Bd. dirs. LIMIT, 1992-94, Nebr. chpt. ACLU, 1965-72; mem. Nebr. Dem. Contact Com., 1973-74, 75-76; chmn. Firt Congl. Dist. Dem. Party, 1975-76; mem. exec. com. Unitarian Ch., Lincoln, 1965-67. With JAGC, U.S. Army, 1954-57. Mem. AAUP, ABA, Soc. Criminology, Am. Law Inst., Am. Arbitration Assn. Office Phone: 407-254-4044. Personal E-mail: wmr337@hotmail.com.

RUDOLPH, WILLIAM KEYSE, curator; b. Garden City, Kans., May 30, 1969; s. Gerald Allen Rudolph and Donna Jean Keyse. BA with high distinction, U. Nebr., Lincoln, 1991; post graduate diploma, Courtauld Inst. Art, London, 1992; MA, U. Va., Charlottesville, 1995; PhD, Bryn Mawr Coll., Pa., 2003. Sr. lectr. liberal arts U. the Arts, Phila., 1997—2004, adj. asst. prof. liberal arts, 2004; departmental assoc. for European decorative arts Phila. Mus. Art, 1999—2004; Pauline Gill Sullivan assoc. curator Am. art Dallas Mus. Art, 2004—. Author: (short stories) Back in the Day, Boyfriend from Hell; curator (exhibitions) Charle's Sheelers Power Series, Town and Country: The Beginnings of the American Landscape Collection at the Dallas Museum of Art, co-curator There and Back Again: Selections from the Graham D. Williford Collection of American Art, curator From Albright to Zinnias: American Works on Paper from the Permanent Collection, Julian Onderdonk: Bluebonnets and Beyond. Mem.: Assn. Art Mus. Curators (website com. mem. 2005), Coll. Art Assn. Office: Dallas Mus Art 1717 N Harwood St Dallas TX 75201 Office Phone: 214-922-1233. Office Fax: 214-720-0862. Business E-Mail: wrudolph@dallasmuseumofart.org.

RUDOLPHSEN, WILLIAM M., retail executive; BS in Acctg., Marquette U.; MBA, DePaul U. With Walgreen Co., Deerfield, Ill., 1977—, dir. 3d party acctg., 1995—98, divisional v.p. acctg., contr., 1998—2004, sr. v.p., CFO, 2004—. Office: Walgreen Co 200 Wilmot Rd Deerfield IL 60015 *

RUDSTEIN, DAVID STEWART, law educator; b. Leeds, Eng., Sept. 27, 1946; BS, U. Ill., 1968, LL.M., 1975; JD, Northwestern U., 1971. Bar: Ill. 1971, U.S. Supreme Ct. 1977. Teaching asst. U. Ill. Coll. Law, 1971-72; law clk. to Justice Walter V. Schaefer Supreme Ct. Ill., Chgo., 1972-73; asst. prof. law Ill. Inst. Tech.-Chgo. Kent Coll., 1973-76, assoc. prof., 1976-79, prof., 1979—, assoc. dean, 1983-87. Author: Double Jeopardy, 2004, (with C.P. Erlinder and D. Thomas) Criminal Constitutional Law, 1990. Mem. ABA, Chgo. Coun. Lawyers, Order of Coif. Office: Ill Inst Tech-Chgo 565 W Adams St Chicago IL 60661-3613 Home Phone: 773-281-4961; Office Phone: 312-906-5354. E-mail: drudstei@kentlaw.edu.

RUDY, ELAINE KIM, elementary school educator; b. Meadville, Pa., Nov. 5, 1951; d. George David Matteson and Marie Alta Webster; m. Joseph G. Rudy, May 8, 1976; children: Angela Crawford, Julie Riley, Tamara Zwick. AS Early Childhood, Edinboro U., Pa., 1986; BS Edn., Edinboro U., 1987, M Edn. Reading, 1988. Tchr. Penncrest Sch. Dist., Townville, Pa., 1977—88, tchr. Title I, Reading Recovery Cambridge Springs, Pa., 1991—. Tchr. adult edn. Penncrest Sch. Dist., Townville, 1986—, coord. literacy, 2004—, mentor Title I, Cambridge Springs, mem. program improvement team, Saegertown, Pa., mem. strategic planning com.; leader Maplewood Elem. Literacy Leadership Team, 2004—. Named Outstanding Educator, Crawford County Headstart, 1990; named to Chancellor's List, Ednl. Comm. Inc., 2004—05, 2005—06. Avocations: reading, camping. Home: 31150 State Hwy 27 Guys Mills PA 16327 Office: Maplewood Elem Sch 32695 Hwy 408 Townville PA 16360

RUDY, ELLEN BEAM, nursing educator; b. Moundsville, W.Va., May 5, 1936; d. William Henry and Mary Ellen Beam; m. Theodore Rudy, June 13, 1959; children: Richard, Alan, William. BSN, Ohio State U., 1958; MPA, U. Dayton, 1974; MSN, U. Md., 1977; PhD, Case Western Res. U., 1980. Cmty. health staff nurse Columbus (Ohio) Pub. Health Nursing Svc., 1958-60; supr. in-svc. instr. Henry County Hosp., New Castle, Ind., 1960-66; emergency room staff nurse St. Elizabeth Med. Ctr., Dayton, Ohio, 1970-73; instr. critical care Johns Hopkins Hosp., Balt., 1975-76; assoc. prof., program dir. Kent (Ohio) State U. Adult Program, 1978-84; adminstrv. assoc. U. Hosp. Cleve., 1985-90; assoc. prof., chmn. MSN Case Western Res. U., Cleve., 1985-88, prof., chair acute care nursing, 1988-90, assoc. dean rsch., 1990-91; dean, prof. U. Pitts. Sch. Nursing, 1991—2005. Author: (with others) Critical Care Nursing, 1992 (Am. Jour. Nursing Book of Yr. 1993); contbr. articles to profl. jours. Grant reviewer NIH Nursing Student Sect., Washington, 1990-93; provider expert testimony Senate Appropriations Com., Washington, 1993, Health Care Forum, Washington, 1993. Edward J. and Louise Mellen Endowed Chair in Acute Care Nursing, 1989-91; fellow Am. Acad. Nursing, 1988; rsch. grantee NIH Nat. Ctr. for Nursing Rsch., 1989-91, 91-94. Mem. ANA, AACN, Am. Heart Assn., Nat. Kidney Found. (co-chair critical care task force 1988-91), Coun. Nurse Researchers. Office: Univ Pitts Sch Nursing 350 Victoria Building Pittsburgh PA 15261-2403 Home: 7815 Lydia Dr Lewis Center OH 43035-8076

RUDY, FRANK R., pathologist; b. Harrisburg, Pa., Jan. 23, 1949; s. Burton B. and Blanch T. (Rhoads) R.; m. Debra R. Bromberg, Dec. 27, 1970; children: Allison, Nicole. BA, Franklin & Marshall Coll., 1970; MD, U. Pitts., 1974. From assoc. pathologist to chmn. lab. Polyclinic Hosp., Harrisburg, 1979-95; chmn. Pinnacle Health Lab., Harrisburg, 1996-99, vice-chmn., 2000—. Regional mem. Commn. for Lab. Accreditation, 1996—2002; pres. Pathology Assocs. Ctrl. Pa., Harrisburg, 1997—. Author: Uropathology, 1989, Principles and Practices of Surgical Pathology; contbr. articles to profl. jours. Fellow Coll. Am. Pathology, Am. Soc. Clin. Pathologists; mem. Internat. Acad. Pathology, Am. Pathology Found., U.S. Acad. Pathology, Canadian Acad. Pathology. Avocation: scuba diving. Office: Pinnacle Health Labs Med Scis Bldg 100 S 2d St PO Box 8700 Harrisburg PA 17105-8700 Business E-Mail: frudy@pinnaclehealth.org.

RUDY, JANET FAYE WALKER, science educator; b. Meridian, Miss., Feb. 26, 1963; d. John Edwin and Pam Anne Walker (Stepmother); life ptnr. Jonathan Mark Gray; children: Tasha Brooks Edwards Veazey, Zachory Adam Edwards, Crystal Faye. AD, Ark. State U., 1989; B in Edn., U. Ctrl. Ark., 1991. Cert. profl. educator Ark., 1991. Tchr. 4th grade Cabot Sch. Dist., Ark., 1992—2001, 2003—04, tchr. 3d grade, 2001—03, sci. lab. specialist, 2004—. Educator art, health, literacy, math, and counseling Twenty First Century Cmty. Learning Coll. Yale U., Cabot, Ark., 2002—. Mem.: Cabot Tchrs. Assn. (v.p. 2005—06, pres. 2006—), NEA, Ark. Edn. Assn. (assoc.; v.p., pres. 2005—). Baptist. Achievements include development of science curriculum. Home: 23 Timber Ln Cabot AR 72023 Office: Ward Ctrl 1570 Wilson Loop Ward AR 72176 Home Phone: 501-541-2514; Office Phone: 501-843-9601. Business E-Mail: janet.rudy@cps.k12.ar.us.

RUDY, KATHLEEN VERMEULEN, small business owner; b. Grand Rapids, Mich., Dec. 29, 1931; d. John Weston and Geneva (Swiet) Vermeulen; m. Fredrick Albers Yonkman, June 9, 1953 (div. Sept. 1980); children: Sara Yonkman Davis, Margriet Yonkman Finnegan, Nina Yonkman Tower; m. Raymond Bruce Rudy, Nov. 14, 1981. BA, Hope Coll., 1953. Owner Kate's Antiques, 1974—2000. Editor mag. Jr. League of Boston, 1960's, Scarsdale Jr. League, 1960's. Bd. dirs. Jr. League of Boston, 1960s, Greenwich Cmty. for Human Svcs., 1970s-80s, Neighbor to Neighbor, Greenwich, 1980-98; trustee Hope Coll., 1986-96; chmn. Mary Fund com. Ladies Golf Tournament, 1985; mem. Women's Nat. Rep. Club, N.Y.C., 1995—, bd. govs., 1997-2004, 06—; mem. Hope Coll. Pres.'s Task Force, 1997-99; treas. Women's Nat. Rep. Club, 2000-02, chmn. nominating com. 2000—. 2d v.p., 2002-04, mem. internat. affairs com., 2004—. Mem. Jr. League of Phoenix, Greenwich Country Club, Boulders Golf Club (Scottsdale), Dorset Field Club, Doubles Club, Kappa Alpha Theta. Republican. Congregationalist. Avocations: tennis, golf, antiques, travel, art. Home and Office: 37 Lismore Ln Greenwich CT 06831-3741 Personal E-mail: RayRudy@worldnet.att.net.

RUDY, MONICA ELAINE, small business owner, music educator; b. Goshen, Ind., June 18, 1976; d. John C. and Rebecca Lee Pappas; m. John Ervie Rudy, Sept. 5, 1998; children: Nicholas Gus children: Clara Isabella. BA, Ohio State U., Columbus, 2000. Cert. tchr. Music Fun. Owner Monica Rudy's Music Studio, Grove City, Ohio, 1998—; pvt. instr. music. Musician: Pappas Family Recorder Quartet, 2002, The Early Interval, 2007—. Mem. Christian edn. bd. S.W. Grace Brethren Ch., Grove City, Ohio, 2001—, mem. missions bd., 2001—, coord.children's worship, 2004—, tchr., 2005—. Mem.: Nat. Guild Piano Teachers (assoc.), Ohio Music Tchrs. Assn. (assoc.), Music Tchrs. Nat. Assn. (assoc.). Republican. Avocations: music, gardening, reading, interior decorating, painting. Office: Monica Rudy's Music Studio 3214 Angela Dr Grove City OH 43123 Home Phone: 614-277-9505.

RUDY, RAYMOND BRUCE, JR., retired food company executive; b. LA, Apr. 24, 1931; s. Raymond Bruce and Wrena Margaret (Higgins) R.; m. Kathleen Vermeulen; children: Bruce Rudy, Alice M.R. Price, Barbara R. Frith. BS, UCLA, 1953; MBA, Xavier U., Cin., 1960. Brand mgr. Procter & Gamble, Cin., 1956-62; product mgr. Hunt-Wesson Foods, Fullerton, Calif., 1962-63; group v.p. Gen. Foods Corp., White Plains, NY, 1963-79; pres. Oroweat Foods Co. subs. Continental Grain Co., NYC, 1979-83; chmn., pres. Arnold Foods Co., Inc., Greenwich, Conn., 1984-86; pres. Affiliates of Best Foods subs. CPC Internat., Englewood Cliffs, NJ, 1987-89; ret., 1989; chmn., CEO, New Hampton, Inc., 1993-94; dep. chmn. Snapple Natural Beverages, Inc., 1992-94; mng. dir. J.W. Childs Assoc., 1995—; chmn. Personal Care Group, Inc., 1996-98. Chmn. Beltone Electronics Corp., 1997-2000, Internat. Diverse Foods, 1998-99, Empire Kosher Poultry, Inc., 1997-2000, Am. Safety Razor, 2000-05, Hartz Mountain Corp., 2001-04, The Meow Mix Co., 2002-03, The Sunny Delight Beverage Co., 2004—; bd. dirs. Widmer Bros. Brewing, Inc. With US Army, 1954—56. Mem. Greenwich Country Club, Dorset Field Club, The Links, The Boulders. Congregationalist.

RUDY, YORAM, biomedical engineer, biophysicist, educator; b. Tel Aviv, Feb. 12, 1946; arrived in U.S., 1973; s. Nahum and Yaffa (Krinkin) R. BSc, Technion/Israel Inst. Tech., Haifa, 1971, MSc in Physics, 1973; PhD in Biomed. Engring., Case Western Res. U., 1978. Asst. prof. dept. biomed. engring. Case Western Res. U., Cleve., 1981-86, assoc. prof., 1986-89, prof., 1989—2004, prof. dept. of physiology and biophysics, 1991—2004, prof. dept. medicine, 1992—2004, dir. cardiac bioelectricity rsch./tng. ctr., 1994—2004; Fred Saigh disting. prof. engring., prof. biomed. engring., cell biology and physiology, medicine, radiology and pediat. Washington U., St. Louis, 2004—, dir. Cardiac Bioelectricity and Arrhythmia Ctr., 2004—. Vis. prof. Technion/Israel Inst. Tech., 1982-83, U. Parma, Italy, 1986-87, U. Utah, Salt Lake City, 1990, Tel Aviv U., 1991, Russian Acad. of Scis., St. Petersburg, 1997, U. Berne, Switzerland, 1998, Johns Hopkins U., 2005, Columbia U., 2005; cardiovascular and pulmonary study sect. NIH, 1984-88; lectr., spkr. in field. Mem. editl. bd. Jour. Electrocardiology, Jour. Cardiovasc. Electrophysiology, Cardiovasc. Rsch., Cardiac Electrophysiology Rev.; Heart Rhythmn Jour. contbr. articles to profl. jours. Grantee NIH, 1985—, Am. Heart Assn., 1990-95, NSF, 1987-94; recipient Gordon K. Moe Prof. award, 1997, NIH-Nat. Heart, Lung and Blood Inst. Merit award, 1998. Fellow IEEE, Am. Physiol. Soc., Am. Inst. Med. and Biol. Engring., Am. Heart Assn., Heart Rhythm Soc., Biomed. Engring. Soc. (Disting. Lectr. award 2001); mem. NAE, Biophys. Soc., Cardiac Electrophysiology Soc. (pres. 2006—). Achievements include development of a novel imaging modality for non-invasive imaging of cardiac electrical events from electrical potentials measured on the body surface (electrocardiographic imaging, ECGI), of theoretical models of cardiac excitation at the cellular, sub-cellular and tissue levels; elucidation of the cellular mechanisms of cardiac arrhythmias and the role of tissue architecture in arrhythmogenesis. Office: Washington U St Louis Cardiac Bioelectricity Ctr 290 Whitaker Hall Campus Box 1097 Saint Louis MO 63130-4899

RUE, DOUGLAS MICHAEL, solutions engineer; b. Pensacola, Fla., Apr. 9, 1964; s. Barbara J. Rue; m. Andra O'Neal, 1995; 1 child, Christian Michael Rue. AA in Bus., Pensacola Jr. Coll., Fla., 1984, AA in Computer Sci., 1984; BS in Computer Sci. cum laude, St. Augustine's Coll., 1988; MS in Telecomms., DePaul U., 1990. Cert. Adtran Data Sales Solutions, 2004. Data sys. analyst Internat. Paper, Memphis, 1990-91, project analyst, 1991-94; tech. cons. Sprint, Universal City, Calif., 1994—98, sr. tech. cons. Universal City, Calif., Jacksonville, Fla., 1998—2000; sr. sales engr. Teleglobe Bus., Atlanta, 2000; solutions engr. Global Crossing Telecom., 2000—01, US LEC Telecom., Memphis, 2004—, solutions engr. CMAC Charlotte, NC, 2003—04; account exec. Allegiance Telecom., 2001—02, Network Telephone, Atlanta. Adj. prof. telecom. sys. adminstrn., DeVry U., Pomona, Calif., 1995, adj. prof. telecom. enterprise networks design and data comm., 2002-03. Active Habitat for Humanity, 1999; with U.S. Army Res., 1985-91. Office: 3150 Lenox Park Blvd Ste 417 Memphis TN 38115 Home Phone: 901-853-8425. Personal E-mail: douglasrue@aol.com.

RUEBENSON, GEORGE E., insurance company executive; BS, Bradley Univ. Mgmt. positions Allstate Ins. Co., Northbrook, Ill., 1970—90, v.p. fin. & planning bus. ins. div., internat. ops., 1990—97, v.p. procurement governance, 1997—2000, v.p. property & casualty claims svc. org., 2000—03, sr. v.p., 2003—06, pres. Allstate Protection, 2006—. Bd. mem. Bradley Univ.; St. Laurence HS. Office: Allstate Corp 2775 Sanders Rd Northbrook IL 60062 *

RUECKERT, ROLAND RUDYARD, retired virologist, educator; b. Rhinelander, Wis., Nov. 24, 1931; s. George Leonard and Monica Amelia (Seiberlich) R.; m. Ruth Helen Ullrich, Sept. 5, 1959; 1 child, Wanda Lynne. BS in Chemistry, U. Wis., 1953, PhD in Oncology, 1960. Fellow Max Planck Inst. for Biochemistry, Munich, 1960-61, Tübingen, Fed. Republic Germany, 1961-62; asst. rsch. virologist virus lab. U. Calif., Berkeley, 1962-65; asst. prof. biophysics lab. U. Wis., Madison, 1965-69, assoc. prof. biophysics lab., 1969-73; prof. Inst. for Molecular Virology, Madison, 1973-85, dist. rsch. prof., 1985-96, prof. emeritus, 1996-97. Mem. viology study sect. NIH, Bethesda, Md., 1981-85; pres. Am. Soc. Virology, 1989-90. With U.S. Army, 1953-55. Recipient William D. Stovall award, U. Wis., 1953, Marie Christine Kohler award U, Oneida County Tree Farmer of the Yr., 2001, Tree Farmer Yr., Wis. 5th Dist., 2007. Achievements include research in dodecahedral model for picornavirus structure and assembly, molecular biology of picornaviruses (polio 8 common cold), structure 8 biology of small insect viruses, mechanism of neutralization by antibodies and antivirals. Home: 2234 W Lawn Ave Madison WI 53711-1952 Business E-Mail: rrruecke@facstaff.wisc.edu.

RUEDA, GUILLERMO, architect, researcher; b. Barranquilla, Atlantico, Colombia, July 12, 1965; m. Luisa Duran; children: Camila Rueda Duran, Nicolas Rueda Duran, Felipe Rueda Duran. Degree in Indsl. and Computer Sci. Engring. cum laude, U. Automa de Bucaramanga, Colombia, 1991; MS in Computer Sci., Monterrey Technol. Inst., Mexico, 1995; MS in Engring. and Tech. Mgmt., Portland State U., Oreg., 2003, candidate in Engring. and Tech. Mgmt., 2003—07. Dean computer sci. dept. U. Automa de Bucaramanga, Santander, Colombia, 1996—2000, info. tech. dir., 2000—01; global teams collaboration rschr. Intel Corp., Hillsboro, Oreg., 2006, enterprise arch., 2007—. Named Outstanding Grad. Student, Engring. and Tech. Mgmt. Dept. Portland State U., 2005; fellow, Maseeh Coll. Engring. and Computer Sci., 2005—07. Mem.: Sys. Dynamics Soc. (assoc.), Omega Rho (past pres., v.p., sec.-treas. 2004—07). Office: Intel Corp 2111 NE 25th Ave Hillsboro OR 97006 Office Phone: 503-712-6125. Personal E-mail: grueda@pdx.edu.

RUEDENBERG, KLAUS, theoretical chemist, educator; b. Bielefeld, Germany, Aug. 25, 1920; came to U.S., 1948, naturalized, 1955; s. Otto and Meta (Wertheimer) R.; m. Veronika Kutter, Apr. 8, 1948 (dec. Jan. 2004); children: Lucia Meta, Ursula Hedwig, Annette Veronika, Emanuel Klaus. Student, Montana Coll., Zugerberg, Switzerland, 1938-39; licence es Scis., U. Fribourg, Switzerland, 1944; postgrad., U. Chgo., 1948-50; PhD, U. Zurich, Switzerland, 1950; PhD (hon.), U. Basel, Switzerland, 1975, U. Bielefeld, Germany, 1991, U. Siegen, 1994. Research assoc. physics U. Chgo., 1950-55; asst. prof. chemistry, physics Iowa State U., Ames, 1955-60, assoc. prof., 1960-62, prof., 1964-78, disting. prof. in sci. and humanities, 1978-91, disting. prof. emeritus, 1991—, sr. chemist Ames Lab., U.S. Dept. Energy, 1964-91, assoc., 1991—. Prof. chemistry Johns Hopkins, Balt., 1962-64; vis. prof. U. Naples, Italy, 1961, Fed. Inst. Tech., Zurich, 1966-67, Wash State U. at Pullman, 1970, U. Calif. at Santa Cruz, 1973, U. Bonn, Germany, 1974, Monash U. and CSIRO, Clayton, Victoria, Australia, 1982, U. Kaiserlautern, Germany, 1987; lectr. univs., rsch. instns. and sci. symposia, 1953—. Contbr. articles to profl. jours.; assoc. editor: Jour. Chem. Physics, 1964-67, Internat. Jour. Quantum Chemistry; Chem. Physics Letters, 1967-81, Lecture Notes in Chemistry, 1976-2003, Advances in Quantum Chemistry, 1987-2004; editor-in-chief Theoretica Chimica Acta, 1985-97; hon. editor Theoretical Chemistry Accounts, 1997—. Co-founder Octagon Center for the Arts, Ames, 1966, treas., 1966-71, also bd. dirs. Guggenheim fellow, 1966-67; Fulbright sr. scholar, 1982. Fellow: AAAS, Internat. Acad. Mathematical Chemistry, Internat. Acad. Quantum Molecular Scis., Am. Inst. Chemists, Am. Phys. Soc.; mem.: AAUP, Am. Chem. Soc. (Midwest award 1982, Nat. Award in Theoretical Chemistry 2002), Phi Lambda Upsilon, Sigma Xi. Office: Dept Chemistry Iowa State Univ Ames IA 50011-0001

RUEDRICH, RANDY, political party official; BS, Tex. A&M U., M in Engring., PhD. Commr., formerly Alaska Oil & Gas Conservation Commn., 2003—; gen. mgr. Doyon Drilling; sr. drilling engr. Arco's Alaska; from fin. chmn. to state chmn. Alaska Rep. Party, 1986—2000, chmn., 2000—. Office: Alaska Rep Com 1001 W Fireweed Ln Anchorage AK 99503 *

RUEGG, DONALD GEORGE, retired rail transportation executive; b. LaJunta, Colo., Sept. 11, 1924; s. George Albert and Cecilia Corrine (Decker) R.; m. Ruth Carson, June 27, 1946 (dec. 1963); m. Mary Ann Eichelberger, June 24, 1964. BA, Dartmouth Coll., 1947; MBA, U. Chgo., 1972. Sec. to trainmaster, trainmaster's clk. Atchison, Topeka & Santa Fe Ry. Co., 1942—50, traveling car agt. Chgo., 1950—51, transp. inspector, 1951—52; safety supr. Atchison Topeka & Santa Fe Ry. Co., Emporia, 1952—53, trainmaster, 1953—68; asst. to v.p. info. sys. Atchison, Topeka & Santa Fe Ry. Co., Topeka, 1968—69, asst. to v.p. operation, 1969—72, gen. mgr. LA, 1972—73, asst. v.p. ops., 1973—78, v.p. ops., 1978—83, exec. v.p., 1983—86; ret., 1986. Personal E-mail: donruegg@aol.com.

RUEGGER, PHILIP T., III, lawyer; b. Plainfield, NJ, Oct. 14, 1949; s. Philip T. Jr. and Gloria Marie (McLaughlin) R.; m. Rebecca Lee Huffman, Aug. 3, 1974; children: Sarah, Britt, Michael. AB magna cum laude, Dartmouth Coll., 1971; JD, U. Va., 1974. Bar: N.Y. 1975. Assoc. Simpson Thacher & Bartlett, NYC, 1974-81, ptnr., 1981—, ptnr., exec. com., 1993—, head corp. dept., 2002—, chmn. exec. com., 2004—. Bd. dirs. Natural Resources Def. Coun. Bd. dirs. Henry St. Settlement. Mem. Assn. Bar City NY, Manursing Island Club (Rye, NY), Apawamis Club (Rye), Phi Beta Kappa. Office: Simpson Thacher & Bartlett 425 Lexington Ave New York NY 10017-3954 Home Phone: 914-967-2812; Office Phone: 212-455-3220. Business E-Mail: pruegger@stblaw.com.

RUEGSEGGER, DONALD RAY, JR., radiological physicist, educator; b. Detroit, May 29, 1942; s. Donald Ray and Margaret Arlene (Elliot) R.; m. Judith Ann Merrill, Aug. 20, 1965 (div.); children: Steven, Susan, Mark, Ann; m. Patricia Ann Mitchell, Oct. 16, 1999. BS, Wheaton Coll., 1964; MS, Ariz. State U., 1966, PhD (NDEA fellow), 1969. Diplomate Am. Bd. Radiology. Radiol. physicist Miami Valley Hosp., Dayton, Ohio, 1969—, chief med. physics sect., 1983—. Physics cons. X-ray dept. VA Hosp., Dayton, 1970-73; adj. asst. prof. physics Wright State U., Fairborn, Ohio, 1973-74, clin. asst. prof. radiology, 1976-81, clin. assoc. prof. radiology, 1981—, group leader in med. physics, dept. radiol. scis. Med. Sch., 1978-85. Mem. AAAS, Am. Assn. Physicists in Medicine (pres. Ohio River Valley chpt. 1982-83, co-chmn. local summer sch. arrangements com. 1986), Am. Coll. Radiology, Am. Coll. Med. Physics (founding chancellor), Am. Phys. Soc., Ohio Radiol. Soc. Home: 6252 Donnybrook Dr Centerville OH 45459-1837 Office: Radiation Therapy Miami Valley Hosp 1 Wyoming St Dayton OH 45409-2722 Home Phone: 937-433-6668; Office Phone: 937-208-4058. E-mail: drruegsegger@mvh.org.

RUEHLE, CHARLES JOSEPH, pathologist, military officer; b. May 26, 1943; s. John Donald and Alta (Brown) R.; m. Nellie Backus, Aug. 5, 1972 (div.). DVM, Iowa State U., 1967; MD, U. Iowa, 1973; MS, 1973. Diplomate Am. Bd. Preventive Medicine, Am. Bd. Pathology. Commd. 2d lt. USAF, 1964; advanced through grades to col., sr. flight surgeon, 1984; chief flight surgeon, 1987; chief Vet. Svc., Grissom AFB, Ind., 1967-69; resident in aerospace medicine Brook AFB, Tex., 1973-75; resident in pathology Wilford Hall USAF Med. Ctr., Lackland AFB, Tex., 1975-79; with div. aerospace pathology Armed Forces Inst. Pathology, Washington, 1979-88; chief div. aerospace pathology, 1982-85; chmn. dept. forensic scis., 1985-88; sec. Joint COm. Aviation Pathology, 1984-88; exec. asst. to fed. air surgeon FAA, Washington, 1988—93, sr. aviation med. examiner, 1989—, mgr. appeals & special projects branch, 1993—2003, prin. liasion, 2004—; spl. asst. fed. Surgeon, 2003—. Adj. asst. prof. prevetive medicine Uniformed Services U. Health Scis. lectr. aerospace pathology; cons. USAF Sugeon Gen., 1987; chmn, Airliner Cabin Environ. Report Team, 2002- Fellow Am. Soc. Clin Pathologists, Aerospace Med. Assn.; mem. Am. Acad. Forensic Scis. AMA, USAF Flight Surgeons, Nat. Sojourners, Assn. Mil. Surgeons U.S., Internat. Soc. Air Safety Investigators, Air Force Assn., Alpha Zeta, Gamma Sigma Delta, Omega Tau Sigma (gov. 1967-

75). Republican. Presbyterian. Home: 1000 Lower Pindell Rd Lothian MD 20711-2704 Office: Fed Air Surgeon FAA 800 Independence Ave SW Washington DC 20591-0001 Office Phone: 202-493-4580. E-mail: charles.ruehle@faa.gov.

RUEMMLER, KATHRYN H., lawyer, former prosecutor; b. Richland, Wash., 1971; BA cum laude, U. Wash., Seattle, 1993; JD, Georgetown U., 1996. Law clk. to Hon. Timothy K. Lewis US Ct. Appeals (3rd Cir.), 1996—97; assoc. Zuckerman Spaeder, LLP, Washington, 1997—2000; assoc. counsel to Pres. The White House, Washington, 2000—01; asst. US atty. DC US Dept. Justice, Washington, 2001—07; ptnr. Latham & Watkins LLP, Washington, 2001, 2007—. With Enron Task Force, US Dept. Justice, 2003—06, dep. dir., 2005—06. Named one of Litigation's Rising Stars, The Am. Lawyer, 2007; recipient Atty. Gen's award for Exceptional Svc., US Dept. Justice, 2006. Office: Latham & Watkins LLP 555 Eleventh St NW Ste 1000 Washington DC 20004 *

RUESINK, ALBERT WILLIAM, biologist, plant sciences educator; b. Adrian, Mich., Apr. 16, 1940; s. Lloyd William and Alberta May (Foltz) R.; m. Kathleen Joy Cramer, June 8, 1963; children: Jennifer Li, Adriana Eleanor. BA, U. Mich., 1962; MA, Harvard U., 1965, PhD, 1966. Postdoctoral fellow Swiss Fed. Inst. Tech., Zurich, 1966-67; prof. biology Ind. U., Bloomington, 1967—, spl. asst. to Pres. for Faculty Rels., 1999—2005. Recipient Amoco Teaching award Ind. U., 1980 Mem. AAUP (pres. chpt. 1978-79, 90-91), Am. Soc. Plant Physiologists, Bot. Soc. Am. Democrat. Mem. United Ch. of Christ. Home: 2605 E 5th St Bloomington IN 47408-4286 Office: Ind U Dept Biology 1001 E 3d St Bloomington IN 47405 Home Phone: 812-336-8366; Office Phone: 812-855-5555. Business E-Mail: ruesink@indiana.edu.

RUESTERHOLZ, VIRGINIA P., telecommunications industry executive; m. Kevin Ruesterholz; 2 children. B in Chem. Engring., Stevens Inst. Tech., 1983; MS in Telecom. Mgmt., Bklyn. Poly. Inst., 1991. Mgr. NY Tel., 1984, market area v.p., gen. mgr. svc. delivery and field ops., 1993; v.p. complex installation and maintenance for network svcs. Bell Atlantic, v.p. ops. assurance, sr. v.p. wholesale markets; pres. Verizon Ptnr. Solutions Verizon Comm., pres. Verizon Telecom. Mem. bus. and tech. bd. Stevens Inst. Tech. Bd. dirs. Manhattan Theater Club. Recipient 40 Under 40 award, Crain's NY Bus., Rising Star award, NY Women's Agenda. Mem.: Edwin A. Stevens Soc. (chair). Office: Verizon Comm 140 West St New York NY 10007

RUETTER, GUNTER H., surgeon; b. Worms on Rhine, Germany, Apr. 19, 1953; s. Elli Ruetter; 1 child, Jan-Frederik H. MD, U. Heidelberg, 1982; PhD, German Cancer Rsch. Ctr., 1989. Medical License State of Baden-Wuerttemberg, Germany, 1982, Specialist in Emergency Medical Services (EMS) Hesse Med. Assn., Germany, 1987, Specialist in Sports Medicine Hesse Med. Assn., Germany, 1988, Specialist in Surgery (general and trauma surgery) Hesse Med. Assn., Germany, 1989, Qualified Surgeon in Chief for Emergency Medical Services (EMS) Baden-Wuerttemberg Med. Assn., Germany, 1990. Sci. asst. German Cancer Rsch. Ctr., Heidelberg, Germany, 1976—82; resident surgeon, gen. surgery St. Franziska Stift Krankenhaus, Bad Kreuznach, Germany, 1983; sr. surgeon U. Hosp. for Surgery, Marburg, 1984—89; resident surgeon, plastic surgery and hand surgery St. Marien Krankenhaus, Siegen; med. dir. Paul Hartmann Corp., Heidenheim; gen. mgr. Serapharm, GmbH, Muenster; pres. Monitoring Force Group, Washington, 1995—. Lectr. Ortenberg Med. Sch., Marburg, Germany, 1984—89; cons., def. and disaster medicine Ind., Washington, 2002—; lectr., med. entrepreneurship and clin. rsch. C. of C., Germany; lectr. Netherlands Def. Coll., The Hague, Netherlands, 2004—; student, european master in disaster medicine program U. of Ea. Piedmont, Novara, Italy, 2005—; col. (med. corps) Joint Med. Svc. Air Forces Reserves, Bonn, Germany, 2002—; br. chief (r), joint med. svc. res. forces Ministry of Def., Bonn, 2005—; chmn. Joint Med. Res. Forces Orgn., Bonn, 2004—; del. Interallied Confederation of Med. Res. Officers, Brussels, 2004—; lectr. U. Marburg, Med. Sch., Germany, 1994—99, Acad. of the German Armed Forces Joint Med. Svc., Munich, 2004—. Contbr. articles to profl. jours. Founding mem. German Am. Bus. Coun., Washington, 2005. Col. Joint Med. Svc. Air Force Res., 2002, Bonn, Germany. Recipient diploma, German Assn. for Sports Medicine, 1998. Master: Interallied Confederation of Med. Res. Officers (del. 2004), Joint Med. Res. Forces Orgn. (chmn. 2004); mem.: World Assn. for Disaster and Emergency Medicine, German Natural Scientists and Physicians Assn., German Disaster Medicine Assn., German Assn. for Trauma Surgery, German Assn. for Surgery, German Assn. for Mil. Medicine and Pharmacy, US C. of C., DC C. of C., Assn. of Mil. Surgeons of the US, German Exec. Round Table, Am. German Bus. Club, German Res. Forces Assn., Army and Navy Club, Wash., German Officers Club, Wash., German Atlantic Coun. Office: Monitoring Force USA Inc 888 Seventeenth Street NW Washington DC 20006-332 Home Phone: 1 (202) 249 1514; Office Phone: 1 (202) 296 5699. Office Fax: 1 (202) 296 2609.

RUFF, KENNETH, management consultant, information technology manager; BS in Computer Sci. and Elec. Engring., U. South Fla., 1986, post grad. Mgmt. cons. FPL Corp., Miami, Fla., 1987—89; managing dir. N.Am. network Telerate, Jersey City, 1989; mgmt. cons. Sandoz, East Hanover, NJ, 1989; mgmt. cons. N.Y. and Tex. IBM, 1986, 1987, 1993; mgmt. cons. GTE, Dallas, 1993, AT&T Solutions, Bridgewater, NJ, 1995, Tokio Marine, NYC, 1995—96, Chase Manhattan Bank, NYC, 1991, 1992, 1997, 2000, Merril Lynch, Princeton, NJ, 1999; project manager Cendant Car Rntal Group, Garden City, N. Y. and Parsippany, NJ, 2000—04; design architect and mgmt. cons. Bank of Am., 2004—05; mgmt. cons. JP Morgan Pvt. Bank, 2005—. Address: 970 Va St Dunedin FL 34697: 22 Elm St Huntington NY 11743-3678

RUFF, LINDY, professional hockey coach; b. Warburg, Alta., Canada, Feb. 17, 1960; m. Gaye Ruff; children: Brett, Eryn, Brian and Madeleine (twins). Defenseman Lethbridge Broncos, 1976—79, Buffalo Sabres, 1979-89, NY Rangers, 1989-91; player/asst. coach Rochester Americans, 1991-92, San Diego Gulls; asst. coach Fla. Panthers, 1993—97; head coach Buffalo Sabres, 1997—. Vol. Children's Hosp., Buffalo, Muscular Dystrophy Assn. Named Buffalo Sabre's Rookie of the Yr., 1980; recipient Jack Adams Award, 2006. Avocations: fishing, boating, golf. Office: c/o Buffalo Sabres HSBC Arena 1 Seymour H Knox III Plz Buffalo NY 14203-3096 *

RUFF, ROBERT LOUIS, neurologist, physiologist, researcher; b. Bklyn., Dec. 16, 1950; s. John Joseph and Rhoda (Alpert) R. BS summa cum laude, Cooper Union, 1971; MD summa cum laude, U. Wash., 1976, PhD in Physiology, 1976. Diplomate Am. Bd. Neurology and Psychiatry, Am. Bd. Phys. Medicine Rehab. Spinal Cord Medicine. Asst. neurologist N.Y. Hosp., Cornell Med. Sch., NYC, 1977—80; asst. prof. physiology and medicine U. Wash., Seattle, 1980—84; assoc. prof. neurology Case We. Res. Med. Sch., Cleve., 1984—92, prof. neurology and neuroscis., 1993—, residency dir., neurology dept., 1994—2003, vice chair neurology dept., 1995—2004; chief dept. neurology Cleve. VA Med. Ctr., 1984—2003, chief phys. medicine and rehab. svc., 1998—2000, mgr. rehab. and spinal cord injury and disorder product line, 1999—2003; med. dir. Functional Elec. Stimulation Ctr., Cleve., 2000—; chief Spinal Cord Injury and Dysfunction Svc., Cleveland VA Med. Ctr., 2003—05; dir. neurology and acting rehab. rsch. svc. Office R & D Dept. VA Ctrl. Office, Washington, 2004—; nat. dir. neurology Dept. Vet. Affairs, Washington, 2006—. Mem. adv. bd. for Neurology Dept. Vets. Affairs, 1989—, mem. study sect. for rehab. rsch. career devel. awards, 1998-, mem. merit rev. bd., rehab. rsch. devel. svc., 1999-2004; mem. NIH adv. couns. NINDS, NICHD, 2006-. Assoc. editor: Neurology, 1994—96, mem. editl. bd.:, 1996—97, Jour. Rehab. and Devel., 1999—, assoc. editor: Jour. Rehab. Rsch. and Devel., 2000—, ad hoc reviewer: various profl. and sci. jours., mem. editl. bd.: Muscle & Nerve, 2006—; contbr. articles to profl. jours., chapters to books. Advisor Child Devel. and Mental Retardation Ctr., Seattle, 1980-84, Burien Devel. Disability Ctr., Wash., 1982-84; med. adv. bd. Muscular Dystrophy Assn., Seattle, 1984, N.E. OH chpt. Multiple Sclerosis Soc.; chmn. med. adv. bd. N.E. OH chpt. Myasthenia Gravis Found., 1987—, mem. state bd. dirs., 1993-, nat. med. adv. bd., 1988-, nat. grant and fellowship com., 1990-2002, mem. nat. bd. dirs., 1990-2002, 2006-. Recipient Tchr. Investigator award NIH, Dr.'s award Periodic Paralysis Assn., 2005; NSF fellow, 1971; NIH grantee, Muscular Dystrophy Assn. grantee, Dept. Vets. Affairs, Rsch. Enhancement Advanced Ctr. awards, 1999—, Dr. award Myasthenia Gravis Found. Am., 2002; NY State Regents med. scholar, 1971. Fellow Am. Heart Assn. (stroke coun.), Am. Acad. Neurology (scientific issues com., legis. action com.); mem. AMA, IEEE, Am. Paraplegia Soc., Am. Soc. Neuro-Rehab., Am. Physics Soc., Neurosci. Soc., Biophys. Soc., Am. Neurol. Assn., N.Y. Acad. Sci., Am. Geriatrics Soc., Am. Physiol. Soc., Sigma Pi Sigma (v.p. 1970-71), Alpha Omega Alpha (v.p. 1975-76). Home: 935 Richmond Rd Lyndhurst OH 44124 Office: VA Med Ctr 10701 East Blvd Ste 128W Cleveland OH 44106-1702 Home Phone: 216-291-1643. Business E-Mail: robert.ruff1@va.gov.

RUFFA, ANTHONY ARMAND, mechanical engineer; s. Anthony R. and Joan R. Ruffa; m. Geraldine S. Skuches, June 30, 1984; children: Elizabeth C., A. Joseph. BS in mech. engring., U. Md., 1981; PhD, Yale U., 1990. Mech. engr. Elec. Boat Divsn. Gen. Dynamics, Groton, Conn., 1981—85; mech. engr. Naval Undersea Warfare Ctr., Newport, RI, 1985—. Adj. prof. physics U. R.I. Named NAVSEA Scientist of Yr., Naval Sea Sys. Command, 2000. Mem.: Am. Soc. Mech. Engrs., Assn. Scientists and Engrs. (Profl. Achievement award 2003). Achievements include 30 U.S. Patents, with 10 pending and others in preparation. Office: Naval Undersea Warfare Center 1176 Howell Street Newport RI 02841 Business E-Mail: ruffaaa@npt.nuwc.navy.mil.

RUFFALO, MARK, actor; b. Kenosha, Wis., Nov. 22, 1967; m. Sunrise Coigney, June 2000; children: Keen, Bella. Actor: (films) Rough Trade, 1993, A Song For You, 1993, There Goes My Baby, 1994, Mirror, Mirror 2:Raven Dance, 1994, A Gift From Heaven, 1994, Mirror, Mirror III: The Voyeur, 1995, The Dentist, 1996, The Last Big Thing, 1996, Blood Money, 1996, Safe Men, 1998, 54, 1998, A Fish in the Bathtub, 1999, Ride with the Devil, 1999, You Can Count on Me, 2000, Committed, 2000, Life/Drawing, 2001, The Last Castle, 2001, XX/XY, 2002, Windtalkers, 2002, My Life Without Me, 2003, View From the Top, 2003, In the Cut, 2003, Eternal Sunshine of the Spotless Mind, 2004, 13 Going On 30, 2004, Collateral, 2004, Just Like Heaven, 2005, Rumor Has It..., 2005, All the King's Men, 2006, Reservation Road, 2007, Zodiac, 2007; (TV films) On the 2nd Day of Christmas, 1997, Houdini, 1998; (TV series) The Beat, 2000; (films) The Destiny of Marty Fine, 1996; writer: films The Destiny of Marty Fine, 1996; exec. prodr., actor: (films) We Don't Live Here Anymore, 2004; (Broadway plays) Awake and Sing!, 2006. Office: c/o Robert Stein 345 N Maple Dr Ste 317 Beverly Hills CA 90210 Office Phone: 310-550-2176. Business E-Mail: robertadamstein@aol.com. *

RUFFIN, HERBERT GEORGE, II, history professor; b. Sacramento, Aug. 17, 1969; s. Herbert George and Sadie Mae Ruffin; m. Veronia Tanya Ruffin, Dec. 18, 2004. AS in Social sci., San Jose City Coll., Calif., 1995; BA in Am. History, U. Calif., Santa Cruz, 1997; MA in Am. History, Claremont Grad. U., 2005, student in Am. History, 2003—; cert. in African Studies, Claremont U., 2004. Cert. computer numerical control machining specialist UAW-Labor Employment and Tng. Corp., Calif., 1991. Tchg. asst. San Jose City Coll., Calif., 1994—95, counseling asst., 1997, vis. prof., 1998—99; supply coord. Smithsonian Instn., Ctr. for Folklife and Cultural Heritage, Washington, 1998—99; web technician Claremont Grad. U., Calif., 1999—2003; tchg. asst. Pitzer Coll., Claremont, Calif., 2000; rsch. asst. Claremont Coll., Calif., 2001—04; vis. prof. Chaffey Coll., Rancho Cucamonga, Calif., 2002, Claremont McKenna Coll., Calif., 2003—05. Cons. folklife festival Smithsonian Instn., Ctr. for Folklife and Cultural Heritage, Washington, 1999—2000; intern Smithsonian Instn., Program in African Am. Culture, Nat. Mus. of Am. History, Washington, 2000, coord. and asst. program developer, 2000—01; cons. African Americans in West conf. Claremont Grad. U., Calif., 2001. Author: (multimedia) Africans on the North American Frontier, 1528-1864; multimedia, Priesthood and Ritual in Ghana: 10th MEHU Anniversary Celebration, 1987-1997, Priesthood and Ritual in Ghana: Musama Disco Christo Church Diamond Jubilee, 1922-1997; author: (multimedia cd) FundaMentals: Part One, A RUFF Assessment of Hip-hop History and Culture, 1965-1986; contbr. multimedia - smithsonian institution; rap album, Who Am I?: Songs From the Ruffunk Experience, multimedia, Ontario Community University Program (OCUP), for Ontario, Pitzer College, CGU, and HUD partnership, Black Graduate Students Association Online, multimedia - pomona college, Latin American Studies at Pomona College Online, multimedia, School of Politics and Economics at CGU; author: (multimedia) African Diaspora Central, (multimedia - smithsonian institution) A Quest for Freedom: The Black Experience in the American West; book reviewer: numerous books. Recipient Outstanding Social Sci./Family Studies Achiever award, San Jose-Evergreen C.C. Dist., 1994-1995, Martin Luther King scholarship, San Jose City Coll., 1994-1995, Leadership Opportunity Award scholarship, U. Calif., 1995-1997, Edn. Abroad award, U. Calif. Edn. Abroad Program, 1996-1997, Acad. Excellence award for African-Am. Student Life, U. Calif., 1996, 1997, Minority Student Internship Program award, Smithsonian Instn., 1997, 2000; Victor Atkins fellowship, Claremont Grad. U., 2001-2002, John McGuire fellowship, 2003-2004. Mem.: Black Grad. Students Assn. (sec. 2002—04), Western Hist. Assn., Assn. for Study of Afro-Am. Life and History, Am. Hist. Assn. Achievements include student activist leader instrumental in desegregating Claremont Graduate University and fighting hate crimes. Avocations: researching history and current affairs, working out, video gaming (sports and strategy games), multimedia production, rebuilding classic Mustang. Home Phone: 909-213-3509. Personal E-mail: herbert.ruffin@cgu.edu.

RUFFIN, JOHN, federal agency administrator, researcher; b. New Orleans, June 29, 1943; s. Wesley and Olivia Ruffin; m. Angela Beverly, Aug. 24, 1968; children: John Wesley, Meeka Dionne, Beverly Alaina. BS, Dillard U., 1965; MS, Atlanta U., 1967; PhD in systematic and devel. biology, Kans. State U., 1971; postgrad., Harvard U., 1975-77. Instr. biology So. U., Baton Rouge, 1967-68; asst. prof. biology Atlanta U., 1971-74; assoc. prof. Ala. A&M U., Huntsville, 1974-75; prof. biology, chmn. dept. NC Ctrl. U., Durham, 1978—90, dean Coll. Arts and Sciences, 1986—90; assoc. dir. rsch. on minority health NIH, 1990—2001; dir. Nat. Ctr. on Minority Health and Health Disparities, NIH, 2001—. Adv. bd. NC Bd. Sci. and Tech., 1983—; chmn. MARC study sect. NIH, Bethesda, Md., 1979-81, com. mem. MARC study sect., 1984-87. Grantee NIH, 1976; Cabot Research fellow, 1976; recipient Presdl. Meritorious Rank Award, 1998. Mem. AAAS, Botanical Soc. Am., NC Acad. Sciences, Assn. Southeastern Biologists, Assn. Environ. and Exptl. Botany. Office: Nat Ctr Minority Health and Health Disparities 6707 Democracy Blvd Ste 800 Bethesda MD 20892-5465 Office Phone: 301-402-1366. Office Fax: 301-402-7040. E-mail: ruffinj@ncmhd.nih.gov.

RUFFIN, RICHARD A., orthopedic surgeon; b. Sept. 29, 1959; BS, U. Notre Dame, South Bend, Ind., 1981; MD, U. Okla., 1985. Cert. Am. Bd. Orthop. Surgery, Am. Bd. Orthop. Hand Surgery. Resident, orthop. U. Iowa, Iowa City, 1985—90; fellow, upper extremity and microsurgery Kleinert Inst., Louisville, 1990—91; with Orthop. Assocs., Inc., Okla., 1991—. Named one of Golf Digest 2006 Top Golf Doctors in Am. Mem.: Arthoscopy Assn. N.Am., Am. Soc. for Surgery of the Hand, Am. Acad. Orthop. Surgeons. Office: Orthop Assocs Inc 3301NW 50th St Oklahoma City OK 73112 Office Phone: 405-947-0911. Office Fax: 405-942-5043.

RUFFING, ANNE ELIZABETH, artist; b. Bklyn. d. John Paul and Ruth Elizabeth (Price) Frampton; m. George W. Ruffing, Mar. 29, 1967; 1 dau., Elizabeth Anne. BS, Cornell U., 1964; postgrad., Drexel Inst. Tech., 1966. One-woman exhbns. include, IBM, 1966, Hall of Fame, Goshen, NY, 1971, exhibited in group shows at Internat. Women's Arts Festival, World Trade Center, NYC, 1975-76, Berkshire Mus., Pittsfield, Mass., 1965, 76, Cooperstown Mus., NY, 1969; represented in permanent collections, Met. Mus. Art, Bklyn. Mus., Library of Congress, Harvard U., Smithsonian Instn., NY Hist. Soc. Johnston Hist. Mus., Atwater Kent Mus., Albany Inst. History and Art, Whitney Mus. Am. Art, Boston Public Library. Recipient 1st place Eric Sloane award, 1974; Internat. Women's Year award Internat. Women's Art Festival, 1976 Address: 1031 Lewis Farm Rd Zebulon NC 27597

RUFFNER, CHARLES LOUIS, lawyer; b. Cin., Nov. 7, 1936; s. Joseph H. and Edith (Solomon) R.; m. Mary Ann Kaufman, Jan. 30, 1966 (div. 1993); children: Robin Sue Donnenfeld, David Robert; m. Nanette Diemer, Feb. 26, 1995. BSBA in Acctg., U. Fla., 1958; JD cum laude, U. Miami, 1964. Bar: Fla. 1964, U.S. Dist. Ct. (so. and Mid. dists.) Fla. 1964, U.S. Ct. Appeals (5th cir.) 1964, U. S. Ct. Appeals (11th cir.) 1984, U.S. Claims Ct. 1966, U.S. Tax Ct. 1966, U.S. Supreme Ct. 1969; cert. in taxation. Trial atty. tax divsn. Dept. Justice, Washington, 1964-67; pres. Forrest, Ruffner, Traum & Hagen, P.A., Miami, Fla., 1967-78, Ruffner, Hagen & Rifkin, P.A., Miami, 1978-81; tax ptnr. Myers, Kenin, Levinson, Ruffner, Frank & Richards, Miami, 1982-84; pres. Charles L. Ruffner, P.A., 1984—. Lectr. Fla. Internat. U., Miami. Author: A Practical Approach to Professional Corporations and Associations, 4 edits., 1970, (column) Tax Talk, Miami Law Rev.; editor Miami Law Rev., 1963-64; contbr. numerous articles on taxation to law jours. Named One of Best Lawyers in Am., 1999—. Mem. ABA, Fed. Bar Assn., Fla. Bar (exec. coun. tax sect. 1967-92, 95—, amicus curiae in test case of validity profl. corps.), Dade County Bar Assn., South Fla. Tax Litigation Assn. (chmn. 1986-00), Phi Alpha Delta, Phi Kappa Phi. Office Phone: 305-669-1904. Personal E-mail: cruff7117@aol.com.

RUFFNER, FREDERICK G., JR., book publisher; b. Akron, Ohio, Aug. 6, 1926; s. Frederick G. and Olive Mae (Taylor) R.; m. Mary Ann Evans, Oct. 8, 1954; children: Frederic G. III, Peter Evans. BS, Ohio State U., 1950. Advt. mgr. Jim Robbins Co., Royal Oak, Mich., 1950-52; research mgr. Gen. Detroit Corp., 1953-54; pres. Gale Research Co., Detroit, 1954-87, Omnigraphics, Inc., 1987—. Editor: Ency. of Assns, 1956-68, Code Names Dictionary, 1963, Acronyms and Initialisms Dictionary, 1965, Allusions Dictionary, 1985; pub. Gold Coast Mag., 1992—; patentee in field. Bd. dirs. Friends of Detroit Pub. Libr., pres., 1975-76; mem. exec. bd. Detroit coun. Boy Scouts Am., 1974—, v.p., 1976-82; pres. Coun. for Fla. Librs., 1979—; trustee Bon Secours Hosp., Grosse Pointe, Mich., 1980-81; v.p. Etruscan Found., Florence, Italy, 1980—; pres. Mich. Ctr. for the Book, 1990, Literary Landmarks Assn., Gold Coast Jazz Soc., Ft. Lauderdale, 1992—; bd. dirs., v.p. Ohio State U. Found., Bonnet House, Ft. Lauderdale, 1992. 1st lt. AUS, 1944-46. Decorated Bronze Star, Combat Inf. award; recipient Centennial award Ohio State U., 1970, Benjamin Creativity award Assn. Am. Pubs., 1985, Career medal Ohioana Libr. Assn., 1988, Lifetime Achievement award Am. Libr. Trustees Assn., 1992; named to Entrepreneurs Hall of Fame, Nova U. Mem. Am. Antiquarian Soc., ALA (hon. life), Am. Mgmt. Assn., Am. Assn. Mus., Detroit Hist. Soc., Am. Hist. Print Collectors Soc., Bibliog. Soc. Am., Sierra Club, Pres. Assn., Audubon Soc., Am. Name Soc., Early Am. Industries Assn., Nat. Press Club (Washington), Ephemera Soc., Johnny Appleseed Soc., Navy League, Newcomen Soc., Cen. Bus. Dist. Assn. Detroit (vice-chmn. 1985-87), Jazz Forum (Grosse Pointe Farms, Mich.), Nat. Trust Hist. Preservation, Fairfield Heritage Soc., Archives Am. Art, Pvt. Librs. Assn., Friends Ft. Lauderdale Pub. Libr. (pres. 1974-78), Phileas Soc. (pres. 1985—), Ohio State U. Club (pres. Detroit club 1958, nat. chmn. Ohio State U. campaign, 1985-88), Masons, Shriners, Book Club, Detroit Athletic Club, Econ. Club, Prismatic Club (pres. 1990), Fontenada Soc. (pres. 1990-91), Detroit Club, Country Club Detroit, Ocean Reef Club, Grosse Pointe Yacht Club, Coral Ridge Yacht Club, Lauderdale Yacht Club, Princeton Club, Salmagundi Club, Grolier Club, Century Assn., Marco Polo Club, Faculty Club Ohio State U., Old Club, Commonwealth Club (San Francisco), Gross Pointe Club, Wawetonong Club, Tau Kappa Epsilon. Republican. Presbyterian. Home: 17111 E Jefferson Ave Apt 18 Grosse Pointe MI 48230-1942 Address: Omnigraphics Inc PO Box 31-1640 Detroit MI 48231-1640 : 936 Intracoastal Dr PH 1 Fort Lauderdale FL 33304

RUFFO, MICHAEL, painter; b. S.I., Mar. 9, 1954; s. Thomas Anthony and Marie (Papa) Ruffo; m. Lorelei Ann Perez, July 5, 1995. BFA, Sch. Visual Arts, NYC, 1991. Exhibited in group shows at Salmagundi Club, 1992—93, 1995—99, Agora Gallery, 1998—99, World Fine Art, 1999, Knickerbocker Gallery, 1999, Hiram Blauvelt Mus., 1999, Nexus Gallery, 1999—2001, NYU, 2000, Green County Coun. Arts, 2002, Gordon Green Gallery, 2002, Mountaintop Gallery, 2003—04, Bklyn. Waterfront Artists Coalition Silver Anniversary Show, 2005, Bklyn. Waterfront Artists Coalition, 2007, Represented in permanent collections US Dept. State, Bklyn. Waterfront Artists Coalition. Recipient Excellence award, Manhattan Arts Internat. Competition, 1997—98, 1999. Mem.: Bklyn. Waterfront Artists Coalition, Nurture Art (reigstry), Orgn. Ind. Artists, NY Artists Equity Assn. Roman Catholic. Achievements include patents for lockable lid support. Personal E-mail: mruffo@verizon.net.

RUGABER, WALTER FEUCHT, JR., retired publishing executive, academic administrator; b. Macon, Ga., Nov. 29, 1938; s. Walter Feucht and Edith Almeda (Maynard) R.; m. Sally Sanford, Oct. 6, 1962; children— Leslie, Christopher, Mark BS, Northwestern U., 1960. Corr., editor N.Y. Times, 1965—78; v.p., exec. editor Greensboro Daily News & Record, NC, 1978—82; pres., pub. The Roanoke Times, Va., 1982—2000; pres. Landmark Pub. Group, 1995—99; interim pres. Hollins U., Roanoke, Va., 2001—02; presdl. fellow Va. Tech. U., 2003—06. Mem. Pulitzer Prize Bd., 1990-99. Bd. dirs. United Way of Roanoke Valley, Va., 1982—88, Roanoke Sympony Soc., 1985—91, pres., 1986—88; trustee Hollins U., 1993—2002, 2004—. Mem. Am. Newspaper Pubs. Assn., Am. Soc. Newspaper Editors, So. Newspaper Pubs. Assn. E-mail: wrugaber@swva.net.

RUGEN, KAREN, retail executive, corporate communications specialist; Head corp. comm. Hyatt Hotels Corp., 1978—94; chief comm. officer Boston Chicken Co., Boston, 1994—98; sr. v.p. corp. comm. and pub. affairs Rite Aid Corp., Camp Hill, Pa., 1999—. Treas. Rite Aid Found. Office: Rite Aid Corp 30 Hunter Ln Camp Hill PA 17011 Office Phone: 717-730-7766. *

RUGGERI, ROBERT EDWARD, lawyer; b. NYC, Sept. 16, 1952; s. Mario Philip and Margaret Gloria (Pascale) R.; m. Mary Beth Thackeray, June 6, 1981. BA, Union Coll., 1974; JD, Antioch U., 1980. Bar: D.C. 1981, N.Y. 1993, U.S. Dist. Ct. D.C. 1982, U.S. Ct. Internat. Trade 1982, U.S. Ct. Appeals (fed. and D.C. cirs.) 1982, U.S. Supreme Ct. 1984. Trainee Commn. European Communities, Brussels, 1980-81; legal cons. Secretariat, OECD, Paris, 1981-82; assoc. Stewart & Stewart, Washington, 1982-83, Graham and James, Washington, 1984-85, Rogers & Wells, Washington, 1985-92; dep. dir. legal affairs N.Y. State Dept. Environ. Conservation, 1993-94; assoc. counsel SUNY System, Albany, 1994—2006, mng. counsel, 2006—. Arbitrator NAFTA panels apptd. by U.S., Can., and Mex. govts., 1992—; adj. prof. Georgetown U. Law Ctr.,

1988-92. Editor comments Antioch Law Jour., 1979-80. Trustee Schenectady County CC, 1999— (chmn. bd. 2006-). Fulbright scholar, 1980-81. Mem. ABA, D.C. Bar Assn., Washington Fgn. Law Soc. (sec., treas. 1985-87, bd. govs. 1987-88), Am. Soc. Internat. Law. Roman Catholic. Home: 1846 Union St Niskayuna NY 12309-4502 Office: SUNY Office U Counsel Univ Plz Rm Albany NY 12246-0001

RUGGIERO, DAVID L., music educator, accountant; s. Elide M. and Lorenzo Ruggiero. B in Bus. Adminstrn., Bryant U., 1985; M in Edn., Lesley U., 2003. Cert. music pre-K-9 profl. Mass., 2004, music 5-12 prof. Mass., 2004. Sr. auditor State RI Auditor Gen., Pawtucket, RI, 1985—99; music educator k-5 Newton Pub. Schs., Mass., 2000—01; music tchr. Sharon Pub. Schs., Mass., 2001—02; music tchr. pre-k to 1 Medfield Pub. Schs., Mass., 2003—. Avocation: skiing. Home Phone: 781-320-3701; Office Phone: 508-359-5135.

RUGGIERO, KENNETH JOSEPH, psychologist; b. Lewiston, NY, Jan. 28, 1972; s. Kathleen Ann and Kenneth Joseph Ruggiero; m. Deana Irene Burbee, June 29, 2002; 1 child, Justin Kenneth. PhD, W.Va. U., 1996—2001. Lic. in clin. psychology SC, 2004. Rschr. Med. U. S.C., Charleston, 2001—, asst. prof., 2003—. Recipient Psychiatry Golden Apple award for Outstanding New Tchr., Med. U. SC, 2002, Cir. of Excellence in Tchr. award, 2004, Faculty Mentorship Excellence award, 2005. Mem.: Assn. for Advancement of Behavior Therapy (pres., disaster and trauma sig; chair, pub. edn. com. 2002—05, Student Rschr. award 1999). Office: Med Univ of South Carolina 165 Cannon St 3rd Floor Charleston SC 29403 Office Phone: 843-792-2945. Office Fax: 843-792-3388. E-mail: ruggierk@musc.edu.

RUGGIERO, MATTHEW JOHN, bassoonist; b. Phila., Sept. 18, 1932; s. Pompeo and Theresa (Ciampa) R.; m. Nancy Cirillo, Apr. 2, 1961; children: Eleanor, Claudia, Lisa. Diploma, Curtis Inst. Music, 1957; AA, Harvard U., 1982, BA cum laude, 1984, MA, 1987; PhD, Boston U., 1993. Second bassoonist Nat. Symphony Orch., Washington, 1957-60; asst. prin. bassoonist Boston Symphony Orch., 1961-89; prin. bassoonist Boston Pops Orch., 1974-89; ret., 1989. Mem. faculty Boston U., 1963—, New Eng. Conservatory Music, 1963— Served with U.S. Army, 1954-57. Boston U. Profs. Program scholar and fellow, 1989.

RUGGLES, RUDY LAMONT, JR., international security advisor; b. Evanston, Ill., Nov. 11, 1938; s. Rudy Lamont and Ruth (Cain) R.; m. Cecelia Ann Consorte, July 20, 1974 (div. 1996); m. Nancy Orbison, June 1965 (div. 1972); m. Sara Joyce Silbernagel, Feb. 3, 1998; children—Rudy, Christopher, Daniel, Andrew. BA, Harvard U., 1960, MBA, 1966. Sr. assoc. physicist IBM Rsch. Labs., Poughkeepsie, NY, 1960-64; corp. planning cons. corp. hdqrs. IBM, Armonk, NY, 1966-71; sr. mem. profl. staff Hudson Inst., Croton-on-Hudson, NY, 1971-75, pres., 1975-79, also dir.; prin. Cresap, McCormick & Paget, Inc., 1979-82; ptnr. The Phila. Mgmt. Cons. Group, Inc., 1982—; mng. dir. New China Group, Inc., 1982—. Chmn. residential solicitation United Fund, Pound Ridge, N.Y., 1969; mem. parents com. St. Paul's Sch., Concord, N.H.; dir. Danbury Hosp. and Danbury Hosp. Devel. Fund, Conn., 1978—, med. affairs com.; chmn. fin. com. Pound Ridge Community Ch., 1969-70; bd. dirs. Harry Frank Guggenheim Found., 1982—; bd. visitors Sch. Langs. and Linguistics Georgetown U.; trustee New Canaan Country Sch.; charter mem. bd. trustees The Newberry Libr., Chgo.; mem. coun. fellows Pierpont Morgan Libr., NYC; mem. Ridgefield (Conn.) Drug and Alcohol Commn.; mem. steering com. Ridgefield Coalition Against Alcohol and Substance Abuse; treas., bd. dir. Nat. Coun. Alcoholism and Drug Dependence; chmn. bd. dir. Midwestern Conn. Coun. on Alcoholism; adv. bd. Founders Hall, Ridgefield Sr. Ctr.; mem. bd. visitors Orgn. for Tropical Studies, Duke U. With C.E., U.S. Army, 1962. Recipient John Carroll Disting. medal, Georgetown U., 1986, hon. cert. Order of Lenin, Russian Nat. Acad. Sci., 1999. Fellow Explorers Club; mem. Hudson Inst. (hon.), N. Am. Soc. Corp. Planning (dir. 1966-72), Internat. Inst. Strategic Studies, Internat. Map Collectors Soc., James Caird Soc., Ends of the Earth (hon.), Hummingbird Soc. (life), Am. Antiquarian Soc. (hon.), Harvard Club N.Y.C., Carnegie Club at Skibo Castle (Scotland), Grolier Club, Sigma Xi (hon.)

RUGMAN, ALAN MICHAEL, international business educator; b. Bristol, Eng., June 9, 1945; arrived in Can., 1968, naturalized, 1973; s. Kenneth M. and Dorothy Irene Rugman; m. Helen Scruton, 1970; 1 child, Andrew. BA in Econs. with honors, U. Leeds, Eng., 1966; MSc in Econ. Devel., U. London, 1967; PhD in Econs., Simon Fraser U., Can., 1974; MA, Oxford U., Eng., 1998. Lectr. econs. U. Winnipeg, Manitoba, Canada, 1970—73, asst. prof. econs., 1973—78, assoc. prof. econs., 1978—79; assoc. prof. fin. Concordia U., Montreal, Canada, 1979—80; assoc. prof. bus. adminstrn. Dalhousie U., Halifax, NS, Canada, 1980—82, prof., 1982—87; dir. Ctr. Bus. Studies, 1980—87; prof. internat. bus. U. Toronto, 1987—98; rsch. dir. Ont. Internat. Bus. Ctr., 1988—92; Thames Water fellow in strategic mgmt. Templeton Coll., U. Oxford, 1998—2001; prof. internat. bus., bus. econs., public policy Indiana U., 2001—; L. Leslie Waters Chair Internat. Bus. Kelley Sch. Bus., Indiana U.; dir. IU CIBER. Outside advisor on free trade, fgn. investment, internat. competitiveness two Canadian prime ministers, 1986—93; mem. internat. trade advisory com. Govt. of Can., 1986—88; vis. prof. Columbia U., Columbia Bus. Sch., Ctr. for internat. Affairs, Harvard U., London Sch. Bus., U. Hawaii, U. Alberta, UCLA, MIT, Warwick Bus. Sch., U. Paris-La Sorbonne; lectr., cons. in field. Author: International Diversification and the Multinational Enterprise, 1979, Multinationals in Canada: Theory, Performance and Economic Impact, 1980, Inside the Multinationals: The Economics of Internal Markets, 1981, Outward Bound: Canadian Direct Investment in the United States, 1987, Multinationals and Canada: United States Free Trade, 1990, The Theory of Multinational Enterprises, 1996, Multinational Enterprises and Trade Policy, 1996, International Business, 2000, rev. edit., 2003, The End of Globalization, 2000, rev. edit., 2001; co-author: International Business: Firm and Environment, 1985, Megafirms: Strategies for Canada's Multinationals, 1985, Administered Protection in America, 1987, Global Corporate Strategy and Trade Policy, 1990, International Business, 1985, rev. edit., 1995, Environmental Regulations and Corporate Strategy, 1999, Multinationals as Flagship Firms: Regional Business Networks, 2000, Analysis of Multinational Strategic Management, 2005, The Regional Multinationals, 2005; editor: New Theories of the Multinational Enterprise, 1982, Multinationals and Technology Transfer: The Canadian Experience, 1983, International Business in Canada, 1989, Research In Global Strategic Management, 1990, 2d edit., 1991, Foreign Investment and North American Free Trade, 1994, Leadership in International Business Education and Research, 2003, Free Trade in the Americas, 2004, North American Economic and Financial Integration, 2004; co-editor: Multinationals and Transfer Pricing, 1985, Business Strategies and Free Trade, 1988, The Oxford Handbook of International Business, 2001, The World Trade Organization in the New Global Economy, 2001, Real Options and International Investment, 2005, European-American Trade and Financial Alliances, 2005, International Business, 4th edit., 2006; referee, reviewer in field:, mem. editl. bd.: Strategic Mgmt. Jour., Jour. Internat. Bus. Studies, others; contbr. articles to profl. jours, chapters to books. Grantee Soc. Scis. and Humanities Rsch. Coun. Can., 1983, 1984. Fellow: Royal Soc. Arts, Acad. Internat. Bus. (v.p. 1989—90, pres. 2004—06), Massey Coll. (sr.); mem.: Acad. Mgmt., North Am. Econ. Fin. Assn. (bd. dirs. 1979—91, pres. 1984). Office: Ind Univ Kelley Sch Bus BU 752 1309 E 10th St Bloomington IN 47405

RUGOFF, RALPH, curator; BA in Semiotics, Brown U. Pew Arts Journalism fellow Columbia U., NYC; rsch. fellow Goldsmiths Coll., London; dir. Calif. Coll. Arts Wattis Inst. for Contemporary Art, San Francisco, 2000—, founding chair Curatorial Practice Program. Guest lectr. Royal Coll. Art; guest lectr., Goldsmith Coll. U. London, U. Calif., LA, Otis Art Inst., Art Ctr., Pasadena, Calif. Contbr. articles to profl. journals and magazines; curator (exhibitions) Just Pathetic, Am. Fine Arts Gallery, NY and Rosamund Felsen Gallery, LA, 1990—92, Scene of the Crime, Armand Hammer Mus. and Cultural Ctr., LA, 1997, At the Threshold of the Visible: Minuscule and Small-Scale Art 1964-1996, 1997—99, The Greenhouse Effect, Serpentine Gallery and Nat. History Mus., London, 2000, Sudden Glory: Sight Gags and Slapstick in Contemporary Art, CCA Wattis Inst., 2002, Capp Street Project: 20th Anniversary Exhbn., 2003, Baja to Vancouver: The West Coast and Contemporary Art, 2004, Monuments for the USA, 2005, Irreducible: Contemporary Short Form Video, 2005. Recipient Ordway prize, Penny McCall Found., 2005. Office: Wattis Inst for Contemporary Art California College of Arts 1111 Eighth St San Francisco CA 94107

RUH, EDWIN, ceramic engineer, consultant, researcher; b. Westfield, NJ, Apr. 22, 1924; s. Harry John and Martha A. (Grasing) R.; m. Elizabeth J. Mundy, June 14, 1952; children: Edwin Jr., Elizabeth Jeanne. BS in Ceramic Engring. with honors, Rutgers U., 1949, MS in Ceramic Engring., 1953, PhD in Ceramics, 1954. Registered profl. engr., Pa. Rsch. engr. Harbison Walker Refractories Co., Pitts., 1954-57, asst dir. rsch., 1957-70; dir. rsch. Harbison Walker Refractories Div. Dresser Ind., Pitts., 1970-73, dir. advanced tech., 1973-74; v.p. rsch. Vesuvius Crucible Co., Pitts., 1974-76; adj. prof. Carnegie Mellon U., Pitts., 1976-84; rsch. prof. Rutgers U., New Brunswick, NJ, 1984—94. Pres. Ruh Internat., Inc., Pitts., 1976-2003. Author: Refractories for the Chemical Process Industries, 1984; editor Metallurgical Transactions, 1979-84; author chpts. to books; contbr. articles to profl. jours. With U.S. Army, 1943-46, ETO. Fellow: Am. Ceramic Soc. (disting. life mem., pres. 1985—86, Founders award Phila. sect. 1989, Bleininger award Pitts. sect. 1990); mem.: AIME, AAAS, Keramos (nat. pres. 1970—72, Greaves-Walker Roll of Honor 1976), Australasian Ceramic Soc., Acad. Ceramics (prof.), Iron and Steel Soc., Minerals, Metals and Materials Soc., Ceramic Assn. NJ (pres. 1991—92, Ann. award 1988), Nat. Inst. Ceramics Engrs. (P.A.C.E. award 1963, Greaves-Walker award 1999). Republican. Presbyterian. Avocations: antiques, antique autos. Home: 892 Old Hickory Rd Pittsburgh PA 15243-1112 Office Phone: 412-561-6994. E-mail: edemruh@adelphia.net.

RUH, MICHAEL A., JR., lawyer; b. Fort Mitchell, Ky., May 27, 1968; BBA, U. Ky., 1990, MBA, 1991; JD, U. Cin., 1996. Bar: Ohio 1996, Ky. 1997. Ptnr. Strauss & Troy, Cin. Named one of Ohio's Rising Stars, Super Lawyers, 2006. Mem.: ABA, Ky. Bar Assn., Ohio State Bar Assn., Cin. Bar Assn. Office: Strauss & Troy Federal Reserve Bldg 150 E Fourth St Cincinnati OH 45202-4018 Office Phone: 513-621-2120. Office Fax: 513-241-8259.

RUHL, SARAH, playwright; b. 1974; m. Tony Charuvastra; 1 child, Anna Beatrice Ruhl Charuvastra. BA in English, Brown U., 1997, MFA in Playwriting, 2001. Author: (plays) Melancholy Play, 2002, Eurydice, 2003, Late: A Cowboy Song, Orlando, 2003, The Clean House, 2004 (Susan Smith Blackburn Prize, 2004, Pulitzer Prize finalist, 2005), Dead Man's Cell Phone, 2005, Passion Play: A Cycle, 2005. Recipient Helen Merrill award, 2003, Whiting Writers' award, 2003; Kennedy Ctr. Fellow, Sundance Theatre Lab., 2000, MacArthur Fellow, John D. and Catherine T. MacArthur Found., 2006.

RUHM, THOMAS FRANCIS, retired lawyer; b. Bridgeport, Conn., June 8, 1935; s. Herman David and Martica (Sturges) R.; m. Michele Wood, Oct. 5, 1974; children: Wendy Sturges, Thomas Wood. BA, Yale U., 1957; JD, Havard U., 1962. Bar: N.Y. 1963, U.S. Dist. Ct. (so. and ea. dists.) N.Y. 1964, U.S. Ct. Appeals (2d cir.) 1969. Assoc. Shearman & Sterling, NYC, 1962-70; asst. gen. counsel Bessemer Securities Corp., NYC, 1970-96, v.p., 1981-96; ret., 1996. Chmn. legal aspects venture capital investing Practicing Law Inst., NY and San Francisco, 1979-81; lectr. on venture capital NYU Grad. Sch., 1986-90, Concordia Coll., Bronxville, NY, 1999-2001; expert on fed. securities law, venture capital legal matters, investment tax policy, Fed. Res. monetary policy; witness during 1980s fed. tax hearings; adj. prof. fin. St. John's U., 2000-03, Concordia Coll, 2005. Contbg. author Technology and Economic Policy, 1986; author: (bi-monthly newsletter) Fed. Reserve Monetary Policy, 1997—; contbr. articles to profl. jours. Commr. upper div. Eastchester (NY) Youth Soccer League, 1990-91, coach, 1985-91, dir. coaching 1995-94; sr. warden Christ Ch., Bronxville, NY, 1991-94; chmn. fin. com. 1982-1986, Vestry mem., 1981-1986 and 1990-1994, past v.p. and treas. Bronxville Sch. PTA; treas., bd. dir. Friends of Bronxville Pub. Libr., 1997-2000; mem. Quogue (NY) Cultural Com., 1998-2003; treas. Quogue Hist. Soc., 2003; mem. Blue Hill Troupe, Ltd., 1972—. Lt. (j.g.) USNR, 1957—59, lt. USNR, 1961—64. Mem. Naval Order of U.S., N.Y. Commandery, St. Andrew's Soc., Am. Scottish Found., Univ. Club N.Y.C. (mem. coun. 2000—2004), Bronxville Field Club, Quogue Field Club, Quogue Beach Club, Men's Book Club (Bronxville), Geezer Bridge (Bronxville). Republican.

RUINA, JACK PHILIP, electrical engineer, educator; b. Rypin, Poland, Aug. 19, 1923; arrived in U.S., 1927, naturalized, 1932; s. Michael and Nechuma (Warshaw) R.; m. Edith Elster, Oct. 26, 1947; children: Ellen, Andrew, Rachel. BEE, CCNY, 1944; MEE, Poly. Inst. Bklyn., 1949, DEE, 1951. Rsch. fellow Microwave Rsch. Inst., Poly. Inst. Bklyn., 1948-50; from instr. to assoc. prof. elec. engring. Brown U., 1950-54; rsch. assoc. prof. coordinated sci. lab. U. Ill., 1954-59, rsch. prof., prof. elec. engring., 1959-63; prof. elec. engring. MIT, 1963—, v.p. for spl. labs., 1966-70. U.S. observer Antarctica, 1964; on leave to U.S. Govt., 1959-63, pres. Inst. Def. Analysis, 1964-66; dep. for rsch. to asst. sec. air force, 1959-60; asst. dir. for def. rsch. and engring. Office Sec. Def., 1960-61; dir. Advanced Rsch. Projects Agy., Dept. Def., 1961-63; mem. panel Presdl. Sci. Adv. Commn., 1963-72, sci. adv. bd. USAF, 1964-67, adv. bd. and panels for Dept. Def., HEW, Dept. Transp., ACDA, Office Tech. Assessment, NSF, NSC, 1963—; mem. gen. adv. com. ACDA, 1969-74; sr. cons. Office Sci. and Tech. Policy, The White House, 1977-80; chmn. com. on environ. decision making NAS, 1974-77; bd. dirs. Mitre Corp. Recipient Fleming award, 1962, Disting. Alumnus award Poly. Inst. Bklyn., 1970, One Hundred and Twenty Fifth Anniversary medal CCNY, 1973. Fellow IEEE, AAAS, Am. Acad. Arts and Scis.; mem. Internat. Sci. Radio Union. Office: MIT Dept Elec Engring 292 Main St Cambridge MA 02142-1014 Home: 130 Mount Auburn St Apt 409 Cambridge MA 02138-5779 E-mail: ruina@mitre.org.

RUIZ, CARLOS LEON, nuclear scientist, physicist; b. El Paso, Sept. 21, 1943; s. Pedro Luis and Maria Elida Ruiz; m. Cynthia Ann Stuart, Aug. 2; children: Christopher Leon, Theresa Ann. BS, U. Tex., El Paso, 1966; MS, U. Kans., 1969, PhD, 1975. Rsch. assoc. La. State U., Baton Rouge, 1974—76, sr. rsch. assoc., 1976—78; mem. tech. staff Sandia Nat. Lab., Albuquerque, 1981—96, prin. mem. tech. staff, 1996—. Vis. asst. prof. La. State U., Baton Rouge, 1979—81. Coach, referee Am. Youth Soccer Assn., Albuquerque, 1981—88. Recipient Nova award, Lockheed-Martin, Albuquerque, 2004. Mem.: Toastmasters Internat. Achievements include being an inventor in the field of nuclear physics. Avocation: guitar. Office: Sandia Nat Labs PO Box 5800 Albuquerque NM 87185 Office Phone: 505-845-7550. E-mail: clruiz@sandia.gov.

RUIZ, HECTOR DE JESUS, information technology executive; b. Piedras Negras, Mex. B of Elec. Engring., M of Elec. Engring., U. Tex., Austin; D in Electronics, Rice U., 1973. Various positions Tex. Instruments, Dallas; pres. Motorola's Semiconductor Products Sector; COO Advanced Micro Devices, Inc., Sunnyvale, Calif., 2000—02, pres., 2000—06, CEO, 2000—, chmn. bd. dirs., 2004—. Bd. dirs. Eastman Kodak Co., Semiconductor Indus. Assn. Apptd. by Pres. Adv. Com. Trade Policy and Negotiations; mem. Govs. Task Force Econ. Growth; apptd. by Gov. G.W. Bush Tex. Higher Edn. Coord. Bd.; mem. adv. coun. Coll. Engring. U. Tex.; mem. adv. bd. Tsinghua Sch. of Econ. and Mgmt.; Nat. Sec. Telecommunications Adv. Com. Named one of 50 Most Important Hispanics in Tech. & Bus., Hispanic Engr. & Info. Tech. mag., 2005; named to, Hispanic Engr. Nat. Awards Conf. Hall of Fame, 2000; fellow, Internat. Engring. Consortium, 2002. Mem.: Hispanic Profl. Engrs. (apptd. bd. dirs.). Office: Advanced Micro Devices Inc 1 AMD Pl Sunnyvale CA 94088 *

RUIZ, MIRIAM, secondary school educator; b. San Lorenzo, Puerto Rico, May 15, 1968; d. Margaro Ruiz and Salvadora Vázquez; m. Pedro J. Mañón, Dec. 1995. B in Edn. and secondary Spanish (magna cum laude), U. Puerto Rico, 1992, M in Edn. Adminstrn. and Supervision, 2005. Lic. secondary edn. Tex. Tchr. Spanish Nuestra Senora la Providencia Acad., Rio Piedras, PR, 1992—94, Panamerica Lang. Inst., Guaynabo, PR, 1992—98, Caribbean Preparatory Sch., Hato Rey, PR, 1994—2004, Sam Rayburn HS, Pasadena, Tex., 2004—. Com. mem. sch. accreditation Middle State Assn., Hato Ray, PR, 2003—04. Mem.: Curriculum and Supr. Assn., Nat. Tchrs. Assn., Tex. State Tchrs. Assn., Fgn. Lang. Tchrs. Assn. Avocations: diving, reading, music, travel, writing. Home: 103 Marina Oaks Dr Kemah TX 77565 Office: Sam Rayburn HS 2121 Cherrybrook Pasadena TX 77502 Office Phone: 713-477-3601.

RUIZ, PEDRO, psychiatrist; b. Cuba, Dec. 31, 1936; MD, U. Paris VI, 1964. Intern Jackson Meml. Hosp., Miami, Fla., 1965, resident in psychiatry, 1966-68; prof. psychiatry U. Tex./Houston Health Sci. Ctr., 1969—. Mem.: Am. Psychiat. Assn. (v.p. 2003—), Am. Assn. Social Psychiatry (pres. 2000—02), Am. Coll. Psychiatrists (pres. 2000—01), Am. Bd. Psychiatry and Neurology (past pres.). Office: U Tex-Houston Health Sci Ct Mental Sci Inst 1300 Moursund St Houston TX 77030-3406 Office Phone: 713-500-2799. Business E-Mail: pedro.ruiz@uth.tmc.edu.

RUIZ, PEDRO JAVIER, education educator; b. San Juan, July 16, 1959; s. Pedro J. Ruiz and Carmen M. Gonzalez; life ptnr. Thomas G. Clark, Oct. 25, 1957. BS in Psychology, Cath. U. PR, Ponce, 1982; MS in Bilingual Spl. Edn., Adelphi U., Garden City, NY, 1993; PhD in Bilingual Edn., NYU, 2003. Mgr., avp Citibank NA, Internat. Pvt. Banking, NYC, 1982—91; bilingual spl. edn. tchr. PS 94, Dist. 75/Citywide Programs, NYC, 1991—95; coord., project mas, title vii N.Y.C. Bd. of Edn.-Ctrl. Office, 1996—97; asst. dir. Dist. 75/Citywide Programs-Ctrl. Office, NYC, 1997—99; adminstr. k-12, bilingual, ESL Mt. Vernon City Sch. Dist., NY, 1999—2005; coord. NY State Edn. Dept., Office Bilingual Edn. and Fgn. Lang. Studies, Albany, 2005—. Dir. Bilingual Spl. Edn. Acad., NYC, 1996—97; past-pres. NY State Assn. Bilingual Edn., NYC, 2001—02; exec. bd. mem. Nat. Assn. Bilingual Edn., Washington, 2004—, pres., 2005—. Recipient Svc. Excellence Award for Outstanding Performance, Citibank NA, 1985, Remunda Cadoux Leadership in Fgn. Lang. Supervision Award, NY State Assn. of Fgn. Lang. Tchrs., 2004, 2005 Dissertation award, Nat. Assn. for Bilingual Edn., 2005, Ednl. Leadership Scholarship Project award, Dr. Ramon S. Velez award, Nat. P.R. Day Parade, 2006; fellow Ph.D. - Fed. - Title VII Fellowship, NY U., NY, 1995-1998; scholar Masters Program in Bilingual Spl. Edn., NYC Bd. Edn., 1991-1993. Mem.: NY State Assn. Bilingual Edn., Nat. Assn. Bilingual Edn., Latino Children Ednl. Network, Coun. for Exceptional Children, Assn. Supervision and Curriculum Devel. Democrat. Roman Catholic. Avocations: furniture restoration, travel, reading, gardening. Home: 729 Belvidere Ave Plainfield NJ 07062 Home Phone: 908-625-6696; Office Phone: 518-474-8775. Personal E-mail: pedrojruiz@aol.com.

RUIZ, RAMÓN EDUARDO, history professor; b. Sessions Ranch, Calif., Sept. 9, 1921; s. Ramon and Dolores (Urueta) R.; m. Natalia Marrujo, Oct. 14, 1944; children: Olivia, Maura. BA, San Diego State Coll., 1947; MA, Claremont Grad. Sch., 1948; PhD, U. Calif., Berkeley, 1954. Asst. prof. U. Oreg., Eugene, 1955-57, So. Meth. U., Dallas, 1957-58; prof. Smith Coll., Northampton, Mass., 1958-69; prof. Latin Am. history U. Calif. at San Diego, 1969-91, prof. emeritus, 1991—, chmn. dept. history, 1971-76, chmn. divsn. humanities, 1972-74; mem. project grant com. NEH, 1972-73, 75-77, dir. pub. programs divsn., 1979-80; Ralph Chase lectr. San Angelo State U., 2000. Vis. prof. Facultad de Economia, Univ. de Nuevo Leon, Mexico, 1965-66, Coll. de Sonora, Mexico, summer 1983, Pomona Coll., 1983-84, Coll. de Michoacan, Mexico, summer 1986, 87, Univ. Nacional Autonoma de Mexico, fall 1992; scholar-in-residence Colegio de la Frontero Norte, Mexico, 1994-96; MacArthur Found. nominator, 1981-82; mem. project grant com. Ford Found. Author: Cuba: The Making of A Revolution, 1968 (One of Best History Books, Book World Washington Post 1968), Mexico: The Challenge of Poverty and Illiteracy, 1963, An American in Maximillians's Mexico, 1865-1866, 1959; (with James D. Atwater) Out From Under; Benito Juarez and Mexico's Struggle for Independence, 1969; (with John Tebbel) South by Southwest: The Mexican-American and His Heritage, 1969, Interpreting Latin American History, 1970, Labor and the Ambivalent Revolutionaries: Mexico, 1911-23, 1975, The Mexican War: Was it Manifest Destiny?, 1963, The Great Rebellion: Mexico, 1905-1924, 1980 (Hubert C. Herring prize), The People of Sonora and Yanqui Capitalists, 1988, Triumphs and Tragedy: A History of the Mexican People, 1992 (named One of Five Best History Books 1991-92, L.A. Times, Gold Medal award Commonwealth Club San Francisco 1993, History Book Club selection); (with Olivia Teresa Ruiz) Reflexiones Sobre la Identidad de los Pueblos, 1996, On the Rim of Mexico: Encounters of the Rich and Poor, 1998, Memories of a Hyphenated Man, 2003. Served to lt. USAAF, 1943-46. William Harrison Mills traveling fellow in internat. rels., 1950; John Hay Whitney Found. fellow, 1950; Fulbright fellow Mex., 1965-66; fellow Ctr. for Advanced Study in Behavioral Scis., 1984-85, Rockefeller Resident, Bellagio Study Ctr., 2003, Ena H. Thompson lectureship, Pomona Coll., 1995; recipient Am. Philos. Soc. grant in aid, 1959, Nat. medal Humanities Pres. U.S., 1998. Mem. Am. Hist. Assn. (Beveridge prize com. 1974-76), Conf. Latin Am. History, Chicano-Latino Faculty Assn. U. Calif. (pres. 1989-91), Phi Beta Kappa, Sigma Delta Pi. Home: PO Box 1775 Rancho Santa Fe CA 92067-1775

RUIZ, VANESSA, judge; b. San Juan, Mar. 22, 1950; d. Fernando and Irma (Bosch) Ruiz-Suria; married; m. David E. Birenbaum, Oct. 22, 1983; stepchildren: Tracy, Matthew. BA, Wellesley Coll., 1972; JD, Georgetown U., 1975. Bar: D.C. 1972. Assoc. Fried, Frank, Harris, Shriver & Kampelman, Washington, 1975—83; sr. mgr., counsel Sears World Trade Inc., Washington, 1983—87; founding ptnr. Sloan, Lehner & Ruiz, Washington, 1987—89; ptnr. Pepper, Hamilton & Scheetz, Washington, 1989—91; dep. corporation counsel, legal counsel div. State of DC, Washington, 1991—93, prin. dep. corp. counsel, 1993—94, corporation counsel, 1994; assoc. judge DC Ct. of Appeals, Washington, 1994—. Spkr. in field; adjunct prof. Georgetown U. Co-author: Europe Without Frontiers: A Lawyers' Guide, 1989. Recipient Judge of the Yr. award, Hispanic Nat. Bar Assn., 2001. Mem.: Hispanic Bar Assn., DC, Am. Law Inst., Coun. Ct. Excellence, Nat. Assn. Women Judges (immediate past pres.), Internat. Assn. Women (bd. mem.). Office: DC Ct of Appeals 500 Indiana Ave NW Fl 6 Washington DC 20001-2131 Office Fax: 202-626-8868.

RUIZ-BRAVO, NORKA, federal agency administrator; B in biology, Goucher Coll., Towson, Md., 1975; M in biology, Yale U., PhD in biology, 1983. Post-doctoral fellow in physiol. chemistry Johns Hopkins U.; post-doctoral fellow in biochemistry and molecular biology U. Tex. MD Anderson Cancer Ctr., mem. faculty, 1983—89, Baylor Coll. Medicine, Houston, 1983—89; sci. rev. adminstr. Office Rev. Activities Nat. Inst. Gen. Med. Sciences, NIH, 1990, program dir. Divsn. Genetics and Biology, 1992, acting dep. dir. Divsn. Minority Opportunities in Rsch., spl. asst. Office Extramural Activities; sci. rev. adminstr. Nat. Ctr. Human Genome Rsch., NIH; dep. dir. Divsn. Cancer Biology Nat. Cancer Inst., NIH,

1997—98, acting dir. Divsn. Cancer Biology, 1998—99; dep. assoc. dir. extramural activities Nat. Inst. Gen. Med. Sciences, NIH, 1999—2000, assoc. dir. extramural activities, 2000—03; dep. dir. extramural rsch. NIH, 2003—. Mem.: AAAS, Soc. Devel. Biology, Am. Soc. Cell Biology. Office: NIH 9000 Rockville Pike Bethesda MD 20892 Office Phone: 301-496-1096. Office Fax: 301-402-3469. E-mail: nb9b@nih.gov.

RUIZ-DEYA, GILBERTO, urologist; s. Jose A. Ruiz and Gloria Deya; m. Beliza Iaizawy-Vendell; children: Isabel, Ricardo, Ana Patricia. Degree in indsl. microbiology, U. PR, Mayaguez, 1985—87; degree in microbiology & cell scis., U. Fla., Gainesville, 1987—89; MD, Ponce Sch. Medicine, PR, 1994. Lic. urologist Tulane Medical U., 2000, laparoscopic surgery Tulane Medical U., 2001, diplomate FACS. Fellowship in laparoscopy & endourology dept. urology Tulane U., New Orleans, 2000—01, asst. prof. urology, 2001—02, clin. asst. prof. urology, 2002—; asst. prof. urology Ponce Sch. Medicine, 2003—. Ednl. program dir. PR Urology Assn., San Juan, 2003—04; presenter & spkr. in field. Contbr. chapters to books, articles to profl. jours. Cath.

RUIZ GUTIERREZ, CARLOS HUMBERTO, professional soccer player; b. Guatemala City, Sept. 15, 1979; m. Laura Ruiz Gutierrez; children: Andrea, Samantha. Mem. CSD Municipal, Guatemala Football League; forward LA Galaxy, Major League Soccer, 2002—. Mem. Guatemala Nat. Team, 2001—. Named MLS Player Month (two times), Major League Soccer, 2002, MLS Player Week (three times), 2002, MLS MVP, 2002. Achievements include tied for league leader in goals (15 goals), Major League Soccer, 2003. Office: L A Galaxy 18400 Avalon Blvd Ste 200 Carson CA 90746-2181

RUIZ MADAS, YESENIA, educational counselor; b. Bklyn., Oct. 17, 1976; d. Federico and Margarita Ruiz, Adrian Feliciano (Stepfather); m. Timothy C. Madas, May 5, 2001. BA, Mercy Coll., NY, 2000, MS, 2003. Job coach Lifespire, NY, 1994—99; social worker St. Christopher's Inc., NY, 2000; academic advisor Mercy Coll., Bronx, NY, 2001—04; student devel. specialist Brookdale C.C., Lincroft, NJ, 2004—. Mem. vol. rels. com. Habitat for Humanity. Recipient Humanitarian award, Jane Addams Vocat. H.S., 1994. Mem.: NJ Edn. Assn., NJ CC Counselors Assn. Roman Catholic. Avocations: reading, sewing, carpentry, bicycling, oragami. Office: Brookdale Community College 765 Newman Springs Rd Lincroft NJ 07738 Home Phone: 732-840-4247; Office Phone: 732-224-2556. Business E-Mail: ymadas@brookdalecc.edu.

RUIZ-VARGAS, YOLANDA, finance educator; b. Mayagüez, PR, Apr. 24, 1968; d. Samuel Ruiz and Isabel Vargas. BSBA cum laude, U. P.R., Mayagüez, 1990, MBA, 1994; PhD, U. of Tex., Edinburg, 2000. Acctg. officer Calzados HQ, Inc, Mayagüez, 1990—93; planner trainee Cutler Hammer of PR, Cabo Rojo, PR, 1994; tchg. asst. U. of Texas-Pan Am., Edinburg, 1996—99; instr. U. P.R., Mayagüez, 1994—96, asst. prof., 2000—03, assoc. prof., 2003—, assoc. dean for rsch. and grad. affairs, 2004—. Co-coordinator UPR- Ctr. for Profesional Enhancement, Mayagüez, PR, 2002—02; faculty rep. Grad. Coun. - UPR Mayagüez, Mayagüez, PR, 2001—03; faculty advisor 2002 Ph.D. Project Fin. Doctoral Students Assn. Conf., San Antonio, —, 2001 Ph.D. Project Fin. Doctoral Students Assn. Conf., Toronto, Canada; liaison 2000 PhD Project Fin. Doctoral Students Assn. Conf., Seattle; planning com. mem. 1999 PhD Project Fin. Doctoral Students Assn. Conf., Orlando; mem. 2002 FMA Ann. Meeting Program Com., San Antonio; vis. asst. prof. Tex. A&M Internat. U., Laredo, 1999—2000. Scholar acad. scholar, U. P.R., 1996—2000. Mem.: Am. Fin. Assn., Internat. Coun. for Small Bus., Fin. Mgmt. Assn. Internat., Alpha Delta Kappa, Beta Gamma Sigma. Avocations: reading, travel. Office: U PR COBA - PO Box 9009 Mayaguez PR 00681-9009 Business E-Mail: yruiz@caribe.net. E-mail: yruiz@uprm.edu.

RUKEYSER, M.S., JR., television consultant, writer; b. NYC, Apr. 15, 1931; s. Merryle Stanley and Berenice (Simon) Rukeyser; children: Jill Victoria, Patricia Bern. Student, U. Va., 1948-52. Reporter Albany (N.Y.) Times-Union, 1949, Internat. News Service, NYC, 1951; TV publicist Young & Rubicam, Inc., NYC, 1952-57; with NBC, 1958-80, 81-88, dir. news info. Washington, 1962, v.p. press and publicity NYC, 1963-72, v.p. corp. info., 1972-74, v.p. pub. info., 1974-77, exec. v.p. pub. info., 1977-80, 81-84, exec. v.p. corp. communications, 1984-88; v.p. comm. Newsweek Inc., 1980-81; sr. v.p. GTG Entertainment, 1988-90; pres. Rukeyser Communications, NYC, 1990—. Sr. fellow Freedom Forum Media Ctr., 1991-92. Author (with Grant Tinker): Tinker in Television: From General Sarnoff to General Electric, 1994. With US Army, 1953—54. Office: Ste 1213 616 Clearwater Park Rd West Palm Beach FL 33401-6250 Personal E-mail: budruk@gmail.com.

RUKEYSER, ROBERT JAMES, manufacturing executive; b. New Rochelle, NY, June 26, 1942; s. Merryle Stanley and Berenice Helene (Simon) R.; m. Leah A. Spiro, July 26, 1964; children: David Bern, Peter Lloyd. BA, Cornell U., Ithaca, NY, 1964; MBA with distinction, NYU, 1969. Bond analyst Dun & Bradstreet, NYC, 1964-65, Standard & Poors, NYC, 1965-66; mktg. rep. data processing div. IBM, NYC, 1967-72, regional mktg. staff, 1973-74, mktg. mgr., 1974-76, corp. mgr. internal comm. and editl. programs Armonk, NY, 1976-79, mgr. comm. ops. Franklin Lakes, NJ, 1979-81; pub. affairs dir., asst. to chmn. Fortune Brands, Inc. (formerly Am. Brands, Inc.), NYC, 1981-83, v.p. pub. affairs, asst. to chmn., 1983-85, v.p. office products Old Greenwich, Conn., 1986-87, v.p. ops., 1987-89, sr. v.p. corp. affairs, 1990-99. Bd. dirs. Fortune Brands (formerly Am. Brands Inc.); mgmt. cons. and author, 2000-. Vice chmn., chair fin. com., mem. exec. com. The Hole in the Wall Gang Camp; bd. dirs. Assn. Hole in the Wall Camps, treas., exec. com., chair budget and fin. com. Mem.: Assn. Hole in Wall Camps.

RUKEYSER, WILLIAM SIMON, journalist; b. NYC, June 8, 1939; s. Merryle Stanley and Berenice (Simon) R.; m. Elisabeth Mary Garnett, Nov. 21, 1963; children: Lisa Rukeyser Burn, James William. AB, Princeton U., 1961; rsch. student, Cambridge U., Eng., 1962—63; LittD (hon.), Maryville Coll., 2002. Copyreader Wall St. Jour., 1961-62, staff reporter Europe, 1963-67; assoc. editor Fortune mag., 1967-71, mem. bd. editors, 1971-72; founding mng. editor Money mag., NYC, 1972-80; mng. editor Fortune mag., 1980-86; dir. internat. bus. devel. Time Inc., 1986-88; editor in chief, exec. v.p. Whittle Communications, Knoxville, Tenn., 1988-91; chmn., CEO, Whittle Books, Knoxville, 1991-94; pres. William Rukeyser, Inc., Knoxville, 1994—; editl. dir. Corporate Board Member mag., 1998—; contbg. editor CNN, 1995-97. Commentator Good Morning America, ABC-TV, 1978-85, CBS Radio Stations News Svc., 1979-86; mem. nat. adv. coun. Maryville Coll., Tenn., 1998-2007, chmn. nat. adv. coun., 2007-; mem. adv. bd. Ctr. of Inquiry in Liberal Arts Wabash Coll., Crawfordsville, Ind., 2001—. Jud. com. Union County (NJ) Med. Soc., 1977-80; co-chair capital campaign Nat. Mental Health Assn., 1984-85; liaison com. U. Tenn. Med. Ctr., 1992-99; vice chmn. U. Health Sys. Inc., 1999—; chmn. bd. dirs. Knoxville Jazz Orch., 2001—; mem. alumni adv. bd. Univ. Press Club, Princeton, 2005—. Office: 1001 First Tennessee Plz Knoxville TN 37929 Personal E-mail: wsr@finehand.com.

RULAND, MILDRED ARDELIA, retired retail executive, retail buyer; b. Draketown, Ga., Aug. 11, 1918; m. Harry Morse Ruland, Aug. 19, 1947; children: Hal Morse, Judy Lee Ruland Rigas. BS, West Ga. Coll., 1966. Elem. tchr., New London, Conn., 1947-48, Atlanta, 1948-51, Rome, Ga., 1951-81; mgr. McBrayer Bros. Furniture Co., Rome, 1981—; ret., 2006. Rosenwald Found. scholar, 1941-42. Mem. NEA, Nat. Fedn. Ind. Bus. (corr. sec. 1975—), Ga. Edn. Assn. (del. 1964-74), Ga. Home Furnishings Assn., Twickham Garden Club, Rome Pride Assn., Rome C. of C., Alfa Delta Kappa. Republican. Baptist. Avocations: dance, swimming, bowling, hiking, singing.

RULAND, RICHARD EUGENE, literature educator, critic, historian; b. Detroit, May 1, 1932; s. Eugene John and Irene (Janette) R.; m. Mary Ann Monaghan; children: Joseph, Michael, Paul, Susan; m. Birgit Noll. BA, Assumption Coll. U. Western Ont., Can., 1953; MA, U. Detroit, 1955; PhD, U. Mich., 1960. Instr., then asst. prof. English and Am. studies Yale U., New Haven, 1960-67, Morse rsch. fellow, 1966-67; prof. English and Am. lit. Washington U., St. Louis, 1967—, chmn. dept. English, 1969-74; chmn. comparative lit. program, 1993-94. Vis. Bruern prof. Am. lit. Leeds (Eng.) U., 1964-65; vis. Fulbright prof. U. Groningen, The Netherlands, 1975, Sch. of English and Am. Studies U. East Anglia, Eng., 1978-79; vis. disting. prof. Am. lit. Coll. of William and Mary, 1980-81. Author: The Rediscovery of American Literature: Premises of Critical Taste, 1900-1940, 1967, America in Modern European Literature: From Image to Metaphor, 1976, (with Malcolm Bradbury) From Puritanism to Postmodernism: A History of American Literature, 1991 (paperback 1992), translation into Czech and Hungarian, 1997; editor: Walden: A Collection of Critical Essays, 1967, The Native Muse: Theories of American Literature, Vol. I, 1972, 76, A Storied Land: Theories of American Literature, Vol. II, 1976; contbr. articles to profl. jours. Guggenheim Rsch. fellow, 1982-83. Mem. Assn. Depts. English (pres. 1974). Avocation: jazz musician. Office: Washington U Dept English Saint Louis MO 63130

RULE, ANN, author; 4 children. Degree in English, U. Washington, 1958, PhD in Humane Letters, Willamette U., 2004, postgrad. in police sci. Former policewoman, Seattle; speaker on subject of serial killers. Author (non-fiction books): The Stranger Beside Me, 1980, The I-5 Killer, Want-Ad Killer, Lust Killer, Beautiful Seattle, 1984, Small Sacrifices, 1987, If You Really Loved Me, 1991, Everything She Ever Wanted, 1992, (novel): Possession, 1983, A Rose for Her Grave, 1993, You Belong to Me, 1994, Dead by Sunset, 1995, A Fever in the Heart, 1995, Green River, Running Red, 2004, Kiss Me Kill Me: And Other True Cases, 2004; exec. prodr. ABC mini-series Small Sacrifices, 1989 (Peabody award), NBC mini-series Dead by Sunset, 1995, CBS mini-series And Never Let Her Go, 2000, USA Network mini-series The Stranger Beside Me, 2003; contbr. over 1400 articles to newspapers and mags. including True Detective, Cosmopolitan, and others. Vol. Seattle Crisis Clinic. Recipient: Washington State Governor's award. Address: PO Box 98846 Seattle WA 98198-0846

RULE, CHARLES FREDERICK (RICK), lawyer; b. Nashville, Apr. 28, 1955; s. Frederick Charles and Mary Elizabeth (Malone) R.; m. Ellen Friedland, May 13, 1976 BA, Vanderbilt U., 1978; JD, U. Chgo., 1981. Bar: U.S. Ct. Appeals. (D.C. cir.) 1983. Law clk. US Ct. Appeals (Fed. Cir.), Washington, 1981-82; spl. asst. to asst. atty. gen. Antitrust divsn. US Dept. Justice, Washington, 1982-83, dep. asst. atty. gen. policy planning, 1984-85, acting asst. atty. gen., then dep. asst. atty. gen. regulatory affairs, 1985-86, asst. atty. gen., 1986-89; ptnr. Covington & Burling LLP, Washington, 1989-2001, Fried, Frank, Harris, Shriver & Jacobson LLP, Washington, 2001—07, Cadwalder, Wickersham & Taft LLP, Washington, 2007—. Legal, econ. analyst Lexecon, Inc., Chgo., 1979-80 Mem. Bar of D.C. Ct. Appeals, Phi Beta Kappa, Phi Eta Sigma. Republican. Presbyterian. Office: Cadwalder Wickersham & Taft LLP 1201 F St NW Washington DC 20004 Office Phone: 202-862-2420. E-mail: rick.rule@cwt.com.

RULE, SHEILA, editor; m. Gerald Boyd (div.). BA in Journalism, Univ. Mo., 1972. Reporter St. Louis Post-Dispatch, 1972—77; from reporter to fgn. corr., Nairobi, London NY Times, NYC, 1977—94, sr. editor, career devel., 1994—. Bd. dir. UN Assn. NY. Bd. dir. Good Shepherd Services, NYC. Office: Career Devel NY Times 229 W 43rd St New York NY 10036 Office Phone: 212-556-4143. Office Fax: 212-556-4401.

RULIS, CHRISTOPHER C., lawyer; b. Cheswick, Pa., Apr. 15, 1956; s. Casmer Rulis and Margaret Thimons; m. Lisa Ross, Sept. 26, 1992; children: Marisa, Amanda. BA, Indiana U., Pa., 1978; JD, U. Akron, 1981. Bar: U.S. Supreme Ct., Pa. Supreme Ct., U.S. Tax Ct., Allegheny County Ct. Common Pleas. Assoc. atty. Brandt, Milnes, Rea, Pitts., 1983—90, Rothman Gordon P.C., Pitts.; mng. ptnr. O'Brien, Rulis, Bochicchio, Sosso, LLC, Pitts., 1996—2005. Spl. master Allegheny County Ct. Common Pleas, 1996—. Mem. Gov.'s Club, Harrisburg, Pa., 1996—2000. Fellow, Million Dollar Advocate's Forum, 1997—. Fellow: Acad. Trial Lawyers; mem.: Pa. Def. Inst., Allegheny County Bar Assn., Pa. Bar Assn. Republican. Roman Catholic. Home: 2762 Brunton Ct Allison Park PA 15101 Business E-Mail: crulis@orbslaw.com.

RULIS, RAYMOND JOSEPH, manufacturing executive, consultant; b. New Britain, Conn., June 2, 1924; s. James Alexander and Eva (Ragauskas) R.; m. Thelma Pelchat, June 16, 1949 (dec.); children: Elaine, Jeffery, Catherine, Elizabeth, Amy, Daniel, Jean; m. Virginia Kleene, Oct. 9, 1999. BSME, U. Conn., 1949; postgrad., U. Conn., Ohio State U., Northeastern U., 1949-58; student, Fed. Exec. Inst., Charlottesville, Va., 1976. Devel. engr. Hamilton Standard, U.T.C., Windsorlocks, Conn., 1951-55; mgr. fuel controls Lycoming Textron, Stratford, Conn., 1955-59; mgr. controls and accessories GE, Lynn, Mass., 1959-62; successively program mgr. sert spacecraft, chief spacecraft engr., chief launch vehicle engr., chief engring design, program mgr. QCSEE program NASA Lewis Rsch. Ctr., Cleve., 1962-81; v.p. rsch. and devel. Textron Turbocomponents Group, Walled Lake, Mich., 1981-92; cons., 1992—. Cons. Joint FAA/NASA Civil Aero Rsch. Document Study, 1972, Cruise Missile PRogram, 1977-78, C-17 Aircraft Source Selection Bd., 1978, Tri-Svcs. Propulsion Group, 1976-78; chmn. Conf. on Short Haul Systems, NASA, 1976; mem. exec. coun. Aerospace Industries Tech. Coun., 1988-89. Contbr. articles to profl. jours.; patentee in field. Chmn. Boy Scouts Am. Fund Drives, Cleve., 1976-78; mem. Coun. on World Affairs, Cleve., 1976-81. With US Army, 1943—46. Decorated Combat Infantryman's badge, Bronze Star medal, Purple Heart. Mem. Am. Helicopter Soc. (chmn. tech. session 1970), AIAA (chmn. tech. session 1965), Detroit Engring Soc., KC. Roman Catholic. Avocation: golf. Office: RJR Cons 9 Outpost Ln Hilton Head Island SC 29928-3820

RULISON, JOSEPH RICHARD, investment banker; b. Syracuse, NY, May 14, 1956; s. Laurence M. and Catherine (Fox) R.; m. Karen Richards, Sept. 6, 1980; children: Elizabeth, Mallorie, Morgan, Abigail. BA, St. John Fisher Coll., 1978, LLD, Doctorate, St. John Fisher Coll., 2006. Account exec. Prudential-Bache Securities, Rochester, NY, 1982—84; investment exec. Tucker Anthony & R.L. Day, Inc., 1984—89; ptnr., exec. v.p. Marsh Capital Mgmt., 1989—96; pres., CEO Rulison & Co., Inc., 1996—2001; founder Muniflow, 2001—; market exec., sr. v.p. cash flow solutions Bank of Am., 2001—. Trustee, past chmn. bd. trustees, past pres., hon. trustee Geva Theatre; chmn. bd. trustees St. John Fisher Coll.; chmn. County Monroe Indsl. Devel. Agy., Monroe County Greater Outdoor Sports Facility-Frontier Field, Monroe County Mid-Sized Arts Com.; past councilman Brighton Town Bd.; past mem. Brighton Planning Bd., Master Plan Com., Archtl. Rev. Bd.; past vice-chmn. Empire Zone of Monroe County; former treas. Monroe County Rep. Com.; bd. dirs. Monroe County Water Authority; bd. mem. Greater Rochester Visitors Assn., Greater Rochester Enterprise. Mem. Genesee Valley Club (former gov., house chmn.), Oak Hill Country Club, The Oldfield Club. Roman Catholic. Avocations: politics, theater, art, wine, golf. Office: Bank America NY7-144-08-02 1 East Ave Rochester NY 14638 Business E-Mail: joseph.r.rulison@bankofamerica.com.

RUMAKER, MICHAEL, writer, language educator; b. Phila., Mar. 5, 1932; s. Michael Joseph and Winifred Marvel Rumaker. Degree in writing (hon.), Black Mountain Coll., 1955; MFA, Columbia U., 1970. Lectr. writing New Sch. for Social Rsch., NYC, 1967-71; tchr. writer, mem. intellectual resources pool Tappan Zee H.S., Orangeburg, NY, 1965-69; instr. writing workshops Rockland Ctr. for Arts, West Nyack, NY, 1975-78; adj. lectr. Rockland C.C., Suffern, NY, 1978-87; writer-in-residence CCNY, CUNY, 1969-71, adj. prof., 1985—98. Author: (novels) The Butterfly, 1962, English edit., 1968, Russian edit., 2002, A Day and a Night at the Baths, 1979, German edit., 1997, My First Satyrnalia, 1981, To Kill a Cardinal, 1992, Pagan Days, 2000, (non-fiction) An Immodest Proposal, 2004, (short stories) Gringos and Other Stories, 1967, 2nd edit., 1991, German edit., 1968, English edit. (Exit 3), 1966, (memoir) Robert Duncan in San Francisco, 1996, Black Mountain Days, 2003, (poems) Pizza Selected Poems, 2005, The Fairies are Dancing All Over the World, 2006, (plays) Queers (Schwul), 1970, 2004, (poem) The Fairies Are Dancing All Over the World, 2006. Mem. Nat. Writers Union. Literary Agent: Harold Ober Assocs 425 Madison Ave Rm 1001 New York NY 10017-1183 Business E-Mail: mr6213@tco.com.

RUMAN, SAUL I., lawyer; b. Chgo., May 12, 1925; s. James A. and Pauline (Scharfer) R.; m. Beverlee Mahan, June 17; children: Loral Ruman Conrad, Melissa Ruman Stewart, Elizabeth Ruman Plumlee. BS, Ind. U., 1949, JD with distinction, 1952. Bar: Ind. 1952, U.S. Supreme Ct. 1963, U.S. Dist. Ct. Ind. 1952, U.S. Ct. Appeals (7th cir.) 1962. Atty. pvt. practice, Hammond, Ind., 1952—; mng. ptnr. Ruman, Clements & Holub, P.C., 1990. Former lectr. bus. law Ind. U. N.W.; mem. faculty numerous insts. on law; mem. com. on rules of practice and procedure Supreme Ct. Ind., 1983-92, Ind. Jud. Nominating Commn., 1990; mem. Ind. Supreme Ct. character and fitness com., 1975—. Pres. Ind. U. Sch. Law Alumni Assn., 1972-73, bd. visitors, 1973; bd. advisors N.W. Campus Ind. U., 1973-85, class rep., 1983; faculty Nat. Inst. Trial Advocacy, 1984-86; trustee Ind. Legal Svcs. Fund, 1978, 84. With usn, 1942-45. Fellow Internat. Acad. Trial Lawyers (dir. 1980-86); mem. Ill. Trial Lawyers Assn., Ind. Bar Assn. (chmn. trial lawyers sect. 1970-71), Ind. Trial Lawyers Assn. (emeritus dir., pres. 1980-81, lifetime achievement award 1997), Coll. Fellows, Assn. Trial Lawyers Am., Am. Bd. Trial Advocates, Order of Coif. Office: 5261 Hohman Ave Hammond IN 46320-1721 Home Phone: 219-864-3980; Office Phone: 219-933-7600.

RUMBAUGH, CHARLES EARL, arbitrator, mediator, educator, lawyer; s. Max Elden and Gertrude R.; m. Christina Carol Pinder; children: Eckwood, Cynthia, Aaron, Heather. BS, UCLA, 1966; JD, Calif. Western Sch. Law, 1971; cert. in advanced mgmt., U. So. Calif., 1993. Bar: Calif. 1972, U.S. Dist. Ct. (cen. dist.) Calif. U.S. Ct. Appeals (9th cir.), U.S. Supreme Ct. Engr. Westinghouse Electric Corp., Balt., 1966-68; legal counsel Calif. Dept. of Corps., LA, 1971-77, Hughes Aircraft Co., LA, 1977-84, asst. to corp. dir. contracts, 1984-89, asst. to corp. v.p. contracts, 1989-95; corp. dir. contracts/pricing Lear Astronics Corp., 1995-97; pres. Ctr. for Conflict Resolution, 1998-99; pvt. practice in pvt. dispute resolution as arbitrator, mediator, pvt. judge, dispute resolution cons. Former EEOC mediator, adminstrv. law judge; mem. arbitration and mediation panels ArbitrationWorks, 1994—2002, Franchise Arbitration & Mediation, Inc., L.A. County Superior Ct., Santa Barbara County Superior Ct.; mem. panel pvt. alt. dispute resolution neutrals U.S. Ct. Fed. Claims; armed svcs. bd. of contract appeals panel of pvt. alt. dispute resolution neutrals, DLA panel of dispute neutrals, also settlement officer U.S. Dist. Ct.; alternative dispute resolution panel World Bank; adj. prof. Calif. State U.; lectr. Naval Postgrad. Sch. and U. Calif.; spkr. in field. Mem. editl. bd. Nat. Contract Mgmt. Jour., 1996-00; contbr. articles to profl. jours. Counselor Boy Scouts Am., LA, 1976—; mem. City of Palos Verdes Estates (Calif.) Citizen's Planning Com., 1986—90; judge pro tem L.A. County Superior Ct., LA, 1991—2000. Fellow: Nat. Contract Mgmt. Assn. (pres. L.A./South Bay chpt. 1991—92, nat. dir. 1992—93, nat. v.p. southwestern region 1993—95, founder, chmn. alt. dispute resolution com., cert. profl. contracts mgr., nat. bd. advisors, Fellow of Yr. award 1994, Nat. Achievement award 2001); mem.: FBA (pres. Beverly Hills chpt. 1992—93), ABA (founder fed. contracts dispute resolution com. dispute resolution sect, forum on franchising, pub. contract law sect., vice chair strategic alliance com. 1999—2007, internat. law sect.), IEEE (sr.), Inst. Supply Mgmt. (former chmn. fed. acquisitions, subcontract mgmt. group), Am. Arbitration Assn. (arbitrator, mediator), Christian Legal Soc., Aerospace Industries Assn. (chmn. procurement techniques com. 1987—88, 1993—94), Soc. Profls. in Dispute Resolution (chmn. internat. sector com. 1996—2000, past bd. dirs. L.A. chpt.), State Bar Calif. (vice chmn. ADR com. 2001—04, chmn. franchise law com. 2002—03, co-chair ADR com. litig. sect. 2006—, Wiley W. Manual pro bono award 1992), Nat. Def. Indsl. Assn. (vice-chmn. west coast legal subcom. 1994—2000, procurement planning com. 1994—), Calif. Dispute Resolution Coun. (cons. to qualifications com. 1997—99). Avocations: camping, skiing, jogging, equestrian. Office: PO Box 2636 Rolling Hills CA 90274 E-mail: adroffice@rumbaugh.net.

RUMBAUGH, JEFFREY ARLIN, neurologist, neuroscientist; b. Lansing, Mich., Jan. 8, 1971; s. Stanley A. and Marcia L. Rumbaugh; m. Y. Nan Park, May 25, 1996. BS, Haverford Coll., Pa., 1993; MS, U. Rochester, NY, 1996, PhD, 1998, MD, 2000. Lic. physician Md., 2004, diplomate Am. Bd. Psychiatry and Neurology, 2005. Intern Johns Hopkins U., Balt., 2000—01, resident neurology, 2001—03, chief resident neurology, 2003—04, asst. prof. neurology Divsn. Neuroimmunology and Neuro-Infectious Diseases, 2004—. Founder, dir. neuroimmunolgy, neuro-infectious disease consult svc. Johns Hopkins U., 2004—. Contbr. articles to profl. jours. Mem. humanism in medicine com., Rochester, 1999—2000; vol. outreach for AIDS awarenes Students Rochester, 1993—2000. Recipient Analytical Chemistry award, Am. Chem. Soc., 1993, Travel award, Am. Soc. Clin. Investigation, 2006; fellow, Elmer Stotz Found., 1995, Louis and Molly Wolk Found., 1996, NIH Genetics, 1996, E. H. Hooker, 1997; scholar, U. Rochester, 1993. Achievements include discovery of a possible new host defense mechanism involving matrix metalloproteinases and viral proteins; research in several new biochemical mechanisms involved in DNA replication and repair; a possible biochemical pathway involved in HIV replication. Avocation: running. Office: Johns Hopkins University 600 N Wolfe Street Baltimore MD 21287 Home Phone: 410-653-6471; Office Phone: 443-287-4656. Office Fax: 410-502-8075.

RUMBAUGH, MAX ELDEN, JR., professional society administrator; b. Ada, Okla., Dec. 11, 1937; s. Max E. and Gertrude (Gulker) R.; m. Joan E. Brockway; children: Maria Rumbaugh Gross, Max E. III. BS in Engring., U.S. Mil. Acad., 1960; MS in Engring. Scis., Purdue U., 1965, MBA, 1972. Instr. Purdue U., West Lafayette, Ind., 1964-65; corp. officer Midwest Applied Sci. Corp., West Lafayette, 1965-72; chief engr. advanced tech. Schwitzer div. Wallace-Murray Corp., Indpls., 1972-77, dir. research, 1977-81; mgr. engring. activities div. Soc. Automotive Engrs., Warrendale, Pa., 1981-84, v.p., asst. gen. mgr., 1984-86, exec. v.p., 1986—2002, exec. v.p. emeritus, 2002—; pres. Performance Rev. Inst., 1991—2001. Pres. Soc. Rsch. Adminstrs. Internat., 1973-74; chmn. Ind. sect. Soc. Automotive Engrs., 1978-79; bd. dirs., exec. com. Am. Nat. Standards Inst., NYC, 1986-02; bd. dirs. Intelligent Transp. Soc. Am., 1992-04, mem. exec. com., 1998-04, Scottsdale Sister Cities Assn., 2006-; internat. spkr. Automotive Engring., 1997-. Author mag. column Focus, 1986-2002. Bd. dirs. Jr. Achievement Western Pa., Pitts., 1986-98, YMCA, North Hills, Pitts., 1985-94, Scottsdale Sister Cities, 2006—; sec. Intelligent Transp. Soc. Am. Bd. Dirs., 2000-04. 1st lt. US Army, 1960—63. Mem. ASME, Am. Soc. Assn. Execs., Coun. Engring. and Sci. Soc. Execs. (bd. dirs. 1990-97, sec. 1993-94, v.p. 1994-95, pres. 1995-96), Soc. Automotive Engrs. of China (hon.), Soc. Automotive Engrs. of India (hon.), Russian Internat. Acad. Engring., Intelligent Transp. Soc. Am. (bd. dirs. 1992-03, sec. 2000-03, chmn. fin. com. 2000-03), Russian Acad. Quality Problems, Rotary (bd. dirs. 1982-84, 93-97, v.p. 1994-95, pres. 1995-96, chmn. youth exch. 2003-). Avocations: skiing, photography. Home: 8731 E San Pablo Dr Scottsdale AZ 85258- Office: Soc of Automotive Engrs Inc 400 Commonwealth Dr Warrendale PA 15086-7511 Office Phone: 480-991-3059.

RUMBERG, ORLY ROBIN, lawyer; b. Cleve., Aug. 28, 1968; d. Dov and Rina Hazony; m. Steven Mantle Rumberg; children: Eliana Rose, Olam Neal. BA in English and Natural Sci., Case Western Res. U., Cleve., 1990; JD., Case Western Res. U. Sch. Law, Cleve., 1993. Chair, health care law group Schwartz Manes Ruby & Slovin, Cin., 2003—. Fundraising chair Fernside: Ctr. for Grieving Children, Cin.; trustee Ctr. Children and Families, Cin., 1998—2006, Cin. Children's Hosp. Med. Ctr. Adolescent Health Ctr. Greater Cin., 2005—; chair, leadership devel. com. Jr. League Cin., 2001—02, chair, mindpeace signature project, 2004—05. Recipient President's award, Jr. League Cin., 2005. Mem.: Ohio State Bar Assn., Am. Health Lawyers Assn., Cin. Bar Assn. (chair, health care law com. 2001—02). Home: 309 Caprice Ct Loveland OH 45140 Office: Schwartz Manes Ruby & Slovin 441 Vine St Ste 2900 Cincinnati OH 45202-3090 Home Phone: 513-697-7669; Office Phone: 513-345-1416.

RUMBOUGH, STANLEY MADDOX, JR., industrialist; b. NYC, Apr. 25, 1920; s. Stanley Maddox and Elizabeth (Colgate) R.; m. Nedenia Hutton, Mar. 23, 1946 (div. 1966); children: Stanley H., David P. (dec.), Nedenia Colgate; m. Margaretha Wagstrom, Dec. 21, 1967 (div. 1990); m. Janna Herlow, Mar. 8, 1990. AB, Yale U., 1942; postgrad. in bus. adminstrn., NYU, 1947-51. Vice pres., dir. Willis Air Service, Teterboro, NJ, 1946-47; v.p., dir. White Metal Mfg. Co., Hoboken, NJ, 1945-61, pres., 1960-61; pres., dir. Metal Container Corp., 1950-59, Am. Totalisator, Balt., 1956-58; chmn. bd. Extrusion Devel. Corp., 1959-61; co-founder, chmn. bd. Elec. Engring. Ltd., 1960-69; co-founder, dir. Trinidad Flour Mills, 1961-72; dir. Dart Industries, 1961—83; chmn. bd. Wallace Clark & Co., 1962—69; co-founder Jamaica Flour Mills, 1963-66. Spl. asst. to sec. Dept. Commerce, 1953; spl. asst. White House charge exec. br. liaison, 1953-55; founder Washington D.C. Tennis Patrons Found. Chmn. U.S. Com. for UN, 1957-58; co-founder Citizens for Eisenhower, 1951; vice chmn. Citizens for Eisenhower-Nixon Com., 1952; bd. dirs. Young Pres. Orgn., 1958-65, 69-80; trustee Young Pres. Found., 1957-70, pres., 1962-65; bd. dirs. N.Y. World's Fair Corp., 1961-70, Nat. Conf. on Citizenship, 1973-2003, Population Resource Ctr., 1978-92, Planned Parenthood of Palm Beach Area, 1979-95, Planned Parenthood Fedn. Am., 1981-84, life trustee Kravis Ctr. Performing Arts; bd. dirs. Palm Beach Civic Assn., chmn. 2005—, co-chmn., 1997-2005; trustee Libr. for Presdl. Papers, 1966-70, Fgn. Policy Assn., 1961-70, Am. Health Found., 1972-76; life trustee Internat. House 1959—. Capt. USMCR, 1942-46. Decorated Air medal (8), D.F.C. (2). Mem. Chief Execs. Orgn., World Pres.'s Orgn. (founding), Young Pres.'s Orgn. (founding), Def. Orientation Conf. Assn., Racquet and Tennis Club, Internat. Lawn Tennis Club, Maidstone Club, Seminole Club, Bath and Tennis Club, Everglades Club, Zeta Psi. Republican. Home: 655 Island Dr Palm Beach FL 33480-4744 Office: 44 Cocoanut Row Ste B103 Palm Beach FL 33480-4069

RUMLER, ROBERT HOKE, agricultural products executive, consultant, retired trade association administrator; b. Chambersburg, Pa., Apr. 4, 1915; s. Daniel Webster and Jennie (Sellers) R.; m. Frances Jeannette Montgomery, June 7, 1939 (dec. 1983); children: Craig M. (dec. 2006), Karen A. Loden; m. Hazel Miller-Karper, Aug. 23, 1986 (dec. 1998). BS, Pa. State U., 1936. Asst. county agt. U. Mo., 1936-37; county agrl. agt. Pa. State U., 1937-45; asst. mgr., editor agrl. promotion divsn. E. I. duPont de Nemours & Co., Inc., Wilmington, Del., 1945-48; asst. exec. sec., COO, Holstein-Friesian Assn. Am., 1948-53, 53-75, exec. sec., CEO, 1975-81, exec. chmn., 1981-82, chmn. emeritus, 1982—. Pres. Holstein-Friesian Svcs., Inc., 1968-81; agribus. cons., 1982—; hon. mem. Holstein-Firesian de Mex. (C.A.); bd. dirs., chmn. Vt. Nat. Bank, Vt. Fin. Svcs., Inc., 1957-88; mem. U.S./USSR Joint Com. Agrl. Cooperation; past chmn. U.S. Agrl. Export Devel. Coun., FAS-USDA; mem. coordinating group Nat. Coop. Dairy Herd Improvement program USDA, 1964-80; mem. agrl. policy adv. com. USTR/USDA Multilateral Trade Negotiations, 1973-87, mem. agrl. tech. adv. com., 1987-95. Contbg. editl. writer Holstein World. Trustee Ea. States Expn., trustee emeritus, 1993—; trustee Assoc. Industries Vt.; past bd. dirs. Internat. Stockmans Ednl. Found.; chmn. adv. bd. Pa. State U., Mont Alto, 1988-98, chmn. 1990-94, emeritus 1998, Centennial fellow, 2004; bd. advisors Pa. State U., Harrisburg, 1990-94. Recipient Disting. award Nat. Dairy Herd Improvement Assn., 1974, Disting. Svc. award Nat. Agrl. Mktg. Orgn., 1977, Cert. of Appreciation, USDA, 1982, Disting. Svc. award Holstein Assn., 1985; named Disting. Alumnus, Pa. State U., 1978, Coll. Agr., 2000, Dairy Industry Man of Yr., World Dairy Expo, 1979, Headliner-of-Yr. Livestock Publs. Coun., 1995, Internat. Person of Yr. World Dairy Expo, 1996, 1st Disting. Alumnus AZ Frat., Pa. State U., 1996; Centennial fellow Pa. State Mont Alto Campus, 20054; named to Internat. Livestock Hall of Fame, 1987; Robert H. Rumler scholarhip founded in his name. Fellow Agr. Adventures; mem. Purebred Dairy Cattle Assn. (dir., exec. com.), Nat. Soc. Livestock Record Assns. (past pres., dir., Disting. Svcs. award 1981), Am. Dairy Sci. Assn. (Disting. Svc. award 1977), Agri-Bus. Found. (All-Time Gt. award 1981), Nat. Dairy Shrine (Dairy Hall of Fame 1976), N.E. Master Farmers Assn. (hon. master farmer 1999, Pa. Farm Bur. Disting. Svc. to Agr. award 1999), U.S. Animal Health Assn., Kiwanis, Masons, Elks, Alpha Zeta (hon. roll 1997), Gamma Sigma Delta. Mem. United Ch. of Christ. Home: 937 Wallace Ave Chambersburg PA 17201-3884 Personal E-mail: bobrumler@pa.net.

RUMMAGE, STEPHEN MICHAEL, lawyer; b. Massillon, Ohio, Dec. 27, 1955; s. Robert Everett and Kathleen Patricia (Newman) R.; m. Elizabeth Anne Seivert, Mar. 24, 1979; children: Everett Martin, Carter Kevin. BA in History and English, Stanford U., 1977; JD, U. Calif., Berkeley, 1980. Bar: Wash. 1980, U.S. Dist. Ct. (we. dist.) 1980, U.S. Ct. Appeals (9th cir.) 1983, U.S. Supreme Ct. 1985. Assoc. Davis, Wright et al, Seattle, 1980-85; ptnr. Davis Wright Tremaine, Seattle, 1986—. Co-author: Employer's Guide to Strike Planning and Prevention, 1985. Mem. Wash. Athletic Club. Democrat. Roman Catholic. Office: Davis Wright Tremaine 1201 Third Ave Ste 2200 Seattle WA 98101-3045 Home Phone: 206-726-8433; Office Phone: 206-622-3150. Business E-Mail: steverummage@dwt.com.

RUMMEL, HAROLD EDWIN, travel company, retail executive; b. Youngstown, Ohio, Oct. 4, 1940; s. Harold Edward and Florence Louise (Hill) R.; children: Timothy B., Jonathan S., Briana. BS, U. Fla., 1963. Writer, editor President's coun., Fla., 1958-70; polit. campaign mgr. various state and congressional campaigns, Tallahassee, 1971-79; sr. v.p. Fla. Fed. Saving Bank, St. Petersburg, Fla., 1979-86; pres., CEO Rummel Co. including The Rummel Real Estate Group, Inc., HardwareUSA.net, St. Petersburg, Fla., 1986—2003, Woodland Bay Group Inc., Mobile, Ala., 1986—2003, Rummel Group Inc., 1986—2003, Global Quest, Inc., Sahara Quest. Active in civic and polit. orgns. Democrat. Avocations: nature, wildlife photography, travel. Home: 1002 Charleston St Mobile AL 36604 Office Phone: 727-204-1187. Personal E-mail: rumgroup@bellsouth.net.

RUMMEL, ROBERT WILAND, aeronautical engineer, writer; b. Dakota, Ill., Aug. 4, 1915; s. William Howard and Dora (Ely) R.; m. Marjorie B. Cox, Sept. 30, 1939; children: Linda Kay, Sharon Lee, Marjorie Susan, Robert Wiland, Diana Beth. Diploma in Aero. Engring., Curtiss Wright Tech. Inst. Aerosci., 1935. Stress analyst Hughes Aircraft Co., Burbank, Calif., 1935-36, Lockheed Aircraft Corp., Burbank, 1936; draftsman Aero Engring. Corp., Long Beach, Calif., 1936, Nat. Aircraft Co., Alhambra, Calif., 1936-37; chief engr. Rearwin A/C & Engines, Inc., Kansas City, Kans., 1937-42; chief design engr. Commonwealth A/C, Inc., Kansas City, 1942-43; v.p. engring. Trans World Airlines, Inc., Kansas City, Mo., 1943-59, v.p. planning and rsch., 1959-69, v.p. tech. devel., 1969-78; pres. Robert W. Rummel Assocs., Inc., Mesa, Ariz., 1978-87; aerospace cons., 1987—. Commnr. Presdl. Commn. Space Shuttle Challenger Accident, 1986; chmn. nat. rsch. coun. Aero Space Engring. Bd. Fellow Inst. Aero. Scis., Soc. Automotive Engrs.; mem. NAE, Masons (32 deg.), Shriners. Home and Office: 1189 Leisure World Mesa AZ 85206-3067 Office Phone: 480-396-9030. Personal E-mail: rwrummel@aol.com.

RUMNEY, HELENE VOSBURGH, retired poet, peace activist; b. SI, NY, July 19, 1928; d. William Henry Vosbrugh and Charlotte Louise (Roehrig) Vosburgh; m. Eward John Rumney, Jan. 27, 1948 (div. 1968); children: Bruce, Marilyn Walenga, John, William, Stephen, Kathleen Rinehart. Diploma, Grand Rapids C.C., Mich., 1972. Cert. Con-Edison cooking sch. cert. SI, 1948. Restaurateur Eddie's Pizza Palace, Grand Rapids, 1960—64; sales rep. Avon Cosmetics Co., Grand Rapids, 1965; distributor Amway Corp., Grand Rapids, 1966; membership dir. G.R. C. of C., Grand Rapids, 1967—74; adv. promoter Art Optical, Grand Rapids, 1980—86; contact lens mfr. H. & R Optical, Grand Rapids, 1987—93; ret. Author: (poetry books) Red Roses White Tears, 1977, Politics and Poetry, 2007. Mem., letter writer Amnesty Internat., NYC, 2000—; demonstrator Peace Presence, Grand Rapids, 2002—; supporter World Wildlife, Earth Justice, Mary Knoll Missions, Paralyzed Vets.; vol. feed poor Cath. Svcs., Mich., 1990—. Served in Civil Air Patrol, 1946—48. Recipient Patriot Yr. award, Help Hospitalized Vets., 2007. Mem.: DAV (Bronze Leader award 2007), VFW, St. Alphonsus Found., St. Christopher's Inn, Sacred Heart League, Co-Redemptorist Assn., Friends Pub. Mus., Internat. Libr. Poetry (Editor's Choice award 2006), Greenpeace Soc. Propagation of Faith, Missionary Assn. Mary Immaculate, Soc. Little Flower, St. Jude League, Missionaries of Africa, Am. Lung Assn. Independent. Roman Catholic. Avocations: reading, writing, walking, knitting, sewing.

RUMP, MARJORIE, library director; b. St. Joseph, Mo., Jan. 19, 1919; d. Edward August and Adeline Amelia Gummig; m. John S. Rump, July 25, 1943 (dec. Sept. 29, 1996); children: Jack, Susan, Marilyn. BA, U. Redlands, Calif., 1941; MLS, U. So. Calif., 1957. Book buyer Sierra Book Store, Bakersfield, Calif., 1953—66; libr. Kern County Libr., Bakersfield, Calif., 1961—66, Ea. Bakersfield H.S., Calif., 1966—68; br. supr. to dep. dir. Kern County Libr., Bakersfield, Calif., 1968—88, dep. dir., 1988—2001. Bd. durs. Kern Cmty. Found., Bakersfield, Calif., 1995—2003, mem. grants com., 2000—; ptnr. Easter Hill Assocs., 1996—2006; trustee Conf. of Calif. Hist. Soc. Trust, Stockton, Calif., 1998—, Rocky Heights, LLC, 2001—. Editor: Inside Historic Kern, 1982; contbr. articles in the California Historian, 1997. Recipient Citizen's Recognition Award, City of Bakersfield, 1983, Jubilee Medallion, U. Redlands, 1984, Soroptimist Women of Distinction Award, Soroptimist Internat., 1990. Mem.: Petroleum Prodn. Pioneers, Conf. Calif. Hist. Soc. (pres. 2000—02), Am. Soc. Pub. Adminstr. (pres. 1980, Doubenmeir Award for Pub. Adminstrn. 1979), Kern County Hist. Soc. (pres. 1981), Soroptimist Internat., Bakersfield (pres. 1978—79), Greater Bakersfield C. of C., Wakayama Sister City (treas. 1984—94). Presbyterian. Avocations: gardening, travel.

RUMSCHITZKI, DAVID SHELDON, chemical engineering educator; BS in Chem. Engring. and Math., Cooper Union, 1978; MS in Chem. Engring., U. Calif., Berkeley, 1979, PhD in Chem. Engring., 1984. Process engr. Stauffer Che. Co., Dobbs Ferry, NY, summer 1978; rsch. engr. Mobil R&D Corp., Paulsboro, NJ, summer 1984; asst. prof. dept. chem. engring. CCNY, 1983-84, 85-89, assoc. prof., 1990-96, prof., 1997—2004, Herbert G. Kayser prof. chem. engring., 2004—. Vis. scientist Max Planck Inst. fur Biophys. Chemistry, Gottingen, Germany, 1985, dept. molecular biology Rsch. Inst. Scripps Clinic, La Jolla, Calif., 1988-89, dept. biophysics Rohr U. Bochum, Germany, 1996-97. Alexander von Humboldt fellow, 1996-97; recipient Frederick Urban Meml. scholarship for excellence in chem. engring., 1978, Harry W. Reddick Fund prize and medal for math., 1978, Standard Oil Co. fellowship, 1978, 79, Presdl. Young Investigator award NSF, 1987-93, Best Papter award ASME Bioengring. Divsn., 1995-96, Melville medal ASME, 1996. Mem. Sigma Pi Sigma, Tau Beta Pi, Sigma Xi.

RUMSEY, VICTOR HENRY, electrical engineering educator emeritus; b. Devizes, Eng., Nov. 22, 1919; s. Albert Victor and Susan Mary (Norman) R.; m. Doris Herring, Apr. 2, 1942; children: John David, Peter Alan, Catherine Anne. BA, Cambridge U., 1941, DSc in Physics, 1972; DEng, Tohoku U., Japan, 1962. With U.K. Sci. Civil Service, 1941-48; asst. to asso. prof. Ohio State U., 1948-54; prof. U. Ill., 1954-57, U. Calif., Berkeley, 1957-66, prof. elec. engring. and computer scis. San Diego, 1966-87, prof. emeritus, 1987—, dept. chmn., 1977-81. Author: 1 book in field; contbr. articles to profl. jours.; patentee in field. Guggenheim fellow, 1965-66; recipient George Sinclair award Ohio State U., 1982, John Kraus Antenna award IEEE Antennas and Propagation Soc., 2004. Fellow IEEE (Morris Liebman prize, John Kraus award Antennas and Propagation), Union Radio Scientifique Internationale, Internat. Astron. Union; mem. Nat. Acad. Engring. Home: 1171 Bohemian Ln Occidental CA 95465-9115

RUMSFELD, DONALD HENRY, former secretary of defense; b. Chgo., July 9, 1932; AB, Princeton U., 1954; degree (hon.), De Paul U. Coll. Commerce, Ill. Coll., Lake Forest Coll., Park Coll., Tuskegee Inst., Nat. Coll. Edn., Bryant Coll., Claremont Grad. Sch., Calif., Ill. Wesleyan U., RAND Grad. Sch., Hampden-Sydney Coll. Adminstrv. asst. to Rep. David Dennison US Congress, 1957-59, mem. staff Rep. Robert Griffin, 1959; investment broker A.G. Becker & Co., Chgo., 1960-62; mem. US Congress from 13th Ill. dist., Washington, 1963—69; dir. Office of Econ. Opportunity & asst. to the Pres. The White House, Washington, 1969—70, counsellor to the Pres., 1970—73, dir. Cost of Living Coun., 1971—73; US amb. & permanent rep. to NATO US Dept. State, Brussels, 1973-74; chair transition to the presidency of Gerald R. Ford The White House, Washington, 1974, chief of staff to Pres., 1974-75; sec. US Dept. Def., Washington, 1975—77, 2001—06; pres., CEO G.D. Searle & Co., Skokie, Ill., 1977-85, chmn. CEO, 1985; spl. presdl. amb. to Mid. East The White House, 1983-84; sr. advisor William Blair & Co., Chgo., 1985-90; chmn., CEO General Instrument Corp., Chgo., 1990-93; chmn. bd. dirs. Gilead Scis., Inc., Foster City, Calif., 1997—2001. Mem., Gen. Advisory Com. on Arms Control & advisor to the govt. on nat. security affairs, 1983-84, US Joint Advisory Commn. on US/Japan Relations, 1983-84, Nat. Commn. on Pub. Svc., 1987-90, Nat. Econ. Commn., 1988-89, Commn. on US/Japan Relations, 1989-91; spl. presdl. envoy on the Law of the Sea Treaty, 1982-83, sr. advisor to the Pres. panel on Strategic Systems, 1983-84, chmn. U.S. Commn. to Assess the Ballistic Missile Threat to the U.S., 1998; commr. U.S. Fed. Trade Deficit Rev. Commn., 1999-2000; U.S. Commn. to Assess Nat. Security Space Mgmt. & Orgn., 2000; bd. visitors, Nat. Def. U., 1988-92. Aviator, flight instructor USN, 1954—57 USNR, 1957—75. Recipient Disting. Eagle Scout award, 1975, Presdl. Medal of Freedom, The White House, 1977, Outstanding Chief Exec. Officer in the Pharmaceutical Industry award, 1980, George Catlett Marshall award, 1984, Woodrow Wilson award, 1985, Dwight David Eisenhower medal, 1993, James H. Doolittle award, 2003, Ronald Reagan Freedom award, 2003, Gerald R. Ford medal, 2004. Republican. the only person to hold the position of secretary of defense twice, 1975-77, 2001-06.

RUNCO, MARIO, JR., astronaut, meteorologist, researcher; b. Bronx, NY, Jan. 26, 1952; s. Mario and Filomena (Ragusa) Runco; m. Susan Kay Friess; 2 children. BS in Meteorology and Phys. Oceanography, CCNY, 1974, DSc (hon.), 1999; MS in Atmospheric Physics, Rutgers U., New Brunswick, NJ, 1976. Rsch. hydrologist US Geol. Survey, LI, NY, 1976—77; state trooper NJ State Police, 1977—78; commd. ensign USN, 1978; rsch. meteorologist Naval Rsch. Lab., Monterey, Calif., 1978—81; watch and meteorol. officer USS Nassau (LHA-4), 1981—83; lab. instr. Naval Postgrad. Sch., Monterey, 1984—85; commdg. officer Oceanographic Unit USNS Chauvenet, 1985—86; fleet environ. svcs. officer Naval Pacific Meterology and Oceanography Command, Pearl Harbor, Hawaii, 1986—87; astronaut NASA Johnson Space Ctr., Houston, 1987—; mission specialist Space Shuttles Atlantis (STS-44), 1991, Space Shuttle Endeavour (STS-54), 1993, Space Shuttle Endeavour (STS-77), 1996; space shuttle flight software avionics lab. test pilot Lyndon B. Johnson Space Ctr. NASA, Houston, 1987—92, capsule communicator Mission Control Ctr. (CAPCOM), 1989—94, lead sci. and utilization Internat. Space Sta. Sci. Window/Window Rsch. Facility, 1993—, Earth and planetary scientist, 1994—, project mgr. Lunar Habitation Sys. project, 2004—, lead spacecraft window optical requirements, 2005—. Decorated Def. Superior Svc. medal NASA, Def. Meritorious Svc. medal, Exceptional Svc. medal, Three Space Flight medals, Two Navy Sea Svc. Deployment Ribbons, Navy Battle Efficiency Ribbon, Navy Achievement medal, Navy Pistol Expert medal; recipient Class of 1938 Athletic Svc. award, CCNY, 1973, Townsend Harris medal, 1993, John Cardinal Spellman award, Cardinal Hayes HS, 1993. Achievements include three space flights, 551 hours in space and one 4.5 hour spacewalk, and designation as Naval Surface Warefare Officer. Avocations: ice hockey, antique cars, collecting toy trains, model railroads, baseball. Office: Human Exploration Sci Office NASA Lyndon B Johnson Space Ctr 2101 NASA Rd 1 Houston TX 77058-3696

RUND, DOUGLAS ANDREW, emergency physician; b. Columbus, Ohio, July 20, 1945; s. Carl Andrew and Caroline Amelia (Row) Rund; m. Sue E. Padavana, 1980; children: Carie, Emily, Ashley. BA, Yale U., 1967; MD, Stanford U., 1971. Lic. physician Ohio, diplomate Nat. Bd. Med. Examiners, Am. Bd. Family Practice, Am. Bd. Emergency Medicine. Intern U. Calif. San Francisco-Moffett Hosp., 1971—72; resident in gen. surgery Stanford U., 1972—74, Robert Wood Johnson Found. clin. scholar in medicine, 1974—76; med. dir. Mid-Peninsula Health Svc., Palo Alto, Calif., 1975—76; clin. instr. dept. medicine and preventive medicine Stanford U. Med. Sch., 1975—76; assoc. prof., dir. divsn. emergency medicine Ohio State Coll. Medicine, 1982—87, dir. emergency medicine residency program, assoc. prof. dept. 1976—87, prof., chmn. dept. preventive medicine, 1988—90, prof., chmn. dept. emergency medicine, 1990—, prof., interim chmn. dept. family medicine, 1994—95, assoc. dean, 2001—; pres. Ohio State Univ. Physicians, 2002—. Attending staff Ohio State U. Hosps., 1976—; med. dir. CSCC, Emergency Med. Svcs. Dept.; pres. Internat. Rsch. Inst. Emergency Medicine; sr. rsch. fellow NATO: Health and Med. Aspects of Disaster Preparedness, 1985—87; vis. epidemiology and injury control U. Edinburgh, Scotland, 1987; working group, emergency and critical care in space NASA, 2001—; bd. dirs. Am. Bd. Emergency Medicine, 1988—97, sr. editor in tng. exam., 1989—, pres., 1995—; pres., chmn. bd. dirs. Physicians of the Ohio State U. (POSU), 2002—; med. dir. Worthington Fire Dept. Author: Triage, 1981, Essentials of Emergency Medicine, 1982, 2d edit., 1986, Emergency Radiology, 1982, Emergency Psychiatry, 1983, Environmental Emergencies, 1985; editor: Emergency Medicine Ann., 1983—84, Emergency Medicine Survey, Annals of Emergency Medicine, Annals of Emergency Medicine Symposium, 1986; editor: (in chief) Ohio State Series on Emergency Medicine, Emergency Medicine Observer, 1986—87; mem. editl. bd.: Physician, Sports Medicine, Emergency Med. Svcs., Jour. Urgent Care Medicine; co-author: Family Medicine Priciples and Practice, 1978, 2d edit., 1983; contbr. articles to profl. jours. Recipient Faculty Tchg. award, Ohio State U., 1999, Douglas A. Rund Disting. Faculty award, Dept. Emergency Medicine, 2003. Fellow: Am. Coll. Emergency Physicians (task force on substance abuse and injury control, Outstanding Contbn. to Edn. award 1992); mem.: IAAA, Columbus Med. Review, Internat. Soc. for Emergency Med. Svcs. (med. dir.), Columbus Med. Forum (pres. 1993—), Soc. Acad. Emergency Medicine (chmn. internat. com. 1991—), Assn. Acad. Chairs Emergency Medicine (pres. 1992—93), Nat. Inst. on Alcohol Abuse and Alcoholism, Alpha Omega Alpha. Office: Ohio State U 146 Means Hall 1654 Upham Dr Columbus OH 43210-1240

RUND, REX BENJAMIN, music director; b. Urbana, Ill., Aug. 20, 1960; s. Benjamin Joseph and Marie Theresa Rund; m. Cathy Berns Rund, Mar. 19, 1988; children: Jacob Simon, Emma Sophie, Marian Rose. B in Music Edn., Ea. Ill. U., Charletson, 1984, MA, 1985. Peace corps vol. US Peace Corps, Leogane, Haiti, 1985—87; grad. asst. Ea. Ill. U., Charleson, 1988—88; asst. headmaster Salzburg Internat. Prep. Sch., Salzburg, Austria, 1989—91; mid. sch. coord. & tchr. Danube Internat. Sch., Vienna, 1991—95; music tchr. Marshall Cmty. Schs., Ill., 1995—97; dir. of music and liturgy Our Lady of Mt. Carmel Ch., Ind., 1997—. Leadership bd. Nat. Assn. of Pastoral Musicians Indpls. Chpt., 1998—2000. Composer: (liturgical songs) O God, You Are My Rock, 1998, God's Caring Love Makes the Difference, 2002, As a Family, We Build God's Kingdom, 2003, Color the World with the Light of Christ, 2004, Journey with Jesus, 2005, Do All For the Glory of God, 2006; author: Liturgical Chants for the Deacon: A Practical Manual, 2007; soloist Carmel Symphony Orch., 2007. Participant Boston Marathon, 2007; co-founder, mission trip leader, and translator Our Lady of Mt. Carmel, St. Antoine Haiti Parish Twinning Program, Ind. Recipient Disting. Young Alumnus award, Ea. Ill. U., 1988, Villa Grove H.S. Hall of Fame Charter Mem., Villa Grove H.S., 1988, Peace Corps Vol. of the Yr. award for Ams. and Caribbean, US Peace Corps, 1987; scholar Warner Presdl. award, Ea. Ill. U., 1983, Talented Student award, 1981—84. Mem.: Choristers' Guild, Am. Choral Dirs. Assn., Nat. Assn. of Pastoral Musicians. Roman Catholic. Avocations: running marathons, travel. Office: Our Lady of Mt Carmel Ch 14598 Oakridge Rd Carmel IN 46032 Home Phone: 317-758-6009; Office Phone: 317-663-4007. Office Fax: 317-846-3475. Business E-Mail: rundr@olmc1.org.

RUNDIO, LOUIS MICHAEL, JR., lawyer; b. Chgo., Sept. 13, 1943; s. Louis Michael Sr. and Germaine Matilda (Pasternack) R.; m. Ann Marie Bartlett, July 10, 1971; children: Matthew, Melissa. BS in Physics, Loyola U., Chgo., 1965, JD, 1972. Bar: Ill. 1972, U.S. Dist. Ct. (no. dist.) Ill. 1972, U.S. Ct. Appeals (7th cir.) 1974, U.S. Dist. Ct. (ea. dist.) Mich. 1983. Assoc. McDermott, Will & Emery, Chgo., 1972-77, ptnr., 1978—. Served to 1st lt. U.S. Army, 1965-68, Vietnam. Mem. ABA, Chgo. Bar Assn. Home: 676 Skye Ln Barrington IL 60010-5506 Office: McDermott Will & Emery 227 W Monroe St Ste 3100 Chicago IL 60606-5096

RUNDLETT, ELLSWORTH TURNER, III, lawyer; b. Portland, Maine, Jan. 12, 1946; s. Ellsworth Turner II and Esther (Stevens) R.; m. Lisa Warren, Oct. 25, 1964 (div. June 1967); 1 child, Ellsworth Turner IV; m. Jamie Donnelly, June 7, 1982 (div. 1986); m. Marilyn DeJenzano, Aug. 17, 1994. AB cum laude, Bowdoin Coll., 1968; JD, U. Maine, 1973. Bar: Maine 1973, U.S. Dist. Ct. Maine 1973, U.S. Ct. Appeals (1st cir.) 1973; cert. civil trial specialist, Nat. Bd. Trial Advocacy; diplomate Nat. Coll. Advocacy. Bowdoin Coll. intern U.S. Senate, Washington, 1967; law clk. Superior Ct. Maine, Portland, 1972-73; asst. corp. counsel City of Portland, 1973-76; ptnr. Childs, Rundlett, Fifield, Shumway and Altshuler, Portland, 1980—. Author: Maximizing Damages in Small Personal Injury Cases, 1991; contbr. legal articles to Maine Bus. Digest, 1978-84. Pres. Pine Tree Alcohol Treatment Ctr., Windham, Maine, 1978-80; trustee Portland Players, Inc., South Portland, Maine, 1977-84, pres., 1985-87. Mem. ATLA, Cumberland County Bar (trustee 1983-84, 86-87, v.p. 1988-90, pres. 1990), Maine Bar Assn. (bd. govs. 1991—), Maine Trial Lawyers Assn. (pres. 2000-01), U. Maine Law Alumni (bd. dirs. 1984-87, v.p. 1988, pres. 1989, bd. govs. 1991—), Cumberland Club, Portland Club (gov.

1983-86), Bowdoin Club of Portland (pres. 1978). Office: Childs Rundlett & Fifield 257 Deering Ave Portland ME 04103-4858 Home Phone: 207-767-4331; Office Phone: 207-773-0275. Business E-Mail: derry@maine.rr.com.

RUNESTAD, KURT S., music educator; b. Fargo, ND, Mar. 1, 1968; s. Cornell Jesse and Diana Cecilia (Rogovin) Runestad; m. Carly Michelle Woythaler, July 20, 1996. BA in Music Edn., St. Olaf Coll., Northfield, Minn., 1990; MA in Choral Conducting, U. Iowa, Iowa City, 1993, DMA in Choral Conducting, 2003. Pub. sch. music tchr., Iowa and Minn., 1996—2003; asst. prof. music Doane Coll., Crete, Nebr., 2003—. Mem.: Music Educators Nat. Conf., Am. Choral Dirs. Assn. (life). Home: 1931 Garret Ln Lincoln NE 68512 Office: Doane Coll 1014 Boswell Ave Crete NE 68333

RUNGE, DONALD EDWARD, food wholesale company executive; b. Milw., Mar. 20, 1938; s. Adam and Helen Teresa (Voss) R.; divorced; children: Roland, Richard, Lori. Grad., Spencerian Coll., Milw., 1960. Fin. v.p. Milw. Cheese Co., Waukesha, Wis., 1962-69; dir. Farm House Foods Corp., Milw., 1966-89, pres., 1966-89, CEO, treas., 1984-89, chmn., pres., 1985-89; chmn., CEO Retailing Corp. Am., Milw., 1982-89; CEO, treas. Drug Sys. Inc., Milw., 1984-89; chmn. Drug Sys. Inc. (now Retailing Corp. of Am.), Milw., 1985-89; pres. TDC, 1987-89; chmn., pres. Runge Industries, Gen. Growth, Inc., 1989—. Bd. dirs. Convenient Food Mart, CasaBlanca Industries, Inc., City of Industry, Calif., Palm Beach Opera, 1992—; sec. The Diana Corp., Milw., 1985-86, treas. 1986—, pres. 1987-96; chmn. Economy Dry Goods Co. Inc.; treas. Fairbanks Farms Inc.; chmn., CEO Internat. Diamond Exch., LLC, 2006—. Adventist. Address: 111C Palm Point Cir Palm Beach Gardens FL 33418-4032 Office Phone: 561-625-4844. *I believe there is very little in life that cannot be accomplished if a person truly wants to attain the goal.*

RUNGE, JEFFREY WILLIAM, former federal agency administrator; b. Oct. 20, 1955; m. Ginny Runge; children: Emily, Will. BA, U. South, 1977; MD, U. S.C., 1981. Diplomate Am. Bd. Emergency Medicine. Resident Charlotte Meml. Hosp. and Med. Ctr., 1984; faculty emergency medicine residency Carolinas Med. Ctr., Charlotte, NC, 1984; dir. Carolinas Ctr. Injury Prevention and Control; adminstr. Nat. Hwy. Traffic Safety Adminstrn. US Dept. Transp., Washington, 2001—06; chief med. officer US Dept. Homeland Security, Washington, 2005—07, acting under sec. for sci. & tech., 2006. Mem.: N.C. Med. Soc. (spkr.), N.C. Coll. Emerency Physicians (past pres.), Am. Coll. Emergency Physicians (trauma care and injury control com., rsch. com.). *

RUNGE, KAY KRETSCHMAR, library consultant; b. Davenport, Iowa, Dec. 9, 1946; d. Alfred Edwin and Ina (Paul) Kretschmar; children: Peter Jr., Katherine. BS in History Edn., Iowa State U., Ames, 1969; MLS, U. Iowa, Iowa City, 1970. Pub. svc. libr. Anoka County Libr., Blaine, Minn., 1971-72; cataloger Augustana Coll., Rock Island, Ill., 1972-74; dir. Scott County Libr. Sys., Eldridge, Iowa, 1974-85, Davenport (Iowa) Pub. Libr., 1985—2001, Des Moines Pub. Libr., 2001—07, KKRunge Assoc., 2007—. V.p. Quad-Cities Conv. and Visitors Bur., 1992—97, Quad-Cities Grad. Study Ctr., 1992—2001, Downtown Davenport Devel. Corp., 1992—2000, Hall of Honor Bd., Davenport Ctrl. H.S., 1992—95, Brenton Bank Bd., 1995—2001, Wells Fargo Bank Bd., 2001; steering com. Quad-Cities Vision for the Future, 1987—91, Humanities Iowa, 1993—2000, chair, 1998—99; bd. govs. Iowa State U. Found., 1991—; dean's adv. bd. Liberal Arts and Sci. Coll. Iowa State U., 2004—, citizens adv. coun., 1998—2000, Leadership Iowa, 1998—99; adv. bd. U. Iowa Sch. Libr. Sci., 1999—, chair, 2006—, adj. prof., 2000—01; devel. bd. Iowa State U. Found., 2000—, Greater Des Moines Leadership, 2002—03; bd. regents Iowa Pub. Radio Exec. Coun., 2005—; bd. dirs. River Ctr. for Performing Arts, Davenport, 1983—97, Iowa State U. Rsch. Pk., 1998—2000, Davenport One, Downtown Devel., 2000—01, Des Moines Operation Downtown, 2004—; chmn. bd. dirs. Am. Inst. Commerce, 1989—98; mem. Qwest Coll. Bd., 1998—2000, Kaplan U. Bd., 2000—. Recipient Svc. Key award Iowa State U. Alumni Assn., 1979, ALA/ALTA Nat. Advocacy Honor Roll award, 2000, Des Moines Women of Influence award, 2004, Carrie Chapman Catt Pub. Advancement award Iowa State U. Alumni Assn., 2006; named Quad City Panhellenic Woman of Yr., 1998. Mem. ALA (chmn. libr. adminstrs. and mgrs. div., fundraising sect. 1988, bd. dirs., Exhibits Round Table 2003-, councilor 2007-), Iowa Libr. Assn. (pres. 1983, Mem. of Yr. award 2000), Pub. Libr. Assn. (bd. dirs. 1990-99, pres. 2000-01), Iowa Edn. Media Assn. (Intellectual Freedom award 1984), Alpha Delta Pi (alumni state pres. 1978). Lutheran. Home and Office: KKRunge Assoc 126 Forest Rd Davenport IA 52803 Home Phone: 563-355-7667; Office Phone: 515-669-1610. Business E-Mail: kkrunge@libraryconsulting.org.

RUNGE, PAUL E., ophthalmologist, educator; b. Milw., June 7, 1946; m. Cheryl Runge; children: Sarah, Megan. AA in Liberal Arts, Orange Coast Coll., Costa Mesa, Calif., 1970; BS in Biology and Immunology, U. Calif., Irvine, 1972, MS in Cellular Immunology, 1974; B Medicine B Surgery, Flinders U., Adelaide, Australia, 1979. Diplomate Am. Bd. Pediat., Am. Bd. Ophthalmology. Rotating intern Flinders Med. Ctr., Adelaide, 1979—80; pediat. resident Hosp. Sick Children, Toronto, Ont., Canada, 1980—82; sr. pediat. resident U. Calif. San Diego Med. Ctr., Children's Hosp., 1982—83; pediat. ophthalmology fellow Hosp. Sick Children and Inst. Ophthalmology, London, 1983—85; resident in ophthalmology Cook County Hosp., Chgo., 1985—88; med. retina fellow U. Calif. Jules Stein Eye Inst., Harbor/UCLA Med. Ctr., LA, 1988—89; surg. retina and vitreous fellow U. Tenn. Ctr. Retina Vitreous Surgery, Memphis, 1989—90; assoc. Ctr. Retina Vitreous Surgery, Memphis, 1990—92; clin. instr. U. Tenn. Health Scis. Ctr., Memphis, 1992—93; clin. prof. So. Ill. U., Carbondale, 1993—96; ptnr. Ophthalmic Cons., Sarasota, Fla., 1996—; clin. asst. prof. dept. ophthalmology U. South Fla., Tampa, 1998—. Presenter in field. Contbr. articles to med. jours. With US Army, 1965—67, Vietnam. Scholar, Given Inst. Pathobiology, 1972; rsch. fellow, NIH, 1973, Brit. Retinitis Pigmentosa Soc., 1984, ARVO traveling fellow, Nat. Eye Inst., 1989. Fellow: ACS, Ont. Coll. Physicians and Surgeons, Am. Acad. Pediat., Am. Acad. Ophthalmology, Am. Ophthal. Soc.; mem.: Royal Coll. Ophthalmology London, Royal Soc. Medicine, Alpha Gamma Sigma. Office: 1700 S Tuttle Ave Sarasota FL 34239

RUNK, FRED J., retired insurance company executive; CFO Am. Fin. Group, Inc., Cin. Office: American Financial Group Inc 1 E 4th St Cincinnati OH 45202 Office Fax: (513) 579-2113.

RUNKEL, PHILLIP M., archivist; b. Waukesha, Wis., Nov. 4, 1946; s. Joseph E. and Lydia R. Runkel. BA, Carroll Coll., 1969; MA, Marquette U., 1972; MLS, Peabody Coll., 1973. Archivist Marquette U., Milw., 1977—. Author: Alfred Lunt and Lynn Fontanne: A Bibliography, 1978; editor: Dorothy Day and the Catholic Worker Movement: Centenary Essays, 2001. Iraq Peace Team del. Voices in the Wilderness, Baghdad, 2003. Mem.: Midwest Archives Conf., Soc. Am. Archivists. Home: Apt 121 100 Corrina Blvd Waukesha WI 53186 Office: Marquette Univ Archives 1355 W Wis Ave Milwaukee WI 53233 Office Phone: 414-288-5903. Office Fax: 414-288-6709. E-mail: phil.runkel@marquette.edu.

RUNKLE, MARTIN DAVEY, library director; b. Cin., Oct. 18, 1937; s. Newton and Ilo (Neal) R.; m. Nancy Force, Aug. 7, 1965; children: Seth, Elizabeth. BA, Muskingum Coll., 1959; MA, U. Pitts., 1964, U. Chgo., 1973. Library systems analyst U. Chgo., 1970-75, head cataloging librarian, 1975-79, asst. dir. tech. services, 1979-80, dir. library, 1980—2004. Sr. lectr. grad. library sch. U. Chgo., 1977-90. Fulbright grantee, 1965-67. Mem. ALA. E-mail: mrunkle183@comcast.net.

RUNNELS, DAVID G., lawyer; b. Woodbridge, Eng., 1961; BBA with high honors in Fin., U. Tex., 1983, JD with honors, 1986. Bar: Tex. 1986. Ptnr., Energy Transactions Andrews Kurth LLP, Houston, mem. mgmt. com. Mem.: Tex. Gen. Counsel Forum (bd. dir.), Houston Bar Found. (bd. dir.), Tex. Young Lawyers, State Bar Tex., Phi Delta Phi. Office: Andrews Kurth LLP 600 Travis St Ste 4200 Houston TX 77002-3090 Office Phone: 713-220-4161. Office Fax: 713-238-7191. Business E-Mail: drunnels@andrewkurth.com.

RUNNER, JACK CHARLES, health facility executive; b. Sandusky, Ohio, Mar. 31, 1955; s. Kenneth Earl and Mary Margaret Runner; m. Kathleen Marie Kahle, July 15, 1978; children: Kristen Marie, Kelly Marie. BS in Microbiology, Bowling Green State U., 1977; MBA, Ashland U., 1984. Staff technologist Sandusky Meml. Hosp., 1978-84; supr. microbiology dept. Firelands Cmty. Hosp., Sandusky, 1984-86; adminstrv. dir. North Coast Clin. Lab. Inc., Sandusky, 1985—. Mem. Am. Soc. for Microbiology, Drug. Info. Assn., Assn. Clin. Rsch. Profls., Am. Assn. Clin. Chemistry, Clin. Lab. Mgrs. Assn., U.S. Power Squadron (dist. comdr. 1999—), Kiwanis Internat., Sandusky Yacht Club, Boat U.S. Office: North Coast Clin Lab Inc 2215 Cleveland Rd Sandusky OH 44870-4485 Office Phone: 419-626-6012. Business E-Mail: jack@northcoastlab.com.

RUNNER, JEFFREY THOMAS, linguist; b. Aberdeen, SD, Feb. 9, 1963; s. Joseph Thomas and Patricia Dawson Runner; life ptnr. Javier Bautista. PhD, U. Mass., Amherst, 1995. Vis. asst. prof. U. Rochester, NY, 1994—98, asst. prof., 1998—2004, assoc. prof., 2004—. Mem.: Linguistics Soc. Am. Avocations: genealogy, genealogy, swimming. Home Phone: 585-802-2602; Office Phone: 585-275-2626.

RUNNICLES, DONALD, conductor; b. Edinburgh, Nov. 16, 1954; Student, Edinburgh U., Cambridge U., London Opera Ctr.; DMus (hon.), U. Edinburgh, 1995. Music dir., prin. condr. San Francisco Opera, 1992—; prin. condr. NY Orch. of St. Luke's. Prin. guest condr. Atlanta Symphony Orch., 2005—06. Repetiteur Nat. Theatre, Mannheim, Germany, 1980—, Kapellmeister, 1984—, prin. condr., Hanover, 1987—, numerous appearances with Hamburg Staatsoper, former gen. music dir. Stadtische Buhnen, Freiburg/Breisgau, appearances with Met. Opera include Lulu, 1988, The Flying Dutchman, 1990, The Magic Flute, condr. Vienna Staatsoper, 1990—91, Sonome, 1996, debut Don Giovanni, Glyndebourne, 1991, Salzburg Festival, 1996, condr. London Symphony Orch., La Scale Milan Freischutz, Orch. Paris, Israel Philharm., Rotterdam Philharm., Seattle Symphony, Pitts. Symphony, St. Louis Symphony, Chgo. Symphony, San Francisco Symphony, Cleve. Orch., New World Symphony, Bavarian Radio Symphony, Billy Budd and the Ring, Vienna State Opera, 2001, Katya Kabanova, San Francisco, 2002, Schoenberg's Gurrelieder, London Proms, 2002, Tristan und Isolde, BBC Symphony Orch., 2002—03, (world premier) Doctor Atomic, John Adams, 2005, rec. artist Hansel and Gretel, Gluck's Orphée with San Francisco Opera Orch., 1995, Tannhäuser-Bayreuth Festspick, 1995, Harvey Milk with San Francisco Opera, 1996, Mozart Requiem, 2005—, opened Edinburgh Festival, 1994, 1996. Recipient Officer of Brit. Empire. Office: San Francisco Opera War Meml Opera House 301 Van Ness Ave San Francisco CA 94102-4509

RUNNING, ANDREW RICHARD, lawyer; b. Lincoln, Nebr., Sept. 5, 1957; s. Donald Richard and Phyllis Iris (Franklin) R.; m. Laura Beth Anderson, Oct. 6, 1990. AB in econs., U. Chgo., 1979; JD, Yale U., 1982. Bar: Ill. 1982, US Dist. Ct. (no. dist.) Ill. 1982, US Ct. Appeals (7th cir.) 1982, US Dist. Ct. Nebr., US Dist. Ct. (ea. dist.) Wis., US Ct. Appeals (8th & 9th cir.). Assoc. Kirkland & Ellis, Chgo., 1982-88, ptnr., 1988—. Recipient Thurman Arnold Moot Ct. prize, Am.'s Leading Lawyers for Bus. in Environment, Chambers USA, 2005. Mem. ABA, U. Club Chgo., Phi Beta Kappa. Office: Kirkland & Ellis 200 E Randolph St Ste 6100 Chicago IL 60601-6436 Office Phone: 312-861-2000. Office Fax: 312-861-2200. Business E-Mail: arunning@kirkland.com.

RUNOWICZ, CAROLYN DILWORTH, physician; b. Willimantic, Conn., May 1, 1951; d. S. Robert and Aline (Bergeron) Dilworth; m. Sheldon H. Cherry. BA, U. Conn., 1973; MD, Thomas Jefferson Med. Coll., Phila., 1977. Diplomate in ob-gyn. and gynecol. oncology Am. Bd. Ob-Gyn. Resident, ob-gyn. Mt. Sinai Sch. Medicine and Med. Ctr., NYC, 1977-81, fellow gynecol. oncology, 1981-83; instr., dir. divsn. ob-gyn. Albert Einstein Coll. Medicine, NYC, 1983-88, asst. prof. dept. ob-gyn., 1988-93, assoc. prof., 1993—98; dir. gynecologic and oncology, divsn. ob-gyn. Our Lady of Mercy, Bronx, NY, 1988; prof., dir. gynecol. oncology dept. ob-gyn. Montefiore Med. Ctr., NYC, 1998—2001; prof. clin. obstetrics and gynecology Columbia U. Coll. Physicians and Surgeons, 2001—03; vice chmn. ob-gyn. St. Luke's Roosevelt Hosp., 2001—03; dir. Carole and Ray Neag Comprehensive Cancer Ctr., prof. ob-gyn. divsn. gynecologic oncology, NE utilities chair exptl. oncology U. Conn. Health Ctr., Famington, NY, 2003—. Presdl. appointee Nat. Cancer Adv. Bd., 2004—, chair, 2006—; testified at Senate hearings advocating cancer screening as rep. Am. Coll. Obstetricians and Gynecologists; spkr., President's Cancer Panel, Meeting the Challenges of Older Adult Cancer Survivors, 2004; lectr. in field. Author: To Be Alive: A Women's Guide to a Full Life After Cancer, 1995, Answer to Cancer, 2004; co-author (with husband): Menopause Book: A Guide to Women's Health After 40, 1994; co-author: (with Jeanne Petrek) Woman and Cancer: A Through and Compassionate Resource for Patients and Their Families, 1999; contbr. chapters to books, articles to profl. jours. Galloway fellow Sloan Kettering Meml. Hosp., NYC, 1980. Fellow: Am. Coll. Ob-Gyn.; mem.: AMA, ACS (pres. 2005—06), Am. Soc. Clinical Oncology, Am. Gynecol. Club, Am. Cancer Soc. (pres. 2005—06), NY Obstet. Soc., Am. Gynecol. Obstetrics Soc., Soc. Gynecologic Oncologists (pres. 2000), Am. Med. Women's Assn. (Local Legend award), Alpha Omega Alpha, Phi Beta Kappa. Office: Carole & Ray Neag Comprehensive Cancer Ctr U Conn Health Ctr 263 Farmington Ave Farmington CT 06030-2875 Office Phone: 860-679-2809, 860-679-2100, 800-579-7822. Office Fax: 860-679-4815. Business E-Mail: crunowicz@uchc.edu. *

RUNQUIST, LISA A., lawyer; b. Mpls., Sept. 22, 1952; d. Ralf E. and Violet R. BA, Hamline U., 1973; JD, U. Minn., 1976. Bar: Minn. 1977, Calif. 1978, U.S. Dist. Ct. (ctrl. dist.) Calif. 1985, U.S. Supreme Ct. 1995. Assoc. Caldwell & Toms, LA, 1978-82; ptnr. Runquist & Flagg, LA, 1982-85; pvt. practice Runquist & Assocs., LA, 1985-99, 2005—, Runquist & Zybach LLP, LA, 1999—2005. Mem. adv. bd. Exempt Orgn. Tax Rev., 1990—, Calif. State U. L.A. Continuing Edn. Acctg. and Tax Program, 1995—. Mem. editl. bd.: ABA Bus. Law Today, 1994—2002; author: The ABCs of Nonprofits, 2005; contbr. chapters to books. Recipient Outstanding Lawyer award, ABA Bus. Law Sect., 1999. Mem. ABA (bus. law sect. counsel 1995-99, com. on nonprofit corps. 1986—, chair 1991-95, subcom. current devels. in nonprofit corp. law 1989—, chair 1989-91, subcom. rels. orgns. 1989—, chair 1987-91, 95-98, subcom. legal guidebook for dirs. 1986—, partnerships and unincorp. bus. orgns. com. 1987—, state rep. sect., ad hoc com. on info-tech., corp. laws com., liason ALI/ABA, state regulation of securities com. 1988-99, ad hoc com. info. tech. 1997-2003, chmn., 1997-98, co-chmn. 1998-2002, sect. liaison to tech. coun. 1997-2000, sec. of taxation exempt orgns. com. 1987—, subcom. religious orgns. 1989—, chair 1995-97, 2005—, subcom. model nonprofit corp. act, co-chmn. subcom. non-exempt orgns. 1997-2003, co-chair state and local regulation subcom. 2003-05, corp. laws com. 1999-2005, subcom. guidebook for dirs. of closely held corps. chair 2000-04, liaison ALI/ABA principles of law of nonprofit orgns. project 2003—, standing com. solo and small firm practitioners 2004-05, ABA liason to NCCUSL project to create legal framework for Unicorp. NP Assn. in N. Am., 2005-), Calif. Bar Assn. (bus. law sect., nonprofit and unincorp. orgns. com. 1985-92, 93-96, 97—, chair 1989-91, 2006—), Christian Legal Soc., Ctr. Law and Religious Freedom, Christian Mgmt. Assn. (dir. 1983-89). Office: 17554 Community St Northridge CA 91325 Office Phone: 818-760-8986. Business E-Mail: lisa@runquist.com.

RUNTE, ROSEANN, academic administrator; b. Kingston, NY, Jan. 31, 1948; arrived in Can., 1971, naturalized, 1983; d. Robert B. and Anna Loretta O'Reilly; BA summa cum laude, SUNY, New Paltz, 1968; MA, U. Kans., Lawrence, 1969, PhD, 1974; DLitt (hon.), Acadia U., Wolfville, NS, Can., 1989, Meml. U., St. John's Newfoundland, 1990, U. Vest Timisoara, 1996, U. Arad, 2001; Assoc. (hon.), Moraine Valley C.C., 2003. Lectr. Bethany Coll., W.Va., 1970—71, St. Mary's U., Halifax, N.S., Canada, 1971—72, Dalhousie U., Halifax, 1972—83, asst. dean, 1980—82, chmn. dept. French, 1980—83; pres. U. Sainte-Anne, Pointe-de-l'Eglise, N.S., Canada, 1983—88; prin. Glendon Coll., Toronto, Canada, 1988—94; pres. Victoria U., 1994—2001, Old Dominion U., 2001—. Bd. dirs. Banque Nat., Va. Advanced Carrier and Shipbldg. Integration Ctr., Va. Nat. Def. Indsl. Authority; mem. hon. bd. Chesapeake Arts Coun., Va. Symphony; adv. bd. Sungard Sgt.; chair edn. com. Army ROTC. Author: Brumes Bleues, 1982, Faux-Soleils, 1984, Birmanie Blues, 1993; editor: Studies in 18th Century Culture, vols. VII, VIII, IX, 1977—79, A Canadian in Love, 2000, The Passionate Mind, 2000; lit. rev. editor: French Rev., 1988—94; editor: Lit. Rsch., 1994—97; co-editor: Man and Nature, 1982, Le Development Regional, 1986—87, From Orality to Literature, 1991, Lectures Canadiennes, 1993, Visions of Beauty, 1995, The Foundation for International Training: 25 Years of International Development, 2001; co-translator: Local Development, 1987; mem. editl. bd. Purdue Romance Lang. Series, 2001—. Can. commn. UNESCO, 1991—92, pres., 1992—96; vice-chair exec. bd. Found. for Internat. Tng., 1994—95, chair bd., 1995—2000; internat. adv. bd. Expo 2000, 1995—2000; v.p. Assn. Internat. des études québecoises, 1999—2001; mem. Internat. Women's Forum, 1998—; chair comm. internat. edn. Am. Coun. on Edn., 2004—06; chair accreditation com. visit NCAA, 2004, 2005, 2006; commr. Southeastern Accreditation Commn., 2004—06; chair Gottschalk Prize Com., 1994; chair publs. com. Hannah Found., 1989—92; vice-chair bd. Gardiner Mus., 1994—2001; mem. Commn. Langs. Instrn., Ontario, Canada, 1999—2001; chair prix du salon Livre Com., 1998; hon. life mem. UNESCO, 2003; adv. coun. Assn. Governing Bds.; bd. dirs. Assn. Med. Svcs., 1989—92; adv. bd. Nat. Libr., 1984—91; bd. dirs. Urban League, United Way, Va. Stage Co., Second Wind Dance Co., Hampton Roads Partnership, Greater Norfolk Corp. Decorated Order of Can., Ordre du Mérite France, Order Acad. Palmes; named Sportsperson of Yr., Norfolk Sports Club, 2007; recipient Fr. Coppée award, French Acad., 1989, Queen Elizabeth Jubilee medal, 2002, Woman of Distinction award, Zonta Group, 2004, Environ. award, Norfolk Environment Commn., 2004, WFXN Trailblazer award, 2004, Lighthouse award, Elizabeth River Project, Women of Distinction award, YWCA, 2006, Humanitarian award, NCCJ, 2006, Billbro award Servant Leadership, 2006, Toast of Town award, Alpha Kappa Alpha, 2007; Regents scholar, SUNY, 1965, Title IV grantee, NDEA, 1968. Fellow: Royal Soc. Can., Soc. Study Values in Edn., World Acad. Arts and Scis.; mem.: Royal Coll. Physicians and Surgeons (exec. com. 1998—2002), Soc. for Study Higher Edn. (bd. dirs. 1988—90), Can. Soc. 18th Century Studies (pres. 1975—76), Atlantic Soc. 18th Century Studies (pres. 1972—76), Can. Fedn. Humanities (pres. 1982—84), Internat. Assn. of Comparative Lit. (treas. 1985—91, sec. 1991—94), Internat. Soc. 18th Century Studies (assoc. treas. 1983—87), World Parliament of Cultures, Club of Rome (exec. com. 1999—2006), Knights of Malta (grande dame 1991—), Phi Delta Kappa, Delta Kappa Gamma. Home: 5000 Edgewater Dr Norfolk VA 23508 Office: Old Dominion U Norfolk VA 23529 Office Phone: 757-683-3159. Business E-Mail: rrunte@odu.edu.

RUNYON, BRETT L., lawyer; b. Fresno, Calif., Oct. 20, 1959; AA, Fresno City Coll., 1981; BS, Calif. State U., Fresno, 1982; JD, San Joaquin Coll. Law, 1986; MS, Syracuse U. Bar: Calif. 1988, D.C., U.S. Dist. Ct. (ea. dist.), U.S. Ct. Appeals (Fed. cir.) 1998. Arbitrator Fresno County Superior Ct., Fresno County Farm Bur. Mem. ABA, ATLA, Fed. Bar Assn., No. Calif. Assn. Def. Counsel, Fresno County Bar Assn., Delta Theta Phi (meritorious svc. award 1986). Office: Marderosian Runyon Cercone & Lehman 1260 Fulton Mall Fresno CA 93721-1916

RUNYON, KEITH LESLIE, lawyer, editor; b. Louisville, Oct. 3, 1950; s. Leslie Thomas and Marjorie Fillmore (Fisher) R.; M. Amelia Payne Sweets, Dec. 29, 1979; children; Amelia Brown Payne, Keith Leslie Jr. Student, U. London, 1971; BA summa cum laude, U. Louisville, 1972, JD, 1982. Staff writer Courier-Jour., Louisville, 1972-77, staff atty., 1984-86; staff atty., assoc. editor Louisville Times and Courier Jour., 1977-86, forum editor, 1986-90; editl. page editor, 1990-92; editor opinion pages, 1992-96; opinion editor, 1996—. Moderator Ky. Author Forum, 1996-. Editor: The Forum and Book Editor, 2001—. Nat. bd. dirs. English-Speaking Union U.S., N.Y., 1976-79, pres. Ky. br., Louisville, 1986-87; pres., dir. U. Louisville Alumni Assn., 1987-93; mem. exec. com. Louisville com. on fgn. rels., 1985-87, Leadership Louisville, 1990-91; clk. Session Calvin Presbyn. Ch., Louisville, 1986-88; mem. St. Francis in the Fields Episcopal Ch., Harrods Creek, Ky.; bd. dirs. Walden Theatre, Louisville, 1999-2001; mem. alumni bd. U. Louisville Brandeis Sch. of Law, 2001—. Recipient William E. Leidt award The Episc. Ch. of U.S., 1975, Roy Howard award (shared) Scripps Howard Journalists Nat. for Pub. Svc., 1976; named Alumnus of Yr., U. Louisville, 1991, disting. alumnus U. Louisville Sch. Law, 1996; Ctr. Fgn. Journalists fellow, 1993, Bingham fellow, 1995-96. Mem. ABA, Ky. Bar Assn., Louisville Bar Assn., Nat. Conf. Edit. Writers (editor The Masthead, 1994-96), Soc. Profl. Jours. (Outstanding Editl. Writing award, 1983, 84, 85, Outstanding Criticism award 1997, 98). Home: Nitta Yuma Harrods Creek KY 40027 Office: Courier-Jour and Louisville Times Co 525 W Broadway Louisville KY 40202-2206 Home Phone: 502-228-5373. Business E-Mail: krunyon@courier-journal.com.

RUO, BERNICE, physician, researcher; d. Hank Hang-Ching Ruo. AB, Harvard/Radcliffe Coll., 1994; MD, Yale U., New Haven, Conn., 1998; MA, U. Calif., San Francisco, 2004. Diplomate Am. Bd. Internal Medicine, 2001. Clin. instr. medicine U. Calif., San Francisco, 2003—04; asst. prof. medicine Northwestern U., Chgo., 2004—. Grantee, Am. Heart Assn., 2006—07, NIH, 2007—. Mem.: ACP, Soc. Gen. Internal Medicine. Office: Northwestern Med Faculty Found 675 N St Clair St 18th Fl Chicago IL 60611 Home Phone: 312-751-9331; Office Phone: 312-695-8630.

RUOFF, A. LAVONNE BROWN, language educator; b. Charleston, Ill., Apr. 10, 1930; d. Oscar and Laura Alice (Witters) Brown; m. Milford Anthony Prasher, Aug. 19, 1950 (div. 1964); m. Gene W. Ruoff, June 10, 1967; children: Stephen Charles, Sharon Louise(dec.). Student, U. Ill., Chgo., 1948—50; BS in Edn., Northwestern U., Evanston, Ill., 1953, MA in English, 1954, PhD in English, 1966. Instr. to asst. prof. Roosevelt U., Chgo., 1961—66; asst. prof. English U. Ill., Chgo., 1966—69, assoc. prof., 1969—81, prof., 1981—94, prof. emerita, 1994. Interim dir. D'Arcy McNickle Ctr. for Am. Indian History, Newberry Libr., 1999-2000; editor Am. Indian Lives series U. Nebr. Press, Lincoln, 1985—; mem. Am. lit. com. Internat. Exch. of Scholars, Washington, 1987-90, chair, 1989-90; NEH dir. Summer Seminars for Coll. Tchr. on Am. Indian Lit., 1979, 83, 89, 94. Author: American Indian Lit., 1990; Lit. of the Am. Indian, 1990; editor: The Moccasin Maker, 1987, 2d edit., 1998; Wynema, 1997; From the Deep Woods to Civilization and Indian Boyhood, 2001; (with Jerry W. Ward, Jr.) Redefining Am. Lit. History, 1990; (with Donald Smith) Life, Letters and Speeches of George Copway, 1997. Bd. dir. Am. Indian Coun. Fire Chgo., 1980-88. Recipient Lifetime Achievement award Before

Columbus Found., 1998, Lit., MLA and Assn. for Study of Am. Indian Lits. award for Outstanding Contbn., 1993; MELUS award for Outstanding Contbn. to Multiethnic Lit., 1986; named Writer of Yr. for Annotation/Bibliography, Wordcraft Circle of Native Writers and Storytellers, 1999; Writer of Yr. for Series Editing Am. Indian Lives; Svc. award Wordcraft Cir. of Native Writers, 2003; NEH fellow, 1992-93, U. Ill. Chgo. Inst. for Humanities fellow, 1990-91; NEH Rsch. Divsn. grantee, 1981. Mem.: MLA (chair discussion group Am. Indian lit. 1990, co-chair lit. of people of color com. 2000—01, exec. coun. 2002—05, del. assembly organizing com. 2004—05, radio com. 2006—, chmn. radio com. 2007—, award for lifetime scholarly achievement 2002), Multi Ethnic Studies Europe and the Ams., Assn. for Study of Am. Indian Lits., Multi-Ethnic Lit. in the U.S., Am. Studies Assn. Personal E-mail: lruoff@uic.edu.

RUPERT, DONALD WILLIAM, lawyer; b. Clearfield, Pa., Oct. 15, 1946; s. Donald Lee and Dorothy Mae (Bonsall) R.; m. Patricia A. Rupert, June 21, 1969. BS in Chemistry, Miami U., Ohio, 1968; JD, Washburn U., Topeka, 1976. Bar: Tex. 1976, Ill. 1978, US Ct. Appeals (Fed. cir.) 1978, US Dist. Ct. (so. dist.) Tex. 1977, US Ct. Appeals (7th cir.) 1981, US Dist. Ct. (no. dist.) Ill. 1979, US Supreme Ct., 1992. Assoc. Arnold, White & Durkee, Houston, 1976-78, Kirkland & Ellis, Chgo., 1978-83, ptnr., 1983-86, Neuman, Williams, Anderson & Olson, Chgo., 1986-90, Mayer, Brown, Rowe & Maw, LLP, Chgo., 1996—2007, Marshall, Gerstein and Borun LLP, Chgo., 2007-; founding ptnr. Roper & Quigg, 1990-93; ptnr. Keck, Mahin & Cate, Chgo., 1993-96; ptnr. cons. USAF, Dayton, Ohio, 1974-81. Contbr. articles to profl. jours. Served to capt. USAF, 1968-74. Miami U. Undergrad. Rsch. fellow, 1967, Grad. Rsch. fellow, 1968. Mem. ABA, Am. Intellectual Property Law Assn., Tex. Bar Assn., Phi Kappa Phi. Democrat. Presbyterian. Home: 2310 Marcy Ave Evanston IL 60201 Office: Marshall, Gerstein & Borun LLP 233 S Wacker 6300 Sears Tower Chicago IL 60606

RUPERT, ELIZABETH ANASTASIA, retired dean; b. Emlenton, Pa., July 12, 1918; d. John Hamilton and Eva Blanche (Elliott) R. Diploma, Altoona Sch. Commerce, 1936; BS in Edn., Clarion State Coll., 1959; MSLS, Syracuse U., 1962; PhD, U. Pitts., 1970. Sec. Sterling Oil divsn. Quaker State Oil Refining Corp., 1939-56; tchr., libr. Oil City Area Schs., 1959-61; libr. Venango campus Clarion (Pa.) U., 1961-62, prof. Sch. Libr. Sci., 1962-70, dean Sch. Libr. Sci., Coll. Libr. Sci., 1971-85; prof. emeritus, 1994. Interim pres. Clarion U., spring, 1977; acct. William Rupert Mortuary, Inc., 1948—88. Author: Pennsylvania Practicum Program for School Librarians: An Appraisal, 1970; mem. ad hoc edit. com. Pa. Media Guidelines, Pa. Dept. Edn., 1976, author (with others) Encyclopedia of Library and Information Science, 1984. Bd. dirs. Knox Pub. Libr., 1991-97; mem. Abscurf; mem. numerous bds. and couns. Church of God. Recipient Disting. Faculty award, Clarion U. Alumni Assn., 1976, Disting. Svc. award, 1986, Disting. Alumni award, 1987, Leadership citation, Coun. of Deans Clarion U., 1985, Zonta Internat. Women of Achievement award, 1987. Mem.: Pi Gamma Mu, Beta Phi Mu. Republican. Home: PO Box H Knox PA 16232-0608

RUPERT, HOOVER (LYNN HOOVER RUPERT), minister, writer; b. Madison, NJ, Nov. 3, 1917; s. Lynn Hoover and Hazel L. (Linabary) R.; m. Hazel Pearl Senti, June 22, 1941 (dec. Jan. 2007); children: Susan Newbry, Elizabeth Wright. AB, Baker U., 1938; A.M., Boston U., 1940, M.Div. cum laude, 1941; student (summers), Garrett Bibl. Inst. and Northwestern U., 1942, Union Theol. Sem., 1943; D.D., Adrian Coll., 1952, Baker U., 1966; L.H.D., Milliken U., 1974. Ordained to ministry Methodist Ch., 1940; asst. pastor First Meth. Ch., Baldwin, Kans., 1936-38, St. Mark's Meth. Ch., Brookline, Mass., 1938-41; pastor Thayer-St. Paul, Kans., 1941-43, First Ch., Olathe, Kans., 1943-45; dir. youth dept. Gen. Bd. Edn. Meth. Ch., Nashville, 1945-50; pastor 1st Meth. Ch., Jackson, Mich., 1950-59, 1st United Meth. Ch., Ann Arbor, Mich., 1959-72, Kalamazoo, 1972-83; faculty dept. religion Fla. So. Coll., Lakeland, 1983-89; adj. faculty Wesley Theol. Sem., Washington, 1989-93. Dean Mich. Meth. Pastors Sch., 1959-65; mem. Jud. Coun. United Meth. Ch., 1968-88, sec., 1976-88, sec. emeritus, 1988; chaplain Epworth Summer Assembly, Ludington, Mich., 1984-98; Bible lectr. Asbury Meth. Village, 1990-2004. Author: Prayer Poems on the Prayer Perfect, 1943, Christ Above All (editor), 1948, Youth and Evangelism, 1948, Youth and Stewardship, rev. edit., 1960, Your Life Counts (editor), 1950, What Methodists Believe, rev. edit., 1959, John Wesley and People Called Methodists, 1953, I Belong, 1954, And Jesus Said, 1960, Enjoy Your Teen-Ager, 1962, A Sense of What is Vital, 1964, The Church in Renewal, 1965, Divine Demands: God's Commandments, 1966, My People are Your People, 1968, Where is thy Sting?, Christian Perspectives on Death, 1969, What's Good About God?, 1975 God Will See You Through, 1976, An Instrument of Thy Peace, 1982, The High Cost of Being Human, 1986, Why Didn't Noah Swat Both Mosquitoes, 1993; writer, syndicated weekly mag. column Accent on Living; newspaper feature Talking to Teens; other publs., periodicals, and newspapers. Trustee Bronson Hosp., 1972-88, Adrian Coll., 1952-67, Asbury Meth. Village, 1996-2000; pres., bd. dirs. Youth for Understanding, 1970-83, Ann Arbor United Fund, YMCA-YWCA. Recipient Distinguished Alumnus award Boston U., 1969; Lucinda Bidwell Beebe fellow Boston U., 1941 Mem. World Meth. Council, Nat. Council Chs., Mark Twain Soc., Nat. Forensic League, Pi Kappa Delta, Alpha Psi Omega. Lodges: Mason, Rotary (Paul Harris fellow 1983), Chi Rho. Home: 403 Russell Ave Gaithersburg MD 20877-2811

RUPLEY, JERRY T., lawyer; b. Lima, Ohio, Dec. 20, 1948; BA polit. Sci. and Econs. with high honors, Mich. State U., 1971; JD cum laude, Harvard U., 1974. Bar: Mich. 1974. Assoc. Miller, Canfield, Paddock & Stone, Detroit, 1974—80, prin., 1981—. Contbr. articles to profl. journs. V.p. Advs. Quality edn., past chair adminstrv. bd. First United Meth. Ch. Northville, trustee and treas. bd edn. Northville Pub. Schs., 1999-2003. Recipient Best Lawyers in Am., Pub. Fin. Law Sect., 2005—07, Mich. Super Lawyers, Bonds/Govt. Fin. Sect., 2006. Mem. ABA, Mich. Bar Assn., Detroit Met. Bar Assn., Phi Beta Kappa, Phi Kappa Phi, Nat. Assn. Bond Lawyers, Nat. Assn. Coll. and U. Attys., Am. Coll. Bond Counsel. Office: Miller Canfield Paddock & Stone 150 W Jefferson Ave Ste 2500 Detroit MI 48226-4416 Office Phone: 313-963-6420, 313-496-7521. Office Fax: 313-496-8451. Business E-Mail: rupley@millercanfield.com.

RUPP, GEORGE ERIK, international relief organization executive; b. Summit, NJ, Sept. 22, 1942; s. Gustav Wilhelm and Erika (Braunoehler) R.; m. Nancy Katherine Farrar, Aug. 22, 1964; children: Katherine Heather, Stephanie Karin. Student, Ludwig Maximilians U., Munich, Germany, 1962-63; AB, Princeton U., 1964; BD, Yale U., 1967; post grad., U. Sri Lanka, Peradeniya, 1969-70; PhD, Harvard U., 1972. Ordained to ministry Presbyn. Ch. USA, 1971; faculty fellow in religion, vice chancellor Johnston Coll., U. Redlands, Redlands, Calif., 1971-74; asst. prof. Harvard Div. Sch., Harvard U., Cambridge, Mass., 1974-76, assoc. prof., 1976-77, prof., dean, 1979-85; prof., dean acad. affairs U. Wis., Green Bay, 1977-79; prof., pres. Rice U., Houston, 1985-93, Columbia U., NYC, 1993—2002; pres. Internat. Rescue Com., NY, 2002—. Bd. dir. Com. for Econ. Devel., Inst. Internat. Edn., InterAction. Author: Christologies and Cultures: Toward a Typology of Religious Worldviews, 1974, Culture Protestantism: German Liberal Theology at the Turn of the Twentieth Century, 1977, Beyond Existentialism and Zen: Religion in a Pluralistic World, 1979, Commitment and Community, 1989, Globalization Challenged: Conviction, Conflict, and Community, 2006; contbr. articles to profl. jour. Recipient Alexander Hamilton medal, Columbia U., 2002, Centennial medal for contbn. to soc., Harvard U. Grad. Sch. Arts and Scis., 2004, Gold medal, Nat. Inst. Social Scis., 2005, Woodrow Wilson award, Princeton U., 2006; Danforth Grad. fellow, 1964—71. Mem.: AAAS, Soc. Values in Higher Edn., Coun. Fgn. Rels., Am. Acad. Religion. Office: International Rescue Committee 122 East 42nd Street New York NY 10168 *

RUPP, JOSEPH D., metal products executive; BS Metallurgical Engineering, U. MO. With Olin Corp., 1972—, v.p., manufacturing and engineering, 1985—96; pres. Olin Brass, Olin Corp., 1996—2001; v.p. Olin Corp., 1996—2001, exec. v.p., operations, 2001—02, pres. CEO, 2002—, chmn., 2005—. Office: c/o Olin 190 Carondelet Plaza Clayton MO 63105 *

RUPP, KALMAN, economist; b. Budapest, Hungary, Apr. 7, 1948; s. Kalman and Ethel Rethy Rupp; m. Kathryn Schiavone Nelson, Oct. 22, 2004; children: Kristen Schiavone, Erin Schiavone; m. Agnes Romhanyi (div.); children: Susan, Judith. PhD, U. Econs., Budapest, Hungary, 1971, Columbia U., NYC, 1982. Rsch. analyst Ctrl. Statis. Bur., Budapest, Hungary, 1971—72; rsch. fellow Inst. Econs. Hungarian Acad. Scis., Budapest, 1972—75; postdoctoral fellow Albert Einstein Coll. of Medicine, NYC, 1978—79; sr. economist Westat, Rockville, Md., 1980—88, U.S. GAO, Washington, 1988—90, U.S. DHHS, Washington, 1990—95, U.S. Social Security Adminstrn., Washington, 1995—. Rsch. cons. European Ctr. Social Welfare Tng. and Rsch., Vienna, 1975—76; lectr. Columbia U., NYC, 1979, rsch. analyst, 1979—80. Author: Entrepreneurs in Red: Structure and Organizational Innovation in the Centrally Planned Economy, 1983, The Youth Labor Force, 1945-1995: A Cross-National Analysis, 1981 (named Disting. Book in Labor Econs., Princeton U., 1982); author and editor: Paying for Results in Vocational Rehabilitation: Will Provider Incentives Work for Ticket to Work?, 2003, Growth in Disability Benefits: Explanations and Policy Implications, 1998; contbr. articles to profl. jours. Recipient Commissioner's citation, Commr. Social Security, 1998, 2001, Excellence in Fed. Career award, Fed. Exec. Bd., 2001; fellow, NIMH, 1978; grantee, Ford Found., 1976. Mem.: Am. Econ. Assn., Soc. Govt. Economists (bd. mem. 1990—91), Nat. Acad. Social Ins. Achievements include design of first large-scale randomized social experiment to study effects of vocational rehabilitation on social security disability insurance beneficiaries; research in the economics of the Social Security Administration's disability programs; design of the methodology of randomized social experiments; one of the first to use administrative record data for policy evaluations. Office: Social Security Administration 500 E Street SW Suite 930 Washington DC 20254 Home Phone: 301-519-1453; Office Phone: 202-358-6216. Business E-Mail: kalman.rupp@ssa.gov.

RUPP, RALPH RUSSELL, retired audiologist, educator, author; b. Saginaw, Mich., Apr. 12, 1929; s. Martin Carl and Veronica Marie (Riethmeier) R. BA, U. Mich., 1951, MA, 1952; PhD, Wayne State U., 1964. Speech and hearing cons. Detroit Pub. Schs., 1955-60; exec. dir. Detroit Hearing and Speech Center, 1960-62; assoc. in audiology Henry Ford Hosp., Detroit, 1962-65; prof. audiology U. Mich., Ann Arbor, 1965-89; coord. audiology Eastern Mich. U., 1985-93, cons. in audiology, 1994—, U. Mich., 1994—2006, ret., 2006. Cons. St. Joseph Mercy Hosp., Ann Arbor, Ann Arbor VA Hosp., Mott Children's Health Ctr., Flint, Mich., Pontiac (Mich.) Gen. Hosp., U. Mich. Health Svcs.; pres. Detroit Hearing Ctr., 1966. Author: (with James Maurer) Hearing and Aging: Tactics for Intervention, 1979, (with Kenneth Stockdell) Speech Protocols in Audiology, 1980; contbr. articles to profl. jours. Served with Med. Service Corps, U.S. Army, 1953-55. Named Disting. Alumnus, Saginaw HS, 1981, Outstanding Grad., Wayne State U. Fellow Am. Speech, Lang. and Hearing Assn. (Editor's award); mem. Acad. Rehab. Audiology (past editor Jour.), Mich. Speech and Hearing Assn. (pres. 1954, Disting. Service award, past editor Jour, honor award). Home: 3163 Plymouth Rd Ann Arbor MI 48105-3203

RUPP, SHERON ADELINE, photographer, educator; b. Mansfield, Ohio, Jan. 14, 1943; d. Warren Edmund Rupp and Frances (Hanson) Christian. BA in Sociology and Psychology, Denison U., Granville, Ohio, 1965; MFA in Photography, U. Mass., Amherst, 1982. Teaching asst. in photography Hampshire Coll., Amherst, Mass., 1981; instr. photography Northfield Mt. Hermon Sch., Mass., 1982-83, U. Mass., Amherst, 1984, Holyoke C.C., Mass., 1986, 87-88; vis. asst. prof. photography Hampshire Coll., 1985, 87; vis. lectr. photography Amherst Coll., Mass., 1994. Guest artist, lectr. Boston Mus. Sch., Portland Sch. Art, Maine, NYU, U. Mass., Hartford Sch. Art/U. Hartford-Conn., Springfield Mus. Fine Arts, Mass., Bard Coll, NY, Mass. Coll. Art, Boston, others; guest lectr. Carpenter Ctr., Harvard U., Cambridge, Mass., 2000. One-woman shows include Tisch Sch. Arts NYU, 1987, Portland Sch. Art, 1989, O.K. Harris Gallery, NYC, 1992, Cleve. Mus. Art, 2000; two-person shows include Columbus Mus. Art, Ohio, 1997—98; Springfield Tech. C.C., Mass., 1997, exhibited in group shows at Mus. Modern Art, NYC, 1991, 1999—, Springfield Mus. Fine Art, 1993, U. Mass., Amherst, 1993, Dirs. Guild, LA, 1994, Manchester Inst. Arts and Scis., NH, 1995, Weber State U., Utah, 1995, Photog. Resource Ctr. 3d Biennial, Boston, 1995, DeCordova Mus., Lincoln, 2000—, Smithsonian Arts and Scis., Washington, 2001, Denison U. Art Gallery, Granville, Ohio, 2002, Around the House, A.N. Bush Gallery, Salem, Oreg., 2002, Boston Mus. Fine Arts, 2002—03, Guild Hall, East Hampton, N.Y., 2003, Smith Coll. Mus. Art, Northampton, Mass., 2004; photographer (group shows) Berman Collection, Getty Mus., LA, 2006—07; Represented in permanent collections De Cordova Mus., Mus. Modern Art, NYC, Fogg Art Mus. at Harvard U., Hallmark Collection of Photography, Kansas City, Columbus Mus. Art, The J. Paul Getty Mus., L.A., Mus. Fine Arts, Boston, Rose Art Mus. Brandeis U., Mead Art Mus. Amherst Coll., Smith Coll. Mus. Art, Danforth Mus. Art, Springfield Tech. C.C. Found., Carpenter Ctr. for Visual Arts Harvard U., The Smithsonian, Corcoran Galley of Art, Washington; photographs (including cover photo) in Double-Take Mag., winter 1998; publ. and exhibit, Where We Live: Photographs of America from the Berman Collection, 2006. Recipient Mass. Fellowship award in photography Artist Found., 1984, 87; visual artist fellow Nat. Endowment for the Arts, 1986, 94, Guggenheim fellow, 1990. Avocations: bicycling, writing. Home and Office: 3 The Lope Haydenville MA 01039 Office Phone: 413-268-9035. E-mail: sheron@crocker.com.

RUPPE, ARTHUR MAXWELL, retired lawyer; b. Boone, NC, Dec. 15, 1928; s. Arthur Monroe and Floye (Robinson) Ruppe; m. Ruth Marie Ledford; children: Ruth Carol, Sharon Marie, Arthur Maxwell, Jr., Susan Lunette. AA, Gardner Webb Coll., 1947; AB, U. N.C. Law Sch., 1950, LLB, JD, 1952. Bar: N.C. 1952, U.S. Dist. Ct. (ea. dist. N.C.) 1955, U.S. Ct. Mil. Appeals 1968, cert.: (mediator). Asst. staff, judge adv. U.S. Army, Ft. Bragg, NC, 1952—55; pvt. practice Fayetteville, NC, 1955—98; mediator, 1997—2003; ret., 2003. Served to 1st lt. US Army, 1952—55. Mem.: ABA, Cumberland County Bar Assn. (pres. 1982—83), 12th Jud. Dist. Bar Assn., N.C. Bar Assn. (patron), K.P. Democrat. Baptist. Avocations: travel, reading, investing. Home: 336 Summertime Rd Fayetteville NC 28303-4658

RUPPEL, EDWARD THOMPSON, geologist; b. Fort Morgan, Colo., Oct. 26, 1925; s. Henry George and Gladys Myrtle (Thompson) R.; m. Phyllis Beale Tanner; children: Lisa, David, Douglas, Kristin. BA in Geology, U. Mont., 1948, Doctorate (hon.), 1996; MA in Geology, U. Wyo., 1950; PhD in Geology, Yale U., 1958. Geologist U.S. Geol. Survey, Denver, 1950-68, rsch. geologist, 1968-86; dir., state geologist Mont. Bur. Mines and Geology, Butte, 1986-94; consulting geologist Twin Bridges, Mont., 1994—. Author and co-author of approximately forty-five maps and reports; contbr. articles to profl. jours. Dir., v.p. Virginia City (Mont.) Preservation Alliance, 1997-98. Lt. (j.g.) USNR, 1943-50. Fellow Geol. Soc. Am. (sr.), Soc. Econ. Geologists; mem. Am. Inst. Profl. Geologists (cert. profl. geologist), Mont. Geol. Soc., Geol. Soc. Washington, Tobacco Root Geol. Soc. (Excellence in Field Work award 1993). Home and Office: 326 S Main St PO Box K Twin Bridges MT 59754-0402

RUPPENTHAL, KARL M., author, educator; b. Russell, Kans., Oct. 5, 1917; s. John P. and Viola (Whitaker) Ruppenthal; m. Irja Alice Autio, May 30, 1942 (dec. Mar. 1999); children: Sara, Stephen, Brian; m. Josephine Maxon, Nov. 18, 2000. AB, U. Kans., 1939, LL.B., 1941, JD, 1968; MBA, U. Calif.-Berkeley, 1950; PhD, Stanford U., 1959. Bar: D.C., Kans., U.S. Tax Ct., U.S. Ct. Appeals (9th cir.), U.S. Supreme Ct. Reporter Russell County News, 1934-35; owner bookstore and restaurant, 1940-41; pilot TWA, 1942-68; UPS Found. prof., dir. Centre Transp. Studies U. B.C., Vancouver, 1971-84. Mem. TWA/ALPA System Bd. Adjustment, 1947-49; exec. v.p. Airline Pilots Assn., 1950; prof., dir. transp. mgmt. program Stanford, 1958-69, dir. European logistics mgmt. program, summers, 1969-71; Ryder prof. transp. U. Miami (Fla.), 1970; founder, editor Farwest Press Ltd.; dir. Aero Air, Inc., Hazleton Labs., Hazleton Nuclear Sci., Karloid Corp.; cons. Can. Ministry Transport, Am. Airlines, Alltalia, C.P. Air, Saudi Arabian Airlines, VASP, TWA, Air Transport Assn., Ethiopian Air Lines, Pacific Western Airlines, NASA, Boeing Co., World Bank, Govts. of Alta. and B.C. Author: Regulation, Competition and the Public Interest, Case Problems in Air Transportation, Canada's Ports and Waterborne Trade; founder, editor: Logistics and Transp. Rev.; cons. editor New Can. Ency.; contbg. editor The Nation, Ency of Mgmt. Pres. Palo Alto Friends of Library, 1952-58; mem. Palo Alto City Council, Calif., 1953-59, Unitarian-Universalist Ch. of Berkeley; pres. Karl and Alice Ruppenthal Found. Arts. Stanford Sloan fellow; recipient Nathan Burkham award in copywright law; Wilton Park fellow. Fellow Chartered Inst. Transport; mem. NAS (com. mem.), Acad. Logistics (founding), Am. Econ. Assn., Indsl. Relations Research Assn., Transp. Research Forum, Canadian Transp. Research Forum, Am. Judicature Soc., Am. Arbitration Assn. (nat. panel), Peninsula Funeral Soc. (founding bd. dirs.), Univ. Club, Masons, Phi Beta Kappa, Sigma Phi Epsilon, Beta Gamma Sigma. Home: 820 Euclid Ave Berkeley CA 94708

RUPPERSBERGER, CHARLES ALBERT, III, (DUTCH), congressman; b. Balt., Jan. 31, 1946; s. Charles Albert Jr. and Margaret (Wilson) R.; m. Kay Murphy, Dec. 28, 1968; children: Charles Albert, Jill Ann. BA, U. Md., 1967; JD, U. Balt., 1970. Bar: Md. 1972, US Supreme Ct. 1977. Social worker Balt. City Schs., 1967-69; claims adjuster US Fidelity and Guaranty Co., Balt., 1969-70; law clk. to presiding justice Balt. County Cir. Ct., Towson, 1970-72; asst. state's atty. Balt. County State's Atty., Towson, 1972-80; ptnr. Ruppersberger, Winter, Clark & Mister, Timonium, Md., 1980—94; mem. US Congress from 2nd Md. dist., 2003—. Chief of investigation div. State's Atty.'s Office, Towson, 1972-80; liaison Balt. County Police Dept. and Md. State Police, 1973-80. Coach, v.p. Cockeysville (Md.) Recreation Council, 1978—; campaign mgr. for senator Francis X. Kelly, Annapolis, Md., 1980-85; councilman Balt. County Council, 1985-94; legal council Balt. County Athletic League; pres. Topfield condominium Assn., Cockeysville, 1975-78, Greater Timonium Community Council, 1980—, co-chmn. fundraising U. Hosp.; bd. dirs. Timonium (Md.) Meth. Ch., 1984—. Recipient Appreciation award Balt. County Order of Fraternal Police, 1977, Cert. of Appreciation Balt. County Police, 1979; named one of Outstanding Young Marylanders Jaycees, 1979. Mem. Md. Bar Assn. (grievance com.), Balt. County Bar Assn. (chmn. bench-bar com.), Nat. Coll. Dist. Attys. (advisor 1974-80), U. Md. Alumni Assn. (v.p.), US Lacrosse Team. Lodges: Masons. Democrat. Methodist. Office: US Ho Reps 1630 Longworth Ho Office Bldg Washington DC 20515-2002 *

RUSCH, DENISE MARIE, school system administrator; MA, Marian Coll., Fond du Lac, Wis., 1998. Cert. in ednl. leadership Cardinal Stritch U., 2003. Coord. dist. assessment Wausau Sch. Dist., Wyo., 2005—; dean student svcs. West H.S., Wausau, 2006—. Office: Wausau School Dist 415 Seymour St Wausau WI 54402 Office Phone: 715-261-0583.

RUSCH, GERALD ALLEN, financial representative; b. Milw., July 8, 1937; s. Herman A. and Martha H. (Gebauer) R.; m. Joan R. Ruehlman, Dec. 29, 1961; children: Susan, Heidi. BA, U. Wis., 1960. Area rep. Wis. Heart Assn., Milw., 1960-61, Tex. Heart Assn., Austin, 1961-63; comms. cons. Wis. Telephone, Milw., 1963-74; sole proprietor Rusch Ins., Eau Claire, Wis., 1974—; fin. rep., 1974—. Contbr. articles to mags. 1st lt. USAR, 1960-67. Named Agent of Yr. Eau Claire Gen. Agents and Mgrs. Assn., 1980. Mem. Nat. Assn. Fin. Profls., Million Dollar Roundtable, Phi Sigma Epsilon. Avocations: photography, walking, reading, classical music. Office: Northwestern Mut Fin Network 4233 Southtowne Dr Ste 1 Eau Claire WI 54701 Home (Winter): 14071 Brant Point Cir 621 Fort Myers FL 33919 Home (Summer): 4224 W Robin Meadows Ln Eau Claire WI 54701

RUSCH, JONATHAN JAY, lawyer; b. Nyack, NY, Oct. 16, 1952; s. Thaddeus David and Alice Marjorie Rusch; m. Doreen Evelyn Lacovara, Aug. 10, 1974; children: Rachel Madeline, Catherine Elizabeth. AB in Pub. Affairs with honors, Princeton U., 1974; MA, U. Va., 1978, JD, 1980. Bar: DC 1981, US Dist. Ct. DC 1981, US Ct. Appeals (DC cir.) 1981, US Ct. Appeals (7th cir.) 1985, US Ct. Appeals (9th cir.) 1990, US Ct. Appeals (5th cir.) 1992, US Supreme Ct. 1992. Assoc. Cleary, Gottlieb, Steen & Hamilton, Washington, 1980-83; spl. asst. to atty. gen. US Dept. Justice, Washington, 1983-84; counsel Pres. Commn. on Organized Crime, Washington, 1984-86; acting dir., then dir. office of fin. enforcement US Dept. Treasury, Washington, 1986-88; trial atty. fraud sect., criminal divsn. US Dept. Justice, Washington, 1988-93, asst. spl. counsel House banking facility, 1992, sr. litigation counsel fraud sect., criminal divsn., 1993—2005, spl. counsel for fraud prevention, criminal divsn., 1998—. Adj. prof. law ctr. Georgetown U., 1996—; lectr. law U. Va. Law Sch., 2007. Recipient Atty. Gen.'s Disting. Svc. award, 1995, Chief Postal Insp.'s award, 2004, Asst. Atty. Gen.'s award for inter-agy. cooperation, 2005, Atty. Gen.'s award for fraud prevention, 2006. Mem. ABA (mem. admin. law sect., sec. 2002-05), Tower Club. Home: 4600 Connecticut Ave NW Apt 207 Washington DC 20008-5702 Office: US Dept Justice Bond Bldg Rm 4300 10th and Constitution Ave NW Washington DC 20530 Home Phone: 202-362-5766; Office Phone: 202-514-0631. E-mail: Jonathan.Rusch2@usdoj.gov.

RUSCH, THOMAS WILLIAM, manufacturing executive; b. Alliance, Nebr., Oct. 3, 1946; s. Oscar William and Gwen Falerne (Middleswart) R.; m. Gloria Ann Sutton, June 20, 1968 (div. Oct. 1979); children: Alicia Catherine, Colin William; m. Lynn Biebighauser, Jan. 17, 1981. BEE, U. of Minn., 1968, MSEE, 1970, PhD, 1973; MS in Mgmt. of Tech., U. Minn., 1993. Sr. physicist cen. rsch. 3M Co., St. Paul, 1973-77, rsch. specialist cen. rsch., 1977-79; project scientist phys. electronics div. Perkin Elmer Corp., Eden Prairie, Minn., 1979-83, sr. project scientist phys. electronics div., 1983-85, lab mgr. phys. electronics div., 1985-87, product mgr. phys. electronics div., 1987-88, sr. product mgr. phys. electronics div., 1988-93; v.p. product devel. Chorus Corp., St. Paul, 1993-94; pres. Creekside Techs. Corp., Plymouth, Minn., 1994—; co-founder Xoft MicroTube, Inc., Plymouth, 1998, chief tech. officer Fremont, Calif., 2001—02; prin. engr. Xoft, Inc., 2002—. Editor: X-rays in Materials Analysis, 1986; co-author: Oscillatory Ion Yields, 1977; patentee in field. Recipient IR100 award for transfer vessel Rsch. and Devel. mag., 1981, IR100 award for energy analyser, 1985. Office: 49000 Milmont Dr Fremont CA 94538

RUSCH, VALERIE WILLIAMS, thoracic surgeon; b. NYC, Oct. 16, 1951; AB in Biochemistry, Vassar Coll., 1971; MD, Columbia U., 1975. Diplomate Nat. Bd. Med. Examiners, Am. Bd. Surgery, Am. Bd. Thoracic Surgery. Intern in gen. surgery U. Wash., Seattle, 1975-76, resident in gen. surgery, 1975-80, resident in cardiothoracic surgery, 1980-82; faculty assoc. dept. of thoracic surgery M.D. Anderson Cancer Ctr., Houston, 1982-83; thoracic surgeon Harborview Med. Ctr., Seattle, 1983-86, assoc. staff mem., 1986-89; thoracic surgeon Group Health Coop. of Puget Sound, Seattle, 1983-84; chief cardiothoracic surgery VA Hosp., Seattle, 1986-87; thoracic surgeon Univ. Hosp., Seattle, 1983-89; mem. courtesy med. staff Pacific Med. Ctr., Seattle, 1987-89; assoc. attending surgeon thoracic svc. Meml. Sloan-Kettering Cancer Ctr., NYC, 1989-94, attending surgeon, 1994—, chief thoracic surgery, 2000—. Asst. prof. div. cardiothoracic surgery U. Wash., 1983-88, assoc. prof., 1988-89; asst. mem. divsn. clin. rsch. Fred Hutchinson Cancer Rsch. Ctr., Seattle, 1985-89; assoc. mem. Meml. Hosp., Meml. Sloan-Kettering Cancer Ctr., N.Y.C., 1989-94, mem., 1994—; assoc. prof. surgery Cornell U. Med. Coll., N.Y.C., 1989-95, prof. surgery Cornell U. Med. Coll., 1995—; mem. cancer clin. investigations rev. com. Nat. Cancer Inst., 1991-98. Mem. editl. bd. Jour. Thoracic and Cardiovasc. Surgery, 1992-, Jour. Clin. Oncology, 2004-; contbr. articles to profl. publs.; author abstracts in field. Grantee NIH, 1985-89, Deknatel Corp., 1986-87, Bard Electro Med. Systems, 1989, NeoRx Corp., 1989-90, Pfizer Corp., 1995-98. Fellow ACS (mem. bd. govs. 2002-), Am. Coll. Chest Physicians; mem. Am. Assn. Thoracic Surgery (mem. coun. 2006-), Soc. Thoracic Surgeons, Assn. Acad. Surgery, Soc. Surg. Oncology (mem. com. tng. 1993-95, mem. edn. com. 1993-95), Am. Soc. Clin. Oncology, (mem. program com. 1993, 96, bd. dirs. 2002-05), Am. Thoracic Soc., NY Cancer Soc., Internat. Assn. Study of Lung Cancer, Am. Med. Women's Assn., Am. Bd. Thoracic Surgery (mem. bd. dirs. 2003-), Henry Harkins' Surg. Soc., M.D. Anderson Assocs., Gen. Thoracic Surg. Club, Alpha Omega Alpha. Office: Meml Sloan-Kettering Cancer Thoracic Surgery Svc 1275 York Ave New York NY 10021-6094 Office Phone: 212-639-8695. Business E-Mail: ruschv@mskcc.org.

RUSCH, WILLIAM GRAHAM, religious organization administrator; b. Buffalo, Dec. 23, 1937; s. William Godfrey and Hope (French) R.; m. Thora Joan Ellefsen, Sept. 2, 1967. BA, SUNY, Buffalo, 1959, MA in Classical Langs., 1960; MDiv, Luth. Theol. Sem., Phila., 1963; PhD, Oxford U., Eng., 1965; DD (hon.), Yale U., 1995. Ordained to ministry Evang. Luth. Ch., 1966. Assoc. pastor Evang. Luth. Ch. of the Holy Trinity, NYC, 1966-68; asst. prof., chmn. dept. classical langs. Augsburg Coll., Mpls., 1968-71; assoc. exec. dir. div. Theol. Studies Luth. Coun. in the USA, 1971-78; adj. prof. The Gen. Theol. Sem., NYC, 1978-82, 95; exec. dir., asst. to Bishop Evang. Luth. Ch. in Am., Chgo., 1987-96; dir. Commn. on Faith and Order Nat. Coun. of Chs. of Christ USA, NYC, 1996-2001; exec. dir. Found. for Faith and Order, NYC, 2001—. Vis. lectr. Waterloo Luth. Theol. Sem., 1969; adj. prof. theology Fordham U., N.Y.C., 1984-86, Luth. Theol. Sem., Phila., 1998—, St. John's Disting. prof., 2002-03; prof. Angelicum Pontificia U. San Tommaso, Rome, 2005-; mem. cen. com. World Coun. Chs., 1991-98, mem. standing com. faith and order commn., 1991—; adj. faculty Yale Div. Sch., 1999—;; scholar-at-large Graymoor Ecumenical Inst., 2002-03; Jean-Marie Tillard disting. prof. Angelicum Pontificia U., San Tommaso, Rome, 2005-2006. Author: The Trinitarian Controversy, Ecumenism: A Movement Toward Church Unity; contbr. articles to profl. jours. Samuel Trexler fellow of N.Y. Synod Luth. Ch. in Am., 1964, 65. Mem. Am. Acad. Religion, Am. Soc. Christian Ethics, Am. Soc. Ch. History, Internat. Assn. Coptic Studies. Lutheran. Avocations: book collecting, chess, tennis. Office: Found for Faith and Order 77 Park Ave New York NY 10016 Home Phone: 212-725-7435. Personal E-mail: ruschgrif@worldnet.att.net.

RUSCHA, EDWARD, artist; b. Omaha, Dec. 16, 1937; m. Danna Knego, 1967; children: Edward Joseph. Studied at, Chouinard Art Inst., Los Angeles, 1956-60. Numerous vis. artist positions including UCLA, 1969-70; US Rep., Venice Biennale, 2005. Author: Twentysix Gasoline Stations, 1962, Various Small Fires, 1964, Some Los Angeles Apartments, 1965, The Sunset Strip, 1966, Thirtyfour Parking Lots, 1967, Royal Road Test, 1967, Business Cards, 1968, Nine Swimming Pools, 1968, Crackers, 1969, Real Estate Opportunities, 1970, Records, 1971, A Few Palm Trees, 1971, Colored People, 1972, Hard Light, 1978; noted for numerous graphite, gunpowder and pastel drawings, over 200 limited-edit. prints; producer, dir.: films Premium, 1970, Miracle, 1974; began showing works, Ferus Gallery, LA, 1963; first internat. show Galerie Rudolf Zwirner, Cologne, Germany,1968; works include (paintings) Standard Station, Amarillo, Tex., 1963; Annie, 1963, Smash, 1963, Electric, 1964, (mural) Miami-Dade Pub. Library, Fla., 1985; one-man exhbns. include Minn. Inst. Arts, 1972, Nigel Greenwood Ltd., London, 1970, 73, 80, Leo Castelli Gallery, N.Y.C., (10 shows) 1973—, Albright-Knox Art Gallery, Buffalo, 1976, Stedelijk Mus., Amsterdam, 1976, Ft. Worth Art Mus., 1977, San Francisco Mus. Modern Art, 1982, Whitney Mus. Am. Art, 1982, Vancouver Art Gallery, 1982, Contemporary Arts Mus., Houston, 1983, Los Angeles County Mus. Art, 1983, James Corcoran Gallery, Los Angeles, 1985, Gagosian Galleries, Chelsea, 2002, Beverly Hills, 2003, also others; exhibited in group shows at 64th Whitney Biennial, 1987, Centre Pompidou, Paris, 1989, Mus. Boymans—van Beuningen, Rotterdam, The Netherlands, 1990, Ghislaine Hussenot, Paris, 1990, Fundacio Caixa, Barcelona, Spain, 1990, Serpentine Gallery, London, 1990, Mus. Contemporary Art, L.A., 1990-91, Robert Miller Gallery, N.Y.C., 1992, Thaddaeus Ropac, Salzburg, Austria, 1992; represented in permanent collections including Mus. Modern Art, Los Angeles County Mus. Art, Whitney Mus., Hirshhorn, Washington, Miami-Dade Pub. Libr., Denver Pub. Libr., J. Paul Getty Mus., L.A., also others; restrospective of works on paper J. Paul Getty Mus., L.A., 1998; paintings exhibited, Gagosian Gallery, Beverly Hills, 1999, Metro Plots, N.Y., 1999; retrospective of career Hirshhorn Mus., 2000, Sculpture Garden, Washington, D.C., 2000, Mus. Contemporary Art, Chgo., Miami Art Mus., Modern Art Mus., Ft. Worth, Tex. Trustee Mus. Contemporary Art, LA. Guggenheim fellow; Nat. Endowment Arts grantee. Fellow: Am. Acad. Arts & Sci.; mem.: Am. Acad. Arts and Letters (mem. dept. art). Office: 90 Gagosian Gallery 980 Madison Ave New York NY 10021-1848 also: 35 S Venice Blvd Venice CA 90291

RUSCHE, MARK C., lawyer; b. Marietta, Ga., Jan. 19, 1959; BA, Furman Univ., 1981; JD cum laude, Univ. SC, 1985. Bar: Ga. 1986. Ptnr., leader, real estate, fin. and investment group Alston & Bird LLP, Atlanta. Bd. of editors Comml. Leasing Law & Strategy. Mem.: Order of Coif. Office: Alston & Bird LLP One Atlantic Ctr 1201 W Peachtree St NW Atlanta GA 30309-3424 Office Phone: 404-881-7281. Office Fax: 404-253-8798. Business E-Mail: mark.rusche@alston.com.

RUSCIO, KENNETH PATRICK, academic administrator, political science professor; b. Red Bank, NJ; BA, Washington and Lee U., 1976; MPA, Syracuse U., 1979, PhD, 1983. Asst. prof. social sci. and policy studies Worcester Polytechnic Inst., 1985—87; asst. prof. politics Washington and Lee U., 1987—94, dean Freshman, 1987—94, assoc. dean Williams Sch. Commerce, Econs. and Politics, 1991—98, assoc. prof., 1994—2000, prof., 2000—02, acting assoc. dean, 2001—02, pres., 2006—; dean Jepson Sch. Leadership Studies, U. Richmond, 2002—06. Contbr. articles to profl. jours. Mem.: Am. Conf. of Academic Deans, Assn. Am. Colls. and Univs., Internat. Leadership Assn., Am. Polit. Sci. Assn. Office: Washington and Lee U Office of Pres Lexington VA 24450-0303 *

RUSCONI, PAOLO, pediatric cardiologist; arrived in U.S., 1989; s. Camillo Rusconi and Enrica Bodega. MD, U. Pavia, Italy, 1982. Lic. cardiology U. of Milan, pediats. Am. Bd. Pediats., pediat. cardiolgy Am. Bd. Pediat. Cardiology, Flex, cert. Fgn. Med. Grad. Exam. in Med. Sci. Intern Ospedale di Lecco, 1982—83; cardiology resident Ospedali Riuniti di Bergamo, Italy, 1984—87; rsch. fellow Brompton Hosp., London, 1987—88; sr. ho. officer in pediats. Riverside Health Authority, London, 1988—89; pediat. resident Riley Hosp. Children Ind. U. Med., Indpls., 1990—93; pediat. cardiology fellow U. Miami, Fla., 1993—96, asst. prof. pediats., 1996—2006; assoc. prof. pediats. Miller Sch. Medicine U. Miami, 2006—. Med. dir. pediat. heart failure and cardiac transplant Miller Sch. of Medicine, U. of Miami, 1996—. Contbr. scientific papers to profl. jours. Lt. Italian Med. Corps., 1983—84. Mem.: Am. Coll. of Cardiology, Internat. Soc. of Heart and Lung Transplantation. Roman Catholic. Achievements include development of new treatment in the management of heart failure in children. Office: Univ of Miami PO Box 016960 (R-76) Miami FL 33101 Home Phone: 305-865-8963; Office Phone: 305-585-8115. Office Fax: 305-324-6012. Business E-Mail: p.rusconi@miami.edu.

RUSH, ANDREW WILSON, artist; b. Detroit, Sept. 24, 1931; s. Harvey Ditman and Mary Louise (Stalker) R.; m. Jean Cochran, Apr., 1957; children: Benjamin, Samuel, Joseph, Margaret; m. Ann Woodin, Oct., 1978. B.F.A. with honors, U. Ill., 1953; M.F.A., U. Iowa, 1958. Asso. prof. art U. Ariz., 1959-69; co-dir. Rockefeller Found. Indian Arts Project, 1960-64; vis. artist, artist-in-residence Ohio State U., 1970, U. Ark., 1972, Colo. Coll., 1973-74; resident mem. Rancho Linda Vista, Community of the Arts, Oracle, Ariz., 1969—; founder, dir. The Drawing Studio, Tucson, 1992—. One-man shows include Carlin Galleries, Ft. Worth, 1973, Graphics Gallery, Tucson, 1972, 75, Tucson Art Inst., 1984, Cruzitas Gallery, San Antonio, 1996, U. Ariz. Mus. Art, 2003, Davis-Dominguez Gallery, Tucson, 2003; exhibited in group shows at World's Fair, N.Y.C., 1964, USIS exhbns., Europe, Latin Am., 1960-65; represented in permanent collections Libr. of Congress, Uffizzi Mus., Dallas Mus., Ft. Worth Mus., Seattle Mus., Free Libr., Phila.; illustrator: Andrew Rush on Oliver Wendell Holmes, 1973, Rule of Two (Ann Woodin), 1984, Voice Crying in the Wilderness (Edward Abbey), 1990, Ask Marilyn, 1992 (pub. art winner 1995), Voice of the Borderlands, 2005; designer The Tucson Gateway Project, 1998. Served with USMC, 1953-55. Fulbright grantee, 1958-59; recipient Lifetime Achievement award Tucson-Pima Arts Coun., 2006. Address: Rancho Linda Vista O M Star Rte 2360 Oracle AZ 85623 E-mail: awrush@earthlink.net.

RUSH, AUGUSTUS JOHN, psychiatrist; b. Glen Ridge, NJ, Dec. 15, 1942; m. Dee Miller; children: Matthew, Augustus John III. AB in Biochemistry cum laude, Princeton U., 1964; MD, Columbia U., 1968. Internship Northwestern U., Chgo., 1968—69; resident U. Pa., Phila., 1972—75; asst. prof. U. Okla. Health Scis. Ctr., Okla. City, 1975—78; assoc. prof. U. Tex. Southwestern Med. Ctr., Dallas, 1978—83, Betty Jo Hay prof., 1983—88, Betty Jo Hay disting. chair in mental health, 1988—. Chair biomedical sci. Rosewood Corp., 1996—; vice-chair dept. clin. scis. U. Tex., Dallas, 2006—. Editor: (book) Short-Term Psychotherapies for Depression, 1982; author: Beating Depression, 1983; co-author: Cognitive Therapy of Depressed Adolescents, 1994; co-editor: Depression: Basic Mechanisms Diagnosis & Treatment, 1986; contbr. over 425 articles to profl. jours., chapters to 10 books. Capt. US Army, 1971—73. Named one of Best Doctor's in Dallas, D Mag., 2003; recipient Charles Burlingame award, 1992, Gerald Klerman award, 1994, Paul Hoch award, 1999, Edward Sachar Vis. Scholar award, 2000, Nola Maddox Falcone prize, Nat. Alliance for Rsch. on Schizophrenia and Affective Disorders, 2000. Fellow: Am. Coll. Neuropsychopharmacology, Am. Coll. Psychiat. (Mood Disorders Rsch. award 2007), Am. Psychiat. Assn. (Rsch. award 2007); mem.: Soc. Biol. Psychiatry (sec.-treas. 1990—94, v.p. 1994, pres. 1996—97, treas. 1998—, George Thompson Founders award 2002), Soc. Psychotherapy Rsch. (pres. 1984—85). Avocations: woodworking, skiing. Office: U Tex Southwestern Med Ctr Dept Clin Scis 5323 Harry Hines Blvd Dallas TX 75390-9066 Office Phone: 214-648-4832. Business E-Mail: john.rush@utsouthwestern.edu.

RUSH, BOBBY L., congressman; b. Albany, Ga., Nov. 23, 1946; m. Carolyn Rush; 5 children. BA in Polit. Sci., Roosevelt U., 1974; MA in Polit. Sci., U. Ill., 1992; MA in Theology, McCormick Theolocal Seminary, 1998. Fin. planner Sanmar Fin. Planning Corp.; assoc. dean Daniel Hale Williams U.; ins. agent Prudential Ins. Co.; city alderman Chgo., 1984-93; dem. committeeman Chgo. 2nd ward, 1984, 88, Central Ill., 1990; dep. chmn. Ill. Dem. Party, 1990; mem. US Congress from 1st Ill. Dist., 1993—. Chmn. Environ. Protection, Energy and Pub. Utilities com., Budget and Govt. Operations com., Capitol Devel. com., Hist. Landmark Preservation Com.; mem. Commerce com. Former mem. Student Non-Violent Coordinating com.; founder Ill. Black Panther Party; past coord. Free Breakfast for Children, Free Med. Clinic. With US Army, 1963-68. Recipient Ill. Enterprise Zone award Dept. Commerce and Community, Operation PUSH Outstanding Young Man award, Henry Booth House Outstanding Community Svc. award, Outstanding Bus. and Profl. Achievement award South End Jaycees, Chgo. Black United Communities Disting. Polit. Leadership award; named one of Most Influential Black Americans, Ebony mag., 2006. Democrat. Office: US Ho Reps 2416 Rayburn Ho Office Bldg Washington DC 20515-1301 Office Phone: 202-225-4372. Office Fax: 202-226-0333. *

RUSH, CURT STEFAN, lawyer; b. 1955; BA in Philosophy, Hunter Coll., 1981; JD cum laude, Bklyn. Law Sch., 1984. Bar: NY 1985. Assoc. Shereff, Friedman, Hoffman & Goodman, P.A., NYC; corp. counsel Image Bank, Inc., 1990—93, Globe Comm. Corp., Boca Raton, Fla., 1993—96; gen. counsel Global DirectMail Corp., Port Washington, NY; gen. counsel, sec. Systemax, Inc., Port Washington, NY, 1996—. Office: Systemax Inc 11 Harbor Park Dr Port Washington NY 11050 Office Phone: 516-608-7000. Office Fax: 516-625-0038. *

RUSH, DANIEL SCOTT, vascular surgeon, educator; b. Louisville, Jan. 2, 1949; s. Everett Neil Rush, Jr. and Dorothy Benton Carrell Rush; m. S. Colleen O'Keefe, July 14, 1984; children: John Everett, Rebekah Eileen, Mary Catherine. AB, Centre Coll., Danville, Ky., 1971; MD, U. Ky., Lexington, 1976. Lic. Ky., 1977, SC, 1988, Tenn., 1997. Vascular fellow, dept. surgery U. Chgo., 1981—82; asst. prof. surgery Tulane U., New Orleans, 1982—88; assoc. prof. surgery U. SC, Columbia, 1988—97; prof. surgery E.Tenn. State U., Johnson City, Tenn., 1997—. Chief vascular surgery U. SC, 1988—97; med. dir. vascular lab. Richmond Meml. Hosp., Columbia, 1995—97; chief divsn. vascular surgery E.Tenn. State U., 1997—, Mountain Home VA Med. Ctr., Johnson City, 1997—; med. dir. vascular lab. Johnson City Med. Ctr., 1999—. Contbr. chapters to books, articles to profl. jours. V.p. SC chpt. Am. Diabetes Assn., Columbia, 1986—87; pres. Palmetto chapt. Juvenile Diabetes Found., Columbia, 1995—96. Grantee Rsch. grant, Am. Heart Assn., 1986—87; scholar Student Rsch. scholarship to Nat. Cancer Inst., Am. Cancer Soc., 1975; Traveling Scholar, Fredrick A. Collar Soc., 1981. Fellow: ACS; mem.: SC Vascular Surg. Soc. (sec., treas. 1989—95, pres. 1995—96), Soc. Vascular Surgery, So. Assn. Vascular Surgery (chmn., archives com., exec. coun. 2003—07). Independent. Presbyn. Avocations: writing, book collecting, travel, painting, drawing. Office: E Tenn State Univ Dept Surgery PO Box 70575 Johnson City TN 37614 Business E-Mail: rush@etsu.edu.

RUSH, DEBORAH L., art educator, artist; d. Victor L. and Judith Rosier; widowed; children: Matthew J., Eric J., Bonnie R. Rush Lukaszewski. Grad., Iroquois Ctrl. HS, Elma, NY, 1970. Owner Art by Rush, 1987—; tchr. drawing and painting Wellsville Creative Arts Ctr., Wellsville, NY, 2006—07. Vol. bible educator Jehovah's Witnesses, Wellsville, 1980—2007. Mem.: Arabian Horse Assn. NY (hon.). Avocations: horseback riding, gardening, travel, hiking, horsebreeder. Office: Art By Rush 5533 County Rd 48 Belmont NY 14813 Home: 5533 County Rd 48 Belmont NY 14813

RUSH, DOMENICA MARIE, health facilities administrator; b. Gallup, N.Mex., Apr. 10, 1937; d. Bernardo G. and Guadalupe (Milan) Iorio; m. W. E. Rush, Jan. 5, 1967. Diploma, Regina Sch. Nursing, Albuquerque, 1958. RN N.Mex.; lic. nursing home adminstr.; cert. legal nurse cons., 2004. Charge nurse, house supr. St. Joseph Hosp., Albuquerque, 1958-63; dir. nursing Cibola Hosp., Grants, 1960-64; supr. operating room, dir. med. seminars Carrie Tingley Crippled Children's Hosp., Truth or Consequences, N.Mex., 1964-73; adminstr. Sierra Vista Hosp., Truth or Consequences, 1974-88, pres., 1989—90; clin. nursing mgr. U. N.Mex. Hosp., 1990—94; adminstr. Nor-Lea Hosp., Lovington, N.Mex., 1990-94; with regional ops. divsn. Presbyn. Healthcare Svcs., Albuquerque, 1994—, regional ops., 1994—2003; adminstr. Sierra Vista Hosp., Truth or Consequences, N.Mex., 1995—2003; regional adminstr. Presbyn. Healthcare Svcs., 2003—04, intern adminstrn. and spl. projects, 2004—06; founder Rush Health Consulting Svc., 2004—; CEO Trans Health, Inc., Balt., 2006—07. Bd. dirs. N.Mex. Blue Cross/Blue Shield, 1977-88, chmn. hosp. relations com., 1983-85, exec. com. 1983—; bd. dirs. Region II Emergency Med. Svcs. Originating bd. SW Mental Health Ctr., Sierra County, N.Mex., 1975; chmn. Sierra County Personnel Bd., 1983—. Recipient Frank Gabriel award N.Mex. Hosp. Health Sys. Assn., 2003, Govenor's award Emergency Med. Svcs., 2003, Govs.award for Outstanding Woman, N. Mex., 2004; Named Lea County Outstanding Woman, N.Mex. Commn. on Status of Women, Woman of Yr. for Lea County, N.Mex.; 1993. Mem. Am. Coll. Health Care Adminstrs., Sierra County C. of C. (bd. dirs. 1972, 75-76, svc. award 1973, Businesswoman of the Yr. 1973-74), N.Mex. Hosp. Assn. (bd. dirs., sec.-treas., pres.-elect, com. chmn., 1977-88, pres. 1980-81, exec. com., 1980-83, 84-85, recipient meritorius svc. award 1988), N.Mex. So. Hosp. Coun. (sec. 1980-81, pres. 1981-82), Am. Hosp. Assn. (N.Mex. del. 1984-88, regional adv. bd. 1984-88). Republican. Roman Catholic. Avocations: raising thoroughbred horses, cooking. Home: 1100 N Riverside Dr Truth Or Consequences NM 87901-9789 Office Phone: 505-740-2334. Personal E-mail: domrush@gmail.com.

RUSH, DORIE MAE, nursing educator; b. Assiniboia, Sask., Can., May 3, 1970; d. June and Steve Yorga (Stepfather); m. Tark Morgan Rush, Mar. 22, 2003; children: Hailey Madison Caragata, Stone Morgan, Brooke Ashlyn Caragata, Austin Talon. DON, Sask. Inst. Applied Arts and Sci., Regina, 1990; BSN, U. Phoenix, Tucson, 2003; postgrad., U. Phoenix, Yuma, Ariz., 2004—. Cert. inpatient OB, NCC, Ariz., fetal monitoring, NCC, Ariz. Unit-based educator Yuma Regional Med. Ctr., 2000—, resource coord., 1997—2000, staff nurse, 1993—97; OB flight nurse Suncare Air Ambulance, Yuma, 1999—2002; part-time Ariz. Western Coll., Yuma, 2002—. Fetal monitor instr. Assn. Women's Health Obstetric and Neonatal Nurses, Yuma, 2003—. Author: (poster presentation) Dynamic New Grad Orientation to Labor and Delivery. Named Yuma's Best Nurse, City of Yuma, 2002. Mem.: Assn. Women's Health Obstetric and Neonatal Nurses. Office: Yuma Regional Med Ctr 2400 S Ave A Yuma AZ 85364-7127 Home Phone: 928-329-7706; Office Phone: 928-336-3020. Office Fax: 928-336-7453; Home Fax: 928-329-7706. Personal E-mail: dmrush@adelphia.net. E-mail: drush@yumaregional.org.

RUSH, GEOFFREY, actor; b. Toowomba, Queensland, Australia, July 6, 1951; m. Jane Menelaus, 1988; children: Angelica, James. diploma, LittD, U. Queensland. Actor: (plays) Wrong Side of the Moon, 1971, Lock Up Your Daughters, 1972, Assault With a Deadly Weapon, 1972, Twelfth Night, 1972, 1983, 1984, Ruling Class, 1972, You're a Good Man Charlie Brown, 1972, Puss in Boots, 1972, Juno and the Paycock, 1973, Expresso Bongo, 1973, National Health, 1973, The Imaginary Invalid, 1973, Suddenly at Home, 1973, Aladdin, 1973, Hamlet on Ice, 1973, Godspell, 1974, The Rivals, 1974, The Philanthropist, 1974, Present Laughter, 1974, Jack and the Beanstalk, 1975—77, King Lear, 1978, 1988, Point of Departure, 1978, Clowneroonies, 1978, Waiting for Godot, 1979, On Our Selection, 1979, Teeth and Smiles, 1980, Revenger's Tragedy, 1981, No End of Blame, 1982, You Can't Take It With You, 1981, A Midsummer Night's Dream, 1982, 1983, Mother Courage, 1982, Silver Lining, 1982, The Prince of Homburg, 1982, Royal Show, 1983, Blood Wedding, 1983, Netherwood, 1983, 1984, The Marriage of Figaro, 1983, Pal Joey, 1983, The Blind Giant is Dancing, 1983, Sunrise, 1983, Benefactors, 1986, On Parliament Hill, 1987, Shepherd on the Rocks, 1987, The Winter's Tale, 1987, Tristram Shandy-Gent, 1988, Les Enfants du Paradis, 1988, The Importance of Being Earnest, 1988, 1990—91, 1992, Troilus & Cressida, 1989, The Diary of a Madman, 1989, 1990, 1992 (Variety Club award for Stage Actor of Yr., 1989, Sydney Theatre Critics Cir. award for Most Outstanding Performance, 1989, Victorian Green Rm. award for Best Actor, 1990), Marat/Sade, 1990, The Comedy of Errors, 1990, The Government Inspector, 1991, Uncle Vanya, 1992, The Dutch Courtesan, 1993, Oleanna, 1993, Hamlet, 1994, 1995; (films) Hoodwink, 1980, Starstruck, 1981, Twelfth Night, 1985, On Our Selection, 1994, Five Easy Pizzas, 1994, Children of the Revolution, 1996, Shine, 1996 (BAFTA award Best Actor, 1997, Golden Globe award for Best Performance in Motion Picture, 1997, Screen Actors Guild award for Outstanding Performance, 1997, Oscar award for Best Actor, 1997), Oscar & Lucinda, 1997, Shakespeare in Love, 1998 (BAFTA award Best Supporting Actor, 1999), Elizabeth, 1998, Mystery Men, 1999, House on Haunted Hill, 1999, Quills, 2000 (NY Film Critics Online award for best actor, 2000), The Tailor of Panama, 2001, Lantana, 2001, Frida, 2002, The Banger Sisters, 2002, Swimming Upstream, 2003, Ned Kelly, 2003, Finding Nemo (voice), 2003, Pirates of the Caribbean: The Curse of the Black Pearl, 2003, Intolerable Cruelty, 2003, The Life and Death of Peter Sellers, 2004 (Golden Globe award for best actor miniseries or TV movie, 2005, Screen Actors Guild Award for best actor in a TV movie or miniseries, 2005, Emmy award for outstanding lead actor in a miniseries or a movie, 2005), Munich, 2005, Candy, 2006, Pirates of the Caribbean: Dead Man's Chest, 2006, Pirates of the Caribbean: At World's End, 2007; (TV series) Consumer Capers, 1979—81, Menotti, 1980—81, The Burning Piano, 1992, Mercury, 1996; dir.: (plays) Clowneroonies, 1978—80, Animal Acts, 1984—86, Teen Ages, 1984—86, Carols-By-Lazerlight, 1984—86, The 1985 Scandals, 1986, Pearls Before Swine, 1986, Pell Mell, 1986, 1987, 1988, The Merry Wives of Windsor, 1987, The Popular Mechanicals, 1987, 1988, 1992, Les Enfants du Paradis, 1989, The Wolf's Banquet, 1989, Popular Mechanicals 2, 1992, Aristophane's Frogs, 1992; co-translator The Government Inspector, 1991, writer (with George Whaley) (TV film) Clowning Around, 1992, (with John Clarke) (play) Aristophane's Frogs, 1992, Call Me Sal, 1996, Children of the Revolution, 1997, Les Misérables, 1998. Office: Creative Artists Agy 9830 Wilshire Blvd Beverly Hills CA 90212-1804

RUSH, HERMAN E., television executive; b. Phila., June 20, 1929; s. Eugene and Bella (Sacks) R.; m. Joan Silberman, Mar. 18, 1951; children: James Harrison, Mandie Susan. BBA, Temple U., 1950. With Ofcl. Films, 1951-57; owner Flamingo Films, 1957-60; with Creative Mgmt. Assocs., NYC, 1960-71, pres. TV divsn., 1964-71, exec. v.p. parent co., dir., 1964-71; ind. prodr., 1971-75; prodr. Wolper Orgn., 1975-76; pres. Herman Rush Assocs., Inc. (Rush-Flaherty Agy. subs.), 1977-78, Marble Arch TV, LA, 1979-80, Columbia Pictures TV, Burbank, Calif., 1980-87; chmn., CEO Coca-Cola Telecom., 1987-88, Rush Assocs., Inc., Burbank, 1988—, Katz/Rush Entertainment Group, Beverly Hills, Calif., 1990-96, New Tech. Entertainment, LLC, Beverly Hills, 1996—, Internet Content Provider East Cap. Fin. Corp., chmn. emeritus; mng. ptnr. Media Consulting Assocs. CEO Infotainment Internat., Inc.; pres., chmn. Royal Animated Art, Inc.; Entertainment Industries Coun.; co-owner, exec. prodr. The Montel Williams Talk Show, 1991-2006; mem. bd. advisors Smart Video Techs., Inc.; CEO Creative Conteal Providers, LLC Trustee Sugar Ray Robinson Youth Found., 1967-75; pres. Retarded Infant Svcs., N.Y.C., 1957-63; bd. dirs. U.S. Marshall's Svc. Found., Just Say No Found.; conferee White House Conf. for a Drug Free America, 1987, 88. Mem. Acad. TV Arts and Scis., Hollywood Radio and TV Soc., Producers Caucus. Clubs: Friars, Filmex. Office: Rush Entertainment Group 2222 Ave of the Stars Los Angeles CA 90067 Office Phone: 310-553-6145. Personal E-mail: hermanrush@aol.com.

RUSH, JAMES EDWARD, retired information scientist; b. Warrensburg, Mo., July 18, 1935; s. Alexander Edward Rush and Verna Lavena Pollock; m. Delores Ann Lee, June 9, 1958; children: Susan Diane Wittenauer, Pamela Elaine, Adam Jay, Jennifer Lee. BS in Chemistry and Math., Ctrl. Mo. State U., 1957; PhD, U. of Mo., 1962. Asst. editor, organic index editing dept. Chem. Abstracts Svc., Columbus, Ohio, 1962—65, asst. head, chem. info. procedures dept., 1965—67, tech. liaison officer, 1967—68; adj. prof., libr. and info. sci. U. of Ill., Ill., 1980—83; pres. James E. Rush Assocs., Inc., Powell, Ohio, 1969—88; exec. dir. PALINET, Phila., 1988—99; adj. prof., coll. of info. sci. and tech. Drexel U., Phila., 2000—; asst. prof., computer and info. sci. The Ohio State U., Columbus, 1965—67, assoc. prof., computer and info. sci., 1969—73, adj. prof., computer and info. sci., 1973—85; dir. R&D Online Computer Libr. Ctr., Inc., Dublin, Ohio, 1973—80; dir. of rsch. Online Computer Libr. Ctr., 1980; adj. prof., libr. and info. sci. U. of South Fla., Tampa, 1992—97. Del., Pa. gov.'s conf. on libr. and info. svcs. Office of the Gov., Harrisburg, 1990; chair, bd. of dirs. Pa. Preservation Consortium, Phila. Author: (book) Information Retrieval and Documentation in Chemistry, Guide to Information Science, (eight-volume set of books) Library Systems Evaluation Guide, Vols. 1-8, (update service (serial) Microcomputers for Libraries: Product Review and Procurement Guide, (book) Optical Disk Storage: Technology and Applications, Information Science and Technology: An Introduction. With Army N.G., 1952—60. Mem.: Am. Chem. Soc. (chmn. divsn. of chem. lit. 1973), Am. Soc. for Info. Sci. and Tech. (pres. 1994—95, gen. chmn. 1980—82). Independent-Republican. Presbyterian. Avocations: construction, woodworking, gardening, photography. Home: 673 Old Eagle School Rd Wayne PA 19087-2042 Home Phone: 610-964-1875. Home Fax: none. Personal E-mail: rush_jamese@hotmail.com.

RUSH, JULIA ANN HALLORAN (MRS. RICHARD HENRY RUSH), artist, writer; b. St. Louis, Oct. 25, 1927; d. Edward Roosevelt and Flavia Hadley (Griffin) Halloran; m. Richard Henry Rush, Aug. 15, 1956; 1 child, Sallie Haywood. Student Washington U., St. Louis, 1945-47; B.A., George Washington U., 1949. One-woman shows: Fort Amador Officers Club, Panama Canal Zone, El Panama Hotel, Panama, George Washington U., Statler Hotel, Roosevelt Hotel, Washington, Newspaper Women's Club, Washington, Waukegan Library, Ill., Epworth Heights Hotel, Ludington, Mich.; exhibited in group shows: Panama Art League, Corcoran Gallery; represented in permanent collections: U. Panama; also pvt. collections; model John Robert Powers Agy., 1950; sec.-treas., dir. N.Am. Acceptance Corp., 1956-58; v.p. Rush and Halloran, Inc., 1957-58, ptnr., 1954-57; research asst. to husband's bi-weekly newsletter Art/Antiques Investment Report, 1973—, articles in Wall St. transcript, 1971—. Illustrator: Antiques As An Investment (author Richard H. Rush), 1968; research asst.: Investments You Can Live With and Enjoy (author: Richard H. Rush), 1974, 2d, edit., 1975, 3d edit., 1976; Photographer: Automobiles as an Investment, 1982; Investing in Classic Cars, 1984. Recipient 1st prize (Panama) Newspaper Women's Club, 1953; First Prize Panama Art League, 1953. Mem. DAR, Nat. League Am. Penwomen, Florence Crittenton Circle (rec. sec. 1968-69), Kappa Kappa Gamma. Club: Washington, Royal Palm Yacht (No. Ft. Myers, Fla.), Boca West Golf and Country (Boca Raton, Fla.)

RUSH, KENT THOMAS, art educator, artist; b. Hayward, Calif., Jan. 16, 1948; MFA, U. Tex., Austin, 1979. One-man shows include Montalvo Ctr. Arts, Saratoga, Calif., 1976, McNay Art Mus., San Antonio, 1977, Dorothy Katz Gallery, 1979, U. Wis., Superior, 1982, Bluxome Gallery, San Francisco, 1984, U. Wis., La Crosse, 1985, Art Space, LA, 1986, Koehler Cultural Ctr., San Antonio, 1987, Galeria Del Taller De Las Artes Plasticas, Mex., 1988, Coke Gallery, U. N.Mex. Art Mus., Albuquerque, 1990, Dowd Fine Arts Ctr., NYC, 1992, Richard Levy Gallery, Albuquerque, 1993, Martin Mus. Art, Waco, Tex., 1994, ArtPace, San Antonio, 1995, Milagros Contemporary Art, 1996, Parchman-Stremmel Galleries, 1998, Ctr. Spirituality and Arts, 2001, Legion Arts/CSPS, Cedar Rapids, Iowa, 2002, Amarillo Mus. Art, Tex., 2003, Art Gallery, Ctr. Fine and Performing Arts, Tex. A&M Internat. U., Laredo, 2006, others, exhibited in group shows at Indpls. Mus. Art, 1970, Oakland Mus., Calif., 1971, San Jose Mus. Art, 1972, U. No. Ill., DeKalb, 1974, So. Conn. State Coll., New Haven, 1975, U. Tex. Health Sci. Ctr., San Antonio, 1976, Madison Art Ctr., Wis., 1977, U. Union Gallery, Calif., 1978, White Meml. Gallery, Santa Barbara, Calif., 1979, Art Space, 1980, Kaiser Ctr., Oakland Calif., 1981, Bradford Galleries, England, 1982, World Print Coun. Gallery, San Francisco, 1983, Olin Fine Arts Gallery, Washington, Pa., 1985, Haggerty Art Ctr. Gallery, Irvine, Tex., 1984, Adams/Middleton Gallery, Dallas, 1986, Laguna Gloria Art Mus., Austin, 1987, San Antonio Art Inst., 1988, Baylor U. Gallery, Austin, 1989, Blue Star Art Space, San Antonio, 1990, Emison Art Ctr., Greencastle, Ind., 1992, Calif. State U., Chico, 1984, Diverse Works, Houston, 1994, Art Chgo., 1995, Southeast Mus. Photography, Daytona Beach, Fla., 1996, North Light Gallery, Tempe, Ariz., 1997, Gerhard Wurzer Gallery, Houston, 1998, Southwest Sch. Art and Craft, San Antonio, 1999, San Antonio Art League Mus., 2000, 808 Gallery, Boston, 2001, 416 West Gallery, Denison, Tex., 2002, Tex. State U., San Marcos, 2003, Midwestern State U. Art Gallery, Wichita Falls, Tex., 2004, Ft. Worth Cmty. Art Ctr. Gallery, 2005, U. Toledo Visual Art Gallery, Toledo, 2006, Northlight Gallery, Tempe, Ariz., 2007, others, Represented in permanent collections Albuqierqie Mus., Auchenbach Found. Graphic Arts, San Francisco, Ctr. Fine Print Rsch., Bristol, England, Longview Mus. Fine Arts, Tex., New Orleans Pub. Libr., others. Mem. exhbn. com. Blue Star Art Space, San Antonio, 1986—88. Fellow Fulbright Sr. Lectr., 1988. Avocations: small boat building, fly fishing, canoeing. Home: 142 Irvington Dr San Antonio TX 78209 Office: U Tex San Antonio Art & AH Dept 6900 N Loop 1604 W San Antonio TX 78249-0642 Home Phone: 210-826-5863; Office Phone: 210-458-4352.

RUSH, KEVIN ARLAND, music educator; b. Franklin, Pa., July 29, 1983; s. Terry Arland and Emily Darlene Rush. MusB, Westminster Coll., 2005. Cert. profl. tchr. music K-12 Pa. Music educator, Clarion County, Pa., 2005—; dir. choral activities Patuvent HS, Calvert County, Md. Sr. organist, choir dir. Good Hope Luth. Ch., Oil City, Pa., 2004—. Mem.: Pa. Music Educators Assn., Phi Kappa Tau, Mu Pi Epsilon (chaplin 2003—). Republican. Presbytertian. Home: 11211 Rt 68 Rimersburg PA 16248

RUSH, NORMAN, author; b. San Francisco, Oct. 24, 1933; s. Roger and Leslie (Chessé) R.; m. Elsa Scheidt; children: Jason, Liza. BA, Swarthmore Coll., 1956. Dealer antiquarian books, 1960-78; instr. English, history Rockland C.C., Suffern, NY, 1973-78; co-dir. Peace Corps, Botswana, 1978-83; freelance writer, 1983—. Author: Whites, 1986, Mating, 1991 (Nat. Book award for fiction 1991, Internat. Fiction prize Irish Times and Aer Lingus 1992), Mortals, 2003. Recipient Rosenthal award Nat. Acad. and Inst. Arts and Letters, 1987; fellow Nat. Endowment for Arts, 1986, Guggenheim fellow, 1987, Bellagio residency fellow Rockeller Found., 1990. Mem. PEN Am. Ctr.

RUSH, RICHARD HENRY, finance company executive, educator, writer; b. NYC, Mar. 6, 1915; s. Henry Frederick and Bessie (Vreeland) R.; m. Julia Ann Halloran, Aug. 15, 1956; 1 dau., Sallie Haywood. *Dr. Rush is the great grandson of Philip Freneau, The Poet of the American Revolution who is credited as having saved the country from monarchy through his publication of the National Gazette. He is the great grandnephew of General Phil Kearny, Civil War general and New Jersey's most prominent soldier. The grandnephew of America's first Consul General and Minister to Japan, Townsend Harris, who through his determined negotiating of the American Japanese trade treaty, signed in 1858, opened Japan to trade with the west. Harris, before going to Japan, founded the free College of the City of New York as President of the New York Board of Education.* BA summa cum laude, Dartmouth Coll., 1937, MCS, 1938; MBA with highest distinction, Harvard U., 1941, DCS (Littauer fellow), 1942. Chief economist, chmn. planning com. All Am. Aviation (U.S. Air), 1943—45; dir. aviation U.S. Bur. Fgn. and Domestic Commerce, 1945—46; dir. aircraft divsn. Nat. Security Resources Bd., 1948—51; Washington rep. to J. Paul Getty, 1951—52; ptnr. Rush & Halloran, 1953—58; pres., chmn. bd. N.Am. Acceptance Corp., Atlanta, Washington, 1956—59; owner Richard H. Rush Enterprises, Greenwich, Conn., Washington, 1953—73; prof., chmn. dept. finance and investments Sch. Bus. Adminstrn., Am. U., Washington, 1967—70, Sch. Bus. Adminstrn. Am. U., Washington, 1977—79. Author: Art as an Investment, 1961, A Strategy of Investing for Higher Return, 1962, The Techniques of Becoming Wealthy, 1963, Antiques as an Investment, 1968, The Wrecking Operation: Phase One, 1972, Investments You Can Live With and Enjoy, 1976, Techniques of Becoming Wealthy, 1977, Automobiles as an Investment, 1982, Selling Collectibles, 1982, Collecting Classic Cars for Profit and Capital Gain, 1984, Collector Cars: Classics for the New Century, 2001; contbr. over 700 articles to newspapers, mags. and profl. jours.; editor series of books on starting businesses for U.S. Dept. Commerce; contbg. editor Wall St. Transcript, 1971-97, Art/Antiques Investment Report, 1972-97. Trustee, exec. com. Finch Coll., 1968-72. Recipient Pres.'s med., CCNY, 1997. Mem. AAUP, Am. Mktg. Assn. (chmn. nat. com.), Am. Econ. Assn., Am. Statis. Assn., Internat. Platform Assn., Harvard Club N.Y.C., Royal Palm Yacht Club (Ft. Myers), Phi Beta Kappa, Phi Kappa Phi, Omicron Delta Kappa. Episcopalian.

RUSH, RICHARD R., academic administrator; Pres. Calif. State U. Channel Islands, Camarillo. Office: Calif State U Channel Islands 1 University Dr Camarillo CA 93012 Business E-Mail: richard.rush@csuci.edu.

RUSH, W. MARVIN, trucking executive; children: W.M. (Rusty), Robin. CEO, chmn. Rush Enterprises Inc., San Antonio, 1965—2006, chmn., 2006—; founder World Wide Tires, several leasing companies, insurance agy., fin. co., hunting ranch. Office: Rush Enterprises Inc PO Box 34630 San Antonio TX 78265-4630 *

RUSH, W.M. (RUSTY), trucking executive; V.p. to exec. v.p. Rush Enterprises, New Braunfels, Tex., 1990—95, pres., 1995—2001, pres., COO, 2001—06, pres., CEO, 2006—. Office: Rush Enterprises 555 IH-35 S New Braunfels TX 78130 *

RUSHANAEDY, AGUSTINUS, urologist; b. Apr. 30, 1947; MD, Cath. U. Leuven, Belgium, 1975. Bd. cert. urology 1985. Surgical resident Rutgers Med. Sch. Affiliated Hosp., Plainfield, NJ, 1977—79; urology resident Wright State, Dayton, Ohio, 1979—82, Ohio State U., Columbus, 1979—82; staff urologist VA Med. Ctr., Lincoln, 1982—84, Clarksburg, W.Va., 1984—85, Kaiser Permanente, Portland, Oreg., 1985—. Mem.: ACS, Endourological Soc., Am. Urology Assn. Office: 9427 SW Barnes Rd Portland OR 97225-6652 Office Phone: 503-203-2130. Office Fax: 503-203-2190. Business E-Mail: agustinusrushanaedy@kp.org.

RUSHDIE, SALMAN (AHMED SALMAN RUSHDIE), writer, educator; b. Mumbai, June 19, 1947; s. Anis Ahmed and Negin (Butt) R.; m. Clarissa Luard, 1976 (div. 1987); child, Zafar; m. Marianne Wiggins, 1988 (div. 1993); m. Elizabeth West (div.); child, Milam; m. Padma Parvati Lakshmi, Apr. 17, 2004. Student, Cathedral Sch., Bombay; MA in History with honors, King's Coll., Cambridge U., Eng., 1968. Disting. writer in residence English Dept. Emory U., Atlanta, 2007—. Hon. prof. MIT. Author: Crimus, 1975, Midnight's Children, 1981 (Booker prize for Fiction, 1981, English Speaking Union Literary award, 1981, James Tait Black Meml. prize, 1982, Booker of Bookers spl. award, 1993), Shame, 1983 (Prix de Meilleur Livre Etranger, 1984), The Jaguar Smile: A Nicaraguan Journey, 1987, The Satanic Verses, 1988 (Whitbread award 1988, shortlist Booker prize for fiction, 1988, German Author Yr. award, 1988), Is Nothing Sacred? (Herbert Read Meml. lectr. 1990), Haroun and the Sea of Stories, 1990 (Writer's Guild prize for children's fiction 1991), Imaginary Homelands, 1991, East, West, 1994, The Moor's Last Sigh, 1995 (Whitbread Novel award, 1995, Brit. Book awards Author of Yr., 1995, shortlist Booker prize, 1995), Burning Your Boats: The Collected Short Stories, 1996, The Ground Beneath Her Feet, 1999, Fury, 2001, Shalimar the Clown, 2005 (shortlist Whitbread Novel award, 2005). Recipient: Kurt Tucholsky prize, 1992, Prix Colette, 1993, State Prize for European Lit., 1994, Aristeion Lit. prize, 1996, Mantova Lit. prize, 1997, Budapest Grand prize lit., 1998, Commandeur de l'Ordre des Arts et des Lettres, 1999, Freedom of the City, Mexico City, 1999. Fellow Royal Soc. Lit. Address: Author Mail Random House UK 20 Vauxhall Bridge Rd London SW1V 2SA England Office: Emory U English Dept 1535-003-1AA 201 Dowman Dr Atlanta GA 30322 E-mail: salman.rushdie@emory.edu. *

RUSHER, MARY NASH KELLY, lawyer; b. Norfolk, Va., May 25, 1958; BA in Polit., German, magna cum laude, Wake Forest Univ., 1980; JD, Univ. Va., 1984. Bar: NC 1985. Law clk., Hon. John D. Butzner, Jr. U.S. Court of Appeals, 4th Cir., 1984—85; with Hunton & Williams LLP, Raleigh, NC, 1985—, ptnr., capital fin., real estate, 1993—, and mem. exec. com., 2002. Mem.: ABA, NC Bar Assn., Nat. Assn. Bond Lawyers, Mortar Board, Omicron Delta Kappa, Phi Beta Kappa, Order of Coif. Office: Hunton & Williams LLP Ste 1400 421 Fayetteville St Mall Raleigh NC 27601 Office Phone: 919-899-3066. Office Fax: 919-899-3160. Business E-Mail: mnrusher@hunton.com.

RUSHER, WILLIAM ALLEN, writer, commentator, columnist; b. Chgo., July 19, 1923; s. Evan Singleton and Verna (Self) R. AB, Princeton U., 1943; JD, Harvard U., 1948; DLit (hon.), Nathaniel Hawthorne Coll., 1973. Bar: N.Y. 1949. Assoc. Shearman & Sterling & Wright, NYC, 1948-56; spl. counsel fin. com. N.Y. Senate, 1955; assoc. counsel internal security subcom. U.S. Senate, 1956-57; pub., v.p. Nat. Review mag., NYC, 1957-88, also bd. dirs.; Disting. fellow The Claremont Inst., 1989—. Mem. Adv. Task Force on Civil Disorders, 1972. Author: Special Counsel, 1968, (with Mark Hatfield and Arlie Schardt) Amnesty?, 1973, The Making of the New Majority Party, 1975, How to Win Arguments, 1981, The Rise of the Right, 1984, The Coming Battle for the Media, 1988; editor: The Ambiguous Legacy of the Enlightenment, 1995; columnist Universal Press Syndicate, 1973-82, Newspaper Enterprise Assn., 1982—; played role of Advocate in TV program The Advocates, 1970-74. Chmn., bd. dirs. Media Rsch. Ctr., Washington, 2001—, Nat. Rev. Bd., 1957-88, 90—; bd. advisors Ashbrook Ctr., Ashland, Ohio, past chmn.; past vice chmn. Am. Conservative Union; past trustee Pacific Legal Found., Sacramento. Served as 2d lt. to capt., USAAF, 1943-45, India-Burma Theater. Recipient Disting. Citizen award NYU Sch. Law, 1973. Mem. ABA, Univ. Club (NYC), Met. Club (Washington). Anglican. Home and Office: 1661 Pine St Apt 933 San Francisco CA 94109

RUSHFORTH, ANN FAY, artist, educator; b. Tampa, Fla., July 17, 1944; d. Robert George Rushforth and Alla Petrovna Riordan; m. Reid Johnson Perryman, May 13, 2000; m. John William Semko, Nov. 11, 1971 (div.); 1 child, Tao Alexandre Semko. BA, George Wash. U., 1966—66; MFA, Antioch U., 1980. Asst. to dir. of film and broadcasting Smithsonian Instn., Washington, 1967—68; adminstrv. asst. Am. Craft Council-Bennington Exhbns., Bennington, Vt., 1972; asst. mgr. Am. Craft Council-Rhinebeck Exhbns., Rhinebeck, NY, 1973—74; dir. pub. rels. Scope Gallery, Torpedo Factory, Alexandria, Va., 1975, pres., 1976—77, bd. dirs., 1978; chmn. dept. art Stoneridge H.S., Bethesda, Md., 1981—84; v.p. Foundry Gallery, Washington, 1986; dir. Pavo Real Gallery, Washington, 1987—88; gallery dir. Arise Gallery of Asian Art and Antiques, Washington, 1988—90; spl. projects photographer Woodrow Wilson Ho. Mus., Washington; arts instr. Duke Ellington Sch. of Arts, Washington, 1990—91, Visual Systems, Rockville, Md., 1991, Fillmore Art Ctr., Washington, 1991; executive dir. The Art Barn Assn., Washington, 1991—93; freelance master paintings copyist Nat. Gallery of Art, Washington, 1993—94; arts instr., 2005—. Rep. Dupont Cir. Consortium of Galleries, Washington, 1986; art instr. Md. Coll. of Art and Design, Dept. Continuing Edn., Rockville, 1990—91; dir., devel. officer R St. Gallery, Washington, 1992—93; conservator, appraiser Artsserve, Ltd., Newnan, 1995—; co-founder Contemporary Arts Alliance, Newnan, 2003—; art instr. The Pottery Wheel, Newnan, Ga., 2005—. Dir.: Carrollton Arts Guild Exhbns.; art critic: Eyewash Newpaper, 1990—91; editor: (exhibition catalog) Sculpture to Touch: For the Sight Impaired, 1987, Md. Craft Coun. News, 1976—78; Wash. Post Mag., 1977, Woodrow Wilson House Mus. Annual Report, Nat. Trust Hist. Preservation, 1987, Greater Chattanooga Artists, The Bureau, 1999, CABIA Arts Calendar, 1999, one-woman shows include Everson Mus. Art Gallery, Syracuse, NY, 1978, Montpelier Cultural Ctr., Md., 1981, Foundry Gallery, Washington, DC, 1986, In Town Gallery, Chattanooga, 2000, exhibited in group shows at NE Juried Exhbn. 12, Rhinebeck, NY, 1974—77, Frederick Wholesale Fair 3, Md., 1975—77, Fairtree Gallery, NYC, 1976, Inc. Gallery, 1976, Concepts Gallery, Ridgewood, NJ, 1976, Scope Gallery, Alexandria, Va., 1976 (Best in Show), 1977, 1984, Montgomery Coll. Gallery, Rockville, Md., 1977, US Govt. Svc. Adminstrn. Invitational Exhbn., Washington, DC, 1977, Westlake Gallery, White Plains, NY, 1977, 1980, 1983, Coqui Galleries, Westport, Conn., 1977, 1978, 1979, Fredericksburg Gallery of Modern Art, Va., 1977, Jelly Mill Gallery, Manchester, Vt., 1981, Md. Nat. Capitol Park and Planning Commn., 1980, VAC Gallery, Columbia, Md., 1981, Visual Arts Ctr., 1982, WWAC Gallery, Washington, DC, 1982, 1985, 1985, 1986, Nat. Capital AMCCAP Festival, 1984 (Second Place, Hon. Mention in Sculpture), 1993, Design Ctr., 1984, Art League Gallery, Alexandria, 1985, Art Barn Gallery, Washington, DC, 1985, 1992, 1992, 1993, Signature Galleries Invitational, Boston and Hyannis, Mass., 1985, Concepts '85, Margate, NJ, 1985, Martin Luther King Libr. Gallery, Washington, DC, 1986, R St. Gallery, 1989, Rockland Ctr., Ellicott City, Md., 1989, Foundry Gallery, Washington, DC, 1989, Jackson Sch. Studios, 1990, 1991, 1992, 901 E St. Gallery, 1991, 1993, Capital Arts Inc. Georgetown Visitation Sch., 1992, 1993, Georgetown Holiday Inn, 1992, The Spy Club, 1993, Universal N. Gallery, 1993, 1993, Washington Project for the Arts, 1993, Jackson Art Ctr., Studio #21, 1993, Gallery West, Alexandria, 1993, Corcoran Sch. Gallery, Washington, DC, 1993, Avery Gallery, Atlanta, Ga., 1995, Blair Voltz Exhbns., Atlanta, 1997, The Stalls, Bennett St., 1997, Grandview Gallery, 1997, Waterhouse Pavilion, Chattanooga, 1998, AVA Gallery, 1998, 1999, Urban Art Inst., 2000, Panoply Showhouse, Newnan, Ga., 2001, Tenn. Valley Art Mus., Tuscumbia, Ala., 2002, Arts Clayton Gallery, Jonesboro, Ga., 2002, Atlanta Arts Club, 2002, Forum Gallery at Defoor Centre, Atlanta, 2002, 2004, Atlanta Coll. Art, Coweta County, Ga., 2003, Keptever Gallery, Peachtree City, Ga., 2004, Mandeville Gallery, Carrollton, Ga., 2004, Jackalope's Gallery, Carrollton, 2004, MECCA Festival for the Arts, 2004, Carrollton Artists Guild, 2004, Carrollton Arts Ctr., 2005, exhibitions include HMR Engring. Inc., Alexandria, 1993, Meml. Hosp. Foyer, Chattanooga, 1999, UTC Faculty Club, 1999, Ga. State Fair, Perry, 2001, prin. works include St. John the Wonderworker, Patron St. Altarpiece and Icon of St. Brigid, Abess & Healer, St. John the Wonderworker Ea. Orthodox Ch., Atlanta, 1996, Christus Rex, Ceramic bas Relief Altarpiece, St. Paul's Episc. Ch., Newnan, 2006. Lector St.Paul's Episcopal Ch., Newnan, 2004—06. Mem.: Am. Ceramic Soc. Potter's Coun., Womens Caucus for Arts, Portrait Soc. Atlanta (edn. dir. 2005), Nat. Coun. Edn. for Ceramic Arts, Newnan-Coweta Artist Assn., Carrollton Artist Guild (exhbn. dir. 2005). Libertarian. Episcopalian. Avocations: physical fitness, dog shows, travel, art history. Home Phone: 678-423-1623; Office Phone: 678-634-6360. E-mail: annfayrushforth@hotmail.com.

RUSHING, JOHN ALAN, business educator; s. Thomas Jefferson and Mary Emma Rushing; m. Sherre Lynn Garvin, Nov. 23, 1963; children: John Alan Jr., Laura Ann. M internat. bus. adminstrn., Nova U., 1990; D in Bus. Adminstrn., Nova Southeastern, 2001. Pres. Kiwi Rsch. and Devel., Ft. Lauderdale, Fla., 1987—89; adj. faculty Broward C.C., Davie, Fla., 1992—99; corp. sec. Geep Corp., Oxford, Miss., 1989—2005; asst. prof. Barry U., Miami Shores, Fla., 1989—2003, asst. dean for academic affairs, 2003—, regional dir., 2006—. Author: Adventure Capital, 2001. Chair bus. devel. Davie C. of C., Davie, Fla., 1997, chair edn. conf., 1999, mem., 1990—99. Mem.: Am. Soc. of Devel., Acad. of Internat. Bus., Sigma Beta Delta Internat. Bus. Honor Soc., Gold Key Honor Soc. Avocation: radio controlled boats and airplanes. Office Phone: 850-385-2279. Office Fax: 850-385-7576. Business E-Mail: jrushing@mail.barry.edu.

RUSHING, PHILIP DALE, retired social worker; b. Carbondale, Ill., Mar. 15, 1932; S. Paul and Beulah Myrl (Benton) R.; m. Linda North, July 5, 1958 (div. July 1964); 1 child, Lisa Anne Rushing Burrow; m. Rosalie Anne Sturm, Aug. 20, 1966. BA, So. Ill. U., 1958; MSW, Washington U., St. Louis, 1960. Diplomate Am. Bd. Clinical Social Workers, Nat. Assn. Social Workers; LCSW Ill. Child welfare worker Ill. Dept. Pub. Welfare, Salem, East St. Louis, 1958-60, child welfare supr. East St. Louis, 1960-63; field rep. Nat. Assn. for Retarded Children, Dallas, Denver, 1963-65; dir. social svcs. A.L. Bowen Children's Ctr., Harrisburg, Ill., 1965-68; asst. zone dir. for mentally retarded Ill. Dept. of Mental Health, Harrisburg, 1968-74; regional coord. for devel. disabilities Ill. Dept. of Mental Health & Devel. Disabilities, Marion, 1974-83; social work adminstr. Choate Mental Health & Devel. Ctr., Anna, Ill., 1983-95; ret., 1995. Adj. asst. prof. So. Ill. U. Rehab. Inst., Carbondale, Ill., 1968-78; bd. dirs. Southeastern Ill. Pastoral Counseling Ctrs., chmn. pers. com., 1996-98. Bd. deacons First Presbyn. Ch., Harrisburg, 1974-77, bd. trustees, 1978-80, bd. elders, 1980-83, 96-98, 2003-06. With USN, 1951-55, Korea Fellow Am. Assn. Intellectual and Devel. Disabilities (life, chmn. social work divsn. Ill. chpt. 1973-74); mem. NASW (chmn. East St. Louis br. 1962). Home: 6542 Hwy 13 W Harrisburg IL 62946-4142 Personal E-mail: pr.rushing@juno.com.

RUSHING, TONNIE AUSTIN PAGE, musician, educator; b. Hartwell, Ga., Mar. 6, 1940; d. George Wilson and Ruth Smith Page; m. Roger Kendall Vichery, June 18, 1960; children: George Kendall, Carol Page; m. Charles Maynard Rushing, Aug. 18, 1979; stepchildren: Joan E., Brian C., Susanne E. BS in Edn., Athens State Coll., Ga., 1973; cert. in Computer Tech., Trident Tech. Coll., 1992, Sylvan Learning Ctr., 1996; cert. in Sign Lang., Trident Tech. Coll., 1997. Musician, Ga., 1958—; prin., owner Opus 11 George Bed & Breakfast, 1988—97; afternoon activities dir. O'Quinn Preschool-Kindergarten, 2001. Dir. music Summer Stock Theater, Morristown, Tenn., 1969; music educator Covenant Sch. Fine Arts Enrichment, 1976—79; music dir. Young Charleston Theatre Co., 1988, 96; mem. founding com. Covenant Fine Arts Enrichment Sch., Decatur, 1976; mem. adv. com. Coun. Arts John C. Calhoun State Coll., Decatur; mem. GAMAC Concert and Chamber Choir, Anderson, SC, 2006. Singer: North Ala. Charleston Symphony, St. Micheal's Ch., Grace Episc. Ch., Choir Eng. Tour, 1981—2002; musician: French Protestant Ch., 1988—96; author: Huguenots and the Legacy, 1994; dir.: (recording) Huguenot Psalter, 1991; jacket cover, Huguenot Psalter, 1991. Pres. Decatur Civic Chorus; vol. Crisis Ctr. Mental Health Ctr., Decatur, 1971—79; mem. comprehensive planning com. City Hartwell, Ga., 2003; bd. dirs. Preservation Soc., 2004, Hart County Hist. Soc., 2004; with Hartwell Christmas Tour of Homes, 2006; chair Olde Time Singing, Hartwell Hist. Soc. Fundraiser, 2006; mem. Greater Anderson Musical Consortium Concert Choir, 2006—07, Greater Anderson Musical Consortium Chamber Choir, 2006—07; music asst. 2d Presbyn. Ch., Charleston, SC, 1988; sect. leader St. Michaels Ch., Charleston, 1998—2001; elder Hartwell 1st Presbyn. Ch., 2004; bd. dirs. Charleston Symphony Orch. Chorus. Mem.: PTA, Greater Anderson Musical Arts Consortium, Am. Guild Organists, Presbyn. Assn. Musicians,

Nat. Assn. Mental Illness, Charleston County Med. Aux., Hartwell Women's Club (v.p. 2006—07), Sigma Alpha Iota. Republican. Home: 175 E Johnson St Hartwell GA 30643 Personal E-mail: cmandtpr@hartcom.net.

RUSHNELL, SQUIRE DERRICK, writer, speaker, television executive; s. Reginald Grant and Erica Mafauna Redwood Sedgemore (Squire) R.; m. Louise DuArt, Oct. 28, 2000; children: Robin Tracy, Hilary Adair, Squire Grant Sedgemore. Student, Syracuse U., 1956-60. Disc jockey Stas. WOLF, WHEN and WFBL, Syracuse, NY, 1958-61, Sta. WTRL, Bradenton, Fla., 1961-62; exec. prodr. Sta. WBZ AM-TV, Boston, 1962-67; program dir. KYW News-Radio, Phila., 1968; exec. prodr. Kennedy & Co. Sta. WLS-TV, Chgo., 1969-71, program dir., 1971-73; v.p. programs ABC-owned TV stas., NYC, 1973-74; v.p. children's TV ABC Entertainment Network, NYC, 1974-78; v.p. Good Morning Am. and children's programs ABC-TV Network, NYC, 1978-81, v.p. long range planning and children's TV, 1981-87; v.p. late night and children's TV ABC Entertainment, NYC, 1987-89; pres. Rushnell Comm. & Pub., Inc., 1990-96; pres., CEO GoodLife TV Network, Washington, 1996—2001; author, motivational spkr., TV producer, 2001—. Author: The Kingdom Chums Greatest Stories, 1986, When God Winks: How the Power of Coincidence Guides Your Life, 2001, When God Winks on Love, 2004, When God Winks at You, 2006; co-author: Broadcast Programming, 1981, Broadcast/Cable Programming, 1985, rev. edit., 1989, 1993. Recipient Emmy awards, 1975-88, TV Critics Circle award, 1976, all for outstanding children's TV programming, Am. Children's TV Festival award, 1985, 87. Business E-Mail: squire@whengodwinks.com.

RUSHTON, ALAN R., physician, medical researcher, historian; b. Oak Park, Ill., Mar. 10, 1949; s. Raymond H. and D. Loree (Swan) R.; m. Nancy Spencer, May 5, 1973; children: Andrew, Daniel. AB in Chemistry, Earlham Coll., Richmond, Ind., 1971; PhD in Genetics, U. Chgo., 1975, MD, 1977. Diplomate Am. Bd. Pediatrics, Am. Bd. Med. Genetics. Resident, intern Yale U.-New Haven Hosp., Conn., 1977-80; physician Hunterdon Med. Ctr., Flemington, NJ, 1980—; assoc. clin. prof. pediatrics Robert Wood Johnson Med. Sch., New Brunswick, NJ, 1980—. Lectr. genetics Princeton U., NJ, 1980-84; adj. prof. Med. U. Ams., Nevis, West Indies. Author: Genetics and Medicine in the United States 1800-1922, 1994. Fellow Am. Acad. Pediatrics, Am. Coll. Med. Genetics, NY Acad. Medicine, Royal Soc. Medicine; mem. Am. Assn. History Medicine, History Sci. Soc. Office: Hunterdon Pediatric Assocs 6 Sand Hill Rd Ste 202 Flemington NJ 08822-4600 Office Phone: 908-788-6468. Personal E-mail: arrdoc@aol.com.

RUSHWORTH, MICHELE D., artist; b. Oct. 16, 1958; Student, Queen's U., Kingston, Ont., Can., 1976—78, Ont. Coll. Art and Design, Toronto, Can., 1978—80. Exhibitions include The Early Show, CBS-TV, 2002, Safeco Field Stadium, 2005, McCaw Hall, Seattle, 2005, Represented in permanent collections Wash. State Capitol, Nev. State Capitol, Nev. State Mus., U. Wash. Recipient profl. devel. program grant, Wash. State Arts Comm., 2006. Mem.: Portrait Soc. Am.

RUSI, EDUARD, engineering educator; b. Korca, Albania, Nov. 17, 1978; s. Nihat and Flutur Rusi. Grad. in Elec. Engring., U. Wis. Tchr. asst. U. Wis., Manitowoc, Wis., 2002—04. Project outreach leader Campus Crusade for Christ, Tirana, Albania, 1998—2000. Mem.: U. Wis. Alumni Assn., Phi Theta Kappa Honor Soc. Home: 2302 University Ave Apt 114 Madison WI 53726 Home Phone: 608-658-5078. Personal E-mail: rusi@wisc.edu.

RUSKIN, JOSEPH RICHARD, actor, director; b. Haverhill, Mass., Apr. 14, 1924; s. Ely and Betty Edith (Chaimson) Schlafman; m. Patricia Herd, 1959 (div. 1976); m. Barbara Greene; 1 child, Alicia Schlafman. Grad., Carnegie Inst. Tech., 1949. Founder Rochester Arena Theatre, NY, 1949-52. Actor: NY stage plays, 1949—52; (plays) Theater Group, UCLA, Mark Taper Forum, 1959; (films) Fall of Legs Diamond, 1959, Magnificent Seven, 1960, Escape from Zahrein, 1963, Robin and the Seven Hoods, 1965, Prizzi's Honor, 1985, Longshot, 1987, Indecent Proposal, 1992, Spider-Man, 1994, (voice) Star Trek: Insurrection, 1998, King Cobra, 1999, The Scorpion King, 2002, The Streetsweeper, 2002, IceMaker, 2003, Smokin' Aces, 2006; (TV series) Untouchables, Land of the Giants, The Twilight Zone, Mission Impossible, Charlie's Angels, Knight Rider, Spider-Man, Star Trek, Alias; dir.: (plays) Houston Alley, 1965—69. With USNR, 1943—46. Mem.: SAG, AFTRA, Actors Equity Assn. (mem. nat. coun.). Home: 1326 Devon Ave Los Angeles CA 90024-5346

RUSKIN, ROBERT STERLING, educational association administrator; b. Washington, Nov. 27, 1945; s. Robert Edward and Thelma (Gipe) R.; m. Rebecca Lynne Wilson, Aug. 11, 1967; 1 child, Brant Edward. BA, Washington Coll., Chestertown, Md., 1967; MA, W.Va. U., 1969, PhD, 1971. Lic. psychologist Va., D.C. Prof. dept. psychology Georgetown U., Washington, 1971-86, chmn. dept. psychology, 1976-85, dir. Ctr. for Personalized Instrn., 1977-80, dir. Teaching Resource Ctr., 1985-86; chief psychol. assessor leadership devel. U. Md., College Park, 1984—; prin. investigator and project dir., consortium univs. rsch fellows program U.S. Army Rsch. Inst., Washington, Alexandria, 1985—; nat. rsch. fellow U.S. Dept. Edn., Washington, 1986-87; affiliate prof. psychology George Mason U., Washington, 1989—; prin. investigator Consortium & Office of Substance Abuse Prevention, Washington, 1990-93; dir. programs and rsch. Consortium of Univs. of Washington Metro. Area, 1987-88, v.p., 1989—. Psychol. cons. DuPont Corp., Seaford, Del., 1986-88; psychol. cons. Consortium of Univs. of D.C., 1984—; cons. in field; rep. of U.S. to UNESCO Planning Meeting, Paris, 1979. Co-author: Behavioral Instruction: An Evaluative Review, 1977; editor manuscript: Consortium Research Fellows Program; editor The Jour. of Personalized Instrn., 1975-81, Revista a Tecnologia Educativa, 1976-83. Battelle Inst. Disting. Acad. Rsch. fellow U.S. Army Rsch. Inst., 1984-86. Fellow APA, Am. Psychol. Soc. (charter); mem. AAAS, D.C. Psychol. Assn., Va. Psychol. Assn., Psi Chi. Methodist. Avocations: golf, fishing. Home: 309 W Alex Ave Alexandria VA 22302 Office: Consortium of Univs of Wash 1 Dupont Cir NW Washington DC 20036-1110 E-mail: robert.ruskin@ari.army.mil.

RUSKIN, RYAN SCOTT, packaging company executive; b. Pitts., Jan. 31, 1968; s. Stanley C. and Judith Anne (Blitzstein) R. BA, Princeton U., 1990; MBA, Northwestern U., 1994. Dir. tng. and devel. The Princeton Rev., 1987—90, dir. nat. tng., 1987—92; mgr. Vail Assocs., Colo., 1990—92; dir. strategic planning Sterling Lebanon Packaging Corp., Jeannette, Pa., 1992—94; assoc. A.T. Kearney, Chgo., 1994—96, sr. mgr., 1996—98; exec. v.p. Sterling Packaging Corp., Pitts., 1998—2000, pres., 2004—, Jeanette Paper Co., Pitts., 2001—. Advisor Coro Ctr. for Civi Leadership, Pitts., 1999—, J.L. Kellogg Sch. Northwestern U., 1994—. Mem. alumni coun. Shady Side Acad., Pitts., 1998; speech writing team, media coord. Rep. Nat. Conv., 1988; dir. Open Hand Chgo., 1999—; nat. faculty U.S. Sailing, Newport, 1990-94. Mem. Am. Soc. for Quality Control, Inst. Packaging Profls., Chgo. Yacht Club, Univ. Club Chgo. Avocations: sailing, skiing, tennis, golf. Home: 823 W Junior Ter Chicago IL 60613-1607 Office: Ste 304 1330 Old Freeport Rd Pittsburgh PA 15238 Home Phone: 773-525-5586; Office Phone: 412-696-0035. Business E-Mail: rruskin@ruskingroup.com.

RUSLING, BARBARA N(EUBERT), real estate broker; b. St. Louis, Nov. 27, 1945; d. Ralph L. and Rosemary (Stroot) Neubert; m. Randolph H. Wieser, Apr. 23, 1966 (div. Nov. 1983); children: Keith, Steve, Eric; m. Robert Best Rusling, Aug. 2, 1985 (dec. Oct. 2004). BA, Vanderbilt U., 1966; postgrad., Baylor U., 1975. Lic. real estate broker, cert. justice of the peace. Appraisal intern Smith Real Estate, Waco, Tex., 1975; resident real estate broker Sanger Suburban Realty, Waco, 1975-81, sales mgr., 1981-83; pres., gen. mgr. Coldwell Banker Hallmark Realty, Waco, 1983-99; with Coldwell Banker Jim Stewart, Realtors, 1999—; commr. Tex. Gen. Svcs. Commn., 1997—2002; regent Tex. State Tech. Coll., 2002—. Mem. from dist. 57 Tex. State Ho. Reps., 1995-97. Chmn. bd. dirs. YWCA, Waco, 1976—79; dir. Leadership Waco Program, 1986—87; various positions Hist. Waco Found.; bd. dirs. Waco Civic Theatre, treas., 1999—2001; bd. dirs. Family Counseling Ctr., 1991—96, United Way, 1992—98, Family Abuse Ctr., 1993—2002, 2004—06, Waco BBB, 1994—99; Justice of the Peace, 2004—. Mem.: Waco C. of C. (bd. dirs. 1990—93), Waco Bd. Realtors (past bd. dirs., Salesman of Yr. 1979), Realtors Nat. Mktg. Inst. (cert.), Tex. Assn. Realtors (edn. com., strategic planning com. 1983—95, realtor lawyer com. 1985—93), Am. Heart Assn. (McLennan County bd. dirs. 1997—, pres. 1999—2000), Kappa Delta. Home: 1635 Meandering Way China Spring TX 76633-2905 Office: Coldwell Banker 500 N Valley Mills Dr Waco TX 76710-6007 Home Phone: 254-836-4681; Office Phone: 254-776-0000. Personal E-mail: brusling@aol.com.

RUSMISEL, STEPHEN RAYMOND, lawyer; b. NYC, Jan. 27, 1946; s. R. Raymond and Esther Florence (Kutz) R.; m. Beirne Donaldson, Sept. 6, 1980 (div. Jan. 1984); 1 child, Margo Alexander; m. Melissa J. MacLeod, Aug. 24, 1985 (div. Oct. 1996); children: Benjamin William, Eric Scot Kunze, Erin Lea Kunze; m. Teresa R. Paterniti, June 28, 1997; 1 child, Sarah J. Lamendola. AB, Yale U., 1968; JD, U. Va., 1971. Bar: NY 1972, US Ct. Appeals (2d cir.) 1974, US Dist. Ct. (so. dist.) NY 1975. Assoc. Winthrop, Stimson, Putnam & Roberts, NYC, 1971-80, ptnr., 1980-2000, Pillsbury Winthrop Shaw Pittman LLP, NYC, 2001—. Aux. officer Bedminster Twp. Police, NJ, 1976—. Mem. Practicing Law Inst., Am. Arbitration Assn. (arbitrator 1976—), Far Hills Polo Club (Annandale, NJ), Ausable Club (St. Huberts, NY), Phi Delta Phi. Republican. Avocations: flying, carpentry, gardening, poetry. Home: Shadowline Farm Bedminster NJ 07921 Office: Pillsbury Winthrop Shaw Pittman LLP 1540 Broadway New York NY 10036-4039 Home Phone: 908-722-6172; Office Phone: 212-858-1000. Business E-Mail: stephen.rusmisel@pillsburylaw.com.

RUSPINI, ENRIQUE HECTOR, research scientist; b. Buenos Aires, Dec. 20, 1942; s. Arnoldo Ruspini and Carlota Julia Gasparini; m. Susana Alicia Carbone, May 22, 1965; children: Gabriel Jorge Agustín, Diego Cristián, Verónica María, Daniel Arnoldo. PhD in Engring., UCLA, 1977. Rsch. asst. Instituto de Cálculo, Universidad de Buenos Aires, Buenos Aires, 1962—66; lectr. dept. math. U. Buenos Aires, 1964—66, invited prof., 1988, 1992, U. Río Cuarto, 2003; vis. prof. Instituto de Física José A. Balseiro, Argentine Nat. Atomic Commn., San Carlos de Bariloche, Río Negro, 1966; rsch. assoc. U. So. Calif. Sch. Med., LA, 1966—68; head computer applications Space Biology Lab., U. Calif., LA, 1968—73; sr. staff engr. TRW Def. and Space Systems Group, Redondo Beach, 1973—78; sr. staff scientist Oper. Systems, Inc., Woodland Hills, 1979—82; prin. scientist Artificial Intelligence Ctr., SRI Internat., Menlo Park, 1982—; rsch. scientist Hewlett-Packard Laboratories, Palo Alto, Calif., 1982—84; vis. prof. U. Granada, Spain, 1989; vis. scholar NASA Ames Rsch. Ctr., Mountain View, Calif., 1994—95. Cons. Centro de Investigaciones Neurológicas Torcuato DiTella, Buenos Aires, 1964—66, TRW, Lockheed, GTE Sylvania, Calif., 1978—86; tech. program chair, ann. meeting Sociedad Argentina de Informática e Investigación Operativa, Buenos Aires, 1994; faculty mem., advanced inst. soft computing NATO, Antalya, Turkey, 1996. Mem. editl. bd. various tech. jours.:. Recipient King-sun Fu award, North-American Fuzzy Info. Processing Soc., 1985, Exceptional Achievement award, SRI Internat., 1987, Meritorious Svc. award, IEEE Computational Intelligence Soc., 2005; fellow, SRI Internat., 1992, Internat. Fuzzy Systems Assn., 1998; vis. scholar, U. Calif., 1986—87, 1989; Fulbright Scholar, Coun. Internat. Exch. Scholars, 1989. Fellow: IEEE (gen. chmn., second ieee internat. conf. on fuzzy systems 1993, gen. chair internat. conf. on neural networks 1993, tech. program co-chair internat. conf. on fuzzy systems 1994, pres. neural networks coun. 2001, distinguihed lectr., computational intelligence soc. 2001—, gen. co-chair internat. workshop on intelligent signal processing 2003, dir. divsn. x 2003—04, mem. audit com. 2003—04, program co chair on computational intelligence and homeland security 2004, mem., adminstrv. com., computational intelligence soc. 2006—, mem. nominations and appointments com. 2005—). Avocations: travel, astronomy, photography, woodworking. Office: SRI International 333 Ravenswood Ave Menlo Park CA 94025 Home Phone: 650-494-0862; Office Phone: 650-859-2314. Personal E-mail: ruspini@ai.sri.com.

RUSS, EDMOND VINCENT, JR., marketing professional; b. Washington, Feb. 14, 1944; s. Edmond V. and Thayer Kennedy (Thompson) R.; m. Tena Marie Loveland, Dec. 26, 1982; children: Jamie Russ Solanics, E.V. Russ III, Christina T. Russ, Cory S. Russ. BA, Kent State U., Ohio, 1966; MBA, U. Pitts., 1967. Dir. mktg. Borg-Warner Ednl. Systems, Niles, Ill., 1969-74; v.p. mktg. Rusty Jones Inc., Chgo., 1974-83; gen. mgr. Signed, Sealed and Delivered, Melrose Park, Ill., 1983-86; v.p. mktg. Merchant Network Inc., Chgo., 1986-90; dir. mktg. Am. Appraisal Assocs., Milw., 1990-93, Pricewaterhouse Coopers, 1993-2001; ptnr., chief mktg. officer Grant Thornton LLP, 2001—. Mem. Am. Mktg. Assn., Assn. Acctg. Marketers, Bus. Mktg. Assn., Strategic Mgmt. Assn., Vintage Sports Car Drivers Assn., Porsche Club Am. Avocations: tennis, community theater, sports car racing. E-mail: planetera@comcast.net.

RUSS, JAMES MATTHIAS, lawyer; b. Duluth, Minn., Sept. 20, 1929; s. Matthias James and Agnes Margaret (Jerina) R.; m. Nanelle Davis, June 27, 1953; children: Tanya, Robin, Sarah, Claudia, Janine, Monica, Matthias James, Kateri. AB cum laude, Spring Hill Coll., 1955; JD, Georgetown U., 1957. Bar: D.C., 1957, Fla., 1958, U.S. Dist. Ct. (no., so. and mid. dists.) Fla., U.S. Ct. Appeals (5th and 11th cirs.), U.S. Supreme Ct.; cert. criminal trial lawyer 1987, criminal appellate lawyer 1992. County solicitor Orange County, Fla., 1961-65; pvt. practice Orlando. Lectr. criminal law and legal ethics seminars. Contbr. articles to profl. jours. Trustee Orange County Legal Aid Soc.; chmn. The Chester Bedell Meml. Found., 1997-98. Recipient Tobias Simon Pro Bono Svc. award Fla. Supreme Ct., 1997, Joseph W. Durocher award Ctrl. Fla. Criminal Def. Lawyers Assn., 2003. Master, Am. Inns of Ct.; fellow Am. Coll. Trial Lawyers, Am. Bd. Criminal Lawyers; mem. ABA (criminal justice sect.-speedy trial com. 1976-77, com. on privacy 1982-83, def. function com. 1983-89, chmn. 1987-89), The Fla. Bar (chmn. criminal law com. 1964-65, 66-67, exec. coun. trial lawyers sect., 1967-68, mem. criminal law cert. com. 1988-91, recipient President's Pro Bono Svc. award, 9th jud. cir. 1993), Orange County Bar Assn. (exec. coun. 1967-70, sec. 1984-88), Nat. Assn. Criminal Def. Lawyers (2d v.p. 1992-93, 1st v.p. 1993-94, dir. 1984—, chmn. Lawyers' Assistance Strike Force 1987-89, Robert C. Heeney Meml. award 1988), Fla. Assn. Criminal Def. Lawyers (chmn. Lawyers' Assistance Strike Force 1988-89, Steven M. Goldstein Criminal Justice award 2002), Nat. Bd. Trial Advocacy (cert. 1982). Office: Tinker Bldg 18 W Pine St Orlando FL 32801-2612 Home Phone: 407-869-0093; Office Phone: 407-849-6050. E-mail: tinkerjmr@covad.net.

RUSS, JOANNA, author; b. NYC, Feb. 22, 1937; d. Evarett and Bertha (Zinner) R. BA high honors in English, Cornell U., Ithaca, NY, 1957; MFA in Playwriting and Dramatic Lit., Yale U., New Haven, Conn., 1960. Lectr. English Cornell U., 1967—70, asst. prof., 1970—72; asst. prof. English Harpur Coll. SUNY Binghamton, 1972—75; asst. prof. English U. Colo., 1975—77; assoc. prof. English, U. Wash., 1977—90, prof., 1984—90. Author: Picnic on Paradise, 1968, And Chaos Died, 1970, The Female Man, 1975, We Who Are About To, 1977, Kittatinny: A Tale of Magic, 1978, The Two of Them, 1978, On Strike Against God, 1980, The Adventures of Alyx, 1983, The Zanzibar Cat, 1983, How To Suppress Women's Writing, 1983, Extra (Ordinary) People, 1984, Magic Mommas, Trembling Sisters, Puritans and Perverts: Feminist Essays, 1985, (collection) The Hidden Side of the Moon, 1987, To Write Like a Woman, 1995, (nonfiction) What Are We Fighting For, 1998; also numerous short stories Mem. Sci. Fiction Writers Am. (Nebula award Best Short Story 1972, Hugo award for Best Novella 1983)

RUSSACK, JOHN A., federal official; Grad., U. Kans., 1970, Nat. War Coll., 1991. Dep. to assoc. dir. of ctrl. intelligence for military support CIA, exec. asst. to dep. dir., military dep. dir. nonproliferation ctr., dep. asst. dir. for collection, dep. chief external ops., cover divsn. for counterintelligence; dir. office of intelligence US Dept. Energy, Washington, 2003—05; program mgr. Information-Sharing Environment Office Dir. Nat. Intelligence, Washington, 2005—.

RUSSEL, WILLIAM BAILEY, engineering educator; b. Corpus Christi, Tex., Nov. 17, 1945; m. 1972; 2 children. BA, Rice U., 1969, MS in Chem. Engring., 1969; PhD in Chem. Engring., Stanford U., 1973. NATO fellow applied math. Cambridge U., 1973-74; from asst. prof. to assoc. prof. chem. engring. Princeton U., NJ, 1974-83, prof. chem. engring. NJ, 1983—, chmn. dept. chem. engring. NJ, 1987-96, dir. Materials Sciences Inst. NJ, 1996-98, dean graduate sch. NJ, 2002—; faculty Princeton Inst. for the Sci. and Tech. of Materials; assoc. faculty, Princeton Environ. Inst. Olaf A. Hougen vis. prof. U. Wis., 1984, Debye vis. prof., U. Utrecht, 2001. Mem.: Am. Acad. Arts & Sciences, Materials Rsch. Soc., Am. Chem. Soc. (award in colloid and surface chemistry 2007), Soc. Rheology (pres. 2001—03, Bingham award 1999), NAE, AIChE (William H. Walker award 1992). Office: Princeton U A 225 Engring Quadrangle 205 Nassau Hall Princeton NJ 08544 Home Phone: 609-921-1863; Office Phone: 609-258-4590. Business E-Mail: wbrussel@princeton.edu. E-mail: graddean@princeton.edu. *

RUSSELL, ALLAN DAVID, lawyer; b. Cleve., May 6, 1924; s. Allan MacGillivray and Marvel (Codling) R.; m. Lois Anne Robinson, June 12, 1947, m. Patricia A. Ellis, March 8, 2003; children: Lisa Anne, Robinson David, Martha Leslie BA, Yale U., 1945, LLB, 1951. Bar: N.Y. 1952, Conn. 1956, Mass. 1969, U.S. Supreme Ct. 1977. Atty. Sylvania Electric Products, Inc., NYC, 1951-56, div. counsel Batavia, NY, 1956-65, sr. counsel, 1965-71; sec., sr. counsel GTE Sylvania Inc., Stamford, Conn., 1971-76; asst. gen. counsel GTE Svc. Corp., 1976-80, v.p., assoc. gen. counsel, 1980—83; pvt. practice Redding, Conn., 1983—2004. Sec., dir. mktg. subs. Sylvania Entertainment Products Corp., 1961-67; sec. Wilbur B. Driver Co Dist. leader Rep. Party, New Canaan, Conn., 1955-56; sec. bd. dirs. Youth Found., Inc., 1981-83, bd. dirs., 1985-2001, pres., 2000-01; mem. planning commn., Redding, Conn., 1987-89; mem. Redding Bd. Ethics, 1990-96, chmn., 1992-96; warden Christ Ch. Parish, Redding, 1987-89; bd. dirs. Mark Twain Libr., 1988-94, 2002-2004, v.p., 1988-89, pres., 1990-92 With USAAF, 1943—46. Mem. SAR, Assn. of Bar of City of N.Y., Conn. Bar Assn. (exec. com. corp. counsel sect. 1986-90), Am. Soc. Corp. Secs., St. Nicholas Soc., Collie Club Am. Found., Inc. (v.p., dir. 1986-89, pres. 1989-90), Soc. Colonial Wars, Yale Alumni Assn. (sec. local chpt. 1953-56), Yale Club of Danbury (pres. 1990—), Phi Delta Phi Home: 33 Old Field Hill Rd Unit #32 Southbury CT 06488-3837

RUSSELL, ALLEN STEVENSON, retired metal products executive; b. Bedford, Pa., May 27, 1915; s. Arthur Stainton and Ruth (Stevenson) R.; m. Judith Pauline Sexauer, Apr. 5, 1941. BS, Pa. State U., 1936, MS, 1937, PhD, 1941. With Aluminum Co. Am., 1940-82, assoc. dir. rsch., 1973-74; v.p. Alcoa, Pa., 1974-78; v.p. sci. and tech. Pitts., 1978-81; v.p., chief scientist, 1981-82. Adj. prof. U. Pitts., 1981-86 Contbr. articles to profl. jours.; patentee in field. Named IR-100 Scientist of Yr., 1979; Pa. State U. alumni fellow, 1980; K.J. Bayer medalist, 1981; recipient chem. Pioneer award Am. Inst. Chemists, 1983 Fellow Am. Soc. Metals (Gold medal 1982), AIME (James Douglas gold medal 1987), Am. Inst. Chemists; mem. NAE (coun. 1978-84), Am. Chem. Soc., Sigma Xi. Republican. Presbyterian. Home: 27 Meadowlark Ln Hilton Head Plantation Hilton Head Island SC 29926 Home Phone: 843-682-3455. Personal E-mail: alsrus@msn.com.

RUSSELL, ANDREW BENJAMIN, historian, educator; b. Oxnard, Calif., June 27, 1960; s. Leonard Russell and Sylvia Bergdal; m. Tona Hughes (div.); m. Rose T. Díaz, Jan. 14, 2001. BA in History, U. Nev., Las Vegas, 1988, MA in History, 1996; PhD in History, Ariz. State U., Tempe, 2003. Seasonal park ranger Nev. Divsn. State Parks, Spring Valley, 1988—90; svc. worker Las Vegas Convention Authority, 1991—96; tchg. asst. U. Nev., Las Vegas, 1994; tchg. asst., assoc. Ariz. State U., Tempe, 1996—98; part-time instr. Albuquerque Tech. Vocat. Inst./Cmty. Coll. (now Ctrl. N.Mex. CC), 1999—2003; history instr. Albuquerque TVI/Cmty. Coll., 2003—. Rsch. historian Ariz. Humanities Coun., Phoenix, 1997; vol. rschr. Ariz. Am. Indian Movement, Phoenix, 1998; presenter in field. Contbr. chapters to books. Recipient Phoenix One Hundred award, City of Phoenix, 1997; grantee, Civil Liberties Pub. Edn. Fund., 1998—99. Mem.: SW Oral History Assn., Albuquerque Hist. Soc. (bd. dirs. 2004—), Oral History Assn. (workship facilitator 1997—, nominating com. 2005). Achievements include research in Japanese-American history. Avocations: guitar, songwriting, camping, travel. Business E-Mail: aruss@cnm.edu.

RUSSELL, ANNE M., editor-in-chief; Editor book divsn. Billboard Publ.; editor Photo Dist. News; reporter Adweek; assoc. editor Am. Photographer; sr. editor Working Women; exec. editor Folio: Pub. News, editor-in-chief, 1992—97, Living Fit, 1997—99, Vegetarian Times, 1999; editl. dir. Fox TV's Health Network, Shape mag., 2001—03, editor-in-chief, 2003—. Office: Shape 21100 Erwin St Woodland Hills CA 91367 *

RUSSELL, BILL, former professional basketball team executive, former professional basketball player; b. Monroe, La., Feb. 12, 1934; Grad., San Francisco State Coll., 1956. Player, NBA Boston Celtics Profl. Basketball Club, 1956-69, coach, 1966-69; sportscaster ABC-TV, 1969-80, CBS-TV, 1980-83; coach NBA Seattle Supersonics, 1973-77, Sacramento Kings, 1987-88, v.p. basketball ops., then exec. v.p., 1988-89. Mem. U.S. Olympic Basketball Team (Gold medal), 1956 Appeared in: TV series Cowboy in Africa; also commls.; co-host: The Superstars, ABC-TV, 1978-79; Author: Second Wind: Memoirs of an Opinionated Man, 1979. Inducted into Basketball Hall of Fame, 1974, Nat. Collegiate Basketball Hall of Fame, 2006; mem. 11 NBA championship teams.

RUSSELL, C. EDWARD, JR., lawyer; b. Portsmouth, Va., Aug. 19, 1942; BA, Hampden-Sydney Coll., 1964; LLB, Washington & Lee U., 1967. Bar: Va. 1967. Law clk. to Hon. John A. MacKenzie U.S. Dist. Ct. (ea. dist.) Va., 1967-68; atty. Kaufman & Canoles, Norfolk. Mem. ABA (bus. law sect., real property, probate and trust law sect.), Va. State Bar (bus. law sect., real property sect.), Va. Bar Assn. (bus. law sect., real estate sect., chmn. young lawyers sect. 1977), Omicron Delta Kappa, Phi Alpha Delta. Office: PO Box 13368 Norfolk VA 23506-0368 Home Phone: 750-428-0652; Office Phone: 757-624-3108. E-mail: cerussell@kaufcan.com.

RUSSELL, CAROL ANN, city council member, retired company executive; d. Billy and Iris Koud; m. Victor Rojas (div.). BA in English, CUNY-Hunter Coll., 1993. Registered employment cons. Various exec. positions in staffing/workforce devel. svcs., NYC, San Francisco Bay, 1964—82; v.p. Wollborg-Michelson, San Francisco, 1974-82; co-owner, pres. Russell Staffing Resources, Inc., San Francisco, Marin and Sonoma, 1983-98; ret.; elected mem. City Coun. Cloverdale, 2006. Media guest, spkr., workshop and seminar leader in field; host/cmty. prodr. Job Net program for TCI Cable T.V. Pub. Checkpoint Newsletter; feature writer/columnist The Slant; contbr. articles to profl. publs. Founding v.p. The Friends of the Frank Lloyd Wright Civic Ctr. Libr. Marin County; vice chair Sonoma County Commn. on Status of Women, 2003—06; mem. cmty. action com. Sonoma County Commn. on Human Rights; founding cmty. prodr. Northbay Pride Music Festival, 2005, 2006; mem. employee rels. policy com. Calif. League of Cities, 2007—; elected city coun. mem. Cloverdale, Calif., 2006; bd. dirs. Sonoma County Libr. Found., 2003—. Named to Inc. 500, 1989—90. Mem. Am. Women in Radio and TV, No. Calif. Human Resources Coun., Soc. Human Resource Mgmt., Calif. Assn. Pers. Cons. (pres. Golden State chpt. 1984-85), Calif. Assn. Temp. Svcs., Bay Area Pers. Assn. (pres. 1983-84), Pers. Assn. Sonoma County, Scowerers and Molly Maguires (bd. dirs., editor The Herald), Sherlock Holmes Soc. London, Nat. Women's Polit. Caucus (comms. chair Marin chpt. 2002, pres. Marin chpt. 2003), Mayors and Coun. Mem.s Assn., Sherlockian Soc. (Scowers and Molly Maguires), Churchill Soc., Sisters in Crime. Business E-Mail: incloverdale@comcast.net.

RUSSELL, DAVID L., federal judge; b. Sapulpa, Okla., July 7, 1942; s. Lynn and Florence E. (Brown) R.; m. Dana J. Wilson, Apr. 16, 1971; 1 child, Sarah Elizabeth BS, Okla. Bapt. U., 1963; JD, Okla. U., 1965. Bar: Okla. 1965. Asst. atty. gen. State of Okla., Oklahoma City, 1968-69, legal adviser to gov., 1969-70; legal adviser Senator Dewey Bartlett, Washington, 1973-75; U.S. atty. for Western dist. Okla. Dept. Justice, 1975-77, 81-82; ptnr. Benefield & Russell, Oklahoma City, 1977-81; judge U.S. Dist. Ct. (we. dist.) Okla., Oklahoma City, 1982—, chief judge, 1994—2002. Lt. comdr. JAGC, USN, 1965-68. Selected Outstanding Fed. Ct. Trial judge Okla. Trial Lawyers Assn., 1988, The Jour. Record award Okla. County Bar Assn., 2005. Mem. Okla. Bar Assn., Fed. Bar Assn. (pres. Oklahoma City chpt. 1981), Order of Coif (alumnus mem.), Jud. Conf. US (mem. exec. com. 2003-06). Republican. Methodist. Office: US Dist Ct US Courthouse 200 NW 4th St Oklahoma City OK 73102-3026 Home Phone: 405-478-1990; Office Phone: 405-609-5100.

RUSSELL, DAVID O., film director, film producer, scriptwriter; b. NYC, Aug. 20, 1958; m. Janet Grillo. Grad., Amherst Coll., 1981. Dir., writer, prodr. (films) Bingo Inferno, 1987, I Heart Huckabees, 2004, dir., writer, exec. prodr. Spanking the Monkey, 1994, dir., writer Flirting with Disaster, 1996, Three Kings, 1999; dir.: (films) Hairway to the Stars, 1990; exec. prodr.: Anchorman: The Legend of Ron Burgundy, 2004, Wake Up, Ron Burgundy: The Lost Movie, 2004; prodr.: The Slaughter Rule, 2002; actor: Adaptation, 2002; dir., prodr. (documentaries) Soldier's Pay, 2004. Office: Apt 2B 250 W 99th St New York NY 10025-5442

RUSSELL, DAVID W., molecular geneticist; BA in Biology, U. Tex., Austin, 1975; PhD in Chemistry, U. NC, Chapel Hill, 1980. Damon Runyon Cancer Rsch. Found. postdoctoral fellow U. British Columbia, 1980—82; mem. faculty U. Tex. Southwestern Med. Ctr., Dallas, 1982—90, prof. dept. molecular genetics, 1990—, Eugene McDermott disting. chair molecular genetics, 1992—. Contbr. articles to profl. jours.; mem. editl. bd.: Cell Metabolism, Trends in Biochemical Scis., assoc. editor: Jour. Biol. Chemistry. Recipient Rsch. Career Devel. award, NIH, 1984, Louis N. Katz award, Am. Heart Assn., 1985, Kilby Sci. Place award, Tex. Instruments, 1993, Adolph Windhaus prize, Falk Found., Germany, 2002. Fellow: NAS; mem.: Am. Soc. Mass Spectrometry, Endocrine Soc. (Ernst Oppenheimer award 1999), Am. Soc. Biol. Chemistry, AAAS. Office: Dept Molecular Genetics U Tex Southwestern Med Ctr 5323 Harry Hines Blvd Dallas TX 75390 E-mail: david.russell@utsouthwestern.edu.

RUSSELL, DAVID WILLIAMS, lawyer; b. Lockport, NY, Apr. 5, 1945; s. David Lawson and Jean Graves (Williams) R.; m. Frances Yung Chung Chen, May 23, 1970; children: Bayard Chen, Ming Rennick. AB, Dartmouth Coll., 1967, MBA, 1969; JD cum laude, Northwestern U., 1976. Bar: Ill. 1976, Ind. 1983. English tchr. Talledega Coll., Ala., 1967; math. tchr. Lyndon Inst., Lyndonville, Vt., 1967-68; asst. to pres. for planning Tougaloo Coll., Miss., 1969-71, bus. mgr., 1971-73; law clk. Montgomery, McCracken, Walker & Rhoads, Phila., 1975; with Winston & Strawn, Chgo., 1976-83; ptnr. Klineman, Rose, Wolf & Wallack, Indpls., 1983-87, Johnson, Smith, Pence, Densborn, Wright & Heath, Indpls., 1987-99, Bose McKinney & Evans, Indpls., 1999—2004, Harrison & Moberly, Indpls., 2004—. Cons. Alfred P. Sloan Found., 1972-73; dir. Forum for Internat. Profl. Svcs., 1985—, sec., 1985-88, pres. 1988-89; U.S. Dept. Justice del. to U.S. China Joint Session on Trade, Investment & Econ. Law, Beijing, 1987; leader Ind. Products Trade Fair, Kawachinagano, Japan, 1996; lectr. Ind. law Ind. Gov.'s Trade Mission to Japan, 1986, internat. law Ind. CLE Forum, 1986-96, 2000-03, chmn., 1987, 89, 91, 2001-03; adj. prof. internat. bus. law Ind. U., 1993-95; nat. selection com. Woodrow Wilson Found. Adminstrv. Fellowship Program, 1973-76; vol. Lawyers for Creative Arts, Chgo., 1977-83; dir. World Trade Club of Ind., 1987-93, 2005—, v.p., 1987-91, pres., 1991-92; dir. Ind. Swiss Found., 1991-2002; dir. Writer's Ctr., Indpls., 1999—, treas., 2001—07; dir. Asian Am. Alliance, 1999—, treas., 2006; dir. Indpls. Peace Games, Inc., 2000—, Friends of Taiwan Assn., Inc., 2001-, African U. Found., 2005-, vice chmn., 2006-; dir. Ind. Soviet Trade Consortium, 1991-99, sec., 1991-92; v.p., bd. dirs. Ind. Sister Cities, 1988—; dir. Internat. Ctr. Indpls., 1988-92, v.p. 1988-89; Ind. dist. enrollment dir. Dartmouth Coll., 1990-99; dir. Carmel Sister Cities, 1993—, v.p. 1995-96, pres. 1997-99, chmn., 1999—; v.p., gen. coun. Lawrence Durrell Soc., 1993—; internat. adv. bds. Supply Chain & Global Mgmt. Acad. Kelley Grad Sch. Bus., Ind. U., 2001—; mem. internat. adv. bd. Ind. U. Law Sch., 2003—, Ind. Econ. Devel. Corp, 2005-; bd. advisors Ctr. for Internat. Bus. Edn. and Rsch. Krannert Grad. Sch. Mgmt. Purdue U., 1995—; dir., v.p., gen. coun. Global Crossroads Found., Inc., 1995-2003; mem. bd. arbitrators NASD, 1999—; dir. Ind. Dist. Export Coun., 1999—, chmn. 2005-. Named Hon. fellow, Ctr. for Internat. Legal Studies, 2002—, Internat. Bus. Person of Yr., World Trade Club of Ind., 2002, Sagamore of the Wabash, 2002, Ind. Super Lawyer, Ind. Monthly Mag. and Ind. Law and Politics, 2004, 2005, 2006, 2007; Adminstrv. fellow, Woodrow Wilson Found., 1969—72, David Williams Russell Day named in his honor, Jan. 15, 2002, Indpls. Mem. ABA, ACLU, Ill. Bar Assn., Ind. Bar Assn. (vice chmn. internat. law sect. 1988-90, treas. 2002-, chmn. 1990-92, 2002-04, co-chmn. written publs. com. 1997-99), Indpls. Bar Assn., Dartmouth Lawyers Assn., Indpls. Assn. Chinese Ams., Chinese Music Soc., Dartmouth Club of Ind. (sec. 1986-87, pres. 1987-88), Internat. Bar Assn., Zeta Psi. Presbyterian. Home: 10926 Lakeview Dr Carmel IN 46033-3937 Office: Harrison & Moberly LLP 2100 First Ind Plz 135 N Pennsylvania St Indianapolis IN 46204-2400 Office Phone: 317-639-4511. Business E-Mail: drussell@h-mlaw.com.

RUSSELL, DIANE ELIZABETH HENRIKSON, career counselor; b. Chgo., July 18, 1952; d. Arthur Allen and Lois Elizabeth (Wessling) H.; m. Darrell Lee Slider, May 31, 1975 (div. Dec. 1992); m. Thomas Lee Russell, July 27, 1999. BA in Spanish, U. Ill., 1974; MA in Counselor Edn., U. South Fla., 1996. Employment counselor Crown Personnel Inc., Mt. Prospect, Ill., 1974-75; bilingual tchr.'s aide Sch. Dist. #21, Wheeling, Ill., 1975; sec., asst. registrar Yale U., New Haven, 1975-77; asst. to personnel dir., personnel coord. Housing Authority New Haven, 1977-79; benefits specialist Profl. Pensions Inc., New Haven, 1980-81, Chloride Inc., Tampa, Fla., 1981-83; personnel technician II human resources dept. U. South Fla., Tampa, 1984-86, personnel technician III, personnel svcs. specialist, 1986-90, coord. human resources dept., 1990-96, career specialist Career Ctr., 1996—2002, 2004—, counselor, advisor honors coll., 2002—04. Mem. choirs St. Mark United Ch., Valrico, Fla., 1987-99, 2003-, dir. Caregivers, 2001-2003; mem. chorus U. South Fla., 1986-88, women's chorale, 1993-95. Mem. AAUW (treas. 1976-78, 80-81), Am. Assn. Employment in Edn., Fla. Career Profls. Assn., Phi Kappa Phi, Phi Beta Kappa, Alpha Lambda Delta, Lambda Delta, Zeta Tau Alpha Soc. Avocations: singing, theater, going to theme parks, travel. Home: 723 Herlong Ct Brandon FL 33511-7920 Office: U South Fla Fla Career Ctr 4202 E Fowler Ave Stop SVC 2088 Tampa FL 33620-6930 E-mail: dhenrik718@aol.com.

RUSSELL, ELBERT WINSLOW, neuropsychologist; b. Las Vegas, N.Mex., June 4, 1929; s. Josiah Cox and Ruth Winslow Russell; children from previous marriage: Gwendolyn Marie Harvey, Franklin Winslow, Kirsten Nash, Jonathan Nash; m. Sally Lynn Kolitz, Apr. 2, 1989. BA, Earlham Coll., Richmond, Ind., 1951; MA, U. Ill., 1953; MS, Pa. State U., 1958; PhD, U. Kans., 1968. Lic. psychologist Florida, 1973. Clin. psychologist Warnersville (Pa.) State Hosp., 1959-61; clin. neuropsychologist VA Med. Ctr., Cin., 1968-71, dir. neuropsychology lab. Miami, Fla., 1971-89, rsch. psychologist, 1989—. Adj. prof. Nova U., Ft. Lauderdale, 1980-87, U. Miami Med. Sch., 1980-94, U. Miami, 1979—. Author: (with C. Neuringer and G. Goldstein) Assessment of Brain Damage, 1970; (with R.I. Starkey) Halstead Russell Neuropsychology Evaluation System (manual and computer program), 1993, rev. 2001; contbr. articles to profl. jours. Recipient Life Time Achievement award, Am. Bd. Psychol. Assessment, 1999, Halstead award, Reitan Soc., 2000. Fellow APA., Am. Psychol. Soc., Nat. Acad. Neuropsychology; mem. Sigma Xi. Democrat. Mem. Soc. Of Friends. Home: 6091 SW 79th St Miami FL 33156-2944 Office: 9350 S Dixie Hwy Ste 1260 Miami FL 33156-2944 Home Phone: 305-667-3821; Office Phone: 305-670-2284. Personal E-mail: ewr@bellsouth.net.

RUSSELL, FINDLAY EWING, physician; b. San Francisco, Sept. 1, 1919; s. William and Mary Jane (Findlay) R.; m. Janet Louise Thiel. Feb. 14, 1950; children: Christa Ann, Sharon Jane, Robin Emily, Constance Susan, Mark Findlay. BA, Walla Walla Coll., Wash., 1941; MD, Loma Linda U., Calif., 1950; postgrad. (fellow), Calif. Inst. Tech., 1951-53; postgrad., U. Cambridge, Eng., 1962—63; PhD, U. Santa Barbara, Calif., 1974, LLD (hon.), 1989. Intern White Meml. Hosp., Los Angeles, 1950-51; practice medicine specializing in toxinology and toxicology Los Angeles, 1953—; mem. staff Los Angeles County-U. So. Calif. Med. Center, Loma Linda U. Med. Center, U. Ariz. Med. Ctr.; physiologist Huntington Inst. Med. Research, 1953-55; dir. lab. neurol. research Los Angeles County-U. So. Calif. Med. Center, 1955-80; mem. faculty Loma Linda U. Med. Sch., 1955—; prof. neurology, physiology and biology U. So. Calif. Med. Sch., 1966-81; prof. pharmacology and toxicology U. Ariz. Health Scis. Coll. Pharmacy, 1981—. Cons. USPHS, NSF, Office Naval Rsch., WHO, U.S. Army, Walter Reed, USAF, Brooks AFB. Author: Marine Toxins and Venomous and Poisonous Marine Animals, 1965, Poisonous Marine Animals, 1971, Snake Venom Poisoning, 1980; co-author: Bibliography of Snake Venoms and Venomous Snakes, 1964, Animal Toxins, 1967, Poisonous Snakes of The World, 1968, Snake Venom Poisoning, 1983, Bibliography of Venomous and Poisonous Marine Animals and Their Toxins, 1984, Venomous and Poisonous Marine Invertebrates of the Indian Ocean, 1996; editor: Toxicon, 1962-70. Served with AUS, 1942-46. Decorated Purple Heart, Bronze Star; recipient award Los Angeles County Bd. Suprs., 1960; award Acad. Medicine Buenos Aires, 1966; Skylab Achievement award, 1974; Jozef Stefan medal Yugoslavia, 1978; U.S. State Dept. medallion, 2006. Fellow A.C.P., Am. Coll. Cardiology, Royal Soc. Tropical Medicine, N.Y. Acad. Scis.; mem. Internat. Soc. Toxinology (pres. 1962-66, Francisco Redi medal 1967), Royal Soc. Medicine, Am. Soc. Physiology, Western Soc. Pharmacology (pres. 1973) Office: U Ariz Health Scis Coll Pharmacy Pharm/Tox Tucson AZ 85721 Office Phone: 520-626-4047.

RUSSELL, FLORENCE L., elementary school educator; d. Helmer Russell, Jr. and Alma D. Russell. BS, Albany State Coll., Ga., 1972; MS, Nova U., Fort Lauderdale, Fla., 1995. Cert. tchr. Fla., 1972. Tchr. Lee County Sch. Dist., Fort Myers, Fla., 1972. Orgn. head Boy Scout #217, 2005—07; recording sec. St. Mary's Program M.B. Ch., 1980—2005; fin. sec. First Missionary Baptist Fellowship Assn., 1997—; grade level chmn./team leader Tanglewood Riverside Sch., Fort Myers, Fla., 1977—2003; dir. Tanglewood Riverside After Sch. Program, Fort Myers, Fla., 1988—96; pres. Tanglewood Riverside Sch. PTA, Fort Myers, Fla., 2002—04; chmn. sch. adv. com. Tanglewood Riverside Sch., Fort Myers, Fla., 2004—06, environ. edn. tchr. laison Fla., 1973—2006. Recipient Outstanding Vol. award, Tanglewood Riverside PTA, 2004. Mem.: Fla. PTA, Nat. PTA. Democrat. Home Phone: 239-694-5651; Office Phone: 239-936-0891. Personal E-mail: florenrss@aol.com. Business E-Mail: florencelr@leeschools.net.

RUSSELL, FRANCIA, retired ballet director, educator; b. LA, Jan. 10, 1938; d. W. Frank and Marion (Whitney) R.; m. Kent Stowell, Nov. 19, 1965; children: Christopher, Darren, Ethan. Studies with, George Balanchine, Vera Volkova, Felia Doubrouska, Antonina Tumkovsky, Benjamin Harkarvy; student, NYU, Columbia U.; degree (hon.), Seattle U., 2003. Dancer, soloist NYC Ballet, 1956-62, ballet mistress, 1965-70; dancer Ballets USA/Jerome Robbins, NYC, 1962; tchr. ballet Sch. Am. Ballet, NYC, 1963-64; co-dir. Frankfurt (Fed. Republic Germany) Opera Ballet, 1976-77; dir., co-artistic dir. Pacific N.W. Ballet, Seattle, 1977—2005; dir. Pacific N.W. Ballet Sch., Seattle, 1977—2005. Affiliate prof. of dance U. Wash. Dir. staging over 100 George Balanchine ballet prodns. throughout world, including Russia and China, 1964—. Named Woman of Achievement, Matrix Table, Women in Comm., Seattle, 1987, Gov.'s Arts award, 1989, Dance Mag. award, 1996, Brava award Women's U. Club, 2003, ArtsFund Lifetime Achievement in the Arts award, 2004, Ernst & Young Entrepreneur of Yr. award, 2004, Seattle Mayor's Arts award for Lifetime Achievement, 2004. Mem. Internat. Women's Forum. Home: 2833 Broadway E Seattle WA 98102-3935 Office: Pacific NW Ballet 301 Mercer St Seattle WA 98109-4600

RUSSELL, FRANK ELI, retired newspaper publishing executive; b. Kokomo, Ind., Dec. 6, 1920; s. Frank E. and Maude (Wiggins) R.; children: Linda Carole Russell Atkins, Richard Lee, Frank E. III, Rita Jane Russell Eagle, Julie Beth Russell; m. Nancy M. Shover, Oct. 5, 1991 AB, Evansville Coll., 1942; JD, Ind. U., 1951; LLD (hon.), U. Evansville, 1985; HHD (hon.), Franklin Coll., 1989. Bar: Ind. 1951; CPA, Ind. Ptnr. George S. Olive & Co., Indpls., 1947—53; exec. v.p. Spickelmier Industries, Inc., Indpls., 1953—59; bus. mgr. Indpls. Star & News, 1959—77; v.p., gen. mgr. Ctrl. Newspapers, Inc., Indpls., 1977—79, pres., 1979—95, chmn., bd. dirs., 1996—98; ret., 1998; also bd. dirs. Ctrl. Newsprint; pres. Bradley Paper Co., also bd. dirs. Past chmn. adv. bd. Met. Indpls. TV Assn., Inc.; trustee retirement trust Ctrl. Newspapers, Inc.; chmn. retirement com. Hoosier State Press. Bd. dirs. Ariz. Cmty. Found., 1992-96, Eiteljorg Mus., 1994—; trustee, chmn. bd. Nina Mason Pulliam Charitable Trust, 1997—. Recipient Disting. Alumni award Ind. U. Sch. Law, 1989, Life Trustee award U. Evansville, 1991, Ralph D. Casey award, 1997 Mem. ABA, AICPA, Ind. Bar. Assn., Indpls. Bar Assn. (past bd. dirs., past treas.), Ind. Assn. CPA (past dir.), Tax Execs. Inst. (past pres.), Ind. Assn. Credit Mgmt. (dir., v.p.), Inst. Newspaper Controllers and Fin. Officers (dir., past pres.), Ind. Acad. Ind. Assn. Colls., Midwest Pension Conf. (Ind. chpt.), Newspaper Advt. Bur. (bd. dirs.), Salvation Army (life, award 1989), Columbia Club, Meridian Hills Country Club, Masons, Shriners, Order of Coif, Phi Delta Phi, Sigma Alpha Epsilon Methodist. Office: Nina Mason Pulliam Charitable Trust 135 N Pennsylvania St Ste 1200 Indianapolis IN 46204-1956

RUSSELL, GEORGE HAW, video production company executive; b. Neosho, Mo., May 22, 1945; s. Kenneth L. and Marjorie (Haw) R.; m. Suzanne Bennett, June 1, 1967; children: Margaret Anne, Marjorie Jane, Karen Lee, George Andrew. BA, La. State U., 1967. Exec. Ednl. Video Network, Huntsville, 1990—; ptnr. Sam Houston Group Ltd. Liability Partnership, Huntsville, 1991—. Prodr. ednl. videos Nombres et Couleurs, 1988 (Silver Apple award 1988), Napoleon, 1989 (Silver Apple award 1989), Bullfight, 1990, The French Revolution, 1990; exec. prodr. Spain's Historic Cities, 1992, Munich's Oktoberfest, 1992, The New Nutriton Pyramid, 1992, The Visual Language of Design, 1992, Florence, 1993, Joan of Arc, 1993, New Food Guide Pyramid, 1993, Cleaning and Maintaining Your VCR, 1993, Arts and Crafts of Mexico, 1993, Understanding Geysers and Hot Springs, 1993, Thoreau at Walden Pond, 1993, French Markets, 1993, Great Zimbabwe, 1993, Longpig. Bd. govs. Tex. Com. on Natural Resources, Dallas, 1979—; bd. dirs. Gibbs-Powell House Mus., Huntsville, Natural Area Preservation Assn., Dallas; chmn. forest practices Lone Star Sierra Club, Austin, Tex., 1984—; chmn. Fed. Forest Reform, Washington, D.C., 1991—; founder, bishop Universal Ethician Ch., 2000—; founder Ethician Family Cemetery; founder Talking Eagle Preserve, Russell Beaver Sanctuary, Russell River Otter Sanctuary, Russell Frog Sanctuary, 2000-2005. 1st lt. U.S. Army, 1971-74. Recipient spl. achievement award Sierra Club, San Francisco 1985, chpt. conservation award 1987, environ. heroes for centennial 1991; named Citizen of Month, Huntsville Item 1988. Democrat. Methodist. Avocations: environmental advocacy, historic building restoration, collecting antiques and folk art. Home: 1409 19th St Huntsville TX 77340-5056 Office: Ednl Video Network 1401 19th St Huntsville TX 77340-5057 Office Phone: 936-295-5767. Personal E-mail: ghr@cyberclone.net.

RUSSELL, IRMA S., lawyer, educator; b. Pratt, Kans., Mar. 22, 1947; d. Vernon V. and Vesta (Coleman) Stephens; m. Thomas Russell; children: Nathaniel, Anna. BA, U. Kans., 1969, BS in Edn., 1974, MA in English, 1972, JD, 1980. Bar: Kans. 1980, Mo. 1982, Tenn. 1985, U.S. Dist. Ct. Tenn. 1985, U.S. Ct. Appeals (10th cir.) 1981. Jud. clk. Hon. James K. Logan, U.S. Ct. Appeals, 10th Jud. Dist., 1980-81; assoc. Hillix, Brewer, Hoffhaus and Whittaker, Kansas City, Mo., 1981-82; pvt. practice Olathe, Kans., 1982-84, Memphis, 1985-89; assoc. Glankler Brown Gilliland Chase Robinson & Raines, Memphis, 1989; prof. law U. Tulsa Coll. Law, 2006—, dir. Nat. Energy-Environ. Law & Policy Inst., 2006—. Vis. asst. prof. Cecil C. Humphreys Sch. of Law, Memphis State U., 1986-89; lectr. in field. Author Issues of Legal Ethics in the Practice of Environmental Law; contbr. articles to profl. jours.; note and comment editor Kans. Law Rev., 1978-79; editor Unified Sch. Dist. 497 publs., 1975-76; tech. writer Golf Course Supts. Assn. of Am., 1974-75; assoc. editor Squire Pubs., Kans., 1969. Legal counsel Shelby Farms Park Conservancy, Med. Pers. for Triathlon Fedn. U.S.A.; commr. Memphis City Beautiful Commn. U.S. Bicentennial Commn. Bill of Rights Project grantee 1990, 91; recipient Scripps-Howard Journalism award, 1968, Mpls. Tribune award, 1968-69, others. Mem. ABA (mem. Com. on Global Oil & Gas, Sect. of Environ., Energy and Resources), Tenn. Bar assn., Memphis Bar Assn., Jud. Conf. for 10th Jud. Cir., Memphis Assn. Women Attys., Tenn. Nature Conservancy, Wolf River Conservancy. Avocations: triathlons, racquetball. Office: Nat Energy-Environ Law & Policy Inst U Tulsa Coll Law 3120 E 4th Pl Tulsa OK 74104-2499 Office Phone: 918-631-2431. Office Fax: 918-631-2194. E-mail: irma-russell@utulsa.edu.

RUSSELL, JAMARCUS, professional football player; b. Mobile, Ala., Aug. 9, 1985; s. Bobby Lloyd and Zina Russell-Anderson. Attended, La. St. U., 2003—07. Quarterback Oakland Raiders, 2007—. Named Sugar Bowl MVP, 2007; named to First Team All-Southeastern Conference, 2006; recipient Manning award, 2006. Achievements include most passing yards in Alabama high school football history; being first overall selection in the 2007 NFL Draft. Office: Oakland Raiders 1220 Harbor Bay Pkwy Alameda CA 94502 *

RUSSELL, JAMES ALVIN, JR., college administrator; b. Lawrenceville, Va., Dec. 25, 1917; s. Dr. James Alvin and Nellie M. (Pratt) R.; m. Lottye J. Washington, Dec. 25, 1943; children: Charlotte Justyne, James Alvin III. BA, Oberlin Coll., 1940; BS, Bradley U., 1941, MS, 1950, spl. insts.; EdD, U. Md., 1967; spl. insts., Wayne U., U. Mich., U. Ill., NSF. Prof., dir. div. engring., also prof. edn. div. grad. studies Hampton Inst., 1950-71; pres. St. Paul's Coll., Lawrenceville, 1971-81; dir. instructional programs and student services Va. C.C. System, 1981-82; chmn. div. profl. studies W.Va. State Coll., 1982-86, acting pres., 1986-87, exec. asst. to pres., 1987-88; pres. So. W.Va. C.C., 1988-89, ret., 1989. Pres. Peninsula Council Human Relations, 1961-65. United Negro Coll. Fund fellow, 1966-67. Mem. IEEE, Am. Soc. Engring. Edn., Am. Assn. Univ. Adminstrs., Am. Vocat. Assn., Am. Tech. Edn. Assn., Nat. Assn. Indsl. Tech., Am. Assn. for Higher Edn., Nat. Assn. for Equal Opportunity in Edn., Brunswick C. of C., Sigma Pi Phi, Alpha Kappa Mu, Iota Lambda Sigma, Omega Psi Phi. Home: 811 Grandview Dr Dunbar WV 25064-1175 E-mail: Drjarusdun@aol.com.

RUSSELL, JAMES BENJAMIN, microbiologist, educator, research scientist; s. Lincoln A. and Mary M. Russell; 1 child, Aaron T. BS, Cornell U., Ithaca, NY, 1973; MS, U. Calif., Davis, 1974, PhD, 1978. Asst. prof. U. Ill., Urbana, 1978—81; rsch. microbiologist Agrl. Rsch. Svc., USDA, Ithaca, 1981—; prof. Cornell U., Ithaca, 1981—. Author: Rumen Microbiology and Its Role in Ruminant Nutrition, 2002; contbr. more than 200 articles, revs. to profl. publs., chpts. to books. Named North Atlantic Area Scientist of Yr., USDA, 1993, 2005; recipient Outstanding Tchr. award, U. Ill., 1981, Am. Feed Industry award, USDA, 1993, 2005. Fellow: Am. Acad. Microbiology; mem.: Am. Soc. Animal Sci., Am. Dairy Sci. Assn., Am. Soc. Microbiology. Achievements include patents for rumen fluid for calves to prevent needless diarrhea; patents pending for carbonated cow manure to kill pathogenic bacteria. Avocation: swimming. Business E-Mail: jbr8@cornell.edu.

RUSSELL, JAMES BRIAN, broadcast executive, media consultant; b. Hartford, Conn., Jan. 30, 1946; s. Seymour and Marian (Kamins) R.; m. Kathleen Anne Schardt, Dec. 28, 1968; children: Theodore, Jennifer, Kimberly. BA in Journalism, Am. U., 1968; postgrad. Wharton Sch. Bus., U. Pa.; postgrad., Stanford U. Reporter, prodr. WAMU FM, Washington; news dir. Sta. WPIK-AM, Arlington, Va., 1965-66; editor, anchorman Sta. WAVA-AM/FM, Washington, 1966-68; editor, corr. UPI, Washington, Cambodia and, Vietnam, 1968-71; from reporter to exec. prodr. All Things Considered Nat. Pub. Radio, Washington, 1971-78; sta. dir., sr. v.p. programming Stas. KTCA/KTCI-TV, Mpls./St. Paul, 1978-88; v.p. nat. prodns., exec. prodr. Marketplace U. So. Calif., LA, 1988-97; v.p. USC Radio and GM Marketplace Prodns., LA, 1990—99; sr. v.p. Minn. Pub. Radio, Am. Pub. Media & GM Marketplace Prodns., LA, 2000—06; pres. Jim Russell Prodns., 2006—, The Program Dr. Mem. steering com. Radio Hall of Fame. Program inventor/creator: Marketplace; Weekend America; The World; Newton's Apple. Mem. prison visitor program AMICUS, St. Paul, 1984-85. Postgrad. fellow in journalism U. Mich.; recipient Nat. Headliner award 1972, 74, Ohio State award, 1973, 75, duPont Columbia awards Columbia U., 1979, 81, 97, Peabody award 2001, Nat. TV Emmy award Acad. TV Arts and Scis., 1989, William Kling award for Innovation and Entrepreneurship, 1998, Mo. Honor medal for disting. svc. in journalism, 2000. Home Phone: 919-942-6950; Office Phone: 919-942-6950. E-mail: jim@programdoctor.com.

RUSSELL, JAMES FRANKLIN, lawyer; b. Memphis, Mar. 21, 1945; s. Frank Hall and Helen (Brunson) R.; m. Marilyn Land, June 1, 1968 (div. May 1976); children: Mary Helen, Myles Edward; m. Linda Hatcher, July 9, 1977; 1 child, Maggie Abele. BA, Rhodes Coll., 1967; JD, Memphis State U., 1970. Bar: Tenn. 1971, U.S. Dist. Ct. (we. dist.) Tenn. 1971, U.S. Ct. Appeals (6th cir.) 1971, U.S. Dist. Ct. (no. dist.) Miss. 1976, U.S. Ct. Appeals (5th cir.) 1977, U.S. Ct. Appeals (8th cir.) 1987. Assoc. Nelson, Norvell, Wilson, McRae, Ivy & Sevier, Memphis, 1971-75; ptnr. Stanton, Russell & Challen, Memphis, 1975-78, Russell, Price, Weatherford & Warlick, Memphis, 1978-82, Price, Vance & Criss, Memphis, 1982-85, Apperson, Crump, Duzane & Maxwell, Memphis, 1985-97, 1985-97; cir.

ct. judge Divsn. II 30th Jud. Dist., 1997—. V.p. mid-south chpt. Am. Red Cross, Memphis, 1992-94; treas. Epilepsy Found. West Tenn., Memphis, 1992-94. Mem. ABA, Nat. Assn. R.R. Trial Counsel, Internat. Assn. Def. Counsel, Tenn. Bar Assn., Tenn. Def. Lawyers Assn., Memphis Bar Assn. (pres. 1992). Episcopalian. Avocations: golf, skiing. Home: 1045 Reid Hooker N Eads TN 38028-6958 Office: Shelby County Courthouse 140 Adams Ave Memphis TN 38103-2000

RUSSELL, JAMES WEBSTER, JR., editor, columnist; b. Shreveport, La., Nov. 30, 1921; s. James Webster and Aline (Faulk) R.; m. Jean Buck, June 29, 1949 (dec. Sept. 2002); children: Nancy Russell Dearr, Eileen Russell Goure; m. Sylvia Swogger Sheldon, Aug. 17, 2004. BA, La. State U., 1942. Fla. mgr. Internat. News Service, 1946-51; bur. chief UPI, Tallahassee, 1951-52; regional editor U.P.I., Atlanta, 1953-57; asst. city editor Miami (Fla.) Herald, 1957-58, bus.-fin. editor, 1958-74, fin.-econ. columnist, 1974—99. Guest lectr. U. Miami, Fla. Internat. U., Miami-Dade Community Coll., La. State U. Contbr. articles to: Fla. Trend, Times of London, N.Y. Times, Gentlemen's Quar. Trustee Fla. So. Coll. Served with USAAF, 1942-45. Recipient Eagle award Invest-in-Am. Nat. Coun., 1976; decorated Air medal with eleven oak leaf clusters; inducted La. State U. Sch. of Mass Comms. Hall of Fame, 1998. Mem. Soc. Am. Bus. Writers, Lambda Chi Alpha, Sigma Delta Chi. Republican. Methodist (chmn. ch. council on ministries 1971-72). Home: 4800 SW 64th Ct Miami FL 33155-6133

RUSSELL, JEFFREY BURTON, historian, educator; b. Fresno, Calif., Aug. 1, 1934; s. Lewis Henry and Ieda Velma (Ogborn) R.; m. Diana Emily Mansfield, June 30, 1956; children: Jennifer, Mark, William, Penelope. AB, U. Calif., Berkeley, 1955, A.M., 1957; PhD, Emory U., 1960. Asst. prof. U. N.Mex., Albuquerque, 1960-61; jr. fellow Soc. of Fellows, Harvard U., Cambridge, Mass., 1961-62; mem. faculty U. Calif., Riverside, 1962-75, prof. dept. history, 1969-75, assoc. dean grad. div., 1967-72; dir. Medieval Inst.; Michael P. Grace prof. medieval studies U. Notre Dame, South Bend, Ind., 1975-77; dean grad. studies Calif. State U., Sacramento, 1977-79; prof. history U. Calif., Santa Barbara, 1979—, prof. religious studies, 1994—. Author: Dissent and Reform in the Early Middle Ages, 1965, Medieval Civilization, 1968, A History of Medieval Christianity: Prophecy and Order, 1968, Religious Dissent in the Middle Ages, 1971, Witchcraft in the Middle Ages, 1972, The Devil: Perceptions of Evil from Antiquity to Primitive Christianity, 1977, A History of Witchcraft: Sorcerers, Heretics, and Pagans, 1980, Medieval Heresies: a Bibliography, 1981, Satan: The Early Christian Tradition, 1981, Lucifer: The Devil in the Middle Ages, 1984, Mephistopheles: The Devil in the Modern World, 1986, The Prince of Darkness, 1988, Ruga in Aevis, 1990, Inventing the Flat Earth: Columbus and the Historians, 1991, Dissent and Order in the Middle Ages, 1992, A History of Heaven: The Singing Silence, 1997, Essays in Honor of Jeffrey B. Russell, 1998, Paradise Mislaid: How We Lost Heaven and How We Can Regain It, 2006, A New History of Witchcraft, 2007; contbr. articles to profl. jours. Fulbright fellow, 1959-60; Am. Council Learned Socs. grantee, 1965, 70; Social Sci. Research Council grantee, 1968; Guggenheim fellow, 1968-69; Nat. Endowment for Humanities sr. fellow, 1972-73 Fellow Medieval Acad. Am.; mem. Am. Soc. Ch. Histor Am. Acad. Religion, Astron. Soc. Pacific. Home: 4798 Calle Camarada Santa Barbara CA 93110-2053 Office: U Calif Dept History Santa Barbara CA 93106 Business E-Mail: russell@history.ucsb.edu.

RUSSELL, JEFFREY SCOTT, engineering educator; b. Alliance, Ohio, June 14, 1962; s. Ronald Francis Russell and Georgia Ann (Charleston) Holmes; m. Vicki Carolina Radford, Aug. 17, 1985; children: Nicole Lynne, Jacob Thomas, Matthew David, Rachel Marie. BS, U. Cin., 1985; MS, Purdue U., 1986, PhD, 1988. Grad. tchg. asst. Purdue U., West Lafayette, Ind., 1985-87, grad. rsch. asst., 1987-88, postdoctoral rsch. assoc., 1988-89; from asst. to assoc. prof. civil engring. U. Wis., Madison, 1989—. Lectr. Tex. A&M U., College Station, 1988—, U. Tex., Austin, 1992—, U. Wis., Madison Ext., 1990—. Editor Jour. Mgmt. in Engring., 1996—. Mem. Wis. Right to Life, Madison, 1989-94; project coord. U. Wis. Coll. Testament Distbn., Gideon's Internat., Madison West Camp, 1990—; dir. evangelistic ministries First Ch. of Nazarene, Madison, 1992-93. Recipient Presdl. Young Investigator award NSF, 1990, Edmund Friedman Young Engr. award for profl. achievement, 1993. Mem. ASCE (assoc., sec. constrn. div. 1989-92, Collingwood Prize 1991, Outstanding Profl. Civil and Environ. Engring. 1991, Walter L. Huber Civil Engring. Rsch. prize 1996, bd. dirs. 1998—), Am. Assn. Cost Engrs. (assoc.), Am. Soc. Engring. Edn., Constrn. Mgmt. Assn. Am., Sigma Xi, Tau Beta Pi. Achievements include identification of causes of constrn. contractor failure; devel. of analytical models to assist in predicting contractor failure prior to contract award. Office: U Wis-Madison 2304 Engring Hall 1415 Johnson Dr Madison WI 53706-1607

RUSSELL, JOHN FRANCIS, retired librarian; b. Mt. Carmel, Ind., Apr. 30, 1929; s. David Freeman and Bertha (Major) R.; m. Edith Raymond Hyde, June 27, 1953; 1 child, Anne Marie. BA, DePauw U., 1951; postgrad., Ind. U., 1951-52; MA, Johns Hopkins U., 1954; student, Cath. U. Am., summer 1955; MS, Grad. Sch. Libr. Sci./Drexel, U., 1977. Tchr. English Park Sch. Balt., 1954-75, chmn. dept., 1957-75; tchr. speech, dir. Ira Aldridge Players Morgan State Coll., fall 1965-66; tchr. drama Loyola Coll., 1964, 66. Editor: The Secondary School Theatre, 1972-74. Pres. Tchrs.'s Assn. Ind. Sch. Balt. Area, 1960-62, adv. bd., 1966-67, chmn. com. on English, 1966-68; exec. com. Assn. Ind. Md. Sch., 1967-68; dir., costumer Johns Hopkins U. Playshop, 1963-64, 1990-2006, hon. bd. chmn., 2006—; lectr. Lecture Group, Woman's Club Roland Park, others, 1964—; bd. dirs. Balt. area coun. World Federalists U.S.A., 1961-67, vice chmn., 1964-67, nat. exec. coun., 1963-65; bd. dirs. Ctr. Stage, 1964-77; dir. Blvd. Players, pres., 1960-67; dir. Pasadena Little Theatre, v.p., 1979-83, pres., 1983-85, 2d v.p., 1990—; dir. Center Stage Players, New Image Theatre, Theatre Network of Houston, U.S.A. Theatre, Actors Conservatory Tex., v.p., 1990-91, Glenbrook United Meth. Ch. Drama Ministry; bd. dirs. Unicorn Sch. Acting, 1996-2003, v.p., 1997-2003; adv. com. Am. H.S. Theatre Festival, 1975; mem. adminstrv. bd. St. Mark's United Meth. Ch., 1957-67, Towson United Meth. Ch., 1967-77, First United Meth. Ch., Houston, 1980-89; adminstrv. coun., vice-chmn. Glenbrook United Meth. Ch., 1997, chmn. pastor-parish rels. com., 1998, lay del., 1999, 2000, 03, 04, lay leader 1999—; sec. Festival Angels, 1982-2001 (Outstanding Svc. award 1991); cmty. vol. svcs. com., ARC, 1985-90; comprehensive volunteerism adv. com., Sheltering Arms, 1986-89. Recipient Nat. Citation of Merit Am. Shakespeare Festival, 1961, Theatre Goddess award U.S.A. Theatre, 1998, Critics Choice award Houston Post, 1984; certs. of appreciation Sheltering Arms, 1986-89, cert. of recognition, 1988. Mem. Am. Assn. Cmty. Theatre, Harris County Heritage Soc., Am. Film Inst., Drama League, Am. Theatre Assn. (v.p. Mid-Atlantic dist. 1967-68, pres. 1968-69, nat. dir. 1970-73, Mid-Atlantic chpt. award for achievement and contbn. to theatre 1973), Secondary Sch. Theatre Assn. (v.p. devel. 1974-75), Tex. Non-Profit Theatre, Nat. (bd. dirs. 1969), Md. Coun. Tchrs. English (pres. 1969-70), Capital Area Media Educators Orgn. (exec. com. 1970-73, screening chmn. 1971-73), ALA, Tex. Libr. Assn. (audiovisual chmn. conv. planning com. 1981), Coun. Info. and Referral Svcs. (newsletter editor 1984-86), Tex. Alliance Info. and Referral Svcs. (conv. speaker 1981, 83, 84, 85), Alliance of Info. and Referral Svcs. (conv. speaker 1985), Houston Pub. Libr. Staff Assn. (pres. 1981-82), Literacy Vols. Am. (sec. Houston 1984-87, adv. bd. 1989-91, 95-96, bd. dirs. 1992-95, chmn. program com. 1991-93), Reading, Edn. and Devel. Coun. (recruitment chmn., exec. com. 1984-86), Cultural Arts Coun. of Houston/Harris County, Park Pl. Civic Club (exemplary svc. award 1991), AARP (bd. dirs. chpt. 1172 1998—, v.p. 1999-2000, 01-02, pres. 2003-04), Phi Beta Kappa, Phi Eta Sigma, Beta Phi Mu. Home: 7817 Grove Ridge Dr Houston TX 77061-1405 E-mail: jrussell10@houston.rr.com.

RUSSELL, JOHN JOSEPH, English educator; b. Orange, NJ, Dec. 4, 1949; s. James Francis and Catherine Mary Russell. BA, Seton Hall U., 1973; MA, U. Chgo., 1979, Seton Hall U., 1982; PhD, Fordham U., 1991. Asst. prof. English Union County Coll., Cranford, NJ, 1991—97, assoc. prof. English, 1997—2005, sr. prof. English, 2005—. Author: (book) Hamlet and Narcissus, 1995. Office: Union County Coll 1033 Springfield Ave Cranford NJ 07016 Business E-Mail: russell@ucc.edu.

RUSSELL, JOYCE ANNE ROGERS, retired librarian; b. Chgo., Nov. 6, 1920; d. Truman Allen and Mary Louise (Hoelzle) Rogers; m. John VanCleve Russell, Dec. 24, 1942; children: Malcolm David, John VanCleve. Student, Adelphi Coll., 1937; BS in Chemistry, U. Ky., 1942; M.L.S., Rosary Coll., 1967; postgrad., Rutgers U., 1970-71. Research chemist Sherwin Williams Paint Co., Chgo., 1942-45; reference librarian Chicago Heights (Ill.) Pub. Library, 1959-61; librarian Victor Chem. Works, Chicago Heights, 1961-62; lit. chemist Velsicol Chem. Corp., Chgo., 1964-67; chemistry librarian U. Fla., Gainesville, 1967-69, interim assoc. prof., 1967-69; librarian Thiokol Chem. Corp., Trenton, N.J., 1969-73; supr. library operations E.R. Squibb Co., Princeton, N.J., 1973-80, sr. research info scientist, 1980-91. Mem. library adv. commn. Mercer Community Coll., 1979—; adv. asso. Rutgers U. Grad. Sch. Library and Info. Scis., 1978— Editor: Bibliofile, 1967—69; contbr. articles to profl. jours. Mem. PTA, 1950-66; den mother Cub Scouts, 1952-59. Mem. Spl. Libraries Assn. (sec., dir., v.p., pres. Princeton-Trenton 1971, 75-80), Am. Chem. Soc. (bus. mgr., sec., dir. Trenton sect. 1969-78), AAUW, Mortar Board, Beta Phi Mu, Sigma Pi Sigma, Chi Delta Phi, Pi Sigma Alpha. Home: 1189 Parkside Ave Trenton NJ 08618-2625

RUSSELL, JUDITH, librarian, dean; BA cum laude, Dunbarton Coll. of Holy Cross; MLS, Cath. U. Am. Dir. Office of Electronic Info. Dissemination Svcs. US Govt. Printing Office, Washington, 1991—96, dir. Fed. Depository Libr. Program, supt. documents, 2003—06; dean univ. librs. U. Fla., Gainesville, 2007—. Former dep. dir. Nat. Commn. on Librs. and Info. Sci. (NCLIS). Mem.: ALA. Office: George A Smathers Librs U Fla PO Box 117001 Gainesville FL 32611-7001 Office Phone: 352-273-2505. E-mail: judruss@uflib.ufl.edu. *

RUSSELL, KENNETH CALVIN, metallurgical engineering educator; b. Greeley, Colo., Feb. 4, 1936; s. Doyle James and Jennie Frances (Smith) R.; m. Charlotte Louise Wolf, Apr. 13, 1963 (div. 1978); children: David Allan, Doyle John. Met.E., Colo. Sch. Mines, 1959; PhD, Carnegie Inst. Tec., 1963. Engr. Westinghouse Rsch. and Devel. Ctr., 1959-61; NSF postdoctoral fellow Physics Inst., U. Oslo, 1963-64; asst. prof. metallurgy M.I.T., Cambridge, 1964-69, assoc. prof., 1969-78, prof. metallurgy, 1978—, prof. nuc. engring., 1979—. Contbr. articles to profl. publs. Served as 2d lt. U.S. Army, 1959-60. DuPont fellow, 1961-62; NSF fellow, 1962-63 Mem.: Metallurgical Soc. Am. Inst. Mining, Metallurgical and Petroleum Engrs., Am. Phys. Soc. Office: MIT Rm 13-5050 Cambridge MA 02139 Office Phone: 617-253-3328. E-mail: kenruss@mit.edu.

RUSSELL, KERI, actress; b. Fountain Valley, Calif., Mar. 23, 1976; d. David and Stephanie Russell; m. Shane Deary, Feb. 14, 2007; 1 child, River Russell. Actress: (films) Honey, I Blew Up the Kids, 1992, Eight Days a Week, 1997 Dead Man's Curve, 1998, Mad About Mambo, 2000, We Were Soldiers, 2002, The Upside of Anger, 2005, Mission Impossible III, 2006, Rohtenburg, 2006, Waitress, 2007; (TV series) MMC, 1989, Mickey Mouse Club, 1991-93, Emerald Cove, 1993, Daddy's Girls, 1994, Malibu Shores, 1996, Roar, 1997, Felicity, 1998-2002 (Golden Globe for Best Performan by an Actress in a TV series 1999); (TV films) MMC in Concert, 1993, Clerks, 1995, The Babysitter's Seduction, 1996, The Lottery, 1996, When Innocence Is Lost, 1997, Cinderelmo, 1999, The Magic of Ordinary Days; (TV mini-series) Into the West, 2005; (TV appearances) Boy Meets World, 1993, Married...with Children, 1987, 7th Heaven, 1996, Roar, 1997. Winner Golden Globe for best performance by an actress in a TV series for Felicity, 1999. Office: The Gersh Agy 232 N Canon Dr Beverly Hills CA 90210-5302 *

RUSSELL, KURT, actor; b. Springfield, Mass., Mar. 17, 1951; s. Bing Oliver and Louise Julia (Crone) R.; m. Season Hubley, Mar. 17, 1979 (div. 1984), 1 child, Boston; 1 child (with Goldie Hawn), Wyatt Russell. Student, pub. schs. Profl. baseball player Calif. Angels-AA, 1971-73; co-head (with Goldie Hawn, Kate Hudson, Oliver Hudson) Cosmic Entertainment, 2003—. Actor: (films) The Absent Minded Professor, 1961, It Happened at the World's Fair, 1963, Guns of Diablo, 1964, Follow Me Boys!, 1966, Mosby's Marauders, 1967, The One and Only Genuine Original Family Band, 1968, The Horse in the Grey Flannel Suit, 1968, Guns in the Heather, 1969, The Computer Wore Tennis Shoes, 1970, The Barefoot Executive, 1971, Fools' Parade, 1971, Now You See Him Now You Don't, 1972, Charley and the Angel, 1972, Superdad, 1974, The Strongest Man in the World, 1975, Used Cars, 1980, (voice only) The Fox and the Hound, 1981, Escape from New York, 1981, The Thing, 1982, Silkwood, 1983, Swing Shift, 1984, The Mean Season, 1985, The Best of Times, 1986, Big Trouble in Little China, 1986, Overboard, 1987, Tequila Sunrise, 1988, Winter People, 1989, Tango and Cash, 1989, Backdraft, 1991, Unlawful Entry, 1992, Captain Ron, 1992, Tombstone, 1993, (voice only) Forrest Gump, 1994, Stargate, 1994, Executive Decision, 1996, Breakdown, 1997, Soldier, 1998, 3000 Miles To Graceland, 2001, Vanilla Sky, 2001, Interstate 60, 2002, Dark Blue, 2002, Miracle, 2004, Sky High, 2005, Dreamer: Inspired by a True Story, 2005, Poseidon, 2006, Grindhouse (Death Proof segment), 2007; actor, prodr., writer (films) Escape from L.A., 1996; actor (TV series) Travels with Jamie McPheeters, 1963-64, The New Land, 1974, The Quest, 1976; (TV movies) Dad, Can I Borrow the Car?, 1970, Search for the Gods, 1975, The Deadly Tower, The Quest, 1975, Christmas Miracle in Caulfield U.S.A., 1977, Elvis, 1979, Amber Waves, 1980; (TV appearences) Sam Benedict, 1963, The Eleventh Hour, 1963, Our Man Higgins, 1963, The Man from U.N.C.L.E., 1964, Gilligan's Island, 1965, The Virginian, 1964-65, The Legend of Jesse James, 1966, Laredo, 1966, Lost in Space, 1966, The F.B.I., 1966, The Fugitive, 1964-66, Daniel Boone, 1965-69, Then Came Bronson, 1969, Love, American Style, 1970, The High Cahaparral, 1970, Storefront Lawyers, 1970, The Road West, 1967, Room 222, 1971, Disneyland, 1967-72, Love Story, 1973, Gunsmoke, 1964, 1974, Hec Ramsey, 1974, The New Land, 1974, Harry O, 1975, Police Story, 1974-75, Hawaii Five-O, 1977; exec. prodr. (TV films) 14 Hours, 2005 Served with Calif. Air N.G. Recipient The Disney Legends award, 1998 Mem. Profl. Baseball Players Assn., Stuntman's Assn. Achievements include being the World championship Class Modified Stock, 1959 Race of Champions, Las Vegas. Office: Creative Artists Agy 9830 Wilshire Blvd Beverly Hills CA 90212-1825 *

RUSSELL, LIANE BRAUCH, retired geneticist; b. Vienna, Aug. 27, 1923; came to U.S., 1941; d. Arthur and Clara (Starer) Brauch; m. William Lawson Russell (dec.), Sept. 23, 1947; children: David Lawson, Evelyn Ruth. AB, Hunter Coll., 1945; PhD, U. Chgo., 1949; ScD (hon.), Hunter Coll., NYC, 1999; LHD (hon.), Berea Coll., 2005. Fellow U. Chgo., 1945-46, teaching asst., 1946-47; rsch. asst. Jackson Lab., Bar Harbor, Maine, 1945, 46; rsch. staff mem. Oak Ridge (Tenn.) Nat. Lab., 1947-75, sect. head., 1975-95, sr. rsch. fellow, 1988—2001; ret., 2002. Sci. advisor U.S. Del. at 1st Atoms for Peace Conf., Geneva, Switzerland, 1955; mem. numerous sci. bds. including Nat. Research Council com. on energy and environment, 1975-77, com. on biol. effects of ionizing radiation, 1977-80, bd. on environ. studies and toxicology, 1981-90, Nat. Council on Radiation Protection and Measurement Task Group, Washington, 1975-77, Genetox Program EPA, Washington, 1979—, Internat. Com. for Protection Against Environ. Mutagens and Carcinogens, Lausanne, Switzerland, 1977-83, Internat. com. on standardized genetic nomenclature for mice, 1977-91, office of tech. assessment, scientific adv. panel, 1985-86; mem. task group Internat. Agy. for Research on Cancer, Hanover, Fed. Republic of Germany, 1979, EPA review panel on mutagenicity guidelines, 1985-86; adj. faculty U. Tenn., 1980-. Assoc. editor Mutation Rsch., 1976-96, Environ. Mutagenesis, 1980-83; editor TCWP Newsletter, 1966—; editor: (book) Genetic Mosaics and Chimeras, 1979; contbr. more than 165 articles to profl. jours. Founder Tenn. Citizens for Wilderness Planning, Oak Ridge, 1966, pres. 1967-70, 86-87; active numerous environ. groups. Corp. fellow Union Carbide, 1983; corp. fellow Martin Marietta, 1985, sr. corp. fellow, 1988; recipient Merit award Mademoiselle, 1955, Roentgen medal City of Remscheid-Lennep, 1973, Disting. Assoc. award U.S. Dept. Energy, 1987; named to Hunter Coll. Hall of Fame, 1979, Sol Feinstone Environ. Achievement award SUNY, 1987, Lifetime Achievement award Tenn. Environ. Coun., 1990, Vocational Svc. award Oak Ridge Rotary, 1992, Marjorie Stoneman Douglas award Nat. Parks Conservation Assn., 1993, Enrico Fermi award U.S. Dept. Energy, 1993, Lifetime Conservation Achievement award So. Appalachian Forest Coalition, 1999, Lifetime Environ. Conservation award Tenn. Dept. Environment and Conservation, 2000. Fellow AAAS, Environ. Health Inst.; mem. Nat. Acad. Scis., Environ. Mutagen Soc. (pres. 1984-85, EMS award 1993), Genetics Soc. Am., Tenn. Environ. Honor Soc. Avocation: environmental activism.

RUSSELL, LOUISE BENNETT, economist, educator; b. Exeter, NH, May 12, 1942; d. Frederick Dewey and Esther (Smith) B.; m. Robert Hardy Cosgriff, May 3, 1987; 1 child, Benjamin Smith Cosgriff. BA, U. Mich., 1964; PhD, Harvard U., 1971. Economist Social Security Adminstrn., Washington, 1968-71, Nat. Commn. on State Workmen's Compensation Laws, Washington, 1971-72, Dept. Labor, Washington, 1972-73; sr. economist Nat. Planning Assn., Washington, 1973-75; sr. fellow Brookings Instn., Washington, 1975-87; rsch. prof. Inst. for Health, Health Care Policy and Aging Rsch. Rutgers U., New Brunswick, N.J., 1987—, prof. econs., 1987—. Chmn. health care policy divsn. Rutgers U., 1988—. Author: Technology in Hospitals, 1979, The Baby Boom Generation and the Economy, 1982, Is Prevention Better Than Cure, 1986, Evaluating Preventive Care: Report on a Workshop, 1987, Medicare's New Hospital Payment System: Is It Working, 1989, Educated Guesses: Making Policy About Medical Screening Tests, 1994, (with MR Gold, JE Siegel and MC Weinstein) Cost-Effectiveness in Health and Medicine, 1996, also numerous articles; assoc. editor Med. Decision Making, 2004—. Mem. U.S. Preventive Svcs. Task Force, 1984-88; co-chair Panel on Cost Effectiveness in Health and Medicine DHHS, USPHS, 1993-96. Mem. Inst. Medicine of NAS (elected mem., com. to study future pub. health 1986-87, bd. on health scis. policy 1989-91, com. on clin. practice guidelines 1990-91, com. on setting priorities for practice guidelines 1994, nat. cancer policy bd. 2001-05). Office: Rutgers U Inst for Health Care Policy 30 College Ave New Brunswick NJ 08901-1293 Business E-Mail: lrussell@rci.rutgers.edu.

RUSSELL, MARK, comedian; b. Buffalo, Aug. 23, 1932; s. Marcus Joseph and Marie Elizabeth (Perry) Ruslander; m. Alison Kaplan, Dec. 17, 1978; children: Monica, John, Matthew. Student, George Washington U., 1952; LittD, Union Coll., 1987; LHD, Canisius Coll., 1988; LHD (hon.), Goucher Coll., 1990; LLD (hon.), D'Youville Coll., 2004. Lectr., public speaker. Polit. comedian, featured performer Shoreham Hotel, Washington, 1961-81; prin. Mark Russell Comedy Spls., Pub. Broadcasting Svc., 1975—, Mark Russell's 25th Anniversary Special, 2000 (Silver Telly award 2000); host Mark Russell's England, PBS-TV, 1988, Mark Russell's Irish Fling, 1993, Mark Russell's Great Ala. Trek, 1994, Mark Russell's Tour de France, 1995, Mark Russell's Viva Italia, 1996; co-host NBC's Real People, 1979-84; regular contbr. Good Morning Am., ABC-TV, Inside Politics Weekend, CNN; author: Presenting Mark Russell, 1980; syndicated columnist via Tribune Media Svcs., 1975. Mem. father's day coun., Washington. With USMC, 1953—56. Recipient Mark Twain award Internat. Platform Assn., 1980, 86, 4th Ann. Lucy award Shea's Buffalo, 1992, Nat. Humor Treasure award Nat. Humor Conf., 1995, SOAR St. Elizabeth Ann Seton award Washington, 1995, Washingtonian of the Yr. Washingtonian Mag., 1996, Disting. Washingtonian award Univ. Club, 2001, Theodore Roosevelt Exemplary Citizenship award T. R. Inaugural Site Found., 2005; named Father of Yr., Am. Diabetes Assn., 2005 Mem. AFTRA, Am. Fedn. Musicians. Office: PO Box 9904 Washington DC 20016-8904 Office Phone: 202-362-5045. E-mail: mail@markrussell.net.

RUSSELL, MARY RHODES, state supreme court justice; b. Hannibal, Mo., July 28, 1958; d. Cleveland Jerome and Mary Elisabeth (Stewart) Rhodes; m. James Lowell Russell, Nov. 25, 1995. BA in Mass. Comms., BS in Home Econs., Truman State U., 1980; JD, U. Mo., Columbia, 1983. Bar: Mo. 1983, Ill. 1984, U.S. Dist. Ct. (ea. dist.) 1984, U.S. Supreme Ct. 1992. Adminstrv. asst. Mo. Senate, Jefferson City, 1980-83, law clk., 1983-84; ptnr. Clayton & Rhodes, Hannibal, 1984-95; judge Mo. Ct. Appeals (ea. dist.), St. Louis, 1995—2004, Mo. Supreme Ct., 2004—. Author: Enforcement of Discovery Sanctions, 1994. Bd. dirs. Comm. on Ret., Removal and Discipline of Judges, St. Louis, 1994-95, Matthews-Dickey Boys & Girls Club; mem. urban campout project Girl Scouts USA, St. Louis, 1996; mem., past pres. PEO, Hannibal, 1993-95, Jefferson City, 1995—. Recipient Equal Justice award Legal Svcs. Ea. Mo., 1994, Citation of Merit award U. Mo. Sch. Law, 1997; Henry Toll fellow, 1997. Mem. Bar Assn. St. Louis (chair bench/bar rels. 1996-97), Woman Lawyers Assn. St. Louis, Nat. Assn. Women Judges, Kansas City Met. Bar Assn., Mo. Lawyer Trust Account Found. (vice chmn., bd. dirs. 1990-95), Rotary (program chmn. 1996-97). Episcopalian. Avocations: cardinal baseball, travel, cooking. Office: Supreme Ct Mo PO Box 150 Jefferson City MO 65102 Office Phone: 573-751-6880. Business E-Mail: mary.russell@courts.mo.gov. *

RUSSELL, MARYANNE, photographer; Grad., NYU; student, Internat. Ctr. Photography. Staff photographer Time Inc.; owner Maryanne Russell Photography Inc., 1986—. Photographer (works appeared at) Acad. Art Coll., San Francisco, Lobet Gallery, NYC, Grant Gallery, Chelsea Art Gallery, (group exhbns.) Sephora's Flagship store. Mem.: Am. Soc. Media Photographers, NY Women in Comm. (Liz Hoover award 1994). Achievements include photography clients AT&T, Christian Dior, HBO, NY Giants, Paramount Pictures, People mag., Time Warner Inc., Viacom, and many others. Office Phone: 212-308-8722.

RUSSELL, MICHAEL K., psychology professor, consultant; s. Alice P. Russell. PhD, U. Conn., Storrs, 1997. Asst. prof. Washburn U., Topeka, Kans., 2001—. Cons. Spring, Kansas City, Kans., 2001—03. Home Phone: 785-233-2369; Office Phone: 785-670-1566. Office Fax: 785-231-1010. Business E-Mail: mike.russell@washburn.edu.

RUSSELL, NAS'NAGA R., illustrator; b. Dayton, Ohio, Apr. 13, 1941; s. Willard Dudly and Kathryn Louise (Pangborn) R.; m. Harriet Ann Russell, June 1967 (div. 1973); 1 child, Jamie Noelle; m. Barbara Jane Mullins, Sept. 14, 1984. Grad. h.s. Mgr. AAAirlines, Ft. Worth, 1970-74; writer Harper & Rowe, NYC, 1974-75; owner, dir. Art Gallery, Kettering, Ohio, 1979-83. Dir., owner Nas'Naga Enterprises, Inc. Pro., Centerville, Ohio, 1980-83; lectr., spkr. in field. Author, illustrator: Indians' Summer, 1975, Western Writers of America, 1975-1980, Dayton's Society of Painters and Sculptors, 1978-1980, Faces Beneith The Grass, 1979, Darker Side of Glory, 2000; columnist Western Mag., Oslo, Norway, 1976-79; co-author: Poetry Anthology, 2004. Airlines rep. Okla. for Indian Opportunity, Tex., 1970—74; steering com. Newark state mound project Ohio Hist. Soc.,

2000. With USN, 1959—63. Recipient Humanitarian Svc. award Oklahomians for Indian Opportunity, Norman, Okla., 1973, United Cerebeal Palsy, Dayton, 1984, Outstanding Artistic Achievement award Green County Ohio, Xenia, 1975. Avocations: archery, painting, research. Home: 3000 B E Main St #359 Columbus OH 43209

RUSSELL, PAUL EDGAR, electrical engineering educator; b. Roswell, N.Mex., Oct. 10, 1924; s. Rueben Matthias and Mary (Parsons) R.; m. Lorna Margaret Clayshulte, Aug. 29, 1943; children: Carol Potter, Janice Russell Cook, Gregory. BSEE, N.Mex. State U., 1946, BSME, 1947; MSEE, U. Wis., 1950, PhDEE, 1951. Registered elec. engr., Ariz. From instr. to asst. prof. elec. engring. U. Wis., Madison, 1947-52; sr. engr., design specialist Gen. Dynamics Corp., San Diego, 1952-54; from prof. to chmn. elec. engring. dept. U. Ariz., Tucson, 1954-63; dean engring. Kans. State U., Manhattan, 1963-67; prof. Ariz. State U., Tempe, 1967-90; dir. engring. Ariz. State U. West, Phoenix, 1985-88; dir. Sch. Constrn. and Tech. Ariz. State U., Tempe, 1988-90. Cons. in field, 1954—; programs evaluator, mem. engring. commn. Accreditation Bd. for Engring. and Tech., N.Y.C., 1968-81. Contbr. articles to jours. and chpts. to books. Served as sgt. U.S. Army, 1944-46. Recipient Disting. Service award N.Mex. State U., 1965. Fellow IEEE (life, chmn. Ariz. sect. 1960), Accreditation Bd. Engring. and Tech.; mem. Am. Soc. Engring. Educators. Home: 5902 E Caballo Ln Paradise Valley AZ 85253 Office Phone: 480-948-0716.

RUSSELL, PAUL SNOWDEN, surgeon, educator; b. Chgo., Jan. 22, 1925; s. Paul Snowden and Carroll (Mason) R.; m. Allene Lummis, Sept. 24, 1952; children: Katherine Swift, Paul Snowden, Allene, Laura Rice. PhB, U. Chgo., 1944, BS, 1945, MD, 1947; MA (hon.), Harvard U., 1962. Diplomate Am. Bd. Surgery, Am. Bd. Thoracic Surgery. From surg. intern, to resident Mass. Gen. Hosp., 1948-56, asst. surgery, 1957-60, chief gen. surg. svcs., 1962-69, chmn. com. on rsch., 1973-76; postdoctoral fellow USPHS, 1954-55; from tchg. fellow to clin. assoc. surgery Harvard Med. Sch., 1956-60, John Homans prof. surgery, 1962-98, John Homans Disting. prof. surgery, 1998—; assoc. prof. surgery Columbia Coll. Phys. and Surg., 1960-62; assoc. attending surgeon Presbyn. Hosp., NYC, 1960-62; assoc. vis. surgeon Francis Delafield Hosp., NYC, 1960-62, 74-94. Mem. com. tissue transplantation NRC-Nat. Acad. Scis., 1963-71, com. trauma, 1963-68; ad hoc com. to study clin. investigation and edn. in USN, 1971-73; allergy and immunology study sect. USPHS, 1963-65, chmn. allergy and immunology study sect. B, 1965-67; mem. transplantation and immunology com. Nat. Inst. Allergy and Infectious Diseases, 1967-69, chmn., 1970; mem. com. on cancer immunotherapy Nat. Cancer Inst., 1974-79. Contbr. papers in field.; Editorial bd.: Archives Surgery, 1963-72, Surgery, 1963-71, Transplantation, 1965-79, Annals of Surgery, 1966—, Transplantation Procs, 1966—, Jour. Immunology, 1977-80. Trustee Pine Manor Coll., Chestnut Hill, Mass., 1963-76, Groton Sch., 1964-79, The Conservation Law Found., 1997—; bd. dirs. Boston Fulbright Com., 1968, pres., 1980—; vice chmn. bd. govs., trustee corp. Jackson Lab. With USAF, 1951-53. Recipient Roche Pioneer award, Am. Soc. Transplant Surgeons, 2005. Fellow AAAS, ACS, Royal Soc. Medicine, Am. Acad. Arts and Scis., Assn. Immunologists, NY Acad. Scis., Mass. Med. Soc., New Eng. Surg. Soc., Boston Surg. Soc. (pres. 1994), Soc. Univ. Surgeons, Soc. Exptl. Biology and Medicine, Halsted Soc., Whipple Soc., Internat. Soc. Surgery, Am. Surg. Assn., Transplantation Soc. (pres. 1970, Medawar Prize 2005), Polish Acad. Sci. (fgn.), Sigma Xi. Home: 10 Longwood Dr Apt 148 Westwood MA 02090 Office: Dept Surgery Mass Gen Hosp Boston MA 02114 Office Phone: 617-726-2801.

RUSSELL, RICHARD A., lawyer; b. 1952; BS, Pa. State U., 1974; JD, U. Pitts., 1979. Bar: Pa. 1979. Assoc. atty. May & Long, Pitts., 1979—86; corp. counsel Giant Eagle Inc., Pitts., 1986—90, sr. corp. counsel, 1990—98, v.p., gen. counsel, 1998—. Mem.: Allegheny County Bar Assn. Office: Giant Eagle Inc 101 Kappa Dr Pittsburgh PA 15238-2809 Office Phone: 412-963-2598. Office Fax: 412-963-3522. E-mail: rick.russell@gianteagle.com.

RUSSELL, RICHARD DONCASTER, geophysics educator, academic administrator; b. Toronto, Ont., Can., Feb. 27, 1929; s. Richard Douglas and Ada Gwennola (Doncaster) R.; m. Virginia Ann Reid Clippingdale, Aug. 11, 1951; children: Linda Jean, Morna Ann, Mary Joyce. BA, U. Toronto, 1951, MA, 1952, PhD, 1954. Asst. prof. physics U. Toronto, 1956-58, prof., 1962-63; assoc. prof. physics U. B.C., Vancouver, Canada, 1958-62, prof. geophysics, 1963-91, prof. emeritus, 1991—, head dept. geophysics, 1968-72, head dept. geophysics and astronomy, 1972-79, bd. govs., 1978-81, assoc. dean sci., 1980-83, assoc. v.p. acad., 1983-86. Sec.-gen. Inter-Union Commn. on Geodynamics, 1976—80; profl. geoscientist. Author (with John Arthur Jacobs and J. Tuzo Wilson): Physics and Geology International Series in the Earth Sciences, first edit., 1959, Physics and Geology McGraw-Hill International Series in the Earth and Planetary Science, 2d edit., 1973; author: (with Ronald McCunn Farquhar) Lead Isotopes in Geology Interscience, 1960. Fellow Royal Soc. Can.; mem. Am. Geophys. Union, Can. Geophys. Union (J. Tuzo Wilson medal 1992). Home: 226-4955 River Rd Delta BC Canada V4K 4V9 Office Phone: 604-940-1164.

RUSSELL, RICHARD LEAVITT, political science professor; b. Poughkeepsie, NY, Aug. 2, 1961; BA in Econ., cum laude, Union Coll., Schnectady, 1983; MA in Internat. Affairs, Am. U., Washington, DC, 1987; PhD in Fgn. Affairs, U. Va., Charlottesville, 1997. Polit.-mil. analyst CIA, Langley, Va., 1984—2001; adj. assoc. prof. security studies Georgetown U., 2005—, rsch. assoc., inst. study diplomacy, 2000—; prof. nat. security affairs Nat. Def. U., Washington, 2001—. Author: George F. Kennan's Strategic Thought, Weapons Proliferation and War in the Greater Middle East, Sharpening Strategic Intelligence. Mem.: Internat. Inst. Strategic Studies. Home: 20484 Ashley Terr Sterling VA 20165 Office: Nat Defense U Fort Lesley J McNair Washington DC 20319 Home Phone: 703-421-9437; Office Phone: 202-685-2163. Office Fax: 202-685-4999. Business E-Mail: russellr@ndu.edu.

RUSSELL, RICHARD MATHER, federal official; b. 1966; m. Lynley Ogilvie; 1 child, George. BS in Biology, Yale U., 1988. Dir. Assn. Calif. Water Agencies; staff mem. subcom. on oceanography, Gulf of Mexico and Outer Continental Shelf U.S. Ho. of Reps. Com. on Merchant Marine and Fisheres, 1993—94; from profl. staff for the subcom. on energy and environment, staff dir. for subcom. on tech. to dep. chief of staff for sci. com. U.S. Ho. Reps. Com. on Sci., 1995—2001; chief of staff Office Sci. & Tech. Policy, Exec. Office of the Pres., Washington, 2001—02, assoc. dir., 2002—; sr. dir. for tech. & telecom. Nat. Econ. Coun., Washington, 2002—. US Amb. World Radiocommunications Conf., Geneva, 2007. Office: Office Sci & Tech Policy EEOB 17th & Pennsylvania Ave NW Washington DC 20502 *

RUSSELL, RICHARD OLNEY, JR., retired cardiologist; b. Birmingham, Ala., July 9, 1932; s. Richard Olney and Louise (Taylor) R.; m. Phyllis Hutchinson, June 15, 1963; children: Scott Richard, Katherine Hutchinson, Meredith Cooper, Stephen Wilbon. AB cum laude, Vanderbilt U., Nashville, 1953, MD, 1956. Diplomate Am. Bd. Internal Medicine, 1964, Am. Bd. Cardiovascular Disease, 1967. Intern Peter Bent Brigham Hosp., Boston, 1956-57, resident, 1959-60, 63-64; fellow in cardiology Med. Coll. Ala., Birmingham, 1960-62, instr., 1962-63; instr. medicine U. Ala., Birmingham, 1964-65, asst. prof., 1965-70, assoc. prof., 1970-73, prof., 1973-81, clin. prof., 1981—2006; pvt. practice medicine specializing in cardiology Birmingham, 1981—2006; ret., 2006. Mem. Jefferson County Bd. Health, 1977—81, chmn., 1979. Author: (with Charles Edward Rackley) Hemodynamic Monitoring in a Coronary Intensive Care Unit, 1974, 2d rev. and enlarged edit., 1981, Coronary Artery Disease: Recognition and Management, 1979, (with others) Radiographic Anatomy of the Coronary Arteries: An Atlas, 1976, Acute Ischemic Syndromes in American College of Cardiology Self Assessment Program, 1993; mem. editl. bd. Circulation, 1976-80, Am. Jour. Cardiology, 1977-82, Heart and Lung, 1978-83, Chest, 1978-83, Ala. Jour. Med. Scis, 1977-80, Jour. Am. Coll. Cardiology, 1987-90; sect. editor for Case Studies for Cardiosource for Am. Coll. Cardiology, 2001-06, assoc. editor, 2006—; contbr. articles to profl. jours. Distbn. com. Greater Birmingham Found., 1984-90; exec. bd. Birmingham area coun. Boy Scouts Am., 1987-1998, v.p., 1990-96, coun. commr., 1996-98; vice chmn. Vulcan dist., 1988-89, chmn., 1989-91, bd. dirs. S.E. region, 1990-92, bd. dirs. southern region, 1992—; bd. dirs. Ctrl. Ala. United Way, 1988-92; mem. Newcomen Soc., 1988—; chmn. exec. com. Birmingham Bapt. Med. Ctr., Montclair, 1995, pres.-elect med. staff, 1998-99, pres. 1999-2000; chmn. Nat. Eagle Scout Assn. Scholarship Com. So. Region, 2001-03; asst. coun. cmmr. Greater Ala. coun. Boy Scouts Am., 1998-2000, coun. commr., 2001-04, v.p. bd., 2006, pres., 2007; mem. Am. Bd. Cardiovasc. Disease, 1991-96. Capt. U.S. Army. Decorated Commendation medal; recipient Dist. Award of Merit, Boy Scouts Am., 1991, Silver Beaver award, 1990, Disting. Eagle Scout, 1999, Silver Antelope award 2001; NIH rsch. fellow, 1966-67. Fellow: ACP, Am. Coll. Cardiology (bd. govs. 1979—81, trustee 1984—85, 1989—94, ann. sci. session program chmn. 1994, disting. fellowship 2001, Ala. chpt. named lectureship in honor); mem.: Med. Assn. State Ala. (spkr. house counselors dels. 1989—94, Laureate award 1999), Birmingham Soc. Internists (pres. 2001—03), Birmingham Cardiovascular Soc. (pres. 1981), Jefferson County Med. Soc. (v.p. 1982, pres. 1984), So. Soc. Clin. Investigation, Am. Fedn. Clin. Rsch., Am. Coll. Chest Physicians (bd. regents 1985—91), Am. Heart Assn. (pres. Ala. affiliate 1975—76, v.p. so. region 1986—87, task force on practice guidelines 1998—2000), Royal Soc. Medicine, NY Acad. Scis., Kiwanis (Brimingham sec. 1984—85, disting. pres. 1994—95), Leadership Birmingham, Omicron Delta Kappa, Alpha Omega Alpha, Phi Beta Kappa. Home: 4408 Kennsaw Dr Birmingham AL 35213-1826 Personal E-mail: rorussell@charter.net.

RUSSELL, ROBERT HILTON, Romance languages and literature educator; b. Oak Park, Ill., Dec. 26, 1927; s. Melvin Alvord and Gladys (Hilton) R.; m. June Adele Thayer, Oct. 27, 1956. AB, Knox Coll., 1949; A.M., Harvard U., 1950, PhD, 1963; A.M., Dartmouth Coll., 1968. Instr. Romance langs. and lits. Dartmouth Coll., 1957-61, asst. prof., 1961-63, assoc. prof., 1963-67, prof., 1967-91, prof. emeritus, 1991—. Vis. prof. Spanish, U. San Diego, 1989, 90, 91, Knox Coll., 1993; guest lectr. Trinity Coll., Dublin, 1967, U. Salamanca, 1977, U. Leeds, 1978, Oxford U., 1978, U. P.R., 1987. Author: The Christ Figure in Misericordia, 1968; translator: Our Friend Manso, 1987, Misericordia, 2007. Corporate mem. United Ch. Bd. Homeland Ministries, 1963-69; N.H. del. Gen. Synod, United Ch. Christ, 1973, 75; corporator Internat. Inst. in Spain. Mem. MLA, Asociación Internacional de Hispanistas, Asociación Internacional de Galdosistas, Phi Beta Kappa. Democrat. Home: 17 Willow Spring Cir Hanover NH 03755-2901 Office: 6072 Dartmouth Hall Hanover NH 03755-3511

RUSSELL, ROBERT L., real estate appraiser; b. Monroe, La., Mar. 4, 1954; s. Howard M and Mary M Russell; m. Joanne Vera Dearing, Nov. 19, 1977; children: John D, Jacob H. BS, La. State U., 1975. Real estate cons., appraiser Robert L Russell, MAI, Shreveport, La., 1976—. Pres. La. Chpt. Appraisal Inst., Shreveport, 2001. Socio political editorial writer various newspaper columns. Independent. Episcopalian. Avocations: golf, martial arts, tennis, travel, creative writing. Office: Robert L Russell MAI P O Box 52075 Shreveport LA 71135-2075 Home Phone: 318-797-8895; Office Phone: 318-798-6993. Office Fax: 319-798-6995; Home Fax: 318-798-6995. Business E-Mail: rob@rrussellmai.com.

RUSSELL, RODNEY E., school system administrator; b. Knoxville, Tenn., Feb. 3, 1964; s. Howard Wade and Lucille Annette Russell; m. Jamie Renee Humphrey, Apr. 7, 1990; 1 child, Daniel Thomas. BS, East Tenn. State U., 1986; EdS, Lincoln Meml. U., Harrogate, Tenn., 1997; EdD, Trevecca Nazarene U., Nashville, 2005. Supr. staff devel. and extended learning Knox County Schs., Knoxville, 2003—, evening alternative sch. prin., 2005—06. Non-daycare facility mgr. Boys Club of Knoxville, 1985—87; lang. devel. specialist Knox County Schs., 1987—97, tchr. 4th grade, 1989—96, sci. specialist, 1996—2003; min. of youth Smithwood Bapt. Ch., Knoxville, 1999—. Bd. dirs. Tenn. Staff Devel. Coun., Tenn., 2000—06. Named Tchr. of the Yr. Bldg. Level, Tenn. Dept. of Edn., 1993; named to Leadership Edn. Class, Knoxville C. of C., 1993; recipient Beacon in the Classroom award, Apple Computers, 1994, 21st Century grant for computer tech., Knox County Schs., 1992; grantee, Jr. League of Knoxville, 1995. Mem.: NEA (assoc.), NSTA (assoc.), Tenn. Staff Devel. Coun. (assoc.; bd. dirs. 2000—06), Nat. Staff Devel. Coun. (assoc.; co-chair conf. exhibits 2004—06), Phi Delta Kappa, Pi Lambda Theta. Baptist. Achievements include research in impact of content reading strategies impact on achievement; development of new teacher academy and mentor program for teachers in Knox County. Avocations: golf, swimming, skiing. Home: 4910 Shannon Run Drive Knoxville TN 37918 Office: Sarah Simpson Prof Dev Center 810 Tipton Avenue Knoxville TN 37918 Home Phone: 865-689-6489; Office Phone: 865-579-8018 1051. Office Fax: 865-579-8191; Home Fax: 865-579-8191. Personal E-mail: russell_rodney@bellsouth.net.

RUSSELL, SABIN, newswriter; m. Ashley Wolff; 2 children. Grad., Yale U., 1974. Writer Venture Mag., Electronic News, various cmty. newspapers Vermont and NH; med. writer San Francisco Chronicle. Recipient Sci. in Soc. Journalism award, Nat. Assn. Sci. Writers, Inc., 2001; grantee, Kaiser Family Found. Primary responsibilities include coverage of science and health policy, focusing on topics such as HIV/AIDS, bioterrorism, SARS, West Nile virus, mad cow, and other infectious diseases. Office: San Francisco Chronicle 901 Mission St San Francisco CA 94103-2988 Office Phone: 415-777-8447. Office Fax: 415-896-1107. Business E-Mail: srussell@sfchronicle.com.

RUSSELL, STELLA PANDELL, artist, author, educator; b. NYC, June 14, 1927; d. James C. and Dorothy (Ross) Pandell; m. George Russell, Aug. 10, 1951 (dec.); children: Janna, Jonathan, Loriann. BA, Hunter Coll., 1948; MA, Columbia U., 1950, PhD, 1972; M in Comml. Arts, NY Inst. Tech., 1986. Animator, Loucks and Norling Co., 1948; dir. art Alexander's Dept. Stores, NYC, 1948-51; tchr. art pub. schs., NYC, 1951-53; co-dir. Russell-Pandell Art Studies, NYC, 1953-61; lectr. art Hunter Coll., NYC, 1961-65; chmn. art Nassau CC, NY, from 1965; one-woman shows include: Oyster Bay Library, NY, 1962, 63, Huntington Library, 1970, Nassau CC, 1971, South Nassau Library, 1973, 83, Firehouse Gallery, 1975, 84, Country Art Gallery, 1977; group shows include: NY State U. traveling exhbn., 1969, St. John's U., 1975, Central Hall Gallery, 1976, C.W. Post Coll., 1977, Royal Acad., Stockholm, 1978, 82, Islip Mus., 1985, Fine Art Mus. of Lit., 1987; represented permanent collections Hunter Coll., Sallskapet Mus., Sweden, Zimmerli Coll., Rutgers U.; host Art in World sta. WHPC, Garden City, 1972—, Art and Religion, 2005-. Author: Art in the World, 1975, 84, 89, 94; contbr. articles to profl. jours. Winner Chancellor's award excellence in teaching, 1982. Mem. Profl. Artists Guild, NY State Ann. Jr. Colls., Nat. Assn. Women Artists, NY State African Studies Assn. Unitarian. Club: Mensa. Home: 29 Tiffany Rd Oyster Bay NY 11771-1907 also: 90 Lawton Rd Hilton Head Island SC 29928 Office: Stewart Ave Garden City NY 11530 Personal E-mail: drstellarrussell@aol.com.

RUSSELL, STEPHEN RICHARD, medical educator; s. William Richard and Karen Malinquist Russell; m. Trudy Foster, May 12, 1981; children: Christopher Stephen, Jonathan Foster, Carolyn Rebecca. BS in Elect. Engring., Biology, Stanford U., Palo Alto, 1978; MD, UCLA, Calif., 1982. Intern Harbor Gen. Hosp., UCLA, Torrence, Calif., 1982—83; ophthalmology resident U. Miami, Buscom Palmer Eye Inst., Miami, 1983—86; retina fellowship U. Iowa, Iowa City, 1986—88; rsch. asst. Stanford U. Ophthalmology Dept., Palo Alto, Calif., 1976—78, La. State U. Ophthalmology Dept., New Orleans, 1979—80; attending physician Iowa City Vets. Hosp., Iowa City, 1987—88; asst. prof. St. Louis U., 1988—94, assoc. prof., 1994—96, U. Iowa, 1996—2005, prof., dir. retina svc., 2005—. Contbr. articles various profl. jours. Mem.: Am. Bd. Ophthalmology (assoc. examiner 1995—2000), Iowa Acad. Ophthalmology, Am. Acad. Ophthalmology (com. positions 2001—06). Avocations: fly fishing, golf. Office: U Iowa 200 Hawkins Dr Iowa City IA 52242 Business E-Mail: steve-russell@uiowa.edu.

RUSSELL, SUE ANN, clinical psychologist; b. Connersville, Ind., Apr. 14, 1949; d. Hugh B. Russell and Martha Jane Meyer. BS, U. Colo., 1971; MDiv, Abilene Christian U., 1981; PhD in Clin. Psychology, U. N.D., 1992. Intern Psychol. Svcs. Ctr. U. N.D., Grand Forks, 1986-92; intern Stone Ctr. Wellesley Coll., Wellesley, 1991-92; rsch. psychologist women's drinking project U. N.D., Grand Forks, 1986-92; pvt. practice Grand Forks, 1993—. Founding fellow Jean Baker Miller Tng. Inst. of Wellesley Coll., 1996. Contbr. articles to profl. jours. Missionary to Tonga Tribe, Africa, 1972—74. Fellowship Nat. Inst. on Alcohol Abuse and Alcoholism Nat. Inst. of Mental Health, 1991-92, Nat. Rsch. Svc. award 1988-91; predoctoral rsch. fellow Stone Ctr. of Wellesley Coll., 1991-92. Mem. Am. Psychol. Assn., N.D. Psychol. Assn., Assn. of Prevention and Cruelty to Animals Avocations: American Eskimo dogs, creating wildlife sanctuary and natural prairie habitat on 290 acres. Office: 628 7th Ave S Ste B Grand Forks ND 58201-4854 Office Phone: 701-746-8737.

RUSSELL, TERRENCE JOSEPH, lawyer; b. Jacksonville, Fla., Sept. 26, 1944; AA, St. Leo Coll., 1964; BA, U. Fla., 1966; JD, Fla. State U., 1968. Bar: Fla. 1969. Law clk. to Hon. W.O. Mehrtens U.S. Dist. Ct. (so. dist.) Fla., 1969; atty. Ruden, McClosky, Smith, Schuster & Russell, P.A., Ft. Lauderdale, Fla. Mem. appellate restructure commn. Fla. Supreme Ct., 1985—86, mem. nominating com., 1994—, chmn. nominating com., 1997, 98; mem. Fed. Magistrate's merit selection panel, 1985; vice-chmn. 17th Jud. Cir. Nominating Com., 1982—84, chmn., 1985—86; mem. spl. com. representation of death sentenced inmates Fla. Bar, bd. govs., 1987—91, pres., 2001—02. Bd. govs. Nova U. Law Sch., 1981, chmn., 1993—97; bd. dirs. Broward County Legal Aid Svcs., 1985—86. Mem.: ATLA, ABA (ho. of dels. 2000—04, sects. litig., legal edn.), Fla. Jud. Qualifications Commn., Fla. Bar Found. (bd. dirs. 1992—98, pres. 2004—), Fla. State U. Law Sch. Alumni Assn. (pres. 1985), Am. Bd. Trial Advs., Am. Bar Found., Acad. Fla. Trial Lawyers (coll. diplomates), Broward County Trial Lawyers Assn., Broward County Bar Assn. (chmn. spl. com. legal malpractice ins. 1978, bar-bench liaison com. 1978, jud. selection and tenure com. 1978—79, exec. com. 1980, 1981, pres. 1984—85), Gold Key, Delta Theta Phi. Office: Ruden McClosky et al PO Box 1900 Fort Lauderdale FL 33302-1900 Home Phone: 954-753-1125; Office Phone: 954-527-2460. Business E-Mail: terrence.russell@ruden.com.

RUSSELL, THEODORE EMERY, diplomat; b. Madras, India, Nov. 21, 1936; s. Paul Farr and Phyllis Hope R.; m. Sara Mather Stedman, Sept. 3, 1960; children: Douglas Richmond, Richard Mather. BA, Yale U., 1958; MA, Fletcher Sch. Law & Diplomacy, 1960, MALD, 1961; sr. tng., Nat. War Coll., 1980—81. Fgn. svc. officer Dept. State, Italy, Czechoslovakia, Washington, 1963-80, dep. office dir. (EUR/RPE) Washington, 1981-83; dep. chief mission Copenhagen, 1983-87, Prague, Czechoslovakia, 1988-91; dep. asst. adminstr. for internat. activities EPA, Washington, 1992-93; amb. to Slovak Republic Bratislava, Slovakia, 1993-96; dep. comdt. internat. affairs Army War Coll., Carlisle, Pa., 1996-99; dir. internat. rels. MHz Networks, 2001—03; internat. security affairs cons., 2001—. Adj. fellow CSIS. Founding chmn. Friends of Slovakia. Mem. Army-Navy Club, Fgn. Svc. Assn., Nat. War Coll. Alumni Assn. Avocations: hiking, fishing, history. Home and Office: 1833 Briar Ridge Ct Mc Lean VA 22101-4233

RUSSELL, THERESA LYNN, actress; b. San Diego, Mar. 20, 1957; d. Jerry Russell Paup and Carole (Mall) Platt; m. Nicholas Jack Roeg, Feb. 12, 1982 (div.); children: Statten Jack, Maximilian Nicolas Sextus. Appeared in films including The Last Tycoon, 1976, Straight Time, 1978, Bad Timing, 1980, Eureka, 1984, Razor's Edge, 1984, Insignificance, 1985, Aria, 1987, Black Widow, 1987 (Nat. Assn. Theater Owners award 1985), Track 29, 1988 (Newcomer of Yr. award), Physical Evidence, 1989, Impulse, 1990, Cold Heaven, 1991 (Best Actress award Viareggio Film Festival 1991), Whore, 1991, Kafka, 1991, Thicker Than Water, 1992, The Trade Off, 1993, (narrator) Being Human, 1993, Flight of the Dove, 1994, Grotesque, 1995, The Proposition, 1995, A young connecticut Yankee in King Arthur's Court, 1995, Public Enemies, 1996, The Proposition, 1997, Running Women, 1998, Wild Things, 1998, Luckytown, 2000, The Believer, 2001, The House Next Door, 2002, Project Viper, 2002, Passionada, 2002, Now & Forever, 2002, Save It for Later, 2003, Chinaman's Chance, 2007, Spider-Man 3, 2007; TV films Blind Ambition, 1979, Women's Guide to Adultery, 1993, Hotel Paradise, 1995, Once You Meet a Stranger, 1996, Trade Off, 1996, Earth vs. the Spider, 2001, Love Comes Softly, 2003, Blind Injustice, 2005, Empire Falls, 2005; (TV miniseries) Blind Ambition, 1979; guest appearances Nash Bridges, 2000, Law & Order: Criminal Intent, 2006; BBC radio play Double Indemnity, 1993. *

RUSSELL, THOMAS WILLIAM FRASER, chemical engineer, educator; b. Moose Jaw, Sask., Can., Aug. 5, 1934; s. Thomas D. and Evelyn May (Fraser) R.; m. Shirley A. Aldrich, Aug. 1956; children: Bruce, Brian, Carey. BChe, U. Alta., Canada, 1956; MChe, U. Alta., 1958; PhD, U. Del., 1964. Registered profl. engr., Del. Rsch. engr. Rsch. Coun. of Alta., Edmonton, Alberta, Canada, 1956—58; process design engr. Union Carbide Can., Montreal, Quebec, Canada, 1958—61; Allan P. Colburn prof. of chem. engring. U. Del., Newark, Del., 1961—; acting dean Coll. of Engring., U. Del., 1978—79; dir. Inst. of Energy Conversion, U. Del., 1979—95; chmn. Dept. Chem. Engring., U. Del., 1986—91; vice provost for rsch. U. Del., 2000—05. Cons. E.I. duPont de Nemours & Co., Inc., Wilmington, Del., 1968—. Author 2 books; contbr. articles to profl. jours., patentee in field. Recipient award, NAE, 1990 to present, 3M Lectureship award, Am. Soc. of Engring. Edn., 1984, Thomas H Chilton award, AIChE, Wilmington Sect., 1988. Mem. NAE, Am. Inst. Chem. Engring. (Thomas H. Chilton award 1988, Chem. Engring. Practice award 1987), Am. Chem. Soc., Am. Soc. Engring. Edn. (3M Lecture award chem. engring. divsn. 1984). Achievements include patents for method for the manufacture of thin film solar cells; method for the continuous deposition by vacuum deposition; first to development of a continuous process for the manufacture of thin film solar modules. Avocations: hiking, skiing, windsurfing. Office: U DE Dept Chem Engring Newark DE 19716 Home Phone: 302-731-4293; Office Phone: 302-831-1714. Personal E-mail: twfr@udel.edu.

RUSSELL, WALTER DALLAS, JR., diversified financial services company executive; b. Culver City, Calif., Oct. 31, 1979; s. Walter Dallas and Leann Marie Russell. BBA in Fin., U. Houston, 2005. Sr. mgr. MRG, Inc., Houston, 2000—03; escrow officer Land Am. Ptnrs. Title, 2003—. Mem.: AARP (assoc.), Am. Mensa. Office Phone: 713-426-4949. Personal E-mail: drussell2028@yahoo.com.

RUSSELL, WAYNE DELANO, activist, educator, poet; s. Arthur Ismael and Edna Alberta Russell; children: Dayon Antoni Lorreen, Niani Simone, Taylor Audrey Delana, Nicholas Wayne Whittington. BS in Aerospace Engring., Poly. U., Bklyn., 1999, MS in Fin. Engring., 2002; postgrad.,

Walden U., Minn., 2004—. CEO World Youth Movement Global Peace, Bklyn., 1992—; lectr. math. CUNY, Bklyn., 2002—; exec. dir. LyricSurge, Bklyn., 2006—. Del. People To People Amb. Program, Bejing, 2007. Author: (poetry) Truly Pertinent Questions, In My heart.On My Mind; poetry, Carmen. Recipient Spirit award, Nat. Soc. Black Engrs., 1997, 1998; fellow, Medgar Evers Coll. CUNY, 2005; grantee, The Sloan Found., 2006; scholar, Dept. Def., 1994—98, Lemelson Found. - Poly. U., 2001—02. Mem.: Soc. Econometrics, Global Assn. Risk Profls., Am. Inst. Aero. and Astronautics, Nat. Soc. Black Engrs., Inst. Ops. Rsch. and Mgmt. Scis., Am. Ednl. Rsch. Assn., Acad. Am. Poets, Bros. Acad. None. Achievements include research in metacognition, developmental mathematics; system theory analysis of schools and the prison industrial complex; minority polymer. Avocations: writing, travel, soccer, reading, painting. Home: 233 Maple St Brooklyn NY 11225 Office: Medgar Evers College - CUNY 1650 Bedford Ave Brooklyn NY 11225 Office Phone: 718-270-4959. Personal E-mail: wrusse01@aol.com. E-mail: wrussell@mec.cuny.edu.

RUSSELL, WILLIAM JOSEPH, educational association administrator; b. Boston, Sept. 23, 1941; s. Stanley Whiteside and Helen Rita R.; m. Frances Marie Chapdelaine, June 25, 1967; 1 son, Scott David. BS, Boston Coll., 1963; M.Ed., Northeastern U., 1966; PhD, U. Calif., Berkeley, 1971. Head math. dept. Oceana, Pacifica, Calif., 1966-71; asst. for fed. and profl. affairs Am. Ednl. Research Assn., Washington, 1971-73, dep. exec. dir., 1973-74, exec. dir., 1974—2002. Adv. bd. Edn. Resource Info. Center Ednl. Testing Center, Princeton, N.J., 1975-87; exec. officer Nat. Council on Measurement in Edn., Internat. Assn. Computing in Edn., 1987-89. Editor: Ednl. Researcher, 1979-90. Mem. Am. Ednl. Research Assn., Phi Delta Kappa. Roman Catholic. Home: 1443 Creekside Ct Vienna VA 22182-1701 Office: AERA 1230 17th St NW Washington DC 20036-3078 E-mail: bfrussell@gmail.com.

RUSSELL, WILLIAM STEVEN, finance executive; b. Evanston, Ill., Aug. 5, 1948; s. John W. and Lillian H. Russell; m. Susan M. Hanson, Aug. 20, 1972. BS, So. Ill. U., 1970. CPA, Ill. Sr. staff auditor Arthur Andersen & Co., Chgo., 1972-76; acctg. mgr., controller, asst. sec. and treas. Lawter Internat., Inc., Northbrook, Ill., 1976-86, treas., sec., 1986-87, v.p. fin., treas. and sec., 1987-96, pvt. investor, 1996—. Served with U.S. Army, 1970-72. Mem. Am. Inst. CPA's, Beta Alpha Psi, Beta Gamma Sigma. Roman Catholic. Home and Office: 51 Park Lane Park Ridge IL 60068-2834

RUSSELL, YVONNE WILLIAMS, history educator; d. Gene P. Williams and Norma Richardson WIlliams; m. Norman Russell; 1 child, Hope Elizabeth. BA in History, U. Houston, Clear Lake, 1999. Social studies composite Tex. State Bd. Educator, 2001. Tchr. US history Pearland Jr. High East, Tex., 2001—02; tchr. advanced placement US history Sam Rayburn HS, Pasadena, Tex., 2002—. Vacation bible sch. craft leader Sunset United Meth. Ch., Pasadena, Tex., 2003—07. Mem.: NEA, Nat. Coun. History Edn., Nat. Coun. Social Studies. Office: Sam Rayburn HS 2121 Cherrybrook Ln Pasadena TX 77502 Personal E-mail: ywr317@yahoo.com.

RUSSELL-TYSON, PEARL LEONIE, elementary school educator; b. Kingston, Jamaica, July 10; d. Claudius Sylvester and Daisy Ann Cox; m. Kenneth Lee Tyson; children: Jermeth Angella Fothergill, Rosemary Tyson, Cheryl Andrea Russell, Laurel Emansea Robinson. BA, Mico U., Jamaica, 1977; BS, NSU, Davie, Fla., 1997, MS, 1999; EdD, Nova Southeastern U., Ft. Lauderdale, Fla., 2005. Cert. nurse, Fla. State Bd. Nursing, 1986; personnel mgmt. U. of Arts, Sci. & Tech., 1978. Literacy facilitator Palm Beach Schol Dist./ Belle Glade Elem. Sch., Fla., 1999—; pres. Tyson Ednl. & Cmty. Resources, Inc., Loxahatchee, Fla., 2000—. Tchr. Ministry Edn., Kingston, Jamaica, 1970—85; presenter in field. Pres. Home Owners' Assn., St Catherine, Jamaica, 1972—80; Cub Scout leader Jamaica, 1972—78; Sunday sch. tchr. Hope of the World Christian Ctr. Ministries, 1990—92; min. Hope of the World Christian Ministry, Pembroke Pines, Fla., Hope of the World Christian Ctr. Ministries, Loxahatchee, Fla. Recipient Distinction in Edn., Mico U., 1973—76. Mem.: Internat. Reading Assn. Conservative. Avocations: travel, evangelism, reading. Office: Tyson Ednl & Cmty Resources I 16218- 83 Pl N Loxahatchee FL 33470 Home Phone: 561-333-9123; Office Phone: 561-386-8929. Personal E-mail: leonie710@aol.com.

RUSSERT, TIMOTHY JOHN, broadcast journalist and executive; b. Buffalo, May 7, 1950; m. Maureen Orth; 1 child, Luke. BA, John Carroll U., 1972; JD, Cleve. State U., 1976. Bar: NY, DC. Spl. counsel US Senate, 1977—82; counselor NY Gov.'s Office, 1983—84; with NBC News, 1984—; moderator, mng. editor Meet the Press, 1991—; anchor The Tim Russert Show CNBC, 1994—; sr. v.p., Washington bureau chief NBC News. Nat. polit. analyst Today program and NBC Nightly News with Tom Brokaw; supr. NBC News Today program live broadcasts from Rome, 1985; overseer prodn. prime time spl. A Day in the Life of Pres. Bush, 1990, A Day in the Life of Pres. Clinton, 1993; has covered 8 U.S./Russian Summits, Geneva, Malta, Washington, Moscow, Vancouver; lectr. at more than 30 univs. Author: Big Russ and Me: Father and Son-Lessons of Life, 2004, Wisdom of Our Fathers: Lessons and Letters from Daughters and Sons, 2006. Recipient Alumni Spl. Achievement award, Cleve.-Marshall Coll. Law, Pres.'s medal, Trocaire Coll., John Peter Zenger award, N.Y. State Bar Assn., 1992, Disting. Grad. award, Nat. Cath. Educator's Assn., 1995, Spl. Achievement Alumni medal, John Carroll U., Joan S. Barone award, 2000, Annenberg Center's Walter Cronkite award, 2000, Edward R. Murrow award overall excellence in TV journalism, 2001, News Media award, VFW, 2005, The Cath. Acad. Comm.'s Gabriel award, 2005, Am. Legion Journalism award, Congl. Medal of Honor Soc. Journalism award, Allen H. Neuharth award excellence in journalism, David Brinkley award excellence in communication, Emmy coverage Pres. Reagan's funeral, Golden Plate award, Acad. Achievement, 2005. Fellow: Commn. European Cmtys. Office: NBC News Meet the Press 4001 Nebraska Ave NW Washington DC 20016-2733 *

RUSSETT, BRUCE MARTIN, political science professor; b. North Adams, Mass., Jan. 26, 1935; s. Raymond Edgar and Ruth Marian (Martin) R.; m. Cynthia Margaret Eagle, June 18, 1960; children: Margaret Ellen, Mark David, Lucia Elizabeth, Daniel Alden. BA magna cum laude, Williams Coll., 1956; diploma in econs., Cambridge U., Eng., 1957; MA, Yale U., 1958, PhD, 1961; PhD (hon.), Uppsala U., 2002. Instr. MIT, Cambridge, 1961-62; asst. prof., then assoc. prof. Yale U., New Haven, 1961-68, prof., 1968—, Dean Acheson prof. internat. rels. and polit. sci., 1985—, chair dept. polit. sci., 1990-96, dir. UN studies, 1993—2006. Vis. prof. Columbia U., 1965, U. Mich., 1965-66, U. Libre Brussels, 1969-70, U. N.C., 1979-80, Richardson Inst., London, 1973-74, Netherlands Inst. Advanced Study, 1984, Tel Aviv U., 1989, U. Tokyo, 1996, Harvard U., 2001; prin. cons. pastoral letter on peace Nat. Conf. Cath. Bishops, Washington, 1981-83; co-dir., secretariat ind. working group Future of the UN, 1993-96. Author: World Handbook of Political and Social Indicators, 1964, What Price Vigilance?, 1970 (Kammerer award Amn. Polit. Sci. Assn. 1971), Interest and Ideology (with E. Hanson), 1975, Controlling the Sword, 1990, Grasping the Democratic Peace, 1993, The Once and Future Security Council, 1997, (with John Oneal) Triangulating Peace, 2001, (with Francis Oakley) Governance, Accountability, and the Future of the Catholic Church, 2004, (with Alex Mintz) New Directions for International Relations, 2005, Purpose and Policy in the Global Community, 2006, others; editor: Jour. Conflict Resolution, 1972—; contbr. articles to profl. jours. Grantee NSF, 1964, 65, 69, 77, 79, 85, 88, 89, 90, 95, 98, Ford Found., 1993, 94, 97, John and Catherine MacArthur Found., 1988, 91; Fulbright-Hays fellow, Belgium and Israel, 1969, 89; John Simon Guggenheim Found. fellow, 1969, 77; German Marshall Fund fellow, 1977. Fellow Am. Acad. Arts and Scis.; mem. AAUP, Am. Polit. Sci. Assn. (coun. 1984-86), Internat. Studies Assn. (pres. 1983-84), Peace Sci. Soc. Internat. (pres. 1977-79). Avocations: tennis, classical music, hiking. Home: 70 Martin Ter Hamden CT 06517-2333 Office: Yale U Dept Polit Sci PO Box 208301 New Haven CT 06520-8301 Home Phone: 203-248-2364; Office Phone: 203-432-5233. E-mail: bruce.russett@yale.edu.

RUSSIANO, JOHN See MILES, JACK

RUSSIN, JONATHAN, lawyer, consultant; b. Kingston, Pa., Oct. 30, 1937; s. Jacob S. and Anne (Wartella) R.; m. Antoinette Stackpole, Oct. 6, 1962; children: Alexander, Andrew, Benjamin, Jacob. BA, Yale U., 1959, LLB, 1963. Bar: DC 1964. Guide interpreter Am. Nat. Exhibit, Moscow, 1959; rsch. asst. Law Faculty U. East Africa, Dar es Salaam, Tanganyika, 1961-62; regional legal adviser for Caribbean AID, 1967-69; ptnr. Kirkwood, Kaplan, Russin & Vecchi, Santo Domingo, Dominican Republic, 1969-74, Washington, 1974-78, Kaplan Russin & Vecchi, Madrid, 1978-81, Washington, 1981-92; ptnr., dir. Russian practice group Russin & Vecchi, Moscow, 1992—. Washington rep. Moscow Patriarchate of Russian Orthodox Ch.; convener adv. coun. Inst. European, Russian and Eurasian Studies, George Washington U.; mem. adv. bd. Caribbean Am. Directory; trustee St. Nicholas Cathedral, Washington, St. Vladimir's Orthodox Theol. Sem., Crestwood, NY, 1985-93; legal adviser Orthodox Ch. Am., 1985-2006. Contbr. articles to profl. jours. Bd. dirs. Nat. Coun. Internat. Visitors, Washington, 1987—93, Fund for Democracy and Devel., Washington, 1993—, MUCIA Global Edn. Group, Inc., 1996—2000, Delphi Internat., Washington, 1988—2000, Dominican Am. Cultural Inst., Santo Domingo, 1988—92. Recipient Order of St. Vladimir, Moscow Patriarchate, Russian Orthodox Ch., 1991. Mem.: Russian Assn. Internat. Law, DC Bar, Yale Club Washington, Yale Club NY, Inter-Am. Bar Assn., ABA. Office: 1000 Potomac St NW 5th Fl Washington DC 20007-3501 Office Phone: 202-822-6100. E-mail: jonathan.russin@russinvecchi.com.

RUSSO, ALEXANDER PETER, artist, educator; b. Atlantic City, June 11, 1922; s. Peter Joseph and Lillian Mary (Soma) R.; 1 child, Eugenie. Student, Pratt Inst., 1940-42, Swarthmore Coll., 1946-47; S.S., Bard Coll., 1947; B.F.A. (Breevort-Eickenmeyer fellow), Columbia U., 1952; postgrad., Acad. Fine Arts, Rome, 1952-54, Inst. Advanced Fine Arts, 1977-79. Instr. New Orleans Acad. Art, 1948-49; asst. prof. art U. Buffalo, 1955-58; instr. in graphic design Parsons Sch. Design, 1958-60; chmn. dept. drawing and painting Corcoran Sch. Art, 1961-70, chmn. faculty, acting dean, 1967-70; lectr., thesis adv. George Washington U., 1961-70; prof. Hood Coll., Frederick, Md., 1970-90, prof. emeritus, 1990—, chmn. dept. art, 1970-87. Vis. guest prof. art Instituto Allende, San Miguel de Allende, Mexico, 1993-94; panelist Md. State Coun. Arts, Balt., 1981-82; reviewer art programs Md. State Bd. Edn., 1981—; guest art critic Southampton Press, N.Y., 1989, 91; cons. in field. One-man shows include Corcoran Gallery Art, Washington, 1946, 64, Chiurazzi Gallery, Rome, 1953, Cavallino Gallery, Venice, Italy, 1954, U. So. Ill., 1955, Frank Rehn Gallery, N.Y.C., periodic exhbns., 1954-74, Phoenix II Gallery, Washington, 1983, Ingber Gallery, N.Y.C., 1983, Washington Gallery Art, 1963, Franz Bader Gallery, Washington, 1967, Internat. Monetary Fund, Washington, 1968, 79, Agra Gallery, Washington, 1971, Benson Gallery, Bridgehampton, L.I., 1976, Phoenix Fine Arts, Frederick, 1981, Benton Gallery, Southampton, N.Y., 1985, 86, 88, 90-91, Arlene Bujese Gallery, East Hampton, N.Y., 1994-95, 97-98, to 2006, Hood Coll., Frederick, Md., 1991, Western Md. Coll., Westminster, 1991, Bell Gallery, Seattle, 1991-92, Gettysburg (Pa.) Coll., 1989, Nabi Gallery, N.Y.C., 2006; group exhbns. include Salon de la Marne, Paris, 1945, Met. Mus. Art, N.Y.C., 1948, Bordighera Internat., Italy, 1953-54, Mus. Modern Art, Madrid, 1953, Sala di Esposizione delle Biblioteca Americano, Rome, 1953, Whitney Mus. Am. Art, N.Y.C., 1960, Mus. Modern Art, N.Y.C., 1969, Guild Hall, East Hampton, N.Y., 1976, 2007, East Hampton Avant-Garde, A Salute to the Signa Gallery, 1990, NAS, Washington, 1984, Bell Gallery, Seattle, 1990, Illustrator's Club, N.Y.C., 1991, Armory Exhbn., N.Y.C., 1991, Inst. Alleude, San Niguel de Allende, Mex., 1994, Fulbright Assoc. 20th Anniv. Art Exhibition, 1997, Josh Kligerman Gallery, San Miguel de Allende, Mex., 1994, Spanierman Gallery, East Hampton, 2007, deCordova Gallery, Greenport, NY, 2007; represented in permanent collections Albright-Know Gallery, Buffalo, Columbia U., N.Y.C., Delgado Mus. Art, New Orleans, Corcoran Gallery Art, Fiat Automobile Co., Rome, Nat. Collection Smithsonian Inst., Washington, Fed. Ins. Deposit Corp., Washington, Gettysburg Coll. Pa.; author: Profiles on Women Artists, 1985, The Challenge of Drawing, 1986, (poetry) Vignettes, 1996. Served with USNR, 1942-46. Fellow Guggenheim Found., 1947-48, 49-50,Edward McDowell Found., 1956, Hood Coll. Hodson teaching fellow, 1983; Fulbright grantee for painting and research, Rome, 1952-54, U.S.-Indo Subcommn. on Edn. and Culture grantee, India, 1984. Office: PO Box 1377 Wainscott NY 11975-1377 also: Arlene Bujese Dealer 40 Whooping Hollow Rd East Hampton NY 11937-2400 Office Phone: 631-324-4914. E-mail: cmdrusso@hotmail.com. *Success is an equivocal matter. "Outward success", no doubt, is meaningful and necessary to most people in terms of fulfilling goals or for some similar reason. "Interior success" is more difficult to achieve, for it means the labor of a developing soul, and, more often than not, the relinquishing of what most would consider to be "material success." Whatever I have achieved in the way of outward or material success, therefore, is but a minute reflection of that which I would wish to achieve on the spiritual level. There is a long way to go.*

RUSSO, ANTHONY, film director; b. Cleve. Co-dir., writer, prod. with Joe Russo (films) Pieces, 1997, The Kiss, 2001, Co-dir., writer, with Joe Russo Welcome to Collinwood, 2002, You, Me and Dupree, 2006, co-dir. with Joe Russo (TV series) Lucky, 2002, Arrested Development, 2003 (Emmy award Outstanding Directing for a Comedy Series, 2004), co-dir., exec. prod. with Joe Russo LAX, 2004, What About Brian, 2006—. Office: c/o Jason Burns United Talent Agy 9560 Wilshire Blvd #500 Beverly Hills CA 90212 also: c/o Section 8 Films 10866 Wilshire Blvd #1100 Los Angeles CA 90024

RUSSO, ANTHONY JOSEPH, public relations professional; b. NYC, Oct. 23, 1953; s. Lucio and Tina (Iarossi) R. BA cum laude, Alfred U., 1974; MA, Columbia U., 1975; PhD, Claremont Grad. Sch., 1982. Asst. to chmn. Mocatta Metals, NYC, 1982-83; account exec. Gavin Anderson and Co., NYC, 1983-85; sr. account exec. Adams and Reinhart, NYC, 1985; dir. corp. rels. Geto and DeMilly, NYC, 1985-86; v.p. Cameron Assocs., NYC, 1986-88; chmn., CEO Russo Ptnrs. LLC, NYC, 1998—; chmn. Madison Life Scis., 1999—2003. Mem. editl. bd.: Jour. Comml. Biotech., Bio People. Bd. dirs. March of Dimes, Target Autism Genome. Mem. APA, Pub. Rels. Soc. Am., Psi Chi. Democrat. Office: Russo Ptnrs Headquarters 729 Seventh Ave 17th Fl New York NY 10019 also: 550 W C St Ste 2000 San Diego CA 92101 also: Maitland Russo Ptnrs 5 Upper St Martins Ln London WC2H 9EA England Business E-Mail: tony.russo@russopatnersllc.com.

RUSSO, CHRISTINE FIORELLA, language educator; b. NYC, July 24, 1931; d. Anthony Joseph and Assunta Mary (Moroni) Fiorella; m. Victor Donald Russo, Jr., Apr. 30, 1960. BA, Marymount Manhattan Coll.; MS, Fordham U., 1959; diploma in reading, Hofstra U., 1978, PhD, 1987, postgrad., 1987—; cert. in litigation, Adelphi U. and Nat. Ctr. for Paralegal Tng., 1980. Cert. elem. and secondary English tchr., N.Y., reading specialist, N.Y. Tchr. St. Margaret's Sch., Bronx, N.Y., 1955-56, Sacred Heart, NYC, 1956-57, Bd. Edn., NYC, 1957-60, Harborfields Dist. 6, LI, 1960—; instr. English, Marymount Manhattan Coll., 1990-96, mem. alumni adv. coun., 1985-96, 1st v.p., bd. dirs., 1995-97, L.I. rep. recruitment program, 1992. Bd. dirs. Sch. Edn., Fordham U., 1995—. Bd. dirs. president's coun. Fordham U., Bronx, 1985-87, active recruitment program, 1983-87, mem. alumnae/i adv. bd. coun., 1994—; campaign worker Dem. Party, N.Y.C., 1990, 92; Marymount rep. N.Y. State Bundy/Affairs Fund, 1982-83; chmn. Ft. Salong Assn., L.I., 1979-83; vol. St. John's Hosp., L.I.; co-dir. Just Say No, Thomas J. Lahey Sch. Recipient Tchr.-Student Participation award Suffolk Reading Coun., 1991—, Tchr.-Student Participation award N.Y. Senate Earth Day Competitions, 1994—, Alumni Achievement award Fordham U., 1998, cert. of participation reflections progam in humanities N.Y. State PTA, 1996-98. Mem. APA, Guilford Internat. Soc. Intelligence Edn. (v.p. 1991—, bd. dirs. 1990—), N.Y. Acad. Scis., N.Y. Orton Dyslexia Soc., Nat. Dyslexia Rsch. Found., Coun. for Exceptional Children, World Coun. for Gifted and Talented Children, Children and Adults with Attention Deficit Disorder, Am. Assn. Higher Edn., Marymount Manhattan Coll. (1st v.p. 1995-97), Fordham U. Alumni Assn. (bd. dirs. adv. coun. Sch. Edn. 1995—), Phi Delta Kappa (1st v.p. chpt. 1995-97). Roman Catholic. Home: 7 Bonnie Dr Northport NY 11768-1448

RUSSO, IRMA HAYDEE ALVAREZ DE, pathologist; b. San Rafael, Mendoza, Argentina, Feb. 28, 1942; came to U.S, 1972; d. Jose Maria and Maria Carmen (Martinez) de Alvarez; m. Jose Russo, Feb. 8, 1969; 1 child, Patricia Alexandra. BA, Escuela Normal MTSM de Balcarce, 1959; MD, U. Nat. of Cuyo, Mendoza, 1970. Diplomate Am. Bd. Pathology. Intern Sch. Medicine Hosps., Argentina, 1969-70; resident in pathology Wayne State U. Sch. Medicine, Detroit, 1976-80. Rsch. asst., instr. Inst. Histology and Embryology Sch. Medicine U. Nat. of Cuyo, 1963-71, assoc. prof. histology Faculty Phys., Chem. and Math. Scis., 1970-72; rsch. assoc. Inst. Molecular and Cellular Evolution U. Miami, Fla., 1972-73; rsch. assoc. exptl. pathology lab. divsn. biol. scis. Mich. Cancer Foun., Detroit, 1973-75, rsch. scientist, 1975-76, vis. rsch. scientist, 1976-82, asst. mem., pathologist, 1982-89, assoc. rsch. mem., 1989-91, co-dir. pathology reference lab., 1982-86, chief exptl. pathology lab., 1989-91; co-dir. Mich. Cancer Found. Lab. Svcs., 1986-91; mem. Fox Chase Cancer Ctr., 1991—, active staff mem. dept. surgery med. scis. divsn., 2004—; dir. anatomic pathology Am. Oncologic Hosp. Dept. Pathology, 1991-92; dir. Lab. Svcs., 1992-94; chief molecular endocrinology sect. Breast Cancer Rsch. Lab. Fox Chase Cancer Ctr., 1994—; chief resident physician dept. pathology Wayne State U. Sch. Medicine, 1978-80, asst. prof., 1980-82; mem. staff Harper-Grace Hosps., Detroit, 1980-82; adj. prof. Pathology and Cell Biology Jefferson Sch. Medicine/Thomas Jefferson U., 1992—, chairperson Basic Breast Biology Study Sect. U. Calif. Breast Cancer Program, 1997, mem. endocrinology panel peer rev. com. breast cancer rsch. program U.S. Army R & D Command, 1994, 95, 96, 2002, 03, chairperson endocrinology peer rev. com., 1996; ad-hoc mem. biochem. endocrinology study sect. NIH, DHHS, 1994, metabolic pathology study sect., 1996-97; mem. European Commn. Cancer Prevention, 1994—; mem. bd. sci. counselor, sec. health and human svcs. Nat. Toxicology Program Bd., 1994-98; mem. Internat. Life Scis. Inst.-Risk Sci. Inst. Mammary Working Group, 1992—; pres., founder League of Women Against Cancer, Rydal, Pa., 1994—; guest lectr. dept. obstetrics Sch. Medicine U. Nat. of Cuyo, 1965-71; mem. resource devel. subcommittee of the profl. advisory com., Latinas Living Beyond Breast Cancer, 2000—; mem. Breast Cancer Res. Sci. Review Panel, N.J.commr. on cancer rsch., Trenton, N.J., 1997, 2000. Editor-in-chief Jour. Women's Cancer, 1997—; contbr. articles to profl. jours. Rockefeller grantee, 1972-73; Nat. Cancer Inst. grantee, 1978-81, 84-87, 94-99, 2003—, Am. Cancer Soc. grantee 1988-89, 91-94, U.S. Army Med. R&D Command grantee, 1994-99, 2003—; recipient Shannon award Nat. Cancer Inst./NHHSS, 1992-94, Gold medal Inst. U. Dexeus, Barcelona, Spain, 2000. Mem. AAAS, Soc. Española Senología y Patología Mamaria, Nat. Cancer Inst. (breast cancer working group, breast cancer program 1984-88), Nat. Alliance Breast Cancer Orgns. (med. adv. bd. N.Y.C. chpt. 1986—), Ea. Coop. Oncology Group, Coll. Am. Pathologists, Am. Soc. Clin. Pathologists, Am. Assn. Cancer Rsch., Am. Assn. Clin. Chemistry, Internat. Coll. Physicians and Surgeons, Women in Cancer Rsch., The Endocrine Soc., Internat. Assn. Against Cancer, Sigma Xi, Food Quality Protection Act, Sci. Review Bd., Fed. Insecticide Fungi and Rodenticide Act, Adivsory Panel, EPA. Roman Catholic. Office: Fox Chase Cancer Ctr 333 Cottman Ave Philadelphia PA 19111 Office Phone: 215-728-4781. Personal E-mail: Lowac@msn.com. Business E-Mail: Irma.Russo@fccc.edu.

RUSSO, JOE, film director; b. Cleve. married. Co-dir., writer, prod. with Anthony Russo (films) Pieces, 1997 (Best Actor award, Am. Film Inst.), The Kiss, 2001, co-dir., writer with Anthony Russo Welcome to Collinwood, 2002, You, Me and Dupree, 2006, co-dir. with Anthony Russo (TV series) Lucky, 2002, Arrested Development, 2003 (Emmy award Outstanding Directing for a Comedy Series, 2004), co-dir., exec-prod. with Anthony Russo LAX, 2004, What About Brian, 2006—. Office: c/o Jason Burns United Talent Agy 9560 Wilshire Blvd #500 Beverly Hills CA 90212 also: c/o Section 8 Films 10866 Wilshire Blvd #1100 Los Angeles CA 90024

RUSSO, JOSE, pathologist; b. Mendoza, Argentina, Mar. 24, 1942; came to US, 1971; s. Felipe and Teresa (Pagano) R.; m. Irma Haydee, Feb. 8, 1969; 1 child, Patricia Alexandra. BS, Agustin Alvarez Nat. Coll., 1959; MD, U. Nat. Cuyo, 1967. Instr. Inst. Gen. and Exptl. Pathology Med. Sch., Mendoza, 1961-66; asst. prof. Inst. Histology and Embryology, 1967-71; Rockefeller Found. postdoc. fellow Inst. Molecular and Cellular Evolution U. Miami, 1971—73; chief exptl. pathology lab. Mich. Cancer Found., Detroit, 1973-81; assoc. clin. prof. pathology Wayne State U., Detroit, 1979-91, chmn. dept. pathology, 1981-91; chmn. dept. pathology, sr. mem. Fox Chase Cancer Ctr., Phila., 1991-94, sr. mem., dir. Breast Cancer Rsch. and Environ. Ctr., 1994—, dir. med. outreach and minority affairs; sci. dir. League of Women Against Cancer. Mem. Mich. Cancer Found., 1982-91; adj. prof. pathology Jefferson Sch. Medicine, U. Pa. Sch. Medicine, Phila. Author: Tumor Diagnosis by Electron Microscopy, vol. 1, 1986, vol. 2, 1988, vol. 3, 1990, Immunocytochemistry in Tumor Diagnosis, 1985, Molecular Basis of Breast Cancer, 2004; editor-in-chief Jour. of Women's Cancer; contbr. over 380 articles to profl. jours USPHS grantee, 1978, 80, 84, 88, 90, 93-95, 98, 2000, 02, grantee Am. Cancer Soc., 1982, Dept. of Def., 1999-2003; NRC Argentina fellow, 1967-71 Mem. Am. Assn. Cancer Rsch., Am. Soc. Cell Biology, Soc. Exptl. Biology and Medicine, Tissue Culture Assn., Am. Soc. Clin. Pathology, Internat. Acad. Pathology, Am. Coll. Pathology, Sigma Xi Roman Catholic. Office Phone: 215-728-4782. Business E-Mail: j_russo@fccc.edu.

RUSSO, LINDA M., pediatric cardiologist; BA in Biology, Immaculata Coll., Pa., 1990; MD, Creighton U., Omaha, 1998. Cert. pediat. Am. Bd. Pediat., 2001, pediat. cardiology Am. Bd. Pediat., 2006. Pediat. cardiologist Childrens Hosp. Pitts., 2004—. Asst. med. dir. Dr. Bill Neches Heart Camp for Kids, Pitts., 2005—. Office: Childrens Hospital Pittsburgh 3705 Fifth Ave Pittsburgh PA 15213 Office Phone: 412-692-5540.

RUSSO, MARISA NATALINA, educational consultant; b. Fullerton, Calif., Mar. 4, 1969; d. Ralph and Nelia (Burdi) Russo. B, Calif. State U., 1992. Sales assoc. The Broadway, Brea, Calif., 1985—95; tchr. Bennett-Kew Sch., Inglewood, Calif., 1996—2000; regional cons. McGraw Hill, Calif., 2000—02, nat. cons. Calif., 2002—. Speaker various ednl. confs. Mem.: One, Internat. Reading Assn. Democrat. Roman Cath. Home: 11381 Parkfield Ct Riverside CA 92505

RUSSO, PATRICIA F., telecommunications company executive; b. Trenton, NJ, June 12, 1952; m. Frank Russo. BA, Georgetown U., 1973; postgrad. in advanced mgmt., Harvard U., 1989; DEng (hon.), Steven Inst. Tech.; D in Entrepreneurial studies (hon.), Columbia Coll., SC. Sales and mktg. mgmt. exec. IBM, 1973-81; with AT&T (now Lucent Techs. Inc.),

1981; pres., Bus Comm. Sys. Unit AT&T (now Avaya Inc.), 1992-96; pres., COO Eastman Kodak Co., 2000—02; exec. v.p. strategy bus. devel. and corp. ops. Lucent Techs. Inc., Murray Hill, NJ, 1997-99, exec. v.p., CEO svc. provider networks Warren, NJ, 1999—2000, pres., CEO Murray Hill, NJ, 2002—03, chmn., CEO, 2003—06; CEO Alcatel Lucent, Paris, 2006—. Bd. dirs. Lucent Techs. Co., 2002—, Schering-Plough Corp., NJ Mfrs. Ins. Co., Avaya Inc.; chair Nat. Security Telecom. Adv. Com., 2004—06. Bd. dirs. Georgetown U.; mem. Network Reliability Interoperability Coun.; mem. appointed by Gov. James McGreevey NJ Commn. on Jobs Growth and Econ. Develop. Named one of 100 Most Powerful Women in Bus., Fortune mag., 1998—2006, 100 Most Influential People, Time mag., 2006, 10 Most Powerful Women in NJ Bus., Newark Star-Ledger, 2006, 50 Who Matter Now, CNNMoney.com Bus. 2.0, 2006, 50 Women to Watch, Wall St. Jour., 2006. Office: Alcatel-Lucent 600 Mountain Ave New Providence NJ 07974 also: Alcatel-Lucent 54 rue la Boétie 75008 Paris France Business E-Mail: execoffice@lucent.com. *

RUSSO, PAUL M., electronics executive; B in engring., McGill U.; MEE, U. California, Berkeley, PhD Computer Sci. and Electrical Engring. Mem. of the technical staff, head Microsystems Rsch., RCA, Princeton, NJ, 1970—80; sr. mgr. Indsl. Electronics Grp., General Electronics (GE), Charlottesville, Va., 1980—83; gen. mgr. Microelectronics Ctr. in Rsch., Triangle Park, NC, 1983—85; founder, CEO, dir. Genesis Microchip Inc., 1987—2000, chmn., 1987—2001; founder, pres., CEO, chmn. Silicon Optix, San Jose, Calif. Outside dir. ATI Technologies. Office: Silicon Optix Hdqs 2025 Gateway Pl Ste 360 West San Jose CA 95110 Office Phone: 1-408-487-9290. Office Fax: 1-408-487-9298.

RUSSO, RENE, actress; b. Burbank, Calif., Feb. 17, 1954; m. Dan Gilroy, Mar. 14, 1992; 1 child, Rose. Fashion model Eileen Ford Agy. Actor: (films) Major League, 1989, Mr. Destiny, 1990, One Good Cop, 1991, Freejack, 1992, Lethal Weapon 3, 1992, In the Line of Fire, 1993, Major League 2, 1994, Outbreak, 1995, Get Shorty, 1995, Tin Cup, 1996, Ransom, 1996, Buddy, 1997, Lethal Weapon 4, 1998, The Thomas Crown Affair, 1999, The Adventures of Rocky and Bullwinkle, 2000, Showtime, 2002, Big Trouble, 2002, Two for the Money, 2005, Yours, Mine and Ours, 2005, (TV series) Sable, 1987-88. Address: 8046 Fareholm Dr Los Angeles CA 90046

RUSSO, RICHARD, writer; b. Johnstown, NY, July 15, 1949; m. Barbara Marie Russo; children: Emily, Kate. BA, U. Ariz., 1967, Ph.D, 1979, MFA, 1980. Writer, Camden, Maine; prof. english Colby Coll., Waterville, Maine, 1991—96. Author: Mohawk, 1994, The Risk Pool, 1994, Nobody's Fool, 1994, Straight Man, 1998, Empire Falls, 2002 (Pulitzer Prize Fiction, 2002, named Best Novel of Yr. Time Mag., 2002), The Whore's Child, 2003; writer: (films) Twilight, 1998; (TV films, teleplay) The Flamingo Rising, 2001; Brush with Fate, 2003; exec. prodr., writer: (films) The Ice Harvest, 2005.

RUSSO, ROY LAWRENCE, retired electronics engineer; b. Kelayres, Pa., Nov. 6, 1935; s. Peter John and Mary (Fudge) R.; m. Elizabeth Jean Tautkus, Dec. 26, 1959; children: Mark, Keith, Aileen, Linda. BSE.E., Pa. State U., 1957, MSE.E., 1959, PhD.E.E., 1964. Asst. prof. elec. engring. Pa. State U., University Park, 1964-65; mgr., staff mem. IBM Research, Yorktown Heights, NY, 1965-77, mem. research staff, 1983-85, mgr. design automation lab., 1985-94; sr. engr. Gen. Tech. div. IBM, Hopewell Junction, 1977-81, mgr. strategy, 1981-82; cons. prof. elec. engring Stanford U., 1982-83; retired, 1994. Editor-in-chief IEEE Computer Soc., 1983-85; co-inventor ink jet printer correction system. Treas. St. Patrick's Ch., Yorktown Heights, 1975-77. Recipient Invention Achievement award IBM, 1978, Outstanding Contbn. award IBM, 1968, 89, Outstanding Writing award Pa. State U., 1967 Fellow IEEE (dir. computer disvn. 1989); mem. IEEE Computer Soc. (pres. 1986-87, Svc. award, Centennial medal 1984, Richard E. Merwin award 1992), Eta Kappa Nu.

RUSSO, ROY R., lawyer; b. Utica, NY, July 26, 1936; BA, Columbia U., 1956; LLB cum laude, Syracuse U., 1959. Bar: N.Y. 1959, D.C. 1967, U.S. Supreme Ct. 1969. Atty. FCC, 1959—66; ptnr. Cohn and Marks LLP, Washington, 1966—. Mem. Order of Coif, Phi Alpha Delta. Democrat. Home: 6528 Bowie Dr Springfield VA 22150-1309 Office: Cohn and Marks LLP 1920 N St NW Ste 300 Washington DC 20036-1622 Office Phone: 202-293-3860. Business E-Mail: roy.russo@cohnmarks.com.

RUSSO, THOMAS ANTHONY, lawyer; b. NYC, Nov. 6, 1943; s. Lucio F. and Tina (Iarossi) R.: m. Nancy Felipe, June 18, 1966 (div. 1974); m. Janice Davis, June 10, 1977 (div. 1979); m. Marcy C. Appelbaum, June 16, 1985; children: Morgan Danielle and Alexa Anne (twins), Tyler James. BA, Fordham U., 1965; MBA, JD, Cornell U., 1969. Bar: NY 1970, U.S. Ct. Appeals (2d cir.) 1971, U.S. Dist. Ct. (so. and ea. dists.) NY 1971, U.S. Ct. Appeals (7th cir.) 1982. Staff atty. SEC, Washington, 1969—71; assoc. Cadwalader, Wickersham & Taft, NYC, 1971—75, ptnr., mem. mgmt. com., 1977—92; dir. divsn. trading and markets Commodity Futures Trading Commn., Washington, 1975—77; vice chmn., chief legal officer, mem. exec. com. Lehman Bros., NYC, 1993—. Vice-chmn. bd. trustees, exec. com. Inst. Fin. Markets; trustee, chmn. exec. com., devel., vision and outreach com., exec. compensation com., scholar rescue fund com., scholar rescue fund selection com. Inst. Internat. Edn.; treas., nat. bd. trustees, fin. com. chmn., exec. com., nominating com., chmn. pension investment com. March of Dimes; mem. US Coun. Internat. Bus., Com. Capital Markets Regulation; mem. Cornell U. Coun., internat. adv. com. Fed. Res. Bank NY. Author: Regulation of the Commodities Futures and Options Markets; co-author: Regulation of Brokers, Dealers and Securities Markets with Supplement; mem. editl. bd. Jour. Fin. Regulation and Compliance, Futures and Derivatives Law Report; practitioner bd. advs. Stanford Jour. Law, Bus. and Fin. Named to Hall of Fame, Futures Industry Assn., 2003. Mem.: ABA, Fgn. Policy Assn., DC Bar Assn., Assn. Bar City NY (chmn. com. commodities regulations 1981—82, chmn. internat. law subcommittee of the com. on commodities regulation 1984—85), Econ. Club NY, Fellows of Phi Beta Kappa Soc. Office: Lehman Bros Inc 745 7th Ave 31st Fl New York NY 10019-6801 E-mail: trusso1@lehman.com.

RUSSO, VINCENT JOSEPH, surgeon; b. Phila., Apr. 15, 1939; s. Joseph Vincent Russo and Yolanda Italia D'Ambrosio; m. Sheila Kay Roos, June 8, 1963; children: Teresa, Joseph, Katrina, Anita. AB, Columbia U., 1960; MD, Boston U., 1964, MPH, 1983. Diplomate Am. Bd. Surgery. Staff surgeon Anna Jaques Hosp., Newburyport, Mass., 1971-88; clin. instr. surgery Harvard Med. Sch., Boston, 1984-98; med. dir. Blue Cross/Blue Shield, Methuen, Mass., 1990-98; sr. staff surgeon Lawrence (Mass.) Gen. Hosp., 1990-2000; med. dir. Ea. Mass. Health Ctrs., 1999—2000; clin. instr. Sch. Medicine Boston U., 2001—04; seaterm ship's physician Mass. Maritime Acad., 2001—. Cons. surgeon Manchester (N.H.) VA Med. Ctr., 1985-98; pres. Essex North Med. Soc., Newburyport, 1988-89, 2002-04; dist. 3 med. examiner Essex County, 1986—; ship's doctor Mass. Maritime Acad., 2001—. Bd. trustees, corporator, mem. auditing com. Newburyport Savings Bank, 1987—; mem. UNICO, Andover, Mass., 1994-97. Lt. cmdr. USN, ships surgeon USS Forrestal Aircraft Carrier, 1969-71; chmn. bd. selectmen Town of Newbury, Mass, 2004—; field rep., surveyor Joint Commn. on Accreditation of Health Orgns., 2004—; commr. mosquito control Commonwealth of Mass., 2005—; chmn. auditing comm. Newburyport Five Cents Savings Bank, 2006-; corporator Anna Jaques Hosp., Newburyport, Mass., 1985—. Lt. col. U.S. Army, 1990-91, Desert Storm. Fellow ACS (councilor Mass. chpt. 1995-98); mem. AMA, Soc. Am. Gastrointestinal Endoscopic Surgeons, Mass. Med. Soc. (legis. com. 1990—, del. 2000—), Boston Surg. Soc., Essex North Dist. Med. Soc. (exec. com. 1986—, pres. 2002-04), Rotary (sr. active), Mass. Med. Soc. (reference com. 2002-04, bd. trustees 2004—), U.S. Naval Inst. Roman Catholic. Avocations: theater, downhill skiing, automobiles, swimming, symphony. E-mail: vjrusso@massmed.org.

RUSSOMANNO, FRANK P., information technology executive; B in History, Seton Hall U., South Orange, NJ; grad. student, U. Okla., Norman, Monmouth Coll. Sales coord. to sales rep. Magnetic/Audio/Video Recording bus. 3M Co., 1973, European Bus. unit dir.; global sales and mktg. dir. Photo Color Products Imation Corp., various exec. and managerial positions including v.p. Data Storage Media and Svcs., gen. mgr. Advanced Imaging Program, corp. sales and mktg. dir., pres. Data Storage and Info. Mgmt. businesses, COO, acting CEO, 2006, pres., CEO, bd. dirs. Bd. dirs. Content Delivery & Storage Assn. Bd. mem. Merrick Cmty. Ctr., St. Paul. Artillery officer (rank of Capt.) US Army. Office: Imation Corp 1 Imation Pl Oakdale MN 55128 *

RUSSONIELLO, JOSEPH PASCAL, lawyer; b. Jersey City, Oct. 12, 1941; s. Sabin G. and Justine B. (Terraciano) Russoniello; m. Moira F. Ward, Aug. 29, 1969. B in Social Sci., Fairfield U., 1963; JD, NYU, 1966. Bar: N.J. 1967, Calif. 1969. Spl. agt. FBI, Washington, 1966—67; dep. dist. atty. City and County San Francisco Dist. Atty. Offices, 1969—75; assoc. Cooley Godward Castro Huddleson & Tatum, San Francisco, 1975—78; ptnr. Cooley Godward L.L.P., San Francisco, 1978—82, 1990—2001; sr. counsel Cooley Godward Kronish L.L.P., San Francisco, 2002—; U.S. atty. US Dept. Justice (no. dist.) Calif., San Francisco, 1982—90. Pres., bd. dirs. San Francisco Law Sch., 1996—2001, dean, 2002—07; analyst Sta. KTVU-Ch. 2, Oakland, 1994—. Pres. Northgate Cottages, Napa, Calif., 1988—; chmn. Silverado Property Owners Assn., 2004—; v.p. Mid-Pacific region Nat. Italian Am. Fedn., 1996—99; mem. nat. rev. bd. U.S. Conf. Cath. Bishops, 2004—; chmn. Caths. Truth and Justice, San Francisco, 1991—. Named Alumni of the Yr., Pub. Sector, NYU Law Sch., 1991; recipient Man of the Yr. award, NIAF, 1986, St. Thomas More Soc., San Francisco, 2000, Italian Am. Cmty. Svc. Agy., San Francisco, 2004, Assumpta award, Trustees St. Mary's Cathedral, 2000, Papal Pro Ecclesia medal, 2000, Landsman award, 2005. Fellow: Am. Coll. Trial Lawyers; mem.: Am. Law Inst., Am. Bd. Trial Lawyers (adv.), McFetridge Inn of Ct. (barrister). Republican. Avocations: tennis, golf, reading, saxophone. Office: Cooley Godward Kronish LLP 101 California St 5th Fl San Francisco CA 94111-5800 Office Phone: 415-693-2014. Business E-Mail: Russonielloj@cooley.com.

RUSSOTTI, PHILIP ANTHONY, lawyer; b. NYC, Mar. 24, 1948; s. Philip Armond and Yolanda (Morelli) R.; m. Mary Wolfe, Jan. 20, 1973 (div. Mar., 1996); children: Thomas, Matthew, Peter; m. Kathleen Kettles, May 25, 1996. BA, Columbia U., 1970; JD, St. John's U., Queens, NY, 1973. Bar: N.Y. 1974, U.S. Dist. Ct. (so. dist.) N.Y. 1974, U.S. Dist. Ct. (ea. dist.) N.Y., 1980, U.S. Ct. Appeals (2nd cir.) 1982, U.S. Ct. Appeals (D.C. cir.) 1989, U.S. Ct. Internat. Trade 1986, U.S. Ct. Fed. Claims, 2000, U.S. Supreme Ct., 1997; bd. cert. civil trial atty. Nat. Bd. Trial Advocacy, 1997, U.S. Ct. Fed. Claims, 2000. Bur. chief, Supreme Ct. trial bur. asst. dist. atty. N.Y. County Dist. Atty.'s Office, NYC, 1973-80; pvt. practice NYC, 1980-84; partner Russotti & Barrison, NYC, 1985-89, Wingate, Russotti & Shapiro, NYC, 1990—. Lectr. in the field. Gen. counsel Italian Am. Repertory Theatre, N.Y., 1985-90; mem. Prospect Park Alliance, Bklyn., 1996—. Recipient Am. Jurisprudence awards Bancroft Whitney & Lawyers Co-op, 1971, 73. Mem. ABA, ATLA, N.Y. State Bar Assn., N.Y. State Trial Lawyers Assn. Roman Catholic. Office: Wingate Russotti Shapiro 420 Lexington Ave Rm 2750 New York NY 10170-2793 Home: 180 Sterling Pl Apt 12 Brooklyn NY 11217-3300 E-mail: prussotti@yahoo.com.

RUSSOTTO, PAUL, artist, educator; b. NYC, May 28, 1944; s. John and Margaret Russotto; m. Ellen Russotto, Aug. 30, 1969; children: Vita, Luca. Student, Art Students League, NYC, 1962-63. Painting and drawing instr., MFA program Parsons Sch. Design, NYC, 1978—80, N.Y. Studio Sch. Drawing, Painting and Sculpture, NYC, 1980—82, Vt. Studio Ctr., Johnson, 1985—, Internat. Sch. Art, Montecastello di Vibio, Italy, 1993, 94; painting and drawing instr. Beijing (China) Art Ins., 1987—88, Shanghai (China) Art Mus., 1987—88; painting and drawing instr., MFA program Pa. Acad. Fine Arts, Phila., 1997, SUNY, Binghamton, 1997, Nat. Acad. Design, NYC, 1999—2000. One-man shows include Forty-year Drawing Survey 1960-2000, traveling to U.N.C. and Italy, exhibited in group shows at Mus. Chateau de Rochefort-en-Terre, Brittany, France, 1995, Omaggio a Marino Marini, Venice, Florence, Rome, Paris, 2000, Heckscher Mus. Fine Art, Huntington, N.Y., 2000, 8 Artists da New York, Florence, Rome, Montecatini Terme, Italy, 2001, Angeli, Rome, Florence, Montecatini Terme, Venice, Romania, 2001—02, Omaggio a Magnelli, Italy, France, Romania, 2005, numerous others, Represented in permanent collections Met. Mus. Art, N.Y.C., Heckscher Mus. Fine Art, GE Corp., Novartis Corp., East Hanover, N.J., Mus. of Art, Bates Coll., Lewiston, Maine, N.Y. Pub. Libr., Tokai Bank, Chgo., Asheville (N.C.) Art Mus., Bklyn. Mus. Art, Accademia d'Arte Moderna Dino Scalabrino, Montecatini Terme, Italy, Circolo La Scaletia, Matera, Italy, City of Todi, Italy. Recipient Purchase award, AAAL, N.Y.C., 1997, Found. award, Rochefort-en-Terre Found., 1995. Mem.: Nat. Acad. Design (cert. of merit 1996, Palmer Meml. prize 2000, Henry Ward Ranger award 2001). Office: P O Box 385 Canal St Sta New York NY 10013-0385

RUST, EDWARD BARRY, JR., insurance company executive, lawyer; b. Chgo., Aug. 3, 1950; s. Edward Barry Sr. and Harriett B. (Fuller) R.; m. Sally Buckler, Feb. 28, 1976; 1 child, Edward Barry III. Student, Lawrence U., 1968-69; BS, Ill. Wesleyan U., 1972; JD, MBA, So. Meth. U., 1975. Bar: Tex. 1975, Ill. 1976. Mgmt. trainee State Farm Ins. Cos., Dallas, 1975-76, atty. Bloomington, Ill., 1976, sr. atty., 1976-78, asst. v.p., 1978-81, v.p., 1981-83, exec. v.p., 1983-85, pres., CEO, 1985—87, CEO, chmn., 1987—. Pres. and bd. dirs. State Farm Investment Mgmt. Corp., State Farm Internat. Services, Inc., State Farm Cos. Found.; bd. dirs. exec. and investment coms. State Farm Annuity and Life Ins. Co., State Farm Mut. Automobile Ins. Co., State Farm Life Ins. Co., State Farm Fire and Casualty, State Farm Gen. Trustee Ill. Wesleyan U., 1985—; mem. adv. coun. Grad. Sch. Bus. Stanford U., 1987-94; mem. bus. adv. coun. Coll. Commerce and Bus. Adminstrn. U. Ill. Mem. Am. Enterprise Inst., Bus. Roundtable (chmn. edn. task force), Tex. State Bar Assn., Ill. Bar Assn., Am. Inst. Property and Liability Underwriters (trustee 1986-96), Ins. Inst. Am. (trustee 1986-96), Ins. Inst. for Highway Safety (vice chmn.), Nat. Alliance of Bus. (chmn. 1998—), Ill. Bus. Roundtable (chmn. 1998—), Bus. Advisory Coun. Univ. Ill. Coll. Commerce and Bus. Admin. Office: State Farm Ins Cos 1 State Farm Plz E-12 Bloomington IL 61710-0001 *

RUST, JOHN HOWSON, JR., lawyer, state legislator; b. May 21, 1947; s. John Howson and Laura Jeanne (Johnson) R.; m. Susan Byrne, Aug. 15, 1970; children: John W., Thomas A., Robert B. BA, U. Va., 1969, JD, 1972. Bar: Va. 1972, U.S. Dist. Ct. (ea. dist.) Va. 1973, U.S. Ct. Appeals (4th cir.) 1975, U.S. Supreme Ct. 1976. Mem. firm Rust & Rust, P.C. Mem. Ho. of Dels., Commonwealth of Va., 1980-82, 97-2001. Office: PO Box 460 10370 Main St Fairfax VA 22030-0460 Office Phone: 703-273-0583. E-mail: johnhr@erols.com.

RUST, NEIL W., lawyer; b. Haslemere, Surrey, Eng., Aug. 14, 1957; BS, U. of London, 1978, LLB, 1985; JD, U.of Penn., 1987. Bar: California, Associate of the Royal School of Mines, London. With White & Case LLP, 1987—. Named Atty. of Yr., Calif. Lawyer Mag., 2002; named one of 12 Dealmakers of Yr., Am. Lawyer Mag., 2004. Office: c/o White & Case 633 West Fifth St ste 1900 Los Angeles CA 90071

RUST, WILLIAM DAVID, JR., retired structural engineer; b. Washington, Oct. 11, 1931; s. William David and Anna Mae (Lyles) R.; m. Eunice Charles Williams, Oct. 24, 1953; children: Diann Yvonne Rust-Tierney, Cheryl Frances, William Douglas. BS in Civil Engring., Howard U., 1954; postgrad., Cath. U. Am., 1956-57; MS in Engring., George Washington U., 1962; postgrad., U. Va., 1973-74. Registered profl. engr., Mass. Naval architect Phila. Naval Shipyard, 1954; structural engr. U.S. Gen. Svcs. Adminstrn., Washington, 1956-92; ret. 1992. Lectr. civil engring. Fed. City Coll. (now U. D.C.), Washington, 1973; mem. com.Interagency Seismic Safety, Washington, 1978-90, ASCE, Found. and Excavation Stds., N.Y.C., 1978-95, AISC, Steel Specification Simplification, Chgo., 1980-81; mem. coms. Fed. Constrn. Coun., Washington, 1978-90. Pack com. chmn. Boy Scouts Am., Washington, 1968; clk. session Northminster Presbyn. Ch., Washington, 1972; commr. genn. assembly Presbyn. Ch. U.S., Ft. Worth, 1973. Lt. C.E., U.S. Army, 1954-56. Fellow ASCE; mem., NSPE, Structural Stability Rsch. Coun. (mem.-at-large), Tau Beta Pi (life). Achievements include administration of development of first nationwide microfilming of design and construction drawings system for the U.S. General Services Adminstration. Home: 7600 Alaska Ave NW Washington DC 20012-1469 E-mail: w.rustjr@worldnet.att.net.

RUSTAND, KAY, lawyer; Ptnr. Lawler, Felix & Hall, Arter & Hadden LLP, 1989—2001; v.p., gen counsel Reliance Steel & Aluminum Co., LA, 2001—. Office: Reliance Steel & Aluminum Co 350 S Grand Ave Ste 5100 Los Angeles CA 90071 Office Phone: 213-687-8792.

RUSTAY, JENNIFER BETH, lawyer; b. Kansas City, Mo., Jan. 30, 1973; m. Allen Harrington Rustay, Sept. 29, 2001. BA, Baylor U., 1995, JD, 1997. Bar: Tex. 1997, U.S. Dist. Ct. (all dists. Tex.), US Dist. Ct. (dist. Colo.), US Ct. Appeals (5th cir.). Law clk. Hon. Sam Johnson US Ct. Appeals (5th cir.), Austin, Tex., 1997—98; atty. Bracewell & Patterson, Houston, 1998—2001, Hagans Burdine Montgomery Rustay & Winchester P.C., Houston, 2001—. Mem. bd. trustees Houston Lawyer Referral Svc. Notes and comments editor: Baylor Law Rev., 1996—97. Named a Rising Star, Tex. Super Lawyers mag., 2006. Fellow: Houston Bar Assn.; mem.: Assn. Women Lawyers (chair jud. screening com.), Houston Trial Lawyers Assn., Assn. Trial Lawyers of Am., Tex. Trial Lawyers Assn., Houston Young Lawyers Assn. Office: Hagans Burdine Montgomery Rustay & Winchester PC 3200 Travis 4th Fl Houston TX 77006

RUSTHOVEN, PETER JAMES, lawyer; b. Indpls., Aug. 12, 1951; s. Richard and Henrietta (Iwema) R.; children: Julia Faith, David James, Mark Bennett, Matthew Boyd. AB magna cum laude, Harvard U., 1973, JD magna cum laude, 1976. Bar: Ind., 1976. Assoc. Barnes, Hickam, Pantzer & Boyd, Indpls., 1976-81; assoc. counsel to Pres. of U.S., White House, Washington, 1981-85; of counsel Barnes & Thornburg, Indpls., 1985-86; ptnr. Barnes & Thornburg LLP, Indpls., 1987—. Counsel Presdl. Commn. on Space Shuttle Challenger Accident, 1986; spl. cons. U.S. Atty. Gen.'s Adv. Bd. on Missing Children, 1988; with Transition Counsel's Office, Bush-Cheney Presdl. Transition, 2001. Contbr. monthly column The Am. Spectator mag., 1973-79; mem. bd. editors Harvard Law Rev., 1974-76, case editor, 1975-76; contbr. articles to nat. mags. Bd. dirs. Ednl. Choice Charitable Trust, 1994—; Legal Svcs. Orgn. Indpls., 1977-79; precinct committeeman Marion County Rep. Ctrl. Com., Indpls., 1978-81; state media dir. Ind. Reagan for Pres. Com., 1979-80, Ind. Reagan-Bush Com., 1980; speechwriter nat. Reagan for Pres. Campaign, 1980; mem. legal policy adv. bd. Washington Legal Found., 1989—; candidate for Rep. nomination for US Senate, Ind., 1998; Republican analyst, Indpls. NBC affiliate, 2000-; mem. merit selection com. for US Naval Acad., US Senator Richard G. Lugar, 2000-; mem. bd. dir. Indpls. Lawyers Chpt. of Federalist Soc., 2007-. Lt. cmdr. JAG corps. USNR, 1982—96. Grantee Inst. Politics, Harvard U., 1972. Mem.: Phi Beta Kappa. Republican. Roman Catholic. Avocations: golf, contract bridge. Office: Barnes & Thornburg LLP 11 S Meridian St Indianapolis IN 46204-3535 Home Phone: 317-341-0143; Office Phone: 317-231-7299. Business E-Mail: peter.rusthoven@btlaw.com.

RUT, WANDA E., artist, educator, writer; b. Lwow, Poland, Jan. 5, 1923; arrived in U.S., 1976, naturalized; d. Adam Edmunt and Langmoier Anna Binder; m. Roman Smoleniec, 1977 (dec. 1979); m. Tadewsz Rut, 1958 (div. 1968); 1 child, Tomasr. BA in Textile Design, Inst. Indsl. Arts, Lwow, Poland, 1943; BA in Econs., Sch. Higher Edn. in Econ., Wroclaw, Poland, 1950; MFA, Acad. Fine Arts, Warsaw, Poland, 1957; student, Polish Acad. Scis., 1975. Chmn. Art Tchg. Divsn. Polish Assn. Artists and Designers, Warsaw, 1966—75; coord. Tailoring Mus. Fashion and Modeling Sch., Warsaw, 1975; editor art column Polish-Am. Weekly Newspaper, NYC, 1978—80; art dir. Polish Inst. Arts and Scis., NYC, 1983; cons. Polish Mus. Found., Port Washington, NY, 1984; art therapist NYC, 1984—85; freelance clothing designer. Tchr. various schs., Poland; costume designer Motion Picture Studios, Wroclaw, Opera House, Prague, Czech Republic; bd. jurors Artist Craftsmen of N.Y., 1980—82. One-woman shows include 40 shows in various international cities including, Avery Fisher Hall Lincoln Ctr., N.Y.C., N.Y., 1977, Suffolk County Hist. Mus., Riverhead, L.I., N.Y., 1978, Mus. of Sci. and Industry, LA, Calif., 1979, Guild Hall Mus., Moran Gallery, East Hampton, N.Y., 1977, Cepelia Salons, San Francisco, Calif., 1977, Interchurch Ctr., N.Y.C., N.Y., 1980, Pen & Brush Club, 1980 (1st prize, 1980), Donnell Libr., 1984, exhibited in group shows at Student Art Show, Moscow, Russia, 1953 (award, 1953), numerous others totalling near 100, exhibitions include Polish Art Weaving, Dresden, East Germany, 1969 (award, 1969), Tchrs. Head Club, Warsaw, Poland, 1973 (award, 1973), Internat. Book & Press Clubs, Poland, 1974 (award, 1974), Womanart Gallery, N.Y.C., N.Y., 1978 (1st prize, 1978), Slavic-Am. Cultural Assn., 1983 (award, 1983), numerous others, Represented in permanent collections Polish Inst. Arts and Scis., N.Y.C., N.Y., Old Warsaw (Poland) Gallery, Alexandria, Va., Polish Mus. Found., Port Washington, N.Y., Slavic Gallery, Glen Cove, N.y., Mus. Textile Industry, Lodz, Poland, Sport Mus., Warsaw, Poland, Brno, Czech. Republic, Stockholm, Sweden, Parliament of Polish People's Republic, Warsaw, Poland, Phys. Edn. Ctr., Cairo, Egypt, City Coun. of Warsaw and Wroclaw, Nat. Tchrs. Club, Warsaw, Poland, Forum Hotel. Recipient 1st prize, Cepelia Art Contest, Warsaw, Poland, 1976, Polish Art Competition, Doylestown, Pa., 1977. Achievements include invention of cylindrical loom enabling weaving in the round. Avocations: poetry, writing. Home: 1660 NE 191 St Apt 402 North Miami Beach FL 33179 Office: Am Inst Polish Culture 1440 79th St Causeway Ste 117 Miami Beach FL 33141

RUTA, FRANK A., chef; b. McKeesport, Pa., 1957; Grad., Am. Culinary Fedn., Pitts., 1978. Sauce cook William Penn Hotel, Pitts.; working chef Lincoln Hills County Club, Irwin, Pa.; asst. chef The White House, Washington, 1980—82, personal lunch and dinner chef to Reagan, Bush families, 1982—87, exec. sous chef, 1982—87, 1988; chef Andrea restaurant, Merano, Italy, 1987—88; sous chef Le Pavillon; grill chef Ritz-Carlton, Arlington, Va.; chef Yannick's, Alexandria, Va.; exec. chef River Club, Cap. Mgmt. Grp., Washington; exec. chef, owner Palena Restaurant, Washington. Named Best Chef: Mid-Atlantic, James Beard Found., 2007; named one of Best New Chefs in Am., Food & Wine mag., 2001. Avocations: gardening, winemaking. Office: Palena 3529 Connecticut Ave NW Washington DC 20008 Office Phone: 202-537-9250. *

RUTA, THOMAS V., professional sports team and accounting executive; married. BS summa cum laude, Fordham U., 1966; MBA with distinction, Pace U.; postgrad. in law, Fordham U. CPA, N.Y., N.J., Minn. Founding ptnr. Behan, Ling & Ruta CPAs, P.C., NYC, 1974, former chmn., pres.;

currently ptnr. in charge NY office Wiss & Co. LLP; ltd. ptnr. Pitts. Penguins; mem. Baldwin Sports Group. Office: 475 Park Ave S 31st Fl New York NY 10016 Office Phone: 212-695-7003. Business E-Mail: truta@wiss.com.

RUTAN, BURT (ELBERT LEANDER RUTAN), aircraft designer, aircraft company executive; b. Portland, Oreg., June 17, 1943; s. George and Irene R. BS in Aero. Engring., Calif. State Polytech. U., 1965; attended, Space Tech. Inst., Calif. Inst. Tech.; attended academic portion of Aerospace Rsch. Pilots Sch., Edwards Air Force Base. Flight test project engr. Air Force Flight Test Ctr., Edwards AFB, Calif., 1965-72; dir. Bede Test Ctr., Kans., 1972-74; pres. Rutan Aircraft Factory, Mojave, Calif., 1974—; founder, CEO Scaled Composites Inc., Mojave, Calif., 1982—; v.p. Beech Aircraft, 1985. Designer more than 100 aircraft including BD-5J jet (world's smallest private jet aircraft), VariViggen, VariEze (a stall-proof kit airplane with a propeller at the back and winglets on the nose), Solitaire, Defiant, Raytheon Beechcraft Starship, Proteus (high altitude long endurance aircraft being used for everything from cellular communications to suborbital space launches), Boomerang, Virgin Atlantic GlobalFlyer (set a world record for the first solo, non-stop, non-refueled circumnavigation of the world, piloted by Steven Fossett, 2005), White Knight (an airborne launch aircraft) and other kits; designer Voyager aircraft (a superlight plane that could carry 10 times its weight in fuel, first to fly around-the-world without stopping, refueling in 1986); company made history with first private manned mission to space in SpaceShipOne (a two-passenger, high altitude research rocket); SpaceShipOne achieved two record flights (broke 62.5-mile barrier) and won the Ansari X prize on October 4, 2004; SpaceShipOne donated to Smithsonian Inst. on October 6, 2005; pilot for EZ-Rocket (XCOR), which made a record-setting point-to-point flight, departing from Mojave California Spaceport and gliding onto a neighboring airport in California City in 2005. Recip. Spirit of St. Louis medal, Am. Soc. Mech. Engrs., 1987, Best Design award, Exptl. Aircraft Assn.; Air medal, 1970, Stan Szik design contbn. trophy, 1972, EAA Outstanding New Design, 1975-76, 78; Dr. August Raspet Meml. award, 1976, ABC World News Tonight Person of the Week, 1986, Collier trophy for ingenious design and devel., Nat. Aeronautic Assn., 1986, Presdl. Citizens medal for design/develop. of the voyager "around-the-world" aircraft, 1986, FAI gold medal for Voyager Constrn., 1987, medal for the City of Paris, 1987, NASA langley Rsch. Ctr. dirs. award, 1987, Soc. of NASA Flight Surgeons, W. Randolph Lovelace award 1987, medal of Outstanding Achievement and disting. leadership, 1987, Soc. of exptl. test pilots, 1987, Aviation Man of the Yr, 1987, Lindbergh Eagle award, 1987, USAF 40th anniversary award, 1987, The City of Genoa, Italy, Christopher Columbus Internat. Communications medal, 1987, British gold medal, 1987, Outstanding Engring. achievement awards, 1988, Franklin medal, 1987, Disting. inventor award 1988, Meritorious Svc. award, 1988, Internat. Aerospace Hall of Fame Honoree, 1988, medal of achievement, 1989, Crystal Eagle award, 1989, Meritorious Civilian Svc. medal, 1989, Leroy Randle Grumman medal, 1989, Structures, Structural Dynamics and Materials award AIAA, 1991, Bus. Leader in Aerospace, Scientific Am., 2003, Ansari X prize, 2004, NAS Award in Aero. Engring., 2005, Breakthrough Leadership award, Popular Mechanics Breakthrough Awards, 2006; co-recipient with Paul Allen, Smithsonian's Nat. Air and Space Mus. Trophy, 2005; named Innovator of Yr., R&D Mag., 2004; named one of 100 Most Influential People of 2005, Time mag., Rave award in indsl. design, WIRED, 2005. Mem. NAE, Exptl. Aircraft Assn., Soc. Exptl. Test Pilots, Am. Inst. Aeronautics & Astronautics (recipient Reed Aeronautics award, 2001), Soc. Flight Test Engrs., Acad. Model Aeronautics, Internat. Order Characters, Aircraft Owners and Pilots Assn.; Fellow Am. Acad. Arts & Sciences Holds 3 US patents: Grizzly wide-chord flap suspension system; variable geometry high lift system incorporated in the Beech Starship (foreign patents also held); Rutan Model 115 Starship configuration (foreign patents also held). Office: Scaled Composites Inc Mojave Airport 1624 Flight Line Mojave CA 93501-1663 Office Phone: 661-824-4541. Office Fax: 661-824-4174. *

RUTAN, CHARLES R., musician; b. May 10, 1966; s. Frank and Peggy (Hendry) Rutan; m. Catherine Mayer, May 29, 1999; children: Gwendolyn, Sophia. MusB in Composition summa cum laude, U. Arts, Phila., 1992; postgrad. in music instrn., Chestnut Hill Coll., 1994; postgrad., Piping Ctr., Glasgow, Scotland, 1998. Cert. tchr. Pa. CEO, founder Bagpipes FAO and Zampoqnari Filadelfia, Phila.; mgr., prin. oboist Chestnut Hill Orch. Performed for Pres. George Bush, Mrs. Tom Ridge, Queen Noor, Regent of Jordan; opened for Rod Stewart Trump Taj Majal, Atlantic City; piper MiGaea Yacht; prin. bagpipe Reading Symphony Orch.; performed USMC, U.S. Army and USN Ceremonies, Guiness Stout and U.S. Airways Promotions, Tom Polis Golf Classic; featured on various TV programs, mags., newspapers, including Phila. Weddings, Modern Bride mags., ABC, NBC, CBS, CNN, FOX, Finnish Nat. TV, Irish Am. Newspaper; ceremonial piper retirement ball for Phila. Episcopal Bishop; piper installation ceremonies Phila. Archdiocesan parishes, Presbytery ofcls., organ dedication ceremonies; performer Irish Uilleann (Union) Pipes, World Bagpipes, Villanova Coll. of Engr., 2004—04, EMS Today Conv., Bingshangm Realestate Conv. Composer (symphonic music): 3 symphonies, numerous choral works, works for bagpipes. Mem.: ASCAP (spl. composer award 1994), Friends of Scotland's Classic Malts, Music Educators Nat. Conf., Eastern U.S. Pipeband Assn., Am. Fedn. Musicians, Internat. Double Reed Soc. Office Phone: 800-544-4028.

RUTENBERG, JIM, journalist; Reporter New York Daily News, 1996—99, NY Observer, 1999, The New York Times, 2003—. Author: (articles) Critics Say Coverage Helped Lead to War, 2003, Shaping Reactions - After First Debate, Both Sides Work Hard to Sway Perceptions, 2004, Mayor Seeking Major Changes at Ground Zero, 2005. Office: The New York Times 229 W 43rd St New York NY 10036

RUTENBERG-ROSENBERG, SHARON LESLIE, retired journalist; b. Chgo., May 23, 1951; d. Arthur and Bernice (Berman) Rutenberg; m. Michael J. Rosenberg, Feb. 3, 1980; children: David Kaifel and Jonathan Reuben (twins), Emily Mara. Student, Harvard U., 1972; BA, Northwestern U., 1973, MSJ, 1975; cert. student pilot. Reporter-photographer Lerner Home Newspapers, Chgo., 1973—74; corr. Medill News Svc., Washington, 1975; reporter-newsperson, sci. writer UPI, Chgo., 1975—84; ret., 1984. Interviewer: exclusives White House chief of staff, nation's only mother and son on death row; others. Vol. Chgo.-Read Mental Health Ctr. Recipient Peter Lisagor award for exemplary journalism in features category, 1980, 81; Golden Key Nat. Adv. Bd. of Children's Oncology Svc. Inc., 1981; Media awards for wire svc. feature stories, 1983, 84, wire svc. news stories, 1983, 84, all from Chgo. Hosp. Pub. Rels. Soc. Mem. Profl. Assn. Diving Instrs., Nat. Assn. Underwater Instrs., Hon. Order Ky. Cols., Hadassah, Sigma Delta Chi, Sigma Delta Tau Home: 745 Marion Ave Highland Park IL 60035-5123

RUTER, ALLAN J., literature and language educator; b. Grundy Center, Iowa, May 28, 1954; s. Eugene T. and Thelma Okones Ruter; m. Jill Lynne Mussay, July 2, 1983; children: Karl Allan, Edward Eike. B of Spl. Studies, Cornell Coll., 1976; MA in Tchg., Northwestern U., Evanston, Ill., 1978, MA in English, 1997. Asst. to dean of students Lake Forest Coll., Ill., 1976—77; instr. of English Glenbrook Acad. for Internat. Studies, Ill.; co.-dir., instr. of English Glenbrook North H.S., Northbrook, Ill., 2005—; instr. of English Glenbrook South H.S., Glenview, Ill., 1977—2005, coord. of pub. info., 1980—81, asst. instrnl. supr. of English, 1984—99, instr. of history, 1984—90, sch. accreditation team chair, 2000—05; instr. of humanities Northwestern U. Ctr. for Talent Devel., Evanston, Ill., 1998—2000. Leader/trainer/designer Glenbrook Peer Counseling Program, Glenview/Northbrook, Ill., 1982—2003; ednl. travel leader Am. Coun. for Internat. Studies, Boston, 1992—; editl. cons. Wonderlic Pers. Inventory, Inc., Libertyville, Ill., 1995—95; product devel. cons. Scott Foresman Co., Glenview, Ill., 1997—97; cert. trainer Ctr. for Performance Assessment, Denver, 2002—05; consulting writer McDougal Littell, Inc., Evanston, Ill., 2005—. Author: (poetry) 1964: The Hardy Boys, 1984, (non-fiction) A Short History of Wellsburg, Iowa (Archived in the State Hist. Libr. of Iowa, 1976), (travel writing) Guernica: Home at Last, 1994; contbr. articles to profl. jours. Vice-chair Glenview Sch. Dist. 34 Caucus, Ill., 1989—93; bd. dirs. Glenview Soccer Club, Ill., 1996—99; appearance commn. Village of Glenview, Ill., 2002—05, downtown plan commr., 2005—; Independence Day Celebration commr. Glenview Pk. Dist., Ill., 2002—04; planning com. Village Glenview, 2005—; exec. bd. mem., youth ministries bd. chair, choir mem., confirmation instr., lector, substitute organist Glenview Cmty. Ch., Ill., 1981—; exec. bd. mem. Cornell Coll. Alumni Assn., Mount Vernon, Iowa, 2002—. Recipient Outstanding Tchr. award, U. Chgo., 1989; Summer Seminar fellow, NEH, 1987, 1991, Ind. Study fellowship, Coun. for Basic Edn., 1990, Columbia U. Summer Seminar fellow, Gilder-Lehrman Inst., 2005. Mem.: ASCD, Glenbrook Edn. Assn. (v.p. 2003—05), Nat. Coun. of Teachers of English (conv. presenter 1983—2004, commn. on lit. 1994—97, com. instrnl. tech. 1992—95), Rotary (Glenview, Ill.) (hon.), Phi Delta Kappa. United Church Of Christ. Avocations: gardening, travel, running. Home: 2349 Fir St Glenview IL 60025 Office: Glenbrook North HS 2300 Shermer Rd Northbrook IL 60062 Home Phone: 847-729-2368; Office Phone: 847-509-2433. Personal E-mail: aruter@comcast.net. Business E-Mail: aruter@glenbrook.k12.il.us.

RUTER, RUTH EVELYN, elementary school educator; b. Louisville, Apr. 24, 1923; d. Thurston Lowell and Ida Lee (Shaw) Wise; m. Charles M. Ruter, Apr. 15, 1944. BA, We. Ky. U., Bowling Green, 1948; MA, George Peabody, Nashville, 1953. Tchr. elem. Bullitt County Pub. Schs., Sheperdsville, Ky., 1943, Jefferson County Pub. Schs., Louisville, 1943—79. Pres. 15th Dist. PTA, Louisville, 1981—83; pres. Fern Creek Women's Club, Ky., 1983—85, 1991—93, 2000—02; worthy matron Order Ea. Star, Louisville, 1962—63, 1984—85, 1987—88; coord. meals Ky. Fedn. Women's Club, Louisville, 1994—2006. Named to Hall of Fame, Heritage Festival, 2000, Fern Creek Traditional H.S., 2005. Presbyterian. Home: 9801 Hillock Dr Louisville KY 40291

RUTFORD, ROBERT HOXIE, geologist, educator; b. Duluth, Minn., Jan. 26, 1933; s. Skuli and Ruth (Hoxie) R.; m. Marjorie Ann, June 19, 1954; children: Gregory, Kristian, Barbara. BA, U. Minn., 1954, MA, 1963, PhD, 1969; DSc (hon.), St Petersburg State Tech U., Russia, 1994. Football and track coach Hamline U., 1958-62; rsch. fellow U. Minn., 1963-66; asst. prof. geology U. SD, 1967-70, assoc. prof., 1970-72, chmn. dept. geology, 1968-72, chmn. dept. physics, 1971-72; dir. Ross Ice Shelf Project U. Nebr., Lincoln, 1972-75, vice chancellor for research and grad. studies, prof. geology, 1977-82, interim chancellor, 1980-81; dir. divsn. Polar Programs NSF, Washington, 1975-77; pres., prof. geoscis. U. Tex., Dallas, 1982-94, Excellence in Edn. Found. prof. of geoscis., 1994—2007, pres. emeritus, 2007. US del. to Sci. Com. on Antarctic Rsch., 1986-02, v.p., 1996-98, pres., 1998-02, exec. com., 2002-04, hon mem, 2004—; chmn. NRC Polar Rsch. Bd., 1991-95; bd. trustees Geol. Soc. Am. Found., 2005—, vice chmn., 2006—; bd. govs. US Corp., 1988—, Arctic Inst. N.Am., Mem. editl. bd. Issues in Sci. and Tech., 1991-94. Trustee Baylor Coll. Dentistry, 1989-96. 1st lt. U.S. Army, 1954-56. Recipient Antarctic Svc. medal, 1964, Disting. Svc. award NSF, 1977, Ernie Gunderson award for svc. to amateur athletics S.D. AAU, 1972, Outstanding Achievement award U. Minn., 1993, "M" Club Lifetime Achievement award, 1995, Commemorative medal Polish Acad. Scis., 2004. Fellow Geol. Soc. Am.; mem. Antarctican Soc. (pres. 1988-90), Arctic Inst. N.Am. (mem. bd. govs. US corp. 1996-), Explorers Club, Am. Polar Soc. (hon.), Philos. Soc. Tex., St. Petersburg Acad. Engring. (Russia), Tex. Acad. Sci., Sigma Xi. Lutheran. Office: Univ Tex Dallas Geosciences Program Richardson TX 75083-0688

RUTGARD, LORRAINE LEVIN, hearing impaired educator; b. Chgo., May 29, 1925; d. Sam and Rhea Levin; m. Meyer David Rutgard; children: Marlan Beth Globerson, Jeffrey Jay. BA, U. Wis., 1946; MA in Spl. Edn., Northeastern Ill. U., 1974. Social worker Hebrew Immigrant Aid Soc. (HIAS), Chgo., 1946-50; tchr. Chgo. Bd. Edn., 1959-72; adminstr. pvt. practice physician Med. Office, Skokie, Ill., 1972-81; ret., 1981. Vol. St. Mary's/Westside Food Bank Alliance, Area Agy. on Aging; docent West Valley Art Mus.; mem. Planned Parenthood; charter mem. Holocaust Mus., Washington. Mem. NOW, Hadassah, Temple Beth Shalom and Sisterhood (mem. CARE com.). Avocations: yoga, hiking, aerobics, snorkeling, sports.

RUTH, JAMES PERRY, financial planner; b. Washington, Feb. 27, 1946; s. Robert Walker and Virginia Null Ruth; m. Kathleen McHugh, Aug. 10, 1968; children: Heather Lynn, Michael James. BS in Bus. and Public Adminstrn., U. Md., 1970; postgrad., Am. Coll., Bryn Mawr, 1971-83. CLU, CFP, chartered fin. cons. agt., Northwestern Mutual Life Ins. Co., Washington, 1967-74. Gen. agt. Indpls. Life, Rockville, Md., 1974-82; partner Fox, Ruth & Middledorf, Rockville, 1975-82; mgr. Mfrs. Fin. Svcs., Rosslyn, Va., 1982-84; pres. Potomac Fin. Group, 1984—. Contbr. articles to profl. publs.; quoted in N.Y. Times, U.S. News and World Report, USA Today, others. Past pres. Jelleff Boys' Club; past pres. Montgomery County Police Boys' and Girls' Club; past chmn. bd. dirs. Asbury Meth. Village Found. Named Outstanding Young Man Am., U.S. Jaycees, 1979. Mem. Nat. Assn. Ins. and Fin. Advisors (pres. Md. chpt. 1995-96), Nat. Assn. Securities Dealers, Suburban Md. Assn. Ins. and Fin. Advisors (past pres., H.L. Meyer Meml. award 1980), Fin. Planning Assn., Suburban Md. Estate Planning Coun. (past pres.), Million Dollar Round Table. Lutheran. Home: 508 Lawson Way Rockville MD 20850 Office: Ste 420 18310 Montgomery Village Ave Gaithersburg MD 20879-3553 Business E-Mail: jruth@pfgroup.org.

RUTH, RODNEY, musician, music consultant, contractor, educator; b. Robesonia, Pa., Sept. 12, 1934; s. Herbert J. and Pearl (Rentz) R.; m. Gloria Mae Kauffman, Nov. 14, 1953; 1 child, Tiffany Tunisia. MusB, Manhattan Sch. Music, 1960; MA, Columbia U., 1964. Freelance musician; music cons., contractor Meadowlands Sports Complex, various theaters and performing arts ctrs., individual conductors and performers, bands, orchs., festivals, NJ, NY, Pa., 1957—; tchr. Paterson (N.J.) Bd. Edn., 1961-98. Performed with USAF Band, 1953-57; music contractor for world premiers (musicals) Lucifer, Laugh a Little, Cry a Little, Shoemakers Holiday, Love Games, Las Vegas Laugh-In '75. Scholar Manhattan Sch. Music, N.Y.C., 1958-60. Mem. Nat. Edn. Assn., Music Educators Nat. Conf., Am. Fedn. Musicians, Air Force Musicians Assn. Avocations: travel, gardening, golf. Home and Office: Rod Ruth Music 129 Schuyler Rd Allendale NJ 07401-1836 Office Phone: 201-327-7374. E-mail: rodruthmusic@aol.com.

RUTHBERG, MILES N., lawyer; BA summa cum laude, Yale Univ., 1973; JD magna cum laude, Harvard Univ., 1976. Bar: DC 1979, Calif. 1979. Law clk. Justice Thurgood Marshall, US Supreme Ct., Judge Carl McGowan, US Ct. of Appeals, DC Cir.; former nat. chair, securities litigation and profl. liability practice group Latham & Watkins, former global dept. chair, litigation dept., exec. com. mem. Former bd. governors Assn. Bus. Trial Lawyers. Developments editor Harvard Law Rev., 1976; author: numerous articles in profl. publications. Mem.: ABA, NY State Bar Assn., DC Bar Assn., Calif. State Bar Assn. Office: Latham & Watkins Ste 4000 633 W Fifth St Los Angeles CA 90071-2007

RUTHCHILD, GERALDINE QUIETLAKE, training and development consultant, writer, poet; d. Nathan and Ruth (Feldman) Stein; m. Neil Wolinsky, Dec. 31, 1993; 1 child, Nathaniel Gideon Wolinsky. BA summa cum laude, Queens Coll., 1977; MA in Am. Lit., Johns Hopkins U., 1980, PhD in Am. Lit., 1983. Asst. prof. Albion (Mich.) Coll., 1982-84; assoc. Investor Access Corp., NYC, 1984-85; program dir. Exec. Enterprises, Inc., NYC, 1985-86; pres. Ruthchild Assocs., NYC, 1987-90, Exemplar, NYC, 1991-95, Exemplar, Ltd., NY, 1995—. Cons. J.P. Morgan & Co., Inc., MetLife, U.S. Army, Bankers Trust Co., MasterCard Internat., GreenPoint Bank, Koch Industries, Inc., Chase Manhattan Bank N.A., Merrill Lynch, TIAA-CREF, Drake Beam Morin, Trans Union Corp, NatWest Bank, U.S.A., Citibank N.A., Robert Morris Assocs., Goldman, Sachs & Co., Dean Witter Reynolds, Inc., also others, 1987—. Contbr. articles, poems to profl. and lit. jours. Vol. handicapped children N.Y. Foundling Hosp., N.Y.C., 1988-90, Fgn. Visitors Desk, Met. Mus. Art, N.Y.C., 1989-97. Hopkins fellow Johns Hopkins U., 1979-80, Andrew Mellon Found. fellow, 1980-81, 81-82. Mem. ASTD, Internat. Soc. Philos. Enquiry, Phi Beta Kappa. Avocations: foreign languages, needlecrafts, gardening. Office: Exemplar Ltd Ste 9 One Alderwood Syosset NY 11791-4711 Home Phone: 516-496-3119. Business E-Mail: GQR@exemplar-ltd.com.

RUTHENBERG, KIRK R., lawyer; b. Blue Island, Ill., Dec. 31, 1952; BA, U. Ill., 1975; JD, Georgetown U., 1979. Bar: Ill. 1979, DC 1989, Md. 1991, US Dist. Ct. No. Dist. Ill. 1979, US Dist. Ct. DC 1991, US Dist. Ct. Dist. Md. 1992, US Ct. Appeals 4th Cir. 1993. Named ptnr. Sonnenschein Carlin Nath & Rosenthal (now Sonnenschein Nath & Rosenthal LLP), Chgo., 1986, now ptnr. Washington, head DC litig. & bus. regulation practice group. Office: Sonnenschein Nath & Rosenthal LLP Ste 600, E Tower 1301 K St NW Washington DC 20015 Office Phone: 202-408-6410. Office Fax: 202-408-6399. Business E-Mail: kruthenberg@sonnenschein.com.

RUTHERFORD, ALAN W., manufacturing executive; b. 1944; With Crown Cork Co. Belgium N.V., 1974-86, European contr. Antwerp, 1986-89; with Crown Cork & Seal Co., Inc., Phila., 1989-90, contr., 1990-91, sr. v.p. fin. and adminstrn., CFO, 1991-92, exec. v.p., CFO, 1992—, bd. dirs., 1991—, and vice chmn. Bd. trustees Thomas Jefferson U. Fellow Chartered Inst. Mgmt. Accts. U.K. Office: Crown Cork and Seal Co Inc One Crown Way Philadelphia PA 19154-4599 *

RUTHERFORD, BARRY D., cardiologist; b. Gore, New Zealand, Aug. 24, 1938; MB, BChir, U. Otago, 1963; MD, Otago Med. Sch., Dunedin, 1964. Diplomate Am. Bd. Internal Medicine, Am. Bd. Cardiology. Intern Dunedin Pub. Hosp., Otago, 1964-65; fellow U. Utah, 1970-71; pvt. practice Cardiovasc. Cons., Kansas City, Mo.; John. B. Simpson asst prof. Interventional Cardiology and Genomic Sci.; dir., Interventional Cardiology and Genomic Sci.; dir. Mid Am. Inst. Heart/Saint Luke's Hosp., Kans. City. Named a Kans. City Super Doctor, Kans. City mag., 2007. Fellow Royal Coll. Cardiologists; mem. Sigma Xi. Office: Cardiovasc Cons PC 4330 Wornall Rd Ste 2000 Kansas City MO 64111-3217 also: 12330 Metcalf Ave Ste 280 Overland Park KS 66213 Office Phone: 816-931-1883, 913-491-1000. Business E-Mail: brutherford@cc-pc.com. *

RUTHERFORD, BOYD KEVIN, federal agency administrator; BA, Howard U., 1979; MA, JD, U. So. Calif., 1990. Atty. analyst Bankers Trust Co., 1979—81; mktg. rep. Data Control Corp., 1981—86; sr. acct. exec. Telenet Comm. Corp., 1986—87; litigation assoc. Carlsmith Wickman Case Mukai & Ichiki, 1990—91; atty. Daihatsu Am., Inc., 1991—92; of counsel Mitsubishi Motor Sales of Am., Inc., 1992—94; assoc. Van Ness Feldman, P.C., 1994—98, Tydings & Rosenberg, LLP, 1998—2000; delegate Rep. Party Nat. Convention, 2000; dir. bus. devel. Kelly Law Registry, 2000—01; assoc. adminstr. office enterprise devel. Gen. Svcs. Adminstrn., 2001—03, assoc. adminstr. office performance improvement, 2002—03; acting sec. Md. Dept. Gen. Svcs., 2003, sec., 2003—06; asst. sec. departmental adminstrn. USDA, 2006—. Office: USDA S Agr Bldg 1400 Independence Ave SW Rm 209A Washington DC 20250 Office Phone: 202-720-3291.

RUTHERFORD, GEORGE WILLIAMS, III, preventive medicine physician; b. San Diego, Apr. 6, 1952; s. G. Williams and Anna Gwyn (Dearing) R.; m. Lisa Anderson, Aug. 24, 1974 (div. 1984); children: Alicia Gwyn, George Williams IV; m. Mary Workman, Feb. 23, 1985; children: Alexandra Catherine, Anne Elizabeth Martha, Hugh Thomas Gwyn, Amanda Frances Julia. AB in Classics, Stanford U., 1974, BS in Chemistry, 1975, AM in History, 1975; MD, Duke U., 1978. Diplomate Am. Bd. Pediat., Am. Bd. Preventive Medicine, Nat. Bd. Med. Examiners. Intern in pediat. U. Calif. Med. Ctr., San Diego, 1978-79; resident in pediat. U. Calif. Med. Ctr., Hosp. for Children, San Diego, 1979-80; resident Hosp. for Sick Children, Toronto, 1980-81; chief resident Children's Hosp. and Health Ctr., San Diego, 1981-82; EIS officer divsn. viral diseases, divsn. field svcs Epidemiology Office Ctrs. for Disease Control, Atlanta, 1982-84; dir. divsn. immunization, acting dir. divsn. tropical disease N.Y.C. Dept. Health, 1983-85; med. epidemologist AIDS program Ctrs. for Disease Control, San Francisco Dept. Pub. Health, 1985-87; from med. dir. to dir. AIDS office San Francisco Dept. Pub. Health, 1986-90; chief, infectious disease br. and state epidemiologist Calif. Dept Health, Berkeley, 1990-92, dep. dir. prevention svcs. and state epidemiologist, 1992-95, state health officer, 1993-95; assoc. dean adminstrn., prof. epidemiology/health adminstrn. Sch. Pub. Health, U. Calif., Berkeley, 1995-97; prof. epidemiology and preventive medicine U. Calif., San Francisco, 1997—, dir. Inst. Global Health, 2004—. Transport physician Children's Hosp. and Health Ctr., San Diego, 1981; clin. asst. prof. pediatrics Emory U., Atlanta, 1982-83, Cornell U., N.Y.C., 1984-85, U. Calif., San Francisco, 1986-92, asst. clin. prof. epidemiology and biostats., 1987-92, family and cmty. medicine, 1988-90; assoc. adj. prof. epidemiology, biostats. and pediatrics, 1992-95, adj. prof., 1996—; assoc. clin. prof. cmty. health u. Calif., Davis, 1991-95; cons. Pan-Am. Health Orgn., S.Am., 1986-89, Ctrs. Disease Control, Atlanta, 1987—, WHO, 1988-90. Contbr. numerous articles to profl. jours., chpts. to books; co-translator cardiology teaching manual, other Spanish med. articles; editor in chief Calif. Morbidity, 1990-92; mem. editl. bd. Calif. AIDS Update, 1988—, Current Issues in Pub. Health, 1993-97; referee: AIDS, 1988—, Am. Jour. Pub. Health, 1989—, Brit. Med. Jour., 1994—, Internat. Jour. Epidemology, 1991—, Jour. Acquired Immune Deficiency Syndrome, 1989—, New Eng. Jour. Medicine, 1989—, Western Jour. Medicine, 1989—. Mem. numerous profl. adv. coms., task forces, etc. which aid govt. and charitable orgns. in work against infectious disease, especially AIDS. Capt. USPHSR, 1982—. Fellow Am. Acad. Pediatrics; mem. APHA, Am. Assn. for History of Medicine, Am. Soc. Tropical Medicine and Hygiene, Bay Area Communicable Disease Exch., Calif. Med. Assn., Infectious Diseases Soc. Am., No. Calif. Pub. Health Assn., Internat. AIDS Soc., Soc. for Epidemiol. Rsch., Assn. State and Territorial Health Ofcls. Republican. Episcopalian. Avocation: tennis. Office: U Calif San Francisco Global Health Inst Ste 1200 50 Beale St San Francisco CA 94105 Office Phone: 415-597-8200. E-mail: grutherford@psg.ucsf.edu.

RUTHERFORD, JIM, professional sports team executive; b. 1948; 1 child, Andrea. Goalie Detroit Red Wings, 1970—71, 1973—80, 1982—83, Pitts. Penguins, 1971—73, Toronto Maple Leafs, 1980—81, LA Kings, 1981—82; dir. hockey ops Compuware Sports Corp., 1982-84; gen. mgr. Windsor Spitfires, Ont., 1984-88, head coach Ont., 1986-87; dir. hockey ops. Detroit Ambassadors, 1989-91, coach, dir. hockey ops., 1991-92, Detroit Jr. Red Wings (formerly Ambassadors), 1992-94; COO KTR Hockey Ltd. Partnership, Hartford, Conn., 1984—; pres., gen. mgr., COO Carolina Hurricanes (formerly Hartford Whalers), 1994—. Mem. Team Can. hockey world championships, Vienna, 1977, Moscow, 79; player rep. 5 seasons Red Wings. Named Exec. of Yr., Can. Hockey League, 1993,

Ont. Hockey League, 1994, The Hockey News, 2002. Achievements include being the general manager of Stanley Cup Champion Carolina Hurricanes, 2006. Office: Carolina Hurricanes 1400 Edwards Mill Rd Raleigh NC 27607-3624

RUTHERFORD, JOHN SHERMAN, III, (JOHNNY RUTHERFORD), professional race car driver; b. Coffeyville, Kans., Mar. 12, 1938; s. John Sherman and Mary Henrietta (Brooks) R.; m. Betty Rose Hoyer, July 7, 1963; children: John Sherman Rutherford IV, Angela Ann Rutherford-Price. Student, Tex. Christian U., 1956. Profl. race car driver, 1959-94; ret., 1994; driver super-modified race cars, sprint cars, stock cars, midgets, sports cars, Indy cars, Trans-Am cars and formula 5000. Mem. Indy Car Racing Inc.; dir. spl. events Indy Racing League, 1995—; pace car driver for Championship Auto Racing Teams, 1992-95; auto racing cons. Pennzoil Products-Racing Divsn.; lectr. in field. Author: (autobiography) Lone Star J.R., 2000; host: TV show The Racers; race commentator TV show, NBC, ESPN, CBS, ABC; appeared in numerous TV commercials; art work included in traveling exhbn. Art and Athletes; TV and radio pub. services messages for Nat. Safety Council, Calif. Hwy. Patrol, U.S. Marines, Muscular Dystrophy Assn., Cystic Fibrosis Assn., Boy Scouts, Camp Fire, Jewel Charity, Shriner's Hosp., Tex. Soc. to Prevent Blindness, Air N.G. Hon. state chmn. Am. Cancer Soc., Tex., Tarrant County Soc. to Prevent Blindness, Emergency Medicine Found., Ft. Worth Kidney Assn., Ft. Worth Burn Ctr.; Ind. chmn. Am. Heart Assn.; hon. mem. bd. dirs. Tex. chpt. Speedway Children's Charities, 1998—. CARA Charities, 2000--; bd. dirs. Indy HOF and Oldtimers, 2002—. With USMC Res., 1955—61. Named Ft. Worth Newsmaker of Yr., 1974, Driver of Yr. Sport Mag., 1976, Driver of Yr. Auto Race Writers and Broadcasters Am., 1974, 80, Olsonite Driver of Yr., 1980, Corvette Challenge's Sportsman of Yr., 1988, Motorsports amb., 1993; recipient Jim Clark award, 1969, Extra Mile award, 1973, Jim Malloy award, 1974, Eddie Sachs award, 1975, Louie Meyer award, 1992; chosen for Internat. Race of Champions, 1974, 76-79, 84, chosen Fast Masters, 1993; named to Tex. Sports Hall of Fame, 1981, Indy 500 Hall of Fame, 1987, Boys Clubs Am.'s Celebrity Hall of Fame, 1987, Tex. Auto Racing Hall of Fame, 1988, Nat. Sprint Car Hall of Fame, 1995, Internat. Motorsports Hall of Fame, 1996, Tex. Motorsports Hall of Fame, 2003, Philanthropy Hall of Fame, 2006. Mem. Fedn. Internat. Automobile, Internat. Motors Sports Assn., Exptl. Aircraft Assn., Warbirds of Am., Confederate Air Force, Internat. Aerobatic Club, League Auto Racing (sec., bd. dirs.), Championship Drivers Assn. (bd. dirs.), Nat. Rifle Assn., Air Force Assn., Air Power Coun., Blue Angels Assn., Ft. Worth Boat Club, Shady Oaks Country Club, Speedway Club, Lions. Republican. Disciples Of Christ. Achievements include winning 27 championship car races; winner Indianapolis 500, 1974, 76, 80, second place, 1975; set new world's record for stock cars, Daytona Beach, Fla., 1963; set record at Indpls. 500, 1973; at Mich. Internat. Raceway, 1984; U.S. Auto Club Nat. Sprint Car champion, 1965; Nat. Driving champion USAC and CART, 1980; oldest driver (48) to win a 500 mile Indy Car Race, 1986. Personal E-mail: bettyr4tx@msn.com. *I am a firm believer in the fact that a person can do anything in this world he or she wants to as long as you have desire. People have to set goals, things to achieve. No one ever remembers who finished second. Luck is where preparation meets opportunity.*

RUTHERFORD, PAUL HARDING, physicist; b. Shipley, Yorkshire, Eng., Jan. 22, 1938; came to U.S., 1965, naturalized, 1976; s. Joseph William and Annie (Harding) R.; m. Audrey Jones Irvine, Oct. 31, 1959; children— Andrea Christine, Julia Irvine. BA, Cambridge U., Eng., 1959, MA, PhD, Cambridge U., Eng., 1963. Research asso. Princeton (N.J.) U. Plasma Physics Lab., 1962-63, mem. research staff, 1965-68, research physicist, 1968-71, sr. research physicist, 1971-99, head theoretical div., 1972-80, dep. asso. dir. for research, 1978-80, asso. dir. research, 1980-95. Chair tech. adv. com. Internat. Thermonuclear Exptl. Reactor, 1992-99; rsch. assoc. U.K. Atomic Energy Authority Culham (Berkshire, Eng.) Lab., 1963-65; lectr. astrophys. scis. Princeton U. Co-author: (with R.J. Goldston) Introduction to Plasma Physics, 1995; mem. editl. bd. Physics of Fluids, 1973-75, Nuc. Fusion, 1980-99. Recipient E.O. Lawrence award U.S. Dept. Energy, 1983, Disting. Career award Fusion Power Assocs., 1998. Fellow Am. Phys. Soc. Home: 10 Burr Dr Princeton NJ 08540-1950 Office: Plasma Physics Lab PO Box 451 Princeton NJ 08543-0451 Business E-Mail: prutherford@pppl.gov.

RUTHERFORD, SCOTT, marketing professional, consultant; BS, Emerson Coll., Boston, 2002; MBA, Babson Coll., Babson Park, Mass., 2004. News reporter, anchor Berkshire Broadcasting Corp., Danbury, Conn., 1994—99; mktg. mgr. Thomson CompuMark, North Quincy, Mass., 2001—. Recipient Hon. Mention, Conn. AP Broadcasters Assn., 1996, 1997. Mem.: Pub. Rels. Soc. Am. Office: Thomson CompuMark 500 Victory Rd North Quincy MA 02171 Home Phone: 617-852-6222; Office Phone: 617-376-7667. Personal E-mail: sjrutherford@gmail.com.

RUTHERFORD, THOMAS TRUXTUN, II, state legislator, municipal official; b. Columbus, Ohio, Mar. 3, 1947; s. James William and Elizabeth Whiting (Colby) R.; m. Linda Sue Rogers, Aug. 28, 1965 (div.); 1 child, Jeremy Todd; m. Charlene Beth Smith, July 22, 2007. BBA, U. N.Mex., 1970, JD, 1982. Page, reading clk. N.Mex. State Legislature, 1960-65; mem. N.Mex. Atty. Gen. Environ. Adv. Commn., 1972; radio broadcaster Sta. KOB Radio and TV, 1963-72; mem. N.Mex. Senate, Albuquerque, 1972-96, majority whip, 1978-88. Chmn. rules com. N.Mex. State Senate, chmn. econ. devel. and new tech. interim. com., mem. sci. and new tech. oversight com., majority fl. leader, 1996; pres. Rutherford & Assocs., Albuquerque, 1978—83; pvt. practice, Albuquerque, 1983—; gen. counsel Nat. Fraternal Order of Police, 1996—2001; commr., chair Bernalillo County Commn., 1996—2004; lobbyist The Rutherford Group, 1996—; bd. dirs. Hispano C. of C., Kirtland Partnership Com., Albuquerque Econ. Devel., Camp Sierra Blanca Youth Detention Ctr., N. Mex. Bus. Weekly Top 100 Power Brokers, 1996—2004; past chmn. Albuquerque Cable TV Adv. Bd.; mem. S.W. Regional Energy Coun., N.Mex. Gov.'s Commn. on Pub. Broadcasting; bd. dirs., v.p. Rocky Mountain Corp. for Pub. Broadcasting; mem. Am. Coun. Young Polit. Leaders; del. mission to Hungary, Austria, Greece, 1983; mem. Fgn. Trade Adv. Com. Bd. Econ. Devel. and Tourism; trade del. People's Republic of China, 1985; local govt. del. Switzerland, 2001. Mem. Leadership N.Mex. Class of 2004; bd. dirs. Nat. Assn. Counties, N.Mex. Assn. Counties. N.Mex. Broadcasting Assn. scholar, 1970. Home: 1016 monroe NE Albuquerque NM 87110

RUTHERFORD, VICKY LYNN, special education educator; b. Florence, SC, Sept. 12, 1947; BS, Hampton U., Va., 1969, MA, 1971; PhD, Mich. State U., East Lansing, 1991. Cert. tchr. French, spl. edn., reading specialist, Va., tchr. spl. edn., SC. Social worker day care Hampton Dept. Social Svc., Va., 1970-72; reading therapist, asst. dir., dir. Bayberry Reading Clinic, Hampton, 1973-77; tchr. reading, English, counselor York County Schs., Yorktown, Va., 1977-85; staff advisor, asst. to course coord. Mich. State U., East Lansing, 1985-90; tchr. autism/emotionally impaired Florence Dist. 1 Sch. Sys., SC, 1996—2004; tchr. emotionally impaired Long Beach Unified Sch. Dist., 2004—. Instrnl. designer: Addiction Severity Index #1, 1987, #2, 1988, Managing a Diverse Workforce, 1990; designer, trainer: Project Teach, 1991; designer, developer: (video) Camp Takona Summer Experience, 1992. Bass guitarist, Sunday sch. sec., youth worker, Sun. sch. supt. Progressive Ch. of Jesus, Florence, 1992-98, Greater Zion Tabernacle Apostolic Ch., Florence, 1998-2004, City of Refuge Gardena, Calif., 2004-. Fellow Mich. Dept. Edn., 1987-89. Mem. Internat. Reading Assn. Office: Rogers Mid Sch 365 Monrovia Ave Long Beach CA 90803

RUTHERFORD, WILLIAM DRAKE, investment executive; b. Marshalltown, Iowa, Jan. 14, 1939; s. William Donald and Lois Esther (Drake) R.; m. Janice W. Rutherford, Feb. 4, 1965 (div. Mar. 1982); children: Wayne Donald, Melissa Drake; m. Karen Anderegg, Jan. 2, 1994. BS, U. Oreg., 1961; LLB, Harvard U., 1964. Bar: Oreg. 1964, U.S. Dist. Ct. Oreg. 1966. Assoc. Maguire, Kester & Cosgrave, Portland, Oreg., 1966-69; house counsel May & Co., Portland, 1969-70, pvt. practice, 1970-71, McMinnville, Oreg., 1971-84; mem. Oreg. Ho. of Reps., Salem, 1977-84; state treas. State of Oreg., Salem, 1984-87; chmn. Oreg. Investment Coun., Salem, 1986-87; exec. v.p., dir. U.S. and Australia ops. ABD Internat. Mgmt. Corp., NYC, 1987-88, pres., chief exec. officer, bd. dirs., 1988-89; pres., bd. dirs. Societé Gen. Touche Remnant, 1990-93; dir. spl. projects Metallgesellschaft Corp., NYC, 1994-95; mng. dir. Macadam Capital Ptnrs., Portland, 1995-96; CEO Fiberboard Asbestos Compensation Trust, Portland, 1997; prin. Rutherford Investment Mgmt. LLC, 1998—. Past chmn. bd. dirs. Metro One Telecomms. Author: Who Shot Goldilocks?, 2006. Trustee The Nature Conservancy, 2005—; bd. dirs. Portland Opera Assn., 1995—99; mem. investment bd. Oreg. Cmty. Found., 2006—. Recipient Contbn. to Individual Freedom award ACLU, 1981 Mem. Nat. Assn. State Treas. (exec. v.p. 1985, 86, pres. western region 1985, 86), Nat. Assn. State Auditors, Comptr. and Treas. (exec. com. 1987). Office: 10300 S W Greenburg Rd Ste 115 Portland OR 97223 Office Phone: 503-452-1210. Business E-Mail: WRutherford@rutherfordinvestment.com.

RUTHERFURD, JOHN, financial information company executive; LLB, Harvard Law Sch., 1966; AB, Princeton U., 1962. V.p., chief of staff Chase Info. Svcs. Group, 1980—85; founder Interactive Data Corp., 1968, pres., 1985—89, 1990—95; exec. v.p. Dun & Bradstreet Fin. Info. Svcs., 1989—90; mng. dir., new bus. develop. Moody's Investors Svc., NYC, 1995-96, chief adminstr. officer, 1996-98, pres., 1998—2000; pres., CEO Moody's Corp., NYC, 2000—, chmn., 2003—. Office: Moodys Corp 99 Church St New York NY 10007

RUTHMAN, THOMAS ROBERT, manufacturing executive; b. Cin., May 24, 1933; s. Alois H. and Catherine (Gies) R.; m. Audrey J. Schumaker, Mar. 17, 1979; children: Thomas G., Julia C., Theresa K. Grad., LaSalle U., 1970. With Ruthman Pump and Engring. Inc. (formerly Ruthman Machinery Co.), Cin., 1953—, gen. mgr., 1964-70, v.p., 1970-74, pres., 1974—, pres., owner, 1981—. Pres. Gusher Pumps, Inc., Fulflo Spltys. Co., Gusher Pumps of New Castle, Cin., Williamstown (Ky.), Dry Ridge, Calif.; pres., owner, dir. Great Lakes Pump & Supply, Mich.; owner BSM Pump Corp, North Kingston, R.I., Negel Pump Co.; pres., owner Birmingham (Eng.) Pump Supply, Ruthmann Pumpen, GMBH, Germany. Office: 1212 Streng St Cincinnati OH 45223-2643

RUTHVEN, JOHN A., wildlife artist; b. Cin., 1924; m. Judy Ruthven; 1 child, Kevin. Student, Cin. Art Acad., Jack Storey Ctrl. Acad. Comml. Art. Opened comml. art studio, 1946; founder Wildlife Internationale Inc., 1971; major exhibits include Famous Figureheads Series, Nat. Mariner Mus., Washington, Cin. Mus. Natural History, 1994, Artist of Am. exhbn., Denver, Leigh Yawkey Woodson Mus., Wausau, Wis., Soc. Animal Artists nat. tours, 1992—2000, Hiram Blauvelt Art Mus., Oradell, NJ, Rory Tory Peterson Inst. Natural History, Jamestown, NY, 1998, 2004—05, The Smithsonian Instn.'s Preservation and Rsch. Ctr., 1998; major commissions include Proctor & Gamble, Cin. Bengals, John Deere & Co., WILDS Internat. Ctr. for the Preservation of Wild Animals, Armco Steel Corp., Bankers Life & Casualty, Mead Corp., Colonial Williamsburg, Classical Music Hall of Fame. Co-author, illustrator (with William Zimmerman) Top Flight Speed Index to Waterfowl of N.Am., 1965, paintings featured in (books) An Instrument of Your Peace, Eyes of Tenderness, John A. Ruthven, In the Audubon Tradition. Served USN, WWII. Named Winner of Fed. Duck Stamp competition for "Redhead Ducks", 1960, Artist of Yr., Ducks Unlimited, 1972, First Ohio Duck Stamp/Print Artist, 1982, 25th Anniversary Artist, Trout Unlimited, 1984, First Ohio Animal Stamp/Print Artist, 1988, Pacific Flyaway Artist, Ducks Unlimited, 1989; recipient Irma Lazarus Award for sustained arts excellence, Ohio Gov.'s Awards for the Arts, 2001, Nat. Medal of Arts, 2004. Mem.: Soc. Animal Artists (past pres.), Nat. Audubon Soc., Am. Ornithological Assn., Cin. Bird Club, Outdoors Writers Assn. Achievements include painting unveilings at The White House, Hermitage Mus., St. Petersburg, Russia, Pres.'s Palace, Philippines, for Crown Prince Henri, Luxemborg, Neil Armstrong Space Mus., Ohio State Capital Rotunda. Office: Wildlife Internationale Inc 202 E Grant Ave PO Box 59 Georgetown OH 45121

RUTKOFF, ALAN STUART, lawyer; b. Chgo., May 31, 1952; s. Roy and Harriet (Ruskin) R.; m. Mally Zoberman, Dec. 22, 1974; children: Aaron Samuel, Jordana Michal, Robert Nathaniel. BA with high distinction, U. Mich., 1973; JD magna cum laude, Northwestern U., 1976. Bar: Ill. 1976, U.S. Dist. Ct. (no. dist.) Ill. 1976, U.S. Ct. Appeals (7th cir.) 1977, U.S. Ct. Appeals (3d cir.) 1978, U.S. Supreme Ct. 1981, U.S. Ct. Appeals (5th cir.) 1983, U.S. Ct. Appeals (8th cir.) 1990, U.S. Dist. Ct. (we. dist.) Wis. 1996, U.S. Ct. Appeals (6th cir.) 2003. Assoc. Altheimer & Gray, Chgo., 1976-80; ptnr. Kastel & Rutkoff, Chgo., 1980-83, Holleb & Coff Ltd., Chgo., 1983-84, McDermott Will & Emery LLP, Chgo., 1984—, gen. coun., 2005—. Pres. N. Suburban Synagogue Beth El, Highland Pk., Ill., 1999-2001. Mem. ABA, Chgo. Bar Assn., Order of Coif. Home: 801 Timberhill Rd Highland Park IL 60035-5148 Office: McDermott Will & Emery LLP 227 W Monroe St Ste 4400 Chicago IL 60606-5096 Home Phone: 847-432-2242; Office Phone: 312-984-7751. Business E-Mail: arutkoff@mwe.com.

RUTKOVE, SEWARD BRIAN, neurologist, educator, neuroscientist; b. Bklyn., May 18, 1964; s. Lowell Jay and Edith (Botwinick) R.; m. Elena Ruehr, Sept. 2, 1989. BA, Cornell U., Ithaca, NY, 1985; MD, Columbia U., NYC, 1989. Diplomate Am. Bd. Psychiatry and Neurology, 1996, spl. qualification in clin. neurophysiology Am. Bd. Psychiatry and Neurology, 1997. Internship, residency, internal med. St Joseph Mercy Hosp., Ann Arbor, Mich., 1989—91; residency in neurology Brigham and Women's Hosp., Boston, 1991—94, fellowship in clin. neurophysiology, 1994—95; neurologist Beth Israel Deaconess Med. Ctr., Boston, 1995—2003; assoc. prof. neurology Med. Sch. Harvard U., Boston, 2003—; chief Divsn. Neuromuscular Disease Dept. Neurology Beth Israel Deaconess Med. Ctr., Boston, 2004—. Contbr. articles to profl. jours. Grantee, NIH, 2003, 2005. Mem. Am. Acad. Neurology, Physicians for Nat. Health Plan. Achievements include development of electrical impedance myography-a new approach to evaluating muscle and nerve diseases; novel approaches to using temperature for the evaluation of peripheral nerve diseases. Avocations: double bass, piano, skiing. Office: Beth Israel Deaconess Medical Center 330 Brookline Avenue TCC-810 Boston MA 02446 Office Phone: 617-667-8130. Business E-Mail: srutkove@bidmc.harvard.edu.

RUTKOWSKI, DUANE JOSEPH, social studies educator; b. Phila., Aug. 20, 1956; s. Edward Joseph and Dorothy Lucille Rutkowski. BA, U. Pa., 1978; postgrad., U. Arts, 1978—82. Dean students, tchr. social studies Performing Arts Sch., Phila., 1978—89; dir. music, organist, dir. choir St. Laurentius Ch., 1968—, tchr. 7th grade social studies, music, lang. arts, 1990—. Asst. dir. Acad. Boys Choir, Phila., 1976—89; guest soloist, organist various area chs., 1990—. Chmn. pastoral coun., fundraiser St. Laurentius Ch., Phila., 1993—. Named Tchr. of Yr., Fox 29 TV Sta. Phila., 1992, 1993, Celebrate Fishtown Assn., Phila., 1998, Fishtown Civic Assn., Phila., 2005; recipient Tchg. Excellence award, Phila. (Pa.) Flag Day Assn., 2005. Mem.: Met. Opera Guild, Nat. Cath. Educators Assn., Phila. Flag Day Assn. Roman Catholic. Avocations: travel, gourmet cooking. Home: 2651 E Huntington St Philadelphia PA 19125 Office: St Laurentius Sch 1612 E Berks St Philadelphia PA 19125 Office Phone: 215-423-8834.

RUTKOWSKI, JOSEPH A., manufacturing executive; Mgr. Cold Finish Nucor Corp., Norfolk, Nebr., 1989-91, mgr. melting & casting steel divsn. Plymouth, Utah, 1991—92, gen. mgr. steel divsn. Darlington, SC, 1992—98, Hertford, NC, 1998, v.p., 1993—98, exec. v.p. steel mills Charlotte, NC, 1998—. Office: Nucor Corp 1915 Rexford Rd Charlotte NC 28211 Office Phone: 704-366-7000. Office Fax: 704-362-4208. *

RUTLEDGE, CHARLES OZWIN, pharmacologist, educator; b. Topeka, Oct. 1, 1937; s. Charles Ozwin and Alta (Seaman) R.; m. Jane Ellen Crow, Aug. 13, 1961; children: David Ozwin, Susan Harriett, Elizabeth Jane, Karen Ann. BS in Pharmacy, U. Kans., 1959, MS in Pharmacology, 1961; PhD in Pharmacology, Harvard U., 1966. NATO postdoctoral fellow Gothenburg (Sweden) U., 1966-67; asst. prof. U. Colo. Med. Ctr., Denver, 1967-74, assoc. prof., 1974-75; prof., chmn. dept. pharmacology U. Kans., Lawrence, 1975-87; dean, prof. pharmacology Purdue U., West Lafayette, Ind., 1987—2002, exec. dir. Discovery Park, 2001—05, interim vice provost rsch., 2002—05, v.p. rsch., 2005—. Contbr. articles on neuropharmacology to profl. jours. Grantee NIH, 1970-87. Mem. AAAS, Am. Soc. Pharmacology and Exptl. Therapeutics (councillor 1982 84, sec.-treas. 1990-93, pres. 1996-97), Am. Assn. Coll. Pharmacy (chmn. biol. scis. sect. 1983-84, chmn. coun. faculties 1986-87, chmn. coun. deans 1993-94, com. implement change pharm. edn. 1989-92, pres. 1996-97), Soc. for Neurosci., Am. Pharm. Assn. Avocations: gardening, skiing. Home: 40 Brynteg Est West Lafayette IN 47906-5643 Office: Purdue U Hovde Hall Rm 338 610 Purdue Mall West Lafayette IN 47907-2040 Home Phone: 765-583-2869; Office Phone: 765-494-6209. Business E-Mail: chipr@purdue.edu.

RUTLEDGE, JOANNE, artist, consultant; b. Indpls., Dec. 17, 1941; d. Edward John and Dorothy Louise (Bachelor) Underwood; m. Kenneth Clay Smith, Sept. 7, 1963 (div. May 1990); children: Elizabeth, Kenneth Clay, Jr., Andrew; m. Mark Alan Rutledge, July 31, 1993. RN, St. Vincent's Sch. Nursing, Indpls., 1962; BSN, Ind. U., Indpls., 1979. RN Ind. Staff RN Children's Hosp., Washington, 1962—63, St. Vincent's Hosp., Indpls., 1963—64, Women's Hosp. Spl. Care Nursery, Indpls., 1990—97; nurse cons. Hosp. Care for Indigent Ind. State Program, Indpls., 1995—. Exhibitions include Ind. State Fair, Ind. Heritage Arts, Southside Art League Regional Show. Docent Indpls. Mus. Art, 1983—; reading tutor Kiwanis Project, 2002—; active various coms. Children's Mus. Guild, 1975—; v.p. Indpls. Athletic Club Art Bd. Found., 1990—. Recipient Billy Cothran Landscape award, Indpls. Art Ctr., 1985. Mem.: Ind. Plein Art Painters Assn., Stutz Artist's Assn., Ind. Artist's Club (assoc.), Proctor Club (pres. 1994—95). Roman Catholic. Avocations: travel, photography, hiking, attending concerts and theater, scuba diving. Home: 1019 W 75th St Indianapolis IN 46260-3408 Office: Ind Hosp Care for the Indigent 402 W Washington St Indianapolis IN 46204

RUTLEDGE, ROGER KEITH, lawyer; b. Knoxville, Tenn., Dec. 27, 1946; s. Joseph P. and Jean Mae (Karnes) R.; m. Lily Mee Kin Hee, June 6, 1970; children: Amelia Leilani, Sarah Elizabeth. BA in History with honors, U. N.C., 1968; JD cum laude, Am. U., 1977. Bar: Tenn. 1977, U.S. Dist. Ct. (we. dist.) Tenn. 1978, U.S. Supreme Ct. 1982. Served in U.S. Peace Corps, Nepal, 1968-70; fgn. service officer U.S. Dept. State, Washington and Italy, 1971-76; ptnr. Rutledge & Rutledge, Memphis, 1977—. Pres. Jabez Burns, Inc., 1998-99; sec., treas. R-Track Tech., Inc., 2003—. Editor fiction Carolina Quar., 1967-68; assoc. editor Am. U. Law Rev., 1976-77. Mem. campaign com. Albert Gore Jr. U.S. Senate, Shelby County, 1984, for pres. campaign, 1988, 2000; bd. chmn. United Meth. Neighborhood Ctrs., Inc., 1992. Mem. ABA, Tenn. Bar Assn., Memphis Bar Assn. (editor Bar Forum 1986, asst. editor 1987). Democrat. Methodist. Office: 1083 W Rex Rd No 102 Memphis TN 38138 *Notable cases include: Fite vs. First Tenn. Prodns. Credit Assn., which involved age discrimination in employment, 1988; Capital Tool & Mfg. vs. Maschinenfabrik Herkules, which involved trade secret law and internat. injunction, 1988.*

RUTLEDGE, VALERIE COPELAND, education educator; b. Alexandria, Va., Feb. 23, 1953; d. David Young and Mary Leamon Copeland; m. Paul Jackson Rutledge, Apr. 14, 1985; 1 child, Ashley Marie. EdD, U. Tenn., Knoxville, 1997. Cert. secondary English, Latin tchr., adminstr., supr. Tenn., 1974. Prof., tchr. preparation acad. U. Tenn., Chattanooga, 1995—, tchr. preparation acad., dept. head, 2003—. Cons. Reading First Cadre, Nashville, 2004—. Contbr. articles to profl. publs. Sec. Freedoms Found. at Valley Forge, Chattanooga, 2006—07; mem. congl. dist. 3 Tenn. State Bd. Edn., Nashville, 1999—; state pres. Tenn. Reading Assn., Nashville, 2000—01, Tenn. Coun. Tchrs. English, Nashville, 2000—01. Named HS Tchr. of Yr., Tenn. State Dept. Edn., 1987. Mem.: Alpha Soc. (v.p. 2006—07), Alpha Delta Kappa (pres. Alpha Pi chpt. 2006—). Republican. Methodist. Office: U Tenn Dept 4154 615 McCallie Ave Chattanooga TN 37403 Home Phone: 423-344-0503; Office Phone: 423-425-5374. Office Fax: 423-425-5380. Business E-Mail: valerie-rutledge@utc.edu.

RUTSALA, VERN A., poet, writer, language educator; b. Feb. 5, 1934; s. Ray Edwin and Virginia Mae (Brady) R.; m. Joan Merle Colby, Apr. 6, 1957; children: Matthew, David, Kirsten. BA, Reed Coll., Portland, 1956; MFA, U. Iowa, Iowa City, 1960. Instr. Lewis and Clark Coll., Portland, 1961-64, asst. prof., 1964-69, assoc. prof., 1969-76, prof., 1976—2004. Vis. prof. U. Minn., Mpls., 1968-69, Bowling Green State U., Ohio, 1970; vis. writer Idaho, Moscow, 1988, Redlands U., Calif., 1979; chmn. English dept. Lewis and Clark, Portland, 1986-89, MWC/Pacific MFA program, 2005. Author: The Window, 1964, Laments, 1975, The Journey Begins, 1976, Paragraphs, 1978, Walking Home from the Icehouse, 1981, Backtracking, 1985, Ruined Cities, 1987, Selected Poems, 1991, Little-Known Sports, 1994, Greatest Hits: 1964-02, 2002, A Handbook for Writers, 2004, The Moment's Equation, 2004, How We Spent Our Time, 2006. With U.S. Army, 1956-58. Guggenheim Found. fellow, 1982-83, NEA fellow, 1975, 79, Masters fellow Oreg. Arts Commn., 1990; recipient Carolyn Kizer prize Western Oreg. State Coll., 1988, N.W. Poets prize N.W. Rev., 1975, Hazel Hall award Oreg. Inst. Lit. Arts, 1992, Juniper prize U. Mass. Press, 1993, Duncan Lawrie prize Arvon Found., 1994, Carolyn Kizer prize, 1997, Richard Snyder prize, 2004, Akron Poetry prize, 2004, Kenneth O. Hanson award, 2005; finalist Nat. Book award, 2005. Mem. AAUP, AWP, PEN, Poetry Soc. Am. Avocations: drawing, painting, sports.

RUTSTEIN, DAVID C., United States public health service administrator; Student, Morehouse Coll. Sch. Medicine; MD, Brown Univ., 1983; MD (hon.), Moreshouse Sch. Medicine. Internal med. physician Salem Hosp., Mass., 1983—84; family med. residency Natividad Medical Center, Salinas, Calif., 1984—87; family physician Nat. Health Svc. Corps, Pohnpei and Yap, Federated States of Micronesia, 1987—2000, chief clin. officer to chief med. officer Washington, 2000—03; dep. assoc. adminstr. for Health Professions Health Resources and Svcs. Adminstrn., Washington, 2003—05; dir. Off.of Internat. Health Affairs, sr. adv., HRSA Adminstr., Washington, 2005; chief. med. officer US Public Health Service, Washington, 2005—; and dep. dir., Off. Disease Prevention and Health Promotion Off. Sec. Health and Human Svcs., Washington, 2005—; also family physician East of the River Cmty. Health Ctr., Washington; capt. US Pub. Health Svc.; acting dir. Office of Force Readiness and Deployment, US Pub. Health Svc., 2007—; chief profl. officer Physicians Profl. Adv. Com. Recipient Disting. Alumnus award, Morehouse Sch. Medicine, Medal of Valor for leadership in pub. health after 2005 Indonesian Island of Nias earthquake, AMA, 2006. Mem.: Pacific Basin Med. Assn., Res. Officers Assn., Commissioned Officers Assn., Am. Pub. Health Assn., Am. Acad. Family Physicians. Office: US Dept Health and Human Svcs Off

Disease Prevention and Health 1101 Wootton Pkwy Ste LL 100 Rockville MD 20852 Office Phone: 240-453-8280. Office Fax: 240-453-8282. Business E-Mail: david.rutstein@hhs.gov. *

RUTSTEIN, DAVID W., lawyer, food products executive; b. NYC, July 7, 1944; s. David and Mazie (Weissman) R.; m. Rena E. Bergsmann, July 19, 1967; children: Sara E., Charles B. BA, U. Pa., 1966; JD with honors, George Washington U., 1969. Bar: Pa. 1969, D.C. 1969. Dep. atty. gen., Pa., 1969-70; ptnr. firm Danzansky, Dickey, Tydings, Quint & Gordon, Washington, 1970-78; sr. v.p., gen. counsel Giant Food, Inc., Washington, 1978—2000; of counsel Bus. Transactions, Mergers & Acquisitions practices Venable LLP, Washington, 2001—. Bd. dirs., chmn., treas. Washington Met. Bd. Trade, Fed. City Coun. Bd. dirs., pres. Washington Hebrew Home for Aged (Hyman Goldman award), 1989-91; mem. exec. com. Fed. City Coun.; chmn. Agnes and Eugene Meyer Found., Wash. Met. Bd. Trade; trustee Greater Washington Rsch. Ctr. Named Washingtonian of the Year, Washingtonian Mag.; recipient award for Disting. Svc. to Washington Theater Cmty., KPMG. Mem. D.C. Bar Assn., Washington Met. Area Corp. Counsel Assn. (pres. 1986). Jewish. Home: 9 Greentree Ct Bethesda MD 20817-1440 Office: Venable Law Firm 575 7th St NW Washington DC 20004-1601 Office Phone: 202-344-4000. Office Fax: 202-344-8300. Business E-Mail: dwrutstein@venable.com.

RUTSTEIN, ELEANOR H., psychologist; b. NY, Dec. 26, 1933; d. Louis Morris and Sarah Rutstein; m. Gilbert Sussman, Aug. 17, 1971; 1 child, Susanna Beth Sussman. BA in psychology summa cum laude with honors, Cornell U., Ithaca, NY, 1955; MA with honors, Boston U., 1956; PhD in Clin. Psychology, NYU, 1970. Lic. psychologist 1971. Training fellow Rsch. Ctr. for Mental Health, NYC, 1965—66; psychologist Bronx Psychiatric Ctr., Bronx, NY, 1966—70; clin. psychologist Beth Israel Hosp., NYC, 1970—72; clin. asst. prof. Cornell Univ. Med. Coll., White Plains, NY, 1980—89; vis. asst. prof. Albert Einstein Coll. of Medicine, Bronx, NY, 1987—91; adj. clin. supr. Yeshiva Univ., Bronx, NY, 1991—; pvt. practice New Rochelle, NY, 1971—. Contbr. scientific papers pub. to profl. jour. Group facilitator Group Mothers of Pre-Schoolers, recently div. woman, White Plains, 1976—; mem. Move On, 2004—. Mem.: APA, N.Y. State Psychol. Assn., Psi Chi, Phi Kappa Phi, Phi Beta Kappa. Democrat. Avocations: piano, photography, theater, music, gourmet cooking. Home and Office: 597 Pinebrook Blvd New Rochelle NY 10804 Office Phone: 914-576-4866. Personal E-mail: eleanorhrutstein@aol.com.

RUTSTEIN, STANLEY HAROLD, apparel retailing company executive; b. Wilkes-Barre, Pa., July 1, 1941; s. Sydney D. and Bessie H. (Cohen) R.; m. Jo Ella Rutstein; children: Wendy Sue, Michael Scott, Lynne Elizabeth. Student, Wilkes Coll., 1959-61; grad., Advanced Mgmt. Program, Harvard U., 1975. Buyer Barbara Lynn Stores, Inc., NYC, 1961-63; buyer, then mdsg. mgr. Casual Corner div. U.S. Shoe Corp., Enfield, Conn., 1963-71, pres., 1971-76; pres., cons., dir. U.S. Shoe Corp., Cin., 1976-79; pres. Commonwealth Trading, Inc., Stoughton, Mass., 1979-85, Chadwick's of Boston Ltd., 1983-85; cons. Commonwealth Trading, Inc., 1985—; pres. Trim Trends, Inc., Boston, 1986-87, chmn., 1987-91; chmn., chief exec. officer, pres. Narragansett Clothing Co., Tiverton, RI, 1987-90, also bd. dirs.; bd. dirs. Reynolds Bros. Inc., 1989-95; pres., CEO S/J Designs Inc., 1989—2002, DBA, Northeast Knitters, Wagner Realty, Bradenton, Fla., 2002—; sales exec. Remax Gulfstream Realty, Bradenton, Fla., 2007—. Bd. dirs. The Icing, Inc., Sycamore Shops, Inc. Bd. dirs. Ptnrs. for Disabled Youth, 1992. Mem. Young Pres. Orgn. Home: The Water Club 1281 Gulf of Mexico Dr #203 Longboat Key FL 34228 Office: Remax Gulfstream Realty 3007 Manatee Ave W Bradenton FL 34205 Office Phone: 941-758-7777. Personal E-mail: nextmoveboston@aol.com.

RUTTAN, VERNON WESLEY, agricultural economist, educator; b. Alden, Mich., Aug. 16, 1924; s. Ward W. and Marjorie Ann (Chaney) R.; m. Marilyn M. Barone, July 30, 1945; children: Lia Marie, Christopher, Alison Elaine, Lore Megan. BA, Yale U., 1948; MA, U. Chgo., 1950, PhD, 1952; LLD (hon.), Rutgers U., 1978; D Agrl. Sci. ((hon.), U. Kiel, Germany, 1986, Purdue U., 1991. Economist TVA, 1951-54; prof. agrl. econs. Purdue U., 1954-63; staff economist President's Council Econ. Advisers, 1961-63; economist Rockefeller Found., 1963-65; head dept. agrl. econs. U. Minn., St. Paul, 1965-70, Regent's prof., 1986-99, Regent's prof. emeritus, 2000—. Pres. Agrl. Devel. Council, N.Y.C., 1973-77 Author (with Y. Hayami): Agricultural Development: An International Perspective, 1971, 1985; author: U.S. Development Assistance Policy, 1996, Technology, Growth and Development, 2001, Social Science Knowledge and Economic Development, 2003, Is War Necessary for Economic Growth, 2006. Recipient Alexander von Humboldt award, 1985. Fellow AAAS, Am. Acad. Arts and Scis., Am. Agrl. Econs. Assn. (pres. 1971-72, Publ. award 1956, 57, 62, 66, 67, 71, 79, 85, 97); mem. NAS. Home: 1666 Coffman St Apt 112 Saint Paul MN 55108-1326 Office: Dept Applied Econs U Minn Saint Paul MN 55108 Business E-Mail: vruttan@umn.edu.

RUTTENBERG, CHARLES BYRON, lawyer; b. Reading, Pa., Nov. 16, 1922; s. Abraham David and Mollie Belle (Rabinowitz) Ruttenberg; m. Arden Honore Suk, July 29, 1955; children: Victoria Arden, Valerie Honore, Alexandra Anne. Student, Yale U., New Haven, Conn., 1941—42; BA, U. Va., Charlottesville, 1946; LLB, U. Pa., Phila., 1949. Bar: DC. With Covington & Burling, Washington; gen. counsel NSF, Washington, Nat. Found. Arts Humanities, Washington, 1949-69; ptnr. Arent, Fox, Kintner, Plotkin & Kahn, Washington, 1969—; fed. mediator US Dist. Ct., 1998—, DC Superior Ct., 2000—. Chmn. legis. bur., mem. exec. com., bd. dirs., gen. counsel Greater Washington Bd. Trade, 1983—92, Nat. Assn. Rec. Merchandisers, Video Software Dealers Assn., 1980—95. Editor, mem. mng. bd.: U. Pa. Law Rev., 1947—49. Gen. counsel Nat. Opera Inst., 1985—95; co-chmn. U. Pa. Law Sch. Alumni Fund, Washington, 1983—91; chmn. lawyers com. DC Comm. Arts, 1972—75; gen. counsel People to People Music Program, Washington, 1970—91; trustee, gen. counsel Wolf Trap Found. Performing Arts, Vienna, Va., 1981—91, Nat. Inst. Music Theatre, Washington, 1969—90; gen. counsel, bd. dirs. Am. Film Inst., 1969—91; trustee, mem. exec. com. U. DC, 1990—94; bd. dirs., pres. Cosmos Club Hist. Preservation Found., 1987—; bd. dirs., v.p., exec. com. Iona Sr. Svcs., 1997—; bd. dirs. Washington Area Lawyers for Arts, 1984—95, Greater Washington Rsch. Ctr., 1980—95; mem. adv. bd. DC Lottery, 2002—. With USAF, 1942—46, capt. USAFR, 1946—55. Recipient Outstanding Svc. awards, US Govt., 1967, 1968. Mem.: ABA, Arts Internat. (gen. counsel), U. Pa. Law Alumni Assn. (pres. 1967—71, bd. dirs. 1967—78), Washington Athletic Club (bd. govs. 1969—74), Mitchell Law Club, St. Alban's Club, Cosmos Club (bd. mgmt. 2000—03, gen. counsel 2003—06, v.p. 2006—07, pres. 2007—, Disting. Svc. award 2005), Phi Beta Kappa. Home: 4735 Butterworth Pl NW Washington DC 20016-4459 Office: Arent Fox Kintner Plotkin & Kahn 1050 Connecticut Ave NW Ste 500 Washington DC 20036-5303 Office Phone: 202-857-6082. Personal E-mail: cbruttenberg@aol.com. Business E-Mail: ruttenbc@arentfox.com.

RUTTENBERG, FRANK Z., lawyer; b. San Antonio, June 4, 1954; BBA, U. Tex., 1976; JD, St. Mary's U., 1979; LLM in Taxation, NYU, 1982. Bar: Tex. 1979. Lawyer Strasburger & Price, L.L.P., San Antonio; ptnr. Bracewell & Patterson, San Antonio, 1999—. Office: Bracewell & Giuliani One Alamo Ctr 106 S Saint Marys St Ste 800 San Antonio TX 78205-3603 Office Phone: 210-226-1166, 210-299-3467. Business E-Mail: frank.ruttenberg@bgllc.com.

RUTTENCUTTER, BRIAN BOYLE, manufacturing company executive; b. Long Beach, Calif., June 15, 1953; s. Wayne Andrew and Florence Mae (Heckman) F.; m. Marilyn Ruth Grubb, Sept. 9, 1978; children: Christi Anne (dec.), Melissa Lyn. BS in Bus. Adminstrn. and Acctg., Biola U., 1976; MBA, Calif. State U., Long Beach, 1983. Cert. mgmt. acct. Controller Fuller Theol. Sem., Pasadena, Calif., 1976-80; dir. gen. acctg. Air Calif., Newport Beach, 1980-84; corp. controller PBS Bldg. Systems, Inc., Anaheim, Calif., 1984-88, v.p. fin. and adminstrn., 1988-93; CFO, v.p. fin. For Better Living, Inc., and The Quikset Orgn., Auburn and Irvine, Calif., 1993-95; v.p. fin., CFO, bd. dirs. Phillips Industries Inc., Commerce, Calif., 1996—2003; CFO ABC Window Co., Inc., Ontario, Calif., 2004—05, pres., CEO, 2005—06. Chmn., vice chmn., fin. commn. City of Irvine, Calif., 1990—94, vice-chmn. cmty. svcs. commn., 1996—98; active Drivers for Hwy. Safety, Irvine, 1986; trustee Fin. Execs. Rsch. Found., 2004—06; v.p. Greater Irvine Rep. Assembly, 1990, treas., 1991; bd. dirs. Grace Brethren Ch., Long Beach, 1978—80, Woodbridge Cmty. Ch., Irvine, 1986—88, 1991—92, vice chmn., 1991, chmn., 1992. Mem. Inst. Cert. Mgmt. Accts., Inst. Mgmt. Accts., Fin. Execs. Internat. (chpt. bd. dirs., nat. bd. dirs., area v.p., nat. v.p. at large 2006—, past chpt. pres.), Assn. Corp. Growth (chpt. bd. dirs., v.p., treas., pres.-elect), Fin. Execs. Rsch. Found. (bd. dirs. 2004-06). Republican. Avocations: tennis, golf, flying stunt kites, performing contemporary christian music. Home: 1071 Castlerock Ln Cowan Heights CA 92705-6110

RUTTER, FRANCES TOMPSON, retired publisher; b. Arlington, Mass., Apr. 12, 1920; d. Harold F. and Mildred F. (Wheeler) Tompson; m. John H. Ottemiller, Mar. 24, 1943; children: Joan Tompson Gillum, John Tompson Ottemiller; m. William D. Rutter, Oct. 26, 1970. AB magna cum laude, Pembroke Coll., Brown U., 1941; postgrad., Mt. Holyoke Coll., 1942—43. Res. book librarian Brown U., 1941-42; annotator ship's papers John Carter Brown Library, Providence, 1943-44; librarian Sci. Service, Washington, 1944-45; ptnr. Shoe String Press, Hamden, Conn., 1952-58; sec., treas. Shoe String Press, Inc., 1958-68, pres., treas., 1968-80, also bd. dirs.; sec.-treas., dir. Tompson-Malone, Inc., book mfrs., 1967-80; pres., treas., dir. Tompson & Rutter, Inc., 1980-89; ret., 1989. V.p. class 1941 Pembroke Coll., 1967-73, 76-91, pres., 1973-76, head class agt., 1979-85, bequests and trust chmn., 1979-90, 40th reunion gift com., 1980, co-chair 50th reunion gift com., 1990-91, 55th reunion gift com., 1995-96, 65th reunion gift com., 2006; spl. projects adv. panel N.H. Commn. on Arts, 1980-84; mem. natural resources com. Grantham, 1980; mem. Grantham Planning Bd., 1981-87, sec., 1981-83, chmn., 1985-87; chmn. Grantham Recycling Com., 1988-89, Grantham Hist. Soc., 1992-96, Habitat for Humanity-Kearsarge/Sunapee chpt., 1989-94; mem. Diocesan Altar Guild Bd., 1990-93, sec., 1991-92; vol. Mary Hitchcock Meml. Hosp. Aux., 1991-2003; mem. vestry St. Paul's Episc. Ch., 1997-2000, jr. warden, 1998-2000; assoc. Holy Cross Monastery, West Park, N.Y. Mem. Friends of Fernald Libr. of Colby-Sawyer Coll., ACLU (life), LWV (editor newsletter 1987-89), Assoc. Alumni Brown U. (bd. dirs. 1981-83), Nicholas Brown Soc., Pembroke Ctr. Assocs. (coun. 1984-86), Soc. for Preservation N.H. Forests, Episcopal Peace Fellowship, Phi Beta Kappa. Episcopalian. Home: 222 S Yale Ave # 217 Tulsa OK 74137 Personal E-mail: franbill@webb.com.

RUTTER, JEREMY BENTHAM, archaeologist, educator; b. Boston, June 23, 1946; s. Peter and Nancy Kendall (Cornstock) Rutter; m. Sarah Robbins Herndon, Jan. 31, 1970; children: Benjamin Ryerson, Nicholas Kendall. BA in Classics with honors, Haverford Coll., 1967; PhD in Classical Archaeology, U. Pa., 1974; MA, Dartmouth Coll., 1993. Vis. asst. prof. dept. classics UCLA, 1975-76, from asst. prof. to prof. dept. classics, 1976—, prof. humanities, 2001—, chmn. dept. classics, 1992-98, 2003—. Participant excavations, Germany, 1966, Italy, 1968—69, Greece, 1972—75, Greece, 1977, Greece, 78, Greece, 1980—81, Greece, 1984—86, Greece, 1988—89, Greece, 1991—; mem. numerous coms. Am. Sch. Classical Studies, Athens. Author: Lerna III: The Pottery of Lerna IV, 1995; mem. editl. adv. bd. Hesperia, Am. Jour. Archaeology; contbr. articles, revs. to profl. jours. With US Army, 1969—71, Vietnam. Woodrow Wilson fellow, 1967—68, NDEA fellow, U. Pa., 1968—69, 1971—73, NEH Rsch. grantee, 1979—81, Travel grantee, Am. Coun. Learned Socs., 1982, Sr. Faculty grantee, 1985—86, 1991—92, 2001—02. Mem.: Classical Assn. New Eng., Archeol. Inst. Am. (mem. numerous coms., Olivia James Traveling fellow 1974—75), Am. Schs. Oriental Rsch., Phi Beta Kappa. Home: 47 Eagle Rdg Lebanon NH 03766-1900 Office: Dept Classics Dartmouth College Hanover NH 03755-3506 Home Phone: 603-448-1650; Office Phone: 603-646-2910. E-mail: jeremy.rutter@dartmouth.edu.

RUTTER, MARSHALL ANTHONY, lawyer; b. Pottstown, Pa., Oct. 18, 1931; s. Carroll Lennox and Dorothy (Tagert) R.; m. Winifred Hitz, June 6, 1953 (div. 1970); m. Virginia Ann Hardy, Jan. 30, 1971 (div. 1992); children: Deborah Frances, Gregory Russell, Theodore Thomas; m. Terry Susan Knowles, Dec. 19, 1992. BA, Amherst Coll., Mass., 1954; JD, U. Pa., 1959. Bar: Calif 1960. Assoc. O'Melveny & Myers, Los Angeles, 1959-64, Flint & MacKay, Los Angeles, 1964-67, ptnr., 1967-72, Rutter Hobbs & Davidoff, Los Angeles, 1973—. Bd. dirs. Ojai Festivals Ltd., 2001, treas., 2004—. Gov. The Music Ctr. of L.A. County, 1978-86, 89-92; bd. dirs. Music Ctr. Operating Co., 1992-96; bd. dirs. Chorus Am., Washington, 1987-96, pres., 1993-95; bd. dirs. L.A. Master Chorale Assn., 1964—, pres., 1980-92, chmn. 1992-96, vice chmn., 1996-2001; vestryman All Saints Ch., Beverly Hills, Calif., 1983-86, 88-90. Mem. ABA, Assn. Bus. Trial Lawyers (bd. dirs. 1980-82), L.A. County Bar Assn., Beverly Hills Bar Assn., Century City Bar Assn., English-Speaking Union (various offices L.A. chpt. 1963-91), L.A. Jr. C. of C. (bd. dirs. 1964-67). Democrat. Episcopalian. Avocations: classical and choral music, golf, stamp collecting/philately. Home: 1045 S Orange Grove Blvd Apt 10 Pasadena CA 91105-1795 Office: Rutter Hobbs & Davidoff Ste 1700 1901 Ave of Stars Los Angeles CA 90067-6018 Home Phone: 626-441-1588; Office Phone: 310-286-1700. Fax: 310-286-1728. Business E-Mail: mrutter@rutterhobbs.com.

RUTTER, MICHAEL LLEWELLYN, child psychology educator; b. Brummanna, Lebanon, Aug. 15, 1933; arrived in Eng., 1936; s. Llewellyn Charles and Winifred Olive (Barber) Rutter; m. Marjorie Heys, Dec. 27, 1958; children: Sheila Carol, Stephen Michael, Christine Anne. MB, BChir, U. Birmingham, Eng., 1955, MD with honors, 1963; diploma in psychol. medicine, U. London, 1961; degree (hon.), U. Leiden, 1985, Cath. U., 1990, U. Birmingham, 1990, U. Edinburgh, 1990, U. Chgo., 1993, U. Minn., 1993, U. Ghent, 1994; degree, U. Warwick, 1999, U. East Anglia, 2000, U. North London, 2000, U. York, 2005, U. Oxford, 2005; EdD (hon.), U. Dublin, 2007. Various tchg. positions in pediat., neurology, internal, 1955-58; registrar then sr. registrar Maudsley Hosp., London, 1958-62; mem. sci. staff MRC Social Psychiatry Rsch. Unit, London, 1962-65; sr. lectr. then reader U. London Inst. Psychiatry, 1966-73, prof. child psychiatry, 1973-98, hon. dir. MRC Child Psychiatry unit, 1984-98, with Social Genetic and Devel. Psychiatry Rsch. Ctr., 1994—98; prof. devel. psychopathology Inst. Psychiatry, 1998—. Nuffield med. traveling fellow Albert Einstein Coll. Medicine, N.Y.C., 1961-62; fellow Ctr. for Advanced Study in Behavioral Scis., Stanford, Calif., 1979-80; hon. prof. U. Amsterdam, 2001. Author: Helping Troubled Children, 1975, Maternal Deprivation Reassessed, 2nd edit., 1981, (with H. Giller) Juvenile Delinquency: Trends & Perspectives, 1983, (with M. Rutter) Developing Minds: Challenge and Continuity Accross the Lifespan, 1993, (with H. Giller, A. Hagell) Antisocial Behavior by Young People, 1998, (with T. Moffitt, A. Caspi and P. Silva) Sex Differences in Antisocial Behavior: Conduct Disorder, Delinquency and Violence in the Dunedin Longitudinal Study, 2001, (with M. Tienda) Ethnicity and Casual Mechanisms, 2005, Genes & Behavior: Nature-Nurture Interplay Explained, 2006; co-editor: Autism: A Reappraisal of Concepts and Treatment, 1978, Stress, Risk and Resilience In Children and Adolescents: Processes, Mechanisms and Interventions, 1994, Development Through Life: A Handbook For Clinicians, 1994, Psychosocial Disorders in Young People: Time Trends & Their Causes, 1995, Antisocial Behavior by Young People, 1998, Child and Adolescent Psychiatry, 4th edit., 2002, Ethnicity and Casual Mechanisms, 2005; editor: Scientific Foundations of Developmental Psychiatry, 1980, Developmental Neuropsychiatry, 1983. Recipient Goulstonian lectr. award, Royal Coll. Physicians, 1973, rsch. award, Am. Assn. Mental Deficiency, 1975, Salmon lectr. award, N.Y. Acad. Medicine, 1979, C. Anderson Aldrich award, Am. Acad. Pediat., 1981, Adolf Meyer ward lectr. award, APA, 1985, Disting. Sci. Contbn. award, 1995, Castilla del Pino prize for achievement in psychiatry, Spain, 1995, Lifetime Achievement award, IMFAR, 2002, G. Stanley Hall award, APA, 2003, Marmor award, 2003, Arnold Lucius Gesell prize, 2004, Bronfenbrenner award, 2005, Camille Cosby World of Children award, 2005; fellow, Royal Soc., 1987; Belding travelling scholar, 1963, Rock Carling fellow, 1979. Fellow Royal Soc. Medicine (London, hon.), Royal Coll. Pediat. and Child Health (hon. founding fellow 1996), Royal Coll. Psychiatrists (London, hon.), Kings Coll. London, Brit. Acad.; mem. AAAS (fgn. hon.), Internat. Soc. Rsch. in Child and Adolescent Psychiatry (pres. 1997-99), U.S. Nat. Acad. Edn. (fgn. assoc.), Brit. Pediat. Assn. (hon.), Assn. Child Psychology and Psychiatry (chmn. 1973-74), Brit. Psychol. Soc. (hon. fellow), Am. Acad. Child Psychiatry (hon. membership), NAS (fgn. assoc. Inst. Medicine, Sarnat Internat. prize in mental health 2001), Soc. Rsch. in Adolescence (John P. Hill award for excellence in theory devel. and rsch. 1992), Soc. Rsch. Child Devel. (pres. 1999-2001), Inst. Child Health (London, hon. fellow 1996), Internat. Acad. Rsch. in Learning Disabilities, Academia Europaea (founding mem.), Acad. Med. Scis. (founder, clin. v.p.). Home: 190 Court Ln London SE21 7ED England Office: SGDP Rsch Centre P080 Inst Psychiatry DeCrespigny Park London SE5 8AF England Office Phone: 44 2078480882. Business E-Mail: j.wickham@iop.kcl.ac.uk.

RUTTER, NATHANIEL WESTLUND, geologist, educator; b. Omaha, Nov. 22, 1932; s. John Elliot and Karleen (Ludden) R.; m. Mary Marie Munson, Sept. 11, 1961; children: Todd, Christopher. BS, Tufts U., 1955; MS, U. Alaska, 1962; PhD, U. Alta., 1965, DSc honoris causa, 2001. Geologist Venezuelan Atlantic Refining Co., 1955-58; research scientist Geol. Survey Can., Calgary, Alta., 1965-74, head urban projects sect. Ottawa, Ont., 1974; environ. advisor Nat. Energy Bd., Ottawa, 1974-75; assoc. prof. dept. geology U. Alta., Edmonton, 1975-77, 77-80, prof., chmn. dept., 1980-89, 77-96, prof. dept. atmospheric scis., 1996-97, univ. prof., 1997—, assoc. dean. faculty sci.; pres. Can. nat. com. Internat. Geol. Correlation Program, UNESCO, 1996-97. Pres. Internat. Union Quaternary Rsch. Congress, 1982-87; mem. Internat. Geosphere-Biosphere Program: A Study of Global Change, 1988-94; mem. rsch. com. Can. Global Change Program, 1992-94; chmn. global change com. INUQA, 1991-95; hon. prof. Chinese Acad. Sci., Beijing, 1994—; disting. lectr. Sigma Xi, 1995-97; mem. sci. bd. Internat. Union of Geol. Scis.-UNESCO, 1997—. Contbr. numerous articles to profl. jours.; assoc. editor Arctic, Geosci. Can. Quaternary Rsch.; mem. editl. bd. Quaternary Sci. Revs., Quaternary Rsch., Estonia Jour. Sci., Arctic; editor-in-chief Quaternary Internat. Named Officer Order of Can., 2001; recipient Queen's Golden Jubilee medal, 2003, Alberta Centennial medal, 2005; grantee Natural Scis. and Engring. Rsch. Coun. Can., grantee Energy, Mines and Resources. Fellow Royal Soc. Can.; mem. Assn. Profl. Engrs., Geologists and Geophysicists of Alta., Internat. Union Quaternary Rsch. (v.p. 1982-87, pres. 1987-91, hon. 1999), Can. Quaternary Assn. (v.p. 1981-82, Johnston medal 1997), Geol. Soc. Am. (mgmt. bd. dirs. quaternary geol. and geomorphology divsn. 1982-84, Disting. Career award 2003), Geol. Assn. of Can. (J. Willis Ambrose medal 1998), Internat. Assn. Quaternary Rsch. (hon.), Explorer's Club, Cosmos Club. Home: Rural Route 3 Stony Plain AB Canada T7Z 1X3 Office: U Alta Dept Earth & Atmospheric Scis Edmonton AB Canada T6G 2E3 Office Phone: 780-492-3085. E-mail: nat.rutter@ualberta.ca.

RUTTINGER, GEORGE DAVID, lawyer; b. Detroit, Jan. 17, 1948; s. George Jacob and Margaret Mary (Smith) R.; m. Camille Ann Larson, Oct. 4, 1975; children: Jacob Charles, David Hayes, Philip George. AB with high distinction and honors, U. Mich., 1970, JD magna cum laude, 1973. Bar: Calif. 1975, D.C. 1975, U.S. Dist. Ct. D.C. 1975, U.S. Dist. Ct. Md. 1987, U.S. Ct. Appeals (D.C. and 4th cirs.) 1984, U.S. Ct. Appeals (1st cir.) 1988, U.S. Supreme Ct. 1984, U.S. Dist. Ct. (ea. dist.) Mich. 1995, U.S. Ct. Appeals (6th cir.) 1996, U.S. Ct. Appeals (3d cir.) 1999, U.S. Ct.Appeals (9th cir.) 2002. Law clk. to Hon. Malcolm R. Wilkey U.S. Ct. Appeals, Washington, 1973-74; assoc. Latham & Watkins, LA, 1974, Crowell & Moring LLP (formerly Jones, Day, Reavis & Pogue), Washington, 1975-79, ptnr., 1980—. Author: (with others) Containing Legal Costs: ADR Strategies for Corporations, Law Firms and Government, 1988; contbr. articles to profl. jours. Fellow Am. Bar Found. Office: Crowell & Moring LLP 1001 Pennsylvania Ave NW Fl 10 Washington DC 20004-2595 Business E-Mail: gruttinger@crowell.com.

RUTZEN, DOUGLAS, lawyer, educator; BA, Cornell U., 1987; JD, Yale U., 1990. With Coudert Brothers; legal advisor Czechoslovak Parliament; prof. law Charles U., Prague; pres., CEO Internat. Ctr. for Not-for-Profit Law, Washington, 2004—. Mem. adv. group Civil Soc. Watch; chair East-West Mgmt. Inst.; steering com. mem. US Internat. Grantmaking (USIG) Project; lectr. law U. Pa. Law Sch. Editl. bd. World Competition: Law and Economics Review; contbr. articles to profl. jours. Office: ICNL 1126 16th St, NW Ste 400 Washington DC 20036 Office Phone: 202-452-8600. Office Fax: 202-452-8555. E-mail: drutzen@icnl.org, drutzen@law.upenn.edu.

RUTZICK, MARK CHARLES, lawyer; b. St. Paul, Sept. 6, 1948; s. Max Arthur and Bertha (Ward) R.; children by previous marriage: Elizabeth Leslie, Karen Deborah; m. Cynthia Lombardi, Jan. 16, 1994; children: Samuel Ryan, Joshua Benjamin, Jacob Louis. BA, U. Mich., 1970; JD, Harvard U., 1973. Bar: N.Y. 1974, U.S. Supreme Ct. 1977, U.S. Ct. Appeals (9th cir.) 1982, Oreg. 1984, Wash. 1987. Spl. asst. corp. counsel N.Y.C. Housing Adminstrn., 1973-75; assoc. Alexander Hammond P.C., NYC, 1975-76; asst. atty. gen. Office N.Y. State Atty. Gen., NYC, 1976-78; atty. Dept. Justice, Washington, 1978-82, spl. litig. counsel, 1982-83, atty.-in-charge field office Portland, Oreg., 1983-86; counsel Preston, Thorgrimson, Shidler, Gates & Ellis, Portland, 1986-87, ptnr., 1988-94, LeBoeuf, Lamb, Greene & MacRae, L.L.P., Portland, 1996-99; shareholder Mark C. Rutzick Law Firm, P.C., Portland, 1994—96, 1999—2003; sr. adv. to gen counsel Nat. Oceanic Atmospheric Adminstrn., U.S. Dept. Commerce, Wash., 2003; pvt. practice Portland, Oreg. Mem. Oreg. Bar Assn., Wash. State Bar Assn. Office: US Dept Commerce Rm 5814A 14th & Constn Ave Washington DC 20230 Home: 3407 SW Stonebrook Dr Portland OR 97239-1269 Home Phone: 503-244-3030. Home Fax: 503-244-3030. Personal E-mail: mark_rutzick@comcast.net.

RUUD, CLAYTON OLAF, engineering educator; b. Glasgow, Mont., July 31, 1934; s. Asle and Myrtle (Bleken) Ruud; m. Paula Kay Mannino, Feb. 24, 1990; children: Kelley Astrid, Kirsten Anne. BS in Metallurgy, Wash. State U., Pullman, 1957; MS in Materials Sci., San Jose State U., 1967; PhD in Materials Sci., U. Denver, 1970. Registered profl. engr., Calif., Colo. Asst. remelt metallurgist Kaiser Aluminum & Chem. Corp., Trentwood, Wash., 1957-58; devel. engr. Boeing Airplane Co., Seattle, 1958-60; mfg. rsch. engr. Lockheed Missiles & Space Corp., Sunnyvale, Calif., 1960-63; rsch. engr. FMC Corp., San Jose, 1963-67; sr. rsch. scientist U. Denver, 1967-79; prof. indsl. engring. Pa. State U., University Park, 1979—. Founder, developer, and co-director of quality and manufacturing management masters degree Pa. State U.; cons. in field; bd. dirs. Denver X-Ray Inst. Inc., Altoona, Pa. Editor series: Advances in X-Ray Analysis, Vol. 12-22, 1970-80, Nondestructive Character of Materials, Vol. 1-6, 1983-1996; editor X-Ray Spectometry, 1975-87; editl. com. Nondestructive Testing and Evaluation, 1991-1995; contbr. chpts. to books. Chmn. Nat. Acad. Sci. Safe Drinking Water Com., Washington, 1976-78.

Recipient IR 100 award, 1983, Gov.'s New Product Award, Pa. Soc. Profl. Engrs., 1988. Fellow ASM Internat. (chmn. Resid. Stress Conf. 1989-91); mem. Internat. Ctr. for Diffraction Data, Soc. Mfg. Engrs., Metall. Soc. of AIME. Achievements include patents in x-ray analysis and residual stress measurement; invention of fiber optic based position sensitive scintillation X-ray detector, instrument for simultaneous stress and phase composition measurement; development of an X-ray diffraction instrument for manufacturing process quality control. Business E-Mail: corl@psu.edu.

RUVIELLA-KNORR, JEANNE L., music educator, consultant, clinician; d. Jean and Marion Post Ruviella; m. H. Richard Knorr, May 26, 1962 (div. Dec. 24, 1993); children: Richard Post Knorr, Michelle Renee Mitchell. MusB, Boston U., 1962; MA, U. So. Calif., 1966; PhD, U. Md., 2004. Cert. advanced profl. cert. tchg. Md., Dalcroze cert. Longy Sch., Dalcroze-Orff-Kodaly cert. Manhattan Sch. Music. Music tchr. L.A. Pub. Schs., 1962—66, Burlington Pub. Schs., Vt.; prof. music edn. Shelton Coll., Cape Canaveral, Fla., 1968—74; music tchr., cons. Anne Arundel County Pub. Schs., Severna Park, Md., 1974—79; prof. music edn. Towson (Md.) U., 1979—97, prof. emerita, 1997—; prof. music edn. Frostburg State U., Md., 1999—2000; tchr. music Harford County Schs., Abingdon, Md., 2000—. Clinician Towson U., 1994—, developer Grad. Dalcroze-Orff-Kodaly Cert. program, co-dir. Dalcroze-Orff-Kodaly Cert. program, 1981—97, adj. faculty Dalcroze-Orff-Kodaly Cert. program, 1997—; cons. in field. Contbg. author: music series Share the Music, Grades 7-8, 1996—2005, Music and You, Grades 7-8, 1989—2005, co-compiler: keyboard proficiency packet for Towson U., rev. Leader women's support groups Chapelgate Ch., Marriottsville, Md., 2000—. Mem.: Md. Music Educators Assn., Music Educators Nat. Conf. (clinician 1983—87, 2000, 2005). Avocations: travel, music. Personal E-mail: ruviella@comcast.net.

RUWE, BRADLEY N., lawyer; b. Fort Lee, Va., Nov. 18, 1970; BSBA, Xavier U., 1992; JD, Salmon P. Chase Coll. Law, 1996. Bar: Ohio 1997. Worked in Tax Dept. Peck, Shaffer & Williams LLP, Cin., ptnr. Named Cincy Leading Lawyer, Cincy Bus. Mag., 2006; named one of Ohio's Rising Stars, Super Lawyers, 2005, 2006. Mem.: Assn. Govtl. Leasing and Fin. (bd. mem.), Ohio Govt. Fin. Officers Assn., Ohio State Bar Assn., Cin. Bar Assn., Potter Stewart Inns of Ct., Moot Ct., Cin. Acad. Leadership for Lawyers. Office: Pack Shaffer & Williams LLP 201 E 5th St Ste 900 Cincinnati OH 45202 Office Phone: 513-621-3394. Office Fax: 513-621-3813.

RUWE, ROBERT PAUL, federal judge; b. Ohio, 1941; Grad., Xavier U., 1963; JD, No. Ky. U., 1970. Spl. agent intelligence divsn. IRS, US Dept. Treasury, Washington, 1963—70, chief counsel, 1970-87; judge US Tax Ct., Washington, 1987—2002, sr. judge, 2002—. Office: US Tax Ct 400 2nd St NW Washington DC 20217-0002

RUXIN, PAUL THEODORE, lawyer; b. Cleve., Apr. 14, 1943; s. Charles and Olyn Judith (Koller) R.; m. Joanne Camy, May 25, 1965; children; Marc J., Sarah. BA, Amherst Coll., 1965; LLB, U. Va., 1968. Bar: Ill. 1968, U.S. Dist. Ct. (no. dist.) Ill. 1968, U.S. Ct. Appeals D.C. 1972. Assoc. Isham, Lincoln & Beale, Chgo., 1968—73, ptnr., 1974—77; ptnr., chmn. energy utilities sect. Jones Day, Cleve., 1977—2005, of counsel, 2006—. Mem. editl. com. Yale U. edit. Boswell Papers, 2003—. Mem. Hudson Archtl. and Hist. Bd. Rev., 1981-81; chmn. bd. govs. Folger Shakespeare Libr., 2007—; exec. bd. Greater Cleve. Boy Scouts Am., 1978-90; bd. dirs. Cleve. chpt. ARC, 1991-97. Recipient Eminent Svc. medal, Amherst Coll., 2007. Mem. ABA, Chgo. Bar Assn., Rowfant Club, Chgo. Club, Caxton Club, Grolier Club, Chgo. Lit. Club. Office: Jones Day 77 W Wacker Dr Fl 35 Chicago IL 60601-1662 also: 901 Lakeside Ave Cleveland OH 44114-1116 Home Phone: 312-915-0533; Office Phone: 312-782-3939. E-mail: paultruxin@jonesday.com.

RUYLE-HULLINGER, ELIZABETH SMITH (BETH RUYLE), municipal financial advisor, consultant; b. Oct. 26, 1946; d. Daniel Lester and Mae (Coley) Smith; m. Craig Harlan Hullinger, Oct. 24, 1985; children: Leigh Ann Ruyle, Clint (dec.), Bret AA, St. Petersburg Jr. Coll., Fla., 1966; BA English, U. Fla., Gainesville, 1968; MPA, U. Ga., Athens, 1975. Rsch. asst. Emory U., Atlanta, 1969—70; health planner Met. Coun. for Health, Atlanta, 1960—72; coord. govtl. rels. Atlanta Regional Commn., 1972—76, coord. govtl. affairs, 1976—78; exec. dir. South Suburban Mayors' and Mgrs. Assn., East Hazel Crest, Ill., 1978—2000; pres. Chgo. Southland Econ. Devel. Alliance, 1999—2000; exec. v.p., dir. Ehlers & Assocs., Lisle, Ill., 2000—. Exec. dir. South Towns Agy. Risk Mgmt., 1980-98, South Towns Area Benefits Coop., 1983-89, South Towns Bus. Growth Corp., 1983-90; cons. Planning Devel. Svc., Tinley Park, Ill., 1986— Contbr. articles to profl. and devel. mags Mem. World's Fair Adv. Com., Chgo., 1986, Met. Planning Coun., 1990-2000, Cook County Tax Reform adv. coun., South Suburban Arts Coun., 1987, Coun. Urban Econ. Devel., 1986; adv. coun. Urban Innovations, Chgo., 1995-2000, Chgo. Assembly Project, 1995-2000; mem. Regional Partnership, 1985-2000; bd. dirs. South Suburban Hosp., 1987-96, mem. governing coun., 1999-2006; bd. dirs. Fin. Cmty. Devel. Corp., 1998-2000. Mem. Internat. City Mgmt. Assn., Ill. City Mgmt. Assn., Met. City Mgrs. Assn., Ill. Govtl. Fin. Officers Assn., Ill. Tax Increment Assn., Lambda Alpha Methodist. Office: Ehlers & Assocs 550 Warrenville Rd Ste 220 Lisle IL 60532-5500 Office Phone: 630-271-3330, 630-271-3332. Business E-Mail: bruyle@ehlers-inc.com.

RUYTER, NANCY LEE CHALFA, dance educator; b. Phila., May 23, 1933; d. Andrew Benedict Chalfa and Lois Elizabeth (Strode) McClary; m. Ralph Markson (div.); m. Hans C. Ruyter, Dec. 7, 1968 (dec. Jan. 1998). BA in History, U. Calif., Riverside, 1964; PhD in History, Claremont Grad. Sch., 1970. Tchr. theater dept. Pomona Coll., 1965-72; instr. dance program U. Calif., Riverside, 1972-76, acting chair dance program, 1974-75; instr. dance dept. UCLA, 1976; instr. phys. edn. dept. Orange Coast Coll., 1976-77; asst. prof. dept. phys. edn. and dance Tufts U., 1977-78; asst. prof. phys. edn. dept. Calif. State U., Northridge, 1978-82; from asst. prof. to full prof. dance dept. U. Calif., Irvine, 1982—, assoc. dean Sch. Fine Arts, 1984-88, 95-96, chair dept. dance, 1989-91. Presenter in field. Appeared with Jasna Planina Folk Ensemble, 1972-77, 78-79, Di Falco and Co., 1955-57; choreographer, dir. numerous coll. dance prodns.; contbr. articles, revs. to profl. publs.; author: Reformers and Visionaries: The Americanization of the Art of Dance, 1979, The Cultivation of Body and Mind in Nineteenth-Century American Delsartism, 1999. Mem. Am. Soc. Theatre Rsch., Bulgarian Studies Assn., Congress on Rsch. in Dance (bd. dirs. 1977-80, 2003-, pres. 1981-85), Folk Dance Fedn., Internat. Fedn. Theatre Rsch., Soc. Dance Rsch., Soc. Ethnomusicology, Soc. Dance History Scholars (steering com. 1980-81), Spanish Dance Soc., Theatre Libr. Assn. Office: U Calif Dept Dance Irvine CA 92697-2775 Office Phone: 949-824-7284. Business E-Mail: nlruyter@uci.edu.

RUZAIRI, ABDUL RAHIM, engineer, educator, director; b. Sungai Petani, Kedah, Malaysia, Jan. 31, 1967; s. Abdul Rahim Lajat and Che Tom Puteh; m. Hafidzah Othman, Oct. 30, 1992; children: Khairulhafiy Muhammad, Raudhatunnadzifah, Raudhatunadiah, Raudhatusyahirah, Raudhatusoufwah. B in Electronic Sys. and Control Engring. with honors, Sheffield City Poly., UK, 1992; PhD in Electronic Instrumentation, Sheffield Halam U., UK, 1996. Dept. head elec. engring. U. Tech. Malaysia, Skudai, Johor, 1998—2006, dep. dean Rsch. Mgmt. Ctr., 2006—. Mem. various coms. U. Tech. Malaysia; electronic engr. Advanced Cutting Sys. Ltd, 1990—91; test engr. Sgs Thomson Microelectronics, Muar, Malaysia, 1991. Author: (books) Sensors & Transducers (Best Book award U. Tech. Malaysia, 2002), Introduction to Control System; contbr. articles to profl. jours. Named an Excellece Scientist, Ministry Higher Edn., 2005; recipient Best paper in Nat. Jour. Category, Publications Day held by Universiti Teknologi Malaysia, 1997. Paper title Optical fibre sensors for process, Universiti Teknologi Malaysia, 1998, Excellence Job Performance award, U. Tech. Malaysia, 1998, Excellence Job Performance of the Yr. 99 awards by Universiti Teknologi Malaysia, Universiti Teknologi Malaysia, 1999, Consolation Prizes - Indsl. Art & Tech. Exhbn. (INATEX '01) at Universiti Teknologi Malaysia, Universiti Teknologi malaysia, 2001, Gold medal, Ministry Sci., Tech. & Environment, Malaysia, 2002, 31st Internat. Exhbn. Invention, New Techniques and Products, Geneva, Switzerland, 2003, 33rd Internat. Exhbn. Invention, New Techniques and Products, Geneva, Switzerland, 2005, Spl. Jury award, 2005; grantee, U. Tech. Malaysia, 1997—2004, Opto Sensors, 1997-1998, Malaysian Govt., 1999—. Mem.: IEEE (assoc.), Inst. Elec. Engrs. UK (assoc.), Instrumentation and Control Soc. Malaysia (sr.). Office: U Tech Malaysia Rsch Mgmt Ctr Skudai 81310 Malaysia Home Fax: 44 7 5566177. Business E-Mail: ruzairi@fke.utm.my.

RUZICKA, ALEXANDER MARION, geologist, educator; b. Owatonna, Minn., Aug. 20, 1960; s. Rudolph and Maria Ruzicka; m. Melinda Lee Hutson, 1986; children: Christopher Ryan, Catherine Marie. BS in Geology, U. Minn., Mpls., 1982, BS in Geophysics, 1982; MS in Earth and Space Scis., SUNY, Stony Brook, 1985; PhD in Planetary Scis., U. Ariz., Tucson, 1996. Postdoctoral rsch. assoc. U. Tenn., Knoxville, 1996—99; instr. Portland CC, Oreg., 1998—2002; asst. prof. Portland State U., 2000—. Dir. Cascadia Meteorite Lab., Portland, 2001—. Bd. editors Astrobiology jour., Portland, 2001—07. Recipient Gerard P. Kuiper Meml. award, Dept. Planetary Scis., U. Ariz., 1996; grantee, NASA, 2003—. Mem.: Sigma Xi (bd. dirs. Columbia-Willamette chpt. 2001—). Avocations: photography, hiking. Office: Portland State U 1721 SW Broadway 17 Cramer Hall Portland OR 97207-0751 Office Phone: 503-725-3372. Office Fax: 503-725-3025. E-mail: ruzickaa@pdx.edu.

RYALL, JO-ELLYN M., psychiatrist; b. Newark, May 25, 1949; d. Joseph P. and Tekla (Paraszczuk) R. BA in Chemistry with gen. honors, Rutgers U., 1971; MD, Washington U., St. Louis, 1975. Diplomate Am. Bd. Psychiatry and Neurology. Resident in psychiatry Washington U., St. Louis, 1975-78, psychiatrist Student Health, 1978-83, asst. prof. clin. psychiatry, 1983—2003, assoc. prof. clin. psychiatry, 2003—. Inpatient supr. Malcolm Bliss Mental Health Ctr., St. Louis, 1978-80, pvt. practtice medicine specializing in psychiatry, St. Louis, 1980—. Bd. dirs. Women's Self Help Ctr., St. Louis, 1980. Fellow: APA (pres. ea. Mo. dist. br. 1983—85, sect. coun. AMA 1986—99, dep. rep. to assembly 1994—97, rep. 1997—2001, chair bylaws com. 2000—03, dep. rep. area 4 2001—06, rep. area 4 2006); mem.: AMA (alt. del. Mo. 1988—90, 1993—94, del. 1995—, mem. coun. on constn. bylaws 1998—2006, vice chair 2002—04, chair 2004—06), Manic Depressive Assn. St. Louis (chmn. bd. dirs. 1985—89), Mo. State Med. Assn. (vice spkr. ho. of dels. 1986—89, spkr. 1989—92), St. Louis Met. Med. Soc. (del. to state conv. 1981—86, councilor 1985—87, v.p. 1989, del. to state conv. 1993—), Am. Med. Women's Assn. (pres. St. Louis dist. br. 1981—82, regional gov. VIII 1986—89, pres. St. Louis dist. br. 1992, spkr. ho. of dels. 1993—96), Washington U. Faculty Club. Office: 12166 Old Big Bend Rd Ste 210 Saint Louis MO 63122 Office Phone: 314-909-0121.

RYAN, ALLAN ANDREW, JR., lawyer, director, educator, writer; b. Cambridge, Mass., July 3, 1945; s. Allan Andrew and Anne (Conway) Ryan; m. Nancy Foote, June 30, 1978; children: Elisabeth, Andrew. AB, Dartmouth Coll., 1966; JD magna cum laude, U. Minn., 1970. Bar: DC 1972, Mass. 1985. Law clk. to assoc. justice Byron R. White U.S. Supreme Ct., 1970-71; assoc. Williams, Connolly & Califano, Washington, 1974-77; asst. to Solicitor Gen. U.S., Washington, 1977-80; dir. office of spl. investigations, Dept. Justice, Washington, 1980-83, spl. asst. to atty. gen., 1983; pvt. practice law, 1983-85; with office of gen. counsel, Harvard U., 1985—2001, dir. intellectual property bus. sch., 2001—. Presenting counsel Internat. Commn. Inquiry on Kurt Waldheim, London, 1988; adj. prof. law sch. Boston Coll., 1990—; adj. prof. divsn. continuing edn. Harvard U., 1997—. Author: Quiet Neighbors: Prosecuting Nazi War Criminals in America, 1984; pres., editor-in-chief: Minn. Law Rev., 1969—70. Mem. exec. com. New Eng. region Anti-Defamation League, 1990—, mem. nat. commn., 2004—; chair Ctr. Civil Rights and Pub. Policy, 2003—; bd. dirs. Facing History and Ourselves Nat. Found., 1985—92; mem. adv. bd. Holocaust and human rights rsch. project Boston Coll. Law Sch., 1984—. Capt. USMC, 1971—74. Recipient Internat. Human Rights award, Anti-Defamation League, 1986, Leadership award, 1997, 2005. Mem.: ABA, Boston Bar Assn. Office: Harvard Bus Sch Publ 60 Harvard Way Boston MA 02163 Home Phone: 781-659-1342; Office Phone: 617-783-7849. Business E-Mail: allan_ryan@harvard.edu.

RYAN, ANTHONY WILLIAM, federal agency administrator; b. 1963; m. Ann Ryan; 4 children. Grad., U. Rochester, 1985; master's degree, London Sch. Econ. and Polit. Sci., 1986. Portfolio mgr. various firms including State Street Corp., The Boston Co.; ptnr. Grantham, Mayo, van Otterloo & Co., LLC; sr. adv. to sec. US Dept. Treasury, Washington, sr. mem. treas. fin. group, asst. sec. for fin. markets, 2006—. Office: US Dept Treasury 1500 Pennsylvania Ave NW Washington DC 20220 *

RYAN, ANTONY L., lawyer; b. July 21, 1971; BA summa cum laude, Yale Univ., 1992; JD magna cum laude, Harvard Univ., 1995. Bar: Mass. 1995, NY 1997. Law clk., Hon. Judith W. Rogers US Ct. of Appeals, DC Cir.; assoc. Cravath Swaine & Moore LLP, NYC, 1996—2003, ptnr., litig., 2003—. Supervising editor Harvard Law Rev. Mem.: Fed. Bar Coun. Am. Inn of Ct., Phi Beta Kappa. Office: Cravath Swaine & Moore LLP Worldwide Plz 825 Eighth Ave New York NY 10019-7475 Office Phone: 212-474-1296. Office Fax: 212-474-3700. Business E-Mail: aryan@cravath.com.

RYAN, ARTHUR FREDERICK, diversified financial services company executive; b. Bklyn., Sept. 14, 1942; s. Arthur Vincent and Gertrude (Wingert) R.; m. Patricia Elizabeth Kelly; children: Arthur, Kelly Ann, Kevin, Kathleen. BA in Math., Providence Coll., 1963, D (hon.) of bus. adminstrn., 1994; student, Am. Coll., 1963—65; LHD (hon.), Dowling Coll.; DSc, NJ Inst. Tech., 2005. Area mgr. Control Data Corp., Washington, 1965-72; project mgr. data processing divsn. Chase Manhattan Corp., NYC, 1972-73, 2d v.p., 1973-74, v.p., 1974—77, sr. v.p., 1977—82, ops. exec., 1978-82, exec. v.p. corp. ops. and systems, 1982—84, exec. v.p. individual banking, 1984, head worldwide retail bank, 1984—90, vice chmn., 1985—90, pres., COO, 1990—94; pres., CEO, chmn. Prudential Ins. Co. Am., Newark, 1994—99; (Prudential Ins. Co. Am. incorporated to become Prudential Fin., Inc., 1999); dir. Prudential Fin., Inc., Newark, 1999—, pres., CEO, chmn., 2000—. Bd. dirs. Regeneron Pharmaceuticals, 2003—. Bd. trustees Providence Coll., 1992—, NY Presbyn. Hosp.; nat. bd. Local Initiatives Support Coalition; bd. dirs. New Am. Schools; co-chair Achieve, Inc., NJ United for Higher Sch. Standards, NJ Performing Arts Ctr. Lt. US Army, 1963—65. Co-recipient (with wife) Pelican award for Corp. and Cmty. Leadership, St. Vincent's Acad., 2001, (with wife) Inaugural Cmty. Leadership award, NJ Performing Arts Ctr. Women's Bd. Assn., 2002; recipient Nat. Alumni Personal Achievement Award, Providence Coll., 75th Anniversary Alumni Services Award, Diamond Anniversary Award, Keeper of the Dream award, Nat. Action Network, 2000, Patterson award, United Negro Coll. Fund/The Coll. Fund, 2000, Pub. Svc. award, NJ State CofC, 2001, Medal of Life award, PIUS XII Found., 2001, Cir. of Life Award, Million Dollar Round Table Found., 2002. Mem.: Am. Bankers Assn. Office: Prudential Fin Inc Prudential Plaza 24th Fl 751 Broad St Newark NJ 07102-3714 *

RYAN, BO (WILLIAM F. RYAN JR.), men's college basketball coach; b. Chester, Pa., Dec. 20, 1947; s. Butch Ryan; m. Kelly Ryan; children: Megan, Will, Matt, Brenna, Mairin. BBA, Wilkes U., Pa., 1969; grad. student, Villanova U. Asst. coach Coll. Racine, Wis.; head coach Sun Valley HS, Phila.; asst. coach U. Wis., Madison, 1976—84, head coach, 2001—, Platteville, 1984—99, Milw., 1999—2001. Mem. Divsn. I Men's Basketball Issues Com. NCAA. Author: Passing and Catching: A Lost Art, How to Run the Swing Offense, Applying and Attacking Pressure. Named Delaware County Coach of Yr., Coach of Yr. (6 times), Wis. Intercollegiate Athletic Conf., Divsn. III Coach of Yr. (4 times), Nat. Assn. Basketball Coaches, Big Ten Coach of Yr., 2002, 2003; named to Wilkes Athletic Hall of Fame, 2003; recipient Guardians of the Game award for Svc., Nat. Assn. Basketball Coaches, 2004. Office: U Wis Men's Basketball Kohl Ctr 601 W Dayton St Madison WI 53715 Office Phone: 608-262-4597. E-mail: bfr@athletics.wisc.edu. *

RYAN, CANDACE L., writer, director, editor; d. Lilburn Terry and Maureen Adell Ryan; children: Elizabeth Maureen Solomon, Virginia Violet Hildenbrand. AA in human rels., Bridgeport U., 1976—79; BBA in journalism, Rice U., 1965—68. Human Relations-Death & Life. Abused Woman & Children of CT, 1978. Adv. bd. Barrington Rev. of the Arts, Westport, Conn., 1976—85; councilor Inner Cities Volunteers of CT., Stamford, Conn., 1976—89; asst dir. & advisor CT. Commn. on the Arts, Westport, Conn., 1977—89. Roving writer Family & Moral Issues, Sacremento, Calif., 1993—. Author: Detecting! The Midnight Tattler, over 20 novels, 14 short stories. Travel industry rep. State Dept. Amb. of Peace, India, Africa, China, numerous countries, Madagascar, 1978—89; sec. World Wildlife Found., San Diego, 1990—93; asst. advisor Women & Children Outreach Org., Sacramento, 1991—2003; asst. editor Wolferts Retreat Ctr. for the Arts, Stamford, Conn., 1980—90. Recipient Journalism Excellence, Fairfield U., 1982, 6 Poetry awards, 1976—2004; Louis Webber grant, Century Acceptance Assoc., 1990—92. Fellow: Mystery Writers Assoc. (corr.; sr. writer 2000); mem.: Beta Corp. Agy. Consortium (v.p. 1981—91), US Travel Industry (rep. China 1984, Israel 1985, France 1986), Quota Club Internat. (sec. 1984—88), Eagles Club of Am. (corr.; mem. 2000, Volunteers above and Beyond the Call of Duty 2001). Republican. Bapt. Achievements include research in Human Relations-Death & Survivors. Avocations: writing, reading, camping, travel. Home: 1419 Eckman Ave Chula Vista CA 91911 Office: Ghost & Creative Writers Co 1419 Eckman Ave Chula Vista CA 91911

RYAN, CLARENCE AUGUSTINE, JR., biochemistry professor; b. Butte, Mont., Sept. 29, 1931; s. Clarence A. Sr. and Agnes L. (Duckham) R.; m. Patricia Louise Meunier, Feb. 8, 1936; children: Jamie Arlette, Steven Michael (dec.), Janice Marie, Joseph Patrick (dec.). BA in Chemistry, Carroll Coll., 1953; MS in Chemistry, Mont. State U., 1956, PhD in Chemistry, 1959; PhD (hon.), Wash. State U., 2005, Carroll Coll., Helena, Mont., 2007. Postdoctoral fellow in biochemistry Oreg. State U., Corvallis, 1959-61, U.S. Western Regional Lab., Albany, Calif., 1961-63; chemist USDA, Albany, 1963-64; asst. prof. biochemistry Wash. State U., Pullman, 1964-68, assoc. prof., 1968-72, prof., 1972—, Charlotte Y. Martin disting. prof., 1991—, chmn. dept. agrl. chemistry, 1977-80, fellow Inst. Biol. Chemistry, 1980—. Faculty athletics rep. to PAC-10 & NCAA Wash. State U., 1991-94, 96-97; vis. scientist dept. biochemistry U. Wash., 1981; vis. scientist Harvard U. Med. Sch., 1982, Bert and Natalie Vallee vis. prof., 1997; res. adv. bd. Kemin Industries, Des Moines, 1981—, Plant Genetics, Davis, Calif., 1987-89; rsch. adv. bd. Frito-Lay, Inc., Dallas, 1982, Plant Genetic Engring. Lab., N.Mex. State U., Las Cruces, 1986-89, Noble Found., 1996-02; mem. NRC rev. bd. Plant Gene Exptl. Ctr., Albany, 1990-93; mgr. biol. stress program USDA Competitive Grants Program, Washington, 1983-84; former mem. adv. panels for H. McKnight Found., Internat. Potato Ctr., Lima, Peru, Internat. Ctr. Genetic Engring. and Biotech., New Delhi, Internat. Ctr. Tropical Agr., Cali, Colombia, Internat. Tropical Agr., Ibandan, Africa; mem. grant rev. panels NSF, USDA, DOE, NIH; co-organizer Internat. Telecom. Symposium on Plant Biotech.; mem. adv. bd. Bert and Natalie Vallee Found., Harvard Med. Sch., 1997—; bd. dirs. New Biology, San Francisco, 2006-. Mem. editl. bd. several biochem. and plant physiology jours.; contbr. articles to profl. publs., chpts. to books; co-editor 2 books. Trustee Carroll Coll., Helena, Mont., 1998-2002; mem. rsch. adv. bd. Danforth Plant Sci. Ctr., St. Louis, 1998-2005. Grantee USDA, NSF, NIH, Rockefeller Found., McKnight Found.; recipient Merck award for grad. rsch. Mont. State U., 1959, Alumni Achievement award Carroll Coll., 1986, Pres.'s Faculty Excellence award in rsch. Wash. State U., 1986; named to Carroll Coll. Alumni Hall of Fame, 1981, Carroll Coll. Basketball Hall of Fame, 1982; named 1 of 100 centennial disting. alumni Mont. State. U., 1993; Career Devel. grantee NIH, 1964-74, non-resident fellow Noble Found., 1996-2002. Fellow Am. Acad. Microbiology, Am. Soc. Plant Biol.; mem. AAAS, NAS (elected 1986), Am. Chem. Soc. (Kenneth A. Spencer award 1992), Am. Soc. Plant Physiologists (Steven Hales prize 1992), Am. Soc. Exptl. Biology, Biochem. Soc., Am. Peptide Soc., Internat. Soc. Chem. Ecology (Silverstein-Simione award 1997), Internat. Soc. Plant Molecular Biology (bd. dirs.), Phytochem. Soc. N.Am., Nat. U. Continuing Assn. (Creative Programming award 1991), Phi Kappa Phi (Recognition award 1976). Democrat. Avocations: fishing, golf, ice skating. Office: Wash State Univ Inst Biol Chemistry Pullman WA 99164-0001 Office Phone: 509-335-3304. Personal E-mail: cabudryan@hotmail.com.

RYAN, DANIEL JOHN, university administrator; b. Buffalo, June 5, 1960; s. Michael E. and Joan F. R.; m. Sandra Suffoleto, Aug. 19, 1989. BA in Pol. Sci., Canisius Coll., Buffalo, 1982, MS in Edn., 1992; PhD in Edn., SUNY, Buffalo, 1997. Fin. cons. First Albany Corp., Buffalo, 1982-84; confidential investigator County of Erie, Buffalo, 1984-87; econ. mkt. analyst City of Buffalo, Buffalo, 1987-90; asst. dir. career planning Canisius Coll., Buffalo, 1990-97, asst. dean students svcs., 1997—; dir. career planning and placement SUNY, Buffalo. Lectr. Buffalo and Erie County Pub. Libr., Buffalo, 1990—; dir. career planning and placement SUNY Buffalo. Author: A Job Search Handbook for People with Disabilities. Pres. Univ. Dist. N. Buffalo Civic Assn., Buffalo, 1990-91; v.p. Kiwanis Club of N. Buffalo, 1987-88; vice chmn. City of Buffalo rep. Com., 1989-91, sec. 1993-95; chmn. Delaware Ward Rep. Com., 1985-91. Recipient Edward A. Parish award, Ea. Assn. Colls. and Employers. Mem. Nat. Assn. Student Personnel Admininstrn.(region II Outstanding New Profl.), N. Buffalo Community Devel. Corp., Assn. for Higher Edn. and Disabilities. Republican. Avocations: reading, raquetball. E-mail: dryan@buffalo.edu.

RYAN, DAVID ALAN, systems analyst; b. Cin., Nov. 13, 1961; s. James Patrick and Virginia Ann (Stewart) R. BS, Wright State U., 1983; MS, Tex. A&M U., 1988. Statistician U.S. Bur. of Census, Washington, 1988-92, computer specialist, 1992—. Vol. math. modeling Soil Conservation Svc., Washington, 1991-96; math. and. probability vol. Washington Opera, 1992—; data entry/programming vol. Opera Am., Washington, 1990-91; hist. rschr. Gasby's Tavern Mus., Alexandria, Va., 1991-94; mem. Bravo! for the Washington Opera, 1991-95. Recipient Vol. Svc. award Soil Conservation Svc., 1992, 93. Mem. Am. Statis. Assn., Capitol PC Users Group, Ballston-Va. Square Civic Assn. (exec. com. 1995—, sec. 1996—, NCAC rep. 1997-98), The Washington Opera Guild, The Washington Opera Camerata, The DC Wagner Soc., Opera Guild of No. Va. (bd. 2006-). Achievements include building a supercomputer at home in 2000. Avocations: classical music, ethnomusicology, history, geography, travel. Office: Bur of Census/CES Ste 208 Washington Plz II Washington DC 20233-6300

RYAN, DAVID THOMAS, lawyer; b. Torrington, Conn., Apr. 18, 1939; s. Edward John and Margaret (Murphy) R.; m. Dale Anderson, Aug. 21, 1965; children: Rachael Anderson, Conor Anne. BS, U. Md., 1961; LLB, Georgetown U., 1965. Bar: Conn. 1966, U.S. Dist. Ct. Conn. 1967, U.S. Ct. Appeals (2d cir.) 1969, U.S. Ct. Appeals (fed. cir.) 1982, U.S. Claims Ct. 1983, U.S. Supreme Ct. 1992. Ptnr. Cooney, Scully & Dowling, Hartford,

Conn., 1966-77, Robinson & Cole, Hartford, 1977—. Fellow Am. Coll. Trial Lawyers; mem. Am. Bd. Trial Advs., Conn. Trial Lawyers Assn. (bd. dirs., mem. Gov.'s commn. on jud. reform). Home: 126 Westerly Ter Hartford CT 06105-1117 Office: Robinson & Cole 280 Trumbull St Ste 26 Hartford CT 06103-3509 Office Phone: 203-275-8200. E-mail: dryan@rc.com.

RYAN, DEBBIE (DEBORAH A. RYAN), women's college basketball coach; BPE, Ursinus Coll., Collegeville, Pa., 1975; MPE, U. Va., Charlottesville, 1977. Asst. basketball and field hockey coach U. Va., 1975-77, head women's basketball coach, 1977—. Lectr. in field; adv. coach Nike; head coach US Jr. Nat. Team, 1988, Jr. World Championship Team, 1989, USA Basketball Sr. Nat. Women's Team, 2001, 03; mem. USA Basketball Women's Games Com. for 1989-92 quadrennium; dir. West team US Olympic festival, Chapel Hill, NC, 1987 (gold medal). Author: Virginia Defense, Virginia Summer Development Program, Women's Basketball Drills-Conditioning. Named Va. Assn. Intercollegiate Athletics for Women Coach of Yr., 1981, Converse Dist. III Coach of Yr., 1986, 87, Nat. Coach of Yr., Shreveport Jour., 1986, Outstanding Woman of Yr. Va. Women's Forum, 1991, Naismith Coach of Yr., Atlanta Tipoff club, 1991, Devel. Coach of Yr., USA Basketball, 2001; recipient Atlantic Coast Conf. Coach of Yr. award, 1984, 86, 87, 91, 93, 95, 2000, Women's Basketball Coaches Assn. Victory Club award, 2005; named to Women's Basketball Hall of Fame, 2007. Avocations: fishing, golf. Office: U Va University Hall PO Box 400827 Charlottesville VA 22904-4827 Office Phone: 434-982-5800. Office Fax: 434-982-5822. E-mail: dar2h@d.mail.virginia.edu. *

RYAN, DENNIS M., lawyer, construction executive; BA, U. Mass., Amherst; JD cum laude, New England Sch. Law. Asst. atty. gen. Commonwealth of Mass.; ptnr. Hinckley, Allen and Snyder, Boston; corp. counsel Perini Corp., Framingham, Mass., 1998—99, v.p., gen. counsel, 1999—. Mem.: Mass. Bar Assn. (former chmn. Construction and Pub. Contract Com.). Office: Perini Corp 73 Mt Wayte Ave Framingham MA 01701

RYAN, DENNIS NEIL, lawyer; b. Enid, Okla., Oct. 10, 1945; BA, Iowa State U., 1967; JD, So. Meth. U., 1974. Bar: Tex. 1974, admitted to practice: US Supreme Ct., US Ct. Appeals (5th Cir.), US Dist. Ct. (No. Dist.) Tex., US Dist. Ct. (Ea. Dist.) Tex. Law clk. to Hon. William M. Taylor Jr. US Dist. Ct. (No. Dist.) Tex., 1974-76; atty. Jackson & Walker LLP, Dallas; ptnr., Litig. Andrews Kurth LLP, Dallas, mem. mgmt. com. Capt. USAF, 1968—71. Mem.: Dallas Bar Assn., Tex. Assn. Def. Counsel, State Bar Tex., ABA (Litig. Sect., Bus. Law Sect.). Office: Andrews Kurth LLP 1717 Main St Ste 3700 Dallas TX 75201 Office Phone: 214-659-4428. Office Fax: 214-659-4791. Business E-Mail: dryan@andrewskurth.com.

RYAN, EDWARD A., lawyer, hotel executive; b. Newark, Oct. 24, 1953; AB summa cum laude, Univ. Pa., 1975, JD cum laude, 1978. Bar: DC 1978, Md. 1985. Atty. Crowell & Moring, Washington, 1978—84, Hogan & Hartson, 1984—89, ptnr., 1989—96; corp. atty. Marriott Internat., Washington, 1996—2006, exec. v.p., gen. counsel, 2006—. Editor (assoc.): Univ. Pa. Law Review. Mem.: ABA, Md. State Bar Assn., D.C. Bar, Phi Beta Kappa. Office: Marriott Internat 1 Marriott Dr Washington DC 20058-0001 *

RYAN, EDWARD F., lawyer; b. Chgo., Sept. 14, 1943; BA magna cum laude, U. St. Thomas, 1965; JD, Georgetown U. Law Ctr., 1968. Bar: Ill. 1968, Fla. 1984, US Dist. Ct. (No. Dist. Ill.), US Ct. Appeals (7th, 8th, 11th cirs.), US Supreme Ct. Ptnr. Holland & Knight LLP, Chgo., mem. dir. com. Lectr. in the field. Fellow: Am. Bar Found.; mem.: Fla. Bar, ABA, Chgo. Bar Assn. Office: Holland & Knight LLP 131 S Dearborn St 30th Fl Chicago IL 60603 Office Phone: 312-578-6552. Business E-Mail: edward.ryan@hklaw.com.

RYAN, EDWARD W., economics professor; b. Plainfield, NJ, Aug. 23, 1932; s. Edward A. and Helen R. (Shannon) R.; m. Georgian Hurley, Dec. 17, 1966; children: Sarah, Jennifer. BS, U. Pa., 1955; MA, Duke U., 1957; LHD (hon.), Manhattanville Coll., 2003. Lectr. Fordham U., NYC, 1956-57; instr. Iona Coll., New Rochelle, NY, 1958-60; Ryan-Bacardi prof. econs. Manhattanville Coll., Purchase, NY, 1958—, Doc. of Humane Letters (L.H.D.), 2003. Dir. Econ. Freedom Inst. Author: In the Words of Adam Smith: The First Consumer Advocate, 1990, Liberty, Virtue and Happiness: The Story of Economic Freedom in America, 2000. Mem.: Econ. History Assn., Assn. Pvt. Enterprise Edn., Am. Econ. Assn. Roman Catholic. Home: 25 Jefferson Rd Scarsdale NY 10583-6411 Office: Manhattanville College 2900 Purchase St Purchase NY 10577-2132 E-mail: edwryan1@aol.com.

RYAN, ELLEN BOUCHARD, psychology professor, gerontologist; b. Holyoke, Mass., 1947; arrived in Can., 1982; d. Raoul Rosario and Etiennette Marie Bouchard; m. Patrick J. Ryan, July 12, 1969; children: Loraine Yvette, Dennis Patrick, Kevin Myles. BA, MA, Brown U., 1968; PhD, U. Mich., 1970. From asst. prof. psychology to prof. U. Notre Dame, 1970—82, chmn. dept., 1978-82; prof. psychiatry McMaster U., Hamilton, Ont., Canada, 1982—, dir. Ctr. for Gerontol. Studies, 1985-95, prof. gerontology, 1987—. Editor: Attitudes Toward Language Variation, 1982, Language Communication and The Elderly, 1986, Intergenerational Communication, 1994, Language Attitudes, 1994, Communication, Aging and Health, 1996. Grantee NICHD, 1972-75, NSF, 1976-79, Nat. Inst. Edn., 1979-82, Natural Scis. and Engring. Rsch., 1983-89, Gerontol. Rsch. Coun. of Ont., 1983-85, Ont. Ministry Health, 1986-89, Soc. Sci. and Humanities Rsch. Coun., 1986—. Fellow APA, Gerontol. Soc. Am., Can. Psychol. Assn.; mem. Internat. Assn. of Lang. and Social Psychology, Can. Assn. Gerontology. Roman Catholic. Home: 71 Sulphur Springs Rd # 14 Ancaster ON Canada L9G 5C1 Office: McMaster U Dept Psychiatry 1200 Main St W Hamilton ON Canada L8N 3Z5 Office Phone: 905-525-9140 ext. 24449. Business E-Mail: ryaneb@mcmaster.ca.

RYAN, FRANK HARRY, plastic surgeon; b. May 21, 1960; BS, U. Mich., Ann Arbor, 1982; MD, Ohio State U. Coll. Medicine, Columbus, 1986. Surgical residency Cedars-Sinai Med. Ctr., U. Mo. & UCLA Med. Ctr., 1986—94; plastic surgeon priv. practice, Beverly Hills, 1994—. Mem. adv. bd. A. Craig Matthias Found. Founder Bony Pony Ranch Found., Malibu. Avocations: boating, fishing, golf, skiing, tennis. Office: 9675 Brighton Wy Ste 340 Beverly Hills CA 90210 also: Bony Pony Ranch Found 9663 Santa Monica Blvd Ste 785 Beverly Hills CA 90210 Office Phone: 310-275-1075. Personal E-mail: drryand@drfrankryan.com.

RYAN, GEORGE WILLIAM, manufacturing executive; b. Sinking Springs, Ohio, Oct. 13, 1939; s. Winson Mark and Mary Edith (Smalley) R.; 1 child: Gina Kristin. Student, Wilmington Coll., Ohio, 1962. Process engr. B.F. Goodrich Co., Marietta, Ohio, 1962-66; product dev. mgr. Chrysler Corp., Sandusky, Ohio, 1966-70; asst. tech. mgr. Inmont Corp., Toledo, 1970-72; tech. mgr. Occidental Petroleum, Burlington, NJ, 1973; owner Ryan Devel. Corp., Peebles, 1973-88; prin. Ironwood Valley Ranch, Ohio, 1986—. Substitute tchr. Adams County Sch. Dist.; cons. Hooker Chem. Corp., Burlington, NJ, 1973; expert Internat. Exec. Svc. Core. Bd. dirs., pres. Missionary Evang. Ch. of Christ; active Adams County Workforce Commn.; mem. Rep. Inner Cir. Mem. Soc. Plastic Engrs., Peebles Ind. Inc. (sec., treas., bd. dirs., 1984-88), Lions Club. Republican. Office Phone: 937-587-2266. Personal E-mail: rydevryan@aol.com.

RYAN, GRETCHEN MARGARETE FRIEDA, art educator; b. Niederschona, Saxony, Germany, Nov. 2, 1929; arrived in U.S., 1952; d. Paul Robert Lutzner and Frieda Gertrud Lutzner-Kupsch; m. Raymond Andrew Ryan, May 12, 1952; children: Michael D., Ralph T., Robert P., Ronald J., Rex W., Renee G. Student, Berlin Art Acad., 1970; AA, Am. River Coll., Sacramento, 1975. Instr. art McClellan AFB, Sacramento, 1967—68, Am. Women's Club, Berlin, 1969—72, Edwards AFB, Calif., 1972—74, Am. River Coll., Sacramento, 1975—2005, Gretchen's Studio, Carmichael, Calif., 1986—. Tchr. art San Juan Sch. Dist., Sacramento, 1975—95; instr. art City of Sacramento, 1980—2006. California's Gold, 2000, Ancient Book of Future, 2002, Decorating 2 Life size Elk, Elk Grove, Calif., 2002, Decorating 1 Life size Lion, Sacramento, 2004. Recipient Restoring Meml. Auditorium resolution, Sacramento City Coun., Recognition award, Shriners Children's Hosp. Sacramento, Purchase award, USAF, 1976, award, Berlin Air Force, 1971, Cmty. Svc. award, Comdr. Air Force Berlin, 1972. Mem.: Sacramento Fine Arts Ctr., Valley Sculpture Artists (bd. dirs., v.p. 1998—), No. Calif. Arts Assn. (bd. dirs.). Avocations: crafts, exercise. Home and Studio: 6225 Luna Ln Carmichael CA 95608

RYAN, HALFORD ROSS, speech educator; b. Anderson, Ind., Dec. 29, 1943; AB, Wabash Coll., 1966; MA, U. Ill., 1968, PhD, 1972. Prof. Washington and Lee U., Lexington, Va., 1970—. Author: FDR's Rhetorical Presidency, 1988, Harry Emerson Fosdick, 1989, Henry Ward Beecher, 1990, Classical Communication for the Contemporary Communicator, 1992, Harry S. Truman, 1993; editor: Oratorial Encounters, 1988, Inaugural Addresses of Twentieth-Century American Presidents, 1993, U.S. Presidents as Orators, 1995; also articles. Recipient awards Eleanor Roosevelt Inst., 1979, Herbert Hoover Inst., 1986, Maurice Mednick Found., 1991; Rockefeller Theol. fellow, 1967. Mem. Speech Communication Assn. Office: Washington and Lee U Robinson Hall Lexington VA 24450 Home Phone: 540-463-2055; Office Phone: 540-458-8812.

RYAN, HEATHER VICKERS, marketing professional; b. Newton, Mass., Jan. 11, 1964; d. William Ward and Vivian Phillips Vickers; m. Joseph John Ryan, July 9, 1994; children: Ashley Vivian, Katherine Jeanne, Connor Vickers. BA in Internat. Rels., Mt. Holyoke Coll., 1986; MBA, MA, NYU, 1994. Cert. competitive intelligence profl. Fuld Acad. Competitive Intelligence. Trustee liaison Mus. of Sci., Boston, 1989—90; project mgr. NYU Film Sch., Mexico, 1991—91; mktg. spl. projects Tohoku Electric Power Co., Sendai, Japan, 1992—92; sr. bus. devel. mgr. Lotus Devel. Corp., Cambridge, Mass., 1994—98; sr. market and competitive analyst IBM, Armonk, NY, 1998—. World econ. forum summit attendee Lotus Devel. Corp., Cambridge, Mass., 1996—98. Fellow, Tohoku Electric Power Co., 1992. Mem.: Soc. Women Geographers (assoc.), White Mountain Ski Runners (life; bd. mem. 1995—98). Avocations: travel, sailing, skiing, horseback riding, archaeology. Home: 140 Miles River Rd South Hamilton MA 01982 Home Phone: 978-468-2283. Personal E-mail: heather_ryan@yahoo.com.

RYAN, J. BRENDAN, advertising executive; BA in History, Fordham U.; MBA, Wharton U. V.p. mktg. Citibank; product mgmt. Gen. Foods; head account mgmt. dept., bd. dirs. OMW, NYC; with Ogilvy & Mather; pres., CEO Foote Cone & Belding NY, 1991—96; CEO FCB Worldwide, NYC, 1996—2004, chmn., 1996—2006; now chmn. emeritus Draftfcb. Bd. dirs. FreshDirect, 2006—. Mem. Citizens Crime Commn., NYC; bd. dirs. Citymeals-On-Wheels, Regis H.S., exec. com. The Quills. Office: Draftfcb 633 N St Clair Chicago IL 60611 Office Phone: 212-885-3000. Office Fax: 212-885-2803. *

RYAN, J. BRENNAN, lawyer; b. Nashville, Apr. 15, 1969; BA in History, U. Fla., 1993, MBA, 1997, JD with honors, 1997. Bar: Ga. Ptnr. Nelson Mullins Riley & Scarborough LLP, Atlanta. With USN, 1985—97. Mem.: ABA, Atlanta Bar Assn. Office: Nelson Mullins Riley and Scarborough LLP Ste 1400 999 Peachtree St Atlanta GA 30309-3964 Fax: 404-817-6050.

RYAN, J. BRUCE, healthcare management consulting executive; b. Southbridge, Mass., Mar. 28, 1944; s. Charles J. and Doris (Olney) R.; m. Sarah E. Pattison, Aug. 16, 1993. BSBA in Fin., U. Mass., 1972, MSBA, 1975; MA in Econs., U. Wash., 1976. Regional v.p. Amherst Assocs. Inc., Atlanta, 1976—85; exec. v.p. Jennings Ryan & Kolb, Inc., Atlanta, 1985—2005; CFO Cross Country Cons., 2002—05; pres. JBR Cons. Inc., 2005—. Contbr. articles to profl. jours. With U.S. Army, 1968-70. Mem. Healthcare Fin. Mgmt. Assn. (Helen M. Yerger/L. Van Seawell best article award 1990), Fin. Mgmt. Assn. Avocation: sailing. Home: 1060 Kentucky Ave NE Atlanta GA 30306-3534

RYAN, J. RICHARD, lawyer; b. NYC, Oct. 23, 1929; s. Peter Leon and Mary Martha (Franklin) R.; m. Diana Louise Gambarelli, Nov. 6, 1954 (dec. Feb. 1988); children: Christopher, Claudia; m. Joan Frances Revelle, Jan. 21, 1995. BA, Georgetown U., 1951; JD, Fordham U., 1954. Bar: N.Y. 1956, U.S. Dist. Ct. (so. dist.) N.Y. 1957, U.S. Supreme Ct. 1987. Assoc. Engel, Judge, Miller, Sterling & Reddy, NYC, 1956-63, ptnr., 1963-66, Kantor, Shaw & Ryan, NYC, 1966-71, Ryan & Silberberg, NYC, 1971-84, Ryan & Fogerty, 1984-88, Ryan, Botway, Reddy & Mesrop, 1988-90; sole practitioner, 1990-99; ptnr. Ryan & Stanton LLP, NYC, 1999—. Bd. dirs. Am. Health Capital Ins. Co. Bd. dirs. Guiding Eyes for the Blind, Inc., pres., 1973-77; trustee Cooper Inst. for Advanced Studies in Medicine and Humanities; Copyright Soc. candidate for Mayor of Pelham, N.Y., 1963. Served with AUS, 1954-56. Mem. ABA, N.Y. State Bar Assn., Assn. Bar City N.Y. (sports law com. 2000—), Soc. Friendly Sons of St. Patrick, Pelham Country Club (past pres.), Union League, Winged Foot Golf Club. Office: 516 5th Ave Ste 805 New York NY 10036-7511 E-mail: lojrrlaw@aol.com.

RYAN, JAMES, insurance company executive; b. Pitts., Jan. 21, 1937; s. Martin Charles and Lucy Elizabeth (Misklow) r.; m. Marlene Sullivan Ryan, Jan. 27, 1973. BA, U. Pitts., U. Louisville. Cert. ins. wholesaler. Chmn. Market Finders Ins. Corp., Louisville, 1972—. Com. chmn. Am. Assn. Mng. Gen. Agts., 1988-89; pres. Ky. Lloyd's Agts. Assn., 1985—; bd. dirs. Nat. Assn. Profl. Surplus Lines Office, Inc., 1983-86; pres. Ky. Surplus Lines Assn., Louisville, 1988-89; mem. adv. coun. Essex Ins. Co., 1991-93, Am. Equity Ins. Co., Scottsdale, Ariz., 1999. Pub. in Best Rev., 1995. Mem. Ky. Thoroughbred Owners & Breeders, Inc., Hon. Order of Blue Goose Internat., Kosair Shrine Temple, Hon. Order of Ky. Col. Named Adv. Coun. Colony Ins. Co., Glen Allen, Va., 1991-93, Hamilton Ins. Co., 1993, Cardinal Ins. Co., 1991-93. Mem. Profl. Ins. Agts., Ind. Ins. Agts. Assn., Am. Assn. Mng. Gen. Agts. (cert., chmn. adv. com. 1991-92, bd. dirs. 1994-96, v.p. zone 2 1995-96, pres.-elect 1996-97, pres. 1997-98), Nat. Assn. Profl. Surplus Lines Offices (chmn. legis. com. 1988-89, Published Best Rev. 1995), Am. Assn. of Gen. Agts. Republican. Roman Catholic. Avocations: breeding and racing thoroughbred horses, golf. Office Phone: 502-423-1800. E-mail: jryan@mfic.com.

RYAN, JAMES JOSEPH, retired lawyer; b. Cin., June 17, 1929; s. Robert J. and Marian (Hoffman) R.; m. Mary A. Noonan, Nov. 25, 1954; children: Kevin, Timothy, Nora, Daniel. AB, Xavier U., 1951; JD, U. Cin., 1954. Bar: Ohio 1954. Tchr. assoc. Northwestern U., Chgo., 1954-55; ptnr. Dolle, O'Donnell & Cash, Cin., 1958-71, Taft, Stettinius & Hollister, Cin., 1971-99. Lectr. U. Cin. Coll. Law, 1960-65. Chmn. Health Planning Assn. Ohio River Valley, Cin., 1978-85; bd. dirs. Hamilton County Bd. of Mentally Retarded, 1968-80; trustee Resident Home for Mentally Retarded, 1980-97, St. Francis-St. George Hosp. Devel. Coun., 1989-99. Mem. ABA, Ohio Bar Assn., Cin. Bar Assn., Queen City Club, Western Hill Club. Republican. Roman Catholic. Avocations: reading, sports. Home: 5316 Cleves Warsaw Pike Cincinnati OH 45238-3602 Office: 1800 Firstar Tower 425 Walnut St Cincinnati OH 45202-3923

RYAN, JAMES LEO, federal judge; b. Detroit, Nov. 19, 1932; s. Leo Francis and Irene Agnes Ryan; m. Mary Elizabeth Rogers, Oct. 12, 1957; children: Daniel P., James R., Colleen M. Hansen, Kathleen A. LLB, U. Detroit, 1956, LLD (hon.), 1986, BA, 1992; LLD (hon.), Madonna Coll., 1976, Detroit Coll., 1978, Thomas M. Cooley Law Sch., Lansing, Mich., 1986. Atty. Waldron, Brennan & Maher, 1960—62; pvt. practice Redford Twp., Mich., 1962—66; Justice of peace, 1963—66; judge 3d Cir. Ct. of Mich., 1966—75; justice Mich. Supreme Ct., 1975—86; judge US Ct. Appeals (6th cir.), 1985—2000, sr. judge, 2000—. Faculty Nat. Jud. Coll., Reno; adj. faculty, bd. dirs. Ave Maria Sch. Law; adj. prof. Thomas M. Cooley Law Sch., 1979—85, U. Detroit, 1974—. Contbr. articles to profl. jours. Capt. JAGC USNR, 1957—92, ret. mil. judge USNR. Mem.: USNR Lawyers Assn., Detroit Bar Assn., Fed. Bar Assn., State Bar Mich., Fed. Judges Assn., K.M., K.C. Office: US Ct Appeals US Courthouse 231 W Lafayette Blvd Detroit MI 48226-2700 *

RYAN, JAMES M., cardiologist, educator; b. 1954; MD, Ohio State U. Coll. Medicine and Pub. Health-, 1979. Cert. Internal Medicine, Cardiovascular Disease, Med. Examination. Intern, internal medicine U. Va. Sch. Medicine, Charlottesville, Va., 1979—80, resident, cardiology, 1980—82, fellow, 1982—83; practicing medicine, 1982—; asst. prof. Ohio State U., Columbus, 1983—85, assoc. prof., internal medicine, 1992—; dir., nuclear cardiology, divsn. cardiovascular medicine Ohio State U. Med. Ctr.; med. dir. Ohio State U. Heart Ctr. at Mill Run; dir. and radiation safety officer Nuclear Cardiology Lab. at Mill Run. Med. dir. First Aid at Jack Nicklaus' Meml. Tournament; presenter in field. Contbr. articles to Circulation, American Journal Non-invasive Cardiology & Journal Cardiology; author: Risk Stratifications Post Myocardial Infarction in Contemporary Internal Medicine Clinical Case Studies. Named one of America's Best Doctors, Midwest Region, Cardiology, Golf Digest 2006 Top 250 Golfers in Am. Fellow: Am. Coll. Cardiology; mem.: Am. Soc. Nuclear Cardiology, Alpha Omega Alpha. Office: Ohio State U 244 Davis Heart Lung Rsch Inst 473 W 12th Ave Columbus OH 43210 Office Phone: 614-293-4984. Office Fax: 614-293-5614. E-mail: James.Ryan@osumc.edu. *

RYAN, JAMES T., wholesale distribution executive; BS, Miami Univ., Ohio; MBA, DePaul Univ. Mgmt. positions W.W. Grainger Inc., Lake Forest, Ill., 1980—94, pres. parts div., 1994—96, v.p. info. services, 1996—2000, pres. grainger.com, 2000—02, exec. v.p. mktg., sales & svc., 2002—04, group pres., 2004—06, pres., 2006—07, pres., COO, 2007—. Trustee Mus. Sci. & Industry, Chgo. Mem.: Econ. Club Chgo. Office: WW Grainger Inc 100 Grainger Pkwy Lake Forest IL 60045-5201 *

RYAN, JAMES WALTER, physician, researcher; b. Amarillo, Tex., June 8, 1935; s. Lee W. and Emma E. (Haddox) R.; children: James P.A., Alexandra L.E., Amy J.S. AB in Polit. Sci., Dartmouth Coll., 1957; MD, Cornell U., 1961; D.Phil., Oxford U., Eng., 1967. Diplomate Nat. Bd. Med. Examiners. Intern, Montreal (Que.) Gen. Hosp., McGill U., Can., 1961-62, asst. resident in medicine, 1962-63; USPHS research asso. NIMH, NIH, 1963-65; guest investigator Rockefeller U., NYC, 1967-68, asst. prof. biochemistry, 1968; investigator Howard Hughes Med. Inst., 1968—71; assoc. prof. medicine U. Miami (Fla.) Sch. Medicine, 1968-79, prof. medicine, 1979-95, mem. vasc. biology ctr., 1995-00; prof. anesthesiology, pharmacology and toxicology Med. Coll. Ga., Augusta, 1995-00; sr. cons. ntGen, 2000—; chief scientist Ryogen, LLC, 2005—. Sr. scientist Papanicolaou Cancer Rsch. Inst., Miami, 1972-77; hon. med. officer to Regius prof. medicine Oxford U., 1965-67; vis. prof. Clin. Rsch. Inst. Montreal, 1974; mem. vis. faculty thoracic disease divsn., dept. internal medicine Mayo Clinic, 1974; vis. prof. Montreal Gen. Hosp./McGill U., 1985. Contbr. numerous articles on biochem. rsch. and pathology to sci. jours.; patentee in field. Rockefeller Found. travel awardee, 1962; William Waldorf Astor traveling fellow, 1966; USPHS spl. fellow, 1967-68; Pfizer travelling fellow, 1972; recipient USPHS Rsch. Career Devel. award NIH, 1968, Louis and Artur Luciano award for research of circulatory diseases McGill U., 1984-85. Fellow Am. Heart Assn. (mem. coun. cardiopulmonary diseases 1972—, coun. for high blood pressure rsch. 1976—); mem. AAAS, Am. Physiol. Soc., Am. Chem. Soc., Biochem. Soc., Am. Soc. Biochemist and Molecular Biology, Oxford and Cambridge Club (London), Sigma Xi. Baptist. Home: 3047 Lake Forest Dr Augusta GA 30909-3027 Office: ntGen Ryogen LLC 3047 Lake Forest Dr Augusta GA 30909

RYAN, JANE FRANCES, corporate communications executive; b. Bronxville, NY, Nov. 1, 1950; d. Bernard M. and Margaret M. (Griffith) R.; m. Kevin Horan, Dec. 26, 1982; 1 child, Kevin. BS in Journalism, Ohio U., 1972; MBA in Mktg., Golden Gate U., 1990. Asst. promotion mgr. Fawcett Publs., Greenwich, Conn., 1972-75; mktg. coordinator Fawcett Mktg. Services div. CBS, Greenwich, Conn., 1975-78; dist. sales mgr. CBS Publs., San Francisco, 1978; prodn. mgr. Cato Inst., San Francisco, 1979-81; account supr. Bus. Media Resources, Mill Valley, Calif., 1981-90, dir. mktg. svcs., 1990-93; dir. publs. RAND Corp., Santa Monica, Calif., 1993—. Office: RAND 1700 Main St Santa Monica CA 90401-3297

RYAN, JASON MICHAEL, lawyer; b. Wharton, Tex., Oct. 30, 1975; m. Megan A. Ryan, Dec. 30, 2000. BBA with honors, U. Tex., 1998, JD with honors, 2001. Bar: Tex. 2001, US Dist. Ct. (So. Dist.) Tex., US Ct. Appeals (5th cir.), US Ct. Appeals (11th cir.), US Ct. Appeals (Armed Forces), US Tax Ct. Assoc. Baker Botts LLP, Houston, 2001—; reserve officer USN, 2005—. Editor-in-chief Am. Jour. Criminal Law; contbr. articles to law jours. Decorated Nat. Def. Svc. medal, Global War on Terror Svc. medal; named Outstanding Young Houstonian, Houston Jaycees, 2007, Outstanding Young Texan, Tex. Jaycees, 2007; recipient Pro Bono award, Nat. Law Jour., 2005. Mem.: ABA, Mil. Officers Assn. of Am., Houston Mil. Affairs Com., Houston World Affairs Coun. (coun. cabinet), Houston Vol. Lawyers Program (bd. dirs.), Pro Bono Coll. of State Bar Tex., Houston Young Lawyers Assn. (bd. dirs.), Houston Bar Found., Houston Bar Assn., Energy Bar Assn. (v.p. Houston Chap., mem. Alternative Dispute Resolution Com.), Alpha Phi Omega. Office: Baker Botts LLP One Shell Plaza 910 Louisiana St Houston TX 77002 Office Phone: 713-229-1820. Office Fax: 713-229-2820. Business E-Mail: jason.ryan@bakerbotts.com. E-mail: jason.m.ryan@navy.mil.

RYAN, JOAN, columnist; b. Sept. 20, 1959; m. Barry Tompkins; 1 child. BS in Journalism with honors, U. Fla., 1981. Copy editor Orlando (Fla.) Sentinel, 1981-82, copy editor sports, 1982-83, sports writer, 1983-85; sports columnist San Francisco Examiner, 1985—2000; columnist San Francisco Chronicle, 2000—06, features writer, 2006—. Author: Little Girls in Pretty Boxes: The Making & Breaking of Elite Gymnasts & Figure Skaters; co-author: Shooting from the Outside: How a Coach & her Olympic Team Transformed Women's Basketball. Recipient Fla. Sports Columnist of Yr. award, 1984, numerous AP Sports Editors awards, AP 1st place enterprise reporting award, 1993, Nat. Headliner award for sports writing, 1990, Women's Sports Found. Journalism award, 1992, Excellence in Journalism award for Feature Writing, Northern Calif. ch. Soc. Profl. Journalists, 2004, 2007, Gideon Equal Justice award, San Francisco Pub. Defender's Office, 2004, AP News Execs. Coun. award for Feature Writing, 2007, Edgar A. Poe award, White House Corrs. Assn., 2007. Office: San Francisco Chronicle 901 Mission St San Francisco CA 94103 Office Phone: 415-777-1111. E-mail: jryan@sfchronicle.com. *

RYAN, JOHN, lawyer; BS, Loyola U.; JD, Harvard U., Cambridge, Mass. Former chief admin. officer, corp. devel. leader Hewitt Assoc., CEO, Fin. Svc. Ltd., pres., holding corp., sr. v.p., chief legal officer. Bd. dir. Chgo. Coun. Global Affairs, Legal Club Chgo.; formerly with Ill. Governor's

Task Force on Judicial Merit Selection; former dir. Children's Memorial Hosp. (Chgo.) Rsch. Found. Office: Hewitt Assoc 100 Half Day Rd Lincolnshire IL 60069-3342 Office Phone: 847-295-5000. *

RYAN, JOHN DUNCAN, lawyer; b. Portland, Oreg., Dec. 20, 1920; s. Thomas Gough and Virginia Abigail (Hadley) R.; m. Florence A. Ryan, Jan. 30, 1970 (dec. 1987); m. Virginia Kane Wilson, June 15, 1996 BS, Fordham U., Bronx, NY, 1943; JD, Lewis & Clark Coll., Portland, 1950. Bar: Oreg. 1950. Pvt. practice, Portland, 1950—. Adj. instr. Northwestern Sch. Law Lewis & Clark Coll., 1953-70 Author: (poems) Expressions, 1993, Expressions II, 1995, No Road without a Turning, 2005, (book) Expressions, 1988, 1999, Cooking with John Ryan, 2002 Sgt. Air Corps, U.S. Army, 1942-46, ETO Recipient St. Thomas More award Catholic Lawyers for Social Justice, 1993 Mem. ABA (Oreg. del. 1985-93, chmn. spl. com. on law & literacy 1991-93), ATLA, Am. Coll. Trial Lawyers, Oreg. State Bar (bd. govs. 1963-67), Oreg. Trial Lawyers Assn. (Trial Lawyer of Yr. 1993), Multnomah County Bar Assn. (Professionalism award 1997), Washington County Bar Assn Home and Office: 503 SW Colony Dr Portland OR 97219-7763 Office Phone: 503-293-2207.

RYAN, JOHN JOSEPH, physician; b. Columbus, Ga., Sept. 5, 1957; s. Joseph Vincent and Annie Elizabeth R.; m. Sonia Francisca Ryan, Nov. 17, 1984; children: Annie, Joseph, Catherine. BS in Med. Tech., Columbus U., Ga., 1978; MD, Nuevo Leon U., Mex., 1990. Diplomate Am. Bd. Family Practice. Intern Anderson Family Practice, Anderson, SC, 1991—92, resident, 1991—94; physician Lowry's Family Medicine, Chester, SC, 1994—98; pvt. practice Chester, 1998—2003; physician Thomas Moore Health Clinic, Fort Hood, Tex., 2005—06, McAllen Primary Care Clinic, 2005—06, Mediplex Health Clinic, 2006—. Bass Brownsville Diocese Choir, Holy Spirit Parish Choir. Fellow: Am. Acad. Family Practice; mem.: AMA, Tex. Acad. Family Practice, Rotary, KC (Grand Knight). Roman Catholic. Avocations: fishing, golf, gardening.

RYAN, JOHN M., lawyer, human resources company executive; BS, Loyola U.; JD, Harvard U. Chief adminstrv. officer Hewitt Associates, Inc., Lincolnshire, Ill., 1988, corp. devel. leader, 2001, sr. v.p. strategy, counsel, 2005—06, sr. v.p., chief legal officer, 2006—. CEO Hewitt Fin. Svcs. LLC; pres. Hewitt Holding Corp.; bd. dirs. Chgo. Coun. on Global Affairs. Former dir. Children's Meml. Hosp. Rsch. Found., Chgo. Mem.: Legal Club Chgo. (bd. dirs.). Office: Hewitt Assocs, Inc 100 Half Day Rd Lincolnshire IL 60069 *

RYAN, JOHN MORGAN, lawyer; b. Glen Ridge, NJ, May 18, 1936; AB, Dartmouth Coll., 1958; LLB, U. Va., 1963. Bar: Va. 1964. Lectr. at law Marshall-Wythe Sch. Law Coll. William and Mary, 1976-86; ptnr. Vandeventer Black LLP, Norfolk, Va.; gen. counsel Va. Internat. Terminals, Inc. Trustee Contemporary Art Ctr. Va.; chair Arts and Humanities Commn., Va. Beach, Va.; bd. dirs. Children's Health Sys., Inc., Greater Norfolk Corp. Fellow: Va. Law Found. (mem. coun.), Am. Bar Found., Am. Coll. Trial Lawyers; mem.: ABA (labor rels., litigation sect.), So. Conf. Bar Pres., Nat. Conf. Bar Pres., Va. State Bar, Norfolk-Portsmouth Bar Assn., Maritime Law Assn. US (bd. dirs. 2005—), Va. Bar Assn. (pres. 1988), S.E. Admiralty Law Inst., James Kent Am. Inn of Ct. (past pres.), 4th Cir. Jud. Conf., Hampton Rds. Maritime Assn. (legis. com.). Office: Vandeventer Black LLP 500 World Trade Ctr Norfolk VA 23510-1679 Office Phone: 757-446-7600. Business E-Mail: jryan@vanblk.com.

RYAN, JOHN R., educational association administrator, former academic administrator, career military officer; m. Diane L. Ackerman; children: Tricia, Kelly, Julie. Graduate, USN Acad., 1967; MSc in Adminstrn., George Washington U., 1975. Enlisted USN, 1968, advanced through grades to vice adm.; naval aviator Patrol Squadron 8, 1969-72; various assignments Naval Acad., 1972-75; served on USS Nimitz, 1975-77; adminstrv. officer Commander Patrol Wing Five, 1977-80; ops. officer Patrol Squadron Twenty-Six, 1980-81; various assignments Patrol Squadron Eleven, 1981-83, Office of Chief of Naval Ops., 1983-85; military asst. to exec. sec. Immediate Office of Sec. Defense, 1985-86; comdr. Patrol Squadron Thirty-One, Moffett Field, 1986-87; exec. asst. to dep. chief naval ops. Office of Chief of Naval Ops., 1987-88; comdr. Patrol Wing Ten, Moffett Field, 1988-90; various assignments U.S. Pacific Command, 1990-93; commdr., patrol wings US Pacific Fleet/Commdr., Anti-Submarine Warfare Forces, U.S. Pacific Fleet, 1993-95; commdr., maritime surveilance and reconnaissance force, us sicth fleet commdr., fleet air mediterranean/commdr. Maritime Air Forces, 1995-98; supt. USN Acad., 1998—2002; pres. SUNY Maritime Coll., 2002—04; interim pres. SUNY, Albany, 2004; acting chancellor SUNY Sys., 2005, chancellor, 2005—07; pres., chief exec. Ctr. for Creative Leadership, Greensboro, NC, 2007—. Decorated D.S.M., Legion of Merit with two gold stars, Meritorious Svc. medal with two gold stars. Office: Ctr For Creative Leadership 1 Leadership Pl Greensboro NC 27410 *

RYAN, JOHN WILLIAM, academic administrator; b. Chgo., Aug. 12, 1929; s. Leonard John and Maxine (Mitchell) R.; m. D. Patricia Goodday, June 20, 1949; children: Kathleen Elynne Ryan Acker, Kevin Dennis Mitchell, Kerrick Charles Casey. BA, U. Utah, 1951; MA, Ind. U., 1958, PhD, 1959; D Pub. Adminstrn., Nat. Inst. Devel. Adminstrn., Thailand, 1991; DLitt (hon.), U. St. Thomas, 1977; LLD (hon.), Ind. U., 1988, U. Notre Dame, 1978, Oakland City Coll., 1981, St. Joseph Coll., 1981, Hanover Coll., 1982, DePauw U., 1983, Manchester Coll., 1983, U. Evansville, 1985, Wabash Coll., 1986, Ind. U., 1988, U. Md., 1994, SD State U., 2005, S.Dakota State U., 2004. Rsch. analyst Ky. Dept. Revenue, Frankfort, 1954-55; vis. rsch. prof. U. Thammasat, Bangkok, 1955-57; asst. dir. Inst. Tng. for Pub. Svc. Ind. U., 1957-58; successively asst. prof., assoc. prof. polit. sci., assoc. dir., Bur. Govt. U. Wis., 1958-62; exec. asst. to pres., sec. of univ. U. Mass., Amherst, 1962-63, chancellor Boston, 1965-68; v.p. acad. affairs Ariz. State U., 1963-65; v.p., chancellor regional campuses Ind. U., Bloomington, 1968-71, pres., 1971-87, pres. emeritus, 1987—, prof. polit. sci., 1968-95, prof. pub. and environ. affairs, 1981-95, prof. emeritus, 1995—; cons. AID, 1991-92; chancellor SUNY, Albany, 1996—2000, chancellor emeritus, 2000—; hon. prof. Moscow State U., 1999. Interim pres. Fla. Atlantic U., 1989, U. Md., Balt., 1994; bd. dirs. Ind. U. Found., chmn. 1972-87; chmn. Nat. Adv. Bd. on Internat. Edn. Programs, 1985-89; chancellor SUNY System, 1996-2000. Contbr. articles to profl. jours. Bd. govs. Pub. Broadcasting Svc., 1973-82; bd. visitors Air U., 1974-81; chmn. Air Force Inst. Tech Subcom., 1976-81; mem. univ. adv. com. Am. Coun. Life Ins.; bd. dirs. Corp. Community Coun., 1976; mem. nat. adv. coun. Pan Am. Games, 1985; mem. adv. bd. Assocs. for Religious and Intellectual Life, 1984—; active United Way Ind. Centennial Commn. Mem. Am. Soc. Pub. Adminstrn. (pres. Ind. chpt. 1969-70, nat. chpt. 1972-73, nat. coun. from 1970, Ind. Soc. Chgo. (non-resident v.p. from 1976, Am. Polit. Sci. Assn., Assn. Asian Studies, Am. Coun. Edn., Assn. Am. Univs. (chmn. 1981-82), Nat. Acad. Public Adminstrn., Ind. Acad., Explorers Club, Adelphia (hon.), Columbia Club (Indpls.), Skyline Club, Cosmos Club (Washington), Athenaeum (London), KC, Equestrian Order of Holy Sepulchre, Elks, Phi Kappa Phi, Phi Alpha Theta, Pi Sigma Alpha, Beta Gamma Sigma, Kappa Sigma (worthy grand master 1985-87). Office: Ind U SPEA 415 1315 E 10th St Bloomington IN 47405-1701 Home Phone: 812-824-9071; Office Phone: 812-855-5780. Personal E-mail: chancem123@aol.com. Business E-Mail: ryan@indiana.edu.

RYAN, JOHN WILLIAM, educational association administrator; b. Manchester, NH, Sept. 16, 1937; s. William Charles and Mary Ann (Marcoux) R.; m. Carol Jean Battaglia, Sept. 17, 1960; children: James, Kathleen, John, Michael. AB, St. Anselm Coll., 1959; MA, Niagara U., 1960; PhD, St. John's U., 1965. Asst. prof. history Gannon U., Erie, Pa., 1965-66; edn. specialist, div. grad. programs U.S. Office Edn., Washington, 1966-68, regional coordinator, grad. acad. programs, 1968-70; dir. univ. programs Univ. Assos., Inc., Washington, 1970-72; asst. to pres., sec. Council of Grad. Schs. in U.S., Washington, 1972-80; exec. v.p. Renewables Research Inst., Annandale, Va., 1980-81; exec. dir. Worcester (Mass.) Consortium Higher Edn., 1981-89, N.H. Coll. and Univ. Coun., Manchester, 1989-93; cons.; exec. dir. Mass. Vet. Med. Assn., Marlborough, Mass., 1995-98; cons., 1998—. Contbr. articles to profl. jours. Bd. dirs. No. Va. C.C., 1999—, Loudoun Healthcare, Inc., 2000—, Loudoun County Econ. Devel. Commn., 2000. Personal E-mail: jwryan@belmontcc.com.

RYAN, JOYCE ETHEL, writer, artist; b. Atlanta, Aug. 29, 1949; m. Jim Cyril Klar, Apr. 5, 1975 BFA, U. Ga., Athens, 1972. Instr. Marsh Draughon Coll., Atlanta, 1972—73; mgr. retail store Army & Air Force Exch. Svc., Dallas, 1974; illustrator U.S. Army Logistics Ctr., Ft. Lee, Va., 1975—77; mgr. graphics Ecosystems Internat., Millersville, Md., 1980—82; dir. freelance art studio Seoul, 1983—85; pres. Butterfly Books, Ariz., 1985—. Instr. Cochise Coll., Sierra Vista, 1986 Illustrator, author: Seoul Sketches, 1985, Scenes of Southern Arizona, 1986, Seoul Travel Guide, 1987, Traveling with Your Sketchbook, 1990, The Happy Camper's Gourmet Cookbook, 1992, Calligraphy: Elegant and Easy, 1994, Drawing at Home, 1996, America's Best Cheesecakes, 1998, Fifty Years of Excellence: Texas Watercolor Society, 1999, America's Best RV Cookbook, 2003; contbr. to RV America mag., 2003— Mem.: San Antonio Watercolor Group. Avocations: drawing, painting. Home Phone: 210-494-0077; Office Phone: 210-494-0077. Personal E-mail: texaswavelady@hotmail.com.

RYAN, JUDITH ANN, dean; d. Thomas Patrick and Ann Patricia Ryan. BA, Queens Coll., Flushing, NY, 1993; MS, Coll. Mt. St. Vincent, Riverdale, 1998. Cert. English 7-12 NY, Sch. Dist. Adminstr. NY. Coom. art tchr. IS204 NYC Bd. Edn., Long Island, NY, 1993—96, title I reading specialist, 1996—2000, title I dept. coord. Jackson Heights, 2000—03, dean of students, 2003—. Advisor liaison IS230, Jackson Heights, NY, 2004—06, fin. officer, 2006. Mem. NYC 2012 Campaign, NYC, 2003—05. Mem.: Nat. Coun. Tchrs. English, Assn. for Supr. and Cirrculum Devel. Office: IS230 73-10 34th Ave Jackson Heights NY 11372

RYAN, JUDITH W., geriatrics nurse, educator; b. Waterbury, Conn., Dec. 8, 1943; d. James Patrick Ryan and Edna (Swanson) Billings. BS, U. Conn., 1965; MS, Boston U., 1967; PhD, U. Md., 1984. RN, Md., Conn.; cert. adult nurse practitioner ANCC. Instr. U. Conn., Storrs, 1967-69; asst. prof. Ind. U., Purdue U., Indpls., 1969-73, U. Md., Balt., 1973-82, dir. primary care adult nurse pracitioner cert. program, dept. medicine, supportive care project, 1985-87, asst. prof. sch. nursing, 1987-95, asst. prof., 1976-82; clin. dir. EverCare, Balt., 1995-99; pres. Nurse Practitioners and Cons., P.C. of Prime Health Group, 2000—. Arbitrator Health Claims Arbitration Program, Md., 1976—; bd. mem. Md. Bd. Nursing, Balt., 1991-98, pres., 1993-96; trustee Md. Nurses Assn. Polit. Action Com., Balt., treas., 1989-91. Contbr. articles to profl. jours. Named Distinguished Practitioner Nursing, Nat. Acad. Practice, 1984-99. Mem. Am. Coll. Nurse Practitioners, Md. Nurses Assn. (2d v.p. 1986-88), Nurse Practitioner Assn. Md., Sigma Theta Tau, Phi Kappa Phi. Office: 20 New Plant Ct Ste 204 Owings Mills MD 21117 Home: 1514 Woodside Ave Baltimore MD 21227 Office Phone: 410-654-8602 Ext. 103. Personal E-mail: jwryan128@comcast.net.

RYAN, KENNETH EUGENE, engineer; b. Guilford, NY, Apr. 3, 1936; s. Julian Nichols and Irene M. Ryan; m. Nancy Race, Aug. 29, 1959; children: Patrick, Kathleen, Timothy, Maureen. BS, Cornell U., 1958, MS, 1959. Registered profl. engr., N.Y. With various mobile equipment mfrs., 1959-66; rsch. assoc. Cornell U., Ithaca, N.Y., 1966-69; sr. project engr. Raymond Corp., Greene, N.Y., 1969—. Chmn. Zoning Bd. Appeals, Oxford, N.Y., 1973-83; chmn. com. North Guilford (N.Y.) Ch., 1989-91; mem. Oxford Planning Bd., 1970—; chmn. Chenango County Planning Bd., 2003—. Mem. NSPE, ASME, Soc. Exptl. Stress Analysis. Achievements include patents in field. Avocation: photography. Home: 221 Ryan Rd Oxford NY 13830-9801

RYAN, KENNETH J., immunologist, educator; MD, U. Wash., 1966. Cert. pathologist. Mem. staff Univ. Med. Ctr., Tuscon; prof. pathology, microbiology, immunology U. Ariz. Coll. Medicine, 1972—, dean acad. affairs Tuscon, 2002—04, interim dean, 2002—04. Avocations: golf, tennis. Office: U Ariz Sch Medicine Rm 2205 PO Box 245017 1501 N Cambell Ave # C 206 Tucson AZ 85724-0002

RYAN, KEVIN VINCENT, lawyer, former prosecutor; b. 1957; m. Anne Ryan; 2 children. BA in History, Dartmouth Coll.; JD, U. San Francisco. Prosecutor Alameda County Dist. Atty.'s Office; judge San Francisco Mcpl. Ct., 1996—98; mem. San Francisco Superior Ct., 1999, presiding judge criminal divsn.; US atty. (no. dist.) Calif. US Dept. Justice, San Francisco, 2002—07; ptnr. Allen Matkins Leck Gamble Mallory & Natsis LLP, San Francisco, 2007—. Bd. dirs. No. Calif. High Intensity Drug Trafficking Area Working Group; mem. Pres. Bush's Corp. Fraud Task Force; apptd. mem. subcom. Controlled Substances and Terrorism and Nat. Security, appointed to Jud. Coun.'s Exec. Legis. Action Network, Chief Justice of Calif. Supreme Ct.; appointed to Criminal Law Planning Com. of Calif. Continuing Jud. Studies Program, Governing Com. of Calif. Ctr. for Jud. Edn. and Rsch.; appointed to Adult Probation Dept.'s Oversight Com., Presiding Judge for Cts.; mem. exec. com. San Francisco Superior Ct.; mem. exec. com. Am. Inn of Cts., U. San Francisco Sch. Law; bd. govs. U. San Francisco Law Soc.; bd. trustees Schs. of Sacred Heart, San Francisco; mem. faculty Intensive Trial Advocacy Program, U. San Francisco Sch. Law; lectr. in field. Recipient Mcpl. Ct. Trial Judge of Yr., San Francisco Trial Lawyers' Assn., 1998. Office: Allen Matkins 3 Embarcadero Ctr 12th Fl San Francisco CA 94111-4074 *

RYAN, KEVIN WILLIAM, virologist, clinical research administrator; s. Joseph Michael Ryan and Etoile Evelyn Werth; m. Mary Ellen Lyman, June 1, 1974; children: Matthew Lyman, Mark Joseph. BS, U. Iowa, 1978; PhD, U. Mich., 1984. Staff fellow Nat. Inst. Allergy and Infectious Diseases, NIH, Bethesda, Md., 1984-86; rsch. asst. dept. virology and molecular biology St. Jude Children's Rsch. Hosp., Memphis, 1986-89, asst. mem., 1989-98; asst. prof. pathology U. Tenn. Coll. Medicine, Memphis, 1994-98; sci. rev. adminstr. Nat. Inst. Allergy and Infectious Diseases, NIH, Rockville, Md., 1998-2000; program officer virology vaccine and prevention rsch. prog. divsn. AIDS, Nat. Inst. Allergy and Infectious Diseases, NIH, Bethesda, Md., 2000—05; deputy chief Prevention Scis. Br., 2001—02, chief, 2002—05, lead program officer grant-supported internat. clin. rsch. in HIV/AIDS prevention, 2001—05; mem. working group NIAID, Comprehensive Internat. Program for Rsch. in AIDS (CIPRA), 2001—05; dep. dir. pediatrics, adolescent and maternal AIDS, Ctr. for Rsch. for Mothers and Children, Nat. Inst. Child Health and Human Devel., NIH, Rockville, Md., 2005—. Prin. investigator Nat. Inst. Allergy and Infectious Diseases, 1992—98; lead program officer HIV prevention trials network HPTN, 2002—05; govt. project officer HIV Network Prevention Trials Internat. (HIVNET) Master Contract for AIDS Rsch. NIAID, 2002—04; NIAID program officer Clin. Trials of Male Circumcision for HIV Prevention, 2002—05, Topical Microbicides Clin. Trials, 2002—05; NIAID Rep. HPTN Prevention Leadership Group, 2002—05; dep. chief Pediat., Adolescent and Maternal AIDS br. Ctr. for Rsch. Mothers and Children, Nat. Inst. of Child Health and Human Devel., NIH, 2005—; lead NICHD program officer Adolescent Medicine Trials Network, 2005—, Women and Infants HIV Transmission Study, 2005—; program officer Pediatric HIV-AIDS Cohort Study, 2005—; NICHD program officer Microbicide Trials Network, 2006—; NICHD rep. on Internat. Working Group on Microbicides, 2007—. Contbr. articles to profl. jours., chpts. to tech. manuals. Recipient Merit award, NIH, 2000, Dir. award, 2002; fellow postdoctoral Mich. Cancer Rsch. Inst., U. Mich., 1982. Mem.: Am. Soc. for Microbiology. Roman Catholic. Avocations: woodworking, golf. Office: Nat Inst Child Health and Human Devel PAMA 6100 Executive Blvd Rockville MD 20852-0001 Business E-Mail: kr90p@nih.gov.

RYAN, L. THOMAS, JR., lawyer; b. Binghamton, NY, Feb. 10, 1952; s. Lawrence T. and Rita Ryan; children: L. Thomas III, Michael I. BS, U. Ala., Tuscaloosa, 1975, JD, 1978. Bar: Ala. 1979, U.S. Dist. Ct. (no. dist.) Ala. 1979, U.S. Ct. Appeals (11th cir.) 1985. Assoc. Lammons Bell & Sneed, Huntsville, Ala., 1978-80; ptnr. Ryan & Robins, Huntsville, 1980-84, Simpson Hamilton & Ryan, Huntsville, 1984-87, Hamilton & Ryan, Huntsville, 1987-89; owner The Ryan Law Firm, Huntsville, 1989—. Bd. dirs. Nat. Children's Advocacy Ctr., Huntsville, 1984-88; bd. dirs., pres. Foster Children's Alliance, Huntsville, 1988-90; bd. dirs. Lawyer Referral and Info. Svc. Madison County, Ala., Huntsville, 1992—. Mem. Am. Acad. Estate Planning Attys., Nat. Acad. Elder Law Attys., Masons, Elks, Eagles. Democrat. Roman Catholic. Avocations: reading, boating, computers, golf. Office: The Ryan Law Firm 2319 Market Pl SW Ste B Huntsville AL 35801-5250 Office Phone: 256-533-1103.

RYAN, L. TIMOTHY, chef, educator, academic administrator; b. Pitts. m. Lynne Ryan; 2 children. BS, U. New Haven; MBA, U. New Haven Sch. Bus. Adminstrn.; graduated, Culinary Inst. Am., 1977; EdD, U. Pa., Pa. Graduate Sch. Edu., Phila. Cert. Master Chef 1985. Asst. chef Ben Gross' Restaurant, Irwin, Pa.; exec. chef La Normande, Pitts.; joined Culinary Institute Am., Hyde Park, NY, 1982, exec. v.p., v.p. edu., dir., culinary edu., dept. head, culinary edu., chef-instructor, pres., 2001—. Developer Am. Bounty Restaurant. Author: The Culinary Olympics Cookbook, 1984, 1988, New Professional Chef, Techniques of Healthy Cooking, An American Bounty; editl. adv. com. mem.: Cheers, Seafood Bus., Take Out Bus. magazines, former chmn. editl. coun.: Nat. Culinary Review; contbr. to videos and television shows. Named Entrepretuer of Yr., Internat. Assn. Culinary Professionals, 2007; named to Am. Acad. Chefs, 1990; recipient Gold medals, Pitts. Culinary Arts Salon, 1981, Eastern Regional Olympic Tryouts, 1982, Gourmet Fair, Japan, 1983, Honor Roll Am. Chefs, Food & Wine magazine, 1983, Chef Yr. award, Am. Culinary Fedn., 1998, Presdl. medal, World Assn. Cooks Societies, 1998, Hon. Doctorate Foodservice medallion, N.Am. Assn. Food Equipment Manufacturers, Grand prize of show, Internat. Feinschmecker Parade, Austria. Mem.: Am. Culinary Fedn. (Pitts. chpt. bd. dirs. 1981—82, pub. rels. chair 1982—83, apprenticeship chair, Mid-Hudson chpt. 1982—84, culinary com. 1983—, team capt., US culinary team 1984, master chef com. 1985—, team capt., US Team, Culinary World Cup Competition 1986, team mgr., US team, Salon Culinaire Mondial 1987, team capt., US culinary team 1988, N.E. v.p. 1991—93, nat. pres. 1995—96, chmn. bd. 1996—97, team mgr., US team, Internat. World Culinary Arts Festival, four Gold Medals and World Championship (Hot Food Competition), Internat. Culinary Competition, Germany 1988, two team Gold medals, Salon Culinaire Mondial, Basel, Switzerland 1987, Team grand prize, Culinary World Cup Competition, Luxembourg 1986, Team medal for culinary excellence, Salon Culinary Art, NY 1985, Two gold medals and silver cup, Internat. Culinary Competition, Germany 1984). Achievements include launching the world's first bachelor's degree program in Culinary Arts Management and Baking and Pastry Arts Management; developing a highly successful publishing program; expanding the continuing education programs. Office: Culinary Inst Am 1946 Campus Dr Hyde Park NY 12538-1499 *

RYAN, LEO VINCENT, business educator; b. Waukon, Iowa, Apr. 6, 1927; s. John Joseph and Mary Irene (O'Brien) Ryan. BS, Marquette U., 1949; MBA, DePaul U., 1954; PhD, St. Louis U., 1958; postgrad., Catholic U. Am., 1951-52, Bradley U., 1952-54, Northwestern U., 1950; LLD, Seton Hall U., 1988; DHL, Ill. Benedictine U., 1997. Joined Order Clerics of St. Viator, Roman Cath. Ch., 1950. Faculty Marquette U., Milw., 1957-65, dir. continuing edn. summer sessions, coord. evening divsns., 1959-65, prof. indsl. mgmt., 1964; prof., chmn. dept. mgmt. Loyola U., Chgo., 1965-66; dep. dir. Peace Corps, Lagos, Nigeria, 1966-67, dir. Western Nigeria Ibadan, 1967-68; asst. superior gen. and treas. gen. Clerics of St. Viator, Rome, 1968-69, dir. edn. Am. province Arlington Heights, Ill., 1969-74; pres. St. Viator H.S., 1972-74; dean, prof. mgmt. U. Notre Dame Coll. Bus. Adminstrn., Ind., 1975-80; dean DePaul U. Coll. Commerce, 1980-88, prof. mgmt., 1980-99; Wicklander prof. ethics DePaul U., 1993-94; prof. emeritus, 1999. Dir. Peace Corps tng. programs Marquette U., 1962-65; adj. prof. human devel. St. Mary's Coll., Winona, Minn., 1972-74; sch. bd. Archdiocese Chgo., 1972-75, vice-chmn., 1973-75, nat. edn. com. US Cath. Conf., 1971-75, exec. com., 1973-75; nat. adv. bd. Benedictine Sisters Nauvoo, 1973-83; nat. adv. coun. SBA, 1982-85, vice-chmn. minority bus., 1982-85, exec. com. Chgo. chpt., 1982-84; vis. prof. U. Ife, Ibadan, 1967-68,; chmn. trust audit com. First Bank-Milw., 1980-85, chmn. audit and exam. com., 1985-90, adv. coun., 1991-93; bd. dirs. Henricksen & Co., Inc.; fin. commn. Clerics of St. Viator, 1978-, provincial chpt., 1985-97, 2001-03, devel. adv. bd. 1996-2001, new foundations com. 1996-98, alt. mem., 1997-2001, provincial coun., 2001-03, coord. coun., U.S., Belize, Columbia, 2001-03, comprehensive devel. coun., 2004; Fulbright prof. Adam Mickiewicz U., Poland, 1993-95; vis. prof. Helsinki Sch. Econs., 1992-2002, Polish-Am. Ctr., U. Lodz, 1998, Poznan Acad. Econs., 1991, 1999—; co-chair bus. and profl. com. Archdiocese of Chgo. Sesquetennial Com. Out Reach Divsn. Ctrl. Planning Group, 1993-94; vis. prof. Notre Dame, 2000, Helsinki Sch. Econs., 2000; vis. scholar U. St. Thomas, Houston, 2006; mem. adv. bd. Sch. Bus. U. Kiev, Ukraine, 2001; vis. adv. bd. DePaul U. Gallery and Mus., 2005—; vis. rsch. scholar U. St. Thomas, Houston, 2006. Author: Human Action in Business, 1996, Etyka Biznesu, 1997, 4th edit., 2000, From Autarcy to Market: Polish Economics and Politics, 1945-1995, 1998, 2d edit., 1999, Students Focus on Business Ethics, 2000, Praxiology and Pragmatism, 2002, Poland: A Transformational Appraisal, 2003; mem. editl. bd. Internat. Jour. Value Based Mgmt., 1983-2003, Bus. Ethics Quar., 1983-2004, European Bus. Jour., 1990-2002, Mid Atlantic Jour. of Bus., 1990-2002, European Jour. Econs. Fin. and Adminstrv. Studies, 2006, Clerics of St. Viator Quar. Mem. Pres.'s Com. on Employment Handicapped, 1959-65, Wis. Gov.'s Com. on Employment Handicapped, 1959-65, Wis. Gov.'s Com. on UN, 1961-64, Burnham Park Planning Commn., 1982-88; bd. dir. Ctr. Pastoral Liturgy U. Notre Dame, 1976-79; trustee Lake Forest Grad. Sch. Mgmt., 1989-91, St. Mary of Woods Coll., 1978-81, Cath. Theol. Union, U. Chgo., 1992-95, Divine Word Coll., 1997-2006; regent Seton Hall U., 1981-87, mem. acad. affairs com., 1981-87, chmn., 1983-87; dir. Ctr. for Enterprise Devel., 1992-95; elected fellow St. Edmunds Coll. Cambridge U., 1992—; mem. Cath. Commn. Intellectual and Cultural Affairs, 1992—, Cath. Campaign for Am., 1994-98; bd. dir. Internat. Bus. Ethics Inst., Am. Grad. Sch. Internat. Mgmt., 1995-97; mem. adv. com. Mgmt. Edn. in Poland, U. Md., College Park, 1995-2000; mem. Iowa Gov. Heartland Leadership Coun., 2000-06. Recipient Freedom award Berlin Commn., 1961, chieftancy title Asoju Atoaja of Oshogbo Oba Adenle I, Yorubaland, Nigeria, 1967, B'nai B'rith Interfaith award, Milw., 1963, Disting. Alumnus award Marquette U., 1974, DePaul U., 1976, Tchr. of Yr. award Beta Alpha Psi, 1980, Centennial Alumni Achievement award Marquette U., 1981, Boland Meml. Disting. Alumni award, St. Louis, 1989, Disting. Alumni and Bicentennial awards Jesuit Bus. Schs., 1989, Pres.' award St. Viator H.S., 1992, Medal of Merit Adam Mickiewicz U., 1995, Excellence in Tchg. award Adam Mickiewicz U., 1997, Ill. Ernst and Young Entrepreneur Supporter award, 1999, Vincentian U. Ethics Scholar award, 2000, Centennial award Dominican U. Sch. Bus., 2002; Brother Leo V. Ryan award named in his honor Cath. Bus. Edn. Assn., 1962; Ryan Scholars in Mgmt. established in his honor DePaul U., 1989, Outstanding Svc. award, 1991-93, Commerce Alumni award of merit, 1997; DePaul Creativity Ctr. named in his honor, 1997, trustee; named hon. life chmn. Nat. Adv. Com., Ryan Creativity Ctr.,

Creative Cutting Edge award, 1999; Ryan Scholarship named in his honor St. Viator H.S., 1992, Lion award, 1997, trustee, 2000-01, gov., 2001-03; named Man of Yr. Jr. C. of C., Milw., 1959, Marquette U. Bus. Adminstrn. Alumni Man of Yr., 1974; named Disting. Vis. Term Prof. Seton Hall U., 2001, Alumnus of Yr., St. Patrick Grade and HS, Waukon, Iowa, 2006; Milw. Bd. Realtors traveling fellow, 1964, Nat. Assn. Purchasing Agts. faculty fellow, 1958, German Am. Acad. Exch. Coun. fellow, 1983, Presdl. fellow Am. Grad. Sch. Internat. Mgmt., 1989, vis. scholar, 1995, Malone fellow in Islamic studies, Bahrain and Saudi Arabia, 1990, fellow Kosciuszko Found. Adam Mickiewicz U., 1990; scholar-in-residence Mgmt. Sch. Imperial Coll. Sci. and Tech. U. London, 1988; vis. scholar U. Calif., Berkeley, 1989; USIA Acad. Specialists grantee, Poland, 1991-93; fellow St. Edmund's Coll. Cambridge U., 1992; named vis. rsch. fellow Von Hugel Inst., 1992-93; scholar-in-residence Am. Grad. Sch. Internat. Mgmt., 1995; guest scholar Kellogg Inst. Internat. Studies U. Notre Dame, 1997; vis. rsch. scholar U. St. Thomas, Houston, 2006, Trustee award Divine Coll., 2006, Distinguished Svc. award Poznan U., 2006, Civic award City of Poznan, 2007. Mem. Cath. Bus. Edn. Assn. (nat. pres. 1960-62, nat. exec. bd. 1960-64), Assn. Sch. Bus. Ofcls. (nat. com. chmn. 1965-67), Am. Assembly Collegiate Schs. Bus. (com. internat. affairs 1977-84, chmn. 1981-84, bd. dirs. 1981-87, program chmn. 1979-80, exec. com., chmn. projects/svc. mgmt. com. 1984-86), Am. Fgn. Svc. Assn., Am. Assn. Profl. Ethics (bd. dir. 1996-98), Am. Philat. Soc., Allamakee County Hist. Soc. (charter life), Ancient Order of Hibernians, Atomic Vets. Assn., August Derleth Soc., Econ. Club Chgo., Chgo. Coun. Fgn. Rels., Coun. Fgn. Rels. (diplomat cir. 1980-2000), European Bus. Ethics Network Poland (hon. 1998), Soc. Bus. Ethics, (mem. exec. com. 1991—, pres. 1993-94, adv. bd. 1995-97), Assn. Social Econs. (life), Iowa Hist. Soc., Iowa Postal History Soc., Iowa Geneological Soc., Fulbright Assn. (life), Iowa Geneal. Soc.,Internat. Assn. for Bus. and Soc. (founder), Internat. Soc. for Bus., Econs. and Ethics (charter), Internat. Trade and Fin. Assn. (founder, bd. dir. 1989-92, 96-98, v.p. membership 1991-92, 96-97), Internat. Learned Soc. Praxiology, (hon. life, internat. adv. bd. praxiology ann.), Polish Inst. Arts and Scis. in Am., Postal History Soc., Polish Am. Historical Assn., DePaul Inst. Bus. and Profl. Ethics (founder 1984, adv. bd. 1984-94, mus. adv. com., 2005—), Founders award 1999), USS Mt. McKinley Reunion Assn. (life, hon. chaplain AGC-7 1989-96, Disting. Svc. award 1991, 96), Friends of Nigeria, Alpha Sigma Nu, Alpha Kappa Psi (bd. dir. found. 1985-91, vice-chmn. 1987-91, chmn. scholarship com. 1987-91, chmn. devel. com. 1987, exec. com. 1990-91, Bronze Disting. Svc. award 1949, Silver Disting. Svc. award 1958, Recognition medal, 2001), Beta Alpha Psi, Beta Gamma Sigma (co-chair 75th Anniversary com. Ill., faculty advisor DePaul chpt. 1986-92), Century Travel Club (Silver award), Delta Mu Delta, Pi Gamma Mu, Tau Kappa Epsilon. Home Phone: 847-870-4903; Office Phone: 847-870-4903. Business E-Mail: leovryan@viatorians.com.

RYAN, LEONARD EAMES, judge; b. Albion, NY, July 8, 1930; s. Bernard and Harriet Earle (Fitts) R.; m. Ann Allen, June 18, 1973; 1 child, Thomas Eames Allen-Ryan. Grad., Kent Sch., 1948; AB, U. Pa., 1954; JD, NYU, 1962. Bar: D.C. 1963, N.Y. 1963, U.S. Ct. Appeals (D.C. cir.) 1963, U.S. Dist. Ct. (so. and ea. dists.) N.Y. 1965, U.S. Ct. Appeals (2nd cir.) 1966, U.S. Supreme Ct. 1967. Field engr. constrn. U.S. Steel Fairless Works, Morrisville, Pa., 1951-52; reporter Upper Darby (Pa.) News, 1954; newsman AP, Pitts., Phila., Harrisburg, NYC, 1955-62; reporter, spl. writer on law N.Y. Times, 1962-63; info. adviser corp. hdqrs. IBM, NYC, 1963; trial atty. firm Perrell, Nielsen & Stephens, NYC, 1964-66; trial atty. civil rights div. Dept. Justice, Washington, 1966-68; asst. to dir. bus. affairs CBS News, NYC, 1968; program officer Office Govt. and Law, Ford Found., NYC, 1968-74; pvt. practice law, cons. pub. affairs, NYC, 1974-91; v.p., sec. W. P. Carey & Co., Inc., NYC, 1977—82; impartial hearing officer Edn. for All Handicapped Children Act of 1975, 1976-91; per diem adminstrv. law judge N.Y. State Agys., 1976-91; hearing examiner N.Y. State Family Ct., 1980-81; apptd. U.S. adminstv. law judge, 1991; adminstv. law judge Office Hearings and Appeals, San Rafael, Calif., 1991—93, Phila., 1993-94, NYC, 1994—. Arbitrator Small Claims Ct., N.Y.C., 1974-84; bd. dirs. Community Action for Legal Svcs. Inc., N.Y.C., 1971-77, vice-chmn., 1975-77; co-chmn. Citizens Com. to Save Legal Svcs., N.Y.C., 1975-76; bd. dirs. Lower East Side Svc. Ctr., N.Y.C., 1977-89. Author: (with Bernard Ryan Jr.) So You Want to Go Into Journalism, 1963; contbr. articles to profl. jours. Served with USAR, 1950-57. Mem. Am. Judicature Soc., Assn. of Bar of City of N.Y., N.Y. State Bar Assn., St. Elmo Club (Phila.), Heights Casino (Bklyn.). Home: 32 Orange St Brooklyn NY 11201-1634 Office: 111 Livingston St Brooklyn NY 11201-5078

RYAN, LISA KATHLEEN, environmental and medical science educator; b. Morgantown, W.Va., July 9, 1958; d. Richard Stoetzer and Ellen Stewart Wagner; m. Gill Diamond, Aug. 31, 1997; m. Niall Patrick Ryan, Oct. 3, 1981 (dec. Oct. 1, 1993); children: Allison Kathleen, Michael Richard Diamond, Sara Elana Diamond. BS in microbiology, Penn State U. Coll. of Sci., University Pk., 1980; MS in med. microbiology, W.Va. U. Med. Sch., Morgantown, 1983; PhD in toxicology, U. Pitts. Grad. Sch. Pub. Health, 1992. Rsch. biologist, immunotoxicology br. U.S. EPA, Rsch. Triangle Pk., NC, 1995—2000; asst. prof., dept. of pathology UMDNJ-New Jersey Med. Sch., Newark, 2000—03; asst. prof. dept. oral biology UMDNJ-N.J. Dental Sch., Newark, 2003—. Devel. Enzyme-Linked ImmunoSorbent Assay endotoxin detection Hyclone Diagnostics/Travenol Labs., 1981—82; rsch. fellow in medicine Mass. Gen. Hosp./Harvard Med. Sch., Boston, 1992—95; ORD regional sci. advisor EPA region 2 US EPA Office Sci. Policy, Washington, 1998—2000. Contbr. articles to profl. jours. Recipient Individual Nat. Rsch. Svc. award, NIH Nat. Heart, Lung and Blood Inst., 1994—97; grantee, Allegheny-Erie Regional chpt. Soc. Toxicology, 1991, NIH Nat. Inst. Allergies and Infectious Diseases, 2000—03, NIH Nat. Heart, Lung and Blood Inst., 2003—, 2007—. Mem.: AAAS, Sigma Xi, Am. Conf. of Govtl. Indsl. Hygenists, Am. Thoracic Soc., Am. Soc. for Microbiology, Soc. for Leukocyte Biology, Am. Assn. Immunologists, Soc. Toxicology. Achievements include patents for polymyxin agarose-lipopolysaccharide antigen and associated method. Avocations: swimming, ice skating, piano, clarinet, skiing. Office: UMDNJ-NJ Dental Sch Dept Oral Biology 185 South Orange Ave Newark NJ 07101 Office Phone: 973-972-2624. Personal E-mail: lkryan@aol.com. Business E-Mail: ryanlk@umdnj.edu.

RYAN, LUCILLE FRANCIS See LAWLESS, LUCY

RYAN, MARGARET A., federal judge; b. May 23, 1964; BA cum laude, Knox Coll., 1985; JD summa cum laude, U. Notre Dame. Bar: Va. 1995, Colo. 2003, DC 2005, U.S. Supreme Ct., U.S. Dist. Ct. Appeals (4th cir.), U.S. Dist. Ct. Colo., U.S. Ct. Fed. Claims, U.S. Supreme Ct. Va., U.S. Supreme Ct. Colo. Comm. officer, co. comdr., platoon comdr. USMC, II and II Marine Expeditionary Forces, 1988—92; chief trial counsel USMC, Quantico, Va., 1995—97, Okinawa, Japan, 1995—97, aide de Camp to 31st comdt., 1997—99; with Cooper Carvin & Rosenthal, 1999—2000; law clk. to Hon. J. Michael Luttig US Ct. Appeals (4th Cir.), 2000—01; law clk. to Justice Clarence Thomas U.S. Supreme Ct., 2001—02; with Bartlit Beck Herman Palenchar & Scott, 2002—04; ptnr. Wiley, Rein & Fielding LLP, 2004—06; judge US Ct. Appeals for the Armed Forces, 2006—. Office: US Ct Appeals for the Armed Forces 450 E St NW Washington DC 20442 *

RYAN, MARIANNE ELIZABETH, lawyer; b. Ft. Knox, Ky., Nov. 15, 1964; d. John L. and Frances J. (McIntosh) R. BA, Trinity Coll., Hartford, Conn., 1986; JD, Yale U., New Haven, Conn., 1991; MS in Info., U. Mich., Ann Arbor, 2003, grad. cert. in Sci., Tech. and Soc., 2006. Bar: Ill. 1991, US Dist. Ct. (no. dist.) Ill. 1991. Assoc. Pattishall, McAuliffe, Newbury, Hilliard & Geraldson, Chgo., 1991—93; internet editor Law Jour. EXTRA! The N.Y. Law Pub. Co., NYC, 1994—95; rsch. scholar Nat. Ctr. for Philanthropy and Law NYU Sch. Law, 1996—99; coord. tech. Americorps/Project F.I.R.S.T., NYC, 1999—2000; VISTA svc. leader Americorps/Ohio Campus Compact, Yellow Springs, 2000—01; resident fellow Lloyd Hall Scholars Program, U. Mich., Ann Arbor, 2002—03, Cmty. Info. fellow Alliance for Cmty. Tech., 2002—06, mem. behavioral sci. instl. rev. bd., 2006—. Adj. prof. trademark and copyright law John Marshall Law Sch., Chgo., 1993. Exec. editor Yale Jour. on Regulation. Recipient Margaret Mann award, Sch. of Info., U. Mich., 2003; Olin fellow, U. Mich. Law Sch., 2004—05, Rackham Regents' fellow, U. Mich., 2004—06, Jacob Javits fellow, U.S. Dept. Edn., 2005—, Margaret Dow Towsley scholar, U. Mich., 2001—02, USA Funds Access to Edn. scholar, 2005—, Microsoft summer fellow, U Mich., 2002. Mem.: Internat. Assn. Sci., Tech. and Soc., Soc. Social Studies of Sci., Soc. Philosophy and Tech., Internat. Soc. Ethics and Info. Tech., Assn. Internet Rschrs., Assn. Practical and Profl. Ethics, Phi Beta Kappa. Home: 1150 Paddock Pl Apt 107 Ann Arbor MI 48108 Business E-Mail: meryan@umich.edu.

RYAN, MARK ANTHONY, architect, lawyer; b. Council Bluffs, Iowa, Sept. 6, 1964; s. Paul Elmer and Darreline Kay (Wyland) Ryan; m. Shelli Ann Hagerbaumer, Sept. 26, 1992. BA in Architecture with distinction, Iowa State U., Ames, 1987; JD summa cum laude, Creighton U., Omaha, 2003. Registered profl. arch., Wis.; bar: Iowa, 2003, Nebr. 2004, U.S Patent and Trademark Office 2005. Project arch. U.S. Army C.E., Omaha, 1987-90, arch., security engr., 1990-91, environ. project mgr., 1991-96; owner, arch. Ryan Designs, Omaha, 1987—; project mgr. Bovis Constrn. Corp. and Bovis Lend Lease, Omaha, 1997-2000; CEO Ad Hoc Comm. Resources, LLC, Omaha, 1999—, gen. counsel, 2004—; pvt. law practice Ryan Patent Law, 2004—. Bd. advisors Fitness Plus, Council Bluffs, Iowa, 1990—92; expert witness, Iowa, Nebr., 1991—; law clk. West Corp., 2002; intern law clk. U.S. Dist. Ct., Nebr., 2003. Chmn. City Devel. Commn., Council Bluffs, Iowa, 1992; trustee San. and Improvement Dist. No. 142, Douglas County, Nebr., 1995—96. Scholar, State of Iowa, 1982; Valentino scholar, 2001, Lane Found. scholar, 2002, Abrahams scholar, 2002. Mem.: ABA, AIA (sec. S.W. Iowa sect. 1991, treas. 1992, v.p. 1993, pres. 1994—96), Omaha Bar Assn., Nebr. State Bar Assn., Iowa Bar Assn., Golden Key, Phi Delta Phi, Tau Sigma Delta, Phi Kappa Phi. Avocations: bicycling, tennis. Office: Ryan Patent Law 9030 Raven Oaks Dr Omaha NE 68152-1759 Business E-Mail: mark@adhoccr.com.

RYAN, MARLEIGH GRAYER, language educator; b. NYC, May 1, 1930; d. Harry and Betty (Hurwick) Grayer; m. Edward Ryan, June 4, 1950; 1 child, David Patrick. BA, NYU, 1951; MA, Columbia U., 1956; postgrad., Kyoto U., 1958-59; PhD, Columbia U., 1965, cert. in Japanese Lit., 1968. Research assoc. Columbia U., NYC, 1960-61, lectr. Japanese, 1961-65, asst. prof., 1965-70, assoc. prof., 1970-72; vis. asst. prof. Yale U., New Haven, 1966-67; assoc. prof. U. Iowa, Iowa City, 1972-75, prof., 1975-81, chmn. dept., 1972-81; prof. Japanese SUNY, New Paltz, 1981-98, dean liberal arts and scis., 1981-90, prof. emeritus, 1999—; assoc. in rsch. Reischauer Inst. for Japanese Studies Harvard U., Cambridge, Mass., 1999—, chair study group on Asian Am. Lit., 2000—02; study group leader Harvard Inst., 2003—. Vice chmn. seminar on modern Japan, Columbia U., 1984-85, chmn., 1985-86; co-chmn. N.Y. State Conf. on Asian Studies, 1986, editor, 1993-99, mem. exec. com., 1993-96, sec., 1993-99, co-chmn., 1998. Co-author: (with Herschel Webb) Research in Japanese Sources, 1965; author: Japan's First Modern Novel, 1967, The Development of Realism in the Fiction of Tsubouchi Shoyo, 1975; assoc. editor: Jour. Assn. Tchrs. Japanese, 1962-71, editor, 1971-75. East Asian Inst. fellow Columbia U., 1955; Ford Found. fellow, 1958-60; Japan Found. fellow, 1973, Woodrow Wilson Ctr. Internat. Scholars fellow, 1988-89; recipient Van. Am. Disting. Book award Columbia, 1968 Mem. MLA (sec. com. on teaching Japanese Lang. 1962-68, mem. del. assembly 1979-87, mem. exec. com. div. Asian lit. 1981-86), Assn. Tchrs. Japanese (exec. com. 1969-72, 74-77), Assn. Asian Studies (bd. dirs. 1975-78, N.E. asian coun. 1975-78, coun. of confs., 1993-96), Midwest Conf. Asian Studies (pres. 1980-81) Personal E-mail: marleighryan@earthlink.net. *Studying the most difficult language in the world has taught me patience and tact. One learns what it is to sit completely still at the Japanese No theatre and absorb wondrous sights and sounds in an atmosphere of absolute peace. Discovering the stillness in movement is perhaps the most important lesson we in the West can derive from our Asian experience.*

RYAN, MEG (MARGARET MARY EMILY ANN HYRA), actress, film producer; b. Fairfield, Conn., Nov. 19, 1961; m. Dennis Quaid, Feb. 14, 1991 (div. July 16, 2001); 1 child, Jack Henry; 1 adopted child, Daisy True. Student, NYU. Established Fandango Films (then called Prufrock Pictures), 1994—2000. Mem. of jury Festival Internat. de Cannes, 2003. Appearences include (TV) One of the Boys, 1982, As The World Turns, 1982-84, Wild Side, 1985, (films) Rich and Famous, 1981, Amityville 3-D, 1983, Top Gun, 1986, Armed and Dangerous, 1986, Innerspace, 1987, Promised Land, 1987, D.O.A., 1988, The Presidio, 1988, When Harry Met Sally, 1989, Joe Versus the Volcano, 1990, The Doors, 1991, Prelude to a Kiss, 1992, Sleepless in Seattle, 1993, Flesh and Bone, 1993, When a Man Loves a Woman, 1994, Restoration, 1994, I.Q., 1994, French Kiss, 1995 (also prodr.), Two for the Road, 1996 (also prodr.), Courage Under Fire, 1996, Addicted to Love, 1997, Anastasia (voice), 1997, City of Angels, 1998, Hurlyburly, 1998, You've Got Mail, 1998, Hanging Up, 2000, Proof of Life, 2000, Kate & Leopold, 2001, In the Cut, 2003, Against the Ropes, 2004, In the Land of Women, 2007; prodr. Lost Souls, 2000, Desert Saints, 2002; exec. prodr. Northern Lights, 1997, The Wedding Planner, 2001. Vol. CARE humanitarian orgn. Recipient Golden Apple award Hollywood Women's Press Club, 1989, Woman of Yr. award Hasty Pudding Theatricals, 1994, ShoWest Conv. Actress of Yr. award, 1999, Am. Comedy Award, 1990, 1994, Women in Film Crystal Award, 1995; named one of the Top 100 Movie Stars of All Time, Empire (UK) Magazine, 1997, The Most Powerful People in Hollywood, Premiere (USA) Magazine, 1999, Most Powerful People in Hollywood, Entertainment Weekly's, 1998. Office: Creative Artists Agy 9830 Wilshire Blvd Beverly Hills CA 90212 *

RYAN, MELBAGENE T., retired food service and nutrition director; b. Arkadelphia, Ark., Jan. 6, 1927; d. Horace Samuel and Eunice Bridges (Moorman) Tull; m. Wayne Stuart Ryan, Dec. 26, 1954. BS in Edn., Henderson U., 1948; M in Edn., Tex. Women's U., 1951. Tchr. Eudora Pub. Schs., Ark., 1948-52; dir. food services Tex. Christian U., Ft. Worth, 1952-53, Tex. Women's U., 1953-58; dir. food and nutriton service Irving Ind. Sch. Dist., Tex., 1958-85. Project dir. to develop stds. excellence with a self study and evaluation Tex. Sch. Food Svc. Assn., 1985-88; cons. in field. Co-author and project dir.: (with others) Youth Advisory Council Resource Manual, 1978-79, Effective Food Service Management Using Computers, 1982. With child nutrition Tex. Sch. Food Svc. Assn., Washington, 1974-79; with legis. Am. Sch. Food Svc. Assn., Irving, 1980-85; mem. Denton Co. Hist. Commn., 1997—, Denton Co. Courthouse-on-the Square Mus., chmn. 1998—; mem. adv. bd. Lake Forest Good Samaritan Village, 1998—, Tex. Woman's U. Centennial Celebration, 2001, planning com., 1998-99, Denton Good Samaritan Village, 2003; chmn. Bayless Selby House Mus., 2002—. Recipient Food Facilities Design award Instns. Volume Feeding Awards Program, New Orleans, 1977, Trend Setter award, North Tex. Brokers Assn., Dallas, 1978; Melbagene Ryan Scholarship named in her honor by Dallas Profl. Friends, 1985. Mem. Denton Dietetic Assn. (pres. 1977-78), Tex. Dietetic Assn., Am. Dietetic Assn. (chmn. joint com. 1979-82), Tex. Sch. Food Svc. Assn. (pres. 1975-76, nutrition edn. 1975), Am. Sch. Food Svc. Assn. (conf. com. 1977-78, 1982-83), Tex. Women's U. Alumni Assn. Methodist.

RYAN, MICHAEL D., state supreme court justice; BA, St. John's U., Collegeville, Minn., 1967; JD, Ariz. State U., 1977. Dep. county atty. Maricopa County Atty.'s Office, 1977—85; judge pro tempore Superior Ct. State of Ariz., Maricopa County, 1985—86, judge Maricopa County, 1986—96, assoc. criminal presiding judge Maricopa County, 1993—96; judge Ariz. Ct. Appeals, Divsn. 1, 1996—2002, vice chief judge, 2001—02; justice Ariz. Supreme Ct., 2002—. Chair Scottsdale Jud. Appts. Adv. Bd., 1999—2002; vice chair Ariz. State Bar Task Force on Persons with Disabilities, 2002—; mem. Maricopa County Resource Site Team for Ctr. for Sex Offender Mgmt., 1996—2000, Ariz. Atty. Gen.'s Capital Case Commn., 2000—02; mem. adv. com. Nat. Ctr. for State Cts., Ctr. for Effective Pub. Policy, also State Justice Inst.'s Nat. Solutions Project, 2003—; chair Ariz. Supreme Ct. Com. on Keeping Record, 2004—. Infantry platoon comdr. USMC, 1968, Vietnam. Recipient Semper Fi award, First Marine Divsn. Assn., Phoenix chpt., 2001, Outstanding Alumnus award, Ariz. State Univ. Coll. Law, 2003, Disting. Achievement award, 2003, James A. Walsh Outstanding Jurist award, State Bar Ariz., 2005. Mem.: State Bar of Arizona (Judicial award of Excellence 2001), Maricopa County Bar Assn. (bd. dirs. 1987—91, 1997—2002, chair task force recruitment and retention of women and minorities 1997—2004, Henry S. Stevens Judge of the Yr. award 2001). Office: Ariz Supreme Ct 1501 W Washington Phoenix AZ 85007-3231 *

RYAN, MICHAEL LOUIS, controller; b. Corning, Iowa, Feb. 22, 1945; s. Leo Vincent and Elda May (Lawrence) R AAS Constrn. Tech., Iowa State U., 1985; BS Acctg., Drake U., 1972. CPA, Iowa, Wyo. Acct. Ernst & Ernst, Des Moines, 1972—75, Becker, Herrick & Co., Pueblo, Colo., 1975—78; pvt. practice acctg. Gillette, Wyo., 1979—81; acct. Karen M. Moody, CPA, Sheridan, Wyo., 1981—85; contr. T-C Investments, Inc., Sheridan, 1985—; ptnr. WHG Partnership, Sheridan, 1991—; v.p. Bosley-Ryan Constrn., Inc., Sheridan, 1993—. With spl. forces U.S. Army, 1966-68, Vietnam Mem. AICPA (tax divsn.), Wyo. Soc. CPA, Am. Legion (fin. officer 1977-81), Lodge (sec. Sheridan club 1982-90, pres. 1989), Phi Kappa Phi, Beta Alpha Psi, Beta Gamma Sigma Democrat. Roman Catholic. Home: 735 Canby St Sheridan WY 82801-4907 Office: 566 Turner Ln Sheridan WY 82801 Personal E-mail: mkryan@wavecom.net.

RYAN, NOLAN, former professional baseball player; b. Refugio, Tex., Jan. 31, 1947; s. Lynn Nolan and Martha (Hancock) Ryan; m. Ruth Elsie Holdruff, June 26, 1967; children: Reid, Reese, Wendy. Student, Alvin Jr. Coll., Tex., 1966—69. Pitcher N.Y. Mets, NYC, 1966—71, Calif. Angels, 1972—79, Houston Astros, 1980—88, Texas Rangers, 1989—93; cattle rancher, China Grove, Ray and Gonzalvez Tex.; owner The Bass Inn, Waterfront Steakhouse and Grill, Express Bank (sold to First Community Capital in 2002); owner, Texas league farm club team The Round Rock Express, Round Rock, Tex.; investor, ptnr. The Express Bank of Texas, Round Rock, Tex., 2003—; owner Corpus Christi Hooks (Houston Astros AA Affiliate), 2004—. Commr. Tex. Parks and Wildlife Commn., 1995—2001, vice chmn., 1995—97. Author (with Steve Jacobson): Nolan Ryan: Strike-Out King, 1975; author: (with Bill Libby) Nolan Ryan: The Other Game, 1977; author: (with Joe Torre) Pitching and Hitting, 1977; author: (with Harvey Frommer) Throwing Heat: The Autobiography of Nolan Ryan, 1988; author: (with Tom House) Nolan Ryan's Pitcher's Bible, 1991; author: (with Jerry Jenkins) Miracle Man: Nolan Ryan, The Autobiography, 1992; author: (with others) Kings of Hill, 1992. Founder, bd. dirs. The Nolan Ryan Found.; bd. dirs. The Justin Cowboy Crisis Fund, Texas Water Found., Natural Resources Found., Tex. With AUS, 1967. Named Am. League Pitcher of Yr., Sporting News, 1977; named to All-Star Team, Am. League, 1972, 1973, 1975, 1979, Nat. League, 1981, 1985, Baseball Hall of Fame, 1999. Achievements include holding over 50 Major League records including most seasons pitched (27), most strikeouts (5,714) and most no-hit games (7). Office: Round Rock Express 3400 E Palm Valley Blvd Round Rock TX 78664 *

RYAN, PATRICK G., diversified financial services company executive, director; b. Milw., May 15, 1937; m. Shirley Welsh, Apr. 16, 1966; children: Patrick Jr., Robert J., Corbett M. BS, Northwestern U., 1959. Sales agt. Penn Mut., 1959-64, Pat Ryan & Assocs. Chgo., 1964-71; chmn., pres. Ryan Ins. Group Inc., Chgo., 1971-82; pres., chief exec. officer Combined Internat. Corp. (now Aon Corp.), Northbrook, Ill., 1982—, bd. dirs., 1982—; pres., CEO Aon Corp., Chgo., 1990—2005, exec. chmn., 1990—. Bd. dirs. Sears Roebuck and Co., Chgo., Tribune Co., Chgo. Life trustee, past chmn., Rush Univ. Med. Ctr., Chgo.; chmn., trustee Northwestern U.; past trustee Field Mus. Natural History, Chgo. Recipient Lifetime Achievement award, The Review-Worldwide Reinsurance, 2005, Internat. Exec. of the Yr., Brigham Young Univ., 2002, Golden Plate award, Acad. of Achievement, 2002; named to Chgo. Bus. Hall of Fame. Mem., past pres., Econ. Club Chgo. Office: Aon Corp Aon Ctr 200 E Randolph St Chicago IL 60601 *

RYAN, PATRICK MICHAEL, lawyer; b. Chgo., May 26, 1944; s. Edward Michael and Kathleen Teresa (Crimmins) R.; m. Holly Ann Daleske, Aug. 31, 1968; children: Rebecca Eileen, Brendan Patrick, Abigail Christine, Lucas Christopher. BA, St. Mary's Coll., Winona, Minn., 1966; JD, Marquette U., 1969. Bar: Wis. 1969. Law clk. Wis. Supreme Ct., Madison, 1969-70; ptnr. Quarles & Brady LLP, Milw., 1970—2001, chmn., mng. ptnr., 2002—. Dir. and officer several pvt. bus. corps. Mem. ABA, Wis. Bar Assn., Milw. Bar Assn. Avocations: reading, sports. Home: 363 Huntington Dr Cedarburg WI 53012-9507 Office: Quarles & Brady LLP 411 E Wisconsin Ave Ste 2550 Milwaukee WI 53202-4497 Office Phone: 414-277-5000. E-mail: pmr@quarles.com.

RYAN, PAUL, congressman; b. Janesville, Wis., Jan. 29, 1970; s. Paul and Betty Ryan; m. Janna Ryan; 3 children. BS in Econs. and Polit. Sci., Miami U., Ohio, 1992. Aide Staff of US Senator Bob Kasten of Wis., Washington; econ. adv., speechwriter Empower Am., Jack Kemp, Bill Bennett, Washington; legis. dir. US Senate, Washington; mktg. cons. Ryan Inc., Ctrl., Janesville; mem. US Congress from 1st Wis. dist., 1999—, mem. ways and means com., mem. joint econ. com., mem. budget com. Defeated former Kenosha City Coun. Pres. Lydia Spottswood in 1998 to succeed two-term Rep. Mark Neumann, who ran unsuccessfully for the Senate. Mem. Janesville YMCA, Janesville Bowmen Inc. and Ducks Unlimited. Republican. Roman Catholic. Office: US Ho Reps 1113 Longworth Ho Office Bldg Washington DC 20515 Office Phone: 202-225-3031. *

RYAN, RAY DARL, JR., academic administrator; b. Joliet, Ill., Dec. 2, 1945; s. Ray D. and Oral Ada (Smiley) R.; m. Marianne Rossetto, Aug. 28, 1965; children: Kimberley, Kristin, Matthew. BS, U. Wis., Menomonie, 1970; MEd, U. Mo., 1973, EdD, 1975; Doctorate (hon.), Tomsk Poly. Inst., Russia, 1992. Cert. vocat./tech. tchr., adminstr., chief sch. officer. Dep. supt. pub. instrn. Nev. Dept. Edn., Carson City; dep. supt. spl. programs Ariz. Dept. Edn., Phoenix, state dir., vocat. educator; exec. dir. Ctr. Edn. and Tng. for Employment Ohio State U., Columbus, assoc. dean rsch., internat. affairs. Bd. dirs., vice-chair Coun. Ednl. Devel. and Rsch.; pres., CEO Nat. Occup. Testing Inst., 1999. Mem. OTT, ASTD, Phi Delta Kappa, Epsilon Pi Tau, Omicron Tau Theta. Office: NOCTI 500 N Bronson Ave Big Rapids MI 49307

RYAN, RAYMOND D., retired steel and insurance company executive; b. Big Timber, Mont., Feb. 7, 1922; s. Robert Allen and Elsie (Beery) R.; m. Eunice Dale Burnett, Jan. 17, 1943; children: Raymond Brant, Brenda Ruth, Ronald Dale. BA, U. Mont., Missoula, 1948, JD (hon.), 1970; LLM, NYU, 1949. Bar: Mont. 1948. Various fin. officer positions U.S. Steel and subsidiaries in U.S. and Venezuela, 1949-75; v.p., treas. U.S. Steel, 1975-83; pres. The Evergreen Group Inc., Stamford, Conn., 1984-94, chmn., 1995-96, Evergreen Benefits Inc., 1996-99, The Money Suite Co., Missoula, Mont., 1999—. With mil. police AUS, 1943-45, ETO. Mem. ABA, Met. Club (N.Y.C.), Phi Sigma Kappa, Phi Delta Phi. Home: PO Box 160601 Big Sky MT 59716-0601 Office Phone: 406-995-3397. Personal

E-mail: rayd@moneysuite.com. *Although luck and ambition are the basis of many apparently successful careers, true success comes from hard work, ethical relationships, dedication, and a willingness to accept responsibility.*

RYAN, REGINA CLAIRE (MRS. PAUL DEUTSCHMAN), editor, literary agent; b. NYC, June 19, 1938; d. Edward F.X. and Kathryn Regina (Gallagher) R.; m. Paul Deutschman, Apr. 11, 1970 (widowed, 2002). BA, Trinity Coll., 1960; postgrad., New Sch. for Social Research, 1960-61, N.Y. U. Film Sch., 1961, N.Y. U. Grad. Sch. English, 1962-63. Copywriter trainee, sec. J. Walter Thompson Co., NYC, 1960-64; asst. to mng. editor Alfred A. Knopf, Inc., NYC, 1964-67, editor, 1967-75; editor-in-chief, v.p. Gen. Books div. Macmillan Pub. Co., NYC, 1975-76; pres. Regina Ryan Pub. Enterprises, Inc., NYC, 1976—. Co-author: Janice LaRouche's Strategies for Women at Work, 1984, 1987. Active Larchmont-Mamaroneck Young Reps., 1960-64; campaign worker, speech writer mayoralty campaign, Larchmont, 1962, 64; mem. Manhattan Women's Polit. Caucus, 1972-74; mem. com. Jimmy Carter Presdl. Campaign; mem., chmn. Sherman Dem. Town Com., Conn., 1985-86; mem. Jewish Cmty. Ctr. for Sherman, 1998-2001; Justice of the Peace, Sherman, 1986-96. Mem. AARP, PEN Am. Ctr., Women's Media Group, Agts. Roundtable, Assn. Authors Reps., Internat. Women's Com. on Human Rights, Linnaean Soc., NY Audubon Soc., NY Mycological Soc., Vet. Feminists Am. Democrat. Home and Office: 251 Central Park W New York NY 10024-4134 Office Phone: 212-787-5589.

RYAN, ROBERT DAVIS, lawyer; b. Lynbrook, NY, Aug. 14, 1941; s. Thomas Francis and Agnes Frances (Davis) R.; children: John, Daniel, Carolyn. BBA, St. John's U., 1962; JD, Fordham U., 1972. Bar: N.Y. 1973, U.S. Dist. Ct. (so. and ea. dists.) N.Y. 1973, U.S. Ct. Appeals (2d cir.) 1975, U.S. Supreme Ct. 1984. Asst. dist. atty. Westchester County, White Plains, N.Y., 1972-77; assoc. Clark, Gagliardi & Miller, White Plains, 1977-82; ptnr. Rende, Ryan & Downes, White Plains, 1982—. Adj. prof. law St. John's U., 1992-95, 99—. Chmn. Cable TV Adv. Com., Lewisboro, N.Y., 1983-99. Mem. Assn. Trial Lawyers Am., N.Y. State Trial Lawyers Assn., Westchester County Bar Assn., N.Y. State Bar Assn. (continuing legal edn. com. trial lawyers sect.), No. Westchester Bar Assn. (bd. govs. 1987-92, pres. 1986-87), White Plains Bar Assn. Republican. Roman Catholic. Home: 1039 Rt 35 Cross River NY 10518 Office: Rende Ryan & Downes 202 Mamaroneck Ave Ste 600 White Plains NY 10601-5312 Business E-Mail: rryan@rrd-law.com.

RYAN, ROBERT LESLIE, oil company executive; b. Detroit, Apr. 15, 1943; s. Henry and Venicee (Beavers) R.; m. Sharon Goode, July 3, 1971; children: Lesley M., Eric A. BSEE, Wayne State U., 1966; MSEE, Cornell U., 1968; MBA, Harvard U., 1970. Mgmt. cons. McKinsey and Co., NYC, 1970-75; v.p. Citibank N.A., NYC, 1975-82; v.p., treas. Union Tex. Petroleum Corp., Houston, 1982-83, v.p., controller, 1983-84, v.p. fin., 1984-93; sr. v.p. & CFO Medtronic Inc., Minneapolis, 1993—2005. Bd. dir. The Black & Decker Co., Gen. Mills Inc., Hewlett-Packard Co., UnitedHealth Group Inc., Citigroup Inc. Dir. Tex. Opera Theatre, Houston; trustee Cornell UNiv.; mem. bd. vis. Harvard Bus. Sch. Mailing: Citigroup Inc Bd Directors 399 Park Ave New York NY 10043 *

RYAN, SEAN T., lawyer; b. Worcester, Mass., May 17, 1969; BA, Wesleyan U., Middletown, Conn., 1991; JD cum laude, Suffolk U. Law Sch., 1999. Bar: Mass. 1999. Sr. aide Staff of Congressman John Joseph Moakley, Washington, Boston campaign mgr.; assoc. Donoghue, Barrett & Singal, P.C., Boston. Bd. dirs. John Joseph Moakley Charitable Found. Named a Rising Star, Mass. Super Lawyers mag., 2005, 2006, 2007. Mem.: Mass. Bar Assn., Boston Bar Assn. Office: Donoghue Barrett & Singal PC One Beacon St Boston MA 02108-3113 Office Phone: 617-720-5090. Office Fax: 617-720-5092.

RYAN, SHEILA A., retired dean, nursing educator; Diploma in Nursing, Creighton Meml. St. Joseph's Hosp. Sch. Nursing, 1967; BSN, U. Nebr., 1969; MSN in Psychiat. Nursing, U. Calif., San Francisco, 1971; PhD in Clin. Nursing Rsch., U. Ariz., 1981. Asst. prof. nursing Creighton U., Omaha, 1971—76, dean nursing, 1977—86; dean Sch. Nursing, dir. Med. Ctr. Nursing U. Rochester, NY, 1986—99; prof., Charlotte Peck Lienemann and Alumni Disting. Chair Coll. Nursing U. Nebr. Med. Ctr., Omaha. Fellow: Am. Acad. Nursing; mem.: Inst. for Healthcare Improvement, Nat. League Nursing (treas. 1993, pres. 1996—97), Inst. Medicine (treas.-sec.), Am. Internat. Health Alliance (bd. dirs. 1999—). Office: UNMC Coll Nursing Rm 4030 985330 NE Medical Ctr Omaha NE 68198-5330

RYAN, SHELLI ANN, public relations executive; b. Blair, Nebr., Dec. 8, 1968; d. Gorlyn Lew and Ruthie Ann Hagerbaumer; m. Mark Anthony Ryan, Sept. 26, 1992. BS, Bellevue U., 1992; MPA, U. Okla., 1997. Accredited Pub. Rels., Pub. Rels. Soc. Am. Mgr. mktg. svcs. Electronic Display Sys., Grand Island, Nebr., 1988-90; mktg. rep. Keeler/Raynor/Hinz, Bellevue, Nebr., 1990-92; mktg. coord. Accent Svc. Co., Omaha, 1992-95; corp. comm. specialist Applied Comm., Inc., Omaha, 1995-96; prin. Ryan Designs, Omaha, 1996-98; pres. Ad Hoc Comm. Resources, Omaha, 1999—. Media spokesperson Am. Heart Assn., Omaha, 1990-95; pub. rels. judge Jr. Achievement, Omaha, 1990, 96. Recipient 40 under 40 award Midlands Bus. Jour., 2002; named Woman Yr. Am. Women's Bus. Assn., Omaha, 1996, Gold Citation of Excellence, Am. Mktg. Assn., 2004, Best of Show and Pinnacle award Am. Mktg. Assn., 2002, Profl. Achievement award Am. Women's Assn., 2005, Bronze award Vision awards League Am. Comms. Profls., 2005. Mem. Pub. Rels. Soc. Am. (sec. 1998, treas. 1997, pres. 2001, dir. 1996—), Am. Bus. Women's Assn. (pres. 1995-96, Profl. Achievement award 2005). Avocations: weightlifting, bicycling. Home: 9030 Raven Oaks Dr Omaha NE 68152-1759

RYAN, STEPHEN JOSEPH, JR., ophthalmologist, educator; b. Honolulu, Hawaii, Mar. 20, 1940; s. S.J. and Mildred Elizabeth (Farrer) Ryan; m. Anne Christine Mullady, Sept. 25, 1965; 1 child, Patricia Anne. AB, Providence Coll., 1961; MD, Johns Hopkins U., 1965. Intern Bellevue Hosp., NYC, 1965—66; resident Wilmer Inst. Ophthalmology, Johns Hopkins Hosp., Balt., 1966—69, chief resident, 1969—70; fellow Armed Forces Inst. Pathology, Washington, 1970—71; instr. ophthalmology Johns Hopkins U., Balt., 1970—71, asst. prof., 1971—72, assoc. prof., 1972—74; Grace and Emery Beardsley prof. ophthalmology Keck Sch. Medicine, U. So. Calif., LA, 1974—, chmn. dept. ophthalmology, 1974—95, dean, 1991—2004, sr. v.p. for med. care, 1993—2004, Grace and Emery Beardsley Chair in Ophthalmology, med. dir. Doheny Eye Inst. (formerly Estelle Doheny Eye Found.), 1977—86, pres. Doheny Eye Inst., 1987—, chief of staff Doheny Eye Hosp., 1985—88; acting head ophthalmology divsn. dept. surgery Children's Hosp., 1975—77. Mem. adv. panel Calif. Med. Assn., 1975—. Editor (with M.D. Andrews): A Survey of Ophthalmology--Manual for Medical Students, 1970; editor: (with R.E. Smith) Selected Topics on the Eye in Systemic Disease, 1974; editor: (with Dawson and Little) Retinal Diseases, 1985; editor: (with others) Retina, 1989; editor:, 2000, 4t edit., 2005; assoc. editor: Ophthalmol. Surgery, 1974—85, mem. editl. bd.: Am. Jour. Ophthalmology, 1981—, Internat. Ophthalmology, 1982—, Retina, 1983—, Graefes Archives, 1984—; contbr. articles to med. jours. Recipient cert. of merit, AMA, 1971, Louis B. Mayer Scholar award, Rsch. to Prevent Blindness, 1973, Rear Adm. William Campbell Chambliss USN award, 1982, Mildred Weisenfeld Award for Lifetime Achievement in Vision Rsch., Fight for Sight, 2000. Mem.: AMA, Inst. Medicine NAS (home sec. 2006), Jules Gonin Club, Rsch. Study Club, Nat. Eye Care Project, Retina Soc., Macula Soc., Pan-Am. Assn. Microsurgery, L.A. Acad. Medicine, Pacific Coast Oto-Ophthal. Soc., Los Angeles County Med. Assn., Calif. Med. Assn., L.A. Soc. Ophthalmology, Assn. Univ. Profs. of Ophthalmology, Pan-Am. Assn. Ophthalmology, Am. Ophthal. Soc., Am. Acad. Ophthalmology and Otolaryngology (award of Merit 1975), Wilmer Ophthal. Inst. Residents Assn., Soc. Scholars of Johns Hopkins U. (life). Office: 1450 San Pablo St Los Angeles CA 90033 Business E-Mail: sryan@doheny.org.

RYAN, STEPHEN M., lawyer; s. Alex L. Ryan and Lynda A. Turner; m. Christine M. Ryan, Dec. 31, 1988; children: Travis A., Caroline A., Taylor R. BA, U. Tex., 1988; JD with honors, U. Mich., 1997. Bar: Tex. 1997. B-52 navigator/electronic warfare officer USAF, 1988—94, active duty law student Ann Arbor, Mich., 1994—97, asst. staff judge adv. Barksdale AFB, La., 1997—2002; atty. Nathan Sommers Jacobs & Gorman, Houston, 2002—05, LeBoeuf Lamb, Greene, & MacRae LLP, Houston, 2005—; staff judge adv. 147th Fighter Wing, Tex. Air N.G., Houston, 2002—. Maj. USAF, 1988—2002, lt. col. Tex. ANG, USAFR, 2004—. Decorated Achievement medal USAF, Commendation medal, Meritorious Svc. medal, Air medal US Ctrl. Command, Humanitarian Svc. medal; recipient Corpus Juris Secundum award, Torts, 1995. Mem.: Res. Officers Assn., VFW, Delta Sigma Phi. Roman Catholic. Avocations: scouting, world travel, aviation. Office: LeBoeuf Lamb Greene & MacRae LLP 1000 Main St Ste 2550 Houston TX 77002 Office Phone: 713-287-2000. Office Fax: 713-287-2100. Business E-Mail: smryan@llgm.com.

RYAN, T. TIMOTHY (THOMAS TIMOTHY RYAN JR.), diversified financial services company executive, former federal agency administrator; b. Washington, June 13, 1945; s. Thomas Timothy and Elizabeth (Ockershausen) R.; m. Judith Rush, June 13, 1970; children: Kathryn, Michael. AB, Villanova U., Pa., 1967; JD, Am. U., 1973. Bar: D.C. 1973. Atty. NLRB, Washington, 1973-74, Balt. and Washington, 1974-75, 76-80; dep. gen. counsel Pres. Ford Com., 1975-76; solicitor US Dept. Labor, 1981-83; assoc., ptnr. Reed, Smith, Shaw & McClay and predecessor Pierson, Ball & Dowd, Washington, 1978-81, 83-90; dir. Office Thrift Supervision US Dept. Treasury, Washington, 1990-93; mng. dir. Global Govt. Institutions Group JP Morgan Chase & Co., NYC, 1993—. Adj. prof. Georgetown U. Law Sch., 1979-83; mem. bd. overseas Pvt. Investment Corp., 1981-83; mem. bd. Program for Advancement of Tech. in India, 1985-90; bd. dirs. FDIC, RTC, Neighborhood Re-investment Corp., 1990-93. 1st lt. USAR, 1967-70. 1st lt. USAR, 1967-70. Mem. ABA, D.C. Bar Assn., Am. Coun. Young Polit. Leaders (bd. dirs. 1983-89, pres. 1985-88), Congl. Country Club, Army and Navy Club. Republican. Roman Catholic. Office: JPMorgan Chase & Co 270 Park Ave New York NY 10017 *

RYAN, TERRY, professional sports team executive; b. Janesville, Wis., Oct. 26, 1953; m. Karilyn Ryan; children: Tim, Kathleen. Diploma in Phys. Edn., U. Wis., 1979. Profl. baseball player Minn. Twins, 1972-76; profl. scout NY Mets, 1980-86; scouting dir. Minn. Twins, 1986-91, v.p. player pers., asst. gen. mgr., 1991-94, v.p., baseball pers., asst. gen. mgr., 1994, v.p., gen. mgr., 1994—. Named Major League Baseball Exec. of the Yr., The Sporting News, 2002, 2006. Office: Minnesota Twins 34 Kirby Puckett Pl Minneapolis MN 55415-1596

RYAN, THOMAS F., lawyer; b. Detroit, Nov. 4, 1943; BS, Ferris State U., 1965; JD magna cum laude, Wayne State U., 1971. Bar: Ill. 1972, US Ct. of Appeals (7th cir.) 1972, US Dist. Ct. (no. dist.) Ill. 1972, U.S. Supreme Ct. 1978. Joined Sidley & Austin (now Sidley Austin, LLP), Chgo., 1972—; ptnr. antitrust and bus. counseling Sidley Austin, LLP, Chgo., 1978—. Exec. com. Sidley Austin, LLP; adv. com. on cir. rules 7th Fed. Ct. Appeals. 1st lt. U.S. Army, 1966-68. Decorated Bronze star. Fellow Am. Coll. Trial Lawyers; mem. Chgo. Bar Assn. (mem. jud. evaluation com.), 7th Cir. Bar Assn. (bd. govs. 1986-89, 2nd v.p. 1990-91, pres. 1991-92). Office: Sidley Austin LLP 1 S Dearborn St Chicago IL 60603 Office Phone: 312-853-7497. Office Fax: 312-853-7036. Business E-Mail: tryan@sidley.com.

RYAN, THOMAS JOHN, cardiologist; b. Manhasset, NY, Dec. 19, 1928; s. Mark J. Ryan and Margaret M. Rooney; m. Nancy Therese Cooney, June 12, 1954; children: Kathie Steinberg, Amy, Beth Ryan Walter, Thomas John Jr., Paula, Jennifer Brown. BA, Holy Cross Coll., Worcester, Mass., 1950; MD, Georgetown Med., Washington, DC, 1954. Diplomate Nat. Bd. of Med. Examiners Pa., 1954, cert. Am. Bd. of Internal Medicine Pa., 1962, Subspecialty Bd. Cardiovascular Disease Pa. Chief cardiology St. Elizabeth's Hosp., Boston, 1961—71; instr. in medicine Harvard Med. Sch., Boston, 1961—71; asst. prof. of medicine Tufts Med. Sch., Boston, 1963—68, assoc. prof. medicine, 1968—71; chief cardiology Boston U. Med. Ctr., Boston, 1971—94; prof. medicine Boston U. Sch. of Medicine, Boston, 1971—, sr. cons. in cardiology, chief emeritus, 1994—. Author: (265 articles pub.) In Peer Reviewed Med. Jours., 24 book chpts. in medical texts. Advisor Dept. of Pub. Health, Boston, 1979—96, med. N.Y. State adv. com. NYC, 1991—2003; med. adv. panel Tech. Assessment Group-Blue Cross, Chgo., 2001—03. Capt. Med. Corps. US Army, 1955—57, Ft. Banks, Mass. Recipient Disting. Leadership award, Am. Heart Assn., 1980, Paul Dudley White award, 1982, Alpha Omega Alpha, Nat. Med. Honor Soc., 1985, Lawrence B. Ellis Lectureship, Harvard Med. Sch., 1986, Gold Heart award, Am. Heart Assn., 1991, The Best Doctors in Am., Woodward/White, Inc., 1994, James B. Herrick award, Coun. on Clin. Cardiology, Am. Heart Assn., 1996, The Stokes Lectureship, Irish Cardiac Soc. Royal Coll. of Physicians and Surgeons, Dublin, Ireland, 1996, Chairman's award, Am. Heart Assn., 2001; fellow Fullbright Scholar, Fullbright Com., Washington, DC, 1990—91, Fogarty Sr. Internat. Fellowship, Oxford U., 1990—91. Master: Am. Coll. Cardiology (bd. govs. 1980—83, bd. trustees 1986—93, Disting. Fellowship award 1998), ACP; fellow: European Soc. Cardiology, Soc. Geriatric Cardiology, Irish Cardiac Soc. (hon.); mem.: NIH (mem. cardiology adv. com. 1990), Am. Heart Assn. (pres. 1984—86), Am. Bd. Internal Medicine (mem. subspecialty bd. cardiovasc. medicine 1986—92), Cardiovasc. Health Initiative Developing Countries (mem. sci. adv. com.), Internat. Health, Inst. Medicine (mem. bd. 1995—98), InterAm. Soc. Cardiology (pres. 1992—95), Assn. Profs. Cardiology, Assn. Univ. Cardiologists, New Eng. Cardiovasc. Soc. (pres. 1973), Roxbury Soc. Med. Improvement, Am. Fedn. Clin. Rsch., Am. Clin. and Climatol. Assn., Mass. Med. Soc. Independent. Roman Catholic. Achievements include early contributor to development of coronary arteriography and the conduct of randomized clinical trials and is internat. recognized as an authority on ischemic heart disease. Avocations: history of western civilization and medicine, classical music, sailing, skiing, golf. Office: Boston U Sch Medicine 88 East Newton St Boston MA 02118 Business E-Mail: thomas.ryan@bmc.org.

RYAN, THOMAS L., funeral company executive; BBA, U. Tex. CPA PricewaterhouseCoopers, 1988—96; fin. mgmt. positions Service Corp. Internat., Houston, 1996—2000, CEO European ops., 2000—02, pres. & COO, 2002—05, pres. & CEO, 2005—. Mem.: Young Presidents Org. Office: Service Corporation Internat 1929 Allen Pkwy Houston TX 77019 *

RYAN, THOMAS M., pharmaceutical company executive; b. NJ, Aug. 15, 1952; m. Cathy H. Ryan; 4 children. BS in Pharmacy, U. RI, 1975. Pharmacist CVS Corp., Woonsocket, RI, from 1975, numerous managerial positions v.p. pharmacy ops., sr. v.p. pharmacy, exec. v.p. pharmacy, exec. v.p. stores; pres., CEO CVS Pharmacy, Inc. (then part of Melville Corp.), Woonsocket, RI, 1993—96; vice chmn., COO CVS Corp., Woonsocket, RI, 1996—98, pres., CEO, 1998—2007, chmn., 1999—2007; pres., CEO CVS Caremark Corp., Woonsocket, RI, 2007—. Bd. dirs. Fleet Fin. Group, Reebok Internat. Ltd., Yum Brands!, Inc.; bd. trustees Healthcare Leadership Coun. Office: CVS Caremark Corp One CVS Dr Woonsocket RI 02895 *

RYAN, THOMAS WILLIAM, lawyer; b. Tulsa, Feb. 16, 1953; s. Dean Lawrence and Helen Ladeen Ryan; m. Mary Ellen Poxon, Jan. 30, 1973; children: Matthew Alan, Jennifer Erin. BA, U. Houston, 1975, JD, 1978. Bar: Tex. 1978. Ptnr. Hart, Ryan & Pfeffer, Houston, 1978-80; contracts adminstr. Texaco Inc., Houston, 1980-85; asst. gen. counsel Total Minatome Corp., Houston, 1985-99; gen. counsel, corp. sec. Total Exploration Prodn. USA, Inc., Houston, 1999-2001; v.p., gen. counsel, corp. sec. Total E&P USA, Inc., Houston, 2001—, v.p., Human Resources, Comm. and Law, gen. counsel & Corp. sec., 2003—, v.p. corp. divsn., gen. counsel, 2003—. Adv. bd. Inst. for Energy Law. Coach youth sports YMCA, Houston, 1990-94. Mem. KC (adv. 1985-87), State Bar Tex., admitted to US Supreme Ct. of Appeals (5th cir.). Avocations: golf, bowling. Office: Total E&P USA Inc One Memorial City Plz 800 Gessner Ste 700 Houston TX 77024

RYAN, TIMOTHY, publishing executive; b. 1959; m. Trish Ryan; children: Tim, Kelly. B. in Polit. Sci., U. Notre Dame; MBA, Northwestern U. Kellogg Sch. Mgmt. Circulation mgr. Chgo. Tribune, 1982—93, v.p. circulation & consumer mktg., 2005—07; v.p. circulation Phila. Inquirer, Phila. Daily News, 1993—2000; v.p. ops. & circulation Balt. Sun, 2000—05, pub. & CEO, 2007—. Recipient Tribune Co. Mgmt. award, 1992. Office: Baltimore Sun Co 501 N Calvert St PO Box 1377 Baltimore MD 21278 Office Phone: 410-332-6000. *

RYAN, TIMOTHY J., congressman; b. Niles, Ohio, July 16, 1973; s. Rochelle Ryan. Student, Youngstown State U., 1991—92; BA in Polit. Sci., Bowling Green State U., 1995; JD, Franklin Pierce Law Ctr., Concord, NH, 2000. Congl. aide Staff of US Rep. James A. Traficant of Ohio, 1995—97; intern Trumbull County Prosecutor's Office; mem. Ohio State Senate from 32nd dist., Columbus, 2001—02, US Congress from 17th Ohio dist., 2003—, mem. appropriations com., 2006—, co-chair Mfg. Caucus, mem. Dem. steering and policy com., 2006—. Trustee Found. Extended. Recipient Legis. Leadership award on Domestic Mfg., US Bus. and Industry Coun., 2004, Friend of Nat. Pks. award, Nat. Pks. Conservation Assn., 2005. Mem. KC, Sons Italy, Internat. Narcotic Enforcement Officers Assn., Ancient Order Hibernians, Elks. Democrat. Office: 197 W Market St Warren OH 44481 Office Phone: 202-225-5261, 330-373-0074. Office Fax: 330-373-0098. *

RYAN, TIMOTHY PATRICK, investment company executive; BS in Mgmt. cum laude, Suffolk U., Boston, 1990. Fund acct. State St. Bank & Trust, Boston, 1990—92; analyst to sr. analyst John Hancock Advisors, 1992—96; sr. statistical analyst Putnam Investments, 1996—97; attribution analyst Fidelity Mgmt. and Rsch., 1997—2000, mgr., attribution analyst, 2000—03, dir., attribution analyst, 2004—05; v.p., performance mgmt. Hartford Investment Mgmt., 2005—. Adv. bd. mem. Jour. of Performance Measurement, 2001—; founder and owner Ryan Tax Prep & Advisory, 1995—2005. Editor: Portfolio Analysis, 2006; contbr. articles to profl. jours. Co-recipient Top Reviewer, Jour. of Performance Mgmt., 2002, 2003, 2004, 2005, 2006; recipient Article of Yr. award, Dietz award for Performance Measurement Lit., 2004. Mem.: Golden Key. Avocations: reading, exercise, golf, carpentry.

RYAN, TOM, reporting applications platform company executive; BS in Computer Sci., San Francisco State U.; MBA in Internat. Bus., U. Notre Dame de Namur. Sr. mgmt. positions at Informix, Illustra, Oracle and Amdahl; dir. customer support Actuate Corp., South San Francisco, Calif., 1997—2002, CIO, sr. v.p. customer svc., 2002—. Mem. adv. bd. AppMail, San Mateo County Cmty. Coll. Dist. Computer Sci. Divsn. Office: Actuate Corp 701 Gateway Blvd South San Francisco CA 94080-7084 Office Phone: 650-837-2000. Office Fax: 650-827-1560.

RYAN, UNA SCULLY, health science association administrator, medical educator; b. Kuala Lumpur, Malaysia, Dec. 18, 1941; d. Henry and Amy (Yee) Scully; m. Allan Dana Callow, May 26, 1989; children: Tamsin Randlett, Amy Jean Susan Ryan. BSc in Zoology, Chemistry & Microbiology, Bristol U., Eng., 1963; PhD in Cell Biology, Cambridge U., Eng., 1968. Fellow dept. biology U. Va., Charlottesville, 1964-66; fellow dept. medicine U. Miami, Fla., 1966-67, adj. asst. prof. biology Fla., 1968-71; dir. lab. for ultrastructure studies Howard Hughes Med. Inst., Miami, 1967-71; from instr. to assoc. prof. medicine U. Miami Sch. Medicine, 1967-80, prof. medicine, 1980-89; sr. scientist Papanicolaou Cancer Rsch. Inst., Miami, 1972-77; rsch. prof. surgery Washington U. Sch. Medicine, St. Louis, 1990—; dir. health scis. Monsanto Co., St. Louis, 1990-93; pres., CEO T Cell Scis., Needham, Mass., 1993-98; rsch. prof. medicine Boston U. Sch. Medicine, 1993—; pres., CEO AVANT Immunotherapeutics, Needham, Mass., 1998—. Dir. course W. Alton Jones Cell Sci. Ctr., 1979-81; dir. Hybridoma Facility, U. Miami, 1986-89; chair local organizing com. Internat. Coun. on Thrombosis and Hemostasis, 1984; chair Rev. Com. for Extracellular Matrix Interactions in Lung, 1983; chair various revs. NHLBI; chair Mass. Biotech. Coun., 2004-06; mem. various rev. and adv. coms.; bd. dirs. Albany Molecular Rsch. Inc., 2006- Author: J. Tissue Culture Methods, 1987, Pulmonary Endothelium in Health Disease, 1987, Endothelial Cells, 1988, Vascular Endothelium: Receptors and Transduction Mechanisms, 1989; editor: Tissue & Cell, 1981-87; rev. editor: In Vitro, 1986; reviewer profl. jours.; contbr. articles to profl. jours. UK state scholar, 1960, Country Major scholar, 1960; D.S.I.R. rsch. fellow, 1964, 65, Ethel Sargant Rsch. fellow, 1964-65, Sci. Rsch. Coun. fellow, 1966; recipient Louis and Artur Lucian award for rsch. in circulatory diseases, 1984, Merit award Nat. Heart, Lung and Blood Inst., 1986, Lillie award Woods Hole, Marine Bill, Lab., 1989, Order of Brit. Empire, 2002. Mem. Am. Soc. Cell Biology, Soc. Neurosci., Tissue Culture Assn., Internat. Soc. Heart Rsch., Am. Heart Assn. (coun. on basic rsch., coun. on circulation, cardiopulmonary coun.), Am. Physiol. Soc., Am. Microcirculatory Soc., European Soc. Microcirculation, Am. Thoracic Soc. (dir. course on culture of pulmonary endothelial cells), Internat. Soc. Applied Cardiovascular Biology, N.Y. Acad. Scis., Fla. Soc. Electron Microscopy, Sigma Xi. Office: AVANT Immunotherapeutics 119 4th Ave Needham MA 02494-2725

RYAN, VINCE, lawyer; b. Houston, Aug. 12, 1947; m. Teresa Pamela Rodriguez; 3 children. BA in English, U. Houston, 1969, JD, 1974; MA in History, Rice U., 1979. Bar: Tex. 1974. Assoc. James Patrick Smith, 1974—75, Thomas P. Duncan, Houston, 1975—76, Smith and Conner, Houston, 1976—79, Watrous, Joyce and Ryan, Houston, 1980—81; divsn. chief commrs. ct. divsn. Office of Harris County Atty., Houston, 1981—83, first asst., 1984—88; of counsel Sinex & Stephenson, Houston, 1988—95; regional mng. atty. Calame Linebarger, Houston, 1996—98; of counsel Linebarger Goggan, Houston, 1998—2004, Travis Law Firm, Houston, 2004—. Dir. legal rsch. svc. U. Houston; adj. faculty U.S. Army Command and Gen. Staff Coll., 1988—. Mem. Dist. C Houston City Coun., 1988—94; alt. City of Houston rep. Houston-Galveston Area Coun., 1989—94; pres. Region 14, Tex. Mcpl. League, 1993—94; bd. dirs. Panama Canal Commn., 1995—99. With US Army, 1969—72, Vietnam, with US Army, 1990, lt. col. USAR. Grad. fellow, 1977—78, Rsch. fellow, 1978—79. Mailing: 3720 Blue Bonnet Houston TX 77025 Office: Travis Law Firm Ste 900 2700 Post Oak Blvd Houston TX 77056-5707 Office Phone: 713-661-1941.

RYAN, WILLIAM FRANCIS, priest; b. Renfrew, Ont., Can., Apr. 4, 1925; s. William Patrick Ryan and Helen Mary Doneg BA, Montreal U., 1951; MA in Labor Rels., St. Louis U., 1953; postgrad., Heythrop Coll., Oxon, Eng.; STL, St. Albert Coll., Louvain, 1958; PhD in Econs., Harvard U., 1964. Ordained priest Roman Catholic Ch., 1957. Asst. prof. econs. Loyola Coll., Montreal, Que., Canada, 1963-65; nat. dir. Social Justice Office Can. Conf. Cath. Bishops, Ottawa, Ont., 1964-70, gen. sec.,

1984-90; founding dir. Ctr. of Concern, Washington, 1970-78; nat. supr. Jesuit Order, Toronto, Ont., Canada, 1978-84; chancellor Sch. Theology Regis Coll., Toronto, 1978-84; vis. sr. rsch. fellow Can. Inst. for Internat. Peace and Security, Ottawa, 1990-91; chair on Cath. social thought St. Paul U., Ottawa, 1991-92; 2001dir. Jesuit Project on Ethics in Politics, Ottawa, 1992. Exec. sec. Inter-religious Peace Colloquium, Washington, 1975-78; bd. dirs. Roncalli Internat. Found., Montreal, 1979-83, North/South Inst., Ottawa, 1979-91; spl. advisor to Internat. Devel. Rsch. Ctr., Ottawa, 1993-2000; coord. Jesuit Ctr. for Social Faith and Justice, 1997—; lectr. in field. Author: The Clergy and Economic Growth in Quebec, 1966, Culture, Spirituality and Economic Development—Opening a Dialogue, 1995, Our Way of Proceeding, in the Lab, The Temple and The Market: Reflections at the Intersection of Science, Religion and Development, 2000; co-author: Religious as Contemplatives in the 80's, 1984, The Lab, The Temple and The Market: Expanding the Conversation, 2001; translator: The Primacy of Charity in Moral Theology, 1961; co-editor: Globalization and Catholic Social Thought--Present Crisis, Future Hope, 2005; subject of biography Faith and Freedom—The Life and Times of Bill Ryan sj, by Jamie Swift and Bob Chodos, 2002; contbr. articles to profl. jours. Mem. Am. Econs. Assn. Roman Catholic. Avocations: hiking, skiing. Office: 169 Sunnyside Ave Ottawa ON Canada K1S 0R2 Office Phone: 613-730-4569, 613-730-6029 ext. 2. Personal E-mail: wfxrsj@web.ca.

RYAN, WILLIAM J., bank executive; b. 1943; With All Allstate, White Plains, N.Y., 1964-72, Essex Bank, Peabody, Mass., 1973-82, Bank New Eng. Corp., 1982-89, People's Heritage Bank, Portland, Maine, 1989-90; pres., CEO People's Heritage Bank (became Banknorth), Portland, Maine, 1990—2000; chmn., pres., CEO Banknorth, Portland, Maine, 2000—05; pres., CEO TD Banknorth, Inc. (formerly Banknorth), Portland, Maine, 2005—07, chmn., 2005—. Office: TD Banknorth Inc 2 Portland Sq 7th Fl Portland ME 04112 *

RYANS, JOHN KELLEY, JR., marketing educator; s. John Kelley and Alta Mae Ryans; m. Cynthia Collis, Jan. 5, 1957. AB in Journalism, U. Ky., 1954; MS in Bus. Adminstrn., U. Tenn., 1958; DBA, Ind. U., 1965. Asst. prof. mktg. U. Md., College Park, 1964—68; assoc. prof. mktg. U. Ky., Lexington, 1968—69; prof. mktg. Kent State U., Ohio, 1970—94, Bridgestone prof., 1994—2003, emeritus Bridgestone prof., 2003—; Good chair global strategy Bowling Green State U., Ohio, 2003—04. Vis. prof. internat. bus. Columbia U., NYC, 1977; cons. in field. Co-author (with D. Peebles): The Management of International Advertising, 1983; co-author: (with W. Shanklin) Marketing High Technology, 1984, Thinking Strategically, 1985, Essentials for Marketing High Technology, 1987; co-author: (with J. Baker and D. Howard) International Business Classics, 1988; co-author: Marketing Strategy for New Europe, 1990; co-author: (with S. Paliwoda) International Marketing Reader, 1995; co-author: India Business, 2002, author 11 other books. 1st lt. USAF, 1955—57. Named Disting. Scholar, Kent State U., 1999, Ohio Commodore, Gov. of Ohio, 2000; recipient 12-yr, award, No. Ohio US Dist. Export Coun., 2002. Fellow: Acad. Internat. Bus.; mem.: Am. Mktg. Assn. Found., Cleve. World Trade Assn. (bd. dirs. 1972—2006). Avocations: sports, writing, travel, cruises. Office: Kent State U Coll Bus Dept Mktg Kent OH 44240 Personal E-mail: jkryans@juno.com.

RYBAK, R. T., mayor; m. Megan O'Hara; 2 children. BA polit. sci. and comm., Boston Coll., 1978. Gen. mgr. WCCO TV & WCCO Radio; v.p. Internet Broadcast Sys.; pub., mgr., bus. ops. Twin Cities Reader; mayor City of Minneapolis, Minn., 2001—. Founder, mem. bd. Save the Water in Mpls.; served Minn. Soc. Architects, Night of the Penguin, Hennepin Ave. Adv. Com., Adv. Fedn. Minn., Eiji Oue Inaugural Com.; coach Little League Baseball, Youth Soccer; vol. reader Minn. Pub. Sch.; co-coord. Bill Bradley for Pres., 2000; co-chair Tony Bouza for Gov., 1994; bd. dir. Residents Opposed to Airport Racket. Democrat. Office: City Hall Rm 331 350 S Fifth S Minneapolis MN 55415 Office Phone: 612-673-2700. Office Fax: 612-673-2305. *

RYBCZYK, JOSEPH ANTHONY, physicist, researcher, writer, inventor; b. Phila., Oct. 19, 1935; s. Frank Rybczyk and Isabella Slivak; life ptnr. Dolores Brannan; m. Ruth Diane Menendez, Dec. 30, 1955 (div.); children: Brian Keith, Deborah Gale, Karen Marie. Tech. diploma, DeVry Inst. Tech., Chgo., 1976. Tech. cert. USAF, Air Training Command, Francis E. Warren Air Force Base, Cheyenne, Wyo., 1956, NASA cert. instr./examiner George C. Marshall Space Flight Ctr., Huntsville, Ala., 1965. Various positions Lockheed Martin Tactical Def. Systems, Horsham, Pa., 1959—96; ind. rschr. in theoretical physics, 1996—. Author: Millennium Theory of Relativity. With USAF, 1955—59. Achievements include research in theory of natural motion; millennium theory of relativity; time and energy; the laws of acceleration; time and energy, inertia and gravity; millennium relativity velocity composition; relativistic motion perspective; millenium relativity acceleration composition; integrated relativisitc velocity and acceleration compostion; millenium theory of inertia and gravity; the four principal kinetic states of material bodies; patents for encoding printing device, 1978; man-powered propulsion device, 1986. Personal E-mail: jrybczyk@comcast.net.

RYBCZYNSKI, WITOLD MARIAN, architect, educator, writer; b. Edinburgh, Mar. 1, 1943; arrived in Can., 1953; s. Witold Kasimir and Anna Jadwiga (Hofman) Rybczynski; m. Shirley Hallam, Nov. 15, 1974. Diploma, Loyola Coll., Montreal, 1960; B.Arch., McGill U., 1966, M.Arch., 1972, DSc (hon.), 2002. Pvt. practice architecture, Montreal, 1970-82; research assoc. McGill U., Montreal, 1972-75, asst. prof. architecture, 1975-80, assoc. prof., 1980-86, prof., 1986-93; Meyerson prof. of Urbanism U. Pa., 1994—. Cons. UN, Manila, 1976, Internat. Devel. Rsch. Ctr., Ottawa, 1977, Banco de Mex., 1979—80; sr. fellow Design Futures Inst., 2003; mem. Meml. and Mus. Cons. Group. Author: Paper Heroes: A Review of Appropriate Technology, 1980, Taming the Tiger: The Struggle to Control Technology, 1983, Home: A Short History of an Idea, 1986, The Most Beautiful House in the World, 1989, Waiting in the Weekend, 1991, Looking Around: A Journey Through Architecture, 1992, A Place for Art, 1993, City Life: Urban Expectation in a New World, 1995, A Clearing in the Distance, 1999 (J. Anthony Lukas Book Prize, Christopher award), One Good Turn, 2000, The Look of Architecture, 2001, The Perfect House, 2002; co-author (with Laurie Olin): Vizcaya, 2005; co-author: Last Harvest, 2007; contbg. editor: Saturday Night, 1990—2001; contbg. author Booknotes: Stories from American History, mem. adv. bd. Ency. Americana; founding editor: Wharton Real Estate Rev., 1996—; Slate, 2005—. Mem. adv. coun. Inst. Classical Arch., 2003—; mem. adv. bd. Chgo. Humanities Festival, 2003—; advisor Libr. Am. Landscape History, 2002—, mem. U.S. Commn. Fin. Arts, 2004—. Recipient QSPELL Lit. prize for nonfiction, 1988, 1989, Prix Paul-Henri Lapointe, 1988, Progressive Arch. Design award, 1991, Jurzykowski Found. award, 1993, Athaneum Lit. prize, 1997, 2001, Christopher award, 2000, J. Anthony Lukas prize, 2000, Vincent Scully prize, 2007, Seaside prize, 2007; Ballard Real Estate scholar, 1994—95. Fellow: AIA (hon.); mem.: Am. Soc. Landscape Archs. (hon.). Office: Sch Design Meyerson Hall Philadelphia PA 19104 Office Phone: 215-573-0985. Business E-Mail: rybczyns@design.upenn.edu.

RYBERG, WILLIAM A., orchestra executive; BMus, Western Wash. State U., 1980; MMus, Ind. U., 1983. Teller, loan officer, br. mgr., regional mgr. Ranier Nat. Bank; v.p., area mgr. West One Bank, Tacoma; v.p., dist. mgr. Key Bank, Wash., 1993-96; exec. dir. Bellingham (Wash.) Festival of Music, 1996-98; pres. Grand Rapids (Mich.) Symphony, 1998—2004, Oreg. Symphony Orch., Portland, 2004—. Office: 921 SW Wahington Ste 200 Portland OR 97205

RYCE, DONALD THEODORE, JR., lawyer; b. New Orleans, Dec. 15, 1943; s. Donald Theodore Sr. and Martha (Herndon) R.; m. Claudine Dianne Walker, July 8, 1984; children: Ted, Martha, Jimmy. BA, U. Fla., Gainesville, 1966, JD, 1968. Bar: Fla. 1968, U.S. Dist. Ct. (so. dist.) Fla. 1972, U.S. Ct. Appeals (5th and 11th cirs.) 1973. Jud. law clk. Fla. Dist. Ct. Appeals (4th cir.), West Palm Beach, 1968—70; ptnr. Hogg, Allen, Ryce, Norton & Blue, Miami, Fla., 1970—89, Donald T. Ryce, P.A., Miami, 1989—. Co-chmn. liaison com. labor and employment sect. NLRB, Fla., 1990-92, mem. publs. com., 1990-91, exec. coun. labor and employment sect., 1994-98, 2003—; apptd. missing children adv. bd. Fla. Dept. Law Enforcement, 1996—; hearing examiner Miami Dade County. Dir. Jimmy Ryce Ctr. for Victims of Predatory Abduction. Named to Policeman Hall of Fame, 1996, Grand Knight of Order of Michael the Archangel; recipient Leadership award Fla. Police Chiefs Edn. Rsch. Found., 1993. Mem. AAA (arbitrator employment law, 2003—, labor law, 2003—, comml. law 2003—), Fla. Bar Assn., Nat. Assn. Securities Dealers (arbitrator), Microcomputer Edn. for Employment of Disabled (bus. adv. coun.), Winter Haven C. of C. (Cmty. Leadership award 1994), Miami Rotary. Episcopalian. Avocations: tennis, gourmet cooking, bicycling, travel. Office: 908 Coquina Ln Vero Beach FL 32963-5326 Office Phone: 772-492-0200. Office Fax: 772-492-0210. Business E-Mail: employerlawyer@yahoo.com.

RYCHLAK, JOSEPH FRANK, psychologist, educator; b. Cudahy, Wis., Dec. 17, 1928; s. Joseph Walter and Helen Mary (Bieniek) R.; m. Lenora Pearl Smith, June 16, 1956; children: Ronald, Stephanie. BS, U. Wis., 1953; MA, Ohio State U., 1954, PhD, 1957. Diplomate Am. Bd. Examiners in Profl. Psychology. Asst. prof. psychology Fla. State U., Tallahassee, 1957-58, Washington State U., Pullman, 1958-61; assoc. prof., then prof. psychology St. Louis U., 1961-69; prof. psychology Purdue U., West Lafayette, Ind., 1969-83, interim dept. head, 1979-80; prof. Loyola U. Chgo., 1983-99, Maude C. Clarke prof. humanistic psychology, 1983—, prof. emeritus, 1999—. Dir. Human Relations Ctr., Pullman, Wash., 1958-61; research cons. AT&T, 1957-82. Author: The Psychology of Rigorous Humanism, 1977, 2d edit., 1988, Discovering Free Will and Personal Responsibility, 1979, A Philosophy of Science for Personality Theory, 2d edit., 1981, Personality and Life Style of Young Male Managers, 1982, (with N. Cameron) Personality Development and Psychopathology, 2d edit., 1985, Artificial Intelligence and Human Reason: A Teleological Critique, 1991, Logical Learning Theory: A Human Teleology and Its Empirical Support, 1994, In Defense of Human Consciousness, 1997, The Human Image in Postmodern America, 2003; assoc. editor Psychotherapy: Theory, Rsch. and Practice, 1965-76, Jour. Mind and Behavior, 1985-94. With USAF, 1946-49. Named Outstanding Contbr. to Human Understanding, Internat. Assn. Social Psychiatry, 1971. Fellow Am. Psychol. Assn. (div. 24 pres. 1977-78, 86-87), Am. Psychol. Soc.; mem. Soc. Personality Assessment, Phi Beta Kappa. Roman Catholic. Home: 12974 Abraham Run Carmel IN 46033 Office Phone: 317-816-0073. E-mail: jrychlak@sbcglobal.net. *From my father I learned to have a sense of purpose, work hard, and assume responsibility. From my mother I learned not to take myself too seriously, and to realize that my achievements are never entirely up to me.*

RYDALCH, ANN, federal agency administrator, former state senator; m. Vernal Rydalch. BS in Business Educ., Idaho State U. Mem. Idaho Senate, 1983—1990, chmn. Fed. Lab. Consortium Tech. Transfer, 2001-, state repr. Idaho, 2004-. Past mem. Idaho Bicentennial Commn.; former vice chmn. Idaho Republican Com. Office: ID Natl Energy & Envrn Lab PO Box 1625 MS 3810 2525 N Fremont Ave Idaho Falls ID 83415-3810

RYDBERG, MARSHA GRIFFIN, lawyer; b. Tampa, Fla., Dec. 11, 1946; d. Jack and Nibia (Santana) Griffin; m. Thomas Henry Rydberg; children: Kristen Elizabeth, Nancy Marshall. BA, Emory U., Atlanta, 1968; JD cum laude, Stetson U., DeLand, Fla., 1976. Bar: Fla. 1976, US Dist. Ct. (mid. dist.) Fla. 1977, US Dist. Ct. (so. dist.) Fla. 1984, US Ct. Appeals (11th cir.) 1977, US Supreme Ct. 1983. Christian youth worker Young Life Campaign, 1968-70; youth dir. First Presbyn. Ch., Tampa, 1970—72; assoc. Gibbons, Tucker, McEwen, Smith Cofer & Taub, Tampa, 1976-79, Taub & Williams, Tampa, 1979-83, ptnr., 1983-89, Rydberg & Goldstein, P.A., 1989-97, Foley & Lardner, 1997-2000; pvt. practice, 2000—. Bd. fellows U. Tampa; adj. prof. banking law and real property finance Stetson U. Coll. Law, 2000—. Contbr. articles to profl. jours. Bd. dirs. YMCA, 1977-79, Jr. League Tampa (atty. 1983-85), 1979-80, Leadership Tampa, 1993, 97, U. Club Tampa, 2000, 05, 06; pres. Tampa-Hillsborough County Drug Abuse Comprehensive Coord. Office, Inc., 1988-90, chmn. Tampa Downtown Partnership, 1995-96, bd. dirs. 1992-2005; elder Temple Terrace Presbyn. Ch., Fla., 1982-85; mem. local rules adv. com. US Mid. Dist. Ct., 1995-97; bd. dirs. Fed. Res. Bd. of Atlanta, Jacksonville, 1997-2002, chmn. 1999, 2002; commr. Tampa Housing Authority Bd., 1994-99, Prison Crusade Bd., 2000-05; mem. Tampa Young Life Com., 1992-2000, chmn., 1994-96; mem. Fla. Commn. on the Status Women, 1993-2001, chmn., 1996-98; bd. trustees The Spring, 1996-98, Eckerd Coll., 2000-06; chmn. NFL-Youth Edn. Town Ctr. Tampa Bay, Inc., 2000—; trustee Tampa Bay History Ctr., 2001—, vice chmn., 2007, Stetson U., 2004-06. Recipient Bob Sikes Incentive award, Judge Joe Morris award; named Woman of Distinction Girl Scouts US, Women in Bus., Tampa Bay Bus. Jour., 2002, Am. Jurisprudence awards for Excellence in evidence and constl. law. Fellow Am. Bar Found., Fla. Bar Found; mem. ABA (com. commendation zoning & property use 1985-88, chair bus. law sect. fin. instn. litig. com. 1992-2003), Am. Bankruptcy Inst., US Supreme Ct. Hist. Soc., Fla. Supreme Ct. Hist. Soc., Fla. Bar (bd. govs. 1993-99, exec. com. 1994-95, 97-98, coun. sects. chmn. 2004-05, exec. com. bus. law sect. 2001—, exec. com. real property, probate and trust law sect. 2002—, sec. 2002-03, v.p. 2003-04, chmn. 2004-05, Tradition of Excellence award 2000), Fla. Assn. Women Lawyers, Ferguson White Inn of Ct., Tampa Bay Bankruptcy Bar Assn., Hillsborough Assn. Women Lawyers, Hillsborough County Bar Assn. (pres. 1991-92, James M. Red McEwen award 1984-85, 87-88, 96-97), Athena Soc., Stetson U. Coll. Law Alumni Assn. (pres. 1993, bd. overseers 1994, chmn. 2003-05), Greater Tampa C. of C. (bd. dirs. 1995-2000, chair com. of 100 1998), Am. and Fla. Land Title Assn., Exch. Club of Tampa (pres. 1998), Phi Alpha Delta (Outstanding Scholastic Achievement award). Democrat. Home: 2606 W Prospect Rd Tampa FL 33629-5358 Office: 201 N Franklin St 1625 Tampa FL 33602 Office Phone: 813-221-2800. Business E-Mail: mrydberg@rydberglaw.com.

RYDÉN, BENGT GUNNAR, retired stock exchange executive; b. Stockholm, Oct. 30, 1936; s. Gunnar H. and Ragnhild L. (Soederbaum) Rydén; m. Monica I.H. Tillberg, May 18, 1961. MBA, Stockholm Sch. Econs., 1960, PhD, 1972. Dep. chief economist Fedn. Swedish Industries, Stockholm, 1965-66; editor-in chief Swedish "Veckans Affärer", Stockholm, 1971-73; chief exec. Ctr. Bus. and Policy Studies, Stockholm, 1974-84, Stockholm Stock Exch., 1985-98, exec. chmn., 1998-99; vice chmn. Swedish Acctg. Stds. Coun., 1989—2002; ret., 2002. Chmn. Internat. Fedn. Stock Exchs., 1995—97, Mus. Nat. Antiquities, Sweden, 1998—2005, Hallvarsson & Halvarsson AB, Sweden, 1999—, Seventh Swedish Nat. Pension Fund, 1999—, Pantor Engring. AB, 2000—; bd. dirs. Found. Fin. Rsch., Sweden, Svenskt Rekonstruktionskapital AB, Sweden, 2003—, Autobalance Svenska AB, 2004—, Nordic Investor Svcs. AB, 2006—; mem. Com. of Wise Men on the Regulation of European Securities Mkts., 2000—01, Govt. Commn. on Restoration Pub. Trust in Bus., 2002—04. Fellow, Indsl. Inst. Econ. and Social Rsch., 1966—70. Fellow: Swedish Acad. Auditing, Royal Swedish Acad. Engring. Scis. Business E-Mail: bengt.ryden@halvarsson.se.

RYDER, EDWARD FRANCIS, secondary school educator; b. Lynn, Mass., Mar. 25, 1931; s. Edward W. and Theresa (Callahan) R. BSBA, Salem State U., Winston-Salem, NC, 1954, EdM in Edn., 1973; EdM in Bus. Edn., Boston U., 1956. Cert. tchr., Mass. Bus. tchr. North Quincy (Mass.) H.S., 1968—98. Owner, pub. Sunnyside Pub. Co., 1975—. Author: The Art of Playing Bingo and Winning Consistently, 1980, The Art of Entering Sweepstakes and Winning Consistently, 1981, How To Save a Fortune Using Refunds and Coupons, 1983, How to Unlock the Secrets of Winning and Good Luck, 1983, How You Can Achieve Total Success Through Self-Hypnosis, 1984, Where to Buy Everything Wholesale--A Book of Lifetime Savings, 1984, A Guide to Over 1,000 Things You Can Get--For Free!, 1984, The Art of Betting Horses and Winning Consistently, 1985, Blackjack: How to Play and Win Like an Expert, 1985, Hot Dice! How to Leave the Table a Winner, 1986, Winning Secrets of a Poker Master, 1986, Picking Winners at the Harness Races, 1987, Winning Consistently at the Greyhound Races, 1987, Lucky Slots!! How to Beat the Casino Bandits, 1988, Secrets of Winning at Casino Roulette, 1988, Keno: The Art of Playing and Winning, 1989, How to Play and Win at Casino Baccarat, 1989, Secrets of Winning at Video Poker, 1990, Winning Secrets of a Master Sports Bettor--Football, 1991, Winning Secrets of a Master Sports Bettor--Basketball, 1992, Winning Secrets of a Master Sports Bettor--Baseball, 1992; all publs. updated, 1997. Roman Catholic. Home: 28 Sunnyside Rd Lynn MA 01905-1105 Office: Sunnyside Pubs 51 Willow St # 165 Lynn MA 01901-1108 Business E-Mail: gambleandwin@verizon.net.

RYDER, HARL EDGAR, economist, educator; b. Mt. Vernon, Ill., July 11, 1938; s. Harl Edgar and Pearl (Kirkpatrick) R.; m. Mary Irene Kingsolver, June 30, 1970; children: Jonathan Harl, David Eugene, Benjamin James. AA, Mt. Vernon Community Coll., 1958; BA, U. Ill., 1960, MS, 1961; PhD, Stanford U., 1967. Asst. prof. econs. Brown U., Providence, 1965-69, assoc. prof., 1969-73, chmn. dept. econs., 1974-81, prof., 1973—2005, prof. emeritus, 2005—. Office: Brown Univ Dept Econs 64 Waterman St Providence RI 02912-9079 E-mail: harl_ryder@brown.edu.

RYDER, HENRY CLAY, lawyer; b. Lafayette, Ind., Feb. 18, 1928; s. Raymond Robert and Mina Elizabeth (Arnold) R.; m. Ann Sater Clay, Nov. 29, 1952 (dec.); children: David C., Sarah Paige Hugon, Anne Ryder O'Keefe; m. Velma Iris Dean, Aug. 27, 1976 (dec.). BS, Purdue U., 1948; LLB, U. Mich., 1951; LLD, Hanover Coll., 1998. Bar: Mich. 1951, Ind. 1952, U.S. Dist. Ct. (so. dist.) Ind. 1953, U.S. Ct. Appeals (7th cir.) 1957, U.S. Supreme Ct. 1981. Assoc. Buschmann, Krieg, DeVault & Alexander, Indpls., 1953-57, ptnr., 1957-60, Roberts & Ryder and successor firms, Indpls., 1960-86, Barnes & Thornburg (merger), Indpls., 1987-95, of counsel, 1996—. Pres. Ind. State Symphony Soc. Inc., 1979-82, bd. dirs., 1972-91, trustee, 1991—; chmn. United Way of Greater Indpls., 1984; vice chmn. Greater Indpls. Progress Com., 1979-86, chmn., 1987-89, mem. exec. com., 1979-2000; trustee Purdue U., 1983-89; trustee Hanover Coll., 1979-2003, chmn., 1988-98; bd. dirs. Hist. Landmarks Found. of Ind., 1985-96, chmn., 1992-95; bd. dirs. Purdue Rsch. Found., 1990-2006; hon. v.p. Ind. Soc. Chgo.; mem. cmty. bd. IUPUI U. Libr., 1998—, chmn. 2003-04; bd. govs. Heartland Film Festival, 2000—04. Lt. U.S. Army, 1951-53. Recipient Jefferson award Indpls. Star, 1983, Whistler award Greater Indpls. Progress Com., 1989; Sagamore of the Wabash, 1984; named Man of Yr., B'nai B'rith Soc., 1984, Ind. Acad., 1992, Lifetime Achievement award Nat. Soc. Fund Raising Execs., 1999, Spirit of Philanthropy award Ind. U. Purdue U. Indpls., 2005. Fellow: Ind. Bar Found., Am. Bar Found.; mem.: ABA, Indpls. Bar Assn., Ind. Bar Assn., Ind. C. of C. (bd. dirs. 1991—94), Purdue U. Alumni Assn. (pres. 1975—77, Alumni Svc. award 1982, Citizenship award 1989), Columbia Club Found. (trustee 1990—), Indpls. Lit. Club (pres. 2004—05), Kiwanis (Downtown Indpls. pres. 1983, Civic award 1981), Columbia Club (bd. dirs. 1987—90, sec. 1988, Benjamin Harrison award 1983, Columbian of Yr. award 2002), USAC Benevolent Found. (bd. dirs., pres. 1999—), USAC Properties (sec., bd. dirs. 1986—), U.S. Auto Club (bd. dirs. 1982—, Pres.'s award 1989, Eddie Edenburn award 2000), Lawyers Club of Indpls. (pres. 1966). Republican. Presbyterian. Office: Barnes & Thornburg 11 S Meridian St Indianapolis IN 46204-3535 Office Phone: 317-231-7521.

RYDER, SUSAN R., elementary school educator; b. Ala. m. David Ryder. Lang. arts tchr. Estes Park (Colo.) Middle Sch., 2001—. Named Colo. Tchr. of Yr., 2007; grantee Nat. Writing Project Fellow, Dept. Edn., 2006. Office: Estes Park Middle Sch 1500 Manford Ave Estes Park CO 80517 Office Phone: 970-586-4439 ext 3278. Business E-Mail: susan_ryder@psdr3.k12.co.us.

RYDER, WINONA (WINONA LAURA HOROWITZ), actress; b. Winona, Minn., Oct. 29, 1971; d. Michael and Cynthia (Istas) Horowitz. Founder Roustabout Studios, 1999. Films include: Lucas, 1986, Square Dance, 1987, Beetlejuice, 1988, Great Balls of Fire, 1989, Heathers, 1989, Edward Scissorhands, 1990, Mermaids, 1990, Welcome Home, Roxy Carmichael, 1990, Night On Earth, 1992, Bram Stoker's Dracula, 1992, Age of Innocence, 1993 (Golden Globe for Best Supporting Actress, 1994, Academy award nominee, Best Supporting Actress, 1993), The House of the Spirits, 1994, Reality Bites, 1994, Little Women, 1994 (Acad. Awd. nom., Best Actress), How to Make An American Quilt, 1995, Looking for Richard, 1995, The Crucible, 1996, Boys, 1996, Alien Resurrection, 1997, Celebrity, 1998, Girl, Interrupted, 1999, Autumn in New York, 1999, Lost Souls, 2000, Mr. Deeds, 2002, S1mOne, 2002, The Day My God Died (narrator), 2003, The Heart Is Deceitful Above All Things, 2004, The Darwin Awards, 2006, A Scanner Darkly, 2006, The Ten, 2007. Named one of Top Players Under 35, People mag., 1996; named to Hollywood Walk of Fame, 2000. *

RYDHOLM, RALPH WILLIAMS, advertising executive; b. Chgo., June 1, 1937; s. Thor Gabriel and Vivian Constance (Williams) R.; m. Jo Anne Beechler, Oct. 5, 1963; children: Kristin, Erik, Julia. BA, Northwestern U., Evanston, Ill., 1958, postgrad. in bus. adminstrn, 1958-59; postgrad. Advanced Mgmt. Program, Harvard U., Cambridge, Mass., 1982. Acct. trainee, copywriter Young & Rubicam Advt., Chgo., 1960-63; copywriter Post-Keyes-Gardner Advt., Chgo., 1963, E. H. Weiss Advt., Chgo., 1963-65; copy group head BBDO Advt., Chgo., 1965-66; with J. Walter Thompson Advt., Chgo., 1966-86, creative dir., v.p., 1969-76, exec. creative dir., 1976-86, sr. v.p., 1972-80, exec. v.p., dir., 1980-86; exec. v.p., chief creative officer, dir. Ted Bates Worldwide, NYC, 1986-87; mng. ptnr., chmn. mgmt. com., chief creative officer, chmn., CEO, EURO RSCG Tatham Advt., Chgo., 1987-98; bd. dirs. Euro RSCG, USA; pres. R2 Cons., 1999—; spl. counsel J. Walter Thompson, 1999-2000. Bd. dirs., ops. com., chmn. creative com., vice chmn., 1996, chmn., 1997-98; Am. Assn. Advt. Agys. guest spkr. Ad Age Workshop, 1969, 77, 86, Adweek Seminar, 1993, CLIO awards, 1995; keynote spkr. Stephen B. Kelly Awards, 1993, CEBA Awards, 1997; chmn. CEBA Awards, 1997. Friends com. Northwestern U.; Prin. for a Day, Chgo. Pub. Schs., 1998—; mem. assoc. bd. Newberry Libr. Assn.; bd. dirs., adv. coun. leadership coun. Chgo. Pub. Edn. Fund; bd. dirs. PRO AD PAC, 1998—; former chmn. bd. dirs. Am. Scandinavian Coun.; dir. Am. Assn. Advt. Agys. Found., 1997—99; cons., bd. dirs. Exec. Svc. Corp., 2003—. Staff sgt. USAFR, 1959—65. Recipient Clio awards, Internat. Broadcast award, Lion awards, Cannes Film Festival, Addy awards; named one of Top 100 Creative Ad People Ad Daily, 1972, Advt. Exec. of Yr. Adweek, 1991, Best Man in Advt. McCalls and Adweek, 1992; named to Creative Leader Hall of Fame, Wall St. Jour., 1994. Mem.: ASCAP, Chgo. Advt. Fedn., Am. Advt. Fedn. (Silver medal lifetime svc. 1997), Lincoln Park Zoo, Friends of Chgo. River, Art Inst. Chgo., Fernwood, Friends of the Pks., Hon. Order Ky. Cols., Chgo. Com. Coun. on Global Affairs, Openlands, Internat. Club, Dunes Club (Mich.), Carlton Club, Tavern Club, Harvard Club NYC, Northwestern Club Chgo., Saddle and Cycle Club, Econ. Club Chgo. (bd. dirs. 1996—98), Harvard Club

Chgo., Execs. Club Chgo., Club Internat., Chikaming Country Club (Mich.), Lost Dunes Club (Mich.), Phi Delta Theta. Office Phone: 312-280-7726. Personal E-mail: rydholm@aol.com.

RYERSON, DENNIS, editor; b. Ames, Iowa, Apr. 20, 1948; children: Carey, Kirsten. Student, Iowa State U., U. No. Iowa. Announcer, news dir. Sta. KWBG, Boone, Iowa; reporter, then city editor Cedar Falls Record, 1969—73; news editor Scottsbluff (Nebr.) Star-Herald, 1973—74; editl. page editor Vancouver (Wash.) Columbian, 1974—83; chief editl. writer, then editl. dir. Cleve. Plain Dealer, 1983—88; mng. editor news Denver Post, 1988—89; editor editl. pages Des Moines Register, 1989-94; exec. editor Great Falls (Mont.) Tribune, 1994-95; v.p., editor Des Moines Register, 1995—2001; editl. page editor San Jose Mercury News, 2001—03; v.p., editor The Indianapolis Star, 2003—. Appeared on TV shows including Good Morning America, MacNeil/Lehrer News Hour, CBS Morning News, NPR's All Things Considered. Mem. Nat. Conf. Editl. Writers (past pres.), Am. Soc. Newspaper Editors. Office: Indianapolis Star PO Box 145 Indianapolis IN 46206-0145 Office Phone: 317-444-6169. E-mail: dennis.ryerson@indystar.com. *

RYERSON, LISA M., academic administrator; BA in English cum laude, Wells Coll., Aurora, NY, 1981; MS, SUNY. Asst. dir. admissions Wells Coll., Aurora, NY, 1981—84, assoc. dean of students, 1984—87, dean of students, 1991—94, v.p. to exec. v.p., 1994—95, pres., 1995—. Vice chair bd. of mng. dir. Ind. Coll. Funf of N.Y.; chair exec. bd. Pub. Leadership Edn. Network, Washington; bd. mem. Women's Coll. Coalition, Washington. Mem. exec. com. Cayuga County C. of C., Auburn, NY. Office: Wells Coll 170 Main St Aurora NY 13026

RYERSON, PAUL SOMMER, lawyer; b. Newark, Oct. 2, 1946; s. Robert Paul and Audrey Mae (Sommer) R.; m. Susan Jean Duckrow, Aug. 7, 1971 (div. Apr. 1995); children: James Sommer, Jill Carin; m. Kenswynn Black, Jan. 26, 2002. BA, Wesleyan U., 1968; JD, Columbia U., 1971. Bar: N.Y. 1972, D.C. 1972, U.S. Ct. Appeals (D.C. cir.) 1973, U.S. Dist. Ct. D.C. 1973, U.S. Supreme Ct. 1976, U.S. Ct. Appeals (5th cir.) 1979, U.S. Ct. Appeals (4th cir.) 1980. Law clk. to judge Jack B. Weinstein U.S. Dist. Ct. ea. dist. N.Y., 1971-72; assoc. Arnold & Porter, Washington, 1972-79, ptnr., 1980-89, Jones Day, Washington, 1989—. Contbr. articles to profl. publs. Mem. ABA, D.C. Bar Assn. Home: 5809 Nicholson Ln North Bethesda MD 20852-5719 Office: Jones Day 51 Louisiana Ave NW Washington DC 20001-2113 Home Phone: 301-230-0278; Office Phone: 202-879-3939. E-mail: psryerson@jonesday.com.

RYERSON, WILLIAM NEWTON, non profit organization executive; b. Phila., Mar. 9, 1945; s. W. Newton and Jean (Hamilton) R.; m. Leta C. Finch, Dec. 6, 1975. BA, Amherst Coll., 1967; M.Phil., Yale U., 1971. Dir. student intern program Population Inst., Washington, 1971-73, dir. youth and student div., 1973-79; dir. devel. Planned Parenthood Southeastern Pa., Phila., 1979-81; assoc. dir. Planned Parenthood No. New Eng., Burlington, Vt., 1981-86; pres. Ryerson & Assocs., fundraising counsel, Shelburne, Vt., 1986-2000; exec. v.p. Population Comm. Internat., NYC, 1986-98; pres. Population Media Ctr., Shelburne, Vt., 1998—. Co-author: Population Activist's Handbook, 1974, Communicating Sustainability, 2000, Entertainment-Education and Social Change-History, Research and Practice, 2003. NASA trainee in biology, Yale U., 1967-70. Mem.: Phi Beta Kappa, Sigma Xi (assoc.). Home: PO Box 580 Shelburne VT 05482-0580 Office: PO Box 547 Shelburne VT 05482-0547 Office Phone: 802-985-8156. Business E-Mail: ryerson@populationmedia.org.

RYGG, GLENN, retired music educator; b. Mayville, ND, Aug. 8, 1944; s. Conrad Ingemann Rygg and Helen Marie Vinje; m. Susan Gay Meidinger (div.); children: Jonathan, Jason. BSc in Instrnl. Music, Mayville State U., ND, 1966. Band, choir tchr., Fessenden, ND, 1966—76; band tchr. Rugby, ND, 1976—81; band, choir, English tchr. Rolla, ND, 1984—88; band tchr. Devils Lake, ND, 1988—2007; ret., 2007. Dir. Devils Lake Elks Cmty. Band, 1988—. Mem. Jaycees, Fessenden, 1968—76. Recipient 25 Yr. Svc. award, ND Music Educators Assn., 2000, Meritorious and Disting. Svc. award, VFW, Devils Lake, 2003. Mem.: Music Educators Nat. Conf., Elks Club. Lutheran. Avocations: painting, music. Home: 1113 4th Ave NE Devils Lake ND 58301-1822

RYLAND, JANE N., educational association administrator; BA, U. Richmond, Westhampton Coll., 1966; MPA, U. Colo., 1980. Systems engr. IBM Corp., Richmond, Va., 1966—70; project mgr., library systems devel. Va. Poly. Inst. & State U., Blacksburg, 1970—72, database adminstr., 1972—73; dir. computing & database adminstr. Va. Cmty. Coll. Sys., Richmond, 1973—76; dir. SHEEO/NCES Comm. Network, Boulder, Colo., 1976—81; mgr. optical systems planning & implementation Storage Tech. Corp., Louisville, Colo., 1981—83; dir. sales & mktg. support Reference Tech., Inc., Boulder, Colo., 1983—86; pres. CAUSE, Boulder, Colo., 1986—98; cons. in higher edn. tech., 1998—; membership cons. Internet2, Ann Arbor, Mich., 1998—. Bd. dirs. CAUSE, 1974—76, Nat. Conf. chair, 1975, ex officio bd. mem., 1986—98; steering com. Coalition Networked Info., 1990—98; coord. coun. Higher Edn. Info. Resources Alliances, 1989—98; mem. Coun. Higher Edn. Mgmt. Assns. (CHEMA), 1986—98; governing bd. Westhampton Coll. Alumnae Assn., Richmond, Va., 1988—90; commn. on learning & comm. tech. Am. Assn. Cmty. Colls., 1996—98; bd. dirs. Assn. Higher Edn. Facilities Officers, 1996—99, VTLS, Inc., 1988—91, COLLEGIS, 1998—, Online Computer Libr. Ctr. (OCLC), 2000—. Office: Internet2 Ste 300 1000 Oakbrook Dr Ann Arbor MI 48104 Office Phone: 303-588-1595. E-mail: jryland@internet2.edu.

RYLAND, WALTER H., lawyer; b. Richmond, Va., Jan. 23, 1943; s. John William and Evelyn (Quillin) R.; m. Madelaine Aerni, July 10, 1976; children: Mark Vanley, Caroline Aerni. BA, Washington & Lee U., 1965, LLB, 1967. Chief dep. atty. gen. Office of the Atty. Gen. of Va., Richmond, 1978-82; ptnr. Williams, Mullen, Christian & Dobbins, Richmond, 1983—. Counselor, Va. Mus. Fine Arts, Richmond, 1983—; pres. J. Sargeant Reynolds Found., Richmond, 1990. Co-editor: Racial Preferences in Government Contracting (Nat. Legal Ctr. for the Pub. Interest), 1993. Sec. bd. trustees Washington Internat. U. Va., 1989-91; bd. dirs. Coun. for Am. First Freedom, Richmond, 1988-92; pres. Theatre Va., Richmond, 1987-88; sec. Communication Disorders Found., Richmond, 1986-88; chmn. Cultural Art Ctr. at Glen Allen Found., 2004-05. Mem. ABA, Va. Bar Assn., Richmond Bar Assn. Office: Williams Mullen Clark & Dobbins 2 James Ctr 1021 E Cary St Richmond VA 23218-4000

RYLANDER, HENRY GRADY, JR., mechanical engineering educator; b. Pearsall, Tex., Aug. 23, 1921; married; 4 children. BS, U. Tex., 1943, MS, 1952; PhD in Mech. Engring., Ga. Inst. Tech., 1965. Design engr. Steam Div., Aviation Gas Turbine Div., Westinghouse Elec. Corp., 1943-47; from asst. to assoc. prof. mech. engring. U. Tex., Austin, 1947-68, research scientist, 1950, prof. mech. engring., 1968—, Joe J. King prof. engring., 1980—. Cons. engr. TRACOR, Inc., 1964-69; founding dir. Ctr. for Electromechanics, U. Tex., 1977-85, chmn., mech. engring. dept., 1976-86. Named Disting. Grad. Coll. Engring., U. Tex., Austin, 1989. Fellow ASME (Leonardo da Vinci award 1985); mem. ASME. Office: U Tex Coll Engring C2200 Austin TX 78712 Office Phone: 512-471-3044. Business E-Mail: hgr@mail.utexas.edu.

RYLANDER, ROBERT ALLAN, financial service executive; b. Bremerton, Wash., Apr. 8, 1947; s. Richard Algot and Marian Ethelyn (Peterson) R.; children: Kate, Erik, Meagan. BA in Fin., U. Wash., 1969; postgrad., U. Alaska, 1972-74. Controller Alaska USA Fed. Credit Union, Anchorage, 1974-77, mgr. ops., 1977-80, asst. gen. mgr., 1980-83, exec. v.p., COO, 1983—; pres., CEO Alaska Option Svcs. Corp., Anchorage, 1983—97, Alaska USA Trust Co., Anchorage, 1997—2004. Chmn. Alaska USA Mortgage Co., Anchorage, 1992—2007, Alaska Option Svcs. Corp., Anchorage, 1997—; bd. dirs. Alaska USA Ins. Brokers, Anchorage, Alaska USA Found., Alaska USA Trust Co., Alaska USA Mortgage Co. Served to capt. USAF, 1969-74. Avocations: audio electronics, music, home theater. Home: PO Box 220587 Anchorage AK 99522-0587 Office: Alaska USA Fed Credit Union PO Box 196613 Anchorage AK 99519-6613 Business E-Mail: r.rylander@alaskausa.org.

RYLES, GERALD FAY, investor, finance company executive; b. Walla Walla, Wash., Apr. 3, 1936; s. L. F. and Janie Geraldine (Bassett) R.; m. Ann Jane Birkenmeyer, June 12, 1959; children— Grant, Mark, Kelly. BA, U. Wash., 1958; MBA, Harvard U., 1962. With Gen. Foods Corp., White Plains, NY, 1962—66, Purex Corp., Ltd., Lakewood, Calif., 1966-68; cons. McKinsey & Co., Inc., Los Angeles, 1968-71; with Fibreboard Corp., San Francisco, 1971-79, v.p., 1973-75, group v.p., 1975-79; with Consol. Fibres, Inc., San Francisco, 1979-88, exec. v.p., 1979-81, pres., dir., 1981-86, chief exec. officer, 1986-88; cons. Orinda, Calif., 1988-90; with Interchecks Inc., 1990-92, pres., CEO, 1990-92; bus. exec., pvt. investor, 1992-94; chmn. bd., CEO Microserv, Inc., Kirkland, Wash., 1994—2001, chmn. bd., 2001—03. Bd. dirs. Halifax Corp., Giant Campus, Inc., Zumiez, Inc., Wash. State Bd. Accountancy. Capt. U.S. Army, 1958-66. Mem.: Harvard Bus. Sch. Assn., U. Wash. Alumni Assn. Republican. Episcopalian. Home: 127 3rd Ave Apt 301 Kirkland WA 98033-6177 Home Phone: 425-827-3519. Personal E-mail: g.ryles@verizon.net.

RYMAN, ROBERT TRACY, artist; b. Nashville, May 30, 1930; s. William Tracy and Nora (Boston) R.; m. Lucy Lippard, 1961 (div. 1966); children: Ethan, Ryman; m. Merrill Wagner, Jan. 31, 1969; children: William Tracy, George Corydon. Exhibited one man shows: Paul Bianchini Gallery, 1967, Solomon R. Guggenheim Mus., NYC, 1972, Kunsthalle, Basel, Switzerland, 1975, Palais des Beaux-Arts, Brussels, 1974, Stedelijk Mus., Amsterdam, Netherlands, 1974, Whitechapel Gallery, London, 1977, Centre Pompidou, Paris, 1981, Sidney Janis Gallery, NYC, 1981, Kunsthalle, Dusseldorf, Germay, 1982, Bonnier Gallery, NYC, 1983, Daniel Weinberg Gallery, LA, 1983, Galerie Maeght LeLong, Paris, 1984, Rhona Hoffman Gallery, Chgo., 1985, Leo Castelli Gallery, NYC, 1986, Galerie Maeght LeLong, NYC, 1986, Pace Gallery, NYC, 1990, DIA Art Found., NYC, 1988-89, Konrad Fischer Gallery, Dusseldorf, Fed. Republic Germany, 1987, Pace Gallery, NY, Tate Gallery, London, MMA, N.Y., San Francisco Mus. Modern Art, Walker Arts Ctr., Mpls., Whitney Mus. Am. Art, 1999-2000, Richard Gray Gallery, NYC, 2001-02, James Cohan Gallery, 2001-02; group shows: Biennal Whitney Mus. Am. Art, NYC, 1977, Stedelijk Mus., Amsterdam, 1978, Art of the 70's, Venice Bernnale, Italy, 1976, 78, 80, Haus der Kunst, Munich, 1981, Stedelijk Mus., Amsterdam, 1983, Whitney Mus. Am. Art, 1983, Skowhegan Sch. of Painting and Sculpture Medal, 1987, Whitney Biennal Exhbn, 1987, Mus. Modern Art, NYC, 1985, Carnegie International, 1988, Peter Blum Gallery, NYC, 1995-96, PaceWildenstein, 1995-96, Galerie Lelong, 1997-98; represented permanent collections: Mus. Modern Art, NYC, Milw. Art Center, Stedelijk Mus., Amsterdam, Whitney Mus. Am. Art, Nat. Gallery Art, Washington, Phila. Mus. Art, San Francisco, Mus. Modern Art, Tate Gallery, London, Whitney Mus. Am. Art, NYC, Mus. Contemporary Art, LA, others; apptd. commr. City of NY Art Commn. With US Army, 1950—52. Recipient Praemium Imperiale award for painting, Japan Art Assn., 2005. Mem. AAAL, Am. Acad. Arts and Scis., Mcpl. Art Soc. NY (bd. dirs. 1991—). Studio: 637 Greenwich St New York NY 10014-3306 *There is never a question of what to paint, but only how to paint. The "how" of painting is the image.*

RYMAR, JULIAN W., manufacturing executive, director; b. Grand Rapids, Mich., June 29, 1919; m. Margaret Macon Van Brunt, Dec. 11, 1954; children: Margaret Gibson, Gracen Macon, Ann Mackall. Student, Grand Rapids Jr. Coll., 1937—39, U. Mich., 1940—41, Wayne State U., 1948—52, Rockhurst Coll., 1952—53, Naval War Coll., 1954—58. Entered as aviation cadet USN, 1942; comdg. officer Naval Air Res. Squadron, 1957—60, staff air comdr., 1960—64; advanced through grades to capt. USN, 1964; chmn. bd., CEO, dir. Grace Co., Belton, Mo., 1955—90; chmn. bd. dirs. Shock & Vibration Rsch. Inc., 1956—66; chmn. bd., CEO Bedtime Story Fashions. Bd. dirs. Am. Bank & Trust. Mem. Kans. City Hist. Soc.; trustee Missouri Valley Coll., 1969—74; pres. Rymar Found.; active Sch. Am. Rsch., Inst. Am. Arts, Mus. N.Mex. Found., Spanish Colonial Art Soc.; active various positions Episcopal Ch.; bd. dirs. Bros. of Mercy, St. Luke's Hosp. Mem.: Soc. Profl. Journalists, Friends of Art (exec. bd. 1971—74, pres., chmn. bd. govs.), Spanish Colonial Arts Soc., Mus. Indian Arts and Culture, Mus. Internat. Folk Art, Mus. Fine Arts, Mus. N.Mex. Found., Santa Fe Symphony, Soc. Fellows of Nelson Gallery Found. (exec. bd. 1972—77), Mil. Order World Wars, Navy League U.S. (pres. 1959—60, dir. 1960—70), Rockhill Homes Assn. (v.p.), Sch. Am. Rsch., Inst. Am. Indian Art, Quiet Birdman Club, Arts Club of Washington, Press Club, Univ. Mich. Club, Sigma Delta Chi. Episcopalian. Personal E-mail: rymarvb@nets.com.

RYMER, JON T., federal agency administrator; b. Apr. 2, 1955; m. Debra Rymer; 1 child, Thomson. BA, U. Tenn., 1981; MBA, U. Ark., 1996. Exec. v.p. First Am. Nat. Bank (now AmSouth Bank), Knoxville and Nashville, 1981—92, Boatman's Bank Ark. (now Bank of Am.), Little Rock, 1992—97; dir., practice leader assurance based adv. svcs. KPMG LLP, Chgo. and Cinn., 1997—2004; insp. gen. FDIC, 2006—. Served with USAR, 2004—. Mem.: Inst. Internal Auditors, Am. Legion. Office: FDIC 3501 Fairfax Dr Rm E9070 Arlington VA 22226

RYMER, PAMELA ANN, federal judge; b. Knoxville, Tenn., Jan. 6, 1941; AB, Vassar Coll., 1961; LLB, Stanford U., 1964; LLD (hon.), Pepperdine U., 1988. Bar: Calif. 1966, US Ct. Appeals (9th cir.) 1966, US Ct. Appeals (10th cir.), US Supreme Ct. Dir., polit. rsch. and analysis Goldwater for President Com., 1964; v.p. Rus Walton & Assoc., Los Altos, Calif., 1965—66; assoc. Lillick McHose & Charles, LA, 1966—75, ptnr., 1973—75, Toy and Rymer, LA, 1975—83; judge US Dist. Ct. (ctrl. dist.) Calif., LA, 1983—89, US Ct. Appeals (9th cir.), LA, 1989—. Faculty The Nat. Jud. Coll., 1986-88; mem. com. summer ednl. programs Fed. Jud. Ctr., 1987-88, mem. com. appellate judge edn., 1996-99; chair exec. com. 9th Cir. Jud. Conf., 1990; mem. com. criminal law Jud. Conf. US, 1988-93, Ad Hoc com. gender-based violence, 1991-94, fed.-state jurisdiction com., 1993-96; mem. commn. on structural alternatives Fed. Cts. Appeals, 1997-98. Mem. editorial bd. The Judges' jour., 1989-91; contbr. articles to profl. jours. and newsletters. Mem. Calif. Postsecondary Edn. Commn., 1974-84, chmn., 1980-84; mem. LA Olympic Citizens Adv. Commn.; bd. visitors Stanford U. Law Sch., 1986-99, trustee, 1991-2001, chair, 1993-96, exec. com., chmn. bd. trustees com. acad. policy, planning and mgmt. and its ad. hoc. com. athletics., chmn. bd. visitors Sch. Law, 1987—; bd. visitors Pepperdine U. Law Sch., 1987—; mem. Edn. Commn. of States Task Force on State Policy and Ind. Higher Edn., 1987-89, Carnegie Commn. Task Force Sci. and Tech. Jud. and Regulatory Decisionmaking, 1990-93, Commn. Substance Abuse Coll. and Univ. Campuses, 1992-94, commn. substance abuse high schs. Ctr. Addiction and Substance Abuse Columbia U.; bd. dirs. Constnl. Rights Found., 1985-97, Pacific Coun. Internat. Policy, 1995—, Calif. Higher Edn. Policy Ctr., 1992-97; Jud. Conf. US Com. Fed.-State Jurisdiction, 1993, Com. Criminal Law, 1988-93, ad hoc com. gender based violence, 1991-94; chair exec. com. 9th cir. jud. conf., 1990-94. Recipient Outstanding Trial Jurist award LA County Bar Assn., 1988; named David T. Lewis Disting. Jurist-in-Residence U. Utah, 1992. Mem. ABA (task force on civil justice reform 1991-93, mem. coord. com. agenda civil justice reform in Am. 1991), State Bar Calif. (antitrust and trade regulation sect., exec. com. 1990-92), LA County Bar Assn. (chmn. antitrust sect. 1981-82, mem. editl. bd. The Judges Jour. 1989-91, mem. com. professionalism 1988—, numerous other coms.), Assn. of Bus. Trial Lawyers (bd. govs. 1990-92), Stanford Alumni Assn., Stanford Law Sch. Soc. Calif., Vassar Club So. Calif. (past pres.). Office: US Ct Appeals 9th Cir US Court of Appeals Bldg 125 S Grand Ave Rm 600 Pasadena CA 91105-1621 *

RYN, CLAES GÖSTA, political science professor; b. Norrköping, Sweden, June 12, 1943; permanent resident of U.S., 1979, naturalized, 2002; s. Gösta Karl and Cecilia Edit (Blom) R.; m. Marianne Carin Tedhagen, Aug. 30, 1969; children: Charlotte, Viveka, Elisabet. MA, Uppsala U., Sweden, 1967, postgrad., 1969—71, Syracuse U., 1968—69; PhD, La. State U., 1974. Asst. prof. politics Cath. U. Am., Washington, 1974-78, assoc. prof. politics, 1978-82, prof. politics, 1982—, asst. dean Sch. Arts and Scis., 1977-79, chmn. dept. politics, 1979-85. Adj. prof. govt. Georgetown U., 2002-05; vis. assoc. prof. U. Va., Charlottesville, 1981; co-founder, chmn. Nat. Humanities Inst., Washington, 1984—; referee, evaluator NEH, Dept. Edn., USIA, others; dir. confs. and lecture series; Richard M. Weaver fellowship selection com., 1980—; faculty sponsor Earhart Found., 1989—; awards com. Ingersoll Prizes, 1990; Salvatori doctoral fellowship selection com. Intercollegiate Studies Inst., 1990—; lectr. in field. Author: (with Bertil Häggman) Nykonservatismen i USA, 1971, Democracy and the Ethical Life, 1978, 2d rev. edit., 1990, Will, Imagination and Reason, 1986, 2d rev. edit., 1997, Individualism och gemenskap, 1986, The New Jacobinism, 1991, Unity Through Diversity (in Chinese), 2001, A Common Human Ground, 2003, America the Virtuous, 2003, Peter Viereck and Conservatism, 2005; editor: Humanitas, 1992—; co-editor (with George Panichas), co-author: Irving Babbitt in Our Time, 1986; editor, author introduction for other volumes; contbr. articles to profl. jours.; mem. edit. bd. Modern Age, 1981—, Marknadsekonomisk Tidskrift, Sweden, 1986-92, This World, 1992—; editl. columnist Svenska Dagbladet, Sweden, 1996—. Mem. vestry St. Francis Episcopal Ch., Potomac, Md., 1986-88. Served with Swedish Army, Royal Life Company I 4 Regt., 1963, Signal Corps, 1967-68. Rsch. fellow Earhart Found., 1980-81, 87-88, Wilbur Found., 1980-81, 90, 93-94, others; Disting. Fgn. scholar Peking U., 2000; recipient award King of Sweden, 1983, Will Herberg award Disting. Faculty Svc. Intercollegiate Studies Inst., 2003; named Outstanding Grad. Prof., Cath. U. Am., 1992, Hon. mem. Heimdal Uppsala U. Mem. Phila. Soc. (trustee 1999, 2d v.p. 2000-01, pres. 2001-02), Acad. Philosophy and Letters (co-founder, mem., bd. dirs. 2006—, pres., 2007—). Episcopalian. Home: 10008 Crestleigh Ln Potomac MD 20854-1820 Office: Cath Univ Am Dept Politics Washington DC 20064-0001

RYNKIEWICZ, STEPHEN MICHAEL, journalist; b. Sheboygan, Wis., Oct. 20, 1955; s. Walter Paul and Ruth Catherine (Van Hercke) R.; m. Brenda Gail Russell, Sept. 27, 1986. BA, U. Wis., 1976. Various staff assignments Chgo. Sun-Times, 1979-97, real estate editor, 1990-97; Internet prodr. Chgo. Tribune, 1997—. Pres. Ill. Freedom of Info. Coun., 1991-93; mem. profl. faculty Columbia Coll., Chgo., 1998. Pres. Chgo. Headline Club, 1991-92, treas., 2001-02; chmn. Peter Lisagor Awards for Exemplary Journalism, 2002-06; sec. Headline Club Found., 2004—. Recipient Web Site award, Nat. Assn. Real Estate Editors, 1997—2000, Editor and Pub. Best Newspaper Classified Site award, 2000, award for pub. svc., Online Journalism Assn., 2002, Pub. award, Chgo. Tribune, 2006. Mem. Soc. Profl. Journalists (regional dir. 1992-95, sec.-treas. 1995-96, membership chair 1997-98, diversity chair 1996-97, Peter Lisagor award 2003), Nat. Soc. Real Estate Editors (bd. dirs. 1999-2000), Toastmasters Internat. (area gov. 2007—), Sigma Delta Chi Found. (bd. dirs. 1995-96). Office: Ste 400 435 N Michigan Ave Chicago IL 60611-4001

RYNN, NATHAN, physics professor, consultant; b. NYC, Dec. 2, 1923; s. Meyer and Rose (Wolkerwiczer) Rynkowsky; m. Glenda Brown, June 24, 1989; children by previous marriage: Jonathan, Margaret, David. BSEE, CCNY, 1944; MS, U. Ill., 1947; PhD, Stanford U., 1956. Rsch. engr. RCA Labs., Princeton, NJ, 1947-52; rsch. asst. Stanford U., Palo Alto, Calif., 1952-56, rsch. assoc., 1958; mem. tech. staff Ramo-Woolridge, LA, 1956-57; supr. Huggins Labs., Menlo Park, Calif., 1957-58; rsch. staff physicist Princeton U., 1958-65; prof. physics U. Calif.-Irvine, 1965-94, prof. physics emeritus, rsch. prof. physics, 1994—. Vis. prof. Ecole Polytechnique Fed. of Lausanne, Switzerland, 1984-90, Ecole Polytechnique, Paris, and other European univs. and labs., 1973-80; indsl. sci. advisor/cons., 1964—; com. mem. Plasma Sci. Com. Nat. Rsch. Coun.; founder and leader plasma physics rsch. facility (the Q-Machine). Contbr. articles and revs. to profl. jours. With USN, 1944-46. Grantee NSF, U.S. Dept. Energy, Air Force Geophys. Lab.; Fulbright sr. fellow, 1978. Fellow Am. Phys. Soc., IEEE, AAAS; mem. Sigma Xi. Avocation: woodworking. Office: U Calif Dept Physics & Astronomy Irvine CA 92697-4575 Office Phone: 949-824-5944. Business E-Mail: nrynn@uci.edu.

RYSKAMP, CHARLES ANDREW, museum director, educator; b. East Grand Rapids, Mich., Oct. 21, 1928; s. Henry Jacob and Flora (DeGraaf) R. AB, Calvin Coll., 1950; MA, Yale U., 1951, PhD, 1956; postgrad., Pembroke Coll., Cambridge U., 1953-54; Litt.D., Trinity Coll., Hartford, 1975; L.H.D., Union Coll., 1977. Nathan Hale fellow Yale U., 1954-55; instr. English Princeton U., 1955-59, asst. prof., 1959-63, assoc. prof., 1963-69; curator English and Am. lit. Univ. Library, 1967-69, prof., 1969—. Procter & Gamble faculty fellow, 1958-59; jr. fellow Coun. of Humanities, 1960-61, John E. Annan preceptor, 1961-64; dir. Pierpont Morgan Libr., N.Y.C., 1969-87, dir. emeritus, fellow (hon.), 1997—; dir. Frick Collection, N.Y.C., 1987-97, dir. emeritus, fellow (hon.), 1997—; dir. vis. Inst. Advanced Study, Princeton, 1997-99; exhbn. of collection of drawings, Pierpont Morgan Libr., 2001; adv. bd. Skowhegan Sch. Painting and Sculpture, Pvt. Papers of James Boswell, Yale U.; vis. com. dept. drawings and printed books Pierpont Morgan Libr. Coun. and Libr. Com., Frick Collection; bd. adv. Princeton U. Art Mus. Author: William Cowper of the Inner Temple, Esq, 1959, William Blake, Engraver, 1969; editor: (with F.A. Pottle) Boswell: The Ominous Years, 1963, The Cast-Away, 1963, Wilde and the Nineties, 1966, William Blake: The Pickering Manuscript, 1972, (with J. King) The Letters and Prose Writings of William Cowper, vol. I, 1979, vol. II, 1981, vol. III, 1982, Vol. IV, 1984, Vol. V, 1986, (with R. Wendorf) The Works of William Collins, 1979, (with J. Baird) The Poetical Works of William Cowper, vol. I, 1980, vols. II-III, 1995, (with J. King) William Cowper: Selected Letters, 1989, Report to the Fellows of the Pierpont Morgan Library, vols. 16-21, 1969-89, Charles Ryskamp and Friends, 1999, (with Scott Westrem) The Works of John Chalkhill, 1999, Of Cabbages and Kings, 2004. Trustee, exec. com. Mus. Broadcasting, 1977-87; trustee John Simon Guggenheim Meml. Found., Libr. of Am.; trustee emeritus Corning Mus. Glass, Amon Carter Mus.; past vis. com. dept. paintings conservation Met. Mus. Art; patron William Blake Trust; bd. mgrs. Lewis Walpole Libr., Yale U.; bd. dirs., v.p. Gerard B. Lambert Found.; past v.p. Frederick R. Koch Found.; trustee Venetian Heritage. Decorated Order St. John of Jerusalem, comdr. Order Orange Nassau, The Netherlands, officer Order Leopold II, Belgium, comdr. Order of Falcon, Iceland; recipient Peter Stuyvesant award Dutch Am. West-India Co., 1987, Gold medal Holland Soc., 1991. Mem. Am. Philos. Soc., Museums Coun. N.Y.C. (past v.p.), Keats-Shelley Assn. Am. (past v.p.), Master Drawings Assn. (past pres.), Met. Opera Assn. (bd. adv., chmn. arts and archives com.), Drawing Soc. (nat. com.), Am. Assocs. Royal Nat. Theatre, Bibliog. Soc. Am., Acad. Am. Poets, Am. Antiquarian Soc., Assn. Art Mus. Dirs. (past pres.), NY Geneal. and Biog. Soc. (spl. corr.), Neuropathy Assn. (nat. adv. coun.), Cowper Soc., Assn. Internat. Bibliophilie (com. of Honor), Found. French Mus. (adv. bd.), Wordsworth Rydal Mount Trust, Grolier Club, Century Assn., Lotos Club, Knickerbocker Club, Elizabethan Club (New Haven), Roxburghe Club (London)

RYTHER, STEPHEN GLENN, military officer, protective services official; b. Columbus, Ohio, Sept. 12, 1970; s. Stephen K. and Annette T. Ryther; m. Tracie Leigh Kehoe, Oct. 2, 1994; children: Cailey Paige, Justin Glenn. Student, Orange County C.C., Middletown, NY, 1988—89; grad. with honors, Lloyd Police Acad., 1992; degree in Warrant Officer, Basic Sch., Quantico, Va., 2002. Lic. police officer NY State, 1992, cert. basic police officer NY State Divsn. Criminal Justice, 1992, 6060 advanced life support sys. USMC, 1992, scout/sniper FBI, 1998, firearms instr. FBI, 2000, lic. anti-terrorism/force protection officer USMC, 2000, cert. instr. NY State Dept. Criminal Justice, 2000, 6004 aviation maintenance officer USMC, 2003, criminal investigator NY State, 2003. Commd. ensign USMC, 1989, advanced through grades to chief warrant officer, prodn. control officer in charge Newburgh, NY, 2005—; dispatcher Town of Newburgh Police Dept., Newburgh, NY, 1990—95; police officer Town of Crawford Police Dept, Pine Bush, NY, 1995—96, Newburgh Police Dept., NY, 1996—2006, detective, 2006—. Scout/sniper Newburgh Police Dept., 1998—, mem. tactical team, 1997—; instr. in field. Decorated Navy Achievement medal USMC, Commendation cert., Operation Iraqi Freedom Expeditionalry medal, Global War on Terrorism medal; named Officer of Yr., Town of Newburgh, 1999; recipient High Shooter award, Town of Lloyd Police Acad., 1992, Excellent Police Duty award, Town of Newburgh, 1996, Meritorious Police Duty award, 1999, Commendation cert., 2005, Unit citation, 2005. Mem.: Internat. Assn. Law Enforcement Firearms Instrs., Am. Sniper Assn., NY Tactical Assn., Nat. Tactical Assn., Boy Scouts Am. Republican. Avocations: travel, good food, shooting sports, outdoor activities. Home Phone: 845-566-0506 334; Office Phone: 845-564-1100. Office Fax: 845-564-1870. Personal E-mail: sgryther@aol.com.

RYTKONEN, JUHA KALEVI, corporate financial executive; b. Vantaa, Finland, Jan. 27, 1973; s. Esko Kalevi and Ilta-Sirkka Rytkonen; m. Mervi Susanna Koistinen, Mar. 17, 2006. BBA, Mercuria Bus. Sch., Finland, 1996—99. Contr. Scan-Group, Helsinki, Helsinki, Finland, 2001—05; fin. mgr. Multibrands Oy, Helsinki, Helsinki, Finland, 2005—06, Vintura Oy, Helsinki, Helsinki, 2005—07, Solera Finland Oy, Helsinki, Helsinki, Finland, 2006—07, cfo, 2007—; ceo Vintura Oy, Helsinki, Helsinki, Finland, 2007—. First seaman SLLAIV, 1994—95, Finland. Decorated Navy Guild Medal Finnish Navy Guild, Nat. Defence Medal Nat. Defence Medal Com.; grantee Scholarship for Studies, Finnish Cultural Fund, 1995. Mem.: The Finnish Club in Helsinki (assoc.). Conservative. Avocations: travel, sports.

RYU, HO JIN, materials researcher; b. Seoul, Republic of Korea, May 21, 1971; s. Do Hyeon Ryu and Mae Ja Kim; m. Sun Mee Lee, Dec. 5, 1998; children: Sina, Hana. PhD, Korea Advanced Inst. of Sci. and Tech., 1995—2000. Sr. rschr. Korea Atomic Energy Rsch. Inst., Daejeon, Republic of Korea, 2000—; vis. scholar Argonne Nat. Lab., 2005—07. Project mgr. Korea Atomic Energy Rsch. Inst., Daejeon, Republic of Korea, 2003—05. Contbr. scientific papers. Youth group leader Yuseong Ctrl. Bapt. Ch., Daejeon. Mem.: Korea Powder Metallurgy Inst., Korean Nuc. Soc., Korean Inst. of Metals and Materials. Christianity. Achievements include patents for. Avocations: tennis, mountain climbing, soccer. Office: Korea Atomic Energy Rsch Inst 150 Deokjin-dong Yuseong-gu Daejeon 305-353 Republic of Korea Office Phone: 82-42-868-8845. Office Fax: 82-42-868-8824. Business E-Mail: hjryu@kaeri.re.kr.

RYU, KYOO-HAI LEE, physiologist; b. Seoul, Sept. 5, 1948; came to US, 1972; d. Hee Soon and Jung Ock Lee; m. David Tai-Hyung Ryu, May 13, 1978; children: Eugenia, Christina, John. BS, Yonsei U., Seoul, 1971; PhD, U. Minn., Mpls., 1981. Postdoctoral fellow U. Minn., Mpls., 1980-81, staff scientist, 1981-82; sr. rsch. assoc. Wright State U., Dayton, Ohio, 1985-91; adminstr. Ohio Ctr. of Cosmetic Surgery, Bellefontaine, Ohio, 1991—. Home: 15 Bexley Ave Springfield OH 45503-1103 Office Phone: 937-390-3277. Personal E-mail: k@ryunet.com.

RYU, MANHO, application developer; b. Sochungdo, Kyungido, Korea, Mar. 23, 1957; arrived in U.S., 1983; s. Bongoh Ryu and Youngah No; m. Michelle M. Ryu, May 28, 1960; children: Angie L., Jason C. BS in Computer Sci., Abilene Christian U., Tex., 1986; BS in Applied Math., U. Tex. at Dallas, Richardson, 1988; MS in Applied Math., U. Tex. at Dallas, 1993; MS in Computer Sci., Kennedy-Western U., Boise, Idaho, 1992; PhD in Computer Sci., Kennedy-Western U., 1996. Programmer Korea Inst. Sci. and Tech., Seoul, 1976—82; computer operator Electrospace Sys., Richardson, 1988; lead programmer Info. Mgmt. Group, Plano, Tex., 1989—90; analyst, sys. supr. Epsilon Data Mgmt., Inc., Dallas, 1990—92; mgr. MIS dept. MB Direct, Inc., Dallas, 1992—93; dir. IS dept. Skyking Freight Sys., Dallas, 1993—94; sr. software engr. Spectra Vision Inc., Richardson, 1994—97, Estech Sys., Plano, 1997—98; sr. software devel. engr. Alcatel-Lucent NA, Plano, 1998—. Author: (software) Clean Man TXU, Cash Man TXU. Mem.: IEEE, Assn. Computing Machinery, Math. Assn. Am. Home: 7902 Bow Ct Frisco TX 75035 Office: Alcatel Lucent NA 3400 W Plano Pkwy Plano TX 75075 Office Phone: 972-477-9660. Personal E-mail: mmryu@yahoo.com. Business E-Mail: man.ryu@alcatel-lucent.com.

RYUN, JIM (JAMES RONALD RYUN), former congressman; b. Wichita, Kans., Apr. 29, 1947; m. Anne Carol Snider, 1969; children: Ned, Drew, Catharine, Heather. BA, U. Kans., 1970. Founder, pres. Jim Ryun Sports, Inc.; mem. US Congress from 2nd Kans. dist., 1996—2007, mem. armed svcs. com., budget com., fin. svcs. com. Participant Olympic Games, 1964, 68, 72. Recipient James E. Sullivan award, 1966, Silver medal 1500 meter run Olympic Games, 1968; Named Sportsman of Yr., SI mag., 1966, Athlete of Yr., ABC Wide World of Soprts, 1966; Named to the US Tack & Field Hall of Fame, 2003, Nat. Distance Running Hall of Fame Republican. *

RZEPKOWSKI, JAMES EDWARD, state agency administrator; b. Annapolis, Md., Mar. 8, 1971; s. Walter Jerome and Veronica Catherine (Gnacyk) R.; m. Laura E. Green, Aug. 23, 1997; 1 child, Brian Myer. BA, U. Md., 1993. Computer aide Nat. Security Agy. U.S. Dept. Defense, 1988-89; office mgr. Md. Dept. Housing and Cmty. Devel., 1990; legis. intern to Sen. John A Cade Md. State Senate, 1992; state del. dist. 32 State of Md., 1995—2003; ins. office rep. State Farm Ins. Agy., 1993—; assoc. dep. sec. Md. Dept. Bus. and Econ. Devel., 2003—. Adminstrv. asst. Crofton Convalescent Ctr., 1991; cashier Latelas Discount Liquors, 1992-93. State mem. Md. State Rep. Ctrl. Com., Annapolis, 1992; ofcl., player intramural sports U. Md.; pastoral coun. Cath. Student Ctr., 1992-93. Recipient Legis. Leadership award, The ARC of Md., 2000, Legislator of Yr. award, Anne Arundel County C. of C., 1996. Mem. K.C., Md. Medallion Soc. (charter), Eta Epsilon Alumni Assn. (pres. 1994—), Phi Beta Kappa, Omicron Delta Kappa, Alpha Lambda Delta, Golden Key, Pi Kappa Phi. Office: 217 E Redwood St Baltimore MD 21202 Home: 8109 Huntmaster CT Glen Burnie MD 21061-6343

RZEZNIK, JOHNNY, singer, musician; b. Buffalo, Dec. 5, 1965; Lead singer, guitarist Goo Goo Dolls, 1985—. Guitarist: (albums) First Release, 1987, Goo Goo Dolls, 1987, singer, guitarist: (albums) Jed, 1989, Hold Me Up, 1990, Superstar Car Wash, 1993, Boy Named Goo, 1995, Dizzy Up the Girl, 1998, Gutterflower, 2002, Let Love In, 2006, (songs) Iris, City of Angels soundtrack, 1998 (nominated for three Grammy Awards.), I'm Still Here, Treasure Planet soundtrack, 2002, Before It's Too Late, Transformers soundtrack, 2007; guest appearance (TV series) Charmed, 2000, (albums) Birdland (with the Yardbirds), 2003; singer, composer: (TV series) Good Morning Miami, 2002. Recipient Artist of Yr. (with Goo Goo Dolls), Radio Music Awards, 2005. Office: Warner Brothers Records 3300 Warner Blvd Burbank CA 91505

SAAB, DEANNE KELTUM, real estate broker, appraiser; b. Allentown, Pa., Jan. 27, 1945; d. James A. and Agnes G. (Hanzlik) S. BA, Cedar Crest Coll., 1966; MS, U. Calif., Santa Barbara, 1973; realtors cert., Pa. State U., 1978. Cert. appraiser Assoc. Appraisal Inst., Pa., 1991; cert. sales profl. Nat. Assn. Home Builders, 1994. Tchr. Ojai (Calif.) Unified Sch. Dist., 1966-74; pvt. practice Allentown, 1978—; owner Heritage Gardens, Allentown, 1981—; pres., treas. DeAnne & Assoc., Inc., Allentown, 1987—. Co-founder, treas. performance group Lehigh Valley Folk Music Soc., 1996. Mem. AAUW (various offices, Best State Newsletter award 1987), Nat. Assn. Realtors, Pa. Assn. Realtors, Allentown Lehigh Valley Assn. Realtors, Cedar Crest Coll. Alumnae Assn. (class rep., various offices), Lehigh Valley Guild Craftsmen (various offices). Avocations: gourd, herbal crafting, painting, folk music performance. Home and Office: 1360 Dorney Ave Allentown PA 18103-9731 Personal E-mail: dksaab@ptd.net.

SAAD, FAWZY ALI, molecular geneticist; b. Shabas Emir, Egypt, Feb. 11, 1956; s. Ali Mohamed and Hanim Ibrahim (Abduh) S. BSc in Genetics, U. Tanta, Egypt, 1978, MSc in Genetics, 1986; PhD in Molecular Genetics, U. Padua, Italy, 1995. Demonstrator dept. genetics U. Tanta, 1979-86, asst. lectr. genetics, 1986-96, lectr. molecular genetics, 1996—. Cons. dept. pathology, U. Padua, Italy, 1994-96. Contbr. articles to profl. jours. Fellow Italian Ministry Fgn. Affairs, 1989-94, 94-96. Mem. AAAS. Muslim. Home: 225 E Maple Ave Mocksville NC 27028-2619 Office: Dept Genetics Sakha Rd ET-33516 Kafr el Sheikh Egypt

SAAD, MICHAEL D., lawyer; b. Zanesville, Ohio, 1941; BS, Ohio State U., 1963, JD summa cum laude, 1966. Bar: Ohio 1966. Law clk. to Chief Justice Ohio State Supreme Ct., 1966—67; ptnr. Squire, Sanders & Dempsey LLP, Columbus, Ohio. Chmn. real estate & hospitality practice group Squire, Sanders & Dempsey LLP. Bd. dir. Ohio Housing Coun. Recipient Founder's Award, Ohio Capital Corp., 2002. Mem.: Order of Coif, Columbus Bar Assn. (fin. institutes com., real estate com., bankruptcy com.), Ohio State Bar Assn., Devel. Com. Ctrl. Ohio, ABA. Office: Squire Sanders & Dempsey LLP 1300 Huntington Ctr 41 South High St Columbus OH 43215-6197 Office Phone: 614-365-2735. Office Fax: 614-365-2499. Business E-Mail: msaad@ssd.com.

SAAD, THEODORE SHAFICK, retired microwave company executive; b. Boston, Sept. 13, 1920; s. Wadie Assad and Mary (Shalhoub) S.; m. Afeefi Abdelnour, May 5, 1943; children: Karen Jeanne, Janet Elaine. BSEE, MIT, 1941. Engr. Sylvania Electric Products, Danvers, Mass., 1941-42; rsch. assoc. radiation lab. Radiation Lab. MIT, Cambridge, 1942-45; sr. engr. Submarine Signal Co., Boston, 1945-49; v.p., chief engr. Microwave Devel. Labs., Waltham, Mass., 1949-53; engring. specialist Sylvania Electric Products, Woburn, Mass., 1953-55; pres., chmn. Sage Labs. Inc., Natick, Mass., 1955-93; ret., 1993. Cons. Horizon House Microwave, Norwood, Mass., 1958—. Editor: Microwave Engineers Handbook, 1971, Historical Perspectives of Microwave Technology, 1984; patentee in microwavetech. and passive components fields. Chmn. Concert Opera, Boston, 1997—. Fellow IEEE (life; Richard M. Emberson award 1996), AAAS; mem. Microwave Soc. of IEEE (hon. life; nat. lectr. 1972, Disting. Svc. award 1983, Centennial medal 1984, Career award 1992). Avocations: photography, reading, travel, music. Home: 52 Doublet Hill Rd Weston MA 02493-2331 E-mail: t.saad@ieee.org.

SAADA, ADEL SELIM, civil engineer, educator; b. Heliopolis, Egypt, Oct. 24, 1934; came to U.S., 1959, naturalized, 1965; s. Selim N. and Marie (Chahyne) S.; m. Nancy Helen Hernan, June 5, 1960; children: Christiane Mona, Richard Adel. Ingénieur des Arts et Manufactures, École Centrale, Paris, 1958; MS, U. Grenoble, France, 1959; PhD in Civil Engring, Princeton U., 1961. Registered profl. engr., Ohio. Engr. Société Dumez, Paris, 1959; research assoc. dept. civil engring. Princeton (N.J.) U., 1961-62; asst. prof. civil engring. Case Western Reserve U., Cleve., 1962-67, asso. prof., 1967-72, prof., 1973—, chmn. dept. civil engring., 1978-98, Frank H. Neff prof. civil engring., 1987. R.J. Carroll Meml. lectr. Johns Hopkins U., 1990; cons., lectr. soil testing and properties Waterways Expt. Sta. (C.E.), Vicksburg, Miss., 1974-79; cons. to various firms, 1962—. Author: Elasticity Theory and Applications, 1974, 2d edit., 1993; contbr. numerous articles on soil mechanics and foundation engring. to profl. jours. Recipient Telford Prize Instn. of Civil Engrs., U.K., 1995, Disting. Leadership award Cleve. Tech. Socs., 2001. Fellow ASCE (named Outstanding Civil Engr. of Yr. Cleve. sect. 1992); mem. Internat. Soc. Soil Mechanics, ASTM, One Two One Athletic Club. Achievements include invention of pneumatic analog computer and loading frame. Home: 3342 Braemar Rd Shaker Heights OH 44120-3332 Office: Case Western Res U Dept Civil Engring Case Sch Engring Cleveland OH 44106 Office Phone: 216-368-2427. Business E-Mail: axs31@case.edu.

SAADEH, CONSTANTINE KHALIL, internist, educator, health facility administrator; b. Beirut, Sept. 6, 1957; came to U.S., 1982; s. Khalil Constantine and Angel Janet (Iskendarian) S.; m. M. Celeste Gaylor; 2 children: Charles, McKenzie. BS in Biology-Chemistry, Am. U. Beirut, 1978, MD, 1982. Diplomate Nat. Bd. Med. Examiners, Am. Bd. Internal Medicine, Am. Bd. Allergy and Immunology, Am. Bd. Internal Medicine, Am. Bd. Rheumatology, Am. Bd. Geriatrics, Am. Acad. Pain Mgmt. Intern U. Miami, Jackson Meml. Hosp., Fla., 1982-83, resident in medicine Fla., 1983-85; fellow in clin. immunology Baylor Coll. of Medicine, Houston, 1985-87; fellow in rheumatology U. Colo. Health Sci. Ctr., Denver, 1987-88, instr. dept. internal medicine, 1988-89; acting chief med. svc. VA Med. Ctr., Amarillo, Tex., 1989, med. svc. staff physician, 1989—; asst. prof. dept. internal medicine Tex. Tech U. Health Scis. Ctr., Amarillo, 1989-91, assoc. prof. internal medicine and pediatrics, dir., 1991—, regional chair internal medicine, dir. residency program, 1992-98, assoc. prof. dept. microbiology and immunology, 1992—, clin. prof. dept. microbiol./immun., internal med., pediats., 1998—; pvt. practice Allergy ARTS, Amarillo, Tex.; pres. Amarillo Ctr. for Clin. Rsch., 2000—. Chief medicine N.W. Tex. Hosp., Amarillo, 1999-2001; lectr. in field. Contbr. articles to profl. jours. Fellow ACP, Am. Acad. Allergy and Immunology, Am. Coll. Rheumatology; mem. AMA, So. Med. Assn. (chmn. rheumatology sect. 1996-97, sec. internal medicine sect. 1997-99, assoc. councilor 1998-99). Home: 3000 S Hughes St Amarillo TX 79109-3515 Office: 6842 Plum Creek Dr Amarillo TX 79124 Home Phone: 806-374-8055; Office Phone: 806-353-7000. Business E-Mail: aarts@allergyarts.com.

SAADEH, SHERIF NABIL, gastroenterologist, hepatologist, researcher; b. Amman, Jordan, Nov. 29, 1969; s. Nabil Ibrahim Saadeh and Helen Aziz Ibrahim; m. Claudia-Aghareed Jamal Haddad; children: Omar, Kareem, Celina. MBBS, U. Jordan Faculty Medicine, MD, 1993. Cert. internal medicine Am. Bd. Internal Medicine, 1999, gastroenterology Am. Bd. Internal Medicine, 2003, hon. diplomate Am. Bd. Hosp. Physicians, Am. Coll. Ethical Physicians. Staff gastroenterologist/hepatologist Baylor U. Med. Ctr., Dallas, 2003—. Contbr. Recipient Rsch. award, North Am. Conf. Gastroenterology Fellows, 2002, fellowship, Am. Bd. Hosp. Physicians, 2002, America's Top Physician award, Consumer's Rsch. Coun. Am., 2003; grantee medical rsch. grant-subinvestigator, Nat. Insts. Health, 2001, medical rsch. grant, Cleve. Clinic Hepatology Inst., 2001. Fellow: Am. Coll. Hosp. Physicians; mem.: ACP, Jordan Med. Assn., European Assn. for Study of Liver, Tex. Soc. Gastroenterology and Endoscopy, Am. Coll. Gastroenterology, Crohn's & Colitis Found. Am., Am. Liver Found., AMA (Physician's recognition award 2004—07), Am. Soc. Gastrointestinal Endoscopy, Am. Gastroenterol. Assn., Am. Ass. Study Liver Diseases. Roman Catholic. Office: Al-Khalidi Medical Plz PO BOX 5321 11183 Amman Jordan Personal E-mail: saadeh@lycos.com.

SAAL, HOWARD MAX, clinical geneticist, pediatrician, educator; b. NYC, Aug. 20, 1951; s. Josef and Ester S.; m. Cara Tina Schweitzer, May 3, 1987; 1 child, Rebecca. BS, U. Mass., Amherst, 1973, MS, 1975; MD, Wayne State U., 1979. Intern pediatrics U. Conn. Med. Ctr., 1979-80; resident pediatrics U. Conn. Health Ctr., 1980-82; fellow med. genetics U. Wash. Sch. Medicine, 1982-84; dir. cytogenetics U. Conn. Health Ctr., Farmington, 1984-87; vice chmn. med. genetics Children's Nat. Med. Ctr., Washington, 1987-93, head clin. genetics Cin., 1993—. Asst. prof. pediats. George Washington U., Washington, 1987-93, assoc. prof. pediats., 1993; assoc. prof. clin. pediats. U. Cin. Sch. Medicine, 1993—, prof. pediats., 2000—. Contbr. articles to profl. jours. Mem. med. adv. com. Nat. Neurofibromatosis Found., N.Y.C., 1987-93; mem. health profl. adv. com. March of Dimes, Arlington, Va., 1991-93; bd. dirs. Capital Area March of Dimes, 1993. Tng. grantee NIH, 1979-82. Fellow Am. Acad. Pediats. (chmn. exec. com. for sect. on genetics and birth defects 1999-2003, com. genetics 2003—, chmn. com. on genetics 2007—), Am. Coll. Med. Genetics; mem. Am. Soc. Human Genetics, Soc. Craniofacial Genetics (sec.-treas. 1990-96), Accredidation Coun. for Grad. Med. Edn. (med. genetics residency com). Avocation: photography. Home: 3715 Monets Ln Cincinnati OH 45241-3847 Office: Cin Childrens Hosp Med Ctr 3333 Burnet Ave Cincinnati OH 45229-3026 Home Phone: 513-563-0916; Office Phone: 513-636-4760. Business E-Mail: saalhm@cchmc.org.

SAALFELD, FRED ERICH, science educator, researcher; s. Eric Arthur and Milla (Kessler) S.; m. Elizabeth Renner, Nov. 22, 1958; 1 child, Fred E. Jr. (dec.). BS cum laude, So. East Mo. State U., 1957; MS in Phys. Chemistry, Iowa State U., 1959, PhD in Phys. Chemistry, 1961. Instr. Iowa State U., Ames, 1961—62; chemist Naval Rsch. Lab, Washington, 1962—63, head mass spectrometry sect., 1963—74, head phys. chem. br., 1974—76, supt. chem. divsn., 1976—82; chief scientist Office Naval Rsch., London, 1979—80, dir. rsch. Arlington, Va., 1982—87, dir., 1987—93, dep. chief naval rsch., tech. dir., 1993—98, exec. dir., tech. dir., 1998—2002; disting. rsch. prof. Ctr. for Tech. and Nat. Security Policy Nat. Def. U., 2003—04; sr. fellow Potomac Inst. for Policy Studies, 2002—, bd. regents, 2007—. Author more than 500 publications, reports, presentations on applications of mass spectrometry to fields of combustion, laser, environ. analysis. Recipient Disting. Rank awards U.S. Pres., Washington, 1989, 96, Meritorious Rank award U.S. Pres., Washington, 1986, Robert Conrad award Sec. USN, Washington, 1988, Disting. Civilian Svc. award Sec. of Def./Dept. Def., 1999; named Fed. Exec. of Yr., Fed. Exec. Inst., Washington, 1991, named Fred E. Saalfed award for lifetime achievement in sci., Chief Naval Rsch., 2001. Fellow AAAS, Potomac Inst. Policy Studies (sr.); mem. Am. Chem. Soc. (councilor 1973-89), Am. Soc. Mass Spectrometry (sec. 1970-74), Combustion Inst., Chem. Soc. Washington (pres. 1972). Achievements include provision for science base for life support systems used in enclosed environments; development of educational programs used by USN for scientist training. Office Phone: 703-887-2197. Personal E-mail: fsaalfeld@cox.net.

SAAM, ROBERT HARRY, human resources specialist, consultant; b. Toledo, Mar. 7, 1947; s. Robert J. and Dorothy H. (Kinney) Saam; m. Pamela Soder, Oct. 30, 1982; children: Robert C., Cara B., Stacia J. BA, U. Toledo, 1970; MS in Ednl. Psychology, U. Wis., 1993. Investigative supr. Ohio Civil Rights Commn., Cleve., 1973—76; councillator U.S. EEO Commn., Cin., 1976—79; mgr. labor rels. Internat. Minerals and Chems., Mundelein, Ill., 1979—85; dir. human resources svcs. Rexnord, Inc., Brookfield, Wis., 1985—87; v.p., owner Thompson Cons. Ltd., Brookfield, 1987—2000; sr. v.p. Lee Hecht Harrison, Brookfield, 2000—. Contbr. articles to profl. jours. Mem.: Am. Assn. Counseling and Devel. Home and Office: 646 N 77th St Milwaukee WI 53213-3512 Business E-Mail: Rob.Saam@LHH.com.

SAARI, DAVID JOHN, retired law educator; b. Va., Minn., Jan. 12, 1934; s. William Willard Saari and Amelia Haapala, Helmi Pesola (Stepmother); m. Madeleine Belanger (div.); children: Glenna, Lenore, Peter, Gail; m. Martha Elizabeth Sullivan, July 16, 1987. BA, U. Minn., Mpls., 1955, JD, 1959. Bar: Oreg. 1962, D.C. 2007. Legal rschr. League Oreg. Cities, U. Oreg., Eugene, 1959—64; ct. adminstr. Circuit Ct. Portland Oreg., 1964—67; rsch. assoc. Am. Bar Found., Chgo., 1967—68; dir. Ct. Mgmt. Study, Washington, 1968—70; mgr. LEX Computer Sys., Bethesda, Md., 1970—72; dir. sch. justice Am. U., Washington, 1972—75, faculty, prof. emeritus, 1972—99. Pres. Western Trial Ct. Adminstr., Portland, 1967, Nat. Assn. Trial Ct. Adminstr., Portland, 1968. Author: (books) American Court Management, Theories and Practices, 1982, Management of Court Reporters, 1985, Too Mock Liberty, Perspectives on Freedom and the American Dream, 1995, Global Corporations and Sovereign Nations, Collision or Cooperation, 1999; contbr. articles various profl. jours. Mem. Eugene City Club, 1963—64, Nat. Assn. Ct. Mgrs., Williamsburg, Va., 1980—90. With USAR. Grantee monetary, Am. U., 1972—85. Independent. Unitarian. Avocations: sailing, skiing, travel, hiking. Home and Office: Funky Farm and Arts de Calif 1451 Branch Mill Rd Arroyo Grande CA 93420

SAARI, DONALD GENE, mathematician, department chairman, economist; b. Ironwood, Mich., Mar. 9, 1940; s. Gene August and Martha Mary (Jackson) S.; m. Lillian Joy Kalinen, June 11, 1966; children: Katri, Anneli. BS, Mich. Technol. U., 1962; PhD, Purdue U., 1967, DSc (hon.), 1989, U. Caen, France, 1998, Mich. Tech. U., 1999. Research astronomer Yale U., New Haven, 1967-68; prof. dept. math. Northwestern U., Evanston, Ill., 1968-2000, prof. econs., 1988-2000, Pancoe prof. math., 1995-2000, chmn. dept., 1981-84; prof. U. Nanjing (China), 1995; disting. prof. econ., math U. Calif., Irvine, 2000—, dir. Ctr. for Decision Analysis, 2002—05, dir. Inst. Math. Behavioral Sci., 2003—. Cons. Nat. Bur. Standards, Gaithersburg, Md., 1979-86, Commn. 9, Internat. Astron. Union, 1985-91; nat. com. math. Nat. Rsch. Coun., 1997-2003, chair 2001-03, math./sci. edn. bd., 2001—, Bd. Internat. Sci. Orgns., 2001-03, NRC com. on Internat. Inst. Applied Sys. Analysis, 2004—; chair trustees Math. Sci. Rsch. Inst., 2004-07. Assoc. editor Jour. Econ. Behavior and Orgn., 1988-94, Celestial Mechanics and Dynamical Astronomy. 1989-97, Econ. Theory, 1990—, Social Choice and Welfare, 1997—, Qualitative Theory of Dynamical Sys., 1999—, Positivity, 2000—. Recipient Duncan Black award, Pub. Choice Soc., 1991, Chauvenet prize Math. Assn. Am., 1995, Ford prize Math. Assn. Am., 1985, Allendorfer award Math. Assn. Am., 1999; Guggenheim fellow, 1988-89. Fellow AAAS, Am. Acad. Arts and Scis.; mem. NAS, Am. Math. Soc. (chief editor bull. 1999-2005, mem. coun. 1999-2005), Am. Astron. Soc., Soc. Indsl. and Applied Math. (editor jour. 1981-88), Econometric Soc. Office: U Calif Inst Math Behavorial Scis SSPA 2119 Irvine CA 92697-5100 Office Phone: 949-824-5894. Business E-Mail: dsaari@uci.edu.

SAARI, JOHN WILLIAM, JR., lawyer; b. Jersey City, Oct. 12, 1937; s. John William, Sr. and Marie (Bain) Saari; m. Susan Jo Olson, Aug. 27, 1967 (div. June 1971); m. Marjorie Ann Palm, Nov. 16, 1973. Student, Duke U., 1955-58, U. N.C., 1962-63; JD with honors, Ill. Inst. Tech., Chgo., 1972. Bar: Ill. 1972, U.S. Dist. Ct. (no. dist.) Ill. 1972, U.S. Ct. Appeals (7th cir.) 1972, Wis. 1980, U.S. Supreme Ct. 1997. Assoc. Yates, Goff, Gustafson & Been, Chgo., 1972-76, Hubbard, Hubbard, O'Brien & Hall, Chgo., 1976-78; atty. Ill. Bell Telephone Co., Chgo., 1978-79; assoc. Cirilli Law Office, Rhinelander, Wis., 1979-83; pvt. practice Rhinelander, 1983-90, 2002—; ptnr. Mouw, Saari, Krueger, Paulson & Smith, Rhinelander, 1990—2002. Bd. dirs Northwoods United Way, 1980—88, pres., 1983—84. With US Army, 1958—61, ETO. Mem.: ABA, Oneida-Vilas-Forest Bar Assn. (pres. 1996—97), Wis. Bar Assn., Ill. Bar Assn., Lions (pres. Sugarcamp 1983—84). Avocations: hunting, fishing, baseball, reading, golf. Home and Office: 6998 Wildwood Ln Rhinelander WI 54501 Home Phone: 715-282-6099; Office Phone: 715-282-8282. E-mail: saarilaw@frontiernet.net.

SAATY, THOMAS LORIE, science educator; b. Mosul, Iraq, July 18, 1926; s. David Saaty and Dola Hayali; m. Bernadine Lucia Wearner; children: Linda, Michael, Emily; m. Rozann Waldron; children: John, Daniel. BA, Columbia Union Coll., 1948; MSc in Physics, Cath. U. Am., 1949; MA in Math., Yale U., 1951, PhD in Math., 1953; attended, U. Paris, 1952-53. Sci. analyst, submarine def. Melpar, Inc., 1953—54; sci. analyst, ops. evaluation group MIT, 1954-57; sci. analyst Navy Mgmt. Office, 1957-58; sci. liaison officer US Embassy, London, 1958-59; dir. advanced planning Office Naval Rsch., Washington, 1959-61, head math. br., 1961-63; sci. analyst Arms Control and Disarmament Agy., Washington, 1963-69; exec. dir. Conf. Bd. Math. Scis., Washington, 1965-67; prof. grad. groups ops. rsch., social sys. scis., grad. groups applied math., energy mgmt. and power, peace sci., civil engring., decision scis. Wharton Sch., U. Pa., Phila., 1969-79, chair, grad. groups ops. rsch., 1969—71; prof. chair., philosophy of sci., ops., decision scis. and artificial intelligence, math., sociology Joseph M. Katz Grad. Sch., Sch. Engring., U. Pitts., 1979—. Cons. govts., France, Egypt, Sudan, Kuwait, Tanzania, China, Indonesia, UN, 1958—; cons. bus., Westinghouse, US Steel, RCA, Woods Gordon Can., R.J. Reynolds, Ford Found., Am. Cyanimid, Colonial Penn Ins., Pan Am. Airlines, Monsanto, Conoco, N.Am. Rockwell, Xerox, Kodak, Martin Marietta, IBM, Booz Allen Applied Rsch., Logistics Mgmt. Inst., Urban Inst., Electric Power Rsch. Inst., NASA, AID, LEAA, NIH, Nat. Bur. Stds., Bur. of Census, Dept. Def., Dept. Air Force; invited lectr., 1972-76. Author: Mathematical Methods of Operations Research (with Japanese and Russian transls.), 1959, Elements of Queueing Theory with Applications (with Russian, Spanish, and German transls.), 1961, Modern Nonlinear Equations, 1967, reprinted edit., 1982, Mathematical Models of Arms Control and Disarmament (Russian transls.), 1968, Optimization in Integers and Related Extremal Problems (Russian transls.), 1970, Topics in Behavorial Mathematics, 1973, The Analytic Hierarchy Process (Russian, Portuguese, and Chinese transls.), 1980, revised edit., 1996, Decision Making for Leaders; The Analytical Hierarchy Process for Decisions in a Complex World (French, Indonesian, Spanish, Korean, Arabic, Persian, Thai transls.), 1982, rev. edit., 2000, Fundamentals of Decision Making with the Analytic Hierrchy Process, 1994, rev. edit., 2000, The Analytic Network Process: Decisions Making with Dependence and Feedback, 1996, rev. edit., 2001, Decision Making with Dependence and Feedback: The Analytic Network Process (ANP) and SuperDecisions Software, Guide, Manual, and Examples, 1997, The Brain, Unraveling the Mystery of How it Works: The Neural Network Process, 2000, Creative Thinking, Problem Solving & Decision Making, 2001, Theory and Applications of the Analytic Network Process, 2005; (with J. Bram) Nonlinear Mathematics, 1964, reprinted edit., 1981, (with R. Busacker) Finite Graphs and Networks (Japanese, Russian, German and Hungarian transls.), 1964-65, (with George B. Dantzig) Compact City (Russian transls.), 1973, (with Paul C. Kainen) The Four-Color Problem; Assaults and Conquest, 1977, reprinted edit. 1986, (with L. Klein) The Unthinkable and the Possible in the Middle East, 1975, (with Joyce Alexander) Thinking with Models, 1981, (with Luis G. Vargas) The Logic of Priorities; Applications in Business, Energy, Health, and Transportation), paperback edit., 1991, (with Kevin P. Kearns) Analytical Planning; The Organization of Systems (Russian transls.), 1985, paperback edit., 1991, (with Joyce Alexander) Conflict Resolution: The Analytic Hierarchy Process, 1989, (with Larry W. Boone) Embracing the Future, 1990, (with Luis G. Vargas) Prediction, Projection and Forecasting, 1991, (with Ernest H. Forman) The Hierarchon-A Dictionary of Hierarchies, 1993, (with L.G. Vargas) Decision Making in Economic, Political, Social and Technological Environments: The Analytic Hierarchy Process, 1994, (with L.G. Vargas) Models, Methods, Concepts and Applications of the Analytic Hierarchy Process, 2000, (with M. Ozdemir) The Encyclicon, 2005; editor, Lectures on Modern Mathematics, vols. I, II, III, Japanese trans., 1964-65, (with F.J. Weyl) The Spirit and Uses of the Mathematical Sciences, 1969; inventor multi-criteria decision making process: Analytic Hierarchy Process; reviewer: Math. Revs., 1954-75; editor, originator, Newsletter Math. Scis., 1965-67; assoc. editor: Naval Rsch. Quar., Jour. Ops. Rsch., 1958-63, Nonlinear Analysis with Applications, Socio-Economic Planning Scis., Internat. Jour. Sys., Measurement and Decisions, Jour. Math. Modeling, Info. Tech. and Decision Making, Jour. Multi-Criteria Decision Analysis, Jour. Sys. Sci. and Sys. Engring., Internat. Jour. Orgnl. Analysis, Applied Math. Letters; contbr. 250 papers in field. Recipient award Inst. Mgmt. Scis., 1977, Gold medal Internat. Soc. Multicriteria Decision Making, 2000; named Alumnus of Yr. award Columbia Union Coll., 1982; established Thomas L. Saaty prize in Math. and Mgmt., 1982. Fellow AAAS; mem. NAE, NAS, Math. Assn. Am. (Lester R. Ford prize 1973), Am. Math. Soc., Ops. Rsch. Soc. Am., Internat. Inst. for Strategic Studies, World Future Soc., Internat. Peace Sci. Soc., Internat. Acad. Mgmt. (elected mem.), Beta Gamma Sigma. Mem. Soc. Of Friends. Achievements include development of the mathematical theory of the Analytic Network Process for decisions with dependence and feedback to decisions with benefits opportunities, costs, and risks; research in neural networks and how the synthesis of firing of neurons is intimately related to decision making using ratio and proportion. Office: U Pitts 322 Mervis Hall Pittsburgh PA 15260-7503 Office Phone: 412-648-1539. E-mail: saaty@katz.pitt.edu.

SAAVEDRA, ABELARDO, school system administrator; b. Feb. 18, 1951; m. Myrna Saavedra; children: Lisa, Elizabeth. BS, Texas A&I Univ., 1972, MS, 1974; PhD in sch. admin., Univ. Michan. Teacher Corpus Christi Pub. Schools, asst. prin., prin., admin.; dist. supt. Houston Pub. Schools, 2001, exec. dep. supt., 2002—04, supt., 2004—. Adj. prof. Univ. Houston, Texas A&M Univ.; mem. Gov. Task Force Juvenile Justice. Chmn. bd. Greater Houston Chapter Red Cross, March of Dimes; with WorkSource Bd. Dir. Recipient state and national recognition for development and adoptio of "real-world academic standards" in all grade levels. Mem.: Tex. Bus. Edn. Coalition (co-chmn.), South Tex. Ed. Research and Develop. Ctr. Office: Houston Independent Sch Dist 3830 Richmond Ave Houston TX 77027 Office Phone: 713-892-6300, 713-892-6061. *

SAAVEDRA, CHARLES JAMES, banker; b. Denver, Nov. 2, 1941; s. Charles James and Evangeline Cecilia (Aragon) S.; m. Ann Helen Taylor, 1967; children: Michael, Kevin, Sarah. BSBA, Regis U., Denver, 1963; postgrad., U. Calif., San Francisco, 1964-66. V.p. Western States Bankcard Assn., San Francisco, 1969-77; dir. info. systems World Airways, Inc., Oakland, Calif., 1977-79; v.p. computer svcs. First Nationwide Bank, San Francisco, 1979-83; sr. v.p. Wells Fargo Bank, San Francisco, 1983-92, Union Bank Calif., San Francisco, 1992—. Instr. Programming & Systems Inst., San Francisco, 1968-69; lectr. Am. Mgmt. Assn., 1984-2005. Pres. Richt Direction Project Contra Costa County; bd. dirs. No. Calif. Family Ctr. With USNR, 1963-64. Mem. Data Processing Mgrs. Assn. (bd. dirs., chmn. program com. 1981), Am. Nat. Stds. Inst., Am. Bankers Assn., San Francisco Jaycees, Commonwealth Club Calif., Lake Lakewood Assn., Alpha Delta Gamma. Home: 210 Lakewood Rd Walnut Creek CA 94598-4826 Office Phone: 925-980-0911. Personal E-mail: jim_saa@yahoo.com.

SABA, SHOICHI, electronics executive, director; b. Tokyo, Feb. 28, 1919; Grad., Imperial U., Tokyo, 1941. With Toshiba Corp., Tokyo, 1942-87, mng. dir., 1972-74, exec. v.p., 1974-76, sr. exec. v.p., 1976-80, pres., CEO, 1980-86, chmn., exec. officer, 1986-87, adviser to bd., 1987—2005, sr. exec. adviser, 2005—; pres. Japanese Indsl. Stds. Com., 1994—2001. Chmn. nat. bd. govts. Nat. Scout Assn. Japan, 1994—; chmn., bd. trustees Internat. Christian U., 1998-2004. Office: Toshiba Corp 1-1 Shibaura 1-chome Minato-ku Tokyo 105-8001 Japan

SABAN, HAIM, investment company executive, television producer; b. Alexandria, Egypt, 1944; arrived in Israel, 1952, arrived in France, 1975, arrived in USA, 1983; m. Cheryl Saban, 1987; children: Ness, Tanya. TV series composer, 1975—95; chmn., CEO Saban Entertainment, LA, 1988—97, Fox Family Worldwide, LA, 1997—2001, Saban Capital Group, Inc., LA, 2001—; founder Saban Music Group, LA, 2002—. Dir. DirectTV Group, Inc., El Segundo, Calif.; bd. regents U. Calif., 2002—; founder Saban Ctr. Middle East Policy Brookings Inst., Washington, 2002, trustee. Composer: (TV series) Heathcliff, He-Man & the Masters of the Universe, The Littles, Inspector Gadget, Mister T, Punky Brewster, Kissyfur, Rainbow Brite, She-Ra: Princess of Power, MASK, Popples, The Real Ghost Busters, Zoobilee Zoo, Dennis the Menace, Maxie's World, Beverly Hills Teens, C.O.P.S., Dragon Quest, The Super Mario Bros. Super Show!, Samurai Pizza Cats; exec. prodr.: (TV series) Kidd Video, 1984—87, Rambo, 1986, Mighty Morphin' Power Rangers, 1993—96, V.R. Troopers, 1994, Sweet Valley High, 1994—98, Power Rangers Zeo, 1996—97, Big Bad Beetleborgs, 1997, Breaker High, 1997—98, Power Rangers Turbo, 1997, Beetleborgs Metallix, 1997, Diabolik, 1997, Power Rangers in Space, 1998, Mystic Knights of Tir Na Nog, 1998, Power Rangers Lost Galaxy, 1999, Power Rangers Lightspeed Rescue, 2000, Power Rangers Time Force, 2001; (films) Mighty Morphin' Power Rangers: The Movie, 1995, Turbo: A Power Rangers Movie, 1997, Rusty: A Dog's Tale, 1998, Addams Family Reunion, 1998; (TV films) The Phantom of the Opera, 1990, Casper: A Spirited Beginning, 1997, Casper Meets Wendy, 1998; writer (TV series) Around the World in 80 Dreams, 1992. Active in Israeli Cancer Rsch. Fund, John Wayne Cancer Inst., U. Tel Aviv, Nat. Park Found., United Friends of the Children, Children's Hosp. LA, Milken Cmty. High Sch. Served in Israeli Def. Force. Named one of Forbes' Richest Americans, 2006. Office: Saban Capital Group Ste 1050 10100 Santa Monica Blvd Los Angeles CA 90067 Office Phone: 310-557-5100.

SABAN, NICK LOU, college football coach, former professional football coach; b. Fairmont, W. Va., Oct. 31, 1951; m. Terry Constable, Dec. 18, 1971; children: Nicholas, Kristen. BS in Bus., Kent State U., 1973, MA in Sports Adminstrn., 1975. Grad. asst. Kent State U., 1973—74, linebackers coach, 1975—76; outside linebackers coach Syracuse U., 1977; secondary coach W. Va. U., Morgantown, 1978—79, Ohio State U., Columbus, 1980—81, U.S. Naval Acad., Annapolis, 1981; secondary coach & defensive coord. Mich. State U., 1983—87; secondary coach Houston Oilers, 1988—89; head coach Toledo U., 1990; defensive coord. Cleve. Browns, 1991—94; head coach Mich. State U., East Lansing, 1995—2000, La. State U., Baton Rouge, 2000—05, Miami Dolphins, 2005—07, U. Ala., Tuscaloosa, 2007—. Co-author (with Sam King): Tiger Turnaround: LSU's Return to Football Glory, 2001. Founder Nick's Kids. Named Nat. Coach of Yr., AP, 2003; recipient Paul "Bear" Bryant award, Nat. Sportscasters & Sportswriters Assn., 2003, Eddie Robinson award, 2003. Achievements include coaching LSU to the BCS Nat. Championship, 2003. Avocation: golf. Office: U Ala Athletics Box 870393 Tuscaloosa AL 35487-0393 *

SABANADZOVIC, SEAD, virologist, educator; b. Podgorica, Montenegro, Aug. 26, 1963; s. Dervis and Aisa Sabanadzovic; m. Nina Abou Ghanem, Sept. 23, 1999; 1 child, Elvin. BS, U. Sarajevo, Bosnia and Herzegovina, 1989; Diploma, Mediterranean Agronomic Inst. Bari, Italy, 1992; MS, Mediterranean Agronomic Inst. Bari, 1993; PhD, U. Bari, 1997. Sci. tutor Mediterranean Agronomic Inst., 1997—2003; postgrad. rschr. U. Calif., Davis, 2003—04; assoc. prof. Miss. State U., 2004—. Postgrad. scholarship, Ministry Fgn. Affairs Italy, 1991—93. Mem.: Internat. Coun. Study Virus and Virus-like Diseases Grapevine, Am. Phytopathological Soc. Achievements include research in a new plant virus species, development of detection methods and plant virus taxonomy. Office: Miss State Univ 103 Clay Lyle Bldg Mail Stop 9775 Mississippi State MS 39762 Office Fax: 662-325-8837. Business E-Mail: ss501@msstate.edu.

SABAT, ROBERT HARTMAN, magazine editor; b. Newark, Aug. 28, 1957; s. Charles and Marilyn Ruth (Hartman) S.; m. Jessica Schilling Fine, Oct. 15, 1989; children: Nathaniel, Olivia. BA, Brandeis U., 1980. Mng. editor Penthouse mag., NYC, 1986—91, Connoisseur mag., NYC, 1991—92, Lear's mag., NYC, 1994—94, Interview mag., NYC, 1994—95, Smart Money mag., NYC, 1995—99, exec. editor, 1999—2002; dep. editor US Weekly mag., NYC, 2002—03; mng. editor GQ mag., NYC, 2003—04; news editor Wall St. Jour., NYC, 2004—. Office: The Wall St Jour 200 Liberty St New York NY 10281 Personal E-mail: robertsabat@hotmail.com.

SABATHIA, C.C. (CARSTEN CHARLES SABATHIA), professional baseball player; b. Vallejo, Calif., July 21, 1980; m. Amber Sabathia; children: Carsten Charles III, Jaeden Arie. Draft pick Cleve. Indians, 1998, pitcher, 2001—. Named to Am. League All-Star Team, 2003—04, 2007. Achievements include leading the Am. League in fewest hits allowed per 9 innings pitched (7.44), 2001; led Am. League in complete games (6) and shutouts (2), 2006. Mailing: Cleve Indians Jacobs Field 2401 Ontario St Cleveland OH 44115-4003 *

SABATINI, DAVID DOMINGO, cell biologist, biochemist; b. Bolivar, Argentina, May 10, 1931; came to U.S., 1961; m. Zulema Lena Sabatini, 1960; children: Bernardo L., David M. MD, U. Litoral, Rosario, Argentina, 1954; PhD in Cell Biology, Rockefeller U., 1966. Instr., lectr., assoc. prof. cell biology Inst. Gen. Anatomy and Embryology, U. Buenos Aires, 1957-60; dir. admissions Sch. Medicine U. Buenos Aires, 1957-60; Rockefeller Found. fellow Sch. Medicine Yale U., 1961—63; rsch. assoc. cell biol. lab Rockefeller U., NYC, 1961-63, from asst. prof. to assoc. prof. cell biology, 1966-72; prof., chmn. dept. cell biology Sch. Medicine NYU, 1972-74, Frederick L. Ehrman prof., chmn. dept. cell biol. Sch. Med., 1975—, dir. MD-PhD program, 1987-97. Wendell Griffith Meml. lectr. St. Louis U., 1977; Mary Peterman Meml. lectr. Meml.-Sloan Kettering Inst., N.Y., 1977; 25th Robert J. Terry lectr. Wash. U., 1978; 3d ann. Keith R. Porter lectr. cell biology, 1994; vis. prof. Coll. France, Paris, 1986, George Washington U., 1986; 7th Ann. Kenneth F. Naidorff Meml. lectr. Columbia U., 1989; fellow Nat. Acad. Medicine, Argentina, 1956; UNESCO fellow Biophysics Inst., Rio de Janeiro, 1957; Pfizer traveling fellow, 1972; mem. molecular biology study sect. NIH, 1973-77, chmn., 1976-77; mem. bd. basic biology Nat. Rsch. Coun., 1986-89. Editor Jour. Cell Biology, 1971—, Jour. Cellular Biochemistry, 1980-84, Molecular & Cellular Biology, 1980-82, Procs. NAS USA, 1985—, Biol. Cell, 1986—, Current Opinions Cell Biology, 1990—; mem. editl. bd. Procs. NAS, 1993-96. Mem. sci. adv. com. Irma T. Hirshcl Charitable Trust, 1979-85; bd. dirs. Pub. Health Rsch. Inst., 1980-88; bd. sci. dirs. Jane Coffin Childs Meml. Fund, 1980-86, Nat. Inst. Diabetes Digest Kidney Disease, 1982-86; sci. adv. com. Robert Wood Johnson Found. Minority Med. Faculty Devel. Program, 1987—, Human Frontier Sci. Program, 1991—, chair molecular grants, 1994—; mem. sci. rev. com. Pew Internat. Fellows Program, 1990—, med. adv. bd., 1989-93, internat. program, 1994—; mem. sci. adv. com. Inst. d'Embryologie Cellular Mol., Coll. France, 1994—;, Ctr. Adv. Biotech. and Medicine, 1996—; mem. Alfred P. Sloan Jr. award selection com. GM Cancer Rsch. Found., 1996—. Recipient Samuel Roberts Noble Rsch. Recognition award, 1980. Fellow AAAS, Am. Acad. Microbiology, NY Acad. Sci.; mem. NAS (chmn. cell and devel. biology sect. 1994-96), Am. Soc. Cell Biology (pres. 1978-79, coun. mem. 1974-77, E. B. Wilson award 1986), Harvey Soc. (v.p. 1985-86, pres. 1986-87), Argentine Med. Assn. (hon.), French Acad. Sci. (fgn. assoc., Charles Leopold Mayer prize 1988, grande médalle, 2003), Am. Soc. Biol. Chemistry, Am. Soc. Microbiology, NY Soc. Electron Microbiology ((pres. 1971), Am. Assn. Anatomy (chair cell biology, neurobiology, exec. coun. 1992—), Inst. Medicine. Business E-Mail: david.sabatini@med.nyu.edu.

SABATINI, NELSON JOHN, healthcare executive; b. Rochester, NY, Jan. 20, 1940; s. John R. and Ida M. (Ceconi) S.; m. Marilyn Jean Gromala, Jan. 19, 1963; children— John Nelson, Michael Christopher Student, Lewis Coll., Lockport, Ill., 1958-62; BA in Psychology, George Washington U., 1971, postgrad. Claims rep. Social Security Adminstrn., Chgo., 1962-65, various positions Balt., 1965-79, dep. dir. disability programs, 1979-81, exec. asst. to commr., 1981-82, assoc. commr., 1982—, dep. commr., 1983-88; dep. sec. health and mental hygiene State of Md., 1988, sec. health and mental hygiene, 1991—95, 2003—05; v.p. Univ. Md. Med. Systems, 1995, exec. v.p., 1995—2003; CEO Sabatini Cons. Group, 2005—; pres. Md. Care Improvement Plus, 2005—. Named Disting. Marylander of Yr. 1993; recipient Sec.'s cert. HHS, 1975; Commr.'s citation Social Security Adminstrn., 1977, 81; Presdl. Merit Rank award Pres. of U.S., 1984 Roman Catholic. Avocations: sailing, tennis. Office Phone: 443-827-3332. Business E-Mail: sconsultinggroup@comcast.net.

SABATINI, SANDRA, physician; b. NYC, Dec. 1, 1940; BS in Chemistry, Millsaps Coll., 1962; MS in Pharmacology, Marquette U., 1966; PhD in Pharmacology, U. Miss., 1968; MD in Internal Medicine, Tex. Med. Sch., 1974. Lic. physician, Ill., Tex. Intern in medicine U. Ill. Hosp., Chgo., 1974-75; asst. prof. U. Tex. Med. Sch., San Antonio, 1968-70; assoc. dir. U. Ill. Hosp., Chgo., 1977-78; asst. prof. U. Ill. Coll. of Medicine, Chgo., 1977-83, assoc. prof. medicine and physiology, 1983-84; attending physician in nephrology VA, Chgo., 1977-84; med. dir. Dialysis Unit U. Ill., Chgo., 1978-84; prof. internal medicine and physiology Tex. Tech. U. Health Sci. Ctr., Lubbock, 1985—, chmn. dept. physiology, 1993-96; attending physician in nephrology U. Med. Ctr., Lubbock, 1985—. Lab. instr. Millsaps Coll., Jackson, Miss., 1961-62; instr. pharmacology Bapt. Hosp. Sch. Nursing, Jackson, 1966-68; merit rev. mem. NSF, 1987, 91, 92; rev. mem. several orgns. including Chgo. Heart Assn., 1984, NIH, 1983, 86, 89-93, 96, Nat. Kidney Found., 1987, 89—, Am. Heart Assn., 1981-84, others; cons. U.S. Med. Licensing Exam/Nat. Bd. Med. Examiners, Step 1 Physiology Test Com., 1996-99. Editl. referee Am. Jour. Kidney Disease, Am. Jour. Physiology, Am. Jour. Nephrology, Annals of Internal Medicine, others; mem. editl. bd. Am. Jour. Nephrology, 1989-93, Seminars in Nephrology, 1984—; co-editor Am. Jour. Kidney Diseases, 1997—; author numerous publs. and abstracts in field; contbr. articles to profl. jours. Bd. dirs. YWCA of Lubbock, 1994-99; mem. Leadership Tex., 1994. Predoctoral fellowship grantee Marquette U., 1963-66; pub. health predoctoral fellow U. Miss. Med. Sch., 1967-69, gen. medicine sci. rsch. grantee U. Tex. Med. Sch., 1968-70, post-grad. fellow Karolinska Inst., Swedish Med. Coun., 1971, 73, NIH grantee, 1979-82, 84-99, Chgo. Heart Assn. grantee-in-aid, 1979-85, 99; grantee Nat. Eye Inst., 1979-80; recipient Banes Charitable trust award U. Ill., 1984-85, U.S. Olympic com. Rsch. Foudn., 1986-87; recipient Outstanding Alumnus award Tex. Med. Sch., 1994, numerous other awards in field. Fellow: ACP; mem.: AAUP, AAAS, ADA (hon.), Lubbock Arts Alliance, Leadership Tex. Alumnae Assn., Nat. Kidney Found. West Tex. (bd. dirs. 1993—99, Outstanding Vol. 1995, 2001, Disting. Svc. award 1996), Nat. Kidney Found. (numerous offices including chmn. several coms.), Italian-Am. Nephrologists, Inc., Internat. Soc. Nephrology, Ill. Kidney Found., Ctrl. Soc. Clin. Rsch., So. Soc. Clin. Rsch. (councillor 1997—99, pres.-elect 1999, pres. 2000), Assn. Chairs Dept. Physiology (councillor 1995—97), Am. Soc. Renal Biochemistry and Metabolism (pres.-elect 1994), Am. Soc. Pharmacology and Exptl. Therapeutics, Am. Soc. Nephrology, Am. Physiol. Soc., Am. Heart Assn., Am. Fedn. Med. Rsch., Lubbock Women's Club, Rotary Internat. Office: Tex Tech U Health Sci Ctr 3601 4th St Lubbock TX 79430-0001

SABATINO, THOMAS JOSEPH, JR., lawyer, pharmaceutical executive; b. Norwich, Conn., Dec. 3, 1958; s. Thomas J. and Germaine (Clement) S.; m. Joan Kathryn Turnbull, June 4, 1983. BS cum laude, Wesleyan U., Middletown, Conn., 1980; JD, U. Pa., 1983. Bar: Mass. 1983, Ill. 1985, Calif. 1989. Assoc. Testa, Hurwitz & Thibeault, Boston, 1983-85, Coffield Ungaretti Harris & Slavin, Chgo., 1985-86; corp. counsel Baxter Healthcare Corp., Deerfield, Ill., 1986-90; pres., CEO Secure Med. Inc., Mundelein, Ill., 1990-92; assoc. gen. counsel Am. Med. Internat., Dallas, 1992-93, v.p., gen. counsel, 1993-95; v.p., assoc. gen. counsel Tenet Healthcare Corp., Dallas, 1995—97; v.p., assoc. gen. counsel, asst. sec. Baxter Healthcare Corp., Deerfield, Ill., 1997—2004, sr. v.p., 1997—2004; exec. v.p., gen. counsel Schering-Plough Corp., Kenilworth, NJ, 2004—. *

SABATO, LARRY JOSEPH, political science professor, director; b. Norfolk, Va., Aug. 7, 1952; s. N.J. and Margaret F. (Simmons) S. BA, U. Va., 1974; postgrad., Princeton U., 1974-75; DPhil, Oxford U., 1977. Lectr. politics New Coll. Oxford U., 1977-78; Robert Kent Gooch prof. politics U. Va., Charlottesville, 1978—, founder, dir. Ctr. for Politics, 1998—. Guest scholar Brookings Instn., 1980; Thomas Jefferson vis. prof. Downing Coll., Cambridge U., 1982. Author: The Rise of Political Consultants: New Ways of Winning Elections, 1981, Goodbye to Goodtime Charlie: The American Governorship Transformed, 1983, PAC Power: Inside the World of Political Action Committees, 1984, The Party's Just Begun: Shaping Political Parties for America's Future, 1988, Feeding Frenzy: How Attack Journalism Has Transformed American Politics, 1991, American Government: Roots and Reform, 1992, Dirty Little Secrets: The Persistence of Corruption in American Politics, 1996, Midterm Madness: The Elections of 2002, 2002, Toward the Millennium: The Elections of 1996, 1997, Overtime!, 2001, The Election 2002, Thriller, 2001, Get In The Booth: A Citizen's Guide to the 2004 Election, 2004, Divided States of America: The Slash and Burn Politics of the 2004 Presidential Election, 2005, Get in the Booth! A Citizen's Guide to the 2006 Election, 2006, The Sixth Year Itch: The Rise and Fall of the George W. Bush Presidency, 2007, A More Perfect Constitution, 2007. Danforth fellow, 1975; Kellog fellow, 1983; Rhodes scholar; recipient Thomas Jefferson award U. Va., 2001. Mem. Am. Polit. Sci. Assn., Phi Beta Kappa. Office: U Va Dept Politics 240 Cabell Charlottesville VA 22904

SABAT-RIVERS, GEORGINA, Latin American literature educator; b. Santiago, Oriente, Cuba; came to U.S., 1962; d. José and Balbina (Mercadé) Sabat; m. Armando A. Guernica (div.); children: Armando A., Antonio J., Rodolfo M., Georgina M.; m. Elias L. Rivers, Sept. 19, 1969. MA in Romance Langs., Johns Hopkins U., 1967, PhD in Romance Langs., 1969. Instr. U. Oriente, Santiago de Cuba, 1956-61; asst. prof. Georgetown Visitation Coll., Washington, 1962-63, Western Md. Coll., Westminster, 1963-69, assoc. prof., 1969-73, prof., 1973-78, chair dept., 1974-78; assoc. prof. SUNY, Stony Brook, 1978-86, prof., 1986—, chair dept., 1981-84. Vis. prof. U. Calif., Irvine, 1989, U. Iowa, Iowa City, 1994, UNAM, Mexico City. Author: El Sueño de Sor Juana Inés de la Cruz: tradiciones literarias y originalidad, 1976, Sor Juana Inés de la Cruz Inundación castálida, 1982, Literatura Femenina conventual: Sor Marcela de San Félix Hija de Lope, 1992, others; mem. editl. bd. Colonial L.Am. Rev., 1990—, Calíope, En busca de Sor Juana, 1998, others; contbr. articles to profl. jours. Fellow NEH, 1984-85, Fulbright, 1987; Soviet Union Internat. Rsch. and Exch. Bd. grantee, 1986, Summer seminar grantee NEH, 1995. Fellow Am. Philos. Soc.; mem. MLA (del. 1988-93), AAUW, Inst. Internat. Revista Iberoamericana Lit. (editl. bd. 1987-90). Home and Office: 1532 Zoreta Ave Coral Gables FL 33146-2433 Personal E-mail: elias-n-georgina@worldnet.att.net.

SABAU, CARMEN SYBILE, retired chemist; b. Cluj, Romania, Apr. 24, 1933; naturalized U.S. citizen; d. George and Antoinette Marie (Chiriac) Grigorescu; m. Mircea Nicolae Sabau, July 11, 1956; 1 child, Isabelle Carmen. MS in Inorganic and Analytical Chemistry, U. C.I. Parhon, Bucharest, Romania, 1955; PhD in Radiochemistry, U. Fridericiana, Karlsruhe, Fed. Republic of Germany, 1972. Chemist Inst. Atomic Physics, Bucharest, Romania, 1956—74, Joint Inst. of Nuclear Rsch., Dubna-Moscow, 1974—75, Argonne (Ill.) Nat. Lab., 1976-98; ret., 1998. Author: Ion-exchange Theory and Applications in Analytical Chemistry, 1967; contbr. articles to profl. jours. Active Romanian World Coun.; del. NGO/DPI Conf. on Human Rights. Internat. Atomic Energy Agy. fellow,

1967-68, Humboldt fellow, 1970-72. Mem. Am. Romanian Acad. Arts and Sci., Internat. Soc. Intercomm. of New Ideas, Alexander von Humboldt Assn. Am., Alpha Friends of Antiquity, Rocky Mountain MLA. Home: 689 Banbury Way Bolingbrook IL 60440-1057 Personal E-mail: carmen_sabau@hotmail.com.

SABB, ANNMARIE LOUISE, retired chemist; b. New Brunswick, NJ, Sept. 21, 1942; d. Frank John and Marianne Previte; m. Frederick Joseph Sabb, Aug. 1, 1965; children: Frederick William, Jacqueline Marie. BA, Douglass Coll., New Brunswick, NJ, 1964; MS, Rutgers U., 1974; PhD, Princeton U., 1986. Sci. info. chemist FMC Corp., Balt., 1965—68; rsch. chemist Am. Cyanamid, Princeton, NJ, 1969—74; sr. scientist Ayerst Rsch., Princeton, NJ, 1986—88; sr. rsch. scientist Wyeth-Ayerst Rsch., Princeton, NJ, 1989—90, prin. scientist, 1991—2001; prin. rsch. scientist Wyeth Rsch., Princeton, NJ, 2002—06; ret., 2006. Grad. coll. faculty fellow Princeton U., NJ, 1992—93; conf. chair, co-organizer Strategic Rsch. Inst., NYC, 1997—99; grant reviewer NIH, Washington, 1999—2001; sci. adv. bd. Inst. for the Study of Aging, NYC, 1999—2005; editl. adv. bd. Bentham Sci. Publishers, Hilversum, Netherlands, 2002—05; panelist careers in sci. and lab. rsch. Princeton U., 2005; cons., reviewer, spkr. in field. Editor: Current Topics in Medicinal Chemistry; contbr. articles to profl. jours. Recipient Patent award, Wyeth-Ayerst Rsch., 1997—2005. Mem.: Soc. for Neuroscience, Am. Chem. Soc. (pres. of Princeton sect. 1990—91, Phoenix award 1991), Sigma Xi, Iota Sigma Pi, Phi Beta Kappa. Achievements include patents for antidementia agents, drugs for neurological illness, antipsychotic agents, others; discovery of heterocyclic ring system with activity at the human 5-HT2C receptor drugs for schizophrenia; patents for 1,4 diazocino, 7,8,1-hi indole derivatives as antipsychotic and anti obesity agents; research in treatment of psychiatric disorders using 5-HT2C agonist. Office Phone: 609-737-9388. Personal E-mail: annmarie_sabb@yahoo.com.

SABBAGHA, RUDY ELIAS, obstetrician, gynecologist, educator; b. Oct. 29, 1931; arrived in U.S., 1965, naturalized; s. Elias C. and Sonia B.S.; m. Asma E. Sahyouny, Oct. 5, 1957; children: Elias, Randa. BA, Am. U., Beirut, 1952, MD, 1958. Diplomate Am. Bd. Ob-Gyn. Sr. physician Tapline, Saudi Arabia, 1958-64, ob-gyn specialist, 1969-70; tchg. fellow U. Pitts./Magee Women's Hosp., 1965-68; fellow diagnostic ultrasound U. Glasgow, Scotland, 1970; asst. prof. ob-gyn U. Pitts., 1970-75; prof. Northwestern U., Chgo., 1975-94; med. dir. Obstet. and Gynecol. Ultrasound S.C., 1994—; clin. prof. U. Chgo. Pritzker Sch. Medicine, 1995-2000; prof. emeritus Northwestern U., Ill., 1995—. Obstetrician, gynecologist Prentice Women's Hosp., Chgo., 1975—. Editor: Ultrasound Applied to Obstetrics and Gynecology, 1980, 3d edit., 1994; co-editor: Fetal Anomalies: Ultrasound Diagnosis and Postnatal Management, 2001; contbr. articles to profl.jours. Fellow Am. Coll. Obstetricians and Gynecologists, Am. Inst. Ultrasound in Medicine; mem. Soc. Gynecol. Investigation, Am. Gynecol. and Obstet. Soc., Ctrl. Assn. Obstetricians and Gynecologists. Research on diagnostic ultrasound, obstetrics and gynecology. Office: 680 N Lake Shore Dr Ste 1430 Chicago IL 60611-8702 E-mail: rsabbagha@comcast.net.

SABBAJ, STEFFANIE, research scientist; b. Guatemala City, Guatemala, May 19, 1964; d. Jacobo and Perla Sabbaj; children: Gabriel Sabbaj Spieler, Daniel Sabbaj Spieler. BA, Brandeis U., Waltham, Mass., 1986; PhD, Ohio State U., Columbus, 1994. Rsch. asst. Ohio State U., Columbus, 1986—87, grad. rsch. assoc., 1987—93; post-doctoral fellow Vanderbilt U., Nashville, 1994, U. Ala., Birmingham, 1994—2002, rsch. assoc., 2002—. Contbr. articles to profl. jours. Travel grant, AIDS Vaccine Conf., 2001, Conf. on Retroviruses and Opportunistic Infections, 2002. Mem.: Am. Assn. Immunologists. Office: Univ Ala 908 20th St S Birmingham AL 35294 Office Phone: 205-975-7612. Office Fax: 205-975-0495. Business E-Mail: sabbaj@uab.edu.

SABBATINI, MARCELLO, journalist, motor sports weekly director; b. Teramo, Abruzzo, Italy, Oct. 20, 1926; s. Ezio and Norina (Guerrieri) S.; m. Maria Pia Fiore, Jan. 23, 1956. Student Faculty of Law, U. Rome, 1945-49. Head sports Il Paese, Rome, 1949-54, Paese e Paese/Sera, Rome, 1954-58; dir. Autorama, Rome, 1959-60; head sports Telesera, Rome, 1960-61, chief staff, 1961-62; asst. editor Corriere dello Sport, Rome, 1963-65; dir. Automondo, Milan, 1965; direttore zesponsabile Autosprint, Bologna, Italy, 1966—81, gen. mgr., 1969-81, Motosprint, Bologna, 1976-81, Rombo, Rombo TV, Bologna, 1981-90; anchorman weekly motormagazine TV Cuore Rosso di TLRC, Modena, 2003—04; anchor Processo F.1 weekly TV show ODEON-TV, 2005. Editor news articles in field. Recipient numerous awards. Roman Catholic.

SABEAN, BRIAN R., professional baseball team executive; m. Barbara Sabean; childrne: Colin, Sean, Brendan, Darren. Grad., Eckerd Coll., St. Petersburg, Fla., 1978. Asst. baseball coach St. Leo (Fla.) Coll., 1978-79, Tampa (Fla.) U., 1980-82, head baseball coach, 1983-85; dir. scouting N.Y. Yankees farm sys., 1986-90, v.p. player devel./scouting, 1990-92; asst. to gen. mgr., v.p. scouting/player pers. San Francisco Giants, 1993-95, sr. v.p., player pers., 1995-96, sr. v.p., gen. mgr., 1996—. Achievement: San Francisco Giants won divisional flag in 1997. Office: c/o San Francisco Giants 24 Willie Mays Plz San Francisco CA 94107-2134 *

SABEL, BRADLEY KENT, lawyer; b. Charleston, Ill., Oct. 6, 1948; s. Walter Bernard and Charlotte (Ahlstrom) Sabel; m. Nancy Jean Parker, Apr. 4, 1984. BA, Vanderbilt U., 1970; JD, Cornell U., 1975; MS in Bus. Policy, Columbia U., 1983. Bar: NY 1976. Atty. Fed. Reserve Bank NY, NYC, 1975-80, asst. counsel, 1980, sec., asst. counsel, 1981-85, assoc. counsel, 1985-87, counsel, 1988-93, counsel, v.p., 1993-94; counsel Shearman & Sterling, NYC, 1994-97, ptnr., 1997—. Contbr. articles to profl. jours. Bd. dirs., treas. NY Chamber Orch., NYC, 1985—87. With US Army, 1970—72. Mem.: N.Y.C. Bar Assn. (former chmn. banking law com.). Home: 2 Midland Gdns Apt 4E Bronxville NY 10708-4727 Office: 599 Lexington Ave Fl C2 New York NY 10022-6030 Office Phone: 212-848-8410. E-mail: bsabel@shearman.com.

SABER, ALAN A., surgeon; arrived in U.S., 1992; s. Abb A. and Sue A. Saber; m. Dalia D. Saber; children: Sara S. children: Jason S., Angie S. MD, Alexandria U., 1984, MChir, 1988. Surg. resident Mt. Sinai Sch. Medicine, NYC, 1993—95, surg. rsch. fellow, 1995—97, surg. resident, 1997—99, chief surg. resident, 1999—2000; clin. fellow minimally invasive surgery Cleve. Clinic Fla., Ft. Lauderdale, 2000—01; asst. prof. surgery Mich. State U., Kalamazoo, 2001—, chief sect. minimally invasive surgery, 2001—. Dir. bariatric surgery Mich. State U., 2001—. Author: (book) eMEDICINE; reviewer Jour. Investigative Surgery, 2001—. Fellow: ACS, Am. Soc. Bariatric Surgery (assoc.); mem.: Am. Soc. Gastrointestinal Endoscopic Surgeons. Achievements include research in minimally invasive surgery, bariatraic surgery, computer tomographic mapping of anatomical landmarks during laparoscopy. Avocations: fishing, swimming, reading. Office: Michigan State Univ 1000 Oakland Dr Kalamazoo MI 49008 E-mail: saber@kcms.msu.edu.

SABERS, RICHARD WAYNE, state supreme court justice; b. Salem, SD, Feb. 12, 1938; s. Emil William and Elrena Veronica (Godfrey) S.; m. Colleen D. Kelley, Aug. 28, 1965 (dec. Feb., 1998); children: Steven Richard, Susan Michelle, Michael Kelley; m. Ellie Schmitz, June 9, 2000. BA in English, St. John's U., Collegeville, Minn., 1960; JD, U. S.D., 1966. Bar: S.D. 1966, U.S. Dist. Ct. S.D. 1966, U.S. Ct. Appeals (8th cir.) 1983. From assoc. to ptnr. Moore, Rasmussen, Sabers & Kading, Sioux Falls, SD, 1966-86; justice SD Supreme Ct., Pierre and Sioux Falls, 1986—. Mem. editorial bd. U. S.D. Law Rev., 1965-66. State rep. March of Dimes, Bismarck, N.D., 1963; bd. dirs. St. Joseph Cathedral, Sioux Falls, 1971-86; trustee, bd. dirs. O'Gorman Found., Sioux Falls, 1978-86; active sch. bd. O'Gorman High Sch., Sioux Falls, 1985-86. Lt. US Army, 1960—63. Named Outstanding Young Religious Leader, Jaycees, Sioux Falls, 1971. Mem. ABA, S.D. Bar Assn., Inst. Jud. Adminstrn., St. John's Alumni Assn. (pres. Sioux Falls chpt. 1975-91). Republican. Roman Catholic. Avocations: tennis, skiing, sailing, sports, wood carving. Office: SD Supreme Ct 500 E Capitol Ave Pierre SD 57501-5070 Home: 5218 S Sweetbriar Ct Sioux Falls SD 57108-2855 Office Phone: 605-367-5926.

SABERSKY, ROLF HEINRICH, mechanical engineer; b. Berlin, Oct. 20, 1920; came to U.S., 1938, naturalized, 1944; s. Fritz and Berta (Eisner) S.; m. Bettina Sofie Schuster, June 16, 1946; children— Carol, Sandra. BS, Calif. Inst. Tech., 1942, MS, 1943, PhD, 1949. Devel. engr. Aerojet Gen. Co., 1943-46, regular cons., 1949-70; asst. prof. Calif. Inst. Tech., Pasadena, 1949-55, asso. prof., 1955-61, prof. mech. engring., 1961-88, prof. emeritus, 1988—. Cons. various indsl. orgns. Author: Engineering Thermodynamics, 1957, Fluid Flow, 4th edit., 1999; contbr. articles to profl. jours. Fellow ASME (Heat Transfer Meml. award 1977, 50th anniversary award Heat Transfer Div 1988); mem. Sigma Xi, Tau Beta Pi. Home: 1135 Calle De Los Amigos Santa Barbara CA 93105-5467 Office: Calif Inst Tech Divsn Engring & Applied Sci Pasadena CA 91125-0001 E-mail: sabersky@cox.net.

SABETI, MIKE A., endodontist, periodontist, educator; s. Hass and Mas Sabeti; m. Parvin Sabeti; children: Sara, Ali Sabet. MA, DDS, U. Tex., Houston, 2003. Cert. Periodontist Tufts Sch. Dental Medicine, Mass., 1995, endodontics U. So. Calif., 2002. Asst. clin. prof. U. Tex. Dental Sch., Houston, 1995—2000; asst. prof. U. So. Calif., LA, 2002—. Reviewer Jour. Endodontics. Author: (clinical reasech) Role of herpesviruses in apical pathosis. Grantee, Am. Acad. Endodontics, 2001. Office Phone: 281-359-3636. Office Fax: 281-359-3680. Personal E-mail: sabeti2001@yahoo.com.

SABETI, PARDIS CHRISTINE, researcher; b. Tehran, Iran, Dec. 25, 1975; BS, MIT, Cambridge, 1997; MS, U. Oxford, 1998, DPhil, 2002; MD summa cum laude, Harvard Med. Sch., Boston, 2006. Grad. rsch. fellow U. Oxford, 1997—2000; post-doctoral fellow genomics and infectious disease Broad Inst. of MIT and Harvard, Cambridge, Mass., 1999—2004. Musician (writer, singer): (five-song cd) Headlight Waves (Billboard Songwriting Contest Hon. Mention, 2006). Named Trailblazer, Sci. Spectrum Mag., 2006; recipient award in biomed. sci., Burroughs Wellcome Career, 2006; fellow, Paul and Daisy Soros Fellowships, 2001—03, L'Oreal For Women in Sci., L'Oreal U.S.A., 2004, Damon Runyon Cancer Rsch. Found., 2004—; Scholarship, Rhodes Trust, 1997—2000. Mem.: ASCAP (assoc.). Office: Broad Inst of MIT and Harvard 7 Cambridge Ctr Cambridge MA 02142 Home Phone: 617-872-7514. Business E-Mail: pardis@broad.mit.edu.

SABHARWAL, RANJIT SINGH, mathematician; b. Dhudial, India, Dec. 11, 1925; came to U.S., 1958, naturalized, 1981; s. Krishan Ch and Devti (An) S.; m. Pritam Kaur Chadha, Mar. 5, 1948; children— Rajinderpal, Amarjit, Jasbir. BA with honors, Punjab U., 1944, MA, 1948; MA U. Calif, Berkeley, 1962; PhD, Wash. State U., 1966. Lectr. math. Khalsa Coll., Bombay, India, 1951-58; teaching asst. U. Calif., Berkeley, 1958-62; instr. math. Portland (Oreg.) State U., 1962-62, Wash. State U., 1963-66; asst. prof. Kans. State U., 1966-68; assoc. prof. math. Calif. State U., Hayward, 1968-74, prof. math., 1974-92, prof. emeritus math., 1992—. Author papers on non-Desarguesian planes. Mem. Am. Math. Soc., Math. Assn. Am., Sigma Xi. Address: 25179 Old Fairview Ave Hayward CA 94542-1355

SABIN, WILLIAM ALBERT, writer; b. Paterson, NJ, May 29, 1931; s. David and Esther (Goodman) S.; m. Marie Frances Noonan, May 31, 1958; children— Margaret, John, Katherine, Christopher, James BA in English, Yale U., 1952, MA in English, 1956. Pub. bus. and office edn. McGraw Hill Book Co., NYC, 1973-78, editor in chief bus. books, 1979-86, pub. bus. books, 1987-90. Author: The Gregg Referance Manual, 10th edit., 2005, The Gregg Reference Manual Online, 10th edit., 2007; co-author: College English: Grammar and Style, 1967. Served as cpl. U.S. Army, 1952-54, ETO Home: 540 Fogler Rd Bristol ME 04539-3101 Office Phone: 207-563-3266.

SABISTON, DAVID COSTON, JR., surgeon, educator; b. Onslow County, NC, Oct. 4, 1924; s. David Coston and Marie (Jackson) S.; m. Agnes Foy Barden, Sept. 24, 1955; children: Anne Sabiston Leggett, Agnes Sabiston Butler, Sarah Coston. BS, U. N.C., 1944; MD, Johns Hopkins U., 1947; DSc (hon.), U. Madrid. Successively intern, asst. resident, chief resident surgery Johns Hopkins Hosp., Balt., 1947—53; successively asst. prof., assoc. prof., prof. surgery Johns Hopkins U. Med. Sch., Balt., 1955—64; Howard Hughes investigator Johns Hopkins Med. Sch., Balt., 1955—61; Fulbright rsch. scholar U. Oxford, England, 1960; rsch. assoc. Hosp. Sick Children, U. London, 1961; James B. Duke prof. surgery, chmn. dept. Duke Med. Sch., Durham, NC, 1964—94, chmn. dept. thoracic surgery, 1964—94; chief of staff Duke U. Med. Ctr., Durham, 1994—96, dir. internat. programs, 1996—. Chmn. Accreditation Coun. for Grad. Med. Edn., 1985—86. Editor: Textbook of Surgery, Essentials of Surgery, Atlas of General Surgery, Atlas of Cardiothoracic Surgery, A Review of Surgery; co-editor: Gibbon's Surgery of the Chest, Companion Handbook to Textbook of Surgery; chmn. editl. bd.: Annals of Surgery, mem. editl. bd.: Annals Clin. Rsch., ISI Atlas of Sci.: The Classics of Surgery Libr., Surgery, Gynecology and Obsetrics, Jour. Applied Cardiology, Jour. Cardiac Surgery, World Jour. Surgery. Capt. M.C., AUS, 1953—55. Named named Disting. Physician, U.S. Va., 1995; recipient Career Rsch. award, NIH, 1962—64, N.C. award in Sci., 1978, Disting. Achievement award, Am. Heart Assn. Sci. Coun., 1983, Michael E. DeBakey award for Outstanding Achievement, 1984, Significant Sigma Chi award, 1987, Coll. medalist, Am. Coll. Chest Physicians, 1987. Mem.: ACS (chmn. bd. govs. 1974—75, regent 1975—82, chmn. bd. regents 1982—84, pres. 1985—86), James IV Assn. Surgeons (bd. dirs. U.S. chpt.), Soc. Internat. De Chirurgie, Soc. Thoracic Surgeons Gt. Britain and Ireland, Soc. Surg. Chairmen (pres. 1974—76), Johns Hopkins U. Soc. Scholars, Soc. Surgery Alimentary Tract, Soc. Thoracic Surgery, Surg. Biology Club II, Halsted Soc., Soc. Univ. Surgeons (pres. 1968—69), Soc. Vascular Surgery (v.p. 1967—68), Internat. Soc. Cardiovasc. Surgery, Soc. Clin. Surgery, Am. Assn. Thoracic Surgery (pres. 1984—85), So. Surg. Assn., Am. Surg. Assn. (pres. 1977—78, sec. 1969—73, pres. 1973—74), Inst. Medicine of NAS, Am. Bd. Surgery (chmn. 1971—72, diplomate), Philippine Coll. Surgeons (hon.), Surg. Congress Assn. Espanola de Cirujanos (hon.), French Surg. Assn. (hon.), Japanese Coll. Surgeons (hon.), Brazilian Coll. Surgeons (hon.), Colombian Surg. Soc. (hon.), German Surg. Soc. (hon.), Royal Australasian Coll. Surgeons (hon.), Royal Coll. Surgeons Ireland (hon.), Royal Coll. Physicians and Surgeons Can. (hon.), Asociación de Cirugía del Litoral (Argentina) (hon.), Royal Coll. Surgeons Eng. (hon.), Royal Coll. Surgeons Edinburgh (hon.; editl. bd. jour.), Phila. Acad. Surgery (hon.), Ill. Surg. Soc. (hon.), University Club, Cosmos Club (Washington), Alpha Omega Alpha (Disting. Tchr. award 1992), Phi Beta Kappa. Office: Duke U Med Ctr PO Box 2600 Durham NC 27715-2600 Home: 622 Cedar Club Cir Chapel Hill NC 27517-7215

SABL, JOHN J., lawyer; b. LA, June 16, 1951; AB with distinction, Stanford U., 1973, JD, 1976. Bar: Calif. 1976, Ill. 1977. Assoc. Sidley & Austin, Chgo., 1977-83; ptnr. Sidley Austin Brown & Wood, Chgo., 1983-97, 2000—; exec. v.p., gen. counsel, sec. Conseco, Inc., Carmel, Ind., 1997-2000. Editorial bd. Stanford U. Law Review, 1974-75, assoc. mng. editor, 1975-76. Mem. ABA, Calif. Bar Assn., Ill. Bar Assn., Chgo. Bar Assn. (chmn. securities law commn. 1985-86), Phi Beta Kappa. Office: Sidley & Austin Bank One Plz 10 S Dearborn St Chicago IL 60603 E-mail: jsabl@sidley.com.

SABLE, BARBARA KINSEY, retired music educator; b. Astoria, NY, Oct. 6, 1927; d. Albert and Verna (Rowe) Kinsey; m. Arthur J. Sable, Nov. 3, 1973. BA, Coll. Wooster, 1949; MA, Tchrs. Coll. Columbia U., NYC, 1950; DMus, U. Ind., 1966. Office mgr., music dir. Sta. WCAX, Burlington, Vt., 1954; instr. Cottey Coll., 1959-60; asst. prof. N.E. Mo. State U., Kirksville, 1962-64, U. Calif., Santa Barbara, 1964-69; prof. music U. Colo., Boulder, 1969—, prof. emeritus, 1992—. Author: (novels) The Vocal Sound, 1982; contbr. poetry and short stories to lit. jours. Mem.: Colo. Music Tchrs. Assn., AAUP, Nat. Assn. Tchrs. Singing (past state gov., assoc. editor bull.). Democrat. Avocation: poetry. Home: 3430 Ash Ave Boulder CO 80305-3432 Office: U Colo PO Box 301 Boulder CO 80309-0301 Business E-Mail: bks@sable-boulder.com.

SABLE, ROBERT ALLEN, gastroenterologist; b. Bklyn., June 21, 1948; s. Benjamin and Sara S.; m. Valerie P. Kubie Kopelman, July 1, 1969 (div. Mar. 1982); 1 child, Jesse; m. Ellen Sue Finer, May 29, 1982; children: Scott, Eric. BS, MIT, 1969; MD, Albert Einstein U., 1973. Bd. cert. in internal medicine, gastroenterology and geriatrics Am. Bd. Internal Medicine. Staff physician N.Y. Telephone Co. Mid Manhattan Med. Dept., NYC, 1978-81; physician Riverdale Gastroenterology Cons., Bronx, 1981—; med. dir. Advanced Endoscopy Ctr., Bronx, 2007—. Chief gastroenterology St. Barnabas Hosp., Bronx, 1982-2003, pres. med. bd., 1985-90; pres. divsn. coun. Montefiore Med. Ctr., 2001-03, pres. med. staff, 2005—. Contbr. articles, reports, revs. to profl. jours. Fellow ACP, Am. Coll. Gastroenterology; mem. AMA, Am. Gastroenterologic Assn., Am. Soc. for Gastrointestinal Endoscopy. Avocations: stamp collecting/philately, coin collecting/numismatics. Office: Advanced Edocsopy Ctr 5525 Broadway Bronx NY 10463 Home Phone: 914-591-6147; Office Phone: 718-549-4267. Personal E-mail: ra.sable@verizon.net.

SABLIK, MARTIN JOHN, research physicist; b. Bklyn., Oct. 21, 1939; s. Martin C. and Elsie M. (Fuzia) S.; m. Beverly Ann Shively, Nov. 26,1965; children: Jeanne, Karen, Marjorie, Larry. BA in Physics, Cornell U., 1960; MS in Physics, U. Ky., 1965; PhD, Fordham U., 1972. Jr. engr. The Martin Co., Orlando, Fla., 1962-63; instr. half-time U. Ky., Lexington, 1963-65; rsch. assoc. Fairleigh Dickinson U., Teaneck, NJ, 1965-67, instr. physics, 1967-72, asst. prof., 1972-76, assoc. prof., 1976-80; sr. rsch. scientist Southwest Rsch. Inst., San Antonio, 1980-87, staff scientist, 1987—2005; ret., 2005. Local chmn. Intermag. Conf., San Antonio, 1995; mem. adv. bd. Conf. on Properties and Applications of Magnetic Materials, 1990—, Workshop on advances in Measurement Techniques and Instrumentation for Magnetic Properties Determination, 1994, Magnetic Materials, Measurements and Modeling Symposium, 1996, Magnetic Materials, Measurements and Microstructure Symposium, 1998, Symposium Magnetic Materials for Magnetoelectronic Devices, 2000; mem. exec. bd. Topical Group on Magnetism and Its Applications, 1996-97; mem. program com., assoc. editor Intermag 2000, Toronto. Mem. editl. bd.: Nondestructive Testing and Evaluation, 1989—; contbr. articles to profl. jours.; mem. editl. bd.: IEEE Transactions on Magnetics, 2002—, assoc. editor:, 2003—. Recipient Imagineer award Mind Sci. Found., 1989. Fellow Am. Soc. Nondestructive Testing (chmn. So. Tex. sect. 1983-84, 2001-02); mem. IEEE (sr.), Am. Phys. Soc. Roman Catholic. Office Phone: 210-522-3342. Business E-Mail: msablik@swri.org.

SABLIOV, CRISTINA MIRELA, humanities educator; m. Dorin Boldor, July 29, 2000; 1 child, Emily Boldor. PhD, NC State U., Raleigh, 2002. Grad. rsch. asst. NC State U., 1998—2002, rsch. assoc., 2002—03; asst. prof. La. State U., Baton Rouge, 2003—. Office: La State Univ 141 E B Doran Bldg Baton Rouge LA 70820 Office Fax: 225-578-3492. Business E-Mail: csabliov@lsu.edu.

SABLOFF, JEREMY ARAC, archaeologist; b. NYC, Apr. 16, 1944; s. Louis and Helen (Arac) S.; m. Paula Lynne Weinberg, May 26, 1968; children: Joshua, Saralinda. AB, U. Pa., 1964; MA, PhD, Harvard U., 1969. From asst. prof. to assoc. prof. Harvard U., Cambridge, Mass., 1969—76; assoc. prof. anthropology U. Utah, Salt Lake City, 1976-77; curator anthropology Utah Mus. Natural History, Salt Lake City, 1976-77; prof. anthropology U. N.Mex., Albuquerque, 1978-86, chmn. dept., 1980-83; Univ. prof. anthropology and the history and philosphy of sci. U. Pitts., 1986-94, chmn. dept. anthropology, 1990-92; Charles K. Williams II dir. U. Mus., U. Mus. Term prof. anthropology U. Pa., Phila., 1994—2004, prof. anthropology, curator Mesoamerican archaeology, 1994—2004, Edmund J. and Louise W. Kahn endowed term prof. social scis., curator Mesoamerican archaeology, 2004—05, Christopher H. Browne disting. prof. anthropology, curator Mesoam. archaeology, 2006—. Sr. fellow for Pre-Columbian Studies, Dumbarton Oaks, 1986-92, chmn. 1989-92. Author: (with G.R. Willey) A History of American Archaeology, 1974, 2d edit., 1980, 3d edit., 1993, Excavations at Seibal: Ceramics, 1975, (with C.C. Lamberg-Karlovsky) Ancient Civilizations: The Near East and Mesoamerica, 1979, 2d edit., 1995, (with D. A. Freidel) Cozumel: Late Maya Settlement Patterns, 1984, The Cities of Ancient Mexico, 1989, rev. edit., 1997, The New Archaeology and the Ancient Maya, 1990, (with G. Tourtellot) The Ancient Maya City of Sayil: The Mapping of a Puuc Region Center, 1991; editor(with C.C. Lamberg-Karlovsky) The Rise and Fall of Civilizations, 1974, (with C.C. Lamberg-Karlovsky) Ancient Civilization and Trade, 1975, (with W.L. Rathje) A Study of Changing Pre-Columbian Commercial Systems, 1975, American Antiquity, 1977-81, (with G.R. Willey) Scientific American Readings in Pre-Columbian Archaeology, 1980, Simulations in Archaeology, 1981, Supplement to the Handbook of Middle American Indians: Archaeology, 1981, Archaeology: Myth and Reality: A Scientific American Reader, 1982, Analyses of Fine Paste Ceramics, 1982, (with D. Meltzer and D. Fowler) American Archaeology: Past and Future, 1986, (with E.W. Andrews V) Late Lowland Maya Civilization: Classic to Postclassic, 1986, (with J.S. Henderson) Lowland Maya Civilization in the Eighth Century A.D., 1993, Tikal: Dynasties, Foreigners, and Affairs of State, 2003, Gordon R. Willey and American Archaeology, 2007. Pres. Kolb Found., 1995-2004; chair Smithsonian Coun., 1999-2001, chair sci. adv. commn., 2001-03; bd. mgrs. Sch. Am. Rsch. Grantee Nat. Geog. Soc., 1972-74, NSF, 1983-88, 2004-07, NEH, 1990-91. Fellow AAAS (sec. H. chair 1994-95), Am. Anthrop. Assn., Soc. Antiquaries London; mem. NAS, Am. Philos. Soc., Soc. Am. Archaeology (pres. 1989-91), Am. Acad. Arts and Sci., Internat. Soc., Comparative Study of Civilizations, Sigma Xi Office: U Pa Mus Archaeology and Anthropology 33d and Spruce Sts Philadelphia PA 19104-6324

SABO, MARTIN OLAV, former congressman; b. Crosby, ND, Feb. 28, 1938; s. Bjorn O. and Klara (Haga) S.; m. Sylvia Ann Lee, June 30, 1963; children: Karin, Julie. BA cum laude, Augsburg Coll., Mpls., 1959; postgrad., U. Minn., 1961-62. Mem. Minn. Ho. Reps. from 57B Dist., 1960-78, minority leader Dem.-Farmer-Labor party, 1969—73, speaker, 1973-78; mem. US Congress from 5th Minn. Dist., 1979—2006; chmn. Dem. Study Group; dep. majority whip 96th to 103rd Congresses; mem. permanent select com. on intelligence 102d Congress; chmn. Ho. Budget Com. 103d Congress; ranking minority mem. house budget com. 104th-106th Congress, mem. standards of official conduct com., appropriations com., ranking minority mem. subcom. on homeland security. Former mem. Nat. Adv. Commn. on Intergovtl. Rels.; past pres. Nat. Legis. Conf.; bd. regents Augsburg Coll. Mgr., player Dem. Congl. Baseball Team, 1987—. Recipient Disting. Alumni citation Augsburg Coll., Arms Control Leadership award Employees Union, Local 113, SEIU, AFL-CIO; named One of 200 Rising Young Leaders in Am. Time mag., 1974; Man of Yr. Mpls. Jr.

C.of C., 1973-74, One of Ten Outstanding Young Men of Yr. Minn. Jr. C. of C., 1974; inducted Scandinavian Am. Hall of Fame, 1994. Mem. Nat. Conf. State Legis. Leaders (past pres.). Democrat. Office Phone: 202-225-4755. *

SABOL, STEVE, film company executive; b. Moorestown, NJ, Oct. 2, 1942; s. Ed Sabol. Attended, Colo. Coll. Cinematographer, co-founder, writer NFL Films, Inc., Mt. Laurel, NJ, 1964—, pres., 1982—. Co-founder NFL Network, 2003. Host, NFL Films Presents, 1979- (longest running syndicated sports series in TV history) Recipient 23 Emmys for sports writing, 65 Emmys for NFL Films; former All-Rocky Mountain Conf. Running Back. *

SABOL, STUART J., otolaryngologist; b. Indpls. m. Michala J. Sabol; children: Nicole, Taylor. BA in Biology and Chemistry, Ind. U., Indpls., 1983, MD, 1990. Resident U. Tex., San Antonio, 1990—95; physician Stuart, Fla., 1995—. Fellow: Am. Acad. Otolaryngology, Head and Neck Surgery; mem.: AMA, Martin County Med. Soc. (pres.), Fla. Med. Assn. Office: 2221 E Ocean Bldg Ste 300 Stuart FL 34996

SABSAY, DAVID, library director, consultant; b. Waltham, Mass., Sept. 12, 1931; s. Wiegard Isaac and Ruth (Weinstein) S.; m. Helen Glenna Tolliver, Sept. 24,1 966. AB, Harvard U., 1953; BLS, U. Calif., Berkeley, 1955. Circulation dept. supr. Richmond (Calif.) Pub. Library, 1955-56; city libr. Santa Rosa (Calif.) Pub. Library, 1956-65; dir. Sonoma County Library, Santa Rosa, 1965-92; libr. cons., 1992—. Coordinator North Bay Coop. Library System, Santa Rosa, 1960-64; cons. in field, Sebastopol, Calif., 1968—. Contbr. articles to profl. jours. Commendation, Calif. Assn. Library Trustees and Commrs., 1984. Mem. Calif. Library Assn. (pres. 1971, cert. appreciation 1971, 80), ALA. Clubs: Harvard (San Francisco). Home: 667 Montgomery Rd Sebastopol CA 95472-3020 E-mail: dsabsay@sonic.net.

SABUNDAYO, BEULAH PERDUE, pharmacist, researcher; b. Bedford, Va., Oct. 29, 1966; d. Ervin Sanford and Edna Jane Perdue; m. Roland Paul Sabundayo, June 6, 1998; children: Chloe Lane, Sophia Pearl. PharmD, Campbell U., Buies Creek, NC, 1992; MPH, Johns Hopkins U., Balt., 1999. Cert. pharmacy state lic. NC Bd. Pharmacy, 1992, Md. Bd. Pharmacy, 1993, bd. cert. pharmacotherapy specialist Am. Coll. Clin. Pharmacy, 1995. Pharmacy practice resident Med. Sys. U. Md., Balt., 1992—93, infectious diseases fellow, 1993—94, clin. instr. Sch. Pharmacy, 1992—94, antimicrobial coord. Med. Sys., 1994—97, clin. specialist, 1994—97; rsch. assoc. Bloomberg Sch. Pub. Health Johns Hopkins U., Balt., 1998—, rsch. assoc. Sch. Medicine, 2002—. Coord. Am. Soc. Cons. Pharmacists, Alexandria, Va., 2000—05; clin. asst. prof. Sch. Pharmacy U. Md., Balt., 2003—; cons. Medimax Comm., Princeton, NJ, 2005—06. Contbr. articles to profl. jours. Recipient Hoechst-Roussel Excellence in Clin. Pharmacy award, Campbell U., 1992. Mem.: Am. Soc. Pub. Health, Omicron Delta Kappa, Alpha Chi. Democrat. Roman Catholic. Avocations: travel, swimming, reading. Home Phone: 410-785-1017; Office Phone: 443-287-6404.

SABY, JOHN SANFORD, physicist, consultant; b. Ithaca, NY, Mar. 21, 1921; s. Rasmus S. and Maude Emily (Sanford) S.; m. Mary Elizabeth Long, June 9, 1945; children: Arthur D., Thomas S., Joseph A., Jean E. BA, Gettysburg Coll., Pa., 1942, Sc.D. (hon.), 1969; MS, Pa. State U., 1944, PhD, 1947. Lab. instr. Gettysburg Coll., 1940-42; instr. Cornell U., 1947-50; with Gen. Electric Co., 1951-82, mgr. semicondr./solid state Syracuse, NY, 1954-56, mgr. lamp phenomena research Cleve., 1956-82; cons., 1982—; mem. vis. com. biol. and phys. scis. Case Western Res. U., chmn., 1969. Co-author: Principles of Transistor Circuits, 1953; patentee in field. Fellow: IEEE (past com. officer); mem.: Cleve. Assn. Rsch. Dirs. (pres. 1963—64), Am. Phys. Soc., Nat. Assn. Watch and Clock Collectors, Phi Sigma Kappa, Phi Kappa Phi, Sigma Xi, Phi Beta Kappa. Home: 600 Carolina Village Rd # 295 Hendersonville NC 28792-3898

SACASAS, RENE, lawyer; b. NYC, July 10, 1947; s. Anselmo and Orlanda (Soto) S.; m. Cathy Lee Van Natta, Jan. 24, 1970. BA, Am. U., 1969; JD, Emory U., 1975. Bar: Fla. 1976, US Dist. Ct. (so. dist.) Fla. 1976, US Ct. Appeals (5th cir.) 1976, US Supreme Ct. 1980, US Ct. Appeals (11th cir.) 1983. Law clk. McLarty and Aiken, Atlanta, 1974-76; assoc. Welbaum, Zook, Jones, Williams, Miami, Fla., 1976-79; ptnr. Darrach, Merkin and Sacasas, Miami, 1979-83, Merkin & Sacasas, Miami, 1984-86; of counsel Welbaum, Zook & Jones, Miami, 1986-95; Welbaum, Guernsey, Hingston, Greenleaf & Gregory, Miami, 1996-04; asst. prof. bus. law U. Miami, 1985-91, assoc. prof., 1991-02, prof., 2002—, chmn. bus. law dept., 1992—; head master Hecht Residential Coll., 1995-97. Mem. ABA, Fla. Bar Assn. (vice chmn. grievance com. 1981-84), Dade County Bar Assn., Latin Am. C. of C., US Jaycees, Cuban Am. Bar Assn., Iron Arrow, Leadership Fla., Phi Sigma Kappa (ET chpt. pres. 1968), Omicron Delta Kappa, Phi Kappa Phi. Contbr. articles profl. jours. Office: U Miami Jenkins 321 Coral Gables FL 33124 Home: 357 Almeria Ave Apt 1406 Coral Gables FL 33134

SACCHI, JOHN, film company executive; b. Feb. 14, 1971; m. Suzanne Fritz; 1 child, Owen Bennett. Student, Pepperdine U., Malibu, Calif. Intern with prodr. Chuck Gordon Universal; sr. v.p. prodn. and devel. Lionsgate. Co-prodr.: (films) Confidence, 2003, See No Evil, 2006; prodr.: In The Mix, 2005; exec. prodr.: The Cookout, 2004, Employee of the Month, 2006, Pride, 2007, Rogue, 2007, Lionsgate World Wrestling Entertainment films. Office: Lionsgate 2700 Colorado Ave Santa Monica CA 90404 *

SACCHI, TERRENCE J., cardiologist; b. Bklyn., July 16, 1952; m. Rita Sacchi; children: Terrence, Alexandra. BS in Biology magna cum laude, Fairfield U., 1972; MD, Albany U., 1976. Bd. cert. Am. Bd. Internal Medicine, Am. Bd. Cardiovasc. Disease; lic. physician, N.Y. Intern in internal medicine St. Vincent's Hosp. and Med. Ctr., NYC, 1976-77, resident in internal medicine, 1977-79; fellow in cardiovasc. disease Georgetown U. Med. Ctr./Washington VA Hosp., Washington, 1979-81; interventional cardiology fellow Mercy Hosp., Des Moines, 1987; clin. instr. dept. medicine SUNY Health Scis. Ctr., Bklyn., 1982-85, clin. asst. prof. dept. medicine, 1985—; assoc. attending divsn. cardiology St. Vincent's Hosp. and Med. Ctr., NYC, 1982—; physician-in-charge coronary care unit L.I. Coll. Hosp., Bklyn., 1986—, physician-in-charge catheterization lab. divsn. cardiology, 1991—, chief divsn. cardiology dept. medicine, 1991—, med. dir. N.Y. Ctr. for Bloodless Medicine and Surgery, 1998—, vice-chmn. dept. internal medicine, 1998—. Asst. attending divsn. cardiology Maimonides Med. Ctr., Bklyn, 1988—; presenter in field. Contbr. numerous articles to med. jours., including New Eng. Jour. Medicine, Chest, Annals of Thoracic Surgery. Fellow Am. Coll. Chest Physicians, Coun. Clin. Cardiology, Am. Heart Assn., Am. Coll. Cardiology, N.Y. Cardiol. Soc.; mem. ACP, Med. Soc. Kings County, Alpha Omega Alpha. Office: Terrence J Sacchi Md 506 6th St Brooklyn NY 11215-3609 Fax: 718-780-1619.

SACCO, AMY, restaurant and nightclub owner; b. NJ, Dec. 30, 1967; d. Eugene and Bette Sacco. Grad., Johnson and Wales Culinary Sch., Providence, R.I., 1990. Former hostess Boulay, NYC; owner Lot 61, NYC, 1998—, Bungalow 8, NYC, 2001—, Bette, NYC, 2005—, Bungalow 8, London, 2006—. Author: Cocktails, 2005. Office: Lot 61 550 W 21st St New York NY 10011 *

SACCO, JOHN MICHAEL, accountant; b. NYC, Oct. 17, 1952; s. Anthony Carmine and Angelina (Pellegrino) Sacco. BS, St. John's U., 1974. CPA. Staff acct. Price Waterhouse & Co., NYC, 1974-75; semi-sr. acct. Seidman & Seidman, CPAs, White Plains, NY, 1976-77; sr. acct. Diamond Internat. Corp., NYC, 1977-79, Burns Internat. Security Svcs., Inc., Briarcliff Manor, NY, 1979-81; acctg. mgr. Burns Integrated Sys., Inc., Briarcliff Manor, NY, 1981-83; pvt. practice White Plains, NY, 1978—. Mem.: AICPA, NY Soc. CPA (mem. peer rev. com., mem. bus. valuations com., mem. cooperation with bankers and credit grantors, mem. acctg. and auditing com., mem. acctg. & rev. svcs. com.). Republican. Roman Catholic. Home: 197 Upper Shad Rd Pound Ridge NY 10576-2237 Office: 108 Corporate Park Dr White Plains NY 10604 Office Phone: 914-253-8757. Business E-Mail: jmsaccocpa@verizon.net.

SACCO, KARI LYNN, psychologist; b. New Haven, Conn., July 21, 1980; d. Louis and Barbara Sacco. BA in Psychology, Quinnipiac U., Hamden, Conn., 1998—2002; MA in Sch. Psychology, So. Conn. State U., New Haven, Conn., 2002—04. Cert. sch. psychologist Conn. State Dept. Edn., 2005. Sch. psychologist W.Haven Bd. Edn., 2005—. Mem.: NASP. Home: 239 W Walk West Haven CT 06516 Home Phone: 203-937-5523. Personal E-mail: klsacco21@comcast.net. Business E-Mail: karisacco@whschools.org.

SACCO, TONY, cinematographer, television director, film director; Prin. ABS Prodns., North Hollywood, Calif. Cinematographer: (TV series) Dream Builders, 1997, Treasures in Your Home, 1999, The Bachelor, 2002, EX-treme Dating, 2002, Last Comic Standing, 2003, Project Runway, 2004—, Project Greenlight 3, 2005; (documentaries) Behind the Action: Stuntmen in the Movies, 2002, Posse, 2003, Great White Shark Uncaged, 2004, Shark Hunter: Chasing the Great White, 2005, Air Guitar Nation, 2006; (films) Save the Mavericks, 2005; dir.: (TV series) R U the Girl, 2005, Tuesday Night Book Club, 2006, Last Comic Standing 4, 2006, Get This Party Started, 2006; prodr.: Project Runway, 2006; dir., prodr.: (TV series) Treasure Hunters, 2006. Office: ABS Prodns 5756 Craner Ave North Hollywood CA 91601-2015 Office Phone: 310-614-6473. *

SACHA, ROBERT FRANK, osteopath, educator; b. East Chgo., Ind., Dec. 29, 1946; s. S. Frank John and Ann Theresa S.; m. Linda T. LePage, 1988; children: Joshua Jude, Josiah Gerard, Anastasia Levon, Jonah Bradley. BS, Purdue U., 1969; DO, Chgo. Coll. Osteo. Medicine, 1975; PharmD, Creighton U., 2004. Diplomate Am. Bd. Pediatrics, Am. Bd. Allery and Immunology. Pharmacist, asst. mgr. Walgreens Drug Store, East Chicago, Ind., 1969-75; intern David Grant Med. Ctr., San Francisco, 1975-76, resident in pediatrics, 1976-78; fellow in allergy and immunology Wilford Hall Med. Ctr., 1978-80; staff pediatrician, allergist Scott AFB (Ill.), 1980-83; practice medicine specializing in allergy and immunology Cape Girardeau, Mo., 1983—. Assoc. clin. instr. St. Louis U., 1980—; clin. instr. Purdue U., 1971-72, Pepperdine U., 1975-76, U. Tex.-San Antonio, 1978-80, assoc. clin. instr. So. Ill. U. Pres., Parent Tchrs. League; bd. gov. Chgo. Coll. Osteopathic Medicine. Maj. M.C. USAF, 1975-83, comdr. USNR. Named one of Top Pediatricians 2002-2003, Pediatric Allergy, Immunology. Fellow Am. Coll. Allergy, Am. Coll. Chest Physicians, Am. Acad. Pediatrics, Am. Acad. Allergy-Immunology, Am. Assn. Cert. Allergists; mem. ACP, AMA, Am. Acad. Allergy, Assn. Mil. Allergists, Am. Coll. Emergency Physicians, Mil. Surgeons and Physicians. Republican. Lutheran. Office: 351 Kelley Ct Cape Girardeau MO 63701 Office Phone: 573-651-4155. E-mail: bsacha@charter.net.

SACHAR, DAVID BERNARD, gastroenterologist, educator; b. Urbana, Ill., Mar. 2, 1940; s. Abram Leon and Thelma (Horwitz) Sachar; m. Joanna Maud Belford Silver, Aug. 29, 1961; children: Mark Benson, Kenneth Hulbert Belford(dec.). BA magna cum laude, Harvard Univ., 1959, MD cum laude, 1963. Cert. Am. Bd. Internal Medicine, diplomate Am. Bd. Gastroenterology. Intern Beth Israel Hosp., Boston, 1963-65, resident in internal medicine, 1967-68; asst. chief clin. rsch. Pakistan SEATO Cholera Rsch. Lab., Dhaka, Bangladesh, 1965-67; resident in gastroenterology Mt. Sinai Hosp., NYC, 1968-70, dir. divsn. gastroenterology, 1983-99, vice chmn. dept. medicine, 1992-99, dir. emeritus, 1999—, Arnold P. Gold Found. prof. medicine, 2005—; instr. to prof. medicine Mt. Sinai Sch. Medicine, NYC, 1970-92, first Burrill B. Crohn prof. medicine, 1992-99. Co-chmn. work group on inflammatory bowel disease NIH, 1973—75; expert adv. panel gastroenterology and nutrition U.S. Pharmacopeial Conv., 1980—85; co-founder, sec., treas. Burrill B. Crohn Rsch. Found., NYC, 1984—; chmn. rsch. devel. com. Nat. Found. Ileitis and Colitis, 1984—89; K. H. Koster meml. lectr. Danish Soc. Gastroenterology, 1992; mem. Gastroenterology Leadership Coun. Task Force Fellowship Curriculum, 1994; internat. state art lectr. Falk Symposia, Germany, 1996; twentieth ann. Norman Tanner meml. lectr. St. George's Hosp. Med. Sch., London, 1997; internat. state art lectr., Belgium, 98, Brit. Soc. Gastroenterology, 1998, World Congresses Gastroenterology, Austria, 1998, Turkish Soc. Gastroenterology, 1998, World Congresses Gastroenterology, Italy, 1999, Hungarian Soc. Gastroenterology, 1999, Hellenic Soc. Gastroenterology, 1999; chmn. GI adv. bd. Solvay Pharm., Inc., 2000—02; internat. state art lectr. Falk Symposia, Germany, 2000—02; 25th ann. Nana Svartz meml. lectr., Örebro, Sweden, 2000; co chmn. 40th ann. post grad. course Portuguese Soc. Gastroenterology, 2000; internat. state art lectr., Italy, 01, Portuguese Soc. Gastroenterology, 2003; mem. GI adv. com. FDA, 2004—, chmn., 2005—. Editor: seven books and monograms on gastroenterology; contbr. chapters to books, articles to profl. jours. Trustee Bangladesh Coun. Asia Soc., NYC, 1972—75, Englewood Cliffs Bd. Edn., 1973—75. Capt. USPHS. Recipient Jacobi Medallion for Disting. Achievement, Mt. Sinai Alumni Assn., 1994, Alexander Richman Commemorative award for Humanism in Medicine, 1996, Norman Tanner medal, St. George's Hosp. Med. Sch., 1997, Gold Headed Cane award, 1997. Master: Am. Coll. Gastroenterology (program dir. com. 1991, Henry Baker Presdl. Lectr. 1989, Berk/Fise clin. achievement award 2005); fellow: ACP, Am. Gastroent. Assn. (first chmn. clin. tchg. project 1984—90, nominating com. 1993—94, chmn. immuno inflammatory disorders sectional nominating com. 1995, Disting. Educator award 1996, Found. Mentors Rsch. Scholar award honoree 2007); mem.: Gold Humanism Honor Soc., Internat. Orgn. Study of Inflammatory Bowel Disease (first Am. elected chmn. 1989—92, chmn. task force clin. phenomics 1992—2007), Crohn's and Colitis Found. Am. (grant rev. com. and coun. 1990—94, Disting. Svc. award 1991, NY Gov. medal 1992), Brazilian Soc. Gastroenterology (patron 2003), Internat. Guild Miniature Artisans (trustee 2004—07), Alpha Omega Alpha, Phi Beta Kappa. Achievements include co developer of oral rehydration therapy for diarrhea; development of resources and standards for clin. tchg. in gastroenterology; established Joanna and David B. Sachar International Award and Visiting Professorship in Inflammatory Bowel Disease. Office: Mt Sinai Med Ctr One Gustave L Levy Pl New York NY 10029 Business E-Mail: david.sachar@mountsinai.org.

SACHAR, HOWARD MORLEY, history educator; b. St. Louis, Feb. 10, 1928; s. Abram Leon and Thelma (Horwitz) S.; m. Eliana Steimatzky, July 23, 1964; children: Sharon, Michele, Daniel. BA, Swarthmore Coll., 1947; MA, Harvard U., 1950, PhD, 1953; LHD (hon.), Hebrew Union Coll. Jewish Inst. Religion, 1996. Instr. history U. Mass., 1953-54; dir; dir. Hillel Found. UCLA, 1954-57, Hillel Found., Stanford (Calif.) U., 1959-61, Hiatt Inst. in Israel, 1961-64; assoc. prof. history George Washington U., Washington, 1964-66, prof. history and internat. affairs, 1966—2004, prof. emeritus, 2004—. Author: The Course of Modern Jewish History, 1958, Aliyah, 1961, From the Ends of the Earth, 1964, The Emergence of the Middle East, 1969, Europe Leaves the Middle East, 1972, A History of Israel, 1976, 3d edit., 2007, The Man on the Camel, 1980, Egypt and Israel, 1981, Diaspora, 1985, A History of Israel Vol. II, 1987; A History of the Jews in America, 1992, Farewell España, 1994, Israel and Europe, 2000, Dreamland: Europeans and Jews in the Aftermath of the Great War, 2003, A History of the Jews in the Modern World, 2005, gen. editor Rise of Israel: A Documentary History, 39 vols., 1988; contbr. articles to NY Times, Washington Post, LA Times, Commentary, others. Charles Brown fellow, 1957-58; NEH fellow, 1970-71, DAAD fellow, 1983; recipient Nat. Jewish Book award, 1976, 81. Mem. Am. Hist. Assn., Am. Jewish Hist. Soc., Phi Beta Kappa. Democrat. Jewish. Office: Elliot Sch Internat Affairs Emeriti George Washington U 1957 E St NW Washington DC 20052 Office Phone: 301-942-7595. Office Fax: 202-994-6231. Business E-Mail: sachar@gwu.edu.

SACHAR, LOUIS, writer; b. East Meadow, NY, Mar. 20, 1954; married, 1985; 1 child. Student, Antioch Coll.; BA, U. Calif., Berkeley, 1976; JD, Hastings Coll. Law, San Francisco, 1980. Part-time atty. Author: (children's books) Sideways Stories From Wayside School, 1978 (1979 Children's Choice Book), Johnny's in the Basement, 1981, Someday Angeline, 1983, Sixth Grade Secrets, 1987, There's A Boy in the Girls' Bathroom, 1987, The Boy Who Lost His Face, 1989, Wayside School is Falling Down, 1989, Dogs Don't Tell Jokes, 1991, Marvin Redpost: Kidnapped at Birth?, 1992, Marvin Redpost: Is He a Girl?, 1993, Marvine Redpost: Why Pick on Me?, 1993, Alone in His Teachers' House, 1994, Wayside School Gets a Little Stranger, 1995, Holes, 1998 (Newbery award, finalist Nat. Book Award), Class President, 1999, Stanley Yelnat's Survival Guide to Camp Green Lake, 2003, Small Steps, 2006 (Schneider Family Book award, 2007). Mem. Soc. Children's Book Writers and Illustrators, Authors Guild. Office: c/o Farrar Straus & Giroux 19 Union Sq W New York NY 10003-3304 Mailing: c/o Ellen Levine Trident Media Group Fl 36 41 Madison Ave New York NY 10010 *

SACHDEO, AMIT, dentist, researcher; b. Allahabad, India, Feb. 07; s. Jogesh and Kiran Sachdeo. B in Dental Sci., Magadh U., 1997; MS, U. Bristol, 2000; postgrad., Harvard U., 2002—. CAD-CAM Training, Nobel Biocare, 2005; Esthetic Dentistry NY U., 2002, Human Participant Protections for Research Teams Nat. Cancer Inst., 2005, Cpr Am. Heart Assn., 2004, Public Oral Health Glasgow University-UK, 2001. Chief dental resident Sir Ganga Ram Hosp., India, 1997—98; resident Bristol Dental Sch., Bristol, England, 1998—2000; rsch. fellow-public oral health Glasgow U., Scotland, 2000—01; resident NYU, NYC, 2001—02; fellow Harvard U., Boston, 2002—. Contbr. articles to profl. jours. Fellow, Acad. Prosthodontics, 2005; grantee, ACP/P&G, 2004; scholar, Straumman, 2003. Mem.: ARC (life), Internat. Acad. Dental Rsch., Am. Acad. Dental Rsch., Am. Acad. Cosmetic Dentistry (life), Acad. Osseointigration (life), Am. Coll. Prosthodontists (life). Achievements include research in Biofilm formation in the Edentulous. Avocations: swimming, skiing, reading, rollerblading, writing, horseback riding. Home: 1191 Boylston St Apt 59 Boston MA 02215 Office: Harvard U Dental Sch 188 Longwood Ave Boston MA 02115 Home Phone: 617-266-5993. Home Fax: 617-432-0901. Personal E-mail: amit_sachdeo@hsdm.harvard.edu.

SACHER, STEVEN JAY, lawyer; b. Cleve., Jan. 28, 1942; s. Albert N. and Cecil P. (Chessin) S.; m. Colleen Marie Gibbons, Nov. 28, 1970; children— Alexander Jerome, Barry Elizabeth, William Paul. BS, U. Wis., 1964; JD, U. Chgo., 1967. Bar: D.C. 1968. Assoc. solicitor Employee Retirement Income Security Act U.S. Dept. Labor, Washington, 1974-77; spl. counsel com. on labor and human resources U.S. Senate, Washington, 1977-79, gen. counsel, 1980-81; ptnr. Pepper Hamilton, Washington, 1982-88; shareholder Johnson & Gibbs, Washington, 1988-94; ptnr. Kilpatrick Stockton LLP, Washington, 1994—2007, Jones Day, Washington, 2007—. Adj. prof. law Georgetown U. Law Ctr., 1977; co-chair sr. editors Employee Benefits Law and Annual Supplements, Bur. Nat. Affairs, Washington, 1991-2000. Mem. adv. bd. BNA Pension and Benefits Reporter; mem. editorial bd. Benefits Law Jour., Jour. Pension Planning and Compliance. Founding mem. ERISA Roundtable, Washington. Fellow Coll. Labor and Employment Lawyers, Am. Coll. Employee Benefits Counsel (charter); mem. ABA (mgmt. co-chmn. com. on employee benefits, sect. on labor and employment law 1988-91, chmn. prohibited trans. subcom., com. on employee benefits, sect. on taxation 1986-91), D.C. Bar Assn. Office: Jones Day 51 Louisiana Ave NW Washington DC 20001-2113 Office Phone: 202-879-5402. Business E-Mail: sjsacher@jonesday.com.

SACHS, ALAN ARTHUR, lawyer; b. Bklyn., Feb. 7, 1947; s. Herman and Clara Sachs; m. Marilyn Mushlin, May 19, 1974; children: David Henry, Stephen Edward. BA, Columbia U., 1967; JD, Harvard U., 1970. Bar: NY 1971, Wis. 1983, Mo. 1989. Law clk. to judge U.S. Dist. Ct. (ea. dist.) N.Y., 1970-71; assoc. Cleary, Gottlieb, Steen & Hamilton, NYC, 1971-79, Paskus, Gordon & Hyman, NYC, 1979-81; sec., gen. counsel The Trane Co., LaCrosse, Wis., 1981-85; sr. v.p., gen. counsel, sec. Edison Bros. Stores Inc., St. Louis, 1985—2001; ptnr. Haar & Woods, LLP, St. Louis, 2001—. Mem.: ABA, Bar Assn. Met. St. Louis. Office: Haar & Woods LLP 1010 Market St Saint Louis MO 63101 Office Phone: 314-241-2224. Business E-Mail: alansachs@haar-woods.com.

SACHS, DAVID HOWARD, surgeon, immunologist, educator; b. NYC, Jan. 10, 1942; s. Elliot and Elsie (Hurvitz) S.; m. Kristina Olsson, Mar. 15, 1969; children: Michelle, Jessica, Karin, Teviah. AB, Harvard U., 1963; DES, U. Paris, 1964; MD, Harvard U., Boston, 1968. Intern in surgery Mass. Gen. Hosp., Boston, 1968-69, resident in surgery, 1969-70, dir. transplantation biology rsch. ctr. surgery dept., 1991—; chief immunology br. Nat. Cancer Inst., Bethesda, Md., 1982-90; prof. surgery and immunology Harvard U. Med. Sch., 1991—. Capt. PHS, 1970-91. Recipient Roche Ernest Hodge Meml. award, Am. Soc. Transplantation, 2005. Avocations: gardening, fishing, windsurfing, skiing. Office: Mass Gen Hosp East Bldg 149-9019 13th St Boston MA 02129

SACHS, GEORGE, biology professor, physician; b. Austria; BSc, U. Edinburgh, 1957, MB, ChB, 1960, DSc, 1980; MD, U. Gothenburg, 1987. Instr. Albert Einstein Coll., 1961—62; rsch. assoc. Columbia U., 1962—63; asst. prof. medicine and physiology U. Ala., Birmingham, 1963—65, assoc. prof., 1965—70, prof., 1970—82, dir. membrane biology, 1974—82; prof. medicine and physiology, Wilshire chair in medicine UCLA, 1982—, co-dir. ctr. ulcer rsch. and edn., 1987—2002, dir. membrane biology lab., 1987—; sr. med. investigator VAGLAHS, LA, 1984—99, staff physician, 1999—. Contbr. articles to profl. jours. Named Dr. Norman Frankel Scholar, U. Chgo., 2005, Evans Scholor, Boston U., 2005; recipient Beaumont Prize in Gatroenterology, Am. Gastroenterological Assn., 1985, Hoffman LaRoche award, 1982, Gairdner award, Gairdner Found., 2004, Ismar Boas Vorlesung Medal, German Gastroenterological Assn., 1992, others. Office: UCLA 405 Hilgard Ave Los Angeles CA 90095 Office Phone: 310-268-3923. E-mail: gsachs@ucla.edu.

SACHS, JEFFREY DAVID, economist, educator; b. Detroit, Nov. 5, 1954; s. Theodore and Joan Sachs; m. Sonia Ehrlich Sachs; children: Lisa, Adam, Hannah. BA summa cum laude, Harvard U., 1976, MA in Econs., 1978, PhD in Econs., 1980; degree (hon.), St. Gallen U., Switzerland, 1990, Lingnan Coll. Hong Kong, 1998, Varba Econs. U., Bulgaria, 2000, Iona Coll. N.Y., 2000. Prof. internat. trade Harvard U., Cambridge, Mass., 1984—2002; prof. sustainable devel. Columbia U., NYC, 2002—, dir. Earth Inst., 2002—. Dir. Harvard Inst. Internat. Devel. Harvard U., 1995—99; chmn. commn. on macroecons. and health WHO, 2000—01; dir. Ctr. for Internat. Devel. Harvard U., 1998—2002; spl. advisor to sec. gen. Kofi Annan UN, NYC, 2002—; cons. in field. Co-author: Macroeconomics in the Global Economy, 1992; author: Poland's Jump to the Market Economy, 1993, The End of Poverty: Economic Possibilities for Our Time, 2005, Development Economics, 1997, Macro Economics in the Global Econ., 2003, The End of Poverty: Economic Possibilities of Our Times, 2005. Named one of 100 Most Influential People of 2005, Time mag., New

York's Influentials, New York Mag., 2006. Mem.: Inst. Medicine. Office: The Earth Inst at Columbia Univ 314 Low Libr MC 4327 535 West 116th St New York NY 10027 Office Phone: 212-854-8704. *

SACHS, JOHN PETER, carbon company executive; b. Duesseldorf, Germany, 1926; married. BAChemE, Ill. Inst. Tech., 1948, MAChemE, 1950, PhDChemE, 1952. Various mgmt. positions in research and devel., engring. and ops. Union Carbide Corp., 1951-66; v.p. ops. then group v.p. Great Lakes Carbon Corp., NYC, 1966-78; pres., chief exec. officer Gt. Lakes Carbon Corp., NYC, 1978-86; chmn. bd., dir. Gen. Refractories Co., 1978-85; mng. ptnr. J.P. Sachs Assocs., Mgmt. Cons., New Canaan, Conn., 1987—99. Trustee Fairfield U., 1978-92; bd. dirs. Kneissl-Dachstein 1992-2004, Peridot, 1989-98. Mem. Am. Inst. Chem. Engrs. (pres. 1985) Home and Office: JP Sachs Assocs 67 Dunning Rd New Canaan CT 06840-4009

SACHS, KATHERINE STEIN, art historian; m. Keith L. Sachs. Grad., Univ. Pa., 1969. Rsch. coord. Phila. Mus. Art. Mem. contemporary collector's com. Harvard Univ. Art Museums; council mem. Tate Internat.; chmn. bd. gov. Ferkauf Grad. Sch. Psychology, Yeshiva Univ.; mem. Trustees Council Penn Women, 2000—; chmn. bd. overseers Inst. Contemporary Art, Univ. Pa., 1998—. Named one of Top 200 Collectors, ARTnews Mag., 2004, 2005, 2006. Avocation: Collector of Contemporary Art. Mailing: Philadelphia Museum of Art Benjamin Franklin Pkwy Philadelphia PA 19130

SACHS, KEITH L., manufacturing executive; m. Katherine Stein. Grad., Univ. Pa., 1967; PhD (hon.), Hebrew Univ., Jerusalem, 2003. Chmn. Saxco Internat. Inc., Horsham, Pa. Trustee Phila. Mus. Art; chmn. bd. Am. Friends of Hebrew Univ. Named one of Top 200 Collectors, ARTnews Mag., 2004, 2005, 2006. Avocation: Collector of Contemporary Art. Office: Saxco International Inc 200 Gibraltar Rd Ste 101 Horsham PA 19044-2333

SACHS, LEO, geneticist, educator; b. Leipzig, Germany, Oct. 14, 1924; s. Elijah and Louise (Lichtblau) S.; m. Pnina Salkind; 4 children. BSc, U. Wales, Bangor, 1948; PhD, Trinity Coll., Cambridge U., 1951; DHC (hon.), Bordeaux U., 1985; MD (hon.), Lund U., 1997. Rsch. scientist John Innes Inst., 1951-52; mem. sci. staff Weizmann Inst. Sci., Rehovot, Israel, 1952—, prof., chmn. genetics dept., 1962—, Otto Meyerhof prof. molecular biology, 1968. Mem. Israeli Acad. Sci. and Humanities, 1975; hon. fellow U. Wales, Bangor, 1999. Contbr. articles to sci. jours. Recipient Israel prize for natural sci., 1972; named Fogarty Internat. scholar NIH, 1972, Harvey Lecture, 1972; recipient Rothschild prize in biol. scis., 1977, Wolf prize in medicine, 1980, Bristol-Myers award for disting. achievement in cancer rsch., 1983, Royal Soc. Wellcome Found. prize, 1986, Sloan prize GM Cancer Rsch. Found., 1989, Warren Alpert prize Harvard Med. Sch., 1997, Emet prize in life scis., 2002. Fellow Royal Soc., 1997; mem. U.S. Nat. Acad. Scis. (fgn. assoc. 1995), Academia Europaea (fgn. 1998), Internat. Cytokine Soc. (hon. life 2001). Office: Weizmann Inst Sci Dept Molecular Genetics Rehovot 76100 Israel Business E-Mail: leo.sachs@weizmann.ac.il.

SACHS, MARILYN STICKLE, writer, educator, editor; b. NYC, Dec. 18, 1927; d. Samuel and Anna (Smith) Stickle; m. Morris Sachs, Jan. 26, 1947; children: Anne, Paul. BA, Hunter Coll., 1949; MSLS, Columbia U., 1953. Children's libr. Bklyn. Pub. Libr., 1949-60, San Francisco Pub. Libr., 1961-67. Author: Amy Moves In, 1964, Laura's Luck, 1965, Amy and Laura, 1966, Veronica Ganz, 1968, Peter and Veronica, 1969, Marv, 1970, The Bears' House, 1971 (Austrian Children's Book prize 1977, Recognition of Merit award George C. Stone Ctr. for Children's Books 1989), The Truth About Mary Rose, 1973 (Silver Slate Pencil award 1974), A Pocket Full of Seeds, 1973 (Jane Addams Children's Book Honor award 1974), Matt's Mitt, 1975, Dorrie's Book, 1975 (Silver State Pencil award 1977, Garden State Children's Book award 1978), A December Tale, 1976, A Secret Friends, 1978, A Summer's Lease, 1979, Bus Ride, 1980, Class Pictures, 1980, Fleet Footed Florence, 1981, Hello...Wrong Number, 1981, Call Me Ruth, 1982 (Assn. Jewish Librs. award 1983), Beach Towels, 1982, Fourteen, 1983, The Fat Girl, 1984, Thunderbird, 1985, Underdog, 1985 (Christopher 1986), Baby Sister 1986, Almost Fifteen, 1987, Fran Ellen's House, 1987 (award Bay Area Book Reviewers Assn. 1988, Recognition of Merit award George C. Stone Ctr. for Children's Books 1989), Just Like A Friend, 1989, At the Sound of the Beep, 1990, Circles, 1991, What My Sister Remembered, 1992, Thirteen, 1993, Ghosts in the Family, 1995, Another Day, 1997, Suprise Party, 1998, Jo Jo & Winnie, 1999, Jo Jo & Winnie Again, 2000, The Four Ugly Cats in Apartment 3D, 2002, Lost in America, 2005, First Impressions, 2006; co-editor: (with Ann Durell) Big Book for Peace, 1990 (Calif. Children's Book award 1991, Jane Addams Children's Book prize 1991); reviewer San Francisco Chronicle, 1970—. Mem. PEN, ACLU, Sierra Club, Authors' Guild. Democrat. Jewish. Avocations: reading, walking, baseball. Home: 733 31st Ave San Francisco CA 94121-3523

SACHS, MURRAY, French language and literature educator, researcher; b. Toronto, Ont., Can., Apr. 10, 1924; came to U.S., 1946, naturalized, 1955; s. Thomas and Sarah (Roth) S.; m. Miriam Blank, Sept. 14, 1961; children: Deborah Ruth Sachs Gabor, Aaron Jacob. BA with 1st class honours, U. Toronto, 1946; AM in French and Romance Philology, Columbia U., 1947, PhD in French, 1953. Lectr. Sch. Gen. Studies Columbia U., NYC, 1946-48; lectr. U. Calif., Berkeley, 1948-50, U. Detroit, 1951-52, Williams Coll., Williamstown, Mass., 1954-57, asst. prof., 1957-60; asst. prof. French and comparative lit. Brandeis U., Waltham, Mass., 1960-61, assoc. prof., 1961-66, prof., 1966-96; emeritus Brandeis Univ., 1996—; chmn. dept. Brandeis U., Waltham, Mass., 1963-64, 67-71, 81-84, 90-91. Presenter, lectr. in field; mem. editl. adv. bd. 19th century French studies, 1974—, Purdue U. Monographs in Romance Langs., 1980-90, Cin. Romance Rev., 1988-2, Romance Quar., 1989—; mem. Nat. Humanities Faculty, Concord, Mass., Atlanta, cons., 1978-81; cons. humanities projects NEH, 1982-84, 92, rev. panelist, 1983, 89, 91; manuscript referee various jours. and univ. presses, others; cons. NEH Summer Inst. on Francophonie, 1993, 94, 97. Author: (with E.M. and R.B. Grant) French Stories, Plays and Poetry: A First-Year Reader, 1959; The Career of Alphonse Daudet: A Critical Study, 1965, The French Short Story in the Nineteenth Century: A Critical Anthology, 1969, Anatole France: The Short Stories, 1974; also articles and revs. to profl. jours. and reference works. Recipient Palmes Académiques, Govt. of France, 1971; Reuben Wells Leonard and Edward Blake scholar U. Toronto, 1942; Henry Alfred Todd fellow Columbia U., 1946-48; rsch. and travel grantee Williams Colls., summers 1955, 59. Mem. MLA (del. assembly 1971, 72, 76-78, exec. com. French 6 group 1970-73, 19th Century French lit. sect. 1975-76), Assn. Depts. Fgn. Langs. of MLA (rep. PhD granting depts. to exec. com. 1983-85, pres. 1985), Greater Boston Fgn. Langs. Collaborative (co-chmn. 1992-93, 93-94), Phi Beta Kappa (hon.). Jewish. Home: 280 Highland Ave West Newton MA 02465-2514 Office: Brandeis U Dept Romance and Comparative Lit 415 South St Waltham MA 02454-9110

SACHS, RICHARD GREGORY, cardiologist; b. Orange, NJ, Mar. 5, 1941; m. Barbara Sachs; children: Eric, Chris, Kevin, Liz, Blair. MD, Georgetown U. Sch. Medicine, Washington, DC, 1966. Diplomate Am. Bd. Internal Medicine, Am. Bd. Cardiovascular Disease. Intern, medicine Georgetown Hosp., Washington, 1966-67, resident, cardiology, 1967-68; fellow, cardiology Emory U. Hosp., Atlanta, 1968-70, Inst. Cardiology, London; mem. staff Overlook Hosp., Summit, NJ, Morristown Meml. Hosp., NJ; clin. instr. Columbia Physicians and Surgeons; pvt. practice cardiology Summit, NJ. Recipient Lifetime Achievement award for Med. Svc., Overlook Hosp., Summit, NJ, 2006. Fellow Am. Coll. Cardiology; mem. FCCAHA. Office: Summit Med Group 95 Madison Ave Morristown NJ 07960 also: 1 Diamond Hill Rd Berkeley Heights NJ 07922

SACHTLER, WOLFGANG MAX HUGO, chemistry professor; b. Delitzsch, Germany, Nov. 8, 1924; arrived in US, 1983; s. Gottfried Hugo and Johanna Elisabeth (Bollmann) S.; m. Anne-Lore Luise Adrian, Dec. 9, 1953; children: Johann Wolfgang Adriaan, Heike Kathleen Julia, Yvonne Rhea Valeska. Diplomchemiker, Tech. U., Braunschweig, Ger., 1949; Dr.rer.nat. (Ph.D), 1952. Rsch. chemist Kon/Shell Lab., Amsterdam, Netherlands, 1952-71; dept. head Kon-Shell Lab., Amsterdam, 1972—83; extraordinary prof. chemistry U. Leiden, Netherlands, 1963-83; V.N. Ipatieff prof. Northwestern U., Evanston, Ill., 1983-96; chmn. Gordon Research Conf. Catalysis, NH, 1985. Rideal lectr. Faraday div. Royal Soc. Chemistry, 1981; F. Gault lectr., 1991. Mem. editl. bd. Jour. Catalysis, 1976-88, Applied Catalysis, 1983-87, Catalysis Letters, 1987—, Advances in Catalysis, 1987—, Catalysis Today, 1996—, Catalysis Reviews, 1997—; contbr. numerous articles to sci. jours. Recipient Deutsche Gesellschaft Mineraloel und Kohle Kolleg award, 1991. Fellow AAAS; mem. Royal Netherlands Acad. Scis., Internat. Congress Catalysis (pres. coun. 1992-96), Am. Chem. Soc. (E.V. Murphee award 1987, Petroleum Chemistry award 1992), Catalysis Soc. N.Am. (Robert L. Burwell award 1985, E. Houdry award 1993). Home: 2141 Ridge Ave Apt 2D Evanston IL 60201-2788 Office: Northwestern Univ 2137 Campus Dr Evanston IL 60208 Business E-Mail: wmhs@northwestern.edu.

SACK, EDGAR ALBERT, electronics company executive; b. Pitts., Jan. 31, 1930; s. Edgar Albert and Margaret Valentine (Engelmohr) S.; m. Eugenia Ferris, June 7, 1952; children: Elaine Kimberley, Richard Warren. BS, Carnegie-Mellon U., 1951, MS, 1952, PhD, 1954. Dept. mgr. Westinghouse Rsch. Lab., Pitts., 1960-63; engring. mgr. Westinghouse Microelectronics, Balt., 1963-65, ops. mgr., 1965-67, divsn. mgr., 1967-69; div. v.p. Gen. Instrument Corp., Hicksville, NY, 1969-73, group v.p., 1973-77, sr. v.p., 1977-84; pres., CEO Zilog Inc., Campbell, Calif., 1984-98, also chmn. bd. dirs.; pres. Productivity Assocs., Coronado, Calif.; founder, chmn. CDT, Inc., San Jose, Calif., 1998-99. Bd. dirs. Enfo-Web, Inc., Mountainview, Calif., LXi, Inc., Mountainview; vis. com. elec. engring. dept. Carnegie-Mellon U., 1969-74; mem. indsl. adv. coun. SUNY, Stony Brook, 1979-83; mem. adv. com. on solid state electronics Poly. Inst. Tech., 1981-83. Author: Forward Controllership Business Management System, 1989, 2nd edit., 1993, Development of the Coronado Shores-A History, 2005; patentee in field. Mem. Action Com. L.I, 1982-84; bd. dir. Coronado Shores Assn. # 7, 2000-, landscaping and recreational com., 2000-, chair, 2002-03, treas., 2004-07; mem. Sharp Coronado Hosp. Aux.; sec. San Diego Imperial Coun. of Vols., 2002; bd. dirs. Coronado Hosp. Found., 2003-04, chair projects and allocations com., 2004. Recipient 2nd Ann. Hammerschlag Disting. Lectr. award Carnegie Mellon U., 1995. Fellow IEEE, Poly. Inst. Tech.; mem. Semicondr. Industry Assn. (dir. 1982-85), Carnegie Mellon Alumni Assn. (Merit award 1981), Eta Kappa Nu (Outstanding Young Elec. Engr. 1959), Huntington Yacht Club (vice comdr. 1977), Tau Beta Pi (finalist San Francisco Entrepreneur of Yr. award 1991), Phi Kappa Phi. Home and Office: 1780 Avenida Del Mundo Unit 404 Coronado CA 92118-4011 Personal E-mail: esack@pacbell.net.

SACK, GEORGE HENRY, JR., molecular geneticist; b. Balt., Apr. 17, 1943; s. George Henry and Sophia Ann (Philippi) S. BA, Johns Hopkins U., 1965, MD, 1968, PhD, 1974. Diplomate Bd. Med. Genetics, Bd. Med. Examiners. Intern Johns Hopkins Hosp., Balt., 1968-69, asst. resident, 1969-70, fellow genetics, 1975-76; rsch. fellow Johns Hopkins Sch. Medicine, Balt., 1970-73; asst. prof. dept. medicine Johns Hopkins U., Balt., 1976-84, assoc. prof. dept. medicine and biol. chemistry, 1984—; molecular biologist Kennedy Inst., Balt., 1982-93, dir. exec. health program, 1996—2006; med dir. Hopkins USA, 2007—. Contbr. articles to profl. jours. Maj. USAR, 1973-75. Andrew W. Mellon scholar Johns Hopkins U., 1976, Kennedy Found. scholar, 1982-85. Fellow Am. Coll. Med. Genetics; mem. AMA, AAAS, Am. Soc. Human Genetics, Phi Beta Kappa. Office: Johns Hopkins Sch Medicine Dept Biol Chemistry P-615 Baltimore MD 21205 Office Phone: 410-955-4621. Business E-Mail: gsack@jhmi.edu.

SACK, JAMES M., lawyer; b. Buffalo, May 26, 1951; BA with honors, U. Chgo., 1972; JD, Boston U., 1975; LLM in Taxation, Georgetown U., 1978. Bar: DC 1976, US Ct. Appeals, DC 1977, US Supreme Ct. 1981, Va. 1985. Atty. advisor US Dept. State, Washington, 1975—77; shareholder Sack Harris & Martin, PC, McLean, Va.; v.p., gen. counsel, sec. NVR, Inc., McLean, Va. Office: Sack Harris & Martin, PC Ste 810 8270 Greensboro Dr Mc Lean VA 22102 also: NVR Inc 7601 Lewinsville Rd Mc Lean VA 22102 *

SACK, JOHN R., library and information scientist; b. 1952; BA in English & Philosophy, U. Va., 1974; MA in English, Stanford U., 1976. Programming supr, programmer/analyst Stanford U., 1975—78, assoc. dir. for systems, 1978—79, dir., planning & schedules, 1979—80, dir., data base mgmt. group, 1980—83; dir. Stanford U. Data & Tech. Resources, 1983—87, Stanford U. Data Ctr., 1987—95; assoc. pub., dir. HighWire Press Stanford U. Libraries & Acad. Info. Resources, 1995—. Mem.: User Alliance for Open Systems, Stanford Fed. Credit Union. Office: 1454 Page Mill Rd Palo Alto CA 94304 E-mail: sack@stanford.edu.

SACK, ROBERT DAVID, federal judge, educator; b. Phila., Oct. 4, 1939; s. Eugene J. and Sylvia I. (Rivlin) Sack; BA, U. Rochester, 1960; LLB, Columbia U., 1963. Bar: NY 1963. Law clk. to judge Fed. Dist. Ct. of NJ, 1963—64; assoc. Patterson, Belknap & Webb, NYC, 1964—70; ptnr. Patterson, Belknap, Webb & Tyler, NYC, 1970—86, Gibson, Dunn & Crutcher, NYC, 1986-98; sr. assoc. spl. counsel US Ho. of Reps. Impeachment Inquiry, 1974; judge US Ct. Appeals (2d cir.), 1998—. Lectr. Practising Law Inst., 1973—97, Columbia U. Law Sch., 2001—, mem. bd. visitors, 2000—; adv. bd. Media Law Reporter. Author: Libel, Slander, and Related Problems, 1980, 2d edit., 1994, CD-ROM edit., 1995, Sack on Defamation-Libel, Slander, and Related Problems, 3d edit., 1999; co-author: Advertising and Commercial Speech, a First Amendment Guide, 1999; contbr. articles to profl. jours. Chmn. bd. dirs. Nat. Council on Crime and Delinquency, 1982—83; trustee seminars on media and society Columbia U. Sch. Journalism, 1985—92, NYC Commn. on Pub. Info. and Comm., 1995—98; v.p., bd. dirs. William F. Kerby and Robert S. Potter Fund. Fellow: Am. Bar Found.; mem.: ABA (bd. govs. forum com. on comm. law 1980—88), Fed. Bar Counsel, Assn. Bar City NY (chmn. comm. law com. 1986—89). Office: US Circuit Ct for 2d Circuit 40 Foley Sq New York NY 10007-1502 *

SACK, ROBERT DAVID, geography professor; PhD, U. Minn., 1971. Clarence J. Glacken prof. geography U. Wis., Madison, 1994—, John Bascom prof. geography, 1997—, prof. Integrated Liberal Studies. Contbr. articles to profl. jours., chapters to books; author: Conceptions of Space in Social Thought: A Geog. Perspective, 1980, Human Territoriality: Its Theory and Hist., 1986, Place, Modernity, and the Consumer's World: A Relational Framework for Geog. Analysis, 1992, Homo Geographicus: A Framework for Action, Awareness, and Moral Concern, 1997, A Geog. Guide to the Real and the Good, 2003; editor: Progress: Geog. Essays, 2002. Recipient Hilldale award, Social Studies, 1993, Honors award, Disting. Rsch., Assn. Am. Geographers, 1994; grantee John Simon Guggenheim Meml. Found. fellowship, 1975—76, Fulbright Sr. Rsch. fellowship, 1979—80. Fellow: Am. Acad. Arts & Scis. Office: Dept Geography U Wis 550 N Park St Madison WI 53706-1404 E-mail: rdsack@facstaff.wisc.edu.

SACK, SEYMOUR, nuclear scientist; b. 1929; BS in Physics, MS in Physics, PhD in Physics, Yale U. Scientist Lawrence Livermore Nat. Lab., 1955—90, lab. assoc., 1990—. Specialist in nuclear weapon design; participant JASON (study on maintaining nuclear stockpile under a comprehensive test ban), 1995. Recipient Fleet Ballistic Missile Achievement award, Strategic Sys. Program, US Navy, 1997, Enrico Fermi award, US Dept. Energy, 2003. Office: Lawrence Livermore Nat Lab 7000 East Ave Livermore CA 94550

SACK, SYLVAN HANAN, lawyer; b. Phila., Dec. 26, 1932; s. Isidore F. and Mollye (Bellmore) S.; m. Ellen L. Foreman, Aug. 13, 1972; children: Reuben H., Sara I. MS in Bus. Adminstrn, Pa. State U., 1956; JD, U. Balt., 1964. Bar: Md. 1964, US Tax Ct. 1967, Ct. Appeals (4th cir.), US Supreme Ct. 1970; CPA, Md. With U.S. Treasury Dept., IRS, 1956—66; pvt. practice Balt., 1967—; assoc. counsel Safety First Club of Md., 1975—78, spl. counsel, 1979—2000; asst. city solicitor City of Balt., 1978—79. Gov. Md. chpt. Retinitis Pigmentosa Found., 1974-75 Contbr. articles to profl. jours. Chmn. Indsl. Toxicology NIOSH Function, 1977, Occupational Disease Forum, 1979, OSHA and Diseases in Workplace Seminar, 1981. Mem. Fed. Bar Assn. (gov. chpt. 1968—, chmn. bd. govs. 1969-70, chmn. environ. law program 1984), ABA (chmn. subcom. sect. taxation 1972-75), Md. Bar Assn., Assn. Trial Lawyers Am.; mem. Md. Trial Lawyers Assn. (lectr. toxic torts 1983 conv.) Office Phone: 410-484-1484.

SACKETT, BARNARD (BARNEY), actor, film producer, director, scriptwriter; Personal mgr. Bret Morrison "The Shadow" of Mutual Network Blue Coal Radio, jazz artist Sylvia Syms, 1950; press agt. summer stock co. Quarterdeck Theatre, Atlantic City, N.J., 1952—55; drama critic, celebrity interviewer Sta. WDAS and Metromedia WIP, Phila., 1953—68; owner/operator Wayne Ave. Playhouse, Phila., 1957—69, Aarde Cinema and Sackett's Screening Room, Phila., 1970—73, Onstage Theatre, Phila., 1986—89; liaison/coord. pvt. fin. placements West Hollywood, Calif. Opened TV prodn. agy. Empire State Bldg., NYC, Knickerbock Hotel, Hollywood, Banker's Securities Bldg., Phila., 1947; writer, prodr., dir. first TV live action film prodn. The Closed Affair Dumont TV Closed Circuit, NYC, 1948; writer, prodr., dir. comedy series The Penn Family WFIL-TV, 1949; concert impresario, 49; dir., prodr. all-star mil. prodn. Death of a Salesman, Earle Theatre, Phila., 1952; originator/operator Silent Movie Nickelodeon Theater, NYC; film actor Eroticon, Bad Girls Go To Hell; personal rep. Erlanger Theater, New Locust Theatre; entertainment dir. Carlos 'n Charlies Night Club, Hollywood. Writer, prodr., dir.: (weekly musical comedy) What a Show; Playtime; (weekly satirical soap opera) Rough in the E.T.; writer, prodr. (weekly satirical soap opera) Bette, Hedy, Mae & Who?; writer, prodr., dir.: (weekly TV series) The Gypsy Markoff Show; Bret Morrison and Lucille Manner Musical Review; Rehearsal with Maggie Teyte; writer, prodr.: (films) Eroticon; All Men Are Apes; Nickelodeon Days; Sweet Smell of Sex; talent coord.: United Nations Musical Review; presenter: concerts Acad. of Music, Witherspoon Concert Hall; presenter: (concerts) Town Hall; author: Rough in the E.T., Hedy, Bette, Marlene & Me. Mem. Hollywood C. of C., Beverly Hills C. of C., West. Hollywood C. of C. Served with US Army, 1943—45, WWII. Achievements include designing world's only three-stage musical theatre, Music-Go-Round Playhouse; interviewed hundreds of famous people from world of sports, theater, film and politics including Debbie Reynolds, Joan Crawford, Sugar Ray Robinson, Bette Davis, Charlton Heston, Otto Preminger, Alfred Hitchcock, Gary Cooper, John Wayne, Sammy Davis, Jr., Henry Fonda, and Hedy Lamarr; exclusive on-stage celebrity interviewer for Stanley Warner Motion Picture Theatres, Phila.; writer, prodr., dir. 71st Annual Easter Sunrise Svc. Office: 1311 N Fairfax Ave Ste 15 West Hollywood CA 90046 Office Phone: 323-851-8842. E-mail: promethean@sbcglobal.net.

SACKETT, SUSAN DEANNA, writer; b. NYC, Dec. 18, 1943; adopted d. Maxwell and Gertrude Selma (Kugel) S. BA in Edn., U. Fla., 1964, MEd, 1965. Tchr. Dade County Schs., Miami, Fla., 1966-68, L.A. City Schs., 1968-69; asst. publicist, comml. coord. NBC-TV, Burbank, Calif., 1970-73; asst. to Gene Roddenberry, creator Star Trek, 1974-91; prodn. assoc. TV series Star Trek: The Next Generation, 1987-91, writer, 1990-91. Lectr. and guest spkr. Star Trek convs. in U.S., Eng., Australia, 1974-. Author, editor: Letters to Star Trek, 1977; co-author: Star Trek Speaks, The Making of Star Trek--The Motion Picture, 1979, You Can Be a Game Show Contestant and Win, 1982, Say Goodnight Gracie, 1986; author: The Hollywood Reporter Book of Box Office Hits, 1990, 2d edit., 1996, Prime Time Hits, 1993, Hollywood Sings, 1995, Inside Trek: My Secret Life with Star Trek Creator Gene Roddenberry, 2002. Mem. ACLU, Writers Guild Am., Am. Humanist Assn., Humanist Soc. Greater Phoenix (pres. 2000—), Mensa, Sierra Club, Am. Humanist Assn. (bd. dir., 2005—). Democrat.

SACKHEIM, ROBERT LEWIS, aerospace engineer, educator; b. NYC, May 16, 1937; s. A. Frederick and Lillian L. (Emmer) S.; m. Babette Freund, Jan. 12, 1964; children: Karen Holly, Andrew Frederick. BSChemE, U. Va., 1959; MSChemE, Columbia U., 1961; postgrad., UCLA, 1966—72. Project engr. Comsat Corp., El Segundo, Calif., 1969-72; project mgr. TRW, Redondo Beach, Calif., 1964-69, sect. head, 1972-76, dept. mgr., 1976-81, mgr. new bus., 1981-86, lab. mgr., 1986-90, dep. ctr. dir., 1990-93, ctr. dir., 1993-99; asst. dir, chief engr. for space propulsion systems Marshall Space Flight Ctr, NASA, Huntsville, Ala., 1999—2006; adj. prof. mech. and aerospace engring. U. Ala., Huntsville, 2006—; ind. cons. in space and launch vehicles and propulsion sys. and tech. Instr. UCLA engring. ext., 1986, Continuing Engring. Edn., U. Ala., Huntsville, 2001; mem. adv. bds. NASA, Washington, 1989—; mem. peer rev. bd. various univs. and govtl. agys., 1990—; mem. Nat. Rsch. Coun./Aeronautics and Space Engring. Bd., 1994—; mem. NRC com. propulsion evaluation, 2003; mem. various NASA investigation teams; guest lectr. various univs. and AIAA short courses. Author: Space Mission Analysis and Design, 1991, Space Propulsion Analysis and Design, 1994, Space Launch and Transportation Systems, 2004; contbr. chpt. to book, more than 250 articles to profl. jours., confs. Mem. adv. bd. L.A. Bd. Edn., 1990-92; fund raiser March of Dimes, L.A., 1970-90, YMCA, San Pedro, Calif., 1974-86. Capt. USAF Reserve, 1960-63. Recipient 16 Group Achievement awards NASA, 1970, 78, 86, 2000, 2001, 2003, 2005, Sustained Svc. award AIAA, 2000, medal for outstanding tech. leadership NASA, Propulsion Outstanding Contbns. award French Acad. Aero/Astro., 2002, NASA/Dir.'s commendation, 2003, Presdl. Rank award for disting. fed. civil svc., 3 ann. TRW Chmn. awards, TRW PAtent of Yr. award, 1992, Govs. award for disting. svc. state Ala., 2004. Fellow AIAA (chmn. com. 1980-83, chmn. L.A. sect. 1997, chmn. Ala./Miss. sect. 2000, 2001, J.H. Wyld Propulsion award 1992, Shuttle Flag award 1984, Martin Schilling award 2001, Hermann Oberth award 2002, Holgar Toftoy award 2003), Internat. Acad. Astronautics, Nat. Acad. Engring., Sigma Xi. Achievements include 9 patents in field. Office: U Alabama Rm N249 Huntsville AL 35812 Office Phone: 256-824-5121. Business E-Mail: sackheir@uah.edu.

SACKS, CHARLES BERNARD, psychiatrist, educator; b. Cleve., May 14, 1939; s. Jerry and Frances (Shifrin) S.; m. Lora Jane Glickman, May 2, 1993; children: Eliza, Aaron. BA, Ohio State U., 1961, MD, 1965. Staff psychiatrist Washington Vets. Hosp., 1971-77; asst. clin. prof. Georgetown U., Washington, 1971—; staff psychiatrist Reston Clinic, Fairfax City, Md., 1976-77, Drug Treatment Adminstrn., Washington, 1971-72, Washington Free Clinic, 1971-73, Arlington & Fairfax City Hosp., 1977-88, Group Health Assocs., Washington, 1984-86; psychiatrist pvt. practice, McLean, Va., 1977—, Greenbelt, Md., 1977—; dir. Chevy Chase Psychiat. Clinic, Washington, 1987-89; Mt. Vernon Mental Health Ctr., 1994—. Maj. U.S. Army, 1969-71. Decorated Bronze medal with Oak Leaf Cluster. Mem.

Am. Psychiat. Assn. Avocations: sailing, photography, music, reading, sports. Office: 6201 Greenbelt Rd College Park MD 20740-2354 also: 1313 Vincent Pl Mc Lean VA 22101-3615 Office Phone: 703-821-1017.

SACKS, HERBERT SIMEON, psychiatrist, educator, consultant; b. NYC, Nov. 29, 1926; s. Maxwell Lawrence and Anne (Edelstein) S.; m. Helen Margery Levin, Dec. 26, 1948; children: Eric Livingston, Katharine Bird, Douglas Lowell, Russell Avery AB magna cum laude, Dickinson Coll., 1948; MD, Cornell U., 1952. Diplomate Am. Bd. Psychiatry and Neurology and subspecialty Child and Adolescent Psychiatry. Clin. assoc. Western New Eng. Psychoanalytic Inst., New Haven, 1955-63; intern in pediatrics Yale-New Haven Med. Ctr., 1952-53; jr. asst. resident in psychiatry Yale Psychiat. Inst., 1953-54; sr. asst. resident in psychiatry, USPHS fellow Yale-New Haven Med. Ctr., psychiat. out patient dept., 1954-55; USPHS fellow in child psychiatry Yale U. Child Study Ctr., 1955-57; clin. dir. Mid-Fairfield Child Guidance Ctr., Norwalk, Conn., 1957-59; cons. Expt. in Internat. Living, Putney, Vt., 1962-69; sr. cons. U.S. Peace Corps, Washington, 1962-69; cons. AID, U.S. Dept. State, Office of Sahel, West Africa, 1974-84, Neurosci. Consultation Group, Grosse Point Farms, Mich., 1984-94; clin. prof. child and adolescent psychiatry Child Study Ctr., Yale U. Sch. Medicine, New Haven. Co-investigator, co-dir. Senegal River pilot health research program, New Haven and West Africa, 1976-78, co-investigator, co-dir. health sector, design team Senegal River integrated devel. project, 1981-83; vis. lectr. Yale Coll., 1969-71; mem. com. reviewers Dept. Commerce Nat. Bur. Standards, Inst. for Computer Scis. and Tech., Washington, 1975-77; mem. exec. com. Nat. Commn. on Confidentiality of Health Records, 1975-80 Author: Hurdles: The Admissions Dilemma in American Higher Education, 1978; contbg. author chpts. in books, articles on confidentiality, juvenile justice, higher edn., issues of youth in transition, other topics; author monographs Mem. Conn. Juvenile Justice Commn., Hartford, 1975-80; bd. advisors Dickinson Coll., Carlisle, Pa., 1980-85. Served to lt. (j.g.) U.S. Navy, 1944-46; PTO Fellow AMA, ACPO, Am. Psychiat. Assn. (trustee 1988-94, v.p. 1994-96, pres. 1997-98), Am. Acad. Child and Adolescent Psychiatry, Am. Orthopsychiat. Assn., Am. Coll. Psychiatrists; mem. Conn. Psychiat. Soc. (pres. 1976-77), Conn. Coun. Child and Adolescent Psychiatrists (pres. 1972-73), World Fedn. for Mental Health, Phi Beta Kappa. Avocations: farming, photography, fishing, lawn bowling. Home: 110 Laurel Rd New Haven CT 06515-2426 Office: 260 Riverside Ave Westport CT 06880-4804 also: Yale U Child Study Ctr PO Box 207900 New Haven CT 06520-7900 Office Phone: 203-227-0996.

SACKS, IRA STEPHEN, lawyer; b. NYC, Dec. 6, 1948; s. Marvin Leonard and Mildred (Finkelstein) S.; m. Deborah DiNolfo; children: James, Jennifer, Allison, Gillian. BS, MIT, 1970; JD, Georgetown U., 1974. Bar: N.Y. 1975, U.S. Dist. Ct. (so. and ea. dists.) N.Y. 1975, U.S. Ct. Appeals (2d cir.) 1975, U.S. Ct. Appeals (3d cir.) 1984, U.S. Supreme Ct. 1985, U.S. Ct. Appeals (9th cir.) 1986, U.S. Ct. Appeals (11th cir.) 1987, U.S. Ct. Appeals (D.C. and fed. cirs.) 1993. Assoc. Kaye, Scholer, Fierman, Hays & Handler, NYC, 1974-82, ptnr., 1983-87, Fried, Frank, Harris, Shriver & Jacobson, NYC, 1988—2003, Gursky and Ptnrs., NYC, 2003—05, Dreier LLP, NYC, 2005—. Contbr. articles to profl. jours. NSF fellow, 1970. Mem. ABA, Supreme Ct. Hist. Soc., N.Y. State Bar Assn., Assn. of Bar of City of N.Y. Democrat. Jewish. Avocations: tennis, skiing. Home: 105 Old Colony Rd Hartsdale NY 10530-3610 Office: Dreier LLP 499 Park Ave New York NY 10022 Office Phone: 212-652-3730. Business E-Mail: isacks@dreierllp.com. E-mail: isacks@aol.com.

SACKS, OLIVER WOLF, neurologist, writer; b. London, July 9, 1933; Came to U.S., 1960; s. Samuel and Muriel Elsie (Landau) S. BA, U. Oxford, 1954; MA, BM, BCh, Middlesex Hosp., London, 1958; DHL (hon.), Georgetown U., 1990, Coll. Staten Island, CUNY, 1991; DS (hon.), Tufts U., 1991, N.Y. Med. Coll., 1991; DS (hon.), Med. Coll. Pa., 1992, Bard Coll., 1992, U. Turin, 2003. Intern in medicine, surgery and neurology Middlesex Hosp., 1958-60; rotating intern Mt. Zion Hosp., San Francisco, 1961-62; resident in neurology UCLA, 1962-65; I.D. fellow in neuropathology and neurochemistry Albert Einstein Coll. Medicine, NYC, 1965-66, instr. neurology, 1966-75, asst. prof., 1975-78, assoc. prof., 1978-85, clin. prof. neurology, 1985—. Adj. prof. psychiatry NYU, 1992-; sci. advisor Inst. Music and Neurologic Function, Beth Abraham Hosp., 1995-; cons. neurologist Comprehensive Epilepsy Ctr., Mt. Sinai Med. Ctr., 1999-; cons., speaker, lectr. in field; hon. lectureships in field. Author: Migraine, 1970, Awakenings, 1973, rev. paperback edit., 1990 (Hawthornden prize 1975), A Leg To Stand On, 1984, The Man Who Mistook His Wife for a Hat, 1985, Seeing Voices: A Journey into the World of the Deaf, 1989 (Mainichi Pub. Culture award 1996), An Anthropologist on Mars, 1995 (George S. Polk award for mag. reporting 1994, Nat. Assn. Sci. Writers award 1994, Esquire Apple Waterstone's Book of Yr. 1995), The Island of the Color Blind, 1996, Uncle Tungsten, 2001, Oaxaca Jour., 2002. Bd. mem. N.Y. Bot. Garden. Recipient Oskar Pfister award APA, 1988, Harold D. Vursell Meml. award Am. Acad. and Inst. Arts and Letters, 1989, Communicator of Yr. Royal Nat. Inst. Deaf, 1991, Lewis Thomas prize Rockefeller U., 2002, Sloan Found. award, 2002, Pub. Comm. award NSF, 2004; Guggenheim fellow, 1989, others. Fellow Am. Acad. Arts and Scis., Am. Acad. Arts and Letters, NY Acad. Scis. (hon.); mem. Am. Acad. Neurology (presdl. citation 1991), Am. Fern Soc., Am. Neurological Assn. (hon.), Assn. Brit. Neurologists (hon.), Brit. Pteridological Soc., NY Mineralogical Club, NY Stereoscopic Soc., Soc. Neurosci., NY Inst. Humanities, Alpha Omega Alpha. Office: 2 Horatio St Apt 3G New York NY 10014-1638

SACKS, PATRICIA ANN, librarian, consultant; b. Allentown, Pa., Nov. 6, 1939; d. Lloyd Alva and Dorothy Estelle (Stoneback) Stahl; m. Kenneth LeRoy Sacks, June 27, 1959. AB, Cedar Crest Coll., 1959; MS in Libr. Sci., Drexel U., 1965. News reporter Call-Chronicle, Allentown, 1956-59, 61-63; reference libr. Cedar Crest Coll., Allentown, 1964-66, head libr., 1966-73; dir. librs. Muhlenberg and Cedar Crest Colls., Allentown, 1973-94; dir. libr. svcs. Cedar Crest Coll., 1994; sr. fellow Lehigh Valley Assn. Ind. Colls., 1994-97, Ctr. Agile Ptnrs. in Edn., 1997-98; info. svcs. cons., 1998—. Del. On Line Computer Library Ctr. Users Council, Columbus, Ohio, 1977-84; cons. colls./health care groups, libr. orgns. 1981—. Author: (with Whildin Sara Lou) Preparing for Accreditation: A Handbook for Academic Librarians, 1993; mem. editl. bd. Jour. Acad. Librarianship, 1982-84. Mem. United Way Lehigh Valley Coms., 1993—97; trustee Cedar Crest Coll., 1985—89; bd. dirs. John and Dorothy Morgan Cancer Ctr., 1994—96; mem. bd. Allentown Cmty. Concert, Pa., 2003—06. Named Outstanding Acad. Woman, Lehigh Valley Assn. Acad. Women, 1984, Muhlenberg Coll. Outstanding Adminstr., 1987, Alumni Tricorn award Muhlenberg Coll., 1989, Alumnae Achievement award Cedar Crest Coll., 1994. Mem. ALA (chmn. copyright com. 1985-87), Assn. Coll. and Rsch. Librs. (chmn. stds. and accreditation com. 1976-78, 81-84), Lehigh Valley Assn. Ind. Colls. (chmn. librs. sect. 1967-81, 88-92), AAUW, LWV, Wildlands Conservancy, Appalachian Mountain Club (Echo Lake naturalist 1997—), Phi Alpha Theta, Phi Kappa Phi, Beta Phi Mu. Democrat. Home: 2997 Fairfield Dr Allentown PA 18103-5413 Personal E-mail: sackspa@ptd.net.

SACKS, ROBERT A., lawyer; b. Long Beach, NY, 1957; AB, Harvard U., 1979; JD, U. Tex., 1982. Bar: NY 1983, Calif. 1990. Assoc. Sullivan & Cromwell, NYC, 1984—90, ptnr. litig. LA, 1990—, now ptnr.-in-charge LA office. Mem.: ABA. Office: Sullivan & Cromwell 1888 Century Pk E Los Angeles CA 90067-1725 Office Phone: 310-712-6600. Office Fax: 310-712-8800. Business E-Mail: sacksr@sullcrom.com.

SACKS, TEMI J., public relations executive; b. Phila. d. Jule and Adeline (Levin) S. BA, Temple U. Pubs. editor Del. Valley Regional Planning Commn., Phila.; comms. assoc. Fedn. Jewish Agys., Phila.; exec. v.p., mng. dir. consumer and healthcare divsns. Lobsenz-Stevens Inc., NYC; exec. v.p., dir. nat. healthcare practice Shandwick, NYC; sr. v.p. Noonan-Russo, NYC; pres. T.J. Sacks & Assocs. Inc., NYC. Mem. Healthcare Businesswomen's Assn., Healtcare Mktg. Assn., Women Execs. in Pub. Rels. Avocations: painting, skiing, jewelry design, antiques. Office Phone: 212-787-0787. Personal E-mail: tjsacks@tjsacks.com.

SACKSTEDER, THOMAS MICHAEL, corporate financial executive, entrepreneur, writer; b. Dayton, Ohio, July 27, 1950; s. Harry Pius and Mary Kay (Liebhardt) S.; children: Lori Ann, Kristi Marie, Julie Kay. Student, Sinclair CC, 1968-72, Wright State U., 1972-73, Grand Valley State Coll., 1978-79, Lourdes Coll., 1996—96. Installer Western Electric, Dayton, 1968-69; sales rep. Smith Corona Mcht., Dayton, 1969-70; office mgr. Indsl. Machinery, Dayton, 1970-71; advisor Bell Pub. Rels., Dayton, 1972-73; sales mgr. Washington Nat. Ins., Grand Rapids, 1974-81, Am. Fidelity Assurance Co., Indpls., 1982—95; gen. ptnr. Innovative Benefits Resource Ltd., 1995—. Gen. ptnr., Annuity Compliance Specialists LTD, 1995-; benefits cons. Ind. State Tchrs. Assn. Ins. Trust, Indpls., 1986-91. Bd. dirs. Mental Health Assn., Dayton, 1971-75, Good Samaritan Mental Health Ctr., 1972-75; campaign mgmt. for polit. candidates and issue oriented policies, 1972—. Mem. Ohio Assn. Sch. Bus. Ofcls. (legis. com. 1993-95), Assn. of Sch. Bus. Ofcls., Natl. Tax Shelter Annuity Assn., Employers Counc. on Flexible Compensation, Natl. Assn. of Life Underwriters, Buckeye Assn. Sch. Adminstrs., Jaycees, Kiwanis. Roman Catholic. Avocations: golf, swimming, writing, research, martial arts. Office: Innovative Benefits Resource Ltd Annuity Compliance Specialists PO Box 70 Holland OH 43528-0070 Business E-Mail: ibr125@aol.com.

SACKTON, FRANK JOSEPH, public affairs educator; b. Chgo., Aug. 11, 1912; m. June Dorothy Raymond, Sept. 21, 1940. Student, Northwestern U., Evanston, Ill., 1936, Yale U., New Haven, Conn., 1946, U. Md., College Park, 1951—52; BS, U. Md., 1970; grad., Command and Gen. Staff Coll., 1942, Armed Forces Staff Coll., 1949, Nat. War Coll., 1954; MPA, Ariz. State U., 1976, DHL (hon.), 1996. Mem. 131st Inf. Regt., Ill. N.G., 1929-40; commd. 2d lt. U.S. Army, 1934, advanced through grades to lt. gen., 1967; brigade plans and ops. officer (33d Inf. Div.), 1941, PTO, 1943-45; div. signal officer, 1942-43; div. intelligence officer, 1944; div. plans and ops. officer, 1945; sec. to gen. staff for Gen. MacArthur Tokyo, 1947-48; bn. comdr. 30th Inf. Regt., 1949-50; mem. spl. staff Dept. Army, 1951; plans and ops. officer Joint Task Force 132, PTO, 1952; comdr. Joint Task Force 7, Marshall Islands, 1953; mem. gen. staff Dept. Army, 1954-55; with Office Sec. Def., 1956; comdr. 18th Inf. Regt., 1957-58; chief staff 1st Inf. Div., 1959; chief army Mil. Mission to Turkey, 1960-62; comdr. XIV Army Corps, 1963; dep. dir. plans Joint Chiefs Staff, 1964-66; army general staff mil. ops., 1966-67; comptroller of the army, 1967-70; ret., 1970; spl. asst. for fed./state relations Gov. Ariz., 1971-75; chmn. Ariz. Programming and Coordinating Com. for Fed. Programs, 1971-75; lectr. Am. Grad. Sch. Internat. Mgmt., 1973-77; vis. asst. prof., lectr. public affairs Ariz. State U., Tempe, 1976-78; founding dean Ariz. State U. Coll. Public Programs, 1979-80; prof. public affairs Ariz. State U., 1980—, finance educator, v.p. bus. affairs, 1981-83, dep. dir. intercollegiate athletics, 1984-85, dir. strategic planning, 1987-88. Contbr. articles to public affairs and mil. jours. Mem. Ariz. Steering Com. for Restoration of the State Capitol, 1974-75, Ariz. State Personnel Bd., 1978-83, Ariz. Regulatory Coun., 1981-93. Decorated D.S.M., Silver Star, also Legion of Merit with 4 oak leaf clusters, Bronze Star with 2 oak leaf clusters, Air medal, Army Commendation medal with 1 oak leaf cluster, Combat Inf. badge. Mem.: Ariz. Acad. Public Adminstrn., Army-Navy Club (Washington), Arizona Country Club (Phoenix), Pi Alpha Alpha (pres. chpt. 1976—82). Home: 12000 N 90th St Unit 3072 Scottsdale AZ 85260-8643 Office: Ariz State U Sch Pub Affairs Tempe AZ 85287-0603 Business E-Mail: frank-sackton@asu.edu.

SACOFF, ROBERT W., lawyer; m. Mary Colnon; children: Colin, Lydon. BA, U. Notre Dame, 1969; JD, Northwestern U., 1973. Bar: Ill. Ptnr. Pattishall, McAuliffe et al., Ill., 1987—. Mem.: ABA (chair intellectual property law sect. 2003—04). Office: Pattishall McAuliffe et al 311 S Wacker Dr Chicago IL 60606 Office Phone: 312-554-7934. Office Fax: 312-554-8015. Business E-Mail: rws@pattishall.com.

SACRIPANTI, PETER JOHN, lawyer; b. 1955; BA summa cum laude, Fordham U., 1982; JD, Pace U., 1984. Fed. prosecutor U.S. Dept. Justice; ptnr., mem. firm exec. mgmt. com. McDermott Will & Emery LLP. Recipient Ellis Island Medal Hon., 2001. Mem.: N.J. Bar Assn., D.C. Bar Assn., N.Y. Bar Assn. Office Phone: 212-547-5583. Office Fax: 212-547-5444. Business E-Mail: psacripanti@mwe.com.

SADAO, SHOJI, architect; b. Los Angeles, Jan. 2, 1927; s. Riichi and Otatsu (Kodama) S.; m. Tsuneko Sawada, Apr. 8, 1972. B.Arch., Cornell U., 1954; Fulbright scholar, Waseda U., Tokyo, 1956-57. Designer Geodesics, Inc., Raleigh, N.C., 1954-56; job capt. Edison Price, Inc., NYC, 1959-64; v.p. Fuller & Sadao (P.C.), Long Island City, N.Y., 1965—. Assoc. prof. archtl. design Sch. Architecture and Environ. Design, SUNY, Buffalo, 1976-77. Works include Dymaxion World Map, 1954; co-designer works include, U.S. Pavilion at Montreal Expo 67. Trustee Isamu Noguchi Found., Long Island City, N.Y., 1967—, exec. dir., 1989-2003; trustee Buckminster Fuller Inst. With AUS, 1945-49. Mem.: The Century Assn., Japan Soc. Address: Fuller & Sadao 33-38 10th St Long Island City NY 11106-4926

SADDLEMYER, ANN (ELEANOR SADDLEMYER), humanities educator, critic, theater historian; b. Prince Albert, Sask., Can., Nov. 28, 1932; d. Orrin Angus and Elsie Sarah (Ellis) S. BA, U. Sask., 1953, DLitt, 1991; MA, Queen's U., 1956, LLD (hon.), 1977; PhD, U. London, 1961; DLitt (hon.), U. Victoria, 1989, McGill U., 1989, Windsor U., 1990, U. Toronto, 1999, Concordia U., 2000. Lectr. Victoria Coll., BC, 1956-57, instr. BC, 1960-62, asst. prof. BC, 1962-65; assoc. prof. U. Victoria, 1965-68, prof. English, 1968-71, Victoria Coll. U. Toronto, 1971-95; prof., dir. Grad. Ctr. for Study of Drama, U. Toronto, 1972-77, 85-86, prof. emerita dept. English, comparative lit., drama, 1995—; sr. fellow Massey Coll., 1975-88, master, 1988-95, master emerita, 1995—; Berg prof. NYU, 1975. Adj. prof. U. Victoria; dir. Hedgerow Press; mem. heritage adv. commn. North Saanich, 2004—06. Dir. Theatre Plus, 1972-84; dir. Colin Smythe Pubs.; author: (with Robin Skelton) The World of W.B. Yeats, 1965, In Defence of Lady Gregory, Playwright, 1966, Synge and Modern Comedy, 1968, J.M. Synge Plays Books One and Two, 1968, Lady Gregory Plays, 4 vols., 1970, Letters to Molly: Synge to Maire O'Neill, 1971, Letters from Synge to W.B. Yeats and Lady Gregory, 1971, Collected Letters of John Millington Synge, Vol. 1, 1983, vol. II, 1984, Theatre Business, The Correspondence of the First Abbey Theatre Directors, 1982, (with Colin Smythe) Lady Gregory Fifty Years After, 1987, Early Stages: Theatre in Ontario, 1800-1914, 1990, J.M. Synge: The Playboy of the Western World and Other Plays, 1995; (with Richard Plant) Later Stages: Theatre in Ontario, 1914-1970s, 1997, Becoming George--The Life of Mrs. W.B. Yeats, 2002; co-editor Theatre History in Canada, 1980-86, Selected Irish Drama; co-gen. editor Cornell Yeats series; editorial bds. Modern Drama, 1972-82, English Studies in Can., 1973-83, Themes in Drama, 1974-93, Shaw Ann., 1977—, Research in the Humanities, 1976-90; Irish Univ. Rev., 1970—, Yeats Ann., 1982-86; Studies in Contemporary Irish Lit., 1986—, Irish Studies Rev., 1997—; contbr. articles to profl. jours. Recipient Brit. Acad. Rose Mary Crawshay award, 1986, Disting. Svc. award Province of Ont., 1985, U. Toronto Alumni award of excellence, 1991, award yeats Soc. NY 2001; named Disting. Dau. of Pa., 1992, Woman of Distinction in Letters, Toronto, YWCA, 1994; Officer of Order of Can., 1995; Can. Coun. scholar, 1958-59, fellow, 1968, Guggenheim fellow, 1968, 77, sr. rsch. fellow Connaught, 1985. Fellow Royal Soc. Can., Royal Soc. Arts; mem. Internat. Assn. Study Irish Lit. (chmn. 1973-76), Internat. Shaw Soc. (corr. scholar festival), Assn. Can. Theatre Rsch. (pres. 1976-77), Can. Assn. Irish Studies, Assn. Can. Coll. and Univ. Tchrs. English. Home: 10876 Madrona Dr North Saanich BC Canada V8L 5N9 Personal E-mail: saddlemy@uvic.ca.

SADDLER, DONALD EDWARD, choreographer, dancer; b. Van Nuys, Calif., Jan. 24, 1920; s. Elmer Edward and Mary Elizabeth (Roberts) Saddler. Student, Los Angeles City Coll., 1939; dance pupil of, Carmalita Maracci, Anton Dolin, Anthony Tudor, Madame Anderson Ivantzova. Mem. Ballet Theatre, NYC, 1940-43, 46-47; asst. dir., then artistic dir. Harkness Ballet, NYC, 1964-70. Exec. v.p. Rebekah Harkness Found., 1967—69; mem. exec. bd. Internat. Ballet Corp., 1979; prodr. Delacorte Theatre NY Dance Festival; guest artist Valerie Bettis Co. Dancer Grand Canyon Suite, 1937, High Button Shoes, 1947, Dance Me a Song, 1950, Bless You All, 1950, The Song of Norway, 1951, Winesburg, Ohio, 1958, The Golden Round, 1960, The Castle Period, 1961, Happy Birthday, Mr. Abbot!, 1987, with Ballet Theatre, NYC Bluebeard, Billy the Kid, Swan Lake, Aurora's Wedding, Les patineus, Lilac Garden, Gala Performance, Romeo and Juliet, Peter and the Wolf, Follies, 2001; dir.: (TV films) Holiday Hotel, 1950; choreographer theatre Blue Mountain Ballads, 1948, Wish You Were Here, 1952, Wonderful Town, 1952, John Murray Anderson's Almanac, 1953, Tobia la Candida Spia, 1954, La patrona di raddio di luna, 1955, Shangri-La, 1956, Buona notte Bettina, 1956, L'adorabile Giulio, 1957, Winesburg, Ohio, 1958, This Property is Condemned, 1958, Un trapezio per Lisistrata, 1958, When in Rome, 1959, Un manderino per Teo, 1959, Dreams of Glory, 1961, Milk and Honey, 1961, Sophie, 1963, Morning Sun, 1963, To Broadway, With Love, 1964, No, No, Nanette, 1971, Much Ado About Nothing, 1972, Fanfare Gala, 1973, Good News, 1973, Tricks, 1973, The Merry Wives of Windsor, 1974, Miss Moffat, 1974, A Midsummer Night's Dream, 1975, A Doll's House, 1975, A Gala Tribute to Joshua Logan, 1975, Rodgers and Hart, 1975, The Robber Bridegroom, 1975, 1976, Koshare, 1976, Vaudeville, 1976, Dear Friends and Gentle Hearts, 1976, Icedancing, 1978, The Grand Tour, 1979, A Long Way to Boston, 1979, Happy New Year, 1980, Hey Look Me Over!, 1981, Pardon, Monsieur Moliere, 1982, On Your Toes, 1983, The Loves of Anatol, 1985, The Golden Land, 1985, Broadway, 1987, The Student Prince, 1987, Teddy and Alice, 1987, My Fair Lady, 1993, tours The Boys from Syracuse, Aida, La Perichole, The Merry Widow, Tropicana, We Take This Town, 1962, Knickerbocker Holiday, 1971, No, No, Nanette, 1971—73, Good News, 1973—74, Hellzapoppin', 1976—77, On Your Toes, 1984, (films) April in Paris, 1952, By the Light of the Silvery Moon, 1953, Young at Heart, 1954, The Main Attraction, 1963, The Happy Hooker, 1973, Radio Days, 1987, (TV films) Holiday Hotel, 1950, (TV series) The Perry Como Show, 1950, Canozionissima, 1959—60, Bell Telephone Hour, 1961—64, (TV films) Much Ado About Nothing, 1973, (TV miniseries) Tony Award Broadcasts, 1973, 1975—78, 1983, Verna: U.S.O. Girl, 1978; dir., choreographer tour Oh, Kay!, 1978, dir., choreographer theatre Wonderful Town, 1955, A Celebration for Sir Anton Dolin, 1984, 100 Years of Performing Arts at the Met., 1984, Kiss Me Kate, 1989, Am. Ballet Theatre's 40th Anniversary, Tribute to Lucille Lortel, Tribute to Richard Rodgers, Merman-Martin Gala, Tribute to Cy Coleman, An Evening with Kurt Weill, Jo Sullivan in Concert, Tribute to George Abbott, Tribute to Lerner and Loewe, Stratford Shakespeare Festival Gala, Am. Guild of Musical Artists 100th Anniversary Gala, dir., choreographer operas Bitter Sweet, Weiner Blut, Abduction from the Seraglio, Washington Opera Follies; dir.(theatre): Berlin to Broadway with Kurt Weill, 1972, George Abbott...A Celebration, 1976, Life with Father, 1982, I Hear Music...of Frank Loesser and Friends, 1984, State Fair Music Hall, 1957, 1959, Carousel Theatre, 1958, Stratford Shakespeare Festival, 1979; prodr.(theatre): The Sol Hurok Birthday Gala, 1973, The 30th Anniversary of City Center Theatre, 1975, (with Martin Feinstein): The Pre-Inaugural Ballet-Opera Gala, 1981,: The Dance Collection Gala, 1972, The 35th Anniversary of the Am. Ballet Theatre, 1975, The Cynthia Gregory Gala. Recipient Dance Mag. award, 1984, Lifetime Achievement award, Theatre Development Fund, 2001, Living Legend of Dance award, Dance Libr. Israel, 2001, Capezio Dance award, 2006. Address: Coleman-Rosenberg Apt 5D 155 E 55th St New York NY 10022-4051

SADE, DONALD STONE, anthropology educator; b. Charleston, W.Va., July 17, 1937; s. Samuel and Charlotte Tracy (Stone) S.; m. Bonita Diane Chepko, Dec. 24, 1971 (div. Feb. 1994); children: Irony Cuervo del Norte, Omen Ondatra; m. Kerry L. Knox, Nov. 24, 1994. Grad., N.Y. State Ranger Sch., 1957; student, Hamilton Coll., 1957-60; AB, U. Calif., Berkeley, 1963, PhD, 1966. Instr. anthropology Northwestern U., Evanston, Ill., 1965-66, asst. prof., 1966-70, assoc. prof., 1970-75, prof., 1975-95, sr. lectr., 1995—97; scientist-in-charge Cayo Santiago, U. P.R., 1970-77; prof. emeritus Northwestern U., 1997—. Founder, pres. North Country Inst. for Natural Philosophy, Inc., Mexico, N.Y., 1980—. Sr. author: Basic Demographic Observations on Free-Ranging Rhesus Monkeys, 3 vols., 1985; editor: The North Country Naturalist, Vol. 1, 1987. Recipient Merit cert., Eastman Sch. Music., 2002, 2005, 2006, 2007; grantee, NSF, 1967—2006. Mem. Animal Behavior Soc., Guild Am. Luthiers, Nature Conservancy, Adirondack Mountain Club, Adirondack Coun., Classical Guitar Soc. Upstate NY. Office: North Country Inst for Natural Philosophy Inc 18 Emery Rd Mexico NY 13114-3311...*and all I've done for want of wit, to memory now I can't recall. (Irish ballad).*

SADEGH, ALI M., mechanical engineering educator, researcher, consultant; b. Tehran, Iran, Sept. 1, 1950; came to U.S., 1974; s. Saleh S. Mir-Mohamad-Sadegh and Asam Lotfi; m. Guita Miremadi, July 10, 1980; children: Mietra, Cameron, Mona, Jasmin, David. BSME, Arya-Mehr U. Tech., Tehran, 1972; MSME, Mich. State U., 1975, PhD in Mechanics, 1978; postgrad., U. Mich., 1979. Registered profl. engr., Mich.; cert. mfg. engr. Design engr. Nat. Radio engring. sect., Tehran, 1972-74; rsch. and teaching asst. Mich. State U., East Lansing, 1975-78; asst. prof. Arya-Mehr U. Tech., 1979-81; vis. asst. prof. Mich. State U., 1981-82; asst. prof. CUNY, NYC, 1982-87, assoc. prof., 1987-91, prof., 1991—, chmn. dept. mech. engring., 1992-96, tchr. courses in solid mechanics, design and CAD/CAM, 1996—. Cons. Devel. Iranian Heavy Industries, Tehran, 1979-81; tech. cons. AC Rochester Gen. Motors Co., 1986-92; forensic engr., 1990—; cons. and presenter in field. Contbr. over 120 articles to profl. jours.; 10 patents in field. U. Mich. scholar, Ann Arbor, 1978-79; recipient 46 Rsch. awards NSF, AT&T Found., PSC-CUNY, others. Fellow ASME (Best Paper award 1992, Melville medal 1993), Soc. Mfg. Engrs. (chmn. chpt. 320); mem. Am. Acad. Mechanics, Biomed. Engrs. Soc., Sigma Xi. Achievements include patents in field. Home: 787 Oneida Trl Franklin Lakes NJ 07417-2216 Office: CUNY Dept Mech Engring 140th St and Convent Ave New York NY 10031 Business E-Mail: sadegh@ccny.cuny.edu.

SADEGHI-NEJAD, ABDOLLAH, pediatrician, educator; b. Meshed, Iran, Apr. 29, 1938; s. Abdolhossein and Azizeh (Jabbari) S.-N.; m. Marion M. Marquardt, Jan. 26, 1974; children: Nathan R., Adrienne R. BA, Beloit Coll., 1960; MS in Pathology, U. Chgo., 1964, MD, 1964. Diplomate Am. Bd. Pediatrics. Intern then resident U. Chgo., 1964-67; fellow pediatric endocrinology Tufts-New Eng. Med. Ctr., Boston, 1967-69, U. Calif., San Francisco, 1969-70; from asst. prof. to prof. pediatrics Tufts U., Boston, 1970—; chief pediatric endocrinology and metabolism divsn. Tufts-New Eng. Med. Ctr., Boston, 1989—. Author and co-author books and articles. Mem. town meeting Town of Brookline, Mass., 1987-2001, 2005—, mem. adv. com., 1993-99; founder, mem. Friends of Lost Pond. Fellow Am. Acad. Pediatrics; mem. Am. Pediatric Soc., Am. Diabetes Assn., Endocrine

Soc., European Soc. Pediatric Rsch., Lawson Wilkins Pediat. Endocrine Soc., Soc. Pediat. Rsch. Office: Tufts-New Eng Med Ctr 750 Washington St Boston MA 02111-1526 Office Phone: 617-636-5335.

SADER, CAROL HOPE, former state legislator; b. Bklyn., July 19, 1935; d. Nathan and Mollie (Farkas) Shimkin; m. Harold M. Sader, June 9, 1957; children: Neil, Randi Sader Friedlander, Elisa Sader Waldman. BA, Barnard Coll., Columbia U., 1957. Sch. tchr. Bd. Edn., Morris, Conn., 1957-58; legal editor W. H. Anderson Co., Cin., 1974-78; freelance legal editor Shawnee Mission, Kans., 1978-87; mem. Kans. Ho. of Reps., 1987-94. Chair Ho. Pub. Health and Welfare Com., 1991-92; chair Joint Ho. and Senate Com. on Health Care Decisions for the 90's, 1992; vice chair Ho. Econ. Devel. Com., 1991-92; policy chair Ho. Dem. Caucus, 1993-94; appointee Kans. jud. qualifications commn. Kans. Supreme Ct., 1995-2004; apptd. Kans. Racing and Gaming Commn., 2003-, chmn., 2005—. Kans. State Bd. Healing Arts, 2003—. Pres. LWV, Johnson County, 1983—85; mem. State of Kans. LWV Bd., 1986—87; pres. Johnson County Found. Aging, 2002—04; mem. Johnson County Charter Commn., 1999; mem. exec. bd. Johnson County C.C. Found., 2000—03; mem. adv. group Kans. Gov.'s B.E.S.T. Team, 2002; cmty. adv. com. Kans. REACH Found., 2003—07; Dem. candidate for Kans. Lt. Gov., 1994; mem. Jewish Cmty. Rels. Bd., 1999—2006; adv. bd. Jewish Cmty. Rels. Adv. Bd., 2007—; mem. Jewish Heritage Found. Bd., 2007—; chmn. bd. trustees Johnson County C.C., Overland Park, Kans., 1984—86, trustee, 1981—86; bd. dirs. United Cmty. Svcs. of Johnson County, Shawnee Mission, 1984—92, Jewish Vocat. Svc. Bd., 1983—92, House of Menuha, 1998—99, Appleseed Found. Kans., 1999—2001, Midwest Ctr. Holocaust Edn., 1999—2004, 2006—, exec. bd., 1999—2004, 2006—, v.p. cmty. rels., 2007—; chmn. Kans. State Holocaust Commn., 1991—94; pres. MAINstream Coalition, 1995—97, vice chair, 1998—2003; v.p. Kans. Advocates for Better Care, 1998—2001. Recipient Trustee award Assn. of Women in Jr. and C.C., 1985, awards Kans. Pub. Transit Assn., 1990, AARP, 1992, Assn. Kans. Theater, 1992, Nat. Coun. Jewish Women, 1992, Kans. Assn. Osteo. Medicine, 1992, Kans. Chiropractic Assn., 1992, United Com. Svcs. Johnson County, 1992, Disting. Pub. Svcs. award Johnson County, 1993, Hallpac Kans. Pub. Svc. award Hallmark Cards, Inc., 1993, Eddie Jacobsen award B'nai B'rith, 1994, Cmty. Svc. award House of Menuha, 1998, The Pillar award Greater K.C. Women's Political Caucus, 2003, Stand-Up, Speak-Out award Mainstream Coalition, 2003. Mem.: Phi Delta Kappa. Democrat. Avocations: theater, travel. Home: 8612 Linden Dr Shawnee Mission KS 66207-1807

SADICK, NEIL SCOTT, dermatologist; b. Bronx, NY, June 1, 1951; s. Harry and Shirley (Tompkins) Sadick; 1 child, Sydney Kamin. BA, SUNY, Binghamton, 1973; MD, SUNY, Syracuse, 1977. Diplomate Am. Bd. Internal Medicine, 1980, Am. Bd. Dermatology, 1983, Am. Acad. Cosmetic Surgery, 2000, Am. Bd. Hair Restoration Surgery, 2001. Pvt. practice, NYC, 1983—; mem. adv. bd. Dermatologic Soc. Greater NY, 1994—; clin. prof. dermatology Cornell U, Monroe Coll. Surg. advisor Archives Dermatology. Author: (book) Your Hair, Helping to Keep It, 1994; asst. editor (jour.) Jour. Am. Acad. Dermatology, 1994—; author: (book) Sclerotherapy of Varicose Veins, 1996; asst. editor (jour.) Jour. Aesthetic and Cosmetic Surgery, —. Mem.: Am. Soc. Dermatological Surgery (bd. dirs.), Am. Cancer Soc. (summer fellow 1977), Manhattan Met. Dermatology Soc. (pres. 1995—96), NY Acad. Medicine, Dermatology Found. (vice chmn. 1993—), Am. Soc. Cosmetic Surgery (bd. dirs.,), Am. Acad. Dermatology (adv. bd. 1995—), Dermatologic Soc. Greater NY (adv. bd. 1994, pres. 1995—96), Am. Coll. Phlebology. (pres. 2002—04, bd. dir., Jobst award 1990), LI Dermatology Soc. Avocations: tennis, travel, antique pens. Office: 911 Park Ave New York NY 10028 Home Phone: 212-288-8502; Office Phone: 212-772-7242. Business E-Mail: nssderm@sadickdermatology.com.

SADIK, MARVIN SHERWOOD, art historian, consultant, retired museum director; b. Springfield, Mass., June 27, 1932; s. Harry Benjamin and Florence (Askinas) S. AB magna cum laude, Harvard U., 1954, A.M., 1960; D.F.A. (hon.), Bowdoin Coll., Brunswick, Maine, 1978. Curatorial asst. Worcester (Mass.) Art Mus., 1955-57; curator Mus. Art Bowdoin Coll., 1961-64, dir., 1964-67, Mus. Art U. Conn. at Storrs, 1967-69, Nat. Portrait Gallery, Washington, 1969-81. Author: Colonial and Federal Portraits at Bowdoin College, 1966, The Drawings of Hyman Bloom, 1968, The Paintings of Charles Hawthorne, 1968, Edith Halpert and the Downtown Gallery, 1968, The Life Portraits of John Quincy Adams, 1970, Christian Gullager: Portrait Painter to Federal America, 1976, Portraits of George Bellows, 1981; co-author: American Portrait Drawings, 1980. Decorated knight Order Dannebrog Denmark; recipient Detur prize Harvard Coll., 1952, Maine State Art award, 1975, gold medal for exceptional svc. Smithsonian Instn., 1981; Harris fellow, 1957-61; Barr fellow, 1957-61; fellow Belgian Art Seminar, 1956. Fellow Pierpont Morgan Library; mem. Am. Antiquarian Soc., Colonial Soc. Mass. (corr.) Clubs: Century Assn, Grolier. Home: PO Box 6360 Scarborough ME 04070-6360 Office Phone: 207-885-9644.

SADIK, NAFIS, United Nations administrator; b. Jaunpur, India, Aug. 18, 1929; d. Iffat Ara and Mohammad Shoaib; m. Azhar Sadik, 1954; 5 children. Student, Loretto Coll., Calcutta, India, Dow Med. Coll., Karachi, Pakistan, Johns Hopkins U., LHD (hon.), 1989, Brown U., 1993, Duke U., 1995; LLD, Wilfrid Laurier U., 1995; DSc (hon.), U. Mich., 1996, Claremont U., 1996; LHD (hon.), Philippines U., 1997; DSc (hon.), Long Island U., 1997; LHD (hon.), Nepal Tribhuvan U., 1998; DSc, Tulane U., 1999. Intern ob-gyn. City Hosp., Balt., 1952-54; civilian med. officer in charge of women's and children's wards various Pakistani armed forces hosps., 1954-63; resident physiology Queens U., Kingston, Ont., Can., 1958; head health sect. Planning Commn. on Health and Family Planning, Pakistan, 1964; dir. planning and tng. Pakistan Ctr. Family Planning Coun., 1966-68, dep. dir.-gen., 1968-70, dir.-gen., 1970-71; tech. advisor UN Fund for Population Activities, 1971-72, chief programme divsn., 1973-77, asst. exec. dir., 1977-87, exec. dir., 1987—; under-sec.-gen. UN, 1987—. Sec.-gen. Internat. Conf. on Population and Devel., 1994, Soc. for Internat. Devel. (pres. 1994-97). Writings include: Population: National Family Planning Programme in Pakistan, 1968, Population: the UNFPA Experience, 1984, Population Policies and Programmes: Making a Difference: Twenty-five Years of UNFPA Experience, 1994, Lessions learned from Two Decades of Experience, 1991, Making a Difference: Twenty-Five Years of UNFPA Experience, 1994; contbr. articles to profl. jours. Recipient Hugh Moore award; Paul Harris fellow Rotary, 1997. Fellow Royal Coll. Ob-Gyn. Avocations: bridge, reading, theater, travel. Office: UN Population Fund 220 E 42nd St Fl 19 New York NY 10017-5806

SADIK-KHAN, JANETTE I., city manager, former federal agency administrator; b. San Francisco, Apr. 28, 1960; d. Orhan and Jane (McCarthy) Sadik-Khan; m. Mark Geistfeld, July 14, 1990. BA, Occidental Coll., 1982; JD, Columbia U., 1987. Bar: N.Y. Dep. dir. govtl. affairs Children's Def. Fund, Washington, 1982-83; co-dir. Found. for Youth Involvement, NYC, 1983-84; litigation assoc. Kaye, Scholer, Fierman, Hays & Handler, NYC, 1987-88; dir. Mayor's Office of Transp.; spl. counsel to the commr. NYC Dept. Transp., 1990-92; assoc. adminstr. budget & policy Fed. Transit Adminstrn., US Dept. Transp., dep. adminstr.; sr. v.p. Parsons Brinckerhoff, pres., CEO, Company 39, 2000—07; commr. NYC Dept. Transp., 2007—. Presenter in field. Contbr. articles to profl. jours. Recipient Harry S. Truman scholarship Occidental Coll., L.A., 1980; named Woman of Yr., Women Transp. Seminar, 2005 Office: City Hall 52 Chambers St Rm 203 New York NY 10007-1222 *

SADINENI, SURESH BABU, research scientist; b. Ongole, Andhra Pradesh, India, Aug. 22, 1975; s. RamaRao and Ramanamma Sadineni; m. Padmaja Chilukuri, May 22, 2003; 1 child, Saanvi. PhD, U. Nev., Las Vegas, 2005. Grad. tchg. asst. dept. mech. engrng. U. Nev., Las Vegas, 2001—02, grad. rsch. asst. dept. mech. engrng., 2002—05, rsch. faculty dept. mech. engrng., 2005. Mem.: Am. Nuclear Soc. Achievements include development of Code to Predict Transient Behavior of a Nuclear Reactor Coupled to an Accelerator. Office: Univ Nev Dept Mech Engring 4505 Maryland Pkwy Las Vegas NV 89154 Home: 4255 Tamprus St Apt 421 Las Vegas NV 89119 Office Phone: 702-895-1331. Personal E-mail: sbsadineni@yahoo.com.

SADINSKY, RACHAEL, curator, art appraiser; b. Elmira, NY, Feb. 28, 1958; BA, SUNY, Binghamton, 1981; MA, U. Del., Newark, 1985. Cert. in Appraisal Studies NYU, 2004. Curator collections Arnot Art Mus., Elmira, NY, 1987—94; curator collections and exhibitions Art Mus. U. Ky., Lexington, Ky., 1995—2004. Author: A Collector's Vision: The 1910 Bequest of Matthias H. Arnot. Andelot fellowship, U. Del., 1983. Mem.: Appraisers Assn. Am., Am. Assn. Museums, Coll. Art Assn. Business E-Mail: rachael@blueone.net.

SADIQ, AAMIR, investment banker, engineer; s. Kamil and Shamim Sadiq. BChemE, Royal Mil. Coll. Can., Kingston, 1997, MChemE, 2000; MBA, Cornell U., Ithaca, NY, 2005. Registered profl. engr., Ont., 1997; cert. project mgmt. profl. Project Mgmt. Inst., 2000. Officer Dept. Nat. Def., Kingston, 1993—2000; project mgr. DuPont - Advanced Rsch. Ctr., Kingston, 2000—01; exec. asst. to CEO Reveo, Hawthorne, NY, 2001—03; investment banking intern Lehman Bros. Investment Bank, NYC, 2004; investment banking assoc. Nomura Securities, NYC, 2005—. With Can. Mil., 1993—97. Mem.: Mensa USA. Achievements include design of proton exchange membrane fuel cell system for the Department of National Defense. Avocations: skydiving, jogging, weight training, golf. Home: 504 Orchard Hill Ln Brewster NY 10509 Office: Nomura Securities 2 World Financial Center Building B New York NY 10281 Home Phone: 914-262-4578; Office Phone: 212-667-9857. Office Fax: 646-587-9857. Personal E-mail: as434@cornell.edu. Business E-Mail: asadiq@us.nomura.com.

SADJADPOUR, HAMID REZA, engineering educator; s. Mahmoud and Zahra Sadjadpour; m. Mariam Akhavan; 1 child, Taraneh. BSc, MSc, Sharif U. Tech., Tehran; PhD, U. So. Calif., LA, 2005. Prin. tech. staff mem. AT&T Shannon Lab., Florham Park, NJ, 1996—2001; assoc. prof. U. Calif., Santa Cruz, Calif., 2001—. Contbr. over 100 sci. articles to profl. jours. Grants, US Army Dept Def., 2003—. Mem.: IEEE. Achievements include over 12 patents in field. Office: Univ Calif 1156 High St Santa Cruz CA 95064 Business E-Mail: hamid@soe.ucsc.edu.

SADLER, DAVID G(ARY), manufacturing executive; b. Iowa City, Mar. 14, 1939; s. Edward Anthony and Elsie June (Sherman) S.; m. Karen Sadler; children: Michael Robert, Katherine Louise. Student, St. Ambrose Coll., 1957—59; BS in Indsl. Adminstrn. and Prodn., Kent State U., 1961. Various mgmt. positions Ford Motor Co., Lorain, Ohio, 1962—67, Sperry-New Holland, Lebanon, Ohio, 1967—71; mgr. mfg. Allis Chalmer, Springfield, Ill., 1971—72; dir. mfg. Purolator, Inc., Fayetteville, NC, 1972—73; v.p. mfg. farm equipment and ops. truck divsn. White Motor Co., Eastlake, Ohio and Chgo., 1973—78; corp. v.p. mfg. Massey Ferguson Ltd., Toronto, Ont., Canada, 1978—80, Internat. Harvester, Chgo., 1980—81, sr. v.p. ops. staff, 1981—82, v.p. bus. devel., 1982, pres. diversified group, 1982—83, pres. internat. group, 1983—85; pres. AMI, Inc., Chgo., 1985—86; vice chmn., CEO Savin Corp., Stamford, Conn., 1986, chmn., CEO, 1986—89, also bd. dirs.; pres. Asset Mgmt. Internat., Westport, Conn., 1989—95; chmn., CEO Rowe Internat., Grand Rapids, Mich., 1995—2000, also bd. dirs., 2000—01; CEO Merisel, Inc., El Segundo, Calif., also bd. dirs.; chmn., CEO, bd. dirs. Global Motorsport Group, Inc., Morgan Hill, Calif., 2002—04. Bd. dirs. greater Chgo. Safety Coun., 1981-84,Hellmold Assocs. Opportunity Fund II. Roman Catholic. Home: 751 Bradford Farms Ln NE Grand Rapids MI 49525-3348 Personal E-mail: davidsadler@comcast.net.

SADLER, ROBERT E., JR., bank executive; b. Miss. Grad., Wash. and Lee U., Lexington, Va.; MBA, Emory U. Various nat. and internat. positions Chemical Bank, 1970—83; joined M&T Bank, 1983, pres., 1996—2003, chmn., 2003—05; exec. v.p. M&T Nat. Bank; pres., CEO M&T Bank Corp., 2005—06; CEO M&T, 2005—06; vice-chmn. M&T Bank Corp., 2007—. Mem. bd. Security Mutual Life Ins. Co., NY, Del. N. Companies, Inc., Gibraltar, 2004—. Bd. managers Buffalo Soc. Natural Sciences. Mem.: Fin. Services Roundtable. Office: M&T Bank Corp One M&T Plaza Buffalo NY 14203-2399 *

SADOCK, BENJAMIN JAMES, psychiatrist, educator; b. NYC, Dec. 22, 1933; s. Samuel William and Gertrude S.; m. Virginia Alcott, Oct. 20, 1963; children: James William, Victoria Anne. AB, Union Coll., 1955; MD, N.Y. Med. Coll., 1959. Rotating intern Albany (N.Y.) Hosp., 1959-60; resident Bellevue Psychiat. Hosp., NYC, 1960-63; instr. psychiatry Southwestern Med. Sch., Dallas, 1964-65, N.Y. Med. Coll., NYC, 1965-67, asst. prof., 1967-71, assoc. prof., 1972-74, prof., 1975-80, dir. student health psychiatry, 1980—; prof. psychiatry NYU Sch Medicine, 1981-99, Menas S. prof. psychiatry, 2000—, vice chmn. dept. psychiatry, 1984—, faculty scholar, 2000—. Attending physician Lenox Hill Hosp.; attending psychiatrist Tisch Univ. Hosp. of NYU Med. Ctr., Bellevue Hosp.; cons. psychiatrist Franklin Delano Roosevelt VA Hosp., 1970-78, U.S. Dept. State, 1980-81, P.R. Inst. Psychiatry, 1976-80; examiner Am. Bd. Psychiatry and Neurology, 1970-80; mem. conf. on recert. Am. Bd. Med. Spltys.-Am. Psychiat. Assn., 1974; mem. Commn. on Continuing Edn. in Psychiatry, NIMH-Am. Psychiat. Assn., 1974-75. Co-author: Comprehensive Group Psychotherapy, 1971, 3d edit., 1993, The Sexual Experience, 1976, Pocket Handbook of Clinical Psychiatry, 1991, Comprehensive Glossary of Psychiatry and Psychology, 1991, Pocket Handbook of Drug Treatment in Psychiatry, 1992;: 4th edit., 2005, Pocket Handbook of Psychiatric Emergency Medicine, 1993, Pocket Handbook of Primary Care Psychiatry, 1996, Comprehensive Textbook of Psychiatry, 8th edit., 2005, Synopsis of Psychiatry, 10th edit., 2007; contbr. articles to profl. jours., chapters to books. Fellow Am. Psychiat. Assn. (treas. N.Y. County dist. br. 1973-76, mem. conf. on psychiatry and med. edn. 1967), N.Y. Acad. Medicine, A.C.P.; mem. AMA, Med. Soc. County and State N.Y., Am. Group Psychotherapy Assn., World Psychiat. Assn., Psychiat. Soc. N.Y. Med. Coll. (founder, pres. 1975-79), N.Y. Med. Coll. Alumni Assn. (gov. 1965-90), NYU-Bellevue Psychiat. Soc. (pres. 1981—), Alpha Omega Alpha. Achievements include research in psychiatric education, individual and group psychotherapy, sexual disorders. Office: 4 E 89th St New York NY 10128-0636 also: NYU Med Ctr 550 1st Ave New York NY 10016-6402 E-mail: bjs6@nyu.edu.

SADOCK, GEOFFREY JOHNSTON, English professor; b. NYC, Sept. 30, 1942; s. Jules Bertero and Rosabelle Johnston Sadock; m. Karen Nauta, Sept. 4, 1971; 1 child, Katharine Cordelia Johnston Sadock. BA with honors, Bklyn. Coll., NYC, 1964; MA, Tufts U., Medford, Mass., 1966; PhD, Brown U., Providence, 1973. Instr. Fairleigh-Dickinson U., Madison, NJ, 1971—72; prof. Bergen CC, Paramus, NJ, 1972—. Dir. honors program Bergen C.C., Paramus, NJ, 1996—2001. Contbr. articles to profl. jours. Recipient Presdl. Recognition award, SGC, 2004; fellow CCNY Grad. Ctr., NYC, 1991; Mid-Career fellow, Princeton U., 1994. Mem.: ALSC, NAS, NJCEA, KC (3d degree), NEA, Am. Coun. Trustees and Alumni, Internat. Walter Pater Soc., Victorian Soc. Am. Avocations: Victorian architecture and restoration, antique lighting. Home: 67 West Shore Ave Dumont NJ 07628 Office Phone: 201-447-7168. Personal E-mail: geoffreyjsadock@optonline.net. Business E-Mail: gsadock@bergen.edu.

SADOFF, JOAN HANDLEMAN, film producer, social worker; b. Detroit, Feb. 25, 1938; d. Joseph and Sally Handleman; m. Robert Leslie Sadoff, June 21, 1959; children: Debra, David, Julie, Sherry. BS, U. Minn., 1959; MEd, Temple U., 1971, MSW, 1979. Clin. social worker Norristown (Pa.) State Hosp., 1977—78, Bartram HS for Human Svc., Phila., 1978—79, Family Svc. Phila., 1977, Northwestern Inst., Ft. Washington, Pa., 1980—92. Prodr.: (documentaries) Philadelphia, MS-Untold Stories, 1994 (Best Video for Edn., 1995); prodr.: (documentaries) Standing on My Sisters' Shoulders, 2001 (13 awards, appeared in 28 film festivals). Mem. adv. bd. LaSalle U., Phila., 1996—; bd. dirs., co-chmn. forum com. Cheltenham (Pa.) Twp. Adult Sch., 1996—; bd. dirs. Rittenhouse Sq. Com. fundraiser for Phila. Orch., Phila., 2003—, Cmty. Women's Edn. Project, Phila., 2002—, Inst. So. Jewish Life, Jackson, Miss., 2000—, Jewish Joint Distbn. Com., NYC, 2003—. Named Social Worker of Yr., Pa. chpt. NASW, 2005; recipient Gallery of Success award, Temple U., 2004, Alumni Fellow award, Temple U. Sch. Social Adminstrn., 2004, Making a Difference for Women award, Soroptimist, 2005. Home: 441 Wingate Rd Huntingdon Valley PA 19006

SADOFF, ROBERT LESLIE, psychiatrist, educator; b. Mpls., Feb. 8, 1936; s. Max and Rose C. (Karroll) S.; m. Joan A Handleman, June 21, 1959; children: Debra, David, Julie, Sherry. BA, U. Minn., 1956, BS, 1957, MD, 1959; MS, UCLA, 1963. Intern L.A. VA Hosp., 1959—60; resident in psychiatry UCLA, 1960—63; asst. prof. psychiatry Temple U., Phila., 1966—72; clin. prof. U. Pa., Phila., 1972—; pvt. practice Jenkintown, Pa., 1965—. Lectr. law Villanova U., 1972-85. Author: (with Marvin Lewis) Psychic Injuries, 1975, Forensic Psychiatry, 1975, 2d edit., 1988, Legal Issues in the Care of Psychiatric Patients, 1982, Violence and Responsibility, 1988, (with Robert I. Simon) Psychiatric Malpractice, 1992; editor: Psychiatric Clinics of North America, 1984. Bd. dirs. Joseph T. Peters Inst., Phila., 1980-92. Capt. M.C., U.S. Army, 1963-65. Recipient Earl Bond award U. Pa., 1979, VII ann. Nathaniel Winkelman award Phila. Psychiat. Ctr., 1988, Manfred Guttmacher award, 2993, Isaac Ray award, 2006. Fellow: Am. Coll. Legal Medicine, Am. Psychiat. Assn. (Manfred Guttmacher award 1993); mem.: Internat. Acad. Law and Mental Health (Philippe Pinel award 1995), Internat. Soc. for Philos. Enquiry (mentor 1987—), Am. Acad. Psychiatry and Law (pres. 1971—73), Am. Coll. Psychiatrists, Am. Red Magen David for Israel (nat. pres. 1986—2001). Avocation: collecting antique books in law and medicine. Office: The Pavilion Ste 326 261 Old York Rd Jenkintown PA 19046 Office Phone: 215-887-6144. Personal E-mail: bobsadoff@aol.com.

SADOH, GODWIN SIMEON, music educator; b. Lagos, Nigeria, Mar. 28, 1965; arrived in US, 1994; s. Anthony Sadoh and Taiwo Akinsanya. BA in Piano Performance and Composition, Obafemi Awolowo U., Ile-Ife, Nigeria, 1988; MA in Ethnomusicology, U. Pitts., 1998; MusM in Organ Performance, U. Nebr., 2000; MusD in Organ Performance and Composition, La. State U., 2004. Lectr. dept. music Obafemi Awolowo U., Ile-Ife, 1988—94; tchg. asst. U. Pitts., 1994—96; part-time faculty Sch. Music U. Nebr., Lincoln, Nebr., 1998—2000; music faculty Baton Rouge Coll., 2003—06; asst. prof. music LeMoyne-Owen Coll., Memphis, 2006—, dir. Sacred Music Program, 2006—, dir. concert choir, 2006—; prof. music Talladega Coll., Ala., 2007—. Organist, choir dir. Eko Boys' HS, Lagos, 1980—82, St. Stephen's Episc. Ch., Wilkinsburg, Pa., 1996—98; assoc. dir. music ministries First United Meth. Ch., Lincoln, Nebr., 1999—2000; founder and dir. Ile-Ife (Nigeria) Choral Soc., Nigeria, 1990—94; asst. organist Cathedral Ch. Christ, Lagos, Nigeria, 1980—90. Author: (book) Joshua Uzoigwe: Memoirs of a Nigerian Composer-ethnomusicologist, 2007, Intercultural Dimensions in AYO Bankole's Music, 2007; composer: Nigerian Suite No. 1 for Organ Solo (ASCAP PLUS Award, 2004), Impressions from an African Moonlight, The Misfortune of a Wise Tortoise for Organ and Narrator, 2005, Nigerian Suite No. 2 for Organ Solo, 2005, Five African Dances for Solo Ogran, 2007, Kabiyesi Hosana, 2005, Ise Oluwa, 2005, Ose Baba, 2005, Gbo Ohun Awon Angeli, 2005, Akoi Wata Geri, 2005, Keresimesi Odun de, 2005, Five African Marches for Organ Solo, 2006, (songs) Lord Send Your Power, 2006, Ose Jesu, 2006, A Bi Jesu, 2006, Open Your Mouth, 2006, Ope Lo Ye O, 2006, (hymn book) E Korin S'Oluwa (Sing Unto The Lord): Fifty Indigenous Church Hymns from Nigeria, 2005, 25 preludes on Yoruba Ch. Hymns for Organ; contbr. articles to profl. jours. Organist, choirmaster Eko Boys' H.S., Lagos, Nigeria, 1980—82; preacher St. Stephen's Episc. Ch., Wilkinsburg, Pa., 1996—98, Christ Luth. Ch., Lincoln, 1999—2000; vis. preacher Redeeming The Time Ministries Internat., Baton Rouge. Scholar, La. State U., 2000—03, U. Pitts., 1997; Dora Dean Emerson Meml. Music fellowship, Sch. Music, U. Nebr., Lincoln, 1998, Alvin Hatton Organ scholarship, 2000—03. Mem.: ASCAP (See Honor's awards 2004, Plus award 2005, 2006), Musicological Soc. Nigeria, Soc. Ethnomusicology, Am. Guild Organists (scholarship 1998—2000), Organ Hist. Soc., The Hymn Soc., Nat. Assn. Composers, USA, The Coll. Music Soc., Pi Kappa Lambda. Evang. Achievements include first African to earn a doctorate degree in organ performance from any institution in the world. Avocations: cooking, movies, travel. Home Phone: 225-757-0135. Business E-Mail: gsadoh1@lsu.edu.

SADOVE, STEPHEN IRVING, retail executive; b. Washington, July 25, 1951; s. A. Robert and Harriet (Tenenbaum) S.; m. Karin Sadove; children: Stacy, David, Laurie. BA, Hamilton Coll., 1973; MBA, Harvard U., 1975. Asst. product mgr. desserts divsn. Gen. Foods Corp., White Plains, N.Y., 1975-76, assoc. product mgr., 1976-77, product mgr., 1977-80, group product mgr., 1980-82, category mgr., 1982-84, mktg. mgr., 1984-86, bus. unit mgr. meals divsn., 1986-88, v.p., gen. mgr., 1988-89, exec. v.p., gen. mgr. desserts divsn., 1989-91; pres. Clairol, Inc., Stamford, Conn., 1991-96, Bristol-Myers Squibb Beauty Care, Stamford, 1996-97, Bristol-Myers Squibb Beauty Care and Nutritionals, Stamford, 1998—2001; vice-chmn. Saks Inc., NYC, 2002—06, CEO, 2006—07, chmn., CEO, 2007—. Bd. dirs. Saks Inc., Ruby Tuesday Inc. Trustee Hamilton Coll., Hazelden, A Better Chance. Avocations: tennis, golf, reading, arts. Office: Saks Inc 12 E 49th St New York NY 10017 Home: 7 Hickory Pine Ct Purchase NY 10577

SADOW, HARVEY S., healthcare company executive; b. NYC, Oct. 6, 1922; s. Nat. and Frances Donna (Saveth) S.; m. Sylvia June Riber, Dec. 22, 1944 (div. 1966); children: Harvey Jr., Suzanne Gail, Todd Forrest, Gay Summer; m. Jacqueline Lucille Clavel, Jan. 24, 1969 (div. 1993); 1 adopted child, Daniel Jean Marie; m. Mary Morrissey McSwiggan, July 13, 1995. BS, Va. Mil. Inst., Lexington, 1947; MS, U. Kans., 1949; PhD, U. Conn., 1953, DSc (hon.), 2000. Intelligence officer CIA, Washington, 1951-53; assoc. dir. rsch. Lakeside Labs., Inc., Milw., 1953-56; med. rsch. cons. Milw., 1956; dir. clin. rsch. U.S. Vitamin & Pharm. Corp., NYC, 1957-64, v.p. R & D, 1964-68; sr. v.p. scientific affairs USV Pharm./Revlon Corp., NYC, 1969-71; pres., CEO Boehringer Ingelheim, Ltd. (named changed to Boehringer Ingelheim Pharms., Inc. 1984), Ridgefield, Conn., 1971-88, Boehringer Ingelheim Corp., Ridgefield, 1984-88, chmn. bd., 1988-90. Chmn. bd. Roxane Labs., Inc., Columbus, Ohio, 1981-88, Boehringer Ingelheim Animal Health, Inc., St. Joseph, Mo., 1981-88, Henley Co., N.Y.C., 1986-88, U. Conn. Rsch. and Devel. Corp., Storrs, 1984-87; bd. dirs. Anika Therapeutics, Inc., Trega Bioscis., Inc., chmn. 2000-01, Cortex Pharms., Inc., Irvine, Calif., chmn. bd., 1991-99; bd. dirs. Cholestech Corp., Hayward, Calif., chmn. bd. 1992-2000; adv. bd. Salk Inst. Biotechnology-Indsl. Assocs., Inc., La Jolla, 1988-90; chmn. bd. dirs. Acacia Bioscis. Inc., 1996-99, Rosetta Inpharmatics, Inc., 1999-2001.

Co-author: Oral Treatment of Diabetes, 1967; contbr. articles to profl. jours. Bd. dirs. Pharm. Mfrs. Assn., 1983-90; chmn. Pharm. Mfrs. Assn. Found., 1988-90; bd. dirs. Conn. Bd. Higher Edn., Hartford, 1977-83, Govs. Tech. Adv. Bd., Hartford, 1984-87; mem. Conn. Commn. on Bus. Opportunity, Def. Diversification and Indsl. Policy, 1991-93; mem. bd. visitors Va. Mil. Inst., Lexington, 1987—, pres. bd., 1991-95; chmn. bd. Conn. Law Enforcement Found., Hartford, 1981-86, 92-97, U. Conn. Found., Storrs, 1984-87; chmn., pres.' coun. Am. Lung Assn., N.Y.C., 1986-87, York Sch., Monterey, Calif., 1988-89; trustee Conn. Coll., Groton, 1991-96, Aldrich Mus. Contemporary Art, Ridgefield, Conn., 1991-98. Capt. US Army, 1943—46. Decorated Disting. Svc. Cross, Fed. Republic of Germany, 1987; recipient Univ. medal U. Conn., 1987, Citizen of Yr. Conn. Chief of Police Assn., 1988, Recognition award Nat. Hypertension Assn., 1990, Humanitarian award Am. Lung Assn. Conn., 1993, Disting. Svc. award Conn. Innovations, Inc., 1996, Va. Mil. Inst. Found., 1998. Mem. Am. Soc. for Clin. Pharmacology and Therapeutics, Am. Fedn. for Clin. Rsch., Am. Diabetes Assn., Danbury C. of C. (Abraham Ribicoff Community Svc. award City of Danbury 1987, bd. dirs. 1978-81), Union League (N.Y.C.), Masons, Sigma Xi, Sigma Pi Sigma, Phi Lambda Upsilon. Avocations: art collecting, photography, music, writing. Personal E-mail: hssadow@aol.com.

SADOWAY, DONALD ROBERT, materials science educator; b. Toronto, Mar. 7, 1950; s. Donald Anthony and Irene Mary (Romanko) S.; m. Sandra Lynn Mary Babij, Sept. 8, 1973 (div. Sept. 1996); children: Steven, Laryssa, Andrew; m. Anne Marie Mayes, Jan. 4, 1997 (div. June 2003); m. Rebecca Rosenberg, Dec. 19, 2004. BASc, U. Toronto, 1972, MASc, 1973, PhD, 1977. Cert. in chem. metallurgy. Asst. prof. materials engring. MIT, Cambridge, 1978-82, assoc. prof., 1982-92, prof. materials chemistry, 1992—, MacVicar faculty fellow, 1995—2005, John F. Elliott prof. of chem. metallurgy, 1999—. Assoc. editor Jour. Materials Rsch., 1995-2005; contbr. over 125 articles on electro and phys. chemistry to profl. jours.; patentee in field, U.S., Can., and Europe. Recipient Grad. Student Coun. Tchg. award MIT, 1982, 84, 87, 88, 93, Prof. T.B. King Meml. award dept. materials sci. and engring. undergrad. students MIT, 1986, Bose award, 1997; NATO postdoctoral fellow Nat. Rsch. Coun. Can., 1977, AT&T Faculty fellow in indsl. ecology, 1993-95. Mem. AAAS, Minerals, Metals and Materials Soc., Electrochem. Soc., Internat. Soc. Electrochemistry, Materials Rsch. Soc., Norwegian Acad. Tech. Sci. (elected). Office: MIT 77 Massachusetts Ave #8-203 Cambridge MA 02139-4307 Home Phone: 617-393-1844; Office Phone: 617-253-3487. Business E-Mail: dsadoway@mit.edu.

SADOWSKI, CAROL JOHNSON, artist; b. Chgo., Mar. 20, 1929; d. Carl Valdamar Johnson and Elizabeth Hilma (Booth) Johnson Chellberg; m. Edmund Sadowski, July 9, 1949; children: Lynn Carol Mahoney, Christie Sadowski Cortez. AAS, Wright Coll., Ill., 1949. Tchr. art Malverne H.S., NY, 1968-69; artist Valley Stream, NY, 1968-76, Hollywood, Fla., 1976—. Guest spkr. Mus. Art, Ft. Lauderdale, Fla., 1991; Libr. League, Oakland Park, 1985; Boca Raton, Fla. Mus., others; TV appearances on WCGB, Gainesville; WSVN, Miami; Storer and Hollywood Cable; Artist Guild, Boca Raton Mus.; Broward C.C., Hollywood, Fla. One woman shows include Mus. Fla. History, Tallahassee, 1984-85, 87; Hist. Mus. South Fla., Miami, 1986; Thomas Ctr. Arts, Gainesville, Fla., 1985, 87; Elliott Mus., Stuart, Fla., 1987; Hemingway Mus. and Home, Key West, Fla., 1986; I.G.F.A. Fishing Hall of Fame Mus., Dania, Fla., 1999, Alliance Francaise de Miami, 1995; commd. painting St. Agustin Antigua Found., St. Augustine, Fla., 1985, Atlantic Bank, Ft. Lauderdale, Fla., Bonnet House Fla. Trust, Ft. Lauderdale, Hollywood Art & Culture Ctr., Hemingway Mus., San Francisco de Paula, Presdl. Palace, Havana, Tropical Art Gallery, Naples, Fla., 1981-83, Tequesta (Fla.) Art Gallery, 1985-89, Gingerbread Square Gallery, Key West, 1990—, Wally Findlay Galleries, Inc., Palm Beach and N.Y.C., DeBruyne Fine Arts Gallery, Naples, 1998—, Patricia Cloutier Gallery, Tequesta, Fla., 1992-. Mem. Ft. Lauderdale Mus. Art; Hollywood Art and Culture Ctr. Recipient Hemingway medal, Ernest Hemingway Mus., Cuba, 1990; appreciation award City of Hollywood; Chgo. Art Inst. scholar; Salmagundi Club N.Y. scholar. Mem. Internat. Platform Assn., Broward Art Guild, Fla. Hist. Assn., Ernest Hemingway Soc., Chopin Found., Am. Inst. for Polish Culture, Alliance Francaise de Miami, Women in the Arts Nat. Mus. (charter mem.), Nat. Women's History Mus. (charter mem.). Avocations: travel, bicycling, swimming, reading. Home and Office: 1480 Sheridan St Apt B 17 Hollywood FL 33020-2295 Home Phone: 954-925-7482. Personal E-mail: esadowski@msn.com. *I try to do my best at what I love to do; not for money or fame, but for self satisfaction.*

SADOWSKI, CHESTER PHILIP, JR., real estate executive; b. Pensacola, Fla., May 28, 1946; s. Chester P. and Florence Edna (Perry)S.; m. Jerriann Gibson Steller, Oct. 4, 1975; children: Julie K., Charles P., Robert T., David A. BSBA, U. Fla., 1968. CPA, Fla. Sr. auditor Arthur Andersen & Co., Tampa, Fla., 1969-74, U.S. Home Corp., Clearwater, Fla. and Houston, 1974-77, audit mgr., 1977-81, sr. audit mgr., 1981-82, audit dir., 1982-85, controller, 1985-87, sr. v.p., controller, chief acctg. officer, 1987—2003; cons., 2003—. Mem.: AICPA (real estate com. N.Y.C. 1986—89), Inst. Mgmt. Accts., Fla. Inst. CPA's. Office: 6445 Sweet Gum St Katy TX 77493 Office Phone: 713-818-3486.

SADOWSKI, PETER T., lawyer; b. Warsaw, Oct. 30, 1954; came to U.S., 1968; s. Fryderyk and Maria (Jaklinska) S.; m. Denise A. Decker, Oct. 13, 1979; children: Katherine, Rachel. BA, St. Louis U., 1976; JD, St. Louis U. Law Sch., 1979. Asst. atty. gen. Mo. Atty. Gen.'s Office, Jefferson City, 1979-81; ptnr. The Stolar Partnership, St. Louis, 1981-96; shareholder Goldberg, Katz, Sadowski & Croft, St. Louis, 1996—99; exec. v.p., gen. counsel Fidelity Nat. Fin. Inc., Jacksonville, Fla., 1999—. Chmn. bd. dirs., greater needs com. YMCA, St. Louis, 1995—. Office: Fidelity National Financial 601 Riverside Ave Jacksonville FL 32204 Office Phone: 888-934-3354. *

SADOWSKI, RAYMOND, electronics executive; married. BS in Acctg., Hunter Coll., NY, 1976. Acct. F. Schumacher; corp. acctg. supr. Avnet, Inc., 1978, acctg. mgr., asst. contr., contr., 1986, v.p., 1987—92, sr. v.p., 1992—, CFO, 1993—, asst. sec. Office: Avnet Inc 2211 S 47th St Phoenix AZ 85034-6403 Office Phone: 480-643-2000. Office Fax: 480-643-7370. *

SADOWSKY, MICHAEL J., microbiologist, educator; married; 2 children. BS, U. Wis., Madison, 1977; MS in Biology/Microbiology, U. Wis., Oshkosh; PhD in Microbiology, U. Hawaii, 1983. Rschr. McGill U., 1983—85; molecular biologist Allied Corp.; biologist Nitrogen Fixation and Soybean Genetics Lab. USDA-ARS, Beltsville, Md.; asst. prof. Dept. Soil Sci. and Microbiology U. Minn., St. Paul, 1989, prof. Dept. Soil, Water, and Climate and Biotechnology Inst., dir. grad. studies Microbial Engring. Program, U. McKnight Disting. prof., 2005—. Co-creator Agricultural Microbe Genomes Confs. Editor: (jour.) Applied and Environ. Microbiology; assoc. editor Symbiosis and Microbes and the Environment; contbr. articles to profl. jours. NSF Grant, 2003. Fellow: Am. Acad. Microbiology; mem.: Am. Soc. Microbiology (Region V Coord. and Branch Archivist). Avocations: woodworking, amateur radio electronics. Office: U Minn 439 Borlaug Hall 1991 Upper Buford Cir Saint Paul MN 55108 Office Phone: 612-625-1244. Office Fax: 612-625-2208. E-mail: sadowsky@soils.umn.edu.

SADR, ALI, neurosurgeon; BS, Tufts U., Medford, Mass., 1990; MD, Boston U. Sch. Medicine, 1996. Intern Mt. Sinai Med. Ctr., NY, 1996—97; resident W.Va. U. Hosps., Morgantown, W.Va., 1997—2002; asst. prof. neurosurgery SUNY, Downstate Med. Ctr., Brooklyn, 2003—. Mem.: Congress Neurol. Surgeons, Am. Assn. Neurol. Surgeons, Alpha Omega Alpha. Office: SUNY Downstate Med Ctr 450 Clarkson Ave Brooklyn NY 11203 Office Phone: 718-270-2111.

SADRAIE, HAMID REZA, civil engineer, researcher; b. Tehran, Iran, Jan. 28, 1975; arrived in US, 2000; s. Abbas Sadraie and Seddigheh Ghassemieh. BS, U. Tehran, Iran, 1996, MS, 1998; PhD, U. Minn., Mpls., 2006. Rsch. asst. U. Minn., Mpls., 2002—06; transp. engr. Caltrans, LA, 2006—. Contbr. articles to profl. jours. Mem.: Sigma Xi. Home: 11030 Hartsook St 127 North Hollywood CA 91601 Office: Caltrans 100 South Main St MS-16 Los Angeles CA 90012 Home Phone: 612-205-2806; Office Phone: 213-897-9605. Business E-Mail: sadra002@umn.edu.

SADRI, AHMAD, sociologist, educator; b. Tehran, Iran, Nov. 17, 1953; PhD, New Sch. Social Rsch., NYC, 1988. Prof. sociology Lake Forest Coll., Ill., 1988—. Author: Max Weber's Sociology of Intellectuals (Acad. Book of the Yr. Choice Mag., 1993); co-translator: Reason, Freedom and Democracy in Islam; translator: (novels) Saddam City. Office: Lake Forest Coll 555 N Sheridan Rd Lake Forest IL 60045 Home Phone: 847-735-5251; Office Phone: 847-735-5251. Business E-Mail: sadri@lakeforest.edu.

SADRUDIN, MOE, humanitarian organization executive; b. Hyderabad, India, Mar. 3, 1943; arrived in U.S., 1964; m. Azmath Qureshi, 1964; 3 children. BSME, Osmania U., Hyderabad, 1964; MS in Indsl. Engring., NYU, 1966; IE, MBA, Columbia U., 1970. Cons. project engr. Ford, Bacon & Davis, NYC, 1966; staff indsl. engr. J.C. Penney, NYC, 1966-68; sr. cons. Drake, Sheahan, Stewart & Dougall, NYC, 1968-70, Beech-Nut Inc. subs. Squibb Corp., NYC, 1970-72; founder, pres. Azmath Constrn. Co., Englewood, NJ, 1972-77; crude oil cons., fgn. govt. rep.; 1977—88; pres. A-One Petroleum Co., Fullerton, Calif., 1985—95; chmn., CEO, Universal Humanitarian Found., Fullerton, 1989—. Govt. advisor Puerto Rico, 1980-82, Dominica, 1983-84, St. Vincent, 1981-82, Kenya, 1983-84, Belize 1984-85, Costa Rica 1983-86, Paraguay 1984-87. Chmn. Universal Humanitarian Found., 1989—; active LA World Affairs Coun. Mem.: Internat. Platform Assn. Address: Universal Humanitarian Found 2656 Camino Del Sol Fullerton CA 92833-4806 Office Phone: 714-526-0633. Personal E-mail: unihumfound@aol.com. *Personal philosophy: I learned from a young age that acquisition of knowledge, developing honesty and integrity and service to humanity in the form of charity, love and struggle to help the poor and needy, are the main foundation stones of a successful life. I believe that acquisition of wealth is only a means to an end and not an end in itself. With accumulation of wealth, one has to care for the underprivileged and try to improve their lot.*

SADYKOVA, VERA PHILIPPOVNA, librarian, educator; b. Dneprostroy, Zaporozhie, Ukraine, Mar. 4, 1933; arrived in Kazakhstan, 1947; d. Yabtchenko and (Phesik) Philipp; m. Albert Sadykov, May, 13, 1956; children: Aleksey, Gennady. Grad., Kazakh State U., Alma-Ata, 1957, Inst. Culture, Leningrad, Russia, 1966. Cert. libr., philologist. Libr. Sci. and Tech. Libr. Kazakhstan, Almaty, 1960-62, asst. dir., 1964-65, dir., 1965-88, chief libr., 1988-94, mgr. sci.-methodical dept., 1962-64, 94—, instr. advanced courses, 1962—, head sci. rsch. sector, 1998. Instr. advanced courses Kazakh State Inst. Sci. and Tech. Info., Almaty, 1962—, Sci. and Tech. Libr. Ctr. Profl. Devel., Kazakhstan, Kirgizia, Tadzhikistan, Uzbekistan, 2000-. Author brochures; mem. editl. bd. Nautchnie i Technitcheskie Biblioteki, 1990-91, New Jour. Libr. World, 2002-; contbr. articles to profl. jours. Mem. presidium Trade Unions Com. of State Instns. Ofcls., Almaty, 1971-86. Recipient medals and hon. degree Honoured Worker of Kazakh Soviet Socialist Republic, Presidium of Supreme Soviet USSR, 1970, 83, 84, bronze medals Exhbn. Econ. Achievements of USSR, 1969, 74, 81. Avocations: collecting books, gardening. Office: Sci & Tech Libr Kazakhstan S Mukanov 223B 050026 Almaty Kazakhstan Office Phone: 68-28-70. E-mail: rntbb@nursat.kz, orb@os.kz.

SAEED, FAIZA J., lawyer; BA with highest distinction, U. Calif., Berkeley, 1987; JD magna cum laude, Harvard Law Sch., 1991. Bar: NY 1992, Calif. 1993, DC 1993. Assoc. Cravath, Swaine & Moore LLP, 1991—98, ptnr., corp., 1999—. Named a Young Global Leader, World Econ. Forum, 2006; named one of 45 Under Forty-Five, Am. Lawyer, 2003, Top 40 Lawyers Under 40, Nat. Law. Jour., 2005. Mem.: Harvard Law Sch. Vis. Com., Calif. State Bar Assn., Internat. Bar Assn., ABA, NY State Bar Assn., Assn. Bar City of NY, Phi Beta Kappa. Office: Cravath Swaine & Moore LLP Worldwide Plaza 825 Eighth Ave New York NY 10019-7475 Office Phone: 212-474-1454. Office Fax: 212-474-3700. Business E-Mail: fsaeed@cravath.com.

SAEGER, JAMES SCHOFIELD, history professor, writer; b. Columbus, Ohio, Aug. 19, 1938; s. James Louttit and Elizabeth (Schofield) Saeger; divorced; children: James P., Edwin S. BA, Ohio State U., 1960, MA, 1963, PhD, 1969. V.p., dealer Jim Saeger Rambler Co., Columbus, Ohio, 1960—62; instr. history NC State U., Raleigh, 1965—67; from instr. to assoc. prof. history Lehigh U., Bethlehem, Pa., 1967—85, prof. history, 1985—. Co-dir. Gipson Inst. for 18th Century Studies, Bethlehem, 1979—91. Author: The Chaco Mission Frontier, 2000, Francisco Solano Lopez and the Ruination of Paraguay, 2007. Fellow, Orgn. Am. States, Paraguay, 1973—74, Fulbright Commn., 1981, NEH, 1988. Mem.: Conf. on Latin Am. History (com. mem. 0991—2005), Soc. Mil. History, Am. Hist. Assn. Avocations: golf, fishing, hiking, bicycling. Home: 239 Uncas St Bethlehem PA 18018 Office: Dept History Maginnes Hall 9 W Packer Ave Bethlehem PA 18015 Office Phone: 610-758-3366.

SAEGER, REBECCA, advertising executive; B in Psychology and Polit. Sci., Muhlenberg Coll., 1976; MBA, U. Pa., 1980. Various positions including sr. v.p., group dir. for Lever Bros. and Am. Express Ogilvy & Mather, NY, 1980—91; sr. v.p., group mgmt. supr., dir. account mgmt. Foote, Cone & Belding, San Francisco, 1991—97; exec. v.p. advt. and brand mktg. svcs. Visa USA, 1997—2001; exec. v.p. brand mgmt. and mktg. comm. Charles Schwab Corp., San Francisco, 2004—06, exec. v.p., chief mktg. officer, 2006—. Mem. exec. mgmt. com. Visa USA. Mem. mktg. com. San Francisco Symphony; mem. adv. bd. World Congress Sports. Mem.: Assn. Nat. Advertisers (bd. dirs.). Office: The Charles Schwab Corp 101 Montgomery St San Francisco CA 94104 *

SAEKS, ALLEN IRVING, lawyer; b. Bemidji, Minn., July 14, 1932; m. Linda J. Levin; 1 child, Adam Charles. BS in Law, U. Minn., 1954, JD, 1956. Bar: Minn. 1956, U.S. Dist. Ct. Minn. 1956, U.S. Ct. Appeals (8th cir.) 1957, U.S. Ct. Appeals (fed. cir.) 1959, U.S. Supreme Ct. 1959, U.S. Ct. Appeals (11th cir.) 1997; cert. civil trial specialist. Asst. U.S. atty. Dept. Justice, St. Paul, 1956-57; assoc. Leonard St. and Deinard, Mpls., 1960-63, ptnr., 1964—. Adj. prof. law U. Minn. Law Sch., 1960-65; chmn. lawyer trust acct. bd., Interest on Lawyers Trust Accounts, 1984-87; nat. bd. dirs. Equal Justice Works, Washington, 2002-05. Pres. Jewish Cmty. Rels. Coun of Minn. and the Dakotas, 1994—96; bd. dirs. Citizens League, Mpls., 1984—87, chmn. property tax com., 1986—87. 1st lt. JAGC US Army, 1957—60. Named one of Best Lawyers Am., 2006; recipient City of Mpls. award, 1996, Lifetime Commitment award, Cardozo Soc., 2001. Fellow Am. Bar Found. (life); mem. ABA (commn. on interest on lawyers trust accts. 1990-93), Minn. State Bar Assn. (ethics task force, 2003, Pres. award 2003), Fund for the Legal Aid Soc. (chmn. 1997-98, Law Day Testimonial award 1996), Hennepin County Bar Assn. (pres. 1983-84), Order of Coif, Phi Delta Phi. Office: Leonard St and Deinard 150 S 5th St Ste 2300 Minneapolis MN 55402-4238 Office Phone: 612-335-1548. Business E-Mail: ais1548@leonard.com.

SAEKS, RICHARD EPHRAIM, engineering executive; b. Chgo., Nov. 30, 1941; s. Morris G. and Elsie E. S. BS, Northwestern U., 1964; MS, Colo. State U., 1965; PhD, Cornell U., 1967. Registered profl. engr., Tex. Elec. engr. Warwick Mfg. Co., Niles, Ill., 1961-63; asst. prof. dept. elec. engring. U. Notre Dame, 1967-71, assoc. prof., 1971-73; assoc. prof. depts. elec. engring., math. Tex. Tech U., Lubbock, 1973-77, prof., 1977-79, Paul Whitfield Horn prof. elec. engring., math. computer sci, 1979-83; prof., chmn. elec. engring. Ariz. State U., 1983-88; dean Armour Coll. Engring. Ill. Inst. Tech., 1988-91, Motorola prof., 1991-92; v.p. engring. Accurate Automation Corp., 1992-2000, chief tech. officer, 2000—. Cons. Research Triangle Inst., 1978-80, Marcel Dekker Inc., 1978-80. Author: Generalized Networks, 1972, Resolution Space Operators and Systems, 1973, Interconnected Dynamical Systems, 1981, System Theory: A Hilbert Space Approach, 1982, Shock Structure Analysis and Aerodynamics in a Weakly Ionized Gas, 2006; contbr. articles to profl. jours.; Editor: Large-Scale Dynamical Systems, 1976, Rational Fault Analysis, 1977, The World of Large Scale Systems, 1982. Recipient Disting. Faculty Research award Tex. Tech U., 1978, INC 500 award, 1994, SBA Rolnd Tibbets award, 1996, Joeseph G. Wohl Outstanding Career award, IEEE Systems, Man, and Cybernetics Society, 2004 Fellow: AIAA, IEEE (life), IEEE Systems Men and Cybernetics Soc. (pres. 1998—99, Joseph G. Wohl Outstanding Career award 2004). Achievements include patents in field. Business E-Mail: richard@saeks.org.

SAENGER, BRUCE WALTER, consulting firm executive; b. Hanover, NH, July 16, 1943; s. Werner Hugo and Natalie Bertha (Brown) S.; m. Cheryl Jeanne Bouchard, Nov. 6, 1976. BA, Pa. State U., 1969; postgrad., Am. Coll., Bryn Mawr, Pa., 1979, Coll. Fin. Planning, Denver, 1980. CPCU; ChFC; CLU; CFP; RHU; REBC; CIC. Agt. Nationwide Ins., Lansdale, Pa., 1969-73, dist. sales mgr. Springfield, Mass., 1973-75, Am. Mut., Braintree, Mass., 1975-77; dir. mktg. Bankers LIfe & Casualty, Chgo., 1977-78; pres., founder Sales Tng. Techniques, Southboro, Mass., 1979-81, The Saenger Orgn., Medway, Mass., 1981—2004; owner, pres. Saenger Consulting Group, Waterville Vallet, NH, 2004—. Mem. faculty Notre Dame U., South Bend, Ind., 1977-78, Northeastern U., Boston, 1984-92; mem. RHU Commn., Washington, 1979-81; dir. Northeastern U. Inst. Inst., Boston, 1985-93; mem. Mass. Ins. Dept. Continuing Edn. Rev. Com., 1985—; program dir. U. Del. Ins. Program, 1989-91; acad. cons. Mass. Soc. Lic. Ins. Advisers, 1995—; cons. in field. Author: Series 6 Study Book, 1983, Series 22 Study Book, 1984, Tax Shelter Market Guide, 1985, Marketing Mutual Funds, 1985, also articles. Bd. dirs. Lansdale Gen. Hosp., 1971-73, New Directions Theater Co., 1988-91, Penn State U. Alumni Assn., 2005-, Waterville Valley Resort Assn., 2006-; mem. Medway Bus. Coun., 1989-94, pres., 1990-92; chmn. Penn State U. Friends of Abington/Ogontz ROTC, 2004-; town moderator Waterville Valley, NH, 2006-. With U.S. Army, 1960-66. Recipient Ednl. Achievement award Profl. Ins. Agts. Assn., 1983, Alumni Achievement award Pa. State Alumni Assn., 2005; named Outstanding Fin. Exec. of Yr., Fin. Mgmt. Assn., 1993. Fellow Soc. CLUs (ednl. adv., bd. dirs. 1987-91), Soc. CPCUs (ednl. adv.), Life Mgmt. Inst. (Outstanding Lectr. award 1984); mem. Internat. Assn. Fin. Planners (ednl. adv., bd. dirs. 1986-92, pres. 1989-91), Internat. Assn. for Fin. Planning (chmn. bd. dirs. 1990-92), Soc. Cert. Ins. Counselors, Life Underwriters Assn., Inst. CFP (v.p. edn., bd. dirs. 1990-91), Mass. Assn. Health Underwriters (pres. 1992-93, Boston Bus. Ethics award 2001), Pa. State U. Alumni Soc. (bd. dirs. 2005—). Republican. Roman Catholic. Avocations: skiing, golf. Home: 1 Village Rd PO Box 304 Waterville Valley NH 03215-1018 Office: Saenger Consulting Group 6 Village Rd PO Box 350 Waterville Valley NH 03215 Office Phone: 603-236-3300. Business E-Mail: bsaenger@saengerconsulting.com.

SAENZ, CECILIA SONIA, education educator; d. Justo Valdez and Ruth Martinez Molina; m. Lloyd Neal Smith, Sept. 14, 1984; 1 child, Michael Robert. BS, Sam Houston U., 1964; MEd, U. Houston, 1975; student, Tex. So. U., 1989; PhD Capella U., 2005—. Adminstrv. cert. 1977, supt. cert. Ariz., Tex., 2003. Second grade tchr. Houston I.S.D., 1972—78, prin., 1978—98, dir. dist. 13, 1989—91; asst. supt. Phoenix Elem. Sch. Dist. 1, Phoenix, 1998—2003; master tchr. U. Houston, 1974—78; prof. online U. Phoenix, 2004—. Prin. ACET (Assn. Compensating Edn.) Conf., Houston, 1995—98; state mem. Tex. Sch. Improvement Initiative Tex. Edn. Agy., 1997—99; asst. supt. Proposition 301 P.E.S.D., Phoenix Elem., Phoenix, 2002—03; dir./cons. Montessori Magnet Program Com., Phoenix, 2003; spkr. and presenter in field. Lobbyist Phoenix Elem., 2002—03, advocate/legis., 2003, spirit program coord., 2003. Named Helping Schs. Outstanding Prin., Tex. Soc. Cert. Pub. Accountants, 1996, Houston Prin. of Yr., Cert. Pub. A Schs., 1996; recipient Tex. Prin. of Yr., 1996, Best Prin. in Tex. award, 1997, Hispanic Prin. of Yr., Houston Independetn Sch. Dist., 1996, Tex. Assn. Hispanic Adminstrv. Exemplary Educator award, Houston Independent Sch. Dist., 1998, Edn. Recognition award, Tex. Assn. Hispanic Adminstrs., 1998, Spirit 2006 award, City of Phoenix, 2004. Mem.: Tex. Retirement System, Ariz. Sch. Adminstr., Am. Assn. U. Women. Democrat. Roman Catholic. Achievements include created, developed, structured Montessori Program for public schools; implemented school improvement process "Eight Steps" as trainer; initiated school reform process "Success for All" Alignment. Avocations: hiking, camping, gardening, travel, tree triming. Office Fax: 623-572-4219. Personal E-mail: soniamaui@aol.com.

SAENZ, MICHAEL, college president; b. Laredo, Tex., Oct. 25, 1925; s. C.A. and Pola R. Saenz; m. Nancy Elizabeth King; children: Michael King, Cynthia Elizabeth. BS in Acctg. with honors, Tex. Christian U., 1949, MEd, 1952; PhD in Econs., U. Pa., 1961. Dep. collector IRS, Ft. Worth, Dallas, 1949-52; adminstr. United Christian Missionary Soc., Bayamon, PR, 1954-57, 59-65, exec. sec. Indpls., 1965-71; acad. dean Laredo (Tex.) Jr. Coll., 1971-74; pres. N.W. campus Tarrant County Coll., Fort Worth, Tex., 1975—. Founder Nat. Comm. Coll. Hispanic Coun., 1985, bd. dirs., 1985—, pres., 1989-91; founder, co-dir. Nat. Hispanic Leadership Inst., 1989—; trustee Tex. Christian U., Brite Div. Sch., 1973-2001. Bd. dirs. Civic Ballet of Laredo, Ft. Worth chpt. NCCJ, Juliette Fowler Homes, Dallas; chmn. Aztec dist., dir. Gulf Coast coun. Boy Scouts Am., 1971-75; gov. Career Devel. Ctr., Arlington, Tex.; chmn. Laredo's Bicentennial Com., 1973-76; trustee, bd. dirs. United Way Ft. Worth, 1979-88; mem., vice moderator gen. bd. Christian Ch. (Disciples of Christ), 1991-93. Mem. Am. Assn. Cmty. Colls. (bd. dirs. 1991-94), Commn. Internat. Edn. Am. Coun. Edn., Tex. Jr. Coll. Tchrs. Assn., Tex. Assn. Jr. Coll. Instructional Adminstrs., Am. Acad. Polit. and Social Scis., Urban Ministries in Higher Edn., Civic Music Assn. Laredo, Rotary. Home: 4427 Tamworth Rd Fort Worth TX 76116-8127 Office: Tarrant County Coll NW Capmus 4801 Marine Pkwy Fort Worth TX 76179 E-mail: michael.saenz@teed.edu.

SAENZ, NANCY ELIZABETH KING, civic worker; b. Greenville, Tex., Jan. 28, 1930; d. Henry M. and Vallie (Wheatley) King; m. Michael Saenz, July 28, 1950; children: Michael King, Cynthia Elizabeth. Saenz Ward. AB with honors, Tex. Christian U., 1950, BS magna cum laude, 1952; postgrad. Hartford Sem. Found., 1952-53, Escuela de Idiomas, 1953, Lexington Theol. Sem., 1953. Missionary, United Christian Missionary Soc., Indpls., serving in PR, 1954-65; bd. dirs. Adminstrv. Bd. Christian Chs., PR, 1950-65; chmn. dept. Christian edn. Christian Chs., PR, 1962-64, sec., 1959-61, state dir., 1963; dept. Christian edn. PR Coun. Chs., 1959-64, sec., 1959-60; sec. and counsellor State Christian Women Fellowship of Christian Chs., PR, 1955-57, 59-63, dist. chmn. Ind. and Tex., 1968-75, adminstrv. com. Tex., 1971-74; mem. Internat. Christian Women's Fellowship Quadrennial Coms., 1974-82; mem. gen. bd. Christian Ch. in U.S. and Can., 1974-78, 80; pres. Christian Ch. in SW, 1976-78. Sec., Disciples of Christ Acad. PTA, Bayamon, PR, 1962-63; mem. state com. Home for Aged, United Ch. Women, PR, 1963; women's com. Ind. State Symphony Soc., 1967—; women's com. Internat. Christian U. Japan, 1962-64, 65-72, pres. Indpls. chpt. 1967-68; mem. vocational-tech. adv.

council Laredo Ind. Sch. Dist., 1971—; vol. coordinator Am. Bible Soc., 1971—; dir. Vol. Center Met. Tarrant County, 1982-93. Bd. dirs. Greater Indpls. Fedn. Chs., 1970-71; bd. dirs. Planned Parenthood Assn. Webb County, 1972-74, pres.-elect, 1974-75; bd. dirs. Civic Ballet Laredo, 1972-75; mem. adv. com. Tarrant County Vol. Center, 1976-81, chmn., 1980; mem. Mercy Hosp. Aux., 1973-75, pres.-elect, 1974-75; interim dir. Ft. Worth Council Chs., 1979, pres., 1981; pres. Ch. Women United, Fort Worth, 1980; bd. dirs. ch. fin. council Christian Ch. (Disciples of Christ) US and Can., 1979-83. Mem. Irvington Union of Clubs (exec. bd. 1966—, 2d v.p. 1968-70), Young Mothers Club Irvington (v.p. 1965, pres. 1967), Marion County Guardian Home Guild (pres. 1968-70), Art Assn. Indpls., Art League, Civic Music Laredo, AAUW, Laredo and Fort Worth Pan Am. Roundtable, Thistle Hill, Docent Guild, Tex., Tex. Christian U., Tex. Christian U. Alumni Assn. (life), Ft. Worth Women's Club, Assn. Vol. Ctrs. (pres. 1990-91), Alpha Chi, Phi Sigma Iota. Clubs: Rotary Anns, Women's College (R.P.); Irvington Women's Laredo Tuesday Music and Lit. (pres. 1973-74), Women's City. Author: Winds of Change, 1968; Step by Step, 1984. Home: 4427 Tamworth Rd Fort Worth TX 76116-8127

SAENZ, SILVIA PATRICIA, special education educator; b. Chihuahua, Mexico, Mar. 8, 1980; arrived in U.S., 1999; d. Alvaro Saenz and Patricia Wong De Saenz. BA, U. Tex., El Paso, 2003. Cert. classroom tchr., spl. edn. grades earlychildhood-12th Tex., 2005, bilingual generalist, generalist early childhood-4th Tex. Rsch. asst. U. Tex., El Paso, 2002—04; spl. edn. tchr. El Paso Ind. Sch. Dist., 2004—. Contbr. articles to profl. jours. Recipient Outstanding Rsch. award, U. Tex. El Paso, 2003, Oustanding Student Achievement award, 2004; Benito Juarez scholar, Marguerite Loya Pearson Scholarship Fund for the Arts, 2000—01, EPCF-Marguerite Pearson scholar, 2001—03. Mem.: Golden Key (life), Psi Chi (life). Roman Catholic. Avocation: photography. Home Phone: 915-256-3140; Office Phone: 915-231-2820. Personal E-mail: pattysanz@yahoo.com.

SAFADI, M. OUSSAMA, engineering educator; arrived in U.S., 1978; BSE, Calif. State U. Northridge, 1982; MSE, UCLA, 1985, PhD in Civil Engring., 1991. Lectr. UCLA, 1991—95; sr. lectr. U. So. Calif., LA, 1991—. Pres. Applied Math. and Engring. Rsch. Industry of Calif., LA, 1991—. Home: PO Box 24344 Los Angeles CA 90024 Office Phone: 310-288-3431. Business E-Mail: safadi@usc.edu.

SAFAI, BIJAN, physician, investigator; b. Ardestan, Iran, Mar. 26, 1940; came to U.S., 1968; s. Abdol-Khalegh Safai and Kanom-Sadat Sadjaddi; m. Vera Plaskon, Sept. 16, 1978; 1 child: Matthew. MD, Tehran U., Iran, 1965; DSc, U. Gutenburg, Sweden, 1981. Diplomate Am. Bd. Dermatology, Am. Bd. Internal Medicine. Intern Nassau County Med. Ctr., East Meadow, NY, 1968-69; resident N.Y.U. Med. Coll. VA Hosp., NYC, 1969-70; resident in dermatology N.Y.U. Med. Coll., NYC, 1971-73; fellow in immunology Sloan-Kettering Inst. for Cancer & Allied Diseases, NYC, 1973-74; from asst. attending physician to chief dermatology svc. Meml. Hosp., NYC, 1974-93; from assoc. to attending physician in dermatology N.Y. Hosp., NYC, 1980-93; dir. dermatology Westchester County Med. Ctr., Valhalla, NY, 1993—; from asst. prof. to prof. in medicine/dermatology Cornell U. Med. Coll., NYC, 1974-93; prof., chmn. dept. dermatology N.Y. Med. Coll., NYC, 1993—, prof. dept. microbiology and immunology, 1994—. Teaching clin. asst. in dermatology NYU Med. Coll, N.Y.C., 1973-74; adj. mem. Rockefeller U., N.Y.C., 1982-84; rsch. assoc. Sloan-Kettering Inst. for Cancer and Allied Diseases, N.Y.C., 1977-79, asst. mem., 1979-83, assoc. mem., 1983-88; assoc. mem. Memorial Sloan-Kettering Cancer Ctr., N.Y.C., 1983-88, mem. 1988-93; mem. grad. sch. med. scis. N.Y. Med. Coll., Valhalla, 1994—; mem. adv. bd. Skin Cancer Found., 1982—; sec. dermatology sect. N.Y. Acad Medicine, 1988-89, chmn. 1989-90; mem. med. adv. bd. Cancer Rsch Instn., 1997—. Mem. editl. bd. Cancer Investigation, 1984-88, AIDS Rsch. and Human Retroviruses, 1986-90, Jour. of Acquired Immune Deficiency Syndromes, 1988—; contbr. numerous articles on immunodermatology to profl. jours. Mem. AIDS adv. task force, NCI/NIH, 1982-85; mem. AIDS Etiology task force, NCI, 1982-85; mem. ad hoc study sect. for AIDS, NIH, 1982-88; mem. spl. dermatology rev. group, GM2 study sect., NIH, 1990-96; mem. spl. rev. team NCI Intramural Rev., Lab. of Tumor cell Biology, 1987, 92, Medicine br., NCI, 1996; mem. study sect. on HIV, NCI, 1996; mem. spl. rev. group FDA Intramural Rev., 1995. Mem. AMA, Internat. Soc. Tropical Dermatology, Am. Fedn. for Clin. Rsch., Am. Acad. Dermatology (mem. AIDS com. 1989-91, task force on cutaneous oncology 1988-9, mem. adv. coun. 1988-91), Am. Dermatol. Soc. for Allery and Immunology, Soc. for Investigative Dermatology, Med. Soc. of State of N.Y., Med. Soc. of County of N.Y., N.Y. State Soc. Dermatology, Dermatol. Soc. of Greater N.Y., N.Y. County Health Svs. Rev. Orgn., N.Y. Acad. Scis., N.Y. Dermatol. Soc. (pres 1990-91, sec., treas. 1989-90), Dermatology Found., Z & E Fisher Med. Found. (pres. 1993—). Home: 340 E 64th St New York NY 10021-7503 Office: NY Med Coll Dept Dermatology Valhalla NY 10595 also: 625 Park Ave New York NY 10021-6545 Office Phone: 212-988-8918. Personal E-mail: safai@aol.com.

SAFARS, BERTA See FISZER-SZAFARZ, BERTA

SAFER, JOHN, artist; b. Washington, Sept. 6, 1922; s. John M. and Rebecca (Herzmark) S.; m. Joy Scott; children: Janine Whitney, Thomas. AB, George Washington U., 1947; LLB, Harvard U., 1949; LittD (hon.), Lees-McRae Coll.; DPhil (hon.), Daniel Webster Coll. Chmn. NationsBank/DC, 1980-92; chmn. exec. com. Fin. Gen. Bankshares, 1977-80; bd. dirs. Nat. Air and Space Mus., The Shakespeare Guild, Materia. Represented in permanent collections at Smithsonian Am. Art Mus., Balt. Mus. Art, Corocoran Gallery Art, Dayton Art Inst., Frederik Meijer Sculpture Gardens, Folger Shakespeare Libr., Nat. Air and Space Mus., Washington Tennis Ctr., High Mus. Art, Atlanta, Milw. Mus. Art, Harvard Law Sch., Harvard Bus. Sch., Hofstra U., Mayo Clinic, Jacksonville, Fla., Phila. Mus. Art, San Francisco Mus. Art, Duke U. Med. Ctr., Embry-Riddle Aero. U., Georgetown U., George Washington U., Williams Coll., Scripps Rsch. Inst., Daniel Webster Coll., Am. Hosp., Paris, Embassy of U.S., London, Nassau, Beijing, New Delhi, Fayetteville (NC) Mus. Art, Nat. Jewish Mus., Nat. Peace Inst., Ponce (PR) Mus. of Art, UN, N.Y.C., corps. including Celanese Corp., NY, Crown Equipment Corp., New Bremen, Ohio, First Union Bank of Md., Bank of Am. Ctr., Norfolk, Va., Gen. Mills Corp., Mpls Rosemont Co., Atlanta, West Chase Corp., Houston, Nat. Air Traffic Controller, numerous others; author: John Safer, Sculptor, Art in Flight, 1990, The Sculpture of John Safer, 1982 1st lt. USAAF, 1942-46. Mem.: Cosmos, Burning Tree, Harvard, Woodmont (Washington), Lyford Cay (Nassau), Linville Ridge (N.C.). Office: PO Box 6720 Mc Lean VA 22106-6720 Office Phone: 703-276-7766. Personal E-mail: johnsafer@mac.com.

SAFF, EDWARD BARRY, mathematics professor, dean; b. NYC, Jan. 2, 1944; s. Irving H. and Rose (Koslow) Saff; m. Loretta Singer, July 3, 1966; children: Lisa Jill, Tracy Karen, Alison Michelle. BS with highest honors, Ga. Inst. Tech., 1964; PhD, U. Md., 1968. Asst. prof. U. Md., 1968; post-doctoral rschr. Imperial Coll., London, 1968-69; from asst. prof. to assoc. prof. math. U. S. Fla., 1969—76, prof., 1976-86, disting. rsch. prof., 1986—2001, dir. Ctr. Math. Svcs., 1978-83, dir. Inst. Constructive Math., 1985—2001, dir. Ctr. Constructive Approximation, 2001—04; exec. dean Coll. Arts and Sci. Vanderbilt U., Nashville, 2004—. Sr. vis. fellow Oxford U., 1978; hon. prof. Zhejiang Normal U. Author (with A. D. Snider): Fundamentals of Complex Analysis, 1976, 3d edit., 2003; author: (with A. W. Goodman) Calculus, Concepts and Calculations, 1981; author: (with A. Edrei and R. S. Varga) Zeros of Sections of Power Series; author: (with V. Totik) Logarithmic Potentials with External Fields, 1997; author: (with R. K. Nagle) Fundamentals of Differential Equations, 1993, Fundamentals of Differential Equations and Boundary Value Problems, 1993; author: (with D. S. Lubinsky) Strong Asymptotics for External Polynomials Associated with Weights on R, 1988; editor: Jour. Approximation Theory, 1990—; editor: (with R. S. Varga) Pade and Rational Approximation: Theory and Applications, 1977; editor: Cambridge U. Press, 1995—2001, Founds. Comp. Math., 1999—2004; editor-in-chief: Constructive Approximation Jour., 1983—, Computational Methods and Function Theory Jour., 2001—. Recipient Chancellor's Rsch. award, Vanderbilt U., 2005; fellow, Fulbright Found., 1968—69, Guggenheim Found., 1978; grantee, NSF, 1970—72, 1980—. Mem.: Math. Assn. Am., Am. Math. Soc., Sigma Xi. Office: Ctr Constructive Approximation Vanderbilt U Dept Math Nashville TN 37240 Office Phone: 615-322-7360. Business E-Mail: ed.saff@vanderbilt.edu.

SAFFAR, JEAN-MARC, healthcare consultant; b. Paris, May 1, 1965; s. Max and Michele S.; m. Claudia Moss, Feb. 13, 1994; children: Etty, Charles. MD, Paris Sch. Medicine, 1991, BS in Biostats., 1995; MS in Health Policy, Dauphine Sch. Mgmt., Paris, 1995; PhD in Pub. Health, Amiens Sch. Medicine, France, 1997; MS in Healthcare Mgmt., Harvard U., 1997; MBA, U. Mich., 2000. Internist Paris Hosp., 1991-93; pub. health rschr. Regional Health Obs., Amiens, France, 1994-96; sr. cons. KPMG Peat Marwick, Boston, 1997-98; sr. mgr. A.T. Kearney, Cambridge, Mass., 1998—2002. Cons. in field. Lt. French Army, 1993-94. Mem. French Med. Bd., French Assn. Pub. Health Profls., Harvard Club N.Y., U. Mich. Bus. Sch. Alumni Assn., Harvard Alumni Assn. Avocations: video editing, french movies, backgammon, skiing. Home: 1365 York Ave #12E New York NY 10021 Office: True North Capital 375 Park Ave Ste 2309 New York NY 10152 E-mail: jean-marc.saffar@post.harvard.edu.

SAFFELS, ANNA WAYNE BROTHERS, retired mathematician, educator; b. Gallant, Ala., Nov. 6, 1928; d. Homer Ervin and Bertie Galloway Brothers; m. George Aaron Saffels (dec.); children: Michael Aaron, Elisabeth Anne. BS in Secondary Edn., Jacksonville State U., 1949; MA in Secondary Edn., U. Ala., Birmingham, 1973. Cert. tchr. Ala., 1949. Tchr. Ivalee Sch., Attalla, Ala., 1949—53, 1956—61, 1964—66; tchr. math. Etowah H.S., Attalla, Ala., 1966—86, ret., 1986. Pres. Etowah County Classroom Tchrs. Assn., 1967—68. Pianist Ivalee Bapt. Ch., 1950—2007, Sunday sch. tchr., 1950—97, dir. sr. activities, 2000—07. Nominee Jacksonville State Tchr. Hall of Fame, 1972, Presdl. award for excellence in math. tchg. Mem.: NEA, Ala. Edn. Assn., Alpha Delta Kappa (past pres. Ala. Alpha Xi chpt.), Kappa Delta Pi. Avocations: genealogy, stamp collecting/philately, photography, music, flower gardening. Home: 3194 Hwy 77 Attalla AL 35954-7140 Personal E-mail: awbsaffels@aol.com.

SAFFIOTTI, UMBERTO, pathologist; b. Milan, Jan. 22, 1928; came to U.S., 1960, naturalized, 1966; s. Francesco Umberto and Maddalena (Valenzano) S.; m. Paola Amman, June 21, 1958; children: Luisa M., Maria Francesca. MD cum laude, U. Milan, 1951, splty. diploma occupational medicine cum laude, 1957. Intern Inst. Pathol. Anatomy U. Milan, 1951-52, asst. to chmn. occupational medicine, chief lab. pathology, Inst. Occupational Medicine, 1956-60, fellow Inst. Gen. Pathology, 1957-60; rsch. asst. oncology, rsch. assoc. Chgo. Med. Sch., 1952-55, from asst. prof. to prof. oncology, 1960-68; mem. staff Nat. Cancer Inst., NIH, Bethesda, Md., 1968—, assoc. dir. carcinogenesis, 1968-76, chief lab. exptl. pathology, 1974-98, acting head Registry of Exptl. Cancers, 1988-98; scientist emeritus, 1998—; adj. prof., Environ. & Occ. Hlth. The George Washington U., Washington, 2000—. Mem. pathology B study sect., NIH, 1964-68; former mem. various adv. coms. govt. agys.; mem. cancer prevention com. Internat. Union Against Cancer, 1959-66, panel on carcinogenicity, 1963-66; chmn. ad hoc com. evaluation low levels environ. carcinogens HEW, 1969-70. Co-editor books; contbr. articles to profl. jours. Bd. dirs. Rachel Carson Trust, 1976-79. Recipient Career Devel. award NIH, 1965-68, Superior Svc. Honor award HEW, 1971, Pub. Interest Sci. award Environ. Def. Fund, 1977, Spl. Recognition award USPHS, 1980 Fellow NYAS; mem. AAAS, Am. Assn. Cancer Rsch. (pres. Chgo. chpt. 1966-67), Am. Soc. Investigative Pathology, Soc. Toxicology, Sigma Xi. Democrat. Home: 5114 Wissioming Rd Bethesda MD 20816-2259 Office: NIH Nat Cancer Inst 6116 Executive Blvd Rm 7212 Bethesda MD 20892-8314 Business E-Mail: saffiotti@nih.gov.

SAFFIR, HERBERT SEYMOUR, structural engineer, consultant; b. NYC, Mar. 29, 1917; s. A.L. and Gertrude (Samuels) S.; m. Sarah Young, May 9, 1941 (dec.); children: Richard Young, Barbara Joan. BSCE cum laude, Ga. Inst. Tech., 1940. Registered profl. engr., Fla., NY, Tex., PR, Miss.; lic. land surveyor, Fla. Civil engr. TVA, Chattanooga, 1940, NACA, Langley Field, Va., 1940—41; structural engr. Ebasco Svcs., NYC, 1941—43, York & Sawyer & Fred Severud, NYC, 1945; engr. Waddell & Hardesty, Cons. Engrs., NYC, 1945—47; asst. county engr. Dade County, Miami, Fla., 1947—59; cons. engr. Herbert S. Saffir, Coral Gables, Fla., 1959—. Adj. prof. civil engring. Coll. Engring., U. Miami, 1964—; adviser civil engring. Fla. Internat. U., 1975-80; chmn. Met. Dade County Unsafe Structures Bd., 1977-92; mem. Bldg. Code Evaluation Task Force after Hurricane Andrew; mem. Am. Nat. Stds. Inst. Com. Bldg. Design Loads, Nat. Adv. Group on Glass Design, Dade County Bldg. Code Com. 1993-96; cmty. rels. com. U. Miami/Coral Gables, 1993-96; reviewer for NSF; bd. adjustment City of Coral Gables, 1994-97, budget bd., 1997-2001; evaluation panel Biltmore, 1982-83; cons., presenter in field Author: Housing Construction in Hurricane Prone Areas, 1971, Nature and Extent of Damage by Hurricane Camille, 1972, Evaluation of Structural Damage Caused by Hurricanes, 1993; contbg. author: Wind Effects on Structures, 1976, Hurricane! Coping with Disaster, 2002; editor: Wind Engr., 1986-92; editor Manual of Wind Damage Investigation; contbr. articles to profl. jours.; designer Saffir/Simpson hurricane scale. With NY Guard, 1942-43, AUS, 1943-44, WWII. Recipient Outstanding Svc. award Fla. Profl. Engrs., 1954, Pub. Svc. award Nat. Weather Svc., 1975, Disting. Svc. award Nat. Hurricane Conf., 1987; named Miami Engr. of Year, 1978, 94, Gov.'s Design award, 1986, Gov. Gilchrist award for Profl. Excellence, 1988, Albert H. Friedman Cmty. Svc. award, 1992, Engring. award Nat. Hurricane Conf., 1997; named to Ga. Tech. Engring. Hall of Fame, 1995; named Herbert S. Saffir Miami-Dade Permitting and Inspection Ctr. in his honor, 2002 Fellow Fla. Engring. Soc. (award for outstanding tech. achievement 1973, Cmty. Svc. award 1980, Lifetime Achievement award 2003, disting. engr. award 2003), Coll. Engrs. P.R. (Disting. Engr. award 2002); mem. ASCE (hon., past pres., sec., aerodynamics com. 1983—, mem. mitigation of wind damage com. 1985—, chmn. com. on damage investigation 1989—, mem. com. A7 on design loads for bldgs. 1972—), Soc. Am. Mil. Engrs., Am. Concrete Inst., ASTM (mem. com. performance bldg. constrn.), Internat. Assn. for Bridge and Structural Engring., Colegio de Ingenieros P.R., Am. Meterol. Soc., Am. Arbitration Assn., Wind Engring. Rsch. Coun. (past bd. dirs., Svc. award 1990), Am. Assn. for Wind Engring., Coral Gables C. of C. (bd. dirs., past pres., past chmn.), Tau Beta Pi, Chi Epsilon (hon.). Clubs: Country of Coral Gables. Home: 4818 Alhambra Cir Coral Gables FL 33146-1643 Office: Consulting Engineers 350 Sevilla Ave Ste 108 Coral Gables FL 33134-6617 Office Phone: 305-444-2611.

SAFFIR, LEONARD, public relations executive; b. NYC, Apr. 19, 1930; s. Abraham and Gertrude S.; m. Patricia Roemer (div. 1980); children: Andrew, Michelle; m. Wendy McConaughy (div. 1992); 1 child, Samantha; m. Eleanor Unger, 1997. Student, Syracuse U., 1948-51. Editor, bur. chief Internat. News Service, Dallas, Tokyo, 1953-58; producer Eng., Australia, Asia, 1958-60; ptnr. Haft, Saffir, Siegel Pub. Relations & Advt., NYC, 1960-62; asst. pub. N.Y. Standard, 1962-63; cons. Ferdinand Marcos, 1964; pub. Latin Am. Times, NYC, 1965; exec. v.p. Franchises Internat., NYC, 1965-69; press sec., chief of staff to Senator James Buckley U.S. Senate, Washington, 1970-76; pub., editor The Trib, NYC, 1977-78, The Sun, Bridgehampton, NY, 1978-84; exec. v.p. Porter/Novelli, NYC, 1984-90; pres. Jay DeBow & Ptnrs., NYC, Fla., 1989-90, Leonard Saffir & Assocs. Pub. Rels., 2000—; investigative reporter, columnist Lake Worth Herald, 2001—03. CEO Adventures One, 1998-2000, Celebrity Stores.com, 1998-2000. Author: Power Public Relations, 1992, Power Public Relations: How to Master the New PR, 2000, PR on a Budget, 2006. Campaign mgr. Marchi for Mayor, N.Y.C., 1973, Buckley for Senator, N.Y., 1976. Served as sgt. USMC, 1951-53. Recipient Silver Anvil and Big Apple awards Pub. Rels. Soc. Am., Mayor's award City of N.Y., others. Mem. Overseas Press Club (pres. 1988-89). Home: 6137 Rainbow Circle Lake Worth FL 33463 Office Phone: 561-289-3100. Personal E-mail: lenpr@bellsouth.net.

SAFFORD, FLORENCE VIRAY SUNGA, travel agent, consultant; b. Masantol, Pampanga, Luzon, Philippines, Mar. 19, 1932; came to U.S., 1953; d. Filomeno Garcia and Dominga (Viray) Sunga; m. Francis Ingersoll Safford, Aug. 4, 1979; children: H. Robert, Erlinda Ann, Ruben Michael. BS in Edn., Adamson U., Manila, 1952; student Hotel Mgmt. and Polit. Sci., Kapiolani C.C., Honolulu, 1975; student, Am. Travel Sch., Honolulu, 1977. Tchr. Cecilio Apostles Elem. Sch., Manila, 1949-51, St. Michael Acad., Masantol, 1951-52; social worker Cath. Social Svc., Honolulu, 1970-77; cons. Travel Cons. of the Pacific, Honolulu, 1977—; social worker Kapiolani C.C., Honolulu. Mem. exec. bd. dirs. Oahu Cmty. Coun., 1994—; elected to Neighborhood Bd., 1982—84, 1993—95; apptd. by mayor of Honolulu to Ethics Commn., 1986—95; v.p. Marbella Home Owners Assn. at Summerlin Resorts, 2001—; bd. dirs., del. Summerlin Resorts Homeowners Assn., 2004—; pres., gen. coord. Miss Internat. Hawaii Pagent, 1973—98; bd. dirs. C. of C. of Hawaii, Small Bus. Assn. Hawaii, Philippine Am. Charity Found., Las Vegas, 2003—. Named Most Outstanding Leader of the Community, Filipino Jaycees of Honolulu, 1976, Donor of Yr., 2006, Help Hospitalized Veterans Orgn. Mem.: Aloha Bus. and Profl. Women's Club (treas., Outstanding award 1981—89), Filipino C. of C. of Hawaii (treas., bd. dirs. 1994, Outstanding award 1991—92), Women's Cmty. Action League of Hawaii (pres. 1972—2001, Outstanding Pres. 1992). Republican. Roman Catholic. Avocation: dance.

SAFFRAN, KALMAN, entrepreneur, venture capitalist; b. Boston, Dec. 28, 1947; s. Max and Marion (Patick) S. BA, Northeastern U., 1971; postgrad., MIT, 1971-72. Lic. real estate broker, Mass. Mgr. sys. MIT, 1972-76; corp. cons. United Brands Co., Boston, 1977-78; CEO Monitrex Corp., Boston, 1977-82; pres. Kalman Saffran Assocs., Inc., Newton, Mass., 1978—2000; bd. advisers Prism Venture Ptnrs. Bd. advisors Blackstone Bank and Trust Co., Boston; mem. network implementation panel U.S. Energy Research and Devel. Adminstrn., Washington, 1975-76; mem. computer com. MIT Lab. for Nuclear Sci., 1975-76. Mem. Data Processing Mgmt. Assn., Assn. Computing Machinery, Soc. for Info. Mgmt., IEEE, Mensa. Republican. Jewish. Home: 1564 Commonwealth Ave W Newton MA 02465-2806 Office: Kalman Saffran Assocs Inc PO Box 66033 Newton MA 02466-0001 Office Phone: 617-527-2000.

SAFIAN, GAIL ROBYN, public relations executive; b. Bklyn., Dec. 12, 1947; d. Jack I. and Harriet S.; m. Jay Mark Eisenberg, Jan. 6, 1979; children: Julia, Eric. BA, SUNY, Albany, 1968; MBA, NYU, 1982. Reporter Albany (N.Y.)-Knickerbocker News/Times-Union, 1969, Athens (Ohio) Messenger, 1969-71; pub. relations asst. Mountainside Hosp., Montclair, N.J., 1971-74; dir. pub. relations Riverside Hosp., Boonton, N.J., 1974-78; consumer affairs coordinator Johnson & Johnson Personal Products Div., Milltown, N.J., 1978-79; v.p., group mgr. Harshe Rotman & Druck, NYC, 1979-82; exec. v.p., dir. Health Care Div. Ruder Finn & Rotman, NYC, 1982-84; v.p., mgr. client services Burson-Marsteller, NYC, 1984-86; v.p., group mgr. health care Cohn & Wolfe, NYC, 1986-90; exec. v.p., gen. mgr. MCS, Summit, N.J., 1990-94; pres. Safian Comm. Inc., Maplewood, N.J., 1994—. Mem. devel. com. Cancer Care, N.Y.C., 1985—. Recipient MacEachern award Am. Hosp. Assn., 1974, Communications Award Internat. Assn. Bus. Communicators, 1976, Creativity in Pub. Rels. award Inside PR, 1992, 93, Big Apple award 2005 Mem. Healthcare Businesswomen's Assn. (mem. bd. dirs.), N.Y. Acad. Scis., Women in Comm. (Clarion award 1974). Jewish. Home and Office: Safian Comm Inc 31 Hickory Dr Maplewood NJ 07040-2107 E-mail: gsafian@safianhealth.com.

SAFIAN, KEITH FRANKLIN, hospital administrator; b. Bklyn., June 22, 1950; s. Jack I. and Harriet S. (Cohen) S.; children: Elizabeth Anne, Alexander William. BS in EE and Indsl. Engring., SUNY, Buffalo, 1972; MBA, U. Pa., 1974. Asst. dir. Kings County Hosp. Ctr., Bklyn., 1974-76; asst. adminstr. NYU Med. Ctr., NYC, 1977-80, assoc. adminstr., 1981-84, sr. assoc. adminstr., 1984-85; adminstr. St. John's Episcopal Hosp., Far Rockaway, NY, 1985-89; pres., CEO Phelps Meml. Hosp. Ctr., Sleepy Hollow, NY, 1989—. Bd. dirs. Addabbo Family Health Ctr., Arverne, N.Y., 1987-89, Rockaway Devel. and Revitalization Corp., Far Rockaway, 1988-89; bd. dirs. The ExcelCare Sys., Bronxville, N.Y., 1993-99, chmn. 1995-98; bd. dirs. No. Met. Hosp. Assn., Newburgh, N.Y., 1989—, mem. exec. com., 1993-98, 2000-05, chmn., 1996, 2003, treas., 2001, vice chmn. 2002. Fellow Am. Coll. Healthcare Execs.; mem. Hosp. Adminstrs. Club of N.Y., Health Care Assn. N.Y. State (trustee 1996-98, 2003-05). Home: 16 Brokaw Ln Great Neck NY 11023-1160 Office: Phelps Memorial Hosp 701 N Broadway Tarrytown NY 10591-1096 Office Phone: 914-366-1001. Business E-Mail: phelpsceo@pmhc.us.

SAFIAN, ROBERT L., executive editor; b. Mount Vernon, NY, Apr. 20, 1964; m. Mary Safian; children: Matthew, Nicholas. BA in History magna cum laude, Brown U., 1987. Summer intern, then reporter, then exec. editor The Am. Lawyer, 1987—94; sr. editor, then articles editor SmartMoney, 1994—97; head personal fin. coverage divsn. Fortune, 1997—98; mng. editor Money Mag., NYC, 1998—2004; exec. editor Time mag., NYC, 2004—. Tchr. legal affairs reporting Columbia U. Sch. Journalism, 1993—96; guest lectr. Harvard Law Sch., 1993. Named one of 40 Under 40, Crain's N.Y. Bus. Office: Time Inc Rockefeller Ctr New York NY 10020-1393

SAFIAN, SHELLEY CAROLE, advertising executive; b. Bklyn., May 29, 1954; d. Jack Israel and Harriet Sara (Cohen) S. BFA, Parsons Sch. Design, 1975; MA, U. Phoenix, 2002. Cert. coding specialist; in health svcs. mgmt. Keller Grad. Sch. Bus., 2005. Asst. art dir. Axelrod and Assocs., NYC, 1975-77; art dir. Sta. WDBO-TV-AM/FM, Orlando, Fla., 1978-80; owner, pres. Safian Comm. Svcs., Inc., Winter Park, Fla., 1981—, Bonté Sportswear, Winter Park, Fla., 1993-97; chair allied health dept. Herzing Coll., Winter Park, Fla., 2004—. Mem. adv. com. Career Edn., Orange County, Fla., 1981—88, chmn., 1982—83; adj. prof. Internat. Acad. Design and Tech., 2000—; adj. prof. City Coll., Casselberry, Fla., 2000—. Author: Insurance Coding & Electronic Claims for the Medical Office, 2005. Exec. producer/dir. March of Dimes Telethon, Orlando, 1984; bd. dirs. Boy Scouts Am., 1987-91; exec. dir. United Cerebral Palsy Telethon, Orlando, 1982-83; pub. rels. liaison United Cerebral Palsy, Orlando, 1983-84; founder Career Dir. for Deaf, Orlando, 1985; trustee, pub. rels. chair Nat. Multiple Sclerosis Soc., 1991-92, bd. dirs., 1990, 91. Recipient 1st pl. Addy awards Orlando ADvt. Fedn., 1981, 87, 88, 89, 1st pl. Addy award, 2d pl. awards, merit awards, 1982, 84, 85, 87, 88, Nat. Telly award Bronze Statue, 1988, Up and Coming award Price Waterhouse/Orlando Bus. Jour., 1988, Pro-Mark 1st pl. awards Fla. Coun. Shopping Ctrs., 1989, 90, merit award, 1990, Telly award Bronze finalist, 1989, 91; named Tchr. of the Quarter, 2001. Mem. Broadcast Promotion and Mktg. Execs. Assn. (Silver Medalion 1983, nat. finalist 2 Silver Microphone awards 1986, 87), Broadcast Designer's Assn. (bd.d irs. 1980-82), Am. Women in Radio and TV (bd. dirs. 1980-81). Republican. Avocation: horseback riding.

SAFIER, PEDRO N., physicist, contractor; b. Buenos Aires, Sept. 17, 1958; s. Mauricio Safier and Leonor Isabel Spilka. BSc, Hebrew U.,

Jerusalem, Israel, 1982, MSC, 1985; PhD, U. Chgo., 1992. Rsch. scientist SAIC, McLean, Va., 1999—2002; owner S&J Solutions LLC, Alexandria, Va., 2002—. Grant proposal referee NASA, College Park, Md., 1995—99. Election officer Fairfax County Bd. Elections, Alexandria, Va., 2003—07. Achievements include research in astronomy and astrophysics. Avocations: crew, photography, action pistol. Office: S&J Solutions LLC 107 S West St PMB 509 Alexandria VA 22314 Home Phone: 703-765-5047; Office Phone: 703-765-5047. Office Fax: 703-997-1401. Business E-Mail: pedro-safier@sj-solutions.com.

SAFIR, PETER OLIVER, lawyer; b. NYC, Apr. 1, 1945; s. Marshall Phillip and Gladys (Weissberger) S.; m. Ellen Beskind, Jan. 2, 1983; children: Jesse Oliver, Roland Smart, Archie Smart. AB in History, Princeton U., 1967; JD, Yale U., 1972. Bar: N.Y. 1973, D.C. 1975. Assoc. Breed, Abbott & Morgan, NYC, 1972—75, Kleinfeld Kaplan & Becker, Washington, 1975—78, ptnr., 1979—2002, Covington & Burling, Washington, 2002—, co-chmn., Food & Drug Regulatory Practice Group. Prof. lectr. food and drug law George Washington U. Law Sch., 1991—; program panelist-moderator Food and Drug Law Inst., Washington, 1979—2004. Contbr. articles to profl., trade, and law jours. With US Army, 1968—71. Mem.: ABA (food and drug law sect.). Democrat. Office: Covington & Burling 1201 Pennsylvania Ave Washington DC 20004-2401 Office Phone: 202-662-5162. Office Fax: 202-662-6291. Business E-Mail: psafir@cov.com.

SAFIRA, BARABARA, science educator; b. Kaprzewnica, Poland, Feb. 18, 1959; d. Regina and Jon Pielecha; m. Hertzel Safira, Jan. 11, 1990; children: Arthur Dov, Ariela. Masters, Acad. Of Mining & Metallurgy, Kracov, Poland, 1986. Cert. phys. sci. tchr. N.J., 2001. Chem. engr. Cement Plant, Ozarow, Poland, 1986—87; rsch. chemist Sika, Lyndhurst, NJ, 1989—98; tchr. phys. sci. Wallington H.S., NJ, 2001—. Head instr. of engrng. club Wallington H.S., NJ, 2002—06; asst. math. team Bergen County Acad., Hackensack, NJ, 2004—06. Office: Wallington HS 234 Main Ave Wallington NJ 07057 Office Phone: 973-777-0808. E-mail: safira@wboe.org.

SAFIRE, WILLIAM, journalist, foundation administrator; b. NYC, Dec. 17, 1929; s. Oliver C. and Ida (Panish) S.; m. Helene Belmar Julius, Dec. 16, 1962; children: Mark Lindsey, Annabel Victoria. Student, Syracuse U., 1947—49. Reporter NY Herald Tribune Syndicate, 1949-51; corr. WNBC-WNBT, Europe and Mid. East, 1951; radio-TV prodr. WNBC, NYC, 1954-55; v.p. pub. rels. Tex McCrary, Inc., 1955-60; pres. Safire Pub. Rels., Inc., 1960-68; sr. White House speechwriter Pres. Richard Nixon, Washington, 1969-73; polit. columnist NY Times, Washington, 1973—2005; columnist On Language, NY Times Mag., 1979—. Trustee Syracuse U.; chmn. Dana Found. Author: The Relations Explosion, 1963, Plunging into Politics, 1964, Safire's Political Dictionary, 1968, rev. edit., 1972—78, Before the Fall, 1975, Full Disclosure, 1977, Safire's Washington, 1980, On Language, 1980, What's the Good Word?, 1982, I Stand Corrected, 1984, Take My Word for It, 1986, Freedom, 1987, You Could Look It Up, 1988, Language Maven Strikes Again, 1990, Fumblerules, 1990, Coming to Terms, 1991, The First Dissident, 1992, Lend Me Your Ears, 1992, 1998, 2004, Good Advice on Writing, 1992, Quoth the Maven, 1993, Safire's New Political Dictionary, 1993, In Love with Norma Loquendi, 1994, Sleeper Spy, 1995, Watching My Language, 1997, Spread the Word, 1999, Scandalmonger, 2000, Let a Simile Be Your Umbrella, 2001, No Uncertain Terms, 2003, The Right Word, 2004; co-author (with Leonard Safir): Good Advice on Writing, 1982, Words of Wisdom, 1989, Leadership, 1990. Mem. Pulitzer Bd., 1995-2004. With AUS, 1952-54. Recipient Pulitzer prize for Disting. Commentary, 1978, Presdl. Medal of Freedom, 2006. Republican. Office: The Dana Foundation 900 15th St NW Washington DC 20005 Business E-Mail: wsafire@dana.org.

SAFIZADEH, M. HOSSEIN, finance educator; BBA, Iran Inst. Banking; MBA, PhD, Okla. State U. Prof. ops. and strategic mgmt. dept. Carroll Sch. Mgmt., Boston Coll., 1997—, interim dean, 2003—. Editl. bd. mem. Prodn. and Ops. Mgmt. Office: Boston Coll Carroll Sch Mgmt Fulton Hall 454A 140 Commonwealth Ave Chestnut Hill MA 02467 Office Phone: 617-552-0476. Business E-Mail: hossein.safizadeh.1@bc.edu.

SAFKA, JIM, information technology executive; BS Accounting, U. So. Ca.; MBA, J.L. Kellogg School of Management, Northwestern U. Mgr. Alberto-Culver, Inc., Warner Bros., Paramount Pictures; with Intuit; v.p. E*Trade, 1997—2002; v.p., gen. mgr. e-commerce AT&T Wireless, 2002—04; CEO Match.com, 2004—. Office: Match.com 3001 George Bush Hwy Ste 100 Richardson TX 75082

SAFLEY, HOLLI EWOLDT, music educator; d. Roy William and Marilyn Hedin Ewoldt; m. William Duane Safley, Aug. 4, 1979; children: Matthew William-Ewoldt, Erin Lynn-Ewoldt. MusB in Edn., Drake U., Des Moines, Iowa, 1974. Instr. vocal and instrumental music edn. Ackely-Geneva (Iowa) Schs., 1974—79; instr. instrumental music edn. Aurelia (Iowa) Cmty. Schs., 1979—88; instr. instrumental music Clay Ctrl. Cmty. Sch., Royal, Iowa, 1989—90, South O'Brien Cmty. Schs., Paulina, Iowa, 1990—96, Storm Lake (Iowa) Cmty. Schs., 1996—. Coach basketball, softball, track Ackley- Geneva (Iowa) Cmty. Schs., 1974—79; head coach volleyball, basketball Aurelia (Iowa) Cmty. Sch. Dist., 1979—84. Musician: Cherokee Symphony Orchestra; dir.: Aurelia (Iowa) H.S. Jazz Band (3rd Pl. award Iowa Jazz Championships, 1987), Jazz Festivals (1st Pl. awards). Recipient Tchr. Tenure award, Iowa Bandmasters, 2007. Mem.: Am. Sch. Band Dirs. Assn., Mu Phi Epsilon (pres. 1973—74), Am. Sch. Band Dirs. Assn. (state chair Iowa chpt. 2005—), N.W. Iowa Bandmasters Assn. (dist. pres. 1990—91), Iowa Bandmasters Assn. (dist. rep. All Iowa 8th Grade Honor Band 2004—), Iowa Music Educators Assn., Music Educators Nat. Conf., Iowa Edn. Assn., Mortar Bd. (treas. 1973—74). Avocations: golf, travel, gardening. Office: Storm Lake Community School 1811 Hyland Drive Storm Lake IA 50588 Home Phone: 712-295-6302; Office Phone: 712-732-8080. Office Fax: 712-732-8084. Personal E-mail: safmusic@iowatelecom.net. E-mail: hsafley@storm-lake.k12.ia.us.

SAFLEY, JAMES ROBERT, lawyer; b. Cedar Rapids, Iowa, Sept. 19, 1943; s. Robert Starr and Jean (Engelman) S.; m. Dianne Lee McInnis; children: Anne Michele, Jamie Leigh. BA, U. Iowa, 1965; JD, Duke U., 1968. Bar: Minn. 1968, U.S. Ct. Appeals (4th, 5th, 6th, 7th, 8th, 9th and 11th cirs.), U.S. Supreme Ct. Law clk. U.S. Dist. Ct. Minn., Mpls., 1968-69; assoc. Robins, Kaplan, Miller & Ciresi, Mpls., 1969-74, ptnr., 1974—. Mem. adv. coun. Women's Intercollegiate Athletics, U. Minn., 1988-94; mem bd. visitors Duke Law Sch, 2004—. Mem. ABA, Minn. State Bar Assn. (antitrust sect. chmn. 1985-87), Hennepin County Bar Assn., Duke Law Alumni Assn. (bd. dirs. 2001-03), Phi Beta Kappa. Office: Robins Kaplan Miller & Ciresi 2800 LaSalle Pla 800 Lasalle Ave Ste 2800 Minneapolis MN 55402-2015 Office Phone: 612-349-8274.

SAFONOV, MICHAEL GEORGE, electrical engineering educator, consultant; b. Pasadena, Calif., Nov. 1, 1948; s. George Michael and Ruth Garnet (Ware) S.; m. Nancy Kelshaw Schorn, Aug. 31, 1968 (div. Oct. 1983); 1 child, Alexander; m. Janet Sunderland, Feb. 25, 1985; 1 child, Peter. BSEE, MSEE, MIT, 1971, EE, 1976, PhDEE, 1977. Electronic engr. Air Force Cambridge Rsch. Lab., Hanscom AFB, Mass., 1968-71; rsch. asst. MIT, Cambridge, 1975-77; prof. elec. engrng. U. So. Calif., LA, 1977—, assoc. chmn. dept., 1989-93, vice chmn. engrng. faculty coun., 2001—02, chmn. engrng. faculty coun., 2003—04. Vis. scholar Cambridge (Eng.) U., 1983-84, Imperial Coll., London, 1987, Calif. Inst. Tech., Pasadena, 1990-91; cons. Honeywell Systems and Rsch. Ctr., Mpls., 1978-83, Space Systems div. TRW, Redondo Beach, Calif., 1984, Northrop Aircraft, Hawthorne, Calif., 1985-91, also numerous others. Author: Stability and Robustness of Multivariable Feedback Systems (hon. mention Phi Beta Kappa 1981); co-author: (book and software) Robust-Control Toolbox, 1988; assoc. editor IEEE Trans. on Automatic Control, 1985-87, Internat. Jour. Robust and Nonlinear Control, 1989-93, Sys. and Control Letters, 1995—. Awards com. chair Am. Automatic Control Coun., 1993-95. Lt. (j.g.) USNR, 1972-75. Rsch. grantee Air Force Office Sci. Rsch., 1978—, NSF, 1982-84. Fellow IEEE; mem. AIAA (sr.), Common Cause. Republican. Office: U So Calif Dept EE Sys MC 2563 3740 McClintock Ave # 310 Los Angeles CA 90089-2563 Home Phone: 310-551-0517; Office Phone: 213-740-4455. Business E-Mail: msafonov@usc.edu. *Consider first only the very simplest problem--but strive for a representation of the simplest problem that generalizes.*

SAFRA, JOSEPH, bank executive; s. Joseph Safra; married; 4 children. Co-owner, chmn. Safra Group; chmn., CEO Banco Safra S.A., Sao Paulo, Brazil; chmn. Safra Nat. Bank NY. Mem. adv. bd. Wharton U. Pa.; chmn. bd. dirs. Banque Jacob Safra (Suisse) S.A. Contbr. New Ctr. Brazilian Studies Oxford U., Hazon Yeshaya Soup Kitchens. Named one of World's Richest People, Forbes Mag., 2000—. Bank holdings span the Caribbean, New York and Europe and include Safra Bank NY, Banque Safra Luxembourg and First Internat. Bank Israel. Office: Safra Nat Bank NY 546 5th Ave New York NY 10036 *

SAFRAN, EDWARD MYRON, financial consultant, bank executive; b. Boston, Oct. 9, 1937; s. Morris and Sophie (Radin) S.; m. Harriet Reva Podolsky, Jan. 15, 1966; children: Steven, Rebecca. BS in Metall., MIT, 1959; MBA, Harvard U., 1961. Pres. Suncrest Corp., Worcester, Mass., 1962-65; exec. asst. Am. Metal Climax, NYC, 1966; sr. auditor Gen. Electric Co., Lynn, Mass., 1966-68; fin. analyst Polaroid Corp., Cambridge, Mass., 1968-70, mgr. banking and investments, 1970-84, asst. treas., 1984-87; pres. Merganser Capital Mgmt. Corp., Cambridge, 1984-2000. Chmn. Direct Fed. Credit Union, Needham, Mass., 1986—. Gleason Works fellow Harvard U., 1959-60. Mem. Harvard Club of Boston Home: 37 Barney Hill Rd Wayland MA 01778-3601 Office: Direct Fed Credit Union PO Box 9123 50 Cabot St Needham MA 02494 Office Phone: 781-433-2900. Business E-Mail: edsafran@directfederal.com.

SAFREN, CHERYL, artist, art educator; d. Abraham Rothberg and Marilyn Pearl Finchler; m. Martin Safren, Jan. 19, 1975; children: Aviva Einhorn, Nathaniel Isaac. BFA, Pratt Inst., 1973; MSc, Hofstra U., 1996. Cert. tchr. N.Y. Edn. Dept., 1997. Tchr. art North Shore Hebrew Acad., Great Neck, NY, 1996—2005, Manhasset (N.Y.) Union Free Sch. Dist., 2005—. Instr. Hofstra U., Hempstead, NY, 1998. One-woman shows include Lawrence Inst. Tech., AAAS, Washington, Great Neck Art Ctr., NY, Discovery Mus., Bridgeport, Conn., Represented in permanent collections City of Aurora, Colo., City of Balatonfored, Hungary, Teleflex Internat., Thyssen Industries, Germany, U. Ga., Athens, U. Maine, Orono, Wyeth Pharms., Fla. State U., Talahassee. Mem.: Williamburg Art and Hist. Ctr. (assoc.), L.I. (N.Y.) Arts Coun. Freeport (assoc.), N.Y. State Art Tchrs. Assn. (assoc.), Art and Sci. Collaborations, Inc. (assoc.), N.Y. Artists Equity (assoc.). Achievements include development of chemistry on metals art techniques and processes. Office Phone: 516-792-0962. Fax: 516-285-8433.

SAFRENO, CASEY, investment banker; b. 1959; m. Lisa Vinella. Mng. dir., investment banking group, co-head, healthcare investment banking Merrill Lynch & Co. Inc., San Francisco; mng. dir., global head, healthcare Lehman Brothers, San Francisco, 2003—. Named Personality of Yr., Corp. Fin. Week, 2004; recipient Rainmaker Prize, Dealmaker mag., 2006. Office: Lehman Brothers--30th fl 555 California St San Francisco CA 94104 Office Phone: 415-263-3300. *

SAFT, STUART MARK, lawyer; b. NYC, Feb. 17, 1947; s. Stanley and Dorothy (Ligerman) S.; m. Stephanie C. Optekman, June 6, 1970; children: Bradley S., Gordon D. BA, Hofstra U., 1968; JD, Columbia U., 1971. Bar: N.Y. 1972, Fla. 1975, U.S. Dist. Ct. (so. dist.) N.Y. 1975, U.S. Supreme Ct. 1990. Ptnr. LeBoeuf, Lamb, Greene & MacRae LLP, NYC. Chmn. bd. dirs. Coun. of NY Coops., NYC, 1981-; mem. Nat. Coop. Bank, NYC Workforce Investment Bd.; chmn. bd. dirs., CEO Pvt. Industry Coun. NYC, 1994-2000. Author: Commercial Real Estate Forms, 3 vols., 1987, Commercial Real Estate Transactions, 1989, Commercial Real Estate Workouts, 1991, Real Estate Development: Strategies for a Changing Market, 1990, Commercial Real Estate Leasing, 1992, Real Estate Investor's Survival Guide, 1992, Commercial Real Estate Financing, 1993, Commercial Real Estate Forms, 3d edit., 8 vols., 2001, Commercial Real Estate Transactions, 2d edit., 1995, Commercial Real Estate Workouts, 2d edit., 1996; contbg. editor: The Real Estate Finance Jour., 1989—; contbr. articles to profl. jours. Capt USAR, 1968—76. Mem. ABA, Am. Coll. Real Estate Lawyers, N.Y. Bar Assn., Fla. Bar Assn. Office: LeBoeuf Lamb Greene & MacRae LLP 125 W 55th St New York NY 10019 Office Phone: 212-424-4285. Business E-Mail: ssaft@llgm.com.

SAFYER, STEVEN MICHAEL, medical association administrator, educator; b. NYC, Feb. 16, 1949; MD, Albert Einstein Coll. of Med., 1982. Cert. internal medicine. Intern Montefiore Med. Ctr., Bronx, NY, 1978—82, resident, 1983—85, v.p. med. affairs, 1997, sr. v.p., chief med. officer, 1998—; assoc. prof., dept. medicine Albert Einstein Coll. Medicine, 1987—, assoc. prof., dept. epidemiology & population health, 1987—. Office: MMC Centennial Bldg 111 E 210 St 4th Fl Bronx NY 10467

SAG, IVAN A., linguist, educator; PhD, MIT, 1976; prof Honoris Causa (hon.), Univ. Bucharest, 2001. V.p. Red White and Blues Prodns., Inc, Rochester, NY, 1969—71; spl. cons., Linguistic Inst. Univ. Mass., 1974; asst. prof., linguistics Univ. Pa., 1977—79, Stanford Univ., 1979—84, assoc. prof., 1984—88, prof., linguistics, symbolic sys., 1986—; affiliated faculty Stanford Symbolic Sys. Program, 1986—. Recipient Victoria Fromkin Prize, for disting. contributions to the field of linguistics, Linguistic Soc. Am., 2005; grantee Andrew Mellon Found. Fellowship, 1978—79. Fellow: Am. Acad. Arts & Scis. Office: Dept Linguistics Stanford Univ Stanford CA 94305 Home Phone: 650-854-6453. Business E-Mail: sag@csli.stanford.edu. *

SAGALOWSKY, ARTHUR I., urologist, educator; b. Indpls., Aug. 19, 1948; s. Meyer and Goldie Sagalowsky; m. Hanne Albaek, June 11, 1972; children: Julie, Jordan. BA, Ind. U., 1970; MD, Ind. U. Med. Ctr., 1973. Intern, resident Ind. U. Med. Ctr., Indpls., 1973—75, resident, 1975—78; clin. asst. prof. surgery and urology U. Tex. Southwestern Med. Ctr., Dallas, 1978—80, asst. prof. urology, 1980—84, assoc. prof. urology and surgery, 1984—89, prof. urology and surgery, 1989—. Surg. dir. renal transplantation U. Tex. Southwestern Med. Ctr., 1983—95, chief urologic oncology, dept. urology, 1995—, co-investigator NIH O'Brien Ctr. Urologic Rsch., 1993—2000, prin. investigator urology, 2000—, prin. investigator urology NIH Cancer Inst. Urologic Cancer Outreach Program, 1989—98. Fellow, Ind. U. Med. Ctr., Krannert Inst. Cardiology, 1967—69, U. Tex. Southwestern Med. Ctr., 1978—80. Avocations: piano, golf, fly fishing. Home: 4450 Cedarbrush Dallas TX 75346 Office: U Tex Southwestern Med Ctr Dept Urology 5323 Harry Hines Blvd Dallas TX 75390-9110 Office Phone: 214-648-3976. Business E-Mail: arthur.sagalowsky@utsouthwestern.edu.

SAGAN, M. J., architectural firm executive; m. Craig L. Haft; children: Nicholas, Claire, Owen. BA in Architecture, Pa. State U., 1982. Lic. NY, NJ, Conn., cert. NCARB. Assoc., staff designer George F. Henschel, Jr., AIA, 1982—83; assoc./project arch. Becker, Becker & Lamont, Inc., New Canaan, Conn., 1983—84; assoc. Shope Reno Wharton Assoc., Greenwich, Conn., 1984—88; sr. assoc. Anderson/Schwartz Arch., NYC, 1988—96; v.p. Anderson Architecture, NYC, 1996—2006; pres. MJ Sagan Architecture, 2006—. Exhibitions include Negotiating Domesticity/ The Greenwich Arts Coun., 2003, Princeton Pub. Libr., 2003. Recipient EDRA/Places Design award, 2003, Bldg. Team Project of the Yr.- Grand award, 2003, Good Design is Good Bus. award, 2002, Project award, Hudson River Pk., 2002, Gold award, 1994, Wallpaper Mag. Design award, 2004, AIA NJ, 2005, numerous other awards, AIA and others. Several selected publications from 1986-2002 in mag. such as: Arch. Record, House & Garden, The New York Times, Interior Design, Vogue, Diseno Interior 70, House Beautiful, Abitare, and Record Interiors. Business E-Mail: admin@mjsaganarchitecture.com.

SAGAWA, YONEO, horticulturist, educator; b. Olaa, Hawaii, Oct. 11, 1926; s. Chikatada and Mume (Kuno) S.; m. Masayo Yamamoto, May 24, 1962 (dec. Apr. 1988); children: Penelope Toshiko, Irene Teruko. AB, Washington U., St. Louis, 1950, MA, 1952; PhD, U. Conn., Storrs, 1956. Postdoctoral rsch. assoc. biology Brookhaven Nat. Lab., Upton, NY, 1955—57, guest in biology, 1958; asst. prof., then assoc. prof. U. Fla., 1957—64; dir. undergrad. sci. ednl. rsch. participation program NSF, 1964; cons. biosatellite project NASA, 1966—67; prof. horticulture U. Hawaii, 1964—; dir. Lyon Arboretum, 1967—91; assoc. dir. Hawaiian Sci. Fair, 1966—67, dir., 1967—68; rsch. assoc. in biology U. Calif., Berkeley, 1970—71; rsch. assoc. Bot. Rsch. Inst. of Tex., 1993—, Hawaii Tropical Bot. Garden, 1995—; external assessor U. Pertanian, Malaysia, 1994—; assoc. sci. Bishop Mus., Honolulu, 2007—. Mem. Internat. Orchid Commn. on Classification, Nomenclature and Registration; fellow Inst. voor Toepassing van Atoomenergie in de Landbouw, U. Agr., Wageningen, The Netherlands, 1979-80; mem. sci. adv. bd. Nat. Tropical Bot. Garden, Kauai, Hawaii; councilor Las Cruces Bot. Garden, Costa Rica; cons. FAO, Singapore, 1971, USAID-Agribus. Assistance Program, Vols. in Overseas Coop. Assistance, UN Devel. Program-UN Internat. Short Term Adv. Resources; dir. Hawaii Tropical Bot. Garden; hon. scientist Rural Devel. Adminstrn., Republic of Korea, 1998—; cons. Fiji-N.Z. Bus. Coun., 1996, 97, 98, 99, 2000; cons. IRETA, Samoa, 1997, 98, 2003, 06; cons. Nat. Hort. Rsch. Inst., Suwon, Republic of Korea, 1998, 2000. Editor: Hawaii Orchid Jour., 1972-99, Pacific Orchid Soc. Bull., 1966-71; mem. editl. bd. Allertonia, 1976; mem. editl. adv. bd. Jour. Orchid Soc. India, 2002—; contbr. numerous articles to profl. jours. Trustee Friends of Honolulu Bot. Gardens, 1973-99. Recipient Disting. Svc. award South Fla. Orchid Soc., 1968, Grand prize for Poster, 1st Nagoya Internat. Orchid Show, 1990, Cert. of Achievement Garden Club Am., 1995, Digest Doer's Profile, 2000, Gold award Hawaii Orchid Growers Assn., 1996; grantee Am. Orchid Soc., Atomic Energy Commn., NIH, HEW, Inst. Mus. Svcs., Stanley Smith Hort. Trust, Honolulu Orchid Soc. Fellow Am. Orchid Soc. (hon. life, Achievement Gold medal 1999); mem. AAAS, Internat. Assn. Hort. Sci., Am. Assn. Hort. Sci., Am. Inst. for Biol. Scis., Bot. Soc. Am., Hawn Bot. Soc. (past v.p.), Internat. Assn. Plant Tissue Culture, Internat. Palm Soc., Am. Anthurium Soc. (hon. life), Pacific Orchid Soc. (trustee 1994), Kaimuki Orchid Soc. (hon. life), Honolulu Orchid Soc. (hon., life), Lyon Arboretum Assn. (trustee 1974-91), Garden Club Honolulu (hon., life), Aloha Bonsai Club, Sigma Xi, Gamma Sigma Delta, Phi Kappa Phi (past pres., v.p., councillor U. Hawaii chpt.). Democrat. Office: U Hawaii TPSS St John Rm 102 3190 Maile Way Honolulu HI 96822-2279 Fax: 808-956-3894. Business E-Mail: yoneo@hawaii.edu.

SAGE, ANDREW GREGG CURTIN, II, former investment banking house executive; b. Bryn Mawr, Pa., Mar. 11, 1926; s. Henry W. and Eleanor (Purviance) S.; m. Sara Wakefield, Sept. 29, 1956; children: Andrew Gregg Curtin III, Sally. Mem. staff DeCoppet & Doremus (odd lot stock house), NYC, 1946-47, Sage & Co., N.Y. Stock Exchange Specialists, NYC, 1947-48; assoc. Lehman Bros., NYC, 1948-60, gen. ptnr., 1960-68, mng. ptnr., 1969, pres., 1970-73, vice chmn., 1973-77, mng. dir., 1977-82, Lehman Bros. Kuhn Loeb, Inc., 1977-82, Shearson Lehman Bros., Inc., 1982-87, sr. cons., 1987-90; pres., CEO, dir. Robertson CECO Corp., Boston, 1992-93, chmn. bd. dirs., 1994—2006, Chgo. Bd. dirs. Am. Superconductor Corp.; pres., treas. Sage Land Devel. Co.; pres., bd. dirs. Sage Capital Corp. Served with USAAF, 1944-46. Home: PO Box 1432 Wilson WY 83014-0937 Office Phone: 307-733-3100. Personal E-mail: andysage@earthlink.net.

SAGE, ANDREW PATRICK, systems engineering and management educator; b. Charleston, SC, Aug. 27, 1933; s. Andrew Patrick and Pearl Louise (Britt) S.; m. LaVerne Galhouse, Mar. 3, 1962; children: Theresa Annette, Karen Margaret, Philip Andrew. BS in Elec. Engring, The Citadel, Charleston, SC, 1955; SM, MIT, Cambridge, Mass., 1956; PhD, Purdue U., Lafayette, 1960; DEng (hon.), U. Waterloo, Can., 1987, Dalhousie U., Halifax, Nova Scotia, Can., 1997. Registered profl. engr., Tex. Instr. elec. engrng. Purdue U., 1956-60; assoc. prof. U. Ariz., 1960-63; mem. tech. staff Aerospace Corp., Los Angeles, 1963-64; prof. elec. engring. and nuclear engrng. scis. U. Fla., 1964-67; prof., dir. Info. and Control Scis. Center, So. Methodist U., Dallas, 1967-74; head elec. engring. dept. So. Meth. U., 1973-74; Quarles prof. engring. sci. and systems U. Va., Charlottesville, 1974-84, chmn. dept. chem. engring., 1974-75, chmn. dept. engring. sci. and systems, 1977-84, assoc. dean, 1974-80; First Am. Bank prof. info. tech. George Mason U., Fairfax, Va., 1984—, assoc. v.p. for acad. affairs, 1984-85, dean Sch. Info. Tech. and Engring., 1985-96, univ. prof., founding dean emeritus, 1996—. Cons. Martin Marietta, Collins Radio, Atlantic Richfield, Tex. Instruments, LTV Aerospace, Battelle Meml. Inst., TRW Sys., NSF, Inst. Def. Analyses, Planning Rsch. Corp., MITRE, Engrng. Rsch. Assocs., Software Productivity Consortium; gen. chmn. Internat. Conf. on Sys., Man and Cybernetics, 1974, 87; mem. spl. program panel on sys. sci. NATO, 1981-82; trustee, cons. Ctr. Naval Analysis, 1990-94. Author: Optimum Systems Control, 1968, 2d edit., 1977, Estimation Theory with Applications to Communications and Control, 1971, System Identification, 1971, An Introduction to Probability and Stochastic Processes, 1973, Methodology for Large Scale Systems, 1977, Systems Engineering: Methodology and Applications, 1977, Linear Systems Control, 1978, Economic Systems Analysis, 1983, System Design for Human Interaction, 1987, Information Processing in Systems and Organizations, 1990, Introduction to Computer Systems Analysis, Design, and Applications, 1989, Software Systems Engineering, 1990, Decision Support Systems Engineering, 1991, Systems Engineering, 1992, Systems Management for Information Technology and Software Engineering, 1995, Handbook of Systems Engineering and Management, 1999, Introduction to Systems Engineering, 2000; assoc. editor IEEE Transactions on Systems Sci. and Cybernetics, 1968-72; editor: IEEE Transactions on Systems, Man and Cybernetics, 1972-98; assoc. editor: Automatica, 1968-81; editor, 1981-96; mem. editl. bd. Systems Engring, 1968-72, IEEE Spectrum, 1972-73, Computers and Elec. Engring., 1972, Jour. Interdisciplinary Modeling and Simulation, 1976-80, Internat. Jour. Intelligent Sys., 1986—, Orgn. Sci., 1994-2002; editor Elsevier North Holland textbook series in sys. sci. and engring., 1970-88, John Wiley textbook series on sys. engring. and mgmt., 1989—; co-editor-in-chief Jour. Large Scale Sys.: Theory and Applications, 1978-88, Info. and Decision Technologies, 1988-94, Info. and Sys. Engring., 1995-96; editor in chief Sys. Engring., 1998—; co-editor in chief Info., Knowledge and Sys. Mgmt., 1999—; contbr. articles to profl. jours. Recipient Norbert Wiener award, 1980, Joseph G. Wohl career award, 1991, Superior Pub. Svc. award Sec. of the Navy, 1994; Case Centennial scholar, 1980, Award Washington Soc. of Engrs., 1996. Fellow: AAAS (chmn. sect. M 1990), IEEE (life M. Barry Carlton award 1970, Centennial medal 1984, Outstanding Contbn. award 1986, Donald G. Fink prize 1994, Simon Ramo medal 2000), Internat. Coun. on Sys. Engring. (Pioneer award 2002); mem.: NAE, Inst. for Ops. Rsch. and

Mgmt. Sci., Washington Soc. Engrs. (award 1996), Am. Soc. Engring. Edn. (Frederick Emmonds Terman award 1970, Centennial cert. for exceptional contbn. 1993), Internat. Fedn. Automatic Control (Oustanding Svc. award), IEEE Sys./Man and Cybernetics Soc. (pres. 1984—85), Tau Beta Pi, Eta Kappa Nu (eminent mem. award 2002), Sigma Xi. Home: 8011 Woodland Hills Ln Fairfax VA 22039-2433 Office: George Mason U Sch Info Tech Fairfax VA 22030-4444 Office Phone: 703-993-1506. Business E-Mail: asage@gmu.edu.

SAGE, WEBSTER LEGENE, JR., ophthalmologist; b. St. Louis, Oct. 22, 1925; s. Webster LeGene and Alice Virginia (Gollehon) S.; m. Claudine New, May 20, 1952 (dec. June 1986); children: Bryan LeGene, Evan Webster; m. Shirley Barr, Jan. 2, 1988. BS, U. Ariz., 1949; MD, Baylor U., 1953. Diplomate Am. Bd. Ophthalmology. Intern Good Samaritan Hosp., Phoenix; resident Loma Linda (Calif.) U.; pvt. practice Phoenix, 1956—. Chmn. dept. ophthalmology Good Samaritan Hosp., Phoenix, 1960-62, St. Joseph's Hosp., Phoenix, 1971-72; cons. Ariz. Bd. Med. Examiners, Phoenix; owner Surg. Eye Ctr. Ariz., Phoenix, 1985—. Chmn. bd. of elders and deacons Camelback Christian Ch., Scottsdale, Ariz. Maj. U.S. Army, 1962-64. Fellow ACS (life), Am. Acad. Ophthalmology, Internat. Coll. Surgeons; mem. Ariz. Ophthalmological Soc. (pres. 1963-64), Phoenix Ophthalmological Soc. (pres. 1967-68), Kiwanis Club, Paradise Valley Country Club, Phoenix Country Club. Avocations: travel, photography. Home: 8210 N Charles Dr Paradise Valley AZ 85253-2405 Office: 5133 N Central Ave Ste 100 Phoenix AZ 85012-1438

SAGE-GAVIN, EVA MARIE, retail executive; b. Boston, Sept. 26, 1958; d. Ross Francis and Theresa Veronica (Bufalo) S.; m. Dennis Gavin. BS in Indsl. and Labor Rels., Cornell U., Ithaca, NY, 1980. Affirmative action pers. specialist Xerox Corp., Washington, 1980-81, compensation analyst Rochester, NY, 1981-82, sales recruiter Boston, 1982, employment mgr., 1983, systems mktg. rep., 1983-85, pers. mgr. LA, 1985—86, human resources mgr. Irvine, Calif., 1986; dir. human resources PepsiCo, 1991, v.p. corp. human resources Taco Bell; sr. v.p. human resources Disney Consumer Products, 1997—2000, Sun Microsystems, Inc., 2000—03; exec. v.p. human resources and corp. comm. Gap Inc., 2003—. Mem. career adv. bd. Emmanuel Coll., Boston, 1983-85. Named one of Top 25 Most Powerful Women in HR, HR Exec. mag., 2005. Mem. Am. Soc. Pers. Adminstrn., Women in Mgmt., Xerox Women's Network (edn. com. 1988), Kappa Kappa Gamma. Democrat. Roman Catholic. Avocations: skiing, travel, boating, sailing, aerobics. Office: Gap Inc 2 Folsom St San Francisco CA 94105 Office Phone: 650-952-4400. Office Fax: 415-427-2553. *

SAGER, DONALD JACK, librarian, consultant, retired publishing executive; b. Milw., Mar. 3, 1938; s. Alfred Herman and Sophia (Sagan) Sager; m. Sarah Ann Long, May 23, 1987; children: Geoffrey, Andrew. BS, U. Wis., Milw., 1963; MSLS, U. Wis., 1964. Sr. documentalist AC Electronics divsn. GM, Milw., 1958-63; teaching asst. U. Wis., Madison, 1963-64; dir. Kingston (N.Y.) Pub. Libr., 1964-66, Elyria (Ohio) Pub. Libr., 1966-71, Mobile Pub. Libr., 1971-75, Pub. Libr. Columbus and Franklin County, Ohio, 1975-78; commr. Chgo. Pub. Libr., 1978-81; dir. Elmhurst Pub. Libr., Ill., 1982-83, Milw. Pub. Libr., 1983-91; pub. Highsmith Press, Ft. Atkinson, Wis., 1991-2000; pres., CEO Gossage Sager Assocs. LLC, NYC, 2000—. Secy Online Computer Library Ctr, 1977—78, disting vis scholar, 1982; chmn investment comt PLA Pub Library, 1985—89, chmn mus comt, 1989—91, mem hist comt, 1993—95, chmn PLA nat conf comt, 1986—88; bd dirs Coun Wis Libraries, 1982—91, Urban Libraries Coun, 1985—93, secy, 1991—93; adj faculty Univ Wis, Milwaukee, 1984—91; consult in field. Author: Reference: A Programmed Instruction, 1970, Binders, Books and Budgets, 1971, Participatory Management, 1981, The American Public Library, 1982, Public Library Administrators Planning Guide to Automation, 1983, Managing the Public Library, 1984, Small Libraries, 1992, 3d rev. edit., 2000; co-editor: Urban Library Management Trends, 1989; contbg. editor: Public Libraries, 1990—2000; contbr. articles to profl. jours. Pres Milwaukee Civic Alliance, 1990—91; chmn Milwaukee United Way Campaign, 1984; pres Milwaukee Westown Asn, 1987—90; treas. Congl. Ch. Deerfield, Ill., 2002—05, bd. dirs., 2005—; bd dirs Goethe House, 1985—91. With AUS, 1956—58. Mem.: ALA (councilor-at-large 1995—2003, policy monitoring comt, awards comt, chmn core values task force, Joseph Lippincott award 2005), Library Admin Asn Wis (chmn 1987—88), Wis Library Asn Found (chmn 1986—88), Wis Library Asn, Chicago Book Clin, Ill Library Asn, Pub Library Asn (pres 1982—83, bd dirs, vpres, pres-elect), Exchange Club Milwaukee (pres 1988—89). Office Phone: 312-961-5536. Business E-Mail: dsager@gamil.com.

SAGER, KELLI L., lawyer; b. 1960; Attended, U. Southern Calif., 1977—81; BA in Polit. Sci. and Journalism, West Ga. Coll., 1981; JD, U. Utah Sch. Law, 1985. Bar: Calf. 1985. Adj. prof. U. Southern Calif. Law Sch., 2002; ptnr. Davis Wright Tremaine, LA. Mem. adv. com. Donald W. Reynolds Nat. Ctr. for Courts and Media, Nat. Jud. Coll., 2000—; mem. internat. adv. bd. Nat. Inst. Entertainment and Media Law, Southwestern U. Law, 2001—; mem. bd. dirs. Pub. Counsel, 2001—; mem. atty. com. Nat. Ctr. for State Courts, 2002—; bd. mem. LA Copyright Soc., 2002—, treas., 2005—. Bd. dirs. LA Youth News, 1995—2001. Named one of 45 Lawyers Under 45, Am. Lawyer mag., 1995, 40 Professionals Under 40, LA Bus. Jour., 1996, 50 Top Lawyers in LA, 1997, Lawyers of Yr., Calif. Lawyer mag., 1997, The 100 Most Influential Lawyers in Calif., LA Daily Jour., 1998—99, 2001—04, Top 50 Women Litigators in Country, Nat. Law Jour., 2001, 500 Leading Lawyers in Am., Lawdragon, 2005, 500 Leading Litigators in Am., 2006, America's Leading Bus. Lawyers, Chambers USA, 2005—06, Top 75 Women Litigators in Calif., Daily Jour., 2005—07, Southern Calif. Super Lawyers, 2007, The 50 Most Influential Women Lawyers in Am., Nat. Law Jour., 2007; named to Best Lawyers in Am., 1997—99, 2000, 2003, 2005—07; recipient ACLU First Amendment award, 1996, adv. award, Calif. First Amendment Coalition, 1996, Freedom of Info. award, Soc. Prof. Journalists, 1996, First Amendment award, LA Youth/LA Times, 1998. Mem.: ABA (western divsn. chair Forum on Comm. Law 2002—, co-chair litig. sect., 1st amendment com. 2005—), Order of the Coif. Office: Davis Wright Tremaine LLP Ste 2400 865 S Figueroa St Los Angeles CA 90017-2566 Office Phone: 213-633-6800. Office Fax: 213-633-6899. Business E-Mail: kellisager@dwt.com. *

SAGER, LAWRENCE GENE, dean, law educator; b. 1941; AB, Pomona Coll., 1963; LLB magna cum laude, Columbia Coll., 1966. Bar: Calif. 1967. Asst. prof. U. Calif., LA, 1966—68, acting prof., 1968—71; assoc. prof NYU, NY, 1972—74, prof., 1974—95; Robert B. McKay prof. law, 1995—2002; Alice Jane Drysdale Sheffield Regents Chair in Law U. Texas, Austin, 2002—, dean, 2006—. Vis. prof. law and social planning Woodrow Wilson Sch., Princeton, 1974-76; vis. prof. U. Mich., Harvard U., spring 1981, Boston U., 1986-89. Recipient Disting. Alumni Award, Pomona Coll. Mem. N.Y. CLU. Office: University of Texas School of Law 727 E Dean Keeton Street Austin TX 78705 Business E-Mail: lsager@law.utexas.edu.

SAGER, MADELINE DEAN, lawyer; b. Turlock, Calif., Feb. 9, 1946; d. Paul Kenton and Jean Madeline (Ferguson) Dean; m. Gregory Warren Sager, June, 1970; children: Jeannette Carolyn, Robert Dean. BA, Sacramento State U., 1967; JD, U. Calif., Davis, 1970. Bar: Calif. 1971, U.S. Dist. Ct. (ea. dist.) Calif. 1971, U.S. Dist. Ct. (no. dist.) Calif. 1973. Atty. Blackmon, Isenberg, Moulds & Blicker, Sacramento, 1971-72, Redwood Legal Assistance, Ukiah, Calif., 1972-77, Sager & Sager, Ukiah, Willits, Calif., 1977-87, Leonard J. LaCasse, Ukiah, Calif., 1990—2002, Nelson & Riemenscheider, Ukiah, Calif., 2002—03, Law Offices of David Riemenschneider, Ukiah, 2003—. Dir. Law Libr. Bd., Ukiah, 1985. Sec. PTA, Calpella, Calif., 1989-90; mem. sch. site coun. Redwood Valley (Calif.) Mid. Sch., 1992-93; treas., dir. Ukiah Dolphin Swim, 1994-97; meet dir. Soroptimist Swim Meet, Ukiah, 1996. Mem. Mendocino County Bar Assn. (pres. 1986), Pacific Swimming (ofcl. 1995-98), Music Boosters Ukiah H.S. Democrat. Presbyterian. Avocations: hiking, camping, music, travel. Home: PO Box 72 Redwood Valley CA 95470-0072 Office: Law Offices of David Riemenschneider 106 N School St Ukiah CA 95482 Office Phone: 707-462-1351.

SAGER, MARGARET E.W., lawyer; b. Nashville, Nov. 16, 1960; BA summa cum laude, U. Richmond, 1982; JD, U. Va., 1985. Bar: Pa. 1985. Assoc. trust and estate dept. Duane, Morris & Heckscher, 1985—94; shareholder Heckscher, Teillon, Terrill & Sager, P.C., West Conshohocken, Pa. Named one of Top 100 Attys., Worth mag., 2005, 2006. Fellow: Am. Coll. Trust and Estate Counsel; mem.: ABA, Pa. Bar Assn., Montgomery County Bar Assn., Phila. Bar Assn. (chair probate and trust law sect. 2000, chair rules and practice com. 1992—96), Phi Beta Kappa. Office: Heckscher Teillon Terrill & Sager Ste 300 100 Four Falls West Conshohocken PA 19428-2900 Office Phone: 610-940-4171. Office Fax: 610-940-6042. E-mail: mewsager@htts.com.

SAGER, PHILIP TRAVIS, pharmaceutical executive, cardiologist, researcher; b. NYC, Jan. 23, 1956; s. Clifford Julius and Ruth (Levy) Sager; m. Linda Sager. BS in Chemistry and Biology, MIT, 1977; MD, Yale U., 1982. Diplomate Am. Bd. Internal Medicine, Am. Bd. Cardiology, Am. Bd. Cardiac Electrophysiology. Resident, fellow in cardiology and cardiac electrophysiology Yale U., New Haven, 1982—88; asst. prof. medicine Sch. Medicine, U. So. Calif., LA, 1988-90, asst. dir. electrophysiology, 1988-90, dir. Pacemaker Ctr., 1988-90; asst. prof. medicine Sch. Medicine, UCLA, 1990-96, assoc. prof. medicine, 1996—2001; dir. cardiac electrophysiology West L.A. VA Med. Ctr., 1990—2001; sr. dir., U.S. lead physician Astrazeneca Inc., Wilmington, Del., 2004—, med. sci. sr. dir., 2005—, exec. dir., curriculum vitae rsch. and global quality tchg. strategy leader, 2006—; dir. cardiac rsch. Schering-Plough Rsch. Inst., 2001—; clin. prof. medicine UMDNJ Med. Sch., 2002—. Mem. cardiology adv. com. VA, Washington, 1990-94; cons. electrophysiology ACGME, Chgo., 1995-01; vis. prof. Kern Med. Ctr., Bakersfield, Calif., 1991, 94, U. Iowa Sch. Medicine, 1994, Northwestern U. Sch. Medicine, 1994, Yale U. Sch. Medicine, 1995, U. Calif., San Francisco, 1996; topic leader, ICH Expert Working Group on the Clin. Quality Tchg. Initative, 2002-05; mem. ICH E 14 Implementation Group, 2005-; chair Internat. DIA-FDA-HRS Quality Tchg. Conf., 2006; exe. com. mem. FDA Duke Critical Pathway Initiative; cons. pharm. cos.; lectr. in field. Contbr. chpts. to books, numerous articles to profl. jours.; reviewer sci. jours. and sci. mags. Recipient many rsch. grants, including Am. Heart Assn., 1996. Fellow ACP, Am. Heart Assn., Am. Coll. Cardiology, Heart Rhythm Soc.; mem. Am. Fedn. Clin. Rsch., Nat. Assn. Pacing and Electrophysiology (program dirs. com. 1992-01, govt. com. 1994-01, co-chair program dirs. com. 1997-01), Phi Beta Kappa, Alpha Omega Alpha. Avocations: travel, bicycling, scuba diving, reading, movies. Office: AstraZeneca 1800 Concord Pike PO Box 15437 Wilmington DE 19850-5437 Office Phone: 302-885-5669. Personal E-mail: psager@alum.mit.edu.

SAGERHOLM, JAMES ALVIN, retired naval officer; b. Uniontown, Pa., Dec. 23, 1927; s. Frithiof Norris and Margaret Blocher S.; m. Margaret Ann Herrlich, June 7, 1952; children— Lisa Marie, Ann Denise, Jeannine Louise, Mark Christian BS, U.S. Naval Acad., 1952. Commd. ensign U.S. Navy, 1952, advanced through grades to vice admiral, 1983, exec. officer USS Sproston, 1961—63, navigator USS Seadragon, 1965, exec. officer blue crew USS Mariano G. Vallejo, 1966-67, comdg. officer gold crew USS Kamehameha, 1968-71, head gen. purpose warfare forces group Office of Chief Naval Ops., 1971, dep. exec. dir. Chief Naval Ops. Exec. Panel, 1972, exec. sec. Chief Naval Ops. Exec. Bd., 1973, comdr. Naval Intelligence Support Ctr. Washington, 1974-75, dep. dir. naval intelligence Chief Naval Ops., 1975-76, comdr. South Atlantic Force, U.S. Atlantic Fleet, 1976-78, dir. Office of Program Appraisal, Office of Sec. Navy, 1978-81, chief naval edn. and tng. Pensacola, Fla., 1983-85; exec. dir. Pres. Fgn. Intelligence Adv. Bd. White House, Washington, 1981-82; ret., 1985. Chmn. bd. dirs. Piedmont Environ. Coun., 1987-89; v.p. for nat. affairs Gen. George C. Marshall Home Found., 1990-91. Trustee Balt. Polytech. Inst. Found., 2000-03, U.S. Naval Acad. Found., 2005—. Decorated D.S.M., Legion of Merit, Meritorious Service medal; named Disting. Alumnus, Balt. Poly. Inst. Mem. Naval Submarine League, U.S. Naval Inst., K.C. Roman Catholic. Avocations: golf, civil war history. Home: 414 Rockfleet Rd Unit 102 Timonium MD 21093-7582

SAGET, BOB, actor, comedian, writer, television director; b. Phila., May 17, 1956; m. Sherri Kramer, 1982 (div. 1997); children: Aubrey, Lara, Jenny. Grad. film studies, Temple U., 1978. Host 2002 Winter Olympics. Appeared at Carnegie Hall, Las Vegas, Atlantic City, The Comedy Store, The Improv, Calif.; actor (stage) Privilege, 2005; (films) Critical Condition, 1986, 1998, Half Baked, 1998, Dumb and Dumberer: When Harry Met Llody, 2003, (voice) Madagascar, 2005; (TV) Full House, 1987-95, Raising Dad, 2001-02, (voice) How I Met Your Mother, 2005-; actor, exec. prodr. Father and Scout, 1994, Jitters, 1997; dir., exec. prodr. For Hope, 1997; co-host The Morning Program, 1986; host, writer: America's Funniest Home Videos, 1989-97; dir., actor, writer: HBO Comedy Hour: In The Dream State; dir. Dirty Work, 1998, Mind of the Married Man, 2001; dir., actor Becoming Dick, 2000. Address: Brillstein/Grey Entertainment 9150 Wilshire Blvd Ste 350 Beverly Hills CA 90212-3453

SAGHIR, ADEL JAMIL, art educator, painter, sculptor; b. Beirut, May 27, 1930; came to U.S., 1973; s. Jamil Khalil and Aisha Rachid (Mirii) S.; m. Jindriska Antonin Moucka, Aug. 24, 1968; children: Jamil, Ryan. BA, Am. U., Beirut, 1968, diploma in tchg., 1973; MFA, Pratt Inst., 1975; postgrad., NYU, 1976-79. Asst. prof. Fine Arts Inst., Lebanese U., Beirut, 1963-73; lectr. Am. Beirut U. Coll., 1972-73; adj. prof. Western Conn. State U., Danbury, 1988—; instr. sculpture, mural painting, art history Silvermine Sch. Art, New Canaan, Conn., 1989-98. Artist various murals and tapestries. Recipient 4th prize Alexandria Biennale, Egyptian Govt., 1963, 1st prize silk tapestries Nat. Contest Lebanon, 1965, 1st prize major sculpture monuments, 1966, 1st prize City Ctr. Sculpture Contest, 1969; Fine Arts scholar, Germany, Munic Acad., 1958-60; Fulbright-Hayes fellow NYU, N.Y.C., 1973-79. Mem. Internat. Soc. Advancement of Living Traditions in Art, Washington Pl. Artists Assn. (pres. 1977-80), Lebanese Artists Assn. (v.p. 1964-73). Avocations: gardening, fishing, upland hunting. Home: 20 Newfane Rd New Fairfield CT 06812-4721 Office: Western Conn State U 181 White St Danbury CT 06810-6826

SAH, CHIH-TANG, electrical and computer engineering educator; b. Beijing, Nov. 10, 1932; s. Adam Peng-tung and Shu-shen Huang; m. Linda Chang, Nov. 29, 1959; children: Dinah W.Y., Robert L.Y. *Father Adam Pen-tung was President of Amoy University of China; Secretary General of Academia Sinica; a prolific textbook author in physics, calculus, electrical circuits and senior electrical machines; and a visiting professor at Massachusetts Institute of Technology, Stanford University and Ohio State University. Mother Shu-shen Huang was a Chinese Olympian in 1930. Wife Linda Chang was recipient of Barat Cup and graduated magna cum laude at Barat College in Chicago in 1958. Daughter Dinah was head of Neuroscience department at Signal Pharmaceuticals and Biogen, Inc. Now with Alnylam Pharmaceuticals, Inc. Son Robert is a Howard Hughes Professor, vice chair of the bioenginnering department, and Director of Cartilage Tissue Engineering Laboratory at University of California at San Diego.* BS Physics, U. Ill., 1953, BSEE, 1953; MSEE, Stanford U., 1954, PhD, 1956; D honoris causa, U. Leuven, Belgium, 1975; Doctorate (hon.), Nat. Chao-Tung U., Taiwan, 2004. Research assoc. Stanford Electronics Lab., Palo Alto, Calif., 1956; sr. mem. tech. staff Shockley Transistor Corp., Palo Alto, 1956—59; head, mgr. physics dept. Fairchild Semiconductor Lab., Palo Alto, 1959-64; prof. physics and elec. engring. U. Ill., Urbana, 1962-88, dir. Ill. Solid State Electronics Lab.; Pittman Eminent Scholar chair, grad. research prof., chief scientist Coll. Engring. U. Fla., Gainesville, 1988—. Program dir. 1st generation Si VLSI tech. Fairchild Corp., 1959-64; cons. Jet Propulsion Lab., Dept. Energy, Pasadena, Calif., 1976-85, Harry Diamond Lab., Washington, 1974-75, IBM Corp., NY, numerous other electronics firms 1964-88; advisor Intel Corp., Oreg., Calif., other semicondr. mfrs., 1988—; hon. prof. Peking U., 2003, Tsnghua U., 2003, Xiamen U., 2004. Author: Fundamentals of Solid-State Electronics, 1991, Transistor Reliability in Fundamentals of Solid-State Electronics—Solution Manual, 1996; founding editor Internat. Series Advances in Solid-State Electronics and Tech., 1991—; contbr. 300 articles to profl. jours. Recipient first high tech. award Asian Am. Mfg. Assn., 1982, Pioneer Recognition award Com. of the 100, 2002, Disting. Lifetime Achievement award Chinese Inst. Engrs. USA, 2003. Fellow IEEE (life, IRE Browder J. Thompson prize 1963, J.J. Ebers award 1980, Jack Morton award 1989), AAAS, Am. Phys. Soc., Franklin Inst. (life, Cert. of Merit award 1975); mem. US Semicondrs. Industry Assn. (U. Rsch. award, 1998),, Nat. Acad. Engring., Academia Sinica Taiwan (academician), Chinese Acad. Scis. (academician). Achievements include development of complementary metal-oxide semiconductor circuit; Si P-N junction diode phenomena Sah-Noyce-Shockley Theory; MOS transistor compact models, Sah, Pao, Jie; invention of deep-level transient spectroscopy Sah, Tasch, Yau; DCIV diagnosis for deep-submicron transistor design and reliability Sah, Cai, Wang, Jie. Office: 2716 NW 20th St Gainesville FL 32605-2999 Personal E-mail: tom_sah@msn.com.

SAHA, SAMAR KANTI, electronics engineer, educator; arrived in U.S., 1981; s. Phani Bhusan and Mahamaya Saha. PhD, Gauhati U., India, 1981; MS in Engring. Mgmt., Stanford U., Calif., 1992. Asst. prof., elec. engring. So. Ill. U., Carbondale, 1982—84; sr. product engr. Nat. Semiconductor, Santa Clara, Calif., 1984—90; staff engr., R & D LSI Logic Corp., Santa Clara, 1990—92; prin. engr., tech. CAD Nat. Semiconductor, Santa Clara, 1992—95; prin. engr., advanced devel. Tex. Instruments, Santa Cruz, 1995—97; mgr., tech. CAD Philips Semiconductors, San Jose, 1997—2000; mgr., tech. modeling Silicon Storage Tech., Inc., Sunnyvale, 2000—06; adj. prof. Santaclara U., 2004—; sr. mgr. Synopsys Inc., 2006—07, MTS DSM Solutions, 2007—. Contbr. scientific papers to profl. jours. Recipient Outstanding Achievement, Analog Divsn. Nat. Semiconductor, 1988, Tchg. Contbn., EE Dept., U. Nev. Las Vegas, 2002. Mem.: IEEE (mem. compact modeling com. 2001—04, chmn. compact modeling com. 2005—, guest editor). Achievements include patents in field; research in scaling considerations for high performance 25 nm metal-oxide-semiconductor field-effect transistors; effects of inversion layer quantization on channel profile engineering for nMOSFETs with 0.1 m channel lengths; development of efficient approach for integrated circuit fabrication technology; scaling flash memory cells. Home: 286 Aspenridge Dr Milpitas CA 95035 Office: DSM Solutions Inc 130B Knowles Dr Los Gatos CA 95032 Personal E-mail: samar@ieee.org.

SAHAGIAN, ARTHUR H., artist; b. Cleve., Oct. 16, 1924; s. Vartavar and Rose Sahagian; m. Laima Sahagian, Oct. 15, 1980; children: Arthur, Sandra. BS, Western Res. U., Cleve.; postgrad., Cleve. Sch. Art; MA, Northwestern U., Chgo. Supr. art Garfield Hts. Bd. Edn., Cleve.; merchant dealer A&S Utilities, Chgo.; unit mgr. Mutual Omaha, Chgo.; gen. agt., pres. Agy. A&S, Chgo.; tchr. art Chgo. Bd. Edn., Chgo.; artist, owner Arthurian Gallery, Skokie, Ill.; artist, pub. Nat. Art Found., Skokie. Tchr. Skokie Pk. Dist.; bd. dirs. Skokie Art Guild; dir. Nat. Arts Found., Skokie. Mem.: Ret. Tchrs. Assn., Masons. Presbyterian. Home: 8725 Karlov Ave Skokie IL 60076 Office Phone: 847-674-7990.

SAHAGUN, AARON, entrepreneur, Internet company executive; b. 1984; BBA, U. Calif. Berkeley Walter A. Haas Sch. Bus., 2006. Bus. analyst Associated Students U. Calif.; fgn. exch. payments cons. Bank of Am.; with Merrill Lynch; with audit enterprise risk svcs. dept. Deloitte & Touche, LLP; co-founder, CEO Alumwire, LLC, San Francisco, 2006—; mgmt. cons. Sapient Corp. Bus. devel. chair Golden Key Internat. Honor Soc. Bd. dirs. Alumni Scholars Assn. Named one of Best Entrepreneurs Under 25, BusinessWeek mag., 2006. Avocations: guitar, basketball. Mailing: c/o Sapient Corp Ste 3 25 1st St Cambridge MA 02141 E-mail: aaron@alumwire.com. *

SAHAGUN, ALLAN, entrepreneur, Internet company executive; b. 1987; Student, Harvard U., 2005—. Web site programmer AAP Imaging Systems, Inc., 2002; co-founder & exec. v.p. Alumwire LLC, 2006—. Named one of Best Entrepreneurs Under 25, BusinessWeek, 2006; scholar Milken Found., 2005. Office: c/o Sapient Corp Ste 3 25 1st St Cambridge MA 02141

SAHAI, AKHIL, computer scientist, researcher; arrived in US, 1999; s. Harnandan and Rachna Sahai; m. Nina Saxena (dec.); 1 child, Nambita Saxena. BTech with honors, Indian Inst. Tech., Karagpur, 1990; ME in Computer Sci., Indian Inst. Sci., Bangalore, 1995; PhD, U. Rennes I, France, 1999; postgrad., U. Pa., Phila., 2006—. Sr. mgr. Tata Steel, Jamsmedpur, India, 1990—93; sr. R & D engr. ISS, NUS, Singapore, 1995; software engr. Hewlett Packard, Cupertino, Calif., 1999—, sr. rschr. Palo Alto, Calif., 2000—. Chair, organizer various confs. Editor: Utility Computing, 2004; author: Web Services in the Enterprise, 2005; contbr. chapters to books. Achievements include patents for decentralized management of composed digital services; patents pending in field.

SAHAI, HARDEO, medical statistics educator; b. Bahraich, India, Jan. 10, 1942; m. Lillian Sahai, Dec. 28, 1973; 3 children. BS in Math., Stats. and Physics, Lucknow U., India, 1962; MS in Math., Banaras U., Varanasi, India, 1964; MS in Math. Stats., U. Chgo., 1968; PhD in Stats., U. Ky., Lexington, 1971. Lectr. math. and stats. Banaras U., Varanasi, India, 1964—65; asst. stats. officer Durgapur Steel Plant, West Bengal, India, 1965; statistician Rsch. and Planning divsn. Blue Cross Assn., Chgo., 1966; statis. programmer Cleft Palate Ctr. U. Ill., 1967; statis. programmer Chgo. Health Rsch. Found., 1968; mgmt. scientist Mgmt. Sys. Devel. Dept. Burroughs Corp., Detroit, 1971—72; from asst. prof. to prof. dept. math. U. PR, Mayaguez, 1972—82; vis. rsch. prof. Dept. Stats. and Applied Math. U. Ceara, Brazil, 1978—79; sr. rsch. statistician Travenol Labs., Inc., Round Lake, Ill., 1982—83; chief statistician US Army Hqrs., Ft. Sheridan, Ill., 1983—84; sr. math. statistician U.S. Bur. Census Dept. Commerce, Washington, 1984—85; sr. ops. rsch. analyst Def. Logistics Agy. Dept. Def., Chgo., 1985—86; prof. Dept. Biostats. and Epidemiology U. PR Med. Scis., San Juan, 1986—. Cons. PR Univ Cons., PR Driving Safety Evaluation Project, Water Resources Rsch. Inst., Travenol Labs., Campo Rico, PR, US Bur. Census, Washington, Lawrence Livermore Nat. Lab., Calif., others; vis. prof. U. Granada, Spain, U. Veracruzana, Mex., patrimonial prof. stats., 1997—; vis. prof. U. Nacional de Colombia, U. Nacional de Trujillo, Peru, 1993-94, hon. prof. stats., 1994—; adj. prof. dept. math. U. P.R. Natural Scis. Faculty, 1995—; Patrimonial prof. stafs U. Veracruzana, 1997—. Author: Statistics and Probability: Learning Module, 1984; author: (with Jose Berrios) A Dictionary of Statistical Scientific and Technical Terms: English-Spanish and Spanish-English, 1981, (with Wilfredo Martinez) Statistical Tables and Formulas for the Biological Social and Physical Sciences, 1996, (with Anwer Khurshid) Statistics in Epidemiology: Methods, Techniques and Applications, 1996, (with Satish C. Misra and Amwer Khurshid) Quotations on Probability and Statistics with Illustrations, 2004, (with Anwer Khurshid) A Pocket Dictionary of Statistics, 2000, (with Mohammad I. Ageel) The Analysis of Variance: Fixed, Random and Mixed Models, 2000, (with Mario M. Ojeda) A Glossary of

Statistical, Sciebtfic and Technical Terms: English-Spanish, 2004, (with Lucas López Segovia and Hector W. Colón-Rosa) A Glossary of Medical Epidemiologic and Demographic Statistics: English-Spanish, 2003, (with Mario M. Ojeda) Un Manual de Distribuciones t, x2y F Centrales Y No Centrales, 2000, (with Mario M. Ojeda) A Glossary of Computer and Management Terms: English/Spanish, 2004, (with Mario M. Ojeda) Comparisons of Approximations to the Percentiles of Noncentral t, x2 and F Distributions, 2001, (with A. Khurshid) Pocket Dictionary of Statistics, 2001, (with Mario M. Ojeda) Analysis of Variance for Random Models, Vol. 1: Balanced Data and Vol. 2: Unbalanced Data, 2004; mem. editl. bd. Sociedad Colombiana de Matematicas, P.R. Health Scis. Jour.; contbr. editor Current Index to Stats.; reviewer Collegiate Microcomputer, Comm. in Statistics, Indian Jour. Stats., Jour. Royal Statis. Soc. (series D, The Statistician), New Zealand Statistician, Biometrics, Can. Jour. Stats., Technometrics, Problems, Resources and Issues in Math. Undergrad. Studies; contbr. more than 150 articles and papers to profl. and sci. jours., numerous articles to tech. mags. Active Dept. Consumer Affairs Svcs. Commonwealth of PR, San Juan, Dept. Anti-Addiction Svcs., Commonwealth of P.R., San Juan., Inst. of AIDS, Municipality of San Juan, VA Med. Ctr. of San Juan, Caribbean Primate Rsch. Ctr., Ctr. Addiction Studies Caribbean Ctrl. U. Recipient Dept. Army Cert. Achievement award, 1984, U. Ky. Outstanding Alumnus award, 1993, medal of honor U. Granada, 1994, plaque of honor U. Nacional de Trujillo, 1994; fellow Coun. Sci. and Indsl. Rsch., 1964-65, U. Chgo., 1965-68, Harvard U., 1979, Fulbright Found., 1982; U.P. Bd. Merit scholar, 1957-59, Govt. India Merit scholar, 1959-64; grantee NSF, 1974-77, NIMH, 1987-90, 91—, NIDA, 1991—. Fellow AAAS, Am. Coll. Epidemiology, Inst. Statisticians (charter statistician), Inst. Math. and Its Applications (charter mathematician), N.Y. Acad. Scis., Royal Statis. Soc.; mem. Internat. Statis. Inst., Internat. Assn. Tchg. Stats., Soc. Epidemiol. Rsch., Inst. Math. Stats., Bernouilli Soc. for Math. Stats. and Probability, Internat. Biometric Soc., Am. Soc. for Quality Control, Am. Stats. Assn., Japan Statis. Soc., Can. Statis. Soc., Inter-Am. Statis. Inst., Internat. Assn. Statis. Computing, Sch. Sci. and Math. Assn., Sigma Xi. Avocations: religious studies, philosophy, reading, gardening. Home: Urb Mayaguez Terrace 7083 Calle B Gaudier Texidor Mayaguez PR 00682-6617 Personal E-mail: hsahai@hotmail.com.

SAHAKIAN, LILLIAN ZAROUHI, artist, designer; d. Archak Agapov Sahakian and Mariam Zarouhi Zahrbhanelian-Sahakian. Secretarial pool First Nat. City Bank, NYC, 1954—55; sec., sales & mktg. Walker Mktg. Corp., Racine, Wis., 1958—59; typist, purchasing Kollsman Instrument Corp., Elmhurst, NY, 1963—70; supv. stenographer City Hosp. Ctr., 1974—78; exec. sec. Racine/Kenosha Cmty. Action Agy., 1979—80, Butter Buds Corp., Racine, 1989—91; mktg. specialist Johnson Internat., Inc., Racine, 1994—2003. Oil portrait - copy, Victor Choque (2nd Prize, 1955), exhibition, Early Oil Paintings-American Artist, Smithsonian, 1957, altar piece, Madonna & Child, St. Sarkis Ch., 1960, graphite rendering, Viet Nam Refugees - Grandmother & Grandson, 1964, watercolor painting, After Matisse, 1990, graphics logo, Lili Archak Studios, 2004, lifestyle interior designs, Interior Designs LLC. Choir mem. St. Hagop Ch., Wis., 1958—59. Scholar Entrepreneurial Incentive award, State of Wis., 2004. Mem.: NAMI Racine (bd. dirs. 1985—2006), Soc. for Tech. Comm., Kenosha Art Assn., Am. Inst. Graphic Artists. Independent. Avocations: reading, do it yourself home repairs, research on the internet & other, computer generated art, cooking. Office: Lili Archak Studios LLC 1117 Saxony Dr Racine WI 53402 Home Phone: 262-898-9351; Office Phone: 262-898-9351.

SAHID, JOSEPH ROBERT, lawyer; b. Paterson, NJ, Feb. 14, 1944; s. Joseph James and Helen (Vitale) Sahid; m. Serra Yavuz; children: Annunziata, Joseph, Olivia. BS, Rutgers U., 1965; LLB, U. Va., 1968. Bar: NY 1973, US Dist. Ct. NY, US Ct. Appeals (2d and 3d cirs.), US Supreme Ct. Staff mem. Nat. Commn. Causes Prevention Violence, Washington, 1968-69; cons. Pres.'s Commn. Campus Unrest, Washington, 1970; assoc. Cravath, Swaine & Moore, NYC, 1972-77, ptnr., 1977-93, cons., 1994-97; ptnr. Barrack, Rodos & Bacine, NYC, 1995—96; pvt. practice NYC, 1996—. Mediator US Dist. Ct. (so. dist.) NY, NY Civil Ct.; arbitrator NY cts., Nat. Assn. Securities Dealers. Author: (book) Rights in Concord, 1969; co-author: Law and Order Reconsidered, 1969; contbr. articles to profl. jours. Lt. USCG, 1968—72. Mem.: ABA, NY County Lawyers Assn. (arbitrator), NY State Bar Assn. (profl. discipline com.), Bar Assn. City NY (profl. discipline com. 2001—03, 2006—, profl. responsibility com. 2003—06, mem. coop. condo mediation project, coun. children com., legal referral svc.). Address: 845 3rd Ave Fl 20 New York NY 10022-6601 Office Phone: 212-308-5930. Personal E-mail: sahid@nysbar.com.

SAHIMI, MUHAMMAD, engineering educator; b. Tehran, Iran, Jan. 22, 1954; s. Habibollah Sahimi and Fatemeh Fakour Rashid; m. Mahnoush Babaei; children: Ali, Niloofar. BS, U. Tehran, 1977; PhD, U. Minn., Mpls., 1984. Asst. prof. U. So. Calif., LA, 1984—89, assoc. prof., 1989—94, prof., 1994—, chmn. chem. engring., 1999—2005, prof. petroleum engring., 2005—, prof. chem. engring. & materials sci., 2005—. Cons. Nat. Iranian Oil Co., Tehran, 1989—97, Avery Dennison Corp., Pasadena, Calif., 1997—. Commentator Inst. Pub. Accuracy, San Francisco, 2005—07, Kirn 670-Am, LA, 1997—2007. Recipient Humboldt Rsch. Fellowship award, Alexander von Humboldt Found., 1992, Kapitza Gold Medal award, Russian Acad. Natural Scis., 1999, Khwarizmi award, Govt. Iran, UNESCO, 2003. Mem.: Soc. Petroleum Engrs., Materials Rsch. Soc., AIChE, Am. Phys. Soc. Independent. Muslim. Avocations: reading, writing. Office: Univ So Calif 925 Bloomwalk Los Angeles CA 90089-1211 Office Fax: 213-740-8053; Home Fax: 213-740-8053. Personal E-mail: moe@iran.usc.edu. Business E-Mail: moe@usc.edu.

SAHINER, MEHMET ALPER, physics professor, researcher; PhD, Rutgers U., New Brunswick, 1995. Sr. scientist Evans Analytical Group, East Windsor, NJ, 1999—2003; asst. prof. Seton Hall U., South Orange, 2003—. Recipient Cottrell Coll. award, Rsch. Corp., 2005—; grantee, NSF, 2004—06. Mem.: Internat. XAFS Soc., Materials Rsch. Soc., Am. Phys. Soc. Achievements include research in High Tc superconductors structural characteization, High-k dielectrics, semiconductors. Office: Seton Hall Univ Dept Physics 400 S Orange Ave South Orange NJ 07079 Office Phone: 973-761-9060.

SAHL, JACOB, retired technologist, secondary school educator, researcher; b. Phila., Aug. 8, 1925; s. Manuel and Jennie Levitt Sahl; m. Rhea Costilo Sahl, Dec. 9, 1950; children: Marla Sahl Emery, Scott Michael. BA in Earth Scis., Thomas Edison State Coll., Trenton, NJ, 1979. Order assembler Shoemaker and Busch Inc., Phila., 1949—55; TV antenna installer Clearview Inc., Phila., 1946—49; pharm. sales rep. Frank and Black, Phila., 1949—52, Showmaker and Busch, Phila., 1959—79; med. technologist U. Pa. Vet. Sch., Kenneth Sqare, Pa., 1959—79, Smith Kline Med. Lab, King of Prussia, Pa., 1980—91; ret. Med. technologist Franklin Sch. Sci. and Arts, Phila., 1957—59; clin. lab supr. U. Pa. Vet. Hosp. Large Animal Clinic New Boton Ctr., Kenneth Square, 1968—79; lt. Palm Beach County Sheriff Dept. C.O.P., 1999. Sgt. US Army Air Corp, 1943—45, PTO. Decorated Disting. Flyin Cross medal Army Air Corp, 5 Air medals, Air Combat medal. Mem.: Jewish War Vets. (vol. 1996—, comdr. 1996, nat. exec. com. 2006). Jewish. Avocations: classical music, Kung Fu, photography.

SAHLEM, JAMES ROBERT, law librarian; b. Buffalo, Feb. 21, 1948; s. Lee M. and Mildred A. (Hibschweiler) S.; m. Susan Mary Schifferli, Aug. 9, 1969; children: Steven, Andrea, Gregory. BS in Mgmt., Canisius Coll., Buffalo, NY, 1970, MS in Edn., 1995; MLS, SUNY, Buffalo, 1971, ASC, 1985. Cert. pub. libr. profl., NY State Edn. Dept. Libr. trainee Bus. Labor Dept. Buffalo-Erie County Pub. Libr., Buffalo, 1970-71; libr. I Mobile Librs. Buffalo-Erie County Pub. Libr., Buffalo, 1971-74; libr. II Amherst Pub. Librs., Williamsville, NY, 1974-78; libr. III, dir. North Park Crane Brs., Buffalo, 1978-81; prin. law libr. NY State Supreme Ct. Libr. Buffalo, 1981—. Cons. Lippes, Silverstein et al, Buffalo, 1985—06. Co-author: (with Jo Ann M. Wahl and Kevin Bauer) Powers of the New York Court of Appeals 1952-1993 Supplement, 1994. Sec., We. NY Libr. Resources Coun. Mem. Am. Assn. Law Librs. (bd. dirs. Upstate NY), NY State Unified Cts. Law Librs. (pres.). Avocations: history, gardening. Office: NY State Supreme Ct Libr Buffalo 77 W Eagle St Buffalo NY 14202-3408

SAHLENE, singer; b. Soderhamn, Sweden, 1976; Rep. for Estonia Eurovision Song Contest, 2002. Child actress (TV series) The Children of Bullerbyn; singer: (albums) 12 Steps Down the Avenue, 1997, It's Been A While, 2003. Recipient 3rd Place for the song "Runaway", Eurovision Song Contest, 2002. Mailing: Comino Productions Inc 1648 10th Ave Brooklyn NY 11215 E-mail: sahlene@sahlene.com.

SAHMOUDI, MOHAMED, computer scientist; b. Fes, Morocco, May 1, 1977; s. Mohammadine and Habiba Sahmoudi; m. Nassera Zouayni, Mar. 6, 1998. M in Statis. Engring., Paris XI U., 2000; PhD in Signal Processing, Paris II U., 2004. Asst. prof. Ecole Polytech. Sch. Def. Engring., Paris, 2001—03, Paris-Dauphine U., 2003—05; prof. Generation BAC, Paris, 2004—05. Asst. prof. Courr Simon, Paris, 2003—05. Contbr. scientific papers, articles to profl. jours. Grantee, Navy Rsch. Office, 2005—07; scholar, Ministry of Rsch., France, 2000—03. Mem.: EURSAIP, IEEE. Avocations: history, soccer, travel. Home: 4234 Chestnut Ave Philadelphia PA 19104 Office: CAC Dept ECE 800 Lancaster Ave Villanova PA 19085

SAHNER, CHRISTIAN C., historian; s. Ron Sahner and Brigid Casey S. BA in Art and Archaeology, Princeton Univ., 2007; student in History, Oxford Univ., 2007—. Editor: (pub.) Princeton Tory. Rhodes Scholar. Achievements include being founder Elizabeth Anscombe Soc; doing archaeological field world in Greece.

SAHNEY, VINOD K., health care executive; b. Amritsar, India, Nov. 16, 1942; BSc, Ranchi U., 1963; MSME, Purdue U., 1965; PhD in Indsl. Engring., U. Wis., 1970. Asst. prof., then assoc. prof. indsl. engring. Wayne State U., Detroit, 1970-77, prof. indsl. engring., 1979—; assoc. prof. health policy and mgmt. Harvard U., Boston, 1977-79; v.p. corp. planning and mktg. Henry Ford Health Care Corp., Detroit, 1984, sr. v.p. planning and devel., 1992—2006; sr. v.p., chief strategy officer Blue Cross Blue Shield Mass., Boston, 2006—. Vis. prof. exec. program for health policy and mgmt., Harvard U., 1979—; mem. health care tech. study sect. U.S. Dept. HHS, 1980—; cons. Nat. Ctr. Health Svcs. Rsch., 1980—; pres. Fairlane Health Svcs. Corp., also bd. dirs.; founding mem. bd. dirs. Inst. for Health Care Improvement, 1988—. Recipient Dean Connelly award Am. Coll. Healthcare Execs., quality award Healthcare Info. Mgmt. Sys. Soc. Fellow Inst. Indsl. Engrs., Hosp. Info. Mgmt. Sys. Soc.; mem. NAE, Nat. Acad. Scis. Inst. Medicine. Office: Blue Cross Blue Shield of Mass Landmark Ctr 401 Park Dr Boston MA 02215-3326 Office Phone: 617-246-3313. E-mail: vinod.sahney@bcbsma.com.

SAHOTA, AMRIK, medical researcher, educator, lab administrator; s. Sadhu Milkhy and Rao Kaur; m. Nirmala Thapar; children: Aneil, Jessica. BS in Biochemistry, Bath U., 1974; MS in Medicinal Chemistry, Loughborough U., 1976; PhD in Med. Genetics, Guy's Hosp. Med. Sch., London U., 1980. Diplomate in clin. molecular genetics Am. Bd. Med. Genetics; chartered biologist U.K. Postdoctoral fellow dept. molecular scis. Aston U., Birmingham, England, 1980—83; biochemist dept. hematology Gen. Hosp., Birmingham, England, 1983—85; rsch. assoc. dept. biology Ind. U., Bloomington, Ind., 1985—87; lab. dir. dept. med. and molecular genetics Ind. U. Med. Sch., Indpls., 1988—98; prof. genetics Rutgers U., Piscataway, NJ, 1998—; lab. dir. dept. pathology Robert Wood Johnson U. Hosp., New Brunswick, NJ, 2001—. Cons. Indpls.-Marion County Forensic Sci. Lab., 1991—98; adj. prof. dept. pathology Robert Wood Johnson Med. Sch., U. Medicine and Dentistry, NJ, 2001—05, clin. prof., 2005—. Contbr. articles to sci. jours.; editor conf. procs. Fellow: Royal Coll. Pathologists UK, Inst. Biology UK, Am. Coll. Med. Genetics; mem.: AAAS, NY Acad. Scis., Internat. Soc. for Nephrology, Assn. Molecular Pathology, Soc. for Study of Inborn Errors of Metabolism, Brit. Soc. Human Genetics, Am. Soc. Human Genetics, Am. Assn. Clin. Chemistry. Achievements include research in Genetic basis of kidney stone disease. Avocations: travel, reading, health and fitness. Office: Rutgers U Dept Genetics Life Scis Bldg 145 Bevier Rd Piscataway NJ 08854-8082 Business E-Mail: sahota@biology.rutgers.edu.

SAHR, MORRIS GALLUP, financial planner; b. Schenectady, Nov. 28, 1928; s. Nathan and Esther (Gallup) S.; m. Sarah Diane Eisenberg, Dec. 23, 1956; children: Evelyn, David, Janet. AB, U. Oreg., 1951, MA, 1953; PhD, Calif. Open U., Oakland, 1978. Cert. fin. planner, registered fin. cons. Pres. Deposit Mgmt. Svc., Inc., Charlottesville, Va., 1978—. Author: Nine Ways to Beat the High Cost of College, 1999, Annuity Owners' Mistakes, 2002; co-author: Your Book of Financial Planning, 1983, Encyclopedia of Financial Planning, 1984, The Financial Planner, 1986, Financial Planning Can Make You Rich, 1987. Chmn. Fairfax County Planning Commn., Va., 1964-68; del. White House Conf. on Aging, 1980, U.S. Congl. Adv. Bd., 1984-87; bd. dirs. Fairfax Indsl. Devel. Authority, 1985-95; adjudicator Am. Arbitration Assn., 1988-99; del to China, People to People Amb. Program, 2000. Recipient award Danforth Found.; named 1 of Top 200 Planners in U.S., Money Mag.; hon. fellow Kennedy Libr., 1985; Paul Harris fellow, 1989. Mem. Internat. Assn. Fin. Planning (founder, 1st pres. Metro Washington chpt.), Inst. Cert. Fin. Planners (nat. govt. affairs com.), Am. Assn. Practicing Fin. Planners (past pres.), Internat. Assn. of Registered Fin. Cons., Rotary (pres. Fairfax 1984-85, Rotary Srs. Project Internat. award). Home and Office: 1289 Courtyard Dr Charlottesville VA 22903 Office Phone: 434-970-2277. E-mail: sahr-dms@comcast.net.

SAHRAKORPI, SEPPO, physicist, researcher; s. Matti L.S. and Sirpa Sahrakorpi; m. Renate Harrison. MSc, Tampere U. of Tech., 1996, PhD with commendation, 2001. Rsch. asst. Tampere U. Tech., 1996—2001; rsch. assoc. Northeastern U., Boston, 2002—. Sci. computing cons. Advanced Sci. Computation Ctr., Northeastern U., Boston, 2002—07, adj. prof., 2007; docent Tampere U. Tech., 2007; ptnr. tech. engr. Totalview Technologies, 2007—. 2d lt. Finnish mil., 1991—92. Recipient Docent award, Tampere U. Tech., 2007, Adj. Prof. award, Northeastern U., 2007; fellow, Vilho, Yrjo and Kalle Found., Finland, 1999—2000, Tampere U. of Tech. Found., 2000; grantee, Vilho, Yrjo and Kalle Found., Finland, 2002, The Acad. of Finland, 2001—02; scholar, Found. for Advancement of Tech., Finland, 1997—98, Vilho, Yrjo and Kalle Found., Finland, 1998, Jenny and Antti Wihuri Found., Finland, 2000. Mem.: Am. Phys. Soc., European Phys. Soc., Finnish Phys. Soc. Achievements include research in fermiology and angle-resolved photoemission of high-temperature superconductors. Personal E-mail: seppo.sahrakorpi@iki.fi.

SAIAH, SUE LYNN, linguist, educator; b. Savannah, Ga., Dec. 5, 1960; d. Leonard Johnson and Jessie Wade Graham; m. Djamel Saiah, Oct. 22, 1995. BA in Music and Fgn. Langs., Armstong U., Savannah, 1982; student in Bus., Oglethorpe U., Atlanta, 2000—01; MEd, Mercer U., Atlanta, 2006. Cert. Am. TESOL, 2004, tchr. Ga., 2006, in accent reduction ALTA Lang. Svcs., Inc., 2006, Inlingua Internat. Lang. Instrn., 2005, lang. evaluation Ednl. Testing Svc., 2005, in oral proficiency evaluation ALTA Lang. Svcs., Inc., 2006, massage therapy and bodywork Nat., 1994. Pvt. practice sports therapist, Atlanta, 1994—2001; pvt. practice corp. trainer and bus. cons., 2000—. Contbr. articles to profl. jours. Mem.: Voice and Speech Trainers Assn., Nat. Assn. Tchrs. Singing, TESOL, Am. Coun. Tchrs. Fgn. Lang., Internat. Phonetic Assn., Internat. Assn. Applied LInguistics, Am. Assn. Applied Linguistics, Alliance Francaise. Home Phone: 770-458-7254. Personal E-mail: saiah@saiah.net.

SAIBLE, STEPHANIE IRENE, editor-in-chief; b. Mobile, Ala., Sept. 11, 1954; d. Lewis J. Slaff and Phoebe-Jane (Berse) Meiss. Student, Va. Commonwealth U., 1972—75. Editorial asst. Woman's World Magazine, Englewood, NJ, 1980—81, service copywriter, 1981—83, assoc. articles editor, 1983—84, articles editor, 1984—85, sr. editor features dept., 1985—86, sr. editor services dept., 1986, now editor-in-chief, 1994—. Contbr. articles to Woman's World, Modern Bride, New Body, Celebrity Beauty, Trim and Fit, Ladies Home Jour. Named Wonder Woman of the Yr., Bus. Jour., N.J., 1986. Mem.: Women in Comms. Office: Woman's World Mag 270 Sylvan Ave Englewood Cliffs NJ 07632-2521 *

SAIDA, TOYOYASU, chemical and biochemical engineer; b. Tokyo, Jan. 18, 1935; came to US, 1985; s. Tameo and Fukiko Saida; m. Mariko Itano, Jan. 16, 1960; children; Tetsuo, Miyoko Asahi, Takashi Saida. BS, U. Tokyo, 1958. Registered profl. engr., Japan. Ops. engr. Toyo Gas Chems. Corp., Niigata, Japan, 1958-59; rschr. Tokyo Inst. of Tech., 1959-61; rsch. engr. Mitsui-Toatsu Chems. Ltd., Yokohama, Japan, 1961-69, chief rsch. engr., 1969-78; mgr. process rsch. divsn. Toyo Engring. Corp., Mobara, Japan, 1978-84, adv. bd. mem. Chiba, Japan, 1984-85; sr. v.p. BW Biotec, Inc., Chgo., 1985-86; gen. mgr. Hazarmacorp Rsch. Ctr., Tsukuba, Japan, 1987-95; mng. dir. Saida & Assocs., Deerfield, Ill., 1997—. Author: Handbook of Membrane Technology, 1978, Handbook of Bioprocess, 1985, Cellulose, 1986. Recipient Excellent Invention of Yr. Sci. and Tech. Agy., 1965. Mem. Am. Chem. Soc., Soc. of Chem. Engrs. Japan. Achievements include invention of innovative new synthetic method of urea, large scale manufacturing process of single cell protein from n-paraffin, fuel alcohol manufacturing process from lignocellulosics, volume reduction method of radioactive wastes with liquid phase oxidation. Home and Office: 431 Kelburn Rd Apt 315 Deerfield IL 60015-4367 Office Phone: 847-236-1231. Personal E-mail: tomsaida@aol.com.

SAIDI, PARVIN, hematologist, medical educator; b. Teheran, Iran, Mar. 21, 1932; came to U.S., 1946; d. Ahmad and Fatemeh (Ashouri) S.; m. Allahverdi Farmanfarmaian, May 27, 1958; children: Dellara Farmanfarmaian Terry, Kimya Farmanfarmaian Harris. BS, Smith Coll., Northampton, Mass., 1952; MD, Harvard U., 1956. Diplomate Am. Bd. Internal Medicine, subspecialty hematology and med. oncology. Intern medicine UCLA Med. Ctr., 1956-57; resident internal medicine U. Calif., San Francisco, 1957-59; NIH rsch. fellow hematology U. Calif. Hosps. and Children's Med. Ctr., San Francisco, 1959-61, 63-64; asst. prof. medicine U. Medicine & Dentistry N.J.-Rutgers Med. Sch., New Brunswick, 1968-71, assoc. prof., 1971-74; prof. U. Medicine & Dentistry N.J.-Robert Wood Johnson Med. Sch., New Brunswick, 1974—, chief divsn. hematology and oncology, dept. medicine, 1972—. Robert Wood Johnson U. Hosp., New Brunswick, 1981—, Melvyn H. and AB Motolinsky chair hematology, 2000—. Cons. internist, hematologist, oncologist St. Peter's Med. Ctr., New Brunswick, Douglass Coll., Rutgers U., New Brunswick, VA Hosp., Lyons, NJ, Muhlenberg Hosp., Plainfield, NJ, Princeton Med. Ctr., NJ; dir. Melvyn H. Motolinsky Lab. Hematology Rsch., NJ Regional Comprehensive Hemophilia Care Program, chmn. adv. bd.; mem. Gov.'s Adv. Coun. on AIDS; chmn. HHS region II Comprehensive Hemophilia Diagnostic and Treatment Ctrs., 1984-85, 89-90, 94-95, 99-2000, 04-05; chmn. med. adv. bd. Hemophilia Found. NJ; mem. med. adv. exec. com. NJ Blood Svcs. Cons. editor Am. Jour. Medicine; contbr. articles to profl. jours. Recipient Disting. Svc. award for rsch. in leukemia Melvyn H. Motolinsky Rsch. Found., 1977, Humanitarian award Hemophilia Assn. No. NJ, 1978, Physician of Yr. award Nat. Hemophilia Found., 2006. Fellow ACP (mem. sci. program com. N.J. region), Acad. Medicine N.J.; mem. Am. Soc. Hematology (edn. com.), N.J. Hemophilia Assn. (chmn. med. adv. com., spl. award, Dr. L. Michael Kuhn Meml. award 1996), Coop. Oncology Group N.J. (exec. com., chairperson subcom. on lymphoma), Am. Heart Assn. (coun. on thrombosis), Am. Fedn. Clin. Rsch., Royal Soc. Medicine (affiliate), Am. Soc. Clin. Oncology, World Fedn. Hemophilia, Alpha Omega Alpha, Phi Beta Kappa, Sigma Xi. Office: Robert Wood Johnson Med Sch 1 Robert Wood Johnson Pl New Brunswick NJ 08901-1928

SAIFAN, CHADI, physician; b. Amioun, Lebanon, July 10, 1978; MD, Lebanese U., Beirut, 2003. Diplomate SC. Internal medicine resident SI U. Hosp., NY, 2004—07; infectious diseases fellow Med. U. SC, Charleston, 2007—. Achievements include research in Diabetes and pneumonia. Office: Medical University of South Carolina 171 Ashley Ave Charleston SC Home Phone: 718-664-4527. Personal E-mail: chadisaifan@hotmail.com.

SAIFER, MARK GARY PIERCE, pharmaceutical executive; b. Phila., Sept. 16, 1938; s. Albert and Sylvia (Jolles) S.; m. Phyllis Lynne Trommer, Jan. 28, 1961 (dec.); children: Scott David, Alandria Gail; m. Merry R. Sherman, June 26, 1994. AB, U. Pa., 1960; PhD, U. Calif., Berkeley, 1966. Acting asst. prof. zoology U. Calif., Berkeley, 1966, fellow, 1967-68; sr. cancer rsch. scientist Roswell Park Meml. Inst., Buffalo, 1968-70; lab. dir. Diagnostic Data Inc., Palo Alto, Calif., 1970-78; v.p. DDI Pharms., Inc., Mountain View, Calif., 1978-94, Oxis Internat., Inc., 1994-95; v.p., sci. dir. Mountain View Pharms., Inc., Menlo Park, Calif., 1996—, also bd. dirs. Lectr., expert witness in field. Author, patentee in field:, mem. editl. bd.: Current Pharm. Biotechnology Jour. Mem. AAAS (life), Am. Assn. Pharm. Scientists, Parenteral Drug Assn. Office: Mountain View Pharms Inc 3475 Edison Way Ste S Menlo Park CA 94025-1821 E-mail: saifer@mvpharm.com.

SAIFI, JAVID, surgeon; b. Hyderabad, India, June 7, 1957; s. Mansoor Ali and Zalekha Begum Saifi; m. Ruxana Yousouf Husain, Dec. 27, 1985; children: Samira, Almira, Zafar. Diploma, Rutgers U., New Brunswick, 1978; MD, U. Med., NJ, 1982. Diplomate Am. Bd. Surgery, 1989, Am. Bd. Cardiothoracic Surgery, 1992. Cardiac surgeon Ctrl. NY Cardiac Surgery, Elmira, 1991—93, Albany Cardiothoracic Surgeons, 1994—. Fellow: ACS, Soc. Thoracic Surgeons. Home: 4033 Windsor Dr Schenectady NY 12309 Office: Albany Cardiothoracic Surgeons 116 Everett Rd Ste 6 Albany NY 12205

SAIKI, PATRICIA, federal agency administrator, congressman; b. Hilo, Hawaii, May 28, 1930; d. Kazuo and Shizue (Inoue) Fukuda; m. Stanley Mitsuo Saiki, June 19, 1954; children: Stanley Mitsuo, Sandra Saiki Williams, Margaret C., Stuart K., Laura H. BA, U. Hawaii, 1952. Tchr. U.S. history Punahou Sch., Kaimuki Intermediate Sch., Kalani High Sch., Honolulu, 1952-64; sec. Rep. Party Hawaii, Honolulu, 1964-66, vice chmn., 1966-68, 82-83, chmn., 1983-85; rsch. asst. Hawaii State Senate, 1966-68; mem. Hawaii Ho. of Reps., 1968-74, Hawaii State Senate, 1974-82, 100th-101st Congresses from 1st Hawaii dist., Washington, 1987-91; adminstr. SBA, Washington, 1991-93. Mem. Pres.'s Adv. Coun. on Status of Women, 1969-76; mem. Nat. Commn. Internat. Women's Yr., 1969-70; commr. We. Interstate Commn. on Higher Edn.; fellow Eagleton Inst., Rutgers U., 1970; fellow Inst. of Politics, Kennedy Sch. Govt., Harvard U., 1993; bd. dirs. Bank of Am.-Hawaii, Landmark Systems Corp., Internat. Asset Recovery Corp.; mem. nat. selection com. Innovations in Am. Govt., Ford Found., Harvard U., 1999-2002. Mem. Kapiolano Hosp. Aux.; sec. Hawaii Rep. Com., 1964-66, vice chmn., 1966-68, chmn., 1983-85; del. Hawaii Constl. Conv., 1968; alt. del. Rep. Nat. Conv., 1968, del., 1984, Rep. nominee lt. gov. Hawaii, 1982, for U.S. Senate, 1990; Rep. nominee gov. Hawaii, 1994; mem. Fedn. Rep. Women; trustee Hawaii Pacific Coll.; past bd. govs. Boys and Girls Clubs Hawaii; mem. adv. coun.

ARC; bd. dirs. Nat. Fund Improvement of Post-Secondary Edn., 1982-85, East West Ctr., 2003—, Nat. Pacific Ctr. on Aging, 2004-; past bd. dirs. Straub Med. Rsch. Found., Honolulu, Hawaii's Visitors Bur., Honolulu, Edn. Commn. of States, Honolulu, Hawaii Visitors Bur., 1983-85; trustee U. Hawaii Found., 1984-86, Hawaii Pacific Coll., Honolulu. Republican. Episcopalian. Avocation: golf. Home: 784 Elepaio St Honolulu HI 96816-4710 E-mail: pfsaiki@cs.com.

SAILER, RACHEL ANN, secondary school educator; b. Cedar Falls, Iowa, May 26, 1951; d. Charles Herbert and Sarah Bronwen Pinkham; m. John Jacob Sailer, Oct. 26, 1950; children: Amy Bronwen, Jacob Thomas. BA, U. No. Iowa, Cedar Falls, 1974; MLS, Hollins U., Roanoke, Va., 1999. Lic. collegiate profl. tchr. Va. Rsch. asst. Inst. Philosophy and Pub. Policy, College Park, Md., 1980—83; mktg. assoc. Mill Mountain Theatre, Roanoke, Va., 1983—86; tchr. drama Salem H.S., 1986—. Actress in cmty. and profl. local prodns. Tchr. Christ Episcopal Ch., 2000—; vol. Interfaith Hospitality, 2000—; bd. dirs. Showtimers Cmty. Theatre, Roanoke, Va., 1985—88, Character Counts, 2005—. Named Tchr. of Yr., Salem City Schs., 2004—05. Mem.: Va. Edn. Assn. Democrat. Office: Salem HS 400 Spartan Dr Salem VA 24153-5090 Home: 2435 Berkley Ave SW Roanoke VA 24015 Office Phone: 540-387-2437.

SAINDON, MICHAEL, music educator; BFA in Music, U. Wis., Milw., 1988; BFA in K-6 gen. music, Alverno Coll., Milw., 1991. Tchr. Milw. Pub. Schs., 1988—.

SAINER, ARTHUR, writer, theater educator; b. NYC, Sept. 12, 1924; s. Louis and Sadie (Roth) S.; m. Maryjane Treloar, Apr. 18, 1981; children: Douglas M., Stephanie M., Jane M., Ross M. BA, Washington Sq. Coll., NYC, 1946; MA, Columbia U., 1948. Tchr. C.W. Post Coll., Bennington Coll., Vt., 1967-69, Adelphi U., Garden City, NY, 1974-75, S.I. Community Coll., 1974-75; faculty Wesleyan U., Middletown, Conn., 1977-80, Hunter Coll., NYC, 1980-81; assoc. prof. theatre Middlebury Coll., Vt., 1981-83; theater faculty New Sch. for Social Rsch., NYC, 1985—, SUNY, Albany, 2004—, Sarah Lawrence Coll., Bronxville, NY, 1990—2002; play dir. Boat Sun Cavern Middlebury Coll., Vt., 1983; drama critic Village Voice, NYC, 1961—; play dir. Lord Tom Goldsmith at Theatre for New City, NYC, 1979, Witnesses at Open Space, NYC, 1977, Poor Man Rich Man, Theatre for the New City, 1992. Reporter Nat. Endowment for Arts, Washington, 1979—82. Editor: Village Voice, 1962; author: (plays) The Children's Army Is Late, 1974, Carol in Winter Sunlight, 1977, After the Baal-Shem Tov, 1979, Images of the Coming Dead, 1980, Sunday Childhood Journeys to Nobody at Home, 1984 (Berman award, 1984), Cruising Angel, 1984, The Celebration Reclaimed, 1993—95, The Burning Out of 82, 1997, Jews and Christians in the End Zone, 2000 (Nat. Found. for Jewish Culture award, 2006), The Potter's Wheel: To Repair the Soul, 2003, The People Impeach the Bushes, 2004, Conversions and Assassins, 2005, (criticisms) The Sleepwalker and the Assassin, 1964, The New Radical Theatre Notebook, 1975, 1997, Zero Dances, 1998; repor. Panelist Vt. Council on the Arts, Montpelier, 1982, 83; panelist N.Y. State Council on the Arts, 1976-78. Ford Found. grantee, 1979, 80; recipient grant Office for Advanced Drama Research, U. Minn., 1967, award for Grab Your Hat John Golden Found., 1946 Address: 59 Railroad Pl #304 Saratoga Springs NY 12866-2161 Personal E-mail: asainer@earthlink.net. *From the Burning Out of 82: Francis: But finally, who is going to do my work? No one is going to do it. Lev: Each will do his work. But in the end only God's work amounts to anything. Francis: And does that make you happy? Lev: It makes me useful.*

SAINI, SIMARJEET SINGH, electronics engineer; b. Mandi, India, Apr. 12, 1975; s. Balbir Singh Saini and Satish Kaur; m. Manpreet Kaur, Dec. 2, 2001; 1 child, Hardit Singh. PhD, U. Md., College Park, 2001. Lead rschr. Covega, Jessup, Md., 2000—04, lead app engr., 2005—; dir. optoelectronics Altanet Comm., Greenbelt, Md., 2004—05. Cons. BSNL, Jallandhar, Punjab, India, 1994—96; cons. r&d Potomac Optronics, Seoul, 2005—. Vol. Janhith, Patiala, Punjab, India, 2004—06. Recipient Disting. Rschr., ECE, U. Md., 2000; Army Rsch. Lab fellow, U.S. Army Rsch. Lab, 1996—97, Ednl. scholar, SPIE, 2000. Mem.: IEEE. Achievements include patents for resonant coupling for tapered waveguides; design of broadband gain chips for tunablelasers; patents for resonant coupling between waevguides over tapers; highly efficient semiconductor optical devices; patents pending for non-uniform current distribution for increased performance of SOA; method for parametric discrimination in fiber bragg grating sensors; design of highest performing semiconductor optical amplifiers in the world; research in highest sensitivity fiber bragg sensors for chemical and biological sensors; discovery of PARC, a new platform for monolithic integration of photonic devices; design of highest power super-luminiscent diode; first to rural area network for Punjab using TDMA system and frequency hopping. Home: 6110 Good Hunters Ride Columbia MD 21045 Home Phone: 410-730-6635; Office Phone: 240-456-7224. Personal E-mail: simarjeet.saini@gmail.com.

SAINI, VASANT DURGADAS, computer software company executive; arrived in U.S., 1974, naturalized; s. Durgadas D. and Pushpa (Sethi) S.; m. Sonia Juneja, May 20, 1983; children: Isha Seyjal, Kaasha Priyal. B of Tech. in Electronics, Ind. Inst. Tech., Kharagpur, 1974; MSEE, U. Rochester, 1975, PhD in Elec. Enging., 1979. Asst. prof. elec. enging. U. Rochester (N.Y.), 1980-88; pres., CEO Advanced Computer Innovations, Inc., Pittsford, NY, 1988—; CEO AccuDot ColorPrinting, Inc., 2004—. Cons. All-Pro Printers, Rochester, 1986, W. Main Ultrasound Group, Rochester, 1986; software developer numerous orgs. Co-author: Doppler Echocardiography, 1985, 2d edit., 1992; also articles. Grantee, Mae Stone Goode Found., 1979—81. Avocations: indo-jazz music, mathematics of music, squash. Home: 19 Roxbury Ln Pittsford NY 14534-4202 Office: Advanced Computer Innovations Inc 656 Kreag Rd Pittsford NY 14534-3730 Office Phone: 585-385-3810. Personal E-mail: vsaini@rochester.rr.com. Business E-Mail: vs@acii.com.

SAINT, EVA MARIE, actress; b. Newark, July 4, 1924; d. John Merle and Eva Marie (Rice) Saint; m. Jeffrey Hayden, Oct. 28, 1951; children: Darrell Hayden, Laurette Hayden. BA, DFA, Bowling Green State U., 1946; student, Actors Studio, 1950. Actor: various radio and TV dramatic shows, 1947—; (plays) The Trip to Bountiful, 1953 (Outer Cir. Critics award, NY Drama Critics award, 1953), The Rainmaker, 1953, Winesburg, Ohio, 1970, The Lincoln Mask, 1972, Summer and Smoke, 1973, Desire Under the Elms, 1974, The Fatal Weakness, 1976, Candida, 1977, Mr. Roberts, First Monday in October, 1979, Duet for One, 1982—83, The Country Girl, 1986, Death of a Salesman, 1994, Lover Letters, 1994—2005, On the Divide, 1994—2007, Touch the Names, 2005; (films) On the Waterfront, 1954 (Acad. Award for Best Suporting Actress, 1955), That Certain Feeling, 1956, Raintree Country, 1957, A Hatful of Rain, 1957, North by Northwest, 1959, Exodus, 1961, All Fall Down, 1962, 36 Hours, 1963, The Sandpiper, 1964, The Russians are Coming, The Russians are Coming!, 1965, Grand Prix, 1966, The Stalking Moon, 1969, Loving, 1970, Cance My Reservation, 1972, Nothing in Common, 1986, Maritté in Ecstacy, 1995, I Dreamed of Africa, 2000, Because of Winn-Dixie, 2005, Don't Come Knocking, 2005, Superman Returns, 2006; (TV films) The Macahans, 1976 (Emmy nominee), The Fatal Weakness, 1976, Taxill, 1978 (Emmy nominee), A Christmas to Remember, 1978, When Hell Was in Season, 1980, The Curse of King Tut's Tomb, The Best Little Girl in the World, 1981, Splendor in the Grass, 1981, Love Leads the Way, 1983, Jane Doe, 1983, Fatal Vision, 1984, The Last Days of Patton, 1876, A Year in the Life, 1876, Breaking Home Times, 1987, I'll Be Home for Christmas, 1988, Voyage of Terror: The Achille Lauro Affair, 1980, People Like Us, 1990 (Emmy award, 1990), Palomino, 1991, Kiss of the Killer, 1992, My Antonia, 1994, After Jimmy, 1996, Time to Say Goodbye, 1997, Titanic, 1997; (documentaries) Primary Colors: The Story of Corita, 1991, (with Bill Moyers) Children in America's Schools, 1997, Papa's Angels, 2000, Open House, 2003; prodr.: (films) Fences, 2006, Desire Under the Elms, 2007.

SAINT-AMAND, PIERRE NEMOURS, humanities educator; b. Port-Au-Prince, Haiti, Feb. 22, 1957; came to U.S., 1978; s. Nemours and Carmen (Clerveaux) Saint-A. BA, U. Montreal, 1978; MA, Johns Hopkins U., 1980, PhD, 1981. Asst. prof. Yale U., New Haven, 1981-82, Stanford U., Calif., 1982-86; assoc. prof. Brown U., Providence, 1986-90, prof., 1990—, Francis Wayland prof., 1996—. Vis. prof. Harvard U., Cambridge, Mass., 1991-2006, U. Iowa, Iowa City, 2001. Author: Diderot, Le Labyrinthe de La Relation, 1984, Séduire Ou La Passion des Lumières, 1986, Les Lois de L'Hostilité, 1992, The Libertine's Progress, 1994, The Laws of Hostility, 1996; editor: Diderot, 1984, Le Roman au Dix-huitième siècle, 1987, Autonomy in the Age of the Enlightenment, 1993, Thérèse philosophe, 2000, Confession d'une jeune fille, 2005. Fellow Stanford Humanities Ctr., 1985-86, John Simon Guggenheim Meml. Found., 1989; decorated chevalier dans l'Ordre des Palmes académiques, 2001. Office: Brown U PO Box 1961 Providence RI 02912-1961

SAINT-ANTOINE, PAUL HEWITT, lawyer; b. Washington, 1964; AB summa cum laude, Kenyon Coll., 1986; JD, Columbia Univ., 1989. Bar: Pa. 1989, NJ 1989. Joined Drinker Biddle & Reath LLP, Phila., 1989, ptnr., litig. dept., head, antitrust practice group. Editor-in-chief Federal Antitrust Guidelines for the Licensing of Intellectual Property, Origins and Applications, 2nd ed., ABA. Named a Harlan Fiske Stone Scholar. Mem.: ABA, Pa. Bar Assn. Office: Drinker Biddle & Reath LLP One Logan Sq 18th & Cherry Sts Philadelphia PA 19103-6996 Office Phone: 215-988-2990. Office Fax: 215-988-2757. Business E-Mail: paul.saint-antoine@dbr.com.

ST. ANTOINE, THEODORE JOSEPH, retired law educator, arbitrator; b. St. Albans, Vt., May 29, 1929; s. Arthur Joseph and Mary Beatrice (Callery) S.; m. Elizabeth Lloyd Frier, Jan. 2, 1960; children: Arthur, Claire, Paul, Sara. AB, Fordham Coll., 1951; JD, U. Mich., 1954; postgrad., U. London, 1957—58. Bar: Mich. 1954, Ohio 1954, DC 1959. Assoc. Squire, Sanders & Dempsey, Cleve., 1954; assoc., ptnr. Woll, Mayer & St. Antoine, Washington, 1958-65; assoc. prof. law U. Mich. Law Sch., Ann Arbor, 1965-69, prof., 1969—81, Degan prof., 1981-98, Degan prof. emeritus, 1998—, dean, 1971-78. Pres. Nat. Resource Ctr. for Consumers of Legal Svcs., 1974—78; mem. pub. rev. bd. UAW, 1973—, chmn., 2000—; spl. counselor on workers' compensation Gov. of Mich., 1983—85; chmn. UAW-GM legal svcs. plan, 1983—95; reporter Uniform Law Commrs., 1987—92; mem. discipline bd. Mich. Atty., 1999—2005, vice chmn. discipline bd., 2000—02, chmn. discipline bd., 2002—05; life mem. Clare Hall, Cambridge (Eng.) U. Co-author: (with R. Smith, L. Merrifield, C. Craver and M. Crain) Labor Relations Law: Cases and Materials, 4th edit., 1968, 11th edit., 2005; editor: The Common Law of the Workplace: The Views of Arbitrators, 2d. edit., 2005; contbr. articles to profl. jours. Bd. dirs. Nat. Workrights Inst., 2005—. 1st lt. JAGC US Army, 1955—57. Fulbright grantee, U. London, 1957—58. Mem. ABA (past sec. labor law sect., coun. 1984-92), Am. Bar Found., State Bar Mich. (chmn. labor rels. law sect. 1979-80), Nat. Acad. Arbitrators (bd. govs. 1985-88, v.p. 1994-96, pres. 1999-2000), Internat. Soc. Labor and Social Security Law (U.S. br. exec. bd. 1983—, vice chmn. 1989-95), Am. Arbitration Assn. (bd. dirs. 2000—), Nat. Workrights Inst. (bd. dirs. 2005-), Labor and Employment Rels. Assn., Coll. Labor and Employment Lawyers, Order of Coif (life). Democrat. Roman Catholic. Home: 1421 Roxbury Rd Ann Arbor MI 48104-4047 Office: U Mich Law Sch 625 S State St Ann Arbor MI 48109-1215 Office Phone: 734-764-9348. Business E-Mail: tstanton@umich.edu.

ST. CLAIR, DONALD DAVID, lawyer; b. Hammond, Ind., Dec. 30, 1932; s. Victor Peter and Wanda Small; m. Sergine Anne Oliver, June 6, 1970 (dec. June 1974); m. Beverly Joyce Tipton, Dec. 28, 1987. BS, Ind. U., Bloomington, 1955, MS, 1963, EdD, 1967; JD, U. Toledo, Ohio, 1992. Bar: Ohio 1992, US Dist. Ct. (no. dist.) Ohio 1993, US Supreme Ct., 1996. Assoc. prof. Western Ky. U. Coll. Edn., Bowling Green, 1967-68, U. Toledo, 1968-77, prof., 1977-92; atty., ptnr. Garand, Bollinger, & St. Clair, Oregon, Ohio, 1992-97; pvt. practice Toledo, 1997—2006. Mem. Ohio Coun. Mental Health Ctrs., Columbus, 1978-79; dir. honors programs U. Toledo. Author: (poetry) Daymarks and Beacons, 1983, Impressions from an Afternoon in a Paris Courtroom, 1998; contbr. articles to profl. jours. Organizer Students Toledo Organized for Peace, 1970-71; mem. Lucas County Dem. Party, 1990—. With US Army, 1955-57. Mem. ABA, AAU (nat. bd. dirs. 1973-74), Am. Inns of Ct., Ohio Bar Assn., Toledo Bar Assn., Ohio Acad. Trial Lawyers, Toledo Power Squadron (comdg. officer 1981), Bay View Yacht Club, Ohio Criminal Def. Lawyers Assn., Lucas County Bar Assn., Maumee Valley Criminal Def. Lawyers Assn., Ottawa County Bar Assn., Masons (32 degree), Shriners, Ancient Order Friars, Phi Alpha Delta. Personal E-mail: stclairlaw@sev.org.

ST. CLAIR, GLORIANA STRANGE, librarian, dean; b. Tonkawa, Okla., Dec. 13, 1939; d. Glen Leroy and Doris Mildred (Furber) Strange. BA in English, U. Okla., 1962, PhD in Literature, 1970; MLS, U. Calif., Berkeley, 1963; MBA in Mgmt., U. Tex., San Antonio, 1980. Rsch. asst. U. Calif., Berkeley, 1962-63, asst. libr., 1963-65; cataloguer U. Okla., Norman, 1965-68; supervising libr. San Antonio Pub. Libr., 1980-84; head acquisitions divsn. Tex. A&M U. Librs., College Station, 1984-87, humanities bibliographer, 1985, head pers. ops., 1986; asst. dir. tech. automation and adminstrv. svc. Kerr Libr., Oreg. State U., Corvallis, 1987-90; assoc. dean, head info. access svcs. Pa. State U. Librs., University Park, 1990-98; dean univ. libr. Carnegie Mellon U., Pitts., 1998—. Editor Coll. & Rsch. Librs., 1990-96, Jour. Academic Librarianship, 1996—. Bd. dirs. Towers Condo. Bd., State College, 1993-94; mem. vestry, mem. book discussion group St. Andrew's Episcopal Ch., State College, 1991-98; examiner Pa. Quality Leadership, 1994. Sr. fellow UCLA, 1991. Mem. Assn. Coll. and Rsch. Librs. (chair edit. adv. bd. 1990-96). Home: 154 N Bellefield Ave Apt 45 Pittsburgh PA 15213-2640 Office: Univ Librs Carnegie Mellon U 4909 Frew St Pittsburgh PA 15213-3890 Home Phone: 412-683-4920; Office Phone: 412-268-2447. Office Fax: 412-268-2793.

ST. CLAIR, JESSE WALTON, JR., retired savings and loan association executive; b. Phila., Jan. 15, 1930; s. Jesse Walton and Susan Elizabeth (Leath) St. C.; m. Elizabeth Anne Bartlett, Oct. 6, 1951; children: Jesse Walton III, Susan Elizabeth, Bruce Bartlett, Anne Leath. BA, Coll. of William and Mary, 1951; MBA, U. Pa., 1958; postgrad., Harvard U., 1968. Trainee Fed. Res. Bank, Phila., 1955-57; with Girard Trust Bank, Phila., 1957-78, asst. treas., 1960-64, asst. v.p., 1964-67, v.p., 1967-70, sr. v.p., 1970-75, exec. v.p., 1976-78; pres., chief exec. officer First Nat. Bank of Allentown (Pa.), 1978-82; chmn., chief exec. officer Wilmington Savs. Fund Soc., 1982-90, ret., 1990. Trustee emeritus endowment fund Coll. William and Mary; former mem. exec. bd. Delmarva coun. Boy Scouts Am.; past trustee Wesley Coll. With USN, 1951-55. Mem. Wilmington Country Club, Theta Delta Chi. Republican. Methodist.

ST. CLAIR, RICHARD COLLINS, composer, administrative assistant; b. Jamestown, ND, Sept. 21, 1946; s. Foster York and Elna Ruth (Bogen) St. Clair; m. Grace Pearson (div.); m. Janice Irene Ellison, Feb. 3, 1991. AB cum laude, Harvard U., Cambridge, Mass., 1969, MA, 1973, PhD, 1978. Tchg. fellow Harvard U., Cambridge, 1973—77, libr. asst., 1984—90, tech. sec., 1990—94; composer, 1978—; tech. writer MIT, Cambridge, 1994—2003, adminstrv. asst., 2003—. Piano soloist, 1967—; guest composer, soloist Marlboro Festival Music, 1967. Composer: Complete Piano Sonatas, 1968—97, The Lamentations of Shinran, 2000, Collected Ragtime Works for Piano, 1989—2003. Founder, dir. Boston Shinshu Buddhist Sangha, Cambridge, 1999—2003. Recipient commn., Andover Summer Session, 1967, MIT Concert Band, 1973—74, Somerville Arts Coun., 1996—97. Mem.: Am. Music Ctr. Democrat. Avocations: poetry, history, science fiction, literature. Home: 3 Michael Way Cambridge MA 02141

ST. CLAIR, THOMAS MCBRYAR, mining and manufacturing company executive; b. Wilkinsburg, Pa., Sept. 26, 1935; s. Fred C. and Dorothy (Renner) St. C.; m. Sarah K. Stewart, Aug. 1, 1959; children: Janet, Susan, Carol. AB, Allegheny Coll., 1957; MS, MIT, 1958; grad. advanced mgmt. program, Harvard U. With Koppers Co., Inc., Pitts., 1958-88, asst. to gen. mgr. enging. and constrn. div., 1966-69, comptroller, asst. treas., 1969-78, pres. Engineered Metal Products Group, 1978-83, v.p., asst. to chmn., 1983-84, v.p., treas., chief fin. officer, 1984-88; sr. v.p., chief fin. officer Phelps Dodge Corp., Phoenix, 1989-99; retired, 1999. Bd. dirs. Pitts. Theol. Sem.; trustee emeritus Allegheny Coll., Meadville, Pa. Mem. Fin. Execs. Inst., Duquesne Club (Pitts.). Presbyterian.

ST. CLAIRE, FRANK ARTHUR, lawyer; b. Charlotte, NC, June 16, 1949; BS, MIT, 1972; JD, NYU, 1975. Bar: Tex. 1975, U.S. Dist. Ct. (no. dist.) Tex. 1985; bd. cert. in comml. real estate law. Assoc. James H. Wallenstein, Dallas, 1975-78; v.p. Wallenstein & St. Claire, Dallas, 1978-81; pres. Frank A. St. Claire, P.C., Dallas, 1981-84; ptnr. St. Claire & Case, P.C., Dallas, 1984-88, pres., 1988-93; chmn. bd. Sunbelt Empire Title Co., Dallas, 1983-88; pres. St. Claire & Assocs., Dallas, 1993—; chmn. real estate section Godwin & Carlton, P.C., Dallas, 1994-96; ptnr., chmn. real estate sect. Strasburger & Price, L.L.P., Dallas, 1996-2000; pres. StClaireNet, 2001—. Author: Texas Condominium Law, 1986; co-author: Texas Real Estate Guide, 2000; contbr. articles to profl. jours. Ofcl. del. Dallas to Baltic Legal Conf., Riga, Latvia, 1990. Mem. Am. Coll. Mortgage Attys. (chmn. pubs. com. 1998—, mem. programs com. 1998—), Tex. Bar Assn. (study of uniform condominium act com., legis. liaison com. 1981-85, vice chmn. 1981-82, chmn. 1982-85, chmn. condominium and coop. housing com. 1985-89, title ins. com., mem. coun. real estate, probate and trust coun. 1991-95, treas. 1996-97, sec., chair-elect 1997-98, chair 1998-99), Dallas Bar Assn., Cmty. Assn. Inst. (bd. dirs. Dallas-Ft. Worth chpt. 1984-85, 87-89, pres.-elect 1989-90), Real Estate Fin. Exec. Assn. (asst. sec. 1996-97), Real Estate Coun., Am. Coll. Real Estate Lawyers (planning com. 1990-98, chmn. practice tech. com. 1993-96, mem. common interest ownership com. 1986-98, alternative dispute resolution com. 1993-95), Tex. Coll. Real Estate Attys. (chmn. projects com. 1991-92, bd. dirs. 1994-98), Internat. Assn. of Attys. and Execs. in Corp. Real Estate (website com. 1997-2001). Episcopalian.

ST. CYR, MARGARET ANN (PEGGY ST. CYR), writer; b. Phila., May 1, 1932; d. Thomas Russell Reiling and Margaret Mary Cannon; m. Raymond Paul St. Cyr, May 14, 1952; children: Mary Louise, Sharon Ann, Margot Elizabeth, Daniel Paul, Mark Dennis. AA, Mesa CC, Ariz., 1977. Sec. to asst. contr. U. Pa. Hosp., Phila., 1965—67; sec. to chmn. dept. pathology Woman's Med. Coll., Phila., 1967—68; exec. sec. to asst. supt. Mesa Pub. Schs., 1969—81; advt. coord. Latter-day Sentinel, Phoenix, 1981—82; profl. writer, 1982—. Spkr. Family History Soc. Ariz. Author: From Conversion to Commitment, 1996, One Fold, One Shepherd, 1999; contbr. poetry to lit. publs. Sec. MARC Bd., Mesa, 1969—70, Mesa Constn. Week Com., 1972—74; co-founder East Falls Human Rels. Com., Phila., 1966; pres. PTA, 1965, 1966; sec. Dist. 29 Reps., Mesa, 1996, 4th vice chmn., 1997, 2d vice chmn., 1998, 1st vice chmn., 1999; precinct committeeman Dist. 18 Reps., 1994—. Served with Women's Army Corps US Army, 1950—51. Named Vol. of Yr., Maricopa County Reps., 1997; recipient, Chapel of 4 Chaplains, Phila., 1967, cert. appreciation, Maricopa County Reps., 1996, Lincoln Day award, 1999, Best Makeup award, Tempe Little Theatre, 1976, Best Actress, 1976, Best Makeup, 1977, Best Dir., 1977, Most Contbn. Mem., 1977, Best Actress, 1978. Mem. Lds Ch. Avocations: acting, singing, choir directing. Home: 724 S Kachina Mesa AZ 85204 Personal E-mail: pete724x@aol.com.

SAINT-DONAT, BERNARD JACQUES, finance company executive; b. Avignon, France, May 22, 1946; came to U.S., 1971; s. Jean Eugene and Paule Louise (Chastan) S.; m. Ingrid Claire Armstrong, June 6, 1986. PhD in Sci., U. Paris, 1973. Rsch. fellow Harvard U., 1971-74; asst. prof. Columbia U., NYC, 1974-76; assoc. prof. Yale U., New Haven, 1976-81; assoc. Lehman Bros., NYC, 1981-84; v.p. Shearson Lehman Bros., NYC, 1984-86, sr. v.p., 1986-89; mng. gen. ptnr. Knox Parthers, NYC, 1989-93; mng. dir. CCF, NYC, 1993-95, Credit Agricole Lazard Fin. Products, NYC, 1995-96, Lazard Frères & Co. LLC, NYC, 1996—2001, Lehman Bros., NYC, 2001—04; pres. Saint-Donat & Co. Bd. dirs. New Haven Sister Cities, Inc.; mem. overseas vis. com. for maths. Harvard U. Author: Toroidal Embeddings, 1975; contbr. articles to profl. jours. Fellow Berkeley Coll., Yale U. Mem. Elizabethan Club (New Haven), Yale Club. Roman Catholic. Home: 1755 York Ave New York NY 10128 Office: 420 Lexington Ave Ste 300 New York NY 10170 Office Phone: 212-297-6211. Business E-Mail: bernard@saintdonat.com.

ST. EVE, AMY J., federal judge; b. Belleville, Ill., 1965; BA, Cornell U., 1987, JD, 1990. Pvt. practice, NYC, 1990—94; assoc. ind. counsel Whitewater Independent Counsel's Office, Little Rock, 1994—96; asst. U.S. atty. No. Dist. Ill., 1996—2001; sr. counsel Abbott Labs., Abbott Park, Ill., 2001—02; judge U.S. Dist. Ct. (no. dist.) Ill., 2002—. Office: US Dist Ct No Dist Ill Everett McKinley Dirksen Bldg 219 S Dearborn St Chicago IL 60604 *

ST. FLORIAN, FRIEDRICH GARTLER, architect, educator; b. Graz, Austria, Dec. 21, 1932; came to US, 1967, naturalized, 1973; s. Friedrich and Anna Maria (Prassl) G.; m. Livia Campanella, Jan. 12, 1967; children: Alisia, Ilaria. M in Architecture, U. Graz, 1958; MS in Architecture, Columbia U., NYC, 1962; DFA honoris causa (hon.), RI Coll., Kingston, 2005, Brown U., Providence, 2006. Instr. architecture Columbia U., NYC, 1962-63; asst. prof. R.I. Sch. Design, Providence, 1963-70, assoc. prof., 1974-77; principal architect Friedrich St.Florian Architect, Providence, 1978—; prof. architecture R.I. Sch. Design, 1980—2004, prof. emeritus, 2004—, chmn. div. archtl. studies, 1977-78, dean of architecture, 1978-88, chief critic European Honors Program, 1991-93. Vis. asso. prof. MIT, Cambridge, 1970-71, 74-75 Works exhibited Nat. Inst. Architects, Rome, 1967, 14th Triennale, Milan, 1968, Moderna Museet, Stockholm, 1969, Hayden Gallery, MIT, 1973, Mus. Modern Art, NYC, 1975, 96, 2002, Drawing Ctr., NYC, 1979, Walker Art Ctr., Mpls., 1980, Georges Pompidou Ctr., Paris, 1994, Centre de Cultura Contemporania, Barcelona, 1994, Biennale di Venezia, 1996, Inst. d' Art Contemporain, Villeurfranne, 2000, Kunsthalle Frankfurt, 2003. Recipient Nat. Endowment for Arts award, 1972-73, 76-77, 79, 26th ann. Progressive Architecture Mag. award, 1979; Ctr. for Advanced Visual Studies fellow MIT, 1970-77, Rome Prize fellow, fellow Am. Acad. in Rome, 1985, Fulbright fellow, Henry Hering medal Nat. Sculpture Soc., 2007; named to RI Coll. Hall Fame, 2005. Mem. AIA. Design architect for the National World War II Memorial, Washington, D.C. Office: Friedrich St Florian AIA 112 Union St Providence RI 02903 Home Phone: 401-272-3030; Office Phone: 401-831-8400. Business E-Mail: friedrich@fstflorian.com.

ST. GEORGE, ELAINE, art educator; b. Wilkes Barre, Pa., Mar. 11, 1948; d. John and Hilda St. George; m. Jeffrey Michael Roblyer (div.); children: Ginevra Gwen Wilson, Julia Gia Roblyer. BFA, U. Miami, 1970, MEd, 1972; MFA, U. NC, 1972. Prof. Broward CC, Darie, Fla., 1979—99; art tchr. Broward County Sch. Bd., Ft. Lauderdale, Fla., 1988—92; Prof. Palm Beach CC, Lakworth, Fla., 1999—. Restoration appraiser Harvey Brown Ins. Agy., Delray Beach, Fla., 2004—. Paintings, original printmaking, pastel drawings, one-woman shows include Bailey Hall Broward CC, 1966. Mem.: Broward Ctr. Performing Arts, NYC Mus. Modern Art, Boca

Raton Mus. Art, Ft. Lauderdale Mus. Art. Republican. Avocations: deep sea diving, tennis, horseback riding. Home and Office: 5095 Van Buren Rd Delray Beach FL 33484

ST. GERMAIN, FERNAND JOSEPH, retired congressman; b. Blackstone, Mass. s. Andrew Joseph and Pearl (Talaby) St. Germain; m. Rachel O'Neill, Aug. 20, 1953 (dec.); children: Laurene, Lisette. PhB in Social Sci, Providence Coll., 1948, LLD, 1965; LLB, Boston U., 1955; JSD (hon.), Suffolk U., 1976; DCL (hon.), Our Lady of Providence Sem., 1968; DBA (hon.), Bryant Coll., 1981; D in Pub. Svc. (hon.), Roger Williams Coll., 1981; LLB, Brown U., 1985. Bar: R.I. 1956, Fed. 1957, U.S. Supreme Ct. 1983. Mem. R.I. Ho. of Reps., 1952-60, 87th to 100th Congresses from 1st R.I. Dist., 1961-1989, chmn. house com. on banking fin. and urban affairs, 1980-88; ret., 1988. Served with AUS, 1949-52. Recipient Silver Shingle award for disting. public service Boston U. Sch. Law Alumni Assn., 1981, Alumni award disting. pub. service Boston U. Sch. Law, 1982 Mem. ABA, R.I., Bar Assn. Fed. Bar Assn., alumni assns. Our Lady of Providence Sem., Providence Coll., Boston U. Law Sch., Am. Legion. Democrat.

ST. GERMAIN, JEAN MARY, medical physicist; BS, Marymount Manhattan Coll., NYC; MS, Rutgers U. Cert. Am. Bd. Health Physics; lic. med. physicist, N.Y.; cert. Am. Bd. Med. Physics. USPHS fellow radiol. health Rutgers U., New Brunswick, NJ; fellow dept. med. physics Meml. Hosp., NYC; asst. physicist Cornell U. Med. Coll., NYC, 1968—71, instr. radiology (physics), 1971—78, clin. asst. prof., 1979—94; assoc. attending physicist Meml. Sloan-Kettering Cancer Ctr., 1993—2006, attending physicist, 2006—; acting chair dept. med. physics Meml. Hosp., 2007—. Vice chair Am. Bd. Med. Physics, 2004—, chair panel med. health physics, 1993—2000; cons. in field. Author: The Nurse and Radiotherapy, 1978; contbr. articles, chpts. to med. jours Fellow: Health Physics Soc. (Failla Meml. lectr. 1999, pres. NY chpt., pres. med. health physics sect.), Am. Assn. Physicists in Medicine (sec., bd. dirs., Disting. Svc. award 2005); mem.: Nat. Soc. Arts and Letters (regional dir., pres. N.Y. chpt., nat. career awards chair, nat. music chair), Radiol. and Med. Physics Soc. NY (past pres.), Am. Acad. Health Physics (treas. 1996—99), Am. Inst. Physics (govs. bd.), Iota Sigma Pi (treas., pres. V chpt.). Office: 1275 York Ave New York NY 10021-6007 Business E-Mail: stgermaj@mskcc.org.

SAINT-GIRARD, CHRISTIAN, theater director, actor, educator, choreographer, theater producer; b. NYC, May 29, 1954; s. Victoria J. Walter. Student, U. Oslo, 1972, Fordham U., 1972-74, Stella Adler Conservatory, NYC; studied with Uta Hagen and H. Berghof, HB Studios, NYC; studied dance, Joffrey Ballet; student dance, Am. Ballet Theatre; also others. Dir. Merry-Go-Round Playhouse, Auburn, NY, 1990-92; dir. edn. Polka Dot Playhouse, Bridgeport, Conn., 2002; artistic dir. Playhouse-on-the-Green, Bridgeport, Conn., 2002. Mem. bd. advisors Actor's Outlet Theatre Ctr., N.Y.C., 1981-85, chmn. steering com., 1982-83; pres., producing artistic dir. Prodrs.' Assn. Real Theatre for Youth, Darien, Ct., 1986-87; tchr. workshops and classes; guest instr. acting and auditioning for mus. theatre and dance at profl. studios, including Actor's Outlet Theatre, Manhattan Theatre Workshop, N.Y.C., Studio at Once Upon a Time Prodns., Inc., N.Y.C., Phil Black's Dance Studio, N.Y.C., Darien Dance Ctr., Darien Arts Coun., Conn. Conservatory for Performing Arts, Workshop Prodns., Inc., Stratford (Conn.) Acad. Dance, Conn. Dance, Newtown (Conn.) Ctr. for Performing Arts, Showbiz Kids, Conn.; performer on Broadway in A Chorus Line, Grease, Shenandoah; on nat. tours in Camelot, A Light Night Music, Oliver!, title role in Pippin; performer in stock and dinner theatre in Funny Girl, Hello Dolly!, The King & I, Cabaret; also appeared in TV pilots, feature films, commls. and operas. Author: (with Viveca Lindfors) (play) Three Boards and A Passion, 1981; librettist (mus. play) Alice in Wonderland, 1985, (ballet) The Red Shoes, 1987; dir., choreographer Singin' in the Rain, She Loves Me, 42d Street, Cabaret, Mame, Into the Woods, Camelot, Applause, My Fair Lady, Unsinkable Molly Brown, Hello, Dolly!, Shenandoah, Music Man, Gypsy, Forty Carats, Chicago, On the Town, Twelfth Night, Cinderella, A Touch of Spring, West Side Story, Annie, Snow White, Pinocchio, Hansel and Gretel, Sleeping Beauty, The Magic Flute, Arsenic and Old Lace, Babes in Toyland, also others; choreographer Paint Your Wagon, Oklahoma, South Pacific, Fame Mem. SAG, AFTRA, Actors Equity Assn., Cath. Actors Guild. Roman Catholic. Avocations: painting, sketching, tennis.

SAINT-JACQUES, BERNARD, linguistics educator; b. Montreal, Que., Can., Apr. 26, 1928; s. Albert and Germaine (Lefebvre) Saint-J.; m. Marguerite Fauquenoy. MA, Sophia U., Tokyo, 1962; MS, Georgetown U., 1964; Doctorat es Lettres and Scis. Humaines, Paris U., 1975. Asst. prof. linguistics U. B.C., Vancouver, Canada, 1967—69, assoc. prof., 1969-78, prof., 1978-90, prof. emeritus, 1991—; prof. Aichi U., Japan, 1990—2003. Mem. U.S. Citizen Amb. Program. Author: Structural Analysis of Modern Japanese, 1971, Aspects sociolinguistiques du bilinguisme canadien, 1976, Language and Ethnic Relations, 1979, Japanese Studies in Canada, 1985, Studies in Language and Culture, 1995; editor: Intercultural Communication Studies, 1998; co-editor: Contrasting Political Institutions, 1997, (with M. Iwasaki) Democratic Viability in Politics, 2000. Leave fellow Can. Council, 1974; profl. fellow Japan Found., 1981; research fellow French Govt., 1982, Ohira Programme, Japan, 1983 Fellow Royal Soc. Can. Acad., Internat. Acad. Intercultural Rsch.; mem. Linguistic Soc. Am., Can. Soc. Asian Studies, Can. Linguistics Assn., Sietar Japan. Office Phone: 604-987-6319. Personal E-mail: bsaintj@telus.net.

ST. JOHN, ANTHONY PAUL, retired manufacturing executive; b. Washington, Jan. 13, 1937; s. Sterling St. John and Beulah Marston; m. Myra Grace Cornfeld, Oct. 30, 1959; children: James Sterling, Ivy Kemp Hurley, Mary Marston. JD, U. Va., Charlottesville, 1960; postgrad., Harvard U., Boston, 1979. Bar: Md. 1961. Atty. Amco Steel Corp., Balt., 1960—61, Nat. Labor Rels. Bd., Balt., 1961—65; asst. G.C., asst. v.p. law, v.p. union rels. Bethlehem Steel Corp., 1965—84; v.p. employee rels. Chrysler Corp., Auburn Hills, Mich., 1985—93. Adj. prof. Lehigh U., Bethlehem, 1993, 95; bd. dirs. Qualitech Steel Corp., 1999—2000. Bd. dirs. Moravian Acad., Bethlehem, 1978—85; chmn. Greater Detroit Alliance Bus., 1989—90; chmn. indsl. rels. com. Motor Vehicles Mfrs., 1990—92; bd. dirs. Henry Ford Hosp. NE, Bloomfield Hills, Mich., 1991—92, Red Cross of So. Mich., Detroit, 1989—92, Kids Peace Hosp., Bethlehem, 1993—95, Detroit C. of C., 1989—90, Muhlenberg Evening Coll., 1997—98. 1st lt. US Army, 1961—68. Mem.: Sanctuary Golf Club (chmn. legal com.), Saucon Valley Country Club. Republican. Avocation: golf. Home: 1556 Saucon Valley Rd Bethlehem PA 18015 Address: 2957 Wulfert Rd Sanibel FL 33957 Personal E-mail: saintmyty@earthlink.net.

ST. JOHN, EDWARD P., social sciences educator; b. Napa, Calif., July 11, 1950; s. Wesley V. and Gladys L. St. John; m. Angela Collins, Feb. 21, 1981; children: Denis W., Liam E. BS, U. Calif., Davis, 1972, EdM, 1974; EdD in Adminstrn., Planning and Social Policy, Havard U., 1977. Prof. edn. U. Dayton, Ohio, 1996—97; prof. ednl. leadership and policy studies Ind. U., Bloomington, 1998—2004; Algo Henderson prof. edn. Ctr. for the Study of Higher and Postsecondary Edn., U. Mich., Ann Arbor, 2005—. Contbr. numerous articlese to profl. jours. Recipient Leadership award, Assn. for the Study of Higher Edn., 2002, Robert P. Huff Golden Quill award, Nat. Assn. Student Fin. Aid Adminstrs., 1993; grantee, Ind. Commn. for Higher Edn. and Lumina Found. for Edn. grantee, 2002—; Lumina Found. for Edn. grantee. Mem.: Assn. for Study of Higher Edn. (bd. mem. 2001—03). Roman Catholic. Achievements include research that has examined the impact of federal and state education policies on changes in educational opportunity. Office: 210 SEB 610 E University Ave Ann Arbor MI 48109-1259 Personal E-mail: edstjohn@umich.edu.

ST. JOHN, HENRY SEWELL, JR., utility company executive; b. Birmingham, Ala., Aug. 18, 1938; s. H. Sewell and Carrie M. (Bond) St. John; m. J. Ann Morris, Mar. 7, 1959; children: Sherri Ann, Brian Lee, Teresa Lynn, Cynthia Faye. Student, David Lipscomb Coll., 1956—58, U. Tenn., 1958—59, U. Ala., 1962—64. Engrng. aide Ala. Power Co., Enterprise, 1960—62, Birmingham, 1962—66; asst. chief engr. Riviera Utilities, Foley, Ala., 1966—71, sec.-treas., gen. mgr., 1972—2001. Chmn. Baldwin County unit Am. Cancer Soc., 1977; treas. Christian Care Ctr. Inc., 1981—; Deacon Foley Ch. of Christ, 1975—82, elder, 1983—; bd. dirs. AGAPE of Mobile, 1977—80; bd. dirs., pres. South Baldwin Civic Chorus, 1979—82; bd. dirs. Baldwin County Econ. Devel. Alliance, 1997—2001, exec. com., 1999—2001, sec., 1998—99, treas., 1999—2000, chmn., 2000—01. Mem.: IEEE (life), Chevrolet Nomad Assn. (bd. dirs. 1991—2002, v.p. 1993—2002), South Baldwin C. of C. (dir. 1972—75, pres. 1974, dir. 1981—90, 1992—95, amb. 2002—), Pub. Gas Assn. Ala. (bd. dirs. 1987—88), Am. Pub. Power Assn. (com. legis. and resolutions 1972—2001, chmn. State of Ala. mem. com. 1982—2001, com. on coms. 1997—2000, bd. dirs. 1997—2001, exec. com. 1999—2000, chmn. nat. membership com. 1999—2000, chmn. bylaws com. 2000—01, Kramer-Preston Pub. Svc. award 2002), United Mcpl. Distbrs. Group (bd. dirs. 1972—2001), Electric Cities Ala. (bd. dirs. 1983—2001, exec. com. 1989—2001, vice chmn. 2000—01, chmn. 2001, Heritage award 2005), Ala. Mcpl. Electric Authority (vice chmn. 1981—83, bd. dirs. 1981—2001, chmn. 1984—2001), Mcpl. Electric Utility Assn. Ala. (exec. com., dir. 1971—85), Ala. Consumer-Owned Power Distbrs. Assn. (chmn. 1974—75, sec.-treas. 1980, vice chmn. 1981, chmn. 1982—83), S.E. Electric Reliability Coun. (assoc.), South Ala. Power Distbrs. Assn. (life; chmn. 1973—74), Nat. Corvette Mus., Nat. Corvette Owners Assn., Azalea City Classic Chevy (bd. dirs., exec. com. 1989—99, v.p. 1991—92, 1996—99), Gulf Shores Golf (dir. 1974—75), Foley Quarterback (sec.-treas. 1984—85), Classic Chevy, Internat. (life). Home: PO Box 1817 Foley AL 36536-1817 Personal E-mail: stjohn@gulftel.com.

ST. JOHN, JULIE, mortgage company executive; BA in English, U. Mich.; MBA, Fla. State U. CPA, Fla. Prin. Arthur Young & Co.; v.p. info. systems Residence Inn divsn. Marriott; joined Fannie Mae, Washington, 1990, sr. v.p. mortgage bus. tech., now exec. v.p., chief info. officer enterprise systems and ops. divsn. Mem. exec. bd. Boys & Girls Club of Greater Washington. Named one of Premier 100 IT Leaders, Computerworld, 2005. Mem.: AICPA, Women of Washington, Women in Housing and Fin. Office: Fannie Mae 3900 Wisconsin Ave NW Washington DC 20016-2892

ST. JOHN, KRISTOFF, actor; b. NYC, July 15, 1966; s. Christopher Kristoff and Maria St. John; m. Mia St. John, 1991 (div. 1995); children: Julian, Paris; m. Allana Nadal, Nov. 24, 2001; 1 child, Lola. Studied, Actor's Studio, LA. Owner Moonboy Inc. prodn. com. Actor: (TV series) The Young and the Restless, 1991— (Outstanding Younger Actor in Drama Series, Daytime Emmys, 1992, Outstanding Actor in Daytime Drama Series, NAACP Image Awards, 1994, 1995, 1996, 1997, 2003, 2004, 2007); guest appearances (TV series) Happy Days, 1976, The Cosby Show, 1984, A Different World, 1988, Jake and the Fatman, Diagnosis Murder, 1994, Hanging with Mr. Cooper, 1994—95, Martin, 1996, Suddenly Susan, 1998, Family Matters, 1998, For Your Love, 1999, Get Real, 1999; actor: (TV films) Roots II: The Next Generation, 1979, Beulah Land, 1980, Atlanta Child Murders, 1985, Finish Line, 1989; (films) The Champ, 1979, Avatar; dir.: (TV series) CBS Soap Break; host (fitness video) Kick Butt, 1999, host, prodr. (video) Backstage Pass. Avocations: movies, guitar. *

ST. JOHN, TERRI, secondary school educator; b. Battle Creek, Mich., July 17, 1953; d. Donald George and Virginia Beth Kelley. AA, Kellogg CC, 1975; BA, U. Central Fla., 1981; MA in Edn., U. Sarasota, 1995, EdD, 2001. Cert. tchr. Fla. Tchr., debate coach Forest Hill HS, West Palm Beach, Fla., 1983—85; tchr., theatre dir. Lake Weir HS, Ocala, Fla., 1985—89; tchr., debate coach Lake Highland Prep Sch., Orlando, Fla., 1991—97, Sarasota (Fla.) HS, 1997—. Presenter in field. Supporter St. Labre Indian Sch., Ariz., 2001—, Mayo Clinic Rsch., Minn., 2002—. Named Diamond Coach, Nat. Forensic League, 2005, Regional Coach of Yr., Fla. Forensic League Region III, 2005, 2006; recipient Outstanding Speech, Debate and Theatre Educator, NFHS, Fla., 2007. Mem.: ASCD, Fla. Forensic League (v.p. ops. 2004—, 2d v.p. 2000—, mem. com. 2003—, named Region III Coach of Yr. 2005, 2006, named State Coach of Yr. 2006), Cath. Forensic League, Fla. Comm. Assn., Nat. Comm. Assn., Nat. Coun. Tchrs. English. Avocations: movies, golf, reading, theater. Office: Sarasota HS 1000 S Sch Ave Sarasota FL 34237 Business E-Mail: terri_st_john@sarasota.k12.fl.us.

ST. JULIEN, THAIS MARY, soprano, musician; d. George W. St. Julien Jr. and Rosemary Gloria Bourda. Pvt. vocal studies, Charles Paddock, New Orleans, 1973—81, Virginia Mac Watters, Bloomington, Ind., 1978—81, Norma Newton, Houston, 1981—88, Andrea von Ramm, New Orleans, 1986; pvt. recorder studies, Milton G. Scheuermann, Jr., 1975—80; apprentice, Des Moines Metro Opera Festival, Indianola, Iowa, 1987; Opera Workshop, Loyola U., New Orleans, 1977—78; Baroque performance practice, Skip Sempe, 1995. Asst. season ticket sales mgr. New Orleans Opera Guild, 1974—77; ensemble singer New Orleans Musica da Camera, 1974—78, principle vocal soloist, 1978—, asst. music dir., 1980—91, asst. instrument builder, 1981—, co-artistic dir., 1991—, founder/dir. Vox Feminae (women's vocal ensemble), 1994—, chief adminstr., 1999—; mgr. single ticket sales New Orleans Philharm. Orch., 1977—79; founder, soloist Banquette Opera, New Orleans, 1979—84; founding mem., calligrapher Scriptease Calligraphy, New Orleans, 1980—92; founding mem., soloist Ezcudantza (voice/guitar duo), New Orleans, 1982—85; part- time libr. technician Tulane U., Maxwell Music Libr., New Orleans, 1989—2005. Musical advisor Hermann Grima Ho. Mus., New Orleans, 1980—84; sec., adv. bd. Entergy Arts Bus. Ctr., New Orleans, 1997—2002; adv. bd. New Orleans Internat. Music Colloquium, 1998—2001; musical advisor Musica Antiqua, Albany, Oreg., 1998—2005; founding dir. music series Belle Alliance Hist. Plantation, Donaldsonville, La., 2002—; bd. pres. New Orleans Musica da Camera, New Orleans; instr. vocal masterclass S.W. Mo. State U.; presenter in field; founding artistic dir. Thursdays at Twilight Concert Series New Orleans Bot. Garden, 2003—. Musician (co-dir.): (albums) Satires, Desires and Excesses: Songs from the Carmina Burana, Natus Est: A Christmas Celebration, The Cross of Red: Music of Love and War from the Time of the Crusades, Maiden, Mother, Muse: The Women of the Cantigas of Alfonso X, Les Motets d'Arras: Songs and Dances of Medieval Arras, The Play of Robin and Marion, A Christmas Offering (Early Music Am./Millenium of Music Nat. Radio Competition, 1996), Natus Est, 1994, 1995, Now Make We Mirthe; musician: (co-dir., host) Alone of All Her Sex; musician: A Voice Still Heard, Early Jewish Music, (radio spl.) Praises from the Heart, Tristan et Iseult, on Cathedral, Court and Countryside Series, 1981; musician: (dir.) (albums) Medee; musician: Moonrise, Circles, Tristan et Iseult, on Cathedral, Court and Countryside Series, 1982, The Garden of Love; hist. music adv. (films) Interview with the Vampire; musician: Creole Cameos: Music of New Orleans Creoles of Color, Performances throughout the U.S.; prodr.(co-host): Continuum-WWNO2, Continuum; editor, contbr.: newsletter The Cypher (Am. Guild Organists, New Orleans); contbr. articles to profl. jours. Founding mem., pres. bd. dirs. St. Charles Ave. Com., New Orleans, 1972—75. Named Vis. Artist in Residence with Musica da Camera, The Hist. Nat. Shrine of Our Lady of Prompt Succor, New Orleans, 1989—; recipient Lifetime Achievement award, Gambit Newspaper, Tribute to the Classical Arts, 1997, Pioneer in Preservation Honor award, Hist. Dist. Landmarks Commn., 1997, Cert. of Appreciation in Thankfulness for Contributions to the City, City of New Orleans, 2001. Mem.: Soc. Am. Magicians (v.p. local assembly), La. Partnership for the Arts, Southeastern Medieval Assn., Entergy Arts Bus. Ctr., Am. Musicological Soc., Knights of Slights, Internat. Brotherhood Magicians (pres. local ring), Mensa. Avocations: magic, reading, drawing, photography. Office: New Orleans Musica da Camera 1035 Eleonore St New Orleans LA 70115 Business E-Mail: mdc@nomdc.org.

SAINT LAURENT, YVES (HENRI DONAT MATHIEU), couturier; b. Oran, Algeria, Aug. 1, 1936; s. Charles Mathieu and Lucinne-Andree (Wilbaux) Saint L. Student, Lycée d'Oran. Worked with Christian Dior, 1954-57, successor, 1957-60. Adminstr. Société Yves Saint Laurent, 1962—. Costume designer (ballets) Cyrano de Bergerac, 1959, Adage et Variations, Notre-Dame de Paris, 1965, Delicate Balance, 1967, Sheherezade, 1973, (films) The Pink Panther, 1962, Belle de Jour, 1967, La Chamade, 1968, La Sirène du Mississippi, 1969, L'Affaire Stavisky, 1974; stage sets and costumes Spectacle Zizi Jeanmaire, 1961, 63, 68, Les Chants de Maldoror, 1962; costume designer for Mariage de Figaro, 1964; illus. La Vilaine Lulu, 1967; exhbns. include Met. Mus. Art, N.Y., 1983, Beijing Mus. Fine Arts, 1985, Musée des Arts de la Mode, Paris, 1986, Ho. Painters USSR, 1986, Hermitage Mus., St. Petersburg, 1987, Art Gallery NSW, Sydney, 1987, Sezon Mus., Tokyo, 1990. Recipient Neiman-Marcus award for fashions, 1958, Oscar from Harper's Bazaar, 1966, Internat. award Coun. Fashion Designers Am., 1982, Lifetime Achievement award, 1999, Best Fashion Designer Oscar, 1985; named Chevalier de la Légion d'Honneur, 1995, promoted de la Légion d'Honneur. Office: 5 ave Marceau 75116 Paris France

ST. LOUIS, MARTIN, professional hockey player; b. Laval, Que., Can., June 18, 1975; m. Heather St. Louis; 1 child. Grad., U. Vt., 1997. Profl. hockey player Cleve. Lumberjacks (IHL), 1997—98, Calgary Flames, 1998—2000, Tampa Bay Lightning, 2000—. Mem. Team Can., World Cup of Hockey, 2004. Named to, NCAA East First All-Am. Team, 1995—97, NHL All-Star Team, 2003, 2004, Second All-Star Team, NHL, 2007; recipient Lester B. Peterson award, 2004, Hart Meml. Trophy, 2004. Achievements include being a member of Stanley Cup Champion Tampa Bay Lightning, 2004; being a member of World Cup Champion Team Canada, 2004. Office: c/o Tampa Bay Lightning 401 Channelside Dr Tampa FL 33602 *

ST. MARTIN, CHARLOTTE, trade association administrator; b. 1945; BS, U. North Tex., 1967. Office mgr. to rep. James M. Collins U.S. Ho. of Reps., 1970; mgr. sales and catering The Fairmount Dallas, 1971—77; dir. sales and mktg. Loews Anatole Hotel, Loews Corp., 1977—82, pres., CEO, 1989—95; regional v.p. sales and mktg. Loews Hotels, Loews Corp., 1982—87, exec. v.p. sales and mktg., 1996—2005; pres. Dallas Convention and Visitors Bur., 1987—89; pres., CEO Charlotte St. Martin Enterprises, 2005—06; exec. dir. League of Am. Theatres and Producers, Inc., 2006—. Office: League Am Theatres and Producers Inc 226 W 47th St New York NY 10036-1487 Office Phone: 212-764-1122. Office Fax: 212-398-2409. E-mail: league@broadway.org.

ST. MARTIN, JO-MARIE, lawyer; b. Feb. 10, 1960; d. Thomas R. and Jean (Quillen) St. Martin; m. Robert Jeffrey Green, Aug. 9, 1997. BS summa cum laude, Mary Washington Coll., 1982; JD, Univ. Tenn., 1985. Atty. Wilson & Worley, Kingsport, Tenn., U.S. Dept. Labor, 1985—86; minority edn. counsel Com. Edn. & Workforce, US Ho. of Reps, Washington, 1986—92, parliamentary counsel, 1995—98, gen. counsel, 1998—2006; gen. counsel to John Boehner US Ho. of Reps, Washington, 2006—. Office: 1011 Longworth HOB Washington DC 20515

ST. PIERRE, GEORGE ROLAND, JR., materials scientist, engineering executive, educator; b. Cambridge, Mass., June 2, 1930; s. George Rol and Rose Ann (Levesque) St. P.; m. Roberta Ann Hansen, July 20, 1956; children: Anne Renee, Jeanne Louise, John David, Thomas George; m. Mary Elizabeth Adams, Dec. 11, 1976; m. Gretchen Ann Butrick, June 29, 2001; 1 dau., Victoria Harris. BS, MIT, 1951, ScD, 1954; DSc (hon.), Ohio State U., 1998. Rsch. metallurgist Inland Steel Co., 1954-56; faculty Ohio State U., 1956—, prof. metall. engrng., 1957-88, assoc. dean Grad. Sch., 1964-66, chmn. metall. engrng., 1983-88, chmn. mining engrng., 1985-92; dir. Ohio Mineral Rsch. Inst., 1984-92, prof., chmn. material sci. and engrng., 1988-92, Presdl. prof., 1988-92, chmn., disting. u. prof. emeritus, 1992—; chief scientist Materials Directorate, Wright-Patterson AFB, 1995-96. Cons. in field; vis. prof. U. Newcastle, NSW, Australia, 1975; adv. com. materials sci. MIT, 1990-97; adv. bd. Argonne Nat. Lab., 1994-99. Editor: Physical Chemistry of Process Metallurgy, Vols. 7 and 8, 1961, Advances in Transport Processes in Metallurgical Systems, 1992, Transactions Iron and Steel Soc., 1994-2003; contbr. articles to profl. jours. Bd. dirs. Edward Orton Jr. Ceramic Found., 1989-92. With USAF, 1956-57. Recipient Milton (Mass.) Clarence Boylston Sci. prize, 1947; MacQuigg award, 1971; Alumni Disting. Tchr. award, 1978; named Disting. scholar Ohio State U., 1988, Presdl. prof. Ohio State U., 1988. Fellow Minerals, Metals & Materials Soc., AIME (bd. dirs. 1988-91, 93-96, Educator award 1996), Am. Soc. Materials Internat. (Bradley Stoughton Outstanding Tchr. award 1961, Gold medal 1987, Albert E. White award 1997); mem. Am. Inst. Mining Metall. and Petroleum Engrs. (Mineral Industry Edn. award 1987), Iron and Steel Soc. (Elliott lectr. 1994), Am. Contract Bridge League (gold life master), Faculty Club (pres. 1990-92), Sigma Xi. Home: 4906 Stonehaven Dr Columbus OH 43220 Office: Ohio State U Dept Materials Sci/Engrng 2041 N College Rd Columbus OH 43210-1124 Home Phone: 614-893-5287; Office Phone: 614-893-5287. Personal E-mail: gstpierr@columbus.rr.com.

SAINT-PIERRE, GUY, engineering executive; b. Windsor Mills, Que., Can., Aug. 3, 1934; s. Armand and Alice (Perra) Saint-P.; m. Francine Garneau, May 4, 1957; children: Marc, Guylaine, Nathalie. B in Applied Sci. in Civil Engring, Laval U., 1957; diploma, Imperial Coll., London, 1958; MSc, U. London, 1959; LLD (hon.), Concordia U., 1992; degree (hon.), Coll. Militaire Royal de Saint-Jean, 1993; DSc (hon.), Laval U., 1992; degree in Applied Sci. (hon.), Sherbrooke, 1994; DSc (hon.), Montreal U.; degree (hon.), Ottawa U., 2002. Registrar, Corp. Engrs. Que., 1964-66. V.p. Acres Que., 1967-70; minister of edn. Govt. Que., 1970-72, of industry and commerce, 1972-76; asst. to pres. John Labatt Ltd., Montreal, 1977—88, sr. v.p., 1977—88; pres., COO Ogilvie Mills Ltd., Montreal, 1977—88; pres., CEO, bd. dirs. The SNC-Lavalin Group Inc., 1989-96; chmn. bd. The SNC-Lavalin Group, Inc., 1996—2002; dir. Royal Bank of Can., 1990—2004, chmn. bd., 2001—04. Chmn. Bus. Coun. Nat. Issues, 1995—97; dir. Alcan Inc., 1995—2007, GM of Can., 1995—2004, Inst. Rsch. Public. Policy, 2003—. Gov. Conseil du Patronat de Que. Served as officer C.E. Can. Army, 1959—64. Decorated companion Order of Can.; named Canada's CEO of Yr., 1994, Canada's Internat. Exec. of Yr., 1996; recipient Sir John Kennedy Medal, 1993, Can. Engrs. Gold Medal award Can. Coun. Profl. Engrs., 1996; Engring. Inst. of Can.; inducted into Can. Bus. Hall of Fame, 2001. Mem.: Order Engrs. Que., Can. Mfrs. Assn. (chmn. bd., pres. 1987), Engring. Inst. Can., Montreal C. of C., Coun. Can. Unity (v.p.), Hermitage Club, Mt. Bruno Club, Mt. Royal Club, Can. Club Montreal (adv. com.). Liberal. Roman Catholic. Office: Royal Bank of Canada 1 Pl Ville Marie PO Box 6001 Montreal PQ H3C 3A9 Canada Business E-Mail: guy.saint-pierre@rbc.com.

ST. PIERRE, MICHAEL A., lawyer; b. Great Falls, Mont., May 29, 1955; BA magna cum laude, Boston Coll., 1977; JD, Suffolk U., 1980. Bar: R.I. 1980, Mass. 1980, U.S. Dist. Ct. R.I. 1981, U.S. Ct. Appeals (1st cir.) 2001, U.S. Supreme Ct. 1988. Law clk. to Chief Justice, R.I. Supreme Ct., 1980—81; asst. town solicitor Town of North Kingstown, 1980—84; atty. Revens, Revens & St. Pierre, Warwick, RI. Mem. Workers Compensation Bench Bar Com., 1991—, chmn., 1994—97; mem. disciplinary bd. RI Supreme Ct., 1997—2003, chmn., 2002—03. Mem.: ABA, RI Bar Found. (bd. govs. 2004—, v.p. 2005—), RI Bar Assn. (meetings com. 1993—2004,

Ho. of Dels. 1993—, exec. com. 1997—2004, pres. 2002—03), RI Trial Lawyers Assn. (young lawyers adv./clerkship com. 1987—92), Assn. Trial Lawyers Am., Fed. Bar Assn. Office: Revens Revens and St Pierre 946 Centerville Rd Warwick RI 02886

ST. PIERRE, RONALD LESLIE, public health and medical educator, academic administrator; b. Dayton, Ohio, Feb. 2, 1938; s. Leslie Frank and Ruth Eleanor (Rhoten) St.P.; m. Joyce A. Guilford, Apr. 1, 1961; children: Michele Christine, David Bryan. BS, Ohio U., 1961; M.Sc., Ohio State U., 1962, PhD, 1965. Instr. anatomy Ohio State U., Columbus, 1965-67, asst. prof., 1967-69, assoc. prof., 1969-72, prof., 1972—2002, chmn. dept. anatomy, 1972-81, assoc. v.p. health scis., 1981-83, sr. assoc. v.p. health scis. and acad. affairs, 1983—2002, assoc. dean Coll. Medicine and Pub. Health, 1987-96, vice dean Coll. of Medicine and Pub. Health, 1996-2000, exec. vice dean, 2000—02, interim dean pub. health, 1999—2002, assoc. v.p., prof. emeritus, 2002—, spl. asst. to sr. v.p. health scis., 2002—06; assoc. dir. Cancer Rsch. Ctr., 1974-78; acting provost, v.p. for acad. affairs Capital U., Columbus, 2006—. Vis. research asso. Duke U., 1966-67; cons. Battelle Meml. Inst., Columbus. Contbr. articles to profl. jours. Chmn. Ohio Gov.'s Com. on Employment of Handicapped, 1970-78; mem. state exec. com. Presdl. Commn. Employment of Handicapped, 1970-78, chmn., 1971-72; mem. planning and adv. council White House Conf. on Handicapped Individuals, 1975-78; mem. Columbus Mayor's Com. on Internat. Yr. of Disabled. Recipient Lederle Med. Faculty award, 1968-71, prize for basic research South Atlantic Assn. Obstetricians and Gynecologists, 1968, Outstanding Individual award Ohio Rehab. Assn., 1969, Gov.'s award for community service, 1973, Coll. Medicine and Mental Health Alumni Faculty Tchg. award, Ohio State U. Coll. Medicine, 2002, Univ. Disting. Svc. award, 2005. Mem. Am. Assn. Anatomists, Am. Assn. Immunologists, Soc. Exptl. Biology and Medicine, Sigma Xi (pres. Ohio State chpt. 1979-80) Republican. Presbyterian. Home: 8586 Button Bush Ln Westerville OH 43082-8675 Office Phone: 614-236-6108. Business E-Mail: rstpierr@capital.edu. E-mail: rstpierre@insight.rr.com.

SAISSELIN, REMY GILBERT, fine arts educator; b. Moutier, Bern, Switzerland, Aug. 17, 1925; came to U.S., 1938, naturalized, 1944; s. Paul A. and Jeanne (Nydegger) S.; m. Nicole M. Fischer, May 31, 1955; children: Anne, Juliet, Peter. BA, Queens Coll., 1951; MA, U. Wis., Madison, 1952, MA in French, 1953, PhD, 1957. Asst. prof. French Western Res. U., Cleve., 1956-59; asst. curator publs. Cleve. Mus. Art, 1959-65; prof. French lit. U. Rochester, N.Y., 1965-70, prof. fine arts N.Y., 1970-87; prof. humanities Hobart & William Smith Coll., 1987-90. Asst. editor: Jour. Aesthetics and Art Criticism, 1959-62; author: Taste in Eighteenth Centruy France, 1965, Rule of Reason and Ruses of the Heart, 1970, Literary Enterprise in XVIII Century France, 1979, The Bourgeois and the Bibelot, 1984, The Enlightenment Against the Baroque, 1992; exhbns. landscapes, still lifes, and abstractions in France, 1997. Served with U.S. Army, 1944-46. Guggenheim fellow, 1972-73 Mem. Phi Beta Kappa. Home: Route de Sancerre 18220 Saint Ceols France Home Phone: 001 33 248 64 33 36.

SAITO, FRANK KIYOJI, import and export firm executive; b. Tokyo, Feb. 28, 1945; s. Kaoru and Chiyoko S.; m. Elaine Tamami Karasawa, Feb. 22, 1975; children: Roderic Kouki, Lorine Erika. LLB, Kokugakuin U., 1967. With import dept. Trois Co. Ltd., Tokyo, 1967-68; founder import/export dept. Three Bond Co., Ltd., Tokyo, 1968-71; sales mgr. Kobe Mercantile, Inc., San Diego, 1971-76; pres. K&S Internat. Corp., San Diego, 1976-97, K&S Techs., Inc., San Diego, 1997—. Office: 9710 Scranton Rd Ste 150 San Diego CA 92121-1771

SAITO, ROBERT SHUNICHI, writer, poet; b. Alameda, Calif., Sept. 9, 1933; s. Sam Shunji Saito and Yayeko Umegawa; m. Naida Cervantes, Dec. 7, 1966. Cert., Coronado Sch. Fine Arts, 1980. Enlisted USN, 1955, advanced through grades to chief petty officer, 1971, pers. officer USS Camden, 1972-75, ret., 1975. Pres. Mega Travel Inc., La Mesa, Calif., 1983-84. Author of poetry, short stories. Recipient 1st Pl. award for Batik, Coronado Art Assn., 1977. Roman Catholic. Avocations: batik art, photography, fishing, walking, tai-chi.

SAITO, TAKASHI, professional baseball player; b. Miyagi, Japan, Feb. 14, 1970; m. Yukiko Saito; children: Kurumi, Mokoka. Student, Tohoku Fukushi U., Sendai, Japan. Draft pick Taiyo Whales (later Yokohama Baystars), Japan, 1991; pitcher Japanese Ctrl. League Yokohama Baystars, 1992—2005, LA Dodgers, 2006—. Named a Four-time All-Star, Japanese League; named to Nat. League All-Star Team, Maj. League Baseball, 2007. Achievements include leading the Japanese Ctrl. League in strikeouts (206), 1996. Office: LA Dodgers 1000 Elysian Park Ave Los Angeles CA 90012 *

SAITOU, KAZUHIRO, engineering educator; b. Tokyo, Dec. 12, 1966; PhD, MIT, 1996. Asst. prof. U. Mich., Ann Arbor, 1997—2003, assoc. prof., 2003—. Recipient Career award, NSF, 1999. Mem.: IEEE, ASME, Soc. Mfg. Engrs., Sigma Xi. Office: U Mich Mech Engring Dept 2350 Hayward St Ann Arbor MI 48109-2125 Business E-Mail: kazu@umich.edu.

SAITTA, NANCY M., state supreme court justice; b. Detroit; married; 4 children. BS magna cum laude, Wayne State U., 1983, JD, 1986. Criminal def. atty., Detroit; atty. Pearson & Patton, Las Vegas; assoc. Gentile & Porter, Las Vegas; sr. dep. atty. gen., Children's Adv. State of Nev.; judge Las Vegas Mcpl. Ct., 1996—98, 8th Jud. Dist. Ct., 1998—2006; assoc. justice Nev. Supreme Ct., 2007—. Mem. Nev. State Juvenile Justice Commn.; founder Clark County Missing & Exploited Children Comprehensive Action Program (M/CAP), So. Nev. Fatality Rev. Team, Complex Litig. Divsn.; assoc. prof. Wayne State U., Criminal Justice Dept.; litig. instr. Am. Inst. Paralegal Studies; instr. U. Phoenix, Criminal Justice Dept. Mem. Clark County Pub. Edn. Found. Named one of Top 500 Judges in Am., Law Dragon, 2005; recipient For the Children award, Nev. Dist. Atty.'s Office, Dist. Atty. Outstanding Svc. award, Angels in Adoption award, US Congress, 2000, Child Advocate of Yr. award, 2001. Mem.: Clark County Bar Assn. (exec. com.), Ct. Apptd. Spl. Advocate (CASA) Found. Office: Nev Supreme Ct 201 S Carson St Ste 300 Carson City NV 89701-4702 *

SAIZAN, PAULA THERESA, business consultant; b. New Orleans, Sept. 12, 1947; d. Paul Morine and Hattie Mae (Hayes) Saizan; m. George H. Smith, May 26, 1973 (div. July 1976). BS in Acctg. summa cum laude, Xavier U., 1969. CPA Tex. Sys. engr. IBM, New Orleans, 1969—71; acct., then sr. acct. Shell Oil Co., Houston, 1971—76, sr. fin. analyst, 1976—77, fin. rep., 1977—79, corp. auditor, 1979—81, treasury rep., 1981—82, sr. treasury rep., 1982—86; asst. treas. Shell Credit Inc., Shell Leasing Co., Shell Fin. Co., Houston, 1986—88, sr. pub. affairs rep., 1988—89, sr. staff pub. affairs rep., 1990—91, program mgr., 1991—96, sr. program mgr., 1996—97, mgr. constituent rels. and edn. support, 1997—2000, mgr. nat. and cmty. outreach, 2000—03, mgr. stakeholder mgmt., 2003—04, sr. advisor corp. affairs, 2005—. Pres. PTBS, Inc., Houston. Bd. dirs. Greater Houston Conv. and Visitors Bur., Xavier U.; bd. dirs. exec. coun. The Links, Incorporate; vice-chair Nat. Coun. Negro Women, Inc.; adv. bd. Sch. Engring. Tex. So. U.; del. White House Conf. on Small Bus., 1995. Mem. AICPA, NAACP (life mem., bd. dirs., trustee spl. contribution fund), Tex. Soc. CPA, Assn. Governing Bds. of Univs. and Colls., Leadership Houston, LWV Houston, Xavier U. Alumni Assn., Nat. Coun. Garden Clubs (life), Nat. Congress Black Women, Alpha Kappa Alpha, Phi Gamma Nu, Kappa Gamma Phi. Roman Catholic. Home: 7601 Oak Fern Houston TX 77040-4407 Office: PTBS Inc 9105 W Sam Houston N Pkwy Ste 700 Rm 320 Houston TX 77064 Business E-Mail: ptbs3@aol.com.

SAJAK, PAT, television game show host; b. Chgo., Oct. 26, 1946; m. Lesly Brown, Dec. 31, 1989, 2 children. Student, Columbia Coll., Chgo. Newscaster WEDC-Radio, Chicago, IL; disk jockey WNBS-Radio, Murray, Ky., 1971—72; staff announcer, public affairs program host, weatherman WSM-TV, Nashville, 1972—77; weatherman, host The Sunday Show, LA, 1977-81; host Wheel of Fortune, 1981—, The Pat Sajak Show, 1989-90, Pat Sajak Weekend, 2003—. Film appearances include: Airplane II: The Sequel, 1982, Jack Paar is Alive and Well, 1987; NBC television specials, host, The Thanksgiving Day Parade, The Rose Parade. Served with U.S. Army, Vietnam. Recipient 3 Emmys, People's Choice award, star on Hollywood Walk of Fame.

SAK, GILBERT, music educator; b. Hong Kong, Oct. 17, 1967; MusB, Manhattan Sch. Music, NYC, 1991; MusM, Ball State U., Ind., 1992; PhD in Musical Arts, U. SC, Columbia, 2000; MEd, Open U. Hong Kong, 2006. 2d violin prin. SC Philharm. Orch., Columbia, 1994—95, Kalamazoo Symphony Orch., 1995—98; 1st violin tutti Malaysian Philharm. Orch., Kuala Lumpur, Selangor, Malaysia, 1998—2000; asst. prodr. Radio 4, RTHK, Hong Kong, 2000—01; music instr. St. Stephen's Coll., Hong Kong, 2001—04; music dir. Potential Violin Inst., Hong Kong, 2005—, The Hong Kong Civic Youth Orch., 2005—; part-time lectr. Hong Kong Acad. Performing Arts; adj. faculty Hong Kong Bapt. U. Advisor Scout Assn. Hong Kong, 2004—06. Mem.: Chamber Music Am. (assoc.), Phi Kappa Lambda, Mensa. Personal E-mail: gsgeiger67@hotmail.com.

SAKAI, JOSEPH THOMAS, psychiatrist, educator; (parents Am. citizens); s. Dennis and Sara Sakai; m. Nicole Fabean Sakai, July 11, 1998. BA, Pomona Coll., Claremont, Calif., 1989—93; MD, Tulane U., New Orleans, 1993—97. Cert. psychiatrist Am. Bd. Psychiatry & Neurology, 2003, addiction psychiatrist Am. Bd. Psychiatry & Neurology, 2004, interdisciplinary cert. Inst. Behavioral Genetics, 2006. Internship cmty. medicine U. Colo. Health Scis. Ctr., Denver, 1998, residency in psychiatry, 2001, addiction fellowship, 2003; instr., fellow U. Colo. Sch. Medicine, 2002—04, asst. prof., 2004—. Assoc. dir. psychiat. svcs. Addiction Rsch. & Treatment Svcs., Denver, 2003—06; med. dir. Asian Pacific Ctr. Human Devel., Denver, 2004—; dir. adolescent psychiat. svcs. Addiction Rsch. & Treatment Svcs., Denver, 2006—. Recipient Travel award, Am. Acad. Addiction Psychiatry & Nat. Inst. Drug Abuse, 2000, K award, Nat. Inst. Drug Abuse, 2004—, Early Career Investigator Travel award, Coll. Problems Drug Dependence, 2002. Mem.: Colo. Psychiat. Soc., Am. Acad. Addiction Psychiatry (Resident Rsch. award), Am. Psychiat. Assn., Alpha Omega Alpha. Office: Univ Colo Med Sch 4200 E Ninth Ave Box C268-35 Denver CO 80262 Office Fax: 303-315-0394. Business E-Mail: joseph.sakai@uchsc.edu.

SAKAI, PETER A., lawyer; b. McAllen, Tex., Oct. 21, 1954; s. Pete Y. and Rose Marie (Kawahata) S.; m. Raquel M. Dias, Mar. 10, 1982; children: George Y., Elizabeth K. BA, U. Tex., Austin, 1976, JD, 1979. Bar: Tex. 1979. Asst. dist. atty. County of Bexar, San Antonio, 1980-82; pvt. practice San Antonio, 1983-94, 2006; assoc. judge dist. ct. Bexar County Courthouse, San Antonio, 1994—2005, judge 225th Dist. Ct., 2007—. Hearings arbitrator City of San Antonio, 1983-93; judge Mcpl. Ct., City of Elmendorf, Tex., 1985; juvenile assoc. judge 289th Dist. Ct., San Antonio, 1989-94; city atty. City of Leon Valley, Tex., 1986-90. Contbr. to profl. publs. Bd. dirs. Bexar County Juvenile Vols. in Probation, San Antonio, 1983-93; Japan Am. Soc. San Antonio, 1987-89, Cmty. Cultural Arts Orgn., San Antonio, 1987-92, Bexar County Local Devel. Corp., San Antonio, 1989-94. Mem. ABA, State Bar Tex., San Antonio Bar Assn. Avocation: sports. Office: Bexar County Courthouse 100 Dolorosa 2d Fl San Antonio TX 78205 Office Phone: 210-335-2233. Personal E-mail: judgepetersakai@yahoo.com.

SAKAI, TOSHIHIKO, engineer; b. Nagoya, Aichi, Japan, July 17, 1943; s. Saichi and Yoshie (Taguchi) S.; m. Junko Fukuoka, Oct. 7, 1971; children: Eiji, Kenji; m. Natsuko Kamei, Nov. 25, 1989; children: Rei, Rui. B.Sc., Nagoya Inst. Tech., Japan, 1967; M.Sc., Ga. Inst. Tech., 1970; PhD, U.M.I.S.T., UK, 1974. Assoc. engr. Toyota Ctrl. R. & D. Labs., Inc., Aichi, Japan, 1967-75, rschr., 1975-84, sr. rschr., 1984-95. Mgr. tech. secretariat Toyota Ctrl. R & D Labs., Inc., Aichi, 1982—89, CEO staff, 1991—95, gen. mgr., 1989—95; councilor Tsuchiya Co., Ltd., Nagaya, Japan, 1995; dir., bd. dirs. Overseas Ops., 1995—2000; sr. mng. dir. NIC Corp. (Venture Capital), Nagoya, Japan, 2001—; exec. v.p., COO Techno Search, Inc., Nagoya, 2004—. Contbr. articles to profl. jours.; inventor and patentee in field. Submit referee Textile Machinery Soc. Japan. Fellow Textile Inst. (UK); mem. Soc. Fiber Sci. and Tech. Japan, Soc. Automotive Engr., The NPO Rsch. Assn. New Industry Creation (sr. mn. dir. 2001—), Nagoya Jr. Chamber (exec. v.p. 1982). Avocations: travel, driving, golf. Home: City Corp B1003 Ueda 3-1501 Tempaku Nagoya 468-0051 Japan Office: Techno Search Inc Nagoya C of C I Bldg 10-F Sakae 2-10-19 Naka Nagoya 460-0008 Japan Home Phone: 81-52-805-9090; Office Phone: 81-52-205-3021.

SAKAI, YU, pathologist; b. Osaka, Japan, July 10, 1966; s. Kunisuke and Kazuko Sakai; m. Asako Kondo, June 10, 2000. MD, Nat. Def. Med. Coll., Tokorozawa, Japan, 1991; PhD, Juntendo U., Bunkyo-ku, Japan, 2002. Jr. resident Nat. Def. Med. Coll., Tokorozawa, 1991—93, sr. resident, 1995—97; physician Japan Self Def. Force Fukuoka Hosp., Kasuga, Fukuoka, Japan, 1993—94; pathologist Japan Self Def. Forces Ctrl. Hosp., Setagaya-ku, Tokyo, 1994—95, 1997—2005, Japan Self Def. Forces Sapporo Gen. Hosp., Japan, 2005—. Fellow: Japanese Soc. Pathology; mem.: Japanese Soc. Lab. Medicine, Japanese Soc. Clin. Cytology. Avocation: fishing. Office: Dept Pathol Japan Self Def Forces Sapporo Gen Hosp 12-1-32 Hiragishi 1Jo Toyohira-ku Sapporo 062-0931 Japan Home Phone: +8111823-3011. Personal E-mail: zwq04043@nifty.ne.jp.

SAKAMOTO, KATSUYUKI, retired academic administrator, psychologist, educator; b. LA, Oct. 24, 1938; m. Edna Christine Sakamoto; children: David Katsu, Bryce Yoshio. BA in Psychology, Calif. State U., Fresno, 1961, MA in Psychology, 1968; PhD in Exptl. Social Psychology, So. Ill. U., Carbondale, 1971; postgrad., Carnegie Mellon U., 1984. Acting dir. Army Edn. Ctr., Munich, 1962-63; dir. social svcs. Salvation Army, Fresno, Calif., 1964-66; assoc. prof. psychology Keuka Coll., Keyka Park, N.Y., 1971-78; prof. social psychology Ea. Oreg. State Coll., La Grande, 1978-85, assoc. dean, then acting dean, 1980-82, 84, assoc. dean acad. affairs, 1982-85; prof. psychology Ind. U. East, Richmond, 1985-91, vice chancellor for acad. affairs, 1985-90, spl. asst. to chancellor, 1990-91; prof., chancellor Calif. Sch. Profl. Psychology, Alameda, 1991-98, ret., 1998. Lectr. So. Ill. U., 1970-71; vis. prof. SUNY, Binghamton, 1973; adj. prof. Alfred (N.Y.) U., 1972-76, Nazareth Coll. Rochester, N.Y., 1975-78, Eisenhower Coll., Seneca Falls, N.Y., 1975-77; evaluator Western Assn. Schs. and Colls., 1991—; commr.-at-large North Ctrl. Assn. Colls. and Schs., 1989-91, educator, cons., 1986-91; mem. exec. bd. for study ctrs. in Japan, China and Korea, campus dir. Oreg. Sys. Higher Edn., 1980-85; bd. visitors Newark (N.Y.) Devel. Ctr., 1975-77; presenter in field. Contbr. articles to profl. jours. Bd. dirs. troop 119 Boy Scouts Am., Richmond, 1986-91, Project 100001, Townsend Cmty. Ctr., Richmond, 1987-89, Alameda Girls Club, Inc., 1992—, Asian Cmty. Mental Health Svcs., 1991—, Found. for Ednl. Excellence, Alameda, 1993—; pres., bd. dirs. Whitewater Opera Co., Richmond, 1987-91, Leadership Wayne County, Richmond, 1988-91; cons. teaching mini-grant program Richmond Cmty. Schs., 1988-91; mem. citizens adv. bd. Wayne County Sheriff's Dept., 1989-91. Mem. APA, Am. Assn. for Higher Edn., Am. Assn. State Colls. and Univs., Am. Assn. Univ. Adminstrs. (nat. v.p. 1990-92, bd. dirs. Found. 1991—), Am. Assn. for Higher Edn. (founding mem. Asian Am. caucus), Asian Am. Psychol. Assn. (treas., membership officer 1983-91, pres. 1988-91), Calif. Psychol. Assn., Nat. Assn. Acad. Affairs Adminstrs., Nat. Coun. Schs. Profl. Psychology, Rotary (bd. dirs. Alameda 1993—). Home: 5000 S Centinela Ave Apt 109 Los Angeles CA 90066-6947 Office: Calif School Of Prof Psychology 1 Beach St Ste 100 San Francisco CA 94133-1221

SAKAMOTO, NORMAN LLOYD, state legislator, civil engineer; b. Honolulu, May 22, 1947; s. Shuichi and Fusa (Hayashi) S.; m. Penelope A. Hayasaka, July 12, 1970; children: David H., Gregory F., Katherine E. BSCE, U. Hawaii, 1969; MSCE, U. Ill., 1970. Registered profl. engr., Calif., Hawaii; lic. spl. inspector, Hawaii; lic. contractor, Hawaii. Engr. storm drain City of L.A., 1970-71, engr. streets and frwys., 1972-73; engr. hydrology C.E., 1971-72; v.p. S & M Sakamoto, Inc., Honolulu, 1973-85; pres. SC Pacific Corp., Honolulu, 1985—; mem. Hawaii Senate, Dist. 15, Honolulu, 1996—. Bd. dirs. Bldg. Industry Assn., Honolulu, spl. appointee, 1991-92, pres.-elect, 1993, pres., 1994; bd. dirs. City Contractors Assn., Honolulu; trustee Home Builders Inst., 1993-96; del. White House Conf. on Small Bus., 1995; co-chair Hawaii Congress on Small Bus. Scoutmaster Honolulu area Boy Scouts Am., 1989-92, asst. scoutmaster, 1993—; elected to Hawaii State Senate, Dist. 15, 1996—; mem. Aliamanu Clubhouse adv. bd. Boys and Girls Club; exec. com. Edn. Commn. of the States, 2006—. Named Remodeler of Month Bldg. Industry Assn., 1990, 91, 96, Remodeler of Yr., 1991, Legislator of Yr., Bldg. Industry Assn., 2003, Legislator of Yr., Friends of the Libr., 2004; recipient Excellence award U. Hawaii, 2005, Charles Dick Medal of Merit, Nat. Guard Assn. US, 2005, State Dirs. award, Career and Tech. Edn. U. Hawaii, 2006, Legis. Yr. award, Am. Sch. Health Assn., 2007. Mem. ASCE, Nat. Assn. Home Builders, Internat. Fellowship Christian Businessmen, Nat. Fedn. Ind. Bus. (Guardian of Small Bus. award 1999), Constrn. Industry Legis. Assn., C. of C., Nat. Fedn. Ind. Bus. (leadership coun., 2007). Evangelical. Office: SC Pacific Corp 3210-A Koapaka St Honolulu HI 96819

SAKAMOTO, RONALD RIKIO, lawyer, construction executive; b. Honolulu, Oct. 2, 1951; s. Richard Tadashi and Hideko Sakamoto; m. Marie Kanno, Jan. 14, 2006; 1 child, Aaron Naoyuki. B in Econs. with distinction, Whitman Coll., 1973; JD, U. Hawaii, 1979. Bar: Hawaii 1979. Atty. Damon Key Char & Bocken, Honolulu, 1979—89, Char Sakamoto Ishii Lum and Ching, Honolulu, 1989—, pres., 2004—; v.p. Tileco Inc., Kapolei, Hawaii, 1983—, also bd. dirs. Bus. and prodn. mgr. U. Hawaii Law Rev. Chair Friends William S. Richardson Sch. Law, Honolulu, 1982—87; bd. dirs. Hawaii Lupus Found., Inc., Honolulu, 1988—93, Hawaii Health Found., Honolulu, 1996—; sect. referee adminstr. sect. 7 (Hawaii) Am. Youth Soccer Orgn., 2005—; mem. law rev. adv. com. U. Hawaii Sch. Law, Honolulu, 1980—93; nat. referee commn. Am. Youth Soccer Orgn., Hawthorne, Calif., 2005—, regional referee adminstr. region 178 Honolulu, 2003—; pres. Assn. Apt. Owners 855 Olokele, Honolulu, 1980—81. Named Referee of the Yr. Region 178, Honolulu, Am. Youth Soccer Orgn., 2002, Referee Instr. of the Yr. Sect. 7, Hawaii, 2005, Outstanding Farringtonian, Farrington H.S., 1969; M.M. Scott scholar, Hawaiian Trust, 1969—73. Mem.: ABA, Hawaii State Bar Assn. (chmn. bus. law sect. 1985, chmn. tax sect. 1994—95), William S. Richardson Sch. Law Alumni Assn. (bd. dirs. 1979—85). Office: Char Sakamoto Ishii Lum and Ching 841 Bishop St # 850 Honolulu HI 96813 Office Phone: 808-522-5133.

SAKHNOVICH, LEV ARONOVICH, mathematics educator, researcher; b. Lugansk, Ukraine, Feb. 24, 1932; naturalized, US, 2005; s. Aron and Donja (Bycova) S.; m. Olena Melnychenko, Feb. 21, 1954; children: Alexander, Anna. Tchr.'s diploma, Pedagogical Inst., Odessa, Ukraine, 1953; PhD in Math., U. Kharkov, Ukraine, 1958, DSc degree, 1960. Lectr. Pedagogical Inst., Ismael, Ukraine, 1956—57; prof. Tech. Inst., Odessa, Ukraine, 1957—64, Acad. Comm., Odessa, 1964—99. Chmn. dept. math. Tech.-Sci. Soc., Odessa, 1981—; vis. mem. Courant Inst. Math. Sci. Author, reviewer Russian Math. Survey, 1980; author Algebra Analysis Survey, 1993, Integral Equations with Difference Kernels on Finite Intervals, 1996, Interpolation Theory and its Applications, 1997, Spectral Theory of Canonical Differential Systesm, 1999; editor: Matrix and Operator Valued Functions, 1994; contbr. articles to profl. jours. Recipient prize Moscow Math. Soc., 1962; grantee Soros, 1993-99. Mem.: Am. Math. Soc. Home: 735 Crawford Ave Brooklyn NY 11223 E-mail: lev.sakhnovich@verizon.net.

SAKIC, JOE (JOSEPH STEVE SAKIC), professional hockey player; b. Burnaby, BC, Canada, July 7, 1969; m. Debbie Sakic. Center Colo. Avalanche (formerly Que. Nordiques), 1991—, capt., 1992—. Mem. Team Can., World Cup of Hockey, 1996, 2004, Team Can., Olympic Games, Nagano, Japan, 1998, Salt Lake City, 2002. Named to NHL All-Star game, 1990—94, 1996, 1998, 2000—02, 2004, 2007; recipient Conn Smythe Trophy, 1996, Hart Trophy, 2001, Lester B. Pearson Award, 2001, Lady Byng Trophy, 2001, MVP Award, NHL All-Star game, 2004. Achievements include being a member of Stanley Cup Champion Colorado Avalanche, 1996, 2001; being a member of gold medal winning Canadian Hockey Team, Salt Lake City Olympic Games, 2002; being a member of World Cup Champion Team Canada, 2004. Office: c/o Colo Avalanche 1000 Chopper Cir Denver CO 80204-5809 *

SAKIEWICZ, NICK, professional sports team executive; b. Passaic, NJ; m. Isabel Sakiewicz; 1 child, Nick Jr. Grad., U. New Haven. Soccer player F.C. Nantes, French 1st Divsn., 1982, N.Y. Arrows, Major Indoor Soccer League, 1983, F.C. Belenenses, Portuguese 1st Divsn., 1984; sales mgr. TIF Instruments, Miami, Fla., 1985-90; zone mgr. Agy. Svcs., Inc., Atlanta, 1990, dir. sales Tampa, Fla., v.p. sales & mktg. Balt.; asst. coach, goalkeeper coach Coll. Boca Raton (Fla.), 1987; goalkeeper coach Southeast Region, Olympic Devel. Program, 1985-89, Fla. Youth Soccer Assn., 1985-89; dir., then v.p. Providian Bancorp, San Francisco, 1995; past v.p. corp. sales Major League Soccer; pres., gen. mgr. Tampa Bay Mutiny, Major League Soccer, 1996-2000; gen. mgr. N.Y.-N.J. Metro Stars, Major League Soccer, East Rutherford, N.J., 2000—. Office: NY-NJ Metro Stars 3rd Fl 1 Harmon Plz Fl 3 Secaucus NJ 07094-2803

SAKKAB, NABIL YAQUB, research and development company executive; b. Jerusalem, Apr. 30, 1947; arrived in US, 1970. s. Yaqub Yusuf and Anastasia (Nuqleh) S.; children: Billie, Jerry, Grady, Nabil Jr., Stephanie. BSc in Chemistry, Am. U. Beirut, Lebanon, 1970; PhD in Chemistry, Ill. Inst. Tech., Chgo., 1973. Postdoctoral rschr. Tex. A&M U., College Station, 1974; staff scientist Procter & Gamble Co. Asia & L.Am. Divsn., 1974—75, group leader laundry products, 1975—77, sect. head laundry products, 1977—78; sect. head oral care product devel. Procter & Gamble Co. Toilet Goods Divsn., 1978—80, assoc. dir. oral care product devel., 1980—83; assoc. dir. fabric softener product devel. Procter & Gamble Co. Bar Soap & Household Cleaning Products Divsn., 1983—87, dir. product devel., 1987, dir. product devel. hard surface cleaners and personal cleansing products, 1987—89; dir. product devel. Procter & Gamble Co. Bar Soap & Household Cleaning Products Divsn. Europe, 1989—92; mgr. R & D laundry products Procter & Gamble Co. Europe, Mid. East, North Africa and Ea. Europe, 1992—94; mgr. R & D Procter & Gamble Far East, Kobe, Japan, 1994—95, v.p. R & D, 1995—96; v.p. R & D laundry and fabric conditioner products Procter & Gamble Worldwide, 1996—99; v.p. R & D global fabric and home care Procter & Gamble Co., 1999—2001, sr. v.p. R & D global fabric and home care, 2001—05, sr. v.p. corp. R & D, 2005—. Mem. bd. GreenEarth Solutions Inc., 2002—; adv. prof. Tsinghua U., Beijing, 2002—; mem. bd. European Chem. Industry Coun., 2003.

Contbr. articles to profl. jours. Mem.: European Inst. Rsch. Mgmt., Indsl. Rsch. Inst. (bd. dirs. 2000—04, Nat. medal 2007). Avocations: photography, travel, gourmet cooking. Office: Procter & Gamble Co PO Box 599 Cincinnati OH 45201-0599 *

SAKS, GENE, theater and film director, actor; b. NYC; Began career as an actor off-Broadway at Provincetown Playhouse and the Cherry Lane Theatre; played in: Auden's Dog Beneath the Skin, E.E. Cummings' Him, Molière's The Bourgeois Gentilhomme; appeared on Broadway in Mr. Roberts, South Pacific, Middle of the Night, The Tenth Man, A Shot in the Dark, Love and Libel, A Thousand Clowns; debut as dir. on Broadway Enter Laughing, 1963; dir. stage plays Nobody Loves an Albatross, 1964, Half a Sixpence, 1964 (Tony nominee Best Dir. Musical), Generation, 1965, Mame, 1966 (Tony nominee Best Dir. Musical), Same Time, Next Year, 1975 (Tony nominee Best Dir. Play), California Suite, 1972, I Love My Wife (best dir. of Musical award Drama Desk, Tony), 1977, Brighton Beach Memoirs (best dir. award, Tony), 1983, Biloxi Blues (best dir. of play award, Tony), 1985, The Odd Couple (female version), 1985, Broadway Bound, 1986, A Month of Sundays, 1987, Rumors, 1988, Lost in Yonkers, 1991 (Tony nominee Best Dir., Outer Critics Cir. award), Jake's Women, 1992, Barrymore, 1997, Mr. Goldwyn, 2001, Remembering Tennessee, 2001; dir. films Barefoot in the Park, The Odd Couple, Cactus Flower, Last of the Red Hot Lovers, Mame, Brighton Beach Memoirs, A Fine Romance; dir. TV movie Bye, Bye Birdie, 1995; appeared in films including a Thousand Clowns, Prisoner of Second Aveneue, Lovesick, The One and Only, The Goodbye People, 1986, Nobody's Fool, 1994, IQ, 1994. Recipient George Abbott award for lifetime achievement in the theatre, 1990; elected to Theatre Hall of Fame, 1991. Mem. Stage Dirs. and Choreographers (pres.).

SAKS, JUDITH-ANN, artist; b. Anniston, Ala., Dec. 20, 1943; d. Julien David and Lucy-Jane (Watson) S.; m. Haskell Irvin Rosenthal, Dec. 22, 1974; 1 child, Brian Julien. Student, Tex. Acad. Art, 1957-58, Mus. Fine Arts, Houston, 1962, Rice U., 1962; BFA, Tulane U., 1966; postgrad., U. Houston, 1967. Curator student art collection U. Houston, 1968-72; artist Am. Revolution Bicentennial project Port of Houston Authority, 1975-76. One-woman shows include Alley Gallery, Houston, 1969, 2131 Gallery, Houston, 1969; group shows include Birmingham (Ala.) Mus., 1967, Meinhard Galleries, Houston, 1977, Galeire Barbizon, Houston, 1980, Park Crest Gallery, Austin, 1981, Margolis Gallery, 2005-06; represented in permanent collections at L.B. Johnson Manned Space Mus., Clear Lake City, Tex., Harris County Heritage Mus., Windsor Castle, Smithsonian Instn.; commns. include Pin Oak Charity Horse Show Assn., Roberts S.S. Agy., New Orleans, Cruiser Houston Meml. Rm., U. Houston; contbr. popular mags. Recipient art awards including 1st prize for water color Art League Houston, 1969, 1st prize for graphics, 1969, 1st prize for sculpture, 1968, Nat. 1st place award for original print DAR/Am. Heritage Com., 1987, Nat. 1st place award for acrylic painting, DAR, 2000, Nat. Hon. Mention for Acrylics, 2006, Tex. award for Acrylic, 2003, 06, Nat. 3rd place award for painting, 2003, Nat. 3rd prize for acrylic, 2005, Nat. 1st prize for acrylic, 2007, Tex. State 1st prize for drawing DAR, 2002, Shofar award, 2003, Outstanding Svc. award Boy Scout Troop 806, 2002, Tex. award for art, 2005. Mem. Art League Houston, Houston Mus. Fine Arts, DAR (chpt. curator 1983-85, 93-95, 2007-, rec. sec. 2001-03, libr. 2003-2005, counselor, 2005-07, curator 2007—, Tex. Best Chpt. Chmn. award 2003, 06, Tex. award for art 2003, Tex. State 1st prize acrylic 2004, 2005, Tex. Cert. award for acrylic 2006), Daus. Republic of Tex., Magna Charta Dames, Colonial Dames Am.

SAKS, STEPHEN HOWARD, accountant, health organization executive; b. Phila., May 16, 1941; s. Samuel and Edythe (Edelman) S.; m. Ruth Workman, Dec. 22, 1963; children: Amy Meryl, Brian Eric, Joshua Marc. BS in Econs., U. Pa., 1962. CPA, Pa. Staff acct. to ptnr. Peat, Marwick, Mitchell & Co., Phila., 1962-78; ptnr. Laventhol & Horwath, Phila., 1978-91; CFO Northeastern Health Sys., Phila., 1991—2001, Neumann Med. Ctr., Phila., 1992-98, Elkins Park Hosp., Pa., 2002—03; exec. dir. John F. Kennedy Meml. Hosp., Phila., 1998-99; v.p. fin. Cooper Health Sys., Camden, NJ, 1999—2001; interim CFO Whitman-Walker Clinic, Washington, 2004; dir. Shechtman Marks Devor PC, Phila., 2005—. Bd. dirs. Jewish Family and Children's Agy, Phila,. 1979-88; treas. Jewish Employment and Vocat. Svc., Phila., 1984-88; chmn. bd. overseers Gratz Coll., Melrose Pk., Pa., 1987-90; pres. Beth Sholom Men's Club, Elkins Pk., Pa., 1987-90. Mem. AICPA, Pa. Inst. CPAs, Healthcare Fin. Mgmt. Assn. (advanced). Democrat. Avocations: community activities, travel. Home Phone: 610-584-8353; Office Phone: 215-496-9339. Personal E-mail: shsaks@verizon.net. E-mail: ssaks@smd-pc.com.

SAKSENA, MARIAN E., lawyer; BA in Polit. Sci., Grinnell Coll., Iowa, 1993; cert. with high distinction, U. Minn. Grad. Sch. Social Work, 1998; JD, U. Minn. Law Sch., Mpls., 1998. Bar: Minn. 1999, White Earth Band of Chippewa Tribal Ct. 2001. Crisis care provider Mpls. Crisis Nursery, 1993—94; child adv. Cornerstone, Bloomington, Minn., 1993—95; summer law clk. Children's Law Ctr. Minn., 1996; Mansfield fellow, summer law clk. Legal Aid Soc. Mpls., 1997; vol. guardian ad litem Ramsey County Guardian ad Litem Prog., 1997—99; law clk. Office of the Hennepin County Atty., 1998—99; atty. Children's Law Ctr. Minn., 1999—2002, Fredrikson & Byron, P.A., 2002—04; assoc. Walling, Berg & Debele, P.A., Mpls., 2004—. Mem. transitioning from adolescence task force Casey Found./VOA, 2000; mem. juvenile rules com. Minn. Supreme Ct., 2001—, mem. guardian ad litem rules com., mem. adoption rules com.; mem. Uniform Parentage Act Task Force, 2001—02, Statewide Adv. Com. on Long-Term Foster Care, 2002. Youth Support Grp. Facilitator Cornerstone, Bloomington, Minn., 1995—96; bd. dirs. Legal Advocacy for West Bank Women, Mpls., 1995—97. Named Rising Star, Minn. Super Lawyers mag., 2006. Mem.: Nat. Assn. Counsel for Children, Children's Justice Initiative (mem. Hennepin County, state wards subcommittee 2002), Minn. State Bar Assn. (chair children & the law sect. 2001—). Office: Walling Berg & Debele PA 121 S 8th St Ste 1100 Minneapolis MN 55402 Office Phone: 612-335-3233. E-mail: Marian.Saksena@wbdlaw.com. *

SAKUGAWA, JUNE ELIZABETH, music educator; b. Buffalo, June 13, 1953; d. Joseph Bernard Feldmeyer and Anna Mary Stresing; m. Edward Chokin Sakugawa, Apr. 19, 1997. A in Applied Sci. in Music, Onondaga C.C., Syracuse, NY, 1973; MusB in Music Edn., Fredonia State U. Coll., NY, 1975; M in Music Edn., U. No. Colo., 1994. Lic. educator Nev. Orch. dir., gen. music tchr. Holland Patent (N.Y.) Ctrl. Sch. Dist., 1975—76; orch. dir. Sch. Dist. 9-R, Durango, Colo., 1977—81; music tchr. St. Andrew Luth. Sch., Denver, 1981—84, Jefferson County Sch. Dist., Lakewood, Colo., 1984—85; orch. dir. Clark County Sch. Dist., Las Vegas, 1985—. Bd. dirs. Colo. String Tchrs. Assn., Denver, 1979—81. Vol. Las Vegas Basset Hound Rescue. Nominee Disney Am. Tchr. award, 2001, 2004; recipient superior performance ratings for mid. sch. orch., Clark County Mid. Sch. Orch. Festivals, 1985—2005. Mem.: NEA, Nev. State Educators Assn., Music Educators Nat. Conf., Am. String Tchrs. Assn. Avocations: colored pencil and graphite art, astronomy, scrapbooks. Home: 1268 Lime Point St Las Vegas NV 89110-5908 Office: Mike O'Callaghan Mid Sch 1450 Radwick Las Vegas NV 89110-5908 Home Phone: 702-438-3978; Office Phone: 702-799-7340 ext 4063. Office Fax: 702-799-8870. Personal E-mail: ejbassetlovers@aol.com. E-mail: jes335@interact.ccsd.net.

SAKURADA, YUTAKA, retired chemist; b. Kyoto, Jan. 1, 1933; s. Ichiro and Chiyoko (Okumura) Sakurada; m. Keiko Sugimoto, May 10, 1960; children: Kazuhiro, Akihiro. BS, Kyoto U., 1956, MS, 1958, PhD, 1966. Rsch. fellow Cen. Rsch. Lab. Kuraray Co. Ltd., Kurashiki, Japan, 1958-62, 64-66; internat. fellow Stanford Rsch. Inst., Menlo Pk., Calif., 1962-64; tech. rep. N.Y. Office Kuraray Co. Ltd., NYC, 1968-71; mgr. Med. Bus. Devel. Div. Kuraray, Osaka, Japan, 1974-77, gen. mgr. Med. Products Div., 1977-88, gen. mgr. Corp. Rand D Div., 1988-89; mng. dir. Kuraray Plastics Co. Ltd., Osaka, 1989-91. Vice chmn. Japanese Soc. Biomaterials, Tokyo, 1987—96; pres. Haemonetics, Japan, 1991—2001, chmn. and CEO, Japan, 2001—05; pres. Haemonetics Japan/Asia, 2003—05, chmn., 2005—06; ret. Recipient Technology award The Soc. Polymers, 1984, Japanese Chem. Soc., 1985. Achievements include development of ethylene vinyl alcohol copolymer hollow fiber for hemo-dialyzer; development of dental adhesives. Home: GM Ebisunomori 1304 4-23-6 Ebisu Shibuya-ku Tokyo 150-0013 Japan Personal E-mail: ysakurada@star.ocn.ne.jp.

SAKUTA, MANABU, neurologist, educator; b. Ichikawa, Japan, Oct. 31, 1947; s. Jun and Shizuko (Tsuji) Sakuta; m. Yuko Fukushi, June 17, 1973; children: Akiko, Junko, Ken-Ichi. MD, U. Tokyo, 1973, PhD, 1978; MS in Neurology, U. Minn., 1981. Diplomate Japanese Bd. Neurology, Japanese Bd. Internal Medicine. Asst. dept. neurology U. Tokyo, 1980, lectr. dept. neurology, 1984—; from rsch. fellow dept. neurology to asst. prof. U. Minn., Mpls., 1980—82; head dept. neurology Japanese Red Cross Med. Ctr., Tokyo, 1982-2000; prof. Japanese Red Cross Women's Coll. Sch. Nursing, Tokyo, 1983-85, instr., 1986-88; lectr. dept. medicine U. Kobe, 1990—; prof. dept. neurology Kyorin U., Tokyo, 2000—, chmn., 2000—, chmn. 1st internal medicine, 2002—. Cons. Nakayama Hosp., Ichikawa, Japan, 1980—. Contbr. articles to profl. jours. Chmn. bd. trustees Japanese Soc. Tobacco Control, 2006—. Fellow: Royal Soc. Medicine (London); mem.: AAAS, Japaneses Soc. Tobacco Control (pres. 2006—, chmn. 2006—), Am. Acad. Neurology, Japanese Soc. Autonomic Nervous Sys. (coun.), Japanese Soc. Sarcoidosis (coun.), Japanese Soc. Cerebrovascular Disease (coun.), Japanese Soc. Clin. Neurophysiology, Japanese Soc. Diabetology, Japanese Soc. Neurology (pres. Kanto br. 1984, mem. coun. Kanto br. 1984—, mem. coun. 1985—, mem. editl. bd. 1988—), Japanese Soc. Internal Medicine (pres. Kanto br. 1992), N.Y. Acad. Sci., Tetsumon Club, U. Minn. Alumni Club, Chevalier du Tastevin (Burgundy), Chevalier Club (pres. internat. com. 1995—), Clin. Neurology Club. Democrat. Buddhist. Address: 71-7-504 Ichigaya-Yakuoji Shinjuku Tokyo 162 Japan Home Phone: 0332677774. Personal E-mail: sakuta@shimkei.jp, manabu.sakuta@nifty.ne.jp.

SALACUSE, JESWALD WILLIAM, lawyer, educator; b. Niagara Falls, NY, Jan. 28, 1938; s. William L. and Bessie B. (Buzzelli) S.; m. Donna Booth, Oct. 1, 1966; children: William, Maria. Diploma, U. Paris, 1959; AB, Hamilton Coll., 1960; JD, Harvard U., 1963. Bar: NY 1965, Tex. 1980. Lectr. law Ahmadu Bello U., Nigeria, 1963-65; assoc. Conboy, Hewitt, O'Brien & Boardman, NYC, 1965-67; assoc. dir. African Law Ctr., Columbia U., NYC, 1967-68; prof., dir. Rsch. Ctr., Nat. Sch. Adminstrn., Zaire, 1968-71; Mid. East regional advisor on law and devel. Ford Found., Beirut, 1971-74, rep. in Sudan, 1974-77; vis. prof. U. Khartoum, Sudan, 1974-77; vis. scholar Harvard Law Sch., 1977-78; prof. law So. Meth. U., Dallas, 1978-86, dean, 1980-86; dean, prof. internat. law Fletcher Sch. Law and Diplomacy, Tufts U., Medford, Mass., 1986-94, Henry J. Braker prof. comml. law, 1994—. Fellow Inst. Advanced Legal Studies, U. London, 1995; vis. prof. Ecole Nat. Ponts et Chaussées, Paris, 1990-95, Inst. Empressa, Madrid, 1995, U. Bristol, U. London Sch. Oriental and African Studies, 1995—2003; cons. Ford Found., 1978-82, 93, US Dept. State, 1978-80, UN Ctr. on Transnat. Corps., 1988—, Harvard Inst. Internat. Devel., 1990—, Asia Found., 1992, Harvard Law Sch./World Bank Laos Project, 1991-93; with Sri Lanka fin. sector project ISTI/US AID, 1993-94; lectr. Georgetown U. Internat. Law Inst., 1978-94, Panam. U., Mexico City, 1981; chmn. com. on Mid. Ea. law Social Sci. Rsch. Coun., 1978-84; chmn. Asia Tigers Fund Inc., 2005—, Coun. Internat. Exch. Scholars, 1987-91, India Fund Inc., 2005—; bd. dirs. Emerging Markets Income Funds. I & II Inc., Global Ptnrs. Income Fund, Inc., Salomon Bros. Worldwide Income Fund, Inc., Emerging Markets Floating Rate Fund, Inc., Mcpl. Ptnrs. Funds I & II, Salomon Bros. High Income Funds I & II, Salomon Bros. 2008 Worldwide Dollar Govt. Term Trust, Mcpl. Ptnrs. Funds I & II; trustee Southwestern Legal Found., 1992-2004, Am. U. Paris, 1993-97; pres. Internat. Third World Legal Studies Assn., 1987-91; chmn. Inst. Transnat. Arbitration, 1991-93; pres. Assn. Profl. Schs. Internat. Affairs, 1988-89; Fulbright disting. chair in comparative law, Italy, 2000; pres. Internat. Ctr. for Settlement Investment Disputes Arbitration Tribunal, 2004—. Author: (with Kasunmu) Nigerian Family Law, 1966, An Introduction to Law in French-Speaking Africa, Vol. I, 1969, Vol. II, 1976, (with Steng) International Business Planning, 1982, Making Global Deals-Negotiating in the International Marketplace, 1991, The Art of Advice, 1994, (video course) Negotiating in Today's World, 1995, The Wise Advisor, 2000, The Global Negotiator, 2003, Leading Leaders, 2005; contbr. articles to profl. jours. Mem. ABA, Dallas Bar Found. (trustee 1983-86), Coun. on Fgn. Rels., Am. Law Inst., Am. Soc. Internat. Law, Cosmos Club (Washington). Office: Tufts U Fletcher Sch Law-Diplomacy Medford MA 02155 Office Phone: 617-627-3633. Business E-Mail: jeswald.salacuse@tufts.edu.

SALADINI, ROBERT, educational association administrator; b. Hagerstown, Md., Feb. 16, 1951; s. Ralph Joseph Saladini and Rose Cicconi Saladini. BA, Towson U., Md., 1974; MA in Musicology, Cath. U. of Am., Washington, 1984. Sr. music specialist Libr. of Congress, Washington, 1990—2001, program officer Office Scholarly Programs, 2001—. John W. Kluge leadership fellow Libr. of Congress, 2001—02; organist, cons. Mem.: Am. Guild Organists (bd. dirs. 2000—03). Roman Catholic. Achievements include research in Library of Congress Choral Series. Home: 605 N Buchanan St Arlington VA 22203 Office: Libr of Congress 10 First St SE Washington DC 20540-4860 Home Phone: 703-524-1550; Office Phone: 202-707-2692. Business E-Mail: rsal@loc.gov.

SALAH, SAGID, retired nuclear engineer; b. Seoul, Sept. 2, 1932; came to U.S., 1954; s. Galim and Faiza (Sultan) Salahutdin; m. Ravile Almakay, Apr. 2, 1966; children: Shamil, Kamil, Safiye. BChemE, U. Fla., 1958, MS in Nuclear Engring., 1960, PhD in Nuclear Engring., 1964. Nuclear engr. AEC, Bethesda, Md., 1964-66; sr. design engr. Westinghouse Astronuclear Lab., Large, Pa., 1966-70; sr. sys. engr. Westinghouse Nuclear Energy Sys., Pitts., 1970-73; mem. sys. safety engring. staff U.S. Nuclear Regulatory Commn., Bethesda, 1973-93; ret., 1993. Nuclear engring. cons. Oak Ridge (Tenn.) Inst. Nuclear Studies, 1963, 64; instr. U. Md., College Park, 1973-76. Contbr. articles to Nuclear Sci. and Engring. Youth coach Nat. Capital Soccer League, Vienna, Va., 1975-85. Mem. Am. Nuclear Soc. (emeritus, reviewer trans. papers 1972), Sigma Tau. Muslim. Achievements include measurements of neutron energy spectra in heterogeneous media using differential and integral methods, neutron energy spectra measurements and analysis in intermediate spectra reactors, three-dimensional transient analysis of boron dilution in PWR reactors. Home: 9302 Kilport Ct Vienna VA 22182-3426 Personal E-mail: srsalah@cox.net.

SALAHUDDIN, PARVEEN, information scientist, researcher; d. Talat Salahuddin; m. Ziaul Islam. BS, Aligarh Muslim U., India, 1981, MS, 1984, MPhil, 1986, PhD, 1989. Sr. bioinformatics officer Aligarh (India) Muslim U., 1991—. Presenter in field. Contbr. articles to profl. jours. Mem.: AAAS, Protein Soc. Avocations: reading, gardening, travel, music, cooking.

SALAM, ADIL, pulmonary critical care physician; arrived in US, 1997; s. Abdul Shakur ul and Mariam Salam; m. Nadia A. Malik, Aug. 16, 1996; 1 child, Minahil. Fellow of Sci., Govt. Coll., Pakistan, 1989; MBBS, Punjab U., Pakistan, 1995. Intern Atlantic City Med. Ctr., resident, ho. officer, 1997—2000; cardiac rehab. fellow Brigham and Women's Hosp., Boston, 2000—01; pulmonary fellow Bridgeport (Conn.) Hosp., 2001—. Mem.: ACP. Office: Bridgeport Hosp/ Yale U 267 Grant St Bridgeport CT 06610 Office Phone: 203-261-3980. Personal E-mail: adilsalam@optonline.net.

SALAMA, C. ANDRE TEWFIK, electrical engineering educator; b. Heliopolis, Egypt, Sept. 27, 1938; arrived in Can., 1957; s. Tewfik and Sarine (Bigio) S.; m. Rhoda R. Kurtz, Dec. 19, 1974. BASc with honours, U. B.C., Vancouver, Can., 1961, MASc, 1963, PhD, 1966. Registered profl. engr., Ont. Mem. sci. staff Bell No. Rsch., Ottawa, Ont., Canada, 1966-67; asst. prof. elec. engring. U. Toronto, Ont., 1967-70, assoc. prof. Ont., 1970-77, prof. Ont., 1977-92, univ. prof. Ont., 1992—. Chmn., bd. dirs. Can. Microelectronics Corp., Kingston, Ont., 1984-98; program leader, bd. dirs. Micronet, Toronto, 1990—. Mem. editorial bd. Solid State Electronics, 1982-2000; contbr. over 300 articles to sci. jours. Recipient Izaak Walton Killam Meml. prize, 1994, Outstanding Lifetime Achievement award, Can. Semiconductor Tech. Conf., 2003, NSERC Lifetime Achievement award, 2004, Recognition award Rsch. Excellence and Outstanding Leadership Network Cures of Excellence, 2004; Info. Tech. Assn. Can. and Natural Scis. and Engring. Rsch. Coun. fellow U. Toronto, 1989-90. Fellow IEEE (assoc. editor Trans. on Cirs. and Systems 1987-89, Millenium medal 2000), Royal Soc. Can., Can. Acad. Engring.; mem. Electrochem. Soc., Assn. Profl. Engrs. Ont., Engring. Inst. Can. Avocations: swimming, sailing, scuba diving, horseback riding, reading. Office: U Toronto Dept Elec Engring Toronto ON Canada M5S 1A4 Home Phone: 416-482-4225; Office Phone: 416-978-8658.

SALAMAN, ALBAN, lawyer; b. Phila., Dec. 23, 1949; s. David Jacob and Lillian (Resow) S.; m. Leslie Beth Garson, Jan. 5, 1974; 1 child, Carly Melissa. BA, U. Pa., 1971; JD, Temple U., 1974; LLM in Taxation, NYU, 1975. Bar: Pa. 1974, DC 1978; CLU 1978. Atty., asst. br. chief Interpretative Divsn. Office of IRS Chief Counsel, Washington, 1977-83; assoc. to ptnr. Melrod, Redman & Gartlan, Washington, 1983-93; ptnr. Holland & Knight, Washington, 1993—, chair mid-Atlantic region pvt. wealth svcs. grp. Instr. DC Inst. CPA, 1987—. Bd. dirs. Am. Com. of the Weizmann Inst., Washington, 1994—. Named one of Top 100 Attys., Worth mag., 2006. Mem. ABA, Am. Soc. CLUs and ChFCs, DC Estate Planning Coun. Office: Holland & Knight 2099 Pennsylvania Ave NW Ste 100 Washington DC 20006 Office Phone: 202-457-5938. E-mail: alban.salaman@hklaw.com. *

SALAMANCA-RIBA, SUSANA ALICIA, mathematics professor; BA, U. Autonoma Metropolitana, Mexico City; PhD, MIT. Assoc. prof. math NM State Univ., Las Cruces. Achievements include being one of 18 top mathematicians and computer scientists (Atlas of Lie Groups Project) from the US to successfully map E8, one of the largest and most complicated structures in mathematics. Office: Dept Math SH260 NMSU PO Box 30001 Las Cruces NM 88003-8001 Office Phone: 505-646-2305. Business E-Mail: ssalaman@nmsu.edu. *

SALAMON, LESTER MILTON, political science professor; b. Pitts., Jan. 11, 1943; s. Victor William Salamon and Helen (Sanders) Weiss; m. Lynda Anne Brown, June 27, 1965; children: Noah, Matthew. BA in Econs. and Pub. Policy, Princeton U., 1964; PhD in Govt., Harvard U., 1971. Instr. dept. polit. sci. Tougaloo Coll., Miss., 1966-67; asst. prof. Vanderbilt U., Nashville, 1970-73; assoc. prof. policy scis. and polit. sci. Duke U., Durham, NC, 1973-80, dir. Ctr. for Urban and Regional Devel., 1973—77; dep. assoc. dir. U.S. Office Mgmt. and Budget, Washington, 1977-79; dir. Ctr. for Governance and Mgmt. Rsch., Urban Inst., Washington, 1980-86; prof., dir. Inst. for Policy Studies, Johns Hopkins U., Balt., 1987-97, dir. Ctr. Civil Soc. Studies, 1997—. Author: America's Nonprofit Sector: A Primer, 1992, The Emerging Sector: Nonprofit Organizations in Comparative Perspective, 1994, Partners in Public Service: Government Nonprofit Relations in the Modern Welfare State, 1995, Defining the Nonprofit Sector: A Cross-National Analysis, 1996, International Guide to Nonprofit Law, 1997, The Resilient Sector, 2003; editor: Beyond Privatization, 1989, Human Capital and America's Future, 1991, Global Civil Society, 1998, The Tools of Government, A Guide to The New Governance, 2002, The State of Non-Profit America, 2002, Global Civil Society, 2004; mem. editl. bd. Adminstrn. and Soc., 1985—, Voluntas, 1988—, Nonprofit and Voluntary Sector Quar., 1990—, Pub. Adminstrn. Rev., 2000—. Mem. experts com. to ind. sector panel on nonprofit sector Nat. Acad. Pub. Adminstrn. Panel, EPA; mem. Balt. City Planning Commn., 1987—95; mem. adv. com on voluntary fgn. aid USAID; chmn. bd. dirs. Cmty. Found. of Chesapeake. Recipient Laverne Burchfield award Am. Soc. Pub. Adminstrn., 1977, Disting. Book award Assn. of Rschrs. on Nonprofit Orgns. and Vol. Action, Disting. Book award Ind. Sector, 2002, Disting. Achievement award Assn. Rschrs. on Nonprofit Orgns. and Vol. Action, 2004. Mem. Internat. Soc. Third Sector Rsch. (vice chmn. 1991-95), Nat. Acad. Pub. Adminstrn., Social Sci. Rsch. Coun. (nonprofit field com.). Avocations: tennis, swimming, carpentry, sailing. Home: 903 Lynch Dr Arnold MD 21012-1504 Office: Johns Hopkins U Inst Policy Studies 3400 N Charles St Baltimore MD 21218-2680 Business E-Mail: lsalamon@jhu.edu.

SALAMON, LINDA BRADLEY, English literature educator; b. Elmira, NY, Nov. 20, 1941; d. Grant Ellsworth and Evelyn E. (Ward) Bradley; divorced; children: Michael Lawrence, Timothy Martin. BA, Radcliffe Coll., 1963; MA, Bryn Mawr Coll., 1964, PhD, 1971; Advanced Mgmt. Cert., Harvard U. Bus. Sch., 1978; D.H.L., St. Louis Coll. Pharmacy, 1993. Lectr., adj. asst. prof. Eng., Dartmouth Coll., Hanover, NH, 1967-72; mem. faculty lit. Bennington Coll., Vt., 1974-75; dean students Wells Coll., Aurora, NY, 1975-77; exec. asst. to pres. U. Pa., Phila., 1977-79; assoc. prof. English Washington U., St. Louis, 1979—88, prof., 1988-92, dean Coll. Arts and Scis., 1979-92; prof. English George Washington U., Washington, 1992—. Mem. faculty Bryn Mawr Summer Inst. Women, 1979—99; dean Columbian Coll. Arts and Sci., Washington, 1992—95, interim v.p. acad. affairs, 1995—96. Author, co-editor: Nicholas Hilliard's Art of Limning, 1983; co-author: Integrity in the College Curriculum, 1985; contbr. numerous articles to literary and ednl. jours. Bd. dir. Assn. Am. Colls., vice chmn., 1985, chmn., 1986; bd. dir. Greater St. Louis council Girl Scouts U.S.A.; trustee Coll. Bd., St. Louis Coll. Pharmacy. Fellow Radcliffe Inst., 1973-74, Folger Shakespeare Libr., 1986, NEH Montaigne Inst., 1988, Fulbright fellow, Taiwan, 2003, Ringler fellow Huntington Libr, 2004; Am. Philos. Soc. Penrose grantee, 1974. Mem.: MLA, Cosmos Club, Phi Beta Kappa. Office: George Washington U Dept of Eng Rome Hall 760 801 22D St NW Washington DC 20052-0001 Business E-Mail: lbs@gwu.edu.

SALAMON, MYRON BEN, physicist, educator, dean; b. Pitts., June 4, 1939; s. Victor William and Helen (Sanders) S.; m. Sonya Maxine Blank, June 12, 1960; children: David, Aaron. BS, Carnegie-Mellon U., 1961; PhD, U. Calif., Berkeley, 1966. Asst. prof. physics U. Ill., Urbana, 1966-72, assoc. prof., 1972-74, prof., 1974—, program dir. Materials Research Lab., 1984-91, assoc. dean. Coll. Engring., 2000—06; dean natural sci. and math. U. Tex., Dallas, 2006—. Vis. scientist U. Tokyo, 1966, 71, Tech. U. Munich, Fed. Republic Germany, 1974-75; cons. NSF; Disting. Vis. Prof. Tsukuba (Japan) U., 1995-96. Editor: Physics of Superionic Conductors, 1979; co-editor: Modulated Structures, 1979; divisional assoc. editor: Phys. Rev. Letters, 1992-96; contbr. sci. papers to profl. jours. Recipient Alexander von Humboldt Sr. US Scientist award, 1974-75; NSF coop. fellow, 1964-66; postdoctoral fellow, 1966; A.P. Sloan fellow, 1972-73; Berndt Matthias scholar Los Alamos Nat. Lab., 1995-96; visiting scientist CNRS and Inst. Laue-Langevin Grenoble, France, 1981-82. Fellow Am. Phys. Soc. Office: Univ Tex Dallas Sch Nat Sci and Math POB 830688 FN32 Richardson TX 75083 Office Phone: 972-883-2416. Business E-Mail: salamon@utdallas.edu.

SALAMON, RENAY, real estate broker; b. NYC, May 13, 1948; d. Solomon and Mollie (Friedman) Langman; m. Maier Salamon, Aug. 10, 1968; children: Mollie, Jean, Leah, Sharon, Eugene. BA, Hunter Coll., 1969. Licensed real estate borker, N.J. Mgr. office Customode Designs Inc., NYC, 1966-68; co-owner Salamon Dairy Farms, Three Bridges, NJ, 1968-86; assoc. realtor Max. D. Shuman Realty Inc., Flemington, NJ, 1983-85; pres., chief exec. officer Liberty Hill Realty Inc., Flemington, NJ, 1985—. Cons. Illva Saronna Inc. (Illva Group), Edison, N.J. 1985—; real estate devel. joint venture with M.R.F.S. Realty Inc. (Illva Group), 1986—; bd. dirs. Anderson House. Mem. Readington twp. Environ. Commn., Whitehouse Sta., N.J., 1978-87, N.J. Assn. Environ. Commrs., Trenton, 1978—; fundraiser Rutgers Prep. Sch., Somerset, N.J., 1984-95; bd. dirs. Hunterdon County YMCA, 1987-95, Anderson House, 2000-04; mem. N.J.-Israel Commn., 1998—; bd. trustees Rutgers Prep. Sch., 2000—; chair Hunterdon County Bd. Social Svc., 2002, 2004; chair Hunterdon County Health and Human Svcs. Commn., 2004—. Named N.J. Broker Record, Forbes Inc., N.Y.C. 1987. Mem.: Realtors Land Inst. Republican. Jewish. Office: Liberty Hill Realty Inc 415 US Highway 202 Flemington NJ 08822-6021 Office Phone: 908-782-1919.

SALAMONE, JOSEPH CHARLES, polymer chemistry professor; b. Bklyn., Dec. 27, 1939; s. Joseph John and Angela (Barbagallo) S.; children: Robert, Alicia, Christopher. BS in Chemistry, Hofstra U., 1961; PhD in Chemistry, Poly. Inst. N.Y., 1967. NIH postdoctoral fellow U. Liverpool, England, 1966-67; rsch. assoc., Horace H. Rackham postdoctoral fellow U. Mich., Ann Arbor, 1967-70, adminstrv. sec., 1968-70; asst. prof., then assoc. prof. chemistry U. Mass., Lowell, 1970-76, prof., 1976-90, prof. emeritus, 1990—, dean Coll Sci., 1978-84, Disting. Rsch. fellow, 1984-90, chmn. dept. chemistry, 1975-78. Pres. Optimers Inc., Lowell, 1985-99; bd. dirs. Rochal Industries, Inc., Boca Raton, Fla.; cons. editor CRC Press, Inc., Boca Raton, 1992-97; v.p. chem. rsch. Bausch and Lomb, 1997-2000, v.p. rsch., 2000-2005, v.p. and spl. adv., 2006. Author 2 books, 2 encys.; mem. editl. bd. Polymer, 1976-94, Jour. Macromolecular Sci.-Chemistry, 1985-2003, Progress of Polymer Sci., 1987-2002, ChemTech, 1995-99; adv. bd. Jour. Polymer Sci., 1974—; editor-in-chief Polymeric Materials Ency., 1993-97; contbr. over 180 articles to profl. jours.; holder 150 U.S. and internat. patents. Recipient Disting. Alumnus award Poly. Inst. N.Y., 1984, Herman F. Mark award for Recognition of Work in Applied Tech., Poly. U., 2005. Fellow Am. Inst. Med. and Biol. Engring. (chmn. industry coun.); mem. Am. Chem. Soc. (chmn. divsn. polymer chemistry 1982, Indsl. Chemistry award 2004), Polymer Sci., Am. Acad. Ophthalmology (assoc.), Pacific Polymer Fedn. (sec., treas. 1988-90, dep. v.p. 1991-92, v.p., 1993, pres. 1994-95), Soc. Biomaterials (Clemson award for applied rsch.). Office Phone: 561-703-4007. Personal E-mail: jcsalamone@yahoo.com.

SALAND, DEBORAH, psychotherapist, educator; b. Val Dosta, Ga., July 25, 1954; d. Charles and Audrey (Horan) Gianniny. B in Profl. Studies, Barry U., 1990, MSW, 1992; D in Psychology, So. Calif. Sch. Profl. Studies, 1996. Lic. clin. social worker, Fla.; cert. addictions profl.; cert. master addiction specialist; diplomat Am. Psychotherapy Assn.; cert. forensic sentence mitigation specialist; cert. forensic addictions specialist; cert. group psychotherapist. Substance abuse counselor Spectrum Programs, Ft. Lauderdale, Fla., 1974—79; owner Obsession in Time, Miami, Fla., 1984—88; asst. clin. dir. Interphase Recovery, Miami, 1988—89; substance abuse counselor Transitions Recovery, Miami, 1989—91; clin. dir. level II Pathways Treatment, Miami; pvt. practice Inst. Human Potential, Miami, 1993—; founder Eating Disorder Tex. Program, 1997—. Lectr. Addiction Traingin Inst. U. Miami, 1992, mem. faculty, 1993—; clin. supr. Transitions Recovery, Miami, 1993—, Treatment Resources, Miami, 1993-94; adj. faculty N.Y. Inst. Tech., Boca Raton, Fla., 1997—; dir. Am. Family Eating Disorder Tract, 1997-98. Contbr. articles to profl. jours. Named Spl. Alumni Barry U., 1996. Mem. NASW, APA, Am. Group Psychotherapy Assn. (clin.), Med. Psychotherapist Am. (assoc. clin.) Nat. Bd. Cert. Counselors (counselor), Broward County Mental Health Assn. Office: Inst Human Potential 19501 NE 10th Ave Ste 305 Miami FL 33179-3502 Office Phone: 305-653-1716.

SALANS, CARL FREDRIC, lawyer; b. Chicago Heights, Ill., Mar. 13, 1933; arrived in France, 1972; s. Leon and Jean (Rudnick) Salans; m. Edith Motel, Sept. 26, 1956; children: Eric Lee, Marc Robert, Christopher John. AB, Harvard U., 1954; BA, Cambridge U., Eng., 1956, MA, 1958, LLB, 1958; JD, U. Chgo., 1957. Bar: Ill. 1958, D.C. 1973, U.S. Supreme Ct. 1972, (admitted in France as conseil juridique) 1972, (admitted in France as avocat) 1992. With State Dept., 1959-72, dep. legal adviser, 1966-72; practice law Paris, 1972—; ret. ptnr. Salans & Assocs., Paris, 1978—. Legal adviser U.S. del. Vietnam Peace Talks, Paris, 1968—71; vice-chmn. ICC Internat. Ct. Arbitration; arbitrator internat. cases; arbitrator U.S.-Iran Claims Tribunal, The Hague; mem. editl. bd. ICC Arbitration Bulletin. Mem.: ABA (chmn. com. East-West trade and investment 1975—82), French Arbitration Assn., London (Eng.) Ct. Internat. Arbitration, Swiss Arbitration Assn., Am. Arbitration Assn. (panel arbitrators), Am. Soc. Internat. Law, Am. C. of C. in France (bd. dirs. 1977—87, chmn. laws and pub. affairs com. 1980—85). Home: 18 Ave Raphael 75016 Paris France Office: Salans & Assocs 9 Rue Boissy d'Anglas 75008 Paris France Home Phone: 01 45 03 08 44; Office Phone: 33 1 42 68 48 00. E-mail: csalans@salans.com.

SALANS, LESTER BARRY, physician, research scientist, educator; b. Chicago Heights, Ill., Jan. 25, 1936; s. Leon K. and Jean (Rudnick) S.; m. Lois Audrey Kapp, Dec. 21, 1958; children: Laurence Eliot, Andrea Eileen. BA, U. Mich., 1957; MD with honors, U. Ill., 1961. Internal medicine intern Stanford U. Med. Ctr., 1961, resident, 1962-64; USPHS postdoctoral and spl. fellow Rockefeller U., 1964-67, asst. prof., 1967-68; asst. prof. medicine Dartmouth Coll., 1968-70, assoc. prof., 1970-77; assoc. dir. diabetes, endocrinology, metabolism, also chief lab. cellular metabolism and obesity Nat. Inst. Arthritis, Metabolism and Digestive Diseases, NIH, Bethesda, Md., 1976-81; adj. prof. Dartmouth Coll., 1978-79; dir. Nat. Inst. Arthritis, Diabetes, Digestive and Kidney Diseases, NIH, 1981-84; adj. prof. Rockefeller U., 1984—; v.p., head preclin. rsch. Sandoz Rsch. Inst., 1985-92; dean Mt. Sinai Sch. Medicine, 1984, prof. internal medicine, 1984-85, clin. prof. medicine, 1987—; v.p. scientific and acad. affairs Sandoz Rsch. Inst., 1993-97; pres. LBS Advisors, Inc., 1997—; prin. BioPharmAnalysis LLC, 2001—, Biopharmanalysis, LLC, 2001; adj. prof., dept. medicine Columbia U. Med. Ctr., 2005—. Adj. prof. Rockefeller U., 1985—2001; vis. prof. U. Geneva, Switzerland, 1974—75; dir. Forest Labs., 1998—; mem. adv. bd. Naomi Berrie Diabetes Ctr. Columbia-Presbyn. Hosp., NYC, 1999—; adj. prof. medicine dept. medicine physicians and surgeons Columbia U. Med. Ctr., 2005—. Contbr. articles on insulin, diabetes mellitus, obesity to profl. jours., textbooks. Recipient NIH Rsch. Career Devel. award, 1972-76, NIH Dir. award, 1980, Juvenile Diabetes Fedn Pub. Svc. award, 1979 Fellow ACP; mem. AAAS, Am. Soc. Clin. Investigation, Am. Fed. Clin. Rsch., Am. Diabetes Soc., Am. Diabetes Assn. (Charles H. Best award 1985), Endocrine Soc., Assn. Am. Physicians, Am. Soc. Clin. Nutrition. Office: 767 Fifth Ave Ste 11-64 11th fl New York NY 10153

SALANT, JONATHAN D., reporter; b. NYC, Feb. 15, 1954; s. Harry and Claire Leatrice (Weinstock) S.; m. Joan Friedenberg; 1 child, Isaac. BA in Polit. Sci., SUNY, Stony Brook, 1976; MS in Journalism, Columbia U., 1978. Reporter Bergen Record, Hackensack, NJ, 1976-78, Miami Herald, 1978-81; st. capitol reporter Albany (N.Y.) Times Union, 1981-84, Syracuse Herald Jour., 1984-87; Washington reporter Syracuse Newspapers, 1987-94; reporter Congressional Quar., 1994-97, AP, 1997—2004, Bloomberg News, 2004—. Contbg. editor: Capital Region mag., 1986—89; Washington editor: Empire State Report, 1997—2001. Contbr. U.S. Holocaust Mus., Washington, 1994—, United Jewish Appeal Fedn. Greater Washington, 1988—; sec. Standing Com. of Corr., Washington, 1991-92; mem. B;nai Israel Congregation, Rockville, Md. Recipient Reporting awards AP, 1984-85, 89-91, Syracuse Press Club, 1984-87, 89, 91; Paul Miller fellowship Freedom Forum, 1988-89. Mem. Nat. Press Club (speakers com. chair 1992-93, profl. affairs com. chair 1993-95, reporting awards 1990, 92, chair Freedom of Press com. 1996; forums com. vice-chmn. 1997, bd. govs. 1998-2007, vice chmn. 2001, chmn. 2002, treas. 2004, v.p. 2005, pres. 2006), Soc. Profl. Journalists (sec. of chpt. 1991-92, v.p. 1992-93, pres. D.C. chpt. 1993-94), Am. Polit. Items Collectors. pres., Regional Reporters Assn., 1992. Jewish. Avocations: political button collector, softball and baseball coach. Home: 5504 Thornbush Ct Bethesda MD 20814 Office: Bloomberg 1399 New York Ave NW Washington DC 20005 E-mail: jds15@aol.com.

SALANT, NIRA L., geographer, educator; b. Boston, Aug. 27, 1981; d. David J. and Anne Salant. BS, Dartmouth Coll., Hanover, NH, 2003, MS, 2005. Asst. mgr. Dartmouth Coll. Moosilauke Ravine Lodge, Warren, NH, 2002; resource asst. US Geol. Survey, Biol. Divsn., Las Vegas, lab tech. Hanover, 2002—03; field asst. Dartmouth Coll., Dept. Environ. Studies, Hanover, 2003—02; tchg. asst. Dartmouth Coll. Dept. Earth Scis., 2003—05, U. BC Dept. Geography, Vancouver, British Columbia, Canada, 2005—. Mem. U. BC Geography Dept. Safety Com., grad. student rep., 2006—. Contbr. articles to profl. jours. Recipient Howard award, Quaternary Geology and Geomorphology Divsn., 2004—05, Tchg. Asst. award, U. BC, Dept. Geography, 2005—06; grantee, Geol. Soc. Am., 2004, Vt. Geol. Soc., 2004; Izaak Walton Killam Meml. fellow, U. BC, 2006—. Mem.: Geol. Soc. Am., Am. Geophys. Union. Avocations: rock climbing, running, yoga, hiking, gardening. Home Phone: 617-965-1623; Office Phone: (604) 619-1623.

SALANT, RICHARD FRANK, mechanical engineer, educator; b. NYC, Sept. 4, 1941; s. Joseph and Augusta (Dick) S.; m. Barbel Lang, Sept. 9, 1962; children: Scott M., Stephanie. BS, MS, MIT, 1963, DSc, 1967. Registered profl. engr., Ga. Asst. prof. U. Calif. Berkeley, 1966-68; asst. prof., assoc. prof. MIT, Cambridge, 1968-72; mgr. fluid mech. and heat transfer Borg-Warner Rsch. Ctr., Des Plaines, Ill., 1972-87; prof., chair tribology rsch. group Ga. Inst. Tech., Atlanta, 1987—, Ga. Power Disting. prof., 2001—. Cons. fluid sealing tech., Atlanta, 1987—. Assoc. editor Jour. Tribology, 1993-99, Jour. Fluids Engring., 1984-87; mem. editl. bd. Jour. Engring. Tribology, 2006—, Mechanika, 2006—; contbr. articles to profl. jours. Fellow ASME (Henry R. Worthington medal 1996, Machine Design award 2003), Soc. Tribologists and Lubrication Engrs. (Edmond E. Bisson award 2000, Frank P. Bussick award 2002, 05, 07). Achievements include patents in field. Home: 1138 Manning Farms Ct Dunwoody GA 30338-2648 Office: Ga Inst Tech Sch Mech Engring Atlanta GA 30332-0405 Business E-Mail: richard.salant@me.gatech.edu.

SALAPATEK, JOHN (JOHN FRANKLIN), literature and language educator, writer; s. Frank and Sophie Salapatek; life ptnr. David White, Aug. 4, 1996. BFA, U. Ill., Urbana, 1981; diploma, Calif. State U., Northridge, 2004, Nat. U., Sherman Oaks, Calif., 2005. English tchr. Sylmar HS, Calif., 2002—05, Golden Valley HS, Santa Clarita, Calif., 2005—. Writer Connie Steven's Shane Prodns., LA, 1991—98. Co-author: (films) Children of the Corn 666: Isaac's Return; actor: (films) Children of the Corn, The Addam's Family, Addam's Family Values; (TV films) Tower of Terror, The Christmas Secret. Recipient Best Feature Screenplay: Horror, Shriekfest Film Festival, 2004. Mem.: NEA, SAG, Hart Dist. Tchrs. Assn., Calif. Tchrs. Assn.

SALARI SANDER, SHERRY, artist, sculptor; b. McCloud, Calif., July 16, 1941; Instr. Scottsdale Artist Sch., Ariz., 1989. Represented in permanent collections Leanin' Tree Mus. Western Art, Boulder, Colo., Buffalo Bill Mus., Cody, Wyo. (Purchase award, 1987, People's Choice award, 1989, Artist's Choice award, 1995), Benson Park Sculpture Garden, Loveland, Colo., Denver Zoo, Genessee Country Mus, Mumford, NY, High Desert Mus., Bend, Oreg., exhibitions include Hubbard Mus., 1990, Leigh Yawkey Woodson Mus., 1990—2000, Represented in permanent collections Okla. City Zoo, exhibitions include Gerald Ford Found., Vail, Colo., 1993, Nat. Sculpture Soc., Scottsdale, 1999, Nat. Geog. Soc., Washington, 2003, Thomas Gilcrease Mus., Tulsa, 2004, Nat. Mus. Wildlife Art, 2005, Recipient Best of Show, Okla. Art Ctr., 1983, Nat. Acad. Scis., Phila., 1984, Purchase award, Buffalo Bill Hist. Ctr., Cody, Wyo., 1987, Best of Show, C.M. Russel Mus., 1988, Silver medal, Knickerbocker Artists 41st Ann. Exhbn., 1991, Helen Gapen Oehler Meml. award, Allied Artists Am., 1989, Silver medal, 1991, 1993, Raymond H. Brumer Meml. award, 2000, Elliot Liskin Meml. award, 2004, Best of Show, Desert Caballeros Art Mus., 2006, NY Pemco award, Catherine Lorillard Wolfe Art Club, 1985, Animals Art award, 1986, IBM award, 1989, Corp. award, 1993, Paul Manship Meml. award, 1994. Mem.: N.W. Rendezvous Group, Am. Artists Profl. League, Allied Artists Am., N.Am. Sculpture Soc., Nat. Acad. Western Art (Gold medal 1983, Silver medal 1986), Soc. Animal Artists (juror 1993), Nat. Sculpture Soc. (juror 1980—89).

SALAS, GUILLERMO, biologist, educator, medical technician; b. Santa Barbara, Chihuahua, Mexico, June 23, 1959; arrived in U.S., 1972; s. Cristino and Irene Salas; m. Rosa Isela Sanchez, Aug. 16, 1985; children: Joel, Omar. BS in Med. Tech., U. Tex., El Paso, 1982, MS, 1996. Cert. med. tech. Am. Soc. for Clin. Pathology, 1982. Med. technologist chemistry dept. Pathlab - Nichols Inst. Reference Lab., El Paso, 1982—88; med. technologist microbiology dept. Corning - Quest Diagnostics Reference Lab., El Paso, 1988—99; biomedical rsch. asst. U. Tex., El Paso, 1999—2001, clin. microbiology instr., 2001—03; biol. sciences instr. Pk. U., El Paso, 1999—2000, El Paso C.C., 1997—. City coord. World Wide Marriage Encounters (Hispanic version), El Paso, 2001—03. Mem.: Am. Soc. for Microbiology (assoc.), Am. Soc. for Clin. Pathology (assoc.). Roman Catholic. Avocations: reading, swimming, racquetball, softball, scuba diving. Home: 2081 Shadow Ridge Dr El Paso TX 79938 Office: El Paso Community College PO Box 20500 El Paso TX 79998-0500 Home Phone: 915-856-8830; Office Phone: 915-831-7106. Personal E-mail: gisal3733@aol.com. Business E-Mail: gsalas18@cp.epcc.edu.

SALAS, MAX, pediatrician, educator; MD, Nat. U. Mex., Mexico City, 1964. Diplomate Am. Bd. Pediats., 1969, Am. Bd. Pediatric Endocrinology, 1986. Rotating intern St. Luke's Hosp., St. Paul, 1963—64; resident in pediat. Children's Hosp., Boston, 1965—67, Sheffield, England, 1967—68; fellow in pediatric endocrinology Pitts. Children's Hosp., 1977—79, North Shore Univ. Hosp., Manhasset, NY, 1979—80; assoc. prof. pediat. UMDNJ/Robert Wood Johnson Med. Sch., New Brunswick, NJ, 1980—. Office: St Peters Univ Hosp 254 Easton Ave New Brunswick NJ 08901-1977 Home Phone: 732-297-8562; Office Phone: 732-745-8574. Personal E-mail: dr.maxsalas@comcast.net.

SALAT, CRISTINA, writer; b. NYC; Student, L.I. U. Founder Shark Prodns., 1998—, Kulana Affordable Artists Sanctuary, Hawaii, 1999—. Freelance editor, 1987—; author, editor, manuscript cons., workshop facilitator, 1985—. Author: Living in Secret, 1993, Alias Diamond Jones, 1993, Min Mors Koereste hedder Janey, 1995, Peanut's Emergency, 2002; contbr. to anthologies including Sister/Stranger, 1993, Am I Blue, 1994, Once Upon A Time, 1996, Higher Learning, 2001; contbr. to popular publ. Office Phone: 808-985-9055. E-mail: discoverkulana@yahoo.com.

SALATHE, JOHN, JR., retired manufacturing executive; b. Montreal, Sept. 25, 1928; s. John and Ida (Schenk) S.; m. Harriet Edith Styles; children: Linda Paul, Craig. BSME, San Jose State U., 1950. Gen. mgr. Indsl. Steel Tank & Body Co., Berkeley, Calif., 1958-62; project mgr. Pacific Foundry div. PACCAR Inc., Renton, Wash., 1962-66, prodn. mgr., 1966-70, asst. gen. mgr., 1970-71, gen. mgr., 1971-79; asst. v.p. PACCAR Inc., Bellevue, Wash., 1979-81, v.p., 1981-90; ret., 1991. Bd. dirs. Jr. Achievement, Seattle, 1979-85; mem. adv. bd. Seattle Pacific U., 1985-95. Sloan fellow Stanford U., 1970. Mem. Soc. Mfg. Engrs. (sr.), Am. Soc. Quality Control (sr.). Avocations: gardening, boating, reading.

SALAZAR, JOHN PAUL, lawyer; b. Albuquerque, Feb. 6, 1943; s. Henry Houghton and Anita (Chavez) Salazar; m. Terri J. Bestgen, June 12, 1967; children: Monique Michelle, John Paul, Stephen Houghton. BA, U. N.Mex., 1965; JD, Stanford U., 1968. Bar: N.Mex. 1968, U.S. Dist. Ct. N.Mex. 1968, U.S. Ct. Appeals (10th cir.) 1968, U.S. Supreme Ct. 1979. Dir. Rodey, Dickason, Sloan, Akin & Robb, P.A., Albuquerque, 1968—, mem. exec. com., 1984—86, mng. dir., west side office, 1985—88, chmn., environ. law sect., 1989—92, mem. exec. com., 1992—93, chair, environ. and natural resources dept., 1992—95, mem. exec. com., 1999—, chair, bus. dept., 2000—. Bd. visitors Stanford U. Law Sch., Calif., 1973—76; state campaign chmn. Jeff Bingaman for Atty. Gen., 1978, Jeff Bingaman for U.S. Sen., 1982, 88, 94, 2000; mem. presdl. search com. U. N.Mex., 1989—90; co-chmn. Governor's Task Force on Responsible Use of Eminent Domain, 2006; mem. Albuquerque Econ. Forum, past chmn., gov. affairs com., 1990—96, past mem. bd. dirs., 1991—94, past vice chair, 1992—93; past hon. cmdr. Field Command Def. Nuc. Agy., Kirtland AFB. Sr. editor N.Mex. Environ. Law Handbook, 1990, 2d edit., 1991, 3d edit., 1993. Former bd. dirs. N.Mex. Symphony Orch.; vice chmn. City of Albuquerque Charter Revision com., 1970—71; active Albuquerque Unity, 1971—73; chmn. N.Mex. Disting. Pub. Svc. Awards Coun., 1986, 1987; chmn. city affairs com. Greater Albuquerque C. of C., 1972, v.p. govtl. affairs, 1973, pres.-elect, 1974, pres., 1975; active Presbyn. Hosp. Ctr. Assocs.; bd. dirs. Albuquerque Hispano C. of C., 2000—, vice-chair, 2001—04, chair, 2005; bd. dirs. Inter-Am. Found., 2007—. Mem.: ABA (environ. aspects of real estate transactions com., land use regulation com., real property, probate & trust law sect., land use planning & zoning com., state & local govt. sect.), Albuquerque Armed Forces Adv. Assn., U. N.Mex. Alumni Assn. (bd. dirs. 1979—85, exec. com. 1982—85, pres. 1983—84), Nat. Assn. Indsl. and Office Parks (govs. bus. adv. coun. 1991—94, past mem. N.Mex. border commn., past chair com. border devel. and internat. trade, mem. exec. com.), N.Mex. State Bar Assn. (former mem. jud. selection com., mem. Real Property, Probate and Trust sect., mem. Pub. Law sect., mem. Natural Resources, Energy and Environ. Law sect., former sec., treas. Young Lawyers sect.), Albuquerque Bar Assn. (former mem. jud. selection com., former dir.). Roman Catholic. Office: Rodey Dickason Sloan Akin & Robb PA PO Box 1888 Albuquerque NM 87103-1888 Office Phone: 505-768-7220. Office Fax: 505-768-7395. Business E-Mail: jsalazar@rodey.com.

SALAZAR, JOHN T., congressman; b. Alamosa, Colo., July 21, 1953; m. Mary Lou Salazar; children: Jesus, Esteban, Miguel. BSBA, Adams State Coll., 1981; class III grad., Colo. Agrl. Leadership Program, 1993; grad., Rapport Leadership Program, 1997. Owner & operator El Rancho Salazar; state rep. dist. 62 Colo. Ho. of Reps., Denver, 2002—04, mem. agr., livestock and natural resources, and info. and tech. coms.; mem. U.S. Congress from 3d Colo. dist., 2005—; mem. Agriculture com. and Transp. and Infrastructure U.S. Ho. Reps. Youth group co-coord. Mi Esperanza Mentoring Program; chair seed export com. Colo Cert. Seed Growers; commr. Colo. State Agrl. Commn.; bd. dirs. Gov.'s Econ. Devel. Adv. Bd., Rio Grande Water Conservation Dist.; youth leadership athletic dir. St. Joseph's Parish. Served US Army, 1973—76. Democrat. Roman Catholic. Office: US Ho Reps 1531 Longworth Ho Office Bldg Washington DC 20515-0603 also: Dist Office Ste 702 225 N 5th St Grand Junction CO 81501 Office Phone: 202-225-4761. Office Fax: 202-226-9669. *

SALAZAR, KEN(NETH) LEE, senator, former state attorney general; b. Alamosa, Colo., Mar. 2, 1955; s. Henry and Emma Salazar; m. Hope Hernandez; 3 children. BA in Polit. Sci., Colo. Coll., 1977; JD, U. Mich., 1981; LLD (hon.), Colo. Coll., 1993. Bar: Colo. 1981, U.S. Dist. Ct. Colo. 1981, U.S. Ct. Appeals (10th cir.) 1981, U.S. Supreme Ct. 1999. Farmer, rancher, Conejos County, Colo.; law clk. to atty. gen. State of Colo., Denver, 1979, chief legal counsel to gov., 1986—90, exec. dir. Dept. Natural Resources, 1990—94, atty. gen., 1999—2005; assoc. Sherman & Howard, Denver, 1981—86; dir. Parcel, Mauro, Hultin & Spaanstra, Denver, 1994—98; US Senator from Colo., 2005—. Gov.'s rep. State Bd. Equalization, Denver, 1990; mem. com. agr., nutrition, and forestry US Senate, com. energy and natural resources, com. veterans affairs, spl. com. ethics, spl. com. aging. Mem. Israel Friendship League, 1986—89; chair Great Outdoors Colo., Denver, 1993—94, Rio Grande Compact Commn., 1995—97, Sangre de Cristo Land Grant Commn., 1993—95; mem. Colo. Water Conservation Bd., Denver, 1990—, City and County of Denver Ethics Panel, 1993; gov.'s rep. State Bd. on Property Tax Equalization, 1987—91; del. Soviet-Am. Young Leadership Dialogue, 1984; mem. adv. com. Colo. U. Sch. Law Natural Resources Law Ctr., 1989—92; mem. Western Water Policy Rev. Adv. Commn., 1995—97; bd. dirs. Denver Cmty. Leadership Forum, 1988, Servicios de la Raza HUD 202 Project, 1985—89, chair, 1986. Recipient Friend of the First award, Colo. Press Assn., Profiles in Courage award, Conf. West Atty. Generals, Judge Learned Hand Human Relations award, Am. Jewish Com. Colo. Chapter, 2001; scholar Juan Tienda. Mem.: ABA, Am. Judicature Soc., Hispanic Bar Assn. (ABA task force on opportunities for minorities in legal profession, bd. dirs. 1986—87), Denver Bar Assn. (2d v.p. 1989, chair policy-cmty. rels. subcoms. 1982—84), Colo. Bar Assn. (bd. govs. 1989—90, task force to assess the legal profession 1986). Democrat. Roman Catholic. Avocations: basketball, outdoor activities, politics. Office: US Senate B40A Dirksen Senate Office Bldg Washington DC 20510 also: District Office Ste 450 2300 15th St Denver CO 80202-1184 Office Phone: 202-224-5852, 719-328-1100. Office Fax: 719-328-1129, 202-228-5036. E-mail: attorney.general@state.co.us. *

SALAZAR, LAURA ANN, education educator; b. Corpus Christi, Tex., Feb. 14, 1976; d. P. Z. and Lori Padron; m. Eric Adolfo Salazar, May 31, 1994; children: Lyrissa, Eric Jr., Lance. Assoc. in Social Work, Del Mar, Corpus Christi; BS, Corpus Christi, M in Counseling, M in Tech. Elem. tchr. Kastoryz Elem. Sch., Corpus Christi, 1999—2004; instrnl. tchr. advisor Crockett Elem. Sch., Corpus Christi, 2004—. Mem.: Internat. Reading Assn. Home: 10626 Outpost Corpus Christi TX 78410-2126

SALAZAR, OMAR MAURICIO, radiation oncologist, educator; b. Havana, Cuba, Sept. 22, 1942; came to U.S., 1959; naturalized, 1970; s. Aramis Victor and Nelida Raquel (Acosta) S.; m. Margarita Cristina Pedraza, July 7, 1979; children: Omar M.II, Sofia M. BS in Biology, Georgetown U., 1965; MD, U. P.R., 1969; MS, U. Rochester, 1974. Diplomate Am. Bd. Radiology. Intern U. Hosp. U. P.R., Rio Piedras, 1969—70, radiotherapy resident, 1970—73, chief resident, 1972-73; instr., fellow U. Rochester, NY, 1973-74, asst. prof. NY, 1974-78, assoc. prof. NY, 1978-81; prof., chmn. dept. radiation oncology U. Md., Balt., 1981-95; dir. radiation oncology La. State U. Med. Ctr., New Orleans, 1995-99; dir. dept. radiation oncology, dir. Ctr. Cancer Care Oakwood Health Sys., Dearborn, Mich., 1999—; pres. Assoc. in Radiation Oncology, PC, 2000—. Mem. CCIRC Nat. Cancer Inst., Bethesda, Md., 1980-84; prof. clin. oncology Am. Cancer Soc., 1989-1993; coord. USA, Circulo Radioterapeutas Ibero-Latino-Americanos-L.Am. Assn. Radiation Therapy, 1981-98, v.p., 1998-2000, pres. elect, 2000-2002, pres. 2002-2005, chmn., 2005— (Gold medal); expert cons. internat. Atomic Energy Agy., Vienna, Austria, 1996—; examiner Am. Bd. Radiology, Phila., 1983-93; chmn. site cancer visit Nat. Cancer Inst., Bethesda, 1983, site visitor, 1982; co-investigator Whitaker Found., 1983; prof. clin. oncology Am. Cancer Soc., 1989-94.

Author: Moments of Decision/Primary Brain Tumors, 1979, Bronchogenic Carcinoma, 1981, Unveiling Mysteries to Create Miracles, 2002; contbr. articles to profl. jours. Arthur A. Ward Trust grantee, 1981; Am. Cancer Clin. Fellowship award, 1984-86. Fellow: Am. Coll. Radiation Oncology (past pres., past chmn. bd. dirs., chancellor, Gold medal), Am. Coll. Radiology; mem.: AMA, Am. Assn. Cancer Edn., Am. Radiol. Soc., Radiol. Soc. Am., Md. Radiol. Soc., Med. Chirurgical Soc., Tex. Radiol. Soc., Ea. Coop. Oncology Group (chmn. brain and lung com. 1979—80), Radiation Therapy Oncology Group, Mask and Bauble Dramatic Soc., Big Five Club. Roman Catholic. Home Phone: 248-855-6677; Office Phone: 313-593-7335. Business E-Mail: salazaro@oakwood.org.

SALAZAR, RAMIRO S., library director; b. Del Rio, Tex., Mar. 3, 1954; s. Jesus and Juanita (Suarez) S.; m. Cynthia Castillo, Dec. 19, 1976 (div. 1990); children: Ramiro Orlando, Selinda Yvette. BA, Tex. A&I U., Kingsville, 1978; MLS, Tex. Woman's U., Denton, 1979. Asst. libr. dir. Val Verde County Libr., Del Rio, 1975-76; libr. Robert J. Kleberg Libr., Kingsville, Tex., 1977-78; libr. dir. Eagle Pass Pub. Libr., Tex., 1980-84; dir. Main Libr. San Antonio Pub. Libr., 1984-90, dir., 2005—; dir. librs. El Paso Pub. Libr., 1991-93, Dallas Pub. Libr., 1993—2004; interim asst. city mgr. City of Dallas, 2004—05. Chmn. Tex. State Libr. Planning Task Force, 1991-92; mem. adv. bd. Tex. Woman's U. Sch. Libr. and Info. Scis., 1993, U. North Tex. Sch. Libr. and Info. Scis., 1993, Alliance for Higher Edn. Libr. Dirs. Coun., 1993. Trustee AMIGOS Bibliog. Coun.; mem. adv. bd. Booker T. Washington HS of Performing and Visual Arts, 1995-96; chair customer svc. steering com. City of Dallas, 1993; chair coupon book/resident privilege card task force City of Dallas, 1995-96; active home instrn. prog. for preschool children Nat. Coun. Jewish Women, 1996. Recipient H.W. Wilson Staff Devel. award jury, 1995-96, Libr. of Yr. REFORMA, 1998. Mem. ALA (mem. nominations com. 1997), Libr. Adminstrn. and Mgmt. Assn. (bldg. and equipment sect., arch. for pub. libr. com. 1993-95, cultural diversity com. 1995, pres.'s progs. com. 1996), Tex. Mcpl. League (resolutions com. 1995—), Tex. Mcpl. Libr. Dirs. Assn. (Libr. Dir. of Yr. 1996), Pub. Libr. Adminstrs. North Tex., Reforma (exec. bd. dirs.), Tex. Libr. Assn. (chmn. pubs. com. 1992-93, legis. com. 1993-95, ad hoc com. value of pub. librs. 1995, awards com. 1995), Pub. Libr. Assn., Jaycees. Democrat. Roman Catholic. Office: San Antonio Pub Libr 600 Soledad San Antonio TX 78205 Office Phone: 210-207-2644. E-mail: Ramiro.Salazar@sanantonio.gov.

SALCEDO-DOVI, HECTOR EDUARDO, anatomist, educator, surgeon; b. Cordoba, Argentina, Nov. 9, 1958; s. Domingo and Rosa (Dovi) Salcedo; m. Adriana Gomez, Apr. 3, 1993; children: Camila, Marianna. MD, U. Nat. Cordoba, 1984; DO, N.Y. Coll. Osteopathic Medicine, 1995. Asst. prof. anatomy, histology N.Y. Coll. Osteo. Medicine, Old Westbury, 1990—93, prof. anatomy, physiology, 1993; chief intern Good Samaritan Hosp., 1996—, chief resident surgery, 2000. Fellow critical care/trauma, 2001—03. Mem.: ACS, Soc. CCM, Am. Coll. Chest Physicians, Am. Osteopathic Assn., Am. Med. Student Assn. Roman Catholic. Avocations: soccer, bicycling, tennis. Home: 1619 Sam Houston Dr Harlingen TX 78550

SALCETTI, MARIANNE, newswriter, educator; d. Robert Anthony Salcetti and Mary Jane Lusher; m. Michael Mrkvicka, May 21, 1977 (div. Mar. 1985); 1 child, Jacob Gene Mrkvicka; m. Dale Rhines, Mar. 18, 1989 (div. June 1995); 1 child, Amalia Margaret Rhines. BA in Polit. Sci., Ohio State U., 1972, MA in Journalism, 1975; PhD in Mass. Comm., U. Iowa, 1992. Editor Franklinton News, Columbus, Ohio, 1974—76; beat reporter Chillicothe (Ohio) Gazette, 1976—77; investigative and health reporter Colorado Springs Gazette Telegraph, 1977—78; editor, co-owner The Weekly News, Johnson County, Iowa, 1980—82; instr. U. Iowa Sch. Journalism and Mass Comm., Iowa City, 1982—87; adj. faculty John Carroll U. and Ursuline Coll., Cleve., 1988—89; asst. prof. dept. comm. John Carroll U., Cleve., 1990—2000; contbg. writer The Cleve. Free Times, 1995—98; spl. projects editor The Garden City (Kans.) Telegram, 2000—02; comm. cons. Water Preservation Com., Finney County, Kans., 2002; investigator-rschr. Rebein & Bangerter, Attys. at Law, Dodge City, 2002—. Editl. radio commentator KSUI/WSUI, 1984—87; Presdl. election commentator WHK, Cleve., 1992; legis. prodr.-reporter State Capitol Update High Plains Pub. Radio, 2003; asst. prof. journalism Keene (N.H.) State Coll., 2003—; lectr. and presenter in field. Contbr. articles to profl. jours. V.p. Greater Cleve. Labor History Soc., 1997—99. Recipient Investigative Reporting award, Inland Daily Press Assn., 1977, Best News Story of the Yr. award, Iowa Press Assn., 1980, Silver Gavel award, ABA, 1981, Nat. Scholar award, Gannett Found., 1986, 1st pl. consumer reporting, Ohio Soc. Profl. Journalists, 1998, 2nd pl. best explanatory journalism, 1998, two honorable mentions, Enterprise News, 2001, honorable mention, Spot News, 2001, Bus. Reporting, 2002; Grauel Faculty fellow, John Carroll, 1995, John F. Murray Dissertation Rsch. grantee, George Meany Meml. Archives, AFL-CIO, 1987. Mem.: Kappa Tau Alpha. Avocations: reading, kayaking, gardening. Home: 272 South St Troy NH 03465 Office: Keene State Coll 229 Main St Keene NH 03435 Office Phone: 603-358-2724. Business E-Mail: msalcetti@keene.edu.

SALCH, STEVEN CHARLES, lawyer, mediator, arbitrator; b. Palm Beach, Fla., Oct. 25, 1943; s. Charles Henry and Helen Louise (Alverson) S.; m. Mary Ann Prim, Oct. 7, 1967; children: Susan Elizabeth, Stuart Trenton. BBA, So. Meth. U., 1965, JD, 1968. Bar: Tex. 1968, U.S. Tax Ct. 1969, U.S. Dist. Ct. (so. dist.) Tex. 1969, U.S. Dist. Ct. (ea. dist.) Tex. 1972, U.S. Ct. Appeals (5th cir.) 1969, U.S. Ct. Appeals (fed. cir.) 1982, U.S. Ct. Fed. Claims, 1982. Assoc. Fulbright & Jaworski, Houston, 1968-71, participating assoc., 1971-75, ptnr., 1975—. Mem. panel of disting. neutrals CPR Inst. Co-author: Tax Practice Before the IRS, 1994; contbr. articles to legal jours. Pres. Tealwood Owners Assn., 1982—83, Meml. H.S. PTA, 1985—86; hon. life mem. Tex. PTA, 1986—; mem. devel. bd. U. Tex. Med. Br., Galveston, 2002—; adv. dir. 1894 Grand Opera House Soc., 2002—, co-chmn. adv. bd., 2004—05. Mem.: ABA (coun. dir. 1985—88, vice chair tax sect. 1988—91, chair tax sect. 1996—97), Houston Bar Found., Am. Bar Found., Internat. Fiscal Assn., Am. Coll. Tax Counsel (regent 5th cir. 1999—2006, sec.-treas. 2006—), Am. Law Inst., Fed. Bar Assn., Houston Bar Assn., State Bar Tex., Theodore Tannenwald Foundation (trustee 2000—), Colonial Williamsburg Found., Menard Soc., Galveston Artillery Club, Houston Downtown Club, Pelican Club Galveston, Galveston County Club, Yacht Club, Order of Coif, Phi Delta Phi, Phi Eta Sigma, Beta Alpha Psi. Presbyterian. Home: 4600 Caduceus Pl Galveston TX 77551-5719 Office: PO Box 3870 Galveston TX 77552 Home Phone: 409-457-6994; Office Phone: 713-651-5433. Business E-Mail: ssalch@fulbright.com. *Set goals for yourself. Unless you know where you are and where you want to be in life, you will not be able to map a plan to accomplish your goals.*

SALCUDEAN, MARTHA EVA, mechanical engineer, educator; b. Cluj, Romania, Feb. 26, 1934; arrived in Can., 1976, naturalized, 1979; d. Edmund and Sarolta (Hirsch) Abel; m. George Salcudean, May 28, 1955; 1 child, Septimiu E. BEng, U. Cluj, 1956, postgrad., 1962; PhD, U. Brasov, Romania, 1969; DSc (hon.), U. Ottawa, Ont., Can., 1992, U. B.C., Can., 2001. Mech. engr. Armatura, Cluj, 1956-63; sr. rsch. officer Nat. Rsch. Inst. Metallurgy, Bucharest, 1963-75; part-time lectr. Inst. Poly., Bucharest, 1967-75; sessional lectr. U. Ottawa, 1976-77, from asst. prof. to assoc. prof. to prof., 1977-85; prof., head dept. mech. engring. U. B.C., Vancouver, 1985-93, assoc. v.p. rsch., 1993-96, acting v.p. rsch. pro-tem, 1995, Weyerhausen Indsl. Rsch. chair computational fluid dynamics, 1996—2002, prof., Weyerhausen indsl. chair emerita dept. mech. engring., 2002—. Mem. grant selection com. for mech. engring. Natural Scis. and Engring. Rsch. Coun. Can.; mem. Nat. Adv. Panel to Min. Sci. and Tech. on advanced indsl. materials, Can., 1990; mem. governing coun. NRC; mem. def. sci.e adv. bd. Dept. Nat. Def.; chair Sci. Coun. B.C. Contbr. numerous articles to profl. jours. Decorated Order of B.C., 1998; recipient Gold medal B.C. Sci. Coun., Killam Rsch. prize U. B.C.; Rsch. Coun. Can. grantee, 1978—, Commemorative medal 125th anniversary Can. Confederation, 1993, Julian C. Smith medal Engring. Inst. Can., 1994-95, Meritorious Achievement award Assn. Profl. Engrs. & Geoscientists B.C., 1996, Killam Meml. prize engring., 1998. Fellow CSME, Can. Acad. Engring., Royal Soc. Can.; mem. ASME, Assn. Profl. Engrs. Ont., Order of Can. (apptd. officer 2004). Home: 1938 Western Pkwy Vancouver BC Canada V6T 1W5 Home Phone: 604-222-0901; Office Phone: 604-822-2732. Business E-Mail: msal@interchange.ubc.ca.

SALDANA, ALFONSO MANUEL, lawyer; b. Lima, Peru, Sept. 4, 1960; came to U.S. 1969. s. Mario J. and Nelly (Davalos) S. BA, U. Miami, 1983; JD, Thomas M. Cooley Law Sch., 1986. Bar: Fla. 1987, U.S. Dist. Ct. (so. dist.) Fla. 1987, U.S. Dist. Ct. (mid. dist.) Fla. 1993, U.S. Ct. Appeals (11th cir.) 1988, U.S. Ct. Appeals (D.C. cir.) 1989, U.S. Supreme Ct. 1996. Asst. atty. gen. Office Atty. Gen. Fla., West Palm Beach, 1987—93; pvt. practice Miami, Fla., 1993—. Author: How to Write an Effective Appellate Brief, 2006. Office: 801 Brickell Ave 9th Fl Miami FL 33131 Office Phone: 305-371-0066. Personal E-mail: amsattorney@aol.com.

SALE, GEORGE EDGAR, pathologist; b. Missoula, Mont., Apr. 18, 1941; s. George Goble and Ruth Edna (Polleys) S.; m. Joan M. Sutliff, 1989; children: George Gregory Colby, Teo Marie Jonsson. AB, Harvard U., 1963; MD, Stanford U., 1968. Intern U. Oreg., Portland, 1968-69; sr. asst. surgeon USPHS, Albuquerque, 1969-71; resident in pathology U. Wash., Seattle, 1971-75, instr. pathology, 1975-78, asst. prof., 1978-81, assoc. prof., 1981-88, prof., 1988—. Asst. mem. faculty clin. divsn. Hutchinson Cancer Ctr., Seattle, 1975-88, assoc., 1988-91, mem., 1991—. Author, editor: Pathology of Bone Marrow Transplantation, 1984, Pathology of Transplantation, 1990. Mem. AAAS, Internat. Acad. Pathology, Coll. Am. Pathologists, Am. Assn. Investigative Pathologists, Physicians for Social Responsibility. Office: Fred Hutchinson Cancer Rsh Ctr G7-923 1100 Fairview Ave N Seattle WA 98109-4417 Office Phone: 206-288-1352. Business E-Mail: gsale@fhcrc.org.

SALE, LLEWELLYN, III, lawyer; b. St. Louis, May 19, 1942; s. Llewellyn Jr. and Kathleen (Rice) S.; m. Cynthia Jean Bricker, Aug. 17, 1968 (div. Apr. 1995); children: Allyson J., Eryn E. AB cum laude, Yale U., 1964; LLB cum laude, Harvard U., 1967. Bar: Mo. 1967, U.S. Dist. Ct. (ea. dist.) Mo. 1967, U.S. Tax Ct. 1982, U.S. Ct. Claims 1985. From assoc. to ptnr. to mng. ptnr. Husch & Eppenberger, St. Louis, 1967-88; ptnr. Bryan Cave LLP, St. Louis, 1988—2004, of counsel, 2005—. Bd. dirs. Washington U. Child Guidance Clinic, St. Louis, 1978-80, Mental Health Assn. St. Louis, 1988-89. Mem. ABA, Bar Assn. Met. St. Louis (chmn. law econs. subcom. 1982), Noonday Club. Avocations: spectator sports, jogging. Office: Bryan Cave 211 N Broadway Ste 3600 Saint Louis MO 63102-2733 Office Phone: 314-259-2649. Business E-Mail: lsale@bryancave.com.

SALE, MERRITT, classicist, educator, comparatist; b. New Haven, Nov. 27, 1929; s. William Merritt and Helen (Stearns) S.; m. Marilyn Mills, June 13, 1953 (div. Oct. 1967); children: Elizabeth, David; m. Anne Perkins, May 18, 1991. BA, Cornell U., 1951, MA, 1954, PhD, 1958. Engr. U.S. Metals Co., Carteret, NJ, 1951-52; instr. in classics Yale U., New Haven, 1957-58; asst. prof., assoc. prof. Washington U., St. Louis, 1958-75, chmn. classics dept., 1961-69, prof. classics and comparative lit., 1975—, chmn. comparative lit. dept., 1981-90. Author: Sophocles' Electra: Commentary with Introduction and Translation, 1970, Existentialism and Euripides, 1977, Homer and the Roland, 1993, The Government of Troy, 1995, The Oral-Formulaic Theory Today, 2006. Recipient Founder's Day award for Excellence in Teaching Washington U., 1978 Mem. Am. Philol. Assn., London Inst. for Classical Studies Home: 2342 Albion Pl Saint Louis MO 63104-2524 Personal E-mail: aperkins@midwest.net.

SALE, TOM S., III, financial economist; b. Haynesville, La., July 27, 1942; s. Thomas and Mary Belle (Fagg) S.; divorced; children: Jennifer Elizabeth, Sarah Elaine. BA, Tulane U., 1964; MA, Duke U., 1965; PhD, La. State U., 1972. CFA. Faculty mem. La. Tech. U., Ruston, 1965—75, prof. econs., 1975—98, ret., 1998. Head dept. econs. and fin. La. Tech. U., 1974-86, 90-95, dir. grad. studies Coll. Adminstrn and Bus., 1988-89; fin. cons. Contbr. articles to profl. jours. Mem. Southwestern Fin. Assn. (pres. 1985-86), CFA Inst. (exam. com. 1983-92, curriculum com. 1993-2004), Fedn. Bus. Disciplines (v.p. 1988-89, pres. 1989-90), CFA Soc. Dallas Fort Worth, Omicron Delta Kappa, Omicron Delta Epsilon. Episcopalian. Home: PO Box 1365 Ruston LA 71273-1365 Personal E-mail: tomsale3@yahoo.com.

SALEH, BRIAN BEHROOZ, aerospace transportation executive; b. Tehran, Iran, Apr. 25, 1939; came to U.S., 1959; m. Farideh Navidi, May 12, 1983. BSEE, Northrop U., Ingelwood, Calif., 1967; MBA, Golden Gate U., San Francisco, 1973; instr. credential, Calif. Design engr. radio frequency cirs. Space Systems/Loral, Palo Alto, Calif., 1970—, mgr. GOES Comm. Subsys., 1974-76, program engr. NATO-III Satellite, 1976-79, mgr. Insat Program Engring., 1979-85, mgr. GOES Spacecraft Engring., 1985-91, mgr. GOES Spacecraft, 1991-92, dir. GOES Prodn. Program, 1992-95, dir. Telstar Program, 1995-97, sr. dir. Fixed Svc. Satellite Programs, 1997-98, sr. dir. common products and planning, 1998, sr. exec. dir. CD Radio Program, 1998-99, v.p. program mgmt., 1999—2002; pres. Aerospace Tech., San Jose, Calif., 2002—. Recipient Telstar 5 Program Mgmt. award, Loral Skynet, GOES I-M Project Group Achievement award, NASA, 2002. Personal E-mail: brian@saleh.com.

SALEH, DAVID JOHN, lawyer; b. Buffalo, Apr. 24, 1953; s. Donald Thomas and Joan Barbara (Labaki) S.; m. Elizabeth Catherine Abdella, July 2, 1976; children: Anthony Donald, Amy Madeline, Anne Teresa, Andrew David. BA, SUNY, Buffalo, 1975, JD, 1978. Bar: N.Y. 1979, U.S. Dist. Ct. (we. dist.) N.Y. 1980. Assoc. Jeffrey D. Oshlag, Esq., Batavia, NY, 1978-82; ptnr. Oshlag, Saleh & Earl, L.L.P., Batavia, 1982—; chief counsel, sec. Am. Real Time Svcs., Inc., NYC, 1988-91; atty. Town of Stafford, NY, 1994—2003; town atty. Town of Darien, NY, 2000—03, Town of Batavia, NY, 2002—03; corp. counsel, v.p. bus. support ventures Inlighten, Inc., 2003—. Prosecutor Village of Corfu, NY, 1997—; legal counsel City of Batavia Housing Authority, 1982—2003; atty. Village of Corfu, NY, 1981-2003, Pembroke Ctrl. Sch. Dist., 1985-90; chief counsel Intelligent Quotation Sys. Inc., Norwalk, Conn., 1987-93, Network Two Comm. Group, Inc., 1997-99; prosecutor Town of Pembroke, 1988-2003, 2006—; chief counsel, dir., treas. GB's Country Corners Inc., 1991-93; v.p., chief counsel Marine Ptnrs. Funding, Inc., 1994-2002; counsel Corfu Fire Dist., 1995-2003, Weston Info. Techs. Inc., others. Mem. staff Buffalo Law Rev., 1976-78. Active Pembroke Vol. Fire Dept., 1976-79, Corfu Vol. Fire Dept., 1979—; bd. dirs. Corfu Area Bus. Assn., 1986-87; del. Rep. Caucus; trustee Corfu Free Libr. Assn., 1991-2002, pres., 1993-96; bd. dirs. St. Jerome Hosp. Found., 1992-98, treas., 1994-98; treas. Genesee Mercy Healthcare Found., Inc., 1996-98; parliamentarian Genesee County Rep. Com., 2000—; chmn. Town of Pembroke Rep. Com., 2007—; pres. parish coun. St. Francis Roman Cath. Ch., 2006—. Mem. ABA, ATLA, NY Defenders Assn., NY State Bar Assn. (mem. house dels. 2004-05), Genesee County Bar Assn. (chmn. criminal def. com. 1995-2003, mem. jud. nominations com. for 8th jud. dist. NY, treas. 2003-05, sec. 2005-07, v.p. 2007-), Erie County Bar Assn., NY State Housing Renewal Ofcls., U. Buffalo Alumni Assn. (bd. dirs., v.p. fin. 1997-99, exec. v.p., pres.-elect 1999-2000, pres. 2000-02), Lions (pres. 1987-88, 2003-04). Republican. Roman Catholic. Home: 54 E Main St Corfu NY 14036-9601 Office: Inlighten Inc 3370 Walden Ave Depew NY 14043 Personal E-mail: dsaleh@rochester.rr.com.

SALEH, JOHN, lawyer; b. O'Donnell, Tex., June 29, 1928; s. Nahum and Arslie S. BBA, U. Tex., 1950, JD with honors, 1952; cert. U.S. Army Judge Advocate Sch., U. Va., 1953. Bar: Tex. 1952, U.S. Ct. Mil. Appeals, 1953, U.S. Tax Ct. 1954, U.S. Dist. Ct. (no. dist.) Tex. 1956, U.S. Ct. Appeals (5th cir.) 1960, U.S. Supreme Ct. 1961, D.C. 1982. Pvt. practice, Lamesa, Tex., 1954—. Tchg. instr. legal rsch. writing U. Tex. Sch. Law, 1950-52 Mem. editl. bd. Tex. Law Rev., 1951-52. Mem. ABA, ATLA, Tex. Law Rev. Assn. (life), Tex. Bar Assn. (spl. com. to study rev. code criminal procedure 1969-71), D.C. Bar Assn., Tex. Trial Lawyers Assn., Tex. Bar Found., Order of the Coif, The Million Dollar Advocates Forum, Phi Delta Phi. Home: 605 Doak Odonnell TX 79351 Office: PO Box 308 Odonnell TX 79351 Office Phone: 806-872-2171.

SALEH, MOHAMMED, diplomat; b. Manama, Bahrain, Oct. 2, 1967; s. Saleh Mohammed Saleh and Fatima Abdulla (Syed) Hussain; m. Khatoon Adbulla A. Salman, Aug. 11, 1995; children: Jaffer, Ali, Alaa. BA in Polit. Sci. and Law, Kuwait U., 1992; M in Polit. sci., L.I. U., 2003; cert. in diplomatic tng. program (hon.), 1996. Third sec. Ministry Foreign Affairs, Manama, Bahrain, 1993-99; second sec. Bahrain Mission to UN, NYC, 1999—. Cons. UN Security Coun., NYC, 1998—99, UN Econ. and Social Coun., 2000—02. Recipient Hist. award, Bahrain Hist. Archeol. Soc., 1998. Avocation: collection of Poliold Polit. and religious books. Office: Bahrain Mission to the UN 866 E Second Ave New York NY 10017

SALEH, PAUL N., telecommunications industry executive; b. 1956; BSEE, MSEE, U. Mich., MBA in Fin. with distinction, 1985. Various leadership positions to treas. Honeywell, 1985—96; sr. v.p., treas., CFO Walt Disney Co., 1997—2001; exec. v.p., CFO Nextel Commn. (merged with Sprint), 2001—05; CFO Sprint Nextel Corp., Reston, Va., 2005—. Bd. dir. Wolf Trap Found. Named best CFO in telecom svcs./wireless sector, Institutional Investor mag., 2004, 2005; named one of 100 Most Influential People in Fin., Treasury & Risk Mgmt. mag., 2005. Office: Sprint Nextel Corp 2001 Edmund Halley Dr Reston VA 20191 *

SALEM, BAKR IBRAMIM, cardiologist; b. Jordan, Oct. 1, 1944; came to U.S., 1974; MB ChB, Cairo U., 1967. Diplomate Am. Bd. Internal Medicine, Am. Bd. Cardiovascular Diseases. Intern St. Luke's Hosp., St. Louis, 1974-75, resident in medicine, 1978-79, mem. staff; resident in medicine St. Mary's Health Ctr., St. Louis, 1975-76; fellow in cardiology St. Luke's Episcopal Hosp., Houston, 1976-78; pvt. practice Chesterfield, Mo. Fellow ACP, Soc. Cardiac Angiography and Intervension, Am. Coll. Cardiology, Am. Coll. Chest Physicians. Office: 222 S Woods Mill Rd Ste 500 Chesterfield MO 63017-3625 Office Phone: 314-205-6699.

SALEM, GEORGE RICHARD, lawyer; b. Jacksonville, Fla., Dec. 24, 1953; s. Kamel Abraham and Margaret Virginia (Bateh) S.; m. Rhonda M. Ziadeh, June 28, 1980; children: James George, Jihan Camille, Laila Suad, Sarah Rose. BA, Emory U., 1975, JD, 1977; LLM, Georgetown U., 1984. Bar: Ga. 1978, Fla. 1979, DC 1981. Ptnr. Thompson, Mann & Hutson, Washington, 1977-85; dep. solicitor U.S. Dept. Labor, Washington, 1985-86, solicitor of labor, 1986-89; ptnr., head of Middle East and US Dept. of Labor practices group Akin, Gump, Strauss, Hauer & Feld, Washington, 1990—2004; prin. AG Solutions, Law Offices of George R. Salem, 2005—; strategic advisor DLA Piper Rudnick Gray Cary, 2005—. Bd. dirs. Overseas Pvt. Investment Corp. Contbr. articles to profl. jours. Nat. exec. dir. ethnic voters div. Reagan Bush '84; bd. dirs. United Palestinian Appeal, Inc., 1981-85, 86—; co-founder, mem. Arab Am. Inst., Jan.-Mar., 1985, Dec. 1986—, chmn. bd. dirs., 1999—; chmn. Arab-Ams. for Bush-Cheney, 2000; mem. Am. Arab Anti-Discrimination Com. 2000-03; chmn. Arab-Ams. for Bush-Quayle '88, '92; adv. bd. Search for Common Ground in the Mid. East, 2001—; exec. adv. bd. Mid. East Inst., 2002—; bd. dirs. Am. Com. on Jerusalem, 1995—, Emory Law Sch. Coun., 2000-2002, Emory Bd. Govs., 1997-2001. Recipient Ellis Island Medal of Honor, 1992. Fellow College of Labor and Employment Lawyers; mem. ABA (labor and employment law sect.), Ga. Bar Assn. (labor rels. div.), Fla. Bar Assn. (labor rels. div.), DC Bar Assn. (labor rels. div.), Nat. Assn. Arab Ams. (bd. dirs. 1987, pres. 1992-94), Am. Ramallah Club (pres. DC chpt. 1984, Wash. rep. 1982-84), Am. Ramallah Fedn. (chmn. human rights com., Washington rep. 1982-84), Arab Am. Rep. Fedn. (chmn. 1985), Century Club Nat. Rep. Heritage Groups Coun., Delta Theta Phi, Omicron Delta Kappa. Mem. Eastern Orthodox Christian Ch. Office: Ste 200 1200 Nineteenth St NW Washington DC 20036 Office Phone: 202-887-1140. Office Fax: 202-887-5550. Business E-Mail: gsalem@georgesalem.com.

SALEM, KAREN E., information technology executive; BS in Indsl. Engring., Pa. State U.; MBA, U. Cin. Sr. cons. Anderson Consulting; dir. bus. solutions Burger King; v.p. info. tech. Rexall Sundown; IT head AFC Enterprises; sr. v.p. and CIO Corning Cable Sys.; former sr. v.p. and CIO Winn-Dixie Stores, Inc., Jacksonville, Fla., 2002; sr. v.p. and CIO Ingram Micro, Santa Ana, Calif., 2005—. Office: Ingram Micro PO Box 25125 1600 E St Andrew Pl Santa Ana CA 92799-5125 *

SALEM, RICHARD ALLEN, mediator; b. NYC, Aug. 15, 1930; s. Louis H. and Catherine (Levy) S.; m. Greta Waldinger, June 26, 1955; children: Susanne, Peter, Erica. BA in Sociology, Antioch Coll., 1953; MS in Journalism, Columbia U., 1957. Reporter Washington Post, 1957-59; editor, publ. Washington SBIC Newsletter, 1960-62; spl. asst. to dep. dir. for investment Small Bus. Adminstrn., Washington, 1963-64, assoc. dir. Office of Equal Opportunity, 1964-67, regional dir., 1967-68; Midwest dir. Cmty. Rels. Svc. U.S. Dept. Justice, Chgo., 1968-82; pres. Conflict Mgmt. Initiatives, Evanston, Ill., 1982—. Adj. prof. Loyola U., Chgo., 1986-90; mediator Wounded Knee Takeover, 1972, Skokie-Nazi Conflict, 1980. Co-author: Students Guide to Mediation and Law, 1987, Ctr. for Pub. Resources award, 1987; mem. editl. bd. Chgo. Reporter, 1996-2004, Jour. Mediation and Applied Conflict Analysis, 2005—; editor: Witness to Genocide - the Children of Rwanda, 2000; contbr. articles to profl. jours. Bd. dirs. Housing Options for Mentally Ill, Evanston, 1997-2004, Found. Self-Sufficiency Ctrl. Am., 2000—; sec. World Mediation Forum, 1997-2002. With U.S. Army, 1953-55. Recipient Outstanding Performance award, U.S. Sr. Exec. Svc., 1980. Mem. Soc. Profls. in Dispute Resolution (2d v.p. 1988, bd. dirs. 1982-89, Mary Parker Follett award 1993). Home and Office: 1225 Oak Ave Evanston IL 60202-1220

SALEM, THOMAS ERIC, electrical engineer, educator; s. William Fredrick and Marjorie Marie Salem; m. Karen B. Tymann, May 14, 1994; children: Madelyn Grace, Eric Timothy, Benjamin Thomas. BS in Engring., Grove City Coll., Pa., 1988; MSEE, U. Ala., 1993, PhD, 1996. Registered profl. engr., Pa., 1997. Project engr. E.I. Dupont DeNemours & Co., Aiken, SC, 1988—89, Westinghouse Savannah River Co., Aiken, 1989—95; asst. prof. engring. Pa. State U., Mont Alto, Pa., 1996—98, Elizabethtown (Pa.) Coll., 1998—2002; asst. prof. elec. engring. U.S. Naval Acad., Annapolis, Md., 2002—. Rsch. engr. U.S. Army Rsch. Lab., Adelphi, Md., 2004—, U.S. Naval Rsch. Lab., Washington, 2002—03; adj. lectr. Pa. State U., Harrisburg, Pa., 2000—01; sr. staff engr. ATC Diversified Electronics, Lancaster, Pa., 1999—2000; prin. electronics engr. TB Wood's Inc., Chambersburg, Pa., 1997—98. Recipient George Westinghouse Signature Excellence award, Westinghouse Savannah River Co., 1989, Westinghouse Total Quality Achievement award, 1991. Mem.: IEEE. Office: United States Naval Academy Maury Hall Mail Stop 14B 105 Maryland Av Annapolis MD 21402 Home Phone: 410-721-2026; Office Phone: 410-293-6178. Business E-Mail: salem@usna.edu.

SALEMBIER, VALERIE BIRNBAUM, publishing executive; b. Teaneck, NJ; d. Jack and Sara (Gordon) Birnbaum; m. Paul J. Block, Dec. 9, 1990. BA, Coll. New Rochelle, 1973. Advt. dir. Ms. Mag., NYC, 1976-79, assoc. pub., 1979-81; pub. Inside Sports Mag., NYC, 1982; sr. v.p. advt. USA Today, 1983-88; pub. TV Guide, Radnor, Pa., 1988; pres. N.Y. Post, NYC, 1988—90; pub. Family Circle Mag., NYC, 1991-93; sr. v.p. advt. N.Y. Times, 1993-95; sr. v.p., pub. Esquire Mag., 1996—2003; sr. v.p., pub. Harper's Bazaar, NYC, 2003—. Lectr. in field. Author: (book) Rotissereie League Baseball, 1982; freelance mag. writer:. Chmn. N.Y.C. Police Found.; bd. dirs., past pres. Nat. Alliance Breast Cancer Orgns., former bd. dirs.; bd. dirs., past pres. Beneficial Orgn. Aid Ex-Fighters; former trustee Ctrl. Synagogue, Coll. New Rochelle; trustee N.Y.C. Sports Devel. Corp. Mem.: Women in Comm., Com. 200, Womens Forum. Office: Harpers Bazaar 1700 Broadway New York NY 10019

SALENTINE, THOMAS JAMES, pharmaceutical executive; b. Milw., Aug. 8, 1939; s. James Edward and Loretta Marie S.; m. Susan Anne Sisk, Apr. 16, 1966; children: Anne Elizabeth, Thomas James Jr. BS in Acctg., Marquette U., Milw., 1961. CPA, Ind., Wis. Sr. audit mgr. Price Waterhouse, Milw., 1961-74; dir. corp. acctg. Ward Foods Inc., Wilmette, Ill., 1974-78; corp. contr. Johnson Controls Inc., Milw., 1984-85; v.p., contr. Stokely Van Camp Inc., Indpls., 1978-87; exec. v.p., CFO Bindley Western Industries Inc., Indpls., 1987—2001, also bd. dirs.; ptnr. Bindley Capital Ptnrs., LLC, 2001—. Bd. dirs. Priority Healthcare Corp., Nat. Refrigeration Svcs. Inc. Chmn. com. United Way, Indpls., 1989-90. Lt. USN, 1962-65. Mem. AICPA, Fin. Execs. Inst. Republican. Roman Catholic. Home: 3991 Gulf Shore Blvd Naples FL 34103 Office Phone: 317-704-4154.

SALERNO, F. ROBERT, travel company executive; b. Springfield, Mass. married; 2 children. D., Marquette U., 1972. Vice pres. eastern region Avis, 1982—87, v.p. field ops., 1987—90, sr. v.p., gen. mgr., 1990—95, exec. v.p. ops., 1995—96, pres., COO, 1996—2002; CEO Cendant Car Rental Group, 2003—06; pres., COO Avis Budget Group, Parsippany, NJ, 2006—. Office: Avis Budget Group 6 Sylvan Way Parsippany NJ 07054 *

SALERNO, FREDERIC V., retired telecommunications company executive; b. NYC, June 28, 1943; m. Patricia Van Arsdale; 3 children. BSEE, Manhattan Coll., 1965; MBA, Adelphi U.; postgrad. in mgmt., Pace U. With N.Y. Telephone (NYNEX Co.), NYC, 1965—, various positions including staff asst. corp. hdqrs., installation and repair foreman, mgmt. positions, 1965-78, gen. mgr., 1978-83, v.p. transition, 1983-84, v.p. customer service, 1984-85, exec. v.p., chief operating officer New Eng. Telephone sub., 1985-87, pres., chief exec. officer, 1987-91, vice chmn., pres. worldwide svcs., 1991-94, vice chmn. fin. and bus. devel., 1994-97; now sr. exec. v.p., CFO Verizon Communications, Inc.(formerly Bell Atlantic), 1997—2000; vice chmn., CFO Verizon Communications, Inc., 2000—02. Bd. dirs. Akamai Technologies, Inc., The Bear Stearns Companies, Inc., Consolidated Edison, Inc., Gabelli Asset Mgmt., Popular, Inc., Viacom, Inc.

SALERNO, SISTER MARIA, advanced practice nurse, educator; b. Syracuse, NY; d. Joseph and Josephine (Ostrowski) S. Diploma in nursing, St. Joseph's Hosp., Syracuse, 1962; BSN summa cum laude, Cath. U. Am., Washington, 1974, MS in Nursing, 1976, PhD in Nursing, 1981; cert. nurse practitioner, U. Rochester, 1984. RN, N.Y., Md., Washington; cert. adult, geriatric nurse practitioner ANCC; joined Sisters of Third Franciscan Order, Roman Cath. Ch., 1963. Staff nurse St. Joseph Hosp. Health Ctr., Syracuse, 1962-63; sr. charge nurse ICU, gen. med. and surg. units St. Elizabeth Hosp., Utica, NY, 1965-66, head nurse pediat. unit, 1966-69; head nurse ECF Loretto Geriatric Ctr., Syracuse, 1969-72; lectr. Cath. U. Am., Washington, 1977—78, 1980—81, asst. prof. nursing, 1978-79, 81-92, assoc. prof., 1992—, dir. primary care adult/geriatric nurse practitioner programs, 1984—, co-dir. FNP program, 1994-97; dir. Adult CNS Nurse Educator Program, 2004—. Contbr. chpts. to books; contbr. articles to profl. jours. Vol. nurse practitioner Cmty. of Hope, Washington; instl. animal care and use com. George Washington U., 1996-, Cath. U. Am. 2000-, Veteran's Adminstrn. Med. Ctr., 2004-; scholarship com. Franciscan Found. for the Holy Land, 1996-. Grantee NIH, 1984-89, Cath. U. Am., 1989-90. Mem.: AAUP, ANA, D.C. League for Nursing (bd. dirs. 1995—97, 1999—), D.C. Nurse Practitioners Assn. (nom. com. 2006—07), N.Y. Acad. Scis., Nat. League for Nursing, Nat. Orgn. Nurse Practitioner Facilities, Nat. Gerontol. Nurses Assn., Am. Coll. Nurse Practitioners, Am. Acad. Nurse Practitioners, Am. Assn. for History of Nursing, Cath. U. Am. Nursing Alumni Assn. (pres. 1986—87, chpt. exec. bd. 1992—2003, treas. 1998—2003), Nat. Italian Am. Found. (assoc.), Sigma Theta Tau (grad. counselor Kappa chpt. 1985—87, awards com. 1987—89, grad. counselor Kappa chpt. 1991—97, eligibility com. 1991—97, 2002—03, grad. counselor Kappa chpt. 2006—). Roman Catholic. Office Phone: 202-319-6545. Business E-Mail: salerno@cua.edu.

SALERNO, PATRICIA J., elementary school educator; married. BS in Edn., Ohio State Univ.; MA in Edn., Univ. Ariz. Tchr. Izmir Elem. Sch., Turkey, Fort Campbell (Ky.) Schs., Vicenza Elem. Sch., Italy. Named Dept. Def. Dependents Schs. Tchr. of Yr., 2006. Office: Vicenza Elem Sch Unit 31401 Box 11 APO AE 09630 Business E-Mail: Patricia.Salerno@eu.dodea.edu. *

SALERNO, WILLIAM DOUGLAS, cardiologist; b. Passaic, NJ, 1956; MD, U. Autonoma de Guadalajara, 1982. Intern U. Medicine Dentistry N.J./Englewood Hosp., 1982-83, 83-84; resident Hackensack (N.J.) U. Med. Ctr., 1984-86, fellow in critical care medicine, 1987-89, 89-90, Norwalk Hosp./Yale U., New Haven, 1986-87; fellow in cardiovascular disease, 1987-89; fellow in interventional cardiology Hackensack U. Med. Ctr., 1989-90; dir. cardiac ICU, dir. coronary care unit Hackensack Med. Ctr.; clin. asst. prof. medicine to clin. assoc. prof. U. Medicine & Dentistry of NJ, sect. chief, coronary care unit. Clin. asst. prof. medicine U. Medicine and Dentistry N.J.-N.J. Med. Sch. Named NJ Health Sci. Libr. Assn. Clinician of Yr., 2003, Honored Citizen Mem., Honor Legion Police Depts. NJ; named one of Top Doctors in NY, NY mag., 2006, 2007. Mem. AMA, Am. Coll. Cardiology, ACP, Am. Coll. Chest Physicians, ATS, Soc. Critical Care Medicine, Internat. Soc. Endovascular Specialists, Am. Soc. Laser Medicine & Surgery, Am. Soc. Echocardiography, Soc. for Vascular Ultrasound. Office: 38 Mayhill St Saddle Brook NJ 07663-5307 also: Hackensack Univ Med Ctr 30 Prospect Ave Hackensack NJ 07601 Office Phone: 201-489-1766. Office Fax: 201-843-5910. Business E-Mail: wds@heart-care.org. *

SALERNO-SONNENBERG, NADJA, violinist; b. Rome, Jan. 10, 1961; arrived in U.S., 1969; d. Josephine Salerno-Sonnenberg. Grad., Curtis Inst. Music, 1975, Juilliard Sch., 1982; D (hon.), N.Mex. State U., 1999. Profl. debut Phila. Orch., 1971; appeared with Am. Symphony Orch., Balt. Symphony, Chgo. Symphony, Colo. Symphony, Cin. Symphony, Detroit Symphony, Houston Symphony, Indpls. Symphony, Milw. Symphony, Montreal Symphony, N.J. Symphony, Pitts. Symphony, San Diego Symphony, Seattle Symphony, St. Louis Symphony, Utah Symphony, Boston Symphony, Dallas Symphony, Minn. Orch., Phila. Orch., L.A. Philharm.; appeared Cabrillo Festival, Ravinia Festival, Blossom Festival, Meadow Brook Festival, Gt. Woods Festival, Caramoor Festival, Hollywood Bowl Festival; internat. appearances Vienna, Munich, Stuttgart, Frankfurt, Liverpool, England, Geneva, Rotterdam, Netherlands, Lisbon, Portugal, Tokyo. Founder, rec. artist Capital Classics and Jazz Records, 1987—, Nonesuch, 1996—, NSS Music, 2005—. Performer: (recitals) with Anne Marie McDermott, with Regina Carter, with Eileen Ivers, with The Assads; appearances: TV 60 Minutes, CBS Sunday Morning, NBC Nat. News, PBS Live from Lincoln Ctr., CNN Newsstand, Charlie Rose Show, Sesame Street; appearances (TV) The Tonight Show with Johnny Carson, subject (documentaries) Speaking in Strings, 1999 (Oscar nomination, 2000). Recipient 1st prize, Naumburg Violin Competition, N.Y.C., 1981, Avery Fisher prize, 1999; Avery Fisher Career grantee, 1983. Mem.: SAG, AFTRA. Office: care M L Falcone Pub Rels 155 W 68th St Ste 114 New York NY 10023-5808

SALES, JAMES BOHUS, lawyer; b. Weimar, Tex., Aug. 24, 1934; s. Henry B. and Agnes Mary (Pesek) Sales; m. Beuna M. Vornsand, June 3, 1956; children: Mark Keith, Debra Lynn, Travis James. BS, U. Tex., 1956, LLB with honors, 1960. Bar: Tex. 1960. Practiced in, Houston, 1960—; head litig. dept. Fulbright & Jaworski, 1979—99, sr. ptnr., 1960—2000, of counsel, 2000—. Author: Products Liability in Texas, 1985; co-author: Texas Torts and Remedies, 6 vols., 1986; assoc. editor: Tex. Law Rev., 1960; contbr. articles to profl. jours. Trustee South Tex. Coll. Law, 1982—88, 1990—2005, A.A. White Dispute Resolution Ctr., 1991—94; cir. chair membership Supreme Ct. Hist. Soc., 1998—2001; trustee Tex. Supreme Ct. Hist. Soc., 2003—; chair commrs. Tex. Access Justice Commn., 2004—; bd. dirs. Tex. Resource Ctr., 1990—97, Tex. Bar Hist. Found., 1990—2001. Named among Best Lawyers in Am., 1989—; recipient Lifetime Achievement award, U. Tex. Law Sch. Alumni, 2005. Fellow: Houston Bar Found. (chmn. bd. 1982—83, sustaining life), Tex. Bar Found. (trustee 1991—95, vice-chmn. 1992—93, chmn. 1993—94, chair adv. bd. planned giving 1994—2004, sustaining life mem.), Am. Bd. Trial Advocates, Am. Bar Found. (state chmn. 1993—98, sustaining life), Internat. Acad. Trial Lawyers, Am. Coll. Trial Lawyers (state chmn. 1993—96); mem.: FBA, ABA (ho. of dels. 1984—2003, mem. Commn. on IOLTA 1995—97), Bar Assn. 5th Fed. Cir., Gulf Coast Legal Found. (bd. dirs. 1982—85), Houston Bar Assn. (bd. dirs. 1970—79, pres.-elect 1979—80, pres. 1980—81), Tex. Law Rev. Assn. (bd. dirs. 1996—2002, pres. 1999—2000), Tex. Assn. Def. Counsel (v.p. 1977—79), State Bar Tex. (bd. dirs. 1983—88, chmn. bd. 1985—86, pres. 1988—89, Pres.'s award 2006), So. Tex. Coll. Trial Advocacy (dir. 1983—87), So. Conf. Bar, Nat. Conf. Bar Pres. (coun. 1989—92, Fellows award 2006), Internat. Assn. Def. Counsel, The Forum, Order of Coif, Inns of Ct. (bd. dirs. 1981—84), Westlake Club (bd. govs. 1980—85). Roman Catholic. Home: 10803 Oak Creek St Houston TX 77024-3016 Office: Fulbright & Jaworski 1301 McKinney St Houston TX 77010-3095 E-mail: jsales@fulbright.com.

SALES, MITZI S., science educator; b. Toronto, Ontario, Canada, Feb. 1, 1978; d. Argeo Cadiz and Milagros Albano Sales. BA in Sci., Brown U., 2000, MA in Secondary Biology, 2003. Tchr., sci. dept. E. W. Thurston Mid. Sch., Westwood, Mass., 2003—06, Rye Country Day Sch., Rye, NY, 2006—. Choreographer, musical E. W. Thurston Mid. Sch., 2005—06, dir., honoring our voices, 2005—06. Mem.: Nat. Sci. Tchrs. Assoc. Achievements include development of honoring our voices curriculum. Office: Rye Country Day Sch 1 Cedar St Rye NY 10580 Home Phone: 401-742-1023; Office Phone: 914-967-1417. Personal E-mail: mitzi1000@hotmail.com.

SALETTA, MARY ELIZABETH (BETTY SALETTA), sculptor; b. Miami, Fla., Sept. 30, 1941; d. Earl Robert and Alta Florence Cotner; m. Albert Michael Saletta, July 1, 1959; children: Tia Suzanne, Kamber Ann. Graphic artist Moore Bus. Forms Inc., Modesto, Calif., 1960-67, Live Oak Pub. Co., Oakdale, Calif., 1977-80; freelance artist U.S. Forest Svc., Modesto Irrigation Dist., Stanislaus Schs., New Don Pedro Dam Project, Calif., 1967-77; sculptor Saletta Sculpture, Oakdale, 1980—. Mem. adv. bd. Calif. State U. Coll. Arts, Letters and Sci., Turlock, 1999-2002; charter mem., dir. Downtown Arts Project, Modesto, 1992-96. One-woman shows City of Oakdale Redevel. Agy., 1990, Modesto C. of C., 1996; group shows include Calif. State U. Stanislaus, Turlock, 1986, Cowboy Artist Am. Mus., Kerrville, Tex., 1988, Benson Park Sculpture Garden, Loveland, Colo., 1989, 90, 93, Danada Sculpture Garden, Chgo., 1991, 93, Tucson Mus. Art, 1995; represented in permanent collections Tucson Mus. Art, Buckaroo Hall of Fame, cities of Modesto, Oakdale, Ripon, Calif., Stockton, Los Banos, Montery, San Leandro, Calif.; sculptures include life-size pub. sculptures Yesterday Is Tomorrow, 1991, Paperbohy, 1995, Am. Graffiti, 1997, Stockton Firefighters Meml., 1998, World War II Meml., 1999, Nursing, the Finest Art, 2001, Chief Estanislao, 2001, Firefighter Sculpture produced at Laguna Beach Pageant of the Masters, 2002, Henry Miller Meml., 2005, Story Time, 2006. Recipient Excellence in Fine Art award Bank Am., Stockton, Calif., 1959, Best of Show award Western Art Roundup, Winnamucca, Nev., 1987, 88, Excellence in Visual Arts award Stanislaus Arts Coun., Modesto, 1999. Mem. Nat. League Am. Pen Women, Ctrl. Calif. Art League (advisor 1991, Best of Show award 1987), Rotary (bd. dirs. Oakdale 1997-99, pres. 2007-). Democrat. Avocations: horses, skiing, mountain climbing, fishing. Home: 4255 Wellsford Rd Oakdale CA 95361-7930 Fax: 209-572-4089. E-mail: salettasculpture@aol.com.

SALGO, PETER LLOYD, internist, writer, anesthesiologist, journalist, commentator; b. NYC, Nov. 9, 1949; s. Michael Nicholas and Ruth F. Salgo. BA, Columbia U., 1971, MD, 1975. Diplomate Am. Bd. Internal Medicine, Am. Bd. Anesthesiology; lic. physician, N.Y., Calif., Mass.; instrument rated comml. pilot. Internal medicine intern Columbia Presbyn. Med. Ctr., NYC, 1975-76, resident in internal medicine, 1976-78; vis. faculty fellow intensive care medicine and anesthesiology, dept. anesthesiology Columbia U., NYC, 1979-81; lectr. Harvard Med. Sch., Boston; clin. prof. medicine and anesthesiology Columbia P&S; mem. staff in anesthesia and medicine Mass. Gen. Hosp., Boston; attending in anesthesia and internal medicine Presbyn. Hosp., NYC, assoc. vice chmn. dept. anesthesiology, chmn. inter-I.C.U. com., assoc. dir. surg. ICU. Host syndicated TV broadcast Healthcare 2000; aviation med. examiner FAA; comml. pilot. instrument Rated; host nat. radio med. program Sta. PRN, 1979—81; writer, producer, host med. info. broadcast Sta. WCBS-TV, NYC, 1980—; med. corr. Sta. WCBS News, 1981—; corr. CBS Network Radio News, 1982—92; host. Healthtalk, 1982—88; med. corr. Sta. CNBC, 1989—, CNBC TV Network, 1989—93; host The Doctor Is In, Eyada.com, 2000—01; cons. to networks on med. content of TV programs; corr. Patient Info. Network, 1989—; anchor Americas Vital Signs, CNBC TV Network, Med. Crossfire, 2001—; lectr. in field.; expert guest on John F. Kennedy, Jr., crash NTSB Report Discovery Network, 2002; expert guest, med. cons. Fox News, 2001—02; host Second Opinion PBS, 2002—. Author: The Heart of the Matter, 2004. Recipient Leonard Pullman award Columbia U., 1971, Blakesley award Am. Heart Assn., Journalism award Medic-alert Found., Honorable Mention in Journalism, UPI, Alumni Assn. medal Columbia U. P&S, 1975, Emmy award for excellence in broadcast journalism, Journalism award Lions Eye Found. Fellow ACP; mem. AAAS, AMA, AFTRA, N.Y. State Med. Soc., N.Y. County Med. Soc., Am. Soc. Anesthesiologists. Office: Presbyn Hosp Dept Anesthesiology New York NY 10032 Home Phone: 212-327-0133; Office Phone: 212-305-6494. E-mail: pls1@columbia.edu.

SALHANY, LUCILLE S. (LUCY SALHANY), broadcast executive; b. 1946; married; 2 children. LHD (hon.), Emerson Coll., 1992. Program dir. WKBF-TV, Cleve., 1967; program mgr. WLVI-TV, Boston, 1975—79; v.p. television & cable programming Taft Broadcasting Co., 1979—85; pres. Paramount Domestic TV, 1985—91; chmn. 20th Century Television, 1991—93, Fox Broadcasting Co., 1993—94; pres. United Paramount Network (UPN), 1994-97; pres., CEO JH Media, Boston, 1998—2004, HJ Media, LifeFX Networks Inc., 2002—04; co-founder, mng. ptnr. Echo Bridge Entertainment, Needham, Mass., 2004—. Bd. dirs. Hewlett-Packard Co., Am. Media Co., Inc., ION Media Networks, Inc., 2006—. Bd. trustees Emerson Coll.; profl. adv. bd. ALSAC/St. Jude Children's Rsch. Hosp. Named Exec. of Yr., Caucus for Prodrs., Writers & Dirs.; recipient Sherrill C. Corwin Human Rels award, Am. Jewish Com., 1995, Silver Satellite award, Am. Women in Radio and TV, 1995, HELP Humanitarian award, 1997, Avatar award, Cable Fin. Mgmt. Orgn., Silver Circle award, Nat. Acad TV Arts and Sci. Achievements include becoming the first woman to manage an American broadcast television network, 1993. Office: Echo Bridge Entertainment Ste 500 75 Second Ave Needham Heights MA 02494 Office Phone: 781-444-9680.

SALI, ANDREJ, chemistry professor; BSc in Chemistry, U. Ljubljana, Slovenia, 1987; PhD in Molecular Biophysics, U. London, 1991. Postdoctoral fellow dept. chemistry Harvard U., Cambridge, Mass., 1991—94; asst. prof. Rockefeller U., 1995—2000, assoc. prof., 2000—03; prof. step V depts. biopharmaceutical scis. and pharm. chemistry Calif. Inst. Quantitative Biomedical Rsch. U. Calif., San Francisco, 2003—. Cons. Accelrys Inc., San Diego, 1994—, Biogen Inc., Cambridge, Mass., 2000—02, Millennium Inc., Cambridge, Mass., 2001—02; founder, cons. Structural Genomix, Inc. (formerly Prospect Genomics, Inc.), Calif., 1999—2004; vice chair computational biology dept. biopharmaceutical scis. U. Calif., San Francisco, 2003—; mem. adv. com. Protein Data Bank, 2005—; co-founder Tropical Disease Initiative. Contbr. articles to profl. jours.; editor: Structure; mem. editl. bd.: Pub. Libr. Sci. Computational Biology, Jour. Computer Aided Molecular Design, Molecular and Cellular Proteomics, Protein Engring., Design and Selection. Named one of 50 Who Matter Now, CNNMoney.com Bus. 2.0, 2006; recipient Irma T. Hirschl Career award, 2000—03; Alfred P. Sloan Rsch. fellow, 1998—2000. Mem.: AAAS, Protein Soc. (mem. exec. com. 2005—). Office: Dept Biopharmaceutical Scis U Calif San Francisco 1700 4th St Byers Hall Ste 503B San Francisco CA 94158-2330 Office Phone: 415-514-4227. Office Fax: 415-514-4231. E-mail: sali@salilab.org. *

SALI, BILL (WILLIAM THOMAS SALI), congressman, former state legislator; b. Portsmouth, Ohio, Feb. 17, 1954; s. Gregory and Dorothy Hazel (Wilkinson) S.; m. Terry Sue Petersen, Aug. 20, 1976; children: Jennifer, Levi, Micah, Anna, Rachel, Christina. BBA, Boise State U., 1981; JD, U. Idaho, 1984. Bar: Idaho, U.S. Ct. Appeals (9th cir.). Pvt. law practice, Meridian, Idaho, 1984—2006; mem. Idaho State Ho. Reps. from Dist. 21A, Boise, 1990—2006, vice chmn. health and welfare com., 1993—2006; mem. US Congress from 1st Idaho dist., 2007—, mem. oversight & govt. reform, nat. resources com. Named Champion of the Family, Idaho Family Forum, 1992. Mem. Idaho State Bar. Republican. Avocation: country music performance and composition. Office: 508 Cannon House Office Bldg Washington DC 20515 also: 802 W Bannock Ste 101 Boise ID 83702 *

SALIBA, ANIS KHALIL, surgeon; b. Karaoun, Bekaa, Lebanon, Jan. 14, 1933; s. Khalil and Rosa (Sallum) S.; m. Siham Saliba, Nov. 8, 1959; children: Khalil Saliba, Nada Saliba. BA, Am. U., Lebanon, 1952; MD with Distinction, Damascus U., 1960. Diplomate Am. Bd. Surgery, Am. Bd. Thoracic and Cardiovascular Surgery, Am. Bd. Surg. Critical Care. Resident Coney Island, Bklyn., 1960-65, St. Vincent Charity, Cleve., 1965-67; cardiovascular surgeon Beebe Med. Ctr., Lewes, Del., 1980—. Trustee Beebe Med. Ctr., 1989—. Fellow Am. Coll. Surgeons; mem. AMA. Home: 30729 Sassafras Dr Lewes DE 19958 Office: 431 Savannah Rd Lewes DE 19958-1460 E-mail: as.saliba@comcast.net.

SALIERS, EMILY, singer, musician; b. New Haven, Conn., July 22, 1963; d. Don Saliers; life ptnr. Leslie Zweben. Student, Vanderbilt U.; BA, Emory U., 1985. Mem. folk rock duo Indigo Girls, 1983—; represented by Epic Records, 1988—2006, Hollywood Records, 2006—. Co-owner Watershed Restaurant, Decatur, Ga.; co-founder Flying Biscuit Cafe, Atlanta. Singer (with Amy Ray): (albums) Early 45, 1985, Strange Fire, 1987, Indigo Girls, 1989 (Grammy award for Best Contemporary Folk Album, 1990), Nomads Indians Saints, 1990, Rites of Passage, 1992, Swamp Ophelia, 1994, Touch Me Fall, 1995, 1200 Curfews, 1995, Shaming of the Sun, 1997, Come on Now Social, 1999, Retrospective, 2000, Become You, 2002, All That We Let In, 2004, Rarities, 2005, Despite Our Differences, 2006, (songs) Closer to Fine, 1989, Hammer and Nail, 1990, Galileo, 1992, Least Complicated, 1994, Shame on You, 1997; composer: (films) One Weekend a Month, 2004; co-author (with Don Saliers): A Song to Sing, A Life to Live: Reflections on Music as Spiritual Practice, 2004; appearances include (films) Boys on the Side, 1995, (documentaries) Wordplay, 2006. Mem.: Phi Beta Kappa. Office: c/o Russell Carter Artist Mgmt Ste 755 315 W Ponce de Leon Ave Decatur GA 30030 Office Phone: 404-377-9900. E-mail: igfan@rcam.com.

SALIGMAN, HARVEY, retired consumer products and services company executive; b. Phila., July 18, 1938; s. Martin and Lillian (Zitin) S.; m. Linda Powell, Nov. 25, 1979; children: Martin, Lilli Ann, Todd Michael, Adam Andrew, Brian Matthew BS, Phila. Coll. Textiles and Sci., 1960. With Queen Casuals, Inc., Phila., 1960-88, v.p., 1966-68, pres., chief exec. officer, 1968-81, chmn., 1981-88; pres., chief operating officer Interco Inc., St. Louis, 1981-83, chief exec. officer, 1983-85, 1985-89, chmn., 1989-90; ret. Bd. dirs. Ameren Corp. (formerly Union Electric). Trustee Washington U., St. Louis, Nantucket Hist. Assn. Mem. St. Louis Club, Masons.

SALINAS, ELISEO, research and development company executive, psychiatrist, researcher; Gained initial medical qualifications, U. Buenos Aires, Argentina, 1980; M in Pharmacology, France. US Ednl. Commn. for Foreign Med. Graduates cert. 1981. Resident in Psychiatry les Hôpitaux Psychiatriques de Paris, France; staff psychiatrist Hôpital de Gonesse, France; cons. psychiatrist Hôpital Sainte-Anne, Clinque des Maladies Mentales et de l'Encéphale, Paris; internat. project leader (CNS) Synthelabo Récherche, 1991—93; with Wyeth Rsch., 1993—2004, head of global Central Nervous Systems, v.p. for regional clin. R & D, 1997—2004; chief scientific officer, exec. v.p., global R&D Shire Pharm., Wayne, Pa., 2004—. Lectr. Université René Descartes, Paris. Mem.: Am. Coll. Neuropsychopharmacology, Collegium Internat. Neuro-Psychopharamacologicum, Assn. European Psychiatrists. Office: Shire Pharm 725 Chesterbrook Blvd Wayne PA 19087-5637 Office Phone: 484-595-8800, 484-595-8276. Office Fax: 484-595-8900.

SALINAS, MARÍA ELENA, newscaster, columnist; b. LA, 1956; d. Jose Luis Cordero Salinas and Luz Tiznado; m. Eliott Rodriguez, Mar. 1993; children: Julia Alexandra, Gabriela Maria stepchildren: Erica, Bianca. Reporter KMEX-34 TV, LA, 1981—87; co-anchor Noticiero Univisión, Miami, Fla., 1987—; columnist King Features Syndicates. Co-anchor (TV series) Noticiero Univisión, 1987—, co-host Aquí y Ahora, 2000—; author: I Am My Father's Daughter: Living a Life Without Secrets, 2006. Founding mem. Nat. Assn. Hispanic Journalists; active in Nat. Assn. Latino Elected & Apptd. Officials; established Maria Elena Salinas Scholarship for Excellence in Spanish-Language News, 2002—. Named Journalist of Yr., Hispanic Media 100, 2002; named one of 100 Most Influential Hispanics, Hispanic Mag., 1999; named to Nat. Assn. Hispanic Journalists' Hall of Fame, 2006; recipient Edward R. Murrow award, 1997, 2 Nat. News Emmy awards, Nat. Acad. TV Arts & Sciences, 1999, LA Area Emmy award, 2002, Pride award, Hispanic Fedn., 2006, President's award, Nat. Assn. Latino Elected & Apptd. Officials, 2006. Mem.: Nat. Assn. Hispanic Journalists (former v.p.), Office: Univision Communications Inc 9405 NW 41st St Miami FL 33178 also: King Features 15th Fl 300 W 57th St New York NY 10019 Office Phone: 305-471-3900. Office Fax: 305-471-4346.

SALINAS, ORLANDO FRANCO, physician; b. Santa Cruz, Calif., May 4, 1929; s. Julio Salinas and Rogelia Franco; m. Anita Morales, June 29, 1956; children: Ana Maria, Rosita Perry, Pilar Devenge, Orlando Jr., Juan, Marcos. MD, U. St. Simon, Bolivia, 1957. Diplomate Va. Bd. Medicine. Intern Euclid-Glenville Hosp., Cleve., 1957—58, resident, 1957—60; house physician Leigh Meml. Hosp., Norfolk, Va., 1960—62; pvt. practice Tidewater, Va., 1962—74, New River Valley, Va., 1974—96. Pres. New

River Valley Acad. Family Practice. Mem.: Am. Acad. Gen. Practice, Med. Soc. Va., Norfolk Med. Soc., Am. Med. Assn., Masters Wardens Assn., Scottish Rite, Hunter's Masonic. Home: 2550 Meadowbrook Dr Blacksburg VA 24060

SALINAS, RODNEY JAY C., media company executive; b. Philippines; s. Dannie and Trinidad; m. Taryn Costanzo. BA in Internat. Affairs, MA in Polit. Mgmt., George Washington U. Former nat. fin. dir. Jon Amores for Congress Campaign, W.Va.; former comm. coord. Assoc. of Fundraising Professionals; former exec. dir. Asian Pacific Am. Inst. for Congressional Studies; founder, pres. Rainmaker Polit. Group LLC, 2001—; founder, publisher PoliticalCircus.com, 2001—. Contr. editor NetPulse; correspondent Balitang Am.; mem. Human Rights Commn., Alexandria, Va., 2001—. Named Rising Star of Polit., Campaigns & Elections Mag., 2002.

SALINGER, FRANK MAX, lawyer; b. Landau, Isar, Germany, Dec. 4, 1951; s. Karl and Ingeborg F. (Herold) S.; m. Susan Ann Wagner, May 20, 1978. Student, Columbia Union Coll., Takoma Park, Md., 1969-72; JD, U. Balt., 1975. Bar: Md. 1975, U.S. Dist. Ct. Md. 1975, U.S. Ct. Appeals (4h cir.) 1978, U.S. Tax Ct. 1978, U.S. Ct. Mil. Appeals 1978, U.S. Ct. Appeals (5th cir.) 1982, U.S. Supreme Ct. 1983, U.S. Ct. Appeals (11th cir.) 1984, U.S. Ct. Appeals (9th cir.) 1986, D.C. 1986, U.S. Ct. Appeals (3d cir.) 1989. Pvt. practice, Balt., 1975-77; counsel Md. State Senate, Annapolis, 1975-76; assoc. counsel Am. Fin. Corp., Silver Spring, Md., 1977-78; govt. rels. counsel Truck Trailer Mfrs. Assn., Washington, 1978-80; v.p., gen. counsel, dir. govt. affairs Am. Fin. Svcs. Assocs., Washington, 1980-92; v.p. govt. rels. Advanta Corp., Wilmington, Del., 1992—. Co-author: (with Alvin O. Wiese and Robert E. McKew) A Guide to the Consumer Bankruptcy Code, 1989; (with Robert W. Green) State Regulations and Statutes on Consumer Credit, 1989, Federal Consumer Credit Regulations and Statutes, 1989. City councilman, Laurel, Md., 1976-78, zoning commr., 1976-78; chmn. Md. State Young Reps., 1977-78; bd. dirs. Am. Bankruptcy Inst., Washington, 1986-88. Mem. ABA (mem. com. on consumer fin. svcs., subcoms. on interest rate regulation and state regulation), Am. League Lobbyists (chair fin. svcs. sect. 1995-97), Federalist Soc. Law and Pub. Policy, Capitol Hill Club, Ford's Theatre Soc. Republican. Office: Advanta Corp One Righter Pkwy Wilmington DE 19803 Business E-Mail: fsalinger@advanta.com.

SALINGER, J(EROME) D(AVID), author; b. NYC, Jan. 1, 1919; s. Sol and Miriam (Jillich) S.; m. Claire Douglas, 1953 (div. 1967); children: Margaret Ann, Matthew; m. Colleen. Student, Valley Forge Mil. Acad., Columbia U., Ursinus Coll. Author: Catcher in the Rye, 1951, Nine Stories, 1953, Franny and Zooey, 1961, Raise High the Roof Beam, Carpenters; and Seymour: An Introduction, 1963; contbr. stories to New Yorker mag. Sgt. AUS, 1942-46. Address: care Harold Ober Assocs 425 Madison Ave New York NY 10017-1110

SALINGER, MICHAEL ALVIN, economist, educator; b. Cin., Aug. 24, 1956; s. James Alvin and Joyce (Joslin) S.; m. Julie Landsman, July 6, 1985; children: Philip Landsman, David Herbert, Nicholas Andrew. BA, Yale U., 1978; PhD, MIT, 1982. Asst. prof. Grad. Sch. Bus. Columbia U., NYC, 1982-87, assoc. prof., 1987-90, Boston U., 1990—, faculty dir. undergrad. program, 1999-2000, chmn. dept. fin. and econ., 2000—04, prof., 2001—. Economist FTC, Washington, 1985—86, dir. Bur. Econs., 2005—07; acad. advisor Princeton Econs. Group, 1989—94; spl. cons. Nat. Econ. Rsch. Assocs., 1994—2005; vis. assoc. prof. MIT, 1997—98. Assoc. editor: Jour. Indsl. Econs., 1996—2002, mem. editl. bd.:, 2002—06, Rev. Ind. Orgn., 2002—05; contbr. articles to profl. publs. Vol. The Alumni Fund, New Haven, 1978—2004. NSF fellow, 1979-82. Mem. Am. Econ. Assn. Jewish. Avocations: tennis, skiing. Office: Boston U Sch Mgmt 595 Commonwealth Ave Boston MA 02215-1704 E-mail: salinger@bu.edu.

SALINS, PETER D., political science professor, academic administrator; b. Berlin, June 15, 1938; came to U.S., 1939; s. Irwin and Ilse Daisy (Lessler) S.; m. Rochelle Chensky, Apr. 4, 1971; children: Jessica Elizabeth, Jonathan Andrew. BArch, Syracuse U., 1961, M in Regional Planning, 1968, PhD, 1969. Registered architect, Mass. Chmn. dept. urban affairs and planning Hunter Coll., CUNY, 1973-93, 96-97, prof. dept. urban affairs and planning, 1980-97, dir. grad. program in urban planning, 1993-95, dir. urban rsch. ctr., 1995-97; provost, vice chancellor acad. affairs SUNY Sys. Adminstrn., Albany, 1997—2006; prof. dept. polit. sci. Stony Brook U., 1996—, Univ. prof. dept. polit. sci., 2006—. Sr. fellow Manhattan Inst. Policy Rsch., NYC, 1985—; mem. Planning Accreditation Bd., Chgo., 1990—; Catherine Bauer Wurster lectr. U. Calif., Berkeley, 1993; dir. SUNY Rsch. Found., 1997—2006. Author: The Ecology of Housing Destruction, 1980, Assimilation, American Style, 1997; co-author: Scarcity by Design, 1992; editor: Housing America's Poor, 1987, New York Unbound, 1988; co-editor Jour. of Am. Planning Assn., 1988-93 (Excellence award 1992, Journalism award 1994). Mem. planning com. Am. Acad. Sci., Washington, 1971-72; mem. adv. panel White House Domestic Policy Unit, Washington, 1977; dir. Citizens Housing and Planning Coun., NYC, 1988—; trustee Lavanburg Found., NYC, 1987—, chmn., Landmarks Preservation Com., Village of Baxter Estates, Nassau County, NY, 1992-99; mem. mayor's adv. commn. NYC Health and Hosps. Corp., 1995-96. Fellow: Am. Inst. Cert. Planners; mem.: ASPA (v.p. 1982—84, Luther Gulick award for outstanding acad. 1994), Am. Planning Assn. (v.p. 1986—88, policy bd. mem. 1986—, N.Y. met. chpt.), Lambda Alpha. Avocations: golf, reading, hiking. Office Phone: 631-632-7672. Business E-Mail: peter.salins@stonybrook.edu.

SALISBURY, DALLAS L., researcher, director; b. Everett, Wash. BA, U. Wash., 1970; MPA in Pub. Policy and Adminstrn., Syracuse U., 1973. With Employee Benefit Security Adminstrn. US Dept. Labor, 1975—76, Pension Guaranty Corp. US Dept. Labor, 1977—78, U.S. Dept. Justice, 1974, Wash. State Legislature, 1971-72, Employee Benefit Rsch. Inst., Washington, 1978—, pres., CEO, mem. bd. trustees. Bd. dir. Nat. Assn. Securities Dealers Investor Edn. Group; lectr. in field; cons. in field. Mem. editl. adv. bd. Benefits Quar., Employee Benefits Jour., Healthplan; contbr. articles to profl. jours. Mem. Employee Retirement Income Security Act of 1974 adv. coun. US Sec. Labor; pres.'s adv. coun. Pension Benefit Guaranty Corp. Fellow Nat. Acad. Human Resources. Office: Employee Benefit Research Inst 2121 K St NW Ste 600 Washington DC 20037-1800

SALISBURY, EUGENE W., lawyer, mediator; b. Blasdell, NY, Mar. 20, 1933; s. W. Dean and Mary I. (Burns) S.; m. Joanne M. Salisbury, July 14, 1950; children: Mark, Ellen, Susan, David, Scott. BA in History and Govt. cum laude, U. Buffalo, 1959, JD cum laude, 1968. Bar: NY 1960, DC 1973, US Dist. Ct. (we. and no. dists.) 1961, US Ct. Appeals (2d cir.) 1970, US Ct. Appeals (DC cir.) 1973, US Supreme Ct. 1973. Ptnr. Lipsitz, Green, Fahringer, Roll, Salisbury and Cambria, Buffalo, 1960—. Justice Village of Blasdell, 1961-2001; lectr. NY Office Ct. Adminstrn., NYC, 1961—; mem. NY State Commn. on Jud. Conduct, 1989-2001, chmn., 2000-01; mem. NY State Jud. Conf., 1989-2001. Author: Manual for NY Courts, 1973, Forms for NY Courts, 1977. Capt. US Army, 1949-54, Korea. Decorated Bronze Star, Purple Heart; recipient Citizen of Yr. award Indsl. Rels. Rsch. Assn., 2000; named Jurist of Yr., Erie County Judges and Police Conf., 2001, Magistrate of Yr., Erie County Magistrates Assn., 2001. Mem. ABA (del. spl. ct. sect. 1988-2001), DC Bar Assn., Erie County Bar Assn., NY State Bar Assn., World Judges Assn., NY State Magistrates Assn. (pres. 1973, Man of Yr. 1974). Office: Lipsitz Green Scime Cambria 42 Delaware Ave Ste 300 Buffalo NY 14202-3857 Office Phone: 716-849-1333. Business E-Mail: esalisbury@lglaw.com.

SALISBURY, FRANK BOYER, botanist, educator, writer; b. Provo, Utah, Aug. 3, 1926; s. Frank M. and Catherine (Boyer) S.; m. Lois Marilyn Olson, Sept. 1, 1949; children: Frank Clark, Steven Scott, Michael James, Cynthia Kay, Phillip Boyer (dec.), Rebecca Lynn, Blake Charles; m. Mary Thorpe Robinson, June 28, 1991. BS, U. Utah, Salt Lake City, 1951, MA, 1952; PhD, Calif. Inst. Tech., Pasadena, 1955. Asst. prof. botany Pomona Coll., Claremont, Calif., 1954-55; faculty Colo. State U., Ft. Collins, 1955-66, prof. plant physiology, 1961-66; plant physiologist Expt. Sta., 1961-66; prof. plant physiology Utah State U., Logan, 1966-97, disting. prof. Agr., 1987-97, prof. emeritus, 1997—, head dept. plant sci., 1966-70; tech. rep. plant physiology AEC, Germantown, Md., 1973-74. Vis. prof. U. Innsbruck, Austria; Lady Davis fellow Hebrew U. Jerusalem, 1983; mem. aerospace medicine adv. com. NASA, 1988-93, life scis. adv. com., 1986-88, chmn. NASA Controlled Ecol. Life Support System Discipline Working Group, 1989-94; leader of project to grow wheat through a life cycle in Russian space station, Mir, 1990-97. Author: The Flowering Process, 1963, Truth by Reason and by Revelation, 1965, The Biology of Flowering, 1971, The Utah UFO Display, 1974, The Creation, 1976, The Case for Divine Design, 2006; co-author: (with R.V. Parke) Vascular Plants, Form and Function, 2d edit., 1970, (with C. Ross) Plant Physiology, 1969, 4th edit., 1992; (with W. Jensen) Botany: An Ecological Approach, 1972, Botany, 2d edit., 1984, (with others) Biology, 1977; editor Jour. Plant Physiology, Ams. and the Pacific Rim, 1989-96; editor, contbr.: Units, Symbols, and Terminology for Plant Physiology, 1996; editor: Geochemistry and The Biosphere, 2006. Trustee Colo. State U. Rsch. Found., 1959-62; leader People to People bot. del. to South Africa, 1984, to China, 1988, Soviet Union, 1990; fin. sec. Ohio Columbus Mission LDS Ch., 1997-99. NSF sr. postdoctoral fellow Germany and Austria, 1962-63. Fellow AAAS; mem. Am. Soc. for Gravitational and Space Biology (Founders award 1994), Am. Soc. Plant Physiologists (editorial bd. 1967-92), Am. Inst. Biol. Scis. (governing bd. 1976-79), Bot. Soc. Am. (merit award 1982), Sigma Xi, Phi Kappa Phi. Mem. Lds Ch. Home: 2250 Bryan Cir Salt Lake City UT 84108-2711 Home Phone: 801-583-6569; Office Phone: 801-281-1575. *This is an extremely exciting time to live! Science has provided marvelous insight into the cosmos, the earth, and the nature of life. The fact that mankind exists and can contemplate it all cries out that it has purpose and direction. My life is full to overflowing because God's revelation of Himself adds the final capstone to this beautiful structure.*

SALISBURY, MICHEAL WAYNE, education educator; b. Pecos, Tex., Sept. 9, 1971; s. Pat and Jerry Salisbury; m. Tara Katina Collins, July 11, 1992; children: Matthew Wayne, Kimberly D'Ann, Kelly D'Lynn. BS, Angelo State U., San Angelo, Tex., 1994, MS, 1996; PhD, N.Mex State U., Las Cruces, 1996—99. Prof. U. Tenn., Knoxville, 2000—01, Angelo State U., 2001—. Contbr. over 50 papers to profl. jours. and pubs. Mem.: Am. Soc. Animal Scientists. Home Phone: 325-653-1861; Office Phone: 325-942-2027.

SALISBURY, ROBERT HOLT, political science professor; b. Elmhurst, Ill., Apr. 29, 1930; s. Robert Holt and Beulah (Hammer) S.; m. Rose Marie Cipriani, June 19, 1953; children: Susan Marie (dec.), Robert Holt, Matthew Gary. AB, Washington and Lee U., 1951; MA, U. Ill., 1952, PhD, 1955. Mem. faculty Washington U., St. Louis, 1955-65, prof., 1965-97, prof. emeritus, 1997—, chmn. dept. polit. sci., 1966-73, 86-92, dir. Center for Study Pub. Affairs, 1974-77, Sidney W. Souers prof. govt., 1982-97. Vis. prof. SUNY, Buffalo, 1965, So. Ill. U., Edwardsville, 1975; affiliated scholar Am. Bar Found., 1981-95; cons. U.S. Conf. Mayors, 1965, Hartford (Conn.) C. of C., 1964, NSF, 1973. Author: Interest Groups Politics in America, 1970, Governing America, 1973, Citizen Participation in the Public Schools, 1980, Interests and Institutions, 1992, The Hollow Core, 1993; contbr. articles to profl. jours. Mem. St. Louis County Charter Commn., 1967, Gov.'s Commn. on Local Govt., 1968-69. Guggenheim fellow, 1990; Rockefeller Ctr. scholar, 1990. Mem. Mo. Polit. Sci. Assn. (pres. 1964-65), Am. Polit. Sci. Assn. (exec. council 1969-71, v.p. 1980-81), Midwest Polit. Sci. Assn. (pres. 1977-78), Pi Sigma Alpha. Democrat. Methodist. Home: 709 S Skinker Blvd Saint Louis MO 63105-3225 Office: Washington U Dept Polit Sci Saint Louis MO 63130

SALITERMAN, RICHARD ARLEN, lawyer; b. Aug. 3, 1946; s. Leonard Slitz and Dorothy (Sloan) S.; m. Laura Shrager, June 15, 1975; 1 child, Robert Warren. BA summa cum laude, U. Minn., 1968; JD, Columbia U., 1971; LLM, NYU, 1974; grad., FBI Citizens Acad., Mpls. and Washington, 2006. Bar: Minn. 1972, DC 1974. Legal staff subcom. on antitrust and monopoly U.S. Senate, Washington, 1971-72; acting dir., dep. dir. compliance and enforcement divsn. Fed. Energy Office, NYC, 1974; mil. atty. Presdl. Clemency Bd., White House, Washington, 1975; pres. Saliterman & Siefferman, PC, Mpls., 1975—. Adj. prof. law Hamline U., 1976-81. Author: Advising Minnesota Corporations and Other Business Organizations, 4 vols., 1975; chmn. Hennepin County Bar Jour., 1985-87. Trustee, sec. Hopkins Edn. Found.; trustee W. Harry Davis Found., 1990-96; pres. Twin Cities Coun.; nat. bd. dirs. Navy League U.S., Washington, 1997—, nat. judge adv., 2001-02; bd. dirs., sec. The Pavek Mus., 1992—; bd. dirs. Mpls. Urban League, 1983-87. Lt. USN, 1972-75, res., 1975—. Office Phone: 612-339-1400. Business E-Mail: rsaliterman@saliterman-law.com.

SALITERMAN, STEVEN S., internist, educator; b. Mpls., June 6, 1951; s. Leonard S. and Dorothy Saliterman; m. Peg E. Maloney, Aug. 24, 1986; children: David Edward, Paul Wesley. BA in Physiology summa cum laude, U. Minn., 1972; MD, Mayo Med. Sch., Rochester, Minn., 1977; grad., Mayo Grad. Sch. Medicine, 1980. Diplomate Am. Bd. Internal Medicine 1983. Pvt. practice, St. Louis Park, Minn., 1981—; sr. aviation med. examiner FAA, Washington, 1981—. Rsch. com. Pk. Nicollet's Meth. Hosp., St. Louis Park, Minn., 1996—2003, chmn. dept. medicine, 2001—05; dept. biomed. engring. U. Minn., Mpls., 2002—, adj. asst. prof., 2002—, faculty nano & microsystems applications ctr., 2006—; exec. com. Meth. Hosp., St. Louis Park, 2004—05, quality assurance com., 2004—05. Author: (textbook) Fundamentals of BioMEMS and Medical Microdevices, 2006; contbr. articles to profl. jours. Recipient Achievement award, US Army, 1969, Acheivement award, Profl. Engrs. Soc. Minn., 1969, Physician's Recognition award, AMA, 2006; fellow, NASA Johnson Space Ctr., 1973—74, NASA Ames Rsch. Ctr., 1976; Nat. Youth Sci. Camp scholar, Minn. State Sci. Fair, 1969. Fellow: ACP; mem.: Mayo Alumni Assn., Internat. Soc. for Optical Engring., Mayo Plummer Soc., Phi Beta Kappa. Achievements include patents for computerized simulator for critical care training & catheterization; design of 7027 computer system; laser activated amphibian monitor system. Avocations: swimming, hiking, photography, amateur radio. Office: 6490 Excelsior Blvd Ste W-110 Saint Louis Park MN 55426 Office Phone: 952-920-8771. Personal E-mail: stevensaliterman@comcast.net.

SALKIND, ALVIN J., engineering educator, dean, consultant; b. NYC; s. Samuel M. and Florence (Zins) S.; m. Marion Ruth Koenig, Nov. 7, 1965; children: Susanne, James. B.Ch.E., Poly. Inst. N.Y., 1949, M.Ch.E., 1952, D.Ch.E., 1958; postgrad. and mgmt. courses, Pa. State U., 1965, Harvard U., 1976. Registered profl. engr., N.Y., N.J. Sr. scientist Sonotone Corp., Elmsford, NY, 1954—57; rsch. assoc. Poly. Inst. N.Y., 1956-58, adj. prof. chem. engring., 1960-70; with ESB-Ray OVAC Co., Yardley, Pa., 1958-79, dir. tech., 1971-72, v.p. tech., 1972-79; pres. ESB Tech. Co., 1972—79; prof., chief bioengring. divsn., dept. surgery UMDNJ-Robert Wood Johnson Med. Sch., Piscataway, NJ, 1970—2004, prof. emeritus, 2004—; prof. biomed. engring. and materials sci. and engring. Rutgers U., Piscataway, NJ, 1985—2002, assoc. dean Coll. Engring., 1989—2001, prof. emeritus, 2004—; pvt. engring. practice, 1979—. Vis. prof., exec. officer Case Ctr. Electrochem. Sci., 1981—82; vis. prof. U. Miami, 2003—; bd. dirs., cons. various cos., rsch. instns. and govt. orgns.; mem. rev. panels Nat. Rsch. Coun., NIH. Author (with S.U. Falk): Alkaline Storage Batteries, 1969; author: (with Herbert T. Silverman and Irving F. Miller) Electrochemical Bioscience and Bioengineering, 1973; editor (with E. Yeager): Techniques of Electrochemistry, 1971, revised edit., 1978, Russian edit., 1977, History of Battery Technology, 1987; editor: (with F. McLarnon and V. Bogatzky) Rechargeable Zinc Electrodes, 1996; editor: (with A. Landgrebe) Power Sources for Transportation Applications, 2003; contbr. over 200 articles to profl. jours. With USNR, 1945—46. Recipient Alumnus citation Poly. Inst. N.Y., 1975, award Internat. Tech. Exch. Soc., 1992, Frank Booth award Internat. Power Sources Symposium Eng., 1999; Case Centennial scholar Case-Western Res. U., 1980. Fellow Acad. Medicine of NJ, Am. Coll. Cardiology, AAAS, Am. Inst. Med. and Biomed. Engrs.; mem. Electrochem. Soc. (past chmn. new tech. com., past chmn. battery div.), Indsl. Rsch. Inst. (emeritus 1979), NY Acad. Scis., Sigma Xi, Phi Lambda Upsilon. Home: 51 Adams Dr Princeton NJ 08540-5401 Office: Rutgers U Sch Engring 607 Taylor Rd Piscataway NJ 08854 Office Phone: 732-445-6858. Personal E-mail: ajsalkind@verizon.net. Business E-Mail: salkind@rci.rutgers.edu, asalkind@miami.edu.

SALKIND, MICHAEL JAY, science administrator, metallurgical engineer; s. Milton and Esther (Jaffe) S.; m. Miriam E. Schwartz, Aug. 16, 1959 (div. 1979); children: Michael Jay, Elizabeth Jane, Jonathan Hillson, Joshua Isaac; m. Carol T. Gill, Dec. 23, 1990. B in Metall. Engring., Rensselaer Polytech. Inst., Troy, NY, 1959, PhD, 1962. Chief advanced metallurgy United Techs. Rsch. Labs., East Hartford, 1964-68; chief structures and materials Sikorsky Aircraft div. United Techs. Corp., 1968-75; dir. product devel. Avco Systems div., 1975-76; mgr. structures NASA, 1976-80; dir. aerospace scis. Air Force Office of Sci. Rsch., 1980-89; pres. Ohio Aerospace Inst., 1990—2003, Business Tech Network, 2003—; prin. Indus Internat., 2003—. Adj. faculty metallurgy Trinity Coll., Hartford; adj. faculty aerospace U. Md., College Park, 1982-85; adj. faculty materials Johns Hopkins U., Balt., 1985-89; chair Ohio Math. and Sci. Coalition; adj. faculty Kent State U., Ohio, 2007- Cons. editor Internat. Jour. Fibre Sci. and Tech.; editor Applications Composite Materials, 1973; contbr. to profl. jours. and textbooks. Evaluator Accreditation Bd. Engring. and Tech., 1989—1995; mem. Daniel Guggenheim Medal Bd. Awards, 1984-90; mem. Spirit of St. Louis Medal Bd., 1984-89; bd. dirs. Citizens' Acad. Charter Sch., Cleve. Internat. Program, NCCJ, Cleve. Coun. World Affairs, Sustainable Cleve.; co-chair Buckeye F.I.R.S.T. Robotics Competition; chair industry adv. bd. Kent State U., Coll. Tech. Capt. ord. US Army, 1962-64. Recipient Disting. Leadership award, Cleve. Tech. Socs. Coun., 2002. Fellow AAAS, AIAA (assoc.), ASM Internat.; mem. ASME (Disting. lectr. 1989-93), ASTM (chmn. com. D-30 on high modulous fibers and their composites 1968-74), Am. Helicopter Soc., AIME, Brit. Inst. Metals, Rsch. Soc. Am., Plansee Soc., India Ohio C. of C., Cosmos Club, Union Club, 50 Club, Leadership Cleve., Sigma Xi, Alpha Sigma Mu. Personal E-mail: michaelsalkind@adelphia.net.

SALKY, BARRY A., surgeon; b. Memphis, Nov. 10, 1944; s. Jake and Mary Salky; m. Alma Halski; children: Jonathan, Adam. MD, U. Tenn., Memphis, 1970. Diplomate Am. Bd. Surgery. Intern Mt. Sinai Hosp., NYC, 1971—73, resident in internal medicine, 1975—78, clin. prof. surgery, 1996—2004, prof. surgery, 2004—, chief divsn. laparoscopic surgery, 1992—96, 2004—. Author: Laparscopy for Surgeons, 1990, Advanced Laparoscopy for Surgeons, 1994. Maj. US Army, 1973—75. Recipient Ambassador's award, Am. Friends of Rambom Med. Ctr., 1995. Fellow: ACS, Am. Coll. of Gastroenterology; mem.: Soc. Surgery Alimentary Tract, Soc. Am. Gastrointestinal Endoscopic Surgeons (v.p. 1997—98). Jewish. Avocations: golf, travel. Office: Mt Sinai Hosp 5 E 98th St 14th Fl New York NY 10029 Office Phone: 212-241-6156. Business E-Mail: barry.salky@mountsinai.org.

SALL, JOHN, information technology executive; married; 4 children. BS, Beloit Coll.; MS, No. Ill. U. Co-founder, exec. v.p. SAS Inst., Cary, NC; leader JMP Bus. Divsn. Named one of Forbes' Richest Americans, 2006. Office: SAS Inst 100 SAS Campus Dr Cary NC 27513-2414

SALL, LARRY DAVID, library director; b. Portland, Oreg., July 10, 1941; s. David Elmer and Lillian Elisabeth Sall; m. Louise Kuhn, Dec. 13, 1967 (div. Aug. 6, 1978); m. Judy Claire McQuade, Nov. 24, 1978; 1 child, Karl Fredrick. BA, U. Idaho, 1964; exch. fellow, U. Munich, Germany, 1967—68; PhD, Wayne State U., 1971. Assoc. dir. spl. collections U. Tex.-Dallas, Richardson, 1982—99, dir. librs., 1999—2004, dean of librs., 2004—. Translator: (memoir) Pioneer Aviator in China, 1998; contbr.: (biography of Lamar Muse) Encyclopedia of American Business History: The Airline Industry. Friends adv. bd. Dallas Pub. Libr., 2004; libr. adv. bd. So. Meth. U., Dallas, 2003; bd. dirs. Frontiers of Flight Mus., Dallas, 1999. Mem.: Audubon Tex. (bd. dirs. 2004, bd. dirs. Dallas chpt. 2001), Am. Birding Assn. (assoc.), Dallas Com. Fgn. Rels. (assoc.), Tex. Philatelic Assn. (assoc.; pres. 1991—95), Richardson Ctrl. Rotary Club (assoc.; pres. 1989—90), Richardson Rotary Club (assoc.). Achievements include development of History of Aviation collection and others, U. Tex.-Dallas. Avocations: bird watching, mountain hiking, scuba diving, travel, reading. Office: Univ Texas at Dallas PO Box 830643 Richardson TX 75083-0643 Home Phone: 214-520-2312; Office Phone: 972-883-2960. Office Fax: 972-883-2473. E-mail: sall@utdallas.edu.

SALLAH, MAJEED (JIM SALLAH), retired real estate developer; b. Boston, Aug. 5, 1920; s. Herbert K. and Rose (Karem) Sallah; m. Aline C. Powers, Apr. 10, 1970; children: Christopher M., Melissa Rose. Pres., dir. Glo-Bit Fish Co., Gloucester, Mass., 1947—48, Live-Pak of Ohio, Inc., 1947—51, Cape Ann Glass Co., Gloucester, 1950—72, Marias Restaurant, 1960—, Cape Ann Realty Co., 1961—. Pres., treas., dir. Gloucester Hot-Top Constrn. Co., Goucester, 1967—75; pres., bd. dir. SGF Corp., 1983—85, SALFAD, Inc., Rossford, Ohio; pres., treas. Points East, Inc.; trustee Christopher Investment Trust; bd. dir. Lustal, Inc.; bd. dir., ptnr. Barsal, Inc., Toledo, Hamsal, Inc. Pres. Lebanese-Am. Bus. Men's Club; treas. Lebanese-Maronite Soc. With US Army, 1942—45. Decorated Bronze Star. Mem.: Gloucester Assoc., Cape Ann Investment Corp., Gloucester Fraternity Assn., Lions, Am. Legion, Amvets, Loyal Order of Moose, Elks, Ky. Cols. (hon.). Roman Catholic. Home and Office: 56 Hilltop Rd Gloucester MA 01931-0078

SALLAM, ISMAIL AWAD-ALLAH, government agency administrator, educator; b. Monoufeya, Egypt, July 21, 1941; Diploma in surgery, Ain Shams U.; PhD, Glasgow U., 1955. Prof., head dept. heart surgery Ain Shams U., 1992—; head health & population com. Shura Consultative Coun., 1992—; min. health & population Ministry of Health & Population, Egypt, 1996—2002; chmn. Gen. Orgn. Teaching Hosps. & Insts. (GOTHI). Active WHO. Recipient United Arab Emirates Health Found. prize for health devel., 1999. Mem.: IOM (elected 2003). Achievements include established Healthy Egyptians 2010 initiative, 1998. Office: Min Health Sharia Magles al-Sha'ab St Cairo Egypt

SALLAN, STEPHEN E., pediatrician; b. Detroit; MD, Wayne State U., 1967. Cert. pediat. Intern Boston Floating Hosp., 1967-68; resident in pediatrics Children's Hosp., Phila., 1968-69, Hosp. Sick Children, London, 1969-70; fellow in pediatric oncology Children's Hosp. Med. Ctr./Harvard U., Boston, 1973-75; mem. med. staff Dana Farber Cancer Inst., Boston, 1975—, chief of staff, 1995—; prof. pediatrics Harvard Med. Sch., Boston. Mem. AMA, AACR, ASCO, ASH, SPR. Office: Dana Farber Cancer Inst 44 Binney St Boston MA 02115-6084

SALLEE, WANDA JEAN, music educator; b. Seminole, Okla., Nov. 30, 1929; d. John Mordecai Cooper and Mary Blanche Jenkins-Cooper; m. William J. Sallee, Jan. 6, 1951; children: Susan Dwan, Martha Jean. MusB in Piano Theory, Okla. State U., 1950; student in Edn. and Pedagogy, Levine Sch. Music, 1990. Cert. tchr. music Am. Coll. Musicians. Tchr. music Hobart (Okla.) Elem. Schs., 1950—51, Mangum (Okla.) Elem. Schs., 1951—52; dir. ch. music First Bapt. Ch., Mangum, 1952—57, Westover Bapt. Ch., Arlington, Va., 1959—72; pvt. piano tchr. Mangum, 1952—58; tchr. Sallee Music Studio, Arlington, Va., 1959—94, Dallas, 1994—. Dir. music Bapt. Ch., Arlington, 1959—72; bd. trustees Oak Hill Acad., Va., 1965—68; presenter in field. Vol. Reagan-Bush Campaign, Arlington, 1980. Mem.: Music Tchrs. Nat. Assn., Am. Coll. Musicians (adjudicator, nat. guild judge), Richardson (Tex.) Music Tchrs. Assn. (pres., v.p., corr.sec.), Tex. State Music Tchrs. Assn. (chmn. practice student affiliate 2003—, named Piano Tchr. of Yr. 2002), Sigma Alpha Iota (life). Avocations: poetry, writing, reading, painting, eggery. Home and Office: Sallee Music Studio 7615 Cliffbrook Dr Dallas TX 75254-8101 Personal E-mail: wjs6214@airmail.net.

SALLER, RICHARD PAUL, classics educator; b. Ft. Bragg, NC, Oct. 18, 1952; s. George E. and Arthea E. (North) S.; m. Carol Joann Fisher, Jan. 12, 1974 (div. Apr. 18, 2002; children: John E., Benjamin T.; m. Tanya M. Luhrmann, Jan. 4, 2003. BA in Greek and History, U. Ill., 1974; PhD in Classics, U. Cambridge, Eng., 1978. Asst. prof. Swarthmore (Pa.) Coll., 1979-84; assoc. prof. U. Chgo., 1984-89, prof., 1990—, dean of social scis., 1994—2001, provost, 2002—06; dean Sch. Humanities and Sci. Stanford U., 2006—. Author: Personal Patronage, 1982, Patriarchy, Property and Death in the Roman Family, 1994; co-editor: Economy and Society in Ancient Greece, 1981; co-author: Roman Empire, 1987; editor Classical Philology, 1991-93. Rsch. fellow Jesus Coll., U. Cambridge, 1978-79; Ctr. for Adv. Study fellow, Stanford U., 1986-87; Trinity Coll., U. Cambridge fellow commoner, 1991. Mem. Am. Philol. Assn., Am. Hist. Assn., Am. Acad. Arts and Scis. Office: Sch Humanities and Scis Stanford Univ Stanford CA 94305 Office Phone: 773-702-8810.

SALLEY, JOHN JONES, retired academic administrator, oral pathologist; b. Richmond, Va., Oct. 29, 1926; s. Thomas Raysor and Kathryn (Josey) S.; m. Jean Gordon Cunningham, Dec. 21, 1950; children: Katharine Gordon, John Jones, Martha Cunningham. DDS, Med. Coll. Va., 1951; PhD, U. Rochester, 1954; DSc, Boston U., 1975. Research fellow U. Rochester, 1951-54; from instr. to prof., chmn. dept. oral pathology Med. Coll. Va., 1954-63, prof. emeritus, 1991—; prof. pathology, dean Sch. Dentistry U. Md., 1963-74, dean emeritus Sch. Dentistry, 1977—, ret., 1991; v.p. research and grad. affairs Va. Commonwealth U., Richmond, 1974-85; acting pres. Va. Ctr. for Innovative Tech., 1985, v.p., 1985-87. Cons. divsn. rsch. grants NIH, 1962—66; cons. US Naval Hosp., Portsmouth, Va., USPHS Hosp., Balt., 1963—74, VA Hosp., Balt., 1964—74, US Naval Dental Sch., Bethesda, Md., 1966—75, WHO, 1969—75; cons. Sch. Dentistry, San Marcos U., Lima, Peru, 1965—69; spl. cons. Nat. Inst. Dental Rsch., NIH, 1957—64; dental health divsn. USPHS; mem. Md. Adv. Coun. Comprehensive Health Planning, 1968—74, Nat. Health Coun., 1970—71; pres. Am. Assn. Dental Schs., 1971—72, Conf. So. Grad. Schs., 1983—84; sr. program cons. Robert Wood Johnson Found., 1978—84; mem. career devel. rev. com. VA, 1974—78; mem. com. health care resources in VA, NRC, 1974—77; mem. Va. Gov.'s Task Force Sci. and Tech., 1982—83; sci. advisor to Gov. of Va., 1984—86; mem. rsch. com. Va. State Coun. Higher Edn., 1974—84; chmn. task force Coun. Grad. Schs. in US, 1979—82. Contbr. articles in field; editorial rev. bd.: Jour. Dental Edn, 1974-78. Bd. dirs. Md. divsn. Am. Cancer Soc., 1963-70, Am. Fund Dental Health, Rappahannock C.C. Found., 1999—; bd. dirs. Nat. Found. Dentistry for the Handicapped, 1986, pres., 1992-94; mem. adv. bd. Va. Inst. for Devel. Disabilities, 1987-91; bd. trustees Middlesex County Pub. Libr., 1994-98, pres., 1995-97. With USAAF, 1944-46. Recipient Outstanding Civilian Service medal Dept. Army, 1961, Disting. Citizenship award State Md., 1974. Fellow AAAS, Am. Coll. Dentists; mem. ADA, Nat. Conf. Univ. Research Adminstrs., Am. Acad. Oral Pathology, Internat. Assn. Dental Research (Novice award 1953), Internat. Med. Informatics Assn. (chmn. working group 1989-92), Sigma Xi, Sigma Zeta, Omicron Kappa Upsilon. Episcopalian (vestryman). Home and Office: 1500 Westbrook Ct Apt 2140 Richmond VA 23227

SALLIS, JAMES, writer; b. Helena, Ark., Dec. 21, 1944; s. Chappelle Horace and Mildred Clodine (Liming) S. Student, Tulane U., 1961-63, U. Tex., 1985-87. Tchr. intensive writing workshops Clarion (Pa.) Coll., U. Wash., Tulane U., Loyola U., Phoenix Coll., Otis Coll., L.A.; guest lectr. modern poetry, European lit., art; writer short stories, essays, poetry and trans. Editor New Worlds 1966-68; editor: (anthologies) The War Book, 1972, The Shores Beneath, 1973; features writer, reviewer, columnist Tex. Jazz, 1980-83, lead book reviewer Dallas Morning News, 1981-83; book reviewer Washington Post Book World, L.A. Times, 1993—; columnist Mag. of Fantasy and Sci. Fiction, Web Del Sol, Boston Globe, 2000--; author: A Few Last Words, 1972, The Guitar Players, 1982, 94, Jazz Guitars, 1984, The Long-Legged Fly, 1992, Saint Glinglin (translator), 1993, Difficult Lives, 1993, Moth, 1993, Black Hornet, 1994, Limits of the Sensible World, 1994, Renderings, 1995, The Guitar in Jazz, 1996, Ash of Stars: On the Writings of Samuel R. Delany, 1996, Death Will Have Your Eyes, 1997, Eye of the Cricket, 1997, Bluebottle, 1999, Gently into the Land of the Meateaters, 2000, Chester Himes: A Life, 2000, Time's Hammers, 2000, Sorrow's Kitchen, 2000, Ghost of a Flea, 2001, Cypress Grove, 2002, A City Equal To My Desire, 2004, A James Sallis Reader, 2005, Drive, 2005, Cripple Creek, 2006.

SALLQUIST, GARY ARDIN, minister, non-profit executive; b. Sioux City, Iowa, July 7, 1938; s. Hal Thurston and Rosemary (Daggett) S.; m. Joyce Darleen Casey, June 10, 1960; children: Susan L. Rail, Steven P. BA, U. Nebr., Omaha, 1960; MDiv, Princeton Theol. Sem., 1993; D of Ministry, La. Bapt. U., 1997; D, Am. Coll. ChFC, CLU. Pres. Planned Giving Sys., Cin., 1987—90; min. adult edn. Coll. Hill Presbyn. Ch., Cin., 1993—95; dir. planned giving Promise Keepers, Denver, 1995—98; v.p., divsn. higher edn. PhilanthroCorp, Woodland Park, Colo., 1998—2000; headmaster Miami Valley Christian Acad., Cin., 2001—06, headmaster emeritus, 2007—. Author: A Seminary Journey, 1995, The Counsel of Many, 1999, God's Messages/Dr. Gardner Taylor, 2003, For the Love of God/Dr. David Willis, 2004. Pres. Omaha Jaycees, 1966-67; dirs. Creighton-St. Joseph Hosp., Omaha, 1975-81, Leadership Cin. Alumni Assn., 1987-89. Mem. U. Nebr. Omaha Alumni Assn. (pres. 1968-70, Outstanding Alumnus award 1977), Pi Kappa Alpha (nat. pres. 1970-72). Avocations: basketball, running, tennis, reading, public speaking. Home: 5300 Barony Pl Cincinnati OH 45241 Office: Miami Valley Christian Acad 6830 School St Cincinnati OH 45244 Business E-Mail: gsallquist@miamivalleychristianacademy.org.

SALMANS, CHARLES GARDINER, banker; b. Washington, Apr. 23, 1945; s. Marion K. and Agnes A. (Gardiner) S.; m. Robin Elizabeth Wakeman, June 8, 1986; children: Jonathan, Peter, Charles II. BS, Northwestern U., 1967; MBA in Fin., Columbia U., 1970. Account supr. Burson-Marsteller, NYC, 1970-74; v.p. Bankers Trust Co., NYC, 1974-84; sr. v.p., divsn. head Chem. Bank, NYC, 1984-96; global bank mng. dir. Chase Manhattan Bank (merger with Chem. Bank 1996), NYC, 1996; sr. v.p., head of corp. comm. and investor rels. Quick & Reilly/Fleet Securities Inc., NYC, 1996—98; sr. v.p. corp. comms. FleetBoston Fin. (merger), NYC, 1998—2004; sr. v.p. corp. comm. Bank of Am. (merger), NYC, 2005—; dir. global pub. rels. Mercer, Inc., NYC, 2005—. Mem. editl. adv. bd. Grad. Sch. of Bus., Columbia U., NYC, 1984—; chmn. bus. adv. com. Guggenheim Mus., NYC, 1994—. Home: 6 Red Rose Cir Darien CT 06820-4928 Office: Mercer Inc 1166 Avenue of the Americas New York NY 10036-2708 Home Phone: 203-656-0296; Office Phone: 212-345-4512. Business E-Mail: charles.salmans@mercer.com.

SALMASSI, SADEGH, physician; b. Baghdad, Iraq, Aug. 14, 1946; s. Jafar and Kobra (Alavi) S.; m. Tahereh Ali Nazari, Jan. 17, 1970; children: Ali (dec.), Nahal. BS, Pahlavi U., 1966, MD, 1973. Diplomate Am. Bd. Pathology, Am. Bd. Gen. Practice in Medicine and Surgery. Instr. pathology U. Ill. Sch. Medicine, Chgo., 1975-80; asst. prof. pathology, assoc. chmn. dept., dir. blood bank U. Mo., Kansas City, 1980-84; chmn. family practice Delano (Calif.) Regional Med. Ctr., 1984-86; pres. Delano Regional Med. Group, 1989-96. Chief of staff Delano Regional Med. Ctr., 1989. Fellow Am. Coll. Internat. Physicians, Coll. Am. Pathologists, Am. Acad. Family Physicians; mem. AMA, Am. Acad. Gen. Physicians, Calif. Med. Assn. Office: Sadegh Salmassi MD & Assocs Urgent Care Ctr 719 Main St Delano CA 93215-2935 also: Salmassi Cosmetic and Med Inst 719 Main St Delano CA 93215-2935 Home Phone: 661-339-0292; Office Phone: 661-725-5877, 661-725-7060. Business E-Mail: salmassi@salmassimd.com.

SALMELA, DAVID DANIEL, architect; b. Wadena, Minn., Mar. 28, 1945; s. Laurie Fredrick and Lempi Christine (Matti) S.; m. Gladys Elaine Hanka, June 23, 1967; children: Cory, Chad, Tia, Kai, Brit. Grad. high sch., Sebeka, Minn.; LHD (hon.), U. Minn., 2007. Registered profl. architect, Minn., Wis. Draftsman McKenzie Hague & Gilles, Mpls., 1965-66, A.G. McKee, Hibbing, Minn., 1966, ABI Contracting, Virginia, Minn., 1966-69, Archtl. Resources, Hibbing, 1969-70; designer, arch. Damberg Scott Peck & Booker, Virginia, 1970-89; arch. Mulfinger Susanka, Duluth, Minn., 1989-90; prin. Salmela Fospick Ltd., Duluth, 1990-94, Salmela, Arch., Duluth, 1994—. Author: Salmela Architect. Recipient Design award, N.Am. Wood, 1994, 1998, 2 Design awards, 2002, Design award, 2003. Fellow: AIA (17 Minn. Honor awards 1985—2005, WRCL/AIA award 1994, Red Cedar Lumber Hon. award 1994, Record Houses award 1998, Nat. Honor award 1998, AIA/PIA award 2000, Louise Bethune award 2000, ASLA award 2001, 2 Nat. Honor awards 2005); mem.: Nat. Soc. Landscape Artists (Mayo Woodlands award 2004, Jackson Meadow award 2001). Home and Office: Salmelaarchitect 630 W 4th St Duluth MN 55806 Office Phone: 218-724-7517. E-mail: ddsalmela@charter.net.

SALMEN, CHARLES R., medical research scholar; Student, Am. Univ., Cairo, 2004; BA in English, Duke Univ., 2007; MSc. student in Med. Anthropology, Oxford Univ., 2007—. Contbr. articles to Jour. Urology. Vol. Big Brothers, Big Sisters, Durham, NC, 2003—07. Rhodes Scholar. Jewish. Achievements include organizing Peace or Pieces, an Arab-Jewish Student Coalition, 2006. Avocations: photography, running. *

SALMI, MIKA, information technology executive; b. Finland; BA, U. Wis.; MBA, INSEAD, France. Founder AtomFilms, San Francisco, 1998—2001; CEO Atom Entertainment, Inc., San Francisco, 2001—06; pres. global digital media MTV Networks, 2006—. Office: MTV Networks 1515 Broadway New York NY 10036 Office Phone: 212-258-8000. Office Fax: 212-258-8100.

SALMINEN, JOHN THEODORE, artist, educator; b. Mpls., Jan. 18, 1945; s. Theodore and Eloise Achterhof Salminen; m. Kathleen Jean Whalen, June 15, 1968; children: Nathan, Eric. BS in Art Edn., U. Minn., Duluth, 1968, M in Art Edn., 1974. Art tchr. Duluth Pub. Schs., 1968—2001. Fulbright art exch. tchr., Edinburgh, 1984—85; guest lectr. U. Minn., Duluth, 2005—; judge and juror various watercolor and fine arts orgns. and socs.; presenter and lectr. in field. Book, Expressing The Visual Language of the Landscape, International Artist, painting, Battery Park II (First Pl. award Exptl. Category, Artist's Mag. Internat. Competition, 2000), numerous nat. and internat. exhbns.; contbr. articles to profl. jours. Co-founder Lake Superior Watercolor Soc., Duluth, 1984. Recipient Best of Show, Georgetown Internat. Art Exhbn., 1998, First Pl. award, New Eng. Watercolor Soc. N.Am. Open Exhbn., 2002, Watercolor West Nat. Exhbn., 2005, Watercolor Art Soc. Houston 25th Internat. Exhbn., 2006, many others; Marie Walsh Sharpe Artist's grantee Tchr./Artist Program, Marie Walsh Sharpe Found., 1995, Sylvan Grouse fellow, Pa. Watercolor Soc., 2002. Master: Transparent Watercolor Soc. Am. (life; nominating chair 2000—05); fellow: Am. Watercolor Soc. (dir. 2002—04, Dolphin fellow 1998, Gold medal internat. exhbn. 2006, Invited Presenter award 2006); mem.: Nat. Watercolor Soc. (acquisition chairperson bldg. fund 2006—, Silver Star award internat. exhbn. 2005). Avocations: reading, travel, fishing, jazz. Home and Office: 6021 Arnold Rd Duluth MN 55803 Office Phone: 218-721-3319. E-mail: salminen@cpinternet.com.

SALMOIRAGHI, GIAN CARLO, physiologist, educator; b. Gorla Minore, Italy, Sept. 19, 1924; came to U.S., 1952, naturalized, 1958; s. Giuseppe Carlo and Dina (Rinetti) S.; m. Eva Tchoukourlieva, Dec. 5, 1970; 1 child, George Charles MD, U. Rome, 1948; PhD, McGill U., 1959; DSc (hon.), Hahnemann U., 1995. Sr. med. officer Internat. Refugee Orgn., Naples, Italy, 1949-52; research fellow Cleve. Clinic Found., 1952-55; lectr. dept. physiology McGill U., Montreal, Que., Canada, 1956-58; from neurophysiologist to dir., div. spl. mental health research NIMH, Washington, 1959-73; assoc. commr. research N.Y. State Dept. Mental Hygiene, Albany, 1973-77; assoc. dir. for research Nat. Inst. Alcohol Abuse, HHS, Bethesda, Md., 1977-84; prof. neurology and physiology Hahnemann U., Phila., 1984—94, vice provost for research affairs, 1984-85, chmn. dept. physiology, asst. v.p sci. affairs, 1986-94; clin. prof. psychiatry George Washington U., 1966-73. Contbr. articles to profl. jours. Recipient Superior Service award HEW, 1970 Fellow Am. Coll. Neuropsychopharmacology; mem. AAAS, Am. Physiol. Soc., Am. Soc. Pharmacology and Exptl. Therapeutics, Internat. Brain Research Orgn., Internat. Soc. Psychoneuroendocrinology, Am. Psychiat. Assn., Soc. Neurosci., Royal Soc. Medicine, Soc. Biol. Psychiat., Assn. Research Neurol. and Mental Disease, Research Soc. Alcoholism, Assn. Chmn. Dept. Physiology, Sci. Research Soc., Sigma Xi. Clubs: Cosmos (Washington). Home: 8216 Hamilton Spring Ct Bethesda MD 20817-2714 Personal E-mail: gsalmoiraghi@pol.net.

SALMON, DENIS R., lawyer; b. St. Paul, Sept. 20, 1951; BA magna cum laude, Hamline U., 1973; JD magna cum laude, U. Minn., 1976. Bar: Calif. 1976. Assoc. Brobeck, Phleger & Harrison, Palo Alto, Calif., 1976—83, ptnr., 1983—95; ptnr., co-chair intellectual property group Gibson Dunn & Crutcher LLP, Palo Alto, Calif., 1995—, and ptnr.-in-charge Palo Alto office. Mem.: ABA (litig. section), Fed. Cir. Bar Assn., State Bar of Calif. (intellectual property section), Am. Intellectual Property Law Assn. Office: Gibson Dunn & Crutcher LLP 1881 Page Mill Rd Palo Alto CA 94304 Office Phone: 650-849-5301. Office Fax: 650-849-5001. Business E-Mail: dsalmon@gibsondunn.com.

SALMON, EDWARD DICKINSON, cell biologist, educator; BS, Brown U., 1967; PhD, U. Pa., 1973. Mem. faculty to James Larkin and Iona Mae Ballou disting. prof. cell biology U. NC, Chapel Hill, 1976—. Mem. sci. adv. bd. U. Wash. Ctr. Cell Dynamics. Contbr. articles to profl. jours.; assoc. editor: Molecular Biology of the Cell. Fellow: Am. Acad. Arts & Scis. Office: Dept Biology U NC CB 3280 Coker Hall Chapel Hill NC 27599-3280 E-mail: tsalmon@email.unc.edu.

SALMON, EDWARD LLOYD, JR., bishop; b. Jan. 30, 1934; s. Edward Lloyd Sr. and Helen Bernice (Burley) S.; m. Louise Hack, 1972; children: Catherine, Edward III. BA, U. of the South, 1956; BD, Va. Theol. Seminary, 1960. Ordained to deaconate Episc. Ch., 1960, to priesthood, 1961. Vicar St. Andrew's Ch., Rogers, Ark., rector, 1963-68; vicar St. James Ch., Eureka Springs, Ark., St. Thomas Ch., Springdale, Grace Ch., Siloam Springs; assoc. St. Paul's Ch., Fayetteville, 1968, rector, 1968-78, Ch. St. Michael and St. George, St. Louis, 1978-90; elected bishop Diocese S.C., 1990—. Pres. province IV Episcopal Ch.; chmn. bd. dirs. Speak, Inc., The Anglican Digest, Voorhees Coll., Denmark, S.C.; trustee, regent Univ. of South; pres. Nashotah House Seminary; pres. Kanuga Confs., Inc.; chmn. Anglican Inst. Chmn. bd. trustees Voorhees Coll. Episcopalian. Office: PO Box 20127 Charleston SC 29413-0127 Home Phone: 843-723-3631; Office Phone: 843-722-4075. E-mail: elsalmon@dioceseofsc.org.

SALMON, JOSEPH THADDEUS, lawyer; b. Auburn, Ala., Nov. 13, 1927; s. William Davis and Helen (Bowman) S.; m. Mabel Marie Groves, July 7, 1951; children: Joseph Thaddeus Jr., Bruce Groves. BS, Auburn U., 1949; JD, U. Ala., 1951. Bar: Ala. 1951. Practice in, Montgomery, 1953-93; sec., gen. counsel Alfa Mut. Ins. Co., Alfa Mut. Fire Ins. Co., Alfa Mut. Gen. Ins. Co., Alfa Corp., Alfa Ins. Corp., Alfa Gen. Ins. Corp., Alfa Life Ins. Co.; ret., 1993. Served with USNR, 1946-47; to 1st lt. USAF, 1951-53. Mem. Internat. Assn. Def. Counsel, Ala. Def. Lawyers Assn., Montgomery County Bar Assn., Phi Alpha Delta, Kappa Sigma. Episcopalian. Home: 2731 Lansdowne Dr Montgomery AL 36111-1741

SALMON, MARLA E., nursing educator, dean; b. Vermillion, SD, May 2, 1949; d. Everett Lloyd and Marceline Louise (Adamson) Salmon; m. Jerry Steven Anderson, Aug. 1, 1984; children: Jessica Louise White, Matthew Lawrence White. BA cum laude, U. Portland, 1971, BSN cum laude, 1972; MSN, 1999; ScD, Johns Hopkins U., 1977; DSc (hon.), UNMC, 2003. Dir. patient advocacy program Johns Hopkins U., Balt., 1974-75, instr., 1975-78; asst. prof. U. Minn., Mpls., 1978-82, asst. dir. PRONA, 1978-79, acting dir. PRONA, 1978-80, dir. pub. health nursing programs, 1980-85, assoc. prof., 1982-86; prof. pub. health nursing, chmn. dept. U. N.C., Chapel Hill, 1986-92; dir. nursing div., Bureau Health Professions HHS, Rockville, 1991-97; prof., dean Grad. Sch. Nursing U. Pa., Phila., 1997-99, dir. grad. studies; dean, prof. Nell Hodgson Woodruff Sch. Nursing Emory U., Atlanta, 1999—. Cons. in field. Co-editor: News Outlook, 1989—91; contbr. articles to profl. jours. Trustee Robert Wood Johnson Found., 2002—; mem. Presdl. Task Force Health Care Reform, Washington, 1993; U.S. del. WHO, Geneva, 1995. Recipient Recognition award, Assn. State Territorial Dirs. Nursing, 1993, Achievement award, Nat. Black Nurses Found., 1994, Presdl. award for Meritorious Exec., The White House, 1995; Fulbright scholar, 1972—73, W. K. Kellogg fellow, 1984—87, Reflective Leadership fellow, 1985—86, Rsch. grantee, 1975—78. Mem.: APHA, ANA (v.p. coun. cmty. health nursing 1988—, mem. task froce credentialing 1989), Women's Health Leadership Trust, Assn. Cmty. Healgh Nurses Educators, N.C. Nurses Assn., N.C. Pub. Health Assn., N.C. League Nursing, Nat. League Nursing, Am. Tae Kwon Do Assn., Am. Acad. Nursing, Sigma Xi, Delta Omega, Sigma Theta Tau. Avocations: athletics, gardening. Office: Emory U Nell Hodgson Woodruff Sch 1520 Clifton Rd Ste 402 Atlanta GA 30322-4207 Office Phone: 404-727-7976. Business E-Mail: msalmon@emory.edu.

SALMON, MATT, former congressman, communications company executive; b. Salt Lake City, Jan. 21, 1958; s. Robert James and Gloria (Aagard) S.; m. Nancy Huish, June, 1979; children: Lara, Jacob, Katie, Matthew. BA in English Lit., Ariz. State U., 1981; MA in Pub. Adminstrn., Brigham Young U., 1986. Mgr. pub. affairs U.S. West, Phoenix, 1988-94; mem. Ariz. State Senate, Mesa, 1990-94, U.S. Congress from 1st Ariz. dist., Washington, 1995-2001; mem. internat. rels. and sci. coms., asst. major whip; exec. v.p. APCO Worldwide, Scottsdale, Ariz., 2001—; chmn. Ariz. State Republican Party, 2006—. Bd. dirs. Mesa United Way, 1990—, Ariz. Sci. Mus., 1992—. Recipient Outstanding Svc. award Ariz. Citizens with Disabilities, 1991, Excellence in Govt. award Tempe Ctr. for Handicapped, 1992; named Outstanding Young Phoenician, Phelps Dodge/Phoenix Jaycees, 1990, Outstanding Legislator, Mesa United Way, 1991. Republican. Mem. Lds Ch. Avocations: tennis, racquetball, bicycling. Office: 3501 N 24th St Phoenix AZ 85016 *

SALMON, THOMAS P., musician; b. Oct. 30, 1964; BA, Berklee Coll. Music, Boston, 1986. Ch. organist, choir dir. various chs., Pa., 1990—2006; pvt. music tchr. Henryville, Pa., 1990—2003. Choir dir. Chorus of Poconos, Scotrun, Pa., 2001—06. Mem.: Am. Guild Organists (Northeast Pa. chpt. 2004—06), Barbershop Harmony Soc. (dir. Stroudsburg, Pa. chpt. 2002—06). Home: RR 1 Box 1657 Henryville PA 18332-9115

SALMON, WILLIAM COOPER, mechanical engineer, company executive; b. NYC, Sept. 3, 1935; s. Chenery and Mary (Cooper) S.; m. Josephine Stone, Sept. 16, 1967; children: William Cooper Jr., Mary Bradford, Pauline Alexandra. SB in Mech. Engring., MIT, 1957, SM in Mech. Engring., 1958, Mech. Engr., 1959, SM in Mgmt. Sci., 1969. Registered profl. engr., Mass. Sr. engr. Microtech, Cambridge, 1959—60; 1st lt. US Army Ord. C., Aberdeen, Md., 1960; asst. sci. adv. US Dept. State, Washington, 1961—74, sr. adv. sci. and tech., 1978—86; counselor sci. and tech. Am. Embassy, Paris, 1974—78; exec. officer NAE, Washington, 1986—99, exec. officer emeritus, adv. to pres., 1999—2001; sec., treas. Internat. Coun. Academies Engring. and Technol. Scis., Inc., 2000—. Interim exec. dir. Am. Assn. Engring. Soc., 2005—. Recipient Superior Honor award Dept. State, 1984, Meritorious Svc. award Pres. US, 1968, Kenneth A. Roe award Am. Assn. Engring. Socs., 1996, Chair's award, 2006; Sloan fellow MIT, 1969. Fellow: ASME; mem.: NSPE, Nat. Soc. Sons Colonial New Eng., Jr. Engring. Tech. Soc. (pres. 1998—2001), Mil. Order Loyal Legion of US, Soc. Colonial Wars, Cosmos Club, Masons. Episcopalian. Home and Office: 3601 N Peary St Arlington VA 22207-5345 Office Phone: 703-527-5782. Office Fax: 703-526-0570. E-mail: wsalmon@nae.edu, caets@nae.edu. *

SALOM, ROBERTO, retired finance company executive; b. Bogota, Colombia, July 12, 1944; arrived in US, 1966; m. Estell Kathleen Millard; children: David Andres, Robert W.A. Student, U. Andes, Bogota, 1965; BS, San Francisco State U., 1969, MBA, 1972; postgrad., U. Calif., Berkeley, 1973; PhD in Econs., NYU, 1977. Rsch. assoc. Fed. Res. Bank San Francisco, 1968-70, fin. analyst, 1970-73; mem. staff UN Devel. Program/Fund for Population Activities, NYC, 1973-82, dep. chief program planning, 1982-83, dep. chief fin. br., 1983-87, chief fin. br., 1987-94; sr. officer UN Adv. Com. on Adminstrv. and Budgetary Questions, 1995—2005; ret., 2005. Cons., presenter in field.

SALOMAN, SYD ADAM, lawyer; b. Boston, May 30, 1974; s. Richard S. and Joni J. Saloman. JD, Suffolk U., Boston, 1999. Bar: Mass. 1999, R.I. 1999. Atty. Tucker, Heifetz & Saltzman, LLP, Boston, 2006—. Home: PO Box 650122 West Newton MA 02465 Office: Tucker Heifetz & Saltzman LLP 100 Franklin St Boston MA 02210 Office Phone: 617-557-9696. Business E-Mail: saloman@ths-law.com.

SALOMON, RICHARD E., investment company executive; s. Richard and Edna (Barnes) Salomon; m. Laura Landro. BA, Yale Univ., 1964; MBA, Columbia Univ., 1967. Pres. & mng. dir. Spears Beznak Salomon & Farrell, 1982—2000; pres. Mecox Ventures, NYC, 2000—. Sr. adv. to David Rockefeller; chmn. adv. bd. Blackstone Alternative Asset Mgmt.; dir. Boston Properties. Vice chmn. Mus. Modern Art, NYC; trustee & chmn. investment com. Rockefeller Univ., NYC; trustee N.Y. Public Libr., Alfred P. Sloan Found. Mem.: Council on Fgn. Rels. (dir. & mem. investment com.). Office: Mecox Ventures 610 5th Ave New York NY 10020

SALOMON, ROGER BLAINE, retired language educator; b. Providence, Feb. 26, 1928; s. Henry and Lucia Angell (Capwell) S.; m. Elizabeth Helen Lowenstein, June 14, 1950; children: Pamela, Wendy. BA, Harvard, 1950; MA, U. Calif., Berkeley, 1951, PhD, 1957. Instr. Mills Coll., Oakland, Calif., 1955-57; instr., then asst. prof. Yale U., New Haven, 1957-66; mem. faculty Case Western Res. U., Cleve., 1966—, prof. English, 1969—, Oviatt prof. English, 1990, chmn. dept., 1974-80, part-time prof. English, 1994-99; Oviatt prof. English emeritus, 1999—. Mem. adv. screening com. Am. lit. Sr. Fulbright-Hayes Program, 1973-76, chmn., 1975; mem. grants-in-aid selection com. Am. Council Learned Socs., 1976-78 Author: Twain and the Image of History, 1961, Desperate Storytelling: Post-Romantic Elaborations of the Mock-Heroic Mode, 1987, Mazes of the Serpent: An Anatomy of Horror Narrative, 2002. Served to 1st lt. USAF, 1952-53. Morse fellow, 1960-61; Guggenheim fellow, 1972-73 Mem. AAUP, MLA. Home: 2830 Coventry Rd Cleveland OH 44120-2231 Office Phone: 216-368-2340.

SALOMONSON, VINCENT VICTOR, meteorologist, educator; b. Longmont, Colo., July 19, 1937; s. Victor Philip and Eunice Cole Salomonson; m. Peggy Lucille Swanner, Feb. 11, 1944; children: Scott Houston, Aaron Phillip, Sarah McBride, Karla Canning, Carol Marie. BS in Agrl. Engring., Colo. State U., Ft. Collins, Colo., 1959; BS in Meteorology, U. Utah, Salt Lake City, Utah, 1960; MS in Agrl. Engring., Cornell U., Ithaca, NY, 1964; PhD, Colo. State U., Ft. Collins, Colo., 1968. Weather officer USAF, Washington, 1959—62; from rsch. meteorologist Goddard Space Flight Ctr. to sr. scientist NASA, Greenbelt, Md., 1962—2001, sr. scientist earth scis. directorate Goddard Space Flight Ctr., 2001—05; rsch. prof. U. Utah, Salt Lake City, 2005—. Contbr. over 130 articles to profl. jours. Bishop LDS Ch., Bowie, Md. 1st lt. USAF, 1959—62. Named Meritorious Exec., Sr. Exec. Svc., U.S. Govt., 1993, Disting. Exec. Sr. Exec. Svc., 1998; recipient Exceptional Sci. Achievement medal, NASA, 1976, 1983, William T. Pecora award, NASA and U.S. Geol. Survey, 1987, Honor Alumnus award, Colo. State U., 1987, William Nordberg award, NASA Goddard Space Flight Ctr., 2002; Goddard Sr. fellow, 2002. Fellow: IEEE (mem. com. 1980—87, Disting. Achievement award 1998), Am. Soc. Photogrammetry and Remote Sensing (pres. 1991—92). Mem. Lds Ch. Office: University of Utah 135 S 1460 E Rm 809 Salt Lake City UT 84112-0110 Home Phone: 801-253-6195; Office Phone: 801-585-9492. Office Fax: 801-585-3681. Personal E-mail: vincesalomonson@msn.com. Business E-Mail: vincent.v.salomonson@nasa.gov.

SALONEN, ESA-PEKKA, conductor, music director; b. Helsinki, Finland, June 30, 1958; married; 3 children. Student, Sibelius Acad., Helsinki; studied Composition, Rautavaara; studied Conducting, Panula. Prin. guest condr. Oslo Philharm. Orch., 1985—90, Philharmonia Orch., London, 1985—94; prin. condr. Swedish Radio Symphony Orch., 1985—95; artistic advisor Stockholm Chamber Orch., 1986—; music director LA Philharm. Orch., 1992—; Walt and Lilly Disney chair L.A. Philharm. Orch., 1992—; artistic dir. Helsinki Festival, 1995—96. Guest condr. London Orch., Berlin Orch., Paris Orch., LA Orch., Phila. Orch. Named Musician of Yr., Musical Am., 2006; recipient Opera award, Royal Philharm. Soc., 1995, Conductor award, 1997, Litteris et Artibus medal, Sweden, 1996, Officier Ordre des Arts et des Lettres, France. also: Los Angeles Philharm Orch 151 S Grand Ave Los Angeles CA 90012-3013 Office: Columbia Artists Management Llc 1790 Broadway # 6 New York NY 10019-1412 *

SALONGA, LEA, actress, singer; b. Manila, Feb. 22, 1971; d. Feliciano Genuino and Maria Ligaya (Imutan) Salonga; m. Robert Charles Chien, Jan. 10, 2004. Attended, Ateneo De Manila U., 1988-89. Actress, singer The King and I, Manila, 1978, Annie, Manila, 1980, The Rose Tattoo, Manila, 1980, The Bad Seed, Manila, 1981, The Goodbye Girl, Manila, 1982, Paper Moon, Manila, 1983, The Fantasticks, Manila, 1988, Miss Saigon, London, 1989-90 (Outstanding Performance by Actress in Musical Olivier award 1990), Broadway, 1991-92 (Best Actress in Musical Tony award 1991, Best Actress in Musical Drama Desk award 1991, Best Actress in Musical Outer Critics Circle award 1991, Outstanding Debut Theatre World award 1991), Les Miserables, Broadway, 1993 & 2007, My Fair Lady, Manila, 1994, Into the Woods, Singapore, 1994, Les Miserables, London, 1996, 3rd nat. tour, 1996, also The Sound of Music, Manila, Fiddler on the Roof, Manila, Cat on a Hot Tin Roof, Flower Drum Song, 2002; Philippine films include Bakit Labis Kitang Mahal?, Dear Diary, Pik Pak Boom, Captain Barbell, Ninja Kids, Like Father, Like Son, Tropang Bulilit; Philippine TV: (host) Kulit Bulilit, Love Lea, Naku, Ha!, Sunday Special, Iba Ito!, That's Entertainment!, This is It!, (co-host) Patok Na Patok!; opening act for Stevie Wonder, Menudo; concerts: The Filipinos of Miss Saigon, A Miss Called Lea, Lea Salonga in Concert, L.A., San Francisco, Les Miserables 10th Anniversary Concert, London, 1995; recs. include Small Voice, 1981 (gold record), Lea, Happy Children's Club, Christmas Album, We are the World, (debut album) Lea Salonga, 1993, Miss Saigon original London cast rec. (gold record), The King and I, Aladdin, 1992 (singing voice Princess Jasmine, motion picture soundtrack), Les Miserables 10th Anniversary Concert Album, 1996, Royal Couyabyab: The Silver Album, 1996, The Little Tramp, (singing voice) Mulan, 1998, (Broadway) Flower Drum Song, 2002; TV films include: Redwood Curtain, 1998, (TV series) As the World Turns, 2001, 03; concert, Carnegie Hall, 2005. Recipient AWIT award outstanding svc. Philippings Recording Industry, 1993, ASEAN Industry award performing arts, 1992, Ten Outstanding Young Men award outstanding debut, 1991, AWIT award outstanding performer, 1990, Presdl. Award of Merit Pres. Aquino, 1990, Laurence Olivier award best actress musical, 1990, Cecil award best recording by a child, 1984, Tinig award one of 10 outstanding singers, 1983, 94, 92, ALIW award best child performer, 1980, 81, 82; named Outstanding Manilan by Govt. City of Manila, 1990. Mem.: Screen Actors' Guild, Actors' Equity Assn., AFTRA. Roman Catholic. Avocations: music, reading, collecting raised-trunk elephants, collecting swatches, working on computers. Office: c/o Jeff Hunter 1325 Avenue Of The Americas New York NY 10019-6026 *

SALOPEK, PAUL F., news correspondent; b. Barstow, Calif., Feb. 9, 1962; m. Linda Lynch. BS in environ. biology, U. Calif., Santa Barbara, 1984. Local newspaper reporter, Roswell, N.Mex., 1985—90; bur. chief Gannett News Svc., Mexico City, 1990; reporter El Paso (Tex.) Times; writer Nat. Geographic, 1992—95; fgn. corr. Chgo. Tribune, 1996—. Recipient Pulitzer Prize for Explanatory Reporting, 1998, Pulitzer Prize for Internat. Reporting, 2001, Bob Considine award, Overseas Press Club, 2007. Office: Chgo Tribune 435 N Michigan Ave Chicago IL 60611 *

SALOTTI, KATHRYN E., marriage and family therapist; d. Peter Arthur Floros and Henrietta Judith Albers; m. Richard Vincent Salotti, June 28, 1969; 1 child, Cara Dominique; m. Thomas Lee Moreland (div.); 1 child, Thomas Michael. AA, Pierce Jr. Coll., Calif., 1980; BA in Sociology summa cum laude, Calif. State U., Northridge, 1983, M in Ednl. Psychology, 1986. Lic. marriage and family therapist Calif. Bd. Behavioral Sci., 1989. Marriage and family therapist intern Exceptional Children's Found., Van Nuys, Calif., 1986—87, Tarzana Treatment Ctr., Calif., 1988—89; rschr., writer, editor, tchr. Gerry Grossman Seminars, Santa Monica, Calif., 1989—90; family therapist Crestwood Manor, San Jose, 1990—93; family therapist, treatment coord. Oakview Youth, Santa Barbara, 1993—94; program dir. Sanctuary Psychiatric of Santa Barbara, 1994—98, County of Santa Barbara Children's Svcs., 1998—. Recipient Academic Excellence award, Phi Kappa Phi, 1983. Mem.: Calif. Assn. of Marriage and Family Therapists. Republican. Avocations: writing, genealogy, dance, reading. Home: 1102 Bel Air Dr Santa Barbara CA 93105 Personal E-mail: katcardi_8@msn.com.

SALPETER, ALAN N., lawyer; b. Phila., Oct. 7, 1947; BA with honors, Am. U., 1969; JD, Villanova U., 1972. Bar: Ill. 1972, US Dist. Ct. (no. dist. Ill.) 1972, US Ct. Appeals (5th cir.) 1977, US Ct. Appeals (7th cir.) 1974, US Ct. Appeals (8th cir.) 1981, US Ct. Appeals (11th cir.) 1985, US Ct. Appeals (DC cir.) 1991, US Ct. Appeals (10th cir.) 1998. Assoc. Mayer, Brown & Platt, Chgo., 1972—79; ptnr. Mayer, Brown, Rowe & Maw, Chgo., 1979—2007, LeBoeuf, Lamb, Greene and MacRae LLP, Chgo., 2007—. Adj. prof. Northwestern Law Sch.; lectr. in field. Mng. editor Law Rev., Villanova U.; author in field. Mem. ABA, Chgo. Bar Assn., Chgo. Coun. Lawyers, 7th Cir. Bar Assn. (bd. gov.). Office: LeBoeuf Lamb Greene & MacRae LLP Two Prudential Plaza 180 N Stetson Ave Ste 3700 Chicago IL 60601 Office Phone: 312-794-8088. Business E-Mail: asalpeter@llgm.com.

SALPETER, EDWIN ERNEST, physical sciences educator; b. Vienna, Dec. 3, 1924; came to U.S., 1949, naturalized, 1953; s. Jakob L. and Frieder (Horn) S.; m. Miriam Mark, June 11, 1950 (dec. 2001); children: Judy Gail, Shelley Ruth; m. Antonia L. Shouse, 2004. MS, Sydney U., 1946; PhD, Birmingham U., Eng., 1948; DSc, U. Chgo., 1969, Case-Western Reserve U., 1970, U. Sydney, 1994, U. New South Wales, Sydney, 1996. Research fellow Birmingham U., 1948-49; faculty Cornell U., Ithaca, NY, 1949-97, now J.G. White prof. phys. scis. emeritus. Mem. U.S. Nat. Sci. Bd., 1979-85 Author: Quantum Mechanics, 1957, 77; mem. editorial bd. Astrophys. Jour, 1966-69; assoc. editor Rev. Modern Physics, 1971-92; contbr. articles to profl. jours. Mem. AURA bd., 1970-72. Recipient Gold medal Royal Astron. Soc., 1973, J.R. Oppenheimer Meml. prize U. Miami, 1974, C. Bruce medal Astron. Soc. Pacific, 1987, A. Devaucouleurs medal, 1992, Dirac Meml. medal U. New South Wales, 1996, Crafoord laureate Royal Swedish Acad. Scis., 1997, H. A. Bethe Prize, Am. Phys. Soc., 1999. Mem. NAS, Am. Astron. Soc. (v.p. 1971-73), Am. Philos. Soc., Am. Acad. Arts and Scis., The Royal Soc. (fgn.), Australian Acad. Sci., Deutsche Akademie Leopoldina. Home: 116 Westbourne Ln Ithaca NY 14850-2414 Office: Cornell U 614 Space Science Bldg Ithaca NY 14853-6801 E-mail: ees12@cornell.edu.

SALPETER, SHELLEY, medical educator; d. Edwin and Miriam Salpeter; children: Nicholas Salpeter Buckley, Jacob Salpeter Buckley. MD, U. Calif., San Francisco, 1982. Clin. prof. medicine Stanford U., Sch. Medicine, Stanford, Calif., 1987—. Dir. medicine consultation svcs. Santa Clara Valley Med. Ctr., San Jose, Calif., 1990—. Achievements include research in evidence-based medicine.

SALSBERG, ARTHUR PHILIP, publishing executive; b. Bklyn., Aug. 28, 1929; s. Solomon William and Rae (Miller) S.; m. Rhoda Gelb, Sept. 11, 1960; children: Charles Martin, Solomon William. BBA, CCNY, 1951. Mng. editor Ojibway Press, NYC, 1957-64; advt. and promotion mgr. RCA Corp., Harrison, NJ, 1965-67; editor N.Am. Pub. Co., Phila., 1967-70; v.p., gen. mgr. Lawyers World, Inc., Phila., 1970-72; editorial dir. Ziff-Davis Pub. Co., NYC, 1973-83; editor, assoc. pub. CQ Communications, Inc., Hicksville, NY, 1984—. Mag. and newspaper pub. cons.; electronics instr.; local campaign publicist, speech writer for town mayor, town coun., libr. bd., sch. bd. Author: Complete Book of Video Games, 1977, Collier's Ency. Yearbook, 1977, 78, 79, 80, 81, 82, First Book of Modern Electronics Fun Projects, 1986, Second Book of Modern Electronics Fun Projects, 1986; editor: Audio Mag, 1967-70, Lawyers World, 1970-72, Popular Electronics, 1973-83, Comm. Handbook, 1973-83, Stereo Directory, 1973-83, Tape Recorder Directory, 1973-83, Citizens Band Handbook, 1976-83, Invitation to Electronics, 1972-83, Modern Electronics, 1984-91, Computer Craft, 1992-93, MicroComputer Jour., 1994-96; assoc. pub.: Amateur Radio Equipment Buyers Guide, 1988, 89, 90, 91, 92, Amateur Radio Antenna Buyers Guide, 1989, 90, 91-92. Publicity chmn. Nassau coun. Boy Scouts Am., 1975; mem. adv. com. Bramson OR Tech. Inst., 1975. With AUS, 1951-53, Korea. Recipient Indsl. Mktg. Mag. award, 1959 Home: 7844 Lexington Club Blvd Apt A Delray Beach FL 33446-3426

SALSBURY, MICHAEL H., lawyer; b. Stamford, Conn., Dec. 12, 1949; AB, Dartmouth Coll., 1971; MBA, JD, U. Va., 1975. Bar: D.C. 1975. Mng.ptnr. Jenner & Block, Balt.; exec. v.p. & gen. coun. MCI, 1995—2003; ptnr. Chadbourne & Parke LLP, Washington, 2004—. Office: Chadbourne & Parke LLP 1200 New Hampshire Ave NW Washington DC 20036 E-mail: msalsbury@chadbourne.com.

SALSER, SCOTT A., music educator; b. Oil City, Pa., June 9, 1962; m. Karen Kreiner, July 11, 1992. BS in Music Edn., Indiana U. of Pa., 1984; MEd in Music Edn., Pa. State U., University Park, 1997. Vocal music tchr. State College (Pa.) Area Sch. Dist., 1984—87; choral dir. East Stroudsburg (Pa.) HS, 1987—91, Indiana (Pa.) HS, 1991—. Mem., soloist Bach Choir of Pitts., 2004—06, asst. dir., 2005—06; guest condr. various county chorus festivals, Pa. Mem.: Am. Choral Dir.'s Assn. (chmn. repertoire and stds. com. 2000—01), Pa. Music Educator's Assn. (chmn. choral policy 2005—). Methodist. Avocations: travel, piano, gardening, church activities. Office: Indiana Sr HS 450 N 5th St Indiana PA 15701

SALT, ALFRED LEWIS, priest; b. Hackensack, NJ, Apr. 30, 1927; s. Alfred John and Lily (Tittle) S.; m. Elizabeth May Loveland, June 18, 1949; children: Richard John, Michael Rob, Christopher William, Katharine Anne. BA with honors, Bishop's U., Lennoxville, Can., 1949, MA in History, 1951, BD, 1960; grad. advanced mgmt. program, Harvard U., 1970; D Ministry, Grad. Theol. Found., 1988. Ordained to ministry Episcopal Ch. as deacon, 1951, as priest, 1952. Incumbent St. Philip's, Sawyerville, Que., Canada, 1951—52, St. John the Evangelist, Portneuf, Que., 1952—54; rector Christ Ch., Stanstead, Que., 1954—62, St. Michael's Ch., Sillery, Que., 1962—72, All Saints Ch., Millington, NJ, 1972—93; hon. asst. Grace Ch., Port Huron, Mich., 1993—98, Trinity Ch., Lexington, Mich., 1998—2001, St. Monica's Ch., Naples, Fla., 2002—03, St. John's Ch., Naples, 2004—06, St. Mary's, Bonita Springs, Fla., 2007—. Bishop's chaplain Diocese of Que., 1962, hon. canon, 1970; pres. Morris Convocation. Morris County, N.J., 1974-78, retreat condr., 1979—; with Victorious Ministry Through Christ, Orlando, Fla., 1981-92, dir., 1986-92, v.p., 1989-92; dir. VMTC Can., 1995-2002. Author: Compass Book on Healing, 1996; contbr. articles to religious jour. Mem. Superior Coun. Edn., Que., 1964-70; commr. Que. Protestant Sch. Bd., 1970-72; trustee Heath Village, Hackettstown, N.J., 1974-76; mem. Passaic Twp. Welfare Bd., Millington, 1977-78, 82. With USAAC Res., 1944-45; with USN, 1945-46. Mem. Naples Deanery Clericus, Order St. Luke (chaplain), Harvard Club of Naples, Worker Sisters of Holy Spirit, Worker Brothers of Holy Spirit. Home (Summer): 190 Chemin Du Lac North Hatley QE J0B 2C0 Canada Personal E-mail: alemsalt@comcast.net. *The more I come to know Jesus, the more I come to know myself. The more I submit myself to Him, the less I depend upon myself.*

SALTARELLI, MICHAEL A., priest; b. Jersey City, Jan. 17, 1933; s. Angelo Michael and Caroline (Marzitello) Saltarelli. BA, Seton Hall U., 1956; MA, Manhattan Coll., 1975. Ordained to ministry Cath. Ch., 1960. Assoc. pastor Holy Family Ch., Nutley, NJ, 1960—77; pastor Our Lady of Assumption, Bayonne, 1977—82; exec. dir. Archdiocesan Pastoral Svcs., Newark, 1982—85; pastor St. Catherine Of Siena Ch., Cedar Grove, 1985—90; aux. bishop Archdiocese of Newark, 1990—96; bishop Diocese of Wilmington, Del., 1996—. Vicar for priests Archdiocese of Newark, 1987—96. Office: 1925 Delaware Ave Ste 1-a Wilmington DE 19806-2301

SALTER, EDWIN CARROLL, retired pediatrician; b. Oklahoma City, Jan. 19, 1927; s. Leslie Ernest and Maud (Carroll) S.; m. Ellen Gertrude Malone, June 30, 1962; children: Mary Susanna, David Patrick BA, DePauw U., 1947; MD, Northwestern U., 1951. Intern Cook County Hosp., Chgo., 1951-53; resident in pediatrics Children's Meml. Hosp., Chgo., 1956-58, Cook County Hosp., Chgo., 1956-58; practice medicine specializing in pediatrics Lake Forest, Ill., 1958-97; attending physician Lake Forest Hosp., 1958—97, pres. med. staff, 1981-82. Attending physician Children's Meml. Hosp., Chgo.; clin. faculty mem. dept. pediatrics Northwestern U. Med. Sch. Served to capt. M.C., U.S. Army, 1954-56 Mem. AMA, Ill. State Med. Soc., Lake County Med. Soc. (pres. 1984), Phi Beta Kappa Republican. Methodist. Home: 19 N Maywood Rd Lake Forest IL 60045-3233

SALTER, JAMES, writer; b. Passaic, NJ, June 10, 1925; m. Ann Altemus, June 6, 1951 (div. 1976); children: Allan Conard, Nina Tobe, Claude Cray, James Owen; m. Kay Eldredge; 1 child, Theo Shaw. BS, USMA, 1945; M in Internat. Affairs, Georgetown U., 1950. Author: The Hunters, 1957, The Arm of Flesh, 1961, A Sport and a Pastime, 1967, Light Years, 1976, Solo Faces, 1981, Dusk and Other Stories, 1989 (Pen, Faulkner prize 1989), Burning the Days, 1997, Cassada, 2001, Gods of Tin: The Flying Years, 2004, Last Night, 2005, There and Then: The Travel Writing of James Salter, 2006; Co-Author (with Kay Salter) Life is Meals, 2006. Lt. Col. USAF, 1960. Recipient, Edith Wharton Prize, NY State Author, 1998—, English Speaking Union Prize, Pen/West Prize, John Steinbeck Prize. Office: ICM Literary 40 W 57th St New York NY 10019

SALTER, KEVIN THORNTON, lawyer; b. NYC, Oct. 21, 1947; s. Hershel Fletcher and Elizabeth (Thornton) S.; m. Eleanor Raftery, Aug. 28, 1982. BA, Iona Coll., 1973; JD, St. John's U., 1977. Bar: N.Y. 1978, U.S. Dist. Ct. (so. and ea. dists.) N.Y., 1978. Atty. Nat. Coun. on Compensation Ins., NYC, 1978-80; coun. James G. Barron, NYC, 1980-81; assoc. St. Regis Paper Co./ Champion Internat., NYC and Stamford, Conn., 1981-88; sr. ptnr. Kroll & Tract, NYC, 1988-94; ptnr. Peterson & Ross, NYC, 1994-98, Querrey & Harrow, 1998—2005, Bolan, Jahnsen, Salter & Sachs, 2006—. With US Army, Korea, 1967-69. Mem.: N.Y. State Bar Assn. Office: Bolan Jahnsen Salter & Sachs 1 Liberty Plz New York NY 10006 Office Phone: 212-201-6825. E-mail: ksalter@bjsslaw.com.

SALTER, LESTER HERBERT, lawyer; b. Waterbury, Conn., Apr. 26, 1918; s. Nathan M. and Eva G. (Levy) S.; m. Nina P. Scheftel, Sept. 15, 1951; 1 child, Ellen Lee. BS in Econs, U. Pa., 1940, LLB, 1948. Bar: RI 1948. Trial atty. Office of Chief Counsel, IRS, Newark and Boston, 1949-53; pvt. practice Providence, 1953-57; partner Salter & McGowan, Providence, 1957-70, Salter, McGowan, Arcaro & Swartz, Providence, 1970-74; pres. Salter, McGowan, Swartz & Holden, Inc., Providence, 1974-95, Salter, McGowan & Swartz, Inc., Providence, 1995-97, Salter, McGowan, Swartz & Sylvia, Inc., Providence, 1997-99, Salter, McGowan, Sylvia & Leonard, Inc., Providence, 2000—. Lectr. Northeastern U., 1955-56; chmn. U. RI Fed. Tax Inst., 1972-77; chmn. disciplinary bd. Supreme Ct., RI, 1975-81; mem. RI Adv. Commn. Jud. Appts., 1978-82, ethics adv. panel Supreme Ct., RI, 1987-92. Assoc. editor: RI Bar Jour., 1961-68. Served with F.A. AUS, 1941-46. Decorated Bronze Star. Fellow: ABA, Am. Bar Found; mem.: Am. Judicature Soc., New Eng. Bar Assn. (pres. 1996—97), Am. Law Inst. (life), R.I. Bar Assn. (pres. 1986—87), ABA (ho. of dels. 1987—2000, bd. govs. 1999—2000). Home: Apt 220 355 Blackstone Blvd Providence RI 02906-5413 Office: 321 S Main St Providence RI 02903-7108 Office Phone: 401-274-0300.

SALTER, MARY JO, poet; b. Grand Rapids, Mich., Aug. 15, 1954; d. Albert Gregory and Lormina (Paradise) S.; m. Brad Leithauser, 1980; children: Emily Salter, Hilary Garner. BA cum laude, Harvard U., 1976; MA, Cambridge U., 1978. Instr. Harvard U., 1978-79; instr. English conversation Japan, 1980-83; lectr. English Mt. Holyoke Coll., South Hadley, Mass., 1984—, Emily Dickinson sr. lectr. in humanities, 1995—2007; prof. writing seminars Johns Hopkins U., Balt., 2007—. Staff editor Atlantic Monthly, 1978-80; poet-in-residence Robert Frost Place, 1981; poetry editor The New Republic, 1992-95. Author: Henry Purcell in Japan, 1985, Unfinished Painting, 1989 (Lamont prize in poetry 1988), The Moon Comes Home, 1989, Sunday Skaters: Poems, 1994 (Nat. Book Critics Circle award nomination 1994), A Kiss in Space: Poems, 1999, Open Shutters: Poems, 2003; co-editor: Norton Anthology of Poetry, 5th edit., 2005; contbr. to periodicals including New Yorker, New Republic, Kenyon Rev. Amy Lowell scholar, 1995; recipient Discovery prize Nation, 1983; Nat. Endowment for Arts fellow, 1983-84, Guggenheim fellow, 1993. Mem. Internat. P.E.N. Office: care Alfred A Knopf Inc 1745 Broadway New York NY 10019

SALTIEL, ALAN ROBERT, biochemist; b. New Brunswick, NJ, Nov. 29, 1953; s. Samuel Albert and Betty (Berg) S.; m. Swanna Elizabeth Cameron, May 30, 1981; children: Jason Ariel, Aren David, Jared Robert. AB, Duke U., 1975; PhD, U. N.C., 1980. Rsch. scientist Burroughs-Wellcome Co., Rsch. Triangle Pk., NY, 1980-84; asst. prof. Rockefeller U., NYC, 1984-90; dir. dept. signal transp. Parke-Davis/Warner-Lambert Co., Ann Arbor, 1990—2000; assoc. prof. U. Mich., Ann Arbor, 1990—94, adj. prof., 1994—2001, prof. medicine & physiology, 2001—, John Jacob Abel collegiate prof. life sciences, 2002—, dir. Life Sciences Inst., 2002—. Mem. sci. rev. Juvenile Diabetes Found., N.Y.C., 1988-91, Am. Diabetes Assn., Alexandria, Va., 1990—; diabetes adv. bd. N.Y. State Health Rsch. Coun., Albany, N.Y., 1986-90; scientific adv. bd. Quatrx; editorial bd. Molecular Medicine, Jour. Biological Chemistry, Jour. Clin. Investigation. Contbr. over 100 papers to profl. jours. Recipient New Investigator award NIH, 1984, Rsch. & Devel. award Am. Diabetes Assn., 1984, John Jacob Abel award Am. Soc. Pharm. & Exptl. Therapy, 1990; named Irma T. Hirschl scholar, 1986, Established Investigator, Am. Heart Assn., 1989. Mem. Am. Soc. Biochem. Molecular Biology, Am. Soc. Pharm. & Exptl. Therapy, Endocrine Soc., Harvey Soc., Am. Soc. Clin. Investigation (hon.), Inst. Medicine. Achievements include discovery of the structure of the second messenger of insulin action; rsch. in role of protein phosphorylation in Nerve Growth Factor action; biology of protein-lipid interactions; biology of lipoproteins; patents in field. Office: Life Sciences Inst U Mich 210 Washtenaw Ave Ann Arbor MI 48109-2216 Office Phone: 734-615-9787. Office Fax: 734-763-6492. E-mail: saltiel@umich.edu.

SALTMAN, ROBERT JON, physician, medical educator; b. Holyoke, Mass., Jan. 15, 1954; s. Zailike and Adelaide Saltman; m. Linda Carolynn Eichler; children: Julie, Jane, Zachary. BA, Yale U., 1976; MD, Washington U., 1980. Diplomate internal medicine Am. Bd. Internal Medicine, endocrinology and metabolism Am. Bd. Internal Medicine. Chief resident, instr. medicine Barnes Hosp./Washington U., St. Louis, 1985—86; physician Barnes Jewish Christian Med. Group, St. Louis, 1986—2001; co-ptnr. West County Med. Specialists, St. Louis, 2001—; assoc. prof. clin. medicine Washington U. Sch. Medicine, St. Louis, 2001—. Co-editor: Washington University School of Medicine Manual of Medical Therapeutics, 1986. Mem.: ACP, Internat. Soc. Clin. Densitometry, Endocrine Soc., Am. Diabetes Assn. Avocations: tennis, skiing, wine collecting. Office: West County Med Specialists Ste 145 969 Mason Rd Saint Louis MO 63141 Home Phone: 314-432-6844; Office Phone: 314-878-6008. Personal E-mail: rlsalt@aol.com.

SALTMARSH, SARA ELIZABETH, lawyer; b. Jacksonville, Fla., Nov. 15, 1956; d. Ernest Olmstead and Anne (Frankenberg) S. Student, Randolph-Macon Woman's Coll., 1974-76; BA in English with honors magna cum laude, Fla. State U., 1978; postgrad., Iowa State U., 1980-81; JD, U. Tex., 1986. Bar: Tex. 1987, Fla. 2004; cert. family law, Tex. Assoc. Ausley & Slaikeu, PC, Austin, Tex., 1987-90, Law Offices of Edwin J. Terry, Jr., Austin, 1990-92; pvt. practice Austin, 1992—2004, Ponte Vedra Beach, Jacksonville, Fla., 2004—. Security com. Travis County Commr.'s Ct., 1991-93; mem. Ctrl. Tex. Collaborative Law Family Practice Group, Inc., 2002-03. Editor: Reference Guide to Travis County Practice, 1991,

92, 93, 95, 96, 97. Bd. dirs. Faith Home for Children with AIDS, 1997-98. Givens Disting. scholar, 1974, Lyndon Baines Johnson Meml. scholar, 1976; recipient Am. Jur. award Wills and Estates, 1986, Marital Relations and Divorce, 1986. Fellow: Austin Young Lawyers' Assn. Found., Tex. Bar Found.; mem.: ABA, Jacksonville Bar Assn., Austin Young Lawyers' Assn. (co-chmn. It's the Law com. 1990—91), Tex. Ctr. Legal Ethics Professionalism, Austin Bar Assn. (sec.-treas. family law sect. 1989—90, v.p. 1990—91, pres. 1991—92, bd. dirs. 1991—92, chair mentor program com. 1993—94, chair mentor program com. 1996—98), Tex. Execs., Tex. Acad. Family Law Specialists, Am. Inns of Ct. (barrister 1996—99), Sierra Club, Fla. State U. Alumni Assn. (life), Lambda Iota Tau, Phi Beta Kappa. Democrat. Avocations: writing, Irish dance, yoga, tai chi. Office: The Met Bldg 320 N First St Ste 613 Jacksonville Beach FL 32250 Office Phone: 904-249-9976. Personal E-mail: sestmrsh@aol.com.

SALTUS, PHYLLIS BORZELLIERE, music educator; b. Rochester, NY, Jan. 17, 1931; d. Nicholas and Sadie Veronica (Leone) Borzelliere; m. William Thomas Saltus, Aug. 21, 1965 (div. Apr. 1991); children: Julie Marie Nicole, William Nicholas. AA, Burlington County Coll., Pemberton, NJ, 1987; MEd in Measurement and Guidance, U. Maine, Orono, 1963; BS in Music Edn., SUNY, 1953, MS, 1957. Cert. student personnel svcs., music and guidance, N.J., N.Y., Me. Music tchr., choral dir. Rochester Pub. Schs., 1953-56, 62-63, 1969-70, high sch. guidance counselor, 1963-65; asst. prof. music edn. SUNY, Geneseo and Fredonia, 1956-62; music tchr, choral dir. Concord (Mass.) Pub. Schs., 1965-66; owner, dir. Saltus Music Studio, Medford, NJ, 1982—91. Music tchr., choral dir. Delanco (N.J.) Pub. Schs., 1984-86; prof. voice N.J.Dept. Edn. Sch. Arts, Rowan Univ., Glassboro (N.J.) State Coll., 1987-89; sr. adj. prof. & coordn., piano lab Burlington County Coll., Pemberton, N.J. and Ft. Dix Mil. Post, Cmty. Coll. of the Air Force at McGuire AFB, 1989—, Interactive Classroom Program, 1995—, Power Package Accelerated Program, 1995—, Telecourse for Distance Learners Program WBZC, 1995—; music coord., dist. tchr. for gifted and talented program Mt. Laurel (N.J.) Pub. Schs., 1989-94; music dir., founding mem. Triple Threat Prodns., Cherry Hill, N.J., 1991—, Burlington County Cmty. Chorus, N.J., 1995—, Kosciusko Boys Choir, Rochester, 1959-60, Young Adults Cath. Youth Orgn. Choir, Dunkirk, N.Y., 1960-62; faculty adv. N.Y. Province of Newman Clubs Fedn. SUNY, 1957-62, lectr., researcher in field. Artist: The Fredonia Main Street Diner, 1952-53, Clarence Welcome Wagon Gourmet Cook Book, N.Y., 1973; contbr. poems to various publs.; soloist Rochester Philharm. Orch. Concert Series, Songsters, Inc., 1953-59. Choir dir., organist, soloist St. Philip Neri R.C. Ch., Rochester, 1949-65, St. Peter's Episc. Ch., Medford, 1989-90; choir dir., accompanist Thessalonia Baptist Ch. Sr. and Jr. Choirs, Willingboro, N.J., 1990-91; vocal dir., accompanist Pineland Players of South Jersey Community Theatre, Medford, 1987-89, Cherry Hill East High Sch., N.J., 1991—; team capt. United Way, Rochester, 1953-56; membership chair Rochester Community Theater, 1955-56; founding mem. Sta. WCVF, 1952-58; trip advisor Ski Club, Monroe HS, Rochester, 1963; bd. dirs., founding mem. Rochester Chamber Orch., 1964-65, Medford (N.J.) Newcomers Club, 1977—; vol. Cmty. Companions of Erie County Office of the Aging, N.Y., 1972-76, Medford PTO, 1976-85; judge preliminary Miss Am. contest Jr. C. of C., Jamestown, N.Y., 1962, vocal dir., accompanist Miss Dunkirk (N.Y.) pageant, 1962, vocal coach Miss Burlington County Pageant, Jr. C. of C., 1989,97-99; active Welcome Wagon, Inc., Clarence, N.Y., pres., 1974, historian, 1981; chair Medford (N.J.) Evening Book Review Group, 1978-80; mem. Medford Morning Book Review Group, 1980—; active Meml. Health Alliance, Burlington County Women's Health Network. NDEA grantee, 1964; EEOC scholar, 1986-87; recipient Jr. County Rifle Championship award Monroe County Dept. Health and Recreation, 1948, Womens Student Table Tennis Championship award SUNY, 1952, Outstanding Scholarship award Charlotte Putnam Landers Outstanding Scholarship award SUNY, 1953, Doubles Table Tennis Championship award Monroe HS, Rochester, 1964-65. Mem. AAUP (treas. 1960-62, state del. 1961), Music Educators Nat. Conf., Am. Personnel and Guidance Assn., South Jersey Music Tchrs. Assn., Meml. Health Alliance, Women's Health Network, AARP Medford chpt. of Deborah Heart & Lung Hosp. Found., Red Lion Wildlife Refuge, Cedar Run Wildlife Refuge, Order Sons of Italy in Am., Kappa Delta Pi (del. Barnard Coll., N.Y., 1952, state del., Atlantic City, N.J., 1953). Roman Catholic. Avocations: reading and research, creative writing, golf, painting, crossword puzzles, gourmet cooking. Home: 77 Finchley Ct Southampton NJ 08088-1006 Office Phone: 609-894-9311 ext. 1790. Business E-Mail: d.learn@bcc.edu.

SALTYKOV, BORIS GEORGIEVICH, economist, politician; b. Moscow, Dec. 27, 1940; s. Georgy N. and Evdokia M. (Pukaleva) Saltykov; m. Lubov N. Clochkova; 2 children. Student, Moscow Inst. Physics & Tech. Rschr., chief engr. Ctrl. Econ. Math. Inst. USSR Acad. Scis., Moscow, 1967—73, sr. rschr., 1973—86, head dept. Inst. Econ. Forecasting, 1986—91, vice dir. Analytical Rsch. Ctr. on Problems Social, Econ. and Sci. Tech. Devel., 1991—96; min. for sci. and tech. policy, pub. affairs chmn. commn. to UNESCO, vice premier of Russian govt. Russian Fedn., 1992—93; mem. Russian Parliament, 1993—95. Pres. Russian House for Internat. S & T Coop., 1996—. Contbr. over 70 articles to profl. jours. Trustee Oxford Russia Fund, England, 2004—. Mem.: Am. Acad. Arts and Scis. (fgn.). Avocation: yachting. Office: Russian House for Interna S&T Coop Brusov per 11 125009 Moscow Russia Home Phone: 7(095)241-44-03; Office Phone: 7(495)629-58-40. Business E-Mail: bsaltykov@rd-mnts.ru.

SALTZ, HOWARD JOEL, newspaper editor; b. Bronx, NY, Apr. 11, 1960; s. Fred Raymond and Sheila Lois (Goldberg) S. BA in Liberal Arts, SUNY, Stony Brook, 1983. Reporter Greenwich Time, So. Conn. Newspapers divsn. Times Mirror, 1983-85; with MediaNews Group, 1985—, N.J. Advance, Dover, 1985-87, editor, 1987-88, Hamilton (Ohio) Jour.-News, 1988-89, Fremont (Calif.) Argus, 1989-91, Johnstown Tribune-Democrat, 1991; dep. bus. editor Denver Post, 1996-98, dep. mng. editor features, 1998-2000, multimedia editor, 2000—02, assoc. editor/new media & strategic devel., 2002—06; v.p. content develop. Media News Group Interactive, 2006—. Adv. com. dept. journalism Ohlone Coll., Fremont, Calif., 1990-91. Bd. dirs. YMCA, Fremont-Newark, Calif., 1990-91, Johnstown Area Heritage Assn., 1991-93. Mem. Greater Johnstown C. of C. (bd. dirs. 1991-96), Soc. Profl. Journalists (bd. dirs. Northern Calif. chpt. 1990-91). Avocations: skiing, travel, scuba. Address: 535 Garfield St Denver CO 80206-4513 Office: Media News Group Interactive 1560 Broadway Ste 2100 Denver CO 80202-5177 Business E-Mail: hsaltz@medianewsgroup.com.

SALTZ, JEFFREY S., lawyer; b. Phila., 1953; AB magna cum laude, Princeton U., 1975; JD magna cum laude, Harvard U., 1978. Bar: Pa. 1978. Law clerk to Hon. Harirson L. Winter U.S. Ct. Appeals (4th cir.), 1978-79; litigator Wolf, Block, Schorr & Solis-Cohen, Phila., 1979—86, ptnr., 1986—98; mem. Law Office of Jeffrey S. Saltz, P.C., Phila., 1998—. Contbr. articles to profl. jours. Chair Lower Merion-Narberth Dem. com., 1988—96; vice chair Montgomery County Dem. com., 1998—2002; solicitor Beth David Reform Congregation, Gladwyne, Pa., 1998—2000, v.p., 2000—04, pres.; bd. mem. Montgomery County Industrial Devel. Authority, 2003—. Mem.: ABA, Pa. Bar Assn., Phila. Bar Assn. (chair: bus. litig. com.). Exec. editor: Harvard Law Review. Office: Law Office of Jeffrey S Saltz PC 1515 Market St Ste 1000 Philadelphia PA 19102 Office Phone: 215-523-5317. Office Fax: 215-568-2739. E-mail: jsaltz@saltzlaw.com.

SALTZBURG, STEPHEN ALLAN, law educator, consultant; b. Phila., Sept. 10, 1945; s. Jack Leonard and Mildred (Osgood) Adelman; m. Susan Lee, March 10, 1990; children: Mark Winston, Lisa Marie, Diane Elizabeth, David Lee Mussehl. AB, Dickinson Coll., 1967; JD, U. Pa., 1970. Bar: Calif. 1971, D.C. 1972, Va. 1976. Law clk. U.S. Dist. Ct. (no. dist.) Calif., San Francisco, 1970-71, U.S. Supreme Ct., 1971-72; asst. prof. law sch. U. Va., Charlottesville, 1972-74, assoc. prof., 1974-77, prof., 1977-87, Class of 1962 prof., 1987-90; Howrey prof. trial advocacy, litigation and profl. responsibility George Washington U. Law Sch., Washington, 1990—2004, Wallace and Beverley Woodbury univ. prof., 2004—. Reporter Alaska Rules of Evidence, 1976-77, Alaska Civil Jury Instrns., 1979-81, Adv. Com. on Rules of Criminal Procedure, 1984-89, Va. Rules on Evidence, 1984-85, Civil Justice Act Adv. Group, U.S. Dist. Ct. D.C., 1992-93, chmn., 1994-99, assoc. independant councel, 1987-88; dep. asst. atty. gen. criminal divsn. U.S. Dept. Justice, 1988-89; ex officio mem. U.S. Sentencing Commn., 1989-90; mem. adv. com. on Fed. Rules of Criminal Procedure, 1989-95, on Fed. Rules of Evidence, 1992-95; mediator dispute resolution program U.S. Ct. Appeals, 1993—. Author: Evidence in America, 1987, American Criminal Procedure, 7th edit., 2004, Criminal Law: Cases and Materials, 1994, 2d edit., 2000, Evidence: The Objection Method, 1997, 2d edit., 2000, Federal Rules of Evidence Manual, 1975, 9th edit., 2006, Federal Rules of Evidence Trial Book, 1998, A Modern Approach to Evidence, 2d edit., 1982, Military Rules of Evidence Manual, 5th edit., 2004, Basic Criminal Procedure, 1994, 4th edit., 2005, Military Evidentiary Foundations, 1994, 2d edit., 2000, Trying Cases to Win: Anatomy of a Trial, 1999, Trying Cases to Win: Evidence: Weapons for Winning, Vol. 1, 2000, Vol. 2, 2002, Vol. 3, 2004, California Federal Evidence Trial Book, 1999, Ohio Rules of Evidence Trial Book, 1999, Washington Evidence Trial Book, 1999. Mem.: ABA (chmn. com. on trial advocacy criminal justice sect. 1992—96, co-chmn. task force on civil trial stds. litig. sect. 1996—97, task force on Ind. Counsel Act litig. sect. 1997—99, mem. criminal justice sect. coun. 2000—, task force on terrorism and the law 2001—02, litigation sect. coun. 2001—04, ho. of dels. 2001—05, task force on gatekeeper regulation and the profession 2002—, task force on enemy combatants 2002—, chair ABA Justice Kennedy Commn. 2003—04, co-chair commns. effective criminal sanctions 2005—), Am. Law Inst. Office: George Washington U Law Sch 2000 H St NW Washington DC 20052 Home Phone: 204-797-9028; Office Phone: 202-994-7089. Business E-Mail: ssaltz@law.gwu.edu.

SALTZMAN, IRENE CAMERON, consumer products company executive; b. Cocoa, Fla., Mar. 23, 1927; d. Argyle Bruce and Marie T. (Neel) Cameron; m. Herman Saltzman, Mar. 23, 1946 (dec. May 1986); children: Martin Howard (dec.), Arlene Norma Hanly. Owner Irene Perfume and Cosmetics Lab., Jacksonville, Fla., 1972—. Mem. Cummer Mus. Art, Jacksonville, 1972-. Mem. NAFE, Nat. Assn. Profl. and Exec. Women, Ret. Judge Advocates Assn. of USAF (hon.), Mil. Officers Assn. Am., Aircraft Owners and Pilots Assn., Trade, Cosmetic, Toiletry and Fragrance Assn., Ret. Officers Assn., Soc. Cosmetic Chemists (affiliate), Ponte Vedra Club. Democrat. Episcopalian. Avocations: aviation, painting, travel, swimming, golf. Home: 2701 Ocean Dr S Jacksonville Beach FL 32250 Home Phone: 904-249-5157; Office Phone: 904-641-5171. Business E-Mail: irene@ireneparfums.com.

SALTZMAN, JARED, performing arts educator, lighting designer; b. NYC, Apr. 14, 1950; s. Perle and David Saltzman; m. Marjorie Harris, May 28, 1972; children: Aimee Perle, Arielle Jessica. MA, NYU, 1976. Cert. entertainment electrician Entertainment Tech. Cert. Program Coun. Prof. Bergen CC, Paramus, NJ, 1973—; head electrician IATSE Local 632, NJ, 1978—. Mem.: NEA, Internat. Alliance of Theatrical Stage Employees, US Inst. for Theatre Tech. Office: Bergen Cmty Coll 400 Paramus Rd Paramus NJ 07652 Office Phone: 201-447-7197.

SALTZMAN, JOSEPH, journalist, educator, television producer; b. LA, Oct. 28, 1939; s. Morris and Ruth (Weiss) S.; m. Barbara Dale Epstein, July 1, 1962; children: Michael Stephen Ulysses, David Charles Laertes. BA, U. So. Calif., 1961; MS, Columbia U., 1962. Freelance writer, reporter, prodr., 1960—; reporter Valley Times Today, LA, 1962-64; editor Pacific Palisades Palisadian Post, 1964; sr. writer, prodr. CBS-TV, LA, 1964-74; freelance broadcast cons. LA, 1974—; prof. journalism U. So. Calif., LA, 1974—, acting dir. Sch. Journalism, 1999; assoc. dir. Sch. Journalism U. So. Calif. Annenberg, 1996-99; assoc. dean Annenberg Sch. Comm., 1999—2003; sr. prodr. investigative unit Entertainment Tonight, 1983; dir. Image of the Journalist in Popular Culture project Norman Lear Ctr., Annenberg Sch. Comm., U. So. Calif., 2001—. CFO The Jester & Pharley Phund. Author: Frank Capra and the Image of the Journalist in American Film, 2002; prodr.(writer): (documentaries) Black on Black, 1968, The Unhappy Hunting Ground, 1971, The Junior High School, 1971, The Very Personal: Death of Elizabeth Schell-Holt-Hartford, 1972, Rape, 1972, Why Me?, 1974, Entertainment Tonight, 1983; editor (columnist): USA Today, 1983—; King Features Syndicate, 1983—92; contbg. editor: Emmy Mag., 1986—90, Roberts Reviewing Svc., 1964—95, others. Recipient AP cert. of excellence and merit, 1968, 72, 73, 74, 75, Edward R. Murrow awards for disting. achievements in broadcast journalism, 1969, 72, Alfred I. duPont-Columbia U. award in broadcast journalism, 1973-74, Silver Gavel award ABA, 1973, Ohio State award Am. Exhbn. Ednl. Radio-TV Programs and Inst. for Edn. by Radio-TV Telecom. Ctr., 1974, Broadcast Media awards San Francisco State U., 1974, 75, Media award for excellence in comm. Am. Cancer Soc., 1976, Disting. Alumni award U. So. Calif., 1992, Alumni award Columbia U. Grad. Sch. Journalism, 2005; Seymour Berkson fellow, 1961; Robert E. Sherwood fellow, 1962; alt. Pulitzer traveling fellow, 1962-63. Mem. NATAS (regional Emmy awards 1965, 68, 74, 75), Radio-TV News Assn. (Golden Mike awards 1969, 71, 73, 75), Writers Guild Am., Greater LA Press Club (awards 1968, 74, 75), Columbia U. Alumni Assn., U. So. Calif. Alumni Assn., Skull and Dagger, Blue Key, Phi Beta Kappa, Sigma Delta Chi, Pi Sigma Alpha, Alpha Epsilon Rho. Home: 2116 Via Estudillo Palos Verdes Peninsula CA 90274-1931 Office: U So Calif Annenberg Sch Journalism Univ Park Los Angeles CA 90089-0001 Office Phone: 310-377-8883. Business E-Mail: saltzman@usc.edu.

SALTZMAN, PHILIP, television producer, writer; b. Sonora, Mexico, Sept. 19, 1928; came to US, 1929, naturalized, 1948; s. Louis and Vanya (Liberman) S.; m. Caroline Veiller, Jan. 24, 1960; children: Jennifer, Daniel, Tony. BA, UCLA, 1951, MA, 1953. Free lance writer, 1958-68. Pres. Woodruff Prodns., Inc. Writer: (TV shows) Alcoa Goodyear Theater, 1959, Richard Diamond, 1959, Rifleman, 1961, Perry Mason, 1964, Dr. Kildare, 1964, Fugitive, 1964, Twelve O'Clock High, 1966; prodr., writer: (TV shows) Felony Squad, 1966-69, F.B.I, 1969-73, Barnaby Jones, 1973-77; prodr., writer, creator Intertect, 1973; prodr.: (TV movie) The FBI vs. Alvin Karpis, 1974, Attack on Terror: The FBI vs. the KKK in Mississippi, 1975, Brinks: The Great Robbery, 1976; co-writer: (feature film) The Swiss Conspiracy, 1975; creator, writer, prodr.: (TV movie) Crossfire, 1975; exec. prodr.: (TV series) Barnaby Jones, 1978-80, Escapade, 1978, Colorado C-I, 1978, A Man Called Sloane, 1979, The Aliens Are Coming, 1979, Freebie and the Bean, 1980; prodr.: (TV shows) Bare Essence, 1982; supervising prodr.-writer Partners in Crime, 1984; prodr., writer Crazy Like a Fox, 1985; prodr., co-writer (TV movie) That Secret Sunday, 1986; exec. supervising prodr. The New Perry Mason movies, 1987-88; exec. supervising prodr., writer Jake and The Fatman, 1987-88; supervising prodr. Columbo, 1989-90; creator, writer The Caller, 1991. Mem. dean's coun. Coll. Letters and Sci., UCLA, Friends of English, UCLA. Mem. Writers Guild Am., West, Caucus for Writers, Producers, Dirs., Acad. TV Arts and Scis., PEN Ctr. USA West. Personal E-mail: cpsaltzman@aol.com.

SALUKO, AYODELO V., hospital administrator; b. York, Pa., July 4, 1967; s. R. S. and P. C. Saluko; m. Victoria Leigh Richmond, Aug. 31, 1993; children: Todd V., Kirsten Marie, Mollie Lane. BS in Health Policy and Adminstrn., Pa. State U., State Coll., 1989; MHA, Pa. State. U., State Coll., 1992. Adminstr. Magee-Women's Hosp. U. Pitts. Med. Ctr., 1993—99, adminstr. Hillman Cancer Ctr. Shadyside, Pa., 1999—2006; adminstr. Meriks Cancer Ctr., Washington, 2006—. Contbr. articles to profl. med. jours. Active Washington Animal Rescue, 2007—. Mem.: Am. Cancer Soc., Sigma Alpha Epsilon. Democrat. Presbyterian. Avocations: fishing, travel, reading, chess.

SALVADORE, GUIDO RICHARD, lawyer; b. Norton, Mass., Oct. 14, 1927; s. Michele Salvadore and Maria Grazia Costantino; m. Barbara Ann Camparone, Oct. 25, 1958; children: Peter, Richard, Susan, Stephen, Marisa. AB, Brown U., Providence, 1951; LLB, Harvard U., Cambridge, Mass., 1954. Bar: R.I. 1954, U.S. Dist. Ct. R.I. 1956, U.S. Ct. Appeals (1st cir.) 1996. Atty. Salvadore & Salvadore, Providence, R.I.; ptnr. Higgins, Cavanagh & Cooney, 1960-90. Dir., pres. Great Am. Nursing Ctrs., Inc., Warwick, R.I., 1969-90. Dir., v.p. R.I. Grand Opera Co., Providence, 1985—. With USN, 1946-48. Mem. ABA, ATLA, Am. Trial Lawyers Assn., R.I. Bar Assn., Univ. Club, Metacomet Country Club, Brown Faculty Club. Republican. Roman Catholic. Avocations: golf, basketball, dance, reading. Home: 38 Sunset Dr East Greenwich RI 02818-1915 Office: Salvadore & Salvadore Ste 303 10 Weybosset St Providence RI 02903-2393 E-mail: grsalvadore@aol.com.

SALVAN, SHERWOOD ALLEN, lawyer; b. NYC, Dec. 2, 1942; s. Harry and Marie Ann (Deramo) S. BBA, St. Francis Coll., NYC; MBA, Pace U.; JD, postgrad., NYU. Bar: N.Y. 1969, U.S. Ct. Appeals (2d dist.) 1971, U.S. Dist. Cts. (so. and ea. dist.) N.Y. 1971, U.S. Cir. Ct. (2d cir.) 1972, U.S. Supreme Ct. 1980, D.C. 1981. Tax specialist Haskins & Sells, NYC, 1969-71; sole practice NYC, 1972—. Mem. cen. screening com. first dept. N.Y. Appellate Div., 1977-82; spl. master N.Y. County Supreme Ct., 1977-85; arbitrator Am. Arbitration Assn., 1976-89, N.Y. County and Bronx County Civil Cts., 1976-89; adminstrv. law judge Environ. Control Bd. City of N.Y., 1975-77. Contbr. articles to profl. jours. V.p. N.Y. County Dem. Club, 1980—; jud. del. N.Y. County dems., 1983—. Mem. N.Y. County Lawyers Assn. (chairperson com. word processing 1978-86), Am. Judge Assn., NY Law Sch. Alumni Assn. (bd. dirs. 1984—). Office Phone: 917-699-8416. Business E-Mail: woodmanlaw@aol.com.

SALVANESCHI, LUIGI, real estate developer, management consultant, educator; b. Casale, Italy, 1929; came to U.S., 1959; s. Ernesto and Carolina (Bassignana) S.; m. Lenore M. Rickels, Aug. 20, 1958; 1 child, Margherita Lina. Classical Maturity, Valsalice, Torino, Italy, 1950; PhD, Vatican U., Rome, 1958; cert. in real estate, UCLA, 1965. Restaurant mgr. McDonalds Co., Chgo., 1959-61, restaurant mgr. and supr. Los Angeles, 1961-63, real estate mgr., 1964-68, v.p. real estate Oakbrook, Ill., 1969-83; sr. v.p. real estate and constrn. Kentucky Fried Chicken, Louisville, 1983-88; pres., COO, dir. Blockbuster Entertainment, Ft. Lauderdale, Fla., 1988-91; disting. adj. prof. Barry Univ., 1991—. Adj. prof. Sch. Bus. U. Louisville, 1987; dir. Fla. Fun-Train subs. First Am. Rwys., Hollywood, Fla. Author: Location, Location, Location, 1997, Renaissance 2000: Liberal Arts Essentials for Tomorrow's Leaders, 1998. Dir. Ft. Lauderdale Internat. Movie Festival. Served as 2d lt. in Italian Infantry, 1945-46. Recipient Outstanding Italo-Am. award Italian Am. Fedn., 1991; named Colonel of the Commonwealth of Ky., 1984. Mem. Nat. Assn. Real Estate Execs. (co-founder, bd. dirs.). Roman Catholic. Avocations: mountain hiking, reading. Office: Barry Univ Sch of Bus 11300 NE 2nd Ave Miami FL 33161-6695

SALVATI, EDWARDO A., surgeon; b. Buenos Aires, Nov. 11, 1939; arrived in U.S., 1969; BS, Jose Manuel Estrada, Buenos Aires, 1957; MD, La Platta Med. Sch., Buenos Aires, 1963. Diplomate Am. Bd. Orthopedic Surgery. Intern Hosp. de Quilmes, Buenos Aires, 1962—63; resident U. Florence, Italy, 1963—65; fellow Hosp. Spl. Surgery, NYC, 1969—72, asst. attending orthop. surgeon, 1972—75, chief hip svc., 1975—91, attending orthop. surgeon, 1983—, dir. hip and knee svc., 1991—, assoc. scientist rsch. divsn., 1993—; from instr. to assoc. prof. clin. orthop. surgery Weil Med. Coll. Cornell U., NYC, 1969—83, prof., 1983—. Asst. attending orthop. surgeon N.Y. Hosp., 1972—75, assoc. attending orthop. surgeon, 1976—83, attending orthop. surgeon, 1983—, Presbyn. Hosp., 1983—; lectr. in field. Guest editor: Hip Internat., 1992; cons. reviewer Hip Internat., mem. editl. bd., cons. reviewer Jour. Bone and Joint Surgery, Clin. Orthop. and Related Rsch., Jour. Arthoplasty, mem. editl. bd. Advances Orthop., Jour. Orthop. Techniques, Internat. Orthop., La Chirurgia degli Organi di Movimenti, Long-Term Effects Med. Implants; contbr. articles to profl. jours. Grantee, Hip Soc., 2003, Orthop. Rsch. and Edn. Found., 1998, 2004—05; Rhone-Poulenc Rhorer Rsch. grantee, Hip Soc., 1998, Zimmer grantee, 2002—05. Mem.: AMA, Sociedad Medica Hispanoamericana, Venezuelan Soc. Orthop. Surgery and Traumatology, Columbian Soc. Orthop. Surgery and Traumatology, Argentine Med. Soc., Argentine Soc. Orthop. and Traumatology, N.Y. State Soc. Orthop. Surgeons, N.Y. Acad. Medicine, New York County Med. Soc., Med. Soc. State of N.Y., Latinoamerican Soc. Orthop. and Traumatology, Internat. Hip Soc., Am. Assn. Hip and Knee Surgeons, Am. Hip Soc., Am. Orthop. Assn., Am. Acad. Orthop. Surgery, Assn. Medica Argentina (hon.). Office: Hosp Spl Surgery 535 E 70th St New York NY 10021

SALVATIERRA, OSCAR, JR., transplant surgeon, urologist, educator; b. Phoenix, Apr. 15, 1935; s. Oscar and Josefine S.; m. Pamela Moss; children: Mark, Lisa Marie. BS, Georgetown U., 1957; MD, U. So. Calif., 1961. Intern, resident in surgery and urology U. So. Calif.-Los Angeles County Med. Ctr., 1961-66; practice medicine Pomona, Calif., 1968-72; chief staff Casa Colina Hosp., 1972; post doctoral fellow in transplantation U. Calif.-San Francisco, 1972-73, asst. prof. surgery and urology, 1973-75, assoc. prof., 1975-81, prof., 1981-91, chmn. transplant service, 1974-91; attending surgeon and urologist Moffitt Hosp., 1973—; exec. dir. Pacific Transplant Inst., 1991-94; prof. surgery/pediatrics, dir. pediat. renal transplantation Stanford U. Med. Ctr., 1994—, attending surgeon, urologist and pediat.; advising dean Sch. Medicine Stanford U., 2005—. Chair faculty senate Stanford U. Sch. Medicine, 2002—04; study sect. NIH, 1981-85, nat. adv. bd., 1986-92, chmn. nat. adv. bd. 1990-92, chmn. spl. study sect., 1997, 99 Mem. editl. bd. Transplantation and Immunology, 1984—, Transplantation, 1987—, Transplantation Procs., 1990—, Pediat. Transplantation, 1998—; assoc. editor Am. Jour. Kidney Diseases, 1987-89; contbr. over 280 articles and chpts. to med. lit. Nat. bd. advisors Agent Orange Class Assistance Program, 1988-96. With M.C., U.S. Army, Vietnam, 1966-68. Decorated Army Commendation medal, Grand Ufficiale of Italian Rep. with title His Excellency award; named Oscar Salvatierra Symposium in his honor, 2001; recipient Chancellor's award for pub. svc., U. Calif., 1986, Commendation resolution, Calif. State Legislature, 1990, Presdl. medal and Diploma of Honor, Argentina, 1999, Rambar-Mark award, Stanford U., 1999, Franklin Ebaugh award, 2003, Albion Walter Hewlett award, 2007, Stanford, 2007; grantee, NIH, 1974—76, 1980—83, 1988—90, 2003—, USPHS, 1986—89; Oscar Salvatierra Ann. Lectureship in Transplantation, in his honor, Stanford U., 2005. Fellow ACS (bd. govs. 1986-92); mem. Am. Surg. Assn., Am. Soc. Transplant Surgeons (bd. dirs. 1977-85, pres. 1983-84, chmn. adv. com. on issues 1984-87), Soc. Univ. Surgeons, Soc. Univ. Urologists, N.Y. Acad. Scis., Am. Soc. Nephrology, Internat. Transplantation Soc. (bd. dirs. 1984—, pres.-elect 1996-98, pres., 1998-2000, Contbns. to Soc. medallion 2006), Soc. Pediatric Urology, Am. Urol. Assn., Nat. Kidney Found. (Pioneer award 2004), Renal Physicians Assn. (bd. dirs. 1984-87), Pacific Coast Surg. Assn., San Francisco Surg. Soc., United Network Organ Sharing (bd. dirs. 1984-88, pres. 1985-86), Internat. Soc. for Organ Sharing (bd. dirs. 1991—, pres. 1993-95), Am. Soc. for Multicultural Health and Transplant Profls. (pres. 1992-94, Lifetime Achievement award, 2005), Nafziger Surg. Soc. Achievements include being the principle lay figure in passage and enactment of National

Organ Transplant Act, 1984; introduction of Pope John Paul II to the 18th International Transplantation Congress for Encyclical on Organ Transplantation, 2000. Office: Stanford U Med Ctr 703 Welch Rd Ste H2 Palo Alto CA 94304-1708

SALVATORE, DIANE J., editor-in-chief; BA in Journalism, Pa. State U.; MA in English and Creative Writing, NYU. Rschr., reporter The Soho News, NYC; editl. asst. Met. Home, NYC, Cosmopolitan, NYC; sr. assoc. editor Ladies' Home Jour., NYC, 1985—88; articles assoc. editor Glamour, NYC, 1988—89; sr. editor Redbook, NYC, 1989—94; dep. editor Good Housekeeping, NYC, exec. editor, 1994—99; editor in chief YM, NYC, 1998—2002; exec. dir. Marie Claire, 2001; editor in chief Ladies Home Jour., NYC, 2002—; dir. editl. ops. Hearst Mag., 2002. Contbr. articles and short stories in various nat. periodicals. Mem.: Am. Soc. Mag. Editors. Office Phone: 212-455-1025. Office Fax: 212-455-1313. E-mail: diane.salvatore@meredith.com. *

SALVATORE, LOUIS R., manufacturing executive; Dir. Ford Motor Co.; v.p. procurement MTD Products, Inc.; v.p. global purchasing Lear Corp., Southfield, Mich., 1996—98, v.p., pres. DaimlerChrysler divsn., 1998, pres. Ford and elec. systems divsns., pres. Ford, elec. systems and interior systems divsns., 2004, sr. v.p., pres. Asian Customer Group, 2005—. Mem. adv. bd. William P. Reuther Libr. Office: Lear Corp 21557 Telegraph Rd PO Box 5008 Southfield MI 48086 Office Phone: 248-447-1500. Office Fax: 248-447-1722. *

SALVATY, BENJAMIN BENEDICT, lawyer; b. Chgo., Dec. 22, 1940; s. Benjamin Benedict and Marion Therese (Ryan) S.; m. Patircia Louise Recor, Aug. 29, 1964; children: Paul Benedict, Kathleen Anne. BBA, U. Notre Dame, 1962; JD, U. So. Calif., 1965. Bar: Calif. 1966, U.S. Dist. Ct. (no., cen., ea. and so. dists.) Calif., U.S. Ct. Appeals (9th cir.), U.S. Tax Ct., U.S. Supreme Ct. Sr. trial atty. Calif. Dept. Transp., 1966-79; gen. atty. The Atchison, Topeka and Santa Fe Railway Co., 1980-89; sr. ptnr. Hill, Farrer & Burrill, Los Angeles, 1990—. Chmn. traffic commn. City of San Marino. Mem. ABA (litigation sect. urban, state and local govt. law com. on condemnation, zoning and planning com.), Am. Bd. Trial Advs., Am. Judicature Soc., Internat. Right Way Assn., Irish Am. Bar Assn. (bd. dirs. 1985—, treas. 1991, sec. 1992, v.p. 1992-93, pres. 1993-94), Italian Am. Lawyers Assn., State Trial Attys. Assn. (pres. 1975-79), Calif. State Bar (chmn. condemnation com. 1987-88, vice chmn. 1986-87), Pasadena Bar Assn., L.A. County Bar Assn. (condemnation and land valuation com.). Office: Hill Farrer & Burrill LLP One California Plz 37th Fl 300 S Grand Ave Los Angeles CA 90071-3109 Office Phone: 213-621-0865. Office Fax: 213-624-4840. Business E-Mail: bsalvaty@hillfarrer.com.

SALVENDY, GAVRIEL, industrial engineer, educator; b. Budapest, Hungary, Sept. 30, 1938; came to US, 1968; s. Paul and Katarina (Brown) S.; m. Catherine Vivien Dees, Apr. 1, 1966; children: Laura Dorit, Kevin David. MSc in Indsl. Psychology, U. Birmingham, Eng., 1966, PhD in Indsl. Psychology, 1968; D (hon.), Academia Sinica, 1995, Chinese Acad. Scis., 1995. Asst. prof. indsl. engring. SUNY, Buffalo, 1968-71; assoc. prof. indsl. engring. Purdue U., 1971—77, prof., 1977—84, 1999—, NEC prof. indsl. engring., 1984-99; chair prof., head dept. indsl. engring. Tsinghua U., Beijing, 2001—. Fulbright disting. prof. mech. engring. U. Belgrade, Yugoslavia, 1979-81; chmn. Internat. Commn. Human Aspects in Computing, Switzerland, 1986-91. Co-author: Prediction and Development of Industrial Work Performance, 1973, Human Aspects of Computer Aided Design, 1987; sr. editor: Machine-Pacing and Occupational Stress, 1981, Social, Ergonomic and Stress Aspects of Work with Computers, 1987, Designing and Using Human-Computer Interfaces and Knowledge Based Systems, 1989; editor: Handbook of Industrial Engineering, 1982, 3d edit., 2001, Human Computer Interaction, 1984, Handbook of Human Factors, 1987, 3d edit., 2006, Cognitive Engineering in the Design of Human Computer Interaction and Expert Systems, 1987; founding editor: Internat. Jour. on Human-Computer Interaction, Internat. Jour. Human Factors in Mfg., Human-Computer Interaction, 1st and 2d edits., 2002, 07; co-editor: Work with Computers: Organizational Management, Stress and Health Aspects, 1989, Human Computer Interaction: Software and Hardware Interfaces, 1993, Human-Computer Interaction: Applications and Case Studies, 1993, Design of Work and Development of Personnel in Advanced Manufacturing, 1994, Organization and Management of Advanced Manufacturing, 1994, Advanceds in Applied Ergonomics, 1996, Handbook of Human Factors and Ergonomics, 3rd edit. 2006, Design of Computing Systems (2 vols.), 1997, Ergonomics in Manufacturing, 1998, Handbook of Industrial Engineering, 3d edit., 2001; contbr. articles to profl. jours., chpts. to books. Pres. Lafayette Jewish Sunday Sch., 1980-81. Recipient Friendship award Sci. and Engring., Govt. China, 2006, John Fritz medal, Am. Assn. Engring. Socs., 2007. Fellow APA, Inst. Indsl. Engrs. (sr., Phil Carroll award 1973), Human Factors and Ergonomics Soc. (past officer), Ergonomics Soc. (hon., life mem.), Internat. Ergonomics Assn.; mem. NAE. Office: Sch Indsl Engring Purdue U 315 N Grant St West Lafayette IN 47907-2023 Office Phone: 765-463-2628, 765-494-5426. Office Fax: 765-494-0874. E-mail: salvendy@purdue.edu.

SALVESEN, B. FORBES, artist; b. Elgin, Ill., Nov. 6, 1944; d. Donald Behan and Helen Elaine (Krajacik) Forbes; m. Bruce Michael Salvesen, Sept. 3, 1966. Studied with Elvira Spivey, Barrington, Ill., 1972-74; studied with Peter Schoelch, Cary, Ill., 1975-82; student, Am. Acad. Art, 1976, Sch. Art Inst. Chgo., 1980-82, Kulick-Stark Byzantine Jewelry Sch., 1983. Asst. to purchasing agt. Harnischfeger, Crystal Lake, Ill., 1962-64; rec. sec. Electric Mfrs. Credit Bur., Cary, Ill., 1964-66; student and practicing artist, 1968—. Illustrator: (book) There were Reasons, 1983. Recipient Award of Excellence, Ill.-Arlington Heights Fine Arts Festival, 1995, Best of Show award 20th Ann. Cambridge Art Fair, 1995, 19th Ann. Fine Arts Festival, Downers Grove, Ill., 1995. Democratic. Roman Catholic. Avocations: writing, poetry, jewelry crafting, cross country skiing, hiking. Home: 1312 Whippoorwill Dr Crystal Lake IL 60014-2614 Studio: 1311 Behan Rd Crystal Lake IL 60014 Office Phone: 815-455-0089.

SALVESEN, MAGDA ABERCROMBY, art and garden historian; b. Edinburgh, June 20, 1944; came to US, 1976; d. Harold Keith and Marion Eleanora (Cameron) S.; m. Jon R. Schueler, July 29, 1976 (dec. Aug. 1992). MA, St. Andrews U., Scotland, 1966, U. London, 1968; Cert. in Secondary Edn., Moray House Coll. Edn., Edinburgh, 1976. Asst. Richard Demarco Gallery, Edinburgh, 1968; exhibn. officer Scottish Arts Coun., Edinburgh, 1969-71; tchr. middle sch. The Day Sch., NYC, 1976-81; ESL tchr. Berlitz Sch. Langs., NYC, 1983-85; exec. adminstr. Archs./Designers/Planners for Social Responsibility, NYC, 1985-88; lectr. art history New Sch. U., NYC, 1988—; lectr. garden history and theory N.Y. Botanical Garden, Bronx, 1990—. Lectr. in field. Editor: (manuscript by Jon Schueler) The Sound of Sleat: A Painter's Life, 1999; co-editor: Artists' Estates: Reputations in Trust, 2005; dir. and exec. prodr.: (video) Jon Schueler: A Life in Painting, 1999. Bd. mem. Queens (N.Y.) Bot. Garden. Democrat. Avocations: museuming, reading, travel, gardening. Address: 40 W 22nd St New York NY 10010 Office Phone: 212-929-7614. E-mail: msalvesen@earthlink.net.

SALVESON, MELVIN ERWIN, management sciences company executive, educator; b. Brea, Calif., Jan. 16, 1919; s. John T. and Elizabeth (Green) S.; m. Joan Y. Stipek, Aug. 22, 1944; children: Eric C., Kent Erwin BS, U. Calif. Berkeley, 1941; MS, MIT, Cambridge, 1947; PhD, U. Chgo., 1952. Cons. McKinsey & Co., NYC, 1947—48; asst. prof., dir. mgmt. sci. rsch. UCLA, 1948—54; mgr. advanced data sys., cons. strategic planning GE, Louisville and NYC, 1954—57; pres. Mgmt. Scis. Corp., LA, 1957—67; group v.p. Control Data/CEIR, Inc., 1967—68; pres. Electronic Currency Corp., 1964—; chmn. OneCard Internat., Inc., 1983—92, Uni-Card Sys. Inc., 1992—. Bd. dirs. Diversified Earth Scis., Inc., Eco Rx Inc., Excel Enterprise Inc., Veritas et Justus Inc., Algeran, Inc., Electronic Currency Corp., So. Calif. Econ. Alliance, founder, pres., 1992-96; bd. dirs. Am. Soc. for Edn. and Econ. Devel., founding chair, 1996-98; exec. dir. Am. Found. for Edn. and Econ. Devel.; founder MasterCard Sys., LA, 1966; chmn. Corp. Strategies Internat.; prof. bus. Pepperdine U. 1972-85; adj. prof. U. So. Calif., Webster U., U. Phoenix, 1972—; adviser data processing City of LA, 1962-64; futures forecasting IBM, 1957-61; adviser strategic sys. planning USAF, 1961-67; info. sys. Calif. Dept. Human Resources, 1972-73, City of LA Automated Urban Data Base, 1962-67; tech. transfer NASA, 1965-70; mem. bd. trustees, Long Beach City Coll., 1990-95 Contbr. articles to profl. jours. Served to lt. comdr. USNR, 1941—46. Named to Long Beach City Coll. Hall of Fame; recipient Dist. Alumnus award Calif. Coll. Sys., 1992 Fellow: AAAS, Inst. Mgmt. Sci. (founder, past pres.), Inst. for Ops. Rsch. and Mgmt. Scis.; mem.: CSSP Alumnus, Calif. Yacht Club, Founders Club (LA Philharm. Orch.). Republican. Office: 515 Ocean Ave # 405 S Santa Monica CA 90402-2623 Office Phone: 310-917-1911. Personal E-mail: mesalveson@aol.com.

SALVINI, EMIL ROBERT, publishing executive, writer, historian; b. Jersey City, June 8, 1949; s. Armando and Marie Salvini; m. Nancy Ann Levenstein, Dec. 12, 1971; children: Amy Cara, Beth Lauren. BA, William Paterson U., 1971; degree, Harvard Bus. Sch., 2001. Pres. Wheal-Grace Corp., Belleville, NJ, 1975—. Author: The Summer City by the Sea, 1995, Boardwalk Memories, Tales of the Jersey Shore, 2005, Hobey Baker American Legend, 2005, Jersey Memories, Vintage Images of the Jersey Shore, 2006. Commr. Cape May Hist. Preservation Commn., Cape May, NJ, 2004—06. Mem.: North Jersey Country Club, Harvard Bus. Sch. NY, Harvard Club Boston, Harvard Club NY. Achievements include invention of GreenPrint program. Avocations: writing, golf, travel. Office: Wheal-Grace Corp 300 Ralph St Belleville NJ 07109 Home Phone: 973-839-1467; Office Phone: 973-450-8100 11. Office Fax: 973-450-5950; Home Fax: 973-839-1403. E-mail: esalvini@wheal-grace.com.

SALVO, J. C., lawyer; b. Council Bluffs, Iowa, Dec. 10, 1947; JD, Creighton U. Sch. of Law, Omaha, Neb., 1972. Bar: Iowa 1972, Nebr. 1972, US Dist. Ct. (Dist. Nebr.) 1972, US Dist. Ct. (So. Dist. Iowa) 1972, US Supreme Ct. 1980, US Dist. Ct. (No. Dist. Iowa) 1983, US Ct. Appeals (8th Cir.) 1984. County atty., Shelby County, Iowa, 1977—82; ptnr. Salvo, Deren, Schenck & Lauterbach, PC, Harlan, Iowa, 1972—. Shelby County atty., 1977—82. Fellow: Iowa Acad. of Trial Lawyers (pres. 1998); mem.: Iowa Supreme Ct. Nominating Commn., Iowa Supreme Ct. Grievance Commn., Assn. of Trial Lawyers of Am., Am. Bar Assn., Neb. State Bar Assn., Iowa State Bar Assn. (bd. gov. 1999—2003, v.p. 2003, pres.-elect 2004, pres. 2005), Phi Alpha Delta. Office: Salvo Deren Schenck & Lauterbach PC 711 Court St Harlan IA 51537-0509 Office Phone: 712-755-3141. Office Fax: 712-755-3144. Business E-Mail: jasalvo@sdsllaw.com. *

SALVUCCI, LINDA, history professor; b. Pittston, Pa., Mar. 28, 1951; d. Joseph A. and Helen Shegelski Kerrigan; m. Richard Salvucci, Aug. 25, 1973; children: Martin J., Rosemary C. AB in History, Villanova U., 1973; AM in History, Princeton U., 1979, PhD in History, 1985. Asst. prof. history Trinity U., San Antonio, 1985—91, assoc. prof. history, 1991—. Chmn., mem. coms. various confs. in field. Co-author: (textbook) Call to Freedom, various edits., 2000—05; contbr. articles to profl. publs. Trustee St. Luke's Episc. Sch., 1998—2005, vice chmn., 2002—04; bd. editors The Americas, 2002—06; bd. dirs. Youth Orchs. San Antonio, 2005—06. Recipient Hubert Herring award for best article, Pacific Coast Coun. on L.Am. Studies, 1985, Coll. Tchrs. award, NEH, 1988—89, prize, Conf. on L.Am. History, 2001. Mem.: Hist. Soc. (bd. govs. 2006—), Nat. Coun. History Edn. (trustee 2005—), Omohundro Inst. Early Am. History and Culture, Am. Hist. Assn. Office: Trinity U Dept History 1 Trinity Pl San Antonio TX 78212 Office Phone: 210-999-7628.

SALYARDS BURTON, SHANNON MARIE, voice educator, singer; b. Hastings, Nebr., June 30, 1979; d. Harry Emory and Mary Phyllis Shannon Salyards; m. Sean Michael Burton, Aug. 21, 2004. MusB, St. Olaf Coll., Northfield, Minn., 1997—2001; MusM, Boston U., 2001—03. Visual asst. Banana Rep. Copley Pl., Boston, 2001—03; voice faculty Tanglewood Inst. Boston U., Lenox, 2003, choral scholar Marsh Chapel, 2003—05; adminstrv. asst. Winchester Cmty. Music Sch., Mass., 2003—05; adj. prof. voice U. Nebr., Omaha, 2005—; adj. prof. music Hastings Coll., Nebr., 2005—06; adj. prof. voice Doane Coll., Crete, Nebr., 2006—. Singer (soprano soloist): Haydn: Lord Nelson Mass, Schumann: Das Paradies und die Peri, Bach: St. John Passion, Bach: Cantata 82a; musician: Schutz: Musikalische Exequien, Mendelssohn: Hor mein Bitten, Handel: Judas Maccabaeus, Faure: Requiem, Schubert: Mass in G, Hasse: Te Deum in D (1751), Crumb: Madrigal Book I, Mozart: Solemn Vespers, Purcell: Come Ye Sons of Art, Away, Haydn: Creation, Haydn: Mass in Time of War, Mozart: Requiem, Handel: Messiah, Davidovsky: Song, Monteverdi: Vespers, Orff: Carmina Burana, Bach: Cantatas 150 and 199, Pfoltner: Light from Out of Darkness, Barber: Knoxville: Summer of 1915, Mozart: Exsultate, Jubilate, Mozart: Mass in C Minor. Mem.: Nat. Assn. Tchrs. Singing. Home: 1100 W C St Apt 309 Lincoln NE 68522 Home Phone: 402-742-5410.

SALYER, KENNETH E., surgeon; b. Kansas City, Kans., Aug. 18, 1936; s. Everett A. and Laurene S.; m. Luci Lara-Salyer; children: Kenneth E. Jr., Leigh Green-Salyer. BS, U. Mo., 1958; MD, U. Kans., 1962. Intern Parkland Meml. Hosp., Dallas, 1962-63, resident in gen. surgery, 1963-67; fellow in surgery U. Tex. SW Sch. Med., Dallas, 1965-67, founder, dir. residency tng. program, 1969-78; prof. surgery, chair plastic surgery, 1969-78; resident in plastic surgery U. Kans. Sch. Med., Kansas City, 1967-69; founder, dir. Internat. Craniofacial Inst., Dallas, 1986—. Editl. bd. mem. Annals of Plastic Surgery, 1977-79, Jour. of Speech and Hearing Disorders (editl. cons.) 1982, Tex. Medicine (editl. cons.) 1981-85, Jour. of Craniofacial Surgery, 1990—, Italian Jour. Craniomaxillofacial Surgery, 1990—, Argentinian Jour. Plastic Surgery (internat. consultative coun. 1990—). Author: Techniques in Aesthetic Craniofacial Surgery, 1989, Cleft Lip and Palate Treatment Center: A Booklet for Parents, 1994, (with J. Bardach) Surgical Techniques in Cleft Lip and Palate, 1987, 2d edit. 1991, (with others) The Atlas of Craniomaxillofacial Surgery, 1982; editor: Symposium on Plastic Surgery in the Orbital Region, 1976; author various book chpts. Recipient Nat. Inst. Health award public health svc., sr. clin. traineeship Cancer Control Program 1967-69, Plastic Surgery Resident Program Participation award 2nd place 1967-69, scholar. competition (hon. mention) Edn. Found. Am. Soc. Plastic and Reconstructive Surgeons, 1972, Rsch. Grant award Ednl. Found. Am. Soc. Plastic and Reconstructive Surgeons 1975-76, Hektoen Gold medal for original investigation "Spectrum of Rsch. and Clin. Mgmt. of Craniofacial Anomalies" exhibit at AMA, San Francisco 1977, selected hon. mem. Japanese Soc. Craniofacial Surgery 1993, selected chmn. med. adv. bd. Children's Craniofacial Assn. 1993; grantee Internat. NIH Microvascular Surg. Rsch. 1969, Vets. Admin. Hosp. Maxillofacial Rsch. 1972-78, Sid Richardson Found. med. rsch. 1975-76, Gen. Electric Found. for Craniofacial Deformities 1985-87; recipient various awards for videos. Mem. AMA (mem. various coms.), Am. Acad. Pediat. (exec. com. section on plastic surgery, founding mem., sec.-treas. 1987-90, chmn. 1991—), Am. Assn. of Pediat. Plastic Surgery (founding mem., chmn. 1991—), Am. Assn. Plastic Surgery (mem. various coms.), Am. Burn Assn., Am. Cleft Palate Assn. (mem. various coms.), Am. Coll. Surgeons, Am. Soc. for Aesthetic Plastic Surgery, Am. Soc. Maxiofacial Surgery (mem. various coms.), Am. Soc. Plastic and Reconstructive Surgery (mem. various coms.), Am. Soc. for Reconstructive Microsurgery, Argentine Soc. of Plastic Surgery, Children's Craniofacial Assn. (chmn. med. adv. bd.), Chirugio Soc., Craniofacial Biology Group, Dallas County Med. Soc., Dallas Soc. Plastic Surgery, Euro. Assn. for Craniomaxillofacial Surgery, Internat. Coll. Surgeons, Internat. Confederation for Plastic Reconstructive Surgery (founding mem.), Internat. Craniofacial Club, Internat. Craniofacial Travel Club, Internat. Soc. Clin. Plastic Surgery, Internat. Soc. Cranofacial Surgery (hon. mem.), Lipoplasty Soc. of N.A., Inc., McKorkle Soc., Pan-Pacific Surg. Assn., Physicians Art Assn., Plastic Surgery Rsch. Coun., Soc. for Biomaterials, Soc. Craniofacial Genetics, Soc. Head and Neck Surgery, So. Med. Assn., Southwestern Med. Found., Tex. Soc. Plastic Surgery (mem. various coms., pres.-elect 1982-83, pres. 1983-84), Tex. State Med. Assn., Wound Healing Soc. Avocations: skiing, running, travel. Office: Internat Cranio Inst 7777 Forest Ln Ste C717 Dallas TX 75230-2550

SALYER, STEPHEN LEE, educational program administrator; b. Lexington, Ky., July 20, 1950; s. Ralph Conley Salyer and Margaret Miles; m. Susan D. Moeller; children: Samuel Wilmot, Duncan Davis, Clara Josephine stepchildren: Walden Jeffrey Davis, Sethly Martin Davis. BA, Davidson Coll., 1972; MPA, Harvard U., 1975. Pres. Citizens' Com. on Population and the Am. Future, Washington, 1972-73; cons. Rockefeller Family Assocs., NYC, 1973-75; assoc. pub. issues program Population Coun., NYC, 1977-79; asst. to the pres. Ednl. Broadcasting Corp., Sta. WNET TV, NYC, 1975-76, v.p. corp. affairs, 1979-80, v.p. program devel. and mktg., 1981-82, sr. v.p. edn. divsn., 1982-86, sr. v.p. mktg. and comm., 1986-88; pres., CEO Pub. Radio Internat., Mpls., 1988—2005, Salzurb Sem., Washington, 2005—, also bd. dirs., 2005—. Chmn. bd. dirs. Pub. Interactive, LLC, 1999—2005. Co-author: (with James J. Bausch) Toward Safe, Convenient and Effective Contraceptives, 1978. Mem. Nat. Commn. on Population Growth and the Am. Future, Washington, 1970—72; bd. dirs. Philanthropic Rsch., Inc. Guidestar, 2001—, Davidson Coll., 2004—; fellow Japan Soc. US-Japan Leadership, 1996. Root-Tilden scholar, NYU Sch. Law, 1976—79, Salzburg Seminar fellow, 1974, Brit.-Am. Program fellow, 1990. Mem. Harvard Club (N.Y.C.). Home: 9510 Midwood Rd Silver Spring MD 20910 Office: 1828 L St NW Washington DC 20036

SALZBERG, BARRY, accounting firm executive; Degree in Acctg., Bklyn. Coll.; JD, Bklyn. Law Sch.; LLM in Taxation, NYU. Joined Deloitte & Touche USA LLP, 1977, named ptnr., 1985, tri-state group mng. ptnr., 1996—99, nat. tax dep. mng. ptnr., 1999—2000, nat. tax mng. ptnr., 2000—03, US mng. ptnr., 2003—, also mem. bd. dirs., chmn. exec. com. Chmn. bd YMCA of Greater NY, 2004—07; bd. mem. Jackie Robinson Found. Recipient CEO Diversity Leadership award, Bus. Women's Network, 2004. Mem.: AICPA, NY County Lawyers Assn., NY State Soc. CPAs, NY State Bar Assn. Office: Deloitte & Touche USA LLP 1633 Broadway New York NY 10019-6754 Office Phone: 212-492-3688.

SALZBERG, RUSS, sportscaster; b. NY; m. Vikki Salzberg; 2 children. Sports radio personality Sta. WFAN, Astoria, N.Y., 1993—; sportscaster Sta. WWOR-TV UPN 9 News, Secaucus, N.J. Sports anchor Sta. WOR-TV; former real estate salesman. Office: WFAN-AM Infinity Broadcasting Kaufman Astoria Studios 34-12 36th St Astoria NY 11106 also: Care Sta Wwor-Tv Upn 9 News 9 Broadcast Plz Secaucus NJ 07094-2913

SALZMAN, ARTHUR GEORGE, architect, consultant; b. Chgo., June 20, 1929; s. Russell Harvey Salzman and Mildred Olive (Olsen) Erickson; m. Joan Marie Larson, Aug. 16, 1952; children: Lisa Jo Salzman Braucher, David Ralph. BS in Archtl. Engring., U. Ill., 1952; MArch, Ill. Inst. Tech., 1960. Nat. Coun. Archtl. Registration Bds. Architect Skidmore, Owings & Merrill, Chgo., 1960, Mies van der Rohe, Arch., Chgo., 1960-69; assoc. The Office of Mies Van Der Rohe, Chgo., 1969-81; v.p. FCL Assocs., Chgo., 1981-86; exec. v.p. Lohan Assocs., Chgo., 1986-91; pvt. practice Evanston, Ill., 1992—2007; cons., 2007—. Bldg. code restructuring com. City of Chgo., 1994-96, bldg. code electronic version com., 1997, bldg. code rev. com., 1998-2004; adj. prof. arch. Ill. Inst. Tech., Chgo., 2005-06. V.p. Chgo. area Unitarian-Universalist Coun., Chgo., 1974—76; bd. dirs. Savoy-aires, Evanston, Ill., 1985—88, 1990—93, pres., 1992—93; active Chgo. Com. on High Rise Bldgs. Cpl. US Army, 1952—54. Mem. AIA (bd. dirs. Chgo. chpt. 1992-96, sec. 1994-96, Ill. region bd., alt. del. 1997-98, del. 1999-2000, emeritis 2007—, Disting. Svc. award for profl. excellence 2003), Am. Soc. Testing and Materials Internat., Constrn. Specifications Inst. (emeritus 2007—), Internat. Code Coun. (profl.), Precast-Prestressed Concrete Inst., North Shore Musicians Club. Avocations: acting, singing. Office Fax: 847-332-2441.

SALZMAN, DAVID ELLIOT, entertainment industry executive; b. Bklyn., Dec. 1, 1943; s. Benjamin and Rose Harriet (Touby) S.; m. Sonia Camelia Gonsalves, Oct. 19, 1968; children: Daniel Mark, Andrea Jessica, Adam Gabriel. BA, Bklyn. Coll., 1965; MA, Wayne State U., 1967. Dir. TV ops. Wayne State U., 1966-67; producer Lou Gordon Program, 1967-70; program mgr. Sta. WKBD-TV, Detroit, 1970-71, Sta. KDKA-TV, Pitts., 1971-72, gen. mgr., 1973-75; program mgr. Sta. KYW-TV, Phila., 1972-73; chmn. bd. Group W Prodns., NYC and Los Angeles, 1975—; founder, pres. United Software Assocs., 1980-81; creator News Info. Weekly Service, 1981; exec. v.p. Telepictures Corp., 1980-84, vice chmn., 1984; pres. Lorimar Telepictures Corp. (merger Telepictures and Lorimar, Inc.), 1985-90, Lorimar TV, 1986-90; creator Newscope: Nat. TV News Cooperative, 1983; pres., CEO David Salzman Entertainment, Burbank, Calif., 1990-93; co-CEO Quincy Jones-David Salzman Entertainment (QDE), 1993—; exec. prodr. Jenny Jones Show, 1991—2003. Exec. prodr. Mad-TV, 1995—, The Rerun Show, Jumble, In the House, 68th Ann. Acad. awards, Concert of the Americas, 1995, Vibe-TV, 1997-98, Steel, 1997, Their Eyes Were Watching God, 2005; CEO David Salzman Enterprises, 1998—; co-owner Vibe Mag., 1995-2006, Spin Mag., 1995-2006, Sta. WNOL-TV, 1995, Sta. WATL-TV, 1995, Sta. KCWE-TV, 1995-2006, Sta. WGRB-TV, 1998; guest lectr. at schs.; bd. govs. Films of Coll. and Univ. Students; co-prodr. (Broadway shows) Urinetown, The Dinner Party, 2001, Into the Woods, 2002. Contbr. articles to profl. jours. Bd. dirs. Pitts. Civic Light Opera, Am. Blood Bank, Pitts., Hebrew Inst., Jewish Community Ctr., Harrison, NY, Temple Etz Chaim, USC Sch. Cinema-TV, Emory U. Ctr. Leadership, Emory Bus. Sch., Bklyn. Coll. Found., HELP group; co-founding bd. mem. Tour Calif. Cycling Race, 2006, 07. Recipient award Detroit chpt. Am. Women in Radio and TV, 1969, award Golden Quill, 1971, award Golden Gavel, 1971, local Emmy award, 1972, award AP, 1974, Gold medal Broadcast Promotion Assn., 1983, Lifetime Achievement award Bklyn. Coll., 1990, Disting. Alumnus award, Golden Plate award Am. Acad. Achievement, 1995; BPME Gold medal San Francisco Film Festival, 1984, N.Y., 1985, Chgo., 1986, Tree of Life award Jewish Nat. Fund, 1988. Mem. Acad. TV Arts and Scis., Nat. Assn. TV Program Execs., Radio-TV News Dirs. Assn., Am. Mgmt. Assn., Am. Film Inst., Brooklyn Coll. Found. Office: Hollywood Prodn Ctr 1149 N Gower St Ste 247 Los Angeles CA 90038 Business E-Mail: davids@madtv.com. *"Be prepared."*.

SALZMAN, GARY SCOTT, lawyer; b. Portchester, NY, May 26, 1963; s. David Stuart and Francine (Selenow) S.; m. Suzanne Sansone, Apr. 2, 1990. BBA, U. Miami, 1985, JD, 1988. Bar: Fla. 1988, U.S. Dist. Ct. (so. dist.) 1989, Colo. 1991, U.S. Dist. Ct. (mid. dist.) Fla. 1992, U.S. Ct. Appeals (11th cir.) 1992, U.S. Supreme Ct. 1992; cert. arbitrator and mediator; cert. in bus. litigation, Fla. Assoc. Robinson & Greenberg, PA, Coral Gables, Fla., 1988-89, Buchbinder & Elegant, PA, Miami, Fla., 1989, Mishan, Sloto, Hoffman and Greenberg, PA, Miami, 1989-91, Dempsey & Assocs., Winter Park, Fla., 1991-92; pvt. practice, Orlando and Winter Park, Fla., 1992-95; ptnr. Marlowe, Appleton, Weatherford & Salzman, Winter Park, 1996-98; shareholder Brown, Salzman, Weiss & Garganese, P.A., Orlando, 1998—2004, Gray Robinson, P.A., Orlando, 2004—. Comml.,employment and fin. arbitration panelist Am. Arbitration Assn. Mem. ABA, Fla. Bar Assn. (Fla. Bar BLSE, bus. litig. cert. com. 1995—),

Bus. Exec. Network, Orange County Bar Assn. Office: Ste 1400 301 E Pine St Orlando FL 32801 Office Phone: 407-843-8880. Office Fax: 407-244-5690. Business E-Mail: gsalzman@gray-robinson.com.

SALZMAN, MICHELE RENEE, historian, educator; b. Bklyn., Aug. 2, 1952; d. Aron and Sylvia Salzman; m. Steven Gregory Brint, 1985; children: Juliana, Benjamin. BA, Bklyn. Coll. CUNY, 1973; MA, Bryn Mawr Coll., 1975, PhD, 1981. Classics lectr. Swarthmore (Pa.) Coll., 1980; vis. asst. prof. classics Columbia U., NYC, 1980-82; asst. prof. classics Boston U., 1982-90, assoc. prof. classics, 1990-95; assoc. prof. history U. Calif., Riverside, 1995—2000, prof., 2000—, chair history dept., 1999—2000, mem. steering com. multi-campus rsch. group, 1999—. Project dir. Inst. for Antiquity and Christianity, Claremont Grad. U., 1999—. prof. in charge of Intercollegiate Ctr. for Classified Studies in Rome, 2003-04. Author: (book) On Roman Time: The Codex-Calendar of 354 and the Rhythms of Urban Life in Late Antiquity, 1990, The Making of a Christian Aristocracy: Social and Religious Change in the Western Roman Empire, 2002; mem. editl. bd.: Am. Jour. Archaeology; contbr. articles to profl. jours. Grantee Am. Philol. Soc., 1983; fellow Ctr. for Ideas and Soc., U. Calif., Riverside, 1996, Am. Coun. Learned Socs., 1983; Mellon Fellow in Classical Studies Am. Acad. Rome, 1986-87. Mem. Am. Philol. Assn. (chair Colloquium on Late Antiquity 1993-97), Classical Assn. So. Calif., N.Am. Patristics Soc., Assn. for Ancient History, Phi Beta Kappa. Avocations: tennis, aerobics, reading. Office: U Calif-Riverside Dept History Riverside CA 92521-0001 Home Phone: 909-625-2745; Office Phone: 951-827-1991. Business E-Mail: michele.salzman@ucr.edu.

SALZMAN, ROBERT JAY, accountant; b. Bklyn., Dec. 7, 1941; s. Irving and Sydelle (Feingold) S.; m. Constance A. Freeman, Sept. 16, 1990. BA, Allegheny Coll., Meadville, Pa., 1962; MBA, U. Pa., Phila., 1965; JD, NY Law Sch., 1972. Bar: NY 1973; CPA, NY. Acct., NYC, 1965—; pvt. practice Robert J. Salzman, CPA, P.C., NYC, 1970—. Home: 10 E End Ave New York NY 10021-1106 Office: 82 Sycamore Dr East Hampton NY 11937-1482 also: 2801 NE 183rd St Miami FL 33160-2100 Office Phone: 212-744-2860. Business E-Mail: rsalzman@rjspc.com.

SALZMAN, STANLEY P., lawyer; b. NYC, Jan. 30, 1931; s. George D. and Fanny M. (Pugach) S.; m. Leona Schames, June 18, 1958 (dec. Nov. 1967); m. Marilyn J. Bzura, Feb. 3, 1974; children: Ira J., Mark B., Debra G., Jeffrey M. David, Steven B. David. BA, Bklyn. Coll., 1952; JD, Bklyn. Law Sch., 1955. Bar: NY 1956, US Dist. Ct. (so. and ea. dists.) NY 1960, US Supreme Ct. 1964, US Ct. Appeals (2d cir.) 1966. Assoc. Otterbourg, Steindler, Houston & Rosen, NYC, 1957; ptnr. Venitt, Adler & Salzman, NYC, 1958-66, Friesner & Salzman, Great Neck, NY, 1966—. Bd. dirs. Colora Printing Inks Inc., Linden, NJ. Home Phone: 516-482-3770; Office Phone: 516-487-1300. Personal E-mail: fssps@juno.com.

SALZWEDEL, JACK C., insurance company executive; b. DeForest, Wis. m. Sarah Salzwedel; 4 children. BS, Wartburg Coll., 1982. Ins. sales positions through v.p. Am. Family Mut. Ins. Co., Madison, Wis., 1983—2000, v.p. personal lines div., 2000—03, v.p. life & health ins. ops., 2003—05, exec. v.p., 2005—06, pres., COO, 2007—. Office: Am Family Mut Ins Co 6000 American Pkwy Madison WI 53783 *

SAM, DAVID, federal judge; b. Hobart, Ind., Aug. 12, 1933; s. Andrew and Flora (Toma) S.; m. Betty Jean Brennan, Feb. 1, 1957 (dec. Aug. 2000); children: Betty Jean, David Dwight, Daniel Scott, Tamara Lynn, Pamela Rae, Daryl Paul, Angie, Sheyla; m. Bennie Lynn Malnar, Jan. 5, 2005. BS, Brigham Young U., 1957; JD, Utah U., 1960. Bar: Utah 1960, U.S. Dist. Ct. Utah 1966. Sole practice and ptnr., Duchesne, Utah, 1963-76; dist. judge State of Utah, 1976-85; judge U.S. Dist. Ct. Utah, Salt Lake City, 1985-97; chief judge U.S. Dist. Ct., Salt Lake City, 1997—99, sr. judge, 1999—. Atty. City of Duchesne, 1963-72; Duchesne County atty., 1966-72; commr. Duchesne, 1972-74; adv. com. Codes of Conduct of Jud. Conf. US, 1987-91, Jud. Coun. of 10th Cir., 1991-93; mem. US Del. to Romania, Aug. 1991. Chmn. Jud. Nomination Com. for Cir. Ct. Judge, Provo, Utah, 1983; bd. dirs. Water Resources, Salt Lake City, 1973-76. Served to capt. JAGC, USAF, 1961-63. Named Judge of Yr., Utah State Bar, 1999. Avocations: beekeeping, reading, sports. Office: US Dist Ct US Courthouse 350 S Main St Ste 441 Salt Lake City UT 84101-2180 Office Phone: 801-524-6190. Business E-Mail: david_sam@utd.uscourts.gov.

SAMADI, ALBERT A., urologist; MD, SUNY, Bklyn., 1995. Diplomate Am. Bd. Urology. Asst. prof., dir. robotic and laparoscopic urology dept. urology NYMed. Coll., Valhalla, 2002—06; dir. urology Facey Med. Group, Valencia, Calif., 2006—. Fellow: ACS, Endourology Soc.; mem.: AMA, Soc. Laparoendoscopic Surgeons, Sephardic Am. Med. Soc., Am. Urologic Assn. Achievements include research in robotic and laparoscopic urology. Office: Facey Med Group 25775 McBean Pky Ste 214 Valencia CA 91355 Home Phone: 310-499-8358; Office Phone: 661-424-8872. Office Fax: 661-255-5626.

SAMARTINI, JAMES ROGERS, retired appliance company executive; b. Cleve., Apr. 13, 1935; s. Leonard Henry and Grace Rogers (Tully) S.; m. Irene Ann Kurnava, Sept. 16, 1961 (dec. June 1994); m. Julia S. Rubin, Sept. 8, 1996; children: David L., James F., Patrick R. AB, Dartmouth Coll., 1957; MBA, Harvard U., 1961. Fin. supr. Ford Motor Co., Dearborn, Mich., 1966-72; v.p. fin. and adminstrn. Thonet Industries Inc., York, Pa., 1972-74; from asst. controller to v.p., CFO Mead Corp., Dayton, 1974-86; CFO Whirlpool Corp., 1986-91, exec. v.p., chief adminstrv. officer Benton Harbor, Mich., 1991-95; ret., 1995. Bd. dirs. Peoples State Bank, St. Joseph, Mich., 1987-95. Trustee, treas. Marvelwood Sch., 2004—; mem. adv. bd. Salvation Army; chmn. bd. trustees Whirlpool Found., 1993—95; trustee Dayton Opera Assn., 1977—86, pres., 1985—86; bd. dirs. Epilepsy Assn. We. Ohio, 1986, S.W. Mich. Symphony Orch., 1991—93; mem. bd. fin. Town of Kent (Conn.), 1999—2005, mem. zoning bd. appeals, 2001—. Mem.: Kent. Libr. Assn. (bd. dirs., treas. 2002—05), Fin. Execs. Inst. (bd. dirs. 1983—86). Home: PO Box 129 South Kent CT 06785-0129

SAMBERG, ANDY, actor; b. Berkeley, Calif., Aug. 18, 1978; Grad., U. Calif., Santa Cruz, NYU Film School. Co-founder, mem. The Lonely Island, NYC, 2001—. Writer G-Phoria, 2004, MTV Movie Awards, 2004, 2005; actor: (TV special) Comedy Central Laughs for Life Telethon, 2004; (TV series) Saturday Night Live, 2005—; (films) Hot Rod, 2007; guest appearances (TV series) 40 Most Awesomely Bad Dirrty Songs...Ever, 2004, Arrested Development, 2005, Premium Blend, 2005, The Late Show with David Letterman, 2006, Conan O'Brien, 2006. Recipient WIRED Rave Award - TV, 2006. Office: United Talent Agency Inc 9560 Wilshire Blvd Ste 500 Beverly Hills CA 90212 Office Phone: 310-273-6700. Office Fax: 310-247-1111. *

SAMBERG, ARTHUR J. (ART SAMBERG), investment company executive; BS, MIT; MS, Stanford U.; MBA, Columbia U. Established first Pequot investment fund, 1986; ptnr. Weiss, Peck & Greer, Inc.; CEO Pequot Capital Mgmt. Bd. mem. Coll. Summit's Nat. Bd. Dirs. Mem.: MIT Corp. Office: Pequot Capital Mgmt 500 Nyala Farm Rd Westport CT 06880

SAMBERY, ANDY, actor; b. Berkeley, Calif., Aug. 18, 1978; Grad., UCSC, NYU. Mem. The Lonely Island, 2001—. Actor: (TV series) Saturday Night Live, 2005— (WIRED Rave Award for TV, 2006), (guest appearances) 40 Most Awesomely Bad Dirrty Songs...Ever, 2004—, Premium Blend, 2005, Arrested Development, 2005—, The Late Show with David Letterman, 2006, Late Night with Conan O'Brien, 2006; writer, guest appearances (TV Specials) G-Phoria 2004, 2004—; actor: (TV Specials) Comedy Central Laughs for Life Telethon, 2004; writer (TV Specials) 2004 MTV Movie Awards, 2004, 2005 MTV Movie Awards, 2005—. Office: United Talent Agency Inc 9560 Wilshire Blvd Ste 500 Beverly Hills CA 90212 Office Phone: 310-273-6700. Office Fax: 310-247-1111.

SAMBLIS, KELLEY C., educator, researcher; d. Joseph and Barbara Faye Chaplauske; children: Colton, Maggie, Mary. Bachelor's degree, U. So. Miss., 1987; Master's degree, Nova U., 1990; EdS, U. West Fla., 2003, Doctorate, 2004. Elem. tchr. Brevard Sch. Dist., Melbourne, Fla., 1987—97; asst. prof. U. So. MIss., Long Beach, 2003—. Mem.: ASCD.

SAMBOL, DAVID E., diversified financial services company executive; b. 1959; m. Ellie M. Sambol. BBA in Acctg., Calif. State U., Northridge, 1982. CPA. Acct. Ernst & Whinney; with Countrywide Fin. Corp., Calabasas, Calif., 1985—94, mng. dir. capital markets, 1994—2000, sr. mng. dir., chief prodn., 2000—02, exec. mng. dir. loans & capital markets, 2003, exec. mng. dir. bus. segment operations, pres., COO Countrywide Home Loans, 2004—, pres., COO, 2006—. Bd. dirs. Countrywide Home Loans, Inc., Balboa Life & Casualty, Countrywide Fin. Holding Co., Inc. Office: Countrywide Fin Corp 4500 Park Granada Calabasas CA 91302-1613

SAMBORA, RICHIE (RICHARD STEPHEN SAMBORA), musician, singer, songwriter; b. Perth Amboy, NJ, July 11, 1959; s. Adam and Joan Sambora; m. Heather Locklear, Dec. 17, 1994 (div. Apr. 11, 2007); 1 child, Ava Elizabeth. LHD, Kean U., 2004. Musician of various bands including Screaming Mimis, Mercy, The Next, Message, and Duke Williams & The Extremes; guitarist, vocalist, songwriter Bon Jovi, 1983—. Musician: (solo albums) Stranger In This Town, 1991, Undiscovered Soul, 1994; musician, vocalist (albums) Bon Jovi, 1984, 7800 Fahrenheit, 1985, Slippery When Wet, 1986, Bon Jovi Live, 1987, New Jersey, 1988, Keep the Faith, 1992, Crossroad, 1994, These Days, 1995, Bon Jovi, 1999, Crush, 2000, Bounce, 2002, Distance, 2003, This Left Feels Right, 2003, 100,000,000 Bon Jovi Fans Can't Be Wrong, 2004, Have a Nice Day, 2005, cameo appearances (films) Staying Alive, 1983, On The Line, 2001, guest appearances American Dreams, 2003. Avocations: watching sporting events, including football, basketball, and boxing, jet-skiing, fishing, golf.

SAMBURG, A. GENE, security company executive; b. Indpls., Apr. 25, 1941; s. A. George and Hermine (Wittgenstein) S.; m. Lorrie Silverman, June 26, 1966; children: Kimberly Jill, Thomas Blair. BEE, Cornell U., 1964; OPM, Harvard U., 1985. Engr. Westinghouse Corp., 1964-72; founder, pres. and CEO Kastle Systems, Inc., 1972—. Adv. on bus. programs Cornell U.; lectr. on entrepreneurship Georgetown U.; spl. lectr. for numerous profl. and ednl. courses in field. Patentee in field. Named E&Y Master Entrepreneur of Yr., Washington, 1999. Mem. IEEE, ASME, CPP, Am. Soc. Indsl. Security, Woodmont Country Club, City Club (Washington), Tower Club (McLean, Va.). Home: 1401 N Oak St Arlington VA 22209 Office: Kastle Systems Inc 1501 Wilson Blvd Arlington VA 22209-2403 Office Phone: 703-528-8800. Business E-Mail: gene@kastle.com.

SAMEC, DIANE PATRICIA, retired elementary school educator; b. Oak Pk., Ill., Mar. 17, 1942; d. Albert Vincent Samec and Helen Hrubec. BA, Hope Coll., Holland, Mich., 1964; MSc in edn., No. Ill. U., DeKalb, 1988. Tchr. Interboro Schools, Glenolden, Pa., 1964—65, Sch. Dist. u-46, Elgin, Ill., 1966—2004; ret., 2004. Vol. and mem. Willow Creek Cmty. Ch., South Barrington, 1986—, Sherman Hosp. Aux. Ch., Elgin, 2004—. Mem.: Nat. Audubon Soc., Elgin Ret. Teachers Assn., Elgin Edn. Assn., Ill. Edn. Assn., Nat. Edn. Assn., Willow Creek Comm. Ch., Nat. Wildlife Assn., Environ. Def., Sierra Club, Fox Valley Beaux Arts Women's Club. Avocations: travel, reading, photography.

SAMEK, EDWARD LASKER, medical transcription executive; b. NYC, Oct. 26, 1936; s. Richard E. and Jane L. Samek; m. Marthann Lauver, June 26, 1960; children: Anne, Margaret, Elizabeth. BS in Commerce and Fin., Bucknell U., 1958; MBA, Columbia U., 1960. Brand mgr. Procter & Gamble Co., Cin., 1960-62; dir. new products Johnson & Johnson, New Brunswick, NJ, 1962-67; v.p., gen. mgr. Avon Products Inc., NYC, 1967-75; pres., CEO Childcraft Edn. Corp., Edison, NJ, 1975-78, also dir.; pres. Hudson Pharm. Corp., West Caldwell, 1978-82; CEO, chmn. bd., pres. Secrephone Ltd., Ft. Washington, Pa., 1982-94, exec. v.p., 1994-95; chmn., pres., CEO Medifax SecrePhone, Atlanta, 1995-96; chmn., CEO The MRC Group, Cleve., 1996-98; vice chmn. Medquist Inc., Marlton, NJ, 1998—2000. Bd. dir. A. Gary Shilling & Co., MedPlus, Inc., Cin., VeriText LLC, Alliance Imaging, Inc., Anaheim, Calif., Third Millenniam Health-care, Atlanta, N.Am. Mgmt. Corp., Boston, Caremedic Healthcare, St. Petersburg, Fla., WaterJel Products, Inc., Carlstadt, NJ. Pres. bd. trustees Hartridge Sch., Plainfield, NJ, 1969-76; v.p. bd. trustees Wardlaw-Hartridge Sch., Plainfield and Edison, 1975—; trustee, v.p. bd. Plainfield Symphony, 1976-86; trustee, treas. Friends of Acadia, 2003—; trustee, treas. The Jackson Lab., 2004—, corp. mem., 2005—. Served with Ordnance Corps, U.S. Army, 1958-59. Mem. Young Pres. Orgn., Princeton Club (chmn. NJ chpt.), World Pres. Orgn. (chmn. NJ chpt.), NYC Univ. Club. Home and Office: 1717 Woodland Ave Edison NJ 08820-1039 Personal E-mail: ed@samek.net.

SAMELSON, LAWRENCE ELLIOT, medical researcher; b. Chgo., Apr. 18, 1951; s. Charles F. and Natalie (Rudeis) S.; m. Elizabeth Trosman, June 8, 1980; children: Seth Aaron, Rebecca Ellen. BA, U. Rochester, 1972; MD, Yale U., 1977. Resident in internal medicine U. Chgo. Hospitals, 1977-80; rsch. assoc. Lab. Immunology Nat. Inst. Allergy and Infectious Diseases, NIH, Bethesda, Md., 1980-85; sr. staff fellow Cell Biology and Metabolism Br., Nat. Inst. Child Health and Human Devel., NIH, Bethesda, 1985-87, named sr. investigator, 1988, chief Sect. Lymphocyte Signaling, 1995, dep. branch chief, 1995; chief Lab. Cellular and Molecular Biology Ctr. Cancer Rsch., Nat. Cancer Inst. NIH, Bethesda, 1999—, dep. dir. Ctr. Cancer Rsch., Nat. Cancer Inst., 2006—. Contbr. articles to profl. publs. Achievements include research in T cell structure and function, T cell activation, and biochemistry of signal transduction. Office: Ctr Cancer Rsch Lab Cellular and Molecular Biology 37 Convent Dr Bldg 37 Rm 2066 Bethesda MD 20892-4256 Office Phone: 301-496-9683. Office Fax: 301-496-8479. E-mail: samelson@helix.nih.gov.

SAMENUK, GEORGE C., former software security company executive; b. June 18, 1955; m. Ann Samenuk; children: Anna, Phil, Amy, Jack. BA in Polit. Sci., Brown U., 1977. Various sr. mgmt. positions in the Americas and ASEAN/South Asia regions IBM Corp., 1977—99; pres., CEO Tradeout, 2000—01; chmn., CEO McAfee, Inc. (formerly Network Associates, Inc.), Santa Clara, Calif., 2001—06. Mem. listed co. advisory com. NY Stock Exchange; bd. dir. Symbol Technologies, Inc.; spkr. in field.

SAMER, BILL FRED CARL, writer, filmmaker; b. Elizabeth, NJ, Sept. 2, 1953; s. Fred Carl and Myrtle Edith (Levey) Samer. BA, Concordia Coll., Bronxville, NY, 1994; MA, Kean U. N.J., Union, 1980; AA in Film, Union Coll., Cranford, NJ, 2005; student, NYU. Film writer Big Screen, 2002; filmmaker, screenwriter, 2007—. Author: Moongate, 2003, UK, for Mother, 2003. Walker CROP, Clifton, NJ, 1978; vol. TV ad campaign, NY, 1976; active Interfaith Hospitality Network, 2003, William Samer Activist Orgn., 1987; mem. choir Grace Luth. Ch. Mem.: Creative and Performing Arts Club, TV and Film Prodn. Club (dir.). Avocations: hiking, volleyball. Home Phone: 908-686-6511; Office Phone: 908-577-7733.

SAMET, DEE-DEE, lawyer; BA, U. Ariz., 1962, JD, 1963. Bar: Ariz. 1964. Pvt. practice, Tucson, 1974—. Arbitrator U.S. Dist. Ct. Ariz., Gender Equality Task Force, 1993; judge pro tem Pima County Superior Ct., 1985—; Ninth Cir. Lawyer rep., 1990-93; mem. Jud. Performance Rev. Commn., 1996-99; pres. Casa de los Ninos, 2003-05. Mem. Fed. Bar Assn. (pres. Tucson chpt. 2004—), State Bar Ariz. (family law sect., workers compensation sect., trial law sect., co-chair workers compensation sect. 1988-89, gender bias task force, bd. govs. 1994-97, pres. 1999-2000, chair workers compensation sect. 2004, chair alternative dispute resolution sect. 2005-06), Am. Arbitration Assn. (nat. panel arbitrators, com. on exams., supreme ct. state Ariz. 1984-91), Pima County Bar Assn. (bd. dirs. 1994—), Nat. Assn. Counsel for Children, Ariz. Assn. Counsel for Children, So. Ariz. Women Lawyers Assn. (bd. dirs. 1990, pres. 1994-95, treas. alt. dispute resolution sect. 2003-04), Nat. Orgn. Social Security Claimants' Reps., Inn of Cts. Office: Dee-Dee Samet PC 717 N 6th Ave Tucson AZ 85705-8304 Office Phone: 520-624-8595. Business E-Mail: dee-dee@samet.psemoil.com.

SAMET, JACK I., lawyer; b. NYC, Aug. 6, 1940; s. William and Tillie (Katz) Samet; m. Helen Ray, Feb. 12, 1967; 1 child, Peter Lawrence. BA, Columbia U., 1961; JD, Harvard U., 1964. Bar: N.Y. 1964, Calif. 1973. Assoc. Whitman & Ransom, NYC, 1966-69, Hall, Casey, Dickler & Howley, NYC, 1969-73; ptnr. Ball, Hunt, Hart, Brown & Baerwitz, LA, 1973-81, Buchalter, Nemer, Fields & Younger, LA, 1981-94, Baker & Hostetler, LA, 1994—2006, active ret. ptnr., 2007—, mem. policy com., 1997-98, ptnr.-in-charge, 1997-98. Arbitrator Nat. Assn. Securities Dealers, LA, 1976—; spkr., panelist Calif. Continuing Edn. Bar, 1988. Actor: Playhouse W., 2005—, Good Time Max, (short film): It's Another Beautiful Day, Empty Apartment,: Welcome Home Soldier. Named a So. Calif. Superlawyer, 2004—07. Mem.: ABA, NY Bar Assn., Calif. Bar Assn., Screen Actor's Guild, Am. Bd. Trial Advs., Million Dollar Advs. Forum, Sport Club/LA. Avocations: exercise, reading, acting. Home: 2741 Aqua Verde Cir Los Angeles CA 90077-1502 Office: 333 S Grand Ave Los Angeles CA 90071-1504 E-mail: jsamet@bakerlaw.com, jsamet@belairmail.com.

SAMET, JONATHAN MICHAEL, epidemiologist, educator; b. Va., Mar. 26, 1946; AB in Chemistry and Physics, Harvard Coll., 1966; MD, U. Rochester, 1970; MS in Epidemiology, Harvard Sch. Pub Health, 1977. Diplomate Am. Bd. Internal Medicine, Nat. Bd. Med. Examiners. Intern in medicine U. Ky. Med. Ctr., Lexington, 1970-71; asst. resident in medicine U. N.Mex. Affiliated Hosps., Albuquerque, 1973-74, sr. resident, 1974-75; rsch. fellow in clin. epidemiology Channing lab. Harvard Med. Sch., Boston, 1975-78, rsch. assoc. in medicine, 1978-83; epidemiologist Cancer Rsch. and Treatment Ctr. U. N.Mex., Albuquerque, 1980-87, asst. prof. medicine, 1978-82, assoc. prof. medicine, 1982-88, assoc. prof. family, cmty., and emergency medicine, 1985-88, prof. family, cmty., and emergency medicine, 1986-94, prof. medicine, 1988-94, clin. prof. medicine, 1994—; prof., chmn. dept. epidemiology The Johns Hopkins U., Balt., 1994—, co-dir. risk scis. and pub. policy inst., 1995—. Chief pulmonary divsn. U. N.Mex Hosp., Albuquerque, 1985—94, chief pulmonary and critical care divsn. dept. medicine, 1985—94; mem. indoor air quality and total human exposure com., sci. adv. bd. US EPA, 1987—95; chmn. biol. effects ionizing radiation VI com. NRC, 1994—98, mem. bd. environ. studies and toxicology, 2002, chmn., 03, chmn. com. rsch. priorities airborne particulate matter, 1998—2004; chmn. Inst. Medicine, 1997, chmn. com. asbestos, 2004—06, chmn. com. evaluation presumptive disability decision making process for vets., 2006—; dir. Inst. Global Tobacco Control, 1998—; chmn. epidemiology and disease control study sect. 2 NIH, 2002. Editor pro tem Am. Jour. of Epidemiology, 1991—92; editor: Am. Jour. of Epidemiology, 1992—98; assoc. editor Tobacco Control: An Internat. Jour., 1991—; editor: Epidemiologic Revs., 1994—2002, Epidemiology, 2002—07; co-editor-in-chief: Air Quality, Atmosphere and Health, 2007—. With US Army, 1971—73. Recipient Clinton P. Anderson award, Am. Lung Assn., N.Mex, 1988, Excellence in Environ. Health Rsch. award, Rochester Sch. Medicine and Dentistry, 2006. Fellow: AAAS, Am. Coll. Epidemiology (pres. 2000—01, Surgeon Gen.'s medallion 2006); mem.: Md. Thoracic Soc., Internat. Soc. Indoor Air Quality and Climate, Internat. Epidemiol. Assn., N.Mex. Thoracic Soc. (sec.-treas. 1982—83, v.p. 1983—84, pres. 1984—85), Am. Thoracic Soc. (long range planning com. environ. and occupational health assembly 1992—, program com. behavioral scis. sect. 1994—95, Pub. Svc. award 2006), Soc. for Epidemiol. Rsch. (pres.-elect 1988—89, pres. 1989—90, exec. com. 1988—91), Delta Omega Alpha, Alpha Omega Alpha. Office: Dept Epidemiology The Johns Hopkins U 615 N Wolfe St Ste W6041 Baltimore MD 21205-2103 Home Phone: 410-539-8982; Office Phone: 410-955-3286. Personal E-mail: jsamet@aol.com. Business E-Mail: jsamet@jhsph.edu.

SAMFORD, YETTA GLENN, JR., lawyer, director; b. Opelika, Ala., June 8, 1923; s. Yetta Glenn and Mary Elizabeth (Denson) S.; m. Mary Austill, Sept. 6, 1949; children: Mary Austill Lott, Katherine Park Alford, Yetta Glenn III (dec.). BS, Auburn U., Ala., 1947; LLB, U. Ala., Tuscaloosa, 1949, LLD (hon.), 1995; DHL (hon.), U. Mobile, Ala., 2001. Bar: Ala. 1949, U.S. Dist. Ct. (mid. dist.) Ala. 1950, U.S. Ct. Appeals (5th cir.) 1961, U.S. Ct. Appeals (11th cir.) 1981. Pvt. practice, Opelika, Ala.; ptnr. Samford & Denson LLP and Predessors, 1949—. Mem. Ala. Senate from Lee and Russell counties, 1958-62; mem. bd. edn.Opelike City, 1963-75, pres. 1966-74; mem. State of Ala. Bd. of Corrections, 1969-75; mem. adv. bd. State Docks, 1987-2000. Trustee U. Mobile, 1963-92, life trustee, 1992—, trustee U. Ala., 1972-93, trustee emeritus, 1993—. Mem. Ala. Law Inst. (exec. com.), Ala. Acad. of Honor, Masons, Phi Delta Phi, Omicron Delta Kappa, Alpha Tau Omega. Republican. Baptist. Home: 615 Terracewood Dr Opelika AL 36801-3850 Office: Samford & Denson LLP PO Box 2345 Opelika AL 36803-2345 Office Phone: 334-745-3504. Personal E-mail: sdhpb@mindspring.com.

SAMIE, AMIDOU, microbiologist, educator, molecular biologist; b. Baigom/Foumbot, Cameroon, July 16, 1973; s. Moussa Nchoudoungam and Adama Ngoungoure. BSc in Biochemistry, U. Yaounde, Cameroon, 1995, MSc in Biochemistry, 1997; PhD in Microbiology, U. Venda, Thohoyandou, South Africa, 2007. Rsch. asst. Lab. Microbial Biotech., Yaounde, Cameroon, 1997—2002; rsch. assoc. dept. biol. scis., dept. biochemistry U. Zimbabwe, Harare, 2002—03; rsch. assoc., lectr. dept. microbiology U. Venda, 2003—05; rsch. fellow Ctr. for Global Health, U. Va., Charlottesville, 2005—. Vol. Cameroon Soc. Microbiology, Yaounde, 1995—2001; leader Assn. for Promotion of Sci. and Cultural Exch. in Africa, Yaounde, 1998—2002. Recipient Travel award, Internat. Union Biochemistry and Molecular Biology Socs., 1998, Best Sci. Presentation award, Internat. Union Immunol. Socs., 2003, Best Oral Presentation award, Boreholes/Coun. for US Landcare Initiative, 2004; grantee, Bill and Melinda Gates Found., 2006; Biotechnology Action fellow, UNESCO, 2002—03, rsch. grantee, Nat. Rsch. Found., South Africa, 2004—06, rsch. fellow, Ellison Med. Soc., 2005—06. Fellow: Internat. Soc. Infectious Diseases (rsch. grantee 2004—05); mem.: South African Soc. Microbiology, Zimbabwe Soc. Biochemistry and Molecular Biology, Brit. Soc. Parasitology, Cameroon Soc. Microbiology (corr.; sec. and internat. rels. 2001—05), Soc. Gen. Microbiology, Am. Soc. Microbiology (travel grantee 2003, 2006). Achievements include development of diagnostic method for the detection of Entamoeba histolytica, the causative agent of Amoebic dysentery; research in molecular epidemiology of Entamoeba histolytica in Africa; antimicrobial activity of medicinal plants used by African populations and isolation of active compounds; infectious diarrhea in the Venda region of South Africa, From genetics to control; microbial and physicochemical water quality; microbial and physicochemical quality of treated Sewage in the Mpumalanga Province, South Africa; epidemiology of Shistosomiasis in the Limpopo Province of South Africa. Avocations: gymnastic, nature, dance, Karate, volleyball. Office: U Venda Dept Microbiology Thohoyandou P/B X5050 South Africa Personal E-mail: samieamidou@yahoo.com.

SAMILJAN, KATRIANA, lawyer; b. Sacramento, Oct. 11, 1969; BA magna cum laude, Harvard Coll., Cambridge, Mass., 1991; JD, Harvard Law Sch., 1998. Former bankruptcy atty., Seattle; pvt. practice atty. Bush Strout & Kornfield, Seattle. Contbr. articles to numerous profl. jours. Named Wash. Rising Star, SuperLawyer Mag., 2001—06. Mem.: ABA, Am. Bankruptcy Inst., King Co. Bar Assn., Wash. State Bar Assn., Fed. Bar Assn. Office: Bush Strout and Kornfield 5500 Two Union Sq 601 Union St Seattle WA 98101-2373

SAMIOS, NICHOLAS PETER, physicist; b. NYC, Mar. 15, 1932; s. Peter and Niki (Vatick) S.; m. Mary Linakis, Jan. 12, 1958; children: Peter, Gregory, Alexandra. AB, Columbia U., 1953, PhD, 1957. Instr. physics Columbia U., NYC, 1956-59, adj. prof., 1970—; asst. physicist Brookhaven Nat. Lab., Upton, NY, 1959-62, assoc. physicist, 1962-64, physicist, 1964-68, sr. physicist, 1968—75, group leader, 1965-75, chmn. dept. physics, 1975-81, dep. dir. for high energy and nuclear physics, 1981, dir., 1982-97, disting. sr. scientist, 1997—; dep. dir. RIKEN/BNL Rsch. Ctr., 1998—. Adj. prof. Stevens Inst. Tech., 1969-75 Contbr. articles in field to profl. jours. Bd. dirs. Stony Brook Found., 1989, L.I. Assn., 1989. Recipient E.O. Lawrence Meml. award, 1980, award in physics and math. scis. N.Y. Acad. Scis., 1980, Bruno Pontecorvo prize, Joint Inst. for Nuclear Rsch., 2001; named AUI Disting. Scientist, 1992, W.K.H. Panofsky prize, 1993. Fellow Am. Phys. Soc. (chmn. divsn. of particles and fields 1975-76, chmn. PEP exptl. program com. 1976-78); mem. Internat. Ctr. Future Acceleration, Akademia Athenon (corr.). Achievements include being an expert in field of high energy particle and nuclear physics. Office: RIKEN/BNL Rsch Ctr Bldg 510A, Physics Dept Brookhaven Natl Lab Upton NY 11973-5000 E-mail: samios@bnl.gov.

SAMMARCO, PAUL WILLIAM, ecologist, researcher; b. Hackensack, NJ, Oct. 18, 1948; s. Giacomo and Esther (Galanti) S.; m. Jean Sogioka, May 29, 1971 (div. 1996); children: Mimi Cecile, Dustin Paul, Jack Isao; m. Donna M. Melancon, Aug. 12, 1998; stepchildren: Lindsay Claire, Ben Charles. BA, Syracuse U., 1970, postgrad., 1970—71; cert., Marine Biology Lab., Woods Hole, Mass., 1971, Fairleigh Dickinson U., 1972; PhD, SUNY Stony Brook, 1977. Tchg. asst. Syracuse U., NY, 1970—71; tchg. asst. Discovery Bay Marine Lab. SUNY-Stony Brook Overseas Acad. Program, Jamaica, 1974; tchg. asst. SUNY, Stony Brook, 1971—77; asst. prof. Clarkson U., Potsdam, NY, 1977—79; vis. asst. prof. tropical ecology SUNY Potsdam, St. Croix, V.I., 1979; sr. rsch. scientist Australian Inst. Marine Sci., Townsville, Queensland, 1979—89; coord. Shelf Seas Rsch. Program, 1985—86; dir. environ. rsch. Resource Assessment Commn. Prime Minister's commn. on natural resources, Canberra, Australia, 1989—91; exec. dir. La. Univs. Marine Consortium, Chauvin, 1991—95, prof., 1995—. Adj. prof. La. State U., U. La. at Lafayette, U. New Orleans, Nicholls State U., U. Campinas-Brazil, 1997-99, Ctrl. Queensland U., Australia, 1997-2002, U. Maine at Orono, 2001—03; pres. Endless Shores Music Pubs.; pres. P&J Records, LLC. Composer, arranger, prodr. popular and sacred music; former mem. Australian Chamber Choir, Wesley Choir, Canberra; co-author: (with S. Kolian) Mariculture and Other Uses for Offshore Oil and Gas Platforms: Rationale for Retaining Infrastructure, 2005; editor: (with M.L. Heron) The Bio-Physics of Marine Larval Dispersal, 1994, Marine Biology (Berlin), 2000—, Aquatic Biology, 2007—; contbr. numerous articles to profl. jours.; editl. advisor Marine Ecology Progress Series, 1985-93; co-editor: Procs. 6th Internat. Coral Reef Symposium, 1988, Procs. 8th Internat. Coral Reef Symposium, Procs. Internat. BioIndicators Conf., Jour. Environ. Bioindicators, 2007. Mem. La. State Gov.'s Platform for Mariculture Task Force, 2004-05; mem. chancel choir First United Meth. Ch., Houma, La. Recipient Internat. Sci. Exch. award, 1988-89. Mem. ASCAP, Assn. Marine Labs. Caribbean (exec. dir.-elect), Australian Marine Scis. Assn. (keynote spkr. 1981, counselor 1984-89, chmn., organizer nat. conf. 1987, chmn. Australia Acad. Sci. Boden Conf. 1990), Internat. Soc. Reef Studies (counselor 1997-2000), Australian Coral Reef Soc., Sigma Xi. Office: La Univs Marine Consortium 8124 Highway 56 Chauvin LA 70344-2110 Office Phone: 985-851-2876. Business E-Mail: psammarco@lumcon.edu.

SAMMET, JEAN E., computer scientist; b. NYC; d. Harry and Ruth S. BA, Mt. Holyoke Coll., Sc.D. (hon.), 1978; MA, U. Ill. Group leader programming Sperry Gyroscope, Great Neck, NY, 1955-58; sect. head, staff cons. programming Sylvania Electric Products, Needham, Mass., 1958-61; with IBM, 1961-88; adv. program mgr. Boston, 1961-65; program lang. tech. mgr. IBM, 1965-68; programming tech. planning mgr. Fed. Systems div., 1968-74, programming lang. tech. mgr., 1974-79, software tech. mgr., 1979-81, div. software tech. mgr., 1981-82, programming lang. tech. mgr., 1983-88; programming lang. cons. Bethesda, Md., 1989—. Chmn. history of computing com. Am. Fedn. Info. Processing Socs., 1977-79; mem. exec. com. Software Patent Inst., 1991—, edn. com., 1992—, chair edn. com., 1992-93; bd. dirs. Computer Mus., 1983-93. Author: Programming Languages: History and Fundamentals, 1969; editor-in-chief: Assn. Computing Machinery Computing Revs, 1979-87; contbr. articles to profl. jours. Recipient Fellow award, Computer History Mus., 2001. Fellow Assn. for Computing Machinery, 1994, (charter; pres. 1974-76, Disting. Svc. award 1985), Computer History Mus.; mem. NAE, Upsilon Pi Epsilon. Home and Office: 3124 Gracefield Rd Apt 311 Silver Spring MD 20904-5818

SAMMLER, ANNE MICHELLE, healthcare educator; b. Binghampton, NY, Oct. 1968; d. Robert (Stepfather) and Carol Anne Roach, Fredrick Thaddeus Mastine; m. Sean Edward Sammler, May 2, 1992; children: Aleni, Alexis. BS in Health Edn. summa cum laude, SUNY, Brockport, 2003. CERT coord. Rochester City Fire Dept., cert. instr. ARC, tchr. NY. Co-chmn. Reading is Fundamental, Rochester, NY, 1998—2002; religious edn. instr. Sacred Heart Cathedral, Rochester, 1999—2002; health educator Aquinas Inst, Rochester, 2003—, red ribbon week coord., 2006, prom promise coord., 2007, cert. points of distbn. mass ER vaccination coord., 2007. Team leader breast cancer walks Am. Cancer Soc., Rochester, 2004; team leader, vol. Spl. Olympics, Rochester, 2000; team leader, fund raiser Am. Heart Assn., Rochester, 2005, heart walk leader, 2007. Scholar, Health Sci. Dept., Brockport State U., 2003. Mem.: AAHPERD (corr.), Aquinas Nat. Honor Soc., Eta Sigma Gamma (corr.), Alpha Chi (life). Avocations: running, reading, canoeing. Office: Aquinas Inst 1127 Dewey Ave Rochester NY 14613 Office Phone: 585-254-2020 ext. 1048.

SAMMONS, MARY F., retail executive; b. Portland, Oreg., Oct. 12, 1946; d. Lee W. and Ann (Cherry) Jackson; m. Nickolas F. Sammons, Sept. 12, 1967; 1 child, Peter. BA, Marylhurst Coll., Oreg., 1970. Buyer Fred Meyer Inc., Portland, 1975-80, v.p., merchandiser, 1980-85, sr. v.p., softgoods divsn. mgr., from 1986, sr. v.p. apparel & home electronics group, 1996, exec. v.p., apparel, home & home electronics group, 1997—98; pres. Fred Meyer Stores, Portland, 1998, pres., CEO, 1999; pres., COO Rite Aid Corp., Camp Hill, Pa., 1999—2003, pres., CEO, 2003—07, chmn., pres., CEO, 2007—. Bd. dirs. First Horizon Nat. Corp., Rite Aid Found., Rite Aid Corp., 1999—; chmn. Nat. Assn. Chain Drug Stores. Named Woman of Achievement, YWCA, Portland, 1987; named one of 100 Most Powerful Women, Forbes mag., 2005—06, 50 Most Powerful Women in Bus., Fortune mag., 2006, 50 Women to Watch, Wall St. Jour., 2006. Mem. Am. Mgmt. Assn. Office: Rite Aid Corp 30 Hunter Ln Camp Hill PA 17011 Office Phone: 717-761-2633. *

SAMO, AMANDO, bishop; b. Moch Island, Federated States of Micronesia, Aug. 16, 1948; s. Benito and Esiper Samo. BA in Psychology, Chaminade U., 1973; diploma in religious edn., EAPI, Manila, Philippines, 1982. Ordained priest Roman Cath. Ch. Parish priest Cath. Ch., Truk, Micronesia, Afghanistan, 1977—87; aux. bishop Diocese of the Carolines and Marshalls, Truk, 1987—95, bishop, 1995—. Founder, bd. dirs. Marriage Encounter-Carolines-Marshalls, Truk, 1982—88, dir. ch. leadership tng. programs, 1986—; mem. Bishop's Conf. Oceania, 1988; pontificial commn. Cor Unum, Rome, Rome, 1995. Chmn. Chmn. Bishop's commn. justice and devel., 1995. Roman Catholic. Home: PO Box 939 Chuuk FM 96942-0939 Office: Diocese Caroline Is PO Box 250 Chuuk FM 96942-0250

SAMOJLIK, EUGENIUSZ, medical educator, health facility administrator; b. Kuchmy-Bialystok, Poland, Aug. 20, 1933; s. Michael and Anastazia S.; m. Anna Morozewicz, Apr. 10, 1965; children: Dorothy, Michael. BS in Biomedicine, U. Warsaw, 1958, PhD in Reproductive Endocrinology, 1964. Rsch. asst. Maternity Inst. Dept. Pharmacology, Warsaw, 1958-62, sr. asst., 1962-66; asst. prof., chief reproductive pharmacology & toxicology Inst. Pharmacy Dept. Pharmacology, Warsaw, 1966-70; assoc. prof., chief hormone rsch. lab. Med. Acad. Dept. Clin. Endocrinology, Warsaw, 1970-73; staff rschr. II Syntex, Inc. Rsch. Divsn., Palo Alto, Calif., 1974-75; asst. prof. physiology, dir. radioimmunoassay lab. Milton S. Hershey (Pa.) Med. Ctr., Divsn. Endocrinology, 1975-80; staff endocrinologist VA Med. Ctr. Dept. Medicine, Sect. Endocrinology, East Orange, NJ, 1980-82; dir. endocrine lab. Newark Beth Israel Med. Ctr., Dept. Medicine, 1982-92; assoc. prof. medicine divsn. endocrinology U. Medicine & Dentistry-N.J. Med. Sch., Newark, 1982—; chief endocrine lab. dept. Labs. NBIMC, 1994-96. Vis. researcher UCLA Sch. Medicine, Torrance, Calif., 1973; vis. scientist Nat. Inst. Child Health Human Devel., Reproductive Br., Bethesda, Md., 1973-74; lectr. in field. Mem. internat. adv. bd. Jour. Assisted Reproductive Tech. and Andrology, mem. editorial bd., 1996; contbr. articles to profl. jours. Grantee WHO, 1973-74, Ciba-Geigy, 1982-83, Nat. Cancer Inst., 1983-86, 85-88; tng. program fellow Worcester Found. Experimental Biology, Shrewsbury, Mass., 1967-69. Mem. AAAS, Am. Soc. Andrology, Am. Assn. Clin. Chemistry, Nat. Acad. Clin. Biochemistry, Acad. Medicine NJ, Endocrine Soc. Home: 73 Sykes Ave Livingston NJ 07039-1318 Fax: 973-972-5185. E-mail: samojleu@yahoo.com.

SAMOLE, MYRON MICHAEL, lawyer, management consultant; b. Nov. 29, 1943; s. Harry Lionel and Bess Miriam (Siegel) Samole; m. Sandra Rita Port, Feb. 2, 1967; children: Stacey Ann, Karen Lynn, Rena Marie, David Aaron. Student, U. Ill., 1962—65; JD, DePaul U., 1967. Bar: Ill. 1967, U.S. Dist. Ct. (no. dist.) 1968, U.S. Ct. Appeals (7th cir.) 1968, Fla. 1981, U.S. Dist. Ct. (so. dist.) 1989, U.S. Ct. Appeals (11th cir.) 2001. Sole practice, Chgo., 1967—79, Miami, 1981—. Bd. dirs. The Sports Collection, Inc., pres. Samole Enterprises, Inc. 1986-, Carcand, Inc. 1986-. Pres. Young Israel Kendall. Mem.: Trial Lawyers Assn., Fla. Bar Assn., Ill. State Bar Assn., Chgo. Bar Assn., ABA, Phi Alpha Delta. Office: Samole & Berger PA 9700 S Dixie Hwy Ste 1030 Miami FL 33156-2865 Office Phone: 305-670-5070. Business E-Mail: msamole@samoleberger.com.

SAMOLYK, KEITH ANDREW, cardiovascular perfusionist, director; s. Edward and Margret Samolyk; 1 child, Tyler Andrew. BS, Northeastern U., Boston MA, 1989. Cert. perfusion tech. Northeastern U., Boston, 1989, lic. Cardiovascular Perfusionist Commonwealth of Mass., 2001. Cardiovasc. perfusionist Johns Hopkins Hosp., Balt., 1990—95; pediatric specialist perfusion Hartford (Conn.) Hosp., 1996; supr. QA, staff perfusionist Winthrop U. Hosp., Mineola, NY, 1997—2000; staff perfusionist Boston Med. Ctr., 2001—, St Elizabeths Med. Ctr., Boston, 2001—; staff perfusionist (per diem) Maine Med. Ctr., Portland, 2003—. Pres., CEO Global Blood Resources LLC, Somers, Conn., 2001—. Author journal papers. Recipient Alumni award profl. promise, Northeastern U., 1989, Gold award co. global blood resources, Conn. Quality Innovation award, 2006. Mem.: Windsor Marksmen Assn., Soc. for Advancement of Blood Mgmt. (assoc.), Windsor Club. Achievements include invention of Hemobag Whole Blood Salvaging device for Surgery; 3 patents. Avocations: golf, skiing, hunting, fishing. Office Phone: 800-942-9243. Personal E-mail: ksamolyk@comcast.net.

SAMORS, NEAL, publishing executive, writer; b. Chgo., July 10, 1943; s. Joseph and Bernette (Schulman); m. Frieda Anschel, May 25, 1969; 1 child, Jennifer Laura. BS, U. Wis., 1965; MA, No. Ill. U., 1967; PhD, Northwestern U., 1979, MA, 2000. Lectr. polit. sci. Loyola U., Chgo., 1967-69; instr. polit. sci. Barat Coll., Lake Forest, Ill., 1969-74; profl. assoc. Ednl. Testing Svc., Evanston, Ill., 1974-80, asst. dir., 1980-84, sr. field mktg. rep., 1984-88, asst. dir. field mktg., 1989-93, exec. dir. field mktg., 1993-95, exec. dir. market devel., 1995-97, exec. dir. client acquisition and retention, 1997-99; pres. Samors & Assocs., Inc., Buffalo Grove, Ill., 1999—2003, Chgo.'s Neighborhoods, Inc., Buffalo Grove, Ill., 2003—. Cons. and evaluator Alverno Coll., Milw., 1978-81, Madonna Coll., Livonia, Mich., 1978-81, Coll. St. Scholastica, Duluth, Minn., 1980-81; cons. Ednl. Testing Svc., Chauncey Group Internat., 1999-2002; cons. U. Ga., 2004-05. Author, pub.: Chicago in the Sixties, 2006; co-author, pub.: Downtown Chicago in Transition, 2007; co-author: Chicago's Far North Side: Illustrated History of Rogers Park and West Ridge, 2000, Neighborhoods Within Neighborhoods: Twentieth Century Life on Chicago's Far North Side, 2002, The Old Chicago Neighborhood, Remembering Life in the 1940s, 2003, Real Chicago: Photographs From the Files of the Chicago Sun-Times, 2004, Chicago in the Fifties, 2005, Real Chicago Sports: Photographs From The Files of The Chicago Sun-Times, 2005; pub: End of Watch, 2007. Dir. resource devel. Rogers Pk./West Ridge Hist. Soc., 2001—03; rschr. Stevenson for Senator, Chgo., 1970. Ford Found. fellow, 1967. Mem. Am. Assn. Higher Edn., Am. Hist. Assn., Orgn. Am. Historians, Chgo. Hist. Soc., Phi Delta Kappa (rsch. v.p. Northwestern chpt. 1980). Avocations: photography, sketching portraits, american history. Home and Office: Chgo's Neighborhoods Inc 282 Stanton Dr Buffalo Grove IL 60089-6841 Office Phone: 847-913-8322.

SAMOSHIN, VYACHESLAV VLADIMIROVICH, chemistry professor, science educator, researcher; PhD in Organic Chem., Moscow State U., 1982, D of Chem. Scis., 1991. Prof., head dept. organic chemistry Moscow State Acad. Fine Chem. Tech., 1992—97; prof. U. of the Pacific, Stockton, Calif., 1997—. Contbr. articles to chem. jours. and books. Mem.: Russian Mendeleev Chem. Soc., Am. Chem. Soc. Achievements include research in organic synthesis and stereochemistry. Office: U of the Pacific 3601 Pacific Ave Stockton CA 95211 Office Phone: 209-946-2921. Office Fax: 209-946-2607. Business E-Mail: vsamoshin@pacific.edu.

SAMPLE, ALTHEA MERRITT, retired secondary education educator, conductor; b. Miami, Fla., Apr. 6, 1937; d. Otis and Alma (Carter) S. BS in Music Edn., Fla. A&M U., Tallahassee, 1960; Master in Music Edn., U. Miami, 1971. Tchr. elem. music edn. Dade County, Miami, 1960-65, dir. jr. hs orch., 1965-84, dir. orch. sr. hs, 1984—; dir. orch. Miami Northwestern Performing Arts Ctr., 1984—. Clin. tchr. internship program U. Miami, 1988-90; clinician Broward County Orch. Evaluation, 1986, 87; participant workshops in field, 1965—. Coord. North Area Festival, 1988; conducted Supt.'s Honors Orch., 1988, 92, South Area Festival Orch., 1989, tribute Dr. George Bornoff Concert, 1994, Gov. Fla. Inaugural Concert, 1991; performed Nat. Educator Reception, 1993; sponsor Miami Herald Silver Knight Award winners, 1988, 90, 92. Recipient Black Music Achievement award, 1992, Outstanding Educator award US Rep. Dante Fussell, 1992, Disting. Alumnus award Fla. A&M U., 1997; named Area III Tchr. of Yr., Dade County, 1992; named to Dade County Schs. Music Educators Hall of Fame, 2006. Mem. United Tchrs. Dade, Fla. Orch. Assn., Fla. Music Educators, Dade Music Educators, Nat. Alliance Educators, Eta Phi Beta. Democrat. Episcopalian. Avocations: reading, playing flute, violin, organ, tennis. Home: 15720 E Bunche Park Dr Opa Locka FL 33054-2020

SAMPLE, FREDERICK PALMER, former college president; b. Columbia, Pa., May 22, 1930; s. William Walter and Erna Rebecca (Roye) S.; m. Mary Jane Drager, Aug. 19, 1951; children: Jeffrey Lynn, Roger Lee. AB, Lebanon Valley Coll., 1952; LHD, Lebanon Valley Coll., 2006; MEd, Western Md. Coll., 1956; DEd, Pa. State U., 1968; D in Pedagogy, Albright Coll., 1968. Tchr. Annville (Pa.) High Sch., 1952-53; tchr. Red Lion Area (Pa.) High Sch., 1953-57, prin., 1957-59, supervising prin., 1959-64; supt. Manheim Twp. Sch. Dist., Neffsville, Pa., 1964-68; pres. Lebanon Valley Coll., Annville, Pa., 1968-83; supt. Bellefonte (Pa.) Area Sch. Dist., 1987-92. Ednl. cons.; adminstr. Bucknell U., 1985-87. Mem. Phi Delta Kappa. Republican. Home: 401 Ford Dr Elizabethtown PA 17022-3194 E-mail: fps0522@dejazzd.com. *Despite failures, difficulties, and disappointments I have tried to find the honorable, responsible, productive, true, and humane solutions to problems and make decisions for progress.*

SAMPLE, JOSEPH SCANLON, foundation executive; b. Chgo., Mar. 15, 1923; s. John Glen and Helen (Scanlon) S.; m. Patricia M. Law, Dec. 22, 1942 (div.); children: Michael Scanlon, David Forrest, Patrick Glen; m. Miriam Tyler Willing, Nov. 19, 1965. BA, Yale U., 1947. Trainee, media analyst, media dir. Dancer-Fitzgerald-Sample, Inc., advt. agy., Chgo., 1947-50, v.p., media dir., 1952-53; pres. Mont. Television Network KTVQ, Billings, KXLF-AM-TV, Butte, Mont., KRTV, Great Falls, Mont., KPAX-TV, Missoula, Mont., 1955-84; dir., prodr. Yellowstone Pub. Radio KEMC, Billings, 1993—. Chmn. Wheeler Ctr. Mont State U., 1988—. Served with AUS, 1943-46. With U.S. Army, 1950-52. Mem. Rotary, Yellowstone Country Club, Port Royal Club, Hole in The Wall Golf Club, Hilands Golf Club, Naples Yacht Club. Home: 606 Highland Park Dr Billings MT 59102-1909 Office: 14 N 24th St Billings MT 59101-2422 Office Phone: 406-256-5667. Personal E-mail: scatman01@msn.com.

SAMPLE, STEVEN BROWNING, academic administrator; b. St. Louis, Nov. 29, 1940; s. Howard and Dorothy (Cunningham) Sample; m. Kathryn Brunkow, Jan. 28, 1961; children: Michelle Sample Smith, Elizabeth Ann. BS, U. Ill., 1962, MS, 1963, PhD, 1965; DHL (hon.), Canisius Coll., 1989, Hebrew Union Coll., 1994, Northeasetern U., 2004; LLD (hon.), U. Sheffield, Eng., 1991; EdD (hon.), Purdue U., 1994; EdD, Northwestern U., 2004; DL (hon.), U. Nebr., 1995; DSc, U. Notre Dame, 2005; DSc (hon.), SUNY, 2006. Sr. scientist Melpar Inc., Falls Ch., Va., 1965—66; assoc. prof. elec. engring. Purdue U., Lafayette, Ind., 1966—73; dep. dir. Ill. Bd. Higher Edn., Springfield, 1971—74; exec. v.p. acad. affairs, dean Grad. Coll., prof. elec. engring. U. Nebr., Lincoln, 1974—82; prof. elec. and computer engring. SUNY, Buffalo, 1982—91; pres. U. So. Calif., LA, 1991—, prof. elec. engring., 1991—, Robert C. Packard pres.'s chair, 1995—. Bd. dirs. Santa Catalina Id. Co., Intermec, William Wrigley Jr. Co., Advanced Bionics, AMCAP/Am. Mut. Fund, Inc., Keck Sch. Medicine; vice-chmn. Western NY Tech. Devel. Ctr., Buffalo, 1982—91; chmn. bd. dirs. Calspan-UB Rsch. Ctr., Inc., Buffalo, 1983—91; mem. Calif. Coun. Sci. and Tech., Irvine, Calif., 1998—2003, L.A. Bus. Advisors, Nat. Acad. of Engring., 1998—; cons. in field; chmn. Pacific-10 Conf., 1997—. Author: Contrarian's Guide to Leadership, 2001, (ref. book) New Dictionary of the History of Ideas, 2004; contbr. articles to profl. jour. Timpanist St. Louis Philharm. Orch., 1955—58; chmn. Western NY Regional Econ. Devel. Coun., 1984—91; trustee U. at Buffalo Found., 1982—91, Studio Arena Theatre, Buffalo, 1983—91, Western NY Pub. Broadcasting Assn., 1985—91; chmn. Gov.'s Conf. on Sci. and Engring. Edn., Rsch. and Devel, 1989—91; sr. warden Ch. of Our Savior, 1996—98; mem. Calif. Bus.-Higher Edn. Forum (CBHEF), 1995—97; trustee LEARN, 1991—96; mem. bd. dir. 1st Interstate Bancorp, 1991—96, Galaxy Inst. Edn., 1991—94, Niagara Mohawk Power Corp., 1988—91; vestry Ch. of Our Savior, 1996—2001; mem. bd. gov. LA Annenberg Met. Project (LAAMP), 1994—2000; mem. bd. dir. Western Atlas, Inc., 1994—97, The Presley Co., 1991—; bd. dir. Buffalo Philharm. Orch., 1982—91, Regenstrief Med. Found., Indpls., 1982—, Rsch. Found. SUNY, 1987—91; bd. dir. LA chpt. World Affairs Coun.; bd. dir. Rebuild LA Com., Coalition of 100 Club, LA; mem. bd. dir. Dunlop Tire Corp., 1987—91, Greater Buffalo C. of C., 1985—91, United Way Buffalo and Erie County, 1985—91; bd. dir. U. So. Calif. Keck Sch. Medicine; bd. trustees J. Paul Getty Trust, 2004—06; mem. leadership coun. Literacy Network of Greater L.A., 2004—; mem. Calif. Commn. for Jobs and Econ. Growth, 2004—. Named Engr. of Yr., NY State Soc. Profl. Engrs., 1985; recipient Disting. Alumnus award, U. Ill., 1980, Alumni Honor award, U. Ill. Coll. Engring., 1985, citation award, Buffalo Coun. on World Affairs, 1986, Outstanding Elec. Engr. award, Purdue U., 1993, Humanitarian award, Nat. Conf. Christians and Jews, 1994, Hollzer Meml. award, Jewish Fedn. Coun. Greater L.A, 1994, Eddy award, LA County Econ. Devel. Corp., 2000, Norton medal, SUNY, 2004, Humanitarian award, Alfred Mann Found., 2004, Heart of City award, Ctrl. City Assn. LA, 2005, KCET Visionary award, 2005, Disting. Bus. Leader award, LA Area C. of C., 2006; fellow, Sloan Found., 1962—63, Grad. fellow, NSF, 1963—65, Am. Coun. Edn. fellow, Purdue U., 1970—71. Mem.: NAE, IEEE (Outstanding Paper award 1976), Am. Acad. Arts and Sci., Assn. Pacific Rim Univ. (co-founder, chmn. 1997—2002), Coun. on Fgn. Rels., Nat. Assn. State Univ. and Land-Grant Coll. (ednl. telecomms. com. 1982—83, chmn. coun. of pres. 1985—86, edn. and tech. com. 1986—87, exec. com. 1987—89), Assn. Am. Univ. (exec. com. 1995—2000, vice-chmn. 1997—98, tenure com. 1997—2001, chmn. 1998—99, assessing quality of univ. edn. and rsch. com. 2000—05, co-chair task force on rsch. accountability 2001—02, internationalization com. 2002—). Episcopalian. Achievements include patents in field. Office: U So Calif Office of Pres University Park Adm 110 Los Angeles CA 90089-0012 Office Phone: 213-740-2111. *

SAMPLES, MARK CHRISTOPHER, music editor; b. Bowling Green, Ohio, May 4, 1981; s. Roger Douglas and Cheryl Marie Samples; m. Jennifer Capron Stein, July 14, 2007. BA in Music Theory & Composition, Point Loma Nazarene U., San Diego, 2003. Instrumental music editor Neil A. Kjos Music Co., San Diego, 2003—. Local piano accompanist, San Diego, 2005—06. Co-editor: (jazz ensemble method book) Standard of Excellence Advanced Jazz Ensemble Method, (jazz method book) That's Jazz; editor: Cutting the Changes: Jazz Improvisation via Key Centers; musician: (CDs) Recorder Excellence, Derren Raser Band: King of I'll Tell You Next Week; composer: (recital) Songs for the Asking: A Senior Composition Recital, (jazz choir arrangement) Complainte de la Butte, (jazz combo piece) Bungalow; musician: (band) Derren Raser Band. Child adv. Compassion Internat., Eugene, Oreg., 2005—07. Mem.: Am. Musicological Soc., Phi Delta Lambda. Avocations: table tennis, fishing.

SAMPLES, PHIL LOVIN, pharmacist, military officer; b. Duluth, Ga., Sept. 18, 1957; m. Cindy Lynell Wood, Dec. 15, 1979 (div. Jan. 10, 1999); m. Diana Leigh Flood, Jan. 28, 2000; children: Marie Lynn, Phil Jr., Carolyn Elizabeth. BS in Pharmacy, U. Ga., Athens, 1980; PharmD, U. Ga., Augusta, 1992; MS in Mil. Operational Art, Air U., Montgomery, Ala., 1999, postgrad., 2006—. Lic. pharmacist Ga. Commd. 2d lt. USAF, 1986; pharmacy flight comdr. 96 Med. Group, Eglin AFB, Fla., 1999—2001; advanced through grades to col. USAF; comdr. 377 Med. Support Squadron, Kirtland AFB, N.Mex., 2001—03; pharmacy cons. USAF Surgeon Gen. Staff, Washington, 2003—05; comdr., CEO 17 Med. Group, Goodfellow AFB, Tex., 2005—. Mem. sci. adv. bd. Angelo State U., San Angelo, Tex., 2005—06; USAF sugeon gen. rep. US Pharmacopeia, Washington, 2003—06. Bd. dirs. West TX Rehab. Ctr., San Angelo, 2005—06, San Angelo Adult Day Care Ctr., 2005—06. Decorated Meritorious Svc. medal (with six oakleaf clusters) USAF, Legion of Merit; named Clin. Pharmacist of Yr., 1993, Co. Grade Pharmacist of Yr., 1989,

USAF Pharmacy of Yr., USAF, Eglin AFB, 2001; recipient Cert. Excellence, Dept. Def., 1990. Mem.: Assn. Mil. Surgeons US, Am. Pharmacist Assn. (fed. adv. bd. 2003—05), Soc. Air Force Pharmacy (life; pres. 1995—96). Home Phone: 334-356-6707; Office Phone: 334-953-2299.

SAMPRAS, PETE, retired professional tennis player; b. Washington, Aug. 12, 1971; s. Sam and Georgia Sampras; m. Bridgette Wilson, Sept. 30, 2000, 2 children, Christian Charles, Ryan Nikolaos. Mem. U.S. Davis Cup team., named to Olympic Team Atlanta, 1996 Chmn. ATP Tour Charities program, 1992. Winner tournaments including Phila., 1990, Manchester, 1990, US Open, 1990, 1993, Grand Slam Cup, 1990, L.A., 1991, Indpls., 1991, Lyon, 1991, IBM/ATP Tour World Championship-Frankfurt, 1991, 94, US Pro Indoor, 1992, Lipton Internat., 1993, Wimbledon, 1993, 94, 95, 97, 98, 99, 2000; Australian Open, 1994, 97, Italian Open, 1994, US Open, 1990, 93, 95, 96, 2002, San Jose Open, 1996, Memphis Open, 1996, ATP Tour World Championship/Hannover, Germany, 1996, Australian Open Wimbledon, 1997, Advanta Championships, 1998, Champions Cup, 2007; ranked # 1 during 1993, 94 season, finalist Australian Open, 1995; ret., 2003; named to Tennis Hall of Fame, 2007. Achievements include 1st male to win the US Open, Wimbledon, and Australian Open in succession, mem. US Davis Cup Team, 1991, became only the fourth player to finish as No. 1 three (or more) consecutive years, 1st player to surpass $5 million in a season, all-time leader in career earnings, named ATP Tour Player of the Year, 1993-94, Jim Thorpe Tennis Player, 1993. Office: ATP Tour 420 W 45th St New York NY 10036-3503 *

SAMPSEL, HUNTER, mortgage company executive; b. 1971; Pres., owner Am. Home Mortgage. Involved with Casa de los Ni-os, U. Ariz. Disability Resource Ctr., El Rio Health Ctr., World Care, Salvation Army Adopt-A-Family. Named one of 40 Under 40, Tucson Bus. Edge, 2006. Mem.: Pan Asian Cmty. Alliance, Ariz. Medical Assn., Continental Ranch Little League, AYSO Soccer Teams, Southern Ariz. Golf. Office: American Home Mortgage 5401 N Oracle Rd Tucson AZ 85704 Office Phone: 877-581-9035. Office Fax: 520-531-9468.

SAMPSON, DAVID ALLAN, insurance association executive, former federal agency administrator; b. Washington, Ind., July 2, 1957; s. Beryl Harrel and Laura Evelyn (King) S.; m. Karen Ann Nichols, Dec. 10, 1978. BA, David Lipscomb Coll., Nashville, 1978; MDiv, New Orleans Bapt. Theol. Sem., 1982; D in Ministry, Abilene Christian, 1990. Min. Westchurch Ch. of Christ, Hammond, Ind., 1978-82; sr. min. Park Row Ch. of Christ, Arlington, Tex., 1982—; pres., CEO Arlington (Tex.) C. of C.; chmn. Tex. Coun. on Workforce and Econ. Competitiveness; asst. sec. for econ. devel. US Dept. Commerce, Washington, 2001—05, acting dep. sec., 2005, dep. sec., 2005—07; pres., CEO Property Casualty Insurers Assn. Am., Des Plaines, Ill., 2007—. Bd. dirs. emergency chaplain program Arlington Community Hosp., 1985—, Overseas Private Investment Corp., 2005-; adv. bd. Arlington Meml. Hosp., 1985—; bd. dirs. Neo-natal Bioethics Review Bd., 1986— Contbr. articles to profl. jours. Mem. United Way; bd. dirs. Arlington Ind. Sch. Dists, Communications Bd., 1985—. Named Arlington's Minister of Yr., Kiwanis, 1985. Mem. Arlington C. of C. (bd. dirs. 1985—, chmn. emergency preparedness com. 1985—), Arlington Ministerial Assn. (pres. 1985-86), Soc. Biblical Lit., Internat. Ch. Soc. (chmn. North Tex. chpt.), Phi Alpha Theta. Lodges: Rotary. Republican. Avocations: travel, tennis. Office: Property Casualty Insurers Assn Am 2600 S River Rd Des Plaines IL 60018 *

SAMPSON, DONNA RENE, mathematics educator; b. Columbia, SC, Mar. 26, 1957; d. James Bradford and Celia Meetze Sampson; children: Shoshone Sampson Willis, Shuyon Sampson Willis. BA in Math., Lehman Col., Bronx, NY, 1979; MA in Edn., U.S. Internat. U., San Diego, Calif., 1991. Math. tchr. John Philip Sousa Jr. HS, Bronx, 1979—81, Luther Burbank Jr. HS, Burbank, Calif., 1981—95, Carver Mid. Sch., Sanford, Fla., 1995—96, Croons Acad., Sanford, 1996—98, Southern HS, Guam, 1998—99, North HS, Phoenix, 1999—2005. Mem.: NEA, Tchr. Assn. Avocations: dance, kickboxing, weightlifting, reading, skating.

SAMPSON, EARLDINE ROBISON, education educator; b. Russell, Iowa, June 18, 1923; d. Lawrence Earl and Mildred Mona (Judy) Robison; m. Wesley Claude Sampson, Nov. 25, 1953; children: Ann Elizabeth, Lisa Ellen. Diploma, Iowa State Tchrs. Coll., 1943, BA, 1950; MS in Edn., Drake U., 1954; postgrad., No. Ill. U., Iowa State U., 1965-66, 74. Cert. tchr. Iowa, guidance counselor Iowa. Tchr. elem. sch. various pub. sch. sys., 1943-48; cons. speech and hearing Iowa Dept. Pub. Instrn., Des Moines, 1950-52; speech therapist Des Moines Pub. Schs., 1952-54, 55; lectr. spl. edn. No. Ill. U., DeKalb, 1964-65; tchr. of homebound Cedar Falls (Iowa) Pub. Schs., 1967-68; asst. prof. edn. U. No. Iowa, Cedar Falls, 1968; asst. prof., counselor Wartburg Coll., Waverly, Iowa, 1968-70; instr. elem. edn., then head of advising elem. edn. Iowa State U., Ames, 1972-82; field supr. elem. edn. U. Toledo, 1988, 89; ind. cons. Sylvania, Ohio, 1989—. Cons. Des Moines Speech and Hearing Ctr., 1958-59; cons. Sartori Hosp., Cedar Falls, 1967-69; spkr. in field. Fellow, NDEA, 1965. Methodist. Avocations: poetry, reading, music, photography. Home: 4047 Newcastle Dr Sylvania OH 43560-3450 *My creed is based on the words of Edwin Markham: "There is a destiny that makes us brothers; none goes his way alone. All that we send into the lives of others comes back into our own." Just reward came from a former student who stated "I have never known you to compromise your principles".*

SAMPSON, HUGH ALBERT, JR., medical educator; b. Winnipeg, Man., Nov. 1, 1948; naturalized; BA, Hamilton Coll., 1971; MD, SUNY, Buffalo, 1975. Diplomate Am. Bd. Pediats., Am. Bd. Allergy and Immunology. Resident Children's Meml. Hosp.-Northwestern U., Chgo., 1975—78; fellow in allergy and immunology-pulmonary medicine Duke U. Med. Ctr., Durham, NC, 1978—80, mem. staff, 1980—86; prof. pediat. Johns Hopkins U., Balt., 1986—97; prof., pediat. Mt. Sinai Sch. of Medicine, NYC, 1997—. Co-author: Intestinal immunology and Food Allergy, 1995, Food Allergy: Adverse Reactions to Foods and Food Additives, 1991, Pediatric Allergy: Principles and Practice, 2003 Fellow Am. Acad. Allergy and Immunology; mem. Am. Pediat. Soc., Am. Acad. Pediats. (Brett Ratner award 2004), Am. Assn. Immunologists, Soc. Pediat. Rsch., Henry Kunkel Soc., Sigma Xi, Alpha Omega Alpha. Mem. Soc. Friends. Avocations: jogging, sailing, skiing. Office: Mt Sinai Sch Medicine One Gustave L Levy Pl Box 1198 New York NY 10029 Office Phone: 212-241-5548. Business E-Mail: hugh.sampson@mssm.edu.

SAMPSON, JOHN EUGENE, food products executive, consultant; b. Feb. 25, 1941; s. Delbert John and Mary Etta (Dodrill) S.; m. Mary Margaret Treanor, Aug. 14, 1965; children: J. Mark, Sharon. AB with distinction, Nebr. Wesleyan U., 1963; MBA, Ind. U., 1964. Mgmt. asst., exec. trainee Office Sec. Def., Washington, 1963—64; mem. staff Com. Econ. Devel., Washington, 1964—69; coord. environ. planning Gen. Mills Inc., Mpls., 1969—72, mgr. devel. planning, 1972—74; dir. corp. planning Cen. Soya Co. Inc., Ft. Wayne, Ind., 1974—76, v.p. corp. planning, 1976—80, v.p. corp. planning and devel., 1980—82, v.p. corp. devel., corp. sec., 1982—84; v.p. corp. planning and devel. Internat. Multifoods, Inc., 1984—96; pres. Sampson Assocs., Edina, Minn., 1996—. Author: How to Sell Your Business and Get the Best Price For It, 2003. Mem. bd. govs. Nebr. Wesleyan U., 1974-80; chmn. bd. trustees St. Joseph United Meth. Ch., Ft. Wayne, 1984; bd. dirs., treas. North Ind. United Meth. Found., 1981-84; lay mem. North Ind. Ann. Conf. United Meth. Ch., 1980-84; bd. dirs. Anthony Wayne coun. Boy Scouts Am., 1984; lay mem. Minn. Ann. Conf. United Meth. Ch., 1985-91, 97-00; chmn. conf. bd. devel. Minn. United Meth. Conf., 1986-91; chmn. bd. trustees Hennepin Ave. United Meth. Ch., Mpls., 1990-92, chair adminstrv. coun., 1993-95, lay leader, 1995-98; chair exec. com. North Naples (Fla.) United Meth. Ch., 2002-05, co-chmn. bldg. com., 2002-05, chair bd. trustees, 2005-. Mem. Ind. U. Sch. Bus. Alumni Assn. (pres. 1984-85), Interlachen Country Club, Country Club of Naples (bd. dirs. 2004—). Home: Unit 1701 4451 Gulf Shore Blvd N Naples FL 34103 Office Phone: 952-928-0800.

SAMPSON, JOHN J., law educator; b. St. Paul, Sept. 30, 1935; s. J.E. and Margaret A. Sampson; m. Joyce C., Aug. 6, 1940; children: Margaret J., Eleanor H. LLB magna cum laude, U. Minn., 1966. Bar: Calif. 1967, Tex. 1980. Assoc. Morriston-Foerster, San Francisco, 1966-69; asst. gen. counsel U.S. Commn. on Obscenity and Pornography, 1969-70; asst. prof. U. Tex. Sch. Law, Austin, 1970-73, prof., 1973-82, Ben Gardner Sewell prof. law, 1982-86, William Benjamin Wynne prof., 1986—. Bd. dirs. Legal Aid Soc. Central Tex.; lectr., legis. draftsman; reporter Nat. Conf. Commrs. Uniform St. Laws, 1990—. Pres., Minn. Law Rev., 1965-66; contbr. numerous articles to legal pubs. Mem. State Bar Tex. (editor family law sect. report 1976—). Office: U Tex Sch Law 727 E Dean Keeton St Austin TX 78705-3299 Office Phone: 512-232-1267. E-mail: jsampson@mail.law.utexas.edu.

SAMPSON, KELVIN DALE, college basketball coach; b. Laurinburg, NC, Oct. 5, 1955; s. John W. and Eva (Brewington) S.; m. Karen Sue Lowry, June 16, 1979; children: Lauren Elizabeth, Kellen Matthew. BS, Pembroke State U., 1978; MS, Mich. State U., 1980. Pres. NABC, 2003; head basketball coach Wash. State U., 1988—94, Univ. of Okla., Norman, Okla., 1994—2006, Ind. Univ., 2006—. Contbr. articles to profl. jours. Mem. Nat. Assn. Basketball Coaches (Dist. Coach of Yr. 1991, PAC 10 Coach of Yr. 1991), AAHPERD. Avocations: golf, reading, exercise. Office: Univ Ind Athletics Dept Assembly Hall 1001 E Seventeenth St Bloomington IN 47408-1590

SAMPSON, ROBERT J., sociologist, educator; BA, SUNY, Buffalo, 1977; MA, SUNY, Albany, 1979, PhD, 1983. Sr. staff assoc. Columbia U., 1981—83; postdoctoral fellow sch. urban and pub. affairs Carnegie-Mellon U., 1983—84; asst. prof. dept. sociology U. Ill., 1984—88, assoc. prof., 1988—91; prof. sociology U. Chgo., 1991—99, Lucy Flower Prof. Urban Sociology, 1997—2001, Fairfax M. Cone Disting. Svc. Prof., 2001—02; Henry Ford II Prof. Social Scis. Harvard U., 2003—. Vis. summer scholar Nat. Ctr. Juvenile Justice, Pitts., 1988; sci. dir. Project on Human Devel. in Chgo. Neighborhoods, 1994—; rsch. fellow Am. Bar Found., 1994—99, sr. rsch. fellow, 1999—2002; mem. steering com. Carnegie-Mellon U. Consortium on Violence Rsch., 1996—98, Harvard U. Ctr. Geog. Analysis, 2005—; fellow Ctr. Advanced Study in Behavioral Scis., Stanford, Calif., 1997—98, 2002—03; mem. sci. adv. bd. NSF Ctr. Spatially Integrated Social Sci., 2000—03; chair dept. sociology Harvard U., 2005—. Contbr. articles to profl. jours., chapters to books; asst. editor: Jour. Rsch. in Crime and Delinquency, 1981—84; co-author: Juvenile Criminal Behavior and Its Relation to Neighborhood Characteristics, 1981, Crime in the Making: Pathways and Turning Points Through Life, 1993 (Michael J. Hindelang Book award for Disting. Scholarly Publ., Am. Soc. Criminology, 1994, Disting. Scholar award, Am. Sociol. Assn. Crime, Law and Deviance sect., 1995, Outstanding Book award, Acad. Criminal Justice Scis., 1995), How Neighborhoods Matter: The Value of Investing at the Local Level, 2001, Shared Beginnings, Divergent Lives: Delinquent Boys to Age 70, 2003 (Michael J. Hindelang Book award for Disting. Scholarly Publ., Am. Soc. Criminology, 2004, Albert J. Reiss, Jr. Disting. Book award, Am. Sociol. Assn. Crime, Law and Deviance sect., 2005, named an Outstanding Academic Title: The Best of the Best in Published Scholarship, 2005, Outstanding Book award, Acad. Criminal Justice Scis., 2005); co-editor: Social Ecology of Crime, 1986, Integrating Individual and Ecol. Aspects on Crime, 1993, Explanation of Crime: Context, Mechanisms, and Devel., 2006; mem. editl. adv. bd.: Criminology, 1988—90, Jour. Quantitative Criminology, 1988—90, Am. Sociol. Rev., 1990—92, consulting editor: Am. Jour. Sociology, 1989—91, mem. editl. bd.:, 1991—2003, Law and Soc. Rev., 1997—2000, Social Forces, 1997—2000, Criminology, 2000—, Jour. Rsch. in Crime and Delinquency, 2000—, Theoretical Criminology, 2000—, Contexts, 2000—04, assoc. editor: Am. Jour. Sociology, 1993—96, Law and Soc. Rev., 2000—03. Recipient Investigator award, Robert Wood Johnson Found. Prog. on Health Policy Rsch., 2005—. Fellow: Am. Soc. Criminology (exec. counselor 1991—94, Edwin H. Sutherland award 2001), Am. Acad. Arts and Scis., NAS (Communities and Crime panel mem. 1988—89); mem.: Am. Sociol. Assn. (chair Crime, Law and Deviance sect. 2000—01, coun. mem. Cmty. and Urban sect. 2000—03, mem. exec. coun. Crime, Law and Deviance sect. 1995—98, Robert Park award 2000), Sociol. Rsch. Assn. Office: Harvard U Dept Sociology William James Hall 33 Kirkland St Cambridge MA 02138 E-mail: rsampson@wjh.harvard.edu.

SAMPSON, ROBERT NEIL, professional society administrator, consultant; b. Spokane, Wash., Nov. 29, 1938; s. Robert Jay and Juanita Cleone (Hickman) S.; m. Jeanne Louise Stokes, June 7, 1960; children— Robert W., Eric S., Christopher B., Heidi L. BS in Agr, U. Idaho, 1960; M.Public Adminstrn., Harvard U., 1974. Soil conservationist Soil Conservation Service, Burley, Idaho, 1960-61, work unit conservationist Orofino, Idaho, 1962-65, agronomist Idaho Falls, Idaho, 1967-68, info. specialist Boise, 1968-70, area conservationist, 1970-72, land use specialist Washington, 1974-77, dir. environ. services div., 1977; land use program mgr. Idaho Planning and Community Affairs Agy., Boise, 1972-73; exec. v.p. Nat. Assn. Conservation Dists., Washington, 1978-84, Am. Forestry Assn., Washington, 1984-95; sr. fellow Am. Forests, Washington, 1995-2000; affiliate prof. Dept. Forest Resources U. Idaho, 1997—. Instr. soils and land use Boise State U., 1972; F.K. Weyerhaeuser vis. fellow in comml. forestry Yale Sch. Forestry and Environ. Studies, 2001; pres., The Sampson Group, Inc., 1996—, Vision Forestry LLC, 2000—; rsch. scientist, Yale Sch. Forestry and Environ. Studies, 2001—; land use and forestry cons. Author: Farmland or Wasteland: A Time To Choose, 1981, For Love of the Land, 1985; contbr. articles to profl. and popular publs. Pres. Orofino Golf Assn., 1966, Clearwater County Search and Rescue Unit, 1966-67; chmn. Nat. Commn. on Wildfire Disasters, 1992-94. Recipient President's citation Soil Conservation Soc. Am., 1978; named Boise Fed. Civil Servant of Year Boise Fed. Bus. Assn., 1972 Fellow Soil and Water Conservation Soc. (Hugh Hammond Bennett award 1992); mem. Soc. Am. Foresters. Presbyterian. Office Phone: 703-924-0773. Personal E-mail: rneilsampson@cs.com.

SAMPSON, ROGER, school system administrator; M in Edn. Adminstrn., U. Mont., Missoula. Prin., sch. adminstr. Annette Island Sch. Dist., Metlakatia, Alaska, 1979—84; prin. Kenai Peninsula Borough Sch. Dist., Alaska, 1984—94; supt. Chugach Sch. Dist., Alaska, 1994—99; commr. edn. and early devel. State of Alaska, 2003—. Mem. standards based edn. com. State of Alaska. Named Alaska Prin. of Yr., 1987, Nat. Rural Supt. of Yr., 1997. Office: Dept Edn & Early Devel 801 W 10th St Ste 200 PO Box 110500 Juneau AK 99801 Office Phone: 907-465-2802. Business E-Mail: roger_sampson@eed.state.ak.us. *

SAMPSON, SAMUEL FRANKLIN, sociology educator; b. Malden, Mass., Sept. 22, 1934; s. Samuel Daniel and Margaret Louise (Grimes) S.; m. Patricia Katherine Driscoll, Apr. 8, 1972. BA, U. Okla., 1960, MA, 1961; PhD, Cornell U., 1968. Asst. prof. dept. sociology SUNY, Binghamton, 1965-66; research assoc. dept. sociology Cornell U., Ithaca, NY, 1966-67; lectr., chmn. bd. tutors and advs. Harvard U., Cambridge, Mass., 1967-72; assoc. prof. dept. urban studies and planning MIT, Cambridge, 1971-72; prof. sociology U. Vt., Burlington, 1972-2000, chmn. dept. sociology, 1972-76, 90-96, prof. emeritus, 2000—. Research and policy cons. Public & Community Agys. and Orgns., 1969— Gen. editor: Bobbs-Merrill Studies in Sociology, 1970-77; contbr. articles to profl. jours. Served with USAF, 1954-58. Mem. AAAS, Internat. Sociol. Assn., Am. Sociol. Assn., Am. Acad. Arts and Scis., Ea. Sociol. Soc., Soc. Study Social Problems, New Eng. Sociol. Assn., Soc. Sci. Study Religion. Office: Univ Vt Dept Sociology 31 S Prospect St Burlington VT 05405-1704 Office Phone: 802-338-2737.

SAMPSON, WILLIAM ROTH, lawyer; b. Teaneck, NJ, Dec. 11, 1946; s. James and Amelia (Roth) S.; 1 child, Lara; m. Drucilla Jean Mort, Apr. 23, 1988; stepchildren: Andy, Seth. BA in History with honors, U. Kans., 1968, JD, 1971. Bar: Kans. 1971, Mo. 2004, U.S. Dist. Ct. Kans. 1971, U.S. Dist. Ct. (we. dist.) Mo. 2004, U.S. Ct. Appeals (10th cir.) 1982, U.S. Ct. Claims 1985, U.S. Ct. Appeals (8th cir.) 1992. Assoc. Turner & Balloun, Great Bend, Kans., 1971; ptnr. Foulston & Siefkin, Wichita, Kans., 1975-86, Shook, Hardy & Bacon LLP, Kans. City, 1987. Adj. prof. advanced litig. U. Kans., 1994; mem. faculty trial tactics inst. Emory U. Sch. Law, 1994-97; mem. merit selection panel US Dist. Ct. Kans., 1999; lectr., presenter in field. Author: Kansas Trial Handbook, 1997, 2d edit., 2006; mem. Kans. Law Rev., 1969—71, editor, 1970—71; contbr. articles to profl. jours. Chmn. stewardship com. Univ. Friends Ch., Wichita, 1984-86; bd. dir. Friends U. Retirement Corp., Wichita, 1985-87, Lied Ctr. Kans., 1994-97, Nat. Found. Jud. Excellence, 2004—, program chmn., 2005, 06, pres. elect, 2007; chmn. capital fund drives Trinity Luth. Ch., Lawrence, Kans., 1990-93, mem. ch. coun., 1990-92, stewardship com. Trinity Episcopal Ch., 2002—. Lt., Judge Advocate General's Corps, USNR, 1971-75. Named one of Best Lawyers in Am., Best Lawyers in Mo., Kans. Super Lawyers, 2005, 2006. Fellow: Kans. Bar Found., Am. Bar Found.; mem.: ABA, Lawyers for Civil Justice (bd. dirs. 2003—05), Am. Inn Ct. (Judge Hugh Means chpt. Master of Bench), Kans. U. Law Soc. (bd. govs. 1993—96), Kans. Assn. Def. Counsel (pres. 1989—90, legis. coun. 1991, 1993, William H. Kahrs Disting. Achievement award 1994), Def. Rsch. Inst. (Kans. state rep. 1990—98, nat. bd. dirs. 1998—2000, nat. pres. 2003—04, chmn. strategic planning com. 2006—07, chair commercial litigation program 2007), Internat. Assn. Def. Coun. (faculty mem. trial acad. 1994), Am. Bd. Trial Advs. (pres. Kans. chpt. 1990—91, nat. bd. dir. 1990—91), Wichita Bar Assn. (bd. dirs. 1985—86), Johnson County Bar Assn. (bench-bar com. 1989—, Boss of Yr. award 1990), Douglas County Bar Assn., Kans. Bar Assn. (chmn. Kans. coll. advocacy 1986, CLE com. 1987—88, long-range planning), Assn. Def. Trial Attys., Club at Porto Cima, Order of the Coif, Omicron Delta Kappa, Phi Alpha Theta, Delta Sigma Rho. Republican. Episcopalian. Avocations: jogging, golf, travel, reading. Office: Shook Hardy & Bacon LLP 2555 Grand Ave Kansas City MO 64108-2613 Home Phone: 785-749-5358; Office Phone: 816-474-6550. Office Fax: 816-421-5547. Business E-Mail: wsampson@shb.com.

SAMS, LOUISE S., broadcast executive, lawyer; b. 1957; Grad., Princeton U., 1979, U. Va. Sch. Law. Bar: NY 1986, Ga. 1995. Corp. assoc. White & Case, NYC; exec. v.p., gen. counsel Turner Broadcasting System Inc., Atlanta; pres. Turner Broadcasting System Internat., 2003—. Mem. bd. dirs. Princeton U. Named one of The 50 Most Influential Women Lawyers in Am., Nat. Law Jour., 2007. Office: Turner Broadcasting System Inc 1 CNN Ctr 100 Internat Blvd Atlanta GA 30303 Office Phone: 404-827-1700. Office Fax: 404-827-2437. *

SAMS, RONALD F., career military officer; BA, Mich. State U., 1972; grad., Squadron Officer Sch., 1977; MA in Ednl. Systems Mgmt., Chapman U., 1978; student, Air Command and Staff Coll., Maxwell AFB, Ala., 1984, Air War Coll., 1993. Commd. 2d lt. USAF, 1972, advanced through grades to lt. gen., 2006; squadron co-pilot, aircraft comdr., instr. pilot 9th Air Refueling Squadron USAF, Beale AFB, Calif., 1974-79; from instr. pilot to faculty instr. pilot 93d Air Refueling Squadron, SAC Ctrl. Flight Instr. Course, Castle AFB, Calif., 1979-83; faculty instr. Air Command and Staff Coll. USAF, Maxwell AFB, Ala., 1984-86; chief tanker crew tng. br., Directorate of Tng. Hdqs. Strategic Air Command, Offut AFB, Nebr., 1986-89; comdr. 70th air refueling squadron USAF, Grissom AFB, Ind., 1989-90; asst. dep. comdr. ops. 305th Air Refueling Wing USAF and chief air refueling ops. 1703rd Wing, Grissom AFB, Ind. King, Khalid, Airport, Riyadh, Saudi Arabia, 1990-91; dep. comdr. 305th ops. group USAF, Grissom AFB, Ind., 1991-92; dir. ops. mgmt. Tanker Airlift Control Ctr., USAF, Scott AFB, Ill., 1993-94; comdr. 4409th ops. group (provisional) USAF, Ridyah AFB, Saudi Arabia, 1994-95; mil. asst. to dir. Defense Tech. Security Adminstrn. Defense Threat Reduction Agy. The Pentagon, Washington, 1995-98; comdr. 55th Wing USAF, Offutt AFB, Nebr., 1998—2000; inspector gen. Air Combat Command, Langley AFB, Va., 2000—02; dir. intelligence, surveillance & reconnaissance, dep. chief of staff, Air & Space Ops. USAF, Washington, 2002—06; inspect. gen. Dept Air Force US Dept Def., Washington, 2006—. Decorated Bronze Star medal, Defense Superior Svc. medal, Air medal, Aerial Achievement medal with 2 oak leaf clusters,, Meritorious Svc. medal with 6 oak leaf clusters, Air Force Organizational Excellence award, Combat Readiness medal, Nat. Defense Svc. medal, Armed Fores Expeditionary medal, S.W. Asia Svc. medal with 2 service stars, Kuwait Liberation medal Kingdom of Kuwait, Kuwait Liberation medal Kingdom of Saudi Arabia. Office: USAF 1140 Air Force Pentagon Rm 4E1076 Washington DC 20330 *

SAMSEL, MAEBELL SCROGGINS (MIDGE SAMSEL), paralegal; b. Yazoo City, Miss., Aug. 15, 1940; d. Robert and Lela Estelle (Hammons) Scroggins; m. John Sanders Swain, Dec. 30, 1960 (div. Oct. 1968); 1 child, Stacy Melissa Swain Ramsey; m. Howard Swinehart Samsel, Oct. 8, 1981. BA, Miss. Coll., 1963. Sec. Standard Life Ins. Co., Jackson, Miss., 1963-64; legal sec. Gray & Montague Law Firm, Hattiesburg, Miss., 1964-65; personnel sec. Adj. Gen.'s Office, State of Miss., Jackson, 1965-70; paralegal State of Miss., Atty. Gen.'s Office, Jackson, 1970-79, 84-86; sales agt. Prudential Ins. Co. Am., Jackson, 1979-84. Chmn. acquisitions Miss. Mus. Art, Jackson, 1983, acquisitions vol., 1982, 89, chmn. Vols. at the Palette Restaurant, 1990-99, music chair Miss. Mus. Art Palette Restaurant, 1996, pres. aux., 1991-92, trustee, 1991-92, treas. Gallery Guild, 1998; mem. Jackson Symphony League, 1988—, Miss. Opera Guild, Jackson, 1991—; bd. dirs. Friends of the Internat. Ballet Competition, historian, 1996-97, pres.-elect, 1997, pres. 1998-99. Named Vol. of the Week, Miss. Mus. Art Palette Restaurant, 1989, Vol. of Yr., Miss. Mus. of Art, 1991-92. Mem. AAUW, Jackson Assn. Legal Secs. (pres. 1975-76, 77-78, del. to nat. convs. 1975-77, Outstanding Legal Sec. of Yr. 1975-76), Miss. Assn. Legal Secs., Nat. Assn. Legal Secs. (chmn. nat. spring bd. mtg. 1980), Miss. Coll. Alumni Assn., Petroleum Aux. (v.p. 1986-87, pres. 1988-89, treas. 1989-90, pres. 1994-96), Serendipity Bridge Club (treas. 1989-93, v.p. 1991-92, pres. 1992-93). Republican. Baptist. Avocations: fishing, piano, travel. Home: 1206 Bay Vis Brandon MS 39047-8650

SAMSON, CARL J., artist; b. Sandusky, Ohio, Jan. 7, 1961; s. Roland Joseph and Giselle Amida Samson; m. Carol Ann Cyran, Sept. 9, 1995; children: Maddie, Haley. Studied with, Allan R. Banks, Sandusky, 1975—79, studied with, 1980—83, R.M. Ives Gammell, Boston, 1979—80, Richard F. Lack, Mpls., 1983—85. Curator Cin. Art Club, 1996—2003; mem. Russian-Am. Cultural Exch., Obem Ctr., Moscow, 1996. Contbr. numerous articles to profl. publs.; live portrait demonstration, Met. Mus. Art, 2000. Officer bd. dirs. Valley View Found., Milford, Ohio, 2002—. Mem.: Am. Soc. Portrait Artists (chmn. 2002—05), Wessel Ho. Sketch Group (co-founder, chmn. 2002—). Avocations: gardening, reading. Studio: 2152 Alpine Pl Cincinnati OH 45206

SAMSON, CHARLES HAROLD, JR., (CAR SAMSON), retired engineering educator, consultant; b. Portsmouth, Ohio, July 12, 1924; s. Charles Harold and Gertrude (Morris) S.; m. Ruth Aileen Baumbach, Sept. 12, 1947; children: Peggy Aileen, Charles Harold III. BS, U. Notre Dame,

1947, MS, 1948; PhD, U. Mo., 1953. Registered profl. engr., Tex., Ind. Asst. field rep. Loebl, Schlossman and Bennett (archs. and engrs.), Chgo., 1948-49; structures engr. Convair Aircraft, Ft. Worth, 1951-52, sr. structures engr., 1952-53, project aerodynamics engr., 1956-58, project structures engr., 1958-60; asst. prof. civil engring. U. Notre Dame, 1953-56; office engr. Wilbur H. Gartner & Assocs., South Bend, Ind., 1954; grad. lectr. civil engring. So. Meth. U., Dallas, 1952-53, 56-60; prof. structural engring. and mechanics, depts. aerospace and civil engring. Tex. A&M U., College Station, 1960-64, prof. civil engring., 1964-94, prof. emeritus, 1994—, head dept., 1964-79, assoc. head dept., 1989-92, constrn. area engring. leader, dir. ctr. constrn. edn., 1992-93; rsch. engr. Tex. Transp. Inst., Tex. A&M U., 1960-62, head structural rsch. dept., 1962-65, acting pres., 1980-81, v.p. planning, 1981-82. Varsity tennis coach U. Notre Dame, 1953-56; pres. S.W. Athletic Conf., 1979-81; v.p. NCAA, 1981-83, mem. coun., 1983-85; cons. sys. engring. and quality mgmt.; Tex. Quality Award examiner, 1998-99, sr. examiner, 2000. Contbr. articles to profl. jours. Pres. Brazos Valley Symphony Soc., 2000—02. With USNR, 1943—46, asst. to pub. works officer civil engr. corps USNR, 1946, active USNR, 1955—56, resigned lt. j.g. USNR, 1958. Recipient Gen. Dynamics-Ft. Worth Excellence in Tchg. award, 1962, Engring. hon. award U. Notre Dame, 1982, Outstanding Contbns. to Engring. and Scientific Profession award Calif. Soc. Profl. Engrs., 1987, Mo. Honor award for Disting. Svc. in Engring., 2006, Disting. Alumni award U. Mo. Civil Engring. Acad., 2006; co-recipient Vol. Excellence award Tex. Assn. Symphony Orchestras, 2005. Fellow ASCE (life), Nat. Inst. Engring. Mgmt. and Sys. (pres. 1989-90), NSPE (past v.p., chmn. profl. engrs. in edn., pres. 1987-88, award 2000); mem. Am. Soc. Engring. Mgmt., Am. Soc. Engring. Edn., Tex. Soc. Profl. Engrs. (past nat. dir., pres. 1973-74, Tex. Engring. Dream Team 2000), Nat. Assn. Parliamentarians, Internat. Soc. Sys. Sci., Order of Engr. (chmn., bd. govs. 1989-91), Am. Soc. Quality, Internat. Coun. Sys. Engring., Nat. Eagle Scout Assn., Sigma Xi, Sigma Gamma Tau, Tau Beta Pi, Phi Kappa Phi, Chi Epsilon. Home: 810 Dogwood Ln Bryan TX 77802-1144 Office Phone: 979-779-0424. Personal E-mail: charleshsamson@msn.com.

SAMSON, DAVID, lawyer; BA, Rutgers U., 1961; LLB, U. Pa. Law Sch., 1965. Law sec. Hon. Nathan L. Jacobs, NJ Supreme Court, 1965—66; founding prin. Wolff & Samson, 1972; gen. counsel NJ Turnpike Authority, 1982—90; atty. gen. State of NJ, 2002—03; sr. ptnr. Wolff & Samson, 2003—. Mem. Gov. Commn., 1990—91; chmn. Gov. Task Force, 1987—89; legal cons. Ethics Com., 1981—85, N.J. Supreme Court Com., 1973—77; legal cons. to atty. gen. Adv. com. on Governmental Immunity, 1967—68. Mem.: U.S. Supreme Court, N.Y. Bar Assn., Am. Bar Found., Am. Bar Assn., N.J. State Bar Assn., Essex County Bar Assn. Office: Wolff & Samson One Boland Dr West Orange NJ 07052

SAMSON, LEONA D., biological engineering educator, research center director; BSc in Biochemistry, Aberdeen U., Scotland, 1974; PhD, London U., 1978. Postdoctoral rschr. U. Calif., San Francisco, Berkeley; from asst. prof. to full prof. dept. molecular and cellular toxicology Harvard Sch. Pub. Health, 1983—2001; prof. biol. engring. and toxicology MIT, 2001—, dir. MIT Ctr. for Environ. Health Scis., MIT Toxicogenomics Rsch. Program, 2001—, mem. Cancer Ctr., 2001—, prof. biology, 2004—, affiliate mem. Broad Inst., 2004—. Mem. Computational and Systems Biology Initiative; mem. bd. sci. counselors NIEHS; mem. coun. for extramural grants ACS. Named Am. Cancer Soc. Rsch. Prof., 2001; recipient Burroughs Wellcome Toxicology Scholar award, 1993, Charlotte Friend Women in Cancer Rsch. award, 2000. Mem.: Inst. Medicine. Office: Ctr for Environ Health Scis MIT Bldg 56-235 Cambridge MA 02139 Business E-Mail: lsamson@mit.edu.

SAMSON, RICHARD MAX, theater director, investment company executive; b. Milw., June 13, 1946; s. Harry E. and Rose (Landau) Samson; m. Nancy K. Pinter; children: Gina Shoshana, Alayna Tamar 1 stepchild, Christopher P. BA, U. Wis., 1968. Dir., owner Puppet Co., Jerusalem, 1972-73; pres. Century Hall, Inc., Milw., 1974-75; dir. purchasing Am. Med. Svcs., Inc., Milw., 1973-74, v.p., 1974-82, exec. v.p., 1982-86, pres., 1986-90, Samson Investments, Milw., 1990—2002. Bd. dirs. Liberty Bank, Milw.; sec. Super Sitters, Mequon, Wis., 1987—2004. Dir.(co-prodr.): (plays) Loss of Breath: The Unfinished Life and Death of Edgar Allan Poe, 1999, Stones of Wisdom, 2003, (co-creator) Einstein: Hero of the Mind, 2002, The Apollo of Bellac, 2004, The Trial Adapted from Franz Kafka, 2005, Smoldering Fires, 2006; designer: (mask and puppet design), 2006. Pres. bd. dirs. Theatre X, Milw., 1982, Holton Youth Ctr., Milw., 1994, Children's Outing Assn., 1996, Jewish Found. Econ. Opportunity, 1996—2004; v.p. bd. dirs. ArtReach, Milw., 1987; mem. funding bd. Wis. Cmty. Fund, 1989—93; dir. Mask and Puppet Co. Milw., 1992—; treas. nat. bd. dirs. Am. for Peace Now, 2002—04; bd. dirs. Bnai Or Religious Fellowship, 1988—93, Milw. Jewish Coun., 1992—94. Recipient Humanitarian Peace award, Ecumenical Refugee Coun., 1989, Social Justice award, Wis. Cmty. Fund, 1997, Human Rels. award, Wis. region NCCJ, 1998, Cmty. Svc. Human Rels. award, Wis. chpt. Am. Jewish Com., 2000. Avocations: chess, comic book collecting, puppetry. Office: Samson Investments 100A E Pleasant St Milwaukee WI 53212-3975

SAMSOT, ROBERT LOUIS, editor, consultant; b. New Orleans, July 20, 1943; s. Robert Desposito and Mary Helen (Dohan) S.; m. A. Michael Newton, June 9, 1965; children: Kathleen Anderson Samsot English, Robert Dohan Samsot. BA in Journalism, U. N.C., Chapel Hill, 1965; cert. in Bus. Adminstrn., Rockhurst Coll., 1982. Reporter Rocky Mountain News, Denver, 1965-67, The Comml. Appeal, Memphis, 1967-72; reporter, editor Newsday, LI, N.Y., 1972-80; Gannett profl.-in-residence U. Kans., Lawrence, 1980-81; met. editor The Kansas City (Mo.) Times, 1981-84; city editor The Plain Dealer, Cleve., 1984-87; lifestyle editor, dep. editor N.J., dep. editor nat. The Phila. Inquirer, 1987-97; regional editor Balt. Sun, 1997-98; nat. editor USA Today, 1998-2000; asst. city editor The Washington Post, 2000—06; editor Fairfax Extra, 2006—. Cons. W.K. Kellogg Nat. Fellowship, Battle Creek, Mich., 1984-93; freelance writer, 1965—. Youth soccer coach Northport, N.Y., 1976-80, dir., 1979-80, Shaker Heights, Ohio, 1984-87, Swarthmore (Pa.) Recreation Assn., 1987-88; coach Johnson County (Kans.) Soccer League, 1983-84, U. Kans. Women's Soccer Club, 1980-81; bd. dirs. Suffolk County Heart Assn., L.I., 1974-75. Mem. Nat. Assn. Hispanic Journalists. Democrat. Roman Catholic. Avocations: travel, fitness, outdoor sports, cooking. Home: 10413 Breckinridge Ln Fairfax VA 22030-3417 Office: The Washington Post 1150 15th St NW Washington DC 20071-0002

SAMUEL, CARREN C., hospital administrator; b. Jan. 7, 1959; arrived in U.S., 1977; d. George A. and Ira P. Dundas; m. Boysing Samuel, Sept. 17, 1984; children: Boysing Jr., Michael C. AS, N.Y.C. Tech. Coll., Bklyn., 1981; BS, L.I. U., Bklyn., 1984, MPA, 1991. Registered respiratory therapist Nat. Bd. Respiratory Care, 1984. Respiratory therapist Kingsbrook Jewish Med. Ctr., Bklyn., 1983—86, asst. dir., respiratory care, 1986—94, dir., respiratory care, 1994—2006, adminstrv. dir., cardiopulmonary svcs., 2001—. Mem.: Am. Assn. for Respiratory Care. Office: Kingsbrook Jewish Med Ctr 585 Schenectady Ave Brooklyn NY 11203

SAMUEL, GREG R., lawyer; b. Oklahoma City, June 24, 1960; s. James H. and Jan Margaret (Allen) S.; children: Emily Grace, Margaret Anne, Sara Katherine. BBA, Abilene Christian U., 1982; JD, Vanderbilt U., 1985. Assoc. Haynes and Boone, LLP, Dallas, 1985-92, ptnr., 1993—. Articles editor: Vanderbilt Law Rev. Mem. State Bar Tex. (chmn. corp. com. of bus. law section, 2003-2005). Office: Haynes and Boone LLP 901 Main St Ste 3100 Dallas TX 75202-3789 Office Phone: 214-651-5645. Business E-Mail: greg.samuel@haynesboone.com.

SAMUEL, MAY LINDA, environmental scientist; d. Joe and Elvira Dixon; m. Earl Samuel; children: Annette Heyward, April Heyward. BS in Biology and Chemistry magna cum laude, Benedict Coll., 1977; MPH in Environ. Health Sci., U. SC, 1982; DD, Inst. Christian Works Coll. and Sem., 1996, PhD, ThD, 1999. Broadcaster Radio Sta. WGCV, Columbia, SC, 1984—86; asst. dir. environ. health scis. Benedict Coll., Columbia, 1990—; exec. dir. SC Environ Econ. Justice Network, Columbia, 2003—. Prof. biology Allen U., Columbia, 1984—86; cons. Inst. for Energy and Environ. Rsch., Tacoma Park, Md., 1999—2004. Contbr. articles to profl. jours. Founder, pastor Light of the World Ch., Winnsboro, SC, 1995—. Recipient SC Dept. Health and Environ. Control award, 1990, SC Dept. Corrections award, 1990; grantee, Dept. of Energy, 1995—97, EPA, 1996—99, Assn. Environ. Health, 2002—03, Sierra Club, 2003. Avocations: travel, reading. Office: Benedict Coll 1600 Harden St Columbia SC 29204-1058 Office Phone: 803-788-0370. Personal E-mail: samuelame@hotmail.com. Business E-Mail: samuelm@benedict.edu.

SAMUEL, PAUL, retired cardiologist; b. Janoshaza, Hungary, Feb. 17, 1927; arrived in U.S., 1954, naturalized, 1960; s. Adolf and Magda (Zollner) Samuel; m. Gabriella R. Zeichner, Mar. 27, 1954; children: Robert Mark, Adrianne Jill. Baccalaureat, Kemeny Zsigmond Gymnasium, Budapest, Hungary, 1945; MD, U. Paris, 1953. Intern Queens Hosp. Ctr., NYC, 1954-55; resident LI Jewish Med. Ctr., New Hyde Park, NY, 1959-61; pvt. practice Forest Hills, NY, 1961—2000; adj. prof. Rockefeller U., NYC, 1971-81; adj. prof. medicine Cornell U., NYC, 1979—; ret., 2000. Dir. Arteriosclerosis Rsch. Lab. LI Jewish-Hillside Med. Ctr., New Hyde Park, 1961—2001; chmn. NY Lipid Rsch. Club Rockefeller U., 1977—78; clin. prof. medicine Albert Einstein Coll. Medicine, Bronx, NY, 1981—. Contbr. articles to profl. jours. Fellow: Am. Coll. Cardiology; mem.: ACP, Am. Fedn. Clin. Rsch., Am. Heart Assn. (fellow coun. arteriosclerosis, Disting. Achievement award), Harvey Soc. Home: 25 Nassau Dr Great Neck NY 11021-2163

SAMUEL, RALPH DAVID, lawyer; b. Augusta, Ga., May 8, 1945; s. Ralph and Louise Elizabeth (Wurreschke) S.; m. Lynn Christel Malmgren, June 12, 1971; children: Lynn Britt, Ralph Erik. AB, Dartmouth Coll., 1967; JD, Dickinson Sch. of Law, 1972. Bar: Pa. 1972, U.S. Dist. Ct. (ea. dist.) Pa. 1972, U.S. Ct. Appeals (3d cir.) 1973, U.S. Supreme Ct. 1976. Law clk. to hon. judge John P. Fullam U.S. Dist. Ct. (ea. dist.) Pa., Phila., 1972-74; assoc. MacCoy, Evans & Lewis., Phila., 1974-76; ptnr. Samuel and Ballard, P.C., Phila., 1976-98; pres., CEO Ralph D. Samuel & Co., P.C., Phila., 1998—. Established Samuel Poetry Fellow Dartmouth Coll., Hanover, N.H., 1994. Contbr. articles to profl. jours., poetry to publs. Pres. Cedar Park Neighbors, Phila., 1975-78, West Mt. Airy Neighbors, Phila., 1981-82.; Trustee George Sch., Newtown, Pa., 1983-90; chmn. bd. dirs. Stapeley in Germantown, 1985-90, bd. dirs., mem. fin. com., 2007-; chmn. budget com. Phila. Yearly Meeting of Friends, 1991-93; bd. dirs., mem. fin. com. Phila. Ranger Corps., 1992-94; mem. Chase Fund Com., 2000; mem. ethics com. Friends Hosp., 2007-. Mem. Pa. Soc., Athenaeum of Phila., Sunday Breakfast Club. Mem. Soc. Of Friends. Avocations: music, writing, squash, tennis. Office: PO Box 35185 Philadelphia PA 19128-0185 Home Phone: 215-843-7012; Office Phone: 215-893-9992. Office Fax: 215-701-1085. Business E-Mail: RalphSamuel@RalphSamuel.com.

SAMUEL, ROBERT THOMPSON, optometrist; b. Kansas City, Mo., June 27, 1944; s. Manlius Thompson and Helen Evelyn (Syverson) S. BA, William Jewell Coll., 1966; postgrad., U. Mo., Kansas City, 1967; MS, U. Mo., 1968; DOptometry, U. Tenn., Memphis, 1971; postgrad., U. Mo., St. Louis, 1995, Northeastern State U., 1998. Cert. optometrist Mo. Buyer Recco, Inc., Kansas City, Mo., 1963-67; histology lab. instr. William Jewell Coll., Liberty, Mo., 1965-66; pvt. practice optometry Gladstone, Mo., 1972—; staff doctor O.H. Gerry Optical Clinics, 1996—. Panel doctor Ford Motor Co., Claycomo, Mo., 1985—, Union Pacific R.R., Kansas City, 1985—, TWA Airlines, 1990, Union Carbide, 1990. Publicity coord. Rep. Party, Kansas City, Mo., 1975-76; chmn. Save Your Vision Week, Kansas City, 1977; mem. Theatre League of Kansas City, 1976—, Kansas City Mus., 1986—, Friends of Art, 1985, Friends of Mo. Town 1955, 1980—. Recipient Outstanding Young Men of Am. award Jaycees, 1978, Good Citizens award DAR, 1962. Mem. Am. Optometric Assn., Mo. Optometric Assn., Optometric Soc. Greater Kansas City, Heart of Am. Contact Lens Congress, Am. Acad. Sports Vision, Vol. Optometric Svcs. for Humanity, Smithsonian Assocs., Lions (exec. bd. dir. Lions Eye Clinic 1974-84, bd. dirs. 1982—, Outstanding Svc. award 1973, 74, editor Lions Optometric Ctr. Quar. 1974-84), Kappa Alpha Order (treas. 1966). Republican. Lutheran. Avocations: photography, music, piano, swimming, travel. Home: 6325 N Monroe Ave Kansas City MO 64119-1923 Office: 1170 W 152 Hwy Liberty MO 64068-2035 also: 5601 NE Antioch Rd Kansas City MO 64119-2302 Office Phone: 816-453-7290.

SAMUELI, HENRY, electrical engineer, educator, entrepreneur; b. Buffalo, Sept. 20, 1954; s. Aron and Sala (Traubman) S.; m. Susan Faye Eisenberg, Aug. 22, 1982; children: Leslie Pamela, Jillian Meryl, Erin Sydney. BSEE, UCLA, 1975, MSEE, 1976, PhD in Elec. Engring., 1980. Staff engr. TRW Inc., Redondo Beach, Calif., 1980-83, section mgr., 1983-85; asst. prof. UCLA, 1985-90, assoc. prof., 1990-94, prof., 1994—95, disting. adj. prof., elec. engring. and computer sci., 2003—. Cons. TRW, Inc., Redondo Beach, 1985-89; co-founder, chief scientist PairGain Techs., Inc., Tustin, Calif., 1988-94; co-founder, chief tech. officer Broadcom Corp., Irvine, Calif., 1991-, v.p. rsch. & devel. & co-chmn., 1991-2003, chmn., 2003-; owner Anaheim Ducks (formerly Mighty Ducks of Anaheim), NHL, 2005-. Named one of Top 20 Entrepreneurs of 1997, The Red Herring Mag., 1997, one of Top 50 Cyber Elite, Time Digital Mag., 1997; Schs. Engring. at both U. Calif. Irvine and UCLA named in honor of; recipient Presdl. award, U. Calif., 2000, Irvine medal, 2000, Alumnus of Yr. award, UCLA Sch. of Engring. and Applied Sci., 2000, Golden Plate award, Acad. Achievement, 2006. Fellow: IEEE (Circuits and Systems Soc. Indsl. Pioneer award 2000), Am. Acad. Arts & Sci.; mem.: NAE. Republican. Jewish. Holder of 22 US patents. Office: Broadcom Corp 16215 Alton Pkwy Irvine CA 92618 Address: U Calif Irvine Henry Samueli Sch Engring Elec Engring and Computer Sci 325 Engineering Tower Irvine CA 92697-2625 *

SAMUELL, TIECHERA DAWN, language educator; d. Alvin Enis and Betty Jeanette House; m. Christopher Michael Samuell, May 26, 2001. BA, Western Ill. U., Macomb, 1997—2001; MA, SE Mo. State U., Cape Girardeau, 2001—03. Edn. and career devel. coord. Boys & Girls Club, Cape Girardeau, 2001—04; writing ctr. assoc., adj. faculty SE Mo. State U., 2003—04; faculty Three Rivers CC, Poplar Bluff, Mo., 2004—. Mem.: Mo. Assn. Tchrs. English, Nat. Coun. Tchrs. English. Office: Three Rivers CC 2080 Three Rivers Blvd Poplar Bluff MO 63901 Business E-Mail: tsamuell@trcc.edu.

SAMUELS, BRIAN LOUIS, oncologist, researcher; b. Harare, Zimbabwe, May 6, 1954; m. Lesley Margaret Samuels, Jan. 5, 1979; children: David, Mark, Emma. MBChB, U. Rhodesia, 1976. Asst. prof. U. Chgo., 1988—95; assoc. prof. U. Ill. at Chgo., 1996—; dir. oncology rsch. Luth. Gen. Hosp., Park Ridge, Ill., 1991—; intern U. Rhodesia, 1977; resident internal medicine Albert Einstein Med. Ctr., Philadelphia, 1979—84, U. Witwatersrand, 1981—83; fellowship Hema/Onc U. Chicago, 1984—88. Office: Oncology Specialists SC 1700 Luther Ln Park Ridge IL 60068

SAMUELS, DONALD L., lawyer; b. Washington, May 8, 1961; s. Jack Donald Samuels and Francis Diane (Katcher) Yeoman; m. Sherri Tobin Samuels. AB, Brown U., 1983; JD, Columbia U., 1986. Bar: Calif. 1986, Calif. 1988, Tex. 1998, U.S. Dist. Ct. (cen., no., ea. and so. dists.), U.S. Dist. Ct. Colo. 1997, U.S. Ct. Appeals (9th cir.) 1989, Colo. 1996, U.S. Ct. Appeals (7th cir.) 1996, U.S. Ct. Appeals (10th cir.) 1997, U.S. Supreme Ct. 2004. Law clk. Hon. William D. Keller, LA, 1986-87; assoc. Sidley & Austin, LA, 1987-94, ptnr., 1994-95, Samuels & Samuels, LA, 1995-97; officer, dir., shareholder Ireland & Stapleton, Denver, 1997—2002; ptnr. Holme, Roberts & Owen, LLP, Denver, 2002—. Mem. ABA, Calif. Bar Assn., Colo. Bar Assn., Tex. Bar Assn., Phi Beta Kappa. Home: 5692 S Florence St Greenwood Village CO 80111-3713 Office: Holme Roberts & Owen LLP Ste 4100 1700 Lincoln St Denver CO 80203-4541 Home Phone: 303-770-9119; Office Phone: 303-866-0548. Business E-Mail: donald.samuels@hro.com.

SAMUELS, DOROTHY J., journalist, writer; b. NYC, May 15, 1951; d. Herman and Roz Silver; m. Peter G. Samuels, Dec. 26, 1971; children: Laurah, Tom, Jenny. AB, Bryn Mawr Coll., 1972; JD, Northeastern U., 1975. Bar: NY. Atty. Brown & Wood, NYC, 1975—76; exec. dir. Com. for Pub. Justice, NYC, 1976—79, N.Y. Civil Liberties Union, NYC, 1979—81; cons. Ford Found., NYC, 1981—83. Mem. editl. bd. NY Times, NYC, 1985—. Author: (novels) Filthy Rich, 2001; contbr. book Then and Now, 2000, articles to mags. Office: NY Times 620 Eighth Ave New York NY 10018-1405 Business E-Mail: dosamu@nytimes.com.

SAMUELS, FERN JACQUELINE, artist, educator; b. Chgo., Feb. 16, 1931; d. Noah S. and Ann (Zager) Andrews; m. Howard Stanley Samuels, Sept. 17, 1950 (dec.); children: Mitchell, Paul, David. BFA, Loyola U., Chgo., 1973; MFA, Sch. Art Inst. Chgo., 1983. Instr.-coord. Mundelein Coll., Chgo., 1976-83; faculty Columbia Coll., 1978-2000. Instr. workshops Field Mus., Chgo., 1976, Lake Forest Coll., Chgo., 1976, Lincoln Park Cultural Ctr., Chgo., 1973, Ill. Inst. Tech., Chgo., 1980—, Latin Sch., Chgo., 1976; juror St. Louis Arts Guild, 1998. One-women shows include Northwestern U., 1988, Ea. Ill. U., Chgo., 1989, Countryside Gallery, 1988, Upstart Gallery, 1990, Soho 20, N.Y.C., 1993, Loyola U., 1995, Morraine Valley Coll., 1995, McDonough Mus. Art, 1997, Fyr Place Gallery, 2000, Gallery on Azeele, 2000, Mos Art Gallery, Lake Park, Fla., 2004, Cornell Mus., Del Ray, Fla., 2004 (1st award), City Hall, Palm Beach Gardens, 2007; exhibited in group shows including Smithsonian Air and Space Mus., 1983, Freeport Mus., 1995, Rockford Mus., 1996, Butler Inst. Am. Art, 1998, Lafayette Mus., 1999, Columbus Mus. Art, 2000, So. Ohio Mus., 2000, South Bend Regional Mus., 2000, Univ. Mus. S.D., 2001, Gallery 228, N.Y.C., 2003, Galleria Prinarde, 2007, Northwind U., West Palm Beach, 2007, Amsterdam Whitney Gallery, NYC, 2007, Amory Art Ctr., Fla., 2007. Mem. LWV, Chgo., 1969—; founding mem. Alternative Fibers, Chgo., 1982; chairperson, coord. Seven Ethnic Museums, Chgo., 1986; membership chmn. ARC Gallery, Chgo., 1983-86, pres. 1988-90; bd. dirs. Artist Book Works, Chgo., 1992-93. Recipient Best of Show award Women in the Visual Arts, Boca Raton, Fla., 2001, Judges Recognition award, Boca Raton, 2001, 2nd award Boca Mus. Artists Guild, 2001, 1st award, 2002, 1st prize Women in Visual Arts, Del Ray, Fla., 2002, Mus. Exhibits, 2002, Jewish Mus., Miami, Norton Mus., West Palm Beach, Fla., 2002, 2004, Cornell Mus. of Art and Sci., Del Ray, 2002, Art Club Chgo., 2003, Permanent Collection, Rutgers U., 2003, 1st award Northwood U., West Palm Beach, Fla., 2003, 1st award Boca Mus. Artist Guild, 2003; grantee Columbia Coll., 1981; Fern Samuels Scholarship Fund est. Columbia Coll., Chgo., 1st award Milagro Art Ctr., Del Ray Fla., 2003, 1st award Boca Mus. Artist Guild, 2003, Artist Guild Inc 1st award, 2005, Women in the Visual Arts 1st award, 2005, Fla. Artist's Group, 2nd award, 2005. Mem. Nat. Assn. Women Artists, Internat. Soc. Exptl. Artists, Arts Club Chgo., Chgo. Soc. Artists, City of Hope (Bobby Blechman chpt. founding mem.), Sch. Art Inst. Chgo. Alumni (2d prize 2002). Democrat. Avocations: reading, music, theater, exercise. Home: 114A Palm Bay Dr S Palm Beach Gardens FL 33418 E-mail: ucars1@aol.com.

SAMUELS, JANET LEE, lawyer; b. Pitts., July 18, 1953; d. Emerson and Jeanne (Kalish) S.; m. David Arthur Kalow, June 18, 1978; children; Margaret Emily Samuels-Kalow, Jacob Richard Samuels-Kalow, Benjamin Charles Samuels-Kalow. BA with honors, Beloit Coll., 1974; JD, NYU, 1977. Bar: N.Y. 1978, D.C. 1980. Staff atty. SCM Corp., NYC, 1977-80, corp. atty., 1980-83, sr. corp. atty., 1983-85, assoc. gen. counsel Allied Paper div., 1983-86, corp. counsel, 1986, Holtzmann, Wise & Shepard, 1986-88. Mem. N.Y. State Bar Assn., Mortar Board, Phi Beta Kappa. E-mail: JanetLSamuels@yahoo.com, JLS@creativity-law.com.

SAMUELS, LESLIE B., lawyer; b. St. Louis, Nov. 10, 1942; s. Joseph E. and Dorothy J. (Bernstein) S.; m. Judith B. Thorn, June 19, 1966 (div. Aug. 1976); children: Colin T., Polly B.; m. Augusta H. Gross, Nov. 8, 1980. BS in Econs., U. Pa., 1963; LLB magna cum laude, Harvard U., 1966; postgrad., London Sch. Econs., 1966-67. Bar: N.Y., 1969, U.S. Dist. Ct. (so. dist.) N.Y. 1973, U.S. Tax Ct., 1980, U.S. Supreme Ct. 1994; CPA. Tax analyst Gulf Oil Co., London, 1967-68; assoc. Cleary Gottlieb Steen & Hamilton LLP, NYC, 1968-75, ptnr., 1975-93, 96—; asst. sec. for tax policy U.S. Dept. Treasury, Washington, 1993-96; vice-chair com. fiscal affairs OECD, 1994-96. Mem. Pres.'s Com. on the Arts and the Humanities, Washington, 1994-96. Editor Law Rev.; contbr. articles to profl. jours. Dir. Lower Manhattan Cultural Coun., N.Y.C., 1981-93, Roy Lichtenstein Found., N.Y.C., 1999—; active Carter-Mondale Transition Planning Group, Washington, 1976-77. Fulbright fellow London Sch. Econs., 1966-67. Mem. N.Y. State Bar Assn., Assn. of Bar of City of N.Y., Harvard Club (N.Y.C.). Democrat. Office: Cleary Gottlieb Steen & Hamilton LLP One Liberty Plaza New York NY 10006 Home Phone: 212-535-4209; Office Phone: 212-225-2250. Business E-Mail: lsamuels@cgsh.com.

SAMUELS, MARK A., lawyer; b. LA, 1957; BA, U. Calif., Berkeley, 1979; JD, U. Calif., LA, 1982. Bar: Calif. 1982, US Dist. Ct., Ctrl. Dist. Calif. 1982, US Ct. Appeals, 9th Cir. 1983, US Dist. Ct., So. and No. Districts of Calif. 1984, US Dist. Ct., Ea. Dist. Calif. 1987, US Ct. Appeals, Fed. Cir. 1991. Ptnr. O'Melveny & Myers LLP, LA, chair, intellectual property & technology dept. Mem. LA Superior Ct. Arbitration Panel. Mem. U. Calif LA Law Review, 1980—81, chief mng. editor, 1981—82. Bd. dir. U. Calif. LA Sch. Law Alumni Assn. Named one of Top 25 Intellectual Property Lawyers, LA Daily Jour. Mem.: Calif. State Bar (mem. intellectual property sect.), Assn. of Bus. Trial Lawyers, Fed. Cir. Bar Assn., Am. Intellectual Property Law Assn., LA County Bar Assn., ABA (liaison, lawyers conf. task force on reduction of litig. cost & delay 1993), Order of the Coif, Flintridge Riding Club (bd. dir., treas.), Phi Beta Kappa. Office: O'Melveny & Myers LLP 400 S Hope St Los Angeles CA 90071-2899 Office Phone: 213-430-6340. Office Fax: 213-430-6407. Business E-Mail: msamuels@omm.com.

SAMUELS, MAURICE ANTHONY, French literature educator; b. Chgo., Aug. 9, 1968; s. Richard Arthur and Virginia Corbisella Samuels. BA, Harvard U., Cambridge, Mass., 1990; PhD, Harvard U., 2000. Asst. prof. of French U. of Pa., Phila., 2000—06; prof. of French Yale U., New Haven, 2006—. Author: (book (academic) The Spectacular Past: Popular History and the Novel in Nineteenth-Century France. Home Phone: 917-679-7871; Office Phone: 203-432-4900.

SAMUELS, SANDOR ELI, lawyer, diversified financial services company executive; b. LA, Aug. 22, 1952; m. Claudia Wallack; 3 children. AB summa cum laude, Princeton U., NJ, 1974; JD, UCLA, 1977. Bar: Calif. 1977, US Dist. Ct. (ctrl. dist. Calif.) 1977. Law clk. to Hon. Irving Hill US Dist. Ct. (ctrl. dist. Calif.), 1977—79; atty. Munger, Tolles & Olson, 1979—83, First Interstate Bancorp, 1984—88, sr. v.p., asst. gen. counsel, 1988; sr. v.p., gen. counsel Fox Inc., 1989—90; sr. v.p., gen. counsel, sec. Countrywide Fin. Corp., Calabasas, Calif., 1990—91, mng. dir., legal, gen. counsel, sec., 1991—2000, sr. mng. dir., legal, gen. counsel, sec., 2001—03, sr. mng. dir., chief legal adv., sec., 2003, exec. mng. dir., chief legal adv., asst. sec. Bd. dirs. U. Judaism, Ziegler Sch. Rabbinic Studies,

Shalhevet Sch., Bet Tzedek Legal Svcs., Adat Ari El Synagogue. Mem.: Mortgage Bankers Assn. Am. (chmn. legal services com. 1995—96), State Bar Calif., LA County Bar Assn., ABA, Order of the Coif. Office: Countrywide Fin Corp 4500 Park Granada Calabasas CA 91302-1613 *

SAMUELS, WILLIAM MASON, physiology association executive; b. Dover, Ohio, Jan. 17, 1929; s. William Mason and Anne Frieda (Fankhauser) S.; m. Joanne Gorenflo, Oct. 2, 1971; children: Robert Lee, Ann Frances. AB, U. Ky., 1951; postgrad., Georgetown U., 1952. Mng. editor for Ind., Courier-Jour. & Times, Louisville, 1955-65; dir. office of v.p. U. Ky. Med. Center, Lexington, 1965-70; exec. dir. Am. Soc. Allied Health Professions, Washington, 1973—78; assoc. Schs. Allied Health Professions, 1970—73; exec. dir. Am. Assn. Blood Banks, Washington, 1978-80, Nat. Soc. Med. Research Washington, 1980-84, Am. Physiol. Soc., Bethesda, Md., 1984-92; retired, 1992—. Contbr. articles to profl. jours. Mem. secretarist Nat. Commn. Health Certifying Agys.; v.p. Coalition Health Funding; cons. to fed. agys.; vol. Habitat for Humanity, Boca Raton; elder Presbyn. Ch., corp. dir. With USAF, 1951-53, USAFR, 1954-76, lt. col. ret. Named Ky. Man of Yr. Sigma Phi Epsilon, 1968 Mem.: AMA (coun. on allied health edn. accreditation), Washington Soc. Assn. Execs., Health Staff Soc., Am. Hosp. Assn. (coun. on edn.), Am. Optometric Assn. (coun. on edn., coun. on optimetric clin. care, nat. commn. on paraoptometric cert.), Am. Soc. Assn. Execs., Pinehurst (NC) Country Club, Lions. Presbyterian. Home: 6055 S Verde Trail H-120 Boca Raton FL 33433-4406

SAMUELSON, CECIL O., JR., academic administrator; b. 1942; m. Sharon Giauque; 5 children. BS, MS, MD, U. Utah. V.p. health scis. U. Utah, Salt Lake City, 1970-90; sr. v.p. Intermountain Health Care, Inc., Salt Lake City, 1990—94; dean IHC Hosps. Inc., Salt Lake City, 1990—; pres. Brigham Young U., Provo, Utah, 2003—. Pres. LDS Ch. No. Area, Utah; Pres. LDS Ch. Europe No. Area; mem. First Quorum of the Seventy, Ch. of LDS, 1994—2003. Office: Office of the Pres Brigham Young U Provo UT 84602 Office Phone: 801-422-2521. *

SAMUELSON, DONALD B., former state legislator; b. Brainerd, Minn., Aug. 23, 1932; s. Walter H. and Ellen (Gallagher) S.; m. Nancy O'Brien, 1952; children: Stephen, Laura, Paula, Christine. Chmn. 6th Dist. Com. on Polit. Edn. State of Minn., 1960-66; mem. Minn. Ho. of Reps., St. Paul, 1969-76, 1981-82, Minn. Senate from 12th dist., St. Paul, 1982—; pres. Minn. Senate, St. Paul, 2000—02. Chmn. Health & Human Svc. Fin. Div. Com., mem. Commerce and Consumer Protection, mem. Family Svc. Com., mem. Fin. and Health Care Com.; former foreman Bor-Son Construct Co.; union bus. mgr. Chmn. 6th Dist. Com. on Polit. Edn., Minn., 1960-66; mem. State Ctrl. Com. Dem-Farmer-Labor Party, 1964-66, former chmn. Crow Wing County. Mem. Housing and Redevel. Authority, Minn. AFL-CIO, Bricklayers Union, Am. Legion, Eagles. Democrat. Home: 1018 Portland Ave Brainerd MN 56401-4133

SAMUELSON, DOUGLAS ALAN, information technology executive; b. Reno, Nev., July 27, 1948; s. Norman Harold and Shirley (Leder) Samuelson; m. Francine Ruth Kimel, Jan. 7, 1979 (div. Aug. 7, 2003); children: Andrew, Diane. BA, U. Calif., Berkeley, 1969; MS, George Washington U., 1981, DSc, 1990. Computer systems analyst Bank Am., San Francisco, 1972-73; cons. San Rafael, Calif., 1973-75; ops. rsch. analyst U.S. Govt., Washington, 1975-82; analyst, v.p. Micro-Zeit/Internat. Telesystems Corp., Reston, Va., 1983-88; asst. prof. Memphis State U., 1990-92; pres. InfoLogix, Inc., Annandale, Va., 1988—; prin. scientist Puma Sys., Inc., Falls Church, Va., 1997-98; chief statistician FMAS Dyncorp., Columbia, Md., 2000; sr. analyst Synergia LLC, 2004, Homeland Security Inst., 2005—07; prin. decision scientist Serco, 2007—. Vis. rsch. scholar George Washington U., 1993—95, mem. nat. adv. coun. Sch. Engring. and Applied Sci., 1996—2000, adj. prof. lectr., 1997—; adj. assoc. prof. George Mason U., Fairfax, Va., 1994—96, external rsch. prof. Krasnow Inst. Advanced Study, 2001—03; adj. assoc. prof. U. Pa., Phila., 2001—. Co-editor, author (with others): Human Rights and Statistics: Getting the Record Straight, 1992, Health Information and Ethics: Protecting Fundamental Human Rights, 1997, columnist: The Oracle, 1986—; contbr. articles to profl. jours. Mem.: AAAS, Inst. Ops. Rsch. and Mgmt. Sci. (bd. dirs. 1998—2000), Am. Statis. Assn. (chair com. sci. freedom and human rights 1985—88), Washington OR/MS Coun. (pres. 1989—90, 1996—97), George Washington U. Engr. Alumni Assn. (bd. dirs. 1994—, v.p. 1996—98, pres. 1998—2000). Democrat. Jewish. Achievements include patent for systems for regulating arrivals of customers to servers. Office: InfoLogix Inc 8711 Chippendale Ct Annandale VA 22003-3807 Home Phone: 703-978-5030; Office Phone: 703-978-5030. Personal E-mail: samuelsondoug@yahoo.com.

SAMUELSON, FRED BINDER, artist, educator; b. Harvey, Ill., Nov. 29, 1925; s. Frederick Gustav and Theresa Marie (Binder) S.; children: Fredric Michael, Lisa Maria. BFA, Art Inst. Chgo., 1951, MFA, 1953. Head lithography dept. Instituto Allende, San Miguel Allende, Gauanajuanto, Mex., 1955-63, head grad. studies, 1964—; faculty chmn. San Antonio Art Inst., 1963-64. Condr. seminars Laredo Art Assn., 1964, 71, 78, Hill County Art Found., Ingram Tex., 1967—, Brownsville, Beaumont, Lamesa art leagues, Lubbock Art Assn., San Antonio Watercolor Soc., Carrizo Lodge, Ruidoso, N.Mex., Houston Water Color Soc., Laguna Gloria Mus., Austin, Tex. Represented in permanent collections Galeria Moderna, Banjaluka, Yugoslavia, Ctr. for Arts, Vero Beach; executed mural for Conv. Ctr., Hemisfair, 1968. Served with USAAF, 1943-45. Recipient numerous hon. mentions, 1953—, purchase prizes, including Denver Art Mus., Joslyn Art Mus., Omaha, Mulvane Art Mus., Topeka, Okla. Art Ctr., Hertzberg Gallery, San Antonio, Witte Mus., San Antonio, Ohio U., Athens. Home and Office: 401 Highland Ter Titusville FL 32796

SAMUELSON, KENNETH LEE, lawyer; b. Natrona Heights, Pa., Aug. 22, 1946; s. Sam and Frances Bernice (Robbins) Samuelson; m. Marlene Ina Rabinowitz, Jan. 1, 1980; children: Heather, Cheryl. BA magna cum laude, U. Pitts., 1968; JD, U. Mich., 1971. Bar: Md. 1972, DC 1980, U.S. Dist. Ct. (trial bar) Md. 1984. Assoc. Weinberg & Green, Balt., 1971-73, Dickerson, Nice, Sokol & Horn, Balt., 1973; asst. atty. gen. State of Md., 1973-77; pvt. practice Balt., 1978; ptnr. Linowes and Blocher, Silver Spring, Md., 1979-93, Semmes, Bowen & Semmes, Balt. and Washington, 1993—95, Wilkes Artis, Chartered, Washington, 1995—2001, Deckelbaum Ogens & Raftery, Washington, 2001—, Bethesda, Md., 2001—. Spkr. in field. Bd. govs. Washington Bldg. Congress, 1998—2001; spkr. CoreNet Global, 2006, Harvard Bus. Club Washington, 2006; bd. dirs. DC Assn. Retarded Citizens, Inc., 1986—2001. Mem.: ABA (co-chair tech. com. 1999—2007, coun. mem. sect. real property, probate and trust law 2000—06, moderator various programs), Internat. Assn. Attys. and Exec. in Corp. Real Estate (spkr. in field 2006, CLE spkr. 2006—07, spkr. in field 2007), Am. Inns of Ct. (speaker at bankruptcy programs), Montgomery County Bar Assn. (mem. jud. selections com. 1988—90), Internat. Coun. Shopping Ctrs. (organized co-faculty program "univ." 1988, NAFTA 1992, condemnations 1994, leasing 1997, high tech. effects 1998, pub./pvt. partnerships 1999), E. Coast Builders Conf., Apt. and Office Bldg. Assn. Met. Washington, Civil Code Drafting Com. Russian Legis., Nat. Assn. Corp. Real Estate Execs., Washington Assn. Realtors, Inc., DC Bldg. Industry Assn., Am. Arbitration Assn. (arbitrator, mediator 1995—2003), Md. Inst. Continuing Profl. Edn. Lawyers, Md. Bar Assn. (litig. sect. 1982—84, real property, planning and zoning sect., chmn. comml. trans. com.), DC Bar (mem. comml. real estate com., chmn. legal opinions project), Am. Coll. Real Estate Lawyers (moderator, speaker various programs), Lambda Alpha, Phi Beta Kappa. Office: Deckelbaum Ogens & Raftery Chartered # 165 2020 Pennsylvania Ave NW Washington DC 20006 Office Phone: 301-347-3469. Business E-Mail: ksamuelson@deckelbaum.com.

SAMUELSON, PAUL ANTHONY, economist, educator; b. Gary, Ind., May 15, 1915; s. Frank and Ella (Lipton) Samuelson; m. Marion E. Crawford, July 2, 1938 (dec.); children: Jane Kendall, Margaret Wray, William Frank, Robert James, John Crawford, Paul Reid; m. Risha Eckaus, 1981; 1 stepchild, Susan Miller. BA, U. Chgo., 1935; MA, Harvard U., 1936, PhD (David A. Wells prize 1941), 1941; LLD (hon.), U. Chgo., Oberlin Coll., 1961, Boston Coll., 1964, Ind. U., 1966, U. Mich., 1967, Claremont Grad. Sch., 1967, Seton Hall U., 1971, U. N.H., 1971, Keio U., 1971, Widener Coll., 1982, Cath. U. at Riva Aguero U., Lima, Peru, 1980, Harvard, 1972, Gustavus Adolphus Coll., 1974, U. So. Calif., 1975, U. Pa., 1976, U. Rochester, 1976, Emmanuel Coll., 1977, Stonehill Coll., 1978, Indiana U. of Pa., 1993; DLitt (hon.), Ripon Coll., 1962, No. Mich. U., 1973, Valparaiso U., 1987, Columbia U, 1988; LHD (hon.), Williams Coll., 1971; DSc (hon.), U. Mass., 1972, U. R.I., 1972, Tufts U., 1988, East Anglia U., Norwich, Eng., 1966, Rennselaer Poly. Inst., 1998; D (hon.), U. Catholique de Louvain, Belgium, 1976, City U., London, 1980, New U. Lisbon, 1985, Univ. Nat. de Educacion a Distancia, Madrid, 1989, Univ. Politecnica de Valencia, Spain, 1991; D in Social Scis. (hon.), Yale U., 2005. Prof. econs. MIT, 1940—65, inst. prof., 1966, prof. emeritus, 1986; mem. staff Radiation Lab., 1944—45; prof. internat. econ. relations Fletcher Sch. Law and Diplomacy, 1945; cons. Nat. Resources Planning Bd., 1941—43, WPB, 1945, U.S. Treasury, 1945—52, 1961—74, Bur. Budget, 1952, RAND Corp., 1948—75, Fed. Res. Bd., 1965—; council Econ. Advisers, 1960—68; econ. adviser to Pres. Kennedy; sr. adviser Brookings Panel on Econ. Activity; mem. spl. commn. on social scis. NSF, 1967—68; cons. Congl. Budget Office, Federal Reserve Bd., 1965—; Gordon Y Billard Fellow MIT, Boston, 1986—; vis. prof of polit. econ. Ctr. Japan-U.S. Bus. and Econ. Studies, NYU, 1987—2005. Mem. nat. adv. com. Inst. for Rsch. on Poverty; lectr. in field. Author: Foundations of Economic Analysis, 1947, enlarged edit., 1983, Readings in Economics, 1955; author: (with R. Dorfman and R.M. Solow) Linear Programming and Economic Analysis, 1958; author: Collected Scientific Papers, 5 vols., 1966, 1972, 1978, 1986, Economics 1948-1980; co-author (with William Nordhaus): Economics, 1985—2005; author: numerous other books; columnist Newsweek, 1966—81; assoc. editor: Jour. Pub. Econs., Jour. Internat. Econs., Jour. Fin. Econs., Jour. Nonlinear Analysis, adv. bd.: Challenge Mag.; contbr. articles to profl. jours. Chmn. Pres.'s Task Force Maintaining Am. Prosperity, 1964; mem. Nat. Task Force on Econ. Edn., 1960—61; econ. adviser to Pres. John F. Kennedy, 1959—63; mem. adv. bd. Nat. Commn. Money and Credit, 1958—60. Recipient David A. Wells prize, Harvard U., 1941, John Bates Clark medal, Am. Econ. Assn., 1947, Alfred Nobel Meml. prize, 1970, medal of Honor, U. Evansville, Ill., 1970, Albert Einstein Commemorative award, 1971, Alumni medal, U. Chgo., 1983, Britannica award, 1989, Gold Scanno prize, Naples, Italy, 1990, Paul A. Samuelson Professorship established in his name, MIT, 1991, Nat. Medal of Sci., Washington, 1996; fellow hon. fellow, London Sch. Econs. and Polit. Sci., Guggenheim, 1948—49, rsch. fellow, Ford Found., 1958—59. Fellow: Econometric Soc. (v.p. 1950, pres. 1951), Am. Philos. Soc., Am. Econ. Assn. (hon.; pres. 1961), Brit. Acad. (corr.); mem.: NAS, AAAS, Nat. Assn. Investment Clubs (Disting. Svc. award in Investment Edn. 1974), Leibniz-Akademie der Wissenschaften und der Literatur (corr.), Internat. Econ. Assn. (pres. 1966—68, hon. pres.), Com. Econ. Devel. (commn. on nat. goals, rsch. adv. bd. 1959—60), Club of Econ. and Mgmt. (medal, hon. Valencia, Spain 1990), Omicron Delta Epsilon (trustee), Phi Beta Kappa. Office: MIT E52 # 383C Dept Econs 50 Memorial Dr Cambridge MA 02142 Office Phone: 617-253-3368.

SAMUELSON, PETER A., management consultant; b. Taipei, Taiwan, Feb. 14, 1968; s. David Morris and Millie Marie (Nelson) Samuelson; married; 1 child. BA, Greenville Coll., Ill., 1990; JD, Yale U., 1993. Legal rschr. Lovell White Durrant, Hong Kong, 1993-94; assoc. Hughes Hubbard Reed, NYC, 1994-96, McKinsey & Co., Inc., NYC, 1996; dir. strategic planning Byran Cave, St. Louis; pres. Americans United for Life, Chgo., 2004—. Bd. dirs. Americans United for Life, St. Louis, 2000—; trustee Ctr. Bioethics and Culture. Summer rsch. grantee Ford Found., 1993. Methodist. Office: Americans United for Life 310 S Peoria Ste 500 Chicago IL 60607 E-mail: peter.samuelson@usa.net.

SAMUELSON, ROBERT JACOB, journalist; b. NYC, Dec. 23, 1945; s. Abraham and Joan (Kahn) S.; m. Judith Herr, July 10, 1983; children: Ruth, Michael, John. AB in Govt., Harvard U., 1967. Reporter Washington Post, 1969-73; free-lance writer Washington, 1973-76; reporter, columnist National Jour. mag., Washington, 1976-84; columnist Newsweek, Washington, 1984—. Columnist Washington Post, 1977—. Author: The Good Life and Its Discontents: The American Dream in the Age of Entitlement 1945-1995, 1996, Untruth: Why the Conventional Wisdom is (Almost Always) Wrong, 2001.

SAMUELSSON, MARCUS (KASSHUN TSEGIE), food service executive; b. Ethiopia; Degree, Culinary Inst. Göteborg, Switzerland. Chef Aquavit, NYC, 1991, worked under Jan Sendel, exec. chef & co-owner, 1995—, opened Mpls.; chef Georges Blanc, Lyon, France; exec. chef & co-owner AQ Café at Scandinavia House, NYC. Chosen to cook for Sweden's royal family; chosen to cook at gala dinner honoring the late Patrick Clark at Tavern on the Green; launched new line of traditional Swedish prepared foods; chef's coun. Chefs for Humanity. Featured Gourmet, USA Today, Food and Wine, NY Times, Australian Vogue Entertaining, appeared CNN, Discovery Channel, ABC's Good Morning Am., (numerous local N.Y. TV programs); author: Aquavit: And the New Scandinavian Cuisine, 2003, The Soul of a New Cuisine: A Discovery of the Foods & Flavors of Africa, 2006 (Libr. Jour. Fall Editor's Pick, 2006). Named Best Rising Star Chef, James Beard Found., 1999; named one of Great Chefs Am., Culinary Inst. Am.; recipient three-star restaurant rev. for Aquavit, NY Times, four-star rating, Forbes, three and a half-star rating, Crain's. Avocations: museums, art galleries. Office: Aquavit Inc 424 Madison Ave Rm 1410 New York NY 10017-1160

SANANMAN, MICHAEL LAWRENCE, neurologist; b. Bklyn., Oct. 11, 1939; s. Jack and Sarey (Bykofsky) S.; m. Elisa Joan Freeman, Apr. 12, 1964; children: Amy, Peter. AB, Swarthmore Coll., 1960; MD, Columbia U., 1964. Diplomate Am. Bd. Psychiatry and Neurology. Intern U. Hosp., San Francisco, 1964-65; resident in neurology N.Y. Neurol. Inst., NYC, 1966-69; practice medicine specializing in neurology Elizabeth, N.J., 1972—. Cons. neurologist Rahway (N.J.) Hosp., Trinitas Hosp., N.J., Union Hosp., N.J.; instr. neurology Columbia U., N.Y.C., 1971-75; assoc. clin. prof. neurology U. Medicine and Dentistry N.J., Newark, 1975—. Lt. comdr. M.C., USNR, 1969-71. Mem. AMA, Am. Acad. Neurology, Am. Epilepsy Soc., N.J. Acad. Medicine, Am. Eastern EEG Socs., Am. Assn. EMG and Electrodiagnosis. Office: 700 N Broad St Elizabeth NJ 07208-2310 Office Phone: 908-354-3994. Personal E-mail: Mikesan48@aol.com.

SANBERG, PAUL RONALD, medical educator; b. Coral Gables, Fla., Jan. 4, 1955; s. Bernard and Molly (Spector) Sanberg BS with honors, York U., 1976; MS, U. B.C., 1979; PhD, Australian Nat. U., 1981, DSc, 1998; grad. diploma sci. edn., We. Australia Inst. Tech., 1986. Postdoctoral fellow Johns Hopkins Med. Sch., Balt., 1981—83; asst. prof. Ohio U., Athens, 1983—86; assoc. prof. U. Cin., 1986—89; prof. Brown U., Providence, 1990—92, U. South Fla., Tampa, 1992—2003, disting. prof., 2003—, assoc. dean, assoc. v.p., 2003—06, chair neurosci., 1997—2005, dir. Ctr. of Excellence for Aging and Brain Repair, 2000—. Co-founder Saneron Therapeutics, Inc., 2000—. Recipient award Am. Coll. Neuropsychopharmacology, Tourette Syndrome Assn., Sir. J.G. Crawford medal, Ove Ferno prize Coll. Internat. Neuropsychopharmacology; grantee NIH, Am. Heart Assn., Childrens Med. Rsch. Found., Hereditary Disease Found., Huntington's Disease Found., Outstanding Rschr. award Sigma Xi; named Healthcare Hero, Tampa Bay Bus. Jour., 2006. Mem. APA, Soc. for Neurosci., Psychonomic Soc., Internat. Brain Rsch. Orgn., Internat. Behavioral Neurosci. Soc. (pres. 1994, Outstanding Rschr. award 2004), Am. Soc. for Neural Transplant (pres. 1995), Cell Transplant Soc. (pres. 1996, editor). Home: 11751 Pilot Country Dr Spring Hill FL 34610-7912 Office: U South Fla Coll Medicine Dept NeuroSurgery MDC 78 12901 Bruce B Downs Blvd Tampa FL 33612-4742 Business E-Mail: psanberg@health.usf.edu.

SANBONMATSU, KEVIN Y., molecular biologist, researcher; BA in Physics, Columbia U., NYC, 1992; PhD in Astrophysical, Planetary and Atmospheric Scis., U. Colo., Boulder, 1997. Postdoctoral rschr. Los Alamos Nat. Lab., N.Mex., 1997—98, staff scientist Theoretical Biology and Biophysics Grp., 1999—. Contbr. articles to profl. jours., chapters to books. Recipient Early Career award for Scientist and Engrs., Pres. George W. Bush, 2006—. Office: Los Alamos Nat Lab Theoretical Biology and Biophysics Grp Theoretical Divsn MS K710 Los Alamos NM 87545 Office Phone: 505-665-6522. E-mail: kys@lanl.gov. *

SANBORN, ANNA LUCILLE, pension fund administrator, consultant; b. Bklyn., Mar. 29, 1924; d. Peter Francis and Matilda M. (Stumpp) Galligen; 1 son, Dean Sanborn. BA, Bklyn. Coll., 1945. Head dept. benefit and estate planning Union Ctrl. Life Ins. Co., NYC, 1949—51; adminstr. employee benefits Seaboard Oil Co., NYC, 1952—56; with Frank J. Walters Assocs., Inc., NYC, 1957—, pres., 1982—. Mem. Am. Acad. Actuaries. Republican. Roman Catholic. Office: Frank J Walters Assocs 58-13 Seabury St Flushing NY 11373-4825 Office Phone: 718-779-8404. Personal E-mail: fjwainc@aol.com.

SANBORN, DOROTHY CHAPPELL, retired librarian; b. Apr. 26, 1920; d. William S. and Sammie Maude (Drake) Chappell; m. Richard Donald Sanborn, Dec. 1, 1943; children: Richard Donald, William Chappell. BA, U. Tex., El Paso, 1941; MALS, Peabody Coll., Nashville, 1947; MPA, Golden Gate U., San Francisco, 1982. Asst. cataloger El Paso (Tex.) Pub. Libr., 1954-55, 57-59, Stanford Rsch. Inst., Menlo Park, Calif., 1955-57; libr. Auburn (Calif.) Pub. Libr., 1959-62; cataloger Sierra Coll., Rocklin, 1962-64; reference libr. Sacramento (Calif.) City Libr., 1964-66; county libr. Placer County (Calif.), Auburn, 1966-89, ret., 1989. Chmn. Mountain Valley Libr. Sys., 1970-71, 75-76, 1984-85; cons. county libr. Alpine County Libr., Markleeville, Calif., 1973-80. Vol. US Peace Corps, Thailand, 1991—93; pres. Auburn Friends of Libr. With WAVES, 1944—46. Mem. AAUW (pres. chpt. 1982-84), Calif. Libr. Assn., Auburn Friends of Libr. (pres. 95-97, governing bd. 2005-), Soroptimists. Democrat. Mem. United Ch. Christ. Home: 135 Midway Ave Auburn CA 95603-5415 *Personal philosophy: To strive to make a continuing contribution.*

SANBORN, GEORGE FREEMAN, JR., genealogist; b. Laconia, NH, Jan. 18, 1944; s. George Freeman and Charlotte (Dearborn) S.; m. Melinde Laura Lutz, Mar. 30, 1984 (div.); children: Ruth Alice, Lowell Freeman. AB, Boston U., 1967; AM, U. Ill., 1968; MEd, U. N.H., 1981. French tchr. Souris (P.E.I., Can.) Regional H.S., 1968-69; French and occupational studies tchr. Massey-Vanier H.S., Cowansville, Que., Canada, 1969-70; French and English tchr. Kings Coll. Sch., Windsor, N.S., Canada, 1970-71; translator, revisor Province of N.B., Fredericton, 1971-73; sr. govt. revisor Province of Ont., Toronto, 1973-75; French and Spanish tchr. Tilton (N.H.) Sch., 1978-80; living unit coord. Laconia (N.H.) State Sch., 1982-83; ref. libr. New Eng. Hist. Geneal. Soc., Boston, 1983-85, acquisitions libr., dir. libr. ops., 1985-95, publs. asst., 1996-2000, ref. libr., 2000—05. Editor The N.H. Geneal. Record, 1990-93; co-compiler Vital Records of Hampton, N.H., 1992, 98; compiler: Deaths of Prince Edward Islanders in Massachusetts, 1891-1900, 6 vols., 2006; contbr. articles to profl. jours. Fellow Am. Soc. Genealogists; mem. Soc. Cin., Soc. Mayflower Descs., New Eng. Hist. Geneal. Soc., P.E.I. Geneal. Soc., N.H. Soc. Genealogists (pres. 1988-95), Geneal. Soc. Vt. (chair publs. com. 1992-96), N.B. Geneal. Soc., Cape Breton Genealogy and Hist. Assn. Democrat. Presbyterian. Avocations: gardening, bantam raising, Scottish Gaelic language, antique glass and china. Home: 15 Leslie Crescent 9 Charlottetown PE C1C 1P7 Canada

SANCAR, AZIZ, research biochemist; MD, Istanbul Med. Sch., 1969; PhD in Molecular Biology, U. Tex., Dallas, 1977. Assoc. prof. biochemistry U. N.C., Chapel Hill, 1982—, Sarah Graham Kenan prof., 2001—. Recipient Presidential Young Investigator award, NSF, 1984—89, Am. Soc. for Photobiology award, 1990, Basic Sci. award, Turkish Scientific Rsch. Council, 1995, Merit award, NIH, 1966. Fellow: Am. Acad. Arts & Sci.; mem.: NAS, Third World Acad. of Sci. Office: U NC Sch Medicine Dept Biochem and Biophysics Box 7260 Chapel Hill NC 27599-7260 Office Phone: 919-962-0115. Office Fax: 919-966-2852. E-mail: aziz_sancar@med.unc.edu.

SANCHEZ, ADALIO T., data processing executive; BS in Elec. Engring., Univ. Miami; MBA, Fla. Internat. Univ., 1987. Engr. IBM Corp., Boca Raton, Fla., 1982, gen. mgr., mobile computing, gen. mgr., personal computing divsn., mfg. ops. & bus. transformation unit, gen. mgr., storage networking divsn., v.p. ops., server group, gen. mgr., eServer pSeries. Adv. coun. Fla. Internat. Univ. Sch. Engring. Named one of 50 Most Important Hispanics in Tech., Bus., Hispanic Engineer and Info. Tech. mag., 2005; recipient Disting. Alumni Svc. Medallion, Fla. Internat. Univ., 2004. Office: IBM Corp 1 New Orchard Rd Armonk NY 10504 Office Phone: 914-499-1900.

SANCHEZ, ALITA CASSANDRA, physical education educator, personal trainer; d. John Phillip and Florinda Lou Sanchez; m. Christopher Brendan McManus, July 31, 2006; 1 child, Sarah. BA in English Lit., U. Calif., Santa Cruz, 1991; tchg. credential, San Francisco State U., 1997. Adapted phys. edn. specialist Hayward Unified Sch. Dist., Calif., 1997—98, Oakland Unified Sch. Dist., Calif., 1998—. Vol. adult leader Family Resource Network, Oakland, 2001—05; vol. coach/capt. Students Run Oakland, 2002—05. Mem.: Calif. Assn. Health, Phys. Fitness, Recreation and Dance, Am. Coll. Sports Medicine (cert. health and fitness instr.).

SANCHEZ, CINDI ASBURY, physical education educator; d. Edgar Allen and Idabell Rogers Asbury; m. Sonny Anthony Sanchez, July 12, 1980; children: Erin, Sonny. BS, North Tex. State U., Denton, 1976. Tchr. phys. edn. Poteet (Tex.) Ind. Sch. Dist., 1976—78; tchr. phys. edn., coach Schertz (Tex.), Cibilo, and Universal City Ind. Sch. Dist., 1978—81; tchr. phys. edn. St. Mary's Episcopal Sch., Edmond, Okla., 2000—. Bd. dirs. Parents Helping Parents, Edmond, 2002—. Named Mathews Elem. Vol. of Yr., Plano Ind. Sch. Dist., 1993, Small Sch. State Champion, Pres.' Phys. Fitness Challenge, 2004, 2005; recipient, 2006, 2007. Mem.: AAHPERD, Okla. Alliance for Health, Phys. Edn., Recreation, and Dance. Avocations: softball, soccer, woodworking, landscaping. Office: St Mary's Episcopal Sch 505 E Covell Edmond OK 73034 Office Phone: 405-341-9541.

SANCHEZ, DANMARY, research scientist; b. Havana, Cuba, Dec. 23, 1977; arrived in US, 1991; d. Daniel Sanchez and Mara Haydee Ramirez; m. Roberto Perez Albertini, May 31, 2003. BS in Computer Engring., Fla. Internat. U., Miami, 1999, MS in Computer Engring., 2001, PhD in Elec. Engring., 2006. Software engr. IBM, Research Triangle Park, NC, 1998, Motorola, Plantation, Fla., 1999—; rsch. sci. Fla. Internat. U., Miami Children's Hosp., Miami, 2003—. Catequist St. Cecilia Cath. Ch., Miami,

1999—. Recipient Grad. Rsch. fellowship, NSF, 1999—2004, Motorola scholarship, 1999, IBM scholarship, 1998—99, Fla. Acad. scholarship, State of Fla., 1995—99, Fla.-Ga. Alliance for Minority Participation scholarship, 1997—99, Noel Betancourt scholarship, Assn. of Cuban Am. Engrs., 2006. Mem.: IEEE, Assn. of Cuban Am. Engrs. (sec. 1998—99), Eta Kappa Nu (pres. 1997—98), Tau Beta Pi (pres. 1998—99). Republican. Roman Catholic. Achievements include research in Three Dimensional Brain Fiber Tracking Modeling in Diffusion Tensor Imaging; EEG Analysis for Automatic Detection of Interictal Spikes in Epilepsy. Avocations: travel, photography, dancing. Office: Florida Internat U EAS 2220 10555 W Flagler St Miami FL 33175 Home Phone: 305-829-8541; Office Phone: 305-348-4106.

SANCHEZ, FAUSTO H., advertising executive; b. Camaguey, Cuba, Oct. 21, 1953; came to US, 1966. s. Fausto Rene and Eloisa (Aparicio) S. AA, Miami Dade CC, Fla., 1976; BA, U. Miami, 1979; postgrad., UCLA, 1980-82. Dir., newswriter, anchor Sta. KMEX-TV, Hollywood, Calif., 1980-82; producer, dir. Brighton Comm., Hollywood, 1982-84; dir. mktg. Edward J. DeBartolo Corp., Miami, Fla., 1984-86; chmn., pres., creative dir. Sanchez & Levitan Advt., Miami, 1986—2000; co-chmn., pres. Publicis, Sanchez & Levitan, Miami, 2000—04. Author: Hispanic Market, 1982; prodr. (documentary): Cachao...There's Nothing Like His Rhythm, 1994. Recipient Media award Calif. N.G., 1983, 2 Nat. Addy awards, 2 Radio Mercury awards, TV Campaign of Yr. award CLIO, The Telly, and Se Habla Espanol. Mem. Advt. Fedn. of Greater Miami. Avocations: films, tennis, sailing.

SANCHEZ, HELIODORO TORRES, JR., education educator; b. San Angelo, Tex., Aug. 15, 1974; s. Heliodoro Torres Sánchez Sr. and Sylvia Torres Sánchez; m. Mary Ann Perez, Mar. 19, 1975. BA in English, Angelo State U., San Angelo, 1997; MEd, Sul Ross State U., Alpine, Tex., 2002. Cert. sch. adminstr. Tex. Edn. Assn., Tex., 2002, tchr. Tex. Edn. Agy., 1998. English tchr. San Angelo Ind. Sch. Dist., San Angelo, Tex., 1998—99, Ector County Ind. Sch. Dist., Odessa, Tex., 1999—2001; prin. St. Mary's Ctrl. Cath. Sch., Odessa, Tex., 2001—03; campus adminstr. Lewisville Ind. Sch. Dist., Flower Mound, Tex., 2003—05; prin. Dogan Middle Sch., Tyler, Tex., 2005—. Presenter in field. Contbr. articles to profl. jours. Mem. John Ben Shepperd Leadership Inst., Odessa, Tex., 2003—04. Recipient Top Rsch. award, Tex. A&M U. Sys. Ann. Rsch. Symposium, 2004, Doctoral Student of Yr. for ednl. adminstrn., Tex. A&M U., 2004; Carr Acad. scholar, Angelo State U., 1997, Grad. Acad. scholar, Tex. A&M U. Commerce, 2004. Mem.: Am. Acad. Disting. Students, Am. Ednl. Rsch. Assn. (assoc.), K.C. (3d degree), Alpha Lambda Delta, Sigma Tau Delta, Kappa Delta Pi, Alpha Chi. D-Conservative. Roman Catholic. Avocations: writing, running, weight training, team sports. Office: Tyler Intermediate Sch Dist 2621 N Border St Tyler TX 75702 Office Phone: 903-262-1450. Office Fax: 903-262-1451; Home Fax: 903-279-1821. Personal E-mail: sanchezht@cs.com. Business E-Mail: heliodoro.sanchez@tylerisd.org.

SANCHEZ, KARLA G., lawyer; AB in History, Columbia U., 1992; JD cum laude, Fordham U., 1995. Bar: NY, US Dist. Ct. (So. Dist. NY), US Dist. Ct. (Ea. Dist. NY). Law clk. to Hon. Deborah A. Batts US Dist. Ct. (So. Dist. NY); ptnr. Patterson, Belknap, Webb & Tyler LLC, NYC. Dean's planning coun. Fordham U. Sch. Law, bd. adv. minority mentorship program; bd. dir. Puerto Rican Legal Defense and Edn. Fund. Named one of 40 Under 40, Crain's NY Bus., 2006, 100 most influential Hispanics in US, Hispanic Bus. mag., 2006; recipient Lucero award, Puerto Rican Legal Defense and Edn. Fund, 2004, Andrew J. Rivera Alumni Achievement award, Fordham U. Sch. Law, 2005, Rising Star award, NY Women's Agenda, 2005. Mem.: Fed. Bar Coun. Inns of Ct., Hispanic Nat. Bar Assn., ABA, Assn. Bar City NY, Order Coif. Office: Patterson Belknap Webb & Tyler LLP 1133 Avenue of the Americas New York NY 10036 Office Phone: 212-336-2785. Office Fax: 212-336-2788. E-mail: kgsanchez@pbwt.com.

SANCHEZ, LAURA ANN, music educator; b. Jamaica, NY, Sept. 26, 1959; d. Arthur F. and Audrey M. Crowe; m. David T. Sanchez, Aug. 4, 1990. AAS, Nassau C.C., 1979; BA, Molloy Coll., 1981; MS, LI U. C.W. Post Coll., 1984. Music tchr. Uniondale Pub. Schools, NY, 1985—. Dir.: (performance) Calif. Ave. School Ensemble (First Pl., Dr. Martin Luther King Nassau County award, 2000). Corr. sec. Uniondale Cmty. Coun., NY. Mem.: Nassau Music Educators Assn., Music Educators Nat. Conf., Tech. in Music Edn., N.Y. State Sch. Music Assn. Office: Calif Ave Sch 236 California Ave Uniondale NY 11553 Home Phone: 516-214-4772; Office Phone: 516-918-1886. E-mail: lsanchez@uniondaleschools.org.

SANCHEZ, LEONEDES MONARRIZE WORTHINGTON (HIS ROYAL HIGHNESS DUKE DE LEONEDES OF SPAIN SICILY GREECE), fashion designer; b. Flagstaff, Ariz., Mar. 15, 1951; s. Rafael Leonedes and Margaret (Monarrize) S. BS, No. Ariz. U., 1974; studied, Fashion Inst. Tech., NYC, 1974-75; AA, Fashion Inst. D&M, LA, 1975; lic., La Ecole de la Chambre Syndical de la Couture Parisian, Paris, 1976-78; certificate, La Mason de Couture, Paris, 2000. Lic. in designing. Contract designer/asst. to head designer House of Bonnet, Paris, 1976—; dress designer-in-resident Flagstaff, 1978—; mem. faculty No. Ariz. U., Flagstaff, 1978-80; designer Ambiance, Inc., LA, 1985—; designer Interiors by Leonedes subs. Studio of Leonedes Couturier, Ariz., 1977, Calif., 1978, London, Paris, 1978, Rome, 1987, Milan, Spain, 1989, Palazzo de Leonedes, 1998, designer Liturgical Vesture subs.; CEO Leonedes Internat., Design Consortium, Leonedes Internat. Ltd., 1999—; designer El Castillo de Nuevo Espana, Santa Fe, La Maison de Couture, Paris, 2000, La Maison de Couture DeLeonedes Internat., Paris, 2001, His Royal Highness Duke DeLeonedes Leonedes XIV Global Subs., His Royal Highness Duke DeLeonedes Leonedes XIV Royal Consortium Cartel, London, Mobiliare Europa, 2002, Mobiliare Pan Americano Atlantico, South Am., Caribbean, 2005, Mobiliare Asia Pacifico, Taipei, Hong Kong, Beijing, China, 2005, Mobiliare England, Ireland, Scotland, 2006, Empresa de El Estudio De Leonedes, Empresa Mobiliare Latino, Empresa De H.R.H. Duke De Leonedes; chamber syndicate De Mobiliare Estidio De Leonedes Internat. South Am., El Caribe, Spain, Studio Leonedes, 2005, Studio of Leonedes Consortium Cartel, 2006, Mobiliare Consortium Cartel, 2006, Imperial Consortium Cartel, 2006, Isla De Leonedes, 2006. Owner, CEO, designer Leonedes Internat., Ltd., London, Milan, Paris, Spain, Ambian Ariz, Calif., Appolonian Costuming, Ariz., London, Milan, Paris, El Castillo de Leonedes, Sevilla, Spain, Villa Apollonian de Leonedes, Mykonos, Greece, Palazzo de Leonedes Internat., Sicily; cons. House of Bonnet, Paris, 1976—, Bob Mackie, Studio City, Calif., 1974-75; CEO, designer artistical dir., Leonedes internat.; appointee commn. on religious antiquities Congregation on the Arts, The Vatican, Italy, 1998. Bd. dirs. Roman Cath. Social Svcs., 1985-86, Northland Crisis Nursery, 1985—; bd. dirs., chmn. Pine Country Transit, 1986-88; pres. Chicanos for Edn.; active master's swim program ARC, Ariz., 1979—; eucharistic min., mem. art and environ. com., designer liturgical vesture St. Pius X Cath. Ch.; vol. art tchr., instr. St. Mary's Regional Sch., Flagstaff, 1987-90, vol. art dir.; mem. Flagstaff Parks and Recreation Commn., 1994-96, citizens' adv. com. master plan, 1994-96; mem. cmty. bd. adv. com. Flagstaff Unified Sch. Dist., 1995; active Duke de Leonedes Found. de Nuevo Espana, Santa Fe, Duke de Leonedes Found. de Neuvo Espana, Santa Fe; prin. chair Duke de Leonedes Found., The Netherlands, 1995; de nuevo espana Duke de Leuedes Found., Santa Fe, N.Mex., 1996. Decorated Duke de Leonedes (Spain), 1994, His Royal Highness (Spain, Greece, Sicily), 1998; recipient Camellian Design award 1988, Atlanta, De Nuevo award Duke DeLeonedes Found., Santa Fe, Barcelona, Ireland, 2004, Spain, Greece, Sicily. Mem. AAU (life, chairperson swimming Ariz. 1995, vice chairperson physique, mem. citizen adv. bd. parks and recreation, chairperson state of Ariz. physique, swimming, adv. to Olympic inquiry com., advisor to internat. Olympic com. on physique), Am. Film Inst., Am. Assn. Hist. Preservation, Costume Soc., Am. Nat. Physique Com., Internat. Consortium Fashion Designers, Nat. Cath. Ednl. Assn., La Legion de Honour de la Mode Parisienne, Social Register Assn., Phi Alpha Theta (historian 1972-73, pres. 1973-74), Pi Kappa Delta (pres. 1972-73, historian 1973-74). Republican. Avocations: bodybuilding, swimming. Office: El Castillo de Leonedes Seville Spain also: El Castillo de Nuevo Espana Santa Fe NM 87501 also: Villa de Apollonian de Leonedes Mykonos Greece Mailing: PO Box 61623 Phoenix AZ 85082-1623

SANCHEZ, LINDA T., congresswoman; b. Orange, Calif. m. Mark Sanchez. BA in Spanish Lit., U. Calif., Berkeley; JD, UCLA, 1995. Bar: Calif. 1995. Clk. to Hon. Chief Justice Terry Hatter, Jr. Ctrl. Dist. Ct., Calif.; compliance officer Nat. Elec. Contractors Assn. and Internat. Brotherhood Elec. Workers, 1998—2002; mem. US Congress from 39th Calif. dist., 2003—; mem. judiciary com.; mem. govt. reform com., small bus. com. Lectr. Nat. Assn. Elected and Apptd. Ofcls., 1998—. Exec. sec.-treas. Orange County ctrl. labor coun. AFL-CIO; campaign worker Loretta Sanchez for U.S. Congress, 1996, 1998. Mem.: Internat. Brotherhood Elec. Workers (Local 441). Democrat. Office: US Ho Reps 1007 Longworth Office Bldg Washington DC 20515-0539 also: Dist Office Ste 106 4007 Paramount Lakewood CA 90712 *

SANCHEZ, LORETTA, congresswoman; b. Lynnwood, Calif., Jan. 7, 1960; BA, Chapman U., 1982; MBA, Am. U., 1984. With Orange County Transp. Authority, 1984-87, Fieldman Rolapp & Assocs., 1987-90; strategic mgmt. cons. Booz Allen & Hamilton; owner, operator AMIGA Advisors Inc.; mem. U.S. Congress from 47th Calif. dist., 1997—; former mem. edn. and the workforce com., mem. armed svcs. com.; mem. House Select Com. on Homeland Security, House Blue Dogs. Mem. Anaheim Rotary Club. Democrat. Office: US Ho Reps 1230 Longworth Ho Office Bldg Washington DC 20515-0547 also: Dist Office Ste 101 12397 Lewis St Garden Grove CA 92840 Office Phone: 202-225-2965. E-mail: loretta@mail.house.gov. *

SANCHEZ, MANUEL, retired social services administrator, writer; b. Los Palacios, Cuba, June 6, 1932; s. Emilio and Elena (Lopez) Sanchez. JD, Havana U., Cuba, 1959. Bar: N.J. 1975. Supr. Dept. Social Svcs., NYC, 1964—90; ret., 1990. Author: The Daring Mysteries, 1991, Stories for a Rainy Afternoon, 2005. Avocation: reading. Home: 220W 98th St Apt 12N New York NY 10025

SANCHEZ, MARLA RENA, communications executive; d. Tomas Guillermo and Rose Sanchez; m. Bradley D. Gaiser. BS, MS, Stanford U., 1979; MBA, Santa Clara U., 1983. Rsch. biologist Syntex, Palo Alto, Calif., 1980-81; fin. analyst Advanced Micro Devices, Sunnyvale, Calif., 1983-85; fin. mgr. ultrasound divsn. Diasonics, Inc., Milpitas, Calif., 1985-86, contr. therapeutic products divsn., 1989-93, contr. internat. divsn., 1992-93; contr. Ridge Computers, Santa Clara, Calif., 1986-88; dir. fin. VLSI Tech., Inc., San Jose, Calif., 1993-98; corp. contr. SDL, Inc., San Jose, 1999—2001, interim CFO, 2005; sr. v.p., CFO Avanex Corp., Fremont, Calif., 2006—. Office: Avanex Corp 40919 Encyclopedia Cir Fremont CA 94538

SANCHEZ, MARY ANNE, retired secondary school educator; b. Galesburg, Ill., Aug. 4, 1939; d. Stephen Mingare and M. Margaret Kennedy; m. J. Manuel Sanchez, Dec. 26, 1980. BS in Edn., Western Ill. U., 1961; MA, Ill. State U., 1970. Tchr., Stanford, Ill., 1962-64, Titusville, Fla., 1964-66, Montgomery County Bd. Edn., Chevy Chase, Md., 1969-72, Hillsborough County Bd. Edn., Tampa, Fla., 1972-96; ret., 1996. Mary Anne Sanchez Young Woman scholarship named in her honor by Social Studies Dept. Leto Comprehensive H.S., 1999. Mem. Nat. Coun. for Social Studies, Fla. Coun. for Social Studies, Adult Edn. Assn. Home: 2715 W Ivy St Tampa FL 33607-1922

SANCHEZ, RAYMOND G., former state legislator; b. Albuquerque, Sept. 22, 1941; s. Gillie and Priscilla S.; 1 child, Raymond Michael. BA, U. N.Mex., 1964, JD, 1967. Bar: N. Mex. 1967. Ptnr. Sanchez, Mowrer & Desiderio, P.C., Albuquerque; mem. N.Mex. Ho. of Reps., 1970—; speaker N. Mex. Ho. of Reps., 1983—84, 1987—88, 1992—2000; mem. judiciary com., rules and order of bus. com., voters and elections com.; interim mem. workers compensation, legis. reform study coms., legis. coun.; pres. Naleo Educational Fund, Albuquerque, 2001. Bd. dirs. New Mex. Amigos, N.Mex. Diamond Jubilee/U.S. Constl. Bicentennial Commn., New Mex. First, Albuquerque Com. Fgn. Rels., N. Valley Neighborhood Assn.; bd. regents U. N. Mex. Mem. Nat. Assn. Latino Elected and Apptd. Ofcls. (bd. dirs.), Alameda Optimist Club (bd. dirs., charter mem.), U. N.Mex. Sch. Law Alumni Assn. (bd. dirs.), Elks Club, Sigma Xi. Democrat. Avocations: handball, scuba diving, swimming, sports. also: PO Box 1966 Albuquerque NM 87103-1966 Office Phone: 505-247-4321.

SANCHEZ, STEVEN M., financial executive; m. Marie Vigil, Sept. 11, 1992; children: Nate, Erica, Emily. Diploma in Acctg., San Joaquin Valley U., 1990. Advisor John Hancock Fin., Fresno, Calif., 1991—93; pres., wealth advisor Sanchez and Associates, Phoenix, 1993—. Contbr. fin. articles to profl. jours. Leader marriage ministry U. of the Family, Phoenix, 2004—06. Recipient Ethics and Excellence award, Nat. Ethics Bur., 2002. Mem.: Nat. Assn. Ins. and Fin. Advisors (assoc.). Conservative. Nazarene. Avocations: travel, music. Home and Office: Sanchez & Associates Fin Group 4802 E Ray Rd Ste23 Phoenix AZ 85044 Office Phone: 888-944-6663. Personal E-mail: smnee1061@aol.com.

SANCHEZ, VINCENT A., lawyer; b. Bronx, NY, Dec. 12, 1968; BA, Univ. Notre Dame, 1991, JD, 1994; MBA, Northwestern Univ., 2003. Bar: Ill. 1994. Ptnr., co-chmn. Tech. & Sourcing Group DLA Piper US LLP, Chgo. Adj. prof. Loyola Univ. Sch. Law, 2002—; mem. adv. bd. West Suburban Tech. Enterprise Ctr. Editor (in chief): Notre Dame Jour. of Legislation. Bd. dir. i.c. stars. 1st Lt. USMC Reserve, 1991—95. Named one of 40 Ill. Attorneys under 40 to Watch, Chgo. Lawyer mag., 2004, Leading Lawyers in Ill. for Tech. & IT Outsourcing, Chambers USA, 2005, 2006. Mem.: ABA. Office: DLA Piper US LLP Ste 1900 203 N LaSalle St Chicago IL 60601-1293 Office Phone: 312-368-3420. Business E-Mail: vincent.sanchez@dlapiper.com.

SANCHEZ, WALTER MARSHALL, lawyer; b. Lake Charles, La., July 3, 1959; s. John Augustine Sanchez and Louise Page Dugas Meyer; m. Frances E. Morgan, Oct. 18, 1986; children: Clare, Madeline, Kate, John. BS, La. State U., Baton Rouge, 1981, JD, 1984. Bar: La. 1984, U.S. Supreme Ct. 1984; bd. cert. family law specialist, La. Bd. of Legal Specialization. Assoc. Godwin, Painter, Roddy, Lorenzi & Watson, Lake Charles, 1985-86; ptnr. Godwin, Roddy, Lorenzi Watson & Sanchez, Lake Charles, 1986-90, Lorenzi & Sanchez, LLP, Lake Charles, 1990—2006, Sanchez & Bannatt, LLP, 2006—. Vice chmn. La. Indigent Defender Bd., New Orleans, 1994-96; chmn. 14th Jud. Dist. Indigent Defender Bd., Lake Charles, 1987-96; mem. faculty trial advocacy tng. program La. State U. Law Ctr., 1993—; mem. spl. com. to study reinstatement of fault in divorce La. State Law Inst., 1998-2001; approved for apptd. judge pro tempore City Ct. of Sulphur, 1999—; mem. La. Pub. Defender Bd., 2005-. Named one of Best Lawyers in Am., Woodward/White, Inc., 2007. Mem. La. Assn. Criminal Def. Attys. (bd. dirs. 1990—, pres. 1997-98), Am. Mensa., Order of St. Charles. Democrat. Roman Catholic. Office: Lorenzi Sanchez & Barnatt LLP PO Box 3305 Lake Charles LA 70602-3305 Home Phone: 337-474-4633; Office Phone: 337-436-8401. Business E-Mail: sanchez@lorenzi-sanchez.com.

SANCHEZ-BARNETT, SUSAN LYNN, historian, educator; b. Hollywood, Calif., Aug. 20, 1954; d. James Edwin and Terah May Johnson; m. David Novell Barnett, Dec. 20, 2000; children: Angel Phillip Sanchez, Angela Victoria Sanchez, Alexandra Querida Sanchez, David Matthew Sanchez. BA, Calif. State U., Pomona, 1991; MA, Calif. State U., Fullerton, 1997; PhD, U. Calif., 2003. Cert. tchr. Md., 2000. Secondary tchr. Balt. County Pub. Schs., Balt., 2000—; adj. prof. Strayer U., Millersville, Md., 2005—. Music dir. Marley Pk. Ch. of the Nazarene, Glen Burnie, Md., 2005—. Mem.: Am. Soc. for Ethnohistory, Am. Hist. Assn. Home: 711 Marley Ave Glen Burnie MD 21060 Personal E-mail: sbarnett@bcps.org.

SANCHEZ MILLS, PEGGY, women's association executive; b. Roswell, N.Mex., Aug. 1, 1953; d. Myron and Gloria Carson; children: Jennifer, Jason. BA in Sociology and Psychology, U. South Fla.; MPA, Golden Gate U. Reading specialist Girl's Clubs Pinellas County, Clearwater, Fla., 1979-80, ctr. supr. St. Petersburg, Fla., 1980-81; project adminstr. YWCA St. Petersburg, 1981-84; exec. dir. YWCA Tampa Bay, St. Petersburg, 1984—2004; CEO YWCA USA, Washington, 2004—06. Mem. adv. com. Riviera Mid. Sch., Lealman Discovery; mem. key philanthropic organizations com., ASAE & The Ctr. for Assn. Leadership. Chair edn. com. Community Alliance, 1989-91; chair Dist. Task Force on Child Abuse Prevention, 1988-91; pres. Leadership St. Pete Assn., mem. planning coun., United Way; pres. Coun. of Exec. Dirs.; sec., bd. dirs. Suncoast Tiger Bay Club; mem. steering com. Teen Parent Self Sufficiency Task Force for Pinellas County; mem. Abuse, Neglect, and Dependency Com., Coalition for Homeless/Affordable Housing, Fla. Ctr. for Children and Youth, Human Svc. Coalition; mem. adv. com. Jr. League of St. Petersburg; apptd. to state coord. coun. early childhood svcs. Recipient Up and Comers award Price-Waterhouse, 1990. *

SANCHEZ-RAMOS, JUAN RAMON, physician, medical educator; b. Cabimas, Zulia, Venezuela, July 16, 1945; arrived in US, 1950, naturalized; s. Juan Ramon Sanchez y Sanchez and Carmen F. Ramos de Sanchez; m. Catherine O'Neill, Aug. 19, 1984; children: Zachary, Zoe Allegra, Sofia Isabel. BS, U. Chgo., PhD, 1976; MD, U. Ill., Chgo., 1981. Rsch. assoc. dept. pharmacology U. Chgo., 1976-78; med. intern Michael Reese Hosp., Chgo., 1981-82; resident in neurology U. Chgo., 1982-86; asst. prof. dept. neurology U. Miami, Fla., 1987-92, assoc. prof. dept. neurology, 1992-96; prof. U. South Fla., Tampa, 1996—, Helen E. Ellis endowed chair, 1996. Contbr. chpts. to books and articles to profl. jours. Recipient Clin. Investigator award NIH, Washington, 1988, Vets. Affairs Merit Rev., Washington, 1994, 98. Mem. AAAS, Am. Acad. Neurology, Am. Neurol. Assn., Movement Disorders Soc., Parkinsons Study Group, Oxygen Radical Soc., Huntington Study Group. Avocations: drawing, painting. Office: Univ South Fla MDC55 12901 Bruce Downs Blvd Tampa FL 33620 Office Phone: 813-974-6022. Business E-Mail: jsramos@hsc.usf.edu.

SANCHEZ-RAMOS, ROBERTO J., attorney general; b. 1968; BS in Computer Sci. and Engring., MIT, 1989; JD summa cum laude, U. PR, 1998; LLM, Yale U., 1993. Admitted to practice: PR, Washington, DC, Supreme Ct. US, US Ct. Appeals for the First Cir. Law clk. to Hon. Federico Hernandez Denton Supreme Ct. PR, 1993—94; assoc. Arnold & Porter LLP, Washington, 1994—96; law clk. to Hon. A. Wallace Tashima US Ct. Appeals (9th cir.), Pasadena, Calif., 1996—97; trial atty., civil divsn., fed. programs br. US Dept. Justice, Washington, 1999—2000; solicitor gen. PR, San Juan, 2001—04, atty. gen., 2004—. Recipient West Publishing award for Excellence in the Study of Anglo-Am. Law, Acad. Excellence award, PR Atty. Bar Assn. Mem.: Eta Kappa Nu Assn., Sigma Xi. Office: Office of Atty General GPO Box 902192 San Juan PR 00902-0192 Office Phone: 787-721-2900. *

SANCHEZ-SILKMAN, JENNIFER CHRISTINE, elementary school educator; b. Bronx, NY, Sept. 11, 1974; d. George Peter Sanchez and Lucille Ann Ramirez; m. Jeffrey Howard Silkman, Dec. 22, 2000; 1 child, Julian Michael Silkman. BS in Elem. Edn., Iona Coll., New Rochelle, NY, 1996; MS in Early Childhood Edn., Coll. New Rochelle, 2000; post grad. in curriculum and tchg., Tchrs. Coll. Columbia U., NYC, 2002—04. Lic. (permanent) tchr. K-6 N.Y. State and N.Y.C., spl. edn. K-12 N.Y. State and N.Y.C. Tchr. grade 3 St. Francis de Chantal Sch., Bronx, NY, 1998—2002; tchr. grade 4 Pub. Sch. 182, 2002—. Tchr. rep. St. Francis de Chantal Sch. PTA, 2000—01. Mem.: ASCD. Roman Catholic. Avocations: walking, exercise, dance, music. Home: 737 Hollywood Ave Bronx NY 10465-2303 Office: PS 182 601 Stickball Blvd Bronx NY 10473

SANCHEZ-WAY, RUTH DOLORES, public health administrator; b. NYC, Aug. 8, 1940; d. Manuel and Cruz Maria Sanchez; m. Harley Milton Dirks, Feb. 9, 1974 (dec. Aug. 1986); stepchildren: Timothy, Darcy Kimmel, Marcine Thomas, James, David, Dale; m. David Vincent Way, Apr. 16, 1988. BS in Chemistry, St. John's U., Bklyn., 1962; MSW in Social Work, Fordham U., 1965; PhD in Pub. Adminstrn., NYU, 1978; diploma in Mgmt. Devel., Emory U., Atlanta, 1981; diploma, Inst. Fed. Health Care Execs., Geroge Washington U., 1993; LHD (hon.), Fordham U., NYC, 2006. Cert. social worker, Md.; cert. prevention profl. Spl. asst. to dir. Nat. Inst. Alcohol Abuse and Alcoholism HEW, Rockville, Md., 1971-79, assoc. dep. adminstr. Equal Employment Opportunity, 1979-83, office asst. Sec. Health, 1979—83; dep. dir. Adolescent Pregnancy Programs Health and Human Svcs., Washington, 1983-91; assoc. adminstr. minority health concerns Substance Abuse & Mental Health Svcs. Adminstrn., Health and Human Svcs., Rockville, 1993-96, divsn. dir. Ctr. for Substance Abuse Prevention, 1991-96, acting dep. dir. Ctr. for Substance Abuse Prevention, 1997, acting dir., 1997—2000, dir., 2000—02; assoc. dir. Ctr. for Faith-Based and Cmty. Initiatives, HHS, 2002—03; v.p. tng. and cmty. devel. Mgmt. Scis. for Devel., 2003—. Bd. dirs. Nat. Health Coun., Washington, 1987-94, Nat. Coun. on Alcoholism and Drug Dependence, N.Y.C., 1979-91, Nat. Orgn. Adolescent Pregnancy Parenting and Prevention, Washington, 1991-93. Nat. operational vol. Girl Scouts US, NYC, 1996-; mem. com. lions quest Lions Clubs Internat. Found., 2003-, friends of Pax Lodge World Found. for Girl Guides and Scouts, 2006-; disaster vol. Am. Red Cross, Ctrl. Md., 2005-; mem. pastoral coun., women's guild Our Lady Sorrows Ch., 2003-. Recipient Excellence in Govt. Svc. award Mex.-Am. Legal Def. and Ednl. Fund, 2000, Presdl. Meritorious Exec. Rank award SES, 1998, Sec.'s award for disting. svc. HHS, 2001; primary care policy fellow USPHS. Mem. NASW, APHA, Chesapeake Multihull Assn. (past commodore, Kilmon award 1996). Roman Catholic. Avocations: sailing, skiing, jazzercise. Office: Mgmt Scis for Devel 4301 Connecticut Ave NW Ste 140 Washington DC 20008 Office Phone: 202-537-7410. Business E-Mail: rsanchez@msdglobal.com.

SAND, LEONARD B., federal judge; b. NYC, May 24, 1928; BS, NYU, 1947; LL.B., Harvard, 1951. Bar: N.Y. 1953, U.S. Supreme Ct. 1956, D.C. 1969. Clk. to dist. ct. judge, N.Y., 1952-53; asst. U.S. atty. So. Dist. N.Y., 1953-54; asst. to U.S. Solictor Gen., 1956-59; mem. firm Robinson, Silverman, Pearce, Aronsohn Sand and Berman, NYC, 1960-78; judge U.S. Dist. Ct. (So. Dist.), NY, 1978—, now sr. judge NY. Adj. prof. law NYU. Note editor: Harvard Law Rev, 1950-51. Del. N.Y. State Constl. Conv., 1967; v.p., treas. Legal Aid Soc. Fellow Am. Coll. Trial Lawyers; mem. ABA, Assn. Bar City N.Y. (v.p.), N.Y. State Bar Assn., Fed. Bar Coun. Office: US Dist Ct US Courthouse 500 Pearl St New York NY 10007-1316

SANDAGE, ALLAN REX, astronomer; b. Iowa City, June 18, 1926; s. Charles Harold and Dorothy (Briggs) S.; m. Mary Lois Connelley, June 8, 1959; children: David Allan, John Howard. AB, U. Ill., 1948, DSc (hon.), 1967; PhD, Calif. Inst. Tech., Pasadena, 1953; DSc (hon.), Yale U., New Haven, Conn., 1966, U. Chgo., 1967, Miami U., Oxford, Ohio, 1974, Graceland Coll., Iowa, 1985; LLD (hon.), U. So. Calif., 1971; D (hon.), U.

Chile, 1992. Astronomer Mt. Wilson Obs., Palomar Obs., Carnegie Instn., Washington, 1952—; Peyton fellow Princeton U., 1952; asst. astronomer Hale Obs., Pasadena, Calif., 1952-56; astronomer Obs. Carnegie Instn., Pasadena, Calif., 1956—; sr. rsch. astronomer Space Telescope Sci. Inst. NASA, Balt., 1986—; Homewood Prof. of physics Johns Hopkins U., Balt., 1987-89. Vis. lectr. Harvard U., 1957; mem. astron. expdn. to South Africa, 58; cons. NSF, 1961—64; Sigma Xi nat. astronomer U. Basel, 1985, 92, vis. prof., 94; vis. rsch. astronomer U. Calif., San Diego, 1985—86; vis. astronomer U. Hawaii, 1986; Lindsey lectr. NASA Goddard Space, Durham, England, 1992; Grubb-Parsons lectr. U. Durham, England, 1992. Assoc. editor: Ann. Rev. Astronomy and Astrophysics, 1990—2005. Served USN, 1945—46. Recipient Helen Warner prize, Am. Astron. Soc., 1960, Pope Pius XI Gold medal, Pontifical Acad. Sci., 1966, Rittenhouse medal, 1968, Russell prize, 1973, Adon medal, Obs. Nice, 1988, Crafoord prize, Swedish Royal Acad. Scis., 1991, Tomalla Gravity prize, Swiss Phys. Soc., 1993, Peter Gruber Found. prize for cosmology, 2000; scholar Fulbright-Hays scholar, 1972. Mem.: Astron. Soc. Pacific (Gold medal 1975), Royal Soc. London (fgn.), Franklin Inst. (Elliott Cresson medal 1973, Gruber Cosmology prize 2000), Royal Astron. Soc. Can., Royal Astron. Soc. (Eddington medal 1963, Gold medal 1967), Lincei Nat. Acad. (Rome), Phi Beta Kappa. Home: 8319 Josard Rd San Gabriel CA 91775-1003 Office: 813 Santa Barbara St Pasadena CA 91101-1232 Office Phone: 626-304-0246.

SANDAGE-MUSSEY, ELIZABETH ANTHEA, retired market research executive; b. Larned, Kans., Oct. 13, 1930; d. Curtis Carl and Beulah Pauline (Knupp) Smith; m. H.I. Danner, 1948 (div. 1956); children: Dianna Louise Danner Wilson, David Alan Danner; m. Charles Harold Sandage, July 18, 1971; m. Robert D. Mussey, Oct. 21, 2000. BS, U. Colo., 1967, MA, 1970; PhD in Comms., U. Ill., 1973. Pub. rels. rep., editor Martin News Martin Marietta Corp., Denver, 1960-63, 65-67; retail advt. salesperson Denver Post, 1967-70; instr. advt. U. Ill., 1970-71, vis. lectr. advt., 1977-84; v.p., corp. sec., dir. Farm Rsch. Inst., Urbana, Ill., 1984-95; ret., 1995. Editor: Advertising as a Social Force: Selected Speeches and Essays by Charles H. Sandage, 1998, Occasional Papers in Advertising, 1971, The Sandage Family Cookbook, 1976, 3d edit., 2002, The Inkling (Carle Hosp. Aux. Newsletter), 1975-76. Bd. dirs. U. Ill. Libr. Friends, 1991-95; exec. dir. Sandage Charitable Trust, 1986—. Mem. U. Ill. Alumni Assn. (pres.'s coun.), Champaign Social Sci. Club, The Book Club, Moneymakers Investment Club, Kappa Tau Alpha.

SANDALOW, TERRANCE, law educator; b. Chgo., Sept. 8, 1934; s. Nathan and Evelyn (Hoffing) Sandalow; m. Ina Davis, Sept. 4, 1955; children: David Blake, Marc Alan, Judith Ann. AB, U. Chgo., 1954, JD, 1957. Bar: Ill. 1958, Mich. 1978. Law clk. to judge Sterry R. Waterman U.S. Ct. Appeals (2d cir.), 1957-58; law clk. to justice Potter Stewart U.S. Supreme Ct., Washington, 1958-59; assoc. Ross, McGowan & O'Keefe, Chgo., 1959-61; assoc. prof. law U. Minn., Mpls., 1961-64, prof., 1964-66; prof. law U. Mich., Ann Arbor, 1966-2000, dean Law Sch., 1978-87, Edson R. Sunderland prof. law, 1987-2000, dean emeritus and Edson R. Sunderland prof. law emeritus, 2000—. Author (with F. I. Michelman): (book) Government in Urban Areas, 1970; author: (with E. Stein) Courts and Free Markets, 1982; contbr. articles to legal jours. and periodicals. Mem. Mpls. Commn. Human Rels., 1965—66. Recipient Profl. Achievement award, U. Chgo. Alumni; fellow, Ctr. Advanced Study in Behavioral Scis., 1972—73. Fellow: Am. Acad. Arts Scis.; mem.: Order of Coif (nat. pres. 2001—04), Phi Beta Kappa (hon.). Office: U Mich Law Sch Hutchins Hall Ann Arbor MI 48109-1215 Home Phone: 734-994-4289. Personal E-mail: terrysan@comcast.net. Business E-Mail: sandalow@umich.edu.

SANDBERG, ARLENE, elementary school educator; BS in Elem. Edn., Kans. State Univ.; MS in Spl. Edn., Fitchburg State Univ., Mass. Tchr. Mass., Va., NY, Hawaii, Pa., 1979—98; ESL tchr. Mountain View Elem. Sch., Anchorage, 1998—. Named Alaska Tchr. of Yr., 2006. Office: Mountain View Elem Sch 4005 McPhee Ave Anchorage AK 99508 Office Phone: 907-742-3926 ext. 3013. Business E-Mail: sandberg_arlene@asdk12.org. *

SANDBERG, CRAIG M., lawyer; b. Ill., Oct. 25, 1971; BA, Mich. State U., East Lansing, Mich., 1994; JD, Chgo., 1998. Bar: Ill. 1999. Jud. extern to Hon. Allen A. Freeman Cir. Ct. Cook County, Chgo., 1996; jud. extern to Hon. Ronald A. Guzman U.S. Dist. Ct. (no. dist.) Ill., Chgo., 1997; pvt. practice Chgo., 1999—2004; asst. state's atty. Cook County State's Atty.'s Office, Chgo., 2004—07; ptnr. Muslin & Sandberg, Chgo., 2007—. Mem. young profls. bd. Chgo. Bar Found. Assoc. bd. mem. Gilda's Club Chgo., 2003—05. Named one of 40 Ill. Attys. Under 40 to Watch, Law Bull., 2007; recipient Excellence in Pro Bono and Pub. Interest Svc. award, U.S. Dist. Ct. (no. dist.) Ill. and Chgo. Chpt. FBA, 2004. Mem.: Chgo. Bar Assn. (mem. exec. coun. young lawyer's sect. 2005, Rising Star award 2005), Fed. Bar Assn. (bd. dir. young lawyer's divsn. 2003). Office: Muslin & Sandberg 19 S LaSalle St Ste 700 Chicago IL 60603-1491 Office Phone: 312-263-7249. Office Fax: 312-263-8193. Business E-Mail: craig@muslin-sandberg.com.

SANDBERG, IRWIN WALTER, retired electrical and computer engineering educator; b. NYC, Jan. 23, 1934; s. Ben and Estelle S.; m. Barbara A. Zimmerman, June 15, 1958; 1 dau. Heidi L. B.E.E., Poly. Inst. Bklyn., 1955, M.E.E., 1956, D.E.E., 1958. Tech. aid Bell Telephone Labs., Inc., Murray Hill, NJ, summer 1954, mem. tech. staff, 1958-67, head systems theory research dept., 1967-72, mem. math. and statis. research ctr., 1972-86; prof. elec. and computer engrng. U. Tex., Austin, 1986—, Cockrell Family Regents chair in engrng. emeritus; engr. Wheeler Labs., Great Neck, NY, summer 1955. Vis. prof. U. Calif.-Berkeley, 1965; U.S. del. Union Radio Scientifique Internationale, Munich, Germany, 1966; U.S. nat. inst. rep. Advanced Study Inst. on Network and Signal Theory, NATO, Bournemouth, Eng., 1972; lectr. study inst. NATO (Knokke), Belgium, 1966, Copenhagen, 1970; disting. invited spkr. Asilomar Conf., 1973-74; main lectr. European Conf. on Circuit Theory and Design, The Hague, 1981; advisor Inst. Electronics, Info. and Comm. Engrs., Tokyo; advisor Am. Men and Women of Sci., 1993. Patentee (in field). Recipient Best Paper award Asilomar Conf., 1970, Achievement award IEEE Circuits and Systems Soc., 1986, Classic Paper citation ISI press, 1984, Outstanding Alumnus award Poly. U., 1993. Fellow IEEE (life, adminstrv. com. group circuit theory 1969-70, vice chmn. group circuit theory 1971-72, Centennial medal, Millennial medal, Cirs. and Sys. Soc. Golden Jubilee medal, Cirs. and Sys. Soc. disting. lectr.), AAAS; mem. NAE, Soc. for Indsl. and Applied Math., Acad. Medicine, Engring. and Sci. Tex., Eta Kappa Nu, Sigma Xi, Tau Beta Pi Home: 8505 Hickory Creek Dr Austin TX 78735-1527 Office: Univ Tex Dept Elec Comp Engr Austin TX 78712 Home Phone: 512-328-1004; Office Phone: 512-471-6899. E-mail: sandberg@ece.utexas.edu.

SANDBERG, JOEL S., ophthalmologist; s. Emanuel and Sadie Sandberg; m. Adele Einhonn Sandberg, June 26, 1965; children: Sheryl, David, Michelle. BA, Johns Hopkins U., Balt., 1961, MD, 1967. Intern NY Hosp.-Sloan Kettering Meml. Hosp., Cornell U. Sch. Medicine, NYC, 1967—68; staff assoc. Cancer Chemotherapy Rsch. Nat. Cancer Inst., NIH, Bethesda, Md., 1968—70; cancer chemotherapy fellow Tel Hashomer Hosp., U. Tel Aviv Med. Ctr., 1970—71; ophthalmology resident Bascom Palmer Eye Inst., U. Miami Sch. Medicine, 1971—74; ophthalmologist Eye Surgery Assocs., Hollywood, Fla., 1974—. Vol. prof. ophthalmology Bascom Palmer Eye Inst., U. Miami Sch. Medicine, Fla., 1974—; chmn. dept. ophthalmology Meml. Regional Hosp., Hollywood, 1986—88. Lt. comdr. USPHS, 1968—70. Scholar, Am. Cancer Soc., 1963—67. Fellow: Am. Acad. Opthalmology; mem.: Miami Ophthal. Soc. (pres. 1996), Alpha Omega Alpha. Office: 2740 Hollywood Blvd Hollywood FL 33020

SANDBURG, HELGA, author; b. Maywood, Ill., Nov. 24, 1918; d. Carl and Lilian (Steichen) S.; m. George Crile, Jr., Nov. 9, 1963; children by previous marriage: John Carl Steichen, Paula Steichen Polega. Student, Mich. State Coll., 1939-40, U. Chgo., 1940. Dairy goat breeder, also personal sec. to father, 1944-51; sec. manuscripts div., also for keeper of collections Library of Congress, 1952-56; adminstrv. asst. for papers of Woodrow Wilson, 1958-59; writer, lectr., 1957—. Author: (novels) The Wheel of Earth, 1958, Measure My Love, 1959, The Owl's Roost, 1962, The Wizard's Child, 1967; (non-fiction) Sweet Music, A Book of Family Reminiscence and Song, 1963; (with George Crile, Jr.) Above and Below, 1969; (poetry) The Unicorns, 1965; To A New Husband, 1970, The Age of the Flower, 1994; (young adult novels) Blueberry, 1963; Gingerbread, 1964; (juveniles) Joel and the Wild Goose, 1963; Bo and the Old Donkey, 1965, Anna and the Baby Buzzard, 1970; Children and Lovers: 15 Stories by Helga Sandburg, 1976; (biography) A Great and Glorious Romance: The Story of Carl Sandburg and Lilian Steichen, 1978; "...Where Love Begins", 1989, (recorded poems) From in the Dream: Helga Sandburg Reads her Poems, 2001; also numerous short stories; rep. in collections.; contbr.short stories, poems, articles to popular mags. including Seventeen. Recipient Va. Quar. Rev. prize for best short story, 1959, Borestone Mountain poetry award, 1962, Poetry award Chgo. Tribune, 1970; 2d prize 7th Ann. Kans. Poetry Contest, Florence Roberts Head Ohioana Book award, 1990; grantee Finnish Am. Soc. and Svenska Inst., 1961 Mem. Authors Guild, Poetry Soc., Am. Milk Goat Record Assn., Am.-Scandinavian Found., Nat. Nubian Club, Coun. Save the Dunes, Am. Luxembourg Soc., Acad. Am. Poets. Address: 2060 Kent Rd Cleveland Heights OH 44106-3339 E-mail: helgacrile@steichen.ws.

SANDDAL, NELS DODGE, foundation executive, consultant; b. Salt Lake City, Feb. 17, 1949; s. James Wesley and Charlotte Jean (Ewer) S.; m. Brenda Kay Lille Griffin, Sept. 27, 1970 (div. June 1990); m. Theresa Louise Knipe, Oct. 10, 1992; 1 child, Jami. BA in English, Carroll Coll., Helena, Mont., 1966-70; MS in Psychology, Mont. State U., 1996; student, Walden U., 2002—. In-svc. trainer Boulder River Sch. and Hosp., Mont., 1974-75; group home mgr. REACH, Inc., Bozeman, Mont., 1975-76; community home trainer Devel. Disabilities Tng. Inst., Helena, Mont., 1976-77; tng. coord. emergency med. svcs. bureau State Dept. Health and Environ. Scis., Helena, 1977-82; cons., lead staff Nat. Coun. State Emergency Med. Svcs. Tng. Coords., Inc., Lexington, Ky., 1981-86; account exec., lead staff Nat. Assn. Emergency Med. Techs., Clinton, Miss., 1986-87; pres., CEO Assn. Mgmt. and Cons., Inc., Boulder, 1983-89; writer, prodr., dir. North Country Media Group, Great Falls, Mont., 1990-91; chief conf. planner S.O.S. Conf. Planning Consortium, Great Falls, 1991-92; exec. dir. Critical Illness & Trauma Found., Bozeman, Mont., 1986-91, pres., CEO, 1991—. Season course leader Nat. Outdoor Leadership Sch., Lander, Wyo., 1966—74; mem. exec. com. Nat. Coun. State EMS Tng. Coords., 1977—82, chmn., Ky., 1979—81; mem. adv. com. pediatric emergency med. svcs. tng. project Children's Hosp. Nat. Med. Ctr., Wash., 1985—88, pediatrics emergency instr., 1986—90; mem. grant peer rev. com. divsn. injury epidemiology Ctrs. for Disease Control, Atlanta, 1986—87; mem. injury prevention profls. New Eng. Network to Prevent Childhood Injuries, Newton, Mass., 1988—95; mem. core faculty devel. trauma sys. tng. program US Dept. Transp., Wash., 1989—; tech. assistance team mem. EMS, 1991—93; EMS instr. and program coord. Great Falls Vocat. Tng. Ctr., 1991—93; rsch. asst. inst. for cmty. studies U. Mo., Kansas city, 1983—95; assoc. rsch. prof. psychology Mont. State U., 1999—2003; asst. clin. prof. surgery U. Nev. Sch. Medicine, 1999—2003; exec. com. Intermountain Regional EMS Children Coord. Coun., Bozeman, Mont., 1994—2002; site reviewer Commn. for Accreditation of Ambulance Svcs., Glenview, Ill., 1997—; firefighter/EMS trainer Gallatin Gateway Vol. Fire Dept., Gallatin Gateway, Mont., 1998—2001; asst. chief Gallatin River Ranch Fire Dept., 2001—, med. officer, 2001—; dir. Rural EMS and Trauma Tech. Assistance Ctr., Bozework, Mont., 2003; tech. adv. trauma sys. and evaluation com. Am. Coll. Surgeons; mem. various coms. Inst. Medicine, 2003—06; assoc. rsch. prof. Health Scis. Mont. State U., 2003—; cons. in field. Editor and tech. cons.: Workbook for Prehospital Care and Crisis Intervention, 4th edit., 1992, 5th edit., 1993, Instructor Resource Manual for Prehospital Care and Crisis Intervention, 4th edit., 1992, Workbook for First Responder, 1990; contbg. editor Jour. of Prehospital Care, 1984-85, The EMT Jour., 1980-81; editl. cons. Am. Acad. Orthopaedic Surgeons, 1980-81; contbr. numerous articles to profl. jours.; video prodr. and presenter in field. Mem. Park County DUI Task Force, Livingson, 1993-96; inaugural coord. Mont. Safe Kids Coalition, Big Timber, 1988-90; adv. com. Nat. Significance Project for Respite Care, 1977-78; mem. basic life support com. of Mont., Mont. Heart Assn., 1977-82. Recipient Golden award for humanity ARC, 1976, 500 Hour award, 1976, Outstanding Svc. award Nat. Coun. State EMS Tng. Coords., 1979, Leadership award, 1981, Charter Membership award, 1984, J.D. Farrington award for excellence Nat. Assn. Emergency Med. Technicians, 1981, Jeffrey S. Harris award, 1985, Outstanding Svc. award Am. Heart Assn., 1982, Appreciation cert. for paramedic emergency care US Dept. Transp., 1984, Appreciation award Colo. Trauma Inst., 1993, Healthy Mothers/Healthy Babies, Helena, Mont., 1997, Kans. Bd. of EMS, Topeka, 1996, 98, 2003, Intermountain Regional EMS for Children Coordinating Coun., Inc., 1998; named Provider of Yr., EMS for Children, 2005. Mem. Nat. Registry EMTs (20 yr. recognition), Mont. Bd. Med. Examiners. Democrat. Avocations: mountain climbing, hiking, sailing, golf, skiing. Home: 115 Lay Pass Manhattan MT 59741 Office: 300 N Willson Ave Ste 502E Bozeman MT 59715 Business E-Mail: nsanddal@citmt.org.

SANDE, THEODORE ANTON, architect, educator, foundation executive; b. New London, Conn., Nov. 21, 1933; s. Lars Anton and Viola (Edgcomb) S.; m. Solveig Inga-Maj Imselius, Aug. 6, 1960; children: Susanne Ingrid, Lars Michael. BSc in Architecture, RI Sch. Design, 1956; MArch, Yale U., 1961; PhD, U. Pa., 1972; grad. Cultural Instns. Mgmt. Program, Mus. Collaborative, 1983; postgrad., Attingham (Eng.) Summer Sch., 1980. Vis. prof. history of architecture Rensselaer Poly. Inst., fall 1973-74, U. Pa., 1976-77; adj. prof. Am. studies and history Case-Western Res. U., 1981—92. Vis. lectr. in historic preservation Cleve. State U., summer 1994, spring 1998; lectr. art Williams Coll., 1972-75; attended teleconfs. non-profit orgn. mgmt. Drucker Found., 1992. Designer, Arkitekt, Hakon Ahlberg, SAR, Arkitekt, Stockholm, 1960, designer, Washburn, Luther & Rowley, Architects, Attleboro, Mass., 1961-62, Barker & Turoff, Architects, Providence, 1962-63, jr. partner, Turoff Assocs., Architects, 1964-67, partner, Turoff & Sande, Architects, Providence, 1968-70, prin. Ted Sande, Architect, Cranston, R.I., 1970, Cleve., 1993—, emeritus architect, R.I., 2004— author: Industrial Archaeology: A New Look at the American Heritage, 2d edit, 1978; contbg. author: Guidebook to Philadelphia Architecture, 1974; editor: New England Textile Mill Survey, 1971; co-editor: Historic Preservation of Engineering Works, 1981; contbr. articles to profl. jours.; two-man show drawings, Providence Art Club, 1970. Dir. profl. svcs. office hist. properties Nat. Trust Hist. Preservation, Washington, 1975—77, dir. planning and devel., 1977—78, acting v.p. office hist. properties, 1978—79, v.p., 1979—80; mem. Old Georgetown Bd. Nat. Commn. Fine Arts, 1979—81; co-chmn. Conf. Indsl. Archeology Smithsonian Instn., 1971; active Shaker Heights Landmark Commn., 1982—84, Cleve. Landmarks Commn., 1985—2004; mem. archtl. bd. rev. Village of Hunting Valley, Ohio, 2000—; mem. Leadership Cleve. Class 86/87, Ohio Gov.'s Commn. on Bicentennials the NW Ordinance and U.S. Const., 1986—89, Cleve. Bicentennial Commn., 1992—94, Stan Hywet Hall and Gardens, Akron, Ohio, trustee, 1997—2005; chmn. Schweinfurth Trust, 1999—2006; mem. vis. com. Mandel Sch. Scis., Case We. Res. U., 1993—2003; trustee U. Circl Inc., 1981—93, Nat. Rock and Roll Mus. and Hall of Fame, mem. exec. bdlg. com., 1993—95; instnl. rep. Cleve. Arts Consortium, 1987—93. Fellow: We. Res. Hist. Soc. (life; exec. dir. 1981—93, exec. dir. emeritus 1993—); mem.: SAR, AIA (com. hist. resources 1972—74), Cleve. Restoration Soc. (pres. 1994—97, trustee, hon., life trustee), Ohio Mus. Assn. (trustee 1982—87), Am. Assn. Mus., Internat. Com. for Conservation of Indsl. Heritage (chmn. bd. dirs. 1978—81), Soc. Archtl. Historians (preservation com. 1972—74), Soc. Indsl. Archeology (co-founder, 1st pres. 1971—72, dir. 1973—76, project supr. handbook on adaptive use of indsl. bldgs., gen. chmn. 15th ann. conf.), Philos. Club Cleve. (past pres.), Rowfant Club (past pres. 2002—03, coun. of fellows). Episcopalian. Home: 13415 Shaker Blvd Ste 11-H-4 Cleveland OH 44120-1586

SANDEFER, G(EORGE) LARRY, lawyer; b. Washington, Mar. 2, 1950; s. George Hall and Mary Gray (Babers) S. BS, Auburn U., 1972; JD, U. Fla., 1978. Bar: Fla. 1978, U.S. Dist. Ct. (mid. dist.) Fla. 1978, U.S. Ct. Appeals (5th and 11th cirs.) 1981, U.S. Supreme Ct. 1982; cert. in criminal trial law Fla. Bar. Asst. state atty., criminal divsn., lead trial atty. State of Fla., Clearwater, 1977-86; sole practice Clearwater, 1986-88; assoc. Kimpton, Burke and White, P.A., Clearwater, 1988-90; pvt. practice, Clearwater, 1991—. Mem. Indian Rocks Civic Assn., 1994-2000, Leadership Pinellas; city commr. Indian Rocks Beach, 1994-00. 1st lt. USAF, 1973-75. Mem. ATLA, Pinellas County Trial Lawyers Assn., Fla. Assn. Criminal Def. Attys., Colo. Bar Assn., Fla. Bar Assn., Clearwater Bar Assn., St. Petersburg Bar Assn., Kiwanis. Avocations: tennis, skiing, boating. Address: 711 N Belcher Rd Clearwater FL 33764

SANDELMAN, JONATHAN E. (JON), investment banker; Bachelor's Degree, Adelphia U.; JD, Cardozo Sch. Law. Dep. head global equities, mng. dir. equity derivatives Salomon Bros.; head equity fin. products NationsBank (now Bank Am. Securities), NYC, 1998—2002; head equities Banc Am. Securities LLC, NYC, 2002—04, pres., 2004—, head debt and equities, 2004—. Trustee Whitney Mus. Am. Art. Office: Bank of Am Securities LLC 9 W 57th St New York NY 10019

SANDER, ALISON BISHOP, international consultant; b. Boston, July 28, 1959; d. Frank E.A. and Emily (Jones) S. BA, U. Chgo., 1983; JD cum laude, Harvard U., 1987, MBA, 1987. Assoc. Goldman Sachs, NYC, 1987—89; pres., CEO Cambridge Transnat. Assocs., Boston, 1990—97; mgr., globalization topic leader Boston Cons. Group, 1997—. Mem. bd. mgrs. N.E. Yearly Meeting of Friends, Boston, 1992-94; bd. dirs. Lisle Fellowship, Mich., 1990-94, Harvard Coop., Cambridge, Mass., 1984-87, Boston Ctr. for Internat. Visitors, 1993-94, WRI, 2006—; overseer Boston Sci. Mus., 1998-; globalization commr. State of World Forum, 1998-2001. Recipient Perry S. Herst prize U. Chgo., 1981. Mem. UN Assn. N.Y. (panel), Coun. Fgn. Rels., Asia Soc., World Affairs Coun., Harvard Bus. Sch. Club of Boston, Phi Beta Kappa. Home: 74 Buckingham St Cambridge MA 02138-2229 Office: Boston Cons Group Exch Pl Boston MA 02109

SANDER, CLARENCE ELLIS, JR., retired protective services official; b. Delray, Fla., Dec. 15, 1946; s. Clarence Ellis and Daisy Bell Sanders; m. Theresa Ann Sander (dec.); children: Sharlene Michelle Sanders, Lawrence Ellis Sanders(dec.); m. Susan Virgina Lee. Cert. in drafting, Washinton Drafting. Security guard Smithsonian Inst., Washington; police officer US Treasury Dept., Washington; ret. Author poems. Lance corp. USMC, 1966—69. Recipient Martin Luther King award, Albert Galitan award, Law Enforcement Honor award, Svc. award, US Treasury Dept. Mem.: Fraternal Order of Police (congl. liason), Am. Fedn. Govt. Employees (shape steward). Democrat. Avocations: poetry, singing, dance, fishing, hunting. Home: 7304 Pacella Ct Clinton MD 20735

SANDER, ELLIOT GENE (LEE SANDER), transportation executive; b. May 3, 1956; m. Lisa Ellen Lempel, Oct. 14, 1990. BS in Fgn. Svc., Georgetown U. Dir. transit NY Dept. Transp.; dep. dir. Office Mgmt. & Productivity NYC; dep. commr. & state rent adminstr. NY Divsn. Housing & Community Renewal; asst. gen. mgr. for surface transit & gen. mgr., Manhattan bus divsn. NYC, exec. dir. operational svc., Bur. Traffic Ops., dep. dir. divsn. parking, spl. asst. to city coun. pres., budget analyst Office Mgmt. & Budget, commr. Dept. Transp., 1994—96; with Frederic R. Harris Inc., 1996—2000; commr. NYC Taxi and Limousine Commn., 1997—2000; sr. v.p., dir. corp. strategic develop. DMJM Harris, 2000—06; exec. dir., CEO Met. Transit Authority, 2006—. Dir. Rudin Ctr. for Trans. Policy and Mgmt Robert F. Wagner Sch. of Pub. Svc. at NYU, 1996—; publisher NY Trans. Jour.; former chmn. com. one large U.S. cities Transportation Rsch. Bd.; sr. adv. Nat. Assn. of City Trans. Officials; mem. citizen adv. bd. Lower Manhattan Devel. Corp., 2002—; founder, co-chmn. Empire State Trans. Alliance. Office: Met Trans Auth 347 Madison Ave 5th Fl New York NY 10017 *

SANDER, FRANK ERNEST ARNOLD, law educator; b. Stuttgart, Germany, July 22, 1927; came to U.S., 1940, naturalized, 1946; s. Rudolf and Alice (Epstein) S.; m. Emily Bishop Jones, Apr. 26, 1958; children: Alison Bishop, Thomas Harvey, Ernest Ridgway Sander. AB in Math. magna cum laude, Harvard U., 1949, LLB magna cum laude, 1952. Bar: Mass. 1952, US Supreme Ct. 1952. Law clk. to Chief Judge Magruder U.S. Ct. Appeals, 1st Cir., 1952-53; law clk. to Justice Frankfurter, U.S. Supreme Ct., 1953-54; atty. tax divsn. Dept. Justice, 1954-56; with firm Hill & Barlow, Boston, 1956-59; mem. faculty Harvard Law Sch., 1959—, prof. law, 1962—, Bussey prof., 1981—, assoc. dean, 1987-2000, emeritus, 2006—. Spl. fields fed. taxation, family law, welfare law, dispute resolution; chmn. Coun. on Role of Cts.; mem. panels Am. Arbitration Assn., Fed. Mediation and Conciliation Svc.; chmn. Coun. on Legal Edn. Opportunity, 1968—70; cons. Dept. Treasury, 1968; treas. Harvard Law Rev., 1951—52; mem. dispute resolution standing com. Mass. Supreme Jud. Ct., 1994—2004; drafting com. Uniform Mediation Act, 1998—2001. Author: (with Westfall and McIntyre) Readings in Federal Taxation, 2d edit., 1983, (with Foote and Levy) Cases and Materials on Family Law, 3d edit., 1985, (with Gutman) Tax Aspects of Divorce and Separation, 4th edit., 1985, (with Goldberg, Rogers and Cole) Dispute Resolution, 5th edit., 2007. Mem. tax mission Internat. Program Taxation to Republic of Colombia, 1959; mem. com. on civil and polit. rights President's Commn. on Status of Women, 1962-63; trustee Buckingham Browne and Nichols Sch., 1969-75; chmn. Mass. Welfare Adv. Bd., 1975-79. With AUS, 1946-47. Recipient Whitney North Seymour medal Am. Arbitration Assn., 1988, spl. award for disting. svc. to dispute resolution Ctr. for Pub. Resources Inst. for Dispute Resolution, 1990, Lifetime Achievement award Internat. Acad. Mediators, 2006. Mem. ABA (chmn. standing com. dispute resolution 1986-89, Kutak medal 1993, D'Alemberte-Raven award 1999), Boston Bar Assn., Phi Beta Kappa. Office: Harvard U Sch of Law Cambridge MA 02138 Home: 100 Newbury Ct Apt 113 Concord MA 01742 Office Phone: 617-495-3184.

SANDER, LEE See SANDER, ELLIOT

SANDERCOX, ROBERT ALLEN, academic administrator, minister; b. Akron, Ohio, May 20, 1932; s. Monroe J. and Elverda (Arnold) S.; m. Nancy Lee Wertz, Sept. 13, 1958; children— Alison Grace, Megan Louise, Robert Philip BA, Bethany Coll., W. Va., 1954; M.Div., Yale U., 1957; postgrad., U. Buffalo, W.Va. U.; LittD, Bethany Coll., 1989. Ordained to ministry Christian Ch. (Disciples of Christ). Asst. minister Park Ave Christian Ch., NYC, 1954-57; asst. provost Bethany Coll., 1957-60, v.p., dean students, 1960-75, v.p., dir. devel., 1975-79, interim pres., 1979-80, v.p., provost for coll. advancement, 1980-89, sr. v.p., 1989-95, cons. to the pres., 1995-97, sr. v.p. emeritus, 1997—. Chmn. Brooke County Mus. Bd., 1995—98; trustee Christian Ch. Disciples of Christ in W.Va., Parkersburg, 1984—88; chmn. Brooke County Landmarks Commn., 1988—98; trustee Bethany Coll., 2004—07. Recipient Alumni Disting. Service award Bethany Coll., 1982 Mem. Coun. Advancement and Support Edn., Duquesne Club (Pitts.), Univ. Club Jacksonville, Order of Symposiarch, Rotary, Kiwanis (pres. 1967), Alpha Sigma Phi (nat. treas. 1982-84, v.p. 1984-86, grad. sr. pres. 1986-88, bd. dir., trustee Ednl. Found. 1982-95, chmn. Ednl. Found. 1994-95, Delta Beta Xi svc. award 1960). Republican. Home: 715 Buckwood Ln Lititz PA 17543 Personal E-mail: rsandercox@dejazzd.com.

SANDERLIN, JAMES L., energy executive; s. Linwood and Elsie R. Sanderlin; m. Ginger Sanderlin; children: Meredith, Elaine, Barry. B, Randolph-Macon Coll., Ashland, Va.; law degree, U. Va., 1966. With McGuireWoods, Richmond, Va.; from various positions to sr. v.p. law Dominion, Richmond, 2000—. Bd. dirs. Tredegar Nat. Civil War Ctr. Found., Richmond, Richmond Pub. Libr.; co-chair VCU/MCV Heart Ctr. Fund. Office: Dominion PO Box 26532 Richmond VA 23261-6532 Office Phone: 804-819-2103. Office Fax: 804-273-4271.

SANDERS, ADRIAN LIONEL, retired educational consultant; b. Paragould, Ark., Aug. 3, 1938; s. Herbert Charles and Florence Theresa (Becherer) S.; m. Molly Jean Zecher, Dec. 20, 1961. AA, Bakersfield Coll., 1959; BA, San Francisco State U., 1961; MA, San Jose State U., 1967. 7th grade tchr. Sharp Park Sch., Pacifica, Calif., 1961-62; 5th grade tchr. Mowry Sch., Fremont, Calif., 1962-64; sci. tchr. Blacow Sch., Fremont, Calif., 1964-76; 5th grade tchr. Warm Springs Sch., Fremont, 1977-87, 5th grade gifted and talented edn. tchr., 1987-94; ret., 2006; edn. cons., 1994—2006. Mem. San Diego Hist. Soc., 1999, Mingei Internat. Mus., Balboa Park-San Diego; vol. 7 km. Race for Alzheimer's Disease Willow Glen Founders Day, San Jose, 1988-92. Named Outstanding Young Educator, Jr. C. of C., Fremont, Calif., 1965. Mem. Zoolog. Soc. San Diego, Calif. Ctr. for the Arts (Escondido). Avocations: photography, travel, collecting license plates. Home and Office: 1437 Stoneridge Cir Escondido CA 92029-5514

SANDERS, BARRY, retired professional football player; b. Wichita, July 16, 1968; s. William and Shirley Sanders. Student, Okla. State U., 1986—89. Running back Detroit Lions, 1989—99. Co-author (with Mark E. McCormick): Now You See Him: The Barry Sanders Story, 2003. Named NFL Rookie of Yr., 1990, NFL Offensive Player of the Yr., 1997, 1994, NFL Player of the Yr., 1991, 1997; named to Sporting News Coll. All-Am. team, 1987, 1988, Pro Bowl, 1989—98; recipient Heisman Trophy award, 1988. Achievements include holds NCAA single season record in rushing yards (2,628); led NFL in rushing, 1990, 94, 96, 97; #3 all-time on NFL rushing list (15,269); inducted into the pro and college NFL Hall of Fame, 2004. Office Phone: 305-674-7221. Business E-Mail: jb@barry.sanders.com.

SANDERS, BARRY R., lawyer; b. Oak Park, Ill., July 21, 1957; s. Eugene Haze and Muriel Efty Sanders; m. Diane Gaffney Sanders, Dec. 28, 1985; 1 child, Mattie Maria Murielle. BA, U. Va., 1979, Cambridge U., 1981; LLM, U. Tex., 1983; MA, Cambridge U., 1986. Bar: Calif. 1984, Ariz. 1985, U.S. Dist. Ct. (no. dist.) Calif. 1984, U.S. Dist. Ct. (ea. dist.) Calif. 1985, U.S. Dist. Ct. Ariz. 1987, U.S. Ct. Appeals (9th cir.) 1989, U.S. Supreme Ct. 1996, U.S. Ct. Appeals (8th cir.) 2001. Shareholder Pohlman & Sanders, PA, Phoenix, 1989—91, Ryley, Carlock & Applewhite, PA, Phoenix, 1991—99, Allen, Price, Padden & Sanders PC, Phoenix, 1999—2005, Mariscal Weeks McIntyre & Friedlander, P.A., 2005—. Recipient Henry prize in Moral Philosophy, U. of Aberdeen, Scotland, 1978. Mem.: State Bar Ariz. (chair antitrust sect. 1998—99, 2002—03). Avocation: golf. Office: Mariscal Weeks McIntyre & Friedlander P A 2901 N Ctrl Ave Ste 200 Phoenix AZ 85012 Business E-Mail: barry.sanders@mwmf.com.

SANDERS, BERNARD (BERNIE SANDERS), senator, former congressman; b. Bklyn., Sept. 8, 1941; s. Eli and Dorothy (Glassberg) Sanders; m. Jane O'Meara, 1988; children: Levi, Heather, Carina, David. Student, Bklyn. Coll.; BA, U. Chgo., 1964. Freelance writer, carpenter, youth counselor, 1964-76; dir. Am. People's Hist. Soc., Burlington, Vt., 1976-81; mayor City of Burlington, Vt., 1981-89; mem. faculty Harvard U., Cambridge, Mass., 1989, Hamilton Coll., Clinton, NY, 1990; mem.-at large US Congress from Vt., 1991—2007; US Senator from Vt., 2007—. Mem. Progressive Caucus, US Congress, mem. fin. svcs. com., ranking minority mem. fin. instns. and consumer credit subsommittee, mem. govt. reform com. Co-author: Outsider in the House, 1997. Chmn. Vt. Liberty Union Party, 1975-76, candidate for Vt. gov., 1972, 76, 86, US Senate, 1971, 74. Independent. Jewish. Office: US Senate 2233 Rayburn House Office Bldg Washington DC 20515 *

SANDERS, CARL E., lawyer, former governor; b. Augusta, Ga., May 15, 1925; s. Carl T. and Roberta (Ailey) S.; m. Betty Bird Foy, 1947; children: Betty Foy, Carl E. Jr. LLB, Univ. Ga., 1947. Bar: Ga. 1947. Mem. Hammond, Kennedy & Sanders, Augusta, Ga., 1948—52; sr. mem. Sanders, Thurmond, Hester & Jolles, Augusta, Ga., Sanders, Hester, Holley, Ashmore & Boozer; chmn., mem. exec. com. Troutman Sanders LLP (formerly Troutman, Sanders, Lockerman & Ashmore), Atlanta, 1967—; Ga. State Rep., 1954—56; Ga. State Senator, 1957—62; pres. pro tem Ga. State Senate, 1960—62; Gov. State of Ga., 1963—67. Chmn., rules com. Dem. Nat. Conv., 1964; mem., exec. com. Nat. Gov. Conf., 1964—65; chmn. Appalachian Gov. Conf., 1964—65; vice chmn. Southern Gov. Conf., 1965—66; mem. Nat. Commn. on Urban Affairs, 1967; bd. dir. Pub. Broadcasting Corp., 1968—70; chmn., fin. com. Dem. Party, Ga., 1974—83; bd. dir. Healthdyne, 1986—96, Matria Healthcare, 1996—, Wachovia Atlanta Adv. Bank Bd.; mem. Atlanta Com., Olympic Games, 1996. Served to 1st lt. (first pilot of B-17 heavy bomber) USAF, WWII. Named a Super Lawyer, Atlanta Mag., 2004; recipient Order of Sacred Treasure Gold and Silver award, Emperor and Govt. of Japan, 1989. Mem.: ABA, Lawyers Club of Atlanta, Atlanta Bar Assn., Phi Delta Phi. Democrat. Achievements include being inducted into Athletic Hall of Fame, 1968, Aviation Hall of Fame, 1997. Office: Troutman Sanders LLP One Logan Sq 600 Peachtree St NE Atlanta GA 30308-2216 Office Phone: 404-885-3100. Office Fax: 404-962-6674. Business E-Mail: carl.sanders@troutmansanders.com.

SANDERS, CHARLES FRANKLIN, energy executive, consultant; b. Louisville, Dec. 22, 1931; s. Charles Franklin and Maragret Rhea (Timmons) S.; m. Marie Audrey Galuppo, Dec. 29, 1956; children: Karen Lynn, Craig Joseph, Keith Franklin. B.Chem. Engring., U. Louisville, 1954, M.Chem. Engring., 1958; PhD, U. So. Calif., 1970. Rsch. engr. Exxon Rsch. and Engring. Co., Linden, NJ, 1955-62; asst. prof. engring. Calif. State U., Northridge, 1962-68, assoc. prof., 1968-71, prof., 1971-82, chmn. dept., 1969-72, dean Coll. Engring. and Computer Sci., 1972-81; pres., chief exec. officer, dir. Rusco Industries, Los Angeles, 1981-82; exec. v.p. Energy Systems Assocs., Tustin, Calif., 1982-89, Energeo, San Francisco, 1989-95, also bd. dirs.; v.p. tech. Smith-Bellingham Capital, San Francisco, 1989-91. Bd. dirs. Catalyst Air Tech., Inc. Bd. dirs. San Fernando Valley Child Guidance Clinic, 1979-81. Served to 1st lt. U.S. Army, 1956-57. NSF fellow, 1965-67 Mem. AIChE, NSPE, Calif. Soc. Profl. Engrs., Am. Soc. for Engring. Edn., Combustion Inst. Republican. Office Phone: 949-362-6585. Personal E-mail: cfs@cox.net.

SANDERS, CHARLOTTA ELISABETH, nuclear engineer, educator; b. Vastervik, Sweden, Feb. 14, 1971; d. Hans J. Nilsson and margareta Gunilla Carlsson; m. Mark Callis Sanders, Aug. 24, 1996. BS in Mech. Engring., Brigham Young U., Provo, Utah, 1994; MS in Nuc. Engring., Tex. A&M U., College Station, 1995; PhD in Engring. in Nuc. & Reactor Physics, Royal Inst. Tech., Stockholm, 1999. Cert. profl. nuclear engr., Bd. Profl. Engrs. & Land Surveyors, Nev., 2003. Reactor physicist Studsvik Nuc., Nykoping, Sweden, 1998—2000; rsch. assoc. Oak Ridge Nat. Lab., Tenn., 2000—02; sr. nuc. engring. specialist Bechtel SAIC Co., LLC, Las Vegas, Nev., 2002—. Adj. prof. U. Nev., Las Vegas, 2006—. Contbr. articles to profl. jours. Recipient Riley Bechtel Merit award, Bechtel Nat., Inc., 2004—05. Mem.: Nev. Local Am. Nuc. Soc. Sect. (vice-chmn. 2005), Environmentalists Nuc. Power (vice-chmn. 1998—2000), Women In Nuc. (Las Vegas valley women in nuc. chpt. exec. coun. mem. 2004), Am. Nuc. Soc. (profl. women in ans com. mem. 1999, exec. com. mem. radiation protection & shielding divsn. 2005). Avocations: golf, travel, skiing. Home: 1930 Village Ctr Cir 3-256 Las Vegas NV 89134 Office: Bechtel SAIC Co LLC 1180 Town Center Dr Las Vegas NV 89144

SANDERS, DALE R., lawyer; b. NYC, Feb. 1, 1946; m. Jo-Ann Sanders, Dec. 25, 1967; 1 child. Bar: Fla. 1970, Wyo. 1991, U.S. Dist. Ct. (so. dist.) Fla. 1971, U.S. Tax Ct. 1972. Atty. Kirsch & Druck, P.A., Ft. Lauderdale, Fla., 1970-71, Kirsch, Digiulian, Druck et al, Ft. Lauderdale, Fla., 1971-72, Digiulian, Spellacy, Lyons, Ft. Lauderdale, Fla., 1972-77, Lyons & Sanders, Chartered, Ft. Lauderdale, Fla., 1977—. With USAR, 1969-75. Mem.: Broward County Trial Lawyers Assn. (pres. 1980), Broward County Bar Assn. (pres. 1990), Fla. Bar (bd. govs. 1991—95, mem. 17th cir. jud. nominating commn. 1992—96, vice chair 1996—2002, mem. State of Fla. jud. qualifications commn.). Office: Lyons and Sanders Chartered 600 NE 3rd Ave Fort Lauderdale FL 33304-2618

SANDERS, DAVID AVRAM, biochemist, researcher; b. NJ, Feb. 3, 1961; s. Gabe and Freyda Sanders; m. Miriam Sarah Hasson, Aug. 20, 1986 (dec. Jan. 16, 2006); children: Honi, Akiva, Yinnon. BS magna cum laude with distinction, Yale Coll., New Haven, Conn., 1983; PhD, U. Calif., Berkeley, 1989. Postdoctoral fellow Whitehead Inst. Biomed. Rsch., Cambridge, Mass., 1990—95; assoc. prof. Purdue U., West Lafayette, Ind., 1995—. Vis. scientist U. Calif., San Francisco, 1989—90; sci. collaborator US Def. Threat Reduction Agy., 2002—05; faculty coun. rep. Purdue U. Markey Ctr. Structural Biology, West Lafayette, 2000—06; vis. scientist Weizmann Inst. Sci., Rehovot, Ind., 2003; chmn. Purdue Life Scis. Program Admissions Com., West Lafayette, 2004—05; exec. rep. Purdue U. Virology Tng. Group, West Lafayette, 2006—. Contbr. articles to profl. jours. Candidate US rep. Dem. Party 4th Congl. Dist., Ind., 2004—06. Recipient Career award, Nat. Sci. Found., 2000—06, Cancer Rsch. award, Elks, Ind., 2005; fellow, Cancer Rsch. Inst., 1990—93; Kaiser fellow, U. Calif., 1983—84, Rsch. scholar, Am. Cancer Soc., 2003—07. Achievements include patents for pseudotyped retroviruses and stable cell lines for their production; patents pending for gene therapy vectors. Office: Purdue Univ 915 W State St West Lafayette IN 47906 Office Phone: 765-494-6453. Office Fax: 765-496-1189. Business E-Mail: retrovir@purdue.edu.

SANDERS, DEBRA KAY, curator; b. Denver, Feb. 3, 1954; d. Donald Jack and Doris Lee Sanders. BS, Colo. State U., Ft. Collins, 1972—76. Seasonal pk. ranger Nat. Pk. Svc., 1976—81; mus. technician NPS, Hubbell Trading Post NHS, Ganado, Ariz., 1982—87; dist. interpreter, curator NPS, Mt. Rainier Nat. Pk., Longmire, Wash., 1986—87; dist. ranger NPS, Chiricahua Nat. Monument, Wilcox, Ariz., 1987—90; chief interpretation Nat. Pk. Svc., Grand Portage Nat. Monument, Minn., 1990—91; mus. curator Nat. Pk. Svc., Klondike Gold Rush NHP, Skagway, Alaska, 1991—. Prodr., coordinator (exhibitions) The Moore House (Spl. Achievement award, 1997), supr. Faraway Ranch (Performance award, 1988). Bd. mem. City Mus., Skagway, 1991—2005; sec. Skagway Med. Ctr., 1994—96; treas., grant writer Paws & Claws Animal Shelter, Skagway, 2005—. Recipient Spl. Achievement award, Nat. Pk. Svc., 2002, Performance award, 2004—06. Mem.: Alaska Mus. Assn. (assoc.), Am. Mus. Assn. (assoc.), Nature Conservancy (assoc.), Best Friends Animal Soc. (assoc.). Democrat-Npl. Avocations: hiking, skiing, gardening, crafts. Office: National Park Svc 2nd & Broadway Skagway AK 99840 Home Phone: 907-983-2287.

SANDERS, DOUGLAS CHARLES, horticulturist, researcher, educator; b. Lansing, Mich., May 21, 1942; s. Charles S. and Dorthy Sanders; m. Ellen Joyce, Apr. 26, 1965. BS, Mich. State U., 1965; MS, U. Minn., 1969, PhD, 1970. From rsch. asst. to rsch. assoc. U. Minn., St. Paul, 1965-70; from asst. prof. N.C. State U., Raleigh, 1970-75, assoc. prof., 1975-82, prof., 1982—. Cons. Orgn. of Am. States, others. Contbr. over 185 articles to profl. jours. Recipient Outstanding Ext. award N.C. State U., 1993, Outstanding Ext. Specialist award Epsilon Sigma Phi, 1993; named Covington Outstanding Ext. Educator, 1999. Fellow Am. Soc. Hort. Sci. (Outstanding Extention Educator award, 1993); mem. Am. Soc. Agronomy, Crop Sci. Soc. Am. Achievements include development of drip fertigation systems for vegetables, of cultural systems for vegetables; investigation of integrated aquaculture and vegetable production system, and of nutrient cycling in vegetables; development of new cropping systems for asparagus, carrots, lettuce and onions. Office: NC State U Dept Horticultural Sci PO Box 7609 Raleigh NC 27695-0001 E-mail: Doug_Sanders@ncsa.edu.

SANDERS, DOUGLAS WARNER, JR., lawyer, judge; b. Oklahoma City, Jan. 13, 1958; s. Douglas Warner Sr. and Jane (Livermore) S.; m. Brenda Gail Cox, Apr. 20, 1990; children: Douglas Warner III, Noel Layne, Jonathan Scott, Stephanie Marie. BS, Okla State U., 1980; JD, Oklahoma City U., 1983. Bar: Okla., U.S. Dist. Ct. (ea., no. and we. dists.) Okla., U.S. Dist. Ct. (we. dist.) Ark. Assoc. Stipe Law Firm, Oklahoma City, 1983-85; ptnr. Sanders, Sanders & Sullivan, Poteau, Okla., 1985—. Mcpl. judge City of Poteau, 1994—, City of Spiro, Okla., 1994—, Town of Shady Point, Okla., 1994—; mem. Okla. Bd. Bar Examiners, 2000—. Recipient Outstanding Alumnus award Oklahoma City U. Law Sch., 1999. Fellow ABA; mem. Okla. Bar Assn. (bd. govs. 1992-94, v.p. 1997, pres. 1999, Pres.'s award 1997, Disting. Svc. award 1999), LeFlore County Bar Assn. (Pres.'s award 1997). Democrat. Presbyterian. Avocation: golf. Home: 900 N Witte St Poteau OK 74953-3636 Office: Sanders Sanders & Sullivan 104 S Church St Poteau OK 74953-3344 E-mail: dougal@clnk.com.

SANDERS, FRANKLIN D., retired insurance company executive; b. Newton, Mass., Apr. 24, 1935; s. Franklin and Ethel Shriner (Dulaney) S.; m. Jane Gray Collier, June 18, 1960; children— Cynthia, Franklin D., Nancy, Carolyn. AB, Amherst Coll., 1957; MBA, Harvard U., 1959. With 1st Boston Corp., NYC, 1960-86, mng. dir., 1976-86; pres. Aegis Ins. Services Inc., Jersey City; ret. Treas., bd. dirs. Assoc. Electric & Gas Ins. Services, Ltd., Hamilton, Bermuda, 1986-97. Chmn. Republican Exec. Com., Bernardsville, N.J., 1965-72, Bernardsville Zoning Bd. of Adjustment, 1966-99; trustee Episcopal Diocese of Vt., 2005—. Mem. Harvard Club (N.Y.C.). Avocations: sailing, skiing, golf.

SANDERS, GERALD HOLLIE, communications educator; b. Mt. Vernon, Tex., Dec. 10, 1924; s. Elmer Hugh and Velma Mae (Hollowell) S.; m. Mary Dean Crew, July 18, 1947; children: Michael Dwaine, Rose Ann, Susan Kathleen, Randall Wayne. BA, Southeastern Okla. U., 1947; MA, Tex. Tech U., 1969; PhD, U. Minn., 1974. Program dir. Sta. WEWO, Laurenburg, NC, 1947—49; sports dir. Sta. KFYO, Lubbock, Tex., 1949—50; gen. mgr. Sta. KLVT, Levelland, Tex., 1950—51, 1953—54; sports dir. Sta. KCUL, Ft. Worth, 1954—55; asst. mgr. Sta. KDAV, Lubbock, 1955—57; mgr. Sta. KCBD, Lubbock, 1957—58; owner Sta. KSEL, Lubbock, 1958—67, Sta. KBUY, Amarillo, Tex., Sta. KERB, Kermit, Tex., Sta. KBEK, Elk City, Okla., Sta. KZZN, Littlefield, Tex.; lectr. comm. Coll. of Wooster, 1967—68, asst. prof, 1968—75, assoc. prof., 1975—91, chmn. dept. comm., 1974—81, Miami U., Oxford, Ohio, 1981—92, prof. emeritus comm., 1992—. Disting. lectr. Jinan U., Zhong Shan U., Fudan U., Nanjing U., Beijing U., China, 1989; cons. in field, Oxford, 1982—; polit. and trial cons., 1996—. Author: Introduction to Comtemporary Academic Debate, 1983; contbr. articles. to profl. jours. Active Political Campaigns. Served to col. USMC, 1943-46, PTO, 1951-53, Korea. Recipient Disting. Svc. award Delta Sigma Rho-Tau Kappa Alpha, 1991, Am. Forensic Assn., 1991. Mem. Am. Forensic Assn. (pres. 1978-82), Speech Comm. Assn., Speech Comm. Assn. of Ohio (pres. 1976-77), Disting. Svc. award 1978), Am. Inst. Parliamentarians, Soc. Trial Cons. Presbyterian. Avocations: sports, political campaigns. Home: 200 Country Club Dr Oxford OH 45056-9050 Office: Advocacy Unltd PO Box 457 Oxford OH 45056-0457 Home Phone: 513-523-6948; Office Phone: 513-523-0227. E-mail: gsanders@one.net.

SANDERS, GINA SUSAN, publishing executive; d. Arnold R. and Joyce S.; m. Steven Oliver Newhouse, Feb. 28, 1993; 2 children. BA magna cum laude, Tufts Univ. Account mgr. House & Garden Condé Nast, 1988, advt. dir. Details mag., 1993—94, pub. Details mag., 1994—97, pub. Gourmet mag., 1997—2002, v.p. Gourmet mag., 2000—02; founding pub. & v.p. Teen Vogue, 2003—. Named Pub. of Yr., Condé Nast, 2005. Office: Teen Vogue Condé Nast 4 Times Sq New York NY 10036 Office Phone: 212-286-4316. *

SANDERS, HAROLD BAREFOOT, JR., judge; b. Dallas, Feb. 5, 1925; s. Harold Barefoot and May Elizabeth (Forrester) S.; m. Jan Scurlock, June 6, 1952; children— Janet Lea, Martha Kay, Mary Frances, Harold Barefoot III. BA, U. Tex., 1949, LLB, 1950. Bar: Tex. bar 1950. U.S. atty. No. Dist. Tex., 1961-65; asst. dep. atty. gen. U.S., 1965-66; asst. atty. gen., 1966-67; legis. counsel to President U.S., 1967-69; partner firm Clark, West, Keller, Sanders & Butler, Dallas, 1969-79; U.S. dist. judge for No. Dist. Tex., Dallas, 1979—, chief judge, 1989-95. Mem. Tex. Ho. of Reps., 1952-58; Dem. nominee U.S. Senate, 1972. Lt. (j.g.) USNR, World War II. Mem. ABA (chmn. nat. conf. fed. trial judges 1988-89), Fed. Bar Assn. (Disting. Svc. award Dallas 1964), Dallas Bar Assn., State Bar Tex. (jud. conf. U.S. 1989-92, jud. panel on multidistrict litigation 1992-2000, jud. conf. com. to rev. cir. coun. conduct and disability orders 2001—06), Blue Key, Phi Delta Phi, Phi Delta Theta. Methodist. Office: US Courthouse 1100 Commerce St Dallas TX 75242-1016 Business E-Mail: barefoot_sanders@txnd.uscourts.gov.

SANDERS, JACK THOMAS, religious studies educator; b. Grand Prairie, Tex., Feb. 28, 1935; s. Eula Thomas and Mildred Madge (Parish) S.; m. M. Patricia Chism, Aug. 9, 1959 (dec. Oct. 1973); 1 son, Collin Thomas; m. Susan Elizabeth Plass, Mar. 3, 1979. BA, Tex. Wesleyan Coll., 1956; M.Div., Emory U., 1960; PhD, Claremont Grad. Sch., 1963; postgrad., Eberhard-Karls U., Tuebingen, Germany, 1963-64. Asst. prof. Emory U., Atlanta, 1964-67, Garrett Theol Sem., Evanston, Ill., 1967-68, McCormick Theol. Sem., Chgo., 1968-69; assoc. prof. U. Oreg., Eugene, 1969-75, prof., 1975-97, head dept. religious studies, 1973-80, 85-90, prof. emeritus, 1997—. Author: The New Testament Christological Hymns, 1971, Ethics in the New Testament, 1975, 2d edit., 1986, Ben Sira and Demotic Wisdom, 1983, The Jews in Luke-Acts, 1987, Schismatics, Sectarians, Dissidents, Deviants: The First One Hundred Years of Jewish-Christian Relations, 1993, Charisma, Converts, Competitors: Societal and Sociological Factors in the Success of Early Christianity, 2000; editor: Gospel Origins and Christian Beginnings, 1990, Gnosticism and the Early Christian World, 1990; mem. edit. bd. Jour. Bibl. Lit., 1977-83. Mem. policy bd. Dept. Higher Edn. Nat. Council Chs., N.Y.C., 1971-73. NDEA grad. study fellow, 1960-63; Fulbright Commn. fellow, 1963-64; Am. Coun. Learned Socs. travel grantee, 1981; NEH fellow, 1983-84. Mem. Assn. for Jewish Studies, Soc. Bibl. Lit. (regional sec. 1969-76, sabbatical rsch. award 1976-77). Democrat. Home: 704 NW 3d Dr Pendleton OR 97801-1411 Office: U Oregon Dept Religious Studies Eugene OR 97403 E-mail: jsands@oregontrail.net.

SANDERS, JACKIE WOLCOTT, ambassador; married. BA, Bowling Green State U., 1976. Spl. asst. Congl. affairs Bur. Near Eastern and South Asian Affairs US Dept. State, Washington, 1984—85, White House liaison, 1985—87, dep. asst. sec. for polit. affairs, 1987—89, dep. asst. sec. state Bur. Internat. Orgn. Affairs, 2001—03; assoc. dir. NSC, Washington, 1987—89; US rep. to Conf. on Disarmament, spl. rep. of Pres. of the US for Non-proliferation of Nuclear Weapons Geneva, 2003—; spl. rep. of Pres. for Non-Proliferation of Nuclear Weapons The White House, Washington, 2003—; alt. US rep. spl. polit. affairs, US Mission to UN US Dept. State, NYC, 2006—.

SANDERS, JACQUELYN SEEVAK, psychologist, educator; b. Boston, Apr. 26, 1931; d. Edward Ezral and Dora (Zoken) Seevak; 1 child, Seth. BA, Radcliffe Coll., 1952; MA, U. Chgo., 1964; PhD, UCLA, 1972. Counselor, asst. prin. Orthogenic Sch., Chgo., 1952—65; rsch. assoc. UCLA, 1965—68; asst. prof. Ctr. for Early Edn., LA, 1969—72; assoc. dir. Sonia Shankman Orthogenic Sch., U. Chgo., 1972—73, dir., 1973—93, dir. emeritus, 1993—; curriculum cons. day care ctrs. LA Dept. Social Welfare, 1970—72; instr. Calif. State Coll., LA, 1972; lectr. dept. edn. U. Chgo., 1972—80, sr. lectr., 1980—93, clin. assoc. prof. dept. psychiatry, 1990—93, emeritus, 1993—; instr. edn. program Inst. Psychoanalysis, Chgo., 1979—82. Cons. Osawatomie State Hosp., Kans., 1965—68; reading cons. Foreman HS, Chgo.; treas. Chgo. Inst. Psychoanalysis, 2003—. Author: Greenhouse for the Mind, 1989; editor (with Barry L. Childress): Psychoanalytic Approaches to the Very Troubled Child: Therapeutic Practice Innovations in Residential & Educational Settings, 1989; editor: Severely Disturbed Children and the Parental Alliance, 1992; editor: (with Jerome M. Goldsmith) Milieu Therapy: Significant Issues and Innovative Applications, 1993; editor: The Seevak Family, The Zoken Family; contbr. articles to profl. jours. Mem. vis. com. univ. sch. rels. U. Chgo.; bd. dirs. KAM Isaiah Israel Congregation, 1997—2001; bd. dirs., treas. Chgo. Inst. for Psychoanalysis. Recipient Alumna award, Girls' Latin Sch., Boston, Bettelheim award, Am. Assn. Children's Residential Ctrs., Disting. Svc. award, Radcliffe Assn., 2002; scholar Radcliffe Coll. scholar, 1948—52; Univ. fellow, UCLA, 1966—68. Mem.: Chgo. Inst. for Psychoanalysis, Assn. Children's Residential Ctrs. (past pres.), Harvard Club (bd. dirs. 1986—2001, Chgo.), Radcliffe Club (sec.-treas. 1986—87, pres. 1987—89, Chgo.). Home: 5842 S Stony Island Ave Apt 2G Chicago IL 60637-2033

SANDERS, JAMES ALVIN, retired minister, retired religious studies educator; b. Memphis, Nov. 28, 1927; s. Robert E. and Sue (Black) S.; m. Dora Cargille, June 30, 1951; 1 son, Robin David. BA magna cum laude, Vanderbilt U., 1948, BD with honors, 1951; student, U. Paris, 1950-51; PhD, Hebrew Union Coll., 1955; DLitt, Acadia U., 1973; STD, U. Glasgow, 1975; DHL, Coe Coll., 1988, Hebrew Union Coll., 1988, Hastings Coll., 1996, Calif. Luth. U., 2000. Ordained teacher Presbyn. Ch., 1955; instr. French Vanderbilt U., 1948-49; faculty Colgate Rochester Div. Sch., 1954-65, assoc. prof., 1957-60, Joseph B. Hoyt prof. O.T. interpretation, 1960-65; prof. O.T. Union Theol. Sem., NYC, 1965-70, Auburn prof. Bibl. studies, 1970-77; adj. prof. Columbia, NYC, 1966-77; prof. Bibl. studies Sch. Theology and Grad. Sch., Claremont, Calif., 1977-97, ret., 1997; vis. prof. Union Theol. Seminary and Columbia U., 1997-98. Ann. prof. Jerusalem Sch. of Am. Schs. Oriental Rsch., 1961-62; fellow Ecumenical Isnt., Jerusalem, 1972-73, 85; vis. prof. U. N.Mex., 1992, Southwestern U., 1992, Calif. Luth. U., 1992, 94, Willamette U., 1993, U. So. Ariz., 1993, Jewish Theol. Sem., 2001—; session chair, Internat. Congress for Fifthieth Anniversary of Dead Sea Scrolls, Jerusalem, 1997; mem. internat. O.T. text critical com. United Bible Socs., 1969—; mem. nat. adv. acad. bd. Hebrew Union Coll., 1997—; co-founder, exec. officer Ancient Bibl. Manuscript Ctr. for Preservation and Rsch., 1977-80, pres., 1980-2003, pres. emeritus, 2003—; chmn. bd. Shepherd U., L.A., 2002—, bd. mem. Early Manuscripts Electronic Literacy, 2005-, bd. adv. Mus. of Archeology and the Bible, 2006-,; vis. prof. Yale Divinity Sch., 1998, Jewish Theol. Seminary, 2001; lectr. in field Author: Suffering as Divine Discipline in the Old Testament and Post-Biblical Judaism, 1955, The Old

Testament in the Cross, 1961, The Psalms Scroll of Qumran Cave 11, 1965, The Dead Sea Psalms Scroll, 1967, Near Eastern Archaeology in the Twentieth Century, 1970, Torah and Canon, 1972, 1974, 2d edit., 2005, Identité de la Bible, 1975, God Has a Story Too, 1979, Canon and Community, 1984, From Sacred Story to Sacred Text, 1987, Luke and Scripture, 1993; editor: Paul and the Scriptures of Israel, 1993, Early Christian Interpretation of the Scriptures of Israel, 1993, The Function of Scripture in Early Jewish and Christian Tradition, 1998, The Canon Debate, 2002; contbr. over 280 articles to profl. jours.; mem. editl. bd. Jour. Bibl. Lit., 1970—76, Jour. for Study Judaism, Bibl. Theology Bull., Interpretation, 1973—78, New Rev. Std. Version Bible Com., A Gift of God in Due Season, 1996, The Quest for Context and Meaning, 1997. Trustee Am. Schs. Oriental Research. Fulbright grantee, 1950-51, Lilly Endowment grantee, 1981, NEH grantee, 1980, 91-92; Lefkowitz and Rabinowitz interfaith fellow, 1951-53, Rockefeller fellow, 1953-54, 85, Guggenheim fellow, 1961-62, 72-73, Human Scis. Rsch. fellow, 1989. Mem. Soc. Bibl. Lit. and Exegesis (pres. 1977-78), Phi Beta Kappa, Phi Sigma Iota, Theta Chi Beta. Home: PO Box 593 Claremont CA 91711-0593 Personal E-mail: sandersja@aol.com.

SANDERS, JAMES GRADY, biogeochemist; b. Norfolk, Va., June 10, 1951; s. Allen Buford and Maple Seretha (Myers) S.; m. Dorothea L. Palmer, 2001. BS in Zoology, Duke U., 1973; MS in Marine Scis., U. N.C., 1975, PhD in Marine Scis., 1978. Postdoctoral investigator Woods Hole (Mass.) Oceanog. Instn., 1978-80; vis. scientist Chesapeake Biol. Lab. U. Md., Solomons, 1980-81; asst. curator Estuarine Rsch. Ctr., Md. Acad. Natural Scis., 1981-85, assoc. curator, 1985-89, curator, 1989-99, dir., 1983-99, v.p., 1999; chair dept. ocean, earth and atmospheric scis. Old Dominion U., Norfolk, 1999-2001; dir. Skidaway Inst. Oceanography, Savannah, Ga., 2001—. Cons. EPA Sweden, Stockholm, 1985-90; mem. Md. Sea Grant Adv. Com., College Park, 1983-90, Environ. Commn., Calvert County, Md., 1981-88; mem. environ. biology panel Office R&D EPA, Washington, 1986-95, sci. adv. bd., ecol. processes and effects com., 2003—; regional rep. Coastal Resources Adv. Commn., Md., 1983-86; bd. dirs. Am. Chestnut Land Trust; mem. bd. govs. Consortium for Oceanog. Rsch. and Edn., 1999—, exec. com., 2003-07; mem. adv. bd. SC Sea Grant Program, 2005—; mem. Savannah Innovation Coun., 2005—. Assoc. editor Estuaries, 1996-99; mem. editl. bd. Environ. Toxicology and Chemistry, 2000-03; contbr. more than 70 articles to sci. jours. Grantee NOAA, EPA, NSF. Mem. AAAS, Am. Geophys. Union, Am. Soc. Limnology and Oceanography, Estuarine Rsch. Fedn. (treas. 1993-97), So. Assn. Marine Labs. (pres. 2004-05), Nat. Assn. Marine Labs. (pres.-elect 2006-), Oceanography Soc. Achievements include first identification of relationships between algal growth and chemical transformations of arsenic in aquatic systems. Office: Skidaway Inst Oceanography 10 Ocean Science Cir Savannah GA 31411 Home: 11 Wesley Crossing Savannah GA 31411 Office Phone: 912-598-2400. Business E-Mail: jim.sanders@skio.usg.edu.

SANDERS, JAN W., librarian, Library Association Executive; b. Kansas City, Kans., Sept. 20, 1947; d. Joseph A. and Esther Knierim Wilkes; m. Merritt V. Sanders, Apr. 15, 1972 (div. Apr. 1989); 1 child, Sara Kay. BSEd, N.W. Mo. State U., 1969; MLS, Ind. U., 1970. Libr. S.E. Mo. Libr. System, Cape Girardeau, Mo., 1970-73, Memphis (Tenn.) Shelby County Libr., 1973-78; instr. N.W. Ark. C.C., Harrison, 1978-82; mgr., libr. Springfield (Mo.) Greene County, 1982-87, Pioneer Libr. System, Norman, Okla., 1987-91; dir. libr. City of Bartlesville, Okla., 1991—2001; dir. Spokane Public Libr., 2001—05, Pasadena (Calif.) Public Libr., 2005—. Cons./trainer in field, Bartlesville, 1991—2001. Contbr. articles to profl. jours. Vice-pres. Allied Arts/Humanities Coun., Bartlesville, 1991—2001; bd. dirs. Boy Scouts Am., Bartlesville, 1997—2001, YWCA; active Heart of Town Advocates, Cert. Cities. Recipient Wall of Honor award Office of Intellectual Freedom, ALA, Chgo., 1999. Mem. Okla. Libr. Assn. (various offices, including pres. 1987—2001), Rotary (v.p. Daybreak Club 1999—2001), Bartlesville Leadership, Pub. Libr. Assn. (pres.-elect 2006-07, pres. 2007-) Episcopalian. Office: Pasadena Public Libr 285 E Walnut St Pasadena CA 91101 Office Phone: 626-744-4066. *

SANDERS, JERRY, mayor, former social services executive; b. San Pedro, Calif., July 14, 1950; m. Rana Sampson; children: Jamie, Lisa. AA, Long Beach City Coll., 1970; BA in Pub. Adminstrn., Nat. U., 1988; student, San Diego State U. Cert. P.O.S.T mgmt. Police officer San Diego Police Dept., 1973-93, chief of police, 1993-99; pres. United Way San Diego, 1999—2005; mayor City of San Diego, 2005—. Bd. dirs. The Nat. Conf., San Diego State U. Cmty. Adv. Bd., Children's Initiative, Youth Econ. Enterprise Zones, Am. Red Cross San Diego; mem. cmty. leaders adv. bd. ElderHelp of San Diego. Recipient Headliner of Yr. award San Diego Press Club, 1984, 93, Exceptional Performance citation for SWAT leadership, 1986. Office: Office of Mayor 202 C St 11th Fl San Diego CA 92101 *

SANDERS, JOEL STEVEN, lawyer; b. Mpls., Mar. 25, 1955; s. David M. and Miriam (Gelfand) S.; m. Carol G. Bieri, May 25, 1984; children: Daniel, Elizabeth. BA, Antioch Coll., 1976; JD, U. Calif., Berkeley, 1982. Bar: Calif. 1982, US Dist. Ct. (no. dist.) Calif. 1982, US Dist. Ct. (cen. dist.) Calif. 1984, US Ct. Appeals (9th cir.) 1983. Law clk. to Hon. Procter R. Hug Jr. US Ct. Appeals (9th cir.), 1982-83; atty. antitrust div. US Dept. Justice, San Francisco, 1983-87; assoc. Gibson, Dunn & Crutcher, San Francisco, 1987-91; ptnr. Gibson, Dunn & Crutcher LLP, San Francisco, 1992—, ptnr.-in-charge, Bay Area offices, 1995—2000. Former adj. asst. prof. law Univ. Calif. Hastings Coll. of Law; mem. exec. com. Gibson Dunn & Crutcher. Assoc. editor Calif. Law Rev., 1980-82. Mem. ABA, State Bar of Calif., Bar Assn. of San Francisco, Order of Coif. Office: Gibson Dunn & Crutcher Ste 3100 1 Montgomery St San Francisco CA 94104 Office Phone: 415-393-8200. Office Fax: 415-374-8439. Business E-Mail: jsanders@gibsondunn.com.

SANDERS, JOHN LASSITER, retired academic administrator; b. Four Oaks, NC, June 30, 1927; s. David Hardy and Louie Jane (Lassiter) S.; m. Ann Beal, Aug. 14, 1954; children— Tracy Elizabeth Sanders Justus, Jane Nesbit, William Hardy. AB, U. N.C., 1950, JD, 1954. Bar: NC 1955. Law clk. to judge U.S. Ct. Appeals, 1954-55; pvt. practice Raleigh, NC, 1955-56; mem. faculty Inst. Govt., UNC, Chapel Hill, 1956-94, dir., 1962-73, 79-92, v.p. planning at Univ., 1973-78. Served with USNR, 1945-46. Recipient NC award State of NC, 1996. Democrat. Baptist. Home: 750 Weaver Dairy Rd Apt 102 Chapel Hill NC 27514 Office: U NC CB 3330 Knapp Sanders Bldg Chapel Hill NC 27599-3330 Home Phone: 919-918-3666; Office Phone: 919-843-3287. E-mail: sandersj@email.unc.edu.

SANDERS, JULIUS RAY, music company executive; b. Williamston, Md., Jan. 5, 1956; s. Sanders and Wright. AA, Martin CC, 1980, MS in Bus., 1999. Engineering Of Computer WILLIAMSTON, 1999. Prin., owner Musical And Lyric. Co., Balt., 2000—; promoter sale rep. Ind. Contractor Joint Venture, Balt., 2001—. Gen. ptnr. Am. Majority Trustees Ltd, Balt., 1995—. Singer (producer): (songs) Song Lyric. Home and Office: Musical And Lyric Co Post Office Box 2024 Mailstop Baltimore MD 21203 Home Phone: 410-977-7320; Office Phone: 410-710-2050. Personal E-mail: jrsanders2002@hotmail.com. Business E-Mail: musicalandlyric@netscape.net.

SANDERS, KEITH PAGE, journalism educator; b. Ashland, Ohio, Sept. 25, 1938; s. Merwin Morse and Phyllis Pearl (Snyder) S.; m. Jane Carmel Adams, June 11, 1966; children: Paige Ann, Kevin Scott. BS in Journalism, Bowling Green State U., 1960; MS in Journalism, Ohio U., 1964; PhD in Mass. Comm., U. Iowa, 1967. Sports editor Ashland (Ohio) Times Gazette, 1960-61, Dover (Ohio) Daily Reporter, 1961-62; instr. journalism Bowling Green (Ohio) State U., 1963-64, U. Iowa, Iowa City, 1965-67; prof. journalism U. Mo., Columbia, 1967—2001, assoc. dean grad. studies Sch. Journalism, 1986-87, 90-91, O.O. McIntyre disting. prof., 1993, prof. emeritus, 2002—. Cons. in field. Contbr. articles to profl. jours. including Journalism Quar., Mass Media Rev., Jour. Broadcasting, Electronic Jour. of Comm.; assoc. editor Mass Comm. Rev., 1981-92, mem. editl. bd., 1972-98; mem. editl. bd. Journalism Monographs, 1973-80, Mass Comm. and Soc., 1998-2006. Recipient Award for Outstanding Achievement U. Mo. Alumni Assn., 1986; Joyce Swan Disting. Faculty award U. Mo., 1973; inducted into Columbia Bowling Hall of Fame, 1999. Mem.: Soc. Profl. Journalists, Assn. for Edn. in Journalism/Mass Comm. (Trayes Prof. of Yr. 1987), Internat. Soc. for Sci. Study of Subjectivity (treas. 1990—95), Mo. State-US Bowling Congress (2d v.p. 2006—), Mo. State Bowling Assn. (bd. dirs. 2000—06, Dir. of Yr. 2005), Omicron Delta Kappa, Kappa Tau Alpha (exec. dir. 1991—). Avocations: bowling, golf, fishing. Home: 6551 N Creasy Springs Rd Columbia MO 65202-8093 Office: Univ of Missouri Sch Journalism Columbia MO 65211-1200

SANDERS, LINDA E., psychologist, educator; d. James E. and Madonna Elaine Hoelscher; m. Jim R. Sanders, June 3, 1973; 1 child, Jason R. BA in English and Journalism, U. Ark., 1976; MEd, Northeastern State U., Tahlequah, Okla., 1988; PhD, U. Okla., 2005. Nat. cert. sch. psychologist Nat. Sch. Psychology Certification Bd., 2005. Tchr. Jenks Pub. Schs., Jenks, Okla., 1985—96, psychologist, 1996—; adj. prof. psychology, asst. prof. Northeastern State U., Broken Arrow, Okla., 2003—. Ednl. cons. and reviewer Holt, Rinehart & Winston Pub. Co., Austin, Tex., 1993—98. Team co-leader home bldg. Habitat for Humanity, Nuevo Progreso, Mexico, 1994—95; adult vol. Day Ctr. for the Homeless, Tulsa, Okla., 1993; team leader Asbury United Meth. Ch., Tulsa, 1993—96. Recipient Pioneer in Edn. award, Nat. Bd. for Profl. Tchg. Standards, 1994, Mortar Bd., U. Ark., 1974. Mem.: APA, ASCD, NASP (regional leader 1997—99, Exemplary Mental Health Programs recipient 1997-1998), Okla. Ednl. Studies Assn., Coun. for Exceptional Children, Okla. Sch. Psychol. Assn. (pres. elect 1997—98, state pres. 1998—99, Past Pres. award 1999). Methodist. Avocations: reading, gardening, writing, travel. Home Phone: 918-299-1260; Office Phone: 918-299-4415 ext. 5507.

SANDERS, MARION YVONNE, retired geriatrics nurse; b. St. Petersburg, Fla., Dec. 4, 1936; d. Ira Laurey and Maude Mae (Cherry) Sanders; children: Dwayne Irwin, Princess Charrie. BS, Fla. A&M U., 1959; MS, Nova U., Ft. Lauderdale, Fla., 1992. RN Fla. Staff nurse Lantana (Fla.) TB Hosp., 1960-61, Mercy Hosp., St. Petersburg, 1961; gen. duty nurse VA, Tuskegee, Ala., 1961-62; staff nurse John Andrews Hosp., Tuskegee, 1962-63; gen. duty staff nurse Brewster Meth. Hosp., Jacksonville, Fla., 1963-65, Duval Med. Ctr., Jacksonville, 1965-66; pvt. duty nurse Dist. 2 Registry, Jacksonville, 1966-70; supr. Eartha White Nursing Home, Jacksonville, 1970; staff nurse Bapt. Hosp., Jacksonville, 1971-73, City-County Methadone Clinic, Jacksonville, 1976-78; pvt. duty nurse Home Nursing, Jacksonville, Fla., 1982-86, pvt. duty geriatric nursing and gerontology specialist, 1995—2001, Sr. Companion Svc. Corp., 1997-98; ret., 2001. Mem. Ideas for Am.'s Future, 1997, 1998, NAACP, 1997—98; vol. shelter mgr. ARC, Miami, Fla., 1992—94; vol. cmty. activist, 1994; respite and relief sr. companion vol. Urban Jacksonville Cathedral Found., 1996—98, 2005—07; vol. Jacksonville Cmty. Rels. Bd., 1996, Jacksonville Inc. Cathedral Found., 1997—2006, respite, 2007; sr. companion Svc. Corp., 1997—98, 1999, 2005, 2006; mem. Brewseter's and Cmty. Nurses Alumni, 1998—2000, 2001—02; vol. cmty. svcs., elem. grades tutor, polit. campaigns, tchr. health edn.; vol. Rep. Nat. Com., 1997—2000, 2001—02, 2005, Rep. Senatorial Com., 1999, Rep. Com. Fla., 1997—98, Northside Rep. Club, 1997, 1998, 1999; active St. Stephen AME Ch., Jacksonville, tch. Bible studies for youth, advocate for poor, homeless and prisoners; mem. Prison Fellowship Ministries, 2007. Recipient cert. of Recognition, Rep. Party, Fla. and Washington, 1990, Rep. Congl. Orgn., 1988, 1990, 1999. Mem.: ANA (mem. polit. actions com.), Nova Southeastern U. Alumni Assn., Fla. A&M U. Alumni Assn., Fla. Sheriff's Assn., Fla. Nurses Assn., Women's Missionary Soc. (life). Republican. Methodist. Avocation: reading. Home: 4832 N Main St Apt 14 Jacksonville FL 32206-1458

SANDERS, MARLENE, news correspondent, journalism educator; b. Cleve., Jan. 10, 1931; d. Mac and Evelyn (Menitoff) Sanders; m. Jerome Toobin, May 27, 1958 (dec. Jan. 1984); children: Jeff, Mark. Student, Ohio State U., 1948—49. Writer, prodr. Sta. WNEW-TV, NYC, 1955-60, P.M. program Westinghouse Broadcasting Co., NYC, 1961-62; asst. dir. news and pub. affairs Sta. WNEW, NYC, 1962-64; anchor, news program ABC News, NYC, 1964-68, corr., 1968-72, documentary prodr., writer, anchor, 1972-76, v.p., dir. TV documentaries, 1976-78; corr. CBS News, NYC, 1978-87; host Currents Sta. WNET-TV, NYC, 1987-88; host Met. Week in Rev., 1988-90; host Thirteen Live Sta. WNET-TV, 1990-91; prof. dept. journalism NYU, NYC, 1991-93, adj. prof. journalism, 1996—; adj. prof. journalism, adminstr. Columbia U. Grad. Sch. Journalism, NYC, 1994-95. Profl.-in-residence Freedom Forum Media Studies Ctr., 1997-2000; freelance broadcaster, narrator; bd. dirs. womensenews.org.; chair RSVP, Inc., 1997-. Co-author: Waiting for Prime Time: The Women of Television News, 1988. Mem. NYC Commn. on Women's Issues, 2003—. Recipient award NY State Broadcasters Assn., 1976, award Nat. Press Club, 1976, Emmy awards, 1980, 81, others. Mem. Am. Women in Radio and TV (Woman of Yr. award 1975, Silver Satellite award 1977), Women in Comm. (past pres.), Coun. Fgn. Rels. Office Phone: 212-877-1250. Personal E-mail: sanders110@aol.com.

SANDERS, PHYLLIS MAY, musician; b. Cleve., Aug. 7, 1922; d. Charles Lester and Marjorie (Roof) Flick; m. Roger Fred Sanders, Aug. 3, 1946 (div. 1986); children: William Paul, Richard Allen, Bruce Edward, Patricia Ann. MusB in Edn., Drake U., Des Moines, 1944. Music tchr. Jefferson (Iowa) jr. high schs., 1944-45, Des Moines jr. high schs., 1945-46; organist, choir dir. Columbia U. Meth. Ch., Columbia Station, Ohio, 1963-83; organist Magyar United Ch. of Christ, Elyria, Ohio, 1984—. Dir. Lorain County Community Messiah Chorus, Elyria, 1981, 88-91; dir., founder Choraliers, Columbia Station, 1975-80, Olmsted Singers, Olmsted Falls, Ohio, 1975-80. Mem. Southwest Chorus, Berea, Ohio, 1988-90, Berea Sr. Ctr. Chorus, 1978—; pres. Columbia Rep. Women, Columbia Station; mem. Columbia Mothersingers, Cleve. Messiah Chorus, 1991—. Mem. Sigma Alpha Iota, Beta Gamma Kappa. Republican. Mem. Christian Ch. (Disciples Of Christ). Avocations: ceramics, needlecrafts. Home: 6119 West River Rd S Elyria OH 44035-5431

SANDERS, RICHARD BROWNING, state supreme court justice; b. Tacoma; 1 child: Laura. BA, U. Wash., 1966, JD, 1969. Assoc. Murray, Scott, McGavick & Graves, Tacoma, Wash., 1969, Caplinger & Munn, Seattle, 1971; hearing examiner State Wash., Olympia, 1970; pvt. practice Wash., 1971-95; justice Wash. Supreme Ct., Olympia, 1995—. Adj. prof. U. Wash. Sch. Law; lectr. in field. Contbr. articles to profl. jours. Office: Supreme Court of Washington Temple of Justice PO Box 40929 Olympia WA 98504-0929 Fax: (360) 357-2092. E-mail: j_r.sanders@courts.wa.gov. *

SANDERS, RICHARD HENRY, lawyer; b. Chgo., Apr. 10, 1944; s. Walter J. and Marian (Snyder) Sikorski; m. Sharon A. Marciniak, July 8, 1967 (dec.); child, Douglas Bennett; m. Susan Gerhardt Nielsen, Feb. 19, 2005. BS, Loyola U., Chgo., 1967; JD, Northwestern U., 1969. Bar: Ill. 1969, Ind. 1990, DC 1990, US Dist. Ct. (no. dist.) Ill. 1970, US Dist. Ct. (no. and so. dists.) Ind. 1990, US Ct. Appeals (7th cir.) 1990, US Supreme Ct. 1990. Assoc. Vedder, Price, Kaufman & Kammholz, Chgo., 1969-76, ptnr., 1976—2003, mem. exec. com., 1991-93, health law area leader, 1989—95, 2001—04, 2006—, shareholder, 2003—, chmn. tech. com., 2003—. Adj. prof. Sch. of Law Northwestern U., 1994—; mem. svc. dispute resolver panel Am. Health Lawyers Assn. Alt. Dispute Resolution, 2000—. Bd. trustees Chgo. Acad. for the Arts, 2006—; bd. dirs. Smart Love Parenting Ctr., 2004—, Breath of Life Found., 2007—. Fellow Am. Bar Found.; mem. ABA, Ill. Bar Assn. (chmn. health sect. 1989-90), Chgo. Bar Assn., Ind. Bar Assn., DC Bar Assn., Am. Health Lawyers Assn., Ill. Assn. Health Attys., Univ. Club, Evanston Golf Club (Skokie). Avocations: skiing, diving, photography, golf. Office: Vedder Price Kaufman & Kammholz 222 N La Salle St Ste 2600 Chicago IL 60601-1100 Office Phone: 312-609-7644. Business E-Mail: rsanders@vedderprice.com.

SANDERS, RICHARD KINARD, actor; b. Harrisburg, Pa., Aug. 23, 1940; s. Henry Irvine and Thelma S. BFA, Carnegie Inst. Tech., 1962; postgrad. (Fulbright scholar), London Acad. Music and Dramatic Art, 1962-63. Pres. Blood Star, Inc. Mem. various acting cos., Front St., Memphis, Champlain Shakespeare Festival, Vt., Center Stage, Balt., N.Y. Shakespeare Festival, N.Y.C., Chelsea Theater Center, N.Y.C., Mark Taper Forum, Los Angeles, Arena Stage, Washington; appeared on: (Broadway) Raisin; (TV series) Les Nessman on WKRP in Cincinnati and The New WKRP in Cincinnati, Paul Sycamore in You Can't Take It With You, Mr. Beanley in Spenser; writer of many episodes of WKRP and other situation comedies; writer NBC movie Max and Sam; numerous TV and film appearances. Vol. Peace Corps, Northeastern Brazil, 1966-69. Recipient Buckeye Newshawk award, 1974-79, Silver Sow award, 1979 Mem. Writers Guild Am., Screen Actors Guild, AFTRA, Actors Equity Assn. Office: PO Box 1644 Woodinville WA 98072-1644

SANDERS, RICHARD L., academic administrator; b. Clintonville, Wis., Jan. 2, 1937; s. Claude H. and Lucille B. (Wedde) S.; m. Janice Miles, Aug. 30, 1958; children: Scott, Jennifer, Todd, Zachary, Nicolle. BS, U. Wis., Eau Claire, 1959; MS, U. Wis., Milw., 1966; EdD, Marquette U., 1971. Tchr. music Milw. Pub. Schs., 1959-62, rsch. assoc., 1966-67; tchr. music West Allis (Wis.) Pub. Schs., 1962-66; registrar, asst. prof. Lakeland Coll., Sheboygan, Wis., 1967-71; dean Lakewood CC, St. Paul, 1971-81; pres. Lincoln Trail Coll., Robinson, Ill., 1981-84, Mattatuck CC, Waterbury, Conn., 1984-92, Naugatuck Valley CC, Waterbury, Conn., 1992—; sec. Naugatuck Valley CC Founds., Inc., Waterbury. Mem. United Way Bd. of Greater Waterbury. Disting. Svc. award Charter Oak State U., 1993. Mem. Am. Assn. CC (mem. rsch. coun.), Conn. Coun. Higher Edn., New Eng.Cmty.-Tech. Coun. (editor The Collegian 1992-94), Alliance CC Innovation, Am. Assn. Higher Edn., Am. Assn. Univ. adminstrs., Am. Coun. Edn., CC Humanities Assn., Nat. Coun. Occupl. Edn., Nat. Coun. Instrl. Adminstrs., New Eng. Assn. Schs. and Colls., New Eng. Coll. Coun., Conn. Cmty.-Tech. Coll. Coun. Pres., Conn. Assn. Latin Am. in Higher Edn., Greater Danbury C. of C., Greater Valley C. of C., Cotley Regional C. of C. (bd. mem.), Conn. Cmty. Found., Waterbury Exec. Educators Roundtable, Waterbury Hosp. Health Network, Inc., N.W. Region Workforce Investment Bd., Phi Delta Kappa (cert. outstanding membership 1990). Avocations: music, tennis, public speaking. Office: Naugatuck Valley CC 750 Chase Pkwy Waterbury CT 06708-3011 Office Fax: 203-596-8709. Business E-Mail: rsanders@nvcc.commnet.edu.

SANDERS, ROBERT HAWVER, systems administrator; b. Richlands, Va., Feb. 23, 1967; s. Robert C. and Lula E. Sanders; m. Catherine Ann Finegan; children: Ian Patrick, Erin Grace. Student, East Tenn. State U., Johnson City, 1986—87; cert. in computer scis., PVCC, Charlottesville, Va., 2004. Pharmacy technician U. Va. Med. Ctr., Charlottesville, 1997—2001, info. sys. technician, 2001—, info. tech. trainer. Vol. Santa MCCCC, U. Va., 2006—07. Mem.: VSHP, ASHP. Republican. Unitarian. Avocations: weightlifting, cooking, reading, movies, team sports. Office: U Va Med Ctr Charlottesville VA 22908 Office Phone: 434-982-3848.

SANDERS, ROBIN RENEE, former ambassador; b. Hampton, Va., July 5; d. Robert M. and Geneva (Machoney) Sanders. B.A., Hampton Inst.; M.A., Ohio U., 1979, M.S., 1979. Broadcast lic. FCC 3d class. Editoral assts. Essence Mag., N.Y.C., 1974-76, Fgn. Broadcast Info. Service, Washington, 1976-77; intern account exec. Burson-Marsteller Co., N.Y.C., 1977-78; pub. relations assoc. Seventeen mag., N.Y.C., 1979-80; polit. and counselor officer Am. embassy, Dominican Republic, 1980-83, consular officer Am. consulate, Oporto, Portugal, 1983-86, dep. polit. sect. chief Am. Embassy Khartoum, Sudan, 1986-88; spl. asst. AF Bur., 1989; dir. for pub. diplomacy for Africa, State Dept.; dir. for Africa, Nat. Security Coun. at the White House, 1988-89, 97-99; spl. asst. for L.Am., Africa and internat. crime for the under sec. for polit. affairs Dept. State, Washington; chief of staff, sr. fgn. policy Mem. Ho. Internat. Rels. Com.; U.S. amb. to Republic of Congo, 2002-2005; internat. affairs adv. Indsl. Coll. Armed Forces; cons. Profl. Women's Seminar, 1983, 84; speaker U. Oporto, 1983; researcher dept. internat. relations Ohio U., 1978; TV producer dept. gerontology Hampton Inst., 1976-77. Recipient 1st place award for painting Two Faces, Scholastic Art Bd., 1981, Dept of State Meritorious award, 1989, three State Dept. Superior Honor awards, three State Dept. Meritorious Honor awards; journalism scholar Syracuse U, 1970. Dir. Nat. Security Coun., 1989; political Econ. Officer Namibia, 1989. Mem. Women in Communications, Pub. Relations Soc. Am., Am. Fgn. Service Assn., Nat. Council Negro Women, Black Caucus, Mus. African Art, Coun. on Fgn. Rels., D.C. C. of C.; Alpha Kappa Alpha, Alpha Kappa Mu. Consular Corps (Oporto); Diplomatic (Santo Domingo), Thursday Luncheon Group, Capital Press (Washington). Office: Indsl Coll Armed Forces Ft McNair 408 4th Ave Washington DC 20319 *

SANDERS, SHANNON KAY, professional society administrator; b. Okla. d. Kevin Antony Sanders and Lisa Kay W; m. Brian C Ensley. Degree in Speech Comm., Auburn, Ala., 1997. Regional devel. dir. SPLC, Montgomery, Ala., 2001—. Ex officio Montgomery AIDS Outreach, 2001. Scholar NSFRE, NSFRE/AFP, 1999. Mem.: Assn. Fundraising Profls. Independent. Avocations: reading, travel, gardening, swimming. Business E-Mail: ssanders@splcenter.org.

SANDERS, SUMMER, Olympic athlete, news correspondent, newscaster; b. Oct. 13, 1972; d. Bob and Barbara Sanders; m. Mark Henderson, July 1997. Student, Stanford U. Olympic swimmer, Barcelona, 1992; ret. from profl. swimming, 1993; returned but did not qualify for Olympics, 1995—96; hostess, Sandblast MTV, 1994—95; host game show for children Figure It Out Nickelodeon, 1997—99; broadcaster WNBA Lifetime TV, 1997—98; co-host NBA Inside Stuff, 1997—; host Beg, Borrow or Deal ESPN 2, 2002—. Co-author (with Melinda Marshall): Champions are Raised, Not Born: How my Parents made me a Success, 1999. Achievements include gold medal 200-meter butterfly, 400-meter medley relay preliminaries; silver medal, 200-meter individual medley and bronze medal 400-meter individual medley, 1992 Olympic Games, Barcelona, Spain. Office: NBA Inside Stuff care NBA Entertainment Inc 450 Harmon Meadow Blvd Secaucus NJ 07094-3618

SANDERS, TRAVIS ALLEN, health facility administrator, director; b. Mora, Minn., Feb. 20, 1979; s. Allen Bert Sanders, Jr. and Gladys Elaine Sanders. BA in Athletic Tng., Bethel Coll., St. Paul, Minn., 2001; MA in Exercise Physiology, Coll. St. Scholastica, Duluth, Minn., 2002. Registered athletic trainer Minn. State Bd. Med. Practice, 2005; cert. Nat. Athletic Trainer's Assn., 2002, exercise physiologist Am. Soc. Exercise Physiologists, 2002. Specialist gerontol. fitness Jones-Harrison Residence, Mpls., 2002—05, coord. gerontol. arthritis, 2005—06; dir. wellness ctr. Christian Cmty. Homes and Svcs., Hudson, Wis., 2006—. Dir. strength and conditioning Northstar Lacrosse Co., Hopkins, Minn., 2004—06. Mem.: Am. Soc. Exercise Physiologists, Minn. Athletic Trainers Assn., Nat. Athletic Trainers Assn., Minn. Lakers Lacrosse Club (mem. exec. bd. 2006—07). Home: 5120 44th St West Edina MN 55436 Office: Christian Cmty Homes and Svcs 1320 Wisconsin St Hudson WI 54016 Home Phone: 651-235-

6670; Office Phone: 715-386-4520, Personal E-mail: tsanders3@hotmail.com. Business E-Mail: travis.sanders@cchhudson.org.

SANDERS, VANESSA, journalist, writer; b. Cumming, Ga., Jan. 10, 1976; d. John Brady and Susie Ashmore; m. John Sanders, June 7, 1991; 1 child, Bethany Rain. BS in Holistic Health, RBA, Ga., 2003. Freelance contbr. Associated Content, 2006—; staff contbr. Rainbow Agenda, Worldwide, Ga., 2007—. Cons. in field. Author: (songs) 20/20 Visions, (poetry) The Artist's Hand (Internat. Bronze award, 2000). Vol. World Cant Wait, Dahlonega, Ga., 2007—07; founder organizer Demand Action, Dahlonega, Ga., 2006—07. Mem.: ACLU (local focalizer 2006—07), Answer Coalition (organizer transp. 2007, participant march on Pentagon 2007). Peace Party. Unitarian Universalist. Home Phone: 706-864-0132.

SANDERS, WALLACE WOLFRED, JR., civil engineer; b. Louisville, June 24, 1933; s. Wallace Wolfred and Mary Jane (Brownfield) S.; m. Julia B. Howard, June 9, 1956; children— Linda, David. B.C.E., U. Louisville, 1955; MS, U. Ill., Urbana, 1957, PhD, 1960; M.Engring., U. Louisville, 1973. Research asst., then research assoc. U. Ill., 1955-60, asst. prof., 1960-64; mem. faculty Iowa State U., Ames, 1964-98, prof. civil engring., 1970-98, assoc. dir. engring. research, 1980-91, assoc. dean research, 1988-91, interim asst. vice provost for research and advanced studies, 1991-92. Cons. to govt. and industry. Contbr. numerous papers to profl. jours. Bd. dirs. Northcrest Cmty., Ames, 1976-82, 92-98, pres., 1987-91, 96-2003; bd. dirs. Am. Bapt. Homes of the Midwest, Mpls., 1998—. Mem. ASCE (R.C. Reese research prize 1978), Am. Welding Soc. (Adams Meml. membership award 1971), Am. Ry. Engring. Assn., Am. Soc. Engring. Edn. Baptist. Home and Office: 1924 Northcrest Cir Ames IA 50010-5113 Home Phone: 515-232-7184. Business E-Mail: wsanders@iastate.edu.

SANDERS, WALTER JEREMIAH, III, (JERRY SANDERS), retired computer company executive; b. Chgo., Sept. 12, 1936; m. Tawny Sanders; 4 children. BSEE, U. Ill., Champaign-Urbana, 1958. Design engr. Douglas Aircraft Co., 1958—59; sales engr. Motorola Semiconductor, 1959—61; sales mgr. to group dir. mktg. Semiconductor divsn. Fairchild Camera and Instrument Corp., 1961—69; co-founder Advanced Micro Devices, Inc., Sunnyvale, Calif., 1969, CEO, 1969—2002, chmn., 1969—2004. Recipient Robert N. Noyce award, Semiconductor Industry Assn., 1991, Medal of Achievement, Am. Electronics Assn., 2001. Mem.: NAE. *

SANDERS, WILLIAM EUGENE, marketing executive; b. Asheboro, NC, Nov. 16, 1933; s. Arthur Ira and Picola (Loftin) S.; m. Velna Elizabeth Sumner, June 8, 1957; children: William Eugene Jr., George Herbert Sumner. AB in Polit. Sci., U. N.C., 1956, postgrad. in Law, 1956-57. Marketing rep. Encyclopaedia Britannica, Greensboro, NC, 1957-60, Am. Pubs., Chgo., 1960-66; pres. S&W Distbrs., Inc., Asheboro, NC, 1966—. Little league coach Civitans, Greensboro, 1967—68. With USAR, 1957—63. Named Hon. Amb. Dept. of Labor, Ky., 1976, Ky. Col., 1976, Hon. Mem. La. Lt. Gov. Staff, 1984; recipient Cert. Appreciation Jefferson Davis Parish Libr., Jennings, La., 1986, Top Sales award Am. Media. Corp., 1996, Marshall Cavendish Top Prodn. award, 1990-91, Mktg. award Am. Media, 1995, Gold Cir. award Penworthy Books, 1999, 2000, 01, Marshall Cavendish quota Prodn. award, 1999, 2000, Rosen Prodn. award, 2002. Mem.: Gen. Alumni Assn. (co-chmn. Greensboro chpt. 1979—80, Rosen Prodn. award 2001—02, 2006), State Libr. Assn. S.C., State Libr. Assn. N.C., State Libr. Assn. La., State Libr. Assn. W.Va., State Libr. Assn. Va. Democrat. Methodist. Office: S&W Distbrs Inc 312 Sunset Ave Ste 4 Asheboro NC 27203 Office Phone: 336-633-3900. Personal E-mail: sanders6407@aol.com.

SANDERS, W(ILLIAM) EUGENE, JR., retired internist; b. Frederick, Md., June 25, 1934; s. W(illiam) Eugene and E. Gertrude (Wilburn) Sanders; m. Christine Culp, Feb. 22, 1974. AB, Cornell U., 1956, MD, 1960. Diplomate Am. Bd. Internal Medicine. Intern Johns Hopkins Hosp., Balt., 1960-61, resident, 1961-62; instr. medicine Emory U. Sch. Medicine, Atlanta, 1962-64; chief med. resident, instr. U. Fla. Coll. Medicine, Gainesville, 1964-65, asst. prof. medicine and microbiology, 1965-69, assoc. prof., 1969-72; prof., chmn. dept. med. microbiology, prof. medicine Creighton U. Sch. Medicine, Omaha, 1972-95, prof. emeritus, 1995—. Cons-in-rsch. Fla. Dept. Health and Rehab. Svcs., 1966—. Editor: Am. Jour. Epidemiology, 1974—95; contbr. scientific papers to profl. jours. Med. officer USPHS, 1962—64. Recipient Rsch. Career Devel. award, NIH, 1968—72; John and Mary R. Markle scholar in acad. medicine, 1968—73. Mem.: N.Y. Acad. Scis., Thoracic Soc., Am. Lung Assn., Soc. Epidemiol. Rsch., Infectious Diseases Soc. Am., Am. Soc. Microbiology, Sigma Xi, Phi Beta Kappa, Phi Kappa Phi. Achievements include patents for enocin antibiotic and RBE limonene and perrilyl alcohol. Home: 1901 Pennsylvania Ave Englewood FL 34224-5530 E-mail: ecsanders@gls3c.com. *Each day provides more challenges and more opportunities than the preceding. No individual can possibly cope with each of these in any given day. Success depends upon establishing priorities and maintaining them. Fight only those battles and pursue with fervor only those opportunities that improve both one's self and one's fellow man.*

SANDERS, WILLIAM JOHN, research scientist; b. Detroit, July 10, 1940; s. John William and Charlotte Barbara (Linsday) Steele; m. Gary Roberts, Sept. 12, 1961; children: Scott David, Susan Deborah. BS, U. Mich., 1962; MSEE, U. Calif., Berkeley, 1964. Sr. rsch. scientist Stanford (Calif.) U., 1967-97; pres. Sanders Data Systems, 1991—. Pres. Computers in Cardiology, 1990-93, dir., 2000—, dir. info. svcs., 2001—. Inventor cardiac probe; contbr. articles to profl. jours. Mem. IEEE Computer Soc. Avocation: bicycling. Office: Sanders Data Sys 3980 Bibbits Dr Palo Alto CA 94303-4531 Business E-Mail: bill@sandersdata.com.

SANDERSON, ARTHUR CLARK, engineering educator; b. Providence, Oct. 23, 1946; s. Robert Leroy and Julia Ayer (Oldham) S.; m. Susan Rita Walsh, Aug. 14, 1971; children: Angeline Mirada, Andrew McWain. BS, Brown U., 1968; MS, Carnegie-Mellon U., 1970, PhD, 1972. Rsch. engr. Westinghouse Electric Corp., Pitts., 1968-70; vis. rsch. scientist Delft (The Netherlands) U. Tech., 1972-73; prof. Carnegie-Mellon U., Pitts., 1973-87, co-dir. robotics inst., 1981-87; rsch. dir. Philips Rsch. Labs., Briarcliff Manor, NY, 1985-87; prof., dept. chmn. Rensselaer Poly. Inst., Troy, NY, 1987—; divsn. dir. elec. & comm. systems NSF, Arlington, Va., 1998-2000; v.p. rsch. Rensselaer Poly. Inst., 2000—. Vis. prof. Univ. Iberoamericana, Mexico City, 1975-77, Inst. Info. Sci. & Elecs., U. Tsukuba, Japan, 1996-97. Contbr. 3 books, over 250 articles to profl. jours. Fellow AAAS, IEEE (pres. robotics and automation soc. 1989, 90); mem. AIAA (mem. space automation and robotics tech. com.), Am. Assn. Artificial Intelligence, Soc. Mfg. Engrs. Office: Rensselaer Poly Inst 110 8th St Troy NY 12180-3522 Home: 18 Barberry Coast Rd Newmarket NH 03857 E-mail: sandea@rpi.edu.

SANDERSON, DAVID R., physician; b. South Bend, Ind., Dec. 26, 1933; s. Robert Burns and Alpha (Rodenberger) S.; divorced, 1978; children: David, Kathryn, Robert, Lisa; m. Evelyn Louise Klunder, Sept. 20, 1980. BA, Northwestern U., 1955, MD, 1958. Cons. in medicine Mayo Clinic, Rochester, Minn., 1965—87, chmn. dept. thoracic disease, 1977—87, cons. in medicine Scottsdale, Ariz., 1987—2000, chmn. dept. internal medicine, 1988—96, vice chmn. bd. govs., 1987—94. Assoc. dir. Mayo Lung Project, Nat. Cancer Inst., Rochester. Contbr. articles to profl. jours. Recipient Noble award Mayo Found., Rochester, Chevalier Jackson award Am. Bronchoesophagologic Assn., 1990. Fellow ACP, Am. Coll. Chest Physicians (gov. for Minn. 1981-87); mem. Am. Bronchoesophagologic Assn. (pres. 1986-87), World Assn. for Bronchology, Internat. Bronchoesophagologic Soc., Internat. Assn. Study of Lung Cancer, AMA, Sigma Xi, Sigma Chi (Significant Sig award 1989). Presbyterian. Home: 10676 E Bella Vista Dr Scottsdale AZ 85258-6086 Office: Mayo Clinic Scottsdale 13400 E Shea Blvd Scottsdale AZ 85259-5499 Personal E-mail: dsanderson958@cox.net.

SANDERSON, DEVON LEE, elementary school educator; b. St Elizabeth, Jamaica; s. George Sanderson and Josephine M. Scarlett-Vaccianna; m. Pauline Vinette Harvey. Cert., Bethlehem Moravian Coll. Cert. nursing asst., 2005. Tchr. Goshen and Belle Plain Basic Schools, Clarendon, Jamaica, 1988—91, Ashton All Age Sch., Westmoreland, Jamaica, 1994—2000, Eber Preparatory and Kindergarten Sch., Jamaica, 2001—03; tchr. Caribbean exam. coun. Bethel Town All Age Evening Inst., 2002—04. Freelance writer-elect Inst. Children's Lit., Conn. Former mem. Montego Bay Writer's Club; former writer, contr. Western Mirror Newspaper; student elect Long Ridge Writers Group, West Redding, Conn. Recipient 1st Place Esteem award, Poetry Jamaica, 2003, Merit award cert. for poetry writing, World of Poetry, 1990. Avocations: reading, gardening, writing, singing. Home: 105 Memorial Dr New Castle DE 19720

SANDERSON, DOUGLAS JAY, lawyer; b. Boston, Apr. 21, 1953; s. Warren and Edith S. Sanderson; m. Audrey S. Goldstein, June 6, 1982; children: Scott M.G., Phoebe H.G. BA, Trinity Coll., Hartford, Conn., 1974; JD, George Washington U., 1977. Bar: Va. 1977, D.C. 1978, U.S. Dist. Ct. (ea. dist.) Va. 1978, U.S. Ct. Appeals (4th cir.) 1978. Assoc. Bettius, Rosenberger & Carter, P.C., Fairfax, Va., 1977-82; ptnr. Bettius & Sanderson, P.C. and predecessor firms, Fairfax, 1982-86; prin. Miles & Stockbridge P.C., Fairfax, 1986-95; br. head Miles & Stockbridge, Fairfax, 1989-91; co-owner McCandlish & Lillard, P.C., Fairfax, 1995—. Trustee Cambridge Ctr. Behavioral Studies, Cambridge, 1981-90. Editor: Consumer Protection Reporting Svc., 1976-77. Bd. dirs. Legal Svcs. No. Va., Inc., 1991-97, pres., 1993-95; vol. counsel Arts Coun. of Fairfax County, Inc., 1991--. Mem. ABA, Va. Bar Assn., Fairfax Bar Assn., Ctrl. Fairfax C. of C. (bd. dirs. 1988-93). Avocations: sports, reading. Office: McCandlish & Lillard 11350 Random Hills Rd Ste 500 Fairfax VA 22030-6044 Office Phone: 703-273-2288.

SANDERSON, GEOFF, professional hockey player; b. Hay River, N.W.T., Can., Feb. 1, 1972; m. Ellen Sanderson; children: Benjamin, Jake. Left wing Hartford Whalers, Hartford, 1990—97, Carolina Hurricanes, 1997—98, Vancouver Canucks, 1998, 2004, Buffalo Sabres, 1998—2000, Columbus Blue Jackets, 2000—04, 2005, Phoenix Coyotes, 2005—06, Phila. Flyers, 2006—. Player NHL All-Star Game, 1994, 97. Office: Phila Flyers 3601 S Broad St Philadelphia PA 19148

SANDERSON, JAMES RICHARD, retired naval officer, financial consultant; b. Selma, Calif., Dec. 27, 1925; s. Charles Maxwell and Edith (Wente) S.; m. Betty Lee Bradley, Sept. 19, 1947. Student, U. Calif.-Berkeley, 1943-44, U. Wash., 1944, U. Willamette, 1944-45; grad., USNR Midshipman Sch. at Columbia U., 1945, Nat. War Coll., 1966; student, Gen. Line Sch., Monterey, Calif., 1953, Sr. Officers Ship Material Mgmt. Course, Idaho Falls, Idaho, 1979; BA in Internat. Affairs, George Washington U., 1968. Served as enlisted man U.S. Naval Res., 1943-45; commd. ensign USN, 1946, advanced through grades to vice adm., 1980; gunnery officer U.S.S. Mansfield, 1946-47, U.S.S. Bausell, 1947-48; flight trainee Naval Air Sta., Pensacola, Fla., 1949, Corpus Christi, Tex., 1950; served in Attack Squadron 195, Alameda, Calif., 1950-52; flight instr. Naval Air Sta., Pensacola, 1953-55; served in Attack Squadron 16, 1955-57; air ops. officer on staff Comdr. Carrier Div. Four, U.S.S. Forrestal, 1957-60; ops. officer Attack Squadron 43, Naval Air Sta., Oceana, Va., 1960-62; comdg. officer Attack Squadron 76, 1962-63; comdr. Attack Carrier Air Wing Three in U.S.S. Saratoga, 1963-65; spl. support plans officer, Pacific Area Strategic Plans and Policy Div., Office of Chief of Naval Ops., Washington, 1966-67; exec. asst. and sr. aide to dep. chief. naval ops., 1967-69; comdg. officer U.S.S. Ranier, 1969-70; dep. chief of staff for ops. and plans U.S. Sixth Fleet, 1970-71; comdg. officer U.S.S. Saratoga, 1971-73; dep. comdr. Naval Striking and Support Forces, So. Europe, Naples, Italy, 1973-76; vice dir. ops. Joint Chiefs of Staff, Washington, 1976-77; asst. dep. chief naval ops. for plans, policy and ops., 1977-79; comdr. Task Force Sixty, U.S. 6th Fleet, 1979-80, Carrier Group Two, 1979-80, Battle Force Sixth Fleet, 1979-80, Carrier Striking Force So. Region, 1979-80; dep. and chief staff, comdr. in chief Atlantic/U.S. Atlantic Fleet, Norfolk, Va., 1980-83; ret., 1983; exec. cons. Exec. Planning & Investment Co., Inc., Virginia Beach, Va., 1983-85; sr. v.p. for corp. ops. Computer Dynamics, Inc., 1984-86; asst. to pres. Eastern Computers, Inc., 1986—94; cons., prin. Exec. Planning and Investment Co., Inc., 1986-94; sr. fellow joint and combined warfare course Jt. Forces Staff Coll., 1994—. Decorated 21 campaign medals, including D.S.M., Legion of Merit with 3 gold stars, D.F.C., Meritorious Service medal, Air medal with 4 gold stars, Navy Commendation medal with combat distinguishing device. Mem.: NRA, KT, U. Calif. Alumni Assn., George Washington U. Alumni Assn., Tailhook Assn., Smithsonian Assn., KT Eye Found., Nat. Wildlife Assn., Order of Daedalians, Nat. Assn. Individual Investors, Nat. Eagle Scout Assn. (regent, Disting. Eagle Scout award 1994), The Golden Eagles, Assn. Naval Aviation, Naval Acad. Athletic Assn., Nat. War Coll. Alumni Assn, Nat. Skeet Shooting Assn., Army Navy Country Club (Arlington, Va.), Mystic Shrine, Royal Order of Scotland, Royal Arch, Masons (33 degree), Shriners, Knights Templar, Sojourners.

SANDERSON, JANET A., former ambassador; b. Tucson, Ariz., Apr. 1955; Diploma, Coll. of William and Mary, 1977; MA in Nat. Security Studies, Naval War Coll., 1993. Econ. officer U.S. Fgn. Svc., 1978; various govt. positions, including energy and petroleum advisor Bur. of European Affairs (OECD), 1986—88; various state dept. positions to dept. econ. counselor to min./counselor for econ. affairs U.S. Embassy, Cairo, dept. chief of mission Amman, Jordan, 1997—2000; US amb. to Algeria US Dept. State, Algiers, 2000—03; US State Dept. diplomat-in-residence U. Calif., Berkeley, 2003—05; US amb. to Haiti US Dept. State, 2006—. Recipient Herbert A. Salzman award for Internat. Econ. Performance, U.S. Dept. of State, 1996, numerous honor awards. Mailing: DOS Amb 3400 Port Au Prince Pl Washington DC 20521-3400 *

SANDERSON, KENNETH JEROME, school system administrator, consultant; b. Sandwich, Ill., June 23, 1962; s. Kenneth Lavern and Teresa Ann Sanderson; m. Lisa Marie Buoy, Aug. 5, 1989; children: John Kenneth, Annelise Marie, Katherine Joy, Mary Therese. BA in Polit. Sci., U. Ill., 1984, EdM in Elem. Edn., 1987, Advanced Cert. in Ednl. Adminstrn., 1993. Cert. ednl. adminstrn. Ill., 1993, elem. edn. Ill., 1987. Athletic dir. St. Matthew Sch., Champaign, Ill., 1989—94; prin. St. Anne Sch., East Moline, Ill., 1994—2001; assoc. supt. Office Cath. Schs., Diocese of Peoria, Ill., 2001—. Site coord. Project Lifeline, Champaign, Ill., 1993—94; facilitator Rainbows for God's Children, East Moline, Ill., 1994—99; pastoral coun. Diocese of Peoria, 1997—97; sec. Black Hawk Fedn., Christian Family Movement, Moline, Ill., 2000—01. Recipient Best-Mannered Tchr. award, Champaign County Chpt., Nat. League of Jr. Cotillions, 2002. Mem.: Nat. Cath. Ednl. Assn. (assoc.). Roman Catholic. Avocations: hiking, travel, camping. Home: 2305 W Wagner Ln Peoria IL 61615 Office: Office of Catholic Schools 412 NE Madison Ave Peoria IL 61603 Home Phone: 309-282-0840; Office Phone: 309-671-1550. Business E-Mail: jsanderson@cdop.org.

SANDERSON, MARY LOUISE, medical association administrator; b. Fairmont, W. Va., Oct. 29, 1942; d. Lawrence Oliver and Frances Evelyn (Shuttleworth) Shingleton; m. William W. Olmstead III, Dec. 1966 (div. June 1974); children: William W. IV, Happy; m. Lester F. Davis, III, Oct. 1979 (div. Dec. 1986); m. David S. Sanderson, Sept. 1992. Student, Vassar Coll., 1960-62, Carnegie Mellon, 1962-63. Real estate broker, N.C. Exec. sec. Creative Dining, Raleigh, NC, 1980-83, Sea Pines Plantation Co., Hilton Head, SC, 1973-79; adminstr. Am. Bd. Neurological Surgery, Houston, 1983—. Vol. Interact, Raleigh, 1984-86, M.D. Anderson Cancer Ctr./Camp Star Trails, 1994-96; docent Mordecai House Hist. Preservation, Raleigh, 1981-83; mem./vol. Reach to Recovery, 1995-2001, Houston Symphony, 2002-, Mus. of Fine Arts, Houston, 1999-. Recipient Vol. award N.C. State Gov., 1986. Mem. Am. Soc. Assn. Execs. Democrat. Episcopalian. Office: Am Bd Neurol Surgery 6550 Fannin St Ste 2139 Houston TX 77030-2718

SANDERSON, STEVEN E., science administrator; B in Hist., U. Ctrl. Ark., 1971; M in Polit. Sci., U. Ark., 1973, Stanford U., Calif., 1975, PhD in Polit. Sci., 1978. Asst. prof. polit. sci. to prof. U. Fla., Gainesville, 1979—97; dean Emory Coll., v.p. arts and scis. Emory U., Atlanta; pres., CEO Wildlife Conservation Soc., Bronx, NY, 2001—. Officer Ford Found. Prog., Brazil; chair polit. sci. dept. U. Fla., 1994—97. Contbr. articles to profl. publs.; author: Agrarian Populism and the Mex. State, 1981, Transformation of Mex. Agr., 1986, Politics of Trade in Latin Am. Devel., 1992; co-editor: Parks in Peril: Working with Politics and People to Save Neotropical Biodiversity, 1998. Fulbright scholar. Office: Wildlife Conservation Soc 2300 Southern Blvd Bronx NY 10460 *

SANDFORD, JOHN (JOHN ROSWELL CAMP), writer, journalist; b. Cedar Rapids, Iowa, Feb. 23, 1944; BA in American Studies, U. Iowa, 1966, MA in Journalism, 1971. Journalist Cape Girardeau S.E. Missourian, Miami Herald, 1971—78, St. Paul Pioneer Press, 1978—90; freelance book reviewer Fort Worth Star Telegram. Author: (as John Camp) The Fool's Run, 1989, The Empress File, 1991, (novels) Rules of Prey, 1989, Shadow Prey, 1990, Eyes of Prey, 1991, Silent Prey, 1992, Winter Prey, 1993, Night Prey, 1994, Mind Prey, 1995, Sudden Prey, 1996, The Night Crew, 1997, Secret Prey, 1998, Certain Prey, 1999, The Devil's Code, 2000, Easy Prey, 2000, Chosen Prey, 2001, Mortal Prey, 2002, The Hanged Man's Song, 2003, Naked Prey, 2003, Hidden Prey, 2004, Broken Prey, 2005, Dead Watch, 2006, Invisible Prey, 2007, Dark of the Moon, 2007. Pulitzer prize for feature writing for Life on the Land: An American Farm Family, 1986. Office: c/o Putnam Books 375 Hudson St New York NY 10014 *

SANDHAAS, JILL T., lawyer; b. Manhasset, NY, July 13, 1961; BA, SUNY, Albany, 1983; JD, St. John's U., 1990. Bar: NY 1991. Ptnr. Wilson, Elser, Moskowitz, Edelman & Dicker LLP, Albany, NYC. Past counsel to chmn. NY State Senate Health Com. Mem.: NY State Bar Assn., Nassau County Bar Assn. Office: Wilson Elser Moskowitz Edelman Dicker Ll 677 Broadway Ste 901 Albany NY 12207-2989 Office Phone: 519-449-8893. Office Fax: 518-449-8927. Business E-Mail: sandhaasj@wemed.com.

SANDHU, HARVINDER SINGH, spinal surgeon, educator; b. Jalandhar, Punjab, India, Mar. 18, 1962; s. Jagtar singh and Shivtej Kaur Sandhu; m. Sonia Kaur Chattha, May 25, 1997; 1 child, alexi. BS, Northwestern U., 1982, MD, 1987; MBA, Columbia U., 2001. Diplomate Am. Bd. Orthopedic Surgery, Nat. Bd. Med. Examiners. Attending spine surgeon UCLA, 1994-97, Hosp. for Spl. Surgery, NYC, 1997—. Pres. Sandhu Cons., Scarsdale, N.Y., 1999—. Recipient Outstanding Sci. Exhibit award Internat. Soc. for Study of the Lumbar spine, 1999, Volvo award for Lumbar Spine Rsch., 2002. Mem. Am. Acad. Orthopedic Surgery (biologic implants com. 2000—), Orthopedic Rsch. Soc., N.Am. Spine Soc. (Outstanding Sci. Exhibit award 1996), Scoliosis Rsch. Soc., Beta Gamma Sigma. Office: Hosp for Spl Surgery 535 E 70th St New York NY 10021 Fax: (212) 774-2600. E-mail: sandhuh@hss.edu.

SANDHU, SUKHMINDER KAUR, epidemiologist, researcher; d. Bachittar Singh and Surjeet Kaur Sandhu; m. Haar Singh Sandhu, July 24, 2006. BA, U. Calif., Berkeley, 1996; MS, Hood Coll., Frederick, Md, 1998; MPH, U. Calif., Berkeley, 2000, PHD, 2004. Epidemic intelligence svc. officer DHHS/CDC, Washington, 2004—06; epidemiologist DHHS/FDA, Rockville, Md., 2006—. Lt. USPHS, 2004, Washington. Office Phone: 301-827-6044.

SAN DIEGO, ARMANDO G., retired military officer, pathologist, consultant; b. Manila, Philippines, June 17, 1934; arrived in U.S., 1959; s. Amado Robles San Diego and Vicenta Sanvectores Gonda; m. Lolita Aves Tan, Apr. 20, 1959; children: Eric, Eileen, Jerry. AA, U. Santo Tomas, 1954, MD, 1959. Diplomate Am. Bd. Pathology, Forensic Examiners, and Forensic Medicine, cert. in anatomical and clinical pathology Am. Bd. Pathology, 1969, lic. physician Philippine Republic, 1959, Ill., 1969, NY, 1969, Calif., 1975, cert. forensic examiner Am. Bd. Forensic Examiners, 1995, in forensic medicine Am. Bd. Forensic Medicine, 1996. Intern Du Page County Hosp., Elmhurst, Ill., 1960; pathology resident Ravenswood Med. Ctr., Chgo., 1961, Columbus-Cuneo Med. Ctr., Chgo., 1962—65; pathologist Keesler USAF Med. Ctr., Biloxi, Miss., 1967—70; capt. USAF, 1967—74, advanced through grades to col., 1974—96, ret., 1996; chmn. Dept. Pathology USAF Regional Hosp., Clark AFB, Philippines, 1970—74, USAF Regional Hosp., March AFB, Riverside, Calif., 1974—79, David Grant USAF Med. Ctr., Fairfield, Calif., 1979—85; chief pathology and lab. medicine Sheppard AF, Wichita Falls, Tex., 1985—87; assoc. chief hosp. svcs. Sheppard Hosp., Wichita Falls, 1987—88, comdr. and chief med. staff, 1993—96; ret., 1996. Adv. Solano County Regional Occupl. Program, Calif., 1984—85; assoc. med. examiner U.S. Med. Examiner Sys. Armed Forces Inst. Pathology; med. dir. med. lab. tng. program Sch. Healthcare Scis. USAF; flight surgeon augmentee Aerospace Medicine Dept. Sheppard AFB; cons. in forensic pathology. Contbr. articles to profl. jours. Dir. med. mission Wichita County Med. Alliance, Wichita Falls, 2001, Filipino Am. Club North Tex., Wichita Falls, 2005; vol. physician Annual Hotter "N" Hell Bike Race, Wichita Falls, 1988—2005; mem. appraisal rev. bd. Wichita County, 2000—05. Decorated Nat. Def. Svc. medal USAF, Meritorious Svc. medal, Legion of Merit medal. Fellow: Coll. Am. Pathologists (life; del. 1987—90, inspector lab. accreditation program), Am. Coll. Forensic Examiners (life), Am. Soc. Clin. Pathology (life; adv. coun. 1987—90); mem.: Soc. Med. Cons. to Armed Forces, Soc. Armed Forces Med. Lab. Scientists, Ret. Officers Assn. (life), Assn. Mil. Surgeons U.S. (life), Filipino-Am. Club (pres. 1999—). Avocations: car collecting, painting, bicycling, hunting.

SANDKUHLER, KEVIN M., military officer; b. Queens, NY, Aug. 28, 1953; BA in History, Coll. Holy Cross; JD, Calif. We. Sch. Law, 1981; LLM, George Washington U., 1991; grad., U.S. Army War Coll., 1994. Bar: Calif. 1981. Commd. 2nd lt. NROTC, 1975; advanced through grades to gen. USMC; fire direction officer, platoon comdr., adjutant, 3rd battalion 11th Marines, 1st Marine divsn. Marine Corps, Camp Pendleton, Calif., with office staff judge advocate, head rev. sect., 3rd Force Service Support Group Okinawa, Japan, 1984, staff judge advocate, 35th Marine Amphibious Unit Republic of Korea, 1984, sr. def. counsel Camp Pendeton, Calif., 1985—86, dir. contracting divsn., contracting officer, 1986—89, assoc. counsel systems command, non-proliferation planner, joint staff directorate strategic plans and policy, 1993—97, staff judge advocate III Marine Expeditionary Force, 3rd Marine divsn. Okinawa, Japan, 1997—2000, dir. appellate govt. divsn.Navy-Marine Corps Appellate Activity Washington, chief def. counsel, 2000, staff judge advocate to commandant, 2001—; advanced through ranks to Brigadier General. Decorated Def. Superior Svc. Medal, Legion of Merit Medal, Meritorious Svc. Medal with Gold Star, Joint Achievement Medal, Navy and Marine Corps Achievement Medal.

SANDLER, ADAM, actor; b. Bklyn., Sept. 9, 1966; m. Jackie Titone, June 22, 2003; 1 child, Sadie Madison. Grad., NYU. Actor: (films) Remote Control (also writer), 1987, Shakes the Clown, 1992, Coneheads, 1993, Airheads, 1994, Bullet Proof, 1996, Punch Drunk Love, 2002, Spanglish, 2004, Reign Over Me, 2007; actor, writer: Billy Madison, 1995 (also composer), Happy Gilmore, 1996, Bulletproof, 1996; actor, exec. prodr.: The Animal, 2001, Mr. Deeds, 2002, Anger Management, 2003, The Longest Yard, 2005; actor, exec. prodr., writer: The Waterboy, 1998, Big Daddy, 1999, Little Nicky, 2000; actor (voice), prodr., writer, also writer (songs) soundtrack: Eight Crazy Nights, 2002; actor, soundtrack song(s) Going Overboard, 1989, Mixed Nuts, 1994, The Wedding Singer, 1998, 50 First Dates, 2004; actor, prodr., Click, 2006, I Now Pronounce You Chuck and Larry, 2007; writer actor, prodr.: Deuce Bigalow: European Gigolo, 2005; prodr.: Benchwarmers, 2006; exec. prodr. (films) Deuce Bigalow: Male Gigolo, 1999, Joe Dirt, 2001, The Master of Disguise, 2002, Hot Chick, 2002, Dickie Roberts: Former Child Star, 2003, Grandma's Boy, 2006, Strange Wilderness, 2007; exec. prodr. (TV) The Mayor, 2003, The Dana & Julia Show, 2004, Gay Robot, 2006; TV appearances include Saturday Night Live: The Best of Chris Farley, 1998, Saturday Night Live: The Best of Mike Myers, 1998, Saturday Night Live: The Best of Phil Hartman, 1998, The Cosby Show, 1987-1988, Couch, 2003; actor, writer Saturday Night Live (Emmy award nomination for writing 1991, 92), 1990-95; appeared on TV programs ABC Afterschool Special, Testing Dirty, 1990, Saturday Night Live Mother's Day Special, 1992, MTV Music Video Awards, 1994, Saturday Night Live Presents President Bill Clinton's All-Time Favorites, 1994, The 37th Annual Grammy Awards, 1995, The ESPY Awards, 1996; rec. artist (albums) They're All Gonna Laught at You!, 1993, What the Hell Happened to Me?, 1996 (also exec. prodr.), What's Your Name, 1997, Stan and Judy's Kid, 1999 (set record for most comedy albums sold in first week released), Shhh...Don't Tell, 2004; exec. prodr. (TV series) Rules of Engagement, 2007-. Recipient People's Choice award, 2000, Funny Male Star, People's Choice award, 2006, Choice Comedian, Teen Choice Awards, 2006; named one of 50 Most Powerful People in Hollywood, 2004-06, 100 Most Powerful Celebrities, Forbes-.com, 2007. *

SANDLER, BERNICE RESNICK, women's rights specialist; b. NYC, Mar. 3, 1928; d. Abraham Hyman and Ivy (Ernst) Resnick; children: Deborah Jo, Emily Maud. BA cum laude, Bklyn. Coll., 1948; MA, CCNY, 1950; EdD, U. Md., 1969; LLD (hon.), Bloomfield Coll., 1973, Hood Coll., 1974, R.I. Coll., 1980, Colby-Sawyer Coll., 1984; LHD (hon.), Grand Valley State Coll., 1974; Dr. Pub. Svc. (hon.), North Adams State Coll., 1985; LLD (hon.), Goucher Coll., 1991; LHD (hon.), Plymouth State Coll., 1992, Wittenberg U., 1993, Ripon Coll., 1998; LLD (hon.), U. St. Thomas, 2006. Rsch. asst., tchr. nursery sch., employment counselor, adult edn. instr., sec.; psychologist HEW, 1970; tchr. psychology Mt. Vernon Coll., 1970; head Action Com. for Fed. Contract Compliance, Women's Equity Action League, 1970—71; edn. specialist U.S. Ho. Reps., Washington, 1970; dep. dir. Womens Action program, HEW, Washington, 1971; dir. project on status and edn. of women Assn. Am. Colls., Washington, 1971—91; sr. assoc. Ctr. for Women Policy Studies, 1991—94; sr. scholar in residence Nat. Assn. Women in Edn., Washington, 1994—2000; sr. scholar Women's Rsch. and Edn. Inst., 2000—. Cons., 1991—; expert witness, 1990—; writer, 1971—; vis. lectr. U. Md., 1968-69; adv. bd. Women's Equity Action League Ednl. and Legal Def. Fund, 1980—, trustee, 1974-80, Women's Equity Action League, 1971-78; adv. com. Math./Sci. Network, 1979, Wider Opportunities for Women, 1978-85, Women's Legal Def. Fund, 1978-84; Nat. Coun. for Alternative Work Patterns Inc., 1978-85, Women's Hdqs. State Nat. Bank for Women's Appointments, 1977-78, and others. Mem. adv. bd. Jour. Reprints Documents Affecting Women, 1976-78, Women's Rights Law Reporter, 1970-80; editor: (newsletters) On Campus With Women, 1971-91, About Women on Campus, 1991-99; contbr. articles. Mem. bd. overseers Wellesley Coll. Ctr. for Rsch. on Women, 1975-87; bd. dirs. Ctr. for Women's Policy Studies, 1972-75; mem. exec. com. Inst. for Ednl. Leadership, 1982-87, mem. program adv. com., 1987-88, chair bd. dirs., 1981, chair adv. com., 1975-81; mem. affirmative action com., task force on family, nat. affairs commn. Am. Jewish Com., 1978, bd. dirs. D.C. chpt.; tech. adv. com. Nat. Jewish Family Ctr., 1980-89; adv. coun. Ednl. Devel. Ctr., 1980-85; adv. bd. Urban Inst., 1981-85, Women Employed Inst., 1981-84, Ex-New Yorkers for N.Y., 1978-79; mem. adv. com. Arthur and Elizabeth Schlesinger Libr. History of Women in Am., 1981-85; nat. adv. com. Shelter Rsch. Inst., Calif., 1980-82; chair adv. panel project on self-evaluation Am. Insts. for Rsch., 1980-82; bd. dirs. Equality Ctr., 1983, Evaluation and Tng. Inst., Calif., 1980, Inst. for Studies in Equality, 1975-77; exec. v.p. Bd. Women for Women, 1997—. Recipient Athena award Intercollegiate Assn. Women Students, 1974, Elizabeth Boyer award Women's Equity Action League, 1976, Rockefeller Pub. Svc. award Princeton U., 1976, Women Educators award for activism, 1987, Anna Roe award Harvard U., 1988, Readers Choice honors Washington Woman Mag., 1987, Woman of Distinction award Nat. Assn. Women in Edn., 1991, Georgina Smith award AAUP, 1992, Woman of Achievement Turner Broadcasting System, 1994; named one of 100 Most Powerful Women Washingtonian Mag., 1982, one of the nation's 100 Most Important Women, Ladies Home Jour., 1988, Leadership Matters award Inst. Ednl. Leadership, 1997, Medal of Honor, Vet. Feminists, 2001, Donna Shavlik award Am. Coun. Edn., 2003, Mary Keetz award Women's Consortium Pa. State Sys., 2004, Am. Fedn. Tchrs. Women's Rights award Mem. Assn. for Women in Sci. Found. (bd. dirs. 1977—), Am. Soc. Profl. and Exec. Women (adv. bd. 1980). Avocations: birding, music, swimming, hiking. Office: Women's Rsch and Edn Inst 1350 Connecticut Ave NW Ste 850 Washington DC 20036-1740

SANDLER, BETTY MOORE, lawyer; b. Martin, Ky., Dec. 10, 1947; BA, U. Ky., 1969; JD, U. Ky. Coll. Law, 1981. Bar: Ky. 1981, US Supreme Ct. 1985, Commonwealth of Va. 1986, US Bankruptcy Ct., E Dist. of Va. 1990. Lobbyist & fed. legislative analyst US Congress; Commr. in Chancery, 31st Judicial Circuit, Va.; prin. Nichols Zauzig Sandler P.C. Founding pres. Prince William County Bar Found. Contbr. articles to profl. law guides, books, publ. Fellow: Am. Acad. of Matrimonial Lawyers (AAML), Internat. Acad. of Matrimonial Lawyers (IAML); mem.: No. Va. Bankruptcy Bar Assn. Office: Nichols Zauzig Sandler PC 12660 Lake Ridge Dr Woodbridge VA 22192-2335 Office Phone: 703-492-4200. Office Fax: 703-492-4201. *

SANDLER, GERALD HOWARD, computer scientist, information technology executive, educator; b. NYC, Sept. 17, 1934; s. Irving and Sally S.; m. Ann Sandler; children: Eric, Steven. BS, CUNY, 1956, MS, 1957. With Grumman Aerospace, 1963-83; past pres. Grumman Data Systems & Svcs., Bethpage, NY, 1983-95; pres. GHS Enterprises, 1995—; prof. computer sci. Poly. U., Farmingdale, NY, 1995—. Author: System Engineering, 1963. Home: 46 Bonnie Dr Westbury NY 11590-2804

SANDLER, HAROLD, retired cardiologist, research scientist, consultant; b. Cin., Ohio, Nov. 24, 1929; s. Hyman and Cecelia Sandler; m. Norma Joan Holloway, Apr. 16, 1961; children: Beth Allison Dunn, Margaret Aline. BS, U. Cin., 1951; MD, 1955. Lic. physician Ohio, 1955. Asst. prof. medicine U. Wash., Seattle, 1963—64; chief biomedical rsch. divsn. Ames rsch. ctr. NASA, Moffett Field, Calif., 1972—85; clin. prof. medicine Stanford U., Palo Alto, Calif., 1978—91, ret., 1991; pvt. practice cons. Bainbridge Island, Wash., 1991—. Author: 8 books; contbr. over 150 articles to profl. jours. Founder Beyond War, Palo Alto, Calif., 1980—90. Capt. USN, 1961—63. Fellow: Am. Coll. Cardiology, Aerospace Med. Assn. (Eric Liljencrantz award 1980), Am. Heart Assn. (chmn. basic sci. coun. 1974—76). Democrat. Jewish. Achievements include research in quantitation left ventricular volume and its mechanics. Use of bedrest to simulate effects of space flight in humans. Avocations: bridge, making stained glass lampshades. Home Phone: 206-842-0176; Office Phone: 206-842-9176. Office Fax: 206-842-9282; Home Fax: 206-842-9282.

SANDLER, IRVING HARRY, art critic, art historian; b. NYC, July 22, 1925; s. Harry and Anna (Robin) S.; m. Lucy Freeman, Sept. 4, 1958; 1 child, Catherine Harriet. BA, Temple U., 1948; MA, U. Pa., 1950; PhD, NYU, 1976. Instr. in art history NYU, 1960-71; prof. emeritus art history SUNY, Purchase; art critic N.Y. Post, NYC, 1960-65. Author: The Triumph of American Painting: A History of Abstract Expressionism, 1970, The New York School: Painters and Sculptors of the Fifties, 1978, Alex Katz, 1979, Al Held, 1984, American Art of the 1960s, 1988; editor (with Amy Newman) Defining Modern Art: Selected Writings of Alfred H. Barr Jr., 1986, Mark di Suvero at Storm King Art Ctr., 1996, Art of Postmodern Era: From Late 1960s to Early 1990s, 1996, Natvar Bhavsar, 1998, Stephen Antonakos, 1999, A Sweeper-Up After Artists: A Memoir, 2003, From Avant-Garde to Pluralism: An On-The-Spot History, 2006, Esteben Vicente: The Aristocratic Eye, 2007. John Simon Guggenheim fellow, 1965; Nat. Endowment for Arts fellow, 1977. Mem. Coll. Art Assn., Internat. Assn. Art Critics. Home: 60 E 8th St Apt 19E New York NY 10003 Office Phone: 212-533-7447.

SANDLER, LUCY FREEMAN, art history educator; b. NYC, June 7, 1930; d. Otto and Frances (Glass) Freeman; m. Irving Sandler, Sept. 4, 1958; 1 child, Catherine Harriet. BA, Queens Coll., 1951; MA, Columbia U., 1957; PhD, NYU, 1964. Asst. prof. NYU, 1964-70, assoc. prof., 1970-75, prof. fine arts, 1975-86, Helen Gould Sheppard prof. art history, 1986—2003, chmn. dept., 1975-89; editorial cons. Viator, UCLA, 1983-97; Helen Gould Sheppard prof. emerita, 2003—. Author: The Peterborough Psalter in Brussels, 1974, The Psalter of Robert De Lisle in the British Library, 1983, new edit., 1999, Gothic Manuscripts 1285-1385, 1986, 'Omne Bonum': A Fourteenth-Century Encyclopedia of Universal Knowledge, 1996, The Ramsey Psalter, 1999, Der Ramsey-Psalter (Glanzlichter der Buchkunst 12), 2003, Der Bestiarium aus Peterborugh/The Peterborough Bestiary, 2003, The Lichtenthal Psalter and the Patronage of the Bohun Family, 2004, (with Jonathan J.G. Alexander and James H. Marrow) The Splendor of the Word, Medieval and Renaissance Illuminated Manuscripts, NY Pub. Libr., 2005; editor: Essays in Memory of Karl Lehmann, 1964, Art the Ape of Nature: Studies in Honor of H.W. Janson, 1981, Coll. Art Assn. Monograph Series, 1970-75, 86-89, Gesta, 1991-94; asst. editor Art Bull., 1964-67, mem. editl. bd., 1994; mem. editl. bd. Jour. Jewish Art, 1978, Speculum, 1994. Trustee Godwin-Ternbach Mus., Queens Coll., 1982-94; chair dels. exec. com. Am. Coun. Learned Socs., 2002-04. NEH fellow, 1967-68, 77; fellow Pierpont Morgan Library; Guggenheim fellow, 1988-89. Fellow: Medieval Acad. Am. (councillor 2002—05), Soc. Antiquaries (London); mem.: AAUP, Coll. Art Assn. (pres. 1981—84), Internat. Ctr. Medieval Art (adv. bd., bd. dirs. 1976—80, 1984—87, 1989—92, 1995—2001). Home: 60 E 8th St Apt 19E New York NY 10012 Office: NYU Dept Fine Arts New York NY 10003

SANDLER, RICHARD H., pediatric gastroenterologist; MD, Mich. State U. Coll. Human Medicine. Resident, pediatrics Mich. State U., Lansing; fellow, pediatric gastroenterology, hepatology, and nutrition Harvard Med. Sch., Boston Children's Hosp.; fellow, human metabolism and nutrition Mass. Gen. Hosp., Boston; asst. in medicine, instr., divsn. of gastroenterology and nutrition The Children's Hosp., Harvard Med. Sch., Boston, 1989—90; dir. Biomed. Acoustics Rsch. Group, Evanston, Ill., 1990—, pres., CEO, 1997—; assoc. prof., pediatrics Rush Med. Coll., Chgo., 1990—; adj. assoc. prof., biomed. engring. U. Ill., Chgo., 2002—. Office: Rush Univ Med Ctr 1725 W Harrison St Chicago IL 60612 Address: 1725 W Harrison St Ste 946 Chicago IL 60612 Office Phone: 312-942-2889.

SANDLER, RICHARD JAY, lawyer; b. NYC, Aug. 26, 1947; s. Albert and Ruth (Marcus) S.; children: Elizabeth, Russell, Victoria. BA summa cum laude, Princeton U., 1969; JD cum laude, Harvard U., 1972. Assoc. Davis, Polk & Wardwell, NYC, 1972-79, ptnr., 1979—, Paris, 1982-85, head capital markets practice group. Mem.: ABA. Avocation: winemaking. Office: Davis Polk & Wardwell 450 Lexington Ave Fl 19 New York NY 10017-3982 Office Phone: 212-450-4224. Office Fax: 212-450-3224. Business E-Mail: sandler@dpw.com.

SANDLER, ROBERT MICHAEL, insurance company executive; b. NYC, Apr. 20, 1942; s. Albert and Ruth (Marcus) S.; m. Annette L. Marchese, Aug. 18, 1963; children: David, Glenn. BA in Math., Hofstra U., 1963. Various actuarial positions Met. Life, NYC, 1963-68; various actuarial positions Am. Internat., NYC, 1968-80; v.p., casualty actuary American Internat. Group, Inc., NYC, 1980-84, sr. v.p., sr. actuary, sr. claims officer, 1984-95, exec. v.p., 1995—, dir. various subs. Mem. Casualty Actuarial Soc. (assoc.), Am. Acad. Actuaries, Internat. Actuarial Assn. Republican. Office: Am Internat Group 70 Pine St New York NY 10270-0002

SANDLER, ROSS, law educator; b. Milw., Jan. 31, 1939; s. Theodore T. and Laurette (Simons) S.; m. Alice R. Mintzer, Sept. 15, 1968; children: Josie, Jenny, Dorothy. AB, Dartmouth Coll., 1961; LLB, NYU, 1965. Bar: N.Y. 1965, Fla. 1965. Assoc. atty. Cahill Gordon Reindel & Ohl, NYC, 1965-68; asst. U.S. atty. So. Dist. N.Y., 1968-72; assoc. atty. Trubin Sillcocks Edelman & Knapp, NYC, 1972-75; sr. staff atty. Natural Resources Def. Coun., NYC, 1975-81, 83-86; spl. advisor to mayor City of N.Y., 1981-82; exec. dir. Hudson River Found., NYC, 1983-86; commr. N.Y.C. Dept. Transp., 1986-90; ptnr. Jones Day Reavis & Pogue, NYC, 1991-93; law prof. N.Y. Law Sch., 1993—, dir. Ctr. for N.Y.C. law, 1993—; pres. N.Y. Legis. Svc., 1998—. Mem. N.Y.C. Procurement Policy Bd., 1994—; vis. lectr. Yale Law Sch., New Haven, 1977; adj. prof. law NYU Law Sch., 1976-94; chair, mem. N.Y.C. Taxi and Limousine Commn., 1980-90. Co-author: A New Direction in Transit, 1978, Democracy by Decree, 2003; columnist Environ. Mag., 1976—80; editor: (jour.) City Law, City Land; contbr. chapters to books, articles. Trustee Woods Hole (Mass.) Rsch. Ctr., 1983—; mem. exec. com. Hudson River Found., 1986-96; mem. adv. coun. Ctr. Biodiversity and Conservation Am. Mus. Nat. History, 1996—. Recipient Pub. Interest award NYU Law Alumni, 1987, Louis J. Lefkowitz award Fordham Law Sch. Urban Law Jour., 1989, Lifetime Achievement award N.Y. State Bar Assn., 1998. Mem. City Club of N.Y. (chair 1992-93, trustee). Office: NY Law Sch 57 Worth St New York NY 10013-2959

SANDLER, STANLEY IRVING, chemical engineering educator; b. NYC, June 10, 1940; s. Murray C. and Celia M. (Kamenetsky) S.; m. Judith Katherine Ungar, June 17, 1962; children: Catherine Julietta, Joel Abraham, Michael Howard. BChemE, CCNY, 1962; PhD, U. Minn., 1966. Chartered engr., European Union. NSF postdoctoral fellow Inst. Molecular Physics U. Md., College Park, 1966—67; successively asst. prof., assoc. prof., prof. dept. chem. engring. U. Del., Newark, 1967-82, H.B. du Pont prof., 1982—2000, chmn. dept., 1982—86, dir. Ctr. Molecular and Engring. Thermodynamics, 1992—, interim dean Coll. Engring., 1992, H.B. duPont chair, 2000—; hon. professorial fellow U. Melbourne, Australia, 2004—; Exxon Mobil prof. Nat. U. Singapore, 2006—. Vis. prof. Imperial Coll., London, 1973—74, U. Nat. del Sur, Bahia Blanca, Argentina, 1985, Tech. U., Berlin, 1981, Berlin, 1988—89, U. Queensland, Brisbane, Australia, 1989, Brisbane, 96, U. Calif., Berkeley, 1995, U. Melbourne, Australia, 2003, hon. professorial fellow dept. chem. and biomolecular engring., 2004—; cons. maj. oil and chem. cos. Author: Chemical and Engineering Thermodynamics, 1977, 3d edit., 1998, Modeling Vapor-Liquid Equilibrium, 1998, Chemical, Biochemical and Engineering Thermodynamics, 2006; editor: Fluid Properties and Phase Equilibria, 1977, Chemical Engineering Education in a Changing Environment, 1989, Kinetic and Thermodynamic Lumping of Multicomponent Mixtures, 1991, Models for Thermodynamic and Phase Equilibria Calculations, 1993, AI Chem E. Jour., 2000—; mem. adv. bd. Jour. Chem. Engring. Data, Chem. Engring. Edn., Indsl. Engring. Chem. Rsch., Indian Chem. Engr., Engring. Sci. and Tech. (Malaysia); also numerous articles. Mem. adv. bd. chem. engring. La. State U., Carnegie-Mellon U., Princeton U. Recipient U.S. Sr. Scientist award Alexander von Humboldt Found., 1988, Francis Alison award U. Del., 1993, Ashton Cary award Ga. Tech. U., 1994, Phillips Lecture award Okla. State U., 1993, Rossini Lectureship award Internat. Union Pure Applied Chemistry, 1998; Mieguny ah fellow U. Melbourne, Australia, 2003, hon. professorial fellow, 2004—; Hikal Chemcon Dist. Spkr. award, Indian Inst. Chem. Engrs., 2004. Fellow Inst. Chem. Engrs. (Britain), AIChE (jour. adv. bd., editor 2000—, Profl. Progress award 1984, Warren K. Lewis award 1996, Del. Soc. award 1998, Founders award, 2004), U.S. Nat. Acad. Engring., Am. Chem. Soc. (award Del. sect. 1989, E.V. Murphree award 1997), Am. Soc. Engring. Edn. (lectr. chem. engring. div. 1988), Cosmos Club (Washington). Jewish. Avocations: jogging, stamp collecting/philately. Home: 202 Sypherd Dr Newark DE 19711-3627 Office: U Del Dept Chem Engring Newark DE 19716 Office Phone: 302-831-2945. Business E-Mail: sandler@udel.edu.

SANDLER, THOMAS R., accountant, director; b. Mt. Kisco, NY, Dec. 16, 1946; s. Louis and Susan (Rosen) S.; m. Alison G. Corneau, Aug. 26, 1972; children: Justin C., Shawn A. BS summa cum laude, Ithaca Coll., 1968; MS, SUNY-Binghamton, 1972. C.P.A., NY, Colo. 1982. Asst. acct. KPMG Peat Marwick, White Plains, N.Y., 1972, mgr. Phoenix, 1975, sr. mgr. NYC, 1978, ptnr. Denver, 1981-92, ptnr. in-charge corp. recovery svcs. NYC, 1993-94; mng. ptnr. BDO Seidman, Denver, 1994-95; CFO, treas., sec. Samsonite Corp., Denver, 1995-98; pres. Samsonite Am., 1998—2004; CEO Case Logic, Inc., Longmont, Colo., 2004—. Contbr. articles to profl. jours. Past trustee, past pres. Colo. Children's Chorale; treas., past pres., gov., mem. exec. com., committeeman Colo. Golf Assn.; committeeman US Golf Assn. bd. dirs. Pacific Coast Golf Assn.; chmn. Travel Goods Assn. Mem. AICPA, Colo. Soc. CPAs (chmn. real estate and govt. acctg. com.), Bear Creek Golf Club, Country Club at Castle Pines, Colo. Golf Club. Home: 896 Anaconda Ct Castle Rock CO 80108-9044 Office: Case Logic Inc 6303 Dry Creek Pkwy Longmont CO 80503

SANDLER, TODD MICHAEL, economist, political scientist, educator; b. Mt. Kisco, NY, Dec. 16, 1946; s. Louis and Susie Sandler; m. Jean Marie Murdock, June 28, 1985; 1 child, Tristan Jon. BA, SUNY, Binghamton, 1968, MA, 1969, PhD, 1971. Asst. prof. Ariz. State U., Tempe, 1971-76; assoc. prof. U. Wyo., Laramie, 1976-79, prof., 1979-85, U. S.C., Columbia, 1985-86; prof. econs. and polit. sci. Iowa State U., Ames, 1986-2000, Disting. prof., 1995—2001; Dockson prof. U. So. Calif., LA, 2000—; Shukla prof. U. Tex., Dallas, 2006—. Author: Collective Action: Theory and Applications, 1992, Global Challenges, 1997, Economic Concepts for the Social Sciences, 2001, Global Collective Action, 2004; co-author: The Theory of Externalities, Public Goods and Club Goods, 1986, The Economics of Defense, 1995, (book) The Theory of Externalities, Public Goods and Club Goods, 2d edit., 1996, International Terrorism in 1980s, 1989, The Political Economy of NATO, 1999, The Future of Development Assistance: Common Pools and International Public Goods, 1999, Regional Public Goods: Typologies, Provision, Financing, and Development Assistance, 2002, The Political Economy of Terrorism, 2006; co-editor: Defense Economics, 1989—94, Handbook of Defense Economics, 1995;: Handbook of Defense Economics, 2007, Economics of Defense, 2001, Economics of Conflict, 2003; assoc. editor: Jour. Environ. Econs. and Mgmt., 1988—89, Jour. Pub. Econ. Theory, 1999—2005; assoc. editor Rev. Internat. Organizations; mem. editl. bd.: Social Sci. Quar., Pub. Fin. Rev., Fiscal Studies, Bull. Econ. Rsch., Internat. Studies Quar., Terrorism and Political Violence; mem. editl. bd. Am. Jour. Polit. Sci., Internat. Studies Perspective, Rev. of Internat. Orgns., chmn. editl. bd. Jour. Conflict Resolution, 2004—; spl. adv. editor: Def. and Peace Econs., 2000—, reviewer: numerous internat. orgns. Co-recipient Rsch. Related to Prevention of Nuc. War award, Nat. Acad. of Scis., 2003; recipient Duncan Black award, Pub. Choice Soc., 2005; fellow NATO postdoctoral, 1977, 1998—2000, Australian Nat. U., 1981, 1994, Sr., Inst. Policy Reform, 1990—91, 1992—94, Hon., U. Wis.-Madison, 1990; grantee NSF, 1989, 1993. Mem.: Pub. Choice Soc., So. Econ. Assn., Assn. Environ. and Resource Econs., Royal Econ. Soc., Am. Econ. Assn., Internat. Def. Econs. Assn. (exec. bd.). Office: U Tex Dallas Sch Econ Polit and Policy Scis 800 W Campbell Rd Richardson TX 75080 Business E-Mail: tsandler@utdallas.edu.

SANDLIN, MAX ALLEN, JR., former congressman; b. Texarkana, Ark., Sept. 29, 1952; s. Max Allen and Margie Beth (Barnett) S.; children: Hillary, Max III, Emily, Christian. BA, Baylor U., 1975, JD, 1978. Bar: Tex. Assoc. Huffman & Palmer, Inc., Marshall, Tex., 1978-82; ptnr. Sandlin & Buckner, Marshall, 1982-96; judge County of Harrison, Marshall, 1986-89, county ct. judge, 1989-96; v.p., gen. counsel Howell & Sandlin, Inc., 1990-96; mem. US Congress from 1st Tex dist., 1997—2005, mem. ways & means com.; co-chmn. Fleishmin-Hillard Govt. Rels., Washington, 2005—. Mem. exec. com. Tex. Supreme Ct. Jud. Edn. Com., Austin, 1987—; bd. dirs. Security State Bank, Elysian Fields, Tex., East Tex. Legal Svcs., Nacogdoches; bd. dirs., treas. East Tex. Housing & Fin. Corp., Marshall, 1990—. Chairman Harrison County Dem. Party, Marshall, 1982-88; mem. exec. com. Marshall-Harrison County Industries, Marshall, 1986-89; founder, sponsor, mem. Michelson-Reves Mus. Art; post supr. Boy Scouts Am., 1982-86; mgr. Marshall Youth Baseball, 1980. Recipient Appreciation award Tex. Dept. Human Resourcs, 1985. Mem. Harrison County Bar Assn. (pres. 1982-84), Baylor U. Alumni Assn. (bd. dirs.), Marshall Symphony Soc. (bd. dirs. 1988-90), Marshall Rotary. Democrat. Baptist. Avocations: politics, hunting, fishing, baseball, classical cars. Office: Fleishman-Hillard Govt Rels 17175 Eye St NW Ste 700 Washington DC 20006 *

SANDLIN, STEPHANIE HERSETH, congresswoman, lawyer; b. Aberdeen, SD, Dec. 3, 1970; d. Ralph Lars and Joyce Herseth. BA summa cum laude in Polit. Sci. and Govt., Georgetown U., 1993, MA in Polit. Sci., 1996; JD, Georgetown U. Law Ctr., 1996. Bar: SD. Law clerk Staff of US Dist. Ct. Judge Charles Kornmann, Pierre, 1998—99, Staff of US 4th Cir. Ct. Appeals Judge Diana Gribbon Motz, Balt., 1999—2000; atty. Skadden, Arps, Slate, Meagher & Flom LLP, Washington, 2001; exec. dir. SD Farmers Union Found., 2003—04; mem. US Congress from SD at-large, 2004—, mem. Blue Dog Coalition, mem. agr. com., mem. resources com., mem. vets. affairs com., ranking minority mem. econ. opportunity subcommittee. Prof. Georgetown U. Law Ctr., 1997, Augustana Coll., 2003, SD State U., 2003; tchr. Fund for Am. Studies; counsel on energy and telecom. issues SD Pub. Utilities Commn., Pierre; bd. dir. First Nat. Bank, Brookings, SD. Sr. editor Georgetown U. Law Rev. Mem. Rotary Internat., Brookings, SD; co-chair Rural Working Grp.; legal counsel for the elderly. Recipient Small Bus. Adv., Small Bus. Survival Com., 2004. Mem.: SD Bar Assn., Phi Beta Kappa. Democrat. Lutheran. Office: US Ho Reps 331 Cannon Ho Office Bldg Washington DC 20515-4101 Office Phone: 202-225-2801. *

SANDLOW, LESLIE JORDAN, gastroenterologist, educator; b. Chgo., Jan. 7, 1934; s. Harry H. and Rose (Ehrlich) S.; m. Joanne J. Fleischer, June 16, 1957; children: Jay, Bruce, Lisa. BS, U. Ill., 1956; MD, Chgo. Med. Sch., 1960. Intern Michael Reese Hosp. and Med. Ctr., Chgo., 1961, med. resident, rsch. fellow gastrointestinal rsch., 1961-64, physician-in-charge clin. gastroenterology lab., 1963-74, asst. attending physician, 1964-67, assoc. attending physician, 1967-72, vice chmn. divsn. gastroenterology, dir. ambulatory medicine, 1968, dir. ambulatory care, 1969-76, attending physician, 1972—, assoc. med. dir., 1972-73; clin. asst. Chgo. Med. Sch.,

1963-68, clin. instr., 1966; asst. prof. dept. medicine Pritzker Sch. Medicine, U. Chgo., 1973-76, assoc. prof., 1976-85, prof., 1985-90; prof. clin. medicine and med. edn. U. Ill. Coll. Medicine, Chgo., 1990-91, prof. medicine and med. edn., 1992—, sr. assoc. dean for grad. and continuing med. edn., 1993—, head dept. med. edn., 1993—, sr. assoc. dean for med. edn. affairs, 1994—. Dep. v.p. profl. affairs Michael Reese Hosp. and Med. Ctr., 1973-78, dir. Office Ednl. Affairs, 1976-81, assoc. v.p. acad. affairs, 1978-82, dir. quality assurance program, 1981-91, v.p. planning, 1982-83, v.p. profl. affairs and planning, 1983-88, dir. divsn. internal medicine, 1986-93, v.p. profl. and acad. affairs, 1988-91, med. dirs. acad. and med. affairs, 1992-94; med. dir. Michael Reese Health Plan, Inc., 1972-74, interim exec. dir., 1976-77; cons. gastroenterologist Ill. Ctrl. Hosp., 1978-80; vis. prof. Pontifica U. Catolica Rio Grande do Sul, Brazil, 1978, U. Fed. Espirito Santo, Brazil, 1978, Nordic Fedn. for Med. Understanding, Akureyri, Iceland, 1978, Seoul Nat. U. Sch. Medicine, 1981, Coll. Physicians and Surgsons, Kharachi, Pakistan, 1994, U. Tex., Ft. Worth, 1977, U. Ariz., Tucson, 1977, Loyola U. Med. Sch., Maywood, Ill., 1979; cons. in field; coord. Health Scis. Librs. in Ill.; mem. Midwest Med. Libr. Network; mem. subcom. on delivery of ambulatory med. care Inst. Medicine Chgo.; mem. cmty. resources task force Interinstnl. Cardiovascular Ctr.; chmn. steering group Ill. Regional Med. Program; past co-chmn. curriculum com. U. Chgo. Reviewer Rsch. in Med. Edn./Assn. Am. Med. Colls., 1985—, Acad. Medicine/Assn. Am. Med. Colls., 1989; contbr. numerous articles to profl. publs. Mem. Skokie (Ill.) Bd. Health, 1973-85, chmn., 1976-85; bd. dirs. Group Health Assn. Am., 1976-78, Portes Ctr., 1980—; bd. dirs. Good Health Program Skokie Valley Hosp., 1978-80; bd. dirs., exec. com. Rsch. and Edn. Found. of Michael Reese Hosp. Med. Staff, 1992—; pres.-elect Inst. Medicine Chgo., 2003-04, pres., 2004-06. Recipient numerous grants, including NIH 1988, Michael Reese Hosp. Found. 1994-95, Chgo. Cmty. Trust 1994-95, AOA faculty award 2007. Fellow Am. Coll. Gastroenterology; mem. N.Y. Acad. Scis., Inst. Medicine, Assn. Am. Med. Colls., Am. Coll. Physician Execs. (co-chair resource mgmt. com. of quality assurance forum), Soc. Dirs. Med. Coll. Continuing Med. Edn., Soc. Dir. Rsch. in Med. Edn. Home: 2314 N Lincoln Park W Chicago IL 60614-3455 Office: U Ill Coll Medicine Med Edn MC 784 1819 W Polk St Chicago IL 60612-7331

SANDMAN, BRADFORD AARON, coach, educator; b. Omaha, Dec. 11, 1957; s. Darrel Alfred and Alice Sandman; m. Beth Marie Bokorney; children: Keegan Gregary, Colton Bradford. BS, Stephen F. Austin State U., Tex., 1980; Med, Prairie View A&M U. of Tex., 2004. Tchr., coach Sealy HS, Tex., 1985—90, Langham Creek HS, Houston, 1990—. Master: Sr. Men (sponsor), Fellowship of Christian Athletes (sponsor), Unity Club (sponsor); mem.: Honor Soc. Com., Gang Task Com. Home: 303 Briar Ridge Bellville TX 77418 Office: Langham Creek HS 17610 Fm 529 Houston TX 77095 Home Phone: 979-865-3479; Office Phone: 281-463-5480. Personal E-mail: bradford.sandman@cfisd.net.

SANDMAN, DAN D., lawyer; b. Cin., May 1, 1948; m. Bonnie A Sandman. BA cum laude, Ohio State U., 1970, JD cum laude, 1973. Bar: Ohio 1973, Pa. 1995. With Marathon Oil Co., Findlay, Ohio, 1973—78, London, 1978—81, sr. mktg. counsel Findlay, 1981—83, gen. atty. refining and mktg., 1983—86, gen. atty. US exploration and prodn. law, 1986, gen. counsel, sec., 1986-92; sec., asst. gen. counsel US Steel Corp. (formerly USX Corp.), Pitts., 1992—93, sec., gen. counsel, 1993, mem. corp. policy com., 1993—, sr. v.p. human resources, 1996, vice chmn., chief legal & adminstrv. officer, gen. counsel, sec., bd. dirs., 2002—07. Bd. dirs. Roppe Corp., Fostoria, Ohio, 1988—, Marathon Oil Co., 1992—; bd. mgrs. Marathon Ashland Petroleum, 2000—. Bd. trustees US Steel Found. (formerly USX Found.), 1990—, Pitts. Symphony Orch., 1993—98; bd. mem. Senator John Heinz Pitts. Regional Hist. Ctr., Carnegie Sci. Ctr., Pitts. Regional Alliance; mem. exec. com. Carnegie Hero Commn.; co-chair Pa. Corp. Counsel Roundtable, 2006; vol. United Way Houston, Houston Grand Opera, Big Bros., Hancock County Mental Health Soc. Mem.: Ohio Bar Assn., Pa. Bar Assn., ABA. *

SANDMAN, JAMES JOSEPH, lawyer; b. Albany, NY, June 16, 1951; s. Edgar A. and Margaret M. (Dugan) S.; m. Elizabeth D. Mullin, June 2, 1985; children: Joseph M., Elizabeth D. AB summa cum laude, Boston Coll., 1973; JD cum laude, U. Pa., 1976. Bar: Pa. 1976, D.C. 1977, U.S. Supreme Ct. 1980, Colo. 1982. Law clk. to judge U.S. Ct. Appeals (3d cir.), Wilkes-Barre, Pa., 1976-77; assoc. Arnold & Porter, 1977—83, ptnr., 1984—, mng. ptnr., 1995—2005, sr. pro bono ptnr., 2007—. Exec. editor U. Pa. Law Rev., 1975-76. Mem. bd. overseers U. Pa. Law Sch., 1998—2007; trustee Wilkes U., NALP Found.; bd. dirs. Washington Performing Arts Soc., Whitman-Walker Clinic, Internat. Sr. Lawyers Project. Fellow Am. Bar Found.; mem. ABA (house of dels., 2006-07, standing com. on pro bono and public svc., 2007—), DC Bar., (bd. gov. 2003-, pres. 2006-07), Order of Coif, Phi Beta Kappa. Democrat. Office: Arnold & Porter 555 12th St NW Washington DC 20004-1206 Home Phone: 202-363-1320; Office Phone: 202-942-5758. Office Fax: 202-942-5999. Business E-Mail: james.sandman@aporter.com.

SANDMAN, PAUL WILLIAM, lawyer; b. Albany, NY, June 21, 1947; s. Edgar Augustus and Margaret Mary (Dugan) Sandman; m. Mary Elizabeth O'Brien, Aug. 28, 1971; children: Katherine M., Margaret M., William A. AB, Boston Coll., 1969; JD, Harvard U., 1973. Bar: Mass. 1973, US Dist. Ct. (dist. Mass.) 1974, US Ct. Appeals (1st cir.) 1974. Assoc., Goodwin, Procter & Hoar, Boston, 1973-81; corp. counsel Wang Labs., Inc., Lowell, Mass., 1981-84, v.p., corp. counsel, 1984—92, sr. v.p., gen. counsel, sec., 1992-93, Boston Sci. Corp. 1993-. Bd. dirs. AMC of Mass. Bay, Boston, 1987—. Mem. Am. Corp. Counsel Assn. (bd. dirs. 1987—). Office: Boston Sci Corp One Boston Scientific Pl Natick MA 01760-1537 *

SANDMAN, PETER M., risk management consultant; b. NYC, Apr. 18, 1945; s. Howard Edwin and Gertrude Leah (Orgel) S.; m. Susan Marie Goertzel, June 18, 1967 (div. 1975); m. Jody Sue Lanard, June 10, 1990; children: Alison, Jennifer; 1 stepchild, James Sachs. BA in Psychology, Princeton U., 1967; MA in Comm., Stanford U., 1968, PhD, 1971. Reporter Toronto (Ont.) Star, Canada, 1966; stringer Time, 1966-67; instr. comm. Stanford (Calif.) U., 1968-70; instr. journalism Calif. State Coll., Hayward, 1970; sr. editor The Magazine, 1970; asst. prof. Ohio State U., Columbus, 1971-72; asst. prof. natural resources, journalism U. Mich., Ann Arbor, 1972-75, assoc. prof. natural resources, 1975-77; assoc. prof. comm., coord. Cook Coll. comm. program Rutgers U., New Brunswick, NJ, 1977-83, prof. journalism, 1983-94, prof. dept. human ecology, 1992-94; adj. prof., 1994—. Adj. prof. TV, radio Ithaca (NY) Coll., 1976, grad. program in pub. health Rutgers U., 1986—, dept. environ. and cmty. medicine Robert Wood Johnson Med. Sch., Rutgers U., 1987—; adv. com. environ./occupl. health info. program 1984-89; founder, dir. environ. comm. rsch. program NJ Agrl. Exptl. Sta., Rutgers U., 1986-92; vis. scholar urban and environ. policy Tufts U., Medford, Mass., 1990-91; rsch. prof. George Perkins Marsh Inst., Clark U.; comm. coun. Environ. Def. Fund, 1985—; bd. advisors grad. program in tech. and sci. comm. Drexel U., Phila., 1988—; cons. on comm. ACP, 1976-79, Cousteau Soc., 1977-79, Pres. Com. on the Accident at Three Mile Island; specialist in comm. coop. ext. svc. U.S. Dept. Agr., 1977-86; cons. risk commn. office policy analysis EPA, 1986-88; exec. com. Sci. Writing Educators Group, 1978-81; cons. ARCO Chem., Boise Cascade, Chevron, Ciba-Geigy, Consumers Power, Dow, Du Pont, Johnson and Johnson, Johnson Wax, Procter and Gamble, Union Carbide, others. Cons. editor Random House, 1982-89, McGraw-Hill, 1989-94, Holt, Rinehart and Winston, 1978-81; contbg. editor Apt. Life, 1971-75; freelance writer, 1966—; editl. bd. Pub. Rels. Rsch. Ann., 1981-91, Jour. Pub. Rels. Rsch., 1991-94; editl. adv. bd. Environ. and Behavior, 1976-86; contbr. articles to profl. jours. Bd. dirs. N.J. Environ. Lobby, 1984-90, Nuclear Dialogue Project, 1985-90, pres. 1986-90; pub. info. com. N.J. chpt., Am. Cancer Soc., 1981-86, vice-chmn., 1983-86; comm. coord. N.J. Campaign for a Nuclear Weapons Freeze, 1982-85; socioeconomic subcom., com. on biotechnology agr. divsn. Nat. Assn. State Univs. and Land Grant Colls., 1988-90; bd. advisors Environ. Scientists for Global Survival, 1988-91; sci. review panel, radium/radon adv. bd. N.J. Dept. Environ. Protection, 1987-88; com. to survey the health effects mustard gas and lewisite Inst. Medicine, NAS, 1992. Mem. AAUP, ACLU (bd. dirs. N.J. chpt. 1984-87), Environ. Def. Fund, Nat. Assn. Profl. Environ. Communicators, Sci. Writing Educators Group, Soc. for Risk Analysis, Soc. Environ. Journalists, Internat. Assn. Pub. Participation Practitioners, Sigma Delta Chi. Home: 59 Ridgeview Rd Princeton NJ 08540-7601 Office Phone: 609-683-4073. Personal E-mail: peter@psandman.com.

SANDNESS, PAUL K., lawyer, energy executive; b. 1954; BA, Valley City State U.; JD, U. ND. Bar: 1979. Various positions including sr. atty. MDU Resources Group, Inc., 1980—2004, gen. counsel, sec., 2004—. Office: MDU Resources Group Inc 1200 W Century Ave PO Box 5650 Bismarck ND 58506-5650 *

SANDORSEN, CASSIOPEIA, public health service officer; b. East Chicago, Ind., July 30, 1958; Health info. mgmt. cons. Wash. U. Sch. Medicine, St. Louis, 2001—; clin. analyst cons. Sisters Saint Mary DePaul Health Ctr., Bridgeton, Mo., 2002—; special corr. Pulitzer, Inc., St. Louis, 2004—. Clin. analyst cons. Gateway Health Info. Mgmt. Project, St. Louis, 2002—. Audio tape and cd series, Sound of Poetry, poetry, Half-Dimension, anthology, Essence of a Dream, Diamonds and Pearls, The Fourth Dimension, New Dawnings, Dreams Gone By, Theatre of The Mind, 2003, Autumn Necklace, Best Poems and Poets of 2003, 2004. Founder Nat. Law Enforcement Mus., Washington, 2003—03; mem. Republican Presdl. Task Force, 2003—04. Recipient Poetic Achievement award, Creative Arts and Sci. Enterprises, 1997, Amherst Soc., 1998, Malcolm Baldridge Nat. Quality award, Bush Adminstrn., 2002, award, Robert Wood Johnson Found., 2003; scholar, Esperanto League of N.Am., 2003. Mem.: Am. Acad. Poets, Internat. Soc. Poets, Mo. Bot. Garden, St. Louis Art Mus., Mo. Hist. Soc., Am. Mus. Natural History, St. Louis Symphony Orch. Vivaldi Soc. Republican. Avocations: nature walks, gardening, fiber arts, travel.

SANDOVAL, ARTURO ALONZO, artist, educator; b. Espanola/Cordova, N.Mex., Feb. 1, 1942; s. Lorenzo Sandoval and Cecilia Eulalia (Archuleta) Harrison; (div. Sept. 1982); 1 child, Avalon Valentine Galaglorial. Student, U. Portland, 1959; BA, Calif. State Coll., LA, 1964, MA, 1969; MFA, Cranbrook Acad. Art, Bloomfield Hills, Mich., 1971. Designer, illustrator Western Lighting Corp., LA, 1964-66; advt. designer, adult edn. instr. spl. svcs. USN, Yokosuka, Japan, 1966; interior design asst. Walter B. Broderick & Assocs., La Mesa, Calif., 1967; asst. prof. art dept. U. Ky., Lexington, 1974—76, assoc. prof., 1976—86, prof., 1986—, dir. art dept. Barnhart Gallery, 1976—, curator, 1979—. Teaching asst. Calif. State Coll., L.A., 1969, Cranbrook Acad. Art, Bloomfield Hills, 1969-71; fiber art demonstrator Mus. Art, Grand Rapids, Mich., 1970; batik and tie-dye demonstrator Gwynn's Fabric Shop, Birmingham, Mich., 1970; instr. Calif. State Coll., L.A., 1970, So. Ill. U., Carbondale, 1971, Edwardsville, 1971, 72, 73, asst. prof., 1971-73; presenter various lectures and workshops throughout the U.S., 1973—; juror Mo. Women Festival Arts, St. Louis, So. Ill. U., East St. Louis, 1974, Paramount Arts Assn., Ashland, Ky., 1975, Ind. Weavers Guild, Indpls., 1979, Fed. Corrections Inst., Lexington, 1979, Hawaii Craftsman Hui and Art Dept. U. Hawaii, Manoa, Honolulu, 1982, art dept. Va. Intermont Coll., Bristol, 1982, Arrowmont Sch. Arts and Crafts, Gatlinburg, Tenn., 1984, Ctr. Contemporary Art, U. Ky., Lexington, 1984, Guild Greater Cin., Carnegie Art Ctr., Covington, Ky., 1989, S.C. Arts Commn., Charleston, 1990, Adams Art Gallery, Dunkirk, N.Y., 1994; visual arts cons. Ky. Arts Commn., Frankfort, 1977; curator Visual Arts Ctr. Alaska, Anchorage, 1982, Ky. Art and Crafts Found., Inc., Louisville, 1985; mem. artist adv. panel Ky. Art and Crafts Found., Louisville, 1986, 87, 92-2000; visual arts cons. Arts Midwest, 1987; artistic advisor Ky. Guild Mktg. Bd., Berea, 1988, 91, 92, 93; bd. trustees Ky. Guild 1995-98, Am. Craft Coun., N.Y.C., 1996—; vis. artist/critic Allen R. Hite Inst., U. Louisville, 1992; vis. artist Coll. Human Environ. Scis., U. Ky., Lexington, 1993; vis. artist/ lectr. fiber dept. Cranbrook Acad. Art, Bloomfield Hills, Mich., 1994, Art. Dept. St. Louis Comm. Coll.-Florissant Valley, 2001, U. Ariz., 2001; curator Art Quilts 2001, River Oaks Square Art Ctr., Louisiana, 2001; alumni-endowed rsch. prof. U. Ky., 2007-. Exhibited in group shows at Yeiser Art Ctr., Paducah/Paramount Arts Ctr., Ashland/S.E. Cmty. Coll., Cumberland, 1994, Textile Arts Centre, Chgo., 1994, Winnipeg (Man., Can.) Art Gallery, 1994, Riffe Gallery, Ohio Arts Coun., Columbus, 1994, Royal Hiberian Acad., Gallagher Gallery, Dublin, Ireland, Cooper Gallery, Barnsley, South Yorks, Gt. Britain, Shipley Art Gallery, Gateshead, Gt. Britain, 1994, Grand Rapids (Mich.) Art Mus., 1994, Whatcom Mus. History and Art, Bellingham, Wash., The Rockwell Mus., Corning, N.Y., Mus. Art, Washington State U., Pullman, The Hyde Collection, Glen Falls, N.Y., 1994, U. Art Galleries, U. S.D., Vermillion, 1994, Barnhart Gallery, U. Ky., Lexington, 1994, Sawtooth Ctr. Visual Art, 1994, Santa Fe Gallery, Santa Fe Cmty. Coll., Gainesville, Fla., 1994, Liberty Gallery, Louisville, 1994, Asahi Shimbun Gallery, Tokyo, Takashimaya Gallery, Osaka, 1994, Minn. Mus. Art, Landmark Ctr., St. Paul, 1994, S.C. State Mus., Columbia, 1994, Galbreath Gallery, Lexington, 1994, U.K. Art Mus., 1998, Giles Gallery, Richmond, Ky., 2004, Ky. Mus. of Art and Design, 2004, Ronald Barr Gallery, New Albany, Ind., 2004, City Gallery, S.C., 2004, Tuska Gallery, Ky., 2004, Pres. Room. Ky., 2004, numerous others; represented in permanent collections at Wabash Coll., Crawfordsville, Ind., Greenville County Mus. Art, Greenville, S.C., Mus. Modern Art, N.Y.C., St. Mary's Coll., Notre Dame, Ind., Coll. St. Rose, Albany, N.Y., Bowling Green (Ohio) StateU., U. Notre Dame, Transylvania U., Lexington, U. Ky. Mus. Art, Lexington, Mid-Am. Rare Coin Auction Galleries, Lexington, Henry Luce Found., N.Y.C., Lexington Ctrl. Libr., UK Art Mus., Nat. Mus. Am. Art, Renwick Gallery, J.B. Speed Art Mus., Louisville, Linda Schwartz Gallery, Tuska Gallery, Pres.'s Room, KY, Shands Gallery, Friedman Gallery, KGAG Offices, Actor's Theater, Ronald Barr Gallery, Opera House Gallery, Waltron Ltd., Whitehouse, N.J., Nat. Hispanic Cultural Arts Ctr., Albuquerque, N.Mex., Rocky Mt. Quilt Mus., Golden, Colo., Mus. Art and Design, N.Y. Recipient Alexandra Korsakoff Galston Meml. prize St. Louis Artist's Guild, 1971, Mus. Merit award Mus. Arts and Scis., Evansville, 1972, Creative Rsch. Grant So. Ill. U.-Edwardsville Rsch. Found., 1972, Craftsman fellowship Nat. Endowment Arts, Washington, 1973, Friend of Mus. award Mus. Arts and Scis., Evansville, 1973, Clay Eugene Jordan ann. bequest prize crafts St. Louis Artist's Guild, 1973, Teaching Improvement grant U. Ky. Rsch. Found., 1974, Travel grant U. Ky. Rsch. Found., 1977, Judges Choice award Berea (Ky.) Coll., 1978, Handweaver's Guild Am. award, 1978, Fiber award LeMoyne Art Found., Tallahassee, 1981, Elise Strout Merit award Mus. Arts and Scis., Evansville, 1981, Handweavers Guild Am. award, 1983, Martha Ryan Merit award Mus. Arts and Scis., Evansville, 1984, Best of Show award Gayle Willson Galleries, Southampton, 1984, Juror's merit award Brenau Coll., Gainesville, Ga., 1985, Installation Grant Ind. Arts Commn., Ft. Wayne, 1985, All Smith fellowship Ky. Arts Coun., Frankfort, 1987, Merit award Spotlight '88 Am. Craft Coun. Southeast Conf., Tuscaloosa, Ala., 1988, Merit award Mus. Arts and Scis., Evansville, 1989, Design Grant, Arts and Cultural Coun. for O.A. Singletary Ctr. Arts, Lexington, 1990, Visual Arts fellowship Nat. Endowment for Arts, Washington, 1992, Hon. award Ky. Crafts Mktg. Bd., Frankfort, 1994, Rude Osolnik Craftsman award Ky. Crafts Mktg. & KAC Fund, 1998, 1st pl. Lexington Art League, Reverse Raffle, Lexington, 1999, Art-in-Arch. Program commn. Gen. Svcs. Adminstrn., London, Ky., 2002; Artist award Ky. Gov.'s award in the arts, 2003, Merit award ACCSE, 2006, Kirwan Meml. prize U. Ky., 2007; grantee NEA, Pyramid Atlantic Press, Riverdale, Md., 1996; Gen. Svcs. Adminstrn.; Al Smith fellow Ky. Arts Coun., 1987, 2006; Kirwan prize, U. Ky, 2007, Alumni professorship, 2007—. Mem. Lexington Fiber Guild Inc., Louisville Visual Arts Assn., Ky. Art and Craft Found., Inc., Ky. Guild Artists and Crafstmen, Am. Craft Coun., Friends of U. Ky. Mus. Art, Friends of Fiber Art, Surface Design Assn. Home: PO Box 25153 Lexington KY 40524-5153 Office: U Ky Dept Art 207 Fine Arts Bldg Lexington KY 40506-0022 Office Phone: 859-230-9635. Personal E-mail: a.sandoval@insightbb.com.

SANDOVAL, BRIAN EDWARD, federal judge, former state attorney general; b. Redding, Calif., Aug. 5, 1963; s. Ronald L. and Gloria Sandoval; m. Kathleen T. Sandoval; children: James, Madeline, Marisa. B in English & Econ., U. Nev., 1986; JD, Ohio State U., 1989. Bar: Nev., Calif., DC. Mem. Nev. State Assembly, 1995—97; atty. McDonald, Carano, Wilson, McCune Bergin, Frankovich & Hicks, Reno, 1989—91, Robinson, Belaustegui, Robb & Sharp, Reno, 1991—95, Gamboa, Sandoval & Stovall, Reno, 1995—99, Sandoval Law Office, Reno, 1999—2003; atty. gen. State of Nev., Carson City, 2003—05; judge US Dist. Ct. Dist. Nev., Reno, 2005—. Mem. Nev. Gaming Commn., 1998—2001, chmn., 1999—2001; mem. State and Local Officials' Adv. Com. US Dept. Homeland Security. Bd. trustees Children's Cabinet, Reno, St. Jude's Ranch for Children, Washoe County Law Libr., Nev. Named Public Lawyer of the Yr., Nevada St. Bar Assoc., 2004; recipient Torch of Liberty, Anti-Defamation League, 2003. Republican. Office: US Dist Ct 400 S Virginia St Reno NV 89501

SANDOZ, GEORGE ELLIS, JR., political science educator; b. New Orleans, Feb. 10, 1931; s. George Ellis and Ruby (Odom) S.; m. Therese Alverne Hubley, May 31, 1957; children: Ellis III, Lisa, Erica, Jonathan. BA in History, La. State U., 1951, MA in Polit. Sci., 1953; D in Polit. Sci., U. Munich, Germany, 1965. Capitol Hill policeman U.S. Ho. of Reps., Washington, 1952-53; instr. to prof. La. Poly. Inst., Ruston, 1959-68; prof., head dept. polit. sci. East Tex. State U., Commerce, 1968-78; prof. polit. sci., chmn. La. State U., Baton Rouge, 1978—, dir. Eric Voegelin Inst., 1987—, Hermann Moyse Jr. disting. prof. polit. sci., 2006—. Mem. Nat. Coun. on the Humanities, Washington, 1982-88; lectr. in field. Author: Political Apocalypse, 1971, 2d edit., 2000, Conceived in Liberty, 1978, The Voegelinian Revolution, 1981, 2nd edit., 2000, A Government of Laws, 1990, 2d edit., 2000; editor: The Collected Works of Eric Voegelin, 1986—; author introduction, editor: Political Sermons of the American Founding Era, 1730-1805, 1991, Roots of Liberty, 1993, Politics of Truth, 1999, Republicanism, Religion and the Soul of America, 2006. Nat. co-chair Reagan-Bush Presidency, Washington, 1984. Pvt. 1st lt. USMC, 1953-56. Fulbright scholar Bd. Fgn. Scholarships, Washington, 1964-65, Fulbright 40th Anniversary Disting. Am. scholar USIA, Italy, 1987. Mem. Am. Polit. Sci. Assn., So. Polit. Sci. Assn. (coun. 1982-85), Southwestern Polit. and Social Sci. Assn. (pres. 1987-88). Republican. Baptist. Avocations: hunting, fishing, tennis. Home: 2843 Valcour Aime Ave Baton Rouge LA 70820-4424 Office: La State U Eric Voegelin Inst 240 Stubbs Hall Baton Rouge LA 70803-0001 Business E-Mail: esandoz@lsu.edu.

SANDQUIST, GARY MARLIN, engineering educator, researcher, consultant, writer, military officer; b. Salt Lake City, Apr. 19, 1936; s. Donald August Sandquist and Lillian (Evaline) Dunn; m. Kristine Powell, Jan. 17, 1992; children from previous marriage: Titia, Julia, Taunia, Cynthia, Carl; stepchildren: David, Michael, Scott, Diane, Jeff. BSME in Mech. Engring., U. Utah, 1956—60; MS in Engring. Sci., U. Calif., Berkeley, 1960—61; PhD in Mech. Nuclear Engring., U. Utah, 1961—64, MBA Exec. MS, 1993—95. Registered profl. engr., Utah, N.Y., Minn., Calif.; cert health physicist, quality auditor; diplomate Am. Acad. Environ. Engring. Staff mem. Los Alamos (N.Mex.) Sci. Lab., 1966; postdoctoral fellow MIT, 1969-70; rsch. prof. surgery Med. Sch., U. Utah, Salt Lake City, 1974—85, prof., dir. nuc. engring. dept. mech. engring., 1975—, acting chmn. dept., 1984-85, adj. prof. civil engring., 1996—; expert in nuc. sci. Internat. Atomic Energy Agy., UN, 1980—; chief scientist Rogers and Assocs. Engring. Corp., Salt Lake City, 1980—90, sr. nuclear engr., 1998—; sr. health physicist URS Corp., 1990—; mgr., owner Applied Sci. Profls., LLC, Salt Lake City, 1998—. Vis. scientist MIT, Cambridge, Mass., 1969-70; advisor rocket design Hercules, Inc., Bachus, Utah, 1962; sr. nuc. engr. Idaho Nat. Engring. Lab., Idaho Falls, 1963-65; cons. nuc. sci. State of Utah, 1982—; vis. prof. Ben Gurion U., Beer Sheva, Israel, 1985, disting. vis. prof. U.S. Mil. Acad., West Point, N.Y., 2003-05; affiliate faculty Idaho State U., 1998-; cons. various cos.; spkr. Nuc. Energy Inst., 1990—; mem. radiation adv com., EPA. Author: Geothermal Energy, 1973, Introduction to System Science, 1985, over 650 pub. presentations, reports in sci. and tech. Comdr. USNR, 1954-56, Korea; ret. Comdr. USNR, 1954—56, Intel officer USNR. Recipient Glen Murphy award in nuc. engring. Am. Soc. Engring. Edn., 1984. Fellow ASME, Am. Nuc. Soc.; mem. Am. Soc. Quality (sr.), Am. Health Physics Soc., Am. Soc. Engring. Edn., Alpha Nu Sigma, Sigma Xi, Tau Beta Pi, Pi Tau Sigma. Republican. Mem. Lds Ch. Achievements include development of 17 major computer codes; participated in 192 tech. meetings, confs., govt. hearings. Home: 2564 E Neffs Cir Salt Lake City UT 84109 Office: U Utah 2232 Merrill Engring Bldg Salt Lake City UT 84112 Home Phone: 801-273-0200. Personal E-mail: gms@asp-llc.com.

SANDRESKY, MARGARET VARDELL, retired composer; b. Macon, Ga., Apr. 28, 1921; d. Charles Gildersleeve Vardell and Eleanor Matilda Ferrill; m. Clemens Harold Sandresky; children: Eleanor, Paul(dec.), Charles. MusB, Salem Coll., Winston-Salem, NC, 1942; MusM, U. Rochester, NY, 1944; cert., Hochschule für Musik, Frankfurt, Germany, 1956. Instr. music theory Oberlin Coll. Conservatory, Ohio, 1944—46, U. Tex., Austin, 1948; head organ dept. Salem Coll., Winston-Salem, 1948—56, prof. music, 1967—86; founder organ dept. NC Sch. Arts, Winston-Salem, 1965—67; ret., 1986. Co-founder NC Composers Symposium, Winston-Salem, 1970. Organist Centenary Meth. Ch., Winston-Salem, 1961—69; bd. dirs. Winston-Salem Symphony. Recipient NC Symphony award, 1952, Disting. Alumna award, Salem Acad. and Coll., 1993, Sam Ragan award, St. Andrews Coll., 2006; Fulbright scholar, Germany, 1955—56. Mem.: ASCAP (Stds. award), Am. Guild Organists (dean local chpt., Disting. Composer award 2004), Col. Dames Am. Home: 1244 Arbor Rd # 443 Winston Salem NC 27104

SANDRICH, JAY H., television director; b. LA, Feb. 24, 1932; s. Mark R. and Freda (Wirtschafter) S.; m. Nina Kramer, Feb. 11, 1952 (div.); children: Eric, Tony, Wendy; m. Linda Green Silverstein, Oct. 4, 1984. BA, UCLA, 1953. Prodr. (TV show) Get Smart, 1965; dir. (TV shows) He and She, 1967, Mary Tyler Moore Show, 1970-88, Soap, 1977-79, Cosby Show, 1984-92; dir. (films) Seems Like Old Times, 1980, For Richer, For Poorer (HBO), 1992, Neil Simon's London Suite (NBC), 1996. Served to 1st lt. Signal Corps U.S. Army, 1952-55. Mem. Dirs. Guild Am. (award 1975, 85, 86), TV Acad. Arts and Scis. (Emmy award 1971, 73, 85, 86). Office: care Andy Elkin Creative Artists Agy 9830 Wilshire Blvd Beverly Hills CA 90212

SANDRIDGE, WILLIAM PENDLETON, JR., lawyer; b. Winston-Salem, NC, Jan. 27, 1934; m. Jane Carolyn Yeager, Dec. 10, 1966; children: Jane, William. AB, U. N.C., 1956; LLB, U. Va., 1961. Bar: N.C. 1961. Mem. Womble Carlyle Sandridge & Rice, PLLC, Winston-Salem, 1962—. Chmn., bd. dirs. Horizons Residential Care Ctr., 1980, Food Bank N.W. N.C., Inc., 1988-89, Data Max Corp., 1996. Office: Womble Carlyle Et Al One W Fourth St Winston Salem NC 27101

SANDROK, RICHARD WILLIAM, lawyer; b. Evergreen Park, Ill., July 8, 1943; s. Edward George and Gertrude Jeanette (Van Stright) Sandrok; m.

Rebecca Fittz, June 19, 1973; children: Richard William, Jr., Alexander Edward, Philip Robert, Erika Joy. BA, Wheaton Coll., Ill., 1965; JD, U. Ill., 1968. Bar: Ill. 1968, U.S. Dist. Ct. (no. dist.) Ill. 1971, ct. apptd. arbitrator: Cook, DuPage, Kane and Will counties. Assoc. Hinshaw Culbertson Moelmann Hoban & Fuller, Chgo. and Wheaton, 1971-75, ptnr. Wheaton, 1976-89, Lisle, Ill., 1989—2001; sole practice Glen Ellyn, Ill., 2001—. Arbitrator Ill. State Mandatory Arbitration. Reviewer: Legal Checklists. Capt. US Army, 1969—71. Mem.: Ill. Ct. Sys. Arbitrator, Assn. Def. Trial Attys., DuPage County Bar Assn. (chmn. med./legal com. 1978—79), Am. Arbitration Assn. (arbitrator). Home: 818 Revere Rd Glen Ellyn IL 60137-5537 Office: Richard W Sandrok Atty at Law 818 Revere Rd Glen Ellyn IL 60137 Office Phone: 630-790-1583. E-mail: RWS283@yahoo.com.

SANDS, DARRY GENE, lawyer; b. Charleston, Ark., Jan. 4, 1947; s. Anthony Wayne and Marjorie (Elkins) S.; m. Charlotte Moore, Dec. 28, 1968; 1 child, Spencer Justin. BS, U. Ark., 1969; JD, U. Kans., 1974. Bar: Mo. 1974, U.S. Dist. Ct. (we. dist.) Mo. 1974. Dir. Davis, Sands & Collins, P.C., Kansas City, Mo., 1991—. Spkr. in field. Contbr. articles to profl. jours. Former mem. bd. dirs. Hope House. Mem. ABA, Mo. Bar, Kansas City Met. Bar Assn. (chmn., past chair coll. and univ. law com., local govt. com.), Order of Coif, Lake Quivira Country Club. Democrat. Home: 5341 Canterbury Rd Shawnee Mission KS 66205-2612 Office: Davis Sands & Collins PC 1720 Commerce Tower 911 Main St Kansas City MO 64105-2105 Home Phone: 913-722-4451; Office Phone: 816-221-8188. Business E-Mail: dsands@ddsc-law.com.

SANDS, DAWN M., lawyer; BA magna cum laude, U. Wis., Eau Claire, 1985; JD cum laude, William Mitchell Coll. Law, 1993. Aide to U.S. Senator Robert Kasten, Wis., Washington; aide to U.S. Senate Fgn. Rels. Com.; mem. exec. staff. Nat. Rep. Senatorial Com.; adminstr. Campaign America PAC; v.p., gen. counsel Menard Inc., Eau Claire, Wis., 1999—. Office: Menard Inc Legal Dept 4777 Menard Dr Eau Claire WI 54703-9604

SANDS, HAROLD WINTHROP, banker, financial planner; b. NYC, Aug. 25, 1926; s. Harold Aymar and Muriel Winthrop Sands; m. Joan Hodges Baker, Sept. 6, 1961; children: Harold, Serena. Grad., St. George's Sch., 1946; student, CBS-NBS Tellers' Acad., 1950—52, Am. Inst. Banking, 1967—69; postgrad., Miami Dade U., 1968—71. V.p., devel. officer, regional mgr. S.E. Banks, Miami, London, Europe, Caribbean, 1967-79; v.p. Marine Midland Bank N.V., London, 1979-85; sr. cons., fin. adviser Sun Life Assurance Soc., London, 1985-87; U.K. rep. Wright Investment Svc., London, 1987-92; v.p. Kreditbank Global Mgmt., Miami, 1993-94; dir., trustee Kapok Bermuda Ltd., London, 1994-96; gen. ptnr. The Winthrop Group L.P., Newport, RI, 1996-2001; assoc. v.p. Pre-paid Legal Svcs., Inc., Newport, RI, 2001—; gen. mgr. Peace Mgmt. Group LLC, Newport, RI, 2002—. Founder Lorimex Internat., N.Y.C., 1952-60; CEO acctg., sales Paramount Pictures Corp., N.Y.C., 1950-52; founder, CEO Distbrs. for Mexico Rex Chain Belt, Ampudia A.S. Mex., 1960-67. Chair N.Am. com. London C. of C., 1985-88, chmn. Caribbean com., 1988-91; hon. treas. European Atlantic Group, 1980—; mem. Rep. Com.; mem. Woolnoth Soc. Coun., City of London, 1980-93; trustee La Farge Restoration Fund of Newport, 1996—; trustee Preservation Soc. Newport, mem. fin. and edn. coms., 1994-2000; com. mem. Tall Ships Salute, 1995; bd. dirs. Newport Hist. Soc., 2001—. Master sgt. U.S. Army, 101st Armed Cav., 1949-54. Decorated Imperial House of David, 1995, Comdr. of Most Revered Order of the Star of Ethiopia, Freeman of the City of London. Mem.: SAR (Newport chpt.), Order of Founders and Patriots R.I. (gov.), The Guild of Internat. Bankers London (liveryman), Order of 1st Families of R.I., Soc. Colonial Wars (Providence and Boston chpts.), RAC Club London, Ida Lewis Club (Newport, R.I.), Clambake Club (gov. reading club), Reading Rm. Club, Ends of the Earth Club London, Broad St. Ward Club London, Rotary Internat., Pilgrim's London. Avocations: sailing, tennis, skiing, boating, chess. Home: 10 Cherry Creek Rd Newport RI 02840 Fax: 401-846-1066. Personal E-mail: hss6518@aol.com.

SANDS, HARRY, psychologist, health administrator, researcher; b. NYC, Jan. 6, 1917; s. Morris and Lena Sandrowitz; m. Helene Purl, June 24, 1945; children: Jeffrey, Richard. AB, NYU, 1941, PhD in Psychology, 1952. Diplomate Am. Bd. Profl. Psychology; lic. psychologist, N.Y. Rsch. fellow dept neurology Neurol. Inst./Columbia U. Phys. and Surg., NYC, 1941-42, rsch. chief psychophysiologist Head Injury Project, 1942-44; assoc. dir., chief psychologist Baird Found. Clinic for Children with Epilepsy/Beth David Hosp., NYC, 1944-46; instr. Washington Sq. Coll./NYU, 1947-50, Bklyn. Coll., 1950-52; exec. dir. Com. Pub. Understanding of Epilepsy, NYC, 1952-53, United Epilepsy Assn. Am., NYC, 1953-56; dir. and clin. psychologist Psychol. Lab., Inc., NYC, 1955-61; dir. Epilesy Asn. N.Y., Epilepsy Found. Am., NYC, 1956-68; dir. program planning and evaluation Epilepsy Found. Am., Washington, 1972-74; assoc. staff adult therapy clinic Postgrad. Ctr. for Mental Health, NYC, 1962-66, assoc. staff supervision therapeutic process, 1971-73, assoc. supr., sr. supr. psychoanalysis, psychotherapy, 1974—85, tng. analyst, psychoanalysis, psychotherapy, 1993-98, exec. v.p., CEO, 1979—87, exec. dir., CEO, 1987—88. Pvt. practice pyschoanalysis and psychotherapy, N.Y.C., 1952-98; cons. divsn. resource devel. Nat. Inst. on Drug Abuse, Rockville, Md., 1978-79, Commn. for Control of Epilepsy and its Consequences, HEW, Washington, 1977, legal and protective svcs. project, Harvard U. Sch. of Pub. Health, Boston, 1974, cons. classification exceptional children, adequacy of classification for physically and sensorially handicapped, Vanderbilt U., Knoxville, 1974, bd. trustees, exec. com., 1988—; bd. dirs. Postgrad. Ctr. Residences, I, II, and III, N.Y.C., 1991-96, sec., 1991-2000, 2002—, pres. Editor: (book) Epilepsy: A Handbook for the Mental Health Professional, 1982 (Book of Yr. award ANA, 1982); co-author: (books) Epilepsy Fact Book, 1979, Education and Training Beyond the Doctoral Degree, 1995, Impact of Managed Care on Psychodynamic Treatment, 1996, The Guide to Pastoral Counseling and Care, 2000; contbr. chpts. in books, articles to profl. jours. Mem. tech. adv. com. on epilepsy N.Y. Dept Health, N.Y.C., 1945, planning com. advisory com on epilepsy, N.Y. State Dept. Mental Hygiene, Albany, 1952, joint legis. com. of State of N.Y. on program of pub. health, medicaid and compulsory health and hosp. ins., Albany, 1953; mem com. on Neurol. Disorders in Industry and com. on Emergency Med. Identification, AMA, Chgo., 1953, com. of info. svcs. and employment com., handicapped sect., Comty. Coun. of Greater N.Y., N.Y.C., 1954, joint legis. com. on mental retardation and physical handicaps, State of N.Y., Albany, 1956. Recipient fellowship Internat. Rehab. Rsch. Program of Social and Rehab. Svcs., HEW, Washington, 1972, Gold medal award for lifetime achievement in practice of psychology, Am. Psychol. Found., Washington, 1995; grantee Social Rehab. Svcs, HEW, Washington, 1968, 78. Fellow APA (bd. govs. coll. profl. practice 1994-99, co-chair nat. conf. on postdoctoral edn. and tng., Washington, 1992-94, bd. govs. coll. profl. practice, 1994-99, coun. reps. 1988-91, 1994, treas. com. for advancement profl. practice, practice directorate, 1992-94, cons. 1995, Karl F. Heiser Presdl. award 1993, Disting. Psychologist award Divsn. Psychotherapy 1995); mem. Am. Acad. Psychology, N.Y. State Psychol. Assn. (pres. 1978-79, 1985-86, coun. of reps. 1957-60, 1986-91, Allen J. Williams Jr. Meml. award 1993), Postgrad. Psychoanalytic Soc., Nat. Acad. of Practices (Disting. Practitioner in Psychology 1995), Psi Chi, Sigma Xi. Democrat. Jewish. Avocations: travel, theater, music, ballet. Home and Office: 219 E 69th St Apt 7 D New York NY 10021-5455

SANDS, JEFF MICHAEL, medical educator; s. Joseph and Jean Lillian Sands; m. Abbe Maureen Zorn, Nov. 23, 1986; children: Jared Samuel, Jenna Shari. BA summa cum laude, Harvard Coll., Cambridge, 1977; MD, Boston U., Mass., 1981. Diplomate internal medicine Am. Bd. Internal Medicine, 1984, nephrology Am. Bd. Internal Medicine, 1992. Asst. prof. medicine Emory U., Atlanta, 1989—93, assoc. prof. medicine, 1993—98, prof. medicine and physiology, 1998—, assoc. dean clinical and translational rsch., 2006—. Renal divsn. dir. Emory U., 2002—. Editor-in-chief Am. Jour. Physiology, Bethesda, 2001—07. Rsch. grants, NIH, 1989—. Mem.: Am. Physiol. Soc. (councillor 2003—06), Am. Soc. Nephrology (program com. chmn. 2003—04), Am. Soc. Clin. Investigation, Am. Assn. Physicians. Achievements include research in renal physiology. Office: Emory U Renal Divsn WMB Rm 338 1639 Pierce Drive Atlanta GA 30322 Home Phone: 404-727-3425. Business E-Mail: jeff.sands@emory.edu.

SANDS, MATTHEW LINZEE, physicist, researcher; b. Oxford, Mass., Oct. 20, 1919; m. Freya Kidner, 1978; children: Michael, Richard, Michelle. BA, Clark U., 1940; MA, Rice U., 1941; PhD, MIT, 1948. Physicist U.S. Naval Ordnance Lab., 1941-43, Los Alamos Sci. Lab., 1943-46; research asso., then asst. prof. physics Mass. Inst. Tech., 1946-50; sr. research fellow, asso. prof., prof. physics Calif. Inst. Tech., 1950-63; prof., dep. dir. Linear Accelerator Center, Stanford, 1963-69; prof. physics U. Calif.-Santa Cruz, 1969-85, prof. emeritus, 1985—, fellow Kresge Coll.; vice chancellor for sci., 1969-72; pres. Sands-Kidner Assocs., Inc., 1986-90. Vis. prof. U. Paris-Sud, spring 1976; mem. Commn. Coll. Physics, 1960-66, chmn., 1964-66; cons. Office Sci. and Tech., ACDA, Inst. Def. Analyses, 1962-67; mem. Pugwash Conf. Sci. and World Affairs, 1960-63; cons. on accelerator physics, 1975-93. Author: (with W.C. Elmore) Electronics-Experimental Techniques, 1948, (with R.P. Feynman and R.B. Leighton) The Feynman Lectures on Physics, 3 vols, 1965, (with others) Physical Science Today, 1973; mem. editl. bd.: Il Nuovo Cimento, 1972-85; contbr. articles to profl. jours. Fulbright scholar Italy, 1952-53. Fellow Am. Phys. Soc. (Robert R. Wilson prize 1998); mem. Am. Assn. Physics Tchrs. (Disting. Service award 1972), Fedn. Am. Scientists, AAAS. Achievements include research in electronic instrumentation for nuclear physics; electron storage rings; science and public affairs; science education; high-energy physics; accelerators; cosmic rays. Home: 160 Michael Ln Santa Cruz CA 95060-1704

SANDS, RICHARD E., food products executive; b. Canandaigua, NY, Mar. 3, 1951; s. Marvin Sands and Marilyn Alpert; m. Sharon Gillick, Apr. 1991. BA, Univ. Vt., 1974; MA, Univ. NC, 1978, PhD, 1979. Teaching rsch. asst. psychology dept. U. N.C., Chapel Hill, 1974-79; exec. trainee Canandaigua Wine Co. Inc., 1979; exec. v.p. Constellation Brands, Inc., Fairport, NY, 1982-86, pres., COO, 1986—93, pres., CEO, 1993—2002, chmn., CEO, 2002—07, chmn., 2007—. Office: Constellation Brands Inc 370 Woodcliff Dr Fairport NY 14450 *

SANDS, RICK (RICHARD SANDS), film company executive; BA with honors in Economics and Film, Syracuse U. From regional sales to head domestic distbn. divsn. Columbia Pictures; exec. v.p., CFO Miramax Films, 1990—93, RHI Entertainment (sold to Hallmark Entertainment), 1993—95; pres. internat. Miramax Films, 1995—97, chmn. worldwide distbn., 1997—2002, COO, 2002—04; pres., COO DreamWorks SKG, 2005—06; COO MGM (Metro-Goldwyn-Mayer Inc.), LA, 2006—. Recipient Humanitarian award, Variety Boys and Girls Club of Queens, 2003. Office: Metro-Goldwyn-Mayer Inc 10250 Constellation Blvd Los Angeles CA 90067-6241 Office Phone: 310-449-3000. Office Fax: 310-449-8750.

SANDS, ROBERT, food products executive; b. Canandaigua, NY, June 10, 1958; B., Skidmore Coll., 1981; JD, Pace U. Sch. Law, 1984. Assoc. Harter, Secrest & Emery; gen. counsel Constellation Brands, Inc., Fairport, NY, 1986—90, v.p., gen. counsel, 1990—93, exec. v.p., gen. counsel, 1993—2000, CEO, internat., 1998—2000, group pres., 2000—02, pres., COO, 2002—07, pres., CEO, 2007—. Pres. bd. trustees Harley Sch.; bd. trustees F.F. Thompson Health Sys.; chmn. bd. trustees ViaHealth Sys. Office: Constellation Brands Inc 370 Woodcliff Dr Ste 300 Fairport NY 14450 *

SANDS, SHARON LOUISE, graphics designer, artist; b. Jacksonville, Fla., July 4, 1944; d. Clifford Harding Sands and Ruby May MacDonald; m. Jonathan Michael Langford, Feb. 14, 1988. BFA, Ctrl. Washington U., 1968; postgrad, UCLA, 1968. Art dir. East West Network, Inc., LA, 1973-78, Daisy Pub., LA, 1978; prodn. dir. L.A. mag., 1979-80; owner, creative dir. Carmel Graphic Design, Carmel Valley, Calif., 1981-85; creative dir., v.p The Video Sch. House, Monterey, Calif., 1985-88; graphic designer ConAgra, Omaha, 1988; owner, creative dir. Esprit de Fleurs, Ltd., Carmel, Calif., 1988-99; owner Sweden by the Sea, Carmel, 1999—2001; owner, dir. Sands Art Studios, Penn Valley, Calif., 1999—. Lectr. Pub. Expo, LA, 1979; panelist Women in Mgmt., LA, 1979; designer corp. ID Carmel Valley CC, 1981, 90; redesign of local newspaper, Carmel, Calif., 82. One-woman shows include Ananda Retreat Ctr., Nevada City, Calif., 2004, Nevada City Winery, 2004; contbr. articles to profl. mags. Recipient 7 design awards, Soc. Pub. Designers, 1977, 1978, Maggie award, LA, 1977, 5 Design awards, Ad Club Monterey Peninsula, 1983, 1985, 1987, Design awards, Print Mag. N.Y., 1986, Desi awards, N.Y., 1986, 1988, Oil Painting awards, Monterey Jazz Festival, 1999. Mem.: Sierra Club. Democrat. Avocations: oil painting, interior decorating, hiking, kayaking. Home and Studio: Lake Wildwood 18807 Chaparral Dr Penn Valley CA 95946-9688

SANDS, VELMA AHDA, lawyer; d. John T. and Thelma Jane (Davis) Carlisle BS, Calif. State U., Dominguez Hills, 1976; JD, Southwestern U., 1985. CPA. Cons. KPMG Peat Marwick Main, LA, 1980—81; v.p. Security Pacific Bank, LA, 1981—86; contr. L.A. Investors, 1986; mgr. IRC divsn. FN Realty Svcs., Pasadena, Calif., 1986—88; mgr. fin. reporting Luz Internat. Ltd., LA, 1988—89; pvt. practice law LA, 1990—; temp. judge L.A. Superior Ct., 1996—. Instr. Fame Entrepreneurial Tng. Program; co-pres. Multicultural Bar Alliance, 2001-02 Participant career day programs for local high schs.; mem. United We Stand Scholar Black Woman Lawyers Assn., 1982; recipient Commendation City of L.A., 2001, Cert. of Commendation, Gov. Calif. 2001, U.S. Senate 2001, Cert. of Recognition, Calif. State Assembly, 2001, Cert. Spl. Recognition, U.S. Rep. 2001, Cert. Congratulations Black Woman Lawyers Assn., 2002; Cert. Appreciation, Superior Ct. Calif., RBD Comm., Inc. award - 1st Ann., Samuel L. Williams Spirit of Law award for outstanding contbn. in field of law, 2001 Mem. ABA, NAFE, Nat. Assn. Bank Women (chair ways and means com. of scholarship fund 1986, scholar 1984), So. Calif. Chinese Lawyers Assn., L.A. County Bar Assn., John M. Langston Bar Assn. (pres. 2000, Pres.' Spl. Recognition award 1997, Appreciation award 2000, 2002), L.A. Bench and Bar Affiliates (scholarship com., meeting host, scholar 1983), Am. Bridge Assn., Phi Alpha Delta Office: 300 E Esplanade Dr 9th Fl Oxnard CA 93036 Home: 154 E Carmel Green Port Hueneme CA 93041 Home Phone: 805-612-0891; Office Phone: 800-281-1622.

SANDSTEAD, HAROLD HILTON, physician, researcher, educator, director; b. Omaha, May 25, 1932; s. Harold Russel and Lula Florence (Hilton) S.; m. Kathryn Gordon Brownlee, June 6, 1959 (dec. May 13, 1989); m. Victoria Regan Liddle, Feb. 14, 1990 (div. Oct. 1993); m. Wilma Helen Carter Streaker, Sept. 25, 2004; children: Eleanor McDonald, James Brownlee, William Harold. BA in Pre-Medicine, Ohio Wesleyan U., 1954; MD, Vanderbilt U., 1958. Cert. Am. Bd. Internal Medicine, 1967, Am. Bd. Nutrition, 1967, Am. Bd. Physician Nutrition Specialists, 2001; lic. physician Tex. Intern, internal medicine Barnes Hosp. Washington U., St. Louis, 1958—59, asst. resident, internal medicine, 1959—60; asst. resident, pathology Vanderbilt Hosp., Nashville, 1960-61; asst. surgeon USPHS U.S. NAMRU 3, Cairo, 1961-63; rsch. resident, internal medicine Thayer VA Hosp., Vanderbilt U., Nashville, 1963-64; chief med. resident, internal medicine Vanderbilt U. Hosp., Nashville, 1964-65; instr. internal medicine, asst. prof. biochemistry Med. Sch. Vanderbilt U., Nashville, 1965-70, asst. prof. internal medicine, assoc. prof. biochemistry in nutrition, 1970-71; dir. USDA-ARS Human Nutrition Rsch. Ctr., Grand Forks, ND, 1971-84; adj. prof. biochemistry and internal medicine Sch. Medicine U. N.D., Grand Forks, 1971-84; dir. USDA-ARS Human Nutrition Rsch. Ctr. on Aging at Tufts U., Boston, 1984-85; prof. nutrition Tufts U., Medford, Mass., 1984-85; prof. preventive medicine and community health U. Tex. Med. Br., Galveston, 1985—2006; chmn. preventive medicine and community health Med. Br. U. Tex., Galveston, 1985-90, prof. internal medicine, biochem. and molecular biology, 1986—2006, prof. emeritus preventative medicine and cmty. health and internal medicine, 2006—. Cons. IAEA, FAO, WHO, IPCS, UNEP, AID, NCI, NICHD, NEI, NHLBI, OIR, NIH, FDA, EPA, USDA, FNB, NRC, IOM, NAS, LSRO, FASEB, USP, AAP, ACS, ASPEN, AHF, Mead Johnson Company, Internaional Lead Zinc Research Organization, National Cattlemen's Beef Association, NeuroBioTex; Clinician, Nutrition Survey of Panama, Interdepartmental Committee for Nutrition & National Development, NIH, 1967, Field Team Director, Texas Nutrition Survey, 10 State Nutrition Survey, US Nutrition Program, NIH, 1968, Clinician, Kentucky Nutrition Survey, 10 State Nutrition Survey, US Nutrition Program, NIH, 1969, Panel Member, White House Conference on Food, Nutrition & Health, 1969, American Board of Nutrition, 1975-81, USDA, ARS, Human Studies Review Committee (Chairman, 83-5), 1976-85, Research Advisory Committee, NSLS X-Ray Microprobe, Brookhaven National Laboratory, 1984-90, Advisor, American Council on Science & Health, 1988-, FASEB Wellcome Vis. Prof. in Basic Med. Sci., Pa. State U., 1988, Zinc Information Nutrition Center Advisory Board, American Zinc Association, 1999-, Permanent Commn. on Occupl. Health, 2004-. Mem. editl. bd. Jour. Nutrition, 1972-76, 81-85, Am. Jour. Clin. Nutrition, 1975-78, Annual Rev. Nutritional Rsch., 1975-1991, Jour. Lab. Clin. Medicine, 1978-1983, Biol. Trace Element Rsch., 1979—, Nutrition Rsch., 1981-85, Nutritional Reports Internat., 1981-88, Trace Elements Medicine Biology, 1983-98, Jour. Trace Elements Exptl. Medicine, 1982-2004, Jour. Am. Coll. Nutrition, 1987-88, Nutrition Rsch. Newsletter, 1989-98, Cancer Prevention, 1990-1994; contbr. over 270 articles to profl. jours., chapters to books. Asst. surgeon USPHS, 1961—63. Recipient Future Leader award, Nutrition Found., 1968—71, Hull Gold medal, with HC Meng, AMA, 1970, Special Recognition award, Vanderbilt U. Sch. Medicine, 1971, Mead Johnson award, Am. Inst. Nutrition, 1971, WO Atwater award medal and lecture, US Dept. Agr., 1984, Ellen Swallow Richard Meml. Lecture, U. NC Inst. Nutrition, 1985, Sam & Mary Roberts Nutrition medal and Lecture, U. Kans. Sch. Medicine, 1985, Raymond Ewell Meml. lecture, U. Buffalo, SUNY Sch. Medicine, 1985, Special Recognition award, USDA Agrl. Rsch. Svc., 2004. Fellow ACP, Am. Soc. Nutrition (Mead Johson award 1972, fellow 1998); mem. Am. Soc. Clin. Nutrition (pres. 1982-83), Internat. Soc. for Trace Element Rsch. in Humans (pres. 2002-04, Raulin award 2007), Cosmos Club, Sigma Xi, Alpha Omega Alpha. Achievements include description of adverse effects of lead poisoning on renin-aldoserone function, pituitary-adrenal function, and pituitary-thyroid function; description of zinc deficiency in Egyptian adolescents, endocrine functions, and effects of zinc treatment; confirmation in rat of essentiality of zinc for nucleic acid and protein synthesis; confirmation in rats of the essentiality of zinc for wound healing; demonstration of some effects of zinc deficiency on development and function of rat on brain and on function later in life; demonstration of essentiality of zinc for neuropsychological functions of children and premenopausal women; demonstration of associations between iron status and zinc status in premenopausal women. Office: U Tex Med Br Ewing Bldg Galveston TX 77555-1109 Home: 5100 San Felipe Rd 351E Houston TX 77056 Office Phone: 409-772-4661. Business E-Mail: hsandste@utmb.edu.

SANDSTEDT, J. ERIK, lawyer; b. New Brunswick, NJ, Nov. 6, 1970; BA with distinction, Univ. NC, Chapel Hill, 1992; JD, Columbia Univ., 1995. Bar: NJ 1995, NY 1996, US Dist. Ct. (NJ 1995, so. & ea. dist. NY 1996), US Ct. Appeals (3d cir. 1998, 1st cir. 2004). Assoc. Latham & Watkins, 1995—98; asst. U.S. atty. U.S. Dept. Justice, NJ Dist., 1998—2001; dep. chief of staff U.S. Dept. Justice, criminal div., 2001—02; ptnr., securities litigation Bernstein Litowitz Berger & Grossmann LLP, NYC & NJ, 2002—, mng. ptnr. NJ office. Assoc. Edward Bennett Williams Inn of Ct.; instr. Columbia Univ. Law Sch.; adj. prof. Seton Hall Univ. Law Sch. Editor: Columbia Jour. Law & Social Problems. Harlan Fiske Stone scholar. Mem.: ABA, NJ State Bar Assn. Office: Bernstein Litowitz Berger & Grossmann 1285 Ave of the Americas New York NY 10019 also: Bernstein Litowitz Berger & Grossmann 220 St Paul St Westfield NJ 07090 Office Phone: 212-554-1495, 908-928-1700. Office Fax: 212-554-1444. Business E-Mail: erik@blbglaw.com.

SANDSTROM, ALICE WILHELMINA, accountant; b. Seattle, Jan. 6, 1914; d. Andrew William and Agatha Mathilda (Sundius) S. BA, U. Wash., 1934. CPA, Wash. Mgr. office Star Machinery Co., Seattle, 1935—43, Howe & Co., Seattle, 1943—46; pvt. practice acctg. Seattle, 1945—85; ret., 1985. Contr. Children's Orthop. Hosp. and Med. Ctr., Seattle, 1948-75, assoc. adminstr. fin., 1975-81; lectr. U. Wash., Seattle, 1957-72 Mem. Wash. state Title XIX Adv. Com., 1975-82, Wash. State Vendors Rate Adv. Com., 1980-87, Mayor's Task Force for Small Bus., 1981-83; bd. dirs. Seattle YWCA, pres., 1986-88; bd. dirs. Sr. Svcs. Seattle King Co., 1985, 1989-95, 2003, treas., 1986, pres., 1988-90; bd. dirs. Children's Orthop. Hosp. Found., 1982-90; rsch. team Children's Hosp., Seattle, 2003 Recipient Jefferson award for vol. svcs., 1997, Alumnus award, U. Wash. Bus. Sch., 2002, Leadership award, 2002—03, Isabel Coleman Pierce award, YWCA, 2003. Fellow Hosp. Fin. Mgmt. Assn. (charter, state pres. 1956-57, nat. treas. 1963-65, Robert H. Reeves Merit award 1970, Frederick T. Muncie award 1985; mem. LWV, Wash. State Hosp. Assn. (treas. 1956-70), Am. Soc. Women Accts. (pres. Seattle chpt. 1946-48), Am. Soc. Women CPA, Wash. Soc. CPA, Seattle Women's Voters League, Women's Univ. Club (Seattle), City Club (Seattle, charter), Beta Alpha Psi (Outstanding Alumnus award 2001) Home and Office: 5725 NE 77th St Seattle WA 98115-6345 Personal E-mail: sandstromaw@hotmail.com.

SANDSTROM, DALE VERNON, state supreme court justice; b. Grand Forks, ND, Mar. 9, 1950; s. Ellis Vernon and Hilde Geneva (Williams) S.; m. Gail Hagerty, Mar. 27, 1993; children: Jack, Carrie, Anne. BA, N.D. State U., 1972; JD, U. N.D., 1975. Bar: ND 1975, US Dist. Ct. ND 1975, US Ct. Appeals (8th cir.) 1976. Asst. atty. gen., chief consumer fraud and antitrust div. State of ND, Bismarck, 1975-81, securities commr., 1981-83, pub. svc. commr., 1983-92, pres. public svc. commn., 1987-91; justice ND Supreme Ct., Bismarck, 1992—. Chair ND Commn. on Cameras in the Courtroom, 1993—, Joint Procedure Com., 1996—, mem. adminstrv. coun., 2005-; mem. exec. com. ND Jud. Conf., 1995—, chair-elect, 1997-99, chair, 1999-2001; mem. Gov.'s Com. on Security and Privacy, Bismarck, 1975-76, Gov.'s Com. on Refugees, Bismarck, 1976; chmn. Gov's Com. on Comml. Air Transp., Bismarck, 1983-84. Mem. platform com ND Reps., 1972, 76, exec. com., 1972-73, 85-88, dist. chmn., 1981-82; former chmn. bd. deacons Luth. Ch.; mem. ch. coun., exec. com., chmn. legal and constl. rev. com. Evang. Luth Ch. Am., 1993—; mem. exec. bd. dirs., No. Lights Coun., dist. chair Boy Scouts Am., 1998-2000. Named Disting. Eagle Scout, Boy Scouts Am., 1997, Master of the Coll. Arts, Humanities, and Social Scis., N.D. State U., 2002; recipient Cmty. Svc. award, N.D. State Bar Assn., 2002. Mem. ABA, ND Bar Assn., Big Muddy Bar Assn., Nat. Assn. Regulatory Utility Commrs. (electricity com.), N.A. Assn. Securities Adminstrs., Order of De Molay (grand master 1994-95, mem. Internat. Supreme coun., Legion of Honor award), Nat. Eagle Scouts Assn. (regent for life), Shriners, Elks, Eagles, Masons (33d degree, chmn. grand youth com. 1979-87, Youth Leadership award 1986), Bruce M. VanSickle Am. Inn of Court (pres. 1999-2001), ND Judges Assn. (v.p. 2005-). Office: State ND Supreme Ct Judicial Wing 1st Fl 600 E Boulevard Ave Bismarck ND 58505 Office Phone: 701-328-2221. *

SANDT, CAROL HARGIS, microbiologist, researcher; b. Phoenix, Nov. 14, 1941; d. Ira Calvin and Marie (Roberts) H.; m. Roger William Sandt, 1963 (div. 1978); children: Severn, Evan, Claire. BS, Roanoke Coll., 1963; MS, Rutgers U., 1968; PhD, U. Del., 1990. Instr. Trenton (N.J.) State Coll., 1973-74, Franklin and Marshall Coll., Lancaster, Pa., 1974-76; microbiologist Wilson L. Miller Lab., Lancaster, 1978-80; rsch. assoc. Sch. of Life and Health Scis. U. Del., Newark, Del., 1988-90; postdoctoral rsch. assoc. biochemistry and molecular biology Pa. State Coll. Medicine, 1990-99, rsch. assoc., 1999—. Contbr. articles to profl. jours. Mem. missions com. Grace Bapt. Ch., Millersville, Pa., 1985—, pastoral search com., 1997-99; chmn. PTO scholarship com. Martic Elem. Sch. PTO, Holtwood, Pa., 1977-81. Mem. Am. Soc. for Microbiology, Phi Kappa Phi. Achievements include discovery and characterization of proteins present in some E-coli which bind antibodies in a non-immune manner and contribute to virulence. Home: 382 River Rd Pequea PA 17565-8802

SANDVICK, JANET ROSE, history educator; b. Cleve., Oct. 30, 1959; d. Thomas John and Judith Diane Leonti; m. Scott Joseph Sandvick, June 13, 1984; children: Maureen, Stephanie, Scott M. BE, Baldwin Wallace Coll., Berea, Ohio, 1993, MEd, 1997. Cert. tchr. 1-8, elem. adminstrn. Ohio, mid. adminstrn. Ohio. 6th grade tchr. Applewood Elem., Brunswick, Ohio, 1993—97; 7th grade history tchr. Willetts Mid. Sch., Brunswick, 1997—99, at risk 8th grade tchr., 2000—01, 8th grade history tchr., 2001—; adminstrv. intern Brunswick City Schs., 1999—2000, subject area coord., 2003—06. Mem.: Ohio Mid. Sch. Assn., Ctrl. Ohio Saddle Club Assn., Appaloosa Horse Club. Home: 6751 Spring Glen Dr Valley City OH 44280 Office: Willetts Mid Sch 1045 Hadcock Rd Brunswick OH 44212

SANDWEISS, JACK, physicist, researcher; b. Chgo., Aug. 19, 1930; s. Charles Ray and Florence (Hymovitz) S.; m. Letha Ann Boeck, Jan. 16, 1956; children: Daniel Howard, Anne Florence, Benjamin Lewis. Student, UCLA, 1948-50; BS, U. Calif., Berkeley, 1952, PhD, 1957. Research assoc. Radiation Lab., U. Calif., Berkeley, 1957; instr. Yale U., New Haven, 1957-59, asst. prof., 1959-62, assoc. prof., 1962-64, prof. physics, 1964—, Donner prof. physics, 1980—, former chmn. dept. physics. Cons. Brookhaven Nat. Lab., Fermi Nat. Accelerator Lab.; chmn. high energy physics adv. panel Dept. Energy-NSF, 1982-86. Editor Phys. Rev. Letters, 1988—; contbr. articles to profl. jours. Fellow Am. Phys. Soc. (chmn. div. particles and fields 1980); mem. NAS, AAAS. Home: 248 Ogden St New Haven CT 06511-1221 Office: Yale Univ Physics Dept Sloane Physics Lab PO Box 2081-21 New Haven CT 06520-8121. E-mail: sandweiss@hepmail.physics.yale.edu.

SANDWEISS, MARTHA ANN, writer, history professor; b. St. Louis, Mar. 29, 1954; d. Jerome Wesley and Marilyn Joy (Gilk) S. BA magna cum laude, Radcliffe Coll., 1975; MA in History, Yale U., 1977, MPhil in History, 1981, PhD, 1985. Smithsonian-Nat. Endowment Humanities fellow Nat. Portrait Gallery, Washington, 1975-76; curator photographs Amon Carter Mus., Ft. Worth, 1979-86; adj. curator photographs, 1987-89; dir. Mead Art Mus. Amherst Coll., 1989-97, adj. assoc. prof. of fine arts and Am. studies, 1989-94, assoc. prof. Am. studies, 1994-97, assoc. prof. Am. studies and history, 1997-2000, prof. Am. studies and history, 2000—. Author: Carlotta Corpron: Designer with Light, 1980, Masterworks of American Photography, 1982, Laura Gilpin: An Enduring Grace, 1986, (catalogue) Pictures from an Expedition: Early Views of the American West, 1979, Print the Legend: Photography and the American West, 2002; co-author: Eyewitness to War: Prints and Daguerreotypes of the Mexican War, 1989; editor: Historic Texas: A Photographic Portrait, 1986, Contemporary Texas: A Photographic Portrait, 1986, Denizens of the Desert, 1988, Photography in Nineteenth Century America, 1991; co-editor: Oxford History of the American West, 1994. Fellow Ctr. for Am. Art and Material Cultures, Yale U., 1977-79, NEH, 1988, 2000-01, Am. Coun. Learned Socs., 1996-97, Weatherhead, 2000-01, Rockefeller Found., 2007; Beinecke fellow Yale U., 2004-05. Office: Amherst Coll Am Studies Dept Box 2225 Amherst MA 01002-5000

SANDWELL, KRISTIN ANN, special education educator; b. Topeka, Kans., Jan. 13, 1955; d. Edwin C. and E. Maxine (Nelson) Henry; m. Steve Sandwell, Dec. 27, 1997; children: Dustin Grimm, Chris Creek, Brandon Grimm, Sarah Sandwell, Paul Sandwell. AA, Hutchinson CC, Kans., 1986; BS, McPherson Coll., Kans., 1989; MEd, Wichita State U., 1992. Cert. tchr. elem., gifted. Math/parenting tchr. Flint Hills Job Corps Ctr., Manhattan, Kans., 1992; gifted facilitator Unified Sch. Dist. 353, Wellington, Kans., 1993-94, Unified Sch. Dist. 260, Derby, Kans., 1995-97; tchr. City of Wichita Summer Youth Employment Program-Edn., 1997—98; gifted facilitator Unified Sch. Dist. 259, 1998—. Head injury counselor, life skills trainer Three Rivers Ind. Living Ctr., Wamego, Kans., 1992; facilitator Summer Youth Employment Edn. Program, 1997-98. Epiphany Festival prodr. Trinity Luth. Ch., McPherson, 1991, 93; CASA organizer McPherson Coll., 1988-89; vol. Coun. on Violence Against Persons, McPherson, 1990-92. Mem. ASCD. Avocations: reading, travel, working with disability issues. Office Phone: 316-973-6450. Personal E-mail: ksandwell@yahoo.com.

SANDY, LEWIS GORDON, physician, healthcare executive; b. Detroit, July 18, 1958; s. William Haskell and Marjorie Mindel (Mazor) S.; m. Kathleen Anne Morgan, June 17, 1984; children: Matthew, Natalie, Jonah. BS, U. Mich., 1979, MD, 1982; MBA, Stanford U., 1988. Diplomate Am. Bd. Internal Medicine, Nat. Bd. Med. Examiners. Intern Beth Israel Hosp., Boston, 1982-83, resident, 1983-85; Robert Wood Johnson clin. scholar U. Calif., San Francisco, 1985-86, clin. fellow in medicine, 1986-88; instr. Harvard Med. Sch., 1988-91; assoc. chief internal medicine Harvard Community Health Plan, Boston, 1988-89, dir. Health Ctr., 1989-91; v.p. Robert Wood Johnson Found., Princeton, NJ, 1991—96, exec. v.p., 1997—2003, UnitedHealthcare, Edina, Minn., 2003—07; sr. v.p. UnitedHealthcare Group, Minnetonka, Minn., 2007—; sr. fellow U. Minn. Sch. Pub. Health, 2004—. Cons. Kaiser Found. Health Plan, Oakland, Calif., 1987-88. Fellow ACP; mem. AMA, Soc. Gen. Internal Medicine, Acad. Health, Alpha Omega Alpha. Home: 4800 Sunnyslope Rd E Edina MN 55424 Office: 9900 Scen Rd E Minnetonka MN 55343

SANDY, SANDRA V., psychologist; d. Eugene Leon and Ruby Elizabeth Sandy. BA, W.Va. U., 1967; MA, New Sch. U., 1974; MPhil, Columbia U., 1983, PhD, 1985. Evaluation assoc. NYC Bd. Edn., Bklyn., 1985—87; sr. rsch. assoc. Cornell U. Med. Coll., NYC, 1987—94; dir. rsch. Internat. Ctr. Coop. & Conflict Resolution Columbia U., NYC, 1995—2001; dir. rsch. Ctr. Social & Emotional Edn., NYC, 2001—06; dir. Educating Com. Social Emotional Learning Inst., New York, NY; exec. dir. Peaceful Kids ECSEL, NYC. Cons. NY Acad. Medicine, NYC, 1995—2000, NJ Health Decisions, Verona, NJ, 2000—02; presentations, workshops in field. Author: (curriculum manual) Peaceful Kids Educating Communities in Social Emotional Learning, 2000; contbr. chapters to books. Grantee Homeless Children co-grant, William T. Grant Found., 1988—91, Parent Child Conflict Resolution grant, William & Flora Hewlett Found., 1996—99, Peaceful Kids ECSEL grant, 1999—2002. Mem.: APA, Internat. Assn. Conflict Mgmt., Assn. Conflict Resolution (editl. bd. 2001—). Office: Peaceful Kids ECSEL 444 E 82d St Ste 6P New York NY 10028 Office Phone: 212-772-9908. Business E-Mail: sandrasandy@earthlink.net.

SANDY, WILLIAM HASKELL, training and communication systems executive; b. NYC, Apr. 28, 1929; s. Fred and Rose S.; m. Marjorie Mazor, June 15, 1952; children: Alan, Lewis, Barbara. AB, U. Md., 1950, JD, 1953; postgrad. Advanced Mgmt. program, Harvard Bus. Sch., 1970—71. Bar: Md. 1953. From planner-writer to acct. supr. Jam-Handy Orgn., Detroit, 1953—64, v.p., 1964—69, sr. v.p., 1969—71; pres. Sandy Corp., Troy, Mich., 1971—88, chmn., 1988—96; pres. Rudgate Corp., Bloomfield Hills, Mich., 1996—. Bd. dirs. U. Mich. Press, Asolo Repertory Theatre. Author: Forging the Productivity Partnership, 1990. Bd. govs. Northwood Inst., 1976-80; bd. dirs. Cranbrook Sci. Inst., Met. Ctr. High Tech., 1993, Birmingham (Mich.) Cmty. House, 1997-2003, Mich. Opera Theatre; pres. Graphic Arts Coun., 1992-93; trustee Detroit Inst. Arts, 1992-93; v.p. nat. exec. coun. Harvard Bus. Sch., 1985-89; mem. Bloomfield Hills Zoning Bd., Walsh Coll. Leader in Residence, Pres.'s Adv. Coun.; mayor City of Bloomfield Hills, 1996-97; mem. Troy Downtown Devel. Authority, 1996-99; Inst. for Humanities trustee U. Mich Mem. ASTD, Am. Mktg. Assn. (pres. Detroit chpt. 1975), Nat. Found. Am. Mktg. Assn (bd. dirs. 1998), S.E. Mich. BBB (bd. dirs. 1999), Adcraft Club, Nat. Assn. Ednl. Broadcasters, Harvard Bus. Sch. Club (pres. Detroit chpt. 1983-85). Home (Summer): 596 Rudgate Rd Bloomfield Hills MI 48304 Home (Winter): 535 Sanctuary Dr B404 Longboat Key FL 34228-3852 Personal E-mail: sandyfamily@aol.com.

SANES, JOSHUA RICHARD, neurobiologist, researcher, educator; b. Buffalo, Sept. 5, 1949; s. Irving and Carlyn (Mildred) S.; m. Susan Corcoran, Dec. 27, 1982; children: Jesse, Amelia. BA, Yale U., 1970; MA, PhD, Harvard U., 1976. With US Congress, Office of Tech. Assessment, 1976—77, U. Calif., San Francisco; asst. prof., dept. physiology Washington U. Med. Sch., St. Louis, 1980-85, assoc. prof., 1985-89, alumni endowed prof. neurobiology, dept. anatomy and neurobiology, 1989; prof. molecular and cellular biology Harvard U., Cambridge, Mass., Paul J. Finnegan Family dir., Ctr. for Brain Neuroscience, Dept. Molecular and Cellular Biology, 2005—. Mem. neurology study sect. NIH, Washington, 1988; mem. nat. adv. coun., Nat. Inst. Neurological Disorders and Stroke, NIH, 1999-2003; mem. adv. com., human embryonic stem cell rsch., NRC and Inst. Medicine, 2006-; mem. scientific adv. bd. Stowers Inst. for Med. Rsch., 2006-, Searle Scholar program, Max-Planck Inst. for Neurobiology in Munich, Howard Hughes Med. Inst. Contbr. articles to profl. jours.; mem. editl. bd. Cell, Journal of Cell Biology, Neuron Fellow AAAS, Am. Acad. Arts & Scis.; mem. NIH (bd. sci. counselor 1993—), Soc. for Neurosci. (councilor 1990—), Muscular Dystrophy Assn. (scientific adv. bd. 1991—), NAS. Office: Harvard U Sherman Fairchild Bldg 7 Divinity Ave Rm 143 Cambridge MA 02138 Office Phone: 617-496-8683. Office Fax: 617-496-9590. Business E-Mail: sanesj@mcb.harvard.edu. *

SANETO, RUSSELL PATRICK, pediatric neurologist, epileptologist, neurobiologist; b. Burbank, Calif., Oct. 10, 1950; s. Arthur and Mitzi (Seddon) S.; m. Kathleen D. Saneto. BS with honors, San Diego State U., 1972, MS, 1975; PhD, U. Tex. Med. Br., 1981; DO, U. Osteo. Medicine and Surgery, 1994. Tchg. asst. San Diego State U., 1969-75; substitute tchr. Salt Lake City Sch. Dist., 1975; tchg. and rsch. asst. U. Tex. Med. Br., 1976-77, NIH predoctoral fellow, 1977-81, postdoctoral fellow, 1981; Jeanne B. Kempner postdoctoral fellow UCLA, 1981-82, NIH postdoctoral fellow, 1982-87; asst. prof. divsn. neurosci. Oreg. Regional Primate Rsch. Ctr., Beaverton, 1987-89; asst. prof. dept. cell biology and anatomy Oreg. Health Scis. U., Portland, 1988-90, U. Osteo. Medicine and Surgery, 1991-94, Cleve. Clinic, 1994-2001; assoc. prof. neurology and pediat. U. Wash. Children's Hosp. and Regional Med. Ctr., Seattle, 2001—. Lectr. rsch. methods Grad. Sch., 1982; vis. scholar in ethics So. Bapt. Theol. Sem., Louisville, 1981; sci. advisor United Mitochondrial Disease Found. Mem. editl. bd. Epilepsy.com, Pediat. Neurology; contbr. articles to profl. jours. Mem. scientific adv. bd. United Mitochondrial Disease Found., Northwest Epilepsy Found. Recipient Merit award Nat. March of Dimes, 1978; named one of Outstanding Young Men in Am., 1979, 81, one of Men of Significance, 1985. Mem. AAAS, Am. Acad. Pediats., Am. Acad. Neurology, Am. Epilepsy Soc., Bread for World, Winter Confs. Brain Rsch., Neuroscis. Study Program, N.Y. Acad. Scis., Am. Soc. Neurochemistry, Soc. Neurosci., Sigma Sigma Phi. Democrat. Mem. Evangelical Free Ch. Office: Childrens Hosp and Regional Med Ctr Neurology B-5552 4800 Sand Point Way NE Seattle WA 98105 Business E-Mail: russ.saneto@seattlechildrens.org.

SANETTI, STEPHEN LOUIS, lawyer; b. Flushing, NY, June 25, 1949; s. Alfred Julius Sanetti and Yolanda Marie (DiGioia) Boyes; m. Carole Leighton Koller, Sept. 21, 1974; children: Christopher Edward, Dana Harrison. BA in History with honors, Va. Mil. Inst., 1971; JD, Washington and Lee U., 1974. Bar: Conn. 1975, U.S. Ct. Mil. Appeals 1975, U.S. Dist. Ct. Conn. 1978, U.S. Ct. Appeals (2d cir.) 1979, U. S. Supreme Ct. 1980. Litigation atty. Marsh, Day & Calhoun, Bridgeport, Conn., 1978-80; gen. counsel Sturm, Ruger & Co., Southport, Conn., 1980—, v.p., 1993-2000, also bd. dirs., 1998—, vice chmn., sr. exec. v.p., 2000—03, pres., COO, 2003—. Dir. Product Liability Adv. Coun., 1988-2002; tech. advisor Assn. Firearm and Toolmark Examiners; chmn. Legis. and Legal Affairs com. Sporting Arms and Ammunition Mfrs. Inst., 1993-2001; bd. govs. Nat. Shooting Sports Found., 2002-. Served to capt., chief criminal law 1st Cavalry Div. Staff Judge Advocate, U.S. Army, 1975-78. Mem. Am. Acad. Forensic Sci., Def. Rsch. Inst. Republican. Roman Catholic. Office: Sturm Ruger & Co Inc 1 Lacey Pl Southport CT 06490-1241

SANFELICI, ARTHUR H(UGO), editor, writer; b. Haledon, NJ, May 23, 1934; s. Hugo and Anna (Schilder) S.; m. Betty Louise Van Riper, Aug. 10, 1957; children: Brian Arthur, Amy Elizabeth, Gary Hugh, Bruce Richard. Attended, Lehigh U., 1952-55. Assoc. editor Flying Mag., NYC, 1961-64; mng. editor Am. Aviation Mag., Washington, 1964-68; dist. sales mgr. Gates Learjet Co., NYC, 1969-71; exec. editor Airport World Mag., Westport, Conn., 1971-74; spl. project editor Aircraft Owners & Pilots Assn., Washington, 1974-75, mng. editor Pilot mag., 1975-79, editor AOPA Newsletter, AOPAirport Report, Gen. Aviation Nat. Report, 1979-88; pub. cons., 1989-90; sr. editor Flight Safety Found., Washington, 1989-92; editor S-Cubed divsn. Maxwell Labs., Alexandria, Va., 1992-95; comms. dir. Helicopter Assn. Internat., Alexandria, 1996-97; editor Shooting Sports USA, 1997-98. Editor, compiler: Yesterday's Wings; editor emeritus Aviation History Mag., Leesburg, Va., 1990—; author: 135 Ways to Get Even With Your Kids, 2003. Pilot USAF, 1955—60. Mem. Nat. Aeronautic Assn., Aero Club of Washington, Soc. Aerospace Comms. Home: 44476 Oakmont Manor Sq Ashburn VA 20147

SANFILIPPO, ALFRED PAUL, dean, medical educator, pathologist; b. Racine, Wis., Aug. 30, 1949; s. Paul Joseph and Therese (Rhode) Sanfilippo; m. Janet Lee Thompson, 1973; children: Lisa, Joseph. Student, Max Planck Inst. Exptl. Medicine, Gottingen, Germany, 1966—68; BA in Physics, MS in Physics, U. Pa., 1970; PhD in immunology, Duke U., 1975, MD, 1976. Diplomate Am. Bd. Pathology, lic. physician NC, Md. Intern in anatomic pathology Duke U. Hosp., 1976—77, resident in anatomic and clin. pathology, 1977—79, postdoctoral rschr. divsn. tumor virology dept. surgery, 1976—79; asst. prof. pathology and exptl. surgery, lectr. immunology Duke U., 1979—84, from assoc. prof. to prof. pathology, 1984—93, from assoc. prof. to prof. exptl. surgery, 1985—93, prof. immunology, 1990—93; attending pathologist Duke U. and Durham VA Hosps., 1979—93; staff mem. Duke Surg. Pvt. Diagnostic Clinic, 1979—93; dir. Transplantation Lab Durham VA Hosp., 1979—93; dir. immunopathology Duke U. Med. Ctr., 1982—93, exec. com. dept. pathology, 1989—91; Baxley Prof. and chair pathology dept. John's Hopkins U., Balt., 1993—2000; pathologist-in-chief Johns Hopkins Hosp., Balt., 1993—2000; sr. v.p. health scis. Ohio State U., Columbus, 2000—, exec. dean health scis., 2004—, dean. coll. medicine; CEO Ohio State U. Med. Ctr. Mem. Duke Comprehensive Cancer Ctr., 1979—93; dir. rsch. Johns Hopkins Comprehensive Transplant Ctr.; mem. Third Frontier Commn. Adv. Bd., Ohio, 2004—; cons. Battelle Human Affairs Rsch. Ctrs., Seattle, 1985—93, NSF of Switzerland, 1992—93, numerous US govt. adv. coms.; mem. editl. bd. Transplantation, 1985—, Pathobiology, 1989—, Transplantation Now, Japan, 1989—, Pathology, Rsch. and Practice, 1990—, Human Immunology, 1992—, Lab. Investigation, 1993—, Xeno, 1994—, Virchows Archiv, 1998—, Transplant Immunology; reviewer Am. Jour. Kidney Diseases, Am. Jour. Ophthalmology, Am. Jour. Pathology, New Eng. Jour. Medicine, Jour. of AMA, Jour. Am. Soc. Nephrology, Jour. Clin. Investigation, Jour. Leukocyte Biology, Kidney Internat., others; contbr. numerous articles to prof. jours.; speaker and presenter in field. Bd. trustees Omeris, Columbus, Ohio, 2004—. Recipient Kermit G. Osserman Award, Myasthenia Gravis Found., 1976, Wiley D. Forbus Award, NC Soc. Pathologists, 1979, Reach for Sight Physician Investigator Award, 1990; grantee numerous, NIH. Fellow: Am. Soc. Clin. Pathologists (coun. on edn. and rsch. 1994—96); mem.: Southeastern Organ Procurement Found. (exec. com 1992—97, sec. 1992—93, treas. 1993—94, v.p. 1994—95, pres. 1995—96), Assn. for Rsch. in Vision and Ophthalmology, Am. Soc. Nephrology, Am. Soc. Transplant Physicians (pres. 1985—86), Am. Soc. Histocompatibility and Immunogenetics, Transplantation Soc., US-Can. Acad. Pathology, Am. Assn. Med. Colls., Am. Assn. Immunologists, AMA, Am. Soc. Investigative Pathology (pres. 2002—03), Intersociety Pathology Coun., Assn. Pathology Chairs (sr. fellow), Am. Soc. Transplantation (past pres.), Alpha Omega Alpha. Office: Office Dean Ohio State U Coll Medicine 370 W 9th Ave 200 A Meiling Columbus OH 43210

SANFILIPPO, JON, lawyer, court clerk; b. Milw., Nov. 10, 1950; s. Joseph Salvator and Jeanne Catherine (Lisinski) S.; m. Pamela Joy Jaeger, July 8, 1972; children: Kerri, Jessica, Jennifer. AS, U. Wis., West Bend, 1972; BS, U. Wis., Milw., 1974, MS, 1978; JD, Marquette U., 1988; postgrad., Nat. Jud. Coll., 1999. Bar: Wis. 1988, U.S. Dist. Ct. (ea. dist.) Wis. 1988, U.S. Ct. Appeals (7th cir.) 1988, U.S. Dist. Ct. (we. dist.) Wis 1989. U.S. Supreme Ct. 1994; cert. elem. tchr., ednl. adminstr., Wis. Educator, athletic dir., coach St. Francis Cabrini, West Bend, 1974-77; clk. cir. ct. Washington County, West Bend, 1976-89; ptnr. Schowalter, Edwards & Sanfilippo, S.C., West Bend, 1989-94; sch. prin.K-8 Campbellsport Sch. Dist., Wis., 1994-95; chief dep. clk. Cir. Ct. Milw. County, Milw., 1995—2007, acting clk., 1997-98; jud. ct. commr. Milw. County, 1997—2007; clerk ct. US Dist. Ct. (ea. dist.) Wis., Milw., 2007—. Judo tchr. City of West Bend, 1967—; phys. edn. instr., judo coach U. Wis., West Bend, 1992—. Author: Judo for the Physical Educator, 1981. Sch. bd. West Bend Sch. Dist., 1979-80. Recipient cert. study internat. and Chinese law, East Chinese Inst. Politics and Law, Willamette U. Law Sch., Shanghai, 1998; fellow ct. exec. devel. program, Inst. Ct. Mgmt. Nat. Ctr. State Cts., 1999. Mem.: Washington County Bar Assn., Milw. Bar Assn. (cts. com. 1995—, criminal bench/bar com., family bench/bar com. 1997—2007, civil bench/bar com. 2000—07), Wis. Bar Assn. (bench/bar com. 1986—88, 1997—2005), Nat. Assn. for Ct. Adminstrn., Nat. Jud. Coll., Justinian Soc., U.S. Martial Arts Assn. (8th degree Black Belt Judo 2003, 7th degree black belt Jujitsu 2003, named to Hall of Fame 2002, 2003), U.S. Judo Assn. (6th degree Black Belt 1995), Universal Tae Kwon Do Assn. (3d degree Black Belt 1988), Rotary (bd. dirs. West Bend Sunrise Club 1990—91, Paul Harris fellow). Roman Catholic. Avocations: Tae Kwon Do, Judo, photography, model railroading, tai chi. Office: US Dist Ct Ea Dist Wis US Courthouse 517 E Wisconsin Ave Milwaukee WI 53202 Business E-Mail: jon_sanfilippo@wied.uscourts.gov.

SANFILIPPO, JOSEPH SALVATORE, gynecologic endocrinologist, educator; b. Bklyn., Feb. 21, 1948; s. Joseph Philip and Elena Teresa (Canepa) S.; m. Patricia M. Cantwell, June 21, 1974; children: Angela, Andrea, Luke. BS, St. John's U., NYC, 1969; MD, Chgo. Med. Sch., 1973. Diplomate Am. Bd. Ob-Gyn., spl. qualification in reproductive endocrinology. Intern Mil. County Gen. Hosp.; resident in ob-gyn. SUNY Upstate Med. Ctr., Syracuse; instr. dept. ob-gyn. U. Louisville Sch. Medicine, 1977—79, asst. prof., 1979—83, assoc. prof., 1983—89, prof., 1989—97, dir. divsn. reproductive endocrinology, 1993—97; James and Marilyn Gilmore prof. ob-gyn. MCP Hahnemann Sch. Medicine, 1998—2001; vice chmn. reproductive sci. Magee-Women's Hosp., Pitts., 2001—, dir. reproductive endocrinology and infertility, 2003—, dir. residency program, 2004—05; chmn. ob-gyn. Allegheny Gen. Hosp., 1998—2001; prof. ob-gyn. and reproductive sci. U. Pitts. Sch. Medicine, 2001—. Pres. med. staff Alliant Health System/Norton Hosp. and Alliant Med. Pavilion, Louisville, 1994—; dir. gynecology Kosair-Children's Hosp., Louisville, 1979—. Editor: Risk Management for Healthcare Professionals, 2001, MBA Handbook for Healthcare Professionals, 2002, Clinical Gynecology, 2026; editor-in-chief: Jour. Pediat. Adolescent Gynecology, 1989—. Named Disting. Alumnus, Chgo. Med. Sch., 1990. Fellow: N.Am. Soc. for Pediat. Adolescent Gynecology (exec. dir.), Am. Soc. for Reproductive Medicine (pres.); mem.: ACOG (chair sci. program com. 2006, chair gynecol. prolog fifth edit.). Avocations: jogging, boating, fishing, amateur radio. Office: Univ Pitts Sch Medicine Dept Ob-gyn and Reproductive Scis 300 Halket St Pittsburgh PA 15213-3180 Office Phone: 412-641-1204. Business E-Mail: jsanfilippo@mail.magee.edu.

SANFORD, DAVID BOYER, journalist, editor; b. Denver, Mar. 4, 1943; s. Filmore Bowyer and Alice Irene (Peterson) S. BA with honors, U. Denver, 1964; MS in Journalism with honors, Columbia U., 1965. With New Republic mag., Washington, 1965-76, mng. editor, 1970-76, Politics Today (formerly Skeptic), Santa Barbara, Calif., 1976-78, contbg. editor, 1978-79; editorial writer Los Angeles Herald Examiner, 1978-79; mng. editor Harper's mag., NYC, 1979-80; editor Wall St. Jour. mag., 1980-81; sr. spl. writer Wall Street Jour., 1981—. Syndicated columnist, 1970-71; commentator Can. Broadcasting Corp., 1967-76; judge Heywood Broun award Newspaper Guild, 1971; mem. print screening com. Champion-Tuck awards, 1985, 86, Judge Wuxtry award, 1990. Author: Who Put the Con in Consumer?, 1972, Me and Ralph, 1976; editor, co-author: Hot War on the Consumer, 1970. Recipient Sackett Law prize, Columbia, 1965, Eckenberg prize, 1965, Gold award, NY Art Dirs. Club, 1977, Wuxtry award for disting. achievement in headline writing, Internat. Soc. for Gen. Semantics, 1989, Pulitzer prize, 1997, Sci.-in-Soc. award, Nat. Assn. Sci. Writers, 1997, disting. headline writing award, NY Newspaper Publisher award, 2007; Centennial scholar, 1960—64, NY Newspaper Guild fellow, 1964—65. Mem. Phi Beta Kappa, Omicron Delta Kappa. Democrat. Home: 118 Prospect Park W Brooklyn NY 11215-4270 Office Phone: 212-416-2597. Personal E-mail: david.sanford@wsj.com.

SANFORD, DIANNE H., lawyer; b. Pittston, Pa., July 29, 1948; BA, Cornell U., 1970, MA, 1973; JD cum laude, Harvard U., 1976. Bar: DC 1977, Mass. 1977. Asst. U.S. atty., D.C., 1977-81; atty. Office of the Solicitor U.S. Dept. Interior, 1981-82; trial atty. wildlife and marine resources U.S. Dept. Justice, 1982-86, asst. chief environmental enforcement sect., 1987-91; ptnr. Akin, Gump, Strauss, Hauer & Feld, LLP, Wash., 2019; atty. Antimicrobial Therapy Inc, Hyde Park, Vt. Author: Assault with a Deadly Weapon: The Autobiography of a Street Criminal, 1977. Office: Antimicrobial Therapy Inc 229 Main St PO Box 70 Hyde Park VT 05655 Office Phone: 540-547-9340. Office Fax: 540-547-9343. Business E-Mail: dhs@sanfordguide.com.

SANFORD, IRENE W., lawyer; b. Framingham, Mass., Apr. 25, 1930; d. Donald F. and Johanna B. Watson; m. Harry E. Sanford (dec.); children: Glenn, Donald, Scott. BS in Polit. Sci., Northwestern U., Evanston, Ill., 1954; JD, Pace U., White Plains, NY, 1980. Bar: NY. Exec. Pharm. Advantage Assocs., NYC, 1956—60; rsch. dir. Hoff, Canny and Bowen, NYC, 1960—63; office mgr. Paul Charry Inc., NYC, 1972—77; trust adminstr. Duke and Benedict Inc., White Plains, NY, 1977—80; atty. Irene W. Sanford Esq., Armonk, NY, 1981—, Somers, NY, 1981—. Cons. Chase Manhatten Bank, White Plains, 1981—82; arbitrator, mediator Am. Arbitration Assn., NYC, 1985—2006; judge nat. environ. law moot ct. competition Pace Law Sch., White Plains, 1995—. No charge tax preparation AARP, 1985—; mem. Town Planning Bd., North Castle, NY, 1974—92; rep., chmn. Westchester County Airport Adv. Bd., 1977—79; dir., 2nd. v.p. Westchester Mucpl. Planning Fedn., 1991—94; mem.

Neibhbors United Justice Housing, Newburgh, NY, 1983—93; founder Habitat for Humanity, New Rochelle, NY, 1985—2000, chair constrn. com., 1996—2000; mem. Heritage Hills. Residential Assn., 2005—, mem. condo. com., 2007—; mem. master plan update com. Town Somers, 2003—. Named to Sr. Citizen Hall Fame, Westchester County, 2002. Mem.: Medicare Rights Orgn., Arthritis Found. (bd. dirs. White Plains chpt. 1983—96, bd. dirs. NYC chpt. 1984—96, Nat. Vol. Svc. citation 1992), Westchester County Bar Assn., Westchester Women's Bar Assn., NY State Women's Bar Assn., NY State Bar Assn. Avocations: golf, tennis, reading, travel.

SANFORD, JAMES KENNETH, public relations executive; b. Clyde, NC, Jan. 23, 1932; s. James Edward S. and Bernice (Crawford) Peebles; m. Judith Bullard Longshore, 2001; children: Timothy, Scott, Jeannette. AA, Mars Hill Coll., NC, 1952; AB, U. N.C., 1954, MA, 1958. Pub. rels. officer Asheville (N.C.) United Appeal, 1954; reporter, copy editor Winston-Salem (N.C.) Jour., 1957-59, asst. state editor, 1959-61, news editor, 1961-63, editorial writer, 1963-64; dir. pub. info. and publs. U. N.C., Charlotte, 1964-94; pub. rels. cons. Charlotte, N.C., 1994—. Cons. Commn. on Future of Mars Hill Coll., 1990-91, City of Charlotte, 1991. Author: Charlotte and UNC Charlotte: Growing Up Together, 1996, Building Future From the Past: The History of Gaston College 1964-99, 1999, The Mystique of Mars Hill: Stories of the College's 150 Years of Struggles, Survival and Triumph, 2007; co-author: Fifty Favored Years, 1972; contbg. author: The North Carolina Century: Tar Heels Who Made a Difference, 1900-2000, 2002; contbr. numerous articles to mag. and newspapers. Attractions com. Charlotte Conv. and Visitors Bur., 1994; pres. elect Internat. House, 2001-2002, adv. com. Sta. WTVI Pub. TV, Charlotte, 1986-94; chmn. bd. deacons local ch., 1994-95; gen. bd. Bapt. State Conv. NC, 2000-2003; active Coun. on Christian Higher Edn., 2000-2003; pres. Mars Hill Coll. Nat. Alumni Bd., 2001; bd. trustees Mars Hill Coll., 2005; bd. dirs. Lions Club Cmty. Found. Named to NC Pub. Rels. Hall of Fame, 1995; recipient Alumnus by Choice award U. NC, Charlotte, 1996. Fellow Pub. Rels. Soc. Am. (chmn. S.E. dist. 1991); mem. Coll. News Assn. Carolinas (Lewis Gaston award 1982), Charlotte Pub. Rels. Soc. (pres. 1974, Infinity award 1986), Coun. for Advancement and Support Edn. (asst. dist. chmn. 1975-76), Phi Kappa Phi. Baptist. Avocations: writing, hiking, photography. Home and Office: 74 Fairway Rdg Lake Wylie SC 29710-9209 Office Phone: 803-831-2999. E-mail: sanf2058@bellsouth.net.

SANFORD, JO ANNE, state agency administrator; b. Laurinburg, NC, Oct. 18, 1950; m. William E. Brewer, Jr.; 1 child, Charlotte Brewer. BA Polit. Sci., N.C. State U., 1972; JD, U. N.C. Sch. Law, 1975. Spl. deputy atty. gen. N.C. Atty. Gen.'s Office, 1975—95; chair N.C. Utilities Commn., Raleigh, 1995—2006; bd. dirs. Universal Svc. Adminstrv. Co., 2001—. Apptd. to N.Am. Numbering Coun. FCC; bd. dirs. Nat. Regulatory Rsch. Inst. Master: N.C. Bar Assn.; mem.: Women Execs. in State Govt., Wake County Bar Assn. Office: 4325 Mail Svc Ctr Raleigh NC 27699-4325

SANFORD, LINDA S., information technology executive; b. Jan. 21, 1953; d. William J. and Catherine A. Sanford; 2 children. BA, St. John's U.; MS in Ops. Rsch., Rensselaer Poly. Inst. From mem. staff to gen. mgr. IBM, Westchester, NY, 1975—98, gen. mgr., global industries, 1998—2000, sr. v.p., group exec., storage systems group, 2000—03, sr. v.p. enterprise on demand transformation and info. tech. Somers, 2003—. Mem. bd. dirs. ITT Industries, 1998—. Bd. dirs. St. John's U., Rensselaer Poly. Inst., The Bus. Coun. of N.Y. State. Named one of 50 Most Influential Women in Bus., Fortune Mag., Top 10 Innovators in Tech. Industry, Info. Week Mag., 10 Most Influential Women in Tech., Working Woman Mag.; named to Women in Tech. Internat. Hall of Fame. Mem.: NAE. Office: IBM Corp Rte 100 Somers NY 10589 *

SANFORD, MARSHALL (MARK SANFORD), governor, former congressman; b. Ft. Lauderdale, Fla., May 28, 1960; m. Jenny Sullivan; children: Marshall, Landon, Bolton, Blake. BA, Furman U., 1983; MBA, U. Va., 1988. With Goldman Sachs, 1988, CRC Realty, 1988-89; prin. Southeastern Ptnrs., 1989—, Norton & Sanford, 1993—95, 2001—02; mem. U.S. Congress from 1st Dist. S.C., 1995-2001; mem. govt. reform and oversight com., internat. rels. com., sci. com., joint econ. com.; gov. State of SC, 2003—. Republican. Episcopalian. Office: Office of the Governor PO Box 12267 Columbia SC 29211 Office Fax: 803-734-5167. *

SANFORD, MELANIE S., chemist, educator; BS/MS cum laude with distinction in Chemistry, Yale U., New Haven, 1996; PhD in Chemistry, Calif. Inst. Tech., Pasadena, 2001. NIH NRSA postdoctoral fellow Princeton U., NJ, 2001—03; asst. prof. chemistry U. Mich., Ann Arbor, Mich., 2003—. Contbr. articles to profl. jours., chapters to books. Recipient New Faculty award, Camille and Henry Dreyfus Found., 2003—, Beckman Young Investigator award, 2004—, New Investigator award in Organic Chemistry, Boehringer Ingelheim, 2005, Young Investigator award, Amgen, 2005, Grantee award, Eli Lilly, 2005—06, Freedom to Discover award, Bristol Myers Squibb, 2006, CAREER award, NSF, 2006, Cottrell Scholar award, Rsch. Corp., 2006, Excellence in Chemistry award, AstraZeneca, 2006, Presdl. Early Career award for Scientists and Engrs., Pres. George W. Bush, 2006, Abbott Young Investigator award, 2006, Chemistry Scholars award, GlaxoSmithKline, 2006; Alfred P. Sloan Rsch. fellow, 2006. Office: Dept Chemistry U Mich Ann Arbor MI 48109 Office Phone: 734-615-0451. Office Fax: 734-647-4865. E-mail: mssanfor@umich.edu. *

SANFORD, ROBERT MELVIN, environmental scientist, educator; b. Waltham, Mass., Aug. 7, 1956; s. Richard Seldon Sanford and Rosemary Elizabeth Hunter (Stepmother), Loramel Patricia Shurtleff; m. Robin Adaire Ruhl, May 28, 1978; children: Corey Elizabeth, Daniel Robert, Morgan Richard. BA, SUNY, 1982, MS in Environ. Scis., 1984; PhD in Environ. Sci. and Forestry, SUNY, Syracuse, NY, 1989. Registered profl. archaeologist Register Profl. Archaeologists, 2002. Cons. archaeologist Neumann & Sanford, Syracuse, NY, 1983—86; environ. coord. Environ. Bd., Springfield, Vt., 1986—96; prof. U. So. Maine, Gorham, 1996—. Author: (book) Site Plan and Development Review, 2004; co-author: Cultural Resources Archaeology, 2001, Practicing Archaeology, 2005, Environmental Science, 2005; editor: Profiles of Intentional Teaching and Liberal Learning, 2006. Bd. dirs. Friends Presumpscot River, Windham, Maine, 1997. Decorated Marksmanship medal USN, Battle Efficiency medal, Good Conduct medal; fellow, U. So. Maine, 2005; Champion Internat. fellowship, SUNY, 1982. Mem.: Maine Environ. Edn. Assn. (bd. dirs. 1997—2006, past pres.), Am. Planning Assn. Avocations: kayaking, gardening, woodworking. Office: Univ So Maine 37 College Ave Gorham ME 04038 Home Phone: 207-892-1196; Office Phone: 207-780-5756.

SANFORD, T. DENNY (THOMAS DENNY SANFORD), bank executive; b. Dec. 23, 1935; s. William B. and Edith C. Sanford; m. Colleen Anderson Sanford, 1995 (div. 2003); children: Scott, William. BA in Psychology, U. Minn., 1958. CEO First Premier Bank, 1986—, Premier Bankcard; CEO, chmn. United Nat. Corp. Named one of 50 Most Generous Philanthropists, Business Week, 2006. Donated several million dollars to Sioux Valley Hospitals & Health Systems to transform the facility into a major research institution for children's health. The hospital has promised to rename the institution in his honor Sanford Health. Other recent donations include several millions to convert an abandoned mine into a science laboratory, for the children's hospital, and to the health system to expand projects involving the University of South Dakota's School of Medicine. Office: United National Corp 601 South Minnesota Ave Sioux Falls SD 57104 *

SANGER, DAVID E., news correspondent; b. White Plains, NY, July 5, 1960; Grad. magna cum laude, Harvard Coll., 1982. With NY Times, 1981—, corr. Tokyo, bur. chief, chief Washington econ. corr., 1994—99, chief White House corr., 1999—. Mem. Coun. Fgn. Rels., Aspen Strategy Group. Co-recipient Pulitzer Prize for Nat. Reporting, 1987, 1999, Weintzal prize for Diplomatic Reporting, Georgetown Inst. for the Study of Democracy, 2004, Deadline News Reporting award, Am. Soc. Newspaper Editors, 2004. Mem.: White House Corrs. Assn. (Aldo Beckman award 2003, Merriman Smith Meml. award 2007, 2003). Office: NY Times Washington Bur 1627 I St NW Ste 700 Washington DC 20006 Office Phone: 202-862-0300. *

SANGER, FREDERICK, retired molecular biologist; b. Rendcomb, Gloucestershire, Eng., Aug. 13, 1918; s. Frederick and Cicely Sanger; m. Margaret Joan Howe, 1940; children: Robin, Peter Frederick, Sally Joan. BA, St. John's Coll., Cambridge U., 1940, PhD, 1943; D.Sc. (hon.), Leicester U., 1968, Oxford U., 1970, Strasbourg U., 1970, Cambridge U. Beit Meml. Med. Research fellow U. Cambridge, 1944-51, rsch. scientist dept. biochemistry, 1944-61, rsch. scientist, div. head Med. Rsch. Coun. Lab. of Molecular Biology, 1962-83. Contbr. articles in field to sci. jours. Fellow King's Coll., Cambridge U., 1954; recipient Corday-Morgan Medal and Prize, Chem. Soc., 1951, Nobel prize for chemistry, 1958, 80; Gairdner Found. ann. award, 1971, 79, William Bate Hardy prize Cambridge Philos. Soc., 1976, Copley medal Royal Soc., 1977, Hon. Fellow, Royal Coll. Pathologists, 1993, Commander, Order Brit. Empire, 1963, Order of Merit, 1971, Companion of Honour, 1981, Millenium Fellow, Royal Soc. Chemistry, 2000. Mem. Am. Acad. Arts and Scis. (hon. fgn. mem.), Am. Soc. Biol. Chemists (hon.), Fgn. Assn., Acad. Sci. Argentina, Acad. Sci. Brazil, Japanese Biochemical Soc. (hon.) Assn. Qulmica Argentina (corr.), NAS. Two time Nobel Prize winner in chemistry for work on amino acids and gene sequencing.

SANGER, LAWRENCE MARK, editor-in-chief; b. Bellevue, Washington, July 16, 1968; BA in Philosophy, Reed Coll., 1991; MA in Philosophy, Ohio State Univ., 1995, PhD in Philosophy, 2000. Ran website Sanger's Review of Y2K News Reports, 1998—2000; editor-in-chief Nupedia; editor Wikipedia, 2001—02; lectr. Ohio State Univ., 2002—05; dir. distributed content prog. Digital Universe Found. (leave of absence in 2006), 2005—06; founder, editor-in-chief Citizendium.org, Citzendium Found., 2006—. Presenter in field. Controversy as to whether co-founder "chief organizer" of Wikipedia and its name. *

SANGER, ROBERT MARSHALL, lawyer; b. Arlington, Va., Jan. 7, 1949; s. Ned and Julia Sanger; m. Catherine Jeanne Swysen; children: Charles Andrew, Jeffrey Scott, Paul Michael, Sarah Swysen. BA, U. Calif., Santa Barbara, 1970; JD, U. Calif., LA, 1973. Bar: Calif. 1973, U.S. Supreme Ct. 1979, U.S. Ct. Appeals (9th cir.) 1981, U.S. Ct. Appeals 10th cir. 1998, U.S. Tax Ct. 1975, U.S. Dist. Ct. No. Cen. Ea. & So. Dist. Calif. 1974, U.S. Dist. Ct. Ariz. 1997, U.S. Dist Ct. We. Okla. 1998; cert. criminal law specialist, Calif. Ptnr. Sanger & Swysen, Santa Barbara, Calif., 1973—. Adj. prof. Santa Barbara Coll. Law, 1975-76. Contbr. articles to profl. jours. Chair legal com. Santa Barbara ACLU, 1985-87, 89-91, pres. 1987-89, 1991-93; bd. mem. Death Penalty Focus Calif. 1999-. Recipient Gov.'s award for pro bono legal svcs. Calif. State Bar, 1982, ACLU Civil Liberties award, 1994. Mem. ABA, FBA, Calif. Attys. for Criminal Justice, State Bar Calif., Calif. Pub. Defender's Assn., Santa Barbara Criminal Def. Lawyers Assn. (co-chair 1994-95, Order of Reasonable Doubt 1993), Santa Barbara County Bar Assn. (bd. dir. 1977), Nat. Assn. Criminal Def. Lawyers, Criminal Cts. Bar Assn., William L. Gordon Inn Ct. (Master 2000-). Avocation: golf. Office: Sanger & Swysen 233 E Carrillo St Ste C Santa Barbara CA 93101-7163 Business E-Mail: rsanger@sangerswysen.com.

SANGER, STEPHEN W., consumer products company executive; b. 1945; BA in History, DePauw U., 1986; MBA, U. Mich., 1970. Marketing and sales positions Procter & Gamble, 1970—73; with Gen. Mills, Inc., Mpls., 1974—, v.p., gen. mgr. Northstar Divsn., 1983—86, v.p., gen. mgr. new bus. devel., 1986, pres. Yoplait USA, 1986—88, pres. Big G Divsn., 1988, sr. v.p., 1989—92, vice chmn. bd., 1992-96, pres., 1993-95, CEO, chmn. bd., 1995—. Bd. dirs. Donaldson Co., Inc., Mpls., Target Corp., Wells Fargo & Co., Grocery Manufacturers of Am.; mem. Bus. Council, Bus. Roundtable; bd. adv. Retail Food Industry Ctr. Treas. Guthrie Theatre Found., Mpls.; bd. mem. Catalyst, Minnesota Bus. Partnership. Office: Gen Mills Inc One General Mills Blvd Minneapolis MN 55426 *

SANGESLAND, ODD EINAR, mechanical engineer, consultant; b. Bklyn., Aug. 7, 1929; s. Erling and Olga S. (Sorensen) Sangesland; m. Ellen Marie Piene, June 27, 1953; children: David William, Marianne Louise, Steven Michael, Laura Ellen Wardwell. BS summa cum laude in Mech. Engring., Poly. U., Bklyn., 1956, MME, 1960, student, 1962. Registered profl. engr., NY, 1962. Clk. indsl. sales Gen. Electric, NY, 1952—55; engr. Grumman Aerospace Corp., Bethpage, NY, 1955—90; pvt. practice cons. Plainview, NY, 1991—. Presenter in field. Scoutmaster Boy Scouts Am., Plainview, 1965—75. Sgt US Army, 1950—52, Korea. Mem.: Profl. Engring. Soc., Am. Soc. Heating, Refrigeration and Air Conditioning Engrs. (life), Greater LI Running Club, Sons Norway (trustee 1982—2006). Independent. Lutheran. Achievements include patents for solar energy collector; heat pipes to use heat from light fixtures; first to thermal control of orbiting astronomical observatory the 1st space telescope; configuration & thermal control of Pegasus the 1st satellite to measure size, direction, quantity of micrometeorites. Home: 17 Felice Ln Plainview NY 11803-6413 Personal E-mail: eosang@aol.com.

SANGIULIANO, BARBARA ANN, tax consultant; b. Bronx, NY, Dec. 28, 1959; d. Patrick John and Mildred (Soell) Gallo; m. John Warren Sangiuliano, Aug. 28, 1982. BA, Muhlenberg Coll., Allentown, Pa., 1982; MST, Seton Hall U., South Orange, NJ, 1989, JD, 1997. Bar: NJ 1997, NY 2006; CPA, NJ, 1987; CMA. Sr. tax cons. Ernst & Young LLP, Iselin, NJ, 1998—2003; tax cons. Deloitte Tax LLP, Parsippany, NJ, 2003—06, Smolin, Lupin & Co. PA, Fairfield, NJ, 2006—07, RSM McGladrey, NYC, 2007—. Mem. AICPA, ABA, NJ Soc. CPAs (past pres. Union County chpt.), NJ Bar Assn., Inst. Mgmt. Accts., Mensa, Omicron Delta Epsilon, Phi Sigma Iota. Republican. Roman Catholic. Avocations: reading, bicycling, fencing. Home: 340 William St Scotch Plains NJ 07076-1430 Office: RSM McGladrey 750 Third Ave New York NY 10017 Office Phone: 212-297-4850. Business E-Mail: barbara.sangiuliano@rsmi.com.

SANGMEISTER, GEORGE EDWARD, lawyer, consultant, congressman; b. Joliet, Ill., Feb. 16, 1931; s. George Conrad and Rose Engaborg (Johnson) S.; m. Doris Marie Hinspeter, Dec. 1, 1951; children: George Kurt, Kimberley Ann. BA, Elmhurst Coll., 1957; LLB, John Marshall Law Sch., 1960, JD, 1970. Bar: Ill. 1960. Ptnr. McKeown, Fitzgerald, Zollner, Buck, Sangmeister & Hutchison, 1969-89; justice of peace, 1961-63; states atty. Will County, 1964-68; mem. Ill. Ho. of Reps., 1972-76, Ill. Senate, 1977-87, 101st-103rd Congresses from 4th (now 11th) Dist. Ill., 1989-95; ret., 1995; cons. McKeown, Fitzgerald, Zollner, Buck, Hutchison, Ruttle and Assocs., 1990—. Chmn. Frankfort Twp. unit Am. Cancer Soc., Will County Emergency Housing Devel. Corp.; past trustee Will County Family Svc. Agy.; past bd. dirs. Joliet Jr. Coll. Found., Joliet Will County Ctr. for Econ. Devel., Silver Cross Found., Silver Cross Hosp. With inf. AUS, 1951-53. Mem. ABA, Ill. Bar Assn., Assn. Trial Lawyers Am., Am. Legion, Frankfort (past pres.), Frankfort C. of C., Old Timers Baseball Assn., Lions. Achievements include establishing Abraham Lincoln National Cemetery for Veterans in 1992. Home: 20735 Wolf Rd Mokena IL 60448-8927 Office Phone: 815-469-2176.

SANGREE, WALTER HINCHMAN, social anthropologist, educator; b. NYC, June 15, 1926; s. Carl Michael and Constance (LaBoiteaux) S.; m. Mary Lucinda Shaw, June 14, 1952 (div. Jan. 1986); children: Margaretta Elizabeth, Mary Cora; m. Ilse Michaelis, Dec. 31, 1988. AB, Haverford Coll., 1950; MA, Wesleyan U., 1952; PhD, U. Chgo., 1959. Asst. prof. anthropology U. Rochester, NY, 1957-64, assoc. prof., 1964-73, prof., 1973-95, prof. emeritus, 1995—, chmn. dept. anthropology, 1974-77, acting chmn. dept., 1990; vis. scholar dept. anthropology Harvard U., 1979-80. Vis. scholar Ctr. for Population Studies, Harvard U., 1986-87; rsch. fellow Ctr. for African Studies, Boston U., 1998—. Author: Age, Prayer & Politics in Tiriki, Kenya, 1966; contbr. articles to profl. jours. Co-clk. Rochester Friends Meeting, 1977-79. Fulbright scholar U.K. and Kenya, 1954-56; NSF research fellow Nigeria, 1963-65 Mem. Am. Anthrop. Assn., African Studies Assn., Sigma Xi. Democrat. Mem. Soc. Of Friends. Home and Office: 11 Hilltop Rd Wellesley MA 02482 Home Phone: 781-237-1962. Personal E-mail: sangree@comcast.net. E-mail: waltersangree@verizon.net.

SANGSTER, PAUL EDWARD, radiologist; b. Washington, June 14, 1939; s. George Edward and Leona Jacqueline (Yoder) Sangster; m. Sandra Lucille Shaum, June 1, 1980; 4 children. BS, U. Mich., Ann Arbor, 1962; MS, U. Ariz., Tucson, 1968, MD, 1974. Diplomate Am. Bd. Radiology. Surg. internship U. Calif., San Diego, 1974—75; radiol. residency U. Ariz., 1975—78. Pres. Coconino County Med. Soc., Flagstaff, Ariz., 1988—89; lectr. physiology dept. No. Ariz. U., Flagstaff, 1992—98. Mem.: Am. Roentgen Ray Soc., Am. Coll. Radiology. Achievements include research in metapyrochatechase study of an oxygenase. Avocations: hiking, golf, reading, racquetball.

SANI, ROBERT LEROY, chemical engineering professor; b. Antioch, Calif., Apr. 20, 1935; m. Martha Jo Marr, May 28, 1966; children: Cynthia Kay, Elizabeth Ann, Jeffrey Paul. BS, U. Calif.-Berkeley, 1958, MS, 1960; PhD, U. Minn., 1963. Postdoctoral researcher dept. math Rensselaer Poly. Inst., Troy, NY, 1963-64; asst. prof. U. Ill., Urbana, 1964-70, assoc. prof., 1970-76; prof. chem. engring. U. Colo., Boulder, 1976—, assoc. dept. chair, 2007—; co-dir. Ctr. for Low-g Fluid Mechanics and Transport Phenomena, U. Colo., Boulder, 1986-89, dir., 1989—. Assoc. prof. French Ministry Edn., 1982, 84, 86, 92, 94, 95, 96, 97; cons. Lawrence Livermore Nat. Lab., Calif., 1974-84. Contbr. numerous chpts. to profl. publs.; co-author three books; mem. editorial bd. Internat. Jour. Numerical Methods in Fluids, 1981—, Revue Européenne des Éléments Finis, 1990—, Internat. Jour. Computational Engring. Sci., 1998—, Internat. Jour. Computational & Numerical Analysis & Applications, 2000-. Guggenheim fellow, 1970 Mem. AICE, Soc. for Applied and Indsl. Math., World User Assn. in Applied Computational Fluid Dynamics (bd. dirs.). Democrat. Office: U Colo Dept Chem & Biol Engring UCB 424 Boulder CO 80309-0424 Office Phone: 303-492-5517. Business E-Mail: robert.sani@colorado.edu.

SANISLO, PAUL STEVE, lawyer; b. Cleve., Feb. 8, 1927; s. Paul and Bertha (Kasa) S.; m. Mary Ellen P. Conroy, May 7, 1949; 1 child, Susan J. BA, Baldwin-Wallace Coll., 1948; JD, Cleve. State U., 1961. Bar: Ohio 1961, U.S. Dist. Ct. (N.E. dist.) Ohio 1964. Order clk. Am. Agrl. Chem. Co., Cleve., 1948-52; safety engr. Park Drop Forge Co., Cleve., 1952-62, personnel mgr., 1954-62; assoc. then ptnr. Spohn & Sanislo, L.P.A., Cleve., 1962-81; pres., 1981-86; ptnr., pres. Sanislo, Bacevice & Assocs. LPA, Cleve., 1987-98; pres. Sanislo & Assocs. Co. LPA, 1998-2000; of counsel Stewart & Dechant, Cleve., 2000—. Spl. counsel Atty. Gen. Ohio, 1971; arbitrator Am. Arbitration Assn., 1972-78. Mem. Cleve. City Coun., 1964-67; trustee Cleve.-Marshall Law Sch., 1962-63; trustee Cleve.-Marshall Ednl. Found., 1963-68, pres., 1980-83; mem. Solon city Bd. Edn., Ohio, 1972-83, pres., 1974-83; chmn. Solon Charter Rev. Commn., 1971, mem., 2000—; past mem., organizer, legal adv. Solon Drug Abuse Ctr.; mem. Cuyahoga County Dem. Exec. Com.; ward leader 29th Ward Dem. Club, 1965-71, also past pres.; trustee Solon Dem. Ward Club, 1972-75. Recipient Disting. Svc. award City of Solon, 1984, Solon Bd. Edn., 1984, Solon Edn. Assn., 1984. Mem. Bar Assn. Greater Cleve. (Merit Svc. award 1978-79, chmn. workers compensation sect. 1975-96), Ohio Bar Assn., Cuyahoga County Bar Assn., Assn. Trial Lawyers Am., Cleve.-Marshall Law Sch. Alumni Assn. (pres. 1967-68), Hungarian Bus. and Tradesmen's Club (pres. 1967-68), Cleve. Assn. Compensation Attys. (pres. 1973-86). Democrat. Roman Catholic. Avocations: golf, travel. Office: Stewart & DeChant 1440 Standard Bldg Cleveland OH 44113 Office Phone: 216-781-2258. Business E-Mail: psanislo@stewartdechant.com.

SANKARANARAYANAN, JAYASHRI, medical educator; d. Sankaranarayanan Sivaramakrishnan and Chandra Sankaranarayanan. BPharm, Prin. K.M. Kundnani Coll. Pharmacy, Mumbai, India, 1989; MPharm, Prin. K.M. Kundnani Coll. Pharmacy, 1992; PhD, Purdue U., W. Lafayette, Ind., 2004. Med. svcs. exec. Burroughs Wellcome India, Ltd., Mumbai, 1993—96; med. svs. sr. exec. Glaxo India, Ltd., Mumbai, 1996—97; med. svcs. mgr. RPG, Mumbai, 1997—2000; asst. prof., coll. pharmacy U. Nebr. Med. Ctr., Omaha, 2004—; med. svcs. mgmt. trainee Burroughs Welcome India, Ltd., Mumbai. Faculty mentor, designer State-wide Cmty. Svc. Medicare, Omaha. Recipient Best Podium Presentation award, 2006; grantee Cancer and Smoking Disease Rsch. grant, Nebr. State HHS, 2006—07, Colorectal Cancer Screening Assessment Rsch. grant, Cancer Awareness, Rsch., Edn. & Svc., 2006—07. Mem.: Acad. Health, Am. Assn. Colls. Pharmacy, Am. Pharmacists Assn., Internat. Soc. Pharmacoeconomics and Outcomes Rsch., Sci. Rsch. Soc. (assoc.), Omicron Delta Kappa (hon.), Alpha Zeta (life). Home: 5102 Grover St #6 Omaha NE 68106 Office: Univ Nebr Med Ctr 986045 Nebraska Medical Center Omaha NE 68198-6045

SANKOVITZ, JAMES LEO, retired development director, lobbyist; b. St. Paul, July 3, 1934; s. John L. and Mabel A. (Hanrahan) S.; m. Margaret E. Mathews, Aug. 3, 1957; children: Richard, Therese, Patrick, Margaret, Katherine. BS in Journalism, Marquette U., 1956; MA in Speech, U. Denver, 1963. Dir. pub. rels. Coll. of St. Mary of the Wasatch, Salt Lake City, 1956-57; dir. pub. info. Colo. Sch. of Mines, Golden, 1957-63; assoc. dir. devel. Marquette U., Milw., 1963-66, dir. alumni fund, 1966-67, dir. alumni rels., 1967-69, asst. v.p. univ. rels., 1969-70, v.p. univ. rels., 1970-78, v.p. govtl. rels., 1978-86, v.p. govtl. and community affairs, 1986-97; ret., 1997. Contbr. articles to profl. jours. Founding dir. Univ. Nat. Bank, Milw., 1971-74; bd. dirs. St. Coletta Sch., Jefferson, Wis., 1970-76, 86-93, chair, 1974-76. Mem. Nat. Assn. for Ind. Colls. and Univs. (bd. dirs. Washington 1986-90), Disting. Svc. award 1986), Assn. Jesuit Colls. and Univs. (fed. affairs cons. Washington 1974-90), Assn. Cath. Colls. and Univs. (fed. affairs cons. Washington 1974-85, Blue Key, Alpha Sigma Nu. Roman Catholic. Avocations: woodworking, reading. Home: 4057 N Prospect Ave Milwaukee WI 53211-2121 E-mail: jsankovitz@wi.rr.com.

SANKS, ROBERT LELAND, environmental engineer, retired educator; b. Pomona, Calif., Feb. 19, 1916; s. John B. and Nellie G. (Church) Sanks; m. Mary Louise Clement, May 16, 1946 (dec. Oct. 1994); children: Margaret Russell, John Clement; m. Edith Millen Harrington, Dec. 2, 1999. AA, Fullerton Jr. Coll., Calif., 1936; BS, U. Calif., Berkeley, 1940; MS, Iowa State Coll., Ames, 1949; PhD, U. Calif., Berkeley, 1965. Registered profl. engr., Mont. Draftsman City of La Habra Calif., 1940; asst. engr. Alex Morrison cons. engr., Fullerton, Calif., 1941; jr. engr. US Army Engrs., LA, 1941-42; asst. rsch. engr. dept. civil engring. U. Calif.-Berkeley, 1942-45; structural engr. The Austin Co., Oakland, Calif., 1945-46; instr. dept. civil engring. U. Utah, Salt Lake City, 1946-49, asst. prof., 1949-55, assoc. prof., 1955-58; structural engr. The Lang Co., Salt Lake City, 1950; instrument man Patti McDonald Co., Anchorage, 1951; checker Western Steel Co., Salt Lake City, 1952; structural engr. Moran,

Proctor, Meuser and Rutledge, NYC, 1953, F.C. Torkelson Co., Salt Lake City, 1955; soils engr. R.L. Sloane & Assocs., Salt Lake City, 1956; prof., chmn. dept. civil engring. Gonzaga U., Spokane, Wash., 1958-61; prof. dept. civil engring. Mont. State U., Bozeman, 1966-82, prof. emeritus, 1982—; vis. prof. U. Tex.-Austin, 1974-75; part-time sr. engr. Christian, Spring, Sielbach & Assoc., Billings, Mont., 1974-82. Cons. engr., 1945—; lectr. at pumping sta. design workshops, 1988—; assoc. specialist San. Engring. Research Lab., 1963-65, research engr., 1966. Author: Statically Indeterminate Structural Analysis, 1961; co-author: (with Takashi Assano) Land Treatment and Disposal of Municipal and Industrial Wastewaters, 1976, Water Treatment Plant Design for the Practicing Engineer, 1978; editor-in-chief: Pumping Station Design, 1989 (award Excellence profl. & scholarly pub. div. Assn. Am. Pubs. 1989), 2d edit., 1998, co-editor 3d edit., 2006; contbr. articles on civil engring. to profl. publs. Mem. Wall of Fame, Fullerton H.S., 1987, Hall of Fame, Mont. Profl. Engrs., 2005; NSF fellow, 1961-63 Mem. ASCE (life, chmn. local qualifications com. intermountain sect. 1950-56, pres. intermountain sect. 1957-58), Am. Water Works Assn. (pres. Mont. sect. 1981-82, George Warren Fuller award), Mont. Water Environ. Fedn., Assn. Environ. Engring. Profs., Rotary, Sigma Xi, Chi Epsilon. Home: 1201 Highland Blvd Apt D309 Bozeman MT 59715 Personal E-mail: bsanks@mcn.net.

SAN MIGUEL, MANUEL, painter, historian, composer, poet; b. Guayama, P.R., Sept. 29, 1930; s. Manuel and Luisa (Griffo) San M.; m. Sandra Bonilla, July 12, 1969; children: Manuel, Ana. Student, U. P.R., 1947-51, U. Pa., 1966-68, Arts Students League, NYC, 1968-69. Historian San Juan Nat. Historic Site, Nat. Park Svc., 1953-63; exec. sec. Acad. Arts and Scis., San Juan, 1963-64. Founder mus. and study collection El Morro Castle San Juan Nat. Hist. Site; co-founder Caribbean Art Gallery, San Juan, PR, Galeria Campeche, NYC; cons. in field. Exhibited in U. P.R., 1958, 62, Ateneo de P.R., 1962, Pan-Am. Union, Washington, 1963, Bienal Mex., 1972, Bienal Rio de Janeiro, 1976, Orange County Schs. Mus. Art, Orlando, Fla., 1992, Mus. Modern Art, Paris, 1994, Expo of the Americas, Orlando, 1996, 98, Galeriá Santiago, San Juan, P.R., 2000, Galeria Campeche, San Juan, P.R., 2001, Simon Bolivar Gallery, Caracas, 2001, Galerie Santiago, 2003, Galeriá Colibri, Santo Domingo, numerous other nat. and internat. exhbns.; contbr. monographs on historical work in San Juan Nat. Historic Site to U.S. Nat. Archives, Washington; contbr. poetry to anthologies including Anthology of Latin American Poets, vol. III, 1987; rec. artist popular music of P.R.; soloist U. P.R. choir, Carnegie Hall, N.Y.C., 1949. Capt. U.S. Army, 1951-53, Korea. Decorated Bronze Star with valor clasp and oak leaf cluster, Purple Heart, Combat Infantryman Badge, others; named One of Ten Outstanding Hispanic Men, Orlando, Fla., 1991; recipient Recognition award for contbns. to Hispanic Am. Culture, Govt. P.R., 1996, Hispanic Heritage Found., medal Painters & Designers 20th Century, Cambridge, Eng., 2000; Coqui de Oro award for contbns. to Puerto Rican arts Casa de P.R., Inc., 1999. Mem. AAAS, VFW (life), Disabled Am. Vets. (life), Am. Legion, Ateneo de P.R. (bd. govs. 1959-60), Am. Biog. Inst. (bd. advisors, life mem. bd. govs.), Am. Philatelic Soc. (postal commemorative soc.), Inst. P.R. Culture (cons.), P.R. Philatelic Assn. (charter), Internat. Platform Assn., Lions (Lion of Yr. 1962-63). Achievements include documentary research in the restoration of Castillo San Marcos, St. Augustine, Fla., Castillo San Felipe de Barajas, Colombia, South Am., and restoration of San Juan fortifications and city walls. Personal E-mail: sanmiguel1969@earthlink.net.

SAN MIGUEL, SANDRA BONILLA, social worker; b. Santurce, PR, May 23, 1944; d. Isidoro and Flora (Carrero) Bonilla; m. Manuel San Miguel, July 12, 1969. BA, St. Joseph's Coll., 1966; MS in Social Work, Columbia U., 1970. Cert. social work mgr., sch. social work specialist. Case worker Dept. Labor, Migration Divsn., NYC, 1966—68; clin. social worker N.Y.C. Housing Authority, NYC, 1968—69, Children's Aid Soc., NYC, 1969—71; sr. social worker Traveler's Aid Soc., San Juan, 1971—74; coord., supr. Dept. Addiction Control Svcs., San Juan, 1974—77; substance abuse div. dir. Seminole County Mental Health Ctr., Altamonte Springs, Fla., 1978—81; cons. pvt. practice Hispanic Cons. Svcs., Winter Springs, Fla., 1982—2004; adj. prof. Seminole C.C., Lake Mary, Fla., 1986—90; sch. social worker Seminole County Pub. Schs., Sanford, Fla., 1986—91, lead sch. social worker, 1991—. Pres.'s minority adv. coun. U. Ctrl. Fla., 1982—, vice-chair, 1982-86, chair, 1986-90; bd. regents EEO adv. com. State U. Sys. Fla., 1985-89; bd. dirs. Seminole Cmty. Mental Health Ctr., 1986-94, 95-2001, v.p., 1988-90, pres., 1990-91; adv. bd. Nat. Devereux Found. Ctrl. Fla., 1993-98, women's adv. bd. South Seminole Hosp., Fla., 1994-96; mem. multicultural cmty. adv. com. Seminole County Pub. Schs., 1993-2004; mem. Fla. Consortium on Tchr. Edn. for Am. Minorities, 1990-96; mem. local com. Hispanic Info. and Telecomms. Network, 1990; mem. Seminole County (Fla.) Juvenile Justice Coun., 1993-96; mem. statewide student svcs. adv. com. Dept. Edn. Fla., 1993-96, student svcs. adv. group, 1996-97; cmty. adv. com. sch. social work U. Ctrl. Fla., 2000—. Named Ednl. Support Ctr. Tchr. of Yr., Seminole County Pub. Schs., 2000; recipient Pres.'s Outstanding Svc. award, UCF, 1991, Ponce de Leon Hispanic Cmty. award, 1992, Bd. Svc. Recognition Plaque, Seminole Cmty. Mental Health Ctr., 1991, Outstanding Contribution to Student Svcs. cert., Fla. Dept. Edn., 1995, Manuel Martinez award for Outstanding Contbns. to Puerto Rican Cmty. in Ctrl. Fla., La Casa de Puerto Rico, 1999. Mem.: NASW (appt. nat. sch. social work credential com. 1996—99), Nat. Network Social Work Mgrs., Collegiate Social Workers P.R., Fla. Assn. Student Svcs. Adminstrs. (pres-elect 2006—07, pres. 2007—), Sch. Social Work Assn. Am. (founding mem.), Fla. Assn. Sch. Social Workers (co-founder minority caucus 1988, columnist quar. newsletter article Minority Corner 1988—92, bd. dirs. 1989—, sec. 1990—92, v.p. 1992—93, pres. 1993—94, chmn. legis. com. 1994—, website article From the Gallery 2001—, Leadership Plaque 1994, Adminstr. of Yr. 1999), Nat. Network Social Work Mgrs., St. Joseph's Coll. Alumni Assn., Columbia U. Alumni Assn. (nat. bd. dirs. 1997—2001). Mailing: PO Box 195933 Winter Springs FL 32708 Personal E-mail: sanmiguel1969@earthlink.net.

SANNER, GEORGE BRADLEY, bank executive; b. Balt., Sept. 20, 1953; s. George E. and Marjorie (Hohman) S.; m. Ann Margaret Tehan, Aug. 31, 1991 (div.); children: Anne, Meredith, Kimberly. BA, U. Va., 1974; MBA, Loyola Coll., Balt., 1978. Asst. v.p. Union Trust Co., Balt., 1974-82; v.p. Am. Security Bank, Washington, 1982-86; sr. v.p. Bank of Md., Towson, 1986-87; mng. dir. Provident Bank of Md., Balt., 1987-94; sr. v.p. FCNB Bank, Frederick, Md., 1994-95; pres./CEO Regal Bancorp, Owings Mills, Md., 1995—; also bd. dirs. Bd. dirs. Md. Bank Svcs., Inc.; bd. dirs., vice chmn. Atlantic Ctrl. Bankers Bank; pres., CEO, bd. dir. Regal Bank and Trust. Airman USAF, 1973-75. Mem. Md. Bankers Assn., Alpha Sigma Nu. Republican. Presbyterian. Avocations: golf, tennis, amateur radio. Office: Regal Bancorp 10123 Reisterstown Rd Owings Mills MD 21117-3814 E-mail: gsanner@regalbank.com.

SANNER, JOHN HARPER, retired pharmacologist; b. Anamosa, Iowa, Apr. 29, 1931; s. Lee Michael and Helen (Grace) S.; m. Marilyn Joan Eichorst, Dec. 28, 1958; children: Linda Leigh, Steven Bradley. BS, U. Iowa, 1954, MS, 1961, PhD, 1964. Rsch. investigator G.D. Searle & Co., Skokie, Ill., 1963-69, sr. rsch. investigator, 1969-75, rsch. fellow, 1975-86, ret., 1986—. Contbr. articles to profl. jours. Mem. Deerfield (Ill.) Cable and Telecomm. Commn. 1st lt. USAFR, 1955-57. Mem.: Ill. Videographers Assn. Democrat. Achievements include pioneering research in prostaglandin antagonists. Avocation: video photography and production. Office: Sanner Video Svc PO Box 199 Deerfield IL 60015-0199 Personal E-mail: johnsanner@comcast.net.

SANO, EMILY JOY, museum director; b. Santa Ana, Calif., Feb. 17, 1942; d. Masao and Lois Kikue (Inokuchi) S. BA, Ind. U., 1967; MA, Columbia U., 1970, MPhil, 1976, PhD, 1983. Lectr. Oriental Art Vassar Coll., Poughkeepsie, NY, 1974-79; curator Asian Art, asst. dir. programs Kimbell Art Mus., Ft. Worth, 1979-89; dep. dir. collections and exhbns. Dallas Mus. Art, 1989-92; dep. dir., chief curator Asian Art Mus., San Francisco, 1993-95, dir., 1995—. Author: Great Age of Japanese Buddhist Sculpture, 1982; editor: The Blood of Kings, 1986, Weavers, Merchants and Kings, 1984, Painters of the Great Ming, 1993. Active Assn. Art Mus. Dirs.; vis. com. Harvard U. Art Mus. Woodrow Wilson Fellow, 1966-67; grantee Carnegie, 1963-64, Fulbright-Hays, 1977-78. Office: Asian Art Museum 200 Larkin St San Francisco CA 94102-4734

SANSALONE, WILLIAM ROBERT, biochemist, educator, biomedical researcher; b. Vineland, NJ, Feb. 16, 1931; s. Fortunato and Rosa (Pelle) Sansalone; m. Alice E. Koury, June 25, 1960; 1 child, Catherine. BS, Rutgers U., 1953, PhD, 1961; MS, U. NH, Durham, 1955. Biochemistry rsch. asst. U. Conn., Storrs, 1955-56; instr. biochemistry SUNY Downstate Med. Ctr., Bklyn., 1961-64, asst. prof. biochemistry, 1964-70, assoc. prof., 1970-71; project scientist NIH, Bethesda, Md., 1971-72, sr. project scientist, 1972-73, exec. sec. biochemistry study sect., 1973-74, program dir. rev., 1974-83, assoc. dir. sci. program ops., 1983-87, dir. office of program planning and evaluation, 1987-96; sr. fellow Georgetown U., Washington, 1999—2002, adj. prof. biochemistry, 2002—. Vis. assoc. prof. physiology and biophysics Med. Coll. Pa., Phila., 1970. Contbr. articles to profl. jours. Served to 1st lt. USAF, 1956—58. Mem.: AAAS, Soc. Exptl. Biology and Medicine, Am. Soc. Nutritional Scis., Biophys. Soc., Harvey Soc., Sigma Xi, Alpha Gamma Rho (chpt. treas. 1968—70). Roman Catholic. Home: 6835 Old Stage Rd Rockville MD 20852-4359 Personal E-mail: ws31@prodigy.net. Business E-Mail: ws23@georgetown.edu.

SANSEVERINO, RAYMOND ANTHONY, lawyer; b. Bklyn., Feb. 16, 1947; s. Raphael and Alice Ann (Camerano) S.; m. Karen Marie Mooney, Aug. 24, 1968 (dec. 1980); children: Deirdre Ann, Stacy Lee; m. Victoria Vent, June 6, 1982 (div. 1995); m. Kimberley Frank, May 11, 2002. AB in English Lit., Franklin & Marshall Coll., Lancaster, Pa., 1968; JD cum laude, Fordham U., Bronx, NY, 1972. Bar: NY 1973, US Dist. Ct. (so. and ea. dists.) NY 1973, US Ct. Appeals (2d cir.) 1974, US Supreme Ct. 1986. Assoc. Rogers & Wells, NYC, 1972—75, Corbin & Gordon, NYC, 1975—77; ptnr. Corbin Silverman & Sanseverino LLP, NYC, 1978—2001, mng. ptnr., 1985—2001; ptnr. Brown Raysman Millstein Felder & Steiner LLP, NYC, 2001—06, chair comml. real estate leasing group, 2001—06, mem. exec. com., 2003—06; ptnr. Loeb & Loeb LLP, NYC, 2006—, chair comml. real estate leasing group, 2006—, chmn. NY real estate dept., 2007—. Contbr. articles to profl. jours.; articles editor Fordham Law Rev., 1971-72. Bd. trustees Franklin & Marshal Coll., 2006—. Recipient West Pub. Co. prize, 1972. Mem. ABA, Assn. Bar City NY, NY State Bar Assn., Twin Oaks Swim and Tennis Club (bd. dirs. 1981-2002, pres. 1993-2001), Alumni Assn. Franklin & Marshall Coll. (bd. dirs., chair devel. and philanthopy com. 2003-04, treas. 2004-05, exec. com. 2004-, v.p. 2005-06, pres. 2006-07, past pres., 2007—). Republican. Roman Catholic. Office: Loeb & Loeb LLP 345 Park Ave New York NY 10154 Office Phone: 212-407-4008.

SANSOM, WILLIAM B., consumer products executive; BS in Civil Engring., The Citadel. Commr. transp., commr. fin. and adminstrn. Tenn. State Govt., 1979—83; CEO H.T. Hackney Co., Knoxville, Tenn., 1983—, also chmn. bd. dirs. Mem. bd. dir. Martin Marietta Materials, NC, 1994—, First Tenn. Nat. Corp. Address: PO Box 238 Knoxville TN 37901-0238 Fax: 423-456-1291.

SANSONE, HEIDI L., primary school educator; b. Suffern, NY, Oct. 19, 1971; d. Richard L. and Karen A. Brightenback; m. Robert P. Brightenback, Apr. 30, 1999; children: Emily P., Madeline J. BA in Economics & Mgmt. Sci., SUNY, Cortland, 1989—93; MS in Childhood Edn. & Literacy, LI U., Orangeburg, 2003—06. Cert. childhood edn. tchr. NY State Dept. Edn., 2007, literacy tchr. NY State Dept. Edn., 2007. Assoc. JPMorgan Chase & Co., New York, NY, 1998—2006; student tchr. Ramapo Ctrl. Sch. Dist., Suffern, NY, 2006—07, instr. reading, 2007—. Mem.: Internat. Reading Assn. Home: 8 Temple Dr Tuxedo Park NY 10987 Home Phone: 845-351-2386. Personal E-mail: bobandheidisansone@yahoo.com.

SANSONETTI, THOMAS L., lawyer, former federal agency administrator; b. Hinsdale, IL, May 18, 1949; BA in Fgn. Affairs, with distinction, U. Va., 1971, MBA, 1973; JD, Washington and Lee U., 1976. Chief of staff, legis. dir. to Congressman Craig Thomas US Ho. Reps; assoc. solicitor on energy and natural resources US Dept. Interior, 1987—89, solicitor, 1990—93; ptnr. Holland & Hart LLP, Cheyenne, Wyo., 1993—2001, 2005—; asst. atty. gen. Environment and Natural Resources Divsn. U.S. Dept. Justice, Washington, 2001—05. Founder Wyo. Tennis Assn., 1978; mem. Wyo. Rep. Nat. Com., 1996—2002; chmn. Wyo. Rep. Party, 1983—87; gen. counsel Rep. Nat. Com., 2001; leader Bush-Cheney transition team Interior Dept., 2001. Republican. Office: Holland & Hart LLP 2515 Warren Ave Cheyenne WY 82001-3162 Office Phone: 307-778-4200. Office Fax: 307-778-8175. E-mail: tlsansonetti@hollandhart.com.

SANSTEAD, WAYNE GODFREY, school system administrator; b. Hot Springs, Ark., Apr. 16, 1935; s. Godfrey A. and Clara (Buen) S.; m. Mary Jane Bober, June 16, 1957; children: Timothy, Jonathan. BA in Speech and Polit. Sci, St. Olaf Coll., 1957; MA in Pub. Address and Group Comm., Northwestern U., 1966; EdD in Secondary Edn., U. ND, 1974. Tchr., Luverne, Minn., 1959-60; dir. forensics Minot High Sch., ND, 1960-71, tchr. social sci. ND, 1960-78; mem. ND Ho. of Reps., 1965-70, 83-85, ND Senate, 1971-73; lt. gov. State of ND, Bismarck, 1973-81, supt. pub. instrn., 1985—. Served with AUS, 1957-59. Recipient Disting. Alumnus award St. Olaf Coll., 1991, Literacy award, Internat. Reading Assn., 1993, Nat. Fedn. Outstanding Speech Educator award, 1995; named Outstanding Freshman Senator A.P., 1971, Outstanding Young Educator, N.D. Jr. C. of C., 1967, Outstanding Young Man, Minot Jr. C. of C., 1964, Communicator of the Yr., Nat. Forensic League, 1992, Advocate of Yr., Am. Sch. Counselor Assn., 1994; James J. Hill Found. scholar, Coe Family Found. scholar, 1963, Eagleton scholar Rutgers U., 1969. Mem. ND Edn. Assn., NEA (legis. com. 1969—), Central States Speech Assn., Am. Forensic Assn., Jr. C. of C., Sons of Norway, Elks, Toastmasters. Democrat. Lutheran. Home: 1120 Columbia Dr Bismarck ND 58504-6514 Office: State Supt ND Dept Pub Instrn 600 E Boulevard Ave Dept 201 Fl 9-10-11 Bismarck ND 58505-0440 Office Phone: 701-328-4570. Business E-Mail: wsanstead@nd.gov. *

SANSWEET, STEPHEN JAY, journalist, writer, marketing executive; b. Phila., June 14, 1945; s. Jack Morris and Fannie (Axelrod) S. BS, Temple U., Phila., 1966. Reporter Phila. Inquirer, 1966-69; reporter Wall Street Jour., Phila., 1969-71, Montreal, Que., Canada, 1971-73, LA, 1973-84, dep. bur. chief, 1984-87, bur. chief, 1987-96; dir. specialty mktg. Lucasfilm Ltd., San Francisco, 1996—97, dir. content mgmt. and fan rels., 1997—; sr. editor Star Wars Galaxy Mag., 1996-2000; columnist Star Wars Insider, 1994—. Lectr. bus. journalism U. So. Calif., LA, 1984-87. Author: The Punishment Cure, 1976, Science Fiction Toys and Models, 1981, Star Wars: From Concept to Screen to Collectible, 1992, Tomart's Price Guide to Worldwide Star Wars Collectibles, 1994, 2d edit., 1997, The Quotable Star Wars, 1996, Star Wars Scrapbook: The Essential Collection, 1998, Star Wars Encyclopedia, 1998, Star Wars Collectibles: A Pocket Manual, 1998, Anakin Skywalker: The Story of Darth Vader, 1998, Star Wars: The Action Figure Archive, 1999, The Star Wars Vault, 2007; co-author: The Star Wars Poster Book, 2005, Star Wars Chronicles: The Prequels, 2005; cons. editor: Star Wars Galaxy card sets, 1993, 2d series, 1994, 3d series, 1995; editor: Star Wars Trilogy Spl. Edn. card sets, 1997. Recipient award for best fire story Phila. Fire Dept., 1968, Pub. Svc.-Team Mem. award Sigma Delta Chi, 1977; finalist Loeb award, 1990. Mem. Soc. Profl. Journalists. Avocation: collecting toys and movie memorabilia. Office: Lucasfilm Ltd PO Box 29901 San Francisco CA 94129

SANT, ROGER W., retired energy executive; M, Harvard U. Instr. corp. fin. Stanford U. Grad. Sch. Bus.; founder several businesses; asst. adminstr. energy conservation & environ. U.S. Fed. Energy Adminstrn., Washington; dir. Mellon Inst.'s Energy Productivity Ctr.; co-founder AES Corp., Washington, 1981, CEO, 1981—93, chmn. bd., 1981—2003, chmn. emeritus, 2003—06. Bd. dir. Marriott Internat. Inc. Author: The Least-Cost Energy Strategy; co-author: Creating Abundance-America's Least-Cost Energy Strategy; contbr. articles to profl. jours. Chmn. Summit Found., Summit Fund, Washington; bd. dir. World Wildlife Fund, chmn., 1994—2000; regent, chmn. exec. com. Smithsonian Institution; bd. dir. Anacostia Waterfront Corp., Nat. Symphony Orch., DC Coll. Access Prog., Tudor Place. Mailing: Summit Foundation Ste 525 2100 Pennsylvania Ave NW Washington DC 20037

SANT, VICTORIA P., museum administrator; BA, Stanford U. Docent Nat. Gallery Art, Washington, DC, 1983—85, chmn. trustees coun., 2001—02, immediate past chmn., The Phillips Collection, pres., 2003—. Co-founder, pres. The Summit Found., The Summit Fund of Washington. Bd. mem. Stanford U., Cmty. Found. for Nat. Capitol Region, Nat. Campaign to Prevent Teen Pregnancy, DC Campaign to Prevent Teen Pregnancy, Population Action Internat., Vital Voices for Global Partnership. Office: The Summit Found Ste 525 2100 Pennsylvania Ave, NW, Washington DC 20037 Office Phone: 202-912-2900.

SANTA-COLOMA, BERNARDO, retired secondary school educator; b. NYC, May 31, 1934; s. Bernardo Santa-Coloma Sr. and Belma Remotti; m. Sofia A. Santa-Coloma, Dec. 22, 1981; childen: Ananda, Anita. BA in Humanistic Psychology, U. Calif., Santa Cruz, 1973; MA in Integral Counseling Psychology, Calif. Inst. Integral Studies, San Francisco, 1976; MEd in Secondary Edn., U. Nev., Las Vegas, 1979; 3 level cert., Feuerstein's Instrumental, Enrichment Program; postgrad., U. Sarasota and U. Houston. Cert. secondary edn. tchr. ESL, history, English Tex., guidance counselor Tex. Edn. Agy., nat. cert. counselor, lic. marriage and family therapist Tex., profl. counselor Tex., bd. approved supr., Medicaid provider, children's health ins. program, child/family protective svcs. Mem. tchr. corps., vol. VISTA, Las Vegas, Nev., 1976-79; family counselor, English tutor Diocese of Matamoros and Valle Hermoso Tamps, Mexico, Cath. Family Svcs. and Vol. Ednl. and Social Svcs., Amarillo, Tex., 1980-82; grad. asst. Pan Am. U., Brownsville, Tex., 1983-84; at-risk program, low-level reading instr. Brownsville Ind. Sch. Dist., 1984-94; basic skills instr. James Pace High Sch., Brownsville; lang. arts, ESL, reading instr. Alternative Edn. Ctr./Brownsville Ind. Sch. Dist., 1994—2005; ESL/inclusion tchr. Dr. Juliet V. Garcia Middle Sch., 2005—06; ret., 2006. Counselor and psychotherapist Family Effectiveness and Devel. Program, Kids in Crisis, Teenage Crisis Hotline, La Casa Esperanza Home for Boys; basic adult reading instr. Southmost Coll.; ESL, lang. arts tchr. Alternative Ctr.; at-risk tchr., pvt. practice counselor, Brownsville Ind. Sch. Dist. Family Ctrs., 1994—1998; part-time counselor Holistic Mind and Health Inst., Brownsville, 1998; counselor, psychotherapist, contract worker, counselor supr., chem. dependency counselor Recovery Ctr., Cameron County Housing Authority, 1999-2001, Citadel Group, 2000-03; Medicaid provider, approved supr. LPC interns, LMFT assocs.; supr. Weslaco, Deer Oaks Mental Health Assocs., 2002-04, Fed. Bur. Prisons, Tex. Commn. Alcohol/Drug Prevention prog. counselor, supr. recovery ctr., 2003—. Contbr. articles to profl. jours. in U.S. and Mex. including Integracion Integral, Journey in Matamoros. Vol. VISTA, 1976-79, VISTA Tchr. Corps, Las Vegas, Peace Corps, Thailand, 1979, Vol. Edn./Soc. Svc., Tex., Mex., 1980-82. With USN, 1952-56, medic neuropsychiatric wards San Diego and Guam. Recipient scholarship U. Calif.-Santa Cruz, 1971-73, U. Nev. tchr. corps scholar, 1977-79; named grad. asst. Calif. Inst. Integral Studies, 1974-76. Home: PO Box 3941 Brownsville TX 78523-3941 also: Country Club 2009 Madero Dr Brownsville TX 78526-1734 Office Phone: 956-548-0028 ext. 110. Personal E-mail: berniesanta@sbcglobal.net. *Waking up is really the seed of perfection, of personal and transpersonal realization - involution precedes evolution! to remain asleep, 'waking-sleep' (inconscience) leads to complacency, dry rot, and moral decay. To be is to do and to do IS. In the final analysis, last judgment, what shall we - yes, you and I contribute to our fellowman, to posterity? - we often die before giving birth to ourselves - truly to be reborn is not easy; we create, instead, an intense paradox, toward life, toward our destiny (i.e., a paradoxical process of self denial instead of one of genuine self interest, self-realization,-actualization, ad infinitum, in tune with spirit, the cosmos-...'Like trees', we begin with a seed. Some do not develop at all. Some die young. And some grow into towering heights with many flourishing branches).*

SANTANA, CARLOS, guitarist; b. Autlan de Navarro, Mexico, July 20, 1947; Guitarist Santana Mgmt., San Rafael, Calif., 1987—. Prin. Guts and Grace Records, 1993. Played guitar in Tijuana nightclubs, recorded with Mike Bloomfield and Al Kooper's Super Session, founder, guitarist rock band Santana, 1966—, appeared at Woodstock Festival, 1969, rec. artist Columbia Records, 1969—97, albums include Santana, 1968, Abraxas, 1970, Santana III, Caravanserai, 1972, Welcome, 1973, Greatest Hits, 1974, Barboletta, 1974, Lotus, 1975, Amigos, 1976, Festival, Moonflower, 1977, Inner Secrets, 1979, Marathon, 1979, Swing of Delight, 1980, Zebop, 1981, Shango, 1982, Havana Moon, 1983, Beyond Appearances, 1985, Freedom, 1987, Viva Santana!, 1988, Doin' It, 1990, Spirits Dancing In the Flesh, 1990, Milagro, 1992, Brothers, 1994, Sacred Fire: Live in South America, 1995, Dance of the Rainbow Serpent, 1995, Supernatural, 1999 (Grammy award for Song of Yr., 2000, Grammy award for Record of Yr., 2000, Grammy award for Album of Yr., 2000), Shaman, 2002, All That I Am, 2005, solo albums include Devadip Carlos-Oneness: Silver Dreams, Golden Reality, 1979, Blues for Salvador, 1987 (Grammy award for Best Instrumental Rock Performance, 1989), appeared in film Soul to Soul, 1971, Love and Music, 1971, Fillmore, 1972, Dominoes: An Uncensored Journey Through the 60s, The All-Star Reggae Session, 1988, Santana: Viva Santana (A Conversation with Carlos), 1989, Carlos Santana: Sacred Fire: Live in Mexico, 1993, History of Rock 'N' Roll, Vol. 6, History of Rock 'N' Roll, Vol. 7, 1995, Blue Note-A Story of Modern Jazz, 1996, Ricky Martin: One Night Only, 1999, 1999, world-wide concert tours with Santana Band, performed and recorded with Buddy Miles, Herbie Hancock, McCoy Tyner, John McLaughlin, Jose Feliciano, Wayne Shorter and Alice Coltrane, Aretha Franklin, Olatunji; rec. artist: Arista Records. Named to Hall of Fame, NAACP Image award, 2006, Rock and Roll Hall of Fame, 1998; recipient Gold Medal award, 1977, Century award Billboard Mag., 1996, Spl. Achievement award ALMA, 1999, Legend Award, World Music Awards, 2005. Office: Santana Mgmt PO Box 10348 San Rafael CA 94912-0348 *Keep an open heart, focus on the positive, be true to your innermost feelings, but most of all make time to visit the Lord within.*

SANTANA, JOHAN ALEXANDER, professional baseball player; b. Tovar Merida, Venezuela, Mar. 13, 1979; m. Yasmile Santana; children: Jasmily, Jasmine. Pitcher Minn. Twins, 2000—. Named Am. League Pitcher of Yr., The Sporting News, 2004, 2006, Player of Yr., Baseball Am., 2006; named to Am. League All-Star Team, 2005—07; recipient Am. League Cy Young award, Maj. League Baseball Writers Assn., 2004, 2006, Player's Choice award for Am. League's Most Outstanding Pitcher, 2004, 2006, Am. League Triple Crown, 2006. Achievements include leading the

Am. League in strikeouts (265) and ERA (2.61), 2004; led Maj. League Baseball in strikeouts (245) and ERA (2.77), 2006. Office: c/o Minnesota Twins Metrodome 34 Kirby Puckett Place Minneapolis MN 55415 *

SANTANA, LYMARI JEANETTE, lawyer; b. Augusta, Ga., 1968; married. BA with honors in Polit. Sci., U. PR, Rio Piedras, 1991; JD with honors, Mich. State U. Detroit Coll. Law, 1994. Bar: Mich. 1994, Minn. 2000. With James M. Hacker, P.C., Mt. Clemens, Mich.; asst. prosecutor Village of New Haven, Mich.; asst. US atty. No. Dist. Ala.; founding shareholder Mack & Santana Law Offices, P.C.; of counsel Mansfield, Tanick & Cohen, P.A., Mpls. With Judge Adv. Gen. Corps US Army, 1995—2000, criminal trial def. counselor 82nd Airborne Divsn. US Army, 1998. Decorated Meritorious Svc. medal; named a Rising Star, Minn. Super Lawyers Mag., 2005, 2006, 2007. Mem.: Nat. Hispanic Bar Assn., Minn. Hispanic Bar Assn. (pres. 2004—05, sec. 2001—03), Hennepin County Bar Assn. Avocations: reading, sports, movies. Office: Mack & Santana Law Offices PC 1700 US Bank Plz South 220 S 6th St Minneapolis MN 55402 Office Phone: 612-605-0967. Business E-Mail: lymari@macksantanalaw.com.

SANTANGELO, MARIO VINCENT, retired dentist; b. Youngstown, Ohio, Oct. 5, 1931; s. Anthony and Maria (Zarlenga) S. Student, U. Pitts., 1949-51; DDS, Loyola U., Chgo., 1955, MS, 1960. Instr. Loyola U., 1957-60, asst. prof., 1960-66, assoc. prof., 1966-70, chmn. dept. radiology, 1962-70, dir. dental aux. utilization program, 1963-70, chmn. dept. oral diagnosis, 1967-70, asst. dean, 1969-70; pvt. practice Chgo., 1960-70; ret., 1970. Cons. Cert. Bd. Am. Dental Assts. Assn., 1967-75, VA Rsch. Hosp., 1969-75; counselor Chgo. Dental Assts. Assn., 1966-69; mem. dental student tng. adv. com. divsn. dental health USPHS, HEW, 1969-71; cons. dental edn. rev. com. NIH, 1971-72; cons. region IV, USPHS, HEW, Atlanta, 1973-76, region V, Chgo., 1973-77; mem. Commn. on Dental Edn. and Practice, Fedn. Dentaire Internat., 1984-92; mem. bd. visitors Washington U. Sch. Dental Medicine, St. Louis, 1974-76; mem. project staff Dental Edn. in the U.S., 1976. Contbr. articles to dental jours. 1st Lt. USAF, 1955—56, Capt. USAF, 1956—57. Recipient Dr. Harry Strusser Meml. award NYU Coll. Dentistry, 1985. Fellow Am. Coll. Dentists (life); mem. ADA (life, asst. sec. coun. dental edn. 1971-81, acting sec. 1981-82, sec. 1982-90, dir. 1990-92, asst. sec. commn. on dental accreditation 1975-81, acting sec. 1981-82, sec. 1982-90, dir. 1990-92, acting sec. commn. continuing dental edn. 1981-82, sec. 1982-90, dir. 1990-92), Ill. State Dental Assn. (life), Chgo. Dental Assn. (life), AMA (edn. work group 1982-86), Assembly Specialized Accrediting Bodies (coun. on postsecondary accreditation 1981-92, award of merit 1992), Am. Assn. Dental Schs., Odontographic Soc. Chgo. (life), Am. Acad. Oral Pathology, Am. Acad. Dental Radiology, Can. Dental Assn. (commn. on dental accreditation award of merit 1992), Am. Acad. Oral Medicine, Am. Assn. Dental Examiners (hon.), Blue Key Honor Soc., Omicron Kappa Upsilon, Xi Psi Phi. Home: 1440 N Lake Shore Dr Chicago IL 60610-1626

SANTAOLALLA, GUSTAVO, musician, composer, record producer; b. Buenos Aires; Founder Surco Records, LA, 1997. Recordings: Santaolla, 1982, GAS, 1995, Roncoco, 1998; composer of movie soundtracks of Amores perros, 2000, 21 Grams, 2003, Diarios de motocicleta (Motorcycle Diaries), 2004, Brokeback Mountain, 2005 (Oscar award for best original score, Acad. Motion Pictures Arts & Sciences, 2006), North Country, 2005, Babel, 2006 (Anthony Asquith award for Achievement in Film Music, British Acad. Film and TV Arts, 2007, Oscar award for best original score, 2007); producer for Carnabailito (Gary Kerpel), Nuevo (Kronos Quartet). Named one of 25 Most Influential Hispanics, Time Mag., 2005. Mailing: Surco Records 1501 Baxter St Los Angeles CA 90026 *

SANTEE, DALE WILLIAM, lawyer, air force officer; b. Washington, Pa., Mar. 28, 1953; s. Robert Erwin and Elsbeth Emma (Bantleon) S.; married; 1 child, Enri De'Von; m. Junko Mori, June 2, 1992. BA, Washington & Jefferson Coll., 1975; MA, U. No. Ariz., 1982; JD, U. Pitts., 1978. Bar: Pa. 1978, US Ct. Mil. Appeals 1979, Calif. 1989. Floor mgr., commn. salesman J.C. Penney Co., Washington, Pa., 1971-76; asst. mgr. Rach Enterprises, Charleroi, Pa., 1977-78; legal intern Washington County Pub. Defender; commd. 2d lt. USAF, 1979, advanced through grades to col., 2001; from asst. staff judge advocate to area def. counsel Luke Air Force Base, Ariz., 1979-81; claims officer 343 Combat Support Group/Judge Advocate, Eielson AFB, Alaska, 1981-83; sr. staff legal adviser Dept. Vet. Affairs, Washington, 1983-89; asst. staff judge advocate Mil. Justice div. Air Force Judge Advocate Gen.'s Office, Washington, 1986-89, 63CSG/Judge Advocate, Norton Air Force Base, Calif., 1989-91; dep. pub. defender Juvenile div. San Diego County, 1990-93, dep. alt. pub. defender, 1993-98; asst. staff judge advocate 452 AMW, March Air Res. Base, Calif., 1991-99, staff judge advocate, 1999-2001; supervising dep., alt. pub. defender Conflict Parent-Child Office, 1998-2001, dep. alt. pub. defender, 2001—; sr. IMA 21 AF/JA, Mc Guire AFB, NJ, 2001—03, HQ Air Res. Pers. Ctr., Denver, 2003—04, HQ PACAF/JA, Hickam AFB, 2004—. V.p. Neuer Enterprises, Nanjemoy, Md., 1983-89; participant Mgmt. Devel. Seminar, 1988. Mem. San Diego County Rep. Party; pres., co-chmn. legis. com. PTA Zamorano Elem. Sch., San Diego, chmn. SITE com.; mem. San Diego County Child Abuse Coord. Coun., San Diego County Commn. on Children and Youth, San Diego County Juvenile Ct. Mental Health Task Force, San Diego County Unified Sch. Dist. Parent Adv. Coun.; bd. dirs. San Diego County Youth Ct. Program, Pub. Defenders Assn., Train Ct. Apptd. Spl. Advocates for Voices for Children, McGill Ctr. Creative Problem Solving Youth Curriculum Com. Decorated Air Force Commendation medal, 1981, 89, Air Force Meritorious Svc. medal, 1991, 96, 99, 2001, 2003, 06, Air Force Achievement medal, 2000; named Outstanding Young Man of Am., U.S. Jaycees, Montgomery, Ala., 1981; acad. scholar Washington & Jefferson Coll., 1971-75, Beta scholar Washington & Jefferson Coll., 1974, Pa. Senatorial scholar Pa. Senate, 1975-78; named Juvenile Justice Commn. Atty of Yr., 1997; recipient Clara Shortridge Foltz award ABA/Nat. Legal Aid and Defender Assn., 1999, Judge Advocates Assn. Outstanding Career Armed Svcs. Atty. award, 2000. Mem. Pa. Bar Assn., Calif. Bar Assn., San Diego County Bar Assn., San Diego County Psych-Law Soc. Avocations: swimming, softball, stamp and coin collecting, foreign travel. Office: 8525 Gibbs Dr Ste 201 San Diego CA 92123 Home Phone: 619-656-2717; Office Phone: 858-974-5819. E-mail: Dale.Santee@sdcounty.ca.gov.

SANTELLE, JAMES LEWIS, prosecutor; b. Milw., Sept. 10, 1958; s. James Nathaniel and Carol Jean (Hasley) S. BA, Marquette Univ., 1980; JD, Univ. Chgo., 1983. Bar: Wis. 1983, U.S. Dist. Ct. (ea. and we. dist.) 1983, U.S. Ct. Appeals (7th cir.) 1983. Clerk Hon. Judge Robert W. Warren, Milw., 1983-85; asst. U.S. atty. Ea. Dist. Wis., Milw., 1985—, civil divsn. chief, 1993—99, interim U.S. atty., 2001—02; prin. dep. dir. Exec. Office U.S. Attys., U.S. Dept. Justice, Washington, 1999—2001, exec. asst. U.S. atty., 2002—03; civil divsn. chief We. Dist. Mich., Grand Rapids, 2003—04. Mem. profl. responsibility com., investigator Wis. Bd. of Attys., 1993-99. Editor: The Milw. Lawyer, 1986-92. Bd. dirs. Waukesha County Coun. Alcoholism and Other Drug Abuse, 1993-99; citizen counselor Badger Boys State, 1986—; coach Wis. Bar Found. High Sch. Mock Trial Tournament, 1986-99. Mem.: Milw. Bar Assn., 7th Cir. Bar Assn. (liaison 2001—), Ea. Dist. Wis. Bar Assn. (sec. 2001—02). Avocations: running, swimming. Office: US Atty Office 517 E Wisconsin Ave Rm 530 Milwaukee WI 53202-4580 Office Phone: 414-297-1700. Business E-Mail: james.santelle@usdoj.gov.

SANTER, BENJAMIN DAVID, atmospheric scientist; b. Washington, June 3, 1955; BS Environ. Scis. with 1st class honors, U. East Anglia, Norwich, Eng., 1976; NATO Rsch. Studentship, U. East Anglia, 1977, PhD in Climatology, 1987. Jr. rsch. assoc. Sch. Environ. Scis. U. East Anglia, Norwich, Eng., 1978-79, rsch. assoc. climatic rsch. unit, 1983-87; project engr. dept. new techs., air pollution and Dornier Sys. GmbH, Friedrichshafen, Germany, 1980-83; postdoct., rsch. scientist Max-Planck Inst. Meteorologie, Hamburg, Germany, 1987-92; physicist earth and environ. scis. directorate Lawrence Livermore Nat. Lab., Livermore, Calif., 1992—. Expert witness German Bundestag Enquete Commn. Hearings on Greenhouse-Gas-Induced Climate Change, Bonn, Germany, 1992; cons. Battelle Pacific Northwest Lab., 1992-93, mem. sci. adv. panel climate change, data and detection program NOAA, 1995—; mem. Climate Variability and Predictability Numerical Experimentation Group, 1995—; participant numerous confs., workshops; lectr. in field. Co-author: Proceedings of NATO Advanced Study Institute on Physically-Based Modelling and Simulation of Climate and Climatic Change, 1988, Science and Engineering on Supercomputers, 1990, Supercomputer '90, Greenhouse-Gas-Induced Climate Change: A Critical Appraisal of Simulations and Observations, 1991, Global Warming: Concern for Tomorrow, 1993, Agricultural Dimensions of Global Climate Change, 1993, Dahlem Workshop on Global Changes in the Perspective of the Past, 1993, Climate Change int the Intra-American Sea, 1993, Communicating About Climate: the Story of the Model Evaluation Consortium for Climate Assessment, 1997; mem. editl. bd. Climatic Change, 1996—; contbr. numerous articles to profl. jours., chpts. to books. MacArthur fellow John D. and Catherine T. MacArthur Found., 1998; Ford Travel scholar, 1974; recipient Outstanding Scientific Paper award U.S. Dept. Commerce Environ. Rsch. Lab. Nat. Oceanic and Atmospheric Adminstrn., 1997, Norbert Gerbier-MUMM Internat. award World Meteorol. Orgn., 1998, E.O. Lawrence award U.S. Dept. Energy, 2002. Mem. Am. Geophys. Union. Achievements include research in climate modeling and greenhouse-gas effects supporting the hypothesis that human activity contributes to global warming. Office: Lawrence Livermore Nat Lab PCMDI PO Box 808 L-264 Livermore CA 94551-0808 Home: 2160 Goldenrod Ln San Ramon CA 94583-5555 Fax: (925) 422-7675. E-mail: santer1@llnl.gov.

SANTHANAM, KALATHUR S. V., chemist, researcher; b. Tirupati, Andhra, India, Sept. 11, 1938; s. Kalathur and Kalathur (Vijayalaxmi) Duraiswamy; m. Santhanam Chari Komalavalli; children: Rohini, Shalini. BSc with honors, Sri Venkateswara U., Tirupati, India, 1958, PhD, 1964; postdoctoral, Tex. U., Austin, 1964-68. Sr. prof. Tata Inst. Fund. Rsch., Mumbai, India, 1968—98; dir., prof. Rochester Inst. Tech., NY, 2001—. Vis. scientist U. Mich., Ann Arbor, 1971-73, Brookhaven Nat. Lab., Upton, NY, 1986, CNRS, Hevdon, France, 1989, 1990, 1994, 1996, PSI Switzerland, 1991, 1992; rsch. assoc. U. Tex., Austin, 1976, 80-81; vis. prof. U. Guelph, Can., 1979, U. Victoria, Can., 1982-90, Rochester Inst. Tech., NY, 1999; cons. Ctrl. Electrochem. Rsch. Inst., Karikudi, India, 1975-76, Nehru Sci. Centre, Mumbai, India, 1983-86, Chemapol, Mumbai, 1993-96. Author: Photoelectrochemical Solar Cells, 1988, Ion-sensing Electrodes and Electrochemical Instrumentation, 1990; contbr. articles to profl. jours., papers in field, chpts. to books. Chmn. Bombay Assn. Sci. Edn., Mumbai, 1982, Bioelectrochem. Soc. India, Mumbai, 1990-96. With Indian mil., 1951-53. Univ. Grants Commn. scholar, New Delhi, 1961-63, Nat. Inst. Sci. India Acad., New Delhi, 1964. Fellow SAEST India (chmn. 1983-89); mem. ACS, Nat. Res. Soc., Saxon Acad. (corr.), Sigma Xi. Office: Rochester Inst Tech Ctr Materials Sci Engring Rochester NY 14623 Office Phone: 585-472-2920. Personal E-mail: santhanam@localnet.com. Business E-Mail: ksssch@rit.edu.

SANTI, E. SCOTT, engineering executive; BS in Acctg., U. Ill., 1983; M in Mgmt., Northwestern U., 1992. Sales rep. Buildex divsn. Ill. Tool Works (ITW), 1983, various sales and mktg. mgmt. positions Buildex and Paslode divsn., 1985—94, gen. mgr. Vortec divsn., 1995—97, v.p., gen. mgr. Hobart Ground Power bus., 1997—98, v.p., gen. mgr. Hobart Bros. businesses, 1998, group v.p. Welding Products, 2002—03, pres. Welding Products Focus Markets Group, 2003—04, exec. v.p., 2004—. Office: Ill Tool Works 3600 W Lake Ave Glenview IL 60026-1215 Office Phone: 847-724-7500. Office Fax: 847-657-4572. *

SANTIAGO, JOSE E., film producer, writer, director, educator; s. Diego Santiago and Angela Falcon; m. Louise Colon, Jan. 12, 1960; children: Angela Rebecca, Margaret Linda. BA, Holy Names U., Oakland, Calif., 2001. Tchr. MIT Acad., Vallejo, Calif., 1999—; writer, prodr., dir. Image 8 Films, Vallejo, Calif., 2004—. Prodr.: (film) Nemesis. Vol. Wheel Chair Found., Danville, Calif., 2004—04. Sgt. US Army, 1977—83. Mem.: Amateur Radio Relay League (licentiate). Home Phone: 707-334-0793; Office Phone: 707-334-0793. E-mail: josesantiago@image8films.com.

SANTIAGO, RAYMOND, library director, educator; b. NYC, July 13, 1949; s. Raymond and Livia Santiago; m. Crystal C. Capelis, May 15, 1979; 1 child, Jason Esrael. BFA, Rochester Inst. Tech., NY, 1974; MLS, SUNY, Buffalo, 1975. Co-chair, head non-print svcs. World U., San Juan, 1978—84; libr. Tampa-Hillsborough Pub. Libr. Sys., Fla., 1984—88, sect. mgr. Fla., 1988—90; supr. libr. svcs. Miami-Dade Pub. Libr. Sys., Fla., 1990—91, asst. dir. Fla., 1991—98, dir. Fla., 1998—. Adj. faculty Sch. Libr. and Info. Sci., U. South Fla., 1994—. Named Libr. of Yr., Libr. Jour., 2003. Mem. ALA, Pub. Libr. Assn., Fla. Libr. Assn. Office: Miami-Dade Pub Libr Sys 101 W Flagler St Miami FL 33130-1504 Office Phone: 305-375-5184. Business E-Mail: santiagor@miamidade.gov. *

SANTINA, DALIA, nutritionist, writer, skin care specialist; b. Amman, Jordan, Sept. 24, 1954; d. Mahmoud Daoud Abbasi, Widad Abbasi; m. Mohammed Shafiq Santina. BA in English Lit., U. Riyadh, Saudi Arabia, 1977; diploma in computer programming, Western Bus. Coll., 1980; diploma in Skin Aesthetics, Career Acad. Beauty, 1989; PhD in Holistic Nutrition, Clayton Coll. Natural Health, 1994. Cert. paramedical acne 1990, glycolic acid services 1991, mgmt. aging and sun-damaged skin 1992, natural pharmacology 1992, aesthetic peeling 1992, oxygenation of the skin 1993, lymphatic drainage massage techniques 1994, homeopathic esthetiocology 1994, iridology diploma 1995, cert. chem. peels 1996, hydrotherapy 1997, glycolic treatments 1998, diploma in iridology 2003, cert. in herbology 2003. Exec. asst. to v.p. Am. Health Ctr., Newport Beach, Calif., 1988—89; skin care co. Skinclub, Huntington Beach, Calif., 1991—96; lectr. holistic nutrition/skin health issues, 1999—. Translator computer sys. tng. manuals, Dallas, 1983—84; tech. translator England and No. Ireland, 1984. Author: Holistic Skin Is...In, 2001, Super Supplements for Skin, Body & Mind, 2004; contbr. articles to profl. jours. Recipient Gold medal in Table Tennis, Sports Bd., Kuwait, 1972. Avocations: horseback riding, reading, antiques. Home Phone: 949-786-0672. Personal E-mail: dalia4skin@msn.com.

SANTINI, GINO, pharmaceutical executive; b. Cesena, Italy; Grad. in Mech. Engring., U. Bologna, Italy, 1981; MBA, U. Rochester, NY, 1983. Pres. SERM and skeletal products; fin. planning assoc. Eli Lilly and Co., Italy, 1983, pharm. dir. Belgium, 1990—91, gen. mgr. Eli Lilly Compania de Mex. Mexico City, 1991, area dir. L.Am., 1994—95, v.p. corp. stategy and bus. devel., 1996—97, pres. women's health bus. unit, 1997—99, pres. US ops., 1999—2004, sr. v.p. corp. strategy and policy, 2004—, mem. policy and strategy com., 2004—, mem. sr. mgmt. coun., 2004—. Bd. trustees Healthcare Leadership Coun.; assoc. mem. bd. Nat. Assn. Chain Drug Stores. Chmn. Nobel of Ind.; mem. exec. com. Indpls. C. of C. Office: Eli Lilly and Co Lilly Corp Ctr Indianapolis IN 46285 Office Phone: 317-276-2000. *

SANTINI, JORGE, mayor; b. San Juan, 1960; BA, U. P.R.; law degree cum laude, Interam. U. Ptnr. Miranda Cardenas & Córdova, 1986—93; legal advisor Gov. of P.R., 1994—96; mem. Sen. of P.R., 1996—99; mayor City of San Juan, 2001—. Chmn. Sen. Jud. Com.; vice-chmn. Govt. and Fed. Affairs Com., Banking, Consumer Affairs, and Pub. Corps. Com. Lt. col. Puerto Rico Nat. Guard. New Progressive Party. Office: PO Box 70179 San Juan PR 00902-4100 *

SANTIS, JORGE HILKER, curator; b. Havana, Cuba, May 4, 1947; arrived in U.S., 1963; s. José Ramón Santis and Prudencia Andrea Forte. BA, Hunter Coll., NYC, 1971, MA, 1975. Asst. curator edn. Mus. Art/Ft. Lauderdale, Fla., 1979—85, registrar, 1985—91, curator collections, 1991—. Co-author: William Glackens, 1996, Breaking Barriers, 1997, Unbroken Ties, 2006. Bd. dirs. Broward Ho., Ft. Lauderdale, 2004—, Hispanic Unity Fla., Hollywood, 2003—06, Sansom Found., Ft. Lauderdale, 2001—, dir. edn., 2002—. Mem.: Am. Assn. Museums. Office: Mus Art/Ft Lauderdale 1 E Las Olas Blvd Fort Lauderdale FL 33301-1807

SANTISI, TERRI M. (THERESA M. SANTISI), multi-media company executive; b. Mar. 5, 1954; BS magna cum laude, Boston Coll., 1976. With Ernst & Young; CFO EMI Music Publishing Worldwide; exec. v.p., gen. mgr. EMI Music N.Am.; mng. ptnr. KPMG; CFO Interpublic Group of Cos.; exec. v.p., chief fin. & adminstrv. officer IMG, 2006—. Mem. adv. bd. She Made It program Mus. TV and Radio; bd. dirs., mem. exec. com. NYC Outward Bound. Office: IMG 1360 E 9th St Ste 100 Cleveland OH 44114 *

SANTISTEBAN, JOSEPH HENRY, human resources specialist; b. NYC, July 15, 1946; s. Mario Santisteban and Antonia (dec.) Rivera; m. Evangelista Pilapil, Oct. 26, 1969 (dec. Dec. 1998); children: Jason, Damien. BA, Chapman U., 1972—74; BS, U. of Nebr., 1982—84; MA, Embry-Riddle Aero. U., 1986—90; PhD, U. of the Philippines, 1988—90. Cert. tchr. Ariz. State Bd. Edn., 1993. Chief master sgt. USAF, 1963—94; sr. staff recruiter Swift Transp. Co., Phoenix, Ariz., 1993—99; recruiting and tng. mgr. ATC Leasing Co. Inc., Kenosha, Wis., 1999—2000; human resources dir. Ill. Auto Truck Co. Inc., Des Plaines, 2000—. Chief enlisted mgr. U.S. Air Force, Phoenix, 1963—93; coll. instr. Embry-Riddle Aero. U., Phoenix, 1990—93. Translator. Leader Boy Scouts of Am., 1979—2003, CAP, 1986—92, 2003—. Maj. Civil Air Patrol. Decorated Bronze Star Medal w/V Dept. of Def.; recipient Outstanding Cmty. Svc. Award, Ariz. C. of C., 1992, Outstanding Svc. Award, Mayor of Mayaguez, PR, 1998, Presdl. Humanitarian Award, Republic of the Philippines, 1970, Outstanding Leader of the Yr., CAP, 1992, Cert. of Recognition, U.S. Sec. of Def., 1994. Mem.: VFW, York Rite Coll., Philalethes Soc., Air Force Security Police Assn., Smithsonian Inst. (assoc.), Air Force Assn., Shriners, Masons. Home: 2465 Forest View Rd Lindenhurst IL 60046-8720 Office: Illinois Auto Truck Co Inc 1669 Marshall Dr Des Plaines IL 60018-1840 Office Phone: 847-299-1100. Personal E-mail: joe_sandy2000@yahoo.com.

SANTMAN, LEON DUANE, lawyer, former federal government executive; b. Phila., July 29, 1930; s. Elmer William and Anna Mary (Moffitt) S.; m. Juliet Gloria Peacock, June 16, 1952; 1 dau., Lorri Leigh Santman Myers. BS, U. S., COAST Guard Acad., 1952; LLB, U. Houston, 1953; LLM, George Washington U., 1968. Bar: Tex. 1963, Md. 1974. Commd. ensign U.S. Coast Guard, 1952, advanced through grades to comdr., 1967, ret., 1972; assoc. gen. counsel Cost of Living Council, Washington, 1972-74; asst. gen. counsel U.S. Dept. Transp., Washington, 1974-77, dir. Materials Transp. Bur., 1977-85; dir. ship ops. Maritime Adminstrn., 1985-88. Episcopalian.

SANTO, FRED M., lawyer; b. Bronx, NY, Oct. 24, 1947; BA, SUNY, Binghamton, 1969; JD, Washington Coll. Law, 1973; LLM, Gerogetown U., 1978. Bar: DC 1973, NY 1979. Law clerk to Chief Judge DC Ct. Appeals, 1973; sr. atty. Div. Corp. Fin., SEC, 1974—76; asst. gen. counsel Commodity Futures Trading Commn., 1976—78; with Katten Muchin Zavis Rosenman, NYC, 1979—, ptnr. Mem.: ABA, Managed Futures Assn., Assn. Bar of City NY. Office: Katten Muchin Zavis Rosenman 575 Madison Ave New York NY 10022 Office Phone: 212-940-8720. Office Fax: 212-940-5663. E-mail: fred.santo@kmzr.com.

SANTOMERO, ANTHONY M., financial consultant, former bank executive, public policymaker; b. NYC, Sept. 29, 1946; s. Camillo and Jean (Oddo) Santomero; m. Marlena Belviso, Aug. 21, 1971; children: Jill Renee, Marc Anthony. AB, Fordham U., 1968; PhD, Brown U., 1971; EDhe (hon.), Stockholm Sch. Econs., 1992; LHC, U. Rome, 2003. Cert. risk profl., Bank Administrn. Inst., 2001. Asst. prof., then assoc. prof., then prof. fin. Wharton Sch., U. Pa., Phila., 1972-84, R.K. Mellon prof. fin., 1984—2002, R.K. Mellon prof. fin. emeritus, 2002—, vice dean, dir. grad. div., 1984-87, dep. dean, 1990-94; dir. Wharton Fin. Instns. Ctr., 1995-2000; pres. Fed. Res. Bank Phila., 2000—06; sr. advisor McKinsey & Co., 2006—. Asst. prof. econs. Baruch Coll., CUNY, 1971—72; vis. prof. European Inst. Advanced Studies Mgmt., Brussels, 1977—78, Stockholm Sch. Econs., 1989—90, U. Rome, Tor Vergata, 1994—97, Ecole Superieure des Scis. Economiques and Commerciales, France, 1977—78; trustee Drexel U.; mem. adv. bd. Penn Inst. Econ. Rsch. Author: Financial Markets, Instruments and Institutions, 1997, 2001, Challenges for Modern Central Banking, 2001; adv. editor Jour. Banking and Fin., 1978—, assoc. editor Jour. Money, Credit and Banking, 1980—2002, Jour. Fin. Svc. Rsch., 2000—, bd. editors Jour. Econs. and Bus., 1979—, European Fin. Mgmt., 1996—, Advances in Internat. Banking and Fin., 1993—, founding co-editor Brookings-Wharton Papers on Fin. Svcs., 1997—2000, adv. bd. European Banking Report, 1994—, Jour. Internat. Econ. Law, 1997—, editl. bd. Open Econs. Rev., 1990—, mem. faculty adv. bd. Jour. Internat. Econ. Law, 1997—, mem. bd. advisory editors Advances in Fin., Investment and Banking, 1992, editl. adv. bd. Jour. Fin. Stability, 2003—; contbr. articles to profl. jours. Mem. Fin. Economists Roundtable; bd. mem. Mann Ctr. Performing Arts, Union League Phila., Drexel U.; chmn. Econ. Adv. Bd., Stockholm Inst. Fin. Rsch.; mem. adv. bd. Wharton Fin. Institutions Ctr.; chmn. Mayor's Coun. Econ. Advisors, 2000—03. Decorated hon. knighthood Republic of Italy; recipient Global Citizen award, Global Interdependence Ctr., 2005. Mem.: Am. Econs. Assn., Am. Fin. Assn. Roman Catholic. Office Phone: 212-446-7551. Business E-Mail: anthony_santomero@mckinsey.com.

SANTONA, GLORIA, lawyer, food products executive; b. Gary, Ind., June 10, 1950; d. Ray and Elvira (Cambeses) S.; m. Douglas Lee Frazier, Apr. 12, 1980; 1 child, Daniel BS in Biochemistry, Mich. State U., 1971; JD cum laude, U. Mich., 1977. Bar: Ill. 1977. Atty. McDonald's Corp., Oak Brook, Ill., 1977-82, dir., 1982-86, assoc. gen. counsel, 1986-92, asst. v.p., 1989-93, v.p., sec., dep. gen. counsel, 1996-99, v.p., US gen. counsel, sec., 1999-2001, sr. v.p., gen. counsel, sec., 2001—03, exec. v.p., gen. counsel, sec., 2003—. Bd. dirs. Aon Corp. Bd. trustees Rush U. Med. Ctr. Mem. ABA, Chgo. Bar Assn., Am. Corp. Counsel Assn., Am. Soc. Corp. Secs., Constl. Rights Found. Chgo. Office: McDonalds Corp 1 McDonalds Plz Oak Brook IL 60523-1911 *

SANTONI, RONALD ERNEST, philosophy educator; b. Arvida, Que., Can., Dec. 19, 1931; s. Fred Albert and Phyllis (Tremaine) S.; m. Marguerite Ada Kiene, June 25, 1955; children: Christina, Marcia, Andrea, Juanita, Jonathan, Sondra. BA, Bishop's U., Lennoxville, Que., 1952; MA, Brown U., 1954; PhD, Boston U., 1961; postgrad., U. Paris-Sorbonne, 1956-57. Asst. prof. philosophy U. Pacific, Stockton, Calif., 1958-61; postdoctoral rsch. fellow Yale U., New Haven, 1961-62; asst. prof. philosophy Wabash Coll., Crawfordsville, Ind., 1962-64; faculty Denison U., Granville, Ohio, 1964—, prof. philosophy, 1968—2002, chmn. dept., 1971-73, 82-84, 92, Maria Theresa Barney chair in philosophy, 1978—, prof. emeritus, 2002—. Peace lectr. Bethel Coll., 1985; vis. scholar in philosophy Cambridge U., Eng., 1986, 90, 94, 97, 99, 2001, vis. lectr. in philosophy, 1990; vis. fellow Clare Hall, Cambridge U., 1986, life mem., vis. scholar, 1990, 94, 97, 99, 2001, 03, 04, 06; vis. fellow in philosophy Yale U., 1975, 81, 93-94, 97; keynote spkr. 2d Internat. Conf. on Nuclear Free Zones, Cordoba, Spain, 1985; Internat. Studies Assn., London, 1989, spkr. and U.S.A. co-chair Internat. conf. Internat. Philosophers for Prevention of Nuclear Omnicide, Moscow, 1990; del. and raporteur UN meeting of Peace Messenger Orgns., Dagomys, Sochi, USSR, 1991; invited participant Colloquium on Technological Risks to Environment, Montreal, 1993; invited spkr. U. Paris (Sorbonne), 2004, Internat. Conf. Honoring Centenary of J.P. Satre, U. Amiens, France, 2005; spkr. in field. Contbg. author: Current Philosophical Issues: Essays in Honor of C.J. Ducasse, 1966, Towards an Understanding and Prevention of Genocide, 1984, Nuclear War: Philosophical Perspectives, 1985, Genocide: A Critical Bibliographic Review, 1988, Just War, Nonviolence and Nuclear Deterrence: Philosophers on War and Peace, 1992, The Institution of War, 1991, Violence and Human Co-Existence, 1994, Hiroshima's Shadows, 1998, The Encyclopedia of Genocide, 1999, Human Coexistence and Sustainable Development, 2001, Das Sein und das Nichts, 2003, Global Studies Encyclopedia, 2003, Dictionnaire Sartre, 2004, Sartre Today: A Centenary Celebration, 2006, Pourquoi Sartre? 2006, Uber Sartre: Perspektiven und Kritiken, 2005, Sartre: le philosophe, l'intellectuel, et la politique, 2007; author: Bad Faith, Good Faith and Authenticity in Sartre's Early Philosophy, 1995, Sartre on Violence: Curiously Ambivalent, 2003; editor, contbr. Religious Language and the Problem of Religious Knowledge, 1968; co-editor Social and Political Philosophy, 1963; contbg. editor Internet on the Holocaust and Genocide; mem. editl. bd. Jour. Peace and Justice Studies; contbr. over 135 publ. in profl. jours. V.p. NAACP, Licking County, 1967; co-organizer Crawfordsville (Ind.) Human Rights Coun., 1962-64; nat. exec. com. Episcopal Peace Fellowship, 1968-78; internat. coun. Internat. Inst. on the Holocaust and Genocide, 1985—; nat. coun. Fellowship of Reconciliation, 1988-89; trustee Margaret Hall Sch., Versailles, Ky., 1972-74; nat. bd. dirs. Promoting Enduring Peace, 1982-2002, 06—. Canadian Govt. Overseas fellow Royal Soc. Can., 1956-57; Church Soc. for Coll. Work faculty fellow, 1961-62; Yale postdoctoral rsch. fellow, 1961-62; Danforth assoc., 1963-64; Soc. for Religion in Higher Edn. postdoctoral fellow, 1972—; Yale rsch. fellow, 1975; guest fellow Berkeley Coll., Yale U., 1975, 81, 93-94, 97, elected assoc. fellow, 1994—; vis. fellow in philosophy Yale U., 1981, 93-94, 97; Robert C. Good faculty fellow Denison U., 1985-86, 2000-01, Robert C. Good faculty fellow, 1993-94; elected life mem. Clare Hall, Cambridge (Eng.) U., 1986; elected mem. High Table, King's Coll., Cambridge U., 1999; recipient Mellon award for disting. faculty Denison U., 1972, Crossed Keys Faculty of Yr. award Denison U., 1986-87; Philosophy, Freedom and Action Conf. held in his honor, 2002. Mem. Am. Philos. Assn., Ch. Soc. for Coll. Work, Soc. for Phenomenology and Existential Philosophy, Internat. Philosophers for Peace (v.p. 1983-85, v.p. cen. div. 1990-91, internat. pres. 1991-96, internat. exec. com. 1996—), Sartre Soc. of N.Am. (exec. com. 1994—), Sartre Circle (coord. 1997—), le groupe d'Etudes Sartriennes, Gandhi-King Soc., Union of Bi-Nat. Profls. Against Omnicide (v.p. 1978—), Institut fuer Axiologische Forschungen (exec. com.), Concerned Philosophers for Peace (founding 1980—, pres. 1996-97), Fellowship of Reconciliation, Radical Philosophers Assn., Amnesty Internat., OxFam Am., ACLU. Episcopalian. Home: 500 Burg St Granville OH 43023-1005 Office Phone: 740-587-6318. Business E-Mail: santoni@denison.edu. *Gratitude for what one has been given, commitment to personal growth and integrity, some "gracious gall", listening to the world's humiliated, and a recognition that any genuine success is a gift of grace, never fully deserved.*

SANTOPIETRO, ALBERT ROBERT, lawyer; b. Providence, Oct. 18, 1948; s. Alfred and Marie (Epifanio) Santopietro; children: Hope, Spencer, Anna. BA, Brown U., 1969; JD, U. Va., 1972. Bar: R.I. 1973, Conn. 1983, Mass. 1997, U.S. Dist. Ct. R.I. 1973, Ill. 1974, U.S. Dist. Ct. Mass. 1997. Atty. Met. Life Ins. Co., Oak Brook, Ill., 1974—75, Seligman Group, NYC, 1975—76, Mut. Benefit Life Ins. Co., Newark, 1976—78, asst. counsel, 1978—81; counsel Aetna Ins. Co., Newark, 1982—91; assoc. counsel Conn. Mutual Life Ins. Co., Hartford, 1991—95; 2d v.p. and assoc. gen. counsel Mass. Mutual, 1995—; spl counsel Babson Capital Mgmt. LLC, 2006—. Home: 142 Pond Brook Rd Huntington MA 01050-9620 Office: 1500 Main St Ste 2800 Springfield MA 01115 Home Phone: 413-210-2741; Office Phone: 413-667-0245. Office Fax: 413-226-2068. E-mail: asantopietro@massmutual.com.

SANTORA, ELLEN DURRIGAN, education educator; b. Utica, NY, July 20, 1945; d. John Francis and Maude Henrietta Durrigan; m. John Anthony Santora, Apr. 1, 1967. BA in Polit. Sci., LeMoyne Coll., 1966; MS in Edn., SUNY, Oswego, NY, 1982; PhD, Pa. State U., 1997. Cert. secondary social studies tchr. NY. Am. studies and world history tchr. Liverpool Ctrl. Sch. Dist., 1974—75; mid. sch. social studies and reading tchr. Altmar Parish Williamstown Ctrl. Sch. Dist., Parish, NY, 1975—76, Baldwinsville Acad. and Ctrl. Sch. Dist., 1976—85; mid. sch. social studies and English tchr. Whisman Elem. Sch. Dist., Mountain View, Calif., 1985—91, Winston Dillard Sch. Dist., 1991—93; grad. rsch. and tchg. asst. Pa. State U., State College, 1993—96; asst. prof. edn. U. Ala., Tuscaloosa, 1997—2000; asst. prof. Warner Sch. Edn. and Human Devel. U. Rochester, NY, 2000—06. Contbr. articles to profl. publs. Advisor Marshall H.S., Law, Govt. and Justice Acad., Rochester, 2001—05. Named Tchr. of Yr., Crittenden Mid. Sch., 1989—90; recipient Dean Betty Poole Jr. Faculty Svc. award, Warner Grad. Sch. Edn., U. Rochester, 2002; grantee, US Dept. Edn., 2001—05, Susan B. Anthony Inst. for Gender and Womn's Studies, 2001; Regents scholar, NY State, 1962, Fulbright-Hays Seminars Abroad fellow, US Dept. Edn., 1990, Instrnl. Tech. grantee, U. Ala., 1999. Mem.: AAUW, Coll. and U. Faculty Assembly (bd. dirs. 2002—05), Am. Ednl. Rsch. Assn. (Outstanding Dissertation award 1999, Outstanding Paper award 1999, 2005), Nat. Coun. Social Studies, Pi Lambda Theta, Phi Gamma Mu, Phi Delta Kappa. Roman Catholic. Avocations: travel, gardening, showing and breeding St. Bernards and briards. Office Fax: 585-473-7598. Business E-Mail: esantora@warner.rochester.edu.

SANTORA, KATHLEEN CURRY, lobbyist, lawyer; b. Hazelton, Pa., Sept. 14, 1958; d. Joseph Anthony and Irene Mary C.; m. Hugo Gary Santora, Jan. 6, 1990. BS in Polit. Sci., U. Scranton, 1980; JD, Cath. U. Am., 1983. Bar: Pa. 1984; lic. emergency med. technician. Assoc. dir. govt. rels., assoc. gen. counsel Nat. Assn. Ind. Colls. and Univs., Washington, 1984—86, exec. dir., counsel for state rels., 1987—89, v.p. ops., counsel, 1989; dir. pub. policy Assn. Governing Bds. Colls. and Univs., Washington, 1986—87; v.p., COO Am. Assn. Higher Edn., Washington; CEO Nat. Assn. Coll. and Univ. Attys., Washington, 2001—. Mem. nat. adv. bd. Ctr. Constl. Studies Baylor U., Waco, Tex., 1987—; various positions, Georgetown U. Trustee Western New Eng. Coll., Springfield, Mass., 1986—; emergency med. technician Fairfax County, Annondale, Va., 1991. Mem. ABA, Pa. Bar Assn. Democrat. Roman Catholic. Avocation: skiing. Office: Nat Assn Coll and Univ Attys One Dupont Cir Ste 620 Washington DC 20036 Office Phone: 202-833-8390. Office Fax: 202-296-8379. E-mail: ksantora@nacua.org. *

SANTORO, ANTHONY RICHARD, history professor; b. Feb. 2, 1939; m. Carol Lynne; 1 child, Melissa. AB, Coll. of the Holy Cross, 1960; MA, U. Calif., 1962; PhD, Rutgers U., 1978. Instr. history Monmouth Coll., West Long Branch, N.J., 1963-67; v.p. for adminstrn., chair depts history and philosophy, registrar Briarcliff Coll., Briarcliff Manor, N.Y., 1967-77; v.p. Devel. and Coll. Rels. Ladycliff Coll., Highland Falls, NY, 1977—78; pres. St. Joseph's Coll., Standish, Maine, 1979-87, Christopher Newport U., Newport News, Va., 1987-96, pres. emeritus, disting. prof. history, 1996—. Author: Theophanes Chronograhia: A Chronicle of 8th Century Byzantium, 1982; co-author: An Eyewitness to History: The Short History of Nikephoros the Patriarch of Constantinople, 1991, (4-track DVD) Triumph of the Will (Leni Riefenstahl), 2001. Office: Christopher Newport U McMurran Hall 217 1 University Pl Newport News VA 23606-2998 Home Phone: 757-875-1212; Office Phone: 757-594-7709. Office Fax: 757-594-7718. Business E-Mail: santoro@cnu.edu.

SANTORO, ELISSA JEANNE, breast oncology surgeon; b. Newark, Oct. 18, 1938; d. James and Jean Santoro. AB in Chemistry and Honors in Theology, Coll. St. Elizabeth, Convent Station, NJ, 1960; MD, Woman's Med. Coll. Pa., 1965; LLD (hon.), Coll. St. Elizabeth, 2004. Diplomate Am. Bd. Surgery, Nat. Bd. Med. Examiners. Straight surg. intern Hosp. of Woman's Med. Coll. Pa., Phila., 1965-66; asst. resident surgery Hosp. of Woman's Med. Ctr., NYC, 1966-67, St. Vincent's Hosp. and Med. Ctr., NYC, 1967-68, sr. asst. resident surgery, 1968-69, chief surg. resident, 1969-70; assoc. attending in surgery and oncology Irvington (N.J.) Gen. Hosp., 1971-77; asst. attending in surgery and oncology St. Barnabas Hosp. and Med. Ctr., Livingston, 1973-80, assoc. attending in surgery and oncology, 1980-81, attending physician, 1983—, clin. chief surg. oncology, 1984—, founder, head, Breast Care and Treatment Ctr., 1977—. Summer student rsch. fellow pathology Woman's Med. Coll. Pa., Phila., 1963; Am. Cancer Soc. fellow St. Vincent's Hosp. and Med. Ctr., NYC, 1968-69; postdoctoral fellow in cancer tng. NIH, NY Med. Coll. and Met. Hosp. Ctr., 1970-71; instr. surgery NY Med. Coll., NYC, 1970-72, assoc. clin. investigator cen. oncology group, 1970-72; clin. asst. prof. surgery Coll. U. Medicine and Dentistry, Newark, 1973-82; med. advisor Ruth Estrin Goldberg Meml. Cancer Rsch., Reach to Recovery; bd. dirs. Susan G. Komen Breast Cancer Found., 2004-05, 06-, also med. adv. bd. mem.; spkr. in field. Appeared on several televised ednl. programs regarding breast health issues; contbr. articles to profl. jours. Vice-chmn. svc. and rehab. com. State N.J. Am. Cancer Soc., 1976-78, chmn., 1978-80, chmn. exec. com., 1983, chmn., 1984, vice-chmn. nominating com., chmn. svc. and rehab. com. Essex County div., 1977-80, chmn. exec. com., 1981-83, v.p., 1983, bd. mgrs.; bd. trustees Regional Coun. Women in Medicine, Inc., 1984, Coll. St. Elizabeth, Convent Station, N.J., 1985-90. Recipient Physician of Yr. award N.J. div. Am. Cancer Soc., 1983, The Mother Xavier award, Coll. St. Elizabeth, 1983, Friends of Hospice award Karen Ann Quinlan Ctr. of Hope, Newton, N.J., 1984, Hon. Chairperson of Yr. award N.J. Fedn. Bus. and Profl. Women's Clubs, Inc., 1984, Woman of Yr. award Irvington Bus. and Profl. Women's Club, 1985, Sister Miriam Teresa Demjanovich medal award N.J. Ladies Aux. Dept., Cath. War Vets., 1985, Woman of Yr. award Italian-Am. Columbus Day Celebration Com., 1986, Med. Appreciation award Reach to Recovery, 1988, Christie Todd Whitman Nat. Women's History Celebration award for Outstanding Women in the Field of Medicine; named one of Top Docs, NJ Monthly, Best Doctors in N.Y./N.J., NY Mag. Mem. AMA (Physician Recognition award for Continuing Edn.), Am. Med. Women's Assn., Am. Med. Writer's Assn., Am. Soc. Contemporary Medicine and Surgery, Assn. Am. Med. Colls., Assn. Acad. Surgery, Am. Assn. Cancer Edn., Am. Soc. Preventive Oncology, Am. Soc. Clin. Oncology, Acad. Medicine N.J., Surg. Soc. N.Y. Med. Coll., Inc., Essex County Med. Soc. (bd. mgrs.), N.J. Med. Women's Assn., N.J. Gastroent. Soc., N.Y. State Cancer Programs Assn., Inc., Oncology Soc. N.J., N.Y. Met. Breast Cancer Group, Inc., Am. Cancer Soc. N.J.(former chmn., former pres., chmn. Essex County Chpt., med. advisor to rsch. and recovery, post mastectomy program), Internat. Soc. Women Educators (hon.), Am. Soc. Breast Diseases, Am. Soc. Breast Surgeons, Alpha Kappa Delta. Office: 200 S Orange Ave Livingston NJ 07039-5817 *

SANTORO, FRANK ANTHONY, lawyer; b. Plainfield, N.J., Dec. 14, 1941; s. Frank V. and Nancy M. (Scavuzzo) S.; m. Patricia Ferrante, Oct. 10, 1964; children— Frank, Jennifer. B.S. in Chemistry, Seton Hall U., 1963, J.D., 1970. Patent atty. Exxon Corp., Linden, N.J., 1970-73; sole practice, South Plainfield, N.J., 1973—; atty. Planning Bd. Borough South Plainfield, 1971-73; mcpl. prosecutor Borough South Plainfield, 1972. Councilman Borough South Plainfield, 1977-79, mcpl. atty., 1985-93; mcpl. chmn. South Plainfield Republican Orgn., 1981-84. Mem. Middlesex County Bar Assn., UNICO Nat. Roman Catholic. Office: 304 Maple Ave South Plainfield NJ 07080-0272 Office Phone: 908-561-6868.

SANTORUM, RICK (RICHARD JOHN), lawyer, former senator; b. Winchester, Va., May 10, 1958; s. Aldo and Catherine (Dughi) S.; m. Karen Garver, June 2, 1990; children: Elizabeth Anne, Richard John Jr., Daniel James, Sarah Maria, Peter Kenneth. BA in Polit. Sci., Pa. State U., 1980; MBA, U. Pitts., 1981; JD, Dickinson Sch. Law, 1986. Bar: Pa. 1986. Adminstrv. asst. to Sen. Doyle Corman Pa. State Senate, Harrisburg, 1981-86, exec. dir. local govt. com., 1981-84, exec. dir. transp. com., 1984-86; assoc. Kirkpatrick & Lockhart LLP, Pitts., 1986-90; mem. US Congress from 18th Pa. dist., Washington, 1991-95; US Senator from Pa., 1995—2007; mem. agr., nutrition, & forestry com., fin. com., rules & adminstrn., banking, housing, & urban affairs, spl. com. on aging; chmn. Senate Republican Conf., 2001—07; cons. Eckert Seamans Cherin & Mellott, LLC, Pitts., 2007—. Sr. fellow The Ethics & Pub. Policy Ctr., 2007—; polit. contr. Fox News Channel, 2007—; bd. dirs. Universal Health Services, Inc., 2007—. Author: Rick Santorum: A Senator Speaks Out on Life, Freedom and Responsibility, 2005, It Takes A Family: Conservatism and the Common Good, 2005. Bd. dirs. Mt. Lebanon Extended Day Program, 1987-91; mem. Child Advocacy Project, 1987-91. Recipient Award for Legis. Excellence, Am. Soc. Consultant Pharmacists, 1997, Award for Manufacturing Legis. Excellence, Nat. Assn. Manufacturers, 1999, Disting. Svc. award, Brent Soc. of Arlington, VA Diocese, 1999, Medical Miracle award, Healthcare Leadership Coun., 2000, John Paul II award, Inst. Psychological Sciences, 2003, Legis. of the Yr., Nat. Multiple Sclerosis Soc., 2003, Friend of Seniors award, Bucks County, PA Area Agy. on Aging, 2004, Higher Edn. Leadership award, Washington Ctr. Internships and Academic Studies, 2005. Mem. KC, Italian Sons and Daus. Assn., Allegheny County Bar Assn. Child Advocacy Program. Republican. Roman Catholic. Avocations: golf, racquetball. Office: Eckert Seamans Cherin & Mellott LLC 1747 Pennsylvania Ave NW Ste 1200 Washington DC 20006 also: Ethics & Pub Policy Ctr 1015 15th St Ste 900 Washington DC 20005 E-mail: rsantorum@eckertseamans.com. *

SANTOS, ADÈLE NAUDÉ, architect, educator; b. Cape Town, South Africa, Oct. 14, 1938; came to U.S., 1973; d. David Francois Hugo and Aletta Adèle Naudé. Student, U. Cape Town, South Africa, 1956-58; diploma, Archtl. Assn., London, 1961; MArch in Urban Design, Harvard U., 1963; MArch, M in City Planning, U. Pa., 1968. Registered arch., Pa., Mass. Pvt. practice architecture with Antonio de Souza Santos, 1966-73; ptnr. Interstudio, Houston, 1973-79; assoc. prof. architecture Rice U., Houston, 1973-78, prof., 1979; prof. architecture, grad sch. design Harvard U., Cambridge, Mass., 1979—81; prof. architecture and urban design, dept. architecture U. Pa., Phila., 1981-90; founding dean Sch. Architecture U. Calif., San Diego, 1990-94; pvt. practice architecture and urban design Adele Naude Santos, Arch., Phila., 1979-90, Adele Naude Santos and Assocs., San Diego and Phila., 1991—2002; prof. architecture Coll. Environ. Design U. Calif., Berkeley, 1994—2003; dean Sch. Architecture and Planning, MIT, Cambridge, 2004—. Project dir., co-filmmaker for 5 part series, 1979-80; works include Albright Coll. Ctr. for the Arts, Reading, Pa., 1991, Franklin-LaBrea Housing, Hollywood, Calif., 1995, Inst. of Contemporary Art, Phila., 1991, Yerba Buena Gardens, San Francisco, 1998. Wheelwright Travelling fellow, Harvard U., 1968; NEA grantee, 1976, Tex. Com. for Humanities grantee, 1979; recipient (with Hugo Naudé) Bronze medal for House Naudé Capt. Inst. South African Architects, 1967, award for public TV program So. Ednl. Communications Assn., 1980, 3d place award Inner city Infill Competition, 1986; winner Internat. Design Competition, Hawaii Loa Coll., hon. mention Cin. Hillside Housing Competition and City Visions, Phila., 1986; winner competition for Franklin/La Brea Affordable Housing Project Mus. Comtemporary Art and Community Redevel. Agy. City L.A., 1988, Pa. Soc. Architects design award for Franklin/La Brea Multi-Family Housing, 1988; winning entry collaborative competition for amphitheater, restaurant and natural history mus., Arts Pk., La., 1989; winner competition for 24-unit residential devel., City of Camden, N.J., 1989, for New Civic Ctr., City of Perris, Calif., 1991, children's mus. The Zeum, 1998, child care facility Yerba Buena Gardens, San Francisco, 1998, Please Touch Mus., Phila., 1998, winner design competition ChildCare Ctr. U. Pa., 1999. Fellow Am. Inst. Archs.; mem. Pa. Soc. Archs., Archs. Registration Coun. (U.K.). Office: Dean Sch Architecture 77 Massachusetts Ave Cambridge MA 02139-4307

SANTOS, ARTHUR MAGNO, thoracic cardiovascular surgeon; b. Pasay City, Philippines, May 15, 1946; BS in Pre-medicine, Far Eastern U., Manila, Philippines, 1967; MD, U. of the East, 1972. Diplomate Am. Bd. Surgery, Am. Bd. Thoracic Surgery. Intern St. Francis Gen. Hosp., Pitts., 1973-74, resident in gen. surgery, 1974-77; resident McKeesport (Pa.) Hosp., 1977-79; resident in thoracic and cardiovascular surgery Shadyside Hosp., Pitts., 1979-81; pvt. practice Assn. of Thoracic Surgeons, Pitts., 1981—. Fellow ACS.

SANTOS, HERBERT JOSEPH, JR., lawyer; b. Reno, Feb. 17, 1963; s. Herbert Joseph Sr. and Jeanette Dorothy (Olivera) S.; m. Kimberly Ellen Saylors, Mar. 8, 1986; children: Herbert Joseph III, Jarred Adam, Hannah McKenzie. BA in Sociology, U. Nev., Las Vegas, 1985; JD, U. of the Pacific, 1991. Bar: Nev. 1991, Calif. 1992, U.S. Dist. Ct. Nev. 1992, U.S. Supreme Ct. 1999. Head social worker Cmty. Welfare, Inc., Reno, 1986-87; inspector Nev. Athletic Commn., Reno, 1986-87; sr. legal rsch. asst. County Sacramento, Calif., 1987-91; assoc. Law Offices of Terry A. Friedman, Ltd., Reno, 1991-98; owner The Law Firm of Herb Santos Jr., 1999—. Mem. State Bar Law Office Mgmt. and Procedures Com., 1996-98; chair election canvassing com. Nev. Bd. Govs, access to justice com., 1998, temp. apptd. jud. selection com. Author (instrn. manual) ORR, County of Sacramento Bankruptcy Forms and Procedures Manual with Practice Pointers, 1990; editor: The Writ, 1997-98; appeared in: (films) Kingpin, Father's Day, (TV miniseries) The Last Don, The Cheater's Partner in Mafia!, Body and Soul, Diamonds. Mem. Cmty. Coalition, Reno, 1986-87; mentor U. Nev., Reno, 1993—. Recipient Am. Jurisprudence award, 1991, Mem. ABA (young lawyers divsn., del. for State of Nev. 1996, 97, 98, 99), ATLA, Nev. Trial Lawyers Assn., State Bar Nev. (exec. coun. mem. young lawyers sect. 1993—, pres. young lawyers sect. 1996-97, com. chair Ask-a-Lawyer young lawyers sect. 1994—. chair pub. com. 1996-97, Pro-Bono award 1997, apptd. alternate dispute resolution sect.-long range planning 1998), Washoe County Bar Assn. (exec. coun., sgt.-at-arms 1997-98, treas. 1998-99, sec. 1999—, Bar Leader award 1998), Am. Inns of Ct. (Hon. Bruce Thompson chpt. 1995-97). Republican. Roman Catholic. Avocations: boxing, basketball, golf. Office: The Law Firm of Herb Santos Jr Liberty Ctr 350 S Center St Ste 350 Reno NV 89501-2113 Home: 14205 Prairie Flower Ct Reno NV 89511-6710

SANTOS, ISABEL RODRIGUEZ, high school marketing educator; Mktg. tchr. Lorenzo Coballes Gandia H.S., Hatillo, PR. Named PR Tchr. of Yr., 2007. Office: Lorenzo Coballes Gandia High Sch PO Box 1357 Hatillo PR 00659 E-mail: isaymario99@yahoo.com. *

SANTOS, LEONARD ERNEST, lawyer; b. Caracas, Venezuela, Aug. 5, 1946; s. Paul Joseph and Frieda (Epstein) S.; m. Jeannie Bernadette Niedermeyer, Oct. 28, 1978; children: Jonathan, Matthew, Andrew. BA cum laude, Tufts U., 1967; JD, NYU, 1971. Bar: Ariz. 1972, D.C. 1972, U.S. Dist. Ct. D.C. 1972, U.S. Ct. Appeals (9th and 5th cirs.) 1972, U.S. Supreme Ct. 1972. Law clk. to cir. judge US Ct. Appeals (9th cir.), San Francisco, 1971-72; assoc. Hogan & Hartson, Washington, 1972-76; sr. atty. internat. affairs US Dept. Treasury, Washington, 1976-83; internat. trade counsel US Senate Fin. Com., Washington, 1983-87; ptnr. Verner, Liipfert, Bernhard, McPherson & Hand, Washington, 1987-89, Perkins Coie, Washington, 1989-98; ptnr., exec. dir. Santos Family Found., Washington, 2000—; pres. Martin Santos Properties, LLC, 2001—, JMA Properties, LLC, 2003—. Note and comment editor NYU Law Jour., 1970; contbr. legal publs.; editor ABA Compendium of Foreign Trade Remedy Laws, 1998. Exec. dir. Dole for Pres. campaign, Washington, 1988, 96. Mem. NAFTA (chpt. 19 dispute settlement panels) Republican. Roman Catholic. Avocations: architecture, economics. Office: Martin Santos Prop LLC 900 Seventeeth St NW Ste 900 Washington DC 20006 Office Phone: 202-833-2559. Personal E-mail: santlen@aol.com.

SANTOS, NADINE, music director; Grad., Full Sail Coll. Phone op. WWPR-FM Clear Channel Comm., 2002—03, programming asst., 2003—05; exec. asst. Warner Music Group, Atlantic Records, 2005—06; music dir. WWPR NY (Power 105.1) Clear Channel Comm., 2006—. Office: Power 105.1 FM 11206th Ave New York NY 10036 Office Phone: 212-704-1051.

SANTOS, NICOLE MARIE, elementary school educator; b. Mayfield Hts., Ohio, Apr. 27, 1978; d. Charles Leon Nipros and Carol Ann Amos; m. Ron Santos (div.). BA, Purdue U., W. Lafayette, Ind., 2000. Lic. standard elem. edn. Ariz. 1st grade tchr. M.C. Cash Elem., Phoenix, 2002—. Mem. sch. improvement team, team leader M.C. Cash Elem., 2002—. Mem.: Purdue Alumni Assn., Kappa Delta Pi.

SANTOS, SHARON LEE, parochial school educator; b. Perth Amboy, NJ, June 23, 1955; d. John Anthony Santos and Dolores Estelle Barrett. BA in History, Kean U., 1978, MA in Guidance and Counseling, 1985; MA in Systematic Theology, Seton Hall U., 1998. Religious sr. Franciscan of Our Lady of Guadalupe; cert. tchr. K-12, guidance counelor N.J., religion tchr. Diocese of Metuchen, N.J. Tchr. Archdiocese of Newark, Diocese of Metuchen, Perth Amboy, Fords, NJ, Woodbridge, NJ; dir. religious edn. Vicariate of Perth Amboy, St. Mary Parish, New Monmouth, NJ. Adv. bd. on evangelization Diocese of Metuchen, 1999; spkr. in field. Mem.: Fellowship of Cath. Scholars, St. Edith Stein Guild (life), Kappa Delta Phi. Avocations: astronomy, gardening. Office: St Mary Cath Ch 26 Leonardville Rd New Monmouth NJ 07748 Home: 17 Cherry Tree Farm Rd Middletown NJ 07748 Office Phone: 732-671-8550.

SANTOSA, FADIL, mathematics professor; b. Bandung, Indonesia, July 31, 1955; naturalized; married; 2 children. BSME, U. N.Mex., 1976; MS in Theoretical and Applied Mechanics, U. Ill., Urbana-Champaign, 1977, PhD in Theoretical and Applied Mechanics, 1980. Post-doctoral rsch. assoc. Cornell U., Dept. Theoretical and Applied Mechanics, 1980—82, lectr., rsch. assoc., 1982—83, asst. prof., 1983—85, U. Del., Dept. Math. Scis., 1985—87, assoc. prof., 1987—92, prof., 1992—96, dir. grad. studies, 1992—94; prof. U. Del., Dept. Mech. Engrng., 1993—96, U. Minn., Sch. Math., 1995—; assoc. dir. Minn. Ctr. for Indsl. Math., U. Minn., Sch. Math., 1995—2000, dir., 2000—; assoc. dir. Inst. for Math. and its Applications, U. Minn., 1997—2001, dep. dir., 2001—04. Vis. assoc. prof. U. Md., Dept. Math., 1987—88, Rutgers U., Dept. Math., 1991—92; vis. prof. U. Trieste, Dept. Math. Svcs., 1993; vis. prof. II Dept. Math. U. Florence, 2004; invited lectr. in field; cons. Symbol Technolgies (acquired by Motorola in 2006), U. No. Iowa, Invarium Inc., GMAC RFC, Hong Kong Shanghai Banking Corp., Vision Ease Lens. Contbr. articles to profl. jours.; co-author (W.W. Symes): An Analysis of Least-Squares Velocity Inversion, The Soc. of Exploration Geophysics, Geophysical Monograph Series No. 4, 1989; co-author: (with Stakgold) Analytical and Computational Methods in Scattering and Applied Math., 2000; co-editor: several Soc. for Indsl. and Applied Math. publications; mem. editl. bd. Soc. for Indsl. and Applied Math., Jour. Applied Math., 1994—2002, (Springer-

Verlag book series) Mathematics in Industry, 2002—, Control, Optimisation and Calculus of Variation, 1995—2002, Numerische Mathematik, 2004—, Inverse Problems, 2005—, European Jour. Applied Math., 2005—, Inverse Problems and Imaging, 2006—, Math-in-Industry Case Studies, 2007—, editor, Industry Corner Column IEEE Computational Sci. and Engring., 1995—2000; co-editor: Springer-Verlag series Inst. Math. and its Applications Volumes, 2001—04; sect. editor, survey and review Soc. for Indsl. and Applied Math. Review, 2006—. Mem.: Soc. for Indsl. and Applied Math. (membership com. 1995—96, indsl. math. com. 1999—2002, nominating com. 2001—03, com. on com. and appointments 2007—). Achievements include patents for Multifocal Optical Device Design with J. Wang and R. Gulliver. Office: Sch Math U Minn 127 Vincent Hall 206 Church St SE Minneapolis MN 55455 Office Phone: 612-626-0528. Business E-Mail: santosa@math.umn.edu, santosa@ima.umn.edu. *

SANTOS DE ALVAREZ, BRUNILDA, lawyer; b. 1958; BSFS, Georgetown U.; JD, Boston Coll. Bar: P.R. 1983. Sr. v.p. Popular, Inc., San Juan, 1996—2001, chief legal officer, 1997—, exec. v.p., 2001—. Sec. of bd. Popular Internat. Bank, Inc., Banco Popular N. Am., Popular Cash Express, Inc., Banco Popular, Popular Insurance, Inc., Popular Securities, Inc., Levitt Mortgage Corp., Popular Insurance Agy. USA, Inc., Popular Mortgage, Inc., P.R. Investor Tax Free Fund, Inc., P.R. Tax Free Target Maturity Fund, Inc., P.R. Investors Flexible Allocation Fund, Inc., Popular Fin. Holdings; asst. sec. of bd. Popular Auto, Inc., Popular Finance, Inc.; mem. bd. of regents Colegio Puertorriqueno de Ninas, 2002—. Office: Popular Inc Popular Ctr Bldg 209 Munoz Rivera Ave San Juan PR 00918

SANTOS PICO, JOSE V., neurosurgeon; s. Jose Santos Grillo and Catina Pico; m. Carol Ilene Spahn, Mar. 25, 2006; children: Jose Santos Martinez, Maria Cecilia Santos Martinez. B, U. PR, Mayaguez, 1976; MD, Caribbean U., San Juan, 1980. Diplomate Am. Bd. Neurol. Surgery, 2003. Intern Detroit Macomb Hosp., 1980—81; resident U. PR, San Juan, 1981—86; neurosurgeon Pavia Hosp., San Juan, 1986—, Hima San Pablo Med. Ctr., PR. Mem.: Cyberknife Soc., Congress Neurol. Surgeons. Office: 712 Ponce de Leon Ave San Juan PR 00918 Office Phone: 787-764-7011. Business E-Mail: jvsantosmd@aim.com.

SANTRY, BARBARA LEA, venture capitalist; b. Key West, Fla., Jan. 20, 1948; d. Jere Joseph and Frances Victoria (Appel) S. BS in Nursing, Georgetown U., 1969; MBA, Stanford U., 1978. Program analyst, br. chief U.S. Dept. HEW, Washington, 1973-76; mgr. cons. div. Arthur Andersen and Co., San Francisco, 1978-80; asst. v.p. Am. Med. Internat., Washington, 1980-83; v.p. Alex Brown and Sons, Inc., Balt., 1983-86; ptnr. Wessels, Arnold and Henderson, Mpls., 1986-88; v.p. Dain Bosworth Inc., Mpls., 1988-90, sr. v.p., 1990-91; ptnr. Pathfinder Venture Capital Funds, Menlo Park, Calif., 1991—2005, Capstone Ventures, Menlo Park, Calif., 1996—. Sr. cons. Quorum Consulting, San Francisco. Trustee Stanford Bus. Sch. Trust, 1996-2002. Served to lt. USNR, 1967-72.

SANTULLI, RICHARD T., air transportation executive; b. Aug. 14, 1944; m. Peggy Santulli; 4 children. BS in Applied Math, MS in Applied Math, Bklyn. Polytechnic Inst., MS in Operations Rsch. Joined Shell Oil Co.; investment banker Goldman Sachs & Co., 1969—80; founder RTS Capital Services Inc.; chmn., CEO NetJets Inc. (formerly Exec. Jet, Inc.), NJ, 1986—. Co-founder Jayeff Stables, 1982—. Bd. dirs. Andre Agassi Charitable Found.; chmn. Intrepid Fallen Heroes Fund, 2001—. Recipient Vision award, Bus. & Comml. Aviation, 2003. Avocations: golf, horse-racing. Office: NetJets Inc 581 Main St Woodbridge NJ 07095 *

SANYOUR, MICHAEL LOUIS, JR., diversified financial services company executive; b. Richmond, Va., Aug. 24, 1930; s. Michael Louis, Sr. and Betty (Toobert) Sanyour; m. Therese Marie McCarthy, June 1, 1951 (dec. Sept. 25, 2002); children: Jeffrey, Mark, Jennifer, Florence, Norman, Ned. AA, Union Coll., 1952; SB, Rutgers U., 1954, postgrad., 1978-82; MBA, Harvard U., 1956; postgrad., Am. Coll., 1987-92. CLU; ChFC. V.p. Harbridge Ho., Inc., Boston, 1956-63, also dir.; corp. v.p. mktg. Volkswagen Am., Inc., Englewood Cliffs, NJ, 1963-70; pres., CEO Subaru Am., Pennsauken, NJ, 1970-75, also dir., Wofac Co., Bridgewater, NJ, 1975-82; exec. v.p., dir. Sci. Mgmt. Corp., 1975-82; pres., CEO, dir. Metrologic Instruments Inc., Blackwood, NJ, 1982-85; pres., COO, dir. Avant-Garde Computing, Inc., Mt. Laurel, NJ, 1985-86; prin., dir. CMS Cos., Phila., 1986—. Bd. dirs. Phila. Film Soc., Phila. Shakespeare Festival, 1995—2006. Co-author: (book) Chief Executive's Handbook, 1975, Am. Mgmt. Assn.'s Publs., 1990. Trustee West Jersey Chamber Music Soc., 1983—, pres., 1987—88; councilman Moorestown, NJ, 1988—98; dep. mayor, 1999—2002; mayor, 2003—04; bd. dirs. Meml. Health Alliance, 1992—97, ARC Burlington County, 1989—94, Coriell Inst. Med. Rsch., 1992—, v.p., 2002—; bd. dirs. World Affairs Coun., Phila., 1992—98, Moorestown Cmty. House, 2000—06, Phila. Pres.'s Orgn., 1994—97, vice chmn., 1992—93, chmn., 1993—94; class sec. HBS Class of '56, 1986—96. With USNG, 1948—56. Decorated knight of St. John's of Jerusalem; recipient Alumni award, Rutgers U., 1954, award, Am. Cancer Soc., 1978—79. Mem.: World Affairs Coun. Phila., Automotive Orgn. Team, World Pres.'s Orgn., South Jersey C. of C. (v.p., dir.), Am. Mensa Ltd., Harvard Club (N.Y.C.), Union League (Phila.) (bd. dirs. 1993—97), Harvard Bus. Sch. Club (Phila.) (pres. 1980—81, chmn. 1983—84, dir. 1984—), Rotary (pres. Moorestown 1987—88, bd. dirs.), Legatus, Delta Sigma Pi, Beta Gamma Sigma. Home: 201 E Maple Ave Moorestown NJ 08057-2011 Office: 308 E Lancaster Ave Ste 300 Wynnewood PA 19096-2145 Office Phone: 610-896-3009. Business E-Mail: mls@cmsco.com. E-mail: mlsanyour@aol.com.

SANZ, LUIS E., gynecologist, educator; b. Camaguey, Cuba; m. Miriam D. Sanz; 1 child, Monica G. MD, Georgetown U., 1976. Uro-gynecology and vaginal reconstruction surgery dept. ob-gyn. Georgetown U. Sch. Medicine, Washington, 1980, prof. dept. ob-gyn., 1980—. Author: Gynecologic Surgery, 1995; contbr. over 40 articles to profl. jours., chapters to books. With US Army, 1966—68, Vietnam. Decorated Vietnam Campaign medal U.S. Army. Fellow: ACOG (assoc.; memberr). Roman Catholic. Avocations: biking, reading, travel, weightlifting. Office: 1625 N George Mason Dr #475 Arlington VA 22101 Office Phone: 703-717-4000. E-mail: lsanz@virginiahospitalcenter.com.

SANZONE, DONNA S., publishing executive; b. Bklyn., Apr. 4, 1949; d. Joseph J. Seitz and Faye (Brooks) Rossman; m. Charles F. Sanzone, Jan. 2, 1972; children: Danielle, Gregory. BA magna cum laude, Boston U., 1970; MA, Northeastern U., 1979. Grad. placement specialist Inst. Internat. Edn., NYC, 1970-72; adminstr. AFS Internat. Scholarships, Brussels, 1972-74; editor Internat. Ency. Higher Edn., Boston, 1974-76, G.K. Hall & Co., Pubs., Boston, 1977-81, exec. editor, 1981-91, editor-in-chief, 1991-96; v.p. Oryx Press, Boston, 1996-2000; editor-in-chief Grolier Acad. Reference, Danbury, Conn., 2000—04; exec. editor Collins Reference, Harper Collins, NYC, 2004—. Contbg. author: Access to Power, 1981. Mem.: ALA, Libr. and Info. Tech. Assn., Assn. Coll. and Rsch. Librs., Soc. for Scholarly and Profl. Pub., Assn. Am. Pubs. Office: Collins Reference 18 Pine St Weston MA 02493-1116

SAPARETO, FRANK VINCENT, II, investment advisor, state legislator; b. Haverhill, Mass., Jan. 12, 1960; s. Frank Vincent and Alice Lambert S.; children: Frank V. III, Justin John. BS, U. Mass., 1982. Cert. IAFP; registered investment adviser; lic. ins. profl., Mass., N.H., securities regulation profl., Mass., N.H.; cert. fund specialist. Fin. planner Eastcorp., Inc., Springfield, Mass., 1989-93; pres. FVS Fin., Inc., Derry, N.H., 1993—; state rep. dist. 13, mem. gen. ct. N.H. Ho. of Reps., Concord, 1997—2002; state senator N.H. Sen., Concord, 2003. Vice-chmn. Derry Taxpayers Assn., 1994-96, chmn., 1995-96; mem. zoning bd. Town of Derry, 1994-96. Mem. several profl. orgns. Avocations: kayaking, scuba diving, skydiving, chess. Home: 14 Oxbow Ln Derry NH 03038-4533 Office: FVS Financial Inc 14 Oxbow Ln Derry NH 03038-4533

SAPER, CLIFFORD BAIRD, neurology educator; b. Chgo., Feb. 20, 1952; s. Julian and Susan Menkin S.; m. Barbara Susan Farby, Aug. 26, 1973; children: Rebecca Michelle, Leah Danielle, Sean Zachary. BS, MS, U. Ill., 1972; MD, PhD, Washington U., 1977. Diplomate Am. Bd. Psychiatry and Neurology. Intern Jewish Hosp., St. Louis, 1977-78; resident New York Hosp., NYC, 1978-81; asst. prof. Washington U., St. Louis, 1981-84, assoc. prof., 1984-85, U. Chgo., 1985-88, prof., 1988-92, chmn. com. on neurobiology, 1987-92; James Jackson Putnam prof. neurology and neurosci. Harvard Med. Sch., 1992—; chmn. dept. neurology Beth Israel Deaconess Med. Ctr., Boston, 1992—. Editor-in-chief Jour. of Comparative Neurology, 1994—; contbr. articles to profl. jours. Fellow: Royal Coll. of Physicians (London); mem.: Soc. for Neurosci., Am. Physiol. Soc., Am. Acad. Neurology, Am. Neurol. Assn. Office: 330 Brookline Ave Boston MA 02215-5400

SAPER, JOEL R., neurologist, educator; b. Joliet, Ill., Feb. 6, 1943; s. Leonard and Jeanette (Kristal) S.; children: Lisa, Justin, Lauren. BS in History, U. Wis., 1965; MD, U. Ill., Chgo., 1969. Diplomate Am. Bd. Psychiatry and Neurology, Am. Bd. Pain Medicine. Intern Michael Reese Hosp., Chgo., 1969-70; resident U. Mich. Med. Ctr., Ann Arbor, 1970-73; instr. U. Mich. Med. Sch., Ann Arbor, 1973-75, asst. prof., 1975-78; founder, dir. Mich. Head Pain and Neurol. Inst., Ann Arbor, 1978—; dir. Head Pain Treatment Program, Chelsea, Mich., 1978—; clin. prof. neurology Mich. State U., Lansing, 1989—. Author: Freedom from Headaches, 1978, Clinical and Basic Neurology for Health Professionals, 1981, Help for Headaches, 1983, Headache Disorders, 1983, Controversies and Clinical Variants of Migraine, 1987, Handbook of Headache Management, 1993, 2nd edition, Handbook of Headache Management, 1999; Topics in Pain Mgmt., 1985—2001; contbr. chapter to book. Chair physicians' subcom. State of Mich. House Health Care Task Force, 1993-94; chair Mich. Coun. on Pain, 1995-96; nat. chmn. Pain Care Coalition, 1995-2001, 2004-06. Recipient John Graham Sr. Clinician award, Am. Headache Soc., 1995, Phillip M. Lippe MD award, 1996. Fellow: ACP; mem.: Am. Coun. on Headache Edn. (chmn. 1994—95), Am. Pain Soc. (cons. to bd. 1992—), Am. Headache Soc. (pres. 1992—94, bd. mem.), Am. Acad. Neurology (edn. com. 1992—), Am. Acad. Pain Medicine (bd. mem. 1992, 1998—). Office: Mich Head Pain and Neurol Inst 3120 Professional Dr Ann Arbor MI 48104-5131

SAPERS, CARL MARTIN, lawyer, educator; b. Boston, July 16, 1932; s. Abraham E. and Anne (Herwitz) Sapers; m. Judith H. Thompson, Nov. 29, 1959; children: Jonathan Simonds, Rachel Elizabeth, Benjamin Lovell. AB, Harvard U., 1953, JD, 1958. Bar: Mass. 1958. Assoc. Hill, Barlow, Goodale & Adams, Boston, 1958—65; ptnr. Hill & Barlow, 1965—96, of counsel, 1997—2002. Spl. asst. atty. gen. criminal divsn. Commonwealth of Mass., 1963—65; spl. cons. Mass. Ethics Commn., 1978—79; adj. prof. Harvard Grad. Sch. Design, 1983—; mem. Mass. Bd. Registration Medicine, 1995—98, vice chair, 1997—98. Moderator Town of Brookline, 1982—91. With US Army, 1953—55. Mem.: AIA (hon. Allied Professions medal 1975), Am. Coll. Constrn. Lawyers (bd. dirs. 1989—, pres. 1993), Am. Arbitration Assn. (bd. dirs. 1987—2000, Whitney North Seymour medal 1991), Boston Bar Assn. (coun. 1970—73, 1991—94). Home: 26C Bradbury St Cambridge MA 02138 E-mail: csapers@gsd.harvard.edu.

SAPERSTEIN, DAVID, writer, film director, television personality; b. Bklyn. s. Louis and Celia S.; m. Ellen Mae Bernard; children: Ivan, Ilena. Student, CCNY Film Inst., CCNY. With CBS-TV Ed Murrow Show-Person To Person; writer, prodr., dir. Skyline Films, Inc., 1963-83. Asst. prof. film NYU Grad. Sch., Tisch Sch. Arts, 1992-93; instr. screenwriting Manhattan Marymount Coll., 1996-99, N.Y. Film Acad., 1997. Lyricist 90 pub. songs; theatrical prodns. include musicals Blue Planet Blue, Clowntown; author: Cocoon, 1985 (bestseller), Fatal Reunion, 1987 (Book of the Month selection), Metamorphosis: The Cocoon Story Continues, 1988, Red Devil: The Book of Satan, 1989, Funerama, 1994, Dark Again, 1999, Retribution, 2003, A Christmas Visitor, 2004, 07, Butterfly: Tomorrow's Children; movies include Cocoon (Best Original Story for Screen 1985, 2 Acad. awards); writer, dir. My Sister's Keeper, Personal Choice (Beyond the Stars), Hearts & Diamonds; writer Torch, Sara Deri, Queen of America, Italian Ices, Joshua's Golden Band, Roamers, Vets, Do Not Disturb, Snatched, Jack in the Box, (with Joe Cacaci) SchoolHouse, Point of Honor, Roberto!, The John Gill Story: In Defense of Ivan the Terrible, Joshua's Golden Band, Fighting Back, Babs' Labs, Silyan, (nonfiction) Woman in the Year 2000, 1975; writer, prodr. Hallmark channel (with George Samerjan) A Christmas Visitor, 2002; co-author (with James Rush) Magi Magic, (with George Samerjan) Christmas Passage, 2006; writer, dir. music videos Dr. Bill, Teenage Mutant Ninja Turtles, Fallow Angel, Wowii; segment prodr. for Northstar Ent./PBS Reppies; dir. over 300 TV commls.; writer dir. over 200 documentaries, corp. and indsl. films, videos including Dance of the Athletes (Emmy nomination), Explorers in Aqua-Space, Rodeo: A Matter of Style; creator first interactive internet publishing at www.darkagain.com. Recipient Cine Golden Eagle award, N.Y. Film Festival award, San Francisco Film Festival award, Venice Film Festival award, Melbourne Film Festival award, N.Y. Art Dirs. award, Chgo. Film Festival award, Townsend Harris medal CCNY, 1998, Daniel Perle award, Pocono Film Festival, 2007. Mem. Writer Guild Am., Dir. Guild of Am., BMI, Nat. Honor Soc. Office: Ebbets Field Prodns Ltd Wykagyl Station PO Box 42 New Rochelle NY 10804-0042

SAPERSTEIN, DAVID NATHAN, rabbi, lawyer, educator; b. NYC, Aug. 5, 1947; s. Harold Irving and Marcia Belle Saperstein; m. Ellen Robin Weiss; children: Daniel, Ari. BA, Cornell U., 1969; MHL, Hebrew Union Coll., 1972; JD, Am. U., 1978; DHL (hon.), Lafayette Coll., 1997, Hebrew Union Coll., 1998. Rabbi Temple Rodeph Sholom, NYC, 1973-74; dir., counsel Religious Action Ctr. of Reform Judaism, Washington, 1974—. Adj. prof. Georgetown U. Law Ctr., Washington, 1980—. Author, editor: (books) Tough Choices, 1993, Jewish Dimensions of Social Justice, 1998, others. Bd. dirs. NAACP, 1987—, People for Am. Way, 1990—, Common Cause, 1988-89, also others; chmn. U.S. Commn. on Internat. Religious Freedom, 1999—. Named one of The Top 50 Rabbis in America, Newsweek Mag., 2007. Office: Religious Action Center 8720 Georgia Ave Silver Spring MD 20910-3638 E-mail: dsaperstein@uahc.org. *

SAPERSTEIN, LEE WALDO, mining engineering educator; b. NYC, July 14, 1943; s. Charles Levy and Freda Phyllis (Dornbush) S.; m. Priscilla Frances Hickson, Sept. 16, 1967; children: Adam Geoffrey, Clare Freda. BS in Mining Engring., Mont. Sch. Mines, 1964; DPhil in Engring. Sci., Oxford U., 1967. Registered profl. engr., Ky., Mo., Pa. Laborer, miner, engr. The Anaconda Co., Butte, Mont., and N.Y.C., 1963-64; asst. prof. mining engring. Pa. State U., University Park, 1967-71, assoc. prof., 1971-78, prof., 1978-87, sect. chmn., 1974-87; prof., chmn. dept. mine engring. U. Ky., Lexington, 1987-93; dean Sch. Mines and Metallurgy U. Mo., Rolla, 1993—2004, prof. mining engring., 1993—2006, prof. emeritus, 2007—, cons., dean emeritus Sch. Mines and Metallurgy, 2004—. Chmn. engring. accreditation commn., 1989-90, bd. dirs. Accreditation Bd. for Engring. and Tech., 1992-2001, sec. of bd., 1995-98, pres.-elect, 1998-99, pres. 1999-2000, ABET fellow. Contbr. articles to refereed jours. Rhodes scholar Oxford U., 1964-67; recipient Linton E. Grinter Disting. Svc. award, 2004. Mem. NSPE, ASEE, Soc. Mining, metallurgy and Exploration, Inc. (disting. mem. AIME-Soc. Mining Engrs.), Am. Assn. Rhodes Scholars. Home: PO Box 1408 Nantucket MA 02554-1408 Office: 20 New St Nantucket MA 02554 Office Phone: 573-578-7750. Personal E-mail: leesaperstein@comcast.net.

SAPERSTEIN, RICHARD S., financial consultant; MBA, NYU. With E.F. Hutton & Co., Janney Montgomery Scott LLC; mem. nat. adv. com. and chmn.'s coun. Oppenheimer & Co.; sr. mng. dir., CMG sr. portfolio mgr. Bear Stearns, NYC, 2003—. Contbr. articles to profl. publs. Bd. dirs. Israel Venture Network, 2005—. Named one of Top 100 Brokers, Barron's, 2004—05. Office: Bear Stearns 383 Madison Ave New York NY 10179 Office Phone: 212-272-0800. E-mail: richard.saperstein@bear.com. *

SAPHIR, RICHARD LOUIS, pediatrician; b. NYC, May 1, 1933; s. Samuel and Grace (Greenberg) Saphir; m. Judith Schwartz, Dec. 6, 1958; 1 child, Steven. BA, NYU, 1954; MD, SUNY, NYC, 1958. Diplomate Nat. Bd. Med. Examiners, Am. Bd. Pediat. Asst. attending pediatrician Mt. Sinai Hosp., NYC, 1965—71, asst dir., pediat. acute care clinic, 1970—78, 1971—82, assoc. clin. prof. pediat., 1982—88, attending pediatrician, 1982—; chief. pediatric svcs. U.S. Naval Hosp., Newport, RI, 1967—69; clin. prof. pediat. Mt. Sinai Sch. Medicine, NYC, 1988—. Bd. dirs. Mt. Sinai Children's Ctr. Found., NYC, 1987—. Contbr. articles to profl. jours. Chmn. cmty. and adv. com. N.Y.C. Info. and Counseling Program for Sudden Infant Death Syndrome, 1979—81; med. bd. YMHA, NYC, 1982—86. Comdr. USNR, 1967—69. Fellow: NY County Med. Soc. (vice chmn. com. child welfare 1974—85), NY Pediat. Soc. (pres. 1978—79), Am. Acad. Pediats. (com. sci. meetings 1985—97, chmn. prep course 1991—96, editl. adv. bd. Continuing Med. Edn. audiotapes 1991—2001, ednl. program rep. ambulatory care quality improvement program 1992—2002, ednl. advisor proficiency testing program 1996—99, editl. bd. Pediat. in Rev. 1997—2003, ednl. adv. Uniformed Svcs. pediat. seminar 1997—, mem. super cont. med. edn. planning com. 2000—06, chmn. super cont. med. edn. planning com. 2002—06, com. on continuing med. edn. 2002—06), NY Acad. Medicine (treas. 1987—89). Office: BSM Pediatrics PC 55 E 87th St New York NY 10128-1043 Home Phone: 212-362-8486; Office Phone: 212-722-4950.

SAPIANO, MATHEW RAYMOND PAUL, meteorologist; BSc in Stats., U. Reading, Eng., 2000, MSc in Biometry, 2001, PhD in Meteorology, 2005. Postdoctoral rschr. Earth Systems Sci. Ctr., U. Reading, 2005, Earth Systems Sci. Interdisciplinary Ctr., College Park, Md., 2005—. Office Phone: 301-405-4887. E-mail: msapiano@essic.umd.edu.

SAPIENZA, DAVID VICTOR, social studies educator; s. Rebecca Sue Bacon; m. Stephanie Ann Varga, June 23, 2001; 1 child, Joshua Stephen. BA, St. Louis U., 1996; EdM, U. Mo., Columbia, 2001. Provisional tchg. lic. Colo., 2005. Tchr. U. Denver H.S., 2002—06, Rock Canyon H.S., Highlands Ranch, Colo., 2006—. Chpt. pres. St. Louis U. Alumni Assn., Denver, 2004—06; past pres. Karis Cmty., Denver, 2002—06; asst. coord. Alum Svc. Corps, St. Louis, 1998—2004. Independent. Roman Catholic. Avocations: travel, cooking, skiing, hiking, snowshoeing. Office: Rock Canyon High Sch 5810 McArthur Rd Highlands Ranch CO 80124-9121 Home Phone: 303-683-5730.

SAPIENZA, MADELINE, historian, researcher; b. Washington, Jan. 27, 1950; d. Angelo Frank and Elaine Madeline (Cipriano) Sapienza. BS in Language, Georgetown U., Washington, 1972, MA, 1975; PhD in Am. History, Cath. U. Am., 1990. History, French HS tchr., Washington, 1976—80; adult ESL tchr. Lado Internat. Coll., Washington, 1979—80, 1994; legis. sec. US House Reps., Washington, 1980—83; part-time adminstrv. asst. and rschr. CBS News, Washington, 1983—92; adminstrv. coord. Wash. law dept. CBS, Inc., Washington, 1988—94; historian, rschr. US Army Ctr. Mil. History, Washington, 1986—88; docent Stephen Decatur Mus. House Nat. Trust for Hist. Preservation, Washington, 1997—99. Contbr. articles to profl. jours. and reference books. Bd. dirs. Rep. Women Capitol Hill, Washington, 1982—83, mem. various coms., 1982—83. Recipient Letter of Commendation, US Army, 1986, Dept. of Army Commendation award, US Army Ctr Mil. History, 1987. Mem.: John Carroll Soc. Washington, Assn. US Army (life), Phi Beta Kappa. Roman Catholic.

SAPIENZA, TONY, public relations executive; With Hewlett-Packard; sr. counsel Miller/Shandwick, Boston, pres. Office: Miller/Shandwick Technologies 101 Main St Cambridge MA 02142-1519

SAPIR, TAMIR, entrepreneur; b. Russia, 1948; arrived in USA, 1973; Former owner New York City Electronics Store; supt. 2 Broadway Bldg. Office: Two Broadway New York NY 10011

SAPIRIE, STEPHEN ALAN, public health administrator; b. Milw., June 17, 1938; s. Samuel Ralph and Florence Katheryn (Canatsey) Sapirie; m. Manana Gagua; children: Mark, Nicholas. BSc, U. Tenn., 1960; MBA, Am. U., Washington, 1968; D in Pub. Health, U. N.C., 1980. Chief mgmt. sys. Naval Command Sys., Washington, 1966—68; computer sys. analyst WHO, Geneva, 1968—70, health sys. analyst, 1970—74, health planner Burma, Thailand, 1974—75, program mgmt. officer New Delhi, 1978—85, scientist family health divsn. Geneva, 1985—90, chief strengthen county health info., 1990—98. Dir. INFORM Mgmt. Scis. for Health, Boston, 1999—. Co-author: Health Project Management, 1974. Lt. USN, 1960—66. Avocations: tennis, skiing. Office: Mgmt Scis Health 784 Memorial Dr Cambridge MA 02139 Business E-Mail: ssapirie@msh.org.

SAPIRO, VIRGINIA, academic administrator, political science professor; b. East Orange, NJ, Feb. 28, 1951; m. Graham K. Wilson; 1 child, Adam. AB, Clark U., 1972; MA in Polit. Sci., PhD in Polit. Sci., U. Mich., 1976. Asst. prof. polit. sci. and women's studies program U. Wis., Madison, 1976-81, assoc. prof., 1981-86, prof., 1986—, Sophonisba P. Breckinridge prof., 1995—, assoc. vice chancellor teaching and learning, 2002—, interim provost, vice chancellor academic affairs, 2005—06. Vis. lectr. dept. govt. U. Essex, 1979-80, lectr., 1981, 82-83, vis. prof., 1989. Author: Women in American Society: An Introduction to Women's Studies, 1986, 3d edit., 1994, Women, Biology and Public Policy, 1985, The Political Integration of Women: Roles, Socialization and Politics, 1983, A Vindication of Political Virtue: The Political Theory of Mary Wollstonecraft, 1992; contbr. articles to profl. jours. Mem. bd. trustees Clark U., Worcester, Mass., 2001—. CIC Academic Leadership fellowship, 2003-04. Mem. Am. Acad. Arts and Scis., Am. Polit. Sci. Assn. (v.p. 1999-2000, pres. sect. elections, pub. opinion, voting behavior), Midwest Polit. Sci. Assn. (exec. coun. 1984-86), Internat. Soc. Polit. Psychology (governing coun. 1988-90, 2000-03), Phi Beta Kappa. Office: Univ Wisconsin 117 Bascom Mall 500 Lincoln Dr Madison WI 53706-1380 Office Phone: 608-262-5246. Office Fax: 608-265-3353. E-mail: vsapiro@wisc.edu.

SAPOFF, MEYER, retired electronics executive; b. NYC, June 2, 1927; s. Benjamin and Mary (Charney) Sapoff; m. Lynn Joy Sapoff; children: Robert J., Judy B. Schiffman. Student, Mohawk Coll., 1946—48; BSEE magna cum laude, Poly. Inst. Bklyn., 1950, postgrad., 1952—53, MIT, 1951, U. Pa., 1951—52; MSEE, Drexel Inst. Tech., 1952. Rsch. engr. Franklin Inst. Labs., Phila., 1950-52; rsch. fellow sr. grade Poly. Inst. Bklyn., 1952-53; dir. rsch. Victory Engring. Corp., Springfield, NJ, 1953-57, dir. engring., 1957-63, v.p., 1963-69; cons., sr. staff scientist Keystone Carbon Co., St. Mary's, Pa., 1969-70; pres. Thermometrics, Inc., Edison, NJ, 1970-86, chmn. bd. dirs., 1986-93, sr. staff cons., 1993-96; pres. MS Cons., Princeton, NJ, 1993—96; ret., 1996. Chmn. E20 temperature com. 6th Symposium Temperature, Measurement and Control in Sci.

and Industry; U.S. del. to tech. com. 65th Internat. Electrotech. Commn.; cons. in field. Contbr. articles to profl. jours.; patentee in field. Active West Orange (NJ) PTA, 1960—76, Citizens League West Orange, 1962—75; trustee George St. Playhouse, New Brunswick, NJ, 1993—2001; bd. dirs. Jewish Ctr., Princeton, 1995—98, fin. chmn., 1995—96, v.p. fin., 1996—98; bd. dirs. United Jewish Fedn. Princeton Mercer Bucks, 1998—, treas., 2001—03. Recipient Indsl. Rsch. IR-100 award, 1974; fellow, Poly. Inst. Bklyn., 1953; scholar, NYU, 1948—50. Mem.: AAAS, ASTM (1st vice-chmn. E20 com. temperature measurement 2000—05, award of merit 1998), IEEE, Am. Ceramic Soc., Poly. Inst. Bklyn. Alumni Assn., Tau Beta Pi, Eta Kappa Nu.

SAPOLSKY, HARVEY MORTON, political scientist, educator; b. Haverhill, Mass., Feb. 21, 1939; s. Abraham and Anne Betty (Selig) S.; m. Karen P. Stenbo, Aug. 27, 1966. BA, Boston U., 1961; MPA, Harvard U., 1963, PhD, 1967. Mem. faculty MIT, 1966—2006, prof. polit. sci., 1977—2006, dir. comm. forum, 1987-95, dir. security studies program, 1989—2006; dep. dir. Univ. Health Policy Consortium, 1978-83, assoc. chmn. faculty, 1981-83. Vis. prof. U. Mich., 1971—72; cons. Artificial Heart Assessment Panel Nat. Heart and Lung Inst., Washington, 1972—73; mem. Ethics and Health Policy Panel Hastings (N.Y.) Ctr., 1979—80; mem. com. on Fed. Rsch. on Effect of Ionizing Radiation NRC, Washington, 1980—81, mem. com. on Risk Perception and Comm., 1987—88; mem. com. on tech. alternatives to anti-pers. mines, 1999—2001; mem. Sec. of Energy's Task Force on Alternative Futures for Dept. of Energy Labs, 1994—95; mem. adv. com. U.S. Army Command and Gen. Staff Coll., 2005—. Author: The Polaris System Development, 1972, (with D. Altman and Richard Greene) Health Planning and Regulation, 1981, (with A. Drake, S. Finkelstein) The American Blood Supply, 1982, Science and the Navy, 1990; editor: Consuming Fears: The Politics of Product Risks, 1986; co-editor: Federal Health Programs, 1981, (with S. Altman), 1981, (with R. Crane, W.R. Newman and E. Noam) The Telecommunications Revolution, 1992; contbr. articles to profl. jours. Mem. AAAS (sec. sect. social and econ. scis. 1968-73), Am. Polit. Sci. Assn., Nat. Acad. Social Ins., Coun. on Fgn. Rels. Home: 37 Edgemoor Rd Belmont MA 02478-3916 Office: MIT Security Studies Program E38-600 Cambridge MA 02139 Home Phone: 617-489-2449; Office Phone: 617-253-5265. Business E-Mail: sapolsky@mit.edu.

SAPORTA, JACK, psychologist, educator; b. NYC, Oct. 21, 1927; s. David and Victoria (Fils) S.; m. Judith Hammond, May 28, 1967 (div. 1979); children: David J., Victoria Johnson. AB cum laude, Adelphi U., 1951; PhD, U. Chgo., 1962. Diplomate Am. Bd. Profl. Psychology; lic. clin. psychologist. Pvt. practice, 1962-99; supt. Tinley Park (Ill.) Mental Health Ctr., 1975-78; chief manpower tng. and devel. Ill. Dept. Mental Health, Chgo., 1978-82; dean, prof. Forest Inst. Profl. Psychology, Des Plaines, Ill., 1982-85; mem. faculty Fielding Grad. U., Santa Barbara, Calif., 1984—2005, Ill. Sch. Profl. Psychology, Chgo., 1985-97. Mem. adj. faculty psychology Lake Forest Grad. Sch. Mgmt., 1987-97; mem. Ill. State Clin. Psychology Lic. and Disciplinary Com., Springfield, 1984-93; profl. staff Forest Hosp., Des Plaines, 1977-96; mem. attending doctoral profl. staff Luth. Gen. Hosp., Park Ridge, Ill., 1986-2000, emeritus, 2000—. Served with U.S. Army, 1946-47, Germany. Named Educator of Yr., Forest Inst., 1982, Outstanding Faculty Mem. Lake Forest Grad. Sch. Mgmt. Fellow Acad. Clin. Psychology, NTL-Inst. (faculty); mem. APA (accreditation site vis. team), Ill. Psychol. Assn., Chgo. Psychol. Assn. (cert. recognition 1999, mem. exec. bd.). Avocations: tennis, computers, do-it-yourself home projects. Home: 13077 Stone Creek Court Huntley IL 60142

SAPP, ERIC, religious organization executive; m. Julie Sapp. Grad., Davidson Coll.; MDiv, Duke U., MA Pub. Policy. Youth pastor First Presbyn. Ch., Durham; part-time dir. Christian Edn. at Heritage Presbyn. Ch., Alexandria, Va.; aide Senate Health, Edn., Labor, and Pensions Com., Rep. David Price's (NC-04) Washington D.C. office, 2004; sr. ptnr. Common Good Strategies. Mem.: Heritage Presbyn. Ch. Office: Common Good Strategies 949 North Pitt St Alexandria VA 22314 Office Phone: 703-863-6403. E-mail: eric@cg-strategies.com. *

SAPP, JOHN RAYMOND, lawyer; b. Lawrence, Kans., June 18, 1944; s. Raymond Olen and Amy (Kerr) S.; m. Linda Lee Tebbe, July 3, 1965; children: Jeffrey, Jennifer, John. BA, U. Kans., 1966; JD, Duke U., 1969. Bar: Wis. 1969, U.S. Dist. Ct. (ea. dist.) Wis. 1969, U.S. Ct. Appeals (7th cir.) 1974, U.S. Ct. Appeals (4th cir.) 1984, U.S. Supreme Ct. 1974. Assoc. Michael, Best & Friedrich, Milw., 1969-76, ptnr., 1976-90, mng. ptnr., 1990—2004, sr. ptnr., 2004—. Dir. Roadrunner Freight Sys., Milw., 1992-2004, J.J. Keller Co., 2003-. Bd. dirs. Milw. Symphony, 1981-95, mem. exec. com., 1993-95; bd. dirs. Boy Scouts Am., Milw., 1986—, pres. 1990-92; mem. Milw. Arts Bd., 1990, Greater Milw. Com.; bd. dirs. Zool. Soc., 1995-, v.p., 2000-05, chmn., 2005-; bd. dirs. Lex Mundi, 1997-2000, mem. exec. com., 1997-2001; bd. dirs. Jr. Achievement Greater Milw., 2001—04. Avocations: golf, curling, print collecting. Office Phone: 414-271-6563, 414-271-6560. Business E-Mail: jrsapp@michaelbest.com.

SAPP, R. LACHANZE See LACHANZE

SAPP, WARREN CARLOS, professional football player; b. Orlando, Fla., Dec. 19, 1972; m. Jamiko Sapp, Jan. 29, 1998; children, Mercedes, Warren Carlos II. Student, U. Miami. Defensive tackle Tampa Bay Buccaneers, 1994—2003, Oakland Raiders, 2004—. Named NFL Defensive Player of the Yr., 1999; named to Pro-Bowl, 1997—2003. Achievements include being a member of Super Bowl XXXVII Champion Tampa Bay Buccaneers, 2002. Avocation: swimming. Office: c/o Oakland Raiders 1220 Harbor Bay Pkwy Alameda CA 94502

SAPPENFIELD, CHARLES MADISON, architect, educator; b. Columbia, SC, Mar. 17, 1930; s. Charles Madison and Elizabeth Olive (Moss) S.; m. Mary Frances McGowan Dec. 14, 1963 (div. June 1990); children—Charles Ross, Sarah Kathleen B.Arch., N.C. State U., 1956; Cert., Denmark's Royal Acad., Copenhagen, 1961. Asst. prof. N.C. State U., Raleigh, 1956-57, asst. prof., 1961-63; head archtl. firm C.M. Sappenfield, Asheville, N.C. and Muncie, Ind., 1961—; assoc. prof. Clemson U., SC, 1963-65; prof. architecture Ball State U., Muncie, Ind., 1965-94, prof. emeritus, 1994—, dean, 1965-81, dean emeritus, 1994—, dir. Design Indiana, 1983-88. Awards juror Interfaith Forum on Religious Art and Architecture, 1981, Am. Cons. Engrs. Council, 1982; mem. accreditation teams Nat. Archtl. Accrediting Bd., 1967-82. Archtl. works include: Dormitories, U. N.C., Gumpert residence, Dave residence. Pres. Asheville Art Mus., N.C., 1964-65; chmn. Ind. Commn. on Aging, Indpls., 1983-85; pres. Alpha Day Care Ctr. for Elderly, Muncie, 1985; mem. State Planning Adv. Commn., Indpls., 1974-82. Served with U.S. Army. Recipient Gold medal for svc. Ball State U., 1983; named Sagamore of the Wabash, Gov. of Ind., 1982 Fellow AIA (dir. nat. bd. dirs. 1989-92); mem. Ind. Soc. Archs. (pres. 1976), Ind. Archtl. Found. (chmn. 1975), Am. Soc. Landscape Archs. (awards juror 1983), Danish Fedn. Archs. (hon., Aeresmedallion 1987), Fulbright Alumni Assn., Alpha Rho Chi. Lodges: Rotary, Civitan. Democrat. Episcopalian. Avocations: bicycling, boating, photography. Home and Office: 11607 Oakmont Ct Fort Myers FL 33908

SAPPINGTON, SHARON ANNE, retired school librarian; b. West Palm Beach, Fla., Sept. 15, 1944; d. A.D. and Laura G. (Jackson) Chambless; m. Andrew Arnold Sappington III, June 11, 1966; children: Andrew Arnold IV, Kevin Sean. Student, Fla. So. Coll., 1962—64; BA in Edn., U. Fla., 1966; postgrad., U. Ala., 1980. Tchr. 5th grade Tates Creek Elem., Lexington, Ky., 1966—68; tchr. 4th grade Sadieville Elem., Ky., 1968—69; libr. media specialist A.H. Watwood Elem., Childersburg, Ala., 1980—98, ret., 1998. Guest storyteller Young Author's Conf., Winterboro, Lincoln, Sylacauga, and Fayetteville, Ala., 1982-94; vis. com. Southeastern Accreditation Assn.; program presenter Internat. Reading Assn., Birmingham, Ala., 1983; guest spkr. rare children's books By the Way TV talk show, 1983; pres. Tale Tellers of St. Augustine, 2003—05; chmn. RSVP Read Aloud Program, 2002-04. Creator, presenter: (slide presentation) Tellers of Tales and Sketchers of Dreams, 1983, (multimedia programs) Dinosaurs, Teddy Bears, and Wild Things, 1990, Shanghaied in the Beijing Airport, 1994. Circle chmn., Sunday tchr. Grace United Meth. Ch., Birmingham, 1973, 92-95; delivery mem. Meals on Wheels, Birmingham, 1975-76; radio reader for the blind WBHM Pub. Broadcasting, Birmingham, 1980; guest spkr., program presenter Jaycees, Kiwanis, and C. of C., Childersburg, 1993-94. Grantee Title I grantee, 1991, Stutz Bearcat grantee, 1992. Mem. AAUW (lit. chmn. St. Augustine chpt., 2005-07), ALA, Internat. Platform Assn., Am. Assn. Sch. Librs., Ala. Libr. Assn. (children's and sch. divsn. publicity chmn. 1991-93, chmn. Nat. Libr. Week in Ala. 1993-94, Outstanding Youth Svcs. award 1989), People to People Internat. (libr. del. to China 1993), Kappa Delta Pi. Democrat. Methodist. Avocation: book collecting. Home: 5131 Shore Dr Saint Augustine FL 32086-6473

SAPSOWITZ, SIDNEY H., entertainment and media company executive; b. NYC, June 29, 1936; s. Max and Annette (Rothstein) Sapsowitz; m. Phyllis Skopp, Nov. 27, 1957; children: Donna Dawn Chazen, Gloria Lynn Aaron, Marsha Helene Gleit. BBA summa cum laude, Paterson State U., NJ, 1980. Various fin. and oper. systems positions Metro Goldwyn Mayer, Inc., NYC, 1957-68; exec. v.p., dir. Penta Computer Assoc. Inc., NYC, 1968-70, Cons. Actuaries Inc., Clifton, NJ, 1970-73; exec. v.p., CFO Am. Film. Theatre, NYC, 1973-76, Cinema Shares Internat Dristb. Corp., NYC, 1976-79; sr. cons. Solomon, Finger & Newman, NYC, 1979-80; exec. v.p., CFO Metro Goldwyn Mayer, LA, 1980-82; various positions leading to sr. exec. v.p. fin. and adminstrn., chief fin. operating and adminstrv. officer MGM/UA Entertainment Co., Culver City, Calif., 1982-86, mem. bd. dirs., exec. com., 1982—89; fin. v.p.; chief adminstrv. and ops. officer, Office of Pres., dir. United Artists Corp., Beverly Hills, Calif., 1986-87; chmn. bd., CEO MGA/UA Telecommunications Corp., Beverly Hills, 1986-89; sr. exec. v.p., bd. dirs., mem. exec. com. MGA/UA Communications Co., 1986-89; chmn., CEO Sid Sapsowitz & Assocs., Inc., 1989—. Pres., Wayne Conservative Congregation, N.J., 1970-77; mem. bd. govs. exec. com. City of Hope, 1990-. Mem. Am. Mgmt. Assn., Am. Film Inst., Acad. Motion Picture Arts and Scis., Fin. Exec. Inst., TV Acad. Arts and Scis., KP (chancellor comdr.).

SARACEVIC, TEFKO, information science educator; married; 2 children. MS in Libr. Sci., Case Western Reserve U., 1962, PhD in Info. Sci., 1970. Prof. comm., info. and libr. studies Rutgers U., New Brunswick, NJ. Editor-in-chief: Info. Processing and Mgmt., 1985—. Avocations: reading, skiing. Office: Rutgers U Sch Comm Info & Libr Studies 4 Huntington St New Brunswick NJ 08901-1071 Office Phone: 732-932-7500 Ext. 8222. E-mail: tefko@scils.rutgers.edu.

SARACHIK, MYRIAM PAULA MORGENSTEIN, physics professor, condensed matter physicist; b. Antwerp, Belgium, Aug. 8, 1933; arrived in US, 1947; d. Solomon and Sarah (Segal) Morgenstein; m. Philip Sarachik, Sept. 6, 1954; 1 child, Karen Beth. AB, Barnard Coll., 1954; MS, Columbia U., 1957, PhD, 1960. Rsch. assoc. IBM Watson Labs., Columbia U., NYC, 1960-61; mem. tech. staff Bell Telephone Labs., Murray Hill, NJ, 1962-64; asst. prof. physics CCNY (CUNY), 1964-67, assoc. prof., 1967-70, prof., 1971—, Disting. prof. physics, 1995—. Advisor NSF, NRC. Contbr. articles to profl. jours. Recipient NYC Mayor's award for excellence in sci. and tech., 1995, Sloan Pub. Svc. award, 2004, Oliver E. Buckley prize in Condensed Matter Physics, 2005, L'Oreal/UNESCO for Women in Sci. (N.Am.) Laureate, 2005. Fellow AAAS, Am. Phys. Soc. (pres. 2003), N.Y. Acad. Scis.; mem. NAS, Am. Acad. Arts and Scis. Office: CCNY (CUNY) Divsn Sci MR429 Physics Dept Convent Ave and 138 St New York NY 10031 Office Phone: 212-650-5618. Business E-Mail: sarachik@sci.ccny.cuny.edu.

SARAF, PETER NATANIEL, film producer, executive; m. Erika Ann Greene, May 30, 1992. Prodr.'s asst. to ptnr. Clinica Estetico; co-founder Big Beach Films, NYC, 2004—. Adv. bd. Woodstock Film Festival. Exec. prodr.: (films) The Complex Sessions, 1994, The Opportunists, 2000, Adaptation, 2002; prodr.: One Foot on a Banana Peel, the Other Foot in the Grave: Secrets from the Dolly Madison Rm., 1994, Into the Rope, 1996, Courage and Pain, 1996, Storefront Hitchcock, 1998, The Truth About Charlie, 2002, The Agronomist, 2003, Everything is Illuminated, 2005, Little Miss Sunshine, 2006 (Darryl F. Zanuck Prodr. of Yr. award in Theatrical Motion Pictures, Prodrs. Guild of Am., 2007); co-prodr.: Mandela, 1996, Ulee's Gold, 1997. Office: Big Beach Films 5th Fl 41 Great Jones New York NY 10012 *

SARAKATSANNIS, LEONIDAS NICHOLAS, musician, concert pianist, music educator, composer, conductor; b. Newport, Ky., May 30, 1929; s. Nicholas Demetrius Sarakatsannis and Melanthia Leonidas Kazangi; m. Frances Charles Nicholas, Jan. 22, 1956; children: Demetrius Leonidas, Nicholas Leonidas, Melanie Leonidas. MusB, Coll. Music, 1951; MusM, Coll.-Conservatory of Music, 1956; D in Musical Arts, U. Cin., 1968; postgrad., U. Mich., 1964. Cert. piano Ohio, 1949. Chmn. piano dept. U. Fla., 1959—63; dir. piano program So. Ill. U., Edwardsville, 1964—65; tchg. asst. U. Cin. Coll. Conservatory Music, 1965—68; chmn. dept. music U. Ctrl. Fla., Orlando, 1968—72; dir. applied music No. Ky. U., Highland Heights, Ky., 1972—77; pianist in residence Bloomsburg (Pa.) U., 1979—80; pianist, prof. music, chmn. music dept. U. Guam, Mangilao, Guam, 1981—93; adj. prof. music Manatee C.C., Bradenton, Fla., 1994—. Coll. recital chmn. Fla. State Music Tchrs. Assn., 1962; adjudicator chmn. World Piano Competition, Cin., 1981—88; condr. Guam Symphony Orch., Mangilao, GM, 1981—85. Composer: (musical composition) Twelve Excursions For The Young Pianist, (voice and piano composition) A Communion Hymn; One Is Holy, (piano composition) Six Guam Sketches for Piano, (various compositions) Sonata for Piano, (musical composition) Hymns for Voice and Piano Entitled Praise the Lord, One is Holy, Yia Tin Photini; musician: (solo) Fla. Symphony, (piano soloist) Three performances with the Cincinnati Symphony Orchestra under Eric Kunzel and Thor Johnson, North Port (Fla.) Orchestra, Delius Festival in Jacksonville, Asolo Theater, Sarasota, Fla., Taft Mus., Cin., Manatee C.C., Saipan, Guam, Hawaii, and 5 Concerts in Japan, Carnegie Libr. Recitals, Xavier U., Coll. Mount Joseph, others, North Port Orchestra. Bd. dirs. Guam Symphony Orch., Mangialo, 1982—86, Ctrl. Fla. Civic Music Assn., Orlando, 1968—72; v.p. Ctrl. Fla. Music Tchrs. Assn., Orlando, 1970—72. Acting sgt. US Army, 1951—53. Recipient Composition award, Fla. Composers League, 1962, Musical Contbn. to the Cultural Life of our Cmty. award, U. Guam, 1983, Concerto Competition, Coll. Conservatory Symphony Orch. Mem.: Coll. Music Soc., Pi Kappa Lambda (hon.), Phi Mu Alpha Sinfonia (recital chmn. 1950—56). Home: 4539 Hamlets Grove Dr Sarasota FL 34235

SARANDON, SUSAN ABIGAIL, actress; b. NYC, Oct. 4, 1946; d. Phillip Leslie and Lenora Marie (Criscione) Tomalin; m. Chris Sarandon, Sept. 16, 1967 (div. 1979); children: Eva Maria Livia Amurri, Jack Henry Robbins, Miles Guthrie Robbins. BA in Drama and English, Cath. U. Am., 1968. Actress: (plays) include An Evening with Richard Nixon, 1972, A Coupla White Chicks Sittin' Around Talkin', 1980-81, A Stroll in the Air, Albert's Bridge, Private Ear, Public Eye, Extremities, 1982, (films) Joe, 1970, Lady Liberty, 1972, The Rocky Horror Picture Show, 1975, Lovin' Molly, 1974, The Front Page, 1974, The Great Waldo Pepper, 1975, Dragon Fly, 1976, Crash, 1976, The Other Side of Midnight, 1977, The Last of the Cowboys, 1978, Checkered Flag or Crash, 1978, Pretty Baby, 1978, King of the Gypsies, 1978, Something Short of Paradise, 1979, Loving Couples, 1980, Atlantic City, 1980 (Prix Genie Best Fgn. Actress award 1981, Acad. award nominee 1981), Tempest, 1982 (Best Actress award Venice Film Festival 1982), The Hunger, 1983, Buddy System, 1984, Compromising Positions, 1985, The Witches of Eastwick, 1987, Bull Durham, 1988, Sweet Hearts Dance, 1988, A Dry White Season, 1989, The January Man, 1989, White Palace, 1990, Thelma and Louise, 1991 (Acad. award nominee for best actress 1992, Golden Globe award nominee 1992), The Player, 1992, Light Sleeper, 1992, Bob Roberts, 1992, Lorenzo's Oil, 1992 (Acad. award nominee 1993), The Client, 1994 (Acad. award nominee for best actress), Little Women, 1994, Safe Passage, 1994, Dead Man Walking, 1995 (Golden Globe award nominee for best actress 1996, Acad. award for best actress 1996), James and the Giant Peach (voice), 1996, 187 (voice), 1997, Illuminata, 1998, Twilight, 1998, Stepmom (also producer), 1998, Joe Gould's Secret, 1999, Baby's in Black, 1999, Cradle Will Rock, 1999, Anywhere But Here, 1999, (voice) Rugrats in Paris: The Movie - Rugrats II, 2000, Moonlight Mile, 2002 (also exec. prodr.), The Banger Sisters, 2002, Igby Goes Down, 2002, Noel, 2004, Shall We Dance?, 2004, Alfie, 2004, Jiminy Glick in La La Wood, 2004, Elizabethtown, 2005; TV appearances: The Haunting of Rosalind, 1973, F. Scott Fitzgerald and The Last of the Belles, 1974, Who Am I This Time, 1982, A.D., 1985, Mussolini: The Decline and Fall of Il Duce, 1985, Earthly Possessions, 1999, Friends, 2001 (Emmy nominee), Malcolm in the Middle, 2002 (Emmy nominee), Ice Bound, 2003., The Exonerated, 2005; (TV series) A World Apart, 1970-71, Search for Tomorrow, 1972-73; TV miniseries: Children of Dune, 2003. Mem. AFTRA, Screen Actors Guild, Actors Equity, Acad. Motion Picture Arts and Scis., NOW, MADRE, Amnesty Internat., ACLU Office: Internat Creative Mgmt care Samuel Cohen 40 W 57th St New York NY 10019-4001

SARANGAN, VENKATESH, computer scientist, educator; B in Elec. Engring., Anna U., Chennai, India, 1997; PhD, Pa. State U., Univ. Pk., 2003. Rschr. Telcordia Techs. Inc., Morristown, NJ, 2001; rsch. asst. dept. computer sci. and engring. Pa. State U., University Park, 2001—02; asst. prof. Okla. State U., Stillwater, 2003—. Contbr. articles to profl. jours. Recipient Employee Recognition award, Telcordia, 2001; grantee, Fed. Dept. Transp., Okla., 2006—. Mem.: IEEE, Assn. Computing Machinery. Achievements include research in protocol for service negotiation in wireless networks. Office: Okla State Univ Computer Sci Dept Stillwater OK 74078 Home Phone: 405-372-3508; Office Phone: 405-744-5672. Office Fax: 405-744-9097.

SARAPH, PRASAD VAMAN, research scientist, industrial engineer; arrived in U., 1998; BSME, Govt. Engring. Coll., Aurangabad, India, 1992; MS, Indian Inst. Tech., 1995; MS Engring., U. Calif., Berkeley, 1999. Prodn. supr. Universal Luggage Mfg. Co., Aurangabad, Maharashtra, India, 1992—93; rsch. assoc. Inst. Devel. Studies U. Sussex, Brighton, England, 1995—96; cons. A.F. Ferguson & Co, Mumbai, Maharashtra, India, 1996—97; grad. rsch. asst. U. Calif., Berkeley, 1998—99; sr. engr. Bayer Corp., Berkeley, 2000—01, project mgr., 2001—02; head Dept. Long Term Planning Bayer Biol. Products, Berkeley, 2003—05, supply chain excellence lead, 2006—. Track coord. healthcare and biotechnology Winter Simulation Conf., 2004—05. Author: Corporate Restructuring: Crompton Greaves and the Challenge of Globalization, 1998; contbr. articles to profl. jours. Recipient First Pl. award, Indian Inst. Tech., 1993, Inst. Indsl. Engrs., 1999. Mem.: YWCA, Capoeira Narahari (capoeirista 2000—). Achievements include first to implement mixed integer programming based supply chain planning in biopharma industry; introduce and successfully implement of discrete event simulation techniques in the biopharmaceuticals industry; analysis methodology for impact of regulatory strategy on biopharmaceutical product and process life cycle management; successfully introduce optimization tools in supply chain planning for biopharmaceuticals; implement mixed integer program in biotech for production planning; research in use of dynamic simulation for risk analysis in biopharmaceuticals industry; development of hierarchical strategic capacity analysis methodology for biopharmaceutical manufacturing; and implementation of organizational decision support structure for biopharmaceutical industry; and implementation of world's largest mixed integer program and the first MIP for supply chanin planning in biopharmaceuticals industry. Avocations: martial arts, classical music, stamp collecting/philately, reading. Office: Bayer HealthCare LLC Biological Products 800 Dwight Way Berkeley CA 94710 Home Phone: 510-548-8628; Office Phone: 510-705-4703. Personal E-mail: psaraph@yahoo.com. Business E-Mail: prasad.saraph.b@bayer.com.

SARASON, IRWIN G., psychology professor; b. Newark, Sept. 15, 1929; s. Max and Anna Sarason; m. Barbara June Ryrholm, Sept. 19, 1953; children: Suzanne, Jane, Donald. BA, Rutgers U., Newark, 1951; MS, U. Iowa, 1953; PhD, Ind. U., 1955. Intern clin. psychology VA Hosp., West Haven, Conn., 1955-56; from asst. prof. psychology to prof. emeritus U. Wash., Seattle, 1956—2003, prof. emeritus, 2003—. Co-author: Abnormal Psychology, 1972, 11th edit., 2005; editor: Jour. Personality and Social Psychology, 1985-91; author over 275 articles. The Netherlands Inst. for Advanced Study fellow, Wassenaar, 1975, 85. Fellow APA, Japan Soc. for Promotion of Sci., AAAS, Western Psychol. Assn. (pres. 1978-79), Wash. State Psychol. Assn. (pres. 1965). Avocations: travel, music, reading. Home: 13516 42nd Ave NE Seattle WA 98125-3826 Office: U Wash Dept Psychology Box 351525 Seattle WA 98195-0001 Business E-Mail: isarason@u.washington.edu.

SARAT, AUSTIN D., jurisprudence and political science educator; b. Fall River, Mass., Nov. 2, 1947; s. Joseph George and Lillian (Sock) S.; children: Lauren, Emily. BA in Polit. Sci., Providence U., 1969; MA in Polit. Sci., U. Wis., 1970, PhD in Polit. Sci., 1973; JD, Yale U., 1988. Rsch. assoc. Yale Law Sch., 1976-81; sr. staff civil litigation rsch. project U. Wis. Sch. Law, 1979-81; rsch. assoc. U. Wis. Law Sch., 1981-83; William Nelson Cromwell prof. jurisprudence and polit. sci. Amherst (Mass.) Coll., Amherst, Mass., 1974—. Cons. Nat. Adv. Commn. on Small Claims Cts., 1976-77, Pub. Mgmt. Svcs., 1977-78, Law Enforcement Assistance Adminstrn., 1977-78, Nat. Ctr. for State Cts., 1977-78, NAS, 1979, Yankelovich, Skelley & White, 1980, Hampshire Coll., 1983, Vt. Law Sch., 1983, Modern Media Inst., 1983-84, Porter, Morris, Arthur and Wright, 1984; dir. NEH summer seminar for coll. tchrs., 1986; vis. asst. prof. Dept. Polit. Sci. Yale U., 1976-77, Johns Hopkins U., 1977-78, vis. lctr. Yale Law Sch., 1993, 1996, O'Bryne disting. vis. prof. Law and Soc. U. Indiana, 1998-99, Cornell Law Sch., 2000, UCLA Law Sch., 2001, U. Conn., 2001, Georgetown Law Ctr., 2002, Mass. Inst. Tech., 2002, 2003, 2004, Harvard U., 2004, Clason lctr. We. New Eng. Law Sch., 1999, Henry Adams lctr. Collegiate Sch., NY 2002, Henry Steele Commager lctr. Greenfield Cmty. Coll., 2002. Author: (with Malcolm Feeley) The Policy Dilemma: Federal Crime Policy and the Law Enforcement Assistance Administration 1968-78, 1980, (with Stan Wheeler and Ken Mann) Sitting in Judgment: The Sentencing of White Collar Criminals, 1988; editor and co-author: American Court Systems, 1978, 2d edit., 1988; also numerous articles and rev. essays, book revs.; sr. editor Yale Law Jour., 1987-88; co-editor Studies in Law, Politics and Society; assoc. editor Justice Quar., 1986—; mem. editorial bd. Law and Society Rev., 1977-78; editorial adv. bd. Yale Jour. of Law and the Humanities, Co-editor, Spl. Issue of Law Text Culture, 2001, editor Law Culture, and Humanities, 2004-, gen. editor Intewrnational Library of Essays Law and Soc., 2004-, The Place of Law, with Lawrence Douglas and Martha Umphrey, 2003, Law in the Liberal Arts, Cornell U. Press, 2004, Dissent in Dangerous Times, U. Mich. Press, 2004, Blackwell Companion to Law and Society, Blackwell Pub., 2004. Woodrow Wilson fellow, 1969-70, Russell Sage fellow Yale Law Sch., 1973-74, Karl Lowenstein fellow in polit. sci. and jurisprudence, 1985-86, vis. fellow

Centre for Socio-Legal Studies, Oxford U., 1985-86, vis. sr. rsch. fellow Am. Bar Found., 1987-88; NSF grantee, 1972-73, 81, 85. Mem. Am. Polit. Sci. Assn. (Corwin award com. 1981, 87), Law and Society Assn. (program com. for 1986 ann. meeting, trustee 1987-81, 86-88, exec. com. bd. trustees 1986-88), Am. Judicature Soc. (program com. 1978-80), Internat. Sociol. Assn., 1992, Assn. Study of Law, Culture, and Humanities (pre.) 2001-04. Office: Amherst Coll PO Box 5000 Amherst MA 01002 Office Phone: 413-542-2308, 413-542-2318.

SARAVOLATZ, LOUIS DONALD, epidemiologist, medical educator; b. Detroit, Feb. 15, 1950; s. Samuel and Saya Betty (Chonich) S.; m. Yvette Susanne Braymer, Oct. 6, 1990; children: Samuel Francis, Louis Donald II, Stephanie Nicole. BS, U. Mich., Ann Arbor, 1972, MD, 1974. Fellow Am. Coll. Epidemiology. Intern Henry Ford Hosp., Detroit, 1974-75, 1975-77, fellow, 1977-79, dir. hosp. epidemiology, 1979-82, divsn. head infectious diseases, 1982-96, dir. infectious diseases rsch. lab., 1982-96; prof. medicine Case-Western Res. U., 1993-96, Wayne State U. Sch. Medicine, Detroit, 1996—. Clin. prof. medicine U. Mich. Med. Sch., Ann Arbor, 1986-96; mem. AIDS clin. drug devel. com. NIH, 1990-95; chmn. dept. internal medicine St. John Hosp. and Med. Ctr., 1996—. Contbr. over 170 articles to profl. publs. Active Blue Ribbon Com. on AIDS State of Mich., Detroit, 1990; chmn. physician com. on AIDS Greater Detroit Health Coun., 1989. Master: ACP, Am. Coll. Physicians; fellow: Royal Soc. Medicine (London), Infectious Diseases Soc. Am. (chmn. antimicrobial use and clin. trials com. 2000—03). Office Phone: 313-343-3362. Business E-Mail: louis.saravolatz@stjohn.org.

SARAZIN, CRAIG LEIGH, astronomer; b. Milw., Aug. 11, 1950; s. Valley V. and Martha V. (Gustafson) Sarazin; children: Stephen N., Andrew T. BS in Physics, Calif. Inst. Tech., 1972; MA in Physics, Princeton U., 1973, PhD in Physics, 1975. Millikan fellow Calif. Inst. Tech., Pasadena, 1975; mem. Inst. Advanced Study, Princeton, NJ, 1975-77; asst. prof. U. Va., Charlottesville, 1977-79, assoc. prof. dept. astronomy, 1979-86, prof., 1986-96, W.H. Vanderbilt prof. astronomy, 1996—, chmn. dept., 1992-95. Vis. asst. prof. U. Calif., Berkeley, 1979; vis. scientist Nat. Radio Astronomy Obs., Charlottesville, 1977-82; vis. prof. physics Inst. Advanced Study, 1981-82, Joint Inst. Lab. Astrophysics vis. fellow U. Colo., Boulder, 1985-86; mem. com. on Space Astronomy Astrophysics, Washington, 1984-86, mem. x-ray astronomy working group, 1989-99, mem. Heineman prize com., 1995-98; chmn. Chandra users com., 1993-01, Advanced Satellite for Cosmology and Astrophysics users com., 1995-2000; mem. High Energy Astrophysics from Space Panel, 1999-2000; chmn. USRA Sci. Coun., 2000-06; mem. program assessment com. Beyond Einstein, 2006-07. Author: X-ray Emission from Clusters of Galaxies; contbr. numerous articles to profl. jours. NSF grantee, 1981-86, NASA grantee, 1979-82, 86—; recipient Haren Fischer Physics prize Calif. Inst. Tech., 1971. Mem. Am. Astron. Soc., Internat. Astron. Union. Home: 664 Courtyard Ct Charlottesville VA 22903-7876 Office: U Va Dept Astronomy PO Box 400325 Charlottesville VA 22904-4325 Home Phone: 434-293-3270; Office Phone: 434-924-4903. Business E-Mail: sarazin@virginia.edu.

SARBANES, JOHN PETER SPYROS, congressman, lawyer; b. Balt., May 22, 1962; s. Paul S. and Christine (Dunbar) Sarbanes; m. Dina Eve Caplin, 1988; 3 children. AB cum laude, Woodrow Wilson Sch. Public & Internat. Affairs, Princeton U., 1984; JD, Harvard U., 1988. Bar: Md. 1988, DC. Law clk. to Hon. J. Frederick Motz, US Dist. Ct. Md., 1988—89; assoc. through ptnr. Venable LLP, Balt., 1989—2006, mem. hiring com., 1992—96, chmn. health care practice, 2000—06; mem. US Congress from 2nd Md. dist., 2007—, mem. edn. & workforce com., resources com., govt. oversight com. Pres. Pub. Justice Ctr., Balt., 1994—97; spl. asst. to supt. schools State of Md. Spl. asst. State Supt. Schools, Md.; bd. mem. Inst. for Christian & Jewish Studies. Fulbright Scholar, 1985. Mem.: ABA, Md. Bar Assn., DC Bar. Democrat. Greek Orthodox. Office: 426 Cannon House Office Bldg Washington DC 20515 also: 600 Baltimore Ave Ste 303 Towson MD 21204 also: Arundel Ctr Ste 349 44 Calvert St Annapolis MD 21401 *

SARBANES, PAUL SPYROS, former senator; b. Salisbury, Md., Feb. 3, 1933; s. Spyros P. and Matina (Tsigounis) S.; m. Christine Dunbar, June 11, 1960; children: John Peter, Michael Anthony, Janet Matina. AB in Public and Internat. Affairs, magna cum laude, Princeton, 1954; BA in Philosophy, Politics and Economics, Rhodes Scholar, Oxford U., Eng., 1957; LLB, Harvard, 1960. Bar: Md. 1960. Law clk. to Hon. Morris A. Soper US Ct. Appeals (4th Cir.), 1960-61; assoc. Piper & Marbury LLP, Balt., 1961-62; adminstrv. asst. to chmn. Walter W. Heller Coun. Econ. Advisors, Exec. Office of the Pres., Washington, 1962—63; exec. dir. Charter Revision Commn., Balt., 1963-64; assoc. Venable, Baetjer & Howard LLP, Balt., 1965-70; mem. Md. Ho. of Dels., 1967-71, US Congress from 3rd Md. dist., 1971—77; US Senator from Md., 1977—2007; mem. banking com., fgn. rels. com., 1977—2007, joint econ. com., 1979—2007, budget com., 1993—2007. Mem. budget com. U.S. Senate, 1993—. Co-author (with David R. Obey): The Changing American Economy: Papers from the Fortieth Anniversary Symposium of the Joint Economic Committee of the US Congress, 1986. Recipient Nat. Disting. Svc. award, Am. Pub. Transit Assn., 1999, Paul H. Douglas Ethics in Govt. award, Inst. Govt. & Pub. Affairs, U. Ill., 2003, Restore Am. Hero award, Nat. Trust for Historic Preservation and HGTV, 2005. Fellow: Am. Acad. Arts & Sci. Democrat. Greek Orthodox. *

SARD, SUSANNAH ELLEN, non-profit executive; b. Boston, May 10, 1944; d. Russell Ellis and Miriam Clark Sard. AB, Bryn Mawr Coll., 1966. Devel. adminstr. Ky. Ednl. TV, Lexington, 1978—88; dir. found. and corp. rels. Sarah Lawrence Coll., Bronxville, NY, 1991—96; dir. devel. The Town Hall, NYC, 1998—2002; exec. dir. Women's City Club NY, NYC, 2002—04; edn. liaison R.J. & S.H. Kaplan Family Found., NYC, 2004—. Alumni bd. Rippowam Cisqua Sch. Mem.: Blue Hill Troupe. Office: Kaplan Family Found 866 UN Plz Ste 306 New York NY 10017 Business E-Mail: owlkap@aol.com.

SARDEGNA, VERÓNICA GABRIELA, language educator; b. Buenos Aires, Dec. 16, 1971; arrived in US, 2002; d. Miguel Angel Sardegna and Juana Luisa Gargiulo; m. Alexis Kwasinski, June 24, 1995; 1 child, Alexander. Licenciatura in English Lang., U. Museosoual Argentino, Buenos Aires, 2002; MA in TESOL with distinction, U. Ill., Urbana-Champaign, 2005. Tchr. English Colegio Nuetra Senora de la Misericordia, Buenos Aires, 1992—2003, head tchr. English dept., 1995—2003; assoc. prof. English grammar U. Museo Social Argentino, Buenos Aires, 1995—2002, assoc. prof. English lit., 1997—2002, assoc. prof. bus. English, 1998—2000; tchg. asst. pronunciation course U. Ill., Urbana-Champaign, 2003—, tchg. asst. acctg. dept., 2003—, coord., supr. TAS, 2005—. Co-author: ESL/EFL Business Communications Handbook for Accountancy Students, 2006. Recipient The Deil Mary A. Hussey award for excellence in ESL tchg., U. Ill., Urbana Champaign, 2006; Liberal Arts and Scis. fellow, 2004. Mem.: TESOL, Phi Kappa Phi.

SARDER, PINAKI, research scientist; b. Kolkata, W.Bengal, India, July 22, 1980; s. Amiya and Chhaya Sarder. BTech, Indian Inst. Tech., Kanpur, 1999—2003. Rsch. asst. Signal & Image Rsch. Labl, ECE Dept. U. Ill., Chgo., 2004—05; rsch. asst. Ctr. Sensor Signal & Info. Processing Lab., ESE Dept. Wash. U., St. Louis, 2006—. Home: 740 W Gate Ave Apt 2S Saint Louis MO 63130 Office: Wash Univ ESE Dept One Brookings Dr Campus Box 1127 Saint Louis MO 63130-4899 Office Phone: 314-935-4146. Office Fax: 661-460-4229; Home Fax: 661-460-4229. Business E-Mail: psardel@ese.wustl.edu.

SAREMBOCK, IAN JOSEPH, internist, cardiologist; b. Cape Town, South Africa, June 9, 1951; arrived in US, 1982, naturalized, 1986; m. Ghita Marueen Sarembock; children: Craig Murray, Kerri Lauren. MD, U. Cape Town, 1975, PhD, 1988. Diplomate Am. Bd. Internal Medicine, Am. Bd. Cardiovasc. Medicine, Am. Bd. Interventional Cardiology. Sr. house officer dept. internal medicine U. Cape Town and Groote Schuur Hosp., Cape Town, 1979-80, resident in internal medicine, 1980-83, sr. registrar Cardiac Clinic, 1985-86; Velva Schrire meml. rsch. fellow Cardiac Clinic Groote Schur Hosp., 1983-85; postdoctoral rsch. assoc. divsn. cardiology Yale U., New Haven, 1986-88; attending cardiologist divsn. cardiology VA Ctr., West Haven, Conn., 1987-88; asst. prof. internal medicine cardiovasc. divsn. U. Va. Health Scis. Ctr., Charlottesville, 1988-93, assoc. prof. internal medicine cardiovasc. divsn., 1993-99, dir. coronary care unit, 1988—2007, prof. internal medicine cardiovasc. divsn., 1999—2007; interventional cardiologist, 1988—2007; cardiology cons. Salem VA Med. Ctr., Va., 1988—2000; dir. Ctr. Interventional Cardiology, U. Va. Health System, 2005—07, Ohio Heart & Vascular Ctr., Cin., 2007—. Lectr., presenter in field; invited prof. Heart-Lung Inst., Utrecht, Netherlands, 1992; mem. faculty restenosis summits, Cleve. Clinic, 1992, 93, 97. Contbr. articles to profl. publs. Mem. policy working com., house staff supervision Commonwealth of Va., 1990-2007. With South African Def. Force, Med. Corps, 1977—78. Grantee U. Va. Sch. Medicine, 1989, Beecham Labs., 1989-90, Am. Heart Assn., 1989-91, 91-92, 95-98, NIH, 1991-94, 2000-05; named Harrison DFisting. Tchg. Prof. Internal Medicine, 2006-07. Fellow ACP, Coll. Physicians South Africa, Am. Coll. Cardiology (allied health profls. com. 1993—), Coun. Thrombosis Atherosclerosis and Vascular Biology; mem. AAAS, Am. Heart Assn. (bd. dirs. Charlottesville/Albermarle divsn. 1991—, mem. Va. affiliate rsch. peer rev. subcom. 1992—, thrombosis coun. 1987, fellow coun. on clin. cardiology 1989), South African Med. and Dental Coun. Jewish. Office: Ohio Heart Vascular Ctr 2123 Auburn Ave Ste 136 Cincinnati OH 45219 E-mail: ijs4s@virginia.edu.

SAREYAN, ANDY, publishing executive; m. Nancy Marshall; children: Alex, Eliza. Graduated summa cum laude in Econ., Middlebury Coll.; MBA, Stanford U. Various consumer mktg. positions Time Inc., 1987—91; consumer mktg. dir., Can. and Latin Am. Time Internat., 1991—93; v.p., consumer mktg. and develop. Entertainment Weekly, 1993—97; v.p., assoc. pub. In Style, 1997—99; founding pub. Real Simple, 1999; pres. Parenting Group, 2001—02, Entertainment Weekly, NY, 2002—05; pub. Better Homes & Gardens Mag., NYC, 2006—; and exec. v.p. Meredith Pub. Group, NYC, 2006—. Office: Meredith Publishing 125 Park Ave New York NY 10017 *

SARFATY, WAYNE ALLEN, insurance agent, financial planner; b. Rochester, NY, Apr. 18, 1951; s. Benjamin and Grace (Rowan) S.; m. Karen Nugent, July 12, 1957 (div. Apr. 2004); children; Melissa A., Gabrielle M. Student, Parsons Coll., 1971-74. Cert. ins. agt. Sales rep. Met. Life, Rochester, N.Y., 1979-81; register rep. Prudential Fin. Svcs., Rochester, 1981-92; owner, broker Wayne A. Sarfaty & Assocs., Rochester, 1992—. Dir. tng. films. Mem. Eagle Club. Recipient Nat. Quality award Nat. Assn. Life Underwriters, 1982-90; named to Million Dollar Round Table, NALU, 1987. Mem.: Eagle Club, Am. Legion. Avocations: camping, auto racing, darts. Home: 8 Rosencrans St Cohocton NY 14826-0182 E-mail: was2@frontiernet.net.

SARGEANT, ERNEST JAMES, lawyer, educator; b. Spokane, Wash., Sept. 26, 1918; s. Ernest Edward and Louise (McWhinnie) S.; m. Helene Sophie Kazanjian, Jan. 29, 1944 BA cum laude, Harvard U., 1940, LL.B. magna cum laude, 1947. Bar: Mass. 1947. Assoc. Ropes & Gray, Boston, 1947, 52-56, ptnr., 1956-90, of counsel, 1991—. Lectr. law Harvard U. Law Sch., Cambridge, Mass., 1961-62, 65-92; adj. prof. Boston Coll. Law Sch., 1990-98. Grad. treas. Harvard Law Rev., Cambridge, 1971-98. Capt. U.S. Army, 1942-46, 51-52. Mem. Am. Law Inst. (council), ABA, Boston Bar Assn. Clubs: Union (Boston); Country (Brookline, Mass.). Home: 24 Highgate Wellesley Hills MA 02481-1420 Office: Ropes & Gray 1 International Pl Boston MA 02110-2624

SARGENT, ANNEILA ISABEL, astrophysicist; b. Kirkcaldy, Fife, Scotland; came to US, 1964; d. Richard Anthony and Annie (Blaney) Cassells; m. Wallace Leslie William Sargent, Aug. 5, 1964; children: Lindsay Eleanor, Alison Clare. BSc with honors in Physics, U. Edinburgh, 1963; MS, Calif. Inst. Tech., 1967, PhD in Astronomy, 1977. Postdoctoral rsch. fellow Calif. Inst. Tech., Pasadena, 1977-80, mem. profl. staff, 1980-88, sr. rsch. fellow, 1988-90, sr. rsch. assoc., 1990—98; assoc. dir. Owens Valley Radio Obs., 1992—96, exec. dir., 1996—98, dir., 1998—, prof., assoc. dir, 1998—, Benjamin M. Rosen prof. astronomy, 2004—. Dir. Michelson Interferometry Sci Ctr., 2000—03, dir. combined array for rsch. in millimeter wave astronomy, 2003—. Contbr. articles to profl. jours. Recipient NASA Pub. Svc. medal, 1998, Alumna of Yr., U. Edinburgh, 2002; grantee, NASA, NSF. Fellow Am. Acad. Arts & Scis.; Mem. Royal Astron. Soc. (assoc.), Am. Astron. Soc. (pres. 2000-02), Internat. Astron. Union Roman Catholic. Office: Dept Astronomy Calif Inst Tech MC 105-24 1200 E Calif Blvd Pasadena CA 91125 E-mail: afs@astro.caltech.edu.

SARGENT, CHARLES LEE, manufacturing executive; b. Flint, Mich., Mar. 22, 1937; s. Frank T. and Evelyn M. (Martinson) S.; m. Nancy Cook, June 9, 1962; children: Wendy L., Joy A., Candace L. B ME, GM Inst., 1960; MBA, Harvard U., 1962; D in Engring. (hon.), Kettering U., 2004. Reliability engr. AC Spark Plug div. GM, Flint, 1962-63; with Thetford Corp., Ann Arbor, Mich., 1962-95, pres., chmn. bd. dirs., 1974-95, Thermassan Corp., 1969-72; pres., owner Quality Boat Lifts, Inc., Fort Myers, Fla., 1996—. Trustee Lincoln Cons. Schs., 1973-77, Ketterine U., 1989-2004, chmn. 1995-97. Patentee in field. Elder Presbyn. Ch. Recipient Entrepreneurial Achievement award GMI, 1989; named Entrepreneur of the Yr., Harvard Bus. Sch. Club of Detroit, 1981, Engring. Achievement award Kettering U., 1999. Mem. Barton Hills Country Club (bd. dirs. 1985-87, pres. 1987), Harvard Bus. Sch. Club of Detroit (bd. dirs. 1983-93). Avocations: travel, golf. Home: 4931 Bonita Bay Blvd 602 Bonita Springs FL 34134

SARGENT, JOHN, psychiatrist; MD, U. Rochester, 1973. Diplomate in psychiatry, child and adolescent psychiatry Am. Bd. Psychiatry and Neurology; diplomate Am. Bd. Pediats.; approved clin. supr. Am. Assn. Marriage and Family Therapy. Intern and resident pediat. U. Wis., Madison, 1973—77; resident child and adolescent psychiatry Phila. Child Guidance Ctr., 1978—80; resident gen. psychiatry Hosp. U. Pa., Phila., 1984—87; dir. child and adolescent psychiatry U. Pa. Med. Sch., 1989—97, dir. adult residency program, 1989—97; mem. staff Children's Hosp. Phila., Phila. Child Guidance Ctr., 1980—97; dir. edn. and rsch., dean Karl Menninger Sch. Psychiatry & Mental Health Svcs., Topeka, 1997—2001; prof. psychiatry Baylor Coll. Medicine, Houston, 2001—; dir. child and adolescent psychiatry Ben Taub Hosp., Houston, 2001—. Assoc. prof. psychiatry and pediat. U. Pa. Med. Sch., 1987-97; Pfeiffer/Adams prof. psychiatry Karl Menninger Sch. Psychiatry. Mem. editl. bd. Jour. Am. Acad. Child and Adolescent Psychiatry, Family Process, Bull. of Menninger Clinic; co-author: Madness, Chaos and Violence: Therapy with Families at the Brink; co-editor: Primary Care Pediatrics; contbr. over 60 articles to profl. jours. Dep. dir. Ea. European Child Abuse and Child Mental Health Program, Soros Found. and Children's Mental Health Alliance, 1997-2003. Office: Baylor Coll Medicine One Baylor Plaza BCM 350 Houston TX 77030 Home Phone: 713-661-8940; Office Phone: 713-798-7889. Business E-Mail: asargent@bcm.edu.

SARGENT, JOSEPH DENNY, insurance executive; b. West Hartford, Conn., Sept. 11, 1929; s. Thomas Denny and Elizabeth (Owen) S.; m. Mary A. Tennant, June 25, 1955; children: Robert Tennant, Thomas Denny II, Mary Diane, Suzanne Davis. BA, Yale U., 1952. Ptnr. Conning & Co., Inc., Hartford, Conn., 1957-86, mng. ptnr., 1986-92; chmn., CEO Conning & Co., Hartford, Conn., 1986-91, chmn., 1992, vice-chmn., 1993-95; chmn. Conning Internat., London, 1986-92; vice chmn. Conning & Co., 1993-95; chmn. Bradley, Foster & Sargent, 1995—. Bd. dirs. Bristol, Conn., Tenwick Reins., Stamford, Conn.; past trustee MMI Co., Chgo., Mut. Risk, Bermuda, Policy Mgmt. Sys., Columbia, S.C.; chmn. Conn. Surety Corp., Hartford, 1993-97, Bradley, Foster & Sargent, Hartford, Beazley Furlonge Holdings, Ltd., London; trustee McLean Fund; chmn., treas. SKI Ltd, 1956-96. Past trustee Wadsworth Atheneum, Children's Svcs. of Conn.; trustee Hartford Hosp. Mem.: Yale Club (Hartford), Hartford Club, Hartford Golf Club. Home: 25 Colony Rd West Hartford CT 06117-2215 Office: City Place II 185 Asylum St Hartford CT 06103-3408

SARGENT, MARK A., dean, law educator; b. New London, Conn., 1951; m. Joan Taranto; 1 child, Alexander. BA magna cum laude, Wesleyan U., 1973; MA Medieval & Renaissance Hist., Cornell U., 1975, JD, 1978. Bar: Mass. 1978. Atty. Csaplar & Bok, Boston, 1978—80; asst. prof. law U. Baltimore Sch. Law, 1980—83, assoc. prof., 1983—87, prof., 1987—89, U. Maryland Sch. Law, 1989—97, dir. Law and Entrepreneurship prog., 1989—97, Piper & Marbury Prof. Law, 1993—97, assoc. dean, 1994—97; dean, prof. law Villanova U. Sch. Law, 1997—. Vis. prof. law Washington Coll. Law, Am. U., 1987; vis. assoc. prof. law So. Methodist U. Sch. Law, 1988; arbitrator Am. Arbitration Assn., 1998—. Editor: The Business Lawyer, 1991—97; mem. editl. bd. The Business Lawyer, 1997—99, co-editor-in-chief Villanova Jour. Law and Investment Mgmt., 1998—; contbr. articles to profl. law jours. Mem. bd. trustees Wilmington Trust Mutual Funds, 2002—; mem. bd. dirs. Saint Thomas More Soc. of Pa., 1998—; independent gen. ptnr. Fiduciary Capital Ptnrs. SBIC, 1998—2002. Mem.: Am. Law Inst., Phi Beta Kappa. Office: Villanova U Sch Law 113 Garey Hall 800 Lancaster Ave Villanova PA 19085-1603 Office Phone: 610-519-7007. Office Fax: 610-519-6472. E-mail: sargent@law.villanova.edu. *

SARGENT, MILDRED CROW, retired history educator, writer; b. Nashville, Feb. 4, 1922; d. Edward Martin and Alpha Eunice Black; m. Arnold Dale Crow, Dec. 10, 1938 (dec. Aug. 18, 1988); children: Larry Wayne Crow, David Hardin Crow, Gerald Dale Crow(dec.), Richard Clayton Crow(dec.); m. John Wesley Sargent, Oct. 25, 1993; stepchildren: Ladonna Clary, John Wesley Jr., Ronald. BS in Social Studies and English, Mid. Tenn. State Coll., Murfreesboro, 1965; MA in History and Libr. Sci., Mid. Tenn. State U., Murfreesboro, 1967, postgrad., 1971—82. Cert. tchr. Tenn. Bd. Edn., geneal. cert. State of NC Archives. Dist. mgr. World Book Ency., Nashville, 1959; English tchr. Antioch HS, Tenn., 1965—66; history tchr. Two Rivers HS, Nashville, 1967—70; libr. Gladeville Elem., Wilson County Bd. Edn., Lebanon, Tenn., 1982—83, libr. West Elem., 1983—86. Author: William Few: A Founding Father, 2 vols., 2006; editor Cmty. News, Donelon, Tenn., 1966—68; contbr. V.p. PTA Mc Garoch Elem. Sch., 1966—68; floor mgr., conv. del. NEA, 1969. Mem.: AAUW, Am. Legion Aux., Phi Alpha Theta, Kappa Delta Pi, Pi Gamma Mu. Democrat. Achievements include unveiling the Women Support the War stamp in Washington, DC. Avocations: bridge, ballroom dancing, golf, symphony performances, travel. Home: 2309 Dundee Ln Nashville TN 37214 Home Fax: 615-882-9275. Personal E-mail: johnsrsargent@bellsouth.com.

SARGENT, PAMELA, writer; b. Ithaca, NY, Mar. 20, 1948; BA, SUNY, Binghamton, 1968, MA, 1970. Mng. editor, Binghamton, 1970-73; asst. editor, 1973-75; Am. editor Bull. Sci. Fiction Writers Am., Johnson City, NY, 1983-91. Author: Cloned Lives, 1976, Starshadows, 1977, The Sudden Star, 1979, Watchstar, 1980, The Golden Space, 1982, The Alien Upstairs, 1983, Earthseed, 1983, Eye of the Comet, 1984, Homesmind, 1984, Venus of Dreams, 1986, The Shore of Women, 1986, The Best of Pamela Sargent, 1987, Alien Child, 1988, Venus of Shadows, 1988, Ruler of the Sky, 1993 (Nebula best novelette award 1992, Locus best novelette award 1993, Electric Sci. Fiction award 1993), Climb the Wind: A Novel of Another America, 1999, (with Ron Miller) Firebrands: The Heroines of Science Fiction and Fantasy, 1998, Child of Venus, 2001, Behind the Eyes of Dreamers and Other Short Novels, 2002, The Mountain Cage and Other Stories, 2002, Eye of Flame: Fantasies, 2003, Thumbprints, 2004, Farseed, 2007; editor: (anthology) Women of Wonder, 1975, Bio-Futures, 1976, More Women of Wonder, 1976, The New Women of Wonder, 1978, (with Ian Watson) Afterlives, 1986, Women of Wonder, The Classic Years, 1996, Women of Wonder, The Contemporary Years, 1995, Nebula Awards 29, 1995, Nebula Awards 30, 1996, Nebula Awards 31, 1997, Conqueror Fantastic, 2004. Office: care Richard Curtis Assocs Inc 171 E 74th St New York NY 10021-3221 Personal E-mail: psdel2003@yahoo.com, pamsargent@gmail.com.

SARGENT, ROBERT GEORGE, engineering educator; b. Port Huron, Mich., June 14, 1937; s. George O. and Marie L. (Roome) S.; m. Dorothy Baum, 1970; 1 dau., Tiffany. BSE, U. Mich., 1959, MS, 1963, PhD, 1966. Elec. engr. Hughes Aircraft Co., Culver City, Calif., 1959-61; faculty mem. Syracuse U., 1966—, asst. prof., 1966-70, assoc. prof., 1970-81, prof. indsl. engring. and ops. research, 1982-96, chmn. dept., 1982-85, prof. elec. and computer engring., 1994-96, prof. elec. engring. and computer sci., 1996—. Vis. faculty Cornell U., 1981-82, Ctr. Econ. Rsch. Tilburg U., 1996; bd. dirs. Winter Simulation Conf., 1974-84, chmn. bd., 1979-81, gen. chmn., 1977, TIMS Coll. on Simulation and Gaming, 1978-80; pres. WSC Found., 2003-. Dept. editor Comms. of Assn. Computing Machinery, 1980-85; mem. editl. adv. bd. ACM Transactions on Modeling and Simulations, 1989-98; mem. adv. bd. Jour. of Simulation, 2005—; contbr. articles to profl. jours. Recipient Svc. award Winter Simulation Conf., 1984. Fellow Inst. Ops. Rsch. and Mgmt. Scis. (Disting. Svc. award for Simulation 1988, Lifetime Profl. Achievement award 2002); mem. Assn. Computing Machinery (nat. lectr 1985-89, Svc. award 1985), Inst. Indsl. Engrs. (Svc. award 1985), Soc. Computer Simulation (bd. dirs. 1984-87), Computer Soc. IEEE (mem. exec. com. simulation 1985-99). Office: Syracuse U Dept Elec Engring and Computer Sci Syracuse NY 13244-0001

SARGENT, RONALD L., retail office and business products executive; m. Jill Sargent; 2 children. BS, Harvard U., MBA, 1979. Various mgmt. and planning positions Kroger Co., 1974-89; regional v.p. ops. Staples Inc., 1989—92, v.p. Staples Direct, 1992—94, pres. Staples Contract and Comml., 1994—98, COO, 1998—2002, pres., 1998—2005, CEO, 2002—, chmn. bd. dir., 2005—. Bd. dir. Aramark Corp., Yankee Candle Corp., Mattel Inc. Office: Staples Inc PO Box 9265 Framingham MA 01701-9265 *

SARGENT, THOMAS ANDREW, retired political science professor; b. Indpls., Apr. 24, 1933; s. Thomas Edward and Inez (Secrest) S.; m. Cecily Constance Fox-Williams, 1965 (dec.); children: Sarah Beatrice, Andrew Fox; m. 2d Frances Petty, 1987. BA, DePauw U., Greencastle, Ind., 1955; MA, Fletcher Sch. Law and Diplomacy, Tufts U., 1959, MA in Law and Diplomacy, 1968, PhD, 1969. With First Nat. City Bank, NYC, 1959-64, asst. accountant, 1963-64; asst. sec. Irving Trust Co., NYC, 1964-66; mem. faculty Ball State U., Muncie, Ind., 1969-89, dir. London Ctr., 1973-74, chmn. polit. sci. dept., 1977-80, prof. polit. sci., 1979-89, prof. emeritus, 1989—, acting asst. to dean Coll. Scis. and Humanities, 1981-82, assoc. dean Coll. Scis. and Humanities, 1982-85, dir. spl. programs Minnetrista Ctr., 1985-87; dir. E.B. Ball Ctr., Muncie, 1987-89, dir. emeritus, 1989—. Contbg. editor Ripon Forum, 1973-78. Bd. dirs., exec. v.p. Ea. Ind. Cmty. TV, Muncie, 1974-76, pres., 1976-77; mem. nat. bd. govs. Ripon Soc.,

Washington, 1976-84; mem. Indpls. Com. Fgn. Rels., 1977-2004, com. fgn. rels. Ctrl. Ind., 2004—, bd. dirs., 2005—; bd. dirs. Hist. Muncie, Inc., 1979-85, pres., 1980; bd. dirs. Muncie Civic Theatre Assn., 1978-81, 90-96, 1st v.p., 1992-96; exec. dir. Ind. Consortium for Internat. Programs, 1982-88; mem. Ind. Real Estate Commn., 1983-91; trustee DePauw U., 1983—; bd. dirs. Muncie Symphony Orch., 1985-95, pres., 1991-93; mem. bd. govs. Minnetrista Cultural Ctr., Muncie, 1989-94, chmn., 1992-94; trustee Malpas Trust, 1990—, pres., 1997—; bd. dirs. Arts Ind., Inc., 1992-99, Muncie Children's Mus., 1994-2000, v.p., 1996-97, pres. 1997; trustee Ind. Colls. Ind., 1996—, United Meth. Meml. Home, Warren, Ind., 1997-2006; mem. strategy coun. North Ind. Conf. United Meth. Ch., 2000—. 1st lt. USAF, 1955-58. Named Sagamore of Wabash, 1988. Mem. Am. Polit. Sci. Assn., Delaware County Hist. Alliance (bd. dirs. 1980-86, 87-95, pres., 1987-91), Soc. Profl. Journalists, Delaware Country Club, Columbia Club (Indpls.), Maxinkuckee Yacht Club (Culver, Ind.), Rotary, Phi Delta Theta. Republican. United Methodist. E-mail: tsarg123@aol.com.

SARGENT, WALLACE LESLIE WILLIAM, astronomer, educator; b. Elsham, Eng., Feb. 15, 1935; naturalized, 2004; s. Leslie William and Eleanor (Denniss) S.; m. Anneila Isabel Cassells, Aug. 5, 1964; children: Lindsay Eleanor, Alison Clare. B.Sc., Manchester U., 1956, M.Sc., 1957, PhD, 1959. Research fellow Calif. Inst. Tech., Pasadena, 1959-62; sr. research fellow Royal Greenwich Obs., 1962-64; asst. prof. physics U. Calif., San Diego, 1964-66; mem. faculty dept. astronomy Calif. Inst. Tech., 1966—, prof., 1971-81, Ira S. Bowen prof. astronomy, 1981—, dir. Palomar Obs., 1997-2000. Miller prof. U. Calif., Berkeley, 1993; Thomas Gold lectr. Cornell U., Ithaca, NY, 1995; Sackler lectr. Harvard U., Cambridge, Mass., 1995, U. Calif., Berkeley, 1996; Icko Iben lectr. U. Ill., 2002. Contbr. articles to profl. jours. Alfred P. Sloan fellow, 1968-70. Fellow Am. Acad. Arts and Scis., NAS, Royal Soc. (London); mem Am. Astron. Soc. (v.p. 2004—, Helen B. Warner prize 1969, Dannie Heineman prize 1991, Henry Norris Russell Lectureship, 2001), Royal Astron. Soc. (George Darwin lectr. 1987, assoc. 1998), Astron. Soc. Pacific (Bruce Gold medal 1994), Internat. Astron. Union. Clubs: Athenaeum (Pasadena). Home: 400 S Berkeley Ave Pasadena CA 91107-5062 Office: Calif Inst Tech Astronomy Dept 105-24 Pasadena CA 91125-0001 Office Phone: 626-395-4055.

SARGENT, WALTER HARRIMAN, II, lawyer; b. Norfolk, Va., Aug. 26, 1958; s. Richard E. and Martha F. (Bassett) S. BS in Philosophy, MIT, 1980, BS in Computer Sci. and Engring., 1980; JD, Harvard U., 1987. Bar: Colo. 1987, U.S. Dist. Ct. Colo. 1988, U.S. Ct. Appeals (3d, 6th, 9th and 10 cirs.), U.S. Supreme Ct. 1992. Assoc. Holme Roberts & Owen, Colorado Springs, 1987-95; pvt. practice Colorado Springs, 1995—; bd. trustees Colorado Legal Aid Found., 1998—2004. Bd. dirs. ARC of the Pikes Peak Region, 1991-97, Coalition for Adult Literacy, Colorado Springs, 1989-93. Recipient John M. Olin prize in law and econs. Harvard Law Sch., 1987, John M. Olin fellow, 1987, fellow Am. Acad. Appellate Lawyers, 2004—. Mem. ABA (appellate practice com.), Colo. Bar Assn. (appellate practice subcom.), Am. Acad. Appellate Lawyers. Avocation: distance running. Home: 1632 N Cascade Ave Colorado Springs CO 80907-7409 Office: Walter H Sargent A Profl Corp 1632 N Cascade Ave Colorado Springs CO 80907-7409 Home Phone: 719-632-2319; Office Phone: 719-577-4510. Personal E-mail: wsargent@wsargent.com.

SARGENT, WILLIAM WINSTON, retired anesthesiologist; b. Oshkosh, Wis., Feb. 28, 1933; s. Sprague Spencer and Lila Jane (Gjermundson) S. BS in Medicine, U. Ill., Chicago, 1955, MD, 1957; MS in Anesthesiology, U. Minn., 1967. Diplomate Am. Bd. Anesthesiology. Staff anesthesiologist St. Anthony Hosp., Rockford, Ill., 1960-61, Swedish Am. Hosp., Rockford, 1960-61; instr. anesthesiology U. Minn., Mpls., 1967-74, asst. prof. anesthesiology, 1974-80; staff anesthesiologist St. Luke's Hosp., Duluth, Minn., 1980-95, ret., 1995. Contbr. articles to profl. jours. Capt. USAF, 1961-64, France. Fellow Am. Coll. Anesthesiologists; mem. AMA, Am. Soc. Anesthesiologists, Minn. Soc. Anesthesiologists, Minn. State Med. Assn., St. Louis County Med. Soc. Presbyterian.

SARGSYAN, DAVID, library director; b. Yerevan, Armenia, Oct. 6, 1957; s. Mkrtich Sargsian and Elena Davidian; m. Valentina Alaverdian, Apr. 19, 1956. Diploma, Yerevan State U., 1979; D in Social Scis. (hon.), Internat. Acad., 2006. Philologist, jr. editor Sovetakan Grogh pub. House, 1980-82, sr. editor, 1982-90; officer CC of CP of Armenia, 1990-91; dir. Hayastan Pub. House, 1991-98; head of apparatus Min. of Culture, Republic of Armenia, 1998; dir. Nat. Libr. of Armenia, 1998—. Founder newspaper Spiritual Fatherland; co-pres. sci. and creative intelligentsia forum CIS, rep. RA. Recipient F. Nansen Golden medal, 2005. Mem. Union Armenian Writers, Union Armenian Journalists, Libr. Assn. Armenia (pres. 2005). Mem. Armenian Rev. Con. Party. Mem. Apostolic Ch. Avocations: reading, hunting. Office: Nat Libr Armenia Terian 72 Yerevan 375009 Armenia Office Phone: 584259. Personal E-mail: nla@arm.r.am, dsargsyan@mail.ru.

SARHAN, MANSOOR MOHAMED, library director; b. Nuwidrat, Bahrain, Jan. 1, 1945; s. Mohamed Abdulla and Sukainah Ahmed (Ismail) S.; m. Zahra Abul Kassim Dashti, Aug. 22, 1971; children: Nazha, May, Mohamed. BA in History, Beirut U., Lebanon, 1972; B in Libr. Sci., U. Bombay, India, 1980; MA in Librarianship, Leeds Poly. U., Eng., 1985; diploma exec. mgmt., U. Bahrain, Isa Town, 1990; PhD in Hist. Documentary Studies, Universal Acad., London, 2003. Tchr. for English lab. Ministry of Edn., Manama, Bahrain, 1963-73, libr. Manama (Bahrain) Pub. Libr., 1973-82, head pub. librs. Manama, 1982-88, dir. pub. librs., 1989—. Gen. organizer Bahrain Internat. Book Fair, Manama. Author: The Book and the Libraries, 1983, Cultural Movement in Bahrain 1940-90, 1993, Bahrain National Bibliography, 1995, Libraries in Islamic Dynasties, 1997, Survey of Cultural Movement in Bahrain during Twentieth Century, 2000, Pioneers of Bookshops in Bahrain, 2000, Libraries in Bahrain, 2001, in Memory of Ebrahim Al-arrayed, 2002, Selections from Ebrahim Al-arrayed's Poetry, 2002, The Education in Bahrain Kingdom, 2003, Shaikh Ahmed Mohamed Al-khalifa: The Poet of Nature and Beauty, 2003, Bahrain Journalism 1939-2003, 2004, Children and Mothers Welfare Society in its 50th Anniversary, 2004, Hassan Jawad Al-Jishi: A Pioneer in Enlightenment, 2005, History of Cinema in Bahrain, 2005, Ali Sayar The Doyenn of Bahrain Journalism, 2005, Literary Criticism in Bahrain During the 20th Century, 2006. Lectr. schs., clubs and assns., Bahrain, 1975—; gen. organizer yearly piano concert Ministry of Edn., Bahrain, 1988—. Mem. Bahrain Libr. Assn. (pres. 1994—), Arab Fedn. for Librs. and Info., Nuwidrat Club (pres. 1966—). Avocations: reading, music, tennis, chess. Home: House 46 Rd 4301 Nuwidrat 643 Bahrain Office: Ministry of Edn PO Box 43 Manama Bahrain Office Phone: (973) 17231105. E-mail: mansoorsarhan@hotmail.com.

SARI, DANA, psychologist; b. Apr. 15, 1973; BA, U. NC, Chapel Hill, 1994; MS, Drexel U., Phila., 1998, PhD, 2001. Lic. clin. psychologist. Neuropsychologist Behavioral Medicine Inst., Newport News, Va., 2002—06, Comprehensive Mental Health Assoc., Chesapeake, 2006—. Contbr. articles to profl. jours. Recipient Nat. Leadership award, NRCC, 2006. Mem.: APA, Internat. Neuropsychological Soc., Tidewater Acad. Clin. Psychologists, Nat. Acad. Neuropsychology, Va. Assn. Clin. Psychologists, Va. Psychol. Assn. Office: Ste B 2010 Old Greenbrier Rd Chesapeake VA 23320

SARI, ROBERT B., lawyer, retail executive; b. 1956; BA, U. Mich.; JD, Cleve.-Marshall Coll. Law. Bar: Calif. 1981. V.p. legal affairs Thrifty PayLess, Inc., 1994—97; assoc. counsel Rite Aid Corp., Camp Hill, Pa., 1997—2000, v.p. legal affairs, 2000, sr. v.p., dep. gen. counsel, sec., 2000—02, sr. v.p., gen. counsel, sec., 2002—05, exec. v.p., gen. counsel, sec., 2005—. Office: Rite Aid Corp 30 Hunter Lane Camp Hill PA 17011 Office Phone: 717-975-5833. E-mail: rsari@riteaid.com. *

SARIC, WILLIAM SAMUEL, aerospace engineering educator; b. Chgo., Sept. 28, 1940; s. Sam and Antonia (Cerovac) S.; m. Carol Powlick, Aug. 25, 1962 (div. Aug. 1987); 1 child, William George; m. Helen L. Reed, Mar. 17, 1990. BSME, Ill. Inst. Tech., 1963, PhD in Mechanics, 1968; MSME, U. N.Mex., 1965. Registered profl. engr., Va. Instr. Ill. Inst. Tech., Chgo., 1966-68; assoc. prof. Va. Poly. Inst. and State U., Blacksburg, 1975-79, prof., 1979-84, Tohoku U., Sendai, Japan, 1991-92; prof. mech. engring. Ariz. State U., Tempe, 1984—2005, prof. emeritus, 2005—; prof. aerospace engring. Tex. A&M U., College Station, 2005—. Mem. fluid dynamics panel AGARD/NATO, 1989-95. Contbr. over 100 articles to profl. jours., chpts. to books. Recipient Sci. Achievement award AGARD/NATO, 1996, G.I. Taylor medal Soc. Engring. Sci., 1993, Alumni award for rsch. excellence Va. Poly. Inst. and State U., 1984. Fellow AIAA (assoc., mem. tech. com. fluid dynamics 1975-78), AMSE (chmn. applied mech. divsn. 1991-92), Am. Phys. Soc. (exec. com. divsn. fluid dynamics 1985-86); mem. NAE. Office: Tex A&M U Engring 3126 TAMU College Station TX 77843 Office Phone: 979-862-1749. E-mail: saric@tamu.edu.

SARICH, DREW, actor; b. St. Louis, Mo., Aug. 24, 1975; m. Ann Mandrella; 2 children. BFA in Musical Theatre, concentration in Directing, Boston Conservatory, 1993—97. Actor: (Broadway plays) Lestat, 2006, Les Miserables, 2006; (plays) Pirates of Penzance, 1995, Forever Plaid, 1996, Hello, Dolly!, 1997, Joseph and the Amazing Technicolor Dreamcoat, 1997, Joan of Arc, 1997, Sugar Suite, 1998, Tony 'n' Tina's Wedding, 1998, Hunchback of Notre Dame, 1999, Rhythm of Life, 2001, Hair, 2002, Tommy, 2002, Leading Man, 2002, Fever, 2002, Hedwig and the Angry Inch, 2002, Lap Dog 'n' Wild Cat, 2003, Jekyll and Hyde, 2003, Barbarella, 2004, Jesus Christ Superstar, 2005, Dracula, 2005, Iz, 2005, Lestat, 2005, Jacques Brel is Alive and Well and Living in Paris, 2006; performer: (albums) Say It, 2000; lead singer (punk/rock band) International Victim. *

SARICKS, CHRISTOPHER LEE, retired transportation analyst; b. Columbus, Ohio, Apr. 19, 1948; s. Ambrose and Reese (Pyott) S.; m. Joyce E. Goering, Aug. 21, 1971; children: Brendan James, Margaret Katherine. BA summa cum laude, U. Kans., 1970; MPhil, London Sch. Econs., Eng., 1973. Dir. environ. planning Chgo. Area Transp. Study, 1975-77, regional planning consistency coord., 1977-78; group leader, planning and assessment Pacific Environ. Svcs., Elmhurst, Ill., 1978-79; assoc. transp. systems planner Argonne (Ill.) Nat. Lab., 1979-84, environ. scientist, 1984—2003, ret., 2003; evaluation mgr. NE Ill. ITS Project, 1995-96. Rsch. project rev. and oversight panels Transp. Rsch. Bd., Washington, 1994—, air quality com., 1988—; mem. working group NAS, 1997—. Contbr. articles to profl. jours. Little League coach Downers Grove, Ill., 1991-92; v.p. Artists Showcase West, Downers Grove, 1988-90, 94-96. Recipient Argonne Pacesetter award Argonne Nat. Lab., 1987, Winner Nat. Pub. Radio, 1987; Marshall scholar, 1970-73. Mem. Air Waste Mgmt. Assn. (land use and transp. com. chair 1988-91, mobile sources com. 1991—, chair 1998—, transp. divsn. dir. 2001-03), Delta Upsilon (Outstanding Alumni Kans. chpt. 1994). Avocations: hiking, biking, reading, trivia games, piano playing. Home: 1116 61st St Downers Grove IL 60516-1819 Office: Argonne Nat Lab ES-362/2B 9700 Cass Ave # 2B Argonne IL 60439-4803 E-mail: csaricks@anl.ogv.

SARICKS, JOYCE GOERING, librarian; b. Nov. 8, 1948; d. Joe W. and Lovella Goering; m. Christopher L. Saricks, Aug. 21, 1971; children: Brendan James, Margaret Katherine. BA with highest distinction in English and German, U. Kans., 1970; MA in Comparative Lit., U. Wis., 1971; MA/MAT in LS, U. Chgo., 1977. Reference librarian Downers Grove Pub. Library, Ill., 1977-80, head tech. svcs., 1980-83, coord. lit. and audio svcs., 1983—2004; ret., 2004. Columnist Booklist Mag.; adj. prof. Dominican U., River Forest, Ill; lectr., presenter workshops in field. Author: (with Nancy Brown) Readers' Advisory Service in the Public Library, 1989, revised edit., 1997, 3d edit., 2005, The Readers' Advisory Guide to Genre Fiction, 2001. Mem. Read Ill. adv. com., 1990-91. Woodrow Wilson fellow, 1970; recipient Allie Beth Martin award Pub. Library Assn., 1989, No. Ill. Libr. of Yr. award Windy City Romance Writers, 1995, Libr. of the Yr. award Romance Writers of Am., 2000. Mem. ALA, Ill. Library Assn., Adult Reading Round Table (founder), Phi Beta Kappa, Delta Phi Alpha, Pi Lambda Theta, Beta Phi Mu. Home: 1116 61st St Downers Grove IL 60516-1819 E-mail: saricksj@juno.com.

SARINO, EDGARDO FORMANTES, radiologist, physician; b. Laoag City, Ilocos Norte, Philippines, Nov. 6, 1940; came to U.S., 1965, naturized, 1983; s. Epafrodito Cruze and Esperanza Raval Formantes S.; m. Milagros Felix Ona, Dec. 6, 1965; chldren: Edith Melanie, Edgar Michael, Edenn Michele. MD, U. of the East, 1964; MBA in Healthcare Svcs. Mgmt. Emphasis, W.Va. U., 1999. Diplomate Am. Bd. Radiology. Rotating intern St. Clare's Hosp., NYC, 1965-66; resident in anatomical pathology Coney Island Hosp, NYC, 1966; resident in gen. surgery Manhattan VA Hosp., NYC, 1966-67, U. Bellevue Med. Ctr., NYC, 1967-68; resident in radiology Manhattan VA Hosp., NYC, 1968-71; fellow in diagnostic radiology, 1968-71; staff radiologist Mercer Med. Ctr., Trenton, N.J., 1973-83; chief nuclear medicine svc. Louis Johnson VA Med. Ctr., Clarksburg, W. Va., 1983-93, acting chief radiology svc., 1988-92, chief imaging svc., 1993—, assoc. chief staff imaging, 1998—; clin. assoc. prof. radiology U. W.Va. Sch. Med., 1989—; teaching asst. gen. surgery N.Y.U.-Bellevue Med. Ctr., NYC, 1967-68. Contbr. articles to med. jours. Recipient Cert. of Merit Mallinkrodt Pharm., 1969. Mem. Am. Coll. Physician Execs., Soc. Nuclear Med., Am. Coll. Radiology, Radiol. Soc. N.Am., Harrison County Med. Soc., W. Va. Radiol. Soc., Assn. Phillipine Practicing Physicians in Am. Philippine Radiol. Soc. Am. Office: Louis Johnson VA Med Ctr Clarksburg WV 26301 Home: 12 Canoa Hills Dr Henderson NV 89052-6634 E-mail: efsarino@msn.com.

SARJEANT, WALTER JAMES, electrical and computer engineering educator; b. Strathroy, Can., Apr. 7, 1944; s. Walter Burns and Margaret (Laurie) S.; m. Ann Richards, June 30, 1972; children: Eric, Cheryl. BSc in Math, Physics, U. Western Ont., Can., 1966, MSc in Physics, 1967, PhD in Physics, 1971. Asst. dir. R&D Gen-Tec Inc., Quebec City, Que., Canada, 1971-73; program mgr. Lumonics Rsch. Ltd., Ottawa, Ont., Canada, 1973-75; staff scientist Nat. Rsch. Coun., Ottawa, Ont., Canada, 1975-78; project leader Los Alamos (N.Mex.) Nat. Lab., 1978-81; James Clerk Maxwell prof. elec. engring. SUNY, Buffalo, 1981—. Dir. High Power Electronics Inst. Author: High Power Electronics, 1989. Fellow IEEE; mem. Electromagnetics Acad., Electrostatics Soc., N.Y. Acad. Scis., Rotary, Eta Kappa Nu. Office: SUNY Elec Engring Dept PO Box 601900 312 Bonner Hall Buffalo NY 14260-1900 Home: 5854 Main St Apt 305 Williamsville NY 14221-5745

SARKAR, MALANCHA, research scientist, educator; d. Dhirendranath and Chobbi Sarkar; m. Subbarayan Ramalingam Pochi; children: Shuvam-Bharathy Subbarayan Pochi, Bhargavi Subbarayan Pochi. BSc, Ranchi U., India, 1989; MSc, Banaras Hindu U., India, 1991, PhD, 1995. Rsch. assoc. Miller Sch. Medicine U. Miami, 2006—, lectr. dept. biology, 2007. Sci. specialist Sunshine State Standards, Fla. Dept. Edn. Author research papers. Recipient Indian Scientist, Internat. Union of Biochemistry and Molecular Biology, 1994; Postdoctoral Fellowship, Sci. and Tech. Agy., Japan, 1995. Home Phone: 305-273-0009; Office Phone: 305-284-3879.

SARKAR, RAJABRATA, surgeon; b. Boston, May 23, 1966; s. Satyapriya and Nilima Sarkar; m. Minakshi Bose, Feb. 8, 1992; children: Amrita, Malini. MD, U. Mich., Ann Arbor, 1990, PhD, 1995. Lic. surgeon Am. Bd. Surgery, 1999, vascular surgeon Am. Bd. Surgery, 2000. Resident in surgery U. Calif., LA, 1990—98; fellow in vascular surgery U. Mich., 1998—99; asst. prof. surgery U. Calif., San Francisco, 1999—2006, assoc. prof. surgery, 2006—. Dir. vascular lab. UCSF Med. Ctr., San Francisco, 2006—07. Study sect. mem. NIH, Bethesda, Md., 2006—07. Recipient Wylie Scholar award, Pacific Vascular Rsch. Found., 2005—; grantee K08 Career Devel. award, NIH, 2000—05, Rsch. grant, US Dept. Def., 2005—, R01 Rsch. grant, NIH, 2006—. Fellow: ACS; mem.: Assn. Academic Surgery, We. Vascular Soc., Soc. Vascular Surgery. Achievements include research in in arterial blockages. Office: UCSF Dept Surgery 4150 Clement St 112G San Francisco CA 94121 Office Fax: 415-750-2181.

SARKAR, SANDIP, telecommunications industry executive, researcher; b. Calcutta, India, Feb. 23, 1969; arrived in U.S., 1992; s. Pradip and Purabi Sarkar; m. Mahasweta Ghosh, July 22, 1996; 1 child, Aarjish Neil. B Mus, Calcutta, India, 1985; B Tech, Indian Inst. of Tech., Kanpur, India, 1992; MA, Princeton U., Princeton, NJ, 1994, PhD, 1996. Sr engr. to staff engr., mgr. Qualcomm Inc., San Diego, Calif., 1996—2004, mgr., sr. staff engr., 2004—. Reviewer IEEE, Piscataway, NJ, 1996—; mem., rev. bd. Signal Processing, Lausanne, Switzerland, 1998—; organizing com. ICPWC, New Delhi, 2001—02; chair 3GPP2 Text Group. Editor: (cdma2000 wireless standard) Rev C, Rev D, Band Class Standard, (tia standards) Tia-1030, Is-2000; contbr. articles pub. to profl. jour. Recipient Merit Award, Indian Inst. of Tech., Kanpur, 1990, 1991, Outstanding Achievement award, Qualcomm, Inc., 2000, Qualstar award; fellow, Indian Statis. Inst., 1988; grantee Sci. Talent Search, NSTS, 1986; scholar, Princeton U., 1992-1996. Mem.: IEEE. Achievements include patents for Over 10 US patents, many worldwide patents; patents pending for Over 20 patents pending (USA and worldwide); design of Reverse Link Design of cdma2000; first to Development of 1xEV-DV; development of Globalstar System. Office: Qualcomm Incorp 5775 Morehouse Dr San Diego CA 92131 Home Phone: 858-578-3535; Office Phone: 858-651-2357. Office Fax: 858-658-5006; Home Fax: 858-658-5006. Personal E-mail: ssarkar@qualcomm.com.

SARKAR, SUBRATA, medical educator; m. Indira Bhagat, June 5, 1993; children: Siddhartha, Avishek, Rohan. MBBS, U. Calcutta, 1984; MD, Mt. Sinai Sch. Medicine, Bklyn., 2001. Cert. Am. Bd. Pediat., 2001, sub-bd. neonatal-perinatal medicine Am. Bd. Pediat., 2003. Clin. instr. SUNY, Stony Brook, 2001—03; clin. asst. prof. pediat. U. Mich. Health Sys., Ann Arbor, 2003—. Mentor medical students, residents, fellows U. Mich., Ann Arbor. Mem.: Soc. Pediatric Rsch. (assoc.). Office: Univ Mich Health Sys 1500 E Medical Center Dr Ann Arbor MI 48109-0254

SARKIS, ZIAD JOSEPH, private equity executive; b. Beirut, July 8, 1968; arrived in France, 1975; s. Nicolas and Claude (Moussalli) Sarkis; m. Elisabeth Kalman, June 21, 1997; 4 children. BAS in Anthropology, Econs. and Math. with distinction and honors, Stanford U., 1990, MS in Engring. and Mgmt., 1990; PhD in Econs., Oxford U., Eng., 1998. Cons. McKinsey & Co., San Francisco, 1990, NYC, 1991—92, Paris, 1992; ptnr. AT Kearney, NYC, London, Paris, 1992—94; co-founder, sr. ptnr., bd. dirs. Mitchell Madison Group, NYC, London, Paris, 1992—2000; ptnr. PAI Ptnrs. (formerly Paribas Affaires Industrielles), London, Paris, 2001—. Bd. dirs. Yoplait. Greek Catholic. Office: PAI Ptnrs 28 Old Brompton Rd Ste 320 London SW73SS England Business E-Mail: ziad.sarkis@paipartners.co.uk.

SARKOZY, OLIVIER (PIERRE OLIVIER SARKOZY), investment banker; b. May 26, 1969; Mng. dir. Credit Suisse First Boston, NYC; global head, banks, fin. inst. group UBS Warburg, NYC, 2002—. Recipient Rainmaker prize, Dealmaker mag., 2006. Office: UBS Warburg 1285 Ave of Americas New York NY 10019 Office Phone: 800-221-3260. *

SARLE, CHARLES RICHARD, health facility executive; b. Saratoga Springs, NY, Sept. 21, 1944; s. John Robert and Marjorie Elizabeth (Swick) S.; m. Marion D. Wallace, June 21, 1968; children: Richard Charles, Robert Edmond. BBA cum laude, Northea. U., 1968; MBA, Babson Coll., 1973. CPA, Mass., Vt. Staff acct. Price Waterhouse & Co., Boston, 1968-70, George Kanavich, CPA, Wellesley, Mass., 1970-72; controller Human Resource Inst., Boston, 1972-73, adminstr., 1973-77; controller Brattleboro (Vt.) Retreat, 1977-78, dir. adminstrn., 1978-85, v.p., 1985-88, chief exec. officer, 1988-97; pres., CEO Carrier Clinic, Belle Mead, NJ, 1997—. Speaker in field. Mem. commn. Vt. Health Bldg. Fin. Agy., 1978—90; trustee Austine Sch. for Deaf and Hard of Hearing, 1990—97, pres., 1994—97; trustee Winston Prouty Ctr. for Child Devel., 1982—97, treas., 1983—90, sec., 1991—97; trustee Health Rsch. and Edn. Trust NJ, 1998—99, NJ Hosp. Assn., 2000—06, policy devel. com., 1998—2001, fin. com., 2000—; bd. govs. NCCJ, 1998—2003, exec. com., 1999—2003. Recipient recognition award Brattleboro C. of C., 1985. Fellow AICPA, Mass. Soc. CPA, Am. Coll. Healthcare Execs. (regent Va. br. 1991-95); mem. Am. Hosp. Assn. (del.-at-large 1988-92, del.-at-large to regional policy bd.), Nat. Assn. Pvt. Psychiat. Hosps. (bd. dirs. polit. action com. 1983-93, trustee 1998-2000), Nat. Psychiat. Alliance (trustee 1989-96, pres. 1994-96), Vt. Soc. CPA (Cmty. Svc. award 1984), Hosp. Fin. Mgmt. Assn. (hosp. cost com. 1985-96), Rescue, Inc. (trustee 1982-83), New Eng. Healthcare Assembly (trustee 1995-97). Avocations: skiing, fishing, tennis, photography. Home: PO Box 840 Belle Mead NJ 08502-0840 Office: Carrier Clinic Rt 601 Belle Mead NJ 08502 E-mail: rsarle@carrierclinic.com.

SARLES, RICHARD R., rail transportation executive; b. Passaic, NJ, Mar. 10, 1945; 3 children. B in Engring., The Cooper Union; MBA, Rutgers U. V.p. Amtrak, 1996—2002; profl. engr. Port Authority NY; asst. exec. dir. capital programs and planning NJ TRANSIT, Newark, 2002—07, exec. dir., 2007—. Office: NJ TRANSIT Corp One Penn Plz E Newark NJ 07108 *

SARMA, PALLAV, research scientist; arrived in US, 2001; s. Bhubaneswar Sarma and Rajeswari Devi; m. Nidhi Gupta, Dec. 27, 2003. BTech in Petroleum Engring., Indian Sch. Mines, Dhanbad, 2000; MS in Petroleum Engring., Stanford U., Calif., 2003, PhD in Petroleum Engring., 2006. Internship Oil & Natural Gas Corp., Ahmedabad, Gujrat, India, 1998, Enron Oil & Gas India Ltd., Mumbai, Maharashtra, India, 1999, Schlumberger Abingdon Tech. Ctr., Abingdon, Oxford, 2002, ExxonMobil Upstream Rsch. Co., Houston, 2003—03, Chevron Energy Tech. Co., San Ramon, Calif., 2005; reservoir engr. Schlumberger GeoQuest, Mumbai, 2000—01; rsch. scientist Chevron Energy Tech. Co., San Ramon, Calif., 2006—. Tech. editor SPE Jour., Stanford, 2005, Sci. Tech. and Future, Stanford, 2005; reviewer Jour. Computational Physics, Stanford, 2005, Computational Geoscis., Stanford, 2005. Contbr. articles to profl. jours. Recipient Ann. Rsch. Excellence award, Soc. Indsl. & Applied Math., 2005; grantee Chevron scholarship, Chevron Corp., 2004—05; Miller Fellowship, Stanford U., 2002, Ramey Fellowship, 2006. Mem.: European Assn. Geologists & Engrs., Can. Petroleum Soc., Soc. Petroleum Engrs. Achievements include development of an optimal control software ResOpt in use by many oil companies; research in the application of Kernel PCA to reservoir engineering problems; development of new mathematical models for dual porosity reservoir simulation; new and efficient algorithms for closed-loop control of petroleum reservoirs for maximixing oil and gas recovery. Home Phone: 650-804-2832.

SARNAT, BERNARD GEORGE, plastic surgeon, educator, researcher; b. Chgo., Sept. 1, 1912; s. Isadore M. and Fanny (Silverman) S.; m. Rhoda Elaine Gerard, Dec. 25, 1941; children: Gerard, Joan. SB, U. Chgo., 1933, MD, 1937; MS, DDS, U. Ill., 1940. Diplomate Am. Bd. Plastic Surgery, 1947. Intern Los Angeles County Gen. Hosp., 1936-37; resident oral and plastic surgery Cook County Hosp., Chgo., 1940-41; asst. to Dr. Marshall Davison (gen. surgery) Univ. Hosp., Chgo., 1942-43; asst. to Drs. Vilray P. Blair and Louis T. Byars (plastic and reconstructive surgery), St. Louis, 1943-46; practice medicine specializing in plastic surgery Chgo., 1946-56, Beverly Hills, Calif., 1956-91; asst. histology U. Ill. Coll. Dentistry, 1937-40, prof., head dept. oral and maxillofacial surgery, 1946-56; asst. dept. surgery, divsn. plastic surgery Washington U. Sch. Medicine, St. Louis, 1944-46; prof., dir. dept. oral and plastic surgery St. Louis U. Coll. Dentistry, 1945-46; clin. asst. prof. surgery (plastic surgery) U. Ill. Coll. Medicine, 1949-56; adj. prof. oral biology Sch Dentistry UCLA, 1969—, mem. Dental Rsch. Inst., 1974-95, adj. prof. plastic surgery Sch. Medicine, 1974—; attending staff Cedars-Sinai Med. Ctr., LA, 1956-91, emeritus, 1991—, mem. staff, sr. rsch. scientist, chief plastic surgery, 1961-81. Cons. in gen., plastic and maxillofacial surgery VA Regional Office, Chgo., 1956; lectr. in field. Sr. author: (with Isaac Schour) Oral and Facial Cancer, 2d edit., 1957, (with Daniel Laskin) Surgery of the Temporomandibular Joint, 1964; editor: (with Daniel Laskin) The Temporomandibular Joint A Biological Basis for Clinical Practice, 4th edit., 1991, (with Andrew D. Dixon) Factors and Mechanisms Affecting Growth of Bone, 1982, Normal and Abnormal Bone Growth: Basic and Clinical Research, 1985, Fundamentals of Bone Growth: Methodology and Applications, 1991; contbr. chpts. to books, articles to profl. jours. Co-winner Joseph A. Capps prize for med. rsch. Inst. Medicine, Chgo., 1940, Frederick B. Noyes prize, 1940; recipient Kerbs award for rsch. plastic and reconstructive surgery, 1950, 1st prize, sr. award Found. Am. Soc. Plastic and Reconstructive surgeons, 1957, Beverly Hills Acad. of Medicine award, 1959, Nat. Achievement award medicine Phi Epsilon Pi, 1964, 1st prize Am. Rhinologic Soc., 1980, medal Hebrew U., Jerusalem, 1985, medal Tel Aviv U., 1985, Disting. Svc. Alumni award U. Chgo. Pritzker Sch. Medicine, 1987, hon. award Am. Soc. Maxillofiacial Surgeons, 1990, Dallas B. Phemister Profl. Achievement award Dept. Surgery U. Chgo., 1993, Disting. Alumnus award U. Ill. Coll. Dentistry, 1994, Craniofacial Biology Rsch. award Internat. Assn. for Dental Rsch., 1995, Disting. Scientist award, Pioneer in Medicine award Cedars-Sinai Med. Ctr., L.A., 1999, Profl. Achievement citation U. Chgo. Alumni Assn., 2003, citatioon of excellence in rsch. Plastic Surgery Ednl. Found., 2003, Profl. Achievement award U. Ill. Alumni Assn., 2004. Fellow ACS, AAAS, Am. Assn. Plastic Surgeons (hon. award 1993); mem. Calif. Med. Soc., L.A. Med. Soc., Am. Soc. Plastic and Reconstructive Surgeons, Plastic Surgery Rsch. Coun. (founding mem., chmn. 1957), Am. Soc. Maxillofacial Surgeons (hon.), Calif. Soc. Plastic Surgeons, Beverly Hills Acad. Medicine (pres. 1962-63), Internat. Assn. Craniofacial Biology, Am. Assn. Pediat. Plastic Surgeons (hon.), Am. Assn. Phys. Anthropologists, Internat. Assn. Study Dento-Facial Abnormalities (hon.), Sigma Xi, Omicron Kappa Upsilon, Zeta Beta Tau, Phi Delta Epsilon, Alpha Omega (Internat. Achievement medal 1988). Home: 1875 Kelton Ave Apt 301 Los Angeles CA 90025-8505

SARNE, ANDREW J., lawyer; b. Houston, Jan. 28, 1971; BBA, Tex. Tech U., 1992; JD, South Tex. Coll. Law, 1996. Bar: Tex. 1996, US Dist. Ct. (all dists. Tex.), US Ct. Appeals (5th cir.). Ptnr Godwin, Pappas & Ronquillo, LLP, Houston. Named a Rising Star, Tex. Super Lawyers mag., 2004—06; named one of Houston's Top Lawyers, H Tex. Mag., 2005—07. Mem.: Tex. Young Lawyers Assn., Houston Young Lawyers Assn. Office: Godwin Pappas Ronquillo LLP 5 Houston Ctr Ste 2700 1401 McKinney St Houston TX 77010 Office Phone: 713-425-7400. Business E-Mail: asarne@godwinpappas.com.

SARNEK, PETER CLIVE, mathematics professor; b. Johannesburg, Dec. 18, 1953; BSc, U. Witwatersrand, 1974, BSc with honors, 1975; PhD, Stanford U., 1980. Asst. prof. Courant Inst. Math. Sciences, NYU, 1980—83, assoc. prof., 1983—84, Stanford U., 1984—87, prof., 1987—91; fellow Inst. Advanced Studies, Hebrew U., 1987—88; Sherman Fairchild Disting. Scholar Calif. Inst. Tech., 1989; prof. Princeton U., NJ, 1991—, H. Fine prof. NJ, 1995—96, chair, dept. math. NJ, 1996—99, Eugene Higgins prof. math. NJ, 2002—; mem. Inst. for Advanced Study, Princeton, NJ, 1999—2002, 2005—07; prof. Courant Inst., NYU, 2001—05. Mem. adv. com. NSF, 1988—92; trustee Math. Sciences Rsch. Inst., mem. scientific adv. com., 1990—96; mem. sci. adv. com. Institut des Hautes Etudes Scientifiques, France, 1997—2003; mem. scientific adv. bd. Field Inst., 2000, 03; chair, adv. panel Am. Inst. Math., 2002—06; mem. vis. overnight com., 1993—; lectr. in field. Contbr. scientific papers, articles to profl. jours.; mem. editl. bd. Cambridge University Press, Duke Math. Journal, Geometric & Functional Analysis, Composito Mathematics, Annals of Mathematics, Journal of Experimental Mathematics, Forum Mathematics, Communications in Mathematical Physics, IMRN, Colloquium Series, Am. Math. Soc. Recipient George Polya prize, 1998. Fellow: Royal Soc. (UK); mem.: NAS, Am. Acad. Arts & Sciences. Office: Princeton U Dept Math 1101 Fine Hall Washington Rd Princeton NJ 08544-1000 Fax: (609) 258-1367. *

SARNELLE, JOSEPH R., publishing executive; b. Bklyn., Aug. 24, 1951; s. Alphonse Louis and Julie Lena (Mingarelli) S.; m. Ruth Patricia Cullen, Aug. 5, 1982 (dec.); children: Cullen Joseph, D'Arcy Emilie. BA, Cornell U., 1973; postgrad., Sch. Visual Arts, NYC, 1976—77, The New Sch., 1979—80. Graphic artist Lewahl KC Graphics, NYC, 1974-76; editor United Bus. Publs., NYC, 1976-79; mng. editor Lebhar-Friedman Inc., NYC, 1979-88; assoc. mng. editor HomeOwner Mag., NYC, 1988-90; mgr. online sys. devel. Info. Builders Inc., NYC, 1990—. Cons. video Markham-Novelle Pub. Rels., NYC, 1988—89; cons. Best info. Family Media, NYC, 1990—91. Author, dir. (videos) J. Roland Pepe's Guide to New York City, 1980, Underground Roundup, 1981. McMullen scholar, Cornell U., Regents scholar, State of N.Y., 1969; recipient Best Headline of Yr. award Lebhar-Friedman Inc., 1982. Office: Info Builders Inc 2 Penn Plz New York NY 10121 E-mail: joe_sarnelle@ibi.com.

SARNER, RICHARD ALAN, lawyer; b. Stamford, Conn., Aug. 6, 1955; s. George and Patricia (Sloman) S.; m. Sharyn Frank, Apr. 5, 1986; children: Bryan, Lauren. BA, Dartmouth Coll., 1977; JD, Hofstra U., 1980. Bar: NY 1982, US Dist. Ct. (so. and ea. dists.) NY 1982, US Ct. Appeals (2d cir.) 1985, US Dist. Ct. (no. dist.) NY 1989, Conn. 1990, US Dist. Ct. Conn. 1991, US Supreme Ct. 1991, US Tax Ct. 1997. Assoc. Shea & Gould, NYC, 1980-82, D'Amato & Lynch, NYC, 1982-84, Lowenthal, Landau, Fischer & Ziegler, P.C., NYC, 1984-90; sole practice Stamford, Conn., NYC, Conn., 1990—. Contbg. author Giving: Philanthropy for Everyone, 2002, Love, Money Control: Reinventing Estate Planning-Practical Answers from America's Foremost Estate Plannig Advisors, 2004. Bd. dirs. The Stamford Mus. and Nature Ctr., 1993-99; trustee King & Low-Heywood Thomas Sch., 1994-2005; sec., coun., bd. dirs. JCEF, 2006—. Mem. ABA, N.Y. State Bar Assn., Conn. Bar Assn., Fairfield County Bar Assn., WealthCounsel, LLC. Democrat. Home: 122 Frost Pond Rd Stamford CT 06903-3031 Office: 184 Atlantic St Stamford CT 06901-3518 also: 465 Park Ave Ste 10C New York NY 10022 Office Phone: 203-967-8899. Business E-Mail: rsarner@sarnerlaw.com.

SARNO, CHRISTOPHER ED, writer; b. NYC, Jan. 25, 1932; s. Christopher and Florence (Shanahan) Sarno. Grad. high sch., Medford, 1950. Mem. Medford (Mass.) Police Dept., 1958-80. Contbg. author: Tank Aces: The U.S. Marine Corps in Korea, 1951, Korean Vignettes: Faces of War, 1951, The Red Dragon: Second Round, 101 Seastories, US Marines in Korea, 1952; author (sound recordings): You'll Be Soorree, R&R in Japan, 1954; contbr. 17 articles to mil. history publs.; author: (memoir) You'll Be Soorree (published on www.koreanwar-educator.org). Charter mem. Nat. Mus. Marine Corps. With Fleet Marine Force USMC, 1950—55, Korea, Japan. Named Citizen of Yr., VFW Medford, 1972; recipient Medal of Valor, New Eng. Chief of Police Assn., 1972. Mem.: DAV (life), Nat. Mus. Marine Corps, USMC Tankers Assn., 1st Marine Divsn. Assn. (life), Semper Fidelis Soc. Boston, Disabled Am. Vets. Assn. (life). Republican. Roman Catholic. Avocations: tennis, travel, writing, reading, gardening. Home: 12 Butler St Medford MA 02155-1856 Personal E-mail: gungho_guy@hotmail.com, gungho_guy@lycos.com.

SARNO, MARIA ERLINDA, lawyer, chemist; BS in Chemistry magna cum laude, U. Santo Tomas, Manila, 1967; MS in Chemistry summa cum laude, Calif. State U., Long Beach, 1975; JD cum laude, Western State U., Fullerton, Calif., 1993. Bar: Calif. 1994, U.S. Patent Office, 1993. Instr. U. Santo Tomas, Philippines, 1967—68; sr. chemist, analytical rsch. and quality assurance Rachelle Labs., Long Beach, 1968—74; tchg., rsch. asst. Calif. State U., Long Beach, 1971—73; mgr. in charge of radioisotope sect. Curtis Nuc. Lab., LA, 1974; assoc. chemist, asst. to dir. quality control Nichols Inst., San Pedro, Calif., 1974—75; mgr. R & D Baxter Healthcare, Hyland, Calif., 1975—91; legal coord. sci. affairs Immunotherapy divsn. Baxter Biotech., Irvine, Calif., 1991—93, mgr. regulatory affairs, 1994—95; pvt. practice, 1994—; bd. dirs. Small Bus. Fin. Devel. Corp. Small bus. coun. Calif. Dept. Gen. Svcs. Mem. editl. bd.: (tech. editor) We. State U. Law Rev.; contbr. articles to profl. jours.; patentee in field. Pres. Asian Bus. Assn. Orange County, 2001; coun. mem. Small Bus. Coun., 2006-, Calif. Dept. Gen. Svcs. Mem. ABA, L.A. County Bar Assn., Am. Chem. Soc., Am. Intellectual Property Law Assn., Nat. Coun. Asian Am. Bus. Assn. (bd. dirs., v.p.), Filipino Am. C. of C. Orange County (pres. 2003-05). Office Phone: 310-612-6637. Personal E-mail: lindasarno@aol.com.

SARNOFF, ANN M., publishing executive, former sports association executive; b. Nov. 2, 1961; m. Richard I. Sarnoff; 2 children. BS in Mktg., Georgetown Univ., 1983; MBA, Harvard Bus. Sch., 1987. Strategic consul. Marakon Assoc., Stamford, Conn., 1987—93; v.p. bus. develop. Nickelodeon, 1994, exec. v.p. consumer products, bus. develop.; dir. corp. devel. Viacom, 1993—94, COO, VH1, Country Music Television, 2001—04; COO WNBA, 2004—05; pres. Dow Jones Ventures, NYC, 2006—. Mem. bd. trustees Georgetown Univ. McDonough Sch. Bus. Office: Dow Jones & Co 1 World Fin Ctr 200 Liberty St New York NY 10281

SARNOFF, LILI-CHARLOTTE (LOLO SARNOFF), artist; b. Frankfurt, Germany (as Swiss citizen), Jan. 9, 1916; arrived in U.S., 1940; d. Willy and Martha (Koch von Hirsch) Dreyfus; m. Stanley Jay Sarnoff, 1948; children: Daniela Martha Bargezi, Robert L. Grad., Reimann Art Sch., Germany, 1936, U. Berlin, 1938; student, U. Florence, Italy, 1936—38; DFA (hon.), Corcoran Coll. Art & Design, 2003. With Red Cross Swiss Motor Corps, 1939—40; Red Cross nurse Bellevue Hosp., NYC, 1942—47; rsch. asst. Harvard Sch. Pub. Health, 1950—54; rsch. assoc. cardiac physiology Nat. Heart Inst., Bethesda, Md., 1954—59; pres. Rodana Rsch. Corp., Bethesda, 1959—61; v.p. Catrix Corp., Bethesda, 1959—61; prin., owner Dara's Sr. Pets for Srs., 2003. Inventor Flolite light sculptures under name Lolo Sarnoff, 1968—; one-woman shows include Agra Gallery, Washington, 1969, Corning (N.Y.) Glass Ctr. Mus., 1970, Gallery Two, Woodstock, Vt., 1970, Gallery Marc, Washington, 1971, 1972, Franz Bader Gallery, 1976, Gallery K, 1978, 1981, 1985, 1987, 1991, Retrospective Show, 1995, Alwin Gallery, London, 1981, Galerie von Bartha, Basel, Switzerland, 1982, La Galerie L'Hotel de Ville, Geneva, 1982, Pfalzgalerie, Kaiserslautern, Germany, 1985, Galerie Les Hirondelles, Geneva, 1988, Represented in permanent collections. Founder, chmn. bd. Arts for Aging, Inc., Bethesda, 1988—; chmn. bd. Dara's Canine Found., Inc., 1999—. Recipient Golda Meir award, 1995, Life Commitment to Arts award, Swiss Am. Cultural Exch., 1999, Path of Achievement award for Arts and Humanities, Montgomery County, Md., 2000, Outstanding Citizen award, Iona Sr. Citizen Svcs., Washington, 2002, Chevalier de L'Ordre des Arts et Des Lettres, République Française, 2006. Home: 7507 Hampden Ln Bethesda MD 20814-1331 Personal E-mail: lolos@erols.com.

SARNOFF, THOMAS WARREN, television executive; b. NYC, Feb. 23, 1927; s. David and Lizette (Hermant) S.; m. Janyce Lundon, May 21, 1955; children: Daniel, Timothy, Cynthia. Grad., Phillips Acad., 1939-43; student, Princeton, 1943-45; BS in Elec. Engring., Stanford U., 1948, postgrad. Sch. Bus. Adminstrn., 1948-49; D.H.L., Columbia Coll. Engaged in prodn. and sales with ABC, Inc., 1949-51; prodn. Metro-Goldwyn-Mayer, 1951-52; with NBC, 1952-77; v.p. prodn. and bus. affairs NBC (Pacific div.), 1956-60, v.p. adminstrn. West Coast, 1960-62, v.p. charge West Coast, 1962-65, staff exec. v.p. West Coast, 1965-77; pres. NBC Entertainment Corp., 1972-77, Sarnoff Internat. Enterprises, 1977-81, Sarnoff Entertainment Corp., 1981—; exec. v.p. Venturetainment Corp., 1981-87, pres., 1987—. Bd. dirs. Multimedia Games, Inc., 1998-2006, chmn. bd., 2004-06, cons., 2006—. Exec. producer Bonanza: The Next Generation, 1987, Bonanza: The Return, 1993, Back to Bonanza Retrospective, 1993, Bonanza: Under Attack, 1995. Mem. Calif. Commn. for Reform Intermediate and Secondary Edn. Pres., Research Found., St. Joseph Hosp., Burbank, 1965-73, Permanant Charities Com. of Entertainment Industries, 1971-72; nat. trustee Nat. Conf. Christians and Jews. Served with Signal Corps AUS, World War II. Mem. Acad. TV Arts and Scis. (chmn. bd. trustees 1972-74, chmn. past pres.'s coun. 1989-92), Acad. TV Arts and Scis. Found. (pres. 1990-99, chmn., CEO 1999—2005, chmn. emeritus 2005-), The Caucus for Prodrs., Writers and Dirs. Office: 2451 Century Hl Los Angeles CA 90067-3510 Office Phone: 310-203-9234. Personal E-mail: tsarnoff@aol.com.

SAROFIM, FAYEZ SHALABY, finance company executive; b. Nov. 19, 1928; m. Louisa Stude (div. 1990); m. Linda Hicks (div. 1996); 5 children. BS in Food Technology, U. Calif., Berkley, 1949; MBA, Harvard, 1951. Founder, chmn., pres. Fayez Sarofim & Co., 1958—. Bd. mgr. Meml. Sloan-Kettering Cancer Ctr.; coun. mem. Rockefeller Univ.; bd. dir. Alley Theatre, Houston Ballet Found., Mus. Fine Arts, Houston; dir. Tex. Heart Inst. Named one of Top 200 Collectors, ARTnews, 2004—, 400 Richest Americans, Forbes, 2006. Mem.: Houston Symphony Soc. (former vice chmn. bd. dirs.). Avocation: collector of Coptic sculpture, Old Masters, 19th century art, Am. Impressionism, modern & contemporary art. Office: Fayez Sarofim & Co Ste 2907 Two Houston Ctr Houston TX 77010

SARREALS, SONIA, data processing executive, consultant; b. NYC, Sept. 17, 1938; d. Espriela and Sadie Beatrice (Scales) Sarreals; m. Waldro Lynch, Sept. 18, 1981 (div. Oct. 1983). BA in Langs. summa cum laude, CCNY, 1960; cert. in French, Sorbonne, Paris, 1961. Systems engr. IBM, NYC, 1963-69; cons. Babbage Systems, NYC, 1969-70; project leader Touche Ross, NYC, 1970-73; sr. programmer McGraw-Hill, Inc., Hightstown, NJ, 1973-78; staff data processing cons. Cin. Bell Info. Systems, 1978-89; sr. analyst AT&T, 1989-92; lead tech. analyst Automated Concepts Inc., Arlington, Va., 1992-96; tech. cons. Teksystems, Reston, Va., 1996—. Elder St. Andrew Luth. Ch., Silver Spring, 1992-96. Downer scholar CUNY, 1960; Dickman Inst. fellow Columbia U., 1960-61. Mem.: Assn. for Computing Machinery, Phi Beta Kappa. Democrat. Avocations: needlecrafts, sewing. Home: 13705 Beret Pl Silver Spring MD 20906-3030 Office: Teksystems 12343 Sunrise Valley Dr Reston VA 20191 Business E-Mail: ssarreals@teksystems.com.

SARRIS, ANDREW GEORGE, film critic; b. Bklyn., Oct. 31, 1928; s. George Andrew and Themis (Katavolos) S.; m. Molly Clark Haskell, May 31, 1969. AB, Columbia, 1951. Film critic Village Voice, NYC, 1960-89, N.Y. Observer, 1989—. Editor-in-chief Cahiers du Cinema in English; instr. Sch. Visual Arts, 1965-67; asst. prof. N.Y. U., 1967-69; assoc. prof. films Columbia Sch. Arts, N.Y.C., 1969-81, prof., 1981— Author: The Films of Josef Von Sternberg, 1966, Interviews with Film Directors, 1967, The Film, 1968 The American Cinema, 1968, Confessions of a Cultist, 1970, The Primal Screen, 1973, The John Ford Movie Mystery, 1976, Politics and Cinema, 1978. Served with Signal Corps AUS, 1952-54. Guggenheim fellow, 1969 Mem. Am. Film Inst. (dir.), Soc. Cinema Studies, Nat. Soc. Film Critics, N.Y. Film Critics. *I keep on working toward that last deadline.*

SARRY, CHRISTINE, ballerina; b. Long Beach, Calif., May 25, 1946; d. John and Beatrice (Thomas) S.; 1 child, Maximilian Sarry Varriale. With Joffrey Ballet, 1963—64, Am. Ballet Theatre, 1964—68, prin. dancer, 1971—74; leading dancer Am. Ballet Co., 1969—71; ballerina Eliot Feld Ballet, 1974—81. Dir. faculty Ballet Tech., NYC; also freelance guest tchr. Performed ballets for Agnes DeMille, Antony Tudor, Jerome Robbins, Twyla Tharp, Eliot Feld; appeared at White House, 1963, 67; U.S. Dept. State tours include, Russia, 1963, 66, S.Am., 1964, 76, various tours of N.Am., Orient, Europe, various appearances U.S. nat. TV; partnered by Mikhail Baryshnikov. Office Phone: 212-777-7710 x 307. E-mail: csarry@ballettech.org.

SARSGAARD, PETER, actor; b. Scott AFB, IL, Mar. 7, 1971; 1 child, Ramona. BA in History, Washington U., 1994. Actor: (off-Broadway plays) Kingdom of Earth, Laura Dennis; (films) Dead Man Walking, 1995, Minor Details, 1998, The Man in the Iron Mask, 1998, Desert Blue, 1998, Another Day in Paradise, 1998, Boys Don't Cry, 1999, The Cell, 2000, Housebound, 2000, The Center of the World, 2001, Bacon Wagon: The Movie, 2001, Empire, 2002, The Salton Sea, 2002, K-19: The Widowmaker, 2002, Unconditional Love, 2002, Death of a Dynasty, 2003, Shattered Glass, 2003, Garden State, 2004, Kinsey, 2004, The Dying Gaul, 2005, The Skeleton Key, 2005, Flightplan, 2005, Jarhead, 2005; (TV films) Freak City, 1999. Office: Creative Artists Agy 9830 Wilshire Blvd Beverly Hills CA 90212

SARSON, JOHN CHRISTOPHER, television producer, director, writer; b. London, Jan. 19, 1935; s. Arnold Wilfred and Annie Elizabeth (Wright) S.; m. Evelyn Patricia Kaye, Mar. 25, 1963 (div. 2005); children: Katrina May, David Arnold BA with honors, Trinity Coll., Cambridge, Eng., 1960, MA, 1963. Dir. Granada TV, Manchester, Eng., 1960-63; producer, dir. Sta. WGBH-TV, Boston, 1963-73; pres. Blue Penguin, Inc., Boulder, Colo., 1974—; v.p. TV programming Sta. WYNC-TV, NYC, 1989-90. Dir. Pub. Broadcasting Assocs., Newton, Mass.; cons. to numerous pub. TV stations Creator, producer MAsterpiece Theatre, PBS, 1970-73, Zoom, PBS, 1971-73; producer Live From the Met, PBS, 1977-79, Kid's Writes, Nickelodeon, 1982-83, American Treasure, a Smithsonian Journey, 1986, Spotlight Colorado, 1991, Parenting Works, 1993, 95-97, Club 303, 1994, Videographer Roots of Empathy, 1999—, Coo, 2004-2005. Served with Royal Navy, 1956-57 Recipient Emmy award, 1973, 74, Peabody award Ohio State U., 1978, Internat. Emmy award, 1983, Nat. Acad. TV Arts and Scis. Gov.'s award, 1991. Mem. Dirs. Guild Am., Nat. acad. TV Arts and Scis. (gov. Heartland chpt.), Windows on the Rockies User Group (pres.). Avocations: music, cooking, gardening, travel, computers. Home and Office: 2515 7th St Boulder CO 80304 Office Phone: 303-352-1959, 303-447-6457.

SARSYNSKI, ELAINE A., insurance company executive; Grad. in Econs., Smith Coll., Northampton, Mass.; MBA in Fin. and Acctg., Columbia U., NYC. With Aetna Life and Casualty, 1981—98, head real estate investments and mortgage fin. ops.; CEO Suffield Twp., Conn.; mng. dir., head portfolio mgmt. group Babson Capital Mgmt., 2005; sr. v.p. Mass. Mut. Life Ins. Co., Springfield, 2005—06, chief adminstrv. officer, 2005—, exec. v.p., 2006—; pres., CEO MassMutual Internat. LLC. Mem. Mass. Econ. Devel. Coun.; bd. trustees Baystate Health Inc., Springfield. Office: MassMutual Fin Group 1295 State St Springfield MA 01111-0001 Office Phone: 800-767-1000. *

SARTAIN, JAMES EDWARD, lawyer; b. Ft. Worth, Feb. 9, 1941; s. James F. and May Belle (Boaz) S.; m. Barbara Hardy, Aug. 17, 1962; 1 child, Bethany Sartain Hughes. BA, Tex. A&M U., 1963; LLB, Baylor U., 1966. Bar: Tex. 1966, U.S. Ct. Mil. Appeals, 1971, U.S. Dist. Ct. (no. dist.) Tex. 1974. Staff atty. Dept. Justice, Washington, 1970-72; staff atty. to U.S. Sen. William L. Scott Fairfax, Va., 1972; pvt. practice Ft. Worth, 1973—2001, Abilene, Tex., 2001—. Bd. dirs. Ft. Worth Boys Club, 1980-89, Oakwood Cemetery, Ft. Worth, 1979-84; adv. dir. Grady McWhinney Rsch. Found., Abilene, Tex., 12th Armored Divsn. Meml. Mus., Abilene. Capt. arty. U.S. Army, Vietnam. Fellow Coll. State Bar Tex.; mem. ABA, NRA, VFW, Abilene Bar Assn., Baylor Law Alumni Assn., Masons, Phi Delta Phi. Republican. Presbyterian. Home: PO Box 450 Abilene TX 79604-0450 Home Phone: 325-690-1129; Office Phone: 325-676-2492.

SARTAIN, LIBBY, human resources specialist; BA, So. Methodist U.; MBA, U. North Tex. Various positions Southwest Airlines, 1988—98, v.p. people, 1998—2001; sr. v.p. human resources, chief Yahoo!, Inc., Sunnyvale, Calif., 2001—. Fellow: Nat. Acad. Human Resources; mem.: Soc. Human Resource Mgmt. (former chmn.). Office: Yahoo Inc 701 1st Ave Sunnyvale CA 94089 Office Phone: 408-349-3300. Office Fax: 408-349-3301.

SARTOR, DANIEL RYAN, JR., lawyer; b. Vicksburg, Miss., June 2, 1932; s. Daniel Ryan and Lucy Leigh (Hubbs) S.; m. Olive Guthrie Moss, Oct. 12, 1957; children— Clara M., Daniel Ryan, Walter M. BA, Tulane U., 1952, LL.B., 1955. Bar: La. 1955. Instr. Tulane U., New Orleans, 1955-56, asst. prof., 1956-57; ptnr. Snellings, Breard, Sartor, Inabnett & Trascher, Monroe, La., 1957—2001, of coun., 2002—. Contbr. articles to profl. jours. Fellow Am. Coll. Trust and Estate Counsel, Am. Bar Found., La. Bar Found.; mem. La. State Law Inst. (mem. 1969—, sec. civil law sect. 1969-97, sr. officer 1997—), La. State Bar Assn. (chmn. sect. on trust estate, probate and immovable property 1973-74, bd. govs. 1974-75), Lotus Club, Bayou DeSiard Country Club. Democrat. Methodist. Home: 2405 Pargoud Blvd Monroe LA 71201-2326 Office: Snellings Breard Sartor 1503 N 19th St Monroe LA 71201-4960 Office Phone: 318-387-8000. Business E-Mail: rsartor@snellingslawfirm.com.

SARTOR, DAVID P., composer; b. Nashville, May 25, 1956; s. Grayl Bruce and Kathleen Lipscomb Sartor; m. Nancy White Sartor, Oct. 6, 1984; children: John Russell Laws, Sharon Rebecca Farrell. BMus with highest honors, U. Tenn., 1978. Composer: Veni Emmanuel-Fantasy of Abstractions, 1976, Medieval Manifesto for Unaccompanied Contrabass, 1977, Affectations for Brass Quintet, 1977, Variants For Solo Trombone, 1977, Open Door for Organ, 1977, Thrice Told Tales of the Pomegranate Forest for Trumpet, Violin and Bass Clarinet, 1978 (winner U Tenn.Chamber Music Composition, 1978, Contest award New Music For Young Ensembles, 1978), Illusions for Percussion Ensemble, 1981, O Worship the King for Orchestra, 1982, Synergistic Parable for Concert Band, 1985 (Ostwald award Am. Bandmasters Assn., 1987, Composition Contest award Appalachian State U., 87), Polygon for Brass Quintet, 1987 (Nat. Fine Arts award Ill., 1993), We Will be Glad for Chorus, Brass, Timpani and Organ, 1994, Prelude on William Billings' "When Jesus Wept" for Organ, 1996, Postlude on William Billings' "Paris" for Organ, 1996, Thy Light Is Come for Chorus, Brass, Timpani and Organ, 1997, Psalm 67 for Chorus, Organ and Trumpet, 1998, Metamorphic Fanfare for Orchestra, 2000 (Masterworks award), Concerto For Orchestra, 2001 (Masterworks award), Simple Blessing for Organ, 2002, Welcome, Christmas Day! for

Chorus and Instruments, 2002, Diplomatic Solution for 4 Violoncellos, 2003, Cat's Eye for Brass Ensemble, 2003, Black Ball Counts Double for Strings, 2003 (Masterworks award), Commendation, Oare Internat. Composing Contest, 2003, Fanfare A4 for Brass Quartet, 2003, Crown Him! for Chorus, Orchestra and Organ, 2004, Ascension for Brass and Timpani, 2005, Search Your Heart for Christmas for Chorus and Violoncello, 2005, Parabola for Brass and Timpani, 2006, Reveries for String Orchestra, 2007, Dies Irae for Brass and Timpani, 2007. Mem. Woodmont Christian Ch., Nashville, Tenn. Recipient award, Thor Johnson Meml. Commn., 2007, various nat. and internat. commns., performances and residencies; Meet The Composer grantee, Creative Connections, NY, 2004. Mem.: ASCAP (18 consecutive panel awards 1989—2006), World Assn. Symphonic Bands and Ensembles, Am. Composers Forum, Ctr. for Promotion of Contemporary Composers, Nat. Assn. Composers USA, Am. Fedn. Musicians, Am. Music Ctr., Soc. Composers, Inc., Pi Kappa Lambda, Phi Kappa Phi. Office: PO Box 190308 Nashville TN 37219-0308 Home Phone: 615-883-7638. E-mail: mail@davidsartor.com.

SARTORELLI, ALAN CLAYTON, pharmacologist, educator; b. Chelsea, Mass., Dec. 18, 1931; m. Alice C. Anderson, July 7, 1969. BS, New Eng. Coll. Pharmacy Northeastern U., 1953; MS, Middlebury Coll., Vt., 1955; PhD, U. Wis., 1958; MA (hon.), Yale U., 1967. Rsch. chemist Samuel Roberts Noble Found., Ardmore, Okla., 1958—60, sr. rsch. chemist, 1960—61; mem. faculty dept. pharmacology Yale Sch. Medicine, New Haven, 1961—, prof., 1967—, head devel. therapeutics program Comprehensive Cancer Ctr., 1974—90, chmn. dept. pharmacology, 1977—84, 1998—2000, dir. Comprehensive Cancer Ctr., 1984—93, Alfred Gilman prof. pharmacology, 1987—, prof. epidemiology, 1991—97. Head devel. therapeutics program Comprehensive Cancer Ctr., 1974—90, chmn. dept. pharmacology, 1977—84, 1998—2000, dep. dir., 1982—84, dir., 1984—93, Alfred Gilman prof. pharmacology, 1987—; Charles B. Smith vis. rsch. prof. Meml. Sloan-Kettering Ctr., 1979; William N. Creasy vis. prof. clin. pharmacology Wayne State U., 1983; Mayo Found. vis. prof. oncology Mayo Clinic, 1983; Walter Hubert lectr. Brit. Assn. Cancer Rsch., 1985; Pfizer lectr. in clin. pharmacology U. Conn. Health Ctr., 1985; William N. Creasy vis. prof. clin. pharmacology Bowman Gray Sch. Medicine, 1987; Wellcome vis. prof. basic sci. U. Pitts. Sch. Medicine, 1990; sci. adv. bd. ImmunoGen, Inc., 1981—90, U. Ind. Cancer Ctr., 1992, Cancer Inst. N.J., 1993—, Cell Pathways, Inc., 1993—2003; chmn. cancer sci. adv. bd. ViraChem., Inc., 1986—93, The Liposome Co., 1986—2001, Vion Pharms., 1993—, bd. dirs., chmn. sci. adv. bd.; chmn. vis. sci. adv. com. Columbia U. Comprehensive Cancer Ctr., 1986—99; chmn. pres.'s cancer adv. bd. Fox Chase Cancer Ctr., 1992—; clin. investigation rev. com. Nat. Cancer Inst., 1968—72, mgmt. cons. to dir. divsn. cancer treatment, 1975—77, bd. sci. counselors, divsn. cancer treatment, 1978—81, chmn. com. to establish nat. coop. drug discovery groups, 1982—83, chmn. spl. rev. com. Outstanding Investigator grant applications, 1992, chmn. ad hoc contracts tech. rev. group, 93; instnl. rsch. grants com. Am. Cancer Soc., 1971—76, coun. analysis and projection, 1978—79; cons. in biochemistry U. Tex. M.D. Anderson Hosp. and Tumor Clinic, Houston, 1970—76; cons. Sandoz Forschungs-Institut, Vienna, 1977—80; mem. exptl. therapeutics study sect. NIH, 1973—77, working cadre nat. large bowel cancer project, 1973—76; adv. com. Cancer Rsch. Ctr., Washington U. Sch. Medicine, 1971—75, SLSB Ptnrs., L.P., 1992—96; sci. adv. com. U. Iowa Cancer Ctr., 1979—83; external adv. com. Wis. Clin. Cancer Ctr., 1978—79, Duke Comprehensive Cancer Ctr., 1983—94; external adv. bd. U. Ariz. Cancer Ctr., 1982—92, U. So. Calif. Cancer Ctr., 1983—93, Clin. Cancer Rsch. Ctr., Brown U., 1980—86; nat. program com. 13th Internat. Cancer Congress, 1979—81; cons. Bristol-Myers Co., 1982—93, selection com. prize in cancer rsch., 1977—85, chmn., 1979—81, chmn. selection com. award for disting. achievement in cancer rsch., 1989—92; bd. advisors Drug and Vaccine Devel. Corp. (Ctr. for Pub. Resources), 1980—81, Specialized Cancer Ctr., Mt. Sinai Med. Ctr., 1981—90, Grace Cancer Drug Ctr., Roswell Park Meml. Inst., 1986—89; med. and sci. adv. com. grants rev. subcom. Leukemia Soc. Am., 1983—88; program planning com. Mary Lasker-Am. Cancer Soc. Conf., 1986; external sci. rev. com. Massey Cancer Ctr., 1989—94; bd. visitors Moffit Cancer Ctr. U. South Fla., 1989—92; dep. dir. Cancer Prevention Rsch. Unit for Conn., 1989—93, acting dir., 1991—93; nat. bd. Look Good...Feel Better program Cosmetic Toiletry and Fragrance Assn., 1989—91; organizing com. Conf. on Bioreductive Drug Activation, 1993—94; chmn. bd. spl. cons. Inst. for Cancer Therapeutics, 1993; scientific adv. bd. U. Ill. Cancer Ctr., 2001; chmn. sci. adv. bd. Celator Technologies Inc., 2002—. Regional editor Am. Continent Biochem. Pharmacology, 1968—2003, exec. editor, 1993—2003, editor-in-chief Cancer Comm., 1969—93, Oncology Rsch., 1993—; editor: Handbuch der experimentellen Pharmakologie vols. on antineoplastic and immunosuppressive agts., series on cancer chemotherapy Am. Chem. Soc. Symposium, 1976; founder, exec. editor Pharmacology and Therapeutics, 1975—2003, editl. bd. Internat. Ency. Pharmacology and Therapeutics, 1972—94, Seminars in Oncology, 1973—83, Chemico-Biol. Interactions, 1975—78, Jour. Medicinal Chemistry, 1977—82, Cancer Drug Delivery, 1982—85, Jour. Enzyme Inhibition, 1984—2002, Jour. Liposome Rsch., 1986—92, In Vivo, 1990—2002, Cancer Biotherapy, 1992—97, Cancer Rsch., Therapy and Control, 1993—97, Oncology Reports, 1995—, Molecular and Cellular Differentiation, 1996—, mem. adv. bd. Advances in Chemistry Series, ACS Symposium Series, 1977—80, editl. adv. bd. Cancer Rsch., 1970—71, assoc. editor, 1971—78, Current Awareness in Biol. Scis., Current Advances in Pharmacology and Toxicology, 1983—88, Cancer Cells, 1989—91, Jour. Exptl. Therapeutics and Oncology, 1995—, exec. adv. bd. Ency. of Human Biology, 1987—90, Dictionary of Sci. and Tech., 1989—91, editl. cons. Biol. Abstracts, 1984—88; contbr. articles to profl. jours. Bd. dirs. Schubert Performing Arts Ctr., 1992—2001, Schubert Opera Bd., 1991—2000, chmn., 1993—. Recipient Outstanding Alumni award, Northeastern U., 1987, Mike Hogg award, M.D. Anderson Cancer Ctr., U. Tex., 1989, Alumni Achievement award, Middlebury Coll., 1990, AACR-Bruce F. Cain Meml. award, 2001, Drug Discovery and Devel. award, Glaxo SmithKline, 2002. Fellow: AAAS, N.Y. Acad. Scis.; mem.: Coun. Biology Editors, Conn. Acad. Sci. and Engring., Inst. Medicine NAS (com. on govt. industry collaboration in biomed. rsch. and edn. 1989, mem. Forum on Drug Devel. and Regulation 1989—93), Assn. Am. Cancer Insts. (v.p. 1986, liaison rep. to Nat. Cancer Inst. 1986, bd. dirs. 1986—89, pres. 1987—88, chmn. bd. dirs. 1989), Am. Soc. Pharmacology and Exptl. Therapeutics (award com. 1988, chmn. 1992, award in exptl. therapeutics 1986, Otto Krayer award 2002), Am. Soc. Cell Biology, Am. Soc. Biochemistry and Molecular Biology, Am. Soc. Microbiology, Am. Chem. Soc., Am. Assn. Cancer Rsch. (dir. 1975—78, chmn. publs. com. 1981—88, dir. 1984—87, v.p. 1985—86, fin. com. 1985—88, exec. com. 1985—89, pres. 1986—87, chmn. exec. com. 1987, chmn. awards com. 1987, chmn. nominating com. 1993—95, mem. devel. com. 1995—97). Home: 4 Perkins Rd Woodbridge CT 06525-1616 Office: Yale U Dept Pharmacology 333 Cedar St New Haven CT 06520-8066 Home Phone: 203-387-8925; Office Phone: 203-785-4533. E-mail: alan.sartorelli@yale.edu.

SARTORI, MICHAEL A., lawyer; b. St. Louis; BSEE, Univ. Notre Dame, 1987, MSEE, 1989, PhD, 1991; JD cum laude, Georgetown Univ., 1998. Bar: Va. 1998, DC 1999, US Patent & Trademark Office, US Ct. Appeals (4th, Fed. cir.). Sr. project mgr. USN Naval Surface Warfare Ctr., 1991—94; patent examiner US Patent & Trademark Office, 1994—96; ptnr., Patent Prosecution, Intellectual Property Litigation Venable LLP, Washington, 2003—, chmn. Patent Prosecution group, 2005—. Lectr. Catholic Univ. Am, 1991. Contbr. articles to profl. jours. Mem.: ABA, Am. Intellectual Property Law Assn. Achievements include patents in field of underwater acoustics. Office: Venable LLP 575 7th St NW Washington DC 20004 Office Phone: 202-344-4004. Office Fax: 202-344-8300. Business E-Mail: masartori@venable.com.

SARTORY, THOMAS J., lawyer; b. Pitts., Apr. 7, 1944; BA magna cum laude, Loyola U., 1966; JD cum laude, Harvard U., 1969. Bar: Mass. 1969, Fla. 1975. Dir. civil litig. Goulston & Storrs, P.C., Boston. Mem. com human studies Harvard Med. Sch., 1980-92; spl. counsel to Mass. Jud. Conduct Commn. Fellow: Am. Coll. Trial Lawyers; mem.: Mass. Bar Assn. (mem. com. profl. ethics, past chmn. bus. litig. com.), Boston Bar Assn. (chmn. professionalism & civility com.). Address: Goulston & Storrs 400 Atlantic Ave Boston MA 02110-3333 Office Phone: 617-574-6411. Office Fax: 617-574-7632. Business E-Mail: tsartory@goulstonstorrs.com.

SARUK, MICHAEL, dermatologist, educator; b. Chgo., Nov. 1, 1951; s. Marvin Saruk and Geraldine Ruth Freeman; m. Louise Link, 1991; m. Anne Faulkner, 1977; children: Benjamin Dov, Jonathan Simon, Evan Samuel. BS, U. Ill., 1973; MD, Rush U., 1977. Diplomate Am. Bd. Dermatology, 1983, Am. Bd. Pathology, 1981, Am. Bds. Pathology and Dermatology, 1981. Asst. prof. pathology and dermatology U. Pitts. Sch. Medicine, 1982—83; instr. dermatology U. Pa. Sch. Medicine, Phila., 1984—86; clin. instr. dermatology Mt. Sinai Sch. Medicine, NYC, 1987—92; clin. asst. prof. dermatology U. Pa. Sch. Medicine, 1993—99, clin. assoc. prof., dermatology, 1999—. Cons., advisor Novartis Pharms., 2002—; cons., clin. investigator Aventis Pharms., 2002—04, Astellas Pharms., 2004—, Allergan Pharms., 2002—05, Galderma Pharms., 2004—05, Centocor - subs. of Johnson and Johnson, 2005—; asst. med. examiner Office of Med. Examiner, New Haven County, Conn., 1978—82. Co-author: (medical text) Soft Tissue Tumors; contbr. articles to profl. jours. Founding sponsor Magnolia Speech Sch. Demonstration Program, Berwyn, Pa., 2002. Fellow: Am. Soc. Dermatologic Surgery, Am. Soc. Mohs Surgery, US & Can. Acad. Pathology, Am. Acad. Dermatology, Am. Soc. Dermatopathology; mem.: Dermatology Found. (vice-chair Ea. Pa. 1997—2000), Del. Acad. Dermatology (pres. 1997—98), Pa. Acad. Dermatology, Soc. Investigative Dermatology, Phi Beta Kappa. Achievements include Start of the pigmented lesion clinic for the diagnosis and treatment of pigmented disorders of the skin, including moles and melanoma, in the department of dermatology, University of Pittsburgh, 1982; Start of What Is Now One Of The Largest Private Group Dermatology And Plastic Surgery Practices In The Delaware Valley, Employing A Multidisciplinary Approach To The Treatment Of Cutaneous Diseases. Office: Atlantic Skin & Cosmetic Surgery Group Ste 100 100 Deerfield Ln Malvern PA 19355 Home Phone: 610-399-1816; Office Phone: 610-296-8844. Office Fax: 610-296-3963.

SARUKHAN, ARTURO, ambassador; BA, Coll. Mex.; MA, Johns Hopkins U., 1991. Chief of staff Embassy of Mex., 1993—95, dir. counternarcotics and law enforcement, 1995—98; sr. adv. to sec. Min. Fgn. Affairs United Mexican States, 1998—2000, chief of staff policy planning, 2000—03; consul gen. Consulate Gen. of Mex., NYC, 2003—06; amb. to US Govt. of Mex., Washington, 2007—. Office: 1911 Pennsylvania Ave NW Washington DC 20006 Office Phone: 202-728-1600. Office Fax: 202-728-1698.

SARUKKAI, SEKHAR, information technology executive; MS in Computer Sci., PhD in Computer Sci., Ind. Univ. Sr. rschr. NASA Ames Rsch. Ctr.; sr. rschr. to chief architect Hewlett-Packard; founder, chief tech. officer Confluent Software Inc. (acquired by Oblix 2004); Tech. architect Oblix; founder, chief tech. officer Securent, Mountain View, Calif. Named one of Top 25 Chief Tech. Officers, InfoWorld mag., 2007. Office: Securent 555 Ellis St Mountain View CA 94043 Office Phone: 650-625-9400. Office Fax: 650-625-9401. Business E-Mail: ssarukkai@securent.com.

SARVER, ROBERT G., professional sports team owner; s. Jack Sarver; m. Penny Sanders, Nov. 2, 1996; 3 children. BBA, U. Ariz., 1982. CPA 1983. Founder, pres. Nat. Bank Ariz., 1984—94; lead investor, CEO GB Bancorporation, 1995—97; chmn., CEO Calif. Bank and Trust (formerly Grossmont Bank), San Diego, 1995—2002; dir., mem. credit com. Zions Bancorporation, 1995—2001, exec. v.p., 1998—2001; pres., chmn., CEO Western Alliance Bancorporation, 2002—; chmn., CEO Torrey Pines Bank, 2003—; co-founder S.W. Value Ptnrs.; mng. ptnr. Phoenix Suns, Ariz., 2004—. Bd. dirs. SkyWest Airlines, Meritage Corp., Phoenix. Mem. adv. bd. U. Ariz. Sarver Heart Ctr.; bd. trustees Japanese Am. Nat. Mus., LA. Avocations: golf, tennis, volleyball. Office: Alliance Bank Ariz 2701 E Camelback Rd Ste 110 Phoenix AZ 85016 *

SARWER-FONER, GERALD JACOB, psychiatrist, educator; b. Volkovsk, Grodno, Poland, Dec. 6, 1924; arrived in Can., 1932, naturalized, 1935; s. Michael and Ronia Sarwer-F.; m. Ethel Sheinfeld, May 28, 1950; children: Michael, Gladys, Janice, Henry, Brian. BA, Loyola Coll. U., Montreal, 1945, MD magna cum laude, 1951; DPsychiatry, McGill U., 1955. Diplomate Am. Bd. Psychiatry and Neurology. Intern. Univ. Hosps. U. Montreal Sch. Medicine, 1950-51; resident Butler Hosp., Providence, 1951-52, Hosps. Western Res. U., Cleve., 1952-53, Queen Mary Vets. Hosp., Montreal, 1953-55; cons. psychiatry, dir. psychiatric rsch., 1955-61; lectr. psychiatry U. Montreal, 1953-55; lectr., asst. prof., assoc. prof. McGill U., 1955—70; dir. dept psychiatry Queen Elizabeth's Hosp, Montreal, 1964-71; prof. psychiatry U. Ottawa, Ont., 1971-89, prof., chmn. psychiatry Ont., 1974-86, prof., 1989—; dir. dept. psychiatry Ottawa Gen. Hosp., 1971-87; dir. Lafayette Clinic, Detroit, 1989-92; prof. psychiatry and behavioral Neurosciences Wayne State U., Detroit, 1989—. Cons. in psychiatry Ottawa Gen. Hosp., Royal Ottawa Hosp., Children's Hosp. of Eastern Ont., Ottawa, Windsor (Ont.) Western Hosp. Ctr., Ottawa Sch. Bd.; Z. Lebensohn lectr. Silbey Meml. Hosp. Cosmos Club, Washington, 1991; disting. lectr. XI World Congress Psychiatry, Hamburg, 1999, XII World Congress Psychiatry, Yokohama, Japan, 2002; mem. test com. Nat. Bd. Med. Examiners, 1975-81; pres. Que. Psychiat. Assn., 1966-68; mem. adv. panel on psychiatry Def. Rsch. Bd. Can., Dept. Nat. Def., 1958-62. Editor: Dynamics of Psychiatric Drug Therapy, 1960, Research Conference on the Depressive Group of Illnesses, 1966, Psychiatric Crossroads-the Seventies, Research Aspects, 1972, Social Psychiatry in the Late 20th Century, 1993; founder, editor in chief Psychiat. Jour. U. Ottawa, 1976-90, emeritus editor in chief, 1990—; mem. editorial bds. of numerous internat. and nat. profl. jours.; editor numerous audio-video tapes; contbr. to more than 200 articles to profl. jours. Bd. govs. Queen Elizabeth Hosp., Montreal, 1966-71; life gov. Queen Elizabeth Hosp. Found.; cons. Protestant Sch. Bd., Westmount, Que., 1966-71; advisor Com. on Health, City of Westmount, 1969-71. Served to lt. col. Royal Can. A Med. Corps, 1949-62. Fulbright fellow, 1951-53; recipient Sigmund Freud award Am. Assn. Psychoanalytic Physicians, 1982, William V. Silverberg Meml. award Am. Acad. Psychoanalysis, 1990, Poca award Assn. Psychiat. Out Patient Ctrs. Am., 1990; Simon Bolivar lectr. Am. Psychiat. Assn., New Orleans, 1981; Can. Forces Decoration; Knight of Malta. Fellow: AAAS, Am. Assn. Social Psychiatry (v.p. 1987—89, pres.-elect 1990, pres. 1992—94), World Psychiat. Assn. (v.p. sect. on edn. 1989—, mem. internat. adv. com. 9th World Congress Rio de Janeiro 1993, lectr., organizing com. sci. com. X World Congress in Madrid, mem. nominating com.), Benjamin Rush Soc. (founding mem., councillor), Am. Coll. Psychiatrists (bd. regents 1978—80, pres. com. long range planning and policy 1986—89, emeritus), Am. Psychopath. Assn., Collegium Internat. Neuropsychopharmacology, Internat. Psychoanalytical Assn. (mem. program com. 31st congress NY 1979), Royal Coll. Psychiatry (Found. fellow), Can. Psychiat. Assn. (life; bd. dirs. 1958—62, founder, chair com., sect. psychotherapy 1962—64), Am. Acad. Psychiatry and the Law (sr.; pres. 1977, Silver Apple award), Am. Coll. Neuropsychopharmacology (life; charter founding fellow), Can. Coll. Neuropsychopharmacology (life; hon. found. 1958—), Am. Psychiat. Assn. (life; chair sci. program com., VI World Congress of Psychiatry, Honolulu 1974—77, v.p., chmn. sci. program com. 1974—77, chair com. psychiatry, law 1975—77, chair task force model commitment code 1976—80, VI World Congress of Psychiatry Honolulu 1974—77), Am. Coll. Psychoanalysts (life; pres.-elect 1983, pres. 1984—85, chair by-laws and constn. com. 1994—2001, Henry Laughlin award 1986), Am. Coll. Mental Health Adminstrn. (life), Royal Coll. Physicians and Surgeons (exec. sec. test psychiat. com. 1987—89), Internat. Coll. Psychosomatic Medicine (sec.-gen. 1979—83); mem.: Am. Psychoanalytic Assn. (mem. program com. 1972—76), Alliance for Mental Health Svcs. (pres. 1999—2000), Mich. Psychoanalytic Soc., Soc. Biol. Psychiatry (sr.; pres. 1983—84, H. Azima Meml. lectr. 1963, George M. Thompson award 1997), Can. Assn. Profs. Psychiatry (pres. 1976—77, 1982—86), Can. Psychoanalytic Soc. (pres. 1979—81), Royal Can. Mil. Inst. Club, Cosmos Club. Home and Office: 3220 Bloomfield Shr Dr West Bloomfield MI 48323-3300 Office Phone: 248-855-9080. Office Fax: 248-855-8321. Personal E-mail: sarwfon@aol.com.

SASAHARA, ARTHUR ASAO, cardiologist, educator, researcher; b. Del Rey, Calif., May 11, 1927; s. Harold Hango and Blanche (Takayama) S.; m. Alice Ann Guenther, Apr. 2, 1955; children: Ann Mariko, Claire Michiko, Ellen Reiko, Karen Hideko, Mark Tadao. AB, Oberlin Coll., 1951; MD, Case Western Res. U., 1955; AM (hon.), Harvard U., 1987. Diplomate Am. Bd. Internal Medicine. Intern Boston City Hosp., 1955-56; jr. asst. med. resident Mass. Gen. Hosp., Boston, 1956-57; fellow in cardiology West Roxbury VA Med. Ctr., Mass., 1957-58, Children's Hosp. Med. Ctr., Boston, 1958-59; sr. resident in medicine Yale-New Haven Med. Ctr., 1959-60; asst. chief med. svc., dir. cardiopulmonary lab., dep. chmn. rsch. and edn. com. VA Hosp. West Roxbury, 1960-70, chief cardiopulmonary sect., 1971-74, assoc. chief staff for rsch. and edn., 1970-76, chief med. svc., 1974-82, West Roxbury-Brockton VA Hosp., 1982-87; prof. medicine Harvard Med. Sch., Boston, 1974-93, prof. emeritus, 1993—; cons. cardiovascular-pulmonary diseases Boston, 1965-87; cons. pediatric cardiology Children's Hosp. Med. Ctr., Boston, 1976-86; physician Brigham and Women's Hosp., Boston, 1979-82, sr. physician, 1982—. Dir. thrombolytics rsch. pharm. products divsn. Abbott Labs., Abbott Park, Ill., 1987—95, sr. med. dir., 1995—97; sr. physician cardiovascular divsn. Brigham and Women's Hosp., 1998—. Author-editor: Pulmonary Embolic Disease, 1965, Pulmonary Emboli, 1975, New Therapeutic Agents in Thrombosis and Thrombolysis, 1997, 2d edit., 2002; contbr. articles to profl. jours.; designer constant infusion med. pump, Harvard Apparatus Co., 1973; mem. editl. bd. New Eng. Jour. Medicine, 1971-73, Jour. Nuclear Medicine, 1981-83, Am. Jour. Medicine, 1971-72, Circulation, 1973-78, VASA, 1978-85, Jour. Cardiovasc. Medicine, 1980-86, Primary Cardiology, 1986-89. With U.S. Army, 1945-47. NIH grantee, 1963-82; VA grantee, 1961-87. Fellow ACP, Am. Coll. Chest Physicians, Am. Coll. Cardiology; mem. AAAS, Internat. Soc. Fibrinolysis and Thrombolysis, Am. Fedn. Clin. Rsch., Internat. Soc. Thrombosis and Hemostasis, Am. Heart Assn., Alpha Omega Alpha. Democrat. Episcopalian. Home: 1115 Beacon St # 12 Newton MA 02461-1154 Personal E-mail: aasasahara@comcast.net.

SASAKI, CLARENCE TAKASHI, surgeon, educator; b. Honolulu, Jan. 24, 1941; s. Tsutomu and Carla Harumi (Mirikitani) S.; m. Carolyn Elizabeth Lindahl, June 26, 1967; children: Peter Gordon, John Eric. BA, Pomona Coll., 1962; MD, Yale U., 1966. Diplomate: Am. Bd. Otolaryngology. Intern San Francisco Hosp., U. Calif., 1966-67; resident in surgery Dartmouth Med. Sch., 1967-68; resident in otolaryngology Yale U. Med. Sch. Hosps., New Haven, 1970-73, faculty mem., 1973—, assoc. prof., 1977-82, prof. surgery, 1982—, chief sect. otolaryngology, 1981—, Charles Ohse prof. surgery, 1988—, vice chmn. dept. surgery, 1996. Author: Surgery of the Skull Base, Head and Neck Surgery, Vol. 1 Atlas Otolaryngology, Vocal Fold Physiology, Laryngeal Function in Phonation and Respiration, Neurological Diseases of the Larynx; mem. editl. bd. profl. jours. Served to maj. M.C. U.S. Army, 1968-70. Recipient award Fowler Triological Soc., 1979. Mem. Am. Acad. Otolaryngology (1st prize clin. rsch.), Am. Soc. Head and Neck Surgery (coun.), Assn. Rsch. Otolaryngology, Am. Laryngol. Rhinol. and Otol. Soc. (coun., sec. ea. sect. 1990, v.p. 1998), New Eng. Otolaryngology Soc. (pres. 1987, coun.), Assn. Acad. Depts. Otolaryngology (coun.), Am. Laryngol. Assn. (Casselberry award 1999), Pan Pacific Surg. Assn., Soc. for Neurosci., Soc. Neurovascular Surgery, Soc. for Head and Neck Surgeons, Am. Neurotolog. Soc., Pan Am. Assn. Oto-rhino-laryngology and Bronchoesophagology, Conn. Med. Soc., N.Y. Acad. Scis., Soc. Univ. Otolaryngologists, Collegium ORLAS, Cartesian Soc. (co-dir.), Am. Bronchoesophagological Assn. (mem. coun., treas. 2003, pres. 2007, Broyles-Maloney award 2004), N.Am. Skull Base Soc., Laryngeal. Cancer Assn. (Padua), Am. Otol. Soc., Dysphagia Rsch. Soc. (treas., pres.), Lawn Club, Mory's Assoc., Yale Club, Phi Beta Kappa, Sigma Xi. Office: Yale U Med Sch Dept Surgery PO Box 208041 333 Cedar St New Haven CT 06520-8041 Office Phone: 203-785-2592.

SASAKI, ROBERT J., financial services executive; b. Oakland, Calif., May 7, 1962; s. Joseph and Kimiko (Sakanashi) S.; m. Momoe Shimabukuro; children: Lisa, Lynn. BA, U. Calif., Berkeley, 1984; MA, Harvard U., 1988. Arbitrageur L.F. Rothschild, Unterberg, Towbin, Inc., NYC, 1986-88, Merrill Lynch & Co., Inc., NYC, 1988-89, JP Morgan, Tokyo, 1989-2001, Bear Stearns Co., Inc., Tokyo, 2001—04; mng. mem. Pacific Property Capital, LLC, San Francisco, 2004—; chmn., CEO K and S Co., Inc., 2005—. Co-founder Free Merchant.Com, Inc., Emeryville, Calif.; founder Robert J. Sasaki Fund for Rsch. in Vision Neurosci., U. Calif., Berkeley, 2004—. Mem. Nat. Eagle Scout Assn. (life), Harvard Club of NYC, Young Pres. Orgn., Tokyo Am. Club, Faculty Club Berkeley, Peninsula Golf and Country Club. Republican. Buddhist. Avocations: skiing, tennis, japanese art. Home: 881 Vista Rd Hillsborough CA 94010 Office: 50 California St Ste 1500 San Francisco CA 94111

SASAKI, TSUTOMU (TOM SASAKI), real estate company executive, trade association administrator, consultant; b. Tokyo, July 28, 1945; came to US, 1979; s. Tsuneshiro and Kimiko (Fujiwara) S.; m. Yoko Katsura, Feb. 21, 1971; children: Mari, Tomoko. BA, Sophia U., Tokyo, 1969. Plant export adminstrn. Ataka & Co., Ltd., Osaka, Japan, 1969-76; officer Seattle-First Nat. Bank, Tokyo, 1976-79, AVP bus. mgr., 1982-84, AVP Japan mgr. Seattle, 1979-82, v.p. Japan mgr., 1984-90; owner, pres. BBS Internat., Inc., Seattle, 1990—. Bd. dirs. Japanese Cmty. Svccs. Seattle, Adopt-a-Stream Found., Everett, Wash., 1987—2002; trustee NW Sch., Seattle, 1987—2002, internat. advisor to bd. trustees, 2002—. Am. Field Svc. scholar, 1963-64. Mem. Japan Am. Soc. Wash. (chmn. membership com. 1988, bd. dir. 1997—, chmn. bd. 2006-07), British Am. Bus. Coun., Fairwood Golf & Country Club, Wash. Athletic Club. Avocations: golf, gardening, music, photography. Home: 4625 136th Ave SE Bellevue WA 98006-3007 Office: BBS Internat Inc 2819 Elliot Ave #201 Seattle WA 98121 Office Phone: 206-623-5714. Business E-Mail: sasaki@bbsint.com.

SASAKI, Y(ASUNAGA) TITO, engineering executive; b. Tokyo, Feb. 6, 1938; arrived in U.S., 1967; s. Yoshinaga and Chiyoko Sasaki; m. Janet L. Cline; 1 child, Heather N. Diploma in indsl. design, Royal Coll. Art, London, 1962; MS in Ekistics, Athens Tech. Inst., Greece, 1965. Cert. planner, Am. Inst. Cert. Planners. Tech. officer London County Coun., 1962-63; sr. rschr. Inst. Battelle, Geneva, Switzerland, 1965-67; planning dir. Golden Gate Bridge, San Francisco, 1970-74; pres. Visio Internat., Inc., San Francisco, 1974-85, Quantum Mechanics Corp., Sonoma, Calif., 1981—. Mem.: AIAA, ASME, Am. Welding Soc., Am. Vacuum Soc. Achievements include co-developer of sensitive helium leak detector;

co-developer of the lowest out-gasing stainless steel. Home: PO Box 200 Vineburg CA 95487-0200 Office: Quantum Mechanics Corp 21885 8th St E Sonoma CA 95476-9797 Office Phone: 707-938-5555.

SASENICK, JOSEPH ANTHONY, consumer products company executive; b. Chgo., May 18, 1940; s. Anthony E. and Caroline E. (Smicklas) S.; m. Barbara Ellen Barr, Aug. 18, 1962; children: Richard Allen, Susan Marie, Michael Joseph. BA, DePaul U., 1962; MA, U. Okla., 1966. With Miles Labs., Inc., Elkhart, Ind., 1963-70; product mgr. Alka-Seltzer, 1966-68, dir. mktg. grocery products divsn., 1968-70; with Gillette Corp., Boston, 1970-79, dir. new products/new ventures, personal care divsn., 1977; v.p. diversified cos. and pres. Jafra Cosmetics Worldwide, 1977-79; mktg. dir. Braun AG, Kronberg, W. Ger., 1970-73; chmn. mng. dir. Braun U.K. Ltd., 1973-77; with Abbott Labs., North Chicago, 1979-84, corp. v.p., pres. consumer products divsn., 1979-84; pres., CEO, Moxie Industries, 1984-87; pres., CEO Personal Monitoring Technologies, Rochester, NY, 1987; pres. Bioline Labs., Ft. Lauderdale, Fla., 1988; mng. dir., ptnr. Vista Resource Group, Newport Beach, Calif., 1988-90; pres., CEO, Alcide Corp., Redmond, Wash., 1991-92, chmn., CEO, 1992—2004; founder Board Romm Ltd., 2004. Mem. Columbia Tower Club, El Niguel Club, Wash. Athletic Club, Tech. Alliance, Rainier Club. Home and Office: Board Room Ltd 1301 Spring St # 24J Seattle WA 98104

SASLOW, DEBBIE L., cancer control specialist, director; d. H Arnold and Ann E Weinstat; m. Adam R Saslow, June 2, 1990; children: Kayla M., Rianna N. BS, Brown U., 1983—87; PhD, Yale U., 1987—92. Coord., president's nat. action plan on breast cancer PHS Office on Women's Health, Washington, 1995—97; dir., breast and gynecologic cancers Am. Cancer Soc., Atlanta, 1997—. Spkr. in field. Office: Am Cancer Soc 1599 Clifton Rd Atlanta GA 30329 *

SASMAN, IRENE DEAK HANDBERG, publishing executive; b. Jamaica, NY; d. Paul and Irene (Dyroff) Deak; children: Roger B. Handberg III, Ryan Paul Handberg; m. Timothy Carl Sasman. BS, Fla. State U.; MEd, U. N.C., 1970. Cert. tchr. in reading and math., N.C. Lead tchr., reading specialist Chapel Hill (N.C.) City Schs., 1966-69; dir. learning lab. Seminole Community Coll., Sanford, Fla., 1974-78; basic skills cons. EDL/McGraw-Hill Book Co., Orlando, Fla., 1978-82; regional dir. EDL/Arista Pub., Orlando, 1982-84; mktg. mgr., product mgr. Arista/Regents/EDL-Hachette, NYC, 1984-85; v.p. mktg. and sales Raintree Pubs., Milw., 1985, gen. mgr., pub., 1985-87; dir. spl. projects Simon & Schuster, Englewood Cliffs, NJ, 1987-88, v.p. corp. devel. NYC, 1988-90, sr. v.p., 1990-91; chmn. Irene Handberg Internat., NYC, 1991—; pres. The Learning Connection, New York, NY, 1991—. Co-author: EDL/McGraw-Hill Teacher's Guide. Elected precinct woman com. Dem. County Com., Fla.; capt. Nat. Cancer So., Fla., chmn. Sch. Adv. Com., Fla. NSF fellow U. N.C., 1969; recipient Svc. award Jr. Achievement. Mem. Chief Exec. Officers Group (coun. small bus. execs.), Sales and Mktg. Execs., Profl. Dimensions, Chief Exec. Officers Club. Lutheran. Avocations: spectator sports, art, music, skiing. Office: The Learning Connection 300 E 93rd St Apt 29C New York NY 10128-6109

SASMOR, JAMES CECIL, publishing representative, educator; b. NYC, July 29, 1920; s. Louis and Cecilia (Mockler) S.; 1 child from previous marriage, Elizabeth Lynn; m. Jeannette L. Fuchs, May 30, 1965. BS, Columbia U., NYC, 1942; MBA, Calif. Western U., 1977, PhD, 1979. Fellow, Diplomate Am. Bd. Med. Psychotherapists, Am. Assn. Sex Educators, Counselors and Therapists; lic. healthcare risk mgr., Am. Inst. Med. Law; diplomate Am. Bd. Sexology, Am. Bd. Disability Analysts (sr. analyst); cert. tchr. health scis. Registered rep. Nat. Assn. Security Dealers, 1956—57; founder, owner J.C. Sasmor Assocs., Pub.'s Reps., NYC, 1959—89; co-founder, pres., dir. adminstrn. Continuing Edn. Cons., Inc., 1976—. Pub. cons., 1959—; clin. assoc. U. So. Fla. Coll. Medicine, 1987-89, mem. adj. faculty Coll. Nursing, 1980-89; dir. Ednl. Counseling Comprehensive Breast Cancer Ctr., U. So. Fla. Med. Ctr., 1984-89, client libr. mental health inst., 1979-89; lectr. divsn. allied health nursing and pub. svc. Yavapi Coll.; co-leader study tours to fgn. countries. Author: Economics of Structured Continuing Education in Selected Professional Journals, Perception May Be Reality Vols. I, II and III; contbr. (chpts. to Childbirth Education: A Nursing Perspective); contbr. articles to profl. jours. Team tchr. childbirth edn. Am. Soc. Childbirth Educators; pres. Sedona unit Am. Cancer Soc., Ariz., 1995—2000, co-chmn. adult edn. com., founder Am. Cancer Soc. edn. dept. Sedona Med. Ctr., 1995—2005; county nursing ednl. cons. ARC, chmn. instrnl. com. on nursing and health, 1979—85; founding mem. coun. trustees Ariz. Nurses Found., 1998; co-leader study tours Russia Profl. Seminar Cons., 1986, ICOWHI, New Zealand and Australia, 1990, China People to People Citizen Amb. Program, 1996, Spain, Morocco Yavapai Coll. Health Inst., 1999, France and Eng. U. Tours Comparative Nursing, 2001; bd. dirs. Tampa chpt. ARC; bd. dirs. Ariz. divsn., mem. pub. edn. com. With USN, 1942—58, PTO, lt. USNR, ret. Recipient cert. of appreciation ARC, 1979, Am. Fgn. Svc. Assn., 1988, Dept. Health and Rehab. Svcs. award for Fla. Mental Health Inst. Svc., 1980; Internat. Coun. Sex Edn. and Parenthood fellow Am. U., 1981, Accomplished Elder award Ariz. Coun. of Govts. Mem. NAACOG (bd. dirs. Tampa chpt.), Nat. Assn. Pubs. Reps. (pres. 1965-66), Am. Soc. Psychoprophylaxis in Obstetrics (dir. 1970-71), Am. Soc. Childbirth Educators (co-founder, dir. 1972—), Internat. Coun. Women's Health Issues (chmn. resources com.), Health Edn. Media Assn., Nursing Educators Assn. Tampa, Lions (bd. dirs. Found. Ariz. 1991-2000, past pres. Sedona club, bd. dirs., chair sight, hearing, and scholarship coms.), Phi Theta Kappa (Honors scholar 2000-04, hon., advisor chpt. 1996-2002). Home: 235 Arrowhead Dr Sedona AZ 86351-8900 Office: PO Box 2282 Sedona AZ 86339-2282 Office Phone: 928-284-9897. Personal E-mail: drjcsasmor@msn.com.

SASS, DAWN MARIE, state official; b. Milw. d. Richard and Patricia S. BA in Hist., Polit. Sci., Univ. Wis., 1994. Probation officer to custody placement specialist Milw. Juvenile Detention Ctr.; child welfare worker Milw. County; office asst. III Wis. Parks Dept.; sales assoc. Boston Store, 2001—07; pharmacy tech. St. Luke's Hosp., 2004—07; former treas. Wis. Electrical Contractors' Corp.; state treas. State of Wis., 2007—. Mem.: Am. Fedn. State, County, Mcpl. Employees, The Nature Conservancy, World Wildlife Fund, Milw. County Zoological Soc. Democrat. Cath. Office: State Treas One S Pinckney St Ste 550 PO Box 7871 Madison WI 53707-7871 Office Phone: 608-266-1714. Office Fax: 608-266-2647. Business E-Mail: treasury@ost.state.wi.us. *

SASS, MARY MARTHA, freelance writer, artist; b. Chgo. d. George James and Arbutus Laraine (Schwartz) Harles; m. Roger Edward Sass, June 29, 1968. BS in Edn., U. Ill., 1965; MA in Guidance and Counseling, Northeastern Ill. U., 1977. Cert. secondary educator, guidance counselor, Ill. Tchr. English Kelvyn Park High Sch., Chgo., 1965-83; freelance writer, Skokie, Ill., 1983—. Lectr. North Suburban Libr. Sys., Chgo., 1992; author radio scripts Chgo. Pub. Libr. Broadcasting Sys.; author short stories, essays and articles; illustrator short stories and essays. Author (and illustrator): The Katy Ornament, 2002; editor: Odd Couple of the Constitution, 2005; illustrator Charlie the Chipmunk, 2007; exhibitions include Oakton C.C., 1993, All Chgo. Juried Art Show Skokie Pub. Libr., 1993, 1994, 1995, 1996, 1997 (hon. mention), 1998, 1999, 2000, 2001, Woman's Club Evanston Ann. Art Exhibit, 1994, 1995, 1996, 1997, 1998, 1999, 2000, Skokie Hist. Soc., 1993, 1994 (hon. mention), 1995, 1996, 1997, 1998, 1999, 2000 (First prize, 2000), 2001, 2002, 2003 (First prize), Allstate Ins., 1995, 1996, 1997, Blue Moon Art Gallery, 1999, Devonshire Cultural Ctr., 2002, Morton Grove Pub. Libr., 2002, 2004, Lincolnwood Village Hall Gallery, 2005, Emily Oaks Nature Ctr, 2006, 2007, South Shore Cultural Ctr., 2006, Shore Early Intervention Ctr., 2006—07, Chgo. Cultural Ctr., 2007, Represented in permanent collections Artists Archives, Chgo. Pub. Libr. Vol. Emily Oaks Nature Ctr. Skokie Park Dist., Ill. Recipient Radio Script hon. mention award Take One Nat. Radio Theatre Competition, 1994, Women in Cable award for cable TV documentary, Memoir 2d pl. award Nat. League Am. Pen Women, 2006, Creative Non-fiction 2d pl. award Nat. League Am. Pen Women, 2006, Ill. Assn. Pk. Dist. Cmty. Svc. award, 2007; Nat. Pub. Radio scholar, 1984. Mem. Chgo. Artist's Coalition, Nat. Pks. and Conservation Assn., Greenpeace, Nature Conservancy, Pk. Activist Network, Sr. Artists' Network, Ocean Conservancy, World Wildlife Fund. Avocations: classical guitar, sculpting, cable television writing and production, gardening. Office Phone: 847-674-7118. Personal E-mail: maryhsass@aol.com.

SASS, NEIL LESLIE, toxicologist; b. Balt., Oct. 24, 1944; s. Samuel and Blanche (Radoon) S.; m. Anita Paige Hoswell, June 29, 1984. BS, Wake Forest Coll., 1966; MS, W.Va. U., 1969, PhD, 1971; MS, Johns Hopkins U., 1984. Commd. officer USPHS, 1966, advanced through grades to capt., 1988, comdr. Preventive Medicine unit, 1989; served as rsch. toxicologist med. labs. U.S. Army, Edgewood Arsenal, Md., 1971-74; chief clin. investigations William Beaumont Army Med. Ctr., El Paso, Tex., 1974-77; toxicologist Bur. of Foods FDA, Washington, 1977-82; spl. asst. to dir. Ctr. for Food Safety and Applied Nutrition, FDA, Washington, 1982-99; dir. divsn. toxicological rsch. Ctr. for Food Safety and Applied Nutrition, Washington, 1996-99; chief toxicologist, state counterterrorism coord., chem. lab. dir. Ala. Dept. Pub. Health, Montgomery, 1999—. Jewish. Office: Ala Dept Pub Health The RSA Tower 201 Monroe St Ste 1450 Montgomery AL 36104-3735 Home: 2160 Woodley Rd Montgomery AL 36111-1013 Home Phone: 334-832-2322; Office Phone: 334-206-5973. Business E-Mail: nsass@adph.state.al.us.

SASS, RIVKAH K., library director; d. Richard and Betty Henricksen; m. Abe J. Sass; 1 child, Ilana E. BA in Polit. Sci., Sonoma State Coll., Rohnert Park, Calif., 1974; MLS, U. Wash., Seattle, 1978. Pub. svcs. libr. Spokane County and Spokane Pub. Librs., 1978—83; cmty. libr. coord. Chehalis br. Timberland Regional Libr., Tumwater, Wash., 1983—89; continuing edn. cons. Wash. State Libr., 1989—93; dep. state libr. Md. State Libr., 1994—96; sr. product mgr. Thomson Corp., 1996—99; info. svcs. coord. Multnomah County Libr., Portland, Oreg., 1999—2003; exec. dir. Omaha Pub. Libr., 2003—. Named Libr. of Yr., Libr. Jour., 2006; named one of Movers and Shakers, 2002; recipient Spirit of Literacy award, Literacy Ctr. of Midlands, 2006. Mem.: ALA, Nebr. Libr. Assn., Mountain Plains Libr. Assn., Jane Austen Soc. N.Am., Rotary Internat. Office: Omaha Pub Libr PO Box 241125 Omaha NE 68124 Office Phone: 402-444-4844. E-mail: rsass@omahapubliclibrary.org.

SASSER, ROBERT, retail executive; Various positions to sr. v.p. Roses Stores, Inc., sr. v.p. merchandise and mktg., 1997—99; v.p., gen. merchandise mgr. Michaels Stores, Inc., 1994—96; sr. v.p., COO Dollar Tree Stores, Inc., Chesapeake, Va., 1999—2004, pres., COO, 2001—04, pres., CEO, 2004—. Office: Dollar Tree Stores Inc 500 Volvo Pkwy Chesapeake VA 23320 *

SASSO, GARY L., lawyer; b. Miami, 1952; BS, U. Pa., 1974, JD, 1977. Bar: Fla., DC, Pa., U.S. Dist. Ct. Fla. (middle and so. districts), U.S. Ct. Appeals (3d, 4th, 6th, 9th and 11th cir.), U.S. Supreme Ct. Law clk. to Hon. Spottswood W. Robinson,III U.S. Ct. Appeals, 1977—78; law clk. to Justice Byron R. White U.S. Supreme Ct., 1978—79; litigator Bredhoff & Kaiser, Washington; various positions including mem. exec. com. and bd. dirs. Carlton Fields, P.A., Tampa, Fla., 1987—, pres., CEO, 2006—. Co-chair civil sect. Fed. Bar Assn. Tampa Bay Chpt.; editor-in-chief U. Pa. Law Rev., 1976—77, Litigation Jour. ABA Sect. Litigation, 2000—02. Contbr. articles to profl. jours. V.p., dir. H.B. Plant Mus., Tampa, Fla.; chmn. bd. dirs. Creative Kids Count, Inc. Fellow: Am. Bar Found., Am. Acad. Appellate Lawyers, Internat. Acad. Trial Lawyers; mem.: Am. Law Inst. Office: Carlton Fields PA 4221 W Boy Scout Blvd Ste 1000 Tampa FL 33607-5736 Office Phone: 813-229-4256. Office Fax: 813-229-4133. E-mail: gsasso@carltonfields.com.

SASSON, AARON R., surgeon; MD, U. Medicine and Dentistry NJ, Newark. Assoc. prof. surgery U. Nebr. Med. Ctr., Omaha, 2001—. Mem.: Soc. Surg. Oncology. Achievements include research in surgical oncology. Office: U Nebr Med Ctr 2709 N 159th St Omaha NE 68198 Office Phone: 402-559-8941. Office Fax: 402-559-7900.

SASTRY, SOSALE SHANKARA, electrical engineer, computer scientist, educator; PhD, U. Calif., Berkeley, 1981. Asst. prof. MIT, 1980—82; Gordon McKay prof. Harvard U., 1994; dir. electronics rsch. lab. U. Calif., Berkeley, 1996—99; dir. info. tech. DARPA, 2000; disting. prof. dept. electrical engring., computer sci., bioengring. U. Calif., Berkeley, chair dept. electrical engring., computer sci., bioengring., 2001—04. Co-author: (books) A Mathematical Introduction to Robotic Manipulation, 1994, An Invitation to 3-D Vision From Images to Models; co-editor: Hybrid Systems II: Lecture Notes in Computer Science, 1995, Hybrid Systems IV: Lecture Notes in Computer Science, 1997, Hybrid Systems: Computation and Control, 1998, Essays in Mathematical Robotics, 1998; author: Nonlinear Systems: Analysis, Stability, and Control, 1999; co-author: over 250 technical papers. Recipient David Marr prize, Internat. Conference in Computer Vision, 1999, Presidential Young Investigator award, NSF, 1994, IBM Faculty Devel. award, 1983—85. Fellow: IEEE, Am. Acad. Arts & Sciences; mem.: Nat. Acad. of Engring. Office: U Calif EECS 253 Cory Hall Berkeley CA 94720-1770

SATARINO, F. MICHAEL (MICHAEL SATARINO), principal; b. Sept. 1947; Grad., U. Notre Dame, 1969. Prin. Sch. for Talented and Gifted at Yvonne A. Ewell Townview Ctr., Dallas. Finalist Prin. of Yr., Dallas Sch. Dist., 2004. Office: Sch for Talented and Gifted Yvonne A Ewell Townview Ctr 1201 E Eighth St, Ste 302 Dallas TX 75203 Office Phone: 972-925-5970. Office Fax: 972-925-6018. E-mail: FMSatari@dallasisd.org. *

SATCHER, DAVID, public health service officer, former Surgeon General of the United States; b. Anniston, Ala., Mar. 2, 1941; s. Wilmer and Anna Satcher; m. Nola Satcher; children: Gretchen, David, Daraka, Daryl. BS, Morehouse Coll., 1963; MD, PhD, Case Western Reserve U., 1970; recipient of many honorary degrees and numerous disting. honors. Resident and fellow Strong Mem. Hosp., U. Rochester, UCLA, and King Drew; former faculty UCLA Sch. Medicine and Pub. Health; faculty, chair dept. family medicine King-Drew Med. Ctr., LA, interim dean, 1977—79; dir. King-Drew Sickle Cell Rsch. Ctr.; prof., chmn. dept. cmty. and family medicine Morehouse Sch. Medicine, Atlanta, 1979—82; pres. Meharry Med. Coll., Nashville, 1982—93; dir. Ctrs. for Disease Control and Prevention, Atlanta, 1993—98; adminstr. Agy. for Toxic Substances and Disease Registry, 1993—98; surgeon gen. US Dept. Health & Human Services, Washington, 1998—2002, asst. sec. health, 1998—2001; sr. vis. fellow Kaiser Family Found., Washington, 2002—; dir. Nat. Ctr. for Primary Care at Morehouse Sch. Medicine, Atlanta, 2002—, also interim pres., 2005—. Apptd. mem. Coun. of Grad. Med. Edn., 1986, chmn.; former Robert Wood Johnson Clin. Scholar; former Macy Faculty Fellow; bd. dir. MetLife Inc., 2007—. Named Nashvillian of Yr., 1992; recipient Watts Grassroots award for cmty. leadership, 1979, Nat. Conf. Christians and Jews awards, 1985, Black Achievment award, Ebony Mag., 1994, Brewslow award in pub. health, 1995, Dr. Nathan B. Davis award, AMA, 1996, Lifetime Achievement award, NY Acad. Medicine, 1997, Bennie Mays Trailblazer award, Nat. Found. for Infectious Diseases, Jimmy and Roslyn Carter award, Discovery Health Channel Med. Honors, 2004. Fellow: Am. Acad. of Family Physicians; mem.: Inst. Medicine NAS, Alpha Omega Alpha, Phi Beta Kappa. Focuses on promoting healthly lifestyles and ending disparities in healthcare; has raised childhood immunization rates to 78% in 1996 from 55% in 1992. Office: Kaiser Family Foundation Ste 250 1450 G St NW Washington DC 20005 also: Nat Ctr for Primary Care at Morehouse Sch Medicine 720 Westview Dr SW Atlanta GA 30310 Office Phone: 404-756-5740. Office Fax: 404-756-5767. Business E-Mail: ncpc@msm.edu. *

SATHAYE, JAYANT, research scientist; s. Vasundhara Sathaye; m. Anuradha Sabnis, May 24, 1980; children: Nakuli, Kiran. PhD, U. Calif., Irvine, 1974. Staff scientist Lawrence Berkeley Nat. Lab., Calif., 1974—94, sr. staff scientist, 1994—. Group leader internat. energy studies Lawrence Berkeley Nat. Lab., 1980. Editor: Mitigation and Adaptation Strategies Jour., Energy Policy jour.; contbr. articles to profl. jours. Philanthropher Indian Inst. Tech., Bombay, 1997. Mem.: AAAS, Ops. Rsch. Soc. Am., Internat. Assn. for Energy Econs. Home Phone: 925-376-3582; Office Phone: 510-486-6294. Personal E-mail: jasldc@aol.com.

SATHER, GLEN CAMERON, professional hockey team executive, coach; b. High River, Alta., Canada, Sept. 2, 1943; m. Ann Sather; 2 children. Former professional hockey player; coach Edmonton Oilers, Nat. Hockey League, Alta., Can., 1977-89, gen. mgr., 1981—2000, pres. Alta., 1982—2000, alt. gov., 1990—2000; pres., gen. mgr. NY Rangers, 2000—, head coach, 2003—04. Head coach, Stanley Cup Champions, 1984, 1985, 1987, 1988. Recipient Jack Adams Award for NHL Coach of the Yr., 1986. Office: c/o New York Rangers 2 Pennsylvania Plaza New York NY 10121

SATHY, ANUP, lawyer; BS highest honors, U. Ill., 1992; JD cum laude, Northwestern U., 1995. Bar: Ill. 1995, US Dist. Ct. (no. dist. Ill.), US Bankruptcy Ct. (no. Ill., Del., so. NY, ea. La., Md., so. Ohio, so. Tex.). Ptnr. Kirkland & Ellis, Chgo. Contbg. editor: ABI Jour.; asst. editor: Norton Bankruptcy Law & Practice; contbr. articles in law jours. Office: Kirkland & Ellis 200 E Randolph Dr Chicago IL 60601 Office Phone: 312-861-2046. Office Fax: 312-861-2200. E-mail: asathy@kirkland.com. *

SATHYAMOORTHY, MUTHUKRISHNAN, engineering educator, associate provost; b. Sathanur, Tamil Nadu, India, Feb. 21, 1946; s. Kuppusamy and Visalakshi Muthukrishnan; m. Chitra Subbiah, May 26, 1971; children: Mohanakrishnan, Kumaran. B in Civil Engring., U. Madras, India, 1967; M in Engring. Mechanics, Indian Inst. of Tech., Madras, India, 1969, PhD in Aero. Engring., 1973. Lectr. Indian Inst. of Tech., Madras, India, 1969-74; rsch. fellow U. Birmingham, Eng., 1974-76; asst. prof. Clarkson U., Potsdam, NY, 1979-82, assoc. prof., 1982-92, assoc. prof., exec. officer, 1992-94, prof., exec. officer, 1994-97, prof., chair, 1997-2001; dean engring. W.Va. U. Inst. Tech., 2001—06; assoc. provost U. Tex., Tyler, 2006—. Vis. rsch. faculty U. Calgary, Can., 1977-79. Contbn. author: Handbook of Civil Engineering Practice, 1988; editor: Material Nonlinearity in Vibrations, 1985; author: Nonlinear Analysis of Structures, 1998. Recipient Appreciation cert. U.S. Army, 1990, Outstanding Advisor award Clarkson U., 1993, Tau Beta Pi Faculty award, 1997, Disting. Tchg. award Clarkson Univ., 2001. Fellow ASME (mem. nat. student sect. com. 1992-94, mem. gen. awards com. 1994-99, Nat. Faculty Advisor award 1993, Dedicated Svc. award 1999); AIAA (assoc.), Aero. Soc. India. Avocations: overseas travel, camping, photography, fishing. Office: Office Assoc Provost U Tex at Tyler 3900 University Blvd Tyler TX 75799 Home: 13325 White Tail Dr Tyler TX 75707 Office Phone: 903-566-7447. Business E-Mail: msathy@uttyler.edu.

SATIN, CLAIRE JEANINE, sculptor, artist; b. Bklyn., Jan. 9, 1942; BA, Sarah Lawrence Coll., 1956; MFA, Pratt Inst., 1968. Instr. art edn. dept. edn. Bklyn. Mus., 1958-59; instr. dept. edn. and dept. Fine Arts Broward Cmty. Coll., Ft. Lauderdale, Fla., 1971-83; dir. Broward Cmty. Coll. Gallery, Ft. Lauderdale, 1975-76. Artist rep. Gabriela Herrera, N.Y.C., Art Vitam, Wynwood, Miami, Priscilla Juvelis, Maine, Vamps and Tramps, Birmingham, Ala. Collections include Libr. Congress, Rare Books Collection, Victoria and Albert Mus., London, Getty Ctr. Hist. Art and Humanities, L.A., Mus. Modern Art, N.Y.C., Mus. Art, Ft. Lauderdale, King Stephen Mus., Szekesfeherdr, Hungary, Ruth and Marvin Sackner Archive of Concrete and Visual Poetry, others; commd. works include: Chapman Chronicles, State of Alaska, U. Alaska, Fairbanks, 1992, Alphawalk, New Tampa Regional Libr., Hillsborough County, Tampa, Fla., 1997 (catalog); Alphastory, Pembroke Pines Libr., Pembroke Pines, Fla., Broward County Art in Pub. Places Program (brochure), Am. Ctrs., New Delhi, Bombay, India. Hon. chair Broward County Cultural Affairs Coun., Ft. Lauderdale, 1981-, bd. dirs., 1975-83, Meml. Found. Jewish Culture, N.Y.C. Recipient S. Fla. Cult Consortium award Miami Art Mus., 1997-98; So. Arts Fedn./NEA Regional Visual Arts fellow, 1996; Fla. State Individual Artist fellow Statewide Exhbn., 1978, 97-98; Cult Consortium fellow Miami Art Mus., 1997-98; Tiffany Found. grantee, 1968-69, Meml. Found. for Jewish Culture, 2001-02. Mem. Internat. Sculpture Ctr., Am. Craft. Coun., Ctr. Book Arts, Fonteneda Soc. (bd. dirs. 1997—). Office: c/o Artworks/Artspace 101 SW 1st St Dania Beach FL 33004-3628 Office Phone: 954-923-9117.

SATIN, JOSEPH, language educator, retired dean; b. Phila., Dec. 16, 1920; s. Reuben Philip and Harriet (Price) Satin; m. Selma Rosen (dec. 1978); children: Mark, Diane; m. Barbara Jeanne Dodson (dec. 1987); m. Terrye Sagan, 1992. BA, Temple U., 1946; AM, Columbia U., 1948, PhD, 1952. Instr. integrated studies W.Va. U., Morgantown, 1952-54; prof. English and Comparative Lit. Moorhead (Minn.) State U., 1954-63; chmn. dept. English and Journalism Midwestern U., Wichita Falls, Tex., 1963-73; dean Sch. Arts and Humanities Calif. State U., Fresno, 1973-89. Mgr. concert series Moorhead State U., 1956—61; mem. nat. bd. con. NEH, Washington, 1979—; dir. London semester Calif. State U., Fresno, 1982—92; dir. Frank Lloyd Wright Auditorium Project. Author: (book) Ideas in Context, 1958, The 1950's: America's "Placid" Decade, 1960, Reading Non-Fiction Prose, 1964, Reading Prose Fiction, 1964, Shakespeare and His Sources, 1966, Reading Literature, 1968, The Humanities Handbook (2 vols), 1969, (poems) The Journey Upward, 1999, Poems on the Internet (www.Poetry.com), 2000; editor: (book) Frank Lloyd Wright-Letters to Apprentices, 1982, Letters to Architects, 1984, Letters to Clients, 1986, Treasures of Taliesin, 1985, The Guggenheim Correspondence, 1986, Frank Lloyd Wright: His Living Voice, 1987, Frank Lloyd Wright, The Crowning Decade, 1989; translator: Federico Fellini, Comments on Film, 1987; contbr. Encyclopedia Int Educ, 1978; dir: Univ Press, Calif State Univ, 1982—92. With US Army, 1943—46, ETO. Named Nat Grand Prize Winner, Nat Library Poetry N Am Ann Poetry Contest, 1998. Jewish. Avocations: creative writing, music. Home: 65 Maywood Dr San Francisco CA 94127-2007 Office Phone: 415-661-3121. E-mail: tewilder@juno.com.

SATINE, BARRY ROY, lawyer; b. NYC, July 25, 1951; s. Norman S. and Fay (Mekles) S.; m. Janice Bea Halfond, Aug. 4, 1974; children: David, Leah. BA, CCNY, 1972; JD, George Washington U., 1975. Bar: N.Y. 1976, D.C. 1977, U.S. Dist. Ct. (so. dist.) N.Y. 1978, U.S. Supreme Ct. 1979, U.S. Dist. Ct. (ea. dist.) N.Y. 1982, U.S. Ct. Appeals (2d cir.) 1989. Trial atty. U.S. Civil Svc. Commn., Washington, 1975—78; atty. AT&T, NYC, 1978—81, N.Y. Tel. Co., NYC, 1981—82; mem. assoc. Surrey & Morse, NYC, 1982—84, ptnr., 1985, Jones Day, 1986—. Mem.: Assn. of Bar of City of N.Y. Office: Jones Day 222 East 41st St New York NY 10017 Office Phone: 212-326-3904. Business E-Mail: barryrsatine@jonesday.com.

SATINOVER, JEFFREY B., physicist, psychiatrist, writer; b. Chgo., Sept. 4, 1947; s. Joseph and Sena (Rotman) Satinover; m. Julie Rachel Leff, June 10, 1982; children: Sarah Katherine, Anne-Rebecca, Jenny Leigh. BS, MIT, 1971; EdM, Harvard U., 1973; MD, U. Tex., 1982; Diplomate, C.G

Jung Inst., Zurich, Switzerland, 1976; MS, Yale U., 2002; student in Physics, U. Nice, 2004—. Diplomate Am. Bd. Psychiatry and Neurology, Am. Bd. Geriat. Psychiatry. Fellow dept. psychiatry and child psychiatry Yale U., New Haven, 1982-86; founder, exec. dir. Sterling Inst., Stamford, Conn., 1985-92; med. dir. Temenos Inst., Westport, Conn., 1984—; pvt. practice Westport, 1992—. William James lectr. psychology and and religion Harvard U., 1975; mem. catchment area coun. S. W. Regional Mental Health Bd., 1988—92; mem. Lower Fairfield County Regional Action Coun. Against Substance Abuse, 1990—92; with relativistic heavy ion group dept. physics Yale U., New Haven, 1999—2001, with condensed matter theory group, 2001—03, with theoretical condensed matter physics group, 2002—03; dir. rsch. VKRA Quantitative Fin., 2003—; mem. condensed matter physics group U. Nice, France, 2003—; vis. lectr. Dept. Politics Princeton U., 2004—05. Co-author: Jungian Psychotherapy, 1984, Science and the Fragile Self, 1990, Jungian Analysis, 1993; author: Homesexuality and the Politics of Truth, 1994, The Empty Self: Gnostic Foundations of Modern Identity, 1994, Feathers of the Skylark, 1996, Cracking the Bible Code, 1997, The Quantum Brain, 2001; contbr. articles to profl. jours. Active nat. physician's resource coun. Focus on Family, 1994—97; pres. C. G. Jung Found., NY, 1988—92; founder, mem. exec. bd. com. Save Our Schs., 1994—; bd. dirs. Toward Tradition; bd. advisors Family Inst. Conn., 1996—; bd. dirs. Klingberg Family Ctrs., 1994—96. Capt. N.G. USAR, 1989—94, maj. USAR, 1995—. Recipient Seymour Lustman Residency Rsch. 2d pl. award, Yale U. Psychiatry Dept., 1983, 1985. Mem.: Internat. Assn. Analytical Psychology, Am. Psychiat. Assn. (Burroughs-Wellcome fellow 1983—85), Aspetuck Valley Country Club, Alpha Omega Alpha. Republican. Jewish. Avocations: tennis, harpsichord, jazz keyboard. Business E-Mail: jsatinov@princeton.edu.

SATINSKY, BARNETT, lawyer; b. Phila., June 17, 1947; s. Alex and Florence (Talsky) S.; m. Fredda Andrea Wagner, June 17, 1973; children: Meagen, Sara Beth, Jonathan. AB, Brown U., 1969; JD, Villanova U., 1972. Bar: Pa. 1972, U.S. Dist. Ct. (ea. dist) Pa. 1975, U.S. Dist. Ct. (mid. dist.) Pa. 1975, U.S. Ct. Appeals (3d cir.) 1981. Law clk. Phila. Ct. Common Pleas, 1972-73; dep. atty. gen. Pa. Dept. Justice, Harrisburg, 1973-75; 1st asst. counsel Pa. Pub. Utility Commn., Harrisburg, 1975-77, chief counsel, 1977; assoc. Fox, Rothschild, O'Brien & Frankel, LLP, Phila., 1978-81; ptnr. Fox Rothschild LLP, Phila., 1981—. Children Svcs. Rev. com., United Way Southeast Pa., 1984-86; bd. dirs. ACLU, Harrisburg, 1973-74, Voyage House, Inc., 1994-96. Mem. ABA (pub. utility, labor and employment law sects., employee benefits com. 1984—), Pa. Bar Assn. (labor rels., pub. utility law sects. 1980—, pub. utility law com., governing coun. 1991-93), Phila. Bar Assn. (labor law com. 1980—, chmn. pub. utility law com. 1988-91), Nat. Assn. Coll. and Univ. Attys., Nat. Assn. Regulatory Commrs. (staff subcom. law 1977), Soc. for Human Resource Mgmt., Louis D. Brandeis Law Soc. Democrat. Jewish. Office: Fox Rothschild LLP 2000 Market St Philadelphia PA 19103-3291 Office Phone: 215-299-2088. Business E-Mail: bsatinsky@foxrothschild.com.

SATIR, BIRGIT H., medical educator, researcher; b. Copenhagen, Mar. 22, 1934; Magistra in Biochemistry, U. Copenhagen, 1961. Rsch. assoc. dept. zoology U. Chgo., 1962-66; asst. rsch. physiologist U. Calif. Dept. Physiology-Anatomy, Berkeley, 1967-74, assoc. rsch. physiologist, 1974-76, adj. assoc. prof., 1976-77; sci. dir. Analytical Ultrastructure Ctr., Cancer Rsch. Inst. Albert Einstein Coll. of Medicine, Bronx, NY, 1977-84, prof. dept. anatomy and structural biology, 1977—. Rschr. Phys.- Chem. Inst. Copenhagen, 1956-57, Biol. Inst., Copenhagen, 1958-61; mem. Cellular and Molecular Basis of Disease Rev. Com., Nat. Inst. Gen. Med. Scis., 1977-79; vis. prof. divsn. biology Calif. Inst. Tech., 1984-85. Mem. editl. bd. Jour. Ultrastructural Rsch., 1975-80, Jour. Cell Biology, 1979-81, Modern Cell Biology, 1980-90, Jour. Eukaryotic Microbiology, 1989-95. Rsch. fellow U. Geneva, 1965-66, Spl. fellow USPHS, 1972-73; recipient Outstanding Women Scientist award N.Y. chpt. Assn. Women in Sci., 1990, Rsch. award Am. Diabetes Assn., 1995. Fellow AAAS, Royal Danish Acad. Sci. and Letters; mem. Am. Soc. Cell Biology (coun. 1975-78, minority affairs com. 1987-90, fin. com. 1993—), Am. Assn. Anatomists, Am. Soc. Biochemistry and Molecular Biology, Electron Microscopy Soc. Am. (program vice-chairperson 38th Meeting 1980, program chairperson 39th Meeting 1981), NYSEM (pres. 1979-80), N.Y. Acad. Sci., Biophys. Soc. Office: Albert Einstein Coll of Medicine Jack and Pearl Resnick Campus 1300 Morris Park Ave Bronx NY 10461-1926 E-mail: bsatir@aecom.yu.edu.

SATLOFF, ROBERT B., think-tank executive; BS, Duke U.; MS, Harvard U.; PhD in Oriental Studies, Oxford U. Exec. dir. Washington Inst. for Near East Policy, 1993—2002, 2003—. Author, editor: Troubles on the East Bank: Challenges to the Domestic Stability of Jordan, 1986, Army and Politics in Mubarak's Egypt, 1988, The Politics of Change in the Middle East, 1993, From Abdullah to Hussein: Jordan in Transition, 1994, U.S. Policy toward Islamism, 2000, After Arafat? Succession in Palestinian Politics, 2002, The War on Terror: The Middle East Dimension, 2002; frequent commentator on the Middle East in major Am. newspapers including the Washington Post, N.Y. Times, Wall St. Jour. and L.A. Times; has appeared on various TV and radio programs to offer his analysis of events in the Middle East. Office: The Washington Inst for Near East Policy 1828 L St NW Ste 1050 Washington DC 20036-5128

SATO, EUNICE NODA, former mayor, consultant; b. Livingston, Calif., June 8, 1921; d. Bunsaku and Sawa (Maeda) Noda; m. Thomas Takashi Sato, Dec. 9, 1950; children: Charlotte Patricia, Daniel Ryuichi and Douglas Ryuji (twins). AA, Modesto Jr. Coll., 1941; BA, U. No. Colo., 1944; MA, Columbia U., 1948. Pub. sch. tchr. Mastodon Twp. Schs., Alpha, Mich., 1944-47; ednl. missionary Reformed Ch. Am., Yokohama, Japan, 1948-51; coun. mem. City of Long Beach, Calif., 1975-86; mayor, 1980-82. Sec. corp. bd. LA County Health Sys. Agy., 1978-79. Monthly contbr. articles to 2 neighborhood papers, 1975-86. Bd. dirs. Long Beach chpt. ARC, 1975-00; mem. exec. com. ARC, 1978-91, 93-99, past pres. and v.p., mem. Calif. state svc. coun., 1995-01; bd. dirs. Goodwill Industries, 1978-82; trustee St. Mary's Bauer Med. Ctr., 1977—; pres. Industry Edn. Coun., Long Beach, 1984-86, mem. exec. bd., 1984-2007; bd. dirs. Industry Edn. Coun. of Calif.; treas. So. Calif. Consortium of I.E.C., 1984-86, pres., 1988-89; mem. State Adv. Group on Juvenile Justice and Delinquency Prevention, 1983-91, Calif. Coun. Criminal Justice, 1983-92; legis. com. Girl Scout coun. Calif., 1986-92, chair, 1991-92; bd. dirs. Long Beach coun. Girl Scouts U.S., 1981-92; with Region III United Way, 1974-88; mem. Asian Pacific adv. com. Calif. Dept. Rehab., 1985-87, recreation commn. City of Long Beach, 1985-86, pub. safety policy com. League Calif. Cities, 1981-86; cmty. econ. and housing devel. com. So. Calif. Assn. Govts., 1976-86; with Calif. Task Force to Promote Self-Esteem and Personal and Social Responsibility, 1987-90; Long Beach chpt. pres. NCCJ, 1987-88; pres. Internat. Cmty. Coun., 1986-87, bd. dirs. 1986-01; pres. Japanese Am. Reps., 1987, 88, exec. bd. mem. 1987-03, 04—; presdl. appointee Nat. Adv. Coun. Ednl. Rsch. and Improvement, 1991-94; pres. Aux. to Sch. Theology, Claremont, 1990-91, exec. bd. 1989-91; nat. selective svc. sys. local bd. 138, 1990-01; SCA Edison Co. Equal Opportunity adv. coun., 1990-94; chair selection com. Leadership Long Beach, 1990-91, sec. exec. bd., 1991-92, bd. govs. 2003—; chair adv. bd. AIESEC, 1990-92; chmn. Long Beach Area Rep. Party, 1990-92; asst. sec. cen. com., L.A, 1990-92; sec.-gen. coun. on fin. and administrn. United Meth. Ch., 1992-00; appointed by Gov. to commn. on tchr. credentialing State Calif., 1994; LA coun. svc. coun. ARC, 1995-99; chair adminstrv. bd. Leisure World Cmty. Ch., 1996-02; rep. to South Coast Ecumenical Coun., 1993-02, chair pastor parish rels. com., 2000; chair Parents Day Festival com. Greater LA County, 1996-00; with Blue Ribbon com. Effective Parenting in Long Beach, 1997-99; mem. adult and elder care adv. com. Long Beach City Coll., Calif., 2004—; caregiver Grace First Presbyn. Ch., 2005—. Recipient Outstanding Svc. award Long Beach Coord. Coun., 1969, Mother of Yr. award Silverado United Meth. Ch., 1973, Hon. Svc. award Calif. PTA, 1963, Continuing Svc. award, 1974, Hon. Life Membership award Nat. PTA, 1974, Outstanding Laywoman of Yr. award Long Beach Area Coun. Chs., 1976, Woman of Yr. award State Women's Coun.-C. of C., 1979, Long Beach Internat. Bus. and Profl. Women's Club, Nat. Merit award DAR, 1982, Citizen of Yr. award Los Altos YMCA, 1982, Calif. Cmty. Pool Handicapped award, 1982, Outstanding Citizen award Torch Club of Long Beach, 1983, W. Odie Wright award Industry Edn. Coun., 1990, Humanitarian award NCCJ, 1992, Vol. of Yr. award ARC, 1995, 1st Life Membership award Long Beach chpt. UN Assn., Kunsho award Order of Sacred Treasure, Gold Rays with rosette from Japanese Govt., 1996, Sr. Vol. of Yr. Long Beach C.C., 1999, Al Taucher Rep. of Yr. award, 2001, Excellence in Leadership award Leadership Long Beach, 2004; Ann. Hall of Fame honoree Long Beach Century Club, 2006. Mem. Industry Edn. Coun. Long Beach (hon. life), Long Beach C. of C. (Dewey Smith cmty. svc. award), Lions Club (hon. life, Internat. Found. Melvin Jones fellow 2004, Outstanding Contrbn. award 2000), Boys Club of Long Beach (life), Soroptimist Internat. (Woman of Distinction in Econ. and Social Devel. 2001), Alpha Iota. Republican. Presbyterian. Home: Bixby Village 551 Pittsfield Ct Unit 101 Long Beach CA 90803-6355

SATO, GLENN KENJI, lawyer; b. Honolulu, Jan. 6, 1952; s. Nihei and Katherine (Miwa) S.; m. Donna Mae Shiroma, Apr. 4, 1980 (dec. Aug. 1985); m. Nan Sun Oh, Mar. 27, 1987 (dec. Nov. 1997); children: Gavan, Allison, Garrett; m. Sandra K. Kumagai, Nov. 21, 1999. BBA, U. Hawaii, 1975; JD, U. Calif., San Francisco, 1977. Bar: Hawaii 1978, U.S. Dist. Ct. Hawaii, 1978, U.S. Ct. Claims 1990. Assoc. Fujiyama, Duffy & Fujiyama, Honolulu, 1978-80, 83-87, ptnr., 1987-95; stockholder Law Offices of Glenn K. Sato, Honolulu, 1980-82; pres. ISL Svcs., Inc., Honolulu, 1983; ptnr. Sato & Thomas, Honolulu, 1995-98; pvt. practice Honolulu, 1998—. Vice chmn. Pattern Jury Instrn. Com., State of Hawaii, Honolulu, 1993. Treas. Polit. Action Com., Honolulu, 1993. Mem. Platform Assn., Beta Gamma Sigma. Avocations: golf, hunting, target shooting, surfing. Office: 220 S King St Ste 600 Honolulu HI 96813-4585

SATO, HIROYUKI, materials engineer, researcher; s. T. and M. Sato. PhD, MB in Engring., Tohoku U., Sendai, Japan, 1990. Rsch. assoc. Tohoku U., Sendai, Miyagi, Japan, 1990—97, lectr., 1997—99; assoc. prof. Hirosaki U., Hirosaki, Aomori, Japan, 1999—. Vis rschr. Tech. U. Hamburg, Germany, 1997—98; vis. prof. U. Erlangen, Germany, 2005, U. Tenn., 2005—06. Mem.: Japan Soc. Mech. Engrs., Iron and Steel Inst. Japan, Japan Inst. Light Metals, Minerals, Metals & Materials Soc., Japan Inst. of Metal. Avocations: radio, travel. Office: Hirosaki University Sci and Tech Intell Mech Bunkyo-3 Aomori Hirosaki 0368561 Japan Home Phone: 731-881-7382; Office Phone: +81-172-39-3673.

SATO, KAZUYOSHI, pathologist; b. Shibata, Niigata, Japan, Apr. 3, 1930; came to U.S., 1968; s. Katsueita and Kyo (Sakagawa) S.; m. Ann Marie Farrenkopf, July 5, 1964 (dec. Aug. 1983); children: P.T. Sachiko, P. Miyoko, Michael T., Phillip K. Student, Niigata U., Japan, 1954, MD, 1958. Diplomate Am. Bd. Pathology, Anatomic and Clin. Pathology. Intern USAF Hosp., Tachikawa, Japan, 1958-59, Ellis Hosp., Schenectady, NY, 1959-60, asst. resident in pathology, 1960-61; resident in pathology Free Hosp. for Women, Brookline, Mass., 1961-62, The Children's Hosp. Med. Ctr., Boston, 1962-63, resident in neuropathology, 1963-64; resident fellow in pathology Mayo Grad. Sch. Medicine, Rochester, Minn., 1968-70; dir. labs. Falmouth (Mass.) Hosp., 1972-96; dir. Falmouth Hosp. Service Lab., Sandwich, Mass., 1986-93. Pathologist and rsch. assoc. Atomic Bomb Casualty Commn., Nagasaki, Japan, 1964-68; pathologist, chief of pathology USPHS Hosp., Norfolk Va., 1970-72, Falmouth (Mass.) Hosp., 1972-97. Recipient Fulbright scholarship, 1959. Fellow Coll. Am. Pathologists, Am. Soc. Clin. Pathologists; mem. Assn. Mil. Surgeons U.S. Home: 88 Two Ponds Rd Falmouth MA 02540-2225

SATO, MOTOAKI, geologist, researcher; b. Tokyo, Oct. 11, 1929; came to U.S., 1955, 63. s. Iwazo and Kyoko (Ito) S.; m. Ellen B. Levinson, Feb. 11, 1961 (div. Sept. 1978); children: Emily Coates, Alice Isomé, Thomas Bartlett. BS in Geology, U. Tokyo, 1953, MS in Geology, 1955; PhD in Geology, U. Minn., 1959. Rsch. asst. dept. geophysics Univ. Minn., Mpls., 1956-58; rsch. fellow in geophysics dept. geol. scis. Harvard Univ., Cambridge, Mass., 1958-61; assoc. prof. geology Inst. Thermal Springs Research, Misasa, Tottori, Japan, 1961-63; rsch. geologist U.S. Geol. Survey, Washington, 1963-65, geologist, project chief Washington/Reston, Va., 1965-95; scientist emeritus U.S. Geological Survey, Washington/Reston, 1995—. Prin. investigator Lunar Sample & Sci. Program, NASA, 1971-80. Contbg. author books and articles in profl. jours. Fulbright/Smith-Mundt fellow Inst. Internat. Edn., 1955-57, Gilbert fellow U.S. Geol. Survey, Reston, Va., 1982-83. Mem. Am. Geophys. Union, Geochem. Soc., Geol. Soc. Washington (2d v.p. 1982-83), Am. Chem. Soc. (geochemistry divsn.). Achievements include patents for mitigation of acid mine drainage. Home: 11173 Lake Chapel Ln Reston VA 20191-4308 Office: US Geol Survey 956 National Ctr Reston VA 20192-0001 Home Phone: 703-860-8236; Office Phone: 703-648-6766. E-mail: msato@usgs.gov. *Remember that we did not design the way Nature works; Nature designed us, too. So let's listen ever so carefully, with an open mind, to what Nature is trying to tell us.*

SATO, THOMAS T., surgeon, educator; b. Fontana, Calif., Nov. 10, 1960; s. Tada and Jane Sato; m. Jennifer Sato, July 22, 1990; children: Misa, Eleanor. MD, U. So. Calif., LA, 1988. Asst. prof. surgery Med. Coll. Wis., Milw., 1997—2001, assoc. prof. surgery, 2001—. Dir. assoc. program surgery Med. Coll. Wis., 2005—. Bd. mem. Children's Splty. Group, Milw., 2005—06. Office: Division of Pediatric Surgery 999 N 92nd St Ste C320 Milwaukee WI 53226 Office Phone: 414-266-6550. Office Fax: 414-266-6579. E-mail: ttsato@mcw.edu.

SATORIUS, JOHN ARTHUR, lawyer; b. Berwyn, Ill., Aug. 20, 1946; s. Woodrow Wilson and Frances Jane (Embshoff) S.; m. Linda Kay Grove, Dec. 26, 1968; children: Katherine, Joseph. BA summa cum laude, U. Va., 1968; MA, Harvard U., 1972, JD cum laude, 1975, PhD, 1977. Bar: Minn. 1975. Assoc. Fredrikson & Byron PA, Mpls., 1975-81, ptnr., 1981—, also bd. dirs., mem. exec. com., v.p., 1997—2002, gen. counsel. Bd. dirs. Bellcomb Techs., Mpls. Editor Contract Law in Minn., 1993. Bd. dirs. Childrens Theater Co., Mpls., Minnesota Land Trust, Belwin Found. With US Army, 1968—70, Vietnam. Named Vol. of Yr. Met. Econ. Devel., 1986. Mem.: Phi Beta Kappa, Hennepin County Bar Assn., Minn. State Bar Assn. Avocations: wilderness canoe activities, travel, reading. Office: Fredrikson & Byron PA 200 S 6th St Ste 4000 Minneapolis MN 55402 Office Phone: 612-347-7023. Office Fax: 612-492-7077. Business E-Mail: jsatorius@fredlaw.com.

SATRE, DEREK DAVIES, psychologist, researcher; s. Neal and Jeanne Satre. BA, U. Calif., Berkeley, 1989; MPhil, U. Cambridge, 1990; PhD, U. So. Calif., LA, 2001. Lic. clin. psychologist Calif., 2001. Rschr. Kaiser Permanente Divsn. Rsch., Oakland, 2001—; asst. adj. prof. psychiatry U. Calif., San Francisco, 2004—. Clin. psychologist U. Calif., 2003—. Contbr. scientific papers, chapters to books. Fellow, Nat. Inst. Aging, 1997—2001, Nat. Inst. Drug Abuse, 2001—04, U. Calif., San Francisco, 2001—04; grantee, NIH, 2005. Mem.: APA, Gerontol. Soc. Am. Episcopalian. Avocations: travel, rowing, tennis. Office: U Calif 401 Parnassus Ave Box 0984 San Francisco CA 94143 Home Phone: 415-771-8480. E-mail: dereks@lppi.ucsf.edu.

SATRE, PHILIP GLEN, casino entertainment executive, lawyer; b. Palo Alto, Calif., Apr. 30, 1949; s. Selmer Kenneth and Georgia June (Sterling) S.; m. Jennifer Patricia Arnold, June 30, 1973; children: Malena Anne, Allison Neal, Jessica Lilly, Peter Sterling. BA, Stanford U., 1971; JD, U. Calif.-Davis, 1975; postgrad. sr. exec. program, MIT, 1982. Bar: Nev. 1975, Calif. 1976. Assoc. Vargas & Bartlett, Reno, 1975-79; v.p., gen. counsel, sec. Harrah's, Reno, 1980-83, sr. v.p., 1983-84; pres. Harrah's East, Atlantic City, 1984; pres., CEO Harrah's Hotels and Casinos, Reno, 1984-91; dir., sr. v.p. Gaming Group The Promus Cos., Inc., Memphis, 1988-91, dir., pres., COO, 1991-94, dir., pres. CEO, 1994-95; pres., CEO Harrah's Entertainment, Inc., Memphis, 1995—, chmn., pres., CEO, 1997—; dir. JDN Realty Co., Memphis, 1999—. Dir., treas. Nat. Jud. Coll., Reno. Active The Stanford Athletic Bd., 1996—. Mem. ABA, Nev. Bar Assn., Calif. Bar Assn., Order of Coif, Phi Kappa Phi, Stanford Alumni Assn. (pres. Reno chpt. 1976-77), Young Pres. Orgn., The Bus. Roundtable. Office: PO Box 29526 Las Vegas NV 89126-9526

SATTER, RAYMOND NATHAN, judge; b. Denver, Oct. 19, 1948; s. Charles Herbert and Muriel Vera (Tuller); m. Suzanne Elizabeth Ehlers, May 28, 1977. BA, U. Denver, 1970; JD, Cath. U., 1973. Bar: Colo. 1973, U.S. Dist. Ct. Colo. 1973, U.S. Ct. Appeals (10th cir.) 1973, U.S. Supreme Ct. 1976, U.S. Tax Ct. 1981. Assoc. Wallace, Armatas & Hahn, Denver, 1973-75; ptnr. Tallmadge, Wallace & Hahn, Denver, 1975-77; pvt. practice Denver, 1978-87; Denver County judge, 1987—; presiding judge Denver County Ct., 2001—04. Gen. counsel Satter Dist., Denver, 1977-78; assoc. mcpl. judge City of Englewood, Colo., 1985-86; com. on civil rules Colo. Supreme Ct., 1988-2003. Pres. Young Artists Orch. Denver, 1985-87; sec. Denver Symphony Assn., 1985-86. Mem. Colo. Bar Assn. (ethics com.), Denver Bar Assn. (bd. trustees 1998-2001, Jud. Excellence award 1992, 95). Avocations: sailing, bicycling, classical music, fishing, bridge. Office: Denver County Ct 108 City & County Bldg 1437 Bannock St Denver CO 80202-5337 Office Phone: 303-640-4718. Business E-Mail: rsatter@ci.denver.co.us.

SATTERFIELD, DAVID MICHAEL, ambassador; b. Balt., Dec. 18, 1954; m. Martha Satterfield; 2 children. BA, U. Md., 1976; JD, Georgetown U. Law Ctr., 1978. With US Fgn. Svc., 1980—, dir. Exec. Secretariat staff, 1990—93; dir. Bur. Near East and South Asian Affairs NSC, 1993-96; dir. Office of Israel & Arab-Israeli Affairs US Dept. State, 1996—98, US amb. to Lebanon Beirut, 1998—2001, prin. dep. asst. sec., Bur. Near Ea. Affairs, 2001—04, dep. asst. sec., 2004—05; dep. chief of mission Am. Embassy, Baghdad, 2005—06; sr. adv. for sec., sr. coord. for Iraq US Dept. State, 2006—. Recipient Presdl. Meritorious Exec. Rank award, Disting. Honor award, US Dept. State, Sr. Performance award, Superior Honor award (6). *

SATTERTHWAITE, GEORGE, II, security firm executive; b. San Jose, Costa Rica, Apr. 18, 1935; s. Livingston Lord andAdelaide (Bristol) S.; m. Helen Marie McCann, June 28, 1958 (div. July 1982); children: Patricia Ann, Livingston Lord, Frank Lord; m. Deanna Marie Kelliher, Apr. 30, 1983; 1 child, Kelley Elizabeth. BA in Internat. Rels., U. Pa., 1957; MA in History, Johns Hopkins U., 1965. Commd. 2d lt. U.S. Army, 1957, advanced through grades to col., 1979, retired, 1987; chief indsl. security Planning Rsch. Corp., McLean, Va., 1987-89; corp. dir. security PRC Inc., McLean, 1989-96; cons., 1996-98; cons., contracts officer SSI Inc., McLean, Va., 1998—2000, photography and security cons., 2000—. Mem. County Bd. Elections, Prince George County, 2003—; mem. admissions coun. U. Pa., 2002—. Mem.: SAR, Mil. Officers Assn. Am. (life), Piscataway Citizens Assn. (bd. dirs. 2003—). Republican. Roman Cath. Avocations: photography, music, volks marching, travel. Home and Office: 513 Holly Rd Fort Washington MD 20744-6606 Personal E-mail: GS2nd@aol.com.

SATTERTHWAITE, HELEN FOSTER, retired state legislator; b. Blawnox, Pa., July 8, 1928; d. Samuel J. and Lillian (Schreiber) Foster; m. Cameron B. Satterthwaite, Dec. 23, 1950 (div. July 1979); children: Mark Cameron, Tod Foster, Tracy Lynn, Keith Alan, Craig Evan (dec.). BS in Chemistry, Duquesne U., 1949. Rsch. asst. Gulf R & D, Harmarville, Pa., 1950; rsch. chemist E.I. duPont de Nemours & Co., Wilmington, Del., 1951-53; biol. technician USDA, 1967-68; lab. technician U. Ill. Coll. Agr., 1968-70; rsch. asst. Iowa State U. Coll. Agr., 1971; technician Nat. Sci. Lab., U. Ill. Coll. Vet. Medicine, 1971-74; rep. Ill. Ho. of Reps., Springfield, 1974-92, majority leader, 1991-92, mem. sch. fin. task force, 1990-92, chmn. com. on higher edn., 1983-91, vice chmn. elem. and secondary edn., 1983-91; ret., 1993. Mem. Commn. on Mental Health and Devel. Disabilities, 1975-85, mem. exec. com., 1977-85, vice chmn., 1979-85; mem. Commn. to Visit and Examine State Instns., 1977-85; mem. Task Force on Global Climate Change, 1991-96; treas. LWV, 1995-98, sec., 1998-2001; treas. Bus. and Profl. Women's Club, 1993-94, sec., 1994-95; bd. dirs. East Ctrl. Ill. Health Sys. Agy., 1977-79, Champaign County Mental Health Ctr., 1993-2002, Univ. YWCA, U. Ill., 1987—, Girls Inc., 1992-96; bd. dirs. Champaign County United Way, 1970-74, mem. budget com., 1973-74, mem. joint rev. com. on funding Champaign County mental health programs, 1973; co-chmn. task force on mental retardation Champaign County Mental Health Bd., 1973; mem. Ill. Devel. Disability Advocacy Authority, 1977-85, vice chmn., 1979-80; chmn. Ill. House Dem. Study Group, 1979-81; mem. Edn. Commn. on States, 1985-92, Nat. Conf. State Legis. Commn. on Labor and Edn., 1985-92; bd. govs. U. YMCA, 1995-2003. Recipient Freshman Legislator of Yr. award Ill. Edn. Assn., 1975, commndation Ill. State's Attys. Assn., 1975, Best Legislator award Ind. Voters Ill., 1976, 78, 80, 82, 84, 86, 88, 90, cert. of honor Assn. Student Govts., 1977, Disting. Svc. cert. AMVETS, 1977, Environ. Legislator of Yr. award Ill. Environ. Coun., 1977, 79, 81, 83, Meritorious Svc. award Champaign County Coun. on Alcoholism, 1978, Ill. C.C. Trustees ASsn., 1986, Perfect Voting Record award Ill. Credit Union League, 1979, Ill. Wildlife Fedn., 1979, cert., of spl. recognition Ill. Women's Polit. Caucus, 1979, 80, Pub. Svc. award Izaak Walton League, 1980, Friend of Edn. award Ill. Bd. Edn., 1985, cert. of appreciation Champaign County Urban League, 1987, Resolution of Honor, Ill. Libr. Assn., 1987, 100 Percent award Ill. Coun. Sr. Citizens Orgns., 1989, Dare To Be Great award Ill. Women Adminstrs., 1989; named Person of Yr., Champaign County Mental Health Assn., 1981, Pub. Citizen of Yr., Illino Dist. and Ill. chpt. NASW, 1981, Legislator of Yr., Ill. Assn. Sch. Social Workers, 1989. Mem. Ill. Conf. Women Legislators (co-convenor 1981-83), Nat. Order Women Legislators (bd. dirs. region IV 1982, treas. 1983-84), State Univs. Annuitants Assn. (exec. com. U. Ill. Urbana Champaign chpt. 2003—), Champaign County League Women Voters, Delta Kappa Gamma. Mem. Soc. Of Friends.

SATTERTHWAITE, JANET F., lawyer; b. Washington, Apr. 29, 1960; BA, Yale Univ., 1982; attended, Christ's Coll., Cambridge Univ.; JD, Univ. Va., 1986. Bar: Va. 1986, DC 1988, Wash. 1993. Ptnr., Trademark & Domain Name practice Venable LLP, Washington, 2001—. U.S. corr. Marques newsletter, Assn. European Trademark Owners. Contbr. articles to profl. jours. Office: Venable LLP 575 7th St NW Washington DC 20004 Office Fax: 202-344-4974, 202-344-8300. Business E-Mail: jfsatterthwaite@venable.com.

SATTERTHWAITE, MARK A., economics professor; BS, Calif. Inst. Tech., 1967; MS, Univ. Wis., Madison, 1969, PhD, 1973. Asst. prof. Kellogg Sch. Mgmt., Northwestern Univ., 1972—78, prof., 1978—83, Earl Dean Howard prof., 1983—2003, IBM rsch. prof., 1979—81, Herman Smith rsch. prof., 1981—83, prof. mgmt. strategy, 1985—, dir. Gen. Motors Rsch. Ctr. for Strategy in Mgmt., 1987—, chmn., dept. Mgmt. & Strategy, 1990—92, assoc. dean, 1992—96, A.C. Buehler prof. hosp. & health svc. mgmt., 2003—. Vis. prof. Calif. Inst. Tech., 1989. Editor (assoc.): Journal of Economic Theory, 1987—; contbr. articles to profl. jour. Fellow: Econometric Soc., Am. Acad. Arts & Sci.; mem.: Game Theory Soc. Office: Kellogg School of Management Northwestern University Evanston IL 60208 Business E-Mail: m-satterthwaite@northwestern.edu.

SATTERWHITE, R. SCOTT, computer company executive; b. Albuquerque, Aug. 5, 1962; s. Ramon Stewart and Katherine Pricilla (Holland) S. BSEE, Tex. A&M U., 1984; MBA, U. Houston, Clear Lake, 1991. Registered profl. engr., Tex. Technician So. Avionics Co., Beaumont, Tex., 1976-80; engr. Fairchild Aircraft, San Antonio, 1982-83, IBM, Austin, Tex., 1983-84, staff engr. fed. systems divsn. Houston, 1985-91; CEO TerraSpace Tech., Inc., Houston, 1991-93, Ecologics Engring., Inc., Houston, 1991—2000, also bd. dirs.; regional mgr. Wind River, 2000—. Ceo, bd. dirs. Wave Communications Internat., Houston, 1989—; corporate liason Bus. of Space Symposiums, Houston, 1989—; lectr. Storm Leadership, Houston, 1989—. Editor, author: Spirit of Apollo, 1989; contbr. articles to profl. jours. Chmn. com. Clear Lake Econ. Devel. Found., Houston, 1982-00; vol. Krug Internat. Space Med. Rsch., Houston, 1987-89. Mem. AIAA (sr. mem., exec. councillor 1988-89, chmn. 1987-89, treas. 1987-88, numerous awards), Students for Exploration and Devel. of Space (treas. 1990-91), World Futures Soc., Nat. Space Soc. Avocations: investing, windsurfing, skiing, racquetball, scuba diving.

SATTLER, BRIAN R., lawyer; b. Mpls., Mar. 31, 1963; s. Roger Raymond and Rosemary Sattler; m. Andrea Marie Steinberg, Dec. 8, 1990; children: Grant, Austin, Gretchen. BS, Drake U., 1985, MBA, 1990; JD, Hamline U., 1989. Bar: Minn. 1989, US Dist. Ct. (Minn.) 1990. Assoc. John D. Rice Law Firm, Mpls., 1990-91, Meagher & Geer Law Firm, Mpls., 1991-97; corp. atty. Schwan Food Co., Marshall, Minn., 1997—99, asst. gen. counsel, 1999—2003, sr. v.p., asst. gen. counsel, 2003—05, sr. v.p., gen. counsel, 2005—, mem. exec. com., 2005—. Bd. dirs. Schwan's Risk Mgmt., Inc., Marshall. Mem. Minn. State Bar Assn., Am. Corp. Counsel Assn., Soc. Human Resource Mgmt. Republican. Roman Catholic. Office: Schwan Food Co 115 W College Dr Marshall MN 56258-1747

SATTLER, BRUCE WEIMER, lawyer; b. South Gate, Calif., July 30, 1944; s. LeRoy Edward and Mary Beth (Weimer) S.; m. Earle Martha Ross, July 22, 1972. BA, Stanford U., 1966, JD, 1969. Bar: Colo. 1969, U.S. Dist. Ct. Colo. 1969, U.S. Dist. Ct. Mont. 1982, U.S. Dist. Ct. (no. dist.) Tex. 1989, U.S. Ct. Appeals (10th cir.) 1969, U.S. Ct. Appeals (9th cir.) 1984. Assoc. Holland & Hart, Denver, 1969-75, ptnr., 1975-87; supervising trial atty. Equal Employment Opportunity Commn., Denver, 1973; ptnr. Morris, Lower & Sattler, Denver, 1987-90, Faegre & Benson, Denver, 1990—2004. Bd. dirs. ACLU of Colo., Denver, 1975-80, 88-94, 2003-, Colo. Legal Svcs., Legal Aid Soc. of Metro Denver, 1976—, Colo. Lawyers Com., Denver, 1990-94, Children's Legal Clinic, Denver, 1989-91, Colo. Women's Employment and Edn., Denver, 1986-89. Fellow Coll. Labor and Employment Lawyers; mem. Denver Bar Assn., Colo. Bar Assn. Office Phone: 303-321-5837. Business E-Mail: bruce@mesattler.com.

SATTLER, ROLF, retired plant morphologist, educator; b. Göppingen, Germany, Mar. 8, 1936; arrived in Can., 1962; s. Otto and Emma Sattler; m. Liv Hamann, May 1, 1963 (div. 1985). PhD, U. Munich, 1961; DSc (hon.), Colombo U. Asst. prof. McGill U., Montreal, Que., Canada, 1964-69, assoc. prof., 1969-77, prof., 1977-97, emeritus prof., 1997—. Author: Organogenesis of Flowers, 1973 (Lawson medal 1974), Biophilosophy, 1986; editor: Theoretical Plant Morphology, 1978, Axioms and Principles of Plant Construction, 1981; contbr. articles to profl. jours. NATO fellow, 1962-64. Fellow Royal Soc. Can., Linnean Soc. London; mem. Can. Bot. Assn., Sci. and Med. Network.

SATULOFF, BARTH, accountant, dispute resolution professional, investment strategist, publishing executive, rancher; b. Buffalo, Dec. 13, 1945; s. Bernard and Annette (Lurie) S.; m. Gail Lois Seid Jaffe, Aug. 23, 1992. BBA in Acctg., U. Miami, 1967, MBA, 1969. CPA, Fla., N.Y., Ill., La.; registered securities arbitrator, NYSE, AMEX, NASD; cert. state ct. arbitrator, Fla., Am. Arbitration Assn., 1992-2005; Spl. Master, Fla. pvt. property and land use cases; cert. comml. arbitrator Am. Arbitration Assn., 1992-2005. Staff acct. Price Waterhouse, Miami, Fla., 1969-71; tax specialist Laventhol & Horwath, Miami, 1973-74; mng. dir. Barth Satuloff, CPA, Miami, 1974-99; chief investment officer, pres., chmn. bd. dirs. Caddis & Co., Inc., Reno, 1998—. Pres., bd. dirs. Satuloff Bros., Inc., Buffalo, 1974-94, Miami, 1994-97. Satuloff Bros. Nev., Inc., Reno, 1997—; CEO, dir. Papillon Press, Inc., Miami, 1998-2001, Vero Beach, 2001—. Mem. Ctr. for the Arts, Vero Beach, Fla., 2001—, Met. Mus. Art, NYC, 1997—, Pagosa Springs Art Coun., 2006—; mem. Fla. state com. Nat. Mus. Women in the Arts, Washington, 1997—. With Fla. N.G., 1970—76. Mem.: AICPA (mem. small bus. taxation com. of tax divsn. 1993—96, mem. fed. tax forms com. of tax divsn. 1997—99), Fla. Inst. CPAs, Idaho Rivers United, Audubon Soc., Ducks Unltd., Nat. Wild Turkey Fedn., Trout Unltd. (life), Rocky Mountain Elk Found. (life; founder Indian River chpt., Fla. state chmn. Habitat coun. Trails. Soc.), Safari Club Internat., Antique Automobile Club Am., Cadillac-LaSalle Club, Am. Rivers Club, Nature Conservancy, Miami Country Day Sch. Alumni Assn. (sec. 1987—93, bd. dirs. 1987—2001, treas. 1994—2001). Avocations: hunting, fishing, photography, antique automobiles. Home and Office: 23 Seagull Pl Vero Beach FL 32960

SATZ, LOUIS K., publishing executive; b. Chgo., Ill., Apr. 28, 1927; s. Harry Addison and Faye Satz; m. Janet Maas, Jan. 2, 1952 children: Jay, Jonathan BS in Mktg, U. Ill., 1949. Circulation dir. Pubs. Devel. Corp., Chgo., 1953, Guns mag., Jr. Arts and Activities, 1961; wholesaler sales mgr., then v.p., dir. sales Bantam Books, Inc., NYC, 1962-80, sr. v.p., dir. diversified markets, 1980-84; pub. Passport Books, Lincolnwood, Ill., 1985-88; pres. Louis K. Satz Assocs., Pub. Cons., NYC, 1988-91; ptnr. Scott/Satz Group, Pub. Cons., Walnut Creek, Calif., 1991—. Guest lectr. Sarah Lawrence Coll.Pub. Sch., Pace U.; faculty Hofstra U., Denver Pub. Inst.; cons. World Book Encyclopedia; bd. dirs. NY is Book Country, Brandeis U. Pub. Scholarship Fund, Oscar Dystel Fellowship NYU. Served with AUS, World War II, ETO. Mem. Am. Assn. Pubs. (chmn. small books mktg. div. 1975) Office Phone: 925-934-2919.

SAUCERMAN, ALVERA ADELINE, elementary school educator; b. Colorado Springs, Nov. 29, 1932; d. Alva Arthur and Delpha Adeline (Cole) Gieck; m. James Ray Saucerman; 1 child, James Randall. Student, Stephens Bus. Sch., Denver, 1950—51; AA, Scottsbluff Coll., 1961; BEd, NW Mo. State U., 1965, MEd, 1971. Cert. French, reading specialization and learning disabilities tchr. Tchr. Lake Alice (Nebr.) Sch., 1961-62, West Nodaway Sch., Clearmont, Mo., 1965-67; remedial reading tchr. Maryville (Mo.) R II, 1968-74, dir. learning lab., 1975-88, tchr. learning disabilities, 1974-97; ret. Lectr. spl. edn. N.W. Mo. State U., Maryville, 1978—97. Mem. Maryville State Tchrs. Assn. (sec. 1978-79), AAUW (life, pres. 1981-83 Maryville Br.), Mo. State Tchrs. Assn. (life), Delta Kappa Gamma, Kappa Delta Pi (life). Avocations: travel, photography, reading, dance. Home: 1331 NW 107th Ter Gainesville FL 32606-5489

SAUCIER, GENE DUANE, retired state legislator, import/export company executive; b. Dallas, Sept. 25, 1931; s. Albert L. and Myrtle Irene (West) S.; m. Marilyn Emmy Cox, Dec. 27, 1952 (div. Sept. 1980); children: Alan, Steve, Renee; m. Giulia Riga LaCagnina, Nov. 28, 1981. BS in Agronomy Soils, Miss. State U., 1953; MS in Counseling, U. So. Miss., 1970, EdD in Adult Edn., 1978. Builder, developer Saucier Co., Hattiesburg, Miss., 1957-70; dir. admissions U. So. Miss., Hattiesburg, 1970-74, dean spl. acad. svcs., 1974-84, asst. v.p. bus. and fin., 1984-93; mem. Miss. Ho. of Reps., Jackson, 1993-99; ret., 1999. Mem. conservation and devel. coun. S.E. Mo., 2005. Mem. Fed. Land Coun., 1997—2003; scoutmaster Boy Scouts Am., 1960—70, chmn. camping and activities Pine Burr area, 1970; bd. dirs., founder Hub Coun., 2000; bd. dirs. Miss. Wild Turkey Fedn., Pine Burr chpt., 2000. 1st lt. pilot USAF, 1953—56. Named Forrest County Tree Farmer of Yr., 1996, Miss. Tree Farmer Yr., 1996; recipient Forestry award Miss. Wildlife Fedn., 1997, Legislator of Yr. Coastal Conservation Assn., 1997. Mem. So. Assn. Collegiate Registrars and Admissions Officers (bd. dirs. 1981, local arrangements chmn. 1981, v.p. admissions and fin. aid 1982-83, pres. 1985-86), Miss. Assn. Collegiate Registrars and Admissions Officers, Miss. Forestry Assn. (exec. bd. dirs. 1992-94, bd. dirs. 1992-94), Soc. Am. Foresters (cert. rev. bd. 2003-05), Am. Legion (life), Miss. Nature Conservancy, Forrest/Lamar Forestry Assn. (pres. 1989-92, 2007—), Audobon (v.p. Forest County chpt. 2004), Sigma Chi (life), ODK, Phi Delta Kappa, Omicron Delta Kappa. Personal E-mail: treefarm43@hotmail.com.

SAUCIER, GUYLAINE, corporate financial executive; b. Noranda, Que., Can., June 10, 1946; d. Gérard and Yvette (Thiffault) S. Chartered acct., École Hautes Etudes Commls., Montreal, Can., 1971. Formerly chair Joint Com. on Corp. Governance. Bd. dirs. Petro-Can., Axa Assurances Inc., Bank Montreal, CHC Helicopter Corp., Areva Group. Fellow Inst. Chartered Accts., Inst. Corp. Dirs.; mem. Order Can. Avocation: tennis. Office Phone: 514-397-5494. Business E-Mail: gsaucier@gsaucier.com.

SAUDEK, CHRISTOPHER D., medical educator; b. Bronxville, NY, Oct. 8, 1941; s. Robert and Elizabeth (Koch) S.; m. Susan Saudek; children: Mark S., Deborah M., Christina A., Anthony C. AB, Harvard U., 1963; MD, Cornell U., 1967. Resident in medicine Presbyn. St. Luke's Hosp., Chgo., 1967-69, Boston City Hosp., 1969-70; fellow in metabolism Thorndike Lab. Harvard U., Cambridge, Mass., 1970-72; asst prof. Cornell U., Ithaca, N.Y., 1973-80; assoc. prof. Johns Hopkins U., Balt., 1981-91, prof., 1991—; former pres. American Diabetes Assoc. Author Johns Hopkins Guide to Diabetes, 1997; co-author (with Sandra Woodruff) The Complete Diabetes Prevention Plan, 2004. Named Outstanding Clinician in Diabetes, Am. Diabetes Assn., 1991. Office: Johns Hopkins U Med Sch Osler 576 600 N Wolfe St Baltimore MD 21287-0005

SAUER, DAVID ANDREW, librarian, writer; b. Urbana, Ill., Feb. 25, 1948; s. Elmer Louis and Frances (Hill) S. BA, Northwestern U., 1970; MS, Simmons Coll., 1975. Reference libr. Boston U., 1976-78, bibliographer, 1978-84, sci. bibliographer, 1984-88, founder and head libr. Stone Sci. Libr., 1988-94; v.p. info. svcs. CyberHelp, Inc., 1995-98; sr. tech. editor Qualcomm, Inc., 1997-2000, 2003—04, sr. tech. writer, 2004—06; staff tech. writer Quaalcomm, Inc., 2006—; tech. pubs. supr. QCP Inc., 2000—01, staff tech. writer/libr., 2001—02; librarian San Diego Maritime Mus., 2002—03. Co-author of 12 books including: Access for Windows 95: The Visual Learning Guide, 1995, Windows NT 4.0 Visual Desk Reference, 1997, Discover Netscape Communicator, 1997. Mem. S.W. Corridor Project, Boston, 1977-87, Forest Hills Neighborhood Improvement Assn., Boston, 1977-90, Forest Hills/Woodbourne Neighorhood Group, 1991-94. Mem. ALA, IEEE, Spl. Librs. Assn., Soc. Tech. Comm. Democrat. Home: 2340 29th St San Diego CA 92104 Personal E-mail: dasauer@cox.net.

SAUER, ELISSA SWISHER, nursing educator; b. Williamsport, Pa., Jan. 9, 1935; d. Oliver S. and Emily Louisa (Gehron) Swisher; m. Raymond James Sauer, Nov. 27, 1964. Diploma, Reading Hosp., Pa., 1957; BS, Albright Coll., Reading, 1958; MSN, U. Pa., 1964. Instr. Reading Hosp. Sch. Nursing, 1957—60, 1964—66, 1969—70, Abington Meml. Hosp. Sch. Nursing, 1960—63; nurse Cmty. Health and Civic Assn., Ardmore, Pa., 1966-67; pub. health coord. Albert Einstein Med. Ctr., 1967-68; pvt. duty nurse, 1968-73; clin. faculty Schuylkill County AVTS, 1973-74; prof. nursing Reading Area CC, 1975-80, dir. nursing programs, asst. dean health svcs., 1989-2000, asst. dean emerita, 2001—, adj. instr. nursing, 2003—; oncology nurse adminstr.-educator Comprehensive Cmty. Cancer Ctr., Allentown, Pa., 1981-85; exec. dir. Holy Family Home Health Care, Orwigsburg, Pa., 1985-89. Cons. nursing edn. and continuing edn.; evaluator for nat. nurse aide cert. assessment program, 2000—; adj. instr. nursing Reading Area C.C., 2003—. Author: Procedure Manual to accompany Fundamentals of Nursing: Human Health and Function, 3d edit., 2003. Mem.: Sigma Theta Tau. Home: 1114 Pepper Ridge Dr Reading PA 19606-3803 E-mail: esauer@ptd.net.

SAUER, HARRY JOHN, JR., mechanical engineer, educator, academic administrator; b. St. Joseph, Mo., Jan. 27, 1935; s. Harry John and Marie Margaret (Witt) S.; m. Patricia Ann Zbierski, June 9, 1956; children: Harry John, Elizabeth Ann, Carl Andrew, Robert Mark, Katherine Anne, Deborah Elaine, Victoria Lynn, Valerie Joan, Joseph Gerard. BS, U. Mo., Rolla, 1956, MS, 1958; PhD, Kans. State U., 1963. Instr. mech. engring. Kans. State U., Manhattan, 1960-62; sr. engr., cons. Midwest Rsch. Inst., Kansas City, Mo., 1963-70; mem. faculty dept. mech. and aerospace engring. U. Mo., Rolla, 1957—, prof., 1966—, assoc. chmn., 1980-84, dean grad. study, 1984-92. Cons. in field; mem. Gov.'s Commn. on Energy Conservation, 1977; mem. Mo. Solar Energy Resource Panel, 1979-83; mem. Accreditation Bd. for Engring. and Tech. Co-author: Environmental Control Principles, 1975, 4th edit., 1985, Thermodynamics, 1981, Heat Pump Systems, 1983, Engineering Thermodynamics, 1985, Principles of Heating, Ventilating and Air Conditioning, 1991, 5th edit., 2006; contbr. articles to profl. jours. Pres. St. Patrick's Sch. Bd., 1970-72, St. Patrick's Parish Council, 1975-76. Recipient Ralph R. Teetor award Soc. Automotive Engrs., 1968; Hermann F. Spoehrer Meml. award St. Louis chpt. ASHRAE, 1979; also E. K. Campbell award of merit, 1983; Louise and Bill Holladay disting. fellow, 1999. Mem. ASME, ASHRAE (disting. svc. award 1981, exceptional svc. award 2001), NSPE, Soc. Automotive Engrs., Am. Soc. Engring. Edn., Mo. Soc. Profl. Engrs., Mo. Acad. Sci. (Most Disting. Scientist award 2003), Sigma Xi. Roman Catholic. Home: 10355 College Hills Dr Rolla MO 65401-7726 Office: Dept of Mech Engring U Mo Rolla MO 65401 Home Phone: 573-364-1272; Office Phone: 573-341-4143. Business E-Mail: sauer@umr.edu.

SAUER, JAMES LESLIE, librarian, educator; b. Buffalo, Aug. 7, 1953; s. Edwin C. and Margaret M. (Denne) S.; m. Paula J. Westerling, Aug. 20, 1977; children: Jacob, Adam, Joseph, Ariel, Abigail, Isaac, Mary Denise, Martha. BA, SUNY, Buffalo, 1975, MLS, 1977; MA, Villanova U., 1985. Libr. Buffalo and Erie County Pub. Librs., 1977-78, Masten Park Rehab. Ctr., 1979; dir. libr. Eastern U., St. Davids, Pa., 1980—. Pres. Tri-State Coll. Libr. Coop., 1999—2003. Coun. Biblical Manhood and Womanhood, 1996—. Mem. ALA, Pa. Libr. Assn., Assn. Christian Librs., Evang. Theol. Soc., Timothy Bitterman Soc. Republican. Presbyterian. Avocations: painting, parenting, book collecting. Home: 1207 Stirling St Coatesville PA 19320-3526 Office Phone: 610-341-5957. E-mail: jsauer@eastern.edu.

SAUER, JEFF, university hockey coach; b. St. Paul, Minn. m. Jamie Sauer Adler; children: Chip, Beth. BA in Sociology, Colo. Coll., 1965. Asst. hockey, baseball coach Colo. Coll., Colo. Springs, 1966-68, head coach hockey, 1971-82; asst.coach hockey U. Wis., Madison, 1968-71, head coach hockey, 1980—. Mem. U.S. Olympic Hockey Com., 1984; coach Olympic Festival, 1987, USA Select Team, Pravda Cup, Leningrad, Russia, 1989, Team USA, Goodwill Games, 1990, U.S. Nat. Team World Championships, 1995, U.S. Select Team, Tampere Cup, Finland, 1997, coach, organizer youth hockey camps in summer; asst. coach USA World Jr. Team, 2003—; head coach USA Team TUI Cup, Manheim, Germany, Gold medal-winning hockey team Deaf Olympics, Salt Lake City, 2007. Counselor Stan Mikita's Hockey Camp for Hearing Impaired, Chgo. Named We. Coll. Hockey Assn. Coach of Yr. 1972-73, 74-75 (Colo. Coll.); NCAA championship (Wis.) 1983, 90, WCHA championship 1987-88, 97-98, WCHA Playoff Championship, 1982-83, 87-88, 94-95. Office: Western Collegiate Hockey Assn 559 D'onofrio Dr Ste 103 Madison WI 53719 Personal E-mail: coachjsauer@juno.com.

SAUER, MARY JULIA, special education educator; b. Pitts., Oct. 10, 1949; d. Edward Henry and Julia Ann (Polkabla) Sauer; 1 child, Jason Michael Sauer; m. John Harold Moore, Oct. 27, 1990 (div.); 1 adopted child, Jocelyn Quan. BS in Art Edn., Edinboro State Coll., 1971; MS in Spl. Edn., Clarion State Coll., 1980; postgrad, U. Pitts., 1988—. Cert. art tchr., spl. edn. tchr. for mentally retarded. Tchr. Polk (Pa.) State Sch. & Hosp., 1971-72; vol. VISTA, Bath, NY, 1972-73; tchr. Polk Ctr., 1973-80, program specialist, 1980-92, residential svc. supr., qualified mental retardation profl., 1992—. Lectr., speaker, video on local TV on history of Polk Ctr., 1987. Patentee beer bottle shaped cake pan; cakes displayed in TV videos and in various mags.; creator history video Polk Ctr., Some Leaky Boot Statues, Polk Center--100 Years; creator video A Century of Care-The History of the Evolution of Institional Care of the Devlopment Disabled. Past vol. Big Bros./Big Sisters. Democrat. Roman Catholic. Avocations: cake decorating, reading. Home: PO Box 97 Franklin PA 16323

SAUERBREY, ELLEN ELAINE RICHMOND, federal agency administrator, former ambassador; b. Balt., Sept. 9, 1937; d. Edgar Arthur and Ethel Frederika (Landgraf) Richmond; m. Wilmer John Emil Sauerbrey, June 27, 1959. AB summa cum laude in Biology and English, Western Md. Coll., 1959. Biology instr., chmn. sci. dept. Baltimore County Sch. System, 1959-64; dist. mgr. Baltimore County U.S. Census, 1970; mem. Md. Ho. of Dels., Annapolis, 1978-94, minority leader, 1986-94; radio talk show host Sta. WBAL, Balt., 1996; U.S. amb. to Commn. on the Status of Women UN, 2002—05; asst. sec. Bur. Population, Refugees & Migration US Dept. State, Washington, 2006—. Rep. nominee for Gov., 1994, 98; U.S. del. commn. human rights UN, 2001, 03; head U.S. del. Baltic states conf., 03; U.S. del econ. commn. Latin Am. and Caribbean, 04; mem. adv. com. women in svcs. US Dept. Def., 2004—06. Nat. chmn. Am. Legis. Exec. Coun., 1990—91; trustee Md. Coun. Econ. Edn., Franklin Sq. Hosp.; founder United Citizen's for Md.'s Future; bd. advisors Yorktown University; Rep. Nat. Com. Woman Md., 1996—2003; Rules com., 1996; del. Rep. Nat. Convs., 1968, 1976, 1984, 1988, 1992, 1996, 2000, platform com., chmn. subcom. on economy, 1977, mem. credentials com., 1984; vice chmn. Rep. State Ctrl. Com. of Balt. County, 1966—71; state chmn. Md. chpt. George W. Bush for Pres., 1999—2000. Recipient Pvt. Property award Greater Balt. Bd. Realtors, 1984; named Legislator of Yr., Md. Assn. Builders and Contractors, 1982, Am. Legis. Exec. Coun., 1986, Western Md. Coll. Alum of Yr., 1988, Outstanding Legis. Leader, Am. Legis. Exec. Coun., 1992, Rep. Woman of Yr., Md. Rep. Party, 1995, Nat. Fedn. Ind. Bus., Guardian of Small Bus. award, 1989, Lifetime Svc. award Baltimore County Rep. Party, 2003, Md. State of Mind award, 2004; named one of top 100 Md. Women, The Daily Record, 1998. Mem. DAR, Nat. Fedn. Rep. Women (Margaret Chase Smith award 1995, Md. State of Mind award 2004), Md. Fedn. Rep. Women, Am. Legis. exch. Coun. (chmn. emeritus), Md. Farm Bur., Md. Conservative Union, Beta Beta, Beta, Phi Beta Kappa. Presbyterian. Avocations: gardening, travel. Office: US Dept State Harry S Truman Bldg 2201 C St NW Rm 5824 Washington DC 20520 Personal E-mail: ellen99@erols.com.

SAUERHAFT, STAN, retired public relations executive, consultant; b. NYC; s. Al and Rae S.; m. Rosalie Cynthia Tolkin; children: Richard Craig, Douglas Clark, Robert James. BA, U. Mich., 1948, MA, 1949. Editor, scriptwriter Paramount News, 1950-51; scriptwriter Hearst Metrotone News, NYC, 1951-52; editor Food Bus. Mag., NYC, 1952-53; acct. supr. Selvage, Lee & Chase, NYC, 1953-55; v.p., mem. creative plans bd. Comm. Counselors, Inc. McCann-Erickson, NYC, 1955-59; pres. Chase and Sauerhaft Assocs., NYC, 1959-65; exec. v.p., dir., mem. mgmt. com. Hill & Knowlton, Inc., NYC, 1965-86; vice chmn. bd., dir. Burson-Marsteller U.S., 1987-88; vice chmn., dir. Burson-Marsteller Internat., 1988—2003; ret., 2003. Instr., lectr. Columbia U. Grad. Sch., 1962-65, Wharton Grad. Sch., 1968, U. Mich. Bus. Sch., 1969, NYU Grad. Bus. Sch., 1984-87; initiated pub. rels. course NYU Grad. Bus. Sch. Author: The Merger Game, 1971, (novels) End Game, 2004, Dead Cat Bounce, 2005; co-author: Image Wars, 1989; contbr. numerous bus. articles and chpts. to anthologies. Chmn. West Point Civilian Pub. Affairs Adv. Com., 1986-2003; mem. exec. com. of bd. Inst. for Pub. Rels. Rsch. and Edn., 1984-87; mem. bd. visitors LS&A Coll. of U. Mich., 1990-95. Staff sgt. AUS, 1945-46. Mem. Pub. Rels. Soc. Am. (Coll. of Fellows; nat. accreditation bd. 1981-83), Pub. Rels. Soc. N.Y. (pres. 1983-85), Soc. Profl. Journalists, Authors Guild Inc., Pub. Affairs Coun. (bd. dirs.), Am. Platform Tennis Assn. (v.p.), U. Mich. Alumni Club, Union League Club N.Y. (chmn. pub. affairs com. 1980-84), Burning Tree Country Club (Greenwich, Conn.), Windmill Club (Armonk, N.Y.), Seabrook Island Club (S.C.), Sigma Delta Chi. Republican. Avocations: golf, platform tennis, bridge, writing. Home Phone: 914-273-6849. Personal E-mail: rosauerh@aol.com. *A father's advice to his sons: If you can't outthink them, outwork them. But better yet, try to do both. Also, the best luck seems to befall the hardest workers.*

SAUFER, ISAAC AARON, lawyer; b. Bronx, NY, June 16, 1953; s. Solomon and Beatrice (Kanofsky) S.; m. Debra Edith Goldberg, June 26, 1977; children: Suzanne, Nancy, Scott, Daniel, Jonathan. BA, Yeshiva U., NYC, 1975; JD, Bklyn. Law Sch., 1978; LLM in Taxation, NYU, 1982. Bar: NY 1979, NJ 1986, Fla. 1986, Conn. 1987. Legal editor Prentice-Hall, Inc., Englewood Cliffs, NY, 1979-80; assoc. Kurzman Karelsen & Frank, LLP, NYC, 1980-85, ptnr., 1986—. Adj. assoc. prof. NYU Sch. Continuing and Profl. Studies, NYC, 1988—; lectr. seminars, 1991, 93, 95, 97, 98, 2000, 01, 06, 07. Co-author: (NY real property forms) Bergerman & Roth, 1986-87. Office: Kurzman Karelsen & Frank LLP 230 Park Ave Rm 2300 New York NY 10169-2399 Office Phone: 212-867-9500. Business E-Mail: isaufer@kurzman.com.

SAUFLEY, LEIGH INGALLS, state supreme court chief justice; b. Portland, Maine, June 21, 1954; m. William Saufley; 2 children. BA, U. Maine, Orono, 1976; JD, U. Maine Sch. of Law, 1980. Pvt. practice, Ellsworth; asst. counsel U.S. VA; asst., then dep. atty. gen. Maine, 1981-90; judge Maine Dist. Ct., 1990—93; justice Maine Superior Ct, 1993—97; assoc. justice Maine Supreme Judicial Ct., 1997—2001, chief justice, 2001—. Mem.: ABA. Maine's first female chief justice. Office: Cumberland County Courthouse PO Box 368 142 Federal St Portland ME 04112-0368 E-mail: amanda.j.martin@maine.gov.

SAUL, ANDREW M., investment company executive; b. NYC, 1946; m. Denise Saul; 2 children. BS, Wharton Sch. Fin., Univ. Pa., 1968. Exec. v.p. Brooks Fashion Stores, 1968—80, pres., 1980—85, BR Investors, 1985—86; gen. ptnr. Saul Partners, 1986—; dir. Caché Inc., 1986—, chmn., 1993—2000. Chmn. Fed. Retirement Thrift Investment Bd.; trustee Federation of Jewish Philanthropies, United Jewish Appeal; commr. Met. Transp. Authority, NY, 1996—; mem. exec. com. Mt. Sinai Med. Ctr., chmn. audit com.; trustee Sarah Neuman Nursing Home, Wharton Sch., Univ. Pa.; Manhattan Inst.; trustee & mem. Chmn. Council Met. Mus. Art, NYC. Named one of Top 200 Collectors, ARTnews Mag., 2004, 2005, 2006. Avocation: Collector of Chinese Bronzes, Modern & Contemporary Art, especially Postwar American. Office: Caché Inc 1440 Broadway New York NY 10018

SAUL, B. FRANCIS, II, bank executive, director; b. Washington, Apr. 15, 1932; s. Andrew Maguire and Ruth Clark (Sheehan) S.; m. Elizabeth Patricia English, Apr. 30, 1960; children: Sharon Elizabeth, B. Francis III, Elizabeth Willoughby, Andrew Maguire II, Patricia English Grad., Georgetown Prep. Sch., 1950; BS, Villanova U., 1954, DCS (hon.), 1989; LLB,

U. Va., 1957; LLD (hon.), Nat. U. Ireland, 1998. Bar: D.C. 1959. Chmn., pres. B.F. Saul Co., Chevy Chase, Md., 1957—; chmn., trustee B.F. Saul Real Estate Investment Trust Co., Chevy Chase, 1964—; with Chevy Chase Bank, F.S.B., 1969—, chmn., CEO, founder; chmn. Fin. Gen. Bankshares, Inc., 1978-82; chmn., CEO, trustee Saul Ctrs., Inc., 1993—. Chmn. bd. dirs. 1st Am. Bankshares, Inc., Washington, 1978—85; dir. Colonial Williamsburg Hotel Properties, Inc., 1983—96. Honors com. John F. Kennedy Ctr. Performing Arts, 1995—; trustees coun. Nat. Gallery of Arts, 1995—; dir. bd. visitors and govs. Washington Coll., 1995—; hon. trustee Brookings Inst., 1993—; dir. Nat. Sporting Libr., 1998—; trustee Fed. City Coun., Nat. Geog. Soc., 1985—, Suburban Hosp., 1972—76, Johns Hopkins Med. Bd., 2000—01, Corcoran Gallery ARt, Washington, 1972—90; bd. dirs. Wadsworth Preservation Trust, 1983—91; vis. com. Sch. Arch. U. Va., Greenway, 1985—90, Portsmouth (R.I.) Abbey Sch., 1979—84, United World Coll. of Am. West, Montezuma, N.Mex., 1982—85, D.C. Fund for Creative Space, 1980—82, D.C. chpt. ARC, 1964—86, Cork U. Found., 1997—; mem. Ea. Shore Land Conservancy, 2002—, James Madison Coun., 1997—; trust fund bd. Libr. of Congress, 2003; archdiocese fin. coun. for Archbishop of Washington, 1990—. Mem. Mortgage Bankers Assn. Met. Washington (pres. 1968), Nat. Assn. Real Estate Investment Truste (pres. 1973-74), Internat. Coll. Auditors Prefecture Econ. Affairs Holy See, Alfalfa Club, Alibi Club, Met. Club, Knights of Malta, Chevy Chase Club, Burning Tree Club, Friendly Sons of St. Patrick (pres. 1992), Wianno Club, The Brook Club, Bohemian Club, Md. Club, White's Club (London) Roman Catholic. Home: 1 Quincy St Chevy Chase MD 20815-4226 Office: BF Saul Co 7501 Wisconsin Ave Bethesda MD 20814

SAUL, CHARLIE, small business owner, investor; b. Rangoon, Burma, Sept. 6, 1933; arrived in US, 1950; s. Joseph Robert and Lily Judah Saul; m. Shirley Ann Ara (div.); children: Charles Joseph, Steven Michael, Pamela Ann; m. Marcelina Escobar Saul, Apr. 27, 2002. Flat work dept. mgr. Excelsior Laundry, Albuquerque, 1957—62; mgr., operator One-House Martinizing Cleaners, Houston, 1962—72; owner, operator Sauls Dry Cleaning, Houston, 1972—94; pres. Specific Dynamics Co. Inc., Houston, 1972—, owner, investor Houston and El Paso, 1994—2000, Chutzpah, Inc., El Paso, 2000—, pres., 2006—. Vol. Sr. Day Care Ctr., Houston, 2000, Tex. Human Resources, El Paso, 2001—02, Tex. Food Bank, El Paso, 2003, El Paso Holocaust Mus., 2005—. With USAF, 1953—57. Independent. Jewish. Avocations: stamp collecting/philately, coin collecting/numismatics, history, travel, writing poetry. Home and Office: 9214 Vicksburg Dr El Paso TX 79924-2614

SAUL, IRVING ISAAC, lawyer; b. July 9, 1929; s. Israel Jacob and Jennie (Green) S.; m. Lita Brown, Dec. 29, 1950; children: Joanne Ilene, Sandra Lynn. BA, Washington and Jefferson Coll., 1949; postgrad., Georgetown U., 1949, Ohio State U., 1951; LLB, U. Pitts., 1952. Bar: Ohio 1952, U.S. Dist. Ct. (so. dist.) Ohio 1954, U.S. Supreme Ct. 1961, U.S. Ct. Appeals (6th cir.) 1966, U.S. Dist. Ct. (no. dist.) Ohio 1967, U.S. Dist. Ct. (ea. dist.) Wis. 1973, U.S. Ct. Appeals (7th cir.) 1978, U.S. Ct. Appeals (4th cir.) 1978, U.S. Ct. Appeals (fed. cir.) 1991. Pvt. practice, Dayton, Ohio, 1952—. Cons. in antitrust litigation; bd. advs. Fed. Civil Practice Abstracts, 1986-88, Ohio Dist. Ct. Rev., 1988-2002; adj. prof. complex litigation Sch. of Law U. Dayton, 1996-98; lectr. in field. Contbr. articles to profl. jours. James Gillespie Blaine scholar, 1948. Mem. Ohio Bar Assn. (chmn. fed. cts. and practice com. 1977-79, chmn. pvt. enforcement com. 1979-92, bd. govs. antitrust sect. 1982-94), Dayton Bar Assn. (chmn. fed. ct. practice com. 1976-77, 78-80, chmn. com. on judiciary 1987-88), Am. Judicature Soc., Masons (Shriner), Phi Beta Kappa. Jewish. Office: 113 Bethpolamy Ct Dayton OH 45415-2512 Office Phone: 937-278-4858.

SAUL, MARK E., secondary school educator, consultant; b. NYC, June 17, 1948; s. Sidney and Shura Saul; m. Carol Portnoy, June 26, 1968; children: Susanna, Michael, Peter. BA, Columbia U., 1969; MS, Courant Inst. Math. Scis., NYU, 1975; PhD, NYU, 1987. Tchr. math. and computer sci. Bronx High Sch. Sci., NY, 1969—85; tchg. fellow Adm. Hyman H. Rickover Found., 1985; tchr. Bronxville Schs., NY, 1985—2003; project dir. NSF, 2003—05; dir. curriculum rsch. and innovation Gateway Project, CUNY Rsch. Found., 2003—05; sr. scholar John Templeton Found., West Conshohocken, Pa., 2006—. Dir. Rsch. Sci. Inst. Ctr. Excellence in Edn., McLean, Va., 1987, San Diego, 90, Cambridge, Mass., 1992—99, Shanghai, 2006; cons. computer graphics 1984 Olympics ABC-TV, NYC, 1983—84; pres. N.Y.C. Interscholastic Math. League, NYC, 1979—89, Am. Regions Math. League, 1989—2000; dir. ARML-Soviet Student Exch., 1991—96; cons. Ednl. Testing Svc., Princeton, NJ, 1980—82; panelist/cons. LaGuardia HS Performing Art, NYC, 1977—86; tchr. trainer N.Y.C. Bd. Edn., 1981; tchr.-coord. computer sci. Hollingworth Ctr. for Gifted, Tchrs. Coll., Columbia U., 1984; instr. Lehman Coll., 1984—92, Johns Hopkins U. Ctr. Talented Youth, 1986, Sophie Davis Biomed. Ctr. CCNY, 1986—94, Sarah Lawrence Coll., 1987—94; mem. U.S. del. to Internat. Congress Math. Educators, Budapest, 1988, Quebec, 92, Seville, 96, Tokyo, 2000, Copenhagen, 04; vis. scholar Ednl. Devel. Ctr., Newton, Mass., 1992—2000, 2005—; cons. John Templeton Found., West Conshohocken, Pa., 2005—06, Math. Scis. Rsch. Inst., Berkeley, Calif., 2005—. Ednl. Devel. Ctr., Newton, Mass., 2005—. Co-author: Science/Mathematics Research Programs in the High School, 1982, The New York City Problem Book, 1986, Read the Question: A Thinking Student's Guide to the SAT's, 1992; co-author: (with I.M. Gelfand) Trigonometry, 2001; author: Enrichment Problems in Leadership Manual for High School Supervisors in Mathematics, 1982; assoc. editor edn. Notices of Am. Math. Soc., 1996—, math. field editor Quantum, 1991—2001, mem. editl. bd. Mathematics and Informatics Jour., 1991—, Math. Horizons Jour., 1992—96, mem. editl. panel MAA Anneli Lax New Math. Libr., 1996—2004. Judge Internat. Math. Olympiad, Washington, 1981, chief guide, 2001; author contest questions Mass. Math. League, 1981; authors' com. Educating Tchrs. Sci., Math., and Tech.: New Practices for the New Millennium, 1998—2000. Recipient Presdl. award for Excellence in Teaching Math., NSF, 1984, Paul Erdos award, World Fedn. Nat. Math. Competitions, 1998; Tandy Tech. scholar, 1994, Gabriela and Paul Rosenbaum Found. fellow, 1995. Mem.: Nat. Coun. Tchrs. Math. (bd. dirs. 2001—04), Am. Math. Soc., Math. Assn. Am. (mem. com. on high sch. contests 1981—92), Assn. Tchrs. Math. (exec. bd. mem. 1980—85). Avocation: chamber music. Office Phone: 917-796-8697. Personal E-mail: marksaul@earthlink.net.

SAUL, NORMAN EUGENE, historian, educator; b. LaFontaine, Ind., Nov. 26, 1932; s. Ralph Odis and Jessie (Neff) S.; m. Mary Ann Culwell, June 27, 1959; children: Alyssa, Kevin, Julia. BA, Ind. U.- Bloomington, 1954; MA, Columbia U., 1959, PhD, 1965; postgrad., Leningrad State U., 1960-61. Asst. prof. Brown U., 1965-68; vis. assoc. prof. Northwestern U., 1969-70; assoc. prof. U. Kans., Lawrence, 1970-75, prof. history, 1975—, chmn. dept. history, 1981-89. Inst. Advanced Study, Princeton, 2000. Author: Russia and the Mediterranean 1797-1807, 1970, Sailors in Revolt, 1917, 1978, Distant Friends: The United States and Russia, 1763-1867, 1991, Concord and Conflict: The United States and Russia, 1867-1914, 1996, War and Revolution: The United States and Russia, 1914-1921, 2001, Friends or Foes?: The United States and Soviet Russia, 1921-1941, 2006; editor: Russian-American Dialogue on Cultural Relations, 1776-1914, 1997. Fulbright scholar, London, 1954-55, Helsinki, 1968-69, Soviet Am. Exch. scholar Internat. Rsch. and Exch. Bd., Moscow, 1973-74, 91-92; fellow Ford Found., 1957-59, Hall Ctr. for Humanities, 1989, 95; recipient Byron Caldwell Smith Book award for Distant Friends, 1993, Robert H. Ferrell book award for Concert and Conflict, Soc. Historians Am. Fgn. Rels., 1997, Pub. Scholar award Kans. Humanities Coun., 1997, Higuchi Rsch. award U. Kans., 1997, Steeples award for Svc. to Kans., 2000, Herbert Hoover Libr. Assn. award, 2001, Franklin and Eleanor Roosevelt Inst. award, 2002. Mem. Am. Assn. Advancement of Slavic Studies, Kans. State Hist. Soc., Kans. Assn. Historians, Phi Alpha Theta. Home: 1002 Crestline Dr Lawrence KS 66049-2607 Business E-Mail: nsaul@ku.edu.

SAUL, RALPH SOUTHEY, diversified financial services company executive; b. Bklyn., May 21, 1922; s. Walter Emerson and Helen Douglas (Coutts) S.; m. Bette Jane Bertschinger, June 16, 1956; children: Robert Southey, Jane Adams. BA, U. Chgo., 1947; LL.B., Yale U., 1951. Bar: D.C. 1951, N.Y. 1952. With Am. Embassy, Prague, Czechoslovakia, 1947-48; assoc. Lyeth & Voorhees, NYC, 1951-52; asst. counsel to gov. State of N.Y., 1952-54; staff atty. RCA, 1954-58; with SEC, 1958-65, dir. divsn. trading and markets, 1963-65; v.p. corporate devel. Investors Diversified Services, Inc., Mpls., 1965-66; pres. Am. Stock Exch., NYC, 1966-71; co-chief exec., chmn. mgmt. com. 1st Boston Corp., 1971-74; chmn., CEO, INA Corp., Phila., 1975-82, CIGNA Corp., Phila., 1982-84. Trustee Com. for Econ. Devel., Brookings Inst.; mem. adv. coun. Pub. Co. Acctg. Oversight Bd. With USNR, 1943-46, PTO. Mem. ABA, Union League, Merion Golf Club, Links Club. Office: Cigna Corp One Tower Bridge 100 Front St Ste 1445 West Conshohocken PA 19428 Office Phone: 610-260-1260. Personal E-mail: yobigdad@aol.com.

SAUL, WILLIAM EDWARD, engineering educator; b. NYC, May 15, 1934; s. George James and Fanny Ruth (Murokh) S.; m. J. Muriel Held Eagleburger, May 11, 1976. BSCE, Mich. Tech. U., 1955, MSCE, 1961; PhD in Civil Engring., Northwestern U., 1964. Registerd profl. engr., Wis., Idaho, Mich., profl. structural engr., Idaho. Mech. engr. Shell Oil Co., New Orleans, 1955-59; instr. engring. mechanics Mich. Tech. U., Houghton, 1960-62; asst. prof. civil engring. U. Wis., Madison, 1964-67, assoc. prof., 1967-72, prof., 1972-84; dean, prof. civil engring. U. Idaho Coll. Engring., Moscow, 1984-90; prof. civil engring. Mich. State U., East Lansing, 1990—2000, chmn. dept. civil and environ. engring., 1990-95, chmn. emeritus, prof. emeritus, 2000. Cons. engr., 1961—; vis. prof. U. Stuttgart, Germany, 1970-71. Co-editor Conf. of Methods of Structural Analysis, 1976. Bd. dirs. Idaho Rsch. Found., 1984-90. Fulbright fellow 1970-71; von Humboldt scholar, 1970-71. Fellow ASCE (pres. Wis. sect. 1983-84), NSPE (bd. dirs.), Mich. Soc. Profl. Engrs. (Steinman award 2003); mem. Internat. Assn. Bridge and Structural Engrs., Am. Concrete Inst., Am. Soc. Engring. Edn., Sigma Xi, Phi Kappa Phi, Tau Beta Pi, Chi Epsilon Avocations: hiking, reading, travel, gadgets. Home: 1971 Cimarron Dr Okemos MI 48864-3905 Office: Mich State U 3546 Engring Bldg E East Lansing MI 48824 Business E-Mail: saul@egr.msu.edu.

SAULE, MARA, librarian, dean; b. Cleve. m. Dan Archdeacon; children: Talis, Nick. BA, Bowling Green State U., MA in English; MLIS, U. Calif., Berkeley. Faculty mem. U. Vt., Burlington, 1985—, assoc. dean libr., dir. collection mgmt. svcs. Bailey/Howe Libr., vice provost enrollment mgmt. and internat. activities, exec. asst. to pres., chief info. officer, dean univ. librs. ALA libr./book fellow Nat. Libr. of Latvia, Riga, 1992—93. Mem.: ALA. Office: U Vt Bailey/Howe Libr Burlington VT 05405-0036 Office Phone: 802-656-2003. E-mail: mara.saule@uvm.edu. *

SAUL-GERSHENZ, LESLIE, entomologist, consultant, ecologist, director; d. Ernest Saul and Sylvia Zion; m. Norman E. Gershenz, Aug. 25, 1991. MS, San Francisco State U., 1999—2001. Dir. insect zoo San Francisco Zool. Gardens, 1979—98; dir. coservation & rsch. Ctr. Ecosystem Survival, San Francisco, 1998—. Cons., 1990—2006. Exhibit designer (interactive conservation parking meter) History of Insect Zoos (Internat. Graphis award, 1991). Co-founder Ctr. Ecosystem Survival, San Francisco, 1987—2006. Grantee Internat. Graphics award, NSF. Mem.: Pacific Coast Entomol. Soc. (pres. 1991). Achievements include discovery of the first example of cooperative aggressive mimicry in insects. Avocations: photography, art. Office: Ctr Ecosystem Survival Save Natue 699 Mississippi St Ste 106 San Francisco CA 94107 Office Fax: 415-648-3392. Business E-Mail: lsaul@meer.net.

SAUNDERS, AUDREY J., tax specialist, writer; b. Cin. d. Robert James and Margaret Ann (Philpot) Saunders. BA, U. Cin., 1971; MS, Xavier U., Cin., 1975; postgrad., Lehman Coll., Bronx, 1990—92. Tchr. N.Y.C. Bd. Edn., 1985—94; with IRS, Cin., 1995—2003, tax examining asst. Holtsville, NY, 2003—05. Adult basic edn. tchr. Gen. Edn. Devel. Program Math, 1974—77. Author short stories, Going From Just A Boxer To A Super Bowler, 2005, The Evolutionary War, 2006. With US Army, 1977—81. Methodist. Home: 34 Pauls Path Coram NY 11727-3711

SAUNDERS, BARRY WAYNE, state official; b. Roxboro, NC, June 9, 1944; s. Charlie Clifton and Mary Louise (Mooney) S.; m. Brenda Kaye Bell, Oct. 18, 1987; children: Dara Louise Saunders Lockamy, Erin Elissa (dec.). BA, Campbell u., 1971; MEd, U. N.C., 1974; EdD, N.C. State U., 1990. Tchr. Granville County Sch. System, Oxford, NC, 1966-69; mental health counselor Vocat. Rehab., Henderson, NC, 1971-75; staff devel. specialist John Umstead Hosp., Butner, NC, 1975-82; trainer, asst. mgr., mgr. tng. N.C. Dept. Transp., Raleigh, 1982—; mgr. tng. (on loan from N.C. Dept. Transp.) Gov.'s Office of Quality Improvement, 1995-96; mgr. tng. N.C. Dept. Transp., Raleigh, 1996-2000; ret., 2000. Pres. Omicron Cons., Mill Spring, NC, 1982—. Contbr. articles to profl. jours., poems to N.C. Poetry Soc., 1981. Sec. Dem. Party, Person County, N.C., 1980-84. Mem. Nat. Mgmt. Assn. (bd. dirs. state govt. chpt. 1992-95, v.p. 1997-98), Triangle Quality Coun. (bd. dirs. 1995-96), Nat. Transp. Tng. Dirs. Assn. (v.p. 1997-2000). Methodist. Home: 121 Canoe Dr Mill Spring NC 28756

SAUNDERS, BRYAN LESLIE, lawyer; b. Newport News, Va., Apr. 18, 1945; s. Raymond Hayes and Lois Mae (Pair) S.; divorced; children: Kelly Brooke, Justin Lee; m. Anne Mason Dunbar, July 15, 1995. BS, East Tenn. State U., 1967; JD, U. Tenn., 1973. Bar: Va. 1973, U.S. Dist. Ct. (ea. dist.) Va. 1973, U.S. Ct. Appeals (4th cir.) 1991. Lawyer Cogdill & Assocs., Newport News, Va., 1973—76; pvt. practice Newport News, 1976—; ptnr. Saunders & Lawrence, 2002—05. Commr. in chancerty Cir. Ct. of Newport News, 1990-97. Sgt. U.S. Army, 1968-71. Decorated Bronze star, 1971; recipient Outstanding Svc. to Law Enforcement Newport News and Police Dept., 1986. Mem. Va. Bar Assn., Nat. Assn. Criminal Def. Lawyers, Va. Coll. Criminal Def. Attys., Pi Kappa Phi, Pi Gamma Mu. Avocations: chess, bridge, bowling. Office: 728 Thimble Shoals Blvd Ste C Newport News VA 23606-4546 Office Phone: 757-873-0043. E-mail: bryansaund@aol.com.

SAUNDERS, CHARLES ALBERT, lawyer; b. Boulder, Colo., Jan. 18, 1922; s. Charles and Anna (Crouse) S.; m. Betti Friedel, Oct. 18, 1946; children— Melanie, Stephen, Cynthia, Shelley. BA, U. Houston, 1942; LLB, U. Tex., 1945. Bar: Tex. 1945. Ptnr. firm Fulbright & Jaworski, L.L.P., 1959—. Editor: How To Live-and Die-With Texas Probate, 8 vols., 1968, Texas Estate Administration, 1975. Bd. dirs. Houston Symphony Soc., 1964—; bd. dirs. Am. Lung Assn., San Jacinto, 1965—, pres., 1972-73; past mem. bd. govs. U. Houston. Recipient Leon Jaworski award for cmty. svc., Houston Bar Assn., 1997, U. Tex. Law Sch. Disting. Alumnus award in Cmty. Svc., 1999. Mem. ABA, State Bar Assn., Houston Bar Assn., Am. Coll. Trust and Estate Coun. (regent 1972-80, pres. 1978-79), Internat. Acad. of Estate and Trust Law, Assn. Cmty. TV (bd. dirs. 1970—). Republican. Presbyterian. Home: 19 Willowron Dr Houston TX 77024-7618 Office: Fulbright & Jaworski 1301 Mckinney St Ste 5100 Houston TX 77010-3031 Office Phone: 713-651-5374. Business E-Mail: csaunders@fulbright.com.

SAUNDERS, CHARLES BASKERVILLE, JR., retired association executive; b. Boston, Dec. 26, 1928; s. Charles Baskerville and Lucy (Carmichael) S.; m. Margaret MacIntire Shafer, Sept. 9, 1950; children— Charles Baskerville III, George Carlton, Margaret Keyser, Lucy C., John R. Grad., St. Mark's Sch., 1946; AB, Princeton, 1950. News reporter, polit. columnist Ogdensburg (N.Y.) Jour., 1950-51; edn. reporter Hartford (Conn.) Times, 1951-53; asst. dir. pub. relations Trinity Coll., Hartford, 1953-55; asst. dir. pub. info. Princeton, 1955-57; legis. asst. Sen. H. Alexander Smith, 85th Congress, 1957-58; asst. to asst. sec. for legislation HEW, 1958-59; asst. to sec. Arthur S. Flemming, 1959-61, dep. asst. sec. for legislation, 1969-71; asst. to pres. Brookings Instn., 1961-69; dep. commr. of edn. for external affairs U.S. Office Edn., 1971-72; dep. asst. sec. for edn. HEW, 1973-74; dir. govt. relations Am. Council on Edn., 1975-78, v.p. for govt. relations, 1978-87, sr. v.p., 1987-92. Author: Brookings Institution: A Fifty-Year History, 1966, Upgrading the American Police, 1970, Four Centuries in America, 2000, rev. edit., 2006. Mem. Montgomery County Bd. Edn., 1966-70, Md. Higher Edn. Commn., 1989-2002 (chmn. 1994-95, vice chmn. 1995-2002); chmn. bd. dirs. Md. Higher Edn. Loan Corp., 1994-95. Mem. Jamestowne Soc. Democrat. Presbyterian. Home: 7622 Winterberry Pl Bethesda MD 20817-4848 Personal E-mail: saunders3@earthlink.net.

SAUNDERS, DONALD LESLIE, hotel executive, real estate developer; b. Brookline, Mass., Jan. 28, 1935; s. Irving M. Saunders and Shirley Brown; m. Liv. Ullmann, 1985; children: Lisa M., Pamela R. AB in Econs., Brown U., Providence, RI, 1957; grad., Inst. Real Estate Mgmt., 1963; LLB, Pine Manor Coll., Brookline, Mass., 1989. Cert. property mgr. Inst. Real Estate Mgmt., Ill., lic. real estate broker Mass. Chmn., pres., CEO The D.L. Saunders Real Estate Corp., Boston, 1957—; CEO, chmn. The D.L. Saunders Cos., Boston, The Boston Pk. Plz. Hotel, LLC, 1976—; chmn. Boston Pk. Plz. Hotel & Towers, 1976—, CEO, 1976—; gen. ptnr. SaunStar Land Co.; ptnr. 20 & 50 Park Plaza Complex, LLC. Bd. dirs. Park Sch. Corp., Brookline, Mass., Brown U. Sports Found., 2002—; with Brown U. Comml. Real Estate Devel. Co.; mem. real estate subcom. Brown U.; pres. Farview Inc., 1976—; trustee emeritus Brown U., 1972—, gov. emeritus, 1996—; mem. Better Bus. Bur. of Mass., Inc.; prime ministers coun. Combined Jewish Philanthropies, 2007—. Mem. Nat. Assn. Realtors, Ea. Point Residents Assn. (Gloucester, Mass.), Ocean Reef Club, Ocean Reef Yacht Club, Racquet Club (Key Largo, Fla.), Brown U. Club (Boston), Lotos Club, The Players, Union League Club (NYC), Hope Club (Providence), Boston Tennis and Racquet Club, Ea. Point Yacht Club, Belmont Country Club, Univ. Club, Providence, Union Club, Charles River Yacht Club, The Worcester (Mass.) Club, Harvard Club, Confrerie Chaine des Rotisseurs, N.Y.C. Office: DL Saunders Cos 20 Park Plz Boston MA 02116-4399 Office Phone: 617-728-2700.

SAUNDERS, FLIP (PHILIP D. SAUNDERS), professional basketball coach; b. Cleve., Feb. 23, 1955; m. Debbie Saunders; children: Ryan, Mindy, Rachel and Kimberly (twins). Student, U. Minn. Asst. coach U. Minn., 1981—86, U. Tulsa, 1986-88; head coach Continental Basketball Assn. Rapid City Thrillers, SD, 1988-89, Continental Basketball Assn. La Crosse Catbirds, Wis., 1989-94, gen. mgr., 1991-93, team pres., 1991-94; head coach Continental Basketball Assn. Sioux Falls Skyforce, SD; gen. mgr., head coach NBA Minn. Timberwolves, 1995—2005; head coach NBA Detroit Pistons, 2005—. Head coach US Men's Basketball Team Goodwill Games (gold medal), Brisbane, Australia, 2001. Named Continental Basketball Assn. Coach of Yr., 1990, 92. Achievements include leading the La Crosse Catbirds to the Continental Basketball Association Championship as head coach, 1990, 92. Office: The Detroit Pistons Four Championship Dr Auburn Hills MI 48326 *

SAUNDERS, GARY WILLIAM, biology educator, phycology researcher; b. Halifax, NS, Can., June 30, 1962; s. Earl L. and Fay M. Saunders; m. Dolores J. Fatur, Apr. 29, 1989; children: Karsten Earl Joseph, Davin Liam Tate. BSc with hons., Acadia U., Wolfville, Nova Scotia, Can., 1985, MSc, 1987; PhD, Simon Fraser U., Vancouver, B.C., Can., 1991. Postdoct. fellow Sch. Botany U. Melbourne, Australia, 1991-93, sr. rsch. fellow Sch. Botany, 1993-95; asst. prof. U. New Brunswick, Fredericton, Canada, 1995-97, assoc. prof., 1997—2001, prof., Can. rsch. chair, 2001—. Cons. Dames & Moore, Seattle, 1990; spkr. in field. Assoc. editor: Can. Jour. Bot., Jour. Phycology; contbr. articles to profl. jours.;. Lt. USAR, 1980—86. Recipient Darbaker award, Bot. Soc. Am., 1996; fellow Postdoctoral, Nat. Scis. and Engring. Rsch. Coun. Can., 1991, Queen Elizabeth II Rsch., Australian Rsch. Coun., 1993. Mem.: Internat. Phycol. Soc. (Luigi Provasoli award 1998), Internat. Soc. Evolutionary Protistology (mem. exec. coun.), Phycol. Soc. Am. (assoc. editor). Avocations: nature, physical fitness, wood carving, music. Office: U New Brunswick Dept Biology Fredericton NB Canada E3B 6EI

SAUNDERS, GEORGE LAWTON, JR., lawyer; b. Mulga, Ala., Nov. 8, 1931; s. George Lawton and Ethel Estell (York) S.; children: Kenneth, Ralph, Victoria; m. Terry M. Rose. BA, U. Ala., 1956; JD, U. Chgo., 1959. Bar: Ill. 1960. Law clk. to chief judge U.S. Ct. Appeals (5th cir.), Montgomery, Ala., 1959-60; law clk to Justice Hugo L. Black U.S. Supreme Ct., Washington, 1960-62; assoc. Sidley & Austin, Chgo., 1962-67, ptnr., 1967-90; founding ptnr. Saunders & Monroe, Chgo., 1990—. With USAF, 1951-54. Fellow: Am. Coll. Trial Lawyers; mem.: Law Club, Quadrangle Club, Point-O-Woods Club, Chgo. Club, Order of the Coif, Phi Beta Kappa. Democrat. Baptist. Home: 179 E Lake Shore Dr Chicago IL 60611-1306 Office: Saunders Monroe Law Offices 20 S Clark St Ste 1720 Chicago IL 60603-1847 Personal E-mail: glsaunders@sbcglobal.net.

SAUNDERS, HAROLD HENRY, foundation administrator; b. Phila., Dec. 27, 1930; s. Harold Manuel Saunders and Marian Elizabeth Weihenmayer; m. Barbara Mc Garrigle, May 4, 1963 (dec. Oct. 1973); children: Catherine Elizabeth, Mark Harril; m. Carol Eleanor Jones Cruse, June 2, 1990. AB, Princeton U., 1952; PhD, Yale U., 1956; LittD, New Eng. Coll., 1999; D of Internat. Rels., Dickinson Coll., 2004. With CIA, Washington, 1959—61; sr. staff Nat. Security Coun., Washington, 1961—74; dir. intelligence and rsch., asst. sec. Near East and South Asian affairs Dept. of State, Washington, 1974—81; fellow Am. Enterprise Inst. Brookings Inst., Washington, 1981—91; profl. lectr. Johns Hopkins U., SAIS, George Mason U., 1984—91; dir. internat. affairs Kettering Found., Washington, 1991—; pres. Internat. Inst. Sustained Dialogue, 2002—. Author: The Other Walls: Arab-Israeli Peace Process in Global Perspective, 1985, 91, A Public Peace Process: Sustained Dialogue to Transform Racial and Ethnic Conflicts, 1999, Politics Is About Relationship: Blueprint for the Citizens' Century, 2005. Trustee Princeton U., 1996—2000; pres. Class of '52, 2002—07; ruling elder Lewinsville Presbyn. Ch., McLean, Va., 1971—; bd. dirs. East-West Inst., NYC, 1981—89, Ptnrs. Dem. Change, San Francisco, 1995—2005, InterNews, Arcata, Calif., 1999—2001. Lt. USAF, 1957—59. Recipient Disting. Fed. Civilian Svc. award Pres. U.S., 1978, Disting. Honor award Dept. of State, 1981, First Disting. Achievement award Germantown Acad., Phila., Lifetime Achievement award Search for Common Ground, 2004. Mem. Internat. Soc. Polit. Psychology (gov. coun. 1991-94), Coun. Fgn. Rels., Princeton Club N.Y., Phi Beta Kappa. Avocation: writing. Home: 2101 Lorraine Ave Mc Lean VA 22101 Office: Kettering Found 444 N Capitol St NW Washington DC 20001

SAUNDERS, JAMES ALLEN, secondary school educator; b. Hungtington, W.Va., Dec. 18, 1945; s. Charles Harry and Lillian Saunders; m. Donna Belcher (div.); 1 child, Kellie Lynn Ami Bree; m. Bonnie Sue Stepp; children: Ashley Nicole, David Michael. BA, Marshall U., Huntington, W.Va., 1975, MA, 1978, W.Va. Coll. Grad. Study, South Charleston, 1989. Tchr. Wayne County Bd. Edn., W.Va., 1975—78, Lincoln County Bd. Edn., Hamlin, W.Va., 1978—81, Pike County Bd. Edn., Pikeville, Ky., 2005—; tchr., adminstr. Mingo County Bd. Edn., Williamson, W.Va., 1982—2005. Football, basketball coach Burch Mid. Sch., Delbarton, W.Va., 1990—97;

football coach Lenore Mid. Sch., W.Va., 2000—01, Burch HS, Delbarton, 2001—02. Candidate W.Va. House Dels., 2004, 2006. Sgt. USAF, 1963—69. Mem.: ASCD, Internat. Reading Assn. Republican. Avocations: woodworking, toy repair, auto restoration.

SAUNDERS, JOHN WARREN, JR., biology professor, consultant; b. Muskogee, Okla., Nov. 12, 1919; s. John Warren and Amanda Mary (Schlattweiler) S.; m. Lilyan Clayton, Feb. 27, 1942; children: Sarah Elizabeth Reeder, John Warren, Margaret Ann Geist, Mary Katherine Brown. BS, U. Okla., 1940, MS, 1941; PhD, Johns Hopkins U., 1948. Jr. instr. in biology Johns Hopkins U., Balt., 1941-43, 46-48; instr. zoology U. Chgo., 1948-49; from assoc. prof. to prof. Marquette U., Milw., 1949-66; prof. anatomy U. Pa., Phila., 1966-67; prof. biology SUNY, Albany, 1967-85; author and cons. in pvt. practice Falmouth, Mass., 1985—. Adv. panel devel. biology NSF, Washington, 1961-66; trustee Marine Biol. Lab., Woods Hole, Mass., 1969-72; emeritus prof. biol. scis. SUNY, Albany. Author: Animal Morphogenesis, 1968, Principles of Animal Development, 1970, Developmental Biology, 1982; contbr. numerous articles to profl. jours. Bd. dirs. Milw. divsn. Am. Cancer Soc., 1960-65; elected mem. Town Meeting, Falmouth, Mass., 1988-95. Lt. (s.g.) USN, 1943-46, PTO. Recipient Joseph Rigge Disting. Svc. award Marquette U., 1988, Edwin Grant Conklin medal, 1996 Fellow AAAS; mem. NAS, Assn. Am. Anatomists, Soc. for Devel. Biology (pres. 1968-69), Am. Soc. Zoologists (sec. 1964-66), NAS. Democrat. Roman Catholic. Home and Office: 110 Dillingham Ave Apt 209 Falmouth MA 02540 E-mail: jsaunder@mbh.edu.

SAUNDERS, JOSEPH W., finance company executive; BS, U. Denver, 1967, MBA, 1968. V.p., credit card ops. Bank of Am., 1984—85; with Household Fin. Corp., 1985—97; chmn., CEO Fleet Credit Card Services L.P., 1997—2001; chmn. bd, CEO & pres. Providian Fin. Corp., 2001—05; pres. card services divsn. Washington Mutual, Inc., Seattle, 2005—07; exec. chmn. Visa Inc., 2007—. Office: Visa Inc 900 Metro Ctr Blvd Foster City CA 94404 *

SAUNDERS, LONNA JEANNE, lawyer, newscaster; b. Cleve. d. Jack Glenn and Lillian Frances (Newman) Slaby. Student, Dartmouth Coll.; AB in Polit. Sci. with honors, Vassar Coll.; JD, Northwestern U., 1981; cert., Mass Media Inst., Stanford, Calif., 1992. Bar: Ill. 1981. News dir., morning news anchor Sta. WKBK-AM, Keene, NH, 1974-75; reporter Sta. KDKA-AM, Pitts., 1975; pub. affairs dir., news anchor Sta. WJW-AM, Cleve., 1975-76; helicopter traffic reporter WERE-AM Radio, Cleve., 1976-77; morning news anchor Sta. WBBG-AM, Cleve., 1978; talk host, news anchor Sta. WIND-AM, Chgo., 1978-82; atty. Arvey, Hodes, Costello & Burman, Chgo., 1981-82; host, "The Stock Market Observer", news anchor WCIU-TV, Chgo., 1982-85; staff atty. Better Govt. Assn., Chgo., 1983-84; news anchor, reporter Sta. WBMX-FM, Chgo., 1984-86; pvt. practice law Chgo., 1985—; news anchor Sta. WKQX-FM, Chgo., 1987; arbitrator Cir. Ct. 17th Jud. Dist., Ill., 2005—; tchr. Ill. Pub. Schs., 2006—, Ohio Pub. Schs., 2006—. Instr. Columbia Coll., Chgo., 1987-90; guest talk host Sta. WMCA, NYC, 1983, Sta. WMAQ, Chgo., 1988, Sta. WLS, Chgo., 1989, Sta. WWWE, Cleve., 1989, Sta. KVI, Seattle, 1994, WCBM-AM, Balt., 1996, WRC-AM, Wash., DC, 1997; host, prodr. The Lively Arts, Cablevision Chgo., 1986; talk show host The Lonna Saunders Show, Sta. KIRO-AM, Seattle, 1995-96; news anchor, WTOP-AM Radio, Washington, DC, 1996-97; talk host, "Today and Tomorrow show", WMAL-AM radio, Washington, DC, 1997, freelance reporter, CBS Radio Network, NYC, 1975—; atty. Lawyers for Creative Arts, Chgo., 1985-91; guardian Ad litem and child rep., 2005—; mem. tv production com. Chgo. Bar Assn., 2005-. Mem. editl. bd. Jour. Criminal Law and Criminology, 1979-81; creator pub. affairs program WBBM-AM, Chgo., 1985; law columnist Chgo. Life Mag., 1986-99; sports columnist Indians Ink mag., Cleve., 1998-2000; writer Rock River Times newspaper, 2004; guest columnist Gainesville Sun, Fla., 1998-99, Rockford Register Star newspaper, 1998-2007; contbr. articles to profl. jours.; contbr. columns to mags. and newspapers. Atty., county counsel voter protection project Kerry-Edwards 2004, Inc.; mem. women's action coun. Amnesty Internat., 2000—. Recipient Akron Press Club award for best pub. affairs presentation, 1978; grantee Scripps Howard Found., 1978-81; AFTRA George Heller Meml. scholar, 1980-81. Fellow Am. Bar Found.; mem. ABA (mem. exec. coms. Lawyers and the Arts, Law and Media 1986-92, chmn. exec. com. Law and Media 1990-91, 91-92, Young Lawyers divsn. liaison to Forum Com. on Comm. Law 1991-93, Commn. for Partnership Programs 1993-94, regional divsn. chair Forum on Comm. Law 1995-96). Roman Catholic. Avocations: theater, piano, baseball. Office Phone: 815-218-9773. Personal E-mail: lonnasaunders@yahoo.com.

SAUNDERS, MARTHA DUNAGIN, academic administrator; m. Joseph Bailey; 7 children. BA, U. So. Miss., 1969; MA, U. Ga.; PhD in Comm. Theory, Fla. State U. Asst. prof. comm. U. West Fla., dir. Univ. Honors Prog., dean Coll. Arts and Scis., 1999; v.p. Academic Affairs Columbus State U.; chancellor U. Wis., Whitewater, 2005—07; pres. U. So. Miss., Hattiesburg, 2007—. Author: Eastern's Armageddon: Labor Conflict and the Destruction of Eastern Airlines, 1992. Mem.: Pub. Relations Soc. Am. (Silver Anvil award). Avocations: fishing, gardening. Office: U So Miss Office of Pres 118 College Dr Hattiesburg MS 39406-0001 *

SAUNDERS, MARTIN, chemistry educator, researcher; b. 1931; BS, CCNY; PhD, Harvard U., 1956. Prof. chemistry Yale U., New Haven, 1955—; Kharasch prof. U. Chgo., 1983. Contbr. articles to profl. jours. including Science, Nature, J. Am. Chem. Soc. Recipient Sr. U.S. Scientist award Alexander von Humboldt Found. 1977-78, 85, Arthur C. Cope Scholar award Am. Chem. Soc., 1998-99, James Flack Norris award in Physical Organic Chemistry, 2005. Fellow: Japanese Soc. Promotion of Natural Sci.; mem.: NAS, Am. Acad. Arts and Scis. Achievements include creation of new methods for studying carbocations, one of the three main species of reactive intermediates in organic reactions; discovery of detailed mechanisms and rates of very rapid rearrangement reactions of cation intermediates. Office: Yale U Dept Chemistry 225 Prospect St New Haven CT 06520-8107 Office Phone: 203-432-3974. Business E-Mail: ms@gaus90.chem.yale.edu.

SAUNDERS, MARY JANE, lawyer; b. Waltham, Mass., Oct. 15, 1956; BA, Va. Polytech. Inst., 1978; JD, Mercer Univ., 1981. Bar: Va. 1982, DC 1993, US Supreme Ct. 1992. Ptnr., Copyright & Unfair Trade, Nonprofit Org. practices Venable LLP, Washington. Mem.: DC Computer Law Forum (past pres.). Office: Venable LLP 575 &th St NW Washington DC 20004 also: Venable LLP Suite 300 8010 Towers Crescent Dr Vienna VA 22182 Office Phone: 202-344-8108, 703-760-1950. Office Fax: 202-344-8300. Business E-Mail: mjsaunders@venable.com.

SAUNDERS, PATRICIA GENE KNIGHT, freelance writer, editor; b. Tulsa, Nov. 29, 1946; d. Eugene Merritt and Patricia May (Hough) Knight; m. Joseph Eugene Saunders, June 24, 1989. BA, Baylor U., 1969. Nat. advt. sec. Sta. KTVT-TV, Ft. Worth, 1969-71; tchr. Arlington Ind. Sch. Dist., Tex., 1971-77, Garland Ind. Sch. Dist., Tex., 1977-79; payroll, spl. projects assoc. Electronic Data Systems, Dallas, 1979-81; adminstrv. asst. Diversifield Innovators, Dallas, 1981-82; system ops. mgr. Span Instruments, Plano, Tex., 1982-86; data processing mgr. Claire Mfg., Addison, Ill., 1986-87, Everpure, Inc., Westmont, Ill., 1987-88; software cons. Software Alternatives, Inc., Downers Grove, Ill., 1988-89; sys. ops. asst., cons. J&J Maintenance, Inc., Austin, Tex., 1989-90; pres., computer cons. Cardinal Software Solutions, Inc., Austin, 1990-93; editor Holt, Rinehart & Winston, Austin, 1993-99. Mem.: Writers' League Tex., Soc. Children's Book Writers and Illustrators, Nat. Mus. Women in Arts, Nat. Arbor Day Found., Nat. Wildlife Fedn., NY Met. Mus. Fine Art, Smithsonian Instn. Republican. Baptist. Avocations: cats, gardening, travel, movies, reading. Home: 410 Teal Ln Kyle TX 78640-8888 Office Phone: 512-262-2062. Office Fax: 512-268-1625. E-mail: pgs2508@austin.rr.com.

SAUNDERS, PAUL CHRISTOPHER, lawyer; b. NYC, May 21, 1941; s. John Richard and Agnes Grace (Kelly) Saunders; m. Patricia Newman, Sept. 14, 1968; children: Dr. Paul Christopher, Michael Eagan. AB, Fordham Coll., 1963; JD, Georgetown U., 1966; Certificat, Institut d'Études Politiques, Paris, 1962. Bar: NY 1966, DC 1967, US Supreme Ct 1969. Assoc. Cravath, Swaine & Moore LLP, NYC, 1971-77, ptnr., litig., 1977—; disting. visitor from practice Georgetown U. Law Ctr., 2003—. Mem ed bd: Georgetown Law Jour, 1965—66; editor (editor-in-chief): The Advocate, 1969—70. Trustee Fordham U., 1991—96, 2004—; bd. regents Georgetown U., 1991—96, bd. visitors Law Ctr., 1996—; trustee, vice-chmn Fordham Prep. Sch., 1986—94; v.p., bd. dirs. Legal Aid Soc., 1983—88; bd. dirs., trustee Lawyers Com. Civil Rights Under Law, 1985—, co-chair, 1995—97; trustee Vols. Legal Svc., Inc., 1999—2007; bd. dirs. Office of the Appellate Defender, 1999—; co-chmn. N.Y. State Judicial Inst. on Professionalism in the Law, 2000—; bd. dirs. Constitution Project, 2000—, co-chmn. bd. dirs., 2000—07. Capt JAGC US Army, 1967—71. Decorated Meritorious Svc. medal; recipient John Carroll medal, Georgetown U., 1995, Whitney N. Seymour award, Lawyers Com. Civil Rights Under Law, 2000, Paul R. Dean award, Georgetown U. Law Ctr., 2006. Fellow: Am. Bar Found., Am. Coll. Trial Lawyers; mem.: ABA, London Ct. Internat. Arbitration, Assn. Bar City N.Y., NY State Bar Assn., Westchester Country Club (Rye, NY), Apawamis Club (Rye, NY), Phi Beta Kappa, Pi Sigma Alpha. Democrat. Roman Catholic. Address: 455 Polly Pk Rd Rye NY 10580-1960 Office: Cravath Swaine & Moore LLP Worldwide Plz 825 8th Ave Fl 39 New York NY 10019-7475 Office Phone: 212-474-1404. Office Fax: 212-474-3700. Business E-Mail: psaunders@cravath.com.

SAUNDERS, PETER PAUL, investor; b. Budapest, Hungary, July 21, 1928; emigrated to Can., 1941, naturalized, 1946; s. Peter Paul and Elizabeth (Halom) Szende; m. Nancy Louise McDonald, Feb. 11, 1956; children: Christine Elizabeth McBride, Paula Marie McMullen. Student, Vancouver Coll., 1941-44; B.Com., U. B.C., 1948. Acct. Canadian Pacific Rly. Co., 1948-50; founder, pres. Laurentide Fin. Corp., Ltd., 1950-66, vice chmn., 1966-67; chmn., pres. Coronation Credit Corp. Ltd., Vancouver, B.C., Canada, 1968-78, Versatile Corp. (formerly Coronation Credit Corp. and Cornat Industries Ltd.), Vancouver, B.C., Canada, 1978-87; prin., pres. Saunders Investment Ltd., Vancouver, 1987—. Past pres. Vancouver Symphony Soc., 1968-70, Can. Cancer Soc., B.C. and Yukon Region, 1975-77, Vancouver Art Gallery Assn., 1981-83; chmn. Vancouver Opera Round Table, 1984-92; chmn. Arthritis Rsch. Ctr. of Can. Mem. Vancouver Club, Shaughnessy Golf and Country Club, Royal Vancouver Yacht Club, Thunderbird Country Club (Rancho Mirage, Calif.). Avocations: golf, skiing, hunting, boating. Home: 3620 Alexandra St Vancouver BC Canada V6J 4B9 Office: Saunders Investment Ltd PO Box 49352 Bentall Ctr Vancouver BC Canada V7X 1L4

SAUNDERS, RAYMOND JENNINGS, artist, educator; b. Pitts., Oct. 28, 1934; Student (Nat. Scholastic scholar), Pa. Acad. Fine Arts, U. Pa., Barnes Found.; B.F.A., Carnegie Inst. Tech., 1960; M.F.A., Calif. Coll. Arts and Crafts. Teaching asst. Calif. Coll. Arts and Crafts, 1960-61; resident Am. Acad. in Rome, 1964-66; art and urban affairs cons. N.Y.C. Bd. Edn. and Human Resources Adminstrn., 1967; art faculty Calif. State Univ., Hayward, 1968—88; prof. painting, drawing Calif. Coll. Arts and Crafts, Oakland, 1988—. Vis. artist, R.I. Sch. Design, 1968, artist-in-residence, vis. artist and critic at various art schs., univs., 1968—; subject of profl. articles.; one-man shows include San Francisco Mus. Modern Art, 1971, Seattle Art Mus., 1981, Pa. Acad. Fine Arts, 1990, Tampa Mus. Art, 1992, Stephen Wirtz Gallery, San Francisco, 1979, 1980, 1982, 1989, 1993, 1996, 1999, 2001, 2003, Galerie Resche, Paris, 1993, Oakland Mus., 1994, M.H. de Young Meml. Mus., San Francisco, 1995, Carnegie Mus. of Art, 1996, Galerie Resche, Paris, 1998, Hunsaker/Schlesinger Fine Art, 2001, Centre Jerome Cuzin, France, 2002, Schneider Mus. Art, So. Ore. Univ, 2004; represented in permanent collections, Mus. Modern Art, N.Y.C., Whitney Mus. Am. Art, N.Y.C., Phila. Mus. Art, Chrysler Mus., Va.; author: Black is a Color, 1968. Served with U.S. Army, 1957-59. Recipient Cresson European traveling scholar, 1956, Thomas Eakins prize, Schwabacher-Frey award San Francisco Mus. Art Ann., 1961, award Nat. Inst. Arts and Letters, 1963, Prix de Rome Am. Acad. in Rome, 1964-66, Ford Found. Purchase award, 1964, award City of Phila., Atwater Kent award Soc. Four Arts, 1970, Granger Meml. award Pa. Acad. Fine Arts, 1972, Art award KQED, 1975, Guggenheim Fellow, 1976, Nat. Endowment for Arts award, 1977, 84, Visual Arts award So. Ea. Ctr. for Contemporary Art, 1989. Office: Painting & Drawing Dept Calif Coll Arts & Crafts 5212 Broadway Oakland CA 94618-1426 Office Phone: 510-594-3600.

SAUNDERS, RICHARD HENRY, III, museum director; b. Rochester, NY, Aug. 13, 1949; s. Richard Henry and Betsy (Macmillan) S.; m. Barbara Fox Williams, June 12, 1971; children: Elizabeth, Christopher, Katherine. BA, Bowdoin Coll., 1970; MA, Del. U., 1973; MPhil, Yale U., 1976, PhD, 1979. Curator Wadsworth Atheneum, Hartford, Conn., 1978-81; asst. prof. U. Tex., Austin, 1981-85; dir. Middlebury Coll. Mus. Art, Vt., 1985—; Walter Cerf Disting. Coll. Prof. Middlebury Coll., 1985—. Lectr. Yale U., New Haven, Conn., 1979. Author: Collecting the West, 1988, John Smibert, 1995, Horatio Greenough, 1999, The Brook Collection, 2005; co-author: American Colonial Portraits, 1987. Trustee Williamstown Regional Art Conservation Lab., 1990, The Shelburne Mus., 1997-, Preservation Trust of Vt., 2003-; bd. dirs. Vt. Mus. and Gallery Alliance, Shelburne, 1988—, Vt. State Craft Ctr., Middlebury, 1985-88; adv. panel New Eng. Found. for the Arts, Cambridge, Mass., 1987-88. Named Lamont Dupont Copeland fellow, Winterthur Mus., Del., 1971-73, Deerfield fellow, Historic Deerfield, Mass., 1969, Kress fellow, Courtauld Inst., Samuel Kress Found., N.Y., 1976-77, Andrew Wyeth fellow, Yale U., New Haven, Conn., 1975-76. Mem. Coll. Art Assn., Nat. Trust, Yale Club.

SAUNDERS, ROBERT SAMUEL, venture capitalist; b. Akron, Ohio, Dec. 3, 1951; s. Samuel Robert and Rose Saunders; m. Heidi Ruth Fulkerson, Mar. 18, 1978. AB with distinction, Stanford U., 1973; MSc with distinction, London Sch. Econs., 1974; diploma, U. Stockholm, 1976; MA, Harvard U., 1978. Cons. World Bank, Washington, 1975—77; sr. cons. Boston Cons. Group, 1978—82; dir. competitive strategy analysis Bain and Co., Boston, 1982—86; sr. v.p., chief planning officer Krupp Cos., Boston, 1986—88. Chmn. Saunders Capital Group, Boston, 1988—94, Internat. Mktg. Concepts, Louisville, 1998—2005, Venture Club, Louisville, 2001—05, Compliance & Ethics Learning Solutions, Chgo., 2004—06; mng. dir. Providian Capital Mgmt., Louisville, 1993—97; sr. mng. dir. Chrysalis Ventures, Louisville, 1997—2006; vice chmn. Telemics, Inc., Louisville, 2000—06; fin. com. chmn. Pub. Radio Partnership, Louisville, 1996—2003; investment com. chmn. African Am. Venture Capital Fund, 1993—2006; chmn. adv. bd. computer engring. and computer sci. U. Louisville, 2001—05; bd. dirs. Metacyte, Inc., Louisville, Constrn. Software Tech., Inc., Cin., Ygnition, Inc., Seattle, RAD Electronics, Inc., LA, Tech Skills LLC, Austin, Mobile Armor, St. Louis; chair investment adv. bd. Actor's Theater, Louisville; dev. com. chmn. Walden Theater, Louisville, 2003—06. Editor: Stanford Quar. Rev., 1973. Co-founder Weston Conservation Trust, Mass., 1988; del. Mass. Dem. Nat. Conv., San Francisco, 1984. Named Entrepreneur of the Yr. award for Ky. and S. Ohio, Ersnt and Young, 2004; Marshall scholar, 1973—75, NEH fellow, 1978, Swedish Govt. Fulbright grantee, 1975, U.S. Congress Profl. Devel. grantee, 1976. Mem.: Internat. Union Sci. Study Population, Am. Econ. Assn. Unitarian Universalist. Home: PO Box 99252 Louisville KY 40269-0252 Office: Chrysalis Ventures Ste 1650 National City Tower, 5th St Louisville KY 40202

SAUNDERS, SALLY LOVE, poet, educator; b. Bryn Mawr, Pa., Jan. 15, 1940; d. Lawrence and Dorothy (Love) S. Student, Sophia U., Tokyo, Japan, 1963, U. Pa., Columbia; BS, George Williams Coll., 1965. Tchr. Shipley Sch., Bryn Mawr, 1962-65, Agnes Irwin Sch., Wynnewood, Pa., 1964-65, Montgomery County Day Sch., Wynnewood, 1962, Miquon (Pa.) Sch., Waldron Acad., Merion, Pa., 1965-66, Phelps Sch., Malvern, Pa., 1965-70, Frankford Friends Sch. Phila., 1965-66, Haverford (Pa.) Sch., 1965-66, Friends Sem. Sch., NYC, 1966-68, Ballard Sch., NYC, 1966-67, Lower Merion Sch., Ardmore, Pa., nights 1967-71, Univ. Settlement House, Phila., 1961-63, Navajo Indian Reservation, Fort Defiance, Ariz., 1963, Young Men's Jewish Youth Center, Chgo., 1964-65, Margaret Fuller Settlement House, Cambridge, Mass., 1958-61; poetry therapist Pa. Hosp. Inst., 1969-74, also drug rehab. house Phila.; poet in residence Tyrone Guthrie Ctr., Newbliss, Ireland, Aug. 1988; poetry workshop leader Pendle Hill Quaker Ctr., Wallingford, Pa., Apr. 1988; poetry week leader Ferry Beach, Saco, Maine, summer 1988. Pioneer in poetry therapy. Poet, 1946—; poems pub. in periodicals including others; author: Past the Near Meadows, 1961, Pauses, 1978, Fresh Bread, 1982, Random Thoughts, 1992, Patchwork Quilt, 1993, Quiet Thoughts and Gentle Feelings, 1996, Word Pictures, 1998, Bits of Thought, 2006; contbr. poems to newspapers. Mem. Acad. Am. Poets, Nat. Fedn. State Poetry Socs., Am. Poetry League, Nat. League Am. Pen Women, Poetry Therapy Assn. (v.p.), Avalon Orgn., Authors Guild, Nat. Writers Club, Pen and Brush Club, N.H.Poetry Soc., Pa. Poetry Soc., Cath. Poetry Soc. (asso.), Fla. State Poetry Soc. (asso.) Episcopalian. Home: 2030 Vallejo St Apt 501 San Francisco CA 94123-4854 Office Phone: 610-356-0849. E-mail: slovesndrs@aol.com. *So often during my life I have found great comfort and strength in writing and reading poetry. With my poetry I want to help others to get in touch with their own powers. Poetry, to me, is a rare and beautiful freedom and this is what I want to share with others.*

SAUNDERS, STACY DAWN, journalist, music educator, vocalist; b. West Union, Ohio, Dec. 8, 1975; d. Russell Caskey and Linda Darlene Glasgow; m. Russell Edwin Saunders, Jr., Aug. 30, 1996; 1 child, Catherine Joy. AA in Arts and Scis., So. State C.C., Hillsboro, Ohio, 1995; BA in English and Humanities summa cum laude, Shawnee State U., 1996. Cert. tchr. Ohio Dept. Edn., profl. educator Assn. Christian Schs. Internat. Tchr. Adams County Christian Sch., West Union, Ohio, 1996—97; min. music Farmersville (Ohio) United Meth., 1997—2000; tchr. Ridgeville Christian Schs., Springboro, Ohio, 1998—2003, Christian Cmty. H.S., White House, Tenn., 2003—05; accompanist The Ch. at Grace Pk., White House, 2004—05; accompanist, song leader Hendersonville (Tenn.) Cumberland Presbytn., 2003—06; pianist White House 1st United Meth. Ch., 2006—. Pvt. music instr. Stacy's Studio, White House, 1998—2007; youth music dir. St. Timothy Luth. Ch., Hendersonville, 2005—06; sponsor music/drama club Christian Cmty. H.S., White House, Tenn., 2003—04; del. Assn. Christian Schs. Internat., Birmingham, Ala., 2004, Birmingham, 05; journalist Browser Pub. Author: (novels) Dark Knight, 2000; author/artist: record Come With Me, 2005, Time to Fly, 2007. Sponsor/ptnr. Compassion Internat., Colorado Springs, Colo., 1996—; Capitol Hill ptnr. Concerned Women for Am., Washington, 2004—; active Am. Conservative Union, Alexandria, Va., 2004—; Bible-A-Month Club mem. Am. Bible Soc., NYC, 2005—; choir mem. Solid Rock Ch., Monroe, Ohio, 2003. Recipient Outstanding Grad. award, Shawnee State U., 1996. Republican. Avocations: writing, hiking, aerobics, yoga.

SAUNDERS, TERRY ROSE, lawyer; b. Phila., July 13, 1942; d. Morton M. and Esther (Hauptman) Rose; m. George Lawton Saunders Jr., Sept. 21, 1975. BA, Barnard Coll., 1964; JD, NYU, 1973. Bar: D.C. 1973, Ill. 1976, U.S. Dist. Ct. (no. dist.) Ill. 1976, U.S. Ct. Appeals (7th cir.) 1976, U.S. Supreme Ct. 1983. Assoc. Williams & Connolly, Washington, 1973-75, Jenner & Block, Chgo., 1975-80, ptnr., 1981-86, Susman, Saunders & Buehler, Chgo., 1987-94; pvt. practice Law Offices of Terry Rose Saunders, Chgo., 1995—2002; ptnr. Saunders & Doyle, Chgo., 2002—. Author: (with others) Securities Fraud: Litigating Under Rule 10b-5, 1989. Recipient Robert B. McKay award NYU Sch. Law. Mem. ABA (co-chair class actions and derivative suits com. sect. litig. 1992-95, task force on merit selection of judges, co-chair consumer and personal rights litig. com. sect. litigation 2000-02), Chgo. Bar Assn., Order of Coif, Union League Club. Office Phone: 312-551-0051. Business E-Mail: trsaunders@saundersdoyle.com.

SAUNDERS, WILLIAM ARTHUR, management consultant; b. Ottawa, Ont., Can., Oct. 13, 1930; BS with honors, McGill U., Montreal, 1954; MBA in Econs. and Fin., U. Western Ont., 1956; M Commerce in Econs. and Mktg., U. Toronto, 1960. Econ. analyst Imperial Oil Ltd., Toronto, Ont., 1956-63; supr. distbrn. Polysar Ltd., Sarnia, Ont., 1963-69; venture mgr. Polysar Plastics, Inc., Westport, Conn., 1969-77; adv. strategy devel. Gulf Oil Chems. Co., Houston, 1977-82; mgmt. cons. Houston, 1982—; pres. William A. Saunders Co., 1987—. Methodist. Home and Office: 8585 Woodway Dr Apt 112 Houston TX 77063-2438

SAUNDERS, WILLIAM HUNDLEY, JR., retired chemist, educator; b. Pulaski, Va., Jan. 12, 1926; s. William Hundley and Vivian (Watts) S.; m. Nina Velta Plesums, June 25, 1960 (dec. June 1982); children: Anne Michele, Claude William; m. Barbara Andrews, Apr. 27, 2002 (dec. May 2005) BS in Chemistry, Coll. William and Mary, 1948; PhD in Organic Chemistry, Northwestern U., 1952. Rsch. assoc. MIT, 1951-53; instr. U. Rochester, 1953-56, from. asst. prof. to assoc. prof., 1956-64, prof. chemistry, 1964-91, faculty sr. assoc., 1991-95, chmn. dept., 1966-70, prof. emeritus, 1996—. Author: Ionic Aliphatic Reactions, 1965; (with A.F. Cockerill) Mechanisms of Elimination Reactions, 1973; (with L. Melander) Reaction Rates of Isotopic Molecules, 1980; contbr. numerous articles to profl. jours. With US Army, 1944—45, ETO. Guggenheim fellow, 1960—61, Sloan Found. fellow, 1961—64, NSF sr. postdoctoral fellow, 1970—71. Mem. Am. Chem. Soc., Royal Soc. Chemistry, Phi Beta Kappa, Sigma Xi, Phi Lambda Upsilon. Democrat. Unitarian Universalist. Avocations: bicycling, cross country skiing, travel. Home: 15 Parkwood Ave Rochester NY 14620-3401 Office: U Rochester Dept Chemistry River Sta Rochester NY 14627 Office Phone: 585-275-4235. Business E-Mail: saunders@chem.rochester.edu.

SAURO, JOSEPH PIO, physics professor; b. New Rochelle, NY, Apr. 4, 1927; s. Francesco Giovanni and Lucia (Arrivebene) S.; m. Elizabeth Joann Schellman, May 2, 1948; children: Brian, Michael, Joseph. BS, Poly Inst. Bkyn., 1955, MS, 1958, PhD in Physics, 1966. Dir. coll. sci. improvement program U. Mass., North Dartmouth, 1969-71, dean grad. sch., 1969-71, interim dean Coll. of Engring., 1978-80, dean Coll. Arts and Scis., 1969-80, prof. physics, 1965-93, prof. emeritus, 1995—. Participant Symposium on Devel. of Physicist's Conception of Nature, Trieste, 1972. With USN, 1944-46. Sci. Faculty fellow NSF, 1964; State War Svc. scholar State of N.Y., 1953. Mem. Am Assn. Physics Tchr., Sigma Xi, Sigma Pi Sigma. Avocations: photography, travel, music. Office: U Mass North Dartmouth MA 02747 E-mail: jsauro@capecod.net.

SAUSMAN, KAREN, zoological park administrator; b. Chgo., Nov. 26, 1945; d. William and Annabell (Lofaso) S. BS, Loyola U., 1966; student, Redlands U., 1968. Keeper Lincoln Park Zoo, Chgo., 1964-66; tchr. Palm Springs (Calif.) Unified Sch., 1968-70; ranger Nat. Park Svc., Joshua Tree, Calif., 1968-70; zoo dir. The Living Desert, Palm Desert, Calif., 1970—. Natural history study tour leader internat., 1974—; part-time instr. Coll. Desert Natural History Calif. Desert, 1975-78; field reviewer conservation grants Inst. Mus. Svcs., 1987—, MAP cons., 1987—, panelist, 1992—; internat. studbook keeper for Sand Cats, 1988-2001, for Cuvier's Gazelle, Mhorr Gazelle, 1990-2000; co-chair Arabian Oryx species survival plan propogation group, 1986-95; spkr. in field. Author Survival Captive

Bighorn Sheep, 1982, Small Facilities- Opportunities and Obligations, 1983; wildlife illustrator books, mags, 1970—; editor Fox Paws newsletter Living Desert, 1970—, ann. reports, 1976—; natural sci. editor Desert Mag., 1979-82; compiler Conservation and Management Plan for Antelope, 1992; contbr. articles to profl. jours. Past bd. dirs., sec. Desert Protective Coun.; adv. coun. Desert Bighorn Rsch. Inst., 1981-85; bd. dirs. Palm Springs Desert Resorts Convention and Visitors Bur., 1988-94; bd. dirs., treas. Coachella Valley Mountain Trust, 1989-92. Named Woman Making a Difference Soroptimist Internat., 1989, 93, 97, Woman of Distinction, Riverside Bus. Press, 2000. Fellow Am. Assn. Zool. Parks and Aquariums (bd. dirs., accredation field reviewer, desert antelope taxon adv. group, caprid taxon adv. group, felid taxon adv. group, small population mgmt. adv. group, wildlife conservation and mgmt. com., chmn. ethics com. 1987, mem. com., internat. rels. com., ethics task force, pres'. award 1972-77, outstanding svc. award 1983, 88, editor newsletter, Zool. Parks and Aquarium Fundamentals 1982); mem. Internat. Species Inventory System (mgmt. com., policy adv. group 1980-96, trustee 1997-2004), Calif. Assn. Mus. (v.p. 1992-96), Calif. Assn. Zoos and Aquariums, World Assn. Zoos and Aquariums (coun. 2002-, governing coun. 200—, pres. 2005—), Western Interpretive Assn. (so. Calif. chpt.), Am. Assn. Mus., Arboreta and Bot. Gardens So. Calif. (coun. dirs.), Soc. Conservation Biology, Nat. Audubon. Soc., Jersey Wildlife Preservation Trust Internat., Nature Conservancy, East African Wildlife Soc., African Wildlife Found., Kennel Club Palm Springs (past bd. dirs., treas. 1978-80), Scottish Deerhound Club Am. (editor Scottish Deerhounds in N.A., 1983, life mem. U.K. chpt.), Internat. Bengal Cat Soc. (pres. 1994-96). Avocations: pure bred dogs, cats, dressage, painting, photography. Office: The Living Desert 47 900 Portola Ave Palm Desert CA 92260 E-mail: kastld@aol.com.

SAUVAGEAU, YVON, application developer; b. Montreal, Que., Can., Dec. 10, 1961; arrived in US, 1998; s. Yvon Sauvageau and Huguette Bergeron. BSc in Computer sci., McGill U., Montreal, 1986. Cert. Java developer Sun Microsystems. Software engr. NSK Technologies, Paris, 1997—99, Merrimac Interactive Media, Cocoa, Fla., 1999—2000, Cisco Sys., Inc., San Jose, Calif., 2000—. Mem.: IEEE. Achievements include patents for method and apparatus for drawing line graphs; development of compression algorithm for the Java language binaries; software tool for the evaluation of binary compatibility between Java language binaries; graphical user interface of network topology maps; event notification subsystem of a network management system. Office: Cisco Sys Inc 3550 Cisco Way SJC19/3/3 San Jose CA 95134 Personal E-mail: ysauv@ieee.org.

SAVA, VASYL, education educator; b. Zelene, Ukraine, May 16, 1951; arrived in U.S., 2002; s. Mykhail and Galyna Sava; m. Alla Krivich, Aug. 25, 1973; children: Yuri, Dmytro. BS, Odessa State U. Ecology, Ukraine, 1973; PhD, Inst. of Bioorganic Chemistry, Minsk, USSR, 1985. Cert. Sr. Scientist Higher Certifying Bd. of Ukraine, 1993. Investigator Internat. Rsch. Program INTAS, Parma, Italy, 1995—97; assoc. prof. Odessa State U. Ecology, 1997—99; sr. scientist and group leader Bogatsky Physico-Chemical Inst. NAS of Ukraine, Odessa, Ukraine, 1989—99; rsch. assoc. Pig Rsch. Inst., Miaoli, Taiwan, 1999—2000, China Med. Coll., Taichung, Taiwan, 2000—01; vis. asst. prof. Inst. of Botany, Academia Sinica, Taipei, Taiwan, 2001—02; rsch. assoc. U. South Fla., Tampa, 2002—04, asst. prof., 2004—. Head of soc. of inventors and rationalizers Bogatsky Physico-Chemical Inst. NAS of Ukraine, Odessa, Ukraine, 1984—89. Recipient Rank of Sr. Scientist, Higher Certifying Bd. of Ukraine, 1993, Zelinsky Prize, Bd. of Odessa Br. of Mendeleev Chem. Soc., 1978, 1983; grantee Intas 94-0839, Consiglio Nazionale dele Richerche, Italy, 1995-1997. Mem.: AAAS (assoc.), Am. Soc. for Neurochemistry (assoc.), Am. Soc. for Neuronal Transplantation and Repair (assoc.), Soc. for Neuroscience (USA) (assoc.), Internat. Soc. for Free radical Biology and Medicine (assoc.). Achievements include patents for Holder of 21. Home Phone: 813-929-1599. Business E-Mail: vsava@hsc.usf.edu.

SAVADOVE, DANIEL C., broadcast executive; b. Phila., Nov. 8, 1958; BA in Speech Comms. with distinction, Pa. State U., 1980. Account exec. Gen. Cinema Corp., Comm. Inc., Sta. WIFI-FM, Phila., 1980-83, Infinity Broadcasting Corp., Sta. WYSP-FM, Phila., 1983-85, local sales mgr., 1985-87; gen. sales mgr. Malrite Comm. Group, Inc., Sta. WEGX-FM, Phila., 1987-91; v.p., gen. mgr. WNNK-FM, Harrisburg, Pa., 1993; CEO Root Comm., Pa., 2001—05; pres. & CEO Main Line Broadcasting LLC, West Conshohocken, Pa., 2005—. Active Big Bros. of Phila.; chair advt. com. Gardenzia's 1994 Benefit Concert. Mem. Ctrl. Pa. Radio Broadcasters Assn. (sec.), Nat. Assn. Broadcasters (radio bd. dirs. 2007-) Avocations: skiing, golf, tennis. Office: Main Line Broadcasting LLC 300 Conshohocken State Rd West Conshohocken PA 19428 *

SAVAGE, CHARLES, news correspondent; b. Ft. Wayne, Ind., 1975; m. Luiza Savage; 1 child, Will. BA, Harvard Coll., 1998; M., Yale Law Sch., 2003. Govt. & politics reporter Miami Herald, 1998—2002; Washington corr. Boston Globe, Washington, 2003—. Recipient Pulitzer Prize for Nat. Reporting, The Pulitzer Board, 2007; Knight Found. journalism fellow, Yale Law Sch., 2002—03. Office: Boston Globe Washington Bur 1130 Connecticut Ave NW Washington DC 20036 Office Phone: 202-857-5123. E-mail: csavage@globe.com. *

SAVAGE, CLARE LEAVY, school psychologist; b. NYC, Mar. 20, 1953; d. Charles Joseph Leavy and Catherine Theresa Frary; m. Paul Jonathan Savage; children: Stephanie, Matthew. BA, Marymount Manhattan Coll., 1975; MSc, Hunter Coll., 1977; Adv. Cert. in Sch. Psychology, CUNY, 1986; PhD, Kennedy Western U., 2003. Cert. sch. psychologist NY, tchr. K-6 NY. Sch. psychologist, spl. edn. tchr. Western Suffolk Bd. Coop. Ednl. Svcs., 1986—99; sch. psychologist Babylon Union Free Sch. Dist., 1999—. Extraordinary min. Eucharist Ch. St. Mary, Manhasset, 1999—; extraordinary min. of Eucharist North Shore Univ. Hosp., Manhasset, 1999—2001; catechist religious edn. program Ch. St. Mary, 1999—2005. Mem.: NY State United Fedn. Tchrs., Nat. Assn. Sch. Psychologists. Roman Cath. Avocations: calligraphy, reading, theater, writing. Home: 24 Stuart Pl Manhasset NY 11030 Personal E-mail: clsavage@optonline.net.

SAVAGE, DANIEL KEENAN, columnist, editor-in-chief; b. Chgo., Oct. 7, 1964; life ptnr. Terry Miller; 1 adopted child, Daryl Jude Pierce. Founder Greek Active Theater, Seattle; syndicated columnist The Stranger, Seattle, 1991—, assoc. editor, 1995—2001, editor-in-chief, 2001—. Author: (columns) Savage Love, 1991—, Dear Dan, 1998—2000, (books) Savage Love: Straight Answers from America's Most Popular Sex Columnist, 1998, The Kid: What Happened After My Boyfriend and I Decided to Go Get Pregnant, 2000, Skipping Towards Gomorrah: The Seven Deadly Sins & the Pursuit of Happiness in America, 2003, The Commitment: Love, Sex, Marriage, and My Family, 2005; host (radio programs) Savage Love Live, KEXP FM 90.3, Seattle, 1994—97, contbr. This American Life; actor: (films) Crocodile Tears, 1998, 20 Gay Stereotypes Confirmed, 2004; author & dir. (plays) Saint Joan, Greek Active Theater, Seattle, 1995, Egguus, 2001. Co-founder Gay City Health Project, Seattle, 1995. Office: The Stranger 3rd Fl 1535 11th Ave Seattle WA 98122 Office Phone: 206-323-7101. Office Fax: 206-323-7203. E-mail: editor@thestranger.com.

SAVAGE, DAVID WILLIAM, lawyer; b. Seattle, Nov. 14, 1944; s. Kenneth and Mary Savage; m. Sally Savage, Aug. 1, 1982; children: Jesse, Erin, Kathryn. BA in Polit. Sci., Wash. State U.; JD, U. Idaho. Bar: Wash. 1973, U.S. Dist. Ct. (ea. dist.) Wash. 1977, Idaho 1991, U.S. Dist. Ct. Idaho 1991, Mont. 1996, U.S. Ct. Appeals (9th cir.) 1997, U.S. Supreme Ct. 1999. Shareholder, pres. Irwin, Myklebust, Savage & Brown, P.S., Pullman, Wash., 1973—. Mem.: ABA, Wash. State Bar Assn. (pres.-elect 2002—03, pres. 2003—04), Idaho State Bar Assn. Office: Irwin Myklebust Savage & Brown PS 1230 SE Bishop Blvd Pullman WA 99163 Office Phone: 509-332-3502. Business E-Mail: savage@imsblaw.com.

SAVAGE, ELDON PAUL, retired environmental health educator; b. Bedford, Iowa, Apr. 4, 1926; s. Paul and Nora (Arthur) S.; m. Ella May, June 5, 1948; children: Steven P., Michael D. BS, U. Kans., 1950; MPH, Tulane U., 1958; PhD, Okla. U., 1968. Coord. environ. sanitation demonstration projects USPHS, Kans., Iowa and Pa., 1950-64; chief state aids sect. pesticide ctr. Ctr. for Disease Control, Atlanta, 1964-70; chief chem. epidemiology sect. Inst. Rural Environ. Health, Colo. State U., Ft. Collins, 1970-84, prof., dir. environ. health divsn., 1984-85, head dept. environ. health, 1985-90, dir. environ. health svcs., 1987-93, prof. emeritus, 1993—. Contbr. articles to profl. jours. Mem. Am. Acad. Sanitarians (sec., treas., diplomate), Nat. Environ. Health Assn., Sigma Xi, Gamma Sigma Delta. Home: Savage EE Arabian Horses 5220 Apple Dr Fort Collins CO 80526-4302 Office: Colo State U Inst Rural Envrion Health Fort Collins CO 80523-0001

SAVAGE, JAMES FRANCIS, editor; b. Boston, July 23, 1939; s. James and Hanora (Enright) S.; m. Sharon Kaye Base, May 29, 1965; 1 son, Sean. AA, Boston U., 1959, BS, 1961. Reporter Quincy (Mass.) Patriot Ledger, 1961-63; reporter Miami (Fla.) Herald, 1963-67, investigative reporter, 1967-78, investigations editor, 1978-84, assoc. editor investigations, 1984—. Investigative reporter Boston Herald Traveler, 1967 Served with AUS, 1962. Recipient Nat. Headliners award, 1969, Fla. Press Assn. award, 1972, George Polk Meml. award for investigative reporting, 1973, 80, Pub. Service award Nat. A.P. Mng. Editors, 1974, 80, award Fla. Soc. Newspaper Editors, 1974, 75, Nat. Disting. Service award Sigma Delta Chi, 1979, 87, Pulitzer Prize Staff award for Nat. Reporting, 1987, Outstanding Investigative Reporting award Investigative Reporters and Editors, 1988, Disting. Alumni award Boston U. Coll. Communications, 1990, Pulitzer Prize Staff Pub. Svc. award, 1993; Profl. Journalism fellow Stanford, 1974-75 Home: 1004 Orange Is Fort Lauderdale FL 33315-1651 Office: 1 Herald Plz Miami FL 33132-1609

SAVAGE, JOHN EDMUND, computer science educator, researcher; b. Lynn, Mass., Sept. 19, 1939; s. Edmund J. and Eldora A. (Guay) S.; m. Patricia Joan Landers, Jan. 29, 1966; children: Elizabeth, Kevin, Christopher, Timothy ScB, ScM, MIT, 1962, PhD, 1965. Mem. tech. staff Bell Telephone Labs., Holmdel, NJ, 1965-67; prof. computer sci. Brown U., Providence, 1967—, chmn. dept. computer sci., 1985-91. Vis. prof. Tech. U. Eindhoven, 1973—74, U. Paris, 1980—81, Warwick U., 1991—92, Ecole Polytechique, 2004—05; vis. Inst. Nat. Rsch. Info. Automatic, Rocquencourt, France; cons. in field. Author: The Complexity of Computing, 1977; author: (with others) The Mystical Machine, 1986; author: Models of Computation: Exploring the Power of Computing, 1996; editor (with Thomas Knight): Advanced Research in VLSI and Parallel Systems, 1992; chmn. editl. bd. Computing Rsch. News, 1990—96, mem. editl. bd. Jour. Computer and Sys. Scis., 1993—, patentee data scrambler, 1970, means and methods for generating permutation of a square, 1976, stochastic assembly of sublithographic interfaces, 2005, sublithographic nanoscale memory architecture, 2005. Mem. MIT Corp. vis. com. dept. elec. engring. and computer sci., 1991-2002. Fulbright-Hays grantee, 1973; NSF fellow, 1961, Guggenheim fellow, 1973 Fellow AAAS, IEEE (life), Assn. Computing Machinery; mem. Computing Rsch. Assn. (bd. dirs. 1990-96), Sigma Xi, Tau Beta Pi. Avocations: reading, bicycling, walking. Office: Brown U Dept Computer Sci 115 Waterman St Providence RI 02912-9016 Home Phone: 401-861-3462; Office Phone: 401-863-7642. Business E-Mail: john_savage@brown.edu.

SAVAGE, JOHN WILLIAM, lawyer; b. Seattle, Oct. 11, 1951; s. Stanley and Jennie Sabina (Siggstedt) S.; m. Rebecca Lee Abraham, Oct. 1, 1983 (div. Oct. 2005); children: Bennett William, James Oliver. Student, Lewis and Clark Coll., 1969-71, JD Northwestern Sch. Law, 1977; BA, U. Wash., 1973. Bar: Oreg. 1977, U.S. Dist. Ct. Oreg. 1977, U.S. Ct. Appeals (9th cir.) 1977, U.S. Supreme Ct., 1985, U.S. Ct. Appeals (fed. cir.) 1998, Wash. 2002, U.S. Ct. Fed. Claims 2003, U.S. Dist. Ct. (we. dist.) Wash. 2005. Pvt. practice law, Portland, Oreg., 1977-79; ptnr. Bailey, Olstad, Rieke, Geil & Savage, P.C., Portland, 1979-80; ptnr., shareholder Rieke, Geil & Savage, P.C., Portland, 1980-95; shareholder Rieke & Savage, P.C., Portland, 1995—2003; pvt. practice, 2003—. Mem. Oreg. Literacy Inc., Portland, 1979-85; mem. standing com. City Club, Portland, 1984-88, chmn. law and pub. safety standing com. 1986-87. Recipient award of merit, Gerry Spence's Trial Lawyers Coll., 1999. Mem. ABA (chairperson young lawyers sect. Nat. Cmty. Law Week 1983-84, inmate grievance com. 1984-88), Assn. Trial Lawyers Am., Trial Lawyers for Pub. Justice, Oreg. Trial Lawyers Assn. (edn. com. 2002-05, bd. mem. 2003—), Oreg. Bar Assn. (def. of indigent accused com. 1985-89), Oreg. Criminal Def. Lawyers Assn. (bd. dirs. 1984-86), Multnomah Bar Assn. (v.p. young lawyers sect. 1980, pres.-elect 1981, pres. 1982, Disting. Svc. award, bd. dirs. 1989-92, task force chair 1992-93, jud. selection com. 1998-99, cir. ct. liaison com. 2002—, Award of Merit 1994). Office: Savage Bowersox Supperstein LLP 620 SW Fifth Ave ste 1125 Portland OR 97204 Home: 5001D Foothills Rd Lake Oswego OR 97034 E-mail: jwsavage@earthlink.net.

SAVAGE, JOSEPH GEORGE, academic administrator; b. Bklyn. s. Joseph George Jr. and Eileen (Schnell) S.; m. Lynn Ann Campbell; children: Kimberly, Patricia, Joseph IV. BA, Oswego Coll., 1977; post-grad., Seton Hall U., 1985. Pub. affairs dir. L.I. chpt. Nat. Multiple Sclerosis Soc., NYC, 1977-79, exec. dir. Conn. chpt., 1979-80; dir. devel., mktg. Clara Mass Meml. Med. Ctr., Belleville, N.J., 1980-81; exec. dir. Found. of St. Joseph's Hosp. Med. Ctr., Paterson, N.J., 1981-89; sr. v.p. St. Francis Hosp. Heart Ctr., Roslyn, N.Y., 1989-92; v.p. St. Vincents Hosp. and Med. Ctr., NYC, 1992-98; exec. v.p. Cathedral Health Care Sys., Newark, 1998—2001, Caldwell (NJ) Coll., 2001—. Commr. health City of Clifton, 1990-94; bd. dirs. N.Y. Heart Coun., 1989-93, Cath. Family and Cmty. Svcs., 1992-2006, Osweo Coll. Alumni, 1992—, St. Mary's Hosp., Passiac, N.J., 1993-99, 2000—; v.p. Caldwell Coll. Fellow Nat. Assn. Hosp. Devel. (communication chair 1982-85, edn. chair 1985-86, bd. dirs., regional dir. 1988-89), Friendly Sons of St. Patrick (N.Y.), Ancient Order of Hibernians, Rotary (past pres. Clifton Club, Paul Harris fellow, Walter Head fellow), Caldwell Club. Roman Catholic. Avocations: swimming, golf. Office: Caldwell Coll 9 Ryerson Ave Caldwell NJ 07006-1558 Home: 300 Alexandria Dr Hackettstown NJ 07840-3804 Home Phone: 973-885-6715; Office Phone: 973-618-3242. E-mail: jsavage@caldwell.edu.

SAVAGE, KIM I., academic administrator; d. William T. and Sylvia V. Savage; 1 child, Nicholas. BA, North Ctrl. Coll., 1977; MEd, Oreg. State U., 1980. Asst. dir., Hermann Hall Ill. Inst. Tech., Chgo., 1977—78; program advisor Oreg. State U., Corvallis, 1978—80; asst. program dir. Ohio State U., Columbus, 1980—81; various positions in student centers adminstrn. U. Ill., Chgo., 1981—2001, campus aux. svcs., 2001—05, asst. to vice chancellor student affairs, 2005—06, assessment coord. for student affairs, 2006—. Contbr. articles to profl. jours. Chmn. Downers Grove Twp. Dem. Orgn., Ill., 2006—, precinct committeeman, 2000—06; mem. Ill. Dem. Women, Springfield; dir. Alford Am. Family Assn., Florrissant, Mo., 2001—04. Recipient Staff Leadership award, Assn. Coll. Unions Internat. Region, 2006. Mem.: AAUW, LWV, Assn. Coll. Unions Internat. (various regional and nat. leadership positions 1980—2003, pub. policy liaison 2005—), Woodridge Toastmasters (v.p. 2005—). Avocations: gardening, genealogy. Home Phone: 630-435-1464.

SAVAGE, MARK RANDALL, lawyer; b. Chicopee, Mass., Mar. 10, 1959; m. Lucia Clara Savage; children: David, Ryan. BA, U. Calif., Berkeley, 1982; JD, Stanford U., 1988. Bar: Calif. Jud. law clk. to Judge James Holden, North Bennington, Vt., 1988-89; mng. atty. Pub. Advs., Inc., San Francisco, 1989—2003; sr. atty. Consumers Union of U.S., Inc., San Francisco, 2003—. Gen. counsel Cmty. Tech. Found. Calif., San Francisco, 1998—; bd. dirs. Family Bridges, Inc., Oakland, Calif. Contbr. articles to profl. jours. Bd. dirs. Unitarian Ch., Oakland, Calif., 2006—, Inst. for Civic Arts and Pub. Spaces, Inc., Albuquerque, 1996—2001. Recipient Drum Maj. award So. Christian Leadership Conf., 1998, Diversity, Innovation and Reform in Edn. award, 1995, El Fuego Nuevo award Assn. Mex. Am. Educators, 1999, Leadership Recognition award Calif. Primary Care Assn., 1999, Screaming Eagle award Calif. Reinvestment Coalition, 2004, Calif. Lawyer Attys. of Yr. award, 2007. Office: Consumers Union 1535 Mission St San Francisco CA 94103-2566 Home Phone: 510-261-8263; Office Phone: 415-431-6747. Business E-Mail: Mark.Savage@pacbell.net.

SAVAGE, MAUREEN WALLS, retired history professor; b. Paterson, NJ, Nov. 16, 1930; d. George A. and Mary Duffy Walls; m. Harry Michael Savage, Nov. 27, 1948; children: Terry, Aileen, Kathleen, Timothy, Russell. BA, Rutgers U., Newark, 1963; MA, Rutgers U., New Brunswick, NJ, 1974. Tchr. social studies, English grades 7-8 pub. schs., Orange, NJ, 1963—66, tchr. social studies, English, world history grades 7-12 Cranford, NJ, 1966—88; prof. polit. sci. Coll. St. Elizabeth, Convent Station, NJ, 1998; prof. Irish history and culture Stockton Coll., Pomona, NJ, 1993—2003. Historian Ctr. for Cmty. Arts, Cape May, NJ, 1996—2006; curator Historic Colonial Ho., Cape May, 2003, African Am. history exhibits, 1996—; pres., v.p., moderator LWV, Cape May County, 1990—, nominating com. state bd., 2002—; leader NJ del. 75th anniversary women's suffrage re-enactment, Washington, 1995. Grantee NJ Hist. Soc., Historic Commn. Cape May County. Mem.: Greater Cape May Hist. Soc. (v.p. 2001—), Irish Am. Cultural Soc. Roman Catholic. Avocations: piano, history, Irish dancing, travel, theater. Home: 916 Columbia Ave Cape May NJ 08204 Home Fax: 609-898-8107. Personal E-mail: hmsavage@verizon.net.

SAVAGE, MICHAEL ALAN (MICHAEL WEINER), radio personality, commentator; b. Bronx, NY, Mar. 31, 1942; s. Benjamin and Rae W.; m. Janet A. Savage (div.); children: Russell, Rebecca; m. Sheila Weiner-Rozzo, 1964 (div. 1967). MS in med. botany, med. anthropology, U. Hawaii, 1970; PhD in epidemiology, nutrition sci., U. Calif. Berkeley, 1978. Talk radio host KSFO, San Francisco, 1995—2003; host The Savage Nation Talk Radio Network, 1999—, MSNBC, 2003. Author: various books on herbal medicine including Weiner's Herbal: The Guide to Herb Medicine, 1980, (book) The Savage Nation: Saving America from the Liberal Assault on Our Borders, Language, and Culture, 2003, The Enemy Within: Saving America from the Liberal Assault on Our Schools, Faith, and Military, 2004, Liberalism is a Mental Disorder, 2005, The Political Zoo, 2006. Mem.: Paul Revere Soc. (founding mem.). Jewish. Address: Talk 910 KNEW 340 Townsend St San Francisco CA 94107 Office Phone: 800-449-8255. E-mail: michaelsavage@paulreveresociety.com. *

SAVAGE, MICHAEL JOHN KIRKNESS, oil industry executive, performing arts company executive; b. Birmingham, Eng., Oct. 28, 1934; arrived in U.S., 1962, naturalized, 1981; s. Leonard W. H. and Hilda C. (Fletcher) Savage; m. Elisabeth Karl, June 21, 1965 (div.); m. Virginia Hooper, Aug. 31, 1978; 1 child, Matthew Nicholas. MA in Econs. and Law with honors, Cambridge U., 1958; postgrad., Manchester Bus. Sch., Eng., 1965; Diploma in Arabic, Middle E. Ctr. for Arab Studies, Shemlan, Lebanon, 1967. Various positions Brit. Petroleum Co. Ltd., 1958-82, internat. dir. London, 1982; pres. BP Alaska Inc., San Francisco, 1977, Sohio Petroleum Co., San Francisco, 1978-82; founder/pres. Merlin Petroleum Co., San Francisco, 1983-88, Savage Petroleum Co., Sausalito, Calif., 1992—95; bd. dirs., mng. dir. San Francisco Opera, 1994-99; exec. dir. bd. dirs. Napa Valley Opera House, Napa, Calif., 2000—04, Lincoln Theater, Napa Valley, Calif., 2004—. Trustee San Francisco Conservatory Music, 1983—, chmn., 1990—94; trustee Alaska Pacific U., 1982—86; dir. Napa Valley Mustard Festival, 2005—. Avocations: music, tennis, skiing, mountain walking. Office: Lincoln Theater California Dr Yountville CA 94599

SAVAGE, MICHAEL PAUL, cardiologist, educator; b. Wilkes-Barre, Pa., Jan. 25, 1955; s. Peter J. and Olga J. (Sekerchak) Savage; m. Kathleen A. Gallagher, June 1989; children: Katherine, Andrew. BA, Wesleyan U., Middletown, Conn., 1976; MD, Jefferson Med. Coll., 1980. Diplomate Am. Bd. Internal Medicine, Am. Bd. Cardiovascular Disease Interventional Cardiology, Nat. Bd. Med. Examiners. Intern, then resident New Eng. Deaconess Hosp.-Harvard U. Med. Sch., Boston, 1980—83; fellow Jefferson Med. Coll., Phila., 1983—86, asst. prof. medicine, 1986—91, assoc. prof., 1991—, dir. cardiac catheterization, 1990—, dir. interventional cardiology sect., 1996—. Cons. Johnson & Johnson Interventional Sys. Co., Warren, NJ, Scimed/Boston Sci., Maple Grove, Minn., GlaxoSmith-Kline, Phila.; lectr. coronary angioplasty and cardiac catheterization. Contbr. articles to profl. jours., chapters to books. Fellow: Am. Fedn. Clin. Rsch., Am. Heart Assn., Pa. Med. Soc., Soc. Cardiac Angiography and Interventions, Am. Coll. Cardiology. Roman Catholic. Achievements include research in interventional cardiology concerning new techniques in treatment of coronary artery disease; culminating in international; propsective trials demonstrating superiority of implantable coronary stents over conventional balloon angioplasty. Office: Jefferson Heart Inst 925 Chestnut St Philadelphia PA 19107-5001 Home Phone: 215-247-8330; Office Phone: 215-955-6478. Business E-Mail: michael.savage@jefferson.edu.

SAVAGE, SUSAN M., state official, former mayor; b. Tulsa, Okla., 1936; married; 2 children. Student, U. Aix-Marseilles, Aix-en-Provence, France, 1969, City of London Poly., Eng., 1972; BA in Sociology with honors, Beaver Coll., 1974. Pre-trial rep. Phila. Ct. Common Pleas, 1974-75; criminal justice planner Montgomery County Criminal Justice Unit, 1975-77; exec. dir. Met. Tulsa Citizens Crime Com., 1977-87; vol. coord. Vote Yes For Tulsa, 1987; chief of staff to mayor City of Tulsa, 1988-92, mayor, 1992—2002; sec. state State of Okla., Oklahoma City, 2003—. Active Lee Elementary Sch. PTA; bd. dirs., treas. Okla. Crime Prevention Assn.; bd. dirs. Youth Svcs. of Tulsa County, 1984-88, pres., 1986-87; co-chair Safe Streets/Enhanced 911 Steering Com., 1987; mem. C. of C. Task Force/Community Edn. Network, 1983. Mem. U.S. Conf. Mayors (chmn. com. energy and environment). Democrat. Office: Office Sec of State State Capitol Rm 101 Oklahoma City OK 73105 Home: 224 NW 33rd St Oklahoma City OK 73118-8614 Office Phone: 405-521-3911. Office Fax: 405-521-3771. Business E-Mail: susan.savage@sos.state.ok.us. *

SAVAGE, TERRY, television personality, journalist, stockbroker; Grad., U. Mich. Registered investment advisor stocks and commodity futures. Founding mem., 1st woman trader Chgo. Bd. Options Exch.; mem. Internat. Monetary Market; columnist Chgo. Sun Times, Chgo.; personal fin. columnist Barron's Online; featured columnist MSN Money website; owner, columnist pvt. website www.TerrySavage.com. Bd. dirs. Devon Energy, Broadway Stores, Chicago Mercantile Exchange; former bd. mem. McDonald's Corp., Pennzoil-Quaker State Corp.; former co-editor Options Trading Strategies newsletter; spkr. in field. Host Money Talks; author: Terry Savage's New Money Strategies for the 90s, 1993, Terry Savage Talks Money: The Common-Sense Guide to Money Matters, 1999, The Savage Truth on Money, 1999; columnist Chgo. Sun-Times. Dir. Chgo. Mus. Sci. and Industry, Northwestern Meml. Hosp. Found., Econ. Club Chgo., Execs. Club Chgo., Jr. Achievement Ill., Ill. Coun. on Econ. Edn., Women's Bus. Devel. Ctr. Recipient Outstanding Consumer Journalism award Nat. Press Club, 1987, Dir.'s Choice award, 1994, 2 Emmy awards,

Outstanding Personal Finance Columnist award, Northwestern U.; Woodrow Wilson fellow in Am. history and econs. Mem. Phi Beta Kappa. Office: Terry Savage Productions 676 N Michigan Ave Ste 3610 Chicago IL 60611 also: Chicago Sun Times 350 N Orleans St Ste 1270 Chicago IL 60654-2148 E-mail: savage@suntimes.com. *

SAVAGE, THOMAS RYAN, lawyer; b. Milw., Dec. 1, 1947; s. John F. and Dorothy R. (Ryan) S.; m. Patricia C. Savage; children: Ryan, Patrick, Molly. BA, Quincy Coll., 1969; JD, Marquette U., 1973. Bar: Wis. 1973, U.S. Dist. Ct. (ea. and we. dists.) Wis. Sr. atty. Clark Oil & Refining Corp., Milw., 1973-82; assoc. Mulcahy & Wherry, Milw., 1982-84; v.p., sec., gen. counsel Sta-Rite Industries, Milw., 1984-92; v.p. adminstrn., gen. counsel Briggs & Stratton Corp., Wauwatosa, Wis., 1992—97, sr. v.p. adminstrn., 1992—. Mem. Dist. Export Coun., Milw., 1983-88, Gov.'s Adv. Coun. on Internat. Trade, Madison, Wis., 1982-85; solicitor United Way, Milw., 1990; bd. dirs. Goodwill Industries Wis., 1995—. Mem. Am. Counsel Assn. (bd. govs. Wis. chpt. 1988-94, pres. 1993-94), Engine Mfrs. Assn. (pres. 2001-02). Office: Briggs & Stratton Corp 12301 W Wirth St Wauwatosa WI 53222-2110 Office Phone: 414-259-5333.

SAVAGE, WILLIAM WOODROW, JR., historian, consultant, social sciences educator; b. Richmond, Va., Oct. 13, 1943; s. William Woodrow and Margaret Savage; m. Sheila Bobalik, July 30, 1983; 1 child, William Woodrow III. BA in Journalism, U. S.C., 1964, MA in History, 1966; PhD in History, U. Okla., 1972. Instr. Coll. Gen. Studies U. S.C., Columbia, 1966; vis. lectr. history Iowa State U., Ames, 1970; asst. editor U. Okla. Press, Norman, 1972-75; from asst. prof. to assoc. prof. history U. Okla., Norman, 1974—89, prof., 1989—. Tech. adviser Korine-Dunlap Prodns., Nashville, 1982—83; adviser Am. Frontier Project, NYC, 1982—85; bd. cons. editors Popular Culture Librs., Binghamton, NY, 1991—99. Author: The Cherokee Strip Live Stock Association, 1973, The Cowboy Hero, 1979, Singing Cowboys and All That Jazz, 1983, Comic Books and America, 1945-54, 1990; editor: Indian Life, 1977, Cowboy Life, 1993; co-editor: The Frontier, 1979; editor (newsletter): Comparative Frontier Studies, 1975—86, Norman and Cleve. County Hist. Mus., 1975; co-prodr., host (TV series) Norman Cable TV, 1986—88; columnist: Okla. Gazette, 1993—95, Jour. Scholarly Publ., 2004—; contbr. articles to profl. jours. Recipient Spl. Recognition award, Okla. Jazz Hall of Fame, 1993. Mem.: Western History Assn., So. Hist. Assn., Okla. Hist. Soc., Phi Alpha Theta, Omicron Delta Kappa, Sigma Delta Chi. Avocations: panelology, mixed media and collage. Office: Univ Okla Dept History 455 W Lindsey Rm 424 Norman OK 73019-6304 Office Phone: 405-325-6001.

SAVANT, DOUG, actor; b. Burbank, Calif., June 21, 1964; m. Dawn Savant, 1983 (div. 1997); 2 children; m. Laura Leighton, 1998; children: Jack Douglas, Lucy Jane. Actor: (films) Swing Shift, 1984, Secret Admirer, 1985, Teen Wolf, 1985, Trick or Treat, 1986, The Hanoi Hilton, 1987, Masquerade, 1988, Paint It Black, 1989, Red Surf, 1990, Shaking the Tree, 1992, Maniac Cop 3: Badge of Silence, 1993, Godzilla, 1998, Dropping Out, 2000, The One, 2001, First Shot, 2002; (TV series, guest appearance) Cagney & Lacey, 1985, Hotel, 1986, Alfred Hitchcock Presents, 1986, The Facts of Life, 1987, Stingray, 1987, In the Heat of the Night, 1988, China Beach, 1990, Jake and the Fatman, 1990, Burke's Law, 1995, The Love Boat: The Next Wave, 2001, The Outer Limits, 1998, Profiler, 1999, Harsh Realm, 2000, That's Life, 2001, The District, 2001, Family Law, 2001, Firefly, 2002, JAG, 2002, According to Jim, 2002, The Guardian, 2004, 24, 2004, Navy NCIS: Naval Criminal Investigative Service, 2004, Nip/Tuck, 2004, CSI: Crime Scene Investigation, 2004; (TV films) The Knife and Gun Club, 1990, Aftermath: A Test of Love, 1991, Columbo: No Time to Die, 1992, Bonnie & Clyde: The True Story, 1992, Fight for Justice: The Nancy Conn Story, 1995, Terminal, 1996, A Face to Kill for, 1999, First Daughter, 1999, First Shot, 2002, Faultline, 2004; (TV series) Melrose Place, 1992—97, Desperate Housewives, 2004— (Screen Actors Guild Award for outstanding performance by an ensemble in a comedy series, 2006). Office: Desperate Housewives Touchtone Television 100 Universal City Plaza Universal City CA 91608

SAVARD, DENIS JOSEPH, professional hockey coach, former professional hockey player; b. Pointe Gatineau, Que., Can., Feb. 4, 1961; m. Mona Savard; 1 child, Tanya. Center Chgo. Blackhawks, 1980—90, 1995—97, Montreal Canadiens, 1990—93, Tampa Bay Lightning, 1993—95; devel. coach Chgo. Blackhawks, 1997, asst. coach, 1997—2006, head coach, 2006—. Player NHL All-Star Game, 1982—84, 1986, 88, 91. Recipient Michel Briere trophy, 1979—80. Achievements include being a member of Stanley Cup Champion Montreal Canadiens, 1993; being inducted into the Hockey Hall of Fame, 2000. Office: Chgo Blackhawks 1901 W Madison St Chicago IL 60612-2459 *

SAVARI, SERAP AYSE, engineering educator, researcher; b. Astoria, NY, Nov. 4, 1968; d. Aykut and Sirin Savari. MS, MIT, Boston, 1991, PhD, 1996. Mem. tech. staff Bell Labs., Lucent Techs., Murray Hill, 1996—2003; acad. guest faculty computer sci. and comm. sys. Swiss Fed. Inst. Tech., 2003; assoc. prof. dept. elec. engring. and computer sci. U. Mich., Ann Arbor, 2004—07. Adj. prof. dept. elec. engring. and computer sci. U. Mich., Ann Arbor, 2003. Contbr. articles to profl. jours. Team leader info. processing Internat. Symposium on Info. Theory, 2005; mem program. com. Info. Theory Workshop, 2004, 2006—07, mem. program com., 2007, Internat. Symposium in Info. Theory, 2001, 2002, 2004; mem. tech. program com. Data Compression Conf., 2000—07; bell labs rep. Ctr. Discrete Math. and Theor. Computer Sci., 2001—03. Mem.: IEEE (program com. data compression conf. 2000—07, program com. symposium 2001, 2002, assoc. editor Source Coding IEEE Transactions on Info. Theory 2002—05, program com. symposium 2004, team leader program com. info. processing 2005), Toastmasters, Tau Beta Pi, Phi Beta Kappa. Home: 3070 Whisperwood Dr Apt 431 Ann Arbor MI 48105 Office: 4225 EECS Bldg 1301 Beal Ave Ann Arbor MI 48109 Business E-Mail: savari@eecs.umich.edu.

SAVAS, EMANUEL S., finance educator, public official; b. NYC, June 8, 1931; s. John and Olga (Limbos) S.; m. Helen Andrew, Dec. 25, 1955; children: Jonathan, Stephen. BA, U. Chgo., 1951, BS, 1953; MA, Columbia U., 1956, PhD, 1960; PhD (hon.), U. Piraeus, Greece, 2000. Control systems cons. IBM, Yorktown Heights and White Plains, NY, 1959-65; urban systems mgr. NYC, 1966-67; 1st dep. city adminstr. Office of Mayor of N.Y.C., 1967-72; chmn. Mayor's Urban Action Task Force, 1969-72; prof. pub. mgmt. Columbia U., NYC, 1972-83, dir. Center for Govt. Studies, 1973-83, assoc. dir. Center for Policy Rsch., 1973-81; asst. sec. for policy devel. and rsch. HUD, Washington, 1981-83; prof. mgmt. Baruch Coll., CUNY, 1981-94, prof. public affairs, 1994—, dir. public policy program, 1994-97, chm. dept. mgmt., 1986-93; dir. Privatization Rsch. Orgn., 1986—. Cons. NSF, HUD, Dept. Transp., Dept. Energy, World Bank, AID, U.S. Dept. State, Pres.'s Commn. on Privatization, UN, UN Devel. Program, ILO, UNIDO, USIA, also others; mem. voting bd. Blue Cross and Blue Shield Greater N.Y., 1976-79, bd. dirs., 1979-81; mem. Pres.-Elect's Urban Affairs Task Force, 1980, N.Y. State Senate Adv. Commn. on Privatization, 1990-95; mem. Gov. Pataki privatization coun., N.Y., 1995-2000; dir. U.S.-USSR Joint Project on Mgmt. of Large Cities, 1973-81; advisor on privatization Govt. Poland, 1990-92, Govt. Lesotho, 1992, Govt. Ukraine, 1993, N.Y.C. Mayor Giuliani, 1994-98, Govt. South Africa, 1996, Govt. Botswana, 1996, Govt. Philippines, 1997, others. Author: Computer Control of Industrial Processes, 1965, Organization and Efficiency of Solid Waste Collection, 1977, Privatizing the Public Sector, 1982, Moscow's City Government, 1985, Privatization, 1987, Privatization and Public-Private Partnerships, 2000, 22 fgn. edits., Privatization in the City, 2005, others; editor: Alternatives for Delivering Public Services, 1977, Privatization for New York, 1992, Managing Welfare Reform in New York City, 2005; co-editor The New Public Management, 2002; mem. editl. bd. Urban Affairs Quar., Privatization Report, Privatization Watch, State and Local Govt. Rev.; contbr. 115 articles to profl. jours. Mem. NYC Mayor-elect Giuliani transition team, 1993, NY Gov.-elect Pataki transition team, 1994; mem. Tenafly (NJ) Borough Coun., 1996. With US Army, 1953-55, Korea. Recipient Systems Sci. and Cybernetics award IEEE, 1968, Louis Brownlow award Am. Soc. Public Adminstrn., 1970, Honor award Templeton Found., 1989, Leadership award Nat. Coun. Pub.-Private Partnerships, 1993, Outstanding Acad. award Am. Soc. Pub. Adminstrn., 1996, Presidential Excellence award for Disting. Scholarship, 2006. Mem. Sigma Xi, Psi Upsilon. Clubs: City of N.Y. (trustee 1974-77, Richard Childs award 1979). Greek Orthodox. Office: CUNY Baruch Coll Box D 901 17 Lexington Ave New York NY 10010-5518 Office Phone: 646-660-6780. Personal E-mail: prisect@aol.com.

SAVEDGE, ANNE CREERY, artist, educator; b. Richmond, Va., Jan. 29, 1947; d. Leslie Roy Jr. and Dorothy (Rakes) C.; m. Edwin Clement Savedge Jr., Aug. 11, 1967; 1 child, Ross Alan. BS, James Madison U., 1969; M in Art Edn., Va. Commonwealth U., 1977. Art instr. Colonial Heights HS, Va., 1969-78; instr. Va. Mus. Robinson House, Richmond, Va., 1983-86; vis. artist Office of Youth and Cmty. Svc., Dinwiddie, Va., 1986-87; artist-in-residence Richmond Children's Mus., 1987-88; instr. Shenandoah Photographic Workshops, 1988; adj. faculty Va. Mus. of Fine Arts, 2000—; founder Savedge Art & Tech. Co., LLC, 2007—. Adj. faculty U. Richmond, 1978-2000—; artist-in-residence Va. Mus. of Fine Arts, Richmond, 1984-86, Richmond Children's Mus., 1987-88; curator Bedford Gallery Photoshow Longwood Coll., Farmville, Va., 1985, Light Images Gallery Photoshow James Madison U., Harrisonburg, Va., 1985, 1708 East Main Gallery Photoshow, Richmond, 1987, 90, New Realities/Digital Transformations show, 1997; artist Fay Gold Gallery, Atlanta, 1985-87; artist-in-edn. gifted program Dinwiddie, Va., 1988; instr. Chesterfield Tech. Ctr., 1989—; grant adv. com. Gov's. Exemplary Standards Award Program, 2007—; presenter in field. One-woman shows include Marsh Gallery, U. Richmond, 1986, 1708 Gallery, 1994, Baton Rouge, 1991, 1912 Gallery, 2000, Bishop Gallery, Longwood Ctr. for the Visual Arts, Farmville, 2003, Cultural Arts Ctr. at Glen Allen, 2002, E3 Gallery, NYC, 2004, Capital One Gallery, 2005, Va. Mus. Architecture, 2005—, Riverviews Artspace, Lynchburg, 2006, Quirk Gallery, Richmond, 2006, exhibited in group shows at Pleiades Gallery, NYC, 1989, Martin Gallery, Washington, 1989, Midwest Invitational, 1993—94, Mars Gallery, Ariz., 1994, Bloom Gallery, Milan, 1995, Longwood Ctr. for Visual Arts, 1997, Chrysler Mus., 1999, Art Mus. Western Va., 2002, Cultural Arts Ctr. Glen Allen, 2002, Daegu Culture and Arts Ctr., Daegu, Korea, 2004, 1708 Gallery, 2004—05, George Mason U., 2005, A.I.R. Gallery, N.Y.C., 2005, C3 Gallery, 2005, Bishop Gallery, 2006, Agora Gallery, NYC, 2006—, Lilly Oncology on Canvas, London, NYC, 2006—07, Youngsan Internat. Art Exhibit, Seoul, 2006, Ptnrs. in The Americas, Va. and Santa Catarina, Brazil, 2006—07, Mariner's Mus., Newport News, Va., 2007, Represented in permanent collections Polaroid Internat. Collection, Fed. Res. Bank, Chrysler Mus., Valentine Mus., Longwood Ctr.for Visual Arts, Va., Art Mus. Western Va., Capital One, Woodstock Ctr. Photography, pub. in, Magic Wand, 1st and 2nd edits., 1998, Agora Gallery pubs., NYC, Exploring Color Photography, 4th edit., 2005, Intro to Digital Photography 2nd edit., 2005, Internat. Exchange Show, Beijing, 2007. Adv. coun. Richmond Arts Coun.; evaluation com. Partners-in-Arts; master tchr. Va. State T&I Skills USA Nat. Conf.; chmn. 1708 Gallery Exhbns., 1995-96, sec. bd. dirs., 2004-2006. Named Art Tchr. of Yr., Chesterfield County, 1997-98, Art Educator of Yr., Va. Art Edn. Assn., 1999, hon. mention Excellence in Photographic Tchg. award Santa Fe Ctr. for the Visual Arts, Tchr. of Year, VATIE, 2007; individual artist fellow Va. Commn. for Arts, 1999, profl. fellow Va. Mus. Fine Arts. Mem. Nat. Art Edn. Assn. (presenter Chgo. chpt. Nat. Conf. 1998, Chgo. chpt. Washington Nat. Conf. 1999, Southeastern Art Educator of Yr. 2000), Richmond Artists Assn. (pres. 1978-80, cert. distinction 1980), Soc. for Photographic Edn., Va. Soc. for Photographic Arts (steering com. 1976—, fundraising chmn. 1978—, mem. chmn. 1980-86). Methodist. Home: 5318 Verlinda Dr Richmond VA 23237-3307 E-mail: asavedge@savedge.com.

SAVEDRA-SCHROEDER, JEANNINE EVANGELINE, artist, educator; b. Montebello, Calif., Dec. 21, 1965; d. Robert Anthony Savedra and April Baroth; m. Nathan Schroeder (Feb. 14, 2007). Student, Pasadena C.C., Calif., 1985—87, Parsons Sch. Design, NYC, 1987—88; BA Studio Art, Calif. State U., LA, 1991; MA Humanities and Art, Calif. State U., Dominguez Hills, 2003; postgrad. IMMEX Inst., UCLA, 1999; postgrad., Otis Sch. Art and Design, 2001—02. Cert. art tchr., Calif. Children's counselor Salvation Army, Pasadena, 1987—88; graphic artist Calif. State U., LA, 1989; pvt. investigator Larry J. Larsen Investigations and Trial Preparations, LA, 1990—93; instr. studio art Visual Arts and Design Acad., Pasadena, 1995—2001; restoration artist, painter St. Gaudens Fine Art Restoration and Conservation, Pasadena, 1999—; tchg. supr. Dept. Edn. Mount St. Mary's Coll., 2002—; visual arts edn. specialist Calif. Living History, Pasadena, Calif., 2001—06. Supr. mural Pasadena Playhouse Improvement Assn., 1995-96; mentor Puente program U. Calif., Berkeley, 1995-2000; educator Nat. Conf. Human Rels., Temescal Canyon, Calif., 1996, Annenberg Inst. Sch. Reform, Brown U., 1998-2000; apptd. to ednl. adv. com. Jack Scott; mem. Assembly, Calif. State Legislature, 1997-99; apptd. to Sierra Madre Arts Commn., 1999-2006; ofcl. assessor tchg. performance Calif. Commn. on Tchr. Credentials. Author: (art curriculum) Me, Myself and Eye, 2006. Bd. dirs. Calif. Living Histories, Pasadena. Calif. Partnership Acad. grantee, 1996—2001; recipient Excellence in Visual Arts award Calif. State U., 1990, VIP award Pntrs. Edn. Pasadena Unified Sch. Dist., 2004 Mem. LA County Mus. Art, Arboretum and Botanic Garden Personal E-mail: jeanninesavedra@yahoo.com.

SAVELL, POLLY CAROLYN, lawyer; b. NYC, Oct. 24, 1960; d. Joel Morton and Elsie Rhea (Crane) S. BA, U. Md., 1982; diploma, Internat. Comp. Law Inst., Paris, 1983; JD, NYU, 1985. Bar: NY 1986. Assoc. corp. and entertainment divsn. Battle Fowler, NYC, 1986-87; atty. Columbia Pictures Entertainment Inc., NYC, 1987-89; counsel Turner Broadcasting Sys. Inc., Atlanta, 1989-91; sole practice Atlanta, 1991-93; asst. gen. counsel WorldCom Inc., NYC, 1993—2001; pvt. practice NYC, 2001—. Bd. dirs. Eviction Intervention Svcs., Homelessness Prevention, Inc. Mem. ABA, Fed. Comm. Bar Assn., Assn. of Bar of City of N.Y. (telecomm. law com.), Task Force Internat. Legal Studies Democrat. Methodist. Office: 410 Park Ave Ste 1530 New York NY 10022

SAVERA, ADNAN TABREZ, surgical pathologist, director; b. Karachi, Sindh, Pakistan, Dec. 18, 1966; s. Tabrez Savera and Nasira Tabrez; m. Noshin Zaib, Jan. 11, 2004; children: Arhum, Aayan. MBBS, Dow Med. Coll., Karachi, 1991. Diplomate Am. Bd. Pathology, 1998. Staff pathologist Henry Ford Health Sys., Detroit, 1998—2006; med. dir., chief gu pathologist LabMD, Inc., Atlanta, 2006—. Assoc. program dir. Henry Ford Health Sys., Detroit, 2001—05. Contbr. scientific papers in field. Named one of Ams. Top Physicians, Consumers' Rsch. Coun. Am., 2005. Fellow: Internat. Soc. Urologic Pathologists, Am. Soc. Clin. Pathologists, Coll. Am. Pathologists (life); mem.: Acad. Pathology, Am. Urol. Assn. Achievements include research in ead and neck and prostate cancers. Office: LabMD 1117 Perimeter Ctr W W-306 Atlanta GA 30338

SAVERCOOL, SUSAN ELISABETH, elementary school educator; b. La Grande, Oreg., Aug. 1, 1947; d. Edwin Gilbert and Francis Gwynne Kirby; m. Niles Seymour Duncan, June 21, 1971 (div. Sept. 1976); m. Lawrence Yeldham Savercool, Aug. 6, 1983; 1 child, David R. BA in Theater/English, Calif. State U., Northridge, 1969; MA in Elem. Edn., No. Ariz. U., 1988. Cert. elem. tchr. Calif., Ariz. Elem. tchr. St. Catherine of Siena Sch., Reseda, Calif., 1969—71; presch. tchr. La Palma E. Preschool, Anaheim, Calif., 1973—74; elem. tchr. Egremont Sch., Encino, Calif., 1977—80, Ganado Intermediate, Ariz., 1980—84, Blue Ridge Elem., Lakeside, Ariz., 1986—98; freelance writer Penn Yan, NY, 2000—03. Presenter poetry for tchrs. workshop Blue Ridge Elem., Lakeside, 1991—96; instr. elem. lang. arts No. Ariz. U., Flagstaff, 1992. Editor: Mountains of Time, vols. 1-5, 1992—97, Saint Bobo and Other Contemporary Short Stories, 1994. Actress, make-up head Theater Mountain, Lakeside, 1993—97; contbg. author Oliver House Mus., Penn Yan, 2000—03; contbr. Internat. Libr. Poetry, Famous Poets Soc., Noble House, 2005. Scholar, Arts Coun., 1968. Mem.: Nat. Acad. Songwriters, Nat. Homer Poet Famous Poets Soc. (outstanding poet/contbr., internat. libr. poetry editions 2004, 2005, 2006, 2007), Phi Kappa Phi. Democrat. Unitarian Universalist. Achievements include development of PhotoLit Posters gift lines; freelance writing (as Glenna MacCauley). Avocations: reading, fishing, community chorus, community theater, writing.

SAVETH, EDWARD NORMAN, historian, educator; b. NYC, Feb. 16, 1915; s. Isidor and Eva (Vasa) S.; m. Harriet Obstler, June 22, 1975; 1 child by previous marriage, Henry. BSS., CCNY, 1935; MA, Columbia U., 1937, PhD, 1946. Prof. history Grad. Faculty New Sch. for Social Research, NYC, 1960-63; Fulbright prof. Kyoto U., Kyoto, Japan, 1964-65; prof. Dartmouth Coll., 1965-66; Disting. vis. prof. Tex. Lutheran Coll., Seguin, 1966-67; Disting. prof. SUNY-Fredonia, 1967-85; adj. prof. SUNY, Buffalo, 1987—; lectr. USIA, Nepal, 1965, Morocco, 1977; Fulbright prof. Hebrew U., Jerusalem, 1981. Vis. prof. U. Rochester, 1972; lectr. Beijing Tchrs. Coll., 1989. Author: American historians and European Immigrants, 1947; author, editor: Understanding the American Past, 1954, Henry Adams, 1963, American History and the Social Sciences, 1964; revisions editor: Ency. Americana, 1962; contbr. numerous articles to mags. Mem. Am. Hist. Assn., Orgn. Am. Historians Home: Blocher Homes 135 Evans St Williamsville NY 14221-5599

SAVIC, JELENA, technologist, educator; d. Johanna Gertrude and Vid Spacoje Savic. BS (hon.), N.E. Ill. U., 1973, M in Math. Edn., 1989. Edn. K-9 Ill., 1973, edn. 9-12 Ill., 1979, bilingual edn. Ill., 1993, ESL edn. Ill., 1993. H.s. math tchr. Ctrl. Jr. H.S., Evergreen Park, Ill., 1973—79, Proviso East H.S., Maywood, Ill., 1979—99; instrnl. technologist Proviso West H.S., Hillside, Ill., 1999—. Workshop presenter - tchr. topics Proviso Twp. 209, Maywood, Ill., 1999—; writer ednl. curriculum Proviso Twp. H.S., Hillside, Ill., 1999—; sch. photographer Proviso West H.S., Hillside, Ill., 2000—; home schooling instr. U. Nebr.-Lincoln, 2002—. Filmmaker (animated short film) The Insect Reaction (Best Film, 1992). Walk animals mem. Humane Farming Assn., Chicago, 2003; humanitarian Serbia orphanages and refugee camps, 2006. Named 1 of Top 10 Tchrs. in US nat. TV documentary, Arnold Shapiro Prodns., 1984, featured spkr. Channel 5 More You Know Edn., Channel 5 Nat. TV, 1984; recipient Larry Stilgebauer Tech. award, West 40 Ednl. Ctr., 1988, 2001. Mem.: Ill. Fedn. Tchrs. Avocations: photography, filmmaking, dance, designing costumes. Home: 3228 N Newland Chicago IL 60634 Office: Proviso W HS 4701 W Harrison St Hillside IL 60162 Office Phone: 708-202-6220. Home Fax: 773-777-7383. Personal E-mail: jxm73@hotmail.com.

SAVILLE, DERRIC JAMES, lawyer; b. Ft. Madison, Iowa, Oct. 2, 1964; s. Jacob Abraham and Brenda K. (Lawrence) S.; m. Jeannene Irene Abbott, Mar. 21, 1987. BS, U. Iowa, 1987; M of Studies in Law, JD cum laude, Vt. Law Sch., 1991. Bar: Minn. 1991, U.S. Dist. Ct. Minn. 1995, Upper Sioux Comty. Tribal Ct. 1996. Atty. Saville Law Office, Mpls., 1991—98; with Saville Title Svcs., Inc., Plymouth, Minn. Chair subcom. Dist. Planning Adv. Commn. #279, Maple Grove, Minn., 1994-96. Articles editor Ferae Naturae, 1991. State del. Reform Party, Maple Grove, 1996; chair mental health adv. bd. Hennepin County Commitment Def. Project, 1998-2002. Mem.: Brain Injury Assn. Minn. (bd. dirs. 1996—2000, chair 1998—99), Minn. Head Injury Assn. (bd. dirs. 1995—96). Avocations: fishing, hiking, golf. Office: Saville Title Svcs Inc 505 Hwy 169 N Ste 230 Plymouth MN 55441 Home Phone: 763-427-2031; Office Phone: 763-398-0377. E-mail: dsaville@savilletitleservices.com.

SAVILLE, PAT, state senate official; b. Marysville, Kans., Sept. 10, 1943; Sec. Kans. Senate, Topeka, 1991—. Mem.: Am. Soc. Legis. Clks. and Secs. (past pres.). Office: Kans Senate State House 374 E Topeka KS 66612 Office Phone: 785-296-2456. E-mail: pats@senate.state.ks.us.

SAVILLE, PAUL C., construction executive; BBA, Coll. William & Mary, Williamsburg, Va., 1977; MBA, U. Pitts. With automotive ops. Rockwell Internat.; with Ryan Homes, 1981, v.p. bus. planning to CFO; sr. v.p. fin., CFO, treas. NVR Inc., McLean, Va., 1993—2002, exec. v.p., CFO, treas., 2002—05, pres., CEO, 2005—. Named to The Va. 100, Va. Bus. mag., 2005. Office: NVR Inc Plaza America Tower 1 11700 Plaza America Dr Ste 500 Reston VA 20190-4792 Office Phone: 703-956-4000. Office Fax: 703-956-4750. *

SAVILLE, ROYCE BLAIR, lawyer; b. Cumberland, Md., Aug. 5, 1948; s. E. Blair and Audrey (Cosner) S.; m. Sharon Ann Brinkman, Apr. 3, 1981; children: Melissa Anne, Lauren Ashley, Meagan Elizabeth, Philip Clarke. BA, W.Va. U., 1970, JD, 1974. Bar: W.Va. 1974, U.S. Dist. Ct. (so. and no. dists.) W.Va. 1974. Assoc. William J. Oates, Jr. Atty. at Law, Romney, W.Va., 1974—75; ptnr. Oates & Saville Attys. at Law, Romney, 1975—78; pvt. practice Romney, 1978—99; mng. ptnr. Saville and Davis, PLLC, 1999—2001, Saville and Stewart, PLLC, 2001—05; pvt. practice Royce B. Saville, PLLC, 2006—. Pres. Potomac Land Co., 1975—; mental hygiene commr. Hampshire County, Romney, 1976—2006; mcpl. judge City of Romney, 1980-90. Mem. W.Va. Jud. Hearing Bd., Charleston, Hampshire County Devel. Authority, Romney, Hampshire County Farm Bur., Nat. Trust Hist. Preservation; dir. Potomac Highlands Travel Coun., Elkins, W.Va., 1984-88; mem. adv. bd. Peterkin Conf. Ctr. of Renewal, Romney, 1988-90; trustee, Indian Mound Cemetery 2003-, Eastern W.Va. Cmty. and Tech. Coll. Found. bd. dirs.; del. W.Va. Dem. Conv., Charleston, 1984; vestryman St. Stephen's Episcopal Ch., Romney, 1984-86; bd. mem. East Cmty. and Tech. Coll. Found., 2006-. Mem. ABA, ATLA, NRA (life), W.Va. Bar Assn., South Branch Valley Bar Assn. (pres. 1996-97), W.Va. Trial Lawyers Assn., Waterfowl U.S.A. (life), N.Am. Hunting Club (life), Hampshire Camp 284 SCV (judge adv.), Civil War Preservation Trust, W.Va. Law Sch. Assn. (life), W.Va. U. Alumni Assn. (life), Am. Legion, Masons, Shriners, Scottish Rite, Order Eastern Star, Rotary (Paul Harris fellow), Phi Alpha Delta (life). Democrat. Episcopalian. Avocations: gun collecting, antiques, local history. Home: Liberty Hall 276 E Main St Romney WV 26757-1821 also: Mill Island Moorefield WV 26836 Office: 95 W Main St PO Box 2000 Romney WV 26757-2000 Office Phone: 304-822-3875.

SAVILLE, THORNDIKE, JR., coastal engineer; b. Balt., 1925; AB, Harvard U., Cambridge, Mass., 1947; MS, U. Calif., Berkeley, 1949. Registered profl. engr., D.C. Rsch. asst. U. Calif., Berkeley, 1947-49; hydraulic engr. Beach Erosion Bd. and Coastal Engring. Rsch. Ctr., Washington, DC and Ft. Belvoir, Va., 1949-81, chief rsch. divsn., 1964-71, tech. dir., 1971-81; cons., 1981—. Contbr. more than 85 articles to engring. and sci. publs. With US Army, 1943—46. Recipient Meritorious Civilian Svc. award, Dept. Army, 1981, Comdr.'s award, 1998, Annual Nat. Cap. award, DC Coun. Engrs. and Archs., 1964, Annual Sci. Achievement in Engring. Scis. award, 1964. Fellow: ASCE (Huber award 1963, Moffatt-Nichol award 1979, Internat. Coastal Engring. award 1991), AAAS, Wash. Acad. Scis. (bd. mgrs. 1962—69); mem.: Am. Shore and Beach Preservation Assn. (bd. dirs. 1976—97, v.p. 1988—95, M. P. O'Brien award 1997), Permanent Internat. Assn., Navigation Congresses (hon.; U.S. commr.

1971—78, U.S. commr. emeritus 1987—, U.S. rep. PTC II 1991—98), Nat. Acad. Engring., Am. Geophys. Union, Cosmos Club (Washington). Home and Office: 5601 Albia Rd Bethesda MD 20816-3304

SAVIN, RONALD RICHARD, chemicals executive; b. Cleve., Oct. 16, 1926; s. Samuel and Ada (Silver) Savin; m. Gloria Ann Hopkins, Apr. 21, 1962; children: Danielle Elizabeth, Andrea Lianne. BA in Chemistry and Lit., U. Cin., 1944-46; BA in Chemistry and Literature, U. Mich., 1948; postgrad., Columbia U., 1948-49, Sorbonne, Paris, 1949-50; grad., Air War Coll., 1975, Indsl. Coll. Armed Forces, 1976. Pres., owner Premium Finishes, Inc., Cin., 1957-91. Cons. aerospace and anti-corrosive coatings; inventor, owner Hyerpseal, Inc. Contbr. articles to profl. jours. With USAF, 1948—55, World War II, Korea, col. USAFR, 1979—96. Mem.: Fedn. Coatings Tech., Fedn. Paint Techs., Nat. Assn. Corrosion Engrs., Steel Structures Painting Coun., Res. Officers Assn., Air Force Assn., Army Navy Club. Achievements include patents in field. Avocations: scientific development, photography, tennis.

SAVINELL, ROBERT FRANCIS, engineering educator; b. Cleve., May 26, 1950; s. Robert D. and Lotte R. Savinell; m. Coletta A. Savinell, Aug. 23, 1974; children: Teresa, Robert, Mark. BSChemE, Cleve. State U., 1973; MS, U. Pitts., 1974, PhD, 1977. Registered profl. engr., Ohio. Rsch. engr. Diamond Shamrock Corp., Painesville, Ohio, 1977-79; assoc. prof. U. Akron, Ohio, 1979-86; prof. Case Western Reserve U., Cleve., 1986—, dir. Ernest B. Yeager Ctr. for Electrochem. Scis., 1991—, assoc. dean engring., 1998—, interim dean of engring., 2000, dean engring., 2001. Divsn. editor Jour. Electrochem. Soc., 1988-91; N.Am. editor Jour. Applied Electrochemistry, 1991-97; contbr. articles to profl. jours. Named Presdl. Young Investigator, NSF, Washington, 1984-89, Outstanding Engring. Alumnus, Cleve. State U., 1984. Fellow Electrochem. Soc., AIChE (program chmn. 1986-92), Am. Inst. Chem. Engrs.; mem. Electrochem. Soc. (divsn. officer 1992—), Internat. Soc. Electrochemistry (v.p. 1995-98). Avocations: sailing, skiing. Office: Case Sch Engring CRWU-500 Nord Hall Cleveland OH 44106-7220 Office Phone: 216-368-4436. Business E-Mail: rfs2@case.edu.

SAVINI, TOM, make-up artist, actor, director; b. Pitts., Nov. 3, 1946; m. Nancy Hare, 1984. Make up artist, actor: (films) Deathdream, 1972, Deranged, 1974, Martin, 1977, Dawn of the Dead, 1978, Effects, 1980, Eyes of a Stranger, 1980, Friday the 13th, 1980, Friday the 13th IV, The Burning, 1981, Maniac, 1981, The Prowler, 1981, Knightriders, 1981, Alone in the Dark, Creepshow, 1982, Midnight, 1983, Friday the 13th-The Final Chapter, 1984, Invasion U.S.A., 1985, Day of the Dead, 1985, The Ripper, 1986, The Texas Chainsaw Massacre, Part II, 1987, Monkey-Shines: An Experiment in Fear, 1988, Red Scorpion, 1989, Two Evileyes, 1990, Heartstopper, 1992, Trauma, 1993, H.P. Lovecrafts Necronomicon, 1994, Ghostwriter, Killing Zoe, 1994, Mr. Stitch, 1996, Children of the Living Dead, 2001, Eyes Are Upon You, 2001, Ted Bundy, 2002, Dawn of the Dead, 2004, The Absence of Light, 2004, Death 4 Told, 2004, Unearthed, 2004, Forest of the Damned, 2005, Land of the Dead, 2005, A Dream of Color in Back and White, 2005, Beyond the Wall of Sleep, 2006, Grindhouse, 2007; dir. Night of the Living Dead, 1990, episodes Tales from The Darkside; writer: Grand Illusions, 1983, Grand Illusions Books II, 1988. *

SAVITS, BARRY SORREL, surgeon; b. Phila., Feb. 14, 1934; s. Frank and Sophia (Cohen) S.; children: George, Frank, Alexander. BA, Princeton U., 1955; MD, U. Pa., 1959; cert. surg. residency, Mt. Sinai Hosp., NYC, 1965. Prof. surgery Project Hope, Ecuador, 1965-66; instr. surgery Albert Einstein Med. Coll., Bronx, NY, 1966-67; surgeon LaGuardia Med. Group, Queens, NY, 1970-72; dir. surgery St. Mary's Hosp., Bklyn., 1973-91, Kingsbrook Jewish Med. Ctr., Bklyn., 1991-2000; attending N.Y. Meth. Hosp., 2000—, SUNY-Univ. Hosp. of Bklyn., 1995—; clin. asst. prof. surgery SUNY Health Scis. Ctr., Bklyn., 1975—. Vis. surgeon Hope-Ecuador, 1965-66, Care-Medico, Afghanistan, 1976. Comdr. USN, 1967-69. Fellow ACS (gov. 1991-97); mem. Soc. Am. Gastrointestinal Endoscopic Surgeons, Assn. Acad. Surgery, Assn. Surg. Program Dirs., Bklyn. Surg. Soc. (pres. 1992-93). Jewish. Avocation: reading. Office: 263 7th Ave Ste 4E Brooklyn NY 11215 Office Phone: 718-832-4992. Office Fax: 718-832-4692. Personal E-mail: bsavits@aol.com.

SAVITSKY, DANIEL, retired structural engineer, educator; b. NYC, Sept. 26, 1921; s. Maxim and Anna (Oleksiw) S.; m. Mary Wysocki; children: Jean, James, Anne. BCE, CCNY, 1942; MSc, Stevens Inst. Tech., 1952; PhD, NYU, 1971. Registered profl. engr., NY. Structural engr. EDO Corp., College Point, NY, 1942-44; aero. rsch. scientist Nat. Adv. Com. for Aero., Langley Field, Va., 1944-47; prof. emeritus Stevens Inst. Tech., Hoboken, NJ, 1947—. Chmn. high speed vehicle com. Internat. Towing Tank Conf., 1978-88; cons. Naval Studies Bd., Nat. Rsch. Coun. Author: (with others) Yearbook of Science and Technology, 1987; patentee hydrofoil controls. Fellow Soc. Naval Architects and Marine Engrs. (hon. mem., Adm. Cochrane award 1967, 2007, Davidson medal 1996), Am. Soc. Naval Engrs., Niantic Bay Yacht Club (Conn.), Sigma Xi. Roman Catholic. Avocations: sailing, skiing, tennis. Home: 597 Delcina Dr Westwood NJ 07675-6111 Office: Davidson Lab 711 Hudson St Hoboken NJ 07030-5953 Office Phone: 201-216-5307. Business E-Mail: dsavitsk@stevens.edu.

SAVITT, KATHY, marketing, apparel executive; b. Scarsdale, NY, 1964; m. Michael Lennon; 2 children. V.p. pub. rels. & bus. devel. Sorensen Roberts & Hansen; pres., co-founder MWW/Savitt; v.p. strategic comm., content & initiatives, Amazon.com; exec. v.p., chief mktg. officer Am. Eagle Outfitters Inc., Warrendale, Pa., 2006—. Named a Woman to Watch, Advt. Age, 2007; recipient MWW/Savitt Best in Show, Galaxy Awards, 2000. Office: Am Eagle Outfitters Inc 150 Thorn Hill Dr Warrendale PA 15086-7528 Office Phone: 724-776-4857. *

SAVITT, STEVEN LEE, computer scientist; b. Mpls., May 25, 1949; s. Leonard Robert and Claire (Hurwitz) S.; m. Gloria Lynn Kumagai; children: Mariko, Leilani, Joshua. BSEE, U. Minn., 1971, PhD in Computer Sci., 1992. Founder, CEO Compmark I Corp., Mpls., 1972-83; rsch. sect. head Honeywell, Inc., Mpls., 1983-89; rsch. staff scientist Alliant Techsystems, Inc., Mpls., 1989-96, engring. sect. head, 1996—. Co-chair database com. Automatic Target Recognizer Working Group, 1985-87. Mem. IEEE, Japanese-Am. Citizens League. Avocations: piano, classic car collecting, canoeing, tennis, swimming. Home: 332 Westwood Dr N Golden Valley MN 55422-5263 Personal E-mail: stevesn.savitt@aik.com.

SAVITT, SUSAN SCHENKEL, lawyer, mediator; b. Bklyn., Aug. 21, 1943; d. Edward Charles and Sylvia (Dlugatch) S.; m. Harvey Savitt, July 2, 1969 (div. 1978); children: Andrew Todd, Daniel Cory. BA magna cum laude, Pa. State U., 1964; JD, Columbia U., 1968. Bar: N.Y. 1968, U.S. Dist. Ct. (so. and ea. dists.) N.Y. 1973, U.S. Tax Ct. 1973, U.S. Ct. Appeals (2d cir.) 1981, U.S. Supreme Ct. 1980, U.S. Dist. Ct. (we. dist.) N.Y. 1996. Atty. Nassau County Legal Svcs., Freeport, N.Y., 1973-74; asst. corp. counsel City Yonkers, 1977-78; from assoc. to ptnr. Epstein, Becker & Green, P.C., NYC, 1978-94; ptnr. Winston & Strawn, NYC, 1994—2004, Schenkel-Savitt Firm, Hastings on Hudson, NY, 2005—. Adj. prof. Elizabeth Seton Coll., Yonkers, 1982-83; mediator Vol. Mediation Panel, US Dist. Ct. (so. dist.) NY, 1997—, US Dist. Ct. (ea. dist.) NY, 1999—. Mem. Hastings-on-Hudson Sch. Bd., 1984-93, v.p., 1986, 87-88, pres., 1989-90, 92-93; mem NYU exec. coun. Met. Ctr. for Ednl. Rsch. Devel. and Tng., 1987-90; bd. dirs. Associated Blind, 1993-95, Nat. Child Labor Com., 2001-04, Liberal Arts Alumni Coun., Pa. State U., 2001—, bd. dirs., 2003-05, Search for Change, 1996—2002, sec., 1998-2002; bd. dirs. Pa. State Profl. Women's Network of NY, 1996-2003, pres., 1998-2000. Mem. ABA (internat. law sect., litigation, dispute resolution and labor law sect.), NY State Bar Assn. (labor law sect.), NY Women's Bar Assn., Westchester Women's Bar Assn., Fed. Bar Coun., Pa. State Alumni Club (v.p. Westchester County 1985-87), Phi Beta Kappa, Alpha Kappa Delta, Pi Gamma Mu. Business E-Mail: sssavitt@optonline.net.

SAVITZ, MAXINE LAZARUS, retired aerospace transportation executive; b. Balt., Feb. 13, 1937; d. Samuel and Harriette (Miller) Lazarus; m. Sumner Alan Savitz, Jan. 1, 1961; children: Adam Jonathan, Alison Carrie. BA in Chemistry magna cum laude, Bryn Mawr Coll., 1958; PhD in Organic Chemistry, MIT, 1961. Instr. chemistry Hunter Coll., NYC, 1962-63; sr. electrochemist Mobility Equipment Rsch. and Devel. Ctr., Ft. Belvoir, Va., 1963-68; prof. chemistry Federal City Coll., Washington, 1968-72; program mgr. NSF, Washington, 1972-74; dir. FEA Office Bldgs. Policy Rshc. U.S. Dept. Energy, Washington, 1974-75, dir. div. indsl. conservation, 1975-76, from dir. div. bldgs. and community systems to dep asst sec., 1975-83; pres. Lighting Rsch. Inst., 1983-85; asst. to v.p. engring. Ceramic Components div. The Garrett Corp., 1985-87; gen. mgr. ceramic components divsn. AlliedSignal Inc., Torrance, Calif., 1987-99; gen. mgr. tech. partnerships Honeywell, Torrance, Calif., 1999—2001, ret., 2001; prin. Washington Adv. Group. Bd. dirs. Am. Coun. Energy Efficient Economy, Draper Corp., Fedn. Am. Scientists, Ceramatec, Inc., Energetics, Inc.; cons. State Mich. Dept. Commerce, 1983, NC Alternative Energy Corp., 1983, Garrett Corp., 1983, Energy Engring. Bd., Nat. Rsch. Bd., 1986—93, Office Tech. Assessment, U.S. Congress Energy Demand Panel, 1987—91; nat. materials adv. bd. NRC, 1989—94, mem. bd. energy and environ. sys., 2002—, bd. dirs. divsn. engring. and phys. sci., 2003—06; chmn. US Advanced Ceramic Assn., 1992; adv. com. divsn. ceramics/materials ORNL, 1989—92, adv. com. dir., 1992—96; mem. lab. adv. com. Pacific NW Nat. Lab., 2000—; adv. bd. Sec. Energy, 1992—2002; mem. Def. Sci. Bd., 1993—96; vis. com. adv. tech. Nat. Inst. Stds. and Tech., 1993—98, Nat. Sci. Bd., 1999—2004; mem. adv. bd. Sandia Sci., 2006—. Contbr. articles to profl. jours. Mem. policy com. NAE, 1994—98. NSF postdoctoral fellow, 1961, 62, NIH predoctoral fellow, 1960, 61. Mem. NAE (v.p. 2006—), AAAS. Office Phone: 310-271-0874. Personal E-mail: maxinesavitz@aol.com.

SAVITZ, SAMUEL J., actuarial consulting firm executive; s. Paul and Ann (Gechman) S.; m. Selma Goldberg, June 15, 1958; children: Jacqueline Beverly, Steven Leslie, Michelle Lynn. BS in Adminstrn., Temple U., 1958; postgrad., 1965, U. Pa., 1960-62. Pension analyst provident Mut. Life Ins. Co., Phila., 1958-61; v.p. The Wirkman Co., Phila., 1961-64; pres. Samuel J. Savitz & Assoc., Inc., Phila., 1964-86; sr. prin. Laventhol & Horwath, Phila., 1986-90; chmn. Savitz Orgn., Inc., Phila., 1990—. Vis. lectr. U. Pa., Phila., 1960, La. State U., 1972-74; faculty Villanova U., 1971-75; cons. in field. Contbr. articles to profl. jours. Bd. dirs. Phila. All-Star Forum, 1987-95; vice chmn. Mann Music Ctr., 1992—2005, Phila. Orch., 2005—; vice chmn., trustee Fgn. Policy Rsch. Inst., 1996—, Pa. Acad. Fine Arts, 1998—2006, Nat. Liberty Mus. and Edn. Ctr., 1999—; chmn. Encore Series, Inc., 1999—, Philly Pops, 1999—, Florentine Festivals USA, Inc., 2000-02, Regional Performing Arts Ctr., 2002—, Kimmel Ctr. for Performing Arts, 2002—, Nat. Mus. Am. Jewish History, 2002—, Abraham Lincoln Found., 2006-. With USAR, 1954—62. Mem. Am. soc. Pension Actuaries (dir. 1969-75), Union League Phila. Jewish. Home: 470 Conshohocken State Rd Bala Cynwyd PA 19004-2639 Office: 1845 Walnut St Philadelphia PA 19103-4708 Business E-Mail: samsavitz@savitz.com.

SAVNER, DAVID A., lawyer; b. Chgo., Mar. 15, 1944; m. Libby Savner; children: Jennifer, Michael. BA, Northwestern U., 1965, JD magna cum laude, 1968. Bar: Ill. 1968. Ptnr. Jenner & Block, Chgo., 1987—98; sr. v.p., gen. counsel, sec. Gen. Dynamics Corp., Falls Church, Va., 1998—. Editor Northwestern U. Law Rev., 1967-68. Mem. ABA, Chgo. Bar Assn., Chgo. Coun. Lawyers, Order of Coif. Office: General Dynamics Corp 2941 Fairview Park Dr Ste 100 Falls Church VA 22042-4513

SAVOIE, BRIETTA DOLORES GIGER, librarian; b. Milw., Aug. 28, 1933; d. Walter and Vera Margaret (Rueger) Giger; m. Edmond Albert Savoie, Oct. 11, 1959; children: Philip Edmond, Raymond Walter, Anne-Marie Margaret. BA, Ohio State U., 1955; MSLS, Columbia U., NYC, 1957. Profl. librarian's cert., NY, NJ Libr., Bklyn. Pub. Libr., 1957-59; cataloger, reference libr. New Sch. Social Rsch., NYC, 1959-60; children's libr. Teaneck Pub. Libr., NJ, 1981-86; asst. reference and circulation libr. River Edge Pub. Libr., NJ, 1986-92, libr. adult svcs., 1992-2002, ret., 2002. Substitute reference libr. Glen Rock Pub. Libr., NJ, 2005-; V.p. United Way of Ridgewood, Glen Rock, Hohokus and Midland Park, NJ, 1980-81; pres. Ridgewood chpt. UN Assn., 1981-85; mem. Fair Housing Coun. Northern NJ. Mem. LWV (chmn. voter registration Glen Rock chpt. 1978-81, chmn. membership Glen Rock chpt. 2004—, co-pres. Glen Rock chpt. 2005—), Am. Libr. Assn., Nat. Arbor Day Soc., So. Poverty Law Ctr. Klanwatch Project, UN Assn., LWV, Native Am. Rights Fund, Sierra Club. Democrat. Unitarian. Avocations: international relations, social justice, environmental protection, bicycling, gardening. Home: 654 Doremus Ave Glen Rock NJ 07452-2033

SAVONENKO, ALENA, neuroscientist, educator; d. Valerji and Elizabeth Savonenko; life ptnr. Amy Huberman. MD, Tomsk U., Russia, 1989; PhD, Lomonosov's Moscow State U., Moscow, Russia, 1994. Post-doctoral fellow Johns Hopkins U., Balt., 1999—2001, asst. prof. Sch. Medicine, 2006—. Grantee, Alzheimer's Assn., 2005—, Adler Found., 2005—. Mem.: Internat. Behavioral Neurosci. Soc., European Brain and Behaviour Soc., Soc. Neurosci. Achievements include research in different experimental treatments to prevent aging-related effects on cognition in rodent models of human diseases. Office: Johns Hopkins University Med School 720 Rutland Ave Ross 558 Baltimore MD 21205 Office Phone: 410-502-5859. Business E-Mail: asavone1@jhmi.edu.

SAVOY, DOUGLAS EUGENE, bishop, writer, religious studies educator; b. Bellingham, Wash., May 11, 1927; s. Lewis Dell and Maymie (Janett) S.; m. Elvira Clarke, Dec. 5, 1957 (div.); 1 son, Jamil Sean (dec.); m. Sylvia Ontaneda, July 7, 1971 (div.); children: Douglas Eugene, Christopher Sean, Sylvia Jamila. Student, U. Portland, 1947—48; DST, D Canon and Sacred Law, Jamilian U. of the Ordained, 1980. Ordained to ministry Internat. Community of Christ Ch., 1962, bishop, 1971. Head bishop Internat. Community of Christ Ch., 1971—; lectr. in ministerial tng. studies, 1972—; pastor Univ. Chapel, Reno, 1979—; founder Jamilian Parochial Sch., 1976; chancellor, founder Sacred Coll. of Jamilian Theology; pres., founder Jamilian U. of the Ordained, 1980; pres. Advs. for Religious Rights and Freedoms; chmn. World Coun. for Human Spiritual Rights, 1984—; head Jamilian Order of Patriarchs, 1990—; engaged in newspaper pub. West Coast, 1949-56; began explorations in jungles east of Andes in Peru to prove his theory that high civilizations of Peru may have had their origin in jungles, 1957; pres., founder Andean Explorers Found & Ocean Sailing Club, Reno. Expedition dir. Grand Ophir Sea Expedition; capt. Feathered Serpent III-Ophir, 1997-98. Author: Antisuyo, The Search for Lost Cities of the High Amazon, 1970, Vilcabamba, Last City of the Incas, 1970, The Cosolargy Papers, vol. 1, 1970, vol. 2-3, 1972, The Child Christ, 1973, Arabic edit., 1976, Japanese edit., 1981, The Decoded New Testament, 1974, Arabic edit., 1981, Millenium Edition, 1983, On The Trail of The Feathered Serpent, 1974, Code Book and Community Manual for Overseers, 1975, Prophecies of Jamil, First Prophecy to the Americas, vol. 1, 1976, Second Prophecy to the Americas, 1976, The Secret Sayings of Jamil, The Image and the Word, vol. 1, 1976, vol. 2, 1977, Project X—The Search For the Secrets of Immortality, 1977, Prophecy to the Races of Man, Vol. 2, 1977, Solar Cultures of The Americas, 1977, Dream Analysis, 1977, Vision Analysis, 1977, Christoanalysis, 1978, The Essaei Document: Secrets of an Eternal Race, 1978, Millennium edit., 1983, The Lost Gospel of Jesus: Hidden Teachings of Christ, 1978, Millennium edit., 1983, Secret Sayings of Jamil, vol. 3., 1978, vol. 4, 1979, Prophecy to The Christian Churches, vol. 3, 1978, The Sayings, vol. 4, 1979, Solar Cultures of Oceania, 1979, Prophecy of The End Times, vol. 4, 1980, Solar Cultures of Israel, vols. 1 and 2, 1980, Solar Cultures of China, 1980, Christotherapy, 1980, Christophysics, 1980, Christodynamics, 1980, Code Book of Prophecy, 1980, The Sayings, vol. 5, 1980, vol. 6, 1981, Solar Cultures of India, 1981, Prophecy on the Golden Age of Light and the Nation of Nations, Vol. 5, 1981, Solar Cultures of Israel, vol. 3, 1981, The Counsels, 1982, Prophecy of the Universal Theocracy, vol. 6, 1982, Prophecy of the New Covenant, vol. 7, 1982, The Book of God's Revelation, 1983, Miracle of the Second Advent, 1984, Clerical Studies in Theology, Book I, Book II, Book III, Book IV, Transformative Theology: The School of Revelation, Transformative Theology: The School of Prophecy, Liturgical Theology: Preparation for Advanced Degrees, 1993; over 400 audio tape rec. lectures, 1974—, numerous others.; dir. documentary film Adventure: Trail of the Feathered Serpent, 1970, Lost City of the Andes, 1987; wrote, dir. videos Royal Roads to Discovery, Mystery of the Essenes of Old Israel, Secrets From the High Andes of Peru, 1993, The Gran Vilaya Expeditions, 1996; contbr. articles on Peruvian cultures to mags., also articles on philosophy and religion; discoverer lost city of Incas at Vilcabamba Cuzco, numerous ancient cities in Amazonia including Gran Pajaten, Gran Vilaya, Monte Peruvia, Twelve Cities of the Condor, Gran Saposoa. Trustee in Trust Head Bishop Internat. Community of Christ. Served with AS USNR, 1944-46. Decorated Order of the Grand Cross Senate of Peru, 1989; recipient Participant's medallion Seawanhaka Yacht Club, 1977; Gold medal Ministry Industry and Tourism Peru, Silver Hummingbird, 1987; Silver medal and scroll City of Ica, Peru; honored with Gene Savoy Day by City of Reno, 1996, numerous exploring awards. Mem. Geog. Soc. Lima, Andean Explorers Found., Ocean Sailing Club (Explorer of the Century 1989, Flag awards), World Coun. for Human Spiritual Rights, Advs. for Religious Rights and Freedoms, Authors Guild, Explorers Club (N.Y.C., Flag awards), L.A. Yacht Club. Home: 2025 La Fond Dr Reno NV 89509-3025 Office: 643 Ralston St Reno NV 89503-4436 Office Phone: 775-786-7827. E-mail: gene@genesavoy.org. *One who makes dreams come true is that person who gets an idea, figures out how to make it work and then throws all of his energy into the project, stopping at nothing.*

SAVOY, SUZANNE MARIE, nursing educator; b. NYC, Oct. 18, 1946; d. William Joseph and Mary Patricia (Moclair) Savoy. BS, Columbia U., 1970; M in Nursing, UCLA, 1978; PhD in Nursing, Loyola U., 2004—. RN, cert. clin. nurse specialist. Staff nurse MICU, transplant Jackson Meml. Hosp., Miami, 1970-72; staff nurse MICU Boston U. Hosp., 1972-74, VA Hosp., Long Beach, Calif., 1974-75; staff nurse MIRU Cedars-Sinai Med. Ctr., LA, 1975-77; critical care clin. nurse specialist Anaheim (Calif.) Meml. Hosp., 1978-81; practitioner, instr. Rush-Presbyn.-St. Luke's Med. Ctr. Coll. Nursing, Chgo., 1982-88; rsch. assoc. dept. neurosurgery Rush U., 1984-88; clin. rsch. assoc. Medtronic, Inc. Drug Adminstrn. Sys., Mpls., 1988-91; staff nurse critical care Harper Hosp., Detroit, 1992-93; clin. nurse specialist, surg./trauma crit. care Detroit Receiving Hosp., 1993-95; clin. instr. Wayne State U. Coll. of Nursing, Detroit, 1991-96; adult crit. care clin. nurse specialist Saginaw (Mich.) Gen. Hosp., 1996—98; cardiac clin. nurse specialist Covenant Healthcare Sys., Saginaw, 1998—2005; asst. prof. Saginaw Valley State U. Coll. Nursing, 2005—. Adj. faculty Wayne State U. Coll. Nursing, 1996—98, program coord. Crit. Care ACNP-CC MSN, 1993—96; neurosci. clinician acute stroke unit Harper Hosp., Detroit, 1989; edn. cons. Critical Care Svcs., Inc., Orange, Calif., 1979—81; mem. staff Convenant Healthcare, 2005—. Contbr. articles to profl. jours. Mem.: Am. Assn. Spinal Cord Injury Nursing (mem. rsch. com. 1993—95), Assn. Health Care Quality (treas. 2002—04), Am. Assn. Crit. Care Nurses (bd. dirs. Long Beach chpt. 1981—82, treas. NEMC chpt. 1999—2001), Am. Assn. Neurosci. Nurses (treas. Ill. chpt. 1983—85, pres. 1986—87, SE Mich. chpt. 1992—96, bd. dirs., treas., program chair), Sigma Theta Tau, Lambda and Gamma Phi (bd. dirs. 1994—96). Roman Catholic. Office Phone: 989-964-7026. Personal E-mail: cardioapn@aol.com. Business E-Mail: smsavoy@svsu.edu.

SAVRIN, LOUIS, lawyer; b. Phila., Jan. 20, 1927; s. William Philip and Anna (Sass) S.; m. Barbara J. Schwimmer, Jan. 16, 1954; children: Jonathan Eric, Philip Wade, Daniel Scott. BS, NYU, 1948; JD, U. Pa., 1951. Bar: N.Y. 1952. Atty. tax dept. Arthur Young & Co., NYC, 1951-55; pvt. practice NYC, 1955—2005. Gen. counsel, sec. Pickwick Internat., Inc., N.Y.C., 1965-77 Assoc. editor: U. Pa. Law Rev, 1949-51. Mem. sch. bd. Dist. 21, Bklyn., 1962-68; docent Whitney Mus. Am. Art. With US Army, 1945—46. Mem. B'nai B'rith (pres. lodge 1957-59, named to lodge Hall of Fame 1967, Torch of Freedom award Anti-Defamation League 1982). Home: 50 Park Ave Apt 17H New York NY 10016-3082 Home Phone: 212-683-3860.

SAVVIDES, MARIOS, electrical and computer engineer, research professor; b. Nicosia, Cyprus, Nov. 11, 1975; arrived in US, 1998; s. Loucas Savvides and Anastasia Savvidou. BE in MicroElectronics Sys. Engring., U. Manchester, 1997; MSc in Robotics, Carnegie Mellon U., 2000, PhD in Elec. and Computer Engring., 2004. Rsch. assoc. Carnegie Mellon U., Pitts., 1998—2004, rsch. faculty, 2004—. Lectr. in field. Contbr. articles to profl. jours. Recipient Best Lectr. award, Carnegie Mellon U., 2004; fellow, 1998—2004. Mem.: IEEE, Soc. of Photo Optical Instrumentation Engrs. Achievements include patents pending for reducing complexity correlation filters for biometric recognition. Office: Carnegie Mellon University 5000 Forbes Ave Pittsburgh PA 15213 Home Phone: 412-367-6189; Office Phone: 412-268-1142. Office Fax: 412-268-6345. Personal E-mail: marios.savvides@ri.cmu.edu.

SAWAI, DAHLEEN EMI, language educator; b. Honolulu, Mar. 13, 1954; d. Kiyoto and Aiko Sawai. BA, U. Hawaii, Manoa, 1975, diploma in elem. edn., 1977, diploma in secondary edn., 1981, MEd, 1984. Cert. tchr. Hawaii. English tchr. Tokyo Family Court, 1977—78; Japanese tchr. Kailua H.S., Honolulu, 1978—80; English tchr. Family Ct. Probation Officer Tng. Sch., Tokyo, 1983—84; Japanese tchr. W. R. Farrington H.S., Honolulu, 1985—; educator Consortium for Tchg. Asia and the Pacific in the Schs., Honolulu, 1989—95; mentor tchr., 1995—. Instr. Sch. Cmty. Based Mgmt., Honolulu, 2000—04; interpreter Star Tanjo, 1976; chmn. dept. world langs. W.R. Farrington H.S., Honolulu, 2001—. Dir. Moanalua Gardens Cmty. Assn., Honolulu, 1976—77, sec., 1978—80; ad hoc com. mem. Sch. Cmty. Coun., 2005. Scholar, Keio Gijuku Daigaku, 1982—84. Mem.: Hawaii State Tchrs. Assn., Hawaii Assn. Tchrs. Japanese, Nat. Coun. Japanese Lang. Tchrs., Farrington Alumni and Cmty. Found., Japanese Cultural Ctr. Hawaii, Temari Ctr. Asian and Pacific Arts, Alliance Drama Edn., Pi Lambda Theta.

SAWALLISCH, WOLFGANG, conductor; b. Munich, Aug. 26, 1923; s. Wilhelm and Maria (Obermeier) Sawallisch; m. S. Mechthild. Student, Wittelsbacher Gymnasium, Munich, Musikalische Ausbildung; pvt. music studies; D (hon.), Curtis Inst. of Music, Westminister Choir Coll. of Rider U., Villanova U. Condr., Augsburg, Germany, 1947-53; musical dir. Aachen, Germany, 1953-58, Wiesbaden, Germany, 1958-60, Cologne Opera, 1960-63; condr. Hamburg Philharm. Orch., 1960-73, hon. mem., 1973—; music dir. Phila. Orch., 1993—2003, condr. laureate, 2003—. Prin. condr. Vienna Symphony Orch., 1960—70, hon. mem.; prof. Staatliche Hochschule fur Musik, Cologne, 1960—63; musical dir. Bayerische Staatsoper Munich, 1971—92; dir. Staatsoper Munich, 1982—92, hon. mem., 1992—; permanent condr. Teatro alla Scala, Milan. Rec. artist U.S. and Britain, hon. condr. NHK Symphony Orch., Tokyo, 1967, artistic dir. Suisse Romande Orch., Geneva, 1973—80. Decorated Osterreichisches

Ehrenkreuz fur Kunst und Wissenschaft, Bundesverdienstkrenz, Bayerischer Verdienstorden, Grosses Bundesverdienstkreuz mit Stern Fed. Republic Germany, Order of Rising Sun Japan; recipient Accademico Onorario Santa Cecilia, 1975, Toscanini Gold Baton, La Scala, 1993, Bruckner-Ring, Vienna Symphony Orch., 1980, Bayerisches Maximiliansorder fur Wissenschaft and Kunst, 1984, Chevalier dans L'ordre Nat. de la Legion d'Honneur de France, 1991, Pa. Gov. Disting. Artist award, Avatar award for artistic excellence, Arts and Bus. Coun., Phila. Mem.: Richard Strauss Gesellschaft Munich (pres. 1976). Office: Phila Orch 260 S Broad St Fl 16 Philadelphia PA 19102-5002 *

SAWCZUK, IHOR S., urologist; b. NYC, Oct. 5, 1952; s. Stefan and Stefania (Mruczkewycz) S. BA, NYU, 1974; MD, Med. Coll. of Pa., 1979. Diplomate Am. Bd. Urology. Chief Allen Pavilion Urology Columbia-Presbyn. Med. Ctr., NYC, 1988—99; prof. urology Columbia U., NYC, 1993—, vice chmn. Dept. of Urology, 1994—2001; chmn. urology Hackensack (NJ) U. Med. Ctr., 2001—, chief urologic oncology Cancer Ctr.; prof. surgery U. Medicine and Dentistry NJ, Newark, 2003—. Adv. bd. Kidney Cancer Assn., 1994—, Kidney and Urology Found., 2002—; dep. dir. Internat. Coop. Urological Edn. Project, 1994-96. Co-editor: (book) Urologic Clinics of North America, 1993. Bd. dirs. Children of Chernobyl, Short Hills, N.J., 1992-98. Recipient Young Investigator award Nat. Kidney Found., 1987, Alpha Omega Alpha Vol. Clin. Faculty award N.J. Med. Sch., 2003. Mem. ACS, Am. Urol. Assn. (scholar 1986), N.Y. Acad. Scis., Soc. Internat. de Urologie, Soc. Urologic Oncology, European Acad. Scis., Minimally Invasive Robotics Assn. Office Phone: 201-336-8090.

SAWERS, SIR JOHN, ambassador; m. Shelley Sawers; 3 children. Student in Physics and Philosophy, U. Nottingham, Eng.; student, U. St. Andrews, U. Witwatersrand, Johannesburg. Prin. pvt. sec. to Fgn. Sec. Douglas Hurd Govt. UK, head embassy's fgn. and def. policy issues team Washington, 1996—98, fgn. affairs advisor to Prime Min. Tony Blair, 1999—2001, amb. to Cairo, 2001—03, polit. dir. Fgn. and Commonwealth Office, 2003—07, spl. rep. Baghdad, Iraq, permanent rep. to UN NYC, 2007—; internat. fellow Harvard U., Cambridge, Mass., 1995—96. Named Knight Comdr. of St. Michael and St. George, UK. Avocations: theater, hiking, tennis, bicycling. Office: UK Mission to UN One Dag Hammarskjold Plz 885 Second Ave New York NY 10017 Office Phone: 212-745-9200. Office Fax: 212-745-9316.

SAWH, RAVI-PERSAD, lab administrator, researcher; s. Sire Persad and Joyce Eileen Sawh; m. Tashi Chetty, Sept. 25, 2004. BS in Physics, U. Houston, 1994. Lab supr. I U. Houston, 1994—98, lab supr. II, 1998—2006, rsch. lab. mgr., 2006—. Mem.: Houston Alumni Orgn., Sigma Pi Sigma, Nat. Physics Honor Soc. Achievements include discovery of a class of double perovskite pinning ceners in high temperature superconductors. Office: U Houston 632 Sci & Rsch Bldg 1 Houston TX 77204 Office Phone: 713-743-3600. Office Fax: 713-747-4526. Business E-Mail: rsawh@uh.edu.

SAWHILL, ISABEL VAN DEVANTER, economist; b. Washington, Apr. 2, 1937; d. Winslow B. and Isabel E. Van Devanter; m. John C. Sawhill, Sept. 13, 1958; 1 son, James W. BA, NYU, 1962, PhD, 1968. Asst. prof. econs. Goucher Coll., Balt., 1969—73; sr. rsch. assoc. Urban Inst., 1973—77, program dir., sr. fellow, 1980—93; dir. Nat. Commn. Employment Policy, Washington, 1977—79; program assoc. dir. Office Mgmt. and Budget, 1993—95; sr. fellow and Arjay Miller chair in pub. policy Urban Inst., 1995—97; sr. fellow Brookings Instn., Washington, 1997—, v.p., dir. econ. studies, 2003—06. Vis. prof. Georgetown U. Law Ctr., 1990-91; chairperson rsch. adv. bd. Com. for Econ. Devel., 1995-98; bd. dirs. Greenhill & Co., Inc. Author: Getting Ahead, 1998, One Percent for the Kids, 2003, Restoring Fiscal Sanity, 2004, 05. Bd. dirs. Manpower Demonstration Res. Corp.; pres. Nat. Campaign Prevent Teen Pregnancy, 1996—. Mem. Am. Econ. Assn., Assn. Pub. Policy Analysis and Mgmt. (pres. 1988), Phi Beta Kappa. Office: Brookings Inst 1775 Massachusetts Ave NW Washington DC 20036-2103

SAWHNEY, MOHANBIR S., finance educator; BSEE, Indian Inst. of Tech., Delhi, India, 1985; MS in Mktg., Indian Inst. Mgmt., Calcutta, India, 1987; MA in Mktg., PhD in Mktg., U. Penn., Wharton Sch., 1993. Asst. prof., mktg. Kellogg Sch. of Mgmt., Northwestern U., 1993—99, McCormick Tribune prof. of tech., 1999—, dir., ctr. for rsch. in tech. and innovation. Former adv. Govt. of Oman, U.S. Jordan Bus. Alliance; bd. dirs. Edmunds.com, IntelliSeek, MarketRx, Confluent Surgical, Autodaq, ConvergeLabs, Instill Corp.; fellow World Economic Forum. Co-author: (books) The Seven Steps to Nirvana: Strategic Insights into eBusiness Transformation, Techventure: New Rules for Value and Profit from Silicon Valley, Kellogg on Technology & Innovation, author numerous jour. articles. Named one of 25 most influential people in e-business, Bus. Week, 40 under 40 bus. leaders, Crain's Chicago Bus. Office: Northwestern U Kellogg Sch of Mgmt Jacobs Ctr Rm 5245B 2001 Sheridan Rd Evanston IL 60208

SAWICKI, MIKOLAJ ZIEMISLAW, physicist; b. Szczecin, Poland, Feb. 2, 1948; came to U.S., 1989; s. Aleksy and Janina Sawicki; m. Krystyna Rynkiewicz, Sept. 4, 1971; children: Magdalena J., Pawel A. MSc, Warsaw U., 1970, PhD, 1975, habilitation, 1986. Fellow Bonn U., Germany, 1976—77; from asst. prof. to assoc. prof. Warsaw U., 1977—91; prof. John A. Logan Coll., Carterville, Ill., 1993—. Owner Nicholas Rsch. and Cons., Carbondale, Ill., 1997—; vis. prof. Hannover (Germany) U., 1983, U. Colo., Boulder, 1997—; vis. asst. prof. Va. Tech., Blacksburg, 1984-85; vis. assoc. prof. Tex. A&M U., College Station, 1990-92, Iowa State U., Ames, 1992-93; vis. physicist U. Ariz., Tucson, 1989-90. Author: Experiments in Electricity, Magnetism and Optics, 1996, Experiments in Mechanics, 1995, Electric Circuits, 1995, Mutual Funds Investor's Guide, 1997; contbr. articles to profl. jours. Rsch. scholar Stanford U., 1983-84. Mem. Am. Phys. Soc. Avocations: hiking, skiing, travel. Business E-Mail: mikolajsawicki@jalc.edu.

SAWICKI, ZBIGNIEW PETER, lawyer; b. Hohenfels, Germany, Apr. 13, 1949; came to U.S., 1951; s. Witold and Marianna (Tukiendorf) S.; m. Katheryn Marie Loman, Aug. 19, 1972; children: James, Jeffrey, Jessica, Jason. BSChemE, Purdue U., 1972; MBA, Coll. St. Thomas, St. Paul, 1977; JD, Hamline U., 1980. Bar: Minn. 1980, U.S. Dist. Ct. Minn. 1981, U.S. Ct. Appeals (8th cir.) 1981, U.S. Patent and Trademark Office 1981, U.S. Ct. Appeals (fed. cir.) 1982, Can. Patent Office 1994, Can. Trademark Office 1995. Process engr. 3-M Co., St. Paul, 1973-75; process engring. supr. Conwed Corp., St. Paul, 1975-77; shareholder, bd. dirs. Kinney & Lange, Mpls., 1980—2003, Westman, Champlin & Kelley, 2003—. Bd. dirs. Orono (Minn.) Hockey Boosters, 1992—2000. With USAF, 1970-76. Mem. Am. Intellectual Property Assn., Internat. Trademark Assn., Minn. Intellectual Property Assn. (past treas.), Licensing Exec. Soc., The Federalist Soc., Am. Legion. Home: 4510 N Shore Dr Orono MN 55364-9602 Office: Westman Champlin & Kelly 900 2d Ave S Ste 1400 Minneapolis MN 55402-1624 Office Phone: 612-330-0581. Business E-Mail: psawicki@wck.com.

SAWOROTNOW, PARFENY PAVLOVICH, mathematician, educator; b. Ust Medveditskaya, Russia, Feb. 20, 1924; came to U.S., 1949, naturalized, 1965; s. Pavel Ivanovich and Anna Davidovna (Soloview) S.; student U. Graz (Austria), 1946-49; MA (Peirce scholar), Harvard U., 1951, PhD (Shattuck fellow), 1955. Teaching fellow Harvard U., 1953-54; instr. math. Cath. U. Am., Washington, 1954-57, asst. prof., 1957-62, assoc. prof., 1962-67, prof., 1967-96, prof. math. emeritus, 1997—. NSF grantee, 1967, 70; with Georgetown U. and George Washington U., 1971-77. Mem. Am. Math. Soc., Math. Assn. Am., Calcutta Math. Soc., N.Y. Acad. Scis., Sigma Xi. Mem. Eastern Orthodox Ch. Contbr. articles to and referred papers for math. rsch. jours. Home: 6 Avon Pl Hyattsville MD 20782-3328 Office: Cath U Am Dept Math 4th And Michigan Ave NE Washington DC 20064-0001

SAWTELLE, CARL S., psychiatric social worker; b. Boston, July 14, 1927; s. Carl Salvador and Martha (Bellamacina) S.; BA, Suffolk U., Boston, 1951; MSW, Simmons Sch. Social Work, 1953; m. Thelma Florence Ramsay, Aug. 20, 1950; children: Tracy Lynn, Lisa June. Social worker Tewksburry (Mass.) State Hosp., 1952; psychiat. social worker, head psychiat. social worker, dir. clin. social work Taunton (Mass.) State Hosp., 1953-74; 1st dir. clin. social work, Plymouth, Mass., 1974-78; co-founder, v.p. 1st legally established War On Poverty program Triumph, Inc., Taunton; co-founder 1st Greater Taunton Coun. on Alcoholism, 1972. With USCG, 1944-46. 1st lic. social worker in Mass., 1980. Mem. Nat. Assn. Social Workers (co-founder Southeast Mass. chpt. 1957, pres. 1957, Spl. Mass. Chpt. award 1978), Acad. Cert. Social Workers (chmn. 1962-72), Am. Legion, Mass. Mental Health Social Workers Assn. (co-founder, pres. 1972-74, other offices). Created innovated programs, resources, opportunities, svcs. to state mental hosp. patients and their families; mentor to young social workers; contbr. advancement of knowledge, practice quality and standards of psychiat. social work; father of licensing and registration of Social Workers in Mass. Home: 9 Tracywood Rd Canton MA 02021-3501

SAWYER, CHARLES F., lawyer; b. 1956; Student, Northwestern U. Sch. Music, 1974—76; AB in Econ. with honors and high distinction, U. Mich., 1978; JD, U. Chgo., 1981. Bar: Minn. 1982. Law clerk, Hon. Charles L. Levin, 1981—82; assoc. Dorsey & Whitney LLP, Mpls., 1982—88, ptnr., corp. dept., 1989—, and co-chair, securitization group. Exec. editor Univ. Chgo. Law Rev., 1980—81. Office: Dorsey & Whitney LLP Ste 1500 50 S Sixth St Minneapolis MN 55402-1498 Office Phone: 612-343-7986. Office Fax: 612-340-8738. Business E-Mail: sawyer.charles@dorsey.com.

SAWYER, DEBORAH, environmental engineering company executive; b. 1957; BA Polit. Sci., Emory U.; MS Petroleum Microbiology, U. New Mexico. Environ. scientist Ohio Environ. Protection Agy.; program mgr. Toxic and Hazardous Waste Grp. at URS Corp., ENR 18; sr. v.p., mem bd. dirs., head Beling Consultants, Solid, Toxic and Hazardous Waste Mgmt. Divsn.; founder, pres. CEO Environ. Design Internat. Inc., 1991—. Mem. bd. dirs. Ill. Inst. of Tech. Rice Campus Adv. Bd., Bradley U., Coll. of Engring., Chicagoland Chamber of Commerce. Appointed City of Chgo. Lake Michigan Commn. Named a Small Bus. Person of the Year, Ill. Gov. Office, 2000, Woman to Watch, Crain's Chgo. Bus., 2007; recipient Minority Small Bus. Person of the Year, US Small Bus. Adminstrn., 1994. Office: Environ Design Internat Inc 200 S Mich Ave Ste 700 Chicago IL 60604 Office Phone: 312-356-5400 x222. Office Fax: 312-356-5499. *

SAWYER, (L.) DIANE, newscaster, journalist; b. Glasgow, Ky., Dec. 22, 1945; d. E. P. and Jean W. (Dunagan) Sawyer; m. Mike Nichols, Apr. 29, 1988. BA, Wellesley Coll., 1967. Reporter Sta. WLKY-TV, Louisville, 1967—70; adminstr. press office White House, 1970—74; rschr. Richard Nixon's memoirs, 1974—78; gen. assignment reporter, then Dept. State corr. CBS News, 1978—81; co-anchor Morning News CBS, 1981—, co-anchor Early Morning News, 1982—84; corr., co-editor 60 Minutes CBS-TV, 1984—89; co-anchor PrimeTime Live (now known as Prime-Time Thursday) ABC News, 1989—; co-anchor Day One, 1995, Turning Point, 1996, Good Morning Am. ABC News, NYC, 1999—. Co-recipient George B. Polk award for TV reporting, 2005; named one of 100 most powerful women, Forbes mag., 2005; named to TV Hall of Fame, 1997; recipient 2 Peabody awards for pub. svc., 1988, Robert F. Kennedy award, 13 Emmy awards, 2 Dupont awards (one Spl.), IRTS Lifetime Achievement award, Robert F. Kennedy Journalism award, 2007. Office: Good Morning America Fl 10 147 Columbus Ave New York NY 10023-5900 *

SAWYER, DOLORES, motel chain executive; b. Shreveport, La., Oct. 16, 1938; d. Orlan B. Greer and Doris Lucile (Sanders) Eckman; m. Raymond Lee Sawyer Jr., June 11, 1960 (dec. Mar. 2007); children: Lisa Kay, Linda Faye. BSN, Northwestern State Coll., 1960; MSN, Tex. Woman's U., 1975. Supr. obstetrics dept. Highland Hosp., Shreveport, La., 1962-64; head nurse (3-11 shift) Scott and White Meml. Hosp., Temple, Tex., 1966-71, dir. of nursing edn., 1975-76; sch. nurse Temple Ind. Sch. Dist., 1971-72; instr. Mary-Hardin Baylor Coll., Belton, Tex., 1972-74; asst. prof., clin. specialist U. Tex. Arlington, 1976-86; v.p. Budget Host Internat., Arlington, Tex., 1986-96, sr. v.p., 1996—, also bd. dirs., chmn. bd., owner. Recipient Amoco Outstanding Tchg. award, 1981. Mem. Sigma Theta Tau. Republican. Methodist. Avocations: reading, scrapbooks, gardening, crafts, piano. Office: Budget Host Internat Ste B 2307 Roosevelt Dr Arlington TX 76016-5865 Home Phone: 817-496-4449; Office Phone: 817-861-6088. Personal E-mail: rsawyerl@airmail.net. Business E-Mail: dsawyer@budgethost.com.

SAWYER, HOWARD JEROME, physician; s. Howard C. and Dorothy M. (Risley) S.; m. Janet Carol Hausen, July 24, 1954; children: Daniel William, Teresa Louise BA in Philosophy, Wayne State U., Detroit, 1952, MD, 1962, postdoctoral, 1969-72. Diplomate Am. Bd. Preventive Medicine in Occupational and Environ. Medicine. Intern William Beaumont Hosp., Royal Oak, Mich., 1962-63, resident in surgery, 1963-64; chief physician gen. parts div. Ford Motor Co., 1964-66; med. dir. metall. products dept. Gen. Electric Co., Detroit, 1966-73, chem. and metal div., 1972-73; staff physician Detroit Indsl. Clinic, Inc., 1973-74; pres., med. dir. OccuMed Assocs., Inc., Farmington Hills, Mich., 1974-84; dir. OccuMed div. Med. Service Corp. Am., Southfield, Mich., 1984-86; dir. occupational, environ. and preventive medicine Henry Ford Hosp., 1987-91; pres. Sawyer Med. Cons., P.C., 1991—. Adj. asst. prof. occupational and environ. health scis. Wayne State U., 1974—, lectr. occpl. and environ. medicine Sch. of Medicine, 1998—; lectr. Sch. Pub. Health, U. Mich., Ann Arbor, 1977-88; cons. med. dir. St. Joe Minerals Corp., 1976-87, Chesbrough Pond's Inc., 1979-83; cons. Anaconda, Bendix, Borg Warner Chems., Fed. Mogul, Gen. Electric, Gt. Lakes Chems., other corps. Contbr. articles to profl. jours., chpts. to textbooks. Fellow Am. Coll. Preventive Medicine, Am. Occupational and Environ. Med. Assn., Mich. Occupational and Environ. Med. Assn. (pres. 1986), Am. Acad. Occupational Medicine; mem. AMA, Detroit Occupational Physicians Assn. (pres. 1984), Mich. State Med. Soc., Oakland County Med. Soc., Am. Indsl. Hygiene Assn., Mich. Indsl. Hygiene Soc. Office: Sawyer Med Cons PC 7072 Edinborough Dr West Bloomfield MI 48322-4025 Home Phone: 248-626-1693; Office Phone: 248-626-8061. Personal E-mail: buzsaw@comcast.net.

SAWYER, JAMES S., manufacturing executive; BS in Geology, Wesleyan U.; MBA, MIT. V.p. Praxair, treasurer, 1992—2000, CFO, 2000—. Office: Praxair 39 Old Ridgebury Rd Danbury CT 06810-5113

SAWYER, JOHN C., lawyer; b. Cherry Point, NC, May 23, 1956; BBA cum laude, U. Ga., 1978; JD magna cum laude, U. Notre Dame, 1981. Bar: Ga. 1981, US Tax Ct. 1992. Ptnr. Alston & Bird, LLP, Atlanta. Contbr. articles to profl. publs. Judge adv. USMC. Named one of Top 100 Attys., Worth mag., 2006. Fellow: Am. Coll. Trust and Estate Counsel. Office: Alston & Bird LLP 1 Atlantic Ctr 1201 W Peachtree St Atlanta GA 30309-3424 Office Phone: 404-881-7886. Office Fax: 404-881-7777. E-mail: jack.sawyer@alston.com.

SAWYER, JOHN WESLEY, retired mathematics and computer science educator, consultant; b. Nov. 2, 1917; s. Joseph Edmond and Inez Avent Sawyer; m. Edna Matthews, Aug. 31, 1939 (dec. Jan. 31, 2002); 1 child, John Wesley Jr. BA, Wake Forest Coll., 1938, MA, 1941, U. Mo., 1948, PhD, 1951. Instr. math. U. Mo., Columbia, 1946—51; assoc. prof. math. Ga. State U., Atlanta, 1951—53, U. Richmond, Va., 1953—56; prof. computer sci. Wake Forest U., Winston-Salem, NC, 1956—88, emeritus prof. computer sci., 1988—. In-house cons. R. J. Reynolds Tobacco Co., Winston-Salem, 1958—86. Contbr. (book) Operations Research Tools for Systems Engineering, articles to profl. jours. Music dir. Wake Forest Bapt. Ch., Winston-Salem, 1964—89; bd. dirs. Salemtowne Retirement Cmty., Winston-Salem, 1999—2004; pres. (4 terms) Atlantic Coast Conf., Greensboro, NC, 1964—86; v.p. NCAA, Kansas City, Mo., 1980—84. Named Tar Heel of Week, Raleigh (N.C.) News & Observer, 1977; grantee NSF, 1960. Fellow: AAAS (life); mem.: Math. Assn. Am., Ops. Rsch. Soc. Am. Achievements include development of computer simulations for business and manufacturing operations; creation and development of computer science department at Wake Forest University. Home: 6113 Salemtowne Dr Winston Salem NC 27106-3497

SAWYER, MALCOLM JAMES, JR., religious studies educator; b. Farmington, Maine, Oct. 31, 1951; s. Malcolm James and Bertha Brindley Sawyer; m. Kay Lynn Fuqua, Dec. 15, 1973; children: James Daniel, Jonathan David, Joel Nathaniel, Joshua William. BA, Biola U., 1973; ThM, Dallas Theol. Sem., 1978, PhD, 1987. Asst. prof. Simpson Coll., San Francisco, 1984—89; prof. Western Sem., Los Gatos, Calif., 1989—2007, Tozer Sem., Redding, Calif., 2007—. Bd. mem. Bay Cities Bible Inst., Oakland, Calif., 1995—97; mem. adv. bd. Christian Counseling Internat., Scott's Valley, Calif., 1999—2002. Author: Charles Augusts Briggs and Tensions in Late Nineteenth Century America Theology, 1994, The Survivor's Guide to Theology, 2006, Taxonomic Charts on Biblical and Theological Studies, 1999; co-author: Reinventing Jesus, 2006; co-editor Who's Afraid of the Holy Spirit?, 2005; contbr. articles to profl. jours. Fellow, Christus Nexus, 2005—. Mem.: Am. Acad. Religion, Soc. for Bibl. Lit., Evang. Theol. Soc. (far west pres. 2001—02). Home: 16485 Severn Rd San Leandro CA 94578

SAWYER, MARGO LUCY, artist, educator; b. Washington, May 6, 1958; d. Eugene Douglas and Joan Imogen (Alford) S. BA hons., Chelsea Sch. Art, London, 1980; MFA, Yale U., 1982. Prof. U. Tex., Austin, 1988—. Vis. artist Chelsea Sch. Art, London, 1982—. One-person shows include Brit. Coun., Bombay, India, 1983, Barbara Toll Fine Arts, N.Y.C., 1989, 91, Sagacho Exhibit Space, Tokyo, 1996, Gallery Gallery, Kyoto, Japan, 1996, Internat. House of Japan, Tokyo, 1996, Austin (Tex.) Mus. Art, 1998, Artplace, 2000, Mattress Factory, Pitts., 2003, Blatter Gallery, Houston, 2004, others; group shows include Whitechapel Gallery, London, 1979, ICA, London, 1979, 80, Leo Castelli Gallery, N.Y.C., 1986, Portland (Maine) Mus. Art, 1987, U. Md. Art Gallery, Balt., 1988, Meyers/Bloom Gallery, Santa Monica, Calif., 1989, Archer M. Huntington Art Gallery, Austin, Tex., 1990, 91, 92, 93, 94, Harn Mus. Art, Gainesville, Fla., 1992, Laguna Gloria Art Mus., Austin, 1994, Abilene (Tex.) Outdoor Sculpture exhbn., 1995-96, Artspace A Found. for Contemporary Art, 2000, Finesilver Gallery, San Antonio, 2002; permanent collections include Hyde Park, London, Cityarts Workshop, Portland Mus. Art, Samuel O. Harn Mus. Art, U. Fla., Prudential Ins., Chem. Bank, Champion Paper, and various pvt. collections. Recipient Louis Comfort Tiffany Found. award, 2001, Am. Acad. Rome fellow, 1986-87, Japan Found. visual arts fellow, 1996; Travel grantee Ford Found., 1981, Fulbright rsch. grantee, India, 1982-83, Japan, 1995-96, N.Y. State Coun. on Arts grantee, 1987, Travel grantee NEA, 1994. Office: U Tex Dept Art and Art History Austin TX 78712-1104

SAWYER, MELVIN WAYNE, psychologist; b. Rock Springs, Wyo., Sept. 24, 1933; m. Sylvia Sawyer. BA, Brigham Young U., 1959, PhD, 1975. Lic. psychologist Utah, 1986. Probation officer Orange County, Calif., 1960—66; med. adminstr., acting supr. mobile counseling, sr. counselor Thiokol Chem., Clearfield (Utah) Job Corps, 1966—68; psychologist Utah State Hosp., Provo, 1988—. Psychol. examiner, instr. Brigham Young U., Provo, 1969—72; dist. dir. State of Utah Juvenile Ct., Provo, 1972—81; program dir., coord. adolescent unit, assessment therapist Charter Canyon Hosp., Provo Charter Canyon Sch, 1981—88; psychologist State of Utah, Divsn. Rehab. Svc., Salt Lake City, 1989. Bishop Brigham Young U. student ward LDS Ch., Provo, 2003—05. With USAR, 1954. Mem.: APA (assoc.). R-Consevative. Mem. Lds Chj. Avocations: fishing, basketball, travel. Home: 709 E 60 N Orem UT 84097 Office: Utah State Hosp 1300 E Center St Provo UT 84603 Home Phone: 801-473-7464; Office Phone: 801-344-4415.

SAWYER, MILDRED CLEMENTINA, retired real estate agent; b. Boston, Nov. 19, 1928; d. Joseph Felix and Assunta (Malone) Volpe; m. Frederick Myles Sawyer, June 15, 1957 (dec. Jan. 1995); children: Frederick G., Bernard G. Clk. Prudential Ins. Co., Brockton, Mass., 1947-57, Clark Bros., Olean, NY, 1957-58; typist NJ, 1958-87, RI, 1958—87; real estate sales rep. JLC & Home Realty, Chepachet, No. Scituate, 1984-97; ins. sales agt. Mass. Indemnity Life Ins. Co., Cranston, RI, 1984-89; security sales rep. First Am. Nat. Securities, Cranston, 1986-89; ret., 1995. Author: A Lifetime of Hints for Everyday Living, 1996, The Path Into Vietnam: An Historical Reflection, 2002; author numerous poems. Sec. Cold Springs Harbor Heights Civic Assn., Huntington, LI, NY, 1961-63, Save All Foster's Environ., Foster, RI, 1969-87, Students for a Dem. Soc., Warwick, 1970-72; mem. RI Coun. for the Humanities. Mem. Soc. Children's Book Writers and Illustrators, Union Concerned Scientists, Noetic Sci. Avocations: reading, exercising, gardening, cooking, sewing. Home: 49A Mount Hygeia Rd Foster RI 02825-1923

SAWYER, NELSON BALDWIN, JR., credit union executive; b. Jacksonville, Fla., Nov. 11, 1948; s. Nelson Baldwin and Nancy (Watson) S.; m. Carla Lee Dowden, Aug. 9, 1986. BA, U. North Fla., 1974. Program cons. State of Fla., Jacksonville, 1974-81; product mgr. Qualified Plan Designs, Inc., Jacksonville, 1981-83, Associated Gen. Contractors, Jacksonville, 1983-86; membership mgr. Calif. Credit Union League, Pomona, 1986-87, comm. mgr., 1987-90; sr. v.p., COO Calif. League Svcs. Corp., Pomona, 1990-93; sr. v.p. Wescorp, San Dimas, Calif., 1994-97; v.p. Travis Fed. Credit Union, Vacaville, Calif., 1997-2000; pres., CEO Chevron Valley Credit Union, Bakersfield, Calif., 2000—. Chmn. bd. dirs. Calif. Ctr. Credit Union, 1996-97, Product Rsch. Orgn. for Credit Unions. Bd. dirs. Jacksonville C. of C., 1983-84, Taft Coll. Found., 2001—; bd. dirs. Am. Heart Assn., Bakersfield, 2002—, chmn., 2005-06; mem. assembly of dels. Calif. Credit Union League, 2002-04. Mem. U.S. Jaycees (pres. Jacksonville 1983-84, chmn. bd. 1984-85, U.S. senator 1984—, internat. senator 1984—, Outstanding Young Man of Am. 1983), Rotary Club of Bakersfield, Fla. Yacht Club. Republican. Episcopalian. Office: Chevron Valley Credit Union 8200 Granite Falls Dr Bakersfield CA 93312-5592

SAWYER, RAYMOND TERRY, lawyer, consultant, theater producer; b. Cleve., Oct. 1, 1943; s. R. Terry and Fanny Katherine (Young) S.; m. Katherine Margaret Schneider, Aug. 5, 1972; children: Margaret Young, John Terry. BA, Yale U., 1965; LLB, Harvard U., 1968. Bar: Ohio 1969, U.S. Dist. Ct. (no. dist.) Ohio 1970, prin., Sawyer LLC, 2002-. Assoc. Thompson Hine LLP, Cleve., 1968-76, ptnr., 1976—83, 1986—2001, chmn. bus. transactions and org. dept., 1998—2001; exec. dir. Ohio Housing Fin. Agy., Columbus, 1983-84; counsel to gov. State of Ohio, Columbus, 1984, chief of staff, 1985-86, chmn. Gov.'s commn. on housing, 1989-90; prin. Sawyer LLC, Cleve., 2002—. Bd. dirs. Premix, Inc., North Kingsville, Ohio. Assoc. prodr.: Frankie and Johnny in the Clair de Lune, 2002—03 (Tony award nomination for best revival of a play); Match, 2004. Vol. VISTA, East Palo Alto, Calif., 1968—69; mem. Tech. Leadership

Coun., 1987—95, Leadership Cleve., 1986—87, Cleve. Found. Study Commn. on Med. Rsch. Edn., 1991—92, George W. Codrington Charitable Found., 1989—, chmn., 1989—2003; mem. Ohio Bd. Regents, Columbus, 1987—96, chmn., 1992—93; trustee Cleve. Ballet, 1987—2000, Cleve. Orch., 1993—, sec., exec. com., 1997—; mem. exec. com. MetroHealth Sys., 1998—; mem. Juilliard Coun. Juilliard Sch.; mem. pres.'s adv. coun. Case Western Res. U. Named Man of Yr. Womanspace, 1982. Mem. Ohio State Bar Assn. (chair corp. law com. 1993-95), Yale U. Alumni Assn. (pres. Cleve. chpt. 1980-81), Assn. Yale Alumni (del. 1996-99). Democrat. Presbyterian. Office: Sawyer LLC 3900 Key Ctr Cleveland OH 44114-1291 Home: 2425 N Park Blvd Apt 3A Cleveland Heights OH 44106-3154 Office Phone: 216-566-5837.

SAWYER, ROBERT MCLARAN, historian, educator; b. St. Louis, Nov. 12, 1929; s. Lee McLaran and Harrie (Alcock) S.; m. Patricia Ann Covert, Nov. 23, 1955; children— Ann Marie, Lee McLaran, Gail Louise. BS, S.E. Mo. State Coll., 1952; MA, U. Ill., 1953; PhD, U. Mo., 1966. Tchr. Rolla Public Schs., Mo., 1955; asst. prof., then asso. prof. history U. Mo., Rolla, 1956-67; mem. faculty U. Nebr., Lincoln, 1967—, prof. history of edn., 1969—2006, chmn. dept. history and philosophy of edn., 1975-81, coun. mem. Coll. Arts and Scis., 1979—2006, emeritus prof., 2007—. Vis. prof. Ark. State U., Jonesboro, 1966; proposal reviewer Nat. Endowment Humanities, 1979 Author: The History of the University of Nebraska, 1929-1969, 1973, The Many Faces of Teaching, 1987, The Art and Politics of College Teaching, 1992, The Black Student's Guide to College Success, 1993, The Handbook of College Teaching, 1994; contbr. articles to profl. jours. With AUS, 1953—55. Mem. Orgn. Am. Historians, History Edn. Soc., Am. Ednl. Studies Assn., Soc. Profs. Edn., Phi Alpha Theta, Phi Delta Kappa. Home: 2640 S 35th St Lincoln NE 68506-6623 Office: Univ Nebr 29 Henzlik Hall Lincoln NE 68588

SAWYER, THOMAS EDGAR, management consultant; b. Homer, La., July 7, 1932; s. Sidney Edgar and Ruth (Bickham) S.; m. Joyce Mezzanatto, Aug. 22, 1954; children: Jeffrey T., Scott A., Robert J., Julie Anne. BS, UCLA, 1959; MA, Occidental Coll., 1969; PhD, Walden U., 1990. Project engr. Garrett Corp., LA, 1954-60; mgr. devel. ops. TRW Systems, Redondo Beach, Calif., 1960-66; spl. asst. to gov. State of Calif., Sacramento, 1967-69; prin., gen. mgr. Planning Rsch. Corp., McLean, Va., 1969-72; dep. dir. OEO, Washington, 1972-74; assoc. prof. bus. mgmt. Brigham Young U., 1974-78; pres., chmn. bd. Mesa Corp., Provo, Utah, 1978-82; pres., dir. Sage Inst. Internat., Inc., Provo, 1982-88; chmn. bd., CEO Pvt. Telecom. Networks, Inc. (name changed to Nat. Applied Computer Techs, Inc.), Orem, Utah, 1988-98; chief tech. officer GST Telecom. (formerly Greenstar Telecom., Inc.), San Francisco, 1993-98, also bd. dirs. Vancouver, Wash., 1995-98; chmn. bd. NeTrue Comm., Inc., Fullerton, Calif., 1998—2002; chmn. bd., CEO Telecom, Inc., Salt Lake City, 2002—06; sr. dir. Econ. Rsch. Inst., AIM Holdings (formerly MMG Holdings), Tokyo, 2003—; consul gen. for Republic of Liberia Monrovia, 2004—; dir. ops. First European Investment Found., Fruitland Park, Fla., 2004—. Bd. dirs. Intechna Corp., HighTech Corp., Indian Affiliates, Inc., Greenstar USA, Inc., San Francisco, 1994-98, GST Global Comm., Inc., Vancouver, Can., 1998-2002, Highpoint Telecom., Inc., Vancouver, 1998-01, World Wide Wireless Comm., Inc., Salt Lake City, 1998-2000, Columbia Hosp., Orem, 1998-05; sr. dir. Econ. Rsch. Inst., AIM Holdings, Ltd., Tokyo, 2003-; consul gen. for Republic of Liberia, Monrovia, 2004—. Author: Assimilation Versus Self-Identity: A Modern Native American Perspective, 1976, The Promise of Funding a New Educational Initiative Using the Microcomputer, 1988, Computer Assisted Instruction: An Inevitable Breakthrough, Current Challenges of Welfare: A Review of Public Assistance as Distributive Justice, 1989, New Software Models for Training and Education Delivery, 1989, New Organizations: How They Deviate from Classical Models, 1989, Increasing Productivity in Organizations: The Paradox, 1989, An Introduction and Assessment of Strategic Decision Making Paradigms in Complex Organizations, 1989, The Future of Technology in Education, 1989, Impact of Failure by Senior Executives to Receive Accurate Critical Feedback on Pervasive Change, 1990, The Influence of Critical Feedback and Organizational Climate on Managerial Decision Making, 1990. Chmn. Nat. Adv. Coun. Indian Affairs, Utah State Bd. Indian Affairs, So. Paiute Restoration Com., Utah Cmty. Mediation Ctrs., 2002-05; trustee Utah Valley State Coll., Orem, 2000-05, Coll. Ea. Utah, Price, 2001—; mem. Utah Dist. Export Coun., Utah dist. SBA Coun.; mem. adv. coun. Nat. Bus. Assn.; mem. Utah Job Tng. Coordinating Coun. Served with USMC, 1950-53. Mem. ASPA, Am. Mgmt. Assn., Utah Coun. Small Bus. (dir.), Utah State Hist. Soc. (bd. dirs. 1993-99), Masons. Republican. Mem. Lds Ch. Home: 548 W 630 S Orem UT 84058-6154 Home Phone: 801-860-9944; Office Phone: 801-944-4090. Business E-Mail: tesawyer@tesawyer.com.

SAWYER, WILLIAM C., lawyer; b. Bangor, Maine, Aug. 26, 1929; s. Frank S. and Linda M. (Makanna) S.; m. Mary A. Eaton (div.); m. Joan N. Gardner; children: William D., Constance, Faith. AB cum laude, Harvard Coll., 1951, JD, 1954. Bar: Mass., U.S. Dist. Ct. Mass., U.S. Ct. Mil. Appeals, U.S. Supreme Ct. Assoc. Palmer & Dodge, Boston, 1958-61; ptnr. Sawyer, Burlingham, Tucker & Salloway, Boston, 1961-85, Dicara, Selig, Sawyer & Holt, Boston, 1985-90, Clarkin, Sawyer & Phillips, P.C., Boston, 1990—. Bd. dirs. Ayer Sales, Inc., others. Contbr. articles to profl. jours. Bd. trustees Mass. Conv. Ctr. Authority, 1991-97; pres., treas., chmn. Metro. Area Planning Coun., 1975-87; pres. Mass. Assn. Regional Planning Agys., 1980, 87; bd. dirs. Nat. Assn. Regional Couns., 1980-86; mem. Mass. Selectman's Assn., 1975—; bd. selectman Town of Action, 1967-75, chmn., 1969, 75; Rep. candidate Mass. Atty. Gen., 1990; pres. New Eng. Rep. Coun.; mem. Rep. State Com.; Rep. candidate Congress, 5th Congl. Dist., Mass., 1980. 1st lt. U.S. Army, 1955. Recipient Regional Leadership award Planning Commns. and Couns. New Eng., 1987, and others. Mem. ABA, Mass. Bar Assn., Boston Bar Assn. Avocations: golf, painting, reading. Office: Clarkin Sawyer & Phillips PC 1 Center Plz Ste 240 Boston MA 02108-1801 Office Phone: 617-742-2525. Business E-Mail: wcs@csplaw.com.

SAWYER, WILLIAM DALE, internist, educator, dean, foundation administrator; b. Roodhouse, Ill., Dec. 28, 1929; s. Cloyd Howard and Eva Collier (Dale) S.; m. Jane Ann Stewart, Aug. 25, 1951; children: Dale Stewart, Carole Ann. Student, U. Ill., 1947-50; MD cum laude, Washington U., St. Louis, 1954; ScD (hon.), Mahidol U., Bangkok, 1988; DPH (hon.), Chiang Mai U., Thailand, 1993, Chulalongkorn U., 1998. Intern Washington U.-Barnes Hosp., 1954-55, resident, 1957-58, fellow, 1958-60; asst. prof. microbiology Johns Hopkins U., Balt., 1964-67; prof., chmn. dept. microbiology Rockefeller Found.-Mahidol U., Bangkok, 1967-73, Ind. U. Sch. Medicine, Indpls., 1973-80; prof. depts. medicine, microbiology and immunology Wright State U., Dayton, Ohio, 1981-87, dean Sch. Medicine, 1981-87; pres. China Med. Bd. N.Y., Inc., 1987-97. Adj. prof. biology Ball State U., Muncie, Ind., 1978-80; hon. prof. microbiology Sun Yat Sen U. Med. Sci., 1987; hon. prof. Peking Union Med. Coll., 1989; hon. advisor Beijing Med. U.; cons. U.S. Army Med. R & D Command, WHO Immunology Ctr., Singapore, 1969-73; mem. bd. sci. advisers Armed Forces Inst. Pathology, 1975-80, chmn., 1979-80; adj. prof. medicine and microbiology and immunology N.Y. Med. Coll., Valhalla, 1990-96; hon. prof. China Med. U., 1995, West China U. Med. Sci., 1995, Zhejiang Med. U., 1995, Jiujang Med. Coll., 1995, Hunan Med. U., 1996, Xian Med. U., 1996, Shanghai Med. U., 1996. Contbr. numerous articles to profl. jours. Mem. Lobund adv. bd. U. Notre Dame; dir. Georgetown Area Cmty. Found., 1998-2002, pres. 1999; mem. exec. com. Georgetown Cmty. Resource Ctr., 2000-03. Served to maj. M.C., USA, 1955-64. Recipient Gold medal of merit Airlangga U., Indonesia, 1992, Pub. Health Recognition award Asia-Pacific Acad. Consortium Pub. Health, 1993, China Health medal, 1996, White Magnolia award, 1996. Fellow ACP; mem. AAAS, Am. Soc. Microbiology (br. pres. 1976), Sci. Rsch. Soc. Am., Am. Fedn. Clin. Rsch., Ctrl. Soc. Clin. Rsch., Infectious Diseases Soc. Am., Soc. Exptl. Biology and Medicine, Am. Acad. Microbiology, Am. Assn. Pathologists, Assn. Am. Med. Colls. (coun. deans 1980-87), Phi Beta Kappa, Sigma Xi, Alpha Omega Alpha. Home: The Summit #313 1034 Liberty Pk Dr Austin TX 78746 E-mail: wllmsawyer@aol.com.

SAWYERS, AL BAKER, lawyer; b. Nashville, Sept. 10, 1960; s. John Lazelle and Julia (Edwards) S.; m. Elise Iekyung Junn, June 17, 1989. BA magna cum laude, Vanderbilt U., 1982; JD, MBA, U. Chgo., 1986. Bar: Ariz. 1986, U.S. Dist. Ct. Dist. Ariz. 1986, Tenn 1987, Ill. 1987, N.Y. 1995. Atty. Snell & Wilner, Phoenix, 1986—87, Chapman & Cutler, Phoenix, 1987—94; ptnr. Orrick Herrington & Sutcliffe LLP, NYC, 1994—. Mem.: N.Y. State Bar Assn., Ariz. Bar Assn., Ill. Bar Assn., Tenn. Bar Assn. Office: Orrick Herrington & Sutcliffe LLP 666 Fifth Ave New York NY 10103 Office Phone: 212-506-5041. Business E-Mail: absawyers@orrick.com.

SAWYERS, ELIZABETH JOAN, librarian, director; b. San Diego, Dec. 2, 1936; d. William Henry and Elizabeth Georgiana (Price) S. AA, Glendale Jr. Coll., 1957; BA in Bacteriology, UCLA, 1959, M.L.S., 1961. Asst. head acquisition sect. Nat. Library Medicine, Bethesda, Md., 1962-63, head acquisition sect., 1963-66, spl. asst. to chief tech. services div., 1966-69, spl. asst. to assoc. dir. for library ops., 1969-73; asst. dir. libraries for tech. services SUNY-Stony Brook, 1973-75; dir. Health Scis. Library Ohio State U., Columbus, 1975-90, spl. asst. to dir. Univ. librs., 1990—. Mem. Assn. Acad. Health Scis. Library Dirs. (sec./treas. 1981-83, pres. 1983-84), Med. Library Assn., Am. Soc. for Info. Sci., Spl. Libraries Assn., ALA Office: Ohio State Univ Librs 1858 Neil Ave Columbus OH 43210-1225 Office Phone: 614-292-4491. E-mail: sawyers.1@osu.edu.

SAWYERS, NORMA ANN, elementary school educator, real estate agent, property manager; b. Detroit, Aug. 10, 1931; d. Austin Sipple and Viola (Anderson) Neeb; m. Thomas J. Stevenson Jr., June 20, 1953 (div. Feb. 1983); children: Mark Stevenson, Lori Ann Smith, Thomas J. Stevenson III; m. Gordon E. Sawyers, July 6, 2003. BS, Mich. State U., 1953; MA, Wayne State U., 1972. Tchr. Grosse Pointe Schs., Mich., 1969—87; real estate sales staff Schweitzer, Prudential, Grosse Pointe, 1979—2000; owner, pres., real estate developer Thompson Marlor Fin. Mgmt. Co., Grosse Pointe, 1980—. Bridge dir. Celebrity Cruise Line, 2001—, Norweigian Cruise Line, 2001—; developer condominium conversion Stevenson Condominium, Grosse Pointe, 1995; lectr., spkr. in field. Treas. PTA, Grosse Pointe, 1968; vol. Hospice, Grosse Pointe, 1990—94, Meals on Wheels, Grosse Pointe, 1999—2003; mem. St. James Luth. Ch., Grosse Pointe, 1940—2006; chair handchimes, dir. of bridge Spirit of Grace Luth. Ch., Surprise, Ariz. Mem.: PEO, Am. Contract Bridge League (dir.), Delta Kappa Gamma (Woman of Distinction 1980). Republican. Avocations: sailing, bridge, bicycling, travel, exercise. Home (Winter): 16236 W Tuscany Way Surprise AZ 85374

SAWYIER, MICHAEL TOD, lawyer; b. Boston, Jan. 6, 1948; s. Calvin Parker and Fay (Horton) S.; m. Judith Puistonen, June 6, 1968; children: Julianne Patricia, Justine Fay, Alexandra Lee, Sydney Anne Helena. BA, Harvard U., 1969; JD, U. Chgo., 1972; LLM, Yale U., 1973, LLM (Tax) John Marshall Law Sch., 2001. Bar: Ill. 1972, D.C. 1974, Calif. 1976, Ind. 1983, Tex. 1989, U.S. Dist. Ct. (no. dist.) Ill. 1979, U.S. Ct. Appeals (7th cir.) 1981, U.S. Dist. Ct. (no. and so. dists.) Ind. 1983, U.S. Supreme Ct. 1984. Atty.-adviser Office of Legal Adviser U.S. Dept. State, Washington, 1974-75; assoc. Pillsbury, Madison and Sutro, San Francisco, 1975-77, Baker and McKenzie, Chgo., 1977-79, Foss, Schuman, Drake & Barnard, Chgo., 1979-87; ptnr. Mathewson, Hamblet & Casey, Chgo., 1987-89; ptnr. Sawyier and Stewart, Chgo., 1989-93, Watt and Sawyier, Chgo., 1993-2002; prin. Law Offices Michael T. Sawyier, 2002—. Bd. dirs. Am. Inst. Sindhulogy, 2006. Recipient Paul Cornell prize Hyde Park Hist. Soc., Chgo., 1982. Mem. ABA, Ill. Bar Assn., Chgo. Bar Assn., Ind. Bar Assn., Tex. Bar Assn., Am. Soc. Internat. Law., Chgo. Rotary Club, Saddle and Cycle Club, Chgo. Club. Home: 424 W Melrose St Apt 15A Chicago IL 60657-3862 Office: 150 N Michigan Ste 2700 Chicago IL 60601-3713 Home Phone: 773-472-9771; Office Phone: 312-856-9741. Business E-Mail: mtsawyier@estateplanningattorneychicago.com.

SAX, DANIEL SAUL, neurologist, educator; b. Balt., Jan. 27, 1935; s. Benjamin and Miriam (Helfgott) S.; m. Joan Atherton Bond, Mar. 25, 1962; children: Karen Bond, John Derek, Diana Atherton. AB, Johns Hopkins U., Balt., 1955; MD, U. Md., College Park, 1959. Diplomate Am. Bd. Psychiatry and Neurology. Intern Boston City Hosp., 1959—60, resident in neurology and neuropathology neurologic unit, 1961—64; resident in neurology N.E. Med. Ctr., Boston, 1961; asst. prof. neurology Northwestern U., Chgo., 1966-67; assoc. prof. neurology Albert Einstein Med. Sch., NYC, 1967-69, Boston U. Sch. Med., 1969-76, prof. neurology, 1976-2000, prof. emeritus neurology, 2000—. Chief neurology svcs. Boston VA Outpatient Clinic, 1974-90; EEG lab. dir., cons. Gifford Med. Ctr., Randolph, Vt., 1977-2003, neurologist, 1977-2003; cons. neurology Boston VA Med. Ctr., 1991-2000, hon. staff, 2002; adj. prof. neurology Dartmouth Med. Sch., Hanover, NH, 2007—. Mem. clin. adv. com. Vt. divsn. Nat. MS Soc., 2001, clin. adv. com. ctrl. N.E. chpt., 1977-03; bd. dirs. Ctrl. Vt.-Upper Valley N.H. chpt. ARC, 2003—. Lt. comdr. USNR, 1964-66. Lt. comdr. USNR, 1964—66. Fellow: Am. Acad. Neurology; mem.: AMA, Internat. Soc. Women Health and Sexuality, Huntington's Study Group, Huntington's Dx Soc. (mem. adv. bd. Mass. chpt. 1980—2000, clin. adv. bd. 2001—03), Multiple Sclerosis Soc. (clin. adv. bd. 1977—2003), Boston Soc. Neurology and Psychiatry (pres. 1982—83, exec. com. 1985—2003, Vt. bd. med. practice 2002—03), Mass. Med. Soc., Am. Assn. for Study of Headache, Am. Neurol. Assn. Avocations: tree farmer, oenology, music. Office: 4142 VT Rte 66 # 185 Randolph Center VT 05061 Personal E-mail: dssax@adelphia.net.

SAX, JOSEPH LAWRENCE, lawyer, educator; b. Chgo., Feb. 3, 1936; s. Benjamin Harry and Mary (Silverman) S.; m. Eleanor Charlotte Gettes, June 17, 1958; children: Katherine Elaine Dennett, Valerie Beth Sax, Amber Sax Rosen. AB, Harvard U., 1957; JD, U. Chgo., 1959; LLD (hon.), Ill. Inst. Tech., 1992. Bar: D.C. 1960, Mich., 1966, U.S. Supreme Ct. 1969. Atty. U.S. Dept. Justice, Washington, 1959-60; pvt. practice law Washington, 1960-62; prof. U. Colo., 1962-65, U. Mich., Ann Arbor, 1966-86; dep. asst. sec. and counselor U.S. Sec. Interior, Washington, 1994-96; prof. U. Calif. Law Sch., Berkeley, 1986—. Fellow Ctr. Advanced Study in Behavioral Scis., 1977-78, Order of the Coif Disting. Visitor, 2004. Author: Waters and Water Rights, 1967, Water Law, Planning and Policy, 1968, Defending the Environment, 1971, Mountains Without Handrails, 1980, Legal Control of Water Resources, 4th edit., 2006, Playing Darts with a Rembrandt, 1999. Fellow: AAAS. Home Phone: 415-346-6221; Office Phone: 510-642-1831. Business E-Mail: saxj@law.berkeley.edu.

SAX, MARY RANDOLPH, speech and language pathologist; b. July 13, 1925; d. Bernard Angus and Ada Lucile (Thurman) TePoorten; m. William Martin Sax, Feb. 7, 1948. BA magna cum laude, Mich. State U., 1947; MA, U. Mich., 1949. Cert. clin. competence in speech and lang. pathology. Supr. speech correction dept. Waterford Twp. Schs., Pontiac, 1949—69; lectr. Marygrove Coll., Detroit, 1971-72; pvt. practice in speech and lang. pathology Wayne and Oakland Counties, Mich., 1973—. Co-investigator Support Pers. Profl. Practice of Speech-Lang. Pathology; counselor to divsn. stroke liaisons Am. Heart Assn. Mich.; liaison between Am. Heart Assn. of Mich. and Am. Heart Assn., Dallas, 1996—98; adj. speech pathologist, Southfield, Mich.; lectr. on stroke Mich. Spkrs. Bur., Am. Heart Assn., 1990—; pub. spkg. coach, 1989—; mem. adj. faculty SS Cyril and Methodius Sem., Orchard Lake, Mich., 1989—90; adj. St. Mary's Prep. Sch., Orchard Lake, 1990—; mem. Met. Detroit Operation Stroke com. Am. Stroke Assn., 1999—2004, mem. med. subcom. to move area hosps. to become primary stroke ctrs. with active stroke teams, 2001—; founder, mem. Stroke Project Task Force for Detroit, 1993—98; com. mem. Charette, study Arch. and Design for phys. restructuring Franklin, Mich., 1993; invited speech pathology del. Internat. Health Programs People to People Citizen Amb. Program, 1996; mem. sci. coun. on stroke Am. Heart Assn., 1980—2002; invited U.S. rep. speech and lang. pathology (cancelled because of 9/11) Med. People to People Amb. Program, neurol. ctrs., Czech Republic, Hungary and Austria; mem. quality improvement and med. edn. subcom. Am. Heart Assn. New Heart and Stroke Network Metro Detroit, 2005—; mem. stroke adv. com./stroke advocacy com. Midwest affiliate Am. Heart Assn., 1995—2005; mem. stroke adv. com./stroke advocacy com. Greater Midwest Affiliate Mich., Ind., Ill., Wis., ND, SD, Minn. Am. Heart Assn., 2005—. Contbr. articles to profl. jours. including Lang. and Lang. Behavior Abstracts, Lang. Speech and Hearing Svcs., Speech Lang. Hearing Jour. Active Franklinites for Responsible Govt.; mem. stroke com. Mich. Heart Assn., 1982—99; founder, pres. Lakeview Assn. Sylvan Lake, Mich., 2006—. Recipient Svc. Recognition award Coll. Edn. Mich. State U.; grantee Inst. Articulation and Learning, 1969, others; Christian svc. commn. St. Owen, Birmingham co-chmn. blood dr. Red Cross, Franklin, Mich., 1991—. Mem.: Founders Soc. of Detroit Inst. Arts, Franklin Found. (mem. natural resources adv. coun. 1991—99, bd. dirs. 1994—98), Pvt. Practitioners Speech-Lang. Pathology (co-founder), Internat. Assn. Logopedics and Phoniatrics (Switzerland), Am. Heart Assn. Mich. (mem. stroke awareness seminars, continuing edn. for physicians and other profls., planning and operation edn.), Mich. Speech-Lang.-Hearing Assn. (pvt. practitioner liaison 1991—, developer structural parameters for State Clin. Svc. award 1999—, com. comty. and hosp. svcs., mem. state award selection com.), Am. Speech-Lang.-Hearing Assn. (clin. competence cert.), Mich. Humane Soc., Gamma Phi Beta, Kappa Delta Pi, Phi Kappa Phi, Theta Alpha Phi. Achievements include research in language and speech acquisition in children in reference to the development of and prediction of biological speech change; research interests in developmental phonatory voice disorders, and in adult acquisition of language and speech relative to central and autonomic nervous systems. Office: 31320 Woodside Dr Franklin MI 48025-2027

SAX, PAUL J., lawyer; b. Sacramento, 1944; AB, Calif. State U., Sacramento, 1965; JD, U. Calif., San Francisco, 1968; LLM in Taxation, NYU, 1969. Bar: Calif. 1969. Mem. Orrick, Herrington & Sutcliffe, San Francisco, ptnr., chmn. tax group. Vice chair pubs. sect. of taxation ABA, 1990—, chair, vice chair standards tax practice com., 1984-88, coun. dir., 1988-90, dept. editor Jour. Taxation, 1990—. Grad. editor Tax Law Rev., 1968-69. Fellow Am. Bar Found.; Am. Coll. Tax Counsel, Am. Tax Policy Inst.; mem. Order of Coif, Thurston Honor Soc., ABA- Sect. Taxation (chmn. 1999-2000, House Delegates 2001-), ABA-Standard Tax Practice Com. (vice chmn./chmn. 1984-1988, coun. dir. 1988-1990), ABA (vice chmn. publ.), Calif. Bd. Legal Specialization (cert. specialist taxation 1975-), Am. Law Inst. (tax adv. group), Office: Orrick Herrington & Sutcliffe LLP The Orrick Building 405 Howard St San Francisco CA 94105 Office Phone: 415-773-5949. Office Fax: 415-773-5759. Business E-Mail: pjsax@orrick.com.

SAXBE, WILLIAM BART, lawyer, former United States attorney general; b. Mechanicsburg, Ohio, June 24, 1916; s. Bart Rockwell and Faye Henry (Carey) S.; m. Ardath Louise Kleinhans, Sept. 14, 1940; children: William Bart, Juliet Louise Saxbe Blackburn, Charles Rockwell. AB, Ohio State U., 1940; LLB, 1948; degree (hon.), Central State U., Findlay Coll., Ohio Wesleyan U., Walsh Coll., Capital U., Wilmington Coll., Ohio State U., Bowling Green State U. Bar: Ohio 1948, DC. Practiced in, Mechanicsburg, Ohio, 1948-55; ptnr. Saxbe, Boyd & Prine, 1955-58; mem. Ohio Ho. Reps., 1947—54, majority leader, 1951-52, speaker, 1953-54; atty. gen. State of Ohio, 1957-58, 63-68; ptnr. Dargusch, Saxbe & Dargusch, 1960-63; mem. US Senate from Ohio, 1969-74; atty. gen. US, 1974—75; US amb. to India, 1975-77; ptnr. Chester, Saxbe, Hoffman & Wilcox, Columbus, Ohio, 1977-81; of counsel Jones, Day, Reavis & Pogue, Cleve., 1981-84, Pearson, Ball & Dowd (merger Pearson, Ball & Dowd and Reed, Smith & McClay), Washington, 1984-93, Chester Willcox & Saxbe, Columbus, Ohio, 1994—; ind. spl. counsel Central States Teamsters Pension Fund, 1982—. Served with 107th Cav. AUS, 1940-42, 107th Cav. USAAF, 1942-45; col. Res. Mem. ABA, Ohio Bar Assn., Am. Judicature Soc., Chi Phi, Phi Delta Phi. Clubs: Mason (Rufus Putnam Disting. Svc. Award), University, Columbus Athletic, Scioto Country, Urbana Country, Burning Tree Country, Bethesda, Md., Country of Fla., Boynton Beach. Republican. Episcopalian. Office: Chester Wilcox & Saxbe LLP 65 E State St Ste 1000 Columbus OH 43215

SAXE, DEBORAH CRANDALL, lawyer; b. Lima, Ohio, July 23, 1949; d. Robert Gordon and Lois Barker (Taylor) Crandall; m. Robert Saxe, June 3, 1989; children: Elizabeth Sara, Emily Jane. BA, Pa. State U., 1971; MA, UCLA, 1973, JD, 1978. Bar: Calif. 1978, D.C. 1979, U.S. Dist. Ct. D.C. 1979, U.S. Dist. Ct. (ea. dist.) Calif. 1981, U.S. Dist. Ct. (ctrl. dist.) Calif. 1982, U.S. Dist. Ct. (no. and so. dists.) Calif. 1987, U.S. Ct. Appeals (4th and D.C. cirs.) 1979, U.S. Ct. Appeals (6th cir.) 1985, U.S. Ct. Appeals (8th and 9th cirs.) 1987, U.S. Ct. Appeals (2nd cir.) 1990, U.S. Supreme Ct. 1982, U.S. Dist. Ct. (no. dist.) Ill. 2001, U.S. Ct. Appeals (7th cir.) 2001. Assoc. Seyfarth, Shaw, Fairweather & Geraldson, Washington, 1978-83, Jones, Day, Reavis & Pogue, Washington, 1983-85, LA, 1985-87, ptnr., 1988-97; shareholder Heller Ehrman LLP, 1997—2005; ptnr. Jones Day, LA, 2006—. Judge pro tem, Small Claims Ct., L.A., 1985-88. Co-author: Advising California Employers, 1990, 3d edit., 2007; contbg. editor Employment Discrimination Law, 1989. Bd. dirs. Constitutional Rights Found., 1997—2002; chair Eisner Pediatric and Family Med. Ctr., LA, 1996—98, bd. dirs., 1990—2003, Los Angeles County Bar Found., 1997—99. Fellow: Coll. Labor and Employment Lawyers; mem.: ABA (labor law sect. 1978—), L.A. County Bar Assn. (labor and employment law sect. 1985—, mem. exec. com. 1988—, chair 2002—03, trustee 2005—), Calif. Bar Assn. (labor law sect. 1985—), Phi Beta Kappa, Pi Lambda Theta. Office: Jones Day 555 S Flower St 50th Fl Los Angeles CA 90071 Office Phone: 213-489-3939. Office Fax: 213-243-2539. Business E-Mail: dsaxe@jonesday.com.

SAXE, LEONARD, social psychologist, educator; b. NYC, June 12, 1947; s. Theodore and Majorie (Mayers) S.; m. Marion Gardner, Aug. 9, 1970; 1 child, Daniel. BS in Psychology, U. Pitts., 1969, MS in Psychology, 1972, PhD in Social Psychology, 1976. Asst. instr. U. Pitts., 1973-75; asst. then assoc. prof. psychology Boston U., 1976-88, assoc. dir. Ctr. Applied Social Sci., 1982-84, dir., 1984-87; rsch. prof. Heller Sch. Social Welfare Brandeis U., Waltham, Mass., 1988-90, adj. prof. psychology, adj. rsch. prof., 1990—; prof. psychology Grad. Ctr. CUNY, 1991—; head social-personality psychology, 1993-95; prof. social policy and mgmt. Brandeis U., dir. Cohen Ctr. Modern Jewish Studies; prof. Jewish Cmty. Rsch., 2006—. Fulbright sr. lectr. U. Haifa, Israel, 1981—82; mem. task force Children's Mental Health Rsch. Inst. of Medicine-NAS, 1988—89; mem. rev. coms. HHS-Healthcare Fin. Adminstrn. NIMH, Nat. Inst. Drug Abuse, Dept. Edn.; cons., contractor Office Tech. Assessment, U.S. Congress, 1980—88; bd. govs. U. Haifa, 1993—; bd. dirs. Steinhardt Social Rsch. Inst. Author: (with others) Children's Mental Health: Problems and Treatment, 1987,)with A. Sales) How Goodly Are Thy Tents, (with M. Fine) Social Experiments: Methods for Design and Evaluation, 1981; editor: (with M.J. Saks) Advances in Applied Social Psychology, Vol. 3, 1986, (with D. Koretz) New Directions for Program Evaluation, 1982, (with D. Bar-Tal) The Social Psychology of Education: Theory and Research, 1978; contbr. chpts. to books, articles to profl. jours.; assoc. and mng. editor Personality and Social Psychology Bull., 1978-81; reviewer in field. Congl. fellow Office Tech. Assessment, 1979. Fellow APA (bd. dirs.

sect. social and ethical responsibility 1985-88, Disting. Contbn. award 1989), AAAS, Soc. Psychol. Study Social Issues (coun. 1982-84, 87-89). Office: Cohen Ctr M5014 Brandeis U Waltham MA 02454 Office Phone: 212-642-2501. E-mail: saxe@brandeis.edu.

SAXENA, ARJUN NATH, physicist; b. Lucknow, India, Apr. 1, 1932; came to U.S., 1956, naturalized, 1976; s. Sheo and Mohan (Piyari) Shanker; m. Veera Saxena, Feb. 9, 1956; children: Rashmi, Amol, Varsha, Ashvin. BSc, Lucknow U., 1950, MSc, 1952, profl. cert. in German, 1954; post MS diploma, Inst. Nuc. Physics, Calcutta, India, 1955; PhD, Stanford U., 1963. Rsch. asst. Stanford U., 1956-60; mem. tech. staff Fairchild Semicondr. Co., Palo Alto, Calif., 1960-65; dept. head Sprague Electric Co., North Adams, Mass., 1965-69; mem. tech. staff RCA Labs., Princeton, NJ, 1969-71; pres., chmn. bd. Astro-Optics, Phila., 1972; pres. Internat. Sci. Co., Princeton Junction, NJ, 1973—. Disting. vis. scientist Centre de Récherches Nucléaires, Strasbourg, France, 1973, 77; sr. staff scientist, mgr. engring. Data Gen. Corp., Sunnyvale, Calif., 1975-80; mgr. process tech. Signetics Corp., Sunnyvale, 1980-81; Gould AMI scientist, dir. advanced process devel. Gould AMI Semicondrs., Santa Clara, Calif., 1981-87; dir. Ctr. for Integrated Electronics, prof. dept. elec. and computer system engring. Rensselaer Poly. Inst., Troy, N.Y., 1987-96, emeritus prof., 1996—; disting. vis. scientist Inst. Microelectronics, Stuttgart, Germany, 1993-94. Contbr. articles to semicondr. tech., optics, nuc. and high-energy physics to sci. jours.; patentee in field. Treas. pack 66 Boy Scouts Am., West Windsor, N.J., 1970-74. Recipient Disting. Citizen award State of N.J., 1975. Mem. IEEE (life, sr.), Stanford U. Alumni Assn. (life). Achievements include establishment of a fellowship in his and his wife's name at Rensselaer Polytechnic Institute. Home: 4217 Pomona Ave Palo Alto CA 94306-4312

SAXENA, BRIJ B., endocrinologist, biochemist, educator; PhD, India; DSc, U. Muenster, W.Ger.; PhD, U. Wis., 1961; DSc (hon.), Bundelkhand U., India, 2002. Asst. prof. biochemistry and endocrinology N.J. Coll. Medicine., 1966-74; assoc. prof. biochemistry Cornell U. Med. Coll., NYC, 1974—, prof. biochemistry, 1974—, prof. endocrinology, 1981—, dir. div. reproductive endocrinology, Harold and Percy Uris endowed prof. reproductive biology, 2000—. Contbr. articles to profl. jours. Recipient Career Scientist award N.Y.C. Health Research Council; Upjohn research award; Campoz da Paz award. Fellow Royal Soc. Medicine (London); mem. Am. Soc. Biol. Chemists, AAAS, Endocrine Soc., Harvey Soc., Am. Physiol. Soc., Am. Chem. Soc. Office: Cornell U Med Coll 515 E 71st St Ste 412 New York NY 10021-4805 Home Phone: 201-569-8612; Office Phone: 212-746-3067. Business E-Mail: brs2003@med.cornell.edu.

SAXENA, ROMIL, pathologist, educator; d. Rajendra Mohan and Rani Saxena; m. Sunil Badve. MBBS, MD, Grant Med. Coll., Mumbai, India. Diplomate Am. Bd. Pathology, 1998. Resident pathologist Sir JJ Group of Hosps., Bombay, 1985—87; sr. registrar, histopathology Tata Meml. Hosp. for Cancer, Bombay, 1987—88, sr. registrar, hematopathology, 1988—90; registrar, dept. pathology, S.E. Thames Regional rotation King's Coll. Hosp., Farnborough Hosp., 1990—91; lectr., dept. pathology King's Coll. Hosp., London, 1991—95; resident, dept. pathology Albert Einstein Sch. Medicine, Bronx, NY, 1995—96; fellow, gene therapy and liver pathology Mt. Sinai Med. Ctr., NYC, 1996—98; fellow, gastrointestinal pathology Yale U. Sch. Med., New Haven, 1998—99; asst. prof., dept. pathology Mt. Sinai Sch. Medicine, NYC, 1999—2002; asst. prof., depts. pathology and lab. med. Ind. U. Sch. Medicine, Indpls., 2002—. Dir., anatomic pathology Richard L. Roudebush VA Med. Ctr., Indpls., 2002—04; lectr. in field in liver transplantation pathology. Contbr. articles to profl. jours., chapters to books. Fellow: Royal Coll. Pathologists (assoc.); mem.: Internat. Acad. Pathology (assoc.), Laennec Hepatopathology Soc. (assoc.), Hans Popper Hepatopathology Soc. (assoc.), US and Can. Acad.Pathology (assoc.). Achievements include expert in liver transplantation pathology. Office: Ind Univ Clarian Health 350 W 11th St Indianapolis IN 46202

SAXER, RICHARD KARL, metallurgical engineer, retired military officer; b. Toledo, Aug. 31, 1928; s. Alexander Albert and Gertrude Minnie (Kuebeler) S.; m. Marilyn Doris Mersereau, July 19, 1952; children: Jane Lynette, Robert Karl, Kris Renee, Ann Luette. Student, Bowling Green State U., 1946-48; BS, U. S. Naval Acad., 1952; MS in Aero. Mechanics Engring., Air Force Inst. Tech., 1957; PhD in Metall. Engring., Ohio State U., 1962; grad., Armed Forces Staff Coll., 1966, Indsl. Coll. Armed Forces, 1971; disting. grad., Air Force Inst. Tech., 2003. Commd. 2d lt. U.S. Air Force, 1952, advanced through grades to lt. gen., 1976; electronics officer, mech. officer (4th Tactical Support Sqadron, Tactical Air Command), Sandia Base, N.Mex., 1953-54; electronics and mech. officer, spl. weapons assembly sect. supr. (SAC 6th Aviation Depot Squadron), French Morocco, 1954-55; project engr. mech. equipment br. Air Force Spl. Weapon's Center, Kirtland AFB, N.Mex., 1957-59; project officer Nuclear Safety div., 1959-60; assoc. prof. dept. engring. mechanics Air Force Inst. Tech., 1962-66; asso. prof., dep. dept. head USAF Acad., 1966-70; comdr., dir. Air Force Materials Lab., Wright-Patterson AFB, Ohio, 1971-74; dep. for Reentry System Space and Missile Systems Orgn., 1974-77; dep. for aero equipment Aero. Systems Div., 1977-80, dep. for tactical systems, 1980, vice comdr., 1981-83; aero. systems div. dir. Def. Nuclear Agy., 1983-85, ret., 1985; pres. R.K. Saxer & Assocs., 1985-91; CEO Universal Tech. Corp., Dayton, Ohio, 1991—96. Research and tech. com. materials and structures NASA, 1973-74; chmn. planning group aerospace materials Interagy. Council Materials, 1973-74; mem. Nat. Mil. Adv. Bd., 1971-74, NATO adv. group for research and devel., 1973-74 Contbr. articles to profl. jours. Decorated Def. Disting. Svc. medal, Legion of Merit, Meritorious Service medal USAF, D.S.M., Joint Svc. Commendation medal, Air Force Commendation medal with 3 oak leaf clusters, Army Commendation medal U.S., Def. Superior Service medal, Cross of Gallantry with palm Vietnam, Def. Meritorious Service medal; recipient Disting. award for systems mgmt. Air Force Assn., 1979; Disting. Alumnus award Ohio State U., 1986, Disting. Alumni award Air Force Inst. Tech., 2003. Mem. Air Force Assn., Am. Def. Preparedness Assn. (pres. Dayton 1977-78), Sigma Xi, Phi Lambda Epsilon, Alpha Sigma Mu, Masons, Shriners. Home: 215 Dalfaber Ln Springboro OH 45066-1571

SAXEY, RODERICK, radiologist, writer; b. Portland, Oreg., May 21, 1950; s. Edward and V'Audrey Willoughby Saxey; m. Mellisa Anne Sprague; m. Linda Karel Haldeman-Julius; children: Caelie Jean Hyde, Roderick II, Leah Mari, Emily Annette, Duncan Alexander, Michelle Celeste. BS magna cum laude, Brigham Young U., Provo, Utah, 1975; MD, George Washington U., Washington, 1980. Diplomate Nat. Bd. Med. Examiners, 1981, Am. Bd. Radiology, 1984. Radiologist Mather USAF Hosp., Mather AFB, Calif., 1984—88; med. dir. diagnostic imaging Woodland Pk. Hosp., Portland, 1988—2001, Pullman Regional Hosp., Wash., 2002—07; radiologist Med. Imaging Northwest, Tacoma, 2007—. Author: (book) The Federalist: Excerpts and Commentary, 1994; editor: (newsletter) The Kithara, 1993—98. Maj. USAF, 1980—88. Decorated Air Force Commendation medal; Hinckley scholar, Brigham Young U., 1968—74, Nat. Merit scholar, 1968, Oreg. scholar, Oreg. Gov.'s Office, 1968, HPSP scholar, USAF, 1976—80. Mem.: Collegium Aesculapium, Am. Roentgen Ray Soc., Radiol. Soc. N.Am., Am. Coll. Radiology, NRA (life). Republican. Mem. Lds Ch. Home: 1901 40th St SE Puyallup WA 98372

SAXL, RICHARD HILDRETH, lawyer; b. Boston, June 3, 1948; BA, U. Pa., 1970; JD, Rutgers U., Camden, NJ, 1975. Bar: Conn. 1976, US Dist. Ct. Conn. 1976, US Ct. Appeals (2d cir.) 1977. Assoc. Jerry Davidoff, Westport, Conn., 1976-78; ptnr. Davidoff & Saxl, Westport, 1979-94; pvt. practice law offices Richard H. Saxl, Westport, 1994—; town atty. Fairfield, Conn., 1997—99, 2001—. Mem. Fairfield Town Plan and Zoning Commn., 1981-93, chmn., 1991-93; chair Fairfield Land Acquisition com., 1997; mem. Fairfield Charter Revision Commn., 1984-85, 92. Recipient Svc. award, Conn. Fedn. Planning and Zoning Agys., 1993, cert. of commendation, Conn. Jud. Dept. Mem. Conn. Bar Assn., Westport Bar Assn., Pequot Yacht Club. Home: 753 Sasco Hill Rd Fairfield CT 06824 Office: 5 Imperial Ave Westport CT 06880-4302 Office Phone: 203-222-8422. Personal E-mail: rhsaxl@sbcglobal.net.

SAXON, BURTON ROY, humanities educator; b. Aurora, Ill., June 22, 1947; s. Samuel and Jennie (Weisman) S.; m. Janet Hunter, June 21, 1969 (div. Dec. 1979); m. Myra Denise Hamburg, June 5, 1983; children: Jeffrey, Rebekah. BA, Carleton Coll., 1969; MAT, Wesleyan U., 1971; EdD, Columbia U., 1977; LHD (hon.), Quinnipiac U., 2006. Tchr. R.C. Lee High Sch., New Haven, 1970-75, 77-80; tchr., facilitator Hillhouse High Sch., New Haven, 1980—2006, New Haven-Yale Internat. Studies Ctr., 1989-93, New Haven-Yale Saturday Sem., 1989—. Vis. instr. edn. Yale U., 1976—. Co-author: Invitation to Psychology, 1980, 89; contbr. articles to profl. jours. Chmn. New Haven Bd. Edn. Family Life Edn. Com., 1979-83; co-founder Children's Coop Daycare, 1970-79. Named New Haven Tchr. of Yr., 2004—05, Conn. Tchr. of Yr., 2005; grantee, NSF, 1974—75. Democrat. Jewish. Avocations: baseball, bridge, movies, plays, tennis. E-mail: burtsaxon@sbcglobal.net.

SAXON, DON B., state agency administrator; Grad., U. Fla., 1975. Investigative supr. Fla. Dept. Banking and Fin., 1979—81, dir. divsn. investigations, 1981—83, asst. dir. divsn. securities and investor protection, 1983—86, dir. divsn. securities and investor protection, 1986—2003; commr. Fla. Office Fin. Regulation, 2003—. Recipient Blue Sky award, North Am. Securities Adminstrs. Assn., 1996, 2006. Office: Fla Office Fin Regulation 200 E Gaines St Tallahassee FL 32399-0370 Office Phone: 850-410-9601. Office Fax: 850-410-9663. E-mail: Ofr@fldfs.com.

SAXON, RANDALL LEE, pastor, author, educator; b. Waverly, NY, Oct. 28, 1947; s. Sherman Kenyon and Velma Marie (Dunning) S.; m. Diane Louise Kennedy, June 23, 1973 (div. Feb. 1985); children: Heather Marie, David Arthur; m. Anna Louise Clock, Mar. 15, 1986; children: Jennifer Elizabeth, Austin Todd. BA, Mansfield U., 1969; MDiv, Princeton Sem., 1973; certificate, Mansfield Coll., Oxford, Eng., 1980, Wadham Coll., Oxford, 2003; D of Ministry, Drew U., 1992. Ordained to ministry Presbyn. Ch. U.S.A., 1973. Asst. pastor United Meth. Ch., Flemington, 1970—71, Fewsmith Presbyn. Ch., Bellville, 1972—73; intern pastor Wattsburg (Pa.) Presbyn. Ch., 1971—72, East Greene Presbyn. Ch., Erie, Pa., 1971—72; asst. chaplain Bayberry State Hosp., Phila., 1973; assoc. pastor Presbyn. Ch., Gettysburg, Pa., 1973—78; sr. pastor 1st Presbyn. Ch., Southampton, 1978—86, Presbyn. Ch. of the Covenant, Port Arthur, Tex., 1986—91, 1st Presbyn. Ch., Wilmette, Ill., 1991—94, Peoria, Ill., 1994—2004; pastor United Presbyn. Ch., Peoria, 2004—; instr. parish nursing program OSF St. Francis Med. Ctr., Peoria, Ill., 1995—99; instr. Inst. Learning in Retirement Bradley U., Peoria, Ill., 1995—; instr. social scis. Ill. Ctrl. Coll., East Peoria, Ill., 1999—. Nat. chaplain Sigma Theta Epsilon, Mansfield, Pa., 1968-72; permanent clk. Presbytery of Carlisle, Camp Hill, Pa., 1975-77, Synod of the Trinity, Camp Hill, 1977-78; jour. clk. Presbytery of L.I., Commack, N.Y., 1980-84; mem. Presbytery of Great Rivers; guest lectr. in field. Author: Voices in the Wilderness, 1985, At the Ffeete of Christe and His Church, 1981, Developing A Ministry of Evangelism With Baby Boomers in A Suburban Setting, 1992, America's Debt to the Native American, 1999, Watch Your Mouth! A Brief History of Everyday Words and Phrases, 2003, Good Grief, Gravestones!, 2005; editor: Special Prayers and Prose for Special People of God, 1998; author articles, poetry, hymns. Program dir. Camp Brule, Boy Scouts Am., Forksville, Pa., 1972; dir. Youth in Govt. Seminar, Harrisburg, Pa., 1977; v.p. Internat. Seamen's Ctr., Houston, 1987-89; chairperson City Task Force on Edn. Summit, Port Arthur, 1990-91; active Presbyn. Hist. Soc.; camp commr. Boy Scouts Am., Forksville, Pa., 1971, dist. commr., Peoria, Ill., 1999 Recipient cert. Shinnecock Indian Tribe, 1981; named an Outstanding Young Man of Am., Jaycees, 1971; Susquehanna Collegiate Inst. grantee, 1972. Mem. Acad. Parish Clergy, Am. Soc. Ch. History, Presbyn. Hist. Soc., Presbyn. Writers Guild, Ctr. Theology and Natural Scis., Presbyn. Assn. Sci, Tech., and Christian Faith, Surrat Soc., Am. Forestry Assn., Presbyns. Renewal Creation, Scottish Soc. S.E. Tex. (pres. 1990-91), Ill. State Hist. Soc., The Co. of Pastors, The Lincoln Party, The Lincoln Project, Abraham Lincoln Assn., Nat. Eagle Scout Assn., Rotary (pres. 1977-78). Democrat. Avocations: coin collecting/numismatics, canoeing, white-water rafting, skydiving, gardening. Home: 3628 N Breckenridge Ct Peoria IL 61614-8034 Office: United Presbyn Ch 2400 W Northmoor Rd Peoria IL 61614-3343 Home Phone: 309-681-9291; Office Phone: 309-693-2002. Business E-Mail: rls@unitedpc.org.

SAXON, WOLFGANG ERIK GEORG, journalist, writer; b. Leipzig, Germany, Sept. 5, 1930; arrived in US, 1952; s. Erich Otto and Klâre (Wochatz) Richter; m. Anna Forti, 1967. BS, Columbia U., 1954; postgrad., Russian Inst., 1960. Newspaper reporter, obituarist New York Times, NYC, 1956—2006; freelance writer, 2006—. Draftee to specialist US Army, 1954—56. Mem.: Phi Beta Kappa, The Silurians. Independent. Agnostic. Avocations: reading, walking, travel. Home Phone: 212-865-0183. Business E-Mail: saxon@nytimes.com.

SAXTON, CATHERINE PATRICIA, public relations executive; b. Sheffield, Eng., July 5, 1944; d. Clifford and Kate Ann Saxton. BA cum laude, Fordham U., 1978. Mgr. corp. comms. Westinghouse Broadcasting & Cable Co., NYC, 1981-82; prin., pres. Saxton & Assocs., NYC, 1983—; CEO Potter/Saxton Assocs., Inc., NYC, 1985-90, The Saxton Group Ltd., 1990—, co-founder, co-chair A-List Strategic affiliate, 2003—. Prof. pub. speaking Katharine Gibbs Coll., N.Y.C., 1977—. Mem. exec. com. Mayor's Commn. for a Vietnam Vets. Meml., 1982-90. Roman Catholic. Home: 325 E 90th St New York NY 10128-5260 Office Phone: 212-672-0509. Business E-Mail: cpsaxton@hotmail.com.

SAXTON, CELESTE DAWN, social studies educator, consultant; b. Balt., Feb. 27, 1958; d. Harvey Lewis and Angela Alice-Attardo Saxton; children: Sara Megan Sciarretta, Natalie Allison-Bianca Sciarretta. AA in Arts & Sci. Transfer, Villa Julie Coll., Stevenson, Md., 1978; BS in History & Secondary Edn., Hood Coll., Frederick, Md., 1980; MS in Sch. Adminstrn. & Supervision, The Johns Hopkins U., Balt., 1993; EdD in Ednl. Leadership & Adminstrn., Nova Southeastern U., Ft. Lauderdale, Fla., 2002. Tchr. social studies Balt. County Pub. Schs., Towson, 1980—86; mid. sch. interdisciplinary team leader Balt. County Pub. Sch., 1986—90, chair social studies dept., 1990—96, mentor tchr. county level, 1996—97, h.s. adminstr., 1997—2002, social studies supr. & educator, 2002—. Sat adminstrv. coord. Balt. County Pub. Schs., 1997—2002, sch.-based minority achievement coord., 1989—93. Advisor for 1st mid. sch. key club Kwanis, Reisterstown, Md., 1987—89; team leader-highway clean-up Md. State Dept. Transp., Westminster, 1998—2001; student govt. advisor Balt. County Pub. Schs., 1989—93. Scholar, Balt. County Pub. Schs., 1999—2001. Mem.: Md. Coun. Social Studies, Nat. Coun. Social Studies. Roman Catholic. Avocations: reading, gardening, swimming, boating, travel. Home: 548 Old Bachmans Valley Road Westminster MD 21157 Office: Carroll County Public Schools 125 N Court Street Westminster MD 21157 Home Phone: 410-751-3096; Office Phone: 410-751-3000. Office Fax: 410-751-3159; Home Fax: 410-751-3159. Business E-Mail: cdsaxto@k12.carr.org.

SAXTON, JIM (HUGH JAMES SAXTON), congressman; b. Nicholson, Pa., Jan. 22, 1943; s. Hugh R. and Helen M. (Billings) Saxton; m. Helen Jean Gadomski, June 9, 1965; children: Jennifer, James Martin. BA in Edn., East Stroudsburg State U., Pa., 1965; grad. student in elem. edn., Temple U., 1967-68. Tchr. Bordentown Pub. Schs., NJ, 1965-68; owner, realtor Jim Saxton Realty Co., Bordentown, NJ, 1968-85; mem. NJ Gen. Assembly, 1976—81, NJ State Senate, 1981-84, US Congress from 3rd NJ dist., 1984—. Asst. minority whip NJ Gen. Assembly, 1980, NJ State Senate, 1981—84; mem. armed svcs. com. US Congress, mem. natural resources com., ranking Rep. mem. joint econ. com. Chair Am. Cancer Com.; mem. Burlington Coun. Boy Scouts Am.; mem. Bordentown C. of C., NJ. Named Outstanding Fed. Legislator of Yr., NJ Vets. of Fgn. Wars, 2000; recipient Henry M. Jackson Disting. Svc. award, Jewish Inst. Nat. Security Affairs, 2003, Leadership award, Nat. Marine Sanctuary Found., 2003. Mem.: USAF Assn., Leadership Found. NJ, Rotary, Elks. Republican. Office: US House Reps 2217 Rayburn Ho Office Bldg Washington DC 20515-3003 Office Phone: 202-225-4765. *

SAXTON, WILLIAM MARVIN, lawyer; b. Joplin, Mo., Feb. 14, 1927; s. Clyde Marvin and Lea Ann (Farnan) S.; m. Helen Grace Klinefelter, June 1, 1974; children: Sherry Lynn, Patricia Ann Painter, William Daniel, Michael Lawrence. AB, U. Mich., 1949, JD, 1952. Bar: Mich. Mem. firm Love, Snyder & Lewis, Detroit, 1952-53, Butzel, Long, Detroit, 1953—, dir., chmn., CEO, 1989-96, dir. emeritus, 1997—. Lectr. Inst. Continuing Legal Edn.; sec., bd. dirs. Fritz Broadcasting, Inc., 1983-97; mem. mediation tribunal hearing panel for 3d Jud. Dist. Mich., 1989—, 6th Jud. Dist., 1994—. Trustee Detroit Music Hall Ctr. Soc. for the Performing Arts, 1984-99; trustee Hist. Soc. US Dist. Ct. (ea. dist.) Mich., 1992-95, pres., 1993-95. Recipient Disting. award Mich. Road Builders Assn., 1987. Master of Bench Emeritus Am. Inn of Court; fellow Am. Coll. Trial Lawyers, Am. Bar Found., Am. Coll. Labor and Employment Lawyers, Mich. Bar Found.; mem. ABA, FBA, Detroit Bar Assn. (dir. 1974-79, Goodnow Pres.'s award 1996), Mich. Bar Assn. (atty. discipline panel, Disting. Svc. award 1998, Champion of Justice award, 2003), Detroit Indsl. Rels. Rsch. Assn. (treas. 1980—, v.p. 1982, pres. 1984-85), Mich. Young Lawyers (pres. 1954-55), Am. Law Inst., Indsl. Rels. Rsch. Assn. Am. Arbitration Assn., U.S. 6th Cir. Ct. Appeals (life, mem. jud. conf., mem. bicentennial com.), Am. Inn Ct., Cooley Club, Renaissance Club, Detroit Golf Club (dir. 1983-89), Detroit Athletic Club. Office: Butzel Long 150 W Jefferson Ave Ste 100 Detroit MI 48226-4416 Office Phone: 313-225-7001. Personal E-mail: saxton214@aol.com.

SAY, ALLEN, writer, illustrator; b. Yokohama, Japan, Aug. 28, 1937; arrived in U.S., 1953; s. Masako Moriwaki; m. Deirdre Myles, Apr. 18, 1974; 1 child, Yuriko. Weekend arts program, Chouinard Art Inst., LA; classes, Art Ctr. Coll. Design, LA; studied arch., U. Calif., Berkeley. Pub. EIZO Pr., Berkeley, 1968. Author, illustrator: Dr. Smith's Safari, 1972, Once Under the Cherry Blossom Tree: An Old Japanese Tale, 1974, The Feast of Lanterns, 1976, The Bicycle Man, 1982, A River Dream, 1988, The Lost Lake, 1989, Tree of Cranes, 1991, Grandfather's Journey, 1993 (Caldecott medal 1994, Boston Globe/Horn Book award 1994), The Stranger in the Mirror, 1995, Emma's Rug, 1996; author: The Innkeeper's Apprentice, 1989, El Chino, 1990, Home of the Brave, 2002; illustrator: A Canticle to the Waterbirds, 1968, Two Ways of Seeing, 1971, Magic and Night River, 1978, The Lucky Yak, 1980, The Secret Cross of Lorraine, 1981, How My Parents Learned to Eat, 1984 (Horn Book honor list 1984, Christopher award 1985), The Boy of the Three Year Nap, 1988 (Boston Globe/Horn Book award 1988, Caldecott honor book 1989), Allison, 1997; retrospective Japanese Am. Nat. Mus., L.A., 2000. Office: care Houghton Mifflin Children's Book Dept 222 Berkeley St Boston MA 02116-3748

SAY, BURHAN, retired physician; b. Istanbul, Turkey, Feb. 26, 1923; came to U.S. 1951; s. Ethem Serif and Ayse Say; m. Elizabeth E. Jackson, Nov. 5, 1955; children: Tony, Daniel Demir. MD, U. Istanbul, 1946. Diplomate Am. Bd. Pediatrics, Am. Bd. Med. Genetics. Asst. prof. pediatrics Hacettepe U., Ankara, Turkey, 1960-64, prof. pediatrics, 1964-73; clin. prof. of pediatrics U. of Okla./Tulsa Med. Coll., 1975—; ret. Dir. H.A. Chapman Inst., Tulsa, 1982—; v.p. Children's Med. Ctr., Tulsa, 1988—. Contbr. articles to profl. jours. Pres. Am. Cancer Soc., Tulsa, 1980-90, Great Plains Genetics Soc., Tulsa, 1993. Lt. Turkish Army, 1946-48, Turkey., Fulbright scholar, Boston, 1966—68. Avocation: sports. Home: 6216 E 99th St Tulsa OK 74137-5503 Office Phone: 918-299-5891. Personal E-mail: mbsay@cox.net.

SAYED, M. GARY, healthcare administrator, educator, scientist; BS in Nuclear Med. Sci., U. of Incarnate Word, San Antonio, 1985; MS in Radiochem., U. Iowa, 1989; PhD in Radiol. Scis., Med. Coll. Ohio, 1993. Med. health physicist U. Iowa, Iowa City, 1989-91; asst. prof. nuclear medicine U. Findlay, Ohio, 1992-97, asst. dir. Nuclear Medicine Inst., 1992-96, acting dir. Nuclear Med. Inst., 1997; assoc. prof. Thomas Jefferson U., Phila., 1998—2003, chmn. dept. diagnostic imaging, 1998—2003, clin. prof., 2002—; prof. Coll. Sci. and Health Charles Drew U. Medicine and Sci., 2003—, dean Coll. Sci. and Health, 2003—. Vis. prof. radiology Dokuz Eylul U., Izmir, Turkey, 1996; vis. prof. nuc. medicine Kuwait U., Kuwait, 2001—02; pres. Am. Bd. of Sci. in Nuc. Medicine. Editor: Nuclear Medicine Science Syllabus, 3d edit., 1999; guest editor: Radiologic Sci. and Edn. Jour. Recipient Leadership award Assn. Schs. of Health Professions, 1998; sr. Fulbright scholar, 1996. Fellow Am. Coll. Nuclear Medicine. Office: Charles Drew U Medicine and Science 1731 E 120th St Los Angeles CA 90059 Home Phone: 856-625-1166; Office Phone: 323-357-3440. Office Fax: 323-357-3433. Business E-Mail: gasayed@cdrewu.edu.

SAYEGH, NABIL, urologist; b. Nafrak, Jordan, May 4, 1949; arrived in US, 1979; m. Jacqueline Sayegh. AA, Westchester C.C., Valhalla, NY, 1970; BA, Lehman Coll., Bronx, 1972; MD, U. Autonoma de Guadalahara, Mex/, 1977. Intern LI Coll. Hosp., 1978, New Rochelle Hosp., 1978—79, NY Med. Coll., 1979—84; attending urologist Nyack Hosp., NY, 1984; urologist Westchester Med. Ctr., Valhalla, 1984—; clin. assoc. prof. surgery, urology NY Med. Coll. Contbr. articles to profl. jours. Fellow: ACS, Am. Coll. Internat. Surgeons; mem.: Am. Urological Assn. Office: 301 N Main St New City NY 10956

SAYER, RONALD J., composer, educator; b. Rochester, NY, Oct. 12, 1961; s. Barbara Sayer. B Music Edn., U. Mo., Kansas City, 1985; MEd, Tex. Wesleyan U., 2002. Instr. vocal music Lansing Unified Sch. Dist., Kans., 1985—97; artistic dir. Marshall (Mo.) Cmty. Chorus, 2000—; instr. vocal music Marshall (Mo.) H.S., 1997—, chmn. fine arts dept., 2000—. V.p. Mid-Mo. Fine Arts Coun., Marshall, 2002—. Mem. music com. St. Peter's Cath. Ch., Marshall, 1999—2003. Recipient Tchr. award, Mo. Fine Arts Acad., 2000, 2002—04, 2006, Sharon Murphy award, Kans. NEA, 1996, Tchr. of the Yr., Marshall HS, 2006;, U. Mo.-Kansas City scholar, 1994. Mem.: Nat. Assn. Tchrs. Singing, Mo. Choral Dirs. Assn. (chmn. cmty. choirs 2002—04), Music Educators Nat. Conf., Am. Choral Dirs. Assn. (chmn. cmty. choirs southwest divsn. 2004—), Pope John Paul II Cultural Ctr., Omicron Delta Kappa, Pi Kappa Lambda, Phi Mu Alpha Sinfonia. Home: 1017 S Ann Drive Marshall MO 65340 Office: Marshall Public Schs 805 S Miami Ave Marshall MO 65340 Office Phone: 660-886-2244.

SAYERS, GALE, computer company executive, retired professional football player; b. Wichita, Kans., May 30, 1943; s. Roger Earl and Bernice (Ross) S.; m. Ardythe Elaine Bullard, Dec. 1, 1973; children: Gale Lynne, Scott Aaron, Timothy Gale, Gaylon, Guy, Gary. Student phys. edn., Kans. U., N.Y. Inst. Finance. Running back Chgo. Bears Profl. Football Team, 1965—72; then asst. to athletic dir. Kans. U.; athletic dir. So. Ill. U., to 1981; v.p. mktg. Computer Suppy by Sayers, Northfield, Ill., 1984—86; pres. Crest Computer Supply Co., Skokie, Ill., 1986—; pres., CEO Sayers Computer Source, Mt. Prospect, Ill., 1983—2006, chmn.; pres., CEO Sayers40, Inc., Mt. Prospect, Ill., 2006—. Columnist Chgo. Daily News;

bd. dir. Global Healthcare Exchange, 2003. Author: (with Al Silverman) I Am Third, 1970. Co-chmn. legal def. fund sports com. NAACP; co-ordinator Reach-Out program, Chgo.; hon. chmn. Am. Cancer Soc.; commr. Chgo. Park Dist. Recipient numerous awards for playing, also holder numerous Nat. Football League records; named to Pro Football Hall of Fame, 1977 Mem. Kappa Alpha Psi. Office: Sayers Computer Source 1150 Feehanville Dr Mount Prospect IL 60056-6007

SAYERS, MARTIN PETER, pediatric neurosurgeon; b. Big Stone Gap, Va., Jan. 2, 1922; s. Delbert Bancroft and Loula (Thompson) S.; m. Marjorie W. Garvin, May 8, 1943; children: Daniel Garvin Sayers, Stephen Putnam Sayers, Julia Hathaway Sayers Bolton, Elaine King Sayers Buck. BA, Ohio State U., 1943, MD, 1945; postgrad., U. Pa., 1948-51. Intern Phila. Gen. Hosp., 1945-46; resident in neurosurgery U. Pa. Hosps., Phila., 1948-51; practice medicine specializing in neurosurgery Columbus, Ohio, 1951—; mem. faculty Ohio State U., Columbus, 1951-87, clin. prof. neurosurgery, 1968-87, emeritus, chief dept. pediatric neurosurgery, 1960-87. Cons. Bur. Crippled Children Services Ohio.; Neurosurgeon Project Hope, Ecuador, 1964, Ceylon, 1968, Cracow, Poland, 1979. Served as lt. jr. grade M.C. USN, 1946—48. Mem. Am. Assn. Neurol. Surgeons (chmn. pediatric sect.), Congress Neurol. Surgeons (pres.), Neurosurg. Soc. Am. (pres.), Am. Soc. Pediatric Neurosurgery, Soc. Neurol. Surgeons. Office: 931 Chatham Ln Columbus OH 43221-2417

SAYKIEWICZ-SAJKIEWICZ, JAN NAPOLEON, marketing educator; b. Lublin, Poland, June 10, 1939; arrived in U.S., 1987; s. Jan Sajkiewicz and Ewa Komorowska; m. Elzbieta Katarzyna Przetacznik, Aug. 27, 1966; children: Jan Rafal, Olaf Xawery, Mateusz Konstanty. MS in Econs., Ctrl. Sch. Planning & Stats., Warsaw, Poland, 1962, PhD, 1969; diploma in African studies, U. Warsaw, 1968; diploma, U. Calif., Berkeley, 1972. Cert. internat. tourism profl. Rsch. assoc. U. Calif., Berkeley, 1972-73; asst., assoc. prof. Ctrl. Sch. Planning & Stats., Warsaw, 1962-75; lectr. in mktg. Exec. Tng. Ctrs., Warsaw, 1969-88; assoc. prof. U. Warsaw, 1974-88; lectr., prof. Warsaw Acad. Arts, 1980-87; prof. Duquesne U. Sch. Bus. Adminstrn., Pitts., 1987—, L. Kozminski Acad. Entrepreneurship and Mgmt., Warsaw, 1998—. Vis. prof. Fordham U., N.Y.C., 1978, Duquesne U., Pitts., 1981, No. Jiaotong U., Beijing, 1997, Rome Campus, Italy, 2005. Duquesne U. Rome Campus Italy, 2005; Fulbright prof., 2000-2001; expert Internat. Labor Orgn., Geneva, 1982; vice-chmn., bd. dirs. Consumer Cooperative Enterprises, Warsaw, 1982-88; mem. Inter-Polcom, Chamber of Industry, Commerce, Warsaw, 1984-86; sec. gen., chief treas. Polish Mktg. Assn., 1974-81, exec. bd., 1985-88 Author: Concentration of Commercial Activities, 1972, Marketing Concept in Business Management, 1975, 2nd edit., 1976, 3rd edit., 1977, Management Systems in Integrated Capitalist Business, 1975; contbr. articles to profl. jours.; transl. profl. lit. Active Solidarity Movement, Poland, 1980-81; social and econ. coun., The Capital City of Warsaw, Poland, 1987-88. Recipient Silver and Gold Crosses of Merit, Coun. of State, Poland, 1980, 1982, Individual award for pedagogical performance, Min. Edn., Poland, 1981, Golden Mermaid Hon. Decoration for svc., Capital City of Warsaw, 1985, Akdeniz Univ. award, Turkey, 2002, award, Fulbright Fgn. Scholarship Bd. and U.S. Dept. State, 2002, Spl. award, Lansbridge U. and Kingston Coll., Can., 2003, Recognition award, Maastricht Sch. Mgmt., The Netherlands, 2004, Fourteenth World Bus. Congress Spl. Svc. award, Internat. Mgmt. Devel. Assn., Fundacion Euroarabe, and Euroarab Mgmt. Sch., Granada Spain, 2005, Internat. Mgmt. Devel. Assn. award, Sixteenth World Bus. Congress, Netherlands, 2007; vis. scholar, U. Calif., Berkeley, 1972—73, Fordham U., N.Y., 1978, No. Jiaotong U., Beijing, 1997, fellow, Ford Found., 1972—73, rsch. grantee, U.S. Dept. Edn., 1993, 1994. Fellow: Am. Acad. Mktg. Sci.; mem.: Polish Inst. Arts and Scis. in Am. (bd. dirs. 1995—97, adv. coun. 2003—, chmn. 2004—), Am. Mktg. Assn. (profl. and exec. mem.), Acad. Internat. Bus., Internat. Mgmt. Devel. Assn. (exec. v.p. 1997, pres. 2002, chmn. bd. regional dirs. 2005, chair bd. regional dirs. 2005, award 2001, Spl. Svc. award 2005). Roman Catholic. Avocations: social studies, books, travel, cognac. Home: 5853 Douglas St Pittsburgh PA 15217-2101 E-mail: saykiewicz@duq.edu.

SAYLER, DONNA L., secondary school educator, director; b. Nov. 2, 1953; BA, Northeastern Ill. U., Chgo., 1975; MA, Alverno Coll., Milw., 2003, Lewis U., Ill., 2004. Tchr. Spanish Milw. Pub. Schs., 1975—97, Shorewood H.S., Shorewood, Wis., 1997—2003; chair dept. world langs. Homewood-Flossmore H.S., Ill., 2003—. Mem.: Am. Assn. Tchrs. Spanish & Portuguese., Am. Coun. Tchrs. Fgn. Langs. Office: 999 Jedzie Ave Flossmoor IL 60422

SAYLER, ROBERT NELSON, lawyer, educator; b. Kansas City, Mo., June 1, 1940; s. John William and Roberta (Nelson) S.; m. Martha Leith, Aug. 1962; children: Christina, Bentley. BA, Stanford U., 1962; JD, Harvard U., 1965. Bar: U.S. Dist. Ct. D.C. 1966, U.S. Ct. Appeals (D.C. cir.) 1966, U.S. Supreme Ct. 1971, D.C. 1972, U.S. Ct. Appeals (2d cir.) 1977. From assoc. to ptnr. Covington & Burling, Washington, 1965—; prof. U. Va., 2003—. Vis. prof. U. Va., 1995, 2002. V.p. Neighborhood Legal Services, Washington, 1980-82; pres. Legal Aid Soc., Washington, 1983-84. Fellow Am. Bar Found., Am. Coll. Trial Lawyers; mem. ABA (dir. programs, program chmn. 1981, 85, coun., chmn. litigation sect., mem. standing com. on fed. judiciary). Democrat. Office: Covington & Burling PO Box 7566 1201 Pennsylvania Ave NW Washington DC 20004-2401 also: U Va Sch Law 580 Massie Rd Charlottesville VA 22903-1789 Office Phone: 434-924-4741. E-mail: rns5b@virginia.edu.

SAYLES, EVA, artist; b. NYC, June 10, 1928; BA, Bklyn. Coll., 1949; studied, Art Students League. Mem. coop. Amos Eno Gallery, NYC, 1989—; pub. spkr. in field. One-woman shows include Pen and Brush Club, NYC, 1971 (1st prize in mems. oil exhibit), St. Bartholomew's Ch., NYC, 1970, Amos Eno Art Gallery, 1992, Port Chester Coun. for Arts, 1992; exhibited in group shows at Queens Mus., NYC, 1983, Knickerbocker Artists Exhibit, NYC, 1970, Pen and Brush Club, 1970, Marcolio Ltd., 1969, Vera Lazuk Galler, Cold Springs Harbor, 1966, Greenwich Art Soc., Conn., 1987, Nat. Assn. Women Artists; represented in private collections; appearances on TV and radio; contbr. articles (newspapers) Greenwich Time, Conn., Jour. News, Westchester, NY; contbr. poetry to anthologies. Bd. dirs. Port Chester Coun. Arts, NY, 1989—. Recipient prize, Art Students League; scholar. Mem. Nat. Assn. Women Artists (publicity, advt., grantwriting chairwoman), Pen and Brush Club (publicity chairwoman, first prize for painting called Life), Greenwich Arts Coun., Greenwich Art Soc., Oratorio Soc. (choir mem.). Achievements include always painting scientific theories of cells and molecules, especially in the sixties. Avocations: music, singing, writing, dance, philosophy. Studio: PO Box 510 Port Chester NY 10573-0510

SAYLES, LEONARD ROBERT, management educator, consultant; b. Rochester, NY, Apr. 30, 1926; s. Robert and Rose (Sklof) S.; m. Kathy Ripin; children: Robert, Emily. BA with highest distinction, U. Rochester, 1946; PhD in Econs. and Social Sci., MIT, 1950. Asst. prof. Cornell U., 1950-53, U. Mich., 1953-56; prof. emeritus Grad. Sch. Bus. Adminstrn., Columbia U., 1956-91, prof. bus. adminstrn., 1962—, head div. indsl. relations and orgnl. behavior, 1960-72; adviser to adminstr. NASA, 1966-71; sr. rsch. scientist Ctr. for Creative Leadership, Greensboro, N.C., 1988-94. Disting. vis. lectr. McGill U., 1974; bd. govs. Center for Creative Leadership, 1984-88. Author: (with G. Strauss) The Local Union, 1953, Managerial Behavior, 1964, Human Behavior in Organizations, 1966, (with E. Chapple) Measure of Management, 1961, Behavior of Industrial Work Groups, 1958, Individualism and Big Business, 1963, (with W. Dowling) How Managers Motivate, 1971, (with M. Chandler) Managing Large Systems; Organizations for the Future, 1971, 2d edit., 1993, (with G. Strauss) Personnel, 4th edit, 1980, Managing Human Resources, 2d edit, 1981, Leadership, 1979, (with R. Burgelman) Inside Corporate Innovation, 1985, Managing in Real Organizations, 1989, The Working Leader, 1993, (with K. Ripin) Insider Strategies for Outsourcing Information Systems, 1999, (with C. Smith) The Rise of the Rogue Executive, 2004; mem. editorial bd. Human Orgn., 1957-62 Trustee Seacrest Sch., 1996-97. Fellow Am. Anthropol. Assn.; mem. Phi Beta Kappa.

SAYLES, WAYNE GERALD, numismatist, writer; b. Waukesha, Wis., Mar. 8, 1943; s. Wayne F. Sayles and Betty Joy Harris; m. Sharon L. Greshay, 1962 (div. 1982); m. Janet M. Foth Olson, 1984 (div. 1993); m. M. Doris Jean Ivey, 1997; children from previous marriage: Scott Allen, Steven Andrew, Stephanie Anne Sayles Bloedorn. B of Gen. Studies, U. Nebr., 1972; MA, U. Wis., 1986. Enlisted USAF, 1961, advanced through grades to capt., 1976, comdr. 2081st comms. squadron Goodfellow AFB, Tex., 1973, comdr. detachment 15, 2140 comm. group Athens, Greece, 1975, AF advisor to air res. forces and Air Nat. Guard, 1976—80, comm. sys., mil. airlift comd. inspector, 1980—82, ret., 1982; pres. Celator, Inc., Lodi, Wis., 1986—; exec. dir. Ancient Coin Collectors Guild, Gainesville, Mo., 2004—. Pub. Clio's Cabinet, Lodi, Wis., 1986—. Editor: (jour.) The Celator; author: Ancient Coin Collecting, vol. I, 1996, 2d edit., 2003, Ancient Coin Collecting, vol. II, 1997, Ancient Coin Collecting, vol. III, 1997, 2d edit., 2007, Ancient Coin Collecting, vol. IV, 1998, Ancient Coin Collecting, vol. V, 1998, Ancient Coin Collecting, vol. VI, 1999, Turkoman Figural Bronze Coins and Their Iconography, 2 vols., 1992—96, The Ned H. and Gloria A. Griner Greek and Roman Coin Collection, Ball State U. Mus. Art, 2002, monographs; contbr. articles to encys. Sec. Ancient Coin Collectors Guild, Gainesville, Mo., 2004—04; bd. edn. Am. Cmty. Schs., Athens, 1974—75; v.p. bd. edn. Lodi Sch. Dist., Wis., 1988—93. Decorated Meritorious Svc. medal with two oak leaf clusters USAF, Commendation medal, Nat. Def. Svc. medal, Armed Forces Expeditionary medal; recipient Minute Man award, Air NG, 1980, Numismatic Ambassador award, Krause Publs., 2006, Exceptional Contbns. Ancient Numismatics award, Ancient Coin Collectors Guild, 2006. Fellow: Royal Numis. Soc. (London), Am. Numis. Soc. (life); mem.: Numis. Lit. Guild (Extraordinary Merit award 1988), Oriental Numis. Soc., Classical and Medieval Numis. Soc., Am. Israel Numis. Assn. (life), Hellenic Numis. Soc. (life). Achievements include founder of The Celator, numismatic journal; founder of the Ancient Coin Collectors Guild. Avocations: coin collecting/numismatics, travel, genealogy. Home and Office: Ancient Coin Collectors Guild PO Box 911 Gainesville MO 65655 Office Phone: 417-679-2142. Personal E-mail: wayne@ancientcoins.ac. Business E-Mail: director@accg.us.

SAYLOR, CHARLES HORACE, lawyer, judge; b. Bethlehem, Pa., Jan. 6, 1950; s. Howard James and Florence M. (Glasser) S.; m. Martha Louise Weaver, July 10, 1971; children: Amy Louise, Matthew Charles. BA, Pa. State U., 1971; JD, Dickinson Sch. Law, 1974. Bar: Pa. 1974, U.S. Dist. Ct. (mid. dist.) Pa. 1979. Law clk. Northumberland County Ct. Common Pleas, Sunbury, Pa., 1974-76; assoc. Wiest & Wiest, Sunbury, 1976-79; ptnr. Wiest, Wiest & Saylor, Sunbury, 1979-85, Wiest, Wiest, Saylor & Muolo, Sunbury, 1985-97, Wiest, Saylor, Muolo, Noon and Swinehart, Sunbury, 1998—2001; judge Court of Common Pleas, Northumberland County, Pa., 2002—. Solicitor Twp. of Rush, Pa., 1979-2001, Twp. of Point, Pa., 1983-2001, County of Northumberland, 1993-95; instr. Pa. State U., Schuylkill Haven, 1986. Asst. editor: Dickinson Law Rev., 1973, Northumberland (Pa.) Legal Jour., 1987—2001. Trustee Northumberland County Law Libr., 1986-2001, Priestley-Forsyth Meml. Libr., Northumberland, 1988-93, v.p., 1990-93; coach Am. Youth Soccer Assn., Northumberland, 1988-90; mem. com. YMCA, Sunbury, 1987-98, bd. dirs., 1991—, pres. of bd. dirs., 1997-98, chmn. sustaining campaign, 1992; asst. coach Girls Track and Field, Shikellamy H.S., 1992-93; profls. co-chair United Way, 2000-01. Mem. Pa. Bar Assn., Northumberland County Bar Assn. (sec.-treas. 1985-2000, pres. 2001), Pa. Trial Lawyers Assn., Sunbury Rotary Club (pres. 2006-07). Republican. Roman Catholic. Avocations: running, golf. Home: 233 Honey Locust Ln Northumberland PA 17857-9679 Office: Northumberland County Courthouse 201 Market St Sunbury PA 17801 Office Phone: 570-988-5445.

SAYLOR, DAVID J., lawyer; b. Johnstown, Pa., Sept. 12, 1945; AB, Williams Coll., 1967; JD, Harvard U., 1970. Bar: Hawaii 1971, D.C. 1972; U.S. Ct. Appeals (D.C. cir. 1973, 2d cir. 1980, 3rd cir. 1987, 11 cir. 1988); U.S. Supreme Ct. 1974. Law clk. to Chief Judge U.S. Dist. Ct., Honolulu, 1970-71; asst. dir. Bur. of Competition Fed. Trade Commn., 1975-78; dep. gen. counsel Fed. Comm. Commn., 1978-81; mem. Hogan & Hartson, Washington, ptnr. Wash., DC. Lectr. in field. Contbr. articles to profl. jours. Mem. DC Bar Assn., ABA (antitrust sect., litig. sect., sci. & tech. sect.), Fed. Comm. Bar Assn. Mem. bd. editors: Harvard Law Review, 1969-70. Office: Hogan & Hartson Columbia Square 555 13th St NW Ste 800E Washington DC 20004-1161 Office Phone: 202-637-8679. Office Fax: 202-637-5910. Business E-Mail: djsaylor@hhlaw.com.

SAYLOR, MAURICE MICHAEL, composer, director, music librarian; b. Neptune, NJ, Aug. 13, 1957; s. Franklin Bertrue Saylor and Gladys Annabelle Schlicting. MusB, The Cath. U. Am., Washington, DC, 1980, MusM, 1984, MS in LS, 2005. Exec. dir. Capital Composers Alliance, Washington, 1987—. Composer: (large choral work) The Hunting of the Snark: An Agony in Eight Fits, (song set) Laudis Corona (Diana Barnhart Am. Song award, 2005), (chamber music) String Quartet #1 in D (David Lloyd Kreeger Creativity award, 1987). Grant, Md. State Arts Coun., The Am. Composer Forum. Mem.: BMI. Home: 644 Franklin St NE Washington DC 20017-1318 Office: The Catholic U Am BTR Sch Music Ward Hall Washington DC 20064 Home Phone: 202-526-2623; Office Phone: 202-319-5424. Personal E-mail: saylor57@bigfoot.com. Business E-Mail: saylor@cua.edu.

SAYLOR, PETER M., architect; b. Phila., July 26, 1941; s. Harry T. and Dorothy (Johnson) S.; m. Caroline Metcalf, Apr. 4, 1970; children: Thomas S., Elizabeth B. BArch, U. Pa., 1963, MArch, 1965. Registered arch., Iowa, Pa., N.J., Ind., Wis., Conn., Ohio, Minn. Architect Mitchell-Giurgola, Phila., 1967-70; ptnr. Dagit-Saylor Architects, Phila., 1970—. Design critic, juror U. Pa., 1975—; bd. dirs. Found. for Architecture, Phila., 1980-90. Bd. dirs. Chestnut Hill Cmty. Assn., Phila., 1976—79, v.p., 1979; bd. dirs. All Saints Hosp., Wyndmoor, Pa., 1981—86, Cathedral Village Retirement Cmty., 1998—2001. Recipient various bldg. design award Fellow AIA (bd. dirs. Phila. chpt. 1973-82, chpt. pres. 1981-82); mem. Pa. Soc. Archs., Chestnut Hill Hist. Soc. (bd. dirs. 1988-95, pres. 1989-92), Phila. Soc. Preservation of Landmarks (bd. dirs. 1989-96, pres. 1993-94), Phila. Mus. Art (friends bd. dirs. 1990-93), Phila. Cricket Club (bd. dirs. 1985-91), Mask and Wig Club (pres. 1980-81, bd. dirs. 1970-84). Republican. Episcopalian. Office: Dagit-Saylor Archs 100 S Broad St Philadelphia PA 19110-1023 Office Phone: 215-972-0500. E-mail: psaylor@dagitsaylor.com.

SAYLOR, THOMAS G., state supreme court justice; b. Meyersdale, Pa., Dec. 14, 1946; BA in Govt., U. Va., 1969; JD, Columbia U., 1972; LLM, U. Va., 2004. Atty. pvt. practice, 1972—82; 1st asst. dist. atty. Somerset County, 1973-76; dir. Pa. Bur. Consumer Protection, 1982-83; 1st dep. atty. gen. Commonwealth of Pa., 1983-87; atty. pvt. practice, 1987—93; judge Pa. Superior Ct., 1993—97; justice Pa. Supreme Ct., 1997—. Contbr. articles to legal publications. Bd. overseers Widener U. Sch. Law. Mem. ABA, Am. Law Inst., Pa. Bar Assn., Cumberland County Bar Assn., Dauphin County Bar Assn., Appellate Judges Conf. Office: Fulton Bldg 16th Fl 200 N 3d St Harrisburg PA 17101

SAYLORS, CHARLES J., educational association administrator, construction executive; m. Teresa Saylors; children: Matthew, Jennifer, Tyler, William. Mktg. exec. Construction Mgmt. Divsn. M.B. Kahn Construction. Trustee Sch. Dist. of Greenville County, SC; bd. mem. Greenville Tech. Coll., Greenville Family Partnership; bd. mem., former pres. Roper Mountain Sci. Ctr.; mem, deacon Hampton Heights Baptist Ch.; exec. bd. mem. Blue Ridge Coun./Boy Scouts of Am. Mem.: Nat. PTA (sec.-treas. 2005—07, pres.-elect 2007—), SC PTA (former v.p., treas., immediate past pres.). Office: PTA Nat Hdqs Ste 1300 541 N Fairbanks Ct Chicago IL 60611-3396 *

SAYRE, DAVID, physicist; b. NYC, Mar. 2, 1924; s. Ralph E. and Sylvia (Rosenbaum) S.; m. Anne Bowns, Dec. 26, 1947. BS, Yale U., 1944; MS, Auburn U., 1948; PhD, Oxford U., Eng., 1951. Staff mem. radiation lab. MIT, Cambridge, 1943-46; rsch. assoc. U. Pa., Phila., 1951-55; mathematician IBM Corp., NYC, 1955-59, corp. dir. programming, 1959-62; mem. rsch. staff IBM T.J. Watson Rsch. Ctr., Yorktown Heights, NY, 1962-90, ret., 1990. Cons. U.S. Office Naval Rsch., London, 1951; mem. U.S.A. Nat. Com. for Crystallography, 1952-55, 81-84, vice chmn., 1984-86; vis. fellow All Souls Coll., Oxford U., 1972-73; guest scientist dept. physics SUNY, Stony Brook, 1980-2004, adj. prof., 2004—; guest rschr. Brookhaven Nat. Lab., Upton, N.Y., 1983—; disting. guest prof. dept. chemistry Rutgers U., 1996-98. Co-author: Waveforms, 1947; editor: Computational Crystallography, 1983; co-editor: Structural Studies on Molecules of Biological Interest, 1983, X-Ray Microscopy II, 1988; contbr. numerous articles to profl. jours. Trustee Village of Head-of-the-Harbor, L.I., N.Y., 1975-95. Named one of Most Notable 20th Century Crystallographers, Hist. Atlas Crystallography. Mem. Am. Crystallographic Assn. (treas. 1952-55, pres. 1983, Fankuchen award 1989) Episcopalian. Achievements include development of atomicity-based direct phasing method for x-ray crystallography; development(with others) of first FORTRAN compiler and first virtual computer system; research in x-ray microscopy; measurement of (with others) x-ray diffraction pattern from single biol. cell; research in extension of x-ray crystallographic methods into field of non-crystals; obtaining with others of first diffraction microscopy images of yeast cell.

SAYRE, DONNA, elementary school educator; b. Goshen, NY; d. Wesley and Dorothea Sayre. BS summa cum laude in Edn., Bloomsburg U., 1995, MEd in Reading, 1997. Reading tchr. Port Jervis City Sch. Dist., NY, 1998—. Participant Relay for Life Am. Cancer Soc.; bd. mem. Amy Bull Crist Reading Coun., 2005—07; Sunday sch. tchr. Craigville Bible Ch., Chester, NY, 2005—07, nursery provider, 2005. Mem.: NY State Reading Assn., Internat. Reading Assn., Amy Bull Crist Reading Coun. (v.p. 2005—06).

SAYRE, EDWARD VALE, chemist; b. Des Moines, Sept. 8, 1919; s. Edward Agnew and Audrey (Vale) S.; m. Virginia Nelle Rogers, Oct. 20, 1943. BS, Iowa State U., 1941; AM, Columbia U., 1943, PhD, 1949. Mgr. rsch. sect. Manhattan Dist. project Columbia U., 1942-45; rsch. chemist Eastman Kodak Rsch. Labs., Rochester, N.Y., 1949-52; sr. chemist Brookhaven Nat. Lab., Upton, N.Y., 1952-84; rsch. phys. scientist Smithsonian Instn., Washington, 1984—. Dir. rsch. Museum Fine Arts, Boston, 1975-80, sr. scientist, 1980-84; sr. scientist Alexander von Humboldt Found., 1980; vis. lectr. Stevens Inst. Tech., 1955-61; adj. prof. fine arts Inst. Fine Arts, N.Y. U., 1960-74; disting. vis. prof. Am. U. Cairo, 1970; Regents prof. U. Calif., Irvine, 1972; mem. sci. adv. coun. Winterthur Mus. Contbr. numerous rsch. articles to profl. jours.; assoc. editor Archaeometry, 1969-93, Art and Archaeology Tech. Abstracts, 1970-87, Jour. Archaeol. Sci., 1971-77. Guggenheim fellow, 1969; recipient U.S. sr. scientist award Alexander von Humboldt Found., 1980-81, George von Hevesy medal, 1984, Alumni Disting. Achievement citation Iowa State U., 1996, Pomerance award Archaeol. Inst. Am., 1999. Fellow Internat. Inst. for Conservation of Hist. and Artistic Works, Am. Inst. for Conservation of Hist. and Artistic Works; mem. Am. Chem. Soc. Clubs: Cosmos. Home: Apt 616 1330 Massachusetts Ave NW Washington DC 20005-4152 E-mail: EVSayre@aol.com.

SAYRE, JOHN MARSHALL, lawyer, former government official; b. Boulder, Colo., Nov. 9, 1921; s. Henry Marshall and Lulu M. (Cooper) S.; m. Jean Miller, Aug. 22, 1943; children: Henry M., Charles Franklin, John Marshall Jr., Ann Elizabeth Sayre Taggart (dec.). BA, U. Colo., 1943, JD, 1948. Bar: Colo. 1948, U.S. Dist. Ct. Colo. 1952, U.S. Ct. Appeals (10th cir.) 1964. Law clk. trust dept. Denver Nat. Bank, 1948-49; asst. cashier, trust officer Nat. State Bank of Boulder, 1949-50; ptnr. Ryan, Sayre, Martin, Brotzman, Boulder, 1950-66, Davis, Graham & Stubbs, Denver, 1966-89, of counsel, 1993—; asst. sec. of the Interior for Water and Sci., 1989-93. Bd. dirs. Boulder Sch. Dist. 3, 1951-57; city atty. City of Boulder, 1952-55; gen. counsel Colo. Mcpl. League, 1959-63; prin. counsel No. Colo. Water Conservancy Dist. and mcpl. subdist., 1964-87, spl. counsel, 1987, bd. dirs. dist., 1960-64; former legal counsel Colo. Assn. Commerce and Industry. Lt. (j.g.) USNR, 1943-46, ret. Decorated Purple Heart; recipient William Lee Knous award U. Colo. Law Sch., 1999. Fellow Am. Bar Found. (life), Colo. Bar Found. (life); mem. ABA, Colo. Bar Assn., Boulder County Bar Assn. (pres. 1959), Denver Bar Assn., Nat. Water Resources Assn. (Colo. dir. 1980-89, 93-95, pres. 1984-86), Denver Country Club, Phi Beta Kappa, Phi Gamma Delta, Phi Delta Phi. Home: Park Place 111 Emerson St Apt 1462 Denver CO 80218 Office: Davis Graham & Stubbs 1550-17th St Ste 500 Denver CO 80202 E-mail: john.sayre@dgslaw.com.

SAYRE, PHIL, editor; BA, DePauw Univ., 1971; MA, Boston Univ. Reporter, editor Messenger-Inquirer, Owensboro, Ky., Argus Leader, Sioux Falls, SD, Trenton Times, NJ, The Record, Hackensack, NJ, New York Times, 1989—2002, asst. nat. editor, 2002, dep. political editor, 2003, currently night editor, nat. desk. Office: New York Times 229 W 43d St New York NY 10036 Office Phone: 212-556-7356. Office Fax: 212-556-7614.

SAYRE, RICHARD LAYTON, lawyer; b. Spokane, Wash., May 21, 1953; s. Charles Layton and Elizabeth Jane (Ward) S.; m. Karen Linda Sayre, Mar. 8, 1979; children: Wendi Sue Stoken, Tracey Lynn Turner. BA, U. Wash., 1976; JD, Gonzaga U., 1979. Bar: Wash. 1979, U.S. Dist. Ct. (ea. and we. dist.) Wash. 1979, U.S. Ct. Appeals (9th cir.) 1986; cert. elder law atty. Nat. Elder Law Found. Deputy prosecuting atty. Spokane County, Spokane, 1979-84; shareholder Underwood, Campbell, Brock & Cerutti, Spokane, 1984-92, Sayre & Sayre P.S., Spokane, 1992—. Pres. Nat. Acad. Elder Law Attys., Washington, 1995-96; apptd. by Wash. Supreme Ct., Washington Profl. Guardian Cert. Bd., 1998-2004; adj. prof. law Gonzaga U. Potentate, trustee El Katif Shrine Temple, Spokane, 1997; bd. govs. Shriner's Hosp. for Children, Spokane, 1993-96; exec. officer Order of DeMolay, Washington, 1993-2004, internat. supreme coun. Order DeMolay. Recipient Pro Bono award Spokane County Bar Assn., 1991, 99, 2003, Recognition of Achievement & Contribution award Lutheran Social Svcs. of Washington, Idaho, 1992, 97, Achievement award Spokane Sexual Assault Ctr., 1997, Disting. Svc. award Gonzaga U., 1997; named Super Lawyer, Washington Law & Politics, 2000-05. Mem. Nat. Acad. Elder Law Attys., Spokane Estate Planning Coun. Democrat. Episcopal. Avocations: sailing, skiing. Office: Sayre & Sayre 201 W North River Dr Ste 460 Spokane WA 99201-3203 Office Phone: 509-325-7330. Business E-Mail: dick@sayrelaw.com.

SAYRE, ROBERT FREEMAN, language educator; b. Columbus, Ohio, Nov. 6, 1933; s. Harrison M. and Mary (White) S.; (divorced); children—Gordon, Nathan, Laura; m. Hutha Refle, May 7, 1988. BA, Wesleyan U., Middletown, Conn., 1955; PhD, Yale U., 1962. Instr. English U. Ill., Urbana, 1961-63; Fulbright lectr. Lund (Sweden) U., 1963-65; faculty U. Iowa, 1965-72, prof. English, 1972-98, prof. emeritus, 1998—. Dir. inter-profl. seminars NEH, 1978, 79; Fulbright lectr. Montpellier, France,

1984; exch. prof. U. Copenhagen, 1988-89; mem. adv. bd. Leopold Ctr. for Sustainable Agr., 1994-2004, chair, 1996; pres. Johnson County Heritage Trust, 2000-04. Author: The Examined Self: Benjamin Franklin, Henry Adams and Henry James, 1964, Adventures, Rhymes and Designs of Vachel Lindsay, 1968; Thoreau and the American Indians, 1977; editor: A Week on the Concord and Merrimac Rivers, Walden, The Maine Woods, Cape Cod (H.D. Thoreau), 1985, Take This Exit: Rediscovering the Iowa Landscape, 1989, New Essays on Walden, 1992, American Lives: An Anthology of Autobiographical Writing, 1994, Recovering the Prairie, 1999, Take the Next Exit, 2000; contbr. articles to profl. jours. Guggenheim fellow, 1973-74.

SAYRE, ROBERT MARION, ambassador; b. Hillsboro, Oreg., Aug. 18, 1924; s. William Octavius and Mary Sayre; m. Elora Amanda Moyhihan, Dec. 29, 1951; children: Marian Amanda, Robert Marion, Daniel Humphrey. BA summa cum laude, Willamette U., 1949; JD cum laude (Alexander Welborn Weddell Peace prize 1956), George Washington U., 1956; MA, Stanford U., 1960; LLD, Willamette U., 1965. Bar: D.C. 1956, U.S. Ct. Appeals 1956, U.S. Supreme Ct. 1962. Joined U.S. Fgn. Service, 1949; econ. adviser on Latin Am., dir. Truman Point 4 Program, 1950-52; mil. adviser, 1952-57; officer charge inter-Am. security affairs, 1955-57; polit. counselor embassy Lima, Peru, 1957-59; fin. attache embassy Havana, Cuba, 1960; exec. sec. Task Force Latin Am., State Dept., Kennedy's Alliance for Progress, 1961; officer charge Mexican affairs Task Force Latin Am., State Dept., 1961-63; dep. dir. Office Caribbean and Mexican Affairs, 1963-64; dir. Office Mexican Affairs, 1964; sr. advisor White House, 1964-65; sr. dep. asst. sec. Bur. Inter-Am. Affairs, Dept. State, 1965-68; acting asst. sec. Dept. State, 1968—; Am. ambassador to Uruguay, 1968-69, to Panama, 1969-74; sr. insp. Dept. State, 1974-75, insp. gen., 1975-78; ambassador to Brazil, 1978-81; chmn. U.S. Interdepartmental group on Terrorism, dir. Counter-terrorism and Emergency Planning Dept. State, 1981-84, sr. insp., 1985; ptnr. IRC Group, Inc., 1986-87; from adv. to U.S. rep. to under sec. for mgmt. Orgn. of Am. States, 1987-94; sr. assoc. Global Bus. Access, Ltd., Washington, 1995—; chair Open Forum Working Group on Internat. Econs. U.S. Dept. State, 1995-96. Sr. councilor Atlantic Coun. Washington Inst. Fgn. Affairs. Capt. AUS, WWII; col. Res., ret. Decorated Soc. Cross (Brazil); Cross of Balboa (Panama); recipient Outstanding Employee award Dept. State, 1952, Superior Honor awards, 1964, 75, Disting. Honor award, 1978, Outstanding Performance award, 1982-85, Presdl. Meritorious award, 1986, Fgn. Svc. Cup award, 1990, Sec.'s Cert. of Appreciation, U.S. Dept. State, 1996. Mem. Am. Acad. Diplomacy, Inter Am. Bar Assn., Inter Am. Dialogue, Atlantic Coun. Washington Inst. Fgn. Affairs, Cosmos Club, Dacor House, Blue Key, Phi Delta Theta, Phi Eta Sigma, Tau Kappa Alpha. Episcopalian. Home: 3714 Bent Branch Rd Falls Church VA 22041-1028 Office: Global Business Access Ltd 1825 I St NW Ste 400 Washington DC 20006-5415

SAYRE, SUSAN KATHRYN GREENWALD, musician, educator; b. Mar. 9, 1939; m. Donald R. Sayre (dec.); children: Donald R. Jr., Mark, Kathryn Sayre Williams, Michelle Sayre Sinistore, Suzanne Sayre Lewandoski, Lena Marie. BA in Edn., San Diego State U.; Med, Temple U., Phila. Tchr. grades 3-4 Santee Sch. Dist., Calif., 1963—64; tchr. grade 3 Santee Elem. Sch., 1964—65; sub. tchr. LA City Schs., 1965—68, Somers Ctrl. Sch., 1994—2004; tchr. grade 1 Mt. Gillen Elem. Sch., 1968—70; spl. ed. tchr. Kuser Elem. Sch., NJ, 1970—72, McCombs Jr. High, Bronx, NY, 1982—84, 2004—; music tchr. Asbury Play & Learn, Asbury Meth. Ch., NY, 1973—81; ESL tchr. Japan Internat. Adolescent Autistic Unit, Tokyo, 1984—87, Bedford Hills Correctional Facility, NY, 1987—90, Westchester CC, Yonkers, NY, 1990—94. Organist Cajon Valley Ch., Cold Springs Presbyn. Ch.; choir dir, organist Armonk Meth. Ch. Mem. Asbury Meth. Ch., 1972—. Office: Asbury United Meth Ch Old Post Rd Croton On Hudson NY 10520

SAYRES, EDWIN J., JR., animal welfare organization administrator; b. White Plains, NY, Nov. 25, 1948; s. Edwin J. and Catherine Marie (Phelan) S.; m. Michelle Diane Dimino, May 21, 1978; children: Christopher, Alexander. BA, Calif. State U., Sonoma, 1970, MA, 1972. Dir. Marin Found., San Rafael, Calif., 1970-74; dir. edn. St. Hubert's Giralda, Madison, N.J., 1974-79, v.p., 1978-81, pres., 1982—95; dir. animal protection divsn. Am. Humane Assn., 1995—97; pres. San Francisco SPCA, 1998—2003; pres., CEO ASPCA, NYC, 2003—. Mem. Humane Soc. U.S., Delta Soc. Lodges: Rotary. Office: ASPCA 424 E 92nd St New York NY 10128

SAYSON, JOSELITO, physical therapist, educator; b. Manila, Philippines, June 19, 1963; s. Alfredo Cruz Sayson and Elvina Valcos; m. Nancy Islan Sayson, July 8, 1995; 1 child, Jade Islan. BS in Physical Therapy, U. Santo Tomas, Republic the Philippines, 1984; M in Orthop. Manual Therapy, Ola Grimsby Inst. Consortium, Salt Lake City, 1995, D in Manual Therapy, 2002. Cert. manual therapy part I Ola Grimsby Inst., McHenry, Ill., 1992, manual therapy part II Ola Grimsby Inst. Consortium, San Diego, 1996, lic. physical therapist Ill., Tex., Philippines. Chief physical therapist Cardinal Santos Meml., Metro-Manila, Philippines, 1985—86; dir. physical therapy Stephens Meml. Hosp., Breckenridge, Tex., 1986; temporary dir. physical therapy Continental Hosp. Suburban, Ft. Worth, 1986; dir. physical therapy in-patient svcs. Spohn-Kleberg Meml. Hosp., Kingsville, Tex., 1986; dir. physical therapy Brewster Meml. Hosp., Alpine, Tex., 1986—89; asst. dir. physical therapy St. Mary's Hosp., Kankakee, 1989—90; dir. Pro-Tech. Physical Therapy Ctr., Kankakee, Ill., 1990—91; dir., mgr. Bourbonnais Rehab. Ctr. St. Mary's Hosp., Bourbonnais, 1991—93; dir. Bradley Rehab. Ctr. St. Mary's Hosp., Ill., 1992—93; dir., owner Newsome & Sayson Physical Therapy Specialists, Kankakee, Ill., 1993—2000; instr. orthop. manual therapy part I Ola Grimsby Inst. Consortium, San Diego, 1996—98, instr., physician physical therapy in orthop. manual therapy program, 1999—; mgr. United Physical Therapy, Kankakee, 2003—06; pres. Jojo Sayson's Performance Physical Therapy Svcs. LLC, Bourbonnaise, 2000—06, Jojo Sayson's Flexeon Rehab.: PPTS Clinics, 2006—. Mem. Bradley-Bourbonnais C. of C., 1993—, Kankakee C. of C., 1993—; vol. physical therapist Cardinal Santos Meml. Hosp., Metro-Manila, Philippines, 1984; v.p. internat. affairs U. Santo Tomas Alumni Assn. Inc., Manila, Philippines, 2006—. Fellow: Am. Acad. Orthop. Manual Physical Therapists; mem.: Ill. Physical Therapy Assn., Am. Physical Therapy Assn., Aerospace Med. Assn., Nat. Strength and Conditioning Assn., Kankakee Lions Club Internat. (officer lion tail twister 2006—, officer lion tamer 1997—98, officer lion tail twister 1998—99, officer tail twister 2001—02, mem. presdl. com. 2004—05, officer lion tail twister 2005—06, Lion the Yr. award 1989, 2001), Rotary Internat. Avocations: bodybuilding, comic book collecting, jazz, ballet, dance. Office: Flexeon Rehab 586 William Latham Dr Ste 3 & 4 Bourbonnais IL 60914

SAYWELL, WILLIAM GEORGE GABRIEL, business development and management consultant; b. Regina, Sask., Can., Dec. 1, 1936; s. John Ferdinand Tupper and Vera Marguerite S.; m. Helen Jane Larmer; children: Shelley Jayne, William James Tupper, Patricia Lynn. BA, U. Toronto, 1960, MA, 1961, PhD, 1968; LLD (hon.), U. B.C., 1994, Simon Fraser U., 1997. Asst. prof. dept. East Asian studies U. Toronto, 1963-69, asst. prof., 1969-71, assoc. prof. RDt., 1971-82, prof., 1982-83, chmn. dept., 1971-76; prof. dept. history, pres., vice chancellor Simon Fraser U., Burnaby, B.C., Can., 1983-93; pres., chief exec. officer Asia Pacific Found. of Can., Vancouver, B.C., 1993-99; vice chmn. Intercedent Ltd., 1999—; pres. William Saywell & Assocs., Vancouver, 1999—. Cons. in higher edn.; sinologist and 1st sec. Can. Embassy, Beijing, 1972-73; dir. U. Toronto-York U. Ctr. Modern East Asia, 1974-75; prin. Innis Coll., 1976-79; vice provost U. Toronto, 1979-83; dir. Tokyo-Mitsubishi Bank (Can.), VLinx Ltd. Author articles and revs. on Chinese affairs to profl. jours. Decorated Order of Can., Order of BC.

SAZANT, NEIL S., real estate investor and developer; Degree in fin., U. Fla.; JD, Nova Southeastern Law Sch. Lic. atty. Worked on talent contracts Sony Pictures Entertainment, LA; corp. counsel Universal Studios in Corp. Ops.; pres. Martin W. Taplin & Assocs., Inc. Pres. Harbour Realty Advisors. Martin W. Taplin & Assocs., Inc. is a company who has bought, managed and sold over 6 million dollars of every kind of real estate throughout the US; company was one of several approved by the FDIC to manage troubled real estate portfolios over 1 million dollars. Achievements include developing several key pieces of real estate in South Florida; rehabilitation and development of the boutique hotel, The Sagamore; development of a mixed use project in Bay Harbor Islands, which includes office, retail, residential and the new Starwood Hotel concept, Aloft by W Hotels.

SAZEGAR, MORTEZA, artist; b. Tehran, Iran, Nov. 11, 1933; s. Hassan Ali and Zahra (Frootan) S.; m. Patricia Jean Kaurich, July 13, 1959. BA, U. Tex., El Paso, 1955, BS, 1956; postgrad., Baylor U. Coll. Medicine, 1956-57, Cornell U., 1958-59. One man exhibitions include, Poindexter Gallery, N.Y.C., 1964, 67, 69, 71, 73, 75, 77, group exhibitions include, Detroit Inst. Arts, 1965, Chgo. Art Inst., 1965, Univ. Art Mus., U. Tex., Austin, 1965, 72, Whitney Mus. Am. Art, 1970, Cleve. Mus. Art, 1972, Corcoran Gallery Art, Washington, 1973, Tyler Sch. Art, Temple U., Phila., 1979; represented in permanent collections, Whitney Mus. Am. Art, N.Y.C., San Francisco Mus. Modern Art, Riverside Mus., N.Y.C., U. Mass., Amherst, Corcoran Gallery Art, Prudential Ins. Corp. Am., Mus. Contemporary Art, Tehran, Iran. Mem. Artists Equity Assn. Democrat. Address: 1223 Homeville Rd Cochranville PA 19330-1712

SAZHIN, SERGEY VICTOROVICH, electrochemist, researcher; b. Alma-Ata, Kazakhstan, USSR, Oct. 24, 1953; s. Victor Sergeevich and Vera Kuz'minichna Sazhin; m. Elena Mikhaylovna S., Mar. 20, 1976; children: Victoria Sergeevna, Tat'yana Sergeevna. MS with honors, Kiev Poly. Inst., Ukraine, 1977, PhD, 1981. Rsch. engr. Kiev Poly. Inst., 1977; sr. engr. Inst. Gen. and Inorganic Chemistry, USSR Acad. Scis. Ukraine, Kiev, 1980-82, jr. rsch. scientist, 1982-84, sr. rsch. scientist, 1984-95; prin. rschr. Samsung Display Devices Co., Ltd., Suwon, Republic of Korea, 1995-98; sr. scientist, mgr. electroanalysis group Moltech Corp., Tucson, 1999-2000; mgr. Lithium Sys., prin. investigator Rayovac Corp., Madison, Wis., 2001—. Patentee in field; contbr. over 50 articles to profl. jours. and conf. procs. Recipient Bronze medal Exhbn. Nat. Economy Achievements USSR, 1982, Inventor award USSR, 1985, Samsung Display Devices Paper Contest, 1996. Achievements include development of advanced batteries. Mailing: 25 Laramie Ct Madison WI 53719 Office: Rayovac Corp 630 Forward Dr Madison WI 53711 E-mail: sazhin@hotmail.com.

SCACCHETTI, DAVID J., lawyer; b. Newark, July 13, 1956; s. Edmond and Evelyn Scacchetti; m. Marcia Ellen Gessiness, Aug. 31, 1985; children: Gabriella Elise, Olivia Beth. BA in Polit. Sci. with honors, U. Cin., 1978, JD, 1981. Bar: Ohio 1982, U.S. Dist. Ct. (so. dist.) Ohio 1982, U.S. Dist. Ct. (ea. dist.) Ky. 1986, U.S. Dist. Ct. Ariz. 1997, U.S. Dist. Ct. (so. dist.), 6th Cir. Ct. Appeals, 7th Cir. Ct. Appeals. Sole practitioner, Cin., 1982-98; atty. Scacchetti & Scacchetti, Cin., 1998—. Mem. ATLA, Nat. Assn. Criminal Def. Lawyers, Greater Cin. Criminal Def. Lawyer Assn., Ohio Acad. Trial Lawyers, Ham. County Trial Lawyers Assn., Phi Beta Kappa. Avocations: writing, tennis, tribal art, guitar, travel.

SCACCHI, GRETA, actress; b. Milan, Feb. 18, 1960; m. Vincent D'Onofrio, 1991 (div. 1993); 2 children. Films include Das Zweite Gesicht, 1982, Heat and Dust, 1982, Defence of the Realm, 1985, The Coca-Cola Kid, 1985, White Mischief, 1987, Un Homme Amoureux, 1987, Good Morning, Babylon, 1987, Paura e Amore, 1988, La Donna della Luna, 1988, Presumed Innocent, 1990, Turtle Beach, 1991, Fires Within, 1991, The Player, 1992, Desire, 1993, Country Life, 1994, The Browning Version, 1994, Jefferson in Paris, 1995, Emma, 1996, Bravo Randy, 1996, The Serpent's Kiss, 1997, Tom's Midnight Garden, 1998, The Red Violin, 1998, Ladies Room, 1999, The Manor, 1999, Looking for Alibrandi, 2000, Festival in Cannes, 2001, Baltic Storm, 2003, Beyond the Sea, 2004, Syriana, 2005, The Book of Revelation, 2005; TV movies include The Ebony Tower, 1984, Camille, 1984, Dr. Fischer of Geneva, 1985, Rasputin, 1996 (Emmy award), The Odyssey, 1997, Macbeth, 1998; (TV mini series) Waterfront, 1984, The Farm, 2001, Daniel Deronda, 2002.

SCACCIA, FRANK JOHN, plastic surgeon, otolaryngologist; b. Teaneck, NJ, June 21, 1959; s. Ralph John and Angelina Josephine Scaccia. BS magna cum laude, Duke U., Durham, NC, 1981; MD, Wake Forest U., Winston-Salem, NC, 1985. Diplomate Am. Bd. Facial Plastic and Reconstructive Surgery, Am. Bd. Otolaryngology and Head and Neck Surgery. Resident in gen. surgery Monmouth Med. Ctr., Long Branch, NJ, 1985—88; resident in otolaryngology Case Western Res. U., Cleve., 1988—92; surgeon Otolaryngology Assocs., Red Bank, NJ, 1992—98; surgeon, CEO Riverside Plastic Surgery and Sinus Ctr., Red Bank, 1998—. Mem. staff Riverview Med. Ctr., Red Bank, Bayshore Cmty. Hosp., Holmdel, NJ. Contbr. articles to med. jours. Vol. surgeon Face to Face, 1992—; vol. Parker Clinic, Red Bank. Named Top Beauty Dr., NJ Savvy Living, 2005, Top NY Metro Dr., Castle Connolly, 2006, Am. Top Dr., 2006, Top NJ Beauty Dr., 2006; recipient Jack Anderson prize for scholastic excellence, Am. Bd. Facial Plastic and Reconstructive Surgery, 1995. Fellow: ACS, Internat. Coll. Surgeons, Am. Acad. Facial Plastic and Reconstructive Surgery, Am. Acad. Otolaryngology; mem.: NJ Med. Soc., Monmouth County Med. Soc., Phi Beta Kappa. Avocations: running, bicycling, classical guitar. Home: 700 Ocean Ave Unit # 1 Sea Bright NJ 07760 Office: 70 E Front St Ste 3 Red Bank NJ 07701 Office Phone: 732-747-5300.

SCADDEN, DAVID THOMAS, hematologist, oncologist, research scientist; b. 1953; BA in English Lit., Bucknell U.; MD, Case Western Res. U., 1980. Diplomate Am. Bd. Internal Medicine. Intern Brigham-Women's Hosp., Boston, 1980-81, resident in internal medicine, 1981-83, fellow in hematology/oncology, 1983-86; staff Dana Farber Inst. Brigham & Women's Hosp., Boston, 1986—; prof. medicine Harvard U.; co-dir. Harvard Stem Cell Initiative, AIDS Rsch. Ctr. for Ptnrs. Health Care, Mass. Gen. Hosp., AIDS Rsch. Ctr., Brigham and Women's Hosp.; dir. Center for Regenerative Medicine and Tech., Mass. Gen. Hosp.; chief of hematologic malignancies Mass. Gen. Hosp. Co-chmn. Dept. of Stem Cell and Regenerative Biology; mem. bd. of scientific counselors Nat. Cancer Inst.; bd. of external experts Nat. Heart, Lung and Blood Inst.; assoc. mem. Broad Inst. Contbr. publications in the field. Recipient Clin. Scientist award in Translational Rsch., 2002, Career award, Burroughs Wellcome Fund. Mem.: Internat. Congress of Cell Transplant Soc. Achievements include research in parathyroid hormone (PTH) stimulation of the production of stem cells; adult hematopoietic stem cells with emphasis on their interaction with the microenvironment and cell cycle control. Office: AIDS Rsch Ctr Mass Gen Hosp Fruit St Boston MA 02114 also: Ctr for Regenerative Medicine and Tech Mass Gen Hosp 13th St Bldg 149 Rm 5212D Boston MA 02129 Office Phone: 617-726-5615. Office Fax: 617-724-2662. Business E-Mail: scadden.david@mgh.harvard.edu. *

SCAGNELLI, JOHN MARK, lawyer; b. NYC, Feb. 5, 1951; s. John Paul and Bernice (Aparo) Scagnelli. BA summa cum laude, Yale U., 1972, JD, 1975. Bar: NY 1976 & US Dist. Ct. (so. & ea. dists.) NY, US Ct. Customs and Patent Appeals 1979, 1982 US Ct. of Appeals (fed. & 2nd cirs.), NJ 1984 & US Dist. Ct. (dist. NJ) 1988, US Ct. of Appeals (3rd cir.), 1994 US Ct. of Appeals (8th cir.). Assoc. Townley & Updike, NYC, 1975—77; corp. counsel Chesebrough-Pond's Inc., Greenwich, Conn., 1977—79; assoc. Milgrim, Thomajan, Jacobs & Lee, NYC, 1979—82; v.p., gen. counsel Allied Maintenance Corp., NYC, 1982—86; ptnr., head environ. law dept. Clapp & Eisenberg, Newark, 1986—90; head environ. law group Whitman & Ransom, NYC, 1990; ptnr. Scarinci & Hollenbeck LLC, Lyndhurst, NJ. Exec. dir. Commonwealth of Puerto Rico; editor Environ. Compliance & Litig. Strategy; lectr. U. Wis.; mem. (editl. bd.), editor (domestic articles) Trademark Reporter, 1979—87. Contbr.: articles to profl. jours. Commr. Interstate Sanitation Commn. Recipient 10 Leaders in Environ. Law, Digital Press Internat.'s NJ, 2003—04, top 10 attys. Mem. Water Resources Assn. Del. River Basin (dir.), ABA, NY State Bar Assn. (environ., trade regulation), Assn. Bar NYC, NY County Lawyers Assn., Inst. Environ. Auditing, NJ State Bar Assn., Authorities Assn. NJ, NJ Commr. Interstate Environ. Comm. NY, NJ, Conn. tri-state environ. comm., mem. Spl. Puerto Rico Land Administn. Comm. Asbestos Issues, chmn. WRA/DRB's Prog. & Spl. Edn. Com., mem. NJ Gov. McGreevey's Transition Team for NJ Dept. Environ. Protection 2001, mem. bd. NY State Mediation. Office: Scarinci & Hollenbeck LLC 1100 Valley Brook Ave PO Box 790 Lyndhurst NJ 07071-0790 Office Phone: 201-896-4100. Office Fax: 201-896-8660. Business E-Mail: jscagnelli@njlegalink.com.

SCAIFE, RICHARD MELLON, philanthropist; married; 2 children. Mgr. Scaife Newspapers. Chmn., trustee Sarah Scaife Found., Inc.; donor, chmn., trustee Carthage Found., Allegheny Found. Named one of Forbes' Richest Americans, 2006.

SCALA, JAMES, health facility administrator, consultant, writer; b. Ramsey, NJ, Sept. 16, 1934; s. Edvigi and Lorene (Hendricksen) Scala; m. Nancy Peters, June 15, 1957; children: James, Gregory, Nancy, Kimberly. BA, Columbia U., 1960; PhD, Cornell U., 1964; postgrad., Harvard U., 1968; LHD (hon.), Hofstra U., 1998. Cert. nutrition specialist. Staff scientist Miami Valley Labs., Procter and Gamble Co., 1964-66; head life scis., dir. fundamental rsch. Owens Ill. Corp., 1966-71; dir. nutrition T.J. Lipton Inc., 1971-75; dir. health scis. Gen. Foods Corp., 1975-78; v.p. sci. and tech. Shaklee Corp., San Francisco, 1978-85, sr. v.p. sci. affairs, 1986-87. Lectr. Georgetown U. Med. Sch.; instr. U. Calif., Berkeley; nutritionist U.S. Olympic Ski Team, 1981—87. Author: Making the Vitamin Connection, 1985, The Arthritis Relief Diet, 1987, 2d edit., 1989, Eating Right for a Bad Gut, 1990, 2d edit., 1992, Eating Right for a Bad Gut, new edit., 1999, The High Blood Pressure Relief Diet, 1988, 2d edit., 1990, Look 10 Years Younger, Feel 10 Years Better, 1991, 2d edit., 1993, Prescription for Longevity, 1992, 2d edit., 1994, If You Can't/Won't Stop Smoking, 1993, The New Arthritis Relief Diet, 1998, 25 Natural Ways to Manage Stress and Avoid Burnout, 2000, 25 Natural Ways to Relieve Irritable Bowel Syndrome, 2000, 20 Natural Ways to Reduce the Risk of Prostate Cancer, 2001, 25 Natural Ways to Lower Blood Pressure, 2002; editor: Nutritional Determinants in Athletic Performance, 1981, New Protective Roles for Selected Nutrients, 1989; columnist: Dance mag.; contbr. articles to profl. jours. With USAF, 1953—56. Disting. scholar, U. Miami, Fla., 1977, Atlantic U., 1977. Fellow: Am. Coll. Nutrition; mem.: AAAS, Am. Diabetic Assn., Mt. Diablo Astron. Soc., Eastbay Astron. Soc., Astron. Soc. Pacific (bd. dirs., chmn. devel. coun.), Inst. Food Technologists, Am. Soc. Cell Biology, Sports Medicine Coun., Brit. Nutrition Soc., Am. Inst. Nutrition, Oakland Yacht Club, Olympic Club (San Francisco), Sigma Xi. Libertarian. Avocations: astronomy, photography. Office Phone: 925-283-2753. Personal E-mail: jscala2@comcast.net. *I am in awe of the incredible resiliency of living things, but most of all the human spirit.*

SCALAMANDRE, JILL E., marketing executive; b. June 21, 1958; Joined Revlon, 1980; sr. v.p. global mktg. Revlon; mktg exec. Prada Beauty, 1999—2003; grp. v.p. Avon Products, Inc., 2003—07; chief mktg. officer Chrysallis, 2007—. Chmn. Cosmetic Exec. Women. Office: Cosmetic Exec Women 286 Madison Ave 19th Fl New York NY 10017 Office Phone: 212-685-5955. Office Fax: 212-685-3334. *

SCALERA, MICHELLE, conservator; d. Ciro and Catherine Scalera. BA, Kean U., Elizabeth, NJ, 1978; MA, U. Internazionale dell' Arte, Florence, Italy, 1980. Conservator NC Musuem of Art, Raleigh, 1980—81; fine arts conservator John and Mable Ringling Mus. Art, Sarasota, Fla., 1981—85, chief conservator, 1985—. Author: (restoration publication) Ca' d'Zan: The Restoration of the Ringling Mansion (Gold ADDY award, 2007); contbr. chapters to books. Grants reviewer IMLS, Washington, 2005—07. Mem.: Am. Inst. Conservation Hisotric and Artistic Works (assoc.), Phi Kappa Phi. Home: 8019 Indigo Ridge Terr Bradenton FL 34201 Office: John and Mable Ringling Mus Art 5401 Bayshore Rd Sarasota FL 34243 Home Phone: 941-355-9856; Office Phone: 941-359-5700. Personal E-mail: msfineart@earthlink.net.

SCALES, JOHN THOMAS, state official; b. Cambridge, Mass., July 5, 1935; s. Frank and Louise Adelaide (Gifford) S. Cert.-qualified law libr. Libr. clk. Harvard U. Law Sch. Libr., Cambridge, Mass., 1955—58, Assn. Bar City N.Y., NYC, 1958—60, NYU Sch. Law, NYC, 1960—61; law libr. Paul, Weiss, Rifkind, Wharton & Garrison, NYC, 1961—69, Kelley, Drye & Warren, NYC, 1969—71; editl. asst. N.J. Law Jour., Newark, 1971; reference libr. Law Sch. Libr. Seton Hall U., Newark, 1971; asst. law libr. Essex County Law Libr., Newark, 1972—80; tech. asst. legal activities State N.J. Bd. Pub. Utilities, Newark, 1981—2002; ret., 2002. Roman Catholic. Avocations: opera, professional sports, public affairs. Home: 13 Summit Ave Unit 2 Antrim NH 03440-3613 E-mail: cantabrigia@verizon.net.

SCALES, PAT R., library association executive, library director; MLIS, George Peabody Coll. for Teachers of Vanderbilt U., 1970. Tchr. children's lit. Furman U., 1976; libr. mid. sch.; dir. libr. info. services SC Governor's Sch. of Arts and Humanities. Founder Communicating Through Lit. prog.; chair Newbery Award Com., 1992, Laura Ingalls Wilder Com., 2001; mem. Intellectual Freedom Com., Freedom To Read Found. Author: Teaching Banned Books; contbr. Book Links mag. Named one of Five Most Influential Librarians in 20th Century in SC. Mem.: AASL (Intellectual Freedom award 1983, 2003), Assn. for Libr. Svc. to Children (mem. bd. dirs. 2005—, pres.-elect 2007—), ALA (Grolier award 1997). Office: SC Governor's Sch of Arts 200 Stewart St Greenville SC 29605 Office Phone: 864-282-3694. Office Fax: 864-241-1270. Business E-Mail: pscales@bellsouth.net. *

SCALES, RICHARD LEWIS, retired sales executive; b. Indpls., Nov. 16, 1928; s. Ortho Lorton and Nina L. (Julian) S.; m. E. Jean Rankin, Dec. 21, 1951; children: Richard, Allan, Anne. BSME, Purdue U., 1952. Rsch. and devel. engr. Bell Labs./Western Electric, Chgo., also Whippany, N.J., 1955-58; sales engr. Bodine Electric Co., Chgo., 1958-61; dist. sales mgr. Wabash (Ind.) Magnetics, 1961-66; founder, chmn. bd. (emeritus) Richard Scales Assocs., Wabash, 1966—, RSA Inc., Wabash, 1985—. Contbr. articles to mag. Elder, Presbyn. Ch. Lt. USNR, 1952-55, Korea. Recipient Paul Harris award Rotary Internat. Republican. Avocations: computers, photography. Home: 550 Sommers Ave Wabash IN 46992-2021

SCALES, ROBERT H., JR., former academic administrator, retired army officer; b. Gainesville, Fla., Aug. 5, 1944; m. Diana Weiss; children: Maria, Monica. BS, U.S. Mil. Acad., 1966; MS, Duke U., PhD in History. Commd. 2d lt. U.S. Army, 1966, advanced through grades to maj. gen.; dep. chief staff for base ops./dep. chief staff for doctrine Tng. and Doctrine Command, Ft. Monroe, Va., 60 1997; comdr. U.S. Army War Coll., Carlisle

Barracks, Pa., 1997—2000; pres., CEO Walden Univ., 2000—02; sr. v.p. Sylvan Learning Sys., 2002—. Prin. author: Certain Victory: The U.S. Army in the Gulf War, 1993, Firepower in Limited War, 1995, Yellow Smoke: The Future of Land Warfare for America's Military, 2003. Decorated DSM, Silver Star, Legion of Merit with 4 oakleaf clusters, Bronze Star medl, Air medal, others. Office: Sylvan Learning Sys 1001 Fleet St Baltimore MD 21202

SCALET, J. CHRIS (JAMES CHRISTOPHER SCALET), pharmaceutical executive; BS in Mgmt. Sci. and Computer Systems, Okla. State U.; student Exec. Development Prog. Kellogg Sch. Mgmt., Northwestern U. V.p., info. tech., CIO MAPCO Inc., 1993—97; sr. v.p., info. tech., CIO Internat. Paper, 1998—2003; sr. v.p., info. services., CIO Merck & Co., Inc., 2003—05, sr. v.p. global process and services, CIO, 2006—. Office: Merck PO Box 100 Whitehouse Station NJ 08889-0100

SCALETTA, HELEN MARGUERITE, volunteer; b. Sioux City, Iowa, Apr. 13, 1927; d. Ralph J. and Ruth Cora (Coyle) Beedle; m. Phillip Jasper Scaletta, May 21, 1946; children: Phillip Ralph, Cheryl Diane Kesler. AA in Bus., Edwards Coll. Bus., Sioux City, 1946. Acct. Towners Dept. Store, Iowa City, 1947—48; legal sec. Phillip Scaletta, Sioux City, 1950—74; svc. chmn. Easter Seal Soc., Lafayette, Ind., 1970—88; rec. sec. Home Hosp. Aux., Lafayette, 1989. Danced in Civic Theatre Follies, 1962. Orch. mem. June's All-Girl Ensemble, 1943-50. Pres. Newcomers club YWCA, Lafayette, 1967-68, mem. chmn., bd. dirs., 1979; leader Girl Scouts Am., Ft. Wayne, Ind., 1960-63; chmn. Mental Health Inc., Ft. Wayne, 1960-61, Cancer Crusade, West Lafayette, 1973-74; precinct worker Rep. Cen. Com., West Lafayette, 1974-76; Nat. Missions sec. 1st Presbyn. Ch., 1957. Recipient Citation Easter Seal Soc., 1981, Ernestine Duncan Collins Pearl Ct. award Sigma Kappa, 1997. Mem. Purdue U. Women's Club (pres. 1973-74), Lafayette Country Club (golf chmn. 1971, 90, bowling pres. 1992-93, golf co-chair Battleground 9-hole group 1996), Purdue Women's Bowling League (treas. 1978-79), Cosmopolitan Club, YWCA (Diamond award, 2005), Sigma Kappa (corp. bd., sec., treas. 1971-99), Kappa Kappa Sigma (pres. 1972), Sigma Kappa Lafayette Alumnae (pres. 1970, 1988-93, Ernestine Duncan Collins Pearl Court award 1997). Avocations: collecting dolls, bowling, golf, sports. Home: One Via Verde Lafayette IN 47906

SCALETTA, PHILLIP RALPH, III, lawyer; b. Iowa City, Dec. 18, 1949; s. Phillip Jasper and Helen M. (Beedle) S.; m. Karen Lynn Scaletta, May 13, 1973; children: Phillip, Anthony, Alexander. BSIM, MS, Purdue U., 1972; JD, Ind. U., 1975. Bar: Ind. 1975, U.S. Dist. Ct. Ind. 1975, Ill. 1993. Assoc. Ice Miller, Indpls., 1975-81, ptnr., 1981—. Contbr. articles to profl. jours. Chmn. Ind. Continuing Legal Edn. Found., Indpls., 1989; mem. Environ. Quality Control Water Com., 1988-98. Mem. Ind. Bar Assn., Indpls. Bar Assn., Def. Rsch. Inst., Internat. Assn. Def. Counsel, Gyro Club Indpls. (v.p. 1992-93, pres. 1993-94, bd. dirs. 1990—). Avocations: golf, skiing, tennis. Home: 7256 Tuliptree Trl Indianapolis IN 46256-2136 Office: Ice Miller 1 American Sq Indianapolis IN 46282-0020 Office Phone: 317-236-2330. Business E-Mail: scaletta@icemiller.com.

SCALFANI, CARL, secondary school educator; M of Edn., Dowling Coll., Oakdale, NY, 1997. Cert. secondary edn. NY, 1995. Tchr. Jaqueline Kennedy Onassis H.S., NYC, 1996—2000; tchr., dean students Rocky Point H.S., NY, 2000—. Jr. sr. class advisor Rocky Point H.S., 2000—. Office: Rocky Point High Sch 82 Rocky Point Yaphank Rd Rocky Point NY 11778

SCALFARI, LARRY ALAN, music educator, director; b. Milw., June 13, 1955; s. Jay Alex Scalfri and Antoinette Anne Daddato; m. Desiree Patrice Yoder, Aug. 14, 1981; children: Amber Dawn, Carlee Joy. BA in Sacred Music, CBC, Springfield, Mo., 1978; MusM, Duquesne U., Pitts., 2004—06. Cert. Cago Am. Guild Organists, 2004. Assoc. dir. music & fine arts St. Andrew United Meth. Ch., Highlands Ranch, Colo., 2006—. Mem.: Am. Guild Organists. Office: St Andrew United Meth Ch 3350 White Bay Dr Highlands Ranch CO 80126-5070 Home Phone: 303-953-0765. Personal E-mail: scalfari@aol.com.

SCALIA, ANTONIN GREGORY, United States supreme court justice; b. Trenton, NJ, Mar. 11, 1936; s. S. Eugene and Catherine Louise (Panaro) Scalia; m. Maureen McCarthy, Sept. 10, 1960; children: Ann Forrest, Eugene, John Francis, Catherine Elisabeth, Mary Clare, Paul David, Matthew, Christopher James, Margaret Jane. AB, Georgetown U., 1957; student, U. Fribourg, Switzerland, 1955—56; LLB, Harvard U., 1960. Bar: Ohio 1962, Va. 1970. Assoc. Jones Day Cockley & Reavis, Cleve., 1961—67; assoc. prof. U. Va. Law Sch., 1967—70, prof., 1970—74; gen. counsel Office Telecomm. Policy, Exec. Office of Pres., 1971—72; chmn. Adminstrv. Conf. U.S., Washington, 1972—74; asst. atty. gen. Office Legal Counsel US Dept. Justice, Washington, 1974—77; prof. law U. Chgo., 1977—82; judge U.S. Ct. Appeals (D.C. cir.), 1982—86; assoc. justice U.S. Supreme Ct., Washington, 1986—. Vis. prof. Georgetown Law Ctr., 1977, Stanford Law Sch., 1980—81; resident scholar Am. Enterprise Inst., 1977. Editor: Regulation mag., 1979—82; author: A Matter of Interpretation, 1998. Sheldon fellow, Harvard U., 1960—61. Republican. Office: US Supreme Ct One First St NE Washington DC 20543-0001 *

SCALIA, EUGENE, lawyer; b. Cleve., Aug. 14, 1963; s. Antonin and Maureen (McCarthy) S.; m. Patricia Larsen, Oct. 16, 1993; children: Antonin, Megan McCarthy, John Christie, Bridget Ann, Luke Francis. BA, U. Va., 1985; JD, U. Chgo., 1990. Bar: Calif. 1990, Va. 1993, D.C. 1995. Asst. to chief of staff U.S. Dept. Edn., Washington, 1985-87; assoc. Gibson, Dunn & Crutcher, LA, 1990-92, assoc. ptnr. Washington, 1993—2001, ptnr., 2003—; asst. to atty. gen. U.S. Dept. Justice, Washington, 1992-93; solicitor U.S. Dept. Labor, 2002—03. Mem. vis. com. U. Chgo. Law Sch., 1998—2001. Editor-in-chief U. Chgo. Law Rev., 1989-90, mem. adv. bd., 1996—. Named Lawyer of Yr., Compliance Reporter mag., 2006, Top Washington, DC Lawyer in Employment Litig., Wash. Bus. Jour., 2006; named one of Litigation's Rising Stars, The Am. Lawyer, 2007. Roman Catholic. Office: Gibson Dunn & Crutcher Ste 900 1050 Connecticut Ave NW Washington DC 20036-5306 Office Phone: 202-955-8500. E-mail: escalia@gibsondunn.com.

SCALING, SAM T., obstetrician, gynecologist; b. Fort Monmouth, NJ, Aug. 16, 1945; s. Sam T. and Helen Louise Scaling; m. Lisa Janine Peck, Aug. 6, 1988; 1 child, Micah;children from previous marriage: Traci, Craig, Chad, Chris, Cory, Tiffany. BS, U. N.Mex., Albuquerque, 1967; MD, U. Tenn., Memphis, 1971. Diplomate Am. Bd. Ob/Gyn. Intern Confederate Meml. Med. Ctr., Shreveport, La., 1971—72; resident in ob-gyn. Baylor Coll. Medicine, Houston, 1975—78, chief resident ob/gyn., 1977—78; pvt. practice Obstetrics, Gynecology and Infertility Casper, Wyo., 1978—; founder, pres. Women's Health Assocs. Wyo., Casper, 2001—; med. staff Wyo. Med. Ctr., 1978—; chmn. dept. ob/gyn. Wyo. Med. Ctr., Meml. Hosp. Natrona County, 1981—83, 1986—88, 2001, 2002—05, sec. med. staff, 1989—91, vice chief of staff, 1991—93, chief of staff, 1993—95. Clin. asst. prof., instr. ob/gyn. Wyo. Family Practice Program, Casper, 1978—; v.p. Wyo. State Bd. Med. Examiners, 1984—92, 1989—90, pres., 1990—92; presenter in field; med. dir. Casper Family-Centered League Lamaze Prepared Childbirth, 1980—84, Christ-Centered Childbirth, 1984—87, Caring Ctr., Casper, 1986—90, Wyo. Med. Ctr. PMS Clinic, 1987—90. Mem. Little Dilly Golf Tournament com. Casper Country Club, 1994—96; mem. adv. bd. Caring Ctr., 2001—; mem. Healing Pl. Counseling Ctr. adv. bd. Highland Park Cmty. Ch., 1994—95; v.p. bd. dirs. Casper Children's Chorale, 1981—82; bd. dirs. Wyo. Cmty. Health Care Alliance, 1997—, Christian Solidarity Worldwide-USA, 1997—2000. Maj. USAF, 1972—75. Named to Am.'s Top Obstetricians and Gynecologists, Consumers Rsch. Coun. Am., 2002—03, 2007; NSF summer scholar, N.Mex. Highlands U., 1962. Fellow: ACS, ACOG, Am. Fertility Soc.; mem.: Am. Soc. Reproductive Medicine (mem. nat. adv. coun. 1997), Natrona County Med. Soc., Am. Assn. Pro Life Obstetricians and Gynecologists, Am. Coll. Physician Execs., Soc. Reproductive Surgeons, Am. Assn. Gynecologic Laparascopists, Wyo. State Med. Soc., Ctrl. Assn. Obstetricians and Gynecologists, Found. N.Am. Wild Sheep (life), Alaska Profl. Hunters Assn., Bass Anglers Sportsman Soc. (life), N.Am. Hunting Club (life), Boone and Crockett Club (life), Safari Club Internat. (life), Rocky Mountain Elk Found., Alpha Omega Alpha. Republican. Mem. Ch. Of God. Avocations: hunting, fishing, hiking, gun collecting, coin collecting/numismatics. Office: Women's Health Assocs Wyo 1125 E 2d Casper WY 82601

SCALLEN, THOMAS KAINE, broadcast executive; b. Mpls., Aug. 14, 1925; s. Raymond A. and Lenore (Kaine) S.; m. Bille Jo Brice; children by previous marriage: Thomas, Sheila, Patrick, Eileen, Timothy and Maureen (twins). BA, St. Thomas Coll., 1949; JD, U. Denver, 1950. Bar: Minn. Asst. atty. gen. State of Minn., Mpls., 1950-55; sole practice Mpls., 1955-57; pres. Med. Investment Corp., Mpls., 1957—, Internat. Broadcasting Corp., Mpls., 1977—; owner Harlem Globetrotters. Pres., exec. producer Ice Capades; chmn. bd. dirs. Century Park Pictures Corp., Los Angeles, chmn. bd. dirs. Blaine-Thompson Co., Inc., N.Y.C; chmn. Apache Plastics, Inc., Stockton, Calif. Served with AUS. Mem. World Pres. Orgn., Minn. Club, Calhoun Beach Club, L.A. Athletic Club. Clubs: University (St. Paul, Mpls.), Rochester (Minn.) Golf and Country, Edina (Minn.) Country, Athletic (Mpls.). Home: Heron Cove Windham NH 03087 Office: Internat Broadcasting Corp 80 S 8th St Ste 4701 Minneapolis MN 55402-2207 Office Phone: 612-333-5100.

SCANDARY, E. JANE, special education educator, consultant; b. Saginaw, Mich., Sept. 12, 1923; d. Leonard William and Reva Charlotte (Smith) Leipprandt; m. Theodore John Scandary; children: John S., Robert G. BA, Mich. State U., East Lansing, 1945, EdS, 1963, PhD, 1968; MEd, Wayne State U., 1951. Cert. secondary and spl. edn. tchr., Mich. Therapist speech and lang. Ann J. Kellogg Sch., Battle Creek, Mich., 1945-47; supr. speech therapy programs Wayne County Schs., Detroit, 1948-52; supr. programs for phys., hearing and visually impaired Ingham Intermediate Schs., Mason, Mich., 1960-78; spl. edn. cons. Mich. Dept. of Edn., Lansing, 1978-87, Livingston Intermediate Schs., Howell, Mich., 1987—. Rsch. assoc. Mich. State U., East Lansing, 1965-66, adj. prof., 1969-75, 81-82; mem. adv. com. China-U.S. Sci. Exchange Program Spl. Edn.; guest lectr. seminars spl. edn. Australia, Eng., Iran, Israel, Aruba, Germany, Scotland. Editor Chronicles newsletter, 1987—; contbr. articles to profl. jours. Vol. Mich. Hist. Mus., 1995—, Meals-on-Wheels, 1998-2001, Salvation Army, 2000—; chair futures com. Mich. Dept. Edn., 1992, editor, chair Task Force Futuresin Spl. Edn. 2000 AD and Beyond, 1992; bd. dirs. Delta Dist. Libr., 1998—. 1st Chance Early Childhood grantee, 1972-78; recipient Resolution of Tribute Mich. State Senate, 1986, 3d Pl. award Mid-Mich. Spring Art Show, 1998; Scandary award for outstanding contbrs. early childhood edn. established in her name, 1990. Mem. Nat. Coun. Exceptional Children (field editor 1976-86, pres. div. physically handicapped 1982-83), Mid-Mich. Art Guild, World Future Soc., Capitol Area Quilt Guild. Avocations: painting, writing, reading, creative sewing.

SCANDURA, JOSEPH MICHAEL, neuroscientist, application developer; b. Bay Shore, NY, Apr. 29, 1932; s. Joseph and Lucy S.; m. Alice Baker, Aug. 13, 1960; children: Jeanne, Janette, Joseph, Julie. AB, U. Mich., 1953, MA, 1955; PhD, Syracuse U., 1962; postdoctoral, Stanford U., summer 1964, 68-69, U. Calif.-Berkeley, summer 1968, MIT, summer 1972; postgrad., U. Kiel, W.Ger., 1975, Inst. Ednl. Tech., Italy, summer 1978. Tchr. math., sci. White Plains, Bay Shore, 1953-56; instr. math., head wrestling coach Syracuse U., NY, 1956-63; asst. prof. edn., math. SUNY-Buffalo, 1963-64; research asst. prof. math. edn. Fla. State U., Tallahassee, 1964-66; dir. instructional systems, structural learning U. Pa., Phila., 1966-96; Fulbright prof. U. Koblenz & Dresden, 1998-99. Vis. rsch. prof. Drexel U., 2005; founder, chmn. Intelligent Micro Systems, Narberth, Pa., 1978-2002; chmn. bd. sci. advisors MERGE Rsch. Inst., 1973-2002; prin. investigator NIST Advanced Tech. Program Project on Automating Supply Chain; cons. U.S. Office Edn., NSF, NAS, Tex. Instruments, Borg-Warner, U.S. Army; organizer, lectr., participant profl. confs., 1963—; dir. NATO Advanced Study Inst. on Structural Process Theories of Complex Human Behavior, 1977; coach undefeated Ea. Intercollegiate Wrestling Championship Team, 1963. Author: Mathematics - Concrete Behavioral Foundations, 1971, (with others) An Algorithmic Approach to Mathematics - Concrete Behavioral Foundations, 1971, Structural Learning I - Theory and Research, 1973, Problem Solving - A Structural Process Approach with Instructural Implications, 1977, (with A.B. Scandura) Structural Learning and Concrete Operations - An Approach to Piagetian Conservation, 1980, Cognitive Approach to Software Development, 1988, Prodoc (comprehensive suite of software devel. and maintenance tools), 1989, Cognitive Approach to Software Engineering and Re-engineering, 1991, ongoing projects; Flexys-customizable reengineering automation, Autobuilder-automated specification and implementation component based software while guaranteeing correctness, intelligent tutor authoring of devel. sys. model IT and tutor IT, 1992—, NATO Advanced Study Inst., 1993, Automated Software Conversions and Re-engineering, 1993; contbr. 200 articles to profl. jours.; editor: Research in Mathematics Education, 1967, Structural Learning II - Issues and Approaches, 1976, (with C.J. Brainerd) Structural Process Models of Complex Human Behavior, 1978; developer, producer numerous computer-based instructional systems and software devel. systems; multiple software patents. Recipient Renssalaer award, 1949, Bausch and Lomb award, 1949, Nat. AAU Wrestling Champion and Outstanding Wrestler award, 1955; Fulbright scholar, 1975-76, 1998-99; U.S. Office Edn. fellow, 1978-79. Fellow: APA (chmn. E.L. Thorndike award com. 1974—79), Structural Learning Soc. (sr.; chmn. 1969—80, editor in chief Jour. Structural Learning 1976—90, chmn. 1985—88, Jour. Structural Learning and Intelligent Systems 1990—2001, chmn. 1995—, founder, sr. advisor Tech., Instr., Cognition & Learning 2002—); mem.: IEEE, AAUP, Univ. Profs. for Acad. Order, Psychonomic Soc., Math. Assn. Am., Nat. Coun. Tchrs. Math. (past fed. funds com. chmn.), Am. Ednl. Rsch. Assn. (chmn. tech., instrn., cognition and learning), Assn. Computing Machinery, Phi Delta Kappa, Phi Eta Sigma, Phi Kappa Phi. Home: 1249 Greentree Ln Narberth PA 19072-1219 Office: U Pa Instructional Systems Philadelphia PA 19104 *Accomodation to -- as well as leadership of -- groups, institutions and/or societies is an essential ingredient of success in most walks of life. There are circumstances, however, which require inner direction, whether developing a new scientific paradigm or standing firm against political pressures. Although vindication is rarely complete and often delayed, following one's best instincts yields its own rewards—perhaps the satisfaction of ultimately being proven right but more often simply knowing one did what had to be done.*

SCANIFFE, JOSEPH ALBERT, anesthesiologist, consultant; s. Angelo and Agnes Mary Scaniffe; m. Lidia Brigette Munteanu, Apr. 8, 2006; children: Richard Anthony, Christopher Michael, Brigette Annette Mocan. BS in Engring., US Mil. Acad., West Point, NY, 1972; MBA, U. So. Calif., LA, 1980; MD, Uniformed Svcs. U. Health Scis., Bethesda, Md., 1985. Diplomate Am. Bd. Anesthesiology, 1990. Commd. 2d lt. US Army, advanced through grades to lt. col., 1972; nuc. weapons assembly team chief 9th Inf. Divsn., Ft Lewis, Wash., 1973—75, exec. officer d/1/84th f.a., 1975—76; attack helicopter platoon comdr. 101st Airborne Divsn., Ft Campbell, Ky., 1976—78, task force logistics officer Germany, 1978—78, comdr. a/3/319th f.a. Ft Campbell, 1979—80; instr. advanced ground/air tactics Armor Ctr., Ft Knox, Ky., 1980—81; staff anesthesiologist Madigan Army Med. Ctr., Tacoma, 1989—90, chief clin. svcs./vascular anesthesia Ft Lewis, Wash., 1991—97; asst. chief anesthesia 82d Airborn Divsn. 5th Mobile Army Surg. Hosp., 1990—91; ptnr. Swedish Med. Ctr., Seattle, 1998—2003; ptnr. Milford Anesthesia Assocs. Bristol Hosp., Conn., 2003—. Asst. prof. Uniformed Svcs. U. Sch. Medicine, Bethesda, 1991—97; faculty Acad. Health Scis., San Antonio, 1991—97; clin. instr. U. Wash., Seattle, 2000—03. Physician Med. Aid Mission, Dominican Republic, 2007. Decorated Meritorious Svc. medal US Army, Army Commendation medal, Army Achievement medal, Nat. Def. Svc. medal, SW Asia Svc. medal, Armed Forces medal, Kuwait Liberation medal Kingdom of Saudi Arabia and Kingdom of Kuwait; named one of Am.'s Top Anesthesiologists, Consumers' Rsch. Coun. Am., 2006. Master: Am. Bd. Anesthesiology; mem.: Assn. Mil. Surgeons (life, Outstanding Leadership and Acad. award 1985), Conn. State Soc. Anesthesiology, Soc. Cardiovasc. Anesthesiologists, Internat. Anesthesia Rsch. Soc., Am. Soc. Regional Anesthesia, Am. Soc. Anesthesiologists. Independent. Roman Catholic. Achievements include development of operational/combat anesthesia machine. Avocations: hiking, bicycling, racquetball, fishing, woodworking. Home: 11 Glenmore Dr Farmington CT 06032 Office: Milford Anesthesia Assoc 309 Seaside Ave Ste 201 Milford CT 06460 Home Phone: 860-677-9702; Office Phone: 203-783-1831.

SCANLAN, JAMES PATRICK, philosophy and Slavic studies educator; b. Chgo., Feb. 22, 1927; s. Gilbert Francis and Helen (Meyers) S.; m. Marilyn A. Morrison, June 12, 1948. BA, U. Chgo., 1948, MA, 1950, PhD, 1956. Research fellow Inst. Philos. Research, San Francisco, 1953-55; instr. Case Inst. Tech., Cleve., 1955-56; from instr. to assoc. prof. Goucher Coll., Balt., 1956-68; prof., dir. Slavic Ctr. U. Kans., Lawrence, 1968-70; prof. Ohio State U., Columbus, 1971-91, dir. Slavic Ctr., 1988-91, prof. emeritus, 1992—. Vis. rsch. scholar Moscow State U., 1964-65, 69, 98, Acad. Scis. USSR, Moscow, 1978, 93, Russian State U. for the Humanities, 1995; fgn. vis. fellow Slavic Rsch. Ctr., Hokkaido U., Sapporo, Japan, 1987-88. Author: Marxism in the USSR, 1985, Dostoevsky the Thinker, 2002, Russian trans., 2006; editor: Historical Letters by Peter Lavrov, 1967, Soviet Studies in Philosophy, 1987—92, Russian Studies in Philosophy, 1992—97, Technology, Culture and Development: The Experience of the Soviet Model, 1992, Russian Thought After Communism, 1994; co-editor: Russian Philosophy, 1965, Marxism and Religion in Eastern Europe, 1976. Served with USMC, 1945-46. Woodrow Wilson Internat. Ctr. fellow, 1982; recipient Translation award Nat. Translation Ctr., 1967, Faculty Rsch. award Fulbright-Hays, 1982-83. Mem. Am. Philos. Assn., Am. Assn. Advancement Slavic Studies, Phi Beta Kappa. Home: 1000 Urlin Ave Apt 206 Columbus OH 43212-3324 Personal E-mail: scanlan.1@osu.edu.

SCANLAN, MICHAEL, priest, academic administrator; b. Far Rockaway, NY, Dec. 1, 1931; s. Vincent Michael and Marjorie (O'Keefe) Scanlan. BA, Williams Coll., 1953; JD, Harvard U., 1956; MDiv, St. Francis Sem., Loretto, Pa., 1975; LittD (hon.), Coll. Steubenville, 1972; LLD (hon.), Williams Coll., Williamstown, Mass., 1978; PdD (hon.), St. Francis Coll., Loretto, Pa., 1987; STM, 3d Order Regular of St Francis, 1996. Ordained priest Roman Catholic Ch., 1964; Cross Pro Ecclesia et Pontifice, 1990. Acting dean Coll. Steubenville, Ohio, 1964-66, dean Ohio, 1966-69; rector pres. St. Francis Major Sem., Loretto, Pa., 1969-74; pres. Franciscan U. Steubenville, 1974-2000, chancellor, 2000—. Pres. (FIRE) Cath. Alliance for Faith, Intercession, Repentence and Evangelism, 1984—. Author: The Power in Penance, 1972, Inner Healing, 1974, A Portion of My Spirit, 1979, The San Damiano Cross, 1983, 2007, Turn to the Lord-A Call to Repentance, 1989, The Truth About Trouble, 1989, rev. edit. 2005, What Does God Want: A Practical Guide to Making Decisions, 1996, (with James Manney) Let the Fire Fall, 1997, The Holy Spirit: Holy Desire, 1998, Rosary Companion with Luminous Mysteries, 2002; chmn. editl. bd. New Covenant mag., 1985-92. Mem. Diocese of Steubenville Ecumenical Commn., 1964-69; bd. dirs. Rumor Control Ctr., Steubenville, 1968-69, C. of C., Steubenville, 1976-79; bd. trustees St. Francis Prep. Sch., Spring Grove, Pa., 1969-74; vice-chmn., bd. trustees St. Francis Coll., Loretto, Pa., 1969-74; trustee United Way, Steubenville, 1975-80; chmn. nat. svc. com. Cath. Charismatic Renewal, 1975-78. Staff judge adv. USAF, 1956-57. Named Sacrae Theologiae Magister Third Order Regular St Francis, 1996. Roman Catholic. Avocations: tennis, golf, skiing. Office: Franciscan U Office of Chancellor 1235 University Blvd Steubenville OH 43952-1796 Office Phone: 740-283-6466. *If you are going to change something, you've got to live on vision, before you live on reality. You have to be so inspired by the vision, that you keep telling everybody until it gets in them, and they start living it with you.*

SCANLAN, THOMAS CLEARY, publishing executive, editor; b. Birmingham, Mich., May 18, 1957; s. Thomas Matthew and Emily (Cleary) S.; m. Sally Sachs, June 20, 1981; children: Bridget C., Thomas M., Patrick J. BS, St. Louis U., 1979. Salesman Walter Heller Co., Chgo., 1979-82; pub., editor Surplus Record, Inc., Chgo., 1982—. Office: Surplus Record Inc 20 N Wacker Dr Chicago IL 60606-2806

SCANLAN, THOMAS JOSEPH, college president, educator; b. NYC, Mar. 5, 1945; s. Thomas Joseph and Anna Marie (Schmitt) S. BA in Physics, Cath. U. Am., 1967; MA in Math., NYU, 1972; PhD in Bus. Adminstrn., Columbia U., 1978; LLD (hon.), Coll. Mt. St. Vincent. Prin. Queen of Peace HS, North Arlington, NJ, 1972-75; dir. fin., edn. NY Province, Bros. of Christian Sch., Lincroft, NJ, 1978-81; vice chancellor Bethlehem U., Israel, 1981-87; pres. Manhattan Coll., Bronx, NY, 1987—. Bd. dirs. Am. Coun. on Edn. Trustee Commn. on Ind. Colls. and Univs., 2002, Assn. Cath. Colls. and Univs., 1994—. Recipient Pro Ecclesia et Pontifice medal, Pope John Paul II, Vatican City, 1986. Mem. Bros. of Christian Schs., Am. Coun. Edn., Assn. Cath. Colls. and Univs. (trustee 1994—), Assn. Am. Colls., Nat. Cath. Edn. Assn., Nat. Assns. Ind. Colls. and Univs., Nat. Collegiate Athletic Assn. (exec. com. and divsn. 1), Metro Atlantic Athletic Assn., Equestrian Order of the Holy Sepulchre of Jerusalem, Phi Beta Kappa, Beta Gamma Sigma, Phi Beta Kappa Fellows. Avocations: golf, reading, movies. Office: Manhattan Coll Office of Pres Manhattan Coll Pky Bronx NY 10471-3913 Home Phone: 718-884-0503; Office Phone: 718-862-7301. Business E-Mail: thomas.scanlan@manhattan.edu.

SCANLON, ANDREW, structural engineering educator; b. Bridge of Allan, Scotland, Apr. 16, 1944; BSc with honors, U. Glasgow, Scotland, 1966; PhD, U. Alta., Can., 1972. Civil engr. Pub. Works Can., St. John, N.B., Canada, 1966-67; project engr. N.B. Devel. Corp., Fredericton, Canada, 1967-68; teaching asst. U. Alta., Edmonton, Canada, 1968-71; structural design engr. Duthie Newby and Assocs., Edmonton, 1971-73; structural divsn. head Reid, Crowther and Ptnrs. Ltd., Edmonton, 1973-78; sr. structural engr. structural evaluation sect. Constrn. Tech. Labs., Inc., 1978-80, mgr. analytical design sect., 1980-82; assoc. prof. civil engring. U. Alta., 1982-83, prof., 1983-87, Pa. State U., University Park, 1987—, dir. transp. structures program Pa. Transp. Inst., 1993—2002, assoc. dir. of Inst., 1999—2002, head dept., 2002—. Recipient Le Prix P.L. Pratley award Can. Soc. Civil Engring., 1990. Fellow Am. Concrete Inst., Am. Soc. of Civil Engrs. Office: Pa State U 212 Sackett Bldg University Park PA 16802-1408 Office Phone: 814-863-3084. Business E-Mail: axs21@psu.edu.

SCANLON, CHARLES FRANCIS, retired military officer, writer, publisher; b. Nashville, Jan. 31, 1935; s. Francis James Gordon and Dorothy Rose (Compton) S.; m. Barbara Coddington Wall Scanlon, June 18, 2005; children: Teri, Brett, Ashlyn, Kellie. BA in Polit. Sci., U. Fla., 1960; grad., Command and Gen. Staff Coll., Ft. Leavenworth, Kans., 1970, Naval War Coll., Newport, RI, 1977; MA in Am. Studies, U. Hawaii, 1974; postgrad., Pa. State U., 1982, Harvard U., 1984-92. Commd. 2d lt. U.S. Army, 1960, advanced through grades to maj. gen., 1988; chief collection U.S. Army Europe, Heidelberg, Germany, 1977-78; comdg. officer 66th Mil. Intelligence Brigade, Munich, 1978-80; chief ops. U.S. Army Intelligence and Security Command, Arlington, Va., 1980-82; exec. officer Dept. Army Asst. Chief Staff Intelligence, Washington, 1982-83; dep. commdr. gen. U.S. Army Intelligence and Security Command, Arlington, 1983-85; dir. estimates Def. Intelligence Agy., Washington, 1985-86, dir. attaches, 1986-90; comdg. gen. U.S. Army Intelligence and Security Command, Ft. Belvoir, Va., 1990-93; ret., 1993; pres. Internat. Security, Counterintelligence Cons. Svcs., Fairfax Station, Va., 1993—, Satellite Beach, Fla., 1993—99, Melbourne Beach, Fla., 1999—2004, Indian Harbour Beach, Fla., 2004—. Decorated Def. D.S.M., Army D.S.M., Nat. Intelligence D.S.M., Legion of Merit with 3 oak leaf clusters, Bronze Star with 2 oak leaf clusters; elected to U.S. Mil. Intelligence Hall of Fame, 1995. Mem. Assn. US Army, Nat. Mil. Intelligence Assn. (pres. 1974-76), 101st Airborne Divsn. Assn., Berlin US Military Vets. Assn., Def. Intelligence Alumni Assn., Sigma Nu. Baptist. Avocations: boating, scuba diving, racquetball, soaring, reading. Home and Office: 16F Marina Isles Blvd Indian Harbor Beach FL 32937 Personal E-mail: chuckscanlon@aol.com.

SCANLON, DOROTHY THERESE, history professor; b. Bridgeport, Conn., Oct. 7, 1928; d. George F. and Mazie (Reardon) Scanlon. AB, U. Pa., 1948, MA, 1949, Boston Coll., 1953; PhD, Boston U., 1956; postdoctoral scholar, Harvard U., 1962—64, postdoctoral scholar, 1972. Tchr. history and Latin Marycliff Acad., Winchester, Mass., 1950—52; tchr. history Girls Latin Sch., Boston, 1952—57; prof. Boston State Coll., 1957—82, Mass. Coll. Art, Boston, 1982—95, prof. emerita, 1995—; lectr. Cape Mus. Fine Arts, Dennis, Mass., 1997—. Author: Instructor's Manual to Accompany Lewis Hanke, Latin America: A Historical REader, 1974; contbr. Biographical Dictionary of Social Welfare, 1986. Recipient Disting. Svc. award, Boston State Coll., 1979, Faculty award of excellence, Mass. Coll. Art, 1985, Faculty Disting. Svc. award, 1987. Mem.: AAUW, AAUP, History of Sci. Soc., Am. Assn. History of Medicine., Am. Studies Assn., Orgn. Am. Historians, Am. Hist. Assn., L.Am. Studies Assn., Delta Kappa Gamma, Phi Alpha Theta. Home: 23 Mooring Ln Dennis MA 02638-2321 Office: Mass Coll Art Dept History 621 Huntington Ave Boston MA 02115-5801 Office Phone: 617-739-4770.

SCANLON, JANE CRONIN, mathematics professor; b. NYC, July 17, 1922; d. John Timothy and Janet Smiley (Murphy) Cronin; m. Joseph C. Scanlon, Mar. 5, 1953 (div.); children: Justin, Mary, Anne, Edmund. Student, Highland Park Jr. Coll., 1939-41; BS, Wayne State U., 1943; MA, U. Mich., 1945, PhD, 1949. Mathematician Air Force Cambridge Research Center, 1951-54; instr. Wheaton Coll., Norton, Mass., 1954-55; asst. prof. Poly. Inst. Bklyn., 1957-58, asso. prof., 1958-60, prof., 1960-65; prof. math. Rutgers U., New Brunswick, N.J., 1965-91, prof. emerita, 1991—. Cons. Singer-Kearfott Div., Naval Research Lab. Office Naval Research Fellow Princeton, 1948-49; Horace H. Rockham Postdoctoral fellow U. Mich., 1950-51, Rutgers Research Council fellow, 1968-69, 72-73; NSF vis. professorship for women Courant Inst., NYU, 1984-85. Author: Fixed Points and Topological Degree in Nonlinear Analysis, 1964, Advanced Calculus, 1967, Differential Equations: Introduction and Qualitative Theory, 1980, 2d edit., 1994, Mathematics of Cell Electrophysiology, 1980, Mathematical Aspects of Hodgkin-Huxley Neural Theory, 1987; editor: Analyzing Multiscale Phenomena Using Singular Perturbation Methods, 1999. Mem. Am. Math. Soc., Soc. for Indsl. and Applied Math., Internat. Soc. Chronobiology. Home: 110 Valentine St Highland Park NJ 08904-2106 Office: Rutgers U Dept Math New Brunswick NJ 08903 Personal E-mail: croninscanlon@optonline.net.

SCANLON, JANICE LYNN, retired gifted and talented educator; b. Goodland, Kans., July 28, 1940; d. Milton Parish Jr. and Bertha May Adams Parish. BS, Ft. Hays State U., 1962; MA, U. Denver, 1980. Tchr. kindergarten, music Brewster Pub. Schs., Kans., 1962—63; tchr. kindergarten Jefferson County Pub. Schs., Lakewood, Colo., 1963—81; tchr. gifted Washington Twp. Pub. Schs., Sewell, NJ, 1983—98; ret., 1998. Del. gifted tchrs. to visit China with People to People, 1990; sec. N.J. Tchrs. Gifted, 1990—92; pres. Jefferson County Kindergarten Tchrs. Assn., Lakewood, Colo., 1964—65. Author: Jefferson County Kindergarten Curriculum, 1974; actor: (films) Teaching Children in Remote Areas, 1968; contbg. author (lessons in book) Teaching Children in Remote Areas, 1968; author: Guides for Washington Twp. Schs., 1983—98; co-author: Ruleton and Its School, 2005, Adams and Parrish Family, 2005. Pres. Palm Aire Nine Hole Golf, 2000—03, assoc., 2002—03; active Clare's Sewing Angels, Dem. Party, S.E. Manatee County, Fla., 2003—; presenter Indian hist. Ch. of Incarnation Sch., 2001—. Co-recipient Outstanding Vol. Group award, Haywood County, NC, 2007; recipient Presdl. award, Palms Aire Country Club, 2007; scholar, Kiwanis Club, Goodland, Kans., 1958, Tuition grant, U.S. Edn. Office, U. Denver, 1978—80. Mem.: N.J. Ret. Tchrs. Assn., Clare's Angels, Palm Aire Women's Club (fundraiser 1999—, v.p. 2001—02, pres. 2002—03), Alpha Delta Kappa (treas.). Democrat. Roman Catholic. Avocations: travel, painting, quilting, genealogy, golf. Home: 7222 Coachlight St Sarasota FL 34243 Personal E-mail: josescan@aol.com.

SCANLON, KERRY ALAN, lawyer; AB cum laude, Harvard U., 1973; JD, Antioch Law Sch., 1977. Bar: DC 1977, US Ct. Appeals, 4th Cir. and DC Cir., US Supreme Ct. Ptnr. litig., chair Equal Rights Litig. and Compliance Group Kaye Scholer LLP, Washington, DC. Mem.: ABA, DC Bar Assn. Office: Kaye Scholer LLP McPherson Bldg 901 Fifteenth St NW Ste 1100 Washington DC 20005 Office Phone: 202-628-3660. E-mail: kscanlon@kayescholer.com.

SCANLON, LAWRENCE EUGENE, language educator; b. Montclair, NJ, Sept. 12, 1927; s. Leo Dudley and Margaret Gertrude (Kennedy) S.; m. Anne Maxwell Sherrerd, Aug. 23, 1952; children: Lawrence Francis, Neal Patrick, Heidi Anne. BA, Wesleyan U., 1951; MA, Rutgers U., 1952; PhD, Syracuse U., 1958. Asst. prof. English Mount Holyoke Coll., South Hadley, Mass., 1958-63; prof. Hartford (Conn.). Coll. for Women, 1963-92. Author: First Came Commodore Perry, 1969, A Memorial of Ebensee, 1994, The Story He Left Behind Him Paddy the Cope, 1994. Justice of the peace Town of East Granby, Conn., 1970-72; v.p. Capital Region Libr. Coun., Hartford, 1970-74. With U.S. Army, 1945-46. Fulbright grantee, Austria, 1952-53, Japan, 1964-65, West Germany, 1980-81, summer grantee NEH, 1974. Avocations: writing, travel, gardening, investing. Home: 101 Holcomb St East Granby CT 06026-9531

SCANLON, PAT H., lawyer; b. Houma, La., Aug. 4, 1936; s. Leo Joseph and Mary (Ezell) S.; m. Carlene Myers, June 10, 1961; children: Margaret, Pat, Jr., Cissy, John. BS in Geology, La. State U., 1957; LLB with distinction, U. Miss., 1960. Assoc. Satterfield, Shell, Williams & Buford, Jackson, Miss., 1960-62; ptnr. Young, Scanlon & Sessums, Jackson, 1962—95; mem. Scanlon, Sessums Parker & Dallas PLLC, 1995-2002; mem. Watkins & Eager PLLC, 2003—; chmn., commnr. Miss. Jud. Performance Commn., Jackson, 1980-83; instr. Jackson Sch. Law, 1963-66; chmn. Miss. Law Inst., Jackson, 1970. Mem. editorial bd. Miss. Law Jour., 1959-60; contbr. articles to profl. jours. Mem. vestry St. James Episcopal Ch., Jackson, 1972-75, 79-82). Served to capt. USAR. Fellow Am. Coll. Trial Lawyers, Internat. Soc. Barristers, Am. Bar Found., Miss. Bar Found. (pres. 1986-87, trustee 1980-83); mem. Miss. Bankruptcy Conf. (pres. 1984-85), Miss. Young Lawyers Assn. (pres. 1969-70), Miss. State Bar Assn. (2d v.p. 1970-71, pres. 1988-89), Hinds County Bar Assn. (pres. 1974-75), Fed. Bar Assn. (pres. Miss. chpt. 1972-73), Am. Arbitration Assn. (panel mem.), Nat. Arbitration Forum (panel mem.). Office: 1650 Mirror Lake Plaza 2829 Lakeland Dr Jackson MS 39232 Business E-Mail: pat@ms-adr.com.

SCANLON, PETER REDMOND, retired accountant; b. NYC, Feb. 18, 1931; s. John Thomas and Loretta Dolores (Ryan) S.; m. Mary Jane E. Condon, Mar. 7, 1953; children: Peter, Barbara, Mark (dec.), Brian, Janet. BBA in Acctg., Iona Coll., 1952, LLD (hon.), 1992. CPA, N.Y. Mem. profl. staff Coopers & Lybrand, NYC, 1956-66, ptnr., 1966-91, vice chmn., 1976-82, chmn., CEO, 1982-91, ret. chmn., 1991—. Hon. ptnr. N.Y.C. Partnership, 1991. Mem. fin. coun. Diocese of Palm Beach, 1995-2002. Lt. USN, 1952-56. Decorated Knight of Malta, Knight Holy Sepulchre; recipient Arthur A. Loftus award Iona Coll., 1974, Trustee award, 1990, Crain's N.Y. All Star award, 1990, Best in Class award Conf. Bd. Youth Edn., 1991. Mem.: AICPA, NY State Soc. CPAs, Jupiter Inlet Beach Club, NY Athletic Club. Roman Catholic. Personal E-mail: prsmjes3179@aol.com. E-mail: prs-mjes.3179@aol.com.

SCANLON, ROSEMARY, economist; b. Dec. 25, 1939; d. Donald Angus and Mary Agnes (MacDonald) MacLellan; m. Michael Scanlon, Apr. 24, 1965 (div. 1979); children: Sean Donald, Jennifer. AB, St. Francis Xavier U., NS, 1959; MA (Ford Found. scholar), U. New Brunswick, 1960; PMD, Harvard Bus. Sch., 1981. Instr. econs. Coll. of William and Mary, Williamsburg, Va., 1960—63; asst. prof. Old Dominion U., Norfolk, Va., 1963—65; econ. analyst Port Authority N.Y. and N.J., 1969—93, sr. economist for regional rsch., 1977—80, mgr. econ. devel. planning, 1980—83, chief economist, 1983—. Asst. dir. Planning and Devel. Dept., 1985; apptd. dep. state contr., NYC, 1993—97; vis. rsch. fellow London Sch. Econ., 1997—2000; cons. urban and regional econs., 2000—; assoc. prof. econs. Real Estate Inst. NYU, 2001—. Co-author: The Arts as an Industry, 2007; editor: The London-NY Study, 2000; author: Bldg. for Growth, A Development Strategy, 2002. Bd. dirs. Transit Ctr. Inc., Accion, NY, 2005—. Recipient Outstanding Achievement award, Exec. Dirs. award, 1987, de Luca award for lifetime achievement in econ. devel., 1999, Disting. Alumnus award, St. Francis Xavier U., 2001. Home: 10 Clinton St Apt 9T Brooklyn NY 11201-2710 Office: 11 W 42nd St New York NY 10036 Personal E-mail: rosemaryscanlon@msn.com.

SCANLON, TERRENCE MAURICE, foundation administrator; b. Milw., May 1, 1939; s. Maurice John and Anne (Hayes) S.; m. Judy Ball, June 14, 1969; children: Michael Mansfield, Justin Ball, Brendan Hayes. BS, Villanova U., 1961. Staff asst. The White House, Washington, 1963-67; with SBA, Washington, 1967-69, Dept. of Commerce, Washington, 1969-83, mem. office Minority Bus. Enterprise, 1969-80, with Internat. Trade Adminstrn., 1980-81, with Minority Bus. Devel. Agy., 1981-83; mem. Consumer Product Safety Commn., Washington, 1983-89, vice chmn., 1983-84, chmn., 1985, 86-89; v.p., treas. The Heritage Found., Washington, 1989-91, v.p. corp. rels., 1991-94; chmn., pres. Capital Rsch. Ctr., Washington, 1994—. Am. Polit. Sci. Assn. Congl. fellow, 1967-68 Mem. Sovereign Mil. Order of Malta, University Club. Office: Capital Rsch Ctr 1513 16th St NW Washington DC 20036-1401 Home: 2425 L St NW Apt 240 Washington DC 20037 Office Phone: 202-483-6900. Business E-Mail: tscanlon@capitalresearch.org.

SCANLON HOBBS, LAURIE ANN, public relations professional; b. Flint, Mich., Jan. 6, 1961; d. James Francis and Angeline (Lubinski) Scanlon; m. William Walter Hobbs, Aug. 1994; 1 child, William James Hobbs. BA in Journalism, No. Ill. U., 1983. Asst. v.p. Fin. Shares Corp., Chgo., 1984-85; account exec., then sr. account exec. Edelman Pub. Rels. Worldwide, Chgo., 1985-87, account supr., then sr. account supr., 1987-90, v.p., 1991-96, prin. Milw., 1996—98; cons. GE Med. Sys. a unit of Gen. Electric Corp., 1999—. Mem. adv. coun. Early Childhood Family Edn.; lectr. on pub. rels. Mem. Chgo. Symphony Orch. Bus./Profl. Orgn., 1990—93. Recipient Silver Trumpet award Publicity Club Chgo., The Tower award The Bus. Profl. Adv. Assn., Golden Bell award The Hotel Sales and Mktg. Assn., Clarion award Women in Comms. Mem. Pub. Rels. Soc. Am. (com.), Northern Ill. U. Exec. Club (charter). Roman Catholic. Avocation: teaching figure skating. Home: 23193 High Ridge Rd Barrington IL 60010-1816 E-mail: lhobbs@execpc.com.

SCANNELL, HERB, broadcast executive; m. Sarah Scannell; 1 child, Caroline. BA in English and History, Boston Coll. Dir. program promotion Showtime/The Movie Channel; dir. programming Nickelodeon, NYC, 1988—89, v.p. programming, 1989—90, sr. v.p. programming; exec. v.p. Nickelodeon Networks, pres., 1996—2006; group pres. MTV Networks, NYC, 2003—06.

SCANNELL, WILLIAM EDWARD, aerospace transportation executive, consultant, psychologist; b. Muscatine, Iowa, Nov. 11, 1934; s. Mark Edward and Catharine Pearson (Fowler) S.; m. Barbara Ann Hoemann, Nov. 23, 1957; children: Cynthia Kay, Mark Edward, David Jerome, Terri Lynn, Stephen Patrick. BA in Gen. Edn., U. Nebr., 1961; BS in Engring., Ariz. State U., Tempe, 1966; MS in Systems Engring., So. Meth. U., Dallas, 1969; postgrad. in law, Western State U., 1977, 81-82; PhD, US Internat. U., San Diego, 1991. Commd. 2d lt. USAF, 1956, advanced through grades to lt. col., 1972; B-47 navigator-bombardier 98th Bomb Wing, Lincoln Air Force Base, Nebr., 1956-63; with Air Force Inst. of Tech., 1963-65, 68-69; chief mgmt. engring. team RAF Bentwaters, England, 1965-68; forward air contr. 20th Tactical Air Support Squadron, Danang, Vietnam, 1970-71; program mgr. Hdqrs. USAF, Washington, 1971-74, staff asst. Office of Sec. Def., 1974-75, ret., 1975; account exec. Merrill Lynch, San Diego, 1975-77; program engring. chief Gen. Dynamics, San Diego, 1977-79, engring. chief, 1979-80, program mgr., 1980-83; mgr. integrated logistics support Northrop Corp., Hawthorne, Calif., 1984-88, mgr. B-2 program planning and scheduling Pico Rivera, Calif., 1988-91; pres. Scannell and Assocs., Fredericksburg, Tex., 1991—. Author: The Nature of Motivation in Aerospace Executives, 1991. Cpl. USNG, 1952-54. Decorated DFC with three oak leaf clusters, Air medal with 11 oak leaf clusters, Vietnamese Cross Gallantry with palm, Meritorious Svc. medal. Mem. APA, Psi Chi, Calif. Psychol. Assn. Republican. Roman Catholic. Business E-Mail: william@scannell.net.

SCANTLEBURY, VELMA PATRICIA, surgeon; b. Barbados, West Indies, Oct. 6, 1955; came to U.S., 1970; d. Delacey Whitstanley and Kathleen (Jordan) S.; 2 children. BS, LI U., 1977; MD, Columbia U., 1981; DS (hon.), LI U., 1998, Seton Hall Coll. PA. Intern in surgery Harlem Hosp. Ctr., NYC, 1981-82, resident in surgery, 1982-86; fellow in transplantation U. Pitts., 1988, assoc. prof. surgery, 1998—2002; prof. surgery, dir. transplantation U. South Ala. Med. Ctr., Mobile, 2002—. Mem. med. advisory bd. Nat. Kidney Found. Vol. King County Hosp., Bklyn., 1972. Recipient Martin Luther King Sch. award, 1973-74, Am. Fedn. Tchrs. Sch. award, 1973-75, Nat. Med. Found. award 1977-78, Joseph Collins Found. Sch. award 1978, Gift of Life award Nat. Kidney Found., OMNI Life Models award, Women of Spirit award Carlow Coll.; named Outstanding Young Women of Am. 1988. Fellow, ACS; mem. AMA (listed by AMA as nation's first African-Am. female transplant surgeon), P&S Alumni Assn., Black and Latin Students Orgn. (treas. N.Y.C. 1979-80), Slpha Epsilon Delta, Phi Sigma Soc. (sec. Bklyn. chpt. 1976-77), Am. Soc. Transplantation, Am. Soc. Transplant Surgeons, Soc. Black Academic Surgeons, Am. Soc. Minority Health and Transplant Professionals (bd. dirs.), Internat. Women's Forum We. Pa., Nat. Assn. Negro Bus. and Profl. Women. Democrat. Office: Univ S Ala Med Ctr 2451 Fillingim St Mobile AL 36617-2293

SCARANO, FRANCISCO A., humanities educator; b. Humacao, PR, Feb. 24, 1952; s. Domingo Antonio Scarano Scarano and Lidia Fiol Bigas; m. Olga M. Maldonado, July 3, 1971; children: Héctor Francisco, Cristina Sofía, Francisco Javier. PhD, Columbia U., NYC, 1978. Asst. prof. U. Sagrado Corazón, Santurce, PR, 1975—79, U. PR, Río Piedras, 1979—80; asst. to full prof. U. Conn., Storrs, 1980—89; prof. U. Wis., Madison, 1989—, dir. L.Am., Caribbean and Iberian studies, 1998—2002. Author: (monograph) Sugar and Slavery in Puerto Rico: The Plantation Economy of Ponce, 1800-1850 (Elsa Goveia award New Eng. Coun. on Latin Am. Studies award, 1985), (textbook) Puerto Rico: cinco siglos de historia, Puerto Rico: una historia contemporánea; editor: (anthology) Cuba: contrapuntos de cultura, historia y sociedad, Inmigración y clases sociales en el Puerto Rico del siglo XIX. Mem.: Assn. Caribbean Historians, Latin Am. Studies Assn., Am. Hist. Assn. Office: U Wis 3211 Humanities Bldg 455 N Park St Madison WI 53706 Home Phone: 608-467-7095; Office Phone: 608-263-3945. Business E-Mail: fscarano@wisc.edu.

SCARBOROUGH, ANN BARLOW, secondary school educator; Tchr. sci. Farmville (N.C.) Mid. Sch., South Ctrl. HS, Winterville, NC. Recipient Outstanding Earth Sci. Tchr. award, 1992. Mem.: N.C. Sci. Tchrs. Assn. (pres. 2003).

SCARBOROUGH, CHUCK (CHARLES BISHOP SCARBOROUGH III), newscaster; b. Pitts., Nov. 4, 1943; s. Charles Bishop and Esther Francis (Campbell) S.; m. Linda Anne Gross, Dec. 14, 1972; children: Charles Bishop IV, Elizabeth Anne; m. Anne Ford Uzielli, Oct. 2, 1982; m. Ellen Carol Ward, Sept. 25, 1994. BS, U. So. Miss., 1969, LittD (hon.). Prodn. mgr. Sta.-WLOX-TV, Biloxi, Miss., 1966-68; reporter, anchorman Sta.-WDAM-TV, Hattiesburg, Miss., 1968-69; reporter, anchorman, mng. editor Sta.-WAGA-TV, Atlanta, 1969-72; reporter, anchorman Sta.-WNAC-TV, Boston, 1972-74, NBC News, NYC, 1974—. Author: (novels) Stryker, 1978, The Myrmidon Project, 1981, Aftershock, 1991. Served with USAF, 1961-65. Recipient awards for journalism AP (9), 1969-72, Emmy awards (30), 1974-2006, award Aviation/Space Writers Assn., 1977, 78, 88, UPI award for journalism N.Y. Press Club award, 1988, 89, Sigma Delta Chi award, Deadline Club award, Terry Anderson Journalism award Working Press Assn. N.J., 1992, Best in Bus. award, Washington Rev. Journalisam, 1994, Humanitarian award, Juvenile Diabetes Found., 2005; named NYC's Best Anchor Team (with Sue Simmons), NY Daily News, 2003 Mem.: Phi Kappa Phi. Office: NBC News 30 Rockefeller Plz Rm 723 New York NY 10112-0036

SCARBOROUGH, MARION NICHOLS, nutritionist, recreational facility executive; b. Enosburg Falls, Vt., July 26, 1915; d. George Leonard and Clara May (Woodward) Nichols; m. Mat. Scarborough, Aug. 30, 1950 (dec. Mar., 1960); 1 child Mary Anne Scarborough O'Donnell Adams. ASS, Green Mountain Coll., Poultney, Vt., 1935; BS, Kans. State U., 1937; MPH, Harvard U., 1947. Chief dietitian Newton (Mass.) Wellesley Hosp., 1938-43, 182d Gen. Hosp., U.S. Army, 1943-45; nutritionist, author food exch. list U.S. Pub. Health Diabetes Sect., Boston, 1947-50; nutritionist Fla. Bd. Health, Jacksonville, 1950-52; owner Happy Acres Ranch, Inc., Jacksonville, 1953—. Sec. Fla. Assn. Children Under Six ECA, 1965, pres., 1966, 67. Commd. officer USPHS, 1948-50. Mem. APHA, Am. Dietetic Assn., Am. Camping Assn., Nat. Assn. Edn. of Young Children. Episcopalian. Avocations: childrens' day care, summer camp. Home and Office: Happy Acres Ranch Inc 7117 Crane Ave Jacksonville FL 32216-9012

SCARBOROUGH, ROBERT HENRY, JR., entrepreneur; b. Hawkinsville, Ga., Mar. 12, 1923; s. Robert Henry and Janet Augusta (Burton) S.; m. Walterene Brant, July 1, 1946; children— Robert Henry, James Burton BS, U.S. Mcht. Marine Acad., 1944; BBA, U. Hawaii, 1969, MBA, 1971; MS, George Washington U., 1971, Armed Forces Staff Coll., 1963, Nat. War Coll., 1971. Commd. lt. (j.g.) USCG, 1949; advanced through grades to vice adm., 1978; chief Office of Ops. USCG, 1974-75, chief of staff, 1975-77, comdr. 9th Coast Guard Dist., 1977-78, vice comdt. Washington, 1978-82, ret., 1982; exec. dir. Navy League U.S., 1982-84; pres. Polaris Potomac Corp., 1985-96. Entrepreneur, 1996—. With USNR, 1942-49 Decorated DSM, Legion of Merit. Mem. Beta Gamma Sigma Office: 5357 37th St N Arlington VA 22207-1312

SCARBOROUGH, STEPHEN J., construction executive; Pres. Orange County div. Std. Pacific Corp., Irvine, Calif., 1981—96, exec. v.p., 1996, pres., 1996—2000, pres., CEO, 2000—01, chmn., CEO, 2001—07, chmn., pres., CEO, 2007—. Named Builder of the Yr., Bldg. Ind. Assn. So. Calif., 2004. Office: Standard Pacific Corp 15326 Alton Pkwy Irvine CA 92618 *

SCARBOROUGH, WILLIAM KAUFFMAN, historian, educator; b. Balt., Jan. 17, 1933; s. James Blaine and Julia Irene (Kauffman) Scarborough; m. Patricia Estelle Carruthers, Jan. 16, 1954; children: Catherine Krohn, William Bradley. AB, U. N.C., 1954; MA, Cornell U., 1957; PhD, U. N.C., 1962. Asst. prof. history Millsaps Coll., Jackson, Miss., 1961—63, N.E. La. U., Monroe, 1963—64; assoc. prof. history U. So. Miss., Hattiesburg, 1964—76, prof. history, 1976—, chair and prof. history, 1980—90, Charles W. Moorman Disting. Alumni Prof. in the Humanities, 1996—98. Author: (book) The Overseer: Plantation Management in The Old South, 1966, Masters of the Big House, 2003 (Landry award, 2003); editor: The Diary of Edmund Ruffin, 3 vols., 1972—89 (Landry award, 1989). Lt. (j.g.) USNR, 1954—56. Recipient Grand Marshal award, 2003, Wright Lit. Excellence award, 2004. Fellow: St. George Tucker Soc. (pres. 2002—03); mem.: AAUP (chpt. pres. 2002—03), The Hist. Soc., S.C. Hist. Soc., Agr. History Soc., Miss. Hist. Soc. (pres. 1979, Willie D. Halsell prize 1993, B.L.C. Wailes award 2005), So. Hist. Assn., Phi Beta Kappa. Avocations: golf, gardening, football, basketball. Home: 1120 Estelle St Hattiesburg MS 39402 Office: Univ So Miss Dept History 118 College Dr # 5047 Hattiesburg MS 39406 Office Phone: 601-266-4336. Business E-Mail: william.scarborough@usm.edu.

SCARCHUK, LYNN NETTLETON, retired music educator; b. Hartford, Conn., July 25, 1950; d. Russell Chaffee Nettleton and Katharine Risley Chaffee; 1 child, James Paul. BS, Western Conn. State U., 1968—72; MS, Ctrl. Conn. State U., 1978. Tchr. Meriden Bd. Edn., Meriden, Conn., 1972—, Jefferson Mid. Sch., Meriden, 1972—84, Washington Mid. Sch., Meriden, 1984—87; choral dir., tchr. Maloney HS, Meriden, 1988—2007; ret., 2007. Dir.(and prodr.): (sch. prodn.) Oklahoma, 1990, My Fair Lady, 1992, Anything Goes, 1994, South Pacific, 1996, 42d St, 1998, Hello Dolly, 2000, Crazy for You, 2002, Footloose, 2004 (hon. mention for set building, Mag.), Seussical, 2006. Music dir. Kiwanis Club Kapers, Meriden, Conn., 2000—01. Mem.: Conn. Music Educators Assn. (25 Yrs. Svc. award). Avocations: travel, bicycling.

SCARDAMALIA, MARLENE, education educator, researcher; PhD, U. Toronto, 1973. K-12 theme leader TeleLearning Network of Centres of Excellence, 1996—2002; pres.' chair in edn. & knowledge technologies Ontario Inst. for Studies in Edn., U. Toronto, 2002—; dir. Inst. for Knowledge Innovation and Tech. Contbr. articles to profl. jours. Named Rschr. of Yr., Telelearning Network of Centres of Excellence, 1997; recipient Jose Vasconcelos World Award of Edn., 2006; fellow Ctr for Advanced Study in the Behavioral Scis., 1992—93. Fellow: Can. Psychological Assn.; mem.: Can. Inst. for Advanced Rsch., Human Devel. Program, US Nat. Acad. Edn. Office: Ontario Inst for Studies in Edn 252 Bloor Street W Toronto Canada M5S 1V6 Office Phone: 416-923-6641 2264. E-mail: mscardamalia@kf.oise.utoronto.ca. *

SCARDINO, DAME MARJORIE MORRIS, publishing executive; b. Flagstaff, Ariz., Jan. 25, 1947; d. Robert Weldon and Beth (Lamb) Morris; m. Albert James Scardino, Apr. 19, 1974; children: Adelaide Katherine Morris, William Brown, Albert Henry Hugh. BA, Baylor U.; JD, U. San Francisco. Ptnr. Brannen Wessels & Searcy, Savannah, Ga., 1976-85; pub. Ga. Gazette Pub. Co., Savannah, 1978-85; pres. The Economist Newspaper Group, Inc., NYC, 1985-93; chief exec. The Economist Group, London,

1993-97, Pearson P.L.C., London, 1997—. Non-exec. dir. Nokia Corp. Trustee Carter Ctr.; bd. dir. MacArthur Found., Atlantic Council of U.S.; trustee Victoria and Albert Mus. Named Dame Comdr. British Empire, 2002; named one of Most Powerful Women, Forbes mag., 2005, 50 Women to Watch, Wall St. Jour., 2005, 2006, 50 Most Powerful Women in Global Bus., Fortune mag., 2005. Office: Pearson PLC 80 Strand London WC2R ORL England

SCARDINO, PETER T., urologic oncologic surgeon; b. Portsmouth, Va., Sept. 28, 1945; m. Alice Barrow ("Barrie") Myrick, 1965; children: Allison Kelly, Peter Daniel Robinson, Elizabeth Barrow. BA, Yale U., 1967; MD, Duke U., 1971. Diplomate Am. Bd. Urology. Resident in surgery Mass. Gen. Hosp., Boston, 1971-73; clin. assoc. surgery br. Nat. Cancer inst., NIH, 1973-76; resident in urology UCLA Sch. Medicine, 1976-79, instr., 1978-79; asst. prof., then assoc. prof. Baylor U. Coll. Medicine, Houston, 1979-86, prof. urology, 1986-98, Russell and Mary Hugh Scott prof., chmn. dept. urology, 1989-98; chmn. dept. urology Alfred P. Sloan chair, head prostate cancer program Meml. Sloan-Kettering Cancer Ctr., NYC, 1999—, mem. Inst. for Cancer Rsch. prostate cancer program, 1999—; prof. Weill Med. Coll. Cornell U., NYC, 1998—. Co-author (with Judith Kelman): Dr. Peter Scardino's Prostate Book, 2005. Recipient Eugene Fuller Triennial Prostate award 1995, Pres.'s award Am. Found. Urolog. Disease, 1996, Alumnus award Duke U. Med. Ctr., 1999, Gordon Wilson lectr. Am. Clin. and Climatological Assn., 1999. Fellow ACS, Am. Surg. Assn.; mem. Am. Urology Assn. (Gold Cytoscope award 1989), Clin. Soc. Genitourinary Surgeons, Am. Assn. Genitourinary Surgeons, Am. Soc. Clin. Oncology, Am. Assn. Cancer Rsch., Inst. Medicine Nat. Acad. Sci., N.Y. Acad. Sci.

SCARINGELLO, NINA MARIA, literature and language professor; m. Patrick C. Scaringello, Aug. 26, 1978; children: Charles, Carolyn. BA, Queens Coll., Flushing, 1975, MA, 1981. Cert. in rhetoric and composition studies SUNY, Stony Brook, 2005. Asst. and adj. prof. English Grant campus Suffolk County CC, Brentwood, NY, 1994—. Mem.: Nat. Coun. Tchrs. English.

SCARLETT, AUSTIN, apparel designer; Degree in fashion design, Fashion Inst. Tech., NYC. With Fashion Inst. Tech. Mus.; costume designer NY Theatre, MGM and Paramount studios, 2001; designer Austin Scarlett line; bridal designer, Kenneth Pool Collection Amsale, NYC. Design contestant Bravo's Project Runway, season 1. Office: Amsale 625 Madison Ave New York NY 10022 E-mail: Austin@AustinScarlett.com. *

SCARLETT, (PATRICIA) LYNN, federal agency administrator; b. Pitts., Dec. 8, 1949; d. James Miles and Virginia (Young) S.; m. James R. Trotter, May 6, 1978; 1 child, Rachel Scarlett Trotter. BA, U. Calif., Santa Barbara, 1970, MA, 1972. Vis. lectr. U. Calif., Santa Barbara, 1980-81; book rev. editor Reason Mag., Santa Barbara, 1982-85; dir. rsch. Reason Found., Santa Monica, Calif., 1985-89, v.p. rsch., 1990—2001, pres., CEO, 2001; asst. sec. policy, mgmt. & budget US Dept. Interior, Washington, 2001—05, dep. sec., 2005—, acting sec., 2006. Mem. task force Calif. Joint Legis. Com. on Surrogate Parenting, Calif., 1989-90; panel reviewer Project 88 Phase II, 1990; chmn. issues com. Citizens for Balanced Community, Santa Barbara, 1989—; chmn. "How Clean Is Clean" Working Group, Nat. Environmental Policy Inst., 1993-98; bd. dirs. Laguna Blanca Sch., Santa Barbara. Author: (chpt.) Food Politics, 1982; contbr. articles to profl. jours. Chmn. Jim Trotter for City Coun., Carpinteria, Calif., 1990—; mem. parents aux. Laguna Blanca, 1986-88. Geneva Inst. of Internat. Studies fellow, 1974-75. Mem. Friends of Girls Club Corp. (2d v.p. 1986-87). Republican. Avocations: birdwatching, drawing, swimming. Office: US Dept Interior 1849 C St NW Rm 5110 Washington DC 20240

SCARNATI, JOSEPH B., III, state senator; b. Brockway, Pa., Jan. 2, 1962; s. Joseph II and Yvonne Scarnati; m. Sheryl Hetrick, Dec. 1, 1990; 3 children BBA, Pa. State U., DuBois, 1982. Mem. Brockway Borough Coun., Pa., 1986—96, Pa. Senate from 25th Dist., Harrisburg, 2001—, pres. pro tempore, 2007—, vice chmn. environ. resources and energy, 2001—, mem. appropriations com., mem. agr. and rural affairs com., 2001—, mem. econ. devel. com., 2001—, mem. game and fisheries com. Harriburg, 2001—, mem. intergovtl. affairs com. Harrisburg, 2001—. Office: State House 187 Capitol Bldg Senate Box 203025 Harrisburg PA 17120-3025

SCARNECCHIA, SUELLYN, dean, law educator; BA, Northwestern U., 1978; JD, U. Mich., 1981. Bar: Mich. Ptnr. McCroskey, Feldman, Cochrane & Brock, Battle Creek, Mich.; clin asst. prof. U. Mich. Sch Law, 1987, clin. prof. law, 1993, clin. coord., 1994—96, assoc. dean clin. affairs, 1996—2002, assoc. dean adminstrn., 1999—2001, asst. provost academic and faculty affairs, 2002; dean, prof. law U. N.Mex, 2003—; chair Jud. Nominating Commn. Govt. N.Mex. Atty. U. Mich. Child Advocacy Law Clinic, 1987; bd. dirs. Clin. Legal Edn. Assn.; panelist Mich. Atty. Disciplinary Bd.; tech. adv. Mich. Supreme Ct. Task Force on Gender and Race Bias. Mem.: Women Lawyers Assn. Mich. (past pres.), Battle Creek Area Orgn. Against Domestic Violence (past bd. pres.). Office: U NMex Sch Law 1117 Stanford NE Albuquerque NM 87131-1431 Office Phone: 505-277-4700. Home Fax: 505-277-0068. E-mail: scarnecchia@law.unm.edu.

SCAROLA, JOHN MICHAEL, dentist, educator; b. NYC, Nov. 18, 1934; s. Michael Fidelis and Filomena Mary (Turso) S.; m. Theodora Mary Marty, June 15, 1963; children: Michael A., John P., Stephen A., Robert M., Mary E. BS, Fordham Coll., 1956; DDS, Columbia U., 1960. Instr. Columbia Dental Sch., NYC, 1962-68, 1969-72, 1969-72, assoc. clin. prof., 1973-86, course dir. prosthodontic elective, 1977-91, clin. prof., 1986—; ethics facilitator Columbia U., Sch. Dental and Oral Surgery, 1992—. Lectr., clin. prof. postgrad. prostodontics Columbia U., N.Y.C., 1986—, AEGD-Columbia U., N.Y.C., 1990-92, Luth. Med. Ctr., Bklyn., 1993—; cons. in prosthodontics Northport VA Hosp., East Northport, N.Y., 1970-91. Scoutmaster Boy Scouts Am., Port Washington, NY, 1976-78; chmn. spl. gifts Bishop's Annual Appeal, St. Peter's-Port Washington, 1977-78; KC (4th degree) sports coach St. Paul the Apostles Coun., Brookville, NY, 1980-83; fundraising com. The Yard, Martha's Vineyard, Mass., 1990; concert com. Musician's Emergency Fund, NYC, 1992. Lt. USNR, 1960-62. Fellow Am. Coll. Dentists (chmn. NY sect. 1994, v.p. 2005-06, Regent of Regency 1998-2002, pres.-elect 2006—), NY Acad. Dentistry (pres. 1989-90), Greater NY Acad. Prosthodontics (dir. 1993-97); mem. Greater NY Acad. Prosthodontics Found. (dir., pres. 1989-97), NY Acad. Dentistry Endowment Fund (dir., pres. 1992-93), Am Coll. Dentists (pres., 2007—). Republican. Roman Catholic. Avocations: golf, opera, classical music, gardening. Home: 83 Fruitledge Rd Glen Head NY 11545-3317 Office: 501 Madison Ave New York NY 10022-5602 Office Phone: 212-758-9690. Personal E-mail: jscaroladds@aol.com.

SCARPA, A. MICHAEL, apparel and corporate financial executive; Degree in Acctg., 1982. CPA 1982. Fin. analyst Krementz & Co.; from budget mgr. to CFO Liz Claiborne, NYC, 1983—2000, CFO, 2000—, sr. v.p., 2002—. Office: Liz Claiborne 1441 Broadway New York NY 10018-1805

SCARPA, MICHAEL, apparel executive; b. 1956; Budget mgr. Liz Claiborne, Inc., NYC, 1983, v.p., divisional controller, 1991—95, v.p., fin. planning and ops., 1995—2000, v.p., CFO, 2000—02, sr. v.p., CFO, 2002—05, sr. v.p., fin. & distbn., CFO, 2005—07, CFO, COO, 2007—. Office: Liz Claiborne Inc 1441 Broadway New York NY 10018 Office Phone: 212-354-4900. Office Fax: 212-626-3416. *

SCARPELLI, BOB, advertising executive; Copywriter Needham Harper, Chgo., 1977—80, named creative dir., 1980; chief creative officer DDB Chgo., 1994, vice chmn., 1995, chmn., 2001; chief creative officer DDB Worldwide (U.S), 2000; elected bd. dirs. DDB Worldwide, 1998, chief creative officer, 2005—, chmn., 2006—. Mem. bd. Chgo. Internat. Film Festival, The Va. Commonwealth Univ. AdCenter, The Chgo. Creative Club, The Off the Street Club, Partnership for a Drug-Free Am.; chmn. Internat. ANDY Awards, 2000, Radio Mercury Awards, 2001, Irish Internat. Advt. Festival, 2001, Clio Festival, 2003. Office: DDB Worldwide 437 Madison Ave New York NY 10022 Office Phone: 212-415-2000. *

SCARR, SANDRA WOOD, retired psychology educator, researcher; b. Washington, Aug. 8, 1936; d. John Ruxton and Jane (Powell) Wood; m. Harry Alan Scarr, Dec. 26, 1961 (div. 1970); children: Phillip, Karen, Rebbecca, Stephanie; m. James Callan Walker, Aug. 9, 1982 (div. 1994). AB, Vassar Coll., 1958; AM, Harvard U., 1963, PhD, 1965. Asst. prof. psychology U. Md., College Park, 1964-67; assoc. prof. U. Pa., Phila., 1967-71; prof. U. Minn., Mpls., 1971-77, Yale U., New Haven, 1977-83; Commonwealth prof. U. Va., Charlottesville, 1983-95, chmn. dept. psychology, 1984-90; CEO, chmn. bd. dirs. KinderCare Learning Ctr., Inc., 1995-97; ret., 1997. Mem. nat. adv. bd. Robert Wood Johnson Found., Princeton, N.J., 1985-91; coord. coun. psychology SUNY Bd. Regents, N.Y.C., 1984-92; prof. Kerstin Hesselgren, Sweden, 1993-94. Author: Race, Social Class and Individual Differences in IQ, 1981, Mother Care/Other Care, 1984 (Nat. Book award APA 1985), Caring for Children, 1989; editor Jour. Devel. Psychology, 1980-86, Current Directions in Psychol. Sci., 1991-95. Fellow Ctr. for Advanced Studies, Stanford U., Calif., 1976-77; grantee NIH, NSF, others, 1967-95. Fellow AAAS, APA (chmn. com. on human rsch. 1980-83, coun. of reps. 1984-89, bd. dirs. 1988-90, Award for Disting. Contbn. to Rsch. on Pub. Policy 1988), Am. Psychol. Soc. (bd. dirs. 1992—, pres. 1996-97, James McKeen Cattell award 1993); mem. Am. Acad. Arts and Scis. (coun. mem. 1995-2000), Behavior Genetics Assn. (pres. 1985-86, exec. coun. 1976-79, 84-87, Dobzhansky award 2004), Soc. for Rsch. in Child Devel. (governing coun. 1974-76, 87-93, chmn. fin. com. 1987-89, pres. 1989-91), Internat. Soc. for Study of Behavioral Devel. (exec. bd. 1987-94). Avocations: dogs, gardening. Home: 77-6222 Kaumalumalu Dr Holualoa HI 96725-9757 Office Phone: 808-322-9445. Personal E-mail: sandrascar@aol.com.

SCARRITT, THOMAS VARNON, newspaper editor; b. Tuscaloosa, Ala., Jan. 28, 1953; s. Charles Wesley and Valerie (Varnon) S.; m. Kathryn Rush Hubbard, Dec. 28, 1973; children: Sara Kathryn, Thomas Varnon Jr. BA in Journalism, U. N.C., 1974; MBA, Samford U., 1995. Reporter The Birmingham (Ala.) News, 1975-79, Washington corr., 1979-83, news editor, 1983-85, editl. page editor, 1986-89, exec. editor, 1989-97, editor, 1997—. Bd. dirs. Workshops Inc. Mem. Am. Soc. Newspaper Editors, Soc. Profl. Journalists, Kiwanis (Birmingham), Phi Beta Kappa. Episcopal. Home: 4240 Clairmont Ave S Birmingham AL 35222-3724 Office: The Birmingham News 2201 4th Ave N Birmingham AL 35203-3840 Home Phone: 205-591-4109; Office Phone: 205-325-2205. E-mail: tscarritt@bhamnews.com.

SCARWID, DIANA ELIZABETH, actress; b. Savannah, Ga. d. Anthony and Elizabeth Scarwid. Grad., Am. Acad. Dramatic Arts, 1975; degree in Theater Arts, Acting, Pace U., 1975. Appeared in films including Pretty Baby, Honeysuckle Rose, Inside Moves, (Oscar award nomination Best Supporting Actress), Mommie Dearest, Rumble Fish, Strange Invaders, Silkwood, Psycho III, Extremeties, Heat, Neon Bible, The Cure, Gold Diggers: The Secret of Bear Mountain, What Lies Beneath, The Angel Doll, A Guy Thing, Party Monster, The Clearing; TV films include Thou Shalt Not Kill, Studs Lonigan, Guyana Tragedy: The Story of Jim Jones, Desperate Lives, A Bunny's Tale, After the Promise, Night of The Hunter, Critical Choices, Bastard Out of Carolina, Angel of Pennsylvania Avenue, Truman (Emmy nomination), If These Walls Could Talk, Ruby Bridges Story, also mini-series From the Earth to the Moon, Before He Wakes; theater prodns. include Key Exchange, Toronto, Can., A Thousand Clowns, Jupiter, Fla., Gethsamanie Springs, Mark Taper Forum, LA, Spoon River Anthology, Ring 'round the Moon, NYC, Nat. Shakespeare Conservancy, NY; (TV films) Down Will Come Baby, Dirty Pictures, Path to War, (series) WonderFalls. Avocations: reading, bicycling, crabbing, walking.

SCATENA, LORRAINE BORBA, retired rancher, women's rights advocate, researcher; b. San Rafael, Calif., Feb. 18, 1924; d. Joseph and Eugenia (Simas) de Borba; m. Louis G. Scatena, Feb. 14, 1960, dec. Nov. 1995; children: Louis Vincent, Eugenia Gayle. BA, Dominican Coll., San Rafael, 1945; postgrad., Calif. Sch. Fine Arts, 1948, U. Calif., Berkeley, 1956—57. Cert. elem. tchr. Calif. Tchr. Dominican Coll., 1946; tchr. of mentally handicapped San Anselmo (Calif.) Sch. Dist., 1946; tchr. Fairfax (Calif.) Pub. Elem. Sch., 1946—53; asst. to mayor Fairfax (Calif.) City Recreation, 1948—53; tchr., libr. U.S. Dependent Schs., Mainz am Rhine, Germany, 1953—56; translator Portugal Travel Tours, Lisbon, 1954; bonding sec. Am. Fore Ins. Group, San Francisco, 1958—60; rancher, farmer Yerington, Nev., 1960—98. Hostess com. Caldecott and Newbury Authors' Awards, San Francisco, 1959; mem. Nev. State Legis. Commn., 1975; coord. Nevadans for Equal Rights Amendment, 1975-78, rural areas rep., 1976-78; testifier Nev. State Senate and Assembly, 1975, 77; mem. adv. com. Fleischmann Coll. Agr. U. Nev., 1977-80, 81-84; speaker Grants and Rsch. Projects, Bishop, Calif., 1977, Choices for Tomorrow's Women, Fallon, Nev., 1989. Poetry presenter World Congress on Arts and Comm., Lisbon, Portugal, 1999, Washington, 2000, St. John's Coll.-Cambridge U., 2001, Vancouver, B.C., Can., 2002. Trustee Wassuk Coll., Hawthorne, Nev., 1984-87; mem. Lyon County Friends of Libr., Yerington, 1971—, Lyon County Mus. Soc., 1978—; sec., pub. info. chmn. Lyon County Rep. Women, 1968-73, program v.p., 1973-75; mem. Lyon County Rep. Ctrl. Com. 1973-74, Marin County Soc. Artists, San Anselmo, Calif., 1948-53; charter mem. Eleanor Roosevelt Edn. Fund for Women and Girls, 1990, sustaining mem., 1992—; Nev. rep. 1st White House Conf. Rural Am. Women, Washington, 1980; participant internat. reception, Washington, 1980; mem. pub. panel individual presentation Shakespeare's Treatment of Women Characters, Nev. Theatre for the Arts, Ashland, Oreg., Shakespearean Actors local performance, 1977; mem. Nev. Women's History Project, U. Nev., 1996—; mem. pres.'s circle Dominican U. Calif., 1997-; mem. Bancroft Libr.'s coun. U. Calif., Berkeley, 2002-. Recipient Outstanding Conservation Farmer award Mason Valley Conservation Dist., 1992, Soroptimist Internat. Women Helping women award 1983, invitation to first all-women delegation to U.S.A. from People's Republic China, U.S. House Reps., 1979; Public Forum Travel grantee Edn. Title IX, Oakland, Calif., 1977; Internat. Biog. Ctr. (Cambridge) fellow World Lit. Acad., 1993. Mem. AAUW (life mem. nat. br. 1975—, Leaders Circle 1998-), Lyon County Ret. Tchrs. Assn. (unit pres. 1979-80, 84-86, v.p. 1986-88, Nev. State Outstanding Svc. award 1981, state conv. gen. chmn. 1985), Rural Am. Women Inc., AAUW (br. pres. 1972-74, 74-76, chair edn. found. programs 1983—, state conv. gen. chmn. 1976, 87, state sec. 1970-72, state legis. program chmn. 1976-77, state chmn. internat. rels. 1979-81, state pres. 1981-83, br. travelship, discovering women in U.S. history Radcliffe Coll. 1981, State Humanities award 1975, Future Fund Nat. award 1983, Lorraine Scatena endowment gift named in her honor for significant contbns. to AAUW Ednl. Found. 1997), Mason Valley Country Club, Italian Cath. Fedn. (pres. 1986-88), Uniao Portuguesa Estado da Calif., Nat. Mus. of Women in the Arts (charter mem., 1987, assoc., mem. mus. coun. 2000—). Roman Catholic. Avocations: writing, photography, travel, Azores history. Home: PO Box 247 Yerington NV 89447-0247

SCATES, ALICE YEOMANS, retired federal official; b. Pitts., Jan. 21, 1915; d. William E. and Georgiana L. (Lloyd) Yeomans. BS, State Tchrs. Coll., Glassboro, NJ, 1936; MEd, Duke U., 1949; EdD, George Washington U., 1963. Tchr. elem. sch., Haddon Heights, N.J., 1937-43; civilian personnel officer Sedalia Army Airfield, Mo., Greenfield Army Airfield, S.C., 1944-46; pers. tng. officer VA Ctr., Dayton, Ohio, 1947—48; rsch. assoc., dir. Am. Coun. on Edn. Staff for Office Naval Rsch. Projects, 1949-53; asst. dir. Nat. Home Study Coun., 1954; editor, rsch. asst. Office of Edn. HEW, 1955, rsch. analyst, coord. coop. rsch. program, 1956-64, program planning officer occupl. rsch. program, 1965-66, dir. basic rsch. br. secondary edn., 1967-69; program planning and eval. officer Nat. Ctr. Ednl. R & D, 1969-71; eval. specialist Office Program Eval., 1971-80; eval. officer Office of Mgmt. U.S. Dept. Edn., 1980-82, cons., 1982-91; mem. continuing care adv. com. Md. State Office on Aging, 1994-99. Contbr. articles to profl. jours.; editor: Life Line, 1998—. Mem. Nat. Continuing Care Residents Assn.; bd. dirs. Town Ctr. Cmty. Assn., Columbia, Md., 1997-2001. Capt. U.S. Army, 1943-46. Fellow AAAS; mem. LWV, Am. Sociol. Assn., Am. Ednl. Rsch. Assn., Adult Edn. Assn., Kappa Delta Pi, Phi Delta Gamma. Home and Office: Vantage House # 1006 5400 Vantage Point Rd Columbia MD 21044-2667 Personal E-mail: ayscates@msn.com.

SCATES, ALLEN EDWARD, coach; BA, UCLA, 1961, MS, 1962. Coach volleyball UCLA, 1970—. Coached UCLA to 18 NCAA championships. Recipient All Time Great Coach awrd USA Volleyball, 1995, Alumnas of Yr. in Profl. Devel., UCLA, 2003; inducted Volleyball Hall of Fame, 1993, Calif. Beach Volleyball Hall of Fame, 1998, UCLA Hall of Fame, 2003; named Coach of Yr., 5 times, U.S. Olympic Com. Coach Yr., 1998. Office: UCLA Morgan Ctr PO Box 24044 Los Angeles CA 90024-0044 E-mail: ascates@athletics.ucla.edu.

SCATURRO, PHILIP DAVID, investment banker, academic administrator; b. Newark, Dec. 8, 1938; s. Charles and Rose (Montino) Scaturro. BA, Williams Coll., 1960; JD, MBA, Columbia U., 1963. Analyst Ladenburg, Thalmann & Co., Inc., NYC, 1964-67; v.p. Sellin, Forbes & Smith, NYC, 1967, Allen & Co. Inc., NYC, 1967-71, mng. dir., exec. v.p., 1977—; gen. ptnr. R&S Assocs., NYC, 1972-76; pvt. investor, NYC, 1976-77; chmn. bd. trustees New Sch U, NYC, 1999—. Bd. dirs. Wilmorite, Inc., Rochester, NY, 2000—05, Mass. Mus. Contemporary Art Found., Inc., North Adams, 1997—, NYC Opera, 1985—2005, mem. exec. com., 1985—2005, chmn. fin. com., 1985—2005, treas., 1985—2005, trustee, 1985—, mem. exec. com., 1985—; trustee New Sch. U., 1989—. Mem.: Century Assn., Univ. Club (N.Y.C.). Avocations: opera, music, theater, wine, fly fishing. Office: Allen & Co 711 Fifth Ave 9th Fl New York NY 10022-3111

SCAVARDA, DONALD ROBERT, composer, artist; b. Iron Mountain, Mich., June 18, 1928; m. Barbara Janet Regner, Nov. 13, 1965. MMus, U. Mich., 1953. Co-founder, organizer Once Festival Musical Premieres, Ann Arbor, Mich., 1960-65. Composer: Groups For Piano, 1959, Sounds for Eleven, 1961, (Haiku song cycle) In the Autumn Mountains, 1961, Matrix for Clarinetist (widely recognized as the pioneering work in discovery and development of clarinet multiphonics), 1962, (piano, clarinet, 8mm film) Landscape Journey, 1963, (film score for electronic realization) Greys, 1963, (multiple film projection and tape) Caterpillar, 1965; paintings include Chamber Music, 1997, Portrait of Helen P., 1998; video films: Cinamatrix, 2002, Colorscapes, 2007; composed recs. named to Top 10 List, Art Forum Mag., 2003; boxed CD-set, Music From the Once Festival-1961-1966, 2003. Fulbright scholar, 1953; recipient 1st prize for Fantasy For Violin And Orchestra BMI Inc., 1954. Mem.: World Wildlife Fund, Humane Soc. U.S. Home: PO Box 1908 Ann Arbor MI 48106-1908

SCEARSE, PATRICIA DOTSON, nursing educator, dean; b. Wabash, Ind., Sept. 4, 1931; d. Claude Richard and Lilly Etta (Colvill) D.; m. Vernon Quinton Scearse, June 26, 1955 (dec. Mar. 1990); 1 child, Victoria Lynn Lenderman. BS, Earlham Coll., 1955; MS, U. Colo., 1968; D in Nursing Sci., U. Calif., San Francisco, 1974. RN. Staff nurse Reid Meml. Hosp., Richmond, Ind., 1954-55; head nurse, instr. Hillcrest Bapt. Hosp., Waco, Tex., 1955-56; instr. Sch. Nursing Candler Hosp., Savannah, Ga., 1956-60; adminstrv. asst., edn. cons. Wyo. State Bd. Nursing, Cheyenne, 1964-68; asst. prof. San Diego State U., 1969, Ball State U., Muncie, Ind., 1969-71; assoc. prof., area chairperson U. Mich., Ann Arbor, 1974-80; prof., dean Coll. Nursing Tex. Christian U., Ft. Worth, 1980-95, emeritus dean, prof., 1995—. Pub. policy editor Jour. Profl. Nursing, Phila., 1986-89; editorial cons. Jour. Pub. Health Nursing, New Haven, 1984-89; contbr. articles to profl. jours. Recipient Outstanding Nurse award Sigma Theat Tau, Beta Alpha, Ft. Worth, 1986; Kennedy Inst. Ethics postdoctoral fellow, Georgetown U., 1978. Mem. ANA, APHA (bd. govs. 1976), Am. Assn. Colls. of Nursing (bd. dirs. 1982-84, 85-87), Nat. League for Nursing, Coun. Baccalaureate and Higher Degree Programs (bd. rev.), Assn. Community Health Nurse Educators (named Great 100 Nurses 1992). Home: 3301 Quail Run Dr High Point NC 27265-2589

SCELFO, CHRIS, university football coach; b. Abbeville, La., Sept. 30, 1963; m. Nancy Caldwell; children: Sarah Beth, Joseph II. BS, N.E. La. U., 1986, MEd, 1988. Asst. coach River Oaks H.S., Monroe, La., 1986; asst. offensive line and tight ends coach N.E. La. U., 1986-87; offensive line grad. asst. coach U. Okla., Norman, 1988, receiver coach, 1989; offensive line coach Marshall U., 1990-95, offensive coord., 1993-95; asst. head coach, offensive line coach U. Ga., Augusta, 1996-98; head football coach Tulane U., New Orleans, 1998—. Office: Tulane U Dept Athletics 6823 Saint Charles Ave New Orleans LA 70118-5665

SCELSA, JOSEPH VINCENT, sociologist, educator, dean; b. NYC, Dec. 7, 1945; s. Albert John and Katherine Mary S.; m. Joyce Ann Tisi, Nov. 13, 1981; 1 child, Jonathan. AA, LIU, 1966, BA, 1968; MA, CUNY, 1973, MSEd, 1978; MA, Columbia U., 1983, EdD, 1984. Lic. mental health counselor, NY, 2006; cert. sch. counselor, NY. Counselor, tchr. NYC Bd. Edn., 1970-78, coord. career and occupational edn., 1979; coord. specialized counseling CUNY, 1979-81; pvt. practice counseling, NYC, 1975—; lectr. grad. faculty Herbert H. Lehman Coll., CUNY, 1980—; dean Calandra Inst., CUNY, 1994—; prof. student pers. Queens Coll., CUNY, 1999, v.p., 2000. Consul gen. of Italy in NY; pres. Italian Am. Mus., 2001—. Active Coun. of 1000 nat. Italian-Am. Found.; past cive chair multi cultural adv. bd. NYC Bd. Edn., 1990-91; NY State Mentoring Program Adv. Bd., 1990—; bd. dirs. Nat. Ethnic Coalition Orgns., 1990—, Coalition Italo-Am. Assn., 2000—; Italian Apostalate, NY, 1993. Decorated cavaliere Order of Merit Republic of Italy; recipient Disting. Alumni award LIU, 1985, Organizational Leadership award Coalition Italo-Am. Assns., Inc., 1988, Americus award Bronx Community Coll., 1989, Role Model award Club DaVinci, 1990, Inte I-A Student Assn. award, CUNY, 1991, Intergroup Rels. Chancellor's award, 1994, FIERI Leadership award, 1993, Philip Mazzei award, 1993, Ellis Island medal of honor, 1997, N.Y. State Govs. award for Excellence, 1999, Medal for 3d Millennium, 2000, Good Shapers Award, Woman & Work Program, 2005; named House of Savoy, 1997; Italian fellow John Jay Coll., 1993; inductee St. Lucy's Hall of Fame, 1996. Mem. Am. Counseling Assn., Am. Mental Health Counselors Assn. (cert. of recognition 1979, counselor of yr. 1983-84), Nat. Acad. Cert. Clin. Mental Health Counselors, Nat. Bd. for Cert. Counselors, Am.-Italian Hist. Assn., NY State Mental Health Counselors Assn. (past pres., Outstanding Work award 1980), Ill. Club. Home: 41 Carwall Ave Mount Vernon NY 10552-1211 Office: CUNY 555 W 57th St Ste 1137 New York NY 10019

SCEPER, DUANE HAROLD, lawyer; b. Norfolk, Va., Nov. 16, 1946; s. Robert George and Marion Eudora (Hynes) S.; m. Sharon Diane Cramer, July 4, 1981; stepchildren: Karin Stevenson, Diane Stevenson. BS in Law, Western State U., 1979, JD, 1980. Bar: Calif. 1982, U.S. Dist. Ct. (so. dist.) Calif. 1982. Field engr. Memorex/Tex. Instruments, San Diego, 1968-70; computer programmer San Diego, 1970-81; atty. Allied Ins. Group, San Diego, 1981-85; sole practice San Diego, 1985-87; ptnr. Paluso & Sceper,

San Diego, 1987—. Cons. computers 1980—; lectr. estate planning various orgns. Patentee in field. Active Com. to Elect King Golden to Congress, San Diego, 1978. Served with USAF, 1965-68. Recipient Am. Jurisprudence award, 1979. Mem. ABA, San Diego County Bar Assn., Assn. Trial Lawyers of Am., Calif. Trial Lawyers Assn., San Diego Trial Lawyers Assn., Am. Subrogation Attys., Assn. of Ins. Def. Counsel, So. Calif. Def. Counsel, Air Commando Assn. (life), Delta Theta Phi. Democrat. Home: 2641 Massachusetts Ave Lemon Grove CA 91945-3149 Office: Paluso & Sceper 1010 2d Ave Ste 1350 San Diego CA 92101 Office Phone: 619-232-8917. Business E-Mail: dhs@thelegalway.com.

SCERNO, JOSEPH BENEDICT, management consultant executive, arbitrator; b. Bklyn., Dec. 25, 1936; s. Benedict Joseph and Mary Laura (Demartini) Scerno; children from previous marriage: Joseph B. III, George P. BS, NYU, 1962; MA in Counseling, Marywood U., Scranton, Pa., 1977. Cert. sr. practitioner human resource mgmt. Human Resource Accreditation Inst., Washington, 1975. V.p., gen. mgr. Express Haulage Corp., NYC, 1959—62; asst. v.p. indsl. rels. Tech. Materials Corp., Mamaroneck, NY, 1962—66; v.p. indsl. rels. Occidental Petroleum Corp., LA, 1966—72; v.p. pers. Hosp. Joint Diseases ad Med. Ctr., NYC, 1972—74; v.p., dir. employee cmty. rels. Intext, Inc., Scranton, 1674—1979; v.p. human resources GBP Industries, Buffalo, 1979—84; v.p., pres. human resources Coastal Corp., Bklyn., 1984—88; commr. Fed. Mediation and Councilation Svcs., Washington, 1988—97; pres. SJM Holdings, Ltd., Clarks Summit, Pa., 2002—; mng. dir. Jospeh B. Scerno Assocs., Internat. Mgmt. Consultancy, Clarks Summit, 1997—. Arbitrator NY State Panel Arbitrators, NYC, 1966—88; cons. City Scranton, Pa., 1976—79; arbitrator Joseph B. Scerno Arbitrators, Clarks Summit, 1997—. With USAF, 1954—57, Korea. Named Col., Hon. Order Ky. Cols., 1990. Mem.: VFW, MENSA, Pa. Soc., NY Acad. Scis., Am. Legion, Zeta Beta Tau (charter pres. 1960—). Avocations: golf, travel, sailing.

SCEUSA, NICHOLAS A., pharmacologist; b. Bklyn., July 22, 1948; s. Nicolo Sceusa and Maria Rita Anastasi; m. Donna Lynn Klein, Feb. 23, 1973; children: Amanda, Nicholas. BS in Biology, Syracuse U., 1971; BS in Pharmacy, L.I. U., 1977; PharmD, U. Ill., Chgo., 1996. Registered pharmacist, N.Y. Sr. staff pharmacist King Khalid Univ. Hosp., Riyadh, Saudi Arabia, 1984-86, Tawam Hosp., Al Ain, United Arab Emirates, 1986-87; staff pharmacist II St. Luke's - Roosevelt Hosp., NYC, 1987—90; staff pharmacist St. Clare's Hosp., 1990—95; pres., CEO Gelsus Rsch. and Consulting, Inc., 1997—. Author (with others): The Secret History of Italian-American Evacuation and Internment during World War II; contbr. articles to profl. jours. Advisor to Sch. Bd. Dist. 3, N.Y.C., 1996-98. Mem.: Am. Assn. Pharm. Scientists, Masons (treas.). Episcopalian. Achievements include patents for biofiltration and (Teorell-Meyer) dosage forms; invention of RAPID drug delivery system; rechargeable cardiac stent; new forms of surgical bandages and novel nutraceutical products. Avocations: hunting, fishing, outdoors, science, invention. Home and Office: 145 W 96th St Ste 1A New York NY 10025-6449 Home Phone: 212-663-7905; Office Phone: 212-663-7905. Office Fax: 212-280-1255. Personal E-mail: gelsus@verizon.net.

SCHAAB, ARNOLD J., lawyer; b. Newark, 1939; s. Robert George and Pauline Schaab; m. Marcia Stecker, 1964 (div. 1978); children: Emily Diana, Genevieve; m. Patricia Caesar, 1981 (div. 1996); m. Susan McGlamery, 2000. BA, New Sch. U., 1962; LLB, Harvard U., 1965. Bar: NY 1967, US Dist. Ct. (so. and ea. dists.) NY 1967. Assoc. Chadbourne & Parke, NYC, 1966-69; ptnr. Anderson, Kill & Olick, NYC, 1969-78; sr. ptnr. Pryor Cashman LLP, NYC, 1978—. Chmn. Literacy Ptnrs., Inc. Fulbright scholar Law Faculty U. Paris. Fellow NY Bar Found., Am. Bar Found.; mem. ABA (vice chair internat. fin. transactions com., sections bus. law, dispute resolution internat. law practice), NY State Bar Assn. (chmn. internat. law practice sect., chmn. spl. com. free trade Ams., mem. com. alternative dispute resolution, house dels., fin. com., long range planning com., by-laws com.), Assn. Bar City NY (com. pvt. investment funds, com. internat. trade, com. fgn. comparative law), Univ. Club (treas., chmn. fin. com., chmn. audit com., mem. coun.), Archaeol. Inst. Am., Bibl. Archaeology Soc. Office: Pryor Cashman LLP 410 Park Ave New York NY 10022-4441

SCHAAF, DOUGLAS ALLAN, lawyer; b. Green Bay, Wis., Nov. 18, 1955; s. Carlton Otto and Fern (Brunette) S.; m. Kathlyn T. Bielke, Feb. 23, 1988. BBA magna cum laude in Internat. Bus., St. Norbert Coll., DePere, Wis., 1978; JD, U. Notre Dame, 1981. Bar: Ill. 1981, Calif. 1987. Assoc. McDermott, Will & Emery, Chgo., 1981-84, Skadden, Arps, Slate, Meagher & Flom, 1984-89; ptnr. Paul Hastings, Janofsky & Walker, LA, 1989—, chair tax dept., 2006—. Adj. faculty mem. John Marshall Law Sch., 1984-87. Atty. Chgo. Vol. Legal Services, 1984-87; bd. dirs. Orange County Alzheimer's Assn., 1993—. Mem. Orange County Bar Assn. (chair tax sect. 1994-96). Office: Paul Hastings Janofsky & Walker 695 Town Center Dr Ste 1700 Costa Mesa CA 92626-7191 Office Phone: 714-668-6221. Office Fax: 714-668-6441. Business E-Mail: dougschaaf@paulhastings.com.

SCHAAL, BARBARA ANNA, evolutionary biologist, educator; BS in Biology with honors, U. Ill., Chgo., 1969; MPhil in Population Biology, Yale U., 1971, PhD in Population Biology, 1974. spkr. in field. Assoc. prof. biology Washington U., St. Louis, 1980-86, prof., 1986—; prof. genetics Wash. U. Sch. Medicine, Spencer T. Olin prof. biology in arts and scis., chair dept. biology, 1993-97, mem. various coms. Assoc. editor Molecular Biology and Evolution, Am. Jour. Botany, Molecular Ecology, Conservation Genetics. Trustee St. Louis Acad. Scis. Fellow AAAS, Am. Acad. Arts & Sciences; mem. NAS (v.p. 2005-), Bot. Soc. Am. (pres. 1995-96, Merit award 1999), Nature Conservancy (trustee Mo. chpt.). Achievements include research on the evolutionary process within plant populations. Office: Washington U Dept Biology Campus Box 1229 1 Brookings Dr Saint Louis MO 63130-4899 Office Phone: 314-935-7230.

SCHAB, DANIEL J., mathematics educator; B in Math., Grand Valley State Univ., 1981; M in Ednl. Adminstrn., Mich. State Univ., 1991. Math. tchr. Lansing (Mich.) Cath. Ctrl. H.S., 1981—94, Williamston (Mich.) H.S., 1994—. Named Mich. Tchr. of Yr., 2006; recipient Outstanding Alumni K-12 Tchr. award, Coll. Edn., Mich. State Univ., 2006, Lansing Regional C. of C. Excellence in Edn. award, 1987, 1994; grantee Einstein Fellowship, Wash., 2003—04; Toyota Internat. Tchr. Program participant, 2000. Mem.: Mich. Assn. Mid. Sch. Educators, Mich. Coun. Tchrs. Math., Nat. Coun. Tchrs. Math. Office: Williamston High Sch 3939 Vanneter Rd Williamston MI 48895 Business E-Mail: schabd@michigan.gov. *

SCHACHT, HENRY MEVIS, writer, consultant; b. Pasadena, Calif., Feb. 28, 1916; s. Henry and Amelia (Claussen) S.; m. Mary Joan Turnbull, Dec. 30, 1937; children: Henry John, Linda Joan. BA, U. Calif., Berkeley, 1936. Info. specialist U. Calif., Berkeley, 1936-42; dir. agr. NBC, San Francisco, 1942-59, ABC, San Francisco, 1959-60; agrl. columnist San Francisco Chronicle, 1959-93. Dir. agrl. info. U. Calif., 1961-65; v.p. corp. relations, corp. sec. Calif. Canners & Growers, San Francisco, 1965-81; freelance writer, 1936—; cons. radio-TV to FAO of UN, Cairo, 1963, Mexico City, 1965, Tokyo, 1966; dir. Calif. Co. for Internat. Trade; dir. Agrl. Issues Ctr., U. Calif. Author: (books) To the 21st Century - Study of Agribusiness to the Year 2000, 1983, History of the San Francisco Engineers Club, 1987, The Long and Winding Trail (History of the California Cattlemen's Association), 1991, Vision Solo - California Agriculture Report to State Dept. of Food and Agriculture, 1999, The California Cowboy, 2000. Pres. U.S. Fruit Export Coun., 1972-75; exec. sec. Commn. Calif. Agr. and Higher Edn., 1993-95; adv. bd. Agrl. Issues Ctr. U. Calif., 1990—2002. Mem. Pub. Rels. Soc. Am., Pub. Rels. Roundtable San Francisco, Nat. Assn. Farm Broadcasters, Agrl. Rels. Coun., Nat. Canners Assn. (dir. 1966-81) Home: 60 Hiller Dr Oakland CA 94618-2351

SCHACHT, JOCHEN HEINRICH, biochemistry educator; b. Königsberg, Fed. Republic Germany, July 2, 1939; arrived in U.S., 1969; s. Heinz and Else (Sprenger) S.; m. Helga Hildegard Seidel, Jan.27, 1967; children: Miriam Helga, Daniel Jochen. BS, U. Bonn, Fed. Republic Germany, 1962; MS in Chemistry, U. Heidelberg, Fed. Republic Germany, 1965, PhD in Biochemistry, 1968. Asst. research chemist, Mental Health Research Inst. U. Mich., Ann Arbor, 1969-72, from asst. prof. to assoc. prof. biochemistry, Dept. Biol. Chemistry & Otolaryngology, 1973-84, prof., 1984—, chmn. grad. program in physiol. acoustics, 1981—; hon. prof. Med. Acad. of the Chinese PLA, Beijing, 1998. Vis. prof. Karolinska Inst., Stockholm, 1979-80; acting dir. Kresge Hearing Rsch. Inst., U. Mich., 1983-84, assoc. dir., 1989-99, dir., 2000—; mem. hearing rsch. study sect. USPHS, NIH, Nat. Inst. Neurol. and Communicative Disorders and Stroke, 1986-89, Task Force Nat. Strategic Rsch. Plan, Nat. Insts. Deafness and Communication Disorders, USPHS, NIH; hon. prof. Hunan Med. U., Changsha, China, 1999—, Tonghi Med. U., Wuhan, China, 1999—; guest prof. Fourth Mil. Med. U., Xian, China, 1999—. Mem. editl. bd. Hearing Rsch., 1990—; assoc. editor Audiology & Neuro-Otol., 1995—; contbr. more than 200 articles to profl. jours., book chpts., revs.; co-editor Neurochemistry of Cholinergic Receptors, 1974. Fogarty Sr. Internat. fellow NIH, 1979, Sen. J. Javitz Neurosci. investigator, 1984; recipient Chercheur Etranger rsch. award INSERM, Paris, 1986, 94, Animal Welfare award Erna-Graff Found., Berlin, 1987, Disting. Faculty Achievement award U. Mich., 1989, Employer of Yr. award Nat. Capital Assoc. Coop. Edn. and Gallaudet U., Washington. Mem. Am. Soc. Neurochemistry, Internat. Soc. Neurochemistry, Soc. for Neurosci., Assn. for Rsch. in Otolaryngology, Am. Soc. Biol. Chemists, Assn. Espanola de Audiologia Exptl. Avocations: photography, travel, birding. Office: U Mich Kresge Hearing Rsch Inst Ann Arbor MI 48109-0506 Home Phone: 734-665-7101; Office Phone: 734-763-3572. Business E-Mail: schacht@umich.edu.

SCHACHTER, JAMES ROBERT, editor; b. Glendale, Calif., July 20, 1959; s. Stanley Herman and Margot (Lipiner) S.; m. Pamela Haag, May 19, 1985; children: Ariel Shira, Miriam Rachel, Naomi Tikvah, Benjamin Lev. BA, Columbia U., 1980. Reporter Jacksonville Jour., Fla., 1980-82, Kansas City Star, Mo., 1982-84, labor writer, 1984-85; reporter LA Times, San Diego, 1985-87, bus. writer LA, 1987-90, asst. bus. editor, 1990-93, Sunday bus. editor, 1993-94, sr. asst. bus. editor, 1994-95; enterprise editor Bus. Day NY Times, NYC, 1995—97, editor Sunday Money and Bus., 1997—2000, dep. editor Bus. Day Desk, 2000—04, dep. culture editor, 2004—06; dep. editor NY Times Mag., 2006—. Recipient award of Distinction, Soc. Newspaper Design, 1992, Cert. of Merit, Greater L.A. Press Club, 1989, 90, Bus. and Fin. Journalism award John Hancock Ins. Co., 1988, Best News Article award San Diego Press Club, 1987, Best Local News Reporting award Inland Daily Press Assn., Chgo., 1984. Mem. Investigative Reporters and Editors. Office: NY Times 229 W 43rd St New York NY 10036-3959 Office Phone: 212-556-1144. Business E-Mail: jims@nytimes.com.

SCHACHTER-SHALOMI, ZALMAN, rabbi; b. Poland, 1924; Studied, Boston U.; studied Near Eastern and Judaic Studies Dept., Univ. Manitoba, in Winnipeg. Co-founder Havurah Congregation; founder B'nai Or Congregation, Boston; World Wisdom Chair Prof., prof. emeritus Naropa Inst., Boulder, Colo.; prof. emeritus Temple U., Phila.; founder ALEPH Ordination Program. ALEPH: Alliance Jewish Renewal. Author: Jewish with Feeling: a guide to Meaningful Jewish Practice, The First Step, 1983, Gate to the Heart, 1993, Paradigm Shift, 1993, Wrapped in a Holy Flame, 2003. Named one of The Top 50 Rabbis in America, Newsweek Mag., 2007. Jewish Renewal. Office: Havurah Shir Hadash PO Box 1262 Ashland OR 97520 *

SCHACHTMAN, NATHAN A., lawyer; b. 1953; AB, Rutgers U., 1975, JD magna cum laude, 1982. Bar: NJ 1984, Pa. 1984, US Ct. of Appeals, Third Circuit, US Dist. Ct., NJ, US Dist. Ct., Pa (Ea. Dist.). Law clerk to Judge H. Emory Widener, Jr. US Ct. of Appeals, Fourth Circuit, NJ, 1982—83; ptnr., litigation, products liability & toxic torts McCarter & English, Phila. Mem. Defense Rsch. Inst.; peer reviewer Federal Judicial Ctr. Mem.: ABA, Pa. State Bar Assn., NJ State Bar Assn. Office: McCarter & English Mellon Bank Ctr 1735 Market St Ste 700 Philadelphia PA 19103 Office Phone: 215-979-3876. Office Fax: 215-988-4323. Business E-Mail: nschachtman@mccarter.com.

SCHACTER, BRENT ALLAN, oncologist, health facility administrator; b. Winnipeg, Man., Can., June 1, 1942; s. Irvin C. and Claire (Easton) S.; m. Sora Ludwig, Dec. 20, 1981; children: Isanne, Jennifer, Miriam. BSc, U. Man., 1965, MD with honors, 1965. Intern Winnipeg Gen. Hosp., 1965-66, jr. asst. resident, 1967-68; asst. resident in internal medicine Barnes Hosp., St. Louis, 1968-69; clin. fellow hematology Barnes Hosp. and Washington U., St. Louis, 1969-70; rsch. fellow, asst. in medicine U. Tex. Southwestern Med. Sch., Dallas, 1970-72; asst. prof. internal medicine U. Man., Winnipeg, 1972-77, assoc. prof. medicine, 1977-87, prof., 1987—; pres., CEO CancerCare Manitoba, Winnipeg, 1993—2003; CEO Can. Assn. Provincial Cancer Agys., 2003—. Lectr. in field; sci. officer grant panel C, Nat. Cancer Inst. Can., 1978, mem., 1979-82; mem. Man. Health Rsch. Coun. grant panel, 1982-84, 89-91; mem. Coun. for Canadian Strategy for Cancer Control, 2002-07, vice chair, 2005-07; mem. adv. bd. Can. Porphyria Found., 1988—; mem. steering com. Can. Strategy For Cancer Control, 1999-2002, co-chair steering com., 2000-02, mem. coun., 2002—; mem. steering com. Can. Cancer Stats., 2000—; chair stds. task force Coun. for Can. Strategy for Cancer Control, 2002—; provisional bd. mem. Can. Partnership Against Cancer, 2007; mem. Man. Health Rsch. Coun., 2005—. Contbr. numerous articles and abstracts to profl. jours. Bd. dirs. Nat. Cancer Inst. Can., 2000—. Recipient Med. Rsch. Coun. Can. Vis. Scientist award, 1986; fellow Muscular Dystrophy Assn., 1964, John S. McEachern Meml. fellow Can. Cancer Soc., 1969-70, Med. Rsch. Coun. Can. fellow, 1970-72, Nat. Cancer Inst. of Can. rsch. fellow, 1966-67; Isbister scholar, 1962, 63, Med. Rsch. Coun. Can. scholar, 1975-80. Fellow Royal Coll. Physicians; mem. AAAS, Royal Coll. Physicians and Surgeons of Can. (specialty com. in med. oncology 1985-94, bd. med. examiners in med. oncology 1987-90, specialty com. in hematology 1989-93, core com. mem. 1990-96, chmn. bd. examiners med. oncology 1990-93, mem. regional adv. com. Sask./Man. dist. 1992-97), Am. Fedn. for Clin. Rsch., Can. Soc. for Clin. Investigation (awards com. 1980-82, chmn. 1981-82), Am. Soc. Hematology, Can. Soc. Hematology, Am. Soc. Clin. Oncology, Can. Bone Marrow Transplant Group, Can. Assn. Provincial Cancer Agys., Can. Hemophilia Soc. (mem. clinic dirs. group 1990-93, sec-treas. 1991-93, Golden Jubilee medal Queen Elizabeth II 2002). Avocations: cross country skiing, scuba diving, model railroading. Home: 224 Lamont Blvd Winnipeg MB Canada R3P 0E9 Office: CancerCare Manitoba 675 McDermot Ave Winnipeg MB Canada R3E 0V9 Office Phone: 204-787-2128. E-mail: brent.schacter@cancercare.mb.ca.

SCHACTER, IRA JASON, lawyer; b. Bklyn., Jan. 31, 1960; s. Herbert Elliot and Barbara Rochelle (Douglas) S.; m. Janice Lynn Landis, Jan. 2, 1988. BA, SUNY, Stony Brook, 1981; JD, Nova Southeastern U., 1984; LLM Corp. Law, NYU, 1985. Bar: N.Y. 1985. Assoc. to ptnr., structured fin. Cadwalader, Wickersham & Taft, NYC, 1985—. Editor (notes & comments): Nova Law Rev. Mem. ABA, NY State Bar Assn. Office: Cadwalader Wickersham & Taft 1 World Financial Ctr New York NY 10281 Office Phone: 212-504-6035. Office Fax: 212-504-6666. Business E-Mail: ira.schacter@cwt.com.

SCHADOW, KAREN E., public speaking trainer, educator; b. Mar. 1949; 1 child, Kelby. BA in comm. and humanities magna cum laude, Fla. State U., 1971, MA in theatre magna cum laude, 1973. Previous cameraperson numerous programs, ABC TV, previous prodn. staff mem.; pres. The Voice of Success!, NYC. Adj. asst. prof. NYU, 1990—; instr. Bergen Cmty. Coll., NJ; creator, presenter various lectures and seminars for sch. and orgn. including Nat. Acad. TV Arts & Scis., NY Coalition Women in Arts and Media, Ctr. Arts Edn., The Learning Annex, nationwide; prodr. student career conf. NY Women in Comm., 2002—05; nominating judge Drama League. Mem.: Nat. Acad. TV Arts & Scis. (past mem. bd. govs., Emmy award 1984), Fla. State U. Theatre Project, New England Soc., Univ. Film & Video Assn., Screen Actors Guild, Actors' Equity, NY Women in Comm. (v.p. student affairs). Office Phone: 212-563-2615. Business E-Mail: karen@thevoiceofsuccess.com.

SCHADT, JAMES PHILLIP, investment and software executive; b. Saginaw, Mich., Aug. 7, 1938; s. Phillip Jr. and Jean D. (Cardy) S.; m. Barbara L. Soldmann, Aug. 16, 1959; children: Lauren C., Andrew F. BA, Northwestern U., 1960. With Procter & Gamble USA, 1960-65, Glendinning Cos., 1965-70, Squibb Corp., 1971-73, Pepsi Co., 1973-77, Sara Lee, 1977-80; pres., CEO Cadbury Schweppes Inc., 1981-91; dir., pres., COO Reader's Digest Assoc. Inc., Pleasantville, NY, 1991-94, pres., CEO, 1994—97, chmn., pres., CEO, 1995-97; chair Dailey Capital Mgmt., L.P., Southport, Conn., 1997—; chmn. Mercator Software, Inc., Wilton, Conn., 2000—03. Trustee Northwestern U. Mem. Blind Brook Club (Purchase, N.Y.), Chgo. Club, Am. Enterprise Inst. (trustee), Country Club of Fairfield, Conn., John's Island Club, Lotos Club N.Y.C.

SCHADY, KATHLEEN, pharmaceutical executive; d. Mildred Schady; m. Paul Gaynor; children: Pryce Gaynor, Pierce Gaynor. BA in Biology, Adelphi U., Garden City, NY, 1974; MS in Cell Biology, C.W. Post Coll., Greenvale, NY, 1975; PhD in Microbiology and Biochemistry, Rutgers U., New Brunswick, NJ, 1978. Cert. med. technologist Am. Soc. Clin. Pathology. Scientist, microbiology dept. Ethicon, Inc., Somerville, NJ, 1978—80, mgr., 1980—86; project mgr. Johnson & Johnson Sterilization Sci. Grp., Somerville, 1986—89; dir. pharmceutical quality assurance Ortho Pharm. Corp., Raritan, NJ, 1989—91; exec. dir., quality assurance Ortho Pharm., Raritan, 1991—93, Ortho-McNeil Pharm., Raritan, 1993—93; v.p. quality Ortho Biotech, Raritan, 1993—2000; v.p. qa biologics & parenterals Pharm. Sourcing Group Americas Bd., Raritan, 2000—02; v.p. bulk quality ops. Centocor, Malvern, Pa., 2002—03; v.p. Purdue Pharma, West Paterson, NJ, 2004—. Contbr. articles to profl. jours. Mem.: Quality Exec. Bd., Internat. Soc. Pharm. Engring. Achievements include development of a tech transfer process that was part of a continuous improvement initiative; supporting the optimization of a clinical supplies program to ensure availability of supplier for critical clinical studies. Office: Purdue Pharma 3 Garret Mountain Plz Ste 303 West Paterson NJ 07424 Office Fax: 973-247-9902. Business E-Mail: kathleen.schady@pharma.com.

SCHAECHTER, MOSELIO, microbiology educator; b. Apr. 26, 1928; children: Judy, John. Student, Cen. U., Ecuador, 1947-49; MA, U. Kans., 1952; PhD, U. Pa., 1954. Postdoctoral fellow State Serum Inst., Copenhagen, 1956-58; from instr. to asst. prof. to assoc. prof. U. Fla., Gainesville, 1958-62; from assoc. prof. to disting. prof. dept. microbiology Tufts U., Boston, 1962-95, prof. emeritus, 1995—. Adj. prof. San Diego State U., 1995—, U. Calif., San Diego, 2004—. Editor: Molecular Biology Bacterial Growth, 1985, Escherichia coli and Salmonella Typhimurium, 1987, 95, Mechanisms of Microbiol. Disease, 1989, 92; author: In the Company of Mushrooms, 1997, Microbe, 2005. Mem. Am. Soc. Microbiology (pres. 1985-86, chmn. internat. activities), Am. Soc. Med. Sch. Microbiology Chmn. (pres. 1984-85), Soc. Gen. Microbiology, Boston Mycol. Club, Sigma Xi. Avocations: field mycology, hiking. Business E-Mail: mschaech@sunstroke.sdsu.edu.

SCHAEDELIN, PIERRE, chef; Apprentice, commis Auberge de l'Ill, Illhaeusern, France, Le Louis XV, Monaco; with Le Grill, France, Fer Rouge, France, Monte's, London, Caesar's Palace, Las Vegas; exec. sous chef Le Cirque, NYC, 1999—2000, exec. chef, 2000—05, 2006—07; personal chef to Martha Stewart, 2005. Office: Le Cirque One Beacon Ct 151 E 58th St New York NY 10022 *

SCHAEFER, BARBARA W., rail transportation executive; B, U. Nebr., Lincoln; JD, U. Nebr. Coll. Law; grad. in Mgmt. Devel. Program, Harvard U. Pvt. practice atty., Omaha; sr. v.p. human resources Union Pacific Corp., 1997—, corp. sec., 2004—. Bd. trustees Weitz Funds. Bd. mem. Children's Hosp., Lauritzen Bot. Gardens, U. Nebr. Found. Named a Woman of Vision, YWCA Omaha, 2001; recipient Welcome T. Bryant Bd. Mem. of Yr. award, Urban League, 2000, 2001, Light of Wellness Leadership award, Wellness Coun. Midland, 2004. Fellow: Nebr. State Bar Assn. Found. Office: Union Pacific Corp 1400 Douglas St Omaha NE 68179 Office Phone: 402-544-5000. *

SCHAEFER, BONNIE (E. BONNIE SCHAEFER), retail executive; b. Chgo., Mar. 16, 1963; d. Rowland Schaefer. From sales assoc. to store mgr. Claire's Stores, Inc., 1987—90, v.p. real estate, 1994—2002, co-vice chmn., 1999—2002, co-chmn., 2002—, co-CEO, 2002—. Bd. dirs. Claire's Stores, Inc., 1998—, Claire's Nippon. Office: Claires Stores Inc 3 SW 129th Ave Pembroke Pines FL 33027 Office Phone: 954-433-3900. Office Fax: 954-433-3999.

SCHAEFER, C. BARRY, rail transportation executive, investment company executive; b. Elizabeth, NJ, Feb. 23, 1939; s. Carl H. and Evelyn G. (Conk) S.; m. Carol Ann Craft, July 11, 1970; children: Sara Elizabeth, Susan Craft. BS in Engring., Princeton U., 1961; MS in Engring., U. Pa., 1962; LLB, Columbia U., 1965; MBA, NYU, 1970. Bar: N.Y. 1966, Nebr. 1972. With Kelley, Drye, Warren, NYC, 1966-69; asst. gen. counsel Union Pacific Corp., NYC, 1969-72; western gen. counsel Union Pacific R.R. Co., Omaha, 1972-74, v.p., western gen. counsel, 1974-77, v.p. law, 1977-82; sr. v.p. planning and corp. devel. Union Pacific Corp., NYC, 1984-88, exec. v.p. Bethlehem, Pa., 1988; sr. advisor Dillon Read & Co. Inc., 1989-91; mng. dir. The Bridgeford Group, 1992-97, 2001—06, Beacon Group, 1997-01. Nat. bd. dirs. Jr. Achievement, Colorado Springs, Colo., 1986-2004. Mem. Racquet and Tennis Club (N.Y.C.), Round Hill Club (Greenwich, Conn.), Desert Mountain Club (Scottsdale, Ariz.). Office Phone: 212-705-0886.

SCHAEFER, CHARLES JAMES, III, advertising executive, consultant; b. Orange, NJ, Dec. 17, 1926; m. Eleanor Anne Montville, Apr. 8, 1961; 1 child, Charles James IV. AB, Dartmouth Coll., 1948, M in Comml. Sci., 1949. Mgr. foods promotion Beech-Nut, 1949—52; v.p. Dickie-Raymond, 1952-67; sr. v.p. Metromedia, 1968-69; exec. v.p., treas. The DR Group, Boston and NYC, 1969-76, pres., 1976-87; exec. v.p., dir. Needham Harper Worldwide Inc., NYC, 1984-87; chmn. bd. Marcoa DR Group, Inc., NYC, 1987-88; cons. Rapp Collins Marcoa, NYC, 1989-92; advt. cons., 1992—. Pres. Dartmouth Class of 1948, 1998-2000; trustee, mem. exec. com. Direct Mktg. Ednl. Found., 1983-89; campaign chairperson United Way Millburn-Short Hills, 1994, 95, trustee, 1991-98, 2000—, v.p., 2004—. With USN, 1945—46. Mem. Direct Mktg. Assn. (chmn. awards com. 1971-76, Hall of Fame com. 1978-81, ethics com. 1981-86), Assn. Direct Mktg. Agys. (pres. 1980-82, gen. chmn. Caples awards 1985, chmn. Direct Mktg. Days NY 1988, NY Direct Marketer of Yr. award 1987, Silver Apple award 1989, contbr. to jour.), Dartmouth Club of NY (pres. 1968-70), Lotos Club (bd. dirs. 1985-88, treas. 1987-88), Canoe Brook Country Club (Summit, NJ). Home and Office: 307 Hobart Ave Short Hills NJ 07078-2207

SCHAEFER, DAVID ARNOLD, lawyer; b. Cleve., May 3, 1948; s. Leonard and Maxine V. (Bassett) S.; m. Riki C. Freeman, Aug. 8, 1971; children: Kevin, Lindsey, Traci. BS, Miami U., Oxford, Ohio, 1970; MA, Northwestern U., 1971; JD, Case Western Res. U., 1974. Bar: Ohio 1974, U.S. Dist. Ct. (no. dist.) Ohio 1974, U.S. Ct. Appeals (6th cir.) 1978, U.S. Supreme Ct. 1978. Ptnr. Guren, Merritt et al, 1980-84, Menexch. Friedlander et al, Cleve., 1984-93, McCarthy, Lebit, Crystal & Haiman, Cleve., 1993—. Author: Deposition Strategy, 1981, 2d edit., 1984; contbr. articles to profl. publs. Mem. ABA, Internat. Assn. Def. Counsel, Fed. Bar Assn. (pres. 1992-93), Nat. Inst. Trail Advocacy (faculty), 8th Cir. Jud. Conf. (life). Office: McCarthy Lebit Crystal & Haiman 1800 Midland Bldg 101 W Prospect Ave Ste 1800 Cleveland OH 44115-1027

SCHAEFER, ELEANOR MONTVILLE, retired publishing executive; b. Worcester, Mass., June 27, 1926; d. Joseph Samuel and Monica Savage Montville; m. Charles James Schaefer; 1 child, Charles James IV. AB, Trinity U., 1949. Radio/tv dept. Sullivan Staufer Colwell & Bayles, Inc., NYC, 1949—50; promotion dept. staff Life Mag., NYC, 1951—52; asst. promotion mgr. Sports Illustrated, NYC, 1953—59; promotion mgr. Glamour mag., NYC, 1960. V.p. League Women Voters, 1971—77; found. dir. Summit Coll. Club; vol. auxilliary mem. Assn. U. Women, Summit, NJ, 1998—99. Mem.: Trinity U. Alumni Assn. (past pres. 1959—60), Summit Coll. Club, Canoe Brook Country Club. Achievements include being first woman staffer on "Project X" which eventually became Sports Illustrated. Avocations: golf, interior decorating. Home: 307 Hobart Ave Short Hills NJ 07078 E-mail: montvilles@aol.com.

SCHAEFER, FRANK WILLIAM, III, microbiologist, researcher; b. Dayton, Ohio, Sept. 1, 1942; s. Frank William Jr. and Irene Josephine (Krouse) S. BA, Miami U., Oxford, Ohio, 1964; MS, U. Cin., 1970, PhD, 1973. Rsch. assoc. parasitologist U. Notre Dame, South Bend, Ind., 1973-78; U.S. EPA EPA, Cin., 1978—. Mem. ASTM, AAAS, Am. Soc. Parasitology, Am. Soc. Microbiology, Am. Water Works Assn., Soc. Protozoologists, Sigma Xi. Home: 9948 McCauley Woods Dr Sharonville OH 45241-1489 Office: US EPA 26 Martin Luther King Dr Cincinnati OH 45268 Office Phone: 513-569-7222. Personal E-mail: f.schaeferiii@att.net. Business E-Mail: schaefer.frank@epa.gov.

SCHAEFER, GEORGE A., JR., bank executive; b. Cincinnati, Ohio, 1945; BS Engineering, U.S. Mil. Acad., West Point, 1967; MBA, Xavier U., 1974. Joined as mgmt. trainee Fifth Third Bancorp, Cin., 1971, pres., 1990—2006, CEO, 1990—2007, chmn., 2006—. Bd. dirs. Fifth Third Bancorp, Fifth Third Bank, Anthem, Inc, Ashland, Inc, Greater Cin./N. Ky. Internat. Airport, Cin. Bus. Com. Chmn., bd. trustees U. Cin.; bd. dirs. Children's Hosp. Med. Ctr., Greater Cin. C. of C., Health Alliance Greater Cin. Served US Army, 1967—70, Europe and Vietnam. Recipient Bronze Star. Office: Fifth Third Bancorp Fifth Third Center 38 Fountain Square Plz Cincinnati OH 45263-0001 *

SCHAEFER, GORDON EMORY, food products executive; b. 1932; married. BS, Marquette U., 1956. CPA Wis. With Peat, Marwick, Mitchell & Co., 1955-59; contr., sec. Wells Badger, Badger Carton Co., 1960—64; treas. Pabst Brewing Co., Milw., 1965-72, v.p. adminstrn., 1972-75, v.p. ops., 1975—80, exec. v.p. ops, 1980—85, dir.; pres., dir. Krier Foods Inc., Belgium, Wis., 1981-85, Corrs Beverages, Chgo., 1985-86; dir. bus. devel. Lakeside Packing Co., Manitowoc, Wis., 1989-92; mng. dir. Robertson Assocs., Mfg. Europe Ltd., Cardiff, Wales, 1993-94. Bd. dirs. Fox Fin. Co., Berg Industries, Inc.; fin. and ops. cons.; owner, operator Schaefer's Orchards. Home: 1626 Vivian Ct West Bend WI 53090-8961 Office Phone: 262-675-0318.

SCHAEFER, HENRY FREDERICK, III, chemistry professor; b. Grand Rapids, Mich., June 8, 1944; s. Henry Frederick Jr. and Janice Christine (Trost) S.; m. Karen Regine Rasmussen, Sept. 2, 1966; children: Charlotte, Pierre, Theodore, Rebecca, Caleb. BS in Chem. Physics, MIT, 1966; PhD in Chem. Physics, Stanford U., 1969; D (hon.), U. Plovdiv, 1998, U. Sofia, 1999, Beijing Inst. Tech., 1999, Huntington U., 2002, North-Eastern Hill U., Shillong, India, 2007. From asst. prof. to prof. chemistry U. Calif., Berkeley, 1969—87; Graham Perdue prof., dir. Ctr. for Computational Chemistry U. Ga., Athens, 1987—. Apptd. Professeur d'Echange U. Paris, 1977, Gastprofessor Eidgenössische Technische Hochshule, Zürich, 1994, 95, 97, 2000, 02, 04, 06; Wilfred T. Doherty prof., dir. Inst. Theoretical Chemistry, U. Tex., Austin, 1979-80; lectr. in field. Author: Science and Christianity: Conflict or Coherence? 2003; contbr. articles to profl. jours. including Electronic Structure of Atoms and Molecules: A Survey of Rigorous Quantum Mechanical Results, 1972, Modern Theoretical Chemistry, 1977, Quantum Chemistry, 1983, A New Dimension to Quantum Chemistry, 1994; editor Molecular Physics, 1991-94, editor in chief, 1995-2005. Recipient Pure Chemistry award Am. Chem. Soc., 1979, Leo Hendrik Baekeland award, 1983, Schrödinger Medal, 1990, Centenary medal Royal Soc. Chemistry, London, 1992, Gold medal Comenius U., Bratislava, Slovakia, 2000; Sloan fellow, 1972, Guggenheim fellow, 1976-77; named one of 100 Outstanding Young Scientists in Am., Sci. Digest, 1984, named 3d Most Highly cited chemist in world Science Watch, 1992. Fellow AAAS, Am. Phys. Soc., Am. Sci. Affiliation, Am. Acad. Arts and Scis., Royal Soc. Chemistry (London); mem. Internat. Acad. Quantum Molecular Sci., Am. Chem. Soc. (chmn. divsn. phys. chemistry 1992, award in theoretical chemistry 2003, Ira M. Remsen award 2003), World Assn. Theoretical and Computational Chemists (pres. 1996-2005, Joseph O. Hirschfelder prize, 2005). Presbyterian. Office: U Ga Ctr Computational Chemistry Athens GA 30602 Office Phone: 706-542-2067. Business E-Mail: hfs@uga.edu.

SCHAEFER, JAMES THEODORE, writer, editor, educator; s. Walter Charles and Louise Petersen Schaefer; m. Karen Elaine Moon, Sept. 16, 1972; children: Patrick Charles, Theodore Glen, Daniel John, Marie Louise. AA, Grand Rapids Jr. Coll., Mich., 1963—65; BA in English & Writing, Mich. State U., E.Lansing, 1965—69; MA in Tchg. Writing, summa cum laude, Ea. Mich. U., Ypsilanti, 2003—05, MA in Comm., summa cum laude, 2007. Cert. tchr.cons. Nat. Writing Project, 2004. Regional editor Muskegon Chronicle, Mich., 1969—70; freelance writer, editor & rschr. Ann Arbor, Mich., 1970—74; publisher/editor Shining Waters Press, 1974—88; sr. editor Comparative Studies Soc. & History, Ann Arbor, 1988—99; prof. Washtenaw CC, Ann Arbor, 1999—, Wayne County CC, Detroit, 2003—. Founder, exec. prodr. & host Riprap: The Academic Book TV Program, Ann Arbor, 1997—; co-founder Orchard Internet Radio, Ann Arbor, Mich., 1999, coord., 2000—02; cons. Wayne County CC, 2003—04. Editor: (book) The Magical State: Nature, Money, and Modernity, by Fernando Coronil; author: Breathe/Exhale; editor: (manuscript) Food in Global History, The Construction of Minorities, States of Violence; prodr.: (video) Falling Leaves; cons. (book) Two Dreams in One Bed: Empire, Social Life, and the Origins of the North Korean Revolution in Manchuria. Co-chair peace project task force Ea. Mich. U., 2006; jr. warden, vestry mem. St. Andrew's Episcopal Ch., Ann Arbor, 2000—03. Mem.: Am. Ednl. Rsch. Assn., Nat. Comm. Assn., Nat. Coun. Tchrs. English (assoc.), Phi Kappa Phi. Avocations: reading, writing, music. Office: Wayne CC 9555 Haggerty Rd Belleville MI 48111 also: Washtenaw CC LA 178 4800 E Huron River Dr PO Box 1610 Ann Arbor MI 48106-1610 Office Phone: 734-973-1425. Office Fax: 734-973-1425.

SCHAEFER, JOHN FREDERICK, lawyer; b. Detroit, Apr. 10, 1943; s. Gilbert Frederick and Mary Cathryn (Henderson) S.; m. Sharon Kathleen Chalmers, May 22, 1976; children: Kimberly Megan, Kelly Leigh, John Frederick, Charles Frederick. Student, U. Notre Dame, 1961-63; BA, Mich. State U., 1965, LLD, 1996; JD, Detroit Coll. Law, 1968. Bar: Mich. 1969. Ptnr. Buesser, Buesser, Snyder & Blank, Detroit, 1968-73, Williams, Schaefer, Ruby & Williams, Birmingham, Mich., 1973-89; propr. Law Firm of John F. Schaefer, Birmingham, 1989—. Adj. prof. domestic rels. Detroit Coll. Law, 1971—; instr. domestic rels. Mich. Jud. Inst., 1980-81; lectr. in field. Contbr. articles to legal jours. Trustee Detroit Coll. Law, Mich. State U., 1985—, William Beaumont Hosp., 2000; chair Detroit Coll. Law at Mich. State U. Found., 1995—; mem. ICLE Legal Edn. Inst. Fellow: Oakland Bar Found., Mich. State Bar Found. (jud. rev. com. 1997—), Am. Acad. Matrimonial Lawyers (pres. Mich. chpt. 1986—87), State Bar Mich. (family law com. 1972—73, com. on character and fitness 1972—75, coun. family law sect. 1974—, mem. fee abritration grievance bd. 1976—, chmn. 1978—79); mem.: Oakland County Bar Assn. (mem. character and fitness com. 1973, family law com. 1973—, chmn. com. 1974—77, cir. ct. com. 1985—88, bd. dirs. 1995—, pres.), Detroit Bar Assn. (friend of ct. and domestic rels. com. 1972—, chmn. com. 1975—76, mem. pub. adv. com. 1976—), ABA (family law sect. 1969—, jud. rev. com. 1997—). Roman Catholic. Office: Law Firm of John F Schaefer Ste 320 380 N Old Woodward Ave Birmingham MI 48009-5347 Office Phone: 248-642-6655. *

SCHAEFER, JOHN H., finance company and security firm executive; b. 1952; BS in Chemistry, Polytechnic Inst. of Brooklyn, 1955; PhD, U. Ill., 1958. Chief strategic and adminstrv. officer, exec. v.p. Morgan Stanley & Co., Inc., NYC, 1998—2000, pres., COO, individual investor group, 2000—. Office: Morgan Stanley & Co Inc 1585 Broadway New York NY 10036 Office Phone: 212-761-4000.

SCHAEFER, KATHERINE L., medical researcher, educator; BS with Distinction, Univ. Ill.-Urbana, 1988; PhD, Carnegie-Mellon Univ., 1996. Rsch. asst. prof., dept. medicine U. Rochester Med. Ctr. Contbr. articles to profl. jours. Mem.: Phi Kappa Phi. Achievements include discovery of a new way to attack tumors that have learned how to evade existing drugs with colleagues. Office: U Rochester Med Ctr 2400 S Clinton Ave Bldg F Rochester NY 14618 *

SCHAEFER, KIM, high school music educator; married; 2 children. Student, Utah State Univ., Colo. State Univ., SD State Univ. Cert. Nat. Bd. Tchg. Standards. Music tchr. Whitehorse High Sch., Navajo Reservation, Montezuma Creek, Utah, 1998—. Dist. arts coord., 2004—. Named Utah Tchr. of Yr., 2007. Mem.: Music Educator's Nat. Conf., Utah Music Educator's Assn. (Superior Accomplishment award 2004), Tri-M Honor Soc. (chair). Achievements include being fluent in Navajo. Office: Whitehorse High Sch PO Box 660 Montezuma Creek UT 84534 Home Phone: 801-633-6755; Office Phone: 435-678-1887. *

SCHAEFER, M. ELAINE, music educator, conductor; b. Frederick, Okla., Apr. 13, 1945; d. Arthur Lloyd and Mary Ellen Bush; m. Edward T. Vrable, July 28, 2001; children: Joel, Anne Marie, Scott Patrick Gillespie. Student, Diablo Valley Coll., Pleasant Hill, Calif., 1961—63, Chico State Coll., Calif., 1963—64; BA, Calif. State U. Hayward, 1967; MusM, U. Regina, Sask., Can., 1988. Tchrs. cert. Calif., 1967. Instrumental music tchr. Kenilworth Jr. HS, Petaluma, Calif., 1967—72; music tchr. Incline Village HS, Nev., 1972—78; instrumental and choral tchr. Humboldt HS, Sask., Canada, 1978—86; music tchr. Balgonie HS, Sask., Canada, 1988—96; music instr., condr. Coll. Siskiyous, Weed, Calif., 1996—. Adjudicator Sask. Music Festivals, 1985—96; condr. Holy Rosary Cathedral Choir, Regina, Sask., 1987—96, Royal Can. Mounted Police Choir, 1987—89; pres. Sask. Choral Dirs., 1989—90. Bd. mem. Sask. Coun. Cultural Orgns., 1990—96. Sgt. US Army, 1974—78. Named Tchr. of Yr., Coll. of Siskiyous, 2006, Faculty Mem. of Yr., 2006; recipient award of Appreciation, Sask. Music Educators, 1982. Fellow: Nat. Assn. Jazz Educators, Calif. Music Educators Assn., Am. Choral Dirs.; mem.: Internat. Fedn. Choral Music, Assn. Can. Choral Dirs. (bd. mem.), Nat. Assn. Jazz Educators, Calif. Music Educators Assn., Am. Choral Dirs. Roman Catholic. Home: 5925 Mule Deer Ct Weed CA 96094 Office: College Siskiyous 800 College Ave Weed CA 96094 Office Phone: 530-938-5315. Business E-Mail: schaefer@siskiyous.edu.

SCHAEFER, MARILYN LOUISE, artist, writer, educator; b. Cedar Rapids, Iowa, Apr. 22, 1933; d. Henry Richard and Maria Augusta (Dickel) S. AA, Monticello Coll. for Women, 1953; BFA, Cranbrook Acad. Art, 1956, MFA, 1960; MA cum laude, U. Chgo., 1958; MA, St. John's Coll., Santa Fe, 1979. Rsch. asst. editor Encyclopaedia Britannica, Chgo., 1960-63; humanities editor Encyclopedia Americana, NY, 1964-68; acquisitions editor Litton Ednl. Pub., NY, 1968-70; from instr. to prof. emeritus art and advt. design dept. N.Y.C. Tech. Coll. CUNY, 1970—. Contbg. editor Encyclopedia Americana, 1979—, Coll. Teaching jour., 1979. Contbr. articles to profl. jours. including Art and Auction mag., Art and Antiques mag., Am. Artist mag., Encyclopedia Americana, 1970—. Luce Found. postgrad. study fellow St. John's Coll., 1976-79; Ingram Merrill Found. grantee, 1983-84. Mem. AAUW, CUNY Acad. Arts and Scis. Home: 306 W 76th St New York NY 10023-8065 Office: NYC Tech Coll CUNY 300 Jay St Brooklyn NY 11201-1909

SCHAEFER, MARLA L., retail executive; b. Chgo., May 19, 1949; d. Rowland Schaefer; 2 children. BA, Fla. Internat. U., 1973; MA in Orgnl. Psychology, Columbia U., 2003. Resident buyer NY Office Claire's Boutiques, 1986, v.p. fashion merchandising, 1990—98, sr. v.p., 1998—, sec., 2002—; vice chmn. bd. dirs. Claire's Stores Inc., Pembroke Pines, Fla., 1998—99, co-vice chmn., 1999—2003, acting co-chmn., co-CEO, 2002—03, co-chmn., co-CEO, 2003—. Office: Claire's Stores, Inc 3 SW 129th Ave Pembroke Pines FL 33027 Office Phone: 954-433-3900. Office Fax: 954-433-3999. E-mail: marla.schaefer@claires.com.

SCHAEFER, PATRICIA, retired librarian; b. Ft. Wayne, Ind., Apr. 23, 1930; d. Edward John and Hildegarde Hartman (Hormel) S. MusB, Northwestern U., 1951; MusM, U. Ill., 1958; AMLS, U. Mich., 1963; DLS (hon.), Ind. Inst. of Tech., 2003. With U.S. Rubber co., Ft. Wayne, 1951-52; sec. to promotion mgr. Sta. WOWO, Ft. Wayne, Ind., 1952, sec. to program mgr., 1953-55; coord. publicity and promotion Home Telephone Co., Ft. Wayne, 1955-56; sec. Fine Arts Found., Ft. Wayne, 1956-57; libr. asst. Columbus (Ohio) Pub. Libr., 1958-59; audio-visual libr. Muncie (Ind.) Pub. Libr., 1959-86, asst. libr. dir., 1981-86, libr. dir., 1986-95; ret. Chmn. Ind. Libr. Film Cir., 1962-63; treas. Ind. Libr. Film Svc., 1969-70, 83-85; mem. trustee adv. coun. Milton S. Eisenhower Libr., Johns Hopkins U.; mem. presdl. counsellors Johns Hopkins U., 1994—; cons. Franklin Electric Co., 2004—. Weekly columnist Libr. Lines, Muncie Evening Press, 1981-83; program annotator Muncie Symphony Orch., 1963-2003, Masterworks Chorale, 1982-2003; contbr. articles to profl. jours. Bd. dirs. Muncie Symphony Assn., 1964-74, 85-91, Ctrl. City Bus. Assn., 1986-92, Ind. Inst. Tech., Ind. Humanities Coun., 1996-2002, 05—, Sta. WIPB-TV, 1996-2002, Muncie Ctr. for the Arts, 1999-2001, Nature Conservancy Ind., 2007—; mem. adv. coun. Coll. Fine Arts, Ball State U.; adv. com., bookshop dir. Midwest Writers Workshop, 1976-77; sec. Del. County Coun. for the Arts, 1978-79, pres., 1979-81, bd. dirs., 1985-86; pres.'s coun. Berea Coll., 1990-2001; bd. dirs. Muncie YWCA, 1977-82, 85-89, 95-2001, treas. 1981-82, 88-89; bd. govs. Minnetrista Cultural Ctr., 1998-2001; gen. chmn. Ind. Renaissance Fair, 1978-79; pres. Muncie Matinee Musicale, 1965-67; mem. adv. bd. Cornerstone Ctr. for the Arts; past pres. Ind. Film and Video Coun.; adv. bd. Cmty. Found. Muncie and Delaware County; bd. dirs. Wapehani coun. Girl Scouts U.S., 1989-96, Hoosier Heartland chpt. ARC, 1997-2003, Ball State U. Found., 2006—. Named Woman Achievement Pub. Svc., 1986; recipient Sagamore of the Wabash award Gov. State of Ind., Outstanding Libr. award Ind. Libr. Fedn., 1995, Cert. of Congrl. Recognition, 1995, Cert. of Achievement, Women's Coalition, 1996, Cert. of Appreciation, Masterworks Chorale, 1998. Mem. ALA, Ind. Libr. Assn. (pres. 1987-88), Nat. League Am. Pen Women (pres. Muncie br. 1974-78), Altrusa (pres. 1986-87, cmty. svc. award 2000), Art Students League, Del. Country Club, Delta Zeta, Mu Phi Epsilon. Republican. Roman Catholic. Home: 5400 W Deer Run Ct Muncie IN 47304-5775

SCHAEFER, PATRICIA ANN, retired librarian; b. Lebanon, Ohio, Jan. 22, 1933; d. Riley Ray and Louise Collette (Fraher) Freeze; m. William H. Schaefer, Aug. 11, 1956; children: Susan P., Nancy A., William H. III(dec.). BS, Miami U., Oxford, Ohio, 1954. Med. technologist Mercy Hosp., Hamilton, Ohio, 1954-58, Middletown (Ohio) Hosp., 1958-62; libr. Middletown City Schs., 1979-93; intermediate libr. McKinley Sch., 1982-93; ret., 1993. Hon. bd. dirs. Am. Cancer Soc., 1961—; chmn. legis. City Charter Rev. Com., 1970, charter revision com., 1989; active YMCA, pres., 1977—79; bd. dirs. Middletown Symphony, 1974—78, Arts in Middletown, 1983—, Middletown Symphony Women, 1992—, exec. bd., 1995—; residential chmn. United Way, 1976, residential-retiree chmn., 1990; chmn. Sch. Tax Levy, 1978; co-chmn. Luncheon Style Show, 1998—2003; exec. com. Ohio-Ky.-Ind. Regional Coun., 1986—88; mem. Bicentennial Com., Middletown; pres. Middletown Needy Youth Bd.; adv. bd. Manchester Tech. Ctr., Drug Task Force Bd., Middletown Schs.; bd. dirs. Citizens Adv. Bd. Manchester Tech., Middletown Fine Arts, 1993—, Dental Emergency Fund Area Children, 1994—; exec. bd. Leadership Middletown; pres. Care View Home Health, 2000, 2003—; co-chmn. Mary Alice Mack City Golf Tournament, 1998; mem. Middletown City Commn., 1983—88, chmn., 1986—88; adminstrv. bd. Meth. Ch.; mem. fin. com., sec. bd. trustees 1st United Meth. Ch., 1999—; exec. bd. United Meth. Women; mem. citizen's adv. com. Miami U., Middletown, co-chair major capital campaign, 2003—. Named Outstanding Woman of Butler County, 1997, hon. chmn., Charity Ball, 1998, Woman of Distinction, Soroptomists Internat., 2000; recipient Stuart Ives Svc. to Youth award, 1980. Mem.: PEO (pres. 1995—, co-chair state conv. 1997), LWV (pres. 1962—63), Am. Bus. Women's Assn. (pres. 1961—62), Registry Med. Technologists, Am. Soc. Clin. Pathologists, Miami U. Hughes Soc., Middletown C. of C., Miami U. Pres. Club, Browns Run Country Club, Sigma Sigma Sigma. Methodist. Home: 1909 Antrim Ct Middletown OH 45042-2901

SCHAEFER, ROBERT WAYNE, banker; b. Balt., Feb. 28, 1934; s. Roland Elmer and Lillian (Reid) S.; m. Elaine Lennon, May 18, 1963; children: Linda, Karen. Student, Balt. City Coll., 1949-51; BS in Acctg., U. Balt., 1955; MBA in Fin., Loyola Coll., 1971. C.P.A., Md. With First Nat. Bank of Md., Balt., 1951-55, 59—, comptroller, 1961—, v.p., 1965-69, sr. v.p., 1969-73, exec. v.p., 1973-96; exec. dir. France-Merrick Founds., Balt., 1996—. Instr. accounting N.C. State Coll., 1956-58; instr. accounting, econs., taxes, credit Balt. chpt. Am. Inst. Banking, 1960-66, Investment Com. State of Md. Retirement System and Baltimore Fire, Police Retirement System. Mem. Balt. City Sch. Bd., 1973-75, Balt. City Bd. Fin.; bd. dirs., treas. Balt. Area United Fund, 1964-79; past bd. dirs. Balt. coun. Boy Scouts Am., Balt. chpt. ARC, Boys Latin Sch.; trustee, pres. Wesley Home for Aged; bd. dirs. Balt. City Aquarium, Roland Park Country Sch., Md. Gen. Hosp., Western Md. Coll., 1981-92, Lyric Theatre, 1985—, Enoch Pratt Libr., 1986-93, Ind. Coll. Fund Md., 1990—. Coun. on Econ. Edn., YMCA Ctrl. Md., 1992, U. Balt. 1st lt. USMCR, 1956-58. Mem.: Fin. Execs. Inst., Md. CPA Assn., Bank Adminstrn. Inst. (past pres., bd. dirs. Balt. chpt.), U. Balt. Found., U. Balt. Alumni Assn. (bd. dirs. 1972—), Ctr. Club, Johns Hopkins Club, L'Hirondelle Club, Valley Country Club. Republican. Methodist (bd. dirs., mem. finance com.). Home: 5903 Meadowood Rd Baltimore MD 21212-2436 Office: Village of Cross Keys Quadrangle E Ste 302 2 Hamill Rd Baltimore MD 21210-1813 Office Phone: 410-464-2004. Personal E-mail: rwsels@aol.com. Business E-Mail: rschaefer@france-merrickfdn.org.

SCHAEFER, RONALD DEAN, secondary school educator; s. Russell Earl and Jewell Dean Schaefer; m. Jeanette Rozanne Bradshaw, Sept. 1, 1962; children: Ronald David, Christian Ann. BA, So. Ill. U., Edwardsville, 1963; MS, So. Ill. U., Carbondale, 1965, PhD, 1969. Analytic chemist Dow Chemical Co., Midland, Mich., 1969—72; mgr. quality control Dow Diagnostics, Indpls., 1972—77; dir. quality assurance/quality control HYCEL Corp., Houston, 1977—79; rsch. scientist Boehringer-Hennheim Corp., Tustin, Calif., 1979—81; dir. quality assurance/quality control Ciba Corning Diagnostics, Irvine, Calif., 1981—99; educator Santa Ana HS, 1999—. Home: 5 Fulton Irvine CA 92620 Personal E-mail: ronald_schaefer@yahoo.com.

SCHAEFER, SAUL, cardiologist; b. Tel Aviv, Dec. 6, 1947; came to U.S., 1952; s. Rudi and Gertrude S.; m. Sylvia Lopez, July 14, 1985; children: Jonathan, Adam. B of Engring., The Cooper Union, 1968; postgrad., U. So. Calif., 1968-69, UCLA, 1970-76; MD, U. Calif., Davis, 1981. Diplomate Am. Bd. Internal Medicine, Am. Bd. Internal Medicine (Cardiovasc. Disease), Nat. Bd. Med. Examiners; lic. physician, Calif.; profl. cert. in bioengring.; Calif. State teaching credential. Tchr. secondary level L.A. Unified Sch. Dist., 1970-76; residency internal medicine U. Calif., San Francisco, 1981-84; fellow cardiology U. Tex. Southwestern Med. Ctr., Dallas, 1984-87; asst. dir. echocardiography VA Med. Ctr., San Francisco, 1987-90; asst. prof. medicine and radiology in residence U. Calif., San Francisco, 1987-91; dir. interventional cardiology VA Med. Ctr., San Francisco, 1990-91, U. Calif., Davis, 1991-94, assoc. prof. medicine, 1991-97, prof., 1997—, acting chief divsn. cardiovasc. medicine, 1998. Co-chair cardiology dept. of vets. affairs No. Calif. Health Care Sys. Contbr. numerous articles to profl. jours. and chpts. to books. Recipient award for excellence in diagnostic radiology, 1981, clin. investigator award NIH, 1987, Hibbard E. Williams rsch. award, 1992; N.Y. State Regents scholar, 1964, Mosby scholar, 1981; grantee Calif. affiliate Am. Heart Assn., 1988, 90, 93, 96, dean's grantee U. Calif., Davis, 1993. Fellow Am. Coll. Cardiology; mem. AAAS, Am. Coll. Cardiology (mem. editl. bd. jour.), Am. Fedn. Clin. Rsch., Soc. Magnetic Resonance in Medicine, Am. Physiologic Soc., Am. Heart Assn. Office: U Calif Cardiovascular Medicine TB 172 Bioletti Way Davis CA 95616 Office Phone: 530-752-0717. Business E-Mail: sschaefer@ucdavis.edu. *

SCHAEFER, THEODORE PETER, retired chemistry professor; b. Gnadenthal, Man., Can., July 22, 1933; s. Paul Jacob and Margarethe (Wiebe) S.; m. Nicola Caroline Sewell, Dec. 26, 1960; children: Catherine, Dominic, Benjamin. BS with Honors, U. Man., 1954, MS, 1955; D.Phil. (Shell scholar), Oxford U., Eng., 1958; D.Sc. (hon. causa), U. Winnipeg, 1982. Prof. chemistry U. Manitoba, Winnipeg, Can., 1958—, Univ. Disting. prof., 1982-97, emeritus, 2000—; researcher NRC, Ottawa, Can., 1959, 62, Nat. Phys. Lab., Teddington, U.K., 1960, 65, Argonne Nat. Lab., Chgo., 1967, 68; sr. fellow, mem. grants com. NRC, Ottawa.; mem. council Nat. Scis. and Engring. Research Council, Ottawa., 1980-85. Contbr. articles on nuclear magnetic resonance to sci. jours. Recipient Herzberg award Spectroscopy Soc. Can., 1975. Fellow Chem. Inst. Can. (Noranda award 1973), Royal Soc. Can.; mem. Order of Can. Home: 210 Oak St Winnipeg MB Canada R3M 3R4 *Persistence can sometimes emulate perspicacity.*

SCHAEFER, WILLIAM DAVID, language educator; b. Dighton, Mass., May 11, 1928; s. Louis and Elsie K. (Otterbein) S.; m. Josephine R. Lamprecht, Aug. 8, 1958; 1 dau., Kimberly. BA, NYU, 1957; MS, U. Wis., 1958, PhD, 1962. Mem. faculty UCLA, 1962-90, prof. English, 1970-90, chmn. dept., 1969-71, exec. vice chancellor, 1978-87. Author: James (BV)

Thomson: Beyond the City, 1965, Speedy Extinction of Evil and Misery, 1967, Education Without Compromise: From Chaos to Coherence in Higher Education, 1990; contbr. articles to profl. jours., short stories to literary mags. Served with AUS, 1954-56. Fulbright fellow Eng., 1961-62 Mem. MLA (exec. dir. 1971-78). Home: 164 Stagecoach Rd Bell Canyon CA 91307-1044 Office: UCLA 405 Hilgard Ave Los Angeles CA 90095-9000 Personal E-mail: wschae444@aol.com.

SCHAEFER, WILLIAM GOERMAN, lawyer; b. Kansas City, Mo., June 16, 1941; m. Sharon Saylor, Dec. 21, 1963; children: James, Kristen. BA, U. Kans., 1963; JD, Harvard U., 1966. Bar: Ill. 1966, D.C. 1978, Md. 1984. Ptnr. Sidley & Austin, Chgo. and Washington, 1966-74, 78-93; v.p., gen. counsel DeKalb Genetics Corp., Ill., 1974-77; spl. counsel Bechel Corp., Gaithersburg, Md., 1993-96; sr. v.p. corporate affairs Vertis, Inc., Balt., 1996-2000; cons., 2000—.

SCHAEFFER, ANDREW, lawyer; b. Cin., July 31, 1974; BA in Economics, Thomas More Coll., 1996, BA in Hist., 1996, AA in Pre-legal Studies, 1996; JD, U. Ky. Coll. of Law, 1999. Bar: Western Dist. Ky. 1999, Ky. 1999, US Dist. Ct. Eastern Dist. Ky. 2000. Atty. Geenebaum Doll & McDonald PLLC, Cin. Vol. firefighter Burlington Fire Protection Dist., 1990—2000, vice chair, 2002—; trustee Thomas More Coll., 1994—96, mem., Found. Bd. Exec. Com., 1999—; fundraiser United Way Ann. Campaign, 2001; mem., Adv. Com. Conrad and Gunpower Creek Park, 2001—02; fundraiser Muscular Dystrophy Assn., 2002; pres. LEGACY, 2003; co-chair Vision 2015. Named one of 40 Under 40, Cin. Bus. Courier, 2005, Ohio's Rising Stars, Super Lawyers, 2005, 2006. Mem.: Cin. Bar Assn., Northern Ky. Bar Assn., Ky. Bar Assn. (mem., Exec. Com. 2000—, chair, Young Lawyers Sect., mem., Ann. Conv. Planning and CLE Com. 2001—02), ABA (mem., The Young Lawyer Editl. Bd. 2001, vice-chair, Ethics & Professionalism Com. 2001, mem., Del. Credentials Com. 2002—, mem., Resolutions Com. 2002—, chair, Young Lawyers Divsn. Nat. Conf. Team 2004, mem., Leadership Adv. Bd. 2004—, prog. dir., Young Lawyers Divsn. Affiliate Outreach 2005—06). Office: Greenebaum Doll & McDonald PLLC RiverCenter I 50 E RiverCenter Blvd Ste 1800 Covington KY 41012-2673 Office Phone: 859-655-4200. Office Fax: 859-655-4239.

SCHAEFFER, CHARLES PERRY, writer, editor; b. Cumberland, Md., Mar. 20, 1926; s. Charles Perry and Dorothy Frances Schaeffer; m. Eliza Ann Riggins, June 16, 1950; children: Sally Ann Canepa, John, Jennifer Bartell. BA, U. Md., 1950. Writer U.S. Info. Agy., Washington, 1950—53; news picture writer UPI, NYC, 1953—54; reporter Balt. Evening Sun, 1954—55, Am. Aviation Publs., Md., 1955—61; sci. writer Newhouse Newspapers, Washington, 1961—65; writer, exec. editor Kiplinger Personal Fin. Mag. (formerly Changing Times) Kiplinger Washington Editors, Inc, 1966—89. Mem. profit sharing bd. Kiplinger Washington Editors. Contbg. author: anthology Esquire's World of Humor, 1964, Saturday Review's Phoenix Nest, 1965; author: short mystery fiction, 2002—; contbr. articles to mags. Chmn. scout troop Walter Reed Army Med. Ctr., Silver Spring, Md., 1971—72; pres Neighborhood Civic Assn., Silver Spring, 1963—64; bd. dirs. Woodlin Elem. Sch., Silver Spring, 1963—64. EM 3/C USN, 1943—46, PTO. Decorated Phillippine Liberation Ribbon, 2 Stars USN, Pacific Theater Ribbon, Six Stars, Victory medal, Am. Theater ribbon; recipient Blakeslee Nat. Sci. Writing award, Am. Heart Assn., 1965. Mem.: Soc. Profl. Journalists, Nat. Assn. Sci. Writers (life), Nat. Press Club (1st pl. consumer journalism 1987). Home: 6036 Chatsworth Ln Bethesda MD 20814 Personal E-mail: schaeffer528@cs.com.

SCHAEFFER, GLENN WILLIAM, casino corporate financial executive; b. Pomona, Calif., Oct. 11, 1953; s. William Donald and Mary Louise (Miller) S.; m. Deborah Lynn Helfer, Sept. 6, 1974 (div. Apr. 1981); m. Renee Sue Riebel, May 25, 1985 AB summa cum laude, U. Calif., Irvine, 1974, MA, 1975; MFA, U. Iowa, 1977. Fin. cons. Dean Witter, Los Angeles, 1977-78; assoc. Hill and Knowlton, Inc., Los Angeles, 1978-81; v.p. Ramada Inns, Inc., Phoenix, 1981-84; exec. v.p., chief fin. officer Circus Circus Enterprises, Inc., Las Vegas, Nev., 1984-91, pres., 1991-93, also bd. dirs. Las Vegas; ptnr. Gold Strike Resorts, Jean, Nev., 1993-95; pres. Mandalay Resort Group, 1995—. Wine grower and estate bottler, N.Z. Founder and patron Internat. Inst. Modern Letters. Pres. Hitch fellow U. Calif.-Irvine, 1973-74 Mem. Phi Beta Kappa. Avocations: reading, bicycling. Office: Mandalay Resort Group 3950 Las Vegas Blvd S Las Vegas NV 89119

SCHAEFFER, LEONARD DAVID, health insurance company executive; b. Chgo., July 28, 1945; s. David and Sarah (Levin) Schaeffer; m. Pamela Lee Sidford, Aug. 11, 1968; children: David, Jacqueline. BA, Princeton U., 1969. Mgmt. cons. Arthur Andersen & Co., 1969—73; dep. dir. mgmt. Ill. Mental Health/Devel. Disability, Springfield, 1973—75; dir. Ill. Bur. of Budget, Springfield, 1975—76; v.p. Citibank, N.A., NYC, 1976—78; asst. sec. mgmt. and budget HHS, Washington, 1978, adminstr. HCFA, 1978—80; exec. v.p., COO Student Loan Mktg. Assn., Washington, 1980—82; pres., CEO Group Health, Inc., Mpls., 1983—86; chmn., CEO Blue Cross of Calif., Woodland Hills, 1986—96, WellPoint Health Networks Inc., Thousand Oaks, Calif., 1992—2004; chmn. WellPoint Inc., 2004—05; sr. advisor Tex. Pacific Group, 2006—; chmn. Surg. Care Affiliates, 2007—. Bd. dirs. Allergan, Inc., Irvine, Calif., Amgen, Inc., Thousand Oaks; bd. councilors U. So. Calif. Sch. Policy, Planning & Devel., 1988—; bd. dirs., exec. com. Blue Cross-Blue Shield Assn., Chgo., 1986—2004; mem. Congl. Prospective Payment Assessment Commn., 1987—93, Pew Health Professions Com., Phila., 1990—93; chmn. bd. trustees Nat. Health Found., LA, 1992—2001; chmn. bd. dirs. Nat. Inst. Health Care Mgmt., 1993—2006; mem. Coun. on the Econ. Impact of Health Sys. Change, 1996—; co-chair adv. coun. dept. of health care policy Harvard Med. Sch., 1998—; founding chmn. Coalition for Affordable and Quality Healthcare, 2000; regents lectr. U. Calif., Berkeley, Calif., 2005—06; sr. advisor Tex. Pacific Group, 2006—. Bd. govs. Town Hall, LA, 1989—2006; trustee The Brookings Inst., Nat. Health Mus., 2000—; adv. coun. Dept. Econs. Princeton U., NJ; adv. group Coun. on Health Care Econs. and Policy. Recipient Citation for Outstanding Svc., Am. Acad. Pediat., 1981, Disting. Pub. Svc. award, HEW, Washington, 1980; fellow, Kellogg Found., 1981—89; Internat. fellow, King's Fund Coll., London, 1990—. Mem.: Am. Assn. Health Plans (bd. dirs. 2001—04), Health Ins. Assn. Am. (chmn. 1999), Inst. Medicine NAS, Regency Club, Princeton Club, Cosmos Club. Office: 1733 Ocean Ave Ste 325 Santa Monica CA 90404 E-mail: lds@northbp.com.

SCHAEFFER, RICHARD, mercantile exchange executive; Grad., U. Md. Sr. v.p., dir. Chgo. Grp., 1992—97; exec. dir. global energy futures ABN Amro Inc., 1997—2006; treas. NY Mercantile Exch. Inc., 1993—2004, vice chmn., 2004—06, chmn., 2006—, NYMEX Holdings Inc., 2006—. Owner, Class A membership NY Mercantile Exch. Inc., 1981, mem. bd. dirs., 1990—, exec. com., 1992—. Office: NY Mercantile Exch World Fin Ctr One N End Ave New York NY 10282 Office Phone: 212-299-2000. *

SCHAEFFER, ROBERT, educational association administrator; Grad., MIT. Rsch. asst. Edn. Rsch. Ctr., MIT; talk show host Nat. Pub. Radio; rsch. dir., joint com. Human Services and Elderly Affairs Mass. Legislature; editl. writer NBC TV affiliate, Boston; pub. edn. dir. Nat. Ctr. Fair & Open Testing, Cambridge, Mass., 1985—, treasurer, clerk, bd. dirs. Co-author: Standing Up to the SAT, 1989; author: Standardized Tests and Teacher Competence, 1996. Office: FairTest 342 Broadway Cambridge MA 02139 Office Phone: 617-864-4810. Office Fax: 617-497-2224. *

SCHAEFFLER, GEORG, lawyer, manufacturing executive; b. Oct. 19, 1964; Lic. oec. HSG, U. of St. Gallen, Switzerland, 1990; JD cum laude, Duke U., LL.M. in International and Comparative Law, 1999. Bar: Texas 2000. With INA Schaeffler Group, Herzogenaurach, Germany, 1990—96, owner, 1996—; assoc. fin. and internat. groups Haynes and Boone LLP, Dallas, 2000—. 1st Lt. German Air Force reserves, 1984—86. Named one of World's Richest People, Forbes Mag., 2003—. Mem.: ABA. Office: Haynes and Boone LLP Ste 3100 901 Main St Dallas TX 75202-3789 *

SCHAFER, ALICE TURNER, retired mathematics professor; b. Richmond, Va., June 18, 1915; d. John H. and Cleon (Dermott) Turner; m. Richard Donald Schafer, Sept. 8, 1942; children: John Dickerson, Richard Stone. AB, U. Richmond, 1936, DSc, 1964; MS, U. Chgo., 1940, PhD (fellow), 1942. Tchr. Glen Allen (Va.) High Sch., 1936-39; instr. math. Conn. Coll., New London, 1942-44, asst. prof., 1954-57, asso. prof., 1957-61, prof., 1961-62; prof. math. Wellesley Coll., 1962-80, Helen Day Gould prof. math., 1969-80, Helen Day Gould prof. math. emerita, 1980—, affirmative action officer, 1980-82; prof. math. Marymount U., Arlington, Va., 1989-96; ret., 1996. Instr. U. Mich., Ann Arbor, 1945-46; lectr. Douglass Coll., New Brunswick, N.J., 1946-48; asst. prof. Swarthmore (Pa.) Coll., 1948-51, Drexel Inst. Tech., Phila., 1951-53; mathematician Johns Hopkins Applied Physics Lab., Silver Spring, Md., 1945; lectr. Simmons Coll., Boston, 1980-88, Radcliffe Coll. Seminars, Cambridge, Mass., 1980-85; U.S. chair postsecondary math. edn. U.S./China Joint Conf. on Edn., 1992, co-chair Citizen Amb. program People to People U.S. and China Joint Conf. on Women's Issues, 1995, session women in sci. and math. Contbr. articles on women in math. and other articles to math. jours. Recipient Disting. Alumna award Westhampton Coll., U. Richmond, 1977; NSF sci. faculty fellow Inst. for Advanced Study, Princeton, N.J., 1958-59. Fellow AAAS (math. sect. A nominating com. 1979-83, mem.-at-large 1983-86, chair-elect sect. A 1991, chair 1992, retiring chair 1993, Assn. for Women in Math. rep., 1993—), AAUP (chmn. nat. com. W 1980-83, mem. nat. coun. 1984-87), Am. Math. Soc. (chmn. postdoctoral fellowship com. 1973-76, affirmative action procedures com. 1980-82, chair com. on Human Rights of Mathematicians 1988-94), Soc. Indsl. and Applied Math., Am. Statis. Assn., Inst. Math. Stats., Nat. Coun. Tchrs. of Math. (chair com. on women 1976-81), Math Assn. Am. (adv. com. for Women and Math. program 1987-89, dir. fund raising 1989-92, lectr. 1982—, chair devel. com. 1988-92, Yueh-Gin Gung and Charles Y. Hu disting. svc. to math. award 1998), Internat. Congress Mathematicians (mem. fund raising com. 1986), Assn. for Women in Math. (pres. 1973-75, Alice T. Schafer Prize established 1989, chair fund raising com. 1992-94, leader math. del. women mathematicians to China 1990, Disting. Svc. award 1996), Emily's List (mem. majority coun.), Cosmos Club, Phi Beta Kappa, Sigma Xi, Sigma Delta Epsilon. Achievements include first study of singularities of space curves in projective differential geometry; research on undulation point of a space curve. Home: 1010 Waltham St Apt A404 Lexington MA 02421-8064

SCHAFER, CHARLES J., communications systems company executive; Various sr. fin. mgmt. positions Hazeltine Corp., 1969—84; various positions Loral Corp., 1984—96; pres. Tactical Def. Systems Divsn. Lockheed Martin; v.p. bus. ops. L-3 Comm. Holdings, Inc., NYC, 1998, COO, pres. Products Group, 1999—, sr. v.p., 2002—. Office: L-3 Comm Holdings Inc 600 Third Ave New York NY 10016 Office Phone: 212-697-1111. Office Fax: 212-805-5477. *

SCHAFER, ELIZABETH DIANE, historian, writer; b. Opelika, Ala., Sept. 26, 1965; d. Robert Louis and Carolyn Louise (Henn) S. BA in History cum laude, Auburn U., 1986, MA in History of Sci., 1988, PhD in History of Tech. magna cum laude, 1993; MA magna cum laude, Hollins Coll., 2003; MFA, Hollins U. Archivist Lee County Hist. Soc. Mus., 1988—. Ind. scholar, 1993—; presenter in field. Author: Exploring Harry Potter, 2000, Lake Martin: Alabama's Crown Jewel, 2002, Auburn: Plainsmen, Tigers and War Eagles, 2003, Auburn Football, 2004; co-author: Women Who Made A Difference in Alabama, 1995; cons. editor Ency. of Sci., 1998; freelance editor various tech. docs.; editl. asst. Proceedings of the We. Soc. for French History, 1988-91, Nat. Forum: The Phi Kappa Phi Jour., 1990-91; contbr. History News Svc.; reviewer Children's Lit. database; contbr. articles to profl. jours., encys., mags., chpts. to books. Recipient hon. mention poetry Writer's Digest, 1994 hon. mention children's non-fiction, 1997, children's non-fiction and fiction, 1998, Writer's Digest, Shirley Henn Meml. award Critical scholar, Hollins Coll., 1998. Mem. AAAS, AAUW, Am. Hist. Assn., Orgn. Am. Historians, Soc. History Tech., History Sci. Soc., Women's History Network, N.Y. Acad. Scis., So. Hist. Assn., Soc. Children's Book Writers and Illustrators, Children's Lit. Network, Ala. Poetry Soc., Children's Lit. Assn., Ala. Writer's Forum, Authors Guild, Lancaster Mennonite Hist. Soc., Lee County Hist. Soc. (life mem.), Auburn U. Alumni Assn. (life), Descs. Mex. War Vets., DAR (chpt. historian), Phi Alpha Theta. Home and Office: PO Box 57 Loachapoka AL 36865-0057 Office Phone: 334-821-0580. Personal E-mail: Elizabeth_D_Schafer@yahoo.com.

SCHAFER, GERALD LEWIS (JAY SCHAFER), library director; b. El Paso, Tex., Apr. 20, 1949; s. Norman Oscar and Clarice S. BA, U. Tex., El Paso, 1971; MLS, U. Denver, 1973. Info. specialist Denver Rsch. Inst., 1973-75; area mgr. Denver Pub. Libr., 1975-80; dir. profl. communications Skidmore, Owings & Merrill, Denver, 1981-84; coord. collection devel. svcs. to asst. dir. for rsch. svcs. Auraria Libr., Denver, 1984—97; dir. libr. and info. svcs. Hatch Library, Bay Path Coll., Longmeadow, 1997—2000; coord. collection devel. U. Mass., Amherst, 2000—04, interim dir. librs., 2004—05, dir. librs., 2005—. V.p., pres. elect Mgmt. Coun. Boston Libr. Consortium, 2006—. Editor: Master Plan-U.S. Air Force Academy, 1984. Chair collections task force Colo. State Libr., Denver, 1993-94, Access Colo. Libr. and Info. Network Collection Devel. Com., 1996—. Mem. ALA, Colo. Libr. Assn. Avocation: architecture and library space planning. Office: Dir Librs U Mass Amherst Amherst MA 01003-9275 Office Phone: 413-545-0284. *

SCHAFER, JACQUELINE ELLEN, federal agency administrator; b. Greenport, NY; AB, Middlebury Coll., 1967. Analyst, rsch. asst. Fed. Reserve Bank NY, 1967—70; legis. asst. to Sen. James L. Buckley U.S. Senate, 1971—76; asst. sec. installations and environ. U.S. Navy; regional adminstr. region 2 U.S. Environ. Protection Agy., 1982—93; dir. Calif. Dept. Fish and Game, 1993—99, Ariz. Dept. Environ. Quality, 1999—2002; dep. asst. adminstr. bur. econ. growth US Agy. Internat. Devel., 2002—05, asst. adminstr. for econ. growth agrl. & trade, 2005—. Office: US Agy Internat Devel 1300 Pennsylvania Ave NW Washington DC 20523 *

SCHAFER, JAMES ARTHUR, physiologist; b. Buffalo, Oct. 10, 1941; s. Joseph James and Gladys Lita (Lighty) S.; m. Margaret Anne Schiefer, Aug. 16, 1964; children: James Arthur Jr., Kirsten Ann. BS, U. Mich., 1963, PhD, 1968. Postdoctoral fellow Gustav-Embden Ctr., Frankfurt, Germany, 1968-69, Duke U., Durham, NC, 1969-70; asst. prof. U. Ala., Birmingham, 1970-72, assoc. prof., 1972-76, prof., 1976—2004, prof. emeritus, 2004—, sr. scientist Nephrology Rsch. and Tng. Ctr. Birmingham, 1980—. Author: (with H. Valtin) Renal Function. Mechanisms Preserving Fluid and Solute Balance in Health, 3d edit., 1994; editor Am. Jour. Physiology: Renal, 1983-89, mem. editl. bd., 2001—; assoc. editor News in Physiol. Scis., 1997-03; cons. editor Jour. Clin. Investigation, 1998-03; mem. editl bd. Jour. Gen. Physiology, 1979-97, adv. editor, 1998—; mem. editl bd. Kidney Internat., 1990-95; author textbooks on physiology; editor sci. monographs in Membrane Transport in Biology, 1992, Methods in Membrane and Transporter Research, 1994; contbr. articles to profl. jours. Chmn. rsch. com. Nat. Kidney and Urol. Diseases Adv. Bd. U.S. Dept. HHS, 1987-90. Fellow Jane Coffin Childs Meml., 1968-69; recipient Robert F. Pitts. Meml. award Internat. Union Physiol. Scis., Sydney, Australia, 1983, Homer W. Smith award Am. Soc. Nephrology and NY Heart Assn., 1993, Max Planck-Von Humboldt Rsch. award, Govt. of Germany, 1994. Mem. Am. Physiol. Soc. (councilor 1992-95, pres.-elect 1995-96, pres. 1996-97, past pres. 1997-98, Carl W. Gottschalk award 2001, Robert W. Berliner award 2004), Am. Soc. Nephrology (sec.-treas. 1989-92, councilor 1992-95), Am. Soc. Clin. Investigation (hon.), Fedn. Am. Socs. Exptl. Biology (bd. dirs. 1995-99, exec. com. 1996-97, pub. affairs exec. com. 1997-99), Am. Heart Assn. (Established Investigator award, 1971-76), Biophys. Soc., Int. Soc. Nephrol., Soc. Gen. Physiol. Avocations: classical music, mountain hiking, skiing. Office: U Ala Dept Phys & Biophysics 834 MCLM Bldg 1918 University Blvd Birmingham AL 35294-0005 Home Phone: 205-991-9750; Office Phone: 205-934-7106. Business E-Mail: jschafer@uab.edu.

SCHAFER, JOHN STEPHEN, poet; b. NYC, Sept. 5, 1934; s. Stephen James and Siiri (Halmi) S.; m. Gertrud Rosa Fleischmann, June 14, 1958; children: Sylvia F., John Stephen, Karen D., Kristen H. BA, Rutgers U., 1956, MBA, 1963. Advt. research mgr. Union Carbide Corp., NYC, 1959—65; rsch. mgr. Bus. Week, NYC, 1965—66; v.p. Opinion Rsch. Corp., Princeton, NJ, 1966—80; pres. Am. Econ. Found., Cleve., 1981—2002, trustee, 1975—2002; v.p., dir. Ams. for Competitive Enterprise System, Phila., 1970-82. Editor: Linde Electric Welding Progress, 1959-62, ORC Pub. Opinion Index, 1968-72, AEF Straight Talk, 1981-82, Bellcore Exch., 1993-94; works pub. in Famous Poems of the Twentieth Century, 1996, Perceptions in Harmony, 1998, The Communicator, 2000-07, Best Poems and Poets of 2003, 2004, others. Polit. pollster Ed Clark for U.S. Pres., 1980; chmn. N.J. Libertarian party, 1983; nat. dir. U.S. Jaycees, 1965-66, v.p. N.J., 1964-65. Served to 1st lt. U.S. Army, 1957-59. Mem. Jr. Chamber Internat. (hon. life), Philosophean Soc., Scabbard and Blade, Delta Phi Alpha Presbyterian. Home: 114 Walton Palm Rd Panama City FL 32413-7311

SCHAFER, MARIE, nurse, educator; d. Eric Martelly and Jacqueline Gabriel; m. Raymond Schafer, July 19, 1997. BA, Fla. Internat. U., Miami, 1994; BSN, Barry U., Miami Shores, Fla., 1997, MSN, 2003. Acting nurse mgr. Miami VA Healthcare Sys., 1998—2001, staff nurse, 2001—03, 2003—04, nurse educator, 2003—. Cons. William Sterns & Assoc., Miami, 2003—04; case mgr. Home Health Agy., Miami, 2003—04. Editor (editor-in-chief): (newsletter) Nightingale News; contbr. articles to profl. jours. Named Excellence Award in Tchg. finalist, Nursing Spectrum, 2006. Mem.: Am. Soc. Parenteral Enteral Nutrition, Am. Holistic Nurses' Assn., Fla. Nurses Assn., Sierra Club. Office: Miami VA Healthcare Sys 1201 NW 16th St Miami FL 33125 Home Phone: 305-971-8228; Office Phone: 305-575-7000 ext. 4239. Home Fax: 18772160328. Personal E-mail: mariem@gate.net. E-mail: marie.schafer@med.va.gov.

SCHAFER, MICHAEL FREDERICK, orthopedic surgeon; b. Peoria, Ill., Aug. 17, 1942; s. Harold Martin and Frances May (Ward) S.; m. Eileen M. Briggs, Jan. 8, 1966; children: Steven, Brian, Kathy, David, Daniel. BA, U. Iowa, 1964, MD, 1967. Diplomate Am. Bd. Orthopedic Surgery. Intern Chgo. Wesley Meml. Hosp., 1967-68; resident in orthop. surgery Cook County Program, Northwestern U., Chgo., 1968-72; asst. prof. orthop. surgery Northwestern U., 1977—; Reyerson prof. and chmn. dept. orthopedic surgery; asso. attending orthopedic surgeon Northwestern Meml. Hosp., 1974—. Adj. staff Children's Meml. Hosp., Chgo., 1974—; cons. VA Lakeside Hosp., 1974—; panelist Bur. Health Manpower, HEW, 1976; sec.-treas. Orthop. Rsch. and Edn. Found.; attending orthop. surgeon Northwestern Meml. Hosp., 1980—, exec. dir. Back and Neck Inst. Contbr. articles to profl. jours. Maj. U.S. Army, 1973-74. Fellow Am. Orthopaedic Assn., Am. Acad. Orthopaedic Surgeons; mem. AMA, Am. Orthopedic Soc. Sports Medicine, Ill. Med. Soc., Chgo. Med. Soc., Scoliosis Rsch. Soc. Roman Catholic. Home: 1815 Ridgewood Ln W Glenview IL 60025-2205 Office: Northwestern U Med School Ste 910 645 N Michigan Ave Chicago IL 60611-2876 Home Phone: 847-724-4228. Business E-Mail: m-schafer@northwestern.edu.

SCHAFER, MILTON, composer, pianist, educator; b. NYC, Sept. 24, 1920; s. Abraham and May (Meyerson) S.; div. 1974; 1 child, Nina Kathryn. Cert., Paris Conservatory, 1950; student, Am. Conservatory, Fontainbleu, France; pvt. study, Nadia Boulanger, Paris, 1949-50; BS, Juilliard Sch. Music, NYC, 1952; MA, CCNY, NYC, 1967; studied with, Alfred Mirovitch, Irwin Freundlich, Lonnie Epstein. Lectr. music CCNY, NYC, 1954—56, prof. music John Jay Coll., 1976—96; asst. to Frank Loesser Frank Music Pub., NYC, 1956—58; music. dir. Am. Theatre Wing, NYC, 1962. Mem. So. Hampton Poetry Workshop, 1997—. Piano recitals at Am. Embassy, Paris, 1949, Quaker Ctr. Internat., Paris, 1949, Town Hall, NYC, 1950, 54; composer, lyricist: (children's song cycle) Mommy Gimme a Drinka Water, 1957 (recorded by Danny Kaye and televised by Nathan Lane with Boston Pops 1999), (Broadway musicals) Bravo Giovanni, 1962 (reading revival, Cleve. 2005), Lyrics: Ronny Graham, (Tony award nomination for score), Drat! The Cat!, 1965 (staged revival "Musicals Tonight", NYC, 2005, voted Best Score of Yr. by Walter Kerr, book, lyrics by Ira Levin), (three revivals) He Touched Me, 1965 (recorded by Barbara Streisand), The No-Color Time of the Day (recorded by Frank Pourcel), I'm Five (recorded by The Muppets and Barbara Streisand), I Like Old People, Don't You? (recorded by Michael Feinstein); songs recorded by Peggy Lee, Sarah Vaughn, Jerry Vale, Eddie Fisher, Ah!Camminare, Frank Pourcel,; author: Practical Technique for Popular Piano Playing, 1947; author, composer adaptation Kate Simon's Bronx Primitive 1990 (staged reading at ASCAP 1998, Hell's Kitchen 2005, Jewish Ctr. of Hamptons, 2006); music critic High Fidelity, 1975, Music Jour., 1976-78; author: (children's book) Crazy Barbara, 2003, I'm Big, 2006, numerous poems. Staff sgt. USAAF, 1942-46. Co-winner Nat. Guild Piano Tchrs. Competition, N.Y.C., 1948. Mem. ASCAP, Dramatists Guild, The Bohemians, Nat. Arts Club. Avocations: reading, yoga, swimming, travel, poetry. Home: 33 Riverside Dr New York NY 10023-8012 Office Phone: 212-769-8720.

SCHAFER, OSCAR S., investment company executive; Bachelor's Degree, Harvard Coll.; MBA, Harvard U. Portfolio mgr. Steinhardt Partners, gen. ptnr., Cumberland Associates, 1982—2001; mng. ptnr. OSS Capital Mgmt. Bd. mem. Parker Vision Inc.; dir. Global Healthcare Ptnrs. Office: OSS Capital Mgmt 605 3rd Ave Lobby New York NY 10158

SCHAFER, ROBERT LOUIS, agricultural engineer, researcher; b. Burlington, Iowa, Aug. 1, 1937; s. Marion Louis and Pansy (Head) S.; m. Carolyn Louise Henn, Aug. 1, 1959; 1 child, Elizabeth Diane. BS, Iowa State U., 1959, MS, 1961, PhD, 1965. Agrl. engr. Agrl. Rsch. Svc., USDA, Ames, Iowa, 1959-64, Auburn, Ala., 1964-95. Co-author: Advances in Soil Dynamics, 1994; contbr. articles to profl. jours. Fellow Am. Soc. Agrl. Engrs. (McCormick Case Gold medal 1997). Home: PO Box 189 Loachapoka AL 36865-0189 E-mail: rls1955@gmail.com.

SCHAFER, RONALD WILLIAM, electrical engineering educator; b. Tecumseh, Nebr., Feb. 17, 1938; s. William Henry and Esther Sophia Schafer; m. Dorothy Margaret Hall, June 2, 1960; children: William R., John C. (dec.), Katherine L., Barbara Anne. Student, Doane Coll., Crete, Nebr., 1956-59; BEE, U. Nebr., 1961, MEE, 1962; PhD in Elec. Engring., MIT, 1968. Tech. staff Bell Labs., Murray Hill, NJ, 1968-74; John and Marilu McCarty prof. elec. engring. Ga. Inst. Tech., Atlanta, 1974—2004, Inst. prof., 1991—2004, emeritus prof., 2004—; HP fellow Hewlett-Packard Labs., Palo Alto, Calif., 2004—. Chmn. bd. Atlanta Signal Processors Inc., 1983-2001. Co-author: Digital Signal Processing, 1974, Digital Processing of Speech Signals, 1979, Speech Analysis, 1979,

Discrete-Time Signal Processing, 1989, 2d edit., 1999, Computer-Based Exercises for Signal Processing Using Matlab, 1995, DSP First: A Multimedia Approach, 1998, Signal Processing First, 2003. Recipient Class of 34 Disting. Prof. award Ga. Inst. Tech., 1985. Fellow IEEE (Emanuel R. Piore award 1980, Edn. medal 1992, 3d millennium award 2000), Acoustical Soc. Am.; mem. IEEE Processing Soc. (soc. award 1982, edn. award 2000), Nat. Acad. Engring. Democrat. Office: Hewlett-Packard Labs 1501 Page Mill Rd Palo Alto CA 94304 Office Phone: 650-857-4142.

SCHAFER, SHARON MARIE, anesthesiologist; b. Detroit, Mar. 23, 1948; d. Charles Anthony and Dorothy Emma (Schweitzer) Pokriefka; m. Timothy John Schafer, Nov. 12, 1977; children: Patrick Christopher, Steven Michael. BS in Biology, Wayne State U., 1971, MD, 1975; MBA in Practice Mgmt., Madonna U., 2000. Diplomate Am. Bd. Anesthesiology. Intern, resident Sinai Hosp. Detroit, 1975-78; pvt. practice anesthesiology Troy, Mich., 1988—. Mem. AMA, Am. Soc. Anesthesiologists. Roman Catholic. Home and Office: 5741 Folkstone Dr Troy MI 48085-3154 Office Phone: 248-879-6246.

SCHAFERMEYER, ROBERT WILLIAM, emergency physician, educator, health policy consultant; b. St. Louis, Jan. 9, 1948; s. William Jacob and Virginia Rose (Cumming) S.; m. An-ping Yuan, May 12, 1973; children: Christina, David, Matthew, Joseph. Student, St. Louis U., 1966-69; MD, U. Mo., 1973. Diplomate Am. Bd. Emergency Medicine, Am. Bd. Pediats., sub-bd. pediat. emergency medicine. Mem. dept. emergency medicine East Tenn. Children's Hosp., Knoxville, 1979-81, Carolinas Med. Ctr., Charlotte, NC, 1981—; clin. assoc. prof. pediats. U. N.C. Sch. Medicine, Chapel Hill, 1981-85, clin. prof. emergency medicine and pediats., 1994—; assoc. chair dept. emergency medicine Carolinas Med. Ctr., Charlotte, 1982—. Dir. E.D. Cons. and Lectrs., Charlotte, 90—. Assoc. editor: Pediatric Emergency Medicine Concepts and Clinical Practice, 1992; editor: Pediatric Emergency Medicine: A Comprehensive Study Guide, 1995, 2d edit. 2002; contbr. articles and revs. to profl. jours. including Annals Emergency Medicine Jour.; reviewer Pediat. Emergency Medicine, Acad. Emergency Medicine; past mem. editl. bd. Pediat. Emergency Med. Jour. Com. mem. MEMAC Adv., Mecklenberg County, 1991-93; mem. task force Drug Abuse for County Commrs., Mecklenberg, 1989-90. Lt. commdr. USPHS, 1974—76. EMS-C grantee Maternal and Child Health, 1992-94. Fellow Am. Coll. Emergency Physicians (bd. dirs. 1994-2002, pres.-elect 1999-2000, pres. 2000-01, past pres. 2001-02, Weigenstein Outstanding Leadership award 2004); mem. Am. Acad. Pediats., NC chpt. Am. Coll. Emergency Physicians (councillor 1984-94, bd. dirs. 1983-89, pres. 1986-88, Leadership/Svc. award 1988, George Podgorny Emergency Medicine Svc. award 1996), Soc. Acad. Emergency Medicine (bd. dirs. 2004-07). Roman Catholic. Avocations: tae kwan do, photography, skiing. Office: Carolinas Med Ctr 1000 Blythe Blvd Charlotte NC 28203-5812 Office Phone: 704-355-3181.

SCHAFF, MANYA, foundation administrator; b. Chgo., Mar. 12, 1931; d. Louis Lipkin and Allene Ewing; m. Jay Barash Schaff, Mar. 25, 1951 (div. Jan. 20, 1971); children: Pamela Beth, William Franz Kim, Elizabeth Aline; m. Dimitri Polonsky, PhD, June 27, 1971 (div. Dec. 14, 2000). MusB, Northwestern U., 1953. Tchr. Carnegie-Mellon U., Pitts., 1961—65, Chatham Coll., Pitts., 1964—71, Immaculate Heart Coll., LA, 1972—79; instr. UCLA, 1973—79; program dir. Performing Tree, Inc., LA, 1982—88; program officer The Ahmanson Found., Beverly Hills, Calif., 1988—; tchr., performer Shady Side Acad., Pitts., 1968—71. Panelist L.A. Cultural Affairs Dept., 1983—85, L.A. Ednl. Partnership, Small Grants to Teachers, 1988—98; sr. facilitator Inst. for the Arts, Pitts. Pub. Schs., Pitts., 1985; bd. dir. Vista Del Mar Child Care, LA, 1979—82. Editor: Piano for Two Directory. Bd. dirs. Chamber Music Soc. of L.A., 1990—95. Recipient Drawing prize, Assoc. Artists Pitts., 1963, Pennational Artists Annual, 1964, Fiber Art prize, Annual Ehrman Mansion Show, 1977. Mem.: Pi Kappa Lambda (life), Sigma Alpha Iota (life). Democrat. Home: 2139 Roscomare Rd Los Angeles CA 90077 Office: The Ahmanson Found 9215 Wilshire Blvd Beverly Hills CA 90210 Personal E-mail: mschaff@mindspring.com.

SCHAFFER, AKIVA, writer, director; b. Berkeley, Calif., Dec. 1, 1977; Grad., U. Calif., Santa Cruz. Co-founder, mem. The Lonely Island, 2001—. Writer MTV Movie Awards, 2004, 2005, G-Phoria, 2004, Saturday Night Live, 2005—, guest appearances (TV specials) 40 Most Awesomely Bad Dirrty Songs...Ever, 2004. Recipient WIRED Rave Award - TV, 2006. Office: United Talent Agency Inc 9560 Wilshire Blvd Ste 500 Beverly Hills CA 90212 Office Phone: 310-273-6700. Office Fax: 310-247-1111.

SCHAFFER, ARCHIE, III, food products executive; b. Ft. Smith, Ark., 1948; B in Natural Scis., U. Ark., 1970. Adminstrv. asst. Gov. Dale Bumpers, 1971—75, Senator Bumpers, 1975—77; adminstr. Greenhurst Nursing Home, Charleston, Ark.; owner Schaffer & Assocs., Little Rock; exec. dir. Ark. Bus. Coun., 1987—91; dir. media, pub. and govtl. affairs Tyson Foods Inc., Springdale, Ark., 1991—99, sr. v.p. external rels., 1999—. Mem. Ark. Leadership Acad.; mem. agrl. devel. coun. U. Ark.; mem. adv. bd. Ark. LWV. Mem.: Ark. Nature Conservancy (bd. mem.). Office: Tyson Foods Inc 2210 W Oakland Dr Springdale AR 72762-6999

SCHAFFER, DAVID EDWIN, retired systems administrator; b. Nov. 3, 1929; s. Karl and Jeanette (Gotthelf) S.; m. Ariel Williams Sullivan, May 3, 1951 (dec. Dec. 2004) stepchildren: Adrienne Sullivan Smith, James W. Sullivan; m. Patricia Owen, Feb. 25, 2006; stepchildren: Christopher Owen, Patricia Taylor. Student, Wharton Sch. of U. Pa., 1948-49; BA, New Sch. for Social Rsch., 1959. Spl. edn. tchr. of emotionally disturbed children various schs. and hosps., 1954-65; br. mgr. 1st Westchester Nat. Bank, New Rochelle, NY, 1965-66; v.p. Longines-Symphonette Inc.; spl. asst. to chmn. bd. Longines Wittnauer Inc., Larchmont, NY, 1966-72; pvt. practice mgmt. cons. Franconia, NH, 1973-77; v.p., dir. ops. Carroll Reed Ski Shops, Inc., 1978-80; ret. Instr. econs. Am. Inst. Banking, 1965-66. Moderator, Town of Franconia, 1973-2005; founding trustee emeritus Frost Pl., 1975—; bd. dirs. White Mountain Community Svcs., 1973-77; bd. dirs., past pres. No. N.H. Mental Health Services, 1975-77. Prodr.: numerous record albums. Vol., bd. dirs. Hospice of the Littleton Area, Jansen Hospice; mem. com. St. Mathews Chapel, Sugar Hill, N.H. With Signal Corps, AUS, 1951-53. Mem. Direct Mail Credit Assn. Am. (founding mem.), Assoc. Retail Credit Men of N.Y.C., Direct Mail Assn. Am. (past chmn. subcom. on consumer affairs and regulatory agys.), Profile Club (pres., dir.). Democrat. Episcopalian. Home: 21 River Rd Franconia NH 03580

SCHAFFER, DAVID IRVING, lawyer; b. NYC, Oct. 17, 1935; s. Frank and Edith (Montlack) S.; m. Lois Ann Warshauer, June 16, 1957; children: Susan Edith, Eric Michael. BA, U. Pa., 1956; LL.B., Harvard U., 1959. Bar: N.Y. 1960. Assoc. Shearman & Sterling, NYC, 1960-65; sec., counsel Yale Express System, Inc., NYC, 1965-66; sr. v.p., gen. counsel, sec. Avis, Inc., Garden City, NY, 1966-83; v.p., gen. counsel U.S. Surgical Corp., Norwalk, Conn., 1983-86; of counsel Meltzer, Lippe, Goldstein & Schlissel, LLP, Mineola, NY, 1986-89; ptnr. Meltzer, Lippe, Goldstein & Breitstone, LLP, Mineola, 1989—. Past pres. Nassau County Legal Aid Soc., 1984-86. Bd. dirs. United Cmty. Fund, Great Neck, N.Y., 1980, Great Neck Estates Civic Assn., 1998—, L.I. Venture Group, 1988-2003. With USAR, 1960. Mem. ABA, N.Y. State Bar Assn., Nassau County Bar Assn., L.I. Software Assn., Harvard Club. Democrat. Home: 31 Amherst Rd Great Neck NY 11021-2910 Office: Meltzer Lippe Et Al 190 Willis Ave Mineola NY 11501-2693 Office Phone: 516-747-0300. Personal E-mail: dlefty35@optonline.net. Business E-Mail: dschaffer@meltzerlippe.com.

SCHAFFER, HENRY M., lawyer; b. Bklyn., Aug. 22, 1943; AB, Columbia U., 1964; MA, Wash. U., St. Louis, 1964; JD, U. Calif., Berkeley, 1973. Bar: Ill. 1973, Ohio (inactive) 1980, US Dist. Ct. No. Dist. Ill. 1974, US Dist. Ct. No. Dist. Ohio 1980, US Supreme Ct. 1980, US Ct. Appeals 8th Cir. 1985. Atty. Jenner & Block LLP, Chgo., 1973—77, Rothschild, Barry & Myers, Chgo., 1977—78, Cooper, Straub, Walinski & Cramer, Toledo, 1983—87; co-dir. civil law clinic U. Toledo, Ohio, 1979—83, Ohio, 1987—89; ptnr. Howe & Hutton, Ltd., Chgo., 1989—2003; of counsel Jenner & Block LLP, Chgo., 2003—. Office: Jenner & Block LLP 1 IBM Plz Chicago IL 60611-7603 Office Phone: 312-840-7673. Office Fax: 312-840-7773. Business E-Mail: hschaffer@jenner.com.

SCHAFFER, JOSEPH IRA, physician, educator; b. NY, Nov. 28, 1955; m. Suzanne Yuri Wada. BA, Wesleyan U., Middletown, Conn., 1978; MD, U. Cin., 1987. Fellow Cleve. Clinic Found., 1991—92; asst. prof. Stony Brook U., NY, 1992—. Prof. UT Southwestern Med. Ctr., Dallas, 1997—, chief gynecology & urogynecology, 1997—. Author: (textbooks) Office Urogynecology, Williams Gynecology. Mem.: Am. Urogynecologic Soc. (mem. rsch. and pub. rels. com. 2002—07), Soc. Gynecologic Surgeons (licentiate; chair rsch. com. 2006—07). Office: UT Southwestern Med Ctr 5323 Harry Hines Blvd Dallas TX 75390-9032 Office Phone: 214-648-7211. Office Fax: 214-648-5697. Business E-Mail: joseph.schaffer@utsouthwestern.edu.

SCHAFFER, KENNETH B., communications executive, mechanical engineer, consultant; b. NYC, Oct. 19, 1947; s. Louis and Rose Schaffer; m. Alla Fyodorovna Kliouka, Aug. 26, 1993 (div.); 1 child, Kibo. BA, BCNY, 1969. Pres., founder Sound Images, Inc., NYC, 1969-72; exec. v.p. Douglas Internat., NYC, 1972-75; pres., founder Ken Schaffer Group, Inc., NYC, 1975-82, Orbita Techs. Corp., NYC, 1981-86; v.p., founder Belka Internat. Inc., NYC and Moscow, 1986-91; pres., founder BelCom, Inc., NYC, Moscow, and Almaty, 1991-96, also bd. dirs.; CEO K2B, Inc., NYC. Profiled in The New Yorker, 1991. Recipient Golden Ace award Cable TV Assn., 1989. Mem. Am. Radio Relay League, Aircraft Owners and Pilots Assn., Internet Soc. Achievements include invention of wireless guitar; satellite system to intercept internal Soviet television; TV2Me, a system that enables global access to any cable television system. Avocations: flying, amateur radio. Home: 21 W 58th St New York NY 10019-1604 Office Phone: 212-371-2344. E-mail: ks@tv2me.com.

SCHAFFER, MARTIN DAVID, cardiologist; b. NYC, May 7, 1957; MD, UCLA, 1982. Cert. Internal Medicine, Cardiovascular Disease. Intern, internal medicine UCLA, 1982—83, resident, cardiology, 1983—85, fellow, 1985—87, Daniel Freeman Heart Ctr., LA, 1987—88; founder, cardiologist Nev. Cardiology Associates, 1989—; staff mem. Mountain View Hosp., Las Vegas, Nev., Sunrise Hosp. & Med. Ctr., Las Vegas, Nev., South Hills Hosp., Las Vegas, Nev.; courtesy U. Med. Ctr., Las Vegas, Nev., Desert Springs Hosp., Las Vegas, Nev.; hosp. affliliation Valley Hosp., Las Vegas, Nev. Office: Nev Cardiology Associates 3121 S Maryland Pkwy Ste 512 Las Vegas NV 89109 Office Phone: 702-796-7150. Office Fax: 702-796-9071. *

SCHAFFER, RANDY, lawyer; b. 1950; m. Mollie Schaffer; children: Randy III, Josh. BA with high honors, U. Tex., 1970, JD with honors, 1973. Bar: Tex. 1973, U.S. Dist. Ct. Tex., U.S. Ct. Appeals (4th, 5th, 9th, 10th,11th cir.), U.S. Supreme Ct. Ptnr. The Schaffer Firm, Houston. Fellow: Houston Bar Found.; mem.: NACDL (Pres. Disting. Svc. Award 1993), ABA, Am. Bd. Criminal Lawyers, Tex. Criminal Def. Lawyers Assn. (Pres. Award of Merit 1989), State Bar Tex. (Outstanding Criminal Def. Lawyer 1989), Houston Bar Assn., Order of Coif, Phi Beta Kappa. Office: The Schaffer Firm 1301 McKinney Ste 3100 Houston TX 77010 Office Phone: 713-951-9555. Office Fax: 713-951-9854. E-mail: reesepook@aol.com. *

SCHAFFER, ROBERT (BOB SCHAFFER), former congressman; b. Cin., July 24, 1962; s. Robert James and Florence Ann (Bednar) S.; m. Maureen Elizabeth Menke, Feb. 8, 1986; children: Jenniffer and Emily (twins), Justin, Sarah Mary. BA in Polit. Sci., U. Dayton, 1984; doctorate (hon.), Colo. Tech. U. Speechwriter republican caucus Ohio Gen. Assembly, 1984-85; legis. asst. State of Ohio, Columbus, 1985; majority adminstrv. asst. Colo. State Senate, Denver, 1985-87, mem., 1987-96, U.S. Congress from 4th Colo. dist., Washington, 1997—2003, mem. agr. com., edn. and workforce com., resources com. Mem. Rep. Policy Com., GOP Theme Team; commr. Colo. Advanced Tech. Inst., 1988—; proprietor No. Front Range Mktg. and Distbn., Inc. Mem. Mental Health Bd. Larimer County, 1986-87; mem. com. on human svcs. Nat. Conf. State Legislatures; campain co-chmn. Arnold for Lt. Gov.; Republican candidate for Lt. Gov. of Colo., 1994. Named Nat. Legislator of Yr., Rep. Nat. Legislators Assn., 1995, Taxpayer Champion, Colo. Union of Taxpayers, 1995, Bus. Legislator of the Yr. Colo. Assn. Commerce and Industry, Named Guardina Small Bus. Nat. Fedn. Ind. Bus.; recipient Spirit of Enterprise award U.S. C. of C. Mem. Jaycees (Mover and Shaker award 1989), KC. Republican. Roman Catholic. Avocations: backpacking, skiing, baseball, painting, reading. Home: 5027 Alder Ct Fort Collins CO 80525-5588

SCHAFFER, SANDRA SUE, artist, educator; b. Kansas City, Mo., Jan. 12, 1947; d. Robert William and Marian Frances Effertz; m. Larry Alan Schaffer, Nov. 10, 1972; children: Kristen Noelle, Scott David. BA in Psychology, U. Mo., Columbia, 1969; MSEd in Learning Disabilities, Ctrl. Mo. State U., Warrensburg, 1974. Diagnostician and learning disabilities specialist Cenl. Mo. State U. Artist, Kansas City, Mo., 1997—. Diagnostician, spl. edn. coord. The Plaza Acad., Mercier, Mo., 2003—. One-woman shows include Corridor Gallery, 2005, Park Ctrl. Gallery, 2006, two-peson exhbn., Irene B. French Meml. Gallery, 2007, exhibitions include Finding the Extraordinary in the Ordinary: Works from Peru, Nepal and other Travels, Nepali Matron (MKEC Engring. award Kans. Watercolor Soc. Regional Show, 2004), Ledgemates (Excellence award Red River Watercolor Soc. Nat. Show, 2004), Rooftop Perspective (Past Pres.'s award N.W. Watercolor Soc. Nat. Show, 2001), Village Life (Friends Cash award Miss. Watercolor Soc. Nat. Show, 2001). Newsletter editor Watercolor Honor Soc., Springfield, Mo., 2004—06; bd. dirs. Mattie Rhodes Arts Ctr., Kansas City, Mo., 1994—95. Recipient First Pl. award, Wyo. Watercolor Soc. Nat. Exhbn., 2001, New Orleans Sch. of Fine Art and Daler-Rowney award, La. Watercolor Soc. Internat. Show, 2002, Nielsen-Bainbridge award, Western Colo. Watercolor Soc. Nat. Show, 2001, Colvin Cash award, Baker Arts Ctr. Nat. Show, 2003, Pacific Gallery Artists' award, Pensicola Art League Nat. Show, 2004, Catherine M. Mulkare Cash award, RI Watercolor Soc., 2005, Merit award, Watercolor Art Soc. Houston, 2005, Juror's Art award, Ctr. Nat. Show, 2005, Merit award, Red River Watercolor Soc., 2005, Distinction award, Mo. Watercolor Soc. Nat. Show, 2007, Cash award, Watercolor USA, 2007, others. Mem.: Mo. Watercolor Soc. (bd. dirs. 2007—, George Latta Cash award 2005), Watercolor West Watercolor Soc., N.W. Watercolor Soc. (signature mem.), Tex. Watercolor Soc. (Purple Sage award, signature mem.), Watercolor Honor Soc. (assoc.; bd. dirs. 2004—06, Winsor-Newton award 2004, signature mem.). Democrat. Unitarian-Universalist. Avocations: travel, bicycling, reading. Home: 12700 E 64th Ct Kansas City MO 64133 Office: The Plaza Acad 4232 Mercier Kansas City MO 64111 Home Phone: 816-358-3609; Office Phone: 816-561-0770. Office Fax: NA; Home Fax: 816-373-2112. Personal E-mail: lschaffer@kc.rr.com. E-mail: na.

SCHAFFER, SCOTT R., lawyer; b. Bronx, NY, Dec. 17, 1959; BS, U. Fla., 1981; JD, Bklyn. Law Sch., 1984. Bar: NJ 1985, NY 1986, US Dist. Ct. So. Dist. NY, US Dist. Ct. Ea. Dist. NY, US Dist. Ct. Dist. NJ. Ptnr. Wilson, Elser, Moskowitz, Edelman & Dicker LLP, NYC, coord. nat. D&O (directors & officers) practice team. Mem.: ABA (tort & ins. practice sect., labor & employment sect.), Assn. of the Bar of the City of NY (chmn. D&O ins. com.), NY State Bar Assn. (tort, ins. & compensation law sect.). Office: Wilson Elser Moskowitz Edelman & Dicker LLP 150 E 42nd St 23rd Fl New York NY 10017-5639 Office Phone: 212-490-3000 ext. 2771. Office Fax: 212-490-3038. Business E-Mail: schaffers@wemed.com.

SCHAFFER, SETH ANDREW, lawyer; b. Bklyn., Jan. 7, 1942; m. Karen (Kiki) Cohn, Dec. 1, 1968; children: Amanda, Julia, James. BA in Econs. magna cum laude, Harvard U., 1963, LLB cum laude, 1967; postgrad., Cambridge U., Eng., 1964. Bar: N.Y. 1970, U.S. Dist. Ct. (so. dist.) N.Y. 1973, U.S. Ct. Appeals (2nd cir.) 1973, U.S. Supreme Ct. 1980. Tchr. math. and econs. York (Pa.) Country Day Sch., 1967-68; assoc. dir. Vera Inst. Justice, 1969-72; asst. U.S. atty. U.S. Dist. Ct. (so. dist.) N.Y., 1972-75; chief counsel Moreland Act Commn. on Nursing Homes, NYC, 1975-76; of counsel Stanley S. Arkin, P.C., Attys. at Law, 1976-77; v.p., gen. counsel, sec. of univ. NYU, NYC, 1977-93, sr. v.p., gen. counsel, sec., 1993—2005; deputy commnr. for legal matters NYPD, 2005—. Adj. prof. law NYU Sch. Law. Dir. Nat. Ctr. Philanthropy and the Law, N.Y.C. Henry fellow Cambridge U., 1964. Mem. Nat. Assn. Coll. and Univ. Attys. (past pres.), Assn. of Bar of City of N.Y., Phi Beta Kappa. Home: 3 Washington Mews New York NY 10003-6608 Office: Deputy Commnr for Legal Matters NYPD One Police Plaza New York NY 10038 Home Phone: 212-677-8350; Office Phone: 646-610-8423. Business E-Mail: andrew.schaffer@nyu.edu.

SCHAFFER, STUART F., lawyer; b. NYC, Sept. 14, 1957; BS with high honors, Univ. Fla., 1979; JD with distinction, Duke Univ., 1982. Bar: Tex. 1982. Ptnr. & chmn. global projects dept. Baker Botts LLP, Houston. Mem. editl. bd. Duke Law Jour. Named a Texas Super Lawyer, Texas Monthly mag. & Law & Politics mag., 2003—04. Mem.: ABA, Houston Bar Assn., Internat. Tax Forum of Houston, Order of the Coif. Office: Baker Botts LLP One Shell Plz 910 Louisiana St Houston TX 77002-4995 Office Phone: 713-229-1780. Office Fax: 713-229-7780. Business E-Mail: stuart.schaffer@bakerbotts.com.

SCHAFFNER, ADAM DAVID, plastic surgeon; b. Chgo., Sept. 26, 1971; s. Dorann Cohn, Robert Marc and Marjorie Schaffner (Stepmother); m. Marcie Suzanne Rubin, June 10, 2007. BS in Biology summa cum laude, Emory U., Atlanta, 1993; MD, Rush U., Chgo., 1998. Diplomate Am. Bd. Otolaryngology, 2004, Am. Bd. Facial Plastic and Reconstructive Surgery, 2007, lic. NY, 2000, Calif., 2003, Conn., 2004, Mich., 2007. Clin. asst. inst. SUNY at Stony Brook, 1998—2003, internship surgery, 1998—99, residency otolaryngology-head and neck surgery, 1999—2003; fellowship facial plastic and reconstructive surgery Mittelman Facial Plastic Surgery Ctr., 2003—04; mem. med. staff Stanford Hosp., 2003—04, Sound Shore Med. Ctr. of Westchester, New Rochelle, NY, 2004—, Greenwich Hosp., Conn., 2004—; resident plastic and reconstructive surgery Detroit Med. Ctr. Wayne State U., 2007—. Rsch. assoc. CDC, Atlanta, 1992—93; summer rsch. fellow NCI, Bethesda, Md., 1994; vol. cons. in field ABC News, 2004—; clin. asst. prof. Weill Med. Coll., Cornell U., 2005—; trainer, cons., mem. spkrs. bur. Sanofi-Aventis, 2005—; cons. Pfizer Upper Respiratory New Products N.Am. Market Coun., 2005, BioForm Med., 2005, Gerson Lehrman Healthcare Coun., 2006—, Kythera Pharm., 2007—; med. com. mem. US Open Championship Golf Tournament, 2006; bd. dirs. Electric Pear Prodns., 2006—. Contbr. articles to profl. jours. Participant FACE to FACE Domestic, 2004—, FACE to FACE Internat., 2006—; mem. exec. com. Rush Cmty. Svc. Initiatives Program, Chgo., 1996—98; steering com. co-chmn. St. Basil's Free People's Clinic, Chgo., 1996—98; vol. Egleston Children's Hosp. at Emory U., Atlanta, 1991—93. Recipient The Jack Boozer, Ph.D. award for Social and Religious Ethics, Emory U., 1992, CibaGeneva award for outstanding cmty. svc., 1996; Messing Meml. Merit scholar, Zeta Beta Tau Found., 1993, Humanitarian Efforts Travel grantee, Am. Acad. Otolaryngology-Head and Neck Surgery Found., 2002. Fellow: ACS, Am. Acad. Otolaryngology-Head and Neck Surgery; mem.: AMA, NY State Soc. Otolaryngology, NY Facial Plastic Surgery Soc., Westchester County Med. Soc., Med. Soc. State of NY, Am. Acad. Facial Plastic and Reconstructive Surgery. Avocations: piano, swimming, theater, travel, skiing. Home: 1719 Gardenia Ave Apt 217 Royal Oak MI 48067-2137 Office Phone: 914-309-8300. Personal E-mail: adamdavidschaffner@yahoo.com.

SCHAFFNER, BERTRAM HENRY, psychiatrist; b. Erie, Pa., Nov. 12, 1912; s. Milton and Gerta (Herzog) S. Student, Harvard U., 1928-29, 32-33; AB, Swarthmore Coll., 1932; MD, Johns Hopkins U., 1937; diploma, William Alanson White Inst., 1953. Diplomate Am. Bd. Psychiatry, Am. Bd. Neurology. Intern Johns Hopkins Hosp., Balt., 1937-38; resident in neurology Mt. Sinai Hosp., NYC, 1938-39; resident in psychiatry Bellevue Hosp., NYC, 1939-40, N.Y. State Psychiat. Inst., NYC, 1946-47; pvt. practice psychiatry and psychoanalysis NYC, 1947—. Lectr. Sch. Nursing Cornell U., N.Y.C., 1950-60; mem. faculty, clin. supr. in psychotherapy William Alanson White Inst. Psychoanalysis, 1960—, med. dir. HIV svc., clin. supr. psychoanalysis, 1993—; cons., editor confs. Josiah Macy Jr. Found., 1949, 50, 51; cons. U.S. Children's Bur., 1946-47, Bur. Mental Health, V.I., 1954-60, World Fedn. Mental Health, 1958-68, others; mem. N.Y. County dist. bd. Com. on Gay and Lesbian Issues; cons. WHO, 1960-67; founder, exec. dir. U.S.-Caribbean Aid to Mental Health, Inc., 1960-68; organizer Biennial Caribbean Confs. for Mental Health, 1959-65; organizer, cons. Caribbean Fedn. for Mental Health, 1959-65; mem. rsch. study Pre-Soviet Russian Family in the Research in Contemporary Cultures, Columbia U., 1949-51. Mem. editl. bd. Jour. of Gay and Lesbian Psychotherapy, 1987—; author: Father Land: A Study of Authoritarianism in the German Family, 1948; contbr. numerous articles to profl. publs. Mem. acquisitions com. The Bklyn. Mus. of Art, 1995—; trustee Bklyn. Mus. of Art. Recipient Adolf Meyer award for Disting. Svc. on Behalf of Improved Care and Treatment of the Mentally Ill in the Caribbean, 1961. Fellow AMA (life), Am. Psychiat. Assn. (chmn. 1983-86, mem. com. on AIDS N.Y. County dist. br. 1989-99, life), Am. Acad. Psychoanalysis (life), Caribbean Psychiat. Assn.; mem. Group for Advancement of Psychiatry (chair internat. rels. com. 1960-65, chair com. on human sexuality 1987-98), Internat. Acad. Sex Rsch. Avocation: collecting asian and indian art. Home and Office: 220 Central Park S New York NY 10019-1417 Home Phone: 212-265-5539; Office Phone: 212-265-5539. Personal E-mail: bertschmd@aol.com.

SCHAFFNER, HOWARD SHELDON, lawyer; b. Chgo., Nov. 2, 1943; s. Irving and Frieda Schaffner; m. Gail Schaffner, July 14, 1970; children: Paula, Stacy. JD, John Marshall Law Sch., 1970. Bar: Ill. 1970. Asst. state's atty. Cook County States Atty.'s Office, Chgo., 1970-78; ptnr. Hofeld & Schaffner, Chgo., 1978—. Mem. ABA, Ill. State Bar Assn., Ill. Trial Lawyers Assn. (bd. mgrs. 1980—; author Cont. Legal Edn. 1980—, Ill. Inst. Cont. Legal Edn. 1980, 83, 86), Ill. State Bar Assn., Internat. Soc. Barristers Office: Hofeld & Schaffner 30 N Lasalle St Ste 3120 Chicago IL 60602-2576 Home Phone: 847-433-6517; Office Phone: 312-372-4250.

SCHAFFNER, KAREN ANN See FIELD, KAREN

SCHAFFNER, WILLIAM, medical educator; BA, Yale U., New Haven, Conn.; MD, Cornell U., Ithaca, NY. Hospital Epidemiologist Vanderbilt U. Hospital, Nashville; prof. of Medicine, Divsn. of Infectious Diseases Vanderbilt U. Sch. Medicine, Nashville, prof., chmn. Dept. of Preventive Medicine. Mem. steering com. Nat. Network for Immunization Info.; mem. bd. dirs. Nat. Found. for Infectious Diseases; pub. health policy and communicable disease control cons. Centers for Disease Control and Prevention, World Health Org., Tennessee Dept. of Health, Am. Hospital Assn., Am. Coll. of Physicians. Contbr. scientific papers, chapters to books; co-editor: (scientific journals) Hospital Infection Control, European Journal of Clinical Microbiology, Patient Care. Named a Fulbright Scholar, Albert Ludwigs U., Freiburg, Germany; recipient Epidemiology Lecturer Award, Soc. of Healthcare, 1996. Office: Vanderbilt University Medical Center Suite 2100 37212 21st Ave South and Garland Ave Nashville TN 37232 E-mail: william.schaffner@vanderbilt.edu. *

SCHAFFZIN, JONATHAN A., lawyer; b. NYC, Aug. 4, 1960; BA, Northwestern U., 1982; JD, Columbia Law Sch., 1985. Bar: NY 1986. Assoc. Finley, Kumble, Wagner, Weine, Underberg, Manley, Myerson & Casey, 1985—86, Cahill Gordon & Reindel LLP, 1986—94, ptnr., 1994—. Named Dealmaker of Yr., Am. Lawyer, 2001; named one of Am. Lawyer 45 Under Forty-Five, 2003, Chambers U.S.A. and Global Leading Lawyers, 2004, 2005, 2006; scholar Harlan Fiske Stone scholar, Columbia Law Sch. Office: Cahill Gordon & Reindel LLP 80 Pine St New York NY 10005-1702 Office Phone: 212-701-3000. Business E-Mail: jschaffzin@cahill.com.

SCHAFRICK, FREDERICK CRAIG, lawyer; b. Sept. 20, 1948; s. Rudolph Henry and Patricia Eleanor (Zemer) Schafrick; m. Sharon Lee Halpin, May 23, 1981; children: Michael Nile, Nathaniel Henry. AB, U. Mich., Ann Arbor, 1970, JD, 1973. Bar: D.C. 1973, U.S. Ct. Appeals (D.C. cir.) 1975, U.S. Supreme Ct. 1977. Law clk. U.S. Ct. Appeals (2d cir.), NYC, 1973—74; assoc., then ptnr. Shea & Gardner, Washington, 1974—2004; with Goodwin Procter LLP, Washington, 2004—. Editor (adminstrv.): (law rev.) Mich. Law Rev., 1973. Mem.: ABA, Order of Coif, Phi Beta Kappa. Democrat. Presbyterian. Home: 5416 Nebraska Ave NW Washington DC 20015-1350 Office: Goodwin Procter LLP 901 New York Ave Washington DC 20001 Office Phone: 202-346-4194. Business E-Mail: fschafrick@goodwinprocter.com.

SCHAIBLEY, ANN M., lawyer; b. St. Cloud, Minn. BA in Politics, Cornell Coll., Mt. Vernon, Iowa, 1994; JD, Hamline U. Sch. Law, St. Paul, 1997. Bar: Minn. 1997. Law clk. to Hon. Mary L. Davidson Hennepin County Dist. Ct., Family Ct. Divsn., 1997—99; assoc. pvt. practice, 1999—2002; ptnr. Schaibley & Vicchiollo, L.L.C., Edina, Minn., 2001—. Named a Rising Star, Minn. Super Lawyers mag., 2006. Mem.: Internat. Acad. Collaborative Profls., Collaborative Law Inst. Minn. (bd. dirs. 2004—), ABA, Minn. State Bar Assn., Ramsey County Bar Assn. (mem. family law sect.). Office: Schaibley & Vicchiollo LLC Edinborough Corp Ctr 3300 Edinborough Way Ste 550 Edina MN 55435 Office Phone: 612-333-0803. E-mail: ann@mnlaw.us. *

SCHAIE, K(LAUS) WARNER, human development and psychology educator; b. Stettin, Germany (now Poland), Feb. 1, 1928; came to U.S., 1947, naturalized, 1953; s. Sally and Lottie Luise (Gabriel) S.; m. Coloma J. Harrison, Aug. 9, 1953 (div. 1973); 1 child, Stephan; m. Sherry L. Willis, Nov. 20, 1981. AA, City Coll., San Francisco, 1951; BA, U. Calif., Berkeley, 1952; MS, U. Wash., 1953, PhD, 1956; DPhil (hon.), Friedrich-Schiller U., Jena, Germany, 1997; ScD (hon.), W.Va. U., 2002. Lic. psychologist, Calif., Pa. Fellow Washington U., St. Louis, 1956-57; asst. prof. psychology U. Nebr., Lincoln, Nebr., 1957-64, assoc. prof., 1964-68; prof. chmn. dept. psychology W.Va. U., Morgantown, W.Va., 1964-73; prof. psychology, dir. Gerontology Rsch. Inst., U. So. Calif., 1973-81; Evan Pugh prof. human devel. and psychology Pa. State U., University Park, 1981—, dir. Gerontology Ctr., 1985—2003; affiliate prof. psychiatry and behavioral scis. U. Wash., 1991—. Devel. behavior study sect. NIH, Bethesda, Md., 1970-72, chmn., 1972-74, chmn. human devel. and aging study sect., 1979-84, expert panel in comml. airline pilot retirement, 1981, data and safety bd. shep project, 1984-91. Author: Developmental Psychology: A Life Span Approach, 1981, Adult Development and Aging, 1982, 5th rev. edit., 2002, Japanese, Chinese and Spanish edits., 2003, Intellectual Development in Adulthood: The Seattle Longitudinal Study, 1996, Developmental Influences on Adult Intelligence, 2005; editor: Handbook of Psychology of Aging, 1977, 6th rev. edit., 2006, Longitudinal Studies of Adult Development, 1983, Cognitive Functioning and Social Structure over the Life Course, 1987, Methodological Issues in Research on Aging, 1988, Social Structure and Aging: Psychological Processes, 1989, Age Structuring in Comparative Perspective, 1989, The Course of Later Life, 1989, Self-Directedness: Cause and Effects Throughout the Life Course, 1990, Aging, Health Behaviors and Health Outcomes, 1992, Caregiving Systems: Formal and Informal Helpers, 1993, Societal Impact on Aging: Historical Perspectives, 1993, Adult Intergenerational Relations: Effects of Societal Change, 1995, Older Adults Decision Making and the Law, 1996, Impact of Social Structures on Decision Making in the Elderly, 1997, Impact of the Workplace on Older Persons, 1998, Handbook of Theories of Aging, 1999, Mobility and Aging, 2000, Evolution of the Aging Self, 2000, Effective Health Behavior in the Elderly, 2002, Mastery and Control in the Elderly, 2003, Influence of Technology on Successful Aging, 2003; Independent Aging: Living Arrangements and Mobility, 2003, Religious Influences on Health and Wellbeing in the Elderly, 2004, Historical Influences on Lives and Aging, 2005, Social Structures, Self-Regulation and Aging, 2006, Demographic Influences on Health and Wellbeing in the Elderly, 2007; editor Ann. Rev. Gerontology and Geriat., vol. 7, 1987, vol. 11, 1991, vol. 17, 1997, series editor, 1996—; contbr. articles to profl. jours. Fellow APA (coun. reps. 1976-79, 83-86, Disting. Contbn. award, 1992), Am. Psychol. Soc., Gerontol. Soc. (Kleemeier award 1987, Disting. Mentorship award 1996); mem. Psychometric Soc., Internat. Soc. Study Behavioral Devel., Mensa (Lifetime Achievement award, 2000). Unitarian Universalist. Avocations: hiking, stamps. Home: 425 Windmere Dr Apt 3A State College PA 16801-7670 Office: Pa State Univ Gerontology Ctr 135 E Nittany Ave Ste 405 State College PA 16801 Office Phone: 814-863-9735. Business E-Mail: kws@psu.edu.

SCHAIR, ROBIN A., lawyer; b. Bronx, NY, Sept. 30, 1961; BA, SUNY, Binghamton, 1982; JD, Albany Law Sch., Union Coll., 1985. Bar: NY 1986, US Dist. Ct. Ea. Dist. NY, US Dist. Ct. So. Dist. NY. Asst. dist. atty. Bronx Dist. Atty.'s Office, NY, 1985—93; ptnr. Wilson, Elser, Moskowitz, Edelman & Dicker LLP, NYC. Office: Wilson Elser Moskowitz Edelman & Dicker LLP 150 E 42nd St 23rd Fl New York NY 10017-5639 Office Phone: 212-490-3000 ext. 2209. Office Fax: 212-490-3038. Business E-Mail: schairr@wemed.com.

SCHAITBERGER, HAROLD, protective services official, labor union administrator; From firefighter to lt. Fairfax County, Va., 1966, lt.; from head legis. programs to gen. pres. Internat. Assn. Fire Fighters, Washington, 1976—2000, gen. pres., 2000—. Chmn. bd. trustees Internat. Assn. Fire Fighters Burn Found.; bd. dir. Internat. Assn. Fire Fighter Meml., Nat. Fallen Fire Fighter Meml. Mem.: Am. Fedn. Labor and Congress of Indsl. Orgn. (exec. coun., v.p. transp. trade dept., v.p. maritime trade dept.), Muscular Dystrophy Assn. (v.p.). Office: Federal Firefighters Assn 1750 New York Ave NW 3rd Fl Washington DC 20006

SCHAKE, LOWELL MARTIN, zoology educator, writer; b. Marthasville, Mo., June 6, 1938; s. Martin Charles and Flora Olinda (Rocklage) S.; m. Wendy Anne Walkinshaw, Sept. 11, 1959; children: Sheryl Anne, Lowell Scott. BS, U. Mo., 1960, MS, 1962; PhD, Tex. A&M U., 1967. Asst. prof. Tex. A&M U., College Station, 1965-67, assoc. prof., 1969-72, prof., 1972-84, asst. prof., area livestock specialist Lubbock, 1967-69; prof., head animal sci. dept. U. Conn., Storrs, 1984-92; prof., chmn. animal sci. dept. Tex. Tech. U., Lubbock, 1992—95. Developer applied animal ethology program Tex. A&M U., 1970, New Eng. Biotech Conf. series, 1990, S.W. Beef Forum, 1993; chmn. Am. Registry of Profl. Animal Scientist Com. on Profl. Stds., 1988; chmn. Nat. Com. Exec. Officers of Animal Vet., Dairy and Poultry Sci. Depts., 1992; cons. Alpart, Kingston, Jamaica, 1975, U.S. Feeds Grain Coun., 1970-73, A.O. Smith Products Inc., 1968-92, Humphrey Land & Cattle Co., Dallas, 1980-86; lectr. in field. Author: Growth and Finishing of Beef Cattle, A Class Handbook, 1982, La Charrette: Village Gateway to the American West, 2003; contbr. articles to profl. jours. Recipient Innovative Teaching award Tex. A&M U., 1978. Mem. Am. Soc. Animal Sci., Plains Nutrition Coun. (adv. bd. 1967-80, sec.-treas. 1994-95, founder), Nat. Assn. Colls. and Tchrs. Agr., Am. Registry Profl. Animal Scientists (dir. for Northeast 1987-89), Coun. for Agr. Sci. and Tech. World Conf. on Animal Prodn., Am. Soc. Dairy Sci., Tiger Club (College Station) (pres.), Gamma Sigma Delta. Republican. Avocations: genealogy, fishing, gardening. Home: 142 Five Dove Cir Port Aransas TX 78373 Personal E-mail: wschake1@centurytel.net.

SCHAKOWSKY, JANICE, congresswoman; b. Chgo., May 26, 1944; d. Irwin and Tillie (Cosnow) Danoff; m. Harvey E. Schakowsky, Feb. 17, 1965 (div. 1980); children: Ian, Mary; m. Robert B. Creamer, Dec. 6, 1980; 1 stepchild, Lauren. BS, U. Ill., 1965. Cert. elem. tchr., Ill. Tchr. Chgo. Bd. Edn., 1965-67; organizer Ill. Pub. Action Coun., Chgo., 1976-85; exec. dir. Ill. State Coun. Sr. Citizens, Chgo., 1985-90; mem. Ill. Ho. Reps., 1990-98, US Congress from 9th Ill. dist., 1999—; mem. banking and fin. svcs. com., 1999—2000; mem. govt. reform com., 1999—2000; Ho. Dem. leadership team-deputy whip; mem. energy and commerce Com. Bd. dirs. Ill. Pub. Action, 4 C's Day Care Coun., Evanston, Ill.; steering com. mem. Cook County Dem. Women, 1986-90; del. Nat. Dem. Conv., 1988; governing coun. Am. Jewish Congress, 1990—. Named Outstanding Legislator Interfaith Coun. for Homeless, 1993, Legislator of Yr. Ill. Nurses Assn., 1992, Ill. Assn. Cmty. Mental Health Agys., 1994, Coalition of Citizens with Disabilities and Ill. Coun. Sr. Citizens, 1993, Cmty. Action Assn., 1991, Champaign County Health Care Assn., 1992, Rookie of Yr. Ill. Environ. Coun., 1991. Mem. ACLU, NOW, Nat. Coun. Jewish Women, Ill. Pro-Choice Alliance, Evanston Mental Health Assn., Evanston Hist. Soc., Evanston Friends of Libr., Rogers Park Hist. Soc. Democrat. Jewish. Avocations: travel, horsebackriding, reading. Office: US Ho Reps 1027 Longworth Ho Office Bldg Washington DC 20515-1309 also: Dist Office 5533 Broadway St Chicago IL 60640 Office Phone: 202-225-2111. *

SCHALIT, ROBERT EDWARD, advertising executive; b. Albany, NY, Nov. 19, 1954; s. Samuel and Ann Ethal S.; m. Margaret Foye, Aug. 26, 1989. BA in English Lit., SUNY, Binghamton, 1976. Sr. writer Fairbrother & Co. Advt., Valatie, NY, 1999—2000; sr. copywriter Rueckert Advt. Pub. Rels., Albany, NY, 2000—07. Freelance advt. copywriter Robert Schalit Freelance Copywriter, Schenectady, NY, 1990—. Author: (numerous ads, tv and radio commls.) CDPHP (HMO) Advertising Campaign. Bd. mem. Ind. Living in the Capital Dist., Schenectady, NY, 1983—84; support group facilitator The Samaritans Suicide Prevention, Albany, NY, 1990—93; pres. Creative Club, Albany, NY, 1988—89. Recipient awards, NORI. Mem.: Am. Mktg. Assn. (Capital region chpt.), The Ad Club, Phi Beta Kappa (bd. dirs. Upper Hudson Assn.). Democrat. Jewish. Avocations: reading, poetry, blues harmonica, fitness activities, ship model building. Home: 1133 Van Curler Ave Schenectady NY 12308 Office: Rueckert Advtsg Pub Rels 638 Albany-Shaker Rd Albany NY 12211

SCHALK, GERWIN, research scientist, software engineer; b. Fuerstenfeld, Styria, Austria, July 6, 1971; arrived in US, 1999, permanent resident, 2005; s. Dieter Erwin and Rosina Schalk; m. Renate Eva Brunner, Dec. 19, 1973; children: Erik Christopher, Alexander Tristan. MS, Graz U. of Tech., Austria, 1999, Rensselaer Poly. Inst., Troy, NY, 2001, PhD, 2006. Rsch. scientist Wadsworth Ctr., N.Y. State Dept. of Health, Albany, 1999—. Contbr. articles to sci. jours. Recipient Frontiers of Engring. award, NAE, 2004, Kurt Goedel stipend, Graz U. of Tech., 1997, Altran Tech. Innovation award (mem. of winning group), Altran Corp., 2005, Pirelli Internetional award (mem. of winning group), Pirelli Corp., 2005, Founder's award, Rensselaer Polytechnic Inst., 2006, Commissioner's Recognition award, NY State Dept. Health, 2006. Mem.: IEEE Medicine and Biology, Soc. for Neurosci., Sigma Xi. Achievements include patents for brain computer interface and detection of brain signals. Avocations: cooking, weightlifting. Office: Wadsworth Ctr NY State DOH E1001 Empire State Plz Albany NY 12201 Home Phone: 518-463-2024; Office Phone: 518-486-2559. Office Fax: 518-486-4910. Business E-Mail: schalk@wadsworth.org.

SCHALL, ALVIN ANTHONY, federal judge; b. NYC, 1944; s. Gordon William and Helen Schall; m. Sharon Frances LeBlanc, Apr. 25, 1970; children: Amanda Lanford, Anthony Davis. BA, Princeton U., 1966; JD, Tulane U., 1969. Bar: NY 1970, US Dist. Ct. (so. and ea. dists.) NY 1973, US Ct. Appeals (2d cir.) 1974, DC 1980, US Dist. Ct. DC 1991, US Ct. Appeals (DC cir.) 1991, US Ct. Fed. Claims 1982, US Ct. Appeals (fed. cir.) 1987, US Supreme Ct. 1989. Assoc. Shearman & Sterling, NYC, 1969—73; asst. US atty. ea. dist. NY Borough of Bklyn., 1973—78, chief appeals divsn., 1977—78; trial atty. civil divsn. US Dept. Justice, Washington, 1978—87, sr. trial counsel, 1986—87, asst. to atty. gen., 1988—92; ptnr. Perlman & Ptnrs., Washington, 1987—88; judge US Ct. Appeals (Fed. cir.), Washington, 1992—. Office: 717 Madison Pl NW Washington DC 20439-0002 *

SCHALL, DAVID GORDON, military officer, surgeon; BA in Chemistry and Biology, U. Mo., Kans. City, 1977, MD; MPH, Johns Hopkins U., Balt., 1982. Diplomate Am. Bd. Med. Specialties, 1983, Am. Bd. Otolaryngology, 1990. Commd. lt. USAF, 1978, advanced through grades to col., chief, program dir. otolaryngology head and neck surgery Madigan army med. ctr. Tacoma, 1994—97, dep. comdr. med. ops. office surgeon gen. Washington, 1997—99, vice comdr. wilford hall Lackland AFB, Tex., 1999—2001, command surgeon USAF acad. Colo. Springs, 2001—02, commd. surgeon pacific Honolulu, 2002—06; fellow Ear Found., Nashville, 1993. Recipient Premier award, Omaha Midwest Clin. Soc., 1988, J. Calvin Davis award, U. Nebr. Dept Otolaryngology, 1990; scholar, USAF, 1974—77; Victor Wilson scholarship, U. Mo., Kans. City, 1971—72. Fellow: ACS, Soc. Mil. Otolaryngologists, Am. Acad. Otolaryngology Head & Neck Surgery, Aerospace Medicine Assn. (The Howard R. Tyner Lit. Excellence award 1990). Office: Hq Useucom Unit 30400 / ECJ4-MR APO 09131 Germany Office Phone: (49)-711-680-7460. Office Fax: (49)-711-680-6408. Business E-Mail: schalld@eucom.mil.

SCHALL, JAN JOAN, curator, educator; b. WIllmar, Minn., Sept. 27, 1952; d. Lloyd Marion and Arlice Christine Thorsness; m. Michael Glen Schall, Sept. 29, 1973; 1 child, Maia Lee. BS in Elem. Edn. and Fine Art cum laude, Minn. State U., Moorehead, 1974; BA in Art History magna cum laude, U. N.Mex., Albuquerque, 1977; MA in Art History, Washington U., St. Louis, 1979; PhD in Art History, U. Tex., Austin, 1989. Tchr. Creative Learning Ctr., Albuquerque, 1974—77; instr. Atlanta Coll. Art, 1979—82; asst. prof. art history N.Mex. State U., Las Cruces, 1987—90, U. Fla., Gainesville, 1990—96; curator modern and contemporary art The Nelson Atkins Mus. Art, Kans. City, Mo., 1996—. Com. chair fine arts and culture Shawnee Mission Schs., 1997—2006; lectr. House Menuha, Kans. City, Mo., 2001—06; adv. com. mem. U. Mo. Mus., Columbia, 2002—04; exhbn. juror McKnight Found., Mpls., 2002; art selection com. Mcpl. Arts Commn., Kans. City, Mo., 2004—06. Author: (book) Tempus Fugit: Time Flies, 2000; exhibitions include sculpture The Nelscon Atkins Mus Art, 1999—; co-curator (exhibitions) The Nelscon Atkins Mus Art, 2005—. Fellow, Andrew Mellon Fellowship, 1993—94; Grant, DAAD, 1985—86, Millennium Projects Grant, Nat. Endowments for Arts, 1997—2000. Mem.: Coll. Art Assns., Assn. Am. Mus., Assn. Am. Mus. Curators. Avocations: reading, gardening, yoga, travel, sewing. Office: The Nelson Atkins Mus Art 4525 Oak St Kansas City MO 64111

SCHALLER, BARRY R., judge; BA, Yale U., 1960, JD, 1963. Bar: Conn. 1963, US Dist. Ct. Conn. 1963, US Ct. Appeals (2nd cir.) 1964, US Supreme Ct. 1966. Ptnr. Bronson & Rice, Atty., New Haven, 1963-74; judge Ct. of Common Pleas, Cir., Conn., 1974-78, Superior Ct., Conn., 1978-92, Appellate Ct., Conn., 1992—. Counsel to Ho. of Reps., 1969; bd. pardons State of Conn., 1971-74, chair, 1973-74; exec. com. Conn. Planning Com. on Criminal Adminstrn., 1972-74; chair Superior Ct. Benchbook Com., 1985-92; vis. lectr. Yale Coll., 1986, 88, Trinity Coll., 2003—, Wesleyan (Conn.) U., 2003-, Vt. Law Sch., 2003-04, U. Conn. Sch. Pub. Health, 2005—; clin. instr. evidence and trial practice Yale Law Sch., 1989—; adj. prof., Quinnipiac Law Sch., 2002; lectr. W.Va. Magistrates Conf., 1990, Vt. Jud. Coll., 1992, Fla. Jud. Coll., 1993-94, 96, 99, 2002, 04, 07, Ohio Jud. Coll., 1999, 2002, Mo. Jud. Coll., 2002, hosp. ethics. com., others; faculty Am. Acad. Jud. Edn. Conn. Judges Inst., 1987-90; mem. Superior Ct. Jury Instrn. Com., 1989-92; exec. com. Conn. Ctr. for Jud. Edn., 1989-92; active Superior Ct. Civil Case Mgmt. Task Force; jud. evidence code drafting com.; mem. biochem. com. Middlesex Hosp., 2004—; chair Com. on Jud. Ethics Adv. Opinions. Author: A Vision of American Law: Judging Law, Literature, and the Stories We Tell, 1997, A Legal Prescription for Bioethical Ills, Quinnipiac Law Review, 2002, Understanding Bioethics & Law: The Promise & Perils of the Brave New World of Biotechnology, 2007; contbr. articles to profl. jours. Assoc. fellow Branford Coll., 1990-2005, adminstrv. co-sec. Yale Class of 1960, 1995-2005; mem. adv. com. Fair Haven Mediation Bd., 1980-82; bd. dirs. Russian-Am. Rule of Law Project, 2001-04; mem. working groups Yale Bioethics Project, 2002—; adv. com. Dongahue Found. Yale, chair human rsch. social context writing group, neuroethics group, 2007—; former vestry mem., tchr. Trinity Ch., Branford; mem. bioethics com. Middlesex Hosp., 2004—; mem. instnl. review bd. (IRIB) St. Francis Hosp. and Health Ctr., 2004—; lectr. pub. health emergency edn. Yale U., chair pub. health constraints on liberty working group. Recipient book award Quinnipic Law Sch., 1997; Guggenheim fellow Yale Law Sch., 1975-76, 84, 85-86. Fellow Conn. Bar Found. (charter life, fellows adv. com.); mem. Conn. Bar Assn., Hartford County Bar Assn., New Haven County Bar Assn., Conn. Judges Assn. (dir. 1990-92), Am. Law Inst., Yale Law Sch. Assn. (exec. com. 1990-92), Am. Inns of Ct. (bencher 1989-90), Conn. Russian-Am. Rule of Law Program (founder, co-chair 2001-04), Phi Delta Phi. Office: Appellate Ct State Conn 75 Elm St Hartford CT 06106 Office Phone: 860-713-2192. Business E-Mail: barry.schaller@aya.yale.edu.

SCHALLER, GEORGE BEALS, zoologist; b. Berlin, May 26, 1933; s. Georg Ludwig S. and Bettina (Byrd) Iwersen; m. Kay Suzanne Morgan, Aug. 26, 1957; children: Eric, Mark. BS in Zoology, U. Alaska, 1955, BA in Anthropology, 1955; PhD in Zoology, U. Wis., 1962. Rsch. assoc. Johns Hopkins U., Balt., 1963—66; rsch. zoologist Wildlife Conservation Soc., Bronx, NY, 1966—. Rsch. assoc. Am. Mus. Natural History. Author: The Mountain Gorilla, 1963 (Wildlife Soc. award 1965), The Year of the Gorilla, 1964, The Deer and the Tiger, 1967, The Serengeti Lion, 1972 (Nat. Book award 1973), Golden Shadows, Flying Hooves, 1973, Mountain Monarchs, 1977, Stones of Silence, 1980, The Giant Pandas of Wolong, 1985, The Last Panda, 1993, Tibet's Hidden Wilderness, 1997, Wildlife of the Tibetan Steppe, 1998; co-editor (with E.Vrba) Antelopes, Deer and Relatives, 2000. Decorated Order of Golden Ark, Netherlands, 1978; recipient Gold medal World Wildlife Fund, 1980, Explorers medal Explorers Club, 1990, Cosmos prize Japan, 1996, Tyler Environ. prize, 1997; Ctr. Advanced Study in Behavioral Scis. fellow Stanford U., 1962, fellow Guggenheim Found., 1971. Office: Wildlife Conservation Soc Bronx Park Bronx NY 10460 Business E-Mail: asiaprogram@wcs.org.

SCHALLER, GORDON A., lawyer; b. Aug. 27, 1949; BS with distinction, Iowa State U., 1970; JD magna cum laude, U. Minn., 1973. Bar: Calif. 1973, Washington 1980, US Tax Ct. Ptnr. Gibson, Dunn & Crutcher, Irvine, Calif.; nat. mng. dir. estate, philanthropy and ins. svcs. myCFO, Inc.; mng. dir. WealthAdvisors, LLC; of counsel Greenberg Traurig, LLP, 2003—04, mng. shareholder Costa Mesa, Calif., 2004—. Contbr. articles to profl. publs.; editor: Minn. Law Rev. 1971-73. Named one of Top 100 Attys., Worth mag., 2006. Fellow Am. Coll. Trust and Estate Counsel; mem. Order of the Coif, Wash. State Bar Assn., Calif. Bar Assn. Office: Greenberg Traurig Center Tower 650 Town Center Dr Ste 1700 Costa Mesa CA 92626 *

SCHALLER, JANE GREEN, pediatrician; b. Cleve., June 26, 1934; d. George and May Alice (Wing) Green; children: Robert Thomas, George Charles, Margaret May. AB, Hiram Coll., Ohio, 1956; MD cum laude, Harvard U., 1960. Diplomate Am. Bd. Pediat., Am. Bd. Med. Examiners. Resident in pediat. Children's Hosp.-U. Wash., Seattle, 1960-63; fellow immunology Children's Hosp. U. Wash., 1963-65; faculty U. Wash. Med. Sch., 1965-83, prof. pediat., 1975-83; head divsn. rheumatic diseases Children's Hosp., Seattle, 1968-83; prof., chmn. dept. pediat., pediatrician-in-chief Tufts U. Sch. Medicine/New Eng. Med. Ctr., 1983-98; Karp prof. pediat. Tufts U. Sch. Medicine, Boston, 1983—, disting. prof., 1995—. Vis. physician Med. Rsch. Coun., Taplow, Eng., 1971-72; adj. prof. diplomacy The Fletcher Sch. Law and Diplomacy, Tufts U., 1998-2000. Contbr. articles to profl. jours. Bd. dirs. Seattle Chamber Music Festival, 1982-85; trustee Boston Chamber Music Soc., 1985—; mem. Boston adv. coun. UNICEF, tech. advisor UN Study on the Impact of Armed Conflict on Children, 1995-97; chmn., adv. com. children's rights divsn. Human Rights Watch, 1995—; mem. adv. com. Middle East divsn., 1998—; exec. com. Women's Commn. for Refugee Women and Children Internat. Rescue com., 1989-94, adv. coun. 1994—. Mem.: AAAS, Royal Coll. Pediats. U.K., Internat. Women's Forum, Mass. Women's Forum, Harvard U. Med. Sch. Alumni Coun. (v.p. 1977—80, pres. 1982—83), Physicians for Human Rights (founding pres. 1986—89, exec. com. 1986—), Com. Health in So. Africa (exec. com. 1986—92), Assn. Med. Sch. Pediat. Chmn. (exec. com. 1986—89, rep. to coun. on govt. affairs and coun. acad. socs.), New Eng. Pediat. Soc. (pres. 1991—93), Am. Coll. Rheumatology, Internat. Pediat. Assn. (pres.-elect 1998—2001, pres. 2001—04, exec. dir. 2004—), Am. Acad. Pediat. (exec. com. sect. on internat. child health, head children's rights program, rep. to UNICEF), Am. Pediat. Soc., Soc. Pediat. Rsch., Inst. Medicine of NAS, Saturday Club, Tavern Club, Aesculapian Club (pres. 1988—89). Office: Floating Hosp for Children 750 Washington St # 8683 Boston MA 02111-1526 Business E-Mail: jschaller@tufts-nemc.org.

SCHALLERT, EDWIN GLENN, lawyer; b. LA, Aug. 7, 1952; s. William Joseph and Rosemarie Diane (Waggner) S. AB, Stanford U., 1974; JD, MPP, Harvard U., 1981. Bar: N.Y. 1974, U.S. Ct. Appeals (7th cir.) 1986, U.S. Ct. Appeals (2d cir.) 1989, U.S. Dist. Ct. (so. dist.) N.Y. 1975. Legis. aid to U.S. rep. Les Aspin, Washington, 1975-78; law clk. to Hon. J. Skelly Wright, 1981-82; law clk. to Hon. Thurgood Marshall, 1982-83; assoc. Debevoise & Plimpton LLP, NYC, 1983-89, ptnr., 1989—, mem. litig. dept., 1983—90. Mem. Internat. Inst. for Strategic Studies, Coun. Fgn. Rels. (term mem. 1983-88), Phi Beta Kappa. Democrat. Avocation: tennis. Office: Debevoise & Plimpton LLP 919 Third Ave New York NY 10022 Office Phone: 212-909-6295. Office Fax: 212-909-6836. E-mail: egschallert@debevoise.com. *

SCHALLERT, WILLIAM JOSEPH, actor; b. LA, July 6, 1922; s. Edwin Francis and Elza Emily (Baumgarten) S.; m. Rosemarie Diann Waggner, Feb. 26, 1949; children: William Joseph, Edwin G., Mark M., Brendan C. BA, UCLA, 1946. Co-founder, owner Circle Theatre, Hollywood, Calif., 1947-50. Appeared in motion pictures, TV, stage, radio, 1947—; movies include Lonely Are the Brave, Heat of the Night, Charley Varrick, Red Badge of Courage, Teachers; starred in TV series Patty Duke Show, 1963-66, Nancy Drew Mysteries, 1977-78, Little Women, 1979, The New Gidget, 1986-88, The Torkelson's, 1991-92; starred as judge in stage play and film The Trial of the Catonsville Nine, N.Y.C., Los Angeles, 1971 (Obie award 1971); starred as Dr. Pangloss in Candide, L.A., 1995; recorded voice of Abraham Lincoln for permanent installation at Lincoln Mus., Springfield, Ill., 2004. Trustee Motion Picture and TV Fund, 1977—.

With AUS, 1942-44; with USAAC, 1944-45. Fulbright fellow Brit. Repertory Theatre, 1952-53. Mem. ASCAP, SAG (pres. 1979-81, trustee pension and health plan 1983—, founder Com. for Performers with Disabilities 1981—, Ralph Morgan award 1993). Personal E-mail: schlrt80@yahoo.com.

SCHALLHORN, CHARLES DEAN, social sciences educator, labor union administrator; s. John and Judith Schallhorn. MS in Secondary Edn., Purdue U. Calumet, Hammond, Ind., 1992. Tchg. cert. single subject social studies Calif. Commn. Tchr. Credentialing, 2001. Social sci. divsn. chair San Benito HS, Hollister, Calif., 2004—06, pres. Tchrs. Assn., 2005—. Western regional coord. Tchrs. Psychology Secondary Schs., Washington, 2007—. Author: Lecture Notes for Teachers: Psychology and You. Outstanding Educator fellow, Ind. Acad. Sci., Math. and Humanities, 1998—99. Avocation: video editing. Office: San Benito HS 1220 Monterey St Hollister CA 95023 Home Phone: 831-524-2122; Office Phone: 831-637-5831 366. Business E-Mail: cschallhorn@sbhsd.k12.ca.us.

SCHALLY, ANDREW VICTOR, endocrine oncologist, researcher; b. Poland, Nov. 30, 1926; arrived in U.S., 1957; s. Casimir Peter and Maria (Lacka) Schally; m. Ana Maria Comaru, Aug. 1976 (dec. Sept. 2004). BSc, McGill U., Can., 1955, PhD in Biochemistry, 1957; 29 hon. doctorates. Research asst. biochemistry Nat. Inst. Med. Research, London, 1949—52; dept. psychiatry McGill U., Montreal, Que., 1952—57; rsch. assoc., asst. prof. physiology and biochemistry Coll. Medicine, Baylor U., Houston, 1957—62; assoc. prof. Tulane U. Sch. Medicine, New Orleans, 1962—67, prof., 1967—2006; chief Endocrine Polypeptide and Cancer Inst. VA Med. Ctr., New Orleans, 1962—2006, with Miami, Fla., 2006—. Sr. med. investigator VA, 1973—99, disting. med. rsch. scientist, 1999—; prof. Disting. Leonard Miller Sch. Medicine U. Miami, 2006—. Author: The Hypothalamus and Pituitary in Health and Disease, 1972; contbr. articles to profl. jours. Co-recipient Nobel prize for medicine, 1977; recipient Van Meter prize, Am. Thyroid Assn., 1969, Ayerst-Squibb award, Endocrine Soc., 1970, William S. Middletown award, VA, 1970, Ch. Mickle award, U. Toronto, 1974, Gairdner Internat. award, 1974, Borden award, Assn. Am. Med. Colls. and Borden Co. Found., 1975, Lasker Basic Rsch. award, 1975; fellow sr. rsch. fellow, USPHS, 1961—62. Mem.: AAAS, NAS, Royal Acad. Medicine Spain, Acad. Sci. Mex., Acad. Sci. Russia, Acad. Sci. Hungary, Acad. Medicine Poland, Acad. Medicine Venezuela, Nat. Acad. Medicine Brazil, Mex. Acad. Medicine, Soc. Internat. Brain Rsch. Orgn., Soc. Exptl. Biol. Medicine, Soc. Biol. Chemists, Am. Physiol. Soc., Endocrine Soc. Home: 3801 Cullins Ave Apt 1506 Miami Beach FL 33140 Office: VA Hosp Research 151 1201 NW 16 St Miami FL 33125 Office Phone: 305-575-3477. Office Fax: 305-575-3126. Business E-Mail: andrew.schally@va.gov.

SCHALOW, FRANK HICKEY, philosopher, educator; b. Denver, Feb. 23, 1956; s. Berthold Erich and Frances Schalow. BA summa cum laude, U. Denver, 1978; MA, Tulane U., 1980, PhD, 1984. Vis. asst. prof. Loyola U., New Orleans, 1984-86, asst. prof., 1986-90, assoc. prof., 1990-92; lectr. Dillard U., New Orleans, 1993—; vis. assoc. prof. Xavier U., New Orleans, 1994-97, U. New Orleans, 1995—. Mem. editl. adv. bd. Auslegung U. Kans., Lawrence, 1983-97, Heidegger Studies U. Wis., LaCrosse, 2000—; mem. dissertation adv. bd. Union Inst., Cin., 1999—. Author: Imagination and Existence, 1986, Renewal of the Heidegger-Kant Dialogue, 1992, Language and Deed, 1998, Heidegger and the Quest for the Sacred, 2001, Incarnality of Being, 2006; co-author: Traces of Understanding, 1990. Mem. Am. Philos. Assn., N.Am. Heidegger Conf. (sec. convenor 1992), S.W. Philosophy Soc. (exec. com. 1993), Phi Beta Kappa. Avocation: golf. Home: 7310 Freret St New Orleans LA 70118 Office: U New Orleans Lakefront Campus New Orleans LA 70148 Business E-Mail: fschalow@uno.edu.

SCHAMA, SIMON, historian, educator, author; b. London, Feb. 13, 1945; married; 2 children. BA, Cambridge U., Eng., 1966, MA in History, 1969. Fellow Christ's Coll. Cambridge U., England, 1966—76; fellow and tutor in modern history Brasenose Coll., Oxford, England, 1976—80; prof. history, Mellon prof. social sciences, and William Kenan prof. humanities Harvard U., Cambridge, Mass., 1980—93, sr. assoc. Ctr. European Studies; prof. Ecole des Hautes Etudes en Sciences Sociales; Trevelyan lectr. Cambridge U.; Tanner lectr. on Rubens and Rembrandt Oxford U.; Tanner lectr. Harvard U., 2002; University prof. Columbia U., NYC. Author: Patriots and Liberators: Revolution in the Netherlands, 1780-1813, 1977 (Wolfson prize for history 1977, Leo Gershoy Meml. prize Am. Hist. Assn. 1978), Two Rothschilds and the Land of Israel, 1979, The Embarrassment of Riches: An Interpretation of Dutch Culture in the Golden Age, 1987, Citizens: A Chronicle of the French Revolution, 1989 (NCR prize for non-fiction), Dead Certainties, 1991, Landscape and Memory, 1995, Rembrandt's Eyes, 1999, A History of Britain: At the Edge of the World, 3500 BC - 1603 AD, 2000, A History of Britain: The Wars of the British, 1603-1776, 2001, A History of Britain: The Fate of Empire, 1776-2000, 2002, Rough Crossings: Britain, the Slaves and the American Revolution, 2006 (Nat. Book Critics Circle award for Gen. Nonfiction, 2006); TV series for BBC: Art of the Western World, Rembrandt: The Public Gaze, Landscape and Memory, A History of Britain, The Power of Art, 2004. Office: Columbia U Dept History 522 Fayerweather Hall 1180 Amsterdam Ave New York NY 10027-7039 E-mail: sms53@columbia.edu. *

SCHAMUS, JAMES ALLAN, film producer and company executive, screenwriter; b. Detroit, Sept. 7, 1959; s. Julian John Schamus and Clarita (Gershowitz) Karlin; m. Nancy Jean Kricorian; children: Nona Esther, Djuna Mariam. AB, U. Calif., Berkeley, 1982, MA, 1984. Asst. prof. Columbia U., NYC, 1991-97, assoc. prof., 1997—; co-pres., co-chmn. GOOD Machine (bought by Universal Pictures and merged into new studio, Focus), NYC, 1991—2002; co-pres. Focus Features, NYC, 2002—06, pres., 2006; CEO specialty film divsn. NBC Universal, Inc., 2006—. Assisted in the finding of Independent TV Series, 1988; involved with Apparatus. Actor Keep It for Yourself, 1991; prodr: (films) The Golden Boat, 1991, Chicken Delight, 1991, Roy Cohn/Jack Smith, 1994, Walking and Talking, 1996, She's the One, 1996, Assault on Precinct 13, 2005; assoc. prodr., co-writer (films): Eat Drink Man Woman, 1994; assoc. prodr. In the Soup, 1992; exec. prodr.: (films) Warrior: Poison, 1991, The Life of Leonard Peltier, 1992, Swoon, 1992, What Happened Was..., 1994, Safe, 1995, The Brothers McMullen, 1995, Greetings From Africa, 1996, Arresting Gena, 1997, Office Killer, 1997, The Myth of Fingerprints, 1997, Wonderland, 1997, Happiness, 1998, Lola and Billy the Kid, 1999, Love God, 1999, The Lifestyle: Group Sex in the Suburbs, 2000, Crouching Tiger Hidden Dragon, 2000 (also writer), Buffalo Soldiers, 2001, Auto Focus, 2002; co-prodr. Thank You and Good Night, 1991, Sense and Sensibility, 1995; writer (films) Tortilla Soup, 2001; writer, prodr.: (films) The Wedding Banquet, 1993, Pushing Hands, 1995, The Ice Storm, 1997 (Best Screenplay, Cannes Film Festival 1997), Ride with the Devil, 1999, Hulk, 2003, Brokeback Mountain, 2005 (Best Theatrical Motion Picture, Producer Guild Am., 2006, Best Feature, Spirit Independent award, 2006, Outstanding Film, British Acad. Film and TV Arts, 2006) Recipient Brian Greenbaum award, 1994, NBC Screenwriter's Tribute, Natucket Film Festival, 2002; named one of 50 Most Powerful People in Hollywood, 2006. Mem. Assn. for Ind. Video and Film (bd. dirs.). Office: NBC Universal Inc 30 Rockefeller Plz New York NY 10112

SCHANFIELD, FANNIE SCHWARTZ, community volunteer; b. Mpls., Dec. 25, 1916; d. Simon Zouberman and Mary (Schmilovitz) Schwartz; m. Melvin M. Stock, Oct. 27, 1943 (dec. Apr. 1944); 1 child, Moses Samuel Schanfield; m. Abraham Schanfield, Aug. 28, 1947; children: David Colman, Miriam Schanfield Kieffer. Student, U. Minn., 1962-75. Author: My Thoughts, 1996, Son, I Have Something to Tell You, 1997, Ma, I Wrote It Down, 1997, 20 April 44 WWII, 2001, The Other Family's Kids, 2004, The Duplex: Fran and Dan Lived Upstairs, 2004, I Was There, 2006. Bd. dirs. Jewish Cmty. Ctr., Mpls., 1975-96, chairperson older adult needs, 1982-88; past pres. Bnai Emet Women's League, Mpls., 1988-90; rschr., advocate Hunger Hennepin County, Mpls., 1969-75; sec. Joint Religious Legis. Coalition; v.p., bd. dirs. Cmty. Housing Svc., Mpls., 1971-85. Recipient Citation of Honor, Hennepin County Commn., 1989, Lifetime Achievement award Jewish Cmty. Ctr. Greater Mpls., 1995, Mpls. Jewish Fedn. citation, 2006. Mem. Lupus Found. Minn., Internat. Soc. Poets, Hadassah (pres. 1967-69, Citation 1969, Nat. Leadership award 2006). Jewish. Avocations: needlepoint, rug hooking, writing.

SCHANFIELD, MOSES SAMUEL, geneticist, educator; b. Mpls., Sept. 7, 1944; s. Abraham and Fanny (Schwartz) Schanfield; m. Patricia A. McCarthy. BA in Anthropology, U. Minn., 1966; AM in Anthropology, Harvard U., 1969; PhD in Human Genetics, U. Mich., 1971. Postdoctoral fellow in immunology U. Calif. Med. Ctr., San Francisco, 1971-74, rsch. geneticist, 1974-75; head of blood bank Milw. Blood Ctr., 1975-78; asst. dir. ARC, Washington, 1978-83; exec. dir. Genetic Testing Inst., Atlanta, 1983-85; lab. dir. Analytical Genetic Testing Ctr., Atlanta and Denver, 1985-2000; adminstr. Monroe County Pub. Safety Lab., Rochester, NY, 2000—02; prof., chair dept. forensic sci. George Washington U., 2002—. Adj. asst. prof. Med. Coll. Wis., Milw., 1976—78; adj. assoc. prof. George Washington U., Washington, 1979—83, Emory U., Atlanta, 1984—89, U. Kans., 1992—; affiliated faculty Colo. State U. Ft. Collins, 1992—2000; mem. Nat. Forensic DNA Rev. Panel, Nat. Inst. of Justice, 1996—2000; pres. 1st European-Am. Intensive Course in PCR, Split, Croatia, 1997; co-organizer 2d European-Am. Intensive Course in PCR, Dubrovnik, Croatia. Author, editor: book Immunobiology of the Erythrocyte, 1980, International Methods of Forensic DNA Analysis, 1996, contg. author: book Immunogenetic Factors and Thalassaemia of Hepatitis, 1975; contbr. articles to profl. publs. Recipient Gold medal, Latin Am. Congress Hemotherapy and Immunohematology, 1979, R&D 100 award, 1993. Fellow: Am. Acad. Forensic Sci.; mem.: Human Biology Coun., Am. Soc. Human Genetics, Am. Soc. Crime Lab. Dirs., Phi Kappa Phi. Achievements include discovery of of the biological function of GC protein as vitamin D transport protein; of 2 sources of errors in DNA sizings; detection of the presence of HIV in Africa in the 1950's. Office: Monroe County Pub Safety Labtr Pub Safety Bldg Rm 524 150 Plymouth Ave S Rochester NY 14614-2277 E-mail: mschanfield@netscape.net.

SCHANNEP, JOHN DWIGHT, brokerage house executive; b. Newport News, Va., May 23, 1934; s. Dwight Bahney and Harriet Louise (Quinn) S.; m. Helen Ann Harris, June 21, 1958; children: John Barton, Dwight David, Timothy Michael, Marie Louise. BS, U.S. Mil. Acad., 1956. Commd. 1st lt. U.S. Air Force, 1956, resigned, 1960; acct. exec. Dean Witter Reynolds, Phoenix, 1960-68, v.p., resident mgr. Tucson, 1968-83, sr. v.p., 1983-89; ret. Pres. Tucson Stock/Bond Club, 1971-72; bd. dirs. SNEDCO. Author, pub. Schannep Timing Indicator and the Dow Theory Investment Timing Newsletter (available on Internet), 1980—. Pres. Big Bros. Tucson, 1972-74. Mem. Nat. Assn. Security Dealers (Ariz. committeeman and chmn. 1971-73), Tucson C. of C. (v.p. 1971), Pinetop Lakes Golf and Country Club (treas. 1990-91, pres. 1991-93), West Point Soc. (pres. 1967), Lions (pres. Phoenix chpt. 1966.) Republican. Home: 5191 E Hill Place Dr Tucson AZ 85712-1346 E-mail: jackschannep@theriver.com, editor@thedowtheory.com.

SCHANWALD, STEVE, professional sports team executive; Grad., U. Md., 1977. Dir. sports mktg. USAF Acad., 1978; dir. promotions Pitts. Pirates, 1979—80; asst. v.p. mktg. Chgo. White Sox, 1981—86; exec. v.p. bus. ops. Chgo. Bulls, 1987—; sr. v.p. mktg. United Ctr., Chgo. Guest lectr. U. Chgo. Bus. Sch., Northwestern Kellogg Grad. Sch. Bus., U. Notre Dame Bus. Sch., Am. Mktg. Assn. Founder, pres. CharitaBulls; bd. mem. James Jordan Boys and Girls Club. Recipient local Emmy award. Mem.: Chgo. Econ. Club. Office: Chgo Bulls United Ctr 1901 W Madison St Chicago IL 60612-2459 *

SCHAPER, LOUISE LEVY, library director; b. Utica, NY, July 8, 1950; d. Harry and Helen (Toffler) L. BS, N.Y. State U., 1972; MSW, Syracuse U., 1982, MLS, 1984. Mktg. info. specialist AT&T Bell Labs., Murray Hill, NJ, 1984-87, info. alerting and document supply services mgr., 1987-90, dept. head librs., 1990-91; head systems dept. libr. U. Calif., San Diego, 1991; exec. dir. Fayetteville Public Library, Ark., 1997—. Contbr. articles to profl. jours. Recipient 21st Century Librarian award, Syracuse U., 2003. Mem. Am. Soc. for Info. Sci. (chmn. standards com. 1987-88), Copyright Clearance Ctr. User Group (chair 1990-91). Office: Fayetteville Public Library 401 W Mountain St Fayetteville AR 72701 *

SCHAPIRO, DONALD, lawyer; b. NYC, Aug. 8, 1925; s. John Max and Lydia (Chaitkin) S.; m. Ruth Ellen Goldman, June 29, 1952 (dec. Aug. 1991); m. Linda N. Solomon, Oct. 10, 1993; children: Jane G., Robert A. AB, Yale U., 1944, LL.B., 1949. Bar: N.Y. 1949. Assoc. Paul, Weiss, Rifkind, Wharton & Garrison, NYC, 1949-51; asst. chief counsel subcom. ways and means com. on adminstrn. revenue laws U.S. Ho. of Reps., Washington, 1951-52; assoc. Barrett, Smith, Schapiro, Simon & Armstrong, NYC, 1952-55, partner, 1955-88; ptnr. Chadbourne & Parke, 1988—. Vis. lectr. law Yale U. Law Sch., 1949-78, 94-95, instr. law and econs., 1945-49. Mem. Order of Coif, Phi Beta Kappa, Phi Delta Phi. Home: 1035 5th Ave New York NY 10028-0135 Office: Chadbourne & Parke 30 Rockefeller Plz Fl 32 New York NY 10112-0129 E-mail: dschapiro@chadbourne.com.

SCHAPIRO, MARY L., financial regulatory service executive; b. NYC, June 19, 1955; d. Robert D. and Susan (Hall) S.; m. Charles A. Cadwell, Dec. 13, 1980, 2 children BA, Franklin and Marshall Coll., 1977; JD, George Washington U., 1980. Bar: DC 1980. Trial atty., 1980-81; counsel to chmn. Commodity Futures Trading Commn., 1981-84; sr. v.p. Futures Industry Assn., 1984, gen. counsel, 1984-88; commr. SEC, Washington, 1988-94, acting chmn., 1993—94; chmn. Commodity Futures Trading Commn. (CFTC), Washington, 1994-96; pres. Nat. Assn. Securities Regulation, Inc., Washington, 1996—2002; vice chmn., pres., regulatory policy oversight divsn. Nat. Assn. Securities Dealers, Washington, 2002—06, chmn., CEO, 2006—07; CEO Fin. Industry Regulatory Authority, Inc., Washington, 2007—. Mem. Tech. Com. and the Develop. Markets Com. of the Internat. Org. of Securities (IOSCO); chmn IOSCO Cons. Com., 2001—; bd. dirs. Duke Energy Corp., Kraft Foods Inc. Mem. bd. trustees, vice chmn. audit com. Franklin and Marshall Coll. Named Fin. Women's Assn. Pub. Sector Woman of the Yr., 2000; named one of 50 Women to Watch, Wall St. Jour., 2006. Office: Financial Industry Regulatory Authority Inc 1735 K St NW Washington DC 20006-1516 *

SCHAPIRO, MIRIAM, artist; b. Toronto, Ont., Can., Nov. 15, 1923; d. Theodore and Fannie (Cohen) S. BA, State U. Iowa, 1945, MA, 1946, MFA, 1949; doctorate (hon.), Wooster Coll., 1983, Calif. Coll. Arts Crafts, 1989, Mpls. Coll. Art Design, 1994, Miami U., 1995, Moore Coll. Art, Phila., 1995. Co-originator Womanhouse, Los Angeles, 1972, Heresies mag., N.Y.C., 1975; co-originator feminist art program Calif. Inst. Arts, Valencia, 1971; founding mem. Feminist Art Inst., N.Y.C.; mem. adv. bd. Women's Caucus for Art; assoc. mem. Heresies Collective; lectr. dept. art history U. Mich., 1987. Works in numerous books and catalogues; numerous one-woman shows including, Galerie Liatowitsch, Basel, Switzerland, 1979, Lerner Heller Gallery, N.Y.C., 1979, Barbara Gladstone Gallery, N.Y.C., 1980, Spencer Mus. Art, Lawrence, Kans., 1981, Everson Mus., Syracuse, N.Y., 1981, Galerie Rudolf Zwirner, Cologne, Fed. Republic Germany, 1981, Staatagalerie, Stuttgart, Fed. Republic Germany, 1983, Dart Gallery, Chgo, 1984, Bernice Steinbaum Gallery/Steinbaum Krauss Gallery, N.Y.C., 1986, 88, 90, 91, 94, 97, Brevard Art Ctr. and Mus., Melbourne, Fla., 1991, Guild Hall Mus., East Hampton, N.Y., 1992, ARC Gallery, Chgo., 1993, James Madison U., Harrisburg, Va., 1996, Nat. Mus. Am. Art Smithsonian Inst., Washington, 1997. others; retrospective exhbn., Wooster (Ohio) Coll. Art Mus., 1980; exhibited in numerous group shows, including, Palais de Beaux Arts, Brussels, 1979, Inst. Contemporary Art, Phila., 1979, Delahunty Gallery, Dallas, 1980, Indpls. Mus., 1980, Va. Mus., Richmond, 1980, Laguna Gloria Mus., Austin, Tex., 1980, R.O.S.C., Dublin, Ireland, 1980, Biennale of Sydney, Australia, 1982, Zurich, Switzerland, 1983, Sidney Janis Gallery, N.Y.C., 1984, Am. Acad. Arts and Letters, N.Y.C., 1985, Mus. Modern Art, N.Y.C., 1988, Whyte Mus. Can. Rockies, Banff, Alta., 1991, Nat. Mus. Women in Arts., Wash., 1993, Jane Voorhees Zimmerli art mus. Rutger's U., New Brunswick, N.J., 1994, Mus. of F.A. Boston, 1994, Santa Barbara Mus. of Art, 1994, Hudson River Mus. of Westchester, Yonkers, N.Y., 1995, Mus. of Contemporary Arts, Los Angeles, Calif. Bronx Mus. of the Arts, N.Y., 1995, Columbus (Ga.) Mus., 1996, Parrish Mus., Southampton, N.Y., 1997, Austin (Tex.) Mus., 1997, Whitney Mus., 2000; represented in permanent collections, Hirshhorn Mus., Washington, Bklyn. Mus., Met. Mus. Art, N.Y.C., Mus. Contemporary Art, San Diego, Mpls. Inst. Art, Mulvane Art Center, Topeka, Nat. Gallery Art, Washington, N.Y.U., Peter Ludwig Collection, Aachen, Germany, Stanford U., Palo Alto, Calif., Univ. Art Mus., Berkeley, Calif., Whitney Mus., N.Y.C., Worcester (Mass.) Art Mus., Santa Barbara (Calif.) Mus. Art, Nat. Mus. Am. Art Smithsonian Inst., Washington, also others; author: (books) Women and the Creative Process, 1974, Rondo: An Artists Book, 1988; sculpture Anna and David, Rosslyn, Va., 1987. Guggenheim fellow, 1987, Nat. Endowment for Arts fellow; grantee Ford Found.; recipient numerous other grants and fellowships. Mem. Coll. Art Assn. (past dir.). Office: Elly Flomenhaft Gallery 547 W 27th St Ste 308 New York NY 10001 *Process and ideology in an opulent, multilayered, eccentric and hopeful abstract art: 1. The need for order and stability. 2. The need to destroy order and stability in order to find something else. 3. Finding something else. Pattern, itself an architectural species, reflects order and stability. Then a need to create chaos as though life itself were taking place. Finally the bonding layer by layer, the interpenetration of paint, fabric, photograph, tea towel, ribbon, lace, and glue. A collage: a simultaneity; a visual dazzlement, a multi-layering, a final message for the senses. And the ideology which inspires the work itself? That is feminism, the wish to have the art speak as a woman speaks. To be sensitive to the material used as though there were a responsibility to history to repair the sense of omission and to have each substance in the collage be a reminder of a woman's dreams. All of my works are auto-biographical. They are about the yearnings of a woman who decided a long time ago to become a painter.*

SCHAPIRO, MORTON OWEN, academic administrator; m. Mimi Schapiro; children: Matt, Alissa, Rachel. BA in economics, Hofstra U., 1975; PhD, U. Pa., 1979. Prof. economics, asst. provost Williams Coll., 1980—91; chair, dept. economics U. So. Calif., 1991—94, dean, Coll. Letters, Arts and Sciences, 1994—2000, v.p. planning, 1998—2000; prof. economics Williams Coll., 2000—, pres., 2000—. Commentator Pub. Radio Internat; expert witness on econ. issues in higher edn. U.S. Congress; bd. dirs. Marsh & McLennan Cos. Inc., 2002—. Co-author (with Michael S. McPherson): Keeping College Affordable, 1991, Paying the Piper, 1993, The Student Aid Game, 1998; contbr. articles to profl. jours. Office: Office of the President Williams Coll PO Box 687 Williamstown MA 01267 *

SCHAPPELL, ABIGAIL SUSAN, retired speech, language and hearing specialist, massage therapist, Reiki master; b. York, Pa., May 25, 1952; d. Felix and Ann (Getty) DeMoise; m. Gery Mylan Schappell, Oct. 20, 1979; 1 child, Jonathan Michael. BS with Master's equivalency, Longwood Coll., 1974; postgrad., Bloomsburg U., 1975—77; cert., Lehmann Sch. Massage and Muscle, 1991, East-West Sch. Massage Therapy, 1995—. Lic. speech-lang. pathologist, Pa. Speech-lang.-hearing specialist dept. pub. welfare Hamburg (Pa.) Ctr., 1975—2004; ret., 2004. Judge deaf posters and essays Virginville Grange, Pa., 1990—, Pa. State Grange Conv., 1997, Sign to Song, 2006; tchr. emergency pers. on communicating with deaf and hard of hearing, 1991, 92; leader demonstrations and workshops on sign lang. and dysphagia, non-verbal comm., active listening to various orgns., 1978—; instr. ARC, 1999-2002; bd. dirs. Berks Deaf and Hard of Hearing Svcs., 2000-06, sec., 2005-06; presenter in field. Pub: (Boy Scouts Coun. manual), Scouting for the Handicapped, Hawk Mountain, 1981-82. Sign/del. to conf. Bible Sch. dir., mem. Zion's United Ch. of Christ, Windsor Castle, Pa., 1985—; rep. nat. triann. conv. Penn Laurel coun. Girl Scouts U.S., 1975; mem. Berks Deaf and Hard of Hearing Svcs., 1975—; vol. residential monitoring project Berks County ARC, 1998-99. Named Virginville Grange Cmty. Citizen of Yr., 1994—95; named one of Outstanding Young Women of Am., 1984. Mem.: Berks Deaf and Hard of Hearing Svcs., Pa. Assn. Ret. State Employees (Berks County chpt. del. state conv. 2006, substitute acting sec.), Schuykill Haven Bus. and Profl. Women (Young Careerist local, dist. and state honors 1980—81, pres. 1983—84, asst. dir. dist. 9 1997—99, dist. 9 dir. 1999—2001, state mentoring com. 2001—03, dist. 9 parliamentarian 2002—04, state edn. and svc. funds com. 2003—05, state chair edn. and svc. funds 2005—06, individual devel. leadership program facilitator 2005—, state PAC com. 2006, involvement on dist. and state level, presenter local, dist. and state level workshops, Eleanor Briner award as dist. 9 dir. 2000), Pa. Speech and Hearing Assn., Yorktown chpt. DAR, Young Careerist Alumni Assn. (life), Hamburg Area Soccer Assn. (sec. 1989—94), Order Ea. Star (chaplain Blue Mountain chpt. 1981—82, assoc. conductress 2005—06, conductress 2006—). Republican. Avocations: massage, signing, music. Home: 531 S 4th St Hamburg PA 19526-1307

SCHAR, DWIGHT C., construction executive; b. 1942; With Ryan Homes, Washington, 1986-77, NVLand, 1977—, NVR Inc., 1980-86, pres., CEO, 1986—2005, chmn., 2005—. Bd. dirs. NVCompanies Inc. Office: Dwight Schar 11700 Plaza America Dr Ste 500 Reston VA 20190-4792 *

SCHARF, CHARLES W., bank executive; married; two children. B, Johns Hopkins U., 1987; MBA, N.Y. U. With Comml. Credit Corp., 1987-95; various sr. positions to CFO Smith Barney, 1995-98; CFO global corp. & investment bank Citibank, 1998-2000; exec. v.p., CFO Bank One Corp., Chgo., 2000—02, head retail banking, 2002—04; CEO retail fin. services JPMorgan Chase, NYC, 2004—. Office: JPMorgan Chase 270 Park Ave New York NY 10017 *

SCHARF, MICHAEL PAUL, law educator; b. Pitts., Apr. 25, 1963; s. Harry and Joan (Seder) S.; m. Trina Elizabeth Smith, May 9, 1988; 1 child, Garrett Michael. AB, Duke U., 1985, JD, 1988. Bar: D.C. 1989. Jud. clk. U.S. Ct. Appeals (11th cir.), Jacksonville, Fla., 1988-89; atty.-adviser Office Legal Adviser, U.S. Dept. State, Washington, 1989-93; asst. prof. law New England Sch. of Law, Boston, 1993—96, assoc. prof. law, 1996—98; prof. law New England Sch. Law, Boston, 1998—2002, Case Western U., 2002—; founder, ptnr. Publ. Internat. Law Policy Group, 1995—. Mem. U.S. Del. to 46th and 47th Sessions of UN Gen. Assembly, U.S. Del. to 49th Session of UN Human Rights Commn.; adj. prof. Georgetown U. Law Ctr., Washington, 1992; chmn. bd. dirs. Internat. Model UN Assn. Inc. N.Y.C., 1984-88; dir. New Eng. Ctr. for Internat. Law and Policy, 1996—02; expert commentator Ct. TV, 1996; dir. Frederick K. Cox Internat. Law Ctr., 2003—. Author: An Insider's Guide to the International Criminal Tribunal for the Former Yugoslavia, 1995, International Criminal Law: Cases and Materials, 1996, Balkan Justice: The Story Behind the First International War Crimes Trial Since Nuremberg, 1997, The Internat. Criminal Tribunal For Rwanda (with Morris), 1998, The Law of International Organizations, 2001, Peace with Justice? 2002, Slobodan Milosevic on Trial, 2002, Saddam on Trial, 2006. Nominee Nobel Peace Prize, 2005. Mem. ABA (U.S. Govt. rep. blue ribbon task force on internat. criminal ct. 1991-93), D.C. Bar (chmn. steering com. internat. law sect. 1991-93), Internat. Law Assn. (exec. com. Am. br. 1996—), Internat. Assn. Penal Law (dep. sec. gen.), Order of Coif, U.N. Assn. Greater Boston (bd. dirs. 1993—); Pub. Internat. Law Group (bd. dir., 1996-); Internat. Law Students Assn. (bd. dirs. 1999—). Avocations: skiing, sailing, tennis, softball, guitar. Office Phone: 216-368-3299. E-mail: michael.scharf@case.edu.

SCHARF, STEPHANIE A., lawyer; m. Jeffry Mandell; children: Meredith, Jonathan. BA, Rutgers U.; MA, Stanford U.; PhD, U. Chgo., 1978, JD, 1985. Bar: Ill. 1985, US Dist. Ct. (no., ctrl. and so. dists.) Ill., US Dist. Ct. (no. dist.) Ind., US Dist. Ct. (we. dist.) Mich., US Ct. Appeals (first cir.). Sr. study dir. Nat. Opinion Rsch. Ctr., Chgo.; ptnr. Schoeman Updike Kaufman & Scharf, Chgo. Author: Consumer Fraud Litigation: Law and Defenses in Illinois, 2004, The Business of Drug Development, 2004, Direct-to-Consumer Advertising of Prescription Pharmaceuticals and Medical Devices, 2004, Through the Glass Ceiling: Best Practices for Women Lawyers and Their Firms, 2004, Benchmarking for Success: Introducing NAWL Assessment Questionnaire, 2004, A Business Approach to Minimizing Product Liability Litigation, 2005, New Rulings In Drug Cases Highlight Debate Over Pre-emption, 2006, Punitive Damages in Supreme Court: How Much is Too Much?, 2007, Foreign Plaintiff's Battle to Keep Class Claims in U.S. Courts, 2007; co-author: The Media and Products Litigation, 1996, Communications Specialists Help With Damage Control, 1997, Marketing Pharmaceutical Products on the Internet: Managing Risks and Limiting Liabilities in the World of E-Commerce, 2001, Post-Sale Duties to Warn, Recall, and Retrofit Defective Products in Illinois, 2003, The Evidentiary Impact of Regulatory Action on Product Litigation in the United States, 2004, Immigration Reform and the Federal Law of Employment Discrimination;: FDA's Comments Herald New Strength for Preemption Defense in Drug Product Litigation, 2006, Foreign Plaintiffs Battle to Keep Class Claims in U.S. Courts, 2007; editor: The Use of Epidemiology in Tort Litigation: A Survey of Federal and State Jurisdictions, 2003; co-editor: The Use of Toxicology in Tort Litigation, 2005; contbr. articles to profl. jours. Bd. mem. The Youth Campus, Chgo.; chair, Best Interest of the Child Subcommittee Cir. Ct. Cook County, mem. Chief judge's Pub. Guardian Com. Harper Fellow, Univ. Chgo. Mem.: ABA (co-editor Product Liability newsletter 1997—2000, editor Mass Torts newsletter 2001, co-chair sect. litig. products liability com. 2005—, mem. mass torts com., bd. dirs., mem. spl. com. bioethics), Internat. Assn. Def. Counsel, Spl. Com. Bioethics, Pub. Guardian Com., Best Interest of Child Subcom. of Child Protection Adv. Com. (chair 1995—96), Circuit Ct. Cook County, Def. Rsch. Inst., Ill. Bar Found. (bd. mem. 2005—), Univ. Chgo. Women's Bus. Group, Products Liability Adv. Coun. (mem. case selection com.), Nat. Assn. Women Lawyers (pres. 2004—05, chair, Survey of Retention and Promotion of Women in Law Firms 2006—07, chair, com. for evaluation of Supreme Ct. nominees, bd. dirs. 2000—), U. Chgo. Women's Bus. Group. Office: Schoeman Updike Kaufman Scharf 333 W Wacker Dr Ste 300 Chicago IL 60606 Office Phone: 312-726-6000. Business E-Mail: sscharf@schoeman.com.

SCHARF, WILLIAM, artist; b. Media, Pa., Feb. 22, 1927; s. Lester William and Ebba (Anderson) S.; m. Diana Denny, Mar. 11, 1947 (div. 1951); 1 child, William Denny; m. Sally Kravitch, Mar. 25, 1956; 1 child, Aaron Anderson. Student, Barnes Found., 1946-47; cert. in painting, Pa. Acad. of Fine Arts, 1947. Instr. Mus. Modern Art, NYC, 1964, Sch. Visual Arts, NYC, 1965-73, San Francisco Inst. Fine Arts, 1963, 66, 69, 74, 89. One-man shows include David Herbert Gallery, NYC, 1960, 62, San Francisco Inst. Fine Arts, 1969, Neuberger Mus., Purchase, NY, 1976, High Mus., Atlanta, 1978, Armstrong Gallery, NYC, 1987, U. Mich. Mus. Art, Ann Arbor, 1993, Phillips Collection, Washington, 2000-01, Frederick R. Weisman Mus., Malibu, Calif., 2001, 07, P.S.1., MOMA, Queens, 2002, Richard York Gallery, NYC, 2004, Meredith Ward Fine Art, NYC, 2005; exhibited in group shows at Guggenheim Mus., NYC, 1982, Hirschl-Adler Gallery, NYC, 1980, Smith-Anderson Gallery, Palo Alto, Calif., Nat. Mus. Am. Art, Washington, 1987, 91-92, Am. Acad. and Inst. Arts and Letters, NYC, 1989, 91, Richard York Gallery, NYC, 2002, Nat. Acad. Design Mus., NYC, 2003, 05, Nat. Head Design Mus., 2007; represented in permanent collections Phila. Mus., Boston Inst. Contemporary Art, Bklyn. Mus., Solomon R. Guggenheim Mus., NYC, Newark Mus., Nat. Mus. Am. Art, Smith Coll. Mus., Northampton, Mass., Zimmerli Mus., Rutgers U., New Brunswick, NJ, U. Mich. Mus. art., Phillips Collection, Washington, The Neuroscience Inst., San Diego, The High Mus., Atlanta, Colgate U., Telfair Mus. of Art, Savannah, Ga., Rose Art Mus., Brandeis U., Montgomery (Ala.) Mus. Art, Cath. U., Washington, Fogg Art Mus. Harvard U., Cambridge, Mass., Yale U. Mus., New Haven. Trustee Rothko Found., NYC, 1979—87; instr. Art Students League, NY, 1987—2006. With USAF, 1945—46. Emmlen Cresson fellow Pa. Acad. Fine Arts, 1948. Mem.: Nat. Acad. Design, Soc. of Illustrators, Artist Equity Assn.

SCHARFENBERG, MARGARET ELLAN, retired elementary school educator; b. Lansing, Mich., Mar. 22, 1924; d. John Milton and Florence Lucille (Craig) Amiss; m. Howard Edward Scharfenberg, June 29, 1946; children: Ann Derr Scharfenberg White, Joan Carol Scharfenberg Anderson, John. Student, Oberlin Coll., 1942-44; BA, Mich. State U., 1946; MA in Teaching, Rollins Coll., 1966. Cert. tchr., elem. supr., Fla. Tchr. Hill Elem. Sch., Maitland, Fla., 1964-65, Cheney Elem. Sch., Orlando, Fla., 1965-66; reading lab. tchr. Richmond Heights Elem. Sch., Orlando, Fla., 1966-68; supr. perceptual planning, oral clinician Orange County Schs., Orlando, Fla., 1968-69; reading lab. tchr. Winter Park HS, Fla., 1969-72; from perceptual trainer to exptl. reading lab. tchr. Gateway Sch., Orlando, Fla., 1972-74; tchr. of migrant children Zellwood Elem. Sch., Fla., 1974-93; ret., 1993. Pioneer white/black sch. staffing Richmond Heights Elem. Sch., 1966-68; dir. Learning Skills Profl. Ctr., Orlando, 1971-74; speaker, cons. in field. Author, editor (newsletter) Paper Meeting, 1968-69, (perception package) Patterns for a Purpose, 1968-69; producer films on perceptual tng., 1968-69. Vol. Women of Hospice, Hospice Hope Chest, Sun. sch. tchr; choir mem., chmn. prayer chain Congl. Ch. Mt. Dora. Named Tchr. of Yr., Zellwood Elem. Sch., 1993. Mem.: NEA, AAUW, Internat. Reading Assn. (sec. Orange County coun. 1965, pres. 1969), Lakes & Hills Garden Club (Oleander Garden Cir. chaplain, past sec.), Rosicrucian Order (A.M.O.R.C.), Humane Soc., Lions (staff mem. seminars on perception, recipient various certs. and plaques), Gamma Phi Beta (past pres. alumna group). Republican. Avocations: reading, boating, gardening, choir. Home: 6492 Dora Dr Mount Dora FL 32757-7064

SCHARFF, JOSEPH LAURENT, lawyer; b. New Orleans, Oct. 2, 1935; s. Joseph Roy and Celia Ray S.; m. Mary Susan Greulach, June 29, 1963; children: Catherine Elizabeth, Robert Laurent, Anne Victoria. BS in Journalism, Northwestern U., 1957; JD, Harvard U., 1964. Bar: D.C. 1965, U.S. Supreme Ct. 1970, U.S. Ct. Appeals (D.C. cir.) 1965, U.S. Ct. Appeals (2nd cir.) 1980, U.S. Ct. Appeals (5th cir.) 1973, U.S. Ct. Appeals (10th cir.); U.S. Ct. Claims 1965. From assoc. to ptnr. Pierson, Ball & Dowd, Washington, 1964-89; ptnr. Reed Smith Shaw & McClay, Washington, 1989-95, counsel, 1996. Mem. ABA (fair trial-free press com. 1973-76, com. reps. media 1985-95, co-chmn. 1989-92), Fed. Comm. Bar Assn., Soc. Profl. Journalists, Radio-TV News Dirs. Assn. (counsel 1965-95, Disting. Svc. award 1987, J. Laurent Scharff Legal Internship established 1996), Media Inst. (First Amendment Adv. Coun. 1993-2003). Home and Office: 12000 Turf Ln Reston VA 20191-2123

SCHARFF, MATTHEW DANIEL, immunologist, cell biologist, educator; b. NYC, Aug. 28, 1932; s. Harry and Constance S.; m. Carol Held, Dec. 19, 1954; children: Karen, Thomas, David. AB, Brown U., 1954, DrMed-Sci (hon.), 1994; MD, NYU, 1959. House officer II and IV med. service Boston City Hosp., 1959—61; rsch. assoc. NIH, 1961—63; asst. prof. Albert Einstein Coll. Medicine, Yeshiva U., Bronx, NY, 1963—67, assoc. prof., 1967—71, prof. dept. cell biology, 1971—, chmn. dept., 1972—83, dir. div. biol. scis., 1975—81; assoc. dir. Cancer Ctr., 1975—86, dir., 1986—95, dep. dir., 1995—2002. Served with USPHS, 1961-63. Recipient Alumni Achievement award NYU Sch. Medicine, 1980, N.Y. Acad. Medicine medal, 1990, Commemorative award Albert Einstein Coll. Medicine, 1993, Mayor of NY Lifetime Achievement award in sci. and tech., 2003. Mem. Am. Assn. Immunologists (Mentoring Excellence award 1998), Am. Soc. Clin. Investigation, Nat. Acad. Scis., Am. Acad. Arts and Sci., Phi Beta Kappa, Sigma Xi, Alpha Omega Alpha. Office: Albert Einstein Coll Med Dept Cell Biology 1300 Morris Pk Ave Bronx NY 10461-1926

SCHARFFE, WILLIAM GRANVILLE, academic administrator, educator; b. Saginaw, Mich., Mar. 12, 1942; s. William Edward and Marion Kittie (Granville) S.; m. Mary Jo Whitfield, Sept. 4, 1965; children: Sue L., William W. BA, Mich. State U., 1965, MA, 1969, PhD, 1977. Tchr. English Webber Jr. High Sch., Saginaw, 1965-66; tchr. speech Arthur Hill High Sch., Saginaw, 1966-68; staff asst. for pers. Saginaw City Schs., 1968-73, dir. pers., 1977-94, dir. employee devel. and media ops., 1994-99; prin. Zilwaukee Jr. High Sch., Saginaw, 1973-74; asst. prin. North Intermediate Sch., Saginaw, 1974-75, 1975-77; dir. policy svcs. Mich. Assn. Sch. Bds., Lansing, 1999—. Adj. asst. prof. Mich. State U., East Lansing, 1977; adj. lectr. Ctrl. Mich. U., Mt. Pleasant, 1987, Mich. State U., 1977, Saginaw Valley State U., 1991; cons. in field. Author: Elfred Alanzo & Santa's Surprise, 1987. Bd. dirs. Japanese Cultural Ctr. and Tea House, Saginaw, 1986-97, pres., 1993-95. Recipient Key Man award United Way Saginaw County, 1978, Outstanding Svc. award, 1978. Mem.: Am. Assn. State Policy Svcs. (pres. 2004—05), Soc. For Human Resource Mgmt., Mich. Mid. Cities Pers. and Labor Rels. Task Force (pres. 1980—82), Mich. Assn. Sch. Pers. Assn. (sec., bd. dirs. 1988—90, pres., bd. dirs. 1992—93), Mich. State U. Alumni Club (pres. Saginaw County chpt. 2002—04), Saginaw Club (pres. 1996—97), Exch. Club (Saginaw chpt. pres. 1981), Phi Delta Kappa. Republican. Episcopalian. Avocations: writing, golf, photography, public speaking. Home: 2812 Adams Blvd Saginaw MI 48602-3103 Home Phone: 989-793-7079; Office Phone: 517-327-5928. Business E-Mail: bscharffe@masb.org.

SCHARLEMANN, ROBERT PAUL, theology studies educator, minister; b. Lake City, Minn., Apr. 4, 1929; s. Ernst Karl and Johanna Meta (Harre) Scharlemann. Student, Northwestern Coll., Watertown, Wis., 1946-49; BA, Concordia Coll. and Sem., St. Louis, 1952; BD, MDiv, Concordia Coll. and Sem., 1955; Dr. theol., U. Heidelberg, Germany, 1957. Ordained to ministry Luth. Ch., 1960. Tchr. Luth. parochial sch., Mobridge, SD, 1949—50; instr. philosophy Valparaiso U., 1957-59; postdoctoral fellow Yale U., 1959-60; pastor Bethlehem Luth. Ch., Carlyle, Ill., 1960-62, Grace Luth. Ch., Durham, NC, 1962-63; asst. prof. religion U. So. Calif., 1963-64, assoc. prof., 1964-66; assoc. prof. religion U. Iowa, Iowa City, 1966-68, prof., 1968-81; Commonwealth prof. religious studies U. Va., Charlottesville, 1981-97, prof. emeritus, 1997—. Fulbright-Hays prof. U. Heidelberg, 1975—76. Author: Thomas Aquinas and John Gerhard, 1964, Reflection and Doubt in the Thought of Paul Tillich, 1969, The Being of God, 1981, Inscriptions and Reflections, 1989, The Reason of Following, 1991, L'intemporel et l'éternel, 1993, Can Religion be Understood Philosophically?, 1995, The Mystical Correlate of Symbolic Appearing, 2001, Religion and Reflection, 2004; editor: Jour. Am. Acad. Religion, 1980—85; contbr. articles to profl. jours. Fulbright scholar, U. Heidelberg, 1955—57. Mem.: Soc. Philosophy Religion, Deutsche Paul-Tillich Gesellschaft, Am. Theol. Soc., Am. Acad. Religion, European Soc. Culture. Lutheran.

SCHAROLD, MARY LOUISE, psychoanalyst, psychiatrist, educator; b. Wichita Falls, Tex., Mar. 3, 1943; d. Walter John and Louise Helen (Hartmann) Baumgartner; m. William Ballew McCollum, Aug. 23, 1964 (div. 1981); m. Harry Karl Scharold, June 19, 1982; children: Margaret Louise, Walter Ballew. BA with highest distinction, U. Kans., 1964; attended, U. Kans. Sch. Medicine, 1964—66; MD, Baylor Coll. Medicine, 1968; attended, Houston-Galveston Psychoanalytic Inst., 1974—76; postgrad., Topeka Inst. Psychoanalysis, 1981. Diplomate Am. Bd. Psychiatry and Neurology, 1975, cert. adult psychoanalysis Am. Psychoanalytic Assn., 1982. Intern Meml. Bapt. Hosp., Houston, 1968-69; resident in psychiatry Baylor Coll. Medicine, Houston, 1969—72, chief resident, 1971-72; psychiatrist Houston, 1972—; psychoanalyst, 1981—. Asst. prof. Baylor Coll. Medicine, Houston, 1973-76, asst. clin. prof., 1981-84, assoc. clin. prof., 1984—; dir. Baylor Psychiat. Clinic, Houston, 1973-76; co-dir. Rice U. Psychiat. Svc., Houston, 1981-82; asst. clin. prof. U. Kans. Sch. Medicine, Kansas City, 1977-81; tchg. assoc. Topeka Psychoanalytic Inst., 1984-86; tchg. analyst, Houston-Galveston Psychoanalytic Inst., 1986-90, tng. and supervising analyst, 1990—, v.p., 1994-96, pres., 1996-01, bd. dirs., 2001-04; acting pres. bd. trustees Child Devel. Ctr., 2005, sec. bd. trustees, 2005-. Contbr. articles to profl. pubs. Adv. bd. Leavenworth (Kans.) Mental Health Assn., 1977-81; sec. bd. trustees, Child Devel. Ctr., 2005-. Watkins scholar U. Kans., 1961-64; Grad. Fellowship award, Pi Beta Phi, 1965; recipient Hilltopper, Ten Outstanding Sr. Women, U. Kans., 1963, Greater U. Fund award, 1964, U. Kans., Eugen Kahn award, Outstanding Baylor Psychiatry Resident, 1972, 1st Disting. Svc. award, Houston-Galveston Psychoanalytic Soc., 2004; named Outstanding Woman Med. Student, AMWA, Houston Branch, 1968; named to Best Doctors in Am., 1998-. Mem. Am. Psychiat. Assn. (disting. life fellow, mem. com. quality assurance 1986-87, chair Tex. peer rev. 1984-88), Am. Coll. Psychoanalysts, Am. Psychoanalytic Assn. (cert. 1982, peer rev. com. 1985-90, prof. ins. commn. 1986-93, bd. profl. stds. 1994-2001, CME com. 1994-96, exec. coun. 1994-96, cert. com. 1995-98, preparedness and progress com. 1998-2006, chair preparedness and progress com. 2000-06, coordinating com. bd. profl. stds. 2000-06, bylaws com. 2001—, fin. com. 2003—, councilor-at-large 2005—, chair councillors-at-large, 2007—, hon. membership.com, 2005-, election oversight com., 2005—, compliance task force, 2006-07, com. on coun., 2006—), Am. Group Psychotherapy Assn., Ctr. Advanced Psychoanalytic Studies, Houston Psychiat. Soc. (v.p. 1984-85, pres.-elect 1985-86, pres. 1986-87), Houston-Galveston Psychoanalytic Soc. (sec.-treas. 1984-86, pres.-elect 1986-88, pres. 1988-90, alt. councillor 1994-96), Houston Group Psychotherapy Soc. (adv. bd. 1984-85), Mortar Bd., Phi Beta Kappa, Delta Phi Alpha, Alpha Omega Alpha, Pi Beta Phi Alumni Assn. Republican. Lutheran. Office: 2301 Westheimer Rd Houston TX 77098-1317 Home Phone: 713-590-2301; Office Phone: 713-590-2302. Personal E-mail: mlscharold@mindspring.com.

SCHATTEN, GERALD PHILLIP, stem cell biologist, reproductive biologist, educator; b. NYC, Nov. 1, 1949; s. Frank and Sylvia Schatten; children, Daniel, Madeline, Samantha. BS, U. Calif., Berkeley, 1971, PhD, 1975. Instr. U. Calif., Berkeley, 1975; postdoctoral fellow Rockefeller Found., 1976-77; from asst. prof. to prof. Fla. State U., Tallahassee, 1979-86; prof. molecular biology, zoology and obstetrics gynecology U. Wis., Madison, 1986-97, rsch. dir. women's health rsch., 1997—, dir. integrated microscopy resource for biomed. rsch., 1986-92, dir. gamete and embryo biol. tng. program, 1989-97; program dir. Mellon Ctr. of Excellence in Reproductive Biology, 1996-97, 99—; prof. ob-gyn. and cell-devel. biology, sr. scientist Oreg. Regional Primate Rsch. Ctr. Oreg. Health Scis. U., Portland, 1997-2001; dir. Pitts. Devel. Ctr., dep. dir. Magee-Women's Rsch. Inst., Pitts., 2001—, vice chair, prof. dept. ob/gyn./reproductive scis., prof. cell biology and physiology, 2001—. Dir. gamete and embryo biol. tng. program U. Wis., Madison, 1989-97; exec. bd. UNESCO Internat. Cell Rsch. Orgn., 1995—; co-dir. frontiers in reprodn. course Marine Biol. Lab., Woods Hole, Mass., 1998-2001. Editor Current Topics in Devel. Biology, 1996—. Recipient Rsch. Career Devel. award NIH, 1981-86, Merit award, 1997-, Sadler award, 1998; Purkinge medal of sci. Czech Acad. Scis., 2000, Patrick Steptoe medal, brit. Fertility Socs., 2005, Stem Cell Sci. and Policy award, Genetics Policy Inst., 2005, Pioneer Human Embryonic Stem Cell award, Stanfor U., 2005. Mem.: Nat. Inst. Aging Coun. Office: Univ PItts Pitts Devel Ctr 204 Craft Ave Pittsburgh PA 15213

SCHATTSCHNEIDER, DORIS JEAN, retired mathematics professor; b. NYC, Oct. 19, 1939; d. Robert W. Jr. and Charlotte Lucile (Ingalls) Wood; m. David A. Schattschneider, June 2, 1962; 1 child, Laura E. AB, U. Rochester, NY, 1961; MA, Yale U., New Haven, Conn., 1963, PhD, 1966. Instr. in math. Northwestern U., Evanston, Ill., 1964—65; asst. prof. U. Ill., Chgo., 1965—68; prof. Moravian Coll., Bethlehem, Pa., 1968—2002, prof. emerita, 2003—. Project dir. Fund for the Improvement of Post-Secondary Edn. U.S. Dept. Edn., 1991—93, 1995—97; vis. scholar U. V.I., 2004. Author (with W. Walker): (books and models) M.C. Escher Kaleidocycles, 1977, 1987; co-author: (videos and activities) Visual Geometry Project, 1986—91; author: M.C. Escher: Visions of Symmetry, 1990, 2d edit., 2004; co-author: A Companion to Calculus, 1995, 2d edit., 2005; editor: Geometry Turned On, 1997, M.C. Escher's Legacy, 2003. Exhbn. curator Allentown Art Mus., 1979, Payne Gallery, 1987. Grantee NEH rsch. grantee, 1988—90. Mem.: Assn. for Women in Math., Am. Math. Soc., Math. Assn. Am. (editor 1980—85, gov. 1980—89, 1st v.p. 1994—96, Allendoerfer award 1979, Meritorious Svc. award 1991, Dist. Math. Tchg. award 1993), Pi Mu Epsilon (councillor 1990—96). Mem. Moravian Ch. Office: Moravian Coll Math Dept PPHAC 1200 Main St Bethlehem PA 18018-6650 E-mail: schattdo@moravian.edu.

SCHATZ, BRETT A., lawyer; b. Cin., Aug. 9, 1972; BSME, U. Cin., 1995; JD, Salmon P. Chase Coll. Law, 2000. Bar: Ohio 2000, Ky. 2000, Ind. 2000, US Dist. Ct. Southern Dist. Ohio, US Dist. Ct. Eastern Dist. Ky., US Dist. Ct. Western Dist. Ky. Adj. prof. Salmon P. Chase Coll. Law, 2000—; assoc. Wood, Herron & Evans, L.L.P., Cin. Named one of Ohio's Rising Stars, Super Lawyers, 2006. Mem.: Am. Intellectual Property Law Assn., Ohio State Bar Assn., Cin. Bar Assn. Office: Wood Herron & Evans LLP 2700 Carew Tower Cincinnati OH 45202 Office Phone: 513-241-2324. Office Fax: 513-241-6234.

SCHATZ, GARY STEWART, marketing professional; b. NYC, 1951; s. Irving and Esther Schatz; m. Rita Schatz. BA, Syracuse U., NY, 1973; MBA, Canadian Sch. Mgmt., 1994. Lic. debt collector. With Century 21, Inc., Montvale, NJ, 1975—82; mktg. rep. Centrac Rsch., Bergenfield, NJ, 1982—84; regional field rep. Certified Mktg., Inc., Kinderhock, NY, 1994—99; pvt. practice NYC, 1999—. Mem. consumer panel NPD Group, Fort Washington, NY, 1990—93. Vol. U.S. Army Corps. Engrs., 1996—98. Mem.: Am. Inst. Computer Scis. Home: 353 W 57th St New York NY 10019 Office Phone: 888-240-6089.

SCHATZ, GEORGE C., chemist, educator; b. Watertown, NY, Apr. 14, 1949; married; 3 children. BS in Chemistry, with great distinction, Clarkson U., Potsdam, NY, 1971; PhD in Chemistry, Calif. Inst. Tech., 1976. Rsch. assoc. MIT, Cambridge, Mass., 1975—76; asst. prof. Northwestern U., Evanston, Ill., 1976—80, assoc. prof., 1980—82, prof., 1982—, Dow prof., 1994—96, Morrison prof., 2002—. Specialist editor Computer Physics Communications, 1991—, adv. bd. Jour. Physical Chemistry, 1992—93, sr. editor, 1993—2004, editor-in-chief, 2005—, editl. bd. Jour. Chemical Physics, 1990—92, Chem. Physics Letters, 1994—, Theoretica Chimica Acta (Theoretical Chemistry Accounts), 1995—, Ann. Rev. Physical Chemistry, 2002—05, Accounts Chem. Rsch., 2005—. Recipient Fresenius award, Phi Lambda Upsilon, 1983, Max Plank Rsch. award, 1993; Alfred P. Sloan Rsch. fellow, 1980—82, Japan Soc. for Promotion of Sci. fellowship, 1986. Fellow: AAAS, Am. Physical Soc.; mem.: NAS, Am. Acad. Arts and Sciences, Internat. Acad. Quantum Molecular Sciences. Office: Dept Chemistry Northwestern Univ 2145 Sheridan Rd Evanston IL 60208-3113 Office Fax: 847-491-5657, 847-491-7713. E-mail: SCHATZ@chem.northwestern.edu.

SCHATZ, IRWIN JACOB, cardiologist, educator; b. St. Boniface, Man., Can., Oct. 16, 1931; came to US, 1956, naturalized, 1966; s. Jacob and Reva S.; m. Barbara Jane Binder, Nov. 12, 1967; children: Jacob, Edward, Stephen and Brian (twins). Student, U. Man., Winnipeg, 1951, MD with honors, 1956. Diplomate: Am. Bd. Internal Medicine. Intern Vancouver (B.C.) Gen. Hosp., 1955-56; resident Hammersmith Hosp., U. London, 1957, Mayo Clinic, Rochester, Minn., 1958-61; head sec. peripheral vascular disease Henry Ford Hosp., Detroit, 1961-68; asso. prof. medicine Wayne State U., 1968-71, chief sect. cardiovascular disease, 1969-71; assoc. prof., asso. dir. sect. cardiology U. Mich., 1972-73, prof. internal medicine, 1973-75; prof. medicine John A. Burns Sch. Medicine, U. Hawaii, 1975—, chmn. dept. medicine, 1975-90, interim chmn. dept. medicine, 2003—05. Author: Orthostatic Hypotension, 1986; contbr. numerous articles to med. jour. Mem. jud. coun. State of Hawaii Supreme Ct., 2000—. Rockefeller Found. scholar, 1991. Master ACP (bd. gov. 1984-89, Laureate award Hawaii chpt. 1992); fellow Am. Coll. Cardiology (bd. gov. 1980-84); mem. Am. Heart Assn. (fellow coun. cardiology), Am. Fedn. Clin. Rsch., Asian-Pacific Soc. Cardiology (v.p. 1987-91), Accreditation Coun. for Grad. Med. Edn. (chmn. residence rev. com. internal medicine 1989-95), Hawaii Heart Assn. (pres.), Western Assn. Physicians, Am. Autonomic Soc. (chmn. bd. gov., pres. 1996-98), Pacific Interurban Club. Jewish. Office: 1356 Lusitana St Honolulu HI 96813-2421

SCHATZ, WAYNE ARDALE, district technology coordinator, educator; b. Cody, Wyo., July 27, 1947; s. Albert R. and Leona Mildred (Johnston) S.; m. Roanne Longwith, Dec. 16, 1966; children: Edith, Heidi, Robert, Leon, Dale, Anne. BS, Ea. Mont. Coll., 1969; MEd, Lesley Coll., 1987. Cert. Elem. tchr., Wyo. Tchr. Coffeen Elem. Sch., Sheridan, Wyo., 1969-78, Woodland Park Elem., Sheridan, 1978-87; computer tchr. Cen. Mid. Sch., Sheridan, 1987-94; in-svc. instr. Sch. Dist. #2, Sheridan, 1987—, dist. tech. coord., 1994-97; computer tchr. Sheridan Jr. H.S., Sheridan, 1997—2001, elem. technology tchr., 2001—. Extension instr. U. Wyo., Laramie, 1989—. Bd. dirs. Bighorn Audobon Soc., Sheridan, 1966-77, pres., 1977-80; active Sheridan County Red Cross, Sheridan. Mem. Sheridan Cen. Edn. Assn. (pres. 1979-80, Tchr. of the Month 1988, 92, Tchr. of Yr. 1992), Wyo. Edn. Assn. (bd. dirs. 1980-82, treas. 1982-84), Wyo. Ednl. Computing Coun. (pres. 1989-92), Wyo. Bus. Edn. Assn. (pres. 2002-03), Wyo. Assn. Career & Tech. Edn. (bd. dirs. 2001-03). Republican. Mem. Lds Ch.

SCHATZBERG, ALAN FREDERIC, psychiatrist, researcher; b. NYC, Oct. 17, 1944; s. Emanuel and Cila (Diamand) S.; m. Nancy R. Silverman, Aug. 27, 1972; children: Melissa Ann, Lindsey Diamand. BS, NYU, 1965, MD, 1968; MA (hon.), Harvard U., 1989. Diplomate Nat. Bd. Med. Examiners, Am. Bd. Psychiatry and Neurology. Intern Lenox Hill Hosp., NYC, 1968-69; resident in psychiatry Mass. Mental Health Ctr., Boston, 1969-72; clin. fellow in psychiatry Harvard Med. Sch., Boston, 1969-72, asst. prof. psychiatry, 1977-82, assoc. prof., 1982-88, prof., 1988-91; interim psychiatrist-in-chief McLean Hosp., Belmont, Mass., 1984-86, dir. depression rsch. facility, 1985—, svc. chief, 1982-84, 86-88; psychiatrist adv. panel Eli Lilly & Co., Indpls., 1986-93; clin. dir. Mass. Mental Health Ctr., Boston, 1988-91; Kenneth T. Norris, Jr. prof. psychiatry and behavioral scis. Stanford (Calif.) U., 1991—, chmn. dept. psychiatry and behavioral scis. Sch. Medicine, 1991—. Cons. AMA Videoclinics, Chgo., 1979-83; mem. AMA/FAA panel on health regulations, Chgo., 1984-86; mem. NIH Biol. Psychopathology and Clin. Neuroscis. Intitial Rev. Group, 1991-95, chmn., 1993-94. Co-author: Manual of Clinical Psychopharmacology, 1986, 6th edit., 2007; co-editor: Depression: Biology, Psychodynamics and Treatment, 1978, Hypothalamic-Pituitary-Adrenal Axis, 1988,

Textbook of Psychopharmacology, 1996, 2d edit., 1998, 3d edit., 2004; mem. editl. bd. McLean Hosp. Jour., 1975—88, Jour. Psychiat. Rsch., 1988—, co-editor-in-chief, 2000—, mem. editl. bd. Harvard Rev. Psychiatry, 1992—, Anxiety, 1993, Jour. Clin. Psychopharmacology, 1993—, Archives of Gen. Psychiatry, 1995—, Psychoneuroendocrinology, 1995—, Am. Jour. Psychiatry, 2002—05, assoc. editor-in-chief Depression and Anxiety, 1992—, translational field editor Neuropsychopharmacology, 2002—07; contbr. more than 300 articles to profl. publs., chapters to books. Maj. USAF, 1972-74. Rsch. grantee NIMH, 1984-87, 94—, Poitras Charitable Found., 1985-93, Pritzker Found., 1997—; recipient Mood Disorders Rsch. award Am. Coll. Psychiatrists, 2002, Klerman Lifetime Rsch. award Nat. Depressive and Manic Depressive Assn., 1998, Strecker award U. Pa., 2002, Falcone award Nat. Alliance Rsch. in Schizophrenia and Affective Diseases, 2005. Fellow: APA (Rsch. award 2002), Soc. Biol. Psychiatry (pres. 2005—06), Am. Coll. Psychiatrists (Disting. Svc. award in psychiatry 2005), Am. Coll. Neuropsychopharmacology (coun. 1994—97, pres. 2000—01), Am. Psychopathol. Assn.; mem.: NAS, Inst. Medicine, No. Calif. Psychiat. Soc. (v.p. 1997—99), Mass. Psychiat. Soc. (coun. 1987—90). Avocations: travel, swimming, fine arts, theater, golf. Office: Stanford U Sch Medicine 401 Quarry Rd Rm 300 Stanford CA 94305-5717 Office Phone: 650-723-6811. Business E-Mail: afschatz@stanford.edu.

SCHAUB, MARILYN MCNAMARA, theology studies educator; b. Chgo., Mar. 24, 1928; d. Bernard Francis and Helen Katherine (Skehan) McNamara; m. Thomas Schaub, Oct. 25, 1969; 1 child, Helen Ann. BA, Rosary Coll., 1953; PhD, U. Fribourg, Switzerland, 1957; diploma, Ecole Biblique, Jerusalem, 1967. Asst. prof. classics and Bibl. studies Rosary Coll., River Forest, Ill., 1957-69; prof. Bibl. studies Duquesne U., Pitts., 1969-70, 73-01. Participant 8 archeological excavations, Middle East; hon assoc Am Schs Oriental Research, 1966—67, trustee, 1986—89; Danforth assoc, 1972—80; admin dir expedition to the Southeast Dead Sea Plains, Jordan, 1989—. Author: (book) Friends and Friendship for St. Augustine, 1964; translator (with H Richter): Agape in the New Testament, 3 vols, 1963—65. Mem.: Am Acad Religion, Cath Biblical Asn, Soc Biblical Literature. Democrat. Home: 25 Mckelvey Ave Pittsburgh PA 15218-1452

SCHAUB, ROBERT GEORGE, pharmaceutical executive; b. Bellevue, Pa., Dec. 16, 1947; s. Edward Clarence Schaub and Barbara Marie Zuratovitch; m. Kathy Anne Gates, Apr. 3, 1983; 1 child, Caitlin Elizabeth. BS, U. Nev., Las Vegas, 1970; PhD, Wash. State U., 1973. Postdoctoral fellow Wash. Heart Assn., Pullman, Wash., 1973—75, Temple U. Med. Sch., Philadelphia, 1975—77; asst. to assoc. prof. U.Tenn., Knoxville, 1977—81; rsch. scientist Upjohn Co., Kalamazoo, 1981—90; sr lab. head to dir. Genetics Inst., Cambridge, Mass., 1990—97; sr. dir. to asst. v.p. Wyeth Pharmaceuticals, Cambridge, 1997—2006; v.p. Archemix Corp., Cambridge, 2006—. Adj. prof. Boston U. Sch. Medicine, 2006—. Recipient Outstanding Educator of Yr., U. Tenn., 1978. Mem.: AAAS, NY Acad. Sci., Internat. Soc. Thrombosis and Haemostasis, Am. Soc. Hematology, Soc. Leukocyte Biology, Am. Soc. Investigative Pathology, Am. Physiol. Soc., Sigma Xi. Achievements include patents in field. Office: Archemix Corp 300 Third St Cambridge MA 02142 Office Fax: 617-621-9300. Business E-Mail: bschaub@archemix.com.

SCHAUBLE, JOHN EUGENE, physical education educator; b. Paterson, NJ, Aug. 14, 1949; s. Charles Eugene and Rosemary (White) S.; children: Sarah, Angela. BA, Bemidji State U., 1973, BS, 1974; MA, U. Ala., 1984. Cert. tchr. health, phys. edn., K-12; cert. swimming coach/level 4; cert. aquatic mgr.; cert. pool operator, ARC water safety instr., lifeguard instr., waterfront lifeguard instr., lifeguard mgmt. instr., first aid instr., CPR instr., water safety instr. trainer, AED essentials instr., disease prevention instr., oxygen adminstrn. instr., safety tng. for swim coaches instr.; cert. U.S.A. Track & Field level II. Northeast area dir. Phys. Fitness Inst. of Am., Albany, N.Y., 1974-75; head swim coach Lake Forest (Ill.) Swim Club, 1975-78; asst. swim coach/grad. asst. U. Ala., Tuscaloosa, 1978-79; head swim coach Palm Springs (Calif.) Swim Team, 1979-80; asst. swim coach Ft. Lauderdale (Fla.) Swim Team, 1980-82; aquatic dir., head swim coach Briarwood of Richmond Aquatic Club, Richmond, Va., 1982-83; head swimming coach, intramural coord. William Rainey Harper Coll., Palatine, Ill., 1983-85; boys/girls asst. swim coach Sch. Dist. 211, Palatine, 1985-90; nat. coach Palatine Swim Team, 1983-92; head boys and girls swim coach Adlai E. Stevenson High Sch., Lincolnshire, Ill., 1990-96, aquatic coord., 1990—, asst. girls track and field coach, 1992-99, varsity cross-country coach, 1999—, boys distance track and field coach, 1999—. Head coach Patriot Aquatic Club, 1992-94, head coach sr. team, 1994-99; fund raising com. U.S. Swimming, Inc., Colorado Springs, Colo., 1990-94; coaches rep. Ill. Swimming, Inc., Aurora, 1990-94, bd. dirs., tech. planning com., others. Nominated Coach of Yr., Nat. Jr. Coll. Athletic Assn., Ft. Pierce, Fla., 1984; named Boys Sectional Coach of Yr., Ill. HS Assn., 1992. Mem. Ill. Swimming Assn. (nominated Coach of Yr. coll. divsn. boys 1984), Nat. Interscholastic Swimming Coaches Assn., Am. Swimming Coaches Assn., Am. Coll. Sports Medicine, Nat. Strength and Conditioning Assn., Ill. Track and Cross Country Coaches Assn (Dave Pasquini award, 2006), AAPHERD, NEA. Republican. Roman Catholic. Avocations: computer, running, swimming, tennis, weight tng. Home: 608 Applegate Ln Lake Zurich IL 60047-2363 Office: 1 Stevenson Dr Lincolnshire IL 60069-2824 Office Phone: 847-634-4000 ext. 1226. Personal E-mail: coachswim@aol.com, coachswim@sbcglobal.net.

SCHAUER, FRANZ PETER, civil and nuclear engineer, educator; b. Mankato, Minn., Nov. 29, 1932; s. Albert Franz and Marie Petrich (Nielsson) S.; m. Joan Laurie; children: Marie, Barbara, Franz, Jr., Lisa, Jill. BS, U.S. Mil. Acad., 1955; MSCE, Iowa State U., 1961, MS in Nuc. Engring., 1961, PhD, 1969. Cert. civil engr. Commd. 2d lt. U.S. Army, 1955, advanced through grades to col., 1980, ret., 1989; engr. U.S. AEC, Germantown, Md., 1964-75; exec. U.S. Nuc. Regulatory Commn., Bethesda, Md., 1975-82; prof. Minn. State U., 1982-93; pres. ADU Engring. Assn., Bethesda, 1994—. Engring. cons. Tex-La Power, Stone and Webster, Boston, 1987, Burns and Roe, NYC, 1986, U.S. Army, Washington, 1984, Todd Shipbuilding, Washington, 1983. Author: Advances in Structural Dynamics, 1980. Trustee Christ Luth. Ch. Fellow ASCE (com. mem.); mem. IEEE Computer Soc., ASME (com.mem.), Phi Kappa Phi, Sigma Xi. Lutheran. Avocations: tennis, computers. Home: Unit 261 6860 Gulfport Blvd S Saint Petersburg FL 33707-2108 Office: PO Box 1423 Mc Lean VA 22101-1423 Personal E-mail: franzschauer1000@hotmail.com.

SCHAUER, FREDERICK FRANKLIN, law educator; b. Newark, Jan. 15, 1946; s. John Adolph and Clara (Balayti) S.; m. Margery Clare Stone, Aug. 25, 1968 (div. June, 1982); m. Virginia Jo Wise, May 25, 1985. AB, Dartmouth Coll., 1967, MBA, 1968; JD, Harvard U., 1972. Bar: Mass. 1972, U.S. Supreme Ct. 1976. Assoc. Fine & Ambrogne, Boston, 1972-74; asst. prof. law W.Va. U., Morgantown, 1974-76, assoc. prof., 1976-78, Coll. William and Mary, Williamsburg, Va., 1978-80, Cutler prof., 1980-83; prof. of law U. Mich., Ann Arbor, 1983-90; Frank Stanton prof. of 1st Amendment Kennedy Sch. of Govt., Harvard U., Cambridge, Mass., 1990—, acad. dean, 1997—2002, acting dean, 2001. Vis. scholar, mem. faculty law Wolfson Coll. Cambridge (Eng.) U., 1977-78; vis. prof. Law Sch., U. Chgo., 1990, 05; vis. fellow Australian Nat. U., 1993, 98; William Morton Disting. sr. fellow in humanities Dartmouth Coll., 1991; vis. prof. law Harvard Law Sch., 1996, 97, 00, 04, 05, 06; Ewald Disting. vis. prof. law U. Va., 1996, vis. prof. govt. Dartmouth Coll., 1997; disting. vis. prof. law U. Toronto, 2000; Fischel-Neil Disting. vis. prof. law, 2005. Author: The Law of Obscenity, 1976, Free Speech: A Philosophical Enquiry, 1982 (ABA cert. merit 1983), Supplements to Gunther Constitutional Law, 1983-96, Playing by the Rules: A Philosophical Examination of Rule Based Decision-Making in Law and Life, 1991, The First Amendment: A Reader, 1992, 2d edit., 1995, The Philosophy of Law, 1995, Profiles, Probabilities and Sterotypes, 2003; editor: Legal Theory, 1995-2000; contbr. articles to profl. jours. Mem. Atty. Gen.'s Commn. on Pornography, 1985-86. Served with Mass. Army N.G., 1970-71. NEH fellow, summer 1980, Guggenheim fellow, 2001-02. Fellow Am. Acad. Arts and Scis., Radcliffe Inst. Adv. Studies; mem. Am. Philos. Assn. (chair com. philosophy and law 2006-), Am. Soc. Polit. and Legal Philosophy (v.p. 1996-99), Assn. Am. Law Schs. (chmn. sect. constl. law 1984-86). Office: Kennedy Sch of Govt Harvard U Cambridge MA 02138 Home Phone: 617-354-6967; Office Phone: 617-495-8737. Business E-Mail: fred_schauer@harvard.edu.

SCHAUER, THOMAS ALFRED, insurance company executive; b. Canton, Ohio, Dec. 24, 1927; s. Alfred T. and Marie A. (Luthi) S.; m. Joanne Alice Fay, Oct. 30, 1954; children: Alan, John, David, Susan, William. BSc, Ohio State U., 1950. With Ind. Ins. Svc. Corp., 1964—, Ind. Benefit Svc. Corp., 1984—2003. Dir. Bank One, Akron, N.A., Ohio, 1991-97, mem. adv. bd., 1997-2000. Chmn. Joint Hosp. Blood Com., 1974; bd. dirs. McKinley Life Ins. Co., 1991-95; bd. dirs. Better Bus. Bur., Canton, 1970-81, chmn., 1979-80; bd. dirs. area YMCA, 1974-92, v.p., 1975-82, pres., 1982-84; trustee Canton Cemetery Assn., 1988-91, Stark County Blue Coats, 1987-, Plain Local Schs. Found., 2004-; bd. dirs. Hosp. Bur. Ctrl. Stark County, 1972-78; vice chmn. bd. Aultman Hosp., 1981-84, chmn., 1984-87; chmn. Aultman Health Svcs. Assn., 1990-93; pres. Aultman Hosp. Found., 1987-90, trustee, 1971-98, trustee emeritus, 1998—; pres. Schauer Family Fund, Inc., 1968—; bd. dirs. United Way, 1974-84, pres., 1976-78; mem. distbn. com. Stark County Found., 1977-87, chmn. distbn. com., 1984-87, dir. Dime Bank, Canton, 1965-72, First Nat. Bank of Canton/Ctrl. Trust Co. NE Ohio, N.A., 1972-91; adv. bd. Malone Coll., 1979-92; trustee Kent State U., 1980-88, trustee emeritus, 1988—, N.E. Ohio Univs. Coll. Medicine, 1983-88; past trustee Canton Urban League, Boys Village, Smithville, Ohio, Canton Art Inst., Buckeye Coun. Boy Scouts Am. With USN, 1946-48. Recipient gold key award United Way Ctrl. Stark County, 1981, award of merit Canton C. of C., 1984, red triangle award Canton Area YMCA, 1985. Mem. Chartered Ins. Inst. London, Nat. Assn. Mfg., Am. Soc. CPCUs, Am. Soc. CLUs, Assn., Advanced Life Underwriters, Am. Risk and Ins. Assn., Am. Soc. Pension Actuaries, Stark County Accident and Health Underwriters (past pres.), Canton Club (past pres.), Brookside Country Club, Atwood Yacht Club. Home: 1756 Dunbarton Ave NW Canton OH 44708-1807 Office: Millennium Ctr 200 Market Ave N Ste 100 Canton OH 44702 E-mail: tomschauer@att.net.

SCHAUF, VICTORIA, pediatrician, educator; b. NYC, Feb. 17, 1943; d. Maurice J. and Ruth H. (Baker) Bisson; m. Michael Delaney; 2 children. BS in Microbiology with honors, U. Chgo., 1965, MD with honors, 1969. Intern in pediat. U. Chgo. Hosp., 1969—70; resident in pediat. Sinai Hosp. of Balt., 1970—71; chief resident pediat. Children's Hosp. Nat. Med. Ctr., Washington, 1971—72; rsch. trainee NIH, Bethesda, Md., 1972; adj. asst. prof. microbiology Rush Med. Coll., Chgo., 1972—74; prof. pediat., head pediatric infectious diseases U. Ill., Chgo., 1974—84; med. officer FDA, Rockville, Md., 1984—86; chmn. dept. pediat. Nassau County Med. Ctr., East Meadow, NY, 1986—90; prof. pediat. SUNY, Stony Brook, 1987—94; pvt. practice, 1995—; chief pediatric svcs. Ridgecrest Regional Hosp., 2005—. Vis. prof. Rockefeller U., 1990-92; mem. vis. faculty Chiang Mai (Thailand) U., 1978; mem. ad hoc com. study sects. NIH, Bethesda, 1981-82; bd. dirs. Pearl Stetler Rsch. Found., Chgo., 1982-84; cons. FDA, 1987-88, 93-95, Can. Bur. Human Prescription Drugs, Ottawa, 1990-2004, Biotech. Investors, 1993-95, Calif. Children's Svcs., 2005—; course dir. pediat. infectious diseases rev. course Cornell U. Med. Coll., N.Y.C., 1994, faculty, 1995. Co-author: Pediatric Infectious Diseases: A Comprehensive Guide to the Subspecialty, 1997; prodr. radio and TV programs in field; contbr. articles to profl. jours., chpts. to books. Vol. physician Cook County Hosp., Chgo., 1974-84; mem. adv. com. Nat. Hansen's Disease Ctr., La., 1986, Nassau County Day Care Coun., N.Y., 1988-90; mem. adv. bd. Surg. Aid to Children of World, N.Y., 1986-90; comm., sec. Kern County Children and Families Commn., 1999-2002; sec., bd. dirs. Indian Wells Valley Cmty. Found., 2001-. Am. Lung Assn. grantee U. Ill., 1977; recipient contract NIH, U. Ill., 1978-81, grantee, 1979-84. Fellow Infectious Diseases Soc. Am.; mem. Pediatric Infectious Diseases Soc. (exec. bd.), Soc. Pediatric Rsch., Am. Pediatric Soc., AAAS, Am. Soc. Microbiology, Am. Acad. Pediat., Phi Beta Kappa, Alpha Omega Alpha. Avocation: walking. Home Phone: 760-384-2399; Office Phone: 760-371-2128. Business E-Mail: vschauf@pol.net.

SCHAUMBER, PETER CAREY, federal agency administrator; b. NYC, May 29, 1942; m. Kathleen Charbonnet; children: Kathleen, Drew, Alexandra. BA, Georgetown U., 1964; JD, Georgetown U. Law Ctr., 1968. Asst. corp. counsel Dist. of Columbia; asst. US atty. DC US Dept. Justice; sr. trial atty., assoc. dir. law dept. divsn., Office Comptr. of the Currency US Dept. Treasury; ptnr., dir. litigation dept. Colton & Boykin P.C., 1980—87; of counsel Wickwire Gavin, 1987—93; adj. prof. law Nat. Law Ctr George Washington U.; mem. NLRB, 2002—. Adj. prof. Georgetown U. Sch. Bus. Office: NLRB 1099 14th St NW Washington DC 20570-0001

SCHAUMBURG, HERBERT HOWARD, neurology educator; b. Houston, Nov. 6, 1932; m. Joanna Jane Austin; children: Barnabas Paul, Kristin Elizabeth. AB cum laude, Harvard Coll., 1956; MD, Washington U., 1960. Instr. in neurology Albert Einstein Coll. of Medicine, NYC, 1964-67, asst. prof. neurology, 1967-69, assoc. prof. neurology, 1972-76, prof., 1976—, vice chmn., 1977-84, acting chmn., 1984-86, chmn., 1986—; instr. pathology Harvard Med. Sch., Boston, 1969-71. Mem. Am. Acad. Neurology, Am. Assn. Neuropathologists, Am. Neurol. Assn., Soc. Toxicology, Soc. Neurosci. Home: 616 King Ave City Island Bronx NY 10464 Office: Albert Einstein Coll Medicine 1300 Morris Park Ave Bronx NY 10461-1926 Home Phone: 718-885-1261; Office Phone: 718-430-2002. Business E-Mail: schaumb@aecom.yu.edu.

SCHAUPP, JOAN POMPROWITZ, trucking executive, writer; b. Green Bay, Wis., Sept. 29, 1932; d. Joseph and Helen Elizabeth (VanderLinden) Pomprowitz; m. Robert James Schaupp, Sept. 4, 1956; children: Margaret Schaupp Siebert, Frederick, John Robert, Elizabeth Schaupp Sidles. BS cum laude, U. Wis., 1954; cert. in theology, St. Norbert Coll. Theol. Inst., 1979; MA, U. Wis., Green Bay, 1982; DMin, Grad. Theol. Found., 1996. Woman's editor Green Bay Press-Gazette, 1955-56; freelance writer Green Bay, 1957-75; sec.-treas., dir. L.C.L. Transit Co., Green Bay, 1962-70; chmn., dir. P & S Investment Co., Green Bay, 1982—, mgmt. cons., 1984-89, dir. strategic planning, 1992, vice chmn., 1994—. Pres. The Manna Co., Green Bay, 1992—; adv. com. Women's Ctr. St. Norbert Coll., 1999—; chmn. P&S Investment Co., 2004. Author: Jesus Was a Teenager, 1972, Woman Image of Holy Spirit, 1975 (Thomas More Book award), Elohim: A Search for a Symbol for Human Fulfillment, 1995. Master gardener De Pere Beautification Com., Wis., 1991-92; design cons. Nat. Fedn. Grden Clubs, 2004; lector St. Francis Xavier Cathedral, Green Bay, 1991-92. Recipient Ambassador award, St. Norbert Coll., 1997, Disting. Svc. award, 2004, Disting. Citizenship award, St. Norbert Coll. Alumni Assn., 2004. Mem.: Nat. Press Club, Nat. Fedn. Press Women, Am. Acad. Religion, Franciscan Internat., Secular Franciscan Order (vice min. Assumption Province 1991—92), Equestrian Order of the Holy Sepulchre Jerusalem (lady grand cross), Soc. Bibl. Lit. Avocations: gardening, walking, swimming.

SCHAUT, JOSEPH WILLIAM, retired bank executive; b. Cleve., May 30, 1928; s. Francis Xavier and Emma Gertrude (Urmann) S.; m. Susan Stiver, Apr. 23, 1955; children: Deborah Anne Schaut Payne, Gregory F., Mary Theresa Schaut Bentley, Michael J. B in Social Sci. in Econs., Georgetown U., 1950, JD, 1953. Bar: D.C. 1953, U.S. Mil. Ct. Appeals 1953, U.S. Dist. Ct. D.C. 1953, U.S. Ct. Appeals (D.C. cir.) 1953, Ohio 1954. Tax analyst Republic Steel Corp., Cleve., 1953-60, asst. to sec., 1960—67, asst. sec., 1967—81, dir. corp. properties, 1976—84, corp. sec., 1981—84; bus. cons., 1984-85; sr. trust officer AmeriTrust Co. Nat. Assn., 1986-92; sr. trust officer Soc. Nat. Bank, Cleve., 1992-93, v.p., 1993-96, Mellon Bank F.S.B., 1996-98; ret., 1998. Col. ret. USAR, 1950—78. Recipient award Silver Beaver Greater Cleve. Coun., Boy Scouts Am., 1975. Mem. Am. Soc. Corp. Secs. (dir. 1976-79), Ohio State Bar Assn., Greater Cleve. Growth Assn., Delta Theta Phi, Pi Gamma Mu. Roman Catholic.

SCHECHNER, RICHARD, theater director, educator; b. Newark, Aug. 23, 1934; s. Sheridan and Selma Sophia (Schwarz) S.; m. Carol Martin; children: Samuel MacIntosh, Sophia Martin. BA, Cornell U., 1956; postgrad., Johns Hopkins U., 1957; MA, State U. Iowa, 1958; PhD, Tulane U., 1962. Asst. prof. theatre Tulane U., 1962-66, assoc. prof., 1966-67; prof. performance studies NYU, 1967-91, Univ. prof., 1991—; co-founder, co-dir. New Orleans Group, 1965-67; founder, dir. Performance Group, NYC, 1967-80; founder, artistic dir. East Coast Artists, 1991—; Andrew H. White prof.-at-large Cornell U., 1999—2005; sr. fellow Ctr. for Cultural Sociology, Yale U., 2004—. Hon. prof. Shanghai Theatre Acad., 1995—; prof. titular adj. Instituto Superior de Arte, Havana, Cuba; bd. dirs. Theatre Comms. Group, 1977-78; advisor Internat. Theatre Inst., 1975-77, Ctr. Performance Rsch., Aberwrystwich, Wales, 1993-97; pres. Bunch of Exptl. Theatres, 1975, 77, Fulbright Theatre Discipline Com., 1988-91. Author: Public Domain, 1968, Environmental Theater, 1973 (with others) Theatres, Spaces, Environments, 1975, Essays on Performance Theory, 1977, 2d edit. 1988, 3d edit., 2003, (with others) Makbeth, 1977, The End of Humanism, 1982, Performative Circumstances, 1983, Betweeen Theater and Anthropology, 1985, (with Samuel MacIntosh-Schechner) The Engleburt Stories: North to the Tropics, 1987, The Future of Ritual, 1993, Performance Studies-An Introduction, 2002, 2d edit., 2006, Over, Under and Around, 2004, (with others) Yokastas, 2003; editor: Dionysus in 69, 1970; adv. editor: Asian Theatre Jour., 1985-; co-editor: Free Southern Theater, 1968, Ritual, Play, and Performance, 1976, By Means of Performance, 1990; gen. editor: (series) Worlds of Performance, 1993-2007, (with Lisa Wolford) Grotowski Sourcebook, 1997, (with Carol Martin) Enactments, 2005-; editor: The Drama Rev., 1962-69, 85—, contbg. editor, 1971-85; adv. editor Jour. Ritual Studies, 1987—, Asian Theatre Jour., 1985-; dir. Dionysus in 69, 1968, Macbeth, 1969, Commune, 1970, The Tooth of Crime, 1972, Mother Courage, 1975, The Marilyn Project, 1975, Oedipus, 1977, Cops, 1978, The Balcony, 1979, The Red Snake, 1981, Richard's Lear, 1981, The Cherry Orchard, 1983, Prometheus Project, 1985, Don Juan, 1987, Tomorrow He'll Be Out of the Mountains, 1989, Ma Rainey's Black Bottom, 1992, Faust/Gastronome, 1993, The Oresteia, 1995, Three Sisters, 1997, Hamlet, 1999, Waiting for Godot, 2002, Yokastas, 2003, Yokastas Redux, 2005, Hamlet: That is The Question Shanghai, 2007. Served with AUS, 1958-60. Recipient Modello prize, 1985, Contbns. to Theatre Spl. award New England Theatre Conf., 1991, Work in Theatre award Towson State U., 1991, Lifetime Achievement award Performance Studies Internat., 2002; grantee John D. Rockefeller 3d Fund, 1971-72, 76, Asian Cultural Coun., 1988, 95; Guggenheim fellow, 1976, Fulbright fellow, 1976, 83, N.Y. Inst. Humanities fellow, 1987-94, NEH sr. rsch. fellow, 1988, Humanities fellow Princeton U., 1992, Am. Inst. Indian Studies fellow, 1997, Montgomery fellow Dartmouth Coll., 1998, Am. Coun. Learned Socs. fellow, 2005, Ctrl. Sch. Speech and Drama fellow, London, 2005. Office: NYU 721 Broadway 6th Fl Washington Sq New York NY 10003 Office Phone: 212-998-1638. Business E-Mail: rs4@nyu.edu.

SCHECHTER, ARTHUR LOUIS, lawyer; b. Rosenberg, Tex., Dec. 6, 1939; s. Morris and Helen (Brilling) S.; m. Joyce Proler, Aug. 26, 1965; children: Leslie Schechter Karpas, Jennifer Schechter Rosen. BA, U. Tex., 1962, JD, 1964; postgrad., U. Houston, 1964-65. Bar: Tex. 1964, U.S. Dist. Ct. (ea. and so. dists.) Tex. 1966, U.S. Ct. Appeals (5th cir.), U.S. Supreme Ct. 1976; cert. Tex. Bd. Legal Specialization to Personal Injury Trial Law, 1964-. Pres. Arthur L. Schechter P.C., Houston, 1992-94, Schechter & Marshall, Houston, 1994-96; amb. U.S. to Commonwealth Bahamas, 1998-2000; atty. Schechter, McElwee & Shaffer, LLP, Houston, 2001—05; shareholder Greenberg Traurig, LLP, Houston, 2005—06; sr. counsel Schechter McElwee Shaffer & Harris LLP, Houston, 2006—. Mediator Arthur Schechter Group, 2006—; spkr. Marine Law Sem., 1983; spkr. in field. Contbr. articles to profl. jours. Bd. dirs. Theatre Under the Stars, Houston, 1972—78, Congregation Beth Israel, Houston, 1972—84, pres., 1982—84; bd. dirs. Inst. Internat. Edn., 1996—98, S.E.A.R.C.H., 1996—98; pres. Am. Jewish Com., Houston, 1982—84, chmn. fgn. rels. com., chmn. United Jewish Campaign exec. com., chmn., 1993—94; pres. Jewish Fedn. Ctr. Houston, 1994—96; mem. Deans Coun. U. Tex. Law Sch.; chmn. bd. Harris County Met. Transit Authority, 2002—04; chmn. internat. travelor task force Mayor of Houston, 2005; mng. trustee mem. fin. com. Dem. Nat. Com., 1992, fin. chmn. Tex. Clinton/Gore '96; vice chmn. Clinton/Gore Jewish Leadership Coun., 1996; v.p. exec. com. Nat. Jewish Dem. Coun., 1992, chmn., 2004—06; mem. Leadership Ctr. Dem. Senatorial Campaign Com.; trustee mem. Kerry/Edwards and Dem. Nat. Com.; fin. coun. Nat. Dem. Orgn., 1979; chmn. bd. Met. Transit Authority of Harris County, 2002—04; bd. dirs. U. Tex. Med. Sch. Named a Tex. Super Lawyer, 2006; named one of Houston's Most Fascinating Mems. of the Med. Cmty., 2003; recipient Career and Recovery Resources Barrier Breaker award, United Way Agy., 2003, Search's Outstanding Leadership award, 2003, Israel Bonds Nat. Leadership award, 2004, Lifetime Achievement award, NJDC, 2006, Nat. Jewish Dem. Coun., 2006, Starlight Leadership award, Coun. of Jewish Women, 2006. Home: 19A West Ln Houston TX 77019-1007 Office Phone: 713-757-7811. Personal E-mail: aschechter@qzip.net. Business E-Mail: aschechter@smslegal.com.

SCHECHTER, DANIEL SCOTT, child and adolescent psychiatrist, researcher; b. Miami Beach, Fla., Aug. 15, 1962; s. Harold and Evelyn Iris (Miller) Schechter; m. Christine Breede, June 25, 1996; 1 child, Jan Nikolai Breede-Schechter. BA summa cum laude, Columbia Coll., 1983; MA in Music Theory, Composition, Columbia Grad. Sch. Arts and Sci., 1987; MD, Columbia Coll., 1991. Diplomate Am. Bd. Psychiatry. Med. intern NY Presbyn. Hosp., NYC, 1992—93, clin. fellow child psychiatry, 1996—99, NY State Psychiat. Inst., resident in psychiatry, 1993—96; NIMH T-32 rsch. fellow Columbia U., NYC, Psychol. U., NYC, 1999—2002; med. dir. Infant-Family Svc., NY Pub. Health, NYC, 1998—; asst. prof. clin. psychiatry in pediat. Columbia Coll. P & S, NYC, 2003—. Mem. bd. dirs. NY Zero to Three Network, NYC, 2004—; mem. adv. bd. Columbia Head Start Program, NYC, 2004—. Editor, contbr. September 11: Trauma and Human Bonds, 2003, revised edit., 2004. Mem. NYC Dept. Health and Mental Hygiene Strategic Working Group on Early Childhood Mental Devel., 2003—; early childhood mental health adv. NYC Dept. Health and Early Childhood Mental Hygiene Strategic Working Group, 2003—. Recipient K-23 award, NIMH, Washington, 2003, Significant Contbr. award, Internat. Psychoanalytical Assn., 2005; grantee, 2000, 2002, 2005; Solnit fellow, Zero to Three Nat. Ctr., Washington, 2001, Ruane scholar, Columbia U., 2003. Mem.: APA, Am. Acad. Child Adolescent Psychiatry (mem. infancy com., co-chair subcom. on practice parameters 2003—, Presdl. scholar 1999, Pilot Rsch. award 2001). Avocations: cello, languages. Office: Columbia U NY State Psychiat Inst Unit 40 Rm 6407 1051 Riverside Dr New York NY 10032 also: 1 Milligan Pl 1F New York NY 10011 Home Phone: 212-463-0702.

SCHECHTER, NAOMI R., oncologist; d. Frederick Gary and Roberta Phyllis Schechter; m. Alex Sverdlik, Feb. 14, 1999; children: Elana Rose Sverdlik, Robyn Pearl Sverdlik. BS in Biol. Scis., Stanford U., Palo Alto, Calif., 1988, BA in Psychology, 1988; MD, U. Calif., San Francisco, 1993.

Intern Northshore U. Hosp., Meml. Sloan Kettering Cancer Ctr., NYC, 1993—94; resident Meml. Sloan Kettering Cancer Ctr., 1994—96, 1997—98; clin. instr. U. Tex., MD Anderson Cancer Ctr., Houston, 1998—99, asst. prof., 1999—2004; asst. prof. clin. radiation oncology U. Calif., San Francisco, 2004—06, assoc. prof. clin. radiation oncology, 2006—. Adj. asst. prof. radiation oncology U. Tex., MD Anderson Cancer Ctr., Sch. Health Scis., 2003—04, attending radiation oncology head & neck svc., 1998—2002, attending radiation oncology breast svc., 2002—04; attending radiation oncology head & neck and breast svcs. U. Calif., 2004—; presenter in field. Grantee, Cellpoint LLC, 2001—03, Imclone Sys., 2002—03; Mortimer Lacher fellow, Meml. Sloan Kettering Cancer Ctr., 1996—97. Mem.: Calif. Radiol. Soc., Am. Radium Soc., Am. Soc. Therapeutic Radiology, Am. Coll. Radiology, Stanford Alumni Assn. Avocation: painting. Office: U Calif 1600 Divisadero Ste H1013 San Francisco CA 94143

SCHECHTER, ROBERT SAMUEL, chemical engineer, educator; b. Houston, Feb. 26, 1929; s. Morris S. and Helen Ruth Schechter; m. Mary Ethel Rosenberg, Feb. 15, 1953; children: Richard Martin, Alan Lawrence (dec.), Geoffrey Louis. BS in Chem. Engring, Tex. A&M U., 1950; PhD in Chem. Engring, U. Minn., 1956. Registered profl. engr., Tex. Asst. prof. chem. engring. U. Tex. at Austin, 1956-60, assoc. prof., 1960-63, prof., 1963—; adminstrv. dir. Ctr. Statis. Mechs. and Thermodynamics, 1968-72, chmn. dept. chem. engring., 1970-73, chmn. petroleum engring., 1975-78, E.J. Cockrell, Jr. prof. chem. and petroleum engring., 1975-81, Dula and Ernie Cockrell prof. engring., 1981-83, Getty prof. engring., 1984-85, Getty Oil Centennial chair in Petroleum Engring., 1985-89, W.A. (Monty) Moncrief Centennial Endowed chair in Petroleum Engring., 1989-97; prof. emeritus U. Tex., 1997. Vis. prof. U. Edinburgh, Scotland, 1965-66; Disting. vis. prof. U. Kans., spring 1968; vis. prof. U. Brussels, 1969; Disting. Lindsay lectr. Tex. A&M U., 1993; cons. in field. Author: Variational Method in Engineering, 1967, (with G.S.G. Beveridge) Optimization: Theory and Practice, 1970, Adventures in Fortran Programming, 1975, (with B.B. Williams and J.L. Gidley) Acidizing Monograph, 1979, (with D.D. Shah) Enhanced Oil Recovery by Surfactants and Polymers, 1979; (with Maurice Bourrel) Microemulsions and Related Systems, 1988, Oil Well Stimulation, 1991; contbr. (with D.D. Shah) numerous articles to profl. jours. Served to 1st lt., Chem. Corps AUS, 1951-53. Decorated Chevalier Order Palmes Academique, 1978; recipient Outstanding Teaching award U. Tex., 1969, Outstanding Paper award, 1973, Gen. Dynamics award for Excellence in Engring. Teaching, Gen. Dynamics Corp., 1987, Sr. Rsch. award Engring. Rsch. Coun. of Am. Soc. Engring. Educators, 1991. Mem. AIME (Industry Edn. award 1998), AIChE (Founders award 1998), Am. Chem. Soc., Soc. Petroleum Engrs. (John Franklin Carll award 1994, Improved Oil Recovery Pioneer 1996), Nat. Acad. Engrs., Sigma Xi, Tau Beta Pi. Achievements include developing methods of measuring surface viscosity and ultra low inter-facial tensions; discovering instability of thermal diffusion. Home: 4700 Ridge Oak Dr Austin TX 78731-4724 Office: U Tex Dept Petroleum & Geosystems Austin TX 78712 Office Phone: 512-471-3245. Business E-Mail: rsschechter@mail.utexas.edu.

SCHECHTERMAN, LAWRENCE, lawyer, chef, business consultant; b. Elizabeth, NJ, June 23, 1943; s. Josef and Sylvia (Berger) S.; children: Jill Laura, Danielle Sara, Gregory Jared. BA, U. Miami, Fla., 1966; JD, Suffolk U., 1969; LLM, NYU, 1973; AS in Culinary Arts, Art Inst. Ft. Lauderdale, 2001. Tax assoc. Coopers & Lybrand, NYC, 1969-70; assoc. Bendit, Weinstock & Sharbaugh, Newark, 1970-72; pvt. practice East Brunswick, NJ, 1972-81; gen. counsel Equinox Solar, Inc., Miami, 1981-83; mem. Lawrence Schechterman, P.A., Boca Raton, Fla., 1983—94; pres. Ocean Cons. Group divsn. Securities Arbitration Recovery, Inc., Boca Raton, 1993-97; pvt. chef Delray Beach, Fla., 2000—; bridgetender C&S Engring., Boca Raton, Fla., 2006—. Author: In the Mood with Food, A Bachelor's Guide to Wooing Her with Food, 1998, 2000, 01, 07; (poetry) New Dimensions: An Anthology of American Poetry, 1967, The Harmony of Silence, 2000, Touched by Grace, 1999, Touched by Love, 1999, Surrounded By Dreams, 1998, A Trusting Heart, 2000; contbr. articles to profl. jours. Mem. coun. Twp. of East Brunswick, NJ, 1976—80; pres. B'nai Torah Congregation of Boca Raton Inc., 1987—89, trustee, 1989—91. Mem.: B'nai B'rith (mens lodge no. 2935 charter pres., co-founder 1973—74). Office: 13845 Via Vittoria Delray Beach FL 33446-3729

SCHECHTMAN, SAUL, conductor; b. Winchester, Conn., Sept. 4, 1924; s. Isidore Schechtman and Clara Goodman; m. Carolyn Raney, July 31, 1952; children: Carol, Julia. BA, Bklyn. Coll., 1947; post grad., Juilliard Sch. of Music, NYC, 1949. Music dir. Bronx Symphony Orch., NYC, 1953—56; conductor, music dir. Omnibus Program (CBS), NYC, 1954—57; music dir. Bergen Philharmonic, Teaneck, NJ, 1956—60, Carnival (Broadway show), NYC, 1961—63, Hello Dolly, NYC, 1966—70, Orch. Piccola, Balt., 1976—80; kapellmeister Theatre Oberhausen, Oberhausen, Germany, 1981—84. Composer: Auntie Mame, 1956, Diaspora variations, 1989, German Radio Orchs., 1990—94; dir.: (plays) Kiss Me Kate, 1958, How To Succeed in Business, 1963—64, My Fair Lady, 1960. Pvt. 1st class US Army, 1943—46, Europe. Fellowship in orch. conducting, Juilliard Sch. of Music, 1949—51. Mem.: Am. Soc. Composers, Authors and Publishers. Avocation: tennis. Home: 134 Cathedral Ave Hempstead NY 11550

SCHECK, BARRY C., legal association administrator, educator; b. Queens, NY, Sept. 19, 1949; BS, Yale U., 1971; JD, U. Calif., Berkeley, 1974. Bar: N.Y. 1974. Staff atty. Legal Aid Soc. NYC, 1974—77; prof. Law, dir. Clin. Legal Edn., Trial Advocacy Programs Benjamin N. Cardozo Sch. Law, Yeshiva U., NYC, 1977—, dir. Jacob Burns Ctr. for Study of Law and Ethics, 1977—, lawyer, dir. Innocence Project, 1992—. Former faculty mem. Nat. Inst. Trial Advocacy and Def. Coun.; tchr., organizer trial advocacy programs numerous pub. defender offices, bas assns. and law firms; commn. mem. NY State Commn. on Forensic Sci.; lectr. in field. Co-author: Raising and Litigating Claims of Electronic Surveillance, Actual Innocence: Five Days to Execution and Other Dispatches from the Wrongly Convicted; contbr. articles to profl. jours. Commr. NY Forensic Sci. Rev. Bd.; co-founder, co-dir. Innocence Project, 1992—; bd. dir. Nat. Inst. of Justice's Commn. on the Future of DNA Evidence, 1999. Named one of 100 Most Influential Lawyers, Nat. Law Jour., 2006. Mem.: Assn. Bar NYC (com. on criminal cts.), Nat. Assn. of Criminal Defense Lawyers (life; pres., bd. dirs., co-chair, DNA Task Force, Most Outstanding Criminal Def. Lawyer in Am., Robert C. Heeney award 1996). Office: Innocence Project Benjamin N Cardozo Sch Law 55 5th Ave New York NY 10003-4301 Address: Nat Assn of Criminal Defense Lawyers 1150 18th St NW Ste 950 Washington DC 20036 Fax: 202-872-8690. E-mail: barry@nacdl.org. *

SCHECTER, ARNOLD JOEL, public health physician, researcher; b. Chgo., Dec. 1, 1934; s. Benjamin and Leonore Natalie (Lyon) S.; m. Martha-Jean Berenson, Feb. 14, 1964; children: Benjamin, David, Anna. BA in Liberal Arts, U. Chgo., 1954, BS in Physiology-Neurophysiology, 1957; MD, Howard U., 1962; MPH, Columbia U., 1975. Diplomate Am. Coll. Preventive Medicine; med. lic., Ky., N.Y., N.J., N.C. Postdoc. dept. anatomy Harvard Med. Sch., Boston, 1962—64; instr. dept. medicine Mass. Gen. Hosp., Harvard Med. Sch., Boston, 1964-65; intern Beth Israel Hosp., Boston, 1966; gen. practitioner, sr. aviation med. examiner West Point, Ky., 1969-70; dir. inpatient rehab. ctr., drug and alcohol rehab. program Region Eight Mental Health and Mental Retardation Bd., Inc., Louisville, 1971-72; asst. prof. dept. psychiatry, divisional drug and alcohol abuse SUNY Downstate Med. Ctr., Bklyn., 1973-75; clin. assoc. prof. dept. preventive medicine N.J. Med. Sch., Newark, 1975-79; prof. dept. preventive medicine SUNY, Binghamton, 1979—98; prof. environ. scis. U. Tex. Sch. Pub. Health, Dallas, 1999—; pres. Zumwalt Inst. for Environ. Health Inc., 1996—. Spl. expert Nat. Inst. Environ. Health Scis. NIH, 1997—98; cons. U.S. EPA, Washington, 1985—86, Washington, 1999—2000, WHO, 1986—90; sci. peer reviewer dioxin U.S. EPA, 1995, 2000; peer reviewer A.T.S.D.R. of C.D.C., 1995—2005; dir. clin. rsch. in drug abuse, coord., faculty mem. Career Tchr. Tng. Ctr., SUNY Downstate, 1972—75; assoc. dir. office primary health care edn., office of the dean NJ Med. Sch., 1976—79; advisor Environ. Def. Fund, 1991—92, Nat. Vets. Legal Svcs. Project, 1991—92; co-founder assoc. editor Am. Jour. Drug and Alcohol Abuse, NYC, 1973—78, editl. bd., 1978—86; editl. adv. bd. Substance and Alcohol Actions/Misuse, Elmsford, NY, 1979—85; adj. prof. epidemiology U. N.C. Sch. Pub. Health, 1998—2004; adj. prof. occupl. medicine Duke Med. Ctr., 1998—99. Editor: Rehabilitation Aspects of Drug Dependence, 1977, Treatment Aspects of Drug Dependence, 1978, Biomedical Issues in Drug Abuse, 1981, Sociological Issues in Drug Abuse, 1981, Dioxins and Health, 1994; sr. editor: 2d edit., 2003; editor: Maxcy Rosenau Last Public Health and Preventive Medicine, 14th edit., 1998, 15th edit., 2007; co-editor (with H. Alksne, E. Kaufman): Drug Abuse: Modern Trends, Issues and Perspectives, 1978, Critical Concerns in the Field of Drug Abuse, 1978; contbr. over 300 articles to profl. jours. Maj., physician MC US Army, 1967-69. Recipient Pacesetter award Commonwealth Mass., 1990. Fellow: ACP, Am. Coll. Occupl. and Environ. Medicine, Am. Coll. Preventive Medicine; mem.: AAAS, APHA (chair Vietnam caucus), Soc. Epidemiology Rsch., Tex. Pub. Health Assn., Soc. Epidemiologic Rsch., Am. Occupl. and Environ. Medicine Assn., Am. Coll. Epidemiology. Achievements include discovery of PBDE brominated flame retardant contamination in breast milk of all US mothers tested, and that these levels as well as blood and food are highest in the world; PCB transformer fires can lead to contamination of buildings by dioxins; Agent Orange elevated dioxin body burden exists decades after exposure in Vietnamese and in American Vietnam Veterans; dioxin contamination of body tissues of general population of the US; dioxin hot spots in Vietnam with current contamination of Vietnamese by contaminated food; development of congener specific tissue dioxin analysis as biomarker for dioxin exposure; developed naltrexone, a narcotic antagonist in rehabilitation of opiate addicts. Home: 16606 Loch Maree Ln Dallas TX 75248-1711 Office: U Tex Sch Pub Health 6011 Harry Hines Blvd Dallas TX 75248 Personal E-mail: ajschecter@aol.com. Business E-Mail: arnold.schecter@utsouthwestern.edu.

SCHECTER, WILLIAM H., bank executive; B in Fin., Ohio State U., Columbus; grad., Stonier Grad. Sch. Banking, 1975. Sr. v.p. corp. banking BancOhio, Nat. City Corp., Cleve., 1984, pres. Nat. Fin. Corp., bd. dirs., chmn. emeritus Nat. City Equity Ptnrs., Inc., sr. v.p., sr. advisor, 1989—. Bd. dirs. Boykin Lodging Co. Bd. dirs. Menorah Park. Office: Nat City Corp Nat City Ctr 1900 E 9th St Cleveland OH 44114-3484 Office Phone: 216-222-2000. *

SCHECTMAN, STEPHEN BARRY, pharmaceutical executive; b. Washington, Oct. 20, 1947; s. Samuel and Rae (Tarnef) S.; m. Barbara L. Butcher, Sept. 10, 1969 (div. May 1994); children: Christopher, Matthew. BS, Randolph Macon Coll., 1970; postgrad., U. Tenn., 1974. Pres., CEO Medvac Corp., NYC, 1993-94; spl. cons. Medco Containment Svcs., Montvale, NJ, 1991-93; ptnr. Hudson BioCapital Corp., NYC, 1993-96; sr. dir. Schering-Plough Pharms., Kenilworth, NJ, 1996—2003; v.p. Schering My Health Solutions, Inc., Kenilworth, 2000—03; sr. v.p. strategy CRI, LA, 2003—; pres. NewHealth Solutions Group, N.J. and Calif., 2003; pres., COO Impact Med. Solutions, Inc., Tustin, Calif., 2004—; mng. ptnr. New Health Solutions Group, LLC, Cedar Knolls, NJ, 2003—. Author (with others) Biomedical Innovation, 1980. Fellowship NIMH, NIH, 1969-73, postgrad. fellowship dept. physiology Georgetown U. Sch. of Medicine, 1975-76. Mem. AAAS, N.Y. Acad. Scis., Beta Beta Beta. Jewish. Office: NewHealth Solutions Group LLC 210 Malapardis Rd Ste B2 Cedar Knolls NJ 07927 Office Phone: 973-292-9645. Personal E-mail: medicine55@hotmail.com. Business E-Mail: nhsgllc@hotmail.com.

SCHEEDER, LOUIS, theater producer, director, educator; b. NYC, Dec. 26, 1946; s. Louis W. and Julia H. (Callery) S. BA in English Lit., Georgetown U., 1968; postgrad., Sch. of Arts, Columbia U., 1968-69; MA in Performance Studies, NYU, 1995, PhD in Performance Studies, 2004. Founder, dir. The Classical Studio Tisch Sch. of the Arts, NYU, 1991—, Master Tchr., 1995—2004, assoc. arts prof., 2004—06, arts prof., 2006—, assoc. dean faculty, 2006—. Dir. Shakespeare Ensemble, NYU Tisch Sch. of the Arts, 1989-90; mem. adv. council Nat. Com. on Arts and Edn., 1977-82; mem. D.C. Commn. on Arts and Humanities, 1976-80; bd. advs. New Playwrights' Theatre of Washington, 1975-82; asst. stage mgr. Arena Stage, Washington, 1969-70; assoc. artistic dir., dir., Folger Theatre Group, Washington, 1971-73, dir. producer, 1973-81; cons. Ctr. for Renaissance and Baroque Studies U. Md., 1984-91; asst. dir. Royal Shakespeare Co. Stratford-Upon-Avon, Eng., 1988. Dir., prodr. plays including Creeps (Am. premiere), 1973, The Farm (Am. premiere), 1974, The Collected Works of Billy the Kid (Am. premiere), 1975, Henry V, 1976, The Fool (Am. premiere), 1976, Mummer's End (world premiere), 1977, Teeth 'n' Smiles (Am. premiere), 1977, Two Gentlemen of Verona, 1977, Mackerel (world premiere), 1978, Black Elk Speaks (tour), 1978, Richard III, 1978, Whose Life Is It Anyway? (Am. premiere), 1978, Richard II, 1978, As You Like It, 1979, Custer (Kennedy Ctr.), 1979, Charlie and Algernon (Kennedy Ctr.), 1980, Crossing Niagara (Am. premiere), 1981, Love's Labour's Lost, 1981; also dir. Broadway, Off Broadway, regional prodns. including (Broadway) Charlie and Algernon, 1980, (Off Broadway) Creeps, 1973, Passover, 1986, (Off-Off-Broadway) The Gettysburg Sound Bite, 1989, Brunch at Trudy and Paul's, 1990, The Christmas Rules, 1991, The Monkey Business, 1992, Mankynde, N.Y Fringe Festival, 2005; dir. All's Well That Ends Well, 1990; dance: dir. Near Ruins, Ruby, 1996, Let's Go Thundering, 1997, Give Us a Kiss, Johnny, 1998, Keeper, 1999; prodr. How I Got That Story (Off Broadway), 1982, Diamonds (Off Broadway), 1984, Today, I Am a Fountain Pen (Off Broadway), 1986; dir. Man. Theatre Ctr., 1982, 83, 84, Nat. Arts Ctr., Ottawa, Ont., Can., 1984, Hedda Gabler, Ctr. Stage, Toronto, 1985, Reg: Life in the Trees, GeVa Theatre, 1991; asst. dir. Broadway prodn. Carrie, 1988, Pacific Rep. prodn. Merchant of Venice, 2002, Much About Nothing, Santa Monica Shakespeare Project, 2004, All's Well that Ends Well, Shakespeare Santa Monica, 2005, King Lear, Shakespeare Santa Monica, 2006, Richard III Shakespeare Santa Monica, 2007; author: (with Shane Ann Younts) All the Words on Stage: A Complete Pronunciation Dictionary for the Plays of William Shakespeare, 2002. Bd. advisors Women's Project, 2006—. Recipient Dixon award Georgetown U., 1968, Alumni Achievement award Georgetown U. Alumni Club Met. Washington, 1981, Mayor's Arts award, D.C., 1982, Acad. Excellence award NYU, 1995, Hall of Fame, Georgetown Theatre Alumni, 2005. Mem.: Soc. Stage Dirs. and Choreographers, Episc. Actors' Guild (life; coun. 1990—96, 2002—04, 2006—). Home: 7 Stuyvesant Oval New York NY 10009-1901 Business E-Mail: louis.scheeder@nyu.edu.

SCHEEL, NELS EARL, corporate financial executive, accountant; b. Spencer, Wis., Sept. 25, 1925; s. Roland Edward and Louise Ernestine Scheel; m. Elaine Marie Carlisle, Aug. 28, 1949; children: Thomas W., John E., Martha L., Mark A., Mary E. BA, Youngstown Coll., 1949; MBA, U. Pa., 1950. CPA, Ohio. Staff acct. Lybrand Ross Bros., Cleve., 1950-54; asst. controller Century Foods, Youngstown, Ohio, 1954-62; treas., controller The Bailey Co., Cleve., 1962-63, Golden Dawn Foods, Sharon, Pa., 1963-82; v.p., chief fin. officer Peter J. Schmitt Co., Sharon, 1982-89; cons. to industry Columbiana, 1989—. Part-time faculty Youngstown (Ohio) State U., 1954—94; bd. mem. Sovereign Cirs., Inc., North Jackson, Ohio, 1992—2001, bd. chmn., 1995—99, sec.-treas., 1999—2001. Pres. Crestview Bd. Edn., Columbiana, Ohio, 1970-81; trustee Columbiana Cmty. Found., 2002—. Staff sgt. AUS, 1943-46, PTO, hon. discharge. Mem. Am. Inst. CPA's, Ohio Soc. CPA's.

SCHEELE, ADAM, music educator; b. Monroe, Wis., Oct. 7, 1976; s. Arthur and Karen Scheele; m. Jennifer Tarp, June 11, 2004; children: Annastasia, Seth. AA in Music Edn., Highland C.C., Freeport, Ill., 2001; BS in Music Edn., U. Wis., Platteville, 2004. Substitute tchr. Area SW Wis. Schs., 2004—05; substitute tchr. 5th-12th grade Shullsburg Sch. Dist., Wis., 2004—04; dir. 5th-12th grade band Montello Sch. Dist., Wis., 2005—. Mem.: Wis. Sch. Music Assn. (adjudicator 2006—), Wis. Youth Band Dirs. Assn., Nat. Band Assn., Nat. Assn. Music Edn. Home: 220 Douglas Ave Montello WI 53949 Office: Montello School District 222 Forest Ln Montello WI 53949 Office Phone: 608-297-2126 248.

SCHEELER, JAMES ARTHUR, architect; b. Pontiac, Ill., Dec. 20, 1927; s. Aman B. and Jane (Steele) S.; m. Barbara Jean Lloyd, Sept. 2, 1950; children: James Erich, Carl Aman, Orissa Jane Elizabeth; m. Nancy S. Kneege, June 2, 2007. BS with highest honors, U. Ill., 1951, MS, 1952; postgrad., U. Liverpool, 1952-53. Grad. asst. U. Ill., Urbana, 1950-52; draftsman-designer Lundeen & Hilfinger, Bloomington, Ill., 1952-53; designer Skidmore, Owings & Merrill, Chgo., 1955-59; partner Richardson, Severns, Scheeler & Assos., Inc., Champaign, Ill., 1959-65, v.p., treas., 1965-71; vice chmn. bd., dir. Prodn. Systems for Architects and Engrs., Inc., 1973-81. Vis. critic U. Ill., 1959-60. Mem. Plan Commn., Champaign, 1966—71, chmn., 1969-71; mem. Champaign County Regional Planning Commn., 1967-71; bd. dirs. Nat. Center for a Barrier-Free Environment, 1978—81, pres., 1981. Served with USN, 1946-47. Recipient various archtl. awards.; Francis J. Plym fellow, 1953-54; Fulbright fellow, 1953. Fellow AIA (hon.; treas. Ctrl. Ill. chpt. 1967-68, sec. 1968-69, pres. 1970-71, nat. dep. exec. v.p. 1971-76, pres. corp. 1974-78, exec. v.p. 1977-78, program devel. group exec. 1976-85, sr. exec. 1985-88, v.p. design practice group 1989, resident fellow 1990—, Edward D. Kemper award 2000), Internat. Union Archs. Profl. Practice Commn. (sec., co-dir. 1994-2003, internat. union archs. coun. 2005—), Fedn. Colls. Archs. Republic Mex. (hon.), Royal Australian Inst. Architects (hon.), Korean Inst. Archs. (hon.); mem. Ill. Arts Coun. (archtl. adv. bd. 1966-71), Japan Inst. Architect (hon.), Montessori Soc. Champaign-Urbana (dir. 1964-66), Gargoyle, Scarab, Phi Kappa Phi, Lambda Chi Alpha, Lambda Alpha, Cosmos Club. Episcopalian. Address: 11179 Saffold Way Reston VA 20190-3824

SCHEER, JOHN C., librarian; b. Jeffersonville, Ind., Mar. 28, 1961; s. John H. and Marilyn B. Scheer. BA in History and Geography, U. Louisville, 1984; MLS, Ind. U., 1986. Asst. librarian, archivist Willard Libr., Evansville, Ind., 1988—91, tech. svcs. librarian, 1991—. Author: Patchwork Central: An Urban Ministry, 2005. Mem.: ALA, Evansville Astron. Soc., Soc. Am. Archivists. Mem. United Ch. Of Christ. Avocation: history. Office: Willard Library 21 First Ave Evansville IN 47710 Office Phone: 812-425-4309.

SCHEER, JOSEPH H., artist, education educator; b. Heildeberg, Germany, Sept. 6, 1958; arrived in U.S., 1960; s. James H. and Kathleen M. Scheer. BFA, Alfred Univ., Alfred, NY, 1984; MA, Univ. New Mex., Albuqergue, New Mex., 1986, MFA, 1987. Artist ind., Los Nutrius, N.Mex., 1986—89; prof. print media Sch. Art Design Alfred Univ., Alfred, NY, 1989—; co-dir. Inst. Electronic Art Alfred Univ., Alfred, NY, 1997—. Author: Night Visions: Secret Designs of Moths, 2003, Night Flyers, 2003; one-man shows include over 30; contbr. articles pub. in over 50 profl. jour. Recipient Silver award, 16th Gold Internat., Chgo., 2003, Stiftung Bockkunst Best Book Design award, Frankfurt, Germany, 2003; grantee Project grant, NYSCA, 2001. Mem.: Entomol. Soc. Am., Lepidoptersit Soc., Phi Kappa Phi. Office: Sch of Art & Design Alfred Univ 2 Pine St Alfred NY 14802

SCHEER, MARK JEFFREY, lawyer; b. NYC, Jan. 6, 1962; s. Morton Herbert and Joan Sylvia (Weiss) S.; m. Sheryl Lynn Weinberg, Oct. 24, 1987; children: Matthew Jordan, Danielle Nicole, Lindsay Gayle. BS in Acctg., U. Fla., 1983, M in Acctg., 1984, JD, 1987. Bar: Fla. 1987, U.S. Tax Ct. 1988, U.S. Dist. Ct. (so. dist.) Fla. 1991. Ptnr. Gunster, Yoakley, & Stewart, P.A., Miami, Fla., 1987—. Mem. ABA, AICPA, Fla. Bar Assn., Fla. Isnt. CPAs. Jewish. Office: 2 S Biscayne Blvd Miami FL 33131-1806 Home Phone: 954-424-2730; Office Phone: 305-376-6000. E-mail: mscheer@gunster.com.

SCHEETZ, BERNADETTE ESTELLE, elementary mathematics educator; d. Donald Robert and Joyce Casey (Stepmother); m. William Arthur Scheetz, Feb. 11, 1995; children: Casey Louise, James Richard. BE, Pa. State U., State Coll., 1994. Tchr. Craven County Schs., Havelock, NC, 2003—. Mem.: Nat. Tchrs. Math. Home Phone: 252-444-1639.

SCHEFDORE, RONALD L., dentist; BS in Biology with honors, Southern Ill. U., 1979, DMD, 1983; Implant Cert., Northwestern U., 1985. Author & lectr. Dentist Worldwide, 2001—. Author: Better Service Better Dentistry, 2003. Mem.: ADA, Am. Acad. Cosmetic Dentistry, Ill. Dental Assn., Chgo. Dental Soc. Office: 345 West Ogden Ave Westmont IL 60559 Office Phone: 630-971-0682. Office Fax: 630-971-0072. Business E-Mail: celebritysmiles@aol.com.

SCHEFF, JONATHAN H., health and medical products executive; B, Amherst Coll., Mass.; MD, Tufts U., Boston; MBA, U. San Diego; grad. Advanced Mgmt. Program, Harvard Bus. Sch. Cert. internal medicine. Med. dir. Southbay NavCare Clinic; cons. Milliman & Robertson, San Diego; regional med. dir. CHAMPUS divsn. Aetna Health Plans, San Diego; various positions including v.p. govt. health affairs and sr. v.p. health care ops. Found. Health Corp.; pres., chmn. bd. dirs. Found. Health Med. Group, Inc., Sacramento; chmn. bd. dirs. Thomas Davis Med. Ctrs., Tucson; chief med. officer, sr. v.p. TRICARE Med. Mgmt. for Health Net Fed. Svcs., Inc. Health Net, Inc., sr. v.p., chief med. officer. Office: Health Net Inc 21650 Oxnard St Woodland Hills CA 91367 Office Phone: 818-676-6000. *

SCHEFFEL, KENNETH PAUL, retired archivist; b. Cin., Aug. 18, 1937; s. Edwin Reuben and Ivy Catherine (Happel) Scheffel. AB, Columbia U., NYC, 1959; MS, U. Wis., 1963. Archivist U. Mich., Ann Arbor, 1967—2003, archivist emeritus, 2003—. Mem.: So. Hist. Assn., Orgn. of Am. Historians. Methodist. Home: 7857 Harrison Ave Apt 4 Mount Healthy OH 45231-3151 Personal E-mail: kenschef@umich.edu.

SCHEFFEY, DAVID HAROLD, civil engineer, musician; b. Harrisburg, Pa., Jan. 5, 1929; s. Paul Revere Scheffey and Adaline Margaret Julius Sheffey; m. Letitia Gibboney Plowman, Dec. 29, 1951; children: David Lincoln, Nancy Eileen. BS in Civil Engring., Pa. State U., State College, 1950. Registered civil engr., Calif., 1971. Project estimator Pa. Turnpike Commn., Ephrata, 1950—51; designer bridges and culverts Michael Baker Jr. Engring., Harrisburg, Pa., 1951—52, 1954—56; asst. engr. Lockheed Aircraft Corp., Burbank, Calif., 1956—57, Dept. Water Resources, 1957—62, Palmdale, Calif., 1962—64, asst. civil engr. 1968—70; design engr. Tipton & Kalmbach, Lahore, Pakistan, 1962—64, Leeds, Hill, Deleen, Cather, Dacca, Bangladesh, 1966—68; asst. civil engr. Calif. Dept. Transp., Bishop, 1970—74, US Bur. Land Mgmt., Ukiah, Calif., 1978—95; assoc. civil engr. Pub. Work, Govt. Guam, Agana, 1974—76; supervisory hydraulic engr. US Dept. Indian Affairs, Fort Duchesne, Utah, 1976—78; ret., 1995. Organist 1st Presbyn. Ch., Ukiah, Calif., 1978—2005. 1st lt. US

Army, 1952—54. Decorated Bronze Star, Letter of Commendation US Army Chaplain. Mem.: Am. Guild Organists. Republican. Avocations: hiking, travel. Home: 1382 Yokayo Dr Ukiah CA 95482-6535

SCHEFFLER, ISRAEL, philosopher, educator; b. NYC, Nov. 25, 1923; s. Leon and Ethel (Grünberg) S.; m. Rosalind Zuckerbrod, June 26, 1949; children: Samuel, Laurie. BA, Bklyn. Coll., 1945, MA, 1948; M.H.L., Jewish Theol. Sem., 1949; PhD (Ford fellow 1951), U. Pa., 1952; A.M. (hon.), Harvard U., 1959; D.H.L. (hon.), Jewish Theol. Sem., 1993. Mem. faculty Harvard U., 1952-92, prof. edn., 1961-62, prof. edn. and philosophy, 1962-64, Victor S. Thomas prof. edn. and philosophy, 1964-92, professor emeritus, 1992—, hon. research fellow in cognitive studies, 1965-66, co-dir. Philosophy Edn. Rsch. Ctr., 1983-98, dir. Philosophy Edn. Rsch. Ctr., 1998—2003; scholar-in-residence The Mandel Ctr., Brandeis U., 2003—. Fellow Center for Advanced Study in Behavioral Scis., 1972-73 Author: The Language of Education, 1960, The Anatomy of Inquiry, 1963, Conditions of Knowledge, 1965, Science and Subjectivity, 1967, Reason and Teaching, 1973, Four Pragmatists, 1974, Beyond the Letter, 1979, Of Human Potential, 1985, Inquiries, 1986, In Praise of the Cognitive Emotions, 1991, Teachers of My Youth, 1995, Symbolic Worlds, 1997, Gallery of Scholars, 2004; co-author: Work, Education and Leadership, 1995; editor: Philosophy and Education, 1958, 66; co-editor: Logic and Art, 1972, Visions of Jewish Education, 2003; contbr. articles to profl. jours. Recipient Alumni Award of Merit Bklyn. Coll., 1967, Disting. Svc. medal Tchrs. Coll., Columbia, 1980, Benjamin Shevach award Boston Hebrew Coll., 1995; Guggenheim fellow, 1958-59, 72-73; NSF grantee, 1962, 65. Mem. Am. Acad. Arts and Scis., Am. Philos. Assn., Philosophy Edn. Soc., Nat. Acad. Edn. (charter), Philosophy of Sci. Assn. (pres. 1973-75), Charles S. Peirce Soc. (pres. 1998). Address: Apt 328 125 B Seminary Ave Auburndale MA 02466 Office: Brandeis Univ Mandel Ctr Waltham MA 02454 Business E-Mail: Israel_Scheffler@Harvard.edu.

SCHEFFLER, SAMUEL, philosophy educator; b. NYC, Oct. 20, 1951; s. Israel and Rosalind (Zuckerbrod) S.; m. Kathryn Granzow, Jan. 16, 1983; children: Adam Nathaniel, Gabriel Alexander. BA, Harvard U., 1973; PhD, Princeton U., 1977. Asst. prof. philosophy U. Calif., Berkeley, 1977-79, assoc. prof., 1979-85, prof., 1985—, chmn. dept., 1985-89, Class of 1941 World War II Meml. prof. Vis. fellow All Souls Coll., Oxford, 1990; chmn. adv. bd. Kadish Ctr for Morality Law & Public Affairs. Author: The Rejection of Consequentialism, 1982 (Franklin J. Machette prize Am. Philos. Assn. 1983), Human Morality, 1992, Boundaries and Allegiances; editor: Consequentialism and Its Critics, 1988; adv. editor Philosophy and Public Affairs; contbr. articles to profl. jours. U. Calif. Humanities Research fellow, 1982, Guggenheim Found. fellow, 1984, Pres.'s fellow U. Calif, 1989, NEH fellow, 1989. Fellow Am. Acad. Arts & Sci.; mem. Am. Philos. Assn. Office: Department of Philosophy 314 Moses Hall 2390 University of California Berkeley CA 94720-2390 Business E-Mail: scheffler@berkeley.edu.

SCHEFFLER, STUART JAY, lawyer; b. Phila., Oct. 9, 1950; s. Walter and Fritzy (Salkoff) S.; m. Barbara Jane Green, July 3, 1975. BA cum laude, Pa. State U., 1972, MPA, 1973; JD, Temple U., 1980. Bar: Pa. 1980, US Dist. Ct. (ea. dist.) Pa. 1981, US Ct. Appeals (3d cir.) 1983, US Supreme Ct. 1986. Tchr. Sch. Dist. of Phila., 1974-75; claims authorizer Social Security Adminstrn., HEW, Phila., 1975-76, equal opportunity specialist Office of Civil Rights, 1976-77; paraprofl. Law Offices of Ronald A. Bell., Bala Cynwyd, Pa., 1978-80; assoc. Law Office of Robert B. Mozenter, Phila., 1980-81, Gekoski & Bogdanoff, Phila., 1981-82; ptnr. Rubin & Scheffler, Phila., 1982-94; pvt. practice, Phila., 1994-04; of counsel Solomon, Berschler, Warren & Schatz,PC, Norristown, Pa., 1998—. Councilman Bakers Bay Condominium Assn., Phila., 1982; bd. dirs. Key West Coun. on the Arts, 1999-03. Artist (CD) From the Jukebox of My Mind, 2001. Fellow Acad. Advocacy; mem. ATLA, ABA (tort and ins. practice, sports and entertainment, civil litig. sects.), Pa. Bar Assn. (legis. liaison, medico-legal coms.), Phila. Bar Assn., Phila. Trial Lawyers Assn., Pa. Trial Lawyers Assn., Drug Info. Assn., Internat. Platform Assn., Hartikvah Basketball Assn. (v.p. 1974—), Phi Beta Kappa, Delta Sigma Rho, Tau Kappa Alpha, Zeta Beta Tau. Democrat. Personal E-mail: stukw@bellsouth.net.

SCHEFFMAN, DAVID THEODORE, economist, management educator, consultant; b. Milaca, Minn., Dec. 1, 1943; s. David Theodore and Fern Virginia (Maas) Scheffman; 1 child, Christopher. BA magna cum laude, U. Minn., 1967; PhD, MIT, 1971. Lectr. Boston Coll., 1970-71; from asst. prof. to assoc. prof. Univ. Western Ont., London, Canada, 1971-81; sr. economist FTC, Washington, 1979-82, dep. dir., 1983-86; prof., dir. Inst. Applied Econs. Concordia U., Montreal, Que., Canada, 1982-83; dir., bur. econs. FTC, Washington, 1985-88; Justin Potter prof., adj. prof. bus. strategy and mktg. Vanderbilt U., Nashville, 1989-99, prof. of bus. strategy and mktg., 1999—; dir. LECG, NYC, 1993-2001, 2003—, Bur. Econs., FTC, Washington, 2001—03; adj. prof., dir. bus. strategy Cornell U., 2001—02. Adj. prof. Georgetown U. Law Ctr., Washington, 1986; cons. Ont. Econ. Coun., Toronto, 1973-81, GM, 1977, Ctrl. Oil Inquiry, Ottawa, Ont., 1982-84, Ctrl. Govt., Ottawa, 1979-81, Can. Competition Tribunal, 1987-89, Can. Bur. Competition Policy, 1988-91, U.S. Sentencing Commn., 1988-89, PepsiCo, 1989-2000, Kraft Gen. Food, 1989-2001, PacifiCorp, 1989-93, NERA, 1991-93, Boeing, 1992-96, Berwind Industries, Inc., 1993-95, Comm. Ctrl., Inc., Applied Innovation, Inc., TEC, 1995-98, Nortel, 1995, Coca Cola, 1996-98. Author: Speculation and Monopoly in Urban Development: Analytical Foundations, 1977, An Economic Analysis of Provincial Land Use Policies in Ontario, 1980, Social Regulation in Markets for Consumer Goods and Services, 1982, An Economic Analysis of the Impact of Rising Oil Prices on Urban Structure, 1983, Strategy, Structure, and Antitrust in the Carbonated Soft Drink Industry, 1992. Dissertation fellow NSF, 1967-68; vis. scholar U. Minn., 1978. Office: LECG 1725 I St NW #800 Washington DC 20006 Office Phone: 202-466-4422. Business E-Mail: dscheffman@lecg.com.

SCHEFSKY, LYNN A., lawyer, chemicals executive; BA, Adrian Coll.; JD with honors, U. Mich. Pvt. practice; western div. counsel Dow Chemical Co., joined, 1985, Tex. ops. div. counsel, mgr. product litig., mng. counsel Dow Plastics, global mng. counsel Dow Thermosets Midland, Mich.; sr. v.p., gen. counsel Chemtura Corp., Middlebury, Conn., 2004—. Mem. Adrian Coll. Bd. Trustees. Office: Chemtura Corp 199 Benson Rd Waterbury CT 06749 Office Phone: 203-573-2000. *

SCHEFTER, ED QUEEN, minister; life ptnr. Heather Q. Schefter, June 27, 1989. ThM (hon.), Portland Bible Coll., Portland, 1987. Dist. pastor City Bible Ch., Portland, 1998—2007; sr. pastor NYC Ch., 2007—. Prodr.: (drama) Eternity (Telly award, 2002). R-Conservative. Non-Denominational Christian. Home Phone: 503-252-2222.

SCHEHR, KEVIN JOHN, art gallery owner; b. Tulsa, Mar. 23, 1966; s. Louis Valentine Schehr, Jr. and Bonnie Louise Sadle; m. Melissa Aileen Boeckl, Feb. 4, 1995; m. Melissa Diane Bell, June 1, 1985 (dec. Feb. 22, 1992); children: Kevin John Schehr, Jr., Alicia Katelyn. AS, Fla. C.C. at Jacksonville, 1990; B. of Vocat. Edn., So. Ill. U., 1990; MBA, U. of Phoenix, 1999. Ops. mgr. New Orleans Windustrial, New Orleans, 1992—95; gen. mgr. Source Prodn. & Equipment Co, Inc., St. Rose, La., 1995; pres. Galerie Rouge, Inc, New Orleans, 2002—. Nat. alerting officer Am. Disaster Res., 2003; vol. USA Freedom Corps, Washington, 2003. With USN, 1985—92. Recipient Pres.'s Vol. Svc. award Silver, USA Freedom Corps, 2004, Pres.'s Vol. Svc. award Gold, 2005. Mem.: Am. Soc. for Non-Destructive Testing (assoc.; New Orleans sect. chmn. 1996—2002), Naval Order of the U.S., State Guard Assn. of the U.S. (assoc.), Am. Legion, VFW (life). Roman Catholic. Home: 2658 Hudson Pl New Orleans LA 70131 Office: Galerie Rouge Inc 623 Royal St New Orleans LA 70130 Home Phone: 504-957-9885; Office Phone: 504-586-0061. Personal E-mail: kschehr826@aol.com.

SCHEIB, GERALD PAUL, art educator; b. LA, Dec. 26, 1937; s. Harry William and Olive Bauer (Cartwright) S.; m. Elizabeth Ann Galligan, Dec. 27, 1965 (div. 1978); children: Gregory Paul, Geoffrey Paul; m. Dedra Lynn True, Oct. 1, 1983; 1 child, Adam True. AA, East L.A. Jr. Coll., 1959; BA, Calif. State U., LA, 1962, MFA, 1968. Cert. life teaching credential in fine arts, secondary and coll. tchr., Calif. Secondary tchr. art L.A. Unified Sch. Dist., 1963-77; prof. fine art L.A. Community Coll. Dist., 1977-2001; ret., 2001; pres. faculty senate L.A. Mission Coll., San Fernando, Calif., 1983-84. Bargaining unit rep., AFT Coll. Guild Local 1521; elected Arts and Letters chair L.A. Mission Coll., 1993; owner, mgr. Artificers Bench, Sylmar, Calif., 1976—; cons. to Edward H. Bohlin Co. Custom Silver Works, 1998; adv. student tchg. art charter coll. edn. Calif. State U., LA, 2007. Mem. policy bd. The Calif. Arts Project, 1995-97; chair Los Angeles County Art Edn. Coun., 1997-98; plank owner U.S. Naval Meml., Washington; trustee L.A. Artcore, 2001, LA Judge for Coca Cola's Ann. Art of Harmony Student Art Scholarship Compeition. With USNR, 1955-97, ret. Recipient of tribute City of L.A., 1983, Citizen of Month award, Los Angeles County, 1983, Cold War Cert. of Recognition, Sec. of Def., 2000. Mem. Calif. Art Edn. Assn. (membership chmn. 1985-87, pres.-elect 1989-91, pres. 1991-93, Calif.'s Outstanding Art Educator in Higher Edn. 1994-95), San Fernando Active 20-30 Club (pres. 1981-82), Nat. Assn. Scholars, Sons of Union Vets of Civil War, U.S. Naval Cryptologic Vets. Assn., L.A. Artcore (bd. dirs. 2001--). Republican. Avocations: collecting antiques, Civil War reenacting, creating custom jewelry. Office: 13356 Eldridge Ave Sylmar CA 91342-3200 Office Phone: 818-364-7678. Personal E-mail: geraldart@aol.com.

SCHEIBE, KARL EDWARD, psychology professor; b. Belleville, Ill., Mar. 5, 1937; s. John Henry and Esther Julia (Friesen) S.; m. Elizabeth Wentworth Mixter, Sept. 10, 1961; children: David Sawyer, Robert Daniel. BS, Trinity Coll., 1959; PhD, U. Calif.-Berkeley, 1963; MA (hon.), Wesleyan U., 1973. Faculty mem. Wesleyan U., Middletown, Conn., 1963—73, prof. psychology, 1973—2005, prof. emeritus, 2005—. Vis. prof. U. So. Calif., 1974; dir. rev. panels NSF Sci. Profl. Devel. Program, 1975-81; cons. Am. Council Edn., 1975-81 Author: Beliefs and Values, 1970, Mirror, Masks, Lies and Secrets, 1979, Studies in Social Identity, 1983, Self Studies: The Psychology of Self and Identity, 1995, The Drama of Everyday Life, 2000. Trustee Trinity Coll., Hartford, Conn., 1977-83; moderator congregation First Ch. of Christ, Middletown, 1981-82. Woodrow Wilson fellow, 1959; NSF fellow, 1961; NIMH research grantee, 1964-68; Fulbright fellow Cath. U. Sao Paulo, Brazil, 1972-73, 84. Mem. Am. Psychol. Assn., Eastern Psychol. Assn., Conn. Acad. Arts and Scis., Phi Beta Kappa Congregationalist. Home: 11 Long Ln Middletown CT 06457-4046 Office: Wesleyan U Wasch Ctr for Ret Faculty Middletown CT 06459-0001 Business E-Mail: kscheibe@wesleyan.edu.

SCHEIBEL, ARNOLD BERNARD, psychiatrist, educator, research director; b. NYC, Jan. 18, 1923; s. William and Ethel (Greenberg) Scheibel; m. Madge Mila Ragland, Mar. 3, 1950 (dec. Jan. 1977); m. Marian Diamond, Sept. 1982. BA, Columbia U., NYC, 1944, MD, 1946; MS, U. Ill., 1952. Intern Mt. Sinai Hosp., NYC, 1946-47; resident in psychiatry Barnes and McMillan Hosp., St. Louis, 1947-48, Ill. Neuropsychiat. Inst., Chgo., 1950-52; asst. prof. psychiatry and anatomy U. Tenn. Med. Sch., 1952-53, assoc. prof., 1953-55, UCLA Med. Ctr., 1955-67, prof., 1967—, mem. Brain Rsch. Inst., 1960—, acting dir. Brain Rsch. Inst., 1987-90, dir., 1990-95. Cons. in field. Contbr. numerous articles to tech. jours, chpts. to books.; mem. editl. bd. Brain Rsch., 1967-77, Developmental Psychobiology, 1968—, Internat. Jour. Neurosci., 1969—, Jour. Biol. Psychiatry, 1968—, Jour. Theoretical Biology, 1980—; assoc. editor News Report, 1989—. Mem. Pres.'s Commn. on Aging, Nat. Inst. Aging, 1980—. Served with AUS, 1943-46; from lt. to capt. M.C. AUS, 1948-50. Guggenheim fellow (with wife), 1953-54, 59; recipient Disting. Svc. award Calif. Soc. Biomed. Rsch., 1998. Fellow Am. Acad. Arts and Scis., Norwegian Acad. Scis., Am. Psychiat. Assn. (life, Harriet and Charles Luckman Disting. Tchg. award 1997) AAAS; mem. Am. Neurol. Assn., Soc. Neuorosci., Pyschiat. Rsch. Assn., Soc. Biol. Psychiatry, So. Calif. Psychiat. Assn. Home: 16231 Morrison St Encino CA 91436-1331 Office: UCLA Dept Neurobiology Los Angeles CA 90024 Business E-Mail: scheibel@mednet.ucla.edu. *Intense personal tragedy can embitter life and choke off further personal creativity. It may also offer the opportunity to open new doors in the discovery of self. I am more aware than ever of my good fortune in having the opportunity to teach, to continue investigative work in the structure and function of the brain, and to give love and care to those who need it. I am more than ever convinced that loving and being loved is the greatest good that we can know, the state in which we most nearly fulfill our roles as human beings.*

SCHEIBEL, KENNETH MAYNARD, journalist; b. Campbell, Nebr., May 17, 1920; s. G. Alfred and Rachel Christine (Koch) S.; m. Helen Schmitt, May 14, 1955 (div. Sept. 1977); children: Victor Warren Schmitt, William Becker Schmitt, Kenneth Jr., Sally. Student, George Wash. U., Washington, DC, 1938—41; BA, U. Va., Charlottesville, 1947, MA, 1949. Mag. salesman Periodical Pubs. Svc. Bur., Inc., 1935-38; reporter Internat. News Svc., Washington, 1940-41, Wall St. Jour., Washington, 1949-51; Washington corr. Gannett Newspapers, 1951-63; syndicated columnist N.Am. Newspaper Alliance, 1963-64; chief Washington bur. Donrey Media Group, 1964-67; founder, bur. chief Washington Bur. News, 1967—; founder nat. syndicated column Washington Farm Beat, 1970-85. Washington corr. Wis. State Jour., 1963-66, LaCrosse Tribune, Wis., 1963-66, Billings Gazette, Mont., 1964-71, V.I. Network, 1966-67, Moline Daily Dispatch, Ill., 1967-68, Drovers' Jour., 1967-68, Newport News Daily Press & Times Herald, Va., 1969-71, Packer Pub. Co., 1964-74, Gasoline Retailer, 1966-67, Okla., Farmer Stockman; congl. corr. F-D-C Reports, 1975-77; Washington columnist Farm Jour., 1960-75; dir. Nat. Press Bldg. Corp., 1973, v.p. pres. club and bldg corp., 1974; covered nat. polit. convs., campaigns; v.p. Fraser Assocs. (pub. rels.), Washington, 1976-79; Congl. broadcast interviewer; founder Wash. Broadcast News, Ft. Smith, Ark., Miami, Las Vegas. Contbr. nat. mags., newspaper syndicates. Incorporator War Meml. of Korea, Washington, 1981; editor Nat. Ctr. Fin. and Econ. Info., U.S.-Saudi Arabian Joint Econ. Commn., Riyadh, 1985-86; mem. Nat. Com. Korean War Meml., 1981. Capt. AUS, 1941-46, 755th Tank Bn., 1st armored divsn., 1942-45, Europe, N. Africa, Italy. Decorated Bronze star, US Army Occupation medal, Combat Infantryman badge; co-recipient Croix De Guerre (France), Thoth award for excellence in pub. rels., 1980. Mem. Izaak Walton League Am., White House Corrs. Assn., Overseas Press Club of Am., Am. Radio Relay League, Nat. Press Club (Washington; fin. sec., gov. 1969-73, vice chmn. bd. 1971, v.p., pres., 1974), Sigma Chi. Presbyterian. Avocation: amateur radio. Home: 1325 18th St NW Apt 302 Washington DC 20036-6505 Personal E-mail: kenscheib@earthlink.com. *The greatest sins are timidity and self indulgence, the greatest virtue is to love. Live each day, don't fret about yesterday or tomorrow. Enjoy the senses, learn from others, and never forget that both love and hate are returned.*

SCHEIBER, HARRY N., law educator; b. 1935; BA, Columbia U., 1955; MA, Cornell U., 1957, PhD, 1961; MA (hon.), Dartmouth Coll., 1965; D.Jur.Hon., Uppsala U., Sweden, 1998. Instr. to assoc. prof. history Dartmouth Coll., 1960-68, prof., 1968-71; prof. Am. history U. Calif., San Diego, 1971-80; prof. law Boalt Hall, U. Calif., Berkeley, 1980—. Chmn. jurisprudence and social policy program, 1982-84, 90-93, assoc. dean, 1990-93, 96-99; The Stefan Riesenfeld prof., 1991—; vice chair Univ. Academic Senate, 1993-94, chair 1994-95; dir. Earl Warren Legal Inst., 2002-05, Inst. for Legal Rsch., 2005—, Sho Sato Program, 1993—; co-dir. Law of the Sea Inst., 2002-; Fulbright disting. sr. lectr., Australia, 1983, marine affairs coord. Calif. Sea Grant Coll. Program, 1989-2000; vis. rsch. prof. Law Inst. U. Uppsala, Sweden, 1995, hon. prof. DiTella U., Buenos Aires, 1999; cons. Calif. Jud. Coun., 1992-93; acting dir. Ctr. for Study of Law and Soc., 1999-2001; Cassel lectr., Stockholm U., 2003. Author: The Wilson Administration and Civil Liberties, 1960, Ohio Canal Era, 1970, Inter-Allied Conflicts and Ocean Law (1945-1953), 2001; co-author: American Law and the Constitutional Order, 1988, The State and Freedom of Contract, 1998, American Law and the Constitutional Order, 1978, Law of the Sea: The Common Heritage and Emerging Challenges, 2000, Bringing New Law to Ocean Waters, 2004, Earl Warren and the Warren Court, 2006, Emerging Concepts of Rights in Japanese Law, 2007; editor: Yearbook of the California Supreme Court Historical Society, 1994—2006; contbr. articles to profl. jours. Chmn. Littleton Griswold Prize Legal History, 1985-88, 2006-07, pres. NH Civil Liberties Union, 1969-70; chmn. Project '87 Task Force on Pub. Programs, Washington, 1982-85; dir. Berkeley Seminar on Federalism, 1986-95; cons. judiciary study U.S. Adv. Commn. Intergovernmental Rels., 1985-88, Pew Oceans Commn., 2002-03, Nat. Rsch. Coun., 2002-03, Joint Ocean Commn. Initiative, 2006—; dir. NEH Inst. on Constitutionalism, U. Calif., Berkeley, 1986-87, 88-91. Recipient Sea Grant Colls. award, 1981-83, 84-85, 86-2002; fellow Ctr. Advanced Study in Behavioral Scis., Stanford Calif., 1967, 71; Guggenheim fellow, 1971, 88; Rockefeller Found. humanities fellow, 1979, NEH fellow, 1985-86; NSF grantee 1979, 80, 88-89. Fellow AAAS, Am. Acad. Arts and Scis., U. Calif. Humanities Rsch. Inst., Am. Soc. for Legal History (hon.; pres. 2003—), Japan Soc. for Promotion of Sci. (invitational fellow); mem. Am. Hist. Assn., Orgn. Am. Historians, Agrl. History Soc. (pres. 1978), Econ. History Assn. (trustee 1978-80), Law and Soc. Assn. (trustee 1979-81, 96-99), Nat. Assessment History and Citizenship Edn. (chmn. nat. acad. bd. 1986-87), Marine Affairs and Policy Assn. (bd. dirs. 1991-96), Ocean Governance Study Group (steering com. 1991-2004), Internat. Coun. Environ. Law, Calif. Supreme Ct. Hist. Soc. (bd. dirs. 1993—, v.p. 1997-98). Office: U Calif Berkeley Law Sch Boalt Hall Berkeley CA 94720-7200 Office Phone: 510-643-9788. E-mail: scheiber@law.berkeley.edu.

SCHEIBER, STEPHEN CARL, psychiatrist, director; b. NYC, May 2, 1938; s. Irving Martin and Frieda Olga (Schor) S.; m. Mary Ann McDonnell, Sept. 14, 1965; children: Lisa Susan, Martin Irving, Laura Ann. BA, Columbia Coll., 1960; MD, SUNY, Buffalo, 1964. Diplomate Am. Bd. Psychiatry and Neurology. Intern Mary Fletcher Hosp., Burlington, Vt., 1964-65; resident in psychiatry Strong Meml. Hosp., Rochester, NY, 1967-70; asst. prof. U. Ariz., Tucson, 1970-76, assoc. prof., 1976-81, prof., 1981-86; exec. sec. Am. Bd. Psychiatry and Neurology, Inc., Deerfield, Ill., 1986-89, exec. v.p., 1989—2006. Adj. prof. psychiatry Northwestern U., Chgo. and Evanston, 1986—, Med. Coll. Wis., Milw., 1986-2006, cli. prof. psychiatry, 2006—. Co-editor: The Impaired Physician, 1983, Certification, Recertification and Lifetime Learning in Psychiatry, 1994, Core Competencies for Psychiatric Practice, 2003, Core Competencies for Neurologists, 2003; contbr. articles to profl. jours. Mem. med. adv. com. Casas de los Ninos, Tucson, 1974-86; mem. mental health adv. com. Tucson Health Planning Coun., 1974-75; med. student interviewer Office of Med. Edn., 1975; mem. Glenbrook (Ill.) North H.S. Boosters Club, 1988-91; treas. Robert E. Jones Found., 1988-96. Surgeon USPHS, 1965-67. Recipient Outstanding Tchr. award, U. Ariz., 1986, Lifetime and Career Achievement award, SUNY, Buffalo, 1998; grantee Group Therapy Outcome Studies on Inpatient Svc., 1980, Dialysis and Schizophrenia Pilot Project, NIH, 1978. Fellow: Assn. Acad. Psychiatry (parliamentary sec. 1979—84, treas. 1984—88, pres.-elect 1988—89, pres. 1989—90, Lifetime Educator award 2002, Disting. Life Fellow 2006), Am. Assn. Dirs. Psychiat. Residency Tng. (pres. 1981—82), Am. Coll. Psychiatrists (bd. regents 1992—2001, treas. 1995—2001, Disting. Svc. award 2007), Group for Advancement of Psychiatry (life; invited mem., chmn. mem. edn. com. 1987—91, bd. dirs., sec. 1993—97, pres.-elect 1997—99, pres. 1999—2001), Am. Psychiat. Assn. (life; chmn. impaired physician com. 1985—88, cons. 1988—92, Disting. Life Fellow 2002); mem.: Oracle Heights Club (pres. 1983—84). Democrat. Jewish. E-mail: sscheiber@comcast.net.

SCHEIBERG, SUSAN L., librarian; b. Chgo., Dec. 19, 1962; d. Steven M. Scheiberg, Margo Scheiberg. BA (hon.), Ind. U., 1984; MA, UCLA, 1986; MS in Libr. Sci., U. Ky., 1997. Grad. rsch. libr. U. So. Calif., 1997—98, team leader, serials acquisitions, 1998—2001; head acquisitions and serials, coord. outreach and cost-ctr. svcs. RAND Corp., Santa Monica, Calif., 2001—02, assoc. dir., 2002—. Editor: (book) NASIG 2001: A Serials Odyssey, 2002, Transforming Serials: The Revolution Continues, 2003; contbr. articles to profl. jours. Fellow Univ., UCLA, 1984-1987; grantee Bardin Endowment Rsch., U. So. Calif., 1998, 1999, 2000. Mem.: ALA (Tony B. Leisner grantee 1996), Reference and User Svcs. Assn., Assn. Coll. & Rsch. Librs., N.Am. Serials Interest Group (proceedings editor 2000—), Libr. Adminstrn. and Mgmt. Assn., Assn. Libr. Collections and Tech. Svcs., Spl. Librs. Assn., Beta Phi Mu, Phi Beta Kappa. Home Phone: 310-478-9863; Office Phone: 310-393-0411. Personal E-mail: susanls@rand.org.

SCHEIBLE, DAVID W., paper company executive; BS, MBA, Purdue Univ. V.p., gen. mgr. Avery Dennison Corp., 1993—99; pres. flexible div. Graphic Packaging Internat., 1999, COO, 1999—2003; exec. v.p. comml. ops. Graphic Packaging Corp., Marietta, Ga., 2003—04, COO, 2004—06, pres., CEO, bd. dir., 2007—. Office: Graphic Packaging Corp 814 Livingston Ct Marietta GA 30067 *

SCHEICH, JOHN F., lawyer; b. Bklyn., Aug. 6, 1942; s. Frank A. and Dorothy (O'Hara) Scheich. BA, St. John's U., NYC, 1963, JD, 1966; postgrad., John Marshall Law Sch., Chgo., 1968. Bar: N.Y. 1967, U.S. Ct. Internat. Trade Admission 1969, U.S. Dist. Ct. (ea. and so. dists.) N.Y. 1971, U.S. Ct. Appeals (2d cir.) 1971, U.S. Supreme Ct. 1975, Pa. 1980. Spl. agt. FBI, U.S. Dept. Justice, Washington, 1966-69; asst. dist. atty. Queens County, Kew Gardens, N.Y., 1969-72; pvt. practice Richmond Hill, NY, 1970—76, 1979—91; ptnr. Raia & Scheich, P.C., Richmond Hill, 1976-79; sr. ptnr. Scheich & Goldsmith, PC, Richmond Hill, 1991—95, 2003—, Scheich, Goldsmith & Dreishpoon, PC, Richmond Hill, 1996—2003; mortgage settlement atty. GMAC, N.Y., 1996—. Mem. assigned counsel panel for indigent defendants in major felony and murder cases 9th and 11th jud. dists. N.Y. State Supreme Ct., Queens County, 1972—94; v.p. Ra-Li Brokerage Corp., 1975—, bd. dirs.; lectr. Lawyers in Classroom, 1979—91; chmn. arbitration panel Civil Ct. City of N.Y., 1981—90; trial judge St. John's U. Sch. Law Civil Trial Inst. Student Competition, 1992—; lectr. estate planning Nat. Bus. Inst., 1994; mem. adv. bd. 1st Am. Title Ins. Co. Am., 1995—2004; mortgage settlement atty. Gen. Motors Acceptance Corp. N.Y. State, 1996—. Editor: Conashaugh Courier, 1989-92; mem. editorial bd., 1988-92; contbg. columnist, 1981-89. Active Performing Arts Ctr. Pinellas County, St. Petersburg, 1995—2003; mem. Com. for Beautification of East Norwich, Nassau County, LI, NY, 1983—, bd. dirs., 1993—96, pres., 1996—; mem. Friends of the Arts, Locust Valley, LI, NY, 1985—; chmn. tri-centennial celebration com. Village of East Norwich, 1996—97; mem. St. Edward the Confessor Sch. Bd., Syosset, NY, 1986—90; nat. trust and estate assoc. Meml. Sloane Kettering Cancer Ctr., NYC, 1994—; active Internat. Wine Ctr., 1985—96; mem. Fransiscan Ctr. Guild, Tampa, Fla., 1996—, Tilles Ctr. Performing Arts, Inc., Long Island U., Brookville, NY, 1997—, Lincoln Ctr. Performing Arts, Inc., 1985—, Bravo Soc., 1994—, Concern for Dying, 1984—2002, Sea Cliff Chamber Players, 1992—99; active Pact, Inc. Ruth Eckerd Hall-Richard B. Baumgardner Ctr. for Performing Arts, Clearwater, Fla., 1995—2001, Rep. Nat. Senate Adv. Coun., 1997—2002, Rep. Nat.

Com. Chmn.'s Honor Roll (cert. Achievement 1998), 1997; appointed to Bus. Advisory Coun. by Nat. Repub. Congressional Comm.; mem. East Norwich Rep. Club, 1982—, bd. dirs., 1984—87, 1993—, v.p., 1987—89, pres., 1989—93; mem. Nat. Rep. Senatorial Com., 1988—2004, Nassau County Rep. Com., Town of Oyster Bay, 1993—, Holy Name Soc. of Our Lady of Perpetual Help Ch., 1963—, sec., 1965—67, v.p., 1969—71, pres., 1971—73; parish coun. Our Lady of Perpetual Help Roman Cath. Ch., 1976—82, pres., 1978—80, fin. com., adv. to pastor, 1970—82, chmn. fin. com., 1979—82; active St. Edward the Confessor Ch., Syosset, 1982—90, St. Vincent Ch., Dingman Hills, Pa., 1977—2004, St. Dominic's Ch., Oyster Bay, NY, 1982—, apptd. pastor's adv. coun. on estate planning, 1998—2003, mem. St. Dominic's Legacy Soc., 1998—; mem. St. John Vianney Roman Cath. Ch., St. Petersburg Beach, Fla., 1994—; bd. dirs. Northslope II Homeowners Assn., Shawnee-on-Delaware, Pa., 1988—90, Shawnee-on-Del., Pa., 1992—94, 2000—02, East Norwich Civic Assn., 2002—04, Conashaugh Lakes Cmty. Assn., Milford, Pa., 1981—90; organizing mem. Conashaugh Lakes Lot Owners interim com., 1977—81, sec., 1981—82, v.p., 1982—84, pres., 1984—86, past pres., 1986—88; Non-Resident Fellow, James Beard Found., NYC, 1995—. Recipient J. Edgar Hoover award, 1967, award of appreciation, Civil Trial Inst., St. John's U. Sch. of Law, 1991, 95, Disting. Svc. award, 1992, cert. of appreciaiton Conashaugh Lakes Cmty. Assn., 1990, Dist. Svc. award Kiwanis Club, 1992, Cert. of Merit for Disting. Svc. award Nassau County Exec. Hon. Thomas Gulotta, 1989, Presdl. Order of Merit award Pres. George Bush, 1991, Order of Merit award Nat. Rep. Senatorial Com., 1994, Cert. Achievement, Rep. Nat. Com., 1998; named one of Best Trial Lawyers in the U.S., Town and Country Mag., 1985; non-resident fellow James Beard Found., N.Y.C., 1995—, Blue Ribbon Survey Commn. cert. of recognition, 2002. Mem. ABA (cert. of appreciation Am. Bar Endowment 1992), ATLA, Pa. State Bar Assn., NY State Bar Assn., Queens County Bar Assn., Nassau County Bar Assn., NY State Trial Lawyers Assn., Ciminal Cts. Bar Assn., John Marshall Lawyers Assn. (bd. dirs. 1992—, pres. 1992-97, treas. 1997—), Soc. Former Spl. Agts. of FBI (nat. chpt., L.I. chpt., chmn. L.I. chpt. 2003-06, charter chmn. 2003-06), NY State Assn. Criminal Def. Lawyers, LeGaL Lawyers Assn. (bd. dirs. 2001—, bd. dirs. found. 1995-98, 2001—, sec. 2003-06, v.p., 2006, pres., 2007), St. John's Coll. Alumni Assn., Asst. Dist. Attys. Assn. Queens County, St. John's U. Sch. of Law Alumni Assn., St. John's Prep. Sch. Alumni Assn., Friends of the Arts of Nassau County, Inc., Cath. Lawyers Guild of Queens County, NY, KC, Brookhaven Wine Lovers Soc., East Norwich Civic Assn., Sun Island Assn. (bd. dirs. 2001-02, 2007-), Heritage Soc., St. John's U. McCallen Soc., Business Advisory Coun., Phi Alpha Delta. Avocation: fine wines. Home: 170 Sugar Toms Ln East Norwich NY 11732-1153 Office: Scheich & Goldsmith PC 103-42 Lefferts Blvd South Richmond Hill NY 11419-2012 also: 109 Newbridge Rd Hicksville NY 11801-3908 Office Phone: 718-843-7200. Personal E-mail: jacksesq@aol.com.

SCHEID, STEVEN L., investment company executive; 3 children. BS in acctg., Michigan St. U. CFO The Charles Schwab & Co. Inc., 1996—99, vice-chmn. San Francisco, 1999—2002; CEO Charles Schwab Investment Mgmt., 1999—2002; pres. Schwab Retail Group, 2000—02; chmn. Janus Capital Group, Denver, 2004—, CEO, 2004—06. Fed. Reserve Bank of San Francisco's representative Fed. Advisory Coun., 2001—02; bd. dirs. The PMI Group Inc., Auto Desk Inc. Avocations: piano, clarinet, running, wine collecting. Office: Janus Capital Group Inc 151 Detroit St Denver CO 80206-4923

SCHEIDT, W. ROBERT, chemistry educator, researcher; b. Richmond Heights, Mo., Nov. 13, 1942; s. Walter Martin and Martha (Videtich) S.; m. Kathryn Sue Barnes, Aug. 9, 1964; children: Karl Andrew, David Martin. BS, U. Mo., 1964; MS, U. Mich., 1965, PhD, 1968; postdoctoral studies, Cornell U., 1970. Asst. prof. U. Notre Dame, Ind., 1970-76, assoc. prof., 1976-80, prof., 1980—, William K. Warren prof., 1999—. Vis. prof. U. Wash., Seattle, 1980, U. Paris (Orsay), Paris, 1991, U. René Descartes, 2005, 06, U. Strasbourg, France, 1998; mem. rev. sec. Metallobiochemistry NIH, Bethesda, 1991—96. Contbr. articles to profl. jours. Fellow AAAS; mem. Am. Chem. Soc. (assoc. editor Chem. Revs. jour. 1980-85), Am. Crystallographic Assn., Biophys. Soc., Sigma X. Democrat. Office: U Notre Dame Dept Chemistry Notre Dame IN 46556 Business E-Mail: scheidt.1@nd.edu.

SCHEIER, IVAN HENRY, volunteer, writer, retired cultural organization administrator; b. Plattsburgh, NY, Jan. 7, 1926; s. Joel Henry and Melba Gottlob S. BA in Philosophy, Union Coll., 1948; MA in Psychology, McGill U., Montreal, 1951, PhD in Psychology, 1953. Vol. coord., project dir. Boulder County Juvenile Ct., 1965-69; interim dir. Vol. and Info. Ctr. of Boulder County, 1968; exec. dir. Nat. Info. Ctr. on Volunteerism, 1967-76; pres. Assn. Voluntary Action Scholars, 1973-74; chair Alliance for Volunteerism, 1975-76; pres. Yellowfire Press, 1981-89; dir. Ctr. for Creative Cmty., 1986-95; dreamcatcher-in-residence Voluntas Retreat Ctr., 1991-95; coord. Stillpoint Self-Help Healing Ctr., 1996—2003; ret., 2003. Freelance writer; mem. faculty McGill U., 1950-51, U. Ill., 1953-58, Nat. Coll. Juvenile Justice, 1970, U. Colo. Vol. Mgmt. Cert. Program, 1973-87; mem. White House Conf. on Children and Youth, 1970, Nat. Adv. Commn. Criminal Justice Stds. and Goals, 1971, Nat. Forum Volunteerism, 1979-80; mem. adv. com. U. Colo. Vol. Mgmt. Cert. Program, 1973-87; sr. advisor Resource Devel., Assn. for Vol. Adminstrn., 1979-80, Citizen Advocacy for Devel. Disabled, 1980-82, New Road Map Found., 1990—; mem. adv. bd. Madrid-Cerrillos Med. Clin., 1993-94; mem. youth vol. leadership tng. project Sister Cities Internat., 1979-81. Author: Exploring Volunteer Space: The Recruiting of a Nation, 1980, Making Dreams Come True Without Much Money: The Midwifery of Dreams, 2000, When Everyone's a Volunteer, 1992, Images of the Future, 1994; pub., editor On Background, 1979-81, The Dovia Exchange, 1984-98, The Restless News, 1986-89, Ex Libris, 1987-90, Madrid Muse, 1991-95; hon. editor (e-jour.) e-volunteerism, 2003--. Pres. emeritus Nat. Info. Ctr. on Volunteerism, 1979—; chair com. NAACP, Urbana, Ill., 1956-59; vol. various orgns., U.S., Can., 1963—; mem. Sierra Pride Com. Turning Point, Truth or Consequences, N.Mex., 1999-2002; mem. policy bd. Assn. Voluntary Action Scholars, 1971-74, Nat. Ctr. for Voluntary Action, 1971-76, Nat. Info. Ctr.on Volunteerism, 1971-79, Alliance for Volunteerism, 1974-77, Nat. Orgn. Victim Assistance, 1977-79, Partners, Inc., 1979-82; bd. dirs. Madrid, N.Mex. Landowners Assn., 1993-94. Recipient Nat. Meritorious Svc. award Nat. Coun. Juvenile Court Judges, 1971, Meritorious Svc. award Province of Ont., 1976, Leadership award Alliance for Volunteerism, Inc., 1976, Disting. Svc. award State of Miss., 1982, Nat. Cmty. Svc. award Nat. Assn. on Vols. in Criminal Justice, 1987, Lifetime Achievement award Denver Dirs. of Vols. in Agys., 1997, Shakespeare award for excellence Famous Poets Soc., 2004. Mem. Assn. Vol. Adminstrn. (life, Nat. Disting. Svc. award 1984, editor Volunteer Adminstrn. 1979-81), Phi Beta Kappa. Avocations: tai chi, dance, hiking, reading, gardening. Personal E-mail: ivan@zianet.com.

SCHEIMAN, EUGENE R., lawyer; b. Bklyn., July 15, 1943; BA, L.I. U., 1966; JD cum laude, Bklyn. Law Sch., 1969. Bar: NY 1970, US Dist. Ct. (so. and ea. dists.) NY 1971, US Ct. Appeals (1st cir.) 1972, US Ct. Appeals (5th cir.) 1973, US Ct. Appeals (4th cir.) 1974, US Supreme Ct. 1976, US Ct. Appeals (2nd cir.) 1977, US Ct. Appeals (fed. cir.), US Ct. Appeals (11th cir.) 1989, US Ct. Appeals (3rd cir.) 1990. Formerly shareholder Buchanan Ingersoll, NYC; with McCarter & English LLP, NYC. Rsch. editor Bklyn. Law Rev., 1968, editor-in-chief, 1969. Mem. ABA (sect. on individual rights and responsibilities, franchise forum constrn. forum), ATLA, NY State Bar Assn., Assn. Bar. City of NY, Philonomic Honor Soc., County Bar Assn. (constrn. law forum), Am. Assn. Trial Lawyers. Office: Arent Fox LLP 1675 Broadway New York NY 10019 Office Phone: 212-484-3949. Business E-Mail: eugene.scheiman@arentfox.com.

SCHEIN, EDGAR HENRY, management educator; b. Zurich, Mar. 5, 1928; came to U.S., 1939, naturalized, 1944; s. Marcel and Hilde (Schoenbeck) S.; m. Mary Louise Lodmell, July 28, 1956; children: Louisa, Elizabeth, Peter. PhB, U. Chgo., 1946, BA, 1947, Stanford U., 1948, MA, 1949; PhD, Harvard U., 1953. Tchg. asst. stats. Stanford U., 1947-49; tchg. asst. social psychology Harvard U., 1949-52; rsch. psychologist, neuropsychiatry div. Walter Reed Army Inst. Rsch., also chief social psychology sect., 1952-56; mem. faculty MIT, 1956—, prof. orgnl. psychology and mgmt., 1964—, chmn. orgn. studies group Sloan Sch. Mgmt., 1972-81, Sloan Fellows prof. mgmt., 1978-97, prof. emeritus, 1995—; mem. bd., exec. com. Nat. Tng. Labs., 1962-64; cons. to govt. and industry, 1956—. Author books and articles in field. Capt. AUS, 1950-56. Recipient Aux. Rsch. award Social Sci. Rsch. Coun., 1958. Fellow APA; mem. Acad. Mgmt. Home Phone: 617-497-7515. Business E-Mail: scheine@comcast.net.

SCHEIN, VIRGINIA ELLEN, psychologist; b. June 23, 1943; d. Jacob Charles and Anne Schein; m. Rupert F. Chisholm (dec. 2004); 1 child, Alexander Nikos. BA cum laude, Cornell U., 1965; PhD, NYU, 1969. Lic. psychologist, Pa. Sr. rsch. assoc. Am. Mgmt. Assn., NYC, 1969-70; mgr. personnel rsch. Life Office Mgmt. Assn., NYC, 1970-72; dir. personnel rsch. Met. Life Ins. Co., NYC, 1972-75; assoc. prof. Sch. Mgmt. Case Western Res. U., Cleve., 1975-76; vis. assoc. prof. Sch. Orgn. and Mgmt. Yale U., New Haven, 1977-80; mgmt. cons., 1975—; assoc. prof. psychology Bernard M. Baruch Coll. CUNY, 1982-85; prof. mgmt. and psychology Gettysburg Coll., Pa., 1986—2006, prof. emerita mgmt. and psychology, 2007—. Chair mgmt. dept. Gettysburg Coll., 1993—95. Author: Working from the Margins, 1995; co-author: Power and Organization Development, 1988; mem. editl. rev. bds. Acad. Mgmt. Review, 1979-82, Women Mgmt. Rev., 1991-, Acad. Mgmt. Execs., 1992-98; contbr. articles to profl. jours. Bd. dirs. Family Planning Ctr., 1988-91, Pvt. Industry Coun., 1990-93, Keystone Rsch. Ctr., 1996-98, Women Cmty. Svc., 1997-2003; bd. dirs. Survivors, Inc., pres. bd. dirs., 1991-92, Adams County Children and Youth Adv. Bd., 2003-04. Mem.: APA (coun.rep. 1978—80, com. women 1980—83), Internat. Assn. Applied Psychology (divsn. orgnl. psychology chair sci. program com. 1995—98, pres.-elect 1998—2002, pres. 2002—06), Acad. Mgmt. (rep. orgn.devel. divsn. 1979—81, exec. com. women mgmt. divsn. 1994—97), Met. Assn. Applied Psychology (pres. 1973—74), Psi Chi. Home Phone: 215-625-0175. Personal E-mail: vschein@gettysburg.edu.

SCHEINBERG, PHYLLIS F., federal agency administrator; BA, Simmons Coll.; MS, U. Calif. Sr. budget examiner trasp. and natural resources, office mgmt. and budget Exec. Office Pres., Washington, 1981—90; dir. transp. issues U.S. Gen. Acctg. Office, Washington; acting asst. sec. budget and programs, CFO US Dept. Transp., Washington, dep. asst. sec. budget & programs, 2001—05, asst. sec. budget & programs, CFO, 2005—.

SCHEINDLIN, RAYMOND PAUL, literature educator, religious organization administrator; b. Phila., May 13, 1940; s. Irving and Betty (Bernstein) S.; m. Shira Ann Joffe, 1969 (div. 1981); children— Dov Baer, Dahlia Rachel; m. Janice C. Meyerson, 1986. BA, U. Pa., 1961; M.H.L., Jewish Theol. Sem., NYC, 1963; PhD, Columbia U., NYC, 1971. Ordained rabbi, 1965. Asst. prof. McGill U., Montreal, Que., Canada, 1969-72; asst. prof. Cornell U., Ithaca, NY, 1972-74; assoc. prof. Jewish Theol. Sem. of Am., NYC, 1974-85, prof. Hebrew lit., 1985—, provost, 1984-90; dir. Shalom Spiegel Inst. of Medieval Hebrew Lit., 1996—; rabbi Congregation Baith Israel Anshei Emes, Bklyn., 1979-82; fellow Cullman Ctr. Scholars and Writers, NY Pub. Libr., 2005—06. Mem. publ. com. Jewish Publ. Soc., Phila., 1985-90; mem. internat. adv. com. Ctr. for Judaic Studies U. Pa., 1995—; mem. bd. acad. advisors Catalan Mus. Jewish Culture, Gerona, Spain, 1993—; mem. editl. com. Jewish Quar. Rev., 1995—. Translator: (novella) Of Bygone Days by Mendele Mokher Seforim, 1973, Jewish Liturgy: A Comprehensive History by Ismar Elbogen, 1993; author: Form & Structure in the Poetry of Al-Mu'tamid Ibn 'Abbad, 1974, 201 Arabic Verbs, 1978, Wine, Women, and Death: Medieval Hebrew Poems on the Good Life, 1986, The Gazelle: Medieval Hebrew Poems on God, Israel and the Soul, 1991, Chronicles of the Jewish People, 1996, The Book of Job, 1998, A Short History of the Jewish People, 1998, (libretto) Miriam and the Angel of Death, 1984, The Song of the Distant Dove: Pilgrimage Poems by Judah Halevi, 2007, 501 Arabic Verbs, 2007; mem. editl. com. Prooftexts, 1988—2004, Edebiyat, 1992—, Studies in Muslim-Jewish Rels., 1992—; mem. editl. bd. Arabic and Mid. Ea. Lits., Medieval Iberia; co-editor The Literature of Al-Andalus, 2000. Fellow Cullman Ctr. Scholar and Writers, N.Y Publ. Libr., 2005—. Recipient Jewish Cultural Achievement award Nat. Found. for Jewish Culture, 2004; Guggenheim fellow, 1988, Annenberg Inst. fellow, 1993; sr. assoc. fellow Oxford Centre for Postgrad. Hebrew Studies. Fellow: Am. Acad. Jewish Rsch. (mem. exec. com. 2003—); mem.: PEN Am. Ctr., Jewish Publ. Soc. (bd. dirs. 1987—93), Assn. Jewish Studies, World Union Jewish Studies, Soc. Judeo-Arabic Studies. Home: 420 Riverside Dr New York NY 10025-7773 Office: Jewish Theol Sem Am 3080 Broadway New York NY 10027-4650 Home Phone: 212-866-3372. Personal E-mail: rscheindlin@gmail.com.

SCHEINE, EDWARD ROBERT, lawyer; b. Bklyn., Sept. 12, 1949; s. David Louis and Ruth (Peck) Scheine; m. Ora Rosen, Aug. 19, 1972; children: David, Michael, Jonathan, Amanda. BA with honors, Northeastern U., 1972; JD, Bklyn. Law Sch., 1975. Bar: NY 1976, U.S. Dist. Ct. (ea. and so. dists.) NY 1976, U.S. Supreme Ct. 1982. Atty. VA, NYC, 1975—76; assoc. Jacowitz & Severance, Bklyn., 1976—77; pvt. practice Bklyn., 1977—78; ptnr. Scheine, Fusco, Brandenstein, P.C., 1978—2001, Scheine, Furey & Assocs., LLP, 2001—. Past pres. NY Workers' Compensation Bar Assn. Author: Workers Compensation for the Health Care Provider. Mem.: ABA, NY Social Security Bar Assn. Trial Lawyers Am., Suffolk County Bar Assn., NY County Lawyers Assn., NY State Bar Assn. Home: 2 Carriage Ct Huntington Station NY 11746-5842 Office: Scheine Furey & Assocs LLP 200 Motor Pky Hauppauge NY 11788 also: 175 Fulton Ave Hempstead NY also: 2014 Williamsbridge Rd Bronx NY

SCHEINESON, IRWIN BRUCE, insurance and investment company executive; b. Cin., Aug. 8, 1955; s. Julian and Joan (Klein) Scheineson; married; children: Kate Marie, John Philip. BBA, U. Cin., 1978. Pres., prin. Lang-Kruke Fin. Group, Cin., 1978—97; agt. adv. liaison Community Mut. Ins. Co. (Blue Cross), Cin., 1978—80, Cen. Benefits Mut., Columbus, Ohio, 1986—88; pres. Gt. Am. Filter Co., Norwood, Ohio, 1990—98; pres., CEO Planning Works, Ltd., 1997. Lectr. in field. Contbr. articles to profl. jours. Fund raiser Guilford Sch., Cin., 1985—. Mem. Internat. Assn. Fin. Planning, Nat. Assn. Health Underwriters, Nat. Assn. Life Underwriters (Nat. Sales Achievement award 1979), Cin. Assn. Health Underwriters (bd. dirs. 1984-87), Nat. Soc. CLUs and Chartered Fin. Cons., 2002 Top of the Table Million Dollar Roundtable, Crest Hills Country Club (bd. dirs. 1988-93). Republican. Jewish. Avocations: tennis, skiing, travel, golf, marathon running. Office: Planning Works Ltd Ste 250 11111 Montgomery Rd Cincinnati OH 45249-3305 Office Phone: 513-489-7526. Personal E-mail: runner@cinci.rr.com. Business E-Mail: planningworks@cinci.rr.com. E-mail: irwin@planningworks.net.

SCHEINFELD, JAMES DAVID, retired travel company executive; b. Milw., Wis., Nov. 11, 1926; s. Aaron and Sylvia (Rosenberg) S.; children from previous marriage: John Stephen, Shaina, Robert Alan; m. Elna Magnusson, 1994. BA in Econs. magna cum laude, U. Wis., 1949. With Manpower, Inc., 1948-78, salesman, Chgo., 1949-51, br. mgr., 1951-53, nat. sales mgr., Milw., 1953-56, dir. sales, corp. sec., 1956-59, v.p. sales, 1959-62, exec. v.p. mktg., 1962-65, exec. v.p. (sr.), chief ops. officer, 1965-76, v.p. spl. projects, 1976-78, mem. exec. com., bd. dirs., 1959-76, cons., 1978-84; exec. v.p., chief exec. officer, bd. dirs. Transpersonal, Inc., Any Task Inc., Manpower Argentina, Manpower Europe, Manpower Ltd. (U.K.), Manpower Australia, Manpower Japan, Manpower Germany GmbH, Manpower Norway, Manpower Denmark, Manpower Venezuela, 1966-76; pres. Travway Internat. Inc. - Funway Holidays, Funjet, 1976-81, Aide Svcs., Inc., Tampa, Fla., 1976-81; pres., chief exec. officer Travelpower Inc., 1976-84; sr. v.p. Carlson Travel Network, 1984—2004. Mem. Hickory Travel Systems Inc., 1977-85, bd. dirs., 1978-85, pres., 1980-82, pres. emeritus, 1982—. Contbr. articles to profl. jours. Chmn. Cancer Crusade Milwaukee County, 1970; bd. dirs. Sinai-Samaritan Med. Ctr., Better Bus. Bur. Milw., 1979-90, Found. for Santa Barbara City Coll., 1989—, pres., 1996-2000; trustee U. Wis. Milw. Found., 1981-91, emeritus trustee, 1991—; mem. bus. adv. bd. U. Wis.-Milw., 1987—; chmn. bus. adv. bd. Santa Barbara City Coll., 1988-92; dir. Santa Barbara Trust for Hist. Preservation, 1995—, v.p., 1998-2004, pres. 2004-06; mem. Greater Milw. Com., 1984-97; bd. dirs. Sansum Clinic, 1989—, chmn., 2005-07. With USNR, 1944—46, Pacific Theatre. Decorated Pacific Theatre Ribbon with 1 Star. Mem. Nat. Assn. Temporary Svcs. (bd. dirs. 1969-77, pres. 1975-76), La Cumbre Country Club (Santa Barbara), Rotary Club of Montecito Calif. Home and Office: 129 Rametto Rd Santa Barbara CA 93108-2317 Office Phone: 805-969-5671. Personal E-mail: jimscheinfeld1@cox.net. *I do not often walk or look back where my footprints are. I prefer to walk that part of the beach I have never walked before. I am a person who thinks more about tomorrow than yesterday... more about what can be done than what has been done... more about challenges than accomplishments. Looking back is helpful only if I can find a sign to help me in my future.*

SCHEINHOLTZ, LEONARD LOUIS, lawyer; b. Pitts., June 2, 1927; s. Bernard A. and Marie (Getzel) Scheinholtz; m. Joan R. Libenson, Aug. 16, 1953; children: Stuart, Nancy, Barry. BA, U. Pa., 1948, MA, 1949; LLB, Columbia U., 1953. Bar: Pa. 1954, US Ct. Appeals (3d cir.) 1959, US Ct. Appeals (6th cir.) 1968, US Supreme Ct. 1972, US Ct. Appeals (4th cir.) 1973, US Ct. Appeals (5th cir.) 1981, US Ct. Appeals (11th cir.) 1991, US Ct. Appeals (2d cir.) 1993. Assoc. Reed, Smith, LLP, Pitts., 1953—62, spl. ptnr., 1962—64, gen. ptnr., 1964—97, head labor dept., 1980—86, of counsel, 1997—. Dir. Am. Arbitration Assn., NYC, 1980—96. Author: Exemption Under the Anti-Trust Laws for Joint Employer Activity, 1982, The Arbitrator as Judge and Jury: Another Look at Statutory Law in Arbitration, 1985. Vice-chmn. Pa. AAA Fedn., Harrisburg, 1982—85; chmn. W. Pa. AAA Motor Club, 1979—82; trustee Jewish Healthcare Found., 2004—; bd. dirs. Nat. Aviary, 1999—, United Jewish Fedn., Pitts., 1997—2000; trustee Montefiore Hosp., Pitts., 1976—79. With USN, 1945—46. Mem.: ABA, Allegheny County Bar Assn., Pa. Bar Assn. Republican. Jewish. Home: 746 Pinoak Rd Pittsburgh PA 15243-1153 Office: Reed Smith LLP Mellon Sq 435 6th Ave Pittsburgh PA 15219-1886 Office Phone: 412-288-3178. Business E-Mail: lscheinholtz@reedsmith.com.

SCHEINMAN, NANCY JANE, psychologist; b. NYC, June 23, 1955; d. Norman Sinclair and Vivian Estelle (Goodwin) Tischenkel; m. Stephen Robert Scheinman, June 15, 1990; children: Cassie Leigh, William Mayer. BA, Vassar Coll., 1977; MS, U. Miami, 1986, PhD, 1988. Intern Duke Med. Ctr., Durham, N.C., 1988; pvt. practice Miami, Fla., 1991—. Founder, dir. Hosp. Based Alternative Medicine Ctr. Contbr. to books and articles to profl. jours. U. Miami fellow, 1988-90. Mem. Am. Psychol. Assn., Soc. Behavioral Medicine, Phi Beta Kappa. Independent. Jewish. Avocations: swimming, tennis. Personal E-mail: nancyscheinman@aol.com.

SCHEINMAN, STANLEY BRUCE, corporate financial executive; b. NYC, Nov. 13, 1933; s. Samuel and Sadie (Seiffer) S.; m. Susan L. Elstein (dec.); m. Janet L. Donnely, Dec. 30, 1975 (dec.); children: Catherine Amy, Anthony Paul, Sarah Jean, Norah Jane; m. Maria Shea Burke, Nov. 17, 2000. AB, Cornell U., 1954; MBA, CCNY, 1957; JD (Harlan Fisk Stone scholar), Columbia U., 1960. Bar: N.Y. 1960. Assoc. firm Cravath, Swaine & Moore, NYC, 1960-62; capital projects officer, legis. programs staff coord. AID, Washington, 1962-64; sr. exec. officer Bur. Pvt. Enterprise, AID, 1982-83; v.p. fin. and adminstrn. svcs. industries div., also v.p., counsel internat. div. PepsiCo. Inc., 1965-70; v.p. fin. and adminstrn. pharm. divsn. Revlon, Inc., 1970-72; sr. v.p. MCI Comm., 1972-76; pres., COO FSC Corp., Pitts., 1976-81; pres. New Venture Capital Corp., Washington, 1984-85; prin. Re Venture Assocs., Salisbury, Conn., 1985-86; chmn., CEO Internat. 800 Telcom Corp., Geneva, 1987-88; pres., CEO Zurich Depository Corp., Manhasset, NY, 1988-89; exec. v.p. AMIF&S Ltd., NYC, 1989-91; pres. IT Svc. Corp., Westport, Conn., 1991-92; v.p. ops. and bus. devel. EQ Corp., Westport, 1992-95; exec. v.p., CFO, Computer Products and Svcs. Inc., Wilton, Conn., 1995-96; pres., mng. dir. TTC Internat. Ltd., London, 1996—. Mem.: ABA, Internat. Execs. Assn., Fin. Execs. Inst., Inst. for Dirs. (U.K.), Assn. Bar City NY, Brit.-Am. Club, Cornell Club, Fgn. Svc. Club, Paris-Am. Club. Home and Office: PO Box 2398 Westport CT 06880 Home: H3 Bridge Rd S Weston CT 06883 E-mail: stanbsch@aol.com, stanbsch@btinternet.com.

SCHEINMAN, STEVEN JAY, dean, medical educator; b. Monticello, NY, Oct. 22, 1951; 2 children. AB summa cum laude, Amherst Coll., 1973; MD cum laude, Yale U., 1977. Diplomate Am. Bd. Internal Medicine in Neprology, lic. physician N.Y., Conn. Resident internal medicine Yale-New Haven Hosp., 1977-80; chief resident internal medicine Upstate Med. Ctr., Syracuse, NY, 1980-81, fellow nephrology, 1981-83, Yale-New Haven Hosp., 1983-84; asst. prof. medicine SUNY Upstate Med. U., Syracuse, 1984-90, asst. prof. pharmacology, 1988-90, assoc. prof. medicine and pharmacology, 1990-94, prof. medicine and pharmacology, 1994—, chief nephrology divsn. dept. medicine, 1994—2004, exec. v.p., dean Coll. Medicine, 2004—, officer-in-charge, 2006. Vis. scientist MRC Molecular Medicine Group, Royal Postgrad. Med. Sch. Hammersmith Hosp., London, 1992, London, 95; vis. scholar dept. biochemistry U. Oxford, 1985; attending physician U. Hosp., Syracuse, Crouse-Irving Meml. Hosp., Syracuse, VA Med. Ctr., Syracuse; dir. Nephrology Fellowship Program, 1993—; spkr. seminars, confs., orgns. Assoc. editor: Neph SAP, 2002—; mem. editl. bd. Yale Jour. Biology and Medicine, 1975—77, Jour. Am. Soc. Nephrology, 2000—02, mem. NIDDK Spl. Rev. Group, 1998—; contbr. Recipient Lange award, Yale U. Sch. Medicine, 1976, Resident Merit award, ACP (Conn. chpt.), 1980, Nat. Rsch. Svc. award, NIH, 1981—83, Clin. Investigator award, 1985—90, Charles R. Ross Rsch. award, SUNY-Health Sci. Ctr., 1992, Pres.'s award for Excellence and Leadership in Rsch., SUNY Upstate Med. U., 2001, Chancellor's Rsch. Recognition award, SUNY, 2002; grantee, Nat. Inst. Arthritis Diabetes Digestive and Kidney Diseases, 1981—83, 1985—90, 1995—2002, 2000—04, 2003—, Am. Heart Assn., 1985, 1988—90, 1990—91, 1992—95, 1995—97, NATO, 1995—98. Mem.: Assn. Am. Med. Colls. Coun. Deans, Assn. Subspecialty Profs., Nat. Kidney Found., Am. Heart Assn. Coun. on Kidney, Am. Soc. Bone and Mineral Rsch., Am. Physiol. Soc., Internat. Soc. Nephrology, Am. Soc. Nephrology (mem. editl. bd. Jour. 2000—02), Am. Fedn. Med. Rsch., Am. Soc. Clin. Investigation, Alpha Omega Alpha, Phi Beta Kappa. Office: Office of Dean SUNY Upstate Med Univ 1257 Weiskotten Hall Syracuse NY 13210 Office Phone: 315-464-9720. Business E-Mail: scheinms@upstate.edu.

SCHEIRER, WILLIAM KENNETH, economist, consultant; b. Bethlehem, Pa., Oct. 17, 1937; s. Kenneth Raymond Scheirer and Pansy Elinor Ruch; m. Rita Gertrud Aase Simmersbach (div.); children: Nicola, Erik, Peter, Karl. AB, Princeton U., 1959; student, London Sch. Econs.,

1959—60, MIT, 1960—63. Sr. economist U.S. SBA, Washington, 1980—95. Cons. Lehigh Valley Techonomics, Bethlehem, Pa., 1995—2007. Mem. editl. bd. Jour. Small Bus. Econs., 1988—93; contbr. chapters to books. Life mem., past pres. Kalorama Citizens Assn., 1968—; life mem. Com. 100 on Fed. City, Wash., 1999—; founder Bethlehem Citizens Assn.; mem. City Bethlehem Task Force on Comprehensive Plan and Zoning Ordinance. Mem.: Am. Econ. Assn., Torch Club. Avocations: reading, writing. Home and Office: Lehigh Valley Techonomics 1890 Eaton Ave Bethlehem PA 18018 Office Phone: 610-954-9997. Personal E-mail: bethlehembill@hotmail.com.

SCHEIRING, MICHAEL JAMES, college official; b. Canton, Ohio, Oct. 11, 1949; s. Robert J. and Madonna L. (Geisigi) S.; m. Marcia L. Young, May 13, 1972; children: Kristy L., Lauren M. BA, Kent State U., 1971, MPA, 1972. Sect. supr. N.J. Dept. Treasury, Trenton, 1974-78; policy analyst to gov. Trenton, 1978-80; dir. adminstrn. N.J. Dept. Community Affairs, Trenton, 1980-82; dir. corp. budgeting N.J. Transit Corp., Newark, 1982-83; v.p. adminstrn. and fin. Thomas A. Edison Coll., Trenton, 1983—; exec. dir. Gov. Mgmt. Rev. Com., Gov.'s Office, Trenton, N.J., 1990-93. Trustee N.J. Ednl. Computer Corp., 1984-90; trustee, comptroller Edison Found., Trenton, 1984—; mem. adv. bd. National Ctr. Productivity; past pres. U.D. Dollars for Scholars Found.; pres. Cerebral Palsy of NJ; chmn. Trenton Audit Commn.; mem. citizen's delegation to China; trustee Robert Wood Johnson U. Hosp. Hamilton. Contbg. author: N.J. Zero-Based Budgeting, 1979. Named Vol. of Yr. N.J. United Cerebral Palsy; recipient Libr. Champion award. Mem. ASPA (nat. coun., v.p. programs 1984, v.p. membership 1985, pres. 1987-89), Old Barracks Assn. (trustee, past pres.), Rotary (pres.). Roman Catholic. Home: 2 Lotus Ln Trenton NJ 08648-3211 Office: Thomas Edison State Coll Trenton NJ 08625 Home Phone: 609-883-4651; Office Phone: 609-984-1110 x 2300. E-mail: mscheiring@tesl.edu.

SCHEITHAUER, CHRISTOPHER C., lawyer; JD, Univ. So. Calif., 1996. Bar: Calif., US Dist. Ct. No., Ea., Ctrl., So. Calif. Ptnr., employment litigation McDermott Will & Emory, Irvine, Calif. Author (contrib.): Employee Benefits Law. Named a Rising Star, So. Calif. Super Lawyers, 2005—06. Mem.: ABA, State Bar Calif. Office: McDermott Will & Emery Ste 500 18191 Von Karman Ave Irvine CA 92612-7108 Office Phone: 949-757-7163. Office Fax: 949-851-9348. Business E-Mail: cscheithauer@mwe.com.

SCHEKMAN, RANDY W., molecular biology administrator, biochemist; b. St. Paul, Dec. 30, 1948; married, 1973; 1 child. BA, UCLA, 1970; PhD in Biochemistry, Stanford U., 1975; PhD (hon.), U. Geneva, 1997. Fellow U. Calif., San Diego, 1974-76, from asst. to assoc. prof. Berkeley, 1976-83, prof., 1983—, head divsn. biochemistry and molecular biology, 1990-97, co-chair dept. molecular and cellular biology, 1997—. Fellow Woodrow Wilson Found., 1970, Cystic Fibrosis Found., 1974, John S. Guggenheim Found., 1982-83; recipient Research award in microbiology & immunology, Eli Lilly, 1987, Lewis S. Rosenstiel award in basic biomedical sci., 1994, Gairdner Found. Internat. award, 1996, Albert Lasker award for basic med. rsch., Albert and Mary Lasker Found., 2002, Louisa Gross Horwtiz prize, Columbia U., 2002; named Amgen award lecturer, Protein Soc., 1999, Berkeley Faculty Rsch. lecturer, U. Calif., 1999. Mem. Am. Soc. Microbiology, Am. Soc. Biochemists & Molecular Biologists, Am. Acad. of Arts & Sciences (elected 2000), NAS (elected 1992); hon. mem. Japanese Biochemical Soc.; foreign assoc. EMBO. Achievements include research on molecular mechanism of secretion and membrane assembly in eucaryotic cells. Office: U Calif Dept Molecular Cell Bio 401 Barker Hall Spc 3202 Berkeley CA 94720-3202 Office Phone: 510-642-5686. E-mail: schekman@uclink4.berkeley.edu.

SCHELBERT, HEINRICH RUEDIGER, nuclear medicine physician; b. Wuerzburg, Germany, Nov. 5, 1939; MD, U. Würzburg, Germany, 1964. Diplomate Am. Bd. Nuclear Medicine. Intern Mercy Med. Ctr., Phila., 1966-67, resident, 1967-68, 70-71; resident in cardiology U. Dusseldorf, Germany, 1971-72; fellow in cardiology, resident in nuclear medicine U. Calif., San Diego, 1968-69, asst. rsch. cardiologist, 1972-75, assoc. rsch. radiologist, 1975-76; hosp. assoc. UCLA Med. Ctr., 1977—; prof. radiol. scis. UCLA Sch. Medicine, 1980-90, prof. pharmacol. and radiol. scis., 1993—. Editor-in-chief: Jour. Nuc. Medicine, 2004. Recipient Georg von Hevesy prize 2d Internat. Congress World Fedn. Nuclear Medicine and Radiation Biology, 1978, 3d Internat. Congress World Fedn. Nuclear Medicine and Radiation Biology, 1982, Disting. Sci. award, Acad. Molecular Imaging, 2006. Fellow Am. Coll. Cardiology; mem. Am. Heart Assn. (disting. scientific achievement award 1989), Soc. Nuclear Medicine (Herrman L. Blumgart pioneer lectr. award 1989, George De Hevesy Nuclear Medicine Pioneer award 1998), German Soc. Nuc. Med. (hon.), Swiss Soc. Nuc. Medicine (hon.)(editor-in-chief). Office: UCLA Sch Medicine Dept Molecular Med B2 085J Box 956948 Los Angeles CA 90095-6948 Office Phone: 310-825-3076. Business E-Mail: hschelbert@mednet.ucla.edu.

SCHELD, WILLIAM MICHAEL, internist, educator; b. Middletown, Conn., Aug. 15, 1947; s. William Herman and Lucille Laverne (Houchens) S.; m. Susan Ella Vaughan, June 14, 1969; 1 child, Sarah Walker. BS, Cornell U., 1969, MD, 1973. Diplomate Am. Bd. Internal Medicine. Intern, then resident U. Va. Sch. Medicine, Charlottesville, 1973-76, fellow in infectious diseases, 1976-79, asst. prof., 1979-82, assoc. prof., 1982-88, prof., assoc. chair dept. infectious diseases, 1988—. Chair Inter-sci. Conf. on Antimicrobial Agents and Chemotherapy. Editor: Infections of the Central Nervous System, 1991, 97, 2004; contbr. sci. articles to profl. publs., chpts. to books. Fellow ACP, Infectious Diseases Soc. Am. (pres. 2002-2003); mem. Am. Soc. Clin. Investigation, Nat. Found. Infectious Diseases (pres.), Alpha Omega Alpha. Achievements include research on meningitis and other central nervous system infections, bacterial endocarditis, sepsis, anthrax, etc. Home: 2075 Earlysville Rd Earlysville VA 22936-9634 Office: U Va Health Systems Box 801342 Charlottesville VA 22908 Office Phone: 934-924-5991.

SCHELER, BRAD ERIC, lawyer; b. Bklyn., Oct. 11, 1953; s. Bernard and Rita Regina (Miller) S.; m. Amy Ruth Frolick, Mar. 30, 1980; children: Ali M., Maddie H., Zoey B. BA with high honors, Lehigh U., 1974; JD, Hofstra U., 1977. Bar: N.Y. 1978, U.S. Dist. Ct. (so. and ea. dists.) N.Y. 1978. Assoc. Weil, Gotshal & Manges, NYC, 1977-81; sr. ptnr., chmn. bankruptcy and restructuring practice Fried, Frank, Harris, Shriver & Jacobson, LLP, NYC, 1981—. Contbg. author: Collier on Bankruptcy, 15th edit. revised, Norton Annual Survey of Bankruptcy Law; rsch. editor Hofstra U. Law Rev., 1975-77. Treas., bus. mgr. Trustees of Gramercy Park, NYC, 1979-87; bd. trustees Lehigh U., bd. adv. leadership coun., Linderman Libr. Project, Wall St. Coun., Coll. Bus. and Econs., K&A Register of Restructuring Profls.; bd. dirs. Vol. Lawyers for Arts, inMotion Justice for All Women, vice-chair; bd. dirs. Village Larchmont Libr. Fellow Am. Coll. Bankruptcy; mem. ABA (bus. bankruptcy com. corp. banking and bus. law sect., creditors' rights com. litig. sect.), N.Y. State Bar Assn., Assn. Bar City of N.Y. (com. on bankruptcy and corp. reorgn. 1991-94), Sigma Alpha Mu (v.p. 1973). Jewish. Home: 94 Larchmont Ave Larchmont NY 10538-3723 Office: Fried Frank Harris Shriver & Jacobson LLP 1 New York Plz Fl 23 New York NY 10004-1980 Office Phone: 212-859-8019. Business E-Mail: Schelbr@ffhsj.com.

SCHELL, ALLAN CARTER, retired electrical engineer; b. New Bedford, Mass., Apr. 14, 1934; s. Charles Carter and Elizabeth Schell; m. Shirley T. Sardineer; children: Alice Rosalind, Cynthia Anne. BS, MSE.E., MIT, Cambridge, 1956, Sc.D., 1961; student, Tech. U. Delft, Netherlands, 1956-57. Research physicist Air Force Cambridge Research Labs., Bedford, Mass., 1956-76, Guenter Loeser Meml. lectr., 1965; dir. electromagnetics directorate Rome Air Devel. Ctr., Bedford, 1976-87; chief scientist Hdqrs. USAF Systems Command, 1987-92; chief scientist, dep. dir. sci. and tech. Hdqrs. USAF Materiel Command, 1992-94. Dir. Electro; vis. assoc. prof. MIT, 1974; chair dept. of elec. enging. adv. coun. U. Pa., 1992-94. Contbr. articles to profl. jours. Pres. Aurora Highlands Civic Assn., Arlington, Va. Lt. USAF, 1958—60. Recipient Fulbright award, 1956-57, NSF fellow, 1955-56, 60-61, Presdl. Rank award, Meritorious Exec. award, 1989, two Air Force Meritorious Civilian Svc. awards. Fellow IEEE (John T. Bolljahn award 1966, Centennial Medal, 1984, Third Millennium Medal, 2000, bd. dirs. 1981-82, editor IEEE Press 1976-79, editor-in-chief Procs. of IEEE 1990-92); mem. IEEE Antennas and Propagation Soc. (pres. 1978, editor tran. 1969-71, chair awards and fellows com., 2000-05, APS Disting. Achievement award 2006), Internat. Sci. Radio Union, MIT Alumni Assn. (bd. dirs. 2003-05), Sigma Xi, Tau Beta Pi. Achievements include patents in field. Business E-Mail: a.schell@ieee.org.

SCHELL, BRAXTON, lawyer; b. Raleigh, NC, Feb. 24, 1924; s. Marshall H. and Margaret (Newsom) S.; m. Ann Cooper Knight, Mar. 30, 1951 (div. 1982); children: Braxton, Richard Knight, James Gray (dec.); m. Mary Rehill, Apr. 16, 1983. Student, N.C. State Coll., 1942-43; BS, U. N.C., 1948, JD with honors, 1951. Bar: NC 1951. Since practiced in, Greensboro; assoc. Smith, Moore, Smith & Pope, Greensboro, 1951-56; ptnr. Smith Moore Smith Schell & Hunter, Greensboro, 1956-85, Smith, Helms, Mullis, and Moore, 1986-87, Schell, Bray, Aycock, Abel & Livingston, 1987—. Gen. counsel, dir. Flagler Sys. and The Breakers Palm Beach, Inc. Assoc. editor N.C. Law Rev., 1950—51. Chmn. Special Liason Tax Com. Southeastern Region, 1960-61; bd. dirs. N.C. Outward Bound Sch., 1975-88, chmn., 1977-80; trustee Outward Bound, Inc., 1978-81; bd. dirs. William R. Kenan Funds for Pvt. Enterprise, Arts and Enging., Tech. and Sci. and Ethics. Pilot USAAF, 1943-45. Fellow Am. Bar Found.; mem. ABA, N.C. Bar Assn., Greensboro Bar Assn. (Disting. Svc. award 2005), Order of Coif, Figure Eight Island Yacht Club, Greensboro County Club (pres. 1971-72), Phi Beta Kappa. Presbyterian. Home: 422B Fisher Park Cir Greensboro NC 27401-1615 Office: Schell Bray Aycock Abel & Living 1500 Renaissance Pla Greensboro NC 27420 Business E-Mail: bschell@sbaal.com.

SCHELL, FARREL LOY, transportation engineer; b. Amarillo, Tex., Dec. 14, 1931; s. Thomas Phillip and Lillian Agnes (McKee) S.; m. Shirley Anne Samuelson, Feb. 6, 1955; children: James Christopher, Maria Leslyn Schell Peter. BS, U. Kans., 1954; postgrad., Carnegie-Mellon U., 1974. Registered profl. engr., Calif., Colo. Resident engr. Sverdrup & Parcel, Denver, 1957-61; project engr. Bechtel Corp., San Francisco, 1961-62, Parsons, Brinckerhoff-Tudor-Bechtel, San Francisco, 1962-67; mgr. urban transp. dept. Kaiser Engrs., Oakland, Calif., 1967-78; program dir. San Francisco Mcpl. Rwy I.C., 1978-80; project mgr. Houston Transit Cons., 1980-83, Kaiser Transit Group, Miami, 1983-85; mgr. program devel. Kaiser Engrs., Oakland, 1985-87; project mgr. O'Brien-Kreitzberg & Assocs., San Francisco, 1987-89; sr. project mgr. Bay Area Rapid Transit Dist., Oakland, Calif., 1989—96. Dir./CEO Schelter Devel. Corp., Piedmont, Calif., 1982—. Contbr. articles to profl. jours. Chmn., bd. dirs. Achenbach Graphic Arts Coun., 1996-2002. Lt. (j.g.) USN, 1954-57, PTO. Mem. ASCE, ASME, Nat. Soc. Profl. Engrs., Nat. Coun. Engring. Examiners, Am. Planners Assn., Am. Pub. Transit Assn., Lakeview Club, Scarab Club, Pachacamac Club, Sigma Tau, Tau Beta Pi. Avocations: fly fishing, camping. Home: 100 Bay Pl #1517 Oakland CA 94610 Personal E-mail: fschell2@mac.com.

SCHELL, JAMES MUNSON, finance company executive; b. Kalamazoo, Mich., Mar. 25, 1944; s. Frank John and Shirley I. S.; m. Susan O'Laughlin, Aug. 6, 1966; children: Karen, Michael, Ryan. BA, Vanderbilt U., 1966; MBA, Washington U., 1968. Dir. term and internat. financing Chrysler Fin. Corp., Troy, Mich., 1976-79, v.p., treas., 1980-81; v.p. domestic treasury Am. Express Co., NYC, 1981-82; v.p. fin. resources Hertz Corp., NYC, 1982-83; v.p., chief fin. officer Clabir Corp., Greenwich, Conn., 1983-84; v.p., treas. Fairchild Industries, 1985-87; ind. fin. cons., 1987—. Bd. dirs. Jackson-Jordan Corp., CTI Industries, Country Home Bakers. Republican. Roman Catholic. Home: 40 Stony Brook Rd Darien CT 06820-4326 E-mail: jmsschell@aol.com.

SCHELL, MELVIN FRANK, JR., real estate agent; b. Binghamton, NY, Feb. 3, 1938; s. Melvin Frank and Irene Schell; m. Dollie Sedot Knowles, May 31, 1958; children: Mark Stephen, Jeremy Joel. BA, Tenn. Temple U., 1971; MBA, Ga. State U., 1987. Ordained Minister of the Gospel Briarlake Bapt. Ch., Atlanta GA, 1976; lic. Real Estate Agent Ga. Real Estate Commn., 2002, Fla. Real Estate Commn., 2004. Mktg. rep. Internat. Bus. Machines, Inc., Chattanooga, 1960—73; asst. min. First Alliance Ch., Atlanta, 1973—74; exec. dir. Evangelism Explosion Atlanta, Atlanta, 1974—75; pres. Ch. Growth Ministries, Atlanta, 1976—81, Omega Info. Systems, Inc., Atlanta, 1981—2003; regional mgr., AT&T computers MicroAge, Tempe, Ariz., 1990—91; pres. Aarist Internat., Inc, Atlanta, 1993—2003; real estate agt. Prudential Ga. Realty, Gainesville, Ga., 2002—, Century 21 Prestige Realty, Key West, Fla., 2005—06. Cons. to churches and non-profit organizations Fuller Evangelistic Assn., Pasadena, Calif., 1980—83. Author: (training materials) The Total Church Growth Model. Electronics technician second class USN, 1956—59, Key West, Fla. Decorated Good Conduct medal USN; recipient Class Pres., Internat. Bus. Machines, Inc., 1972. Dedicated Follower Of Jesus Christ.

SCHELL, RICHARD A., federal judge; b. 1950; BA, So. Meth. U., 1972, JD, 1975. Bar: Tex. 1975. Asst. dist. atty. Collin County, Tex., 1976; atty. pvt. practice, 1977—81; judge County Ct. Law Collin County, 1982—86, 219th Jud. Dist. Ct. Tex., 1986—88, U.S. Dist Ct. (ea. dist.) Tex., Beaumont, 1988—2003, U.S. Dist. Ct., Sherman, Tex., 2003—. Instr. rsch. methods and legal writing So. Meth. U., 1975—76. Mem.: State Bar Tex. Office: US Dist Ct 200 N Travis Sherman TX 75090

SCHELLENBERGER, ROBERT EARL, retired management educator, department chairman; b. Janesville, Wis., July 25, 1932; s. Ervin William and Adelaide Louise (Keller) S.; m. Linda Eula Todd, Dec. 30, 1961; children: Brian T., Keith W., Heidi L. BSBA, U. Wis., 1958, MBA, 1959; PhD, U. N.C., 1963. Personnel supr. Libby McNeill and Libby, Janesville, Wis., 1957-58; from asst. prof. to assoc. prof. chmn. div. stats. dept. bus U. Md., College Park, 1963-68; chair dept. mgmt. So. Ill. U., Carbondale, Ill., 1968-70, dir. planning Sch. Human Resources Devel., 1970-71, prof. mgmt., 1968-71; vis. prof., dir. program evaluation Babcock Grad. Sch. Mgmt., Wake Forest U., Winston-Salem, NC, 1971-73; prof. dept. mgmt. Temple U., Phila., 1973-81, from chmn. dept. mgmt. to asst. to acad. vice chancellor, 1975-77; prof. decision scis. dept. East Carolina U., Greenville, NC, 1981-2000, chmn. decision scis. dept., 1989-95; ret., 2001. Pres. Md. Rsch. and Cons., Hyattsville, 1966-67; v.p. Ea. Acad. Mgmt., 1967; cons. Comml. Credit Corp., Balt., 1966. Author: Managerial Analysis, 1967, Policy Formulation, 1978, 2d edit., 1982; co-editor Jour. of Econs. and Bus., 1976; developer (software package) MANYSYM, 1965, 68, 78, 82, 86. Chmn. Utilities Com., Carbondale, 1970-72. Title IV NDEA fellow U. N.C., 1960-62, Earhart Jr. fellow U. Wis. Mem. Assn. for Bus. Simulation, SE Decision Scis. Inst., Decision Scis. Inst. (bd. dirs. 1974-77), Beta Gamma Sigma. Personal E-mail: dcschell@suddenlink.net.

SCHELLER, JOHN C. J., lawyer; b. Jan. 11, 1969; BA, St. Norbert Coll., DePere, Wis., 1991; JD, John Marshall Law Sch., Chgo., 1995. Jud. clk. Ill. Appellate Ct. (2d dist.), Chgo.; assoc. Lord, Bissell & Brook, Chgo., Michael Best & Friedrich, Madison, Wis., ptnr. Mem. Opera for Young, Madison. Office: Michael Best & Friedrich 1 S Pinckney St # 700 Madison WI 53703 Business E-Mail: jcscheller@michaelbest.com.

SCHELLER, RICHARD H., physiologist, science educator; b. Milw., Oct. 30, 1953; BA in Biochemistry with honors, U. Wis., Madison, 1975; PhD in Chemistry, Calif. Inst. Tech., 1980. Postdoctoral fellow divsn. biology Calif. Inst. Tech., 1980—81; postdoctoral fellow in molecular neurobiology Columbia U. Coll. Physicians and Surgeons, 1981—82; asst. prof. dept. biol. scis. Stanford (Calif.) U., 1982—87, assoc. prof. dept. biol. scis., 1987—90, assoc. prof. dept. molecular and cellular physiology, 1990—93, assoc. prof. dept. biol. scis. by courtesy, 1990—93, prof. dept. molecular and cellular physiology, 1993—, prof. dept. biol. scis., 1993; assoc. investigator Howard Hughes Med. Inst., Stanford U. Med. Ctr., 1990—94, investigator, 1994—2001; sr. v.p., research Genentech, Inc., South San Francisco, 2001—03, exec. v.p., research, 2003—. Mem. molecular, cellular and devel. neurobiology rev. com. NIMH, 1993—96; mem. sci. adv. bd. Hereditary Disease Found., 1995—96; mem. neurobiology adv. bd. Cold Spring Harbor Lab., 1995; mem. sr. rev. com. McKnight Endowment Fund, 1995; mem. adv. bd. Nat. Adv. Mental Health Coun., NIH, 1996. Mem. editl. bd. Jour. Neurosci., 1984—90, DNA, 1984—, Ann. Rev. Neurosci., 1985—90, Molecular Brain Rsch., 1985, Cellular and Molecular Neurobiology, 1986, Synapse, 1989—91, Neuron, 1990, Current Opinion in Neurobiology, 1990, sect. editor Jour. Neurosci., 1991—95, monitoring editor Jour. Cell Biology, 1991, assoc. editor Genes to Cells, 1995; contbr. articles to profl. jours. Recipient Basil O'Connor award, March of Dimes Found., 1983, Presdl. Young Investigator award, 1985, Alan T. Waterman award, NSF, 1989, Merit award, NIMH, 1992, W. Alden Spencer award, Columbia U., 1993; fellow, NIH, 1976—80, 1981—82, Alfred P. Sloan Found., 1984, Klingstein fellow in Neuroscis., 1985; scholar, McKnight Found., 1983, Pew scholar in biomed. scis., 1986, Camile and Henry Dreyfus Tchr. scholar, 1986. Mem.: Acad. of Arts and Sciences, NAS (award in Molecular Biology 1997), Soc. for Neurosci. (young investigator award selection com. 1996). Office: Genentech Inc 1 DNA Way South San Francisco CA 94080 Office Phone: 650-225-1000.

SCHELLIE, PETER D., lawyer; b. 1945; BA with honors, Ind. U., 1967; JD, U. Mich. Law Sch., 1970. Bar: DC & Md., US Supreme Ct, US Ct. Appeals (4th cir., 7th cir., DC cir.), DC Cir. Appeals, US Supreme Ct., Ind. Supreme Ct., Md. Ct. Appeals, US Bankruptcy Ct. Md. Ptnr. Bingham McCutchen LLP, Washington. Mem.: ABA, Md. State Bar Assn., Bar. Assn. DC. Office: Bingham McCutchen LLP 2020 K St NW Washington DC 20006 Office Phone: 202-373-6090. Office Fax: 202-373-6390. E-mail: peter.schellie@bingham.com. *

SCHELLING, DONALD LAWRENCE, lawyer; b. Clearwater, Fla., June 5, 1959; s. Dorothy Ann Allen and Donald Anthony Schelling; m. Myrna Ytis Marca, Aug. 11, 1996. BSc, U. Manchester, England, 1985; PhD, Dundee U., Scotland, 1991; JD, No. Ill. U., 2001. USPTO Registration: US Patent Office 2002. Patent atty. Townsend and Townsend and Crew, San Francisco, 2001—04, Polsinelli Shalton Welte Seulthaus, Kans. City, Mo., 2004—, Bozicevic Field & Francis LLP, East Palo Alto, Calif., 2004—. Author: Regulation of Hepatic Phosphatases, Patent Law Primer. Mem.: ABA, Am. Intellectual Property Assn., Calif. Bar Assn., Brit. Biochemical Soc., San Francisco Intellectual Law Assn., Veterans Rugby Club, Carnoustie Golf Club, PAD. Achievements include research in regulation of phosphatases by ancillary proteins. Office: Bozicevic Field & Francis LLP 1900 University Ave East Palo Alto CA 94303 Office Phone: 650-327-3400. Business E-Mail: schelling@bozpat.com.

SCHELLING, THOMAS CROMBIE, economist; b. Oakland, Calif., Apr. 14, 1921; s. John M. and Zelda M. (Ayres) S.; m. Corinne T. Saposs, Sept. 13, 1947 (div. 1991); children: Andrew, Thomas, Daniel, Robert; m. Alice M. Coleman, Nov. 8, 1991. AB in Econ., U. Calif., Berkeley, 1944; PhD in Econ., Harvard U., 1951; Doctorate (hon.), The RAND Grad. Sch. of Policy Analysis; Doctorate Honoris Causa, Erasmus U. Rotterdam. Economist US Bur. of the Budget, Washington, 1945—46, The Marshall Plan, Copenhagen and Paris, 1948—50; economist, Exec. Office of Pres. The White House, Washington, 1951—53; assoc. prof. and prof. econs. Yale U., 1953-58; prof. economics Harvard U., Cambridge, Mass., 1958-90, mem., John F. Kennedy Sch. Govt., 1969—90, Lucius N. Littauer prof. polit. economy emeritus; prof. econs. and pub. affairs U. Md., College Park, 1990—2003, disting. prof., 1990—2003, disting. prof. emeritus. Sr. staff mem. RAND Corp., 1958-59; chmn. rsch. adv. bd. Com. Econ. Devel., 1978-81, 84-85; mem. sci. adv. bd. USAF, 1960-64, def. sci. bd., 1966-70; mem. mil. econ. adv. panel CIA, 1980-85; dir. Inst. for Study of Smoking Behavior and Policy, Harvard U., 1984-90; trustee Aerospace Corp., 1984-93; trustee Ctr. for Advancement of Health. Co-author (with Morton H. Halperin): Strategy and Arms Control, 1961; author: Nat. Income Behavior, 1951, Internat. Economics, 1958, The Strategy of Conflict, 1960, Arms and Influence, 1966, Micromotives and Macrobehavior, 1978, Thinking Through the Energy Problem, 1979, Choice and Consequence, 1984, Strategies of Commitment, 2006. Trustee Ctr. for Advancement of Health. Recipient Frank E. Seidman Disting. award in polit. economy, 1977; Nobel Prize in Econ. Sci., 2005. Fellow AAAS, Assn. for Pub. Policy Analysis and Mgmt., Am. Econ. Assn. (pres. 1991, Disting. Fellow award); mem. NAS (Award Behavioral Rsch. Relevant to the Prevention of Nuclear War, 1993), Inst. Medicine, Ea. Econ. Assn. (pres. 1996). Office: Univ Md Sch Pub Policy College Park MD 20742-0001 Mailing: 4506 Wetherill Rd Bethesda MD 20816 Office Phone: 301-405-3494. E-mail: tschelli@mail.umd.edu.

SCHELLMAN, ELIZABETH TURNEY, vocalist, educator; b. Los Alamos, N.Mex., Apr. 20, 1951; d. John Turney and Donna Mott Turney; m. Mark Schellman, Nov. 18, 1972; children: Heidi, Eric, Gina, Craig, Kevin, Lori George, Kelly. MusB, BYU, Provo, Utah, 1973; MusM, U. Kans., Lawrence, 1996; DMA, U. Kans., 2000. Voice instr. Midwestern Music Camp, Lawrence, 1997—, Washburn U., Topeka, 2000—, Home Studio, Lawrence, 2000—; choir dir. LDS 2d Ward, Lawrence. Program com. mem. Topeka Opera Soc., 2004—06, bd. mem., 2004—06. Mem.: SAI (pres. Lawrence alumnae chpt. 2006—), Pi Kappa Lamba. Office: Washburn Univ 1700 SW College Ave Topeka KS 66621 Personal E-mail: dr_doremi@yahoo.com. Business E-Mail: elizabeth.schellman@washburn.edu.

SCHELLMAN, JOHN A., chemistry professor; b. Phila., Oct. 24, 1924; s. John and Mary (Mason) S.; m. Charlotte Green, Feb. 10, 1954; children: Heidi M., Lise C. AB, Temple U., 1948; MS, Princeton U., 1949, PhD, 1951; PhD (hon.), Chalmers U., Sweden, 1983. USPHS postdoctoral fellow U. Utah, 1951-52, Carlsberg Lab., Copenhagen, 1953-55; DuPont fellow U. Minn., Mpls., 1955-56, asst. prof. chemistry, 1956-58; assoc. prof. chemistry Inst. Molecular Biology, U. Oreg., Eugene, 1958-63, prof. chemistry, rsch. assoc., 1963—. Vis. Lab. Chem. Physics, Nat. Inst. Arthritis and Metabolic Diseases, NIH, Bethesda, Md., 1980; vis. prof. Chalmers U., 1986, U. Padua, 1987. Contbr. articles to profl. jours. Served with U.S. Army, 1943-46. Fellow Rask-Oersted Found., 1954, Sloan Found., 1959-63, Guggenheim Found., 1969-70. Fellow Am. Phys. Soc., Biophys. Soc.; mem. NAS, Am. Chem. Soc., Am. Soc. Biochemistry and Molecular Biology, Am. Acad. Arts and Scis., Phi Beta Kappa, Sigma Xi. Democrat. Business E-Mail: john@molbio.uoregon.edu.

SCHELM, ROGER LEONARD, information systems specialist; b. Kingston, NY, July 29, 1936; s. Frederick G. and Elizabeth M. (Wojciehowski) S.; m. Gloria Mae Dutterer, June 13, 1958; children: Sandra Lee Kern, Theresa Jean Sollitto, Ginger Lisa Shah. BA in Polit. Sci., Western Md. Coll., 1958; MA in Pub. Adminstrn., Am. U., 1970; postgrad., U. Md.,

1960-62. Analytic equipment programmer Nat. Security Agy., Ft. Meade, Md., 1958-60; computer cons. various cons. firms Balt., 1960-68, Washington, 1960—68; mgr. army plans and programs Informatics Inc., Bethesda, Md., 1968; mgr. def. programs Automation Tech. Inc., Wheaton, 1968-69; dir. advanced planning Genasys Corp., Washington, 1969-71; mgr. info. systems Ins. Co. North Am., Phila., 1971-72, sect. mgr. computing ops., 1972-74; mgr. tech. services INA Corp., 1974-75; mem. spl. tech. projects INA Corp. merger with Conn. Gen. Ins. Co. to form CIGNA Corp. 1982, 1975-76, asst. dir. tech. services, 1977, asst. dir. spl. tech. projects, 1977-78, asst. dir. adminstrn., 1978-79, asst. dir. resource mgmt., data ctr. design, contingency planning, 1979-80; dir. corp. info. tech. now CIGNA Corp., 1981-82, dir. planning and control ops. div., 1982-83, v.p. strategic planning, systems div., 1983-84, v.p. applied research/expert systems, systems div., 1984-92; co-founder, pres. Schelm Internat., Inc., Cherry Hill, NJ, 1992—2002. Mem. adj. faculty Camden Coll., N.J., 1978-82; mem. Camden County EDP Adv. Com., 1980-82; mem. faculty Drexel U., Phila., 1983-95. Author: Ednl. Computer mag., 1982; mem. editl. adv. bd., author Small Sys. World mag., 1982-84; mem. editl. adv. bd. Spang-Robinson Report, 1986-87, Machine Intelligence News, 1987-93, AI Expert mag., 1985-88; cons. editor Expert Sys. Jour., 1987-91. Tech. advisor various sch. bds., colls., univs. and non-profit orgns. Served to capt. U.S. Army, 1959. Mem. Am. Assn. Artificial Intelligence, Assn. Computing Machinery (founder Delaware Valley chpt. vice. chmn., program chmn. 1983-84, chmn. 1984-85, founder Del. Valley Spl. Interest Group in Artificial Intelligence, 1985, vice chmn. 1985-87), World Future Soc. Home and Office: 506 Balsam Rd Cherry Hill NJ 08003-3202

SCHENCK, JACK LEE, retired electric utility executive; b. Morgantown, W.Va., Aug. 2, 1938; s. Ernest Jacob and Virginia Belle (Kelley) S.; m. Rita Elizabeth Pietschmann, June 7, 1979; 1 son, Erik. BSE.E., BA in Social Sci., Mich. State U., 1961; MBA, NYU, 1975. Engr. AID, Tunis, Tunisia, 1961, Detroit Edison Co., 1962-63; engr., economist OECD, Paris, 1963-70; v.p. econ. policy analysis Edison Electric Inst., NYC and Washington, 1970-81; v.p., treas. Gulf States Utilities Co., Beaumont, Tex., 1981-92, sr. v.p., CFO, 1992-94. Cons. on electric utility restructuring and privatization in the former Soviet Union, 1994—. Mem. Internat. Assn. Energy Econs., Triangle Club, Eta Kappa Nu. Republican. Office Phone: 281-360-3960. E-mail: schenck1@aol.com.

SCHENCK, JOHN FREDERIC, physician; b. Decatur, Ind., June 7, 1939; s. John C. Schenck and Mildred Blosser; m. Jane Stark, Oct. 12, 1962 (div. 1982); children: Brooke, Kimberly, David; m. Susan J. Kalia, Oct. 8, 1994; 1 stepchild, Tania. BS in Physics, Rensselaer Poly. Inst., 1961, PhD in Physics, 1965; MD, Albany Med. Coll., NY, 1977. Staff scientist electronics lab. GE, Syracuse, NY, 1965-73; assoc. prof. elec. engring. Syracuse (NY) U., 1970-73; intern Albany Med. Ctr. Hosp., 1977-78; staff mem., sr. scientist GE Global Rsch., Schenectady, NY, 1973—; mem. med. staff Ellis Hosp., Schenectady, 1981—98. Adj. asst. prof. dept. radiology U. Pa., 1983-2000; adj. prof. neurology Albany Med. Coll., 2003-; chmn. Workshop on Advances in Magnetic Resonance Imaging Safety and Compatibility, McLean, Va., 1996; dir. Magnetic Resonance Imaging rsch. Neuroscis. Rsch. Ctr., Albany Med. Ctr., 2001-. Contbr. articles pub. to profl. jours. Recipient S.S. Greenfield award Am. Assn. Physicists in Medicine, 1993; Nat. Merit scholar, 1957-61; NSF fellow, 1962-63, Coolidge fellow GE, 2003. Fellow Am. Phys. Soc.; mem. IEEE, AAAS, Internat. Soc. Magnetic Resonance in Medicine, NY Acad. Scis., Sigma Xi. Achievements include 20 patents for magnetic resonance imaging. Home: 22 E Claremont Dr Voorheesville NY 12186-9104 Office: GE Global Rsch Bldg K1 NMR Schenectady NY 12309 Office Phone: 518-387-6543. Business E-Mail: schenck@research.ge.com.

SCHENCK, ROBERT ROY, hand surgeon; s. Isaac Barrett Schenck and Pearl Irene Murnan; m. Ruth Helm (div.); children: Rebecca VanNydeggen, Karen Schmidt, Heidi McCluskey, Robert Paul; m. Marcia Anne Whitney, June 13, 1982. B cum laude, Taylor U., 1952; MD, U. Ill., Chgo., 1955. Diplomate Am. Bd. Plastic Surgery. Asst. attending plastic and orthop. surgery Rush U., Chgo., 1972—80, dir. sect. hand surgery, 1972—, assoc. attending plastic and orthop. surgery, 1980—85, sr. attending plastic and orthop. surgery, 1985—. Cons. orthop. and gen. surgery West Suburban Hosp., Oak Park, Ill., 1973—; pres. Hand Therapy Ltd., Chgo., 1985—95. Bd. dirs. Bishop Anderson House, Chgo., 2004—; founding pres. The Hand Surgery Endowment, 1996—2001. Sr. surgeon USPHS, 1957—59. Mem.: Am. Assn. Hand Surgery. Episcopalian. Achievements include invention of dynamic traction for finger fracture. Avocations: photography, art, sculpting. Home: 1100 N Lake Shore Dr Apt 33-A Chicago IL 60611 Office: Hand Surgery Ltd 1725 W Harrison St #319 Chicago IL 60612 Office Phone: 312-738-3426. Personal E-mail: rschenckmd@aol.com. Business E-Mail: handsurgeryltd@aol.com.

SCHENDEL, DAN ELDON, management consultant, finance educator; b. Norwalk, Wis., Mar. 29, 1934; s. Leonard A. and Marian T. (Koch) S.; m. Mary Lou Sigler, Sept. 1, 1956; children: Suzanne, Pamela, Sharon. BS in Metall. Engring., U. Wis., 1956; MBA, Ohio State U., 1959; PhD (Ford Found. fellow), Stanford U., 1963. With ALCOA, 1956, U.S. Civil Svc., 1959-60, SRI, 1963-65; prof. mgmt., dir. exec. edn. programs Purdue U., Lafayette, Ind., 1965-85, Blake Family endowed chair emeritus in strategic mgmt.; vis. prof. U. Mich., 1988-89, U. Chgo., 1990-91, 1999—2004. Former dean German Grad. Internat. Sch. Mgmt. and Adminstrn., Hannover, Germany, 1999-2005; pres. Strategic Mgmt. Assocs., Inc. Author: (with others) Strategy Formulation: Analytical Concepts, 1978, Divided Loyalties, 1980, Fundamental Issues in Strategy, 1994; editor: (with others) Strategic Management: A New View of Business Policy and Planning, 1979; founding and cons. editor Strategic Mgmt. Jour., 1980-2007; founding editor Strategic Entrepreneurship Jour., 2006—. With USAF, 1956—59. Fellow Acad. Mgmt., Strategic Mgmt. Soc. (founding pres., treas.); mem. Univ. Club Chgo. Home: 1327 N Grant St West Lafayette IN 47906-2463 Office: Krannert Grad Sch Mgmt Purdue U West Lafayette IN 47907 Office Phone: 765-494-4386. Business E-Mail: schendel@purdue.edu.

SCHENDEL, STEPHEN ALFRED, surgeon, educator; b. Mpls., Oct. 10, 1947; s. Alfred Reck and Jeanne Shirley (Hagquist) S.; children: Elliott, Mélisande. BA, St. Olaf Coll., Northfield, Minn., 1969; BS with high distinction, U. Minn., 1971, DDS, 1973; diplome asst. etranger with high honors, U. Nantes, France, 1980; MD, U. Hawaii, 1983. Diplomate Am. Bd. Plastic Surgery, Nat. Bd. Med. Examiners, Nat. Bd. Dental Examiners, Am. Bd. Oral and Maxillofacial Surgery (adv. com., bd. examiner 1991-95). Intern, then resident in oral and maxillofacial surgery Parkland Meml. Hosp., Dallas, 1975-79; resident in gen. surgery Baylor U. Med. Ctr., Dallas, 1983-84, Stanford (Calif.) U. Med. Ctr., 1984-86, resident in plastic surgery, 1986-89, acting assoc. prof. surgery, 1989-91, assoc. prof., 1991-95, head divsn. plastic and reconstructive surgery, 1992—2002, dir. residency tng., 1992-98, chmn. dept. functional restoration, 1994—2001, prof. surgery, 1995—2002; head plastic surgery, dir. Craniofacial Ctr. Lucile Salter Packard Children's Hosp., Stanford, chief pediat. surgery, 1997—2002. Asst. to Dr. Paul Tessier, Paris, 1987-88; asst. dept. stomatology and maxillofacial surgery Centre Hospitalier Regional Nantes, 1979-80; med. bd. Lucile Salter Packard Children's Hosp. at Stanford, 1991—. Assoc. editor Selected Readings in Oral and Maxillofacial Surgery, 1989—; mem. editl. bd. Jour. Cranio-Maxillofacial Surgery; contbr. articles to profl. jours., chpts. to books. Recipient Disting. Alumnus award St. Olaf Coll., 1993; Fulbright fellow, Nantes, 1979-80, Chateaubriand fellow Govt. of France, 1987-88. Fellow ACS, Am. Acad. Pediat.; mem. Internat. Soc. Craniofacial Surgeons, European Assn. Cranio-Maxillofacial Surgeons, Am. Soc. Pediat. Plastic Surgeons, Am. Assn. Plastic Surgery, Soc. Baylor Surgeons (founding), Am. Cleft Palate-Craniofacial Assn., Am. Soc. Plastic Surgeons (sec. 1996—), Am. Soc. Maxillofacial Surgeons (sec., pres. 2000-01), Assn. Acad. Chairmen Plastic Surgery, Zedplast (bd. dirs. 1993—), Omicron Kappa Upsilon. Avocations: fly fishing, painting and sculpture. Office: Stanford U Med Ctr Divsn Plastic Reconstr Surg 770 Welch Rd Ste 400 Palo Alto CA 94304 Home Phone: 650-261-1031; Office Phone: 650-723-5824. Business E-Mail: sschendel@stanford.edu.

SCHENK, SUSAN KIRKPATRICK, nursing educator, consultant, small business owner; b. New Richmond, Ind., Nov. 29, 1938; d. William Marcius and Frances (Kirkpatrick) Gaither; m. Richard Dee Brown, Aug. 13, 1960 (div. Feb. 1972); children: Christopher Lee, David Michael, Lisa Catherine; m. John Francis Schenk, July 24, 1975 (widowed Apr. 1995). BSN, Ind. U., 1962; postgrad., U. Del., Newark, 1973-75. RN, PHN, BCLS; cert. community coll. tchr., Calif.; cert. vocat. edn. tchr., Calif. Staff nurse, then asst. dir. nursing Bloomington Hosp., Ind., 1962-66; charge nurse Newark Manor, Del., 1967-69; charge nurse GU Union Hosp., Terre Haute, Ind., 1971-72; clin. instr. nursing Ind. State U., Terre Haute, 1972-73; clin. instr. psychiatric nursing U. Del., Newark, 1974-75; psychiatric nursing care coord. VA Med. Ctr., Perry Point, Md., 1975-78; from nurse educator to cmty. rels. coord. Grossmont Hosp., La Mesa, Calif., 1978—91; dir. psychiat. svcs. Scripps Hosp. East County, El Cajon, Calif., 1991-97; nursing instr., adult edn. Grossmont Union H.S. Dist., La Mesa, 1996—. Tech. advisor San Diego County Bd. Supervisors, 1987; tech. cons. Remedy Home and Health Care, San Diego, 1988; expert panelist Srs. Speak Out, KPBS-TV, San Diego, 1988; guest lectr. San Diego State U., 1987. Editor: Teaching Basic Caregiver Skills, 1988; author, performer tng. videotape Basic Caregiver Skills, 1988. Mem. patient svcs. com. Nat. Multiple Sclerosis Soc., San Diego, 1986-89; bd. dirs. Assn. for Quality and Participation, 1989. Adminstrn. on Aging/DHHS grantee, 1988. Mem. Ind. U. Alumni Assn. (life), Calif. Coun. Adult Edn., Mensa, Sigma Theta Tau. Avocations: piano, gardening, reading. Home and Office: 9435D Carlton Oaks Dr Santee CA 92071-2582 Personal E-mail: susansks@aol.com.

SCHENK, WILLIAM EARL, III, senior special agent, criminal investigator; b. Fort Worth, July 25, 1952; s. William Earl Schenk II and Hildreth Howells Schenk; m. Carol Jean Kortzendorf, Oct. 17, 1993; children: Wesley Elliot, Amanda Nicole, Amanda Leigh Byers, Mark Christopher O'Neill, William Earl Schenk IV. BA, Auburn U., 1977. Lic. Chemical Agents Instructor FBI, Va., 1991, Criminal Investigator Fed. Law Enforcement Tng. Ctr., Ga., 1981, cert. Self Defense Instructor Kans. City Police Dept., 1985, lic. White Collar Crime Investigator Fed. Law Enforcement Tng. Ctr., Ga., 1985. Grad. criminal justice tchg. asst. U. of Ill., Chgo., 1977—79; police officer, detective U. S. Vets. Adminstrn., Hines, Ill., 1978—80; spl. agt. Insp. Gen., Investigations, U.S. Dept. of Agr., Chgo., 1980—97, sr. spl. agt. Indianapolis, Ind., 1997—. Chpt. pres. Lambda Alpha Epsilon Criminal Justice Honor Soc., Mobile, Ala., 1973—74; spl. investigator Grant County Prosecutor, Marion, Ind., 1983—84; self def. instr. Insp. Gen., Investigations, U.S. Dept. of Agr., 1985—96; chem. agents instr. Insp. Gen., Investigations, US Dept. of Agr., 1991—95; group leader Joint Task Force on Illegal Grain Handling Practices, Indpls., 1994—99. Editor: (book) Songs From the Shelf of Retirement; co-author (federal legislation, US criminal code) Title 7, United States Code, Section 87, Penalties (Superior Svc. Award from U.S. Sec. of Agr., 1988). Recipient Outstanding Prosecutive Achievement, U.S. Justice Dept., 1998, Investigative Excellence, Fed. Law Enforcement Officers Assn., 1999, Group Honor award for Excellence, U.S. Sec. of Agr., 1998, Superior Performance, U.S. Vets. Adminstrn., 1980. Mem.: Fed. Law Enforcement Officers Assn. Avocations: travel, reading, running, cooking, soccer. Office: Inspector Genl Investigations USDA 6039 Lakeside Blvd Indianapolis IN 46278 Home Phone: 317-892-5566; Office Phone: 317-290-3000 305.

SCHENKEL, BARBARA ANN, minister, nurse, social worker; b. Albuquerque, Mar. 17, 1951; d. Richard Henry and Mildred (Voth) S. BSN, U. N.Mex., 1972; MDiv, Iliff Sch. Theology, 1978; MSW, Ariz. State U., 1988. RN, N.Mex.; ordained to ministry Meth. Ch., 1979. Minister intern Christ Ch. U. Meth. Ch., Denver, 1975-77; parish minister Herman (Nebr.) Federated and Riverside Bapt. Ch., 1978-82, Cambridge (Nebr.) Bartley U. Meth. Ch., 1982-85; family minister Red Mountain U.M.C., Mesa, Ariz., 1988-94; nurse Ariz. Health Cost Containment Sys., Phoenix, 1994—; minister Life in the Spirit Ministry, Crossroads, Ariz., 1999—2003; prayer coord., life in spirit leader Sunrise United Meth. Ch., Phoenix, 2005—. Christ Ch. Caring Community Coordinator, Denver, 1975-77; advisor alcohol treatment program Immanuel Hosp., Washington County, Nebr., 1980-82; mem. task group to study Ministry Effectiveness in Nebr., 1981; vis. del. to World Meth. Conf., Honolulu, 1981; registrar for candidacy Bd. or Ordained Ministry, 1980-84, strategy com., 1984-85; drug and alcohol cons. Salvation Army Adult Rehab. Ctr., Phoenix, 1987-88, Adult Protective Svcs., 1988—. Chaplain Jackson-Peck Am. Legion Post, Herman, 1980—82; prayer coord., spiritual life min. Sunrise United Meth. Ch., Phoenix, 2005—. Served to 1st lt. USAF Nurse Corps, 1973—75. Mem. Nebr. Ann. Conf. United Meth. Chs., Cambridge Ministerial Assn. (pres. 1984), Tekamah-Herman Ministerial Assn. (pres. 1981), S.W. Dist. Coun. Ministries (past com. memberships). Avocations: horseback riding, bowling, crochet, needlepoint, crewel. Office: Ariz Health Cost Containment Sys 2830 W Glendale Ave Phoenix AZ 85051-8400 Home: Unit 1134 2150 E Bell Rd Phoenix AZ 85022

SCHENKEL, SUZANNE CHANCE, retired natural resource specialist; b. Phila., Mar. 12, 1940; d. Henry Martyn Chance II and Suzanne (Sharpless) Jameson; m. John Lackland Hardinge Schenkel, June 15, 1963 (div. 2002); children: John Jr., Andrew Chance. BS in Edn., Tufts U., 1962. Tchr. Roland Pk. Country Sch., Balt., 1962-65; exec. dir. Mass. Citizens' Com. for Dental Health, Springfield, 1981-83; pub., editor Women's Investment Newsletter, Longmeadow, Mass., 1985-89; pub. affairs officer USDA's Soil Conservation Svc., Amherst, Mass., 1990-93; resource conservationist conservation & ecosys. assistance divsn. USDA's Natural Resources Conservation Svc., Washington, 1993-97; ops. partnership liaison East Regional Office, Beltsville, Md., 1997—2002; ret., 2002. Staff Merchant Marine and Fisheries com. U.S. Ho. of Reps., Washington, 1993. Author Wetlands Protection and Management Act. Chmn. Longmeadow (Mass.) Conservation Commn., 1984-90; supr. Hampden County (Mass.) Conservation Dist., 1985-90; bd. dirs., v.p. League of Women Voters of Mass., Boston, 1974-85; exec. com. Water Supply Citizens' Adv. Com.; adv. bd. Water Resources Authority, Mass., 1979-90; bd. dirs. Alliance for Chesapeake Bay, 2001. Mem. Soil and Water Conservation Soc., Nat. Assn. Conservation Dists. Episcopalian. Avocations: golf, tennis, sailing. Home: 304 W Coral Trace Cl Delray Beach FL 33445 Home Phone: 561-274-2074.

SCHENKER, ERIC, university dean, economist; b. Vienna, Feb. 24, 1931; came to U.S., 1939, naturalized, 1945; s. Adolph and Olga (Strauss) S.; m. Virginia Martha Wick, Apr. 14, 1963; children: David, Richard, Robert. BBA, CCNY, 1952; MS, U. Tenn., 1955; PhD, U. Fla., 1957. Asst. prof. Mich. State U., 1957-59; mem. faculty U. Wis.-Milw., 1959—, prof. econs., 1965—; dean U. Wis.-Milw. (Sch. Bus. Adminstrn.), 1976—, dean, prof. emeritus, 1997—; dir. Urban Research Center, 1974-76; assoc. dir. Center Great Lakes Studies, 1967-74, sr. scientist, 1974—; asso. dean Coll. Letters and Scis., 1963-69. Bd. dirs. Am. Med. Bldgs., Ampco Metal, Pressed Steel; cons. in field. Author: The Port of Milwaukee: An Economic Review, 1967; co-author: Port Planning and Development as Related to Problems of U.S. Ports and the U.S. Coastal Environment, 1974, The Great Lakes Transportation System, 1976, Port Development in the United States, 1976, Maritime Labor Organizations on the Great Lakes-St. Lawrence Seaway System, 1978, Great Lakes Transportation System in the 80s, 1986; also monographs and articles. Sr. mem. Milw. Bd. Harbor Commrs., 1960-72, chmn., 1965-68; chmn. panel on future port requirements of U.S., Maritime Transp. Research Bd., Nat. Acad. Scis., 1973-76, chmn. panel on reducing tankbarge pollution, 1980-81; mem. pilotage adv. bd. to U.S. sec. transp., 1972-75; trustee Mt. Sinai Med. Ctr, 1984-88; mem. Econ. Progress Authority of Milw. Met. Sewerage Dist., 1983-88, Marine Bd., NAS, 1982-83, Gov.'s Coun. on Econ. Issues, 1983—. Served with AUS, 1952-54. Mem. Am. Econs. Assn., So. Econs. Assn., Phi Kappa Phi, Alpha Kappa Psi, Beta Gamma Sigma, Beta Alpha Psi. Home: 6792 N Melissa Ct Glendale WI 53209-3473 E-mail: esconinc@aol.com, Schenker@uwm.edu.

SCHENKER, LEO, retired utilities executive; b. Vienna, Jan. 3, 1922; came to U.S., 1952, naturalized, 1959; s. Max and Selda Lea (Podhorcer) S.; m. Alda R. Tinson, Jan. 20, 1949; children: Michael Gregory, Deborah Anne. BS with first class honors, U. London, 1942; MA in Sci. (Can. Inst. Steel Constrn. fellow), U. Toronto, 1950; PhD, U. Mich., 1954. Mng. dir. METAG Ltd., London, 1945-48; asst. rsch. engr. Hydro-Electric Power Commn. of Ont. (Can.), Toronto, 1948-52; rsch. assoc. U. Mich., Ann Arbor, 1952-54; with Bell Telephone Labs., 1954-87, various positions, dir. mil. electronic tech., 1968-71; dir. Loop Maintenance Systems Lab., 1971-80, exec. dir. Central Office Ops. div., 1980-83, exec. dir. network system planning div., 1983-84, exec. dir. tech. info. div., 1984-87. Adj. prof. elec. engring. Cooper Union, N.Y.C., 1989-97. Served with RAF, 1942-45. Recipient Duggan medal Can. Inst. Steel Constrn., 1970 Fellow IEEE, Sigma Xi, Phi Kappa Phi. Home: 3228 Fellowship Rd Basking Ridge NJ 07920 Personal E-mail: leoschenker@fvonline.net.

SCHENKER, MARC BENET, preventive medicine physician, medical educator, department chairman; b. LA, Aug. 25, 1947; s. Steve and Dosella Schenker; m. Heath Massey; children: Yael, Phoebe, Hilary. BA, U. Calif., Berkeley, 1969; MD, U. Calif., San Francisco, 1973; MPH, Harvard U., Boston, 1980. Instr. medicine Harvard U., Boston, 1980-82; asst. prof. medicine U. Calif., Davis, 1982-86, assoc. prof., 1986-92, prof., 1992—, chmn. dept. pub. health scis., 1995—. Fellow ACP; mem. Am. Thoracic Soc., Am. Pub. Health Assn., Soc. Epidemiologic Rsch., Am. Coll. Epidemiology, Soc. Occupl. Environ. Health, Internat. Commn. Occupl. Health, Assn. Tchrs. Preventive Medicine, Phi Beta Kappa, Alpha Omega Alpha. Office Phone: 530-752-5676.

SCHENKER, STEVEN, internist, educator; b. Poland, Oct. 5, 1929; came to US, 1943, naturalized, 1946; s. Alfred and Ernestyna S.; m. Sally Ann Wood, May 11, 1956; children: Julie C. Schenker Burn, Steven A., David S., Andrew G., Jennifer E. Schenker Campeggi; m. Jo Ann Neumann, Nov. 24, 1985. BA, Cornell U., Ithaca, NY, 1951, MD, 1955. Intern Harvard Service-Boston City Hosp., 1955-56, resident in medicine, 1956-58; asst. prof. medicine U. Cin. Sch. Medicine, 1961-63; asst. prof. U. Tex., Southwestern Sch. Medicine, 1963-67, assoc. prof. medicine, 1967-70; prof. medicine, biochemistry, dir. div. gastroenterology Vanderbilt U. Sch. Medicine, Nashville VA Hosp., 1970-82; prof. medicine and pharmacology U. Tex. Sch. Medicine, San Antonio, 1982—, dir. divsn. gastroenterology, 1982—2001. Chmn. study sect. Nat. Inst. on Alcohol Abuse and Addiction, 1980-83; chmn. study sects. VA, 1985-88. Editor: Hepatology, 1985-90; contbr. numerous articles in field to profl. jours. Recipient Markle award, 1963; Career Devel. award NIH, 1968; Jurzykowski Found. for Research in Medicine award, 1979, Alcoholism Research Soc. award 1987. Mem. Am. Assn. for Study of Liver Diseases (pres. 1980, Disting. Svc. award 1997), Am. Soc. Clin. Investigation, Assn. Am. Physicians, Am. Gastroent. Soc., Am. Soc. Pharm. and Exptl. Therapeutics, Am. Soc. Clin. Nutrition, Internat. Soc. for Study of Liver Diseases, Alpha Omega Alpha. Home: 26025 Mesa Oak Dr San Antonio TX 78255-3533 Office: U Tex Med Sch San Antonio TX 78284 Personal E-mail: stvschenker@aol.com.

SCHENKKAN, DIRK MCKENZIE, lawyer; b. Durham, NC, Aug. 9, 1949; s. Robert Fredric and Jean (McKenzie) S.; m. Patricia Sinnott, Nov. 11, 1979; children: Jean, Penelope, Victoria. AB highest honors, U. Tex., 1971; JD, Yale U., 1975. Bar: Calif. 1976, U.S. Dist. Ct. (no. dist.) Calif. 1976, U.S. Ct. Appeals (9th cir.) 1978, U.S. Dist. Ct. (ea. dist.) Calif. 1987. Rsch. assoc., tutor Law Sch. Yale U., New Haven, 1975-76; arbitrator Fed. & State Cts. No. Dist., Calif., mediator San Francisco; prin. Howard, Rice, Nemerovski, Canady, Falk & Rabkin, San Francisco, 1976, dir. Contbr. articles to profl. jours. Bd. dirs. San Francisco Neighborhood Legal Assistance Found., 1984—, Assn. Bus. Trial Lawyers, 1994—, San Francisco Girls Chorus, 1994—, Pacific Primary Sch., San Francisco, 1985-88. Named No. Calif. Super Lawyer, by Law & Politics., 2004—06. Mem. ABA, Calif. Bar Assn., Bar Assn. San Francisco, Assn. Bus. Trial Lawyers, Rotary Internat. fellow U. Kent Canterbury, England 1972-1973, Phi Beta Kappa. Office: Howard Rice Nemerovski Canady Robertson & Falk 3 Embarcadero Ctr 7th Fl Ste 7 San Francisco CA 94111-4074 Office Phone: 415-434-1600. Office Fax: 415-217-5910. E-mail: dschenkkan@howardrice.com.

SCHENKKAN, ROBERT FREDERIC, playwright, scriptwriter; b. Chapel Hill, Mar. 19, 1953; s. Robert Frederic Sr. and Jean (McKenzie) Schenkkan; m. Maria Dahvana Headley; children: Sarah Victoria, Joshua McHenry. BA in Theatre Arts, U. Tex., 1975; MFA in Acting, Cornell U., 1977. Author: (plays) Final Passages, 1981, The Survivalist, 1982 (best of the fringe award Edinburgh Festival, 1984), Tachinoki, 1987, Tall Tales, 1988 (Playwrights Forum award, 1988, Best One Act Plays, 1993), Heaven on Earth, 1989 (Julie Harris Playwright award Beverly Hills Theatre Guild, 1989), The Kentucky Cycle, 1991 (Pulitzer prize for drama, 1992, L.A. Drama Critics Circle Best Play award, 1992, Penn Ctr. West award, 1993, Best Play Tony award nominee, 1993, Best Play Drama Desk award nominee, 1993), Conversations with the Spanish Lady and Other One-Act Plays, 1993, The Dream Thief, 1998, Handler, 1999, The Marriage of Miss Hollywood and King Neptune,The Devil and Daniel Webster, 2002, By the Waters of Babylon, 2004, Lewis and Clark Reach the Euphrates, 2005, (TV films) Crazy Horse, (TV miniseries) Spartacus, (films) The Quiet American, 2002. Grantee Vogelstein Found., 1982, Arthur Found., 1988, Fund for New Am. Plays, 1990, Calif. Arts Coun., 1991. Mem.: SAG, Actors Equity, Writers Guild, Ensemble Studio Theatre, Dramatists Guild.

SCHENKMAN, JOHN BORIS, pharmacologist, educator; b. NYC, Feb. 10, 1936; s. Abraham and Theresa (Moses) S.; m. Deanna Owen, June 5, 1960; children: Jeffrey Alan, Laura Ruth. BA in Chemistry, Bklyn. Coll., 1960; PhD in Biochemistry, SUNY Upstate Med. Ctr., Syracuse, 1964. Postdoctoral fellow U. Pa. Johnson Found., Phila., 1964-67, Inst. Protein Research Osaka U., Japan, 1967-68, Inst. Toxicology Tübingen U., Germany, 1968; asst. prof. Yale U. Sch. Medicine, New Haven, 1968-71, assoc. prof., 1971-78; prof. pharmacology U. Conn. Health Ctr., Farmington, 1978-2000, head dept., 1978-87; dir. grad. program cellular and molecular pharmacology U. Conn., Farmington, 1995-99, prof. emeritus, 2000—. Assoc. editor Drug Metabolism and Drug Interactions, 1988—, Xenobiotica, 1990—; mem. editl. bds.; contbr. articles to profl. jours. Served as sgt. US Army, 1953-55. Rsch. grantee NIH, NSF; recipient Rsch. Career Devel award NIH, 1971-76. Mem. Am. Soc. Biochemists and Molecular Biologists, Am. Soc. Pharmacology Exptl. Therapeutics, Am. Med. Sch. Pharmacologists (councilor 1987-88). Jewish. Avocations: fishing, botany, winemaking, acting. Office: U Conn Sch Medicine Dept Pharm Farmington CT 06030-0001

SCHENKMAN, WALTER ALLEN, retired music educator; b. New Market, NJ; s. Max and Ray (Kuntz) Schenkman; m. Anne Marie Woerner, Feb. 7, 1970; m. Libby Yankelewitz (div.); children: Max Alexander, Fay Sara, Rebecca Carol(dec.). BA cum laude, Harvard Coll., Cambridge, Mass., 1948; MusM, Yale Sch. Music, New Haven, Conn., 1955; MusD,

Ind. U. Sch. Music, Bloomington, 1964. Prof. music U. No. Colo. Sch. Music, Greely, Colo., 1956—84, chair piano dept., 1974—83; ret. Performer various coll. campuses through US; contbr. over 60 articles to profl. jours.; recording project: 9 CD's covering entire gamut of paino's lit. Sgt. US Army Air Corp, 1943—46, New Guinea, Philippines. Recipient Dist. Scholar award, U. No. Colo., 1981.

SCHEPARTZ, ALANNA, biochemist, educator; b. NYC, Jan. 9, 1962; m. Thomas E. Schrader; 1 child, Abigail BS, SUNY, Albany, 1982; PhD in Chemistry, Columbia U., 1987. NIH fellow Calif. Inst. Tech., 1988; asst. prof. Yale U., New Haven, Conn., 1988-92, assoc. prof. chemistry, 1992-94, Milton Harris assoc. prof. chemistry, 1994-95, prof., 1995—. And prof. Howard Hughes Med. Inst., 2002—. Contbr. numerous articles to profl. jours. Recipient Presdl. Young Investigator award NSF, 1991, Camille and Henry Dreyfus Teacher-Scholar award, 1993; David and Lucille Packard Found. fellow, 1991, Eli Lilly Biochemistry fellow, 1991, Alfred P. Sloan Rsch. fellow, 1994, Howard Hughes Med. Inst. grantee for chemistry, 2002. Mem. Am. Chem. Soc. (Arthur C. Cope Scholar award 1995, Eli Lilly award 1997). Achievements include rsch. in bioorganic chemistry.

SCHEPIS, ANTHONY JOSEPH, artist, educator; b. Cleve., Mar. 6, 1927; s. Andrew Peter Schepis and Sarah Antonette Miraglia; children: Andrea, Pamela, Roman. Diploma, Cooper Sch. Art, Cleve., 1951; cert. painting, Cleve. Inst. Art, 1955; MA, Kent State U., Ohio, 1977. Instr. drawing and painting Cooper Sch. Art, Cleve., 1957—74; instr. drawing Cuyahoga C.C., Cleve., 1974—75, Lakeland C.C., Kirtland, Ohio, 1975—76; instr. drawing and painting Cleve. Inst. Art, 1976—78, prof. drawing and painting, 1979—96, prof. emeritus, 1999. Chair found. art dept. Cooper Sch. Art, Cleve., 1965—70. Represented in permanent collections Massillon Mus., Butler Inst. Am. Art, Canton Mus. Art, Richmond Art Mus. Recipient Individual Fellowship award, Ohio Arts Coun., 1980, Major Painting award, Cleve. Mus. Art, 1988, Thomas J. Ruddy Meml. award, Associated Artists Pitts.-Carnegie Mus. Art, 1999. Mem.: Cleve. Artists Found. Avocation: collecting recordings early 20th century Italian folk singers. Home: 125 Osprey Heights Dr N Winter Haven FL 33880 Personal E-mail: ajschepis@yahoo.com.

SCHEPP, RICHARD D., lawyer, retail executive; b. July 1960; m. Beth Schepp. BBA, U. Wis., Eau Claire; JD, U. Wis. Atty. Quarles & Brady, Milw.; dir. legal affairs, asst. corp. sec. Shopko Stores, Inc., 1992—96, v.p. legal affairs, corp. sec., 1996—98, sr. v.p., gen. counsel, 1998—2000; sr. v.p. Kohl's Corp., 2000—01, gen. counsel, sec., 2000—, exec. v.p., 2001—. Office: Kohls Corp N56 W17000 Ridgewood Dr Menomonee Falls WI 53051-5660 Office Phone: 262-703-7000. *

SCHEPPKE, JIM, library director; MLS, U. Tex., Austin. Ind. bookseller; with West Tex. Libr. Sys., Tex. State Libr.; adminstr. libr. devel. Oreg. State Libr., Portland, 1986—91, interim dir., 1991, state libr., 1991—. Bd. dirs. Bibliographical Ctr. Rsch., Colo. Mem.: Oreg. Libr. Assn. (pres. 1991, Libr. of Yr. award 1996). Office: Oreg State Libr 250 Winter St NE Salem OR 97301-3950 Office Phone: 503-378-4367. E-mail: jim.b.scheppke@state.or.us. *

SCHER, HOWARD DENNIS, lawyer; b. Ft. Monmouth, NJ, Apr. 23, 1945; s. George Scher and Rita (Eitches) Zar; m. Linda J. Scher; children: Seth Micah, Eli David, Nicholas Earl, Sara Catherine. BA, Brandeis U., 1967; JD, Rutgers U., 1971. Bar: Pa. 1971, U.S. Dist. Ct. (ea. dist.) Pa. 1971, U.S. Ct. Appeals (3rd cir.) 1971, U.S. Supreme Ct. 1975. Asst. city solicitor City of Phila., 1971-73; assoc. Goodis, Greenfield, Henry & Edelstein, Phila., 1973-77, Montgomery, McCracken, Walker & Rhoads, Phila., 1977-80, ptnr., 1980-2001; shareholder Buchanan Ingersoll P.C., Phila., 2001—, mng. ptnr., Phila. office, mem. bd. dir. Trustee Fedn. of Jewish Agys. of Greater Phila., 1994-2002; dir. Akiba Hebrew Acad., Merion, Pa., 1996-98; mem. pres.'s coun. Brandeis U.; chair Jewish Employment and Vocat. Svcs., 1998-02); chmn. Com. of Seventy, 2002. Fellow Am. Coll. Trial Lawyers, Internat. Acad. Trial Lawyers; mem. ABA, Pa. Bar Assn. (dir.), Phila. Bar Assn. (chmn. fed. cts. com. 2001-02), Brandeis U. Alumni Assn. (v.p. 1983-87). Home: 2222 Locust St Philadelphia PA 19103-5511 Office: Buchanan Ingersoll & RooneyPC 1835 Market St 14th Fl Philadelphia PA 19103 Home Phone: 215-985-0692; Office Phone: 215-665-3920. Office Fax: 215-665-8760. Business E-Mail: howard.scher@bipc.com.

SCHER, JORDAN MAYER, pharmacologist, psychiatrist, alcohol/drug abuse services professional; b. Balt. s. Robert Samuel and Marye Kremen Scher; m. Jeanne Nonken, July 20, 1954 (div. June 1960); children: Jan. Jo, Jill, Gabhriel. BS, Wesleyan U., Middleton, Conn., 1945; MD, U. Md., Balt., 1949; PhD in Neuropsychopharmacology, Northwestern U., Evanston, Ill., 1957. Diplomate Am. Bd. Psychiatry and Neurology, Am. Bd. Med. Hypnosis, cert. addiction specialist Am. Acad. Health Care Providers in Addiction Disorders. Resident and fellow in psychiatry U. Md. Psychiat. Inst., Balt., 1953—55; fellow in psychiatry NIMH, Bethesda, Md., 1955—57; fellow in medicine, hypertension studies Cleve. Clinic Found., 1950—51; project dir., rsch. psychiatrist NIMH, 1955-57; dir. narcotics project Cook County (Ill.) Jail and Criminal Ct., 1957—59; coor. undergrad. psychiatry Northwestern U. Med. Sch., 1957—60; pvt. practice psychiatry Chgo., 1957—79; cons. Sheriff's Office and Cook County Jail, 1958—63; from asst. to assoc. prof. dept. neurology and psychiatry Northwestern U. Med. Sch., Chgo., 1960—63; dir. Chgo. Psychiat. Found. and Ontoanalytic Inst., Chgo., 1960—70; prof. dept. neurology and psychiatry Northwestern U., 1963—65; dir. psychiat. svcs. Bd. of Health, 1963—65; exec. dir. Nat. Coun. Drug Abuse, Chgo., 1971—79; dir. sct. on psychiatry and religion Yeshiva Torat Israel, Jerusalem, 1972—74; exec. dir. Methadone Maintenance Inst., Chgo., 1972—79; advisor acupuncture Nat. Inst. Acupuncture and Herbal Medicine, Taiwan, 1974—; psychiatrist cons. Diaspora Yeshiva, Jerusalem, 1980—; pvt. practice psychiatry Jerusalem, 1982—. Vis. prof. psychiatry and drug abuse Hebrew U., 1982-89; cons. psychiatry, Israel and numerous orgns.; rschr. in field; dir. Jerusalem Inst. Drug Abuse, 1980-85, Jerusalem House, Israel, 1989—; dir. drug abuse unit Ezrat Nashim; advisor on drugs and alcohol Min. of Health, Israel; commn. on addiction, chmn. Adult Subcom. on Drug Abuse, City of Jerusalem. Author: Narcotic Detoxification as Acute Induced Panic Disorder: Neuropsychopharmacological Causes, Treatment, and Implications, A Monograph, 1992, (with L. Appleby, J. Cumming) Chronic Schizophrenia, 1959, Theories of the Mind, 1963, Drug Abuse in Industry: Growing Corporate Dilemma, 1973; co-editor: (with M. Segal): Drugs and the Law, vol. 1, Perspectives in Drug Abuse, 1989; founder, editor The Jour. Existential Psychiatry, 1959-70; cons. Am. Psychiat. Assn. Jour., 1963-70, Jour. AMA, 1964-71; mem. editl. bd. Psychosomatics Jour., 1965-67, Human Context Jour., 1970-72, Medica Judaica Jour., 1971-72; editor, founder Nat. Coun. Drug Abuse Drug/Health Alert, 1972-79; co-editor: Perspectives in Drug Abuse, 1989; contbr. numerous articles to profl. jours.; patentee in field. Co-chair bus. adv. coun. Nat. Rep. Congl. Com., 2002-03. Lt. USNR, 1949-57. Recipient Key to City of St. Louis, 1969, Wisdom award of honor, Wisdom Soc., 1972, Pawlowski Peace prize, 1974, Physician's Recognition award, AMA, 1975—2004, De-Quincey prize in addiction rsch., 1993, Cert. of Honor 50 Yrs. of Dedicated Svc. to Med. Profession, AMA, 2002. Fellow AAAS, Royal Soc. Medicine, Am. Acad. Psychosomatic Medicine (program com.), World Med. Assn. (hon.; US com.), Comprehensive Medicine Assn., Am. Assn. Clin. and Exptl. Hypnosis, Nat. Acad. Religion and Mental Health, Am. Geriatric Soc., NY Acad. Scis.; mem. AMA, Am. Coll. Forensic Psychiatry, Am. Acad. Psychiatry and Law, Am. Acad. Psychiatry in Alcohol and Drug Abuse, Am. Soc. Neuroimaging, Am. Soc. Addiction Medicine, Am. Soc. Addiction Psychiatry, Am. Ontoanalytic Assn. for Existential Psychiatry (founder), Am. Soc. Psychoanalytic Physicians, Inc., Am. Med. Soc. Alcoholism, Am. Acad. Orthomolecular Psychiatry, Am. Med. Record Assn., Am. Soc. Group Psychotherapy and Psychodrama, Chgo. Soc. Assn. Execs., Ill. Rehab. Assn., Nat. Rehab. Assn., Nat. Coun. Crime and Delinquency, Chgo. Assn. Commerce and Industry, Assn. Advancement of Psychotherapy, Am. Soc. Group Psychotherapy and Psychodrama, Am. Assn. Psychoanalytic Physicians, Internat. Soc. Med. Hypnosis, Internat. Assn. Group Psychotherapy, Am. Psychiat. Assn., Internat. Ontoanalytic Assn., Vienna Med. Psychol. Soc. (hon.), Assn. Am. Med. Colls., Am. Acad. Neurology, Washington Psychiat. Soc., Am. Humanistic Psychology Assn., Am. Acad. Psychotherapists, Am. Soc. Psychoanalytic Medicine, Am. Group Psychotherapy Assn., Psychosynthesis Rsch. Found., Soc. Advancement of Gen. Systems Theory, Soc. Sci. Study of Sex, Human Ecology Found., Soc. Biol. Psychiatry, Am. Soc. Photobiology, Ill. Med. Soc., Sigma Xi, Phi Delta Epsilon. Jewish. Avocations: Biblical/Jewish-Christian studies, archaeology, cosmology, paleoanthropological studies on the origin and evolution of human mind and communication. Office Phone: 212-245-9585. Personal E-mail: barschaar@yahoo.com.

SCHER, ROBERT SANDER, instrument design company executive; b. Cin., May 24, 1934; m. Audrey Erna Gordon, Oct. 21, 1961; children: Sarahh, Alexander, Aaron. SB, MIT, 1956, SM, 1958, Diploma in Mech. Engring., 1960, ScD, 1963. Rsch. and teaching asst. MIT, Cambridge, Mass., 1957-62; control system engr. RCA, Hightstown, NJ, 1963-65; engring. mgr. Sequential Info. System, Elmsford, NY, 1965-71; tech. dir. Teledyne Gurley, Troy, NY, 1971-78, v.p. engring., 1978-86, pres., 1986-92, Encoder Design Assocs., Clifton Park, NY, 1993—. Co-author patent Linear Digital Readout, 1975. Mem. ASME, Optical Soc. Am. Jewish. Avocation: chamber music. Home: 2 Laurel Oak Ln Clifton Park NY 12065-4712 Home Phone: 518-371-7383; Office Phone: 518-383-4910. E-mail: bobscher@nycap.rr.com.

SCHERAGA, HAROLD ABRAHAM, retired physical chemistry professor; b. Bklyn., Oct. 18, 1921; s. Samuel and Etta (Goldberg) S.; m. Miriam Kurnow, June 20, 1943; children: Judith Anne, Deborah Ruth, Daniel Michael. BS, CCNY, 1941; A.M., Duke U., 1942, PhD, 1946, Sc.D. (hon.), 1961, U. Rochester, 1988, U. San Luis, 1992, Technion, 1993, U. Gdansk, 2005. Teaching, research asst. Duke U., 1941-46; fellow Harvard Med. Sch., 1946-47; instr. chemistry Cornell U., 1947-50, asst. prof., 1950-53, assoc. prof., 1953-58, prof., 1958-65, Todd prof. chemistry, 1965-92, Todd prof. chemistry emeritus, 1992—, chmn. dept., 1960-67. Vis. assoc. biochemist Brookhaven Nat. Lab., summers 1950, 51, cons. biology dept., 1950-56; vis. lectr. div. protein chemistry Wool Rsch. Labs., Melbourne, Australia, 1959; vis. prof. Weizmann Inst., Israel, 1970-80, Soc. for Promotion Sci., Japan, Aug. 1977; Ramachandran prof., India, 2002; mem. tech. adv. panel Xerox Corp., 1969-71, 74-79; mem. biochemistry tng. com. NIH, 1963-65, reviewers res., 1995-98; mem. rsch. career award com. NIGMS, 1967-71, NIH BBCA study sect. mem., 1998-2002; commn. molecular biophysics Internat. Union for Pure and Applied Biophysics, 1965-69, mem. commn. macromolecular biophysics, 1969-75, pres., 1972-75, mem. commn. subcellular and macromolecular biophysics, 1975-81; adv. panel molecular biology NSF, 1960-62; Welch Found. lectr., 1962, Harvey lectr., 1968, Gallagher lectr., 1968, Lemieux lectr., 1973, Hill lectr., 1976, Venable lectr., 1981; co-chmn. Gordon Conf. on Proteins, 1963; mem. coun. Gordon Rsch. Confs., 1969-71. Author: Protein Structure, 1961, Theory of Helix-Coil Transitions in Biopolymers, 1970; co-editor Molecular Biology, 1961-86; mem. editl. bd. Physiol. Chemistry and Physics, 1969-75, Mechanochemistry and Motility, 1970-71, Thrombosis Rsch., 1972-76, Biophys. Jour., 1973-75, Macromolecules, 1973-84, Computers and Chemistry, 1974-84, Internat. Jour. Peptide and Protein Chemistry, 1982-96, Jour. Peptide Rsch., 1997—; corr. PAABS Revista, 1971-73; mem. editl. adv. bd. Biopolymers, 1963—, Biochemistry, 1969-74, 85—, Structural Chemistry, 1989-93, Jour. Computational Polymer Sci., 1991-95, Jour. Biomolecular NMR, 1991—, Computational and Theoretical Polymer Sci., 1996-2000, Jour. Biomed. Sci., 1994—, Jour. Am. Chem. Soc., 1995-2000. Mem. Ithaca Bd. Edn., 1958-59; Bd. govs. Weizmann Inst., Israel, 1970-97; mem. staff Naval Research Lab. Project, Air Force OSRD Project, World War II. Fulbright, Guggenheim fellow Carlsberg Lab., Copenhagen, 1956-57, Weizmann Inst., Israel, 1963; NIH Spl. fellow Weizmann Inst., 1970; Fogarty scholar NIH, 1984, 86, 88-91; recipient Townsend Harris medal CCNY, 1970, Chemistry Alumni Sci. Achievements award, 1977, Kowalski medal Internat. Soc. Thrombosis and Haemostasis, 1983, Linderstrøm-Lang medal Carlsberg Lab., 1983, Internat. Soc. of Quantum Chemistry and Quantum Pharmacology award in Theoretical Biology, 1993, Stein & Moore award Protein Soc., 1995; named Hon. mem. Soc. Polymer Sci. Japan, 1995. Fellow AAAS, Biophys. Soc. (coun. 1967-70); mem. NAS, Am. Peptide Soc. (hon.), Am. Chem. Soc. (chmn. Cornell sect. 1955-56, mem. exec. com. div. biol. chemistry 1966-69, vice chmn. divsn. biol. chemistry 1970, chmn. divsn. biol. chemistry 1971, Eli Lilly award 1957, Nichols medal 1974, Kendall award 1978, Pauling award 1985, Mobil award 1990, Repligen award 1990, IBM award for computers in chem. and pharm. rsch. 1997, Hirschmann award in peptide chem., 1999), Am. Soc. Biol. Chemists, Am. Acad. Arts and Scis., N.Y. Acad. Scis. (hon. life), Hungarian Biophys. Soc. (hon.), Phi Beta Kappa, Sigma Xi, Phi Lambda Upsilon. Home: 212 Homestead Ter Ithaca NY 14850-6220 Business E-Mail: has5@cornell.edu.

SCHERDIN, MARY JANE LISKOVEC, retired librarian, researcher; b. LaCrosse, Wis., Sept. 29, 1940; d. Ambrose John and Martha Marie (Borgmeier) Liskovec; m. Arthur William Scherdin, Apr. 15, 1961 (div. 1976); children: James William, Laurette Therese (dec.), Amy Lynn; m. William A. Wera, July 11, 1998. BS in Elem. Edn., U. Wis., LaCrosse, 1961; MS in Libr. Sci., U. Wis., Madison, 1972, PhD in Edn. Adminstrn., 1989; MEd Profl. Devel. in Audiovisual Media, U. Wis., Whitewater, 1980. Children's libr. LaCrosse Pub. Libr., 1961; sch. libr. LaCrosse Pub. Schs., 1961-64; media dir. Whitewater Pub. Schs., 1971-75; head learning matter ctr. U. Wis., Whitewater, 1979-86, supr. arts media ctr., 1975-79, instr., 1976-78, asst. dean Milw., 1986-88, collection access coord. Madison, 1988-92; libr. dir. Edgewood Coll., Madison, 1992—2004, doctoral advisor, 2004—. Rschr. The Highsmith Co., Ft. Atkinson, Wis., 1983, ALA, Chgo., 1991—96; cons. Consulting Psychologists Press, Palo Alto, Calif., 1991—96, Myers-Briggs Type Indicator, 1992—; vis. prof. U. Wis., Madison, 1992—2005. Co-author: K-12 Library Curriculum, 1974; author of bio-bibliographies of Wis. authors, 1981-83; designer; instructional computer programs 1983, 87, 89; author,editor: Discovering Librarians: Profiles of a Profession, 1994; contbr. articles to profl. jours. Pres. Jefferson (Wis.) Jaycettes, 1968-69; state and internal exec. v.p. Wis. Jaycettes, 1969-71; edn. chair Nat. Found. March of Dimes, Jefferson, 1970-74; vol. Nat. Found. Sudden Infant Death, Wis., 1975-83. Mem. AAUW (v.p. Ft. Atkinson 1974-75), Assn. Coll. and Rsch. Librs. (task force chair 1991-93, coll. libr. sect. nominating com., 1996, chair appts. com. 1997-98), Libr. Adminstrv. and Mgmt. Assn. (pubs. and bibliography com. 1989-91), Wis. Health Sci. Libr. Assn. (long range planning com. 1990-92, bd. dirs. 1992-93), Wis. Libr. Assn. (lit. awards com. 1980-84, chair lit. awards com. 1983, bd. dirs. 1987-88, chair edn. sect. 1993), Wis. Assn. Acad. Librs. (chair conf. planning 1985, 96, chair publs. 1993, chair 1988, info. literacy com. 1996-2001, chair info. lit. nat. immersion conf. 2000-01, ACRL liaison 1997), U. Wis. Sch. Libr. and Info. Studies Alumni Assn. (sec. 1993-95, v.p. 1999-2001, pres. 2002, past pres. 2003), Wis. Fedn. Ind. Colls. (tech planning team 1997-2002), Coun. Wis. Librs. (del. 1994-96), Czechoslovak Geneal. Soc. Internat. (conf. planning co-chair 2006—). Avocation: violin. Home: 6111 Winnequah Rd Madison WI 53716-3459

SCHERER, DONALD JAMES, II, systems administrator, researcher; b. New Orleans, Dec. 26, 1972; s. Donald James and Annetta Kruebbe Scherer; m. Guadalupe Carmona Carmona, July 5, 2003; children: Tatiana Destini-Marie, Raven Elisa, Donald James Scherer, III, Finley Amadeus. BS, U. New Orleans, 1991—2003, MS, 2003—06. Cert. nortel networks support specialist Prometric, Ill., 2006. Network adminstr. St. Charles Parish Pub. Schs., Luling, La., 1997—; physics rsch. asst. Advanced Materials Rsch. Inst., New Orleans, 2003—. Lance cpl. USMC, 1993—94, Marine Corps Air/Ground Combat Center 29 Palms, Calif. Decorated Nat. Def. medal USMC; recipient Employee of Yr. award, St. Charles Parish Pub. Schs., 2004. Mem.: Mensa (assoc.). R-Liberal. Cath. Avocations: movies, travel. Office: St Charles Parish Pub Schs 13855 River Rd Luling LA 70070 Home Phone: 985-307-0043. Office Fax: 985-785-9926; Home Fax: 985-785-9926. Business E-Mail: dscherer@stcharles.k12.la.us.

SCHERER, FREDERIC MICHAEL, economics professor; b. Ottawa, Ill., Aug. 1, 1932; s. Walter King and Margaret (Lucey) Scherer; m. Barbara A. Silbermann, Aug. 17, 1957; children: Thomas, Karen, Christina. AB with honors, U. Mich., 1954; MBA with high distinction, Harvard U., 1958, PhD, 1963; D (hon.), Univ. Hohenheim, 1996. Asst. prof. Princeton (N.J.) U., 1963-66; prof. econs. U. Mich., Ann Arbor, 1966-72; chief economist FTC, Washington, 1974-76; prof. econs. Northwestern U., Evanston, Ill., 1976-82; Joseph Wharton prof. polit. economy Swarthmore (Pa.) Coll., 1982-89; Aetna prof. pub. policy and mgmt. Harvard U., Cambridge, Mass., 1989-2000, emeritus prof., 2000—. Vis. prof. Ctrl. European U., Prague, 1993—94; Arthur Andersen disting. visitor U. Cambridge, 1997; lectr. Princeton U., 2000—05; Ludwig Erhard vis. prof. U. Bayreuth, 2000; vis. prof. Haverford Coll., 2004—06. Author: The Weapons Acquisition Process, 1964, Industrial Market Structure and Economic Performance, 1970, revised edit., 1980, 1990, The Economics of Multi-Plant Operation, 1975, Innovation and Growth, 1984, International High-Technology Competition, 1992, Competition Policies for an Integrated World Economy, 1994, Industry Structure, Strategy and Public Policy, 1996, New Perspectives on Economic Growth and Technological Innovation, 1999, Quarter Notes and Bank Notes, 2004; co-author: Mergers, Sell-Offs and Economic Efficiency, 1987. Mem. adv. panel NSF, Washington, 1980—83, U.S. Office Tech. Assessment, 1989—93, U.S. Bur. of Census, 1997—2000. Recipient Lifetime Achievement award, Am. Antitrust Inst., 2002; grantee, NSF, 1970, 1979, 1982, Sloan Found., 1996; sr. rsch. fellow, Internat. Inst. Mgmt., 1972—74, Census fellow, Am. Stats. Assn., 1989—90, Baker scholar, Harvard U., 1957, Centennial Rsch. grantee, O'Melveny & Myers, 1989. Mem.: Indsl. Orgn. Soc. (pres. 1992), Am. Econ. Assn. (v.p. 1988), European Assn. for Rsch. in Indsl. Econs. (co-founder 1974). Roman Catholic. Avocations: listening to music, musicology. Home: 53 Standish St Cambridge MA 02138 Office: CBG; John F Kennedy Sch Govt Harvard U Cambridge MA 02138 Office Phone: 617-495-1154. Business E-Mail: mike_scherer@harvard.edu.

SCHERER, HAROLD NICHOLAS, JR., electric power industry executive; b. Plainfield, NJ, Apr. 5, 1929; s. Harold Nicholas and Nora (McDonough) S.; m. Jane Neely, Sept. 6, 1952 (div.); children: Anne Scherer McConnell, Peter; m. Patricia Condon, May 4, 1974; stepchildren: James, John, Joseph, Jeffery Ludwig, Jean Ludwig Ransdell. BE, Yale U., 1951; MBA, Rutgers U., 1955. Registered profl. engr., N.J., Mass. Various engring. positions Pub. Svc. Electric and Gas Co., Newark, 1951-63, Am. Electric Power Svc. Corp., NYC, 1963-68, asst. chief. elec. engr., 1968-69, chief elec. engr., 1969-73, v.p. elec. engr., 1973-82, sr. v.p. elec. engring. Columbus, Ohio, 1982-90, also dir., until 1990; pres. Commonwealth Electric Co., Wareham, Mass., 1990-93, Cambridge (Mass.) Electric Light Co., Canal Electric Co., Com/Steam Co., 1990-93. Bd. dirs. Commonwealth Electric Co., Cambridge Electric Light Co., Com/Steam Co., Commonwealth Svcs. Co., Canal Electric Co.; joint U.S.-USSR working group on power transmission, 1975-81, joint U.S.-Italy working group on power transmission, 1979-88; vice-chmn. Am. Nat. Stds., NYC, 1985-87; v.p. U.S. Nat. Com., 1985-93, pres., 1993-99, chmn. U.S. tech. com. Internat. Conf. on Large High Voltage Electric Sys., 1985-91, internat. adminstrv. coun., 1988-99, internat. exec. com., 1993-99; engring. rev. bd. Bonneville Power Adminstrn., 1984-94; chmn. elec. sys. and equipment com. Edison Electric Inst., 1989-90, pres. power engring. edn. found., 1992-96; chmn. blue-ribbon panel Pacific Coast Blackouts, Bonneville-Power Adminstrn., 1996-97; bd. dirs. NY State Ind. Sys. Operator, 1998-, chmn. audit and compliance com., 1998-2006; cons. in field Contbr. articles to profl. jours. Pres. N.J. Jr. C. of C., 1960-61; councilman City of Plainfield, 1963-65; mem. Watchung (N.J.) Hills Regional H.S. Bd. Edn., 1970-72; pres. Woods at Josephinum Civic Assn., Worthington, Ohio, 1983-84; trustee, treas. Beech Leaf Landing Trust, 2001-. Recipient Clayton Frost award U.S. Jaycees, 1961, Young Man of Yr. award Plainfield Jaycees, 1963, Lifetime Achievement award T&D Mag., 1990. Fellow IEEE (v.p. power engring. soc. 1988-89, pres. 1990-91, William Habirshaw award for transmission and distbn. engring. 1986, Disting. Mem. award Internat. Conf. on Large High Voltage Electric Systems 1996, Hon. Mem. award Internat. Conf. on Large High Voltage Electric Systems 2000, Philip Sporn award U.S. nat. com. Internat. Conf. on Large High Voltage Electric Systems 2002); mem. NAE, Yale Club N.Y.C., Tau Beta Pi, Beta Gamma Sigma. Home and Office: 467 Bay Ln Centerville MA 02632-3352 Home Phone: 508-775-6516. Personal E-mail: schererhn@aol.com.

SCHERER, RONALD CALLAWAY, voice scientist, educator; b. Akron, Ohio, Sept. 11, 1945; s. Belden Davis and Lois Ramona (Callaway) S.; children: Christopher, Maria. BS, Kent State U., 1968; MA, Ind. U., 1972; PhD, U. Iowa, 1981. Research asst. U. Iowa, Iowa City, 1979-81, asst. research scientist, 1981-83, adj. asst. prof., 1983-88, adj. assoc. prof., 1988—; adj. asst. prof. U. Denver, 1984-86; asst. adj. prof. U. Colo., Boulder, 1984-93, adj. assoc. prof., 1993-96; rsch. scientist Denver Ctr. Performing Arts, 1983—88, sr. scientist, 1988—96; lectr. voice and speech sci. Nat. Theatre Conservatory, Denver, 1990-94; asst. clin. prof. Sch. Medicine U. Colo., Denver, 1988—96; assoc. prof. Bowling Green State U., Ohio, 1996—2001, prof., 2001—05, 2006—. Adj. assoc. prof. U. Okla., 1992-96; affiliate clin. prof. U. No. Colo., 1993-96; Oberlin Coll. affiliate scholar, 1996—; mem. exec. and legis. bd. Nat. Ctr. Voice and Speech, 1990-96; adj. prof. Drexel U., Phila., 2006-; G. Paul Moore lectr., The Voice Found., 2002; rsch. prof. U. Cin., 2005-06. Author: (with Dr. I. Titze) Vocal Fold Physiology: Biomechanics, Acoustics and Phonatory Control, 1983; contbr. articles to profl. jours. Nat. Inst. Dental Research fellow, 1972-76. Fellow: Internat. Soc. Phonetic Scis. (auditor 1988—91); mem.: Am. Assn. Phonetic Scis. (nominating com. 1985—87, counselor 2000—03, councelor 2000—03), Internat. Assn. Logopedics and Phoniatrics, Acoustical Soc. Am., Am. Speech-Lang.-Hearing Assn., Internat. Arts Medicine Assn., Collegium Medicorum Theatri, Sigma Xi, Pi Mu Epsilon (G. Paul Moore lectr.). Office Phone: 419-372-2515.

SCHERER, VICTOR RICHARD, physicist, computer scientist, consultant, musician; b. Poland, Feb. 7, 1940; came to U.S., 1941; s. Emanuel and Florence B. Scherer; m. Gail R. Dobrofsky, Aug. 11, 1963; children: Helena Cecile, Markus David. BS magna cum laude, CCNY, 1960; MA, Columbia U., 1962; PhD, U. Wis., 1974. Health physics asst. Columbia U., NYC, 1961-63; rsch asst. physics. dep. U. Wis., Madison, 1967-74; project assoc., project mgr. Inst. for Environ. Studies, World Climate-Food Rsch. Group, 1974-78; specialist computer systems U. Wis. Acad. Computing Ctr., 1978—; coord., sr. cons. Divsn. Info. Tech. U. Wis., Madison; concert pianist; tchr.; promoter contemporary composers. Researcher in particle physics, agroclimatology, soil-yield relationships and computer graphics; cons. on computer sys., electronic mail, geographic analysis, help desk and supercomputing applications. Fellow AEC, 1960-61. Mem. AAAS, Am. Phys. Soc., Am. Meteorol. Soc., Am. Soc. Agronomy, Assn. Computing

Machinery, Nat. Computer Graphics Assn., Phi Beta Kappa, Sigma Xi. Office: U Wis-Madison Divsn Info Tech 1210 W Dayton St Madison WI 53706-1613 Office Phone: 608-262-3570. Business E-Mail: scherer@doit.wisc.edu.

SCHERF, DIETMAR, publishing executive, artist, minister; b. Graz, Austria, June 12, 1961; came to US, 1990; s. Friedrich and Maria S.; m. Patricia Michaela Rech, Apr. 9, 1987; children: Alexander, Deborah, Daniel, David. Diploma, trade sch., Graz, 1979. CEO Handelshaus D. Scherf, Vienna, 1987-90; CEO, pres. Scherf, Inc., Las Vegas, Nev., 1990-2000, creative dir., 2001—03; pastor, founder Megagrace Christian Ctr., Las Vegas, 2003—05; chief designer Cascada Design Studies, Creative Consultant, Cascada Resorts, 2005; CEO, pres. Cascada Corp., 2006—. Author: Short Term Trading, 1990, (booklet) Ross Perot, 1992, I Love Me: Avoiding and Overcoming Depressions, 1998, (as Alec Donzi) The Consultant, 2000; composer, producer, performer (CD) Nice to Meet Ya!, 1994. Avocations: movies, reading, contemporary architecture, bible studies, music. Office: Cascada Corp PO Box 80180 Las Vegas NV 89180-0180 Business E-Mail: ds@scherf.com.

SCHERF, JOHN GEORGE, IV, lawyer; b. Tuscaloosa, Ala., Oct. 12, 1962; s. John G. III and Roberta Cannon (Timmons) S.; m. Lorie Lankford, Feb. 12, 1994; 1 child, Austin Tyler. AA, Okaloosa Walton Jr. Coll., Niceville, Fla., 1983; BA in Psychology, U. West Fla., 1987; JD, Samford U., 1991. Bar: Ala. 1992, U.S. Dist. Ct. (no. dist.) Ala. 1994, U.S. Dist. Ct. (mid. dist.) Ala. 1997, U.S. Dist. Ct. (so. dist.) Ala., 1999. Clk., assoc. Taylor & Taylor, Birmingham, Ala., 1992-93; assoc. Frank S. Buck, P.C., Birmingham, 1993-95; pvt. practice Birmingham, 1995—. Mem. ATLA, Ala. Bar Assn., Ala. Trial Lawyers Assn., Birmingham Bar Assn. Democrat. Methodist. Office: PO Box 849 Mary Esther FL 32569-0849 Home: PO Box 1185 Mary Esther FL 32569-1185 Office Phone: 205-939-0000. E-mail: smurflaw@aol.com.

SCHERGER, JOSEPH EDWARD, family physician, educator; b. Delphos, Ohio, Aug. 29, 1950; m. Carol M. Scherger, Aug. 7, 1973; children: Adrian, Gabriel. BS summa cum laude, U. Dayton, 1971; MD, UCLA, 1975. Family practice residency U. Wash., Seattle, 1975-78; clin. instr. U. Calif. Sch. Medicine, Davis, 1978-80, asst. clin. prof., 1980-84, assoc. clin. prof., 1984-90, clin. prof., 1990—, dir. predoctoral program, 1991-92; med. dir. family practice and community medicine Sharp Healthcare, San Diego, 1992-96; assoc. dean primary care, chair dept. family medicine U. Calif., Irvine, 1996—2001, prof. dept. family medicine, 1996—2001, prof. family and preventive medicine San Diego, 2003—; dean Fla. State U., Coll. Medicine, Tallahassee, 2001—03. Med. dir. AmeriChoice, 2006—; consulting med. dir. Lumetra, 2007—. Editor (in chief): (med. jour.) Hippocrates. Recipeient Hippocratic Oath award UCLA, Calif. Physician of Yr. award Am. Acad. Family Physicians. Mem. NAS (mem. Inst. Medicine), Am. Acad. Family Physicians, Soc. Tchrs. Family Medicine. Office Phone: 858-232-8858. Business E-Mail: jscherger@ucsd.edu.

SCHERICH, ERWIN THOMAS, civil engineer, consultant; b. Inland, Nebr., Dec. 6, 1918; s. Harry Erwin and Ella (Peterson) Scherich; m. Jessie Mae Funk, Jan. 1, 1947; children: Janna Rae Scherich Thornton, Jerilyn Mae Scherich Dobson, Mark Thomas. Student, Hastings Coll., 1937—39, N.C. State Coll., 1943—44; BS, U. Nebr., 1948; MS, U. Colo., 1951. Registered profl. engr., Colo. Civil and design engr. U.S. Bur. Reclamation, Denver, 1948—84, chief spillways and outlets sect., 1974—75, chief dams br. divsn. design, 1975—78, chief tech. rev. staff, 1978—79; chief divsn. tech. rev. Office Asst. Commr. Engring. and Rsch. Ctr., 1980—84; cons., 1984—. Mem. U.S. Com. Internat. Commn. Large Dams. With US Army, 1941—45. Fellow: NSPE (nat. dir. 1981—87, v.p. southwestern region 1991—93), ASCE; mem.: Profl. Engrs. Colo. (pres. 1977—78), Jefferson County West C. of C. Republican. Methodist. Home and Office: 3915 Balsam St Wheat Ridge CO 80033-4449

SCHERKENBACH, FRANK EVERETT, lawyer; b. Milw., July 17, 1963; s. Frank Anthony and Donna Mae (Fohr) S. BS with distinction, BA with distinction, Stanford U., 1986; JD, Harvard U., 1989. Bar: Calif. 1989, U.S. Ct. Appeals (fed. cir.) 1990, Mass. Law clk. to judge H. Robert Mayer U.S. Ct. Appeals (fed. cir.), Washington, 1989—91; assoc. Brown & Bain, PA, Fish and Richardson, PC, 1992—2002, prin. Boston, 2002—. Notes and comments editor Harvard Jour. Law & Tech., 1987-88, editor-in-chief, 1988-89. Named recommended lawyer, Chambers USA, 2005; named one of Litigation's Rising Stars, The Am. Lawyer, 2007, 2007 Best Lawyers in Am., Intellectual Property Law. Mem. ABA, State Bar Calif., Fed. Cir. Bar Assn., Am. Intellectual Property Law Assn., Phi Beta Kappa, Tau Beta Pi. Avocations: sports, hiking, history. Office: Fish & Richardson PC 225 Franklin St Boston MA 02110-2804 Office Phone: 617-521-7883. E-mail: scherkenbach@fr.com. *

SCHERLER, KATHY LOUISE, music educator, researcher; b. Okla. City, Aug. 17, 1958; d. Jimmie Mack Cosby and Avis Norvell Cosby (Bailey); m. David Kent Scherler, Jr., Aug. 5, 1978; children: David Kent III, Kale Cosby. BA, Cameron U., 1980; MusM, Tex. A & M, 1982; PhD in Music Edn., U. No. Tex., 2005. Mid. sch. choral dir. Hugo Jr. HS, Okla., 1980—81; choral dir. Valliant HS, Okla., 1981—83; music tchr. Wilson Elem. Sch., Bartlesville, Okla., 1988—90; choral dir. North Lamar HS, Paris, Tex., 1990—94; adj. prof. music Dallas Bapt. U., 1995—2000; tchg. fellow U. North Tex., Denton, 1996—98; music tchr. Walnut Hill Elem. Sch., Dallas, 1998—99; mid. sch. choral dir. Sam Houston Mid. Sch., Irving, Tex., 1999—2001; HS choral dir. Grapevine HS, Grapevine, Tex., 2001—02; asst. prof. music Midwestern State U., Wichita Falls, Tex., 2004—. Author: (jour. article) Southwestern Musician; dir.: (conducted chorus and orch.) Messiah by Handel; musician: (voice recital) Les Filles de Cadix by Leo Delibes, (soprano soloist) Gloria by Vivaldi, Merry Wives of Windsor by Otto Nicolai, Trial by Jury by Gilbert and Sullivan, Help, Help the Globolinks by Menotti, The Prodigal Son by Debussy; author: (paper presentation) 19th Ann. Conf. on Interdisciplinary Qualitative Studies; musician (and lectr.): (recital) Coll. Music Soc., So. Ctrl. chpt., Midwestern State U. Faculty Forum; dir.(co-dir.): (opera) Die Fledermaus; musician: (voice recital) U. North Tex., Dallas Bapt. U., Der Hirt auf dem Felsen, by Schumann. Accompanist Meml. Bapt. Ch., Grapevine, Tex., 2000—06. Finalist, Nat. Assn. Tchrs. of Singing, 1987; recipient Okla. All State Choir, 1974—76, winner Sweepstakes Choral Competition, U. Interscholastic League, 1994, Superior Ratings: Grapevine High Choir, 2001—02, music scholarship, Cameron U., Lawton, Okla., 1976—79, Best Actress award, Okla. Theater Ctr., 1976, Best in Class for Superior Ratings, Blue Bonnet Choral Festival, 2002; grantee, Midwestern State U. Fine Arts Dept., 2005. Mem.: Tex. Assn. Coll. Tchrs., Coll. Music Soc., Am. Choral Dirs. Assn., Phi Delta Kappa, Tex. Music Educators Assn., Nat. Assn. Tchrs. of Singing, Music Educators Nat. Conf. Home: 204 Mineral Springs Keller TX 76248 Office: Midwestern State U 3410 Taft Blvd Wichita Falls TX 76308-2099 Home: 121 Mustang Springs Sunset TX 76270 Home Phone: 817-482-1903. Business E-Mail: kathy.scherler@mwsu.edu.

SCHERMER, JUDITH KAHN, lawyer; b. NYC, Feb. 28, 1949; d. Robert and Barbara Kahn; m. Daniel Woodrough Schermer; 1 child, Sarah Nicole. BA, U. Chgo., 1971; JD, William Mitchell Coll. Law, 1987. Bar: Minn. 1987, U.S. Dist. Ct. Minn. 1987. Advt. and promotion specialist U. Chgo. Press, 1971-75; systems analyst Allstate Ins. Co., Northbrook, Ill., 1975-78, Lutheran Brotherhood, Mpls., 1980-83; polit. aide Mpls. City Coun., 1986-87; ptnr. Schermer & Schermer, Mpls., 1987-99, Schermer & Guy, Mpls., 1999—2001, Judith K. Schermer PLC, 2001—. Assoc chair 5th Congl. dist., state exec. com. Dem. Farm Labor Party. Mem. ATLA, Minn. Trial Lawyers Assn. (bd. govs., chair legis. com., employment com. 1999—), Minn. State Bar Assn., Minn. Women Lawyers, Nat. Employment Law Assn. Home: 4624 Washburn Ave S Minneapolis MN 55410-1846 Office: Lumber Exch Bldg 10 S 5th St Ste 950 Minneapolis MN 55402-1006

SCHERR, ALLAN LEE, computer scientist, software executive; b. Balt., Nov. 18, 1940; s. Morris and Sarah (Kratzmar) S.; m. Marsha Kahn, Sept. 2, 1962 (div. 1974); children: Elise A., Stephanie L.; m. Linda Martin, June 8, 1980; 1 child, Katherine M. B.E.E., M.E.E., MIT, 1962, PhDE.E., 1965. Mgr. time sharing option (TSO) design System Devel. div. IBM, Poughkeepsie, NY, 1967-70, mgr. multiple virtual storage (MVS) project, 1971-74, mgr. distributed systems programming System Communications div. Kingston, NY, 1977-80, dir. communications programming, 1980-81, dir. communications and applications systems corp. staff Armonk, NY, 1981-83, dir. engring. and programming systems products div. White Plains, NY, 1983-86, dir. integrated applications info. systems div. Milford, Conn., 1986-88, v.p. devel. and integration application systems div., 1988-89, application solutions dir. architecture and devel., Application Solutions Line Bus., 1990-91; v.p. tech. World Wide Cons. Practices IBM Cons. Group, Milford, Conn., 1991-93; ind. cons. bus. process engring., info. tech., tech. mgmt. Weston, Conn., 1993-94; sr. v.p. software engring. EMC Corp., Hopkinton, Mass., 1994-2000, sr. v.p. tech., new bus. devel., 2000—01; ind. cons., 2001—; chief tech. officer Mission Control Productivity, Inc., 2000—03. Seminar leader Werner Erhard & Assocs., NYC, 1982-90; co-creator, co-tchr. new course leadership Simon Sch. Bus. U. Rochester, NY, 2005-. Author: An Analysis of Time-Shared Computer Systems, 1966 (Grace Murray Hopper award Assn. Computing Machinery 1975); patentee in field. Mem. The Hunger Project, San Francisco, 1977. IBM fellow, 1984 Fellow IEEE; mem. Sigma Xi, Tau Beta Pi, Eta Kappa Nu Democrat. Home and Office: 18 Wyndclyffe Ct Rhinebeck NY 12572 Office Phone: 845-876-0785. E-mail: scherr@alum.mit.edu.

SCHERR, BARRY PAUL, foreign language educator; b. Hartford, Conn., May 20, 1945; s. Joseph and Helen Lillian (Shapiro) S.; m. Sylvia Egelman, Sept. 8, 1974; children: Sonia, David. AB magna cum laude, Harvard U., 1966; AM, U. Chgo., 1967, PhD, 1973. From acting asst. prof. to asst. prof. U. Washington, Seattle, 1970-74; from asst. prof. to prof. Russian, Dartmouth Coll., Hanover, NH, 1974—, chmn. dept. Russian, 1981-90, 96-97, chmn. program linguistics and cognitive sci., 1989-96, assoc. dean for humanities, 1997—2001, assoc. provost, 2001, provost, 2001—. Co-organizer Internat. Conf. Russian Verse Theory, 1987, Internat. Conf. Anna Akhmatova and the Poets of Tsarskoe Selo, 1989, Internat. Conf. Eisenstein at 100: A Reconsideration, 1998. Author: Russian Poetry: Meter, Rhythm and Rhyme, 1986, Maxim Gorky, 1988; co-trans. The Seeker of Adventure, Alexander Grin, 1989; mem. editorial bd. Slavic and East European Jour., 1978-88; co-editor: Russian Verse Theory: Procs. of the 1987 Conference at UCLA, 1987, O RUS! Studia litteraria Slavica in honorem Hugh McLean, 1995, A Sense of Place: Tsarskoe Selo and Its Poets, 1993, Twentieth-Century Russian Literature, 2000, Eisenstein at 100: A Reconsideration, 2001; co-translator, co-editor Maksim Gorky: Selected Letters, 1997; contbr. articles to profl. jours. Scholar Harvard Coll., 1963-66; fellow NDEA, 1966-69; grantee Internat. Rsch. and Exch. Bd., 1969-70, NEH, 1987, 89, U.S. Dept. Edn., 1987-89, Dartmouth Coll. Sr. Faculty, 1988; summer rsch. grantee Grad. Sch., Inst. Comparative and Fgn. Area Studies U. Wash., 1973. Mem. MLA (mem. exec. com. assoc. dept. fgn. langs. 1983-85, del. assembly 1986-88), Am. Assn. Advancement Slavic Studies, Am. Assn. Tchrs. Slavic and East European Langs. (pres. 1987-88, founder, past pres. No. New Eng. chpt., numerous coms.). Office: Dartmouth Coll Russian Dept Reed Hall Hanover NH 03755-3506 Office Phone: 603-646-2070. Business E-Mail: Barry.scherr@Dartmouth.edu.

SCHERR, LAWRENCE, internist, healthcare educator, historian; b. NYC, Nov. 6, 1928; s. Harry and Sophia (Schwartz) S.; m. Peggy L. Binenkorb, June 13, 1954; children: Cynthia E., Robert W. AB, Cornell U., 1950, MD, 1957. Diplomate Am. Bd. Internal Medicine (bd. dirs., sec.-treas. 1979-86). Intern Cornell Med. divsn. Bellevue Hosp. and Meml. Ctr., NY, 1957-58, asst. resident, 1958-59, rsch. fellow cardiorenal lab., 1959-60, chief resident, 1960-61, co-dir. cardiorenal lab., 1961-62, asst. vis. physician, 1961-63, assoc. vis. physician, 1963-65, dir. cardiology and renal unit, 1963-67, assoc. dir., 1964-67, vis. physician, 1966-68; physician to out-patients NY Hosp., 1961-63, asst. attending physician, 1963-66, assoc. attending physician, 1966-71, attending physician, 1971-2000; asst. attending physician, cons. Sloan-Kettering Cancer Ctr., 1962—2000. Chmn. dept. medicine North Shore Univ. Hosp., 1967-01, chmn. emeritus, 2001-, dir. acad. affairs, 1969-93, sr. v.p. med. affairs, 1993-00; exec v.p. med. and acad. affairs North Shore-LI Jewish Health Sys., 1998-00, trustee, 2000—, chief acad. officer, sr. v.p. acad. affairs, 2000-05, Betsey Cushing Whitney acad. dean emeritus, historian, 2005—; asst. in medicine Med. Coll. Cornell U., 1958-59; rsch. fellow NY Heart Assn., 1959-60; instr. medicine Cornell U. Med. Coll., 1960-63, asst. prof., 1963-66, assoc. prof., 1966-71, David J. Greene disting. prof. medicine Weill Cornell Coll. Medicine, 1971-96, assoc. dean, 1969-96, Betsey Cushing Whitney prof. emeritus medicine, 2006-; prof. medicine NYU Sch. Medicine, 1996-05; career scientist Health Rsch. Coun., NYC, 1962-66; tchg. scholar Am. Heart Assn., 1966-67; pres. NY State Bd. Medicine, 1974-75; chmn. Accreditation Coun. for Grad. Med. Edn., 1988, NY State Coun. on Grad. Edn., 1990-92. Contbr. articles to profl. jours. Mem. US White House Rev. Coun., Nat. Health Policy devel., 1993. Lt. USN, 1950—53, Korea. Decorated NY State Conspicuous Svc. medal, Korean Pres. Unit Citation for Meritorious Svc. Fellow NY Acad. Medicine, Am. Heart Assn. (coun. on clin. cardiology); master ACP (chmn. and gov. Downstate NY region II 1975-80, regent 1980-86, chmn. bd. regents 1985-86, chmn. bd. regents emeritus, nat. pres.-elect 1986-87, pres. 1987-88, pres. emeritus, Alfred Stengel Meml. medal); mem. AMA, Am. Fedn. Clin. Rsch., Harvey Soc., NY Med. Soc., Nassau County Med. Soc., Assn. Am. Med. Colls., Am. Clin. and Climatologic Assn. Office: N Shore LIJ Health Sys 125 Community Dr Great Neck NY 11021-5502 Office Phone: 516-465-2536. Business E-Mail: scherr@nshs.edu.

SCHERY, STEPHEN DALE, physicist; b. Jan. 1, 1945; (parents Am. citizens); s. Robert Walter and Lois (Keller) S.; m. Patricia Cooksey, Nov. 1986. BS cum laude, Ohio State U., 1967; MS, U. Ark., 1970; PhD, U. Colo., 1973. Tchr. Cassville (Mo.) H.S., 1968-70; vis. asst. prof. Kenyon Coll., Gambier, Ohio, 1973-74; asst. prof. Tex. A&M U., Galveston, 1974-79; asst. prof. and rsch. physicist N.Mex. Inst. Mining and Tech., Socorro, 1979—84, assoc. prof. and rsch. physicist, 1984—90, prof. and rsch. physicist, 1990—2000, emeritus prof., 2000—. Cons. Mich. State U., East Lansing, 1975-78, Kerr McGee Corp., Chgo., 1983; vis. sr. scientist Australian Atomic Energy Commn., Sydney, 1986; vis. scientist dept. geology, Yale U., 1987; vis. scholar Australian Nuclear Sci. and Tech. Orgn., Sidney, 1990; investigator U.S. Dept. Energy Rsch. Contract in Natural Radioactivity, 1979—. Contbr. articles to profl. jours. NDEA fellow, 1968; NSF grantee, 1977-79. Mem. Am. Phys. Soc., Am. Geophys. Union, Health Physics Soc., Sierra Club, Phi Beta Kappa, Sigma Chi, Soaring Soc. Am. Office: Dept Physics New Mex Inst Mining Tech Socorro NM 87801 Home: 746 Bounty Dr Apt 4608 Foster City CA 94404-2674

SCHETZ, JOSEPH ALFRED, aerospace engineer, educator; b. Orange, NJ, Oct. 19, 1936; s. Alfred John and Teresa (Zappa) S.; m. Katherine Frances Giorgianni, Jan. 31, 1959; children: Holly, Joseph, Katherine, John. BS, Webb Inst. Naval Architecture, 1958; MS, MA, PhD, Princeton U. Sr. scientist Gen. Applied Sci. Lab., Westbury, NY, 1961-64; assoc. prof. aerospace engring. U. Md., 1964-69; Fred D. Durham chair aerospace and ocean engring. Va. Poly. Inst. and State U., Blacksburg, 1999—, chmn. dept., 1969-93. Cons. Applied Physics Lab., Johns Hopkins, 1964-96, Atlantic Rsch. Corp., Alexandria, Va., 1966-72, Du Pont Corp., Richmond, Va., 1980-85; guest prof. Inst. for Theoretical Gas Dynamics, Aachen, Germany, summer 1970; religious edn. tchr. St. John's Roman Cath. Ch., Colesville, Md., 1965-69; prin. H.S. religion St. Mary's Roman Cath. Ch., Blacksburg, 1970-71; vis. scholar Beijing Rsch. Lab., 1985; vis. scientist Wright Labs., Dayton, Ohio, 1993. Author books; contbr. chpts. to books; contbr. articles to profl. jours. Republican precinct chmn., Montgomery County, Md., 1965-69; mem. Rep. Exec. Com., 1973-86; faculty adviser Va. Poly. Inst. Rep. Club, 1973-76. Fellow AIAA (assoc. editor jour. 1975-77, editor-in-chief edn. book series, publs. com. 1978-84, edn. com. 1978-81, air breathing propulsion tech. com. 1994-97, Pendray Aerospace Lit. award 1997, Air Breathing Propulsion Tech. award 1998, Aerospace Contbn. to Soc. award 1999, J. Leland Atwood award 2004), ASME (life); mem. Soc. Naval Architects and Marine Engrs., Sigma Gamma Tau, Tau Beta Pi, Sigma Xi. Home: 607 Rainbow Ridge Dr Blacksburg VA 24060-5535 Office Phone: 540-231-9056. E-mail: ptiger@vt.edu.

SCHEUER, RALPH H., lawyer; b. Albuquerque, Feb. 23, 1946; BA, U. Colo., 1967; JD, U. Va., 1970. Bar: N.Mex. 1970, US Tax Ct. 1982, US Dist. Ct. (dist. N.Mex.) 1982, US Ct. Appeals (10th cir.) 1982. Ptnr. Scheuer, Yost & Patterson, Santa Fe. Named one of Top 100 Attys., Worth mag., 2005. Mem.: ABA, First Jud. Dist. Bar Assn., Phi Alpha Delta, Pi Sigma Alpha. Office: Scheuer Yost & Patterson PC PO Drawer 9570 125 Lincoln Ave Ste 223 Santa Fe NM 87504 Office Phone: 505-982-9911. Office Fax: 505-982-1621. *

SCHEUERMAN, WALTER GEORGE, retired neurologist, retired surgeon; b. Wheeling, W.Va., Apr. 2, 1918; s. Walter George Scheuerman and Henretta Farber; m. Rosemary Anker, Apr. 15, 1945 (dec.); children: Walter Thomas, Thomas Michael, Nancy William, Carol Ann, Joanne, Christopher Robert; m. Helen Sweeten. BS, U. Mich., Detroit, 1938; MD, U. Mich., Ann Arbor, 1942. Diplomate Am. Bd. Neurol. Surgery, 1952, lic. Mich., 1942, Pa., 1943, NJ, 1943. Intern We. Reserve U. Hosp., Cleve., 1946—50; resident U. Pa., Phila.; pres. Mercer County Med. Sch., Trenton, NJ. Maj. med. corp US Army, 1943—46, Italy. Decorated Disting. Svc. award US Army. Mem.: KC (named Grand Knight), ARC, NJ Neurol. Soc. (pres.). Republican. Roman Catholic. Avocations: tennis, golf, skiing.

SCHEUNEMAN, CHRISTINE A., lawyer; b. Kansas City, Mo., Dec. 30, 1950; BA, Univ. Kansas, 1972; JD, DePaul Univ., 1981. Bar: Ill. 1981, Calif. 1984. Ptnr., chmn. Orange County Litigation group Pillsbury Winthrop Shaw Pittman, Costa Mesa, Calif. Mem. nat. panel of arbitrators Am. Arbitration Assn. Pres. bd. dir. Orange County Chamber Orch. Mem.: Order of the Barristers. Office: Pillsbury Winthrop Shaw Pittman 7th Fl 650 Town Ctr Dr Costa Mesa CA 92626 Office Phone: 714-436-6814. Office Fax: 714-436-2800. Business E-Mail: christine.scheuneman@pillsburylaw.com.

SCHEVILL, JAMES ERWIN, poet, playwright; b. Berkeley, Calif., June 10, 1920; s. Rudolph and Margaret (Erwin) S.; m. Margot Helmuth Blum, Aug. 2, 1966; children (by previous marriage): Deborah, Susanna. BS, Harvard U., 1942; MA (ad eundem), Brown U.; LHD (hon.), R.I. Coll., 1986. Mem. faculty San Francisco State Coll., 1959-68, prof. English, 1968, dir. Poetry Center, 1961-68; prof. Brown U., 1969-85, prof. emeritus, 1985—. Reader various univs., insts., and orgns. Author: New and Selected Poems, 2000. Served to capt. AUS, 1942-46. Ford Found. grantee, 1954, 60-61, R.I. Com. on Humanities grantee, 1975; Fund Advancement Edn., 1953-54, Office for Advanced Drama Rsch. fellow, 1957, Rockefeller fellow, 1964, Guggenheim fellow, 1981, McKnight fellow, 1984; recipient Performance prize Nat. Theatre Competition, 1945, 2d prize Phelan Biography Competition, 1954, 2d prize Phelan Drama Competition, 1958, William Carlos Williams award, 1965, Roadsted Found. award, 1966, Gov.'s award R.I., 1975, Best Story of Yr. award Ariz. Quart., 1977; story selected for O. Henry Awards Prize Stories, 1978; award in lit. Am. Acad. Arts and Letters, 1991; work commd. by Nat. Coun. Chs., 1956-61, Fromm Found., 1959, Trinity Repertory Co., R.I. State Coun. on the Humanities, 1986, Providence Coll., 1986, Magdalena Group, 1992. Home: 1309 Oxford St Berkeley CA 94709-1424 Office: Brown U Dept English Providence RI 02912-0001 Personal E-mail: mschevill@aol.com.

SCHEXNAYDER, BRIAN EDWARD, vocalist, educator; b. Port Arthur, Tex., Sept. 18, 1953; s. Leonard and Dorothy (Carrier) S.; m. Sherri Scallan, Oct. 2, 1976. BA in Music, U. Southwestern La., 1976; postgrad., Juilliard Sch. Music, 1976-80. Vocal instr. Brian Schexnayder Vocal Studio, NYC, 1995-97, Plano, Tex., 1997—. Performances with Met. Opera, N.Y.C., Paris Opera Co., Edmonton (Alta., Can.) Opera Co., New Orleans Opera Co., Santiago (Chile) Opera, Winnipeg (Man., Can.), St. Petersburg (Fla.) Opera, Jackson (Miss.) Opera Co., San Francisco Opera, Frankfurt Opera, Hamburg Staatsoper Opera, Oper der Stadt Bonn, Spoleto (Italy) Festival of Two Worlds, Cin. Opera, Fla. Grand Opera. Mem. Am. Guild Musicians. Avocations: computers, billiards, remote control airplanes.

SCHEXNAYDER, CHARLOTTE TILLAR, state legislator; b. Tillar, Ark., Dec. 25, 1923; d. Jewell Stephen and Bertha (Terry) Tillar; m. Melvin John Schexnayder Sr., Aug. 18, 1946; children: M. John Jr., Sarah Holden, Stephen. BA, La. State U., Shreveport, 1944, postgrad., 1947—48. Asst. editor La. Agrl. Extension, Baton Rouge, 1944; editor The McGehee (Ark.) Times, 1945-46, 48-53; editor, co-publisher The Dumas (Ark.) Clarion, 1954-85, pub., 1985-99; mem. Ark. Ho. of Reps., Little Rock, 1985-99, asst. speaker pro tem, 1995—. Pres. Ark. Assn. Women, 1955, Nat. Newspaper Assn., Washington, 1991-92, Ark. Press. Assn., Little Rock, 1982, Nat. Fedn. Press Women, Blue Springs, Mo., 1977-78, Little Rock chpt. Soc. Profl. Journalists, 1973; mem. pres.'s coun. Winrock Internat., 1990—; chmn. Dumas Area Cmty. Found., 2000-02; pres. Main Street Dumas. Editor: Images of the Past, 1991. 1st woman mem. Ark. Bd. Pardons and Parole, 1975-80; mem. Ark. Legis. Coun., 1985-92; bd. dirs. Women's Found. Ark., sec. 1999—; bd. dirs. Chicot-Desha Port Indsl. Com.; v.p. Desha County Mus., 1989—; dir. Dumas Indsl. Found., 1986—; exec. com. Ark. Ctrl. Radiation Therapy Inst., 1991-92; mem. adv. bd. Ark. Profl. Women Achievement, 1992—; vice chair Ark. Rural Devel. Commn., 1991-96, chair 1996-97; mem. Winrock Internat. Adv. Coun., 1991—; founding incorporator Ark. Waterways Commn., 1996—, bd. dirs.; bd. visitors Manship Sch. Comm., La. State U., 1998—; bd. dirs. Main Street Ark., Hist. Preservation Alliance Ark.; active Ark. Transitional Employment Coun., 1999—, Ark. Transitional Employment Assistance Bd., 2000; sec. Dumas Area Cmty. Fund, 2000—; bd. dirs. Enterprise Corp. for the Delta, 1999-2002, Dumas Main St., v.p.; bd. dirs. Historic Preservation Alliance Ark, 2000—; outstanding bd. mem. Ark. Main St., 2002; outstanding bd. chair Ark. Cmty. Found., 2003. Named Disting. Alumnus Ark. A&M Coll., 1971, Woman of Achievement Nat. Fedn. Press Women, 1970, Outstanding Arkansan C. of C., 1986; recipient Ark. Profl. Women of Distinction award No. Bank, Little Rock, 1990, Emma McKinney award Nation's Top Cmty. Newspaper Woman, 1980, Journalist award Nat. Conf. of Christians and Jews, 1989, Lifetime Achievement award Nat. Fedn. Press Women, 1992, Outstanding Svc. award Ark. Assn. Elem. Prins., Disting. Svc. award Ark. Press Assn., 1993, Disting. Svc. award Internat. Soc. Weekly Newspaper Editors, 1996, Golden Svc. award Ark. Press Assn., 1996, State Leadership award Ark. Waterways Commn., 1996, Horizon award League Women Voters Ark., 1998 Ernie Deane award U. Ark., 2005, Chilcote award Ark. Cmty. Found., 2006; named to La. State U. Alumni Hall of Distinction, 1994, Journalism Hall of Fame La. State U., 1998; named one Top 100 Ark. Women, Ark. Bus., 1995-98; named Outstanding Bd. Mem. of Yr., Main Street Ark., 2002, Outstanding Bd. Mem., Ptnrs. of Ark. Cmty. Found., 2003, Extraordinary Svc. award Ark. Cmty. Found., 2006; honored Outstanding Svc. Women's Found. Ark., 2003. Mem.: Main St. Dumas (pres. 2005), Ark. Delta Coun. (chmn., pres.

Dumas Main St., mem. Main St. Ark. adv. bd.), Pi Beta Phi (Crest award 1992). Democrat. Roman Catholic. Home Phone: 870-382-5255. Personal E-mail: cschexnayder@centurytel.net.

SCHEXNAYDER, RANDALL V., pharmacist, dean; b. Vacherie, La., Apr. 26, 1957; s. John B. and Dolores J. Schexnayder; m. Eva Marie Dumas; children: Christopher Randall, Jessica Nicole. BS in Pharmacy, Xavier U. La., New Orleans, 1980; MS in Pub. Health, Tulane U., New Orleans, 1983. Registered pharmacist La., 1980. Pharmacist intern D & H Drug Store, New Orleans, 1977—80; staff pharmacist Touro Infirmary, New Orleans, 1980—82, West Jefferson Gen. Med. Ctr., Marrero, La., 1982—83; pharmacy supr. Baton Rouge Gen. Med. Ctr., 1983—84; asst. dean student affairs Xavier U. Coll. Pharmacy, New Orleans, 1984—. Interim chmn. Assoc. Minority Health Professions Schs., Atlanta, 1989—90; membership chmn. So. Region Natl. Assn. Minority Med. Educators, SC, 1987—88; reviewer Office Minority Health, Washington, 1998—; mem. adv. bd. La. State U. Med. Ctr. Future Health Profls. Network, New Orleans, 1993—; membership chmn., newsletter editor New Orleans Progressive Pharmacists Assn., 1983—86. Contbr.: (documentary) Reconstruction Creole: Laura Plantation at Vacherie; creator: newsletter NOPPA Dropper. Grand knight Knights Peter Claver, Marrero, 1993, jr. comdr., 2001; mem. parish coun. St. Joseph Worker Cath. Ch., Marrero, 1995—97; faithful scribe KPC EOM 4th Degree Assembly # 4, New Orleans, 2004; pres. St. Joseph Worker PTO, Marrero, 1994—95. Recipient Mem. Activity award, Knights Peter Claver, 1992. Mem.: Am. Assn. Colls. Pharmacy, Phi Lambda Sigma (chpt. advisor 1993), Chi Delta Mu, Alpha Kappa Mu (pres. 1978—79), Alpha Epsilon Delta, Kappa Psi (vice regent 1978—79). Democrat. Achievements include research in SchexDumas ancestry, Vacherie AFAM genealogy. Home: 1525 Alison Dr Gretna LA 70056 Office: Xavier U La Coll Pharmacy 1 Drexel Dr New Orleans LA 70125 Home Phone: 504-391-0341; Office Phone: 504-520-7431. Office Fax: 504-520-7977. Business E-Mail: rschexna@xula.edu.

SCHEXNIDER, VIRGINIA REEVES, school psychologist; d. Curtis Reeves Sr. and Virginia Cundiff Reeves; m. Alvin James Schexnider, July 1, 1978; children: Alvin James, Elena Cundiff. BA, Fisk U., Nashville, 1975; MA, U. Va., Charlottesville, 1978. Dir. student assessment ctr. Va. State U., Petersburg, 1980—81; sch. psychologist Richmond City Pub. Schs., Richmond, 1993—96; lic. sch. psychologist Winston-Salem/Forsyth County Pub. Schs., NC, 1996—2002; cert. sch. psychologist Va. Beach City Pub. Schs., 2002—. Directorship The Richmond Symphony, 1989—94, Reynolda Ho. Mus. of Am. Art, Winston-Salem, NC, 1997—2003. Mem.: NASP (assoc.), Va. Acad. Sch. Psychologists (assoc.), Fisk U. Alumni Assn. (life), U. Va. Alumni Assn. (life), Phi Beta Kappa. Office Phone: 757-263-2700.

SCHEYER, DANIEL, lawyer; b. Bklyn., May 13, 1928; s. Emanuel and Clara (Cohen) S.; m. Audrey C. Deutsch, July 27, 1950; children: Lawrence, Richard. AB, NYU, 1947; JD, Columbia U., 1950. Bar: N.Y. 1950. Assoc. Carb, Luria, Glassner, Cook & Kufeld, NYC, 1957-66, ptnr., 1966—99, counsel, 1999—2005; pvt. practice Port Washington, NY, 2005—. Mem., chmn. Bd. Zoning and Appeals, Village of Sands Point, N.Y., 1987-94, trustee, 1994—. Lt. col. USAR. Fellow Am. Coll. Trust and Estate Counsel; mem. ABA, N.Y. State Bar Assn., Assn. of Bar of City of N.Y., Knickerbocker Yacht Club. Home Phone: 516-883-9029; Office Phone: 516-883-9029. Personal E-mail: dscheyer@verizon.net.

SCHIANO, GREG, college football coach; b. Wyckoff, NJ, June 1, 1966; m. Christy Schiano; 4 children. Grad., Bucknell U. Grad. asst. Rutgers U., 1989—90; defensive backs coach Penn St. U., 1991—95; defensive asst. Chgo. Bears, 1996—97, defensive backfield coach, 1998; defensive coord. U. Miami, 1999—2000; head football coach Rutgers U., New Brunswick, NJ, 2000—, defensive coord., 2005—. Named Big East Coach of Yr., 2006, Nat. Coach of Yr., Home Depot, 2006, Coach of Yr., Walter Camp Football Found., 2006; recipient, Liberty Mutual, 2006. Achievements include leading Rutgers football to first ever win against top 5 opponent, 2006. Office: Rutgers U Dept Athletics Louis Brown Athletic Ctr 83 Rockafeller Rd Piscataway NJ 08854 *

SCHIAVO, PASCO LOUIS, lawyer; b. Hazleton, Pa., June 21, 1937; s. Louis and Josephine (Cortese) S. BA, Lafayette Coll., 1958; JD, U. Pa., 1962. Bar: Pa. 1962, U.S. Dist. Ct. (mid. dist.) Pa. 1965, U.S. Ct. Appeals (3d cir.) 1972, U.S. Supreme Ct. 1970. Assoc. Laputka, Bayless, Ecker & Cohn, Hazleton, 1963-65; asst. dist. atty. Luzerne County, Wilkes-Berre, Pa., 1963-65; pvt. practice Hazleton, 1965—. Mem. disciplinary bd. Supreme Ct. Pa., Harrisburg, 1977-83. Contbr. articles to profl. jours. Pres. Luzerne County Commn. Econ. Opportunity, Wilkes-Barre, 1966-68. Mem. ABA, ATLA, Pa. Bar Assn., Luzerne County Bar Assn., Pa. Trial Lawyers Assn., Am. Judicature Soc., Nat. Bd. Trial Advocacy (diplomate, cert. civil trial advocate). Office: 199 N Church St Hazleton PA 18201-5874 Home Phone: 570-454-7349; Office Phone: 570-454-3583.

SCHIAVONE, JOHN, state agency administrator; b. Phila., Aug. 8, 1924; s. Louis and Sadie Ferrara Schiavone; m. Stanislawa Bober (dec.); children: Mark, John; m. Judith Ann Helm. Grad. h.s., Bangor, Pa. From employment intern to mgr. office Bur. Employment Security, Easton, Pa., 1955—87. Mgr. Bangor Little League, 1958; coach Cath. Youth Orgn. Basketball Team Our Lady Good Coun., 1961; founder, 1st pres. Bangor Booster, 1959; pres. 4th Ward Citizens Club, Bangor, 1965. Sgt. Amphibian Engrs. US Army, 1943—46. Decorated Bronze star (2), Medal of the Jubilee of Liberty French Govt. Avocation: horse breeding and racing. Home: 2530 Delabole Rd Bangor PA 18013-9402

SCHIAZZA, GUIDO DOMENIC (GUY SCHIAZZA), educational association administrator; b. Phila., May 17, 1930; s. Guido and Claudina (DiPrinzio) S.; m. Irmgard Heidi Reissmueller, May 15, 1954. BA, Pa. State U., 1952; postgrad., St. Joseph's U., 1954-55, Villanova U., 1954-55, Temple U., 1955-58. Cert. tchr., Pa.; cert. clinician, ednl. specialist, instructional specialist, sch. psychologist, guidance counselor, reading specialist. Speech therapist, lang. arts instr. Commonwealth of Pa., Dept. Edn., 1956-59; founder, clinician, instr., dir., bd. pres. Communicative Arts Ctr., Inc., Drexel Hill, Pa., 1958, Comm. Skills, Cmty. Resources Ctr., Inc., Drexel Hill, Pa., 1958, 1964—; charter mem. exec. bd., bd. pres. United Pvt. Acad. Schs., Assn. of Pa., Drexel Hill, 1966—; exec. bd. govs., bd. chmn. The Accrediting Commn., Drexel Hill, 1971—. Charter mem. Pa. State Univ. Radio and TV Guild, University Park, Pa., 1951—; mem. legis. action com., Pa. State U., Univ. Park, 1988—; cons. communications skills, The Accrediting Commn., 1971—, United Pvt. Acad. Schs. Assn., Pa., 1966—. Founder, chmn., CEO Am. Ednl. Group, 1991—; chmn. CEO Internat. Ednl. Group, 1991—; CEO Cmty. Resources Ctr., Drexel Hill, 1991—, project coord. Energy Quest, 1992—; active Nat. Com. to Preserve Social Security and Medicare, Washington, 1986—, Am. Immigration Control Found., Monterey, Va., 1987—. English First, Springfield, Va., 1988—; mem. pres.'s coun. Rep. Nat. Com., 1989—, Nat. Rep. Senatorial Com., 1989—, Rep. Presdl. Task Force, 1989—; mem. Congrl. Legis. Agenda steering com. Empower Am., 1999. 1st Lt. Signal Corps, U.S. Army, 1952-54. Recipient Svc. award United Pvt. Acad. Sch. Assn. Pa., Monroeville, Pa., 1978, Disting. Achievement and Svc. award Bd. Govs. of the Accrediting Commn., Downington, Pa., 1980, Dr. Charles Boehm Edn. of Yr. award University Park, Pa., 1990, Loyal and Dedicated Svc. award The Accrediting Commn., 1974. Mem. NEA, Libr. Congress (chartered), Internat. Platform Assn., Pa. Edn. Assn., Jefferson Ednl. Found., World Affairs Coun. Phila., Heritage Found., Nat. Trust for Hist. Preservation, Nat. Congl. Club, Pa. State U. Nittany Lions Club, Pa. State U. Alumni Assn., Pa. State U. Football Lettermen's Club, Pa. State U. Varsity "S" Club. Republican. Roman Catholic. Avocations: music, home and garden design, automotive design, reading, golf. Office: The Accrediting Commn 436 Burmont Rd Drexel Hill PA 19026-3630 Office Phone: 610-623-7890.

SCHICK, EDGAR BREHOB, language educator; b. Phila., June 28, 1934; s. Claude Ernest and Martha Henrietta (Brehob) S.; m. Margaret Barbara Buehl, Feb. 12, 1938; children: Susanne, Christina. AB magna cum laude, Muhlenberg Coll., 1955; MA, Rutgers U., 1962, PhD, 1965. Asst. prof. German SUNY, Binghamton, 1963-68, asst. to pres. Albany, 1968-72, asst. prof., 1968-72; v.p. acad. affairs St. John Fisher Coll., Rochester, NY, 1972-78, exec. v.p., 1978-80, assoc. prof., 1972-80; pres. Nasson Coll., Springvale, Maine, 1980-83; provost, v.p. acad. affairs, prof. Eastern Ill. U., Charleston, 1984-87; exec. dir. Bd. Trustees, Md. State Univs. & Colls., Annapolis, 1987-88; vice chancellor for policy and planning U. Md. System, Adelphi, 1988-91; sr. fellow Am. Assn. State Colls. and Univs., 1991-94; cons. Assn. Governing Bds., 1993-95; interim v.p., dean St. Mary Coll., Lawrence, Kans., 1997-98; pres. Luther Inst., Washington, 1998—2003, pres. emeritus, 2003—. Chmn. visitation team Mid. States Assn. Colls. and Schs., Phila., 1975-79; cons. IBM, Yorkville, N.Y., 1968, Nat. Luth. Campus Ministry, 1968-85, USAID, 1992-95. Author: Metaphorical Organicism in the Early Herder, 1971, Shared Visions of Public Higher Education Governance: Structures and Leadership Styles That Work, 1992, The "Local Board" in Multi-Campus Public Universities, 1994; contbr. articles on German lit. and higher edn. to profl. jours. Bd. dirs. United Way, 1981-82, Maine Ind. Colls. Assn., 1981-93, Deaton Hosp., Balt.; v.p. Christ Luth. Ch. Found., Balt.; mem. Accreditation Bd. for Engring. Tech.; pres. Oakleigh Forest Civic Assn. Fellow Univ. fellow, Rutgers U., New Brunswick, N.Y., 1962—63; grantee, Carnegie Found. Mem. Am. Assn. Higher Edn., Am. Assn. Univ. Adminstrs., Registry for Coll. and Univs. Presidents, Am. Assn. State Colls. and Univs., Am. Assn. Tchrs. German, Assn. for Instl. Rsch., Soc. for Coll. and Univ. Planning, Thomas Mann Soc., Nat. Soc. Fund-Raising Execs. Lutheran. Home: 106 Quinn Rd Severna Park MD 21146-3015 E-mail: ebschick@erols.com.

SCHICK, HARRY LEON, investment company executive; b. NYC, Oct. 24, 1927; s. Martin and Sadie (Spitz) S.; m. Eleanor Alter, Oct. 17, 1982; m. Inge Nussbaum, Oct. 12, 1964 (div. Nov. 1971); 1 child, Susan. AB magna cum laude, Bklyn. Coll., 1947; MS, Columbia U., NYC, 1948; postgrad., NYU, 1948-52. Securities analyst Sutro Bros., NYC, 1948-52; asst. to pres. Clairdale Enterprises, Inc., NYC, 1953-66; mgr. arbitrage dept. First Manhattan Co., NYC, 1966-69, gen. ptnr., 1969-91, mng. dir., 1992—. Lectr. Donaldson Sch. Orgn. and Mgmt., Yale U., New Haven, 1978-88, NYU Grad. Sch. Bus. Adminstrn., NYC, 1977; lectr. in field. Trustee Washington Inst. for Near East Rsch. Mem. Inst. Chartered Fin. Analysts, Am. Fin. Assn., Am. Econ. Assn., N.Y. Soc. Security Analysts (bd. dirs. 1975-76), Beta Gamma Sigma. Jewish. Home: 215 E 68th St Apt 15Y New York NY 10021-5726 Office: First Manhattan Co 437 Madison Ave New York NY 10022-7001 Office Phone: 212-756-3350. Business E-Mail: hschick@firstmanhattan.com.

SCHICK, MICHAEL WILLIAM, public relations executive; b. San Antonio, July 17, 1956; s. Lawrence Martin and Jeanne Frances (McCuen) S.; m. Diana Lynn McGinty, Mar. 14, 1988; children: Tiffany Michele, Jessica Diane. B in Media Arts with honors, U. S.C., 1979. Dir. prodns., asst. v.p. S.C. Savs. & Loan League, Columbia, 1978-81; dep. press sec. to U.S. Sen. Strom Thurmond Washington, 1981-85; sr. assoc. Civic Svc. Inc., Washington, 1985-2000; COO Justice Fellowship, Washington, 2000—01; dir. comm. U.S. Chamber of Commerce Inst. for Legal Reform, 2001—03; sr. v.p. Porter Novelli, 2003—. Co-founder, chmn. First Monday Night, McLean, Va., 1981-94; Fourth Presbyn. Ch., Bethesda, Md., 1988—; chmn. Creative Living Internat., Reston, 1988—. C.S. Lewis fellow C.S. Lewis Inst., 1999-2000. Republican. Avocations: golf, tennis, soccer, guitar. Home: 11560 Brass Lantern Ct Reston VA 20194-1221 Office Phone: 202-419-3246. Business E-Mail: michael.schick@porternovelli.com.

SCHICK, ROBERT MICHAEL, lawyer; b. Elizabeth, NJ, Oct. 3, 1954; s. Donald E. and Virginia (Dotterweich) S.; m. Shelley Woodward, May 26, 1979; children: Cameron, Catherine. AB, Princeton U., 1976; JD, U. Houston, 1981. Bar: Tex. 1981, U.S. Dist. Ct. (so. dist.) 1981, U.S. Dist. Ct. (ea. dist.) 1995, U.S. Dist. Ct. (no. dist.) 2005, U.S. Dist. Ct. (we. dist.) 2006, cert.: Tex. Bd. Legal Specialization (civil trial law), Tex. Bd. Legal Specialization (personal injury trial law). Assoc. Vinson & Elkins LLP, Houston, 1981-88, ptnr., 1989—, co-head Litig. Sect. Fellow: Am. Coll. Trial Lawyers, Tex. Bar Found.; mem.: Product Liability Adv. Coun. Office: Vinsons & Elkins LLP First City Tower 1001 Fannin St Ste 2500 Houston TX 77002-6706 Office Phone: 713-654-4582. Business E-Mail: rschick@velaw.com.

SCHICK, THOMAS, diversified financial services company executive; Sr. exec. v.p. Shearson Lehman Brothers, 1986—92; exec. v.p. pub. affairs and comms. Travel Related Svcs. sub. Am. Express, 1992—93, Am. Express Co., 1993—. Office: Am Express Co World Fin Ctr 200 Vesey St New York NY 10285 *

SCHICKLI, JEANNE HLAVKA, virologist, researcher; BA in Biology, Carleton Coll., Northfield, Minn., 1975; MS in Chem. Engring., Yale U., New Haven, 1981; PhD in Microbiology, U. Colo., Denver, 2000. Sr. scientist Medimmune, Inc., Mountain View, Calif., 2002—. Contbr. articles to profl. jours. Achievements include patents pending for variant of human metapneumovirus. Office: Medimmune Inc 297 N Bernardo Ave Mountain View CA 94043

SCHIEBLER, GEROLD LUDWIG, pediatrician, educator; b. Hamburg, Pa., June 20, 1928; s. Alwin Robert and Charlotte Elizabeth (Schmoele) Schiebler; m. Audrey Jean Lincourt, Jan. 8, 1954; children: Mark, Marcella, Kristen, Bettina, Wanda, Michele. BS, Franklin and Marshall Coll., 1950; MD, Harvard U., 1954. Intern pediat. and internal medicine Mass. Gen. Hosp., Boston, 1954—55, resident, 1955—56; resident pediat. U. Minn. Hosp., Mpls., 1956—57, fellow pediatric cardiology, 1957—58, rsch. fellow, 1958—59; rsch. fellow sect. physiology Mayo Clinic and Mayo Found., 1959—60; from asst. prof. pediatric cardiology to prof. emeritus U. Fla., 1960—2001, prof. emeritus, 2001—. Dir. divsn. Children's Med. Svcs. State of Fla., 1973—74, area med. dir., 1974—2000, cons., 2001—. Author (with L.P. Elliott): The X-ray Diagnosis of Congenital Cardiac Disease in Infants, Children and Adults, 1968, 1979; author: (with L.J. Krovetz and I.H. Gessner) Pediatric Cardiology, 1979. Named Children's Med. Svcs. Pediatrician of Decade, Gov. Jeb Bush, 1999; recipient Lifetime Achievement award, Coll. Medicine, 2004. Mem.: AMA (Benjamin Rush award 1993), AAAS, Fla. Med. Assn. (past v.p., bd. govs., pres. 1991—92), Fla. Heart Assn. (past pres.), Fla. Pediat. Soc. (exec. com.), Soc. Pediatric Rsch. (emeritus), Am. Coll. Cardiology, Am. Acad. Pediat. (Abraham Jacobi award 1993), Inst. Medicine NAS, Alpha Omega Alpha, Phi Beta Kappa. Home: 408 Beachside Villas Amelia Island Plantation Amelia Island FL 32034-6551 Home Fax: 904-277-7211. Business E-Mail: gls@ufl.edu.

SCHIEFFER, BOB, newscaster; b. Austin, Tex., Feb. 25, 1937; m. Patricia Penrose; children: Susan, Sharon. BA in Journalism, Tex. Christian U., 1959. Reporter Ft. Worth Star-Telegram; news anchorman Sta. WBAP-TV, Dallas-Ft. Worth; with CBS News, 1969—, Pentagon corr., 1970-74, White House corr., 1974-79, chief Washington corr., 1982—85; anchorman CBS Sunday Night News, 1973-74, CBS Evening News (Saturday edit.), 1976—96, CBS Morning News, 1979-80, 1985; anchor, Face the Nation CBS News, 1991—; interim anchor CBS Evening News, NYC, 2005—06, weekly commentator, polit. analyst, 2006—; participant CBS news spls. and spl. reports, including Peace and the Pentagon, 1974, Watergate-The White House Transcripts, 1974, The Mysterious Alert, 1974, 1976, Ground Zero, 1981; mem. Emmy award-winning team CBS Evening News with Walter Cronkite, 1971; chief Washington corr. CBS News, 1975; co-anchor CBS Weekend News/Sunday News, NYC. Co-author (with Gary Paul Gates): The Acting President, 1989; author: This Just In: What I Couldn't Tell You On TV, 2003 (NY Times Bestseller). Named Broadcaster of Yr., Nat. Press Found., 2002; named to Broadcasting/Cable Hall of Fame; recipient 2 Sigma Delta Chi awards, 6 Emmy awards, Paul White award, Radio-TV News Directors Assn., 2003, Internat. Radio & TV Soc. Found. award, 2004, Helen Thomas award excellence in journalism, Am. News Women's Club, 2004. Office: Face the Nation with Bob Schieffer 2020 M St NW Washington DC 20036-3304

SCHIEFFER, J. THOMAS (JOHN THOMAS SCHIEFFER, TOM SCHIEFFER), ambassador, former professional baseball team executive; b. Ft. Worth, Oct. 4, 1947; s. John E. and Gladys (Payne) Schieffer; m. Susanne Silber, Sept. 22, 1979; 1 child, Paul Robert. BA in Govt., U. Tex., 1970, MA in Internat. Rels., 1972, JD. Bar: Tex. 1979. Mem. Tex. Ho. of Reps., 1973—79; pvt. law practice, 1979—89; ptnr.-in-charge of ballpark devel. Tex. Rangers Baseball Club, 1990—91, pres., 1991—99, gen. ptnr., 1994—99; pres. J. Thomas Schieffer Mgmt. Co. & Pablo Oper. Co., 1989—2001; US amb. to Australia US Dept. State, Canberra, 2001—05, US amb. to Japan Tokyo, 2005—. Office: DOS Amb 9800 Tokyo Pl Washington DC 20521

SCHIELE, MICHELE M., not-for-profit fundraiser, medical association administrator; b. 1967; Grad., Boston U. Coll. Communication, 1989, Northwestern U. Sch. Communication, 1995. V.p. & assoc. dean devel. U. Chgo. Biol. Sciences Divsn./U. Chgo. Hospitals, 2003—. Active in YWCA, Chgo. Named one of 40 Under 40, Crain's Chgo. Bus., 2006. Office: U Chgo Hospitals 5841 S Maryland Ave Chicago IL 60637-1470 also: U Chgo Divsn Biol Sciences 5812 S Ellis St Chicago IL 60637 Office Phone: 773-702-4767. Office Fax: 773-702-1670. E-mail: mschiele@medmail.uchicago.edu.

SCHIER, DONALD STEPHEN, language educator; b. Ft. Madison, Iowa, Sept. 10, 1914; s. Francis and Marcella (Kenny) S. BA, State U. Iowa, 1936; MA, Columbia U., 1937, PhD, 1941. Mem. faculty State Tchrs. Coll., Bemidji, Minn., 1939-41, 41-42, Ill. Inst. Tech., 1946; mem. faculty Carleton Coll., Northfield, Minn., 1946-80, prof. French, 1953-80. Vis. prof. U. Wis., 1964-65; Brown tutor in French U. of South, Sewanee, Tenn., 1980-81 Author: Louis-Bertrand Castel, 1942; editor: (with Scott Elledge) The Continental Model, 1960, 2d edit., 1970; (Bertrand de Fontenelle), Nouveaux Dialogues des morts, 1965, rev. edit., 1974; translator: Letter on Italian Music (Charles de Brosses), 1978. Mem. selection com. Young Scholar Program, Nat. Found. Arts and Humanities, 1966-67. Served to capt. AUS, 1942-46. Mem. MLA, Am. Assn. Tchrs. French, Am. Soc. Eighteenth-Century Studies Home: 750 Weaver Dairy Rd Apt 1106 Chapel Hill NC 27514-1441

SCHIESEL, SETH, reporter; Grad., Yale Univ., 1994, JD, 1997. Tech., gaming reporter NY Times, NYC, 1996—. Office: Bus Day Desk NY Times 229 W 43rd St New York NY 10036 Office Phone: 212-556-7135. Office Fax: 212-556-1448. Business E-Mail: thegamer@nytimes.com.

SCHIESER, HANS ALOIS, education educator; b. Ulm, Germany, July 15, 1931; arrived in U.S., 1965; s. Alois and Anna (Stegmann) S.; m. Margret H. Schröer, June 6, 1962; children: Peter, Elisabeth. BA, Kepler Gymnasium, Ulm, 1952; MA in Philosophy, U. Passau, Fed. Republic Germany, 1959; EdM, Pedagogic Acad., Weingarten, Fed. Republic Germany, 1962; PhD, Loyola U., Chgo., 1970. Head tchr. Pestalozzischule, Ulm, 1964-65; learning disabilities tchr. Jeanine Schultz Meml. Sch., Skokie, Ill., 1966-67; co-dir. Oak Therapeutic Sch., Evanston, Ill., 1967-70; from assoc. prof. to prof. edn. DePaul U., Chgo., 1969-91, prof. emeritus, 1991—. Cons. in field; program cons. Delphian Soc., L.A., 1977-90; rschr., tchr. in Germany, 1991—; active in tchrs. edn. Midwest Montessori Tchr. Tng. Ctr., Evanston, Ill.; guest prof. State U. Chelyabinsk, State Linguistic U., Irkutsk, Russia, 1998-2005; ord. prof., dean of studies Gustav-Siewerth-Akademie, Germany, 1995-2003. Author chpts. in books; contbr. articles to profl. jours.; adv. bd. Ann. Edits. Sociology, Dushkin Pub. Group, 1985-91. Pres. N.Am. Family Svc. Found., Oak Lawn, Ill., 1974-91; bd. dirs. S.O.S. Children's Villages USA, Washington, 1986-94; pres. emeritus S.O.S. Children's Village Ill., Inc., Chgo.; bd. govs. Invest-in-Am. Nat. Found., Phila., 1988-90. Rsch. grant DePaul U., 1985-86, Rsch. sabbatical, 1989. Mem. Am. Ednl. Studies Assn., Nat. Soc. for Study of Edn., Philosophy of Edn. Soc. U.S.A., Soc. Educators and Scholars (bd. dirs. 1984-90), Am. Montessori Soc., Thomas More Gesellschaft/Amici Mori Europe, Phi Delta Kappa (pres. Zeta chpt., Chgo. 1973-75). Home: Veilchenweg 9 D-89134 Bermaringen Germany also: 400 E Main/6B/DJURI Evanston IL 60202 Office: DePaul U 2320 N Kenmore Ave Chicago IL 60614-3210 Personal E-mail: profschieser@aol.com, prof_schieser@hotmail.com.

SCHIFANO, KATH M., artist; b. NYC; d. John A. and Mary Theiss; m. Carl M. Schifano, Oct. 7, 1972; children: Robin, Charles. BA, SUNY, Fredonia, 1971; MA, U. Buffalo, 1975. Cert. art tchr. K-12 permanent cert. N.Y. State. Art instr. Niagara Falls Bd. Edn., NY, 1974—2005, chair art and music, 1993—2003. Workshop presenter, adviser Niagara Falls Tchr. Resource Ctr., 2000—. Exhibited in group shows at N.Y. State Art Tchrs. Juried Shows, 1987, 1989, 1991, 1992, 1994, Kenan Ctr., Niagara County Art Tchrs. Shows, 1991, 1993, 1995, 2001, Williger Doering Gallery - Fine Arts League, 1997, Grand Island Art Soc., 1999, 2002, Locus Media Gallery, N.Y.C., 2004, Albright Knox Regional Artist Exhibit, 2004, 2006, 2007, SUNY Fredonia Alumni Invitational, 2004, one-woman shows include Earl Brydges Libr., Niagara Falls, 1996, Ransomville Libr., 1997—98, Barnes and Noble Bookstore, 1997. Contbg. artist Castellani Mus., Niagara Arts Coun., Buffalo Philharmonic, 1998—2004; asst. curator Ann. Niagara Falls City Sch. Dist. Art Shows, 1985—2005. Recipient partial fellowship, Global Arts Village, 2006, Corp. Award for Art, Albright Knox Art Gallery, 2004. Mem.: N.Y. State United Tchrs., N.Y. State Art Tchrs. Assn., Buffalo Niagra Art Assn., Internat. Plein Air Painters, Niagra Frontier Plein Air Painters, Coll. Club Niagara Falls. Avocations: reading, travel, gardening.

SCHIFF, ADAM BENNETT, congressman, lawyer; b. Framingham, Mass., June 22, 1960; s. Edward Maurice and Sherrill Ann (Glovsky) S.; m. Eve Schiff; 2 children, Alexa Marion, Elijah Harris. BA, Stanford U., 1982; JD cum laude, Harvard U., 1985. Bar: Calif. 1986. Assoc. Gibson, Dunn & Crutcher, LA, 1986; asst. U.S. atty. U.S. Atty.'s Office, LA, 1987—96; mem. Calif. Senate, 1997—2001; chmn. Senate Judiciary Com.; mem. U.S. Congress from 29th Calif. dist., Washington, 2001—; mem. judiciary com., internat. rels. com. Spl. assignment to Czechoslovakia, Justice Dept., Bratislava, 1992. Democrat. Avocation: creative writing. Office: 326 Cannon HOB Washington DC 20515-0529 Business E-Mail: congressman.schiff@mail.house.gov. *

SCHIFF, DAVID TEVELE, investment banker; b. NYC, Sept. 3, 1936; s. John Mortimer and Edith Brevoort (Baker) Schiff; m. Martha Elisabeth Lawler, May 11, 1963; children: Andrew Newman, David Baker, Ashley Reynolds. B.Engring., Yale U., 1958. Trainee Chem. Bank N.Y. Trust, NYC, 1959-62; analyst Madison Fund, NYC, 1962; assoc., then partner Kuhn, Loeb & Co., NYC, 1963-77; vice chmn. Kuhn Loeb & Co. Inc., 1977; mng. dir. Lehman Bros. Kuhn Loeb Inc., NYC, 1977-83, also dir.;

mng. ptnr. Kuhn, Loeb & Co. (formerly KLS Enterprises), 1984—. Bd. dirs. Crown Life Ins. Co., Toronto, 1971—92; mem. lower Manhattan adv. bd. Chem. Bank, 1977—85; dir., vice chmn. Am. Crown Life Ins. Co., NYC, 1981—95; bd. advisors Venture Capital Fund Am., 1996—; mem. leadership coun. Yale Sch. Forestry and Environ. Studies, 2000—; mem. adv. bd. Yale Ctr. Environ. Law and Policy, 2006—. Trustee, chmn. emeritus Wildlife Conservation Soc., 1965—; trustee Met. Mus. Art, 1971—, Citizens Budget Commn., NYC, 1973—, Greater NY coun. Boy Scouts Am., 1965—91, Beekman Downtown Hosp., 1966—82, chmn., 1975—79; trustee Brooks Sch., North Andover, Mass., 1972—90, treas., 1987—90; bd. govs. Yale U. Art Gallery, 1973—97, Fed. Hall Meml. Assn.; mem. adv. bd. dirs. Outward Bound, Inc., 1983—99; mem. Provident Loan Soc. NY; bd. dirs. Am. Hosp. Paris Found., NYC, 1987—2006. With US Army, 1959. Mem.: Century Assn., Yale Club (NYC), Mill Reef Club (Antigua), Maroon Creek Club (Aspen, Colo.), River Club, Brook Club, Econ. Club (NYC), Pilgrims of US (mem. exec. com.). Episcopalian. Home: 770 Park Ave New York NY 10021-4153 Office: 50 Rockefeller Plz 15th Fl New York NY 10020-1622 Office Phone: 212-655-7044. Personal E-mail: gorilla@kuhnloebco.com.

SCHIFF, DONALD WILFRED, pediatrician, educator; b. Detroit, Sept. 11, 1925; s. Henry and Kate (Boesky) S.; m. Rosalie Pergament; children: Stephen, Jeffrey, Susan, Douglas. Student, Wayne State U., 1943-44, Oberlin Coll., 1944-45; MD, Wayne State U., 1949. Diplomate Am. Bd. Pediatrics. Intern Detroit Receiving Hosp., 1949-50; resident in pediatrics U. Colo., 1954-55, chief resident in pediatrics, 1955-56; instr. U. Colo. Health Scis. Ctr., Denver, 1956-59, asst. clin. prof., 1959-69, assoc. clin. prof., 1969-78, clin. prof., 1978-87, prof., 1987—; pvt. practice Littleton (Colo.) Clinic, 1956-86, chmn. bd., 1973-79; med. dir. HMO Colo., Denver, 1980-86; med. dir. Child Health Clinic The Children's Hosp., Denver. Contbr. articles to profl. jours. Bd. dirs. Sch. Dist. VI, Colo., 1962; pres. Arapahoe Mental Health Clinic, Denver, 1968-70, bd. dirs., 1964-70; adv. coun. State of Colo. Medicaid, Denver, 1981—. With USN, 1944-46, USPHS, 1952-54, Turtle Mountain Indian Reservation, N.D. Recipient 25 Yrs. Teaching award U. Colo. Sch. Medicine, 1981. Mem. Am. Acad. Pediatrics (chmn. Colo. chpt. 1973-79, alternate dist. chmn. 1977-81, chmn. dist. 8 1981-86, nat. pres. 1988-89), Rocky Mountain Pediatric Soc., Colo. Med. Soc. Home: 600 Front Range Rd Littleton CO 80120-4052 Office: The Childrens Hosp Child Health Clinic Box BO32 1056 E 19th Ave Denver CO 80218-1088

SCHIFF, ERIC ALLAN, physics professor; b. LA, Aug. 29, 1950; s. Gunther Hans and Katharine Shepard (MacMillan) S.; m. Nancy Ruth Mudrick, Aug. 12, 1973; children: Nathan, Evan. BS, Calif. Inst. Tech., 1971; PhD, Cornell U., 1979. Rsch. assoc. U. Chgo., 1978-81; asst. prof. Syracuse (N.Y.) U., 1981-87, assoc. prof., 1987-95, prof., 1995—, dept. chair, 1997—2003, assoc. dean sci. and math., 2003—. Vis. Brown U., Providence, 1988-90, Xerox Palo Alto Rsch. Ctr., 1995. Contbr. articles to profl. jours. Rsch. grant NSF, 1983-86, 2002-06. Mem. Am. Phys. Soc. (exec. com. NY state chpt. 1991-94), Materials Rsch. Soc. (symposium organizing com. 1992-97, 2003-04), Internat. Conf. Amorphous and Nanocryst Semicondrs. (organizing com. 1999, 2007). Office: Syracuse U Dept Physics Syracuse NY 13244-1130 Office Phone: 315-443-3901.

SCHIFF, FRANK, investment company executive; BS magna cum laude, U. Colo.; JD cum laude, Cornell Law Sch. Ptnr. White & Case LLP, head corp. dept.; mng. dir. DB Capital Ptnrs.; ptnr. MidOcean Ptnrs. Mem.: NY State Bar. Office: MidOcean Ptnrs 320 Park Ave Ste 1700 New York NY 10022 Office Phone: 212-497-1390. Business E-Mail: fschiff@midoceanpartners.com.

SCHIFF, GUNTHER HANS, lawyer; b. Cologne, Germany, Aug. 19, 1927; came to U.S., 1936; s. Hans and Alice (Goldstein) S.; m. Katharine MacMillan, Jan. 27, 1950 (div. 1957); children: Eric Alan, Mary Alice; m. JoAnn R. Schiff; children: Jage, Hans Judson. BSFS., Georgetown U., 1949, JD, 1952. Bar: D.C. 1952, Calif. 1953. Assoc., ptnr., of counsel various firms, Beverly Hills, Calif., 1954-94; pvt. practice Beverly Hills, Calif., 1994—. Sec. Los Angeles Copyright Soc., Beverly Hills, 1975-76 Contbr. articles to profl. jours. Pres. Beverly Hills Civil Svc. Commn., 1984-85, 88-89; pres. Free Arts for Abused Children, 1993-94, dir.; chmn. Rent Control Rev. Bd., Beverly Hills, 1980-84; trustee Young Musicians Found. With USNR, 1945-46. Mem. ABA, Beverly Hills Bar Assn. (chmn. Resolutions Com. 1977-78), Los Angeles County Bar Assn., Los Angeles Copyright Soc., USCG Aux., Calif. Yacht Club. Avocations: sailing, skiing, golf. Office: 9430 W Olympic Blvd Beverly Hills CA 90212-4552 Home Phone: 310-271-7770; Office Phone: 310-557-9081. Personal E-mail: hgschiff@pacbell.net.

SCHIFF, HOWARD IRWIN, urologist; b. Bklyn., May 15, 1948; s. Frank and Mildred Schiff; m. Debbie Mathews Schiff, Aug. 29, 1970; children: Jonathan, Richard, Robin, Meredith, Amanda. BA, Hofstra U., 1970; MS, W.Va. U., 1973, MD, 1975. Diplomate Am. Bd. Urology, lic. physician N.Y. Intern dept. surgery Montefiore Hosp., Bronx, 1975—77; intern dept. urology Mt. Sinai Med. Ctr. N.Y., 1977—80; asst. attending physician Mt. Sinai Med. Ctr., NYC, 1980—; consulting urologist City Hosp. Ctr., Elmhurst, NY, 1980—2004; attending urologist Beth Israel Med. Ctr., NYC, 1983—2003; asst. attending physician Weill-Cornell Med. Ctr., NYC, 2001—. Asst. clin. prof. urology Mt Sinai Sch. Medicine, NYC, 1982—; adj. asst. clin. prof. urology Weill-Cornell Sch. Medicine, NYC, 2001—. Contbr. articles to profl. jours. Named one of Best Drs. in N.Y., N.Y. Mag., 1998, 2000, 2001, Best Drs. in N.Y. Metro Region, Castle Connelly Guide, 1997—2004; recipient Ferdinand Valentine Residents Essay award, N.Y. Acad. Mag., 1979, Physicians Recognition award, AMA, 1980—. Fellow: ACS; mem.: Med. Soc. State of N.Y., Am. Urol. Assn. Office: 1120 Park Ave New York NY 10128 Office Phone: 212-996-6660. Personal E-mail: hschiffmd@gmail.com.

SCHIFF, JAYNE NEMEROW, underwriter; b. NYC, Aug. 8, 1945; d. Milton E. Nemerow and Shirley (Kaplan) Wachtel; m. Albert John Schiff, Mar. 7, 1971; children: Matthew Evan, Kara Anne. BS in Bus., Marymount Coll., 1981; M.Profl. Studies in Elem. and Spl. Edn., Manhattanville Coll., 1995. Corp. sec., treas. Albert J. Schiff Assocs., Inc., NYC, 1970—78; field underwriter Mut. NY Fin. Svcs., Greenwich, Conn., 1973—90; freelance employee benefit cons. Greenwich, 1990—99; sr. account exec., contr. Nylex Benefits, Stamford, Conn., 1999—2005; dir. exec. benefits The NIA Group. LLC, 2005—. Regional dir. mktg., MONY Fin. Svcs., NYC, 1978-79; tutor HELP program Manhattanville Coll., 1996-2000. Bd. dirs. NY League Bus. Profl. Women, 1976-78, Temple Sinai, Stamford, Conn., 1979-84; cub scout leader Boy Scouts Am., 1977-78; treas. Ann. Mothers Bd. Benefit Greenwich Acad., 1988, upper sch. acquisitions chmn., 1989, chmn. spl. acquisitions Greenwich Acad. Benefit, 1990-91, chmn. advt., 1992; ESL tutor Lit. Vols. Am., ESL tutor, trainer, 1993; co-chair U. Rochester Parents Coun., 1993-96, v.p. alumni bd. Am. Coll. Named Conn.'s Outstanding Young Woman, 1979. Mem. LWV, Am. Soc. Chartered Life Underwriters, NY Ctr. Fin. Studies (bd. dirs.), NYC Life Underwriters Assn. (bd. dirs. 1977-78). Jewish. Avocations: sailing, knitting, playing piano, reading. Office: Nylex Benefits 301 Tresser Blvd Stamford CT 06901-3284 Personal E-mail: jayneschiff@earthlink.net. Business E-Mail: jschiff@niagrup.com.

SCHIFF, JOHN JEFFERSON, JR., finance company executive; BS, Ohio State U., 1965. Chmn., CEO John J. & Thomas R. Schiff & Co., Inc., 1983-96; COO Cin. Fin. Corp., 1998—99, pres., CEO, 1999—2006, CEO, 2006—, also chmn. bd. dirs. Trustee Am. Inst. Chartered Property Casualty Underwriters; dir. Cinergy Corp., Fifth Third Bancorp, Cin. Bengals Inc., John J. & Thomas R. Schiff & Co. Inc., Std. Register Co. Office: Cin Fin Group PO Box 145496 Cincinnati OH 45250-5496 *

SCHIFF, LAURIE, lawyer; b. Newark, Apr. 24, 1960; d. Norman Nathan and Claire Jane (Schott) Schiff. BS in Law, Western State U., Fullerton, Calif., 1987, JD, 1988. Bar: Calif. 1989. Ptnr. Schiff Mgmt., Newport Beach, Calif., 1983-89; pvt. practice Schiff & Assocs., Irvine, Calif., 1989-91; ptnr. Schiff & Shelton, Newport Beach, 1991—, Attys. Equity Law Group, LLP, 2001—06; judge pro tem Orange County Superior Ct., 2006. Probation monitor State Bar Ct. Calif., 1991—97, spl. prosecutor, 1997—; temp. judge Orange County Supreme Ct., 2006—. Prodr.: (Albums) Boys Just Want to Have Sex, 1984; author: Genetics of Pointed Mink and Sepia, 2006. Bd. dirs. Jewish Family Svcs. Orange County, 1994—99. Mem.: Am. Trial Lawyers Assn., Nat. Bus. Women Orgn., Assn. Trial Lawyers Am., Nat. Assn. Women Bus. Owners, Orange County Bar Assn. (arbitrator 1995—), Am. Mensa, Online Feline Fanciers (v.p. 1995—97, bd. dirs. 1997—), Tonkinese Breed Assn., Tonks West (v.p. 1994—96, pres. 1996—97), Internat. Cat Assn. (chair legis. com. 1995—97, 1998—99, legal counsel 1999—, lic. splty. judge 2001—04, chair Tonkinese breed com. 2002—, lic. allbreed judge 2004—), Internat. Politically Correct Cat Club (v.p. 1996—). Democrat. Jewish. Office: Schiff & Shelton 3700 Campus Dr Ste 202 Newport Beach CA 92660-2603 Office Phone: 949-417-2211.

SCHIFF, LAWRENCE ALAN, dentist; b. NYC, June 11, 1954; s. Leonard Julius and Mildred Ruth Schiff; m. Susan Lynn Zemmel, Aug. 17, 1986; children: Chelsea Ann, JonDavid. BA, Colgate U., Hamilton, NY, 1976; DMD, Fairleigh Dickinson U., Hackensack, NJ, 1980; GPR, U. Pa., Phila., 1981. Clin. assoc. instr. U Pa. Sch. Dental Medicine, Phila., 1981—86; pvt. practice Erdenheim, Pa., 1986—. Coach SE Pa. Youth Lacrosse Assn. Fellow: Acad. Gen. Dentistry; mem.: ADA, Phila. County Dental Assn., Montgomery Bucks Dental Assn., Am. Acad. Cosmetic Dentistry, Beta Beta Beta. Achievements include research in effects of estrogen on collagen crosslinking. Avocations: golf, skiing. Office: 813 Bethlehem Pike Erdenheim PA 19038 Home Phone: 610-667-2566; Office Phone: 215-233-1163.

SCHIFF, MARTIN, physician, surgeon; b. Phila., July 16, 1922; s. Isidore and Cecelia (Miller) S.; m. Mildred Tepley, Jan. 5, 1946; children: Denise Schiff Simon, Michael, David BS, Pa. State U., 1943; MD, U. Calif.-Irvine, 1951. Intern L.A. County Gen. Hosp., 1950-51; gen. practice medicine specializing in bariatrics LA, 1951—. Lectr. L.A. area community colls. Author: Eat & Stay Slim, 1972, Miracle Weight-Loss Guide, 1976, One-Day-At-A-Time Weight Loss Plan, 1980, (5 tapes) Weight Loss Plan for Health, Happiness & A Longer Life Span, 1982, The Thin Connection, 1986, Lose Unwanted Pounds Permanently Without Dieting/Trying/Playing Games, 1998, Weight Control-Fact or Fiction?, 1999, The Power of Your Will, 1999, Connections: Feelings and Emotions, 2000, YOU: A Guide to Yourself and a Mental Roadmap to Your Inner Being, 2002, Mental Conditions and Situations-Fact or Fiction?, 2006, An Overview and Understanding of Mental Activity and Action, Conditions and Situations, 2006, Weight Thinkers, 2006. Lt. USN, 1943-45, PTO Mem. AMA, Calif. Med. Assn., L.A. Med. Assn., Am. Soc. Weight Control Specialists.

SCHIFF, MOLLY JEANETTE, artist, researcher; b. Chgo., Oct. 19, 1927; d. David Nathan and Beatrice (Aisenberg) Rice; m. Haskell Schiff, June 12, 1946; children: Darryll Nat, Lesley Nan, Brad Scott, Rae Ellyce Student, U. Chgo., 1958—63, student, 1968—69; BFA, Art Inst., Chgo., 1962, MFA, 1963, MA Edn., 1969. Cert. Art tchr. Ill. Instr. art Chgo. Bd. Edn. and Park Dist., 1962—66, Jewish Cmty. Ctrs., Chgo., 1962—65; pvt. practice Chgo., 1962—; instr. art New Trier Extensions, Winnetka, Ill., 1965—78, Evanston Art Ctr., Ill., 1965, St. Tarsissus Sch., Chgo., 1968, Young Artists Studio Art Inst., Chgo., 1968—69, Ill. Visually Handicapped Inst., Chgo., 1968—73, Govs. State U., Monee, Ill., 1975—76. Cons. Markal Corp., Chgo., 1968-94; cons., presenter, regional rep. Shiva Corp., Chgo., 1984-87 Prin. works include Facades, 1971 (Honors award 1971), Drawn Paintings, 1976 (Honors award 1976), Acapulco Balcony, 1978 (Honors award 1980), Mexican Scenics, 1980 (Honors award 1980), Figures on Paper, 1988-89 (Honors award 1989), Low Seam, 1988 (Honors award), Latest Impressions, 1989 (Honors award), Acapulco Nite View, 1989 (Honors award), Latest Impressions, Mannequin Cut Outs, 1990 (Honors award 1990), Mannequin Soiree 1992 (Honors award 2000), Union League, 1993 (Honors award), Jarvis Still Life, 1993 (Honors award), Blue Moon, 1997 (Honors award), Triplets, 1997 (Honors award 1998), Sunset at Pushkar, 1998 (Honors award 1999), Rain Forest, Brazil, 2003 (Honors award 2003), I'm Not Square, 2003 (Honors award 2003-2004), I Forgot My Sketch Book, 2003 (Honors award 2004), V is For Vashti, 2003 (Honors award 2003-2004); exhibitions include I Remember Purim-A Visual Narrative, Chgo. Sinai Congregation, 2006, Biennale Internat., Florence, Italy, 2003, I Remember Purim, Loyola Univ. Art Mus. Chgo., 2007. Pres. I.G.C. chpt. Am. Jewish Congress, Chgo., 1955 Recipient Cash award Foremost Corp., 1963, Ill. Dept. Energy and Natural Resources, 1988, Purchase award Rotarian Mag., 1978, Ill. State Mus., 1978, Nite View, 1989, Honors award U.S. State Dept., 1996-2000. Mem. Archives, Figurative Art League, Nat. Mus. Women in Arts, Chgo. Artists Coalition, Chgo. Soc. Artists, Am. Jewish Artists Assn. (program dir. 1970-74, 89-93, pres. 2004-2005, exhbn. com. 2006), Dutch Folk Art Assn. (cons., juror 1979), Alumni Assn. Art Inst. Chgo., Am. Jewish Artists Club, Scan Chgo. (bd. dir. 1988-91) Avocations: tour directing, travel. Office Phone: 312-274-0930. Personal E-mail: mollyjart@msn.com.

SCHIFF, RICHARD, actor; b. Bethesda, Md., May 27, 1955; s. Edward and Charlotte Schiff; m. Sheila Kelley, 1996; children: Gus, Ruby Christine. Grad., CCNY, 1983. With Actors Gang; founder, artistic dir. Manhattan Repertory Theatre. Dir.: (plays, off-Broadway) Antigone; actor: (films) Arena Brains, 1988, Medium Straight, 1989, Young Guns II, 1990, Stop! Or My Mom Will Shoot, 1992, Rapid Fire, 1992, The Public Eye, 1992, Malcolm X, 1992, The Bodyguard, 1992, Hoffa, 1992, My Life, 1993, Ghost in the Machine, 1993, The Hudsucker Proxy, 1993, Major League II, 1994, Speed, 1994, Tank Girl, 1995, Skinner, 1995, Rough Magic, 1995, Se7en, 1995, City Hall, 1996, The Arrival, 1996, The Trigger Effect, 1996, Grace of My Heart, 1996, Michael, 1996, Santa Fe, 1997, Touch, 1997, Volcano, 1997, Loved, 1997, The Lost World: Jurassic Park, 1997, Deep Impact, 1998, Doctor DoLittle, 1998, Heaven, 1998, Living Out Loud, 1998, Crazy in Alabama, 1999, Forces of Nature, 1999, Gun Shy, 2000, Whatever It Takes, 2000, Forever Lulu, 2000, Lucky Numbers, 2000, What's the Worst That Could Happen?, 2001, I Am Sam, 2001, People I Know, 2002, With It, 2004, Ray, 2004; (TV films) Trenchcoat in Paradise, 1989, Till Death Us Do Part, 1992, Cruel Doubt, 1992, The Positively True Adventures of the Alleged Texas Cheerleader-Murdering Mom, 1993, Amelia Earhart: The Final Flight, 1994, Saved by the Bell: Wedding in Las Vegas, 1994, Special Report: Journey to Mars, 1996, The Taking of Pelham One Two Three, 1998, The Pentagon Wars, 1998; (TV series) Relativity, 1996—97, The West Wing, 1999—2006 (Emmy award, best supporting actor in drama series, 2000); (plays) Goose and Tom Tom (Dramalogue award, best actor), Urban Folktales (Ovation award), Underneath the Lintel, 2006. Recipient Townsend Harris medal, CCNY, 2000.

SCHIFF, ROBERT, healthcare consulting company executive; b. NYC, Jan. 7, 1942; s. Henry and Jeanette (Levine) S.; m. Adrianne Bendich, Aug. 16, 1964 (div. July 1979); children: Jorden, Debra; m. Joann McTaggart, Aug. 24, 1986. BS, CCNY, 1964; MS, Iowa State U., 1966; PhD, U. Calif., Davis, 1968. Asst. prof. anatomy Tufts U. Sch. Medicine, Boston, 1969-72; mgr. serology rsch. Hyland divsn. Baxter Labs., Costa Mesa, Calif., 1972-74; dir. R & D J.T. Baker Diagnostics, Bethlehem, Pa., 1974-77; dir. diagnostic R & D Hoffmann-LaRoche, Nutley, N.J., 1977-80; group v.p. Warner Lambert Co., Morris Plains, N.J., 1980-82; pres., CEO Schiff & Co., Inc., West Caldwell, N.J., 1982—. Del. Nat. Commn. for Clin. Lab. Stds., 1979-80; vice chmn. R & D Coun. N.J., 1980-82; bd. dirs. E.P.I. subs. E-Z-EM, Westbury, N.Y., 1991-98. Contbr. numerous articles to profl. jours.; patentee in field. Bd. dirs. Pharm. Tng. Inst., 2002. Post Doctoral fellow U. Calif., Davis, 1969; Aid to Cancer Rsch. grantee, Mass., 1970. Mem. N.Y. Acad. Sci., Regulatory Affairs Profl. Soc. (cert., bd. editors Focus 2006), Am. Soc. Quality Control (cert. quality auditor), Am. Assn. Clin. Chemistry, Brit. Inst. Regulatory Affairs, Parenteral Drug Assn., Sigma Xi. Avocation: flying. Office: Schiff & Co 1129 Bloomfield Ave West Caldwell NJ 07006-7123 Office Phone: 973-227-1830. Personal E-mail: rschiff13@aol.com.

SCHIFF, STACY, writer; b. Adams, Mass., Oct. 26, 1960; married. BA, Williams Coll. Sr. editor Simon and Schuster. Author: Saint-Exupery: A Biography, 1994 (Pulitzer prize finalist for Biography, 1995), Véra (Mrs. Vladimir Nabokov): Portrait of a Marriage, 1999 (Pulitzer prize for Biography, 2000), A Great Improvisation: Franklin, France, and the Birth of America, 2005 (George Washington Book prize, 2006); contbr. The New Yorker, The N.Y. Times Book Rev., The Times Literary Supplement, others. Fellow, Guggenheim Found., 1996, Nat. Endowment for the Humanities.

SCHIFFER, CHARLES ALAN, oncologist, educator; b. Bklyn., Apr. 11, 1944; s. Mortimer and Esther (Ginsberg) S.; m. Judy T. Schiffer, June 14, 1970 (dec. Aug. 1992); 1 child, Joshua T. BA, Brandeis U., 1968; MD, NYU, 1968. Diplomate Am. Bd. Internal Medicine, Am. Bd. Med. Oncology. Intern, resident, chief resident NYU Sch. Medicine, 1968-72; staff fellow, sr. investigator Nat. Cancer Inst., Balt., 1972-81; chief divsn. malignancies, hematology U. Md. Cancer Ctr., Balt., 1981—97; prof. medicine and oncology Barbara Ann Karmanos Cancer Inst., Wayne State U. Sch. Medicine, Detroit, 1997—; prin. investigator, clinical trials of Gleevec Wayne State U. Sch. Medicine, Detroit, 1999—. Prof. oncology and medicine U. Md. Sch. Medicine, Balt., 1983-1997; chair oncology drug adv. com. FDA, Rockville, Md., 1992-95; chair leukemia com. Cancer and Leukemia Group B, Chgo.; cons. various pharm. cos.; vis. prof. numerous univs. Editor: Neoplastic Diseases of Blood, Leukemia sect., Current Opinion in Oncology; mem. editl. bds. Blood, Jour. Clin. Oncology, Internat. Jour. Hematology, Transfusion Medicine Reviews and Transfusions; contbr. chpts. in books and articles to profl. jours. Lt. comdr. USPHS, 1972-81. Recipient Humanitarian award Arlene Wyman Guild, 1992, Dr. John J. Kenney award, Leukemia/Lymphoma Soc. Am., 2006, Celegene award for Career Acheivement in Hematology, 2006; named Best Doctor, Am. Health Mag., Best Cancer Specialist in the US, Good Housekeeping Mem. Am. Soc. Hematology (coms.), Am. Soc. Clin. Oncology (coms.). Avocations: skiing, biking, music, reading. Office: Hudson-Webber Cancer Rsch Ctr 4100 John R Detroit MI 48201 Address: Weisberg Cancer Treatment Ctr 31995 Northwestern Hwy Farmington MI 48334 Office Phone: 313-576-8737. Business E-Mail: schiffer@karmanos.org, schiffer@wayne.edu. *

SCHIFFER, CLAUDIA, model; b. Rheinberg, Germany, Aug. 25, 1970; m. Matthew Vaughn, May 25, 2002; 2 children. Model Guess? jeans, 1989, Revlon cosmetics, Chanel; amb., internat. spokesperson L'Oréal; co-owner Fashion Cafe restaurants. Ptnr. Fashion Cafe, N.Y.C., London, New Orleans, Barcelona, Jakarta, Manila, others; host World Music Awards with Luke Perry, Monte Carlo, 1995. Runway debut in Chanel fashion show, 1990; appeared on covers of Mademoiselle, Cosmopolitan, Vogue, and over 100 others; creator series of exercise videos (with Kathy Kaehler) Claudia Schiffer's Perfectly Fit, 1996; pub.: (pictorial book) Memories. Hon. bd. dirs. Dishes AIDS; spokesperson Nat. Breast Cancer Coalition.

SCHIFFER, LOIS JANE, lawyer; b. Washington, Feb. 22, 1945; d. Benjamin and Clara (Goldberg) S. BA, Radcliffe Coll., Cambridge, Mass., 1966; JD, Harvard U., Cambridge, Mass., 1969. Bar: Mass. 1969, DC 1971, US Supreme Ct. 1973. Legal svcs. lawyer Boston Legal Assistance Project, 1969-70; ct. law clk. DC Circuit Ct., Washington, 1970-71; assoc. Leva, Hawes, Symington, Martin, Oppenheimer, Washington, 1971-74; lawyer Ctr. for Law and Social Policy, Washington, 1974-78; chief gen. litig. sect. Land and Natural Resources divsn. U.S. Dept. Justice, Washington, 1978-81, spl. litig. counsel, 1981-84; gen. counsel Nat. Pub. Radio, Washington, 1984-89; ptnr. Nussbaum & Wald, Washington, 1989-93; acting asst. atty. gen. environ. and natural resources divsn. US Dept. Justice, Washington, 1993-94, asst. atty. gen. environ. and natural resources divsn., 1994-2001; sr. v.p. for pub. policy Nat. Audubon Soc., 2001—02; ptnr. Baach Robinson & Lewis, Washington, 2002—05; gen. counsel Nat. Capital Planning Commn., Washington, 2005—. Adj. prof. environ. law Georgetown U. Law Ctr., Washington, 1986—; lectr. Harvard Law Sch., 2004; bd. dirs. DC Appleseed, Lawyers, Internat. Sr. Project, Naturalist Soc. Bd. dirs. Women's Legal Def. Fund, 1975-86, Am. Rivers, 1989-93; bd. dirs. ACLU/NCA, 1982-93, pres., 1988-90. Fellow Am. Bar Found.; mem. ABA (del.), Am. Law Inst., Phi Beta Kappa Democrat. Jewish. Avocations: reading, movies, hiking. Home: 4640 Brandywine St NW Washington DC 20016-4449 Home Phone: 202-363-0841. Business E-Mail: lois.schiffer@ncpc.gov.

SCHIFFER, STEPHEN, philosopher, educator; BA in Philosophy, Univ. Pa., 1962; DPhil, Oxford Univ., 1970. Prof., philosophy, dept. chair NYU. Author: Meaning, 1972, Remnants of Meaning, 1987, The Things We Mean, 2003. Fellow: Am. Acad. Arts & Scis. Office: Dept Philosophy NYU 5 Washington Pl New York NY 10003 Office Phone: 212-998-8227. Office Fax: 212-995-4179. Business E-Mail: ss72@nyu.edu. *

SCHIFFMAN, DANIEL, lawyer, arts advocate; b. NYC, Nov. 7, 1932; s. Jacob and Eva (Katzin) Schiffman; m. P.G. Galex, June 26, 1955 (div.); m. Nancy A. Ozelli, Apr. 7, 1990. BBA, CCNY, 1959; JD, NYU, 1962. Bar: NY 1962, US Dist. Ct. (so. dist.) NY 1966, US Ct. Appeals (3d cir.) 1966, US Dist. Ct. (ea. dist.) NY 1979, US Supreme Ct. 1975, US Ct. Appeals (2d cir.) 1980, US Ct. Appeals (1st cir.) 1988, US Ct. Appeals (4th cir.) 1998. Musician, 1950—55; pub. acct. Morris, Sherwood & May CPA, NYC, 1956—59, Meyerson and Levine, CPA, NYC, 1959—61; legal sec. to chief city magistrate City of NY, 1961—62; assoc. Maxwell and Diamond, NYC, 1962—66; mem. Schiffman and Ellenbogen, NYC, 1975—78, Schiffman and Frank, NYC, 1996—2004; pvt. practice, NYC, 1966—74, 1978—96, 2004—. Cons., lectr. Practising Law Inst., NYC, 1963—68, NYC, 1982; counsel, migration div. Commonwealth of PR Labor Dept., 1970—72; counsel to adminstr. Commonwealth of PR Econ. Devel. Adminstrn., 1971—73; advisor US GSA, 1979; lectr., moderator, panelist World Gaming Congress, 1987—99; panelist Global Gaming Expo., 2006; co-chair, moderator, planning com. mem. ALI-ABA CLE courses, 1998, 2000, 01; moderator and panelist ABA, 1988, 2001; referee, special master, mental hygiene evaluator, guardian ad litem, receiver Supreme and Surrogate's Cts., NY, 1991—; adv. com. Little Hoover Com., Calif., 1997. Mem. staff: NYU Law Rev., 1961—62, contbg. author: Casino Credit and Collection Law, 1989, Internat. Casino Law, 1991, 1993, 1999, 2007, columnist and contbg. author: The Gaming Lawyer, 1998—, Global Gaming Bus. Mag., 2003—, mem. ed. bd.: Gaming Law Rev., 1997—. Bd. dirs. Am. Symphony Orch., 1989—2005, treas., 1990—93, sec., 1997—2004; bd. dirs. MAESTRO Found., London, 1985—87; treas. Citizens for a Responsive Congress, 1978—80; co-founder, exec. prodr., founding pres. (hon.) Cala Records, Inc., 1991—. Recipient Nat. Arts Club Pres. Medal, 1989. Mem.: Am. Fedn. Musicians, NYC Jr. C. of C. (legal advisor 1980—90), Internat. Masters of Gaming Law (bd. dir. membership com., publications com.), Internat. Assn. Gaming Advs. (formerly Internat.

Assn. Gaming Attys.), Assn. Bar City NY, Nat. Arts Club (bd. dirs. 1986—, chmn. music com. 1986—, Pres.'s medal 1989). Home: 903 Park Ave New York NY 10075-0362 Office Phone: 212-628-6433.

SCHIFFMAN, GERALD, microbiologist, educator; b. NYC, May 22, 1926; s. Samuel and Mollie (Brookner) S.; m. Lillian Ebert, July 12, 1951; children: Stewart, Howard. BA cum laude, NYU, 1948, PhD, 1954. Asst. prof. microbiology Coll. Physicians and Surgeons, Columbia U., NYC, 1960—63; asso. prof. dept. research medicine and microbiology U. Pa., Phila., 1963-70; prof. SUNY Health Sci. Ctr., Bklyn., 1970-97, disting. svc. prof., 1995-97, prof. emeritus, 1997. Cons. Contbr. articles to profl. jours. Served in U.S. Army, 1943-45, ETO. Decorated Bronze Star; recipient Nichols award, 1947; Atomic Energy fellow, 1948-52; NIH grantee, 1974-94. Mem. Am. Assn. Immunologists, Am. Chem. Soc., Am. Soc. Microbiology, AAAS, Harvey Soc., Soc. Complex Carbohydrates, Sigma Xi, Phi Beta Kappa, Mu Chi Sigma, Pi Mu Epsilon. Jewish. Office: 450 Clarkson Ave Brooklyn NY 11203-2056 Personal E-mail: gs1246@verizon.net.

SCHIFFMAN, HAROLD FOSDICK, Asian language educator; b. Buffalo, Feb. 19, 1938; s. Merl and Mathilda (Keller) S.; m. Marilyn Gail Hornberg, June 10, 1978; 1 son, Timothy Marc Rajendran. BA, Antioch Coll., 1960; MA, U. Chgo., 1966, PhD, 1969. Lectr. anthropology U. Calif.-Davis, 1966-67; asst. prof. U. Wash., Seattle, 1967-73, assoc. prof., 1973-78, prof., 1978-95, chmn. dept. Asian langs., 1982-87; prof. South Asian studies U. Pa., Phila., 1995—2002, acad. dir. Penn Lang. Ctr., Luce prof. lang. learning, 1995-2000, rsch. dir. Penn. Lang. Ctr., 2000—, prof. emeritus, 2007—; dir. Consortium Lang. Policy and Planning, 2001—, Pedagogical Materials Project South Asia Lang. Resource Ctr., 2002—05. Trustee Am. Inst. Indian Studies, Chgo., 1979-82; lang. dir. Southeast Asian Summer Studies Inst., 1992-93, mem. lang. adv. com., 1993-94. Author: A Grammar of Spoken Tamil, 1979, A Reference Grammar of Spoken Kannada, 1983, Linguistic Culture and Language Policy, 1996, A Reference Grammar of Spoken Tamil, 1999; co-editor: Dravidian Phonological Systems, 1975; co-author: Language and Society in South Asia, 1981. Pres. bd. dirs. Seattle Pro Musica (choral group), 1976-78; mem. Pacific Northwest Chamber Chorus, Seattle, 1983-87. Sr. fellow Am. Inst. Indian Studies, 1976, 78; grantee U.S. Office Edn., 1971, 74, 78, NEH, 1984-87, Smithsonian Inst., 1984-87, Fulbright Rsch., 1993-94. Mem. Assn. Asian Studies (S. Asia council 1982-85), Am. Inst. Indian Studies (trustee 1979-82), Soc. S. Indian Studies (sec.-treas. 1973-75), Internat. Assn. Tamil Research (v.p. 1987-89). Mem. Soc. Of Friends. Office: U Pa Dept South Asia Studies 820 Williams Hall Philadelphia PA 19104-6305 Office Phone: 215-898-5825. Business E-Mail: haroldfs@gmail.com.

SCHIFFMAN, LOUIS F., management consultant; b. Poland, July 15, 1927; s. Harry and Bertha (Fleder) S.; m. Mina R. Hankin, Dec. 28, 1963; children: Howard Laurence, Laura Lea. BChemE, NYU, 1948, MS, 1952, PhD, 1955. Rsch. engr. Pa. Grade Crude Oil Assn., Bradford, 1948-50; tchg. fellow dept. chemistry NYU, 1950-54; rsch. chemist E.I. DuPont de Nemours & Co., Wilmington, Del., 1954-56, Atlantic Refining Co., Phila., 1956-59; project leader, group leader, head corrosion sect. Amchem Products Inc., Ambler, Pa., 1959-70; pres. Techni Rsch. Assocs. Inc., Willow Grove, Pa., 1970—. Bd. dirs. Techno Ventures, Inc., Texchange-.com; real estate developer: ptnr. Bay Properties Co., Bay Club Marina, Margate, N.J., Willow Grove (Pa.) Assocs.; pub., editor Patent Licensing Gazette, 1968—, World Tech., 1975—; panelist on forum patents and inventions Delaware Valley Industry, 1973; mem. adv. oversight com. NSF, 1975, moderator energy conf. ERDA, Washington, 1976, Las Vegas, 1977; mem. adv. group in small bus. R&D programs Dept. Def., 1980. Editor: (with others) Guide to Available Technologies, 1985; contbr. to Encyclopedia of Chemical Technology, 1967; contbr. articles to profl. jours.; patentee in field. Recipient Founders Day award NYU, 1956. Fellow Am. Inst. Chemists; mem. Am. Chem. Soc., N.Y. Acad. Scis., Lic. Exec.s Soc., Tech. Transfer Soc., Assn. Univ. Tech. Mgrs., Assn. Small Rsch. Cos. (editl. contbr. newsletter), Sigma Xi, Phi Lambda Upsilon. Home: 1001 Easton Rd 206M Willow Grove PA 19090 Office: Techni Rsch Assocs Inc PO Box 1036 Willow Grove PA 19090-0922 Personal E-mail: techniresearch@yahoo.com.

SCHIFFNER, ADRIENNE ANITA, art historian, educator; b. Jersey City, June 7, 1947; d. Thomas B. and Anita (Grosvenor) McAndrews; m. Richard Burchett (div.); children: Anita Claussen, Arianne Burchett; m. Charles Robert Schiffner, Jan. 22, 1983. BA in Art History, Ariz. State U., Tempe, 1989, MA in Art History, 2001. Cert. CC tchr. Ariz. Dir. Main Trail Galleries, Scottsdale, Ariz., 1972—73; archivist Frank Lloyd Wright Found., Scottsdale, 1977—83; v.p. Charles Schiffner Arch. Ltd., Phoenix, 1983—2000; program coord. pres. cmty. enrichment programs Ariz. State U., Tempe, 2000—03, instr. art history, 2003—04; tchr. art history Xavier Coll. Prep., Phoenix, 2002—. Lectr. in field; adj. faculty mem. Rio Salado CC, Phoenix, 2003—06. Chmn. living rm. restoration project Taliesin West, Scottsdale; mem. Phoenix Arts Commn.; mem. adv. bd. Ariz. State U. Art Mus., Tempe, 1998—2000; chmn. grants com. Phoenix Arts Commn., 1985—88; bd. dirs. Ariz. chpt. Nat. Soc. Arts and Letters, 1992—95; bd. dirs. Ballet Ariz., Phoenix, 1999—2001. Taliesin fellow, Frank Lloyd Wright Found., 1973—83. Mem.: Coll. Art Assn., Soc. Archtl. Historians, French Heritage Soc. (pres.), Ariz. State U. Coll. Fine Arts Alumni Assn. (co-pres. 2002—). Home: 5202 E Osborn Phoenix AZ 85018 Office: Xavier Coll Prep 4710 N 5th St Phoenix AZ 85012

SCHIFFNER, CHARLES ROBERT, architect; b. Reno, Sept. 2, 1948; Robert Charles and Evelyn (Keck) S.; m. Iovanna Lloyd Wright, Nov. 1971 (div. Sept. 1981); m. Adrienne Anita McAndrews, Jan. 22, 1983. Student, Sacramento Jr. Coll., 1967-68, Frank Lloyd Wright Sch. Architecture, 1968-77. Registered architect, Ariz., Nev., Wis. Architect Taliesin Associated Architects, Scottsdale, Ariz., 1977-83; pvt. practice architecture Phoenix, 1983—. Lectr. The Frank Lloyd Wright Sch. of Architecture, 1994, 95. Named one of 25 Most Promising Young Americans Under 35, U.S. mag., 1979; recipient AIA Honor award Western Mountain Region, 1993, Western Home awards Sunset Mag., 1989, 91, AIA Ariz. Merit award, 1993 and numerous others. Home: 5202 E Osborn Rd Phoenix AZ 85018-6137 Office: 2944 N 44th St Ste 101 Phoenix AZ 85018

SCHIFFNER, ROBERT A., food products executive; BA, Princeton Univ.; MBA, Rutgers Univ. Mgmt. positions through v.p. fin. & planning Nabisco Inc.; v.p., contr. Nabisco Holdings, 1995—97, sr. v.p., treas., 1998—2001; sr. v.p., CFO Campbell Soup Co., Camden, NJ, 2001—. Office: Campbell Soup Co Campbell Pl Camden NJ 08103-3878

SCHIFFRIN, MILTON JULIUS, physiologist; b. Rochester, NY, Mar. 23, 1914; s. William and Lillian (Harris) S.; m. Dorothy Euphemia Wharry, Oct. 10, 1942; children: David Wharry, Hilary Ann. AB, U. Rochester, 1937, MS, 1939; PhD cum laude, McGill U., 1941. Instr. physiology Northwestern U. Med. Sch., Chgo., 1941—45; lectr. pharmacology U. Ill. Med. Sch., 1947—57, clin. asst. prof. anesthesiology, 1957—61; with Hoffmann-La Roche, Inc., Nutley, NJ, 1946—79, dir. drug regulatory affairs, 1964—71, asst. v.p., 1971—79; pres. Wharry Rsch. Assn., Seattle, 1979—. Chmn. Everglades Health Edn. Ctr., 1986—87. Author: (with E.G. Gross) Clinical Analgesics, 1955; editor: Management of Pain in Cancer, 1957. Bd. dirs. Univ. Adult Day Ctr., 1993—; mem. adv. bd. Regional Ombudsman Program, 1998—, Residents Coun. Washington, 1998—. Capt. USAAF, 1942-46. Mem. Am. Med. Writers Assn. (bd. dirs. 1967-70, pres. N.Y. chpt. 1967-68, nat. pres. 1972-73), Am. Physiol. Soc., Internat. Coll. Surgeons, Am. Therapeutic Soc., Coll. Clin. Pharmacology and Therapeutics, Am. Chem. Soc. Home and Office: Unit 308 4400 Stone Way N Seattle WA 98103-7486 Office Phone: 206-284-8809. Personal E-mail: grampared@comcast.net.

SCHIFTER, RICHARD, lawyer; b. Vienna, July 31, 1923; came to US, 1938; s. Paul and Balbina (Blass) S.; m. Lilo Krueger, July 3, 1948; children: Judith, Deborah, Richard P., Barbara, Karen BS in Social Sci. summa cum laude, CCNY, 1943; LLB, Yale U., 1951; DHL (hon.), Hebrew Union Coll., 1992. Bar: Conn. 1951, DC 1952, US Supreme Ct. 1954, Md., 1958. Assoc. Fried, Frank, Harris, Shriver & Jacobson, Washington, 1951-57, ptnr., 1957-84; dep. US rep. with rank of ambassador UN Security Coun., NYC, 1984-85; asst. sec. of state for human rights and humanitarian affairs Dept. State, Washington, 1985-92; US rep. UN Human Rights Commn., Geneva, 1983-86, 93; spl. asst. to pres., counselor Nat. Security Coun., Washington, 1993-97, spl. adviser to Sec. of State, 1997-2001. Head US del. Conf. on Security and Cooperation in Europe Experts Meeting on Human Rights, Ottawa, Ont., Can., 1985, Dem. Insts., Oslo, 1991; bd. dirs. US Inst. Peace, 1986-92; mem. Congl. Commn. on Security and Cooperation in Europe, 1986-92. V.p., pres. Md. Bd. Edn., Balt., 1959-79; chmn. Md. Gov.'s Commn. on Funding Edn. of Handicapped Children, 1975-77, Md. Values Edn. Commn., 1979-83, Montgomery County Dem. Cen. Com., Md., 1966-70; del. Dem. Nat. Conv., 1968; bd. govs. Am. Jewish Com., 1992-93, 01-04, mem. exec. com., 2001-04; chmn. Internat. Rels. Commn., 2001-04; chmn. bd. dirs. Ctr. for Democracy and Reconciliation in Southeastern Europe, 2002-06, Am. Jewish Internat. Rels. Inst., 2005-; bd. trustees Inst. Christian and Jewish Studies, 2000-. With US Army, 1943-46, ETO, office of mil. govt. for Germany, 1946-48. Decorated Austrian Gt. Golden Decoration with star, comdr. Order of the Romanian Star, Bulgarian Stara Planina Order 1st class; recipient Disting. Svc. award, Sec. of State, 1992. Mem. Phi Beta Kappa. Democrat. Jewish. Home: 6907 Crail Dr Bethesda MD 20817-4723 Personal E-mail: rschifter@aol.com.

SCHILD, NANCY LOIS, realtor, music educator; b. Hartford, Conn., May 31, 1947; d. William and Elsie Lena Brusick; m. William Adrian Schild, Mar. 19, 1947. B in Music Edn., Fla. State U., 1967; MS, Portland State U., 1976; MusM in Conducting, U. Wis., Milw., 2001. Music tchr. Orlando (Fla.) Luther H.S. and Middle Sch., 1996—99, Hales Corner (Wis.) Luth. Sch., 1996—99, choir dir., 1997—2002; music tchr. St. Joan Antida H.S., Milw., 1999—2002; accompanist, part-time organist Christ Our Redeemer Luth. Ch., Temple Terrace, Fla., 2002—; music tchr. Christ Our Redeemer Luth. Sch., Temple Terrace, 2004—; realtor Century 21, Tampa, Fla., 2004—05, Exit Realty Advisors, Tampa, 2005—. Founder, condr. Hales Corners Children's Choir, 1997—2001; singer Master Singers Milw., 1997—99, Milw. Choral Artists, 1999—2002. Mem.: Temple Terrace C. of C. (amb. 2005—), Greater Tampa Assn. Realtors, Nat. Assn. Realtors, Temple Terrace Svc. League. Republican. Lutheran. Avocations: golf, oil painting. Office: Exit Realty Advisors 11502 N 56th St Tampa FL 33617

SCHILD, RAYMOND DOUGLAS, lawyer; b. Chgo., Dec. 20, 1952; s. Stanley Martin and Cassoundra Lee (McArdle) S.; m. Kathryn Elizabeth McKaig Schild, June 21, 2004. Attended, U.S. Mil. Acad., 1970; BA summa cum laude, De Paul U., 1974, JD magna cum laude, 1982; M in Life Scis., Order of Essenes, 1996. Bar: Ill. 1982, U.S. Dist. Ct. (no. dist.) Ill. 1982, U.S. Ct. Appeals (7th cir.) 1982, Idaho 1989, U.S. Dist. Ct. Idaho 1989, U.S. Ct. Appeals (9th cir.) 1989, U.S. Supreme Ct. 1990. Law clk. to chief judge law divsn. Cir. Ct. Cook County, Chgo., 1984-85; pres. Martin, Chapman, Schild & Lassaw, Chartered, Boise, 1990—96; mng. assoc. prelitigation divsn. Litster Injury Lawyers, Boise, 2001—05, Goicoechia Law Offices, Boise, 2005—. Lectr. on legal edn. ICLE and NBI, 1993-98. Co-host legal radio talk show KFXD, 1994; legal columnist Idaho Bus. Rev., 1988-96. Mem. adv. bd. Alliance for the Mentally Ill, Boise, 1991—, Parents and Youth Against Drug Abuse, Boise, 1991-92; fair housing adminstr. Sauk Village (Ill.) Govt., 1987-88; instr. Ada County Youth Ct., Boise, 1992—. Schmitt fellow DePaul U., 1974; recipient Merit award Chgo. Law Coalition, 1987. Mem. ATLA, Idaho Trial Lawyers' Assn., Ill. State Bar Assn., Idaho State Bar Assn., Boise Estate Planning Counsel, Shriners (temple atty. 1994—, liaison Crippled Children's Hosp.), Masons (jr. steward 1992). Avocations: tennis, trombone, writing, music.

SCHILIT, MATTHEW TODD, assistant principal; b. July 16, 1978; 1 child, Alexis Elizabeth. MEd in Edn. Adminstrn., U. SC, Columbia. Cert. secondary and elem. prin. SC. Asst. adminstr. Richland Sch. Dist. Two, Columbia, 2003—04, asst. prin., 2004—. Mem.: SC Assn. Sch. Adminstrs. Office: Richland School District Two 2721 Decker Blvd Columbia SC 29206 Home Phone: 803-518-4449; Office Phone: 803-699-2750. Personal E-mail: mschilit@gmail.com. Business E-Mail: mschilit@dm.richland2.org.

SCHILKEN, MICHAEL C., lawyer; BS, U. Colo., Boulder, 1987; JD, Creighton U., 1990. Bar: Nebr. 1990, US Tax Ct. Atty. Gross & Welch, P.C., 1990—2004; ptnr. Blackwell, Sanders, Peper & Martin, LLP, Omaha, 2004—. Bd. dirs. Cantorium Found. Named one of Top 100 Attys., Worth mag., 2006. Mem.: Omaha Estate Planning Coun., Nebr. State Bar Assn., ABA. Office: Blackwell Sanders Peper & Martin 1620 Dodge St Ste 2100 Omaha NE 68102 Office Phone: 402-964-5018. Office Fax: 402-964-5050. E-mail: mschilken@blackwellsanders.com. *

SCHILL, CHARLES F., lawyer; BS in Chemistry, Le Moyne Coll., 1968; JD, Capital Univ. Coll. of Law, 1973. Bar: Ohio 1973, DC 1985, US Supreme Ct. 1985, US Ct. Internat. Trade 1985, US Ct. Appeals, Fed., DC circuits 1985, registered: to practice before US Patent and Trademark Office 1975. Sr. staff atty., Office Legal Svcs. and Office of Gen. Counsel US Internat. Trade Commn.; ptnr., internat. trade & investment tech. dept Steptoe & Johnson LLP, Washington. Frequent lectr. on internat. trade regulation, WTO, intellectual property and litig. Mem.: Fed. Cir. Bar Assn. (pres. 2004—05), Internat. Trade Commn. Trial Lawyers Assn., Am. Intellectual Property Law Assn., Order of the Curia. Office: Steptoe & Johnson LLP 1330 Connecticut Ave NW Washington DC 20036 Office Phone: 202-429-8162. Office Fax: 202-429-3902. Business E-Mail: cschill@steptoe.com.

SCHILL, MICHAEL H., dean, law educator; b. Schenectady, NY, 1958; AB, Princeton U., 1980; JD, Yale Law Sch., 1984. Law clerk Hon. Marvin Katz Ea. Dist. Pa., 1984—85; assoc. Fried, Frank, Harris, Shriver & Jacobson, 1985—87; vis. lectr. Yale Law Sch., 1987; asst. prof. law U. Pa. Law Sch., 1987—91, assoc. prof., 1991—92; prof. law and real estate U. Pa. Law Sch. and Wharton Sch., 1993—95; vis. prof. Harvard Law Sch., 1999; dir. Furman Ctr. for Real Estate and Urban Policy, NYU, 1994—2004; prof. law and urban planning NYU Sch. Law and Robert F. Wagner Grad. Sch. Pub. Svc., 1995—2003, Wilf Family Prof. in property law and prof. urban planning, 2003—04; dean, prof. law UCLA Sch. Law, 2004—. Asst. counsel N.Y. State Assembly, Com. Housing, 1979; dir. Study of Neighborhood Reinvestment Princeton Urban and Regional Rsch. Ctr., 1980—81; vis. faculty U. Miami Law Sch., Grad. Prog. in Real Estate, 1994. Co-author: Revitalizing America's Cities: Neighborhood Reinvestment and Displacement, 1983, Reducing the Cost of New Housing Construction in New York City, 1999, The State of New York City's Housing and Neighborhoods, 2001; author: Housing and Community Development in New York City: Facing the Future, 1999; contbr. articles to law jours. Office: UCLA Sch Law Box 951476 Los Angeles CA 90095-1476 E-mail: schill@law.ucla.edu. *

SCHILLER, BARBARA, retired special education educator; b. NYC, Jan. 1, 1943; d. Harry M. and Lee C. Browner; m. Charles Philip Schiller, July 16, 1967; children: Andrew Barry, Zachary Alan. BS in Edn., SUNY, Cortland, 1964; MS in Edn. of Visually Impaired, Hunter Coll., 1971. Tchr. children with limited vision NYC Bd. Edn., 1964—95. Sculpture exhbns., SUNY, Purchase, 1980—2005, sculpture in two-person show, Gallery at Marmara, N.Y.C., 2003, Cirque d'Art, N.Y., 2003, sculpture juried show, Katonah Mus., N.Y., 2003—06, sculpture in one-woman shows, John C. Hart Libr., Shrub Oak, N.Y., 2003, sculpture in permanent collections, Amsterdam Whitney Gallery, N.Y.C., 2004—. Mem. bd. gov. Temple Beth Shalom, Mahopac, NY, 1995—2004. Named Woman of Yr., Temple Beth Shalom, Mahopac, NY, 2004; recipient NY award for sculpture, Knickerbocker Artists, multiple awards 4 first place, Quilts Along the Bay, Barnegat, NJ, 2003—04. Mem.: Am. Soc. Contemporary Artists, Studio Art Quilt Assn., Pen and Brush, Katonah Mus., Nat. Women in Arts, No. N.Mex. Quilters Guild, State Quilter Guild NJ, No. Star Quilters Guild. Hadassah. Avocations: reading, interior decorating, music, doll making, jewelry making. Home: 3600 Curry St Yorktown Heights NY 10598

SCHILLER, DONALD CHARLES, lawyer; b. Chgo., Dec. 8, 1942; s. Sidney S. and Edith (Lastick) S.; m. Eileen Fagin, June 14, 1964; children— Eric, Jonathan Student, Lake Forest Coll., 1960-63; JD, DePaul U., 1966. Bar: Ill. 1966, US Dist. Ct. (no. dist.) Ill. 1966, US Supreme Ct. 1972. Ptnr. Schiller, DuCanto & Fleck LLP, Chgo., 1966—; lectr. in law U. Chgo. Law Sch., 2001—. Chair domestic rels. adv. com. Cir. Ct. Cook County, 1993—2001, co-chmn. rules revision com., 2003—; spkr. profl. confs. Contbr. chpts. and articles to profl. publs. Mem. steering com. on juvenile ct. watching, LWV, 1980-81. Named one of Am.'s Best Divorce Lawyers, Town and Country, 1986, 1998, Nat. Law Jour., 1987, Best Lawyers in Am., 1987—, Chgo.'s Best Divorce Lawyers, Crain's Chgo. Bus., 1981, Today Chgo. Woman, 1985, Inside Chgo. Mag., 1988, Chgo. Sun Times, 2000, Worth Mag., 2002, Nat. Top 500 Lawyers, Law Dragon Mag., 2005, 2006, 2007, Ill. 10 Top Lawyers, Super Lawyers Mag., 2006, Leading Laws Mag., 2006, 2007; recipient Maurice Weigle award, Chgo. Bar Found., 1978, Disting. Alumni award, DePaul U., 1988, various certs. of appreciation from numerous profl. groups. Fellow Am. Bar Found., Am. Acad. Matrimonial Lawyers (nat. chair continuing legal edn. 1993-94); mem. ABA (bd. govs. 1994-97, chmn. family law sect. 1985-86, Ill. State del. 1980-84, mem. Ho. of Dels. 1984-2003, editor-in-chief Family Law Newsletter 1977-79; mem. editorial bd., assoc. editor Family Adv. Mag. 1979-84, speaker at confs. and meetings), Am. Bar Retirement Funds (pres. 2005-06, adv. bd. mem. 2007—), Ill. Bar Assn. (pres. 1987-88, chmn. family law sect. 1976-77, editor Family Law Bull. 1976-77, bd. govs. 1977-83, treas. 1981-84, v.p. 1984-86, chmn. various coms., lectr., incorporator and pres. Ill. State Bar Assn. Mutual Ins. Co., Inc. 1988-89), Chgo. Bar Assn., Am. Coll. Family Law Trial Lawyers (diplomate). Office: Schiller DuCanto & Fleck LLP 200 N La Salle St 30th Fl Chicago IL 60601-1098 Office Phone: 312-609-5560. Business E-Mail: dschiller@sdflaw.com.

SCHILLER, JOAN HOFF, oncologist, educator; b. Chgo., Ill., Nov. 10, 1954; MD, U. Ill. Coll. Medicine, Chgo., 1980. Diplomate Am. Bd. Internal Medicine, Am. Bd. Internal Medicine, Med. Oncology, cert. Nat. Bd. Med. Examiners. Intern, internal medicine Northwestern Meml. Hosp., Chgo., 1980—81, resident, oncology, 1981—83; fellow, human oncology U. Wis. Clin. Cancer Ctr., Madison, Wis., 1984—86, rsch. assoc.; asst. prof. U. Wis., Madison, Melanie Heald prof., dept. medicine, sect. med. oncology; dep. dir., Harold C. Simmons Comprehensive Cancer Ctr. U. Tex. Southwestern Med. Ctr., Dallas, chair, hematology/oncology, prof., dept. hematology/oncology. Mem. internat. scientific com. 10th World Conf. on Lung Cancer; head, lung cancer disease-orientated working group U. Wis. Hosp. and Cancer Ctr.; spkr. in field. Contbr. articles to profl. jours., chapters to books. Mem. med. com. Joan's Legacy Lung Found.; founder, pres. Women Against Lung Cancer. Mem.: Am. Soc. Clin. Oncology, Eastern Co-operative Oncology Group (chairperson, thoracic oncology com.). Office: U Tex Southwestern Med Ctr at Dallas 5323 Harry Hines Blvd Dallas TX 75390-8852 Office Phone: 214-648-4180. Office Fax: 214-648-1955. *

SCHILLER, JONATHAN DAVID, lawyer; b. Washington, Sept. 25, 1946; s. Irving and Patricia Schiller; m. Margaret I. Miller, July 24, 1976; children: Zachary, Joshua, Aaron. BA, Columbia U., 1969, JD, 1973. Bar: U.S. Dist. Ct. D.C. 1973, U.S. Ct.Appeals (D.C. cir.) 1975, U.S. Dist. Ct. (ea. dist.) Ky. 1985, U.S. Dist. Ct. (ea. dist.) Mich. 1988, U.S. Ct. Appeals (6th cir.) 1988, U.S. Ct. Appeals (2d and 3d cirs.) 1990, U.S. Supreme Ct. 1991. Law clk. U.S. Dist. Ct. D.C., Washington, 1973-74; assoc. Arnold & Porter, Washington, 1974-76; ptnr. Rogovin, Huge & Schiller, Washington, 1976-90, Donovan, Leisure, Rogovin, Huge & Schiller, Washington, 1991—94, Kaye Scholer Fierman Hays & Handler, Washington, 1994—97; mng. ptnr. Boies Schiller & Flexner, Washington, 1997—. Pres. Washington Tennis & Edn. Found., 1993—; dir. Irwin Sweeney Miller Found., Washington, 1976—. Life Fellow, Am. Bar Found.; bd. mem. Washington Council of Lawyers; mem. Jud. Conf. D.C. Cir. (standing com. pro se and pro bono matters); Milan Chamber Nat. & Internat. Arbitration; Club of Arbitrators. Avocations: tennis, golf. Office: Boies Schiller & Flexner LLP Suite 800 5301 Wisconsin Ave NW Washington DC 20015 Business E-Mail: jschiller@bsfllp.com.

SCHILLER, JUSTIN GALLAND, antiquarian bookseller, researcher, editor; b. Bklyn., Sept. 10, 1943; s. S. Gary and Constance Audrey (Galland) S. BA in English Renaissance Lit., Ithaca Coll., 1965; postgrad., SUNY, Binghamton, 1965—66. Prin. Justin G. Schiller, Bklyn., 1960-69; pres. Justin G. Schiller, Ltd., NYC, 1969—. Instr. hist. children's literature Rare Books Sch., Columbia U., 1984-89, U. Va., Charlottesville, 1996—; lectr. in field. Editor: (with A. Lurie) Garland's Classics in Children's Literature, 73 vols.; contbr. articles to Horn Book mag., Am. Book Collector, The Book Collector, others. Mem. coun. Bibliog. Soc. Am., 2001—. Mem Antiquarian Booksellers Assn. Am., Assn. Internat. de Bibliophilie, Am. Antiquarian Soc., Grolier Club. Home: 77 W Chestnut St Kingston NY 12401-5929 Office: Justin G Schiller Ltd Antiquarian Booksellers Ste 302 Rockefeller Ctr 1270 Ave of the Americas New York NY 10020-1702 Home Phone: 845-331-3309; Office Phone: 212-332-7070. E-mail: justin.schiller@usa.net.

SCHILLER, PETER HARKAI, biomedical engineering and physics educator; Dorothy W. Poitras prof. med. engrng. and med. physics MIT, Cambridge, Mass. Contbr. articles to profl. jours. Fellow: Am. Acad. Arts & Scis.; mem.: NAS. Office: MIT E25-634 Bldg 46-6041 77 Massachusetts Ave Cambridge MA 02139 Office Phone: 617-253-9339. Office Fax: 617-253-8943. Business E-Mail: phschill@mit.edu. *

SCHILLER, PHILIP W., information technology executive; BS in biology, Boston Coll., 1982. Former programmer, sys. analyst Mass. Gen. Hosp.; former IT mgr. Nolan, Norton & Co., Lexington, Mass.; mktg. positions Apple Computer Inc., 1986—93, sr. v.p. worldwide product mktg. Cupertino, Calif., 1997—, interim v.p. mktg. Japan, 2006—; dir. product mktg. FirePower Sys., Menlo Park, Calif., 1993—95; v.p. product mktg. Macromedia, Inc., San Francisco, 1995—97. Office: Apple Computer Inc 1 Infinite Loop Cupertino CA 95014 Office Phone: 408-996-1010.

SCHILLER, PIETER JON, retired venture capital executive; b. Orange, NJ, Jan. 14, 1938; s. John Fasel and Helen Roff (Roberts) S.; m. Elizabeth Ann Williams, Nov. 20, 1965; children— Cathryn Ann, Suzanne Elizabeth. BA in Econs. with honors, Middlebury Coll., 1960; MBA, NYU, 1966. Fin. analyst Merck & Co., Inc., NYC, 1960—61; fin. analyst, asst. divsn. contr., dir. auditing, then asst. contr. Allied Chem. Corp., NYC and Morristown,

NJ, 1961—75, treas., 1975—79, v.p. planning and devel., 1979—83; exec. v.p. diagnostic ops. Allied Health & Sci. Products Co., 1983—86; pres. subs. Instrumentation Lab., Lexington, Mass., 1983—86; gen. ptnr. Advanced Tech. Ventures, Waltham, Mass., 1986—2005, ptnr. emeritus, 2006—. Bd. dirs. CytoLogix Corp., Waltham, Mass.; bd. advisors Fresh Tracks Capital, LLC, Middlebury, Vt. Chmn. bd. trustees Newark Boys Chorus Sch., 1976—78, pres. bd., 1974—76; trustee Colonial Symphony Soc., 1978—85, v.p., 1980—82, pres., 1982—83; active Morris Mus., Morristown, Concord Mus., Mass., 1994—96, v.p., 1996—2000, chmn. bd. trustees, 2002—06; pres. Middlebury Coll. Alumni Assn., 1994—96; chmn. allocations com. United Way of Morris County, 1974—79, v.p. bd. dirs., mem. exec. com., 1979—80; trustee Morris Mus. Arts and Scis., 1980—83; bd. dirs. New Eng. Coun., Boston, 1983—86; v.p. Middlebury Coll. Alumni Assn., 1992—94; bd. dirs. John Adams Innovation Inst., Westborough, Mass., 2005—. Mem. Fin. Execs. Inst. Republican. Episcopalian. Avocations: skiing, photography. Home: 18 S Meadow Rdg Concord MA 01742-3051 Home Phone: 978-371-1858; Office Phone: 781-290-0707. Personal E-mail: pjschiller@aol.com. Business E-Mail: pschiller@atvcapital.com.

SCHILLER, ROBERT E., former school system administrator; PhD, U. Pa. Supt. local sch. districts, NJ, 1984—87; state dep. supt. edn. La., 1988—89; state dep. supt. pub. instrn. Del., 1989—91; supt. pub. instrn. Mich. State Dept. Edn., Lansing, 1992—95; interim CEO Balt. Pub. Schs., 1997—98; supt. Caddo Parish Pub. Sch. Dist., Shreveport, La., 1999—2002; state supt. edn. Ill. Dept. Edn., 2002—04.

SCHILLER, VIVIAN, Internet company executive; BA in Russian and Soviet Studies, Cornell U., 1983; MA in Russian, Middlebury Coll., 1984. Russian interpreter, prodn. coord. Turner Broadcasting Systems, Inc., v.p., gen. mgr. Turner Original Productions, exec. v.p. CNN productions; sr. v.p., gen. mgr. Discovery Times Channel The NY Times Co., 2002—05, sr. v.p. TV and video, 2005—06, exec. v.p., gen. mgr. Discovery Times Channel, 2005—06; sr. v.p., gen. mgr. NYTimes.com, 2006—. Bd. govs. Banff TV Festival; mem. Coun. Fgn. Rels., Nat. TV Acad. Exec. Peer Group. Supervising prodr. (TV documentaries) A Century of Women, 1994, Moon Shot, 1994, sr. prodr. Hank Aaron: Chasing the Dream, 1995, Hollywood's Amazing Animal Actors, 1996, Biker Women, 1996, Survivors of the Holocaust, 1996 (Emmy award for Outstanding Informational Spl., 1996), Animal ER, 1996, Pirate Tales, 1997, Twin Stories, 1997, Warner Bros. 75th Anniversary: No Guts, No Glory, 1998, Dying to Tell the Story, 1998, prodn. mgr. Terror's Children, 2003, The New Face of Late Night TV, 2003, exec. prodr. (documentaries) Word Wars, 2004, Off to War, 2005. Recipient five Emmy awards, two Peabody awards, Alfred I. duPont-Columbia U. award, 2007. Office: The NY Times Co 229 W 43rd St New York NY 10036 *

SCHILLER, WILLIAM RICHARD, surgeon; b. Bennett, Colo., Jan. 14, 1937; s. Francis T. and Frances M. (Finks) S.; m. Beverlee Schiller; children from previous marriage: Julie, Lisa. BS, Drury Coll., Springfield, Mo., 1958; MD, Northwestern U., 1962; MA in Liberal Arts, St. John's Coll., 2005. Diplomate Am. Bd. Surgery; cert. of added qualifications in surg. critical care, 1987, recertified in surg. critical care, 1994. Intern Passavant Meml. Hosp., Chgo., 1962-63; resident Northwestern U. Clin. Tng. Program, Chgo., 1963-68; assoc. prof. surgery Med. Coll Ohio, Toledo, 1970-78; prof. surgery U. N.Mex, Albuquerque, 1978-83; dir. Trauma Ctr. St. Joseph's Hosp., Phoenix, 1983-89; dir. burn and trauma ctr. Maricopa Med. Ctr., Phoenix, 1989-98; prof. surgery So. Ill. U., Springfield, 1998—2002; ret., 2002. Clin. prof. surgery U. Ariz. Health Sci. Ctr.; prof. surgery Mayo Grad. Sch. Medicine, Rochester, Minn. Contbr. chpts. to books, articles to profl. jours. Served as maj. M.C. U.S. Army, 1968-70, Vietnam. Recipient Disting. Alumnus award for career achievement, Drury Coll., 2004. Fellow ACS; mem. Am. Assn. Surgery of Trauma, Cen. Surg. Assn., Western Surg. Assn., Soc. Surgery of Alimentary Tract, Am. Burn Assn., Internat. Soc. of Surgery. Republican. Home: 784 Aspen Compound Santa Fe NM 87501 Personal E-mail: wrschiller@hughes.net.

SCHILLING, CURTIS MONTAGUE, professional baseball player; b. Anchorage, Alaska, Nov. 14, 1966; m. Shonda Schilling; children: Gehrig, Grant, Gabriella, Garrison. Student, Yavapal Coll., Ariz. Selected by Boston Red Sox, 1986—88; pitcher Balt. Orioles, 1988—91, Houston Astros, 1991—92, Phila. Phillies, 1992—2000, Ariz. Diamondbacks, 2000—03, Boston Red Sox, 2004—. Named to MLB All-Star game, 1997—99, 2001, 2002, 2004; recipient Lou Gehrig award, Phi Delta Theta, 1996, Nat. League Championship Series Most Valuable Player, 1993, co-World Series Most Valuable Player, 2001, Best Championship Performance, ESPY awards. Achievements include led Nat. League in strikeouts (319), 1997, (300), 1998; led Nat. League in wins (22), 2001, Am. League (21), 2004; being a member of World Series Champion Arizona Diamondbacks, 2004; being a member of World Series Champion Boston Red Sox, 2004; has had over 200 career wins, over 3,000 career strikeouts. Office: c/o Boston Red Sox 4 Yawkey Way Boston MA 02215-3496

SCHILLING, FRANKLIN CHARLES, JR., retail management professional; b. Balt., Apr. 17, 1958; s. Franklin Charles and Shirley Jean (Whitehurst) S.; m. Dana E. Schilling, Apr. 21, 2005; children: Franklin Charles III, Tyler Kyle, Brittany Alexandra Stainbrook. Student, Dundalk C.C., 1975—77. Dept. mgr. Santonis Market, Inc., Balt., 1976-80; store mgr. A&P Plus Food Stores, Balt., 1980-82; area supr. Southland Corp/7-Eleven, Suitland, Md., 1982-85; mgr. retail ops. Moore Oil Co./Makin' Tracks Stores, Washington, NC, 1986, Besche Oil Co./Quik Shop Stores, Waldorf, Md., 1987-89; dist. mgr. Royal Farm Stores, Balt., 1989-97, dir. ops., 1997-98, dir. mktg. and merchandising, 1999—. Lutheran. Avocations: reading, sports, music. Office: Royal Farm Stores 3611 Roland Ave Baltimore MD 21211-2408 Home: 649 Budleigh Cir Lutherville MD 21093 Office Phone: 410-889-0200. Business E-Mail: fschilling@royalfarms.com.

SCHILLING, FREDERICK AUGUSTUS, JR., geologist, consultant; b. Phila., Apr. 12, 1931; s. Frederick Augustus and Emma Hope (Christoffer) Schilling; m. Ardis Ione Dovre, June 12, 1957 (div. 1987); children: Frederick Christopher, Jennifer Dovre. BS in Geology, Wash. State U., 1953; PhD in Geology, Stanford U., 1962. Cert. engring. geologist, Calif.; registered geologist Calif., environ. assessor Calif. Computer geophysicist United Geophys. Corp., Pasadena, Calif., 1955-56; geologist various orgns., 1956-61, U.S. Geol. Survey, 1961-64; underground engr. Climax (Colo.) Molybdenum Co., 1966-68; geologist Keradamex Inc., Anaconda Co., M.P. Grace, Ranchers Exploration & Devel. Corp., Albuquerque and Grants, N.Mex., 1968-84, Hecla Mining Co., Coeur d'Alene, Idaho, 1984-86, various engring. and environ. firms, Calif., 1986-91; prin. F. Schilling Cons., Canyon Lake, Calif., 1991—. Author: Bibliography of Uranium, 1976. Del. citizen amb. program People to People Internat., USSR, 1990—91. With US Army, 1953—55. Fellow: Explorers Club; mem.: Internat. Platform Assn., Soc. Mining Engrs., Am. Assn. Petroleum Geologists, Geol. Soc. Am., Adventurer's Club LA, Kiwanis, Masons, Sigma Xi, Sigma Gamma Epsilon. Republican. Presbyterian. Avocation: track and field. Office: F Schilling Cons 30037 Steel Head Dr Canyon Lake CA 92587-7460 also: 14661 Myford Rd Ste C Tustin CA 92780-7205 Home Phone: 951-244-8999; Office Phone: 714-731-8438. E-mail: faschill@pacbell.net.

SCHILLING, W. A. HAYDEN, history professor; BA, So. Meth. U., 1959; MA, Vanderbilt U., 1961, PhD, 1970. Faculty mem. Coll. Wooster, Ohio, 1964—, Robert Critchfield prof. English history Ohio, 1982—, dir. Advanced Placement Inst. Ohio. Recipient US Professors of Yr. Award for Outstanding Baccalaureate Coll. Prof., Carnegie Found. for Advancement of Tchg. and Coun. for Advancement and Support of Edn., 2005. Office: Coll Wooster 1189 Beall Ave Wooster OH 44691 Office Phone: 330-263-2452. E-mail: hschilling@wooster.edu. *

SCHILLINGS, DENNY LYNN, retired history professor, educational and grants consultant; b. Mt. Carmel, Ill., June 28, 1947; s. Grady Lynn and Mary Lucille (Walters) S.; m. Karen Krek; children: Denise, Corinne. AA, Wabash Valley Coll., 1967; BEd, Ea. Ill. U., 1969, MA in History, 1972; MA in Adminstrn., Govs. State U., 1996; postgrad., Ill. State U., No. Ill. U. Grad. asst. dept. history Ea. Ill. U., Charleston, 1969; tchr. Edwards County High Sch., Albion, Ill., 1969-70, Sheldon (Ill.) High Sch., 1971-73, Homewood-Flossmoor (Ill.) High Sch., 1973—2003, tchr. history, grants and devel. mgr., 1994—2003; supr. history dept. Coll. Liberal Arts and Scis, No. Ill. U., Dekalb, 2003—; ret., 2003; adj. prof. Trinity Christian Coll., 2003—. Participant, con. Atlantic Coun. U.S. and NATO, Washington, 1986, Internat. Soviet-U.S. Textbook Project Conf., Racine, Wis., 1987; moderator Soviet-U.S. Textbook Study: Final Report, Dallas, 1987; chair history content adv. com. Ill. Tchr. Certification Requirements Com. 1986; mem. Ill. State Bd. Edn., Com. to Establish Learner Outcomes, 1984, Joint Task Force on Admission Requirements Ill. State Bd. on Higher Edn., 1986—; mem. adv. com. for Jefferson Found. Sch. Programs, 1987-90, Ill. State Bd. Edn.'s Goals Assessment Adv. Com., 1987-90; chair Ill. Learning Standards Project, 1996-97; pres. Corinne Jeannine Schillings Found., 2004—. Author: (with others) Economics, 1986, The Examination in Social Studies, 1989, Links Across Time and Place: A World History, 1990, Illinois Government Text, 1990, 99, 2003, Challenge of Freedom, 1990; author: The Living Constitution, 1991, 3d edit., 2002; co-editor: Teaching the Constition, 1987; reviewer, cons. for edn. instns. and organizations; chair editorial bd. Social Edn., 1983; contbg. editor Social Studies Tchr., 1987-88. Mem. steering com. Homewood-Flossmoor High Sch. Found., 1983-84; elected bd. edn. Homewood Elem. Dist. 153, 1999—, found. pres., 2005—. Mem. NEA, Am. Hist. Assn. (James Harvey Robinson prize com. 1990-91), Ill. Coun. Social Studies (v.p. 1981, editor newsletter 1979-84, pres. 1983), Ill. Edn. Assn. (Gt. Lakes coord. com. 1982-83), Nat. Coun. Social Studies (publs. bd. 1983-86, bd. dirs. 1987-90, 94-96, exec. com. 1989-90, chair conf. com. 1989-90, pres. 1993-94, program planning com. 1989, 91), Phi Alpha Theta. Avocations: computers, reading. Home and Office: 18447 Aberdeen St Homewood IL 60430-3525 Home Phone: 708-957-3684; Office Phone: 630-886-0507. Personal E-mail: dschillings1@comcast.net.

SCHILLOW, NED WILLIAM, mathematics professor; b. Skippack, Pa., Aug. 3, 1950; s. William James and Doris Elizabeth (Shaffer) S. BS, Ursinus Coll., Collegeville, Pa., 1972; MS, Rutgers U., 1974; MEd, Temple U., Phila., 1976. Sec. tchr. Cherry Hill (N.J.) Sch. Dist., 1974-76; prof. math. Lehigh Carbon C.C., Schnecksville, Pa., 1976—. Assoc. editor the UMAP Jour., 1986—2005; asst. newsletter editor Pa. State Math. Assn. Two Yr. Colls., 1982-90; columnist Mo. Coun. Tchrs. Math. newsletter, 1985-90; contbr. articles to profl. jours. and chpts. to books. Recipient Faculty Appreciation award Student Govt. of Lehigh Carbon C.C., 1987, George Elison Faculty Svc. award, 1988, Employee Recognition award, 1989, Pa. Outstanding Teaching award State Commn. for C.C., 1992, Faculty Excellence award, Lehigh Carbon C.C., 2003; NSF-MSP grantee, 2003—. Mem. Math Assn. Am., Am. Math. Assn. of 2-Yr. Colls., Nat. Coun. Tchrs. Math. (rep. 1988—), Pa. State Math. Assn. of 2-Yr. Colls. (exec. bd. 1982—), Pa. Coun. Tchrs. Math (exec. bd. 1979-84, conv. publicity com. 1991-92), Ea. Pa. Coun. Tchrs. Math. (exec. bd. 1979—, pres. 1980-82). Republican. United Ch. of Christ. Avocations: reading, travel, crystal. Home: PO Box 539 Skippack PA 19474 Office: Lehigh Carbon CC 4525 Education Park Dr Schnecksville PA 18078-2510 Home Phone: 610-584-6448; Office Phone: 610-799-1752. Business E-Mail: nschillow@lccc.edu.

SCHILSKY, RICHARD LEWIS, oncologist, researcher; b. NYC, June 6, 1950; s. Murray and Shirley (Cohen) S.; m. Cynthia Schum, Sept. 24, 1977; children: Allison, Meredith. BA cum laude, U. Pa., Phila., 1971; MD with honors, U. Chgo., 1975. Diplomate Nat. Bd. Med. Examiners, Am. Bd. Internal Medicine (subspecialty med. oncology); lic. physician, Mo., Ill. Intern, resident medicine Parkland Meml. Hosp., Southwestern Med. Sch., Dallas, 1975-77; clin. assoc. medicine br. and clin. pharmacology br. Divsn. Cancer Treatment, Nat. Cancer Inst., Bethesda, Md., 1977-80, cancer expert clin. pharmacology br., 1980-81; asst. prof. dept. internal medicine U. Mo. Sch. Medicine, Columbia, 1981-84; asst. prof. dept. medicine U. Chgo. Pritzker Sch. Medicine and Michael Reese Med. Ctrs., 1984-86, assoc. prof. dept. medicine, 1986-89; assoc. dir. joint sect. hematology and med. oncology U. Chgo. and Michael Reese Med. Ctrs., 1986-89; assoc. prof. dept. medicine, assoc. dir. sect. U. Chgo. Pritzker Sch. Medicine, 1989-91, prof. dept. medicine sect. hematology-oncology, 1991—; dir. U. Chgo. Cancer Rsch. Ctr., 1991-99; chmn. Cancer and Leukemia Group B, Chgo., 1995—; assoc. dean clin. rsch. biol. scis. divsn. U. Chgo., 1999—. Vivian Saykaly vis. prof. oncology McGill U., 1992; sci. com. Internat. Congress on Anti-Cancer Chemotherapy, 2002; adv. panel on hematologic and neoplastic disease U.S. Pharmacopeial Conv., 1991-95; cancer ctr. support grant rev. com. Nat. Cancer Inst., NIH, 1992-95; expert panel on advances in cancer treatment, 1992-93; mem. Cancer Ctrs. Working Group, 1996-97; oncologic drugs adv. com. FDA, 1996-2000, chmn., 1999-2000; mem. clin. trials implementation com. Nat. Cancer Inst., 1997-98, mem. bd. sci. advisors, 1999—, mem. clin. trials working group, 2004-05, mem. translational rsch. working group, 2005-, mem. clin. trials adv. com., 2007—. Mem. editl. bd. Investigational New Drugs, 1988-95, Jour. Clin. Oncology, 1990-93, Contemporary Oncology, 1991-95, Jour. Cancer Rsch. and Clin. Oncology, 1991—, Seminars in Oncology, 1997—; assoc. editor Clin. Cancer Rsch., 1994—, Cancer Therapeutics, 1997-99, Cancer, 2000—; contbr. articles to profl. jours., chpts. to books. With USPHS, 1977-80. Recipient Spl. Advancement for Performance award VA, 1983, Fletcher Scholar award Cancer Rsch. Found., 1989; grantee VA, 1981-87, Am. Cancer Soc., 1983-86, 92-95, Ill. Cancer Coun., 1985-86, Michael Reese Inst. Coun., 1985-86, Nat. Cancer Inst., 1987, 88-90, Burroughs-Wellcome Co., 1987-88, NIH/Nat. Cancer Inst., 1988—. Fellow ACP; mem. AAAS, Am. Soc. Clin. Oncology (bd. dirs. 2002-05, pres.-elect 2007), Am. Assn. Cancer Rsch. (chmn. Ill. state legis. com. 1992—), Am. Fedn. Clin. Rsch. (senator Midwest sect. 1983-84, councilor 1983-86, chmn. 1988-89), Am. Cancer Soc. (bd. dirs. Ill. divsn. 1997—), Am. Assn. Cancer Edn., Am. Soc. Clin. Pharmacology and Therapeutics, Ctrl. Soc. Clin. Rsch., N.Y. Acad. Scis., Assn. Am. Cancer Insts. (bd. dirs. 1995-99), Chgo. Soc. Internal Medicine, Sigma Xi, Alpha Epsilon Delta, Alpha Omega Alpha. Office: U Chgo Biol Scis Divsn 5841 S Maryland Ave Chicago IL 60637-1463 Office Phone: 773-834-3914. Business E-Mail: rschilsk@medicine.bsd.uchicago.edu.

SCHILTZ, PATRICK JOSEPH, federal judge; b. Duluth, Minn., 1960; BA summa cum laude, Coll. St. Scholastica, 1981; JD magna cum laude, Harvard Law Sch., 1985. Bar: Minn. 1985. Summer assoc. Faegre & Benson LLP, 1985, assoc., 1987—92, ptnr., 1993—95; law clk. to Hon. Antonin Scalia, US Ct. Appeals, DC Cir., 1985—86, US Supreme Ct, 1986—87; assoc. prof. law U. Notre Dame Law Sch., 1995—2000; assoc. dean U. St. Thomas Sch. Law, 2000—03, law prof. & St. Thomas More chair in law, 2003—06; judge US Dist Ct. Minn., 2006—. Office: US Dist Ct 778 Fed Bldg 316 N Robert St Saint Paul MN 55101 Office Phone: 651-848-1906. Office Fax: 651-848-1902. *

SCHIMEK, DIANNA RUTH REBMAN, state legislator; b. Holdrege, Nebr., Mar. 21, 1940; d. Ralph William and Elizabeth Julia (Wilmot) Rebman; m. Herbert Henry Schimek, 1963; children: Samuel Wolfgang, Saul William. AA, Colo. Women's Coll., 1960; student, U. Nebr., Lincoln, 1960-61; BA magna cum laude, U. Nebr., Kearney, 1963. Former tchr. and realtor; mem. Nebr. Legislature from 27th dist., Lincoln, 1989—; chmn. govt., mil. and vets. affairs com. Nebr. Legislature, Lincoln, 1993-94, 99—, vice chair urban affairs com., 1995-98. Dem. Nat. committeewoman, 1984-88; chmn. Nebr. Dem. Com., 1980-84; mem. exec. com. Dem. Nat. Com., 1987-88; past pres., sec. bd. dirs. Downtown Sr. Ctr. Found., 1990-96; mem. exec. bd. Midwestern Legis. Conf., 1995—, co-chair health and human svcs. com., 1995-96; exec. dir. Nebr. Civil Liberties Union, 1985; former bd. dirs. Nebr. Repertory Theater, Exon Found., 1997-2000; mem. adv. bd. Martin Luther Home, 1997-2003; chair Midwestern Legis. Conf. Coun. of State Govts., 2000-01, co-chair com. intergovtl. affairs; mem. Midwest Interstate passenger Rail Commn., 2001-05; mem. exec. bd. Coun. State Govts., 2000-05; chair NCSL Task Force on Initiative and Referendum, 2001-02; bd. dirs. Habitat Humanity, 2006—. Recipient Outstanding Alumni award, U. Nebr., 1989, Tribute award, YWCA, 1992, Friend of Psychology award, NE Psychol. Assn., 1998, Woman of Yr. award, Nova Chpt. Bus. & Profl. Women, 1999, Disting. Svc. award, Nat. Guard Assn., 2000, Woman of Distinction award, Soroptimists, 1999, Legis. of Yr. award, NE Dental Hygienists Assn., 2001, Disting. Svc. award, NE League of Municipalities, 2002, Lincoln Interfaith Leadership award, 2003, Harold Steck award, ARC of NE, 2004, Alice Paul award, Lancaster Status of Women Commn., 2006, Civil Libertarian of Yr. award, ACLU Nebr., 2006, Patty Steele Meml. award, Am. Cancer Soc., Ethics in Govt. award, Common Cause, 0207, others; Toll fellow, 1999. Mem. Nat. Conf. State Legislators Women's Network (bd. dirs. 1993-96, 1st vice chmn.), PEO, Mayflower Soc., Delta Kappa Gamma (hon.), Mortar Bd. (cmty. advisor 1998, hon.), Rotary Internat. Democrat. Unitarian Universalist. Home: 6437 Lone Tree Dr Lincoln NE 68512 Office: Dist # 27 State Capital Lincoln NE 68509 Home Phone: 402-423-0262; Office Phone: 402-471-2632. Business E-Mail: dschimek@leg.ne.gov.

SCHIMEK, JOHN BRADLEY, music educator, musician; b. Houston, Tex., July 21, 1955; m. Pamela J. Schimek; 1 child, Joel. MusB in Edn., U. Wis., 1979; MusM in Double Bass Performance, Rice U., 1981; EdD, La Salle U., 1996; student, U. North Tex. Instr. music Sam Houston State U., 1979—82; dir. orch. Oshkosh Pub. Schs., 1982—86; dir. youth symphony U. Wis., Oshkosh, Wis., 1982—86; instr. music U. North Tex., 1986—92; from asst. prof. music to prof. Okla. City U., 1993—95, prof., 1999—. Adv. bd. Classen H.S. Arts, 1993—, De Vinci Inst., 2003—; lectr. in field. Contbr. articles to profl. jours.; musician: Okla. City Philharmonic. Named Outstanding Music Faculty, Okla. City U., 1997. Mem.: AAUP, Coll. Music Soc., Am. Fedn. Musicians, Okla. Music Educators Assn., Music Educators Nat. Conf., Internat. Soc. Bassists, Am. String Tchrs. Assn. Office: Okla City Univ 2501 N Blackwelder Ave Oklahoma City OK 73106

SCHIMEL, DAVID S., ecologist, science administrator; b. 1955; BA, Hampshire Coll., Amherst, Mass., 1977; PhD, Colo. State U., Ft. Collins, 1982. Statis. cons. Rsch. Computing Ctr. U. Mass., Amherst, 1976—77; rsch. assoc. Ecosystems Ctr. Marine Biol. Lab., Woods Hole, Mass., 1977—79; grad. rsch. asst. Nat. Renewable Energy Lab., Golden, Colo., 1979—82, postdoctoral fellow, 1982—83, rsch. assoc., 1983—86, rsch. scientist, 1986—2006, sr. rsch. scientist, 1995; assoc. prof. dept. forest & wood sci. Colo State U., 1989—95; project scientist climate sys. modeling prog. Univ. Corp. Atmospheric Rsch., 1990—2006; sect. head climate and global dynamics divsn. Nat. Ctr. Atmospheric Rsch., Boulder, Colo., 1992—2006, scientist III, 1992—95, sr. scientist, 1995—2006; prof., dir. Max Planck Inst. Biogeochemistry, Germany, 1997; CEO Nat. Ecol. Obs. Network, Washington, 2006—. NRC sr. fellow NASA Ames Rsch. Ctr., 1988—89. Contbr. articles to sci. jours., chapters to books. Mem.: Internat. Ecology Inst., Max Planck Soc., Ecol. Soc. Am., Am. Geophys. Union. Office: Nat Ecol Obs Network 1444 Eye St NW Ste 200 Washington DC 20005 Office Phone: 202-628-1500. *

SCHIMKE, DENNIS J., former state legislator; m. Olive Young, Dec. 1964 (dec. 1998); 3 children. BS, U. N.D., 1968, MS, 1972. Bison rancher, Coteau Hills, ND, 1987—; tchr. h.s. math. and physics LaMoure, N.D., 1975-2000; lectr. math. N.D. State U., 2001—; rep. Dist. 28 N.D. Ho. of Reps., 1991-93, rep. dist. 26, 1995-97, mem. edn. and agr. com., 1991—93, 1995—97. Founding bd. dirs. N.D. Buffalo Assn., 1991—95. Home: PO Box 525 Edgeley ND 58433-0525

SCHIMMEL, PAUL REINHARD, biochemist, biophysicist, educator; b. Hartford, Conn., Aug. 4, 1940; s. Alfred E. and Doris (Hudson) S.; m. Judith F. Ritz, Dec. 30, 1961; children: Kirsten, Katherine. AB, Ohio Wesleyan U., 1962; postgrad., Tufts U. Sch. Medicine, 1962-63, Mass. Inst. Tech., 1963-65, Cornell U., 1965-66, Stanford U., 1966-67, U. Calif., Santa Barbara, 1975-76; PhD, Mass. Inst. Tech., 1966; DSc (hon.), Ohio Wesleyan U., 1996. Asst. prof. biology and chemistry MIT, 1967-71, assoc. prof., 1971-76, prof. biochemistry and biophysics, 1976-92, John D. and Catherine T. MacArthur prof. biochemistry and biophysics, 1992-97; prof. Scripps Rsch. Inst. and The Skaggs Inst. for Chem. Biology, 1997-2001, Ernest and Jean Hahn prof. molecular biology and chemistry, 2001—. Mem. study sect. on physiol. chemistry NIH, 1975-79; indsl. cons. on enzymes and recombinant DNA; bd. dirs. Cubist Pharms., 1993-2002, Repligen Corp., Alkermes, Inc., Alaylam, Inc. Author: (with C. Cantor) Biophysical Chemistry, 3 vols., 1980; mem. editl. bd. Archives Biochemistry, Biophysics, 1976-80, Nucleic Acids Rsch., 1976-80, Jour. Biol. Chemistry, 1977-82, Biopolymers, 1979-88, Internat. Jour. Biol. Macromolecules, 1983-89, Trends in Biochem. Scis., 1984—, Biochemistry, 1989—, Accounts of Chem. Rsch., 1989-94, European Jour. Biochemistry, 1991-96, Protein Sci., 1991-94, Proc. Nat. Acad. Scis., 1993-99. Alfred P. Sloan fellow, 1970-72; recipient Emily M. Gray award Biophys. Soc., 2000. Fellow AAAS, Am. Acad. Arts and Scis. (chmn. Amory prize com. 1995-96); mem. NAS (class II biochemistry sect. rep. 1995-96), Am. Philos. Soc., Am. Chem. Soc. (Pfizer award 1978, chmn. divsn. biol. chemistry 1984-85) Am. Soc. for Biochemistry and Molecular Biology (chmn. nominating com. 1990, awards com. 1995-97), Inst. Medicine, Ribonucleic Acid Soc. Office: The Scripps Rsch Inst 10550 N Torrey Pines Rd La Jolla CA 92037-1000

SCHIMMELBUSCH, WERNER HELMUT, psychiatrist; b. Vienna, Nov. 16, 1937; came to U.S., 1954; s. Hans Mowgli and Anneliese Martha (Koeppe) S.; m. Faye Karina Wrangel, Dec. 29, 1958 (div. Mar. 1967); m. Jeanette Ramona Dyal, Mar. 26, 1971; children: Andre Curt, Anne Ramona. MD, U. Wash., Seattle, 1962; psychiatrist, Yale U., 1968; adult psychoanalyst, Seattle Inst. Psychoanalysis, 1977, child psychoanalyst, 1992. Instr. Dept. Psychiatry and Behavioral Sci. U. Wash., Seattle, 1968-69; pvt. practice Seattle, 1969—. Clin. prof. U. Wash., Seattle, 1984—; tng. and supervising psychoanalyst Seattle Inst. Psychoanalysis, 1990—. Capt. U.S. Army, 1963-65. Mem. AMA, Am. Psychiatric Assn., Am. Psychoanalytic Assn., Seattle Psychoanalytic Soc. and Inst. (pres. 1979-80, 94-96, dir. 2006), Ctr. Adv. Psychoanalytic Studies. Avocations: skiing, hiking, sailing. Office: 4033 E Madison St Seattle WA 98112-3104 Office Phone: 206-322-6219.

SCHIMMENTI, JOHN JOSEPH, lawyer; b. NYC, Mar. 21, 1938; s. John Marcus and Mae M. (Miranti) S.; m. Mary Elizabeth Sleep, Apr. 18, 1964. BA, Columbia Coll., 1959; JD, Georgetown U., Washington, DC, 1962, LLM, 1964. Bar: DC 1962, NY 1964, Calif. 1965, US Dist. Ct. (ctrl. dist.) Calif. 1965, US Ct. Appeals (9th cir.) 1966, US Supreme Ct. 1971. Trial atty. Anti-Trust divsn. US Dept. Justice, Washington, 1962-64, Lands divsn., LA, 1965-67; trial atty. Santa Fe R.R., LA, 1968-70; ptnr. Schimmenti, Mullins & Berberian, El Segundo, Calif., 1971-. Mem. S.W. Dist. Bar Assn. (pres. 1983), LA Bar Assn. (condemnation com. 1983), Columbia U. Alumni of So. Calif. (pres. 1978). Republican. Roman

Catholic. Club: El Segundo Rotary (pres. 1977). Office: Schimmenti Mullins & Berberian Unit 303 5630 Ravenspur Dr Rancho Palos Verdes CA 90275-3535 Home Phone: 310-541-4906; Office Phone: 310-874-4801.

SCHINDEL, DONALD MARVIN, retired lawyer; b. Chgo., Jan. 5, 1932; s. Harry L. and Ann (Schiff) S.; m. Alice Martha Andrews, Apr. 24, 1960; children: Susan Yost, Judith Harris, Andrea Glickman. BS in Acctg., U. Ill., 1953; JD, U. Chgo., 1956. Ptnr. Sonnenschein, Nath & Rosenthal, Chgo., 1956-2000, ret., 2000. Author: Estate Administration and Tax Planning for Survivors, 1987, supplements, 1988-1996. Pres. United Way Highland Park-Highwood, Ill., 2000—03; v.p. campaign United Way of the North Shore, 2004—05; pres. Congregation Beth Or, Deerfield, Ill., 1983—85. Fellow Am. Coll. Trust and Estate Counsel; mem. Chgo. Estate Planning Coun. (Austin Fleming Disting. Svc. award 1999), ABA, Ill. Bar Assn., Chgo. Bar Assn. (chmn. probate practice com. 1981-82). Clubs: East Bank (Chgo.). Avocations: tennis, travel, bridge, golf, running. Home: 636 Rice St Highland Park IL 60035-5012

SCHINDEL, RONNIE M., lawyer; b. NYC, June 12, 1966; Student, Cornell U., 1984—86; BA cum laude, SUNY, Stony Brook, 1989; JD, Bklyn. Law Sch., 1993. Bar: NY 1994, US Dist. Ct. (so. and ea. dists. NY) 2000. Atty. Sheresky, Aronson & Mayefsky, LLP, NYC. Named one of Top 100 Attys., Worth mag., 2005. Mem.: NY County Lawyers Assn. (mem. matrimonial law sect.), NY State Bar Assn. (mem. family law sect.). Office: Sheresky Aronson & Mayefsky LLP 750 Lexington Ave 19th Fl New York NY 10022-1200 Office Phone: 212-521-3518. Office Fax: 212-838-5505. E-mail: schindel@samllp.com. *

SCHINDERLE, ROBERT FRANK, retired hospital administrator; b. Mayville, Wis., Aug. 3, 1923; m. Elizabeth, June 23, 1949; children: David, Gary, Mary, Brian. BS, Marquette U., Milw., 1949; MS, Northwestern U., Evanston, Ill., 1959. Asst. office mgr. Western Leather Co., Milw., 1949-51; mgr. bus. office St. Francis Hosp., Peoria, Ill., 1951-55; credit mgr. Mercy Hosp., Chgo., 1955-59, asst. to adminstr., 1957-58, controller, 1958-59, asst. adminstr., 1959-65, St. Joseph Hosp., Joliet, Ill., 1965-70, assoc. adminstr., 1970-71, adminstr., 1971-76, exec. dir., 1976-86; dir. corp. legis. affairs and devel. Franciscan Sisters Health Care Corp., Mokena, Ill., 1986-89, ret. Chmn. Areawide Hosp. Emergency Svcs. Coun. Bd. dirs. Region IX Health Systems Agy., Our Lady of Angels Retirement Home, Joliet, Joliet YMCA, St. Joseph Coll. Nursing, Joliet. Fellow Am. Coll. Health Care Execs. (life); mem. Am. Hosp. Assn., Ill. Hosp. Assn. (chmn. 1975-76), Ill. Hosp. Licensing Bd. (chmn. 1982-97, vice chmn. 1997-), Catholic Hosp. Assn. (dir.), Ill. Cath. Hosp. Assn. (chmn. 1972-73) Lodges: Rotary, Elks, KC. Roman Catholic. Home: 24017 W Newkirk Dr Plainfield IL 60544-1838

SCHINDLER, ALBERT ISADORE, physicist, researcher; b. Pitts., June 24, 1927; s. Jonas and Esther (Nass) S.; m. Phyllis Irene Liberman, June 17, 1951; children— Janet Mae, Jerald Scott, Ellen Susan. BS, Carnegie Inst. Tech., 1947, MS, 1948, DSc, 1950. Research asst. Carnegie Inst. Tech., Pitts., 1947-50, research physicist, 1950-51; supervisory rsch. physicist Naval Rsch. Lab., Washington, 1951-75; assoc. dir. research for material sci. and component tech. Naval Research Lab., 1975-85; prof. materials engring. and physics Purdue U., West Lafayette, Ind., 1985-92, cons., 1992-97, dir. Ind. Ctr. for Innovative Superconductor Tech., 1988-91, dir. Midwest Superconductivity Consortium, 1990-91; dir. div. materials rsch. NSF, Washington, 1988-90; chief scientist Office Naval Rsch., Arlington, Va., 1997-99; cons., 1999—. Cons. in field. Recipient E.O. Hulburt award Naval Research Lab., 1956, Nat. Capitol award for applied sci., 1962, Pure Sci. award Naval Research Lab.-Sci. Research Soc. Am., 1965, award Washington Acad. Scis., 1965, USN Disting. Achievement in Sci. award, 1975, Alumni Merit award Carnegie Mellon U., 1976, Sr. Exec. Service award Dept. Navy, 1983, Superior Pub. Svc. award Dept. Navy, 1999. Fellow Am. Phys. Soc., Washington Acad. Scis.; mem. Sigma Xi. (dir.) Home: 6615 Sulky Ln Rockville MD 20852-4344 Personal E-mail: al.schindler@verizon.net.

SCHINDLER, DAVID J., lawyer; b. 1962; BA, U. Calif., Berkeley, 1983; JD, U. Calif., LA, 1987. Bar: Calif. Clerk US Dist. Ct., Ctrl. Dist. Calif., US Ct. of Appeals, Ninth Cir.; sr. litig. counsel US Attorney's Office, LA, computer fraud, telecom. coord.; spl. atty. to US Atty. Gen.; ptnr. Latham & Watkins, LA. Named one of Top Lawyers, Calif. Lawyer, 1997, Top 40 Lawyers, Daily Jour., Litigation's Rising Stars, The Am. Lawyer, 2007; recipient Atty. Gen. award for Disting. Svc., Director's award for Superior Performance. Office: Latham & Watkins 633 W 5th St Ste 4000 Los Angeles CA 90071-2007 Office Phone: 213-485-1234. Office Fax: 213-891-8763. *

SCHINDLER, JO ANN, librarian, director; BA, U. Hawaii, Manoa; MLS, U. Calif., Berkeley. With San Francisco Pub. Libr. Sys., LA County Libr. Sys.; head Bus., Sci., and Tech. Sect. Hawaii State Pub. Libr. Sys., dir., state libr. Named Hawaii State Pub. Libr. Sys. Employee of Yr., 1999, MCI Cybrarian of Yr. for State of Hawaii. Mem.: ALA, Hawaii Libr. Assn. Office: Hawaii State Pub Libr Sys 235 S Beretania St Honolulu HI 96813 *

SCHINDLER, JUDI(TH) (JUDITH KAY SCHINDLER), public relations executive, marketing professional, consultant; b. Chgo., Nov. 23, 1941; d. Gilbert G. and Rosalie (Karlin) Cone; m. Jack Joel Schindler, Nov. 1, 1964; 1 child, Adam Jason. BS in Journalism, U. Ill., 1964. Assoc. editor Irving Cloud Publs., Lincolnwood, Ill., 1963-64; asst. dir. publicity Israel Bond Campaign, Chgo., 1965-69; v.p. pub. relations Realty Co. of Am., Chgo., 1969-70; dir. pub. relations Pvt. Telecomm., Chgo., 1970-78; pres. Schindler Comm., Chgo., 1978—2006; prin. Hodge Schindler Integreted Mktg., Chgo., 2007—. Del. White House Conf. on Small Bus., Washington, 1980, 86; mem. adv. bd. Entrepreneurship Inst., Chgo., 1988—92. Appointee small bus. com. Ill. Devel. Bd., 1988—89. Named Nat. Women in Bus. Adv. SBA, 1986, Chgo. Woman Bus. Owner of Yr., Continential Bank and Nat. Assn. Women Bus. Owners, 1989, Ill.; named to Hall of Fame, Nat. Assn. of Women Bus. Owners, 2003. Mem. Nat. Assn. Women Bus. Owners (pres. Chgo. chpt. 1980-81, nat. v.p. membership 1988-89), Publicity Club Chgo., Alpha Epsilon Phi. Office: Hodge Schindler Comms 900 N Franklin Chicago IL 60610 Home Phone: 312-266-6161; Office Phone: 312-666-6662. Business E-Mail: jschindler@hodgeschindler.com.

SCHINDLER, LAURA ANN, piano teacher, accompanist; b. St. Louis, Aug. 17, 1943; d. Francis Joseph and Alice Binkley (Hurtgen) Schindler; m. John Charles Noto, Dec. 27, 1986. BM cum laude, Fontbonne Coll., St. Louis, 1970; MAT, Washington U., St. Louis, 1972; student, Ecole Normale de Musique, Paris, 1973-74. Nat. cert. tchr. of music; cert. Orff Schulwerk, Mozarteum Acad., Salzburg, Austria. Organist, choir dir. St. John's Basilica, St. Louis, 1971-73; piano tchr. Cmty. Music Sch., St. Louis, 1971-73, St. Louis Inst. Music, 1972-73; accompanist Robert McFerrin, Sr., NYC, Chgo.,Springfield, St. Louis, 1974-77; piano tchr., Orff instr. St. Louis Conservatory, 1974-82; pvt. piano tchr. and accompanist St. Louis, 1982—. Vocal accompanist Affiliate Artist Program, St. Louis, 1977; accompanist MTNA West. Ctr. Divsn. Auditions, St. Louis, 1979, Forest Park C.C. Chorus, 1980-82, Ethical Soc. Chorus, 1980-83, Washington U. Music Sch., 1970-72; adjudicator piano competitions, Mo. and Ill., 1978—; clinician Piano Tchr. Workshops, Mo./Ill., 1979—. Contbr. articles to profl. jours.; performer Today Show, NBC, 1976, Capella Soloists Sunset concerts, 1976, Bicentennial Horizons of Am. Music, 1976, Rubinstein Music Club Meetings, 1997—, Benefit for Mo. Com. for Firearms Safety, 1982; performer, composer Am. Composers Concert, 1976. Recipient Mid-Am. Disting. Ind. Piano Tchr. award N.W., 1997, Disting. Piano Tchr. award Cedarhurst Chamber Music and Beethoven Soc., 1992; Acad. fellow Washington U., 1970-72. Mem.: Piano Tchrs. Round Table (pres. 1999—2001, exec. bd. 2001—05), Musical Diversions Soc. (bd. dirs. 1995—2005), St. Louis Area Music Tchrs. Assn. (v.p. for programs 1986—88, pres. 1988—92, chair nominating com. 1996—2000), Rubinstein Music Club (treas. 2007—). Democrat. Mem. Ethical Soc. Avocations: travel, walking, reading, eastern european folk dancing, ballroom dancing. Home: 7567 Lindbergh Dr Saint Louis MO 63117-2173 Office Phone: 314-645-3127.

SCHINDLER, WILLIAM STANLEY, retired public relations executive; b. Detroit, Jan. 4, 1933; s. William Henry and Katherine (Schilling) S. Student, Wayne State U., 1950-53. Sr. v.p. Campbell-Ewald Co., Warren, Mich., 1968-85; v.p. pub. rels. Detroit Med. Ctr., 1985-92; interim v.p. Wayne State U., Detroit, 1993. Cons. to bus., univs., and founds.; v.p. Sandusky Pub. Co., Mich. Editor: Progress Report-New Detroit, Inc, 1969. Past mem. Detroit Hist. Commn., Detroit Fire Commn.; chmn. Detroit CSC; mem. Gov.'s Sesquicentennial Commn., Peoria, Ariz. Fire Pension Bd., Pers. Bd., Hist. Preservation Com.; mem. trans. needs assessment com.; pres. United Churchmen of Detroit; bd. dirs. Adult Well-Being Svcs., Sacred Heart Rehab. Ctr., Brush Park Devel. Authority, Harper Hosp. Aux. With US Army, 1954—56. Decorated Commendation Medal with pendant. Mem. Pub. Rels. Soc. Am., Adcraft Club Detroit, Detroit Press Club, Sons Whiskey Rebellion, Recess Club, Univ. Club, Detroit Athletic Club, Prismatic Club, Box 12 Club, Heard Mus. Coun. Home: 8741 W Wescott Dr Peoria AZ 85382-8773

SCHINK, JAMES HARVEY, lawyer; b. Oak Park, Ill., Oct. 2, 1943; s. Norbert F. and Gwendolyn H. (Hummel) S.; m. Lisa Wilder Haskell, Jan. 1, 1972 (div. 1980); children— David, Caroline, Elizabeth; m. April Townley, Aug. 14, 1982. BA, Yale U., 1965, JD, 1968. Bar: Ill. 1968, Colo. 1982. Assoc. Sidley & Austin, Chgo., 1968; law clk. to judge U.S. Ct. Appeals, Chgo., 1968-69; assoc. Kirkland & Ellis LLP, Chgo., 1969—72, ptnr., 1972—. Sustaining fellow Art Inst. Chgo. Mem. ABA, Ill. Bar Assn., Chgo. Bar Assn., Chgo. Club, Saddle and Cycle Club, Mid-Am. Club, Econ. Club Chgo., Sonnenalp Golf Club, Vail Racquet Club, Vail Mountain Club, Yale Club Chgo., Racquet Club Chgo., Game Creek Club. Republican. Presbyterian. Home: 1530 N State Pkwy Chicago IL 60610-1614 Office: Kirkland & Ellis LLP 200 E Randolph St Ste 6100 Chicago IL 60601-6436 Home Phone: 312-951-0036; Office Phone: 312-861-2258. Business E-Mail: jschink@kirkland.com.

SCHINK, ROBERT KELLY, sales executive; b. Joplin, Mo., Aug. 16, 1921; s. Domonic Charles and Cleo Kelly Schink; life ptnr. James B. Battle. A, Joplin Jr. Coll., 1942; BBA, Western Res. U., Cleve., 1948. Stock contr. RCA TV Svc. Co., Cleve., 1948—57, office mgr., 1957—58; salesman Fullber Brush Co., Plantation, Fla., 1958—. Sgt. USAF, 1942—45, ETO. Named to Honor Roll of Vets., World War II Meml., Washington, D-Day Meml., New Orleans. Mem.: Hollywood Stamp Club. Democrat. Avocations: stamp collecting/philately, travel, theater. Home and Office: 921 W County Club Cir Plantation FL 33317

SCHIOLDAGER, AMY LEE, investment company executive; BSc in Bus. Adminstrn., Fin., Calif. State U., Hayward, 1989. Registered rep. series 7, 63, 24, 3 NASD, 2000. Fund acct. Barclays Global Investors, San Francisco, 1989—2001, mng. dir., chief investment officer, equity indexing, 1991—. Mem. adv. bd. Russell Investment Group, Tacoma, 2002—, Dow Jones Wilshire Index, 2006—. Author: Active Index Investing: The Unique Challenges of US Equity Index Management, Real Estate Investing: The REIT Way. Recipient award, Wall St. Jour., 1989. Mem.: Fin. Women's Assn. Office: Barclays Global Investors 45 Fremont St San Francisco CA 94105 Home Phone: 925-253-1305. Business E-Mail: amy.schioldager@barclaysglobal.com.

SCHIRM, DAVID, art educator, artist; b. Mar. 31, 1945; s. Norman Benjamen Schirm and Myra Virginia Barnhart; m. Elizabeth Gemperlein; children: Riddley, Kateri. BFA, Carnegie Mellon U., Pitts., 1967; MFA, Ind. U., Bloomington, 1972. Art educator Carnegie Mellon U., 1972—75, U. Cin., 1977, UCLA, 1977—80, Otis Art Inst., LA, 1980—81, U. So. Calif., LA, 1981—83, U. at Buffalo, 1985—. Chair dept. visual studies U. at Buffalo, 2004—. Councilman, Batavia, NY, 1994—98. Fulbright fellow, USIA, Sri Lanka, 1994, India and Sri Lanka, 2004. Avocations: running, reading, woodworking. Home: 3602 Rose Rd Batavia NY 14020

SCHIRMEISTER, CHARLES F., retired lawyer; b. Jersey City, June 18, 1929; s. Charles F. and Louise P. (Schneider) Schirmeister; m. Barbara Jean Fredericks, Feb. 9, 1952; children: Pamela, Charles Bradford. BA, U. Mich., 1951; LLB, Fordham U., 1956. Bar: N.Y. 1956, U.S. Dist. Ct. (so. dist.) N.Y. 1961, U.S. Ct. Appeals (2d cir.) 1961, U.S. Supreme Ct. 1961. Asst. dist. atty. New York County, NY, 1956-61; assoc. Thelen, Reid & Priest, NYC, 1961-71, ptnr., 1971-94; ret., 1994. Trustee Ocean Grove (N.J.) Camp Meeting Assn.; deacon Cmty. Congl. Ch., Short Hills, NJ. Capt. USMC, 1951—53. Mem.: Canoe Brook Country Club (Summit, NJ), Univ. Club (NYC), Sigma Alpha Epsilon. Republican. Avocations: tennis, oenology, golf. Home: 15 Beechcroft Rd Short Hills NJ 07078-1648

SCHIROKAUER, CONRAD, history professor; b. Leipzig, Germany, Apr. 29, 1929; s. Arno and Erna Schirokauer; m. Lore Strich, Nov. 26, 1956; children: David Walter, Oliver Arno. BA, Yale U., New Haven, Conn., 1950; PhD, Stanford U., Calif., 1960. Prof. CUNY, NYC, 1962—91; sr. scholar, adj. prof. Columbia U., NYC, 1991—2007. Author: (textbooks) A Brief History of Chinese & Japanese Civilizations. With US Army, 1955—57. Fellow, ACLU, 1967—69. Mem.: Assn. Asian Studies. Home: 340 Lantana Ave Englewood NJ 07631 Office: Columbia U New York NY 10027 Home Phone: 201-567-1387; Office Phone: 212-854-9646. Office Fax: 212-662-7289. Business E-Mail: cs176@columbia.edu.

SCHISGAL, MURRAY, playwright; b. NYC, Nov. 25, 1926; s. Abraham and Irene (Sperling) S.; m. Reene Schapiro, June 29, 1958; children: Jane, Zachary. Student, Bklyn. Conservatory of Music, 1948, L.I. U., 1950; LLB, Bklyn. Law Sch., 1953; BA, New Sch. Social Research, 1959. Playwright, screenwriter and prodr. movies, TV and theatre. Author: The Typists and The Tiger, London, 1960, N.Y.C., 1963, Ducks and Lovers, London, 1961, Knit One, Purl Two, Boston, 1963, Luv (One of the Best Plays of 1964-65), London, 1963, N.Y.C., 1964, Fragments, Windows and other plays, 1965, Best Short Plays, 1981, 83, 85; contbr. to Best Short American Plays 1994-1995; original TV plays The Love Song of Barney Kempinski, 1966, Natasha Kovolina Pipishinski, 1976; off-Broadway Fragments, 1967, The Basement, 1967; Jimmy Shine, 1968, 69, Shooting Towards the Millinneum, 1997, Playtime, 1997; Broadway The Chinese, N.Y.C., 1970 (pub. in Best Short Plays of the World Theatre 1973), Dr. Fish, 1970, An American Millionaire, 1974, All Over Town, 1974 (pub. Best Plays 1974-75); screenplay The Tiger Makes Out, 1967, The Pushcart Peddlers, prod. off-off-Broadway, 1979 (pub. as The Pushcart Peddlers, The Flatulist and other plays); novel Days and Nights of a French Horn Player, 1980, Walter and the Flatulist; prod. off-Broadway The Downstairs Boys, 1980, The Songs of War, 1989; prod. regional theatre A Need for Brussels Sprouts, 1981, Play Time, Denver Ctr. Theatre, 1991, The Japanese Foreign Trade Minister, Cleve. Playhouse, 1992, 74 Georgia Ave., 1992, Circus Life, 1992; prod. Broadway Twice Around the Park, 1982; Other Plays, 1983, Closet Madness and Other Plays, 1984, Popkins, Paris, 1990, Play Time, 1991, The Songs of War, 1989; prod. Off Broadway The New Yorkers, 1984, Circus Life, 1995; prodr. Extensions, 1994; co-author: screenplay Tootsie (Winner Los Angeles Film Critics, N.Y. Film Critics, Nat. Soc. Film Critics, Writers Guild Am. award for best comedy); author Luv and Other Plays, 1983, The Rabbi and the Toyota Dealer, 1985, Jealousy, There are No Sacher Tortes in Our Society, 1985, Old Wine in a New Bottle, 1987, Road Show, 1987, Man Dangling, 1988, Oatmeal and Kisses, 1990, (with others) Best Short American Plays of 1991, 92-93, Sexaholics and Other Plays, 1995, Extensions, 1994, Circus Life, 1995, The Artist and The Model (Best Am. Short Play), 1994-95, Play Time (Published by Dramatists Play Svc., 1997), The Man Who Couldn't Stop Crying (Best Am. Short Plays, 1997-98), We Are Family, 2002, produced regional theaters and Berlin undertitle Warum Nicht and Prague, 2003; produced in Rome Regret Undertitle Tutto in Famiglia, 2004; produced in Paris under title La Regard, 2002; 74 Georgia Ave. produced in regional theater, 2002; First Love (Best Am. Short Plays 1991-2000); prodr. feature films A Walk on the Moon, 1999, (cable TV) The Devil's Arithmetic, 1999, Boys and Girls, 2000, Clubland, 2000 (also exec. prodr.); exec. prodr. (cable TV) A Separate Peace, 2003. Recipient Vernon Rice award otustanding achievement off-Broadway Theatre, 1963; Outer Circle award Outstanding Theatre, 1963; named Outstanding Playwright, 1963. Office: care Arthur B Greene 101 Park Ave 26th Fl New York NY 10178-0002

SCHIZER, DAVID MICHAEL, dean, law educator; b. Bklyn. s. Zevie Baruch and Hazel Gerber Schizer; m. Meredith Wolf; 2 children. BA in History, summa cum laude, Yale U., 1990, MA in History, 1990, JD, 1993. Law clerk for Judge Alex Kozinski US Ct. Appeals, 1993—94; for Justice Ruth Bader Ginsburg US Supreme Ct., 1994—95; tax law atty. Davis Polk & Wardwell, NYC, 1995—98; prof. Columbia U., NYC, 1998—, Wilbur H. Friedman prof. tax law, 1998—2004, chair Columbia appointment com., 2002—04, Lucy G. Moses prof. law, 2004—, dean, 2004—. Chair Columbia U. Clerkship Com., 2000—02. Exec. editor Yale Law Jour.; contbr. articles to law jours. Named one of Top 40 Lawyers Under 40, Nat. Law Jour., 2005, 40 Under 40, Crain's NY Bus., 2006; recipient Willis L.M. Reese Prize for Excellence in Tchg., 2002. Mem.: Tax Forum, Tax Club, N.Y. State Bar Assn. Tax Sec. (exec. com., co-chair Com. on Fin. Insts.). Achievements include becoming youngest dean of Columbia Law School in history. Office: Columbia U Sch Law Dean's Office 8th Fl Jerome L Greene Hall 435 W 116th St New York NY 10027 Office Phone: 212-854-2675. Office Fax: 212-854-9740. E-mail: dschiz@law.columbia.edu.

SCHIZER, ZEVIE BARUCH, lawyer; b. Bklyn., Dec. 19, 1928; s. David and Bertha (Rudavsky) S.; m. Hazel Gerber, Aug. 23, 1962; children: Deborah Gail, Miriam Anne, David Michael. BA magna cum laude, NYU, 1950; JD, Yale U., New Haven, 1953. Bar: N.Y. 1954, U.S. Dist. Ct. (so. and ea. dist.) N.Y. 1959, U.S. Ct. Appeals (2d cir.) 1959, U.S. Supreme Ct. 1959. Assoc. Guzik & Boukstein, NYC, 1953-54; teaching fellow NYU Sch. Law, 1954-55; assoc. Philips, Nizer, Benjamin & Krim, NYC, 1955-56, Aranow, Brodsky, Einhorn & Dann, NYC, 1956-57; asst. counsel jud. inquiry Appellate Divsn. 2nd Dept., Bklyn., 1957-62; assoc. Hays, Porter, Spanier & Curtis, NYC, 1963-68, ptnr., 1968-85; sec. United Aircraft Products, Inc., Dayton, Ohio, 1970-83; ptnr. Schizer & Schizer, NYC, 1985—. Trustee Bklyn. Pub. Libr., 1966—2003, pres., 1985—88, N.Y. Young Dem. Club, NYC, 1960—61; trustee East Midwood Jewish Ctr., Bklyn., 1991—, pres., 2003—06; dir. N.Y. met. region United Synagogue Conservative Judaism, NYC, 2004—. Mem. N.Y. County Lawyers Assn. (mem. profl. ethics com., mem. com. on profl. discipline), Phi Beta Kappa. Democrat. Jewish. Home: 1134 E 23rd St Brooklyn NY 11210-4519 Office: Schizer & Schizer 3 New York Plz New York NY 10004-2442 Office Phone: 212-943-3340.

SCHJERVEN, ROBERT E., manufacturing executive; With McQuay-Perfex Inc., Trane Co.; v.p. mktg. and engring. Heatcraft Inc. (subs. Lennox Internat. Inc.), 1986—88, v.p., gen. mgr., 1988—91; pres., COO Armstrong Air Conditioning Inc., 1991—95, Lennox Industries Inc. (subs. Lennox Internat. Inc.), 1995—2000; COO Lennox Internat. Inc., 2000—01, CEO, 2001—. Office: 2140 Lake Park Blvd Richardson TX 75080

SCHLAERTH, JOHN BURR, oncologist, gynecologist; b. Buffalo, Nov. 1, 1942; s. John Norbert and Margaret Henrietta (Heath) Schlaerth; m. Katherine Regina Dowling, Jan. 27, 1968; children: John Burr Jr., Alan Charles, William Joseph, Elizabeth Catherine, Michael Robin, Mary Christine, James Andrew. BS in Pure Sci. Biology, Lemoyne Coll., Syracuse, NY, 1964; MD, SUNY, Buffalo, 1968. Lic. Physician Calif., 70, surgeon Calif., 70. Intern rotating surgery LA County Med. Ctr., 1968—69; resident ob-gyn Womens Hosp. LA County-USC Med. Ctr., 1969—73; asst. prof. ob-gyn. U. So. Calif. Sch. Medicine, LA, 1977—82, assoc. prof., 1982—87, prof. clin. ob-gyn., 1987—94; gynecologic oncologist Womens Cancer Ctr., Palo Alto, Calif., 1994—97, Pasadena, Calif., 1997—2005, Pacific Gynecologic Specialists, Burbank, Calif., 2005—. Maj. US Army, 1973—75. Fellow, Gynecol. Oncology U. So. Calf. Sch. Medicine, 1975—77. Mem.: Pacific Coast Ob-Gyn. Soc., Internat. Soc. Genecologic Oncology, Soc. Gynecol. Oncologists. Republican. Roman Catholic. Office: Pacific Gynecol Specialists 501 S Buena Vista St Burbank CA 91505

SCHLAFER, DONALD HUGHES, veterinary pathologist; b. Sidney, NY, July 15, 1948; s. Donald Hughes and Mildred (Gamewell) S., Jr.; m. Judith Ann Appleton, Aug. 2, 1980; children: Nathan James, Russell Matthew. BS, Cornell U., 1971, MS, 1975; DVM, N.Y. State Coll. Vet. Medicine, Ithaca, 1974; PhD, Coll. Vet. Medicine, Athens, Ga., 1982. Diplomate Am. Coll. Vet. Pathologists, Am. Coll. Theriogenologists (exec. com. 1993-96), Am. Coll. Vet. Microbiologists. Gen. practice vet. medicine Guilderland Animal Hosp., Altamont, NY, 1975-77; resident dept. vet. pathology U. Ga., Athens, 1977-79; rsch. pathologist USDA Plum Island Animal Disease Ctr., Greenport, NY, 1975-82; asst. prof. dept. vet. pathology Cornell U., Ithaca, 1982-88, assoc. prof., 1988-97, prof. comparative reproductive pathology, 1997—, dir. Bovine Rsch. Ctr., 1982-91. Vis. fellow Oxford (Eng.) U., 1990—91; vis. pathologist San Diego Zoo, 2003; vis. prof. U. Padua, Italy, 2004; cons. in field. Contbr. articles to profl. publs. Named Theriogenologist of Yr., 2004. Mem. AVMA, Soc. for Theriogenology (exec. com. 1993-96). Office: T6020 Coll Vet Medicine Cornell U Ithaca NY 14853 Office Phone: 607-253-3352. Business E-Mail: dhs2@cornell.edu.

SCHLAFF, BARBARA E., lawyer; b. Detroit, Mar. 21, 1950; BA, Brandeis U., 1971; attended, U. Mich. Law Sch.; JD, Boston Coll., 1974. Bar: D.C. 1979, Md. 1980. Ptnr., Employee Benefits, Taxation practices Venable LLP, Balt. Mem. adv. com. Univ. Balt. Law Sch. Officer Ctr. for Jewish Edn.; trustee, past v.p. Har Sinai Congregation. Mem. ABA, Md. State Bar Assn., D.C. Bar, Bar Assn. Balt. City. Office: Venable LLP 1800 Mercantile Bank & Trust Bldg 2 Hopkins Plz Baltimore MD 21201 Office Phone: 410-244-7494. Office Fax: 410-244-7742. Business E-Mail: beschlaff@venable.com.

SCHLAFLY, HUBERT JOSEPH, JR., communications executive; b. St. Louis, Aug. 14, 1919; s. Hubert J. and Mary Ross (Parker) S.; m. Leona Martin, June 12, 1944. BSEE, U. Notre Dame, 1941; postgrad., Syracuse U., 1946—47; DHL (hon.), Sacred Heart U., 2003; LHD (hon.). Electronics engr. Gen. Electric Co., Schenectady, 1941-44, Syracuse, 1946-47; project engr. radiation lab. MIT, 1944-45; dir. TV rsch. 20th Century-Fox Film Corp., NYC, 1947-51; founder, v.p. Teleprompter Corp., NYC, 1951-74, pres., 1971-72, exec. v.p. tech. devel., 1972-74; pres. Transponder Corp., Greenwich, 1977-86; chmn., CEO Portel Services Corp., 1984-86; chmn., pres. Portel Services Network, Inc., 1987-91, chmn. bd., 1991-97, ret., 1998. Cons. in field; industry coord., chmn. exec. com., cable tech. adv. com. FCC, 1972—75; adviser com. telecomm. Nat. Acad. Engring.; adviser Sloan Commn. Cable Comms.; mem. engring. adv. coun. U. Notre Dame, 1977, vice chmn., 83, chmn., 84; bd. dirs., sec. Milbrook Corp., 1994—2001; lectr. in field. Author: Computer in the Living Room, 1977.

Bd. govs. Milbrook Club, 1993-98. Recipient Engring. Honor award, U. Notre Dame, 1976, Emmy award, NATAS, 1992, 1999, Sci. Initiative award, Sacred Heart U., 1997, Discovery award, 2001, David Sarnoff citation award, Radio Club Am., 2004. Fellow Soc. Motion Picture and TV Engrs.; mem. IEEE (life, Delmer Ports award 1979), Nat. Cable TV Assn. (chmn. standards com. 1965-69, chmn. domestic satellite com. 1971-73, chmn. future svcs. com. 1972, assns. com. 1981, Outstanding Tech. Achievements award 1974), Electronic Industries Assn. (chmn. broadband cable sect. 1971-73, founding chmn. broadband comm. com.), Soc. Cable TV Engrs. (sr.), Fairfield Found. (hon.); named Notre Dame alumni Man of Yr., 1992, Rotary (pres. Greenwich club 1991-92), Knights of Malta, Knight St. Gregory the Great. Roman Catholic. Achievements include patents in field. Personal E-mail: hschlafly@aol.com.

SCHLAFLY, PHYLLIS STEWART, writer; b. St. Louis, Aug. 15, 1924; d. John Bruce and Odile (Dodge) Stewart; m. Fred Schlafly, Oct. 20, 1949; children: John F., Bruce S., Roger S., Phyllis Liza Forshaw, Andrew L., Anne V. BA, Washington U., St. Louis, 1944, JD, 1978; MA, Harvard U., 1945; LLD, Niagara U., 1976. Bar: Ill. 1979, DC 1984, Mo. 1985, U.S. Supreme Ct. 1987. Syndicated columnist Copley News Svc., 1976—. Broadcaster Spectrum, CBS Radio Network, 1973—78; commentator Matters of Opinion sta. WBBM-AM, Chgo., 1973—75, Cable TV News Network, 1980—83; pres. Eagle Forum, 1975—. Author, pub.: Phyllis Schlafly Report, 1967—; author: A Choice Not an Echo, 1964, The Gravediggers, 1964, Strike From Space, 1965, Safe Not Sorry, 1967, The Betrayers, 1968, Mindszenty The Man, 1972, Kissinger on the Couch, 1975, Ambush at Vladivostok, 1976, The Power of the Positive Woman, 1977, First Reader, 1994, Turbo Reader, 2001, Feminist Fantasies, 2003, The Supremacists: The Tyranny of Judges and How to Stop It, 2004; editor: (book) Child Abuse in the Classroom, 1984, Pornography's Victims, 1987, Equal Pay for Unequal Work, 1984, Who Will Rock the Cradle, 1989, Stronger Families or Bigger Government, 1990, Meddlesome Mandate: Rethinking Family Leave, 1991. Del. Rep. Nat. Conv., 1956, 1964, 1968, 1984, 1988, 1992, 1996, 2004, alt., 1960, 1980, 2000; 1st v.p. Nat. Fedn. Rep. Women, 1964—67; nat. chmn. Stop ERA, 1972—; mem. Ronald Reagan's Def. Policy Adv. Group, 1980, Commn. on Bicentennial of U.S. Constn., 1985—91, Adminstrv. Conf. U.S., 1983—86; pres. Ill. Fedn. Rep. Women, 1960—64; mem. Ill. Commn. on Status of Women, 1975—85. Named Woman of Achievement in Pub. Affairs, St. Louis Globe-Democrat, 1963; named one of 10 Most Admired Women in World, Good Housekeeping poll, 1977—90, 100 Most Important Women of 20th Century, Ladies Home Jour., 1998; recipient 10 Honor awards, Freedom Found., Brotherhood award, NCCJ, 1975. Mem.: DAR (nat. chmn. Am. history 1965—68, nat. chmn. bicentennial com. 1967—70, nat. chmn. nat. def. 1977—80, 1983—95), ABA, Ill. Bar Assn., Phi Beta Kappa, Pi Sigma Alpha. Office: Eagle Forum 7800 Bonhomme Ave Saint Louis MO 63105-1906 Office Phone: 314-721-1213. E-mail: phyllis@eagleforum.org.

SCHLAGEL, DEBORAH "DEVO" LYNN, chemist, materials scientist; b. Sante Fe, N.Mex., Feb. 18, 1970; d. Paul and Mary Ann Gray; m. Donald Henry Schlagel; children: Jordan Corrina, Taylor Rose. BS with honors, No. Ariz. U., 1993; MSc in Inorganic and Analytical Chemistry, Iowa State U., 1997. Asst. scientist III Ames Lab., Ames, Iowa, 1997—. Contbr. articles to profl. jours. Ch. Of Christ, Christian. Avocations: cooking, sewing, gardening, hiking, travel. Office: Ames Lab 111 Metals Devel Ames IA 50011 Home Phone: 515-233-4144; Office Phone: 515-294-3924. E-mail: schlagel@iastate.edu.

SCHLAGEL, RICHARD H., retired philosophy educator; b. Springfield, Mass., Nov. 22, 1925; BS in Pre-Med cum laude, Springfield Coll., 1949; MA in Philosophy, Boston U., 1952, PhD, 1955. Instr. philosophy Coll. of Wooster, 1954-55; instr. Clark U., 1955-56; asst. prof. George Washington U., 1956-62, assoc. prof., 1962-68, prof., 1968—, chmn. dept., 1965-69, 70-71, 77-83, named Elton prof. philosophy, 1986, Elton prof. emeritus, 2001—. Sabbatical, Paris, with travel throughout Europe, 1962-63, 69-70, 76-77, 83-84, 90-91. Author: The Vanquished Gods: Science, Religion, and the Nature of Belief, 2001, From Myth to Modern Mind: A Study of the Origins and Growth of Scientific Thought, vol. 1, Theogony through Ptolemy, 1995, vol. 2, Copernicus through Quantum Mechanics, 1996; Contextual Realism: A Metaphysical Framework for Modern Science, 1986; contbr. articles and reviews to profl. jours. Borden Parker Browne fellow, 1953-54. Mem. AAUP, Am. Philos. Assn., Washington Philosophy Club (v.p. 1964-65, pres. 1965-66). Personal E-mail: richschlagel@aol.com.

SCHLAGETER, ROBERT WILLIAM, museum administrator; b. Streator, Ill., May 10, 1925; s. Herman Pete and Ida (Ladtkow) S.; divorced; children— David Michael, Robert William Diploma, Karl Ruprecht Univ., Heidelberg, Fed. Republic Germany, 1950; BA, U. Ill., Champaign-Urbana, 1950, MFA, 1957. Asst. prof. U. Tenn., Knoxville, 1952-58; dir. Mint Mus. Art, Charlotte, NC, 1958-66; assoc. dir. Downtown Gallery, NYC, 1966, Ackland Art Ctr., U. NC, Chapel Hill, 1967-76; dir. Cummer Gallery Art, Jacksonville, Fla., 1976-92, dir. emeritus, 1992—. Fine arts cons. corp. and pvt. collecting, 1993—. Author: (exhbn. catalogue) Winslow Homer's Florida, George Inness' Florida, Martin Johnson Heade Florida, Robert Henri-George Bellows. Served with U.S. Army, 1943-45, ETO

SCHLANG, DAVID, retired real estate company executive, lawyer; b. NYC, May 2, 1912; s. Alexander and Blanche (Cohen) S.; m. Arlene Roth, May 9, 1948. LLB, NYU, 1933. Bar: NY 1935, US Dist. Ct. (so. dist.) NY 1940. Pvt. practice, 1935—42; sec., pres. Schlang Bros. & Co., Inc., NYC, 1945—2004. Vice chmn. emeritus Brookdale-Schulman Inst., 2006—. Trustee Brookdale Hosp., Bklyn., 1980—, vice chmn., 1983—2006, emeritus, 2006; vice chmn. Linroc Nursing Home, 1993—; founding mem. US Congl. Adv. Bd.; bd. dirs., vice chmn. Samuel Schulman Inst. Nursing Rehab. Brookdale Hosp., 1973—. With AUS, 1942—45. Decorated Croix de Guerre with palm (France); recipient Conspicious Svc. award State of NY, 1965. Mem.: ABA, Real Estate Bd. NY, NY County Lawyers Assn., NY State Bar Assn., Criminal Investigation Divsn. Agts. Assn., Met. Club. Home: 737 Park Ave New York NY 10021-4256

SCHLAPBACH, DAVID, lawyer; BA summa cum laude, U. Va.; MA, Stanford U.; JD, Yale U. Atty. Blackwell Sanders Peper Martin LLP, St. Louis; joined First Data, 1996, dep. gen. counsel internat. Paris, 2000—04; gen. counsel, sec. Western Union Co., Englewood, Colo., 2004—. Office: Western Union Co PO Box 6992 Greenwood Village CO 80155-6992 Office Phone: 866-405-5012. *

SCHLECHTE, DEBORAH WHITLEY, music educator; d. Norwood and Shirley Whitley; m. Gene Schlechte, Sept. 6, 1980; children: Jennifer, Christopher. BS in Music Edn., U. N.C., Greensboro, 1978. Dir. choral music Wilson County Pub. Sch., NC, 1978—80, Brunswick County Pub. Sch., Leland, NC, 1981—84; dir. music Naval Postgrad. Sch., Monterey, Calif., 1985—86, Seaville UMC, Seaville, NJ, 1987—90, NATO Base Chapel, Keflavik, Iceland, 1990—92; dir. mid. sch. choral music Prince William County Sch., Dale City, Va., 1995—2004, chmn. mid. sch. choral Manassas, Va., 2004—. Dir. Woodbridge Youth Chorale, Manassas, 1995—98; judge All-State Chorus, Va., 1995—; mem. Gifted Edn. Adv. Bd., Prince Williams County, Va., 1992—97. Vice-chmn. Wilson County Dem. Party, NC, 1978—80; basketball rep. Osbourn Pk. Booster Club, Manassas, Va., 2003—; mem. youth salute exec. bd. Prince William County, 2003—. Mem.: Am. Choral Dir. Assn., Music Educators Nat. Conf. Republican. Baptist. Avocations: cooking, basketball, gardening, decorating. Office: Parkside Mid Sch 8602 Mathis Ave Manassas VA 20110

SCHLEEDE, GLENN ROY, marketing professional, consultant; b. Lyons, NY, June 12, 1933; m. Sandra Christine Klafehn, Dec. 27, 1958; children: Kristen M., Kimberly J., Kendall E. BA, Gustavus Adolphus Coll., 1960; MA, U. Minn., 1968; advanced mgmt. program, Harvard U., 1987. Research asst. Indsl. Relations Ctr., U. Minn., Mpls., 1960-61; mgmt. intern, then contractor personnel specialist AEC, Argonne, Ill. and Germantown, Md., 1961-65; asst. chief div. natural resources U.S. Office Mgmt. and Budget, Exec. Office of Pres., Washington, 1965-72, exec. assoc. dir., 1981; dep. assoc. dir. Office of Policy Analysis, AEC, Germantown, 1972-73; assoc. dir. energy and sci. Domestic Council, The White House, Washington, 1973-77; sr. v.p. Nat. Coal Assn., Washington, 1977-81; pres. New Eng. Energy Inc., Westborough, Mass., 1982-92, also bd. dirs.; v.p. New Eng. Power Service Co., Westborough, 1982-92, also bd. dirs.; v.p. New Eng. Electric System, Westborough, 1986-92; pres., CEO, dir. Energy Market and Policy Analysis, Inc., Reston, Va., 1992—2003; freelance analyst, writer Round Hill, Va., 2003—. Author numerous speeches, papers and congl. testimony on various nat. energy policy issues. Recipient Disting. Alumni in Bus. award Gustavus Adolphus Coll. Alumni Assn., St. Peter, Minn., 1987. Republican. Lutheran. Avocations: reading, travel, carpentry. Home: 18220 Turnberry Dr Round Hill VA 20141-2574 Personal E-mail: empainc@aol.com.

SCHLEGEL, FRED EUGENE, lawyer; b. Indpls., July 24, 1941; s. Fred George and Dorothy (Bruce) S.; m. Jane Wessels, Aug. 14, 1965; children: Julia, Charles, Alexandra. BA, Northwestern U., 1963; JD with distinction, U. Mich., 1966. Bar: Ind. 1966. Assoc. lawyer Baker & Daniels, Indpls., 1966-72, ptnr., 1972—; vice chmn. Meridian St. Preservation Commn., Indpls., 1975-90. Contbr. articles to profl. jours. Chmn. Pub. Schs. Edn. Found., Indpls., 1988—90; pres. Festival Music Soc., 1974—75, 1979, 1986—87; bd. dirs. Indpls. Symphony Orch., chmn., 2002—04; bd. dir. Arts Coun., Indpls, 1996—2002. Mem. ABA, Ind. Bar Assn., Energy Bar Assn., Northwestern U. Alumni Club Indpls. (pres. 1992-94). Episcopalian. Office: Baker and Daniels 300 N Meridian St Ste 2700 Indianapolis IN 46204-1782 Office Phone: 317-237-1410. Business E-Mail: fred.schlegel@bakerd.com.

SCHLEGEL, JOHN FREDERICK, management consultant, personal trainer; b. Ogden, Utah, Dec. 18, 1944; s. Max Joseph and Mary Georgia (Whittaker) S.; m. Priscilla Mary Hecht, Sept. 8, 1967. BS in Pharmacy, U. Pacific, 1967; D of Pharmacy, U. So. Calif., 1972, MS in Edn., 1980; ScD in Pharmacy (hon.), Mass. Coll. Pharmacy, 1984, L.I. U., 1985. Lic. pharmacist, Calif., Nev.; cert. assoc. exec. Chief pharmacist U. So. Calif. Sch. Pharmacy, LA, 1967-73, postdoctoral fellow, 1972—73, dir. pharmacy admissions, 1973-75; dir. office student affairs Am. Assn. Colls. Pharmacy, Alexandria, Va., 1975-77, asst. exec. dir., 1977-81, exec. dir., 1981-84; CEO Am. Pharm. Assn., Washington, 1984-89; exec. v.p., CEO Am. Acad. Facial Plastic and Reconstructive Surgery, Washington, 1989-92; pres. Schlegel & Assocs., 1992—. Cons. in field. Contbr. over 100 articles on pharmacy, health care and assn. mgmt.; presenter in field. Nat. del. White House Conf. on Aging, Washington, 1981. Disting. alumnus U. So. Calif. Sch. Pharmacy, 1985, U. the Pacific Sch. Pharmacy, 1987. Fellow Am. Soc. Assn. Execs.; mem. Fla. Soc. Assn. Execs., The Meadows Country Club (bd. govs), Phi Delta Chi (charter, bd. counsellors). Avocations: tennis, classical music, gardening, bridge. Office: 3390 Highlands Bridge Rd Sarasota FL 34235-6859 Office Phone: 941-341-0434. Business E-Mail: jschlegel@comcast.net.

SCHLEGEL, PETER NILES, urologist, educator; b. Malden, Mass., Feb. 17, 1958; s. Niles Matthew and Mary Patricia (McIntyre) S.; children: Andrew Peter, Lucy Filice, Nicholas Halloran. AB, Hamilton Coll., 1979; MD, U. Mass., 1983. Diplomate Am. Bd. Urology, Nat. Bd. Med. Examiners; lic. physician, N.Y. Intern in gen. surgery and resident Johns Hopkins Hosp., Balt., 1983-85, resident, chief resident in urology, 1985-89, instr. urology, 1989; fellow-in-residence The Population Coun., NYC, 1989-91, staff scientist, 1991—; asst. attending surgeon New York Hosp., NYC, 1991-96; assoc. attending surgeon N.Y. Hosp., NYC, 1996—; assoc. vis. physician Rockefeller U., NYC, 1991—; asst. prof. urology Cornell Med. Coll., NYC, 1991-96, assoc. prof. urology, 1996—2004, prof., 2004—, vice chmn. urology, 1999-2001, acting chmn., 2001—03, chmn., 2003—. Vis. prof. Austria, Israel, Indonesia, Saudi Arabia, Brazil, others; vis. fellow Royal Coll. Surgeons, 1993; co-dir. Ctr. for Male Reproduction and Microsurgery, Cornell Inst. for Reproductive Medicine, 2000—03; lectr. in field. Co-editor Jour. of Audiology; mem. numerous editl. bds.; contbr. numerous articles, abstracts to profl. jours., chpts. to books. Recipient Edwin Beer Program award N.Y. Acad. Medicine, 1996-98, New Investigator award Am. Found. for Urol. Disease, 1993-95, fellow, 1989-91; fellow Am. Cancer Soc., 1986-87, NIH, 1989-91; established Clinician award ESHRE, 1996; named one of Medical Marvels, New York Mag., 2006 Mem.: Soc. for Male Reprodn. /Urology (pres.), Soc. for Study of Male Reprodn. (pres.), Am. Urol. Assn., Soc. for Basic Urol. Rsch., Soc. for Study of Reprodn., Am. Soc. Andrology, Am. Soc. Reproductive Medicine (bd. dirs.), Alpha Omega Alpha. Roman catholic. Avocation: sailing. Office: New York Hosp Dept Urology 525 E 68th St New York NY 10021-4885 Office Phone: 212-746-5491. E-mail: pnschleg@med.cornell.edu.

SCHLEICHER, NORA ELIZABETH, bank executive, treasurer, accountant; b. Balt., Aug. 10, 1952; d. Irvin William and Eleanor Edna S.; m. Ray Leonard Settle Jr., July 27, 1985. AA cum laude, Anne Arundel Community Coll., 1972; BS summa cum laude, U. Balt., 1975. CPA, Md. Staff auditor Md. Nat. Bank, Balt., 1975-76, sr. staff auditor, 1976-77, supr. auditing dept., 1977-78; full charge acct. Wooden & Benson, CPA's, Balt., 1978-81; asst. to treas. First Fed. Savs. & Loan Assn., Annapolis, Md., 1981, asst. treas., 1982-83, v.p., 1984; v.p., treas. First Fed. Savs. & Loan Assn. (now First Annapolis Bank), 1984—. Bd. dirs., treas. Coll. Manor Community Assn. Mem. AICPA, Md. Assn. CPA's, Fin. Mgrs. Soc., Coll. Manor Community Assn. (bd. dirs., treas.). Methodist. Office: First Annapolis Savs Bank 1832 George Ave Annapolis MD 21401-4103

SCHLEIFER, STEVEN J., psychiatrist, educator; b. NYC, Mar. 10, 1950; s. Jack and Caroline (Rapps) S.; m. Sarah L. Rosenberg, Dec. 1971; children: Jonathan, Jason, Justin, Tara. MD, Mt. Sinai Sch. of Medicine, 1975; BA, Columbia Coll., 1971. Diplomate Nat. Bd. Med. Examiners, Am. Bd. Psychiatry and Neurology. Asst. prof. of psychiatry Mt. Sinai Sch. of Medicine, New York, NY, 1982—87; assoc. prof. of psychiatry UMDNJ-New Jersey Med. Sch., Newark, 1987—92, prof. of psychiatry NJ, 1992—, chair, dept. of psychiatry NJ, 1992—2001. Cons. NIH, Bethesda, Md., 1984—, Hackensack U. Med. Ctr., NJ, 1988—, Veterans Adminstrn. Med. Ctr., East Orange, NJ, 1988—2002; chief of svc., dept of psychiatry UMDNJ-Univ. Hosp., Newark; chief of svc. UMDNJ-Univ. Behavioral Healthcare, Newark, 1992—2002. Contbr. articles to profl. jours. Grantee NIMH, 1982, Chernow Found., N.Y.C., 1983, Upjohn Co., Kalamazoo, 1989, NIAAA, 1990. Fellow Am. Psychiat. Assn. (disting.); mem. N.J. Psychiat. Assn., Soc. Biol. Psychiatry, Internat. Soc. Psychoendocrinology, Am. Psychosomatic Soc., Psychoneuroimmunology Rsch. Soc., Acad. Psychosomatic Medicine. Avocations: opera, skiing. Office: UMDNJ-New Jersey Med Sch 183 South Orange Ave Newark NJ 07103 E-mail: schleife@umdnj.edu.

SCHLEIFER, THOMAS C., management consultant, author, lecturer; BS in Constrn. Mgmt., E. Carolina U., 1989, MS in Constrn. Mgmt., 1990; PhD, Herriot-Watt U., 1994. Owner Schleifer Bros., Inc., Hanover, NJ, 1964-75; owner, founder, pres., internat. cons. firm CMA Cons. Group, Morristown, NJ, 1976-86; dir. appropriate tech., vol. Habitat for Humanity, Americus, Ga., 1987-88; assoc. prof. Ariz. State U., Tempe, 1990-92; eminent scholar Del E. Webb Sch. Constrn., Ariz. State U., 1993-94; eminent scholar Del E. Webb Sch. Constrn. Ariz. State U., Tempe, 2001—. Vis. prof. East Carolina U., 1989-90; former chmn. continuing edn. com. Associated Gen. Contractors Am.; lectr. and presenter in field. Author: Construction Contractors' Survival Guide, 1990, Glossary of Suretyship and Related Terms, 1981; contbr. articles to profl. jours. Bd. advisors Habitat for Humanity Internat., 1989—. Mem. Am. Inst. Constructors (bd. dirs. 1990-93), Am. Arbitration Assn. (N.J. adv. coun. 1968-75), Am. Concrete Inst. (edn. com. 1972-76), Associated Gen. Contractors Am. (chmn. continuing edn. com. 1970-76), Assn. Advancement 3d World (internat. adv. coun. 1988-91). Home and Office: 5625 N 75th Pl Scottsdale AZ 85250-6471 Personal E-mail: tschleifer@aol.com.

SCHLEIN, MICHAEL EDWARD, diversified financial services company executive; m. Lisa Jordan Tamagni. BS in Econs., MIT, 1984, MS in Polit. Sci., 1984. Assoc., pub. fin. investment banking divsn. Smith Barney; chief of staff N.Y.C. dep. mayor for fin. and econ. devel., U.S. SEC, 1994—97; sr. v.p., global corp. affairs, human resources, and bus. practices Citigroup, Inc., NYC, 1997—. Mem.: Phi Beta Kappa. Office: Citigroup Inc 399 Park Ave New York NY 10043

SCHLENDER, WILLIAM ELMER, management sciences educator; b. Sawyer, Mich., Oct. 28, 1920; s. Gustav A. and Marie (Zindler) S.; m. Lela R. Pullen, June 9, 1956 (dec. June 1983); m. Margaret C. Krahn, Mar. 3, 1987. AB, Valparaiso U., 1941; MBA, U. Denver, 1947; PhD, Ohio State U., 1955. With U.S. Rubber Co., 1941-43, 46; asst. prof., assoc. prof. bus. adminstrn. Bowling Green State U., 1947-53; asst. prof. bus. orgn., prof. Ohio State U., 1954-65, asst. dean, 1959-62; assoc. dean Ohio State U. (Coll. Commerce and Adminstrn.), 1962-63; prof. mgmt. U. Tex., 1965-68, chmn. dept., 1966-68; dean Cleve. State U. Coll. Bus. Adminstrn., 1968-75, prof. mgmt., 1975-76; Internat. Luth. Laymen's League prof. bus. ethics Valparaiso (Ind.) U., 1976-79, Richard E. Meier prof. mgmt., 1983-86, Richard E. Meier prof. emeritus, 1986—. Vis. assoc. prof. mgmt. Columbia U., 1957-58; vis. prof. mgmt. U. Tex., Arlington, 1981-82; cons. in field; bd. govs. Internat. Ins. Soc., 1972-90. Author: (with M.J. Jucius) Elements of Managerial Action, 3d edit., 1973, (with others) Management in Perspective: Selected Readings, 1965; editor: (with others) Management in a Dynamic Society, 1965; mem. editl. bd. Jour. Acad. Mgmt., 1966-72; contbr. articles to profl. jours. Mem. Assn. Ohio Commodores. Served with AUS, 1943-45. Decorated Bronze Star; Exec. Order of Ohio Commodore in recognition of contbn. to econ. devel., Gov. Ohio, 1972. Fellow Acad. Mgmt.; mem. Indsl. Rels. Rsch. Assn. (pres. N.E. Ohio chpt. 1971-72), Am. Legion, Tau Kappa Epsilon, Rotary, Beta Gamma Sigma, Sigma Iota Epsilon, Pi Sigma Epsilon, Alpha Kappa Psi, Phi Kappa Phi. Home (Summer): PO Box 446 Sawyer MI 49125-0446 Office: Coll Bus Adminstrn Valparaiso U Valparaiso IN 46383 Personal E-mail: bschlend@aol.com. *I resolved long ago that where I worked and what I did would be guided not by prestige considerations, but by the answers to three questions: (1) Will my work allow me to grow by discovering and developing my capabilities? (2) Will it make a significant contribution to my profession and to the community? (3) Will I enjoy doing it? My career, and my personal philosophy, have these underlying guidelines.*

SCHLENSKER, GARY CHRIS, landscape company executive; b. Indpls., Nov. 12, 1950; s. Christian Frederick and Doris Jean (Shannon) S.; m. Ann Marie Tobin, Oct. 27, 1979; children: Laura Patricia, Christian Frederick II. Student, Purdue U., 1969-71, 73; A Bus. Adminstrn., Clark Coll., 1979; cert. emergency med. technician, Ind. Vocat. Tech. Inst., Lafayette, 1974. Salesman Modern Reference, Indpls., 1971; orthopaedic technician St. Elizabeth Hosp., Lafayette, 1973-75, asst. mgr. ambulance service, 1975; sales asst. Merck, Sharpe & Dohme, Oakbrook, Ill., 1975-77; v.p. Turfco, Inc., Zionsville, Ind., 1977-84; pres. Turfscape, Inc., Zionsville, 1984—. Speaker Midwest Turf Conf., 1991; del. erosion and sediment control econ. summit Internat. Erosion Control Assn., New Orleans, 2000. With U.S. Army, 1971-73. Mem. ASTM (erosion control subcom.), BBB, Nat. Fedn. Ind. Bus., Midwest Turf Found., Ohio Turf Found., Internat. Erosion Control Assn. (bd. dirs. Gt. Lakes chpt. 1998-2002), U.S. C. of C., Zionsville C. of C., Phi Kappa Psi. Presbyterian. Avocations: woodworking, golf. Business E-Mail: gary@turfscapeinc.com.

SCHLER, MICHAEL LAWRENCE, lawyer; b. NYC, May 6, 1949; m. Joan McClure, 1982. AB, Harvard U., 1970; JD, Yale U., 1973; LLM in Taxation, NYU, 1979. Bar: N.Y. 1974. Law clk. to Judge Max Rosenn U.S. Ct. Appeals (3d cir.), Wilkes Barre, Pa., 1973-74; assoc. Cravath Swaine & Moore, NYC, 1974-82, ptnr., tax dept., 1982—. Contbr. articles to profl. jours. V.p. Am. Tax Policy Inst., trustee. Fellow Am. Coll. Tax Counsel; mem. N.Y. State Bar Assn. (chair tax sect. 1994-95). Office: Cravath Swaine & Moore LLP 825 8th Ave New York NY 10019-7475 Office Phone: 212-474-1588. Office Fax: 212-474-3700. Business E-Mail: mschler@cravath.com.

SCHLESINGER, ADAM, musician; b. Oct. 31, 1967; Grad., Williams Coll. Bassist Ivy, 1994—, Fountains of Wayne, 1995—99, 2001—; prin. Scratchie Records, NYC, 1995—; co-owner Stratosphere Sound, NYC, 1999—. Musician & prodr. (Ivy albums) Lately, 1994, Realistic, 1995, Apartment Life, 1997, Long Distance, 2001, Guestroom, 2002, In the Clear, 2005, (Fountains of Wayne albums) Fountains of Wayne, 1996, I Want an Alien for Christmas, 1997, Utopia Parkway, 1999, Welcome Interstate Managers, 2003, Traffic and Weather, 2007; composer: (songs) Stacy's Mom, 2003 (ASCAP award, BMI Pop award); composer & prodr. (film soundtracks) That Thing You Do!, 1996 (Oscar nomination for Best Original Song, Golden Globe award nominee for Best Original Song, 1997), prodr. There's Something About Mary, 1998, Sweet and Lowdown, 1999, Me, Myself & Irene, 2000, Scary Movie, 2000, Josie & the Pussycats, 2001, Because of Winn-Dixie, 2005, Robots, 2005, composer Music & Lyrics, 2007. Office: c/o MOB Agy 6404 Wilshire Blvd #505 Los Angeles CA 90048 also: Stratospheric Sound 239 11th Ave New York NY 10001 *

SCHLESINGER, ANDREA BATISTA, think-tank executive; b. Bklyn., 1977; AB, U. Chgo., 1999. Student rep. NYC Bd. Edn.; dir. pub. rels. Teach for Am.; edn. adv. to Bronx Borough pres. Fernando Ferrer; exec. dir. Drum Major Inst. Pub. Policy, 2002—. Contbr. Huffington Post; mem. editl. bd. The Nation. Bd. dirs. Sadie Nash Leadership Project; adv. bd. Cmty. Rsch. Coun., Chattanooga. Named one of 40 Under 40, Crain's NY Bus., 2007, 35 Under 40, City Hall Newspaper; recipient Dolores Huerta award, LatinaPAC. Office: Drum Major Inst Pub Policy 28th Fl 110 E 59th St New York NY 10002 Office Phone: 212-909-9674. E-mail: abs@drummajorinstitute.org. *

SCHLESINGER, B. FRANK, architect, educator; b. NYC, Sept. 17, 1925; s. Augustus and Ethel (Brower) S.; m. Draga A. Christy; children: Jeff, Nike, Katherine, Daniel, Christy Anna; 1 stepson, Frances L. Haley Jr. Student, Middlebury Coll., 1946—48; BS, U. Ill., 1950; MArch, Harvard U., 1954. Draftsman Hugh Stubbins Assocs., 1953-55, Marcel Breuer, 1955-56; pvt. practice architecture Princeton, NJ, 1956-59, Doylestown, Pa., 1959-69, Phila., 1969-71, Washington, 1971—. Instr. archtl. design U. Pa., 1957-60; vis. critic Columbia Sch. Architecture, 1962-63, U. Pa., 1965; prof. architecture Sch. Architecture, U. Md., 1971-2001, prof. emeritus, 2001—. With USNR, 1943-46. Wheelwright fellow Harvard U., 1963; AIA fellow, 1970; Disting. Designer fellow Nat. Endowment for the Arts, 1984; recipient Design awards Pa. Soc. Archs., 1960-65, 69, 84, Bronze medal, 1965, Silver medal, 1973; Design awards Progressive Arch., 1966-67, 69, 72, 74; Design awards Interfaith Forum on Religion, Art and Arch., 1987, 92; Design awards Philia. chpt. 1960-61, 1963-65, 1968-69; Design awards No. Va. chpt. 1975, 2001; Design awards Wash. chpt. 1990, 92, 95, 2002, 05; Centennial medal Wash. chpt. 2001. Mem.: Associated Harvard Alumni (dir. 1972), Harvard Grad. Sch. Design Alumni Assn. (pres. 1971—73). Address: 1015 33rd St NW Apt 806 Washington DC 20007-3538 Office Phone: 202-333-0344. E-mail: schlesingerfaia@msn.com.

SCHLESINGER, DEBORAH LEE, retired librarian; b. Cambridge, Mass., Sept. 13, 1937; d. Edward M. and Edith D. (Schneider) Hershoff; divorced; children: Suzanne, Richard. BA, U. Mass., 1961; MS, Simmons Coll., 1974; postgrad., U. Pitts., 1983. Reference librarian Bently Coll., Waltham, Mass., 1964-65; dir. Carnegie Library, Swissvale, Pa., 1973-77, South Park Twp. Library, Library, Pa., 1977-81, Monessen (Pa.) Library, 1981-82, Lewis & Clark Library, Helena, Mont., 1983—88, 1989—2004, ret., 2004; state librarian Mont. State Library, Helena, Mont., 1988-89. Vis. scholar Pitts. Regional Library Ctr., 1982-83. Editor Pa. Union List, 1982-83. Mem. exec. bd. Mont. Cultural Advocacy, 1983-2004. Mem. Mont. Libr. Assn. (chmn. legis. com. 1984-92, lobbyist 1992-2001), AAUW (exec. com. 1985-86). Clubs: Montana (Helena). Democrat. Avocations: flying, painting, reading, rafting, travel. Personal E-mail: dbooks@aol.com.

SCHLESINGER, HARVEY ERWIN, judge; b. June 4, 1940; BA, The Citadel, 1962; JD, U. Richmond, 1965. Bar: Va. 1965, Fla. 1965, U.S. Supreme Ct. 1968. Corp. counsel Seaboard Coast Line R.R. Co., Jacksonville, Fla., 1968-70; chief asst. U.S. atty. Mid. Dist. Fla., Jacksonville, 1970-75, U.S. magistrate judge, 1975-91, U.S. Dist. judge, 1991—. Adj. prof. U. North Fla., 1984-91; mem. adv. com. on Fed. Rules of Criminal Procedure to U.S. Supreme Ct., 1986-93; mem. Jud. Conf. Adv. Com. on Adminstrn. of Magistrate Judges Sys., 1996-2003, chmn., 1998-2003; chmn. U.S. Dist. Ct. Forms Working Group, Washington, 1983—, Jud. Ct. Ad hoc Com. on Long Range Planning, 1998-2003; Jud. Conf. Jud. Officers Resources Working Group, 1998-99; 11th Cir. Dist. Judges Assn., 1991—, sec., treas. 1996- 97, v.p. 1997-98, pres.-elect., 1999-2001, pres., 2001-02. Bd. dir. Pine Castle Ctr. for Mentally Retarded, Jacksonville, 1970-87, pres., 1972-74, chmn. bd. dirs., 1973-74; trustee Pine Castle Found., 1972-76, Congregation Ahavath Chesed, Jacksonville, 1970—, v.p., 1975-80, pres., 1980-82; v.p. S.E. Coun. Union Am. Hebrew Congregations, 1984-88; asst. commr. for exploring North Fla. Coun. Boy Scouts Am., 1983-86, exec. com., 1986-98, adv. bd., 1998—; active Boy Scouts Am. Nat. Jewish Com. on Scouting, Irving, Tex., 1986-93, Fla. Sesquicentennial Commn., 1995-96; trustee River Garden Home for Aged, 1982—, sec., 1985-1990; co-chmn. bd. gov. Jacksonville chpt. NCCJ, 1983-1993, presiding co-chmn. 1984-89; nat. bd. trustees, NYC, 1986-93; trustee Jacksonville Cmty. Found., 2000—, vice-chair, 2003-05, chmn. 2006—. Capt. JAGC, U.S. Army, 1965-68. Recipient Silver Beaver award Boy Scouts Am., 1986; George Washington Medal of Honor, Freedoms Found., Valley Forge, Pa., 1987, Silver Medallion Humanitarian award NCCJ, 1992, Founders award, Fed. Magistrate Judges Assn., 1999, William Green award for profl. excellence U. Richmond Law Sch., 2000, Jurist of Yr. award Am. Bd. Trial Adv., 2001. Mem. ABA (fed. rules of evidence and criminal procedure com. 1979-98, Nat. Conf. Spl. Ct. Judges, 1975-90, conf. newsletter editor, 1988-90, Nat. Conf. Fed. Trial Judges, 1990—, chmn. legis. com., 1996-97, Flascher award 1989), Va. Bar Assn., Fla. Bar Assn., Fed. Judges Assn., Jacksonville Bar Assn.; Fed. Bar Assn. (pres. Jacksonville chpt. 1974, 75, 81-82), Am. Judicature Soc., Chester Bedell Am. Inns of Ct. (pres. 1992-96), Rotary (Paul Harris fellow, pres. S. Jacksonville club), Masons (past master, past venerable master, knights comdr. of Ct. Honour, 33 degree Scottish Rite bodies), Shriners. Office: 300 N Hogan St Ste 11-150 Jacksonville FL 32202-4246 Office Phone: 904-549-1990.

SCHLESINGER, IRWIN D., neurologist; b. Bklyn., Sept. 13, 1935; s. Edward Schlesinger and Eva Parkoff; m. Marcia Rubinstein; 1 child, Lisa. BS, Bklyn. Coll., 1956; MD, SUNY, Med. U., Syracuse, 1961. Diplomate Am. Bd. Psychiatry and Neurology, Am. Bd. Clin. Neurophysiology. Intern then resident medicine Cornell med. divsn. Bellevue Hosp., NYC, 1961—63; resident neurology Albert Einstein Coll. Medicine Bronx Mcpl. Hosp., 1965—68; neurologist Neurol. Specialities L.I., Manhasset, NY, 1968—. Attending neurologist N. Shore Univ. Hosp., Manhasset, 1968—; staff neurologist L.I. Jewish Med. Ctr., Glen Oaks, NY, 1969—; cons. neurologist St. Francis Hosp., Roslyn, NY, 1975—; clin. assoc. prof. neurology Cornell U. Med. Coll., NYC, 1971—95, NYU Med. Sch., NYC, 1995—. Capt. USAF, 1963—65. Fellow: ACP, Am. Acad. Neurology; mem.: AMA, Am. Acad. Sleep Medicine, Am. Clin. Neurophysiology Soc., Am. Assn. Electrodiagnostic Medicine, Alpha Omega Alpha. Office: Neurological Specialties Long Island 170 Great Neck Rd Great Neck NY 11021 Office Phone: 516-487-4464.

SCHLESINGER, LEONARD ARTHUR, retail executive; b. NYC, July 31, 1952; s. Joe and Edith (Smukler) S.; m. Phyllis Barbara Fineman, Dec. 23, 1972; children: Rebecca, Emily, Katharine. BA, Brown U., 1972; MBA, Columbia U., 1973; DBA, Harvard U., 1979. Mgr. Procter & Gamble, Green Bay, Wis., 1973-75; asst. prof., assoc. prof. bus. sch. Harvard U., Boston, 1978-85; exec. v.p., COO Au Bon Pain, Inc., Boston, 1985-88; prof. bus. adminstrn. Harvard U., Boston, 1988-98; sr. v.p. Brown U., 1998-99; exec. v.p., COO Limited Brands, Columbus, Ohio, 1999—2003, vice chmn., COO, 2003—07. Past bd. dir. Limited Brands, Columbus, Ohio Editor: Human Resources Mgmt. Jour., Jour. Mgmt. Inquiry; contbr. articles to profl. jours. Jewish. Avocations: travel, music, bicycling. Home: 3900 Kitzmiller Rd New Albany OH 43054 Home Phone: 614-939-5309. Business E-Mail: lschlesinger@limitedbrands.com.

SCHLESINGER, SANFORD JOEL, lawyer; b. NYC, Feb. 8, 1943; s. Irving and Ruth (Rubin) Schlesinger; m. Lianne Lazetera; children: Merideth, Jarrod, Alexandra. BS in Govt. with hons., Columbia U., 1963; JD, Fordham U., 1966. Bar: NY 1966, US Dist. Ct. (so. and ea. dists.) NY 1967, US Ct. Appeals (2d cir.) 1968, US Ct. Internat. Trade 1969, US Tax Ct. 1993, US Supreme Ct. 1978. Assoc. Frankenthaler & Kohn, NYC, 1966—67; asst. atty. gen. trusts and estates bur. charitable found. div. State of N.Y., NYC, 1967—69; ptnr. Rose & Schlesinger, NYC, 1969—81, Goldshmidt, Oshatz, Powsner & Saft, NYC, 1981—85; ptnr., head trusts and estates dept. Shea & Gould, NYC, 1985—93; ptnr., head wills and estates dept. Kaye Scholer LLP, NYC, 1993—2004, ptnr. co-chair family owned bus. practice group, 1993—2004; founding ptnr. Schlesinger Gannon & Lazetera LLP, NYC, 2004—. Adj. faculty Columbia U. Sch. Law, 1989-94; adj. prof. NY Law Sch., 1978-2003; adj. prof. estate planning grad. program U. Miami Grad. Sch. Law, 1995-2003, NY State Bar Jour., 1995-2005, emeritus, 2005—; dir. NY State Bar Found. 2004; mem. estate planning adv. com. Practising Law Inst., 1990—; bd. advisors and contbrs. Jour. Corp. Taxation, 1989-96; lectr. in field; condr. workshops in field. Author: Estate Planning for the Elderly Client, 1984, Planning for the Elderly or Incapacitated Client, 1993; columnist, mem. editl. bd. Estate Planning mag., 1995—; contbr. articles to profl. jours. Mem. adv. bd. Inst. Fed. Taxation NYU, 1988-96, chmn., 1993-94; mem. legis adv. com. Scarsdale Sch. Bd., NY, 1981-83, mem. nominating com., 1979-82; pres. dist. 17 NYC Cmty. Sch. Bd., 1970-71; mem. fin. and estate planning adv. bd. Commerce Clearing House, 1988-; mem. adv. bd. Tax Hotline, 1997-; mem. profl. adv. coun. Rockefeller U., 1994-, The Metropolitan Mus. of Art, 2006-; mem. NY Presbyn. Hosp. Planned Giving Adv. Coun., 2004-. Fellow Am. Coll. Trust and Estate Counsel (chmn. Downstate NY 2001-07); mem. ABA (chmn. social security and other govt. entitlements com. 1990-91, chmn. probate and trust com.-estate planning, drafting charitable giving coms., 1992-94), Internat. Acad. Estate & Trust Law (Academician 1992—), Nat. Acad. Elder Law Attys., Bklyn. Bar Assn., Bar Assn. City of NY, NY State Bar Assn. (treas. trusts and estates sect. 1991-92, sec. trusts and estates sect. 1992-93, chmn. trusts and estates sect. 1994-95, chmn. exec. com. 1st jud. dist. 1987-91, jour. bd. editors 1995-). Avocations: baseball, writing. Office: Schlesinger Gannon & Lazetera LLP 499 Park Ave New York NY 10022 Home Phone: 212-980-4632; Office Phone: 212-652-3777. Business E-Mail: sschlesinger@sglllp.com.

SCHLESINGER, STEPHEN CANNON, foreign policy consultant; b. Boston, Aug. 17, 1942; s. Arthur Meier and Marian (Cannon) S.; m. Judith Barbara Elster, Mar. 18, 1984; 1 child, Sarah Elizabeth. BA in Am. History and Lit. cum laude, Harvard U., 1964, JD, 1968; cert. study in European History, Cambridge U., 1965. Legal asst. to pres. N.Y. State Urban Devel. Corp., 1968; founder, editor The New Dem., 1969-72; speechwriter Dem. Presdl. Candidate George McGovern, 1972; staff writer TIME Mag., 1974-78; editorial writer, chief polit. corr. N.Y. Post, 1978; spl. asst. to Gov. Mario Cuomo, 1983-90; dir. for internat. orgns. N.Y. State Dept. Econ. Devel., 1990—94; vis. scholar Taub Urban Rsch. Ctr. NYU, 1995-97; spl. advisor UN Ctr. for Human Settlements, 1995-97; dir. World Policy Inst. at New Sch. U., NYC, 1997—2006. With Gore Presdl. Campaign, 2000, Kerry Presdl. Campaign, 2004; mem. internat. election observer teams Nat. Dem. Inst., 1993, 90; tchg. fellow in English composition Harvard U., 1968; adj. prof. Am. politics New Sch. U., 1976-77; lectr. Royce Carlton Agy., 1984-88. Author: The New Reformers, 1975, Bitter Fruit: The Untold Story of the U.S. Coup in Guatemala, 1982, Act of Creation: The Founding of the United Nations, 2003 (Harry Truman Book award 2004); contbr. articles to profl. jours., mags. and newspapers; columnist: Boston Globe, 1973-74. Mem. Coun. Fgn. Rels., Roosevelt Inst., PEN, Author's Guild, Overseas Press Club. Unitarian Universalist. Avocations: bicycling, jogging, skiing, swimming, tennis. Home: 500 W 111th St Apt 4A New York NY 10025-1905 E-mail: scsje@aol.com.

SCHLESS, PHYLLIS ROSS, investment banker; d. Lewis H. and Doris G. Ross; m. Aaron Backer Schless, 1970; 1 son, Daniel Lewis Ross. Cert., Neighborhood Playhouse Sch. of Theatre, 1962, N.Y. Sch. Interior Design, 1964; BA in Econs., Wellesley Coll., 1964; MBA, Stanford U., 1966. Cert. theater prodns. Am. League Theater Owners and Prodrs. Assoc. internat. fin. Kuhn Loeb & Co., NYC, 1966—70; fin. cons., 1971—73; sr. fin. analyst Trans World Airlines, NYC, 1974—75; corp. fin., mergers and acquisitions Lazard Freres & Co., 1976—79; dir. mergers and acquisitions Am. Can Co., Greenwich, Conn., 1979—82; v.p. mergers and acquisitions Bear, Stearns & Co., NYC, 1982—84; sr. v.p. corp. acquisitions Integrated Resources, 1984—85; chmn., CEO Ross Fin. Svcs. Group Inc., 1986—; supervisory dir. Merrill Lynch HYTS Funds, 1991—96. Bd. dirs. Calvary Hosp. Fund Bd., 1990-2000, chair investment com., 1995-99; trustee A.R. Tinker Fund, 1993-2004, hon. trustee, 2004—; trustee Nat. Child Labor Com., 1981-95, chmn., 1992-94; trustee New World Found., 1986-92, chair fin. com., treas. 1988-92; bd. dirs. Stanford Bus. Sch. Assn., N.Y., 1994-2004; adj. asst. prof. NYU, 1996—, Columbia U. Sch. Bus., 2001—; bd. dirs. Nat. Found. Tchg. Entrepreneurship, metro. N.Y. chair, 2000-05. Pres. Greater Bridgeport Nat. Coun. Jewish Women, 1971-73, bd. dirs., 1974-75; bd. dirs. Girls Clubs Am., 1975-89, mem. exec. com., 1982-89, pres., 1984-86; bd. dirs. Pauline Koner Dance Co., 1979-81, So. Conn. Child Guidance Clinic, 1981-83, New Canaan United Way, 1981-83; treas. Wellesley Class '64, 1984-89. Mem. Univ. Club. Office Phone: 212-223-1781.

SCHLESSINGER, JOEL, dermatologist, researcher, entrepreneur; b. Columbus, Ohio, Sept. 14, 1960; s. Bernard S. and June Hirsch Schlessinger; m. Nancy Beth Gordon, Oct. 29, 1989; children: Claire Elizabeth, Daniel Isaac. BA in Biology, U. RI, Kingston, 1977—81; degree in Basic Scis., Brown U., Providence, 1981—83; MD, Baylor Coll., Houston, 1983—85. Lic. MD Fedn. Licensing Exam., 1985, cert. pediatrician Am. Bd. Pediat., 1988, dermatologist Am. Bd. Dermatology, 1992, general cosmetic surgeon Am. Bd. Cosmetic Surgery, 1999. Residency in pediat. U. Ala., Birmingham, 1985—88; residency in dermatology Wash. U., St. Louis, 1989—92; CEO Skin Specialists, PC, Omaha, 1993—, LovelySkin.com, Omaha, 1997—, Advanced Skin Rsch. Ctr., Omaha, 2001—. Nat. dir. clin. rsch. ExCel Cosmeceuticals, Bloomfield Hills, Mich., 1998—; adv. bd. Medicis Corp., Scottsdale, Ariz., 2000—; mem. nat. edn. found. Allergan Corp., Irvine, Calif., 2000—; adv. bd. Stiefel Corp., Coral Gables, Fla., 2005—; presdl. adv. bd. Connetics Corp., Palo Alto, Calif., 2004—; adv. bd. Artes Med., San Diego, 2005—. Contbr. articles to profl. jours. Bd. mem. Beth El Synagogue, Omaha, 2000—06; bd. mem. alumni schools com. Brown U., 1997—; bd. trustees Millard Pub. Schs. Found., 1999—2005; curriculum com. mem. Millard Pub. Schs., Omaha, 2000—. Recipient Best Cosmetic Surgeon in Omaha, Omaha Mag., 2000—07, Best Dermatologist in Omaha, Reader Mag., 2002—06. Fellow: Am. Assn. Cosmetic Surgery (assoc.); mem.: Am. Soc. Dermatologic Surgery (assoc.; post grad. edn. com. 2005—06), Am. Numis. Assn. (assoc.), Am. Soc. Laser Surgery & Medicine (assoc.), Nebr. Med. Assn. (assoc.; bd. pres. 2005—06), Am. Acad. Dermatology (assoc.; polit. unpaid lobbyist 1998—, Model State Soc. award 2005—06), Nebr. Dermatology Soc. (assoc.; pres. 2003—06, Model State Soc. award for first time under my presidency 2005—06), Am. Soc. Cosmetic Dermatology & Aesthetic Surgery (assoc.; pres. 2006—, co-founder 1999, Disting. Svc. award 2003—06), Brown Nebr. Club (pres. 2006—), Classic Thunderbird Club Internat. (assoc.), Nebr. Thunderbird Club (assoc.), Phi Beta Kappa (assoc.). Jewish. Achievements include development of one of the largest skincare websites in the world, LovelySkin.com. Avocations: travel, photography, kickboxing. Office: Skin Specialists PC 2802 OakView Mall Dr Omaha NE 68144 Home Phone: 402-496-2168. Office Fax: 402-334-8627; Home Fax: 402-334-8627. Business E-Mail: skindoc@lovelyskin.com.

SCHLESSINGER, JOSEPH, pharmacology educator; BSc in Chemistry/Physics magna cum laude, The Hebrew U., Jerusalem, 1968, MSC in Chemistry magna cum laude, 1969; PhD, The Weizmann Inst. Sci., Rehovot, Israel, 1974. Postdoctoral assoc. dept. chemistry Sch. Applied Physics, Cornell U., 1974-76; vis. scientist immunology br. Nat. Cancer Inst., NIH, Bethesda, Md., 1977-78; sr. scientist dept. chem. immunology The Weizmann Inst. Sci., Rehovot, 1978-80, assoc. prof. dept. chem. immunology, 1980-84, prof. dept. chem. immunology, Ruth & Leonard Simon prof., 1984-91; dir. div. molecular biology Biotech. Rsch. Ctr. Meloy Labs., Inc., Rockville, Md., 1985-86, dir. Biotech. Rsch. Ctr., 1986-88; rsch. dir. Rorer Biotech., Inc., King of Prussia, Pa., 1988-90; prof., chmn. dept. pharmcology NYU Med. Ctr., NYC, 1990—2001; prof., chmn. pharmcology Yale U. Sch. of Medicine, New Haven, 2001—. Mem. editorial bds. European Molecular Biology Orgn. Jour., Jour. Cell Biology, Cell Regulation, Cancer Rsch., Receptors, Growth Factors, Cell Growth & Differentiation, Protein Engineering, Oncogenes and Growth Factor Abstracts; contbr. articles to profl. jours. Recipient Sara Leedy prize, Weizmann Inst. Sci., 1980, Hestrin prize, Biochem. Soc. Israel, 1983, Levinson prize, 1984, The Drew-Ciba prize (with G. Blobel and A. Levine), 1995, Antoine Lacassagne prize, 1995, Disting. Service award, Miami Nature Biotechnology, 1999, Taylor prize (with T. Hunter and T. Pawson), 2000. Mem. European Molecular Biology Orgn., NAS, Am. Academy of Arts and Sciences, Inst. Medicine. Office: Yale U Sch Medicine Dept Pharmacology PO Box 208066 New Haven CT 06520-8066 Office Phone: 203-785-7395. Office Fax: 203-785-3879. E-mail: joseph.schlessinger@yale.edu.

SCHLESSINGER, LAURA, radio talk show host; b. Bklyn., Jan. 16, 1947; d. Monroe and Yolanda Schlessinger; m. Lewis G. Bishop, 1982; 1 child, Deryk. BS in Biological Sciences, SUNY, Stonybrook; MS in Physiology, M Phil in Physiology, Columbia U., PhD in Physiology, 1974. Lic. in marriage and family therapy; cert. marriage, family and child counseling, U. So. Calif. Psychotherapist in private practice, LA, Calif., 1980—90; nat. syndicated radio talk show host The Dr. Laura Schlessinger Program, 1990—; columnist Santa Barbara News Press, 2006—. Past mem. faculty U. So. Calif., Pepperdine U, instr. UCLA, UC Irvine; founder, pres. Dr. Laura Schlessinger Found., 1998- Author: Ten Stupid Things Women Do to Mess Up Their Lives, 1994, How Could You Do That?! The Abdication of Character, Courage and Conscience, 1996, Ten Stupid Things Men Do To Mess Up Their Lives, 1997, The Ten Commandments: The Significance of God's Law in Everyday Life, 1998, Gods, Dragons, and Regular Guys, 2000, Parenthood by Proxy; Don't Have Them If You Won't Raise Them, 2000, Ten Stupid Things Couples Do To Mess Up Their Relationships, 2002 The Proper Care & Feeding Of Husbands, 2004, Bad Childhood Good Life: How to Blossom and Thrive in Spite of an Unhappy Childhood, 2006; (children's books) Why Do You Love Me?, 1999, But I Waaannt It!, 2000, Growing Up is Hard, 2001, I Hate My Life!, 2001, Where is God?, 2003; featured on The Oprah Winfrey Show, A&E Biography, Larry King Live, Lifetime's Intimate Portrait, 20/20, The Today Show, PBS, Hannity & Colmes, CBS This Morning, 48 Hours, Meet the Press with Tim Russert, Crier Today, Eye to Eye with Connie Chung, ABC This Week, Dateline; featured in Time, U.S. News and World Report, People, USA Today, The New York Times Magazine, The Los Angeles Times, The Wall Street Journal and others; featured spkr. Nat. Congressional Prayer Breakfast, Mus. Radio and Television, Claremont Inst., PBS, Nat. Religious Broadcasters, Country Radio Seminar. Named Woman of the Yr., State of Calif. 19th Dist., 2006; recipient Marconi Award for Network/Syndicated Personality of the Yr., 1997, Genii Award, American Women in Radio & Television, 1998, Israel 50th Anniversary Tribute award, 1998, Crystal Cathedral Academy award, 1998, Love of a Child award, Childhelp USA, 1998, Chairman's award, Nat. Religious Broadcasters, 2000, Nat. Heritage award, Nat. Council of Young Israel, 2001, Conservative Leadership award, Clare Booth Luce Inst., 2001, Woman of the Yr. award, 2002, Women Extrardinaire award, Internat. Women's Conf., 2004, Truth in Media award, Pacific Justice Inst., 2006. Mem.: AFTRA, SAG, Nat. Assn. At-Home Mothers (bd. adv.). Achievements include being broadcasted on approximately 300 stations with 12 million listeners; the second most popular talk show host in the country; show syndicated since June 1994; on air radio career for more than 25 years. Office: Premire Radio Networks 15260 Ventura Blvd Ste 300 Sherman Oaks CA 91403-5337

SCHLEUSE, WILLIAM, retired psychiatrist, psychoanalyst; b. Austin, Oct. 18, 1932; s. Louis W. and Oleta Vivian (Hedgpeth) S.; m. Virginia Walker, 1965 (div. 1977); children: Martin, Stuart, Paul; m. Doris Laird, Apr. 20, 1985 (div. 2004). BA, U. Tex., 1953; MD, U. Tex. Med. Br., Galveston, 1957. Diplomate Am. Bd. Psychiatry and Neurology. Pvt. practice psychiatry and psychoanalysis, Houston, 1962-81, Austin, 1981—2000; pres. med. staff Hedgecroft Hosp., Houston, 1966; ret., 2000. Photography exhibited in numerous shows, 1993—. Pres. Houston Psychiat. Soc., 1967, Austin chpt. Am. Assn. Individual Investors, 1992. Fellow Am. Psychiat. Assn. (life); mem. San Antonio/Austin Psychoanalytic Soc. (pres. 1996-98), Austin Fine Art Photography Group (founding mem.), Houston Yacht Club, Phi Beta Kappa. Avocations: sailing, boating, fine-art photography. Home: 8141 Forest Mesa Dr Austin TX 78759-8746

SCHLEUSENER, RICHARD AUGUST, college president; b. Oxford, Nebr., May 6, 1926; s. August William and Katherine Charlotte (Albrecht) S.; m. Elaine Emma Wilhelm, June 12, 1949; children: Kathryn Jeanne Schleusener Miller, Richard Dennis, Rand Lee, Debra Sue, Jeffrey Thomas. BS, U. Nebr., 1949, DSc (hon.), 1984; MS, Kans. State U., 1956; PhD, Colo. State U., 1958; postgrad., MIT, 1951-52. Rsch. engr. Colo. State U., 1958-64, dir. Inst. Atmospheric Sci.; prof., head dept. meteorology S.D. Sch. Mines and Tech., Rapid City, 1965-74, v.p., dean engring., 1974-75, acting pres., 1975-76, pres., 1976-86, Black Hills Regional Eye Inst. Found., 1987-96, ret., 1996. Cons. weather modification U.S. Dept. Interior, 1964—, U.S. Forest Svc., 1966—, UNESCO, 1971—, also pvt. firms. Contbr. articles to tech. jours. With USAF, 1950-55. Inductee S.D. Hall of Fame, 2000. Mem. Am. Meteorol. Soc., Am. Geophys. Union, Rotary, Sigma Xi, Beta Sigma Psi. Lutheran. Home: Unit 104 4120 Villa Ridge Ct Rapid City SD 57701 Personal E-mail: dickelaine@rushmore.com.

SCHLEY, REEVE, III, artist; b. NYC, Mar. 11, 1936; s. Reeve and Elizabeth (Boies) S.; m. Georgia Terry, Oct. 5, 1968; children: Marie B., Reeve T. BA, Yale U., 1959; M.F.A., U. Pa., 1962; studied with, Josef Buchty, Munich, 1954-55. Instr. watercolor NAD, NYC, 1981—. Exhibited in group shows including Spook Farm Gallery, Farm Hills, N.J., 1958, Hunterdon County Art Ctr. Ann., 1959, Pa. Acad., 1966, NJ State Mus., Trenton, 1967, Tenn. Fine Arts Ctr., Nashville, 1973, Okla. Art Ctr., Oklahoma City, 1974, Butler Inst. Am. Art, Youngstown, Ohio, 1974, Drew U., 1975, Silvermine Guild Artists, 1975, NAD, 1977-78, Bklyn. Mus., 1984; one-man shows Vendo Nubes Gallery, Chestnut Hill, Pa., 1967, 71, Phila. Art Alliance, 1969, Spook Farm Gallery, 1970, Saratoga (N.Y.) Gallery, 1972-75, James Graham Gallery, N.Y., 1973-05, N.J. State Mus., 1978, Hull Gallery, Washington, 1978, 80, Byck Gallery, Louisville, 1979, Peale House Gallery, Pa. Acad. Fine Arts, 1980, Gallerie Arnoldi-Livie, Munich, 1985, New Orleans Acad. Fine Arts, 1985, 96; represented in permanent collections NJ State Mus., Trenton, NAD, Newark Mus., Bklyn. Mus., Yale U. Art Gallery, Met. Mus., Heublein Collection, Somerset County Coll., Tenneco Chems. Recipient Best in Show award Hunterdon County Art Ctr., 1974, Laura M. Gross Meml. award Silvermine Guild Artists, 1975, Purchase prize Somerset County Coll. Tri-State Exhbn., 1975, 2d prize for watercolor Sumerset Art Assn., 1975, Ranger Fund Purchase prize NAD, 1981, 85, Cert. of Merit, 1978, Schweitzer prize NAD, 1999; Cresson travel scholar Pa. Acad. Fine Arts, 1962; fellow NJ Coun. Arts, 1979.

SCHLEY, WAYNE ARTHUR, political scientist, consultant; b. Hamilton, Mont., May 22; AA, Shasta Coll., 1960; BS, Sacramento State U., 1963; MS, Am. U., 1974; postgrad., U. Alaska, 1970, Harvard U. Cert. high sch. tchr. (lifetime), Calif. Dept. Edn. Tchr., admin. Placer H.S., Auburn, Calif., 1963-70; spl. asst. to Sen. Ted Stevens, Washington, 1971-77; staff dir. minority and majority subcom. civil svc. Post Office and Gen. Svcs., Washington, 1977-86; minority staff dir. Senate Com. on Rules and Adminstrn., Washington, 1987-92; commr. U.S. Postal Rate Commn., Washington, 1992-95; cons. on legis. and postal issues Washington, 1995—. Elected bd. dirs. Assn. Postal Commerce, 2003—; chmn. Calif. Teenage Reps., 1963-64; regional v.p. Calif. Young Reps., 1964-66, state sgt. at arms, 1966-67; mem. Placer County Rep. Ctrl. Com., 1965-70. Recipient Cert. of Achievement, JFK Sch. Govt. Harvard U., 1982. Home and Office: 614 Massachusetts Ave NE Washington DC 20002-6006 Office Phone: 202-547-9476. Personal E-mail: was2nat@hotmail.com.

SCHLEY, WILLIAM SHAIN, otolaryngologist; b. Columbus, Ga., Sept. 21, 1940; s. Frances Brooking Schley and Susie (Smith) Mathews. BA, Emory U., 1962, MD, 1966. Intern mixed surg. The Roosevelt Hosp., NYC, 1966-67, resident in surgery, 1967-68; resident in otorhinolaryngology N.Y. Hosp.-Cornell Med. Ctr., NYC, 1970-73; clin. instr. otorhinolaryngology Cornell U. Med. Coll., 1972-75, clin. asst. prof., 1975-81, assoc. prof., 1982—, acting chmn. dept. otorhinolaryngology, 1988-94, chmn. dept. otorhinolaryngology, 1994—2005. Otorhinolaryngologist to outpatients with pvt. patient privileges N.Y. Hosp., 1973-75, asst. attending otorhinolaryngologist with pvt. patient privileges, 1975-81, assoc. attending, 1992—, acting otorhinolaryngologist-in-chief, 1988-94, otorhinolaryngologist-in-chief, 1994-2005; assoc. asst. surgeon otolaryngology Manhattan Eye, Ear, Nose and Throat Hosp., 1988-99; v.p. and sec. med. bd. N.Y. Hosp., 1994-97, pres., 1998-99; pres., v.p. med. bd. The N.Y. and Presbyn. Hosp., 1998, pres., 1998-99, mem. ex officio bd. trustees, 1998-99; mem. co-chmn. vis. day com. The N.Y. Hosp.-Cornell Med. Ctr., 1995-98; pres. N.Y. Hosp.-Cornell Med. Coll. Alumni Coun., 1996-98; course dir. Salzburg Cornell Med. Seminars, 1996—, steering com.,

1999—. Author: (with others) Pulmonary Diseases of the Fetus Newborn and Child, 1978; contbr. numerous articles to profl. publs. Vestry St. James Ch., N.Y.C., 1994-97; mem. ad hoc bd. visitors Emory U., 1994-95; bd. dirs. Health Advs. for Older People, 1997—, v.p., 2000—; mem. adv. bd. Sch. Medicine Emory U., 2000—, chmn. adv. bd., 2002—; chmn. third age coun. St. James Ch., 2007—. Lt. comdr. USNR. Recipient The Emery medal, 2001. Fellow ACS (Manhattan dist. #2 com. on applicants 1991-97, Manhattan Credentials Com. 1991-99); mem. Am. Acad. Otolaryngology-Head and Neck Surgery, Med. Soc. State of N.Y., N.Y. State Soc. Otolaryngology-Head and Neck Surgery (exec. coun. 1974-80, dist. dir. 1980), County Med. Soc. N.Y., N.Y. Laryngol. Soc. (sec.-treas. 1981-84, v.p. 1984-85, pres. 1985-86), N.Y. Bronchoscopic Soc. (v.p. 1986-94, pres. 1994-97), N.Y. Clin. Soc. (v.p. 1998-99, pres. 1999-2000, sec.-treas, 2005-07), Assn. Emory Alumni (bd. govs. 1990-97, pres.-elect 1993-94, pres. 1994-95), Omicron Delta Kappa. Episcopalian. Avocations: astronomy, ornithology. Home: 430 E 63d St Apt 5E New York NY 10021-7927 Office: DS10 449 E 68th St New York NY 10021-6310 Office Phone: 212-746-2223. E-mail: schley@med.cornell.edu.

SCHLEYER, PAUL VON RAGUÉ, chemistry educator; b. Cleve., Feb. 27, 1930; s. Charles Ernest and Hulda Betty (Kamphausen) S.; m. Ingeborg Venema, Dec. 29, 1969; children by previous marriage: Betti, Laura, Karen. AB, Princeton U., 1951; MA, Harvard U., 1956, PhD, 1957; PhD Honoris Causa, U. Lyon, France, 1971. Instr., Princeton U., 1954-58, asst. prof., 1958-63, assoc. prof., 1963-65, prof., 1965-69, Eugene Higgins prof. chemistry, 1969-76; prof. U. Erlangen-Nuremberg, Germany, 1976; sr. fellow U. So. Calif., 1978; Graham Perdue prof. chemistry Univ. Ga., Athens. Vis. prof. U. Colo., 1963, U. Würzburg, Germany, 1967, U. Mich., 1969, U. Munich, 1969, Carnegie Mellon U., 1969, Kyoto (Japan) U., 1970, U. Münster, Germany, 1971, U. Geneva, 1972, U. Groningen, The Netherlands, 1972-73, 90; vis. U. Jerusalem, 1973, U. Paris, 1973, U. Louvain, Belgium, 1974, U. Regensburg, Germany, 1975, Case Western Res. U., 1976-77, U. Western Ont., 1978, Carnegie-Mellon U., 1977-78, U. Copenhagen, 1979-80, U. Utrecht, 1982, 85, U. Barcelona, 1983, Technion, Haifa, Israel, 1993; disting. vis. prof. U. Ga., 1990—; cons. to industry, 1955—. Co-author: The Nonclassical Ion Problem, 1977, AB INITIO Molecular Orbital Theory, 1986; mem. editl. bd. Chem. Revs., 1969-72, Jour. Am. Chem. Soc., 1970-79, Revs. Chem. Intermediates, 1982—, Jour. Phys. Organic Chemistry, 1987—, Heteroatom Chemistry, 1988, Tetrahedron Pubs., 1990—, Chem. Comms., 1990-96; co-editor series Carbonium Ions, vol. 1, 1968, vol. 2, 1970, vol. 3, 1972, vol. 4, 1973, vol. 5, 1977, Lithium Chemistry, 1995, Stable Carbocation Chemistry, 1997; editor Jour. Computational Chemistry, 1981—, Theoretical Structures of Molecules, 1993, 94; editor-in-chief Ency. Computational Chemistry, 1997; contbr. 850 rsch. articles to tech. jours. Mem. rev. com. NIH, 1967-70. Recipient von Humboldt sr. scientist award U. Munich, 1974-75; A.P. Sloan research fellow, 1962-66; Fulbright fellow, also; Guggenheim fellow U. Munich, 1965; von Baeyer prize German Chem. Soc. 1986, J.F. Norris award in Phys. Organic Chemistry Am. Chem. Soc., 1987, Heisenberg medal World Assn. Theoretical Chemists and Hungarian Chem. Soc., 1987, Ingold Medal Royal Soc. Chemistry, 1988; Cope scholar Am. Chem. Soc., 1990. Fellow AAAS, Am. Acad. Arts & Scis., Bavarian Acad. Scis., Merck-Schuchardt Chair (Belgium 1991), World Assn. Theoretical Organic Chemists (pres. 1990-96), Internat. Acad. Quantum Chem. Sci. also: 126 S Stratford Dr Athens GA 30605-3024 *

SCHLEYER, WILLIAM T., cable company executive; b. Phila. BS in Mech. Engring., Drexel U.; MBA, Harvard Bus. Sch. Mgr. IBM, Abbott Labs.; from sys. mgr. to pres., COO US West Media Group Continental Cablevision, 1977-97; pres., COO MediaOne, Boston, 1997—2000; prin. Pilot House Ventures, LLC, 2001; pres., CEO, broadband services unit AT&T Corp., 2001—03; chmn., CEO Adelphia Communications Corp., Greenwood Village, Colo., 2003—. Office: Tele Communications Inc 183 Inverness Dr W Englewood CO 80112-5203

SCHLICHER, RONALD LEWIS, ambassador; With Fgn. Svc., 1982—; min.-counselor sr. fgn. svc.; vice-consul Dhahran, 1982—84; consul Damascus, Syria, 1984—86; staff asst. Bur. Near Ea. Affairs US Dept. State; dep. prin. officer Am. Embassy, Alexandria, Egypt, 1987—89, first sec. Cairo, 1989—91; chief civilian officer Multinational Force and Observers, Israel, 1991—92; dep. dir. regional affairs Office of Coord. Counter Terrorism, 1994—97; dep. chief of mission Am. Embassy, Beirut, 1994—97; dir. office Egyptian and N. African affairs, Bur. Near Eastern Affairs US Dept. State, Washington, 1997—2000; chief of mission, counsul-gen. Am. Embassy, Jerusalem, 2000—02; dir. Iraqi Task Force, 2003; dep. asst. sec. US Dept. State, Washington, US amb. to Cyprus Nicosia, 2005—. Recipient Disting. Honor award, Superior Honor award (3), Meritorious Honor award (2), Nat. Human Intelligence Collector award, Christian A. Herter award. Office: Am Embassy 5450 Nicosia Pl Washington DC 20521

SCHLICHTING, CATHERINE FLETCHER NICHOLSON, librarian, educator; b. Huntsville, Ala., Nov. 18, 1923; d. William Parsons and Ethel Loise (Breitling) Nicholson; m. Harry Fredrick Schlichting, July 1, 1950 (dec. Aug. 1964); children: James Dean, Richard Dale, Barbara Lynn. BS, U. Ala., 1944; MLS, U. Chgo., 1950. Asst. libr. U. Ala. Edn. Libr., Tuscaloosa, summers 1944-45; libr. Sylacauga (Ala.) H.S., 1944-45, Hinsdale (Ill.) H.S., 1945-49; asst. libr. Centre for Children's Books, U. Chgo., 1950-52; instr. reference dept. libr. Ohio Wesleyan U., Delaware, 1965-69, asst. prof., 1969-79, assoc. prof., 1979-85, prof., 1985—, curator Ohio Wesleyan Hist. Collection, 1986—, student pers. libr., 1966-72. Author: Introduction to Bibliographic Research: Basic Sources, 4th edit., 1983, Checklist of Biographical Reference Sources, 1977, Audio-Visual Aids in Bibliographic Instruction, 1976, Introduction to Bibliographic Research: Slide Catalog and Script, 1980; info. cons. (documentary) Noble Achievements: The History of Ohio Wesleyan 1942-1992, 1992, 150 Years of Excellence: A Pictorial View of Ohio Wesleyan University, 1992. Mem. adminstrv. bd. Meth. Ch., 1973-81, chmn. adminstrv. bd., 1985—, mem. coun. on ministries, 1975-81, chmn., 1975-77, trustee, 1999—2003. Recipient Algernon Sidney Sullivan award U. Ala., 1944, Hon. Alumna award Ohio Wesleyan U., 1997; Ohio Wesleyan U.-Mellon Found. grantee, 1972-73, 84-85; GLCA Tchg. fellow, 1976-77. Mem. ALA, Ohio Libr. Assn., Midwest Acad. Libr. Conf., Acad. Librs. Assn. Ohio (dir. 1984-86), AAUP (chpt. sec. 1967-68), United Meth. Women (pres. Mt. Vernon dist. 1994-97, newsletter editor 1998-2002), Ohio Wesleyan Woman's Club (exec. bd. 1969-72, 77-79, 81-84, pres. 1969-70, sec. 1977-78), History Club (pres. 1971-72, v.p. 1978-79, 2003-04) Fortnightly Club (pres. 1975-76, 87-88, 2003-04), Am. Field Svc. (pres. Delaware chpt. 1975-76), Kappa Delta Pi, Alpha Lambda Delta. Democrat. Home: 57 Willow Brook Way S Delaware OH 43015 Office: Ohio Wesleyan U La Beeghly Library Delaware OH 43015

SCHLICHTING, NANCY MARGARET, hospital administrator; b. NYC, Nov. 21, 1954; BA, Duke U., 1976; MBA, Cornell U., 1979. Adminstrv. resident Meml. Hosp. Cancer, NYC, 1978; fellow Blue Cross-Blue Shield Assn., Chgo., 1979-80; asst. dirs. ops. Akron (Ohio) City Hosp., 1980-81, assoc. dir. planning, 1981-83, exec. v.p., 1983-88, Riverside Meth. Hosps., Columbus, Ohio, 1988-92, pres., COO, 1992-93, pres., CEO, 1993-96; pres. Ea. region Cath. Health Initiatives, Aston, Pa., 1996-97; exec. v.p., COO Summa Health Sys., Akron, Ohio, 1997—98; sr. v.p., chief adminstrv. officer Henry Ford Healthcare Sys., Detroit, 1998—99, exec. v.p., COO, 1999—2003, pres., CEO, 2003—, Henry Ford Hosp., 2001—03. Bd. dirs. Fifth Third Bank Corp., First Nat. Bank of Ohio, Mich. Health and Hosp. Assn., Greater Detroit Area Health Council, Walgreen Co., 2006—. Trustee Kresge Found. Office: Henry Ford Health Sys 1 Ford Pl Detroit MI 48202

SCHLICHTING, WILLIAM HENRY, lawyer, writer; b. Austin, Minn., Jan. 24, 1944; s. John Frederick and Frances Amelia (Garbisch) Schlichting. BA, St. Olaf Coll., 1966; MS, U. Chgo., 1970; JD, Columbia U., 1973; LLM in Taxation, NYU, 1979. Bar: NY 1974, Minn. 1981, US Tax Ct. 1982. Assoc. Shea & Gould, NYC, 1973—76; editor Law Jour. Pub. Co., NYC, 1976—79, Matthew Bender & Co., Inc., NYC, 1979—81; assoc. Peterson, Hanson, Schlichting & Davies, Albert Lea, Minn., 1981—83; gen. counsel, sec. Med. Venture, Inc., Mpls., 1983—89; writer Matthew Bender & Co., Inc., NYC, 1989—91; acquisitions editor, classifier West Group, Eagan, Minn., 1991—2002; bd. dirs. The Aliveness Project, Inc., 2004—, pres., chmn., 2005—. Writer Butterworth Legal Pub., Mason divsn., St. Paul, 1983—84. Author, editor Banking Law, 1979—81, Clark's Digest-Annotator, 1976—79; contbr. articles to profl. jours. Mem. investments and fin. com. Philanthrofund Found., 2005—. Fellow, NSF, 1966—70; Erik Hetle scholar, 1966—67. Mem.: Minn. Bar Assn., Phi Beta Kappa, Sigma Pi Sigma. Lutheran. Home: 5901 Laurel Ave #325 Golden Valley MN 55416-1075 Personal E-mail: wmhenrys@comcast.net.

SCHLICHTMANN, JAN RICHARD, lawyer; b. Framingham, Mass., Mar. 16, 1951; BA, U. Mass., 1973; JD, Cornell U., 1977. Bar: DC 1977, Mass. 1978, N.H. 1978, U.S. Dist. Ct. Mass. 1978, U.S. Ct. Appeals (1st cir.) 1978, U.S. Supreme Ct. 1990. Pvt. practice, Boston, 1978—. Staff atty. U.S. Ho. Reps., 1978—79; lectr. U. Wis., Nat. Judiciary Coll., 1990. Mem. com. revise Mass. hazardous waste statute Commonwealth of Mass., 1990—92. Mem.: ATLA, Mass. Acad. Trial Attys., Mass. Bar Assn., Phi Beta Kappa. Office: Jan Schlichtmann PC PO Box 233 Prides Crossing MA 01965 Business E-Mail: jschlichtmann@levinlaw.com. E-mail: info@schlichtmannlaw.com. *

SCHLICK, AUSTIN C., lawyer; b. NYC, 1963; BA in History, magna cum laude, Princeton U., 1985; JD, Yale Law Sch., 1990. Bar: Pa. 1994, DC 1996. Law clk. to Chief Judge Abner Mikva US Ct. Appeals (DC Cir.), 1990—91; law clk. to Justice Sandra Day O'Connor US Supreme Ct., 1991—92; assoc. Klein, Farr, Smith & Taranto, Washington, 1992—93; assoc. to ptnr. Kellogg, Huber, Hansen, Todd & Evans, Phila. & Washington DC, 1993—2000; ptnr. Kellogg, Huber, Hansen, Todd, Evans & Figel PLLC, Washington, 2006—; asst. solicitor gen. Office of Solicitor Gen., US Dept. Justice, Washington, 2000—04; dep. gen. counsel Fed. Communications Commn., Washington, 2004—05, acting gen. counsel, 2005. Office: Kellogg Huber Hansen Todd Evans & Figel Ste 400 1615 M St NW Washington DC 20036 Office Phone: 202-326-7907. Office Fax: 202-326-7999. E-mail: aschlick@khhte.com. *

SCHLICKEISEN, RODGER OSCAR, non-profit environmental organization executive; b. Houston, Jan. 24, 1941; s. Oscar and Elvene Alice (Rennemo) S.; m. Susan Jane Culver, May 23, 1970; 1 child, Derek. BA, U. Wash., 1963; MBA, Harvard U., 1965; DBA, George Washington U., 1978. Loan officer Export-Import Bank of U.S., Washington, 1968-70; pres. Gryphon, Inc., Washington, 1970-74; group dir. com. on budget U.S. Senate, Washington, 1974-79; assoc. dir. econs. and govt. U.S. Office of Mgmt. and Budget, Washington, 1979-80; v.p. Craver, Mathews, Smith & Co., Falls Church, Va., 1980-81, CEO, 1981-87; chief of staff Office of U.S. Senator Max Baucus, Washington, 1987-91; pres., CEO Defenders of Wildlife, Washington, 1991—, Defenders of Wildlife Action Fund, Washington, 2001—. Bd. dirs. Partnership Project, Inc., Washington, League Conservative Voters, Washington, Keystone Ctr., Colo.; bd. advisors Environ. Comms. Orgn., L.A., 1992—, Environ. Media Assn., L.A., 1992—. Contbr. articles to profl. publs. Va. state chmn. Common Cause, 1971-74. Office: Defenders of Wildlife 1130 17th St NW Washington DC 20036

SCHLIEVE, HY C. J., school administrator; b. Mandan, ND, Apr. 4, 1952; s. Calvin L. and Loretta L. (Johnson) S.; m. Terri Ann Hansen, Dec. 30, 1977; children: Derek, Aaron, Jessica. BA, N.D. State U., 1974, MS, 1984; EdD, Calif. Coast U., 1994. Tchr., coach Halliday (N.D.) Pub. Sch., 1974-75, Drake (N.D.) Pub. Sch., 1975-76, Montpelier (N.D.) Pub. Sch., 1976-81; prin. Unity Pub. Sch., Petersburg, N.D., 1981-83, Page (N.D.) Pub. Sch., 1983-85; supt. Wolford (N.D.) Pub. Sch., 1985-87, Garrison (N.D.) Pub. Schs., 1987-93; prin. Buhl Joint Sch. Dist. 412, Idaho, 1993-95, Oconto Falls Area Sch. Dist., Wis., 1995-99; supt. Ellendale (N.D.) Pub. Schs. #40, 1999—. Com. mem. NDASA Rsch. and Evaluation, Garrison, 1988-93; fiscal agt. Mo. Hills Consortium, McLean County, N.D., 1989-93; cons. asbestos Garrison Pub. Sch. Dist., 1987-93. Sec. Govtl. Affairs Com., Garrison, 1987-93; mem. Tourism Com., Garrison, 1988-92, Econ. Devel. Com., 1988-89. Recipient Nat. Superintendent of the Yr. awd., North Dakota, Am. Assn. of School Administrators, 1992. Mem. Nat. Assn. Secondary Sch. Prins. (prin. assessor tng. 1990), NSBA Fed. Policy Coords. Network. Avocations: golf, hunting, fishing, bowling, outdoor activities. Office: Ellendale Pub Schs PO Box 400 321 N 1st St Ellendale ND 58436 Home: 1330 12th St N Apt 18 Wahpeton ND 58075-5028

SCHLISSEL, FRED, management consultant, educator; b. NYC, June 19, 1930; s. Louis and Pauline Schlissel; m. Betty Kreisler Schlissel, June 22, 1952; children: Alan, Laura, Arnold. Student, NYU, 1966; BBA, CCNY, 1952; MBA, Columbia U., NYC, 1960. Cert. Inst. Mgmt. Conssultants. Indsl. engr. Penn Akron Howe HCG, NYC, 1954—56, plant mgr., 1956—60; head mgmt. adv. svcs. Back & Gould CPAs, NYC, 1960—64; mgmt. cons. Knowledge Resources Inc., NYC, 1964—. Adj. prof. various colls., 1960—. Contbr. articles to profl. jours. 1st lt. US Army, 1952—54, Korea. Avocations: sailing, writing. Home: 920 Browers Point Br Woodmere NY 11598 Personal E-mail: fred@42usa.net.

SCHLOERB, PAUL RICHARD, surgeon, educator; b. Buffalo, Oct. 22, 1919; s. Herman George and Vera (Gross) S.; m. Louise M. Grimmer, Feb. 25, 1950; children: Ronald G., Patricia S. Johnson, Marilyn A. Hock, Dorothy S. Hoban, P. Richard. AB, Harvard U., 1941; MD, U. Rochester, 1944. Intern U. Rochester Med. Sch., 1944—45, asst. resident, 1947—48, instr. surgery, 1952; rsch. fellow, resident Peter Bent Brigham Hosp., Boston, 1948—52; faculty U. Kans. Med. Ctr., Kansas City, 1952—79, prof. surgery, 1964—79, 1988—2006, prof. surgery emeritus, 2006—, dean for rsch., 1972—79, dir. nutritional support svc., 1993—2002; prof. surgery U. Rochester (NY) Med Ctr., 1979—88, adj. prof. surgery, 1988—90; surgeon Strong Meml. Hosp., 1979—88, dir. Surg. ICU, 1979—85, dir. surg. nutritional support service. Contbr. over 100 articles to profl. jours. Lt. (j.g.), M.C. USNR, 1944-45; to lt. 1953-55. Mem. AMA, ACS, AAAS, Am. Surg. Assn., Soc. U. Surgeons, Am. Physiol. Soc., Internat. Soc. Surgery, Ctrl. Surg. Assn., Am. Assn. for Surgery of Trauma, Am. Assn. Cancer Rsch., Biomed. Engring. Soc., Am. Inst. Nutrition, Am. Soc. Clin. Nutrition, Sigma Xi. Achievements include first to measure total body water in humans. Office: Dept Surgery U Kansas Med Ctr Kansas City KS 66160-0001 Home Phone: 913-451-8998; Office Phone: 913-588-7565. Business E-Mail: pschloer@kumc.edu.

SCHLOM, JEFFREY BERT, research scientist; b. NYC, June 22, 1942; s. David and Anna Schlom; m. Kathleen; children: Amy Melissa, Steven Michael. BS (Pres.'s scholar), Ohio State U., 1964; MS, Adelphi U., 1966; PhD, Rutgers U., 1969. Instr. Columbia Coll. Phys. and Surg., 1969-71, asst. prof., 1971-73; chmn. breast cancer virus segment Nat Cancer Inst., NIH, Bethesda, Md., 1973-76, chief lab. tumor immunology and biology, 1983—, head exptl. oncology sect., 1976-83; prof. George Washington U., Washington, 1975—. Disting. lectr. Can. Cancer Soc., 1985 Contbr. articles to profl. jours. Recipient Dir.'s award NIH, 1977, 89, Tech. Transfer award NIH, 1994, 95, 96, Disting. Scientist award Turin U., 1996, others. Mem. Am. Assn. Cancer Rsch. (Rosenthal award 1985), Am. Soc. Cytology (Basic Rsch. award 1987). Office: Inst Health Bldg 10 Rm 8B09 Bethesda MD 20892 Business E-Mail: js141c@nih.gov.

SCHLOSS, HOWARD MONROE, financial regulatory service executive; b. Rochester, NY, Jan. 30, 1960; m. Deborah Tawney; children: Michael Austin, Lindsay Taylor, Gabriella Greer. BFA in Journalism, So. Meth. U., 1982. Copy editor Fort Worth Star-Telegram, asst. to the op-ed page editor, 1983-87; writer, editor UPI, Dallas, 1982; dep. comm. dir., comm. dir. Dem. Congl. Campaign Com., 1987-91; acct. supr. Powell Tate, 1991-93; dep. asst. sec. for pub. affairs US Dept. Treasury, Washington, 1993-95, asst. sec. for pub. affairs, 1995—99; v.p. pub. affairs NY Stock Exch., 1999—2000; sr. v.p. comm. & govt. rels. NASD, 2000—07, Fin. Industry Regulatory Authority, 2007—. Office: Financial Industry Regulatory Authority 1735 K St NW Washington DC 20006

SCHLOSS, IRVING STEVEN, lawyer; b. NYC, Feb. 3, 1945; s. Arthur and Bianca (Steinberger) S.; m. Christine Skeeles, June 28, 1970 (div. Mar. 1999); children: Tracy, David; m. Deborah V. Abildsoe, Nov. 21, 1999. AB magna cum laude, Harvard Coll., 1966; LLB, Yale U., 1970. Bar: Conn. 1972, U.S. Dist. Ct. Conn. 1972, U.S. Ct. Appeals (2d cir.) 1973, U.S. Tax Ct. 1985; cert. mediator U. Conn.-Quinnipiack U., 2003. Law clerk for Judge Spottswood Robinson, III (D.C. cir.) U.S. Ct. Appeals, Washington, 1970-71; ptnr. Tyler, Cooper & Alcorn, LLP, New Haven and Madison, 1976—. Co-author: Understanding TIAA-CREF: Planning for a Secure and Comfortable Retirement, 2000; bd. editors Tax Mgmt. Estates, Gift & Trust Jour.; contbr. articles to profl. jours. Bd. dirs. Shoreline Found., Guilford, 1984-93, 1997-2007, Guilford Free Libr., Conn., 1986-92, New Haven Symphony Orch., 1995-2001, Valley-Shore YMCA, Westbrook, Conn., 2007—; vol. CPTV Auction, West Hartford, 1987-88; mem. Rep. Town Commn., Guilford, 1987-91. Recipient Man of Yr. award Guilford YMCA, 1990. Mem. ABA, Conn. Bar Assn. (chmn. sect. corps. and other bus. orgns. 1988-90, mem. exec. com. estates and probate sect. 1996—), Am. Coll. Trust and Estate Counsel (regent and editor ACTEC Studies), New Haven Conn. Bar Assn., Quinnipiack Club. Office: Tyler Cooper & Alcorn PO Box 1936 New Haven CT 06509-0906 also: 23 Woodland Rd Madison CT E-mail: ischlos@attglobal.net, schloss@tylercooper.com.

SCHLOSS, NATHAN, retired economist; b. Balt., Jan. 14, 1927; s. Howard L. and Louise (Levi) S.; m. Rosa Montalvo, Mar. 1, 1958; children: Nina L., Carolyn D. BS in Bus., Johns Hopkins U., 1950. Buyer Pacific Coast gen. merchandise office Sears Roebuck & Co., Los Angeles, 1955-60; staff asst. econ. rsch. dept. Chgo., 1960-63; sr. market analyst corp. rsch. dept. Montgomery Ward & Co., Chgo., 1963-65; rsch. mgr. real estate dept. Walgreen Co., Chgo., 1970-72; v.p. rsch. and planning Maron Properties Ltd., Montreal, Que., Can., 1972-74; corp. economist, fin. analyst Real Estate Rsch. Corp., Chgo., 1974-88, sr. v.p., 1986-88, treas., chief fin. analyst, 1982-88; economist Office of Ill. Atty. Gen., Chgo., 1988-97. Cons. in field, 1965-97. Contbr. articles on fin. and market analysis of real estate to profl. jours. Mem. Plan. Commn., village of Wilmette, Ill., 1975-77, tech. adv. com. on employment and tng. data Ill. employment and Tng. Coun., 1979-82, tech. adv. com. Ill. Job Tng. Coordinating Council, 1983-87; mem. com. on price indexes and productivity fgn. labor Bus. Rsch. Adv. Coun. of Bur. Labor Stats, Dept. Labor, 1979-88, chairperson, 1985-86, com. on employment and unemployment. Recipient Commendable Svc. Citation, Bur. Labor Stats., Dept. Labor, 1987. Mem. Am. Mktg. Assn., Nat. Assn. Bus. Economists, Ill. Econ. Assn., Lambda Alpha. Home and Office: 115 Hollywood Ct Wilmette IL 60091-3122 Office Phone: 847-251-9582.

SCHLOSSER, ANNE GRIFFIN, librarian; b. NYC, Dec. 28, 1939; d. C. Russell and Gertrude (Taylor) Griffin; m. Gary J. Schlosser, Dec. 28, 1965. BA in History, Wheaton Coll., Norton, Mass., 1962; MLS, Simmons Coll., 1964; cert. archives adminstrn., Am. U., 1970. Head UCLA Theater arts Libr., 1964-69; dir. Louis B. Mayer Libr., Am. Film Inst., LA, 1969-88, dir. film/TV documentation workshop, 1977-87; head Cinema-TV Libr. and Archives of the Performing Arts, U. So. Calif., LA, 1988-91; dir. Entertainment Resources Seminar, 1990; dir. rsch. libr. Warner Bros., 1991—2001; part-time libr. Nevada County Libr., 2002—. Project dir. Motion Pictures, Television, Radio: A Union Catalogue of Manuscript and Special Collections in the Wesern U.S., 1977. Recipient numerous grants for script indexing, manuscript cataloging, libr. automation. Mem. Soc. Calif. Archivists (pres. 1982-83), Theater Libr. Assn (exec. bd. 1983-86), Spl. Librs. Assn. Democrat. Episcopalian. Avocations: swimming, reading, dog training.

SCHLOSSER, ERIC, writer; Writer, contributor Atlantic Monthly Mag. Author: (books) Fast Food Nation; television appearances 60 Minutes, CNN, NBC Nightly News, Fox News; contbr. articles to numerous profl. jours. Achievements include several months on new york times best-seller list, 2004-2005; film based on first book produced, 2006. Office: c/o Houghton Mifflin 222 Berkeley St Boston MA 02116

SCHLOSSER, HERBERT S., broadcasting company executive; b. Atlantic City, Apr. 21, 1926; s. Abraham and Anna (Olesker) S.; m. Judith P. Gassner, July 8, 1951; children: Lynn C., Eric M. AB summa cum laude, Princeton, 1948; LL.B., Yale, 1951. Bar: N.Y. 1952. Assoc. firm Wickes, Riddell, Bloomer, Jacobi & McGuire, NYC, 1951-54, Phillips, Nizer, Benjamin, Krim & Ballon, NYC, 1954-57; with NBC, 1957-78; v.p., gen. mgr. Calif. Nat. Prodns., Inc. sub. NBC, 1960-61, dir. talent and program adminstrn., 1961-62, v.p. talent and program adminstrn., 1962-66; v.p. programs West Coast NBC, 1966-72; exec. v.p. NBC-TV Network, 1972-73, pres., 1973-74, mem. bd. dirs., 1973-78; pres. NBC, Inc., 1974-78, CEO, 1977-78; exec. v.p. RCA, 1978-85; sr. advisor broadcasting and entertainment Schroder & Co., Inc., NYC, 1986—2000; sr. advisor, ind. cons. comms. investment banking Citigroup Global Markets Inc., 2000—. Ptnr. Arts and Entertainment Cable Network, RCA/Columbia Home Video. Trustee Internat. Radio and TV Found., 1972-74; former mem. govs. Ford's Theatre Soc.; former trustee Nat. Urban League; chmn. bd. Am. Mus. of the Moving Image; bd. dirs. Chamber Music Soc. of Lincoln Ctr. With USNR, 1944-46. Recipient Humanitarian award NCCJ, 1974, Gold Brotherhood award, 1978 Mem. ABA, Assn. Bar City N.Y., Coun. on Fgn. Rels., Acad. TV Arts and Scis., Advt. Coun. (past dir.), Yale Law Sch. Assn., Internat. Radio and TV Soc. (trustee 1973-74), Hollywood Radio and TV Soc. (trustee 1970-72), Century Assn., Princeton Club (N.Y.), Phi Beta Kappa (pres. alumni assn. So. Calif. 1970-72. Office: Citigroup Global Markets 388 Greenwich St New York NY 10013-2375

SCHLOSSMAN, JOHN ISAAC, architect; b. Chgo., Aug. 21, 1931; s. Norman Joseph and Carol (Rosenfeld) S.; m. Shirley Goulding Rhodes, Feb. 8, 1959; children: Marc N., Gail S. Mewhort, Peter C. Student, Grinnell Coll., 1949-50; BA, U. Minn., 1953, BArch, 1955; MArch, MIT, 1956. Registered architect, Ill. Archtl. designer The Architects Collaborative, Cambridge, Mass., 1956-57; architect Loebl Schlossman & Hackl and predecessors, Chgo., 1959-65, assoc., 1965-70, prin., 1970-98, cons. prin., 1998—. Bd. overseers Coll. Arch. Ill. Inst. Tech., Chgo.; adv. bd. Coll. of Arch. and Landscape Arch. U. Minn., 2003-06; founding bd. dirs. Chgo. Archtl. Assistance Ctr., 1974-79 Chmn. Glencoe Plan Commn., Ill., 1977-82; mem. Village of Glencoe Contextual Design Rev. Commn., 2005-0; trustee Com. for Green Bay Trail, Glencoe, 1970-77, Chgo. Arch. Found., 1971-75, Graham Found. for Advanced Studies in Fine Arts, 1995-99, pres. 1999-2001; adv. bd. dirs. Merit Sch. of Music, Chgo., 1983-93, pres., 1988-90, hon. trustee, 1996; governing mem. Chgo. Symphony Orch.; mem. founders coun. Field Mus., Chgo.; mem. zoning and planning com. Greater North Michigan Ave. Assn., Chgo., 2000-01; mem. Nat. Trust Coun., Nat. Trust for Hist. Preservation, Washington.

Named dir. for life Young Men's Jewish Coun., Chgo., 1971; Rotch travelling scholar, 1957; sustaining fellow Art Inst. Chgo. Fellow AIA (trustee ins. trust 1971-76, chmn. ins. com. 1974-75, v.p. Chgo. chpt. 1975, chmn. architects liability com. 1976, 80-82, hon. found. trustee 1995—), Tavern Club (gov. 1986-88, v.p. 1990), The Club at Symphony Ctr., The Arts Club, Alpha Rho Chi. Office: Loebl Schlossman & Hackl 232 Mary St Winnetka IL 60093-1522 E-mail: jschloss@worldnet.att.net.

SCHLOSSMAN, STUART FRANKLIN, physician, educator, researcher; b. NYC, Apr. 18, 1935; s. Abe and Pearl (Susser) Schlossman; m. Judith Seryl Rubin, May 25, 1958; children: Robert, Peter. BA magna cum laude, NYU, 1955, MD, 1958; MA, Harvard U., 1975; MD (hon.), U. Heidelberg, 2006. Intern in medicine med. divsn. III Bellevue Hosp., NYC, 1958—59, asst. resident in medicine med. divsn. III, 1959—60; Nat. Found. fellow dept. microbiology Coll. Physicians Columbia U., NYC, 1960—62; asst. physician med. svc. Vanderbilt Clinic, Coll. Physician USPHS, Washington, 1960—62; Ward hematology fellow dept. internal medicine Sch. Washington U., St. Louis, 1962—63; rsch. assoc. lab. biochemistry Nat. Cancer Inst. USPHS, Washington, 1963—65; clin. instr. in medicine Sch. of Medicine George Washington U., 1964—65; assoc. in medicine, dir. blood bank Beth Israel Hosp., Boston, 1965—66; instr. Med. Sch. Harvard U., Boston, 1966—68, asst. physician, 1967—68, chief clin. immunology, 1971—73; physician Beth Israel Hosp., Boston, 1968—; from asst. to assoc. prof. medicine Harvard Med. Sch., Boston, 1968—77, prof., 1977—, Baruj Benacerraf prof. medicine, 1990—, chief divsn. tumor immunology and immunotherapy, 1973—; sr. physician Brigham and Women's Hosp., Boston, 1976—. Mem. editl. bd. Jour. of Immunology, 1969—74, Cellular Immunology, 1970—, Human Immunology, 1979—84, Clin. Immunology and Immunopathology, 1979—, mem. editl. bd.Hybridoma Hybridoma, 1980—, Cancer Investigation, 1981—, Stem Cells, 1981—, Cancer Revs., 1984, Internat. Jour. of Cell Cloning, 1983—86, mem. adv. bd. Cancer Treatment Reports, 1976—80, assoc. editor Human Lymphocyte Differentiation, 1980—82; contbr. articles to profl. jours. Recipient Solomon Berson Achievement award, 1984, Robert Koch prize and medal, 1984. Fellow: AAAS; mem.: NAS, Assn. Am. Physicians, Am. Soc. Clin. Investigation, Am. Soc. Immunologists, Am. Soc. Hematology, Inst. of Medicine of NAS, Alpha Omega Alpha. Office: Dana-Farber Cancer Inst Divsn Tumor Immunology 44 Binney St Mayer 557 Boston MA 02115-6084 Office Phone: 617-632-3325. Business E-Mail: stuart_schlossman@dfci.harvard.edu.

SCHLOTHAUER, SHIRLEY NORTON, retired media consultant, writer; b. Denver, Jan. 29, 1925; d. Eldridge Stallard Norton and Fredricka Johanna Erickson; m. David F. Schlothauer, May 4, 1946; children: James (Jay) Norton, Julie Ann Pickering. Student, Washington State Coll., Pullman, 1944—45, Brown U.1974, Providence, RI, Harvard U. Ext., Cambridge, Mass., 1976—82. Passenger agt. Western Airlines, Denver, 1945—46; travel agt. Pentagon Combined Airline Ticket Office, Arlington, Va., 1951; regional and state chair edn. and health Mass. Hosp. Assn., Burlington, Mass., 1976—78, chair hosp. aux., 1978—80; owner S & N Co., Attleboro, Mass., 1982—86; ret. Trustee Sturdy Meml. Hosp., Attleboro, Mass., 1974—80. Of poems;, editor of newsletters and brochures and programs. Bd. mem., chair Coalition Buzzards Bay, New Bedford, Mass., 1990—91; mem. New Bedford YMCA, 1985—; vol. Eisenhower Campaign, 1951—76; candidate Mass. State Rep., Attleboro, 1980, 1982; mem. Attleboro, Mass. Rep. Com., 1975—85; vestryman Grace Ch., North Attleboro; bd. mem. Plymouth Bay Girl Scout Coun., Brockton, Mass., 1980—86, Westport River Water Shed Alliance, Mass., 1988—94; bd. dirs. Barker Found., Washington; com. mem. Am. Hosp. Assn. State Aux. Leaders. Named first woman bd. mem., Mass. Hosp. Assn. Mem.: Boston Mus. Fine Arts (sr. assoc., bd. mem. Ladies Com.), Westport Rivers and Meadows Book Group, Acoaxet Club (Westport, Mass.), Elephant Rock Beach Club (Westport, Mass.), North Purchase Club (past pres.). Achievements include initiated no smoking programs into hospitals; lobbied in US Congress for healthcare costs reform. Avocations: swimming, walking, travel, reading. Personal E-mail: hammerdfs@aol.com.

SCHLOTMAN, J. MICHAEL, food products executive; Grad., U. Ky., Lexington. CPA. With The Kroger Co., Cin., 1985—, v.p. fin. svcs. & control, 1995—2000, CFO, 2000—, sr. v.p., 2003—. Office: Kroger 1014 Vine St Cincinnati OH 45202 *

SCHLOTTERBECK, DAVID L., health products executive; BSEE, GM Inst.; MSEE, Purdue U.; grad., Stanford U. Exec. Inst., 1984. Exec. v.p., COO Nellcor, Inc., 1991—94; pres., CEO Vitalcom, Inc., 1995—97; pres., COO Pacific Sci. Co., 1997—98, ALARIS Med. Systems, 1999; CEO Clin. Technologies and Svcs. Cardinal Health, CEO Pharm. and Med. Products, 2006—. Office: Cardinal Health 7000 Cardinal Pl Dublin OH 43017

SCHLOTTERBECK, WALTER ALBERT, manufacturing executive, lawyer; b. NYC, Dec. 22, 1926; s. Albert Gottlob and Maria Louise (Fritz) S.; m. Pauline Elizabeth Hoerz, Sept. 2, 1951; children— Susan, Thomas, Paul. AB, Columbia U., 1949, LL.B., 1952. Bar: N.Y. 1953. Counsel Gen. Electric Co. (various locations), 1952-87; v.p., corp. counsel Gen. Electric Co., NYC, 1970-77, sec., 1975-76; gen. counsel Gen. Electric Co. (various locations), 1976-87, sr. v.p., 1977-87. Served with USNR, 1944-46. Home: 201 Overlake Dr E Medina WA 98039-5331

SCHLOW, MICHAEL, food service executive; b. Bklyn. Diploma, Acad. Culinary Arts N.J.; trained with Mark Straussman. Chef, owner Radius, Boston; chef Coco Pazzo, Le Madri; exec. chef Sapore di Mare, LI, 75 Main; owner Ariel & Michael; chef, owner Radius, Boston, 1999—. Author: (cookbooks) It's About Time: Great Recipes for Everyday Life, 2005. Named Best Chef (twice), Boston Mag.; recipient Culinary Award of Excellence, Robert Mondavi Winery, 2000, American Express Best Chef: Northeast award, James Beard Found., 2001. Office: Radius 8 High St Boston MA 02110

SCHLOZMAN, BRADLEY J., former prosecutor; b. Overland Park, Kans., Feb. 6, 1971; BA in Hist., U. Pa., 1993; JD, George Washington U. Law Sch., 1996. Clk. Chief US Dist. Judge G. Thomas VanBebber, Dist. Kans., US Ct. Appeals, 10th Cir.; atty. Howrey, Simon, & White, LLP, Washington, 1999—2001; counsel to dep. atty. gen. US Dept. Justice, 2001—03, dep. asst. atty. gen., 2003, acting asst. atty. gen., Civil Rights divsn., prin. dep. asst. atty. gen., Civil Rights divsn., interim US atty. (we. dist.) Mo., 2006—07. *

SCHLUB, TERESA RAE, minister; b. Oak Park, Ill., July 11, 1946; d. Robert Carl and Shirley Rae (Listhartke) Grupe. BA, Westmar Teikyo U., 1971; MDiv, Garrett Evangel. Seminary, Evanston, Ill., 1974. Ordained deacon United Meth. Ch., 1973, elder, 1978. Asst. minister First United Meth. Ch., Morris, Ill., 1974-76; minister Leaf River (Ill.) German Valley United Meth. Ch., 1976-82, East Jordan United Meth. Ch., Sterling, Ill., 1982-86, Paw Paw (Ill.) United Meth. Ch., 1986-89, Community United Meth. Ch., LaMoille, Ill., 1989-95, Capron (Ill.) United Meth. Ch., 1995—2000, North Boone Coop. Ministries, Poplar Grove, Ill., 1998—2000. Mem. alumni coun., sec. Garrett Evangel. Theol. Seminary, Evanston, 1974-76; mem. Conf. Bd. of Evangelism, 1974-76, founder, Schlub Ministries Bd. dirs. Green Hills coun. Girls Scouts U.S., Freeport, Ill., 1986-88, Lee County Red Cross, Dixon, Ill., 1986-89, Crossroads Counseling Ctr., Mendota, 1989-91; bd. dirs. Quad County Counseling Ctr., Princeton, 1991—, treas., 1993-94; mem. Ill. Home Extension Assn., Grundy, Ogle, Whiteside and Lee Counties, 1974-89; sec. DeKalb Dist. Com. Ordained Ministry; mem. Boone County Coun. Aging, 1997-2000, Boone County Planning Commn., 1998-2000; founder Schlub Ministries, Pathways to Paralegal, Kaplan U., 2005. Home: 4027 Albright Ln Rockford IL 61103 *Life becomes meaningful when one is able to become vulnerable and be willing to take risks. This becomes possible when one has faith in God and confidence in the self. It also helps to know and experience the love of others.*

SCHLUETER, DAVID ARNOLD, law educator; b. Sioux City, Iowa, Apr. 29, 1946; s. Arnold E. and Helen A. (Dettmann) S.; m. Linda L. Boston, Apr. 22, 1972; children: Jennifer, Jonathan. BA, Tex. A&M U., 1969; JD, Baylor U., 1971; LLM, U. Va., 1981. Bar: Tex. 1971, D.C. 1973, U.S. Ct. Mil. Appeals 1972, U.S. Supreme Ct. 1976. Legal counsel U.S. Supreme Ct., Washington, 1981—83; assoc. dean St. Mary's U., San Antonio, 1984—89, prof. law, 1986—, Hardy prof. trial advocacy, dir. advocacy programs, 2000—; reporter Fed. Adv. Com. on Criminal Rules, 1988—2005. Chmn. JAG adv. coun., 1974-75. Author: Military Criminal Justice: Practice and Procedure, 1982, 6th edit., 2004; (with others) Military Rules of Evidence Manual, 1981, 6th edit., 2006, Texas Rules of Evidence Manual, 1983, 7th edit., 2005, Texas Evidentiary Foundations, 1992, 3d edit., 2005, Military Evidentiary Foundations, 1994, 2d edit., 2000, Military Criminal Procedure Forms, 1997, 2d edit., 2003, Federal Evidence Tactics, 1997, Texas Rules of Evidence Trial Book, 2000; editor-in-chief: Emerging Problems Under the Federal Rules of Evidence, 3d edit., 1998; contbr. articles to legal publs. Maj. JAGC, U.S. Army, 1972-81. Fellow Am. Law Inst., Tex. Bar Found. (life), Am. Bar Found. (life); mem. ABA (vice-chmn. criminal justice sect. coun. 1991-94, vice-chmn. com. on criminal justice and mil. 1983-84, chmn. standing com. on mil. law 1991-92, mem. standing com. on armed forces law, chmn. editl. adv. bd., Criminal Justice Mag., 1989-91, 2000-), Tex. Bar Assn. Republican. Lutheran. Office: St Marys U Sch Law 1 Camino Santa Maria St San Antonio TX 78228-8603

SCHLUETER, JUNE MAYER, literature educator, writer; b. Passaic, NJ, Nov. 4, 1942; m. Paul Schlueter. BA in English magna cum laude, Fairleigh Dickinson U., 1970; MA in English, Hunter Coll., CCNY, 1973; PhD in English and Comparative Lit., Columbia U., 1977. Asst. prof. Lafayette Coll., Easton, Pa., 1977-84, assoc. prof., 1984-91, prof., 1991-92, Charles A. Dana prof., 1992—, head English dept., 1992-93; asst. to provost, 1986-90; acting provost., 1993-94; provost Lafayette Coll., Easton, Pa., 1994—2006. Fulbright prof. Gesamthochschule Kassel Univ., Fed. Republic Germany, 1978-79; chmn. Shakespeare Seminar Columbia U., 1989-91, 2004-06, exec. bd., 1989—; active NEH summer seminar for coll. profs., 1981, lectr. Commonwealth Partnership Summer Lit. Inst., 1985-87, dir. summer seminar for sch. tchrs., 1988, selection panel, 1989, 91, evaluator Instl. Grant Program, 1990. Author: Metafictional Characters in Modern Drama, 1979, The Plays and Novels of Peter Handke, 1981, Dramatic Closure: Reading the End, 1995; (with James K. Flanagan) Arthur Miller, 1987; (with James P. Lusardi) Reading Shakespeare in Performance: King Lear, 1990; editor: Feminist Rereadings of Modern American Drama, 1989, Modern American Drama: The Female Canon, 1990, Critical Essays: The Two Gentlemen of Verona, 1995; (with Paul Schlueter) The English Novel: Twentieth Century Criticism, Vol. 2: Twentieth Century Novelists, 1982, Modern American Literature, Supplement II, 1985, An Encyclopedia of British Women Writers, 1988, Francis A. March: Selected Writings of the First Professor of English, 2005; (with Enoch Brater) Approaches to Teaching Beckett's Waiting for Godot, 1991; (with Paul Nelsen) Acts of Criticism: Performance Matters in Shakespeare and His Contemporaries, 2006; co-editor Shakespeare Bull., 1983-2003; assoc. editor Stages, 1984-90; editl. bd. Studies in Am. Drama, 1945-Present, 1989—2000; editl. cons. Modern Drama, Theatre Jour., PMLA, Studies in Twentieth Century Lit., Shakespeare Quar., others; contbr. revs., essays to profl. jours. Bd. govs. Fairleigh Dickinson U., Rutherford, N.J., 1985-90, bd. dirs., Madison, N.J., 1997-2005; mem. adv. com. Lehigh Valley Ednl. Coop., 1988-90; selection panel German Acad. Exch. Svc., Bonn, 1979. Rsch. grantee Lafayette Coll., 1977-93, NEH summer rsch. grantee, 1990, DAAD summer rsch. grantee, 1991. Mem. MLA, Shakespeare Assn. Am., Internat. Shakespeare Assn., Coll. English Assn., Samuel Beckett Soc., AAUP, Columbia Shakespeare Seminar. Home: 123 High St Easton PA 18042-1609 Office: Lafayette Coll Lafayette College Easton PA 18042

SCHLUETER, LINDA LEE, law educator; b. LA, May 12, 1947; d. Dick G. Dulgarian and Lucille J. Boston; m. David A. Schlueter, Apr. 22, 1972; children: Jennifer, Jonathan. BA, U. So. Calif., 1969; JD, Baylor U., 1971. Bar: D.C. 1973, U.S. Supreme Ct. 1976, Ct. Mil. Appeals, 1990, Tex. 1997. Govt. rels. specialist hdqrs. U.S. Postal Svc., Washington, 1973-75; staff atty. Rsch. Group, Inc., Charlottesville, Va., 1979-81; pvt. practice Washington, 1981-83; asst. prof. law Sch. Law St. Mary's U., San Antonio, 1983-87, assoc. prof., 1987-90, prof., 1990-94. Presenter law Tex. Women Scholars Program, Austin, 1986, 87; bd. dirs Inst. for Comparative and Internat. Legal Rsch. Author: Punitive Damages, 1981-89, 5th edit., 2005, ann. suppls., Legal Research Guide: Patterns and Practice, 1986, 5th edit., 2006; editor Cmty. Property Jour., 1986-88, Cmty. Property Alert, 1989-90; editor Modern Legal Sys. Cyclopedia, 20 vols., 1990-2005, ann. suppls. Mem. ABA, Bexar County Women's Bar Assn., San Antonio Conservation Soc., Order of Barristers, Phi Alpha Delta. Republican. Lutheran.

SCHLUSSEL, JOSEPH LAZAR, business executive; b. Munkacs, Czechoslovakia, Apr. 19, 1935; came to U.S., 1951; m. Rose Ickowitz, June 16, 1960; children: Fay, Amy. Student, Bklyn. Coll., 1954-55, CCNY, 1956-59. Mgr. Gemcutters, NYC, 1960-61; broker Diamond Dealers Club, NYC, 1961-69; pres. The Diamond Registry Inc., NYC, 1969—. Editor, publisher Diamond Registry Bulletin, 1969—; cons. Nat. Westminster Bank USA, E.A.B., Merchants Bank, Bankers Trust, Solomon Bros.; lectr. in field. Columnist Nat. Jeweler, 1978, Jewel Mag., 1988—; guest on NBC Today, 1978, also CNN, BBC, NPR. Mem. Gemological Assn. Gt. Britain, Jewelers Vigilance Com., Jewelers Bd. of Trade, Diamond Dealers Club. Office: The Diamond Registry Inc 580 5th Ave New York NY 10036-4701 Office Phone: 212-575-0444. Personal E-mail: jschlussel@aol.com.

SCHLUSSEL, SEYMOUR, obstetrician, gynecologist; b. NYC, Mar. 22, 1928; s. Albert and Lilian Schlussel; 1 child, Ralph. BA, Johns Hopkins U., Balt., 1946; MD, NY Med. Coll.; NYC, 1951. Diplomate Am. Bd. Ob-gyn., Internat. Coll. Surgeons. Clin. prof. ob-gyn. NY Med. Coll., NYC, 1975—2006. Capt. US Army, 1952, Korea. Recipient Medal of Honor, NY Med. Coll., 1978. Fellow: ACS. Home: 3850 Hudson Manor Terr Bronx NY 10463

SCHLUTER, PETER MUELLER, electronics executive; b. May 24, 1933; s. Fredric Edward and Charlotte (Mueller) S.; m. Jaquelin Ambler Lamond, Apr. 18, 1970 (div. June 1990); children: Jane Randolph Amitsis, Charlotte Mueller Bashforth, Anne Ambler; m. Christine Moon Van Ness, Feb. 7, 1998. BME, Cornell U., 1956; postgrad., Harvard U. Grad. Sch. Bus. Adm, 1982. Sr. engr. Thiokol Chem. Corp., Brigham City, Utah, 1958-59; assoc. Porter Internat. Co., Washington, 1960-65, v.p., pres., treas., dir., 1966-70; pres., treas., dir. Zito Co., Derry, NH, 1970-72; internat. bus. cons. Washington, 1972-74; v.p., dir. Buck Engrng. Co. Inc. (now Lab-Volt Sys., Inc.), Farmingdale, NJ, 1975, pres., CEO, dir., 1975—. Mem. Rep. Inaugural Book and Program Com., 1969; cmty. adv. bd. Monmouth coun. Girl Scouts US, NJ; adv. coun. Monmouth U. Sch. Bus. Adminstrn.; bd. dirs. United Way of Monmouth County; trustee Monmouth Med. Ctr.; N.Am. rep., mem. presidium WORLDDIDAC, Bern, Switzerland, v.p., 1996—. Recipient Golden Osprey award So. Monmouth County C. of C., 1995. Fellow City and Guilds of London Inst. (hon.); mem. World Assn. Mfrs. and Distbrs. of Ednl. Materials (N.Am. rep.), Met. Club Washington, Sanctuary Golf Club Sanibel, Pi Tau Sigma. Home: 4 Quaker Ln Little Silver NJ 07739-1806 Office: PO Box 686 Farmingdale NJ 07727-0686 Business E-Mail: pschluter@labvolt.com.

SCHMALBECK, RICHARD LOUIS, dean, lawyer; b. Chgo., Dec. 31, 1947; s. George Louis and Betty Jeanne Schmalbeck; m. Linda Michaels; children: Suzanne, Sabine. AB in Econs. with honors, U. Chgo., 1970, JD, 1975. Bar: Ohio 1975, D.C. 1977. Asst. to dir. and economist Ill. Housing Devel. Authority, Chgo., 1971-73; assoc. Vorys, Sater, Seymour & Pease, Columbus, Ohio, 1975-76; spl. asst. to assoc. dir. for econs. and govt. Office of Mgmt. and Budget, Washington, 1976-77; assoc. Caplin & Drysdale, Washington, 1977-80, counsel, 2007—; assoc. prof. law Duke U., Durham, NC, 1980-84, vice chmn. acad. coun., 1984—85; dean U. Ill. Coll. Law, Champaign, 1990-93; prof. law Duke U., Durham, NC, 1984-90, 93—, vice chmn. acad. coun., 2001—02. Prof. U. Mich. Northwestern U, adv. Russian Fedn. Assoc. editor U. Chgo. Law Rev., 1974-75; contbr. articles to profl. jours, co-authored Schmalbeck Zelenak Federal income tax casebook Aspen Publishers. Mem. ABA (articles editor jour. 1977-80), Am. Law Inst., Phi Beta Kappa. assco.editor U. Chgo. Law Review. Office: Duke U Sch Law PO Box 90360 Durham NC 27708-0360

SCHMALE, NEAL E., utilities company executive; BS in Petroleum Engrng., Colo. Sch. Mines; LLD, Loyola U. With UNOCAL, sr. v.p., pres. petroleum products and chem. divsn., CFO; exec. v.p., CFO Sempra Energy, San Diego, 1997—2005, pres., COO, 2006—. Office: Sempra Energy 101 Ash St San Diego CA 92101-3017 *

SCHMALENSEE, RICHARD LEE, dean; b. Belleville, Ill., Feb. 16, 1944; s. Fred and Marjorie June (Veigel) S.; m. Edeth Diane Hawk, Aug. 19, 1967; children: Alexander Clayton, Nicholas Hawk. SB, MIT, 1965, PhD in econs., 1970. Asst. prof. econs. U. Calif., San Diego, 1970—74, assoc. prof. econs., 1974—77; instr. Sloan Sch. Mgmt., MIT, Cambridge, Mass., 1967—69, asst. prof., 1970, assoc. prof. applied econs., 1977-79, prof., 1979—, prof. dept. econs., 1986—, Gordon Y Billard Prof. of Econs. and Mgmt., 1988-99, dep. dean, 1996—98, interim dean, 1998, dean, 1998—2000, John C Head III Dean, 2001—; dir. Ctr. for Energy and Environ. Policy Rsch. MIT, Cambridge, Mass., 1991-99. Vis. prof. Harvard Bus. Sch., 1985—86, U. Louvain, Belgium, 1985, vis. assoc. prof., rsch. fellow, Belgium, 1973—74; vis. scholar dept. econs. Harvard U., 1980—81; editl. bd. Jour. of Econs. and Mgmt. Strategy, 1992—98; assoc. editor Internat. Jour. Indsl. Orgn., 1982—89, Jour. Econ. Perspectives, 1992—98; bd. editors Am. Econ. Review, 1982—86; assoc. editor Jour. Indsl. Econs., 1977—81, bd. editors, 1981—89; founding editor Regulation of Econ. Activity, 1978—89, co-editor, 1989—; mem. Pres.'s Coun. Econ. Advisers, 1989—91; bd. dirs. Am. Coun. for Capital Formation Ctr. for Policy Rsch., 1991—, environ. policy fellow, 1997—98; rsch. assoc. Nat. Bur. Econ. Rsch., 1992—; Internat. Rsch. Fellow Kiel Inst. World Econs., 2001—; spl. cons. NERA Econ. Cons., 1981—89, 1991—2004; bd. dirs. Internat. Securities Exch., 2000—, Internat. Data Group, 2004—; dir. LECG, LLC, 2004—. Author: The Economics of Advertising, 1972, Applied Microeconomics, 1973, The Control of Natural Monopolies, 1979; co-author: An Introduction to Applied Macroeconomics, 1973, Markets for Power, 1983, Economics, 1988, Paying with Plastic, 1999, Markets for Clean Air, 2000, Did Microsoft Harm Consumers? Two Opposing Views, 2000, Paying With Plastic, 2005, Invisible Engines, 2005, Catalyst Code, 2007; co-editor: The Empirical Renaissance in Industrial Economics, 1987, Handbook of Industrial Organization, 1989, Management: Inventing and Delivering Its Future, 2003. NSF grant, 1975-77, 81-83; Co-recipient Edward A. Hewett Prize, Am. Assn. for the Advancement of Slavic Studies, 1995 Fellow: AAAS, Econometric Soc.; mem.: Internat. Acad. Mgmt., Am. Econ. Assn. (nominating com. 1987, exec. com. 1993—95). Office: MIT Sloan Sch Mgmt 50 Memorial Dr Rm E52-473 Cambridge MA 02142-1347

SCHMALSTIEG, WILLIAM RIEGEL, retired Slavic languages educator; b. Sayre, Pa., Oct. 3, 1929; s. John William and Dorothy Augusta (Riegel) S.; m. Emily Lou Botdorf, Mar. 28, 1952; children: Linda, Roxanne. BA, U. Minn., 1950; postgrad., Columbia U., 1952; MA, U. Pa., 1951, PhD, 1956; PhD (hon.), Vilnius U., 1994. Instr. U. Ky., Lexington, 1956-59; asst. prof. Lafayette Coll., Easton, Pa., 1959-63; assoc. prof. U. Minn., Mpls., 1963-64; prof. Pa. State U., University Park, 1964—2002, head dept. Slavic langs., 1969-91. Mem. Internat. Commn. Balto-Slavic Linguistics, 1973—; appointed Edwin Erle Sparks prof. Slavic Lang., 1990. Author: (with L. Dambriunas and A. Klimas) An Introduction to Modern Lithuanian, 1966, 4th edit., 1990, 5th edit., 1993, reprinted as Beginner's Lithuanian, 1999, An Old Prussian Grammar, 1974, Studies in Old Prussian, 1976, Indo-European Linguistics, 1980, An Introduction to Old Church Slavic, 1976, 2d edit., 1983, A Lithuanian Historical Syntax, 1988; (with Warren Held and Janet Gertz) Beginning Hittite, 1988, A Student Guide to the Genitive of Agent in the Indo-European Languages, 1995, An Introduction to Old Russian, 1995, The Historical Morphology of the Baltic Verb, 2000; editor Gen. Linguistics, 1971-82; mem. editl. adv. bd. Jour. Indo-European Studies, Baltistica, Linguistica Baltica, Acta Linguistica Lithuanica, Archivum Lithuanicum, Lietuviu Kalbotyros Klausimai, Baltu Filologija. Served to 1st lt. U.S. Army, 1952-54. NEH grantee, 1978-79, Fulbright grantee and exch. scholar Acad. Scis., Vilnius, USSR, 1986; recipient Humanities medal Pa. State U., 1983, Friend of Lithuania award Knights of Lithuania, 1990, Lithuanian Govt. Mazvydas medal, 1997; named Disting. Alumnus Breck Sch., 1990. Mem.: Lithuanian Acad. Scis. (fgn.), Assn. Advancement Baltic Studies (pres. 1982—84). Episcopalian. Home: 814 Cornwall Rd State College PA 16803-1430 Personal E-mail: emily@leanonemily.com.

SCHMALTZ, DAVID G., lawyer; b. St. Paul, Aug. 2, 1968; BS cum laude in Civil Engring., Marquette U., 1991; JD cum laude, U. Wis., Madison, 1994. Bar: Wis. 1994, Minn. 1994, US Patent and Trademark Office. Ptnr. Merchant & Gould, P.C., Mpls. Named a Rising Star, Minn. Super Lawyers mag., 2006. Mem.: Wis. State Bar Assn., Minn. State Bar Assn., Minn. Intellectual Property Law Assn., Hennepin County Bar Assn., ABA (tech. and patent sects.). Office: Merchant & Gould PC 3200 IDS Ctr 80 S 8th St Minneapolis MN 55402 Office Phone: 612-332-5300. E-mail: dschmaltz@merchantgould.com. *

SCHMALZ, CARL NELSON, JR., artist, educator, art appraiser, printmaker; b. Ann Arbor, Dec. 26, 1926; s. Carl Nelson and Esther Dorothy (Fowler) S.; m. Dolores Irene Tourangeau, Dec. 2, 1950; children: Stephen Theodore (dec.), Mathew Nelson, Julia Irene. AB, Harvard U., 1948, MA, 1949, PhD, 1958; MA (hon.), Amherst Coll., 1969. Teaching fellow in fine arts Harvard U., Cambridge, Mass., 1950-52; asst. prof. Bowdoin Coll., Brunswick, Maine, 1953-62; curator, asst dir. Walker Art Mus., 1953—62; asst. prof. Harvard U., Cambridge, Mass., 1960; prof. Amherst Coll., 1962—95, prof. emeritus, 1995—; prof. Heartwood Coll. Art, Kennebunk, Maine, 2006—. Lectr. in field; workshop tchr. in field. Author: Watercolor Lessons from Eliot O'Hara, 1974, Watercolor Your Way, 1978, Finding and Improving Your Painting Style, 1986, paperback, 1992; co-suthor: Science Education in the United States: Issues, Crises and Priorities, 1990; author numerous essays and reviews; exhibited in one-man shows including Cambridge (Mass.) Art Assn., 1948, Laing Gallery, Portland, Maine, 1955, Amherst (Mass.) Coll., 1963, U. Mass., 1965, W.C. Rawls Mus., Va., 1972, Concord (Mass.) Art Assn., 1974, Govt. House, Hamilton, Bermuda, 1979, Jones Library, Amherst, Mass., 1979, The Arlington, Kennebunkport, Maine, 1980, Harmon-Meek Gallery, Naples, Fla., 1987, 91, 92, 98, Gallery at 6 Deering St., Portland, Maine, 1987, 91, Fretz Gallery, Portland, 1987-88, Marsh Gallery, Amherst Coll., 1995, Kennebunk Free Libr., 2005; exhibited in group shows including Jordan Marsh Co., 1947, 48, 50, 71-73, Colby Coll., 1958, Carnegie Inst., Pitts., 1963, FAR Gallery,

N.Y.C., 1964-68, Am. Watercolor Soc., 1966, 68, 70, Bowdoin Coll. Mus., 1973, Balt. Watercolor Soc., 1976, Boston Atheneum, 1979, Watercolor U.S.A. Honor Soc., 1989, 91, Maine Art Gallery, 1991, Rolly-Michaux Gallery, Boston, 1995, 2007, Kennebunk Free Libr., 2004; represented in permanent collections: Signet Soc., Cambridge, Mass., Walker Art Mus., Brunswick, Maine, Jones & Laughlin Steel Corp., Diners Club Am., Kalamazoo Art Center, Hampshire Coll., Zanesville Art Inst., Blue Cross/Blue Shield, Philharmonic Ctr. for the Arts, Naples, Fla., Springfield (Mo.) Art Mus., Amherst Coll., Bowdoin Coll., Hampshire Coll., Kalamazoo Art Inst., Springfield (Mo.) Art Mus.; work published in various pubs. including The Artist's Guide for Using Color, 1992, The Artist's Mag., 1994, Splash 3: Ideas and Inspirations, 1994. Mem. exec. bd. Interfaith Housing Corp., Amherst, 1966-76; pres. bd. trustees Amherst Day Sch., 1966-69; mem. Pelham Arts Lottery Coun., 1984-90; v.p. bd. dirs. Portland Mus. Art, 1957-62. Bacon fellow, 1951; recipient 1st prize watercolor Cambridge Art Assn. Ann., 1947, 1st prize for traditional watercolor Virginia Beach Boardwalk Show, 1965, South Mo. Trust purchase award Watercolor U.S.A., 1970, 1st prize watercolor 30th Ann. Kennebunk River Club Show, 1985, Purchase prize Watercolor U.S.A., 1997. Mem.: Coll. Art Assn., The Signet Soc., Watercolor U.S.A. Honor Soc. Democrat.

SCHMALZ, DOUGLAS J., agricultural company executive; BS, Univ. Minn. CPA. Public acct. Ernst & Young, 1975—85; fin. mgmt. positions Archer Daniels Midland Co., Decatur, Ill., 1985—86, controller, 1985—94, CFO, 1985—2002, sr. v.p., CFO, 2002—. Bd. mem. Cmty. Found. of Decatur Macon County, Ill., Decatur Mem. Hosp., Boys & Girls Clubs of Decatur, Decatur Area Arts Council. Office: Archer Daniels Midland Co 4666 E Fairies Pkwy PO Box 1470 Decatur IL 62526 Office Phone: 217-424-5200. *

SCHMALZ, ELIZABETH MOODY, cosmetics company executive; b. Pittsburgh, Pa., Feb. 18, 1951; d. Norman F. and Mary Edith (Husted) Moody; m. David A. Forsythe, Sept. 16, 1978 (div. 1988); m. Brian F. Schmalz, Dec. 16, 1989; children: Brian Norman, Elizabeth Mary. Studentt, Rumson Fair Haven, 1969; student, Vermont Coll., 1971, U. Arizona, 1973. Mgr. AGI Inc., NYC, 1974-75; mktg. mgr. Germaine Monteil Cosmetics Inc., NYC, 1976-79; product mgr. Estee Lauder Clinique Inc., NYC, 1980-86; v.p. Revlon Inc., NYC; v.p. corp. product Estee Lauder, NYC, 1986—2006, sr. v.p., 1986—93; prin., owner Elizabeth Forsyth Schmalz & Co., LLC, 1993—98; exec. v.p. Bath & Bodyworks, 1998—, exec. v.p. creative tech. innovations, 1998—; exec. v.p. creative tech. innovation Beauty Avenues, 2006—, exec. v.p. creative, tech., fragrance innovations NYC, 2006—. Mem. Cosmitsi Exec. Women, Fashion Group. Home: 15 Downing Hill Ln Colts Neck NJ 07722-1414 Office Phone: 212-904-8030. Business E-Mail: BSchmalz@beautyavenues.com.

SCHMALZRIED, MARVIN EUGENE, financial consultant; b. Dighton, Kans., Nov. 11, 1924; s. Carl D. and Marie M. (Bahm) S.; m. Jean Landino, Nov. 27, 1946 (dec.); children— Darlene, Candace, Cynthia, Derek, Valerie, Rebecca; m. Judith Reichardt Stuart, Oct. 23, 2004. BBA, Northwestern U., 1949; LL.B., U. Conn., 1955. Bar: Conn. bar 1955; C.P.A., Conn. Acct. Webster, Blanchard & Willard, CPA's (name changed to Price Waterhouse & Co.), Hartford, Conn., 1950-55; contr., asst. treas. J.B. Williams Co., Glastonbury, Conn., 1955-57; treas., sec. Curtis 1000, Inc. (name changed to Am Bus. Products, Inc.), Atlanta, 1957-61; asst. to pres. Wyeth Labs., NYC, 1961-63, comptroller, 1964-67, v.p., 1967-72, sr. v.p., 1972-84; pres. Venda Vid, Inc., NYC, 1986-90; sr. v.p. View-Master Ideal Group, Inc., NYC, 1987-90; exec. v.p. Strategics Inc., 1993-95. Recipient Gold medal Conn. Soc. C.P.A.'s, 1953 Mem. AICPA, ABA, Old Greenwich Friday Evening Reading Soc. (pres.) Clubs: Darien Country, Bent Tree Country. Home and Office: 4874 Cherry Laurel Cir Sarasota FL 34241-6442

SCHMANDT-BESSERAT, DENISE, archaeologist, educator; b. Ay, France, Aug. 10, 1933; came to U.S., 1965, naturalized, 1970; d. Victor and Jeanne (Crabit) Besserat; m. Jurgen Schmandt, Dec. 27, 1956; children: Alexander, Christopher, Phillip. Ed., Ecole du Louvre, 1965. Rsch. fellow in Near Eastern Archaeology Peabody Mus. Harvard U., Cambridge, Mass., 1969-71; fellow Radcliffe Inst., Cambridge, 1969-71; asst. prof. Middle Eastern studies U. Tex., Austin, 1972-81, assoc. prof., 1981-88, prof., 1988—2004; acting chief curator U. Tex. Art Mus., 1978—79. Vis. assoc. prof. U. Calif., Berkeley, 1987-88; curator Legacy of the Middle East exhbn. Jeddah (Saudi Arabia) Hist. Preservation Dept. Author: Before Writing, 1992, How Writing Came About, 1996, History of Counting, 1999, When Writing Met Art, 2007; adv. editor Tech. and Culture, 1978-92; editl. adv. bd. Archaeology Odyssey, 2003-06; mem. editl. bd. Written Communication, 1993-95, Visible Lang., 1985—, Explorations in Media Ecology, 2001-05, Ancient Adminstrn., 2001; mem. editl. bd. Near Eastern Archaology, 2005—; contbr. articles to profl. jours. Recipient Kayden Nat. U. Press Book award, 1992, Robert W. Hamilton Author award, 1998, Walter J. Ong award Media Ecology Assn., 2004; named in Am. Scientist, 1999; Wenner-Gren Found. grant, 1970-71, NEA grant, 1974-75, 77-78, ACLS grant, 1984, Deutscher Akademischer Austauschdienst grant, 1986, NEH grant, 1992; NEH fellow, 1979-80, U. Wis. Inst. for Rsch. in Humanities fellow, 1984-85, USIA, Am. Ctr. Oriental Rsch. fellow, 1994-95, 97, 2001, Malone fellow 1997, 99, 2005, Weeks fellow Humanities Rsch. Ctr. Stanford U., 2003—. Mem. Am. Oriental Soc., Archeol. Inst. Am. (governing bd. 1983-89), Am. Anthropol. Assn., Am. Schs. of Oriental Rsch., Centro Internat. Rsch. Archeologiche Anthropologiche e Storiche (Rome). Business E-Mail: dsb@mail.utexas.edu.

SCHMEISER, CYNTHIA BOARD, educational organization executive; BA in Psychology and Elem. Edn., U. Iowa, MA, PhD in Ednl. Psychology. Rsch. assoc. Am. Coll. Testing Program (ACT), Iowa City, 1973, v.p. devel., sr. v.p. rsch. and devel., 2003—06, pres., COO edn. divsn., 2006—. Bd. trustees Am. Coll. Edn. Chair bd. dirs. United Way of Johnson County; outreach coord. Family Concert Series; bd. dirs. Mercy Hosp.—Iowa City. Office: ACT 500 ACT Dr PO Box 168 Iowa City IA 52243-0168 E-mail: schmeiser@act.org. *

SCHMELTZER, EDWARD, lawyer; b. NYC, Aug. 22, 1923; s. Harry A. and Julia (Hoffman) S.; m. Elizabeth Ann Cooper, June 19, 1949; children: Henry Cooper, Elizabeth Sabine. BA, Hunter Coll., NYC, 1950; MA, Columbia U., NYC, 1951; JD, George Washington U., Washington, 1954. Bar: DC 1954, U.S. Supreme Ct 1958. Economist PHA, 1951-53; econ. cons., 1953-54; trial atty. Fed. Maritime Bd. Maritime Adminstrn., 1955-60; dir. bur. domestic regulation Fed. Maritime Commn., 1961-66, mng. dir., 1966-69; ptnr. Morgan, Lewis & Bockius, 1969-76, Schmeltzer, Aptaker & Shepard, 1976—99, of counsel, 2001—06; sr. v.p., gen. counsel Sea Star Line, Jacksonville, 1999—2001. US rep. 12th Diplomatic Conf. on Internat. Maritime Law, Brussels, 1967, 13th Diplomatic Conf., Brussels, 1968. Mem. bd. editors: Jour. Maritime Law and Commerce; Contbr. articles to profl. jours. Served with USAAF, 1943-46. Recipient Fed. Maritime Commn.; Distinguished Service award, 1969. Mem. Maritime Adminstrv. Bar Assn. (pres. 1971-73), Cosmos Club (Washington). Office: 10412 Buckboard Pl Potomac MD 20854-3805 Office Phone: 301-299-9030. Business E-Mail: eacs@comcast.com.

SCHMELZ, BRENDA LEA, paralegal; b. Washington, Mo., June 13, 1958; d. Edward G. and Wilma D. (Hektor) R.; m. Jan M. Schmelz, Oct. 7, 1978; children: Edward L., Brent T. Secretarial sci. cert. with honors, East Ctrl. Coll., Union, Mo., 1977; AAS in Ct. Reporting, St. Louis CC, 2003. Sec., paralegal Mittendorf & Mittendorf, Union, Mo., 1976-83, Eckelkamp, Eckelkamp, Wood & Kuenzel, Washington, 1983—2002; ct. reporter Franklin County Cir. Ct., Union, 2004—. Mem. legal secretarial adv. bd. East Ctrl. Coll., 1978, chmn., 1987; mem. legal secretarial adv. bd. State Fair C.C., 1995. Mem. Nat. Assn. Ct. Reporters, Nat. Assn. Legal Secs. (mem. certifying bd. 1997-2000, chmn. 1998-2000, Jett award 1999), Mo. Ct. Reporters Assn., Mo. Assn. Legal Secs. (pres. 1994-96, pres-elect 1992-94, v.p. 1986, 89-91, sec. 1984-86, 89-90, dir. pub. rels. 1987-89, parliamentarian 1998-99, Legal Sec. of Yr. 1987), Franklin County Legal Secs. (pres. 1989-92, Legal Sec. of Yr. 1986, 95), Ill. Ct. Reporters Assn., Union of Women Today, Phi Beta Kappa. Republican. Roman Catholic. Home: 1792 Oak Parc Union MO 63084-3607 Office: Franklin County Circuit Ct Div I 300 E Main St Union MO 63084 Home Phone: 636-583-4240; Office Phone: 636-583-6307. Personal E-mail: biendaschmelz@sbcglobal.net.

SCHMELZER, JANET L., history professor, researcher; b. Milw., Dec. 7, 1950; d. Robert Benjamin and Jessie Mae (Brady) Schmelzer; m. Charles H. Woods III, June 28, 1998. BA, Tex. Christian U., Ft. Worth, 1973, MA in History, 1975, PhD in Am. History, 1978. Instr. Temple (Tex.) Jr. Coll., Tex., 1978—79; asst. prof. Sam Houston State U., Huntsville, Tex., 1979—80; vis. asst. prof. Tex. Tech. U., Lubbock, 1980—82; asst. prof. U. Nebr., Lincoln, 1982—83; prof. Tarleton State U., Stephenville, 1983—. Author: Where the West Begins, 1985; co-author: Texas USA, 1996. Pres. Southwestern Hist. Assn., 1992—93, Erath County Women's Plit. Caucus, 1987—88.. Fellow, Eleanor Roosevelt Inst., 1980; Moody fellow, Lyndon Baines Johnson Found., 1979. Mem.: Tex. Faculty Assn. (pres. 2004—), East Tex. Hist. Assn., So. Hist. Assn., Tex. State Tchrs. Assn. (bd. dirs.), Tex. State Hist. Assn. (Disting. Spkr. 2005, Coral H. Tullis award 1993), Southwestern Social Sci. Assn. (pres. 2001—02), Phi Alpha Theta (internat. adv. bd. 1995—99), Delta Zeta. Democrat. Methodist. Office: Tarleton State Univ Stephenville TX 76402

SCHMEMANN, SERGE, journalist; b. Paris, Apr. 12, 1945; arrived in U.S., 1951; s. Rev Alexander and Juliana (Ossorguine) Schmemann; m. Mary Schidlovsky, Sept. 13, 1970; children: Anne, Alexander, Nathalie. BA cum laude, Harvard U., 1967; MA, Columbia U., 1971; LittD (hon.), Middlebury Coll., 1995. Desk editor AP, NYC, 1972—75, UN corr., 1975—77, South Africa corr., 1977—79, Moscow corr., 1979—80; Moscow bur. chief NY Times, 1980—87, 1991—95, Bonn bur. chief, 1987—90, Jerusalem bur. chief, 1995—98, dep. fgn. editor, 1998—2001, UN bur. chief, 2001—02; editor, editl. page Internat. Herald Tribune, Paris, 2003—. Author: Echoes of a Native Land: Two Centuries of a Russian Village, 1997, When the Wall Came Down: The Berlin Wall and the Fall of Communism, 2006; contbr. articles to profl. publs. With US Army, 1968—70, Vietnam. Recipient Hal Boyle award, Overseas Press Club, 1986, Pulitzer Prize for coverage of German reunification, 1991, Emmy award for Outstanding Individual Achievement in a Craft, Nat. TV Acad., 2003. Mem.: Phi Beta Kappa. Avocations: carpentry, piano. Office: NY Times 229 W 43rd St New York NY 10036-3959 also: Internat Herald Tribune, 6 bis, rue des Graviers 92521 Paris France Office Phone: 33 1 4143 91 80. E-mail: serge@nytimes.com.

SCHMERLING, ERWIN ROBERT, counselor, retired physicist; b. Vienna, July 28, 1929; came to U.S., 1955, naturalized, 1962; s. Heinrich H. and Lily (Goldsmith) S.; m. Esther M. Schmerling, Apr. 5, 1957; children: Susan D., Elaine M. BA, Cambridge U., 1950, MA, 1954, PhD in Radio Physics, 1958; grad., Advanced Mgmt. Program, Harvard, 1969, Fed. Exec. Inst., 1975. Asst. prof. elec. engring. Pa. State U., University Park, 1955-60, assoc. prof., 1960-62, 63-64; staff scientist NASA-Hdqrs., Washington, 1962-63, program chief ionospheric physics, magnetospheric physics, space plasma physics, 1964-82; asst. dir. space and earth scis. Goddard Space Flight Ctr., NASA, Greenbelt, Md., 1984-86; chief data system scientist Office Space Science and Applications NASA Hdqrs., Washington, 1986-88; SAIS program scientist NASA, Washington, 1988-89; data system scientist solar system exploration div. NASA Hdqrs., Washington, 1989-90, program mgr. astrophysics data systems, 1991-94; counselor Svc. Corps of Retired Execs. (SCORE), 1995—98. Mem. U.S. coms. III and IV Internat. Sci. Radio Union, 1985—, sec. U.S. Com. III, 1966-69, chmn., 1969-72; chmn. subcom. C1 Com. Space Rsch. (COSPAR), 1984-88; mem. Adv. Group Aerospace R&D, NATO, 1978-85; vis. scholar Stanford U., 1983; cons. RCA, Gen. Electric, 1959-62. Contbr. papers to profl. jours. Recipient medal for contbns. to internat. geophys. programs, Soviet Geophys. Soc., 1985. Fellow IEEE (mem. wave propagation standards com.); mem. Am. Geophys. Union, AAAS, Sigma Xi. Home: 2101 Wind Ln Wilmington DE 19810 E-mail: erwinschmerling@comcast.net.

SCHMERTMANN, JOHN HENRY, civil engineer, educator, consultant; b. NYC, Dec. 2, 1928; s. Johannes Conrad Schmertmann and Margaret Anna-Marie (Carstens) Schmertmann Ottesen; m. Pauline Anne Grange, Aug. 11, 1956; children: Carl, Gary, Neil, Joy. BSC.E., MIT, 1950; MSC.E., Northwestern U., 1954, PhD in Civil Engring., 1962. Registered profl. engr., Fla. Soils engr. Mueser Rutledge Cons. Engrs., NYC, 1951-54; soils engr. C.E., U.S. Army, Wilmette, Ill., 1954-56; asst. prof. civil engring. U. Fla., Gainesville, 1956-62, assoc. prof., 1962-65, prof., 1965-79, adj. prof., prof. emeritus; prin. Schmertmann & Crapps, Inc., Gainesville, 1979-97, LoadTest Inc., Gainesville, 1991—, Office John H. Schmertmann Inc., Gainesville, 1997—. Postdoctoral fellow Norwegian Geotech. Inst., Oslo, 1962-63; vis. scientist div. bldg. research NRC Can., Ottawa Ont., 1971-72 Author numerous profl. papers Fellow ASCE (br. pres. 1972, Collingwood prize 1956, Norman medal 1971, State of the Art award 1977, Middlebrooks award 1981, Terzaghi lectr. 1989), Fla. Engring. Soc.; mem. Nat. Acad. Engring. Lutheran. Avocation: sport fishing. Office: Office John H Schmertmann Inc 4509 NW 23rd Ave Ste 19 Gainesville FL 32606-6570 Home Phone: 352-378-6414; Office Phone: 352-378-2792.

SCHMERTZ, ERIC JOSEPH, lawyer, educator, commissioner; b. NYC, Dec. 24, 1925; married; 4 children. AB, Union Coll., 1948, LL.D. (hon.), 1978; cert., Alliance Francaise, Paris, 1948; JD, NYU, 1954. Bar: N.Y. 1955. Internat. rep. Am. Fedn. State, County and Mcpl. Employees, AFL-CIO, NYC, 1950-52; asst. v.p., dir. labor tribunals Am. Arbitration Assn., NYC, 1952-57, 59-60; indsl. relations dir. Metal Textile Corp. subs. Gen. Cable Corp., Roselle, NJ, 1957-59; exec. dir. N.Y. State Bd. Mediation, 1960-62, corp. dir., 1962-68; labor-mgmt. arbitrator, NYC, 1962—; mem. faculty Hofstra U. Sch. Bus., 1962-70; prof. Hofstra U. Sch. Law, 1970—. Edward F. Carlough disting. prof. labor law, 1981-98, dean Sch. Law, 1982-89, disting. prof. emeritus of law, 1998—; of counsel The Dweck Law Firm, NYC, 1999—; commr. labor rels. City of N.Y., 1990-91. Scholar-in-residence Pace U. Sch. Law, 1998-2000, Disting. Practioner in residence, 2005—; 1st Beckley lectr. in bus. U. Vt., 1981; bd. dirs. Wilshire Oil Co.; mem. N.Y. State Pub. Employment Rels. Bd., 1991-97; cons. and lectr. in field. Co-author: (with R.L. Greenman) Personnel Administration and the Law, 1978; contbr. chpts. to books, articles to profl. jours., to profl. law confs., seminars and workshops. Mem. numerous civic orgns. Served to lt. USN, 1943-46. Recipient Testimonial award Southeast Republican Club, 1969; Alexander Hamilton award Rep. Law Students Assn.; Eric J. Schmertz Disting. Professorship Pub. Law and Pub. Svc. established Hofstra Law Sch., 1993. Mem. Nat. Acad. Arbitrators, Am. Arbitration Assn. (law com., Whitney North Seymour Sr. medal 1984), Fed. Mediation and Conciliation Svc., N.Y. Mediation Bd., N.J. Mediation Bd., N.J. Pub. Employment Rels. Bd., Hofstra U. Club, Princeton Club. Office: The Dweck Law Firm 75 Rockefeller Plz New York NY 10019 Office Phone: 212-687-8200. Business E-Mail: schmertz@dwecklaw.com.

SCHMERTZ, MILDRED FLOYD, editor-in-chief, writer; b. Pitts., Mar. 29, 1925; d. Robert Watson and Mildred Patricia (Floyd) S B.Arch., Carnegie Mellon U., 1947; M.F.A., Yale U., 1957. Archtl. designer John Schurko, Architect, Pitts., 1947-55; assoc. editor Archtl. Record, NYC, 1957-65, sr. editor, 1965-80, exec. editor, 1980-85, editor-in-chief, 1985-90. Vis. lectr. Yale Sch. Architecture, 1979— Editor, contbr.: New Life for Old Buildings, 1982; contbr. articles to profl. jours.; chpts. to books. Bd. mgrs. Jr. League, City of N.Y., 1964-65; commr. N.Y. Landmarks Preservation Commn., 1988-92 Fellow AIA; mem. Mcpl. Art Soc. N.Y., Century Assn. (N.Y.C.) Home and Office: 310 E 46th St Apt 15E New York NY 10017-3002 Office Phone: 212-661-7831.

SCHMETTERER, ROBERT ALLEN, advertising executive; b. NYC, Nov. 23, 1943; s. Robert Mayer and Rosalie (Fernandez) S.; children: Adam, Tyler; m. Stacy Lynn Chiarello, Sept. 26, 1987. BS, Fairleigh Dickinson U., 1967, MBA, 1970. Sales promotion mgr. Brit. Motor Corp., Leonia, NJ, 1963-68; market research dir. Volvo, Rockleigh, NJ, 1968-71; v.p. market rsch. Scali, McCabe, Sloves Inc., NYC, 1971-73, sr. v.p. dir. account service, 1974-79, exec. v.p., chief oper. officer, mng. dir., 1979-84; pres., chief exec. officer/worldwide HCM, NYC and Paris, 1984-87; pres., ptnr. Messner Vetere Berger McNamee Schmetterer, NYC, 1987—97; chmn., CEO Euro RSCG Worldwide, NYC, 1997—2004; pres., COO Havas, 2002—04. Bd. dirs. N.Y.C. Partnership, 1987. Author: Leap: A Revolution in Creative Business Strategy, 2003. Bd. dirs. NYC Partnership, 1985—87, NYC Hist. House Trust, 2005—, J Mandle Performance, Inc., chmn. Mem.: Coral Beach and Tennis Club, Ocean Reef Club, NY Yacht Club. Address: 24 Dockside Ln PMB398 Key Largo FL 33037

SCHMETZER, ALAN DAVID, psychiatrist; b. Louisville, Sept. 3, 1946; s. Clarence Frederick and Catherine Louise (Wootan) Schmetzer; m. Janet Lynn Royce, Aug. 25, 1968; children: Angela Beth, Jennifer Lorraine. BA, Ind. U., 1968, MD, 1972. Diplomate Am. Bd. Psychiatry and Neurology, subsplty. cert. in addiction psychiatry; diplomate Am. Psychotherapy Assn., Am. Bd. Forensic Med. Examiners, Assn. Convulsive Therapy. Intern Ind. U. Hosps., Indpls., 1972-73, resident, 1972-75; dir. clinics PCI, Inc., Anderson, Beech Grove, Kokomo, Ind., 1975-79; psychiat. cons. Cmty. Addiction Svcs. Agy., Indpls., 1975-80; instr. psychiatry in primary care Family Practice Residency Programs St. Francis Hosp., St. Vincent's Hosp. and Ind. U. Hosps., Indpls., 1975-91; med. dir. Child Guidance Clinic of Marion County, Indpls., 1980-81; chmn. psychiatry dept. St. Francis Hosp., Beech Grove, 1980-82; med. dir. Crisis Intervention Unit Midtown Mental Health Ctr., 1980-90, dir., 1990-96, med. dir., 1996-98; coord. emergency psychiat. svcs. Ind. U. Med. Ctr., Indpls., 1980-90, asst. prof. psychiatry, 1975-94, assoc. prof. psychiatry, 1994—2002, prof. psychiatry, 2002—, coord. psychiat. edn. of med. students, 1989-95, asst. chmn. dept. psychiatry, 1993-96, dir. psychiat. edn., 1995-97, vice chmn. edn. dept. psychiatry, 1997—, dir. psychiatry residency tng., 1998—, dir. addiction psychiatry residency tng., 1999—, dir. psychiat. mgmt., 2007—; chief psychiatry Wishard Meml. Hosp., 1990-98; chief rsch. unit Larue D. Carter Meml. Hosp., 2007—. Primary psychiat. cons. Ind. Dept. Mental Health and Addiciton, 1988-89; med. dir. Ind. Divsn. Mental Health, 2001-03; supt. Larue D. Carter Meml. Hosp., 2003-05; examiner Am. Bd. Psychiatry and Neurology; addiction psychiatrist Midtown Mental Health Ctr., 2006-07; dir. rsch. unit Carter Meml. Hosp., 2007—; med. dir. Ind. U. Psychiat. Mgmt., Inc., 2007—. Contbr. articles to profl. jours. Maj. Ind. N.G., 1972-79. Decorated Army Commendation medal, 1978; recipient Residents award for outstanding teaching, 1985, 90, 97, 2003, Roeske Excellence in Teaching award, 1992, Med. Student Psychiatry Clin. Tchg. award, 2000, Irma Bland Residency Tchg. award, 2005, Alumnus of the Yr., Silver Creek H.S., 2005, Eugene E. Levitt svc. award in psychology, 2003, Exemplary Psychiatrist award NAMI, 2004, named one of Best Doctor's in Am., 2003-04, 06-07, Am. Top Psychiatrists, 2006. Fellow Am. Psychiat. Assn., Am. Ortho-psychiat. Assn.; mem. AMA (Physicians Recognition award 1978-), Ind. Med. Assn., Indpls. Med. Soc., Ind. Psychiat. Soc. (pres. 1989-90, 97-98), Am. Orthopsychiat. Assn., Am. Acad. Clin. Psychiatry, Univ. Faculty Club Indpls. (v.p. 1999-2000, pres. 2000-01), Athenaeum Turnverein Club, Alpha Phi Omega, Phi Beta Pi, Psi Chi, Alpha Epsilon Delta. Presbyterian. Office: Dept Psychiatry 1111 W 10th St PB-A212 Indianapolis IN 46202-4800 Office Phone: 317-274-1224. Business E-Mail: aschmetz@iupui.edu.

SCHMID, CHARLES ERNEST, acoustical engineer, academic administrator; b. Jamaica, NY, Oct. 30, 1940; s. Edson Scofield Schmid and Agatha Sofia Zimmermann; m. Linda Dexter, June 18, 1966; children: Andrew, Jenny. BSEE, Cornell U., 1963; MSEE, U. Conn., 1968; PhD, U. Wash., 1977. Systems engr. Gen. Dynamics/Electric Boat, Groton, Conn., 1963-66; fellow Honeywell, Seattle, 1966-90; exec. dir. Acoustical Soc. Am., Woodbury, N.Y., 1990—. With physics vis. com. U. Wash., 1999—. Numerous citizen com., Bainbridge Island, Wash. Congl. Sci. Engring. fellow AAAS, Washington, 1985-86. Fellow Acoustical Soc. Am.; mem. Am. Inst. Physics (gov. bd. 1991—, exec. com. 1993-99, 2003—). Achievements include research in simulation and analysis of underwater sound. Office: Acoustical Soc of Am 2 Huntington Quadrangle Melville NY 11747-4501

SCHMID, JOHN A., musician, voice educator; b. Danville, Ill., Oct. 27, 1944; s. Herman A. and Marjorie E. Schmid; m. Kara Sue Schmid, Sept. 20, 1986; 1 child, Jordan Olivia. MusB, Butler U., 1968; MusM, Jordan Coll., 1969; student of pvt. voice, Indiana U., 1979. Accompanist Butler U., Indpls., 1968—70, voice instr., 1970—87; dir. music and studios Fairview Presbyn., Indpls., 1982—; chorus master Indpls. Opera, 1984—; dir. Indpls. Matinee Musicale Ensemble, 2003—. Voice tchr., coach Butler U., 1970—82; dir. Fairview Studies, 1982—. Mem.: Nat. Assn. Tchrs. of Singing, Nat. Assn. Tchrs. Music, Presbyn. Assn. of Musicians, Nat. Choral Dir. Assn. Presbyn. Avocations: cooking, opera. Office: Fairview Studios 4609 N Capitol Ave Indianapolis IN 46208 Office Phone: 317-253-5982. Business E-Mail: jschmid@fairviewpresbyterian.org.

SCHMID, JOHN HENRY, JR., lawyer; b. Erie, Pa., May 11, 1944; s. John Henry Sr. and Margery (St. Lawrence) S.; m. Carol Christine Imig, July 1, 1967; children: Christine Catherine, Heidi Imig. BA, Beloit Coll., Wis., 1966; JD, U. Wis., 1969. Bar: Wis. 1969, U.S. Dist. Ct. (we. dist.) Wis. 1969, U.S. Ct. Appeals (7th cir.) 1993, U.S. Supreme Ct. 1993. Sr. ptnr. Axley Brynelson, Madison, Wis., 1969—. Emergency med. technician Village of Maple Bluff, Madison, 1977-84, trustee, 1985-89. Mem. Assn. Def. Trial Attys., Civil Trial Counsel Wis. Avocations: fishing, golf, travel. Home: 802 Farwell Dr Madison WI 53704-6034 Office: Axley Brynelson 2 E Mifflin St Madison WI 53703-2889 Office Phone: 608-257-5661. Business E-Mail: jschmid@axley.com.

SCHMID, MARK DANIEL, music educator; s. Rudolf Otto Dimitri and Renate Schmid; m. Jennifer Ann Ness, July 27, 1997. PhD, Northwestern U., Evanston, Ill., 1997. Assoc. prof. Mansfield U., Pa., 1998—. Recipient Tower award, Mansfield U. Libr., 2006; fellow, Searle Ctr. Tchg. Excellence, Northwestern U., 1995. Mem.: Coll. Music Soc. (assoc.), Am. Musicological Soc. (assoc.), Phi Mu Alpha. Home: 140 Wakefield Terr Mansfield PA 16933 Home Phone: 570-662-1328; Office Phone: 570-662-4737.

SCHMID, PATTI A., library director; d. Harold and Anna May Schmid. BA, Drew U., Madison, NJ, 1971, M in Theol. Studies, 1975; MS in Libr. Sci., Cath. U. of Am., Washington, 1980. Libr. ops. cons., procurement analyst Bus. Mgmt. Rsch. Assocs., Arlington, Va., 1980—82, info. and systems mgr., 1983—89; bibliographic and quality assurance profl. Raven Systems and Rsch., Inc., Washington, 1982; dir. rsch. and info. mgmt. ODS Inc., Silver Spring, Md., 1984—92; cost and billings mgr. OAO Corp., Greenbelt, Md., 1989—91; tech. asst. III-libr. Cumberland County Coll. Libr., Vineland, NJ, 1992—97, head libr., 1997—. Adj. faculty Cumberland County Coll., Vineland, 1997—; presenter in field. Editor: (glossary) Federal Contracting Handbook. Mem.: NAFE, AAUW, Cumberland Librs. United Electronic Sys., Virtual Academic Libr. Environment, Coun. NJ

Coll. and Univ. Libr. Dirs., NJ Edn. Assn., NJ Libr. Assn. Office: Cumberland County Coll Libr 3322 College Dr Vineland NJ 08360 Home Phone: 856-692-7269; Office Phone: 856-691-8600. Office Fax: 856-691-1969.

SCHMID, RUDI (RUDOLF SCHMID), retired internist, educator, academic administrator; b. Switzerland, May 2, 1922; arrived in U.S., 1947, naturalized, 1954; s. Rudolf and Bertha (Schiesser); m. Sonja D. Wild, Sept. 17, 1949. BS, Gymnasium Zurich, 1941; MD, U. Zurich, 1947; PhD, U. Minn., 1954. Intern U. Calif. Med. Ctr., San Francisco, 1948—49; resident medicine U. Minn., 1949—52, instr., 1952—54; rsch. fellow biochemistry Columbia U., 1954—55; investigator NIH, Bethesda, Md., 1955—57; assoc. medicine Harvard Med. Sch., 1957—59; asst. prof. Harvard U., 1959—62; prof. medicine U. Chgo., 1962—66, U. Calif., San Francisco, 1966—91, recall prof. medicine, 1991—2004, prof. emeritus, 2005, dean Sch. Medicine, 1983—89, assoc. dean internat. rels., 1989—95. Cons. to U.S. Army surgeon gen. NIH; hon. prof. Peking Union Med. Coll., Shanghai Second Med. U., Xian U. of Med. Sci., Jillin U. Medicine. Mem. editl. bd.: Blood, 1962—75, Jour. Clin. Investigation, 1965—70, Gastroenterology, 1965—70, Jour. Investigative Dermatology, 1968—72, Annals Internal Medicine, 1975—79, Procs. Soc. Exptl. Biology and Medicine, 1974—84, Chinese Jour. Clin. Scis., Jour. Lab. Clin. Medicine, 1991—, Hepatology Rsch. (Japan), 1993—, World Jour. Gastroenterology (China), 2002—, cons. editor: Gastroenterology, 1981—86. With Swiss Army, 1943—47. Master: ACP; fellow: Royal Coll. Physicians, N.Y. Acad. Scis., Am. Acad. Arts and Scis.; mem.: NAS, German-Am. Acad. Coun. (exec. com. 1992—99), Leopoldina/German Acad. Sci., Swiss Acad. Med. Scis., Am. Assn. Study Liver Disease (pres. 1965), Am. Gastroenterol. Assn., Am. Soc. Hematology, Am. Soc. Biol. Chemistry and Molecular Biology, Am. Soc. Clin. Investigation, Assn. Am. Physicians (pres. 1986), Internat. Assn. Study Liver (pres. 1980—82), IOM (sr.). Achievements include research in biochemistry, metabolism of hemoglobin, heme, prophyrins, bile pigments, liver and muscle. Home: 211 Woodland Rd Kentfield CA 94904-2631 Personal E-mail: s.d.schmid@comcast.net.

SCHMID, SIGI, professional soccer coach; b. Tuebingen, West Germany, Mar. 20, 1953; came to U.S., 1962; children: Erik, Kurt, Kyle. BS in Econs., UCLA, 1976; MA in Bus. Adminstrn., U. So. Calif. CPA, Calif. Coach UCLA Bruins, 1980-99; head coach L.A. Galaxy, 1999—. Office: L A Galaxy 18400 Avalon Blvd 200 Carson CA 90746-2172

SCHMIDHAUSER, JOHN RICHARD, retired political science professor; b. NYC, Jan. 3, 1922; s. Richard J. and Gertrude (Grabinger) S.; m. Thelma Lorraine Ficker, June 9, 1952; children: Steven, Paul, Thomas, John C., Martha, Sara, Susan. BA with honors, U. Del., 1949; MA, U. Va., 1952, PhD, 1954. Instr. U. Va., 1952-54; prof. constl. law U. Iowa, 1954-64, prof. polit. sci., 1967-73, U. So. Calif., 1973-92, prof. emeritus, 1993—. Mem. 89th Congress 1st dist. Iowa.; research fellow Research Inst. on Jud. Process, Social Sci. Research Council, 1958; sr. fellow law and behavorial scis. U. Chgo. Law Sch., 1959-60; Talbot vis. prof. govt. U. Va., 1982-83. Author: The Role of Supreme Court as Final Arbiter in Federal-State Relations, 1789-1957, 1958, The Supreme Court; Its Politics, Personalities and Procedures, 1960, Constitutional Law in the Political Process, 1963, (with Berg) The Supreme Court and Congress, 1972, (with Berg and Hahn) American Political Institutions and Corruption, 1976, (with Totten) Whaling in Japan-U.S. Relations, 1978, Judges and Justices, 1979, Constitutional Law in American Politics, 1984, Comparative Judicial Politics, 1987; contbr. chpt. to book; also numerous articles in jours. Chmn. Citizens Action Com. for Fair Representation in Iowa Legislature, 1961; dist. chmn. Operation Support Pres. Kennedy and Johnson, 1961—; chmn. Johnson County Dem. Ctrl. Com., 1961-64; del. Iowa Dem. Convs., 1956, 58, 60, 62; mem. Dem. Nat. Com. Alumni Coun., 1986—; chmn. Santa Barbara, Calif. Dem. Ctrl. Com., 1991-92; mem. exec. com. Los Padres chpt. of the Sierra Club, 1992-96; sec. Santa Barbara Dem. League, 1993-96. With USNR, 1941-45, PTO. Recipient Raubenheimer award U. So. Calif., 1991, Golden Key award for Comparative Rsch, 1991. Mem. Iowa City Mgr. Assn. (bd. reps. 1956-59, chmn. handbook revision 1958), Internat. Polit. Sci. Assn. (chmn. research com. for comparative jud. studies 1980-88), Am. Polit. Sci. Assn., Western Polit. Sci. Assn. (v.p., program chmn. 1980-81, pres.-elect 1981-82), AAUP (sec.-treas. State U. Iowa 1958-59, mem. com. on relationship fed. and state govt. to higher edn., mem. exec. com. U. So. Calif. chpt. 1983-92), Humanities Soc., Raven Soc., Phi Beta Kappa, Phi Kappa Phi. Unitarian (chmn. Iowa City Soc. Men's Club 1960-61). Avocations: French horn, public policy writing, gardening. Home: 726 Arbol Verde St Carpinteria CA 93013-2508 E-mail: jschmidhauser@verizon.net. *For the young today the opportunity for a good education puts them at the threshold of great opportunities. I encourage them to enjoy that with the same spirit that my generation experienced.*

SCHMIDLY, DAVID J., academic administrator, biology professor; b. Levelland, Tex., Dec. 20, 1943; m. Janet Elaine Knox, June 2, 1966; children: Katherine Elaine, Brian James. BS in Biology, Tex. Tech U., 1966, MS in Zoology, 1968; PhD in Zoology, U. Ill., 1971. From asst. prof. to prof. dept. wildlife fisheries scis. Tex. A&M U., College Station, 1971-82, prof., 1982-96, head dept. wildlife, 1986-92, CEO, campus dean Galveston, 1992-96; chief curator Tex. Coop. Wildlife Coll., College Station, 1983-86; v.p. Tex. Inst. Oceanography, 1992-96; v.p. rsch. and grad studies, dean grad. sch., tech. transfer Tex. Tech U., Lubbock, 1996—2002, prof. biol. scis., 1996—2002, pres., 2000—02; sys. CEO, pres. Okla. State U., Stillwater, 2002—07; pres. U. N.Mex., 2007—. Cons. Nat. Park Svc., Wildlife Assocs., Walton and Assocs., Continental Shelf Assn., LGL; lectr. in field; press adv. com. Tex. A&M U., 1983-96; charter mem. Tex. A&M U. Faculty Senate, 1983-85, chmn. Scholarship Com., 1978-82. Author: The Mammals of Trans-Pecos Texas including Big Bend National Park and Guadalupe Mountains National Park, 1977, Texas Mammals East of the Balcones Fault Zone, 1983, The Bats of Texas, 1991, The Mammals of Texas, 1994, Texas Natural History: A Century of Change, 2002; contbr. articles to profl. jours. Trustee Tex. Nature Conservancy, 1991—; mem. adv. bd. Ft. Worth Zoo, 2000. Recipient Dist. Prof. award Assn. Grad. Wildlife and Fisheries Scis., 1985, Donald W. Tinkle Rsch. Excellence award Southwestern Assn. Naturalists, 1988, Diploma Recognition La Universidad Autonoma de Guadalajara, 1989, La Universidad Autonoma de Tamaulipas, 1990. Fellow Tex. Soc. Sci. (bd. dirs. 1979-81); mem. AAAS, Am. Soc. Mammalogists (life, editor Jour. Mammalogy 1975-78), Am. Inst. Biol. Scis. (bd. dirs. 1993—, coun. affiliate socs. 1989—), Am. Naturalist, Soc. Marine Mammalogy (charter mem.), Soc. Systematic Zoology, The Wildlife Soc. Soc. Conservation Biology, Nat. Geog. Sci. Soc., S.W. Assn. Naturalists (life mem., bd. govs. 1980-86, 91—, pres. 1981, trustee 1986—), Tex. Mammal Soc. (pres. 1985-86), Assn. Systematic Collections (bd. dirs.), Chihuahuan Desert Rsch. Inst. (v.p. bd. scientists 1982—, bd. dirs. 1991), Mexican Soc. Mammalogists, Sigma Xi (v.p. 1986-87, pres. 1987-88), Disting. Scientist award 1991), Coun. Pub. Univ. Pres. and Chancellors (exec. com. 2000), Golden Key, Beta Beta Beta, Phi Sigma, Phi Kappa Phi.

SCHMID-SCHOENBEIN, GEERT WILFRIED, biomedical engineer, educator; b. Albstadt, Baden-Wurttemberg, Germany, Jan. 1, 1948; came to U.S., 1971; s. Ernst and Ursula Schmid; m. Renate Schmid-Schoenbein, July 3, 1976; children: Philip, Mark, Peter. Vordiplom, Liebig U., Giessen, Germany, 1971; PhD in Bioengring., U. Calif., San Diego, 1976. Staff assoc. dept. physiology Columbia U., NYC, 1976-77, sr. assoc., 1977-79; asst. prof. dept. applied mechs. & engring. scis. U. Calif., San Diego, 1979-84, assoc. prof., 1984-89, prof., 1989-94, prof. dept. bioengring., 1994—. Editor: Frontiers in Biomechanics, 1986, Physiology and Pathophysiology of Leukocyte Adhesion, 1994, Molecular Basis of Microcirculatory Disorders, 2002; author more than 280 rsch. reports. Recipient Melville medal ASME, 1990, Ratschow medal European Soc. Phlebology, 1999. Fellow Am. Inst. for Med. and Biol. Engring., Am. Heart Assn.; mem. NAE, Biomed. Engring. Soc. (pres. 1991-92), Am. Microcirculatory Soc. (pres. 2003-04), N.Am. Soc. Biorheology (pres. 1989-99), European Microciculatory Soc., Am. Physiol. Soc., Am. Mech. Engring. Soc. Achievements include bioengineering research on cardiovascular disease, microcirulation, bioengineering, and lymphology. Office: U Calif San Diego Dept Bioengineering Gilman Dr 9500 0412 La Jolla CA 92093-0412

SCHMIDT, ALBERT JOHN, retired history professor; b. Louisville, Aug. 27, 1925; s. Christian Carl Schmidt and Mary Margaret Jann; m. Kathryn Estelle Jung, Aug. 25, 1951; children: Christine Elise, Elizabeth Suzanne. AB, DePauw U., Ind., 1949; MA, U. Pa., 1950, PhD, 1953. Asst. prof., assoc. prof., prof. history Coe Coll., Cedar Rapids, Iowa, 1953—65; Arnold Bernhard prof. history U. Bridgeport, Conn., 1965—90; dean U. Bridgeport Coll. Arts and Scis., 1972—76, v.p. acad. affairs, 1976—78, prof. of law, 1979—90, Bernhard prof. of history emeritus, 1990—; prof. law emeritus Quinnipiac U., Hamden, Conn., 1992—; rsch. assoc. George Washington U., Washington, 1992—. Supr. elections Bosnia, Kosovo US Dept. State, Washington, 1997, 98, 2000. Author: The Architecture and Planning of Classical Moscow, 1989; contbr. articles to profl. jours. Sgt. USAF, 1944—46, New Guinea, Philippines. Fulbright scholar, US Dept. State, U. London, 1952—53. Mem.: Am. Hist. Soc. (life). Democrat. Avocations: reading, hiking, bicycling, writing, travel. Personal E-mail: 601alschmidt@comcast.net.

SCHMIDT, BARNET MICHAEL, communications and electronic engineer; b. New Milford, NJ, June 30, 1958; s. Frank Lowell and Lee (Fishkin) S. BSEE, Stevens Inst. Tech., 1980, BS Computer Sci., 1980, MSEE, 1985, PhD, 2003. Cert. comml. pilot/instrument. Electronic engr. Cessna Aircraft Co., Boonton, N.J., 1980-81; sr. sys. engr. Timeplex Corp., Unisys Co., Woodcliff Lake, N.J., 1981-85; tech. staff, cons. AT&T Bell Labs., Holmdel, N.J., 1985-90; tech. staff Bell Comms. Rsch. (now Telcordia Technologies, Inc.), Piscataway, NJ, 1990—95; tech. staff network transmission sys. lab. Lucent Technologies Bell Labs., Holmdel, N.J., 1995-99; sr. tech. staff data arch. divsn. AT&T Corp. R&D, Middletown, NJ, 1999—2000; mem. tech. staff network ops. sys. engring. lab Lucent Tech., Middletown, 2000—02; project engr., comm. sys. analysis BAE Sys. Inc., Totowa, NJ, 2002—; pres. Schmidt and Assocs., PC, Cons. Comms. Engrs., Oradell, NJ, 1999—. Cons. engr. Computer Scis. Corp., El Segundo, Calif., 1986-90; prin. Schmidt & Assocs., LLC Cons. Mem. IEEE (sr.), Sigma Xi (assoc.). Achievements include development of optimal SONET network architectures and routing methods; robust fault tolerant optical transmission system; network surveillance systems; dense wavelength division multiplexing system; invention of novel adaptive filter synthesis techniques, statistical signal identification methods, multiplanar image correlation, parallel image processing systems; neural-network based intelligent systems for isolating hidden troubles in telecommunications networks; performance analysis and tuning of communications networks and operational support systems; spread-spectrum optimal modulation and systems engineering; spread spectrum/secuire wireless system; patents in field; research in wireless network modulation error correcting codes. Office: BAE Sys Inc 18A40 150 Parish Dr Wayne NJ 07474-0975 Office Phone: 973-305-2013.

SCHMIDT, BENNO CHARLES, JR., lawyer; b. Washington, Mar. 20, 1942; s. Benno Charles and Martha (Chastain) S.; children by previous marriage— Elizabeth, Benno III, Christina. BA, Yale U., 1963, JD, 1966; LLD (hon.), Princeton U., 1986; LittD (hon.), Johns Hopkins U., 1987; LLD (hon.), Harvard U., 1987. Bar: D.C. 1968. Law clk. Chief Justice Earl Warren, U.S. Supreme Ct, Washington, 1966-67; spl. asst., asst. atty. gen. Office Legal Counsel U.S. Dept. Justice, Washington, 1967-69; Harlan Fiske Stone prof. constl. law Columbia U., NYC, 1969-86, dean Law Sch., 1984-86; pres., prof. law Yale U., New Haven, 1986-92; chmn. Edison Schs., NYC, 1992—. Author: Freedom of the Press versus Public Access, 1976; (with A.M. Bickel) The Judiciary and Responsible Government 1910-1921, 1984. Dir. Nat. Humanities Ctr., Chapel Hill, N.C., 1985—; chmn. bd. trustees CUNY, 2000—. Office: Edison Schools 521 5th Ave Rm 1100 New York NY 10175-1599

SCHMIDT, CHARLES EDWARD, lawyer; b. NYC, Oct. 6, 1951; s. Donald J. and Yanina S. (Giera) S.; children: John Charles, Michael Joseph. AB cum laude, Boston Coll., 1972; JD, Fordham U., 1975. Bar: N.Y. 1976, U.S. Supreme Ct. 1982. Law clk. Lilly Sullivan & Purcell, P.C., NYC, 1973-76, assoc., 1976-84, Donovan Maloof Walsh & Kennedy, NYC, 1984-86; ptnr. Kennedy & Lillis, NYC, 1986-93, Kennedy Lillis Schmidt & English, 1993—. Mem. N.Y. State Bar Assn., Maritime Law Assn., Assn. Average Adjusters U.S. (assoc.). Episcopalian. Home: 255 W 108th St Apt 8D1 New York NY 10025-2926 Office: Kennedy Lillis Schmidt & English 75 Maiden Ln Ste 402 New York NY 10038-4816 Home Phone: 917-670-3652; Office Phone: 212-430-0802. Business E-Mail: cschmidt@klselaw.com.

SCHMIDT, CHARLES OTTO, military officer, engineer; b. Farmingdale, NY, June 9, 1937; s. Charles McKenzie and Catherine Margaret (McMahon) Schmidt; m. Margaret Ellen McCormick, Jan. 18, 1975; children: James Andrew(dec.), Catherine Margaret, Ellen Elizabeth; m. Mary Jane Naugle (div.); children: Elizabeth Jessie Loporchio, Gretchen Dana Droese. Ordnance prodn. officer USN, 1958—84; project mgr. Los Alamos Tech. Assocs. Inc., Albuquerque, 1984—2004, project mgr., tech. writer, 2005—. Ind. contractor ordnance, logistics Los Alamos Tech. Assocs. & Sandia Nat. Labs., Albuquerque, 2002—05. Co-author (editor): (handbook) Fuse Shock and Vibration Design Handbook, 1997, 2000; co-author: (book) Trace Chemical Sensing of Explosives, 2007. Vol., docent Nat. Atomic Mus., Albuquerque, 2000—; plank owner USN Meml., 2002. Decorated Surface Warfare Officer USN, Navy Unit Commendation, Navy Commendation medal, Def. Meritorious Svc. medal Sec. Def., Joint Meritorious Unit award Dept. Def. Mem.: NRA (life). Republican. Avocations: travel, gardening, gunsmithing. Office: Los Alamos Tech Assocs Inc 2400 Louisiana Blvd NE Ste 400 Albuquerque NM 87110

SCHMIDT, CHAUNCEY EVERETT, banker, director; b. Oxford, Iowa, June 7, 1931; s. Walter Frederick and Vilda (Saxton) S.; m. Anne Garrett McWilliams, Mar. 3, 1954; children: Carla, Julia, Chauncey Everett. BS, U.S. Naval Acad., 1953; MBA, Harvard U., 1959. With First Nat. Bank, Chgo., 1959-76, v.p., gen. mgr. br. London, Eng., 1965-68, v.p. for Europe, Middle East, Africa, 1968-69, sr. v.p. Chgo., 1969-72, exec. v.p., 1972, vice chmn. bd., 1973, pres., 1974-76; chmn. bd., chief exec. officer, dir. Bank of Calif. N.A., San Francisco, 1976—; chmn. bd., pres., chief exec. officer, dir. BanCal Tri-State Corp., 1976—. Dir. Amfac, Inc., Honolulu; mem. Adv. Council Japan-U.S. Econ. Relations; adv. bd. Pacific Rim Bankers Program. Exec. bd. and pres. San Francisco Bay Area council Boy Scouts Am.; council SRI Internat.; bd. dirs. Bay Area Council; bd. govs. San Francisco Symphony; trustee U.S. Naval War Coll. Fedn., Newport, R.I. Served with USAF, 1953-56. Mem. Assn. Res. City Bankers, Am. Bankers Assn., Internat. Monetary Conf., Calif. Bankers Clearing House Assn. (dir.), Calif. Roundtable (dir.), Japan-Calif. Assn. Clubs: Comml. (Chgo.); Bankers (San Francisco), Bohemian (San Francisco). Home: 40 Why Worry Farm Woodside CA 94062-3654 Office: Ste 140 525 Middlefield Rd Menlo Park CA 94025

SCHMIDT, CHRISTINE ALICE, art gallery owner; b. St. Albans, NY, Sept. 1, 1932; d. Paul Joseph and Alice Patricia (McKane) Schmidt. BA magna cum laude, Adelphi U., 1964; MA, Pratt Inst., 1968. Cert. clothing design McDowell Art Sch., 1952, edn. NY, 1964. Asst. buyer May Co., NYC, 1952—54; asst. and designer Finger & Rabiner, Linker, Grioni, NYC, 1955—59; fashion illustrator, freelance clothing designer NYC, 1959—63; parochial sch. art tchr. St. Brigid's, St. Francis, St. Christopher, 1963—64; art tchr. Cold Spring Harbor (NY) HS, 1964—84; owner, operator Christine's Gallery, Southwest Harbor, Maine, 1972—, Lamoine, Maine, 2000—, Christine's Etchings and Prints, Lamoine, 2003—. Etchings and watercolor paintings in numerous collections in Europe and US, 1972—. Ambulance driver Am. Red Cross, Garden City, NY, 1950—65; bd. mem. Southwest Harbor C. of C., Southwest Harbor, Maine, 1994—99. Achievements include various coat and suit designs for the covers and interior of Vogue, Harper's Bazaar, Mademoiselle. Avocations: sewing, photography, european travel. Home and Office: 19 Artists Way Lamoine ME 04605 Office Phone: 207-664-2667.

SCHMIDT, CLAUDE HENRI, retired science administrator; b. Geneva, May 6, 1924; came to U.S., 1935; s. Roger Auguste Schmidt and Lucette (Henriette) Wuhrman; m. Melicent Esther Hane, June 25, 1953; children— Valerie Lynn, Jeffrey Allan AB, Stanford U., 1948, MA, 1950; PhD, Iowa State U., 1956. With Agrl. Rsch. Svc., USDA, 1956-88; rsch. entomologist Orlando, Fla., 1956-62; project leader Fargo, N.D., 1964-67; br. chief Beltsville, Md., 1967-72; area dir. N. Cen. region Fargo, 1972-82; lab. dir., 1982-88; acting dir. Red River Valley Agrl. Rsch. Ctr., 1988; collaborator, 1988-94; with Cass County Vector Control Dist., 1994—2003; ret. Entomologist IAEA, Vienna, Austria, 1962-64; sec. Nat. Mosquito Fish and Wildlife Commn., Washington, 1968-72 Editor Leafy Spurge News, 1994—2005; contbr. articles to profl. jours. Mem. state legis. com. AARP, N.D., 2000-03; mem. Fargo Sr. Commn., 2001-07, chmn., 2003-07; docent Plaines Art Mus., Fargo, 2005—. With AUS, Signal Corps 1942-46, to 1st lt. Med. Service Corps, 1950-53. Fellow Washington Acad. Sci., AAAS; mem. Am. Mosquito Control Assn. (pres. 1981-82), Am. Chem. Soc., Entomol. Soc. Am., Nat. Assn. Ret. Fed. Employees (pres. N.D. fedn., 1988-89). Republican. Home: 1827 3rd St N Fargo ND 58102-2335 E-mail: chs1827@i29.net.

SCHMIDT, CYRIL JAMES, librarian; b. Flint, Mich., June 27, 1939; s. Cyril August and Elizabeth Josephine S.; m. Martha Joe Meadows, May 22, 1965; children: Susan, Emily. BA, Cath. U. Am., 1962; MSLS, Columbia U., 1963; PhD, Fla. State U., 1974. Asst. bus. and industry dept. Flint Pub. Library, 1963-65; reference librarian Gen. Motors Inst., Flint, 1965; asso. librarian S.W. Tex. State U., San Marcos, 1965-67; head undergrad. libraries, asst. prof. Ohio State U., 1967-70; dir. libraries SUNY, Albany, 1972-79; also mem. faculty SUNY (Sch. Library and Info. Sci.); univ. librarian Brown U., Providence, 1979-81; exec. v.p. Rsch. Libraries Group, Stanford, Calif., 1981-89; prin. cons. Schmidt & Assocs., Palo Alto, Calif., 1989—; univ. prof. San Jose (Calif.) State U., 1992—. Author papers in field. Libr. Svcs. Act fellow, 1962-63, Higher Edn. Act fellow, 1970-72 Mem. ALA, ACLU, Pi Sigma Alpha, Beta Phi Mu. Home: 244 Forest Ave Palo Alto CA 94301-2510 Office: San Jose State U 1 Washington Sq San Jose CA 95192-0001 Office Phone: 408-924-2465. Business E-Mail: jim_schmidt@sjsu.edu.

SCHMIDT, DANIEL EDWARD, IV, lawyer, arbitrator; b. NYC, Dec. 17, 1946; s. Daniel Edward III and Mary (Mannion) S.; m. Gail Kennedy, Sept. 5, 1980; children: Kathryn Kennedy, Michael Kennedy. BA, St. Lawrence U., 1971; postgrad., New Sch., 1972; JD, St. John's U., 1975. Bar: N.Y. 1976; cert. arbitrator. From asst. counsel to assoc. gen. counsel Prudential Property & Casualty, Holmdel, NJ, 1978—81, assoc. gen. counsel, divsn. head, 1981—82; v.p., assoc. gen. counsel, asst. sec. Prudential Reins Co., Newark, 1982—84; dir., v.p., gen. counsel, corp. sec. Scor U.S. Group, NYC, 1984—86, dir., sr. v.p., gen. counsel, corp. sec., 1986—89; dir., exec. com., sr. v.p., gen. counsel, corp. sec. Sorema N.A. Group, NYC, 1989—94, dir., exec. com., exec. v.p., group gen. counsel, 1995—99, dir. exec. com., group exec. v.p., chief legal officer, 1999—2000; dep. gen. mgr., gen. counsel, corp. sec. Sorema Internat. Holding, N.V., Netherlands, 1993—96; U.S. counsel Groupama, France, 1996—2000; cons. Sorema NA Group, 2000—03. Pvt. practice comml. arbitrator, umpire, Little Silver, N.J., 1987—; reins. lectr., 1986—; founding dir., 1994-2003; pres., 1999-2002, chmn. 2002-2003, bd. dirs. ARIAS (U.S.), N.Y.C. Assoc. editor Arias-U.S. Quar. Presiding judge Ecclesiastical Trial Ct., 1999—2000, Episcopal Diocese of N.J., 1997—; bd. dirs., exec. com. ARC, Monmouth County, Shrewsbury, NJ, 1981—84. With US Army, 1967—70. Mem. ABA, Am. Arbitration Assn. (panel comml. arbitrators, roster of umpires, panel internat. arbitrators), N.Y. Bar Assn., Assn. Internat. Droit des Assureurs (U.S. chpt.), Bamm Hollow Country Club, Desert Mountain Club, Sands Beach Club. Episcopalian. Avocations: bicycling, golf, skiing. Home and Office: Dispute Resolution Svcs Internat 628 Little Silver Point Rd Little Silver NJ 07739-1737 Home Phone: 732-741-6620; Office Phone: 732-741-3646. Business E-Mail: dschmidt4@comcast.net.

SCHMIDT, DEREK, state legislator; b. Independence, Kans., Jan. 23, 1968; m. Jennifer Shaw, May 23, 1998. Student, Independence C.C.; B, Kans. U., 1990; M in Internat. Politics, U. Leicester, Eng., 1992; JD, Georgetown U., 1996. Bar: Kans. 1996, D.C. 1996, U.S. Supreme Ct. 2003. Mem. legis. staff Senator Nancy Kassebaum, 1992—96; gen. counsel, legis. dir. Senator Chuck Hagel, 1996—98; asst. atty. gen. State of Kans., 1999; legis. liaison, spl. counsel to Kans. Gov. Bill Graves, 2000; pvt. practice Scovel, Emert, Heasty & Chubb, Independence, 2000—; mem. Kans. Senate from 15th dist., Topeka, 2001—, majority leader, 2005—, chmn. agr. com., 2001—05, chmn., post audit com., 2004—05, chmn. confirmation oversight com., 2005—, chmn. spl. com on Medicaid reform, 2005. Bd. dirs. Independence Industries, Inc. Grad. Leadership Kans., 1999; trustee, ea. Kans. br. Nat. Multiple Sclerosis Soc.; active Am. Coun. Young Polit. Leaders. Ralph Kirchner scholar U. Leicester; fellow Bowhay Inst. for Legis. Leadership Devel.; Henry Toll fellow, 2002, Simons Pub. Humanities fellow U. Kans., 2006. Mem.: Kans. State Hist. Soc., Inc. (bd. dirs.), Rotary. Republican. Office: State Capitol Rm 392E Topeka KS 66612 Office Phone: 785-296-2497.

SCHMIDT, EDWARD CRAIG, lawyer; b. Pitts., Nov. 26, 1947; s. Harold Robert and Bernice (Williams) Schmidt; m. Elizabeth Lowry Rial, Aug. 18, 1973; children: Harodl Robert II, Robert Rial. BA, U. Mich., 1969; JD, U. Pitts., 1972. Bar: Pa. 1972, US Dist. Ct. (we. dist.) Pa. 1972, US Ct. Appeals (3d cir.) 1972, US Ct. Appeals (DC cir.) 1975, US Supreme Ct. 1981, US Ct. Appeals (9th and 4th cirs.) 1982, US Ct. Appeals (6th cir.) 1987, US Ct. Appeals (2d cir.) 1992. Assoc. Rose, Schmidt, Hasley & Di Salle, Pitts., 1972—77, ptnr., 1977—90, Jones, Day, Reavis & Pogue, Pitts., 1990—2001, Thompson Coburn LLP, Washington, 2002—06; counsel Edward C. Schmidt LLC, Chautauqua, NY, 2006—. Mem. adv. com. Superior Ct. Pa., 1978—80; instr. NITA Duquesne U., 1998—99. Asst. editor: Antitrust Discovery Handbook, 1980; co-editor: Antitrust Discovery Handbook-Supplement, 1982; contbr. articles to profl. jours. Bd. dirs. Urban League, Pitts., 1974—77. Mem.: Acad. Trial Lawyers Allegheny County (bd. govs. 1980), Internat. Acad. Trial Lawyers, Allegheny County Bar Assn. (pub. rels. com. coun. civil litig. sect. 1977—80), DC Bar Assn., Pa. Bar Assn., Supreme Ct. Hist. Soc., We. Res. Acad. Alumni Assn. (trustee 1998—2000), Duquesne Club (Pitts.), Rolling Rock Club (Ligonier, Pa.). Office: PO Box 1091 20 Hazlett St Chautauqua NY 14722 Office Phone: 716-357-2448. Business E-Mail: eschmidt@ecslaw.net.

SCHMIDT, ELEANORE, library director; Assoc. dir. Long Beach Pub. Libr., Calif., 1989—98, dir. libr. svcs. Calif., 1998—. Bd. dirs. Long Beach Pub. Libr. Found. Office: Long Beach Pub Libr 101 Pacific Ave Long Beach CA 90822 Office Fax: 562-570-6016, 562-570-7408. E-mail: eschmidt@lbpl.org.

SCHMIDT, ERIC EMERSON, information technology executive; b. Washington, Apr. 27, 1955; m. Wendy Schmidt; 2 children. BSEE, Princeton U., 1976; MS in Computer Sci., U. Calif., Berkeley, 1979, PhD in Computer Sci., 1982. With Bell Labs., Zilog; research intern Xerox PARC, Palo Alto, Calif., 1979-80, mem. research staff, 1980-83; software mgr. Sun Microsystems, Mountain View, Calif., 1983-84, software dir., 1984-85, v.p., gen. mgr. software products div., 1985-88, v.p. gen. systems group, 1988-91, chief tech. officer, 1994—97; pres. Sun Tech. Enterprises, Inc., Mountain View, Calif., 1991-94; chmn., CEO Novell, Inc., Provo, Utah, 1997—2001; chmn. exec. com., CEO Google, Inc., Mountain View, Calif., 2001—. Bd. dirs. Google, Inc., 2001—, Apple Computer, Inc., 2006—. Bd. trustee Princeton U. Named one of Forbes' Richest Americans, 2004—, World's Richest People, Forbes Mag., 2006—, 50 Who Matter Now, Business 2.0, 2007. Mem. IEEE, Assn. Computing Machinery, Sigma Xi; fellow Am. Acad. Arts & Scis. Achievements include patents in field. Office: Google Inc 1600 Amphitheatre Pkwy 41 Mountain View CA 94043-1351 Office Phone: 650-623-4000. Office Fax: 650-618-1499. *

SCHMIDT, FRANK BROAKER, executive recruiter; b. Shamokin, Pa., Aug. 8, 1939; s. Frank Wilhelm and Doris (Maurer) S.; children by previous marrage: Susan E., Tracie A.; m. Elizabeth Mallen, Mar. 18, 1989; children: Alexandra M., Frank W.M., Drake M. BS, U. Pa., 1962; MBA, Case Western Res. U., 1969; cert. brewmaster, Siebel Inst. Brewing Tech., Chgo., 1964. With Carling Brewing Co., Cleve., 1964-69, mgr. sales and advt. div., brand mgr., 1969-70; advt. and merchandising mgr. The Pepsi-Cola Co., Purchase, NY, 1970-73, dir. mktg. programs, then dir. mgmt. devel., 1973-74; dir. sales and mktg. The Olga Co., Van Nuys, Calif., 1974-75; mng. dir. Stanton Chase Internat., 1995—2001; pres. F.B. Schmidt, Internat., LA, 1975—95, 2001—. Chmn. Mediterranean Properties, 1994—. Author: Draft Beer Manual, 1967, Assn. Nat. Advertisers Computerized Media System, 1970. Chmn. Morrison Ranch Estates Homeowners Assn., 1993-96. Mem. Calif. Exec. Recruiters Assn., Wharton Alumni Assn., Personnel Cons. Am. (region chmn. 1981-83, chmn. 92-95), Am. Mktg. Assn. Republican. Avocations: sports cars, flying, marathon bicycling, racing. Office: FB Schmidt Internat 5737 Kanan Rd Agoura Hills CA 91301-1601

SCHMIDT, GARY DAVID, language educator; b. Massapequa, NY, Apr. 14, 1957; s. Robert H. and Jeanne A. (Smith) S.; m. Anne E. Stickney, Dec. 22, 1979; six children. BA, Gordon Coll., 1979; MA in Lit., U. Ill., 1981, PhD in Lit., 1985. Teaching asst. U. Ill., Urbana, 1979-85; prof. English Calvin Coll., Grand Rapids, Mich., 1985—. Book reviewer, 1987—. Author: Robert McCloskey, 1990, Hugh Lofting, 1992, Anson's Way, 1999, Straw into Gold, 2001, A Passionate Usefulness: The Life and Literary Labors of Hannah Adams, 2004, Lizzie Bright and the Buckminster Boy, 2005, Mara's Stories, 2005, First Boy, 2005; co-editor: Voice of the Narrator, 1989, Sitting at the Feet of the Past, 1992, Communities of Discourse, 1992. Mem. Early English Text Soc. Avocation: farming. Office: Calvin Coll English Dept Grand Rapids MI 49546 Home Phone: 616-868-0067; Office Phone: 616-526-6540. E-mail: sdg@calvin.edu.

SCHMIDT, GARY P., lawyer, personal care industry executive; b. Youngstown, Ohio, Mar. 25, 1951; BA, Miami U., 1973; JD, U. Akron, 1976. Gen. counsel Lyphomed, Inc., 1988—90; v.p., sec., gen. counsel Fujisawa USA, Inc., 1990—97; v.p., asst. sec., gen. counsel Alberto-Culver Co., Melrose Park, Ill., 1997—2000, sr. v.p., asst. sec., gen. counsel, 2000—. Mem.: ABA, Patent Law Assn., Ill. State Bar Assn., Chicago Bar Assn. Office: Alberto-Culver Co 2525 Armitage Ave Melrose Park IL 60160 *

SCHMIDT, GEORGE, physicist, educator; b. Budapest, Hungary, Aug. 1, 1926; s. Laszlo Schmidt and Katalin Wellisch; m. Katalin Varkonyi, June 26, 1955; children: Franklin R., Ronald W. Diploma in Elec. Engring., Tech. U., Budapest, 1950; PhD in Physics, Hungarian Acad. Scis., Budapest, 1956; M in Engring., Stevens Inst. Tech., 1961. Sr. lectr. Israel Inst. Tech., Haifa, Israel, 1957-58; asst. prof. Stevens Inst. Tech., Hoboken, NJ, 1959-61, assoc. prof., 1961-63, prof. physics, 1963-83, George Meade Bond prof. physics and engring. physics, 1983-92, prof. emeritus, 1992—. Vis. prof. U. Wis., 1965, UCLA, 1972-73; vis. scientist Culham Labs., Culham, Eng., 1965, Ecole Polytechnique, Paris, 1979-80; cons. Sci. Applications Inc., Washington, 1981—, Poly. U. of N.Y., 1984—, Berkeley Assocs., Washington, 1985. Author: Physics of High Temperature Plasmas, 1966, 2nd rev. edit., 1979; contbr. sci. articles to profl. jours. Recipient Research award Stevens Inst. Tech., 1961. Fellow Am. Phys. Soc.; mem. N.Y. Acad. Scis. Office: Stevens Inst of Tech Dept Of Physics Hoboken NJ 07030 E-mail: gschmidt@stevens.edu.

SCHMIDT, HANS R., retired history educator; b. Yonkers, NY, Aug. 1938; m. Joan M. Schmidt; children: Julie, Jenny. PhD, Rutgers U., New Brunswick, NJ, 1968. Author: (book) The United States Occupation of Haiti, 1915-34, Maverick Marine: General Smedley D. Butler and the Contradictions of American Military History. Lt (j.g.) USN, 1960—63. Home Phone: 386-322-0238.

SCHMIDT, HILDRED DORIS, music educator; b. Marion County, Kans., Aug. 13, 1932; d. Rudolf B Schmidt and Susie Voth. B of Music Edn., Coll. Emporia, 1954, BA, 1954; M of music edn. with highest distinction, Ind. U., 1958. Cert. Teacher Kans. State Bd. Edn., Service Playing Certificate Am. Guild Organists. Music tchr. Mullinville Grade Sch., Kans., 1954—57, Zenda Grade and H.S., Kans., 1958—60, Inman Grade Sch., 1960—67, Lyons Jr. High, Mid. and H.S., Lyons, Kans., 1967—96; ret., 1996. Founding mem. The Silver Sounds (flute quartet); organizer music festivals Lyons Jr. High Music Dept. Mem. People to People Lifeline et al., Bob Larson Communicator Club. Recipient Master Teacher award, Discipline and Classroom Mgmt., 1984. Mem.: Kans. Assn. of Retired Sch. Personnel, Kans. Bandmasters Assn., Music Educators Nat. Conf. (50 yr. mem.), Am. Guild Organists (sub-dean, Hutchinson chpt. 1988—93, 1996—98, dean Hutchinson chpt. 1998—2001, sub-dean, Hutchinson chpt. 2001—05), Kans. Music Educators Assn. So. Ctrl. Dist. (exec. sec. 1974—2004, 50 yr. mem.), Tabor Mennonite Ch., Coll. Emporia Alumni Assn. (bd. dirs.), Mu Phi Epsilon (pres. chpt. Phi Epsilon 1952—54). Avocations: gardening, needlecrafts, travel, photography.

SCHMIDT, HOLLIE, secondary school educator; 1 child. BS in Health Sci., Dance cum laude, Calif. State U., Sacramento, 1991. Cert. fitness instr. Am. Coun. Exercise. Tchr. Napa H.S., 1992—. Dir., head coach and dir. NHS dance dept. NHS Spirit Leader Team, Napa, 1992—; fitness instr. Health Quest, Napa, 1992—. Office: Napa HS 2475 Jefferson St Napa CA 94558

SCHMIDT, JAMES CRAIG, retired bank, savings and loan association executive; b. Peoria, Ill., Sept. 27, 1927; s. Walter Henry and Clara (Wolfenbarger) S.; m. Jerrie Louise Bond, Dec. 6, 1958; children: Julie, Sandra, Suzanne. Student, Ill. Wesleyan U., 1945, 48-50, Ph.B. in Bus. Adminstrn, 1952; postgrad., U. Ill. Coll. Law, 1950-52; JD, DePaul U., 1953. Bar: Calif., Calif. Spl. agt. Fidelity & Deposit Co., Chgo., 1956-58; with Home Fed. Savs. & Loan Assn., San Diego, 1958-67; asst. sec. bus. and transp. State of Calif., 1967-69; vice-chmn., pres. Gt. Am. Bank, San Diego, 1969-88. Pres. Conf. Fed. Savs. and Loans of Calif., 1974-75; mem. Calif. Toll Bridge Authority, 1969-74; mem. Calif. State Transp. Bd., 1972-78; past chmn. San Diego Bal. Commn. Task Force. Columnist San Diego Daily Transcript. Pres. San Diego Holiday Bowl Football Game, 1986; bd. dirs. San Diego Internat. Sports Coun., San Diego Hwy. Devel. Assn.; pub. mem. San Diego County Sunset Adv. Bd.; mem. City-County Re-Investment Task Force. Mem. Calif. Bar Assn., Ill. Bar Assn., Calif. League Savs. Instns. (chmn. 1986-87), Calif. C. of C. (bd. dirs. 1987-90), U.S. Savs. Instn. League (exec. com. 1983-86), San Diego East County C. of C. (bd. dirs.), Catfish Club, Sigma Chi, Phi Delta Phi. Office: 8383 Center Dr Ste J La Mesa CA 91942-2913 Home Phone: 619-447-5604.

SCHMIDT, JASON, professional baseball player; b. Lewiston, Idaho, Jan. 29, 1973; Pitcher Atlanta Braves, 1995—96, Pitts. Pirates, 1996—2001, San Francisco Giants, 2001—06, Los Angeles Dodgers, 2006—. Named NL Starting Pitcher MLB All-Star Game, 2003; recipient NL ERA Leader award, MLB, 2003. Office: LA Dodgers 1000 Elysian Park Ave Los Angeles CA 90012-1199 *

SCHMIDT, JEAN, congresswoman; b. Cin., Nov. 29, 1951; m. Peter W. Schmidt; 1 child, Emilie. BS in Polit. Sci., U. Cin., 1974. Tchg. cert. in secondary edn. U. Cin., 1986. Trustee, Miami, Ohio, 1989—2000; mem. Ohio State Ho. Reps. from Dist. 66, 2001—04, US Congress from 2nd Ohio dist., 2005—. Chmn. Clermont County Rep. Party, 1996—98, Taft for Gov., 1998; mem. agr. com. US Congress, mem. transp. and infrastructure com. Mem. Milford Miami Twp. C. of C., 1989—, Ohio Twp. Assn., 1990—, Clermont County Twp. Assn., 1990—, Clermont County 20/20 Com., 1990—, Clermont County League of Women Voters, 1990—, Clermont County Agrl. Soc., 1990—, Clermont County C. of C., 1990—, mem. econ. devel. com., 1995—2005; mem. Leukemia Soc. Team in Tng., 1994—, mentor, 1996—; bd. trustees Clermont County Libr., 1980—92, 1994—2000, 2005—; bd. mem. Clermont County Mercy Hosp. Found., 1997—, Phoenix Pl., 2005—; founder, chmn. Sauls Found. 5K Race, 1995—. Named Marriage & Family Therapy Legislator of Yr., 2003, Empowerment Coalition Legislator of Yr., 2004, Am. Liver Found. Legislator of Yr., 2004, Bioscience Legislator of Yr., 2004; recipient Clermont County Cmty. Devel. of the Greater Cin. Found. Appreciation award, 2003, Clermont County Mental Health Svc. Recognition Award, 2003, Children's Hosp. Award of Distinction, 2003, So. Ohio Agrl. and Cmty. Devel. Found. Disting. Svc. Award, 2004. Republican. Roman Catholic. Avocations: long distance running, auto racing. Office: US House Reps 238 Cannon House Office Bldg Washington DC 20515 Office Phone: 202-225-3164. Office Fax: 202-225-1992. *

SCHMIDT, JOHN CHARLES, music educator; b. Kenedy, Tex., Feb. 19, 1941; s. Bruno Carl and Frances Mae (Schuessler) Schmidt; m. Jacqueline Sue Yetter, June 16, 1973. PhD in Musicology, NYU, NYC, 1978; M. Sacred Music, Union Theol. Sem., NYC, 1963; MusB, Southwestern U., Georgetown, TX, 1961. Instr. NYU, Bronx, 1969—73; prof. Tex. State U., San Marcos, 1976—; organist Covenant Presbyn. Ch., Austin, 1998—. Author: The Life and Works of John Knowles Paine; editor: (scholarly edition) John Knowles Paine Complete Piano Music, John Knowles Paine: Three Chamber Works for Piano and Strings, John Knowles Paine: Vocal Chamber Music, John Knowles Paine: The Nativity, Op. 39; contbr. articles to profl. jours. Recipient John G. Tower Disting. Alumnus award, 2005. Fellow: Am. Guild Organists (S. Lewis Elmer award 2002); mem.: Am. Musicological Soc., Soc. for Am. Music, Coll. Music Soc. (life), Phi Mu Alpha (chpt. faculty advisor 1991—, Orpheus Award 1995), Sigma Alpha Iota (nat. arts assoc. 2005), Kappa Sigma Frat. Presbyterian. Home: P O Box 1373 San Marcos TX 78667-1373 Office: Tex State Univ Sch Music 601 University Dr San Marcos TX 78666-4616 Business E-Mail: js26@txstate.edu.

SCHMIDT, JOHN R., lawyer; b. Chgo., Nov. 24, 1943; s. Edward F. and Josephine (Roggen) S.; m. Janet Gilroy, Apr. 24, 1982; 1 child, Laura. BA, Harvard U., 1964, JD, 1967. Bar: Ill. 1967, U.S. Dist. Ct. (no. dist.) Ill. 1972, U.S. Supreme Ct. 1972. Assoc. Mayer, Brown & Platt, Chgo., 1967-73, ptnr., 1973-84, Skadden, Arps, Slate, Meagher & Flom, Chgo., 1984-93; Amb., chief US negotiator Uruguay Round, 1993—94; assoc. atty. gen. U.S. Dept. Justice, Washington, 1994—97; ptnr. Mayer, Brown, Rowe & Maw, LLP, Chgo., 1998—. Vis. scholar Northwestern U. Sch. Law, 1997—98. Contbr. articles to profl. jours. Chmn. Ill. Guardianship and Advocacy Commn., 1979-82, Met. Pier and Exposition Authority, Chgo., 1989-94; chief of staff City of Chgo., 1989; co-chmn. Citizens for Ct. Reform, Chgo., 1986-92; trustee Ill. Inst. Tech., 1991-93, 1998-, Chgo. Symphony Orch., 1978-93, 1998-. Recipient Judge Learned Hand Human Rels. award Am Jewish Com., 1992. Fellow Am. Bar Found.; mem. ABA, Chgo. Coun. Lawyers (pres. 1974-76). Office: Mayer Brown Rowe Maw LLP 71 S Wacker Dr Chicago IL 60606-4637 Office Phone: 312-701-8597. Office Fax: 312-706-8397. Business E-Mail: jschmidt@mayerbrownrowe.com.

SCHMIDT, JOSEPH DAVID, urologist; b. Chgo., July 29, 1937; s. Louis and Marian (Fleigel) S.; m. Andrea Maxine Herman, Oct. 28, 1962. BS in Medicine, U. Ill., 1959, MD, 1961. Diplomate Am. Bd. Urology. Rotating intern Presbyn. St. Luke's Hosp., Chgo., 1961-62, resident in surgery, 1962-63; resident in urology The Johns Hopkins Hosp., Balt., 1963-67; faculty U. Iowa Coll. Medicine, Iowa City, 1969-76, U. Calif., San Diego, 1976—, prof., head divsn. urology, 1976—2006, vice-chmn. dept. surgery, 1985-97. Cons. U.S. Dept. Navy, San Diego, 1976—; attending urologist Vets. Affairs Dept., San Diego, 1976—; assoc. dir. for clin. rsch. U. Calif. San Diego Cancer Ctr., 1997-98. Author, editor: Gynecological and Obstetric Urology, 1978, 82, 93. Capt. USAF, 1967-69. Recipient Francis Senear award U. Ill., 1961. Fellow ACS; mem. AMA, Am. Urol. Assn. Inc., Alpha Omega Alpha. Avocations: collecting antique medical books, manuscripts. Office: U Calif Med Ctr Divsn Urology 200 W Arbor Dr San Diego CA 92103-8897 Home Phone: 858-459-3625; Office Phone: 619-543-5904. Office Fax: 619-543-6573. Business E-Mail: jdschmidt@ucsd.edu.

SCHMIDT, JOSEPH W., lawyer; b. Jeffersontown, Ky., July 6, 1946; s. A. W. and Olivia Ann Schmidt; m. Angela Petchara Apiradee, Dec. 20, 1969; children: Narissa Ann, Suriya Christine. BA in Psych., Bellarmine Coll., 1969; AB in Commerce, U. Md., 1972; JD, Columbia U., 1975. Bar: NY 1976. Law clk. to presiding judge US Dist. Ct. (so. dist. NY), 1975-76; assoc. Breed, Abbott & Morgan, NYC, 1976-83, ptnr., 1983-93, Whitman, Breed, Abbott & Morgan, NYC, 1993-96, Coudert Bros. LLP, NYC, 1996—2002; v.p., gen. counsel, sec. Dover Corp., NYC, 2003—. Adminstrv. editor: Columbia Jour. Law and Social Problems, 1974—75. Woodrow Wilson fellow, 1968, Harlan Fiske Stone scholar, 1975. Mem.: ABA, Assn. Corp. Coun., Soc. Corp. Secs. and Governance Profls., Assn. Bar City NY. Avocations: travel, skiing, reading. Office: Dover Corp 280 Park Ave Fl 34W New York NY 10017-1292 Office Phone: 212-922-1640. E-mail: jws@dovercorp.com.

SCHMIDT, JULIUS, sculptor; b. Stamford, Conn., June 2, 1923; s. Louis Frank and Susie (Koment) S.; m. Carolyn Marsha Wolf (div.); children: Ania J., Ianos; m. Mary Katherine Powers, 1981 (div.); 1 child, Araan J. Student, Okla. A&M U., 1950-51; BFA, Cranbrook Acad. Art, 1952, MFA, 1955; student, Ossip Zadkine, Paris, 1953, Accademia di Belle Arti, Florence, Italy, 1954. Chmn. sculpture dept. Kansas City Art Inst., 1954-59, R.I. Sch. Design, 1959-60, U. Calif.-Berkeley, 1961-62, Cranbrook Acad. Art, 1962-70, U. Iowa, Iowa City, 1970-93; ret., 1993. Exhibited in 43 one-man shows 1953—; group shows include Allen Meml. Art Mus., Oberlin, Ohio, 1958, Arts Club of Chgo., Mus. Modern Art, N.Y.C., 1960, Whitney Mus., 1960-63, Gallerie Claude Bernard, paris, 1960, Guggenheim Mus., 1962, San Francisco Mus. Art, 1962, Phila. Art Alliance, 1963, Battersea Park, London, 1963, Sai Paolo Bienal, Brazil, 1963, White House Festival of Arts, Washington, 1965, Bienale Middleheim, Belgium, 1971; represented in permanent collections Nelson Gallery-Atkins Mus., Kansas City, Mo., Art Inst., Chgo., Mus. Modern Art, N.Y.C., Mus. U. Nebr., Whitney Mus. Art, N.Y.C., Krannert Art Mus., Urbana, Ill., Washington, U., Walker Art Center, Mpls., Albright-Knox Mus., Buffalo, Detroit Inst. Art, U. Calif. Art Mus., Cranbrook Acad. Art, Mich., Princeton Mus. Art, Hirschhorn Mus., Washington, Numerous others. Served with USNR, World War II. Decorated Air medal (2); recipient Lifetime Achievement award in sculpture edn. Internat. Sculpture Ctr., 1998; Guggenheim fellow, 1963-64. Address: 5 Highview Knl NE Iowa City IA 52240-9149 Home Phone: 319-351-1665; Office Phone: 319-351-1665. Personal E-mail: jfeschmidt@earthlink.net.

SCHMIDT, KARL A., lawyer; b. Stockton, Calif., Sept. 18, 1947; BS, U. Calif., Berkeley, 1969, JD, 1974. Bar: Calif. 1974. Mem. Parker, Milliken, Clark, O'Hara & Samuelian, LA. Contbr. Retaliation Matters, to L.A. Daily Jour. Ann. Employment Update, 1997, USC TAx Inst. 2003: Exec. Terminations. Mem. ABA. Home Phone: 310-544-9685; Office Phone: 213-683-6518. Business E-Mail: kschmidt@pmcos.com.

SCHMIDT, KATHLEEN MARIE, lawyer; b. Des Moines, June 17, 1953; d. Raymond Driscoll and Hazel Isabelle (Rogers) Poage; m. Dean Everett Johnson, Dec. 21, 1974 (div. Nov. 1983); children: Aaron Dean, Gina Marie; m. Ronald Robert Schmidt, Feb. 7, 1987. BS in Home Econs., U. Nebr., 1974; JD, Creighton U., 1987. Bar: Nebr. 1987, U.S. Dist. Ct. Nebr. 1987, U.S. Ct. Appeals (8th cir.) 1989, U.S. Supreme Ct. 1991. Apprentice printer, journeyman Rochester (Minn.) Post Bull., 1978-82; dir. customer info. Cornhusker Pub. Power Dist., Columbus, Nebr., 1982-83; artist Pamida, Omaha, 1983; offset artist Cornhusker Motor Club, Omaha, 1983-84; assoc. Lindahl O. Johnson Law Office, Omaha, 1987-88; pvt. practice Omaha, 1988-90; ptnr. Emery, Penke, Blazek & Schmidt, Omaha, 1990-91; pvt. practice, Omaha, 1992—. Atty. in condemnation procs. Douglas County Bd. Appraisers, Omaha, 1988-99, Sarpy County Bd. Appraisers, Omaha, 1999—; presenter Nebr. Sch. Bd. Assn., 1991, 92. Mem. Millard Sch. Bd., Omaha, 1989-96, treas. 1991, 92; mem. strategic planning com. Millard Sch. Dist., 1990; mem. Omaha Mayor's Master Plan Com., 1991-94; mem. ch. coun. Luth. Ch. of the Master, Omaha, 2005-07, deacon. Named hon. mem. Anderson Mid. Sch., Omaha, 1991; recipient Award of Achievement, Nebr. Sch. Bd. Assn., 1991, 94. Mem.: Nat. Sch. Bd. Assn. (del. fed. rels. network 1991—96, cert. recognition 1991), Omaha Bar Assn. (spkrs. bur. 1992—), Nebr. Bar Assn. (treas. women and law sect. 2005—06, sec. 2007). Republican. Lutheran. Office Phone: 402-330-7733. E-mail: kathleenmschmidt@yahoo.com.

SCHMIDT, KELLY, state official; b. Elmhurst, Ill. married; 4 children. State treas. State of ND, 2004—. Pres. ND Jump$tart Coalition for Personal Fin. Literacy; trustee ND State Hist. Bd. Found. Mem.: Nat. Assn. State Treas. (pres., Midwest State Treas.), Bus. Profl. Women, AmVets Auxiliary, Am. Legion Auxiliary. Republican. Office: State Treas 600 E Blvd Ave 3d fl Bismarck ND 58505-0130 Office Phone: 701-328-2643. Office Fax: 701-328-3002. Business E-Mail: klschmidt@nd.gov.

SCHMIDT, KLAUS DIETER, marketing professional, management consultant, educator; b. Eisenach, Germany, May 8, 1930; came to U.S., 1949, naturalized, 1952; s. Kurt Heinrich and Louise (Kruger) S.; m. Lynda Hollister Wheelwright, June 29, 1950; children: Karen, Claudia. BA in Econs., U. Calif., Berkeley, 1951; MBA, Stanford U., 1953; PhD in Bus. Adminstrn., Golden Gate U., 1978. Buyer, jr. mdse. mgr. Broadway Hale, 1952-54; sales mgr. Ames Harris Neville Co., 1954-56, ops. mgr., 1956-57; gen. mgr. Boise Cascade Corp., 1957-60; pres., chmn. bd. Kimball-Schmidt Inc., San Rafael, Calif., 1960-73, chmn. subs. Kalwall Pacific, 1962-67, chmn. subs. AFGOA Corp., 1966-69; asst. prof. mgmt. and mktg. San Francisco State U., 1970-75, assoc. prof. mgmt., 1975-80, prof. mgmt. and mktg., 1989-85, prof. mgmt., chmn. dept., 1979-85, prof. emeritus, 1989—, assoc. dean emeritus Sch. Bus., 1985-88; chmn. Schmidt Cons. Group, Brooklin, Maine, 1988—. Dir. Ctr. for World Bus., 1976-88, dir. U.S.-Japan Inst., 1981-88, editor-in-chief Sch. Bus. Jours., 1980-88; U.S. negotiator for Pres. Carter White House on Afghanistan issue, 1980-88; mem. Dept. Commerce Dist. Export Council, 1982-88; rsch. cons. SRI Internat. Author: (20 booklet series) Doing Business In..., Stanford Rsch. Inst., 1978-80, A Spy For Life, 2004, Living Your Life, 2005. Mem. Univ. Club (San Francisco), Alpha Delta Phi, Beta Gamma Sigma. Republican. Home and Office: PO Box 269 Brooklin ME 04616-0269 Office Phone: 207-359-4644.

SCHMIDT, KLAUS FRANZ, advertising executive; b. Dessau, Germany, May 25, 1928; came to U.S., 1951; naturalized, 1957; s. Franz and Elfriede (Klamroth) S.; m. Gisela Garbrecht, June 19, 1954; children: Dagmar Schmidt Etkin, Ena Schmidt Reynen. Student, Coll. of Journalism, Aachen, Germany, 1947-48, Sch. of Design and Printing, Bochum, Germany, 1948-50; BA, Wayne State U., 1956. Printer, compositor, 1948-56; type dir. Mogul Williams & Saylor, NYC, 1956-59, Doyle, Dane, Bernbach, NYC, 1959-61, Young & Rubicam, NYC, 1961-68, v.p., dir. print ops., 1968-75, v.p., dir. creative support, 1975-85, sr. v.p., mgr. prodn. svcs., 1985-91; advt./graphic arts cons., 1991—. Co-organizer Vision Congress Internat. Ctr. for Communications Arts & Scis., N.Y.C., 1965, 67, 69, 77; chmn., bd. trustees Internat. Ctr. Typographic Arts, N.Y.C. 1969-70 Author: Signs of the Times, 1997; Am. editor Der Druckspiegel, 1957-64; contbg. editor Print Mag., 1968-01, The Dunn Report, 1991-95 Recipient Typomundus award, 1964, Internat. Book Exhbn. award, Leipzig, Germany, 1965 Mem. Print Advt. Assn. (chmn. N.Y. chpt. 1969-71, nat. sr. v.p. 1971-75), Am. Assn. Advt. Agys. (chmn. subcom. on phototypography 1969-75), Digital Distbn. of Advt. to Publ. Assn. (vice chmn. 1991-95), N.Y. Type Dirs. Club (pres. 1984-86, awards 1962, 64-66, 68, 69), N.Y. Art Dirs. Club (v.p. 1984-86), Advt. Prodn. Club (pres. 1982-84), Gravure Advt. Coun. (chmn. 1970-72) Home and Office: 549 Munroe Ave Sleepy Hollow NY 10591-1333 Personal E-mail: kaschmi@optonline.net.

SCHMIDT, L. LEE, JR., retired university official; b. Mullinville, Kans., Oct. 2, 1937; s. Lester Lee and Mary (Gilliam) S.; m. Sarah Sue Lookingbill, Aug. 12, 1961; children: Suzanne, Jon. BS in Bus. Adminstrn., U. Ark., 1962, PhD, 1971; MBA, Tex. Tech U., 1963. CPA, Colo. Audit sr. Ernst & Young, Fort Worth, 1963-66; mgr. acctg. The Western Co., Fort Worth, 1966-67; asst. prof. U. Tex.-Arlington, 1967-68; instr. U. Ark., Fayetteville, 1968-71; prof. acctg., chmn. dept. Colo. State U., Ft. Collins, 1971-87, assoc. dean Coll. Bus., 1988-92; assoc. dean Coll. Bus. Adminstrn., U. Tex., El Paso, 1992-96; dean Coll. Bus. and Tech. Tex. A&M U., Commerce, 1996-2000; ret., 2000. Speaker in field Contbr. articles to profl. jours. Served with USN, 1955-58. Earhart Found. fellow, 1968-69 Mem. AICPA, Am. Acctg. Assn., Fin. Execs. Inst., Beta Gamma Sigma, Beta Alpha Psi.

SCHMIDT, L(AIL) WILLIAM, JR., lawyer; b. Thomas, Okla., Nov. 22, 1936; s. Lail William and Violet Kathleen (Kuper) S.; m. Diana Gail (div. May 1986); children: Kimberly Ann, Andrea Michelle; m. Marilyn Sue, Aug. 11, 1990; stepchildren: Leland Darrell Mosby, Jr., Crystal Rachelle Mosby. BA in Psychology, U. Colo., 1959; JD, U. Mich., 1962. Bar: Colo. 1962, U.S. Dist. Ct. Colo. 1964, U.S. Tax Ct. 1971, U.S. Ct. Appeals (10th cir.) 1964. Ptnr. Holland & Hart, Denver, 1962-77, Schmidt, Elrod & Wills, Denver, 1977-85, Moye, Giles, O'Keefe, Vermeire & Gorrell, Denver, 1985-90; of counsel Hill, Held, Metzger, Lofgren & Peele, Dallas, 1989-94; pvt. practice law Denver, 1990-2001; ptnr. Schmidt & Horen LLP, Denver, 2001—; of counsel MCGuane & Hogan LLP, 2005—. Lectr. in field. Author: How To Live-and Die-with Colorado Probate, 1985, A Practical Guide to the Revocable Living Trust, 1990, Preserving Your Wealth, 2003, Funding the Revocable Living Trust, 2005; contbr. articles to profl. jours. Pres. Luth. Med. Ctr. Found., Wheat Ridge, Colo., 1985-89; pres. Rocky Mountain Prison and Drug Found., Denver, 1986-2002; bd. dirs. Luth. Hosp., Wheat Ridge, 1988-92, Bonfils Blood Ctr. Found., 1995—, Planned Giving Adv. Group of Nat. Jewish Hosp., Denver,

1996-98, St. Joseph Hosp. Found., 1999-2005; bd. dirs. Goodwill Inds. Denver, 2005—; planned giving adv. Aspen Valley Med. Found., 1997-98; mktg. and gifts adv. com. The Denver Found., 1998—. Recipient Philanthropic Leadership award, Denver Found., 2004, Leadership award, Bonfils Blood Ctr. Found., 2007. Fellow Am. Coll. Trust and Estate Counsel (Colo. chmn. 1981-86); mem. ABA, Am. Judicature Soc., Denver Estate Planning Coun., Rocky Mtn. Estate Planning Coun. (founder, pres. 1970-71), Greater Denver Tax Counsel Assn., Am. Soc. Magicians, Denver Athletic Club, 2% Club, Phi Delta Phi. Republican. Baptist. Avocation: magic. Office: 1050 17th St Ste 1700 Denver CO 80265-2077 also: Law Offices Robert L Bolick Ltd 6060 Elton Ave Ste A Las Vegas NV 89107-0100 Office Phone: 303-436-9121. Personal E-mail: estpln@aol.com.

SCHMIDT, LYNDA WHEELWRIGHT, psychotherapist; b. Beijing, July 29, 1931; came to the U.S., 1931; d. Joseph Balch and Jane Byers (Hollister) Wheelwright; m. Klaus Dieter, May 8, 1930; children: Karen Calley, Claudia Lewis. BA, U. Calif., Berkeley, 1965, MSW, 1968. Cert. Jungian analyst; bd. cert. diplomate Am. Bd. Examiners Clin. Social Work. Staff psychiat. social worker Pacific Med. Ctr., San Francisco, 1968-71; pvt. practice psychotherapy and Jungian analysis San Francisco, 1971-87, Brooklin, Maine, 1985—. Tng. analyst CG Jung Inst., San Francisco, 1978—; mem. certifying com. CG Jung Inst., San Francisco, 1980-84; cons. and lectr. in field. Author: Time Out of Mind: Trekking the Hindu Kush, 1978, The Long Shore, A Psychological Experience of the Wilderness, 1991; contbr. articles to profl. jours. Fellow Calif. Soc. Clin. Social Workers; mem. NASW, Acad. Cert. Social Workers, Inc., CG Jung Inst. (chair certifying com. 1980-84), Alpha Phi Sorority. Democrat. Avocations: reading, horseback riding, travel, music. Home and Office: PO Box 269 Brooklin ME 04616-0269

SCHMIDT, NANCY ANNE, psychotherapist; b. Jersey City, July 18, 1958; d. William John Lawrence and Ruth Martha (Morant) S. BA summa cum laude, Fordham U., 1986; MA summa cum laude, N.J. City State U., 1990; cert. pastoral counselor, World Christianship Ministries, 1994. Cert. social worker, criminal justice specialist, hypnotherapist, addiction counselor, eating disorders specialist; cert. domestic violence counselor, cert. crisis counselor. Adj. prof. N.J. City State U. (formerly Jersey City State Coll.), 1988-91, adj. prof. psychology, 1990-94; pvt. practice West New York, 1990—; counselor Substance Abuse Treatment Ctr., Union City, NJ, 1994-96; substance abuse program dir. Sr. Treatment and Edn. Program, Union City, 1994-96; staff psychotherapist North Hudson Cmty. Action Corp. Mental Health Ctr., West New York, 1996-98, dir. mental health, addictive svcs., social work, psychiatry, 1998—. Bd. dirs. Hudson Health Care Partnership, Jersey City; bd. dirs. Hudson County Healthy Families 2000, mem. Hudson County Task Force on Women & Addiction, co-dir. Union City Police Dept./North Hudson Cmty. Action Corp. Domestic Violence Outreach Program, Union City Police Dept. stress reduction cons.; presenter in field. Mem. APA, Am. Counseling Assn., Am. Assn. Family Counselors (cert.), Nat. Assn. Alcohol and Drug Abuse Counselors, Am. Assn. Christian Counselors, Am. Psychotherapy Assn., Alpha Sigma Lambda, Phi Kappa Phi, Psi Chi. Avocations: swimming, walking, reading, writing, poetry. Office: North Hudson Cmty Action Corp Mental Health Addictive Svc 5301 Broadway West New York NJ 07093-2622

SCHMIDT, PAUL WICKHAM, lawyer; b. Milw., June 25, 1948; s. Edmund Julian and Barbara (Wickham) S.; m. Cathryn Ann Piehl, June 27, 1970; children: Thomas Wickham, William Piehl, Anna Patchin. BA cum laude, Lawrence U., 1970; JD cum laude, U. Wis., 1973. Bar: Wis. 1973, U.S. Dist. Ct. (we. dist.) Wis. 1973, U.S. Supreme Ct. 1982, D.C. 1988. Atty. advisor Bd. Immigration Appeals, Washington, 1973-76; gen. atty. office of gen. counsel Immigration and Naturalization Service, Washington, 1976-78, acting gen. counsel, 1979-81, 86-87, dep. gen. counsel, 1978-87; assoc. Jones, Day, Reavis & Pogue, Washington, 1987-89, ptnr., 1990-92; mng. ptnr. Fragomen, Del Ray & Bernsen, PC, Washington, 1993-95; chmn. Bd. of Immigration Appeals, Falls Church, Va., 1995-2001, mem., 2001—03; judge Arlington (Va.) Immigration Ct., 2003—. Mem. ABA, D.C. Bar Assn., Wis. Bar Assn., Fed. Bar Assn. (immigration sect.). Avocations: crew volunteer, gardening, camping, history. Home: 711 S View Ter Alexandria VA 22314-4923 Office: Arlington Immigration Ct 901 N Stuart St Ste 1300 Arlington VA 22203 Business E-Mail: paul.schmidt@usdoj.gov.

SCHMIDT, PETER GUSTAV, marine engineer; b. Tumwater, Wash., Dec. 3, 1921; s. Peter G. and Clara Louise (Muench) S.; m. Elva Mary Ingalls, Dec. 3, 1945; children: Mimi Schmidt Fielding, Jill Schmidt Crowson, Janet Schmidt Mano, Hans. BSME, U. Wash., 1948; MS in Naval Architecture and Marine Engring., U. Mich., 1950. Naval architect Nat. Steel Shipbldg. Corp., San Diego, 1950-52, Carl J. Nordstrom/P. Spaulding, Seattle, 1952-53; pres. Marine Constrn. & Design Co., Seattle, 1953—, Astilleros Marco Chilena Ltd., Santiago, Chile, 1960—, Marco Peruana S.A., Lima, Peru, 1965—, Campbell Industries, San Diego, 1979-99, Campbell Ship Design & Engring., Seattle, 2000—; chmn. Marco Global, Inc., 2005—. Author papers on fishing gear and vessels. Served to lt (j.g.) USN, 1942-45, PTO. Recipient Puget Sound's Maritime Man of Yr. award Puget Sound Press Assn., 1975, Naval Arch. and Marine Engring. Merit award U. Mich., 1996. Mem. Soc. Naval Architects and Marine Engrs., Wash. State Boatbuilders Assn. (pres. 1956-58), Alpha Delta Phi. Avocations: sailing, classical music. Office: Marine Constrn & Design 4259 22d Ave W Seattle WA 98199 Office Phone: 206-285-3200.

SCHMIDT, RAYMOND PAUL, military officer, historian, government agency administrator; b. Western, Nebr., Sept. 14, 1937; s. Reuben Edward and Angeline Agnes (Kudlik) Schmidt; m. Roberta Ruth Schrom, June 11, 1961; 1 child, Douglas Craig. B in Edn., History and Social Sci., U. Nebr., Lincoln, 1958; postgrad., U. Md., College Park, 1960-62, The Am. U., Washington, 1975-81; M in History, U. Wis., Madison, 1966. Instr. math. and social sci. Sr. High Sch., Bellevue, Nebr., 1958-59; history instr. James Madison Meml. High Sch., Madison, Wis., 1966-68; ensign USN, 1959, historian, archivist Naval Security Group Command Washington, 1968-81, advanced through grades to capt., 1981, sr. congl. security policy rev. officer, Naval Intelligence Washington, 1981-82, sr. res. forces advisor Dept. Def., 1982-88, head Navy info. security policy, 1988-98, mgr. declassification program, 1998-00; cons., 2000—03; freelance rschr., writer, 2001—. Mem. Nat. Disclosure Policy Com. Team, Japan, 1989, Thailand, 89, Germany, 91, leader, Albania, 95. Author (with others): Naval Officers Guide, 1983, And I Was There, 1985; contbr. articles to profl. jours. Pres. North Ashburton Citizens Assn., Bethesda, Md., 1982—; merit badge counselor Boy Scouts Am., 1974—93; info. officer U.S. Naval Acad., Annapolis, Md., 1978—93; spkr. Pearl Harbor Symposium Adm. Nimitz Found., Tex., 1991, symposium moderator, 1992; active Montgomery County Planning Bd. Citizens Adv. Com., Md., 1989—94; ret. pers. adv. coun. Naval Dist. Washington. Named Hon. Adm. Great Navy, State of Nebr., 1983. Mem.: DAV (life), Nat. Cryptologic Mus. Found., U.S. Naval Cryptologic Vets. Assn., Naval Intelligence Profls., Am. Hist. Assn., Nat. Trust Hist. Preservation, Nat. Classification Mgmt. Soc. (editor Viewpoints 1991—96), Nat. Assn. Active and Ret. Fed. Employees, Naval Res. Assn. (life; sec./treas. 1966—68), Mil. Officers Assn. Am. (life), Res. Officers Assn. (life), Nat. Assn. Uniformed Svcs. (life), U.S. Naval Inst. (life; contbr.), Phoenix Soc., Colonial Williamsburg Found., U. Nebr. Alumni Assn. (life). Unitarian. Home: 6205 Lone Oak Dr Bethesda MD 20817-1743

SCHMIDT, ROBERT, retired mechanics and civil engineering educator; b. Reshetylivka, Ukraine, May 18, 1927; arrived in U.S., 1949, naturalized, 1956; s. Alfred and Aquilina (Konotop) S.; m. Irene Hubertine Bongartz, June 10, 1978; 1 child, Ingbert Robert Floyd. Student, UNRRA-Univ., Munich, 1946—47, Technische Hochschule Karlsruhe, Germany, 1947—49, Vorpruefung; BS, U. Colo., Boulder, 1951; MS, U. Colo., 1953; PhD, U. Ill., Champaign-Urbana, 1956. Tech. draftsman, Kalisch, Poland, 1943-45; rsch. asst. U. Ill., Urbana, 1953-56, asst. prof. mechanics, 1956-59; assoc. prof. U. Ariz., Tucson, 1959-63; prof. mechanics and civil engring. U. Detroit, 1963-99, chmn. civil engring. dept., 1978-80; ret., 1999. Lectr. Oakland U., 1997-98; rschr. in linear and nonlinear theory of elasticity, theories of arches, plates, and shells, and approximate methods of analysis. Editor: Indsl. Math., 1969—; book reviewer Applied Mechanics Rev., Indsl. Math. Jour.; contbr. numerous articles to profl. jours. With C.E., U.S. Army, 1951-52. Grantee NSF 1960-78. Mem. AAUP, ASCE, ASME (cert. recognition 1972), Am. Acad. Mechanics (founder), Indsl. Math. Soc. (pres. 1966-67, 81-84, 1st Gold award 1986), Sigma Xi. Avocations: biosophy, walking, bicycling, swimming.

SCHMIDT, ROBERT MILTON, preventive medicine physician, educator, medical association administrator; b. Milw., May 7, 1944; s. Milton W. and Edith J. (Martinek) S.; children Eric Whitney, Edward Huntington. AB, Northwestern U., 1966; MD, Columbia U., 1970; MPH, Harvard U., 1975; PhD in Law, Medicine and Pub. Policy, Emory U., 1982; MA, San Francisco State U., 1999. Diplomate Am. Bd. Preventive Medicine, Am. Bd. Internal Medicine, Am. Bd. Hematology. Resident in internal medicine Univ. Hosp. U. Calif.-San Diego, 1970-71; resident in preventive medicine Ctr. Disease Control, Atlanta, 1971-74; commd. med. officer USPHS, 1971; advanced through grades to comdr., 1973; dir. hematology div. Nat. Ctr. for Disease Control, Atlanta, 1971-78, spl. asst. to dir., 1978-79, inactive res., 1979—; clin. asst. prof. pediatrics Tufts U. Med. Sch., 1974-86; clin. asst. prof. medicine Emory U. Med. Sch., 1971-81, clin. assoc. prof. community health, 1976-86; clin. assoc. prof. humanities in medicine Morehouse Med. Sch., 1977-79; attending physician dept. medicine Wilcox Meml. Hosp., Lihue, Hawaii, 1979-82, Calif. Pacific Med. Ctr., San Francisco, 1983—; dir. Ctr. Preventive Medicine and Health Rsch., 1983—, dir. Health Watch, 1983—; sr. scientist Inst. Epidemiol. and Behavioral Medicine, Inst. Cancer Rsch., Calif. Pacific Med. Ctr., San Francisco, 1983-88; prof. hematology and gerontology, dir. Ctr. Preventive Medicine and Health Rsch., chair health professions program San Francisco State U., 1983-99, prof. medicine, 1983—, prof. emeritus, Calif. State U. Sys., 1999—; founding dir. Health Watch Internat., 1994—, CEO, pres. Cons. WHO, FDA, Washington, NIH, Bethesda, Md., Govt. of China, Mayo Clinic, Rochester, Minn., Northwestern U., Evanston, Ill., Chgo., U. R.I., Kingston, Pan Am. Health Orgn., Inst. Pub. Health, Italy, Nat. Inst. Aging Rsch. Ctr., Balt., U. Calif., San Diego, U. Ill., Chgo., Columbia U., NYC, Harvard U., Johns Hopkins U., U. Chgo., UCLA, U. Calif. Berkeley, Brown U., Providence, U. Calif., San Francisco, Stanford U., Boston, Emory U., Atlanta, Duke U., NC, U. Tex., Houston, Ariz. State U., U. Hawaii, Honolulu, U. Paris, U. Geneva, U. Munich, Heidelberg U., U. Frankfurt, U. Berlin, Cambridge U., England, U. Singapore, others; vis. rsch. prof. gerontology Ariz. State U., 1989—90; mem. numerous sci. and profl. adv. bd., panels, com. Mem. editorial bd. Am. Jour. Clin. Pathology, 1976-82, The Advisor, 1988—, Generations, 1989—, Contemporary Gerontology, 1994—, Alternative Therapies in Health and Medicine, 1995—, Aging Today, 1997—; book and film reviewer Sci. Books and Films, 1988—, many other jours.; author: 17 books and manuals including Hematology Laboratory Series, 4 vols., 1979-86, CRC Handbook Series in Clinical Laboratory Science, 1976—; assoc. editor: Contemporary Gerontology, 1993—; contbr. more than 400 articles to sci. jours. Alumni regent Columbia U. Coll. Physicians and Surgeons, 1980—. Northwestern U. scholar, 1964-66; NSF fellow, 1964-66; Health Professions scholar, 1966-70; USPHS fellow, 1967-70; Microbiology, Urology, Upjohn Achievement, Borden Rsch. and Virginia Kneeland Frantz scholar awards Columbia U., 1970; recipient Am. Soc. Pharmacol. and Exptl. Therapy award in pharmacology, 1970, Commendation medal USPHS, 1973, Meritorious Performance and Profl. Promise award, 1989, Student Disting. Teaching and Svc. award Pre-Health Professions Student Alliance, 1992, Leadership Recognition awards San Francisco State U., 1984-89, 91-96, Meritorious Svc. award, 1992. Fellow: ACPM, AAAS (med. scis. sect.), ACP (commentator ACP Jour. Club/Annals of Internal Medicine 1993—), Internat. Soc. Hematology, Am. Soc. Clin. Pathology, Am. Coll. Preventive Medicine (sci. com.), Am. Geriat. Soc., Royal Soc. Medicine (London), Gerontol. Soc. Am.; mem.: APHA, AMA, Emory Sch. Pub. Health, Calif. Coun. Gerontology and Geriat., Nat. Assoc. Adv. for Health Professions, Internat. Health Eval. Assn. (v.p. for Ams. 1992—94, bd. dirs. 1992—, pres. 1994—96), Calif. Med. Assn., San Francisco Med. Soc., NY Acad. Sci., Am. Soc. Aging (editl. bd. 1990—, Dychtwald Pub. Speaking award 1991), Am. Soc. Microbiology, Assn. Tchr. Preventive Medicine (edn. com., rsch. com.), Am. Coll. Occupl. and Environ. Medicine, Calif. Coun. Gerontology and Geriat., Am. Assn. Med. Info., Nat. Assn. Advisors for Health Professions (bd. dirs.), Am. Assoc. Blood Banks, Acad. Clin. Lab. Physicians and Scientists, Internat. Soc. Thrombosis and Hemostasis, Am. Soc. Hematology (hon.; emeritus), Internat. Commn. Standardization in Hematology, Am. Assn. Med. Info. (chair prevention and health evaln. informatics WG), Nat. Gallery of Art (Washington), Columbia U. Club No. Calif., Circle Club (Washington), Army and Navy Club, Golden Key (hon. faculty mem.), Harvard Club (NY and San Francisco), Northwestern U. Club. No. Calif., Cosmos Club (mem. art com. 1997—), Knights of Malta, Sigma Xi, Phi Beta Kappa. Home: Whaleship Plaza 25 Hinckley Walk San Francisco CA 94111-2303 Office: Health Watch Med Ctr Calif Pacific Med Ctr San Francisco CA 94120-7999 Home Phone: 415-956-5670; Office Phone: 415-956-5670. Personal E-mail: rmschmidtmd@aol.com.

SCHMIDT, ROGER R., engineer; BS, Bradley U.; MS, U. Minn., PhD in Mech. Engring. Disting. engr. IBM Corp., Poughkeepsie, NY; mem. IBM Acad. Tech. Assoc. editor Jour. Electronic Packaging; contbr. articles to profl. jours. Fellow: ASME (mem. Heat Transfer Div. and K-16 Electronic Cooling Com.); mem.: NAE. Office: IBM Server Group 2455 S Rd Poughkeepsie NY 12601 E-mail: c28rrs@us.ibm.com.

SCHMIDT, RONALD HANS, architect; b. Hoboken, N.J., Sept. 9, 1938. BArch., Syracuse U., 1961. Sr. designer Skidmore, Owings & Merrill, N.Y.C., 1963-68; ptnr., dir. archtl. design Grad. Partnership, Newark, 1968-81; pres., chief exec. officer Ronald Schmidt & Assocs., P.A., Englewood, N.J., 1981—. Chmn. Bergen County (N.J.) Econ. Devel. Corp.; mem. bd. regents Felician Coll.; mem. exec. com. Network of Opportunity. Recipient numerous awards. Office: 222 Grand Ave Englewood NJ 07631-4352 E-mail: rschmidt@RSAaia.com.

SCHMIDT, RUSSEL ALAN, II, sales executive; b. Stuttgart-Bad Canstatt, Germany, Nov. 18, 1953; arrived in U.S., 1954; s. Russell Allen and Phyllis (Coty) S.; m. Christie Ellen Duncan, Oct. 18 1975; children: Rachel Lea, Russell Alan III. BS, U. Minn., 1984. Lic. FCC gen. radiotelephone operator; cert. Motorola Effective Presentations, Successful Negotiator. Pres. Electronic Engring. Inds. Co., St. Paul, 1971—77, Dis-Com Inc., St. Paul, 1978—81; sales engr. Motorola Inc., Mpls., 1984—85, dist. sales engr., 1985—86, dist. sales mgr., 1987—89, sr. account sales mgr., 1989—93, sr. acct. sales mgr., 1993—95, market devel. mgr., 1995—2001; v.p. Essential Bus. Svcs. Roseville, Minn., 1986—; pres. Forefront Devel. Inc., 2001—; chief mgr. RAC Schmidt Properties LLC, 2001—. Bd. dirs. Dis-Com Inc. 1978-81; chief TV engr. Renewal Internat. Inc., St. Paul, 1984-87; pres. Forefront Devel., Inc., 2001; chief mgr. R&C Schmidt Properties LLC; v.p. Essential Bus. Svcs. Roseville, 2001. Pub. (music CD) Living In Laodicea, 1999. Mem. Nat. SBA, St. Paul C. of C., North Suburban C. of C., Mpls. C. of C., North Oaks Golf Club. Republican. Lutheran. Avocations: small business or real estate ventures, non-fiction reading, computer programming, travel. Office: Motorola Semiconductor Products 5620 Smetana Dr Minnetonka MN 55343-9611 Business E-Mail: russ2@spacestar.net.

SCHMIDT, RUTH ANN, retired academic administrator; b. Mountain Lake, Minn., Sept. 16, 1930; d. Jacob A. and Anna A. (Ewert) S. BA, Augsburg Coll., Mpls., 1952; MA, U. Mo., 1955; PhD, U. Ill., 1962; LLD, Gordon Coll., 1987. Asst. prof. Spanish Mary Baldwin Coll., Staunton, Va., 1955-58, SUNY-Albany, 1962-67, assoc. prof., 1967-78, dean of humanities, 1971-76; prof. and provost Wheaton Coll., Norton, Mass., 1978-82; pres. Agnes Scott Coll., Decatur, Ga., 1982-94, pres. emerita, 1994—. Interim pres. Lyon Coll., 1998; chair Women's Coll. Coalition, 1986-88. Author: Ortega Munilla y sus novelas, 1973, Cartas entre dos amigos del teatro, 1969. Trustee Gordon Coll., Wenham, Mass., 1980-86, Lyon Coll., 1993-2001; bd. dirs. DeKalb C. of C., 1982-85, Atlanta Coll. Art, 1984-94; mem. exec. com. Women's Coll. Coalition, 1983-88; v.p. So. Univ. Conf., 1993. Named Disting. Alumna Augsburg Coll., 1973 Mem. Assn. Am. Colls. (dir. 1979-82, treas. 1982-83), Soc. Values in Higher Edn., Am. Coun. Edn. (commn. on women in higher edn. 1985-88), AAUW, Assn. Pvt. Colls. and Univs. Ga. (pres. 1987-89), Internat. Women's Forum, Young Women's Christian Assn. Acad. Women Achievers, Women's Action for New Directions. Democrat. Presbyterian. E-mail: ruthschmidt@mindspring.com.

SCHMIDT, SHERRIE, library director, dean; BA, Ohio State U., 1970, MLS, 1974. With Ohio State U.; cataloger U. Fla., 1974—75; head user svcs. AMIGOS Bibliog. Coun., 1975—78; assoc. dir. libr. svcs. U. Tex., Dallas, 1979—82; SW US sales rep. Faxon Co., 1982—84; asst. info. sys. planning U. Tex., Austin, 1984—86; asst. dir. collections and bibliog. svcs. Tex. A&M U., 1986—90; assoc. dean libr. svcs. Ariz. State U., 1990—91, dean univ. librs., 1991—. Contbr. articles to profl. jours. Sr. fellow, UCLA, 1989. Mem.: ALA (mem. Office for Info. Tech. Policy Adv. Com. 2002—04). Office: Ariz State U 113 Hayden Libr PO Box 871006 Tempe AZ 85287-1006 Office Phone: 480-965-3956. Office Fax: 480-965-9169. E-mail: sherrie.schmidt@asu.edu. *

SCHMIDT, STANLEY ALBERT, editor, writer; b. Cin., Mar. 7, 1944; s. Otto Elliott William and Georgia (Metcalf) S.; m. Joyce Mary Tokarz, June 9, 1979. BS, U. Cin., 1966; MA, Case Western Res. U., 1968, PhD, 1969. Asst. prof. physics Heidelberg Coll., Tiffin, Ohio, 1969-78; freelance writer Lake Peekskill, N.Y., 1968—; editor Analog Sci. Fiction and Fact Dell Mags., NYC, 1978—. Mem. bd. advisors Nat. Space Soc., Washington, 1982—, Sci. Fiction Mus. and Hall of Fame, Seattle, 2003-. Author: Newton and the Quasi-Apple, 1975, The Sins of the Fathers, 1976, Lifeboat Earth, 1978, Analog Yearbook II, 1981, Analog's Golden Anniversary Anthology, 1980, Analog: Readers' Choice, 1981, Analog's Children of the Future, 1982, Analog's Lighter Side, 1982, Analog: Writers' Choice, 1983, War and Peace: Possible Futures from Analog, 1983, Aliens from Analog, 1983, Writer's Choice, Vol. II, 1984, From Mind to Mind, 1984, Analog's Expanding Universe, 1986, Tweedlioop, 1986, Unknown, 1988, Unknown Worlds, 1989, Analog Essays in Science, 1990, Writing Science Fiction and Fantasy, 1991, Aliens and Alien Societies, 1995, Roads Not Taken, 1998, Which Way to the Future?, 2001, Generation Gap and Other Stories, 2002, Argonaut, 2002; contbr. stories to sci. fiction mags., articles to mags., chapters to books. Mem. Sci. Fiction and Fantasy Writers Am., Am. Assn. Physics Tchrs., Am. Fedn. Musicians. Avocations: photography, hiking, linguistics, cooking, flying. Office: Analog Sci Fiction 475 Park Ave S New York NY 10016-6901 Personal E-mail: analog@dellmagazines.com.

SCHMIDT, STANLEY EUGENE, retired speech educator; b. Harrington, Wash., Dec. 14, 1927; s. Otto Jacob and Ella Genevieve (Wilson) S.; m. Jayne Brown; children: Randall Lee, Stephen Douglas. BS in Edn., Beta Theta Pi, U. Idaho, 1956; MEd in Adminstrn., U. Oreg., 1958; MA in Speech, Wash. State U., 1975. Supt., tchr., coach Rose Lake (Idaho) Sch. Dist. #35, 1949-55; forensics coach, speech tchr., dir. forensics Jefferson H.S., Portland, Oreg., 1955-65; dir. forensics Portland C.C., 1965-93, lead speech instr., 1979-82, subject area chmn., 1986-90; adj. prof. speech U. Portland, 1987-93; ret., 1993. Parliamentarian faculty senate, 1975-80. Co-author anthology: The Literature of the Oral Tradition, 1963. Chmn., precinct committeeman Rep. Party, Kootenai County, Idaho, 1951-53; pres. Kootenai County Tchrs. Assn., 1953-54, North Idaho Edn. Assn., 1954-55, Oreg. Speech Assn., 1960-61, Oreg. C.C. Speech Assn., 1971-72. Recipient Excellence award U.S. Bank, Portland, 1993, Merit award N.W. Forensic Assn., 1992, Faculty Merit award Portland C.C., 1984. Mem.: Order of Quetzalcoatl (dir. of work 2007—), N.W. Comm. Assn., Am. Forensic Assn., Oreg. Speech Assn. (pres.), Speech Comm. Assn., Western Speech Comm. Assn., Oreg. Ret. Tchrs. Assn, Am. Rose Soc., Portland Rose Soc. (Best Rose Garden in Portland Grand Sweepstakes award 2003), Allied Masonic Degrees, Scottish Rite (comdr. multnomah coun. kadosh 1990—91, pres. found. 2002—, 33 degree), Benevolent and Protective Order of the Elks, Royal Arch Masons, Shriners (dir. of the work 1990—, pres. Tualtin valley shrine club 1991, group leader of the guides 1998—2006), Royal Ark Mariners, Royal Order Scotland, York Rite Sovereign Coll., Red Cross of Constantine (dir. of the work 1989—2001, recorder 1993—97, sovereign 2000—01, St. Laurence Conclave), Order of Ea. Star (Worthy Patron 1953, 1970), Knights Templar (knight comdr. of temple of grand encampment), Cryptic Masons of Oreg. (grand orator 1994—95, illustrious master 1997), Masons (worshipful master 1984—85, dist. dep. 1986—90, jr. grand deacon 1990—91, jr. grand steward 1991—92, grand orator 1992—93, grand lodge edn. com. chmn. 1993—95, chmn. grand lodge programs com. 1996—2007), Royal Rosarian. Baptist. Avocations: gardening, stamp collecting/philately, coin collecting/numismatics, fishing, sports. Home: 5460 SW Palatine St Portland OR 97219-7259 Personal E-mail: stanrosebud@comcast.net.

SCHMIDT, STEFAN, mechanical engineer, economist; b. Darmstadt, Hessen, Germany, 1950; s. Josef and Elisabeth (Urnauer) S.; m. Elizabeth Anne Godwin-Schmidt, 1983; children: Rebecca Elizabeth, Benjamin Stefan Godwin. Diploma mech. engring., Fachhochschule Frankfurt, Germany, 1972; diploma indsl. engring. and mgmt., Technische U. Berlin, Germany, 1980. Profl. mech. engr. Engr. Mech. Engring. Lab., Tokyo, 1973, C & P Telephone Co. of Md., Balt., 1978-79; planning engr. Systemtechnik, Darmstadt, Germany, 1980; rsch. assoc. U. Dortmund, Germany, 1981-84; logistics, strategy, maintenance, quality assurance, and internat. mfg. engr. BMW AG, Munich, 1984—; asst. prof. tech. mgmt. and sustainable devel. Lectr. in field; mgmt. trainer Centre of Technol. Cooperation, Berlin, 1985—; seminar presenter C. of C., Passau and Munich, Germany, 1986—, Sabel Bus. Sch., 2000—, REFA/VDI, 2001, others. Contbr. articles to profl. jours.; pub. bus. books, 1994—. Econ. commentator Internat. Newspapers and Jours., Frankfurt, Munich, Berlin, 1990—. Recipient 1st prize Precision Instrument Maker, 1969. Fellow Verein Deutscher Wirt. ing. Home: Fritzstrasse 41 D-82140 Olching Bayern Germany Office: BMW AG D-80788 Munich Germany E-mail: stefan.sb.schmidt@bmw.de, stefan.schmidt-1@t-online.de.

SCHMIDT, STEPHEN CHRISTOPHER, agricultural economist, educator; b. Isztimer, Hungary, Dec. 20, 1920; came to U.S., 1949, naturalized, 1965; s. Francis Michael and Anne Marie (Angeli) S.; m. Susan M. Varszegi, Dec. 20, 1945; children— Stephen Peter, David William. Dr.Sc., U. Budapest, Hungary, 1945; PhD, McGill U., Montreal, Que., Can., 1958. Asst. head dept. Hungary Ministry Commerce, Budapest, 1947-48; asst. prof. U. Ky., Lexington, 1955-57, Mont. State U., Bozeman, 1957-59, U. Ill., Urbana-Champaign, 1959-63, assoc. prof., 1963-70, prof. agrl. mktg. and policy, 1970-91, prof. emeritus, 1991—. Fulbright grantee Bulgaria, 1992-93; Ford Found. fellow, 1959; Agrl. Devel. Coun. grantee, 1966, U. Man. Rsch. fellow, 1968-69, Ford Found. rsch. grantee, 1973, 74, Whitehall found. grantee, 1979, Internat. Inst. Applied Systems Analyses (Laxenburg, Austria) rsch. scholar, 1976-77, USDA Intergovtl. Personnel

Act grantee, 1983-84. Mem. Am. Agrl. Econs. Assn. (award 1979), Internat. Assn. Agrl. Economists, Am. Assn. Advancement Slavic Studies, Ea. Econ. Assn., Sigma Xi, Gamma Sigma Delta. Office: 1301 W Gregory Dr Urbana IL 61801-9015

SCHMIDT, SUSAN, journalist; m. Glen Nishimura; 2 children. BA, Mary Baldwin Coll., 1975. News asst. Washington Star; reporter Herald Examiner, LA, Patriot Ledger, Quincy, Mass.; metro desk editor to bus. news reporter Washington Post, 1983—92, nat. news desk reporter, 1992—. Co-author: Truth at Any Cost, 2000. Co-recipient Pulitzer Prize for nat. reporting, 2002; recipient Pulitzer Prize for investigative reporting, 2006, Seldon Ring award, 2006, Worth Bingham prize, 2006. Office: Washington Post Nat News Desk 1150 15th St NW Washington DC 20071-0070 Office Phone: 202-334-6157. Office Fax: 202-496-3883. Business E-Mail: schmidts@washpost.com.

SCHMIDT, TERRY L., healthcare executive; b. Chgo., Nov. 28, 1943; s. LeRoy C. and Eunice P. Schmidt; children: Christie Anne, Terry L. II. BS, Bowling Green State U., 1965; MBA in Health Care Adminstrn, George Washington U., 1971; Dr Health Adminstrn., Med. U. S.C., 2001. Resident in hosp. adminstrn. U. Pitts. Med. Center, VA Hosp., Pitts., 1968-69; adminstrv. asst. Mt. Sinai Med. Center, NYC, 1969-70; asst. dir. Health Facilities Planning Council of Met. Washington, 1970-71; asst. dir. dept. govtl. relations A.M.A., Washington, 1971-74; contract lobbyist and govtl. rels. Wash. Reps. in Health, Washington, 1974-87; pres. Terry L. Schmidt Inc. Physician Svcs. Group, San Diego, 1987-99, Washington Actions on Health, 1975-79; partner Washington Coun. Medicine and Health, 1979-81; pres. Recreational Enterprises, Inc., Washington, 1977-78; v.p. Crisis Communications Corp. Ltd., 1982-90; pres. Med. Cons. Inc., 1983-84, Ambulance Corp. Am., La Jolla, Calif., 1984-87; exec. dir., chief operating officer Emergency Health Assocs. P.C., Phoenix, 1989-91, Charleston Emergency Physicians, Inc., S.C., 1990-94, Joplin Emergency Physican Assocs., 1991-92, Big Valley Med. Group, 1991-92, Blue Ridge Emergency Physicians, P.C., 1992-94, Berkeley Emergency Physicians, P.C., 1992-94; chmn., pres. Univ. Inst., Inc., 1992—; asst. dir. dept. emergency medicine Med. U.S.C., 1999—2001. Bd. dirs., Univ. Inst., 1997—, lectr., instr. dept. health svcs. adminstrn. George Washington U., 1969-83, preceptor, 1975-84; adj. prof. grad. sch. Pub. Health San Diego State U., 1996—, preceptor, 1989—, guest lectr. health care adminstrn. Nat. U. San Diego, 1992-93; guest lectr. Bus. Adminstrn. U.S. Internat. U., San Diego, 1994—; instr. Nat. Naval Sch. Health Care Adminstrn., 1971-73; faculty Civil Svc. Commn. Legis. Insts., 1972-76; fac. Am. Assn. State Colls. and U. Health Tng. Insts., 1975-78; mem. adv. com. ambulatory care standards Joint Commn. Accreditation of Hosps., 1971-72, pres., Recreational Enterprises, Inc., Wash., 1977-78, guest lectr. Med. U.S.C., 1998-99, preceptor, 1999—, assoc. prof. Coll. of Health, Med. U.S.C., 1999—. Author: Congress and Health: An Introduction to the Legislative Process and the Key Participants, 1976, A Directory of Federal Health Resources and Services for the Disadvantaged, 1976, Health Care Reimbursement: A Glossary, 1983; mem. editl. adv. bd. Nation's Health, 1971-73; contbr. articles to profl. jours. Bd. dirs. Nat. Eye Found., 1976-78. Mem. Med. Group Mgmt. Assn., Health Care Fin. Mgmt. Assn., Assn. Venture Capital Groups (bd. dirs. 1984-89), Amer. Coll. of Health Execs., Amer. Coll. of Med. Prac. Exec., Assn. of Univ. Progs. in Health Admin., San Diego Venture Group (chair 1984-87), Univ. Club (life), Natl. Rep. Club (life), Nat. Dem. Club (life), Capitol Hill Club (life), Alpha Phi Omega (pres. Bowling Green alumni chpt. 1967-70, sec.-treas. alumni assn. 1968-71). Office: University Inst Inc Ste 113 611 7770 Regents Rd San Diego CA 92122-1967

SCHMIDT, THOMAS CHARLES, biomedical engineer, researcher; b. Jersey City, Feb. 21, 1947; s. Ernest J. and Shirley J. Schmidt; m. Marilyn I. Karcheski, Aug. 3, 1968; 1 child, Thomas M. B in Engring., Stevens Inst. Tech., 1968, M in Engring., 1973. Registered profl. engr., Fla., Calif. Vis. lectr. physiol. psychology Stevens Inst. of Tech., Hoboken, NJ, 1974—76; engr. Perry Techs., Riviera Beach, Fla., 1976—80; sr. rsch. engr., rsch. specialist, staff engr., sr. staff engr. Lockheed-Martin, San Diego, 1980—. Participant NASA Med-Ops. Task Group (Clin. Care Capability Project), Houston, 2000; chair ASME PVHO design sub-com., 2003—. Contbr. The Underwater Handbook: A Guide to Physiology and Performance for the Engineer, 1976, articles to profl. jours.; patentee in field. Dir., pub. safety chair Clairemont Town Coun., San Diego, 1997—; chair Balboa Ave. Citizens Adv. Com., San Diego, 1999—2003; mem. Cmty. Engagement Action Forum County Health and Human Svcs., San Diego, 1999—, participant strategic planning process, 1999—2003; mem. Clairemont-Mesa Planning Com., San Diego, 2000—. Recipient cert. of appreciation, State of Calif. (78th Assembly Dist.), 1999, cert. of recognition, 2000, 2001, State of Calif. (76th Assembly Dist.), 2003, 2004, spl. commendation, City of San Diego (6th Dist. Councilmember), 1998, 1999, cert. of appreciation, County of San Diego (3rd Dist. Supr.), 1999, County of San Diego (Asst Dir. Health and Human Svcs.), 2000, spl. commendation, City of San Diego (6th Dist. Councilmember), 2000, 2001, 2002, 2004, Cmty. Svc. award, City of San Diego (Dir. of Planning), 2001, 2002, commendation, Gov. of Calif., 2003, spl. commendation, City of San Diego (6th Dist. Councilmember), 2004, cert. of recognition, U. S. Congress (Calif. 50th Dist.), 2004, cert. of appreciation, ASME (Codes and Standards), 2004. Mem.: ASME (ANSI/ASME safety code com. - pressure vessels for human occupancy 1987—, chair PVHO design sub-com. 2003—), Calif. Environ. Health Assn. (exec. bd. S.W. chpt. 2000—), Undersea and Hyperbaric Med. Soc. (safety com. 1981—, submarine medicine com. 1984—). Home: 5953 Castleton Dr San Diego CA 92117 Office: Lockheed Martin Services 3853 Calle Fortunada San Diego CA 92123-1824 E-mail: thomas.c.schmidt@lmco.com.

SCHMIDT, WALDEMAR ADRIAN, pathologist, educator; b. LA, Aug. 22, 1941; s. Waldemar Adrian and Mary Charlotte (Parker) S.; m. Karmen LaVer Bingham, Feb. 1, 1963; children: Rebecca, Sarah, Waldemar, Diedrich. BS, Oreg. State U., 1965; PhD, MD, U. Oreg., 1969. Intern U. Oreg. Hosps. and Clinics, Portland, 1969-70, resident, 1970-73; pathologist LDS Hosp., Salt Lake City, 1973-77; prof. pathology U. Tex. Med. Sch., Houston, 1977-91, Oreg. Health and Scis. U., Portland, 1991—2003, prof. emeritus, 2003—; chief pathology and lab. medicine svc. Oreg. Health and Scis. U. and VA Med. Ctr., Portland, 1997—2001, vice chair pathology, 1997—2001; CEO Cascadia Placenta Registry, 1996—2002, dir., 2002—03; pres. Cascadia Med. Consultants, PC, 2004—. Author: Principles and Techniques of Surgical Pathology, 1982; editor Cytopathology Annual, 1991-94, Revs. in Pathology-Cytopathology, 1994-99. Asst. scoutmaster Boy Scouts Am., Houston, 1982-91. Maj. U.S. Army, 1970-76. Fellow Am. Soc. Clin. Pathologists, Coll. Am. Pathologists; mem. Internat. Acad. Cytology, Sigma Xi, Alpha Omega Alpha. Avocation: photography. Office: U Oreg Health and Scis U Sch Medicine Dept Pathology 3181 SW Sam Jackson Park Rd Portland OR 97201-3098 E-mail: cme@ccwebster.net.

SCHMIDT, WILLIAM ARTHUR, JR., lawyer; b. Cleve., Oct. 2, 1939; s. William Arthur and Caroline (Jäger) S.; m. Gerilyn Pearl Smith, Sept. 30, 1967; children: Deborah, Dawn, Jennifer. BSBA, Kent State U., 1962; JD, Cleve. State U., 1968. Bar: Ohio 1968, Ill. 1990. Contract specialist NASA-Lewis, Cleve., 1962-66, procurement analyst, 1967-68; atty. Def. Logistics Agy., Alexandria, Va., 1968-73; assoc. counsel Naval Sea Sys. Command, Arlington, Va., 1973-75; procurement policy analyst Energy R & D Adminstrn., Germantown, Md., 1975-76; sr. atty. U.S. Dept. Energy, Germantown, 1976-78, counsel spl. projects Oak Ridge, Tenn., 1978-83; judge Agr. Bd. Contract Appeals, Wash., 1983-87; judge Bd. Contract Appeals HUD, Wash., 1987; chief legal counsel Fermilab, Batavia, Ill., 1987-92; gen. counsel Univ. Rsch. Assn., Inc., Wash., 1992—, Fermi Rsch. Alliance, Wash., 2007—. Co-author: (NASA handbook) R & D Business Practices, 1968. Founder/dir. DOE Contractor Attys. Assn.; dir. Spotsylvania Crime Solvers. Mem. ABA, Fed. Bar Assn. (past pres. East Tenn. 1978-83, 25 Yr. Svc. award 1994), Ill. Bar Assn., Bd. Contract Appeals Judges Assn. (dir.-sec. 1986-88), Sr. Execs. Assn., Delta Theta Phi (dist. chancellor 1978-83), Sigma Chi. Republican. Lutheran. Avocations: classic cars, M-1 carbines. Home: 10611 King Elder Ct Spotsylvania VA 22553-3666 Office: Fermi Rsch Alliance 1111 19th St NW Ste 400 Washington DC 20036-3627 Business E-Mail: wschmidt@ura.nw.dc.us.

SCHMIDT, WILLIAM C., retired chemicals executive; b. Niles, Mich., Sept. 27, 1938; s. Felix A. and Anna (Reifschneider) S.; m. Bethany Ann Boyd, Dec. 17, 1966; 1 child, Craig W. BBA, U. Mich., 1960, MBA, 1961. Cert. Mgmt. Acct. Various acctg. positions Dow Chem. Co., Midland, Mich., 1961-73; controller Dow Chem. Pacific Ltd., Hong Kong, 1973-78; area controller Dow Chem. Co., Midland, Mich., 1978-82, asst. corp. controller, 1982-98; v.p., chief fin. officer DowElanco, Indpls., 1989-98; chmn. bd. Wolverine Bank, F.S.B., 2004—. Bd. dirs. Midland Hosp., 1982-89, 98—, chmn. bd., 1986-88, 2004-06; bd. dirs. Mid-Mich. Health Corp., 1983-89, 2001—, chmn. bd., 1986-88; treas., bd. dirs. Indpls. Symphony Orch., 1992-98; dir. West Midland Family Ctr., 2000—06; mem., vice chmn. Midland County Bldg. Authority, 2003—. Cpl. U.S. Army, 1962-64. Mem. Inst. Mgmt. Accts., Inst. Cert. Mgmt. Accts. (regent 1985-89), Am. Indsl. Health Coun. (treas. 1986-87), Ind. C. of C. (bd. dirs. 1992-98). Presbyterian. Home: 5908 Londonberrie Ct Midland MI 48640-6965

SCHMIDT, WILLIAM E., editor; b. Detroit, Mar. 15, 1947; s. E. F. and Irene E Schmidt; m. Margo Jean Doble, Nov. 4, 1972 (div. May 11, 2005); children: Jordan Alison, Lindsay Ella, Peter William. BA, U. Mich., Ann Arbor, 1967. Reporter Detroit Free Press, 1968—73; bur. chief Newsweek, Miami, Fla., 1975—76, Cairo, 1976—79, Moscow, 1979—81, corr. Chgo, 1973—75; bur. chief N.Y. Times, Denver, 1981—83, Atlanta, 1983—87, Chgo., 1987—91, corr. London, 1991—95, dep. nat. editor NYC, 1995—97, assoc. mng. editor, 1997—2005, asst. mng. editor, 2005—. Bd. dirs. Maynard Inst. Journalism Edn., Oakland, Calif., 2005—. With USAR, 1968—74. Recipient George Polk award for Nat. Reporting, L.I. U., 1971, Mag. Reporting award, Overseas Press Club, 1976, Pulitzer Prize in Nat. Reporting, Columbia U., 1988. Mem.: Assn. Am. Correspondents in London (pres. 1993—94). Lutheran. Office: NY Times 229 W 43rd St New York NY 10036 Office Phone: 212-556-1211. Office Fax: 212-556-4401. Business E-Mail: schmidt@nytimes.com.

SCHMIDT, WILLIAM MAX, management consultant, marketing and business development executive; b. Danville, Pa., Nov. 23, 1947; s. Frank Wilhelm and Doris Savilla (Maurer) S.; m. Marylea O'Reilly, Sept. 20, 1980. BS, U. Pa., 1969; MBA, Northwestern U., 1971. Mktg. specialist Moody's Investors Svc., Inc., NYC, 1971-72; cons. William E. Hill & Co. Inc., NYC, 1972-74; product supr. Internat. Paper Co., NYC, 1974-79; dir. market analysis U.S. Industries, Inc., Stamford, Conn., 1979-82, mgr. corp. devel., 1982-84; dir. corp. mktg. Combustion Engring., Inc., Stamford, Conn., 1984-86, v.p. mktg., planning Union, NJ, 1986-91; pres. Pragmatics, Basking Ridge, NJ, 1991—2000, 2003—; dir. global mktg. Gemplus Internat., Montgomeryville, Pa., 2000—03. Author (newsletter): Think Again, 1995. Bd. dirs., pres. Curbing Hunger, Inc., Basking Ridge, NJ, 1995—; adv. Jr. Achievement, NYC, 1976-78; mem. governing body St. Mark's Episcopal Ch. Mem. TAPPI, Exec. Forum, Strategic Leadership Forum, Univ. Club, Sons of the Revolution, Wharton Club (N.Y.C.), Sigma Chi. Republican. Mem. United Ch. of Christ. Avocations: tennis, astronomy, canoeing, community service, coin collecting/numismatics. Office: Pragmatics 46 Quincy Rd Basking Ridge NJ 07920 Office Phone: 908-580-1259. Personal E-mail: billprag@optonline.net.

SCHMIDTBERGER, MICHAEL J., lawyer; b. 1959; BA, Columbia Coll., 1982; JD, Columbia Univ., 1985. Bar: NY 1986. Assoc. Sidley Austin Brown & Wood, NYC, 1990—93, ptnr. securities and futures-related funds and corp. transactions, 1993—, and mem. exec com. Editor-in-chief Columbia Human Rights Law Rev., 1985. Mem.: ABA, NYC Bar Assn. (com. on futures regulation 1997—2000), Phi Beta Kappa. Office: Sidley Austin Brown & Wood 787 Seventh Ave New York NY 10019 Office Phone: 212-839-5458. Office Fax: 212-839-5599. Business E-Mail: mschmidtberger@sidley.com.

SCHMIDT-HOLTZ, ROLF, music company executive; b. Martinsreuth, Germany, Aug. 31, 1948; 2 children. Degree in Law, Polit. Sci., Psychology, U. Erlangen, U. Kiel, 1973; JD, U. Kiel, 1976. Paralegal, 1973-76; asst. prof. law U. Kiel, 1976; svc. chief Federal Press Office, 1977-80; contbr. West Deutscher Rundfunk, 1980-84; editor Tageschau und Tagesthemen, 1980-84; TV corr. ARD Studio Bonn, WDR, 1981-84; dir. Federal Press Conf., Bonn, 1984-86; mgr. dirs. bur. info. and publicity Bertelsmann AG, Gütersloh, 1985-86; editor in chief TV program listings WDR, 1986-88; editor Der Stern Mag., Gruner & Jahr AG & Co., 1988—, Hamburger Morgenpost, Gruner & Jahr AG & Co., 1989-90; bus. dir. Gruner & Jahr Zeitschriften TV GmbH, 1990—; editor in chief Der Stern Mag., Gruner & Jahr AG & Co., 1990-94; head TV and Film Europe divsn. Bertelsmann AG, 1994—97; CEO, CLT-Ufa Luxembourg, 1997—2000; chief creative officer, mem. exec. bd. Bertelsmann AG, 2000—; chmn., pres., CEO BMG Entertainment, New York, 2001—04; chmn. Sony BMG Music Entertainment, 2004—06, CEO, 2006—; mem. supervisory bd. Gruner & Jahr AG & Co., 2000—, RTL Group, 2002—. Office: Sony BMG Music Entertainment 550 Madison Ave New York NY 10022

SCHMIDTKE, SUZANNE DE FINE, retired social worker; d. Poul and Else de Fine Lassen; m. Edwin (Ned) C. Schmidtke, June 7, 1964; children: Peter Christian, Elizabeth de Fine Knudsen. MSW, U. Ill., Chgo., 1980. Cert. social worker NASW, 1982, diplomate NASW, 1988, Am. Bd. Examiners in Clin. Social Work, 1988, LCSW Ill. Dept. Profl. Regulation, 1989. Social worker Madden Mental Health Ctr., Ill. Dept. Mental Health, Hines, 1980—84, Ill. State Psychiat. Inst., Chgo., 1984—87, social worker adminstr., 1987—94; mgr., rsch. patient recruitment dept. psychiatry U. Ill., Chgo., 1994—2004; ret., 2004. Adj. instr. art therapy Sch. of Art. Inst. Chgo., Chgo., 1989—93; social work field instr. Jane Addams Coll. Social Work, U. Ill., Chgo., 1992—2004. Bd. mem. Nat. Alliance for Mentally Ill, Chgo., 1996—2003; pres. Nat. Alliance for Mentally Ill of Ill., Springfield, 2001—03, family-to-family tchr.; bd. mem. Nat. Alliance for Mentally Ill San Fernando Valley, 2007. Recipient Vol. of the Yr., Nat. Alliance for Mentally Ill., 2000. Avocations: theater, hiking, travel, films. Personal E-mail: suzned@sbcglobal.net.

SCHMIDT-NIELSEN, BODIL MIMI (MRS. ROGER G. CHAGNON), retired physiologist, educator; b. Copenhagen, Nov. 3, 1918; came to U.S., 1946, naturalized, 1952; d. August and Marie Jorgensen Krogh; m. Knut Schmidt-Nielsen, Sept. 20, 1939 (div. Feb. 1966); children: Astrid, Bent, Bodil; m. Roger G. Chagnon, Oct. 1968 (dec. 2003). DDS, U. Copenhagen, 1941, DOdont, 1946, DPhil, 1955; DS (hon.), Bates Coll., 1983; MD (hon.), U. Aarhus, Denmark, 1997. Mem. faculty Duke U., Durham, NC, 1952-64; prof. biology Case Western Res. U., Cleve., 1964-71, chmn. dept., 1970-71, adj. prof., 1971-74; trustee Mt. Desert Island Biol. Lab., Maine, rsch. scientist Maine, 1971-86, exec. com. Maine, 1978-85, v.p. Maine, 1979-81, pres. Maine, 1981-85; prof. dept. physiology U. Fla., Gainesville, 1985—. Adj. prof. Brown U., Providence, 1971-75, dept. physiol. U. Fla., Gainesville, 1986—; mem. tng. grant com. NIGMS, 1965-71. Author: August and Marie Krogh, Lives in Science, 1995, Danish edit., 1997; editor: Urea and the Kidney, 1970; assoc. editor Am. Jour. Physiology: Regulatory, Integrative and Comparative Physiology, 1978-81. Trustee Coll. of Atlantic, Bar Harbor, Maine, 1972-92. Recipient Career award NIH, 1962-64, John Simon Guggenheim Meml. fellow, 1952-53; Bowditch lectr., 1958, Jacobaeus lectr., 1974. Fellow AAAS (del. coun. 1977-79), NY Acad. Scis., Am. Acad. Arts and Scis.; mem. Am. Physiol. Soc. (coun. 1971-77, pres. 1975-76, Ray G. Daggs award 1989, Orr Reynolds award 1994, August Knogh lectr. 1994, Berliner award 1998), Soc. Exptl. Biology and Medicine (coun. 1967-71). Achievements include research, publications on biochemistry of saliva, water metabolism of desert animals, urea excretion, peristalsis of renal pelvis and concentrating mechanism, comparative kidney physiology, comparative physiology of excretory organs. Office: U Fla Dept Physiology 2015 SW 16th Ave Gainesville FL 32605 Business E-Mail: bodil@gator.net.

SCHMILL, STUART, admissions director; Grad., MIT, 1986. Sr. assoc. dir. admissions MIT, Cambridge, interim dir. admissions, 2007—. Dir. MIT Ednl. Coun.; coach MIT Men's Crew Team, 1987—2000, dir. crew program, 1990—2000. Recipient Harold E. Lobdell '17 Disting. Svc. Award. Office: MIT Rm 3-108 77 Massachusetts Ave Cambridge MA 02139-4307 Office Phone: 617-258-5529. E-mail: stucrew@MIT.EDU. *

SCHMIT, LUCIEN ANDRÉ, JR., retired structural engineer; b. NYC, May 5, 1928; s. Lucien Alexander and Eleanor Jessie (Donley) S.; m. Eleanor Constance Trabish, June 24, 1951; 1 son, Lucien Alexander, III. BS, MIT, 1949, MS, 1950. Structures engr. Grumman Aircraft Co., Bethpage, NY, 1951-53; rsch. engr., aeroelastic and structures lab. MIT, 1954-58; asst. prof. engring. Case Inst. Tech., 1958-60, assoc. prof., 1961-63, prof., 1964-70; prof. engring. and applied sci. UCLA, 1970-91, Rockwell prof. aerospace engring. emeritus, 1991—; ret., 1991. Sci. adv. bd. USAF, 1977-84. Contbr. articles on analysis and synthesis of structural systems, finite elements methods, design of fiber composite components and multidisciplinary design optimization to profl. jours. Fellow AIAA (Design Lecture award 1977, Structures, Structural Dynamics and Materials award 1979, Multidisciplinary Design Optimization award 1994, Walter J. and Angeline H. Crichlow Trust prize 1999), ASCE, Am. Acad. Mechanics; mem. NAE. Home: 545 3rd Ave S Edmonds WA 98020-4103 Personal E-mail: schmit13@comcast.net.

SCHMIT, RANDALL, painter; b. Newark, May 27, 1955; s. Kenneth Howard and Doris Schmit. BFA, Tex. A&M U., College Station, 1977; MFA, Tex. A&M U., Commerce, 1979. Artist, painter, NYC, 1980—. Guest critic, studio program SUNY at Empire State Coll., NYC, 1982; adj. faculty, studio program Empire State Coll., 1983; guest lectr. U. New Orleans, 1984; guest critic & lectr. E.Tex. State U., 1984; guest critic & lectr., Bennington Coll., Vt., 1992, Md. Inst. Grad. Sch. Fine Arts, Balt., 1991, Skidmore Coll., Saratoga Springs, NY, 1992; guest lectr. Parsons Sch. Design, NYC, 1996, SUNY at Purchase Grad. & Undergrad. Schs., NY, 1997, US Consulate Gen., Istanbul, Turkey, 2000, Delgado Coll., New Orleans. Paintings, Mongerson-Wunderlich Gallery, Chgo., 1980, Betty Cuningham Gallery, NYC, 1982, pub. & corp. collections, Met. Mus. Art, NYC, Frederick R. Weisman Collection, LA, New Orleans Mus. Art, LA Ogden Mus. So. Art, New Orleans, Castellani Art Museum, Niagara U., NY, Art Mus. We. Va., Roanoke, Birmingham Mus. Art, Ala., Nasher Mus. Art, Duke U. Bus. adv. coun. Mental Health Assn. Columbia Greene, Hudson, NY, 2000—07; mem. Columbia County C. of C., Hudson, NY, 2003—07. Grantee Rsch. grant, Ludwig Vogelstein Found., 1983, Invitational Travel grant, US Consulate Gen., Istanbul, 2000.

SCHMITT, EDWARD A., manufacturing executive; b. July 25, 1946; BS, La. State Univ., 1969. Gen. mgr. ops. Ga. Gulf Corp., Atlanta, v.p. ops., 1993-97, exec. v.p., COO, 1997—98, chmn., CEO, pres., 1998—. Office: Georgia Gulf Corp Ste 460 115 Perimeter Pl Atlanta GA 30346 Mailing: Georgia Gulf Corp PO Box 105197 Atlanta GA 30348 *

SCHMITT, GEORGE FREDERICK, JR., materials engineer; b. Louisville, Nov. 3, 1939; s. George Frederick and Jane Limbird (Hurst) S.; m. Ann Cheatham, July 31, 1965; 2 children. BS, U. Louisville, 1962, MS, 1963; MBA, Ohio State U., 1966. Advanced engring devel. mgr. USAF Materials Lab., Wright Patterson AFB, Ohio, 1986-90, chief plans and programs br. Wright AFB, Ohio, 1989-90, asst. chief nonmetallic materials divsn., 1990-96, chief integration and ops. divsn., 1997—2005; dir. internat. programs Air Force Rsch. Lab. USAF Materials Directorate, Wright Patterson AFB, Ohio, 1966—. Guest lectr. U. Dayton, 1970, 95, Cath. U., 1973, U. Mich., 1975. Contbr. articles to profl. jours. Mem. Kettering (Ohio) Civic Band, 1965—. Affiliate Socs. Coun. Dayton, 1972-81; mem. Dayton Philharm Chorus, 1999—, Dayton Letter Carriers Band, 2000—, Windjammers Circus Music Preservation Soc., 2001—. 1st lt. USAF, 1963-66. Named Fed. Profl. Employee of Yr., Dayton, 1972; named one of Ten Outstanding Engrs., Engrs. Week, 1975; recipient Meritorious Civilian Svc. award, USAF, 1994, Burton award, Playhouse South Cmty. Theater, 1998, Tech. Transfer award, Fed. Lab. Consortium, 2001, Internat. Program Supr. award, USAF, 2002, Internat. Program Non-Supr. award, 2007, Internat. award, USAF Materiel Command, 2006. Fellow Soc. for Advancement Materials and Process Engrs. (Best Paper award 1973, nat. sec. 1975-76, nat. membership chmn. 1977-79, nat. v.p. 1979-81, nat pres. 1981-82, chmn. long-range planning com. 1983-87, trustee 1991—, chmn. Internat. SAMPE Symposium 1996, chmn. SAMPE Trophy com. 1998-2004, chmn. internat. conf., 2003, adminstr. Fellows program 1997-2007), AIAA (assoc., materials tech. com.); mem. ASTM (rec. sec. 72-75, chmn. com. on erosion and wear 1976-79, chmn. liaison subcom. 1979-83, award of merit 1981), Am. Chem. Soc., Affiliate Socs. Coun. Dayton (chmn. 1978-79). Republican. Lutheran. Home: 1500 Wardmier Dr Dayton OH 45459-3354 Office: AFRL Materials and Mfg Directorate MLO Wright-Patterson AFB 2977 Hobson Way Bldg 653 Dayton OH 45433-7733 Office Phone: 937-656-9209. Business E-Mail: george.schmitt@wpafb.af.mil.

SCHMITT, GLENN RALPH, federal agency administrator; b. Indpls., Aug. 11, 1961; s. Ralph and Barbara Jean (Davenport) S. BS, Ind. State U., 1983; JD, U. Notre Dame, 1986. Bar: Ind. 1986, Ohio 1986, US Dist. Ct. (no. and so. dists.) Ind. 1986, US Dist. Ct. (no. dist.) Ohio 1986, US Dist. Ct. Md. 1991, US Ct. Appeals (7th and 6th cirs. 1986), US Supreme Ct. 1989. Assoc. Thompson, Hine & Flory, Cleve., 1986—92; chief counsel House Judiciary Com., Crime Sub-Com., Washington, 1994—2001; dep. dir. Nat. Inst. Justice, Washington, 2001—05, acting dir., 2005—. Author: The Bankruptcy Code Requirement of Compliance with Lease Obligations- Does "All" Mean Everything?, 10 Northern Ill. U. Law Review 225, 1990. Vice chmn. community wide svcs. allocation panel Cleve. United Way, 1987—; mem. alumni coun. Ind. State U., 1990—. Res. Officer Judge Adv. Gen. Corps US Army, 2004, Iraq. Mem. ABA, Ohio State Bar Assn. (legal ethics and profl. conduct com. banking, comml. and bankruptcy law com.), Ind. State Bar Assn., Cleve. Bar Assn. (profl. ethics com.). Republican. Presbyterian. Avocations: music, photography, golf, tennis. Office: Nat Inst Justice 810 7th St NW Washington DC 20531 Office Fax: 202-307-6394. *

SCHMITT, HARRISON HAGAN, former senator, geologist, astronaut, consultant; b. Santa Rita, N.Mex., July 3, 1935; s. Harrison A. and Ethel (Hagan) S. BA, Calif. Inst. Tech., 1957; postgraduate student, U. Oslo, 1957—58; PhD, Harvard U., 1964; degree (hon.), Franklin Marshall Coll., 1977, Colo Sch. Mines, 1971, Rensselaer Poly. Inst., 1973. Geologist US Geol. Survey, 1964—65; astronaut NASA, 1965; lunar module pilot Apollo 17, 1972, spl. asst. to adminstr., 1974; asst. adminstr. Office Energy Progs., 1974; mem. US Senate from N.Mex., 1977—83; cons., 1983—; founder, chmn. Interlune-Intermars Initiative Inc. Mem. Pres.' Fgn. Intelligence Adv. Bd., 1984-85, Army Sci. Bd., 1985-90, Pres.' Ethics Commn., 1989; chmn. tech. adv. bd. Army Rsch. Lab.; adj. prof. engring. U. Wis., Madison, 1995—; chair, pres. to chair emeritus Annapolis Ctr., 1994—; bd. dirs.

Orbital Scis. Corp.; chair, NASA adv. coun., 2005-. Author: Return to the Moon: Exploration, Enterprise and Energy in the Human Settlement of Space, 2005. Trustee The Lovelace Insts. Recipient MSC Superior Achievement award, 1970, Disting. Svc. medal NASA, 1973, Lovelace award NASA, 1989, Gilbert award GSA, 1989, Eugene Shoemaker Meml. award BEYOND, 2007. Mem. AIAA, AAAS, Geol. Soc. Am., Am. Geophys. Union, Am. Assn. Petroleum Geologists. Home: PO Box 90730 Albuquerque NM 87199-0730 *

SCHMITT, JOHN K., army officer; b. Buffalo, July 17, 1949; m. Mee Ja; children: Charlene, Jeffrey. BS in Chemistry, St. Bonaventure U., 1971; MS in Sys. Mgmt., U. So. Calif. Command. 2d lt. U.S. Army, 1971, advanced through grades to brig. gen.; dep. comdg. gen. Ft. Carson, Colo., to 1998; dep. chief of staff for ops. and plans, dir. Army Digitization Office, Pentagon, Washington, 1998—. Decorated Legion of Merit, Meritorious Svc. medal with 3 oak leaf clusters, Order Nat. Security Merit Samil medal (Korea), Def. Superior Svc. medal, Republic of Korea Order Nat. Security Merit Semil medal, Army Commendation medal, Nat. Def. Svc. medal with Svc. star, Expert Infantryman badge, Master Army Aviator badge, Sr. Parachutist badge, Ranger Tab, Dept. Army Staff Identification badge, Republic of Korea Army Hon. Aviator Wings. Office: Dep Chief Staff Operations and Plans 3A522 400 Army Pentagon Washington DC 20310-0400

SCHMITT, KARL MICHAEL, retired political scientist; b. Louisville, July 22, 1922; s. Edward Peter and Mary Ann (Iula) S.; m. Grace Bernadette Leary, June 18, 1949; children: Karl, Edward, Barbara, William, Michael. BA, Cath. U. Am., 1947, MA, 1949; PhD, U. Pa., 1954. Teaching asst. U. Pa., 1948-50; instr. history Niagara U., 1950-54, asst. prof., 1954-55; research analyst U.S. Dept. State, 1955-58; asst. prof. dept. govt. U. Tex., 1958-63, assoc. prof., 1963-66, prof., 1966-91, prof. emeritus, 1991—, chmn., 1975-80. Vis. prof. U. Calif., LA, 1959, Nat. War Coll., 1970-71; vis. sr. fellow U. Manchester, Eng., 1988-89; cons. Dept. of State, 1962-70 Author: Communism in Mexico; A Study in Political Frustration, 1965, Mexico and the United States, 1821-1973: Conflict and Coexistence, 1974, others. Contbr. articles to profl. jours. With US Army, 1943—45. Decorated Purple Heart. Mem. Tex. Cath. Hist. Assn. (pres. 1976-77). Roman Catholic. Home: 2603 Pinewood Ter Austin TX 78757-2136

SCHMITT, ROBERT LEE, computer scientist; b. Astoria, NY, Oct. 1, 1948; s. Edward and Margaret Louise (Gleason) S.; m. Elsy Evagelene Burnett, June 1999; stepchildren: Eric Jason Marin, Alexis Michelle Marin. AAS in Data Processing, SUNY, Farmingdale, 1972; student, Hofstra U., 1972-73; BS in Computer Sci., SUNY, Stony Brook, 1974, MS in Computer Sci., 1975; postgrad., U. Md., 1979-80, 94-96; grad. diploma in strategic sci., U.S. Naval War Coll., 1991. Cert. computer programmer, data processor. Computer programmer U.S. Army Environ. Hygiene Agy., Aberdeen Proving Ground, Md., 1976; data sys. programmer Dept. Def., Ft. George G. Meade, Md., 1976—78, data sys. analyst, 1978—83, computer sys. analyst, 1983—85, sr. computer sys. analyst, 1985—86, computer scientist, 1986—89, mgr. sys. acquisition, 1989—94, dep. dir. for tech. fellow, 1994—95, sr. computer scientist, 1995—96, stds., tng. and verification engr., 1996—97, sys. engr., 1997—99, mgr. yr. 2000 compliance, 1999, sys. arch. implementation engr., 2000—01, sys. engr., 2001—02, dep. chief engring. divsn., 2002—03, acting dep. chief Sys. Engring Office, engr., 2003, lead sys. engr., 2003—. With Va. Summer Inst. for Math. Tchrs., 1995-96, dir. 1996-2000. With USNR, 1968-79. Home: 3002 Viburnum Pl Olney MD 20832-3073 Office: 9800 Savage Rd Fort George G Meade MD 20755-6000 Personal E-mail: robertleeschmitt@comcast.net.

SCHMITT, ROLAND WALTER, retired academic administrator; b. Seguin, Tex., July 24, 1923; s. Walter L. and Myrtle F. (Caldwell) S.; m. Claire Freeman Kunz, Sept. 19, 1957; children: Lorenz Allen, Brian Walter, Alice Elizabeth, Henry Caldwell. BA in Math, U. Tex., 1947, BS in Physics, 1947, MA in Physics, 1948; PhD, Rice U., 1951; DSc (hon.), Worcester Poly. Inst., 1985, U. Pa., 1985; DCL (hon.), Union Coll., 1985; DL (hon.), Lehigh U., 1986; DSc (hon.), U. S.C., 1988, U. Tech. De Compeigne, 1991; DL (hon.), Coll. St. Rose, 1992, Russell Sage, 1993, Hartford Grad. Ctr., 1995, Ill. Inst. Tech., 1996, Rensselaer Polytechnic Inst., 1997. With GE, 1951-88, R & D mgr. phys. sci. and engring. Schenectady, 1967-74, mgr. energy sci. and engring. R & D, 1974-78, v.p. corp. R & D, 1978-82, sr. v.p. corp. R & D, 1982-86, sr. v.p. sci. and tech., 1986-88, ret., 1988; pres. Rensselaer Poly. Inst., Troy, NY, 1988-93; ret., 1993. Bd. dirs. Blasch Precision Ceramics, GlobalSpec, Logical Net, Value Innovations; chmn. NYSTAR; bd. advisors LearnLinc, 1996-2000; tech. adv. bd. Chrysler Corp., 1990-93; tech. adv. coun. Mobil Corp., 1997-99; mem., past pres. Indsl. Rsch. Inst., 1978-88; energy rsch. adv. bd. U.S. Dept. Energy, 1977-83; mem. Nat. Sci. Bd., 1982-94, chmn., 1984-88; chmn. CORETECH, 1988-93; mem. Com. on Japan, NRC, 1988-90, Comml. Devel. Ind. Adv. Group, NASA, 1988-90; exec. com. Coun. on Competitiveness, 1988-93; chmn. NRC Panel on Export Controls, 1989-91; mem. Dept. Commerce Adv. Commn. on Patent Law Reform, 1990-92; adv. bd. Oak Ridge Nat. Lab., 1993-98; chair Rev. NATO Sci. program, 1998; mem. NRC panel rev. state dept. use sci. tech. and health, 1999; chmn. rsch. priority panel for NRC Future of Space Sci., 1994-95; chmn. Motorola's Sci. Adv. Bd., 1995-99, ICSU, 1997. Trustee N.E. Savs. Bank, 1978-84; bd. advisors Union Coll., Schenectady, 1981-84, Argonne Univs. Assn., 1979-82, RPI, 1982-88; bd. govs. Albany Med. Ctr. Hosp., 1979-82, 88-90; bd. dirs. Sunnyview Hosp. and Rehab. Ctr., 1978-86, Coun. on Superconductivity for Am. Competitiveness, 1987-89; mem. exec. com. N.Y. State Ctr. for Hazardous Waste Mgmt., 1988-89; chmn. Office of Tech. Assessment adv. panel on industry and environment; mem. Nat. Commn. Ill. Inst. Tech., 1993-94; chair NSF Acad. Rsch. Fleet Rev., 1998-99. With USAAF, 1943-46. Recipient Rensselaer Polytechnic Inst. Cmty. Svc. award, 1982, award for disting. contbns. Stony Brook Found., 1985, Disting. Alumni award Rice U., 1985, IRI Medalist award, 1989, Royal Swedish Acad. Engring. Sci., 1990, Arthur M. Bueche award Nat. Acad. Engring., 1995, NY State Bus. Coun.'s Corning award, 2001, Tech Mentor award Ctr. Econ. Growth, 2006; named Fgn. Assn. of Engring. Acad. Japan, U. Albany Found. Acad. Laureate, 1997; named to Jr. Achievement Capital Region Bus. Hall of Fame, 1996, Rensselaer Polytechnic Inst. Hall of Fame, 1999. Fellow AAAS, IEEE (Centennial medal 1984, Engring. Leadership award 1989, Founders medal 1992, Hoover medal 1993), Am. Phys. Soc. (Pake award 1993), Am. Acad. Arts and Scis.; mem. NAE (coun. 1983-89), Am. Inst. Physics (chmn. 1993-98), Coun. Sci. Soc. Pres. (chair 1993-97), N.Y. Acad. Scis. (pres. coun. 1993—2001), Dirs. Indsl. Rsch., Rensselaer Alumni Assn. (Disting. alumni award 1993), Eta Kappa Nu (eminent mem.) Office: PO Box 240 Rexford NY 12148-0240 Office Phone: 518-384-0965. E-mail: roland@schmitt.org.

SCHMITT, WILLIAM ALLEN, lawyer; b. Louisville, Aug. 29, 1909; s. Michael Joseph and Naoma Katherine Schmitt; m. Dorothy S. Turner, June 12, 1936 (dec. Feb. 1998); 1 child, Selene S. Kaelin. Student, U. Louisville, 1933. Bar: Ky. 1936, U.S. Dist. Ct. (we. dist.) Ky. 1936, NC 1997. Pvt. practice law, Louisville, 1936—; assoc. atty. Schmitt & Schmitt, Louisville, 1936-60; judge Jefferson County Probate Ct., Louisville, 1962-70; alcohol beverage control adminstr. Jefferson County Govt., Louisville, 1962-70; law ptnr. Schmitt & Sandmann, Louisville, 1968-74; pvt. practice law Louisville, 1974—, Jamestown, NC, 1997—. Author: Kentucky Probate, 1980, 2nd edit., 1997; contbr. articles to profl. jours. Election poll judge various gen. elections, Louisville; active Muir Chapel United Meth. Ch.; pres. Wildwood Country Club, 1964, Legal Aid Soc., Louisville, 1968. Lt. USN, 1944-46. Named to, Ky. Tennis Hall of Fame, 1993. Mem. ABA, ATLA, Am. Arbitration Assn. (arbitration panelist 1983-2003, cert. mediator 1985-99), Nat. Assn. Securities Dealers (arbitration panelist 1990-2004, cert. mediator 1994-2004), Am. Coll. Trust and Estate Counsel (state chmn. 1978-83), Ky. Bar Assn. (life, spkr. at seminars and convs. 1960-80, pres. 1970-71, probate com. 1970-86, chmn. 1977-81, trustee 1971-86, chmn. 1978-86, clients indemnity fund), N.C. State Bar Assn., N.C. State Bar, Louisville Bar Assn. (spkr. at seminars 1960-80, pres. 1966, chmn. probate com. 1974-79, various meritorious svc. awards 1966-75). Avocation: tennis. Home and Office: 109 Sagewood Rd Jamestown NC 27282-9489 Office Phone: 336-887-1135.

SCHMITT, WOLF RUDOLF, consumer products executive; b. Koblenz, Germany, Mar. 12, 1944; s. Josef H. and M.H. (Baldus) S.; m. Toni A. Yoder, June 30, 1974. BA, Otterbein Coll., 1966; AMP, Harvard U. Bus. Sch., 1986. With Rubbermaid Inc., Wooster, Ohio, 1966—, pres., gen. mgr. housewares products div., 1984-91, exec. v.p., bd. dirs., 1987-91, pres., chief operating officer, 1991-92; chmn., CEO, 1993-99; ret., 1999. Bd. dirs. Parker Hannifin Corp. Bd. dirs. Otterbein Coll., 1992—, Secrest Arboretum, 2002—. Avocations: horticulture, tennis, sailing. Office: Trends 2 Innovation 105 E Liberty St Wooster OH 44691-4345

SCHMITTMANN, BEATE, physics professor; b. 1957; Grad., U. Aachen, 1981; PhD in Physics, U. Edinburgh, 1984. Rsch. assoc. Physics Dept. U. Dusseldorf, Germany, 1984—86, rsch. asst. prof., 1991—97; vis. asst. prof. Va. Tech. U., Blacksburg, 1990—91, assoc. prof., 1991—97, prof., 1997—, chair physics dept., 2006—. Lectr. in field. Contbr. articles to profl. jours. Grantee Pro Renovanda Cultura Hungarica Fellow, Hungarian Ministry of Sci., 1995. Fellow: Am. Physical Soc. Office: Va Tech U 111 Robeson Hall Blacksburg VA 24061 Office Phone: 540-231-6518. Office Fax: 540-231-7511. E-mail: schmittm@vt.edu. *

SCHMITZ, BARBARA, art preservationist; b. Cin., 1936; AM, U. Chgo., 1960; MA, PhD, NYU, 1981. Prof., advisor LCW U., Lahore, Pakistan, 2007—. Author: (illustrated catalogs of Islamic paintings) Islamic Manuscripts, N.Y. Pub. Libr., 1992, Islamic and Indian Manuscripts and Paintings, Pierpont Morgan Libr., 1996; co-author (with Z.A. Desai): Mughal and Persian Painting and Illustrated Manuscripts in the Raza Library, Rampur (U.P.), 2006; editor, contbr.: After the Great Mughals: Painting in Delhi and the Regional Courts in the 18th-19th Centuries, 2004. Fulbright grantee, 1992—93, 1997—98, Indira Gandhi Nat. Ctr. for the Arts grantee, New Delhi, 1995, Am. Inst. Indian Studies grantee, 1998—99, Browniee Grant, Mo. Hist. Soc., 2002. E-mail: barbaraschmitz65016@yahoo.com.

SCHMITZ, DENNIS MATHEW, retired language educator; b. Dubuque, Iowa, Aug. 11, 1937; s. Anthony Peter and Roselyn S.; m. Loretta D'Agostino, Aug. 20, 1960; children: Anne, Sara, Martha, Paul, Matthew. BA, Loras Coll., 1959; MA, U. Chgo., 1961. Instr. English Ill. Inst. Tech., Chgo., 1961-62, U. Wis., Milw., 1962-66; asst. prof. Calif. State U., Sacramento, 1966-69, assoc. prof., 1969-74, prof., 1974-99; ret., 1999. Poet-in-residence, 1966-99. Author: We Weep for Our Strangeness, 1969, Double Exposures, 1971, Goodwill, Inc., 1976, String, 1980, Singing, 1985, Eden, 1989, About Night: Selected and New Poems, 1993, The Truth Squad, 2002. Recipient Discovery award Poetry Center, NYC, 1968; winner First Book Competition Follett Pub. Co., 1969; di Castagnola award Poetry Soc. Am., 1986; Shelley Meml. award Poetry Soc. Am., 1987; NEA fellow, 1976-77, 85-86, 92-93, Guggenheim fellow, 1978-79. Mem. PEN, Assoc. Writing Programs. Roman Catholic.

SCHMITZ, JOHN, energy and food products executive; BS in Acctg., St. Cloud State U., Minn. CPA, Minn. With Harvest States (merged with Cenex, now CHS Inc.), Inver Grove Heights, Minn., 1974—, v.p., contr., 1986—98, sr. v.p., CFO, 1999, exec. v.p., CFO. Bd. dirs. Nat. Coop. Refinery Assn., Cofina Fin., LLC. Mem. AICPA, Nat. Soc. Accts. for Coops., Minn. Soc. CPAs. Office: CHS Inc PO Box 64089 Saint Paul MN 55164-0089 Office Phone: 651-355-3778. E-mail: john.schmitz@chsinc.com. *

SCHMITZ, JOHN J., writer, educator; b. Fond du Lac, Wis., Mar. 9, 1937; s. John L. Schmitz and Josephine Knaus; children: David, Rebecca. BA, St. Francis Sem., 1963. CLU Am. Coll. Life Underwriters, 1975. Pres. John Schmitz Agy., Brookfield, Wis., 1992—; instr. Hondros Coll., Columbus, Ohio, 1994—. Cons. Bryant and Stratton Coll., Milw., 2003—04. Author: A Funny Thing Happened On My Way Out of Church, JoAnn: In Search of N.E.D. Bd. mem., officer Elmbrook Sch. Bd., Brookfield, Wis., 1988—92. Mem.: KC (assoc.; grand knight 1996—97). Achievements include development of Insurance Courses for Continuing Education. Avocations: writing, photography, travel. Home: 405 Lynnwood Lane Brookfield WI 53005-6134 Office: John Schmitz Agency 405 Lynnwood Lane Brookfield WI 53005-6134 Personal E-mail: jschmitz13@wi.rr.com.

SCHMITZ, JOSEPH EDWARD, lawyer, former federal agency administrator; s. John G. Schmitz. BS with distinction, U.S. Naval Acad., 1978; JD, Stanford U., 1986; grad., Naval Inspector Gen. Sch., Army Inspector Gen. Sch. Commd. USN; capt. USNR, dep. sr. inspector for Naval Res. Intelligence program; law clk. to Hon. James L. Buckley US Ct. Appeals (D.C. cir.); spl. asst. to atty gen. US Dept. Justice; inspector gen. US Dept. Def., Arlington, Va., 2002—05; COO, gen. counsel The Prince Group, McLean, Va., 2005—. Adj. prof. law Georgetown U. Law Ctr., 1995—2002; mem. steering com. Washington Lawyers chpt. Federalist Soc. for Law and Pub. Policy Studies. Mem.: Sovereign Mil. Order Malta.

SCHMITZ, ROBERT ALLEN, publishing executive, investor; b. Chgo., Ill., Jan. 19, 1941; s. John and Lee (Zeal) S.; m. Jenny Ann Quest, Aug. 23, 1969 (div.); m. Judith Mair Grey, Oct. 25, 1997; children: Alexander, Nicholas, Lara, Maximilian. BA with distinction, U. Mich., 1963; MBA, MIT, 1965. Asst. to pres. Lima (Peru) Light and Power Co., 1965-67; acquisition analyst W.R. Grace Co., NYC, 1967-69; asst. to chmn. N.W. Industries, NYC, 1969-70; prin. McKinsey & Co., Inc., NYC, 1970-82; v.p. books Dow Jones & Co., NYC, 1982-88; chmn., pres., chief exec. officer Richard D. Irwin, Inc., Homewood, Ill., 1983-89; pres., founder Quest Capital Ltd., 1989—; investment cons. Soros Fund Mgmt., 1990-92; mgn. dir., sr. ptnr. Trust Co. of the West, 1993-97; mng. dir., founder. Quest Turnaround Advisors, 1999—; chmn., founder Headline Media Group, 2001—; COO, PTV Inc., 2003—. Mem. adv. bd. Coll. Commerce De Paul U., Chgo., 1985—; bd. dirs. Two Way Media, London, Premium TV LLC, London, Cablecom GmBH, Zurich, Adams Rite Sabre, Inc., Glendale, Calif., Superior Fireplace Co., Fullerton, Calif., Houston Foods Co., Chgo., Archibald Candy Co., Chgo., US Media Group, Inc., Crystal City, Mo., Ctrl. Valley Publ., Merced, Hobby Products Co., Inc., Penrose, Colo., Automated Bar Controls, Vacaville, Calif., Spectran Techs., Inc., Sturbridge, Mass.; non-exec. chmn. PTV Ltd., London, 2 Way Media Ltd., London. Pres. Cultural Arts Ctr. Found., Homewood, Ill. Mem. Assn. Am. Pubs. (chmn. higher edn. divsn. 1989), Nature Conservancy (trustee N.Y. state chpt.). Office: Quest Turnaround Advisors Ltd 287 Bowman Ave Purchase NY 10577 Home Phone: 914-921-3497; Office Phone: +44-7968285821. E-mail: bob.schmitz@ptvinc.com.

SCHMITZ, ROGER ANTHONY, chemical engineer, educator, academic administrator; b. Carlyle, Ill., Oct. 22, 1934; s. Alfred Bernard and Wilma Afra (Aarns) Schmitz; m. Ruth Mary Kuhl, Aug. 31, 1957; children: Jan, Joy, Joni. BSChemE, U. Ill., 1959; PhD in Chem. Engring., U. Minn., 1962. Prof. chem. engring. U. Ill., Urbana, 1962-79; Keating-Crawford prof. chem. engring. U. Notre Dame, Ind., 1979—2005, prof. emeritus, 2005—, chmn. dept. chem. engring. Ind., 1979-81, dean engring. Ind., 1981-87, v.p., assoc. provost Ind., 1987-95. Cons. Amoco Chems., Naperville, Ill., 1966—77; vis. prof. Calif. Inst. Tech., LA, 1968—69. Contbr. articles to profl. jours. With US Army, 1953—55. Fellow, Guggenheim Found., 1968. Mem.: AIChE (A.P. Colburn award 1970, R.H. Wilhelm award 1981), Am. Soc. Engring. Edn. (George Westinghouse award 1977), Nat. Acad. Engring. Roman Catholic. Home: 16865 Londonberry Ln South Bend IN 46635-1444 Office: U Notre Dame 305 Cushing Hall Notre Dame IN 46556 Office Phone: 574-631-7798. Business E-Mail: schmitz.1@nd.edu.

SCHMITZ, SHIRLEY GERTRUDE, marketing professional, sales executive; b. Brackenridge, Pa., Dec. 19, 1927; d. Wienand Gerard and Florence Marie (Grimm) Schmitz. BA, Ariz. State U., 1949. Tchr., guidance counselor Mesa HS, Ariz., 1949-51; area mgr. Field Enterprises Ednl. Corp., Phoenix, 1951-52, dist. mgr., 1952, regional mgr., 1953-55, br. mgr. Montreal, 1955-61, nat. supr. Chgo., 1961-63, asst. sales mgr., 1963-65, nat. sales mgr., 1965-70; v.p., gen. sales mgr. F.E. Compton Co. divsn. Ency. Brit., Chgo., 1970-71, exec. v.p., dir. sales, 1971-73; pres. CHB Port-A-Book Store, Inc., 1973-76; gen. mgr. Bobbs-Merrill Co., Inc., Indpls., 1976-82; v.p. sales U. S. Telephone Comms. of Midwest, Inc., Indpls., 1982-83; exec. v.p. sales and market devel. Entertainment Publ. Corp., Birmingham, Mich., 1983-89, sr. v.p. mktg. and sales Troy, Mich., 1989-92. Prin. S. G. Schmitz and Assocs., Chgo., 1992—; bd. adv., founder Ctr. Advancement Small Bus. (now Spirit of Enterprise Ctr.), W. P. Carey Sch. Bus. Ariz. State U.; pres.'s cabinet capital fund raising campaign Ariz. State U.; prin. Innovators-Changemakers LLC, Ariz., 2005—. Bd. dir., founder, pres. Shirley G. Schmitz Found., Inc.; founder, managing ptnr. Innovators-Changemakers, LLC, 2005—. Recipient Elizabeth Cutter Morrow award, Internat. Bd. YWCA, 1978, Disting. Achievement award, Ariz. State U., 1995, Angel award, Ariz. chpt. Nat. Assn. Women Bus. Owners, 1996, Nat. Bus. Achievement award, Beta Gamma Sigma, 1998, Impact for Enterprising Women award, 2001. Home: 11899 N 135th Way Scottsdale AZ 85259-3651 Office: SG Schmitz and Assocs Scottsdale AZ 85259-3651 Personal E-mail: reysgs@aol.com.

SCHMOKE, KURT LIDELL, dean, former mayor; b. Balt., Dec. 1, 1949; m. Patricia Schmoke; children: Katherine, Gregory. BA, Yale U., 1971; JD, Harvard U., 1976. Assoc. Piper & Marbury LLP, 1976—78; asst. U.S. atty Dist. Md. US Dept. Justice, Balt., 1978—82; state's atty. State of Md., 1982-87; mayor City of Balt., 1988—99; ptnr. Wilmer Cutler Pickering LLP, Balt., 2000—03; dean Howard U. Sch. Law, Washington, 2003—. Apptd. mem. White House Domestic Policy Staff, 1977-78; former mem. Gov.'s Commn. on Prison Overcrowding; former mem. Md. Criminal justice Coord. Coun. & Task Force to Reform Insanity Def.; founder Balt. Community Devel. Financing Corp., 1988—. Recipient Literacy award, The White House, 1992. Office: Howard Univ Sch Law Office of the Dean 112 Houston Hall 2900 Van Ness St NW Washington DC 20008 *

SCHMOLKA, LEO LOUIS, law educator; b. Paris, Apr. 25, 1939; came to US, 1944; s. Francis and Irene S.; m. Lucille J. Schoenbaum, July 29, 1965; children: Andrew, Gregory. AB, Dartmouth Coll., 1960; LL.B., Harvard U., 1963; LL.M., NYU, 1971. Bar: NY 1964. Assoc. Weil, Gotshal and Manges, NYC, 1964-71, ptnr., 1971-81, of counsel, 1981—; adj. asst. prof. law NYU Sch. of Law, 1971-75; adj. assoc. prof. law NYU Law Sch., 1975-76, adj. prof., 1977-80, assoc. prof., 1981-84, prof., 1985—, mem. faculty, dir. IRS/NYU continuing profl. edn. program, 1987—. Cons. US Treasury Dept. Office Tax Policy, Washington, 1994-95, Am. Law Inst., 1979-86, U. Miami Estate Planning Inst., Fla., 1976-80; vis. adj. prof. law U. Miami Sch. Law, 1977, 80, U. San Diego Sch. Law, 1999; vis. lectr. continuing legal edn. various univs. and tax insts., 1973—. Contbr. articles to legal jours. Fellow Am. Coll. Trust and Estate Counsel; mem. ABA, NY State Bar Assn. (chmn. com. on income taxation estates and trusts 1973-75, estate and gift tax 1976-77, mem. exec. com. tax sect. 1978), Internat. Acad. Estate and Trust Law (academician). Office: NYU Sch Law 40 Washington Sq S Rm 430 New York NY 10012-1099 Personal E-mail: schmolka@optonline.net.

SCHMOLL, EDITH MARGARET, music educator; b. Boston, Mar. 10, 1924; d. William James Pruyn, Sr. and Ida Mary Langan; m. John Arthur Pickering (div.); children: Nancy Pickering, Lois Pickering, Barry Pickering; m. Mariel Theodore Schmoll, Sr., Jan. 10, 1969 (dec. 2002). Grad., Boston Clerical, Mass., 1941; student in Piano Performance, New Eng. Conservatory, Boston, 1945—46; student in Accordian Performance, Conservatory of Music, Kaiserslautern, Germany, 1954—55. Cert. tchr. music Calif. Tchr. music, LA, 1960—; br. mgr. Int. Rectifier Fed. Credit Union, Temecula, Calif., 1991—97. Concert pianist, 1940—; ch. musician, 1965—; pres. Music Songs, Sun City, Calif., 1976—. Editor: (college piano books) Creative Keyboard Experience, 1970. Mem. Legacy Soc., Mt. San Jacinto Coll. Found., Calif., 2006; past pres. Sun City Hermosa Homeowners Assn., Calif., 1995—97. Mem.: Mensa. Avocations: portrait and mural painter, writing. Office: Music Songs 28108 Gardena Dr Ste A Sun City CA 92586 Office Phone: 951-679-4201.

SCHMOLL, HANS JOACHIM, hematology and oncology educator; b. Hannover, Germany, June 21, 1946; s. Johannes and Edeltraut (Schneider) S. MD, Med. U. Hannover, 1970, PhD, 1982. Rsch. assoc. Med. U., Hannover, 1971—84, prof. medicine and hematology-oncology, 1984—95; prof. medicine and hematology, chair hematology/oncology Martin Luther U., Halle-Wittenberg, Germany, 1996—. Author, editor: Kompendium Intern Onkologie, 1986, 4th edit., 2005; assoc. editor Cancer Rsch., 2002—; editor-in-chief Oncologie, 2001—; mem. editl. bd. European Jour. Cancer Annals of Oncology. Recipient German Cancer award, 2001, Sci. award, German Assn. Med. Oncologists, 1998. Mem.: German Assn. Med. Oncology (pres., chmn. 2001—). Home: Ludwig Barnay Strasse 9 D-30175 Hanover Germany Office: Martin Luther Univ Dept Oncol Hematol Int Med IV D-06120 Halle Germany Home Phone: 0049-0171-3141667; Office Phone: 0049-345-557-2924. Business E-Mail: haematologie@medizin.uni-halle.de. E-mail: hjschmoll@yahoo.de.

SCHMOLL, HARRY F., JR., lawyer, educator; b. Somers Point, NJ, Jan. 20, 1939; s. Harry F. Sr. and Margaret E. S.; m. Rita L. Miescier, Aug. 29, 1977. BS, Rider Coll., 1960; JD, Temple U., 1967. Bar: Pa., D.C. 1969, N.J. 1975. With claims dept. Social Security Adminstrn., Phila., 1960-67; staff atty. Pa. State U., State College, 1968-69, instr. criminal justice University Park, 1969-74; regional dir. Pa. Crime Commn., State College, 1969-70; campaign aide U.S. Senator Hugh Scott, Harrisburg, Pa., 1970; pvt. practice law State College, 1970-74, Manahawkin, NJ, 1975-96; prof. criminal justice, prof. emeritus bus. law Burlington County Coll., Pemberton, NJ, 1974—2002; assoc. Mattleman, Weinroth & Miller, P.C., Cherry Hill, NJ, 2003—. Judge mcpl. ct., Stafford Twp., 1982—85. Author: New Jersey Criminal Law Workbook, 1976, 2nd edit., 1979, Absecon Diary of Margie Roth, 1933-37, 2000. Former gen. counsel German Heritage Coun. N.J., Inc.; mem. Barnegat Twp. Rent Control Bd., 1991, Barnegat Twp. Zoning Bd., 1994; mem. fund distbn. com. United Way of Burlington County, N.J., 1987-89; former trustee H.B. Smith Indsl. Village Conservancy; bd. trustees Holiday Village East Cmty. Svcs. Assn., 2003-04; mem. Stafford Twp. Com., 1979-81; dep. mayor, 1979. Mem. Pa. Bar assn., N.J. Bar Assn. (mem. probate/estate planning com. Burlington County), German-Am. Club So. Ocean County (past pres.), Tri-State Jazz Soc. (webmaster). Home Phone: 856-222-9674; Office Phone: 856-429-5507. Personal E-mail: HarrySchmoll2@comcast.net.

SCHMUDDE, LEE GENE, resort executive, corporate lawyer; b. Harvey, Ill., Apr. 13, 1950; s. Kenneth H. and Jean E. (Alexander) S.; m. Mariann Verscharen, June 25, 1976; 1 child, Leighanne K. BA summa cum laude,

Cornell Coll., Mount Vernon, Iowa, 1972; JD, Duke U., Durham, NC, 1975. Bar: Fla. 1975, US Dist. Ct. (ctrl. dist.) Fla. 1975. Law clk. to Chief Judge Joseph P. McNulty 2d Dist. Ct. Appeals, Lakeland, Fla., 1975-76; atty. Peterson, Myers, Lake Wales, Fla., 1976-78; v.p. legal and environ. affairs Walt Disney World Co., Orlando, Fla. Lectr. ABA, Fla. Bar, Orange County Bar Assn., Def. Lawyers Assn. Contbr. articles to Fla. Bar Jour. Bd. dirs., treas. Fla. Symphony Orch., Orlando, 1997; bd. dirs. Children's Home Soc., 1981-85; mem. adv. bd. Jr. Achievement, 1995—; chmn. Fla. Self-Ins. Guaranty Assn., 1985, 93, bd. dirs., 1985—; mem. adv. bd. Western Carolina Sch. Tourism & Hospitality. Mem. Fla. Bar Assn. (lectr.), Am. Zoo and Aquarium Assn., US C. of C. (Outstanding Young Man of Am. 1975), Fla. C. of C. (jud. and tort reform adv. bd. 2000—), Fla. Assn. Self-Insurers (bd. dirs. 1984-85), Ctrl. Fla. Hist. Soc. (bd. dirs. 2000—), United Arts of Ctrl. Fla. (bd. dirs., 2005—), Phi Beta Kappa, Eta Sigma Delta. Avocations: tennis, basketball, sport fishing. Office: Walt Disney World Co PO Box 10 000 Lake Buena Vista FL 32830-1000 Business E-Mail: lee.schmudde@disney.com.

SCHMULTS, EDWARD CHARLES, lawyer; b. Paterson, NJ, Feb. 6, 1931; s. Edward M. and Mildred (Moore) S.; m. Diane E. Beers, Apr. 23, 1960; children: Alison C., Edward M., Robert C. BS, Yale U., 1953; JD, Harvard U., 1958. Bar: N.Y. 1959, D.C. 1974. Assoc. White & Case, NYC, 1958-65, ptnr., 1965-73, 77-81; gen. counsel US Dept. Treasury, Washington, 1973-74, under sec., 1974-75; dep. counsel to Pres. The White House, Washington, 1975-76; dep. atty. gen. US Dept. Justice, Washington, 1981-84; sr. v.p. external rels., gen. counsel GTE Corp., Stamford, Conn., 1984-94; sr. advisor Iraqi Ministry of Justice - Coalition Provisional Authority, 2004. Lectr. securities laws. Served to 1st lt. USMC, 1953-55; capt. USMCR. Mem. Am. Bar Assn., Assn. Bar City N.Y., Adminstrv. Conf. U.S. (council 1977-84), Sakonnet Golf Club, Met. Club. Personal E-mail: eschmults@msn.com.

SCHMUTZ, JOHN FRANCIS, lawyer; b. Oneida, NY, July 24, 1947; s. William L. and Rosemary S. Schmutz; m. H. Marie Roney, June 7, 1969; children: Gretchen, Jonathan, Nathan. BA cum laude, Canisius Coll., 1969; JD cum laude, Notre Dame U., 1972; LLM, George Washington U., 1975. Bar: Ind. 1972, DC 1975, Tex. 1993, U.S. Ct. Mil. Appeals 1972, U.S. Tax Ct. 1973, U.S. Supreme Ct. 1975. Legislation and maj. projects officer Office Judge Adv. Gen., 1972—74; appellate atty. U.S. Army Legal Svcs. Agy., 1974—75; assoc. Ice, Miller, Donadio & Ryan, Indpls., 1976—77; staff atty. Burger Chef Sys., Inc., Indpls., 1977—78, sr. atty., 1979, asst. chief legal counsel, 1978—80, chief legal counsel, 1980, v.p., gen. counsel, sec., 1981—91; v.p.-legal Hardee's Food Sys., Inc., 1983—91; v.p., gen. counsel Sbarro, Inc., 1991—92; v.p., gen. counsel, sec. La Quinta Inns, Inc., 1992—98, gen. counsel, sec., 1998—99; sr. v.p., gen. counsel, sec. Meditrust Cos., Inc., 2000—01, La Quinta Cos., Inc., 2001—02; founding prin. Turtle Creek Group, LLC, 2002—. Dir., v.p. Bursan Credit Union; dir. Food Svc. and Lodging Inst., RIX Sys., Inc., Burger Chef Distributive Corp.; v.p. Hardee's Food Sys., Inc. Exec. editor: Notre Dame Law Rev., 1971—72. Exec. bd. Boy Scouts Am.; bd. dirs. Blessed Sacrament Acad. Found. Mem.: ABA (dir. hospitality com., cmty. recreation and common interest devel. com.), Am. Corp. Counsel Assn. (bd. dirs.), Internat. Corp. Sec. Assn., Am. Hotel and Motel Assn. (gen. counsel com.), Nat. Restaurant Assn., Am. Assn. Corp. Counsel, San Antonio Bar Assn., Tex. Bar Assn., Indpls. Bar Assn., DC Bar Assn., Ind. Bar Assn., Fed. Bar Assn. Republican. Roman Catholic. Home: 17122 Eagle Star San Antonio TX 78248-1548 Personal E-mail: johnschmutz@sbcglobal.net.

SCHMUTZHART, BERTHOLD JOSEF, sculptor, educator; b. Salzburg, Austria, Aug. 17, 1928; came to U.S., 1958, naturalized, 1963; s. Berthold Josef and Anna (Valaschek) S. Student, Acad. for Applied Art, Vienna, Austria, 1956. Cert. fed. tchr., Austria. Prof. Werkschulheim Felbertal, Salzburg, 1951-58; sculptor Washington, 1959-60; tchr. Longfellow Sch., Bethesda, Md., 1960-63; prof., chmn. dept. sculpture Corcoran Sch. Art, Washington, 1963-94, prof. emeritus, 1994—; lectr. Smithsonian Instn., Washington, 1968-84. One-man shows include Fredericksburg Gallery Fine Art, Va., 1967-73, Franz Bader Gallery, Washington, 1978, 81, 83, 86, 88; group shows include Nat. Collection Fine Arts, Washington, 1961-70, High Mus. Art, Atlanta, 1965, Ark. Art Ctr., Little Rock, 1966, Birmingham Mus. Art, Ala., 1967, Hirschhorn Mus. and Sculpture Garden, Washington, 1981, Nat. Gallery Modern Art, New Delhi, 1990; represented in permanent collections Hirschhorn Collection; designer fountain, Gallery of Modern Art, Fredericksburg, 1967; author: The Handmade Furniture Book, 1981; contbr. articles to profl. jours. Fine arts panelist D.C. Commn. for Arts, 1973-79; chmn. bd. Market Five Gallery, Washington, 1978-82; bd. dirs. Franz Bader Gallery, Washington, 1981-86; trustee Arts for the Aging, Inc., Washington, 1990—98; chmn. Franz and Virginia Bader Fund, 2001-06, bd. dirs., 2006-. Recipient 1st prize Washington Religious Arts Council, 1960, for sculpture, Little Rock, 1966, Louisville, 1968, Silver medal Audubon Soc., Washington, 1971 Mem. Guild for Religious Architects, Artists Equity Assn. (pres. D.C. chpt. 1973-75), AAUP, Am. Austrian Soc. (pres. 1968-70, exec. com.), Soaring Soc. Am. Home: 32 Layline Ln Fredericksburg VA 22406-4061 E-mail: gn15bs@earthlink.net.

SCHNABEL, ECKHARD JOHANNES, theologian, educator; b. Stuttgart, Germany, May 9, 1955; s. Paul and Elsbeth (Blattner) S.; m. Barbara Cornelia Duerrschmidt, Sept. 11, 1981; children: Mirjam, Benjamin. ThM, FETA, Basel, Switzerland, 1979; PhD, U. Aberdeen, Scotland, 1983. Asst. prof. N.T. Asia Theol. Sem., Manila, 1985-88; lectr. Wiedenest Bible Coll., Bergneustadt, Germany, 1989-94; head N.T. dept. German Theol. Sem., Giessen, Germany, 1994-98; prof. Trinity Evangelical Divinty Sch., Deerfield, Ill., 1998—. Exec. com. Arbeitskreis für evangelikale Theologie, Germany, 1991-98. Author: Law and Wisdom From Ben Sira to Paul, 1985, Inspiration und Offenbarung, 1986, Das Reich Gottes als Wirklichkeit und Hoffnung, 1993, Sind Evangelikale Fundamentalisten?, 1995, Die Gemeinde des neuen Bundes, 1996, Jesus and the Beginnings of the Mission to the Gentiles, 1994, Studium des Neuen Testaments, 2 vols., 1999-2000, Urchristliche Mission, 2002, Early Christian Mission, 2004, Der erste Brief des Paulus an die Korinther, 2006; assoc. editor Bulletin Bibical Rsch.; contbr. articles to profl. jours. Mem. Soc. N.T. Studies, Tyndale Fellowship, Soc. of Bibl. Lit., Evang. Theol. Soc., Inst. for Bibl. Rsch. Office: Trinity Internat U Half Day Rd Deerfield IL 60015 E-mail: eschnabel@trin.edu.

SCHNABEL, MARTA-ANN, lawyer; b. Butte, Mont., July 15, 1957; m. Kevin O'Bryon; 2 children. BA in History, with honors, Meml. U. Newfoundland, Can., 1978; JD, Loyola U., 1981. Bar: La. 1981, US Dist. Ct. (Ea. Dist. La.), US Dist. Ct. (Mid. Dist. La.), US Dist. Ct. (We. Dist. La.), US Ct. Appeals (5th Cir.). Assoc. Hammett Leake and Hammett, 1981—86, ptnr., 1986; mng. ptnr. Leake & Andersson LLP; shareholder O'Bryon & Schnabel PLC, New Orleans. Mem. Alliance for Good Govt., treas., 2000—03; v.p. La. Client Assistance Found., 2003; bd. dirs. New Orleans Legal Aid Bur., 1990—94, sec., 1994—95, v.p., 1997—99; bd. dirs. New Orleans Legal Assistance Corp., 1996—99; mem. bd. trustees St. Martin's Episcopal Sch., 2001—04. Recipient Gillis Long Pub. Svc. award, Loyola Law Sch. Master: New Orleans Bar Assn. Inn of Ct.; fellow: La. Bar Found.; mem.: Def. Rsch. Inst., Assn. Def. Trial Attys., La. Assn. Def. Counsel, La. State Bar Assn. (bd. gov. 1998—2006, ethics adv. svc. com. 2000, editor-in-chief law jour. 2001—03, pres. 2006—07, practice assistance com., improvement com., co-chair access to justice com., com. rules of profl. conduct, Pres. award 1998, 2004), New Orleans Bar Assn. (pres. 1995). Office: O'Bryon & Schnabel PLC Ste 830 1515 Poydras St New Orleans LA 70112-4541 Office Phone: 504-799-4200. Office Fax: 504-799-4211.

SCHNABEL, ROBERT VICTOR, retired academic administrator; b. Scarsdale, NY, Sept. 28, 1922; s. Frederick Victor and Louise Elizabeth (Frick) S.; m. Ellen Edyth Foelber, June 7, 1946; children: Mark F., Philip P. Student, Concordia Sem., St. Louis, 1943-45; AB, Bowdoin Coll., 1944; MS, Fordham U., 1951, PhD, 1955; LLD (hon.), Concordia Coll., 1988. Tchr. St. Paul's Sch., Ft. Wayne, Ind., 1945-49; prin. St. Matthew's Sch., NYC, 1949-52; assoc. supt. edn. Central Dist., Luth. Ch.-Mo. Synod, 1952-56; asst. prof. philosophy Concordia Sr. Coll., Ft. Wayne, 1956-60, assoc. prof., 1960-65, prof., acad. dean, 1966-71; pres. Concordia Coll., Bronxville, NY, 1971-76; acad. v.p., dean Wartburg Coll., Waverly, Iowa, 1976-78; pres. Valparaiso (Ind.) U., 1978-88. Cons. Luth. Edn. Conf. N.Am., 1977-88. Contbr. articles to profl. jours. Mem. AAUP, Luth. Acad. Scholarship, Assoc. Colls. Ind., Nat. Assn. Ind. Colls. and Univs., Rotary, Phi Delta Kappa. Office: Valparaiso Univ 23 Huegli Hall Valparaiso IN 46383

SCHNABEL, ROCKWELL ANTHONY, former ambassador; b. Amsterdam, Holland, Dec. 30, 1936; s. Hans and Wilhelmina S.; m. Marna Belle Del Mar, 1964; children: Mary Darrin, Christy Ann, Everton Anthony. BS in Bus. Adminstrn., Trinity Coll., The Netherlands, 1951-56; LLD (hon.), Pepperdine U. Pres. Unilife Assurance Group S.H. Luxembourg, 1974-78, Bateman Eichler Hill Richard Group, Los Angeles, 1981-83; U.S. amb. to Finland U.S. Dept. State, Helsinki, 1986—89; under sec. for travel and tourism U.S. Dept. Commerce, Washington, 1989-91, dep. sec., 1991-92, acting sec., 1992-93; U.S. amb. to the European Union U.S. Dept. State, Brussels, 2001—06; sr. ptnr. Trident Capital LLP, Palo Alto, Calif., 1992—2001, advisory dir., 2006—; chmn. Sage Group LLC, 2006—. Bd. dirs. Internat. Game Tech., CSGystems Inc.; chmn. La.-Inc.; bd. trustees U. Calif. Bus. Sch. Co-author (with Francis X. Rocca): The Next Superpower? The Rise of Europe and its Challenge to the United States, 2005. Past pres. L.A. Pension Bd., Calif., 1982; mem. L.A. Olympic Organizing Com., 1983-84. With Air N.G., 1958-64. Decorated comdr. Order of Good Hope, South Africa, Grand Cross of Lion of Finland; recipient Gold medal Dutch Govt., U.S. Dept. Commerce, medal of honor the Netherlands Olympic Com. Mem. L.A. Beach Club, Calif. Club, L.A. Country Club. Office: Trident Capital Ste 200 505 Hamilton Ave Palo Alto CA 94301

SCHNACKENBERG, GJERTRUD CECELIA, poet; b. Tacoma, Aug. 27, 1953; d. Walter Charles and Doris Ione Schnackenberg; m. Robert Nozick, Oct. 5, 1987. BA summa cum laude, Mount Holyoke Coll., 1975, LittD (hon.), 1985. Fellow The Bunting Inst., Radcliffe and Cambridge, Mass., 1979-80; lectr. in writing MIT, Cambridge, 1980-81; Hurst prof. poetry Washington U., St. Louis, 1987; Conkling writer in residence Smith Coll., Northampton, Mass., fall 1994. Vis. fellow St. Catherine's Coll., Oxford U., 1997, Getty Rsch. Inst., 2000. Author: numerous poems. Recipient Rome prize in lit. Am. Acad. Arts and Letters, 1983, Acad. award in lit. Am. Acad. Arts and Letters, 1998, Brandeis citation in poetry, 1989, Berlin prize, 2004; Nat. Endowment for the Arts fellow in poetry, 1986, Guggenheim fellow, 1987; Book Prize in Poetry, L.A. Times, 2000. Fellow: Am. Acad. Rome, Am. Acad. Arts and Scis., Am. Acad. in Berlin. Democrat.

SCHNAITMAN, WILLIAM KENNETH, retired finance company executive; b. Talbot County, Md., May 12, 1926; s. William and Catherine Almeda (Cheezum) S.; m. Beverly June Marshall, July 13, 1963. Student, Strayer Bus. Sch., Balt., 1943. Clk. Comml. Credit Co., Balt., 1946-70, asst. sec., 1970-72, treas., 1972-75, dir. cash mgmt., 1976-87, ret., 1987. With AUS, 1944-46, ETO. Home: 12520 Wye Landing Ln Wye Mills MD 21679-2050

SCHNAKE, RICHARD LANE, lawyer; b. Carthage, Mo., Aug. 3, 1957; s. Ivan Eugene and Phyllis Lea (Stewart) S.; m. Kelly Dawn Barfield, Oct. 9, 1999. BA in History, S.W. Mo. State U., 1979; JD, Washington U., St. Louis, 1982. Bar: Mo., 1982, U.S. Dist. Ct. (we. dist.) Mo. 1982, U.S. Ct. Appeals (8th cir.) 1984, U.S. Supreme Ct., 1986, U.S. Ct. Appeals (7th cir.) 1989. Law clk. to Hon. Warren D. Welliver Supreme Ct. of Mo., Jefferson City, 1982-83; assoc. Neale, Newman, Bradshaw & Freeman, Springfield, Mo., 1983-87; ptnr. Neale, Newman, Bradshaw & Freeman, Neale & Newman, L.L.P., Springfield, Mo., 1988—. Mem. Mo. Supreme Ct. Civil Rules Com., Jefferson City, 1994—2002, mem. Appellate Practice Com., 2002—; spl. asst. Atty. Gen. Mo., Jefferson City, 1990-93; chmn. Springfield Metro. Bar Assn. Law Day Com., 1989-91, 2003—, sec., bd. dirs., 1992-95. Author: Civil Rules Practice, Rules 85-88, 17A Missouri Practice, 1999; contbr. articles to profl. jours. Bd. dirs., pres., sec. Ozark Counseling Ctr., Springfield, Mo., 1987-88, 89-91, 92-94, 95—. Recipient Scribes award for legal writing, 1982, David J. Dixon Appellate Advocacy award Mo. Bar Found., Jefferson City, Mo., 1990; nominee for nonpartisan appt. to Mo. Ct. Appeals, 2003. Mem. ABA, Springfield Met. Bar Assn. (seminar lectr.), Mo. Bar Assn. (seminar lectr.), Order of Coif, Phi Kappa Phi. Mem. Ch. of Christ. Avocation: autograph collecting. Office: Neale & Newman LLP 1949 E Sunshine St Ste 1-130 Springfield MO 65804-1682 Address: PO Box 10327 Springfield MO 65808-0327 Home: 4196 E Gastonbury St Springfield MO 65809 Home Phone: 417-886-7234; Office Phone: 417-882-9090. Business E-Mail: rschnake@nnlaw.com.

SCHNAPP, ROGER HERBERT, lawyer, consultant; b. NYC, Mar. 17, 1946; s. Michael Jay and Beatrice Joan (Becker) S.; m. Candice Jacqueline Larson, Sept. 15, 1979; 1 child, Monica Alexis. BS, Cornell U., 1966; JD, Harvard U., 1969; postgrad. Pub. Utility Mgmt. Program, U. Mich., 1978. Bar: NY 1970, US Ct. Appeals (2d cir.) 1970, US Supreme, 1974, US Dist. Ct. (so. dist.) NY 1975, US Ct. Appeals (4th and 6th cirs.) 1976, US Ct. Appeals (7th cir.) 1977, US Dist. Ct. (so. dist.) NY 1975, US Dist. Ct. (no. dist.) Calif. 1980, US Ct. Appeals (8th cir.) 1980, Calif., 1982, US Dist. Ct. (cen. dist.) Calif. 1982, US Ct. Dist. (ea. dist.) Calif., 1984. Atty. CAB, Washington, 1969-70; labor atty. Western Electric Co., NYC, 1970-71; mgr. employee rels. Am. Airlines, NYC, 1971-74; labor counsel Am. Electric Power Svc. Corp., NYC, 1974-78, sr. labor counsel, 1978-80; indsl. rels. counsel Trans World Airlines, NYC, 1980-81; sr. assoc. Parker, Milliken, Clark & O'Hara, LA, 1981-82; ptnr. Rutan & Tucker, Costa Mesa, Calif., 1983-84, Memel, Jacobs, Pierno, Gersh & Ellsworth, Newport Beach, Calif., 1985-86, Memel, Jacobs & Ellsworth, Newport Beach, 1986-87; pvt. practice Newport Beach, 1987—. Bd. dirs. Dynamic Constrn., Inc., Laguna Hills, Calif., 1986—; commentator labor rels. Fin. News Network; commentator Sta. KOCN Radio, 1990-91; commentator employment law Orange County Register; lectr. Calif. Western Law Sch., Calif. State U.-Fullerton, Calif. State Conf. Small Bus.; lectr. collective bargaining Pace U., NYC; lectr. on labor law Coun. on Edn. in Mgmt.; NE regional coord. Pressler for Pres., 1979-80; adv. bd. manufacturingzone.com.; dir. Orange County Bur. Jewish Edn., Friends of Fertility Found. Author: Arbitration Issues for the 1980s, 1981, A Look at Three Companies, 1982; editor-in-chief Indsl. and Labor Rels. Forum, 1964-66; columnist Orange County Bus. Jour., 1989-91; contbr. articles to profl. publs. Mem. Bus. Rsch. Adv. Coun. US Dept. Labor; trustee Chapman U., 1991-95. Mem. Calif. Bar Assn. (chmn.), Labor Law Consulting Group, Calif. Bd. of Legal Specialization, Balboa Bay Club, The Ctr. Club (chmn. membership com.), Club 33, Jewish Cmty. Ctr. Orange County. Republican. Jewish. Office: PO Box 9049 Newport Beach CA 92658-1049 Office Phone: 949-706-7365. Business E-Mail: rhs@schnapp.com.

SCHNEBELEN, PIERRE, resort planner and developer, consultant; b. Mulhouse, Alsace, France, June 10, 1935; s. Emile and Renee (Gingelwein) S.; children: Stephanie, Mathieu; m. Francois E. Roetynck, June 1, 1985; children: Yvan, Sophie, Wendy, Thomas. Diploma in engring., Ecole Nat. d'Arts et Metiers, Paris, 1958; MS, MIT, 1960. With Mobil Oil Internat., NYC, 1961; founder, chief exec. officer SEFCO, 1965-73, Soc. des Telepheriques de la Grande Motte, 1967-87, SEGMO, 1974-88; founder, pres. SEPARFI, SEGMO IMMOBILIER; founder, dir. Soc. de reprentacoes et de participacoes, Sao Paulo, Brazil, 1977—; pres., chief exec. officer Piersen SA, 1989—; founder, pres. P.S.I. Resorts, Paris, 1988—. Founder, pres. Soc. des telepheriques de Valfrejus, 1983-88, societa delle Funivie del Frejus, 1983-88; founder, dir. SEGMO Vacances; CEO West Rock Assocs. LLC, Boise, Idaho, 1998—; pres., CEO Athlon Fin. Corp., L.A., 1995—. Avocations: skiing, tennis, squash. Home: 820 El Oro Ln Pacific Palisades CA 90272-2813 Office: Athlon Resorts 1801 Ave Of Stars Los Angeles CA 90067-5902

SCHNECK, JEROME M., psychiatrist, historian, medical educator; b. NYC, Jan. 2, 1920; s. Maurice and Rose (Weiss) S.; m. Shirley R. Kaufman, July 24, 1943. AB, Cornell U., 1939; MD, SUNY, Bklyn., 1943. Diplomate Am. Bd. Psychiatry and Neurology, Am. Bd. Psychotherapy. Intern Interfaith Med. Ctr., 1943; psychiat. staff Menninger Clinic, Topeka, 1944-45; chief psychiatry and sociology dept. Fort Missoula, Mont., 1946, Camp Cooke, Calif., 1947; mem. psychiat. staff L.I. Coll. Hosp., 1947-48, Kings County Hosp., 1948-70, SUNY Hosp., Bklyn., 1955-70; assoc. vis. psychiatrist Kings County Hosp., 1949-70; mem. psychiat. staff State U. Hosp., Bklyn., 1955-70; pvt. practice N.Y.C., NYC, 1947—; attending psychiatrist St. Vincent's Hosp. and Med. Ctr. N.Y., 1970—, hon. sr. psychiatrist, 1990—. Psychiat. cons. VA Regional Office, 1947-48, NY State Dept. Social Svcs., 1977-83, NY State Dept. Civil Svc., 1978-84, NY State Office Ct. Adminstrn., 1978-85, NY State Dept. Edn., 1981-83; dir. Mt. Vernon Mental Hygiene Clinic, 1947-52; assoc. chief psychiatrist Westchester County Dept. Health, 1949-50, cons., 1951-52; clin. instr. L.I. Coll. Medicine, 1947-50; clin. assoc. SUNY Coll. Medicine, Bklyn., 1950-53, asst. prof., 1955-58, assoc. prof., 1958-70; supervising psychiatrist Cmty. Guidance Svcs., 1955-70; cons. coun. on mental health AMA, 1956-58; cons. NBC, 1962, Ctr. Rsch. in Hypnotherapy, 1964-70; vis. lectr. N.Y. Med. Coll.-Met. Hosp., 1965; faculty, fellow Am. Inst. Psychotherapy and Psychoanalysis, 1970-85. Author: Hypnosis in Modern Medicine, 1953, 2d edit., 1959, Spanish lang. edit., 1962, 3rd edit., 1963, Studies in Scientific Hypnosis, 1954, A History of Psychiatry, 1960, The Principles and Practice of Hypnoanalysis, 1965 (Best Book award Soc. For Clin. and Exptl. Hypnosis 1965); editor: Hypnotherapy, Hypnosis and Personality, 1951; author over 400 med. and sci. publs., book chpts., articles; mem. bd. editors: Personality: Symposia on Topical Issues, 1960-61, Jour. Integrative and Eclectic Psychotherapy, 1986-89; contbg. editor Psychosomatics, 1961-75; mem. editorial bd. Voices—The Art and Science of Psychotherapy, 1965; features editor The Interne, 1942, co-editor, 1943. Lt. U.S. Army Field Arty. Res., 1939-42; capt. M.C. AUS, 1945-47. Recipient Shirley R. Schneck award to physician making significant contbns. to devel. of med. hypnosis, 1970, Clarence B. Farrar award for history of Am. psychiatry rsch. Clarke Inst. Psychiatry, U. Toronto, 1976, Roy M. Dorcus award for best clin. paper on hypnosis, 1981, Spl. Presdl. award for lifetime contbns. to lit. on sci. hypnosis, 1986. Fellow AAAS, APA (disting. life), Am. Med. Authors, Acad. Psychosomatic Medicine, Am. Psychiat. Assn. (disting. life), Am. Soc. Clin. Hypnosis (life), Soc. for Clin. and Exptl. Hypnosis (life, founder, founding pres. 1949-56, exec. coun. 1949—, assoc. editor jour. 1953—, Merit award 1955, Gold medal 1958, Bernard B. Raginsky award 1966, Shirley Schneck award 1970, Roy M. Dorcus award 1980, Spl. Presdl. award 1986), Am. Acad. Psychotherapists (co-founder, v.p. 1956-58), Am. Med. Writers Assn., Am. Soc. Psychoanalytic Physicians (hon., bd. dirs. 1958-62), Internat. Soc. Clin. and Exptl. Hypnosis (co-founder, bd. dirs. 1958-68, founding fellow), Internat. Acad. Eclectic Psychotherapists (charter); mem. AMA, NY Acad. Scis., Soc. Acad. Achievement (charter), Soc. Apothecaries London, Inst. Practicing Psychotherapists, Pan Am. Med. Assn. (v.p. sect. clin. hypnosis 1960-65, N.Am. v.p. 1966), NY Soc. Med. History (exec. com. 1956-62), Am. Bd. Med. Hypnosis (life, founder, pres. 1958-60, bd. dirs.), Inst. Rsch. in Hypnosis Inc. (bd. dirs., bd. editors 1957-70), Am. Assn. History Medicine, History of Sci. Soc., Assn. Advancement Psychotherapy (charter) Can. Med. History Assn., NY Soc. for Clin. Psychiatry (chmn. com. on history of psychiatry), Charles F. Menninger Soc., Internat. Soc. Hypnosis (hon. life), Brit. Soc. Med. Hypnosis (hon.), Internat. Soc. Hypnosis (hon. life), Sigma Xi. Address: 26 W 9th St New York NY 10011-8971

SCHNECK, STUART AUSTIN, retired neurologist, educator; b. NYC, Apr. 1, 1929; s. Maurice and Sara Ruth (Knapp) S.; m. Ida I. Nakashima, Mar. 2, 1956; children: Lisa, Christopher. BS magna cum laude, Franklin and Marshall Coll., 1949; MD, U. Pa., 1953. Diplomate Am. Bd. Psychiatry and Neurology (bd. dirs., sec. 1990-91, v.p. 1991-92, pres. 1992-93). Intern Hosp. U. Pa., Phila., 1953-54; resident in medicine U. Colo. Med. Center, Denver, 1954-55, 57-58, resident in neurology, 1958-61; instr. neurology U. Colo. Sch. Medicine, 1959-61; instr. neuropathology Columbia U., NYC, 1961-63; vis. fellow in neuropathology Columbia-Presbyn. Med. Ctr., NYC, 1961-63; asst. prof. neurology and pathology U. Colo., 1963-67, assoc. prof., 1967-70, prof., 1970-95, assoc. dean clin. affairs Sch. Medicine, 1984-89, emeritus prof., 1996—. Cons. Fitzsimons Army Hosp., VA, Nat. Jewish Hosp.; pres. med. bd. Univ. Hosp., Denver, 1983-89, bd. dirs., 1989-90; mem. benefits adv. bd. U. Colo., 1999—, v.p. retired faculty assn. health sci. ctr., 1998-99, pres., 1999-2001. Author (with Ida I. Nakashima) The Geezers' Guide to Colo. Hikes, 2002; contbr. articles to profl. jours. Served with USAF, 1955-57. USPHS fellow, 1961-63 Mem. Am. Acad. Neurology, Am. Assn. Neuropathologists, Am. Neurol. Assn., Univ. Srs. Assn. (chmn. bd. dirs. 1997-2002), Rocky Mountain Stroke Assn. (bd. dirs. 1998—2006), Ctr. for Personalized Edn. Physicians (bd. dirs. 1999—), Alpha Omega Alpha (bd. dirs. 1979-89, treas., pres. 1990-93, editl. bd. 1994—2006).

SCHNEEMAN, BARBARA OLDS, nutritionist, educator; m. Paul Schneeman; 1 child, Eric. BS in Food Sci. and Tech., U. Calif., Davis, 1970; PhD in Nutrition, U. Calif., Berkeley, 1974. NIH postdoctoral fellow gastrointestinal physiology Children's Hosp., Oakland, Calif., 1974-76; faculty mem. nutrition dept. nutrition and food sci. & tech. U. Calif., Davis, 1976—, prof. dept. internal medicine divsn. clin. nutrition, 1986—, assoc. dean Coll. Agrl. and Environ. Scis., 1985-88, chair dept. nutrition, 1988-93, dean Coll. Agrl. and Environ. Scis., 1993-99. Pres., bd. dirs. Dannon Inst., 1996—; vis. scientist Cardiovascular Rsch. Inst., U. Calif., San Francisco, 1991-92; lectr. women in sci. series Coll. St. Catherine, St. Paul, 1987; adv. dir. Blue Cross Calif., 1992-95; mem. dietary guidelines for Ams. adv. com. to Secs. of Agr., Health and Human Svcs., 1989-90, 94-95; mem. expert panel on food safety and nutrition Inst. Food Technologists, 1985-91; mem. external adv. bd. Post Ctr. for Nutrition and Health, 1989-90; councilor Soc. for Exptl. Biology and Medicine, 1988-91. Assoc. editor Jour. Nutrition, 1991-94; contbg. editor Nutrition Revs., 1982-90; editl. bd. Jour. Nutrition, 1982-87, Procs. for Soc. Exptl. Biology and Medicine, 1985-91, Acad. Press: Food Sci. and Nutrition, 1988-2001. Fellow NDEA, U. Calif., Berkeley; recipient Outstanding Cmty. Svc. award Tierra del Oro coun. Girl Scouts U.S., 1995, Future Leaders award for rsch. Nutrition Found., 1978-80, Samuel Cate Prescott award for rsch. Inst. Food Tech., 1985, Farma Food Internat. Fibre prize, Copenhagen, 1989, Ethel Austin Martin disting. lectr. on Human Nutrition, S.D. State U., 1999. Fellow AAAS; mem. Inst. Food Technologists (sec.-treas. nutrition divsn. 1988-89), Am. Physiol. Soc., Am. Inst. Nutrition (treas. 1989-92), Am. Heart Assn. (fellow arteriosclerosis coun.), Food and Nutrition Bd. IOM, 2001—. Office: U Calif Davis Dept Nutrition Davis CA 95616

SCHNEIDER, ADELE GOLDBERG, librarian, educator; b. NYC, May 13, 1924; d. Abraham and Anna (Levy) Goldberg; m. Noel Schneider, Jan. 1, 1950; children: Adam Matthew, Tracy Lynn. BA, Bklyn. Coll., 1945; MLS, Pratt Inst., 1965; MA, L.I. Univ., 1971. Field interview Gallup Poll, NYC, 1941-48; social worker N.Y.C. Dept. Social Svcs., 1949-52; editor Bklyn. Coll. Alumni Quar., 1961-65; instr. Kingsborough C.C./CUNY, 1965-70, asst. prof. dept. libr., 1970-72, assoc. prof., 1972-88, prof.,

1988-92, prof. emeritus, 1992—. Contbr. articles to profl. jours. Recipient lifetime achievement award Bklyn. Coll., 2000. Mem. ALA, Libr. Assn. CUNY, N.Y. Tech. Svcs. Librs., Beta Phi Mu. Home: 124 Oxford St Brooklyn NY 11235-2311 Office: 2001 Oriental Blvd Brooklyn NY 11235-2333 Personal E-mail: lordduffy@msn.com.

SCHNEIDER, ADELE SANDRA, clinical geneticist; b. Johannesburg, Mar. 21, 1949; came to U.S., 1976, naturalized, 1981; d. Michael and Annette Schneider; m. Gordon Mark Cohen, July 2, 1978; children: Jeffrey, Brian, Adrienne. MB, BChir, Witwatersrand U., Johannesburg, South Africa, 1973. Intern in internal medicine Baragwanath Hosp., Johannesburg, 1974, intern in gen. surgery, 1974; sr. house officer in pediatrics Coronation Hosp., Johannesburg, 1975; sr. house officer in radiation therapy Johannesburg Gen. Hosp., 1975-76; resident in pediatrics Wilmington (Del.) Med. Ctr., 1976-78; fellow in clin. genetics and metabolic diseases Children's Hosp. of Phila., 1978-81, staff physician Cystic Fibrosis Clinic, 1987-88; staff pediatrician Children's Rehab. Hosp., Phila., 1981-82, dir. pediatrics, 1982-87, acting med. dir., 1984-85; clin. instr. dept. pediatrics Jefferson Med. Coll., Phila., 1982-84, clin. asst. prof. dept. pediatrics, 1984—, clin. assoc. prof. pediats., 2002—; clin. geneticist Hahnemann Univ. Hosp., Phila., 1987-90, asst. clin. prof. dept. pediatrics and neoplastic diseases, 1987-90; clin. geneticist Albert Einstein Med. Ctr., Phila., 1990-92, acting dir. med. genetics, 1992-93, dir. clin. genetics program, 1993—. Mem. courtesy faculty Sch. Medicine Temple U., Phila., 1987; clin. geneticist St. Christopher's Hosp. for Children, Phila., 1987; genetics cons. dept. pediatrics Bryn Mawr (Pa.) Hosp.; genetics cons. Lankenau Hosp., Thomas Jefferson U. Hosp.; presenter, lectr. in field. Contbr. articles to profl. jours. Bd. dirs. Phila. Parenting Associates, 1986-93. Fellow Am. Coll. Med. Genetics; mem. Am. Soc. Human Genetics, Am. Chem. Soc. Office: Albert Einstein Med Ctr Dept Pediatrics 5501 Old York Rd Philadelphia PA 19141-3018 Office Phone: 215-456-8722.

SCHNEIDER, ALLAN STANFORD, biophysics, neuroscience and pharmacology educator, biomedical research scientist; b. NYC, Sept. 26, 1940; s. Harry and Edith (Gonsky) S.; m. Mary-Jane Beekman Tunis, Dec. 14, 1968; children: Henry Seth, Joseph Benjamin B.Chem. Engring., Rensselaer Poly. Inst., 1961; MS, Pa. State U., 1963; PhD, U. Calif.-Berkeley, 1968. Chem. engr. E.I. du Pont de Nemours & Co. Exptl. Sta., Wilmington, Del., 1963-64; postdoctoral fellow Weizmann Inst. Sci., Rehovot, Israel, 1969-71; staff fellow NIH, Bethesda, Md., 1971-73; assoc. Sloan-Kettering Inst. Cancer Rsch., NYC, 1974-80, assoc. mem., 1980-85; asst. prof. Cornell U. Grad. Sch. Med. Scis., NYC, 1974-80, assoc. prof. biochemistry, 1981-83, assoc. prof. cell biology and genetic, 1983-85, chmn. biochemistry unit Sloan-Kettering div., 1982-83; assoc. prof. pharmacology and toxicology Albany Med. Coll., NY, 1985-86, prof. pharmacology and toxicology, 1986-94, prof. pharmacology and neurosci., 1995—, dir. grad. studies, 1987-91. Adjunct prof. Biomedical Sci., Sch. of Public Health, St. U. N.Y., Albany, 1987—; vis. prof. Weizmann Inst. Sci., Rehovot, Israel, 1987; vis. rsch. scholar U. Bergen, Norway, 1989, 95; vis. rsch. scholar, U. of Melbourne, Australia, 1998. Contbr. chpts to books, sci. articles to profl. jours. Rsch. grantee Am. Cancer Soc., 1980-83, Am. Heart Assn., 1977-82, 90-93, NIH, 1982-93, 2001—05, NSF, 1977-79, 1997-2002, Cystic Fibrosis Found., 1980-82; established investigator Am. Heart Assn., 1977-82. Mem. Biophys. Soc., Soc. Neurosci., Soc. of Gen. Physiologist, Am. Heart Assn. (coun. on basic sci. 1977-95), Phi Lambda Upsilon, Tau Beta Pi (internat. com. for chromaffin cell biology 1987-93). Achievements include first isolation and characterization of chromaffin cells of the adrenal gland now widely used as a model neuronal cell culture system; determination of the relation between cytosolic calcium signals and neurohormone (adrenaline) secretion, relevant to cellular mechanism of hormone and neurotransmitter release; determination of hydration of biomembranes; spectroscopic characterization of protein structure in situ in biomembranes and cells; theoretical and experimental analysis of optical activity spectra of turbid biological suspensions; research on neurochemistry of adrenal chromaffin cells, regulation of cell calcium and hormone and neurotransmitter release; mechanisms of nicotine dependence and fetal nicotine syndrome and effects of maternal smoking on fetal brain development. Office: Ctr for Neuropharmacology & Neurosci Albany Med Coll MC 136 Albany NY 12208 Office Phone: 518-262-5837. Business E-Mail: schneia@mail.amc.edu.

SCHNEIDER, AMANDA JEAN, lawyer; d. Peter Albert and Catherine Jean Schneider. BA in English and Sociology, Ind. U., Bloomington, 2001, JD, 2006. Legal intern Legal Aid Soc., Evansville, Ind., 2004, Ind. Legal Svcs., Bloomington, 2004—06; staff atty. Children's Legal Alliance, St. Louis, 2006—. Peggy Browning fellow Cmty. Legal Svcs., Phila., 2005. Big sister Big Bros./Big Sisters, Bloomington, 1999—2001. Mem.: Phi Beta Kappa. Office: Legal Svcs Eastern Mo 4232 Forest Park Ave Saint Louis MO 63108 Home Phone: 812-323-1974; Office Phone: 314-256-8768. Office Fax: 314-534-1075. Business E-Mail: ajschneider@lsem.org.

SCHNEIDER, ANN IMLAH, federal agency administrator, education consultant; b. Boston, Jan. 3, 1934; d. Albert Henry and Helen (Woodbridge) Imlah; m. John Hoke Schneider, Mar. 26, 1966 (div. 1978); children: Helen May, James Christopher. BA, Swarthmore Coll., 1955; MA, Fletcher Sch., 1956; PhD, London Sch. Econs., 1963. Asst. dir. Davis House, Am. Friends Service Com., Washington, 1956-57; adminstrv. asst. Nat. Acad. Scis., Washington, 1957-60; fgn. affairs research analyst U.S. Dept. State, Washington, 1964-70; sr. program specialist U.S. Dept. Edn., Washington, 1970—95; internat. edn. cons., 1995—. Author: Britain and Switzerland 1845-60, 1966, Federal Funding for International Studies: Does It Help? Does It Matter?, 1999, Internationalizing Teacher Education: What Can Be Done?, 2003, To Leave No Teacher Behind: Building International Competence into the Undergraduate Training of K-12 Teachers, 2007; contbr. articles. Sec. Alumni and Friends of London Sch. Econs., Washington, 1983—91, chair scholarship com., 1990—98, pres., 1999—2003. Mem.: AAAS, Soc. for Hist. in Fed. Gov., Am. Hist. Assn., Soc. Woman Geographers (asst. treas. 1987—90, treas. 1990—96, oral history com. 1996—, chair membership com. 2003—), Internat. Studies Assn. (editl bd. for Internat. Studies Perspectives 1979—2005, pres. local chpt. 1980—81, nat. exec. coun. 1981—82). Avocations: hiking, theater, concerts, gardening, needlecrafts. Home: 3319 Fessenden St NW Washington DC 20008-2034 Office Phone: 202-363-0109. Personal E-mail: aimlahs@aol.com.

SCHNEIDER, ARTHUR PAUL, retired videotape and film editor, author; b. Rochester, NY, Jan. 26, 1930; s. Mendell Phillip and Frieda (Bl) S.; m. Helen Deloise Thompson, June 5, 1954; children: Robert Paul, Lori Ann. Student, U. So. Calif., 1948. With NBC, 1951-68, film and videotape editor, 1953-60, developer double system method of editing video tape, 1958; pres. Burbank (Calif.) Film Editing, Inc., 1968-72, Electronic Video Industries Inc., 1977-79; supr. video tape editing Consol. Film Industries Inc., Hollywood, Calif., 1972-76, editorial supr., 1980-83; pvt. practice editing, 1983-88. Cons., lectr., author. Film and tape editor all: Bob Hope shows, 1951-67; supr. NBC kinescope and video tape editors (1966-67); video tape editor: Laugh-In Series, 1967-68; video tape editor: Comedy Shop Series, 1977-80; post-prodn. cons. to Video Systems and Broadcast Engring. mag.; video tape editor: TV series Sonny & Cher, 1973, Sonny Comedy Revue, 1974, Tony Orlando and Dawn, 1974, Hudson Bros., summer, 1974, Dean Martin Series, 1975-76, Mickey Mouse Club Series, Walt Disney Prodns., 1976, Redd Foxx Series, 1977; (author: Electronic Post Production and Videotape Editing, 1989 (pub. in Chinese 1995), Electronic Post Production Terms and Concepts, 1990; contbg. author: Association of Cinema and Video Laboratores (ACVL) Handbook, 5th edit., 1995, Focal Guide to Electronic Media CDRom Version, 1998, Jump Cut: Memoirs of a Pioneer Television Editor, 1997, (autobiography) My 50 Years of Television History: Been There, Done That, 2005; oral history interview for Acad. TV Arts and Scis. Found. Archive of Am. TV First 50 Yrs., 2001; contbr. articles to publs. in field. Recipient Broadcast Preceptor award San Francisco State U., 1975; named hon. Ky. Col. Mem. Acad. Television Arts and Scis. (Emmy nominations and Emmy award for video tape editing 1966, 68, 73, 84, gov. 1977-80, sec. 1980-81), Am. Cinema Editors (life, Life Achievement award 1999), Soc. Motion Picture and TV Engrs., Delta Kappa Alpha (life). Home: 2586 Neptune Pl Port Hueneme CA 93041 Personal E-mail: art2586@earthlink.net.

SCHNEIDER, BENJAMIN, psychology professor, consultant; b. NYC, Aug. 11, 1938; s. Leo and Rose (Cohen) S.; m. H. Brenda Jacobson, Jan. 29, 1961; children: Lee Andrew, Rhody Yve. BA, Alfred U., 1960; MBA, CUNY, 1962; PhD, U. Md., 1967. Lic. psychologist, Md. Asst. prof. adminstrv. scis. and psychology Yale U., New Haven, 1967-71; prof. psychology-mgmt. U. Md., College Park, 1971-79, prof. psychology and mgmt., 1982—2004, prof. emeritus, 2004—; sr. rsch. fellow Valtera Corp., 2003—; John A. Hannah prof. orgnl. psychology Mich. State U., East Lansing, 1979-82. Vis. prof. Inst. Adminstrn. and Enterprise, U. Aix-Marseille, 1993, 99, 2001, Peking U., 1988, Tuck Sch. Bus. Adminstrn., Dartmouth Coll., 1999. Author: (with D.T. Hall) Organizational Climates and Careers, 1973, Staffing Organizations, 1976, (with N. Schmitt) 2d edit., 1986, (with F.D. Schoorman) Facilitating Work Effectiveness, 1988, Organizational Climate and Culture, 1990, (with D.E. Bowen) Winning the Service Game, 1995, (with S.S. White) Service Quality: Research Perspectives, 2004, (with D.B. Smith) Personality and Organizations, 2004, (with R.E. Playhart and N. Schmitt) Staffing Organizations, 3d edit., 2006; mem. editl. rev. bd. Jour. Applied Psychology, 1988-98, 02-, Internat. Jour. Svc. Industry Mgmt., 1989—, Jour. Svc. Rsch., 1998—, Orgnl. Behavior and Human Decision Processes, 2002-, Cornell Quar., 2002-. Fulbright grantee, 1973—74. Fellow APA, Am. Psychol. Soc., Soc. for Indsl. and Orgnl. Psychology (pres. 1984-85, Disting. Sci. Contbns. award 2000, Scholarly Contbn. award 2004), Acad. Mgmt. (pres. orgnl. behavior divsn. 1982-83), Am. Mktg. Assn. (svcs. mktg. spl. interest group, Career Contbns. award 2006), San Diego Indsl. and Orgnl. Profls. (pres. 2005—). Office: 1363 Caminito Floreo Ste G La Jolla CA 92037 Office Phone: 858-488-7594. Business E-Mail: bschneider@valtera.com.

SCHNEIDER, CALVIN, physician; b. NYC, Oct. 23, 1924; s. Harry and Bertha (Green) S.; m. Elizabeth Gayle Thomas, Dec. 27, 1967. AB, U. So. Calif., 1951, MD, 1955; JD, LaVerne Coll., 1973. Intern L.A. County Gen. Hosp., 1955—56, staff physician, 1956—57; pvt. practice medicine West Covina, Calif., 1957—. Staff Inter-Community Med. Ctr., Covina, Calif. With USNR, 1943-47. Republican. Lutheran.

SCHNEIDER, CARL EDWARD, law educator; b. Exeter, NH, Feb. 23, 1948; s. Carl Jacob and Dorothy (Jones) S.; m. Joan L. Wagner, Jan. 6, 1976. BA, Harvard Coll., 1972; JD, U. Mich., 1979. Curriculum specialist Mass. Tchrs. Assn., Boston, 1972-75; law clk. to judge U.S. Ct. Appeals (D.C. cir.), Washington, 1979-80; law clk. Potter Stewart U.S. Supreme Ct., Washington, 1980-81; asst. prof. law U. Mich., Ann Arbor, 1981-84, assoc. prof. law, 1984-86, prof. law, 1986—, prof. internal medicine, 1998—, Chauncey Stillman prof. ethics, morality and practice of law; vis. prof. U. Tokyo, 1998. Disting. vis. prof. US Air Force Acad., 2007. Author: The Practice of Autonomy: Patients, Doctors and Medical Decisions, 1998, (with Margaret F. Brinig) An Invitation to Family Law, 1996, (with Marsha Garrison) The Law of Bioethics, 2003; editor: (book) The Law and Politics of Abortion, 1980, Family Law in Action: A Reader, 1999 (with Margaret F. Brinig and Lee E. Teitelbaum), Law at the End of Life: The Supreme Court and Assisted Suicide, 2000; contbr. articles to profl. jours. Mem. Pres. Coun. Bioethics, 2006—, 2006—. Fellow Am. Council of Learned Socs., Ford Found., 1985, Hastings Ctr.; life fellow Clare Coll., Cambridge. Fellow Am. Coll. Legal Medicine (hon.); mem. Order of Coif. Office Phone: 734-647-4170.

SCHNEIDER, CARL STANLEY, retired physics professor, researcher; b. Balt., Dec. 20, 1942; s. Stanley Samuel and Viola Jeannette Schneider; m. Carole Bottom, Dec. 24, 1971; children: Kathleen Schneider Sollars, James Andrew. BA, Johns Hopkins U., Balt., 1960—63; MS, MIT, Cambridge, 1963—65, PhD, 1963—68. Prof. U.S. Naval Acad., Annapolis, Md., 1968—2007; ret. Dir. sch. U.S. Naval Acad., 1986—96. Pres. Broadneck Fedn. Communities, Annapolis, 1974—76; cmty. program dir. Annapolis Rotary Club, 1995—96. Recipient Outstanding Young Men in Am., Jaycees, 1975, Meritorius Civilian Svc. award, USN, 1986—96, Frank R. Haig prize, Am. Assn. Physics Tchrs., 1998. Mem.: Mine Warfare Assn. (hon. Charles Rowzee award 1996), Phi Kappa Phi, Sigma Xi, Phi Beta Kappa. Liberal. Methodist. Achievements include patents for closed loop degaussing control system. Avocations: singing, photography, travel, hiking, gardening. Home Phone: 410-757-8140. Personal E-mail: carl1047@comcast.net.

SCHNEIDER, CARL WILLIAM, lawyer; b. Phila., Apr. 27, 1932; s. Nathan J. and Eleanor M. (Milgram) S.; m. Mary Ellen Baylinson; children: Eric, Mark, Adam, Cara BA, Cornell U., 1953; LLB magna cum laude, U. Pa., 1956. Bar: Pa. 1957. Law clk. U.S. Ct. Appeals (3d cir.), Phila., 1956-57; sr. law clk. U.S. Supreme Ct., Washington, 1957-58; assoc. Wolf, Block, Schorr and Solis-Cohen LLP, Phila., 1958-65; ptnr. Wolf, Block, Schorr and Solis-Cohen, Phila., 1965-2000, of counsel, 2000—. Spl. advisor divsn. corp. fin. SEC, Washington, 1964; lectr. securities law U. Pa., 1968-70, vis. assoc. prof., 1978-81, acting dir. Ctr. for Study Fin. Instns.; bd. editors and advisors Rev. Securities and Commodities Regulations. Author: SEC Consequences of Corporate Acquisitions, 1971, Pennsylvania Corporate Practice and Forms: The Wolf, Block, Schorr and Solis-Cohen Manual, 1997; also numerous articles. Bd. dirs. Found. Jewish Families and Children's Svc., Abramson Ctr. Jewish Life; chmn. bd. dirs. Jewish Family and Children's Svc. Greater Phila., 2000—03; trustee Jewish Fedn. Greater Phila. Mem. ABA, Pa. Bar Assn., Phila. Bar Assn. (chmn. sect. corp. banking and bus. law 1972), Am. Law Inst. (life). Home: 1601 Locust St Apt 500 Philadelphia PA 19102-3315

SCHNEIDER, CAROL GEARY, educational association administrator; BA in History magna cum laude, Mt. Holyoke Coll., South Hadley, Mass., 1967; postgrad. student, U. London Inst. Hist. Rsch.; PhD in Early Modern History, Harvard U. Instr. Chgo. State U., DePaul U., Boston U., U. Chgo., 1978—88, dir. Midwest Faculty Seminar, founding dir. Inst. Tchg. and Learning; exec. v.p. Assn. Am. Colls. and Univs., Washington, 1988—98, pres., 1998—. Contbr. articles to profl. jours. Bd. trustees Mt. Holyoke Coll. Woodrow Wilson fellow, Harvard U., Kent fellow, Harvard Prize fellow, Mina Shaughnessy fellow, US Dept. Edn., 1982. Mem.: Phi Beta Kappa. Office: Am Assn Colls and Univs 1818 R St NW Washington DC 20009 Office Phone: 202-387-3760 ext. 401. Office Fax: 202-265-9532. E-mail: cgs@aacu.org. *

SCHNEIDER, CAROLYN ALICE BRAUCH, elementary school educator; b. NYC, Dec. 15, 1946; d. Elliott David and Marie Alice (Giroux) B.; m. Thom J. Schneider, Aug. 3, 1978; children: Logan, Whitney, Brock. BS, U. Bridgeport, 1968. Tchr. phys. edn. Westview (Colo.) Elem. Sch., 1968-72, McElwain (Colo.) Elem. Sch., 1972-75; tchr. phys. edn., health Northglenn (Colo.) Mid. Sch., 1975—, coach gymnastics, 1975-84, coach track, 1975—2000, coach softball, 1998—2000, coach volleyball, 1975—96; coach xtreme competitve soccer, 1997—2003; coach explosion soccer, 1988—97. Coach North Area Soccer Assn., Thornton, Colo., 1995-96, 96-97 Rec. (competitive), 97— U-11B/Explosion White coach traveling competitive team, U-12 O-Colo. XTreme -U/17B competitive soccer team, 1997-2003; instr., bldg. supr. Northglenn Recreation Dept., 1969-84, mem. sch. improvement team, rep. Dist. Sch. Improvement Team. Mem. NEA, AAHPERD (Colo. recipient Nat. Pathfinder award for Outstanding Leadership in Girls and Womens Sports, 2002), Colo. Edn. Assn., Am. Health Assn. Roman Catholic. Avocations: sports, reading, travel.

SCHNEIDER, CATHERINE CHEMIN, occupational therapist, consultant; d. Anthony Joseph Chemin and Irma Gema Bizzotto; m. Daniel Patrick Schneider, Sept. 25, 1970; children: David Patrick, Patricia Marie. BS in Occupl. Therapy, Wayne State U., 1970. Staff therapist Henry Ford Hosp., Detroit, 1971, Plymouth Ctr. for Human Devel., 1971—73, Oak Park Devel. Tng. Ctr., Mich., 1973—75; itinerant staff therapist, cons. Ingham Intermediate Sch. Dist., Mich., 1975—76; sch. therapist, cons. Birmingham (Mich.) Pub. Schs., 1978—91; cons., pres. The Positive Difference, LLC, Northville, Mich., 1992—2000; sch. therapist, cons. Bloomfield Hills (Mich.) Sch., 1992—99; presenter in field, 2003—. Author: Sensory Secrets: How to "Jump-Start" Learning in Children, 2001, 2006; co-author (with Carol Poltorak): Your Sensory Brain, 2006. Mem.: Am. Occupl. Therapy Assn. Avocations: reading, music, needlecrafts. Office Phone: 248-344-8188. Fax: 243-344-8188. E-mail: catherine_schneider@msn.com, posdiff@aol.com.

SCHNEIDER, CHARLES IVAN, newspaper executive; b. Chgo., Apr. 6, 1923; s. Samuel Hiram and Eva (Smith) S.; m. Nancy Barrier-Schneider; children: Susan, Charles I. Jr., Kim, Karen, Traci. BS, Northwestern U., 1944. Indsl. engr., sales mgr., v.p. mktg. and sales Curtis-Electro Lighting Corp., Chgo., 1945-54, pres., 1954-62, Jefferson Electronics, Inc., Santa Barbara, Calif., 1962-64; pres. 3 sub., v.p., asst. to pres. Am. Bldg. Maintenance Industries, Los Angeles, 1964-66; group v.p. Times Mirror Co., Los Angeles, 1966-88, ret.; pvt. investor and cons., 1988—. Bd. dirs. Jeppesen Sanderson, Inc., Denver, Graphic Controls Corp., Buffalo, Regional Airports Improvement Corp. Bd. regents Northwestern U., Evanston, Ill.; trustee, past pres. Reiss-Davis Child Study Center, L.A.; bd. govs., past pres. The Music Ctr.; trustee the Menninger Found.; pres. St. John's Hosp. and Health Ctr. Found., Santa Monica, Calif. Served with AUS, 1942-44. Mem. Chief Execs. Orgn. (past pres., bd. dirs.). Clubs: Standard (Chgo.); Beverly Hills Tennis (Calif.); Big. Ten of So. Calif. Avocations: tennis, squash, music, reading. Home: 522 N Beverly Dr Beverly Hills CA 90210-3318 *An individual's growth and success as a manager are in direct proportion to his or her ability to develop, motivate and lead able, capable people.*

SCHNEIDER, CINDY E. GOWER (LONES), financial advisor; b. Springfield, Ohio, Nov. 27, 1960; d. James K. Lones and Catherine May (Dellinger) Oldfield; children: Natasha May, Matthew W.; m. Brian J. Schneider, Nov. 27, 1999. AAS in Electronic Engring., Columbus State C.C., 1993, AAS in Acctg., 1993. HVAC electronic control tech. Creative Control Designs, Inc., Columbus, 1993—96. Owner Schneider's Tax and Bookkeeping Svc., Columbus, 1992—. Mem. Nat. Assn. Tax Profls., Am. Inst. Profl. Bookkeepers, WIBC. Republican. Avocations: pencil drawing, reading, bowling, electronics, philosophy. Home and Office: 1730 Westbrook Dr Columbus OH 43223 E-mail: taxprocindy@aol.com.

SCHNEIDER, CRAIG DAVID, health policy analyst; b. Bklyn., Feb. 6, 1963; s. Nelson Myron Schneider and Marilyn Glaser; m. Tamar Kliger Schneider, July 31, 1988; children: Sarah Bess, Benjamin Samuel. BA, Boston U., 1985, MBA, 1992; PhD, Brandeis U., Waltham, Mass., 2004. Mgr. provider reimbursement br. Ctrs. for Medicare and Medicaid Svcs., Boston, 1992—2006; dir. healthcare policy Mass. Health Data Consortium, Waltham, 2006—. Treas. Temple Hillel B'Nai Torah, West Roxbury, Mass., 2004—07. Presdl. Mgmt. fellow, US Office Pers. Mgmt., 1992. Office: Massachusetts Health Data Consortium 460 Totten Pond Rd Ste 385 Waltham MA 02459 Office Phone: 781-768-2503. Office Fax: 781-768-2510. Business E-Mail: cschneider@mahealthdata.org.

SCHNEIDER, CYNTHIA PERRIN, former ambassador, political science professor; b. Pa., Aug. 16, 1953; m. Thomas J. Schneider; 2 children. BA in Fine Arts magna cum laude, Harvard U., 1977, PhD in Fine Arts, 1984. Asst. curator European paintings Mus. Fine Arts, Boston, unitl 1984; asst. prof. art history Georgetown U., Washington, 1984-90, assoc. prof. art history, 1990—2004; amb. to The Netherlands Am. Embassy, The Hague, 1998-2001; dir., life sciences & society initiative Georgetown U., Washington, 2003—, disting. prof. in practice of diplomacy, Pfizer Med. Humanities Initiative scholar-in-residence. Lectr. on Rembrandt and Dutch art in US and Europe; vice-chair President's Com. on Arts and Humanities. Author: Rembrandt's Landscapes, 1990; organizer, writer (catalog) Rembrandt's Landscape Print and Drawings, Nat. Gallery Art, 1990; contbr. articles to profl. jour. Mem. steering com. Creative Am., chair fed. design subcom.; coord. arts policy Clinton-Gore Campaign, 1992; bd. dir. Nat. Mus. Women in Arts, Australian-Am. Leadership Dialogue; supervisory bd. Royal Ahold, 2001—05; adv. bd. Strawberry Frog, Inc.; bd. dir. Wesley Theological Sem., Coun. Am. Ambassadors; bd. adv. Inst. for Cultural Diplomacy; internat. bd. adv., Inst. for the Study of Europe Columbia U.; Am. bd. Anne Frank House Found. Recipient Exceptional Svc. Order, Office of US Sec. of Def., 2001. Office: Distinguished Prof in Practice of Diplomacy Georgetown Univ 3300 Whitehaven St NW Ste 500 Washington DC 20057 Office Phone: 202-687-0703. Office Fax: 301-924-8715. E-mail: schneidc@georgetown.edu.

SCHNEIDER, DAN W., lawyer, consultant; b. Salem, Oreg., Apr. 28, 1947; s. Harold Otto and Frances Louise (Warner) S.; m. Nancy Merle Schmalzbauer, Mar. 29, 1945; children: Mark Warner, Edward Michael. BA cum laude, St. Olaf Coll., 1969; JD, Willamette U., 1974; LLM, Columbia U., 1975. Bar: Oreg. 1974, D.C. 1978, Ill. 1987. Trial atty. U.S. Dept. Justice Antitrust, Washington, 1975-79; dep. assoc. dir. U.S. SEC, Washington, 1979-86; gen. ptnr. Schiff Hardin & Waite, Chgo., 1986-95; name ptnr. Smith Lodge & Schneider, Chgo., 1995-98; ptnr. Hopkins & Sutter, Chgo., 1998-2000; internat. ptnr. Baker & McKenzie, Chgo., 2000—. Bd. dirs. NygaarArt, Northfield, Minn. Contbr. articles to profl. jours. Trustee, sec. Ill. Acad. Fine Arts, Chgo., 1990-98; mem. adv. bd. Flaten Art Mus., Northfield, 1990—; mem. adv. bd. Hallie Ford Mus. Art, Salem, Oreg., 1999—; pres. adv. group arts in edn. Willamette U., 2004—. Recipient 1st prize Nathan Burkan Law Essay Competition ASCAP, N.Y., 1974, Christie award Securities Transfer Assn., 1987. Mem. Met. Club. Chgo., Monroe Club, Plaza Club. Avocations: art collecting, art writing, music composition. Office: Baker & McKenzie 1 Prudential Plz 130 E Randolph St Ste 3700 Chicago IL 60601-6342 Business E-Mail: dan.w.schneider@bakernet.com.

SCHNEIDER, DANIEL B., reporter; Reporter, bureau asst., UN New York Times. Office: New York Times 229 W 43d St New York NY 10036 Office Phone: 212-556-1510. Office Fax: 212-556-1421.

SCHNEIDER, DAVID C., bank executive; BSBA in Acctg., Babson Coll., Wellesley, Mass.; MBA, Ind. U., Bloomington. CPA. Positions up to CFO Old Kent Fin. Corp., Mich., 1992—97, exec. v.p. retail banking; mng. ptnr. Stratmor Group; positions up to pres., COO CitiMortgage, Inc., St. Louis, 2001; pres. Home Loans Washington Mut., Inc. Pres. Consumer Mortgage Coalition; mem. exec. com. Housing Policy Coun. Office: Washington Mut Inc 1301 Second Ave Seattle WA 98101 Office Phone: 206-461-2000. *

SCHNEIDER, DAVID WALTER, lawyer; b. Chillicothe, Ohio, Sept. 7, 1942; s. August L. and Ruth M. (Sifferd) S.; m. Virginia Glann, Oct. 28, 1967; children: Tanya, Alina, Toby. BA, Gettysburg Coll., 1964; BD, Yale U., 1967, JD, 1971. Bar: Conn. 1971, U.S. Dist. Ct. Conn. 1973, U.S. Ct.

Appeals (2d cir.) 1973, U.S. Supreme Ct. 1975, U.S. Tax Ct. 1992. Clergyman United Ch. of Christ, Stamford, Conn., 1967-68; law clk. to judge U.S. Ct. Appeals (2d cir.), NYC, 1971-73; assoc. Tyler, Cooper & Alcorn, New Haven, 1973-79, ptnr., 1979—, mng. ptnr., 1987-92. Mem.: Conn. Bar Assn. (chmn. liaison with state cts. com. 1985—87). Home: 25 Cassway Rd Woodbridge CT 06525-1214 Office: Tyler Cooper & Alcorn 205 Church St New Haven CT 06510-1805 Home Phone: 203-393-3721; Office Phone: 203-784-8216. Business E-Mail: dschneider@tylercooper.com.

SCHNEIDER, DEENA JO, lawyer; b. 1950; Student, U. Mich.; BA magna cum laude, Yale U., 1971; JD, Harvard U., 1974. Bar: Pa. 1974, Supreme Ct. US, US Ct. of Appeals (3rd, 8th cirs.), US dist. Ct. (ea. dist.) Pa. Mem. Schnader, Harrison, Segal & Lewis, Phila., ptnr. Contbr. Co-dir. Yale Alumni Schs. Com. Phila.; mem. of coun. Yale Club of Phila. Recipient Pa. Super Lawyer, 2004—06. Mem.: ABA (antitrust litig. sect.), Phila. Bar Assn. (appellate cts. com.), Pa. Bar Assn. Office: Schnader Harrison Segal & Lewis LLP 1600 Market St Ste 3600 Philadelphia PA 19103-7286 Office Phone: 215-751-2166, 215-751-2000. Office Fax: 215-751-2205. Business E-Mail: dschneider@schnader.com.

SCHNEIDER, DENNIS EUGENE, manufacturing executive; b. Bellevue, Ohio, Dec. 27, 1957; s. Vernon Edwin and Marquerite Mary (Best) S.; m. Sandra Lynn Seavolt, June 26, 1982; children: Elaina Amanda, Alexander Nikita, Marina Lubov, Jake Ridan. BS, Bowling Green State U., 1981; MBA, Rockford Coll., 1995. Buyer Teledyne Continental Aviation and Engrng. Co., Toledo, 1981-84; div. purchasing mgr. Tappan Appliances, Mansfield, Ohio, 1984-85; corp. purchasing mgr. Marathon Electric Mfg. Corp., Wausau, Wis., 1985-88; materials mgr. Pacific Sci. Corp., Rockford, Ill., 1988-90; group materials mgr. Case Corp., Racine, Wis., 1990-93, ops. mgr., 1993-95, dir. global logistics, 1995-97, dir. supply chain Europe, Africa and Middle East, 1997; v.p. supply chain Allied Signal, Tempe, Ariz., 1998-2000; sr. v.p. supply chain and ops. World Kitchens, Elmira, NY, 2000—02; v.p. global ops. Stanley Tool Works, East Greenwich, RI, 2002—04, Bobcat Cos., Fargo, ND, 2004—. Vol. Toledo Bid Bros./Big Sisters, 1982-85. Mem. Am. Prodn. and Inventory Control Soc., Nat. Assn. Purchasing Mgmt., Coun. Logistics Mgmt., Internat. Platform Assn., Ducks Unltd., Am. Chesapeake Club, KC. Republican. Roman Catholic. Avocations: history, dog tng., music, backpacking, wildlife art. Home: 277 Chestnut Dr Horace ND 58047-4006 Office: Ingersol Rand Compact Vehicles Sector 250 Beaton Dr West Fargo ND 58078 Office Phone: 701-241-8786.

SCHNEIDER, DENNIS RAY, microbiology professor, research and development company executive; b. Sinton, Tex., June 10, 1952; 2 children. BA with honors, U. Tex., 1974, PhD, 1978. Post-doctoral fellow Behringwerke AG, Marburg/Lahn, West Germany, 1978-79; postdoctoral fellow U. Mo. Med. Sch., Columbia, 1980-81; rsch. microbiologist New England Nuc., North Billerica, Mass., 1981-82; dir. R & D Austin (Tex.) Biol. Lab., 1982-88; adj. assoc. prof. U. Tex., Austin, 1986—; dir. R & D devel. Micro-Bac Internat., Austin, 1988-94, v.p. Round Rock, Tex., 1994—. Author: Bioremediation: A Desktop Manual for the Environmental Professional; contbr. chpt. to Microorganism Adaptation to Host Defense. Grantee NASA, 1988, 92, 93. Mem. AAAS, Am. Soc. for Microbiology, Mensa, Profl. Assn. Dive Instrs. Avocations: scuba diving, writing. Office: Micro-Bac Internat 3200 N I H 35 Round Rock TX 78681-2410 Office Phone: 512-310-9000. Personal E-mail: drdiver2001@yahoo.com. Business E-Mail: drdiver@mail.utexas.edu.

SCHNEIDER, DONALD J., trucking company executive; b. Green Bay, Wis., 1935; married; 5 children. BA, St. Norbert Coll., 1957; MBA, U. Pa. Pres. Schneider Transport Inc., Green Bay, Wis., 1957—; CEO, pres. Schneider National, Inc., 1971—2002, chmn. Office: Schneider National Inc PO Box 2545 Green Bay WI 54306-2545

SCHNEIDER, DUANE BERNARD, English literature educator; b. South Bend, Ind., Nov. 15, 1937; s. William H. and Lillian L. (Pitchford) S.; m. Crystal J. Gips; children: Jeffrey, Eric, Lisa, Emily. BA, Miami U., Oxford, Ohio, 1958; MA, Kent State U., 1960; PhD, U. Colo., 1965. Instr. engring. English U. Colo., 1960-65; asst. prof. English Ohio U., Athens, 1965-70, assoc. prof., 1970-75, chmn. Faculty Senate, 1981-83, chmn. dept. English, 1983-86, prof. emeritus, 1998—; dir. Ohio U. Press, 1986-95; part-time faculty New Sch. U., NYC, 2000—05. Editor, pub. Croissant & Co., 1968-2002. Author: (with others) Anais Nin: An Introduction, 1979. Mem. Thomas Wolfe Soc. (trustee, pres. 1979-81). Home: 102 Bay Berry Cir Saint Simons Island GA 31522 E-mail: schneide@ohio.edu.

SCHNEIDER, EDGAR ROLF GOTTFRIED, retired mathematician, application developer, writer; b. Bklyn., Apr. 9, 1932; s. Richard Bernhard Grunewald and Sylvia Goldberg, adopted s. Nathan Schneider; m. Sally Jane Mitchell, Oct. 3, 1959 (div.); children: Elisabeth Sutter, Christian, Eric; m. Alexandra Khan Kazan, June 26, 1999. BA, City Coll. of N.Y., 1954; MA, The Am. U., Washington, 1970. Mathematician, sci. computer programmer Svc. Bur. Corp., NYC, 1959—63, LA, 1963—66, IBM Corp., Bethesda, Md., 1966—70, Atlantic City, 1970—74, Warminster, Pa., 1974—75, Owego, NY, 1975—82. Spkr. Autism Soc. Fla., Fort Lauderdale, 1996—. Author: Discovering My Autism, 1999, Living the Good Life with Autism, 2003. Singer Fla. Philharmonic Chorus, Fort Lauderdale, 1974—2003. 2nd lt. US Army, 1954—58. Mem.: Phi Beta Kappa, Sigma Xi. Roman Catholic. Avocations: art, music, photography, history, literature. Home Phone: 954-724-3571. E-mail: hansachsthegreat@juno.com.

SCHNEIDER, EDWARD LEE, botanist, researcher; b. Portland, Oreg., Sept. 14, 1947; s. Edward John and Elizabeth (Mathews) S.; m. Sandra Lee Alfarone, Aug. 2, 1968; children: Kenneth L., Cassandra L. BA, Ctrl. Wash. U., 1969, MS, 1971; PhD, U. Calif., Santa Barbara, 1974. From asst. to assoc. prof. botany S.W. Tex. State U., San Marcos, 1974-84, prof., 1984-94, chmn. biology dept., 1984-89, dean sci., 1989-92; pres., CEO Santa Barbara (Calif.) Botanic Garden, 1992—. Author: The Botanical World, CEOs and Trustees--Building Working Partnerships; contbr. articles to profl. jours. Bd. dirs. Ctr. for Plant Conservation; bd. dirs. Coun. Sci. Soc. Presidents, 2005-06. Recipient Presdl. Rsch. award S.W. Tex. State U., 1986, Disting. Alumnus award Ctrl. Wash. U., 1996; grantee NSF, 1980, 90. Fellow Tex. Acad. Sci. (pres. 1992-93); mem. Internat. Water Lily Soc. (bd. dirs., sec. 1989-96, inducted into Hall of Fame, Award of Appreciation 1997), Bot. Soc. Am. (bd. dirs., pres.-elect 2004, pres. 2005-06, past pres. 2006-07, Award of Merit 1998, Centennial medallion 2006), Am. Assn. Bot. Gardens and Arboreta (bd. dirs.), Internat. Pollination Congress, Nat. Coun. Deans, Am. Assn. Mus. (assessment program adv. com., nat. program com, Excellence in Peeer Rev. Sev. award 2007). Home: 1140 Tunnel Rd Santa Barbara CA 93105-2134 Office: Santa Barbara Botanic Garden 1212 Mission Canyon Rd Santa Barbara CA 93105-2126 Office Phone: 805-682-4726 ext. 123. Business E-Mail: eschneider@sbbg.org.

SCHNEIDER, EDWARD MARTIN, retired internist, medical educator; b. Cleve., May 12, 1922; s. Sol S. and Beatrice Hilda (Sicherman) Schneider; m. Jane H. Einstein, June 18, 1950 (dec. Aug. 2001); children: Douglas A., Robert S. 1 stepchild, Donald E. Deutsch. Student, Northwestern U., 1940-43; MD, U. Cin., 1946. Diplomate Am. Bd. Internal Medicine. Intern Mt. Sinai Hosp., Cleve., 1946-47, asst. resident medicine, 1947-48, sr. asst. resident medicine, 1950-51; fellow in medicine Cin. Gen. Hosp., 1951-52; asst. prof. of medicine U. Okla. Sch. Medicine, Oklahoma City, 1952-57; sr. physician gastroenterology Miner's Meml. Hosp. Assn., McDowell, Ky., Beckley, W.Va., 1957-61; chief of medicine Cameron Meml. Hosp., Bryan, Ohio, 1961-62; chief medical rsch. sect. Upjohn Co., Kalamazoo, Mich., 1962-67; pvt. practice Woodland Hills, Calif., 1968-81. Author 17 rsch. papers. Capt. M.C., AUS, 1948-50. Recipient Cert. of Recognition, Dept. Def. Fellow ACP, Am. Coll. Gastroenterologists; mem. Assn. Mil. Surgeons (life), Am. Assn. Study Liver Disease (emeritus), Sigma Xi. Avocations: amateur radio, music appreciation. Home: 1521 Lake Forest Dr Charlottesville VA 22901 E-mail: gutdoc22@gmail.com.

SCHNEIDER, EDWIN KAHN, research scientist; b. Philadelphia, Pa., May 6, 1948; s. Abraham and Edna May Schneider; m. Penelope Lee Ganzel, Aug. 5, 1980; children: Andrew Ganzel, Thomas Schmidt. AB, Harvard U., 1970, PhD, 1975. Postdoctoral rsch. assoc. MIT, Cambridge, Mass., 1974—77, prin. rsch. scientist, 1984—84; NATO postdoctoral fellow Reading U., England, 1977—78; rsch. fellow, assoc. Harvard U., Cambridge, Mass., 1978—83; assoc., sr. rsch. scientist U. Md., College Park, Md., 1984—93; sr. rsch. scientist Ctr. for Ocean-Land-Atmosphere Studies, Calverton, Md., 1993—; prof. climate dynamics George Mason U., Fairfax, Va., 2002—; exec. editor Climate Dynamics, 2004—. Author: (book chapter) Climate Change: An Integrated Perspective; contbr. (articles) Encyclopedia of Global Environmental Change; contbr. articles to profl. jours. Fellow, NSF, 1970—72; grantee, NSF, NOAA, NASA, DOE, EPRI, 1985—2007; Nat. Merit scholar, 1966—70. Fellow: Am. Meteorol. Soc.; mem.: Am. Geophys. Union. Achievements include research in Hadley circulation, El Nino/Southern Oscillation, atmospheric and oceanic dynamics, climate change. Avocations: orchestral violinist, golf. Office: Center for Ocean-Land-Atmosphere Studies 4041 Powder Mill Rd Suite 302 Beltsville MD 20705 Office Phone: 301-595-7000.

SCHNEIDER, ELAINE CAROL, lawyer, researcher, writer; b. Mpls., Aug. 28, 1957; d. Allan William and Deborah G. Schneider; m. William Mack Olivé, Oct. 10, 1987 (div. July 1996); 1 child, Vanessa Inez Olivè; m. G.R. Smith, Jan. 2, 2002. BA, U. Minn., 1979; JD, William Mitchell Coll. Law, St. Paul, 1982. Bar: N.Mex. 1984, Minn. 1998, D.C. 1999. Assoc. Settles, Kalamarides & Assocs., Anchorage, 1982, Dickson, Evans & Esch, Anchorage, 1982; legal rschr. John Hanson, Anchorage, 1983; acct. rep. Westlaw Svcs., Inc., Albuquerque, 1984, sales rep. New Orleans, 1985-86; libr. sales rep. West Pub. Co., Spokane, Wash., 1986-87, reference atty. St. Paul, 1988-97, product mgr., 1997-2001; pvt. practice Mpls.; CEO, mem. Coeur à Coeur Fashion Beauty Products, LLC, Minn., 2004. Ethics adv. bd. N.Mex. Bar, Albuquerque, 1984-85; midwest regional conf. com. Am. Immigration Lawyers Assn., 2000. Author: Substantive Judicial Law Outline of Habeas Corpus, 1984, What They Don't Teach You in the Bar Review Course, 1991, Challenging an Incredibility Finding on Appeal, An Incredibility Paradigm, 2001; mem. law rev. staff: William Mitchell Coll. Law, 1980—81. Atty. immigration and naturalization law Minn. Advocates for Human Rights, Refugee and Immigrant Project. Recipient Vol. Pro Bono Atty. award, 15th Ann. Minn. Advocates for Human Rights, 1999. Mem. Phi Beta Kappa. Avocations: ventriloquism, skiing, swimming, travel, languages. Office: 701 4th Ave S Ste 500 Minneapolis MN 55415-1810 Personal E-mail: avocatecs@aol.com.

SCHNEIDER, ELIZABETH KELLEY, law librarian, educator; b. Bloomington, Ill., July 10, 1946; d. George Raymond and Lucille Genviève (Sutter) Kelley; m. John James Schneider, Aug. 21, 1982. BA in History, Wesleyan U., Ill., 1968; MLS, U. Minn., 1969; JD, William Mitchell Coll. of Law, 1973; LLM in Health Law, St. Louis U., 1997. Bar: Minn. 1974, U.S. Dist. Ct. Minn. 1979. Libr. Ramsy County Law Libr., St. Paul, 1971-73; asst. law libr. U. Akron Coll. Law, Ohio, 1973-74; prof. law, libr. Hamline U. Sch. Law, St. Paul, 1974-81; dir. Maricopa County Law Libr., Phoenix, 1981-91; assoc. dir. law libr., asst. prof. Tex. Tech. Sch. Law, 1992-2000. Instr. legal rsch. Ariz. Legal Secs. Assn., 1982, Phoenix Coll., 1982-85, Ariz. State Library Assn., 1984; adj. prof. Sch. Health Mgmt. and Policy Ariz. State U., 2006-07. Mem. ABA, Am. Assn. Law Librs. (chair Legal Info. Svcs. to the Pub. 1988-89), Ariz. Assn. Law Librs. (pres. 1985-86), Ariz. Women Lawyers Assn., Desert Sun Aux., Nat. Assistance League (sec. 1985-86, chmn. 1986-87), Southwestern Assn. Law Libr. (sec. 1987-90, v.p. 1990-91), Alpha Gamma Delta (pres. 1985-86). Office: Plattner Schneidman & Schneider 4201 North 24th St Ste 100 Phoenix AZ 85016 Home Phone: 602-957-1897; Office Phone: 602-274-7955. E-mail: eksphx@yahoo.com.

SCHNEIDER, ERIC C., medical educator, physician; b. East Lansing, Mich., Mar. 25, 1961; BS, Columbia U., 1986; MSc, U. Calif. Berkeley, 1989; MD, U. Calif. San Francisco, 1991. Intern Brigham & Women's Hosp., Boston, 1991—92, resident, 1992—94, fellow gen. medicine, 1994, assoc. physician divsn. gen. medicine; assoc. prof. medicine dept. medicine Harvard Med. Sch., Boston, asst. prof. dept. health policy and mgmt. Co-chair physician consortium workshop on quality measures for emergency medicine AMA; mem. performance measures subcom. ACP, Cancer Quality Coun. Ontario. Contbr. articles to profl. jours. Office: Harvard Sch Pub Health Kresge Bldg Rm 406 677 Huntington Ave Boston MA 02115 Office Phone: 617-432-3124. Office Fax: 617-432-4494. E-mail: eschneid@hsph.harvard.edu. *

SCHNEIDER, GERALD L., plastic surgeon; b. Mechanicsburg, Pa., Oct. 25, 1945; s. Gordon Henry and Pauline Emma (Rife) S.; 1 child, Ross Roberts. BS, No. Ariz. U., 1968; MD, U. Ariz., 1973. Intern Naval Regional Med. Ctr., San Diego, 1973-74; resident in gen. surgery U.S. Naval Hosp., San Diego, 1974-78, resident in plastic surgery Portsmouth, Va., 1978-80, staff surgeon divsn. plastic surgery San Diego, 1981-83, chief divsn. plastic surgery, 1983-84; pvt. practice Flagstaff, Ariz., 1984-90; staff surgeon La Jolla (Calif.) Cosmetic Surgery Ctr., 1990-91; surgeon Scripps Clinic & Rsch. Found., La Jolla, 1991—. Capt. USNR Fellow ACS; mem. Am. Soc. Plastic Surgeons. Avocation: golf. Office: Scripps Clinic & Rsch Found 10666 N Torrey Pines Rd La Jolla CA 92037-1092 Office Phone: 858-554-9606. Business E-Mail: schneider.gerald@scrippshealth.org.

SCHNEIDER, HARRY H., JR., lawyer; b. San Antonio, Jan. 12, 1954; AB, U. Calif., Berkeley, 1976; JD, U. Chgo., 1979. Bar: Wash. 1979, US Ct. Appeals (9th Cir.), US Dist. Ct. (We. Dist.) Wash., US Dist. Ct. (Ea. Dist.) Wash. Clk. Contra Costa County Dist. Atty. Office, Martinez, Calif., 1972—76; with Kobin & Meyer, Portland, 1977, Cooley, Godward, Castro, Huddleson & Tatum, San Francisco, 1978; ptnr. Perkins Coie LLP, Seattle, mem. mgmt. com. Office: Perkins Coie LLP 1201 Third Ave Ste 4800 Seattle WA 98101-3029 Office Phone: 206-359-8508. Office Fax: 206-359-9000. Business E-Mail: hschneider@perkinscoie.com.

SCHNEIDER, HILARY A., Internet company executive; BA in Econs., Brown U., 1982; MBA, Harvard Bus. Sch., 1986. Dir. devel. The Balt. Sun Co., 1992—94, v.p. new bus. devel., 1994—95, v.p. sales, 1996—97, v.p. sales and mktg., 1997—98, gen. mgr., 1998—99; v.p. corp. fin. Drexel Burnham Lambert Inc., 1986—90; dir. bus. devel. Times Mirror Corp., 1990—92; pres., CEO Times Mirror Interactive, Balt., 1999—2000, Red Herring Comm., 2000—02; v.p., Knight Ridder Digital Knight Ridder, Inc., 2002—04, pres., CEO, Knight Ridder Digital, 2002—04, sr. v.p., 2005—06; sr. v.p. marketplaces (now called Local Markets and Commerce) Yahoo! Inc., Sunnyvale, Calif., 2006, exec. v.p., local markets and commerce divsn., Yahoo! Pub. Network, 2006—. Bd. dirs. CareerBuilder.com; exec. sponsor and leader of significant cross-co. partnership with US publishing companies, including several daily newspapers, 2006—. Office: Yahoo Inc 701 1st Ave Sunnyvale CA 94089 *

SCHNEIDER, HOWARD, lawyer; b. NYC, Mar. 21, 1935; s. Abraham and Lena (Pincus) S.; m. Anne Evelyn Gorfinkle; children: Andrea Rose, Jeffrey Winston. AB, Cornell U., 1956, JD with distinction, 1959. Bar: N.Y. 1960, D.C. 1976. Assoc., then ptnr. Stroock & Stroock, NYC, 1959—75; gen. counsel Commodity Futures Trading Commn., Washington, 1975—77, Rosenman & Colin (now Katten Muchin Rosenman LLP), NYC, 1977—2005; sr. v.p. regulatory affairs Man Fin. Inc., NYC, 2005—. Contbr. articles to profl. jours. Served to capt. USAR, 1956-66. Mem.: ABA (chmn., com. on regulation of futures and derivative insts. 1997—2001), Assn. Bar City of N.Y. (chmn. com. 1982—86). Republican. Jewish. Home: 20 E 74th St New York NY 10021 Office: Man Fin Inc 717 Fifth Ave New York NY 10022 Office Phone: 212-589-6266. Business E-Mail: hschneider@mfglobal.com.

SCHNEIDER, HOWARD STEWART, former newspaper editor; b. Bklyn., Oct. 10, 1945; s. Robert and Helen (Friedman) S.; m. Ilene Roberta Weinstein, July 3, 1967; children— Lara Joy, Scott Michael, Jillian Debra BA cum laude in Journalism and Psychology, Syracuse U., 1966; MS in Journalism, Columbia U., 1967. Co-editor, founder weekly newspaper Syracuse U., NY, 1965-66; editor-pub. Poor Howard's Wednesday Afternoon Post, Wellfleet, Mass., 1966-68; reporter Newsday, Long Island, NY, 1969-76, editor, 1976-85, sr. editor, 1985, mng. editor, 1986—2003, editor, exec. v.p., 2003—04. Adj. prof. journalism SUNY, Stony Brook 1983-87, vis. prof. journalism and media ethics, LI, 2005— Author profiles on Luciano Pavarotti, Tom Seaver, Edward Albee, and Johnny Carson Recipient Nat. Hearst award Syracuse U., 1965; editor George Polk award-winning series, 1979, 1st pl. N.Y. State Pub.'s Assn., 1982, (supr. reporting and editing team) Pulitzer prize for local reporting, 1984 Jewish. Business E-Mail: howardschneider@stonybrook.edu.

SCHNEIDER, JAMES M., bank executive, former computer company executive; b. 1952; BS in Acctg., Carroll Coll, Waukesha, Wis., 1974. Mgmt. to ptnr. Price Waterhouse, 1974—93; sr. v.p. fin. MCI Commns., 1993—96; v.p. fin. & chief acctg. officer Dell Computer Corp., Round Rock, Tex., 1996—98, interim chief info. officer, 1999—2000, sr. v.p., CFO, 2000—07; exec. chmn. Frontier Bancshares Inc., Austin, Tex., 2007—. Bd. dirs. Lockheed Martin Corp., 2005—. Office: Frontier Bancshares Inc 4610 Chiappero Austin TX 78731 *

SCHNEIDER, JAMES RICHARD, orthopedist; b. Keansburg, Pa., July 20, 1937; s. Theodore Jacob and Miriam Gertrude Schneider; m. Jeanine Marie Schneider; children: James Jr., Stephen, Patricia, William. BA, Drake U, Des Moines, 1959; MD, U. Iowa, 1970. Orthop. surgeon US Navy Med. Corps, 1970—87; pvt. practice orthop., hand, microvascular surgeon Concord, Calif., 1987—2005. Capt. USN, 1955—87. Grantee Phi Beta Kappa. Mem.: Am. Assn. Tissue Banks, Am. Soc. Surgery of Hand, Am. Bd. Orthop. Surgeons, World Soc. Reconstructive Microsurgery, Am. Acad. Orthop. Surgery, Calif. Med. Assn. Achievements include microvascular rsch. Office: PO Box 1248 Twain Harte CA 95383 Business E-Mail: vasculargrafts@gmail.com.

SCHNEIDER, JAN, retired obstetrics and gynecology educator; b. Prague, Czechoslovakia, Dec. 10, 1933; came to US, 1963, naturalized, 1967; s. Evzen and Erika S.; m. Sandra Wilson, May 20, 1961; children: Hana, Donald, Kathryn, Jonathan. M.B., U. London, 1957; M.P.H., U. Mich., 1967. Prof. ob-gyn, chief obstetric service dept. ob-gyn U. Mich. Med. Sch., Ann Arbor, 1963-77; prof., chmn. ob-gyn. Med. Coll. Pa. and Hahnemann U. (now Drexel U. Coll. Medicine), Phila., 1978-97, assoc. dean, 1997-99, prof. and chmn. emeritus of ob-gyn., 1999—. Editor: (with R. J. Bolognese and R. H. Schwarz) Perinatal Medicine, 2d edit, 1981. Fellow Am. Coll. Obstetricians and Gynecologists, Soc. Perinatal Obstetricians, Am. Gynecol. and Obstet. Soc., Phila. Obstet. Soc. Presbyterian.

SCHNEIDER, JANET M., arts administrator, curator, painter; b. N.Y.C., June 6, 1950. d. August Arthur and Joan (Battaglia) S.; m. Michael Francis Sperendi, Sept. 21, 1985. BA summa cum laude, Queens Coll., CUNY, 1972; spl. study fine arts Boston U. Tanglewood Inst., 1971. With Queens Mus., Flushing, N.Y.C., 1973-89, curator, 1973-75, program dir., 1975-77, exec. dir., 1977-89. Collections arranged include: Sons and others, Women Artists See Men (author catalog), 1975, Urban Aesthetics (author catalog), 1976, Masters of the Brush, Chinese Painting and Calligraphy from the Sixteenth to the Nineteenth Century (co-author catalog), 1977, Symcho Moszkowicz: Portrait of the Artist in Postwar Europe (author catalog), 1978, Shipwrecked 1622, The Lost Treasure of Philip IV (author catalog), 1981, Michaelangelo: A Sculptor's World (author catalog), 1983, Joseph Cornell: Revisited (author catalog), 1992, Blueprint for Change: The Life and Times of Lewis H. Latimer (co-author catalog), 1995. Chmn. Cultural Instns. Group, N.Y.C., 1986-87; mem. N.Y.C. Commn. for Cultural Affairs, 1991-93; bd. dirs. N.Y.C. Partnership, 1987-88, Gallery Assn. N.Y. State 1979-81; exec. dir. Cultural Inst. Group, 1995-06; cons. dir. Flushing Town Hall, 2007. Mem. Artists Choice Mus. (trustee 1979-82), Am. Assn. Mus., Phi Beta Kappa.

SCHNEIDER, JOANNE, artist; b. Lima, Ohio, Dec. 4, 1919; d. Joseph and Laura (Office) Federman; m. Norman Schneider, May 15, 1941; children: Melanie Schneider Tucker, Lois Schneider Oppenheim. BFA, Syracuse U., 1941. One-man shows John Heller Gallery, NYC, 1954, 55, 57, 58, Tirca Karlis Gallery, Provincetown, Mass., 1963, Frank Rehn Gallery, NYC, 1965, 66, 69, 72, 75, Elaine Benson Gallery, Bridgehamton, NY, 1972, 74, 79, 85, St. Mary's Coll., St. Mary's City, Md., 1978, Alonzo Gallery, NYC, 1978, Discovery Art Gallery, Clifton, NJ, 1978; group shows include Whitney Mus., NYC, Pa. Acad. Arts, Corcoran Galleries, Washington, Toledo Mus., U. Nebr., Everson Mus., Syracuse, NY; represented in permanent collections Met. Mus. Art, NYC, Colby Coll., Syracuse U., Butler Inst., St. Mary's Coll., U. Notre Dame, Guild Hall, East Hampton, NY Recipient Audubon Artists Stanley Grumbacher Meml. award, 1972 Address: 35 E 75th St New York NY 10021-2761 *A life spent in pursuit of creative expression is a fuller, more satisfying life.*

SCHNEIDER, JOHN ARNOLD, investor; b. Chgo., Dec. 4, 1926; s. Arnold George and Anna (Wagner) S.; m. Elizabeth C. Simpson, Oct. 20, 1951; children: Richard Ward, William Arnold, Elizabeth Anne. BS, U. Notre Dame, 1948. Exec. assignments with CBS-TV in Chgo. and NYC, 1950-58; v.p., gen. mgr. sta. WCAU-TV, Phila., 1958-64; sta. WCBS-TV, NYC, 1964-65; pres. CBS TV Network, 1965-66, CBS/Broadcast Group, 1966-69, 71-77; exec. v.p. CBS, Inc., 1969-71, sr. v.p., from, 1977; pres., chief exec. officer MTV Networks, Inc., 1979-84. Trustee, mem. exec. com. U. Notre Dame; trustee Com. for Econ. Devel. Served with USNR, 1943-46. Mem.: Indian Harbor Yacht. Roman Catholic. Home: 155 Clapboard Ridge Rd Greenwich CT 06831-3304

SCHNEIDER, JOHN K., financial advisor; b. Bryn Mawr, Pa., June 30, 1964; s. Arnold C. and Dorothy A. Schneider. BS in Fin. summa cum laude, Lehigh U., 1986. Cert. chartered fin. analyst 1989. V.p. Wilmington Capital Mgmt., Del., 1986-91; sr. securities analyst DuPont Pension Fund, Wilmington, 1991; sr. v.p. Newbold's Asset Mgmt., Bryn Mawr, 1991; joined Schneider Capital Mgmt., 1996; sr. portfolio mgr., mng. dir. PIMCO Equity Advisors, 1999—2005; founder, pres., chief investment advisor JS Asset Management, LLC (JSAM), West Conshohocken, Pa., 2005; sub-advisor Touchstone Large Cap Value Fund, 2006—. Mem.: Fin. Analysts of Wilmington, Phila. Fin. Analysts Soc. (speakers com. mem.), Beta Gamma Sigma (v.p. 1986), Kappa Alpha Soc. Republican. Episcopalian. Avocations: sailing, volleyball, photography. Office: JS Asset Mgmt, LLC One Tower Bridge 100 Front St, Ste 501 West Conshohocken PA 19428 Office Phone: 610-234-2202. Office Fax: 610-825-1831. *

SCHNEIDER, KAREN G., freelance writer; BA in English, Barnard Coll., NYC, 1982; MS in Libr. and Info. Sci., U. Ill., Urbana-Champaign, 1992; MFA in Creative Writing, U. San Francisco, 2006. Children's libr., electronic resources libr. Queens Borough Pub. Libr., Jamaica, NY, 1992—93; electronic resources libr. Newark Pub. Libr., 1993—94; CEO Blue Hwys., Wayne, NJ, 1994—96; dir. US EPA Region 2 NY Libr. Garcia Consulting, Inc., NYC, 1996—98; dir. Brunswick Cmty. Libr., NY, 1998—99; dir. tech. Shenendehowa Pub. Libr., Clifton Park, NY, 1999—2001; dir. Librarians' Internet Index, 2001—06. Adj. instr. dept. info. studies SUNY, Albany, NY, 1998—2001; adj. instr. San Jose State U. Sch. Libr. and Info. Sci., Calif., 2002—03. Columnist: Am. Libraries, 1995—2002; contbr. articles to profl. publs. Aircraft maintenance specialist USAF, 1983—91. Decorated Air Force Commendation medal with three oak leaf clusters; recipient Leadership award, U. Ill. Grad. Sch. Libr. and Info. Sci., 1998, Electronic Frontier Found. 2000 Pioneer award.

SCHNEIDER, KIRK J., psychologist, writer; b. Cleve., July 27, 1956; s. Murray Harold Schneider and Laura Siegal; m. Jurate Elena Raulinaitis, Sept. 17, 1989. BA in Psychology, Ohio State U., 1978; MA in Psychology, West Ga. Coll., 1979; PhD in Psychology, Saybrook Inst., 1984. Lic. psychologist Mass., Calif. Suicide prevention staff Columbus Mental Health Ctr., 1977—78; family therapy trainee Ohio State U., 1978—79; counseling intern West Ga. Coll., 1978—79, grad. tchg. asst., 1978; adv. psychology trainee N.E. Cmty. Mental Health Ctr./Fairhill Psychiat. Hosp., East Cleveland, Ohio, 1979—80; intern, supervisee InterLogue-James F.T. Bugental, PhD, Santa Rosa, Calif., 1980—83; post-doctoral trainee Massillon (Ohio) State Hosp., 1984—85; staff psychologist Human Resources Inst., Norton, Fall River, Mass., 1985—87; pvt. practice, founder Ctr. for Existential Therapy, San Francisco, 1987—. Staff psychologist Ctr. for Nutritional Rsch., Quincy, Mass., 1987—88; mem. crisis counseling team Merrill-Lynch & Co., Boston, 1988; staff psychologist South Shore Coun. on Alcohol, Quincy, 1988—89; instr. Existential-Humanistic Inst., San Francisco, 1997—; adj. faculty Lesley Coll., Cambridge, 1986—90, Bentley Coll., Waltham, Mass., 1989, Union Inst., Cin., 1989—90, Calif. Sch. Profl. Psychology, Berkeley, Alameda, 1990—96, The Profl. Sch. Psychology, San Francisco, 1992, Saybrook Grad. Sch., San Francisco, 1995—, Calif. Inst. Integral Studies, San Francisco, 1996—, clin. supr., 1990—; adj. faculty Ctr. for Humanistic Studies, Detroit, 2001—; spkr. in field. Author, editor: The Paradoxical Self: Toward an Understanding of Our Contradictory Nature, 1990, Horror and the Holy: Wisdom-teachings of the Monster Tale, 1993, The Psychology of Existence: An Integrative, Clinical Perspective, 1995, The Handbook of Humanistic Psychology: Leading Edges in Theory, Research, and Practice, 2001, Rediscovery of Awe: Splendor, Mystery and the Fluid Center of Life, 2004, Existential-Integrative Psychotherapy, 2007; contbr. chapters to books, articles to profl. jours. Pres. Existential-Humanistic Inst., San Francisco, 1999—. Fellow: APA (Rollo May award 2004); mem.: AAAS, Assn. for Humanistic Psychology.

SCHNEIDER, LAWRENCE ALAN, lawyer; b. Richmond, Va., Feb. 4, 1949; m. Susan Ness, Oct. 13, 1974; children: Elisabeth, David. BA cum laude, Yale U., 1971; JD cum laude, Harvard U., 1974. Bar: D.C. 1975, U.S. Ct. Appeals (D.C. cir.) 1975, U.S. Supreme Ct. 1982, U.S. Ct. Internat. Trade 1985. Assoc. Arnold & Porter, Washington, 1974-81, ptnr., Internat. Trade Practice Group, 1982—. Mem. D.C. Bar Com. on Pub. Service Activities, 1979-88, chmn. 1985-87; dir. Washington Council of Lawyers, 1981—, pres. 1984-85. Mem. ABA. Office: Arnold & Porter LLP 555 12th St NW Washington DC 20004-1206 Office Phone: 202-942-5694. Office Fax: 202-942-5999. Business E-Mail: lawrence.schneider@aporter.com.

SCHNEIDER, LAZ LEVKOFF, lawyer; b. Columbia, SC, Mar. 15, 1939; s. Philip L. and Dorothy Harriet (Levkoff) S.; m. Ellen Linda Shiffrin, Dec. 12, 1968; 1 child, David Allen. BA, Yale U., 1961, LLB, 1964; LLM, NYU, 1965. Bar: D.C. 1965, N.Y. 1965, Fla. 1970. Assoc. Fulton, Walter & Duncombe, NYC, 1965-67, Roseman, Colin Kaye Petschek Freund & Emil, NYC, 1967-69, Kronish, Lieb, Weiner, Shainswit & Hellman, NYC, 1969-70; ptnr. Ruden Barnett McClosky & Schuster, Ft. Lauderdale, Fla., 1970-80; pvt. practice Ft. Lauderdale, 1980-86; ptnr. Sherr, Tiballi, Fayne & Schneider, Ft. Lauderdale, 1986-91, Berger Singerman, Ft. Lauderdale, 1991—. Bd. dir. Ocean Biochem. Inc. Grad. editor Tax Law Rev., 1964-65. Exec. com. Fla. regional bd. Anti Defamation League, 1972—. Mem. Fla. Bar Assn., Broward County Bar Assn. (chmn. sect. corp. bus. and banking law 1978-80), Yale Club (pres. 1977-79). Jewish. Office: 350 E Las Olas Blvd Ste 1000 Fort Lauderdale FL 33301-4215 Home Phone: 954-566-2591; Office Phone: 954-525-9900. Personal E-mail: lazsch@att.net. Business E-Mail: lschneider@bergersingerman.com.

SCHNEIDER, LISA A., lawyer; b. Bklyn., Apr. 24, 1962; BA cum laude, SUNY, Binghamton, 1984; JD, St. John's U. Sch. Law, 1987. Bar: NJ 1987, NY 1988, US Dist. Ct. (so. and ea. dists. NY) 1988, US Dist. Ct. (dist. NJ) 1988, Fla. 1994, cert.: Fla. Bd. (wills, trusts and estates) 2003. Atty. Shea & Gould; positions to shareholder pvt. wealth svcs. dept. Gunster, Yoakley & Stewart, West Palm Beach, Fla., 1994—. Contbr. articles to profl. publs. Mem. profl. adv. com. United Way of Martin County Found. Named one of Best of the Bar, South Fla. Bus. Jour., 2003—04, Fla. Legal Elite, Fla. Trend mag., 2004, Top 100 Attys., Worth mag., 2005, Top Lawyers, South Fla. Legal Guide, 2006. Mem.: Jewish Women's Found. of Jewish Fedn. of Palm Beach County (founding trustee), Found. of Jewish Fedn. of Palm Beach County (mem. profl. adv. com.), East Coast Estate Planning Coun., Treasure Coast Planned Giving Coun., Fla. Assn. Women Lawyers (mem. treasure coast chpt.), Martin County Estate Planning Coun., ABA, NY State Bar Assn., NJ State Bar Assn., Martin County Bar Assn. (mem. elder law, probate and guardianship com.). Office: Gunster Yoakley & Stewart Phillips Point 777 S Flagler Dr Ste 500 E West Palm Beach FL 33401 Office Phone: 561-650-0680. Office Fax: 561-655-5677. E-mail: lschneider@gunster.com.

SCHNEIDER, LORI BETH, neurologist; b. Bklyn., Jan. 23, 1965; d. Daniel and Eileen Schneider; m. Jean-Pierre Riou, Apr. 30, 1989; children: Jessica Riou, Justin Riou. BS in Biology, NYU, NYC, 1986, MD, 1990. Diplomate Am. Bd. Psychiatry and Neurology, Am. Bd. Geriatrics. Neurologist, pres. Lakeside Neurology, Cornelius, NC, 1994—. Recipient award, Am. Bd. Hosp. Physicians, 2006, Am. Bd. Ethical Physicians, 2006. Fellow: Am. Acad. Neurology; mem.: Am. Assn. Neuromuscular and Electrodiagnostic Medicine, Phi Beta Kappa. Avocations: travel, exercise, movies. Office: Lakeside Neurology 19615 Liverpool Pkwy Ste A Cornelius NC 28031 E-mail: lorijp@bellsouth.net.

SCHNEIDER, MAHLON C., lawyer; b. 1939; BA, U. Minn., 1962, LLB, 1964. Bar: Minn. 1965. Atty. Green Giant Co., 1968—80, Pillsbury, 1980-84, v.p., gen. counsel foods divsn., 1984-89; corp. atty. Hormel Foods Corp., Austin, Minn., 1989-90, v.p., gen. counsel, 1990-99, sr. v.p. external affairs, gen. counsel, 1999—2005. Bd. dirs. HMN Fin. Inc., 2000—. Office: HMN Fin 1016 Civic Center Dr NW Rochester MN 55901 Office Phone: 507-437-5611.

SCHNEIDER, MARK, political science professor; b. NYC, Oct. 28, 1946; s. Irving and Ida Schneider; m. Susan Roth, June 27, 1986; children: Johanna, Elizabeth. BA, Bklyn. Coll., 1967; PhD, U. N.C., 1974. Asst. prof. polit. sci. U. Mich., Ann Arbor, 1973-74, SUNY, Stony Brook, 1974-78, assoc. prof., 1978-85, prof., 1985—2004, chmn. dept., 1986—2004, disting. prof., 2004—. Fulbright sr. lectr., India, 1980—81; dep. commr. Inst. Edn. Scis., 2004—05. Author: The Competitive City, 1989, Public Entrepreneurs, 1995, Choosing Schools, 2000, Charter Schools: Hope or Hype, 2007; contbr. articles to profl. jours. Dep. commr. Inst. Edn. Scis., 2004—05; commr. Nat. Ctr. for Ednl. Stats., 2005—. Mem. Am. Polit. Sci. Assn. (v.p. 2000-01), Midwest Polit. Sci. Assn. Office: Nat Ctr Edn Statis Washington DC 20208

SCHNEIDER, MARK LEWIS, foreign policy executive, retired government agency administrator; b. Newark, Dec. 31, 1941; s. Benjamin and Ruth (Kobran) S.; m. Susan Gilbert, June 20, 1965; children: Aaron Mitchell, Miriam Beth. AB in Journalism with honors, U. Calif., Berkeley, 1963; MA in Polit. Sci., San Jose State Coll., 1965; LLD (hon.), Am. U., 2000. Reporter UPI, San Francisco, 1963-64, San Francisco News Call Bull., 1965; vol. Peace Corps, El Salvador, 1966-68; reporter Washington Daily News, 1969-70; mem. staff U.S. Senate Judiciary Subcom., 1970-71; legis. asst. to Sen. Edward M. Kennedy, 1971-77, 80-81; dep. asst. sec. for human rights Dept. State, Washington, 1977-79; mem. del. UN Gen. Assembly, 1978, UN Human Rights Commn., 1979; coordinator policy planning, sr. advisor Pan Am. Health Orgn., 1981-93; adminstr. for Latin Am. and Caribbean U.S. AID, 1993-99; dir. The Peace Corps, 1999-2001; sr. v.p. Internat. Crisis Group, Washington, 2001—. Lectr. Kennedy Inst. Politics, Harvard U., 1976; adj. prof. Georgetown U., 1996. Trustee Am. U., 2006—; bd. dirs. Internat. Human Rights Law Group, 1981—92. Fulbright fellow, 1976; recipient George W. Eastman medal U. Rochester, 2000, Bernardo O'Higgins medal Govt. Chile, 1993 Mem. Am. Polit. Sci. Assn., Latin Am. Studies Assn. Democrat. Jewish. Home: 3517 Tilden St NW Washington DC 20008-3122 Office Phone: 202-785-1601. E-mail: mschneider@crisisgroup.org.

SCHNEIDER, MARTIN AARON, photojournalist, ecologist, engineer, writer, artist, television director, filmmaker, public advocate, medical researcher, educator; b. NYC, Sept. 23, 1926; s. Morris and Florence (Frohlich) S. Student, Stuyvesant Sci., 1941-44; BC, CUNY, 1948—53. Editor Nocturne; artist, 1941—; photographer, 1954—. Photojournalist Life, Time, Newsweek, Sports Illustrated, NY Times, NBC-TV, Ency. Britannica, Mpls. Tribune, Handball Illustrated, Time Annual Year in Review, Grolier Ency., Crowell-Collier Ency., NBC Startime, Variety, Time-Life: Ecology, Saturday Review of Literature, 1960—; ecologist, USPHS, US Senate, US EPA, NYCEPA, NY State Dept. Environ. Conservation, NYC Dept. Air Pollution, 1964—; product safety engineer, designer, builder, crash-safety, pollution and radiation monitoring, multi-alternate fuel, laboratory vehicle, stereotactic radiosurgery: safer therapy delivery collimator, 1967—, univ. faculties NYU, Cornell U., Ithaca, NY, New Sch. Social Rsch. U., NYC, SUNY, Albany, Cooper Union for Advancement of Sci. and Art, NYC, CUNY, Iowa U., lectr. in field, 1969—; pub. advocate, NYC Health Dept., NY State Health Dept., NY State Dept. Environ. Conservation, Gov. Rockefeller's State Study Commission for NYC (Scott Commission), US District Ct., NY Supreme Ct., People of NYC, NYC Council, NY Atty. Gen., 1970—. TV news guest NBC Today, CBS, ABC, FOX, PBS, 1970—; radio news guest NBC, CBS, NPR, 1970; TV and radio commentator, NBC, CBS, ABC, PBS, Fox, 1970—; author: Breath of Death, 1972, Consumer Genocide: Censored Survival Kit 1992; The Schneider Tapes, 1996, War Against War, ed. 1996, CARnage: 3 Million Killed by Suppressed 100 mph Safety, 1997, The Food You Eat--Eats You: How to Get Safe Food in Same Stores at Same Price, 1998, Cataclysmathon, 2001, Cancerterias, 2002, Scars of Eternity, 2005; co-author: NBC Startime, 1963, America-Photographic Statements, 1972, Eye of Conscience, 1974 (chpt. Martin Schneider); dir., prodr., writer, videographer, cinematographer (TV documentaries) Environment Crusade, CBS, 1970, The Poisoned Air, CBS, 1970, Killers of the Environment, NBC, 1971, Censorship of Pollution Solutions by Media and Government, PBS, 1974, No Justice for Victims-Criminals Only, 1992; contbr. NY Times, Ency. Britannica, Macmillan Ency. of Photographic Artists, NY Village Voice "Whole Earth Ranger: Ecology's Batman", New World Or No World (Frank Herbert) 1970—; photography exhibited at Mus. Modern Art, NYC, 1958—, George Eastman House Mus., Rochester, NY, 1963, 64—, Libr. Congress, 1970, Smithsonian Instn., 1972—, Art Inst. Chgo., 1973—, Whitney Mus., NYC, 1978—; permanent exhibit includes NY Mus. of TV and Radio, 1999; painting exhibited at Guggenheim Mus., NYC, 1943; film exhibited at Am. Mus. Natural History, NYC, 1969-72, network TV guest appearances; dir. documentaries, 1969-. Served with US Army Paratroopers, 1944-46, PTO. Fellowship grantee Creative Artists Pub. Svc., 1977, 78; recipient TV Franny Consumer Advocacy award, 1974, for work that was a basis for the first Clean Air Act of 1970. Jewish. Achievements include advocacy for Mayo Clinic non-toxic patient-derived vaccine cancer theraphy now offered alternative to chemotherapy uniquely in US for all stages, 2004. Office: 545 8th Ave Ste 401 New York NY 10018 Office Phone: 212-840-1234. *Where millions are endangered where my work makes a difference--despite gunfire, vehicle sabotage, seizure of home and all possessions, censorship--I cannot compromise public health for private wealth- for there is no dream for me in moving mere mountains, but only in moving man to move himself.*

SCHNEIDER, MARY LOUISE, retired elementary school educator; b. Waterville, Wash., Oct. 17, 1918; d. John Steve and Alice Ray (Jones) S. BA in Edn., Holy Names Coll., 1940. Cert. elem. tchr. Wash., 1940. Tchr. Mud Springs/Douglas County, Mansfield, Wash., 1941-42; elem. tchr. Mansfield Sch. dist., Douglas County, Wash., 1942-43, Waterville (Wash.) Sch. Dist., Douglas County, Wash., 1943-49, Lewis and Clark Elem. Sch., Wenatchee, Wash., 1949-60; spl. reading tchr. H.B. Ellison Jr. High, Wenatchee, 1960-62, Orchard Jr. High, Wenatchee, 1962-67; lang. arts tchr. Pioneer Jr. High, Wenatchee, 1967-77; retired, 1977. Author lang. arts learning packages for students, 1967; co-author: Name on the Schoolhouse, 1989. Vol. Am. Heart Assn., Wenatchee, 1975-90, Am. Cancer Soc., Wenatchee, 1975-88. Recipient Cert. of Recognition, Wash. State Ct. Cath. Daus. of the Ams., 1970, 72, 74. Mem.: AAUW (treas. 1973—75), PEO (pres. CP chpt. 1980—82, pres. 1988—90), Chelan-Douglas County Sch. Retirees Assn. (com. chmn. 1989—90), Cath. Daus. of the Ams. (local ct. pres. 1958—60, state pres. 1984—86, nat. evangelization chmn. 1986—88, author Wash. State Ct. of Cath. Daus. 1988, local ct. pres. 1999—2001), Delta Kappa Gamma (pres. Zeta chpt. 1966—68). Avocation: sewing.

SCHNEIDER, MATHIEU, professional hockey player; b. NYC, June 12, 1969; married. Defenseman Montreal Canadiens, 1990-95, NY Islanders, 1995-96, Toronto Maple Leafs, 1996-98, NY Rangers, 1998—2000, LA Kings, 2000—03, Detroit Red Wings, 2003—07, Anaheim Ducks, 2007—. Player NHL All-Star Game, 1996, 2003. Achievements include being a member of Stanely Cup Champion Montreal Canadiens, 1993. Office: Anaheim Ducks 2695 E Katella Ave Anaheim CA 92806 *

SCHNEIDER, MATTHEW ROGER, lawyer; b. NYC, Nov. 7, 1948; s. Theodore David Schneider and Rosalind (Schwartz) Werner; m. Marjorie Ann Friedlander, Mar. 6, 1976; children: Adam Benjamin, Emily Beth. BA, Cornell U., 1970; student, Georgetown U., 1971; JD, Cath. U., Washington, 1974. Bar: D.C. 1976, U.S. Dist. Ct. D.C., 1994. Staff asst. U.S. Senate Jud. Com., Washington, 1973-74; counsel U.S. Senate Govt. Ops. Com., Washington, 1974-77; spl. asst. Office of Sec. Def., Washington, 1977-79; dir. legis. affairs SEC, Washington, 1979-81, sr. counsel, divsn. corp. fin., 1981-82; chief of staff U.S. Senator Jeff Bingaman, Washington, 1983-85; prin. Law Office Matthew Schneider, Washington, 1985-87; ptnr. Willkie, Farr & Gallagher, Washington, 1987-95, Garvey Shubert Barer, Washington, 1996—98, mng. dir. DC office, 1998—, mng. dir. NYC office, 2001—, mng. dir. Beijing office, 2005—06. Chmn. govt. and legal affairs com. Nat. Epilepsy Found., Washington, 1997—2003; bd. dirs. Nat. Epilepsy Found., 2000—04, mem. exec. com., 2001—04; bd. dirs Capitol Hill Hosp., Washington, 1987—95. Avocations: physical fitness training, singing, guitar. Office: Garvey Schubert Barer 5th Fl 1000 Potomac St NW Ste 5 Washington DC 20007-3501 Office Phone: 202-965-7880.

SCHNEIDER, PAM HORVITZ, lawyer; b. Cleve., Nov. 29, 1951; m. Milton S. Schneider, June 30, 1973; 1 child, Sarah Anne. BA, U. Pa., 1973; JD, Columbia U., 1976. Bar: N.Y. 1977, Pa. 1979. Assoc. White & Case, NYC, 1976-78, Drinker Biddle & Reath LLP, Phila., 1978-84, ptnr., 1984-2001; founding ptnr. Gadsden Schneider & Woodward LLP, King of Prussia, Pa., 2001—. Contbr. articles to profl. jours. Fellow Am. Coll. Trust and Estate Counsel (past regent); mem. ABA (past chair, real property probate and trust law sect.), Internat. Acad. Estate and Trust Law (academician). Office: Gadsden Schneider & Woodward LLP The Merion Bldg 700 S Henderson Rd Ste 345 King Of Prussia PA 19406 E-mail: pschneider@gsw-llp.com.

SCHNEIDER, PAUL, writer; b. Passaic, NJ, Aug. 4, 1923; s. Solomon Peter and Rose (Levine) S.; m. Margaret Flood Perrin, Apr. 10, 1951; children: Peggy Lee, Peter Lincoln, Ann. BA, Harvard U., 1945. Writer, NYC, Hollywood, Calif., 1954-91; staff writer Universal City Studios, North Hollywood, Calif., 1967-74; head writer Love of Life CBS Studios, NYC, 1974-76. Writer: (TV) Star Trek, 1954-85, Bonanza, 1954-85, Marcus Welby, M.D., 1954-85, (movies) The Looters, 1957, Ride the Wind, 1966, (plays) Effigy, 1983, Acrimonious, 1962. Mem. Writers Guild Am. (chmn. violence com. 1980-81), Harvard Alumni Assn., Dems. for Action. Avocations: hiking, mountain trails, travel, zen. Home: PO Box 65 Idyllwild CA 92549-0065

SCHNEIDER, PAUL ALLAN, federal agency administrator; m. Leslie Schneider. BS, U. Mass. Project engr. submarine propulsion and auxillary machinery systems br. Portsmouth Naval Shipyard, 1965—66; various positions in submarine design, constrn. and overhaul programs, 1966—81; dep. dir. Auxilliary Systems Sub-Group Naval Sea Systems Command, 1981—86, exec. dir. Amphibious, Auxilliary, Mine and Sealift Ships Directorate, 1986—91, exec. dir. Surface Ship Directorate, 1991—94, exec. dir., sr. civilian, 1994—98; prin. dep. asst. sec. Navy rsch., devel., and acquisition, 1998—2002; sr. acquisition exec. Nat. Security Agy., 2002—03; def. and aerospace cons. US Navy; under sec. for mgmt. US Dept. Homeland Security, Washington, 2007—. Mem.: Assn. Old Crows, Naval Inst., Navy League, Assn. Scientists and Engrs., Armed Forces Comm. and Electronics Assn., Am. Soc. Naval Engrs. Office: US Dept Homeland Security Seventh and D Streets SW Washington DC 20528 Office Phone: 202-282-8000. Office Fax: 202-776-9646. *

SCHNEIDER, PAULINE A., lawyer; b. Bridgeton, NJ, May 25, 1943; BA, Glassboro State Coll., 1965; postgrad., Syracuse U., 1966; M Urban Studies, Howard U., 1972; JD, Yale U., 1977. Bar: DC 1978. Staff asst. White House Office Intergovtl. Affairs, 1978—81; dir. Office Intergovtl. Rels., DC Govt., 1983—85; ptnr. Hunton & Williams, Washington, 1985—2006; ptnr., pub. fin. group Orrick, Herrington & Sutcliffe LLP, Washington, 2006—. Bd. dirs. MedStar Health Inc., Potomac Elec. Power Co., Diamond Cluster Internat., MDL Capital Mgmt. Bd. dir. Nat. Partnership for Women and Families; bd. dirs. Access Group, Lab Sch. of Washington; trustee Shakespeare Theatre, U. Md. Balt. Found.; mem. Pres. Adv. Coun. Washington Coll. Named one of Women Who Shape Future, Women's Legal Def. Fund, 1994; recipient Woman Lawyer of Yr., Women's Bar Assn. DC, 1995, Pres. award, Nat. Assn. Women Lawyers, 1998, Margaret Brent Women of Achievement award, ABA Commn. on Women, 1999, Woman of Genius award, Trinity Coll., 2000, Woman of Achievement, Anti-Defamation League, 2001, Outstanding Alumni, Rowan Univ., 2001. Mem.: ABA (bd. govs. 2003—06, mem.exec. com. 2005—, ho. of dels. 1993—, chair coun. sect. on legal edn. 2004—05), Econ. Club of Washington (bd. dirs.), Nat. Bar Assn., DC Bar Assn. (bd. dirs. 1988—94, pres. 1994—95), Am. Bar Found., Am. Law Inst., Nat. Assn. Securities Professionals, Nat. Assn. Bond Lawyers. Office: Orrick Herrington & Sutcliffe LLP 3050 K St NW Washington DC 20007-5135 Home Phone: 202-723-7134; Office Phone: 202-955-1660, 202-339-8483. Business E-Mail: paschneider@orrick.com.

SCHNEIDER, PETER A., urologist, surgeon; BA, Amherst Coll., Mass.; MD, Columbia Uu., NYC. Lic. urologist Yale U., cert. Am. Bd. Urology. Pvt. practice Orinda Urology, Inc., Calif., 1988—. Office: Orinda Urology Inc 25 Orinda Way Ste 100 Orinda CA 94563

SCHNEIDER, PETER RAYMOND, political scientist; b. Muskogee, Okla., Aug. 8, 1939; s. Leo Frederick and Tillie Oleta (Cannon) S.; m. Anne Larason, Jan. 22, 1964 (div. 1983); children: Christopher, Geoffrey; m. Adrienne Armstrong, Dec. 19, 1986; children: Robbie, Samantha. BS, Okla. State U., 1966, MS, 1968; PhD, Ind. U., 1974. News editor No. Va. Sun, Arlington, 1961-62; news writer AP, Balt., 1962, Balt. News-Am., 1962-65; asst. prof. U. Oreg., Eugene, 1974-76; pres. Inst. of Policy Analysis, Eugene, 1976-83; v.p. Am. Justice Inst., Sacramento, 1983; dir. Ctr. for Assessment of The Juvenile Justice Ctr., Sacramento, 1983; v.p. Nat. Partnership, Washington, 1985; sr. rsch. scientist Pacific Inst. for Rsch. and Evaluation, Bethesda, Md., 1984-92, dir. justice div., 1986-89; pres. Inst. of Policy Analysis, McLean, Va., 1992-95; CEO IPA Internat., Inc., Vienna, 1995—. Contbr. numerous articles to profl. jours., chpts. to books. Recipient Julia Lathrop award Am. Criminal Justice Assn., 1985. Mem. Am. Polit. Sci. Assn., Am. Restitution Assn., Pi Sigma Alpha, Sigma Delta Chi, Phi Kappa Phi, Omicron Delta Kappa, Phi Kappa Theta. Avocations: flying, tennis, selling wine. Office: IPA Internat Inc 7291 Jones Branch Dr Ste 501 Mc Lean VA 22102 Home: 1345 Woodside Dr Mc Lean VA 22102-1530 *In a career devoted to the pursuit of knowledge, I have learned that nothing - absolutely nothing - is worth more than lessons learned from painful personal experience. To my regret, I usually learned such lessons after the opportunities to profit from them had already passed. If I could do it over again I would be more daring and venturesome and make my mistakes early, while there was still plenty of time to invest the information.*

SCHNEIDER, PHYLLIS LEAH, writer, editor; b. Seattle, Apr. 19, 1947; d. Edward Lee Booth and Harriet Phyllis (Ebbinghaus) Russell; m. Clifford Donald Schneider, June 14, 1969; 1 child, Pearl Brooke. BA, Pacific Luth. U., 1969; MA, U. Wash., 1972. Fiction, features editor Seventeen Mag., NYC, 1975-80; mng. editor Weight Watchers Mag., NYC, 1980-81; editor YM mag., NYC, 1981-86. Author: Parents Book of Infant Colic, 1990, Kids Who Make a Difference, 1993, Straight Talk on Women's Health: How to Get the Health Care You Deserve, 1993, Hot Health Care Careers, 1993, What Kids Like To Do, 1993; contbr. The Parents Answer Book, 1998; The Prose Reader, 2001, 2004. Recipient Centennial Recognition award Pacific Luth. U., 1990. Democrat. Episcopalian.

SCHNEIDER, RICHARD DURBIN, art educator; b. Toledo, Apr. 5, 1937; s. Richard V. and Josephine D. Schneider; m. Patricia A. Hughes, Dec. 19, 1980; children: Elizabeth, Karl, Owen. BA in Art, U. Toledo, 1963; MA in Art, Bowling Green U., Ohio, 1968. Cert. tchr. Ohio, 1964. Art tchr. Washington Jr. HS, Toledo, 1965—67; asst. prof. art Monroe County CC, Monroe, Mich., 1969—71; assoc. prof. art Cleve. State U., 1971—. Prin. works include wall panels for Kaiser Permanente Hosp., Cleve., 1987, ceramic sculptures Allen, Booz & Hamilton Internat., 1999, ceramic sculptures Cleve. Clinic Internat. Hotel, 1999. Recipient Purchase award for ceramics, Butler Mus. Am. Art, Youngstown, Ohio, 1973, Best of Exhbn. award, Ohio Craft Mus., Columbus, 1996; grantee, Ohio Arts Coun., 1978—80, Cleve. Mus. Art, 1972. Avocations: computers, photography. Home: 2610 Exeter Rd Cleveland Heights OH 44118 Office: Cleve State U 2307 Chester Ave Cleveland OH 44115

SCHNEIDER, RICHARD GRAHAM, lawyer; b. Bryn Mawr, Pa., Aug. 2, 1930; s. Vincent Bernard and Marion Scott (Graham) S.; m. Margaret Peter Fritz, Feb. 15, 1958; children: Margaret W., Richard Graham Jr., John

F. BA, Yale U., 1952; JD, U. Pa., 1957, MLA, 2001. Bar: Pa. 1958. Assoc. Dechert Price & Rhoads, Phila., 1957-66, ptnr., 1966-95; of counsel, 1995—. Case editor U. Pa. Law Rev., 1956-57. Trustee Baldwin Sch., Bryn Mawr, 1971-79, Episcopal Acad., Merion, Pa., 1976-83, Episcopal Cmty. Svcs., Phila., 2003—. 1st lt. USAF, 1952-54, PTO. Mem. ABA, Pa. Bar Assn., Phila. Bar Assn., Order of Coif, Merion Cricket Club, Merion Golf Club (sec. 1997-2002), Yale Club (pres. 1966-68). Republican. Presbyterian. Office: Dechert LLP CIRA Ctr 2929 Arch St Philadelphia PA 19104-2808 Personal E-mail: gladwyne@aol.com.

SCHNEIDER, RICHARD T(HEODORE), optics scientist, researcher, engineer; b. Munich, July 29, 1927; came to U.S., 1961; s. Wilhelm and Martha E. (Hofmann) S.; m. Lore M. Reinhard, May 16, 1950; children: Ursula M. Schneider Long, Richard W. Diploma in physics, U. Stuttgart, Fed. Republic of Germany, 1958, PhD, 1961. Registered profl. engr. Calif. Teaching asst. U. Stuttgart, 1958-61; sect. chief Allison div. Gen. Motors Corp., Indpls., 1961-65; assoc. prof. U. Fla., Gainesville, 1965-68, prof., 1968-88, prof. emeritus, 1988-90; pres. Eye Rsch. Lab., Inc., Alachua, Fla., 1984-90; chief scientist RTS Labs., Inc., Alachua, 1984-92. Cons. Allison div. Gen. Motors Corp., Indpls., 1965-67; IPA assignment Eglin AFB, Ft. Walton Beach, Fla., 1983; liaison scientist USN Office Naval Rsch., London, 1975. Editor: Uranium Plasmas, 1971; patentee in field; contbr. articles to profl. jours. Recipient Medal for Exceptional Sci. Achievement, NASA, 1975, Outstanding Tech. Achievement award, Fla. Engring. Soc., 1978. Mem. Internat. Soc. for Optical Engring., Sigma Xi, Tau Beta Pi (Eminent Engr. 1970). Home: 12903 NW 112th Ave Alachua FL 32615-6520 Home Phone: 386-462-3301; Office Phone: 386-462-2666. Personal E-mail: schneider-labs@worldnet.att.net.

SCHNEIDER, ROB, actor; b. Pacifica, Calif., Oct. 31, 1963; s. Marvin and Pilar Schneider; m. London King, 1988 (div. 1990); 1 child, Chole Autumn. Co-owner restaurant Eleven, San Francisco. Actor: (films) Martians Go Home, 1990, Necessary Roughness, 1991, Home Alone 2: Lost in New York, 1992, Surf Ninjas, 1993, Demolition Man, 1993, The Beverly Hillbillies, 1993, Judge Dredd, 1995, Down Periscope, 1996, The Adventures of Pinocchio, 1996, Knock Off, 1998, Susan's Plan, 1998, The Waterboy, 1998, Deuce Bigalow: Male Gigolo, 1999, Big Daddy, 1999, Muppets From Space, 1999, Little Nicky, 2000, The Animal, 2001, The Hot Chick, 2002, Mr. Deeds, 2002, (voice) Eight Crazy Nights, 2002, 50 First Dates, 2004, Around the World in 80 Days, 2004, The Longest Yard, 2005, Deuce Bigalow: European Gigolo, 2005, Grandma's Boy, 2006, The Benchwarmers, 2006, (TV series) Saturday Night Live, 1990-94, Men Behaving Badly, 1996-97, (TV films) The Mummy Parody, 2001, (voice) The Electric Piper, 2003, Back to Norm, 2005. Office: United Talent Agy 9560 Wilshire Blvd Fl 5 Beverly Hills CA 90212-2400

SCHNEIDER, ROBERT JAY, oncologist; b. Miami, Fla., May 31, 1949; s. Irving and Ethel (Pack) S.; m. Barbara Cunningham, June 1, 1974; children: Matthew, Kirsten. Student, Washington U., 1967-69; BA cum laude, Boston U., 1971; MD, Albert Einstein Coll. Medicine, NYC, 1975. Diplomate Am. Bd. Internal Medicine, Am. Bd. Oncology; lic. physician, N.Y. Intern, jr. and sr. resident internal medicine Bronx Mcpl. Hosp., NYC, 1975-78; fellow med. oncology Meml. Sloan-Kettering Cancer Ctr., NYC, 1978-80, adj. attending physician/cons. dept. medicine, 1981—; asst. prof. medicine N.Y. Med. Coll., Valhalla, 1980-81. Clin. instr. medicine Cornell U. Med. Coll., 1978-80; jr. clin. faculty fellow Am. Cancer Soc., 1980-81; mem. N.Y. Met. Breast Cancer Group, 1990—; cons. cancer program No. Westchester Hosp. Ctr., Mt. Kisco, N.Y., 1981-82; mem. staff Westchester County Med. Ctr., Valhalla, N.Y., No. Westchester Hosp. Ctr., Mt. Kisco, Meml. Sloan-Kettering Cancer Ctr., N.Y.C. Contbr. articles to profl. jours. Mem. adv. bd. Cancer Care, Inc. Conn., 1997-99. Recipient Clin. Fellowship award Am. Cancer Soc., 1978-79. Mem. Am. Soc. Clin. Oncology, Westchester County Med. Soc., Soc. Integrative Oncology, Am. Soc. Breast Disease, N.Y. State Med. Soc., Woodway Country Club. Republican. Presbyterian. Achievements include research in detection and treatment of early breast cancer, the human spirit in the fight against cancer, salvage chemotherapy with etoposide, ifosfamide and cisplatin in refractory germ cell tumors. Office: 101 S Bedford Rd Ste 202A Mount Kisco NY 10549-3456

SCHNEIDER, ROBERT JEROME, lawyer; b. Cin., June 22, 1947; s. Jerome William and Agnes (Moehringer) S.; m. Janice Loraine Eckhoff, Dec. 13, 1968; children: Aaron Haisley, Jared Alan, Margot Laraine. BSME, U. Cin., 1970, JD, 1973. Bar: Ill. 1973, U.S. Dist. Ct. (no. dist.) Ill. 1973, U.S. Ct. Appeals (7th cir.) 1973, U.S. Ct. Appeals (fed. cir.) 1973. Ptnr. Mason, Kolehmainen, Rathburn & Wyss, Chgo., 1973-82; ptnr., asst. chmn. patents, chmn. intellect. property dept. McDermott, Will & Emery, Chgo., 1982-94; chmn. intellectual property dept. Chapman & Cutler, Chgo., 1995—. Mem. ABA, ASME, Ill. Bar Assn., Chgo. Bar Assn., Licensing Execs. Soc., Intellectual Property Law Assn. Chgo. (sec. 1981-83), Fedn. Internat. des Conseils en Proriete Industrielle, Assn. Internationale pour la Protection de la Properitété Industrielle, Internat. Pat-Got Assn. (treas. 2001-05, pres. 2005-), Internat. Trademark Assn., Internat. Trade Commn. Trial Lawyers Assn., Am. Intellectual Property Law Assn., Tower Club (bd. govs. 1988—, v.p. 1994-95, pres. 1995—), Univ. Club Chgo. (bd. dirs. 2001-). Republican. Roman Catholic. Home: 1609 Asbury Ave Winnetka IL 60093-1303 Office: Chapman & Cutler Chicago IL 60601 Office Fax: 312-803-3529. E-mail: iplaw@chapman.com.

SCHNEIDER, RYAN A., lawyer; b. Fort Worth, Tex., May 29, 1968; s. Edward Schneider and Carol Forman; m. Jennifer B. Tourial, Mar. 8, 1997; children: Lily Maya, Gray Salem, Owen Roarke. BME, Ga. Inst. Tech., Atlanta, 1990; JD, U. Ga., Athens, 1995. Bar: US PTO 1995. Assoc. Deveau, Colton & Marquis, Atlanta, 1996—2000; ptnr. Troutman Sanders LLP, Atlanta, 2000—. Home: 2548 Sharondale Ct NE Atlanta GA 30305 Office: Troutman Sanders LLP 600 Peachtree St NE Ste 5200 Atlanta GA 30308 Personal E-mail: ryan.schneider@troutmansanders.com.

SCHNEIDER, SHARON M., systems administrator, information technologist; b. Detroit, Mar. 15, 1958; d. Peter and Mary S.; m. Wesley A. Comes, May 23, 1987. BS, Kutztown U., 1990; MS, MSIS, Drexel U., 1998. Reference and info. asst. Bucks County Free Libr., Doylestown, Pa., 1988-94; computer sys. tech. Cedar Crest & Muhlenberg Colls., Allentown, Pa., 1994-95; sys. adminstr., info. technologist Cedar Crest Coll., 1995—. Mem. Assn. Computing Machinery, World Future Soc., Beta Phi Mu.

SCHNEIDER, STEPHEN HARLEY, medical educator; b. Neptune, NJ, Apr. 1, 1948; s. Joseph and Edith (Himmelman) S.; m. Carole Robin Lowenstein, Aug. 31, 1981; children: Ari, Rachel. BA, MD, Boston U., 1972. Cert. in internal medicine and endocrinology, N.J. Rsch. assoc. Boston City Hosp., 1975-76, fellow divsn. diabetes and metabolism, 1976-77, asst. dir. diabetes clinic, 1976-77, dir. diabetes clinic, 1977-78, dir. diabetes and metabolism svcs., 1978-79; instr. medicine Boston Univ. Sch. Medicine, 1978-79; asst. prof. medicine U. Medicine and Dentistry N.J.-Robert Wood Johnson Med. Sch., New Brunswick, NJ, 1979-85, assoc. prof. clin. medicine, 1985-88, assoc. prof. medicine, 1988-95, prof. medicine, 1995—. Mem. editl. bd. Diabetes Forcast Mag.; contbr. numerous articles to profl. jours. including Jour. Clin. Endocrinology and Nutrition, New Eng. Jour. Medicine, Diabetes Care, Atherosclerosis, Japanese Heart Jour., Diabetologia, Metabolism. Bd. dirs. Juvenile Diabetes Assn., East Brunswick Jewish Ctr. Youth Com.; founding mem. affiliate Internat. Diabetic Athlete's Assn. Recipient McKeen Cattell award Am. Coll. Clin. Pharmacology, 1986; rsch. fellow Am. Heart Assn., 1976. Fellow ACP; mem. Am. Soc. Internal Medicine, Am. Coll. Sports Medicine, Am. Fedn. Clin. Rsch., Begg Soc., Phi Beta Kappa, Alpha Omega Alpha. Jewish. Avocations: football, soccer, history, theology, bicycling. Office: UMDNJ-Robert W Johnson Med Divsn Endocrinology PO Box 19 New Brunswick NJ 08903-0019 Home Phone: 732-390-7429; Office Phone: 732-235-7751. Business E-Mail: schneide@umdnj.edu.

SCHNEIDER, STEVEN JACK, neurosurgeon; b. Bklyn., June 22, 1958; s. Irene Alexandra; children: Samantha, Daniel. BA in Biology cum laude, NYU, 1979; MD magna cum laude, Baylor Coll. Medicine, 1982. Diplomate Am. Bd. Neurological Surgeons, 1992, Am. Bd. Pediatric Neurosurgery, 1997. Intern, pediatric neurological surgery Baylor Coll. Medicine and Affiliated Hosps., Houston, 1982-83, resident, pediatrics, 1983-88; fellow in pediatric neurological surgery NYU Med. Ctr., NYC, 1988-89; asst. attending physician, pediatric neurological surgery Winthrop U. Hosp., Mineola, NY, 1989—; assoc. attending physician, pediatric neurological surgery LI Jewish Med. Ctr., NY, 1989—, dir., neurosurgery residency NY, chief, pediatric neurological surgery NY, 2002—, dir., surgical services, Comprehensive Epilepsy Ctr. NY; chief attending physician neurosurgery Nassau County Med. Ctr., East Meadow, NY, 1989—; asst. attending physician North Shore U. Hosp., Manhasset, N.Y., 1992-93, head sect. pediatric neurological surgery, asst. attending physician, 1989—, chief, pediatric neurological surgery, 2002—, Schneider Children's Hosp., New Hyde Park, NY, 2002—, dir., surgical services, Comprehensive Pediatric Movement Disorder Ctr.; clin. instr., Leo M. Davidoff Dept. Neurological Surgery Albert Einstein Coll. Medicine, Yeshiva U., Bronx, NY, 1989—; clin. instr. Cornell U. Med. Ctr., NY, 1993—; clin. asst. prof. neurosurgery NYU Sch. Medicine; pediatric neurosurgeon, sr. ptnr. LI Neurosurgical Associates, PC, New Hyde Park, NY, 1989—. Contbr. articles to profl. jours.; serves as ad hoc editor for multiple scientific jours., including Pediatric Neurosurgery. Mem. adv. coun. Children's Brain Tumor Found., Epilepsy Found., Think First Found. Fellow Am. Coll. Surgeons, Am. Acad. Pediatrics; mem. Am. Epilepsy Soc., Am. Acad. Pain Medicine, Harris County Med. Soc., Tex. Med. Assn., Congress Neurol. Surgeons, Am. Assn. Neurol. Surgeons (mem. sect. on pain, mem. joint sect. on disorders spine & peripheral nerves), AMA, Am. Modulation Soc., Complex Regional Pain Syndrome Assn., Hydrocephalus Assn., Guardians of Hydrocephalus, Nat. Neurofibromatosis Found., Am. Syringomyelia Alliance Project, Congress Neurological Surgeons, Nassau County Med. Soc., NY State Neurosurgical Soc., NY Soc. Neurosurgery, Alpha Omega Alpha, Beta Lambda Sigma. Office: 410 Lakeville Rd Ste 204 New Hyde Park NY 11042 Office Phone: 516-354-3401. Office Fax: 516-354-8597. Business E-Mail: sschneid@lij.edu. *

SCHNEIDER, THOMAS AQUINAS, surgeon, educator, retired surgeon; b. St. Charles, Mo., Dec. 22, 1934; s. Vincent Augustine and Anna Maria (Marheineke) Schneider; m. Joyce Elaine Diehr, June 7, 1958; children: Lisa, Thomas, Dawn, Tracy. BS, Loras Coll., 1954; MD, St. Louis U., 1958. Diplomate Am. Bd. Surgery. Resident surgery St. Louis City Hosp., 1958—63; pvt. practice St. Charles, 1963—2001; ret., 2001. Clin. instr. St. Louis U., 1966—91, asst. clin. prof., 1991—; med. dir. vascular lab. St. Joseph Health Ct., St. Charles, 1991—, dir. trauma svc., 1981—91. Fellow: ACS; mem.: St. Louis Vascular Soc. (pres. 1993—95), St. Louis Surg. Soc. (councilor 1988—91, v.p. 1996—97), Mo. Com. on Trauma, Hodgen Club (pres. 1988), Alpha Omega Alpha. Roman Catholic. Avocations: golf, music, history. Personal E-mail: opas@sbcglobal.net.

SCHNEIDER, THOMAS PAUL, non-profit agency administrator; b. June 5, 1947; s. Milton and Gloria (Bocaner) S.; m. Susan G. Stein, May 31, 1987; children: Rachel Jenny, Daniel Joshua. BA with honors, U. Wis., 1972, JD, 1972. U.S. atty. U.S. Dist. Dist. Ct. (ea. dist.) Wis., Milw., 1993-2001; exec. dir. youth svcs. COA Youth & Family Ctrs., Milw., 2001—. Mem. Wis. Bar Assn. Democrat. Jewish. Office: COA Youth & Family Ctrs 909 E North Ave Milwaukee WI 53212 Office Phone: 414-263-8383. Business E-Mail: tomschneider@coa-yfc.org.

SCHNEIDER, URSULA WILFRIEDE, author; b. Stuttgart, Germany, June 13, 1936; came to U.S., 1966; d. Kurt and Anna Schneider; children: Kurt Mihran, Yvonne Ulrike. BA in French, CUNY, 1977, MA in French Lit., 1979, ABD in Comparative Lit., 1988, PhD in Comparative Lit., 1992. Mgr. export/import of chems. A.K. Peters Co., NYC, 1967-80; asst. to sales mgr. FBA Pharms., NYC, 1981; pvt. sect. to sr. ptnr., head internat. dept. Bear Stearns, NYC, 1982-84; in-house translator for acquisition Siemens Capital Corp., NYC, 1985-86; adj. lectr. German Hunter Coll./CUNY, 1987-90, Montclair (N.J.) State U., 1991-92. Prof. World Trade Ctr./Internat. Inst. for Langs., 1988-89, UN Internat. Sch., N.Y.C., 1979. Author: Ars amandi: The Erotic of Extremes in Thomas Mann and Marguerite Duras, 1995, The Cross-Eyed God, 1995, Velvet Cages, 2001, Vernal Amours, 2004. Helena Rubinstein Found. grantee, Bd. Higher Edn. grantee; recipient Marta Retzler award. Mem. MLA, Fgn. Lang. Educators of N.J., Northeastern MLA, Am. Coun. Tchrs. English Lang., Phi Beta Kappa. Avocations: running, skiing, swimming, skating, tennis. Home: 1201 River Reach Dr Apt 204 Fort Lauderdale FL 33315-1179 Personal E-mail: uwsftlaud@aol.com.

SCHNEIDER, VALERIE LOIS, retired speech educator; b. Chgo., Feb. 12, 1941; d. Ralph Joseph and Gertrude Blanche (Gaffron) S. BA, Carroll Coll., 1963; MA, U. Wis., 1966; PhD, U. Fla., 1969; CAS, Appalachian State U., 1981. Tchr. English and history, dir. forensics and drama Montello (Wis.) H.S., 1963-64; instr. speech U. Fla., Gainesville, 1966-68, asst. prof. speech, 1969-70, Edinboro (Pa.) State Coll., 1970-71; assoc. prof. speech East Tenn. State U., Johnson City, 1971-76, prof. speech, 1976-97. Instr. newspaper course Johnson City Press Chronicle, 1979, Elizabethton Star, Erwin Record, Mountain City Tomahawk, Jonesboro Herald and Tribune, 1980; mem. investor panel USA Today, 1991-92. Editor East Tenn. State U. evening and off-campus newsletter, 1984-91; assoc. editor Homiletic, 1974-76; columnist Video Visions, Kingsport Times-News, 1984-86; book reviewer Pulpit Digest, 1986-90; contbr. articles to profl. jours. Chmn. AAUW Mass Media Study Group Com., Johnson City, 1973-74. Recipient Creative Writing award Va. Highlands Arts Festival, 1973, award Kingsport Times News, 1984, 85, Tri-Cities Met. Advt. Fedn., 1983, 84, hon. life mem. Tenn. Presbyn. Women, 2000; named Danforth assoc., 1977; finalist Money mag. contest, 1994, Writer's Digest contest, 2000. Mem.: AAUW (v.p. chpt. 1974—75, pres. 1975—76), Tenn. Basic Skills Coun. (pres. 1975—76, exec. bd. 1979—80, v.p. 1980—81), Religious Speech Comm. Assn. (Best Article award 1976), Tenn. Speech Comm. Assn. (exec. bd. 1974—77, publs. bd. 1974—78, pres. 1977—78), So. Speech Comm. Assn., Speech Comm. Assn. (Tenn. rep. to states adv. coun. 1974—75), Mensa, Presbyn. Women (hon.; life mem.), Johnson City Book Club (pres. 2001—03), Bus. and Profl. Women's Club (chpt. exec. bd. 1972—73, v.p. 1976—77), Pi Gamma Mu, Phi Delta Kappa, Tau Kappa Alpha, Delta Sigma Rho. Presbyterian.

SCHNEIDER, VIVIAN I., psychologist, researcher; b. Wichita Falls, Tex., Sept. 6, 1949; d. Robert and Vivian H. Davis; m. Robert Jordan Schneider, June 8, 1972 (dec. Mar. 13, 2002); children: Kayt, Amy J. Kim, Jay Robert. BA in Psychology, Met. State Coll. Denver, 1972; MA in Psychology, U. Colo., Boulder, 1988, PhD in Psychology, 1991. Sr. rsch. assoc. U. Colo., Boulder, 1991—. Co-author: (chpts.) Learning and Memory of Knowledge and Skills: Durability and Specificity, Foreign Language Learning: Psycholinguistic Studies on Training and Retention, The Psychology of Learning and Motivation: Advances in Research and Theory; contbr. articles to profl. jours. Ham radio operator Boulder County Amateur Radio Emergency Svcs., 1995—2007; vol. Lamb's Lunch, Boulder, 2004—07; children's leader Bible Study Fellowship, Boulder, 1975—85, 2006—07; Sunday sch. tchr. Bethany Ch., Boulder, 1976—2007. Mem.: Psychonomic Soc. Avocations: reading, quilting. Home: PO Box 1097 Boulder CO 80306 Office: U Colo Ucb 345 Boulder CO 80309 Home Phone: 303-494-3123; Office Phone: 303-735-6488. Office Fax: 303-492-8895. Business E-Mail: vivian.schneider@colorado.edu.

SCHNEIDER, WESLEY CLAIR, marketing communications company executive; b. Chgo., May 2, 1953; s. Clair A. and Ruth (Jenks) S.; m. Jeanie A. Tomaino, Nov. 23, 1990. BA magna cum laude, Ill. Wesleyan U., 1975. Sales rep. confectionery div. Am. Home Products, Chgo., 1975-77; midwest regional sales mgr. confectionery & snacks div. Beatrice Foods, Denver, 1977-78, mktg. analyst, 1978-80; product mgr. Tootsie Roll Industries, Chgo., 1980-85, mgr. internat. mktg., 1985-88; v.p., gen. mgr. Marden-Kane, inc., Chgo., 1988-91; pres., owner Creative Mktg. Comm., Inc., Chgo., 1991—. Bd. dirs. Wesleyan Co., Inc., Chgo.; speaker Inst. for Internat. Rsch. and Promotion Mktg. Assn. Am., N.Y.C., 1991. Patentee in field. Cubmaster Boy Scouts Am., Chgo., 1991; founder Silver Wicket Chairty Event; mem., chair candidates slating subcom. Kenilworth Citizens Adv. Com.; bd. dirs. Kenilworth Assembly Hall Soc., 2001—; chmn. Am. Leadership Fund., 2003; leadership coun. Ill. Wesleyan U.; asst. committeeman New Trier Rep. Orgn., 2003—, fin. chmn., 1998-2002; founder Christ The King Anglican Ch., 2004, sr. warden, 2005-07. Recipient Best Design award retail food category Nat. Flexible Packaging Assn., 1979, Indian statue Point of Purchase Advt. Inst., 1986, 87, U.S. Senatorial Medal of Freedom, 1999. Mem. Am. Def. Preparedness Assn., Exec. Club Chgo. (comms. com.) Internat. Platform Assn., Masons, Shriners, Sigma Chi. Anglican. Avocations: fishing, reading, politics. Office: Creative Mktg Comm Inc 980 N Mich Ave Ste 1400 Chicago IL 60611

SCHNEIDER, WILLIAM GEORGE, chemist, research consultant; b. Wolseley, Sask., Can., June 1, 1915; s. Michael and Phillipina (Krauschaar) S.; m. Jean Purves, Sept. 2, 1940; children: Judith Schneider Saunders, Joanne Schneider Spurrier. B.Sc., U. Sask., 1937, M.Sc., 1939, D.Sc., 1969; PhD, McGill U., 1941, D.Sc., 1970; D.Sc. (hon.), York U., 1966, Meml. U., 1968, McMaster U., 1969, Laval U., 1969, Moncton U., 1969, U. N.B., 1970, U. Montreal, 1970, Acadia U., 1976, U. Regina, 1976, Ottawa U., 1978; LL.D., U. Alta., 1968, Laurentian U., 1968. Head phys. chemistry sect., div. chemistry NRC Can., Ottawa, Ont., 1946-63, dir. div. pure chemistry, 1963-65, v.p., 1965-67, pres., 1967-80; research cons., 1980—. Author: (with J.A. Pople, H.J. Bernstein) High Resolution Nuclear Magnetic Resonance, 1959; contbr. articles to profl. jours. Decorated Order of Can., 1977 Fellow Royal Soc. Can. (Henry Marshall Tory medal), Royal Soc. London, Chem. Inst. Can. (medal 1969, Montreal medal 1973); mem. Internat. Union Pure and Applied Chemistry (pres. 1983-85)

SCHNEIDER, WILLYS HOPE, lawyer; b. NYC, Sept. 27, 1952; d. Leon and Lillian (Friedman) S.; m. Stephen Andrew Kals, Jan. 21, 1979; children: Peter, Josefine. AB cum laude, Princeton U., 1974; JD, Columbia U., 1977. Bar: NY 1978, US Dist. Ct. (ea. and so. dists.) NY 1978, US Tax Ct. 1979. Law clk. to hon. Jack B. Weinstein US Dist. Ct. (ea. dist.) NY, Bklyn., 1977-78; assoc. Paul, Weiss, Rifkind, Wharton & Garrison, NYC, 1978-83, Kaye Scholer LLP, NYC, 1983-87, 1987—. Articles editor Columbia Law Rev., 1976—77; contbr. articles to profl. jours. Mem.: ABA, Internat. Tax Inst. (pres.), Assn. Bar City of NY, NY State Bar Assn. Home: 320 W End Ave New York NY 10023-8110 Office: Kaye Scholer LLP 425 Park Ave New York NY 10022-3506 Home Phone: 212-580-2124; Office Phone: 212-836-8693. E-mail: wschneider@kayescholer.com.

SCHNEIDER-CRIEZIS, SUSAN MARIE, architect; b. St. Louis, Aug. 1, 1953; d. William Alfred and Rosemary Elizabeth (Fischer) Schneider; m. Demetrios Anthony Criezis, Nov. 24, 1978; children: Anthony, John and Andrew. BArch, U. Notre Dame, 1976; MArch, MIT, 1978. Registered architect, Wis. Project designer Eichstaedt Architects, Roselle, Ill., 1978-80, Solomon, Cordwell, Buenz & Assocs., Chgo., 1980-82; project architect Gelick, Foran Assocs., Chgo., 1982-83; asst. prof. Sch. Architecture U. Ill., Chgo., 1980-86; exec. v.p. Criezis Architects, Inc., Northfield, Ill., 1986—2005; dir. cmty. devel. Village of Kenilworth, 2005—. Graham Found. grantee MIT, 1977, MIT scholar, 1976-78; Prestressed Concrete Inst. rsch. grantee, 1981. Mem. AIA, Chgo. Archtl. Club, Chgo. Women in Architecture, Am. Solar Energy Soc., NAFE, Jr. League Evanston, Evanston C. of C. Roman Catholic. Avocations: tennis, swimming. Office: 419 Richmond Rd Kenilworth IL 60043 Office Phone: 847-251-1666. E-mail: scriezis@villageofkenilworth.org.

SCHNEIDERMAN, ANNE MERCEDES, lawyer, neurobiologist; b. Ithaca, NY; d. Howard Allen and Audrey MacLeod Schneiderman. BS in Biol. Scis. with distinction, Stanford U., Calif., 1977; PhD in Neurobiology, Harvard U., Cambridge, Mass., 1984; JD, Stanford U., Calif., 2000. Registered: US Patent and Trademark Office (patent atty.) 1998, bar: NY 2001, Calif. 2001, Washington, DC 2003; cert. Kripalu Yoga Tchr. Kripalu Ctr. for Yoga & Health, 2005. Post doctoral fellow Yale U., 1984—88; asst. prof. neurobiology Cornell U., Ithaca, 1989—96; law clk. Pennie & Edmonds LLP, NYC, 1996—2000, law clk., patent agt., 1998—2000, assoc. atty. NYC, 2000—03; legal counsel Advanced Design Consulting, USA, Lansing, NY, 2003—04; pvt. practice, 2004—. Contbr. articles to profl. jours. Recipient Best Paper Award, Am. Soc. of Zoologists, Divsn. of Devel. Biology, 1980, Nat. Merit Scholar, 1973—77, award in Neuroethology, Capranica Found., 1987; undergraduate rsch. fellowship, Calif. Heart Assn., 1977, graduate fellowship, Nat. Sci. Foun., 1977—80, fellowship, Helen Hay Whitney Found., 1984—87. Mem.: ABA, Women's Bar Assn. State of NY, Tompkins County NY Bar Assn., Soc. Neuroscience, NY State Bar Assn., Monroe County NY Bar Assn., Kripalu Yoga Tchrs. Assn. Avocation: yoga. Office: 102 East State St Ste 7 PO Box 422 Ithaca NY 14851-0422 Office Phone: 607-227-7263. Office Fax: 815-361-9050. Business E-Mail: anne@schneidermanlaw.com.

SCHNEIDERMAN, DAVID ABBOTT, former publishing executive; b. NYC, Apr. 14, 1947; s. Robert D. and Mary (Torres) S.; m. Peggy Rosenthal, Sept. 19, 1981. BA, Johns Hopkins U., 1969, MA, 1970. Asst. to the editor op-ed page N.Y. Times, 1970-74, dep. editor, 1974-78; editor in chief Village Voice, NYC, 1979-87, pub., 1985—88, 1991—2005, pres., 1985—2005; publ. 7 Days, NYC, 1988-90; pres. Stern Pub., 1995—; chmn. L.A. (Calif.) Weekly Inc., 1995—; pres. digital ops. Village Voice Media, NYC, 2005—06. Mem. libr. coun. Johns Hopkins U.

SCHNEIDERMAN, IRWIN, lawyer; b. NYC, May 28, 1923; s. Meyer and Bessie (Klein) S.; m. Roberta Haig, Nov. 28, 1966; 1 child, Eric T. BA, Bklyn. Coll., 1943; LLB cum laude, Harvard U., 1948; DHL (hon.), Bklyn. Coll., 1993. Bar: NY 1949, DC 1952. Assoc. Cahill Gordon & Reindel, NYC, 1948-59, ptnr., 1959-89, sr. counsel, 1990—. Spl. cons. to chmn. SEC, 1981-82, mem. adv. com. on tender offers, 1983. Trustee Bklyn. Coll. Found., 1983—, NY Ctrl Park Conservancy, 2004; chmn. NYC Opera, 1993-2004, chmn. emeritus, 2004—; bd. dirs. WNYC Radio, 1989—, NARAL-Pro-Choice, NYC, 1990—, Lincoln Ctr. for Performing Arts, Inc., 1994-2004, dir. emeritus, 2004; chmn. NARAL-Pro-Choice NY Found., 1998-2007. Lt. j.g. USNR, 1943—46. Mem. Harvard Club. Home: 203 E 72nd St New York NY 10021-4568 Office: Cahill Gordon & Reindel 80 Pine St Fl 17 New York NY 10005-1790 Home Phone: 212-988-0810; Office Phone: 212-701-3800. Personal E-mail: irwinschneiderman@yahoo.com.

SCHNEIDERS, RICHARD J., food service company executive; b. Remsen, Iowa, 1948; m. Beth Schneiders; 2 children. BA in Maths., U. Iowa, 1970. Dir. supplies and equipment, v.p., exec. v.p. Sysco Corp., Memphis, 1982-88; pres., CEO, chmn. Hardin's-Sysco Food Services, LLC, Memphis, 1988—92; sr. v.p. merchandising svcs. Sysco Corp.,

Houston, 1992—97, sr. v.p. corp. merchandising svcs. and multi-unit sales, 1997—99, exec. v.p. foodservice ops., 1999-2000, pres., COO, 2000—03, chmn., CEO, 2003—, pres., 2005—. Bd. dirs. Aviall, Inc. Office: Sysco Corp 1390 Enclave Pkwy Houston TX 77077-2099 E-mail: schneiders.rick@corp.sysco.com.

SCHNEIDLER, JON GORDON, lawyer; b. Seattle, Oct. 22, 1938; s. J. Gordon and Mary Louise (Bartholomew) S.; m. Linda Gilmore White, June 27, 1964 (div. June 1988); children: Kristina Richards, Jolie Wolcott, Andrew Schneidler, Peter Schneidler; m. Elizabeth Ann Nairn, Apr. 2, 1989; 1 stepdaughter: Jessica Rodriguez. BA, U. Wash., 1962, JD, 1968; student, Carleton Coll., 1957—60. Bar: Wash.; U.S. Ct. Appeals (9th Cir.), U.S. Dist. Ct. (we. dist.) Wash. CEO Schneidler Industries, Inc., Seattle, 1968-70; ptnr. Cartano, Botzer & Chapman, Seattle, 1970-86; pvt. practice Seattle, 1986—2006; mng. agt. Schneidler & Schneidler, PLLC, Seattle, 2006—. Sec. Transiplex Internat., Inc., Seattle; mem. adv. bd. Pacific Legal Found., Sacramento; trustee Ehrlich Donnan Found., Seattle. Co-author: (book) Real Property Deskbook, 1981, 2d edit. 1986; patentee Air Structure Systems, 1969. Bd. dirs. North Kitsap Sch. Bd., Poulsbo, Wash., 1984, Friends of Youth, Renton, Wash., 1974; founder, dir. Tchr. of Yr. Found., Poulsbo, 1988—; mem. U.S. Legal Del. to Russia, People to People, 2004. 1st lt. USAF, 1962-66. Decorated Air Force Commendation medal, Outstanding Unit Citation with oak leaf cluster; Baker scholar, George F. Baker Foun., 1957—60. Fellow Paul Harris Found.; mem. ABA (bus. law sect., vice-chair indsl. lease com.), Wash. State Bar Assn., King County Bar Assn., Coll. Club (pres. 2004—05), Rotary. Avocations: fly fishing, competitive bridge, sailing, gardening.

SCHNEIER, EDWARD VINCENT, political science professor; b. Bronx, N.Y., May 25, 1939; s. Edward Vincent and Lillian (Buhr) S.; m. Janice Bernier, June 16, 1960 (div. Jan. 1974); children: Andrew, Katherine; m. Margrit Russenberger, May 13, 2000. BA, Oberlin Coll., 1960; MA, Claremont Grad. U., Calif., 1961, PhD, 1963. Rsch. fellow Brookings Instn., Washington, 1963; legis. asst. Senator Birch Bayh, Washington, 1963-64; asst. prof. The Johns Hopkins U., Balt., 1964-65, Princeton (N.J.) U., 1965-68; from asst. to assoc. prof. The City Coll., CUNY, 1968-93, prof., 1993—2002, prof. emeritus, 2002—. Ptnr. Grassroots Tavern, N.Y.C., 1975—. Author: Congress Today, 1993, Legislative Strategy, 1993, Vote Power, 1974, Party and Constituency, 1970, New York Politics, 2001, Crafting Constitutional Democracies, 2005. State legis. dir. Am. for Dem. Action, Albany, 1992-2001; commr. Copake (N.Y.) Park Commn., 1991-2001; officer Downtown Ind. Dem., N.Y.C., 1975-90; trustee Roe-Jan Comty. Libr., 2003—, pres., 2005—; candidate for Congress Dem. Primary, N.Y.C., 1976; lobbyist Com. for Equity in Edn., N.Y.C., 1994-2000. Rsch. fellow NEH, U. Chgo., 1978-80, Princeton, 1996, Fulbright Found., 1988-89, 2002. Mem. Am. Polit. Sci. Assn. Avocations: golf, skiing, cooking. Home: 1284 Lake View Rd Copake NY 12516-1028 Office: Dept Polit Sci City College # 138th St New York NY 10031 Office Phone: 518-329-0460. E-mail: nedmarg@earthlink.net.

SCHNEIER, MARC, rabbi; BA, MPhil, Yeshiva U. Cert. ordained Rabbi. Pres., founder Found. Ethnic Understanding; found. rabbi Hampton Synagogue, West Hampton Beach, NY, New York Synagogue, NYC. Author: (books) Shared Dreams, 2000; appearances: (TV and Radio incl. Good Morning America, Today Show, Good Day New York, CBS Sunday Edition, CBS Morning Show, O'Reilly Factor, Fox News, CNN, PBS, NP). Named one of The Top 50 Rabbis in America, Newsweek Mag., 2007. Mem.: Jewish Comm. for Interreligious Consultations, Hebrew Immigrant Aid Soc. (former mem. exec. com.), NY Board Rabbis (past pres.), World Jewish Congress (founder, pres.). Jewish. Office: FFEU Ste 1C 1 East 93rd St New York NY 10128 Office Phone: 917-492-2538. Fax: 917-492-2560. *

SCHNELL, CARLTON BRYCE, lawyer; b. Youngstown, Ohio, Jan. 1, 1932; s. Carlton Wilhelm and Helen Jean (Alexander) S.; m. Dorothy Stewart Apple, Aug. 15, 1953; children: Laura, Margaret, Heidi BA, Yale U., 1953, LL.B., 1956. Bar: Ohio 1956. Assoc. Arter & Hadden, Cleve., 1956-65, ptnr., 1966-96, mng. ptnr., 1977-82, Washington, 1982-84. Exec. comm. mem. Greater Cleve. Growth Assn., Cleve., 1983-97; chmn. Build Up Cleve., 1981-89; profl. chmn. United Way, Cleve., 1983; co-chmn. Charter Rev. Commn., Cleve., 1983-84; pres. Citizen's League Rsch. Inst., 1992-95. Named Vol. of Yr., Leadership Cleve., 1985. Mem. Tex. Club Cleve. (pres. 1972-73), Cleve. Tax Inst. (chmn. 1978), Ohio C. of C. (trustee 1977-80) Clubs: Tavern, Pepper Pike. Republican. Presbyterian. Avocations: golf, tennis. Home: 31450 Shaker Blvd Pepper Pike OH 44124-5153

SCHNELL, GEORGE ADAM, geographer, educator, demographer; b. Phila., July 13, 1931; s. Earl Blackwood and Emily (Bernheimer) S.; m. Mary Lou Williams, June 21, 1958; children: David Adam, Douglas Powell, Thomas Earl. BS, West Chester U., 1958; MS, Pa. State U., 1960, PhD, 1965; postdoctoral study, Ohio State U., 1965. Asst. prof. SUNY, New Paltz, 1962-65, assoc. prof., 1965-68, prof. geography, 1968-99, founding chmn. dept., 1968-94, prof. emeritus, 1999—. Adj. prof. SUNY, 2000-05; vis. assoc. prof. U. Hawaii, summer, 1966; cons. cmty. action programming, 1965; manuscript reader, cons. to several pubs., 1967—; founder, founding bd. dirs., investigator Inst. for Devel., Planning and Land Use Studies, 1986-96; cons. Mid-Hudson Pattern for Progress, 1986, Open Space Inst., 1987, Mid-Hudson Regional Econ. Devel. Coun., 1989, Urban Devel. Corp., 1989-90, 93, Tech. Devel. Ctr., 1991, Catskill Ctr., 1991, Ednl. Testing Svc., 1993-94, 96, 97; cons. editor Exams Unltd., Albany, N.Y., 1995-99; ind. contractor and cons. Excelsior U., 2003—05; founding mem. exec. bd. dirs. Hudson Valley Study Ctr., 1995-98; ind. contractor Excelsior U., 2003; cons., presenter in field. Author: (with others) The Local Community: A Handbook for Teachers, 1971, The World's Population, Problems of Growth, 1972; contbr. Pennsylvania Coal: Resources, Technology, Utilization, 1983, West Virginia and Appalachia: Selected Readings, 1977, Hazardous and Toxic Wastes: Technology, Management and Health Effects, 1984, Environmental Radon: Occurrence, Control and Health Hazards, 1990, Natural and Technological Disasters: Causes, Effects and Preventive Measures, 1992, Conservation and Resource Management, 1993, Medicine and Health Care into the 21st Century, 1995, Forests: A Global Perspective, 1996, (with M.S. Monmonier) Ecology of the Wetlands and Associated Systems, 1998, (with M.S. Monmonier) Renewable Energy: Trends and Prospects, 2002; co-author: (with M.S. Monmonier) The Study of Population: Elements, Patterns, Processes, 1983, Map Appreciation, 1988; editor, contbr.: (with with M.S. Monmonier, G.J. Demko, and H.M. Rose) Population Geography: A Reader, 1970; contbr. articles to profl. and scholarly jours. Appt. mem. local bds. and coms. Town and Village New Paltz, New Paltz Ctrl. Sch. Dist., 1965-2007; elder Reformed Ch. New Paltz; Rep. committeeman Town of Gardiner, Ulster County, NY, 2000-01; trustee Gardiner (NY) Pub. Libr., 2005-07. With AUS, 1952-54; bd. mem. River Park Homeowners Assn., 2007—. Recipient Excellence award NY State/United Univ. Professions, 1994, Disting. Alumnus award West Chester U., 1994; named Disting. Tchr. Emeritus, SUNY New Paltz Alumni Assn., 2006. Mem. Assn. Am. Geographers, Pa. Geog. Soc. (mem. editl. bd. Pa. Geographer, Disting. Geographer award 1994), Pa. Acad. Sci. (assoc. editor jour. 1988-2005), Nat. Coun. for Geog. Edn., Paltz Club. Home: 29 River Park Dr New Paltz NY 12561-2636 Office: SUNY at New Paltz Dept Geography 75 S Manheim Blvd New Paltz NY 12561-2400 Personal E-mail: gschnell123@yahoo.com.

SCHNELL, LAURA S., lawyer; b. Cleve., May 1, 1958; BA magna cum laude, Dartmouth Coll., 1980; JD cum laude, U. Chgo., 1983. Bar: NY, US Dist. Ct. (so. & ea. dists.) NY 1985, US Ct. Appeals (2nd cir.) 1991. Law clk. Hon. Jack B. Weinstein, US Dist. Ct. (ea. dist.) NY, 1983—84; mem. Eisenberg & Schnell LLP, NYC. Mem.: Assn. of the Bar in the City of NY (Fed. Cts. com.), Nat. Employment Lawyers Assn., Phi Beta Kappa. Office: Eisenberg & Schnell LLP 9th Fl 377 Broadway New York NY 10013 Office Phone: 212-966-8900. Office Fax: 212-966-2505. E-mail: lschnell@eisenbergschnell.com. *

SCHNELL, ROBERT LEE, JR., lawyer; b. Mpls., Sept. 20, 1948; s. Robert Lee and Dorothy Mae (Buran) S.; m. Jacqueline Irene Husak, Dec. 19, 1969 (div. Aug. 1988); children: Robert Lee III, Elizabeth Anne, Jennifer Irene; m. Julie Ann Bemlott, Sept. 29, 1989; children: Helen Bridget, Michael Henry. BA cum laude, Princeton U., 1970; JD magna cum laude, Harvard U., 1974. Bar: Minn. 1974, U.S. Dist. Ct. Minn. 1974, U.S. Ct. Appeals (8th cir.) 1975, U.S. Supreme Ct. 1990. Assoc. Faegre & Benson, Mpls., 1974-81, ptnr., 1982—. Bd. dirs. United Way of Mpls., 1992-93. Office: Faegre & Benson 2200 Wells Fargo Ctr 90 S St Ste 2200 Minneapolis MN 55402-1109 Office Phone: 612-766-7225. E-mail: rschnell@faegre.com.

SCHNELL, ROGER THOMAS, small business owner, retired state official; b. Wabasha, Minn., Dec. 11, 1936; s. Donald William and Eva Louise (Barton) Schnell; m. Barbara Ann McDonald, Dec. 18, 1959 (div. Mar. 1968); children: Thomas Allen, Scott Douglas. A in Mil. Sci., Command and Gen. Staff Coll., 1975; A in Bus. Administn., Wayland Bapt. U., 1987. Commd. 2d lt. Alaska N.G., 1959, advanced through grades to col., 1975, shop supt. Anchorage, 1965-71, personnel mgr., 1972-74, chief of staff, 1974-87, dir. logistics, 1987; electrician Alaska R.R., Anchorage, 1955-61, elec. foreman, 1962-64; dir. support personnel mgmt. Joint Staff Alaska N.G., 1988-92, ret.; personnel mgr. State of Alaska, 1992, asst. commr. dept. mil. and vets. affairs Ft. Richardson, 1992-95, dep. commr. dept. mil. and vets. affairs, 1995-98, 2002—06, brig. gen., 2007; owner RTS Enterprises, Anchorage, 1999—. Prin., owner RTS Enterprises, 1999—; adv. bd. state joint armed svc. com. State of Alaska, 2001—06; dep. commr. dept. Mil. and Vet. Affairs, 2003—06. Chmn. Alaska Nat. Guard Mus. Trust Fund, 2001—02; appointed to Gov.'s State Seismic Hazard Safety Commn., 2005—06; chmn. pastor parish rels. com. Meth. 1st Ch., 2001—02, mem. fin. com., 2007—; bd. dirs. Meth. Trust Fund, 2002—04, 2007—. Named Brigadier Gen. (hon.) Alaska NG, Gov. of Alaska, 2007. Mem. Fed. Profl. Labor Relations Execs. (sec. 1974-75), Alaska N.G. Officers Assn. (pres. 1976-78, bd. dirs. 1988—), Assn. U.S. Army (corp.), NG Assn. U.S. (life, retiree rep. from Alaska 1993—), Am. Legion, Amvets, Elks. Republican. Methodist. Avocations: travel, photography. Home and Office: Huntwood Park Estates 6817 Queens View Cir Anchorage AK 99504-5203 Personal E-mail: rogertschnell@gci.net, rtschnellenterprises@gci.net.

SCHNELLE, KARL BENJAMIN, JR., chemical engineering professor, consultant, researcher; b. Canton, Ohio, Dec. 8, 1930; s. Karl Benjamin and Kathryn Emily (Hollingsworth) S.; m. Mary Margaret Dabney, Sept. 8, 1954; children: Karl Dabney, Kathryn Chappell. BS, Carnegie Mellon U., 1952, MS, 1957, PhD, 1959. Registered profl. engr., Tenn. Chem. engr., shift foreman Organics area Pitts. Plate Glass Co., New Martinsville, W.Va., 1952-54; asst. prof. chem. engring. Vanderbilt U., Nashville, 1958—61, assoc. prof., 1961—64, assoc. prof. environ. and air resources engring., 1967—70, prof., 1970—80, chmn. divsn. socio-tech. sys., 1972—75, chmn. environ. and water resources engring., 1975—76; mgr. edn., rsch. Instrument Soc. Am., Pitts., 1964—67; chmn. environ. engring. and policy mgmt. dept. Vanderbilt U., 1976—80, chmn. chem. engring. dept., 1980—88, prof. chem. and environ. engring., 1980—; Alexander Heard disting. svc. prof., 1995-96. V.p. ECCE, Nashville, 1983-88, pres., 1989—; mem. Air Pollution Control Bd., State Tenn., 1978-82, 82-87; Fulbright prof. U. Liege, Belgium, 1977; invited prof. Universite Catholique de Louvain, Belgium, 1982; vis. prof. chem. engring. Danish Tech. Inst., Lyngby, Denmark, 1988-89. Fellow AICE; mem. Air and Waste Mgmt. Assn. (Lyman A. Ripperton Environ. Educator award 2006), Instrument Soc. Am. (mgr. edn. and rsch. 1964-67), Am. Soc. Engring. Edn., Am. Soc. Environ. Engrs., Sigma Xi, Phi Kappa Phi, Tau Beta Pi. Office: Vanderbilt U VU Station B 351604 Nashville TN 37235-1604 Office Phone: 615-322-3370. Business E-Mail: karl.b.schnelle@vanderbilt.edu.

SCHNELLER, EUGENE STEWART, health administration and policy educator; b. Cornwall, NY, Apr. 9, 1943; s. Michael Nicholas and Anne Ruth (Gruner) Schneller; m. Ellen Stauber, Mar. 24, 1968; children: Andrew Jon, Lee Stauber. AA, SUNY, Buffalo, 1965; BA, LI U., 1967; PhD, NYU, 1973; grad. physician assoc. (hon.), Duke U., 2004. Rsch. asst. dept. sociology NYU, NYC, 1968-70; project dir. Montefiore Hosp. and Med. Ctr., Bronx, NY, 1970-72; asst. prof. Med. Ctr. and sociology Duke U., Durham, NC, 1973-75; assoc. prof., chmn. dept. sociology Union Coll., Schenectady, 1975-79, assoc. prof., dir. Health Studies Ctr., 1979-85; prof., dir. Sch. Health Mgmt. and Policy, Ariz. State U., Tempe, 1985—91, assoc. dean rsch. and adminstrn. Coll. Bus., 1992-94; dir. L. William Seidman Rsch. Ctr., Tempe, 1992-94, counselor to pres. for health profl. edn., 1994-96; clin. prof. cmty. and family medicine U. Ariz., 1995-96, clin. prof. prevention, rsch., 1997—2002; prof., dir. Sch. Health Mgmt. and Policy W.P. Carey Sch. Bus. Ariz. State U., 1996—2002, prof. Sch. Health Mgmt. and Policy, 2002—; dir. Health Sector Supply Chain Initiatives, 2002—; prin. Health Care Sector Advances, 2004—, Dean's Coun. of 100 Disting. Rsch. Scholars, 2007—. Mem. health rsch. coun. N.Y. State Dept. Health, 1977—85; vis. rsch. scholar Columbia U., NYC, 1983—84; fellow Accrediting Commn. Edn. Health Svcs. Adminstrn., 1983—84; chmn. Western Network Edn. Health Adminstrn., Berkeley, Calif., 1987—92; commr. Calif. Commn. Future Med. Edn., 1996—97; mem. Ariz. Medicaid Adv. Bd., 1990—92, Ariz. Data Adv. Bd., 1989—91, Ariz. Health Care Group Adv. Bd., 1989; Dean's Coun. 100 Disting. Rsch. scholar Ariz. State U., 2007—. Author: The Physician's Assistant, 1980; mem. editl. bd. Work and Occupations, 1975—93, Hosps. and Health Svcs. Adminstrn., 1989—92, Health Adminstrn. Press, 1991—94, Health Mgmt. Rev., 1996, Electronic Hallway, 1999; contbr. articles to profl. jours., chapters to books. Trustee Barrow Neurol. Inst., Phoenix, 1989—95; chair nat. adv. com. Investigator Awards Health Svcs. Rsch. Robert Wood Johnson Found., 1993—96. Mem.: APHA, Pharm. and Therapeutics Soc. (trustee 1999—2005, sec. 1999—2005), Assn. Univ. Health Programs Health Adminstrn. (bd. dirs. 1990—96, chmn. bd. dirs. 1994—95), Am. Sociol. Assn. Home: 11843 N 114th Way Scottsdale AZ 85259-2609 Office: Ariz State U Sch Health Mgmt and Policy WP Carey Sch Bus Tempe AZ 85287 Office Phone: 602-320-1512. Business E-Mail: gene.schneller@asu.edu.

SCHNELLER, MARINA VELENTGAS, lawyer; b. Portland, Maine, Feb. 24, 1943; d. Peter Constantine and Katherine Rena (Zolotas) Velentgas; 3 children. AB, Smith Coll., 1965; MS, U. Vt., 1968; JD, Am. U., 1972. Bar: Va. 1972, D.C. 1973, U.S. Patent & Trademark Office, U.S. Ct. Appeals (DC cir.), U.S. Supreme Ct. Atty. Cushman Darby & Cushman, Washington, 1974-80; pvt. practice, 1980-82; tech. asst. Hon. Nies US Ct. Appeals Fed. Cir., Washington, 1982—84; counsel Mobil Oil Corp., Fairfax, Va., 1984-98; ptnr., Patent Prosecution, Intellectual Property Group Venable LLP, Washington, 1998—. Lectr. George Mason Univ. Sch. Law. Adv. bd. mem. BNA U.S. Patents Quarterly, Washington; contbr. articles to profl. jours. Coach Alexandria (Va.) Soccer Assn., 1986-89, 91-93. Mem. Am. Chem. Soc. (Am. Chemists Medal 1961), ABA, Am. Intellectual Property Law Assn. (patent law com. 2005-), Patent Lawyers Club, Women Patent Lawyers Club, Hellenic Lawyers Assn. (pres.), Sigma Xi. Office: Venable LLP 575 7th St NW Washington DC 20004 Office Phone: 202-344-4062. Office Fax: 202-344-8300. Business E-Mail: mvschneller@venable.com.

SCHNEPF, HARRY ERNEST, microbiologist, consultant; b. Chula Vista, Calif., Feb. 1, 1952; s. Harry Ernest and Jane Voorhees Schnepf; m. Cameron Lee Fosterling, July 8, 1955; children: Sidney Lee, Kai Dale. BA, U. Calif., La Jolla, Calif., 1977; PhD, U. Wash., Seattle, 1984. Post-doctoral fellow, dept. microbiology and immunology U. Wash., Seattle, 1984—90; from rsch. scientist to sci. fellow Mycogen Corp., San Diego, 1990—99, sci. fellow, 1996; rsch. scientist, sci. leader, subject matter expert Dow AgroSciences, LLC, San Diego, 1999—2002; ind. cons. in field San Diego, 2003—. Fellow, Achievement Rewards Coll. Scientists Found., 1984. Mem.: Am. Soc. Microbiology. Achievements include first to clone insecticidal protein genes from Bacillus thuringiensis, leading ultimately to genetically engineered insect resistant plants, such as cotton and corn; 43 patents in field. Avocations: piano, gardening. Home Phone: 858-271-7867. Personal E-mail: eschnep1@san.rr.com.

SCHNEPS, JACK, physics professor, department chairman; b. NYC, Aug. 18, 1929; s. Elias and Rose (Rephen) S.; m. Lucia De Marchi, Mar. 11, 1960; children: Loredana, Melissa, Leila. BA, N.Y. U., 1951; MS, U. Wis., 1953, PhD, 1956. Asst. prof. physics Tufts U., 1956-60, asso. prof., 1960-63, prof., 1963—, chmn. dept. physics, 1980-89, Vannevar Bush chair, 1995—. Vis. scientist European Orgn. Nuc. Rsch., Geneva, Switzerland, 1965-66; lectr. Internat. Sch. Elementary Particle Physics, Yugoslavia, 1968; vis. rsch. fellow Univ. Coll., London, Eng., 1973-74; vis. prof. Ecole Polytechnique, Palaiseau, France, 1982-83, The Technion, Haifa, Israel, 1989-90, Coll. de France, Paris, 1997; chmn. Internat. Neutrino Com., 2002—; vis. scholar Harvard U., 2005-06. Contbg. author: Methods in Subnuclear Physics, Vol. IV, 1970; editor Proc. of Neutrino 88, 1989; contbr. articles to profl. jours. NSF postdoctoral fellow U. Padua, Italy, 1958-59. Fellow Am. Phys. Soc.; mem. European Phys. Soc., AAUP, Phi Beta Kappa, Sigma Xi. Home: 3 Foxcroft Rd Winchester MA 01890-2407 Office: Dept Physics Tufts U Medford MA 02155 Office Phone: 617-627-3374. E-mail: jacob.schneps@tufts.edu.

SCHNIEDERS, RICHARD J., food products executive; b. Remsen, Iowa; 2 children. BA in Math., U. Iowa, 1970. With exec. devel. program SYSCO Corp., Memphis, 1982, dir. supplies and equipment, v.p. merchandising and exec. v.p., promoted to pres., CEO, 1988, chmn., sr. v.p. merchandising svcs. dept. Houston, 1992, responsible multi-unit sales, dir. corp., 1997, exec. v.p. food svc. ops., 1998, pres., COO, 2000—03, chmn., CEO, 2003—. Mem. Aviall Inc. (bd. dirs.). Office: SYSCO Corp 1390 Enclave Pkwy Houston TX 77077-2099 *

SCHNITZER, ALAN D., lawyer; b. Dallas, Tex., Dec. 6, 1965; BSE magna cum laude, Wharton Sch., Univ. Pa., 1988; JD, Columbia Univ., 1991. Bar: NY 1992. Assoc. Simpson Thacher & Bartlett LLP, NYC, 1991—99, ptnr., corp. law practice, 1999—; vice-chmn., chief legal officer Travelers Companies, Saint Paul, Minn., 2007—. Mem. Columbia Law Rev. Bd. dir., mem. audit com. Legal Aid Soc. Harlan Fiske Stone scholar. Mem.: ABA, NY State Bar Assn, Assn. Bar City of NY. Office: The Travelers Cos 385 Washington St Saint Paul MN 55102 *

SCHNITZER, IRIS TAYMORE, diversified financial services company executive, lawyer, arbitrator, mediator; b. Cambridge, Mass., Aug. 3, 1943; d. Joseph David and Edith (Cooper) Taymore; m. Stephen Mark Schnitzer, Sept. 10, 1966. BA in Econ., Boston U., 1967; JD, Mass. Sch. Law, 1996. CLU; bar: Mass. 1996; lic. real estate broker, registered rep. NASD, CFP, cert. fin. counseling advanced pension planning. Real estate broker Woods Real Estate, Braintree, Mass., 1968; real estate broker, property mgr. Village Gate Realty, Brockton, Mass., 1969; agt. Prudential Ins., Boston, 1970-73, Northwestern Mut. Life, Boston, 1973—78; fin. planning cons. Iris Taymore Schnitzer Assoc., Boston, 1973-79; supr. edn. and advanced underwriting Northwestern Mut. Life, Boston, 1976—78; trainer fin. planners Gerstenblatt Co., Newton, Mass., 1978-79; founder, CEO Fin. Forum, Inc., Boston, 1979-91; CEO TFF, Inc. at Chase Exch., NYC, 1980—83; prin. I&S Assoc., Boston, 1991—; arbitrator Nat. Assn. Securities Dealers Dispute Resolution, 1992—; v.p. Fleet Pvt. Clients Group, Boston, 1993-2000; pvt. practice Boston, 2000—; mediator Mediation Works, Inc., Boston, 2002—, Boston Municipal Ct., Boston Bar Assn., Alternative Dispute Resolution Program, Boston, 2003—. Bd. dirs. Mister Tire, Inc.; arbitrator fee arbitration bd. Mass. Bar. Assn., 2003—. Contbr. articles to profl. jours. Pres. Mass. divsn. Women's Equity Action League, 1977—79; treas., bd. dirs. Festival of Light and Song, 1989—92; bd. dirs. Achievement Rewards Coll. Scientists, Boston, 1991—95; mem. steering com. Fleet Bank Mass. United Way, 1994—95; chair Girls' Bank Patriots' Trail Girl Scout Coun., 1996—98; overseer Boston Lyric Opera, 1999—2004; bd. dirs. Ledgewood, Brookline, Mass., 1967—70, LWV, Brockton, 1968—70, NOW, Boston, 1972—73; chair credit com., bd. dirs. Mass. Feminist Fed. Credit Union, Cambridge, Mass., 1975—77. Named one of Best Fin. Planners in the U.S., Money Mag., 1987; named to Mut. Funds Panel, Silvia Porter's Personal Fin. Mag., 1988, 1989. Fellow: Mass. Bar Found.; mem.: Boston Estate Planning Coun., Boston Bar Assn., Am. Assn. Individual Investors (bd. dirs. 1985—95, pres. Boston chpt. 1987—89), Navy League U.S. (life), Boston Club. Republican. Avocations: horseback riding, sailing, gardening, interior and fashion design, animals. Personal E-mail: itschnitzer@usa.com.

SCHNITZER, STEVEN C., lawyer; b. Balt., Apr. 6, 1962; BA, U. Md., 1984; JD cum laude, Touro Coll., 1988. Bar: Conn. 1988, NY 1989, DC 1990. Assoc. corp. fin. dept. Debevoise & Plimpton, NYC, 1988—94; ptnr. corp. group Crowell & Moring LLP, Washington, 1994—2001; ptnr. Katten Muchin Rosenman LLP, Washington, 2001—. Office: Katten Muchin Rosenman LLP E Lobby Ste 700 1025 Thomas Jefferson St NW Washington DC 20007 Office Phone: 202-625-3605. Office Fax: 202-339-8293. Business E-Mail: steven.schnitzer@kattenlaw.com.

SCHNOBRICH, ROGER WILLIAM, lawyer; b. New Ulm, Minn., Dec. 21, 1929; s. Arthur George and Amanda (Reinhart) Schnobrich; m. Angeline Ann Schmitz, Jan. 21, 1961; children: Julie A. Johnson, Jennifer L. Holmers, Kathryn M. Kubinski, Karen L. Holetz. BBA, U. Minn., 1952, JD, 1954. Bar: Minn. 1954. Assoc. Fredrikson and Byron, Mpls., 1956-58; pvt. practice Mpls., 1958-60; ptnr. Popham Haik, Schnobrich & Kaufman, Mpls., 1960-97, Hinshaw & Culbertson, Mpls., 1997—2004; officer Wayworth, Inc., Wayzada, Minn., 2004—. Bd. dirs. numerous corps. With US Army, 1954—56. Mem.: ABA, Order of Coif. Roman Catholic. Avocations: jogging, reading, golf. Home and Office: Wayworth Inc 530 Waycliff Dr N Wayzata MN 55391-1385 Personal E-mail: rnapana@aol.com.

SCHNOEBELEN, ANNE MARY, musicologist, educator; b. Tomahawk, Wis., Aug. 4, 1933; d. Herman Sabas and Katherine Alma (Yenor) Schnoebelen; m. John Albert Meixner, May 7, 1980. BA, Rosary Coll., 1958; MusM, U. Ill., 1960, PhD, 1966. From chmn. dept. musicology to prof. emerita Shepherd Sch. Music Rice U., Houston, 1974—2004, interim dean, 1981, 2002—03, prof. emerita Shepherd Sch. Music, 2004—. Author: Padre Martini's Collection of Letters in the Civico Museo Bibliografico Musicale: An Annotated Index, 1979; editor: Cantatas by Maurizio Cazzati in the Italian Cantata in the Seventeenth Century, 1985, Solo Motets from the Seventeenth Century, 10 vols., 1987—89, Seventeenth Century Italian Sacred Music, 10 vols., 1995—99; contbr. articles and reviews to profl. jours. Fellow, Fulbright, 1964; grantee, NEH, 1969, 1983; Travel grant, Am. Coun. Learned Societies, 1984. Fellow: AAUW; mem.: Am. Musicol. Soc. (coun. sec. 1986—88). Home: 2001 Holcombe Blvd #702 Houston TX 77030-4214 Office Phone: 713-348-4217. Business E-mail: aschnoeb@rice.edu.

SCHNOEBELEN, IAN, chef; b. 1971; Sous chef Commander's Palace, Las Vegas, Lilette, New Orleans; owner, exec. chef Iris, New Orleans, 2006—. Named one of Best New Chefs, Food and Wine Mag., 2007. Office: Iris 8115 Jeannette St New Orleans LA 70118 Office Phone: 504-862-5848. *

SCHNOLL, HOWARD MANUEL, financial consultant, investment company executive; b. Milw., June 6, 1935; s. Nathan P. and Della (Fisher) Schnoll; m. Barbara Ostach, Dec. 3, 1988; children: Jordan, Terry, Jeffrey, Robert, Tammy, Daniel. BBA, U. Wis., 1958. CPA Wis.; cert. mgmt. cons., registered investment advisor. Mng. ptnr. Nankin, Schnoll & Co., S.C., Milw., 1966-86; mng. ptnr., bd. dirs. BDO Seidman, 1986-90; pres., COO Universal Med. Bldgs., L.P., Milw., 1990, also bd. dirs.; pres. Howard Schnoll & Assocs., Milw., 1991; mng. dir. Grande, Schnoll & Assocs., Milw., 1992-93; exec. mng. dir., COO Glaisner, Schilffarth, Grande & Schnoll, Ltd., Milw., 1993-98; exec. v.p., treas., bd. dirs. GS2 Securities, Inc., Milw., 1998—2004; sr. v.p. B. C. Ziegler and Co., Milw., 1999—, mng. dir., 2005—06; sr. v.p. Shilffarth-Schnoll Group, RBC Dain Rauscher, Milw., 2006—. Bd. dirs. Milw. World Festival, Inc., 1968—, pres., 2003—05, chmn. bd., 2005—; bd. dirs. City of Festivals Parade, Milw., 1983—89, Aurora Health Care Ventures, Milw. Heart Rsch. Found., Milw. Milw. Heart Inst., Arthritis Found.; pres. Impact, 1993—, bd. dirs.; pres., treas. Am. Heart Assn., Milw., 1978—82; capt. United Way, Milw., 1985; mem. greater Milw. com. Nat. Found. Ileitis and Colitis. Served to sgt. US Army, 1956—63. Mem.: AICPA, Acct. Computer Users Tech. Exchange, Wis. Inst. CPAs, B'nai Brith (pres. 1960—62), Boca Grove Golf and Tennis (bd. dirs. 2003—, treas. 2006—, v.p. 2005—), Brynwood Country Club (pres. 1988—2000, bd. dirs., treas.). Jewish. Avocations: golf, tennis. Office: RBC Dain Rauscher 1000 N Water St Milwaukee WI 53202-4298 Office Phone: 414-347-7106. Business E-Mail: howard.schnoll@rbcdain.com.

SCHNOOR, JEFFREY ARNOLD, lawyer; b. Winnipeg, Man., Can., June 22, 1953; s. Toby and Ray. BA, U. Man., 1974, LLB, 1977. Bar: Man. 1978. Assoc. McJannet Weinberg Rich, Winnipeg, 1977-84, ptnr., 1984-86; exec. dir. Man. Law Reform Commn., Winnipeg, 1986-97; dir. criminal justice policy Man. Dept. Justice, Winnipeg, 1998—2002, exec. dir. policy devel. and analysis, 2002—05, asst. dep. min. cts. divsn., 2005—. Pres. Fedn. Law Reform Agys. Can., 1995-98; del. Uniform Law Conf. Can., 1986-2003, exec. com. 1996-2001, chair civil sect., 1996-97, v.p., 1998-99, pres., 1999-2000. Trustee United Way of Winnipeg, 1990-97, 99-2005, exec. com., 1990-97, 2001-05, treas., 1991-92, pres., 1994-95, cmty. rels. com. 1995-98, chmn. 1996-97, chair United Way 2005 com., 1997-98, hon. solicitor, 2001-05, chmn. 211 implementation com., 2001—; mem. R&D 2000 steering com., United Way of Can., 1995-98; bd. dirs. Winnipeg Libr. Found., 1997-2001, St. Boniface Gen. Hosp., 2005—; Man. Voluntary Sector Coun., 2001-04, U. Man. Winnipeg area study adv. group, 2001-04. Named Queen's Counsel Govt. of Man., 1992; recipient Chair's award of distinction United Way of Can., 1997. Mem. Law Soc. Man. (lectr. bar admission course 1981-96), Man. Bar Assn. (life, governing coun. 1988-96, recipient Cmty. Svc. award 1999), Can. Bar Assn. (legis. and law reform com. 1994-2000, 01—03, vice-chair 1997-2000, chair 2001-03, nat mag. editl. bd. 2002—). Avocations: travel, languages, performing arts. Office: 235-405 Broadway Winnipeg MB Canada R3C 3L6 Home Phone: 204-475-9069; Office Phone: 204-945-3027. Business E-Mail: jeffrey.schnoor@gov.mb.ca.

SCHNUCK, CRAIG D., grocery store company executive; b. Apr. 20, 1948; s. Donald Schnuck. BS, Cornell U., 1967, MBA, 1971. With Schnuck Markets, Inc., Hazelwood, Mo., 1971—, v.p., 1975-76, exec. v.p., sec., 1976-83, pres., chief exec. officer, 1983-91, also bd. dirs., 1991, chmn., CEO, 1991—. Office: Schnuck Markets Inc 11420 Lackland Rd Saint Louis MO 63146-3559

SCHNUCKER, ROBERT VICTOR, historian, educator; b. Waterloo, Iowa, Sept. 30, 1932; s. Felix Victor and Josephine (Maasdam) S.; m. Anna Mae Engelkes, Sept. 18, 1955; children: Sarai Ann, Sar Victor, Christjahn Dietrich. AB, NE Mo. State U., 1953; BD, U. Dubuque, 1956; MA, U. Iowa, 1960, PhD, 1969. Ordained to ministry Presbyn. Ch., 1956. Pastor United Presbyn. Ch. USA, Springville, Iowa, 1956-63, Meth.-Presbyn. Ch., Labelle, Mo., 1976-97; asst. prof. N.E. Mo. State U., Kirksville, 1963-65, assoc. prof., 1963-65, prof., 1969—99; interim pastor Bethany Presbyn. Ch., Grundy Center, Iowa, 1999—2001, First Presbyn. Ch., Aplington, 2002—04, Immanuel Presbyn. Ch., Waterloo, Iowa, 2004—05. Dir. Thomas Jefferson U. Press; supr. Bible exam. Presbyn. Ch. USA, Louisville, 1977-89; bd. dir. Ctr. for Reformation Rsch., St. Louis, 1984-99; pres. Conf. of Hist. Jours., 1993; adj. prof. religion U. No. Iowa, 1999—; vis. prof. religion and humanities, 2001-02. Author: A Glossary of Terms for Western Civilization, 1975, Helping Humanities Journal Survive, 1985, History Assessment Test, 1990; editor: Calviniana, 1989, Historians of Early Modern Europe, 1976-93, 97, Network News Exch., 1978-88; pres. 1st and 2d Editing History, Conf. for Hist. Jour., 1985-97; book rev. editor, mng. editor 16th Century Jour., 1972-97; pub. 16th Century Essays and Studies, 1980-97; contbr. articles to profl. jours. Recipient 16th Studies Conf. medal for Significant Achievement in Early Modern Studies, 1997, Presdl. Citation for Contbns. to the Univ., Truman State U., 1997; fellow Soc. Sci. Study of Religion, 1988, Sixteenth Century Studies conf., 1998; NEH grantee for jour. pubs., 1980. Mem. AAUP, Am. Acad. Religion, Renaissance Soc. Am., Am. History Assn. (chmn. Robinson prize com. 1987), Am. Soc. Ch. History, Soc. History of Edn., Soc. Bibl. Lit., Soc. for Reformation Rsch., Soc. Scholarly Pubs., Soc. for Values in Higher Edn., Conf. for Hist. Jour., Am. Coun. Learned Soc. (exec. bd. conf. adminstr. officers 1993-96, sec. 1994, chmn. 1995-96), Conf. Faith and History, 16th Century Studies Cons. (exec. sec. 1972-97), Humanities Iowa (bd. dirs. 1999-2003, pres. 2002-03). Office: Dept Philosophy and Religion U No Iowa Cedar Falls IA 50614-0501 E-mail: rvs@cedarnet.org.

SCHNUR, ROBERT ARNOLD, lawyer, educator; b. White Plains, NY, Oct. 25, 1938; s. Conrad Edward and Ruth (Mehr) S.; children: Daniel, Jonathan. BA, Cornell U., 1960; JD, Harvard U., 1963. Bar: Wis. 1965, Ill. 1966. Assoc. Michael, Best & Friedrich, Milw., 1966-73, ptnr., 1973—. Chmn. Wis. Tax News, 1983-90; adj. prof. tax law U. Wis. Law Sch., 1988—; vis. prof. tax law Cornell U. Law Sch., 2006-. Capt. U.S. Army, 1963-65. Fellow Am. Coll. Tax Counsel; mem. ABA, Wis. Bar Assn. (chmn. tax sect. 1986-88), Milw. Bar Assn. Home: 3093 Timber Ln Verona WI 53593 Office: Michael Best Friedrich 100 E Wisconsin Ave Ste 3300 Milwaukee WI 53202-4108 Business E-Mail: raschnur@michaelbest.com.

SCHOCH, ALEXANDER C., lawyer, energy executive; BA, Kenyon Coll.; JD, Case Western Reserve U. Bar: Ill., Tex., Ohio. Internat. atty. Marathon Oil Co.; v.p., assoc. gen. counsel, sec. Goodrich Corp.; v.p., gen. counsel Emerson Process Mgmt.; exec. v.p., chief legal officer Peabody Energy, St. Louis, 2006—. Mem.: ABA, Am. Soc. Corp. Sec., State Bar Assn., Internat. Bar Assn. Office: Peabody Energy 701 Market St Saint Louis MO 63101

SCHOCHET, BARRY P., health care executive; b. NYC, Mar. 13, 1951; s. George and Freda Schochet. BA in Zoology, U. Maine, 1973; MA in Health Care Adminstrn., George Washington U., 1975. Asst. adminstr. Doctors Hosp., Hollywood, Fla., 1975-76, Cypress Community Hosp., Pompano Beach, Fla., 1976-77, adminstr., 1977-78, exec. dir., 1978-79; asst. regional v.p. Nat. Med. Enterprises, St. Petersburg, Fla., 1979-80, asst. v.p. Los Angeles, 1980-81, v.p. ops. Tampa, Fla., 1981-83, sr. regional v.p., 1984-87, sr. divisional v.p., 1987-89, exec. v.p., 1989-91, sr. exec. v.p. and COO Santa Monica, Calif., 1991-93, pres., COO hosp. group, 1993-95; exec. v.p. operations Tenet Healthcare (formerly Nat. Med. Enterprises), Dallas, 1995—99; vice chmn. Tenet Healthcare, 1999—. Mem. Am. Hosp. Assn., Fedn. Am. Health Care Systems (bd. govs. 1985—, bd. dirs. 1989—, chmn. 2000), Am. Coll. Health Care Execs., Fla. League Hosps. (bd. dirs. 1981—, chmn. 1988-89), bd. dir. Healthcare leadership coun., 1999—. Office: Tenet Healthcare 13737 Noel Rd Ste 100 Dallas TX 75240-2017

SCHOCHOR, JONATHAN, lawyer, educator; b. Suffern, NY, Sept. 9, 1946; s. Abraham and Betty (Hechtor) S.; m. Joan Elaine Brown, May 31, 1970; children: Lauren Aimee, Daniel Ross. BA, Pa. State U., 1968; JD, Am. U., 1971. Bar: D.C. 1971, U.S. Dist. Ct. D.C. 1971, U.S. Ct. Appeals (D.C. cir.) 1971, Md. 1974, U.S. Dist. Ct. Md. 1974, U.S. Supreme Ct. 1986. Assoc. McKenna, Wilkinson & Kittner, Washington, 1970-74, Ellin & Baker, Balt., 1974-84; ptnr. Schochor, Federico & Staton, Balt., 1984—. Lectr. in law; expert witness to state legis. Editor-in-chief: Am. U. Law Rev., 1970—71. Mem. ABA, ATLA (state del. 1991, state gov. 1992-95), Am. Bd. Trial Advs. (membership com. 1994—), Am. Bd. Trial Advs., Am. Judicature Soc., Md. State Bar Assn. (spl. com. on health claims arbitration 1983), Md. Trial Lawyers Assn. (bd. govs. 1986-87, mem. legis. com. 1985-88, chmn. legis. com. 1986-87, sec. 1987-88, exec. com. 1987-92, v.p. 1987-88, pres.-elect 1989, pres. 1990-91), Balt. City Bar Assn. (legis com. 1986-87, spl. com. on tort reform 1986, medicolegal com. 1989-90, cir. ct. for Balt. City task force-civil document mgmt. sys. 1994-95), Bar Assn. D.C., Internat. Platform Assn., Phi Alpha Delta. Office: Schochor Federico & Staton PA 1211 Saint Paul St Baltimore MD 21202-2783 Office Phone: 410-234-1000. Business E-Mail: jschochor@sfspa.com.

SCHOCK, ROBERT NORMAN, geophysicist; b. Monticello, NY, May 25, 1939; s. Carl Louis and Norma Elizabeth (Greenfield) S.; m. Susan Esther Benton, Nov. 28, 1959; children: Pamela Ann, Patricia Elizabeth, Christina Benton. BS, Colo. Coll., 1961; MS, Rensselaer Poly. Inst., 1963, PhD, 1966; postgrad., Northwestern U., 1963-64. Cert. Calif. state wine judge. Jr. geophys. trainee Continental Oil Co., Sheridan, Wyo., 1960; jr. geologist Texaco In., Billings, Mont., 1961; teaching asst. Rensselaer Poly. Inst., Troy, NY, 1961-63, research asst., 1964-66; research assoc. U. Chgo., 1966-68; sr. research scientist Lawrence Livermore Nat. Lab., U. Calif., 1968—2006, group leader high pressure physics, 1972-74, sect. leader geoscis. and engring., 1974-76, div. leader earth scis., 1976-81, head dept. earth scis., 1981-87, energy program leader, 1987-92, dep. assoc. dir. for energy, 1992-98, sr. fellow Ctr. Global Security Rsch., 1998—2006. Pres. Pressure Sys. Rsch. Inc.; faculty Chabot Coll., 1969-71; dir. Alameda County Flood Control and Water Conservation Dist., 1984-86, chmn., 1985; adv. panel on geoscis. US Dept. Energy, 1985-87; chmn. adv. com. U. Calif. Energy Inst., 1992-98; rsch. adv. com. Gas Rsch. Inst., Chgo., 1995-2001; dir. studies World Energy Coun., London, 2005—; chmn. Study Group Energy Tech. in 21st Century, 1999-2004, coord. lead author intergovtl. panel on climate change, UN, 2004-07; instrumentation and facilities rev. panel NSF, 2001-04. Mem. editl. bd. Rev. Sci. Instruments, 1975-77; assoc. editor: Jour. Geophys. Rsch., 1978-80; bd. assoc. editors: 11th Lunar and Planetary Sci. Conf., 1980; mem. adv. bd. Physics and Chemistry of Minerals, 1983-97; rsch. and publs. on high pressure physics, solid state physics, physics of earth interior, rock deformation, energy R&D and energy policy. Fulbright sr. fellow U. Bonn, Germany, 1973; vis. research fellow Australian Nat. U. Canberra, 1980-81 Mem. AAAS, Am. Geophys. Union, Sigma Xi, Commonwealth of Calif. Club, Cosmos Club (Washington).

SCHOECH, STEPHAN JAMES, biology professor; b. Modesto, Calif., Feb. 19, 1949; s. Joseph Wayne and Hazel Moore Schoech; m. Sarah Ellen Kistler, May 23, 1988. BS, Ariz. State U., Tempe, 1989, MS, 1990; PhD, U. Wash., Seattle, 1995. Post doctoral fellow Ind. U., Bloomington, 1995—2000; asst. prof. U. Memphis, 2000—04, assoc. prof., 2004—. Contbr. articles to profl. jours. Vol. NSF, Arlington, Va., 2000—06. Recipient Rsch. Assoc., Archbold Biol. Sta., Fla., 2002—, Early Career Rsch. award, U. Memphis, Coll. Arts and Scis., 2003; Rsch. grants, NSF, 1997—. Mem.: AAAS, Am. Ornithologists Union, Soc. Integrative and Comparative Biology, Brit. Ornithologists Union (assoc. editor 2006), Soc. Behavioral Neuroendocrinology. Democrat. Avocations: travel, cooking, birdwatching. Office: Univ Memphis Dept Biology 3774 Walker Ave Memphis TN 38152 Home Phone: 901-763-1435; Office Phone: 901-678-2327.

SCHOECK, RICHARD J., English and humanities scholar, poet; b. NYC, Oct. 10, 1920; s. Gustav J. and Frances M. (Kuntz) S.; m. Reta R. Haberer, 1945 (div. 1976); children: Eric R., Christine C., Jennifer A.; m. Megan S. Lloyd, Feb. 19, 1977 (dec. Nov. 17, 2005). MA, PhD, Princeton U., 1949. Instr. English Cornell U., 1949-55; from asst. prof. to assoc. prof. U. Notre Dame, 1955-61; prof. English U. Toronto, 1961-71; head dept. English St. Michael's Coll., 1965-70; prof. vernacular lit. Pontifical Inst. Mediaeval Studies, Toronto, 1964-71; dir. rsch. activities Folger Shakespeare Libr., also dir. Folger Inst. Renaissance and 18th Century Studies, 1970-74; adj. prof. English Cath. U. Am., 1972; prof. English, medieval and renaissance studies U. Md., 1974-75; prof. English and humanities U. Colo., Boulder, 1975-89, prof. emeritus, 1987—, chmn. dept. integrated studies, 1976-79; chmn. comparative lit., 1983-84; prof. Anglistik Univ. Trier, 1987-90, head dept. (Geschäftsführer), 1988-89; adj. prof. English U. Kans., Lawrence, 1990—2000. Vincent J. Flynn prof. letters Coll. St. Thomas, 1959; vis. prof. Princeton U., 1964, U. Dallas, 1985; vis. fellow Inst. Advanced Studies in Humanities, Edinburgh, 1984-85; vis. scholar Corpus Christi Coll., Oxford, 1994, Wolfson Coll., Oxford, 1997; fellow Assn. Advancement Edn., 1952-53, Yale U., 1959-60, Can. Coun. 1967-68, Ctr. for the Book, Brit. Libr., 1995-96; cons. NEH: bd. dir. Natural Law Inst. U. Notre Dame; advisor Italian Acad. for Advanced Studies in Am., 1993; presenter in field. Author: The Achievement of Thomas More, 1976, Intertexuality and Renaissance Texts, 1984, Erasmus Grandescens, 1988, (poems) A Raging Against Chaos, 1989, The Eye of a Traveller, 1992, The Knight's Book, 1993, My Hiroshima, 1997, (poems) Laurentian Codicil, 2002, rev. edit., 2004, Prairie Epiphanies, 2003, Childhood and Old Age, 2001, Erasmus of Europe, Vol. I, The Making of a Humanist, 1467-1500, 1990, Vol. II The Prince of Humanists, 1501-1536, 1993; contbr.: The Wakaruska Wetlands in Word and Image, 2005, numerous articles, papers, revs. on edn. to jours. and mags.; editor: Delehaye's Legends of the Saints, 1961, Editing 16th Century Texts, 1966, Roger Ascham: The Scholemaster, 1966, Shakespeare Quar., 1972-74, Acta Conventus Neo-Latini Bononiensis, 1985; gen. editor: The Confutation of Tyndale, 3 vols., 1973; co-editor: Voices of Literature, 2 vols., 1964, 66, Chaucer Criticism, 2 vols, 1960, 61, Style, Rhetoric and Rhythym: Essays by M.W. Croll, 1966, Acta Conventus Neo-Latini Torontonensis, 1991; past gen. editor: Patterns of Literary Criticism; spl. editor Canada vol. Rev. Nat. Literatures, 1977, Sir Thomas Browne and the Republic of Letters, 1982, A Special Number of English Language Notes, 1982; gen. editor: (series) Renaissance Masters, 1992-99; mem. editl. bds. profl. jours. From pvt. to 1st lt. US Army, 1940—46. Guggenheim Found. fellow, 1968-69, Fulbright fellow, 1983; recipient Centennial medal U. Colo., 1976, Falconer Madan award Bibliographical Soc., London, 1997; co-recipient 1st prize Mellen Poetry Competition, 1997; grantee Can. Coun., UNESCO, Am. Coun. Learned Socs., U. Toronto, U. Colo. Fellow Royal Soc. Can., Royal Hist. Soc.; mem. Internat. Assn. Neo-Latin Studies (pres. 1976-79), MLA, Renaissance Soc. Am., PEN, Internat. Assn. U. Profs. English, Princeton Club (NY). Home: 1516 Fountain Drive Lawrence KS 66047 Personal E-mail: rjschoeck@sunflower.com. *More than a thousand years ago Bede summed up what are for me the principles of my professional career: I have always thought it fitting to learn and to teach and to write.*

SCHOELEN, MARY JEANETTE, federal judge; b. Rota, Spain, 1968; BA, U. Calif. Irvine, 1990; JD, George Washington U. Law Sch., 1993. Law clk. Nat. Veterans Legal Services Project; staff atty., veteran's benefits program Vietnam Veterans of Am., 1994; intern, com. veterans' affairs US Senate, 1994, minority counsel, com. veterans' affairs, 1997—2001, minority gen. counsel, com. veterans' affairs, 2001, dep. staff dir. benefits programs and gen. counsel, com. veterans' affairs, 2001—04; judge US Ct. Appeals Vets. Claims, 2004—. Office: US Ct Appeals Veterans Claims 625 Indiana Ave NW Ste 900 Washington DC 20004 Office Phone: 202-501-5970. *

SCHOEN, ALLEN HARRY, retired aerospace engineering executive; b. NYC, Mar. 10, 1936; s. Harry Alfred and Dorothy Julia (Browne) S.; m. Patricia Alice O'Madigan, June 1, 1958 (div. 1989); children: Theresa Mary, James Allen, Karen Linda; m. Lauria Juliette Trahan, Feb. 14, 2001. SB in Aero. Engring., MIT, 1958, postgrad., 1989. Aerodynamicist Douglas Aircraft Co., Santa Monica, Calif., 1958-61, United Aircraft Co., Farmington, Conn., 1961-66; with Boeing Helicopters, Phila., 1966-98, tech. mgr., 1980-84, dir. tech., 1984-86, dep. tech. dir. V-22 Osprey joint program, 1986-88, dir. preliminary design, 1988-92, dir. devel. engring., 1992-95, dir. devel. program, 1995-98; ret., 1998. Aero. adv. com. NASA, Washington, 1985-90. Patentee propulsion sys.; contbr. articles to profl. jours. Fellow AIAA (assoc.), Am. Helicopter Soc. (hon., pres. Phila. chpt. 1983-84, v.p. Mideast region 1986-88, dir.-at-large 1988-90, Paul E. Haueter Meml. award 1999), Brewster Assn. Part-time Residents (founder, pres. 2002-04). Republican. Episcopalian. Avocations: photography, gardening, woodworking, woodcarving.

SCHOEN, CHARLES JUDD, service executive; b. Owatonna, Minn., Sept. 6, 1943; s. John Nicholas and Dorothy Georgine (Jacobson) S.; m. Birgitta Marianne Haggren, Dec. 15, 1972; 1 child, Vanja Karina. BA, U. Minn., 1965. Stockbroker Harris, Upham and Co., Mpls., 1967-70; with Litton Industries, Sydney, Australia, 1970-71; gen. mgr. Westinghouse Electric, Mpls., 1971-77; pres. Westco Security, Wayzata, Minn., 1977—, Automatic Alarm Corp., Wayzata, Minn., 1986-95; pres., chmn. Westec Security Products, Laguna Beach, Calif., 1993—. Bd. chmn. SpyderNet, Minn., 1993—. Author: History of Wayzata, 2004. Past pres. Wayzata Hist. Soc. With USN, 1966-67 Named Alumni Notable Achievement, U. Minn., 1999. Mem. Assn. Former Intelligence Officers, Alarm Dealers Assn. (past pres.). Office: Westco Security 401 Lake St E Wayzata MN 55391-1667

SCHOEN, MARC ALAN, pension and employee benefits executive; b. Worcester, Mass., May 30, 1938; s. A. Robert and Ruth D.Schoen; m. Joanne S. Schultz, June 24, 1962; children: Elliott, Aaron, Jennifer, Matthew. BBA, BS, U. Miami, 1965. Asst. buyer Allied Stores, Miami, Fla., 1965-66; agt. Fidelity Mut. Ins., Miami, 1966-67, Prudential Ins. Co., Miami, 1967-68; pvt. practice registered rep., agt. Miami, 1968-73; pres. A Pension Store, Inc., Miami, 1973—2004. Cons. Criterion Funds, Inc., Houston, 1983-1987, TMG Holding LLC, Chgo., 2004—; newspaper columnist, 1969-1976, 1984. Mem. So. Fla. Employee Benefits Coun., Dade Estate Planning Coun.; scoutmaster Boy Scouts Am., Miami, 1966-90; exec. bd. dirs. Crouse Found. to Pub. Arts at CUNY, N.Y.C., 1983—. With USN, 1957-62. Recipient Cmty. Svc. award Prudential Ins., 1968; CFC Designation, Employers Coun. on Flexible Compensation; named Outstanding Young Man Yr., Optimists, 1967; named to Rollins Coll. Sports Hall of Fame, 1987. Mem. (assoc.) Am. Soc. Pension Actuaries, Internat. Assn. Fin. Planners, Million Dollar Round Table (qualifying life), Nat. Assn. Ins. and Fin. Advisors, Employers Coun. on Flexible Compensation, Rotary, Masons. Avocations: stamp collecting/philately, camping, hiking. Home: 838 Blue Heather Ct Lawrenceville GA 30045 Office Phone: 786-514-1933. E-mail: marc@apensionstore.com, maschoen@bellsouth.net.

SCHOEN, RICHARD MELVIN, mathematics professor, researcher; b. Celina, Ohio, Oct. 23, 1950; s. Arnold Peter and Rosemary (Heitkamp) S.; m. Doris Helga Fischer-Colbrie, Oct. 29, 1983; children: Alan, Lucy. BS, U. Dayton, 1972; PhD, Stanford U., 1976. Lectr. U. Calif.-Berkeley, 1976-78, prof. math., 1980-85; asst. prof. Courant Inst. NYU, 1978-80; prof. math. U. Calif.-La Jolla, 1985-87, Stanford U., 1987—. Contbr. articles to profl. jours. Recipient Bocher prize, 1989; fellow NSF, 1972, Alfred P. Sloan Found., 1979, MacArthur Found. prize, 1983, Guggenheim Found., 1996. Mem. Am. Acad. Arts and Scis., Am. Math. Soc., Nat. Acad. Sci. Office: Stanford U Mathematics Dept Stanford CA 94305 Business E-Mail: schoen@math.stanford.edu.

SCHOEN, STEVAN JAY, lawyer; b. NYC, May 19, 1944; s. Al and Ann (Spevack) S.; m. Cynthia Lukens; children: Andrew Adams, Anna Kim. BS, U. Pa., 1966; JD, Cornell U., 1969; MPhil, Cambridge U., Eng., 1980. Bar: N.Mex. 1970, N.Y. 1970, U.S. Supreme Ct. 1976, U.S. Tax Ct. 1973, U.S. Ct. Internat. Trade 1982. Dir. Vista law recruitment OEO, Washington, 1970-71; atty. Legal Aid Soc. of Albuquerque, 1971-73; chief atty. N.Mex. Dept. Health and Social Svcs., Albuquerque, 1973-77; ptnr. Brennan, Schoen & Eisenstadt, 1979-88, Bingham, Hurst, Apodaca, Wile & Schoen, P.C., 2001—03; prin. Stevan J. Schoen, LLC, Placitas, N.Mex., 2003—; probate judge Sandoval County, 1991—99. Arbitrator NYSE; mem. N.Mex. Supreme Ct. Appellate Rules Com., 1982—92; chmn. rules com. Com. on Fgn. Legal Cons., 1993—95; chmn. N.Mex. Supreme Ct. Com., Probate Ct. Rules and Forms, 1998—; mem. state bd. Profl. Engrs. and Surveyors, 2004—. Mem. Mayor's Albuquerque Abd. Com. on Fgn. Trade Zone, 1992-94; v.p. Placitas Vol. Fir Dept., 1974-86; bd. edn. Bernalillo Pub. Sch. Dist., 1996-97; chair Sandoval County Dem. Party, 2001-03. Recipient Cert. for Outstanding Svc. to Judiciary, N.Mex. Supreme Ct., 1982, Outstanding Svc. award N. Mex. Supreme Ct., 1992, 2003, Cert. of Appreciation, N.Mex. Sec. of State, 1980, Pro Bono Pub. Svc. award, 1989, Cert. of Recognition Legal Aid, 1994, award Las Placitas Assn., 1996; named Outstanding Probate Judge, N.Mex State Senate, 1998. Mem. Am. Judges Assn. (ho. of dels. 1999-2002), Nat. Coll. Probate Judges, State Bar N.Mex. (past chmn. real property, probate and trust sect. 1989, Outstanding Contbn. award 1989, past chmn. appellate practice sect. 1991, past chmn. internat. law sect. 1991-92, commn. on professionalism 1992-95, organizing com. U.S.-Mex. law inst. 1992), N.Mex. Probate Judges Assn. (chmn. 1993-99, award 1998, N.Mex. state bar, chair sr. lawyers sect. 2003-04, dir. 2002-), Bench and Bar Com. (co-chair 2001-2002), Oxford-Cambridge Soc. N.Mex. (sec.), M.Mex. Assn. Counties (adv. bd. 1995-98). Home and Office: 4 Hillside Dr Placitas NM 87043 Office Phone: 505-867-2802. Business E-Mail: schoenlaw@comcast.net.

SCHOEN, WILLIAM JACK, finance company executive; b. LA, Aug. 2, 1935; s. Jack Conrad and Kathryn Mabel (Stegmayer) S.; m. Sharon Ann Barto, Oct. 1, 1966; children: Kathryn Lynn, Karen Anne, Kristine Lea, William Jack. BS in Fin. magna cum laude, U. So. Calif., 1960, MBA, 1963. Mktg. mgr. Anchor Hocking Glass Co., 1964-68; v.p. sales and mktg. Obear-Nester Glass Co., 1968-71; pres. Pierce Glass Co., Port Allegheny, Pa., 1971-73; pres., chief exec. officer, dir. F.&M. Schaefer Brewing Co., NYC, 1973-81; now chmn., pres. Wilshar Mgmt. Co. Inc., Naples, Fla., 1981—; chmn. Health Mgmt. Assocs. Inc., Naples, 1983—, also bd. dirs. Contbr. to indsl. publns. Founder Marine Corp. Heritage Found.; mem. Bus. Coun. of 100 of Fla.; bd. dir. Internat. Coll. Found.; chmn. Schoen Found.; mem. bd. advisors U. So. Calif. Bus. Sch.; trustee U. So. Calif., 2006-. Served with USMC, 1953-56, Korea. Mem. Naples Yacht Club, Port Royal Club, Quail Creek Country Club, Teton Springs Club, Phi Kappa Phi. Republican. Lutheran. Home Phone: 239-261-7170; Office Phone: 239-598-3175.

SCHOENBERG, MARK GEORGE, government agency administrator; b. Bklyn., Nov. 22, 1947; s. Abraham Arthur and Ruth Millie (Dunn) S. BA, Columbia U., 1971, postgrad., 1972-73, N.C. State U., 1971-72. Research asst. NIMH-sponsored project at N.C. State U., Raleigh, 1971-72; asst. to pres. Key Electric Ltd., Glen Oaks, NY, 1973-76, gen. mgr. Los

Angeles, 1976; asst. to pres. Kalsan Electric, Hempstead, NY, 1977; asst. mgr. Lincoln Inn, Rockville Ctr., NY, 1978; expert, cons. EPA, Washington, 1978; assoc. dir. U.S. Regulatory Council, Washington, 1979-82; exec. dir. Regulatory Info. Service Ctr., Washington, 1982-99; sr. advisor to dep. adminstr. Gen. Svcs. Adminstrn., 1999—. Avocations: healthy gourmet cooking, early music, wine collecting, travel, photography.

SCHOENBERGER, JAMES EDWIN, retired federal agency administrator; b. Dayton, Ohio, Sept. 7, 1947; s. Harry Robert and Elizabeth Jane Schoenberger; m. Aura Victoria Montana, June 24, 1977; children: David, Eric. BSCE, Purdue U., 1969; MBA, Harvard U., 1971. V.p. ops. for midwestern housing developer Herman Devel. Group, Indpls., 1971-74; various positions New Communities Adminstrn. and with sec. HUD, Washington, 1974-77, assoc. dep. asst. sec., 1981-83; dir. land utilization Peabody Coal Co., St. Louis, 1977-81; sr. v.p. ops. The Investment Group, Washington, 1983-86; gen. dep. asst. fed. housing commr. HUD, Washington, 1987-89, assoc. gen., dep. asst. sec., 1990-97, ret., 1997. Roman Catholic. Avocations: computers, philanthropy.

SCHOENBERGER, STEVEN HARRIS, physician, research consultant; b. Cleve., Nov. 26, 1950; s. Stanford L. and Irene (Gold) S. BA, Tulane U., 1972; MD, U. Autonoma Guadalajara, Mex., 1976. Diplomate Am. Bd. of Urology. Asst. prof. Tulane U. Sch. Medicine, New Orleans, 1983—. Rsch. assoc. Delta Regional Primate Rsch. Ctr., Covington, La., 1983-85, chief section of urology Lawrence and Meml. Hosp., New London, Conn.; chmn. laser com., Lawrence and Meml. Hosp., New London, Conn., 1989—, chief sect. urology, 2003—; rsch. cons. Pfizer Med. Group, Groton, Conn., 1989—. Fellow ACS, Am. Soc. Laser Medicine and Surgery; mem. Soc. Univ. Urologists, N.Y. Acad. Scis., New Eng. Escadrille. Office: 3 Shaws Cv Ste 206 New London CT 06320-4968 Office Phone: 860-443-0622.

SCHOENDORFER, DONALD W., engineer; b. Albany, NY, Mar. 1949; m. Laurie Schoendorfer; children: Erika, Heidi, Anna. BA, Baldwin Wallace Coll., Berea, 1972; BS, Columbia U.; MS in Mech. Engring., MIT, PhD in Mech. Engring., 1977. Cofounder, v.p. rsch. and devel. Subdormed, Santa Ana, Calif.; cofounder, CEO Free Wheelchair Mission, 2001—. Recipient Beta Gamma Sigma Medallion for entrepreneurship, 2005, Outstanding Alumni award, Baldwin Wallace Coll., 2006, Mayor's award, Orange County, Calif., Feb., 2006. Achievements include 53 US patents for human blood collection and processing equipment, drug testing and fingerprinting materials and procedures; invention of wheelchair made from $3 lawn chair and other inexpensive materials, costing $41 to manufacture; distributed more than 145,000 free wheelchairs in over 57 countries since 2001. Office: Free Wheelchair Mission 9341 Irvine Blvd Irvine CA 92618

SCHOENER, ALLON, museum and organization consultant; b. Cleve., Jan. 1, 1926; s. Harry and Ida (Finkelstein) S.; m. Mary Heimsath, Mar. 27, 1959; children: Abraham, Rebecca. BA, Yale U., 1946, MA, 1949; postgrad. U. London Courtauld Inst., 1947-48. Curator, San Francisco Mus., 1950-55; dir. Contemporary Arts Ctr., Cin., 1955-64; asst. dir. Jewish Mus., NYC, 1966-67; dir. visual arts program. NY State Coun. on Arts, NYC, 1967-72; cons. Smithsonian Instn., Washington, 1972-74. Author: Portal to America, 1967; Harlem On My Mind, 1969; American Jewish Album, 1983; The Italian Americans, 1987. Mem. Union HS Bd., Bellows Falls, Vt., 1977-82. Rsch. grantee Nat. Endowment for Arts, Washington, 1982. Mem. Am. Assn. of Mus., Internat. Com. of Mus.

SCHOENER, THOMAS WILLIAM, zoology educator, researcher; b. Lancaster, Pa., Aug. 9, 1943; BA, Harvard Coll., 1965, PhD, 1969. Asst. prof. Harvard Coll., Cambridge, Mass., 1972-73, assoc. prof., 1973-75, U. Wash., Seattle, 1975-76, prof., 1976-80, U. Calif., Davis, 1980—, chairperson sect. evolution and ecology divsn. biol. scis., 1993-99. Mem. editl. bd. dirs. Oecologia, 1984-93; past mem. editl. bd. Evolution, Am. Naturalist, Sci., Acta Oecologia; contbr. chpts. to books, articles to profl. jours. Recipient MacArthur prize Ecol. Soc. Am., 1987; grantee NSF, 1975—, Nat. Geog. Soc.; jr. fellow Harvard U., 1969-72; Guggenheim fellow, 1992-93. Mem. NAS, Am. Acad. Arts and Scis., Am. Ornithologists Union (elective), Am. Soc. Naturalists, Ecol. Soc. Am., Am. Soc. Ichthyologists and Herpetologists, Cooper Ornithol. Soc., Am. Arachnological Soc., Soc. Study of Amphibians and Reptiles. Avocations: weightlifting, reading. Office: U Calif Sect Evolution Ecology Davis CA 95616 Office Phone: 530-752-8319. Business E-Mail: twschoener@ucdavis.edu.

SCHOENFELD, ALAN HENRY, mathematics education professor, researcher; b. NYC, July 9, 1947; s. Neil Howard and Natalie (Weinberg) S.; m. Jean Snitzer, June 14, 1970. BS in Math., Queens Coll., 1968; MS in Math., Stanford U., 1969, PhD in Math., 1973. Lectr. U. Calif., Davis, 1973-75; from asst. prof. to assoc. prof. Hamilton Coll., Clinton, NY, 1978-81, U. Rochester, NY, 1981-84; lectr. U. Calif., Berkeley, 1975-78, assoc. prof. edn., math., 1985-86, prof., 1986—, chmn. div. edn. in math., sci. and tech., 1987—98, chmn. Sch. Edn., 1994—98. Chmn. Grad. Group in Sci. and Math. Edn., U. Calif., Berkeley, 1985-87; chief organizer IV Internat. Congress Math. Edn., 1984. Author: Mathematical Problem Solving, 1985, Mathematical Association of America Notes # 1, Problem Solving, 1983; editor: Cognitive Science and Mathematics Education, 1987, A Source Book for College Mathematics Teaching, 1990, Mathematical Thinking and Problem Solving, 1994, Research in Collegiate Mathematics Education, vol. 1, 1994, vol. 2, 1996, vol. 3, 1998, vol. 4, 2000, Assessing Mathematical Proficiency, 2007, A Study of Teaching: Multiple Lenses, Multiple Views, 2007. Mem. State Calif. Math. Framework Com., 1988-90; mem. adv. panel Calif. Assessment Program, 1988—; mem. Supt.'s Math. Task Force, 1995. Grantee NSF, 1979, 85, 87, 90-92, 96-97, 2001-06, Sloan Found., 1984, 87, Spencer Found., 1983, 93. Fellow: AAAS; mem.: Nat. Rsch. Coun. (math. sci. edn. bd. task force on K-12 1986—88, bd. testing/assessment 1993—98), Nat. Bd. for Profl. Tchg. Stds. (math. panel 1990—95), Nat. Coun. Tchrs. Math. (rsch. adv. com. 1990—93, chair 1992—93, leader prins. and stds. 1997—2000), Cognitive Sci. Soc., Am. Math. Soc. (com. on edn. 1992—97), Am. Ednl. Rsch. Assn. (exec. com. Spl. Interest Group Math. Edn. 1984—86, chair publs. com. 1994—, pres. 1998—2000), Math. Assn. Am. (chmn. tchg. undergrad. math. com. 1982—89), Nat. Acad. Edn. (exec. bd. 1995—2006, v.p. 2001—06), Kappa Delta Pi (Laureate 2006). Avocations: food, wine. Home: 830 Colusa Ave Berkeley CA 94707-1839 Office: U Calif Dept Edn Berkeley CA 94720-1670

SCHOENFELD, ANDREW JASON, orthopedist, surgeon; b. NYC, May 22, 1978; s. David and Patricia Ann Schoenfeld; m. Erin Marie Zook, Sept. 4, 2004. BS, BA, Kent State U., 1999; MD, Northeastern Ohio U. Coll. of Medicine, 2003. Clin. instr. orthopaedic surgery Northeastern Ohio U. Coll. of Medicine, Akron, Ohio, 2004—. Trauma preceptorship U. Wis., 2007. Contbr. articles to profl. jours. Bd. dirs. Royal Rwandan Assn. 2d lt. US Army Med. Svc. Corps, 1998—2003, capt. United State Army M.C., 2003—, lt. Order of Danilo, 2007. Decorated Grand Cross Order of Lion Rwanda; recipient Nat. Resident Rsch. award, Clin. Orthop. Soc., 2005, Nat. Phys. in Tng. award, Mid.-Am. Orthop. Assn., 2007, Resident Best Paper award, Arthros Assn. N.Am., 2007, Barry Friedman MD Rsch. award, 2007. Mem.: Arthroscopy Assn. N.Am. (recipient Basic Sci. Rsch. award 2007), Mid-Am. Orthop. Assn. (recipient Carl Nelson MD award 2007), ACS (assoc.), Modern Greek Studies Assn., Phi Beta Kappa, Alpha Omega Alpha (lt. order danilo 2007). Jewish. Achievements include research in pullout strength variance among self-tapping screws in normal and osteoporotic bone; the use of Megaprosthetic femoral replacement in orthopaedic trauma; tissue engineering meniscal constructs. Avocation: writing. Office: Akron Gen Med Ctr 224 West Exchange St Akron OH 44302 Home Phone: 330-945-9734; Office Phone: 330-329-2594. Personal E-mail: ajschoen@neoucom.edu.

SCHOENFELD, BARBARA BRAUN, executive recruiter, lawyer, consultant; b. Phila., Apr. 17, 1953; d. Irving Leon Braun and Virginia (Parker) Sand; m. Larry Jay Schoenfeld, June 29, 1975; children: Alexander, Gordon, Max. BA cum laude, U. Pa., 1974, M in City Planning, Social Work, 1977; JD, Boston U., 1982. Bar: R.I. 1982, U.S. Dist. Ct. R.I. 1982. Assoc. planner Del. Valley Hosp. Council, Phila., 1978-79; summer assoc. Tillinghast, Collins & Graham, Providence, 1980, 81; assoc. Edwards & Angell, Providence, 1982-86, Ropes & Gray, Providence, 1986-92; dep. treas., gen. counsel State of R.I., 1993-99; v.p. Brown Bros. Harriman & Co., Boston, 1999—2006; prin. Ligature Ptnrs., 2006—. Chmn., bd. dirs. Com. Women's Health Concerns, Phila., 1978-79; bd. dirs. Jewish Family Svc., Providence, 1982-88, Jewish Fedn. of RI, 1989-91, investment com., 2004-07; assoc. treas. Jewish Cmty. Ctr. of RI; bd. dirs. Alumni Trustees U. Pa.; chmn. admissions com. U. Pa. Alumni Club, Providence, 1982-95; trustee The Wheeler Sch., 1994-2002; trustee Dunn Inst., 2004—. Mem. RI Bar Assn., Ledgemont Country Club (Seekonk, Mass.), Cherrystone Angel Group. Democrat. Jewish. Avocations: skiing, travel, French language. Office: Ligature Partners 60 Ship St Providence RI 02903 Office Phone: 401-521-3997. Personal E-mail: barbara.schoenfeld@gmail.com. Business E-Mail: barbara@ligaturepartners.com.

SCHOENFELD, DAVID ALAN, statistician, educator; b. Ft. Monmouth, NJ, Apr. 19, 1945; s. Robert Louis Schoenfeld and Helene Flapan; m. Ellen Maureen Beeks, Dec. 30, 1973; children: Heather, Elizabeth, Jonathan. BA, Reed Coll., 1967; MA, U. Oreg., 1968, PhD, 1974. Postdoctoral fellow Stanford U., Calif., 1974—75; rsch. asst. prof. SUNY, Buffalo, 1975—77; from asst. to assoc. scientist Dana-Farber Cancer Inst., Boston, 1977—86; from asst. prof. to prof. dept. of biostats., Sch. Pub. Health Harvard U., Boston, 1977—; assoc. prof. to prof. dept. medicine, 1985—; dir. Biostatistics Ctr. Mass. Gen. Hosp., Boston, 1985—. Co-editor: (book) Aids Clinical Trials, 1995. Fellow: American Statis. Assn.; mem.: Assn. of GCRC Statisticians, Internat. Statis. Inst., Biometric Soc., Inst. of Math. Stats. Avocation: skiing. Home: 41 Brook Rd Sharon MA 02067 Office: Mass Gen Hosp 50 Staniford St Boston MA 02114 Personal E-mail: david@schoenfeld.com. E-mail: dschoenfeld@partners.org.

SCHOENFELD, GERALD, performing company executive; BS, Univ. Ill.; LLB, N.Y. Univ.; postgraduate, Mass. Inst. Tech., Columbia Univ.; DHL (hon.), CUNY, 1999, Emerson Coll., 2001. Faculty Yale Drama Sch.; chmn. Schubert Org., NYC, 1972—. Adj. prof. Sch. Arts, Columbia Univ.; chmn. League Am. Theatres & Producers; chmn. bd. gov. League of N.Y. Theatres & Producers. Bd. mem. N.Y. Conv. & Vis. Bureau; chmn. Mayor's Midtown Citizens Com., NYC & Company. Recipient Humanitarian award, N.Y. Soc. Assn. Executives. Fellow: Am. Acad. Arts & Scis. Office: League of American Theatres & Producers 226 W 47th St New York NY 10036

SCHOENFELD, HANNS-MARTIN WALTER, finance educator; b. Leipzig, Germany, July 12, 1928; came to U.S., 1962, naturalized, 1968; s. Alwin and Lisbeth (Kirbach) Schoenfeld; m. Margit Frese, Aug. 10, 1956 (dec. Jan. 21, 2005); 1 child, Gabriele. MBA, U. Hamburg, Fed. Republic Germany, 1952, DBA, 1954; PhD, U. Braunschweig, Fed. Republic Germany, 1966. Pvt. practice acctg., Hamburg, 1948-54; bus. cons. Europe, 1958-62; faculty accountancy U. Ill., Champaign/Urbana, 1962—, prof. acctg., bus. adminstrn. Urbana, 1967—, Weldon Powell prof. acctg., 1976, 80-81, H. T. Scovill prof. acctg., 1985-94; prof. emeritus, 1994—; dir. Office of West European Studies, 1982-84. Lectr., cons. in bus. and acctg., Eng., Belgium, Austria, Denmark, Brazil, Mex., Germany, Poland, Indonesia, Korea, Japan, Switzerland, Hungary, Czechoslovakia, 1962—; vis. prof. Econs. U. Vienna, Austria, 1984-2002, Handelshochschule, Leipzig, Germany, 1996-2002. Author: Management Dictionary 2 vols., 4th edit, 1971, Cost Accounting, 8th edit, 1974-95, Management Development, 1967, Cost Terminology and Cost Theory, 1974, (with J. Sheth) Export Marketing: Lessons from Europe, 1981, (with H.P. Holzer) Managerial Accounting and Analysis in Multinational Enterprises, 1986, (with L. Noerreklit) Resources of the Firm, 1996. With German Army, 1944-45. Recipient Dr. Kausch prize for internat. integration of acctg. U. St. Gall, Switzerland, 1996. Mem. Am. Acctg. Assn. (chmn. internat. sect. 1976-77), Acad. Acctg. Historians (v.p. 1976-77, pres. 1978-79, Hour Glass award for best book publs. 1975), Acad. Internat. Bus., German Profs. Bus. Adminstrn., German Assn. Indsl. Engring., European Acctg. Assn., Coun. of European Studies, Internat. Assn. for Acctg. Edn. and Rsch., Beta Gamma Sigma, Beta Alpha Psi. Home: 1014 Devonshire Dr Champaign IL 61821-6620 Office: U Ill Dept Acctg 360 Wohlers Hall 1206 S 6th St Champaign IL 61820-6915 Business E-Mail: hschoenf@uiuc.edu.

SCHOENFELD, HOWARD ALLEN, management consultant, lawyer; b. NYC, Apr. 17, 1948; s. Irving and Muriel (Levy) S.; m. Paula Simon; 1 child, Haley Rebecca. BA, U. Pa., 1970; JD, Georgetown U., 1973. Bar: Md. 1973, U.S. Dist. Ct. Md. 1973, Wis. 1976, U.S. Dist. Ct. (ea. dist.) Wis. 1976, U.S. Dist. Ct. (we. dist.) Wis. 1987. Law clk. Md. Ct. Appeals, 1973-74; assoc. Gordon, Feinblatt, Rothman, Hoffberger & Hollander, Balt., 1974-76; ptnr. Trebon & Schoenfeld, Milw., 1976-85, Godfrey & Kahn, Milw., 1985—2002; prs. DSC Advisors, Milw., 2002—. Chmn. John Anderson Campaign for Pres., Wis., 1980; pres. Milw. Jewish Coun., 1987-89, mem., 1983—. Recipient Young Leadership award Milw. Jewish Fedn., 1983. Mem. ABA, Wis. Bar Assn., Milw. Bar Assn. Office: DSC Advisors 3805 N Oakland Ave Milwaukee WI 53211 Home Phone: 414-351-1919; Office Phone: 414-967-0579. E-mail: hasreorg@aol.com.

SCHOENFELD, JIM, professional sports team executive, former professional hockey coach; b. Galt, Ont., Can., Sept. 4, 1954; m. Theresa Schoenfeld; children: Katie, Justin, Adam, Nathan. Defenseman Buffalo Sabres, 1972—81, 1984—85, Detroit Red Wings, 1981—83, Boston Bruins, 1983—84; head coach Rochester Americans, 1984, Buffalo Sabres, 1985—86, NJ Devils, 1988—89, Washington Capitols, 1994-97, Phoenix Coyotes, 1997—99; asst. coach NY Rangers, 2002—03, asst. gen. mgr. player personnel, 2007—; gen. mgr. Hartford Wolfpack, 2003—07, head coach, 2005—07. Lead analyst Nat. Hockey Night, ESPN, 1999—2002. Office: NY Rangers 2 Pennsylvania Plaza New York NY 10102 *

SCHOENFELD, MICHAEL P., lawyer; b. Oct. 17, 1935; s. Jack and Anne Schoenfield; m. Helen Schorr, Apr. 3, 1960; childrne: Daniel, Steven, Tracy. BS in Acctg., NYU, 1955; LLB, LLD, Fordham U., 1958. Bar: N.Y. 1959, U.S. Supreme Ct. 1963. Coun. Am. Home Assurance Co., NYC, 1958-62; ptnr. Schoenfeld & Schoenfeld, Melville, N.Y., 1959—. V.p. Interstate Brokerage Corp., 1965-84, pres., 1984-90; ptnr. Melville Realty Co., 1977-90; legal adv. various bus. orgns. V.p., trustee Temple Beth David, Commack, N.Y., 1972-75; chmn. Cmty. Action Com. of Dix Hills and Commack, 1970-72, Dix Hills Planning Bd., 1972-74; treas. Dix Hills Rep. Club, 1976-80; mem. Huntington (N.Y.) Zoning Bd. Appeals, 1980-91, chmn., 1986-89. Recipient United Jerusalem award Israel Bond Drive, 1977, City of Hope Svc. award, George Bacon award Fordham Law Sch. Mem.: Suffolk County Bar Assn., NY State Bar Assn. Home: 14 Clayton Dr Dix Hills NY 11746-5517 Office: 999 Walt Whitman Rd Melville NY 11747-3007 Office Phone: 631-673-5004.

SCHOENFELD, ROBERT LOUIS, biomedical engineer; b. NYC, Apr. 1, 1920; s. Bernard and Mae (Kizelstein) S.; m. Helene Martens, Jan. 22, 1944 (div. 1965); children: David, Joseph, Paul; m. Florence Moskowitz, Dec. 11, 1965 (dec. 1989); children: Nedda, Bethany; m. Shulamith Stechel, July 8, 1990. BA, Washington Square Coll., 1942; BSEE, Columbia U., 1944; MEE, Poly. Inst. Bklyn., 1949, DEE, 1956. Rsch. assoc. Columbia U. Med. Sch., NYC, 1947-51; rsch. fellow Sloan Kettering Cancer Rsch. Inst., NYC, 1951-56; assoc. prof. Poly. Inst. Bklyn., 1957—59; biomed. engr. Rockefeller U., NYC, 1957—59, from asst. prof. to assoc. prof., 1957-90, prof. emeritus, 1990—. Contbr. articles to profl. jours. Lt. Signal Corps, U.S. Army, 1944-46, ETO. Fellow IEEE (mem. editl. bd. 1965-75, Centennial medal 1985), Am. Inst. for Med. and Biol. Engring. Democrat. Jewish. Achievements include pioneering application of computer automation to biological laboratory experiments. Office: Rockefeller U 1230 York Ave New York NY 10021-6399 Business E-Mail: rls@mail.rockefeller.edu.

SCHOENFELD, WALTER EDWIN, manufacturing executive; b. Seattle, Nov. 6, 1930; s. Max and Edna Lucille (Reinhardt) S.; m. Esther Behar, Nov. 27, 1955; children— Lea Anne, Jeffrey, Gary. BBA, U. Wash., 1952. Dir. Reading Railroad, 1964—68; v.p., dir. Sunshine Mining Co., Kellogg, Idaho, 1964-69, First N.W. Industries, Inc. (Seattle Super Sonics), 1968-79; chmn. bd., pres. Schoenfeld Industries, Inc. (diversified holding co.), 1968-93; vice chmn., acting pres., CEO, Vans, Inc., 1993-97, chmn., bd. dirs., 1997—2004; non-exec. chmn. Found. Bank, 2005—06, dir., 2005—, Aritzia, 2007—. Ptnr. Seattle Mariners Baseball Club, 1977-81, Seattle Sounders Soccer Club, 1974-79; bd. dirs. Hazel Bishop Cosmetics. Bd. dirs. Wash. China Rels. Coun., 1980—, Sterling Recreation Orgn., 1985-90; chmn. Access Long Distance of Washington; bd. govs. Weizmann Inst. Sci., Rehovot, Israel, 1980—; trustee Barbara Sinatra Children's Ctr., Eisenhower Hosp., Rancho Mirage, Calif., 1990—. With AUS, 1952-55, Korea. Recipient various service awards. Mem. Chief Execs. Orgn. (v.p., bd. dirs. 1987-93), Rainier Club, Tamarisk Country Club (Rancho Mirage, Calif.), Mission Hills Country Club, Alpha Kappa Psi. Office: 999 3rd Ave Ste 3800 Seattle WA 98104-4023

SCHOENFIELD, RICK MERRILL, lawyer; b. Chgo., July 21, 1951; s. Herbert and Bernice (Krichilsky) S. BA, Northwestern U., 1973, JD cum laude, 1976; cert., Nat. Inst. Trial Advocacy, Chgo., 1979. Bar: Ill. 1976, U.S. Dist. Ct. (no. dist.) Ill. 1977, U.S. Ct. Appeals (7th cir.) 1979, U.S. Ct. Appeals (4th cir.) 1984, U.S. Supreme Ct. 1984, U.S. Dist. Ct. (ea. dist.) Wis. 1987. Assoc. Ettinger & Lake, Chgo., 1976—79, Ettinger & Assocs., Ltd., Chgo., 1979—81; ptnr. Ettinger & Schoenfield, Chgo., 1981—92, Schoenfield, Swartzman & Massin, Chgo., 1992—2002, DiVincenzo Schoenfield Swartzman, Chgo., 2002—. Instr. De Paul Law Sch., Chgo., 1977-78, Chgo.-Kent Coll. Law, 1989—, U. Ill. Chgo., 1991-94. Co-author Legal Negotiations: Gettin Maximum Results, 1988, The McGraw Hill 26 Hour Negotiation Course, 1991. Recipient award for Pro Bono Litigation, Operation Lakewatch, Chgo., 1983. Mem. Nat. Resources Def. Coun. Office: Di Vincenzo Schoenfield Swartzman 33 N LaSalle 29th Fl Chicago IL 60602 Office Phone: 312-334-4800, 312-334-4809. Personal E-mail: rschoenfield@aol.com.

SCHOENHARD, WILLIAM CHARLES, JR., health system executive; b. Kansas City, Mo., Sept. 26, 1949; s. William Charles S. and Joyce Evans (Thornsberry) Bell; m. Kathleen Ann Klosterman, June 3, 1972; children: Sarah Elizabeth, Thomas William. BS in Pub. Adminstrn., U. Mo., 1971; M of Health Adminstrn. with honors, Washington U., St. Louis, 1975. V.p., dir. gen. svcs. Deaconess Hosp., St. Louis, 1975-78; assoc. exec. dir. St. Mary's Health Ctr., St. Louis, 1978-81; exec. dir. Arcadia Valley Hosp., Pilot Knob, Mo., 1981-82, St. Joseph Health Ctr., St. Charles, Mo., St. Joseph Hosp. West, Lake St. Louis, 1982—86; exec. v.p., COO SSM Health Care, St. Louis, 1986—. Adv. bd. dirs. Firstar Bank, 1998-01, Midwest Bank Ctr., 2004, Coll. Bus. Mgmt. U. Mo., Columbia, Mo., 2005-. Contbr. articles to profl. jours. Mem. Mo. Commn. on Patient Safety, 2003—04; mem. adv. bd. St. Louis chpt. Lifeseekers, St. Louis, 1985—94; mem. bd. mgrs. Kirkwood-Webster (Mo.) YMCA, 1990—96, sec., 1996; mem. healthcare adv. bd. Sanford Brown Colls., 1992—94; bd. dirs. St. Andrews Mgmt. Svcs., Inc., 1994—2002, Mid Am. Transplant Svcs., 1995—, sec., 2005—; bd. dirs. Lindenwood U., 1997—, Civic Entrepreneurs Orgn., 1997—2000, Greater St. Louis Boy Scouts Am., 1997—, Benedictine Health Sys., 2002. With USN, 1971—72, Vietnam. Fellow Am. Coll. Health Care Execs. (regent Mo.-Gateway area 1997-01, bd. govs. 2002—, chmn. 2006-07); mem. VFW, Am. Hosp. Assn. (del. regional policy bd. 1999-2005, bd. trustees, 2007—, ops. com. 2007—), Mo. Hosp. Assn. (bd. trustees 1999-2005, chmn. 2000), Am. Heart Assn. (mem. bd. Greater St. Louis chpt. 2001-03), Cath. Health Assn. U.S. (mem. fin. com. 1999-01), Am. Legion, US Navy League, Westborough Country Club, Phi Eta Sigma, Pi Omicron Sigma, Delta Upsilon, Delta Sigma Pi. Roman Catholic. Avocations: reading, walking. Home: 420 Fairwood Ln Saint Louis MO 63122-4429 Office: SSM Health Care 477 N Lindbergh Blvd Saint Louis MO 63141-7832 Office Phone: 314-994-7810.

SCHOENHERR, JOHN (CARL), artist, illustrator; b. NYC, July 5, 1935; s. John Ferdinand and Frances (Braun) S.; m. Judith Gray; children: Jennifer L., Ian G. BFA, Pratt Inst., 1956. Painter, illustrator Owl Moon, 1987 (Caldecott medal, 1988); exhibitions include Hiram Blauvelt Art Mus., 1997. Recipient World Sic. Fiction award, World Sci. Fiction Conv., London, 1965, Silver medal, Phila. Acad. Natural Sci., 1984, purchase award, Hiram Blauvelt Art Mus., 1994. Mem.: Soc. Animal Artists (medal 1979, 1985, 2003), Am. Soc. Mammalogists (emeritus). Home and Office: 135 Upper Creek Rd Stockton NJ 08559-1209

SCHOENHUT, FREDERICK W., stock exchange executive; BEE, Clarkson U. Prin. owner Copia Trading Co., Ltd., 1980; vice chmn. NY Bd. Trade (NYBOT), 2002—03, chmn., 2003—. Mem.: NY Board of Trade (NYBOT) (bd. mem. 1994—97, 1999—), NY Cotton Exchange (NYCE), Coffee, Sugar, and Cocoa Exchange (CSCE), Commodity Floor Brokers and Traders Assn. (CFBTA) (vice chmn. 2003—). Office: NY Bd Trade One N End Ave 13th Fl New York NY 10282 Office Phone: 212-748-4040. Office Fax: 212-748-4156. *

SCHOENL, WILLIAM JAMES, history professor; b. Buffalo, Feb. 15, 1941; s. William and Erma Osborne Schoenl; m. Linda Volker, May 14, 1966; children: Karen Schoenl Carpenter, Lauren Schoenl van Loon, Mark William. BS in Math., Canisius Coll., 1963; MA in History, Columbia U., 1964, PhD in History, 1968. Prof. humanities Mich. State U., East Lansing, 1968-89, prof. history, 1989—. Mem. com. on rsch. Am. Soc. Ch. History, Chgo., 1988-93. Author: Intellectual Crisis in English Catholicism, 1982, C.G. Jung, 1998; editor: Major Issues in Jung, 1996, New Perspectives on the Vietnam War, 2002; author of poetry; contbr. articles and revs. to profl. jours. Mem., chair disbursement com. for dire needs overseas St. John Student Parish, East Lansing, Mich., 1971—; founder scholarship Meridian Non-Traditional HS, 2005—. Rsch. grantee Nat. Endowment for the Humanities, Washington, 1970, Am. Philos. Soc., Phila., 1975, global competence grantee Mich. State U., East Lansing, 1993. Mem. Am. Hist. Assn., Ctr. Jung Studies Detroit (trustee 1991-94), Kiwanis Club Okemos (chair internat. iodine deficiency disorders project 1994-98, chair Salvation Army project 1996—, chair human and spiritual values com. 1999-2002, 2004—. Avocations: fishing, walking, travel, reading mysteries, snowshoeing. Home: 2643 Roseland East Lansing MI 48823 Office: Mich State Univ Dept History East Lansing MI 48824 Office Phone: 517-355-7500.

SCHOENRICH, EDYTH HULL, internist, preventive medicine physician; b. Cleve., Sept. 9, 1919; d. Edwin John and Maud Mabel (Kelly) Hull; m. Carlos Schoenrich, Aug. 9, 1942; children: Lola, Olaf. AB, Duke U., Durham, NC, 1941; MD, U. Chgo., 1947; MPH, John Hopkins U., Balt., 1971. Diplomate Am. Bd. Internal Medicine, Am. Bd. Preventive Medicine. Intern John Hopkins Hosp., Balt., 1948-49, asst. resident medicine,

1949-50, fellow medicine, 1950-51, chief resident, pvt. wards, 1951-52; asst. chief, acting chief dept. chronic and cmty. medicine Balt. City Hosp., Balt., 1963-66; dir. svc. to chronically ill and aging Md. State Dept. Health, Balt., 1966-74; dir. divsn. pub. health adminstrn. Sch. Pub. Health, John Hopkins U., Balt., 1974-77, assoc. dean acad. affairs, 1977-86, dir. part time profl. programs and dep. dir. MPH program, 1986—, prof. dept. health policy and mgmt., 1974—, joint appointment medicine, 1978—. Contbr. articles to profl. jours. Trustee Friends Life Care Cmty., 1984—, Kennedy-Krieger Inst., Balt., 1985—, Vis. Nurses Assn., 1990-95, Md. Home and Cmty. Care Found., 1995—. Recipient Stebbins medal John Hopkins U., 1989, Disting. Med. Alumna award, 1997, Golden Apple award, 2007; named to Md. Women's Hall of Fame, 2005 Fellow ACP, Am. Coll. Preventive Medicine; mem. APHA, Assn. Tchrs. Preventive Medicine, Med. and Chirurg. Soc. Md., Balt. City Med. Soc., Phi Beta Kappa, Alpha Omega Alpha, Delta Omega. Avocations: gardening, music, theater, swimming. Home: 1402 Boyce Ave Baltimore MD 21204-6512 Office: Johns Hopkins Univ Sch Pub Health 615 N Wolfe St Baltimore MD 21205-2103 E-mail: eschoenr@jhsph.edu.

SCHOETTLE, ENID C.B., federal agency administrator; m. Herbert Stuart Okun, Dec. 27, 1990. BA, Radcliffe Coll.; PhD in Polit. Sci., MIT, Cambridge, Mass. Faculty polit. sci. U. Minn., Mpls., Swarthmore Coll.; staff mem. Ford Found., 1976—91, dir. internat. affairs program, 1981—91; sr. fellow Coun. on Fgn. Rels., 1991—93; nat. intelligence officer for global and multilateral issues Nat. Intelligence Coun., 1993—96; chief advocacy and external rels. unit UN Dept. Humanitarian Affairs, 1996—97; spl. advisor Nat. Intelligence Coun., Washington, 1997—. Prof. polit. sci. Univ. Minn., Swarthmore Coll. Office: Central Intelligence Agy Nat Intelligence Coun Washington DC 20505

SCHOETTLER, GAIL SINTON, former ambassador; b. LA, Oct. 21, 1943; d. James and Norma (McLellan) Sinton; children: Lee, Thomas, James; m. Donald L. Stevens, June 23, 1990. BA in Econs., Stanford U., 1965; MA in History, U. Calif., Santa Barbara, 1969, PhD in History, 1975. Businesswoman, Denver, 1975-83; exec. dir. Colo. Dept. of Personnel, Denver, 1983-86; treas. State of Colo., Denver, 1987—95, lt. gov., 1995—99; chmn. bd. Fischer Imaging Corp. U.S. amb. World Radio Comm. Conf., Istanbul, 1999-2000; bd. dirs. AspenBio, Inc., CancerVax Corp., A4S Security, Inc. Active Douglas County Bd. Edn., Colo., 1979-87, pres., 1983-87; trustee U. No. Colo., Greeley, 1981-87; pres. Denver Children's Mus., 1975-85; bd. dirs. Gunnison Ranchland Conservation Legacy, Colo. Conservation Trust, Progress Now, Ctr. for Women's Health Rsch. Decorated chevalier French Legion of Honor; recipient Disting. Alumna award U. Calif., Santa Barbara, 1987, Trailblazer award AAUW, 1997, Childrens Advocacy award Colo. Soc. Sch. Psychologists, 1997. Mem. Internat. Women's Forum (mem. bd. dirs. 1981-89, pres. 83-85), Women Execs. in State Govt. (bd. dirs. 1981-87, chmn. 1988), Leadership Denver Assn. (bd. dirs. 1987, named Outstanding Alumna 1985), Nat. Congress Lt. Govs., Stanford Alumni Assn. Democrat.

SCHOETTLER, JAMES ANTHONY, JR., lawyer; b. Balt., Nov. 3, 1956; s. James Anthony and Ellouise (Diggle) S.; m. Monica Gladys Solorzano, Jan. 14, 1984; children: Juliana Kathryn, Alison Louise. BA, Johns Hopkins U., 1978; MS in Fgn. Svc., Georgetown U., 1982, JD magna cum laude, 1982. Bar: D.C. 1982, Mass. 1982, U.S. Army Ct. Mil. Rev. 1983. Assoc. Dewey Ballantine, Washington, 1987—92, 1993—94, Prague, Czech Republic, 1992—93; asst. gen. counsel USEC Inc., Bethesda, Md., 1994—, acting gen. counsel, 2004—05. Capt. U.S. Army, 1983-87; col. USAR, 1987—. Mem. Bar Assn. D.C. Roman Catholic. Office: USEC Inc 6903 Rockledge Dr Bethesda MD 20817 Office Phone: 301-569-3325. Business E-Mail: schoettlerj@usec.com.

SCHOETZ, DAVID JOHN, JR., colon and rectal surgeon, educator; b. Milw., Oct. 29, 1948; s. David John and Beverly (Rogers) S.; m. Ruthanne Brennan, Mar. 25, 1972; children: Elizabeth Anne, David John III. BA, Coll. of Holy Cross, Worchester, Mass., 1970; MD, Med. Coll. Wis., Milw., 1974. Diplomate Am. Bd. Surgery, Am. Bd. Colon and Rectal Surgery. Resident in surgery Boston U. Med. Ctr., 1974-81; resident in colon/rectal surgery Lahey Clinic Med. Ctr., Burlington, Mass., 1981-82, staff colon-rectal surgeon, 1982—, chmn. dept. colon-rectal surgery, 1987—2002; prof. surgery Med. Sch. Tufts U., Boston, 1999—, chmn. dept. med. edn., 2000—; acad. dean for Tufts Lahey Clinic, 2006—. Fellow ACS (commn. on cancer 1998-2003, gov., 2004—), Am. Bd. Colon and Rectal Surgery (sr. examiner 1996-, assoc. exec. 2005-06, exec. dir. 2006-), Am. Soc. Colon and Rectal Surgeons (sec. 1999-2002, pres.-elect 2002-03, pres. 2003—04). Office: Lahey Clinic Med Ctr 41 Mall Rd Burlington MA 01803-4521

SCHOEWE, THOMAS M., retail executive; BBA in Fin., Loyola U. of Chgo., MBA. CFO, contr. Beatrice Consumer Durables, Inc.; v.p. bus. planning and analysis The Black & Decker Corp., 1986—89, v.p. fin., 1989—93, senior v.p., CFO, 1993—99; exec. v.p., CFO Wal-Mart Stores, Inc., Bentonville, Ark., 2000—. Bd. dirs. Centex Corp., 2001—. Mem.: Fin. Execs. Internat. Office: Wal-Mart Stores 702 SW 8th St Bentonville AR 72716-8611 *

SCHOFER, JOSEPH LANDY, civil engineer, educator; b. Columbus, Ohio, Feb. 19, 1941; s. August and Rose (Landy) S.; m. Nancy Levy, June 29, 1969; children: Susan Jessica, Daniel Abraham. B in engring., Yale U., 1963; MS in civil engring.-transp., Northwestern U., 1965, PhD in civil engring.-transp., 1968. Asst. instr. Yale U., New Haven, 1963-64; asst. prof. sys. engring. U. Ill., Chgo., 1967-70; assoc. prof. civil engring. Northwestern U., Evanston, Ill., 1970-73, prof., 1974—, dir. rsch. transp. ctr., 1979-97, chmn. civil and environ. engring., 1997—2002, assoc. dean for faculty affairs Robert R. McCormick Sch. of Engring. and Applied Sci., 2003—, interim dean, 2004—05. Chmn. Transp. Commn., Wilmette, 1990-98; bd. advisors Inst. Transp. Studies U. Calif.-Davis, 1998-, Transp. Rsch. Bd. Contbr. over 120 articles to profl. jours., chpts. to books on transp. planning, policy analysis, impacts, traveler response and evaluation. Recipient Wilbur S. Smith Transp. Educator of Yr., 2003. Mem. AAAS, ASCE (life), Transp. Rsch. Bd., Inst. Transp. Engrs. (Wilbur Smith Disting. Educator award, 2003), Tau Beta Pi, Sigma Xi, Chi Epsilon Office: Dept Civil Engring Northwestern U 2145 Sheridan Rd Evanston IL 60208-3109

SCHOFF, DENNIS L., lawyer; b. Apr. 17, 1959; m. Nina Schoff. BS in Fin., Ind. U., JD cum laude. Bar: Ind., Ohio, Pa. Atty. Taft, Stettinius & Hollister, Cin.; various positions Lincoln Nat. Corp., Phila., 1990—2000, v.p., assoc. gen. counsel, 2000—01, v.p., dep. gen. counsel, 2001—02, sr. v.p., gen. counsel, 2002—, mem. sr. mgmt. com. Mem.: ABA, Am. Corp. Counsel Assn., Exec. Bd. Gen. Counsel Roundtable, Ind. Bar Assn., Pa. Bar Assn., Allen County Bar Assn. Office: Lincoln Nat Corp Centre Sq West Tower 1500 Market St Ste 3900 Philadelphia PA 19102-2112 Office Phone: 215-448-1400. Office Fax: 215-448-3215. *

SCHOFIELD, ANTHONY WAYNE, lawyer; b. Farmington, N.Mex., Mar. 5, 1949; s. Aldred Edward and Margueriete (Knudsen) S.; m. Rebecca Ann Rosecrans, May 11, 1971; children: Josie, Matthew Paul, Peter Christian, Addie, Joshua James, M. Thomas, Jacob L., Daniel Z. BA, Brigham Young U., 1973, JD, 1976. Bar: Utah 1976, U.S. Dist. Ct. Utah 1976, U.S. Ct. Appeals (7th and 10th cirs.) 1977. Law clk. to hon. judge A. Sherman Christansen U.S. Dist. Ct. Utah, Salt Lake City, 1976-77; assoc. Ferenz, Bramhall, Williams & Gruskin, Agana, Guam, 1977-79; pvt. practice American Fork, Utah, 1979-80; assoc. Jardine, Linebaugh, Brown & Dunn, Salt Lake City, 1980-81; mem., dir. Ray, Quinney & Nebeker, Provo, Utah, 1981—93; judge 4th Jud. Dist. Ct., Provo, 1993—2007; mem. Kirton & McConkie, Orem, Utah, 2007—. Bishop Mormon Ch., American Fork, 1985-88; commr. American Fork City Planning Commn., 1980-85; trustee American Fork Hosp., 1984-93. Mem. Ctrl. Utah Bar Assn. (pres. 1987, 91). Office: Kirton & McConkie 518 West 800 North 204 Orem UT 84057 Home Phone: 801-756-3074; Office Phone: 801-426-2100. Personal E-mail: aschofield@kmclaw.com.

SCHOFIELD, EDMUND ACTON, JR., botanist, academic administrator, conservationist, writer; b. Worcester, Mass., Nov. 26, 1938; s. Edmund Acton and Phyllis Louise (Parslow) Schofield; m. Eileen Kathryn Carroll (div. Oct. 1972). BA in Biology, Clark U., 1962, MA in Biology, 1964; PhD in Botany, Ohio State U., 1972. Sci. editor Battelle Meml. Inst., Columbus, Ohio, 1965—67; postdoc. rsch. fellow Calif. Inst. Tech., 1972—73; ecologist Ohio Dept. Natural Resources, Columbus, 1973—76; dir. rsch. Sierra Club, San Francisco, 1976—77; staff scientist Inst. Ecology, Indpls., 1977—80; assoc. editor Horticulture Mag., Boston, 1982—85; editor Arnold Arboretum Harvard U., Boston, 1986—88; various positions Worcester, Mass., 1989—2002; dir. edn. Tower Hill Botanic Garden, Boylston, Mass., 2002—07. Plant ecologist Clark U., US Antarctic Rsch. Program Hallett and McMurdo Sta., Antarctica, 1963-64, Ohio State U., US Antarctic Rsch. Program McMurdo Sta., 1967-69, Internat. Biol. Program, Barrow and Prudhoe, Alaska, 1971, jet propulsion lab., Calif. Inst. Tech., Internat. Biol. Program, 1973. Editor: Earthcare: Global Protection of Natural Areas, 1978; assoc. editor: Horticulture mag., 1982—85; co-editor: Thoreau's World and Ours, 1993. Pres. Thoreau Country Conservation Alliance, 1992—95, Walden Forever Wild, 1993—95, Friends of Thoreau Country, 2007—; mem. Worcester Hist. Commn., Mass., 1999—2003; docent Preservation Worcester, Mass., 1999—. With USNR, 1956—62. Recipient Antarctic Svc. medal, U.S. Congress, 1972, Resident Rsch. associateship, NASA/NAS, 1972—73; summer fellowship, Nat. Endowment for Humanities, 1979. Mem.: Worcester Hist. Mus., Worcester County Poetry Assn., Friends of Thoreau Country (pres. 2007—), English Lunch Club, Boston, Worcester History Group, Worcester County Horticultural Soc., Thoreau Soc. (pres. 1990—92). Democrat. Congregationalist. Avocations: poetry, walking, reading, scholarly research. Home: 707 Main St Boylston MA 01505 Personal E-mail: edmundschofield@yahoo.com.

SCHOFIELD, JAMES ROY, computer programmer; b. Reedsburg, Wis., Aug. 16, 1953; s. G. C. Schofield and Margaret (Collies) Tverberg. BA, Carleton Coll., 1976. Programmer Brandon Applied Systems, San Francisco, 1977-78, Rand Info. Systems, San Francisco, 1979-83; systems programmer IBM, San Jose, Calif., 1983-91; programmer Office of Instnl. Rsch./U. Calif., Berkeley, 1991-94, Datis Corp., San Mateo, Calif., 1994-95, Compuware Corp., Los Gatos, Calif., 1995-96, Pacific Bell, San Ramon, Calif., 1996—2001, AT&T, San Ramon, Calif., 2002. Mem. Assn. for Computing Machinery, Commonwealth Club Calif., Phi Beta Kappa. Avocations: guitar, reading, swimming. Home: PO Box 25143 San Mateo CA 94402-5143 Office: AT&T 2600 Camino Ramon San Ramon CA 94583-5099

SCHOFIELD, REGINA BROWN, federal agency administrator; b. Natchez, Miss., Jan. 14, 1962; d. Elvia John and Velma Marie (Cameron) Brown; m. Stephen Gerard Schofield, Nov. 2, 1996. BSBA, Miss. Coll., 1983; MBA, Jackson State U., Miss., 1990. Sales rep. Philip Morris, USA, Jackson, 1983-91; spl. asst. U.S. Dept. Edn., Washington, 1991-92, White House liaison, 1992-93; mgr. environ. issues Internat. Coun. Shopping Ctrs., Alexandria, Va., 1993—98; mgr. govt. rels US Postal Svc., 1998—2001; dir., Office of Intergovernmental Affairs US Dept. HHS, 2002—05, White House liaison, 2001—05; asst. atty. gen., Office of Justice Programs US Dept. Justice, Washington, 2005—. Bd. dirs. Nat. Wetlands Coalition, 1997—99, Va. Dept. Agrl. and Consumer Svcs., Richmond, 1995—99, Va. Fedn. Rep. Women, Richmond, 1996-98, 2001-05; bd. visitors Coll. William and Mary, Williamsburg, Va., 1997—2001, The Endowment Assn. of the Coll. of William and Mary, 2004-05; mem. Commonwealth Rep. Women's Club, Alexandria, 1995, Am. Coun. Young Polit. Leaders, 1998-2005. Roman Catholic. Avocation: reading. Office: US Dept Justice 810 7th St NW Rm 6400 Washington DC 20531

SCHOFIELD, ROBERT E. (ROBERT EDWIN SCHOFIELD), historian, educator, academic administrator; b. Milford, Nebr., June 1, 1923; s. Charles Edwin and Nora May (Fullerton) S.; m. Mary-Peale Smith, June 20, 1959; 1 son, Charles Stockton Peale. AB, Princeton U., 1944; MS, U. Minn., 1948; PhD, Harvard U., 1955. Research asst. Fercleve Corp. and Clinton Labs., Oak Ridge, 1944-46; research assoc. Knolls Atomic Power Lab., Gen. Electric Co., 1948-51; asst. prof., then assoc. prof. history U. Kans., Lawrence, 1955-60; mem. faculty Case Western Res. U., Cleve., 1960-79, prof. history of sci., 1963-72, Lynn Thorndike prof. history of sci., 1972-79; prof. history Iowa State U., Ames, 1979-93, prof. emeritus, 1993—, dir. grad. program history tech. and sci., 1979-92. Mem. Inst. Advanced Study, 1967-68, 74-75; Sigma Xi nat. lectr., 1978-80 Author: The Lunar Society of Birmingham, 1963, Scientific Autobiography of Joseph Priestley: Selected Scientific Correspondence, 1966, Mechanism and Materialism: British Natural Philosophy in an Age of Reason, 1970, (with D.G.C. Allan) Stephen Hales: Scientist and Philanthropist, 1980, The Enlightenment of Joseph Priestley: A Study of His Life and Work from 1733 to 1773, 1997, The Enlightened Joseph Priestley: A Study of His Life and Work from 1773 to 1804, 2004. Served with AUS, 1945-46. Fulbright fellow, 1953-54; Guggenheim fellow, 1959-60, 67-68 Fellow Am. Phys. Soc., Royal Soc. Arts; mem. History of Sci. Soc., Soc. History Tech., Midwest Junto History of Sci., Am. Soc. 18th Century Studies, Acad. Internat. d'Histoire des Scis. (corr.)

SCHOGGEN, PHIL H(OWARD), psychologist, educator; b. Tulsa, Aug. 28, 1923; s. Walter B. and Emma F. (Alexander) S.; m. Maxine F. Spoor, June 28, 1944; children: Leida, Christopher, Ann, Susan. AB in Psychology, Park Coll., 1946; MS, U. Kans., Lawrence, 1951, PhD in Psychology, 1954. Asst. prof. psychology U. Oreg., 1957-62, asso. prof., 1962-66; prof., chmn. dept. psychology George Peabody Coll., 1966-75; prof. York U., Toronto, Ont., Can., 1975-77; prof. human devel. and family studies N.Y. State Coll. Human Ecology, Cornell U., 1977-90, prof. emeritus, 1990—, chmn. dept., 1977-82. Author: (with R. G. Barker) Qualities of Community Life, 1973; Behavior Settings: A Revision and Extension of Roger G. Barker's Ecological Psychology, 1989. Served with USNR, 1944-46, 50-51. Mem. APA. Home: 121 Vossland Dr Nashville TN 37205-3617 Personal E-mail: schoggph@comcast.net.

SCHOHL, JOSEPH, lawyer; BA, U. Ill.; JD, Columbia Law Sch.; MBA, Northwestern U. Kellogg Bus. Sch., 2004. Bar: NY, Ill. Atty. Milbank, Tweed, Hadley & McCloy, NYC, Sidley Austin Brown & Wood, NYC; corp. counsel Corp. Sec. Group Baxter Healthcare Corp., Chgo., 1998—2001, corp. counsel Transfusion Therapies Bus., 2001—03, corp. counsel BioScience Bus. and Transactions Group, 2004; v.p., gen. counsel, corp. sec. DaVita, El Segundo, Calif., 2004—. Office: DaVita 601 Hawaii St El Segundo CA 90245

SCHOLEFIELD, PETER GORDON, health facility administrator; b. Newport, Wales, June 26, 1925; emigrated to Can., 1947, naturalized, 1952; s. Tom and Margaret (Bithell) S.; m. Erna Mary Cooper, Sept. 29, 1951; children: David, John, Paul. B.Sc., U. Wales, 1944, M.Sc., 1946, D.Sc., 1960; PhD, McGill U., Montreal, Que., Can., 1949. From research fellow to prof. biochemistry McGill U., 1949-65, dir. cancer research unit, 1965-69; asst. exec. dir. Nat. Cancer Inst. Can., Toronto, 1969-80, exec. dir., 1980-91, spl. adviser to chief exec. officer, 1991-92; dir. grants and awards Alta. Heritage Found. for Med. Rsch., Edmonton, 1992-94; coord. acad. affairs Samuel Lunenfeld Rsch. Inst. Mt. Sinai Hosp., Toronto, 1994-99. Chair rsch. policy com., bd. dirs. Alzheimer Soc. of Can., 1994-2000; mem. health adv. com. Alta. Heritage Found. Med. Rsch, 1994-99; bd. dirs. Ont. Neurotrauma Found., 1999-2004, sec., 2003-04, chmn. rsch. com., 2003-04; mem. adv. bd. Inst. Neuroscis. Mental Health and Addiction, Can. Insts. Health Rsch., 2001-04, mem. standing com. on grants and awards competitions, 2005-07, mem. sub-com. on programs and peer rev., 2007-; chair Can. Tobacco Control Rsch. Initiative, 2007-. Home: 2010 Islington Ave # 1503 Etobicoke ON Canada M9P 3S8 Personal E-mail: peter.scholefield@rogers.com.

SCHOLER, SUE WYANT, retired state legislator; b. Topeka, Oct. 20, 1936; d. Zint Elwin and Virginia Louise (Achenbach) Wyant; m. Charles Frey Scholer, Jan. 27, 1957; children: Elizabeth Scholer Truelove, Charles W., Virginia M. Scholer McCal. Student, Kans. State U., 1954-56. Draftsman The Farm Clinic, West Lafayette, Ind., 1978—79; assessor Wabash Twp., West Lafayette, 1979-84; commr. Tippecanoe County, Lafayette, Ind., 1984-90; state rep. Dist. 26 Ind. Statehouse, Indpls., 1990—2004, ret., 2004; legis. cons. Gov.'s Office, 2007. Asst. minority whip, 1992-94, Rep. whip, 1994-2000, asst. Rep. leader, 2001—04; mem. Tippecanoe County Area Plan Commn., 1984-90; chmn. Midwestern legis. conf. CSG, 1998. Bd. dirs. Crisis Ctr., Lafayette, 1984-89, Tippecanoe Arts Fedn., 1990-99, United Way, Lafayette, 1990-93; mem. Lafayette Conv. and Visitors Bur., 1988-90. Recipient Salute to Women Govt. and Politics award, 1986, United Sr. Action award, Outstanding Legislator award, 1993, Small Bus. Champion award, 1995, Ind. Libr. Fedn. Legislator award, 1995, Disting. Legislator award Nat. Alliance for Mentally Ill, 1997, 2003, West Ctrl. Ind. Advocate award, 2003, Friend of Cmty. Action award, 1999, Disting. Pub. Svc. award Am. Legion, 2004, Family Svcs. Advocacy award Family Svcs., 2004, Sagamore of the Wabash, 2004, Order of the Griffin, Purdue U., 2004. Mem. Ind. Assn. County Commrs. (treas. 1990), Assn. Ind. Counties (legis. com. 1988-90), Greater Lafayette C. of C. (ex-officio bd. 1984-90), LWV, P.E.O., Purdue Women's Club (past treas.), Kappa Kappa Kappa (past pres. Epsilon chpt.)., Delta Delta Delta (past pres. alumnae, house corp. treas.). Republican. Presbyterian. Avocations: golf, needlecrafts, reading. Home: 807 Essex St West Lafayette IN 47906-1534

SCHOLES, EDISON EARL, military officer; b. McCaysville, Ga., Aug. 16, 1939; s. Alvin L. and Marie (Plemmons) S.; m. Elva E. Bussey, June 4, 1961; children: Juana Kimberly Scholes, Tracy Michele Scholes Heller, Michael Lee. BS in Physics cum laude, No. Ga. Coll., 1961; MS in Ops. Rsch., Naval Postgrad. Sch., 1970; postgrad., Army War Coll., 1980, Harvard Def. Policy Seminar, 1991. Commd. 2d lt. U.S. Army, 1961, advanced through grades to maj. gen., 1991; comdr. A Detachment, 10th Spl. Forces Group U.S. ArmyEurope, 1963-66; comdr. Co. D, 2d Bn.(Abn.), 8th Cav., 1st Cav. Divsn. U.S. Army, Republic of Vietnam, 1967-68, sr. adv. I Corps. Ranger Commd. Vietnam, 1970—71, comdr. 1st Bn., 23d Inf., 2d Inf. Divsn. Republic of Korea, 1976-77, comdr. 2d Tng. Bn., Sch. Brigade, U.S. Army Inf. Sch. Ft. Benning, Ga., 1978-79, comdr. 1st Inf. Tng. Brigade, U.S. Army Infantry Tng. Ctr., 1983-85, dep. commanding gen. chief of staff 3d U.S. Army/U.S. Army Cen. Command Ft. McPherson, Ga., 1986-88, asst. divsn. comdr. 82d Airborne Divsn. Ft. Bragg, NC, 1988-89, chief of staff XVIII Airborne Corps, 1989-90, chief of staff joint task force-south, Op. Just Cause, 1989-90, dep. commanding gen. XVIII Airborne Corps, Operation Desert Shield/Desert Storm Saudi Arabia, Iraq, 1990-91, dep. commanding gen. XVIII Airborne Corps Ft. Bragg, 1991-93; dep. comdr. Allied Land Forces, S.E. Europe NATO, 1993-95; program gen. mgr. Saudi Arabia N.G. Modernization Program, Vinnell Arabia, 1996—2002; pvt. contractor numerous countries, 2002—. Decorated Dept. Def. Disting. Svc. medal, Army Disting. Svc. medal with oak leaf cluster, Silver Star, Legion of Merit with oak leaf cluster, Bronze Star with V device and 4 oak leaf clusters, Purple Heart with oak leaf cluster, 6 Air medals, Army Commendation medal with V device and oak leaf cluster, Armed Forces Expeditionary medal, Combat Infantryman badge, Expert Infantry badge; Cross of Gallantry with Silver and Bronze Stars and Palm (Republic of Vietnam); numerous other domestic and fgn. awards; inducted into North Ga.'s Coll. and State U. Hall of Fame. Mem. 82d Airborne Divsn. Assn., Spl. Forces Assn., U.S. Army Ranger Assn., Spl. Ops. Assn. (Ranger Hall of Fame). Baptist. Avocations: reading, camping, fishing. Home Phone: 850-897-9669. Personal E-mail: escholes@cox.net.

SCHOLES, MYRON S., financier, former law and finance educator; b. Timmins, Ont., Can., July 1, 1941; BA, McMaster U., 1959—62, MBA, 1962—64; PhD in finance, U. Chgo., 1964—69; D (hon.), U. Paris-Dauphine, 1989, McMaster U., 1990, U. Leuven, 1998. Rsch. assoc., Ctr. for Math. Studies in Bus. and Econs. U. Chgo., 1966—67, instr. in fin., grad. sch. bus., 1967—68, assoc. prof., 1973—74, prof., 1975—79, dir., Ctr. for Rsch. in Security Prices, 1975—81, Edward Eagle Brown prof. fin., 1979—82; asst. prof. in fin. MIT Mgmt. Sch., Cambridge, 1968—72, assoc. prof., 1972—73; prof. law Stanford U., Calif., 1983—96, Frank E. Buck prof. Grad. Sch. Bus., 1983—96, sr. rsch. fellow, Hoover Instn., 1988—96, Frank E. Buck prof. emeritus fin., 1996—; mng. dir., sr. advisor Salomon Bros., 1990—93; prin. Long-Term Capital Mgmt., Greenwich, Conn., 1994—98; chmn. Oak Hill Platinum Ptnrs., Rye Brook, NY, 1999—2005; mng. ptnr. Oak Hill Capital Mgmt., 1999—2005. Bd. trustees Math. Scis. Rsch. Inst.; bd. dirs. Chgo. Mercantile Exchange, 2000—, chmn. Competitive Markets Adv. Coun., 2004—; bd. dirs. Chgo. Mercantile Exchange Holdings, 2001—, Intelligent Markets, Am Century, FEP/Constellation, UNext Inc., Salomon Swapco Inc. Contbr. articles to profl. jours. Recipient Nobel Prize for econ. scis., 1997. Mem.: Am. Fin. Assn. (v.p. 1989, pres. 1990), Econometrics Soc. Office: Arbor Investors 2775 Sand Hill Rd Ste 220 Menlo Park CA 94025-7019 Address: Oak Hill Platinum Ptnrs Reckson Exec Park 1100 King St Bldg 4 Rye Brook NY 10573 E-mail: mscholes@pacbell.net. *

SCHOLLANDER, WENDELL, III, lawyer; b. East Ridge, Tenn., Oct. 15, 1974; BA, U. N.C., Chapel Hill, 1997; JD, Wake Forest Law Sch., Winston-Salem, NC, 2001. Missionary Presbyn. Ch., Guatemala, 1998; pvt. practice Winston-Salem, NC, 2001—. Co-author: Forgotten Elegance, 2001, Small Business Owner's Guide to Bankruptcy, 2002. Scoutmaster Boy Scouts of Am., Winston-Salem, 2002—04; active Forsyth Soil and Water Commn., 2004—, vice chmn., 2006—. Recipient Point of Light award, Pres. George Bush, 1992, Chevron Conservation award, Chevron Award Program, 1992, Take Pride in Am. award, Dept. of Interior, 1991, 1992. Mem.: NC Bar Assn. (bankruptcy sect. 2001—, sect. coun. 2006—, young lawyers sect.), SAR (awards chair 2002—). Office: Schollander 2000 W 1st St Ste 308 Winston Salem NC 27104 Business E-Mail: schollanderlaw@bellsouth.net.

SCHOLLANDER, WENDELL LESLIE, JR., lawyer; b. Ocala, Fla., May 17, 1943; m. Jayn Cochran; 1 child, Wendell Leslie III. BS, U. Pa., 1966, MBA, 1968; postgrad., Stetson U., 1969-70; JD, Duke U., 1972. Bar: NC 1977, Tenn. 1972, Fla. 1987. With Container Corp. Am., Fernandina, Fla., 1968-69; assoc. Miller, Martin, Chattanooga, 1972-75; asst. counsel R.J. Reynolds Industries, Inc., 1975-78, assoc. counsel, 1978-79, sr. assoc. counsel, 1979-82, sr. counsel, 1982-85; gen. counsel RJR Archer, Inc., Winston-Salem, NC, 1979-85; of counsel Finger, Parker & Avram, Winston-Salem, 1985-87; ptnr. Schollander, Winston-Salem, 1987—. Gen. counsel Splty. Tobacco Coun., 1985-87. Mem. ABA, NC Bar Assn., Forsyth County Bar Assn., Mensa, SAR, Phi Delta Phi, Kappa Sigma. Presbyterian. Office: 2000 W 1st St Ste 308 Winston Salem NC 27104-4225 Office Phone: 336-727-0900.

SCHOLLY, EDWIN, chef; b. South Africa; Master Chef Germany. Corp. chef Ritz-Carlton, Kuala Lumpur, Malaysia; adv., cons. German Embassy, Boston; exec. chef Ivana, Trump yacht; tchr. Scottsdale Culinary Inst.,

Ariz., chef instr.; top chef Tucson Convention Ctr., Ariz., master chef; chef instr. Pima Cmty. Coll., Tucson. Mem. German nat. culinary team Internat. Culinary Olympics, 1995—97. Recipient bronze medal, Internat. Kochkunst Ausstellung, 2004. Achievements include winning 6 gold, 5 silver, 3 bronze medals in culinary arts; cooking for celebrities such as Madonna, Bruce Springsteen, Neil Diamond, and Garth Brooks. Office: Tucson Convention Ctr 260 S Church Ave Tucson AZ 85701 Business E-Mail: masterchefscholly@masterchefscholly.com. *

SCHOLSKY, MARTIN JOSEPH, retired priest; b. Stafford Spring, Conn., Jan. 16, 1930; s. Sigmund Felix and Mary Magdalen (Wysocki) S. BA, St. John's Sem., 1952, MA in History, 1956; MA in Classical Greek, Cath. U. of Am., 1966. Ordained priest Roman Cath. Ch., 1956. Asst. pastor St. Peter's Ch., Hartford, Conn., 1956-61; prin. St. Peter's Sch., Hartford, 1956-58; instr. St. Thomas Sem., Bloomfield, Conn., 1961-67, admissions dir., 1965-67; vocations dir. Archdiocese of Hartford, 1967-78; chaplain Newington (Conn.) Children's Hosp., 1961-78; weekend asst. St. Mary's Ch., Newington, 1961-78; pastor St. Bartholomew Ch., Manchester, Conn., 1978-90; dean Manchester Deanery, 1989-91; spiritual dir. St. Thomas Aquinas HS, New Britain, Conn., 1991—92; pastor St. Mary's Ch., East Hartford, Conn., 1992—2005. Weekend asst. St. Francis of Assis Ch., South Windsor, Conn., 1991-92; instr. Holy Apostle's Sem. & Coll., Cromwell, Conn., 1988-94. Contbr. articles to profl. jours. Home: 36 Griswold St Manchester CT 06040-3928 Personal E-mail: mjscholsky@aol.com. *Conscience is not our own personal feelings about things; rather, it is our innate awareness of the rightness and wrongness of our deeds as God sees them, an awareness, often denied, that still remains the measure by which God will ultimately judge us all.*

SCHOLTEN, GARY P., finance company executive; Grad., U. No. Iowa, 1980. From asst. planning analyst to v.p. retail info. scs. Prin. Fin. Group, Des Moines, 1980—2002, sr. v.p., CIO, 2002—. Fellow: Life Office Mgmt. Inst. (chmn. ind. product sys. com.). Office: Prin Fin Group 711 High St Des Moines IA 50392

SCHOLTEN, MENNO NICO, banking consultant; b. Assen, Drenthe, Netherlands, June 18, 1943; arrived in U.S., 1949; s. Nico Menno and Hennie (Nienhuis) S.; m. Susan Sumnar, Aug. 11, 1973; 1 child, Paul Menno. BArch., U. Calif., Berkeley, 1967; MBA, DePaul U., 1980. Registered architect. Architect various, including Skidmore, Owings & Merrill, others, Chgo., 1968-78, Knight Architects, Engrs. and Planners, Chgo., 1978-81, 1989-92; asst. v.p. constrn. lending adminstr. First Nat. Bank of Chgo., 1981-85; v.p. real estate group First Tex. Savs., Dallas, 1985-87; mgr. constrn. lending Household Internat. (Household Bank), Prospect Heights, Ill., 1992-94; pres. The Mesu Group, Ltd., Evanston, Ill., 1995—. Bd. dirs. Global Med. Relief Program. Patentee chair design, 1979. Bd. dirs. Global Med. Relief Program. Recipient award of merit Chgo. Assn. of Commerce and Industry and Internat. Trade Club of Chgo., 1979. Mem. AIA (Chgo. chpt.), Am. Guild Organists (bd. dirs., treas. 1991-99), Calif. Scholarship Fedn. (life mem.), Inst. Mgmt. Cons., Rotary Internat., Delta Mu Delta. Avocations: tennis, skiing. Home: 3521 Central St Evanston IL 60201-4915

SCHOLTZ, ROBERT ARNO, electrical engineering educator; b. Lebanon, Ohio, Jan. 26, 1936; s. William Paul and Erna Johanna (Weigel) Scholtz; m. Laura Elizabeth McKeon, June 16, 1962; children: Michael William, Paul Andrew. BSEE, U. Cin., 1958; MSEE, U. So. Calif., 1960; PhD, Stanford U., 1964. Co-op student Sheffield Corp., Dayton, Ohio, 1953-58; MS and PHD fellow Hughes Aircraft Co., Culver City, Calif., 1958-63, sr. staff engr., 1963-78; prof. U. So. Calif., LA, 1963—. Vis. prof. U. Hawaii, 1969, 78; cons. LinCom Corp., L.A., 1975-81, Axiomatix Inc., L.A., 1980-86, JPL, Pasadena, 1985, Tech. Group, 1987-89, TRW, 1989, Pulson Comm., 1992-93, Colley-Godward, Palo Alto, 1994-97, Time Domain Corp., 2000-01. Co-author: Spread Spectrum Comm., 3 vols., 1984, Spread Spectrum Communications Handbook, 1994, Basic Concepts in Information Theory and Coding, 1994; contbr. articles to profl. jours. Pres. South Bay Cmty. Concert Orgn., Redondo Beach, Calif., 1975—79. Fellow: IEEE (bd. govs. info. theory group 1981—86, bd. govs. communication soc. 1981—83, chmn. fin. com. NTC 1977, program chmn. ISIT 1981, Leonard G. Abraham award 1983, Donald G. Fink award 1984, Sr. Paper award Signal Processing Soc. 1992, Fred Ellersick Paper award Com. Soc. 1997, Mil. Coms. Conf. award 2001, S.A. Shelkunoff prize Antennas and Propagation Soc. 2003, Eric E. Sumner award 2006). Office: U So Calif Comm Scis Inst Dept Elec Engring Los Angeles CA 90089-2565 E-mail: scholtz@usc.edu.

SCHOLZ, PETER M., surgeon, director; MD, U. Basel, Switzerland, 1970. Diplomate Am. Bd. Surgery, 1983, Am. Bd. Thoracic Surgery, 1985. Intern in Surgery Duke U. Med. Ctr., Durham, NC, 1974—75, resident gen. and thoracic surgery, 1975—83; physician divsn. thoracic surgery Robert Wood Johnson U. Med. Group, New Brunswick, NJ, 1983—, chief divsn. cardiovasc. surgery, 2005—. Office: Clin Acad Bldg Ste 4100 125 Paterson St New Brunswick NJ 08901-1977 Office Phone: 732-235-7642.

SCHONBERG, ALAN ROBERT, personnel director; b. NYC, Oct. 23, 1928; s. Julius and Evelyn (Guzik) S.; m. Carole May Kreisman, Dec. 27, 1975; children: William, Evelyn, David, Jeffrey. Nat. sales mgr. Majestic Specialties, Inc., Cleve., 1953-63; pres. Internat. Personnel, Inc., Cleve., 1963-65; chmn. Mgmt. Recruiters Internat., Inc., Cleve., 1965-98, 1998—2000, chmn. emeritus, 2001—. Pres., bd. dirs. Jewish Vocat. Service, Cleve., 1983—; trustees Mt. Sinai Hosp. (now Mt. Sinai Found.), Cleve., bd. dirs. Cleve. Jewish News; gen. chmn. Welfare Fund Campaign; trustee Am. Jewish Commn., Mt. Sinai Med. Ctr., Hebrew Immigrant Aid Soc. Named one of Cleve.'s 86 Most Interesting People, Cleve. Mag., 1986, Man of Yr. local chpt. Orgn. through Rehab. and Tng., 1996, Entrepreneur of Yr. Inc. Mag., Merrill Lynch Ernst & Young, 1995; recipient Human Rels. award Cleve. chpt. Am. Jewish Com., 1998. Mem. Internat. Franchise Assn., Internat. Confederation Pvt. Employment Agys. Assns., Am. Mgmt. Assn., Assn. Human Resource Cons. (chmn. 1980—), Org. for Rehab. and Training (ORT), Assn. Am.-Israel C. of C. (pres.), Ohio Israel C. of C. (co-chmn.), Jewish Family Svcs. Assn. (v.p., pres. 1998-2002). Avocation: travel.

SCHONBRUN, MICHAEL K., senior housing developer and operator; b. NYC, Jan. 26, 1948; s. Arnold Laurance and Madeline (Courland) Schonbrun; m. Michelle I. Fredson, June 6, 1971 (div. Dec. 1998); 1 child, Ethan F.; m. Susan E. Juroe, Feb. 17, 2001; children: Adam J., Theodore C. BA, Yale U., 1969; JD, U. Pa., 1973. Bar: Ohio 1973, Colo. 1975. Asst. to gov. Ohio Gov.'s Office, Columbus, 1973—74, Colo. Gov.'s Office, Denver, 1974—75; asst. dir. Colo. Dept. Health, Denver, 1976—78; pres., CEO Nat. Jewish Hosp., Denver, 1979—91; sr. v.p. Blue Cross/Blue Shield of Colo., Denver, 1991—93; exec. v.p. Vitas Healthcare Corp. Inc., Miami, Fla., 1994—95; pres. Schonbrun & assocs., Boulder, Colo., 1995—97; founder, pres., CEO Balfour Sr. Care, Boulder, 1997—. Chmn. Young Pres.'s Orgn. Healthcare Focus Forum, Dallas, 1999—2001; bd. dirs. Colo. Assn. Housing and Svcs., Denver, United Bank of Denver, 1985—91; mem. leadership coun. Assisted Living Fedn. Am., Washington, 1999—. Contbr. articles to profl. jours. Chmn. bd. dirs. Rocky Mountain Alzheimers Assn., 2002, Denver Met. Air Quality Coun., 1985—89, Internat. Med. Corp., LA, 1996—2000; mem. Colo. 2002 Winter Olympic Games Com., 1988—90. Democrat. Jewish. Avocation: travel, running, tennis, reading fiction, movies. Home: 10200 Niwot Rd Longmont CO 80504 Office: Balfour Sr Care 1331 Hecla Dr Louisville CO 80027-2325

SCHÖNEMANN, PETER HANS, psychologist, educator; b. Pethau, Germany, July 15, 1929; arrived in U.S., 1960, naturalized, 2003; s. Max Paul Franz and Hertha Anna (Kahle) S.; m. Roberta Dianne Federbush, Jan. 29, 1962; children: Raoul Dieter, Nicole Deborah. Vordiplom in Psychologie, U. Munich, 1956; Hauptdiplom in Psychologie, U. Goettingen, 1959; PhD, U. Ill., 1964. Thurstone postdoctoral fellow U. N.C., 1965-66; asst. prof., then assoc. prof. Ohio State U., 1966-69; postdoctoral fellow Ednl. Testing Service, Princeton, NJ, 1967-68; vis. prof. Technische Hochschule, Aachen, Fed. Republic Germany, 1981; mem. faculty Purdue U., 1969—, prof. psychology, 1971-2001, emeritus, 2001—. Vis. prof. Univs. Munich, Bielefeld and Braunschweig, 1984-85, Nat. Taiwan U., 1992, 96, 97. Author papers in field. Recipient Found. for the Advancement of Outstanding Scholarship award, Taiwan, 1996. Office: Dept Psychol Scis Purdue U Lafayette IN 47907 Home Phone: 765-583-4807. Personal E-mail: phs@psych.purdue.edu.

SCHONFELD, GUSTAV, medical educator, researcher, administrator; b. Mukacevo, Ukraine, May 8, 1934; arrived in US, 1946, naturalized, 1951; s. Alexander Schonfeld and Helena Gottesmann; m. Miriam Steinberg, May 28, 1961; children: Joshua Lawrence, Julia Elizabeth, Jeremy David. BA, Washington U., St. Louis, 1956, MD, 1960. Diplomate Am. Bd. Internal Medicine. Intern. Bellevue Med. Ctr. NYU, 1960—61, resident in internal medicine, 1961—63; chief resident in internal medicine Jewish Hosp., St. Louis, 1963—64; from NIH trainee in endocrinology & metabolism to Kountz prof. medicine Washington U., St. Louis, 1964—96, Busch prof., chair medicine, 1996—99, Samuel E. Schechter prof. medicine, 2002—; rsch. assoc. Cochran VA Hosp., St. Louis, 1965—66, clin. investigator, 1968—70, cons. in internal medicine, 1972—; rsch. flight med. officer USAF Sch. Aerospace Medicine, Brooks AFB, Tex., 1966—68; from asst. physician to physician Barnes Hosp., St. Louis, 1972—96; physician-in-chief Barnes Jewish Hosp., St. Louis, 1996—99; clin. instr. medicine Harvard U. Med. Sch., Boston, 1970—72; assoc. prof. metabolism and human nutrition, asst. dir. Clin. Rsch. Ctr. MIT, Cambridge, 1970—72. Mem. rsch. com. Mo. Heart Assn., 1978-80; expert witness working group on atherosclerosis Nat. Heart, Lung and Blood Inst., 1979, Nat. Diabetes Adv. Bd., 1979; mem. endocrinologic and metabolic drugs adv. com. USPHS, FDA, 1982-86; mem. nutrition study sect. NIH, 1984-88, spl. reviewer metabolism study sect.; mem. adult treatment guidelines panel Nat. Cholesterol Edn. Program, 1986; mem. Consensus Devel. Conf. on Triglyceride, High Density Lipoprotein and Coronary Heart Disease, 1992; cons. Am. Egg Bd., Am. Dairy Bd., Inst. Shortening and Edible Oils, Ciba-Geigy, Sandoz, Fournier, Parke-Davis, Bristol-Meyers Squibb, Monsanto/Searle; adj. prof. medicine Columbia U. Coll. Physicians & Surgeons, 2006. Past editor: Atherosclerosis, past mem. editl. bd.: Jour. Clin. Endocrinology and Metabolism, Jour. Clin. Investigation, Jour. Lipid Rsch., past assoc. editor: Circulation. Recipient Berg Prize in Microbiology, 1957, 58, Faculty/Alumni award Washington U., 1995; named Physician honoree Am. Heart Assn. Mo. Affiliate, 1995; grantee MERIT status NIH, Vascular Biology Spl. Merit award, Am. Heart Assn. Fellow ACP, AAAS; mem. Assn. Am. Physicians, Am. Soc. for Clin. Investigation, Am. Physiol. Soc., Am. Soc. Biol. Chemists, Am. Inst. Nutrition, Am. Diabetes Assn., Am. Heart Assn. (program com. coun. on atherosclerosis 1977-80, 86-88, nutrition com. 1980-84, pathology rsch. com. 1980-83, budget com. 1991, awards com. 1992, exec. com. 2001—, Spl. Vascular Biology award 2005, G.L. Duff lecture award, 2006), Endocrine Soc., Alpha Omega Alpha. Democrat. Jewish. Office: Washington U Sch Medicine Box 8046 660 S Euclid Ave Saint Louis MO 63110-1010 Office Phone: 314-362-8060. Business E-Mail: gschonfe@wustl.edu.

SCHONFELD, WILLIAM ROST, political science professor; b. NYC, Aug. 28, 1942; s. William A. and Louise R. (Rost) S.; m. Elena Beortegui, Jan. 23, 1964; children: Natalie Beortegui, Elizabeth Lynn Beortegui. Student, Cornell U., 1960-61; BA cum laude with honors, NYU, 1964; MA, Princeton U., 1968, PhD, 1970. Research asst. Princeton U., 1966-69, research assoc., 1969-70, vis. lectr., 1970; asst. prof. polit. sci. U. Calif.-Irvine, 1970-75, assoc. prof., 1975-81, prof., 1981—, dean Sch. Social Scis., 1982—2002; sr. lectr. Fond. Nat. de Sci. Politique, Paris, 1973-74; researcher Centre de Sociologie des Organisations, Paris, 1976-78; dir. Ctr. for Study of Democracy, 2004—. Author: Youth and Authority in France, 1971, Obedience and Revolt, 1976, Ethnographie du PS et du RPR, 1985 Recipient Disting. Teaching award U. Calif.-Irvine, 1984, Disting. Faculty Lectureship award for tchg., 1998, Daniel G. Aldrich Disting. Univ. Svc. award, 2000-01; Fulbright fellow Bordeaux, France, 1964-65; Danforth grad. fellow, 1964-69; Fulbright sr. lectr. Paris, 1973-74; NSF-CNRS Exchange of Scientists fellow Paris, 1976-78; Ford Found. grantee France, Spain, 1978-79; finalist Prof. Yr. Council for Advancement and Support of Edn., 1984; Lauds & Laurels Extraordinarious award, U. Calif.-Irvine Alumni Assn., 2002. Mem. Am. Polit. Sci. Assn., Assoc. Francaise de Sci. Pol., Phi Beta Kappa. Office: U Calif Sch Social Scis Irvine CA 92697-0001 Office Phone: 949-824-8801. Personal E-mail: wrschonf@uci.edu.

SCHONHORN, HAROLD, chemist, researcher; b. NYC, Apr. 2, 1928; s. Benjamin and Dorothy (Gitlin) S.; m. Esther Matesky, Jan. 17, 1954; children: Deborah, Jeremy. BS, Bklyn. Coll., 1950; PhD, N.Y. Polytech. U., 1959. Mem. tech. staff Bell Labs., Murray Hill, NJ, 1961-84; v.p. R & D Polyken Tech. div. Kendall Co., Lexington, Mass., 1984-93; pres. Schonhorn Consultants, 1993—. Contbr. over 100 articles to profl. jours. Pres. B'nai B'rith Lodge, Summit, N.J., 1970. With U.S. Army, 1953-55, Korea. Mem. Am. Chem. Soc. Achievements include 15 patents. Office Phone: 617-738-4742. Office Fax: 617-738-4742. Personal E-mail: HaroldSchonhorn@cs.com.

SCHOO, BERNARD JOHN, surgeon; b. Louisville, July 20, 1922; s. Joseph A. and Catherine Schoo; m. Catherine Filburn, Sept. 16, 1944; children: Virginia, Michael, Ann, Patrick, Kenneth, Margaret. BS, Notre Dame U., South Bend, Ind., 1944; MD, U. Louisville, 1946. Intern St. Joseph Infirmary, Louisville, 1946—47, resident, 1949—50, U. Louisville, 1950—54; ret., 1990. Assoc. prof. surgery, Louisville, 1960—; pres. of staff St. Joseph Infirmary, 1977; cheif surgery Humana Audubon Hosp., Louisville, 1974—78. Lt. (jg) USN, 1947—49. Fellow, U. Louisville, 1954—56. Mem.: AMA, Am. Coll. Surgery, Audubon Country Club. Avocations: model railroading, kite flying, golf, travel, motorcycling. Home: 616 Cressbrook Dr Louisville KY 40206

SCHOOLAR, JOSEPH CLAYTON, psychiatrist, pharmacologist, educator; b. Marks, Miss., Feb. 28, 1928; s. Adrian Taylor and Leah (Covington) S.; m. Betty Jane Peck, Nov. 2, 1960; children: Jonathan Covington, Cynthia Jane, Geoffrey Michael, Catherine Elizabeth, Adrian Carson AB, U. Tenn., Knoxville, 1950, MS, 1952; PhD, U. Chgo., 1957, MD, 1960. Diplomate Am. Bd. Psychiatry and Neurology. Chief drug abuse research TRIMS, Houston, 1966-72; assoc. prof. U. Tex. Grad. Sch. Biomed. Scis., Houston, 1968—; prof. psychiatry Baylor Coll. Medicine, Houston, 1975—, prof. pharmacology, 1974—2002, prof. emeritus pharmacology and psychiatry, 2003—, chief div. psychopharmacology, 1973-82; dir. Tex. Research Inst. Mental Scis., Houston, 1972-85. Mem. Nat. Bd. Med. Examiners' Task Force on Drug Abuse and Alcoholism, 1982-; mem. Drug Abuse Adv. Com., FDA, Washington, 1983-85, chmn., 1984; chmn. profl. needs planning task force Nat. Inst. Drug Abuse, Washington, 1977-Editor: Current Issues in Adolescent Psychiatry, 1973, Research and the Psychiatric Patient, 1975, The Kinetics of Psychiatric Drugs, 1979, Serotonin in Biological Psychiatry - Advances in Biochemical Psychopharmacology, 1982. Cons. Parents' League Houston, 1972-74; mem. coordinating com. Citizens Mental Health Service, Houston, 1976; mem. acad. com. for study of violence Houston Police Dept., 1979; bd. dirs. Can-Do-It, Houston, 1982-. Served with U.S. Army, 1945-47, to 1st lt. USAR, 1950-62. Recipient Eugen Kahn award Baylor Coll. Medicine, Houston, 1964, Alumni award for Disting. Svc., U. Chgo., 1995, Psychiat. Excellence award Tex. Soc. Psychiat. Physicians, 1995. Fellow Am. Psychiat. Assn. (disting. life), Am. Coll. Psychiatrists, Am. Coll. Neuropsychopharmacology, Collegium Internationale NeuroPsychopharmacologicum, Am. Soc. Pharmacology and Exptl. Therapeutics. Episcopalian. Home: 1111 Hermann Dr Unit 17E Houston TX 77004-6930 Office: Baylor Coll Medicine PO Box 66575 Houston TX 77266-6575 Home Phone: 713-523-6979; Office Phone: 713-524-9700. E-mail: jschoolar@pol.net.

SCHOOLS, SCOTT N., prosecutor; b. Feb. 26, 1962; Degree in Math., Duke U.; JD, U. Tex. Sch. Law. Clk. US Dist. Ct., 1987—89; asst. US atty. dist SC US Dept. Justice, 1989—92, 1997—2001, interim US atty. dist. SC, 2001, 1st asst. US atty. dist. SC, 2001—05, gen. counsel, Exec. Office for US Attorneys, 2005—07, interim US atty. (no. dist.) Calif. San Francisco, 2007—; lawyer pvt. practice, Charleston, SC, 1992—97. Office: US Atty's Office 450 Golden Gate Ave Box 36055 San Francisco CA 94102 Office Phone: 415-436-7200. Office Fax: 415-436-7234. *

SCHOOMAKER, ERIC B., career military officer; b. Detroit, Sept. 15, 1948; married; 3 children. BS Commd. a 2nd Lt. as a Disting. Mil. Grad., U. Mich., Ann Arbor; MD, U. Mich. Med. Sch., 1975, PhD in Human Genetics, 1979. Cert. Am. Bd. Internal Medicine, 1979, Am. Bd. Hematology, 1982. Intern, internal medicine Duke Univ. Med. Ctr., Durham, NC, 1976—78, fellow, hematology, 1979; rsch. hematologist Walter Reed Army Inst. Rsch., 1979—82; asst. chief, program dir., dept. medicine Walter Reed Army Med. Ctr., Washington, 1982—88, acting comdr., 2007—; med. cons. to hdqs. 7th Med. Command, Heidelberg, Germany, 1988—90; dep. comdr., clin. services Landstuhl Army Regional Med. Ctr., Germany, 1990—92; chief, program dir., dept. medicine, dir. primary care Madigan Army Med. Ctr., Tacoma, 1992—95; dir. med. edn. for the Office of the Surgeon Gen. Hdqs. US Army Med. Command (USAMEDCOM), Washington, DC and Fort Sam, Houston, Tex., 1995—97, dir. clin. ops., 1997; comdr. US Army Med. Dept. Activity (USA MEDDAC)-(Evans Army Cmty. Hosp.), Fort Carson, Colo., 1997—99; attended US Army War Coll., Carlisle Barracks, Pa., 1999—2000; command surgeon US Army Forces Command (FORSCOM), 2000—01; comdr. 30th Med. Brigade, Heidelberg, Germany, 2001—02; chief Army Med. Corps, 2002; commdg. gen. Southeast Regional Med. Command/Dwight David Eisenhower Army Med. Ctr., 2002—05, US Army Med. Rsch. and Materiel Command and Fort Detrick, Va., 2005—07; also comdr. North Atlantic Regional Med. Command, 2007—. Decorated DSM, Legion of Merit with four oak leaf clusters, Meritorious Svc. Medal with two oak leaf clusters, Joint Svc. Commendation Medal, Army Commendation Medal, Army Achiever Medal, Humanitarian Svc. Medal, Order of Mil. Med. Merit, "A" Proficiency Designator. Office: Walter Reed Army Med Ctr 6900 Georgia Ave NW Washington DC 20307-5001 *

SCHOOMAKER, PETER JAN, retired military officer; b. Detroit, Feb. 12, 1946; m. Cynthia A Petroski, Jan. 14, 1980; 3 children. BS in Edn. Adminstrn., U. Wyo., 1969; MA in Mgmt., Ctrl. Mich. U., 1977; grad., USMC Amphibious War Sch., 1976, US Army Command/Gen. Staff Coll., 1982, Nat. War Coll., 1989; LLD (hon.), Hampden-Sydney Coll. Commd. 2d lt. US Army, 1969, advanced through grades to gen., 1997, reconnaissance platoon leader, 2nd Bn., 4th Infantry Ft. Campbell, Ky., 1970—71; comdr., Co. C, 2nd Bn., 4th Infantry US Army Europe, 1970—72, asst. S-3 (Ops.) then S-4 (Logistics), 1st Squadron, 2nd Armored Vavalry, 1972—73; comdr. troop C, 1st Squadron, 2nd Armored Cavalry Regiment US Army Europe & 7th Army, Germany, 1973-74; asst. insp. gen., 2nd Infantry Divsn. US Army, Republic of Korea, 1974, S-3, 1st Bn., 73rd armor, 2nd Infantry Divsn., 1974—75; assignment officer Officer Pers. Mgmt. Directorate US Army Mil. Pers. Ctr., Alexandria, Va., 1976-78; comdr. 1st Spl. Forces Operational Detachment US Army, Ft. Bragg, NC, 1978-81; exec. officer 2d Squadron, 2d Armored Cavalry Regiment U.S. Army Europe and 7th Army, Germany, 1982-83; spl. ops. officer J-3 Joint Spl. Ops. Command Ft. Bragg, N.C., 1984-85; served in various position within 1st Spl. Forces Operational Detachment D, 1985—88; comdr. Combat Applications Group, Ft. Bragg, NC, 1989-92; asst. divsn. comdr. 1st Cavalry Divsn., Ft. Hood, Tex., 1992-93; dep. dir. ops., readiness & mobilization Office of Dep. Chief of Staff Ops. & Plans, US Army, Washington, 1993-94; comdg. gen. Joint Spl. Ops. Command US Army Spl. Ops. Command, Ft. Bragg, NC, 1994-96, comdg. gen., 1996-97; comdg. in chief US Spl. Ops. Command, MacDill AFB, Fla., 1997—2000; chief of staff US Army, Washington, 2003—07. Decorated Disting. Svc. medal, Def. Superior Svc. medal with 3 oak leaf clusters, Legion of Merit with 2 oak leaf clusters, Bronze Star medal with oak leaf cluster, Def. Meritorious Svc. medal with oak leaf cluster, Meritorious Svc. medal with 2 oak leaf clusters, Joint Svc. Commendation medal, Joint Svc. Achievement medal *

SCHOON, KENNETH JAMES, science educator, writer; b. Gary, Ind., Aug. 23, 1946; s. Lester K. and Vivian B. Schoon; m. Margaret Shipley Schoon, Nov. 22, 1969; children: Jacob Kenneth, Robert Kendall. AB in Geology, Ind. U., Bloomington, 1968, MS in Secondary Edn., 1972; PhD in Curriculum and Instrn., Loyola U., Chgo., 1989. Sci. tchr. Sch. City East Chgo., Ind., 1968—90; prof. sci. edn. Ind. U. NW, Gary, 1990—, assoc. dean edn., 1999—. State membership dir. Ind. Sci. Olympiad, 1993—; evaluator for initiative for schools, industries, and scis. Valparaiso (Ind.) U., 2003—; pres. Ind. Dunes Environ. Learning Ctr., Porter, Ind., 2006—. Author: Calumet Beginnings: Ancient Shorelines and Settlements at the South End of Lake Michigan, 2003 (Ind. U. Outstanding Rsch. award, 2004), Portraits of a Ridge Family: The Jacob Schoons. Mem., former dir. Munster (Ind.) Hist. Soc., 1982—; mem., former pres. Munster Bd. Pks. and Recreation, 1994—; chair Munster Centennial Com., 2005—07. Mem.: Munster Lions. Presbyterian. Avocations: Calumet area geology and history, genealogy, travel. Office: Ind U NW 3400 Broadway Gary IN 46408 Home Phone: 219-836-8593; Office Phone: 219-980-7766. Office Fax: 219-981-4208.

SCHOONHOVEN, RAY JAMES, retired lawyer; b. Elgin, Ill., May 24, 1921; s. Ray Covey and Rosina Madeline (Schram White) S.; m. Marie Theresa Dunn, Dec. 11, 1943; children: Marie Kathleen (Kamie), Ray James, Jr., Pamela Suzanne, John Philip, Rose Lynn. BSc, U. Notre Dame, 1943; JD, Northwestern U., 1948. Bar: Ill. 1949, U.S. Supreme Ct. 1954, D.C. 1973, U.S. Ct. Mil. Appeals 1954. Assoc. Seyfarth, Shaw Fairweather & Geraldson, Chgo., 1949-57; ptnr. Seyfarth, Shaw Fairweather & Geraldson now Seyfarth Shaw, Chgo., 1957-92; ret. Chief rulings and ops. br. Wage Stabilization Bd. Region VII, Chgo., 1951-52. Book rev. editor: Ill. Law Rev., 1948. Served to lt.comdr. USNR, 1942-62. Mem. ABA, Ill. State Bar Assn., Chgo. Bar Assn., D.C. Bar Assn., Chgo. Athletic Assn., Univ. Club. Chgo., Fed. Bar Assn., Order of Coif. Republican. Roman Catholic. Home: 1182 Lynette Dr Lake Forest IL 60045-4601 Office: Seyfarth Shaw 131 S Dearborn St Ste 2400 Chicago IL 60603-5577 Office Phone: 312-460-5000. *I work hard to preserve our free enterprise system and, hopefully, to make such contribution to our society that it is better for my having been a part of it.*

SCHOONMAKER, GAIL GRAHAM, voice educator, director; d. Walter Alvin and Betty Griffith Graham; m. Bruce Warder Schoonmaker, Aug. 4, 1973; children: Geoffrey Noel, Richard Graham. MusB, Furman U., 1973; MMus, Northwestern U., Evanston, Ill., 1974. Libr. asst. Northwestern U. Libr., Evanston, 1974—77; prof. voice Furman U., Greenville, SC, 1977—. Coord. chapel music Furman U., Greenville, 2000—, sorority adv., 2002—06. Singer Chgo. Symphony Chorus, 1975—77; pres. Travelers Rest (SC) Elem. PTA, 1989—90; co-pres. Travelers Rest HS PTA,

1995—96; co-dir. music Luth. Ch. of Our Savior, Greenville, 1987—2006. Mem.: Nat. Assn. Tchrs. Singing, Music Club (Greenville). Baptist. Avocations: bridge, music composition. Home: 41 Flatwoods Rd Travelers Rest SC 29690 Office: Furman Univ Poinsett Hwy Greenville SC 29613

SCHOONMAKER, SAMUEL VAIL, III, lawyer; b. Newburgh, NY, Sept. 1, 1935; s. Samuel V. Jr. and Catherine (Wilson) S.; m. Carolyn Peters, Sept. 18, 1965; children: Samuel V. IV, Frederick P. BA magna cum laude, Yale U., 1958, JD, 1961. Bar: Conn. 1961, U.S. Dist. Ct. Conn. 1961, U.S. Dist. Ct. (so. and ea. dist.) N.Y. 1964, U.S. Ct. Appeals (2d cir.) 1964, U.S. Supreme Ct. 1965. Assoc. Cummings & Lockwood, Stamford, Conn., 1961-70, co-mng. ptnr., 1987-90, mng. ptnr., 1990-94, chmn. exec. com., 1987-96; founder, pres. Schoonmaker George & Colin, P.C., Greenwich, Conn., 1996—. State trial referee Conn. Superior Ct., 1989; pres. Schoonmaker Family Assn., New Paltz, N.Y., 1975-77. Sr. topical editor Conn. Bar Jour., 1977-81; mem. editl. bd. Fairshare and Am. Jour. Family Law, 1992—; contbr. articles to profl. jours. Chmn. Conn. Child Support Commn., 1984-86; mem. Conn. Family Support Com., 1986-90; mem. Darien (Conn.) Rep. Town Com., 1974-76, rep. town meeting, 1990-98; pres. Youth Tennis Found. New Eng., Needham, Mass., 1975-77; pres. New Eng. Lawn Tennis Assn., 1977-79 (Man of Yr. award 1979); pres., trustee Huegenot Hist. Soc., 1999—. Fellow Am. Acad. Matrimonial Lawyers Conn. (bd. mgrs., Disting. Svc. award 1988), Internat. Acad. Matrimonial Lawyers, Am. Bar Found.; mem. ABA (chmn. family law sect. 1982-83), Conn. Bar Assn. (chmn. family law sect. 1971-74), Conn. Bus. and Industry Assn. (bd. dirs. 1993-98), S.W. Conn. Bus. and Industry Assn. (bd. dirs. 1990-97), Pub. Defenders Assn. (chmn.), Wee Burn Country Club (Darien, Conn., asst. sec.), Yale Club (N.Y.C.), Phi Beta Kappa. Avocations: tennis, platform tennis. Home: 231 Old Kings Hwy S Darien CT 06820-5931 Office: Schoonmaker George & Colin PC PO Box 5059 81 Holly Hill Ln Greenwich CT 06831-5059

SCHOONMAKER POWELL, THELMA, film editor; b. Algeria, Jan. 3, 1940; m. Michael Powell, May 19, 1984 (dec. Feb. 19, 1990). Editor: (films) Who's That Knocking at My Door, 1968, Woodstock, 1970 (nominee Best Film Editing Acad. award, 1970), Raging Bull, 1980 (Best Film Editing Acad. award, 1980, Best Film Editing award Am. Cinema Editors, 1980, Best Film Editing award Brit. Acad., 1981), The King of Comedy, 1983 (nominee Brit. Acad. award for best film editing, 1983), After Hours, 1985, The Color of Money, 1986, The Last Temptation of Christ, 1988, New York Stories (Life Lessons segment), 1989, GoodFellas, 1990 (nominee Best Film Editing Acad. award, 1990, Best Dramatic Film Editing Brit. Acad. award, 1990, nominee Best Film Editing, Am. Cinema Editors, 1990), Cape Fear, 1992 (nominee Brit. Acad. award for best film editing, 1993), The Age of Innocence, 1993, A Personal Journey with Martin Scorsese Through American Movies, 1995, Casino, 1995 (nominee Best Film Editing Am. Cinema Editors, 1995), Kundun, 1997, Bringing Out the Dead, 1999, Il Mio Viaggio in Italia, 2000, Gangs of New York, 2002 (Best Dramatic Film Editing Am. Cinema Editors award, 2003, nominee Best Film Editing Acad. award, 2003), The Aviator, 2004 (Best Film Editing Acad. award, 2005, Best Dramatic Film Editing Am. Cinema Editor award, 2005), The Departed, 2006 (Best Film Editing Acad. award, 2007, Best Dramatic Film Editing Am. Editors award, 2007).

SCHOONOVER, BRENDA B., ambassador; BA, Morgan State U., Balt.; postgrad., Howard U. Vol. Peace Corps, Philippines, 1961, adminstr. Office Talent Search Washington, assoc. dir. Tanzania, dir. sch. partnership program Washington; affirmative action officer Govt. of Arlington County, Va.; with Fgn. Svc. U.S. Dept. State, Manila, Colombo, Sri Lanka, Tunis, Tunisia, with Bur. Near East and South Asia Washington, 1978-88, chief pers. Bur. European and Can. Affairs, 1988-91, mem. Sr. Seminar, 1996-97; adminstrv. officer, dept. dir. Office Joint Adminstrv. Svcs. Am. Embassy, Brussels, 1992-96; Capstone fellow Nat. Def. U., Washington, 1997; U.S. amb. to Togo Am. Embassy, Lome, 1998-2000; amb.-in-residence Chapel Hill, NC, 2000—01; chargé d'affaires, ad interim min. counselor Am. Embassy, Brussels, 2001—04. Bd. dirs. Am. Diplomacy On-line Mag. Mem. adv. bd. Carolina for Kibera; ex-officio adv. bd. Global Edn., U. N.C., Chapel Hill. Recipient Order of the Mono award, The Togolese Govt., 2000, Presdl. Meritorious award, U.S., 2003, Sec. of State Career Achievement award, 2004. Mem.: LWV (local chpt. bd. dirs.). Office: 108 Ironwoods Dr Chapel Hill NC 27516 E-mail: RCSchoon2@aol.com.

SCHOONOVER, JACK RONALD, senior judge; b. Winona, Minn., July 23, 1934; s. Richard M. and Elizabeth A. (Hargisheimer) S.; m. Ann Marie Kroez, June 18, 1965; children: Jack Ronald, Wayne J. Student, Winona State Coll., 1956-58; LLB, U. Fla., 1962. Bar: Fla. 1962. Atty. Wotitzky, Wotitzky & Schoonover, 1962-69, Schoonover, Olmsted & Schwarz, 1969-75; spl. asst. state's atty. State of Fla., 1969-72; city atty. City of Punta Gorda, Fla., city judge, 1973-74; judge 20th Jud. Cir. Ct., Ft. Myers, Fla., 1975-81, 2d Dist. Ct. Appeal, 1981-97, chief judge, 1990-92, ret., 1997. Atty. Charlotte County Sch. Bd., 1969-75, Charlotte County Zoning Bd., Charlotte County Devel. Authority; mem. unauthorized practice law com. 12th Jud. Cir., mem. grievance com. 20th Jud. Cir.; adj. prof. Edison C.C.; tchr. Charlotte County Adult Edn. Assn. Served with USAF, 1952-56. Home and Office: 14380 Olde Hickory Blvd Fort Myers FL 33912-0816

SCHOONOVER, PHILIP J., retail executive; m. Cindi Schoonover; 2 children. Degree in mktg. and fin., U. N.H.; postgrad., Boston Coll. Former sales and mktg. exec. Sony Corp. Am.; former exec. v.p., gen. merchandise mgr. TOPS Appliances; sr. v.p. digital tech. Best Buy Co., Inc., 1995—2001, exec. v.p. digital solutions, 2001—02, exec. v.p. bus. devel., 2002—04, exec. v.p. customer segments, 2004; exec. v.p., chief merchandising officer Circuit City Stores Inc., Richmond, Va., 2004—05, pres., 2005—, CEO, 2006—. Active Anti-Defamation League, United Jewish Appeal, Chabad Ho., United Way, Wayzata (Minn.) Yacht Club Youth Sailing Program. Avocation: sailing. Office: Circuit City Stores Inc 9950 Maryland Dr Richmond VA 23233-1464 *

SCHOONOVER, STANLEY R., music educator, consultant; b. Bethesda, Md., July 27, 1955; s. William and Martha Schoonover. MusM, West Chester U., 1982. Cert. music edn. K-12 Pa. Dir. of bands Mt. Vernon HS, Alexandria, Va., 1982—92, Robinson Secondary Sch., Fairfax, Va., 1993—98; music specialist Fairfax County Pub. Schs., Fairfax, 1998—. Music cons., Va., 1990—; founding condr. Fairfax Wind Symphony, 1999. Dir.: (internat. band clinic performance) MidWest Band and Orchestra Clinic, 1993 (5 NBA Citations of Excellence). Named to East Stroudsburg Music Hall of Fame, 2004. Mem.: Va. Band and Orch. Dirs. Assn. (pres. 1993—95), Phi Delta Kappa. Office: Alan E Leis Instructional Ctr 7423 Camp Alger Ave Falls Church VA 22042 Office Phone: 703-208-7717. Personal E-mail: stanschoonover@verizon.net. E-mail: stan.schoonover@fcps.edu.

SCHOPF, JAMES WILLIAM, paleobiologist, researcher, educator; b. Urbana, Ill., Sept. 27, 1941; s. James Morton and Esther Julie (Nissen) S.; m. Julie Morgan, Aug. 7, 1965 (div. 1979); 1 child, James Christopher; m. Jane Shen, Jan. 16, 1980. AB with high honors, Oberlin Coll., 1963; A.M., Harvard U., 1965, PhD (Harvard fellow, NSF fellow), 1968. Research chemist NASA, Ames Research Center, Calif., 1967; mem. lunar sample preliminary exam. team Manned Spacecraft Center, Tex., 1968-71; asst. prof. dept. earth and space scis. UCLA, 1968-70, assoc. prof., 1970-73, prof., 1973—, mem. Inst. Evolutionary and Environ. Biology, 1970-76, mem. Inst. Geophysics and Planetary Physics, 1973—, dean honors div. Coll. Letters and Sci., 1983-85, dir. Ctr. for Study Evolution and Origin of Life, 1985—, Sigma Xi Disting. lectr., 1976, Rubey lectr., 1976, Golden Yr. Disting. lectr., 1980, Faculty Research lectr., 1984; Sigma Xi Disting. lectr. U. Cin., 1980; Disting. lectr. Buffalo Mus. Sci., 1982; J.A. Bownocker lectr. Ohio State U., 1982. Vis. lectr. Am. Inst. Biol. Scis. Vis. Biologists Program, 1969-72; faculty rsch. learner, UCLA Acad. Senate, 1984, M.W. Haas vis. disting. prof. geology U. Kans., 1979; extraordinary vis. prof. exobiology U. Nijmegen, Netherlands, 1980-81; C. O'Neal lectr. Ohio Wesleyan U., 1982; Sandia disting. lectr. U. N.Mex., 1985; Sigma Xi disting. lectr. U. Oreg., 1985; Du Pont disting. lectr. U. Ill., 1985; R. Stanier disting. lectr. U. Calif.-Berkeley, 1987; H.P. Mangelsdorf disting. lectr. U. N.C., 1987; mem. Bot. Soc. Am. del., People's Republic China, 1978; Academia Sinica vis. research scientist, People's Republic China, 1981, 82; mem. NASA Terrestrial Bodies Sci. Working Group, 1975-76, space program adv. council NASA Life Scis. Com., 1976-78, NASA Working Group on Origins of Life, 1978-79, NASA Space Sci. Adv. Com., 1979-82, mem. NASA Life Scis. Strategic Planning Study Com., 1985—; Alan T. Waterman Award com. NSF, 1978-81; mem. working group on precambrian biostratigraphy Internat. Geol. Correlation Program, UNESCO, 1975—; mem. Working Group on Cambrian-Precambrian Boundary, 1976—; mem. adv. com. USSR and Eastern Europe, Commn. Internat. Relations NRC, 1981-85, mem. bd. earth sci. Commn. Phys. Scis., Math. and Resources, 1982-85, mem. space sci. bd., 1983-86; mem. com. on guidelines for paleontol. collecting, 1984-86, sub.-com. on evolution and diversity Commn. on Life Scis., 1986; mem. Internat. Congress Systematic and Evolutionary Biology, 1990—; mem. com. space research Internat. Council Sci. Unions; chair Gordon Rsch. Conf. Origin of Life, 1999; mem. sci. coun., Geo-bio Ctr., Ludwig-Maximilians U., 2003; lecturer and spkr. in field, 1980—. Mem. editorial bd.: Origins of Life, 1973-87, Precambrian Research, 1973-91, Evolutionary Theory, 1973-85, U. Calif. Press, 1973-82, Paleobiology, 1974-80, Geomicrobiology Jour., 1977—, Evolutionary Monographs, 1977-85, Quarterly Rev. Biology, 1988—, Artificial Life, 1993—, Astrobiology, 2001—, Geokimiya: Internat. Geochemistry, 2005—; contbr. articles to profl. jours. Bd. dirs. Brentwood Glen (Calif.) Assn., 1972-75; trustee UCLA Found., 1983-85; bd. trustees Oberlin Coll., 1992-97. Recipient N.Y. Bot. Garden award Bot. Soc. Am., 1966; Group Achievement award NASA, 1969; Outstanding Paper award Jour. Paleontology, 1971; Charles Schuchert award Paleontol. Soc., 1974; Disting. Teaching award UCLA, 1977; Alan T. Waterman award NSF, 1977; G. Hawk award U. Kans., 1979; spl. recognition diploma NASA, 1979, Group Achievement award, 1997; Outstanding Vol. in Phys. Scis. award Am. Assn. Pubs., 1983; Mary Clark Thompson medal Nat. Acad. Scis., 1986, Profl. and Scholarly Pub. award, Assn. Am. Pubs., 1983, 1992, Disting Sci. award, IGPP Ctr. for Study of Evoluton & The Origin of Life, 2000; Guggenheim fellow, 1973, John Simon Guggenheim Found. fellow, 1988; U.S. Nat. Acad. Scis. exchange scientist USSR, 1975; named one of So. Calif.'s 50 Leading Scientists of 20th Century, 1999. Fellow Geol. Soc. Am. (vice-chmn. Cordilleran sect. 1983-84, chmn. 1984-85); mem. NAS, AAAS, Bot. Soc. Am. (com. on sci. liaison with People's Republic China 1978—), Paleontol. Soc. (mem. Schuchert Award com. 1978-82), Internat. Soc. Study of Origin of Life (treas. 1977-83, nat. meeting adv. com. 1980, 83, 86, councilor, 1983—), Geochem. Soc. (nominating com. 1980-82), Soc. Study of Evolution (edn. com. 1980-83), Am. Philos. Soc., Linnean Soc. London, Internat. Assn. Plant Taxonomy, Internat. Org. Paleobotany, Psychol. Soc. Am., Am. Assn. Univ. Profs., Am. Inst. Biol. Scis., Internat. Psychol. Soc., Am. Soc. Naturalists, Soc. Econ. Paleontologists and Mineralogists, Paleontological Assn., Am. Soc. Mibrobiology, Soc. Molecular Biology and Evolution, Sigma Xi (treas. UCLA chpt. 1972-74, chpt. v.p. 1984-84, pres. 1984-85). Office: UCLA Dept Earth Space Scis Los Angeles CA 90095-0001 Office Phone: 310-825-1170. Business E-Mail: schopf@ess.ucla.edu.

SCHOPF, WILLIAM GRANT, lawyer; b. Muskegon, Mich., Sept. 7, 1948; s. William G. and June Marie (Bodine) Schopf; children: Brody A., Alexandra J., Anais M.E. AB, Princeton U., 1970; JD, Cornell U., 1973. Bar: Ill. 1973, US Dist. Ct. (no. dist. Ill.) 1973, US Supreme Ct. 1977, Tex. 1989, US Dist. Ct. (so. dist. Tex.) 1995, US Dist Ct. (ea. dist. Tex.) 1998, US Dist. Ct. (so. dist. Ill.) 2001, US Dist. Ct. (we. dist. Mich.) 2005, US Ct. Appeals (3rd, 5th, 7th, 8th, 10th and 11th cirs.). Assoc. Keck, Mahin & Cate, Chgo., 1973-79; ptnr. Reuben & Proctor, Chgo., 1979-86, Isham, Lincoln & Beale, Chgo., 1986-87, Schopf & Weiss, Chgo., 1987—. Adj. prof. John Marshall Law Sch., Chgo., 1977-78; owner Music Box Theatre & Schopf Gallery on Lake, Chgo. Author: Money in the Bank, 1988; contbr. articles, chpts. to legal publs. Named an Top 10 Trial Lawyers in Am., Nat. Law Jour., 2004. Mem. ABA, Chgo. Bar Assn., Union Internationale des Avocats, Union League Club (Chgo.), Princeton Club (NYC). Office: Schopf & Weiss 1 S Wacker Dr 28th Fl Chicago IL 60606-4617 Office Phone: 312-701-9308. E-mail: schopf@sw.com. *

SCHOPPMEYER, MARTIN WILLIAM, education educator; b. Weehawken, NJ, Sept. 15, 1929; s. William G. and Madeleine M. (Haas) S.; m. Marilyn M. Myers, Aug. 9, 1958; children: Susan Ann, Martin William. BS, Fordham U., 1950; EdM, U. Fla., 1955, EdD, 1962. Tchr. Fla. pub. sch., 1955-59; instr., then asst. prof. U. Fla., 1960-63; assoc. prof., then prof. edn. Fla. Atlantic U., Boca Raton, Fla., 1963-68, dir. continuing edn., 1965-67; mem. faculty U. Ark., Fayetteville, Ark., 1968—, prof. edn., 1971-93, Univ. prof., 1993—99, Univ. prof. emeritus, 1999—, program coord. for ednl. adminstrn., 1983-90. Mem. Nat. Adv. Coun. Edn. Professions Devel., 1973-76; exec. sec. Ark. Sch. Study Coun., 1976—; evaluator instructional tng. program Nat. Tng. Fund, 1978; bd. dirs. Women's Ednl. and Devel. Inst., 1977-80, Nat. Sch. Devel. Coun., sec., 1989-90, v.p. 1990, pres., 1990-92; mem. oversight com. South Conway (Ark.) County Sch. Dist.; mem. state commn. to study effect of Amendment 59 to Ark. Constn.; cons. Lake View V. Huckabee, 1994-2002. Author books, monographs, articles in field. Mem. president's coun. Subiaco Acad., 1984-90; chmn. Subiaco Sch. Bd., 1990-93, mem., 1993-97. With U.S. Army, 1951-53, Korea. Recipient numerous fed. grants. Mem. VFW, KC (past grand knight), Ark. Edn. Assn. (past chpt. pres.), Ark. Assn. Ednl. Adminstrs., Am. Legion, Rotary, Kappa Delta Pi, Phi Delta Kappa, Delta Tau Kappa. Roman Catholic. Home: 2950 Sheryl Ave Fayetteville AR 72703-3542 Personal E-mail: mschoppmeyer@yahoo.com. *The only really sound investment for a family, a community, or a society is that money spent for the education of its youth.*

SCHOPPMEYER, MARTIN WILLIAM, JR., school system administrator; b. Ft. Lauderdale, Fla., Nov. 1, 1966; s. Martin William and Marilyn Myers Schoppmeyer; m. Carin Anne Morales. MEd in Ednl. Tech., U. Ark., Fayetteville, 1996, EdD in Ednl. Leadership and Instrnl. Design, 1999. Dir. corp. rels. Coll. Engring., U. Ark., 1999—2003; founder, supt. schs. Haas Hall Acad., Farmington, Ark., 2003—; founder, CEO Digi-Tell ID Sys., Fayetteville, 2000—, chmn., 2001. Adj. faculty U. Ark., 1995—2003. Contbr. articles to profl. jours., chapters to books. Chmn. The Acad., Inc., Fayetteville, 2003—. Recipient Charles and Nadine Baum Tchg. Excellence award, U. Ark., 1999; grantee Roy B. Allen Doctoral scholarship, 1998; Rsch. grant, Ark. Dept. Edn., 2003—04, 2004—05, Fed., 2004—06, Walton Family Found., 2004—06. Mem.: Am. Ednl. Rsch. Assn. (life), Rotary Internat. (life), Am. Ednl. Rsch. Assn. (life), Phi Delta Kappa (life; bd. mem. 2001—02), Rotary Club Internat. (life), Elk's Lodge (life), Phi Delta Kappa (life; bd. mem. 2000—03), Phi Kappa Phi (life; sec. 2000—03). Achievements include development and patent of iCard technology to link our clients to their digital profile; created the first only open-enrollment charter high school in the state of Arkansas. Home: 1156 East Glenn Ln Fayetteville AR 72703 Office: Haas Hall Acad 13370 Rheas Mill Rd Farmington AR 72703 Business E-Mail: martinschoppmeyer@haashall.org.

SCHOR, JOSEPH MARTIN, pharmaceutical executive, biochemist; b. Bklyn., Jan. 10, 1929; s. Aaron Jacob and Rhea Iress (Kay) S.; children: Esther Helen, Joshua David, Gideon Alexander, Eric, Neil; m. Laura Sharon Strumingher, June 14, 1992. BS magna cum laude, CCNY, 1951; PhD, Fla. State U., 1957. Sr. rsch. chemist Armour Pharm. Co., Kankakee, Ill., 1957-59, Lederle Labs., Pearl River, N.Y., 1959-64; dir. biochemistry Endo Labs., Garden City, N.Y., 1964-70; head dept. biochemistry DuPont and Endo Labs., 1970-77; v.p. sci. affairs Forest Labs., NYC, 1977-94, sr. v.p. sci. affairs emeritus, 1995—. Editor, contbr.: Chemical Control of Fibrinolysis-thrombolysis, 1970. Contbr. articles to profl. jours. Patentee in field. USPHS fellow, 1955-57. Fellow Am. Inst. Chemists (cert. prof. chemist); mem. Am. Chem. soc. (chmn. Nassau County subsect. 1971-72), Internat. Soc. on Thrombosis and Hemostasis, N.Y. Acad. Scis., AAAS, Phi Beta Kappa, Sigma Xi. E-mail: joseph.m.schor@verizon.net.

SCHOR, LAURA STRUMINGHER, historian; b. NYC, June 24, 1945; d. David Charles and Esther Rachel (Pearl) Gross; children: Eric Alain, Neil Remy; m. Joseph Martin Schor, June, 1992. BA, Queens Coll., CUNY, 1967; MA, U. Rochester, 1970, PhD, 1974. Asst. prof. SUNY, Fredonia, 1973-79; assoc. prof., dir. women's studies U. Cin., 1979-85, prof., vice provost, 1985-89; prof., provost, v.p. acad. affairs Hunter Coll., CUNY, NYC, 1989-98; exec. dir. Hadassah, The Women's Zionist Orgn. of Am., Inc., NYC, 1998-2000; dean CUNY Honors Coll., 2001—05; prof. history Hunter Coll., 2005—. Author: Women and the Making of the Working Class, 1979, What Were Little Boys and Girls Made Of?, 1984, The Odyssey of Flora Tristan, 1988, Les Jolies Femmes d'Edouard de Beaumont, 1994, The Life and Legacy of Baroness Betty de Rothschild, 2006. Mem.: Internat. Soc. for Study European Ideas, Am. Hist. Assn., French Hist. Assn., Phi Beta Kappa.

SCHOR, LAURENCE, lawyer; b. Bklyn., May 3, 1942; s. Julius and Ruth (Zackowitz) S.; m. Susan Leslie Gurevitz, Dec. 26, 1965; children: Meredith Nan, Joseph Sanford, Wendy Claire, Samuel Julius. BBA, So. Meth. U., 1963; JD, U. Tex., 1966; LLM, George Washington U., 1972. Bar: Tex. 1966, D.C. 1971, Md. 1993.; U.S. Ct. Appeals (D.C., 4th, 5th, 11th cirs.). Atty. NASA, Huntsville, Ala., 1966-68; asst. gen. counsel NASA support U.S. Army C.E., Washington, 1968-70; assoc. Sellers, Conner & Cuneo, Washington, 1970-73; from assoc. to ptnr. Max E. Greenberg, Trayman, Cantor, Reiss & Blasky, Washington, 1974-80; ptnr. Schnader, Harrison, Segal & Lewis, Washington, 1981-91, ptnr.-in-charge, 1986-88; mem. Miller & Chevalier, Washington, 1991-93; ptnr. Smith, Somerville & Case, LLC, Washington, 1993-96, McManus, Schor, Asmar & Darden, LLP, Washington, 1997—. Lectr. George Washington U., others. Author: The Right to Stop Work, 1991; author: (manual) Delays, Suspensions and Acceleration, Workplace Safety and Health in the 1990's, 1992; author: Claims Against Bonding Companys, Construction Contractors' Handbook of Business and Law, 1992, How to File a Federal Contract Claim, 1998, 2007; co-author: Suing a Government: Special Considerations; Construction Disputes: Representing the Contractor, 3d edit., 2001; author, editor 50 State Lien and Bond Laws, 1993—2007, Vol. 3 Form Book rewrite, 2000, editor update, 2001—07; contbr. chapters to books, articles to profl. jours.; commentator MSNBC-TV, 2000. Founder, pres. Manor Lake Civic Assn., Montgomery County, 1969-71; precinct chmn. Montgomery County Dems., 1972-76; mem. D.C. City Coun. Procurement Reform Task Force, 1995-96. Named to Chambers Ams. Leading Lawyers for Bus., 2003—05. Mem. ABA (chmn. region III pub. contract law sect., 1982-88, chmn. constrn. com. 1986-90, sect. budget and fin. 1990-95), D.C. Bar Assn. (chmn. divsn. 10 govt. contracts and litigation, 1981-85), Fed. Bar Assn., Am. Coll. Constrn. Lawyers (founder, bd. govs., treas. 1996-2000, pres. elect 2000, pres. 2001-02), B'nai B'rith Youth Orgn (adult adv. bd. 2001-02), Phi Alpha Delta (pres. T.C. Clark chpt. 1965-66), Nat. Panel Arbitrators Am., Arbitration Assn. Jewish. Avocations: reading, travel. Home: 7021 Mountain Gate Dr Bethesda MD 20817-3913 Office: McManus Schor Asmar & Darden LLP 1155 15th St NW 9th Fl Washington DC 20005 Home Phone: 301-365-2694; Office Phone: 202-296-9260. Business E-Mail: lschor@msadlaw.com.

SCHOR, OLGA SEEMANN, mental health counselor, real estate broker; b. Havana, Cuba, Mar. 2, 1951; came to U.S., 1961; d. Olga del Carmen (Hernandez) S.; m. David Michael Schor, Apr. 22, 1979; 1 child, Andrew. AA, Miami Dade Community Coll., 1971; BA, U. Fla., Gainesville, 1973; M.Edn., U. Miami, Fla., 1976; Psy.D., Nova U., 1981. Cert. Bert Rodgers Sch. Real Estate, Miami, 1981, Gold Coast Sch. Real Estate, 1988; lic. real estate broker. Teaching asst. U. Fla., Gainesville, 1972-73; counselor U. Miami, 1974-79; assoc. psychotherapist Linda H. Jamrozy & Assocs., Miami, 1976-78, Interactive Systems, Miami, 1978-79; psychometrist Jackson Meml. Hosp., Miami, 1979-85, tony Ciminero & Assocs., Miami, 1985-86; lectr. U. Miami, 1976-78, Jackson Meml. Hosp. Sch. Nursing, Miami, 1976; real estate broker The Keyes Co. Realtor, Coral Gables, 1981-88, Keyes Asset Mgmt., Miami, 1988—; CEO My Co. Realty, Inc., 1997—. Sec./treas. bd. dirs. BODS Inc., Miami. Chmn. creative writing Jr. Orange Bowl competition. Recipient Assoc. of Quarter award Keyes Co. Realtors, 1986. Mem. Am. Psychol. and Guidance Assn., Keyes Comml. Roundtable, Keyes Inner Circle, Coral Gables Bd. Realtors, Guilliver Acad.'s Parents Bd., Dade County Mental Health Assn., Million Dollar Sales Club. Clubs: South Fla. Sailing Assn. (Miami). Avocations: sailing, travel, reading, kayaking, theater, acting, tennis. Office: My Company Realty Inc 2050 Coral Way Ste 505 Miami FL 33145-2682 Home: 15000 Old Cutler Rd Miami FL 33158-2116 Office Phone: 305-856-8574. E-mail: artistme@aol.com.

SCHOR, SUZI, lawyer, psychologist; b. Chgo., Feb. 1, 1947; d. Samuel S. and Dorothy Helen (Hineline); 1 child, Kate. BSBA, Ind. U., 1964; JD, Northwestern U., 1970, U. Palmer's Green, London, 1971; PhD in Fine Arts (hon.), U. Nev., PhD in Clin. Psychology, 1989, Kensington U., 1989. Bar: Ill., 1971. Pvt. practice, LA, 1971-80; v.p. legal affairs Little Gypzy Mgmt., Inc., Beverly Hills, Calif., 1980—; trust officer, pvt. fiduciary svcs. Bank of Am., LA. Mem. Pres.'s Coun. on Alcoholism. Author: 13th Step to Death, 1995; contbg. author Wine and Dine Mag.; contbr. articles to profl. jours. Bd. dirs. Nat. Ctr. for Hyperactive Children, L.A., 1989-91, sec. Rainbow Guild Cancer Charity, L.A., 1985-89, ind. cons. Jewish Legal Aid, L.A., 1988—; campaign coord. advisor Dem. Nat. Campaign, L.A., 1990, 94, 2000; donor mem. L.A. Coun. on World Affairs. Recipient Poet of Yr. award Nat. Libr. and Assn. of Poetry, 1995, 98. Mem. ABA (criminal justice com. 1994), AAUW, NAADAC, CAADAC, L.A. Breakfast Club (chmn. entertainment 1988-90), Rotary, Mensa, Beverly Hills Bar Assn., Century City Bar Assn. Jewish. Avocations: singing, skiing, writing.

SCHORER, JOSEPH U., lawyer; b. Baraboo, Wis., June 15, 1953; BA with highest distinction, Northwestern U., 1975; JD cum laude, Harvard U., 1978. Bar: Calif. 1978, US Dist. Ct. (so. dist. Calif.) 1978, Ill. 1981, US Dist. Ct. (no. dist. Ill.) 1981, US Ct. Appeals (7th cir.) 1987, US Ct. Appeals (5th cir.) 1985, US Ct. Appeals (10th cir.) 1984. Law clk. to Hon. Gordon Thompson, Jr. So. Dist. Calif., 1978—80; ptnr. Mayer, Brown & Platt, Chgo., 1985—97; gen. counsel Diamond Homes Svcs., 1997—2000, Globe Bldg. Materials, 1997—2000, Mid-West Spring Mfg. Co., 1997—2000; of counsel Kirkland & Ellis, Chgo., 2000—. Contbr. articles to law jours. Mem.: Chgo. Coun. Lawyers, Chgo. Bar Assn., Phi Beta Kappa. Office: Kirkland & Ellis 200 E Randolph Dr Chicago IL 60601-6636 Office Phone: 312-861-2345. Office Fax: 312-861-2200. E-mail: jschorer@kirkland.com. *

SCHORER, SUKI, ballet teacher; b. Boston; d. Mark and Ruth (Page) S.; 1 child, Nicole. Studied with, George Balanchine. Dancer San Francisco Ballet, 1956-59, N.Y.C. Ballet, 1959-72; prin. dancer N.Y.C. Ballet Co., 1968-72, artistic assoc. lecture demonstration program, 1972-95; mem. faculty Sch. Am. Ballet, 1972—, Brown Found. sr. faculty chair, 1998—. Internat. guest tchr. and lectr. specializing in Balanchine tng. and technique; artist dir., tchr. on Balanchine Essays (videos). Author: Suki Schorer on Balanchine Technique, 1999 (de la Torre Bueno prize 2000), Put Your

Best Foot Forward, 2005; created roles in Balanchine's Harlequinade, Don Quixote, Midsummer Night's Dream, Jewels, La Source, Raymonda Variations; repertory included prin. roles in Apollo, Serenade, Concerto Barocco, Symphony in C, La Sonnambula, Stars and Stripes, Tarantella, Valse Fantaisie, The Nutcracker, Brahams Schoenberg, La Valse, Western Symphony, Ivesiana, Divertimento # 15, Ballet Imperial, others. Recipient Disting. Tchr. in Arts award Nat. Found. Advancement in Arts, 1997, award Dance mag., 1998. Office: Sch of Am Ballet 70 Lincoln Center Plz New York NY 10023-6548 Office Phone: 212-769-6600.

SCHORI, KATHARINE JEFFERTS, bishop; b. Pensacola, Fla., Mar. 26, 1954; m. Richard M. Schori, 1979; 1 child, Katharine. BS in Marine Biology, Stanford U., 1974; MS in Oceanography, Oreg. State U., Corvallis, 1977, PhD in Oceanography, 1983; MDiv, Ch. Div. Sch. of the Pacific, Berkeley, Calif., 1994. Worked in oceanography, including at the Nat. Marine Fisheries Svc. in Seattle; ordained deacon, 1994, priest, 1994; asst. rector Episcopal Ch. of the Good Samaritan, Corvallis, Oreg., 1994—2001; consecrated bishop, 2001; bishop Episcopal Diocese of Nev., Las Vegas, 2001—06; chief pastor, presiding bishop Episcopal Church USA, NYC, 2006—. Author: A Wing and a Prayer: A Message of Faith and Hope, 2007. Achievements include becoming the first woman to lead a church in the worldwide Anglican Communion, 2006. Office: Episcopal Church Ctr Second Ave New York NY 10017 Office Phone: 702-737-9190. Office Fax: 702-737-6488. *

SCHORLING, WILLIAM HARRISON, lawyer; b. Ann Arbor, Mich., Jan. 7, 1949; s. Otis William Schorling and Ruthann (Bales) Schorling Moorehead; m. Lynne Ann Newcomb, June 1, 1974; children: Katherine Pearce, Ann Oury, John Roberts. BA cum laude, Denison U., 1971; JD cum laude, U. Mich., 1975. Bar: Pa. 1975, U.S. Ct. Appeals (3d cir.) 1977, N.J. 1998, Del. 2001, U.S. Dist. Ct. (so. and ea. dists.) N.Y. 2005. Ptnr. Eckert, Seamans, Cherin & Mellott, Pitts., 1984-89, Klett Rooney Lieber & Schorling, PC, Phila., 1989—2006, Buchanan Ingersoll & Rooney, P.C., Phila., 2006—. Lectr. Pa. Bar Inst., Harrisburg, 1983—, Comml. Law League, N.Y.C., 1984—, mem. exec. coun. bankruptcy sect., 2003—, Profl. Edn. Systems, Inc., Eau Claire, Wis., 1986—, Southwest Legal Found., Dallas, 1994—; founders' coun. Comml. Fin. Assn. Edn. Found., 1991—; bd. dirs. Consumer Bankruptcy Assistance Project; adj. prof. Temple U. Beasley Sch. Law, 1999-2004. Contbr. articles to profl. jours. Trustee Pa. Acad. Fine Arts. Fellow Am. Coll. Bankruptcy, Am. Bar Found.; mem. ABA (bus. law section coun. 2000-04, chmn. bus. bankruptcy com. 1996-99, lectr. 1988—, mem. standing com. on fed. jud. improvement 2007-), Am. Banker Inst. (lectr. 1994—), Phila. Bar Assn. (lectr. 1996—), E. Dist. Bankruptcy Conf., Pa. Bar Assn. (lectr. 1983—), Allegheny County Bar Assn. (chmn. bankruptcy and comml. law sect. 1991), The Com. of Seventy (chmn. 2003-04), Longue Vue Club, Duquesne Club, Pyramid Club, Pa. Soc. Presbyterian. Home: 933 S 2nd St Philadelphia PA 19147 Office: Buchanan Ingersoll & Rooney PC 1835 Market St Flr 14 Philadelphia PA 19103-2985 Office Phone: 215-665-5326. Business E-Mail: william.schorling@bipc.com.

SCHORNACK, JOHN JAMES, accountant; b. Chgo., Nov. 22, 1930; s. John Joseph and Helen Patricia (Patrickus) S.; m. Barbara Anne Lelli, June 5, 1965; children: Mark Boyd, Anne Marguerite Schornack Trueman, Erin Keeley Schornack Dickes, Tracy Bevan Schornack Power. BS, Loyola U., 1951; MBA, Northwestern U., 1956; grad., Advanced Mgmt. Program, Harvard Bus. Sch., 1969. With Ernst & Young (formerly Arthur Young & Co.), 1955-91, partner, 1964-91; firm dir. personnel Ernst & Young LLP (formerly Arthur Young & Co.), NYC, 1966-71, asst. mng. ptnr. N.Y.C. office, 1971-72, mng. ptnr., 1972-74, mng. ptnr. Chgo. office, 1976-85, mng. ptnr. Midwest region, vice chmn., 1985-91; mem. mgmt. com. Arthur Young & Co. Mgmt. com. Arthur Young & Co.; vice chmn., mng. ptnr. Midwest region Ernst & Young, 1989-91; bd. dirs., chmn. Ernst & Young Found., 1981-91; chmn., bd. dirs. North Shore Bancorp, Inc., 1992-, Wintrust Fin. Corp., 1996-. Pres. Chgo. Youth Ctrs., 1979-95; bd. govs. Chgo. Symphony, 1979-85, trustee, 1985-2003, life trustee; vol. United Way, 1975-92, dir., 1989-92; vis. adv. com. sch. accountancy DePaul U., 1980-83; mem. Loyola U. Citizens Bd., 1977-94, chmn., 1993-94; mem. adv. com. Northwestern U. Grad. Sch. Mgmt., 1967-91; coun. U. Chgo. Grad. Sch. Bus., 1982-91; bd. dirs. Met. Planning Coun., 1992-95; trustee Kohl Children's Mus., 1994-2005, life trustee, 2005—; trustee Lyric Opera, 1984-92, Cath. Charities Chgo., 2004—, Cath. Theol. Union, 1992-97, Graham Found., 1992-98; trustee Barat Coll., 1983-98, life trustee, 1999-2001, vice chmn., 1985-90, chmn., 1990-97; trustee St. Francis Hosp., 1986-97, vice chmn., 1991-94; trustee Night Ministry, 1998-004 Recipient Order of the Sacred Treas., Emperor of Japan, 1999. Mem. AICPA, Am. Acctg. Assn., Ill. Soc. CPAs, Midwest-Japan Assn. (chmn. 1983-99), Japan Am. Soc., Chgo. Club, Glen View Club, The Little Club. Home: 314 Regent Wood Rd Northfield IL 60093-2762 Office: Ernst & Young LLP Great Lakes Reg Office 233 S Wacker Dr Chicago IL 60606-6306

SCHORNAGEL, KARL WILLIAM, government agency administrator; b. Fremont, Mich., Feb. 15, 1951; s. Jacob Teunis and Nellie Marie (DeWitte) Schornagel; m. Mary Louise Smitten, May 7, 1999; m. Patricia Kay Kartes (div.). BS in Bus. Adminstrn., George Mason U., Va., 1979. CPA. Auditor US Dept. Treasury, Washington, 1979—85, audit dir., 1985—2001; inspector gen. Libr. of Congress, 2001—. Advisor Ctr. for Rsch. Libr., Chgo., 2005—06. Contbr. articles various profl. investigative reports. Recipient Superior Fed. Svc. award, Inspector Gen. US Dept. Commerce, 1988, 2000, Meritorious Fed. Svc. award, Sec. US Dept. Commerce, 1997. Mem.: Exec. Coun. Integrity and Efficiency, A. Inst. Cert. Pub. Accountants. Achievements include directing analyses leading to improved allocation of about $400 million in federal government programs and operations. Avocations: tennis, music, writing, auto racing, golf. Office: Libr of Congress 101 Indep Ave SW Washington DC 20540-1060 Business E-Mail: kasc@loc.gov.

SCHORR, ALAN EDWARD, librarian, publishing executive; b. NYC, Jan. 7, 1945; s. Herbert and Regina S.; m. Debra Genner, June 11, 1967; 1 son, Zebediah. BA, CUNY, 1966; MA, Syracuse U., 1967; postgrad., U. Iowa, 1967-71; MLS, U. Tex., 1973. Tchr., rsch. asst. dept. history U. Iowa, 1967-70; govt. publs. and map libr., asst. prof. Elmer E. Rasmuson Libr., U. Alaska, 1973-78; assoc. prof., dir. libr. U. Alaska, Juneau, 1978-84; prof., dean univ. libr. Calif. State U., Fullerton, 1984-86; pres. The Denali Press, Juneau, 1986—. Freelance indexer and bibliographer; vis. lectr. Birmingham (Eng.) Poly., 1981; mem. Alaska Ednl. Del. to China, 1975. Author: Alaska Place Names, 1974, 4th edit., 1991, Directory of Special Libraries in Alaska, 1975, Government Reference Books, 1974-75, 1976, 1976-77, 1978, Government Documents in the Library Literature 1909-1974, 1976, ALA RSBRC Manual, 1979, Federal Documents Librarianship 1879-1987, 1988, Hispanic Resource Directory, 1988, 3d edit., 1996, Refugee and Immigrant Resource Directory, 1990, 92, 94; editor: The Sourdough, 1974-75, Directory of Services for Refugees and Immigrants, 1987, 3d edit., 1993, Guide to Smithsonian serial publs., 1987; book reviewer, columnist: S.E. Alaska Empire, 1979-82, L.A. Times; contbr. articles to profl. jours. Mem. Auke Bay (Alaska) Vol. Fire Dept., 1978—81, Juneau Borough Libr. Adv. Com., 1981—82, Juneau Borough Cemetery Adv. Com., 1980—81, Am. Book Awards Com., 1980; chmn. program evaluation com., former chmn. facilities com., former chmn. policy com. to v.p. Juneau Bd. of Edn., 2000—; mem. Juneau Bd. Edn., 1991—94, 1995—97, 1997—2000, 2000—03, 2003—04; mem. citizens adv. coun. Juneau Empire Newspaper, 2003—. Mem. ALA (mem. reference and subscription books rev. com. 1975-86, mem. reference and adult svcs. divsn. publs. com. 1975-77, Nat. Assn. Hispanic Publs., Mudge citation commn. 1977-79, 84-86, Dartmouth Coll. Medal Commn., Governing Coun. 1977-84, mem. Dewey medal com. 1984-85, Denali Press award), Alaska Libr. Assn. (mem. exec. bd. 1974-75, mem. nominating com. 1977-79), Pacific N.W. Libr. Assn. (rep. publs. com. 1973-75), Assn. Coll. and Rsch. Librs. (mem. publ. com. 1976-80), Spl. Librs. Assn. (assoc. editor geography and map divsn. bull. 1975-76), Internat. Assn. Ind. Pubs (bd. dirs. 1990-92), True North Fed. Credit Union (bd. dirs. 1997-, treas. 2001-2002, vice chmn., 2002-04, chmn., 2004-), PEN Ctr. USA West, Explorers Club N.Y., Wash. Athletic Club (Seattle). Office: Denali Press PO Box 1535 Juneau AK 99802

SCHORR, BRIAN LEWIS, lawyer, writer; b. NYC, Oct. 5, 1958; s. Philip I. and Hannah Schorr; m. Amy B. Horowitz; 2 children. BA magna cum laude, MA, Wesleyan U., Middletown, Conn., 1979; JD, NYU, 1982. Bar: N.Y. 1983, D.C. 1985, U.S. Supreme Ct. 1988. Assoc. Paul, Weiss, Rifkind, Wharton & Garrison, NYC, 1982-90, ptnr., 1991-94; exec. v.p., gen. counsel Triarc Cos., Inc., NYC, 1994—. Mem. bd. advisors Jour. Ltd. Liability Cos., 1994-98; lectr. CLE programs. Author: Schorr on New York Limited Liability Companies and Partnerships, 1994; contbr. articles to legal jours. Trustee NYU Sch. Law, Wesleyan U.; bd. dir. Bronx HS Sci. Endowment Fund, Inc., NY. Mem. ABA, N.Y. State Bar Assn., Assn. Bar City N.Y. (chmn. com. on corp. law 1993-96, co-chmn. joint drafting com. N.Y. ltd. liability co. law, mem. spl. com. on mergers, acquisitions and corp. control contests 1996—), Tri Bar Opinion Com. Office: Triarc Cos Inc 280 Park Ave New York NY 10017-1216

SCHORR, DANIEL LOUIS, broadcast journalist, author, lecturer; b. NYC, Aug. 31, 1916; s. Louis and Tillie (Godiner) S.; m. Lisbeth Bamberger, 1967; children: Jonathan, Lisa. BSS, CCNY, 1939; doctorate (hon.), Kalamazoo Coll., Columbia Coll., Chgo., Wilkes U., Nebr. Wesleyan U., LI U., Brandeis U., Spartus Coll., Bates Coll., Haverford Coll. Asst. editor Jewish Telegraphic Agy., 1934-41; news editor ANETA (Netherlands) News Agy. in N.Y., 1941-43; freelance corr. N.Y. Times, Christian Sci. Monitor, London Daily Mail, 1948-53; Washington corr. CBS News, also spl. assignments L.Am. and Europe, 1953-55; reopened CBS Moscow Bur., 1955; roving assignments U.S. and Europe, 1958-60; chief CBS News Bur., Germany, 1960-66; Washington corr. CBS, 1966-76; Regents prof. U. Calif., Berkeley, 1977; columnist Des Moines Register-Tribune Syndicate, 1977-80; sr. Washington corr. Cable News Network, 1980-85; sr. analyst Nat. Pub. Radio, 1985—. Author: Don't Get Sick in America!, 1971, Clearing the Air, 1977, Forgive Us Our Press Passes, 1999, Staying Tuned, 2001. With U.S. Army, 1943-46, 47. Decorated officer Orange Nassau (The Netherlands), Grand Cross of Merit (Germany); recipient citations of excellence for radio-TV reporting Soviet Union Overseas Press Club, 1956, Best TV Interpretation of Fgn. News award 1963, ACLU and other awards for pub. suppressed Congsl. intelligence report, Emmy awards for coverage of Watergate, 1972, 73, 74, Peabody award for lifetime of uncompromising reporting of highest integrity, 1992, George Polk award for radio commentary L.I. U., 1994, Disting. Svc. award Am. Soc. Journalism and Mass Comm., 1994, Golden Baton award for lifetime achievement A.I. DuPont Columbia U., 1996; inducted in Hall of Fame Soc. Profl. Journalists, 1991, Comms. Hall of Fame CCNY, 1999. Mem. Am. Acad. Arts and Scis. (elected), Coun. on Fgn. Rels. N.Y.C., Nat. Press Club. Office Phone: 202-513-2277. E-mail: dschorr@npr.org. *Journalism, for more than 60 years, has been both profession and outlook on life. I have always felt myself the observer and nonparticipant, the quintessential outsider. I have pursued the sense of things behind the appearance of things, the meaning behind the manipulation. I have fought, with dubious success, against the blurring of the media line between reality and fantasy.*

SCHORR, LISBETH BAMBERGER, sociologist, researcher; b. Munich, Jan. 20, 1931; d. Fred S. and Lotte (Krafft) Bamberger; m. Daniel L. Schorr, Jan. 8, 1967; children: Jonathan, Lisa. BA with highest honors, U. Calif., Berkeley, 1952; LHD (hon.), Wilkes U., 1991, U. Md., 1994, Bank St. Coll. Edn., 1999, Wheelock Coll., 2000, Lewis & Clark Coll., 2001, Whittier Coll., 2003. Med. care cons. U.A.W. and Community Health Assn., Detroit, 1956—58; asst. dir. Dept. Social Security AFL-CIO, Washington, 1958—65; acting chief CAP Health Svcs., OEO, 1965—66; chief program planning Office for Health Affairs, OEO, Washington, 1967. Cons. Children's Def. Fund, Washington, 1973—79; scholar-in-residence Inst. of Medicine NAS, 1979—80; chmn. Select Panel on Promotion Child Health, 1979—80; adj. prof. maternal and child health U. N.C., Chapel Hill, 1981—85; lectr. social medicine Harvard U. Med. Sch., 1984—; dir. project on effective interventions Harvard U., 1988—2007; founder www.PathwaysToOutcomes.org; nat. coun. Alan Gutmacher Inst., 1974—79, 1982—85; pub. mem. Am. Bd. Pediat., 1978—84; vice chmn. Found. for Child Devel., 1978—84, bd. dirs., 1976—84, 1986—94; mem. coun. Nat. Ctr. for Children in Poverty, 1987—96; mem. children's program adv. com. Edna McConnell Clark Found., 1987—97; bd. dirs. Pub. Edn. Fund Network, 1991—93; co-chair Roundtable on Cmty. Change Aspen Inst., 1992—2006, mem. exec. com. Roundtable on Cmty. Change, 2006—; mem. bd. on children and families NAS, 1993—95; mem. Nat. Commn. State and Local Pub. Svcs., 1992—94; mem. task force on young children Carnegie Corp., 1992—94; mem. sec.'s adv. com. Head Start quality and expansion, 1993—94; mem. nat. selection com. Ford Found./Kennedy Sch. Awards for Innovations in Am. Govt., 1998—2006; dir. Pathways Mapping Initiative, Project on Effective Interventions, 2000—. Author: Within Our Reach: Breaking the Cycle of Disadvantage, 1988, Common Purpose: Strengthening Families and Neighborhoods to Rebuild America, 1997. Co-chmn. Boundaries task force Harvard Children's Initiative, 1998—2000; mem. Brookings Children's Roundtable, 1999—2002; bd. dirs. Nat. Student Partnerships, 2001—03, Eureka Cmtys., 1995—2005, Civic Ventures, 1997—99. Recipient Dale Richmond Meml. award, Am. Acad. Pediat., 1977, 9th ann. Robert F. Kennedy Book award, 1989, Nelson Cruikshank award, Nat. Coun. Sr. Citizens, 1990, Porter prize, 1993, PASS award, Nat. Coun. on Crime and Delinquency, 1997, Marian F. Langer award, Am. Orthopsychiat. Assn., 1999, Empatheia award, Vols. of Am., 1999. Mem.: Nat. Acad. on Social Ins., Inst. Medicine NAS, Phi Beta Kappa. Home and Office: 3113 Woodley Rd NW Washington DC 20008-3449 Home Phone: 202-483-7150; Office Phone: 202-462-3071. Business E-Mail: lisbeth_schorr@hms.harvard.edu.

SCHORR, S. L., lawyer; b. NYC, Feb. 19, 1930; s. Charles and Clara (Lerech) S.; m. Eleanor Daru, Mar. 23, 1956; children: Lewis, Andrew, Emily, Roberta. Student, L.I. U., 1948-50; LLB, Bklyn. Law Sch., 1953. Bar: N.Y. 1955, Ariz. 1962, U.S. Dist. Ct. Ariz. 1962, U.S. Supreme Ct. 1979. Planning commr. Pima County, Tucson, 1959-62; asst. city mgr. Tucson, 1962-63; ptnr. Lewis and Roca, Tucson, 1988—. Co-chair Continuing Legal Edn. Seminar on Ballot Box Zoning, U. Ariz., 1991, Ariz. State Bar Continuing Legal Edn. Seminar on Land Use Regulation and Litigation, 1977, 86, 89, 95. Bd. dirs. Pima Coll., 1966-67, So. Ariz. Leadership Coun., 1997—; mem. Commn. on Improved Govtl. Mgmt., Tucson, 1974-77, Gov.'s Econ. Planning and Devel. Adv. Bd., Phoenix, 1983-85, regional trans. authority; chmn. Gov.'s Task Force on Seriously Mentally Ill, Phoenix, 1989-91; vice chmn. Ariz. State Transp. Bd., 2003-. Mem. Ariz. Bar Assn., Pima County Bar Assn. Democrat. Office: Lewis Roca 1 S Church Ave Ste 700 Tucson AZ 85701-1611 Office Phone: 520-622-2090.

SCHORR-RIBERA, HILDA KEREN, psychologist; b. NYC, May 2, 1942; d. Leon and Rosa Schorr-Ribera; m. Ira Eli Wessler, Aug. 6, 1971; children: Mike, Daniel. BA, Hunter Coll., 1963; MEd, U. No. Fla., 1982; PhD, U. Pitts., 1988. Lic. psychologist, Pa.; diplomate Am. Bd. Forensic Examiners; diplomate, fellow Am. Bd. Med. Psychotherapists and Psychodiagnosticians; diplomate Am. Bd. Forensic Medicine, Am. Acad. Experts in Traumatic Stress; cert. in clin. hypnosis. Psychotherapist South Hills Interfaith Ministries, Bethel Park, Pa., 1989-92, Profl. Psychol. Assn. of Greater Pitts., 1992; pvt. practice psychologist Pitts., 1993—. Child therapist Forbes Hospice, 1993—; group facilitator of adult wellness group and children's support groups Burger King Cancer Caring Ctr., Pitts., 1989—, Allegheny Hospice, Pitts., 1994—96; psychol. evaluator Washington (Pa.) County Ct., 1993—2005, Allegheny County Ct., Pitts., 1995—98; cons. psychologist to sch. dists. Allegheny and Washington Counties. Author (with others): Educating the Child With Cancer, 1993. Keynote spkr. on illness and bereavement to profl. assns., hosps., schs. and agys., Pitts., 1989—. Mem. APA, Internat. Soc. Hypnosis, Am. Soc. Clin. Hypnosis, Am. Acad. Experts in Traumatic Stress, Am. Counseling Assn., Am. Coll. Forensic Examiners, Pa. Psychol. Assn., Greater Pitts. Psychol. Assn. Avocations: music, bilingual activities, reading, walking, travel. Office: 117 Ridgeway Ct Pittsburgh PA 15228-1729 Home Phone: 412-344-0575; Office Phone: 412-344-0222. Personal E-mail: schorrribera@yahoo.com.

SCHORSCH, ISMAR, theology studies educator, rabbi; b. Hannover, Germany, Nov. 3, 1935; m. Sally Korn; children: Jonathan, Rebecca, Naomi. BA, Ursinus Coll., 1957; MA, Columbia U., 1961, PhD, 1969; MHL, Jewish Theol. Sem. Am., 1962; LittD (hon.), Wittenberg U., 1989, Ursinus Coll., 1990, Gratz Coll., 1995, Russian State U., 1996, Tufts U., 2000. Ordained rabbi, 1962. Instr. Jewish Theol. Sem., NYC, 1964-68; asst. prof. Jewish Theol. Sem. Am., NYC, 1970-72, assoc. prof., 1972-76, prof., 1976—, dean Grad. Sch., 1975-79, provost, 1980-84, chancellor, 1986—2006; asst. prof. Jewish history Columbia U., NYC, 1968-70. Bd. dirs. Leo Baeck Inst., 1976, mem. exec. com., 1980, pres., 1985-86, 90—, mem. editorial bd. of yearbook, 1987; participant symposium Spirit and Nature: Religion, Ethics and Environ. Crisis, Middlebury Coll.; organizer Nat. Religious Partnership for the Environment. Author: From Text to Context: The Turn to History in Modern Judaism, 1994, Canon Without Closure, 2007, (monograph) Sacred Cluster: The Core Values of Conservative Judaism, 1995; contbr. articles to profl. publs. Chaplain US Army, 1962—64. Recipient Clark F. Ansley award Columbia U. Press, 1969, Life Achievement award in Jewish history Nat. Found. for Jewish Culture, 2003; NEH fellow, 1979-80 Fellow Am. Acad. Jewish Rsch. Jewish. Office: Jewish Theol Sem 3080 Broadway New York NY 10027-4650 Office Phone: 212-678-8951. E-mail: Isschorsch@JTSA.edu.

SCHORSCH, LOUIS L., metal products executive; b. Chgo. married; 3 children. BA, Georgetown U., 1971; PhD, Am. U. Analyst U.S. Congl. Budget Office; prin. McKinsey & Co., 1985—2000; pres., CEO Global Steel Exchange, 2000—03; with LNM Group, 2003; pres. CEO Ispat Inland, Inc., 2003—05; CEO Mittal Steel USA, 2005—; economist Am. Iron and Steel Inst., vice chmn. Washington, 2006, chmn., 2006—. Co-author (with Donald F. Barnett): (book) Steel: Upheaval in a Basic History, 1983; contbr. articles to profl. jours. Office: Am Iron and Steel Inst 1140 Connecticut Ave NW Ste 705 Washington DC 20036-4011 Office Phone: 202-452-7100. Office Fax: 202-463-6573.

SCHORSKE, CARL EMIL, historian, educator; b. NYC, Mar. 15, 1915; s. Theodore A. and Gertrude (Goldschmidt) S.; m. Elizabeth Gilbert Rorke, June 14, 1941; children: Carl Theodore, Anne (Mrs. J. L. Edwards), Stephen James, John Simon, Richard Robert. AB, Columbia U., 1936; MA, Harvard U., 1937, PhD, 1950; DLitt (hon.), Wesleyan U., 1967, Bard Coll., 1982, Clark U., 1983, New Sch. Social Rsch., 1986, Miami U., 1987, Monmouth Coll., 1994, Princeton U., 1997, SUNY, Stony Brook, 1989; DPhil (hon.), U. Salzburg, 1986, U. Graz, 1996. Prof. history Wesleyan U., Middletown, Conn., 1946-60; prof. history U. Calif.-Berkeley, 1960-69, Princeton U., 1969-80, emeritus, 1980—. Author: (with Hoyt Price) The Problem of Germany, 1947, German Social Democracy 1905-17, 1955, Fin-de-Siècle Vienna, 1980, Thinking with History, 1998. Lt. (j.g.) USNR, 1943-46; with OSS, 1941-46. Recipient Austrian Cross of Honor for arts and scis., 1979, Pulitzer prize gen. nonfiction, 1981, Grand prize cultural edn. City of Vienna, 1985, Harvard Centennial medal, 1999, Wittgenstein prize, 2004, Victor Adler prize, Austria, 2007; named Officer, French Order Arts and Letters, 1987, Great Silver medal of Honor, Austria, 1996, Gold Cross of Honor, City of Vienna, 2000; MacArthur fellow, 1981-86. Fellow Royal Acad. Fine Arts Netherlands (hon.); mem. Am. Acad. Arts and Scis., Austrian Acad. Scis. (corr.), Am. Hist. Assn. (council 1964-68, Disting. Scholar award 1992), Ctr. Advanced Study Behavioral Sci., Inst. Advanced Study., Getty Ctr. Home: 45 Meadow Lakes 01 Hightstown NJ 08520

SCHOTLAND, DONALD LEWIS, retired medical educator, neurologist; b. Orange, NJ, Sept. 21, 1930; s. Joseph Henry and Elsie (Block) S.; m. Marilyn Goldfeder, July 6, 1955 (dec. 1974); m. Estherina Shems, Jan. 11, 1976; children: John, Thomas, Peter. AB, Harvard U., 1952, MD, 1957; spl. student, MIT, 1955-56; MA (hon.), U. Pa., 1973. Diplomate Am. Bd. Psychiatry and Neurology 1964. Intern U. Ill. Research and Edn. Hosp., 1957-58; asst. resident in neurology Columbia Presbyn. Med. Center, NYC, 1958-61, asst. neurologist, 1961-65, asst. attending neurologist, 1965-66; asst. in neurology Coll. Physicians and Surgeons, Columbia U., NYC, 1960-61, vis. fellow in neurology, 1961-64, assoc. in neurology, 1964-66, asst. prof. neurology, 1966-67; assoc. prof. Sch. Medicine, U. Pa., Phila., 1967-72, prof., 1972-98, prof. emeritus, 1998—. Speaker profl. confs., U.S., Can., Italy, Japan, China, France, Israel, Finland; dir. Henry M. Watts, Jr. Neuromuscular Disease Rsch. Ctr., 1974-90. Editor: Diseases of the Motor Unit, 1982; contbr. articles, papers to profl. publs. Served to 1st lt. USAR, 1958-65. NIH postdoctoral fellow, 1961-64; recipient Research Career Devel. award, 1966-67, various grants NIH and Muscular Dystrophy Assn. Fellow Coll. of Physicians of Phila.; mem. Am. Acad. Neurology, Am. Neurol. Assn., Phila. Neurol. Soc., Muscular Dystrophy Assn. (sci. adv. com. 1974-86, chmn. fellowship com. 1974-86, chmn. 6th Internat. Conf. 1980). Home: 1310 Wyngate Rd Wynnewood PA 19096-2455 Office: Hosp of Univ Pa 3400 Spruce St Philadelphia PA 19104-4283 Personal E-mail: dlschotl@mail.med.upenn.edu.

SCHOTT, DONALD KARL, lawyer; b. Lynwood, Calif., Sept. 13, 1955; s. Otto H. and Violet M. (Reiman) S.; m. Cynthia A. Cronkrite, Aug. 9, 1980; children: Nathan Daniel, Anna Katherine, Laura Elizabeth BS in History and Polit. Sci., U. Wis., Madison, 1977; JD, Harvard U., 1980. Bar: Wis. 1980, U.S. Dist. Ct. (ea. and we. dists. Wis. 1980, no. dist. Ill. 1991), U.S. Ct. Appeals (7th cir. 1980, 9th cir. 2003), US Supreme Ct. 1995. Assoc. Quarles & Brady LLP, Milw., 1980-82, 85-87, ptnr., litig. practice Milw. & Madison, Wis., 1987—, mem. exec. com., 1999—; legis. asst. to Gov. State of Wis., Madison, 1983-85. Master: James. E. Doyle Am. Inn. Ct.; fellow: Am. Coll. Trial Lawyers; mem.: ABA, State Bar Wis. (bd. dir., young lawyers div. 1982—83), We. Dist. Bar Assn. (chmn. com. alternative dispute resolution 1992—97), Dane County Bar Assn., Phi Beta Kappa. Office: Quarles & Brady Ste 600 1 S Pinckney St Madison WI 53703-2808 Office Phone: 608-283-2426. Office Fax: 608-294-4923. Business E-Mail: dks@quarles.com.

SCHOTT, JOHN ROBERT, international consultant, educator; b. Rochester, NY, Jan. 30, 1936; s. John and Ellen (Waite) S.; m. Diane Elizabeth Dempsey, June 19, 1963; children: Elizabeth Anne (dec.), Jennifer, Jared Reed, George Kermit Alexander. BA magna cum laude, Haverford Coll., 1957; postgrad., Oxford U., 1957-59; PhD, Harvard U., 1964. Resident tutor in govt. Eliot House, Harvard Coll., Cambridge, Mass., 1960-64; inst. polit. sci. Wellesley (Mass.) Coll., 1964-66; policy planning specialist AID, Washington, 1966-67; chief Title IX div. AID, Washington, 1967-68; vis. prof. polit. devel. Fletcher Sch. Law & Diplomacy, Tufts U., Medford, Mass., 1968-70; sr. v.p. Thunderbird Grad. Sch. Internat. Mgmt., Phoenix, 1970-71; cons. internat. affairs Francestown, NH, 1971-74; pres. Schott & Assocs., Inc., Jaffrey Center, NH, 1974-93. Mem. U.S. Del. World Assembly Internat. Secretariat for Voluntary Service, New Delhi, 1967;

advisor Office Prime Minister Royal Thai Govt., Bangkok, 1978-80, Minister Cooperatives Govt. of Indonesia, Jakarta, 1983-84; research asst. spl. appointment The Brookings Inst., Washington, 1960-61 Author: Kenya Tragedy: European Colonization in East Africa, 1964, Frances' Town: History of Francestown, N.H., 1972, 2d edit., 1998, A Five-Year Comprehensive Plan for Development of Agricultural Cooperatives in Thailand, 1979, Recana-Komprehensip Pengembangan Kud, Jakarta, Indonesia, 1985; editor: An Experiment in Integrated Rural Development, 1978; contbr. articles to profl. jours. Mem. Bd. of Selectmen, Francestown, NH, 1975-78; trustee Spaulding Youth Ctr., Tilton, N.H., 1971-82, 85-89, pres. bd. trustees, 1972-75; trustee Internat. Inst. Rural Reconstrn., NYC, 1979-89, exec. com., 1985-89, bd. trustees NH Pub. Radio, 1990-96, chmn., 1993-95; spl. study commn. Coop. Extension Svc. State of NH, 1980-81, scenic and cultural by-ways com., 1993-96; forestry rep. County Extension Coun., Hillsboro County, NH, 1979-82; pres. NH Timberland Owner's Assn., 1989-90, bd. dirs., 1988-91; chmn. NH chpt. Nature Conservancy, 1990-93, hon. trustee, 1993—, chmn. NH Timber-Tourism Coalition, 1990-94; vice-chmn, Foresters Lic. Bd. State of NH, 1990-95; bd. trustees Cheshire Med. Ctr., 1992-94, RiverMead Retirement Cmty., Peterborough, NH, 1992-2000, chmn., 1996-2000; bd. overseers cmty. econ. devel. program So. NH U., 1997-2001, chmn., 1997-2000; trustee Sharon Arts Ctr., 2001-03; bd. dirs. Granite State Conservation Voters Alliance, 2004—. Recipient The Haverford award, Haverford Coll., Pa., 1999, Global Alumni Svc. to Humanity award, Rotary Internat. Found., 2005—06; fellow, Rotary Found., 1957—58, Harvard U. Arts and Sci., 1959—60; scholar, Coslett Found., 1958—59, Fulbright Found., 1962—63. Home and Office: Schott & Assocs 15 Upper Troy Rd Fitzwilliam NH 03447

SCHOTT, MICHAEL J., library director; b. Atlantic City, Sept. 28, 1950; s. Joseph Louis and Dorothy Theresa Schott; m. Janice Alexander, Aug. 4, 1984; children: Christopher Windsor, Rebecca Katherine. BA in Am. History, LaSalle Coll., Phila., 1972; MA in Libr. Sci., Glassboro State Coll., 1978; MLS, So. Conn. State Coll., 1993. Asst. libr. dir. N.Y. Med. Coll., Valhalla, 1985—86; hosp. libr. dir. Danbury (Conn.) Hosp., 1987—99; med. libr. dir. W.Va. U., Charleston, 2000—06; with Easton Hosp, Pa., 2006—. Author: Medical Library Downsizing; contbr. articles to profl. jours. Recipient Pub. Rels. award, Conn. Libr. Assn., 1982, 1984, 1986. Mem.: Beta Phi Mu. Office: Easton Hosp 250 S 21st St Easton PA 18045 Home: 2747 Queen St Easton PA 18045

SCHOTT, ROBERT JAMES, internist, cardiologist; b. Sept. 15, 1957; MD, U. Mich. Med. Sch., 1981. Cert. Internal Medicine, Cardiovascular Disease. Resident U. Mich.; fellow Mass. Gen. Hosp., Harvard Med. Sch.; dir. med. affairs Sutter Med. Ctr., Sacramento, chief, cardiovascular disease, 2007—, hosp. affiliation: physician Sutter Independent Physicians. Mem. adv. bd. Am. Health Care. Office: Northern Calif Cardiovascular Assocs 5301 F St Ste 117 Sacramento CA 95819 Address: 1004 Fowler Way #4 Placerville CA 95667 Office Phone: 916-733-1788, 916-733-1787, 530-626-9488. Office Fax: 916-561-6818. *

SCHOTT, SALLY MARIA, music publisher, arts education consultant; b. San Antonio, Feb. 7, 1943; d. Valentine Felix Schott, Jr. and Doris Faye. MusB, Okla. Coll. Women, 1964; MusM Edn., North Tex. State U., 1966. Choral dir. Jackson Intermediate, Pasadena, Tex., 1965—74, South Houston H.S., 1974—2004; founding ptnr. Alliance Music Publs., Houston, 1994—. Ednl. cons. Bay Area Chorus, Houston, 2004—; supr. student tchrs. U. Houston, 2004—; text correlations writer McGraw-Hill, Woodland Hills, Calif., 2005—; minority ptnr. AMC Music, Houston, 1975—2006; pres. Quaid/Schott Media Prodns., LLC, 2005—, Schott Bradshaw Publ., LLC, 2006—; cons. choral adjudicators panels, American Classic music festivals. Editor: Something to Sing About, 1981, Howard Swan: Conscience of a Profession, 1987; coord. writing team Sing, 1988. Mem. adv. bd. Am. Classic Festivals, San Antonio, 2004—; ednl. adv. bd. Houston Chamber Choir, 2004—. Named to Hall Fame, U. Sci. & Arts Okla., 1996; recipient Outstanding Young Educator, Pasadena Jaycees, 1974, HS Tchr. Year, Pasadena, 1986, Tchrs. Make a Difference award, KTRK, 1988. Mem.: Tex. Choral Dirs. Assn. (state v.p. 1976—77), Am. Choral Dirs. Assn. (R&S 1994—98, pres. 2000—02, editor newsletter 2002—04), Tex. Music Educators Assn. (pres., state vocal chair 1981—86), Pasadena Area Ret. Sch. Employees, Delta Kappa Gamma, Sigma Alpha Iota (pres. 1966, Leadership award Svc. to Music in Houston 1987). Republican. Methodist. Avocations: photography, travel, sports. Home: Quaid/Schott Media Publ 62 W Thymewood Pl The Woodlands TX 77382

SCHOTT, SARAH E., lawyer; b. Sheboygan, Wis., Oct. 14, 1975; BA in Geology and Economics, magna cum laude, Lawrence U., 1997; JD cum laude, Duke U., 2000. Bar: Ill. 2000, US Dist. Ct. (No. Dist. Ill.) 2000, Wis. 2004. Assoc. Wildman Harrold Allen & Dixon, Chgo., 2000—03; v.p., asst. gen. counsel The Ziegler Cos., Inc., Milw., 2003, sr. mng. dir., gen. counsel. Mem.: Securities Industry Assn. (mem. legal and compliance divsn.), Am. Corp. Counsel Assn., ABA, Chgo. Bar Assn., Ill. Bar Assn. Office: Ziegler Companies Ste 2000 250 East Wisconsin Ave Milwaukee WI 53202 Office Phone: 414-978-6400. Office Fax: 414-978-6401.

SCHOTTENFELD, DAVID, retired epidemiologist, educator; b. NYC, Mar. 25, 1931; m. Rosalie C. Schaeffer; children: Jacqueline, Stephen. AB, Hamilton Coll., 1952; MD, Cornell U., 1956; MS in Pub. Health, Harvard U., 1963. Diplomate Am. Bd. Internal Medicine, Am. Bd. Preventive Medicine. Intern in internal medicine Duke U., Durham, NC, 1956-57; resident in internal medicine Meml. Sloan-Kettering Cancer Ctr., Cornell U. Med. Coll., NYC, 1957-59; Craver fellow med. oncology Meml. Sloan-Kettering Cancer Ctr., 1961-62; clin. instr. dept. pub. health Cornell U., NYC, 1963—65, asst. prof. dept. pub. health, 1965-70, assoc. prof. dept. pub. health, 1970-73, prof. dept. pub. health, 1973-86; John G. Searle prof., chmn. epidemiology sch. pub. health U. Mich., Ann Arbor, 1986—2004, prof. internal medicine, 1986—2004, prof. emeritus internal medicine and epidemiology Sch. Pub. Health, 2004—; adj. prof. dept. family medicine and cmty. health U. Mass. Med. Sch., Worcester, 2006—. Vis. prof. epidemiology U. Minn., Mpls., 1968, 71, 74, 82, 86; W.G. Cosbie lectr. Can. Oncology Soc., 1987. Editor: Cancer Epidemiology and Prevention, 1982, 2d. edit., 1996, 3d edit., 2006; author 10 books; contbr. more than 250 articles to profl. jours. Served with USPHS, 1959-61. Recipient Acad. Career award in Preventive Oncology, Nat. Cancer Inst., 1980-85, Disting. Achievement award Am. Soc. Preventive Oncology, 1992; vis. scholar Nat. Cancer Inst., 2007. Fellow AAAS, ACP, APHA (John Snow award 2007), Am. Coll. Preventive Medicine, Am. Coll. Epidemiology (Abraham Lilienfeld award 2002), Armed Forces Epidemiology Bd.; mem. Soc. Epidemiologic Rsch. (pres. 1998-99), Phi Beta Kappa. Office: U Mich Sch Pub Health Dept Epidemiology 109 Observatory St Ann Arbor MI 48109-2029 Home: 25 River Birch Ln Dalton MA 01226-2104 Business E-Mail: daschott@umich.edu.

SCHOTTENFELD, RICHARD STEVEN, psychiatrist; b. East Orange, NJ, Apr. 27, 1949; s. Alvin Carl and Pearl Natalie (Feller) S.; m. Tanina Rostain. BA, Yale U., 1971, MD, 1976. Diplomate Am. Bd. Psychiatry and Neurology. Intern Mt. Sinai Hosp., NYC, 1976-77; resident Yale U. Sch. Medicine, New Haven, 1979-82, Robert Wood Johnson clin. VA fellow, 1982-84; asst. prof. psychiatry Yale U., New Haven, 1984-90, assoc. prof. psychiatry, 1990—; dir. alcohol treatment Conn. Mental Health Ctr., New Haven, 1984-87, dir. evaluation unit, 1984-87, assoc. dir. substance abuse treatment unit, 1987-89, co-dir. substance abuse treatment unit, 1989-91, dir. substance abuse treatment unit, 1991—; med. dir. APT Found., New Haven, 1987—, acting chief exec. officer, 1989-91, chief exec. officer, 1991—. Mem. Conn. Psychiat. Soc. (co-chair AIDS subcom. 1988-89). Avocations: cross country skiing, backpacking, bicycle riding. Office: Conn Mental Health Ctr 34 Park St Rm S-103 New Haven CT 06519-1187

SCHOTTENHEIMER, MARTY (MARTIN EDWARD SCOTTENHEIMER), former professional football coach; b. Canonsburg, Pa., Sept. 23, 1943; m. Patricia Schottenheimer; children: Kristen, Brian BA in Eng., U. Pitts., 1964. Profl. football player Buffalo Bills, 1965-68, Boston Patriots, 1969-70, Pitts. Steelers, 1971, Portland Storm, World League Football, 1974; real estate developer Miami and Denver, 1971-74; linebackers coach NY Giants, 1975-77, defensive coord., 1977; linebackers coach Detroit Lions, 1978-79; defensive coord. Cleve. Browns, 1980-84, head coach, 1985-88, Kans. City Chiefs, 1989-99, Wash. Redskins, 2001, San Diego Chargers, 2002—07; tv analyst ESPN, 1999—2000. Motivational spkr. IMG Speakers Bureau. Named Coach of the Year, UPI/AFC, 1995, AP, 2004, Pro Football Weekly, 2004.

SCHOTTENSTEIN, JAY L., retail executive; b. 1954; Grad., Ind. U. With Schottenstein Stores, Columbus, Ohio, vice chmn., exec. v.p., CEO, 1992—; chmn. Value City Department Stores, Columbus, Ohio, 1992; CEO Am. Eagle Outfitters, Warrendale, Pa., 1992—2002, chmn., 2002—, Retail Ventures Inc., 2002—. Office: Schottenstein Stores 1800 Moler Rd Columbus OH 43207-1680 Address: Retail Ventures Inc 3241 Westerville Rd Columbus OH 43224 also: American Eagle Outfitters 150 Thorn Hill Dr Warrendale PA 15086-7528

SCHOTTER, ANDREW ROYE, economics professor, consultant; b. NYC, June 6, 1947; s. I. Harvey and Sara (Rothstein) S.; m. Anne Howland, June 7, 1970; children: Geoffrey, Elizabeth. BS, Cornell U., 1969; MA, PhD, NYU, 1974. Asst. prof. Syracuse (N.Y.) U., 1974-75, NYU, 1975-81, assoc. prof., 1981-86, prof., chmn. econs. dept. NYC, 1989-93, 96-99, chmn. C.V. Starr Ctr. for Applied Econs., 1986-89, dir. Ctr. for Experiential Social Sci., 2001—. Vis. asst. prof. Cornell U., Ithaca, 1974-75; vis. prof. U. Venice, 1993, U. Amsterdam; cons. Gulf & Western Corp., N.Y. 1987, Pegalis & Wachsman, Great Neck, N.Y., 1987-88, Nat. Econ. Rsch. Assocs., White Plains, N.Y., 1989—. Author: Economic Theory of Social Institutions, 1981, Free Market Economics: A Critical Appraisal, 1985, 2d edit., 1990, Microeconomics: A Modern Approach, 1993, 3d edit., 2000; mem. editl. bd.: Am. Econ. Rev., 1995—, Exptl. Econs., 1997; assoc. editor: Games and Econ. Behavior; spl. editor: Exptl. Econs. Grantee Office of Naval Rsch., 1980-85, NSF, 1988-90, 97—; recipient Kenan Enterprise award, 1993. Mem. Am. Econ. Assn., Econometric Soc., Econ. Sci. Assn. (pres.-elect 1997), Game Theory Soc. Office: NYU Dept Econs 269 Mercer St New York NY 10003-6633

SCHOTTLAENDER, BRIAN E.C., university librarian; BA in German Studies, U. Tex., Austin, 1974; MSLS, Ind. U., 1980. Past various libr. positions at Firma Otto Harrassowitz, Wiesbaden, Germany, Ind. U., U. Ariz.; from asst. head cataloging dept. to asst. univ. libr. tech. svc. UCLA, 1984—93, assoc. univ. libr. for collections and tech. svc., 1993—99; univ. libr. U. Calif., San Diego, 1999—. ALA rep. to internat. Joint Steering Com. for Revision Anglo-Am. Cataloguing Rules, 1995—2001; chair Program Coop. Cataloguing Libr. Congress, 1997—98; chair Pacific Rim Digital Alliance, 1999—2001, San Diego Libr. Circuit, 1999—. Editor: Retrospective Conversion: History, Approaches, Considerations, 1992. Sr. fellow Palmer Sch. Libr. Sci., Long Island U., 1995. Mem.: Assn. Rsch. Libr. (bd. dir. 2001—, pres. 2006—07), ALA (bd. dir. Assoc. Libr. Collections and Tech. Svc. 1996—, pres. Assoc. Libr. Collections and Tech. Svc. 2003—, recipient Margaret Mann Citation award 2001), Beta Phi Mu. Office: Adminstrv Office Geisel Libr Univ Calif 9500 Gilman Dr #0175G La Jolla CA 92093-0175 Office Phone: 858-534-3060. E-mail: becs@ucsd.edu. *

SCHOULTZ, LARS, political scientist, educator; b. San Gabriel, Calif., Aug. 23, 1942; s. Ture Wilhelm and Bernice (Bowie) S.; m. Jane Volland, Jan. 18, 1969; children: Nils Gibson, Karina Anne. BA, Stanford U., 1964, MA, 1966; PhD, U. N.C., 1973. Prof. Miami U., Oxford, Ohio, 1973—77, U. Fla., Gainesville, 1977—79; William Rand Kenan Jr. prof. polit. sci. U. N.C., Chapel Hill, 1979—. Author: Human Rights and U.S. Policy Toward Latin America, 1981, National Security and U.S. Policy Toward Latin America, 1987, The Populist Challenge, 1983, Beneath the United States, 1998. Sgt. U.S. Army, 1966-67. MacArthur fellow in internat. peace and security MacArthur Found., 1990-91, Fulbright fellow, Rockefeller Found. fellow, Ford Found. fellow, Social Sci. Rsch. Coun., Woodrow Wilson fellow, 1994-95, Nat. Humanities Ctr. fellow, 1999-00. Mem. Latin Am. Studies Assn. (pres. 1991-92, v.p. 1990-91). Democrat. Home: 250 Glandon Dr Chapel Hill NC 27514-3816 Office: U NC Inst Latin Am Studies Chapel Hill NC 27599-0001 Home Phone: 919-929-6087; Office Phone: 919-962-0422. E-mail: Schoultz@unc.edu.

SCHOUMACHER, BRUCE HERBERT, lawyer; b. Chgo., May 23, 1940; s. Herbert Edward and Mildred Helen (Wagner) S.; m. Alicia Wesley (Sanchez), Nov. 4, 1967; children: Liana Cristina, Janina Maria. BS, Northwestern U., 1961; MBA, U. Chgo., 1963, JD, 1966. Bar: Nebr. 1966, U.S. Dist. Ct. Nebr. 1966, Ill. 1971, U.S. Dist. Ct. (no. dist.) Ill. 1971, U.S. Ct. Appeals (7th cir.) 1979, U.S. Supreme Ct. 1982, U.S. Ct. Fed. Claims 1986. Assoc. Luebs, Tracy, and Huebner, Grand Island, Nebr., 1966-67, McDermott, Will, and Emery, Chgo., 1971-76; ptnr. McDermott, Will,and Emery, Chgo., 1976-89, Querrey and Harrow, Ltd., Chgo., 1989—. Instr. bus. adminstrn., Bellevue Coll., Nebr., 1967-70; lectr., U. Md. Overseas Program, 1970. Author: Engineers and the Law: An Overview, 1986; contbg. author: Construction Law, 1986, Construction Law Handbook, 1999, Construction Business Handbook, 2004; co-author: Successful Business Plans for Architects, 1992; contbr. articles to profl. jour. Capt., USAF, 1967-71, Vietnam. Decorated, Bronze Star, 1971. Fellow Am. Coll. Constrn. Lawyers; mem. ABA, AIA (profl. affiliate), Nebr. Bar Assn., Ill. State Bar Assn. (ad hoc com. large law firms 1992-98), chmn. membership and bar activities com. 1988-89, coun. ins. law sect., 1986-91, mem. spl. com. on computerized legal rsch. 1986-87, Chgo. Bar Assn. (chmn. fed. civil procedure com. 1982-83), Def. Rsch. Inst., Ill. Assn. Def. Trial Counsel, Chgo. Bldg. Congress (bd. dirs. 1985—, sec. 1987-89, 95—, v.p. 1989-91), Soc. Ill. Constrn. Attys. (steering com. 2004-2005, sec. 2005-07, treas. 2007—), Western Soc. Engr. (assoc.), The Lawyers Club of Chgo., Tower Club, Chgo., Univ. Club Chgo., Rolling Green Country Club, Pi Kappa Alpha, Phi Delta Phi. Republican. Methodist. Office: Querrey & Harrow Ltd 175 W Jackson Blvd Ste 1600 Chicago IL 60604-2827 Office Phone: 312-540-7046. Business E-Mail: bschoumacher@querrey.com.

SCHOVILLE, DENNIS A(RNOLD), lawyer; b. Richland Ctr., Wis., May 31, 1945; BS, U. Wis., 1967; JD with Distinction, Ill. Inst. Tech., 1973; LLM, Northwestern U., 1974. Bar: Wis. 1973, Ill. 1973, U.S. Dist. Ct. (no. dist.) Ill. 1973, Calif. 1974, U.S. Dist. Ct. (so. dist.) Calif. 1974, U.S. Ct. Appeals (9th cir.) 1985, U.S. Ct. Claims. Ptnr. Schoville & Arnell, LLP, San Diego. Capt. U.S. Army, 1968-73. Recipient Broderick award for professionalism, integrity and ethics, 1996; named Consumer Attys. San Diego Trial Lawyer of the Yr., 1995, 99. Mem. ABA, ATLA, Am. Coll. Trial Lawyers, Am. Bd. Trial Advocates (nat. bd. dirs., past pres. San Diego chpt.), Consumer Attys. San Diego (past pres., Trial Advocacy award 2005, Consumer Adv. of Yr. award 2005), Ill. State Bar Assn., State Bar Wis., State Bar Calif., San Diego County Bar Assn. (chair jud. evaluation com. 2006), San Diego Trial Lawyers Assn. (Outstanding Trial Advocacy award-civil 1984, 89, 94), Am. Inns of Ct. (sr. master), DFC Soc. (gen. counsel, nat. dir.). Office: Schoville & Arnell LLP 1230 Columbia St Ste 800 San Diego CA 92101-3571 Office Phone: 619-232-9901.

SCHOWALTER, JOHN ERWIN, child and adolescent psychiatry educator; b. Milw., Mar. 15, 1936; s. Raymond Phillip and Martha (Kowalke) S.; m. Ellen Virginia Lefferts, June 11, 1960; children: Jay, Bethany. BS, U. Wis., 1957, MD, 1960. Diplomate Am. Bd. Psychiatry and Neurology (com. on cert. in child psychiatry 1983-85, chmn. 1986-87, bd. dirs. 1993-2000, chmn. com. added qualifications forensic psychiatry 1993-97); cert. in adult and child psychiatry also psychoanalysis. Intern in pediat. Yale-New Haven Hosp., 1960-61; asst. resident in psychiatry Cin. Gen. Hosp., 1961-63; fellow in child psychiatry Yale U. Child Study Ctr., New Haven, 1963-65; psychiatrist Mental Hygiene Clinic U.S. Army, Ft. Ord, Calif., 1965-67; asst. prof. Yale U. Child Study Ctr., 1967-70, assoc. prof. Sch. Medicine, 1970-75, dir. tng., 1971-96, prof. pediat. and psychiatry, 1975-89, chief child psychiatry, 1982-90, dir. child psychiatry clin. svcs., 1990—2003, Albert J. Solnit prof. child psychiatry and pediat., 1989—2003, interim chmn., 2001—02, prof. emeritus, sr. rsch. scientist, 2003—. Mem. publ. com. Yale U. Press., 1992-97; mem. sci. adv. bd. Sophia Found. Med. Rsch., Rotterdam, The Netherlands, 1984-89; dir. mental health and substance abuse Yale Preferred Health Plan, 1995-99. Co-author: The Family Handbook of Adolescence, 1979; contbr. numerous articles, book revs.; mem. editl. bd. Pediatrics, 1976-81, Children's Health Care, 1977-2003, Jour. Am. Psychoanalytic Assn., 1978, Pediatrics in Rev., 1978-85; asst. editor: Jour. Am. Acad. Child and Adolescent Psychiatry, 1988-97; co-editor: Yearbook Psychiatry and Applied Mental Health, 1988-97. Capt. U.S. Army, 1965-67. Fellow Am. Acad. Child and Adolescent Psychiatry (sec. 1985-87, pres. 1989-91, Simon Wile award 1996, mem. fin. planning com. 2000-04, chair governance com. 2001-04, chmn. presdl. scholars com. 2005—, chmn. policy statements com. 2005—, chmn. task force policies and procedures, 2007—), Am. Coll. Psychiatrists (chair Laughlin fellowship com. 2000-01, chair membership com. 2002-07), Am. Acad. Pediat.; mem. AMA (residency rev. com. psychiatry 1983-87, 89-94), Am. Pediatric Soc., Am. Psychoanalytic Assn. (cert. adult and child), Group Advancement Psychiatry (life fellow, com. on child psychiatry 1981, bd. dir. 1989-91, pres. 1993-95, chair life fellowship com. 2000—), Assn. Care Children's Health (pres. 1984-86), Am. Psychiat. Assn. (chmn. McGavin award selection com., 2007—, McGavin award, 2006—), Soc. Profs. Child Psychiatry (pres. 1984-86), Western New Eng. Inst. Psychoanalysis (mem. faculty in child psychoanalysis 1984—, pres. 1986-88), Conn. Med. Soc., New Haven Med. Soc., Conn. Coun. Child Psychiatrists (pres. 1979-81), Benjamin Rush Soc. (sec., treas. 1998-99, v.p. 1999-2000, pres. 2000-02), Sigma Xi. Lutheran. Home: 256 Ives St Hamden CT 06518-2200 Office: Yale U Child Study Ctr PO Box 207900 230 S Frontage Rd New Haven CT 06520-7900

SCHOWALTER, WILLIAM RAYMOND, college dean, educator; b. Milw., Dec. 15, 1929; s. Raymond Philip and Martha (Kowalke) S.; m. Jane Ruth Gregg, Aug. 22, 1953; children: Katherine Ruth, Mary Patricia, David Gregg. BS, U. Wis., 1951; postgrad., Inst. Paper Chemistry, 1951-52; MS, U. Ill., 1953, PhD, 1957; PhD (hon.), Inst. Nat. Poly. Lorraine, France, 1996. Asst. prof. dept. chem. engring. Princeton U., 1957-63, assoc. prof., 1963-66, prof., 1966-86, Class of 1950 prof. engring. and applied sci., 1986-89, acting chmn. dept. chem. engring., 1971, chmn. dept. chem. engring., 1978-87, assoc. dean Sch. Engring. and Applied Sci., 1971-77, class of 1950 prof. engring. and applied sci. emeritus, 2000—; dean Coll. Engring. U. Ill., Urbana, 1989-2001, dean, prof. emeritus, 2001—; Mobil prof. chem. engring. Nat. U. Singapore, 1998, sr. advisor to pres., 2001—. Sherman Fairchild disting. scholar Calif. Inst. Tech., 1977-78; vis. fellow U. Salford, Eng., 1974; vis. sr. fellow Sci. Rsch. Coun., U. Cambridge, Eng., 1970; cons. to chem. and petroleum cos.; editl. adv. bd. McGraw-Hill Pub. Co., 1964-92; co-chmn. Internat. Seminar for Heat and Mass Transfer, 1970; vis. com. for chem. engring. MIT, 1979-87, Lehigh U., 1980-87; mem. vis. com. Sch. Engring., Stanford U., 1990-2001; evaluation panelist Ctr. Chem. Engring. Nat. Bur. Standards, 1982-88, chmn., 1986-88; mem. commn. engring. and tech. sys. NRC, 1983-88; engring. rsch. bd., 1984-86; adv. coun. chem. engring. Cornell U., 1983-91; adv. coun. Sch. Engring., Rice U., 1986-92; adv. com. Ill. Inst. Tech., 1992-97; adv. coun. Coll. Engring., U. Calif., Berkeley, 1997-2001, Coll. Engring. U. Mich., 1997-2001, Sch. Engring. and Applied Sci., Princeton U., 1998-2002, Carnegie Inst. Tech., 1999-2001; acad. adv. bd. Sematech Corp., 1992-2001; internat. adv. panel Nat. U. Singapore, 1996, 2002; Reilly lectr. in chem. engring. U. Notre Dame, 1985, Van Winkle lectr. in chem. engring. U. Tex., Austin, 1986, David M. Mason lectr. chem. engring. Stanford U., 1987; Bird Stewart and Lightfoot lectr. chem. engring. U. Wis., 2001; R.H. Wilhelm lectr. in chem. engring. Princeton U., 2002; mem. fellowship program Packard Found. Sci. Adv. Panel, 1998—; mem. sci. adv. bd. Singapore Inst. for Chem. and Engring. Scis., 2003—; mem. panel for U.K., Rsch. Assessment Exercise 2008, 2006—. Author: Mechanics of Non-Newtonian Fluids, 1978; co-author: Colloidal Dispersions, 1989; mem. editl. com. Ann. Rev. Fluid Mechanics, 1974-80, Internat. Jour. Chem. Engring., 1974-94, Indsl. and Engring. Chemistry Fundamentals, 1975-78, Jour. Non-Newtonian Fluid Mechanics, 1976-2001, AIChE Jour., 1979-83; contbr. articles to profl. jours. Mem. Ill. Gov.'s Sci. Adv. Com., 1989-96. Served with U.S. Army, 1953-55. Decorated officier des Palmes Académiques (France); recipient Disting. Svc. citation Coll. Engring., U. Wis., Madison, 1983; Guggenheim fellow, 1987-88. Fellow AIChE (William H. Walker award 1982, bd. dirs. 1992-94), NAS (class membership com. 2000, 2002, class chmn. 2002-05), Am. Acad. Arts and Scis.; mem. Am. Soc. Engring. Edn. (Lectr. award chem. engring. divsn. 1971, exec. com. engr. deans coun. 1992-95, vice-chair, engring. deans coun. pub. policy com. 1998, chair engring. deans coun. pub. policy com. 1999-2001), NAE (awards com. 1986-88, chmn. 1987, acad. adv. bd. 1991-94, chmn. 1992-94, coun. 1994-2000, Draper Award com. 2001-03), Am. Chem. Soc., Soc. Rheology (exec. com. 1977-79, v.p. 1981-83, pres. 1983-85, Bingham medal 1988), Sigma Xi, Tau Beta Pi, Phi Lambda Upsilon, Phi Eta Sigma.

SCHOWEN, RICHARD LYLE, retired scientist; b. Nitro, W.Va., Aug. 29, 1934; s. J. Lyle and Margaret Marie Frances (Stamm) S.; m. Katharine Barbara Jetter, Aug. 10, 1963; children: Susana Katharine, Sarah Veronica. Student, Morris Harvey Coll., 1951-53; BS, U. Calif., Berkeley, 1958; PhD, MIT, 1962; doctorate (hon.), Martin Luther U. Halle-Wittenberg, German Democratic Republic, 1988. Rsch. assoc. M.I.T., 1962-63; mem. faculty U. Kans., Lawrence, 1963—, prof. chemistry, 1971-77, Solon E. Summerfield disting. prof. chemistry, prof. chemistry, molecular biosciences, pharmaceutical chemistry, 1977—2000; prof. emeritus, 2000—. Vis. lectr. Kyoto U., Japan, 1969; fgn. lectr. Tokyo U., 1969; vis. prof. Ind. U., 1976; Univ. disting. vis. prof. Calif. State U., Long Beach, 1978; sci. visitor U. Costa Rica, 1977, U. Sheffield, UK, 1978, U. Freiburg, 1982, Free U. Berlin, 1996; cons. NIH, NSF, publishers and pharm. firms; Kurt Mothes vis. prof. Martin Luther U., Halle-Wittenberg, Germany, 2000; sci. visitor Scripps Rsch. Inst., 2002. Editor: (with Richard Gandour) Transition States of Biochemical Processes, 1978; (with Alfred Barth) Peptides and Proteases: Recent Advances, 1987; (with Alfred Schellenberger) Thiamin Pyrophosphate Biochemistry, 1988, (with J.T. Hymes, J.P. Klinman, H.H. Limbach) Hydrogen-Transfer Reactions, 2006; editl. bd. Jour. Am. Chem. Soc.; editl. adv. bd. Jour. Phys. Organic Chemistry, Jour. Organic Chemistry, Bioorganic Med. Chemistry, Bioorganix Med. Chemistry Lett.; contbr. articles to profl. jours. NIH fellow, 1960-62; Elizabeth Watkins scholar, 1964; NIH Research Career Devel. grantee, 1968-73; Dolph Simons Sr. award, 1982, Humboldt Rsch. prize, 1996; vis. fellow Syntex (Can.), 1988. Fellow Am. Inst. Chemists, AAAS; mem. Am. Chem. Soc. (Midwest award 1992), Fedn. Am. Scientists, Soc. Neurosci., Am. Soc. for Biochemistry and Molecular Biology, Phi Beta Kappa (hon.), Sigma Xi, Chi Beta Phi. Democrat. Office: Dept Chemistry U Kans Lawrence KS 66045-0001 Business E-Mail: rschowen@ku.edu.

SCHRADE, ROBERT WARREN, classical pianist, educator; b. Walden, NY, Dec. 2, 1924; s. Louis J. and Elizabeth M. (Eitner) S.; m. Rolande M. Young, Dec. 21, 1949; children: Robelyn, Rhonda Lee, Rolisa M., Randolph R.A., Rorianne C. MusB, MusM, Manhattan Sch. Music, 1948. Mem. piano faculty Manhattan Sch. of Music, NYC, 1949-56, 68-89; mem. music faculty, artist-in-residence Chapin sch., NYC, 1948-89; pres., artistic dir. Sevenars Concerts, Inc., Worthington, Mass., 1976—. Lectr. in field. Appeared in frequent piano concerts, N.Y.C., Europe, including Carnegie Hall, Lincoln Ctr., 1977, 81, 86, with Schrade Family Pianists, 1980-93, Lincoln Ctr., N.Y.C., 2000; soloist symphony orchs. throughout Europe and South Pacific; ann. solo concerts Sevenars Music Festival, Sevenars Music Festival, Worthington, Mass., Berkshires; featured on radio and TV shows including PM Mag. film, NBC Today Show, Radio New Zealand; 50th anniversary of N.Y. adult debut Liederkranz Found. (Town Hall), N.Y.C; featured in Lifetime TV film, 2000. Cpl. USAAC, 1942-45. Avocations: tennis, fishing. Home: 30 East End Ave New York NY 10028-7053 Address: Rte 112 at Ireland St S Worthington MA 01098

SCHRADER, ALFRED EUGENE, lawyer; b. Nov. 1, 1953; s. Louis Clement and Helen Mae (Eberz) S.; m. Debra Susanne Britt-Garrett, Aug. 12, 1997. BA in Polit. Sci. magna cum laude, Kent State U., 1975; JD, Ohio State U., 1978. Bar: Ohio 1978, U.S. Dist. Ct. (no. dist.) Ohio 1978, U.S. Ct. Appeals (6th cir.) 1985, U.S. Supreme Ct. 1985. Dep. clk. Summit County Clk. of Cts., Akron, 1972-74; pvt. practice law Akron, 1978—; spl. counsel Bath Twp., Ohio, 1980-92, 95-98. Spkr. Akron Bar Assn. Akron Univ. Sch. Law CLE Seminars. Trustee Springfield Twp., Ohio, 1973-2001, pres., 1975, 79, 82, 88, 90, 95-96, 2000-01; v.p. Springfield-Akron Joint Econ. Devel. Dist., 1995-97, pres., 1997-2000; mem. adv. com. Cmty. Devel. Block, Summit County, 1985-97, Twinsburg Twp. tax abatement counsel, 1994—, Summit County Annexation Com., 1981-85; mem. Summit County Jail Study Commn., 1983, 84; mem. adv. bd. Springfield Schs., 1975; acting law dir. City of Streetsboro, Portage County, Ohio, 1997; legal coun. Reminderville Twinsburg JEDD Bd. 2000-; rep. numerous twps. State of Ohio on land use planning, annexation, revenue sharing, joint econ. devel. dist., annexation agreements, co-operative econ. devel. agreements, zoning and local govt. law matters; spl. counsel Harrison Hills Bd. Edn., Warren, Ohio Econ. Devel. Dist., 2002-2004, Lorain Co. Commr., 1999; rep. coun. dist. 8 Summit County, 2003-05, law dir. Twinsburg township, 2006—; law dir. East Union township, Wayne County, 1996—, Chippewa township, 2007—. Mem. ATLA, Akron Bar Assn. (v.p. legis. com. 1981-82, v.p. local govt. sect. 1992-93, chair local govt. sect. 1993-95, v.p. continuing legal edn. com. 2001-04), Ohio Acad. Trial Lawyers, Ohio Bar Assn., Summit County Twp. Assn. (exec. com. 1983-2001), Ohio Twp. Assn., Risk Mgmt. Authority (bd. dirs. 1996-2001, sec. 1997-2000, pres. 2000-01), Nat. Assn. Town and Twp. Attys. (bd. dirs. Ohio chpt. 1986, sec. 1987-93, v.p. 1993-97). Democrat. Roman Catholic. Fax: 330 762 2255. Home: 3344 Brunk Rd Akron OH 44312-3710 Office: Schrader Romanoski Stevenson and Wells 441 Wolf Ledges Pky Ste 400 Akron OH 44311-1039 Home Phone: 330-628-9678; Office Phone: 330-762-0765. Office Fax: 330-762-2255. E-mail: alschrader@choiceonemail.com.

SCHRADER, LAWRENCE EDWIN, plant physiologist, educator; b. Atchison, Kans., Oct. 22, 1941; s. Edwin Carl and Jenna Kathryn (Tobiason) S.; m. Elfriede J. Massier, Mar. 14, 1981 BS, Kans. State U., 1963; PhD, U. Ill., 1967; grad., Inst. Ednl. Mgmt., Harvard U., 1991. Asst. prof. dept. agronomy U. Wis., Madison, 1969-72, assoc. prof., 1972-76, prof., 1976-84; prof., head dept. agronomy U. Ill., Urbana, 1985-89; dean Coll. Agr. and Home Econs. Wash. State U., Pullman, 1989-94, prof. dept. horticulture, 1994—. Chief competitive rsch. grants office Dept. Agr., Washington, 1980-81; trustee, treas. Agrl. Satellite Corp., 1991-94. Contbr. chpts. to books, articles to profl. jours. Active Consortium for Internat. Devel., 1989-94, chair fin. com., vice chair exec. com., 1990-92, trustee 1989-94; mem. exec. com. Coun. Agrl. Heads of Agr., 1992-94. Capt., Rsch. biochemist, US Army, 1967-69. Recipient Soybean Researchers Recognition award 1983, Disting. Service award in Agriculture Kansas State U., 1987; Romnes Faculty fellow U. Wis., 1979 Fellow AAAS (steering group sect. agr. 1991-95, chair-elect sect. on agr., food and renewable resources 1995-96, chmn. 1996-97, past chmn. 1997-98, coun. mem. 1997-98), Am. Soc. Agronomy, Crop Sci. Soc. Am.; mem. Internat. Soc. for Hort. Sci., Am. Soc. for Hort. Sci., Am. Soc. Plant Biologists (sec. 1983-85, pres.-elect 1986, pres. 1987), Am. Chem. Soc., Coun. for Agrl. Sci. and Tech., Blue Key, Sigma Xi, Gamma Sigma Delta (Outstanding Alumnus award, 2003), Phi Kappa Phi, Phi Eta Sigma, Alpha Zeta (named to Centennial Honor Roll 1997). Methodist. Home: 3504 Crestview Rd Wenatchee WA 98801-9668 Office: Wash State U Tree Fruit Rsch & Extension Ctr 1100 N Western Ave Wenatchee WA 98801-1230 Home Phone: 509-662-7301; Office Phone: 509-663-8181 x265. Business E-Mail: schrader@wsu.edu.

SCHRADER, SUSAN RAE, elementary school educator; b. Tucson, Nov. 12, 1972; d. Edward Arthur and Nancy Young Schrader. BS, Nebr. Wesleyan U., Lincoln, 1994; M in Elem. Edn., No. Ariz. U., Phoenix, 2001. Cert. Ariz., 1995. Tchr. Tucson Unified Sch. Dist., 1995—96, Alhambra Sch. Dist., Phoenix, 1997—. Coach Peoria (Ariz.) Sch. Dist., 2004—06. V.p. Catalina Booster Club, Phoenix, 2002—04. Named Dist. Employee of Month, Alhambra Sch. Dist.; named to Athletic Hall of Fame, Nebr. Wesleyan U., 2005; recipient Spirit of Catalina, Catalina Ventura Elem., 2004. R-Consevative. Roman Catholic. Avocations: travel, gardening, home improvements, movies, reading. Office: Catalina Ventura 6331 N 39th Ave Phoenix AZ 85019 Home Phone: 623-266-3978; Office Phone: 602-841-7445. E-mail: sschrader@alhambra.k12.az.us.

SCHRADER, WILLIAM L., communications executive; BS, Cornell U. Exec. dir., co-founder Cornell Theory Ctr.; founder, pres., CEO NYSER-Net; dir., founder N.E. Paralle Archs. Ctr. Syracuse (N.Y.) U.; chmn., CEO, founder PSINet, Inc., Herndon, Va., 1989—. Participant panel discussions of industry trends CNN, CNBC, MSNBC, FNN, First Bur., TechnoPolitics.

SCHRADY, DAVID ALAN, civilian military employee, educator; b. Akron, Ohio, Nov. 11, 1939; s. Marvin G. and Sheila A. (O'Neill) S.; m. Mary E. Hilt, Sept. 1, 1962; children: Peter, Patrick, Matthew. BS, Case Inst. Tech., 1961, MS, 1963, PhD, 1965. Prof., chmn. Naval Postgrad. Sch., Monterey, Calif., 1974-76, dean acad. planning, 1976-80, provost and acad. dean, 1980-87, prof. ops. rsch., 1988—, Disting. prof., ops. rsch. educator, 1995—. Vis. prof. Cranfield Inst. Tech./Royal Mil. Coll. of Sci., Shrivenham, Eng., fall 1987-spring 88. Contbr. articles to profl. jours. Recipient Goodeve medal Ops. Rsch. Soc., U.K., 1992, Navy Disting. Civilian Svc. medal, 2006 Fellow: Inst. for Ops. Rsch. and the Mgmt. Scis., Mil. Ops. Rsch. Soc., (pres. 1978—79, Wanner medal 1984); mem.: Internat. Fedn. Ops. Rsch. Socs. (hon. treas. 1988—97), Ops. Rsch. Soc. Am. (pres. 1983—84, Kimball medal 1994). Avocations: guitar, motor sports. Office: Naval Postgrad Sch Dept Ops Rsch Monterey CA 93943-5000 Business E-Mail: dschrady@nps.edu.

SCHRAFT, SUSAN, radiologist; b. New Rochelle, NY, Mar. 4, 1954; d. William Charles and Mary Masalsky Schraft; m. Richard Berne Schraft, Sept. 7, 1985; children: Marisa, Charles. BA, Wesleyan U., Middletown, Conn., 1976; MD, SUNY, Syracuse, 1983. Attending resident Downstate Med. Ctr., Bklyn., 1989—92, Ctrl. Maine Med. Ctr., Lewiston, Maine, 1992—. Fellow, Hosp. for Spl. Musculoskeletal Surgery, NY, 1984, Mt. Sinai Med. Coll., NY, 1988. Mem.: Coll. Radiology, Maine Med. Assn., Reading Soc. N.Am. Avocations: yoga, gardening, skiing, reading, travel. Home: 5 Thomhunt Rd Falmouth ME 04105

SCHRAG, ADELE FRISBIE, business education educator; b. Cynthiana, Ky., May 7, 1921; d. Shirley Ledyard and Edna Kate (Ford) S.; m. William Albert Schrag, Apr. 6, 1963; 1 stepchild, Marie Carol. BS, Temple U., 1942; MA, N.Y. U., 1944, PhD, 1961. Tchr. Manor Twp. High Sch., Millersville, Pa., 1942-43, Downingtown (Pa.) Sr. High Sch., 1943-50; instr., asst. prof. Temple U. Sch. Bus. and Pub. Administrn., Phila., 1950-60; prof. bus. edn. and vocat. edn. Coll. Edn., 1960-85, sr. prof. edn., 1985-88, prof. emeritus, 1988—. Vis. lectr. N.Y. U.; cons. Phila. Community Coll., 1967-82 Editor: Business Education for the Automated Office, 1964; author: (with Estelle L. Popham and Wanda Blockhus) A Teaching-Learning System for Business Education, 1975, How to Dictate, 1981, Office Procedures Update, 1982, (with Robert Poland) A Teaching System for Business Subjects, 1988; contbr. articles to profl. jours., chpts. to books. Trustee Meth. Hosp., 1981—85, Sun Cities Symphony Assn., 1988—93, Habitat for Humanity West Valley, 1994—2005, co-pres., 1999—2001; trustee Habitat for Humanity Ariz., 1999—2003. Recipient Profl. Panhellenic award, 1963; Kensington High Sch. Alumnae award, 1972 Mem. Soc. Automation in Bus. Edn. (pres. 1969-73, dir. 1974), Nat. Assn. Bus. Tchr. Edn. (pres. 1983-84), Bus. Edn. Certification Council, Phi Gamma Nu (nat. treas. 1952-54, nat. sec. 1954-56), Delta Pi Epsilon (policy commn. for bus. and econ. edn. 1975-78, dir. research found. 1978-83, pres. research found. 1983). Home: 14515 W Granite Valley Dr # 644 Sun City West AZ 85375-6021 E-mail: as107@cox.net.

SCHRAG, DANIEL P., geochemist, educator; BS in Geology/Geophysics and Polit. Sci., Yale U., New Haven, 1988; PhD in Geochemistry, U. Calif., Berkeley, 1993. Asst. prof. dept. geosciences Princeton U., NJ, 1994—97; mem. faculty to prof. geochemistry Harvard U., 1997—, dir. Lab. Geochemical Oceanography. Contbr. articles to sci. jours. Recipient Macelwane medal; grantee MacArthur fellowship, 2000. Fellow: Am. Geophys. Union. Office: Lab Geochemical Oceanography Harvard U Dept Earth and Planetary Scis 20 Oxford St Cambridge MA 02138 E-mail: schrag@eps.harvard.edu.

SCHRAG, EDWARD A., JR., lawyer; b. Milw., Mar. 27, 1932; s. Edward A. and Mabel Lena (Baumbach) Schrag; m. Leslie Jean Israel, June 19, 1954; children: Amelia Marie Schrag Prack, Katherine Allison Schrag Roberts, Edward A. III(dec.). BS in Econs, U. Pa., 1954; JD, Harvard, 1960. Bar: Ohio 1961. From assoc. to ptnr. Vorys, Sater, Seymour & Pease, Columbus, Ohio, of counsel, 1960—. Sec. Ranco Inc., 1972—87; trustee Lake of Woods Water Co., 1972—91; mem. Ohio divsn. Securities Adv. Com. Mem. Downtown Area Com., 1970—74. Served to lt. (j.g.) USNR, 1954—57. Mem.: ABA, Columbus Bar Assn., Ohio Bar Assn., Navy League, Columbus Area C. of C., Ohio State U. Pres.'s Club, Capital Club, Crichton Club, Pi Gamma Mu, Phi Sigma Alpha, Beta Gamma Sigma, Alpha Tau Omega. Episcopalian. Home: 9400 White Oak Ln Westerville OH 43082-9606 Office: Vorys Sater Seymour and Pease PO Box 1008 52 E Gay St Columbus OH 43216-1008 Office Phone: 614-464-6400. Business E-Mail: easchrag@vssp.com.

SCHRAG, PETER, editor, writer; b. Karlsruhe, Germany, July 24, 1931; arrived in U.S., 1941, naturalized, 1953; s. Otto and Judith (Haas) S.; m. Melissa Jane Mowrer, June 9, 1953 (div. 1969); children: Mitzi, Erin Andrew; m. Diane Divoky, May 24, 1969 (div. 1981); children: David Divoky, Benaiah Divoky; m. Patricia Ternahan, Jan. 1, 1988. AB cum laude, Amherst Coll., 1953. Reporter El Paso (Tex.) Herald Post, 1953-55; asst. sec., asst. dir. publs. Amherst Coll., 1955-66, instr. Am. Studies, 1960-64; assoc. edn. editor Sat. Rev., 1966-68, exec. editor, 1968-69; editor Change mag., 1969-70; editor at large Saturday Rev., 1969-72; contbg. editor Saturday Review/Education, 1972-73; editl. adv. bd. The Columbia Forum, 1972-75; editl. bd. Social Policy, 1971—; contbg. editor More, 1974-78, Inquiry, 1977-80, The Am. Prospect, 1995—; editl. page editor Sacramento Bee and McClatchy Newspapers, 1978-96, contbg. editor, 1996—. Vis. lectr. U. Mass. Sch. Edn., 1970-72; fellow in profl. journalism Stanford U., Palo Alto, Calif., 1973-74; lectr. U. Calif., Berkeley, 1974-78, 90—; Pulitzer Prize juror, 1988-89; vis. scholar U. Calif. Inst. Govtl. Studies, Berkeley, 1998—. Author: Voices in the Classroom, 1965, Village School Downtown, 1967, Out of Place in America, 1971, The Decline of the Wasp, 1972, The End of the American Future, 1973, Test of Loyalty, 1974, (with Diane Divoky) The Myth of the Hyperactive Child, 1975, Mind Control, 1978, Paradise Lost: California's Experience, America's Future, 1998, Final Test: The Battle for Adequacy in America's Schools, 2003, California: America's High-Stakes Experiment, 2006; contbr. articles to profl. publs. Adv. com. Student Rights Project, NY Civil Liberties Union, 1970-72; mem. Com. Study History, 1958-72; trustee Emma Willard Sch., 1967-69; bd. dirs. Park Sch., Oakland, Calif., 1976-77, Ctr. for Investigative Reporting, 1979-81, Ed Source, 1998—; bd. adv. Pub. Policy Inst. Calif. Guggenheim fellow, 1971-72; Nat. Endowment for Arts fellow, 1976-77 Office: 5835 Colton Blvd Oakland CA 94611-2204 Business E-Mail: pschrag@sacbee.com.

SCHRAG, PHILIP GORDON, law educator; b. Chgo., Apr. 12, 1943; s. Louis Phillip and Lala D. (Fineman) S.; m. Emily Shiling, June 7, 1964 (div. Aug. 1985); children: David, Zachary; m. Lisa Gabrielle Lerman, Dec. 29, 1985; children: Samuel Lerman, Sarah. AB, Harvard U., 1964; LLB, Yale U., 1967. Bar: NY 1967, D.C. 1981. Asst. counsel NAACP Legal Def. & Edn. Fund Inc., NYC, 1967-70; consumer adv. NYC, 1970-71; assoc. prof. law Columbia U., NYC, 1971-73, prof. law, 1973-77; dep. gen. counsel ACDA, Washington, 1977-81; prof. law Georgetown U., Washington, 1981—, dir., Ctr. for Applied Legal Studies & Pub. Interest Law Scholars Program. Cons. Consumer Protection Bd., N.Y., 1975, Carter-Mondale Transition Planning, 1976, Gov.'s Adv. Coun., P.R., 1970. Author: Counsel for the Deceived, 1972, Behind the Scenes: The Politics of a Constitutional Convention, 1985, A Well-Founded Fear: The Congressional Battle to Save Political Asylum in America, 2000, Repay As You Earn: The Flawed Government Program to Help Students Have Public Interest Careers, 2002; co-author (with M. Meltsner): Reflection on Clinical Legal Education, 1998; co-author: (with Lisa G. Lerman) Ethical Problems in the Practice of Law, 2005. Del. Statehood Constnl. Conv., D.C., 1982; chair Consumer's Adv. Coun., N.Y.C., 1968-70. Office Phone: 202-662-9099. Business E-Mail: schrag@law.georgetown.edu.

SCHRAGE, ROSE, retired academic administrator; b. Montelimar, France, Apr. 15, 1942; came to U.S., 1947; d. Abraham and Celia (Silbiger) Levine; m. Samuel Schrage, Dec. 12, 1935 (dec. 1976); children: Abraham, Leon. BRE, Beth Rivkah Tchrs. Sem., Bklyn., 1968; Paralegal, Manpower Career Devel. Agy., Bklyn., 1973; MS, L.I. U., 1975; Advanced Cert. Ednl. Adminstrn., Bklyn. Coll., 1983. Cert. sch. dist. adminstr., guidance counselor, tchr., asst. prin. Sec., NYC, 1964-68; police adminstrv. aide N.Y.C. Police Dept., 1974-75; coord. state reading aid program Sch. Dist. 14, Bklyn., 1977-78, project dir. Title VII, 1978-81, asst. dir. reimbursable fed. and state programs, 1981-85, dist. bus. mgr., 1985-94, asst. prin., 1994—99, spl. edn. instrn. specialist, adminstr., 1999—; ednl. adminstr. Ctrl. Liaison Office for Impartial Hearings divsn. student support svcs. Dept. Edn., NYC, 2001—04; ret., 2004. Chmn. N.Y.C. Bd. Edn. IMPACT Com., Bklyn., 1986—. Author (poem): Never Again, 1983; contbg. editor Chai Today; contbr. articles to profl. jours. Del. Republican. Jud. Conf., 1968; founder, pres Concerned Parents, Bklyn., 1977; radio co-host Israeli War Heroes Fund-Radiothon, Bklyn.; family counselor local social agys., Bklyn.; co-founder cmty. vol. ambulance Hatzalah, 1977. Recipient Cert. of Appreciation as vol. regional coord. N.Y. State Mentoring Program N.Y. Gov. Cuomo, 1991, Proclamation, N.Y. City Coun., 2003, State of N.Y. Legis. Resolution Proclamation N.Y. State Senate, 2003, U.S. Congress Proclamation, 2003, Excellence in Fiscal Mgmt. award IMPACT. Mem. Am. Assn. Sch. Adminstrs., Assn. Orthodox Jewish Tchrs. (v.p. exec. bd., pres. 2004, Orgn. award 2003), N.Y. State Assn. Sch. Bus. Ofcls., N.Y.C. Assn. Sch. Bus. Ofcls., Coun. Suprs. and Adminstrs. Avocations: piano, reading, composing music.

SCHRAGER, IAN, hotel executive; b. 1946; m. Rita Narona; children: Sophie, Ava. Co-owner (with Steve Rubell) Studio 54 (discotheque), 1977—80, Palladium; owner Royalton Hotels, NYC, Hudson Hotels; founder, pres., CEO Ian Schrager Hotels, LLC; owner Morgans Hotel Group, LLC, studio operator, pres.; chmn., CEO Ian Schrager Co., 2005—. Bd. dirs. Mncpl. Art. Soc., Legal Action Ctr. Office: Ian Schrager Co 818 Greenwich St New York NY 10014 *

SCHRAGER, MINDY RAE, operations research specialist; b. Paterson, NJ, Jan. 18, 1958; d. Julius Maxwell and Miriam (Max) Schrager; m. Jim Flannery, 1993. BA, Dickinson Coll., 1979; MBA, Babson Coll., 1981. Cert. NLP Master Practitioner, NLP and Life Purpose Coach, Aura-Soma Practitioner, Herrmann Brain Dominance Indicator facilitator. Cons. Nolan Norton & Co., Lexington, Mass., 1981—86; mgr. Logos Corp., Dedham, Mass., 1986—87; resource ctr. supr., customer satisfaction mgr., dir. quality Motorola ISG, Mansfield, Mass., 1987—95; dir. quality, dir. bill payment ops., dir. project mgmt. Fidelity Investments, Boston, 1995—99; sr. program mgr., sr. mgr. collaborative product delivery, dir. program and operational excellence Ascential Software, Westboro, Mass., 1999—2005; mgr., program dir. IBM, Westboro, 2005—. Mem.: NAFE, Internat. Coach Fedn., Am. Soc. Quality, Assn. Rsch. and Enlightenment, Internat. Assn. Facilitators. Avocations: gardening, coaching. Home: 10 Magnolia Pointe Ashland MA 01721-2529 Office: IBM 50 Washington St Westborough MA 01581-1013 Office Phone: 508-599-7117.

SCHRAM, HENRY B., insurance company executive; Sr. v.p. Chubb Corp., Warren, NJ, chief acctg. officer. Office: The Chubb Corp PO Box 1615 Plainfield NJ 07061-1615 Office Phone: 908-903-2000. Office Fax: 908-903-2027. *

SCHRAM, JEFFREY SCOTT, music educator; s. John Harlan Schram and Pearl Violet Opel; m. Karen Sue Rutter-Schram, Aug. 10, 1985; children: Kristen, Jacob. BFA in Music Performance, U. Wis., Milw., 1982. Salesman Brass Bell Music Store, Milw., 1982—84; instr. brass various summer camps, Kenosha, Wis., 1980—84, St. John's Conservatory Music, Orange, Calif., 1986—88; dir. band Luth. H.S., Orange, 1984—88, Norway Cmty. Schs., Iowa, 1988—90, Merrill Area Pub. Schs., Wis., 1990—. Performer: (trumpeter) Peoples Choice, 2004—06; prodr.: (trumpeter) River City Jazz, 2004—06. Mem.: Nat. Band Assn., Internat. Assn. Jazz Educators, Music Educators Nat. Conf. Office: Merrill High Sch 1201 N Sales St Merrill WI 54452

SCHRAM, LEE J., manufacturing executive; married; 2 children. BS, Miami Univ., Ohio; MBA, Univ. Dayton. Corp. contr. NCR Corp., Dayton, Ohio, 1999—2000, CFO retail & fin. group, 2000—02, v.p., gen. mgr. fin. solutions div., 2002—03, sr. v.p. retail solutions div., 2003—06; CEO Deluxe Corp., Saint Paul, Minn., 2006—. Mailing: Deluxe Corp PO Box 64235 Saint Paul MN 55164-0235 Office: Deluxe Corp 3680 Victoria St S Saint Paul MN 55126 *

SCHRAM, MARTIN JAY, journalist; b. Chgo., Sept. 15, 1942; s. Marlo Joseph and Charleene Janice (Fidler) S.; m. Patricia Stewart Morgan, May 23, 1964; children— Kenneth Marlo, David Morgan. BA, U. Fla., 1964. Reporter The Miami (Fla.) News, 1964-65; reporter Newsday, Garden City, NY, 1965-67, mem. Washington bur., 1967-69, White House corr., 1969-73, chief Washington bur., sr. editor paper, 1973-79; writer on the presidency Washington Post, 1979-81, nat. affairs writer, 1981-86; assoc. editor, editor Sunday edits. Chgo. Sun-Times, 1986-87; asst. mng. editor, editor Sunday edits. Rocky Mountain News, Denver, 1987-88; commentator Cable News Network, 1988-98; nat. editor Washingtonian Mag., 1988-90; polit. columnist United Feature Syndicate, Newspaper Enterprise Assn., 1989-94, Scripps Howard News Svc., Washington, 1994—; news story edit., columnist Fox News, Washington, 1998-2000; mng. editor Avoiding Armageddon, PBS/Ted Turner Documentaries TV Series, 2001—03. Fellow Gannett Ctr. for Media Studies, Columbia U., 1985-86; guest scholar Woodrow Wilson Internat. Ctr., 1990-91. Author: Running for President, A Journal of the Carter Campaign, 1976, Running for President: 1976, The Carter Campaign, 1977; (with others) The Pursuit of the Presidency, 1980, The Great American Video Game: Presidential Politics in the Television Age, 1987, Speaking Freely, 1995; co-author: Cell Phonex: Invisible Hazards in the Wireless Age, 2001, Avoiding Armageddon: Our Future. Our Choice, 2003; co-editor: Mandate for Change, 1993. Recipient James Wright Brown Meml. award Sigma Delta Chi, 1965, Lowell Mellet award Pa. State U., 1988. Office: Scripps Howard News Svc 1090 Vermont Ave NW Ste 1000 Washington DC 20005-4906 Personal E-mail: martin.schram@gmail.com.

SCHRAM, RONALD BYARD, lawyer; b. Detroit, Sept. 7, 1942; s. Byron Canby and Mary Louise (Byard) S.; m. Carol Lorraine Anderson, July 19, 1969; children: Laura Mary, Alison Leigh. BA, Dartmouth Coll., 1964; MA in Econs., Cambridge U., England, 1966; JD, U. Mich., 1969, LLM, 1970, SJD, 1971. Bar: Mass. 1970. Assoc. Ropes & Gray, Boston, 1970-78, ptnr., 1978—2002. Author: Non-Billable Hours: A Poetic Journey Through the 1st Year of Retirement, 2005. Trustee Dartmouth Coll., Hanover, NH, 1981-92, Dartmouth-Hitchcock Med. Ctr., Lebanon, NH, 1983-93, New Eng. Sports Mus., Cambridge, Mass., 1984-1999, Derby Acad., Hingham, Mass., 1982-89; trustee Ctrl. New Eng. chpt. Nat. Multiple Sclerosis Soc., Waltham, Mass., 2002—, chair, 2004-06; bd. visitors Rockefeller Ctr. of Pub. Policy, Dartmouth Coll., 2003—, chair, 2004—. Keasbey Found. fellow, Cambridge U., 1964-66; George M. Humphrey fellow in law econ. policy, U. Mich. Law Sch., Ann Arbor, 1969-70. Mem.: Phi Beta Kappa. E-mail: cschram1@aol.com.

SCHRAMEK, TOMAS, ballet dancer, educator; b. Bratislava, Czechoslovakia, Sept. 11, 1944; emigrated to Can., 1968, naturalized, 1973; s. Hans and Valeria (Neudorfer) S. BFA, Acad. Mus. and Theatre Arts, Bratislava, 1968. Mem. Sluk, Slovakia folk dance ensemble, 1959-68, prin. dancer, 1964-68; dancer Nat. Ballet Can., 1969-71, soloist, 1971-73, prin. dancer, 1973-91, prin. character artist, ballet master, 1991—. Mem. Actors Equity Assn., Assn. Can. TV and Radio Artists. Home: 125 Rose Park Dr Toronto ON Canada M4T 1R6 Office: Nat Ballet Canada 470 Queens Quay West Toronto ON Canada M5V 3K4 Home Phone: 416-483-6737; Office Phone: 416-345-9686. E-mail: tomaschr@rogers.com.

SCHRAMM, BERNARD CHARLES, JR., retired advertising agency executive; b. Balt., Jan. 23, 1928; s. Bernard C. and Juliet Marie (Barranger) Schramm; m. Florence Mae Fangman, 1950; children: Stephanie Schramm McDaniel, Carol Schramm Molander, Bernard Charles III, Claudia Schramm Smith. Grad., Balt. Poly. Inst., 1946. Prodn. mgr. Van Sant, Dugdale & Co., Balt., 1946-52; media dir. AWL Advt., Balt., 1952-55; dir. prodn. Henry J. Kaufman Assocs., Washington, 1955-58; exec. v.p. Avalon Hill Co., Balt., 1958-64; v.p. Cargill, Wilson & Acree Advt., Richmond, Va., 1964-68; pres. William Cook Advt. Inc. (now William Cook Mktg. Comm.), Jacksonville, Fla., 1968-89, chmn. bd., 1989-97; ret., 1997. Chmn. Otis F. Smith Found., 1991—97. Mem. exec. com., v.p. United Way N.E. Fla., 1982-87, bd. dirs., 1982-93; bd. dirs. N.E. Fla. chpt. ARC, 1976-89, chmn., 1980-81; bd. dirs. Fla. C.C. Found., 1976-89. Mem.: Am. Assn. Advt. Agys. (chmn. Fla. coun. 1984—85, So.

Region Bd. of Govs. 1988—92, chmn. 1989, nat. bd. dirs., agy. mgmt. com. 1989—92), Jacksonville Area C. of C., Rotary Club. Republican. Roman Catholic. Avocations: golf, reading, spectator sports, hunting.

SCHRAMM, PAUL HOWARD, lawyer; b. St. Louis, Oct. 6, 1933; s. Benjamin Jacob and Frieda Sylvia (Goruch) Schramm; m. Sue-Ann Batson; children: Scott Lyon(dec.), Dean Andrew, Thomas Edward(dec.), Jeremy Arthur Savran. AB, U. Mo., 1955, JD, 1958. Bar: Mo. 1958, US Dist. Ct. (ea. dist.) Mo. 1963, US Dist. Ct. (we. dist.) Mo. 2003, US Ct. Appeals (8th cir.) 1967, US Tax Ct. 1970, US Supreme Ct. 1972, US Dist. Ct. (ea. dist.) Wis., 1988. Ptnr. Schramm & Schramm, St. Louis, 1959-61, Schramm & Morganstern, St. Louis, 1970-76, Schramm, Pines & Marshall, St. Louis, 1977-79, Schramm, Newman, Pines & Freyman, St. Louis, 1979-82, Schramm, Pines & Spewak, St. Louis, 1983-85, Schramm & Pines, LLC, St. Louis, 1985-2000, Edwards, Singer, Schramm, Watkins, Spoeneman & Waltrip, LLP, St. Louis, 2000—03, Edwards, Schramm, Watkins, Spoeneman, Waltrip & Beilenson, LLP, St. Louis, 2003—05, Edwards Schramm Young & Beilenson, LLP, 2006—07; of counsel Spoeneman, Watkins Waltrip & Harvell, LLP, St. Louis, 2007—. Pros. atty. City of Ellisville, Mo., 1973-77; judge Ellisville mcpl. div. St. Louis County Cir. Ct., 1977-83; teaching faculty trial advocacy Harvard Law Sch., 1991. Mem. Bar Assn. Met. St. Louis (exec. com. 1976-77, chmn. county sect. 1976-77), St. Louis County Bar Assn. (chmn. lawyers reference service 1971, cir. ct. jud. com. 1970), M-H Bar Register Preeminent Lawyers, Phi Delta Phi. Avocations: music, sports, reading. Home: 7507 Byron Pl Saint Louis MO 63105-2703 Office: Spoeneman Watkins Waltrip Harvell LLP 8000 Maryland Ste 600 Saint Louis MO 63105 Office Phone: 314-862-1110. Office Fax: 314-862-1105. Business E-Mail: pschramm@swwhlaw.com.

SCHRAMM, VERN L., biochemist, educator; B, SD State Coll., Brookings; M in Nutrition, Harvard U., Cambridge, Mass.; PhD, Australian Nat. U., Canberra. Postdoctoral rsch. assoc. NASA Ames Rsch. Ctr., Moffett Field, Calif.; mem. faculty Temple U. Sch. Medicine, Phila.; prof. Albert Einstein Coll. Medicine of Yeshiva U., Bronx, NY, 1987—, chair biochemistry dept., 1987—95, Ruth Merns chair dept. biochemistry, 1995—. Contbr. articles to profl. jours. Recipient George A. Sowell award for Excellence in Tchg., Temple U. Sch. Medicine, Rudi Lemberg award, Australian Acad. Sci., Repligen award, Am. Chem. Soc. (Biol. Chemistry Divsn.), 2006. Fellow: AAAS; mem.: NAS. Office: Albert Einstein Coll Medicine Jack and Pearl Resnick Campus 1300 Morris Park Ave Forchheimer Bldg Rm 316 Bronx NY 10461 Office Phone: 718-430-2813. Office Fax: 718-430-8565. E-mail: vern@aecom.yu.edu.

SCHRAND, RICHARD HENRY, SR., broadcast executive, advertising bureau owner, educator; b. Cin., Nov. 1, 1957; s. Edward August and Jane Marie (Scheib) S.; m. Deborah Fortner, 1979 (div. 1985); 1 child, Cynthia Lanette; m. Sharon Lynn Lassandro, Dec. 24, 1986; children: Courtney Lynne, Richard Jr., Brandon Ian. Student, Ohio State U., 1975-76, No. Ky. U., 1976-77. Intern Sta. WCPO-TV, Cin., 1971-75; producer Sta. WKRC-TV, Cin., 1975-79; pub. affairs dir., reporter, anchor Sta. WCSC-TV, Charleston, SC, 1979-83; actor Phila. Experiment, LA, 1984; asst. promotion dir. Sta. WLWT-TV, Cin., 1983-86; spl. projects coord. Sta. KXAS-TV, Dallas/Ft. Worth, 1986-87; mgr. media svcs. NBC TV Network, Burbank, Calif., 1987-89; pres. Cyn-Court Enterprises, Burbank, 1989-91; mktg. dir. Sta. WPTA-TV, Ft. Wayne, Ind., 1991-92; v.p., gen. mgr. Branson (Mo.) Broadcasting Corp., 1992-95; dir. spl. projects/nat. media, graphics and advt. creator Jim Owens & Assocs., 1995-98; gen. mgr. Jim Owens Radio, Inc., Nashville, 1995-98; pres. GRFX ByDesign, Nashville, 1996—2004, Broadsword Prod., 2002—; v.p. Komodo Studios, LA, 1999-2000; instr. computer graphics and web design Nossi Coll. Art, Nashville, 2001—, chmn. Dept. Computer Graphics, 2001—, mem. adv. bd., 2001—. Instr., spkr. Graphic Design Tour, 2000—; computer design Nossi Coll. Art, 2001—, edu. bd., 2002—, adv. bd., 2003—, instr. graphic art and design, 2004—; demonstrator 3D software Siggraph, MacWorld, 2001—. Author: Canoma Visual Insight 2000, 3D Creature Workshop vol. 2, 2000, Macromedia Web Design Handbook, 2000, Adobe Golive 5F/X & Design, 2000, Adobe Live Motion Visual Jumpstart, 2000, Adobe Photoshop 6 Visual Jumpstart, 2000, Poser 4 Pro Pack F/X & Design, 2001, Final Cut Pro 3: The Complete Reference, 2002, Vue 6 Revealed, 2006; contbr.: Pixels: 3D Book, 1999, Mastering Pixels: 3D, 2001; webmaster Crook & Chase Theater, Mid. Tenn. LightWave Users Group, Nossi Coll. Art, Games Plus, Handshake Productions, Elegant Diamonds. Bd. dirs. Project Graduation, Dallas/Ft. Worth, 1986-87; mem. Muscular Dystrophy Assn., Charleston, 1980-83; publicist Housing Now, L.A., 1988. Recipient Regional Emmy award NATAS, 1975, award Broadcast Promotion and Mktg. Exec., Seattle, 1992. Avocations: guitar, writing, singing, golf. Office Phone: 615-812-2705. Business E-Mail: rschrand@broadswordproductions.com.

SCHRANK, SHIRLEY ANN, artist; b. Nunda, NY, Jan. 30, 1933; d. Ward Donald and Norma Mae (Kelley) Crane; m. John Roberts McKalip Jr., Oct. 8, 1966 (dec. May 1974); children: Catherine, William Ward; m. William Thomas Schrank, Nov. 24, 1976 (dec. Aug. 1993). Degree in nursing, U. Rochester, 1954, BSN, 1960, MS in Nursing Edn., 1961. Staff nurse dept. psychiatry U. Rochester, NY, 1954-56, team leader dept. medicine, 1956-60; instr. in pediatric nursing Genesee Hosp., Rochester, 1960-61; staff nurse eye surgery Children's Hosp. San Francisco, 1961; nurse pvt. duty surg. patients Presbyn. Med. Ctr. Etal SF Hosps., San Francisco, 1962; instr. medicine, surg. and ICU nursing Samuel Merritt Hosp. Sch. Nursing, Oakland, Calif., 1963-67, ret., 1967. With The Blackhawk Gallery, Danville, Calif., 1995—2006, East Bay Women Artists, Oakland, Calif., 1989—99, San Francisco Women Artists, 1989—92, La Junta Artists Assn., 1974—76, 2005, Calif. Watercolor Assn., 2005. Stephen min., Stephen tchg. leader, choir. Republican. Presbyterian. Avocations: camping, travel, singing, needlepoint, gardening. Home: 609 Maureen Ln Pleasant Hill CA 94523-2719 Personal E-mail: shirley-schrank@comcast.net.

SCHREADLEY, RICHARD LEE, newswriter, retired editor; b. Harrisburg, Pa., Jan. 3, 1931; s. Harry Leroy and Flora Rebecca (McQuilken) S.; m. Doris Arlene Sheaffer, Dec. 18, 1952; 1 child, Rhys Leroy. BA, Dickinson Coll., 1952; MA, Tufts U., 1968, MAL.D., 1969, PhD, 1972. Reporter The News and Courier, Charleston, SC, 1975; asso. editor The Evening Post, Charleston, 1975-76, editorial page editor, 1976-77, editor, 1977-81; exec. editor The Evening Post and The News and Courier, 1981-88; assoc. editor and sr. writer mil. and polit. affairs The News and Courier, 1989. Author: From the Rivers to the Sea, The United States Navy in Vietnam, 1992, Valor and Virtue, The Washington Light Infantry in Peace and in War, 1996. Chmn. Fgn. Affairs Forum of Charleston, 1987-88, mem. steering com., 1989. Served to comdr. USN, 1949-52, 56-73. Mem. Navy League, Ret. Officer Assn., Washington Light Infantry, German Friendly Soc. Charleston, Army-Navy Club of Washington, Country Club of Charleston. Home: 812 Clearview Dr Charleston SC 29412-4511 Personal E-mail: rlschrea@bellsouth.net.

SCHRECK, ROBERT A., JR., lawyer; b. Buffalo; BS in Bus. Adminstrn., Georgetown U., 1974; MBA, Northwestern U., 1975, JD, 1978. Bar: Ill. 1978. Ptnr. McDermott, Will & Emery, Chgo., 1978—. Mem. ABA. Office: McDermott Will & Emery 227 W Monroe St Ste 4400 Chicago IL 60606-5096 E-mail: rschreck@mwe.com.

SCHRECKENGAST, WILLIAM OWEN, retired lawyer; b. Greenwood, Ind., Oct. 14, 1926; s. Vernon Edward and Marthena O. (Mullinix) S.; m. Helen Margaret Sheppard, Nov. 11, 1949 (div.); children: Pamela, Sandra, James, John; m. Virginia Thompson, Mar. 14, 1990. LLB, Ind. U., 1956. Bar: Ind. 1956, US Ct. Appeals (7th cir.) 1956, US Dist. Ct. (so. dist.) Ind. 1956, US Supreme Ct. 1967. Ptnr. Kitley, Pontius & Schreckengast, Beech Grove, Ind., 1957-59, Kitley & Schreckengast, Beech Grove, 1959-63, 78-82, Kitley, Schreckengast & Davis, Beech Grove, 1963-78, Schreckengast & Lovern, Indpls., 1982-88, Schreckengast Lovern & Helm, Indpls., 1988—2003, ret., 2003. Chmn. Ind. campaign John Walsh for Sec. of State, Indls., 1958; chmn. ward Beech Grove Dems., 1958-60. Served to 1st sgt. US Army, 1944-46, PTO. Mem. ABA, Ind. Bar Assn. (bd. mgrs. 1973-74, pres. citation 1974, pres. trial lawyer sect. 1977-78), Ind. Def. Lawyers Assn. (diplomat), Am. Judicature Soc., Nat. Inst. Trial Advocacy (teaching faculty 1980-85), Platform Soc. Clubs: Hillview Country (Franklin, Ind.). Lodges: Masons. Republican. Avocations: golf, flying. Home: 8026 Singleton St Indianapolis IN 46227-2568

SCHRECKENGOST, VIKTOR, artist; b. June 26, 1906; Diploma, Cleve. Sch. Art (now Cleve. Inst. Art), 1929; postgrad., Kunstgenerboschule, Vienna, Austria, 1929—30; DFA (hon.), Cleve. Inst. Art, 1995; DHL (hon.), Case Western Res. U., Cleve., 2002. Instr. Cleve. Inst. Art, 1930—2006, prof. emeritus, 2006—; head designer Murray Ohio, Nashville, 1938—72. Recipient Presdl. medal in arts, 2006, Pers. Recognition award, Indsl. Designers Soc. Am., 2002. Fellow: Am. Ceramic Soc. (life). Home: 2265 Stillman Rd Cleveland OH 44118

SCHRECKER, JOHN, historian, educator; b. Rumburk, Czech Republic, Aug. 22, 1937; s. Karl Steiner and Marian Schrecker-Heller, Franz Schrecker (Stepfather); m. Ellen Wolf, Feb. 18, 1962 (div.); m. Janet Barry, May 11, 1992; children: Michael Franz, Daniel Edwin. BA, U. Pa., 1958; MA, Harvard U., Cambridge, Mass., 1959; PhD, Harvard U., 1968. Asst. prof. of history Princeton U., NJ, 1965—71; prof. of history Brandeis U., Waltham, Mass., 1971—. Assoc. in rsch. Fairbank Ctr. for East Asian Rsch., Harvard U., Cambridge, 1971—. Author: (book) Imperialism and Chinese Nationalism, 1971, The Chinese Revolution in Historical Perspective, 1991, 2nd rev. edit., 2004; author: (with Ellen Schrecker) Mrs. Chiang's Szechwan Cookbook, 1976; editor (with Paul Cohen): Reform in Nineteenth-Century China, 1976. Fellow Fulbright, Social Sci. Rsch. Coun., NAS. Mem.: Am. Hist. Assn., Assn. for Asian Studies, Phi Beta Kappa. Avocation: classical piano. Office: History Dept MS 036 Brandeis Univ Waltham MA 02454 Home Phone: 781-894-4062; Office Phone: 781-736-2284. Office Fax: 718-736-2273. E-mail: schrecker@brandeis.edu.

SCHRECKINGER, SY EDWARD, advertising executive, consultant; b. Bklyn., Jan. 10, 1937; s. Robert and Bessie (Gable) S.; m. Linda Fiarman, Mar. 4, 1962; children: Jamie Fran, Jon Gary. B.F.A., Pratt Inst., 1958. Art dir. Sudler and Hennesey, NYC, 1958-61; sr. art dir. Marschalk Co., NYC, 1961-63; group supr. Grey Advt., NYC, 1963-66; v.p., assoc. creative dir. Hicks & Greist, NYC, 1966-69; sr. v.p., assoc. creative dir. Young & Rubicam Inc., NYC, 1969-88; advt. and mktg. cons. Oceanside, NY, 1988—2005; advt.-mktg. dir. Magnificent Muffin Corp., 1995—. Recipient Lion Venice Internat. Film Festival, 1972, Andy Ad Club, N.Y., 1965, 86, award Internat. Bus. Assn., Best award Hollywood Radio & TV Soc., 1971, Clio Am. TV Comml. Festival, 1967, 72, 82, 85, Effy, 1985. Jewish.

SCHREIBER, ALAN HICKMAN, lawyer; b. Muncie, Ind., Apr. 4, 1944; s. Ephriam and Clarrisa (Hickman) S.; m. Phyllis Jean Chamberlain, Dec. 22, 1972; children: Jennifer Aline, Brett Justin. Student, DePauw U., 1962-64; BS in Bus., Ind. U., 1966, JD, 1969. Bar: Fla. 1971, U.S. Dist. Ct. (so. dist.) Fla. Asst. State Atty.'s Office, Ft. Lauderdale, Fla., 1971-76; pub. defender 17th Jud. Cir., Ft. Lauderdale, 1976—. Cons. Fla. Bar News on Criminal Law, 1982; lobbyist for indigent funding, Fla., 1980—; apptd. to Supreme Ct. Com. on Racial and Ethic Bias; co-chair Chiles-MacKay task force on criminal justice. Contbr. articles to profl. jours. Mem. Dem. Exec. Com., Ft. Lauderdale, 1980; mem. Plantation Dem. Club, 1983; campaign chmn. Goldstein for Atty. Gen. Fla., 1982. Named Young Dem. of Yr., Broward County Young Dems., 1980; Man of Yr., Jewish War Vets., 1982; recipient B'nai B'rith Pub. Servant award, 1990, Dem. of Yr. award 2000, Harry Galkin Meml. award 2002. Mem. Fla. Bar Assn., Broward County Bar Assn., ABA, Nat. Legal Aid Defenders Assn., Phi Alpha Delta. Home: 885 Orchid Dr Fort Lauderdale FL 33317-1221 Office: 201 SE 6th St Fort Lauderdale FL 33301-3303 Office Phone: 954-993-5433. Personal E-mail: alschreiber@direcuay.com.

SCHREIBER, BERTRAM MANUEL, mathematics professor; b. Seattle, Nov. 4, 1940; s. Isador and Amy (Hurwitz) S.; m. Rita Ruth Stusser, June 30, 1963; children: Susannah M. Schreiber Bechhofer, Deborah H. Schreiber Shapiro, Abraham D., Elisabeth T. Schreiber Seigel. BA, Yeshiva U., 1962; MS, U. Wash., 1966, PhD, 1968. Asst. prof. Wayne State U., Detroit, 1968-71, assoc. prof., 1971-78, prof., 1978—, chair dept. math., 1987-90. Vis. prof. Hebrew U., Jerusalem, 1975, 2000, 07, Mich. State U., East Lansing, 1982-83, Nat. U. Singapore, 1992, U. NSW, Sydney, 1992, Indian Statis. Inst., New Delhi and Bangalore, 1993, Tata Inst. Fund Res., Bombay, 1993, Bar Ilan U., Ramat Gan, Isreal, 1993, 2007, Tel Aviv U., 1993, U. Utrecht, The Netherlands, 1993, U. Wroclaw, Poland, 1993, 2006, U. Paris VII, 1999, U. Granada, Spain, 1999-2000, U. Wash., Seattle, 2000, Ecole Poly. Féd. Lausanne, Switzerland, 2006, U. Vienna, 2007. Contbr. articles to profl. jours. NSF grantee, 1968-87; Sci. and Engring. Rsch. Coun. Gt. Britain fellow U. Edinburgh, Scotland, 1976. Mem. Am. Math. Soc., Math. Assn. Am., Israel Math. Union, Edinburgh Math. Soc. Achievements include research in the fields of harmonic analysis, topological groups, and probability theory. Office: Wayne State U Dept Math Detroit MI 48202 Home Phone: 248-827-1199; Office Phone: 313-577-8838. Business E-Mail: bschreiber@wayne.edu.

SCHREIBER, CLARE ADEL, journalist; b. Chgo., Feb. 22, 1914; d. Otto Herman Mentz and Martha Toll; m. William I. Schreiber, June 18, 1934 (dec. Jan. 1998); children: William M., James L., Ralph W.(dec.), Stephen T. BS in Journalism, U. Ill., 1935; LHD, Coll. of Wooster, 1985. Freelance writer Fairfield Iowa Ledger, 1937, The Daily Record, Wooster, Ohio, 1956; dir. Coll. of Wooster Nursery Sch., 1956—85; family life educator Cmty. Action Wayne Medina, 1985—. Exec. bd. Wayne Assn. of the Edn. of Young Children, Wooster, Ohio, 1983—. Author, editor (book) Green Grow the Children, 1984; contbr. articles. Mem. human rights group Am. Assn. for Univ. Women, Wooster, Ohio; mem. League of Women Voters, Nat. Assn. for Edn. of Young Children, Philos. Edn. Orgn. Internat. Recipient Child Advocate of the Yr., Wayne County Children's Services, 2002; fellow Paul Harris fellow, Rotary Internat., 2004. Mem.: Theta Phi Alpha, Kappa Tau Alpha. Democrat. Presbyn. Home: 1471 Cleveland Rd Wooster OH 44691 Office: Cmty Action Wayne/Medina 2375 Benden Dr Wooster OH 44691

SCHREIBER, EILEEN SHER, artist; b. Denver, 1925; d. Michael Herschel and Sarah Deborah (Tannenbaum) Sher; m. Jonas Schreiber, Mar. 27, 1945; children: Jeffrey, Barbara, Michael. Student, U. Utah, 1942-45, NYU, 1966-68, Montclair State Coll., NJ, 1975-79; also pvt. art study. Exhibited Morris Mus. Arts and Scis., Morristown, N.J., 1965-73, N.J. State Mus., 1969, Lever House, N.Y.C., 1971, Paramus (N.J.) Mus., 1973, Newark Mus., 1978, 1991-92, Am. Water Color Soc., Audubon Artists, N.A.D. Gallery, N.Y.C., Pallazzo Vecchio Florence, Italy, Art Expo 1987, 1988, India Mus., 1994, 95, Athens (Greece) Mus., 1996, 97, Gaelin Gallery, Whippany, N.J., 2004, Solstice Gallery, Beach Haven, NJ, Municipal Bldg. of West Orange, NJ; represented in permanent collections Tex. A&M U., Telesoft Inc., Phoenix, State of N.J., Morris Mus., Seton Hall U., Bloomfield (N.J.) Coll., Barclay Bank of Eng., N.J., Somerset Coll., NYU, Morris County State Coll., Broad Nat. Bank, Newark, Ind. Cmty. Bank, Consulting Actuaries, Internat., IBM, Am. Tel. Co., RCA, Johnson & Johnson, Champion Internat. Paper Co., Sony, Mitsubishi, Celanese Co., Squibb Corp., Nabisco, Nat. Bank Phila., Data Control, Ind. Cmty. Bank, Sperry Univac, Ga. Pacific Co., Pub. Svc. Co. N.J., Diane Levine Gallery, Boston, S.W. Gallery, Long Beach Island, N.J., Solstice Gallery, Beach Haven, NJ, Town Hall Libr., West Orange, NJ, others; also pvt. collections. Recipient awards N.J. Watercolor Soc., 1969, 72, 1st award in watercolor Hunterdon Art Ctr., 1972, Best in Show award Short Hills State Show, 1976, Tri-State Purchase award Somerset Coll., 1977, Art Expo, N.Y.C., 1987, 88, numerous others. Mem. Nat. Assn. Women Artists (chmn. watercolor jury, Collage award 1983, Marian Halpren Meml. award 1995), Nat., N.Y. Artists Equity, Printmaker Coun. Visual Artists (1st award in printmaking 1996), Women Visual Artists (Fla.). Home and Office: 10 Jackson Dr Egg Harbor Township NJ 08234 Office Phone: 609-927-0440. Personal E-mail: artess25@aol.com.

SCHREIBER, GEORGE RICHARD, publishing executive, writer; b. Ironton, Ohio, July 4, 1922; s. George Joseph and Marie Frances (Heitzman) S.; m. Veva Jeanette Hopkins, May 14, 1945; children: Susan, George, Ellen. AB, St. Joseph's Coll., Rensselaer, Ind., 1943, L.H.D., 1974; MA, U. Chgo., 1944. Exec. editor Billboard mag., 1945-60; editor, pub. Vend mag., 1946-66; editl. dir. Billboard Publs., 1966-70; pres., chief exec. officer Nat. Automatic Mdsg. Assn., Chgo., 1970-88, pres. emeritus, 1988—; pres., chief exec. Sunrise Books, 1994—. Mem. staff and faculty U. Chgo., 1944-46 Author: Verses from the River Country, 1941, What Makes News, 1943, Automatic Selling, 1954, A Concise History of Vending in the U.S.A, 1965, revised 2d edit., 1990, Millenium edit., 1999, The Bobby Baker Affair— How to Make Millions in Washington, 1964, Vending For Investors-How to Spot Phony Deals, 1994, 2d edit., 1996; contbg. author: Handbook of Modern Marketing, 1986. Chmn. Glenview Plan Commn., Ill., 1962-64, mayor, 1964-67; chmn. Region 1, Chgo. Area Transp. Study Group, 1962-63; bd. dirs. Rockefeller Meml. Chapel, U. Chgo., 1944-45; trustee St. Joseph's Coll., 1964—, chmn., 1970-76, life trustee, 1978—. Recipient Jesse H. Neal award for editl. achievement, 1964; dedication of St. Joseph's Coll. G. Richard Schreiber Dept. Humanities, Ind., 1987. Mem. The Authors Guild Inc., Am. Bus. Press (editl. bd.), Assn. Econs. Coun., Am. Soc. Assn. Execs., Tavern Club, Internat. Club, Tower Club. Home: 735 Ravine Ave Lake Bluff IL 60044-2625 E-mail: vevaj@aol.com.

SCHREIBER, HOWARD E., lawyer; b. Balt., May 18, 1959; BA in Polit. Sci., Dickinson Coll., 1981; JD with honors, Duke U., 1984. Bar: Tex. 1984. Shareholder Jenkens & Gilchrist, P.C., Dallas, 1993—, firm leader real estate practice group. Mem.: ABA, Am. Coll. Mortgage Attorneys, Dallas Bar Assn., Tex. State Bar Assn. Office: Jenkens & Gilchrist PC Ste 3200 1445 Ross Ave Dallas TX 75202-2799 Office Phone: 214-855-4370. Office Fax: 214-855-4300. Business E-Mail: hschreiber@jenkens.com.

SCHREIBER, JAY, journalist; Asst. sports editor The New York Times. Author: (articles) Judges Decision Lifts Ban on Sale of Ephedra in Utah, 2005. Office: The New York Times Sports Desk 229 W 43rd St New York NY 10036 Office Phone: 212-556-7371. Office Fax: 212-556-5048.

SCHREIBER, JOHN T., lawyer; b. NYC, Mar. 30, 1960; s. Toby Schreiber and Morley Ann (Perrish) Clark; children: Zoe Cassandra Bloch Schreiber, Alana Nichole Perrish Schreiber. BA Politics, Brandeis U., 1982; JD, Santa Clara U., 1986. Bar: Calif. 1987(cert. specialist appellate law); U.S. Dist. Ct. (no. dist.) Calif. 1987; U.S. Dist. Ct. (ea. dist.) Calif. 1990; U.S. Ct. Appeals (9th cir.) 1989, U.S. Supreme Ct. 1998. Assoc. Law Offices of Wm. D. McHugh, San Jose, Calif., 1987-88, Hallgrimson, McNichols, McCann & Inderbitzen, Pleasanton, Calif., 1989-92; pvt. practice Walnut Creek, Calif., 1993—. Bd. dirs. East Bay Depot for Creative Re-use, Oakland. Field coord. Cen. Contra Costa County, Tom Bradley Campaign for Govs., Concord, Calif., 1982, Clinton-Gore Campaign, Walnut Creek, Calif., 1992; mem. Ask-A-Lawyer Program Contra Costa Legal Svcs. Found., Richmond, Calif., 1992-96; co-chair Clinton-Gore Contra Costa County, 1996. Mem. ABA, Contra Costa Bar Assn. (program dir. appellate sect. 1993-95, 2000—, pres. appellate sect. 1995-96, MCLE com. 1995—), Santa Clara Bar Assn., Am. Israeli Pub. Affairs Com. Avocations: reading, golf, softball, movies, exercising. Office: 2000 Ridgewood Rd Alamo CA 94507-1044

SCHREIBER, KURT GILBERT, lawyer; b. Milw., Aug. 22, 1946; s. Raymond R. and Mildred L. (Kleist) S.; m. Nelda Beth Van Buren, May 3, 1974; children: Katharine Anne, Matthew Edward. AB in Econs., Cornell U., 1968; JD, U. Mich., 1971; M in Theol. Studies, Vanderbilt U., 2003. Bar: Wis. 1971, Tex. 1979, Tenn. 1997. Internat. atty. Tenneco Internat. Holdings Co., London, 1974-78; atty. Tenneco Inc., Houston, 1978-80; 2d v.p., asst. gen. counsel Am. Gen. Corp., Houston, 1980-83, v.p., gen. counsel, 1983-84, sr. v.p., gen. counsel, 1984-93, sr. v.p., corp. sec., 1993-94; pvt. practice Houston, 1994-96; exec. v.p., gen. counsel Direct Gen. Corp., Nashville, 1996-98, pres., 1998—2001. Bd. dir. Cumberland Trust and Investment Co., Urban Housing Solutions. Fellow Tex. Bar Found.; mem. ABA, Wis. Bar Assn., Tex. Bar Assn., Tenn. Bar Assn. Home: 4117 Dorman Dr Nashville TN 37215

SCHREIBER, LIEV (ISAAC LIEV SCHREIBER), actor; b. San Francisco, Oct. 4, 1967; s. Tell and Heather Schreiber. Student, Bklyn. Tech., Royal Acad. Dramatic Arts, London; BA, Hampshire Coll., 1988; MFA, Yale Sch. Drama, 1992. Actor: (Broadway plays) In the Summer House, 1993, Betrayal, 2000—01, Glengarry Glen Ross, 2005 (Tony award for best performance by a featured actor in a play, 2005), Talk Radio, 2007 (Drama League awardd disting. performance, 2007); (films) Mixed Nuts, 1994, Denise Calls Up, 1995, Mad Love, 1995, Party Girl, 1995, Walking and Talking, 1996, The Daytrippers, 1996, Big Night, 1996, Ransom, 1996, Scream, 1996, His and Hers, 1997, Baggage, 1997, Scream 2, 1997, Phantoms, 1998, Sphere, 1998, Twilight, 1998, (voice only) Desert Blue, 1998, A Walk on the Moon, 1999, Jacob the Liar, 1999, The Hurricane, 1999, Spring Forward, 1999, Hamlet, 2000, Scream 3, 2000, Dial 9 for Love, 2001, Kate & Leopold, 2001, The Sum of All Fears, 2002, Spinning Boris, 2003, The Manchurian Candidate, 2004, The Omen, 2006, The Painted Veil, 2006, The Ten, 2007; (TV films) Janek: The Silent Betrayal, 1994, The Sunshine Boys, 1995, Buffalo Girls, 1995, Since You've Been Gone, 1998, RKO 281, 1999, Young Dr. Freud, 2002, Hitler: The Rise of Evil, 2003, Lackawanna Blues, 2005, (voice only) Oil Storm, 2005,; (TV series) CSI: Crime Scene Investigation, 2006; dir.: (films) Everything is Illuminated, 2003. Avocations: basketball, fencing, bicycling. Office: c/o Internat Creative Mgmt Inc 10250 Constellation Blvd Los Angeles CA 90067 *

SCHREIBER, MARK TRAUDT, psychiatrist; b. Denver, Oct. 6, 1947; s. Charles William and Sophie Emily Schreiber; m. Constance Anne Rabe, Nov. 27, 1976; children: Vanessa, Laura, Charles, Anne, John. BS, U. Nebr., Lincoln, 1970; MD, Washington U., St. Louis, Mo., 1975. Diplomate Am. Bd. Psychiatry and Neurology, 1980, Am. Bd. Addictionology, 1986. Resident Barnes Hosp. Washington U., St. Louis, 1975—78; psychiatrist Hearst, Fischer & Schreiber, Virginia Beach, Va., 1978—84, Crossroads Clin., Virginia Beach, 1984—89, Atlantic Psychiatric, Virginia Beach, 1989—. Med. dir. Serenity Lodge, Chesapeake, Va., 1984—91; assoc. med. dir. Va. Beach Psychiat. Ctr., 1991—. Contbr. articles to profl. jours. Elder Bayside Presbyn. Ch., Va. Beach, 1980—, chmn. com., 1980—; vice chmn. internat. partnership com. Presbytery Ea. Va., Portsmouth, 1982—. Named Am.'s Top Psychiatrists, Consumers' Rsch. Coun. Am. Fellow: Am. Soc. Addiction Medicine (regional chmn. 2000—04), Am. Psychiat. Assn. (Disting. fellow 2005). Avocations: ballroom dancing, skiing, reading, camping, travel. Office: Atlantic Psychiatric 780 Lipshua Pkwy Ste 450 Virginia Beach VA 23452

SCHREIBER, PAUL SOLOMON, lawyer; b. Krakow, Poland, Mar. 29, 1941; came to U.S., 1949; s. John and Betty (Silber) S.; m. Joan A. Perlmutter, Mar. 20, 1971; children: Douglas Arun, Stacey Lauren. BS, CCNY, 1963; LLB, NYU, 1966, LLM, 1967; postgrad., U. Paris, 1967-68. Bar: N.Y. 1966. Assoc. Marshal, Bratter, Greene, Allison & Tucker, NYC, 1969-76, ptnr., 1976-82, Kramer, Levin, Naftalis, Nessen, Kamin & Frankel, NYC, 1982-94, Shearman & Sterling LLP, NYC, 1994—. Bd. dirs. Harbor Trust Co., Hoboken, N.J., 1985-92. Editor: Annual Survey Am. Law; co-author articles, papers and revs. Trustee Park Ave. Synagogue, N.Y.C., 1985—, pres., 1998-2003, hon. pres., 2003—; bd. dirs. Am. Friends of the Rambam Med. Ctr., N.Y.C., 1989-99, N.Y.C. chpt. Nat. Multiple Sclerosis Soc., 1991—, Sch. for Strings, 1994-96, Jr. Achievement of N.Y., 2005—; bd. overseers Rabbinical Sch. Jewish Theol. Sem., 1995-96. Arthur Garfield Hayes fellow; Ford Found. fellow. Democrat. Jewish. Office Phone: 212-848-8920. E-mail: pschreiber@shearman.com.

SCHREIBER, ROBERT WALTER, computer scientist; s. Eric Christian and Annelise Marie Schreiber; m. Patricia Valdata, Apr. 21, 1979. Cert. data processor Inst. Certification Computer Profls., 1979. Assoc. dir. sys. engring. NJ Ednl. Computer Network, New Brunswick, 1979—84; prin. Computer Sys. Design and Mgmt., Inc., Annandale, NJ, 1984—88; dir. ops. and tech. svcs. U. Del., Newark, Del., 1988—89; cons. sys. arch. and engring. Lotus Devel. Corp., Wayne, Pa., 1989—2001, arch. enterprise sys. Westford, Mass., 2002—03; sr. programming engr. IBM Corp., Endicott, NY, 2003—. Mem.: IEEE, Am. Guild Organists (assoc.). Achievements include patents in field. Avocation: boating. Office: IBM Corporation 1701 North St 250/2/W013 Endicott NY 13760 Home Phone: 410-392-9553; Office Phone: 607-429-5472. Personal E-mail: rschreiber@zoominternet.net. Business E-Mail: schreib@us.ibm.com.

SCHREIBER, SALLY ANN, lawyer; b. El Paso, Tex., July 23, 1951; d. Warren Thomas and Joyce (Honey) S.; children: Amanda Honey, Ryan Thorp Luther. BBA, U. N.Mex., 1973; JD, Stanford U., 1976. Bar: Calif. 1976, Tex. 1977. Assoc. Johnson & Swanson, Dallas, 1976-81, ptnr., 1981-89; mem. firm Johnson & Gibbs, P.C., Dallas, 1989-93; of counsel Cox & Smith, Inc., Dallas, 1993-94; shareholder Munsch Hardt Kopf & Harr, P.C., Dallas, 1994—. Spkr. in field. Editor Stanford U. Law Rev., 1975-76; co-author paper Internat. Bar Assn., 1986. Bd. dirs. The Lyric Opera of Dallas, 1982-86; law sch. bd. vis. Stanford (Calif.) U., 1981-84, 2004-06; dir. Tex. Bus. Law Found., 1989—, treas. 1994-96, sec. 1996-98. Mem.: ABA, Dallas Bar Assn., Calif. Bar Assn., Tex. Bar Assn. (corp. law com. 1981—, vice-chair corp. law com. 1993—97, chair corp. law com. 1997—2001, partnership law com. 1985—, ltd. liability co. com. 1992—, opinion com. 1989—98, codification com. 1997—, bus. law sect. coun. 1996—2007, vice chmn. 2004—05, chair 2005—06). Home: 2737 Purdue Ave Dallas TX 75225-7910 Office: Munsch Hardt Kopf & Harr PC 500 N Akard St Ste 3800 Dallas TX 75201 Office Phone: 214-855-7598. Business E-Mail: sschreiber@munsch.com.

SCHREIER, BRADLEY, management executive; b. Aug. 19, 1951; m. Marge St. Pierre; children: Ryan, Kyle. BS in Social Studies and Econs., Minn. State U., Mankato, 1973. Letterpress supr. Carlson Craft, Mankato, Minn., 1973-74, custom svc. supr., 1974-76, office mgr., 1976-79; v.p. sales and mktg. Taylor Corp., Mankato, 1980-85, pres., COO, 1985—2001, CEO, 2001—. Bd. dir. Malto Meal Corp., Mpls. Bd. dirs. Mankato Area United Way, 1975-81, v.p., 1979, 80, pres. bd. dirs., 1981; bd. dirs. YMCA, 1983-92, chmn. fin. com., co-chair spl. gifts divsn. 1 million dollar bldg. expansion capital campaign; bd. dirs. Immanuel-St. Joseph's Hosp., 1984-94, treas., 1988, vice chmn., treas, 1989, chmn. med. office bldg. task force, 1990, vice chmn., 1990, chmn. bd. dirs., 1991, 92, mem. exec. com., 1993-94; bd. dirs. Mankato Area Cath. Sch. Found., 1988—; pres. parish coun., mem. coun. Holy Rosary Ch., 1988—, chmn. fin. com., mem. com., 1989—; mem. pers. com. Loyola Cath. High Sch., 1989-90, mem. sch. bd., 1989-90; chmn. Mankato Area Cath. Sch. Bd., 1990—; coach Mankato Area Youth Baseball Assn., 1986—, bd. dirs., 1991—; pres. Mankato Royals Baseball, 1989, 90, bd. dirs., 1989-93; Fitzgerald 7th and 8th grade basketball coach, 1988, mem. Loyola Booster Club; bd. dirs. Mankato Basketball Assn., 1989—, traveling team coach, 1989—; basketball team coach Holy Rosary. Recipient Book of Golden Deeds award for Outstanding Cmty. Svc., Mankato Exch. Club, 1994, Disting. Alumni award Minn. State U., Mankato, 1994. Mem. KC. Office: Taylor Corp 1725 Roe Crest Dr Mankato MN 56003-1807 Office Phone: 507-625-2828.

SCHREIER, KAREN ELIZABETH, judge; b. Sioux Falls, SD, 1956; AB, St. Louis U., 1978; JD, St. Louis U. Law Sch., 1981. Law clk. to Hon. Francis Dunn, SD Supreme Ct., 1981—82; pvt. practice Sioux Falls, SD, 1982—93; US atty. US Dept. Justice, Sioux Falls, SD, 1993-99; judge US Dist. Ct., Rapid City, SD, 1999—. Office: US Dist Ct 515 9th St Rm 318 Rapid City SD 57701-2626 Office Phone: 605-343-3744.

SCHREIER, PETER, tenor; b. Meissen, Germany, July 29, 1935; Student, Dresden Hochschule für Musik, Germany. With Dresden State Opera, Germany, 1959-63, Berlin Staatsoper, Germany, 1963. Appearances include Vienna State Opera, Salzburg Festival, La Scala, Milan, Sadler's Wells, London, Met. Opera, N.Y.C., Teatro Colon, Buenos Aires; recital debut London, 1978; debut as conductor, 1969; has conducted recordings of several choral works by J.S. Bach and Mozart. Office: Kammersänger Calberlastr 13 D-01326 Dresden Germany

SCHREINER, ALBERT WILLIAM, internist, educator; b. Cin., Feb. 15, 1926; s. Albert William and Ruth Mary (Neuer) S.; m. Jean Tellstrom, Dec. 12, 1953; 1 child, David William. BS, U. Cin., 1947, MD, 1949. Diplomate Am. Bd. Internal Medicine, 1958. Clin. investigator VA Hosp., Cin., 1957-59, chief med. svc., 1959-68, dir. dept. internal medicine, 1968-93; dir. resident program internal medicine Christ Hosp., Cin., 1978-87; mem. faculty U. Cin. Coll. Medicine, 1955—, assoc. prof. medicine, 1962-67, prof. internal medicine, 1967-98, emeritus prof. internal medicine, 1998—; attending physician Cin. Gen. Hosp., 1957—95. Cons. to med. dir. Gen. Electric, 1987-96; med. dirs. United Home Care Hospice, 1993-99, United Home Care Agy.; chair instnl. rev. bd. The Christ Hosp., 1988—; subinvestigator Sterling Rsch. Group, 2003—. Contbr. articles to profl. jours. Bd. dirs., chmn. health com. Cmty. Action Commn., 1968-71; trustee Drake Meml. Hosp., 1975-78, Leukemia Found. Southwest Ohio, Cancer Control, Am. Cancer Soc., bd. dirs. Hamilton County unit, 1990; bd. dirs., chair profl. affairs com. United Home Care Agy., 1998; bd. dirs. Gamble Inst. Med. Rsch., Cin., 1991-96. Fellow: ACP; mem.: Am. Soc. Clin. Rsch. Program Dirs. Internal Medicine, Assn. Program Dirs. Internal Medicine, Clin. Soc. Internal Medicine (pres. 1979—80), Ohio Soc. Internal Medicine (trustee 1978, sec.-treas. 1981—85, v.p. 1982—83, pres. 1984—85), Ohio Med. Assn., Am. Fedn. Clin. Rsch., N.Y. Acad. Scis., Am. Cancer Soc. (bd. dirs. Hamilton County unit 1990—92), Am. Leukemia Soc. (med. adv. exec. bd.), Phi Beta Kappa, Sigma Xi. Roman Catholic. Home: 8040 S Clippinger Dr Cincinnati OH 45243-3248 Office: 2139 Auburn Ave Cincinnati OH 45219-2906 Office Phone: 513-585-2742. Business E-Mail: schreia@healthall.com.

SCHREINER, DONALD SCOTT, not-for-profit fundraiser; b. Topeka, Mar. 6, 1963; s. Walter Richard and Genevieve Ragan Schreiner. BGS in Art History, U. Kans., Lawrence, 1986; MPA in Non-Profit Mgmt., U. Mo., Kansas City, 1993. Cert. fund raising exec. Cert. Fund Raising Exec. Internat., 1998. Bus. mgr. Unicorn Theatre, Kansas City, 1991—94; assoc. dir. devel. Cath. Charities Archdiocese Kans. City, 1994—2002; dir. devel. Powell Gardens, Inc., Kingsville, Mo., 2002—. Comm. chmn. Assn. Fund Raising Execs. Mid-Am. Chpt., Kansas City, Mo., 2004; bd. mem. Garden Ctr. Assn., Kansas City, 2007—. Mem.: Garden Ctr. Assn., Assn. Fundraising Profls. Avocations: gardening, architecture, piano, jazz. Home: 9840 Aberdeen Dr Leawood KS 66206 Office: Powell Gardens Inc 1609 NW US Hwy 50 Kingsville MO 64061 Office Phone: 816-697-2600 238. Personal E-mail: dschreiner@everestkc.net. Business E-Mail: dschreiner@powellgardens.org.

SCHREINER, JOHN CHRISTIAN, economics consultant, software publisher; b. Los Angeles, Nov. 2, 1933; s. Alexander and Margaret S.; m. Marie Nielsen, June 19, 1967; children: Christian Alexander, Carl Arthur, Elizabeth, Nathan Alexander. BS in Mech. Engring., U. Utah, 1958; MBA, Harvard U., 1960; PhD, UCLA, 1970. Chartered fin. analyst. Design engr. Eimco Corp., Salt Lake City and NYC, 1957-59; credit exec. James Talcott, Inc., NYC and Boston, 1960-65; lectr. mgmt. U. Utah, 1965-66; mem. faculty Grad. Sch. Mgmt., U. Minn., Mpls., 1969-84, chmn. dept. fin. and ins., 1973-74, 76-81; pres. The Sebastian Group, Inc., 1984—. Cons. to corps. and govt. agys. Co-author: Executive Recruiting: How Companies Obtain Management Talent, 1960; contbr. articles to profl. jours. Mem. Fin. Execs. Inst., Fin. Analysts Fedn., Tau Beta Pi, Phi Kappa Phi. Republican. Mem. Ch. Jesus Christ of Latter-day Saints (missionary, Ger. 1953-56). Club: Harvard Bus. Sch. Minn. Office: The Sebastian Group Inc 2040 Douglas Dr Minneapolis MN 55422

SCHRENK, GARY DALE, foundation executive; b. San Jose, Calif., Apr. 29, 1949; s. Robert Shepard and Katherine Mildred (Grant) S.; m. Rhonda Lynn King, Oct. 9, 1981 (div. Jan. 1989); children: Stephen, Kristen, James. BA in Comm., Am. U., 1970; M in Nonprofit Mgmt., Regis U., 2002. TV dir. WTOP (now WUSA), Washington, 1971-73, KBTV (now KUSA), Denver, 1973-75; with Denver Area Boy Scouts Am., 1975-80; regional dir. St. Jude Children's Rsch. Hosp., Memphis, 1980-83; dir. devel. Denver Art Mus., 1983-85; asst. dir. devel. The Children's Hosp., Denver, 1985-87; pres. North Colo. Med. Ctr. Found., Greeley, 1987—. Dir., instr. Fast Start Course, 1985—; pres. Monfort Children's Clinic, Greeley, Colo., 1994—2001. Pres. Vision Together, Weld County, Colo., 1994—95; chmn., founding dir. Weld Citizen Action Network, 1995—98, 2000—02; founding dir. First Steps Weld County, 1993—99; chmn. Weld Cmty. Health Coalition, 1992—98; bd. dirs. North Colo. Health Alliance, 2002—06; chmn. pub. support com. Team Colo. ARC, 1997—2004; regional svc., area 2 public support com. ARC, 2004—06, bd. dirs. Centennial chpt., 2003—. Recipient Disting. Citizen award Highlanders, Denver, 1974 Mem. Assn. Fundraising Profls. (nat. found. bd. 1998-2003, nat. assembly 1994-98, bd. dirs. Colo. chpt. 1979-2000, 03-, pres. 1984, internat. bd. dirs. 2004—, Colo. Outstanding Devel. Profl. 2004), Colo. Assn. Nonprofit Orgns. (founding dir. 1987-92), Rotary, Greeley Country Club, Tahosa Alumni Assn. (past pres., past chair). Methodist. Avocation: golf. Home: 4956 13th St Greeley CO 80634-2215 Office: North Colo Med Ctr Found 1801 16th St Greeley CO 80631-5154 Office Phone: 970-356-9020. Business E-Mail: gary.schrenk@bannerhealth.com.

SCHREYER, CHARA, foundation administrator, art collector; Chmn. Kadima Found., Mill Valley, Calif. Trustee Mus. Modern Art, San Francisco, Contemporary Jewish Mus. Named one of Top 200 Collectors, ARTnews Mag., 2004, 2005, 2006. Avocation: Collector of Modern & Contemporary Art & Photography. Mailing: Kadima Foundation PMB 200 38 Miller Ave Mill Valley CA 94941

SCHREYER, LESLIE JOHN, lawyer; b. NYC, Apr. 11, 1946; s. Oscar and Greta (Loebl) S.; m. Judith Camps, Sept. 25, 1994; 1 child, Gabrielle. BA, Columbia U., 1967; LLB, Yale U., 1970; LLM in Taxation, N.Y.U., 1977. Bar: N.Y. 1971. Assoc. Chadbourne & Parke, NYC, 1970-78, ptnr., 1978-81, 83—; dep. internat. tax counsel U.S. Treasury Dept., 1981-83; gen. counsel GLG Ptnrs. Svcs. Ltd., 2000—, also bd. dirs. Adj. assoc. prof. law NYU, 1990-97; cons. Am. Law Inst., Fed. Income Tax Project on Internat. Aspects of U.S. Income Taxation, 1983-91. Author: (with others) Foreign Tax Credit, 1980; contbr. numerous articles to profl. jours. Trustee Am. Friends of the Victoria and Albert Mus., Inc. Mem. ABA, Internat. Bar Assn., Internat. Fiscal Assn., N.Y. State Bar Assn., Assn. of Bar of City of N.Y., Phi Beta Kappa. Republican. Home: 60 E End Ave New York NY 10028-7907 Office: Chadbourne & Parke 30 Rockefeller Plz Fl 31 New York NY 10112-0129 E-mail: lschreyer@chadbourne.com, les@glgpartners.com.

SCHREYER, WILLIAM ALLEN, retired finance company executive; b. Williamsport, Pa., Jan. 13, 1928; s. William L. and Elizabeth (Engel) S.; m. Joan Legg, Oct. 17, 1953; 1 child, DrueAnne Frazier. BA, Pa. State U., 1948. With Merrill Lynch, Inc. and predecessors, NYC, 1948-93; CEO Merrill Lynch & Co., NYC, 1984-92, chmn., 1985-93, chmn. emeritus, 1993—. Trustee, chmn. exec. com. Ctr. for Strategic and Internat. Studies, Pa. State U., 1986—, chmn. bd. trustees, 1993—96. With USAF, 1955—56. Mem. River Club, Links Club, Saturn Club, Springdale Golf Club, Bedens Brook Club, Eldorado Country Club, Georgetown Club, Met. Club, Nassau Club, Carnegie Club at Skibo Castle, Bond Club NY, Knights of Malta, Bay Head Yacht Club, Manasquan River Golf Club. Roman Catholic. Office: Merrill Lynch & Co Inc 800 Scudders Mill Rd Plainsboro NJ 08536-1606

SCHRICKER, SCOTT RAYMOND, dental educator; b. Cin., July 29, 1969; s. Don Edwin and Julia Yu Schricker; m. Diane Michele Basso, July 15, 2000; children: Winston Haskell Basso-Schricker, Sienna Raye Basso-Schricker. BS, Pa. State U., University Park, 1991; PhD, U. Calif., Santa Barbara, 1997. Postdoctoral rschr. Ohio State U., Coll. Dentistry, Columbus, 1997—98, rsch. scientist, 1998—2001, asst. prof., 2001—. Mem.: Internat. Assn. Dental Rsch., Am. Chem. Soc. Achievements include patents for synthesis of visible light curable (VLC) acid containing polymers. Office: Ohio State U 305 W 12th Ave Columbus OH 43210 Home Phone: 614-459-4638; Office Phone: 614-688-3367. Office Fax: 614-292-9422. Business E-Mail: schricker.1@osu.edu.

SCHRIEFFER, JOHN ROBERT, physics professor, science administrator; b. Oak Park, Ill., May 31, 1931; s. John Henry and Louise (Anderson) Schrieffer; m. Anne Grete Thomsen, Dec. 30, 1960; children: Anne Bolette, Paul Karsten, Anne Regina. BS, MIT, 1953; MS, U. Ill., 1954, PhD, 1957, ScD, 1974; ScD (hon.), Tech. U., Munich, 1968, U. Geneva, 1968, U. Pa., 1973, U. Cin., 1977, U. Tel Aviv, 1987, U. Ala., 1990. NSF postdoctoral fellow U. Birmingham, England, Niels Bohr Inst., Copenhagen, 1957—58; asst. prof. U. Chgo., 1958—59; asst. prof., then assoc. prof. U. Ill., 1959—62; prof. U. Pa., Phila., 1962—79, Mary Amanda Wood prof. physics, 1964—79; Andrew D. White prof. at large Cornell U., 1969—75; prof. U. Calif., Santa Barbara, 1980—91, Chancellor's prof., 1984—91, dir. Inst. for Theoretical Physics, 1984—89; Univ. prof. Fla. State U., Tallahassee, 1992—, Univ. Eminent Scholar prof., 1995—, chief scientist Nat. High Magnetic Field Lab., 1992—. Pres.'s com. Nat. Medal of Sci., 1996—98. Author: Theory of Superconductivity, 1964. Recipient Comstock prize, NAS, 1968, Nobel prize for Physics, 1972, John Ericsson medal, Am. Soc. Swedish Engrs., 1976, Alumni Achievement award, U. Ill., 1979, Nat. medal of Sci., 1984; fellow Guggenheim, Copenhagen, 1967, Los Alamos Nat. Lab., Exxon faculty, 1979—89. Fellow: Am. Phys. Soc. (v.p. 1994, pres.-elect 1995, pres. 1996, past pres. 1997, Oliver E. Buckley solid state physics prize 1968); mem.: NAS (coun. 1990—), Acad. Sci. USSR, Royal Danish Acad. Scis. and Letters, Am. Acad. Arts and Scis. Office: Fla State Univ NHMFL 1800 E Paul Dirac Dr Tallahassee FL 32310-3748 Business E-Mail: schrieff@magnet.fsu.edu.

SCHRIER, ARNOLD, historian, educator; b. NYC, May 30, 1925; s. Samuel and Yetta (Levine) S.; m. Sondra Weinshelbaum, June 12, 1949; children: Susan Lynn, Jay Alan, Linda Lee, Paula Kay. Student, Bethany Coll., W.Va., 1943-44, Ohio Wesleyan U., 1944-45; BS, Northwestern U., 1949, MA, 1950, PhD (Social Sci. Research Council fellow, Univ. fellow), 1956. Asst. prof. history U. Cin., 1956-61, assoc. prof., 1961-66, prof., 1966-95, dir. grad. studies history, 1969-78, Walter C. Langsam prof. modern European history, 1972-95; Walter C. Langsam prof. history emeritus, 1995—. Vis. asst. prof. history Northwestern U., Evanston, Ill., 1960; vis. assoc. prof. history Ind. U., Bloomington, 1965-66; vis. lectr. Russian history Duke U., 1966; disting. vis. prof. US Air Force Acad., 1983-84; dir. NDEA Inst. World History for Secondary Sch. Tchrs., U. Cin., 1965; Am. del. Joint U.S.-USSR Textbook Study Commn., 1989. Author: Ireland and the American Emigration, 1958, reissued, 1970, paperback edit., 1997, The Development of Civilization, 1961-62, Modern European Civilization, 1963, Living World History, 1964, rev., 1993, Twentieth Century World, 1974, History and Life: the World and Its People, 1977, rev., 1993, A Russian Looks at America, 1979, Irish Immigrants in the Land of Canaan, 2003. Pres. Ohio Acad. History, 1973-74, Midwest Slavic Conf., 1980. Served with USNR, 1943-46, 52-54. Recipient Disting. Svc. award Ohio Acad. History, 1992; Am. Coun. Learned Socs. fgn. area fellow, 1963-64 Mem. World History Assn. (v.p. 1986-88, pres. 1988-90). Home: 10 Diplomat Dr Cincinnati OH 45215-2073 Personal E-mail: arnsond@aol.com.

SCHRIER, ERIC WOODSIDE W., publishing executive; b. San Francisco, Nov. 21, 1951; s. Elliot and Nancy (Gennes) S.; m. Ellen Woodside, Dec. 30, 1978; 3 children. BA in Human Biology, Brown U., 1973; MA in Journalism, U. Calif., Berkeley, 1977. Marine biologist URS Co., San Mateo, Calif., 1973-77; pub., editor Novus mag., San Francisco, 1977-78; co-founder, mng. editor Science mag., Washington, 1979-85; editor-in-chief Hippocrates (now Health mag.), San Francisco, 1985—95, Time Inc. Ventures, 1990—95; pres., CEO Time Inc. Health, 1995—99; editor-in-chief to pres. RD N. Am. The Reader's Digest Assn., Inc., Pleasantville, NY, 2000—05, pres., CEO, 2005—07, cons., 2007—; indsl. ptnr. Ripplewood Holdings, LLC, 2007—. Co-editor: Newton At the Bat, The Science of Sport, 1984, Esquire (mag.) Register, 1985. Regents fellow U. Calif.-Berkeley, 1975 Mem. Am. Soc. Mag. Editors, Sigma Xi Office: Reader's Digest PO Box 200 Pleasantville NY 10572-0200 also: One Rockefeller Plz, 32nd Fl New York NY 10020 *

SCHRIER, ROBERT WILLIAM, physician, educator; b. Indpls., Feb. 19, 1936; s. Arthur E. and Helen M. Schrier; m. Barbara Lindley, June 14, 1959; children: David, Debbie, Douglas, Derek, Denise. BA, Depauw U., Greencastle, Ind., 1957; DSc (hon.), DePauw U., Greencastle, Ind., 2004; MD, Ind. U., 1962; DSc (hon.), U. Colo., 1996, Silesian Acad. Medicine, Katowice, Poland, 1997. Intern Marion County Hosp., Ind., 1962; resident U. Wash., Seattle, 1963-65; asst. prof. U. Calif. Med. Ctr., San Francisco, 1969—72, assoc. dir. renal divsn., 1971-72, assoc. prof., 1972; prof., head renal disease U. Colo. Sch. Med., Denver, 1972-92, prof., chmn. dept. medicine, 1976—. Editor 45 textbooks in internal medicine, geriat., drug usage, and kidney disease; contbr. over 800 sci. articles to profl. jours. Pres. Western Soc. Clin. Investigation, 1981, Nat. Kidney Found., 1984-86. With US Army, 1966—69. Recipient David Hume award Nat. Kidney Found., 1987, Louis Pasteur medal U. Strasburg, 1987, Mayo Soley award Western Soc. Clin. Investigation, 1989, Robert H. Williams award Assn. Profs. Medicine, 1996, Torchbearer award 1997, Edward N. Gibbs Meml. award NY Acad. Medicine, 2000, Alexander von Humboldt Rsch award 2004, Grand Hamdan Internat. Med. Scis. award 2004. Mem. ACP (master, John Phillips award 1992), Am. Soc. Nephrology (treas. 1979-81, pres. 1983, John Peters award 1997), Internat. Soc. Nephrology (treas. 1981-90, v.p. 1990-95, pres. 1995-97, Jean Hamburger award 2003), Am. Clin. and Climatol. Assn. (v.p. 1986), Assn. Am. Physicians (pres. 1994-95, Francis Blake award 1995), Western Assn. Physicians (pres. 1982), Inst. of Medicine of NAS, Alpha Omega Alpha. Achievements include research contributions centered on the pathogenesis of acute renal failure, genetic renal disorders, mechanisms of cell injury, diabetic nephropathy and renal and hormonal control of body fluid volume; advancement of a unifying hypothesis of sodium and water regulation in health and disease which has stimulated world-wide interest in the medical science community. Office: U Colo Health Scis Ctr Renal Divsn PO Box B173 Denver CO 80262-0001 Business E-Mail: Robert.Schrier@uchsc.edu.

SCHRIESHEIM, ALAN, science administrator; b. NYC, Mar. 8, 1930; s. Morton and Frances (Greenberg) Schriesheim; m. Beatrice D. Brand, June 28, 1953; children: Laura Lynn, Robert Alan. BS in Chemistry, Poly. Inst. Bklyn., 1951; PhD in Phys. Organic Chemistry, Pa. State U., 1954; DSc (hon.), No. Ill. U., 1991; Laureate, Lincoln Acad., 1996; PhD (hon.), Ill. Inst. Tech., Chgo., 1992, Pa. State U., 2001. Chemist Nat. Bur. Standards, 1954—56; with Exxon Rsch. & Engring. Co., 1956—83, dir. corp. rsch., 1975—79; gen. mgr. Exxon Engring., 1979—83; sr. dep. lab. dir., COO Argonne Nat. Lab., 1983—84, lab. dir., CEO, 1984—96, dir. emeritus, 1996—; prof. chemistry dept. U. Chgo., 1984—96, lectr. Bus. Sch., 1996—99; prin. Washington Adv. Group, 1996—; pres. Chgo. Coun. Sci. and Technol., 2007—. Karcher lectr. U. Okla., 1977; Hurd lectr. Northwestern U., 1980; Rosenstiel lectr. Brandeis U., 1982; Welsh Found. lectr., 87; com. svc. NRC, 1980—; vis. com. chemistry dept. MIT, 1977—82; mem. vis. com. mech. engring. and aerospace dept. Princeton (N.J.) U., 1983—87, mem. vis. com. chemistry dept., 1983—87; mem. Pure and Applied Chemistry Com.; del. to People's Republic of China, 1978; mem. Presdl. Nat. Commn. on Superconductivity, 1989—91, U.S.-USSR Joint Commn. on Basic Sci. Rsch., 1990—93; mem. U.S. nat. com. Internat. Union Pure and Applied Chemistry, 1982—85; mem. magnetic fusion adv. com. Divsn. Phys. Scis. U. Chgo. Magnetic Fusion adv. com. to U.S. DOE, 1983—86; mem. Dept. Energy Rsch. Adv. Bd., 1983—85, Congl. Adv. Com. on Sci. and Tech., 1985—96; mem. vis. com. Stanford (Calif.) U., U. Utah, Tex. A&M U., Lehigh U.; bd. govs. Argonne Nat. Lab., 1984—96; mem. adv. com. on space sys. and tech. NASA, 1987—93; mem. nuc. engring. and engring. physics vis. com. U. Wis., Madison; mem. Coun. Gt. Lakes Govs. Regional Econ. Devel. Commn., 1987—, rev. bd. Compact Ignition Tomamak Princeton U., 1988—91; advisor Sears Investment Mgmt. Co., 1988—89; bd. dirs. HEICO, Smart Signal Corp.; adv. bd. Batterson Venture Ptnrs., Influx, UHV Aluminum, Valley Indsl. Assn., Coun. on Superconductivity for Am. Competitiveness; mem. State of Ill. Commn. on the Future of Pub. Svc., 1990—92; co-chair Indsl. Rsch. Inst. Nat. Labs./Industry Panel, 1984—87; mem. Nat. Acad. Engring. Adv. Commn. on Tech. and Soc., 1991—92, Sun Electric Corp. Bd., 1991—92, U.S. House of Reps. subcom. on Sci.-Adv. Group on Renewing U.S. Sci. Policy, 1992—96, Chgo. Acad. Scis. acad. coun., 1994—; mem. adv. bd. Chemtech; mem. sr. action group on R&D investment strategies Ctr. for strategic and Internat. Studies, 1995; bd. vis. Astronomy and Astrophysics Pa. State U., 1995—; bd. overseers Fermi Nat. Lab., 2003—. Adv. bd.: Chemtech, 1970—85, editl. bd.: Rsch. & Devel., 1988—92, Superconductor Industry, 1988—95; patentee in field. Mem. spl. vis. com. Field Mus. of Natural History, Chgo., 1987—88; trustee The Latin Sch. of Chgo., 1990—92; adv. bd. WBEZ Chicagoland Pub. Radio Cmty., 1990—96; mem. Conservation Found. DuPage County, 1983—96, Econ. Devel. Adv. Commn. of DuPage County, 1984—88, Ill. Gov.'s Commn. on Sci. and Tech., 1986—90, Inst. for Ill. Coun. Advisors, 1988—, Ill. Coalition Bd. Dirs., 1989—, Inst. for Ill. Adv. Rev. Panel, 1986—88, NASA Sci. Tech. Adv. Com. Manpower Requirements Ad Hoc Rev. Team, 1988—91, Ill. Sci. and Tech. Adv. Com., 1989—, chmn., 1997; mem. U. Ill. Engring. Vis. com., Urbana-Champaign, 1986—95; trustee Tchrs. Acad. for Math. and Sci. Tchrs. in Chgo., 1990—96; bd. visitors astronomy and astrophysics Pa. State U., 1995—; bd. dirs. LaRabida Children's Hosp. and Rsch. Ctr., 1987—95, Children's Meml. Hosp., Children's Meml. Inst. for Edn. and Rsch. Recipient Outstanding Alumni Fellow award, Pa. State U., 1985, laureate, Lincoln Acad. Ill., 1996, Disting. fellow, Poly. U., 1989, Disting. Alumni award, Pa. State U., 2005. Fellow: AAAS (coun. del. chem. sect. 1986—92, sci. engring. and pub. policy com. 1992, standing com. audit

1992, bd. dirs. 1992—96, selection com. to bring FSU scientists to ann. mtg. 1995—), N.Y. Acad. Scis.; mem.: AIChE (award com. 1992—), NAE (adv. com. tech. and soc. 1991—92, mem. program adv. com. 1992—94, chair study fgn. participation in U.S. R&D 1993—96, NRC com. on dual use tech. 1996—97, com. to assess policies and practices of Dept. of Energy to design, ma 1998—99), NASA Com. on Aeronautics Innovation Models (chmn. 2005—), Ctr. Strategic and Internat. Studies (sr. action group 1995—96), Indsl. Rsch. Inst. (co-chmn. Nat. Labs. Indsl. Panel 1984—87, fed. adv. com. to Fed. Sci. and Tech. Com. 1992—96, sr. action group on R&D Investment Strategies), Am. Nuc. Soc., Am. Petroleum Inst. (rsch. coord. coun.), Nat. Conf. Advancement Rsch. (conf. com. 1985—, site selection com. 1994, conf. com. 50th ann. 1996), Am. Mgmt. Assn. (R&D coun. 1988—), Am. Chem. Soc. (joint bd. coun. on sci. 1983—87, chmn. petroleum divsn. 1983—91, councilor, com. on chemistry and pub. affairs 1983—91, petroleum chemistry award 1969, 1995—96), Econ. Club, Comml. Club, Cosmos Club, Carleton Club (bd. govs. 1992—), Phi Lambda Upsilon, Sigma Xi. Home: 1440 N Lake Shore Dr Apt 31ac Chicago IL 60610-5927 Office: Argonne Nat Lab 9700 S Cass Ave Argonne IL 60439-4803 Home Phone: 312-440-9408; Office Phone: 630-252-3872. E-mail: schriesheim@anl.gov.

SCHRIEVER, FRED MARTIN, management consultant, financial investor; b. NYC; s. Samuel and Sara S.; m. Cheri G. Spatt; children: Melissa Ann, Elizabeth Ellen. BME, Poly. U. N.Y., 1956, MME, 1958. Registered profl. engr., N.Y., Wash.; cert. mgmt. cons. Chief engr. divsn. Sperry Corp., NYC, 1956-64; ptnr. Booz, Allen and Hamilton, NYC and Washington, 1964-71; chmn., pres. RCG Internat. Inc., NYC, 1971—96. Investor and cons. in field; dir. Nat. Exec. Svc. Corps., 1998—, Hagler Bailly Inc., 1996-2000. Fellow Inst. of Dirs., Inst. Mgmt. Consultants U.K.; mem. ASME, Inst. Mgmt. Cons., Chemists Club. Home: PO Box 32 Westport CT 06881-0032

SCHRIVER, JOHN T., III, lawyer; b. Evanston, Ill., May 18, 1945; AB, Coll. of Holy Cross, 1967; JD, Georgetown U., 1970. Bar: Ill. 1971, Fla. 1972. Ptnr. Duane Morris LLC, Chgo. Mem. ABA, Chgo. Bar Assn., Fla. Bar. Office: Duane Morris LLC 227 W Monroe St Ste 3400 Chicago IL 60606-5096

SCHROCK, NANCY CARLSON, conservator, consultant; d. John Edward Carlson and Frances Felicia Pogorzelski; m. Richard Royce Schrock, 1971; children: Andrew Richard, Eric Noah. BFA, Brown U., Providence, 1968; MLS, Simmons Grad. Sch. Libr. and Info. Sci., Boston, 1971; MA in Art History, U. Del., Newark, 1976. Rare book libr. Winterthur Mus., Winterthur, Del., 1972—75; visual collections libr. MIT Librs., Cambridge, Mass., 1976—78, Thomas J. Peterson jr. conservator spl. collections, 2006—; pvt. practice conservator Winchester, Mass., 1978—97; chief collections conservator Harvard Coll. Libr., Cambridge, Mass., 1997—2006. Preservation cons. MIT Librs., Cambridge, 1979—94, Harvard U. Libr., Cambridge, 1990—96; cons. Gaylord Bros., Syracuse, NY, 1992—97. Author: Architectural Records in Boston; A Guide to Architectural Resources in Boston, Cambridge, and Vicinity, Records in Architectural Offices; Suggestions for the Proper Organization, Storage, and Conservation of Architectural Office Archives, 1980, Records in Architectural Offices; Suggestions for the Proper Organization, Storage, and Conservation of Architectural Office Archives, 3d edit., 1992; co-author: Preservation: Issues and Planning, Who Wants Yesterday's Papers? Essays on the Research Value of Printed Materials in the Digital Age. Dir. Mass. Com. Preservation Archtl. Records, Cambridge, 1978—95; commr. Mass. Hist. Records Adv. Bd., Boston, 1996—2007; treas. Winchester Hist. Soc., Mass., 2003—07. Mem.: ALA (chair phys. quality materials group 1995—97), Guild Book Workers, Am. Inst. Conservation (treas. 1998—2002). Office: MIT Librs Bldg 14-0513 77 Massachusetts Ave Cambridge MA 02139 Home Phone: 781-721-1229; Office Phone: 617-452-4064.

SCHROCK, RICHARD ROYCE, chemistry professor; b. Berne, Ind., Jan. 4, 1945; m. Nancy F. Carlson, 1971; children: Andrew, Eric. AB, U. Calif., Riverside, 1967; PhD, Harvard U., 1971. Rsch. chemist, Ctrl. R&D dept. E.I. du Pont de Nemours & Co., Wilmington, Del., 1972-75; asst. prof. MIT, Cambridge, 1975-78, assoc. prof., 1978-80, prof., 1980-89, Frederick G. Keyes prof. chemistry, 1989—. Assoc. editor: Organometallics; contbr. articles to profl. jours. Co-recipient Nobel Prize in Chemistry, 2005; recipient Bailar medal, U. Ill., 1998, Sir Geoffrey Wilkinson medal, Royal Soc. Chemistry, 2002, Sir Edward Frankland prize, 2004, August Wilhelm von Hofmann medal, German Chem. Soc., 2005; NSF postdoctoral fellow, Cambridge U., 1971—72. Mem.: NAS, AAAS, Am. Chem. Soc. (award organometallic chemistry 1985, Harrison Howe award 1990, Humboldt award 1994, award inorganic chemistry 1996, Arthur C. Cope Scholar award 2001, F. Albert Cotton award in Synthetic Inorganic Chemistry 2006), Am. Acad. Arts and Scis. Office: MIT Dept Chemistry Rm 6 331 77 Massachusetts Ave Cambridge MA 02139 Office Phone: 617-253-1596. Office Fax: 617-253-7670. E-mail: rrs@mit.edu.

SCHROCK, SIMON, retail executive; b. Oakland, Md., Dec. 28, 1936; s. Noah and Cora (Burkholder) S.; m. Eva Lena Yoder, June 7, 1959 (dec. Apr. 1962); m. Pauline Yoder, Sept. 29, 1963; children: Janice Yvonne, Eldon Laverne, Ivan Dale. With Eastern States Farm Supply Co., Oakland, Md., 1957-59, Children's Hosp., Washington, 1959-61, Copp Properties, Vienna, Va., 1961-75; pres. Choice Books of No. Va., Fairfax, Va., 1975—. Chmn. Lighthouse Lit., 1976-2001. Author: Get on With Living, 1976, Price of Missing Life, 1981, One-Anothering, 1986, Vow-Keepers Vow-Breakers, A Smoother Journey, 1994, What Shall The Redeemed Wear, 2001, Where Has Integrity Gone, 2001, Don't Throw In the Towel, 2003; contbr. articles to ch. jours. Bishop Faith Christian Fellowship, Catlett, Va., 1981—. Avocations: travel, writing, biking. Office: 10100 Piper Ln Bristow VA 20136 Business E-Mail: schrocks@nva.choicebooks.org.

SCHROCK, THEODORE R., surgeon; b. Berne, Ind., Oct. 21, 1939; s. N.J. and M.A. Schrock; married. AB, U. Calif., San Francisco, 1961, MD, 1964. Diplomate Am. Bd. Surgery. Intern U. Calif. Hosps., San Francisco, 1964-65, resident, 1965-67, 69-71; fellow Mass. Gen. Hosp., Boston, 1967-69; chmn. dept. surgery U. Calif. San Francisco Med. Ctr., 1993-99, J. Englebert Dunphy prof. surgery, 1998—, assoc. dean clin. svcs., chief med. officer, 1999—. Fellow ACS; mem. Am. Gastroenterological Assn., Am. Soc. Colon and Rectal Surgery, Am. Soc. Gastroenterological Endoscopy, Am. Surg. Assn., Soc. Surgery Alimentary Tract. Office: UCSF Campus Box 0296 500 Parnassus Ave San Francisco CA 94143-0296

SCHRODER, JACK SPALDING, JR., lawyer; b. Atlanta, July 10, 1948; s. Jack Spalding Sr. and Van (Spalding) S.; m. Karen Keyworth, Sept. 1, 1973; children: Jack Spalding III, James Edward. BA, Emory U., 1970; JD, U. Ga., 1973. Bar: Ga. 1973, U.S. Dist. Ct. (no. dist.) Ga. 1973, U.S. Ct. Appeals (11th cir.) 1982. Assoc. Alston & Bird, Atlanta, 1973-78, ptnr., 1978—2003, sr. counsel, 2004—07, of counsel, 2007—. Author: Credentialing: Strategies for a Changing Environment/BNA's Health Law and Business Series, 1996; co-editor, contbg. author: Georgia Hospital Law manual, 1979, 84, 92. Bd. dirs. Rsch. Atlanta, 1996-00, pres., 1999, co-chair bd. advisors, 2003-06; participant Leadership Ga., Atlanta, 1986. United Way (chmn. legal divsn.), Atlanta, 1980; bd. dir. Good Samaritan Health and Wellness Ctr., Jasper, Ga., 2006-. Decorated comdr. S.E. Commandery Mil. and Hospitaller Order of St. Lazarus of Jerusalem. Mem. ABA (vice chmn. medicine and law com. 1989-90), Am. Health Lawyers Assn. (bd. dirs. 1994-99, chmn. med. staff and physician rels. com. 1991-94, vice chair hosps. and health systems law inst. 2001-07), Ga. Acad. Healthcare Attys. (pres. 1981-82), State Bar Ga. (bd. govs. 1987-89), Atlanta Coun. Younger Lawyers (pres. 1977-78), Atlanta Bar Assn. (pres. 1982-83), Atlanta Bar Found. (pres. 1991-95), Mil. and Hospitaller Order St. Lazarus Jerusalem (comdr. S.E. commandery 2003—). Office: Alston & Bird One Atlantic Ctr 1201 W Peachtree St NW Atlanta GA 30309-3424 Office Phone: 404-881-7685.

SCHRODER, RICK, actor; b. SI, NY, Apr. 13, 1970; s. Richard and Diane Schroder; m. Andrea Bernard, Sept. 1992; children: Holden Richard, Luke William, Cambrey, Faith Anne. Attended and majored in Farm and Ranch Mgmt., Mesa State Coll., Grand Junction, Colo. Actor: (films) The Champ, 1979 (Golden Globe award 1979), The Last Flight of Noah's Ark, 1980, The Earthling, 1981, There Goes My Baby, 1994, Crimson Tide, 1995, I Woke Up Early the Day I Died, 1998, Poolhall Junkies, 2002, Consequence, 2003, Face of Terror, 2003; (TV series) Silver Spoons, 1982-86, NYPD Blue, 1998-2001, Strong Medicine, 2005-; (TV movies) Little Lord Fauntleroy, 1980, Something So Right, 1982, Two Kinds of Love, 1983, A Reason to Live, 1985, Hansel and Gretel, 1982, Too Young the Hero, 1988, Terror on Highway 91, 1989, Out on the Edge, 1989, A Son's Promise, 1990, The Stranger Within, 1990, Blood River, 1991, My Son Johnny, 1991, Across the Tracks, 1991, Miles from Nowhere, 1992, Call of the Wild, 1993, To My Daughter with Love, 1994, Innocent Victims, 1996, Too Close to Home, 1997, Detention: The Siege at Johnson High, 1997, Heart Full of Rain, 1997, Ebenezer, 1997, What We Did That Night, 1999, Lost Battalion, 2001, 14 Hours, 2005; (TV mini series) Lonesome Dove, 1989, Return to Lonesome Dove, 1993; (video) Texas, 1994; (TV spls.) The Jimmy McNichol Special, Doug Henning's World of Magic, An Orchestra is a Team, Too, Walt Disney's Tenth Anniversary Special, Battle of the Network Stars, Circus of the Stars, Missing, Have You Seen this Person?, S.O.S., Secrets of Surviving, Kraft Salutes Walt Disney World's 10th Anniversary; actor, writer, dir. (films) Black Cloud, 2004; dir. (music video) "Whiskey Lullaby" (Music Video of Yr., Country Music Assn., 2004, Video Dir. of Yr., Country Music Television Music award, 2005, Video of Yr., Vocal Event of Yr., Acad. Country Music Awards, 2005); guest appearances (TV) Scrubs, 2003.

SCHRODER, SIGRID CAROLINE, lawyer, consultant; married, 1980; 1 child, Peter; 1 child, John. BA, Columbia U., NYC, 1977; JD, So. Meth. U., Dallas, 1988. Bar: Tex. 1988. V.p. PM Legal Search, Dallas, 1983—85; pvt. practice Dallas and Houston, 1989—2006; prin. Sulgrave Resources, LLC, Houston, 2001—; CEO Bellevue, Mercer Island, Wash., 2007. Sec, chair legal com., bd. Dallas Chamber Orch., 1989—91; dir. bd. Allegro Dallas (formerly known as SPA Dallas), 1989—90; devel. advisor U. Tex., Health Sci. Ctr. Biotech Incubator, Houston, 2001—03; v.p. Houston Planning Forum, 2002—03; cornerstone sponsor Houston Tech. Ctr., 2002—03; dir., adv. bd. Houston Achievement Pl., Houston, 2003. Mission com. St John the Divine, Houston, 2002—04. Recipient Alan R. Bromberg Securities award, Dedman Sch. Law, 1988. Mem.: Coll. State Bar Tex., Pro Bono Coll. Tex. State Bar, State Bar Tex. (chair internat. law com. 2005—07, intellectual property sect.), Columbia U. Alumni So. Tex. (pres. 2005—07), Houston City Club, Barnard Coll. Club Houston (pres 1995—2006), Univ. Club. Avocations: travel, ballet, historic preservation, photography. Office: Sulgrave Resources 800 Bellevue Way NE Ste 400 Bellevue WA 98004 Home Phone: 206-275-0350; Office Phone: 425-462-4035. Business E-Mail: caroline@sulgrave-llc.com.

SCHRODER, WIL, state supreme court justice; b. Ft. Mitchell, Ky., 1946; m. Susan Wahlbrink; children: Stephanie, Lydia, Wil. BA, JD, U. Ky.; LLM, U. Mo. Bar: Ky. 1970, Mo. 1972. Atty. Kansas City Legal Aid Soc., 1971; corp. atty. St. Paul Ins. Co., 1971—72; asst. law prof. Chase Law Sch., Ky., 1972—75; pvt. practice Covington, Ky., 1975—83; trial ct. judge Kenton County Dist. Ct., Ky., 1983—91; judge Ky. Ct. Appeals, 1991—2006; justice for 6th Supreme Ct. dist Ky. Supreme Ct., 2007—. Hearing officer Ky. Personnel Bd., 1981—83. Office: Supreme Ct Ky 700 Capital Ave Rm 235 Frankfort KY 40601 Office Phone: 502-564-5444. *

SCHROEDER, BRIAN S., philosopher, educator; b. Quantico, Va., June 15, 1959; s. Gary Stephen and Faye Mary (Monette) Schroeder; m. Silvia Benso, June 5, 1999; 1 child, Erik Aren. MA, PhD, Stony Brook U.; MDiv, Princeton Theol. Sem. Prof. philosophy Rochester Inst. Tech., Rochester, 2001—. Coord. religious studies Rochester Inst. Tech. Author: (book) Altared Ground: Levinas, History, and Violence, 1995, Pensare ambientalista: Tra filosofia e ecologia, 2000; editor: Thinking Through the Death of God, 2004, Contemporary Italian Philosophy: Crossing the Borders of Ethics, Politics, and Religion, 2006; co-editor: SUNY Series Contemproary Italian Philosophy, 2005—; editor: (journal) Studies in Practical Philosophy. Fellow, J. William Fulbright Scholarship Commn., 2000—01; Miller Rsch. Fellowship, Rochester Inst. of Techology, 2003—04, Sr. Fellowship in Religion and Soc., Princeton Theol. Sem., 1984. Mem.: Levinas Rsch. Seminar (co-dir. 2003—04), Wisdom Rendezvous (bd. dirs. 1992—), Found. for the Philosophy of Creativity (exec. bd. 2000—), Internat. Soc. for Universal Dialogue (treas. 2001—03), Soc. for the Philosophy of Creativity (v.p. ea. divsn. 2000—), Nietzsche Soc. (exec. com. 2001—04), Soc. for Phenomenology and Existential Philosophy, Am. Acad. of Religion, Am. Philos. Assn., Internat. Assn. for Environ. Philosophy (chmn. bd. dirs. 2002—). Independent. Office Phone: 585-475-6346.

SCHROEDER, CHRISTOPHER, literature and language professor, writer; b. St. Louis, Aug. 24, 1970; m. Ranimarie Buen-Schroeder, Dec. 6, 1996; children: Mahal, Mateo. BA in English, SIU; MA in English, U. Mo., St. Louis; PhD with distintion, U. La., Lafayette, 1999. Assoc. prof. English Northea. Ill. U., Chgo., 2002—. Author: ReInventing the University: Literacies and Legitimacy in the Postmodern Academy, 2001; editor: ALT DIS: Alternative Discourses and the Academy, 2002. Office: Northestern Ill U Dept English 5500 N St Louis Ave Chicago IL 60625 Office Phone: 773-442-5483. Business E-Mail: c-schroeder2@neiu.edu.

SCHROEDER, DAVID J. DEAN, psychologist; b. Hutchinson, Kans., Mar. 21, 1942; s. D.J.W. and Louise (Wedel) S.; m. Nevonna Joyce Thomas, May 24, 1964; children: Taryn Dee Schroeder Dye, Anita Joy Fitch. BA, Tabor Coll., 1964; MS, Kans. State Tchrs. Coll., 1967; PhD, U. Okla., 1971. Lic. psychologist, Kans. Rsch. psychologist Civil Aerospace Med. Inst., Oklahoma City, 1970-72, clin. rsch. psychologist, 1980-89, supr., 1989-90, mgr. human factors rsch. lab., 1990-91, mgr. aerospace human factors rsch. divsn., 1991—; intern Norfolk (Nebr.) Regional Ctr., 1972-73; clin. psychologist VA Hosp., Murfreesboro, Tenn., 1973-75, Topeka, 1975-80. Co-author: FAA Employee Survey: National Report, 1984, 86, FAA Employee Survey: Regional/Center Reports, 1984, 86, FAA Job Satisfaction Survey National Report, 1988, FAA Job Satisfaction Survey: Regional/Center/Work Group Reports, 1988; mem. adv. editl. bd. Aviation Space and Environ. Medicine, 1993-95, 99-2001, 2006-. Mem. senate adv. com. Tabor Coll., Hillsboro, Kans., 1987-89; Christian edn. com. chmn. So. Dist. Conf. Mennonite Brethren Ch., Hillsboro, 1989; Sunday Sch. tchr. Western Oaks Christian Ch., Oklahoma City, 1990—; co-chair cmty. investment subcom. Okla. City United Way, 2006, 07. Fellow APA, Aerospace Med. Assn. (chmn. sci. program com. 1990-91, mem. coun. 1992-95, v.p. 1996-97, v.p. edn. and rsch. 1999-2002, pres.-elect, 2002-03, pres. 2003-04, program com. chair APA divsn. applied exptl. and engrng. psychology 1996-97, sec.-treas. 1998-2001, pres.-elect 2001-02, pres. 2002-03, chmn. aerospace human factors com. 1999-2002, Raymond F. Longacre award for outstanding accomplishmnts in psychol. and psychiat. aspects of aerospace medicine 1997), Aerospace Human Factors Assn. (pres. 1994-95, Henry L. Taylor Founders award 2001); mem. Okla. Psychol. Assn. (bd. dirs. 1988-89, pres.-elect 1991, pres. 1992), Internat. Acad. Aviation and Space Medicine. Democrat. Achievements include research in assessing the interactive effects of alcohol, age and drugs on dynamic tracking and cognitive performance, personality characteristics and training success of air traffic control students, biofeedback, anxiety and burnout in government employees, human factors of air traffic control operational errors, fatigue and shiftwork. Home: 2601 NW 23rd St Oklahoma City OK 73107-2209 Office: PO Box 25082 Oklahoma City OK 73125-0082 Personal E-mail: davids20@cox.net.

SCHROEDER, DOUGLAS FREDRICK, architect; b. Omaha, June 12, 1935; s. Walter Elmer and Ellen Ruth (Niles) S.; m. Joanne Vlecides, July 5, 1980. B.Arch., U. Mich., 1959. Registered Architect, Ill., N.C., Mich. Designer, draftsman C.F. Murphy Assocs., Chgo., 1959-63; architect, sr. architect Skidmore, Owings & Merrill, Chgo., 1964-67; architect, ptnr. Schroeder, Yamamoto & Schreiber, Chgo., 1968-69; ptnr. Hinds & Schroeder, Ltd., Chgo., 1972-74; propr. Douglas Schroeder Assocs., Chgo., 1974-83, 93—; ptnr. Siegel & Schroeder, P.C., Chgo., 1983-91; dir. SGA Planning and Constrn. Cons. Co. div. Goforth Group, Chgo., 1991-93; v.p. Yacht Harbor Mgmt. Co., South Haven, Mich., 1983-88. Dir. Inland Architect Mag. Contbr. articles to profl. jours. Bd. dirs. Chgo. Archtl. Assistance Ctr., 1982-84; chmn. Mass. Transp. Crisis Com., Chgo., 1973, Ill. Futures Forum, 1976-77; pres. Ill. Planning and Conservation League, Chgo., 1971-74; ptnr. Burnham & Bennett Plan of Chgo. 1909 Centennial Celebration. Named Outstanding Alumnus Lake Superior State U., 1971. Fellow AIA; mem. Am. Arbitration Assn. (arbitrator) Clubs: Cliff Dwellers (dir. 1971-74). Unitarian Universalist. Home: 700 W Irving Park Rd Apt 4A Chicago IL 60613-3133 Office: Douglas Schroeder Assocs Arch & Planners 980 N Michigan Ave Ste 1277 Chicago IL 60611-4523 Office Phone: 312-280-5376. Business E-Mail: dschroeder@dsa-architects.com.

SCHROEDER, ERIC PETER, lawyer; b. Floral Park, NY, July 21, 1970; s. Fredric G. and Linda M. Schroeder. BA, Duke U., 1992; JD, Vanderbilt U., 1996. Bar: Ga. 1997, U.S. Dist. Ct. (no. dist.) Ga. 1997, U.S. Ct. Appeals (11th cir.) 1998. Law clk. Hon. William C. O'Kelley, U.S. Dist. Ct. (no. dist.) Ga., Atlanta, 1996-97; atty. Powell, Goldstein, Frazer & Murphy, Atlanta, 1997—. Mem. planning com. Ga. Bar Media Jud. Conf., 1999-2002. Articles editor Vanderbilt Law Rev., 1995-96; mem. editl. bd. INTA The Trademark Reporter, 2000-01, 2003-05. Lawyer Anti-Defamation League, Atlanta, 1998. Mem. Atlanta Bar Assn., (chair election com. 2002-03), Internat. Trademark Assn., State Bar. Ga. (mem. com. on the judiciary), Am. Health Lawyers Assn., ABA, Media Law Resource Ctr., Order of Coif, Lamar Inn of Ct. Home: 340 Sutherland Pl Atlanta GA 30307-2346 Office: Powell Goldstein LLP 1201 W Peachtree St Atlanta GA 30309 Business E-Mail: eschroeder@pgfm.com.

SCHROEDER, FRED ERICH HARALD, humanities educator; b. Manitowoc, Wis., June 3, 1932; s. Alfred William and Sissel Marie (Lovell) S.; m. Janet June Knope, Aug. 21, 1954; 1 child, Erich Karl. BS, U. Wis., 1960; MA, U. Minn., 1963, PhD, 1968. Elementary sch. tchr. various locations, Wis., 1952-60; asst. prof. English U. Minn., Duluth, 1968-71, assoc. prof. English, 1971-74, prof. behavioral sci., 1977-82, prof. humanities, 1974-96, dir. Ctr. for Am. Studies, 1986-87, dir. Inst. Interdisciplinary Studies, 1987-90, dir. dept. humanities and classics, 1989-90, dir. grad. liberal studies, 1992-95, prof. emeritus, 1996—. Author: Joining the Human Race: How To Teach Humanities, 1972, Outlaw Aesthetics: Arts and the Public Mind, 1977, Front Yard America: The Evolution and Meanings of a Domestic Vernacular Landscape, 1993; co-author: Encyclopedia of Modern Everyday Inventions, 2003; editor Interdisciplinary Humanities (formerly Humanities Edn. jour.), 1983-95, assoc. editor, 1995—; editor 5000 Years of Popular Culture, 1980, 20th Century Popular Culture in Museums and Libraries, 1981; lectr., writer Nat. Humanities Series, 1969-71; adv. editor Guide to U.S. Popular Culture, 2001. Mem. Minn. Humanities Commn., 1985-90. Woodrow Wilson Nat. Found. fellow, 1960-61, dissertation fellow 1963; NEH scholar, 1969-70; Inst. for Human Values in Medicine fellow, 1976. Mem. Am. Culture Assn. (pres. 1984-87), Nat. Assn. Humanities Edn. (pres. 1987-89, exec. sec.-treas. 1989-96), Am. Assn. for State and Local History (seminar instr. 1978-82), Popular Culture Assn. Avocations: collecting art, woodworking, gardening. Home: 5756 N Shore Dr Duluth MN 55804-9660 E-mail: fschroed@d.umn.edu.

SCHROEDER, GERALD FRANK, retired state supreme court justice; b. Boise, Idaho, Sept. 13, 1939; s. Frank Frederick and Josephine Ivy (Lucas) S.; children: Karl Casteel, Erich Frank. BA magna cum laude, Coll. of Idaho (now Albertson Coll. of Idaho), 1961; JD, Harvard U., 1964. Bar: Idaho 1965. Assoc. Moffatt, Thomas, Barrett & Blanton, Boise, 1965—66; pvt. practice Boise, 1966—67; asst. U.S. atty. Dept. Justice, Boise, 1967—69; judge Ada County Probate Ct., Boise, 1969—71; magistrate State of Idaho, Boise, 1971—75; dist. judge U.S. Dist. Ct. (4th dist.) Idaho, 1975—95; justice Idaho Supreme Ct., 1995—2007, chief justice, 2004—07. Instr. Boise Bar Rev., 1973—; adj. faculty law Boise State U., 1986—95; former mem. Gov. Coun. on Crime and Delinquency. Author: Idaho Probate Procedure, 1971, (Novel) Triangle of the Sons-Phenomena, 1983; contbr. chpt. to history text. Adminstrv. and dist. judge 4th dist. State of Idaho, 1985—95; Bd. dirs. Boise Philharm. Assn., 1979—81. Fellow Toll fellow, Nat. Coun. State Govt., 1990. Mem.: Idaho Bar Assn., Boise Racquet and Swim Club (pres. bd. dirs. 1991—93). Home Phone: 208-375-6139; Office Phone: 208-334-3324. Business E-Mail: gschroeder@isc.state.io.us. *

SCHROEDER, GLENN CARL, lawyer, educator; b. Ann Arbor, Mich., Mar. 21, 1953; s. Glenn A. Schroeder and Monnie C. (Hamling) Phillips; m. Janet S. Wong, Jan. 1, 1990. BA, U. Calif., LA, 1975; MA, U. Ill., 1976; JD, Yale U., 1979. Bar: Calif. 1979. Assoc. Loeb and Loeb, LA, 1979-86, ptnr., 1987; gen. counsel, sr. v.p. Sta. KCET Cmty. TV of So. Calif., LA, 1987; gen. counsel Ednl. Testing Svc., Princeton, NJ. Adj. prof. Loyola U. Law Sch., L.A., 1982, Whittier Coll. Sch. of Law, L.A., 1988—. Bd. dirs. Asian Rehab. Svcs., L.A., 1989-90. Mem. LA County Bar Assn. (exec. com. of intellectual property sect. 1988-92), LA Copyright Soc. Office: Ednl Testing Svc Rosedale Rd MS 23 C Princeton NJ 08541 Office Phone: 609-734-5361. Office Fax: 609-734-1700.

SCHROEDER, HERMAN ELBERT, scientific consultant; b. Bklyn., July 6, 1915; s. Henry W. and Caroline (Schmidt) S.; m. Elizabeth Barnes, June 13, 1938 (dec. July 27, 2002); children: Nancy Schroeder Tarczy (dec.), Edward L., Peter H., Martha L. Schroeder Lewis. AB summa cum laude, Harvard, 1936, A.M., 1937, PhD, 1939. With E.I. du Pont de Nemours & Co., Wilmington, Del., 1938-80, asst. dir. R&D, 1957-63, dir. R&D, 1963-80; pres. Schroeder Sci. Svcs., Inc., 1980—. Sci. cons. Met. Mus. Art, N.Y.C., Smithsonian Instn., Winterthur Mus. Mem. Chester County Sch. Bd., Unionville, Pa., 1950-56; pres. Assn. Harvard Chemists, 1955-57; mem. vis. com. Harvard Chemistry Dept., 1960-72; mem. sci. adv. com. Winterthur Mus.; trustee, chmn. research com. U. Del. Research Found., 1976-84, former v.p. Recipient award Internat. Inst. Synthetic Rubber Producers, 1979, Lavoisier medal DuPont, 1992, Disting. Achievement award PolyPrep, N.Y.C., 1997. Mem. AAAS, Am. Chem. Soc. (Charles Goodyear medal 1984), N.Y. Acad. Scis., Phi Beta Kappa, Alpha Chi Sigma. Home and Office: 74 Stonegates 4031 Kennett Pike Greenville DE 19807-2033 Personal E-mail: her2schro@aol.com. *A life in industrial research has been for me both challenging and rewarding. Forces which impel me are largely the compulsion to look for the new, to change for the better, be it by finding better ways to do things or by inventing products to make the world function better. Gratifyingly, these often make the world aesthetically more pleasant and sometimes cleaner. I am concerned by the growing hostility of society to science and to developments that ensure a more comfortable life and safer food and energy than would otherwise be possible.*

SCHROEDER, JAMES WHITE, retired lawyer; b. Elmhurst, Ill., Apr. 19, 1936; s. Paul W. and Thelma C. (White) S.; m. Patricia N. Scott, Aug.

18, 1962; children: Scott W. and Jamie C. BA, Princeton U., 1958; JD, Harvard U., 1964. Bar: Colo. 1964, U.S. Dist. Ct. Colo. 1964, U.S. Ct. Appeals (10th cir.) 1965, U.S. Supreme Ct. 1972, U.S. Dist. Ct. D.C. 1973, U.S. Ct. Appeals (D.C. cir.) 1974, U.S. Ct. Appeals (8th cir.) 1977, U.S. Ct. Appeals (3d cir.) 1981, U.S. Claims Ct. 1983, U.S. Ct. Appeals (fed. cir.) 1983. Ptnr. Mosley, Wells & Schroeder, Denver, 1965-72, Kaplan Russin & Vecchi, Washington, 1973-92; counsel Whitman & Ransom, Washington, 1992-93; dep. under sec. U.S. Dept. Agr., 1993-2001. Arbitrator Am. Arbitration Assn. Active Ams. for Democratic Action, Smithsonian Instn.; bd. trustees Orlando Opera, 2003—. Lt. USNR, 1958-64. Am. Field Svc. scholar, 1953, NROTC scholar, 1954. Mem. ABA, Fed. Bar Assn., Denver Bar Assn., Colo. Bar Assn., D.C. Bar Assn., Cap and Gown Club, Lincoln's Inn Club, City Club Denver (pres. 1972), Princeton Club Washington (pres. 1982-84). Democrat. Home: 621 Nadina Pl Celebration FL 34747

SCHROEDER, JOHN A., systems engineering consultant, educator; s. John Bruno and Gertrude Dorothy Schroeder; m. Joanne Louise Galt, Mar. 2, 1985; children: Sarah Louise, Jeanette Lynne. BS, Purdue U., Lafayette, Ind., 1963; MS, U. Calif., Berkeley, 1966. Cert. advanced comms. sys. engring. U. Calif., Irvine. Sr. engr. Rockwell Internat., Anaheim, Calif., 1970—80; sys. engr. Boeing Co., San Beach, Calif., 1980—98, dir. sys. engring. Huntington Beach, Calif., 2000—04; COO Maxsys Tech., Irvine, Calif., 1998—2000; sr. cons. Booz Allen Hamilton, LA, 2004—; part time lectr. U. So. Calif., LA, 2005—; pres. Skill Sessions Seminars, Lake Forest, Calif., 1992—96. Mem. City Redevelopment Coun., Huntington Beach, Calif., 1980, 1981; angel supporter Fred Jordan Mission, LA, 2005. Mem.: Internat. Coun. on Sys. Engring., Am. Mensa. Avocation: Bible study. Home: 22621 Manalastas Dr Lake Forest CA 92630 Personal E-mail: jschroeder@mail.com.

SCHROEDER, JOHN H., university chancellor; b. Twin Falls, Idaho, Sept. 13, 1943; s. Herman John and Azalia (Kimes) S.; m. Sandra Barrow; children: John Kimes, Andrew Barrow. BA, Lewis and Clark Coll., Portland, Oreg., 1965; MA, U. Va., 1967, PhD, 1971. Instr. history U. Wis., Milw., 1970-71, asst. prof., 1971-76, assoc. prof., 1976-86, prof., 1986—, Am. Coun. on Edn. fellow, 1982-83, assoc. dean, 1976-82, asst. to vice chancellor, 1982-85, acting vice chancellor, 1985-87, vice chancellor, 1987-90, chancellor, 1990-98, U. Wis. sys. prof., 1998—. Louis M. Sears Meml. lectr. Purdue U., 1978. Author: Mr. Polk's War: American Opposition and Dissent, 1973, The Commercial and Diplomatic Role of the American Navy 1829-1861, 1985, Matthew C. Perry: Antebellum Sailor and Diplomat, 2001 (Theodore and Franklin Roosevelt Naval History prize 2002, John Lyman Naval History award 2002), Commodore John Rodgers: Paragon of the Early American Navy, 2006. V.p. bd. dir. John Michael Kohler Arts Ctr.; bd. dir. Wis. Hist. Soc., We. Golf Assn. Recipient Edward and Rosa Uhrig award U. Wis.-Milw., 1974, Disting. Teaching award AMOCO/U. Wis.-Milw., 1975. Mem. Orgn. Am. Historians, Soc. for History of Early Republic, Soc. for History Am. Fgn. Rels. Office: U Wis Dept History PO Box 413 2310 E Hartford Ave Milwaukee WI 53211-3165 Business E-Mail: jhs@uwm.edu.

SCHROEDER, JONI LYNN, secondary school educator; b. Cheverly, Md., June 20, 1958; d. James Albert and Betty Jean Schroeder. BS, Lipscomb U., Nashville, Tenn., 1983. Cert. tchr. Tenn. Tchr. health and phys. ed. Haynes Design Ctr., Nashville, 1988—. Named Tchr. of Yr., Metro Nashville Bd. Edn., 2002. Mem.: AAHPERD (assoc.). Office: Haynes Design Ctr 510 W Trinity Ln Nashville TN 37207 Home Phone: 615-754-8990; Office Phone: 615-262-6688. Personal E-mail: joni.schroeder@mnps.org.

SCHROEDER, JOYCE KATHERINE, state agency administrator, research analyst; b. Moline, Ill., Apr. 1, 1951; d. Reinhold J. and Miriam May (Schroeder). BS in Math., U. Ill., Champaign-Urbana, 1973; MA in Ops. rsch., U. Ill., Springfield, 1978. Underwriter, programmer, Springfield, Ill., 1973—76; ops. rsch. analyst Ill. Dept. Transp., Springfield, 1976—78, data analyst, 1978—80, team leader, fatal accident reporting sys., 1980—83, mgr. safety project evaluation, 1983—92, mgr. crash studies and investigation, 1992—. Sys. engring. del. to China, China Assn. Sci. and Tech., 1986; mem. staff Driving While Intoxicated Adv. Coun. and Task Force, State of Ill., 1983-86, 89-92, Gov. Task Force on Occupant Protection, 1988-90; Ill. Traffic Safety Info. Sys. Coun., 1993-95; mem. safety engring. tech. adv. group Ill. Ctr. Transp., 2005—; mem. Ill. Traffic Records Coord. Com., 2004-. Vol. Animal Protective League, Springfield; leader bd., co-chair LPGA Rail Classic, Springfield, 1983-87; mem. U. Ill. Sangamon Auditorium Vol. Assn., Springfield, 2007—. Named to Pres.'s Coun., U. Ill., 2004. Mem.: Ill. Traffic Safety Leaders, N. Am. Conf. Lions Found. (ann. conf. steering com. 2001—03, treas. 2005—, bd. dirs. 2004—), Past Dist. Gov. Assn. (sec.-treas. 1993—2006), Lions of Ill. Endowment Fund (trustee 1998—99, coord. meml. and endowments 1999—), Springfield Lincoln Land Lions Club (charter pres. 1988—90, treas. 1993—95, news editor 1995—, treas. 2002—), Lions Ill. Found. (amb. goodwill 1993, trustee 1995—99, treas. found. bd. 1996—97, v.p. found. bd. 1997—98, chmn. long range planning com. 1997—, pres. found. bd. 1998—99, policy ad hoc com. 1999—, chmn. policy ad hoc com. 2002—, fellow 1995, fellow laureate 2002, Disting. Svc. award 2003), Internat. Assn. Lions Clubs (dist. Gov. Ill. 1992—93, state membership coord. 1994—96, Melvin Jones fellow 1993), Kappa Delta Pi, Phi Kappa Phi. Avocations: travel, dogs, music, sports, humanitarian service. Office: Ill Dept Transp 3215 Exec Pk Dr Springfield IL 62703-4514 Home Phone: 217-529-8242. Personal E-mail: jksplus3@sbcglobal.net.

SCHROEDER, JULIAN IVAN, biology professor; b. Summit, NJ, June 11, 1958; s. Manfred Robert and Anny (Menschik) S.; m. Marion G. Spors, Aug. 9, 1991; children: Julia Sofia K., Nicola A.J. Dr. rer. nat., U. Gottingen, Max Planck Inst., 1987. Postdoctoral rschr. dept. physiology UCLA Sch. Medicine, 1988-90; from asst. to prof. dept. biology U. Calif. San Diego, La Jolla, 1990-2000, Novartis Endowed chair in plant scis., 2000—. Dir. U. Calif. San Diego Plant Sys. Biology Grad. Tng. Program, La Jolla, 2005—. Contbr. articles to profl. jours. Named Highly Cited Rschr., Inst. for Sci. Info., 2002; recipient Heinz Meier Leibnitz prize, Deutsche Forschungs Gemeinschaft, 1984, Presdl. Young Investigator award NSF, 1991, Blasker award in environ. sci. and engring., San Diego Found., 2001; vis. scholar guest prof., ETH Zurich, 2005; Alexander von Humboldt fellow, 1988, 1996. Fellow AAAS; mem. Biophys. Soc., Am. Assn. Plant Biologists (Charles Albert Shull award 1997). Achievements include identification of ion channels in higher plant cells, characterization of their functions and regulation in membrane signal transduction; cloning and functional roles of mineral nutrient and heavy metal transport and detoxifying enzymes in plants. Office: U Calif San Diego Div Biology Ctr Molec Gene 9500 Gilman Dr La Jolla CA 92093-0116 Home Phone: 858-459-3097; Office Phone: 858-534-7759.

SCHROEDER, KENNETH L., electronics executive; b. 1946; BSEE, U. Wis.; MBA, U. Pa. Gen. mgr. constrn. sys. divsn. Spectra-Physics; ops. mgr. computer group Hewlett-Packard; pres., COO Genus, Inc.; various KLA-Tencor Corp., San Jose, Calif., pres., COO, 1991-99, CEO, 1999—. Bd. dirs. SEMI, GaSonics Internat. Office: KLA Tencor Corp 160 Rio Robles San Jose CA 95134 Fax: 408-875-3030.

SCHROEDER, LAVERNE, medical/surgical nurse; b. Dover, Colo., Mar. 2, 1925; d. Chester Albert and Thelma May (Warren) Hutchison; m. Herman D. Schroeder, Sept. 5, 1947; children: Gloria, Rodger, Colleen, Darlene. Diploma, St. Anthony Hosp. Sch. Nursing, 1947. RN Colo., Wyo. Head nurse Poudre Valley Hosp., Ft. Collins, Colo., 1948, Longmont (Colo.) Hosp., 1950, Platte County Meml. Hosp., Wheatland, Wyo., 1957—76. Contbr. poetry to anthologies; author: A Blessed Trinity, 2003, The Queen's Secret, 2005. Pres. PTA; pres. bd. dirs. Platte County Meml. Hosp., Wheatland; Platte County del. Wyo.State Rep. Conv. Mem.: Wyo. Nurse Assn., Am. Vet. Med. Assn. Aux. (pres.).

SCHROEDER, MARVIS LYNN, accountant, artist; b. Gary, Ind., June 19, 1946; d. William Isaac and Leva Marcella (Pierce) Marlatt; m. Douglas Eugene Testerman (div.); 1 child, Tiffany Lynn Courtois; m. Charles Edward Schroeder, July 19, 1988. BS in Art Edn., Ind. U., 1969, MSBA, 1984; MA in Spl. Edn., U. Wyo., Laramie, 1975. Cert. in Acctg., 1992; tchr. Wyo., Ind., Calif. Tchr. Glasgow AFB Jr. High, Mont., 1967—68; tchr. art and spl. edn. Cheyenne Pub. Schs., Wyo., 1969—71; tchr. spl. edn. NW Ind. Spl. Edn. Coop., Crown Point, 1974—80; tchr. learning disabilities Riverside Schs., Calif., 1980—81; tchr. art Hobart Schs., Ind., 1981—84; group mgr. softlines Zayre, Merrillville, Ind., 1985; fin. aid counselor Ind. U., Northwest Gary, 1986—2001; acct. Harold Sullivan CPA, Portage, Ind., 2001—03. Exhibitions include Portage Sr. Artists Exhibit, 2002, 2003, 2004, 2005, 2006, 2007, 1st United Meth. Ch., 2003, Chesterton Women's Art Ctr., Ind., 2003, 2005, 2006, Art Barn Gallery, Valparaiso, Ind., 2004, 2006, Valparaiso Art Acad. Gallery, 2005, Porter County Adminstrn. Ctr., Valparaiso, 2005, 2006, 170 note cards from original oil paintings, Chesterton Women's Art Ctr., 2007. Trustee Portage First United Meth. Ch., 2003—07, mem. fin com., 2007. Mem.: Illiana Artists Assn., Chesterton Art Ctr. Home: 2527 Pryor Rd Portage IN 46368 Personal E-mail: chuckandmarvis@comcast.net.

SCHROEDER, MARY MURPHY, federal judge; b. Boulder, Colo., Dec. 4, 1940; d. Richard and Theresa (Kahn) Murphy; m. Milton R. Schroeder, Oct. 15, 1965; children: Caroline Theresa, Katherine Emily. BA, Swarthmore Coll., 1962; JD, U. Chgo., 1965. Bar: Ill. 1966, DC 1966, Ariz. 1970. Trial atty. Dept. Justice, Washington, 1965—69; law clk. to Hon. Jesse Udall Ariz. Supreme Ct., 1970; mem. Lewis and Roca, Phoenix, 1971—75; judge Ariz. Ct. Appeals, Phoenix, 1975—79, US Ct. Appeals (9th cir.), Phoenix, 1979—2000, chief judge, 2000—. Vis. instr. Ariz. State U. Coll. Law, 1976—78. Contbr. articles to profl. jours. Recipient Disting. Achievement award, Ariz. State U. Coll. of Public Programs. Mem.: ABA (Margaret Brent award 2001), Am. Judicature Soc., Am. Law Inst. (coun. mem.), Fed. Bar Assn., Ariz. Bar Assn. (James A. Walsh Outstanding Jurist award 2004), Soroptimists. Office: US Ct Appeals 9th Cir US Courthouse Ste 610 401 W Washington St SPC-54 Phoenix AZ 85003-2156 Fax: 602-322-7320. E-mail: mary_schroeder@ca9.uscourts.gov. *

SCHROEDER, PATRICIA SCOTT, trade association administrator, former congresswoman; b. Portland, Oreg., July 30, 1940; d. Lee Combs and Bernice (Lemoin) Scott; m. James White Schroeder, Aug. 18, 1962; children: Scott William, Jamie Christine. BA magna cum laude, U. Minn., 1961; JD, Harvard U., 1964. Bar: Colo. 1964. Field atty. NLRB, Denver, 1964-66; practiced in Denver, 1966-72; mem. faculty U. Denver, 1969-72, C.C. Denver, 1969-70, Regis Coll., Denver, 1970-72; hearing officer Colo. Dept. Personnel, 1971-72; mem. 93d-104th Congresses from 1st Colo. dist., Washington, 1973-96; co-chmn. Congl. Caucus for Women's Issues, 1976-96; prof. Woodrow Wilson Sch. of Pub. and Internat. Affairs Princeton U., 1997; pres., CEO Assn. Am. Pubs., Washington, 1997—. Mem. Nat. Security Com.; dean Congl. Women; chair Ho. Select Com. Children, Youth and Families, 1991—93. Author: Champion of the Great American Family, 1989, 24 Years of House Work and the Place is Still a Mess: My Life in Politics, 1998. Bd. dirs. Marguerite Casey Found. Named to Nat. Women's Hall of Fame, 1995. Congregationalist. Office: Assn Am Publishers 50 F St NW Fl 4 Washington DC 20001-1530 Office Phone: 202-347-3375. Business E-Mail: pschroeder@publishers.org.

SCHROEDER, PAUL J., JR., lawyer; b. Mo., 1947; BA magna cum laude, U. Notre Dame, 1969; JD, Washington U., 1972. Bar: Mo. 1972. Ptnr. Bryan Cave, St. Louis; vice-pres., sec. and gen. counsel Dillard's Inc., Little Rock. Mem. ABA. Office: Dillard's Inc PO Box 486 1600 Cantrell Rd Little Rock AR 72203-0486 *

SCHROEDER, RAYMOND ERNEST, educational administrator; b. South Bend, Ind., Dec. 8, 1949; s. Marvin Klopsch and Jean (Hirsch) S.; m. Gail Arnsdorf, Mar. 5, 1977; children: Geneva Marie, Mary Lynn. BA in Speech, Augustana Coll., Rock Island, Ill., 1970; MS in Radio-TV, U. Ill., 1972. Reporter Sta. WOWO, Ft. Wayne, Ind., 1969; gen. mgr. Sta. WVIK, Rock Island, 1970; news reporter Sta. WILL-AM-FM, Urbana, Ill., 1971-74; instr. radio-TV U. Ill., Urbana, 1975-77; asst. prof. communication Sangamon State U., Springfield, Ill., 1977-83, assoc. prof. comm., 1983-95, dir. TV Office, 1984-97, faculty assoc. to v.p. for acad. affairs, 1984-94; prof. comm. U. Ill., Springfield, 1995—2001, prof. emeritus comm., 2001—, dir. office of technology-enhanced learning, 1997—; interim exec. dir. Inst. for Pub. Affairs, 1992-93. Part-time photographer Sta. WAND-TV, Decatur, Ill., 1975-77; coordinator community access Dimension Cable, Springfield, 1984-97; vis. scholar in online learning, U. Southern Maine, 2006-. Editor, cons. TV documentary Breadbasket or Dustbowl, 1983; tech. cons. TV documentary Illinois Prairies: Sense of Place, 1986; co-dir. TV documentary Mr. Lincoln of Illinois, 1986 (Spl. Achievement award 1987); creative cons. TV documentary The Lincolns of Springfield, Illinois, 1990 (Spl. Achievement award 1991). V.p. Holy Spirit Frat., 1986-87. Grantee Ill. State Bd. Edn., 1994, Application of Learning Technologies to Higher Edn., 1995; recipient Finalist award Nat. Fedn. Local Cable Programmers, 1987, 88, 93, Most Outstanding Achievement in Online Learning by an Individual award, Sloan Consortium, 2002. Mem. Internat. TV Assn., Broadcast Edn. Assn., Sangamon State U. Faculty Union (pres. 1993). Roman Catholic. Avocations: running, bicycling. Office: U Ill at Springfield OTEL 1 University Plz Springfield IL 62703 Home Phone: 217-629-7324; Office Phone: 217-206-7531. Business E-Mail: schroeder.ray@uis.edu.

SCHROEDER, STEVEN ALFRED, medical educator; b. NYC, July 26, 1939; s. Arthur Edward and Norma (Scheinberg) Schroeder; m. Sally B. Ross, Oct. 21, 1967; children: David Arthur, Alan Ross. BA, Stanford U., 1960; MD, Harvard U., 1964; LHD (hon.), Rush U., 1994; DSc (hon.), Boston U., 1996, U. Mass. Med. Ctr., 1997, Georgetown U., 2000; DSc, Med. Coll. Wis., 2002; DHL (hon.), U. Medicine Dentistry NJ, 2003. Diplomate Am. Bd. Internal Medicine. Intern and resident in internal medicine Harvard Med. Svc., Boston City Hosp., 1964—66, 1968—70; asst. prof., then assoc. prof. George Washington Med. Ctr., Washington, 1971—76; vis. prof. St. Thomas' Hosp. Med. Sch., London, 1982—83; prof. medicine, chief div. gen. internal medicine, mem. Inst. Health Policy Studies U. Calif., San Francisco, 1976—90; pres., CEO Robert Wood Johnson Found., Princeton, NJ, 1990—2002; clin. prof. medicine U. of Medicine and Dentistry N.J., 1990—2002; disting. prof. health and health care U. Calif., San Francisco, 2003—, dir. smoking cessation leadership ctr., 2003—. Conv. various govtl. and philanthropic health orgns.; chair internat. adv. com. faculty medicine Ben Gurion U., Israel. Sr. editor: Current Med. Diagnosis and Treatment, 1987—93, mem. editl. bd.: New Eng. Jour. Medicine Mag.; contbr. numerous articles to profl. jours. Mem. U.S. Prospective Payment Assessment Commn., 1983—88; bd. overseers Harvard Coll., 2000—06; bd. dirs. Am. Legacy Found., 2000—05, vice chair, 2001—03, chair, 2003—05; bd. dirs. Save Ellis Island, 2002—; dir. James Irvine Found., Charles R. Drew U. Medicine and Sci., 2005—. Named a Nat. Pub. Health Hero, U. Calif. Berkeley, 2004. Master: ACP (James Bruce award 2007); fellow: Am. Acad. Arts & Scis.; mem.: AAAS, APHA, Albany Med. Ctr. (Medicine prize 2000—), Soc. Gen. Internal Medicine (past pres.), Inst. Medicine, Assn. Am. Physicians, Physicians for Social Responsibility, Harvard Med. Alumni Assn. (past pres.), Alpha Omega Alpha, Phi Beta Kappa. Office: U Calif San Francisco 3333 California St Ste 430 San Francisco CA 94143-1211 Home Phone: 415-435-3872; Office Phone: 415-502-1881. Business E-Mail: schroeder@medicine.ucsf.edu.

SCHROEDER, THOMAS D., lawyer; b. Atlanta, May 26, 1959; Attended, Conservatory of Music, U. Cin., 1977—78; BS, U. Kans., 1981; JD, Notre Dame Law Sch., 1984. Bar: NC 1984. Jud. clerk for Hon. George E. MacKinnon US Ct. Appeals (DC Cir.), 1984—85; practice group leader, product liability practice group Womble Carlyle Sandridge & Rice, PLLC, Winston-Salem, NC, 1994—2002, mem. firm mgmt. com., 1996—, vice chmn. firm mgmt. com., 2005. Lectr. in field; faculty, trial tng. program Womble Carlyle Sandridge & Rice, PLLC, Winston-Salem, NC. Editor-in-chief Notre Dame Law Review, 1983—84. Mem.: Def. Rsch. Inst., Internat. Ass. Def. Counsel, NC Assn. Def. Attys. (bd. dir. 1997—99, sec. 1999—2001), 21st Jud. Dist. Bar Assn., Forsyth County Bar Assn., NC Bar Assn., Assn. of Trial Lawyers of Am. (assoc.), Phi Alpha Delta. Mailing: Womble Carlyle Sandridge & Rice PLLC PO Box 84 Winston Salem NC 27102 Office: Womble Carlyle Sandridge & Rice PLLC One W 4th St Winston Salem NC 27101 Office Phone: 336-721-3691. Office Fax: 336-733-8354.

SCHROEDER, W(ILLIAM) WIDICK, retired religion educator; b. Newton, Kans., Nov. 12, 1928; s. William Fredric and Irene (Widick) S.; m. Gayle Eadie, Sept. 1, 1956; children: Scott David, Carla Gayle. BA, Bethel Coll., 1949; MA, Mich. State U., East Lansing, 1952; BDiv, Chgo. Theol. Sem., 1955, DD (hon.), 1995; PhD, U. Chgo., 1960. Ordained to ministry Congl. Christian Ch., 1955. Instr. Mich. State U., 1953-54, U. Chgo., 1958-60; from asst. prof. to prof. religion and society Chgo. Theol. Sem., 1960-94, prof. emeritus, 1994—. Vis. fellow Mansfield Coll., Oxford, Eng., 1966; vis. lectr. Yale U., 1970; vis. scholar Ctr. for Process Studies, Claremont, Calif., 1976; vis. lectr. in ethics and soc. Div. Sch. U. Chgo., 1967-71, 76; editor Rev. of Religious Rsch., 1964-69. Author: (with Victor Obenhaus) Religion in American Culture: Unity and Diversity in a Midwestern County, 1964; Cognitive Structures and Religious Research, 1970; (with Victor Obenhaus, Larry A. Jones and Thomas P. Sweetser) Suburban Religion: Churches and Synagogues in the American Experience, 1974; (with Keith A. Davis) Where Do I Stand? Living Theological Options for Contemporary Christians, 1973, rev. edit., 1975, 3d edit., 1978; Flawed Process and Sectarian Substance: Analytic and Critical Perspectives on the United Church of Christ General Synod Pronouncement, Christian Faith: Economic Life and Justice, 1990; Toward Belief: Essays in the Human Sciences, Social Ethics, and Philosophical Theology, 1996; co-editor: (with Philip Hefner) Belonging and Alienation: Religious Foundations for the Human Future, 1976; (with Gibson Winter) Belief and Ethics: Essays in Ethics, the Human Sciences and Ministry in Honor of W. Alvin Pitcher, 1978; (with John B. Cobb, Jr.) Process Philosophy and Social Thought, 1981; (with Perry LeFevre) Spiritual Nurture and Congregational Development, 1984, Pastoral Care and Liberation Praxis: Essays in Personal and Social Transformation, 1986, Creative Ministries in Contemporary Christianity, 1991; (with Franklin I. Gamwell) Economic Life: Process Interpretations and Critical Responses, 1988; co-editor Studies in Religion, Society and Personality, Center for the Scientific Study of Religion, 1972-2001. Mem. Religious Rsch. Assn., Soc. Christian Ethics. *The aims of existence are aesthetic satisfaction and intensity of feeling. In facilitating these aims, the Divine Reality is the locus of potentiality, the mediator of experience, the evoker of feeling and the ultimate recipient of all that has become.*

SCHROEDER-LEIN, GLENNA RUTH, librarian, historian; b. Pasadena, Calif., Sept. 23, 1951; d. Walter A. Schroeder and Ruth L. Mueller; m. Lonnie Keith Lein, Aug. 4, 1990. BA in History, Calif. State U., Fullerton, 1975, MA in History, 1978; MLS, U. Ariz., 1981; PhD in History, U. Ga., 1991. Archivist Southwest Mus., LA, 1977—81; photo libr. World Vision, Monrovia, Calif., 1982—84; vis. asst. prof. Washington Coll., Chestertown, Md., 1990; adj. instr. U. Tenn., Knoxville, 1993—2000; vis. asst. prof. Lincoln Meml. U., Harrogate, Tenn., 2000; manuscript libr. Abraham Lincoln Presdl. Libr., Springfield, Ill., 2005—. Asst. editor: Papers of Andrew Johnson, 1990—2000, Papers of Abraham Lincoln, 2001—03; author: Confederate Hospitals on the Move: Samuel H. Stout and the Army of Tennessee, 1994, Andrew Johnson: A Biographical Companion, 2001; contbr. articles to profl. jours. Office: Abraham Lincoln Presdl Libr 112 N 6th St Springfield IL 62701

SCHROER, GENE ELDON, lawyer; b. Randolph, Kans., Aug. 29, 1927; s. Harry Edward and Florence Lillian (Schwartz) S.; m. Edith Grace Kintner, Apr. 7, 1956 (div.); children: Kenneth G., Rebecca J., Sonya J., Connie J.; m. Anne Oliver, Dec. 21, 1988; child: Paul R., John O., Andrew M., Edward G. AB, LLB, Washburn U., 1957. Bar: Kans. 1957, U.S. Dist. Ct. Kans. 1957, U.S. Ct. Appeals (10th cir.) 1970, U.S. Supreme Ct. 1983. Pvt. practice, Topeka, 1957-68; ptnr. Schroer, Rice, P.A., Topeka, 1968—2004, pres., 1970—2004, also bd. dirs.; pvt. practice, 2004—. Contbr. articles to profl. jours. and chpts. to books. Supr. Shawnee County Soil Conservation Dist., Topeka, 1968-84. With U.S. Army, 1951-53. Mem. ABA, Kans. Bar Assn., Assn. Trial Lawyers Am. (gov. 1976-79, seminar lectr. 1973—, chmn. tort sect. 1974-75, instr. Nat. Coll. Adv. 1978, 81-88), Kans. Trial Lawyers Assn. (gov. 1972—, seminar lectr. 1974—, pres. 1974-75), Nat. Bd. Trial Advocacy (sustaining founder), Am. Bd. Trial Advs. (sec., treas. Kans. chpt. 1990-91, pres. 1991-92), Civil Justice Found. (founding sponsor), Trial Lawyers for Pub. Justice (bd. dirs. 1982-96). Democrat. Methodist. Office: 115 SE 7th St Topeka KS 66603 Office Phone: 785-357-7300. Personal E-mail: gschroer@schroer.kscoxmail.com.

SCHROPP, JAMES HOWARD, lawyer; b. Lebanon, Pa., June 20, 1943; s. Howard J. and Maud E. (Parker) S.; m. Jo Ann Simpson, Sept. 4, 1965; children: James A., John C., Jeffrey M., Jeremy M. BA, U. Richmond, 1965; JD, Georgetown U., 1973. Bar: DC 1973, US Supreme Ct. 1980. Asst. gen. counsel SEC, Washington, 1973-79; ptnr. Fried, Frank, Harris, Shriver & Jacobson, Washington, 1979—2005, of counsel, 2005—. Adj. prof. Georgetown U., Washington, 1982-86; mem. faculty Na.t Inst. for Trial Advocacy. Mem. ABA (discovery com. litigation sect. 1984-86, tender offer litigation subcom. corp. banking and bus. law sect. 1985-86, task force on broker-dealer compliance supervisory procedures 1987-89). Office: Fried Frank Harris Shriver & Jacobson 1001 Pennsylvania Ave NW Washington DC 20004-2505 Office Phone: 202-639-7110. Business E-Mail: schroja@ffhsj.com.

SCHROPP, TOBIN, lawyer; b. 1962; BS in Fgn. Svc., Georgetown U., 1984, JD, 1987, LLM in Taxation, 1991. Bar: 1987. Sr. v.p., gen. counsel Peter Kiewit Sons' Inc., Omaha. Office: Peter Kiewit Sons Inc 1000 Kiewit Plaza Omaha NE 68131

SCHROTH, PETER WILLIAM, lawyer, management, educator; b. Camden, NJ, July 24, 1946; s. Walter and Patricia Anne (Page) S.; children: Laura Salome Erickson-Schroth, Julia James. AB, Shimer Coll., 1966; JD, U. Chgo., 1969; M in Comparative Law, U.Chgo., 1971; SJD, U. Mich., 1979; postgrad., U. Freiburg, Fed. Republic Germany, Faculté Internationale pour l'Enseignement de Droit Comparé; MBA, Rensselaer Poly. Inst., 1988; DHL, Shimer Coll., 2000; MSc, Sch. Oriental and African Studies, 2000. Bar: Ill. 1969, NY 1979, Conn. 1985, Mass. 1990; solicitor Supreme Ct. England and Wales 1995. Asst. prof. So. Meth. U., 1973-77; fellow in law and humanities Harvard U., 1976-77, vis. scholar, 1980-81; assoc. prof. NY Law Sch., 1977-81; prof. law Hamline U., St. Paul, 1981-83; dep. gen. counsel Equator Bank Ltd., 1984-87; v.p., dep. gen. counsel Equator Holdings Ltd., 1987-94, v.p., gen. counsel, 1994-2000. Adj. prof. law U.

Conn., 1985-86, Western New Eng. Coll., 1988-92, adj. prof. mgmt. Rensselaer Poly. Inst., 1988-98, prof., 1999-2005, dir. Ctr. for Global Bus. Studies, 2000-05, pres. Internat. Rsch. and Consulting Group LLC, 2005-. Author: Foreign Investment in the United States, 2nd edit., 1977; author: (with Stiefel) Products Liability: European Proposals and American Experience, 1981; author: Doing Business in Sub-Saharan Africa, 1991; bd. editors Am. Jour. Comparative Law, 1981—84, 1991—, mem. editl. bd. Conn. Bar Jour., 1988—, sr. editor, 1993—2000, 2006—, editor-in-chief, 2000—06, recent decisions editor NY Internat. Law Rev., 1994—, mem. editl. rev. bd. Jour. Bus. in Developing Nations, 1996—2000, editor-in-chief, 2000—, co-editor-in-chief Jour. Legal Studies in Bus., 2003—. Treas., mem. bd. trustees Shimer Coll. Mem. ABA (editor in chief ABA Environ. Law Symposium 1980-82), Am. Soc. Comparative Law (bd. dirs. 1978-84, 91—), Am. Fgn. Law Assn., Internat. Bar Assn., Internat. Law Assn. (com. multinat. banking), Acad. Internat. Bus., Conn. Civil Liberties Union (bd. dirs. 1985-92), Environ. Law Inst. (assoc.), Columbia U. Peace Seminar (assoc.), Hartford Club (bd. govs. 1995-98), Am. Corp. Counsel Assn. (pres. Conn. chpt.1997-2000), Conn. Bar Assn. (chair sect. of internat. law 1997-2000). Office: PO Box 29 South Glastonbury CT 06073-0029

SCHROTH, THOMAS NOLAN, editor; b. Trenton, NJ, Dec. 21, 1920; s. Frank David and Loretta (Nolan) S.; m. Colette Streit, May 1, 1948 (div. 1958); 1 child, Valerie; m. Patricia Wiggins, Sept. 27, 1958; children: Jennifer, Amy, Anne. Student, Tuck Sch. Bus. Adminstrn., 1942; AB, Dartmouth Coll., 1943. Reporter Time, Washington, 1946-47, UPI, Boston, 1947-48; reporter, news editor Bklyn. Eagle, 1948-51, mng. editor, 1951-55; editorial adviser Magnum Photos, Inc., NYC, 1955; exec. editor, pub. Congl. Quar. Inc. and Editorial Research Reports, Washington, 1955-68; founder, editor Nat. Jour. Ctr. Polit. Rsch., Washington, 1969-70; communications adviser Pub. Broadcasting Environment Ctr., Washington, 1970-71; asst. dir. pub. affairs for communications EPA, Washington, 1970-71, cons., 1972; exec. editor The Ellsworth (Maine) American, 1972-77; co-pub.-editor (with Patricia Schroth) Maine Life Mag., Sedgwick, 1977-81; editorial cons. U. Maine, Bangor, 1976-90; mng. editor South-North News Svc., Hanover, N.H., 1987-91; co-pub. New Leaf Pubs., Sedgwick, Maine, 1990—. Mem. Am. Press Inst. Seminar for Mng. Editors, 1953, Regional Transp. Adv. Com., 1996-99. Editor: Congress and the Nation, 1946-64--A Review of Government and Politics in the Postwar Years; editor Improving the U. of Maine trustee's pamphlet. Elected selectman Town of Sedgwick, 1989-94, moderator 1995—; bd. dirs. Blue Hill (Maine) Meml. Hosp., 1978-93, Bangor Symphony Orch., 1981-87, Blue Hill Concert Assn., 1991-2003; bd. dirs., v.p. Island Nursing Home, Deer Isle, Maine, 1985—; mem. Maine State Dem. Com., Augusta, 1985-92, 97—; bd. dirs. Downeast Transp., Inc., 1993—; del. Maine Dem. Nat. Conv., 2000. 1st lt. Army Airways Comm. Sys., USAAF, WWII. Mem. Sigma Delta Chi. Avocations: gardening, walking, music. Home and Office: 16 Reach Rd Sedgwick ME 04676

SCHROYER, MICHAEL KEVIN, healthcare consultant, hospital executive; b. Kewanee, Ill., Sept. 14, 1959; s. Jesse Wayne and Shirley Ann (Brown) S.; m. Joy Anne, June 20, 1987; children: Tiffany Marie, Rebecca Ann, Adam Michael. Diploma, Moline Pub. Hosp. Sch. Nursing, 1980; BSN, Loyola U., 1984; MSN, Seton Hall U., 1987; postgrad., Rush U., 1990-91; MBA, Auburn U., 2006. Cert. hosp. exec. (CHE). Nurse mgr., CCU, ICU, PICU, CCFP Jersey Shore Med. Ctr., Neptune, NJ; assoc. dir., critical care nursing Hyde Park Hosp., Chgo.; adminstrv. dir., transplant svcs. Rush-Presbyn./St. Lukes Med. Ctr., Chgo.; adminstrv. coord., v.p. cardiovascular and med./surg. svcs. United Med. Ctr., Moline, Ill.; adminstrv. leader, v.p. Regional CardioLife Ctr., Tenet Brookwood Med. Ctr., Birmingham, Ala., 1993-96; v.p. clin. svcs. MedCath McAllen (Tex.) Heart Hosp., 1996-98, MedCath Dayton (Ohio) Heart Hosp., 1998-2000, interim CEO, 2000, v.p. ops./COO, 2000—01; pres. / CEO Okla. Heart Hosp., Oklahoma City, 2001—03; prin., cons. TRG Cardiovascular, Denver, 2001—; exec. dir. cardiac and vascular svcs. Meml. Heart & Vascular Inst., Meml. Health Sys., Springfield, Ill., 2004—07; COO St. Vincent Heart Ctr. of Ind., Indpls., 2007—. Author: Emergency Nursing, 1989, Nursing Spectrum, 1989, Comprehensive Nursing Care Plans, 1995. Former bd. dirs. Rock Island County chpt. Am. Heart Assn. Fellow: Am. Coll. Healthcare Execs. (cert. healthcare exec.); mem.: AACN, Am. Coll. Cardiology, Am. Heart Assn. (bd. dirs. Oklahoma City chpt., bd. dirs. Springfield chpt.), Am. Assn. Med. Cardiovasc. Adminstrs., Sigma Theta Tau. Home: 1425 Hunters Glen Zionsville IN 46077 also: 9065 Pebblepointe Cir Zionsville IN 46077 Office: St Vincent Heart Ctr of Ind 10580 N Meridian St Indianapolis IN 46290 Personal E-mail: mschroyer@trqcardiovascular.com.

SCHRUM, JAKE BENNETT, academic administrator; b. Greenville, Tex., Feb. 9, 1946; s. Jake M. and Julia (Bennett) S.; m. Jane Woodman, Dec. 28, 1968; children: Julia Elizabeth, Emily Katharine. BA, Southwestern U., 1968; MDiv, Yale U., 1973; postgrad., Harvard U., 1983. Ordained to ministry Meth. Ch., 1969. Devel. officer Yale U., New Haven, 1973-77; dir. devel. Muhlenberg Coll., Allentown, Pa., 1977-78; v.p. Tex. Wesleyan Coll., Ft. Worth, 1978-82; v.p. univ. rels. Southwestern U., Georgetown, Tex., 1982-85; v.p. Emory U., Atlanta, 1985-91; pres. Tex. Wesleyan U., 1991-2000, Southwestern U., Georgetown, Tex., 2000—. Chmn. CASE, 1995—96, Associated Colls. of the South, 2005—07, Georgetown Project, 2005—06; vice chair higher edn. com. Austin Area Rsch. Orgn.; bd. dirs. Southern U. Conf., Southern Collegiate Athletic Assn., Coun. Pres., Assn. Governing Bds., First Tex. Bank, Edn. and Inst. Insurance Adminstrn., Assn. Tex. Colls. and Univs., Coun. Ind. Colls. Author: Democracy's Last Stand: The Role of the New Urban University, 1999; editor: A Board's Guide to Comprehensive Campaigns, 2000, Justice for All, 2001. Mem. exec. com. Tex. Ind. Coll. Found.; bd. dirs. Georgetown Area Cmty. Found.; chair Georgetown Project. Named Man of Yr., Bnai Brith North Tex., 1995. Mem.: Nat. Assn. Schs. and Colls. of United Meth. Ch., Annapolis Group, Am. Coun. Edn., Philos. Soc. Tex. Avocations: golf, public speaking. Office: Southwestern U Office of Pres 1001 E University Georgetown TX 78626 Office Phone: 512-863-1454. E-mail: schrum@southwestern.edu.

SCHRUMP, DAVID STUART, medical association administrator, researcher; b. New Haven, Conn., Dec. 21, 1956; s. LeRoy Everett and Myra Ruth Schrump; m. Brenda Ann Willett, Mar. 13, 1984; children: Willaim David, Christopher Eldridge, Nathaniel Stuart. BA, NYU, NYC, 1979; MD, Univ. of Conn., Farmington, 1983. Diplomate Am. Bd. Thoracic Surgeons, 1994. Asst. prof thoracic surgery UT-MD Anderson Cancer Ctr., Houston, 1993—97; head thoracic oncology sect. surgery br. Nat. Cancer Inst., Bethesda, Md., 1997—. Contbr. articles to profl. jours. Hockey coach Montgomery Youth Hockey Assn., Rockville, Md., 1998. Recipient NIH Merit award for the Devel. of an Innovative Translational Rsch. Program in Thoracic Oncology, Nat. Cancer Inst., 2005, Bench to Bedside award for Outstanding Translational Lung Cancer Rsch., 2001. Fellow: ACS.; mem.: John Alexander Soc., Am. Soc. of Clin. Oncology, Internat. Assn. for the Study of Lung Cancer, Am. Assn. for Cancer Rsch., Am. Assn. forThoracic Surgery, Soc. of Thoracic Surgeons. Achievements include fundamental research pertaining to lung cancer; expert in lung cancer surgery; expert in esophageal cancer surgery; expert in pleural mesothelioma surgery. Office: National Cancer Institute Building 10 Rm 4-3942 10 Center Drive Bethesda MD 20892-1201 Home Phone: 301-496-2128; Office Phone: 301-496-2128. Office Fax: 301-451-6934. E-mail: david_schrump@nih.gov.

SCHTEINGART, DAVID EDUARDO, internist; b. Buenos Aires, Oct. 17, 1930; came to U.S., 1957; s. Mario and Flora (Garfunkel) S.; m. Monica Naomi Starkman, July 3, 1960; children: Miriam, Judith, M. Daniel. MD, U. Buenos Aires, 1955. Diplomate Am. Bd. Internal Medicine. Fellow Mt. Sinai Hosp., NYC, 1957-58, Maimonides Hosp., Bklyn., 1958-59, U. Mich., Ann Arbor, 1959-62, instr., 1962-63, asst. prof., 1963-68, assoc. prof., 1968-72, prof., 1972—. Contbr. articles to profl. jours., books. Pres. Beth Israel Congregation, Ann Arbor, 1974-79, Hebrew Day Sch., Ann Arbor, 1984-86, Jewish Fedn. Washtenaw County, Ann Arbor. Recipient rsch. grants NIH, Bethesda, Md., 1985—. Fellow Am. Coll. Physicians; mem. Endocrine Soc., N.Y. Acad. Scis., Am. Soc. Clin. Nutrition, Cen. Soc. Clin. Rsch., Am. Fedn. Clin. Rsch. Jewish. Avocations: tennis, running, community activities. Office: U Mich Med Sch 1150 W Medical Center Dr Ann Arbor MI 48109-0726

SCHUBACH, SCOTT LESLIE, cardiac physician; b. Denver, July 21, 1957; m. Lisa; 1 child, Abigail. BS cum laude, Rensselaer Poly. U., 1979; MD, Baylor Coll. Medicine, 1983. Dir. cardiac surg. ICU Winthrop U. Hosp., Mineola, NY, 1991—, chmn., dept. thoracic, cardiac surgery; and asst. prof., clin. surgery SUNY Sch. Medicine, Stony Brook. Fellow Am. Coll. Chest Physicians, Am. Coll. Cardiology, ACS; mem. AMA, Soc. Critical Care Medicine, NY State Med. Soc., NY Soc. Thoracic Surgery, Nassau County Med. Soc. Office: 120 Mineola Blvd Ste 300 Mineola NY 11501 also: Thoracic & Cardiac Surgery Winthrop Univ Hosp 259 First St Mineola NY 11501 *

SCHUBART, CAREN NELSON, psychologist; b. Staten Island, NY, Sept. 26, 1945; d. Kenneth Warwick and Carey Boone Nelson; m. Richard Douglas Schubart, July 5, 1969; children: Darcy, Lindsey, Nelson. BA in Psychology, Wittenberg U., Springfield, Ohio, 1967; MEd in Rehab. Counseling, Kent State U., Ohio, 1968; postgrad., Syracuse U., NYC, 1972—73, Boston U., 1974—88, Plymouth State U., Mass., 2001—. Lic. psychologist NH Bd. Mental Health Practice, nat. cert. sch. psychologist Nat. Assn. Sch. Psychologists; cert. learning disability specialist NH Assn. Sch. Psychologists, lic. sch. psychologist NH Bd. Edn., NY State Edn. Dept. Rehab. counselor Ohio Bur. Vocat. Rehab., Akron, 1967—68, NY Dept. Vocat. Rehab., Syracuse, 1968—73; regional dir. spl. edn. NH Sch. Unions 16, 19, 21, Exeter, 1973—79; sch. psychologist NH Supervisory Sch. Union 16, Exeter Jr. HS, 1979—88, NH Supervisory Sch. Union 16, Exeter HS, 1989—. Contbr. articles to profl. jours. Vol. Rockingham County Family Planning, Exeter, bd. dirs. Recipient full scholarship, U.S. Govt. Dept. Rehab. Edn., 1967—68. Mem.: APA, NH Assn. Sch. Psychologists, NH Psychol. Assn., Nat. Assn. Sch. Psychologists. Independent. Episcopalian. Avocations: photography, genealogy, outdoor activities, travel. Home: 65 Court St Exeter NH 03833 Office: Exeter Regional Coop HS 315 Epping Rd Exeter NH 03833 Office Phone: 603-395-2557. Business E-Mail: cschubart@sau16.org.

SCHUBEL, JERRY ROBERT, marine scientist educator, dean; b. Bad Axe, Mich., Jan. 26, 1936; s. Theodore Howard and Laura Alberta (Gobel) S.; m. Margaret Ann Hostetler, June 14, 1958; children: Susan Elizabeth, Kathryn Ann. BS, Alma Coll., 1957; MA in Tchg., Harvard U., 1959; PhD, Johns Hopkins U., 1968; DSc (hon.), Mass. Maritime Acad., 1997. Rsch. assoc. Chesapeake Bay Inst., Johns Hopkins U., Balt., 1968-69, rsch. scientist, 1969-74, adj. rsch. prof., assoc. dir., 1973-74; dir. Marine Sci. Rsch. Ctr. SUNY, Stony Brook, 1974-83, dean, leading prof., 1983-94, acting dir. Waste Mgmt. Inst., 1985-87, provost, 1986-89, dir. COAST Inst., 1989, disting. svc. prof., 1994-95, prof. emeritus, 1995—; pres. emeritus, CEO New Eng. Aquarium, Boston, 1994—2001; vis. prof. Wash. Coll., Chestertown, Md., 2002—, dir. Alternative Futures Forum, 2002—; pres., CEO Aquarium of Pacific, Long Beach, Calif., 2002—. Hon. prof. East China Normal U., Shanghai, 1985—; sec. exec. com. Commn. on Food, Environ. and Renewable Resources, 1993, chair steering com., 1994; mem. governing bd. Regional Marine Rsch. Program, Greater N.Y. Bight, 1993-94; v.p., founding dir. Gulf of Maine Ocean Observing Sys., 1998-02; adv. panel Nat. Whale Conservation Fund Found., 2001—; mem. Nat. Sea Grant Adv. Panel, 2002—, chair, 2004-05; bd. dirs. Internat. Resources Group, 2002—, rev. panel Census of Marine Life, U.S. Nat. Com., 2003-07, mem. NSF Edn. and Human Resources Adv. Com., 2003-05, South Bay Salt Pond Restoration, Nat. Sci. Panel, 2003-06; nat. assoc. Nat. Acads. Sci. and Engring.; mem. marine bd. NRC, 1989-94, 2002—; bd. dirs. Inst. for Learning Innovation, 2004—; mem. adv. panel Ocean Rsch. and Resources, 2006—, vice chair, 2007—. Author: The Living Chesapeake, 1981, The Life and Death of the Chesapeake Bay, 1 986; (with H.A. Neal) Solid Waste Management and the Environment, 1987, Garbage and Trash: Can We Convert Mountains Into Molehills?, 1992; editor: (with B.C. Marcy Jr.) Power Plant Entrainment, 1978; (with others) The Great South Bay, 1991; sr. editor Coastal Ocean Pollution Assement News, 1981-86; co-editor in chief Estuaries, 1986-88; mem. editl. bd. CRC Revs. in Aquatic Scis.; contbr. articles to profl. jours. Mem. adv. bd. Environ. Sci. Com. Outer Continental Shelf, Minerals Mgmt. Scs., 1984-86, chmn., 1986; bd. dirs. N.E. Area Remote Sensing Sys., 1983-85, L.I. Incubator Corp.; v.p. L.I. Forum for Tech., 1989-92; chair Mass. Outfall Monitoring Task Force, 1995-98; mem. sci. adv. bd. EPA, 1996-98; commr. Nat. Rsch. Coun.'s Commn. on Engring. Tech. Sys., 1996-2000; mem. vis. com. dept. ocean engring MIT, 1995-2002; trustee Natural Heritage Insts., 1995-2001; mem. Boston Artery Bus. Bd. Dirs., 1994-2001; mem. Boston Mcpl. Rsch. Bur. Bd. Dirs., 1994-2001; mem. Annenberg Challenge Adv. Com., 1995-2002; hon. trustee Sci. Mus. L.I., 2000-02. Recipient L.I. Sound Am. Environ. Edn. award, 1987, Stony Brook U. medal, 1989, Matthew Fontaine Maury award, 1990, Ben Gurion U. medal, 1993, sci. achievement award Sci. Mus. L.I., 2000; Alfred P. Sloan fellow, 1959; Wheaton Coll. Disting. fellow, 2000. Mem. NAS (mem. exec. com. 1990, vice chair 1991-94, chair 1992-94, com. on Coastal Ocean 1989-93), Nat. Assn. State Univ. and Land Grant Colls. (bd. dirs. marine divsn., chmn. 1986-88), L.I. Environ. Coun., L.I. Marine Resources Adv. Coun. (chair 1990-94), L.I. Rsch. Inst. (bd. dirs. 1992-94), L.I. Environ.-Econ. Roundtable (co-chair 1991-92), Suffolk County Recycling Commn., (chmn. 1987-88), Estuarine Rsch. Fedn. (v.p. 1982-83, pres. 1985-87), N.Y. Sea Grant Inst. (chmn. governing bd. 1988-90, mem. gov.'s task force on coastal resources 1990-91), Census Marine Life (mem. U.S. nat. com. 2003—), The Nature Conservancy (trustee L.I. chpt. 1991-94), Franklin Electronic Pubs. (bd. dirs. 1991—), Taproot (bd. dirs. 1988-93, vice chair 1990-93), Internat. Resources Group (bd. dirs., 2002—), Sigma Xi, Phi Sigma Pi. Avocation: photography. Office: Aquarium of the Pacific 100 Aquarium Way Long Beach CA 90802 Home Phone: 564-437-5722; Office Phone: 562-951-1608. Business E-Mail: jschubel@lbaop.org.

SCHUBERT, BARBARA SCHUELE, retired performing arts association administrator; b. Cleve., Feb. 21, 1939; d. William Edward and Mildred Marianne (Matousek) Schuele; m. John Dwan Schubert, June 15, 1963; children: William Edward, Christopher John, David Matthew. BS in Social Scis., John Carroll U, 1962, MA in English, 1967; MEd, 1980. Cert. secondary tchr., elem. remedial reading tchr., Ohio. Tchr. Sch. on Magnolia, Cleve., 1980-82, Ruffing Montessori, Cleve., 1982-83; tchr. English U. Sch., Chagrin Falls, Ohio, 1983-86; gen. mgr. Ohio Ballet, Akron, 1987-90, assoc. dir., 1990-99; ret. Bd. trustees Ohio Ballet, 1974-87, 91-99. Bd. dirs. John Carroll U., 1990—; trustee Boys Hope Girls Hope, 2001. Mem.: Cleve. Skating. Roman Catholic. Personal E-mail: BJSchubert@earthlink.net, matousek04@yahoo.com.

SCHUBERT, BLAKE H., lawyer; b. Wheeling, W.Va., Apr. 21, 1939; s. John Arnold and Esther Elizabeth (Masters) Schubert; m. Carol Jean Cramp, Jan. 13, 1962; children: Cheryl Lynn, Charles Bradley, Elisabeth Anne. BA, Ohio Wesleyan U., Deleware, 1961; JD, U. Chgo., 1964. Bar: Ill. 1964, U.S. Dist. Ct. (no. dist.) Ill. 1968, U.S. Tax Ct. 1994. Counsel Brunswick Corp., Chgo., 1964—68; asst. group counsel FMC Corp., Chgo., 1968—73; gen. counsel Dresser Tool Group, Chgo., 1973—79; chmn. Schubert Securities Corp., Oak Park, Ill., 1979—84, Inter-Am. Investmemts, Inc., Oak Park, 1980—, Midwestern Bus. Devel. Corp., Oak Park, 2005—. Gen. ptnr. Investment Trust Ltd., St. Petersburg, Fla., 1981—91, Inter-Am. Fund, Oak Park, 1982—91, Inter-Am. Fund l, Oak Park, 1982—91, Inter-Am. Fund ll, Oak Park, 1984—89; chmn. Compath Video Corp., Oak Park, 1984—85; lectr. Am. Inst. Banking, 1965, Chgo. Inst. Fin. Studies, 1984—85. Author: The Well-Kept Secrets of Investing, 1982. Chmn. Park Forest Co-op., Ill., 1966—70; mem. Chgo. Bd. Options Exch., 1979—83; chmn. 1st United Ch. Endowment Fund, Oak Park, 1975—80. Home and Office: 522 Linden Ave Oak Park IL 60302-1659

SCHUBERT, GUENTHER ERICH, pathologist; b. Mosul, Iraq, Aug. 17, 1930; s. Erich Waldemar and Martha Camilla (Zschitzschmann) Schubert; children: Frank, Marion, Dirk. MD, U. Heidelberg, Germany, 1957; pvt. docent in pathology, U. Tuebingen, Germany, 1966. Asst. med. dir. U. Tuebingen, Germany, 1966—76; prof. pathology, 1972; head Inst. Pathology, Wuppertal, Germany, 1976—96; chair of pathology U. Witten-Herdecke, Germany, 1985—96. Co-author: Coloratlas of Cytodiagnosis of the Prostate, 1975, Pathologie, 1984, 1997, Endoscopy of the Urinary Bladder, 1989, Textbook of Pathology, 1981, 1987. Mem. Wissenschaftlicher Beirat, Bundesarztekammer, Bonn, Germany, 1976—85; pres. Medizinisch Naturwissenschaftliche Gesellschaft, Wuppertal, 1984—85, Onkologischer Schwerpunkt, Wuppertal, 1985—93, OSP Bergisch-Land, 1992—95, Bergische Arbeitsgemeinschaft fur Gastroenterologie, Wuppertal, 1987—88, 1990—91, 1994—95. Mem.: NY Acad. Scis., Internat. Acad. Pathology, Deutsche Gesellschaft fur Urologie, Deutsche Gesellschaft fur Nephrologie, Deutsche Gesellschaft fur Pathologie, Lions. Avocations: music, diving, photography. Office: Inst Pathology Am Anschlag 71 42113 Wuppertal Germany

SCHUBERT, HELEN CELIA, public relations executive; b. Washington City, Wis. d. Paul H. and Edna (Schmidt) S. BS, U. Wis., Madison. Dir. pub. rels. United Cerebral Palsy, Chgo., 1961; adminstrv. dir. Nat. Design Ctr., Chgo., 1962-67; owner Schubert Pub. Rels., Chgo., 1967—. Bd. dirs. Fashion Group, Chgo., 1988—95; adj. prof. comm. Roosevelt U., 1992—. Mem. women's bd. Am. Cancer Soc., Chgo., 1988—, Art Resources in Tchg., Chgo., 1988-92. Recipient Comm. award Am. Soc. Interior Designers, Chgo., 1979, 83, 88, 94; named to Chgo. Women's Hall of Fame City of Chgo., 1990. Fellow Nat. Home Fashion League; mem. Women's Ad Club Chgo. (pres. 1981-83, Woman of Yr. award 1987), Women in Comm. (pres. 1969-70, Matrix award Lifetime Achievement 1996), Am. Advt. Fedn. (lt. gov. 1983-85). Lutheran. Personal E-mail: schube@mail.com.

SCHUBERT, RICHARD FRANCIS, social services administrator, consultant; b. Trenton, NJ, Nov. 2, 1936; s. Yaro and Frances Mary (Hustak) S.; m. Virginia Thomas Austin, Sept. 15, 2000; children: Robyn, David. BA cum laude, Eastern Nazarene Coll., 1958; LLB, Yale U., 1961. Bar: Pa. 1962, U.S. Supreme Ct 1972. Arbitration atty. Bethlehem Steel Corp., Pa., 1961-66, asst. mgr. labor relations, 1966-70; exec. asst. to undersec. labor Washington, 1970; gen. counsel labor, 1971-73; dep. sec. labor, 1973-75; asst. to v.p. indsl. relations Bethlehem Steel Corp., 1973, asst. v.p. public affairs, 1975-77, v.p. public affairs, 1977-79, pres., 1979-80, vice chmn., 1980-82; pres., CEO ARC, 1982-89, Points of Light Found., 1990-95. Bd. dirs. Internat. Ctr. for Religion and Diplomacy, Mgmt. Tng. Corp. Bd. dirs. Women in Cmty. Svc.; exec. v.p. EXCN; chmn. emeritus Internat. Youth Found., chmn., Nazarene Compassionate Ministries; vice chmn. Leader to Leader Inst.; chmn. Nat. Job Corps Assn. Mem.: Ctr. Excellence in Govt., Coun. on Fgn. Rels., Northampton County Bar Assn., Pa. Bar Assn., Ea. Nazarene Alumni Assn. (pres. 1969—73), Phi Alpha Delta. Mem. Ch. of Nazarene. Home: 6615 Madison McLean Dr Mc Lean VA 22101-2425 Office Phone: 703-416-6656. E-mail: rfs@iyfnet.org.

SCHUBERT, RUTH CAROL HICKOK, artist, educator; b. Janesville, Wis., Dec. 24, 1927; d. Fay Andrew and Mildred Wilamette (Street) Hickok; m. Robert Francis Schubert, Oct. 20, 1946; children: Stephen Robert, Michelle Carol. Student, DeAnza Coll., 1972—73; AA Scholarship, Monterey Peninsula Coll., Calif., 1974; BA with honors, Calif. State U., San Jose, 1979. Owner, mgr. Casa De Artes Gallery, Monterey, Calif., 1977—86; dir. Monterey Peninsula Mus. Art Coun., 1975—76; quick-draw artist So. Oreg. Pub. TV, KSYS; leader painting workshops; demonstrator, lectr., judge in U.S., B.C. Can., New Zealand and Loreto, Baja, Mexico. One-woman shows include Aarhof Gallery, Aarau, Switzerland, 1977, Degli Agostiniani Recolletti, Rome, 1977, Wells Fargo Bank, Monterey, 1975, 1978, 1979, Seaside (Calif.) City Hall Gallery, 1979, 1989, Village Gallery, Lahaina, Hawaii, 1983, 1986, 1989, 1994, Portola Valley Gallery, 1984, 1985, Rose Rock Gallery, Carmel, 1984—86, Taupo (N.Z.) Arts Soc., 1988, Geyserland Art Mus., Rotorua, N.Z., 1988, Wanganui (N.Z.) Art Soc., 1988, Hallei Brown Ford Gallery, Roseburg, Oreg., 1991, 1995, Collection of Ann Cunningham, Carmel, 1993—95, Libr. Found., Medford, Oreg., 2005, catalog nat. group juried shows include, Sierra Nev. Mus. Art, Reno, 1980, Bard Hall Gallery, San Diego, 1980, San Diego Nat. Watercolor Show, Mid-West Nat. Watercolor Show, Rahr-West Mus., Manitowoc, Wis., 1980, Rosicrucian Mus., San Jose, 1981, 1984, Calif. State Agri-Images, Sacramento, 1984, XVII Watercolor West, Brea Civic Cultural Ctr., 1985, Watercolor West XXIII, Grand Art Galleries, Glendale, Calif., 1991, Watercolor West XXV, Riverside (Calif.) Art Mus., 1993, Nat. Pen Women at Marjorie Evans Gallery, Carmel, 1986, Monterey County Juried Expo, Monterey Peninsula Mus. Art, 1986, 1987, Am. Artists Group Exhbn., 1993, 1994, 1995, Gallery Hirose, Tsukuba, Ibaragi, Japan, Internat. Art Show and End of World Hunger, Ashland, Oreg., 1990, biann. art exhbn. Sumner Mus., Washington, D.C., 1992, State of the Art, New Eng. Fine Arts, Boston, 1993, N.W. Wildlife, Nightingale Gallery, Ea. Oreg. Coll., La Grande, 1993, N.W. Visual Arts Ctr. 19th Ann., Panama City, Fla., 1993, NW Watercolor Soc. Waterworks N.W. Julie Tolles Gallery, Mercer Island, Wash., 1994, Represented in permanent collections Rogue Valley Manor Spl. Svcs., Medford, Oreg., Monterey Calif. Peninsula Mus. Art, Nat. Biscuit Co. subs. RJR Nabisco, San Jose, Waikato Mus. Art, Hamilton, N.Z., Muscular Dystrophy Assn., San Francisco, Old Sch. Hous Mus., Qualicum Bay, Vancouver Island, B.C., USS George Washington Aircraft Carrier, Adm. Robert Sprigg, Pres. Bill Clinton, Barbara Bush, George Montgomery, Marilyn Horne, Alison Krauss, also numerous pvt. collections. Recipient 1st prize, Monterey County Fair, 1979, Jade Fon Watercolor award, Hall of Flowers, San Francisco, 1980, 1st Nat. Art Show, NY Am. Artist mag., 1980, Nat. Art Appreciation award, 1984, award, Norcal State Art Fair, 1985, Watercolor award, 25 Ann. Aqueous Media Show, Salem, Oreg., 1990, award, Calif. Watercolor Soc., 2001, Silver award mem., Oreg. Watercolor Soc. Portland, 2000, numerous other awards for watercolor paintings. Mem.: NW Watercolor Soc. (hon. signature mem., Watercolor Transparent award, Mercer Island 1994, Waterworks, Seattle 1999), Art Du Jour Gallery (dir. Medford, Oreg.), Watercolor West (hon. signature mem., Calif.), Women Artists Registry N.Am., Nat. Mus. Women in Arts, Art Alumni San Jose State U., Nat. League Am. Pen Women (pres. 1983—84, 1986—87), Cen. Coast Art Assn. (pres. 1982—85), Arts Coun. So. Oreg., Watercolor Soc., Rogue Valley Art Gallery (bd. officer 2004—05), LaHaina Arts Soc., Artists Equity Assn., Nat. Watercolor Soc. (assoc. Nat. award 2005, Viva Sherman Oaks (Calif.) award), Am. Watercolor Soc. (assoc.). Achievements include Artwork selected for inclusion in profl. pubs. including "Best of Watercolor" in Rockport Publr. and "The California Art Preview" Les Krantz. Home: 3533 Southvillage Dr Medford OR 97504-9283 Home Phone: 541-772-0136; Office Phone: 541-772-0136. Personal E-mail: schubert0136@msn.com.

SCHUBERT, WILLIAM HENRY, curriculum studies educator; b. Garrett, Ind., July 6, 1944; s. Walter William and Mary Madeline (Grube) S.; children by previous marriage: Ellen Elaine, Karen Margaret; m. Ann Lynn Lopez, Dec. 3, 1977; children: Heidi Ann, Henry William. BS, Manchester

Coll., 1966; MS, Ind. U., 1967; PhD, U. Ill., 1975. Tchr. Fairmount, El Sierra and Herrick Schs., Downers Grove, Ill., 1967—75; clin. instr. U. Wis., Madison, 1969—73; tchg. asst., fellow U. Ill., Urbana, 1973—75, asst. prof. Chgo., 1975—80, assoc. prof., 1981—85, prof., 1985—, coord. secondary edn., 1979—82, coord. instrnl. leadership, 1979—85, dir. grad. studies Coll. Edn., 1983—85, coord. grad. curriculum studies, 1985—2005, coord. edn. studies, 1990—94, 1996—, chair area curriculum and instrn., 1990—94, 2002—05, Univ. scholar, 2005—, coord. PhD program in curriculum and MEd program in edn. studies, 2006—. Vis. assoc. prof. U. Victoria (B.C., Can.), 1981; disting. vis. prof. U. S.C., 1986; presenter in field. Author (with Ann Lopez Schubert): Curriculum Books: The First Eighty Years, 1980; author: Curriculum: Perspective, Paradigm and Possibility, 1986, with Edmund C. Short and George Willis, 1985; author: (with J. Dan Marshall and James T. Sears) Turning Points in Curriculum: A Contemporary American Memoir, 2000; author: (with others) 2d edit., 2007; author: (with Ann Lopez Schubert, Thomas P. Thomas, Wayne M. Carroll) Curriculum Books: The First Hundred Years, 2002; editor (with Ann Lopez): Conceptions of Curriculum Knowledge: Focus on Students and Teachers, 1982; editor: (with George Willis) Reflections from the Heart of Educational Inquiry: Understanding Curriculum Teaching Through the Arts, 1991; editor: (with William Ayers) Teacher Lore: Learning From Our Own Experience, 1992, 2001; editor: (with George Willis, R. Bullugh, C. Kridel, J. Holton) The American Curriculum: A Documentary History, 1993; assoc. editor, mem. editl. bd. Ednl. Theory, mem. editl. bd. Catalyst: Voices of Chicago School Reform, Taboo: The Jour. of Culture and Edn., former mem. editl. bd. Ednl. Studies, former cons. editor Phenomenology and Pedagogy, adv. bd. Tchg. Edn., Pi Lamda Pubs., 1995—, Jour. Curriculum and Supervision, mem. editl. bd. Curriculum and Teaching, Jour. Curriculum and Pedagogy, emeritus editl. bd. Jour. Curriculum Theorizing, 1999—; editor: (book series) Student Lore, 1990—; cons. editor Jour. Curriculum Discourse and Dialogue, mem. adv. bd. Jour. Critical Issues in Curriculum and Instrn., 2000—, contbr. over 200 articles to profl. jours., chpt. to books. Mem.: ASCD (steering com. curriculum com. 1980—83, publs. com. 1987—90, internat. polling panel 1990—), Internat. Acad. Edn., Am. Assn. for Advancement of Curriculum Studies, Internat. Assn. for Advancement of Curriculum Studies, Soc. Profs. of Edn. (exec. bd. 1988—97, pres.-elect 2000—01, pres. 2001—02, Mary Ann Raywid award 2007), John Dewey Soc. (bd. dirs. 1986—95, chair awards com. 1988—90, co-chair lectures commn. 1989—91, 1989—91, pres.-elect 1990—91, pres. 1992—93), Inst. Dem. in Edn., Nat. Soc. Study Edn., World Coun. Curriculum and Instrn., Am. Ednl. Rsch. Assn. (chmn. creation and utilization of curriculum knowledge 1980—82, program chmn. curriculum studies divsn. 1982—83, sec. divsn. B 1989—91, v.p. 2000—01, Lifetime Achievement award in Curriculum Studies 2004), Am. Assn. Colls. Tchr. Edn., Soc. Study Curriculum History (sec.-treas. 1981—82, pres. 1982—83, founder), Profs. of Curriculum (factotum 1984—85), Internat. Acad. Edn., Scottish Rite, Masons, Phi Kappa Phi (pres. U. Ill. Chgo. chpt. 1981—82), Phi Delta Kappa. Office: U Ill Coll Edn M/C 147 1040 W Harrison St Chicago IL 60607-7129 Business E-Mail: schubert@uic.edu.

SCHUBERT, WILLIAM KUENNETH, hospital medical center executive; b. Cin., July 12, 1926; s. Wilfred Schubert and Amanda Kuenneth; m. Mary Jane Pamperin, June 5, 1948; children: Carol, Joanne, Barbara, Nancy. BS, U. Cin., 1949, MD, 1952; LHD (hon.), Coll. Mt. St. Joseph, Cin., 1997. Diplomate Am. Bd. Pediat. Pvt. practice specializing in pediat., Cin., 1956-63; dir. clin. rsch. ctr. Children's Hosp. Med. Ctr., Cin., 1963-76; dir. divsn. gastroenterology Children's Hosp., Cin., 1968-79; prof. pediat. U. Cin., 1969-96, prof. emeritus, 1997—, assoc. sr. v.p. for children's hosp. affairs Coll. Medicine, 1993-96; chief of staff Children's Hosp. Med. Ctr., Cin., 1972-88; chmn. dept. pediat. U. Cin., 1979-93; dir. Children's Hosp. Rsch. Found., Cin., 1979-93; pres., CEO Children's Hosp. Med. Ctr., Cin., 1983-96, trustee, 1983—. V.p. Ohio Solid Organ Transplant Consortium, Columbus, 1986-87, pres., 1987-88, alt. trustee, 1988-96; trustee med. rsch. James N. Gamble Inst., Cin., 1989-95; bd. dirs. Choice Care Found., Health Found. of Greater Cin.; mem. fetal oversight com. Fetal Care Ctr. Cin., 2005—. Contbr. over 100 articles to profl. jours. Trustee Greater Cin. Hosp. Coun., 1986-96, Assn. of Ohio Children's Hosp., Columbus, 1986-96, The Children's Hosp. Found., 1990—, Springer Sch., Cin., 1994-2003, Children's Convalescent Hosp., 1997—, The Children's Hosp., 2001—; chmn. Greater Cin. Hosp. Coun., 1989; co-chmn. Citizen's Com. for Med. Ctr., Cin., 1980-81; chmn. Hosp. Divsn. 1988 Fine Arts Fund, Cin., 1987; hon. trustee Babies' Milk Fund, Children's and Prenatal Clinics, Cin., 1994-2002. Recipient Disting. Alumni award U. Cin., 1992, Donald Newkirk award Ohio Hosp. Assn., 1997, Health Care Heros Lifetime Achievement award Bus. Courier, Cin., 2003, Great Living Cincinnatian award, 2004. Fellow Am. Acad. Pediat. (Murray Davidson award sect. on gastroenterology/nutrition 2003); mem. Am. Pediatric Soc. (councillor 1986-93), Soc. Pediatric Rsch., Assn. Med. Sch. Pediatric Dept. Chmn., Cin. Acad. Medicine, AMA, Midwestern Soc. for Pediatric Rsch., Am. Assn. for Study of Liver Diseases, Ctrl. Soc. Clin. Rsch., Am. Gastroenterological Assn., N.Am. Soc. Pediatric Gastroenterology, Nat. Reye's Syndrome Found. (med. dir. 1976-87), Internat. Assn. Study Liver Diseases. Clubs: Queen City (Cin.). Office: Children's Hosp Med Ctr Cin ML 5005 3333 Burnet Ave Cincinnati OH 45229-3026 Home Phone: 513-751-6007. Business E-Mail: william.schubert@cchmc.org.

SCHUBKEGEL, JOYCE CATHERINE, music educator, composer; b. New Haven, Ind., Apr. 23, 1937; d. Clarence Frederick Nahrwold and Helen Edith Ross; m. Francis Luther Schubkegel, June 30, 1962; children: Catherine Biedenbender, Timothy, Jean Reiners, David. AA, Concordia Jr. Coll., Ft. Wayne, Ind., 1957; BS in Edn., Concordia U., River Forest, Ill., 1959; MusM, Northwestern U., Evanston, Ill., 1962. Organist Concordia Luth. Ch., Ft. Wayne, Ind., 1956—57; music dir. First Immanuel Luth. Ch., Chgo., 1958—59; tchr., music dir. St. John's Luth. Sch., Wheaton, Ill., 1959—60; music instr. Concordia Tchrs. Coll., River Forest, Ill., 1960—62; music dir. Bethlehem Luth. Ch., River Grove, Ill., 1960—62, Good Shepherd Luth. Ch., Palos Heights, Ill., 1963—66; music instr. Wis. Luth. Coll., Milw., 1966—70; music prof. Dr. Martin Luther Coll., New Ulm, Minn., 1970—95, Martin Luther Coll., New Ulm, Minn., 1995—. Mem.: Am. Choral Dir. Assn. Lutheran. Avocation: gardening. Home: 1303 Southridge Rd New Ulm MN 56073

SCHUCHARD, ROBERT L., lawyer; b. LA, Feb. 14, 1952; BA in Polit. Sci., Stanford U., 1974; JD, Santa Clara U., 1977. Bar: Calif. 1977. Ptnr. Sonnenschein Nath & Rosenthal LLP, LA, 1997—. Office Phone: 213-633-6800. Office Fax: 213-633-6899. Business E-Mail: robertschuchard@dwt.com.

SCHUCHAT, ANNE, health facility administrator; B in Philosophy, with minor in Biology, Swarthmore Coll., 1980; MD, Dartmouth U., 1984. Resident in internal medicine Manhattan VA Hosp.; epidemic intelligence svc. officer Centers for Disease Control, Atlanta, 1988, chief respiratory diseases br., acting dir. Nat. Ctr. Infectious Diseases, dir. Nat. Immunization Program, 2005—; clin. asst. prof. medicine Emory U. Contbr. chapters to books, articles to profl. jours. Office: Nat Immunization Program CDC Mailstop C23 1600 Clifton Rd Atlanta GA 30333 E-mail: aschuchat@cdc.gov.

SCHUCK, PETER HORNER, lawyer, educator; b. NYC, Apr. 26, 1940; s. Samuel H. and Lucille (Horner) S.; m. Marcy Cantor, June 26, 1966; children: Christopher, Julie. BA with honors, Cornell U., 1962; JD cum laude, Harvard U., 1965, MA, 1969; LLM, NYU, 1966; MA (hon.), Yale U., 1982. Bar: N.Y. State 1966, D.C. 1972. Practiced law, NYC, 1965-68; teaching fellow in govt. Harvard U., 1969-71; cons. Center for Study of Responsive Law, Washington, 1971-72; dir. Washington office Consumers Union, 1972-77; dep. asst. sec. for planning and evaluation HEW, Washington, 1977-79; vis. scholar Am. Enterprise Inst. for Public Policy Research, Washington, 1979; assoc. prof. law Yale U., 1979-81, prof., 1981-86, Simeon E. Baldwin prof. law, 1986—, dep. dean, 1993-94. Vis. prof. Georgetown U. Law Ctr., 1986-87, NYU Law Sch., fall 1994, N.Y. Law Sch., spring 1997, 98, 99, Fordham Law Sch., 2007. Author: The Judiciary Committees, 1975, Suing Government, 1983, Citizenship Without Consent, 1985; co-author: Agent Orange on Trial, 1986, enlarged edit., 1987, Citizens, Strangers and In-Betweens: Essays on Immigration and Citizenship, 1998, The Limits of Law: Essays on Democratic Governance, 2000, Diversity in America: Keeping Government at a Safe Distance, 2003, Meditations of a Militant Moderate: Cool Views on Hot Topics, 2006, Targeting in Social Programs: Avoiding Bad Bets, Removing Bad Apples, 2006; editor: Tort Law and the Public Interest, 1991, Foundations of Administrative Law, 1994, 2nd edit., 2004; co-editor: Paths to Inclusion, 1998, Immigration Stories, 2005; contbr. articles and revs. to profl. and popular publs. Recipient Silver Gavel award ABA, 1987; Guggenheim fellow, 1984-85; Fulbright scholar, 2004. Jewish. Office: Yale Law Sch PO Box 208215 New Haven CT 06520 Office Phone: 203-432-4967. E-mail: peter.schuck@yale.edu.

SCHUCK, THOMAS ROBERT, lawyer, farmer; b. Findlay, Ohio, Feb. 7, 1950; s. Robert Damon and Katherine Margaretta (Beynon) S. BA, DePauw U., 1972; MA, U. Kent, UK, 1974; JD, Harvard U., 1976. Bar: Ohio 1976, U.S. Dist. Ct. (no. dist.) Ohio 1977, U.S. Dist. Ct. (so. dist.) Ohio 1979, Ariz. 1990, U.S. Ct. Appeals (6th cir.) 1978, U.S. Ct. Appeals (9th cir.) 1991, U.S. Ct. Appeals Armed Forces, 2000, U.S. Supreme Ct. 2001. Law clk. U.S. Dist. Ct., Cleve., 1976-79; assoc. Taft, Stettinius & Hollister, Cin., 1979-87, ptnr., 1987—; owner, operator Rural Hill Farm. Participant Ohio Bench Bar Conf., Columbus, 1990-91, Glenmoor Justice Inst., 2000; barrister Am. Inn of Ct., 1986-87, LEAD Clermont, 1997-98; bar exam com. US Dist. Ct. (so. dist.) Ohio, nen, panel criminal justice act, mem. criminal justice act atty. panel, 2006—; merit panel for bankruptcy judge selection US Ct. Appeals Sixth Cir., 1998, chair, 2002; life mem. Jud. Conf. of 6th Cir., mem. standing com. Author: Federal Employment Litigation Practice Guide, 2006; contbg. author: Aids and the Law, 2d edit. 1992; contbr. articles to profl. jours. Trustee Mental Health Svcs. East, Inc., Cin., 1985-91; sec. bd. trustees Joy Outdoor Edn. Ctr., Inc., 1999-2005; active May Festival Assocs., Cin., 1984-86, WGUC Radio Cmty. Bd., 1984-86, Clermont County Mental Health Bd., Batavia, Ohio, 1992-2000, vice-chmn., 1997-2000; steering com. Clermont County Mental Retardation Developmental Disabilities Levy, 1996, trustee, 2000-02, vice-chmn., 2002; spl. gifts com. Cin. Art Acad., 1987, Ohio Found. Ind. Colls., 1995-, bd. dir., 2003—; pres. Fed. Bar Assn. Found. Cin. Grad. fellow Rotary Internat. Found., 1972-73. Mem. Fed. Bar Assn. (pres. Cin. chpt. 1994-95, v.p. 6th cir. 1996-99, nat. membership chair 1997-99, nat. sec. 2001-2002, nat. treas., nat. v.p. 2002-03, nat. pres.-elect 2003-04, nat. pres. 2004-05, govt. rels. com., pres. Foun. of Cin.), Potter Stewart Am. Inn of Ct. (barrister 1986-87), U.S. Rowing Assn. (asst. referee), Harvard Club Cin. (pres. 1995-96), Soc. Bacchus Am., Masons (33rd degree, trustee Valley of Cin. 2003-05), Phi Beta Kappa, Delta Chi, Phi Eta Sigma, Sigma Delta Chi. Republican. Methodist. Avocations: reading, photography. Home: PO Box 615 189 State Route 133 Felicity OH 45120 Office: Taft Stettinius & Hollister LLP Ste 1800 425 Walnut St Cincinnati OH 45202-3957 Home Phone: 513-633-1841; Office Phone: 513-381-2838.

SCHUCKENBROCK, STEVE (STEPHEN FRANCIS SCHUCKENBROCK), computer company executive, former information technology executive; b. 1960; BA in Bus. Adminstrn., Elon Coll., 1982. Sales and tech. mgmt. positions IBM, 1983—93; ptnr. Feld Group, 1993—95, COO, 2000—04; chief info. officer Frito-Lay, 1995—98; sr. v.p. info. tech. PepsiCo. Inc., 1998—2000; exec. v.p. global sales & client solutions EDS, Plano, Tex., 2004—06; sr. v.p. global services Dell Inc., Round Rock, Tex., 2007—. Office: Dell Inc 1 Dell Way Round Rock TX 78682 *

SCHUDER, RAYMOND FRANCIS, lawyer; b. Wickford, RI, Dec. 27, 1926; s. Rollie Milton and Selma (Ball) S.; m. Betty Jo Williams, Mar. 14, 1948; children: Gregg Williams, Glen Arva. AB, Emory U., 1949, JD, 1951. Bar: Ga. 1951. With Trust Co. Ga., Atlanta, 1951—54; assoc. firm Wheeler Robinson & Thurmond, Gainesville, Ga., 1954—59; pvt. practice law Gainesville, 1959—70, 1981—96; ptnr. Schuder & Brown, Gainesville, 1971—76, Schuder & Hartness, Gainesville, 1977—80. Mcpl. ct. judge Gainesville, 1956-60, 73-75; magistrate ct. judge, 1985-2000, sr. magistrate, 2001-03. Supr. Upper Chattahoochee Soil and Water Conservation Dist., 1971-74; CEO, bd. dirs. Charles Thompson Estes Found., Inc., Gainesville. Cpl. USMCR, 1944-50; 1st lt. USAR, 1950-56, ret. Mem. State Bar Ga. (gov. 1966-70), Gainesville-Northeastern Bar Assn. (pres. 1969-70), Am. Legion, VFW, Elks. Methodist. Home: 2224 Riverside Dr Gainesville GA 30501-1232 E-mail: xrfs@charter.net.

SCHUELE, DONALD EDWARD, retired physics professor, dean; b. Cleve., June 16, 1934; s. Edward and Mildred (Matousek) S.; m. Clare Ann Kirchner, Sept. 5, 1956; children: Donna, Karen, Melanie, Judy, Rachel, Ruth. BS, John Carroll U., Cleve., 1956, MS, 1957; PhD, Case Inst. Tech., 1962. Instr. physics and math. John Carroll U., 1956-59; part-time instr. physics Case Inst. Tech., 1959-62, instr., asst. prof., assoc. prof., 1962-70; mem. tech. staff Bell Telephone Labs., 1970-72; assoc. prof. physics Case Western Res. U., 1972-74, prof., 1974—, dean undergrad. coll., 1973-76, chmn. dept. physics, 1976-78; vice dean Case Inst. Tech., 1978-83, v.p. for undergrad. and grad. studies, 1983-84, dean, 1984-86, prof. physics, 1986-88, dean math. and natural sci., 1988-89, Albert A. Michelson prof. physics, 1989—2006, Albert A. Michelson emeritus prof. physics, 2006, acting chmn. elec. engring. and applied physics, 1992-93. Cons. in field. Co-editor: Critical Revs. in Solid State Scis, 1969-84; contbr. articles to profl. jours.; patentee in field. Mem. adv. bd. St. Charles Borromeo Sch., 1970-72; pres. Seed Found., 1986-89; trustee St. Mary's Sem., 1980-93; mem. Olympic Sports Equipment and Tech. Com., 1982-93; trustee Newman Found., 1983—, Northeastern Ohio Sci. Fair, 1983—; mem. Diocesan Pastoral Coun., 1992-94; active Rep. Presdl. task force. Recipient Disting. Physics Alumnus award John Carroll U., 1983; NSF Faculty fellow, 1961-63; Sam Givelber fellow Case Alumni Assn., 2001. Mem.: North Coast Thermal Analysis Soc., Am. Assn. Physics Tchrs., Am. Phys. Soc. (vice chair Ohio sect. 1995—96, chair 1996—97), Newman Apostolate, Case Alumni Coun. (life; 3d v.p. 2001—02, 1st v.p. 2002—03, pres. 2003—04, treas. 1992, chair Case Fund Bd. 2004—), Tau Beta Pi, Sigma Xi, Alpha Sigma Nu. Republican. Roman Catholic. Achievements include patents fluid pressure device, impact wrench torque calibrator, detection of wear particles and other impurities in industrial fluids, electrical oil analysis instrument. Home: 4892 Countryside Rd Cleveland OH 44124-2513 Office: Case Western Res U 10900 Euclid Ave Cleveland OH 44106-1712 Home Phone: 216-382-0561; Office Phone: 216-368-4013. Business E-Mail: des3@case.edu.

SCHUELER, JOHN R., newspaper executive; b. Grosse Point, MI; m. Linda Schueler; children: Tracie, Lindsey. BA, W. Mich. U. Dir. sales Atlanta Jour. & Constn., 1979—82; with Miami Herald, Miami, Fla., 1984—89; pres. New England Newspapers, 1989—91; v.p. consumer mktg. & circulation The Orange County Register, Santa Ana, Calif., 1991—92, exec. v.p. & gen. mgr., 1992—95, pres., COO, 1995-98; publisher Star Tribune, Mpls., 1998—2001; pub. Los Angeles Daily News, 2001—04; pres., CEO Los Angeles Newspaper Group, 2004—05; pres. Fla. Comm. Group, 2005—. Office: Media General Broadcast Group 200 S Parker St Tampa FL 33606 Office Phone: 813-221-5757.

SCHUELKE, JOHN PAUL, religious organization administrator; b. Benton Harbor, Mich., Nov. 5, 1934; s. Alwin E. and Martha M. (Schoeneberg) S.; m. Noreta H. Petersen, Sept. 9, 1956; children: Alvin, Mary, Sheryl, Brian. BS in Acctg., U. Wyo., 1957; LLD (hon.), Concordia U., Irvine, Calif., 1983. CPA. From acct. to sr. acct. Colo. Interstate Gas Co., Colorado Springs, 1957-63; staff acct. Arthur Anderson & Co., Denver, 1963-64; mgr. fin. control Colo. Interstate Corp., Colorado Springs., 1964-67, dir. fin. control, 1967-71; adminstrv. v.p. mfg. divsn. Marsh Instrument Co. subs. Colo. Mfg. Corp., Skokie, Ill., 1971-72; exec. officer bd. dirs., CAO Luth. Ch.-Mo. Synod, St. Louis, 1972-98, ret., 1999. Former chmn. Concordia Asia Ednl. Found.; lectr. in field. Asst. scoutmaster Boy Scouts Am., Colorado Springs; former mem. governing bd., sec. Luth. Svcs. in Am.; former mem. governing bd. Luth. Coun.-USA, com. Luth. Coop.; v.p. Faith Luth Ch., Woodland Park; former mem. bd. human care ministries, sec., mem. lic. deacon com. Rocky Mountain dist. Luth. Ch.-Mo. Synod. Recipient God and Country award Eagle Scout. Mem. Alpha Kappa Psi, Gamma Delta (former pres.). Lutheran. Avocations: travel, fishing, reading.

SCHUELLER, GRETEL HELENA, journalist, educator; d. Helmut and Nimmi Joanna Schueller; m. Todd Michael Goff, June 6, 2006; 1 child, Alexander Helmut Goff. BA, Smith Coll., Northampton, Mass., 1992; MA, NYU, NYC, 1996. Freelance writer, editor, Essex, NY, 1996—; assoc. prof. journalism SUNY, Plattsburgh, 2001—. Assoc. editor: Audubon Mag., 1998—2001; contbr. chapters to books, articles to numerous mags. Recipient Investigative Journalism award, Newsletter and Electronic Pub. Found.; fellow, Woods Hole Marine Biological Lab., Scripps Inst. Environ. Mem.: Nat. Assn. Sci. Writers. Avocations: cooking, gardening, travel. Home: PO Box 223 Essex NY 12936 Office: SUNY Plattsburgh Ctr Comm 101 Broadstreet Plattsburgh NY 12901 Home Phone: 802-658-4253; Office Phone: 518-564-2425. Personal E-mail: gretel.schueller@gmail.com.

SCHUENEMAN, DIANE L., diversified financial services company executive; Account exec. instl. sales Merrill Lynch, 1971, head global ops. and infrastructure svcs., 2004—06, sr. v.p., head global infrastructure solutions grp., 2006—. Bd. mgrs. Omgeo; bd. dirs. Depository Trust and Clearing Corpn. Office: Merrill Lynch 4 World Fin Ctr 250 Vesey St New York NY 10080

SCHUEPPERT, GEORGE LOUIS, financial executive; b. Merrill, Wis., July 1, 1938; s. George Henry and Eleanor Natalie (Pautz) S.; m. Kathleen Kay Carpenter, May 6, 1967; children: Steven Andrew, Stephanie Roanne, Stenning Karl BBA, U. Wis., Madison, 1961; MBA, U. Chgo., 1969. Treas., controller Steiger-Rathke Devel. Co., Phoenix, 1964-65; various positions Continental Ill. Nat., Chgo., 1965-76, 1981-86; mng. dir. Continental Ill. Ltd., London, 1977-81; sr. v.p. Continental Ill. Nat. Bank, Chgo., 1982-86; ptnr. Coopers & Lybrand, Chgo., 1986-87; exec. v.p. fin. CBI Industries Inc, Oak Brook, Ill., 1987-95, also bd. dirs., 1987-95; exec. v.p., CFO Outboard Marine Corp., Waukegan, Ill., 1996-97. Bd. dirs. Wells Mfg. Co., Barrington Bank & Trust Co. Pres. Gt. Books Found.; chmn., bd. dirs. De Paul U. Gov. Asst. Program. Lt. (j.g.) USN, 1961-64. Recipient Herfurth award U. Wis., 1960 Mem. Econ. Club Chgo. (bd. dirs., chmn. membership com.). Republican. Avocations: history, architecture, travel, golf. Home: 97 Otis Rd Barrington IL 60010-5129 Office: Great Books Found 35 E Wacker Dr Ste 2300 Chicago IL 60601-2298

SCHUERHOLZ, JOHN BOLAND, JR., professional baseball executive; b. Balt., Oct. 1, 1940; s. John Boland and Maryne (Wyatt) Schuerholz; m. Ellen Louise Lawson, June 21, 1963; 1 child, Regina Marie Reagan; m. Karen Louise Wiltse, Sept. 18, 1978; 1 child, Jonathan Lawrence. BE, Towson State U., 1962; postgrad., Loyola Coll., Md., 1964—66. Tchr. various schs., 1962—66; adminstrv. asst. Balt. Orioles, 1966—68, Kansas City Royals, 1968—70, asst. farm dir., 1970—75, farm dir., 1975, dir. scouting and player devel., 1976—79, v.p. player personnel, 1979—81, exec. v.p., gen. mgr., 1981—90, Atlanta Braves, 1990—. With AUS, 1966—72. Recipient Lifetime Achievement award, Baseball America, 2004. Lutheran. Office: Atlanta Braves PO Box 4064 Atlanta GA 30302-4064

SCHUESSLER, JOHN T. (JACK SCHUESSLER), retired food service executive; b. Dec. 21, 1950; m. Patty A. Schuessler. BS, Spring Hill Coll. Mgr. trainee Wendy's franchise, Atlanta, 1974-76; joined Wendy's Internat., 1976, dist. mgr., dir. area ops., regional dir. various zones US, 1976-83, regional v.p. ea. divsn., 1983-84, zone pres., 1984-86, divsn. v.p., 1986-87, sr. v.p. N.E. region, 1987-95, exec. v.p. US ops., 1995-97, pres., COO US ops., 1997-2000, pres., COO Can., 1999-2000, pres., CEO, 2000—06, chmn., 2001—06. Trustee Wendy's Nat. Advtsg. Program.

SCHUESSLER FIORENZA, ELISABETH, theology studies educator; b. Tschanad, Romania, Apr. 17, 1938; parents German citizens; d. Peter and Magdalena Schuessler; m. Francis Fiorenza, Dec. 17, 1967; 1 child, Chris. MDiv, U. Wuerzburg, Germany, 1962; Lic. Theol., U. Wuerzburg, 1963; DrTheol, U. Muenster, Germany, 1970. Asst. prof. theology U. Notre Dame, South Bend, Ind., 1970-75, assoc. prof., 1975-80, prof., 1980-84; instr. U. Muenster, 1966-67; Talbot prof. N.T., Episcopal Div. Sch., Cambridge, Mass., 1984-88; Krister Stendahl prof. Divsn. Scripture and Interpretation Harvard U., Cambridge, Mass., 1988—. Harry Emerson Fosdick vis. prof. Union Theol. Sem., N.Y.C., 1974-75; guest prof. U. Tuebingen, Federal Republic of Germany, 1987, Cath. Theol. Faculty Luzern, Switzerland, 1990; Stiftungs prof. Humboldt U., Berlin, 1997; Ernst Troeltsch prof. U. Heidelberg, Germany, 1999. Author: Der Vergessene Partner, 1964, Priester für Gott, 1972, The Apocalypse, 1976, Invitation to the Book of Revelation, 1981, In Memory of Her, 1983, Bread not Stone, 1984, Judgement or Justice, 1985, Revelation: Vision of a Just World, 1991, But She Said - Feminist Practices of Biblical Interpretation, 1992, Discipleship of Equals: A Critical Feminist Ekklesialogy of Liberation, 1993, Jesus: Miriam's Child and Sophia's Prophet, Critical Issues in Feminist Christology, 1994, Sharing Her Word, 1998, Rhetoric and Ethic The Politics of Biblical Studies, 1999, Jesus and the Politics of Interpretation, 2000, Wisdom Ways, 2001, Grenzen uberschreiten, 2004; editor: Searching the Scriptures, 2 vols, 1993, 94, The Power of Naming, 1996; founding co-editor Jour. Feminist Studies in Religion; also editor other works. Mem.: Am. Acad. Arts and Scis., Soc. Bibl. Lit. (past pres.), Am. Acad. Religion. Office: Harvard Div Sch 45 Francis Ave Cambridge MA 02138-1911 Office Phone: 617-495-5751.

SCHUETTE, CHARLES A., lawyer; b. Columbus, Ind., Feb. 24, 1942; BBA, U. Okla., 1964, JD, 1967. Bar: Okla. 1967, Fla. 1970, U.S. Supreme Ct. 1979, U.S. Dist. Ct. (so. dist.) Fla. 1982, U.S. Dist. Ct. (mid. dist.) Fla. 1982. With Akerman Senterfitt. Fellow Am. Bar Found.; mem. ABA, Fla. Bar, Okla. Bar Assn., Dade County Bar Assn. Office: Akerman Senterfitt 1 SE 3rd Ave Fl Miami FL 33131-1700

SCHUETTINGER, BRUCE MICHAEL, conservator; b. Frederick, Md., Apr. 15, 1955; s. Arthur George Schuettinger and Shirlee Price; children: Kathryn, Alison. BS in Fine Arts cum laude, Towson State U., 1978. Conservator Antique Restorations, Frederick, Md., 1983—90, Antique Restorations Ltd., New Market, Md., 1990—2007; personal property appraiser Internat. Soc. of Appraisers (Indiana U.), 1985, 1986, U. Md., 1985; conservator Schuetinger Conservation Svcs., Inc., 2007—. Presenter in field. Co-author: (directory) Conservation Resources for Art and Antiques, 2001. Mem. curitorial com. Hist. Soc. of Frederick County, Md., 2002—05. Mem.: Wash. Conservatory Guild, Internat. Soc. Appraisers, Am. Inst. for Conservation of Historic and Artistic Wants (assoc.).

Independent. Episcopalian. Avocations: painting, photography. Home: 13724 Pryor Rd Thurmont MD 21788 Office Phone: 301-865-3009. Personal E-mail: bscheuttinger@verizon.net.

SCHUETZE-COBURN, MARJE, university librarian; BA in German and History, Univ. Calif., Berkeley; MLS, UCLA, MA in History. Cataloger, Feuchtwanger Collection USC, 1989—91, Feuchtwanger Libr. and Curator, 1991—2001, dir., Spl. Libraries and Archival Collections, 2001—, also assoc. dean faculty affairs for Univ. Libraries, interim dean librs., 2006—07. Office: Dir SLAC Univ So Calif Los Angeles CA 90089 Office Phone: 213-740-7119. Business E-Mail: schuetze@usc.edu.

SCHUH, DALE R., insurance company executive; Joined Sentry Ins. Group, Stevens Point, Wis., 1972, v.p. planning, 1988, pres., COO, 1996, CEO, pres., chmn., 1997—. Office: Sentry Ins Group 1800 North Point Dr Stevens Point WI 54481 *

SCHUH, FRANK JOSEPH, oil industry executive, consultant; b. Columbus, Ohio, Feb. 3, 1935; s. Sebastian and Elizabeth (Zorn) S.; m. Alice Virgene Kasler, June 16, 1956; children: Dwain Joseph, Michael James, Barbara Ann. BS in Petroleum Engring., MS in Petroleum Engring., Ohio State U., 1956. Registered profl. engr., Ohio. Drilling and rsch. engr. Atlantic Refining Co., Tex., La., 1956-62; mem. drilling engring. staff, dir. engring. Atlantic Richfield Co., Dallas, 1962-82, mgr. drilling rsch., sr. advisor Plano, Tex., 1982-86; v.p. Enertech Engring. & Tech., Dallas, 1986-87; pres. Drilling Tech., Inc., Plano, 1987—; v.p. Supreme Resources Corp., Dallas, 1988-92. Founder, 1st pres. Drilling Engring. Assn., Dallas, 1983-85; mem. tech. adv. com. Internat. Ocean Drilling Program, 2002—. Author: Drilling Equations, 1975; patentee horizontal drilling, high pressure drilling system, continuous heavy oil production process, 31 other patents. Precinct, region chmn. Rep. Party, Dallas, 1964-74; vol. bldg. com. Mary Immaculate Ch., Dallas, 1965-66; mem. tech. engring. and devel. com. Ocean Drilling Program, Bryan, Tex., 1980-2006. Recipient outstanding achievement in field of engring. award Nat. Engrs. Coun., 1980, Robert Earl McConnell award Am. Inst. Mining Engrs., 1994, Ohio State Univ. Coll. of Engring. Benjamin G. Lamme Meritorious Achievement medel, 1995. Mem. NAE, Soc. Petroleum Engrs. (nat. bd. dirs. 1983-86, Drilling Engring. award 1986, Disting. Mem. award 1989), Am. Petroleum Inst. (chmn. com. 6, 1985-88, svc. citation 1986), Am. Assn. Drilling Engrs., Soc. Ind. Profl. Earth Scientists, Petroleum Engrs. Club (pres. 1974-75), Ohio State U. Alumni Club (pres. 1968-69), Dallas-Ft. Worth Oilman's Club (handicapper 1973-86). Avocations: golf, sailing. Office: Drilling Technology Inc 5808 Wavertree Ln Ste 1000 Plano TX 75093-4513 Office Phone: 972-380-0203. Business E-Mail: schuh1@tx.rr.com.

SCHUH, G(EORGE) EDWARD, dean, agricultural economist; b. Indpls., Sept. 13, 1930; s. George Edward and Viola (Lentz) S.; m. Maria Ignez, May 23, 1965; children: Audrey, Susan, Tanya. BS in Agrl. Edn, Purdue U., 1952, DAgr, PhD, Purdue U., 1992; MS in Agrl. Econs., Mich. State U., 1954; MA in Econs, U. Chgo., 1958, PhD, 1961; prof. (hon.), Fed. U. Vicosa, Brazil, 1965. From instr. to prof. agrl. econs. Purdue U., 1959-79; dir. Center for Public Policy and Public Affairs, 1977-78; dep. undersec. for internat. affairs and commodity programs Dept. Agr., Washington, 1978-79, chair bd. for internat. food and agrl. devel., 1995—2002; prof. agrl. and applied econs., head dept. U. Minn., Mpls., 1979-84; dir. agr. and rural devel, World Bank, Washington, 1984-87; dean Humphrey Inst. for Pub. Affairs U. Minn., 1987—96; Orville and Jane Freeman Endowed chair Humphrey Inst. for Pub. Affairs, U. Minn., 1996—; regents prof. U. Minn., 1998—. Program advisor Ford Found., 1966-72; sr. staff economist Pres.'s Coun. Econ. Advisors, 1974-75; mem. bd. on agr. and natural resources NRC, 1998—2004; trustee Internat. Food Policy Rsch. Inst., 1997-2003, Internat. Potato Ctr., 2004—. Contbr. articles to profl. jours. Trustee Sasakawa Africa Assn., 1998—. Served with U.S. Army, 1954-56. Recipient 60 at 60 award, Internat. Insts. Cooperation in Agr., Order Sci. Merit, Grand Cruz. Fellow: AAAS, Brazilian Acad. Sci., Brazilian Soc. Rural Econs., Am. Acad. Arts and Scis., Am. Agrl. Econs. Assn. (bd. dirs. 1977—80, pres.-elect 1980—81, pres. 1981—82, Thesis award 1962, Pub. Rsch. award 1971, Article award 1975, Policy award 1979, Publ. of Lasting Value award 1988); mem.: Brazilian Soc. Agrl. Economists, Am. Econ. Assn., Internat. Assn. Agrl. Econs. Office: Humphrey Ctr U Minn 301 19th Ave S Minneapolis MN 55455-0429 Office Phone: 612-625-8388. Business E-Mail: geschuh@hhh.umn.edu.

SCHUKER, STEPHEN ALAN, historian, educator; b. NYC, Feb. 16, 1939; s. Louis A. and Millicent (Milchman) S.; m. Elisabeth Glaser, 1998. AB summa cum laude, Cornell U., 1959; AM, Harvard U., 1962, PhD, 1969; children: Lauren, Daniel. Asst. head hist. rsch. naval history div. Office Chief Naval Ops., 1959-61; instr. history Harvard U., Cambridge, Mass., 1968-69, asst. prof., 1969-74, lectr., 1974-75; vis. assoc. prof. European studies Sch. Advanced Internat. Studies, Johns Hopkins U., Washington, 1977, adj. prof., 1978-83; assoc. prof. history Brandeis U., Waltham, Mass., 1977-82, prof., 1982-91; Commonwealth prof. history U. Va., Charlottesville, 1991-92, William W. Corcoran prof., 1992—; syndic U. Press New Eng., 1979-81; cons. Nat. Commn. Documents and Records Federal Ofcls., 1976, Rockefeller Found., 1981. Author: The End of French Predominance in Europe (George Louis Beer prize, Gilbert Chinard prize), 1976, American "Reparations" to Germany, 1919-1933: Implications for the Third World Debt Crisis, 1988; editor: Deutschland und Frankreich vom Konflikt zur Aussöhnung, 2000; mem. bd. editors Internat. History Rev., 2001-2004; contbr. articles to profl. jours. Lt. USNR, 1959-61. NEH fellow, 1972-73; Am. Council Learned Socs. fellow, 1976-77, 85; sr. fellow USIA-Fulbright Commn., 1984, fellow internat. security John D. and Catherine T. MacArthur Found., 1987-89, fellow Historisches Kolleg, Bayerische Akademie der Wissenschaften, 1996—, fellow German Marshall Fund, 1998-99. Mem. Am. Hist. Assn., Soc. Historians Am. Fgn. Relations, Hist. Soc. Office: U Va Corcoran Dept History University Station Charlottesville VA 22904 Home Phone: 434-293-6951; Office Phone: 434-924-6405. Business E-Mail: sas4u@virginia.edu.

SCHULBERG, BUDD, author; b. NYC, Mar. 27, 1914; s. Benjamin P. and Adeline (Jaffe) S.; m. Virginia Ray, July 23, 1936 (div. 1942); 1 dau., Victoria; m. Victoria Anderson, Feb. 17, 1943 (div. 1964); children: Stephen, David; m. Geraldine Brooks, July 12, 1964 (dec. 1977); m. Betsy Anne Langman, June 9, 1979; children: Benn Stuart, Jessica A. Student, Deerfield Acad., 1931-32; AB cum laude, Dartmouth Coll., 1936, LLD, 1960; LittD, Long Island U., 1983; DHL, Hofstra U., 1987, Five Points Coll., 2001. Boxing editor Sports Illustrated; pres., prodr. Schulberg Prodns. Founder, dir. Watts Writers Workshop, L.A., 1965—; founder, chmn. Frederick Douglass Creative Arts Ctr., N.Y.C., 1971—. Screenwriter, Hollywood, 1936-39; writer "The Schulberg Report", Newsday Syndicate; author: What Makes Sammy Run?, 1941, The Harder They Fall, 1947, The Disenchanted, 1950, Some Faces in the Crowd, 1953, Waterfront, 1955 (Christopher award 1955), Sanctuary V, 1969, The Four Seasons of Success, 1972, Loser and Still Champion: Muhammad Ali, 1972, Swan Watch, 1975, Everything that Moves, 1980, Moving Pictures: Memories of a Hollywood Prince, 1981, Writers in America Love, Action, Laughter and Other Sad Tales, 1990, Sparring with Hemingway: And Other Legends of the Fight Game, 1995, La Foret Interdite, including dialogue in Black and White with James Badwin, 1997; editor: From the Ashes: Voices of Watts, 1967; screenwriter: (films) (with Samuel Ornitz) Little Orphan Annie, 1938, (with F. Scott Fitzgerald) Winter Carnival, 1939, (with Dorothy Parker) Weekend for Three, 1941, (with Martin Berkeley) City without Men, 1943, (with Dudley Nichols) Government Girl, 1943, On the Waterfront, 1954 (Academy award best original story and screenplay 1954, N.Y. Critics award 1954, Fgn. Corrs. award 1954, Screen Writers Guild award 1954, Venice Festival award 1954), A Face in the Crowd, 1958 (German Film Critics award 1957), Wind Across the Everglades, 1958, (teleplays) The Pharmacist's Mate, 1951, Paso Doble, Memory in White, The Legend That Walks Like a man, A Question of Honor, A Table At Ciro's; playwright: The Disenchanted: A Play in Three Acts, 1958, What Make's Sammy Run?, 1959, (musical) Senor Discretion Himself, 1985, (play in 2 acts) The Disenchanted, 1999, On the Waterfront, 2001; contbr. to Sports Illustrated, Life, N.Y. Times Book Rev., Esquire, Newsday Syndicate, L.A. Times Book Rev., N.Y. Times Sunday Mag., Playboy, The New Yorker, Vanity Fair. Bd. dirs. Westminster Neighborhood Assn., L.A., 1965-68, Inner City Cultural Ctr., L.A., 1965-68; mem. nat. adv. commn. on black participation John F. Kennedy Ctr. for Performing Arts; trustee Humanitas Prize. Lt. (j.g.) USNR, 1943-46, assigned to OSS. Awarded Army Commendation Ribbon for gathering photog. evidence of war crimes for Nuremberg Trial, 1945-46; recipient Susie Humanitarian award B'nai B'rith, Image award NAACP, Journalism award Dartmouth Coll., Merit award Lotos Club., L.A. Community Svc. award, 1966, B'hai Human Rights award, 1968, spl. award for Watts Writers Workshop, New Eng. Theater Conf., 1969, Heritage award Deerfield Acad., 1986, Amistad award, award for work with black writers Howard U., Prix Literaire, Deauville Festival 1989, 2005, Westhampton Writers Lifetime Achievement award, 1989, World Boxing Assn. Living Legend award, 1990, 97, Southampton Cultural Ctr. 1st Annual Literature award, 1992, Lifetime Achievement award Guild Hall, 2003, Lifetime Achievement award L.A. (Calif.) H.S., 2005, Ann. Achievement award Congresswoman Maxine Waters, 2005; named to Internat. Boxing Hall of Fame, 2003. Mem. Dramatists Guild, ASCAP, Authors Guild N.Y.C. (mem. council), ACLU, Writers Guild East (mem. coun.), Boxing Writers Am. (A. J. Liebling award 1997), P.E.N., Sphinx (Dartmouth), The Players Club, Yale/Dartmouth Club, Phi Beta Kappa. Address: Mr Mickey Freiberg Acme Literary Agy 4727 Wilshire Blvd Los Angeles CA 90064 also: Ms Mirian Altshuler 53 Old Post Rd N Red Hook NY 12571 Office Phone: 631-288-0514. E-mail: bschul@optonline.net.

SCHULEIT, ANNA, artist; b. Mainz, Germany, 1974; BFA, RI Sch. Design, 1998; MFA, Dartmouth Coll., Hanover, NH, 2005. Cons. Met. Transit Authority, NYC, 2005; art instr. Nightingale-Bamford Sch., NYC, 2005. Guest lectr. Dept. Sociology, Brown U., 1999, 2002, 05, Smith Coll., 2000, Conn. River Valley Hospital, Middletown, Conn., 2000, Springfield Coll., 2001, Brattleboro Mus. and Art Ctr., 2001, The Delaney House, Holyoke, Mass., 2001, RI Sch. Design, 2005; presenter Forum on Hist. Records, U. Mass. Amherst, 2001, Nat. Conv. State Art Agencies, 2001, Sch. Arch., McGill U., Montréal, 2003; vis. artist Westborough Sate Hospital, Mass., 2001—04; disting. visitor Sch. Art & Design, U. Mich., 2006. Exhibitions include A Translatlantic Project, Muhle der schoenen Kunste, Germany, 1995, Off the Wall, 16 S. Main St. Gallery, Providence, 1998, National Prize Show, Cambridge Art Assn., Mus. Fine Art, Boston, 1998, Summer Show, Harvard U., 1999, Medfield State Hospital Closing: Projections, Dept. Mental Health, Westborough, Mass., 2004, Amherst Art Show, 2004, The Matzo Files, NYC, 2004—05, one-woman shows include Nada Mason Gallery, Northfield, Mass., 2000, Northampton Ctr. for Arts, 2000, exhibited in group shows at Kaelin Gallery, Boston, 2002, Pioneers of Public, Revolving Mus., Lowell, Mass., 2002, Inch x Inch, Arlington Ctr. for Arts, 2002, CHi of Ancestry, Gallery Luna, Salem, Mass., 2004, 1939 The Missing Year, New Art Ctr., Newton, Mass., 2005, Goliath, Brooklyn, 2006, installations, Habeas Corpus, Northampton State Hospital, 2000, When At Last, Brattleboro Mus. and Art Ctr., 2001, Bloom, Mass. Mental Health Ctr., 2003. Recipient Grad. Alumni award, Dartmouth Coll., 2005, Thesis Rsch. award, 2005; fellow MacDowell Colony, 2002, 2006, Yaddo, 2005, Radcliffe Inst., Harvard U., 2006—07; Artist Grant, Elizabeth Greenshields Found., 1996, Northampton Arts Coun., 2000, Mass. Found. for Humanities, 2000, Chubb Life Am. Fellow, MacDowell Colony, 2000—01, MacArthur Fellow, John D. and Catherine T. MacArthur Found., 2006. Office: HIstoric Northampton 46 Bridge St Northampton MA 01060 Office Phone: 413-584-6011. Office Fax: 413-584-7956.

SCHULENBERG, GARY MICHAEL, social studies educator; b. Buffalo, Feb. 9, 1951; s. Richard Franklin and Virginia Marie Schulenberg; children: Joel, Joshua, Bethany. BS in Social Studies Edn., Buffalo State Coll., 1973; MS in Social Studies Edn., U. Buffalo, 1978. Permanent tchr. cert. NY State Bd. Regents. Tchr. Bishop Neuman HS, Williamsville, NY, 1973—76; tchr. dept. chair social studies Cardinal O'Hara HS, Tonawanda, 1977—83, St. Mary's HS, Lancaster, 1984—. Dean of curriculum St. Mary's HS, 1984—. Organizer Kenton Peace Pilgrims, Kenmore, NY, 1978; vol. coach Kenton Soccer Assn., 1973—; leader Cub Scouts. Named Tchr. of Yr., Diocese of Buffalo, 1978; grantee, NEH, 1984. Mem.: Nat. Assn. Social Studies. Avocations: music, gardening, home improvement. Office: St Marys HS Ste 2 142 Laverack Ave Lancaster NY 14086-1899 Home: 81 Nassau St Kenmore NY 14217 Office Phone: 716-683-4824.

SCHULER, ALISON KAY, lawyer; b. West Point, NY, Oct. 1, 1948; d. Richard Hamilton and Irma (Sanken) S.; m. Lyman Gage Sandy, Mar. 30, 1974, (dec. Mar. 2002); 1 child, Theodore. AB cum laude, Radcliffe Coll., 1969; JD, Harvard U., 1972. Bar: Va. 1973, D.C. 1974, N.Mex. 1975. Assoc. Hunton & Williams, Richmond, Va., 1972-75; asst. U.S. atty. U.S. Atty.'s Office, Albuquerque, 1975-78; adj. prof. law U. N.Mex., 1983-85, 90, 98—; ptnr. Sutin, Thayer & Browne, Albuquerque, 1978-85, Montgomery & Andrews, P.A., Albuquerque, 1985-88; sole practice Albuquerque, 1988—. Bd. dirs. Am. Diabetes Assn., Albuquerque, 1980—85, chmn. bd. dirs., 1984—85; bd. dirs. Chamber Music Albuquerque, 1980—2006, pres., 1983—85, 1993—94; bd. dirs. Albuquerque Conservation Trust, 1986—90, N.Mex. Osteo. Found., 1993—96; chairperson Albuquerque Com. Fgn. Rels., 1984—85; mem. N.Mex. Internat. Trade and Investment Coun., Inc., 1986—; chartered org. rep. troop 444 Boy Scouts Am., 1997—, mem. nominating com., mem.-at-large dist. com. Sandia dist., 1998—, dist. vice chmn., 1999—2002, v.p. Great S.W. coun., 2001—05, pres. Great S.W. coun., 2006—, mem. staff, 2002—04, wood badge course dir., 2005; mem. adv. bd. Care Net Pregnancy Ctr. of Albuquerque, 2003—; mem. coun. St. Lukes Luth. Ch., 1976—80, 1982—84, 1991—96, pres., 1994—95. Named to, Best Lawyers Am., 2006; recipient Award of Merit, Sandia Dist., 2000, Svc. award, Albuquerque Astron. Soc., 2002, Silver Beaver award, Gt. S.W. Coun., 2002. Mem. Fed. Bar Assn. (coord.), ABA, Va. Bar Assn., N.Mex. Bar Assn. (chmn. corp., banking and bus. law 1982-83, bd. dirs. internat. and immigration law sect. 1987-95, chmn. 1993-94), Albuquerque Astron. Soc. (Svc. award 2002), Harvard U. Alumni Assn. (mem. fund campaign, regional dir. 1984-86, v.p. 1986-89, chmn. clubs com. 1985-88, chmn. communications com. 1988-91), Radcliffe Coll. Alumnae Assn. Bd. Mgmt. (regional dir. 1984-87, chmn. comms. com. 1988-91), Harvard-Radcliffe Club (pres. 1980-84). Home: 632 Cougar Loop NE Albuquerque NM 87122-1808 Office: 2155 Louisiana Blvd NE Ste 8500 Albuquerque NM 87110-5483 Office Phone: 505-872-0800. Personal E-mail: akschuler@aol.com.

SCHULER, DOROTHY R., education educator, consultant, retired elementary school educator; b. Tex., May 1, 1947; d. Raymond Lowell and Violet Marie Hayes; m. Robert Dale Schuler, Aug. 17, 1968; children: Christy Anne Bryant, Amy Lynne. BS in Elem. Edn., U. Tex., Austin, Tex., 1968; MS in Edn., So. Ill. U. at Edwardsville, Edswardsville, Ill., 1989. Cert. Nat. Bd. Tchr. Nat. Bd. for Profl. Tchg. Standards, 2001. Third grade tchr. Ashlawn Elem., Arlington, Va., 1968—69; fourth grade tchr. Bret Harte Elem., Cherry Hill, NJ, 1969—70; kindergarten tchr. Dow Elem. Sch., Dow, Ill., 1982—86; second grade tchr. Grafton Elem. Sch., Grafton, Ill., 1986—2004; coll. instr. and cons. Greenville Coll., Greenville, Ill., 2004—. Cons./presenter Schuler's Schoolars Consulting, Elsah, Ill., 1996—; coll. instr. So. Ill. U. at Edwardsville, Edswardsville, Ill., 1998—2000. Contbr. scientific papers to profl. jours. Recipient Tchr. of the Yr., Wal Mart, 1999. Mem.: Nat. Assn. Edn. of Young Children, Ill. Project Support Group. Methodist. Avocations: golf, writing, reading, gardening. Office: 13610 Schuler Ln Dow IL 62022-9721 Home Phone: 618-466-5345; Office Phone: 618-466-5345. Business E-Mail: dorothy.schuler@greenville.edu.

SCHULER, MARY CALLAGHAN, artist, educational association administrator; b. Upper Darby, Pa., Aug. 15, 1938; d. John J. Callaghan and Catherine Graham Callaghan O'Reilly; m. Richard E. Schuler, May 12, 1962; children: Richard E., Anne E., Judith M. Cert. in Oil Painting, RI Sch. Design, Providence, 1972; BS, Cornell U., Ithaca, NY, 1979. Dir. activities Ithacare Ctr., Ithaca, NY, 1979—82; exec. staff asst. Einaudi Ctr. Internat. Studies Cornell U., Ithaca, 1983—93. Exhibitions include Logan Ridge Winery, 2002, Clinton Ho. Artspace, 2002, State of the Art Gallery, 2004—06, Upstairs Gallery, 2005—06, Cmty. Sch. Music and Art, Ithaca, 2005, Tompkins Cmty. Libr., 2005. Bd. dirs. State of the Art Gallery, Ithaca, 2004—07. Mem.: Cornell Alumni Assn. and Club, Cornell Campus Club, Ithaca Garden Club, Sigma Alpha Iota. Avocations: painting, reading, walking. Home: 2 Captains Walk Ithaca NY 14850-8502 Personal E-mail: mcs@lightlink.com.

SCHULER, ROBERT LEO, appraiser, consultant; b. Cin., June 15, 1943; s. Del D. and Virginia D. (Heyl) S.; m. Shelagh J. Moritz, Aug. 11, 1962; children: Robert C., Sherry L. V.p. Comprehensive Appraisal Service, Cin., 1977—. Bd. dirs. Hamilton County Regional Planning Commn., Cin., 1987-88; mem. exec. com., past pres. OKI Regional Coun. Govts., Cin., 1981-92. Councilman City of Deer Park, Ohio, 1979-86; trustee Sycamore Twp., 1988-92; Ohio state rep. 36th dist., 1993—2000; senator, 7th Dist., Ohio, 2003-; active Scarlet Oaks Bus. Adv. Coun. Recipient United Conservatives of Ohio Watchdog of the Treasury award, 1994, 1996, 1998, 2005; Coun. of State Govts. Toll fellow, 2004. Mem. Cin. Bd. Realtors, Ohio Assn. Realtors, Jaycees (v.p.). Republican. Roman Catholic. Home: 3648 Jeffrey Ct Cincinnati OH 45236-1544 Office: State House of Ohio Columbus OH 43215 Office Phone: 614-466-9737.

SCHULER, THEODORE ANTHONY, retired civil engineer; b. Louisville, July 1, 1934; s. Henry R. and Virginia (Meisner) S.; m. Jane A. Bandy, July 29, 1979; children: Marc, Elizabeth, Eric, Ellen. BCE, U. Louisville, 1957, M Engring., 1973. Registered profl. engr., Tenn. Design constrn. engr. Brighton Engring. Co., Frankfort, Ky., 1960—65; design engr. Hensley-Schmidt Inc., Chattanooga, 1965—68, assoc., 1969—73, sr. assoc., 1973—75, prin., asst. v.p., head Knoxville office, 1975—81; chief planning engr. engring. dept. City Knoxville, 1981—96, ret., 1996. Served to lt. (j.g.) USNR, 1957-60. Fellow ASCE. Home: 5907 Adelia Dr Knoxville TN 37920-5801 Personal E-mail: tschu30447@aol.com.

SCHULHOF, MICHAEL PETER, electronics company executive; b. NYC, Nov. 30, 1942; s. Rudolph B. and Hannelore (Buck) Schulhof; m. Paola Nissim, Apr. 17, 1969; children: David Kenneth, Jonathan Nissim. BA, Grinnell Coll., 1964, DSc (hon.), 1990; MS, Cornell U., 1967; PhD, Brandeis U., 1970. Lic. comml. pilot. Am. rsch. fellow Brookhaven Nat. Lab., Uptown, NY, 1969—71; asst. to v.p. mfg. CBS Records, Inc., NYC, 1971—73, exec. com., bd. dirs., 1987—88; from gen. mgr. bus. products divsn. to sr. v.p. Sony Corp., NYC, 1973—86; pres. Sony Industries, NYC, 1978—86; chmn. Digital Audio Disc Corp., Terre Haute, Ind., 1986—96; pres. Sony Software Corp., 1991—96; pres., CEO Sony Corp. Am., 1993—95. Chmn. bd. dirs. Quadriga Art Inc., 1980—, World On Line, 1998—99; bd. dirs. Sony Corp., Japan, Sony Corp. Am., Sony Pictures Entertainment, Materials Rsch. Corp., J2 Global Commn., 1997—, CBS/Sportsline; chmn. Sony Music Entertainment; former chmn. Comml. Electronics, 1998—; chmn., CEO Global Tech. Investments, 2001—; mem., coun. of fgn. rels. and investment; svcs. policy, adv. com. U.S. Trade Rep. Contbr. articles to profl. jours. Trustee Brandeis U., 1990—, Lincoln Ctr. for Performing Arts, Inc., NYC, Brookings Instn., Washington; investment and svcs. policy adv. com. U.S. Trade Rep.; active Coun. Fgn. Rels.; bd. dirs. Ctr. on Addiction and Substance Abuse at Columbia U., NYC, Am. Hosp. of Paris Found. Fellow, NSF, 1970. Master: Am. Phys. Soc. (bd. dirs. 1978); mem.: Am. Radio Relay League, Computer and Bus. Equipment Mfrs. Assn. (bd. dirs.), Whitney Mus., Guggenhiem Mus., Aircraft Owners and Pilots Assn., Atlantic Golf Club, Fenway Golf Club, Profile Club, East Hampton Tennis Club, Gipsy Trail Club, Harmony Club. Achievements include patents for audio disc apparatus. Office: 375 Park Ave New York NY 10152-0002

SCHULHOFER, STEPHEN JOSEPH, law educator; b. NYC, Aug. 20, 1942; s. Joseph and Myrelle S.; m. Laurie Wohl, May 28, 1975; children: Samuel, Jonah. AB, Princeton U., 1964; LLB, Harvard U., 1967. Bar: DC 1968, US Dist. Ct. Ea. Dist. Pa. 1973, US Supreme Ct. 1973. Law clk. to Justice Hugo L. Black, US Supreme Ct., Washington, 1967-69; assoc. Coudert Freres, Paris, 1969-72; asst. prof. law U. Pa., Phila., 1972-77, assoc. prof., 1977-81, prof., 1981-85, Ferdinand Wakeman Hubbell prof., 1985-86; prof. U. Chgo. Law Sch., 1986-2001, dir. Ctr. for Studies Criminal Justice, 1987-2001; prof law NYU Sch. Law, 2001—, Robert B. McKay prof. law, 2002-. Vis. prof. U. Chgo., 1985, NYU Sch. Law, 2001; speedy trial reporter US Dist. Ct. Dist. Del., Wilmington, 1975-80; cons. US EPA, Washington, 1977-78, US Sentencing Commn., Washington, 1987-94. Author: Prosecutorial Discretion and Federal Sentencing Reform, 1979, Unwanted Sex: The Culture of Intimidation and the Failure of Law, 1998, REthinking the Patriot Act, 2005; editor: Criminal Law and its Processes, 1983, 89, 95, 2001, 05; contbr. articles to profl. journals. Trustee, Cmty. Legal Services, Inc., Phila., 1981-86. Walter Meyer grantee Am. Bar Found., 1984. Mem. ACLU (Ill. bd. dirs. 1983-97), Law and Soc. Assn. Office: NYU Sch Law Vanderbilt Hall Rm 319 40 Washington Sq S New York NY 10012-1099 E-mail: schulhos@juris.law.nyu.edu.

SCHULHOFF, KAREN L., information specialist; b. Long Island City, NY, Dec. 11, 1959; d. Edward and Eleanor (Gillespie) S. MLS, CUNY, 1993. Tng. program coord. Chem. Bank, NYC, 1983-90; libr. Katharine Gibbs Sch., NYC, 1990-92; cons. Pfizer, NYC, 1993-2001; info. specialist, rschr. Bear, Stearns Investment Banking, NYC, 2001—; founder, owner Smack Cosmetics, Inc., 2004—. Mem.: NAFE, Am. Mgmt. Assn. Office: Bear Stearns Investment Banking 383 Madison Ave New York NY 10167

SCHULIAN, JOHN (NIELSEN SCHULIAN), screenwriter, author; b. LA, Jan. 31, 1945; s. John and Estella Katherine (Nielsen) S.; m. Paula Lynn Ellis, Aug. 20, 1977 (div. Oct. 1984). BA, U. Utah, 1967; MS, Northwestern U., 1968. Copy editor Salt Lake City Tribune, 1968; reporter Balt. Evening Sun, 1970-75; sportswriter Washington Post, 1975-77; sports columnist Chgo. Daily News, 1977-78, Chgo. Sun-Times, 1978-84, Phila. Daily News, 1984-86; staff writer Miami Vice, Universal City, Calif., 1986-87, story editor, 1987, The Slap Maxwell Story, North Hollywood, Calif., 1987-88; exec. story editor TV series Wiseguy, Hollywood, 1988-89; co-prodr. TV series Midnight Caller, Burbank, Calif., 1989-90, supervising prodr., 1990-91; co-exec. prodr. TV series Reasonable Doubts, Burbank, 1991-92; creative cons. TV series The Untouchables, LA, 1992-93; co-exec. prodr. TV series Hercules, Universal City, Calif., 1994-96; co-creator Xena: Warrior Princess, Universal City, 1995; assoc. prodr. (documentary) Ben Johnson: Third Cowboy on the Right, 1996; co-exec. prodr. (TV series) Lawless, 1996-97; consulting prodr. (TV series) JAG, 1999-2000; exec. prodr. (TV series) The Outer Limits, Vancouver, Canada, 2000-01; culture columnist MSNBC.com, 2001—02; co-exec prodr. (TV series) Tremors, Universal City, 2002—03. Spl. contbr. Sports Illustrated, 1998—; profl. in residence U. Utah, 2004. Author: Writers' Fighters and Other Sweet Scientists, 1983, Twilight of the Long Ball Gods, 2005; contbg. editor Panorama mag., 1980-81; syndicated columnist UP Syndicate; commentator Nat. Pub. Radio, 1985-86; cons. The Reader's Catalog, 1989; contbr. articles to NY Times, Playboy, Gentlemen's Quar.,

Oxford Am.Mag., The National, LA Times; included in The Best Am. Sports Writing, 1994. Mem. Pacific Coast League Hist. Soc. With U.S. Army, 1968-70. Recipient Nat. Headliners Club award, 1980, Column Writing award AP Sports Editors, 1979, 82, Best Sports Stories award, 1983, 84, Nat Fleischer Excellence in Boxing Journalism award Boxing Writers Assn. Am., 1985. Mem. Writers Guild Am., Phi Beta Kappa. Office: Endeavor Talent Agy 9701 Wilshire Blvd 10th Fl Beverly Hills CA 90212 also: Sterling Lord Literistic 35 Bleecker St New York NY 10012 Personal E-mail: jschulian@aol.com.

SCHULKERS, JOAN M., lawyer; Grad., William Mitchell Coll. Law, 1999. Bar: Minn. Ptnr. Borman & Schulkers, P.L.L.P., Mpls. Named a Rising Star, Minn. Super Lawyers mag., 2006. Mem.: Minn. Women Lawyers, Minn. State Bar Assn. (bd. govs. 2001—, chair new lawyers sect. 2003—04, vice chair new lawyers sect. 2002—03, sec. new lawyers sect. 2001—02), Hennepin County Bar Assn. (sec. 2001—02, bd. govs. 2001—04, mem. exec. com. 2002—03, chair new lawyers sect. 2002—03, co-chair litig. sect. 2004—06). Office: Borman & Schulkers PLLP 250 3rd Ave North Ste 530 Minneapolis MN 55401 Office Phone: 612-332-3096. E-mail: joan@bormanschulkers.com. *

SCHULL, NATASHA DOW, anthropologist, educator; b. San Francisco, May 11, 1971; d. Diantha Dow and Walter Bruno Schull. PhD, U. Calif., Berkeley, 2002, BA, 1993. Health and soc. scholar Robert Wood Johnson Found., 2003—05; asst. prof. MIT, Boston, 2007—. Dir.(editor, prodr.): (documentary film) BUFFET: All You Can Eat Las Vegas (Best Short Film award, Am. Anthrop. Assn., 2006). Creative dir. Axis of Eve, NYC, 2003—05. Grantee, NSF, 2006—; Lambda Alpha scholar, Nat. Collegiate Honors Soc., 1993, Charlotte W. Newcombe fellow, Woodrow Wilson Found., 1999, Weatherhead fellow, Sch. Advanced Rsch. on Human Experience, 2002. Mem.: Phi Beta Kappa (scholar 1999). Home Phone: 646-326-3604.

SCHULLER, DAVID EDWARD, cancer center administrator, otolaryngologist; b. Cleve., Oct. 20, 1944; m. Carole Ann Hauss, June 24, 1967; children: Rebecca, Michael. BA, Rutgers U., 1966; MD cum laude, Ohio State U., 1970. Diplomate Am. Bd. Otolaryngology 1975. Intern dept. surgery U. Hosps. Cleve., 1970-71; resident dept. otolaryngology Ohio State U., Columbus, 1971-72; resident dept. surgery U. Hosps. Cleve., 1972-73; fellow head and neck surgery Pack Med. Found. with John Conley, NYC, 1973; resident dept. otolaryngology Ohio State U. Hosps., Columbus, 1973-75; fellow head and neck oncology and facial plastic and reconstructive surgery U. Iowa, Iowa City, 1975-76; trustee Ohio Cancer Found, 1988—; from clin. instr. to prof. and chmn. dept. otolaryngology The Ohio State U., Columbus, 1971—; dir. Am. Bd. Otolaryngology, 1988—2000, Comprehensive Cancer Ctr., Columbus, 1997—; prof. sect. oral biology, Coll. Dentistry The Ohio State U., 1990—; dir. Arthur G. James Cancer Hosp. & Richard J. Solove Rsch. Inst., Columbus, 1988—; chair dept. otolaryngology Ohio State U., Columbus, 1990—; past pres. American Board of Otolaryngology. Mem., chmn. various coms. Ohio State U. Hosps. and Coll. Medicine, 1976—; dir. CCC head and neck oncology program Ohio State U., 1977—, hosps. physician flr. coord. 10th flr., 1977-82, dir. laser-microsurgery teaching and rsch. lab., 1987-88; mem. various coms. Grant Hosp., 1980-84; mem. Accreditation Coun. for the Grad. Med. Edn. Residency Review Com. for Otolaryngology, 1985—, chmn., 1988—; vis. prof., lectr., ACS prof. clin. Oncology, 1989-94. numerous instns. Author: (books) (with others) Otolaryngology-Head and Neck Surgery-4 Vols., 1986, Textbook of Otolaryngology-7th Edit., 1988, Otolaryngology-Head and Neck Surgery-Update I, 1988, Musculocutaneous Flaps in Head and Neck Reconstructive Surgery, 1989, Otolaryngology-Head and Neck Surgery Update II, 1990, Otorinolaringologia-Cirugia de Cabeza y Culleo, 1991, Otolaryngology-Head and Neck Surgery-4 Vols., 1992; contbr. chpts. to books and articles to profl. jours.; mem. editorial bd. New Horizons in Otolaryngology/Head and Neck Surgery, 1982-87, The Laryngoscope, 1986—, Am. Jour. Otolaryngology, 1988—, Facial Plastic Surgery Internat. Quar. Monographs, 1992—; mem. rev. bd. Jour. Head and Neck Surgery, 1985—; mem. editorial rev. bd. Otolaryngology-Head and Neck Surgery, 1990—; reviewer New Eng. Jour Medicine, 1992—. Recipient Cert. of Appreciation, Scioto Meml. Hosp., 1982, Edmund Prince Fowler award Triological Soc., 1984; Henry Rutgers scholar Rutgers U., 1965-66; grantee Nat. Cancer Inst., 1980-88, 90-97, Bremer Found., 1982-83, 87-88, Photomedica Inc., 1986-89, Upjohn Co., 1986-90, others. Mem. AMA (mem. rev. panel Archives of Otolaryngology-Head and Neck Surgery 1984—), Am. Cancer Soc. (mem. instl. grant rev. com. 1980—, chmn. rehab. com. Franklin County unit 1981-82, mem. profl. edn. com. 1981—, chmn. 1982-85, v.p. 1982-83, pres. 1986, 87, trustee Ohio divsn. 1988—), Am. Assn. Cosmetic Surgeons, Am. Acad. Facial Plastic and Reconstructive Surgery (mem. rsch. com. 1977-82, chmn. residency rels. com. 1982-85, mem. program com. 1982-85, v.p. mid. sect. 1983-87, chmn. by-laws com. 1988-90, treas. 1988-90, Honor award 1989), Am. Coll. Surgeons, Am. Cleft Palate Assn., Assn. Am. Cancer Insts., Am. Soc. Head and Neck Injury, Am. Acad. Otolaryngology Head and Neck Surgery (mem. editorial bd. self-instructional package program 1982—, del. bd. govs. 1982-87, Honor award 1983), Am. Soc. Laser Medicine and Surgery, Am. Laryngological, Rhinological, Otological Soc., Inc., Am. Laryngological Assn., Am. Soc. Clin. Oncology (mem. program com. 1989—), Am. Assn. Cancer Researchers, Am. Soc. Head and Neck Surgery (mem. coun. 1983-86, chmn. scholastic and fellowship award com. 1984-86, mem. profl. rels. and pub. edn. com. 1989—), Southwest Oncology Group (chmn. head and neck com. 1983—), Collegium ORLAS, Ohio State Med. Assn. (pres. sect. otolaryngology 1987—), Ohio Soc. Otolaryngology (pres. 1985, 86, 87), Acad. Medicine of Columbus and Franklin County, Columbus E.E.N.T. Soc., Franklin County Acad. Medicine (mem. profl. rels. com. 1982—), Head and Neck Intergroup (vice-chmn. 1984-86, chmn. 1986-89), Assn. Rsch. Otolaryngology, Ohio State U. Med. Alumni Soc. (class rep. 1980—, v.p. 1987-88, pres. 1989-90), Med. Forum, Med. Review Club, Order of Hippocrates (charter), Alpha Omega Alpha. Office: 456 W 10th Ave Columbus OH 43210-1240 also: Ohio State Univ Comp Cancer Ctr 300 W 10th Ave Columbus OH 43210-1240

SCHULLER, GUNTHER ALEXANDER, composer; b. NYC, Nov. 22, 1925; s. Arthur E. and Elsie (Bernartz) Schuller; m. Marjorie Black, June 8, 1948; children: Edwin Gunther, George Alexander. Student, St. Thomas Choir Sch., NYC; MusD (hon.), Manhattan Sch. Music, 1987, Northeastern U., 1967, U. Ill., 1968, Colby Coll., 1969, Williams Coll., 1975, Cleve. Inst. Music, 1977, New Eng. Conservatory Music, 1978, Rutgers U., 1980, Manhattan Sch. Music, 1987, Oberlin Coll., 1989. Tchr. Manhattan Sch. Music, 1950—63; head composition dept. Tanglewood, 1963—84; pres. New Eng. Conservatory Music, 1967—77; artistic dir. Berkshire Music Ctr., Tanglewood, 1969—84, Festival at Sandpoint, 1985—. Founder, pres. Margun Music Inc., 1975, GM Recs., 1980. Author: The Swing Era, 1989; French horn player Ballet Theatre, then prin. horn player Cin. Symphony Orch., 1943—45, prin. French horn Met. Opera Orch., 1945—59, Concerto #1 for Horn, 1945; composer: Concerto for Cello and Orchestra, 1945, Six Early Songs, 1945, Quartet for Four Double Basses, 1947, Jumpin' in the Future for jazz ensemble, 1948, Perpetrum Mobile for Four Horns, 1948, Fantasy for Unaccompanied Cello, 1951, Adago for Flund String Trio, 1952, Recitative and Rondo for Violin and Piano, 1953, Music for Violin, Piano and Percussion, 1957, Contours, 1958, Woodwind Quintet, 1958, Seven Studies on Themes of Paul Klee, 1959, Spectra, 1960, Six Renaissance Lyrics, 1962, String Quartet No. 2, 1965, Symphony, 1965, Capriccio Stravagante, 1972, The Power Within Us, 1972, Tre Invenzioni, 1972, Three Nocturnes, 1973, Four Soundscapes, 1974, Concerto No. 2 for Orch., 1975, Triplum II, 1975, Horn Concerto No. 2, 1976, Violin Concerto, 1976, Diptych for organ, 1976, Sonata Serenata, 1978, Contrabassoon Concerto, 1978, Deaï for 3 orchs., 1978, Trumpet Concerto, 1979, Octet, 1979, Eine Kleine Posaunemusik, 1980, In Praise of Winds (Symphony for Large Wind Orch.), 1981, Symphony for Organ, 1982, Concerto Quaternio, 1983, Concerto for Bassoon and Orch., 1984, On Light Wings (piano quartet), 1984, Farbenspiel (Concerto No. 3 for Orch.), 1985; author: Horn Technique, 1962, Early Jazz: Its Roots and Development, 1968, Musings: The Musical Worlds of Gunther Schuller, 1985; composer: A Bouquet for Collage for chamber ensemble, 1988; premier of Symphony for Brass and Percussion, Cin., 1950, Salzburg Festival, 1957; Dramatic Overture, N.Y. Philharm., 1956; String Quartet, Number 1 Contemporary Arts Festival, U. Ill., 1957, Concertino for Jazz Quartet and Orch., Balt. Symphony Orch., 1959, Seven Studies on Themes of Paul Klee, Ford Found., commn., Minn. Symphony, 1959, Spectra, N.Y. Philharm., 1960, Music for Brass Quintet, Coolidge Found., Libr. of Congress, 1961, Concerto No. 1 for Orch., Chgo. Symphony Orch., 1966, Triplum, N.Y. Philharm. commd. Lincoln Ctr., 1967, Aphorisms for Flute and String Trio commd., Carleton Coll. Centennial, 1967, Eine Kleine Posaunenmusik, 1980, In Praise of Winds, 1983, Concerto Quaternio, N.Y. Philharm., 1983, Duologue for Violin and Piano, Libr. of Congress, 1984, Farbenspiel, Berlin Philharm., 1985, Concerto for Viola and Orch., 1985, String Quartet No. 3, 1986, Chimeric Images, 1988, Concerto for String Quartet and Orchestra, 1988, Concerto for Flute and Orchestra, 1988, On Winged Flight: A Divertimento for Band, 1989, Chamber Concerto, 1989, Concerto for Piano Three Hands, 1989, Phantasmata for Violin and Marinba, 1989, 5 Impromptus Eng. Horn and String Quartet, 1989, Impromptus and Cadenzas, 1990, premier of Hommage à Rayechka for 8 cellos/or multiples thereof, 1990, A Trio Setting for clarinet, violin, piano, 1990, Violin Concert No. 2, 1991, Sonata Fantasia for piano, 1992, Ritmica-Melodia-Armonia for orch., 1992, Of Reminiscences and Reflections for orch., 1993 (Pulitzer prize for music, 1994), Brass Quintet No. 2, 1993, The Past is in the Present for orch., 1994, Sextet for left hand piano and woodwind quintet, 1994, Concerto for organ and orch., 1994, Mondrian's Vision, 1994, Magnificat and Nunc Dimittis (choir), 1994, Headin Out, Movin In (jazz ensemble), 1994, Lament for M (jazz ensemble), 1994, Rush Hour an 23d St., 1994, Blue Dawn into White Heat (concert band), 1995, An Arc Ascending, 1996; composer: Bright and Sassy, 1997, Ohio River Reflections for Piano Trio and Horn, 1998, Sonata for Alto Saxophone, 1999, Fantasie Impromptu for Flutet Hpschd, 2000, Quodlibet - Vln, Cello, Oboe, Horn, and Harp, 2001, The Birth of the Cool Suite, 2001, String Quartet No. 4, 2002, Concerto da Camera No. 2, 2002, rev. Duo Concertante for Cello and Piano, 2002, Four Preludes for Harp, 2002, Encounters for Jazz Band and Large Symphony Orch., 2003, String Trio, 2003, Grand Concerts for Percussion Ensemble and Three Keyboards, 2005, Nature's Way for Band/Wind Ensemble, 2006, Refrains (for ten euphoniums, twelve tubas), 2006, Where the World Ends (for orch.), 2006, (Operas) The Visitation, 1966, Fisherman and His Wife, 1970. Named Guggenheim fellow, 1962, 1963, MacArthur fellow, 1991, Composer of Yr., Mus. Am., 1995; named to Am. Classical Music Hall of Fame, 1998; recipient Creative Arts award, Brandeis U., 1960, Deems Taylor award, ASCAP, 1970, Alice M. Ditson Conducting award, 1970, Rodgers and Hammerstein award, 1971, Friedheim award, 1988, William Schuman award, Columbia U., 1989, Down Beat Lifetime Achievement award, 1993, BMI Lifetime Achievement award, 1994, Gold medal, Am. Acad. Arts and Letters, 1997, Order of Merit Cross, Fed. Republic of Germany, 1997, Max Rudolf award, 1998. Mem.: Am. Acad. Arts and Scis., Nat. Inst. Arts and Letters. Address: 167 Dudley Rd Newton Center MA 02459-2830 Office Phone: 617-332-6328.

SCHULLER, ROBERT HAROLD, minister, writer; b. Alton, Iowa, Sept. 16, 1926; s. Anthony and Jennie (Beltman) Schuller; m. Arvella DeHaan, June 15, 1950; children: Sheila, Jeanne, Carol, Gretchen. BA, Hope Coll., 1947; BD, Western Theol. Sem., 1950; DD, Hope Coll., 1973; LLD, Azusa Pacific Coll., 1970, Pepperdine U., 1976; LittD, Barrington Coll., 1977. Ordained to ministry Reformed Ch. Am., 1950. Pastor Ivanhoe Ref. Ch., Chgo., 1950—55; founder, sr. pastor Garden Grove Cmry. Ch., Calif., 1955—; founder, pres. Hour of Power TV Ministry, 1970—; founder, dir. Robert H. Schuller Inst. for Successful Ch. Leadership, 1970—; chmn. nat. religious sponsor program Religion in Am. Life, NYC, 1975—. Bd. dirs. Freedoms Found. Author: God's Way to the Good Life, 1963, Your Future Is Your Friend, 1964, Move Ahead with Possibility Thinking, 1967, Self Love, the Dynamic Force of Success, 1969, Power Ideas for a Happy Family, 1972, The Greatest Possiboloty Thinker That Ever Lived, 1973, Turn Your Scars into Stars, 1973, You Can Become the Person You Want To Be, 1973, Your Church Has Real Possibilities, 1974, Love or Loneliness - You Decide, 1974, Positive Prayers for Power-Filled Living, 1976, Keep on Believing, 1976, Reach Out for A New Life, 1977, Peace of Mind Through Possibility Thinking, 1977, Turning You Stress Into Strength, 1978, Daily Power Thoughts, 1978, The Peak to Peek Principle, 1981, Living Positively One Day at a Time, 1981, Self Esteen: The New Reformation, 1982, Tough Times Never Last, But, Tough People Do!, 1983, Tough Minded Faith for Tender Hearted People, 1984, The Be-Happy Attitudes, 1985, Be Happy You Are Loved, 1986, Success is Never Ending, Failure is Never Final, 1988, Believe in the God Who Believes in You, 1989; co-author: The Courage of Carol, 1978. Founder Robert H. Schuller Corr. Ctr. Possibility Thinkers, 1976; bd. dirs. Religion in Am. Life; pres. bd. dirs. Christian Counseling Svcs. Named Headliner of Yr. in Religion, Orange County, 1977, Clergyman of Yr., Religious Heritage Am., 1977; recipient Ddisting. Alumnus award, Hope Coll., 1970, Prin. award, Freedoms Found., 1974. Mem.: AIA (bd. dirs. 1986—), Religious Guild Architects (hon.), Rotary. Office: Religion Am Life 12141 Lewis St Garden Grove CA 92840-4627

SCHULMAN, ALAN, lawyer; b. Bklyn., Sept. 7, 1949; BA, NYU, 1971; JD, La. State Univ., 1974. Bar: La. 1974, Tex. 1974, Wash. 1982, Calif. 1986, US Dist. Ct. (so. dist. Calif. 1987, no. & ctrl. dist. Calif. 1989), US Ct. Appeals (5th & 11th cir. 1981, 9th cir. 1982), US Supreme Ct. 1995. Ptnr., Complex Class Action Litigation Bernstein Litowitz Berger & Grossmann, San Diego. Adj. prof. Univ. San Diego Sch. Law, 2000—; co-chmn. so. dist. Calif. Lawyer Reps. Ninth Cir. Judicial Conf., 2000—01, mem. exec. com., 2002—04, Conf. co-chmn., 2005. Editor (assoc.): La. Law Rev. Mem.: ABA (co-chmn. Securities Law com.), Fed. Bar Assn., Wash. State Bar Assn., La. State Bar Assn., State Bar Tex., State Bar Calif., Assn. Bus. Trial Lawyers San Diego (pres. 2001, mem. bd. gov. 1995—2001), Order of the Coif. Office Phone: 858-720-3185. Office Fax: 858-793-0323. Business E-Mail: alans@blbglaw.com.

SCHULMAN, CATHY, film producer; Prodn. and acquisitions exec. Samuel Goldwyn Co.; founder Artists Production Group, 1999, pres.; ptnr. Bull's Eye Enterntainment. Co-dir. Sundance Film Festival, 1989—91. Assoc. prodr. (films) Isn't She Great?, 2000, Tears of the Sun, 2003; prodr.: (films) Sidewalks of New York, 2001, You Stupid Man, 2002, Employee of the Month, 2004, Godsend, 2004, Crash, 2005 (Best Motin Picture of Yr., Acad. Motion Pictures Arts and Sciences, 2006); exec. prodr.: Thumbsucker, 2005. Office: Bull's Eye Entertainment 4th Floor 10850 Wilshire Blvd Los Angeles CA 90024

SCHULMAN, CLIFFORD A., lawyer; b. Dec. 6, 1947; s. George and Henrietta Schulman; m. Michele Weissman, June 28, 1969; 1 child, David Michael. B.S. in Journalism and Communications cum laude, U. Fla., 1969, J.D., 1972. Bar: Fla. 1972, U.S. Supreme Ct. 1981, U.S. Ct. Appeals (5th cir.) 1975. Law clk. to Eugene P. Spellman, Miami, Fla., 1970-71; research aide to Judge Norman Hendry, Miami, 1972-73; asst. county atty. Met. Dade County, Miami, 1973-79; ptnr. Greenberg, Traurig (formerly Greenberg, Traurig, Askew, Hoffman, Lipoff, Rosen & Quentel), Miami, 1979—. Editor-in-chief continuing legal edn. manual Environ. Regulation and Litigation in Fla., 1981 edit. Mem. Gov.'s Task Force on Biscayne Bay Rules, 1978; del. 57th biennial conv. Am. Hebrew Congregations, 1983. Served to capt. USAR, 1969-73. Mem. Fla. Bar (co-editor environ. law sect. newsletter 1977-80; exec. council environ. and land use law sect. 1979-83, sec.-treas. 1981-83, chmn. 1984-85). Office: Greenberg Traurig 1221 Brickell Ave Miami FL 33131-3224 Office Phone: 305-579-0613. Office Fax: 305-961-5613. Business E-Mail: schulmanc@gtlaw.com.

SCHULMAN, HAROLD, obstetrician, gynecologist; b. Newark, Oct. 26, 1930; m. Rosemarie Vincenti; children: Stanley H., Sandra C., Gina M. BS, U. Fla., 1951; MD, Emory U., 1955. Diplomate Am. Bd. Ob-Gyn., Am. Bd. Maternal and Fetal Medicine; registered diagnostic med. sonographer. Intern Jackson Meml. Hosp., Miami, Fla., 1955-56, resident, 1958-61; instr. dept. ob-gyn. U. Miami (Fla.) Sch. Medicine, 1961; instr., asst. prof. dept. ob-gyn. Temple U. Sch. Medicine, Phila., 1961-65; asst. prof. dept. ob-gyn. Albert Einstein Coll. Medicine, Bronx, 1965-67, assoc. prof., 1968-71, prof., 1971—, acting dept. chmn., 1972—80, chmn., 1973-80; assoc. dir. dept. ob-gyn Bronx Mcpl. Hosp. Ctr., 1967-70, dep. dir., 1970-72; chmn. dept. ob-gyn. Winthrop U. Hosp., Mineola, NY, 1984-93; prof. ob-gyn SUNY, Stony Brook, 1984-93; chmn. dept. ob-gyn. Lawnwood Regional Med. Ctr., Ft. Pierce, Fla., 1995-2000. Author: Tipping the Scales, 2005; contbr. articles to profl. publs. Served to capt. U.S. Army, 1956-58. Am. Cancer Soc. fellow, 1959-60; USPHS trainee, 1965-66 Fellow ACOG (vice chmn. Dist. II 1972-75); mem. Bronx County Obstet. Soc. (pres. 1974), AAAS, Obstet. Soc. (sec. 1978-80, pres. 1982-83), N.Y. Obstetrical Soc., Soc. Maternal Fetal Medicine, Am. Gynecologic and Obstetric Soc., Am. Gynecol. Obstetrics, N.Y. Obstetics Soc. (pres. 1982), Phi Beta Kappa, Alpha Omega Alpha; hon. mem. Miami Ob-Gyn. Soc., South Atlantic Obstetricians and Gynecologists Soc., Buffalo Gynecologic and Obstetric Soc. (E.G. Winkler meml. lectr.), Croatian Ultrasound Soc. (hon.). Democrat. Jewish. Office Phone: 914-747-4168. Personal E-mail: hschulman@sprintmail.com.

SCHULMAN, JOSEPH DANIEL, physician, health facility administrator, medical geneticist, educator; b. Bklyn., Dec. 20, 1941; s. Max and Miriam (Grossman) S.; m. Dixie A. King; children: Erica N., Julie K. BA, Bklyn. Coll., 1961; MD, Harvard U., 1966. Diplomate Am. Bd. Pediat., Am. Bd. Ob-Gyn., Am. Bd. Med. Genetics. Intern, then resident in pediat. Mass. Gen. Hosp., Boston, 1966-68; clin. assoc. Nat. Inst. Arthritis and Metabolic Diseases, 1968-70; resident in obstetrics and gynecology and fellow in pediatrics N.Y. Hosp.-Cornell Med. Ctr., 1970-73; Gilbert and Nat. Found. fellow Cambridge (Eng.) U., 1973-74; head sect. human biochem. genetics Nat. Inst. Child Health and Human Devel., NIH, Bethesda, Md., 1974-83; dir. med. genetics program NIH, Bethesda, 1979-1983; prof. ob-gyn., pediat., genetics George Washington U., 1983-84; CEO Genetics & IVF Inst., Fairfax, Va., 1984-98, chmn., 1984—2001, 2004—; prof. human genetics, pediat., ob-gyn. Med. Coll., Va. Commonwealth U., 1984—; with dept. ob-gyn. Fairfax Hosp., 1984—. Affiliate prof. ob-gyn. U. Cal., San Diego, 2003—; advisor to numerous govt. and pvt. orgns. Author 3 books; contbr. numerous articles to med. jours.; editorial bd. Molecular Human Reproduction, 1995—, numerous other sci. jours. With USPHS, 1968-70, 74-83. Fellow ACOG; mem. Soc. Pediat. Rsch., Soc. Gynecologic Investigation, Am. Soc. Clin. Investigation, Am. Soc. Human Genetics, Am. Fertility Soc., Harvard Club, Cosmos Club, Calif. Club, Phi Beta Kappa, Sigma Xi. Office: 3015 Williams Dr Fairfax VA 22031

SCHULMAN, ROBERT S., lawyer; b. NYC, July 9, 1941; s. Donald Benedict and Edythe (Smythe) Schulman; m. Susan Jan Von Helbig, Sept. 18, 1974; children: Elizabeth Jane, Jennifer Lynn. BA, Rutgers U., New Brunswick, 1963; JD cum laude, Rutgers U., Newark, 1966. Bar: NJ 1967, US Dist. Ct. NJ 1967, US Supreme Ct. 1970, Calif. 1976, US Dist. Cts. (ctrl., no., so. and ea. dists.) Calif. 1976, US Ct. Appeals (9th cir.) 1976. With Pitney, Hardin & Kipp, Newark, 1966-74; dep. atty. gen. Office of NJ Atty. Gen., Trenton, 1974-75; assoc. Cox, Castle & Nicholson, LA, 1976-80; ptnr. Zobrist, Garner & Garrett, LA, 1980-83, Stephens, Berg, Lasater & Schulman, LA, 1984-91, Crosby, Heafey, Roach & May, LA, 1991—2002, Fulbright & Jaworski, LLP, LA, 2002—. Atty. Bd. Adjustment, Fairview, NJ, 1971—73, Bd. Edn., Fairview, 1972. Contbr. articles to profl. jours. Dir. Deafwest Theater, LA, 1991—97. Mem.: State Bar of Calif., Calif. Club. Congregationalist. Home: 13600 Marina Pointe Dr Unit 710 Marina Del Rey CA 90292-9250

SCHULMAN, RUTH MERYL ARONSON, research and development company executive; BA, SUNY at Potsdam, Potsdam, NY, 1977—81. Interim regional dir., asst. to dir., interim edn. coord. Anti-Defamation League, NY State Regional Office, Albany, 1987—96; dir. ann. giving United Jewish Fedn. Northeastern NY, Latham, 1996—99; dir. devel. Equinox, Inc., Albany, 1999—2000; dir. resource devel. United Way Schenectady County, NY, 2000—01; dir. devel. Animal Protective Found., Scotia, NY, 2001—05, U. Albany, 2005—. Lead vol. Albany Med. Ctr. Found., 2005—. Bd. dirs. So. Saratoga YMCA, 2004—. Mem.: Women In Devel. of Northeastern NY, Assoc. of Fundraising Professionals, Hudson-Mohawk Chpt. (chapter pres.). Home: 51 Grant Hill Court Clifton Park NY 12065 Office: Univ Albany Sch Edn Rm 246 1400 Washington Ave Albany NY 12222 Office Phone: 518-442-4991. Office Fax: 518-442-4953. Business E-Mail: rschulman@uamail.albany.edu.

SCHULMAN, SIDNEY, neurologist, educator; b. Chgo., Mar. 1, 1923; s. Samuel E. and Ethel (Miller) S.; m. Mary Jean Diamond, June 17, 1945; children— Samuel E., Patricia, Daniel. BS, U. Chgo., 1944, MD, 1946. Asst. prof. neurology U. Chgo., 1952-57, assoc. prof., 1957-65, prof., 1965-75, Ellen C. Manning prof., divsn. biol. scis., 1975-93, Ellen C. Manning prof. emeritus, 1993—. Served with M.C. AUS, 1947-49. Mem. Am. Neurol. Assn., U. Chgo. Med. Alumni Assn. (pres. 1968-69, Norman Maclean award 1997), Chgo. Neurol. Soc. (pres. 1964-65)

SCHULT, THOMAS P., lawyer; b. Great Falls, Mont., Sept. 12, 1954; s. Peter Henry and Louise (de Russy) S.; m. Margo C. Soulé, Sept. 18, 1982. BS in Russian History, U. Va., 1976, JD, 1979. Bar: U.S. Dist. Ct. (we. dist.) Mo. 1979, U.S. Ct. Appeals (10th cir.) 1983, U.S. Ct. Appeals (7th, 8th and llth cirs.) 1984, U.S. Ct. Appeals (5th cir.) 1985, U.S. Supreme Ct. 1987, U.S. Ct. Appeals (9th cir.) 1988. Ptnr. Lathrop Koontz & Norquist, Kansas City, Mo., 1979-89, Bryan Cave, Kansas City, 1989-94; Stinson, Mag & Fizzell, Kansas City, 1994-2001; ptnr. Berkowitz Feldmiller, 2001—. Committeeman Jackson County Reps., Kansas City, 1984—. Mem. ABA (products liability com.), Products Liability Adv. Coun., Mo. Bar Assn. (lectr. continuing legal edn.), Fedn. of Ins. and Corporate Counsel, Def. Rsch. Inst. Episcopalian. Office: Stinson Mag & Fizzell 1201 Walnut St Ste 2800 Kansas City MO 64106-2117

SCHULTE, DAVID MICHAEL, investment banker; b. NYC, Nov. 12, 1946; s. Irving and Ruth (Stein) S.; m. Patricia Gordon, Sept. 5, 1999; children: Michael B., Katherine F. BA, Williams Coll., 1968; postgrad., Exeter Coll., Oxford U., Eng., 1968-69; JD, Yale U., 1972. Bar: DC 1973. Law clk. to Mr. Justice Stewart, US Supreme Ct., 1972-73; spl. asst. to pres. NW Industries, Inc., Chgo., 1973-75, v.p. corp. devel., 1975-79, exec. v.p., 1979-80; sr. v.p. Salomon Bros., Chgo., 1980-84; mng. ptnr. Chilmark Ptnrs., Chgo., 1984—. Editor-in-chief: Yale Law Jour, 1971-72. John E. Moody scholar Exeter Coll., Oxford U., 1968-69. Mem. Washington Bar Assn., Chgo. Club, Racquet Club, Bryn Mawr Country Club, Vineyard Golf Club. Office: Chilmark Ptnrs 875 N Michigan Ave Ste 3460 Chicago IL 60611-1957 Office Phone: 312-984-9711.

SCHULTE, FRANCIS B., retired archbishop; b. Phila., Dec. 23, 1926; Grad., St. Charles Borromeo Sem. Ordained priest Roman Cath. Ch., 1952. Apptd. titular bishop of Afufenia and aux. bishop of Phila., 1981—85; bishop Wheeling-Charleston, W.Va., 1985—88; archbishop Archdiocese of New Orleans, 1989—2002, archbishop emeritus, 2002—. Office: c/o 7887 Walmsley Ave New Orleans LA 70125-3431

SCHULTE, GREGORY L., ambassador; married; 2 children. Grad. magna cum laude, U. Calif. Berkeley, 1980; MPA, Princeton U., 1983. Presdl. mgmt. intern office of sec. def., Washington, 1983—85; dir. strategic forces policy, asst. theater nuc. forces policy, 1985—92; with internat. staff NATO, Belgium, 1992—98; spl. asst. to Pres. for implementation of Dayton Peace Accords NSC, 1998—99; prin. dir. requirements, plans and counter-proliferation policy for sec. US Dept. Def., 1999—2000; sr. dir. S.E. European affairs NSC, 2000—02, exec. sec., 2003—05; permanent rep. to UN US Dept. State, Vienna, 2005—, permanent rep. to IAEA, 2005—. Recipient two Presdl. Rank awards. Address: US Dept State 2201 C Street NW Washington DC 20520

SCHULTE, JEFFREY LEWIS, lawyer; b. NYC, July 24, 1949; s. Irving and Ruth (Stein) S.; m. Elizabeth Ewan Kaiser, Aug. 13, 1977; children: Andrew Riggs, Ian Garretson, Elizabeth Alexandra. BA, Williams Coll., 1971; postgrad., Harvard U., 1971-72; JD, Yale U., 1976. Bar: Pa. 1978, Ga. 1993. Law clk. to hon. John J. Gibbons U.S. Ct. Appeals (3d cir.), Newark, 1976-77; assoc. Schnader, Harrison, Segal & Lewis, Phila., 1977-84, ptnr., 1985-92, founding ptnr. Atlanta, 1992-98, exec. com., 1994-98; ptnr. Morris, Manning & Martin, Atlanta, 1998—. Chair securities law com. Ga. State Bar, 2005—07; mem. exec. com. Business Law Sect., Ga. State Bar, 2005-; nat. steering com. lawyers com. to end "Pay-to-Play."; bd. adv. Michael C. Carlos Mus. Emory U., Cole Sch. Bus. Kennesaw State U. Contbr. articles to profl. jours. Mem.: ABA, Bus. and Tech. Alliance, Atlanta Venture Forum, Atlanta Bar Assn. (chmn. comm. and media rels. com.), Phila. Bar Assn., State Bar Ga., Pa. Bar Assn., Weekapaug Tennis Club, Yale Club of Ga. (bd. dirs. 1996—2002, pres. 2000—01, chmn. of bd. 2001—02), Weekapaug Yacht Club R.I., Williams Club N.Y.C., Williams Club Atlanta, Merion Cricket Club, Phi Beta Kappa. Office: Morris Manning & Martin Atlanta Financial Center 3343 Peachtree Rd NE Ste 1600 Atlanta GA 30326-1044 Office Phone: 404-233-7000. Business E-Mail: jls@mmmlaw.com.

SCHULTE, JOHN C., lawyer; b. Cleve., Jan. 19, 1950; BS, Ohio State U., 1972; JD with honors, U. Mont., 1985. Bar: Mont. 1985. Assoc. Worden Thane and Haines PC, 1987—89; solo pvt. practice Missoula, Mont. Instr. bus. law U. Mont., 1987; mem. clin. bd. visitors U. Mont. Sch. Law, 1994—. Recipient Wall Street Jour. award, 1985. Mem.: Mont. Assn. Criminal Def. Lawyers, Mont. Def. Trial Lawyers, Mont. Trial Lawyers Assn., State Bar Mont. (trustee 1994—, chmn. bd. trustees 2005—06, pres.-elect 2006—07), ABA, Western Mont. Bar Assn. (pres. 1992—93). Office: Atty at Law 2425 Mullan Rd Missoula MT 59808 Office Phone: 406-721-6655. Office Fax: 406-543-5023.

SCHULTE, MELANIE ANN, athletic trainer; b. Omaha, Mar. 8, 1980; d. Clyde Alan and Susan Marie Schulte. BS in Exercise and Sport Sci., Coll St. Catherine, St. Paul, 2002; MS in Athlteic Tng., U. Nebr., Omaha, 2004. Cert. CPR ARC; athletic trainer Nat. Athletic Trainers Assn. Bd. Cert. Asst. athletic trainer S.W. Minn. State. U., Marshall, Minn., 2004—06; head athletic trainer Northland Coll., Ashland, Wis., 2006—. Pres. Maverick Athletic Tng. Students. Mem.: Nat. Athletic Trainer's Assn. Avocations: reading, singing. Office: Northland Coll 1411 Ellis Ave Ashland WI 54806

SCHULTE, STEPHEN JOHN, lawyer, educator; b. NYC, July 7, 1938; s. John and Marjorie (Fried) S.; m. Patricia Walker, June 6, 1962 (div.); children: Susan Jean, Jeffrey David, Elizabeth Ann; m. Margaret Van Doren Cook, Mar. 12, 1975. BA, Brown U., 1960; JD, Columbia U., 1963. Bar: N.Y. 1964. Assoc. Lowenstein, Pitcher, Hochkiss & Parr, NYC, 1963-66, Fried, Frank, Harris, Shriver & Jacobson, NYC, 1966-69; founding ptnr. Schulte Roth & Zabel LLP, NYC, 1969—2005, of counsel, 2005—. Adj. prof. law Benjamin N. Cardozo Law Sch., 1992—2000, vice chmn. bd. dirs., 1995—2000, bd. dirs.; adj. prof. law Columbia U., 2000—04, Fordham U., 1992—97; lectr. securities law field; panelist various forums. Life trustee Choate Rosemary Hall Sch., Wallingford, Conn., 1982—, chmn. investment and fin. com., 1984-85, chmn. devel. com., 1985-86, chmn. nominating com., 1986-89, chmn. bd. trustees, 1990-95; chmn. The York Sch., 2006—; bd. dirs. Innocence Project; vice chmn. Big Sur Band Trust, 2004— Mem. ABA, NY State Bar Assn. (com. on securities regulation), Assn. of Bar of City of NY (chmn. com. on securities regulation 1998-2000) Office: Schulte Roth & Zabel LLP 919 3rd Ave New York NY 10022-4774 Business E-Mail: stephen.schulte@srz.com.

SCHULTHEIS, ADAM JOHN, music educator, consultant; b. Quebec City, Que., Canada, Apr. 23, 1962; s. August Thomas and Joan Helen Schultheis; m. Cynthia Anne Forcey, Dec. 14, 1995; children: Johnathon Michael Bohnet, Caroline Emily, Thomas Gabriel, Christopher Addison, Aidan Patrick. MusB in Edn., U. Ariz., Tucson, 1980—86; MS, Nova U., Ft. Lauderdale, Fla., 1987—89. Cert. elem. tchr. Nev., Nat. Bd. Cert. orch. Orch. tchr. McCall Elem. Sch., North Las Vegas, 1986—92, Orr Mid. Sch., Las Vegas, 1992—97, Boulder City H.S., Nev., 1997—. Music leader, cons. Boy Scouts of Am., Boulder City, Nev., 1998—; hon. composer Vincennes U., Ind., 2001—; advisor U.S. Jr. Congl. Leadership Conf., Washington, 2001—. Composer: Prayer, Vincennes U. Bicentennial, 2001, Vegas Fiddle Dance, 2005. Founder, dir. Boulder City Hometown Fiddlers, Nev., 1999—; vol. Make A Difference Day Found., Las Vegas, 1999—; chmn. Nev. Nat. Anthem Project. Named Tchr. of Yr., VFW, Nev., 2006, Outstanding Am. Tchr., Nat. Honor Roll, 2005—06; named to, Clark County Sch. Dist.'s Hall of Fame, Las Vegas, 2001, Wall of Tolerance, San Francisco State U., 2004; recipient Disney Am. Tchr. Honoree, Disney Corp., 1999, Achievement in Edn award, Rotary Club, Boulder, City, Nev., 2001, Music For 1000 Children Award, U. Hartford, Hart Sch. Music, 2002, Nev. Cmty. award, DAR, 2006, Vol. of Yr. award, Am. Legion, 2005, Cmty. Achievement award, DAR, 2006; grantee Arts in the Cmty., Target Edn. Found., 2002, 2003, 2004; Cuban Music fellow, San Francisco State U., 2001. Mem.: Sons of the Am. Legion, Music Educators Nat. Conf. (life), Am. String Tchr. Assn. (life; advisor, cons. 1986—2003), Music Tchr. Nat. Assn. (life), KC, Pi Lambda Theta, Valley Forge Freedom Found. (hon. Past George Washington Honor Medal Winner 2001). Conservative. Achievements include being Nevada's only participant in the 2001 National Independence Day Parade, Washington, D.C; being Nevada's only music participant in National World War Two Memorial Dedication, Washington, 2004; Las Vegas' centennial committee commissioned composition Vegas Fiddle Dance, 2005. Avocations: fiddling, woodworking, gardening, hiking. Home: 1327 Bayleaf Terr Ave Henderson NV 89014 Office: Boulder City HSI 1101 Fifth St Boulder City NV 89005 Office Phone: 702-799-8200. Personal E-mail: adamschultheis@cox.net.

SCHULTHEIS, ANN LUCIA, curriculum specialist; b. Kalamazoo, Mich., Aug. 22, 1946; d. Mario Salvatore Cioffari and Kathleen Loretta Mahoney; m. Patrick James Schultheis, Aug. 17, 1968 (dec.); children: Michael Patrick, Jennifer Ann O'Donoghue. BS, Western Mich. U., Kalamazoo, 1968. Tchr. elem. sch. Portage Pub. Schs., Mich., 1968—70, Allegan Pub. Schs., 1971—95; dir. arts edn. United Arts Coun., Battle Creek, 1996—98; asst. prin. Nat. Heritage Acads., Grand Rapids, 1998—2000, core knowledge curriculum specialist, 2000—05, state stds. specialist, 2005; ret., 2005. Co-owner, operator Hayloft Farm, Kalamazoo, 1971—2006, Celebration Hall, 1981—2003. Avocations: pottery, painting, poetry, history, gardening. Home: 3950 Mary Rd Bloomingdale MI 49026 Personal E-mail: hayloft@btc-bci.com.

SCHULTHEIS, EDWIN MILFORD, dean, business educator; b. NYC, Apr. 15, 1928; s. Milford Theodore and Lillian May (Hill) S.; m. Joan Edna Bruckner, June 23, 1956. BS, Hofstra Coll., 1950; MBA, NYU, 1958, EdD, 1972. Officer mgr., sales rep. Topton Rug Mfg. Co., NYC, 1950-54; area mgr., trainer Mobil Oil Co., NYC, 1954-62; coord. distributive edn. North Babylon (N.Y.) Pub. Schs., 1962-88, chmn. bus. mktg. and indsl. edn. depts., 1988-91; prof. bus. adminstrn. SUNY, Farmingdale, 1970-91; asst. prof. edn. NYU, 1973—; dir. edn. Syracuse (N.Y.) U., 1973-78; chmn. dept. bus. adminstrn. Five Towns Coll., Seaford, N.Y., 1991-92, divsn. chmn. bus. and tech. Dix Hills, N.Y., 1992-98, dean instrn., 1993-98, dep. dean of faculty, 1993-98, assoc. dean, 1996-97, prof. emeritus, 1998—. Test writer, cons. N.Y. State Dept. Edn., Albany, 1965—; textbook reviewer McGraw-Hill Book Co., N.Y.C., 1967-69; cons. Cornell U., 1975; dist. adviser Distributive Edn. Clubs N.Y., 1970, bd. govs., trustee, 1975-78; mem. curriculum adv. coun. Suffolk County (N.Y.) Distributive Edn. Assn., 1967—. Author: Modern Petroleum Marketing, 1971, Content and Structure of Belief-Disbelief Systems, 1972. Elder Presbyn. Ch., U.S.A. Named N.Y. State Tchr. of Yr., 1976, Outstanding Tchr. in N.Y. State, 1978; recipient Outstanding Svc. award Distributive Edn. Clubs N.Y., Suffolk County Distributive Edn. Assn., Tchr. Excellence award N.Y. State, 1980, Citation for Excellence in Edn. Gov. Mario Cuomo N.Y., 1991, Citation Excellence in Teaching Babylon Twp., 1991. Mem. Acad. Mgmt., Am. Petroleum Inst., Am. Security Coun., Suffolk County Assn. Distributive Edn. Tchrs. (mem. exec. bd. 1962-74), N.Y. State (pres. 1975-78), L.I. Distributive Edn. Assns. (hon. life, exec. bd. 1972-75), N.Y. State Occupl. Edn. Assn. (v.p. 1975-78), L.I. Bus. Edn. Chmns. Assn. (hon. life, exec. bd. 1972-75), N.Y. State Occupl. Edn. Assn. (v.p. 1975-78), L.I. Bus. Edn. Chmns. Assn. (hon. life), Distributive Edn. Clubs Am. (regional leader 1972-75, hon. life 1991), Bellport (N.Y.) Golf Club, Phi Delta Kappa, Kappa Delta Pi, Sigma Alpha Lambda, Phi Sigma Eta. Presbyterian (ordained ruling elder). Home: 14 Thorn Hedge Rd Bellport NY 11713-2616

SCHULTHEIS, PATRICIA ANN, writer, editor; b. Bridgeport, Conn., Aug. 11, 1943; d. Ralph and Clare Podufaly; m. William Christian Schultheis, Oct. 15, 1966; children: Kurt Christian, Matthew Christian. BA, Albertus Magnus Coll., 1965; MA in Liberal Arts, Johns Hopkins U., 1973. Prodn. mgr. Balt. Mag., 1976—77; rschr. Md. Pub. TV, Owings Mills, 1977—79; rsch. assoc. Changing Times Mag., DC, 1979—81; editor U. Md., Balt., 1981—85; dir. publs. CC Balt., 1985—89; copy editor The Balt. Sun, 1990; editor Skills Bank Corp., Baltimore County, 1991—95; freelance writer, 1995—; fiction editor Balt. Review, 2001—. Editor Mt. Wash. Newsletter, Balt., 1973—75, U. Md. Sch. Law Alumni Newsletter, Balt.; contbr. Bread Loaf Writer's Conf.; rschr. Ft. McHenry Nat. Monument. Co-author: Personal Mathematics, Media Materials. Sec. Charles Village Improvement Assn., Balt., 1967—69; mentor Dickey Hill Elem. Sch., Balt., 2002—. Mem.: Hamilton St. Club. Avocations: ice skating, folk art painting, embroidery. Home: 2509 Pickwick Rd Baltimore MD 21207 Personal E-mail: bpschult@yahoo.com.

SCHULTHEIS, PATRICK JOSEPH, lawyer; b. Spokane, Wash., Sept. 3, 1964; s. John Arthur and Catherine Christina (McCann) Schultheis. AB in History, Stanford U., 1986; JD, U. Chgo., 1989. Bar: Calif. 1989, Wash. 1998, US Dist. Ct., No. Dist. Calif., US Ct. Appeals, ninth cir. Assoc. Wilson, Sonsini, Goodrich & Rosati, Palo Alto, Calif., 1989-96, mem., 1997—, Seattle, 1997—. Co-author: The Initial Public Offering: A Guidebook for Executives & Boards of Directors, 2004. Mem.: Federalist Soc., ABA-Bus. Law Sect., Inglewood Golf Club, Bellevue Club, Buck Cardinal Club, Mem. Club Aldarra, Kappa Sigma. Republican. Roman Catholic. Office: Wilson Sonsini Goodrich & Rosati 701 Fifth Ave Ste 5100 Seattle WA 98104-7036 Office Phone: 206-883-2500. Office Fax: 206-883-2699. Business E-Mail: pschultheis@wsgr.com.

SCHULTIS, GAIL ANN, library director; b. Freeport, Ill., May 12, 1951; d. Richard C. and Ida G. Schultis. BA, Cornell Coll., 1973; MLS, U. Mo., 1976; MA, U. Tex., San Antonio, 1989. Reference libr. U. Tex., San Antonio, 1976-79, El Paso, 1979-84, 89, head access svcs., 1984-88; reference libr. Park U., Parkville, Mo., 1989-96, dir. libr. sys., 1996—. Co-author: Best Self-Help & Self-Awareness Books, 1995. Mem. ALA, Am. Hist. Assn., Orgn. Am. Historians. Home: 10307 NW 57th Ter Parkville MO 64152-3396 Office: Park Univ Libr 8700 NW River Park Dr Parkville MO 64152-4358 Office Phone: 816-584-6704. Business E-Mail: ann.schultis@park.edu.

SCHULTS-BERNDT, ELFIE, music educator; Grad. in Piano Performance, SUNY, Buffalo; PhD in Piano Performance, Music Theory and Lit., Mich. State U. Dir. music Lake Mich. Coll., Benton Harbor. Recipient US Prof. of Yr. award, Carnegie Found. for Advancement of Tchg. and Coun. for Advancement and Support of Edn., 2006. Office: Music Prog Lake Mich Coll 2755 E Napier Ave Benton Harbor MI 49022 Office Phone: 269-927-8192. E-mail: berndt@lakemichigancollege.edu.

SCHULTZ, ALBERT BARRY, engineering educator; b. Phila., Oct. 10, 1933; s. George D. and Belle (Seidman) S.; m. Susan Resnikov, Aug. 25, 1955; children: Carl, Adam, Robin BS, U. Rochester, 1955; M.Engring., Yale U., 1959, PhD, 1962. Asst. prof. U. Del., Newark, 1962-65; asst. prof. U. Ill., Chgo., 1965-66, assoc. prof., 1966-71, prof., 1971-83; Vennema prof. U. Mich., Ann Arbor, 1983-99. Contbr. numerous articles to profl. jours. Served to lt. USN, 1955-58 Rsch. Career award NIH, 1975-80; Javits Neurosci. Investigator award NIH, 1985-92 Mem. NAE, Internat. Soc. for Study Lumbar Spine (pres. 1981-82), ASME (chmn. bioengring. div. 1981-82, H.R. Lissner award 1990), Am. Soc. Biomechanics (pres. 1982-83, Borelli award 1996), U.S. Nat. Com. on Biomechanics (chmn. 1982-85), Phi Beta Kappa Business E-Mail: aschultz@umich.edu.

SCHULTZ, ARTHUR LEROY, clergyman, educator; b. Johnstown, Pa., June 14, 1928; s. Elmer Albert Robert and Alice Lizetta (Flegal) S.; m. Mildred Louise Stouffer, Nov. 29, 1948; children: Thomas Arthur, Rebecca Louise. BA, Otterbein Coll., 1949; MDiv, United Theol. Sem., 1952; MEd, U. Pitts., 1955, PhD, 1963. Sr. min. Albright United Meth. Ch., Pitts., 1952-56; dir. pub. rels. Otterbein Coll., Westerville, Ohio, 1956-65, adj. prof. religion and philosophy, 1990-98; pres. Albright Coll., Reading, Pa., 1965-77, Ashland (Ohio) Coll., 1977-80; exec. dir. Cen. Ohio Radio Reading Svc., Columbus, 1980-84; parish min. Ch. Master United Meth., Westerville, 1984-89; min. of visitation Ch. Messiah United Meth., Westerville, 1991—2002. Pres. Pa. Assn. Colls. & Univs., Harrisburg, 1974-75. Trustee Reading Hosp., 1967-77, Wyoming Sem., Kingston, Pa., 1971-80; v.p. Found. for Ind. Colls. Pa., Harrisburg, 1972-73; pres. Pa. Coun. on Alcohol Problems, Harrisburg, 1968-76; pres. Westerville (Ohio) Hist. Soc., 1986-89, Westerville Area Ministerial Assn., 1992-93. Named Outstanding Young Man of the Year Jr. C. of C., Westerville, Ohio, 1960. Mem. Brookstone Cmty. Assn. (sec. bd. trustees 1994-99, v.p. 1999-2000), Rotary (charter pres. 1959, dist. gov. 1965-66, dist. sec.-treas. 1982-93), Masons, Shriners, Torch Club. Republican. Methodist. Avocations: collecting post cards, golf, tennis, travel. Home: 151 Sandstone Loop W Westerville OH 43081-4599

SCHULTZ, ARTHUR WARREN, retired communications executive; b. NYC, Jan. 13, 1922; s. Milton Warren and Genevieve (Dann) S.; m. Elizabeth Carroll Mahan, 1949 (div. 1987); children: Arthur Warren, John Carroll (dec.), Julia Hollingsworth; m. Susan Keefe, 1988. Grad., U. Chgo.; DLitt (hon.), Rosary Coll. With Foote, Cone & Belding Comms., Chgo., 1948-82, v.p., 1957-63, sr. v.p., dir., 1963-69, exec. v.p., 1969, chmn. bd., CEO, 1970-81, chmn. exec. com., CEO, 1981-82; dir. Chgo. Sun-Times Co.; vice chmn. Chgo. Sun-Times Newspaper Co., 1989-94. Lectr. in field. Author: In Praise of America's Collectors, 1997; co-author: Valley Club of Montecito, 1999; editor Caring for Your Collections, 1992. Pres. Cook County Sch. Nursing, 1963-64, Welfare Coun. Met. Chgo., 1965-67; mem. bus. adv. coun. Urban League Chgo., 1971-82; chmn. Nat. Com. to Save Am.'s Cultural Collections, 1990-94; mem. Pres.'s Com. Arts and Humanities, 1984-93; bd. dirs. Chgo. Crime Commn., 1965-71, Cmty. Fund Chgo., 1966-67, Better Bus. Bur., 1970-78, Lyric Opera Chgo., 1967-77, Chgo. Coun. Fgn. Rels., 1977-86, Chgo. Pub. TV, 1978-82, Chgo. Central Area Com., 1978-82; mem. millennium Com. to Save Am.'s Treasures, 1998; trustee YWCA, 1962-74, Calif. Coll. Arts & Crafts, 1985-87; trustee Art Inst. Chgo., 1975-2002, chmn. bd., 1981-84; trustee U. Chgo., 1977—, Santa Barbara Mus. Art, 1988—, pres., 1989-92. 1st lt. USAF, 1943-45. Recipient Alumni Svc. award U. Chgo., 1986. Mem. Am. Assn. Advt. Agys. (dir. 1968-71, 74-76, chmn. Chgo. coun. 1964-65, chmn. Ctrl. region 1970-71), Comml. Club, Valley Club (Montecito, Calif.), Delta Kappa Epsilon. Roman Catholic. Home and Office: 2072 China Flat Rd Santa Barbara CA 93108-2211

SCHULTZ, BARBARA MARIE, investment advisor; b. Chgo., Sept. 9, 1943; d. Edwin and Bernice (Barstis) Legner; m. Ronald J. Schultz, Sr., May 1, 1965; 1 child, Ronald J. Student, Prairie State Coll. Fin. planner Metlife Fin. Svcs., NYC, 1981—2001; fin. advisor Morgan Stanley Dean Witter, NYC, 2001—02; agt., investment advisor rep. Country Ins. and Fin. Svcs., Hickory Hills, Ill., 2002—04; investment advisor Edward Jones Investments, Palm Harbor, Fla., 2004; mature mktg. specialist AIG/Am. Gen., Tampa, 2005—06; fin. advisor Waddell & Reed, Palm Harbor, Fla., 2007—. Qualifier Met. Life Leaders Conf., 1990. Recipient Pres. Trophy Campaign award, AIG, 2005, Eagle award, AIG/AGLA, 2006. Fellow: South Cook County Assn. Life Underwriters (edn. chmn. 1988—91), Life Underwriters Tng. Coun. (chmn. 1986—88), Nat. Assn. Life Underwriters (edn. chmn. 1988—91, citation 1987, nat. quality award, Robert L. Rose award 1990), Country Club (1st pl. award 2002). Roman Catholic. Avocations: boating, aerobics, golf. Office: 35111 US Hwy 19 North Ste 302 Palm Harbor FL 34684 Home Phone: 727-945-9024; Office Phone: 727-785-3195.

SCHULTZ, CARL HERBERT, real estate developer; b. Chgo., Jan. 9, 1925; s. Herbert V. and Olga (Swanson) S.; m. Helen Ann Stevesson, June 6, 1948; children: Mark Carl, Julia Ann BS Gen. Engring., Iowa State U., 1948. With Schultz Bros. Co., 1948—, mdse. mgr. and store planner Chgo., 1962—70, v.p. Lake Zurich, Ill., 1968—72, pres., 1972—2000, Ill. Schultz Bros. Co., Ind. Schultz Bros. Co., Iowa Schultz Bros. Co., Wis. Schultz Bros. Co.; chmn. Schultz Bros. Co., 2000—. Mem. Lake Bluff Zoning Bd. Appeals, Ill., 1976-85, chmn., 1978-85. Served with U.S. Army, 1944-46 Mem. Lake Zurich Indsl. Coun. (sec. 1976), Assn. Gen. Mdse. Chains (dir. 1975-86, exec. com. 1983-86, chmn. nat. conv. 1982), Ill. Retail Mchts. Assn. (dir. 1984-89), Wis. Retail Fedn. (dir. 1981-89). Presbyn. Office: 815 Oakwood Rd Unit I Lake Zurich IL 60047 Home: 1100 Pembridge Dr Apt 242 Lake Forest IL 60045-4219 Office Phone: 847-438-3900. Personal E-mail: chs701@sbcglobal.net.

SCHULTZ, CLARENCE JOHN, minister; b. Morris Twp., Wis., Aug. 4, 1937; s. Clarence John Sr. and Ella Mae (Feavel) S.; m. Doroland Kay King, Aug. 24, 1957 (dec. Jan. 1974); children: Sharon Kay Braun, Susan May Schultz Rogers; m. Martha Ann Aylor, Apr. 5, 1975. BS, Bryan Coll., 1960. Ordained to ministry Conservative Congl. Ch., 1961. Min. 1st Congl. Ch., Herreid, SD, 1961-66, Immanuel Evang. Congl. Ch., Sheboygan, Wis., 1966-77, Hope Congl. Ch., Superior, Wis., 1977-83, Zion Evang. Ch., Scottsbluff, Nebr., 1983-89, 1st Congl. Ch., Buffalo Center, Iowa, 1989-92, Kenosha, Wis., 1992-98, St. Lucas Cmty. Ch., Lake Elmo, Minn., 1998—2007; pastor emeritus St, Lucas Cmty. Ch. Mem. Conservative Congl. Christian Conf. (rec. sec. 1973-82, v.p. 1994-96, pres. 1996-99, Rocky Mountain area rep. 1987-89, endorser of chaplains 1988-2000, mem. credentials com. 1988-2006), Rotary (ch. chaplain com. 1993-95). Congregationalist. Avocations: amateur radio, golf. Personal E-mail: cjsmas@sbcglobal.net.

SCHULTZ, DANIEL R., insurance company executive; Fin. mgmt. positions Am. Family Mut. Ins. Co., Madison, Wis., 1977—99, v.p. contr. div., 1999—2006, v.p., CFO, 2006—. Office: Am Fam Mut Ins Co 6000 American Pkwy Madison WI 53783 *

SCHULTZ, DAVID FRANKLIN, psychologist; b. Pontiac, Ill., June 7, 1952; s. David Franklin Schultz and Bernadine Yvonne Riffey, Marilyn Schultz (Stepmother); m. Lori Dale Edwards, May 15, 2005. PhD, U. Tex., 1991. Master Traumatologist Internat. Traumatology Inst., 2002. Chief psychologist Polk Youth Devel. Ctr., Polk City, Fla., 1996—2000; clin. psychologist D. Franklin Schultz, Ph.D., Lakeland, Fla., 1994—; adj. prof. Webster U., 2001—. Cons., Lakeland, Fla., 2001—. Author: (self help book) A Language of the Heart: Therapy Stories that Heal; co-author (therapist training manual) Trauma Practice: Tools for Stabilization and Recovery. Bd. mem., trainer, team mem. Polk County Critical Incident Stress Mgmt. Team, Bartow, Fla., 2002—05. Master: Masonic Order. Avocations: skiing, golf, fishing, scuba diving. Home: PO Box 717 Auburndale FL 33823 Office: D Franklin Schultz PhD 930 Alicia Rd Lakeland FL 33801 Home Phone: 863-680-1950; Office Phone: 863-680-1950. Office Fax: 863-683-4654; Home Fax: 863-683-4654. Personal E-mail: drfrank@aloth.com.

SCHULTZ, DENNIS BERNARD, lawyer; b. Detroit, Oct. 15, 1946; s. Bernard George and Madeline Laverne (Riffenberg) Schultz; m. Andi Lynn Leslie, Apr. 18, 1967; 1 child, Karanne Anne. BS, Wayne State U., 1970; JD, Mich. State U., 1977. Bar: Mich. 1977, U.S. dist. Ct. (ea. and we. dists.) Mich., U.S. Ct. Appeals (6th cir.), U.S. Dist. Ct. (we. dist.) Pa. V.p. Barkay Bldg. Co., Ferndale, Mich., to 1976; law clk. Hon. George N. Bashara, Mich. Ct. Appeals, Detroit, 1977; shareholder Butzel Long, Detroit, 1978—. Editor: Detroit Coll. Law Rev., 1977. Scholar Detroit Coll. Law Alumni Assn., 1976, Mich. Consol. Gas Co., 1977. Mem.: Mich. Bar Assn., Detroit Bar Assn. Republican. Roman Catholic. Avocations: boating, bicycling, golf. Personal E-mail: dbs77@comcast.net.

SCHULTZ, E. EUGENE, JR., computer engineer, director; b. Chgo., Sept. 10, 1946; s. Earl Eugene and Elizabeth Claire Schultz; m. Cathy Brown Schultz, Aug. 9, 1975; children: Sarah Ardelle, Rachel Elizabeth, Leah Brown. BA, UCLA, 1968; MS, Purdue U., 1973, PhD, 1977. Cert. info. sys. security profl. Internat. Info. Sys. Security Cert. Consortium, info. security mgr. Info. Sys. Audit and Control Assn. Project leader, engr. Lawrence Livermore (Calif.) Nat. Lab., 1986—92; prin. Eugene Schultz and Assocs., Livermore, 1992—93; prin. security engr. ARCA Sys., San Jose, Calif., 1993—94; sr. cons. SRI Internat., Menlo Park, Calif., 1994—98; rsch. dir. Global Integrity Corp., Reston, Va., 1998—2001; prin. engr. Lawrence Berkeley Nat. Lab., 2001—05; chief tech. officer High Tower Software, 2005—. Adj. prof. Purdue U., West Lafayette, Ind., 1998—2001. Author: Internet Security for Business, 1996, Windows NT/2000 Network Security, 2000, Incident Response, 2001, Intrusion Detection and Prevention, 2004; editor-in-chief: Computers and Security, 2002— (Golden Page award, 2003); contbr. articles to profl. jours. Active Livermore (Calif.) Vision 2000, 2001. Recipient Tech. Innovation award, NASA, 1986. Mem.: Info. Sys. Audit & Control Assn., Computer Security Inst., Info. Sys. Security Assn. (Profl. Contbn. award, Hall of Fame). Achievements include development of decluttering method for visual displays; founding the Department of Energy's Incident Response Team. Avocations: bicycling, travel. Home: 2587 Pienza St Livermore CA 94550 Office: Lawrence Berkeley Nat Lab 1 Cyclotron Rd Berkeley CA 94720 Personal E-mail: eeschultz@sbcglobal.net.

SCHULTZ, EILEEN HEDY, creative director; b. Yonkers, NY; d. Harry Arthur and Hedy Morchel) S. BFA, Sch. Visual Arts, 1955. Staff artist C.A. Parshall Studios, NYC, 1955—56; editorial art dir. Paradise of the Pacific, Honolulu, 1956—58; graphic designer Adler Advt. Agy., NYC, 1958-59; art dir. Good Housekeeping Mag., NYC, 1959-82, creative dir. advt. and sales promotion, 1982—86; creative dir. Hearst Corp., 1986—87; pres., creative dir. Design Internat., 1987—. Creative dir. The Depository Trust Co., 1987-99; prof. Sch. Visual Arts, 1974—. Art dir., editor, designer, 50th Art Directors Club Annual, 1973; columnist: Art Direction, 1969-1994. Dir. Sch. Visual Arts, N.Y.C., 1978—; trustee Sch. Art League, 1978—; advisor Fashion Inst. Tech., 1979—; adv. commn. N.Y.C. Cmty. Colls., 1979—. Named Yonkers Amb. of Good Will to Netherlands, 1955; recipient Outstanding Achievement Sch. Visual Arts Alumni Soc., 1976, Sch. Art League Youth award, 1976, Key to City of Osaka, Japan, 1976. Mem. Art Dirs. Club (pres. 1975-77), Soc. Illustrators (pres. 1991-93), Joint Ethics Com. (chmn. 1978-80), Am. Inst. Graphic Arts, Soc. Publ. Designers, Type Dirs. Club. Office Phone: 212-371-0121.

SCHULTZ, FREDERICK HENRY, investor, former government official; b. Jacksonville, Fla., Jan. 16, 1929; s. Clifford G. and Mae (Wangler) S.; m. Nancy Reilly, Aug., 1951; children: Catherine G., Frederick H., Clifford G., John R. BA, Princeton U., 1951; postgrad., U. Fla. Sch. Law, 1954-56. With Barnett Nat. Bank, Jacksonville, 1956-57; owner, operator investment firm, from 1957; mem. Fla. Ho. of Reps., 1963-70, speaker of the house, 1968-70; chmn. bd. Barnett Investment Svcs., Inc.; dir. Barnett Banks Inc., to 1979; vice chmn. bd. govs. Fed. Res. System, Washington, 1979-82; sr. advisor Drexel Burnham Lambert, 1982—90; founder Schultz Ctr. Tchg. & Leadership, 2002—. Served to lt. U.S. Army, 1952-54, Korea Decorated Bronze Star Roman Catholic. Office: PO Box 1200 Jacksonville FL 32201-1200

SCHULTZ, GERALD ALFRED (JERRY SCHULTZ), retired chemicals executive; b. Lockport, NY, Jan. 22, 1941; s. Alfred Henry and Lucy Vivian (Proctor) S.;m. Barbara Joan Beals, July 13, 1962; 1 child, Amy Lynn Schultz-Kessler. AAS, Erie County Tech. Inst., Buffalo, 1961; BA in Chemistry, SUNY, Buffalo, 1969; postgrad., Harvard U., 1979. Rsch. technician Occidential Chem. Corp., Niagara Falls, NY, 1961—63; rsch. engr. Nat. Gypsum Co. Inc., Buffalo, 1963-66; from chemist, devel. mgr., gen. mgr. to v.p. Akzo Chems., Burt, NY and Chgo., 1966-86; CEO VanDeMark Inc. subs. Groupe SNPE, Lockport, NY, 1986—2003; ret., 2003. Cons. in field. Contbr. articles to profl. jours; patentee in field. Fund raiser United Way, Newfane, N.Y., 1982-84; treas., bd. dirs. Newfane Intercommunity Meml. Hosp., 1980-84; bd. dirs. ARC, Lockport, N.Y., 1980-84, 97-2000; mem. United Way Ea. Niagara Allocations Com., 1994-97. Mem. Am. Chem. Soc., Soc. Plastic Engrs., Soc. Plastics Industry (bd. dirs. 1974-76), Organic Peroxide Prodn. Safety Divsn. (chmn. 1974-76), Synthetic Organic Chem. Mfrs. Assn. (bd. dirs. 1991-94), Soc. Plastics Engrs., NY State Bus. Coun., NY State Chem. Alliance, Lockport Indsl. Coun. (treas. 1991-98), Ea. Niagara C. of C. (bd. dirs. 1992-95), Lockport Town and Country Club (bd. dirs. 1995-96), Olcott Yacht Club (past commr. 1975) Republican. Episcopalian. Avocations: golf, gardening, computers, boating. Home: 6846 Lockhaven Dr Lockport NY 14094 Personal E-mail: schultz_gerald@msn.com.

SCHULTZ, GREGORY S., biochemist; b. Enid, Okla., Sept. 30, 1949; BS, Okla. State U., 1971, PhD, 1976; Medicinae Doctoreum, Linkoping U., Sweden, 1996. Postdoctoral fellow Yale U., New Haven, 1976-79; asst. prof. biochemistry U. Louisville, 1979-85, assoc. prof. biochemistry, 1985-89; prof. ob-gyn U. Fla., Gainesville, 1989—, dir. Inst. for Wound Rsch., 1989—; v.p. lab & clinical rsch. Quick-Med Technologies Inc., Gainesville, 2000—. Scientific cons. Chiron Corp., Emeryville, Calif., 1982-85, Ethicon Corp., Summerville, N.J., 1985-86, Santen, Inc., Sonoma, Calif., 1997-98, U.S. Biomaterials, Gainesville, 1998—; bd. dirs. Quick-Med Technologies Inc., 2000—; Everett Kinsey lectr. Contact Lens Assn. Ophthalmologists, 1997. Editor: Exptl. Eye Rsch., 1997—; patentee in field. Named Time Mag. Innovator, 2006. Mem. Wound Healing Soc. (pres.-elect 1997-98, pres. 1999-2001), Am. Soc. Biochemistry and Molecular Biology (Ethicon Endo-Surgery Lectureship 1997), Assn. for Rsch. in Vision and Ophthalmology, Phi Kappa Phi. Avocations: scuba diving, tennis. Office: U Fla Dept Ob Gyn 1600 SW Archer Rd Gainesville FL 32610-0294 also: Quick Med Technologies Inc 3427 42nd Way Gainesville FL 32608 Office Phone: 352-392-4060. E-mail: SchultzG@obgyn.ufl.edu.

SCHULTZ, HARLEY, consulting company executive; b. NYC; s. William and Rose Diane Schultz. MBA, NYU, 1981. Pres. Harley Schultz & Assocs., Cons. in Mktg., Mgmt. and Internet Bus. Devel., Scarsdale, NY, 1987—. Mem. various charitable orgns. Avocations: sailing, golf, French literature, 19th-century art, classical music. Office: Harley Schultz & Assocs 130 Garth Rd # 250 Scarsdale NY 10583-3750 Business E-Mail: harleyschultz@consultant.com.

SCHULTZ, HOWARD, beverage service executive; b. Bklyn., July 19, 1953; m. Sheri Kersch; 2 children. BS, No. Mich. U., 1975. Joined as saleman Xerox Corp.; v.p., gen. mgr. Hammarplast, USA, (divsn. Perstorp); dir. retail ops. & mktg. Starbucks Coffee Co., 1982—85; founder, chmn. Starbucks Corp., 1987—, CEO, 1987—2000, chief global strategist, 2000—04; chmn. & owner Seattle Supersonics, 2001—06. Bd. govs. Nat. Assn. of Securities Dealers, 1998—2001. Author (with Dori Jones Young): Pour Your Heart Into It: How Starbucks Built a Company One Cup at a Time, 1996. Named Exec. of the Year, Restaurants and Institutions mag., 2000. Office: Starbucks 2401 Utah Ave S Seattle WA 98134 *

SCHULTZ, LEANNE, violinist, performer, music educator; b. Topeka, Jan. 15, 1953; d. Ted Wilder Baehni and Lucille Elizabeth Reuter; m. Larry Wayne Schultz, June 30, 1984. BA in Music, Washburn U., Topeka, Kans., 1988. Pvt. music tchr. Marquardt Music Store, Topeka, 1972—73; sec. Inlet Ins. Agy., Homer, Alaska, 1976—78; pvt. piano and violin tchr. Allegro Music Shop, Homer, 1978—80; permanent emergency substitute music dir., tchr., 6th grade elem. band tchr. Homer Alaska Jr. and Sr. H.S., 1978—79; escrow sec. Peninsula Title Ins. Co., Homer, 1979—80; clk. typist II Office Pers. Dept. Adminstrn., State of Kans., Topeka, 1980—81; computer/word-processor divsn. water resources State Bd. Agriculture, Topeka, 1981—84; office adminstrv. asst. III SRS Dept., Topeka, 1985; music condr., tchr. Cair-Paravel/Topeka Latin Sch., Topeka, 1986—88; escrow sec. Lawyers Title Topeka, 1988—94; pvt. violin, viola and piano tchr. Topeka, 1994—. Concert, mem., violinist Topeka Civic Symphony, 1971—74, 1981, Topeka Symphony Orch., 1999—; pvt. traditional classical violin music tchr. Marquardt-Manning Music Store, Topeka, 1985—90, Manning Music Store, Topeka, 1991—2000; student-music tchr., adjudicator Washburn U. Collegiate Music Educators Nat. Conf., Topeka, 1986—88; accompanist/pianist pvt. music students solo performances Collegiate Music Educators Nat. Conf., Kans. State HS Activities Assn., Mid. Sch., Regional, Statewide Solo Fest Contests; adjudicator Topeka Youth Symphony, 1992—2000; violinist Messiah Festivals, 2005—. Musician (violist): 124th Messiah Festival, 2005, 125th Messiah Festival, 2006; musician: (violinist) 126th Messiah Festival, 2007. Mem., sec. Latchkey bd. advisors NE Kans. Music Tchrs. Assn., 1999—2003; mem. Writer for Arts Advocacy. Recipient Scholarship winner, Sitka Music Festival Winter Session, Student-Institute Workshop, Univ. of Alaska at Juneau/Juneau, Alaska, 1980. Mem.: Music Tchrs. Nat. Assn., Topeka Symphony League, Am. String Tchrs. Assn., Kans. Music Tchrs. Assn., N.E. Kans. Music Tchr. Assn. (sec. 1998—2003), Topeka Music Tchr. Assn. (chmn. honors recitals 1999—2001), Washburn Univ. Alumni Assn., Topeka HS Alumni Hist. Soc., Woman's Kans. Day Club, Sigma Alpha Iota (alumnae). Avocations: music literature, music history. Home and Office: 3618 SW 33d St Topeka KS 66614-2812 Office Phone: 785-271-0402. Personal E-mail: schultzstringstorm@sbcglobal.net.

SCHULTZ, LOUIS WILLIAM, retired judge; b. Deep River, Iowa, Mar. 24, 1927; s. M. Louis and Esther Louise (Behrens) S.; m. D. Jean Stephen, Nov. 6, 1949; children: Marcia, Mark, Paul. Student, Central Coll., Pella, Iowa, 1944-45, 46-47; LLB, Drake U., Des Moines, 1949. Bar: Iowa. Claims supr. Iowa Farm Mut. Ins. Co., Des Moines, 1949-55; partner firm Harned, Schultz & McMeen, Marengo, Iowa, 1955-71; judge Iowa Dist. Ct. (6th dist.), 1971-80; justice Iowa Supreme Ct., 1980-93; county atty. Iowa County, 1960-68; ret., 1993. Served with USNR, 1945-46. Mem. Iowa Bar Assn. (bd. govs.), Iowa Judges Assn. (pres.)

SCHULTZ, MARIAN STARR, musician, educator; b. Buffalo, Aug. 4, 1956; d. Joseph Starr and Catherine Marian Haroney; m. Paul Howard Schultz, July 29, 1985; 1 child, Alexandra Louise. MusB, Shenandoah Conservatory, 1979, PhD in Music Arts, 2000; MusM, Cath. U. Am., 1988. Music specialist Green Acres Sch., Rockville, Md., 1983—2003, FCPS, Fairfax City, Md., 2003—. Advisory council mem. Assn. Ind. Md. Schs., 1992—94, conf. chair, 1993. Author: (book) A Study to Determine the Effect..., 2005. Donor St. Louis RC Ch., Buffalo, 2004, St. Anthony's Parish, Buffalo, 2003—04. Mem.: Music Educators Nat. Conf., Sigma Alpha Iota (treas. 1986—88). Avocations: fencing, swimming, gardening, travel.

SCHULTZ, NANCY JANSSON, artist; b. Kanas City, Mo., Apr. 15, 1933; d. Carl Albert Jansson and Lora Elizabeth Wilson; m. Everett Hoyle Schultz, June 24, 1955; children: Susan, Frank, Janet, Sally. Student, Park Coll., Parkville, Mo., 1951—54. Founder Women on Paper, Augusta, Ga., 1987—; exhibit organizer Art of the Sketchbook, Ga., 2005. Exhibitions include Genema Gallery, Altanta, McCormick Arts Ctr., S.C. (Purchase award, 2004, 2005, 2006, 2007), Quinlan Arts Ctr., Gainsville, Ga., Gwinnett Fine Arts Ctr., Duluth, Ga., U. S.C., Aiken, Cotton Exch. Gallery, Augusta, 1998, Clayton St. Gallery, Athens, Ga., 1998, Emory U. Law Sch. Libr., Atlanta, 2000, Barnes & Noble Bookstore, Augusta, 2000, State Capitol Gallery, Ga. Arts Day, Atlanta, 2001, Aiken Ctr. Arts, 2001, State Bot. Gardens, Athens, 2002, Cork Gallery, Avery Fisher Hall, N.Y.C., 2002—05, Birmingham So. Coll. Durbin Gallery, 2006 (Merit award, 2006), Represented in permanent collections Bank Fla., Deloritte & Touche, Charlotte, N.C., Med. Coll. Ga., U. Hosp., Augusta, St. Joseph's Hosp., PAC 2000, N.H., Jud. Ctr., Ocala, Fla., Augusta Nat. Golf, prin. works include Carptenter's Gallery, Augusta, Ann Jacob Gallery, Highlands, NC, The Pheasants Eye, Lynchburg, Va., McCormick Arts Coun., S.C., exhibited in group shows at Broad Strokes Gallery, Augusta, Ga., 2007; artist (represented by) Broad Strokes Gallery, Augusta, Art on Broad. Named to Archives on Women Artists, Nat. Mus. of Women in the Arts, Washington, 1995; recipient Honorable Mention, Eyes for the Art, Augusta, 1992, Merit award, Images in Art, Ocala, 1992, First Pl., Fine Arts for Watercolor, Blue Crab Festival, N.C., 1989, Merit award, Miss. Watercolor Soc., 1989, 1st pl. Watercolor, Columbia County Renaissance Festival, 2005, Honorable Mention, Art on Main Hendersonville, N.C., 2005, Merit award, Ala. Watercolor Soc., 2006, Images Art Festival, New Smyrna Beach, Fla., 2007. Mem.: Gertude Herbert Inst. of Art, Nat. League of Am. Pen Women (1st pl. 1994, 3d pl. 1997, Pres. award. 1997, Marel Brown award 1999, 1st pl. in mixed media 2002, 3d pl. 2002, 2d pl. 2005, 2d pl. Watercolor Spring Juried Show 2006), Ga. Watercolor Soc. (newsletter editor 1990—92, signature mem.). Achievements include development of booklet for newcomers to Augusta area 'A Guide For Visual Artists'. Avocations: aerobics, writing, reading, making hand made books. Home and Studio: 608 Aumond Rd Augusta GA 30909

SCHULTZ, NORBERT J., retired music educator; b. Gardner, Ill., Apr. 25, 1937; s. Lewis H. and Vera Schultz; m. Janet A. Schultz, Aug. 19, 1979; children: Sonia, Shelly Luppen 1 stepchild, John Bracamontes. BS in Music Edn., Ill. State U., 1959. Band, vocal and gen. music tchr., grade and H.S. Kempton and Cabrey (Ill.) Schs., 1959—61; vocal tchr. Piper City (Ill.) Grade and H.S., 1961—63; band and vocal dir. Taft Grade Sch., Lockport, Ill., 1963—67; band dir. Lyons (Ill.) Sch. Dist., 1967—70, Edwardsville (Ill.) elem, jr. high and H.S., 1970—85; gen. music tchr. Shenandoah and Woodward Elem. Schs., St. Louis, 1986—99; beginning and intermediate band dir. St. Paul's Luth. Sch., Troy, Ill., 1999—2001; ret., 2001. Profl. entertainer, band dir. Musical dir. chapel Charles Melvin Price Support Ctr. Army Facility, Granite City, Ill., 1995—2000; deacon Holy Cross Luth. Ch., Collinsville, Ill., 1988—96, elder, 1999, St. Paul's Luth. Ch., Troy, 2002—. Named team mem. in citizen ambassador program elementary edn. del. to Vietnam, Eisenhower award, U. Toledo, 1994; recipient numerous 1st pl. band awards at state competitions. Mem.: Music Tchrs. Nat. Assn., Ill. State Music Tchrs. Assn. Republican. Lutheran. Avocations: fishing, travel, private teaching. Home: Holiday Shores 846 Newport Bay Edwardsville IL 62025 Office Phone: 618-659-8736.

SCHULTZ, PATRICIA BOWERS, vocal music educator, conductor; b. Gomer, Ohio, Apr. 26, 1941; d. Paul Edward and Blodwen (Watkins) Bowers; m. Charles Albert Schultz; children: Todd Matthew, Vaughn Andrew, Cinnamon Paulette. BS in Edn., French & Music, Miami U., Oxford, Ohio, 1963; MEd in Counseling, U. Ill., 1964; D of Musical Arts in Vocal Performance, U. Mo-Kansas City, 1984. Performer freelance USA and Europe, 1964—; music educator, counselor Northmont Pub. Schs., Dayton, Ohio, 1964-66; French educator Bowling Green (Ohio) H.S., 1967-68; instr. music and French Dickinson (N.D.) State U., 1972-74; instr. voice Ctrl. State U., Wilberforce, Ohio, 1975-76; dir. choral activities Savannah (Mo.) H.S., 1979-80; prof. music N.W. Mo. State U., Maryville, 1981—2002. Dir. music First United Meth. Ch., Maryville, 1977—88; tour mgr. Jenny Lind Ensemble, 1978—; musical dir. N.W. MO. State U., Maryville, 1981—2002; vis. prof. Internat. Enrichment, London, 2000, 02, 06, 2004—06, 2006; adjudicator Nat. Assn. Tchrs. of Singing, Mo. H.S. Activities Assn.; co-dir. Summer in London Program Internat. Enrichment, 2006; presenter in field. Author, lead role in music drama Encore for Jenny Lind, 1976— (London Premiere 1992); conductor choral music Welsh Gymanfoedd Ganu, 1989— (Nat. Selection 1992, 1993, 2005); Coloratura soprano recitals and concerts throughout U.S.; soloist European tour Cin. Symphony, 1969. Pres. Univ. Women, Maryville, 1978-79; first judge vocal competition Nat. Glenn Miller Scholarship Competition, Clarinda, Iowa, 1992, 94, 2001; pres. Faculty Senate N.W. Mo. State U., 1993-95, Centennial Soc. 2002-; organizer, charter mem. Mo. Assn. Faculty Senates, Springfield, Mo., 1993-94. Named Faculty Fellow Mo. Coordinating Bd. Higher Edn., 1997-98, Outstanding Alumnae Conservatory of Music, U. Mo.-Kansas City, 1990; grantee Mo. State Coun. on Arts, 1991-95. Mem. AAUW, Coll. Music Soc., Nat. Assn. Tchrs. Singing (Teacher of regional state and chpt. winners in Mo., Nebr. and eight state region 1986, 88, 90, 92, 97, 98), Am. Choral Dirs. Assn., (hon.) Mortar Bd. (Outstanding advisor, 2003), Sigma Alpha Iota (patroness and advisor 1995-2002), Delta Omicron. Avocations: gardening, reading, travel. Home: 1004 W Cooper St Maryville MO 64468-2005

SCHULTZ, RICHARD ALLEN, lawyer, farmer; b. Emporia, Kans., Jan. 3, 1939; s. Ebur Samuel and Opal Mae (Porter) S.; m. Esther Marie Strafuss, May 8, 1971; children: William Allen, Bryan Lee. BS in Indsl. Mgmt., U. Kans., 1961; JD, Washburn U. Topeka, 1970. Bar: Kans. 1971. Sole practice law, Topeka, 1970—. Dep. dir. Kans. Govs. Com. Criminal Adminstrn., 1971-73; asst. jud. adminstr. Kans. Supreme Ct., 1973-76; ct. adminstr. 3d Jud. Dist., Kans., 1976-83; dep. sec. Dept. Corrections State of Kans., Topeka, 1983-88. Exec. bd. Topeka YMCA; dist. officer Jayhawk Area Boy Scouts Am., Nat. Eagle Scout Assn.; dir. Kans. Vets. Found., Inc. Lt. USN, 1961-67. Decorated commendation award USN. Mem. ABA, Topeka Bar Assn. (Liberty Bell award 1983), Kans. Bar Assn., Am. Legion, Vietnam Vets Am., Phi Alpha Delta, Alpha Tau Omega. Democrat. Methodist. Office: 2440 SW Camelot Pl Topeka KS 66614-5623 Office Phone: 785-273-5566.

SCHULTZ, RICHARD CARLTON, plastic surgeon; b. Grosse Pointe, Mich., Nov. 19, 1927; s. Herbert H. and Carmen (Huebner) S.; m. Pauline Zimmermann, Oct. 8, 1955; children: Richard, Lisa, Alexandra, Jennifer. MD, Wayne State U., 1953. Diplomate Am. Bd. Plastic Surgery. Intern Harper Hosp., Detroit, 1953-54, resident in gen. surgery, 1954-55, U.S. Army Hosp., Ft. Carson, Colo., 1955-57; resident in plastic surgery St. Luke's Hosp., Chgo., 1957-58, U. Ill. Hosp., Chgo., 1958-59, VA Hosp., Hines, Ill., 1959-60; practice medicine specializing in plastic surgery Park Ridge, Ill., 1961-96; ret., 1996; clin. asst. prof. surgery U. Ill. Coll. Medicine, 1966-70, assoc. prof. surgery, 1970-76, prof., 1976-96, head divsn. plastic surgery, 1970-87; pres. med. staff Luth. Gen. Hosp., Park Ridge, 1977-79. Vis. prof. U. Pitts., 1972, U. Miss., 1973, U. Pisa, Italy, 1974, Jikei U. Coll. Medicine, Tokyo, 1976, Ind. U., 1977, U. Helsinki, 1977, U. N.Mex., 1978, U. Milan, 1981, So. Ill. Sch. Medicine, 1982, Tulane U. Med. Sch., 1983, Shanghai 2d Med. Coll., 1984, U. Guadalajara (Mex.), 1986, Gazi U., Turkey, 1988, U. Coll. Medicine Tsuksba, Japan, 1996, Taegu (Korea) U., 1996; sr. Fulbright lectr. U. Uppsala, Sweden, 2003; participant, guest surgeon Physicians for Peace, Turkey and Greece, 1988, Israel and Occupied Ters., 1990, Egypt, 1991, Lithuania, Estonia, 1993 (team leader); leader citizen amb. People to People Internat. Del. Plastic Surgeons to Albania & Russia, 1994, del. leader, Tibet and China, 1998. Author: Facial Injuries, 1970, 3d edit., 1988, Maxillo-Facial Injuries from Vehicle Accidents, 1975, Outpatient Surgery, 1979. Mem. sch. bd., Lake Zurich, Ill., 1966-72, pres., 1968-72; pres. Chgo. Found. for Plastic Surgery, 1966-. Served to capt. M.C., AUS, 1955-57. Fulbright Found. scholar, Sweden, 1960-61; recipient Auto Safety award Med. Tribune, 1967, Robert H. Ivy award 1969, Disting. Sci. Achievement award Wayne U. Coll. Medicine Alumni, 1975, Sanvenero-Rosselli award, 1981; McGregor scholar, U. Mich., 1946-49; grantee Ednl. Found. Am. Soc. Plastic and Reconstructive Surgery, 1964-65. Fellow ACS (pres. local commn. on trauma 1985-87); mem. Am. Assn. Plastic Surgeons (trustee 1990-91), Am. Soc. Plastic and Reconstructive Surgeons, Midwestern Assn. Plastic Surgeons (pres. 1978-79), Chgo. Soc. Plastic Surgeons (pres. 1970-72), Midwestern Assn. Plastic Surgeons (pres. 1978-79), Am. Soc. Maxillofacial Surgeons (pres. 1988-89, award of honor 1986), Am. Assn. Automotive Medicine (pres. 1970-71, A. Merkin award 1982), Am. Cleft Palate Assn., Am. Soc. Aesthetic Plastic Surgery, Tord Skoog Soc. Plastic Surgeons (pres. 1971-75), Can. Soc. Plastic Surgery, Chilean Soc. Plastic Surgery (corr.), Japanese Soc. Plastic Surgery (corr.), Cuban Soc. Maxillofacial Surgery (corr.), Korean Soc. Plastic Surgery (corr.). Office: PO Box 357 Northport MI 49670-0357 Office Phone: 231-386-5950. Business E-Mail: schultz5@coslink.net.

SCHULTZ, RICHARD DALE, national athletic organization executive; b. Grinnell, Iowa, Sept. 5, 1929; s. August Henry and Marjorie Ruth (Turner) S.; m. Jacquilyn Lu Duistermars, June 26, 1949; children: Robert Dale, William Joel, Kim Marie. BS, Ctrl. Coll., Pella, Iowa, 1950; EdD (hon.), Ctrl. Coll., 1987; LLD (hon.), Wartburg Coll., 1988, Alma Coll., 1989, Luther Coll., 1991; PhD (hon.), U.S. Sports Acad., 1993; LLD (hon.), Daniel Webster Coll., 1997, Gettysburg Coll., 1998. Head basketball coach, athletic dir. Humboldt (Iowa) High Sch., 1950-60; freshman basketball coach U. Iowa, Iowa City, 1960-62, head baseball coach, assoc. basketball coach, 1962-70, head basketball coach, 1970-74, asst. v.p., 1974-76; dir. athletics and phys. edn. Cornell U., Ithaca, NY, 1976-81; dir. athletics U. Va., Charlottesville, 1981-87; exec. dir. NCAA, Mission, Kans., 1987-94; pres. Global Sports Enterprises, 1994-95; exec. dir. U.S. Olympic Com., Colorado Springs, Colo., 1995—2000; chmn. Mktg. Assocs. Internat., 2000—04; chmn., CEO, Internat. Partnerships, 2002—. Mem. honors ct. Nat. Football Found. and Hall of Fame, Nat. Basketball Hall of Fame, 1992; chmn. bd. NCAA Found., 1989; organizer Iowa Steel Mill, Inc.; trustee Gettysburg Coll., 1996—99; bd. dirs. Hanspree Corp., Tacipe, Twaian. Author: A Course of Study for the Coaching of Baseball, 1964, The Theory and Techniques of Coaching Basketball, 1970; Contbr. articles to mags. Bd. dirs. Fellowship of Christian Athletes, 1986, chmn., 1990; chmn. Multiple Sclerosis, 1974-75; mem. Knight Found. Commn. on Intercollegiate Athletics, 1990—; mem. adv. com. on svc. acad. athletic programs Def. Dept. Recipient Disting. Alumni award Ctrl. Coll., Pella, 1970, 98, Lifetime Svc. award U. Iowa, 1994, Corbett award Nat. Assn. Collegiate Dirs. Athletics, 1994, medal of honor Ellis Island, 1997, Disting. Alumni award Ctrl. Coll., 1998, Casey award, 1999, Pres. and Mrs. Bush Cmty. Impact award 1999; mem. Basketball Hall of Fame Honor Ct., 1992, Sportsman of Yr. award Marine Corp., 1997; inducted into Iowa Baseball Hall of Fame, 1993, Ctrl. Coll. Hall of Honors, 2002, Des Moines Register Hall of Fame, 2003. Mem. Nat. Assn. Coll. Basketball Coaches, Ea. Coll. Athletic Assn. (mem. exec. com. 1980-81), Am. Basketball Coaches Assn. (Award of Honor 1994), Am. Football Coaches Assn. (internat. dir. CEO forum 2005-, lifetime membership award 1995). Home: 3670 Twisted Oak Cir Colorado Springs CO 80904-4720 Home Phone: 719-685-3238; Office Phone: 719-685-3245. Personal E-mail: dschultzprint2@earthlink.net.

SCHULTZ, RICHARD MICHAEL, biochemistry educator, researcher; b. Phila., Oct. 28, 1942; s. William and Beatrice (Levine) S.; m. Rima M. Lunin, Mar. 7, 1965; children: Carl M., Eli J. BA, SUNY, Binghamton, 1964; PhD, Brandeis U., 1969. Rsch. fellow Harvard U. Med. Sch., Boston, 1969-71; asst. prof. Loyola U. Stritch Sch. of Medicine, Maywood, Ill., 1971-78, assoc. prof., 1978-84, prof., 1984—, chmn. dept. molecular and cellular biochemistry, 1984-2000. Mem. adv. med. bd. Leukemia Rsch. Found., Chgo., 1987-91. Co-author: Textbook of Biochemistry; contbr. articles to profl. jours., chapters to books. Recipient Rsch. grants NIH. Achievements include in vivo evidence for the role of protease enzymes and their inhibitors in regulating tumor cell metastasis, ras oncogene pathways in cancer, role of JNK and c-Jun in cancer cell protease expression, obtaining evidence on the nature of the transition-state in serine protease enzyme catalysis. Office: Divsn Molecular & Cellular Biochemistry Loyola U Sch Medicine Maywood IL 60153 Home Phone: 708-383-7026; Office Phone: 708-216-9378. E-mail: rschult@lumc.edu.

SCHULTZ, RICHARD OTTO, ophthalmologist, educator; b. Racine, Wis., Mar. 19, 1930; s. Henry Arthur and Josephine (Wagoner) S.; m. Diane Haldane, Sept. 29, 1990; children: Henry Reid, Richard Paul, Karen Jo. BA, U. Wis., 1950, MS, 1954; MD, Albany Med. Coll., 1956; MSc, U. Iowa, 1960. Diplomate Am. Bd. Ophthalmology. Intern, Univ. Hosps., Iowa City, 1956-57, resident in opthalmology, 1957-60; chief ophthalmology sect. div. Indian health USPHS, Phoenix, 1960-63; practice medicine specializing in ophthalmology Phoenix, 1963; NIH spl. fellow in ophthalmic microbiology U. Calif., San Francisco, 1963-64, clin. assoc., 1963-64, research assoc., 1963-64; assoc. prof., chmn. dept. ophthalmology Marquette U. Sch. Medicine (now Med. Coll. Wis.), Milw., 1964-68, prof., chmn., 1968-97, prof. ophthalmology, 1997—2000, prof. emeritus, 2000—. Mem. nat. adv. eye coun. NIH, 1984-88; cons. Froedert Hosp., Milw. Contbr. articles to profl. jours. Served with USPHS, 1960-63. Fellow: ACS (life), Am. Ophthalmol. Soc. (emeritus), Am. Acad. Ophthalmology (life); mem.: Milw. Acad. Medicine, Oxford Ophthalmol. Congress (Eng.), Rsch. to Prevent Blindness, N.Y. Acad. Scis. (emeritus), Pan Am. Assn. Ophthalmology (life), Assn. Rsch. Vision and Ophthalmology (emeritus), Milw. Ophthal. Soc., Assn. Univ. Profs. Ophthalmology (past pres., trustee). Home: 7505 S Kangaroo Lake Rd Baileys Harbor WI 54202 Office Phone: 414-456-7915. Personal E-mail: eyeotto@aol.com.

SCHULTZ, ROBERT JORDAN, orthopaedic surgeon, educator; b. Bklyn., June 29, 1930; m. Marcie Schultz. Student, Muhlenberg Coll., 1948-49; BS, Bklyn. Coll., 1952; MD, Chgo. Med. Sch., 1957. Diplomate Am. Bd. Orthopedic Surgery (examiner). Intern Meadowbrook Hosp., Hempstead, NY, 1957-58; resident in surgery Mt. Sinai Hosp., Miami, Fla., 1958-59; resident in orthopaedic surgery Charity Hosp., New Orleans, 1959-62; fellow in hand surgery Columbia Presbyn. Med. Ctr., NYC, 1968; instr. dept. orthopaedic surgery Albert Einstein Coll. Medicine, NYC, 1966-73, asst. prof., 1968-73, assoc. prof., 1973-77; lectr. div. prosthesis and orthotics NYU Postgrad. Med. Sch., 1968—; dir. dept. orthopaedic surgery Albert Einstein Coll. Medicine, NYC, 1969-77; prof. dept. surgery N.Y. Med. Coll., Valhalla, 1988-90, prof. dept. anatomy, 1987-90, dir. sports medicine, dept. orthopaedic surgery, 1980—, dir. Sylvester J. Carter Hand Svc., 1980—, prof., chmn. dept. orthopaedic surgery, 1977—; with U. S. Fal. Med. Ctr., Tampa, 1990—. Dir., attending surgeon dept. orthopaedic surgery Westchester County Med. Ctr., Valhalla, 1977—, dir. sports medicine, 1978—; attending orthopaedic surgeon, Met. Hosp., N.Y.C., 1977—, Lincoln Hosp., Bronx, 1977—, Lenox Hill Hosp., N.Y.C., 1982—, Terence Cardinal Cooke Health Care Ctr., N.Y.C., 1977—, Bronx Mcpl. Hosp. Ctr., 1966-77; dir. and attending orthopaedic surgeon Hosp. of Albert Einstein Coll. Medicine, Bronx, 1969-77; presenter papers, exhibits, invited lectr. to numerous nat. and internat. assns., hosps., med. colls., postgrad. courses; spl. orthopaedic del. to People's Republic of China, 1981, chmn. dels., 1983, 86; med. cons. N.Y. State Athletic Commn., chmn. of med. adv. bd.; adv. coun. USN; vis. prof. Haddasah Hosp. and Med. Sch., Jerusalem, 1972, Browley Bristow Orthopaedic Hosp., Surrey, Eng., 1973, U. Colo., 1977, University Cattolica del Sacro Cuore, Rome, 1984, Michael Reese Hosp. & Med. Ctr., Chgo., 1984, Bethesda Naval Hosp., 1986, U. W.Va. Med. Sch., Morgantown, 1988;; adv. com. State of Conn. Higher Edn. Supplemental Loan Authority, 1983—; police surgeon of Westchester County (N.Y.) Police Dept., 1983—, commdg. officer police surgeons, 1984—. Author: The Language of Fractures, 1972; editor Jour. Hand Surgery; mem. editorial bd. Jour. Orthopaedic Surg. Techniques, Surg. Rounds for Orthopaedics; contbr. chpts. to books, articles and abstracts to sci. and med. jours. Mem. grant rev. com. Orthopedic Rsch. and Edn. Found. Career Devel. Awards Com., Fellowsip Grant Com., The Mary and David Hoar Fellowsship Com. N.Y. Acad. Medicine; sr. investigator N.Y. Med. Coll. for Aging and Adult Devel., 1984—. With USN, 1962-66; flight surgeon, 1963-65, capt. USNR, 1980—. Fellow ACS, Am. Acad. Orthopaedic Surgeons, N.Y. Acad. Medicine (sec. sect. orthopaedic surgery 1979-80, chmn. 1980-81); mem. AMA, Am. Orthopaedic Assn., Am. Soc. for Surgery of the Hand, Societe Internationale de Chirurgie Orthopedique et de Traumatologie, Sociedad de Cirugia de la Mano del Caribe (hon.), Amicale Internationale de Chirurgie de la Main (hon.), Soc. Med. Cons. to Armed Forces, Ea. Orthopaedic Assn., Am. Rheumatism Assn., N.Y. Soc. Orthopaedic Surgeons, Westchester Acad. Medicine (chmn. sect. sports medicine, 1979-81), N.Y. Soc. for Surgery of the Hand (sec. 1981-83, v.p. 1983-84, pres. 1985-86).

SCHULTZ, ROGER C., career military officer; b. LeMars, Iowa, Oct. 13, 1945; s. Harry Willis and Sylvia Dorothy (Aronson) S.; m. Barbara J. Kaiser, Feb. 14, 1969. BS, Upper Iowa U., 1988; MPA, Shippensburg U., 1992. Commd. USNG, advanced through grades to brig. gen., 1996; rifle platoon leader Co. A 2d Bn., 133d Inf., Ft. Carson, Colo., 1968-69; scout leader Hdqs. and Hdqs. Co. 2d Bn., 22d Inf., Vietnam, 1969; logistics, personnel, intelligence officer HHC 2d Bn., 133d Inf., Sioux City, Iowa, 1970-75, rifle co. comdr. Co. B Sheldon, Iowa, 1975-76, ops. and tng. officer HHC Sioux City, Iowa, 1976-78; brigade ops. and tng. officer 34th Brigade, 47th Inf., Boone, Iowa, 1978-81, exec. officer, 1981-82; bn. comdr. 1st Bn., 168th Inf., Council Bluffs, Iowa, 1982-84; dir. op. and tng. Iowa Army Nat. Guard, Johnston, Iowa, 1984-88, chief of staff, 1988-95, dep. adjutant gen., 1995—98; dir. Army Nat. Guard, Washington, 1998—. Lobbyist Dept. Pub. Def., Des Moines, 1996. Decorated Silver Star, 1969, Bronze Star, 1969, Purple Heart (2 awards), 1969, Legion of Merit, 1995. Presbyterian. Office: NG Bur 1411 Jefferson Davis Hwy Arlington VA 22202-3231

SCHULTZ, STANLEY GEORGE, physiologist, educator, dean; b. Bayonne, NJ, Oct. 26, 1931; s. Aaron and Sylvia (Kaplan) S.; m. Harriet Taran, Dec. 25, 1960; children: Jeffrey, Kenneth. AB summa cum laude, Columbia U., NYC, 1952; MD, NYU, 1956. Intern Bellevue Hosp., NYC, 1956-57, resident, 1957-59; research assoc. in biophysics Harvard U., 1959-62, instr. biophysics, 1964-67; assoc. prof. physiology U. Pitts., 1967-70, prof. physiology, 1970-79; prof., chmn. dept. physiology U. Tex. Med. Sch., Houston, 1979-96, prof. dept. internal medicine, 1979—, prof. dept. integrative biol. pharm. physiology, 1997—, vice chmn., 1999—2003, Fondren chair in cell signalling, 1999—, dean Sch. Medicine, 2003—06, H. Wayne Hightower Dist. prof. biomed. sci., 2005—. Cons. USPHS, NIH, 1970—; mem. physiology test com. Nat. Bd. Med. Examiners, 1974-79, chmn., 1976-79 Editor Am. Jour. Physiology, Jour. Applied Physiology, 1971-75, Physiol. Revs., 1979-85, Handbook of Physiology: The Gastrointestinal Tract, 1989-91—; mem. editl. bd. Jour. Gen. Physiology, 1969-88, Ann. Revs. Physiology, 1974-81, Current Topics in Membranes and Transport, 1975-81, Jour. Membrane Biology, 1977—, Biochim. Biophys. Acta, 1987-89; assoc. editor Ann. Revs. Physiology, 1977-81; assoc. editor News in Physiol. Scis., 1989-94, editor, 1994-2003; contbr. articles to profl. jours. Served to capt. M.C. USAF, 1962-64. Recipient Rsch. Career award NIH, 1969-74, Solomon Berson award NYU, 2003; overseas fellow Churchill Coll., Cambridge U., 1975-76 Mem. AAAS, AMA (coun. on med. edn.), Am. Heart Assn. (estab. investigator 1964-68), Am. Physiol. Soc. (councillor 1989-91, pres.-elect 1991-92, pres. 1992-93, past pres. 1993-94, Guyton award 1997, Orr Reynolds award 1999, Daggs award 2003), European Acad. Sci., Fed. Am. Soc. Exptl. Biology (exec. bd. 1992-95), Biophys. Soc., Soc. Gen. Physiologists, Internat. Cell Rsch. Orgn., Internat. Union Physiol. Scis. (chmn. internat. com. gastrointestinal physiology 1977-80, chmn. U.S. nat. com. 1992-98), Assn. Am. Physicians, Am. Assn. Ob-Gyn. (hon. fellow), Assn. Chmn. Depts. Physiology (pres. 1985-86), Houston Philos. Soc., Phi Beta Kappa, Sigma Xi. Home Phone: 713-729-7660; Office Phone: 713-500-5012. Business E-Mail: stanley.g.schultz@uth.tmc.edu.

SCHULTZ, T. PAUL, economics professor; b. Ames, Iowa, May 24, 1940; s. Theodore W. and Esther (Werth) S.; m. Judith Hoenack, Sept. 16, 1967; children: Lara, Joel, Rebecca. BA, Swarthmore Coll., 1961; PhD, MIT, 1966; MA (hon.), Yale U., 1974. Cons. Joint Econ. Com., Washington, 1964; rschr. econ. dept. Rand Corp., Santa Monica, Calif., 1965-72, dir. population rsch., 1968-72; prof. econ. U. Minn., Mpls., 1972-75, Yale U., New Haven, 1974—, dir. Econ. Growth Ctr., 1983-96; prof. econ. Malcolm K. Brachman, 1977. Cons. World Bank, Rockefeller Found., InterAm. Devel. Bank; mem. com. on population NAS, Washington, 1987-89, 90-93. Author: Structural Change in a Developing Country, 1971, Economics of Population, 1981; editor: (books) The State of Development Economics, 1988, Investment In Women's Human Capital, 1995, (periodical) Research in Population Economics, 1985, 88, 91, 96; assoc. editor Jour. Population Econs., 1991—, Econ. of Edn. Rev., 1993-2004, China Econ. Rev., 1994-2004. Mem. commn. on behavioral sci. and edn. Nat. Rsch. Coun., 1997-2002. Fellow: AAAS (population resources environ. com. 1985—89, nomination com. 1987—90); mem.: Econ. Rsch. Forum for Arab Countries (trustee 1993—2001), European Soc. for Population Econs. (bd. dirs., pres. 1997), Soc. for Study Social Biology (bd. dirs. 1986—89), Internat. Union for Sci. Study Population, Population Assn. Am. (bd. dirs. 1979—81, Irene B. Taeuber award for rsch. 2007), Econometrics Soc., Am. Econ. Assn. Office: Yale U Econ Growth Ctr PO Box 208269 27 Hillhouse Ave New Haven CT 06520-8269 E-mail: paul.schultz@yale.edu.

SCHULTZ, VICTOR M., physician; b. Pitts., Aug. 14, 1932; s. Irvin and Rose (Reiss) S. BS, Kent State U., Ohio, 1955; MD, Ohio State U., Columbus, 1958. Diplomate Am. Bd. Dermatology. Pvt. practice, Santa Monica, Calif., 1965—. Fellow Am. Acad. Dermatology, Pacific Dermatologic Assn.; mem. AMA, Am. Coll. Physicians, Calif. Med. Assn., L.A. County Med. Assn. Avocations: skiing, tennis, golf, music, swimming. Office: 2461 Santa Monica Blvd Santa Monica CA 90404-2049 Home Phone: 310-826-6832; Office Phone: 310-828-7492.

SCHULTZ, VICTORIA L., harpist, entertainer, music educator; b. Kansas City, Mo., May 12, 1952; d. Kenneth Leroy and Russie Juanita (McIntosh) S. BMusic, U. Mo., Kansas City, 1975; M Music, Drake U., 1977. Opera coach, accompanist, prof. piano U. Ctrl. Fla., Orlando, 1977-80; prof. voice and piano Valencia C.C., Orlando, 1980-86; music dir. Pine Castle (Fla.) Ctr. of the Arts, 1983-84; pianist, harpist Hyatt Regency Grand Cypress, Orlando, 1984-96; pianist Altamonte Springs (Fla.) Hilton and Towers, 1985-89; pianist, harpist Caruso's Palace, Orlando, 1990-94; harpist Sergio's Restaurant, Orlando, 1994-95. Adj. prof. voice Rollins Coll., Winter Park, Fla., 1991-92; entertainer Walt Disney World, Orlando, 1996—; adj. prof. harp U. Ctrl. Fla., Orlando, 1998-2006, adj. prof. voice Valencia CC, Orlando, 2002-04; pvt. tchr. and freelance entertainer, Fla., 1980—; clinician Harpcon, 2003. Composer: (music for piano and voice) Set of Songs, 1979; arranger/composer: albums Orange Blossom Tale, 1996, arranger/performer: albums Harp Dreams, 1997, Harp Favorites, 1998, Soothing Harp, 1999, Victoria Lynn-Live in Concert, 2004, composer, harpist: Harp Meditation for Chakra Attunement, 2001, Celtic Crossings with Tryskelon, 2006; author: (textbook) You CAN Play the Harp, 2002. Sponsor, Riverside Musicale Jr. Music Club, Orlando, 1991—; entertainer fund raising events for AHA, Am. Cancer Soc., Muscular Dystrophy, Am. Diabetes Assn., Cystic Fibrosis; artist-in-residence Fla. Hosp. Recipient Nat. 1st Place award Encore Prodns. Talent Competition, 1985, 86, State Young Artist 1st prize Fla. Fedn. Music Clubs, 1976, Silver medal Internat. Piano Rec. Competition, Am. Coll. Musicians, 1978. Mem. Ctrl. Fla. Musicians Assn. (local 389), Am. Harp Soc., Fla. Harpers and Friends (1st Place Composition award 2002, People's Choice award 2002), Ctrl. Fla. Music Tchrs. Assn. (recital chmn. 1999-2000), Orlando Music Club (founding mem.), Music Tchrs. Nat. Assn., Scottish Harp Soc. of Am. Democrat. Avocations: reading, movies, going to concerts, shopping. Home: 848 River Cove Ave Orlando FL 32825-8107 Office: Harpspun Prodns PMB 306 509 S Chickasaw Trl Orlando FL 32825-7852 Office Phone: 407-381-4440. Business E-Mail: victoria@victoriaschultz.com.

SCHULTZ, WILLIAM B., lawyer; b. Bloomington, Ind., Mar. 16, 1948; BA, Yale U., 1970; JD, U. of Va. Sch. of Law, 1974. Bar: Va., DC 1975, U.S. Supreme Ct. Law clk. Hon. William B. Bryant, Washington, 1974—75; adj. prof. Georgetown U. Law Ctr., Washington, 1983—93, 1996; atty. Pub. Citizen Litigation Grp., 1975—89; counsel Subcommittee on Health and Environ., U.S. Ho. of Reps., 1990—94; asst. commn. Policy, U.S. Food and Drug Adminstrn., 1994—98; asst. dep. Mng. Civil Division's Appellate and Tobacco Litigation, U.S. Dept. of Justice, 1999—2000; atty. Zuckerman Spaeder LLP, 2000—. Named one of 100 Most Influential Lawyers, Nat. Law Jour., 2006; recipient Disting. Svc. and Leadership Award, Food and Drug Law Inst., 2005. Mem.: DC Cir. Historical Soc. (treas.), Keystone Ctr. (bd. mem.), Ctr. for Sci. in Pub. Interest (bd. mem.). Office: Zuckerman Spaeder LLP 1800 M St NW Suite 1000 Washington DC 20036-5802

SCHULWEIS, HAROLD MAURICE, rabbi; b. NYC, Apr. 14, 1925; s. Maurice and Helen (Rezak) S.; m. Malkah Muriel Savod, June 22, 1947; children: Seth, Ethan, Alissa. BA, Yeshiva Coll., 1945; MA, NYU, 1948; MHL, Jewish Theol. Sem., 1950, DD (hon.), 1975; ThD, Pacific Sch. Religion, 1970; HHD (hon.), Hebrew Union Coll., 1983. Rabbi Conservative Jewish Congregation, 1945, Temple Emanuel, Parkchester, N.Y., 1950-52, Temple Beth Abraham, Oakland, Calif., 1952-70, Valley Beth Shalom, Encino, Calif., 1970—. Instr. philosophy CCNY, 1948-51; adj. prof. contemporary civilization U. Judaism, L.A., 1970—; lectr. Jewish theology Hebrew Union Coll., L.A., 1971—; guest of Govt. of Fed. Republic Germany to observe rehab. of German ednl. instns., 1966; mem. nat. rabbinical cabinet Rabbinical Assembly, 1968, sec. assembly, 1978; mem. faculty B'nai B'rith Adult Edn. Commn; founder, dir, Schulweis Inst Author: Evil and the Morality of God, 1983; also articles; co-author: Approaches to the Philosophy of Religion, 1952; mem. editorial bd. The Reconstructionist, 1970—, Moment, 1974—, Davka, 1974—, Sh'ma, 1974—. Founder Inst. for the Righteous Arts, Judah Magnes Mus., Berkeley, Calif., 1961; founder, chmn. Inst. for Righteous Acts—Documentation and Study Ctr. on Rescuers of Jews in the Nazi Era. Recipient Social Actions award United Synagogue Am., 1969, medal Prime Min. of Israel, 1975; named one of The Top 50 Rabbis in America, Newsweek Mag. 2007. Office: 15739 Ventura Blvd Encino CA 91436-2903 *

SCHULZ, DAVID ALAN, lawyer, educator; b. Blue Island, Ill., Mar. 30, 1952; s. Edmund Leonard and Marjorie Ann (Johnson) S. BA magna cum laude, Knox Coll., 1974; MA in Econs., Yale U., 1976, JD, 1978. Bar: NY 1979, DC, US Dist. Ct. (so., no., we. and ea. dists.) NY, US Ct. Appeals (2d, 3rd and DC cirs.), US Supreme Ct, US Ct. Appeals (4th cir.), US Dist. Ct. NY and DC. Assoc. Rogers & Wells, NYC, 1978-86, ptnr., 1986—, Levine Sullivan Koch & Schulz, L.L.P., NYC, 2003—. Adj. assoc. prof. Fordham Law Sch., 1983—, Bklyn. Law Sch., 2006-. Contbr. articles to profl. jours. Mem. N.Y. State Com. on Open Govt., 1988—; trustee Knox Coll., 1976-79, 89—. Recipient The Best Lawyers in Am. Mem. ABA (forum com. on communications law), ACLU, NY City Bar Assn. Office: Levine Sullivan Koch & Schulz LLP 230 Park Ave Ste 1160 New York NY 10169 Office Phone: 212-850-6103. Office Fax: 212-850-6299. Business E-Mail: dschulz@lskslaw.com.

SCHULZ, EKKEHARD, metal products executive; b. Bydgoszcz, Poland, July 24, 1941; PhD in metallurgy, Clausthal U., 1971. Chmn. exec. bd. Thyssen Krupp AG; mem. sci. staff & chief engr. Clausthal U., 1967—72; with Thyssen Group, 1972, appt. dep. mem., 1985—; appt. regular mem., exec. bd. ThyssenStahl AG, 1986—, head tech. directorate, 1988—, appt. chmn. exec. bd., 1991—, mem. exec. bd., 1991—; chmn. exec. bd. Thyssen Krupp Stahl AG, 1997—, Thyssen AG, 1998—; co-chmn. exec. bd. ThyssenKrupp AG, 1999—2001, chmn exec. bd., 2001—, ThyssenKrupp Steel AG, 1999—2001. Bd. dirs. Budd Co.; mem. supervisory bds. Commerzbank AG, Hapag Lloyd AG, MAN AG, Energie AG, Strabag AG; former chmn. MAN AG, second vice chmn., 2007-; pres. Eurofer; com. mem., bd. Wirtschaftsvereinigung Stahl, VDEh. Recipient hon. professorship, Clausthal U., 1999. Office: Thyssen Krupp AG August Thyssen Str 1 40211 Düsseldorf Germany *

SCHULZ, JOHN JOSEPH, communications educator; BA in Journalism, U. Mont., 1962; MPhil, Oxford U., 1979, DPhil, 1981; student, Nat. War Coll., Washington, 1985-86. Newswriter, reporter Voice of Am. News, Washington, 1971-72, corr. Hong Kong, 1972-74, bur. chief Tokyo, 1974-77; commentator BBC, London, 1977-79; coverage editor Voice of Am., 1979-82; dep. dir. Voice of Am. News Divsn., 1982—85; South Asia corr. Voice of Am. News, Islamabad, Pakistan, 1987-89; thinktank analyst Oxford Analytica, 1977-79, 84-88; prof. Nat. War Coll., Washington, 1989-91; sr. corr. Voice of Am. News, 1986—87, 1991—92; assoc. dir. publs. The Arms Control Assn., 1992-95; prof. internat. comm. Coll. Comm. Boston U., 1995—97, 2000—03, 2006—, chair dept. mass. comm., advt., and pub. rels., 1997—2000, dean. Coll. Comm., 2003—06; editor Arms Control Today, 1992-95. Presenter in field. Editor-in-chief Global Beat Syndicate, 2002-06; contbr. articles to profl. jours. With USAF, 1963-71. Decorated 3 DFC, silver star, air medals, gallantry crosses; recipient disting. alumni award U. Mont., 1995. Office: Coll Communication 640 Commonwealth Ave Boston MA 02215-2422 Business E-Mail: jjschulz@bu.edu.

SCHULZ, JUERGEN, art historian, educator; b. Kiel, Germany, Aug. 18, 1927; came to U.S., 1938; s. Johannes Martin Askan Schulz and Ilse (Lebenbaum) Hiller; m. Justine Hume, Sept. 1951 (div. 1968); children: Christoph (dec.), Ursula, Catherine; m. Anne Markham, May 19, 1969; 1 child, Jeremy. BA, U. Calif., Berkeley, 1950; PhD in History of Art, U. London, 1958. Reporter San Francisco Chronicle, 1950-51; copy editor UPI, London, 1952-53; from instr. to prof. history of art U. Calif., 1958-68; prof. Brown, Providence, 1968-90, Andrea V. Rosenthal prof. history art and architecture, 1990-95; Samuel H. Kress prof. Nat. Gallery of Art, 2000-2001. Mem. Inst. for Advanced Study, Princeton, N.J., 1971-72. Author: Venetian Painted Ceilings of the Renaissance, 1968, Printed Plans and...Views of Venice, 1971, La cartografia tra scienza e arte, 1990, The New Palaces of Medieval Venice, 2004; also articles. Staff sgt. U.S. Army, 1945-48. Decorated grande ufficiale Ordine della Stella della Solidarieta della Repubblica Italiana; Guggenheim fellow, 1966-67. Mem. Ateneo Veneto, Centro Internaz. di Studi di Architettura A. Palladio. Office: Brown U Dept History Art and Architecture PO Box 1855 Providence RI 02912-1855 Office Phone: 401-863-1174.

SCHULZ, KEITH DONALD, corporate lawyer, writer; b. Burlington, Iowa, Dec. 20, 1938; s. Henry Carl and Laura Iral (Bowlin) S.; m. Emily Brook Roane, Apr. 19, 1985; children: Keith Jr., Sarah, Christine, Stefan. BA, U. Iowa, 1960, JD, 1963. Bar: Iowa 1963, Ill. 1966, Wis. 1990. Dep. Sec. of State, State of Iowa, Des Moines, 1965-66; atty. AT&T, Chgo., 1966-67; sec., gen. counsel Borg-Warner Acceptance Corp., Chgo., 1967-74; asst. gen. counsel Borg-Warner Corp., Chgo., 1974-84, v.p., gen. counsel, 1984-88; of counsel Bell, Boyd & Lloyd, Chgo., 1988—. Chmn., CEO Downtown Ptnrs., Inc., 1995-96. Author: (novel) Keepers of the River, 2001; contbr. articles to Harvard Bus. Rev., Jour. for Corp. Growth. Mem. Theatre Bldg. Chgo., 1975-85, chair, 1977-82, bd. dirs., 1977-82; chmn. bd. dirs. Vol. Legal Svcs. Found., Chgo., 1984-91, pres.; bd. dirs. S.E. Iowa Symphony Orch., pres., 1998-2000, 03—, Heritage Trust Found.; mem. Capitol Theater Found., 2006-, bd. dirs., 2006-. Mem.: Assn. Gen. Counsel, Wis. Bar Assn., Econ. Club, Univ. Club. Avocations: tennis, bicycling, skiing. Office: Bell Boyd & Lloyd 70 W Madison St Ste 3300 Chicago IL 60602-4284 Home Phone: 312-654-0387; Office Phone: 312-372-1121. Personal E-mail: KDons@aol.com.

SCHULZ, RAYMOND ALEXANDER, medical marketing professional, consultant; b. Paris, June 2, 1946; s. Helmut W. and Colette (Prieur) S.; m. Dixie Lee Suzanne Specht, Apr. 9, 1977 (div. Dec. 1990); children: Christopher, William; m. Casey Elizabeth Watson, Apr. 10, 1999; 1 child, Francis John. BA in Physics, W.Va. U., Morgantown, 1970; MS in Computer Sci., Columbia U., NYC, 1975. Sr. programmer Meml. Sloan Kettering Cancer Ctr., NYC, 1972-74; program coord. Neurol. Inst. Columbia Presbyn. Hosp., NYC, 1974-76; engring. mgr. EMI Med. Systems, Northbrook, Ill., 1976-78; product mgr. Johnson & Johnson (Technicare), Solon, Ohio, 1978-80; group product mgr. Siemens Corp., Iselin, NJ, 1980-82; mktg. mgr. Toshiba Am. Med. Systems (formerly Diasonics MRI), South San Francisco, Calif., 1983-92; dir. mktg. Voxel, Laguna Hills, Calif., 1992—98; v.p. mktg. and customer support Voxel, Inc., Provo, Utah, 1999—2001; prin. RAenterprises, San Mateo, Calif., 2001—; v.p. mktg. and sales Scanis, Inc., Foster City, Calif., 2002—03; tech. dir. Accuray, Sunnyvale, Calif. Bd. dirs. Dynecology, Harrison, NY, 2004—07; presenter in field; mktg. mgr. Varian Med.-Surg. Scis., Palo Alto, Calif., 2007—. Editor (pubs.): Robtoic Radiosurgery, 2005, Robotics Radio Surgery: Treating Tumors that Move with Respiration, 2007; contbr. articles to profl. jours. Mem. vestry St. Matthews Episcopal Ch., San Mateo, Calif., 2006—. Recipient first prize Roentgen Centenary Congress, 1995, Best Paper prize Am. Assn. Neurol. Surgeons, San Francisco, 2000, 06. Mem. Am. Assn. Physicists in Medicine, N.Y. Acad. Scis., Internat. Soc. Magnetic Resonance in Medicine, Med. Mktg. Assn., Larchmont Yacht Club, Commonwealth Club Calif., Eta Kappa Nu. Avocations: skiing, running, hiking, swimming, mountainbiking. Personal E-mail: ras257@columbia.edu.

SCHULZ, RENATE ADELE, German studies and second language acquisition educator; b. Lohr am Main, Germany, Feb. 24, 1940; came to U.S., 1958; 1 child, Sigrid Diane. BS, Mankato State Coll., 1962; MA, U. Colo., 1967; PhD, Ohio State U., 1974. Edn. officer U.S. Peace Corps, Ife Ezinihitte, Nigeria, 1963-65; asst. prof. Otterbein Coll., Westerville, Ohio, 1974-76, State U. Coll. N.Y., Buffalo, 1976-77; from asst. to assoc. prof. U. Ark., Fayetteville, 1977-81; from assoc. to prof. U. Ariz., Tucson, 1981—, head dept. German, 1984-90, chair PhD program in second lang. acquisition and teaching, 1994-97. Disting. vis. prof. USAF Acad., Colorado Springs, Colo., 1990-91; co-dir. Ctr. Ednl. Resources in Culture, Lang. and Literacy, 2006-07. Recipient Creative Tchg. award, U. Ariz. Found., Tucson, 1984, Stephen A. Freeman award, N.W. Conf. Tchg. Fgn. Langs., 1984, Bundesverdienstkreuz, Fed. Govt. Germany, 1990, Anthony Papalia award for excellence in tchr. edn., Am. Coun. on the Tchg. of Fgn. Langs./N.Y. State Assn. Fgn. Lang. Tchrs., 2002, Henry and Phyllis Koffler prize for outstanding accomplishments in tchg., U. Ariz., 2005. Mem.: Nat. Fedn. Modern Lang. Tchrs. Assns. (v.p. 2004—05, pres. 2006—), Am. Assn. Applied Linguistics, Tchrs. of ESL, Am. Assn. Tchrs. German (v.p. 1988—90, pres. 1990—91), Am. Coun. on the Tchg. of Fgn. Langs. (exec. coun. 1979—81, Florence Steiner award 1993). Office: U Ariz Dept German Studies Tucson AZ 85721-0105 Office Phone: 520-621-7388. Business E-Mail: schulzr@u.arizona.edu.

SCHULZ, SALLY ANN, pastoral musician, conductor, educator; b. Red Oak, Iowa, Mar. 12, 1951; d. Robert Lionel and Mary Ellen Evans; m. Thomas Richard Schulz, Dec. 29, 1972; children: Matthew Thomas, Joanne Elizabeth. MusB, U. of Iowa, 1969—73. Indepent piano tchr. Schulz Studio, Bettendorf, Iowa, 1973—77; ind. piano & organ tchr. Freeport, Ill., 1977—88; dir. music St. Thomas Aquinas Ch., Freeport, Ill., 1984—90; elem. vocal music tchr. Freeport Cath. Sch., Freeport, Ill., 1988—90, Trinity Episcopal Day Sch., Baton Rouge, 1991—92; dir. music St. Ann's Ch., Long Grove, Iowa, 1993—95; dir. music & liturgy St. John Vianney Ch., Bettendorf, Iowa, 1995—2005; dir. music Rivermont Collegiate, Bettendorf, 2006—. Mem. Diocesan Liturgical Commn., Davenport, Iowa, 2002—05; prin. organist Christ Episc. Ch., Moline, Ill., 2006—. Mem.: Am. Guild of English Handbell Ringers, Am. Guild of Organists, Nat. Pastoral Musicians, Nat. Soc. Colonial Dames of Am., Delta Gamma. Achievements include Selected as a member of the MASTER CHORALE of the USA for the 2003 Festival Internazionale di Music e Arte Sacra in Rome; Selected by Paul Wilkes for his book Excellent Catholic Parishes published by Paulist Press. Home: 2993 Greenview Dr Bettendorf IA 52722

SCHULZ, WALTER KURT, accountant, information technology consultant; b. Hamburg, Germany, Apr. 9, 1940; came to U.S., 1970; s. Richard and Karla (Halm) S.; m. Beth Ann Edwards, June 21, 1972; children: Alec, Elli, Peter, Andrew, Heidi. MBA, U. Münster, Germany, 1969; M in Acctg., Ohio State U., 1972. Auditor Dr. Kaase, CPA, Bad Oeynhausen, Germany, 1966-71; systems analyst United Airlines, Chgo., 1973-77; v.p. fin. Eickhoff-Nat. Corp., Pitts., 1977-79; div. controller Mobay Corp., Pitts., 1979-86; owner Infotek/Euronet, Inc., Charlotte, N.C., 1986—; cons. Penske Nascar Racing, Charlotte Hornets. Cons. Westinghouse Corp., Mercy Hosp., Pitts, Charlotte Hornets. Lt. German Air Force, 1960-63.

Mem. Am. Mgmt. Assn., Assn. MBA Execs. Republican. Avocation: flying. Home: 301 Sardis Rd N Charlotte NC 28270-2245 Office Phone: 704-442-2414. Personal E-mail: walterkurts@hotmail.com.

SCHULZ, WILLIAM FREDERICK, human rights scholar and advocate; b. Pitts., Nov. 14, 1949; s. William F. and Jean Smith; m. Beth Graham, 1993. AB, Oberlin Coll., 1971; MA, Meadville/Lombard Theol. Sch., 1973, DMin, 1975, DDiv, 1987; MA, U. Chgo., 1974; DHL (hon.), Nova Southeastern U., 1995, Grinnell Coll., 2004, Willamette U., 2005, Oberlin Coll., 2005, U. Cinn., 2005, Lewis and Clark Coll., 2006. Minister First Parish Unitarian Universalist, Bedford, Mass., 1975-78; dir. social responsibility Unitarian Universalist Assn., Boston, 1978-79, exec. v.p., 1979-85, pres., 1985-93; exec. dir. Amnesty Internat. USA, 1994—2006; fellow Carr Ctr. Hunan Rights Policy, Kennedy Sch. Govt., Harvard U., 2006—07; adj. prof. The New Sch., 2006—; sr. fellow Ctr. for Am. Progress, 2006—. Author: Finding Time and Other Delicacies, 1992, In Our Own Best Interest: How Defending Human Rights Benefits Us All, 2001, Making the Manifesto: The Birth of Religious Humanism, 2002, Tainted Legacy: 9/11 and the Ruin of Human Rights, 2003; editor, contbr.: Transforming Words: Six Essays on Preaching, 1984; editor, contbr.: 2d edit., 1996, The Phenomenon of Torture: Readings and Commentary, 2007. Named Humanist of Yr., Am. Humanist Assn., 2000. Mem. ACLU, Unitarian Universalist Mins. Assn., Coun. Fgn. Rels. Democrat. E-mail: williamfschulz@yahoo.com.

SCHULZE, CHAD WILLIAM, lawyer; m. Kelly Schulze. BS in Speech Comm. and Polit. Sci., U. SD, Vermillion; JD, Hamline U. Sch. Law, St. Paul, 2002. Bar: Minn. 2002, US Dist. Ct. (dist. Minn.) 2003. Law clk. Rondoni, MacMillan & Schneider, Ltd., 2000—02; atty. Milavetz, Gallop & Milavetz, P.A., Edina, Minn., 2003—. Named a Rising Star, Minn. Super Lawyers mag., 2006, 2007. Mem.: Minn. Trial Lawyers Assn., Am. Trial Lawyers Assn. (mem. Vioxx litig. grp. 2004—, mem. Hurricane Katrina relief grp. 2005—), Ramsey County Bar Assn., Hennepin County Bar Assn., Minn. State Bar Assn., Am. Civil Liberty Union. Avocations: hunting, fishing. Office: Milavetz Gallop & Milavetz PA 6500 France Ave South Edina MN 55435 Office Phone: 952-920-7777. E-mail: attorneyschulze@netscape.net.

SCHULZE, CHERYL RANEA, secondary school educator; b. Nevada, Mo., Dec. 16, 1959; d. Nelson Ray and Ella Mae Brooks; m. Ron Schulze, June 15, 1979; children: Christopher, Kyle. BS in Edn., Pittsburg State U., Kans., 1982, MS in Secondary Edn., 1995. Tchr. 7th grade English, 8th grade reading Nevada Mid. Sch., 1983—85; tchr. 10th grade English Nevada R-5 Schs., 1986—. Coord. R-5 Drug Free Schs., Nevada, 1997—; bldg. rep. Nevada CTA; bd. dirs. Nevada Pks. Bd., 2000—03. Named Educator of Yr., Vernon County C. of C., 1996, Tchr. of Yr., Nevada R-5 Cmty. Tchrs. Assn., 1997—98, Mo. Wal-Mart Tchr. of Yr., 2006. Baptist. Home: Rte 1 Box 23 Nevada MO 64772 Office: Nevada HS 800 W Hickory Nevada MO 64772 Office Phone: 417-448-2020. Office Fax: 417-448-2039. E-mail: crschulze@nevada.k12.mo.us.

SCHULZE, ERIC WILLIAM, lawyer; b. Libertyville, Ill., July 8, 1952; s. Robert Carl and Barbara (Mayo) Schulze. BA, U. Tex., 1973, JD, 1977. Bar: Tex. 1977, US Dist. Ct. (we. dist.) Tex. 1987, US Ct. Appeals (5th cir.) 1987, US Dist. Ct. (ea. and so. dists.) Tex 1988, US Dist. Ct. (no. dist.) Tex. 1989, US Supreme Ct. 1989, bd. cert. civil appellate law: Tex. Bd. Legal Specialization 1990. Rsch. asst. U. Tex., Austin, 1978; legis. aide Tex. Ho. Reps., Austin, 1979—81; editor Tex. Sch. Law News, Austin, 1982—85; assoc. Hairston, Walsh & Anderson, Austin, 1986—87; ptnr. Walsh, Anderson, Brown, Schulze & Aldridge, Austin, 1988—. Mng. ptnr. Walsh, Anderson, Brown, Schulze & Aldridge, Austin, Tex., 1993—2004; co-pub. Tex. Sch. Adminstrs. Legal Digest, 1991—2005, mng. editor, 1992—2005; editl. adv. com. West's Edn. Law Reporter, 1996—2006. Editor: Tex. Edn. Code Annotated, 1982—85, Tex. Sch. Adminstrs. Legal Digest, 1986—92. Del. Tex. State Dem. Conv., 1982, Travis County Dem. Conv., 1982, 1984, 1986. Recipient Merit award, Internat. Assn. Bus. Communicators (Austin br.), 1983, Coll. State Bar Tex., 1992. Mem.: Tex. Coun. Sch. Attys., Nat. Coun. Sch. Attys., Bar Assn. of 5th Cir., Travis County Bar Assn., Tex. Bar Assn., Fed. Bar Assn., Edn. Law Assn., Def. Rsch. Inst., Toastmasters (pres. Capital City chpt. 1995). Home: 2615 Ave O 1/2 Galveston TX 77550 Office: Walsh Anderson Brown Schulze & Aldridge PO Box 2156 Austin TX 78768-2156

SCHULZE, FRANZ, JR., critic, educator; b. Uniontown, Pa., Jan. 30, 1927; s. Franz and Anna E. (Krimmel) Schulze; m. Marianne Gaw, June 24, 1961 (div. 1975); children: F. C. Matthew, Lukas A.; m. Stephanie Mora, 1992 (div. 1996). Student, Northwestern U., Evanston, Ill., 1943; PhB, U. Chgo., 1945; BFA, Sch. Art Inst. Chgo., 1949, MFA, 1950; postgrad., Acad. Fine Arts, Munich, 1956-57. Instr. art Purdue U., 1950-52; chmn. dept. art Lake Forest (Ill.) Coll., 1952-58, artist-in-residence, 1958-61, prof. art, 1961—, Hollender prof. art, 1974-91, Hollender prof. art emeritus, 1991—; art critic Chgo. Daily News, 1962-78, Chgo. Sun-Times, 1978-85. Chgo. corr. art Christian Sci. Monitor, 1958—62; art. and arch. critic Chicagoan, 1973—74; mem. vis. com. dept. art U. Chgo., 1974—87; adj. prof. U. Ill., Chgo., 1996. Co-author: Art, Architecture and Civilization, 1969; co-author: (with Rosemary Cowler and Arthur Miller) Thirty Miles North, 2000, Philip Johnson: Life and Work, 1994; co-author: (with Kevin Harrington) Chicago's Famous Buildings, 2003; co-author: Mariotti II, 2004; author: Fantastic Images: Chicago Art Since 1945, 1972, 100 Years of Chicago Architecture, 1976, Stealing is My Game, 1976, Mies van der Rohe: A Critical Biography, 1985, The University Club of Chicago: A Heritage, 1987, Mariotti, 1988, Illinois Institute of Technology. Campus Guide, 2005; editor: Mies van der Rohe: Critical Essays, 1989, Mies van der Rohe Archive, 1993; editor: (with Kevin Harrington) Chicago's Famous Buildings, 1993; co-editor: A. James Speyer, Architect, Curator, Exhibition Designer, 1997, The Farnsworth House, 1997, Illinois Institute of Technology, Campus Guide, 2005; contbg. editor: Art News, 1973—, Inland Arch., 1975—94, corr. editor: Art in Am., 1975—. Trustee Ragdale Found., Lake Forest, 1981—. Recipient Harbison award for tchg., Danforth Found. St. Louis, 1971, Disting. Svc. award, Chgo. Phi Beta Kappa soc., 1972, Hon. Mention Hitchcock Book award, Soc. Archtl. Historians, 1987, Excellence in Architecture award, Ill. Inst. Tech., 1999; Adenauer fellow, 1956—57, Ford Found. fellow, 1964—65, Graham Found. for Advanced Studies in the Fine Arts fellow, 1971, 1981, 1993, NEH fellow, 1982, 1988, Skidmore Owings & Merrill Found. fellow, 1983. Mem.: AAUP, Soc. Archtl. Historians (Hon. Mention Hitchcock Book award), Archives Am. Art (mem. adv. com.), Coll. Art Assn. (bd. dirs. 1983—86). Office: Lake Forest Coll Dept Art Lake Forest IL 60045 Office Phone: 847-735-5084. Business E-Mail: schulze@lakeforest.edu.

SCHULZE, PAUL, industrial designer, educator; b. NYC, Feb. 7, 1934; s. Paul and Hilde (Werdin) Schulze; children: Zoe Anne, Tara Anne. Cert. completion, Parsons Sch. Design, NYC, 1960; BS in Design, NYU, NYC, 1960. Freelance designer glass, fixtures, functional and decorative pieces, 1960—; comml. interior designer Bus. Equip Design, 1960—63; tchr. design Parsons Sch. Design, 1960—64; designer, design dir. Steuben Glass, 1962—87. Staff sgt. USAF, 1952—56. Home and Office: 8415 Skunk Ln Cutchogue NY 11935

SCHULZE, RICHARD HANS, environmental engineering executive; b. Buffalo, May 28, 1933; s. Hans Joachim and Lucy (Kawczynska) S.; m. Jacqueline Van Luppen, Nov. 2, 1967 (div. Aug. 1979); children: Richard Hans Jr., Linda Monaco, John; m. Enika Grooters, Aug. 29, 1987. BSME, Princeton U., 1954; MBA, Northwestern U., 1958. Registered profl. engr., Tex. Rsch. analyst U.S. Steel Corp., Pitts., 1958-60; chief engr. G&H Rsch. and Devel., McKeesport, Pa., 1960-62; cons. Mgmt. and Mktg. Inst., NYC, 1962-63, Ill. Inst. Tech. Rsch. Inst. mgmt. consulting divsn., NYC, 1963-64; market analyst Mobil Chem. Co., NYC, 1964-66; market devel. mgr., plastics divsn. Mobil Chem. Co. (now PACTIV), Jacksonville, Ill., 1966-68, dist. sales mgr. Dallas, 1967-71; pres. Ecology Audits, Inc. (Core Labs.), Dallas, 1971-74; pres., CEO, Trinity Cons., Inc., Dallas, 1974-97, chmn. bd. dirs., 1997—, CEO, 2001—. Instr. over 200 short courses on dispersion modeling of air pollutants throughout world; vis. lectr. air quality Princeton U., 1998; adv. bd. Dept. of Environ. Civil Engring, So. Meth. U., 2001—. Contbr. articles to Jour. of Air and Waste Mgmt. Assn., Atmospheric Environ., others; presented papers at sci. symposiums, seminars, confs. Mem. Dallas Symphony Assn., Mus. Art; trustee Dallas Opera, 1993—; elder Preston Hollow Presbyn. Ch., 1996-98; commr. to Grace Presbytery, 1996-98. Lt. (j.g.) USNR, 1954-56. Mem. ASME, Am. Acad. Environ. Engrs. (diplomate, trustee 2001-2003), Am. Chem. Soc., Am. Meteorol. Soc., Air and Waste Mgmt. Assn. (bd. dirs. 1986-89, 90-93, v.p. 1988-89, 1st v.p. 1990-91, pres. 1991-92, past pres. 1992-93, chmn. honors and awards com. 1996-97, vice chmn. planning com. 1999-2000), Soc. Petroleum Engrs. (chmn. environ. health and safety award com. 1994-95), Soc. for Risk Analysis, Verein Deutscher Ingenieure, Assn. Francaise des Ingénieurs et Techniciens Environ., Inst. Profl. Environ. Practice (qualified environ. profl., trustee 1993-95), European Assn. for the Sci. of Air Pollution. Home: 7619 Marquette St Dallas TX 75225-4412 Office: Trinity Cons Inc 12770 Merit Dr Ste 900 Dallas TX 75251 Home Phone: 214-696-5108; Office Phone: 972-419-5606. Business E-Mail: rschulze@trinityconsultants.com.

SCHULZE, RICHARD M., retail executive; b. St. Paul, Minn., 1941; married; 9 children. D (hon.), Univ. of St. Thomas, St. Paul, 1998. With No. States Sales Co., 1962-66; founder, chmn. Sound of Music (now Best Buy Co., Inc.), Eden Prairie, Minn., 1966—; CEO Best Buy Co., Inc., Eden Prairie, Minn., 1983—2002, chmn., 2002—. Mem. Minn. Bus. Partnership; bd. dir. Pentair Inc., Nat. Entrepreneur of Yr. Inst., 1992—; bd. of overseers Carlson Sch. of Mgmt.; bd. trustees Univ. of St. Thomas. With Minnesota Air National Guard. Named Corp. Leader of Yr., Juvenile Diabetes Assn., 1999; named one of Top CEOs, Worth Mag., 1999, Am.'s Richest People, Forbes mag., 1999—, Exec. Pay, 1999—, World's Richest People, 2001—; recipient Nat. Entrepreneur of Yr., Ernst & Young, 1999, America's Promise Red Wagon for Cmty. Svc., Gen. Colin Powell, 1999, Outstanding Mktg. Exec of Yr., Minnesota DECA, 2000, Robert C. McDermond Medal for Excellence in Entrepreneurship, Robert C. McDermond Ctr. for Mgmt. and Entrepreneurship, 2000. Office: Best Buy 7601 Penn Ave S Minneapolis MN 55423-3645 *

SCHULZKE, MARGOT SEYMOUR, artist, author, educator; b. San Francisco; BA in Art, Brigham Young U., 1959; studied with, Roman Andrus and others. Lectr. Brigham Young U. Edn. Weeks., Provo, Utah, 1966-68. Instr. painting workshops; juror numerous exhibits. Exhibited in shows at Nat. Art Club, Salmagundi Club, NYC, New Orleans, San Francisco, Colo., Oreg., Nev., Calif., others, (numerous awards); at Mus. Calif., Ill., NJ, Miss., Utah; featured artist in Pastel Interpretations, Northlight, 1993, Best of Pastel, Rockport, Mass. Pubs., 1996, Landscape Inspirations, Rockport Pubs., 1997, Best of Pastel II, 1998, Pure Color: Best of Pastel, North Light, 2006; author: Painter's Guide to Design & Composition, 2006; contbg. editor, The Pastel Jour., contbr. articles to other profl. jours. Bd. dirs. Friends of Moldova Relief, Sacramento, 1992-93. Recipient Disting. Emeritus award, Brigham Young U., 2000. Mem.: Degas Pastel Soc., Calif. Art Club, Pastel Soc. West Coast (bd. dirs. 1985—, adv. bd. 1988—, founding pres. 1985—88, pres. 1995—97, Pastel Laureate award 2006), Pastel Soc. Am., Am. Artists Profl. League. Mem. Lds Ch. Avocations: photography, travel, gardening, reading. Personal E-mail: schulzke@jps.net.

SCHULZRINNE, HENNING G., computer science educator; b. Cologne, Germany; arrived in US, 1984; BS, Tech. U. Darmstadt, 1984; PhD, U. Mass., 1992. With AT&T Bell Labs., Murray Hill, N.J., 1992-94, GMD Fokus, Berlin, 1994-96; assoc. prof., prof., chair Columbia U., NYC, 1996—. Editor: Jour. Communications and Networks. Fellow: IEEE (editor Transactions on Networking, past mem., chmn. bd. gov. Comm. Soc., past editor Internet Computing Mag.). Office: Dept Computer Sci Columbia Univ New York NY 10027 Office Phone: 212-939-7004. E-mail: hgs@cs.columbia.edu.

SCHUMACHER, BARRET, motion picture propman, writer; b. Boulder, Colo., Sept. 16, 1965; s. Eugene Pierre and Mary Alice Schumacher; m. Beth Alice Edelstein, Mar. 24, 1996; 1 child, Tess Sara. BA screenwriting/film, San Franciso State Univ., Calif., 1990. Model maker Holt, Hinshaw, Peau Jones Arch., San Fransico, 1987—90, Clockwork Apple, Inc., NYC, 1991—94, Cinergy Films "Judge Dredd", Lenox, Mass., 1994—95; motion picture propman I.A.T.S.E. Local 52, NYC, 1995—. Author: (novels) Fear Itself, 2002; propman: (films) In and Out; The Ice Storm; I Am Legend. Avocations: guitar, hiking, skiing, drawing. Office Phone: 917-459-3079.

SCHUMACHER, CYNTHIA JO, retired elementary and secondary education educator; b. Sebring, Fla., Sept. 24, 1928; d. Floyd and Espage S. BA, Fla. State U., Tallahassee, 1950, MA, 1951, postgrad., 1968-69; MS, Nova U., Ftl. Lauderdale, Fla., 1978. English tchr. Grady County Sch. System, Cairo, Ga., 1951-53; elem. tchr. Brevard County Sch. System, Melbourne, Fla., 1953-55; elem. tchr., curriculum generalist, secondary tchr. Lake County Schs., Tavares, Fla. area, 1955-85; retired, 1985. Mem. Edn. Standards Commn., Fla., Fla., 1980—85, Quality Instrn. Incentives Coun., Fla., 1983—84. Author: (poetry) Seeds from Wild Grasses, 1988, Creekstone Crossings, 1993, Soul Candles, 1998, Wellspring Legacies, 2000; (poetry and stories) Butterfly Excursions, 1996; (children's books) Colorful Character, 1998, Searching for S, 1998. Pres. League of Women Voters of Lake County, 1989-91; mem. Lake Conservation Coun., The Nature Conservancy, Habitat for Humanity of Lake County. Named Fla. Tchr. of Yr., Fla. Fedn. Women's Clubs, 1966, Lake County Tchr. of Yr., Lake County Sch. Sys., 1985, East Cen. Fla. Tchr. of Yr. finalist, State of Fla., 1986; recipient Good Egg award, Leesburg Area C. of C., 1991, Lifetime Achievement award, Fla. Edn. Assn. United, 2000. Mem. Lake County Edn. Assn. (pres. 1971-72, cons. 1985—). Democrat. Roman Catholic. Avocations: gardening, creative writing, macrobiotic cooking, environmental support activities.

SCHUMACHER, DIANE KOSMACH, manufacturing executive, lawyer; b. Chgo., Aug. 13, 1953; BA with high honors, So. Ill. U., 1974; JD magna cum laude, DePaul U., 1977. Bar: Mo. 1977, Ill. 1978, Tex. 1983. Corp. atty. Belden Corp. (acquired by Cooper Industries Inc. 1981), 1980-81; sr. counsel Cooper Industries Inc., Houston, 1981-88, corp. sec., 1988-91, corp. v.p., 1991-93, v.p. adminstrn., corp. sec., 1993-95, sr. v.p., gen. counsel, sec., 1995—2003, sr. v.p., gen. counsel, chief compliance officer, 2003—. Bd. dirs. Gardner Denver, Inc. Mem. ABA, Am. Corp. Counsel Assn., Am. Soc. Corp. Secs. (pres. Houston chpt. 1992-93, bd. dirs. 1995-98), Am. Arbitration Assn. (bd. dirs. 1996—), State Bar Tex. Office: Copper Industries Inc Chase Tower 600 Travis St Ste 5800 Houston TX 77002-2912 E-mail: schumach@cooperindustries.com.

SCHUMACHER, H(ARRY) RALPH, internist, rheumatologist, medical educator, researcher; b. Montreal, Canada, Feb. 14, 1933; s. H. Ralph and Dorothy (Shreiner) S.; m. Elizabeth Jean Swisher, July 13, 1963; children: Heidi Ruth, Kaethe Beth. BS, Ursinus Coll., 1955; MD, U. Pa., 1959. Intern Denver Gen. Hosp., 1959-60; resident in medicine Wadsworth VA Hosp., LA, 1960-62, fellow in rheumatology, 1962-63, Robert B. Brigham Hosp. and Harvard U. Med. Sch., Boston, 1965-67; chief arthritis-immunology ctr. VA Med. Ctr., Phila., 1967—2006; faculty mem. U. Pa. Sch. Medicine, Phila., 1967—, prof. medicine, 1979—, acting arthritis divsn. chief, 1978-80, 91-95, prof. orthopaedics, 1998—2002. Vis. scholar NIH, 1994-99; lectr. in field. Author: (books) Gout and Pseudogout, 1978, Essentials of a Differential Diagnosis of Rheumatoid Arthritis, 1981, Rheumatoid Arthritis, 1988, Case Studies in Rheumatology for the House Officer, 1989, Atlas of Synovial Fluid and Crystal Identification, 1991, A Practical Guide to Synovial Fluid Analysis, 1991, The Spondylarthropathies, 1998, Classic Papers in Rheumatology, 2001, Crystal-induced Arthropathies, 2006; editor: Primer on Rheumatic Disease, 1981—97, Jour. Clin. Rheumatology, 1994—, Crystal Diseases Section, 2005—; mem. editl. bd. Jour. Rheumatology, 1973—, Arthritis and Rheumatism, 1981—88, Revue du Rhumatisme (now Joint, Bone, Spine), 1992—, Internat. Jour. Clin. Practice, 1992—, New European Rheumatology, 1993—, Asian Pacific League Against Rheumatism Jour. Rheumatology, 1997—, Current Rheumatology Reports, 1999—, Indian Jour. Rheumatology, 2000—, Portuguese Jour. Rheumatology, 2000—; mem. editl. bd. Resident and Staff Physician, 2001—; mem. editl. bd.: Vojnosanitetski, 2005—, Chinese Jour. Integrative Medicine, 2007—; contbr. articles to profl. jours. Pres. Ea. Pa. chpt. Arthritis Found., 1980-82; chmn., founder Phila. Garden Tours, 1987—95; bd. dirs. Hemochromatosis Rsch. Found., 1984—, Am. Bd. Med. Advancement China, 1983-99. With M.C. USAF, 1963-65. Recipient VanBreeman award Netherland Rheumatism Soc., 1988, Philip Hench award Assn. Mil. Surgeons, 1986, Hollander award Arthritis Found., 1996; named Alumnus of Yr. Ursinus Coll, 1995; named to Sports Hall of Fame, 1997; Deposition VA grantee, 1967-95, NIH grantee, 1981, 94—. Fellow ACP; mem. AAAS, Am. Coll. Rheumatology (master; pres. Southeastern region 1981-82, Klemperer lectr. 2002), Phila. Rheumatism Soc. (pres. 1980), Phila. Electron Microscopy Soc. (chmn. 1975-76), Rheumatism Soc. Mex., Rheumatism Soc. Australia, Rheumatism Soc. Colombia, Rheumatism Soc. Chile, Rheumatism Soc. China, Rheumatism Soc. Argentina, Med. Soc. Argentina, Slovak Soc. Rheumatology, Fedn. Clin. Rsch. Office: VA Med Ctr 151 K University and Woodland Aves Philadelphia PA 19104 also: Hosp U Pa 8 Penn Tower 3400 Spruce St Philadelphia PA 19104-4206 Business E-Mail: schumacr@mail.med.upenn.edu. *I try to teach meticulous observation and questioning of dogma both in daily care of patients and in laboratory investigation of the poorly understood rheumatic diseases.*

SCHUMACHER, HARRY RICHARD, lawyer; b. June 21, 1930; s. Henry Richard and Martha (Hagenbucher) S.; m. Katherine E. Ware, June 8, 1991; children: Richard, Garry. BA, Yale U., 1951; JD magna cum laude, Harvard U., 1958. Bar: N.Y. 1959, U.S. Supreme Ct. 1964. Assoc. firm Cahill Gordon & Reindel and predecessor firms, NYC, 1958—67, ptnr., 1968—97. Chmn. Legal Svcs. for N.Y.C., Inc., 1994—2003; dir. New York Legis. Svcs., 2000—. Mem. Manhattan Borough Pres.'s Cmty. Planning Bd. 6, 1962—66; Dem. candidate N.Y. State Assembly, 1962, 1963; warden Episcopalian Ch.; bd. dirs. Incarnation Camp, Ivoryton, Conn., 1961—72. Lt. (j.g.) USNR, 1951—54. Mem.: ABA, Am. Judicature Soc., N.Y. County Lawyers Assn. (bd. dirs. 1987—93, 1996—99), Fed. Comms. Bar Assn., Assn. Bar City of N.Y., N.Y. State Bar Assn. (mem. ho. dels. 1990—94, 2001—03), Yale (N.Y.C.), Union. Home: 47 E 88th St New York NY 10128-1152 Office: Cahill Gordon & Reindel 80 Pine St Fl 16 New York NY 10005-1790

SCHUMACHER, HENRY JEROLD, museum director, retired military officer; b. Torrance, Calif., June 17, 1934; s. Henry John and Rene S.; m. Barbara Howell, Aug. 24, 1958; children: Sheri Lynn, Henry Jerold II. Student, Stanford U., 1953; BS, U.S. Mil. Acad., 1957; MS, Northeastern U., Boston, 1965; MBA, Auburn U., 1977. Commd. lt. U.S. Army, 1958, advanced through grades to maj. gen., 1982; army attaché Moscow, 1969-71; chief communications ops. Vietnam, 1971-72; exec. officer Office Chief of Staff, 1972-75; comdr. U.S. Army Communications Command, Panama, 1977-79; dir. network integration, Office Asst. Chief of Staff Automation and Communications, Dept. Army, 1979-81; comdr. The White House Communications Agy., Washington, 1981-82; chief U.S. Army Signal Corps, 1981-83; ret., 1983; sr. v.p. Visa Internat., 1983-86; chief oper. officer Fuel Tech., Inc., Stamford, Conn., 1986-87; pres. IMM Systems, Phila., 1987-89; exec. v.p. Cylink Corp., Sunnyvale, Calif., 1990-95; exec. dir. Hiller Mus. of No. Calif. Aviation History, Redwood City, 1995-98; mng. gen. ptnr. Distributed Sys. Ptnrs., 1999—2002, adv. bd. cranite sys., 2003—. Decorated Def. D.S.M., D.S.M., Legion of Merit. Home: 156 Normandy Ct San Carlos CA 94070-1519

SCHUMACHER, JON LEE, lawyer; b. Rochester, NY, Feb. 28, 1937; s. Howard Alexander and Ruth S.; m. Katherine Truesdell, Apr. 22, 1967; children: Sara Wolff, Howard Alexander II. AB, Princeton U., 1959; JD, U. Va., 1964. Bar: N.Y. 1964. With Nixon Peabody LLP and predecessor firms, Rochester, 1964—; mem. mgmt. com. Nixon, Hargrave, Devans & Doyle, Rochester, 1986-90, mng. ptnr., 1988-90. Co-author Charitable Giving and Solicitation. Bd. dirs., officer Rochester Area Found., Inc., 1987-94, United Way, 1986—; pres. estate planning Coun. Rochester, 1986-87; officer Rochester Philharm. Orch. Fund, Inc., 1985-. Fellow Am. Coll. Trusts and Estate Counsel; mem. NY State Bar Assn. (exec. com. trusts and estates law sect. 1985-88, 94—, chmn. 1997, chmn. estate planning com. 1992-94), Monroe County Bar Assn. (found. pres. 1995-97), Country Club Rochester, Genesee Valley Club. Democrat. Presbyterian. Avocation: opera. Home: 550 Allens Creek Rd Rochester NY 14618-3406 Office: Nixon Peabody LLP Clinton Sq PO Box 31051 Rochester NY 14603-1051 Office Phone: 585-263-1263. Business E-Mail: jschumacher@nixonpeabody.com.

SCHUMACHER, LAURA J., lawyer, pharmaceutical executive; Grad. in Bus. Adminstrn./Mktg., U. Notre Dame, 1985; JD, U. Wis., Madison, 1988. Assoc. Schiff, Hardin & Waite, Chgo.; atty. Litig. Dept. Abbott Labs., Abbott Park, Ill., 1990, div. v.p. litig., 2000, v.p., sec., dep. gen. counsel, 2003—05, sr. v.p., sec., gen. counsel, 2005—. Bd. dirs. Chgo. Children's Mus., Clara Abbott Found. Mem.: Chgo. Network, Econ. Club Chgo. Office: Abbott Labs 100 Abbott Park Rd Abbott Park IL 60064-3500 Office Phone: 847-937-6100. *

SCHUMACHER, MARGARET LYNN, not-for-profit fundraiser, director; b. Pitts., Sept. 22, 1963; d. Paul William, Sr. and Margaret Josephine Schumacher; 1 child, Crystal Lynn. BA, Chatham Coll., Pitts., 1992; MS, LaRoche Coll., Pitts., 2000. Dir. sr. programs Citizen Care, Pitts., 1995—99; devel. dir. St. Anthony Sch. Programs, Pitts., 1999—2001; dir. grants and procurement YWCA Greater Pitts., 2001—02; dir. fund devel. Redstone Presbyn. Sr. Care, Greensburg, Pa., 2002—03; devel. dir. Vets. Leadership Program, Pitts., 2003—05; exec. dir. Tampa Bay Trial Lawyers Assn., Fla., 2006—. Vol. Susan B. Koman Found., Pitts., 2001—06, Friends of DaHang, Pitts., 2006—, Voices for Children, Tampa, 2006—. Mem.: Assn. Fundraising Profls. (cert., nominating com. local chpt.), Rotary (Bethel Park Rookie of Yr.). Republican. Avocations: golf, fishing, boating, piano. Office: Tampa Bay Trial Lawyers Assn PO Box 26091 Tampa FL 33623

SCHUMACHER, MICHAEL, retired race car driver; b. Hürth-Hermühlheim, Germany, Jan. 3, 1969; s. Elizabeth and Rolf; m. Corinna Schumacher; children: Gina-Maria, Mick. Race car driver Jordan team, 1991, Benetton team, 1991—95, Ferrari team, 1996—2006; asst. to chief exec. Jean Todt Ferrari S.p.A., 2006; ret., 2007. Named one of 100 Most Influential People, Time Mag., 2005; recipient Best Driver, ESPY awards, 2005. Achievements include winning the Formula 1 Driver's Championship a record 7 times, 1994, 95, 2000-04; 90 career Grand Prix wins since

1992; first to win a Formula 1 Grand Prix event 8 times, French Grand Prix, 1994, 95, 97, 98, 2001, 02, 04, 06; winner, Formula 3 German Championship, 1990. Office: Ferrari SpA Via Ascari 55-57 I-41053 Maranello Italy *

SCHUMACHER, PAUL MAYNARD, lawyer; b. Columbus, Nebr., Apr. 4, 1951; s. Maynard Mathew and Rita Bell (Jarosz) S.; m. Michele Suzanne Gassé, June 26, 1976; children: Nicole Suzanne, Kristen Paulette. AA, Platte Coll., 1971; BS, Fort Hays U., 1973; JD, Georgetown U., 1976. Bar: Fla. 1976, Nebr. 1977, U.S. Dist. Ct. Nebr. 1977. Mem. staff U.S. Senate, Washington, 1974-76; sole practice Miami, Fla. and Columbus, 1976—; v.p. Community Lottery Systems, Inc., Columbus, 1990-92, pres., 1992—. V.p. Megavision Corp., Columbus, 1976—. Treas. prin. Rep. campaign com. U.S. Senate Candidate, Lincoln, Nebr., 1978-79; atty. Platte County, Columbus, 1979-87; chmn. Platte county Reps., 1988-94; mem. Nebr. Rep. State Ctrl. Com., 1994-96, 2000—; CEO Lotto Nebr., 1992—; CEO Cmty. Internet Sys., Inc., 1995-98, bd. dirs., 1995—; bd. dirs. Keep the Money in Nebr. Com. Mem. Nebr. Bar Assn., Fla. Bar Assn., Platte County Bar Assn. (pres. 1992-93), Nat. Republican small bus. adv. council, Nebr. Republican Legis. Com., Rotary, Elks. Roman Catholic. Avocation: physics. Home: 6255 Meyer Rd Columbus NE 68601-8044 Office: PO Box 122 Columbus NE 68602-0122 Home Phone: 402-563-2112. E-mail: pschumac@megavision.com.

SCHUMACHER, ROBERT DENISON, banker; b. Evanston, Ill., Dec. 16, 1933; s. Frank Ade and Dorothy Ormonde (Hilton) S.; m. Mary Ann Montgomery, Aug. 25, 1956; children: Stephen Michael, Jeffrey Hilton. BA, Williams Coll., 1956; postgrad., Grad. Bus. Sch. N.Y. U., 1957-59; P.MD, Harvard Bus. Sch., 1966. With Irving Trust Co., NYC, 1956-89, sr. v.p., 1977-89, mgr. adminstrv. services, 1976—89, ret., 1989. Treas. Calvary, Holy Communion and St. George's Episcopal Ch., 1976-79, warden, 1980-86, 89-93, 2001-05; trustee The Church Club, 1993-2003, treas., 1994-99; mem.summer resident's adv. com. Town of Chatham, Mass., 2001-07. Mem. The Church Club. Home: 431 E 20th St New York NY 10010-7502 Personal E-mail: rschumach@aol.com.

SCHUMAKER, WILLIAM THOMAS, retired insurance company executive; b. Phila., Apr. 14, 1925; s. William John and Julia Ida Schumaker. BSc, Drew U., Madison, NJ, 1964, DD, 1980. Ordained to ministry Meth. Ch., 1974. V.p. New Amsterdam Casualty Co., Phila., 1947—59; gen. mgr. P.L.M. Ins. Co., 1959—79; min. Cortez United Meth. Ch.; chmn. Julia Ida Schumaker Found. Instr. Surety Bonds Ins. Soc. Phila., 1950-52; mem. adv. bd. P.L.M. Ins. Co., Phila., 1954-59. City ofcl. 34th ward City of Phila., 1955. Staff sgt. U.S. Army, 1943-46. Nat. acctg. fellow New Amsterdam Casualty Co., Phila., 1955, Paul Harris fellow Rotary of Nfld., Pa., 1990. Mem. Mensa, 63d Inf. Divsn. US Army (life). Avocations: antiques, stamp collecting/philately. Home: 603 Britt St Georgetown SC 29440-4003 E-mail: karpadopol@aol.com.

SCHUMAN, ALLAN L., chemicals executive; b. 1937; BS, NYU, 1955. With Ecolab Inc., St. Paul, 1957—, v.p. mktg. and nat. acctg., 1972-78, v.p. mktg. devel., 1978-79, pres. svc. group, 1988—92, pres., COO, 1992—95, pres., CEO, 1995—2004, chmn., 2000—06, chmn. emeritus, 2006—. Bd. dir. Tanger Factory Outlet Ctr. Inc., Soap & Detergent Assn. Bd. dir. Ordway Ctr. Performing Arts, Guthrie Theater; bd. overseers Carlson Sch. Mgmt. at U. Minn.; trustee Hamline U., Minn., Culinary Inst. Am., Nat. Restaurant Assn. Office: Ecolab Inc Ecolab Ctr 370 N Wabasha St Saint Paul MN 55102

SCHUMAN, PATRICIA GLASS, publishing company executive, educator; b. NYC, Mar. 15; d. Milton and Shirley Rhoda (Goodman) Glass; m. Alan Bruce Schuman, Aug. 30, 1964 (div. 1973); m. Stanley Robert Epstein, June 14, 1997 (dec. 2005) AB, U. Cin., 1963; MS, Columbia U., 1966. Libr. trainee Bklyn. Pub. Libr., 1964—65; tchr. libr. Brandeis High Sch., NYC, 1966; asst. prof. libr. N.Y. Tech. Coll., Bklyn., 1966-71; assoc. editor Sch. Libr. Jour., NYC, 1970-73; sr. editor R.R. Bowker Co., NYC, 1973-76; pres. Neal-Schuman Pubs., NYC, 1976—. Vis. prof. St. John's U., Queens, N.Y., 1977-79, Columbia U., N.Y.C., 1981-90, Pratt Inst., 1993-2000, Syracuse U., 1997—; cons. N.Y. State Coun. on Arts, 1987, Office Tech. Assessment, U.S. Congress, 1982, 84, Coord. Coun. Lit. Mags., N.Y.C., 1987, NEH, 1980, Temple U., 1978-80; bd. visitors Sch. Libr. and Computer Studies Pratt Inst., 1987-2001; juror Best of Libr. Lit., 1980-88; mem. adv. bd. Sch. Libr. and Info. Studies, Queens Coll., 1989-91. Author: Materials for Occupational Education, 1973, 2d edit., 1983 (Best Edn. Book award 1973), Library Users and Personnel Needs, 1980, Your Right to Know: The Call to Action, 1993; editor: Social Responsibilities and Libraries, 1976; mem. editorial bd. Urban Acad. Libr., 1987-89, Multicultural Review, 1991-95; contbr. articles to profl. jours. Bd. dirs. Women's Studies Abstracts, Albany, N.Y., 1970-74, Pratt Inst. Sch. of Libr. and Info. Studies, 1993—2000, Ctr. for Publ., NYU, 1996—, Am. Libr. in Paris, 2004-; mem. Com. To Elect Major Owens to U.S. Congress, 1983, N.Y.C. Mayor's Com. for N.Y. Pub. Ctr., 1984-85; pres. Met. Reference and Resources Coun./Met. N.Y. Libr. Coun, Neal Schumen Found., Inc. Recipient Fannie Simon award Spl. Librs. Assn., 1984, Disting. Alumni award Columbia U., 1992, Disting. Alumni award U. Cin., 2006; U.S. Office Edn. fellow, 1969. Mem. ALA (councillor 1971-79, 84-88, exec. bd. 1984-88, 90-93, treas. 1984-88, chmn. legis. com. 1989-90, 94-96, chmn. internat. rels. com. 1998, 99, chmn. Libr. Advocacy NOW!, v.p., pres.-elect 1990-91, pres. 1991-92, Disting. Coun. Svc. award 1979, 88, Equality award 1993, hon. mem. Black Caucus, appreciation award 1993, Freedom to Read Found. Honor Roll 1999, Lippincott award for disting. svc. 2001, Eileen Cooke/James Madison award, 2007), Spl. Librs. Assn. Office: Neal-Schuman Pubs Inc 100 William St Ste 2004 New York NY 10038 Business E-Mail: pgs@neal-schuman.com.

SCHUMANN, J. PAUL, retired federal agency administrator; b. Kansas City, Mo., Dec. 10, 1937; s. Fred and Miriam E. (Penzotti) S.; m. Olva Kimmel Dorris, Dec. 23, 1960; 1 child, Robert Reynold. BA, MA, U. Miss., 1960; cert., Indsl. Coll. Armed Forces, 1966; PhD, U. Okla., 1982. Instr. polit. sci. Jacksonville (Ala.) State U., 1961-64; intelligence officer Missile and Space Intelligence Ctr., Huntsville, Ala., 1964-91, sr. intelligence officer, 1991—2006; ret., 2006. Adj. asst. prof. U. Ala., Huntsville, 1981—2000; mem. Tenn dept. Coun. on Am's Mil. Past, Huntsville, 1971—82; adj. instr. Calhoun C.C., Huntsville, 1996, Huntsville, 2006—. Contbr. articles to profl. jours. V.p. external affairs Jaycees, Jacksonville, 1963-64. Recipient achievement medal for civilian svc. U.S. Army, 1992, letter of commendation South Korean Def. Intelligence Agy., 1992, Nat. Intelligence Cert. of Distinction, 2005, superior achievement medal Def. Intelligence Agy., 2006; Dept. Def. scholar, 1971-72. Mem. Nat. Mil. Intelligence Assn., Am. Polit. Sci. Assn., Phi Alpha Theta, Phi Kappa Psi (treas. 1957-58), Pi Sigma Alpha. Avocation: military history. Home: 8204 Willowbrook Cir SE Apt A Huntsville AL 35802-3335 Personal E-mail: paulschumann@comcast.net.

SCHUMANN, JILL, religious organization administrator; b. Pitts. m. Mark W. Oldenburg. BA, Ind. U. of Pa.; MBA, Mount St. Mary's Coll. Dir. outpatient svcs. Ctr. for Addictive Illnesses, Morristown, NJ; substance abuse program developer Gettysburg Coll., Pa.; dir., v.p. Craig and Assocs., York, Pa.; exec., v.p. planning and mktg. Tressler Luth. Svcs., Mechanicsburg; exec. v.p. Kairos Health Sys.; dir. mem. svcs. Luth. Svcs. in Am., Balt., pres., CEO, 2001—. Office: Luth Svcs in Am 700 Light St Baltimore MD 21230-3850 Office Phone: 410-230-2702. Office Fax: 410-230-2710. E-mail: jschumann@lutheranservices.org.

SCHUMANN, NICHOLAS M., elementary school educator; s. Dennis and Beverly Schumann; m. Jennifer Koenig, May 27, 2000; children: Alexa, Allison. BS, Ea. Mich. U., Ypsilanti, 1993—98; MA in Art of Tchg., Marygrove Coll., Detroit, 2001—02. Tchr. Huron Valley Schs., Highland, Mich., 2000—. Football coach Milford HS, Highland, 2000—. Youth min. St. Mary Cath. Ch., Chelsea, Mich., 2003. Mem.: Mich. Football Coaches Assn., Nat. Coun. Tchg. Math., Delta Tau Delta (jud. chair 1996—97, Brother of Yr. award 1997). Home Phone: 517-522-3819.

SCHUMANN, PAULA M. L., writer; b. Phila., Oct. 23, 1938; d. Paschal Francis and Paula Marie Libonati; m. Walter Francis Schumann, June 17, 1967; 2 children. MT, Philadelphia County Med. Soc., 1972. Cert. med. technologist Phila. Gen. Hosp. Sch. Med. Tech., Pa.; admitted to holy profession Secular Franciscan Order, 2004. Author and pub. Renaitre Press, King of Prussia, Pa., 1998—. Author (publisher): A Chapter in the Life of a Poet (a story in verse), 1995, With His Love, Prayers and Poems, 2002; author: (poetry) Les Saisons de la Vie, 1998. Pres. Legion of Mary, King of Prussia, Pa., 2000—02., Franklin Sch. Sci. and Arts scholar, 1960—61. Mem.: Internat. Soc. Poets (disting. mem.), Phila. Writers' Conf., Poetry Soc. Am., Acad. Am. Poets. Roman Catholic. Avocations: cooking, travel, swimming, piano, dance. Office: Renaitre Press P O Box 61163 King Of Prussia PA 19406-1163 Business E-Mail: renaitrepress@yahoo.com.

SCHUMANN, WILLIAM HENRY, III, corporate financial executive; b. Iowa City, Aug. 28, 1950; s. William Henry Jr. and Eunice Vere (Doak) S. BS, UCLA, 1972; MS, U. So. Calif., 1973. Program mgmt. analyst Hughes Helicopters, Culver City, Calif., 1973-75; mgr. fin. planning Sunkist Growers, Sherman Oaks, Calif., 1975-81; dir. N.Am. Ops. Agrl. Products Group, FMC Corp., Chgo., 1981—; treas. FMC Corp., 1987—, exec. dir. corp. development, 1990-93, v.p., 1995—, sr. v.p., CFO, 1999—2001, FMC Techs., 2001—. Bd. dirs. Gt. Lakes Advisors and UAP Holdings. Republican. Office: FMC Technologies 200 E Randolph Dr Chicago IL 60601

SCHUMER, CHUCK (CHARLES ELLIS), senator; b. Bklyn., Nov. 23, 1950; s. Abraham and Selma (Rosen) S.; m. Iris Weinshall, 1980; children: Jessica Emily, Alison. BA magna cum laude, Harvard U., 1971, JD with honors, 1974. Bar: NY 1975. Mem. staff US Senator Claiborne Pell, 1973; assoc. Paul, Weiss, Rifking, Wharton and Garrison, 1974; mem. NY State Assembly, 1975-80, chmn. subcom. on city mgmt. and governance, 1977, chmn. com. on oversight and investigation, 1979; mem. US Congresses from 16th NY Dist., 1981—85, US Congresses from 10th (now 9th) NY Dist., Washington, 1985-98; US Senator from NY, 1998—. Com. banking, housing and urban affairs US Senate, com. fin., com. judiciary, com. rules and adminstrn., joint com. on Liberty of Congress. Author: Positively American: Winning Back the Middle-Class Majority One Family at a Time, 2007. Bd. dirs. NY Philharmonic. Herbert Tenzer award for Pub. Service, Five Towns Jewish coun., 1995, Criminal Justice Legis. award, NY State Bar Assoc., 1999, Leadership in Govt. award, Columbia U. Bus. Sch., 1999, Travers J. Bell Mem award of Distinction, NY Dist. Econ. Edn. Found, Securities Industry, Assoc., 1999, Pub. Policy Achievement award, Amer. Cancer Society, 2000, Sound Guardian award, NY Audobon and Cons. Industry Coun. of Westchester, 2002 Mem. Jewish War Veterans, B'nai Brith, Phi Beta Kappa. Democrat. Jewish. Office: US Senate 313 Hart Office Bldg Washington DC 20515-0001 also: District Office Ste 17-02 757 Third Ave New York NY 10017 Office Phone: 202-224-6542, 212-486-4430. Office Fax: 202-228-3027, 212-486-7693. *

SCHUMER, ROBERT B., lawyer; b. NYC, Mar. 8, 1958; BA magna cum laude, U. Mich., 1979; JD, Columbia U., 1982. Bar: NY 1983. With Paul, Weiss, Rifkind, Wharton & Garrison LLP, NYC, 1989—, ptnr., corp. dept., co-head mergers & acquisitions group, mem. mgmt. com. Named a Dealmaker of the Yr., Am. Lawyer mag., 2006; named one of 40 under 40, Crain mag., 1995, 45 under 45, Am. Lawyer mag., 1995. Mem.: ABA, Phi Beta Kappa. Office: Paul Weiss Rifkind Wharton & Garrison LLP 1285 Ave of the Americas New York NY 10019-6064 Office Phone: 212-373-3097. Office Fax: 212-757-2004. E-mail: rschumer@paulweiss.com.

SCHUMM, DARLA YZONNE, religious studies educator; b. Kitchner, Ontario, Can. d. Claire Floyd and Katie Ann Schumm; m. Jonathan Fisher Harris, Oct. 14, 2000. BA, Goshen Coll., NY, 1987; MA, Pacific Sch. Religion, 1992; PhD, Vanderbilt U., Nashville, 2002. Case mgr. Cath. Charities, Washington, 1987—89; clin. dir. Gould Farm, Monterey, Mass., 1992—94; asst. prof. Hollins U., Roanoke, Va., 2001—. Fellow, Am. Ctr. Oriental Rsch., 2005. Mem.: Menoanite Scholars Network, Am. Acad. Religion, Delta Kappa Gamma. Avocations: knitting, reading, running. Office: Hollins Univ PO Box 9623 Roanoke VA 24020

SCHUMM, STANLEY ALFRED, geologist, educator; b. Kearny, NJ, Feb. 22, 1927; s. Alfred Henry and Mary Elizabeth (Murdock) S.; m. Ethel Patricia Radli, Sept. 3, 1950; children: Brian Murdock, Mary Theresa, Christine Ann. BA, Upsala Coll., 1950; PhD, Columbia U., 1955. Research geologist U.S. Geol. Survey, Denver, 1955-67; prof. geology Colo. State U., Ft. Collins, 1967-86, Univ. disting. prof., 1986-98, acting asso. dean, 1973-74, prof. emeritus, 1998—; prin. geomorphologist Mussetter Engring., Ft. Collins, 1995—. Vis. prof. U. Calif., Berkeley, 1959-60, U. Witwatersrand, South Africa, 1975; fellow U. Sydney, Australia, 1964-65, U. New South Wales, 1988; vice chmn. U.S. Nat. Com. Quaternary Rsch., 1967-70, 75-82; dist. vis. scientist U. tex., 1970; vis. lectr. numerous univs. in U.S., vis. scientist N.Z., Europe, Can., Venezuela, Brazil; vis. scientist Polish Acad. Sci., 1969; cons. to govt. agys., engring. firms; prin. geomorphologist, dir. Water Engring. Tech., Davis, Calif., and Ft. Collins, Colo., 1980-91; sr. assoc. Ayres Assocs., Ft. Collins, 1991-2000; prin. investigator rsch. projects NSF, 1969-92, Colo. Agrl. Expt. Sta., 1970-75, Army Rsch. Office, 1970-80, 82-93, Office Water Rsch. and Tech., 1974-83, Nat. Park Svc., 1975-77, Fed. Hwy. Adminstrn., 1978-80, Soil Conservation Svc., 1980-85, NASA, 1984-88, Smithsonian Inst., 1986-87, Can. Internat. Devel. Agy., 1991-92. Author: The Fluvial System, 1977, To Interpret the Earth, 1991; co-author: Incised Channels, 1984, Geomorphology, 1985, Experimental Fluvial Geomorphology, 1987, Active Tectonics and Alluvial Rivers, 2000; editor: United States Contribution to Quaternary Research, 1969, River Morphology, 1972, Slope Morphology, 1973, Drainage Basin Morphology, 1977, Physical Geography of W.M. Davis, 1980, The Variability of Large Alluvial Rivers, 1994, River Variability and Complexity, 2005; contbr. chpts. to sci. books, articles to profl. jours. Served with USNR, 1944-45. Recipient Disting. Alumnus award Upsala Coll., 1980, L.W. Durrell award Colo. State U., 1980, Linton award Brit. Geomorphology Rsch. Group, 1981, Warren prize NAS, 1986, Outstanding Paper award Soc. Sedimentary Geology, 1996, Hydrology Days award Colo. State U., 2001; Harkness fellow U. Canterbury, N.Z., 1983; fellow Japanese Soc. for Advancement of Sci., 1983, Dept. Agr., Republic of South Africa, 1984, Australian Nat. U., 1988; named honor scientist Colo. State U. chpt. Sigma Xi, 1986, Frost lectr. U. Hull, 1999. Fellow AAAS, Geol. Soc. Am. (asso. editor 1973-75, vice chmn. geomorphology div. 1978-79, chmn. 1979-80, Kirk Bryan award 1979, Disting. Career award 1997); sr. fellow Internat. Assn. Geomorphologists; mem. (hon.) Japanese Geomorphological Union, Am. Geophys. Union (Horton award 1958, assoc. editor 1973-75), ASCE, Internat. Geog. Union, Assn. Am. Geographers, Internat. Assn. Quaternary Research, Am. Quaternary Assn. (councillor), Sigma Xi (pres. Colo. State U. chpt. 1987-88, honor scientist 1987). Home: 1308 Rollingwood Ln Fort Collins CO 80525-1946 also: Mussetter Engring 1730 S College Ave Fort Collins CO 80525-1073 Home Phone: 970-482-0680; Office Phone: 970-224-4612. E-mail: stans@mussei.com.

SCHUNICHT, SHANNON ANTHONY, retired military officer, political scientist; b. Miami, Fla., Nov. 17, 1961; s. Wayne Anthony Schunicht and Suzanne Chatin (Tindell) Fast. BA in Philosophy and Polit. Sci., Fla. State U., 1983; BA in Biology, Tex. A&M U., 1994, BS in Microbiology, 1994. Cert. real estate agt. Tex. Spkr. in field. With U.S. Army, 1983-90. Mem. Internat. Leprosy Assn., Am. Soc. for Microbiology. Home and Office: 408 Eisenhower St College Station TX 77840-1715 Office Phone: 979-218-5764. Personal E-mail: mnemonicmind@alpha1.com.

SCHUNK, DALE HANSEN, dean; b. Chgo., Aug. 14, 1946; s. Elmer Charles and Mildred Augusta Schunk; m. Caryl Sue Cook, June 29, 1984; 1 child, Laura Christine. BS, U. Ill., Urbana, 1968; MEd, Boston U., 1974; PhD, Stanford U., Calif., 1979. Asst. prof. edn. U. Houston, 1979—85, assoc. prof. edn., 1985—86, U. NC, Chapel Hill, 1986—91, prof. edn., 1991—93; head dept. ednl. studies Purdue U., W. Lafayette, Ind., 1993—2001; dean sch. edn. U. NC, Greensboro, 2001—. Cons. chpt. 1 reading Spring Br. Ind. Sch. Dist., Tex., 1981—94; mem. bd. trustees NC Tchr. Acad., Durham, 2002—; mem. task force tchr. retention NC State Bd. Edn., Raleigh, 2004—05. Author: (textbooks) Motivation In Education, 2002, Learning Theories: An Educational Perspective, 2004; editor: (profl. book) Educational Psychology: A Century of Contributions, 2003; contbr. chapters to books, articles to profl. jours. Sec. parent coun. W. Lafayette Sch. Corp., 1997—99; girls' softball coach W. Lafayette Little League, 1997—2000. Capt. USAF, 1968—74, Sewart AFB, Tenn., Naples, Italy. Recipient Disting. Svc. award, Purdue U. Sch. Edn., 1995, Fulbright Scholar award, New Zealand-US Ednl. Found., 1997, Cmty. Honor Roll, W. Lafayette Sch. Corp., 2000. Fellow: APA (pres. divsn. ednl. psychology 1998—99, Early Career award 1982); mem.: Am. Ednl. Rsch. Assn. (program chair 1999—2000). Avocations: tennis, travel. Home: 7007 Morganshire Ct Summerfield NC 27358 Office: Univ NC-Greensboro 1000 Spring Garden St Greensboro NC 27402 Home Phone: 336-644-6031. Office Fax: 336-334-4120. Business E-Mail: dhschunk@uncg.edu.

SCHUNK, ROBERT WALTER, space physics research administrator; b. NYC; BS, NYU, 1965; PhD in Phys. Fluids, Yale U., 1970. Fellow space physics Inst. Sci. and Tech., U. Mich., 1970-71; rsch. assoc. geophysicist Yale U., 1971-73; rsch. assoc. space physics U. Calif., San Diego, 1973-76; assoc. prof. Utah State U., Logan, 1976-79, prof. physics, 1979—. Mem. Com. Solar Terrestrial Rsch., Geophys. Rsch. Bd., Nat. Acad. Sci., 1979-82, Nat. Ctr. Atmospheric Rsch. Computer Divsns. Adv. Panel, 1980-83; prin. invester Solar Terrestrial Theory Program, 1980—. Assoc. editor Jour. Geophys. Rsch., 1977-80. Recipient Gov.'s Medal Sci. & Tech., Utah, 1988. Fellow Am. Geophys. Union (Nicolet lectr. 2002); mem. AAAS. Home: Utah State U Ctr Atmospheric Space Logan UT 84322-4405 Office Phone: 435-797-2978. Business E-Mail: schunk@cc.usu.edu.

SCHUNKE, HILDEGARD HEIDEL, accountant; b. Indpls., Nov. 24, 1948; d. Edwin Carl and Hildegard Adelheid (Baumbach) Schunke. BA, Ball State U., Muncie, Ind., 1971, MA in German, English, 1973, MA in Acctg., 1975. CPA Ind., Calif. Exch. tchg. grad. asst. Padagogische Hochschule, Germany, 1971-72; tchg. grad. asst. in German and acctg. Ball State U., 1972, 74-75, asst. prof. acctg., 1975-78; investing rschr. Family Partnership, Muncie, 1977-83; staff acct. Am. Lawn Mower Co., Muncie, 1984-88, G&J Seiberlich, CPAs, St. Helena, Calif., 1988-89, R.A. Gullotta, MBA, CPA, Sonoma, Calif., 1989-90; plant acct. Napa Pipe Corp., Calif., 1990—2001; sys. engr. Napa Pipe Divsn. Oreg. Steel Mills, 2002—04; freelance acct. Fairfield, Calif., 2004—; sr. accountant Syar Industries, Inc., Napa, 2007—. ESOL instr. Napa County Project Upgrade, 1988—92; mem. ticketing and refreshments com. North Bay Philharm. Orch., Napa, 1988—2004, North Bay Wind Ensemble, Napa, 1988—2004; mem. steering com. Cordelia Cmty. Pk., 2005—. Named Adminstrv. Divsn. Vol. of the Yr., City of Fairfield, Calif., 2006. Mem.: AICPA, Inst. Internal Auditors, Calif. Soc. CPAs (continuing edn. instr. Redwood City 1990, bd. dirs. East Bay chpt. 1998—2000). Avocations: gardening, building computers, networks and websites. Home: 1117 Devonshire Ct Fairfield CA 94534-7443 Office: HH Schunke MA CPA 1117 Devonshire Ct Fairfield CA 94534-7443 Home Phone: 707-864-2640; Office Phone: 707-864-2640. Personal E-mail: hsg_1@juno.com.

SCHUPAK, LESLIE ALLEN, public relations company executive; b. Spokane, Wash., Apr. 5, 1945; s. Leo and Henrietta (Neumann) S.; m. Dianne Barbara Goldin, June 23, 1968; 1 child, Adam J. BS, Boston U., 1967, MS, 1971. Asst. to pres., account exec. Sperber Assocs., Inc., Boston, 1968-69; account supr. Wilcox & Williams, NYC, 1969-70; v.p., mgr. Daniel J. Edelman, Inc., NYC, 1970-72; mng. ptnr. Kanan, Corbin, Schupak & Aronow, Inc. Worldwide, NYC, 1972—. Pres. Whippoorwill Lake Property Owners Assn., Chappaqua, NY, 1984-88; chmn. exec. com. Coll. Comm., Boston U., 1997-2007; dir. First Tee Met. NY, Inc. With US Army, 1968-73. Mem.: Golf Writers Am. Assn., MGA Found. (chmn.), Nat. Investor Rels. Inst., Donald Ross Soc., Met. Golf Writers Assn. (v.p.), Met. Golf Assn. (pres.), US Golf Assn. (comms. com.), Desert Mountain Club (Scottsdale, Ariz.), Metropolis Country Club (White Plains, NY). Avocations: golf, writing. Office: Kanan Corbin Schupak & Aronow Inc Worldwide 800 2nd Ave New York NY 10017-4709 Office Phone: 212-682-6300. Business E-Mail: lschupak@kcsa.com.

SCHUPBACH, TRUDI M. (GERTRUD SCHUPBACH), biologist, researcher; b. Zurich, Switzerland, Feb. 3, 1950; arrived in US, 1981; m. Eric F. Wieschaus. BS in Biology, U. Zurich, PhD, 1978. Rsch. biologist Princeton U., NJ, 1983-90, assoc. prof. NJ, 1990-94, prof. molecular biology; investigator Howard Hughes Med. Inst. Mem.: NAS. Office: Dept Molecular Biology Princeton University Princeton NJ 08544-0001 Office Phone: 609-258-6492. Office Fax: 609-258-1547. E-mail: gschupbach@molbio.princeton.edu.

SCHUPP, ANASTASIA LUKA, retired lawyer; b. Chgo. d. Joseph Anthony and Anastasia Maria (Romel) Luka; m. William Schupp, Apr. 20, 1968 (div. June 1994); 1 child, William Joseph. BS in Social Sci., Loyola U., 1966, JD, 1977; MA, U. Mich., 1968; Jagellonian, U. Sum., Poland, 1993. Bar: Ill. 1982, U.S. Supreme Ct. 1994. Law libr. Seyfarth, Shaw, Fairweather & Geraldson, Chgo., 1979-82; ptnr. Flader & Haces, Chgo., 1982-85; pvt. practice Chgo., 1986—2001; assoc. Hyatt Legal Svcs., Chgo., 1985—86, ret., 2001. Lectr. Chgo. Bd. Realtors, 1988—89, Robert Morris Coll., Orland Park, Ill., 1992, East West U. Chgo., 1992, Montay Coll., Chgo., 1991—, lectr., acad. coun., 1994—95; adminstrv. asst. William Joseph Schupp, 2003; tutor ESL Polish Am. Assn., 2004—; asst. ESL Evang. Ch. Dr. Martin Luther, 2004—05. Editor: An Ethnic Christmaas, 1982; (newsletter) The Overture, 1980-81; contbr. articles to profl. jours. Vol. Chgo. Vol. Legal Svcs., 1991—95; arbitrator Chgo. Archdiocese, 1994—2000; atty. coord. Com. to Elect Richard J. Owens for Judge, Chgo., 1993—94. Recipient Hon. Mention, Polish Arts Club, 1996. Mem.: AARP, Advs. Soc. (historian 1985—87), Chgo. Bar Assn., Womens Bar Assn. Ill. (chair com. 1982—85), Polish Army Vets. Assn. Ladies Aux., First Cath. Slovak Ladies Assn., Midway Carden Soc., Chgo. Artists Coalition, Polish Arts Club of Chgo. (bd. dirs. 1999—2002). Democrat. Roman Catholic. Avocations: reading, writing, exhibiting artist. Home: 5425 S Richmond St Chicago IL 60632

SCHUPP, RUSS, computer professor, web site designer; AA, State Fair C.C., Sedalia, Mo, 1974; MusB in Edn., Ctrl. Mo. State U., Warrensburg, 1976; MA, Webster U., Whiteman Air Force Base, 2003. Lan mgr. State Fair C.C., 1997—2000, coll. tchr., 2000—. Percussionist Sedalia Symphony, Sedalia, 1971—2006; elder Broadway Presbyn. Ch., 2004—06; percussionist Broadway Presbyn. Ch. and Antioch Fellowship Praise and Worship groups, 1996—2006. Achievements include development of new curriculum and course requirements for computer programming, computer programming with emphasis in accounting, and Web development degrees. Home Phone: 660-826-1394; Office Phone: 660-530-5800.

SCHUR, JEFFREY, advertising executive; b. Capetown, South Africa, May 3, 1946; Canadian citizen; came to U.S., 1992; s. Lionel Harry and Dorothy (Siman) S.; m. Lucille Stella Breakey, Nov. 30, 1965; children: David Leon, Cynthia-Jean. Diploma in Mktg., Cape Peninsula U., Capetown, 1970. Account exec. J. Walter Thompson, Capetown and Johannesburg, Republic of South Africa, 1969-71; account dir. Ogilvy & Mather, Johannesburg, 1971-76, internat. vp. Latin Am. base NYC, 1976-78, account dir. Toronto, Ont., Can., 1977-80; gen. mgr., pres. Saatchi & Saatchi, Toronto, 1980-84; pres., chief exec. officer Needham Harper Can., Toronto, 1985-86, Schur Peppler & Assocs., Toronto, 1986-89, Doner Schur Peppler, Toronto, 1989-92; exec. v.p. Earle Palmer Brown, NYC, 1992-94; ptnr. Doig, Elliott, Schur Inc., NYC, 1994—99; dir. integration Omnicom Group, NYC, 1999—2006; dir. integrated mktg. JWT N.Y., 2006—07; sr. client ptnr. Korn Ferry Internat., NYC, 2007—. Dir. Outward Bound, 1980-83, Can. Liver Found., 1984-86, Family Svc. Assn., 1985, York Mills Valley Assn., 1990-92, Cath. Children's Aid, Toronto, 1991-92, S.A. Defence Forces 1st Parachute Bn., 1964-73. Fellow Chartered Inst. Mktg. (lectr. 1971-73, examiner 1973-74, edn. chmn. 1974-75, rsch. award 1970), Vintage Sports Car Club Am., Old Greenwich Yacht Club, Sports Car Vintage Racing Assn., Yale Club N.Y. Avocations: skiing, scuba, vintage racing cars, gardening, sailing. Home: 10 Palmer Ter Riverside CT 06878-2103

SCHUR, WALTER ROBERT, physician; b. Webster, Mass., June 17, 1914; s. Robert O. and Alma L. (Gatzke) S.; m. Delta Jean Newman, June 17, 1944; children: Paul, David, Jonathan, Ruth, Timothy, Peter, Stephen, Mary, Joel, Daniel, Rhoda. Student, Valparaiso U., 1931-34; MD, Middlesex U.Sch. of Med., 1940. Resident Milford (Del.) Meml. Hosp., 1940-41, Grace Hosp., Cleve., 1942-43; intern Luth. Hosp., Cleve., 1941-42; pvt. practice Oxford, Mass., 1944—. Bd. dirs., pres. Doctors Hosp., Worcester, Mass., chmn. bd., 1978-87; bd. dirs. AdCare Hosp., 1987—, chmn. bd. dirs., 1987-91, Atlantic dist. Luth. Ch.-Mo. Synod, 1978-87, mem., sec. edn. com., missions com., 1960-77, mem. stewardship com., youth com., edn. com., 1951-57, chmn. edn. com. Atlantic dist., 1954-57, mem. commn. on mission and ministry in ch., named Dist. Layman of Yr., 1966, chmn. com. on ministry Atlantic dist., 1970; bd. dirs. Luth. Assn. Works of Mercy, assn. Evang. Luth. Chs.; bd. dirs. Valparaiso U., 1969-99, sec., 1984-99; pres., scholarship chmn. N.E. dist. Luth. Laymen's League, 1957; vice chmn. Luth. Hour Oper. Com., 1958, chmn., 1959-61; New Eng. bd. dirs. Assn. Evang. Luth. Chs., 1977-87, trustee East Coast Synod, 1977-87, mem. nat. bd. dirs., 1979-88; mem. coun. New Eng. Synod Evang. Luth. Ch. Am., 1988-94; bd. dirs., vice chmn. French River Edn. Ctr., 1985—; mem. Oxford Sch. Com., 1961-86, Mass. Commn. on Christian Unity; assoc. charter mem. Park Ridge Ctr., 1986. Recipient award of merit Internat. Luth. Laymen's League, 1963, Soli Deo Gloria award New Eng. Synod, Evang. Luth. Ch. Am., 1994. Fellow Am. Acad. Gen. Practice, Am. Acad. Family Physicians (charter); mem. AMA, Mass. Med. Soc., Worcester Dist. Med. Soc., Am. Geriatrics Assn., New Eng. Ob-gyn. Soc., Valparaiso U. Alumni Assn. (past pres.), Luth. Acad. for Scholarship (bd. dirs. 1977-86), Concordia Hist. Inst., New Eng. Luth. Hist. Soc. (charter), Internat. Platform Assn., New Eng. Huguenot Soc., Rotary (past pres.). Home: 168 Charlton St Oxford MA 01540-2008 Office: 367 Main St Oxford MA 01540-1746

SCHURENBERG, ERIC, magazine editor; b. Cin., Aug. 23, 1953; s. Carl Joseph and Lorraine Claire (Willows) S.; m. Judith Margaret Dowd, Apr. 30, 1983; 1 child, Emilie. AB in English, Brown U., 1975. Joined Money mag., NYC, 1984, sr. editor, 1990-95, asst. mng. editor, 1995—97, Fortune mag., 1997—2000; mng. editor Goldman.com, 2000—01; editor-at-large Business 2.0, 2001, deputy mng. editor, 2001—04; mng. editor Money mag., NYC, 2004—. Commentator Nightly Bus. Report, PBS, 1990—; former pers. fin. reporter WCBS News. Former pers. fin. editor Marketplace Radio, Mut. Broadcasting Sys., 1988-96. Author: (books) 401K Take Charge of Your Future, 1995. Recipient Nat. Mag. award Am. Soc. Mag. Editors, 1988, Page One award Newspaper Guild of N.Y., 1989, Gerald Loeb award Anderson Sch., UCLA, 1989. Mem.: Am. Soc. Mag. Editors (bd. dirs. 2007—). Office Phone: 212-522-0119. Office Fax: 212-522-3737. *

SCHURING, ELIZABETH, lawyer; BA in English, Baylor U., 1984; JD, U. Tex. Sch. Law, 1988. Cert.: Tex. Bd. Legal Specialization (estate planning and probate law). Ptnr. Giordani, Schurig, Beckett & Tackett, LLP, Austin. Mem. faculty Investment Mgmt. Consultants Assn. Wealth Mgmt. Prog. Contbr. articles to profl. jours.; author, editor: Asset Protection: Domestic and Internat. Law and Tactics. Named a Tex. Super Lawyer, Tex. Monthly and Law & Politics mag., 2003—06; named one of Top 100 Attys., Worth mag., 2005—06. Fellow: Travis County Bar Found., Tex. Bar Found., Tex. Acad. Probate and Trust Lawyers; mem.: State Bar Tex. (mem. real estate, probate and trust law sect.), ABA (vice chair real property, probate and trust law sect. 2006—07, mem. asset protection com., real property, probate and trust law sect., mem. internat. law and practice sect.), Austin Bar Assn. (dir. estate planning and probate sect. 1995—96), Estate Planning Coun. Ctrl. Tex., Coll. State Bar Tex. Office: Giordani Schuring Beckett Tackett LLP 100 Congress Ave 22nd Fl Austin TX 78701 Office Phone: 512-370-2732. Office Fax: 512-370-2730. E-mail: eschurig@gsbtlaw.com. *

SCHUR KAUFMAN, SUSAN, retired public affairs consultant; b. Feb. 27, 1940; d. Norman and Jeanette (Handelman) Dorfman; m. Clayton Kaufman; children from previous marriage: Diana Elisabeth Schur, Erica M. Rydzewski. BA, Goucher Coll., 1961. Adminstr. fed. housing, fgn. aid, anti-poverty programs, 1961-67; mem. Mass. Housing Appeals Com., 1977-86; mem., v.p. Bd. of Alderman, Newton, Mass., 1974-81; mem. Mass. Ho. of Reps., 1981-94; pvt. pub. affairs cons., 1995—2000. Bd. dirs. Middlesex Bank & Trust Co. Bd. dirs. Newton Cmty. Devel. Found., 1995-99; overseer New Philharmonia Orch., 1997-99; mem. Newton Dem. City Com., 1970-99.

SCHURMAN, DAVID JAY, orthopedic surgeon, educator; b. Chgo., Apr. 25, 1940; s. Shepherd P. and Dorothy (Laskey) S.; m. Martha Ellen Rocker, Mar. 8, 1967; children: Hilary Sue, Theodore Shepherd. BA, Yale U., 1961; MD, Columbia U., 1965. Intern Baylor U., Houston, 1965-67; resident in gen. surgery Mt. Sinai Hosp., NYC, 1966-67; resident in orthop. surgery UCLA, 1969-72; asst. rsch. surgeon UCLA Med. Sch., 1972-73; asst. prof. orthopedic surgery Stanford Med. Sch., 1973-79, assoc. prof., 1979-87, prof., 1987—. Acting chief divsn. orthop. surgery Stanford U. Med. Ctr., 1990-93, fellowship dir. total joint replacement, 1983—, fellowship dir. sports medicine, 1992-95, dir. orthop. rsch. lab., 1973—. Capt. USAF, 1967-69. Fellow NIH, 1972-73; grantee NIH, 1976-96; recipient Top Dr. award, San Francisco Mag., 02, 03, 05. Mem. Am. Orthopaedic Assn. (bd. dirs. 1994-95), Clin. Orthopaedics and Related Rsch. (bd. dirs. 1994-00), Assn. Bone and Joint Surgeons (v.p. 1996-97, pres. 1997-98). Office: Stanford U Sch Medicine R144 Divsn Orthop Surgery 300 Pasteur Dr Palo Alto CA 94304-2203 Office Phone: 650-723-7608.

SCHURZ, SCOTT CLARK, journalist; b. South Bend, Ind., Feb. 23, 1936; s. Franklin Dunn and Martha (Montgomery) S.; m. Kathryn Joan Foley, Aug. 5, 1967; children: Scott Clark, Alexandra Carol, John Danforth. BA, Denison U., 1957; LHD (hon.), Ind. U., 2000. Asst. instr. U. Md., 1957-58; adminstrv. asst. South Bend Tribune, 1960-66; circulation cons. Imperial Valley Press, El Centro, Calif., 1966; pres. Hoosier Times, Inc.; dir., vice chmn. Schurz Comms., Inc., pub. Pres. Bloomington Boys' Club, 1970-71, Jr. Achievement Monroe County, 1971-73; bd. dirs. United Way Monroe County, 1979-81, Cmty. Found. Area Arts Coun. Served with U.S. Army, 1958-60. Mem.: Ind. U. Found. (bd. dirs. 1986—), Newspaper Advt. Bur. (bd. dirs. 1987—92), Internat. Press Inst. (mem. bd. US), World Press Freedom Com. (adv. bd.), Hoosier State Press Assn. (pres. 1989, 1997), Inter-Am. Press Assn. (bd. dirs. 1995—; hon. pres.), Newspaper Assn. Am. (bd. dirs. 1992—95, 2002—, found. bd. trustees), Inland Daily Press Assn. (pres. 1989), Internat. Newspaper Mktg. Assn. (pres. 1986, treas. 1997—2004), World Assn. Newspapers (bd. dirs., exec. com., v.p.). Republican. Presbyterian. Office: Hoosier Times Inc 1900 S Walnut St Bloomington IN 47401-7720 Office Phone: 812-332-4401.

SCHUSSLER, IRWIN, psychiatrist, educator; b. Bklyn., Nov. 14, 1943; s. Jack and Fannie Yetta (Blank) S.; m. Myra Yvette Paget, June 26, 1966; children: Jeffrey Mitchell, Doreen Robyn, Kimberly Beth, Howard Brian. BS, Bklyn. Coll., 1964; DO, Chgo. Coll. Osteopathic Medicine, 1968. Diplomate Am. Bd. Psychiatry and Neurology, Am. Bd. Gen. Psychiatry and Child Psychiatry, Am. Osteopathic Bd. Neurology and Psychiatry, Am. Bd. Sexology. Intern Interboro Gen. Hosp., Bklyn., 1968—69; resident in gen. psychiatry U. Fla. Coll. Medicine, Gainesville, 1972—74, asst. prof. psychiatry and pediatrics, 1976—77, dir. in-patient psychotherapy, 1976—77, fellow in child and adolescent psychiatry, 1974—76; fellow in human sexual medicine U. Pa., Phila., 1975; practice medicine specializing in psychiatry Ft. Worth, 1977—; clin. assoc. prof., vice chmn. dept. psychiatry North Tex. State U. Health Scis. Ctr., North Tex. Coll. Osteo. Medicine, Ft. Worth, 1977—79. Past mem. bd. dirs., former med. dir. psychiatry dept. Osteo. Med. Ctr. Contbr. articles to profl. jours. Bd. dirs. Mental Health Assn. Fellow Am. Coll. Neuropsychiatry, Am. Coll. Sexology; mem. Am. Psychiat. Assn., Am. Acad. Child Psychiatrists, Am. Acad. Clin. Psychiatrists, Am. Assn. Sex Educators, Counselors and Therapists, Tex. Soc. Psychiat. Physicians (pres. Tarrant County chpt.), Am. Osteo. Assn., Tex. Osteo. Med. Assn., Fla. Osteo. Med. Assn., Masters and Johnson Found. Jewish. Home: 3712 Myrtle Springs Rd Fort Worth TX 76116-9213 Office: Psychiat Cons Ft Worth 3704 Mattison Ave Fort Worth TX 76107-2619 also: Austin Psychiat cons 1500 W 38th St Ste 53 Austin TX 78731 Office Phone: 817-732-8441. E-mail: mschussler@charter.net, pcfw@sbcglobal.net.

SCHUSTER, CARLOTTA LIEF, psychiatrist; b. NYC, Sept. 16, 1936; d. Victor Filler and Nina Lincoln (Rayevsky) Lief; m. David Israel Schuster, Sept. 2, 1962; 1 child, Amanda. BA, Barnard Coll., 1957; MD, NYU, 1964. Cert. Am. Bd. Psychiatry and Neurology; cert. addiction psychiatry. Intern Lenox Hill Hosp., NYC, 1964-65; resident St. Luke's Hosp., NYC, 1965-68; fellow Inst. Sex Edn. U. Pa., Phila., 1968-69; instr. N.Y. Med. Coll., NYC, 1969-72; asst. attending Met. Hosp., NYC, 1969-72; assoc. attending St. Luke's-Roosevelt Hosp. Ctr., NYC, 1972-95; staff psychiatrist Silver Hill Hosp., New Canaan, Conn., 1972-95; clin. assoc. instr. Columbia U., NYC, 1990-95. Chief substance abuse svc. Silver Hill Hosp., New Canaan, 1976-95; dir. Recovery Clinic Bellevue Hosp., N.Y.C., 1995-2003; mem. faculty Dept. Psychiatry Sch. Medicine NYU, 1995—. Author: Alcohol and Sexuality, 1988; co-author: Chapter in Advances in Alcohol and Substance Abuse, 1987; contbr. chpts. to books. Mem. Am. Psychiat. Assn., Am. Med. Soc. on Addictions, Am. Acad. Addiction Psychiatry. Democrat. Jewish. Avocations: cooking, attending concerts, opera, films. Home: 130 E 30th St New York NY 10016-8230 Home Phone: 212-725-0978; Office Phone: 212-213-2513. Personal E-mail: carlotta_schuster@msn.com.

SCHUSTER, CAROL JOYCE, special education educator, consultant; d. Samuel Saul and Ruth Edna Levine; m. George M. Schuster, Sept. 18, 1964; 1 child, Robert Churchill. BS in Edn., SUNY, Oswego, 1952; MS in Edn., Queens Coll., SUNY, 1958. Lic. heath conservation for physcially handicapped NYC, 1963, tchr. orthop. handicapped NY, 1976, elem. tchr. NYC. Tchr. NYC Bd. Edn., 1953—62, tchr. physically handicapped, 1963—67, St. Francis Hosp., Roslyn; tchr. in charge Queens Gen. Hosp., Queens, NY; cons. in spl. edn. Dep. for handicapped, Huntington, NY, 1982—86; mem. adv. bd. and founding com. Dolan Family Health Ctr., Huntington, 1997—. Mem. prin. selection com. Half Hollow Hills Dist., Dix Hills, NY, 1979—80; cmty. activist Huntington, 1979—; mem. campaign com. election for US congressman Dix Hills, Huntington, LI, 1986—89; mem. Dem. campaign com. US pres. Huntington, 2003—04; youth edn. mentor AAUW; cert. instr. Literacy Vols. of Am. Recipient Lifetime award for Outstanding Achievement in Career and Cmty. Svc., SUNY, Oswego, 1997. Achievements include invention of an adjustable wheelchair desk in 1963. Avocations: reading, writing poetry and prose, painting, Sherlockian literature, travel.

SCHUSTER, ELAINE, retired civil rights professional; b. Detroit, Sept. 26, 1947; d. William Alfred and Aimee Isabelle (Cote) LeBlanc; m. James William Schuster, Sept. 6, 1969; 1 child, Cambrian James. BA, Wayne State U., 1972, postgrad., 1974-75, paralegal cert., 1991; student, Bay Mills Com. Coll., 2003—. Asst. payments Mich. Dept. Social Svcs., Detroit, 1972-73; rights rep. Mich. Dept. Civil Rights, Detroit, 1973-80, 82-87, 90, asst. dir. div., 1987-90, supr., 1993-97, dir. Svc. Ctr., 1997-99, contract coord., 1999—2002, ret., 2003; ct. adminstr. Chippewa-Ottawa Conservation Ct., Bay Mills, Mich., 1980-82; quality assurance coord. State Mental Health Facility, Southgate, Mich., 1991-93; acting interim dir. Mich. Indian Commn., Detroit, 1995; proprietor Good Things to Share, 2003—; trainer HIV/AIDS health support profls., 2004—. Author: Walking in Two Worlds, Delivering Culturally Competent Care in the American Indian Community, 2004, Critique, An Indian Tours Michilimackinac, 1981, In the Track of the Bear, Discussion, Coordination of Resources to Fight HIV, 2005; contbr. articles and poems to mags. and profl. jours. Bd. dirs. Tri-County Native Ams., Warren, Mich., 1982-89, sec. Native Am. Sesquicentennial subcom., Mich., 1987; mem. Linking Lifetimes, mentor program for Native Am. youth, 1992-93; sec., newsletter editor various civic orgns.; also other polit. and civic activities. Native Am. fellow Mich. State U., 1989. Mem. NAACP (housing com. S. Oakland br. 2000), ACLU (bd. dirs. Union-Oakland county 1987-88, 2002-04). Democrat. Avocations: exploring local historical and natural places of interest, historical re-enactment, research, exercise. E-mail: ikwewe@comcast.net.

SCHUSTER, JAMES EDWARD, defense equipment manufacturing company executive; b. Buffalo, Apr. 28, 1953; s. William Daniel and Donna Mae (Flury) S.; S.; m. Ann Marie Evans; children: Jeremy L., Jesse D., Benjamin T., Christian D. BA, Lockhaven U., 1976; postgrad., Morehead U., 1976-77, Ill. Inst. Tech., 1978; MBA, Lake Erie Coll., 1984. Labor analyst GTE Automatic Electric, Northlake, Ill., 1977-79; mgr. corporate staff Gould Inc., Rolling Meadows, Ill., 1979-80; sr. ops. program mgr. Westinghouse Corp. (formerly Gould Inc.), Cleve., 1980-82, head metal working sect., 1982-84, mgr. electronics assembly, 1984-86, dir., mgr. mfg., 1986-88; mgr. ops. oceanic div. Westinghouse Electronics, Cleve., 1988—95; v.p. operations Aerospace Equipment Sys. Divsn. AlliedSignal Inc., Torrance, Calif., 1995—96; exec. v.p. MagneTek Inc., Nashville, sr. v.p. operations, 1996—98, pres. moters and generators divsn., 1998—99; pres. Raytheon Aircraft Integration Systems (RAIS), 1999—2001; chmn., CEO Raytheon Aircraft Co., 2001—; exec. v.p. Raytheon Co., 2001—. Mem.: Gen. Aviation Mfrs. Assn. (GAMA) (chmn. Security Issues Com. 1999—, mem. bd. dirs. 2001—, elected v.p. 2003—). Lutheran. Avocations: scuba diving, flytying, fishing. Office: Raytheon Co 9709 E Ctrl Wichita KS 67206 *

SCHUSTER, PEGGY LINDNER (PRAVRAJIKA BRAHMAPRANA), sister, nun; b. Seattle, Apr. 7, 1949; d. Philip Frederick Schuster and Ruth Elizabeth Robar. BA in History, Occidental Coll., Calif., 1970, U. Calif., Santa Barbara, 1973; solemn ordination (hon.), Vedanta Soc. So. Calif., 1984. Sr. monastic Vedanta Soc. So. Calif., 1973—. Convent bookstore mgr. Vedanta Soc., 1984—2004, interfaith dialog, 1984—, mem. monastic coun., 1995—2004; nun Ramakrishna Order of India; spkr. and presenter in field. Contbr. articles to religious and profl. jours.; editor: Vivekananda Swami: The Complete Works of Swami Vivekananda, 1997, of numerous works and works in progress. Interfaith seminar participant, Calcutta, India, 1977—98; lectr. Hospice, Santa Barbara, Calif., 1995—2004. Mem.: Amnesty Internat. Avocations: swimming, writing, music, cooking. Home: Vedanta Convent 2027 Vine St Hollywood CA 90068 Personal E-mail: brahmaprana@gmail.com. Business E-Mail: peggylschuster@gmail.com.

SCHUSTER, PHILIP FREDERICK, II, lawyer, writer, educator; b. Denver, Aug. 26, 1945; s. Philip Frederick and Ruth Elizabeth (Robar) S.; m. Barbara Lynn Nordquist, June 7, 1975; children: Philip Christian, Matthew Dale. BA, U. Wash., 1967; JD, Willamette U., 1972. Bar: Oreg. 1972, Wash. 2002, U.S. Dist. Ct. Oreg. 1974, U.S. Ct. Appeals (9th cir.) 1986, U.S. Ct. Appeals (D.C. cir.) 2001, U.S. Supreme Ct. 1986. Dep. dist. atty. Multnomah County, Portland, Oreg., 1972; title examiner Pioneer Nat. Title Co., Portland, 1973-74; assoc. Buss, Leichner et al, Portland, 1975-76; from assoc. to ptnr. Kitson & Bond, Portland, 1976-77; pvt. practice Portland, 1977-95; ptnr. Dierking and Schuster, Portland, 1996—; adj. prof. law Lewis & Clark Coll., 2002. Arbitrator Multnomah County Arbitration Program, 1985—; student mentor Portland Pub. Schs., 1988—, mentor new lawyers divsn. Oreg. State Bar, 2007-. Author: The Indian Water Slide, 1999; contbg. author OSB CLE Publ., Family Law; contbr. articles to profl. jours. Organizer Legal Aid Svcs. Cmty. Clinics, Salem, Oreg. and Seattle, 1969-73; Dem. committeeman, Seattle, 1965-70; judge Oreg. State Bar and Classroom Law Project, HS Mock Trial Competition, 1988—. Mem. ABA, NAACP (exec. bd. Portland, Oreg. chpt. 1979-98), ACLU, Am. Assn. for Justice, Multnomah Bar Assn. (Vol. Lawyers Project), Alpha Phi Alpha. Avocations: river drifting, camping, swimming, walking, writing. Office: 3565 NE Broadway St Portland OR 97232-1820 Office Phone: 503-335-7765. Business E-Mail: schuster@pcez.com. *Hard work and perseverance are the keys to accomplishing any goal. Protecting and nurturing our children and our environment are life's most noble goals. Success is the pursuit of these goals.*

SCHUSTER, REID S., advertising executive; m. Rachelle Schuster; 2 children. BA, U. Md. Founder Insite Strategies Corp., 1992; acct. exec. TDI (now Viacom Outdoor), 1997—99, nat. acct. mgr., 1999—2000, local sales mgr., 2000—02; exec. v.p. sales and mktg. Titan Worldwide, NYC, 2002—06, pres. sales and mktg., 2006—. Office: Titan Worldwide 850 Third Ave New York NY 10022 Office Phone: 212-644-6200. Office Fax: 212-644-2010.

SCHUSTER, ROBERT PARKS, lawyer; b. St. Louis, Oct. 25, 1945; s. William Thomas Schuster and Carolyn Cornforth (Daugherty) Hathaway; 1 child, Susan Michele. AB, Yale U., 1967; JD with honors, U. Wyo., 1970; LLM, Harvard U., 1971. Bar: Wyo. 1971, US Ct. Appeals (10th cir.) 1979, US Supreme Ct. 1984, Utah 1990. Dep. county atty. County of Natrona, Casper, Wyo., 1971-73; pvt. practice Casper, 1973—76; assoc. Spence & Moriarity, Casper, 1976-78; ptnr. Spence, Moriarity & Schuster, Jackson, Wyo., 1978—2002; pvt. practice Jackson, Wyo., 2002—. Trustee U. Wyo., 1985-89; Wyo. Dem. nominee for US Ho. of Reps., 1994; polit. columnist Casper Star Tribune, 1987-94; pres. United Way Natrona County, 1974; bd. dirs. Dancers Workshop, 1981-83; chair Wyo. selection com. Rhodes Scholarship, 1989-98; mem. bd. visitors Coll. Arts and Scis., U. Wyo., 1991-2000; mem. Dem. Nat. Com., 1992-2000; chair Wyo. Pub. Policy Forum, 1992-98; mem. Wind River Reservation Econ. Adv. Coun., 1998-99; bd. dirs. Internat. Edn. Found., 2005—. Ford Found. Urban Law fellow, 1970-71. Mem. ABA, AJA, Wyo. Trial Lawyers Assn. (named one of Best Lawyers in Am.), Yale Club (pres. Wyo. chpt., 2004—). Home: PO Box 13160 Jackson WY 83002 Office: Robert P Schuster PC 250 Veronica Ln Ste 204 PO Box 13160 Jackson WY 83002 Office Phone: 307-732-7800.

SCHUSTER, SEYMOUR, mathematician, educator; b. Bronx, NY, July 31, 1926; s. Oscar and Goldie (Smilowitz) S.; m. Marilyn Weinberg, May 2, 1954; children: Paul Samuel, Eve Elizabeth. BA, Pa. State U., 1947; A.M., Columbia U., 1948; PhD, Pa. State U., 1953; postgrad. (fellow), U. Toronto, 1952-53. Instr. Pa. State U., 1950-52, Poly. Inst. N.Y., 1953-54, asst. prof., 1954-56, assoc. prof., 1956-58; vis. assoc. prof. Carleton Coll., Northfield, Minn., 1958-59, assoc. prof., 1959-63, prof. math., 1968—, chmn. dept., 1973-76, William H. Laird prof. math. and liberal arts, 1992-94, William H. Laird prof. emeritus, 1994—. Vis. assoc. prof. U. N.C., Chapel Hill, 1961; research assoc. math. dept. U. Minn., Mpls., 1962-63, assoc. prof., 1963-65; assoc. prof. Minn. Math Center, 1965-68, dir. coll. geometry project, 1964-74; dir. Acad. Year Inst. for Coll. Tchrs., 1966-67, NSF Faculty fellow, 1970-71; vis. scholar U. Calif., Santa Barbara, 1970-71, U. Ariz., 1990; guest scholar Western Mich. U., 1976, 81; vis. prof. Western Wash. U., 1983, U. Oreg., 1986. Author: (with K. O. May) Undergraduate Research in Mathematics, 1961, Elementary Vector Geometry, 1962, (with P.C. Rosenbloom) Prelude to Analysis, 1966; also research articles on geometry, graph theory, and analysis.; cons. editor Xerox Pub. Co., 1962-71; assoc. editor, editorial bd.: Am. Math. Monthly, 1969-86; assoc. editor: Indian Jour. Math. Edn, 1976-86; co-producer 12 films on geometry. With USNR, 1944—46. Recipient Honor award Am. Film Festival, 1967, Golden Eagle award Cine Film Festival, 1967, 68; named found. fellow Inst. for Combinatorics and Applications. Mem. Math. Assn. Am., Am. Math. Soc., Nat. Assn. Math., Sigma Xi, Pi Mu Epsilon. Home: 316 Sumner St E Northfield MN 55057-2843 E-mail: schusters@charter.net.

SCHUSTERMAN, MARK A., surgeon, plastic surgeon; b. Chgo., Jan. 10, 1955; s. Daniel Ethan Malachi and Margaret Jane (Liggitt) S.; m. Lori Louise Langenbrunner (div. Feb. 1996); children: Asher, Elizabeth. BA in Chemistry, Emory U., 1976; MD, U. Louisville, 1980. Diplomate Nat. Bd. Med. Examiners, Am. Bd. Surgery, Am. Bd. Plastic Surgery. Rsch. fellow U. Louisville Cancer Ctr., 1978-79; gen. surgery intern U. Miami (Fla.) Hosp., 1980-81; asst. resident, chief resident U. Cin. Hosp., 1981-85; resident in plastic surgery, fellow microsurgery U. Pitts. Hosp., 1985-88; asst. prof. plastic surgery U. Tex.-M.D. Anderson Cancer Ctr., Houston, 1988-92, assoc. prof., 1992—, chmn. and assoc. prof., 1993—; clin. asst. prof. plastic surgery U. Tex. Med. Sch., Houston, 1988—; clin. asst. prof. to clin. prof. plastic surgery Baylor Coll. Medicine, Houston, 1989—; and in pvt. practice Houston. Coun. mem. Johnson & Johnson Med., Inc., Arlington, Tex., 1992—; site visit team mem. Joint Coun. for Advanced Tng. in H&N Oncology Surgery, U. Tenn., Memphis, 1995—; oral examiner Am. Bd. Plastic Surgery, 1995—; mem. numerous coms. U. Tex. M.D. Anderson Cancer Ctr., 1988—; mem. craniofacial/maxillofacial subcom of in-svc. exam Mass. Gen. Hosp., Harvard Med. Sch., Boston, 1991-92. Author Microsurgical Reconstruction of the Cancer Patient, 1997; contbr. articles to profl. jours., chpts. to books. Dir. CANCARE, Houston, 1990-93; coach Little League. Recipient awards Pfizer and Ciba-Geigy, 1978-79. Mem. Am. Soc. Maxillofacial Surgeons (mem. sci. program com. 1994-95, constn. bylaws com. 1994—, outcomes study com. 1994—, Am. Soc. Plastic and Reconstructive Surgeons (chmn. med. effectiveness rsch. com. 1994—, task force on outcome and guidelines, 1994—, vice chmn. guidelines com. 1994—, program com. 1994—, mem. EF teleplast com. 1993—), Soc. Head and Neck Surgeons (edn. com. 1993—, Best Rsch. award 1993), Soc. Surg. Oncology (local arrangements com. 1993-94, program com. 1993-94). Avocations: golf, skiing, sailing. Office: O'Quinn Med Tower at St Luke's 6624 Fannin Ste 1420 Houston TX 77030 Office Phone: 713-794-0368. *

SCHUTTA, HENRY SZCZESNY, neurologist, educator; b. Gdansk, Poland, Sept. 15, 1928; came to U.S., 1962, naturalized, 1967; s. Jakub and Janina (Zerbst) S.; m. Henryka Kosmal, Apr. 29, 1950; children—Katharine, Mark, Caroline. M.B., BS, U. Sydney, Australia, 1955, MD,

1968. Jr. resident, then sr. resident St. Vincent's Hosp., Sydney, 1956-58; acad. registrar, house physician Nat. Hosp. Nervous Diseases, London, 1958-62; neurologist Pa. Hosp., Phila., 1962-73; asso. prof. neurology U. Pa. Med. Sch., 1963-73; prof. neurology, chmn. dept. SUNY Downstate Med. Center, Bklyn., 1973-80; prof. U. Wis. Med. Sch., 1980-98, chmn. dept. neurology, 1980-95, prof. emeritus, 1999; prof. neurology U. Ariz., Tucson, 2001—. Achievements include research on bilirubin encephalopathy, cerebral edema, degeneration and regeneration of muscle, history of medicine. Office: U Hosp 600 Highland Ave Madison WI 53792-0001 Home: 506 Addison Street Philadelphia PA 19147-1404 E-mail: hsschutta@comcast.net.

SCHUTTE, RICHARD DAVID, diversified financial services company executive; b. Corona, Calif., Sept. 25, 1954; s. Richard A. and Cory M. Schutte; m. Karen M. Schutte, Sept. 8, 1984; children: Laura M., Michael R. BBA in Acctg., U. Wis., Eau Claire, 1976. CPA. Audit. mgr. Ernst & Young, Milw., 1976-83; contr. Hytek Internat. Corp., Brookfield, Wis., 1983-86; asst. contr. Autotrol Corp., Milw., 1986-89; v.p. fin., CFO Manu-Tronics Inc., Kenosha, Wis., 1989-2000; CFO Accutec, Oak Creek, Wis., 2000—01; pres. RDS & Assocs., Inc., Franklin, Wis., 2001—. Mem. Coun. Small Bus. Execs. Mem. AICPA, Wis. Inst. CPAs, Fin. Execs. Internat. (bd. dirs. 1992-95, treas. 1996, sec. 1997, v.p. 1998, pres. 1999), Kenosha Health Care Ptnrs., Inc. (bd. dirs. 1994-95, treas. 1994, pres. 1995), Metro. Milw. Assn. Commerce, CEO Roundtable, South Suburban C. of C. Avocations: reading, golf. Home: 2954 W Briarwood Dr Franklin WI 53132-9145 Office: RDS & Assoc Inc 2954 W Briarwood Dr Franklin WI 53132 Business E-Mail: richard@rdsassociates.com.

SCHUTZ, DONALD FRANK, geochemist, environmental corporate executive; b. Orange, Tex., Sept. 22, 1934; s. Theodore J. and Mildred Irene S.; m. Beatriz Valera, May 18, 1958; children: Delfino, Celita. BS in Geology cum laude, Yale U., 1956, PhD in Geology, 1964; MA in Geology, Rice U., 1958. Research staff geologist Yale U., New Haven, 1963-64; mgr. nuclear geochemistry dept. Teledyne Isotopes, Westwood, NJ, 1968-70, v.p., 1970-75, pres., 1975-93; engring. group exec. Teledyne, Inc., Westwood, 1989-92; chief scientist Teledyne Environ. Systems, 1992-93; gen. mgr. Teledyne Brown Engring. Environ. Svcs., 1993—99; v.p. Teledyne Environ., Inc., 1996-99; pres. Geonuclear, Inc., 1999—. Low level waste adv. com. N.J. Dept. Environ. Protection, Trenton, 1988-90; chmn. com. on radioactive materials N.J. BIA, Trenton, 1980-88. Pres. Children's Aid and Adoption Soc. N.J. Inc., Bogota, 1976-95, Am. Amateur Judo Found., River Vale, N.J., 1979-89; bd. visitors Berry Coll., 1985—; bd. dirs. Yale U. Alumni Fund, 1989-94; co-chmn. Children's Aid and Family Svcs. Inc., 1995-96, bd. dirs. emeritus, 2000—. Recipient Antarctic Service medal U.S. Congress, 1964. Mem.: World Fedn. Engring. Orgns. (mem. environ. com. 2005—, mem. energy com. 2006—), Am. Assn. Engring. Soc. (engrs. forum on sustainable devel. 1995—, internat. activities com.), Am. Nuc. Soc. (chmn. no. N.J. sect. 1988—89, pub. policy com. 1991—96, coord. climate change and sustainable devel. activities UN 1994—, chair environ. scis. divsn. 1995—96, vice chair 2000—01, chair 2001—02), Am. Assn. Radon Sci. and Tech. (life; pres. 1986—89, treas. 1990—95), Yale Sci. and Engring. Alumni Assn. (bd. dirs. Bergen County and vicinity chpt. 1989—), Sigma Xi. Office Phone: 201-391-2790. E-mail: donald.schutz@aya.yale.edu.

SCHUTZER, KAREN ANN, nurse; b. Detroit, Jan. 22, 1958; d. Melvin and Pauline Gordon; m. Robert Allen Schutzer, Apr. 22, 1989; children: Lauren Jean, Jake Maxwell. BSN, Mercy Coll. Detroit, 1977—81; MS, Fla. Atlantic U., Boca Raton, 1998—2004. RN State of Mich., 1981. Nursing asst. Children's Hosp. Mich., Detroit, 1979—81; med.-surg. nurse Henry Ford Hosp., Detroit, 1981—82; critical care, surg. ICU Jackson Meml. Hosp., Miami, Fla., 1985—88; cardiac rehab staff nurse Meml. Hosp., Hollywood, Fla., 1988—94; dir., cardiac rehab. Glades Gen. Hosp., Belle Glade, Fla., 1996—; adj. faculty, nursing Palm Beach C.C., Lake Worth, Fla., 2004—. Contbr. articles to profl. jours. Mem.: FACVPR. Avocations: travel, camping, running, gardening. Home Phone: 561-753-0904; Office Phone: 561-996-6571.

SCHUUR, DIANE JOAN, vocalist; b. Tacoma, Dec. 10, 1953; d. David Schuur. Singer: (albums) Pilot of My Destiny, 1983, Deedles, Schuur Thing, 1986, Timeless (Grammy award for female jazz vocal, 1986), Diane Schuur and the Count Basie Orchestra (Grammy award for female jazz vocal, 1987), Talkin' 'Bout You, 1988, Pure Schuur, 1991 (#1 on Billboard contemporary jazz chart, 1991, nominated for Grammy award, 1991), In Tribute, 1992, Love Songs, 1993 (Grammy nomination, Best Traditional Vocal, Grammy nomination for The Christmas Song), Love Walked In, 1996, Blues For Schuur, 1997, The Best of Diane Schuur, 1997, Music Is My Life, 1999, Friends for Schuur, 2000; singer: (with B.B. King) Heart to Heart, 1994 (No. 1 on Billboard contemporary jazz chart); singer: (with Maynard Ferguson) 'Swingin' for Schuur, 2001, Midnight, 2003; singer: Schuur Fire, 2005, (performances) White House, Monterey Jazz Festival, Hollywood Bowl, Carnegie Hall, Moscow Symphony, (tours) Japan, Far East, Near East, South Am., Europe, South Africa. Recipient 1st Ella Fitzgerald ann. award, Montreal Jazz Festival, 1999, Helen Keller Personal Achievement award, Am. Found. Blind, 2000. Office Phone: 212-362-5684. Business E-Mail: leftside@bway.net. *"There is no plateau that can't be reached, no obstacle that can't be overcome if you believe in yourself and your higher power".*

SCHUURMAN, WILLEM GERHARD, lawyer; b. June 21, 1940; s. William B. and Rina (Du Preez) S.; m. Karla Arnold, Feb. 15, 2001; children: Greg W., Bruce J., Angus D., D. Geordie. BS, U. Cape Town, South Africa, 1962, LLB, 1964; JD magna cum laude, South Tex. Coll. Law, 1981. Bar: Tex. 1981, U.S. Dist. Ct. (so. dist.) Tex. 1982, U.S. Dist. Ct. (we. dist.) Tex. 1985. Ptnr. Adams & Adams, Pretoria, South Africa, 1967—79; assoc. Arnold, White & Durkee, Houston, 1979—83, ptnr., 1983—98; ptnr., intellectual property sect. head Vinson & Elkins LLP, Austin, Tex., 1998—. Mem.: ABA, Internat. Assn. for the Protection of Indsl. Property, Travis County Bar Assn., Internat. Fedn. Indsl. Property Attys. U.S., Am. Intellectual Property Law Assn., Westwood Country Club. Office: Vinson & Elkins LLP Terrace 7 2801 Via Fortuna Ste 100 Austin TX 78746-7568 Home Phone: 512-327-1859; Office Phone: 512-542-8663. Business E-Mail: bschuurman@velaw.com.

SCHUURS, MARIEKE E., singer, educator, small business owner; b. Apr. 15, 1961; B in Music, U. Calif., Irvine, 1984, MFA, 1986. Voice faculty Concordia Coll., Irvine, Calif., 1988—92, Cerritos Cmty. Coll., 1989—91, Lane Cmty. Coll., Oreg., 1997—2000; dir., owner Cantare Voice Studio, Oreg., 1996—, Yuletime Carolers, Oreg., 2003—; chorus master Eugene Opera, Oreg., 1999—2004. Music dir. St. Anthony Claret Ch., Anaheim, Calif., 1988—91; girl choir condr. Oreg. Festival Children's Choir, Eugene, 1999—2001; active Eugene Opera Ednl. Outreach Program, 2000—04. Singer: (Operas) Die Fledermaus, 1997, Marriage of Figaro, 2000, Susannah, 2001, Little Red Riding Hood, 2003, The Telephone, 2007, Pirates of Penzance, 2006, Afterhours Jazz. Cantor, soloist Holy Family Cathedral, Orange, Calif., 1986—91. Mem.: Oreg. Music Educators Assn. (state adjudicator 2003—07), Voicecare Network, Opera Am., Nat. Assn. Tchrs. of Singing.

SCHVANEVELDT, ROGER WAYNE, science educator, consultant; s. Dee Wayne Schvaneveldt and Betty Mary Latimer; m. Ann West, Sept. 27, 1959 (div. July 1, 1999); 1 child, Susan Hamm. BA, U. Utah, 1963; PhD, U. Wis., Madison, 1967. Asst., assoc. prof. SUNY, Stony Brook, 1967—77; prof. N.Mex State U., Las Cruces, 1977—2000, Ariz. State U., Mesa, 2000—. Author: (book) Pathfinder Associative Networks. Rsch. grants, NSF, 1987—90, 2002—05, Air Force Rsch. Lab., 1980—. Fellow: AAAS; mem.: Human Factors and Ergonomics Soc., Psychonomic Soc., Cognitive Sci. Soc. Achievements include development of psychometric scaling with pathfinder networks; research in semantic priming; memory, attention, human information processing. Office: Ariz State Univ 7001 E WIlliams Field Rd Mesa AZ 85212 Home Phone: 520-219-1431; Office Phone: 480-727-1760. Personal E-mail: schvan@yahoo.com. Business E-Mail: schvan@asu.edu.

SCHWAAB, RICHARD LEWIS, lawyer; b. Oconomowoc, Wis., Nov. 15, 1945; s. Thomas L. and Phyllis N. (Lord) S.; m. Lynn Louise Howie; children: Amy, William, Andrew, Matthew. BSChemE with honors, U. Wis., 1967; JD with honors, George Washington U., 1971, LLM in Internat. Law with highest honors, 1979. Bar: Va. 1971, U.S. Dist. Ct. (ea. dist.) Va. 1979, U.S. Supreme Ct. 1980, U.S. Ct. Appeals (fed. cir.) 1982, D.C. 1998. Ptnr. Stepno, Schwaab & Linn, Arlington, Va., 1972—74, Bacon & Thomas, Arlington, Va., 1974—78, Schwartz, Jeffrey, Schwaab, Mack, Blumenthal & Evans, P.C., Alexandria, 1978-88; mng. ptnr., dept. chair intellectual property and mgmt. com., Tokyo office supervising ptnr Foley & Lardner, 1988—. Lectr. law George Washington U., 1978-88, George Mason U., 1989—. Max Planck Inst. Fgn. and Internat. Patent, Copyright and Competition Law fellow, 1971-72. Co-author Patent Practice, 6 vols., 1976-99, International Patent Law: EPC & PCT, 3 vols., 1978; Intellectual Property Protection for Biotechnology Worldwide, 1987; contbr. articles to profl. jours. Bd. trustees Nashotah House Sem., Wis.; founding bd. mem. Nat. Law Ctr. for Children and Families, Alexandria, Va. Mem. ABA, Am. Intellectual Property Law Assn., Va. State Bar (gov. 1974-78), Internat. Patent and Trademark Assn., Internat. Fedn. Indsl. Property Attys., Christian Legal Soc., Phi Kappa Phi, Tau Beta Pi. Avocation: marathons. Home: 34205 Nashotah Rd Nashotah WI 53058-9534 Office: Foley & Lardner 3000 K St NW Ste 500 Washington DC 20007-5143 Business E-Mail: rschwaab@foley.com.

SCHWAB, ARTHUR JAMES, lawyer; b. Pitts., Dec. 7, 1946; s. Earl Walter and Helen Alice (Gascoine) S.; m. Karen Jenny, Sept. 2, 1967; children: John Arthur, Ellen Katherine, David Earl. Student, Muskingum Coll., 1964-65; AB, Grove City Coll., 1968; JD, U. Va., 1972. Bar: Pa. 1972, N.J. 1985, U.S. Dist. Ct. (we. dist.) Pa. 1972, U.S. Dist. Ct. (ea dist.) Pa. 1978, U.S. Dist. Ct. (no. dist.) Ohio 1979, U.S. Dist. Ct. S.C. 1980, U.S. Dist. Ct. N.Mex. 1981, U.S. Dist. Ct. Mass. 1984, U.S. Dist. Ct. N.J. 1984, U.S. Ct. Appeals (3d cir.) 1972, U.S. Ct. Appeals (11th cir.) 1982, U.S. Ct. Appeals (4th cir.) 1982, U.S. Ct. Appeals (8th cir.) 1991, U.S. Ct. Appeals (9th cir.) 1995, U.S. Supreme Ct. 1975. Ptnr. Reed, Smith, Shaw and McClay, Pitts., 1973-90; ptnr., chair of litigation Buchanan Ingersoll, Pitts., 1990-99, chief counsel complex litig., 2000—. Mem. faculty Grove City Coll., U. Va. Trial Advocacy Program. Mem. editorial bd. Va. Law Rev., Sch. Law U. Va., Charlottesville, 1972. Bd. dirs. Grove City (Pa.) Coll. Mem. Pa. Bar Assn. (past chair civil litigation sect.), Acad. Trial Lawyers Allegheny County (past mem. bd. dirs.), Allegheny County Bar Assn., (past chair civil litigation sect.), Am. Inns of Ct. (past pres. Pitts. chpt.), Duquesne Club. Republican. Presbyterian. Office: Buchanan Ingersoll One Oxford Ctr 301 Grant St Fl 20 Pittsburgh PA 15219-1410 Home: 104 Applehill Ct Gibsonia PA 15044-8064

SCHWAB, CHARLES R., investment company executive; b. Sacramento, July 29, 1937; m. Helen O'Neill; 5 children. BA in Economics, Stanford U., 1959, MBA, 1961. Formerly mut. fund mgr., Marin County, Calif.; founder Charles Schwab Corp., San Francisco, 1971, chmn., CEO, 1971—2003, 2004—. Bd. dirs. The Gap, Inc., 1986—2004, Seibel Systems, Inc.; dir. U.S. Trust Corp., U.S. Trust Co. of NY; chmn. Charles Schwab Bank, N.A.; trustee Charles Schwab Family of Funds, Schwab Investments, Schwab Capital Trust, Schwab Annuity Portfolios. Author: How to be Your Own Stockbroker, 1984, Guide to Financial Independence, 1998, You're Fifty - Now What?, 2001; co-author (with Carrie Schwab Pomerantz): It Pays To Talk. Chmn. All Kinds of Minds Inst.; co-founder (with Helen Schwab) and chmn. Charles and Helen Schwab Found., 2001—; bd. trustees Stanford U. Named one of Forbes' Richest Americans, 1999—, Forbes' Executive Pay, 1999—, World's Richest People, Forbes Mag., 1999—, Top 200 Collectors, ARTnews Mag., 2004, 2005, 2006, 50 Most Generous Philanthropists, BusinessWeek, 2005. Republican. Achievements include pioneer in discount brokerage business since 1974. Avocation: collector of modern & contemporary art. Office: Charles Schwab & Co Inc 101 Montgomery St San Francisco CA 94104-4175 *

SCHWAB, EILEEN CAULFIELD, lawyer, educator; b. NYC, Feb. 11, 1944; d. James and Mary (Fay) Caulfield; m. Terrance W. Schwab, Jan. 4, 1969 (dec. Apr. 25, 2004); children: Matthew, Catherine Welykoridko, Claire. BA, Hunter Coll., 1965; JD, Columbia U., 1971. Bar: N.Y. 1972, U.S. Dist. Ct. (so. and ea. dists.) N.Y. 1975, U.S. Ct. Appeals (2d cir.) 1975, U.S. Tax Ct. 1980, U.S. Ct. Appeals (10th cir.) 1993. Assoc. Poletti Friedin, NYC, 1971-72, Hughes Hubbard & Reed, NYC, 1972-75, Davis Polk & Wardwell, NYC, 1975-81; dep. bur. chief Charities Bur., Atty. Gen. of N.Y., 1981-82; counsel Sidley Austin LLP, NYC, 1983—, ptnr., 1984. Adj. prof. N.Y. Law Sch. Trustee, sec., exec. com. Caramoor Ctr. Music and the Arts; trustee Cath. Communal Fund; chair planned gifts, bequests and endowment com. Archdiocese of NY; mrm. profl. adv. com. Mus. Modern Art, Met. Mus. Art, Cen. Park Conservancy, Calvary Hosp., Mus. Arts and Design, Meml. Sloan-Kettering Cancer Ctr.; co-chmn. profl. adv. com. N.Y. Pub. Libr.; chmn. adv. com. Ascension Sch.; trustee Cooke Ctr. Learning and Devel. Fellow Am. Coll. Trust and Estate Counsel; mem. N.Y. State Bar Assn., Phi Beta Kappa. Democrat. Roman Catholic. Office Phone: 212-839-5300. Business E-Mail: eschwab@sidley.com.

SCHWAB, ERNEST ROE, III, physiology educator, researcher, academic administrator; b. Denver, July 19, 1950; s. Ernest Roe and Mary Ellen (Murray) S.; m. Patty Ann Millspaugh, May 16, 1974. BA, Union Coll., Lincoln, Nebr., 1975; MS, Andrews U., Berrien Springs, Mich., 1978; PhD, Loma Linda U., Calif., 1989. Assoc. prof. allied health studies, assoc. dean academic affairs Sch. of Allied Health Professions, Loma Linda U., Loma Linda, Calif., 1996—; assoc. prof. biology La Sierra U., Riverside, Calif., 1991—96; asst. prof. biology Loma Linda U., 1983—91. Contbr. articles to profl. jours. Planner, grant writer So. Calif. Young Artists Symphony, Redlands, Calif., 1998—2001; judge Calif. State Sci. Fair, L.A., Calif., 1998—2007. Recipient Godfrey T. Anderson award for Excellence in Tchg., Loma Linda U., 1990, Cert. of Merit, Nat. Acad. Advising Assn., 1994, Disting. Svc. award, Loma LInda U. Sch. Allied Health Professions, 2004; grantee Rsch. Opportunity award, NSF, 1989. Mem. Union Concerned Scientists, Scientists Action Network, N.Y. Acad. Scis., Sigma Xi (Grad. Student Research grantee 1979), Nat. Acad. Adv. Assn. (Cert. of Merit 1994), Soc. for Neurosci., Internat. Soc. for Neuroethology, Soc. Integrative and Comparative Biology. Democrat. Seventh-Day Adventist. Avocations: photography, travel, backpacking, piano. Home: 423 Marilyn Lane Redlands CA 92373 Office: Loma Linda University 11234 Anderson St Loma Linda CA 92350-0001 Personal E-mail: achetal@earthlink.net. Business E-Mail: eschwab@llu.edu.

SCHWAB, EVAN LYNN, lawyer; b. Detroit, Apr. 13, 1938; s. Joe Schwab and Vanita Dobbs; m. Heidi Jensen, June 11, 1960 (div. Dec. 1975); children: Mari, Eric, Peter; m. Carole Fuller, Mar. 12, 1976; 1 child, William. BA, U. Wash., 1961, LLB with high honors, 1963. Bar: Wash. 1964, U.S. Dist. Ct. (we. dist.) Wash. 1966, U.S. Supreme Ct. 1967; CPA. Law clk. U.S. Supreme Ct. Justice William O. Douglas, Washington, 1963-64; assoc. Davis, Wright & Jones, Seattle, 1964-69, ptnr., 1969-88, Bogle & Gates, Seattle, 1988—99, co-chair dept. litigation, 1992—99; ptnr. trial group Dorsey & Whitney LLP, Seattle, 1999—; chair Seattle Trial Group, 2005—. 2nd. lt. USAR, 1962-64. Fellow: Am. Coll. Trial Lawyers (chmn. Wash. state com. 2005—); mem.: ABA, Seattle-King County Bar Assn., Wash. State Bar Assn., Fed. Bar Assn. Western Dist. Wash. (pres. 1985—86), Wash. Athletic Club, Seattle Yacht Club (judge adv. 1986, 2005—). Avocations: sailing, skiing. Office: Dorsey & Whitney LLP Ste 3400 US Bank Ctr 1420 Fifth Ave Seattle WA 98101-4010 Office Phone: 206-903-8858. Office Fax: 206-903-8820. Business E-Mail: schwab.evan@dorsey.com.

SCHWAB, FRANK, JR., management consultant; b. Brookline, Mass., Dec. 19, 1932; s. Frank Sr. and Phyllis (Robinson) F. BA, Rutgers U., 1952; MBA, Harvard Bus. Sch., 1956. Cert. mgmt. cons. Internal auditor Champion Paper, Inc., Hamilton, Ohio, 1956-57, mgmt. indsl. engr. Pasadena, Tex., 1957—58; cons., assoc. Booz Allen & Hamilton, NYC, 1958-65; dir. trans. planning Planning Rsch. Corp., LA, 1965; pres., CEO F.R. Schwab & Assocs., NYC, 1965-82; pres., co-CEO Fenvessy & Schwab, NYC, 1982-87; pres., CEO, Anderson & Schwab, NYC, 1987—. Bd. dirs. Sugarland Oil Corp., N.Y.C., Nat. Mining Assn. (mfrs. and svcs. divsn.), Wash., D.C. Trustee Nat. Mining Hall of Fame and Mus., Leadville, Colo., 1992—. 1st lt. U.S. Army, 1952-54, Korea. Decorated Nat. Def. Svc. medal, Korean Svc. medal with bronze star, Commendation ribbon with medal pendant, UN Svc. medal; recipient medal for merit State of NY. Mem. Inst. Mgmt. Cons. (pres. N.Y. chpt. 1975-77), Am. Arbitration Assn. (panel arbitrator), Mil. Order Fgn. Wars (vet. companion), Maidstone Club, Union Club, River Club, King Coal Club, Army and Navy Club. Republican. Avocation: tennis. Office: Anderson & Schwab Inc 444 Madison Ave New York NY 10022-6903 Home Phone: 212-751-0971; Office Phone: 212-758-6800. Fax: (212) 755-9576. Business E-Mail: fschwab@andersonschwab.com.

SCHWAB, GEORGE DAVID, social sciences educator, writer; b. Nov. 25, 1931; s. Arkady and Klara (Jacobson) S.; m. Eleonora Storch, Feb. 27, 1965; children: Clarence Boris, Claude Arkady, Solan Bernhard. BA, CCNY, 1954; MA, Columbia U., 1955, PhD, 1968. Lectr. Columbia Coll., NYC, 1959, CUNY, 1960-68; asst. prof. history, 1968-72; assoc. prof. history, 1973-79; prof., 1980—2000; prof. emeritus, 2001—. Mem. Columbia U. Seminar on Law and Polit. Thought and Institutions; dir. Conf. History and Politics CUNY; with Nat. Com. Am. Fgn. Policy. Author: Dayez: Beyond Abstract Art, 1967, Enemy oder Foe, 1968, Switzerland's Tactical Nuc. Weapons Policy, 1969, The Challenge of the Exception: An Introduction to the Polit. Ideas of Carl Schmitt, 1970, 2nd edit., 1989, Appeasement and Detente, 1975, 81, Carl Schmitt: Polit. Opportunist?, 1975; translator: The Concept of the Polit. with Comments by Leo Strauss (Carl Schmitt), 1976, 96, Legality and Illegality as Instruments of Revolutionaries in Their Quest for Power, Remarks Occasioned by the Outlook of Herbert Marcuse, 1978, The German State in Hist. Perspective, 1978, Ideology: Reality or Rhetoric, 1978, Ideology and Fgn. Policy, 1978, 81, The Decision: Is the Am. Sovereign at Bay?, 1978, State and Nation: Toward a Further Clarification, 1980, Am. Fgn. Politics at the Crossroads, 1980, Carl Schmitt: Through a Glass Darkly, 1980, From Quantity and Heterogeneity to Quality and Homogeneity: Toward a New Foreign Policy, 1980, Toward an Open-Society Bloc, 1980, Eurocommunism: The Ideological and Political Theoretical Foundations, 1981, Am. Fgn. Policy at the Crossroads, 1982, A Decade of the Nat. Com. on Am. Fgn. Policy, 1984, (trans.) Polit. Theology: Four Chapters on the Concept of Sovereignty (Carl Schmitt), 1985, 88, 2005, The Destruction of a Family, 1987, Elie Wiesel: Between Jerusalem and New York, 1990, The Broken Vow, The Good Obtained, 1991, Thoughts of a Collector, 1991, Carl Schmitt Hysteria in the US, 1992, Contextualizing Carl Schmitt's Concept of Grossraum, 1994; (translator) The Leviathan in the State Theory of Thomas Hobbes (Carl Schmitt), 1996, Carl Schmitt, A Note on a Qualitative Authoritarian Bourgeois Liberal, 2000, The Nat. Com. on Am. Fgn. Policy's Focus on Russia, 2000, U.S. National Security Interests Today, 2003; editor Am. Fgn. Policy Interests; series Global Perspectives in History and Politics. Trustee, pres. mem. exec. com. Nat. Com. Am. Fgn. Policy; mem. Coun. on Fgn. Rels. Decorated Order of the Three Stars (Latvia); recipient Ellis Island medal of honor. Office: Nat Com Am Fgn Policy 320 Park Ave New York NY 10022-6815 Office Phone: 212-224-1120. Business E-Mail: george.schwab@ncafp.org.

SCHWAB, HAROLD LEE, lawyer; b. NYC, Feb. 5, 1932; s. Harold Walter and Beatrice (Braverman) S.; m. Rowena Vivian Strauss, June 12, 1953; children: Andrew, Lisa, James. BA, Harvard Coll., Cambridge, Mass., 1953; LLB, Boston Coll., 1956. Bar: NY 1957, U.S. Ct. Mil. Appeals 1958, U.S. Dist. Cts. (so. and ea. dists.) NY 1967, U.S. Dist. Ct. (no. dist.) NY 1974, U.S. Dist. Ct. (we. dist.) NY 1988, U.S. Dist. Ct. Conn. 1995, U.S. Dist. Ct. (ea. and we. dists.) Ark. 2000, U.S. Ct. Appeals (2d cir.) 1971, U.S. Ct. Appeals (DC cir.) 1986, U.S. Ct. Appeals (11th cir.) 1988, U.S. Ct. Appeals (5th cir.) 1991, U.S. Supreme Ct. 1971. V.p. H.W. Schwab Textile Corp., NYC, 1959-60; assoc. Emile Z. Berman & A. Harold Frost, NYC, 1960-67, ptnr., 1967-74; sr. ptnr. Lester Schwab Katz & Dwyer, LLP, NYC, 1974—. Lectr. NY Jud. Seminars, 2000-02, 05, NY State Bar Assn., NY County Lawyers Assn.; examiner, Character and Fitness Com., First Jud. Dept. Contbr. articles to legal jours.; mem. editl. bd. Jour. Products and Toxics Liability, 1976-96. Served to lt. col. USAFR. Fellow Internat. Acad. Trial Lawyers; mem. ABA, ASTM, SAE, Assn. Advancement of Automotive Medicine, NY State Bar Assn. (chmn. trial lawyers sect. 1980-81, editor sect. newsletter 1981-84), Am. Bd. Trial Advs. (pres. NY chpt. 1982-83), Fedn. Ins. and Corp. Counsel (v.p. 1979-80), NY State Trial Lawyers Assn., Def. Assn. NY, Harvard Club NY, Downtown Assn., Ft. Hamilton Officers Club. Home: 205 Beach 142 St Neponsit NY 11694 Office: Lester Schwab Katz & Dwyer LP 120 Broadway Fl 38 New York NY 10271-0071 Office Phone: 212-341-4234. Business E-Mail: hschwab@lskdnylaw.com.

SCHWAB, HERMANN CASPAR, banker; b. NYC, Jan. 8, 1920; s. Hermann Caspar and Ruth (Bliss) S.; m. C. Meteer Shanks, July 5, 1955; children: Henry R., Lesley Schwab Forman, Margery Schwab Weekes, Stuart Taylor, George Bliss, Katharine Lambard Schwab Kimmick. Grad., St. Marks Sch., 1937, Yale U., 1941. With Hanover Bank, 1941-44, 46-55, asst. sec., 1949-53, asst. v.p., 1953-55; ptnr. Dick & Merle Smith, 1956; v.p. Empire Trust Co., 1957-66, sr. v.p., 1965-66; with Bank N.Y., 1966-67; sr. v.p. Schroder Trust Co., NYC, 1967-73, dir., 1970-73; pres., dir. Cheapside Dollar Fund Ltd., NYC, 1970-88; sr. v.p. Schroder Capital Mgmt. Inc., NYC, 1973-84, cons., 1984-88. Chmn., dir. Schroder Capitol Funds Inc., 1988-98, trustee dir., 1998—. Mayor Oyster Bay Cove, N.Y., 1973-85, trustee, 1965-98; trustee St. Lukes-Roosevelt Hosp. Ctr., 1969-99. 2d lt. inf., AUS, 1943-46. Mem. Piping Rock Club (Locust Valley, N.Y.), Knickerbocker Club NY, Order of St. John's Jerusalem. Home: 34 Northern Blvd Oyster Bay NY 11771-4105

SCHWAB, JOHN H., psychologist; b. NYC, Apr. 19, 1952; s. Armand Schwab Jr. and Lois F. Schwab; m. Robin Lynn Smith, Apr. 22, 1982; children: Peter, Rachel. BA in English, Middlebury Coll., Vt., 1975; MFA in Directing, Boston U., 1979; MA in Psychology, Seattle U., 1992; PhD in Clin. Psychology, Seattle Pacific U., 2001. Lic. clin. psychologist Wash., 2004. Pvt. practical clin. psychologist, Seattle, 1992—. Mem.: APA. Office Phone: 206-780-3976. E-mail: jhschwab@mindspring.com.

SCHWAB, JOHN JOSEPH, psychiatrist, educator; b. Cumberland, Md., Feb. 10, 1923; s. Joseph L. and Eleanor (Cadden) S.; m. Ruby Baxter, Aug. 4, 1945; 1 dau., Mary Eleanor. BS, U. Ky., 1946; MD, U. Louisville, 1946; MS in Physiology (Med. fellow), U. Ill., 1949; postgrad., Duke U., 1951-52, U. Fla., 1959-61. Diplomate: Nat. Bd. Med. Examiners. Intern Phila. Gen. Hosp., 1947-48; resident medicine Louisville Gen. Hosp., 1949-50; edn. officer med. coll. U. Yokohama, 1952-54; internist, psychosomaticist Holzer Clinic, Gallipolis, Ohio, 1954-59; resident psychiatry U. Fla. Hosp., 1959-61; NIMH Career tchr. U. Fla., Gainesville, 1962-64, mem. faculty, 1961-73, prof. psychiatry and medicine, 1967-73, dir. cons. liaison program, 1964-67, resident tng. dir., 1965-71; prin. investigator Fla. Health Study, 1969-74; prof., chmn. dept. psychiatry and behavioral scis. Sch. Medicine U. Louisville, 1973-91, prof. psychiatry, 1991-93, prof. emeritus, 1993—, assoc. dir. clin. psychopharm. rsch., 1991—. Chmn. epidemiologic studies rev. com. Ctr. for Epidemiologic Studies, NIMH, 1973-75, cons. psychiatry br., 1975-92; cons. Old Order Amish Study of Depression, 1978—; vol. vis. lectr. Howard U., 1992; ann. vis. lectr. U. Würzburg, Germany, hon. faculty, 1992—; vis. prof. El-Azar U., Cairo, 1991; prin. investigator LSVL Family Health Study, 1982—; dir. U. Fla. Coll. Med. Program: History and Philosophy of Medicine, 1965-72; mem. instn;. rsch. rev. bd. U. Louisville, 2003—. Author: Handbook of Psychiatric Consultation, 1968; also articles; co-author: Sociocultural Roots of Mental Illness: An Epidemiologic Survey, 1978, Social Order and Mental Health, 1979; assoc. editor Psychosomatics, 1965-86; co-editor: Man for Humanity: On Concordance V. Discord in Human Behavior, 1972, Social Psychiatry, vol. l, 1974, The Psychiatric Examination, 1974, first author Family Mental Health History, Epidem, Clinical Health Issues, 1993, first author Family Functioning: The General Living Systems Research Model, 2000; co-edited 9 books, 11 Monographs, and over 250 articles. Capt. USAMC, 1949-54. Recipient Disting. Mental Health award Mental Health Assn. Ky., 1992. Fellow Am. Coll. Psychiatrists (regent 1977-79), Collegium Internat. Neuro-Psychopharmacologicum, World Assn. Social Psychiatry, AAAS, Am. Psychiat. Assn. (chmn. council research and devel. 1974-75); mem. AMA, Acad. Psychosomatic Medicine (exec. 1965-72, pres. 1970-71), Group for Advancement Psychiatry (bd. dirs. 1985-87), So. Assn., Jefferson County Med. Soc., Ky. Psychiat. Assn., Am. Assn. Social Psychiatry (pres. 1971-73), Alpha Omega Alpha, (Outstanding Performance award for Affirmative Action U. Louisville 1986), World Assn. Soc. Psychiatry (internat. adv. com., Rome, 1991), Psychiatrists for Better Psychiat. (pres. 1990-99), U. of the World (co-chair health, edn. com. 1992-98). Achievements include research on applicability of psychiatric concepts to general medicine, sociocultural aspects of mental illness; establishing guidelines for identification and management of medical patients with illnesses complicated by emotional stress; epidemiology of mental illness; depression and the family; clinical psychopharmacology, historical and epidemiologic perspectives on the family. Home: 6217 Innes Trace Rd Louisville KY 40222-6008

SCHWAB, JUDITH, artist, educator, sculptor; b. Phila., Feb. 22, 1935; d. Henry Ellick and Eleanor Adelman; m. Ralph Schwab, 1956; children: Linda Deutsch, Andrea Cohen. BA cum laude, Kean Coll., NJ, 1975; postgrad., Rutgers U., Union, NJ, 1978—79; MFA in Sculpture, U. Del., Newark, 1986. Cert. art tchr. Pa. Substitute art tchr. Manalapan-Englishtown Pub. Schs., Englishtown, NJ, 1970—77, art tchr., 1978—79; artist Sterk Sch. Hearing Impaired, Newark, Del., 1981, art tchr., 1982; vis. artist, facilitator Xian Art Sch., Xian, China, 1998; substitute art tchr. Del. Pub. Schs., Wilmington, 1990—93; art tchr. Shortlidge Elem. Sch., Wilmington, 1994—98. Initiator internat. exchanges Pacem in Terris, 1998; lectr. in field. One-woman shows include No. Ariz. U. Art Gallery, Flagstaff, 1985, Thompson Park Gallery, Lincroft, N.J., 1985, West Gallery and East Gallery, 1995, U. Tenn. Art Galleries I and II, Chattanooga, 1987, Susan Isaacs Gallery, Wilmington, 1990, U. Del. Clayton Hall Conv. Ctr. Gallery, 1990, Ctrl. House of Art, Tbilisi, Ga., Russia, 1991, Del. Ctr. for Contemporary Art, 1991, Jewish Cmty. Ctr. Art Gallery, 1993, Cecil CC Cultural Art Ctr., 2005, Brandeis U. Women's Com., Waltham, Mass., 2007, exhibited in group shows at Del. Art Mus., 1991—92, The Lorelton Gallery, Wilmington, 1999, U. Del., 1992—94, Xian Art Sch., 1998, Artemis Gallery, Richmond, Va., 1999—2001, Synergy Gallery, West Palm Beach, Fla., 2000—01, Del. Art Mus., Wilmington, 2001—04, Grace Gallery, 2005, Cecil Cultural Arts Ctr., Cecil C.C., 2005, East of the Bay Gallery, Md., 2006, Ft. Lauderdale History Mus., 2006, Internat. Ctr. U. Del., 2007, Represented in permanent collections Corp. Holding Svcs., One on One Fitness Ctr., Wilmington, Skadden Arps Slate Meagher and Flom, Salva Profl. Assn., The Arches, Del. History Mus. Mem. Nat. Mus. for Women in the Arts, NOW; bd. dirs. People to People Internat., 1993—2000, Jewish Family Svc., Wilmington, 1983—84. Grantee, U. Del., 1985; Emerging Artist fellowship in Sculpture, Del. Divsn. of the Arts, 1986—87, Established Artist fellow in Sculpture, 1993—94, Art fellow, Del. State Arts Coun., 1993—94, Opportunity grantee in Painting, Del. Divsn. of the Arts, 2005. Mem.: Del. Ctr. for Contemporary Art, Del. Art Mus. Avocations: dance, yoga, music, ceramics, voice. Personal E-mail: j_art_schwab@comcast.net.

SCHWAB, STEPHEN WAYNE, lawyer; b. Washington, Jan. 25, 1956; s. A. Wayne and Elizabeth (Parsons) S.; m. Debora Zellner, May 26, 1979; children: Benjamin Earl, Jason Edward. BA, Northwestern U., 1979; JD, Pa. State U., 1982. Bar: Ill. 1982, U.S. Dist. Ct. (no. dist.) Ill. 1983, U.S. Ct. Appeals (7th cir.) 1985, U.S. Ct. Claims 1986, U.S. Supreme Ct. 1989, U.S. Ct. Appeals (9th cir.) 1991, D.C. 1994. Assoc. Pretzel & Stouffer, Chgo., 1982-85; ptnr. Piper Rudnick LLP, Chgo., 1985—2004; ptnr., chmn. Insurance & Reinsurance practice group DLA Piper US LLP, Chgo., 2005—. Contbr. chapters to books, articles to profl. jours. Scoutmaster Troop 5 Boy Scouts Am., Wilmette, Ill., 1999—2003; chmn.NE Ill. coun. Jamboree Com., 2003—; lay reader Luth. Ch. of the Ascension, Northfield, Ill., 1998—, endowment com., 2002—. Recipient Nat. Scoutmaster award, Nat. Eagle Scout Assn., 2002, Potawatomi Dist. Merit award, 2003, Wood Badge award, 2003. Mem. ABA, Internat. Bar Assn., Chgo. Bar Assn., ARIAS U.S., Internat. Assn. Insurance receivers, Def. Rsch. Inst., Nat. Conf. Insurance Legislators, Nat. Assn. Insurance Commissioners, Order of Barristers, Phi Eta Sigma. Lutheran. Office: DLA Piper US LLP Fl 19 203 N LaSalle St Chicago IL 60601-1293 Home Phone: 847-251-4056; Office Phone: 312-368-2150. Office Fax: 312-630-7343. Business E-Mail: stephen.schwab@dlapiper.com.

SCHWAB, STEWART JON, dean, law educator; b. 1954; BA, Swarthmore U., 1975; MA, Mich. U., 1978; JD econ., magna cum laude, Mich. U. Law Sch., 1980; PhD econ., Mich. U., 1981. Bar: D.C. 1982. Law clk. to Hon. J. Dickson Phillips U.S. Ct. Appeals (4th cir.), 1981-82; law clk. to Hon. Sandra O'Connor U.S. Superior Ct, 1982-83; from asst. prof. to prof. law Cornell U. Law Sch., Ithaca, NY, 1983—2003, dean, 2004—; disting. visiting prof. U. Nebr. Coll. Law, Lincoln, 2003; Fulbright sr. scholar Australian Nat. Univ. Ctr. for Law & Econ., Canberra, 1998. Vis. fellow Centre Socio-Legal Studies Oxford U., 1990; vis. rsch. prof. U. Va. Law Sch., 1991; vis. prof. U. Mich. Law Sch., 1988, Duke Law Sch., 1999-2000; dir. Am. Deans Law Assn., 2005-. Editor: Jour. Empirical Legal Studies, 2004—. Fellow Alcoa Found.; mem. Am. Econ. Assn., Am. Judicature Assn., Order of Coif; City of Ithaca bd. zoning appeals, 1985-88. Office: Cornell Law Sch 263 Myron Taylor Hall Ithaca NY 14853-4901 Office Phone: 607-255-3527. Office Fax: 607-255-7193. Business E-Mail: stewart-schwab@lawschool.cornell.edu, sjs15@cornell.edu. *

SCHWAB, SUSAN CARROLL, ambassador, former academic administrator; b. Washington, Mar. 23, 1955; d. Gerald and Joan Inga (Newton) Schwab. BA in Polit. Economy, Williams Coll., 1976; MA in Devel. Policy, Stanford U., 1977; PhD in Pub. Adminstrn., George Washington U., 1993. US trade negotiator Office of US Trade Rep., Washington, 1977-79; internat. economist & trade policy officer U.S. Embassy, Tokyo, 1980-81; chief economist, legis. asst. for internat. trade for Senator John C. Danforth, Washington, 1981-86, legis. dir., 1986—89; asst. sec. commerce, dir. gen. US and Fgn. Comml. Svc. US Dept. Commerce, Washington, 1989-93; dir. corp. bus. devel. Motorola, Inc., Schaumburg, Ill., 1993-95; dean U. Md. Sch. Pub. Affairs, College Park, 1995—2003; pres., CEO U. Md. Found., Adelphi, Md., 2004—05; vice chancellor U. Md. Sys., Adelphi, Md., 2004—05; dep. US Trade Rep. Exec. Office of the Pres., Washington, 2005—06, US Trade Rep., 2006—. Bd. dirs. Calpine Corp., 1997—2005. Office: US Trade Rep 600 17th St NW Rm 200 Washington DC 20508 Office Phone: 301-445-1941, 202-395-7360. *

SCHWABE, GEORGE BLAINE, III, lawyer; b. Tulsa, Oct. 10, 1947; s. George Blaine Jr. and Marguerite Irene (Williams) S.; m. Jann Lee Schoonover, July 28, 1972; 1 child, George Blaine IV. BBA, U. Okla., 1970, JD, 1974. Bar: Okla. 1973, Maine 2001, U.S. Dist. Ct. (we. dist.) Okla. 1974, U.S. Dist. Ct. (no. dist.) Okla. 1985, U.S. Dist. Ct. (ea. dist.) 1998, U.S. Ct. Appeals (10th cir.) 1974, U.S. Supreme Ct. 1991. From assoc. to ptnr. Crowe & Dunlevy, Oklahoma City, 1974-82; ptnr., dir. Mock, Schwabe, Waldo, Elder, Reeves & Bryant, Oklahoma City, 1982-96; shareholder, dir. Gable Gotwals Mock Schwabe, Oklahoma City, 1996-98; member Mock, Schwabe, Waldo, Elder, Reeves & Bryant, Oklahoma City, 1998—. Adj. prof. law Oklahoma City U.; lectr. in field. Mem. Leadership Oklahoma City. Capt. USAR. Fellow Am. Coll. Bankruptcy; (Class III, 10th cir. regent) mem. ABA (bus. bankruptcy com. sect. bus. law), Okla. Bar Assn., Bankruptcy and Reorganization Sect. (pres. 1987-88, 2004-05, bd. dirs. 1985—), Okla. City Golf & Country Club, Rotary. Republican. Mem. Christian Ch. Avocation: golf, snow and water skiing, tennis. Office: Mock Schwabe et al 2 Leadership Sq 14th Fl 211 N Robinson Ave Oklahoma City OK 73102-7109 Office Phone: 405-235-1110. Business E-Mail: gschwabe@mswerb.com.

SCHWABE, JOHN BENNETT, II, lawyer; b. June 14, 1946; s. Leonard Wesley and Hazel Fern (Crouch) Schwabe. AB, U. Mo., Columbia, 1967; JD, U. Mo., Columbia, 1970. Bar: Mo. 1970, U.S. Dist. Ct. (we. dist.) Mo. 1970, U.S. Ct. Mil. Appeals 1971, U.S. Supreme Ct. 1973; ordained minister. Pvt. practice, Columbia, Mo., 1974—96, St. Louis, 1984—96. Mem. N. Am. Boxing Fedn., 1997—; minister, founder John Schwabe Ministries. Capt. JAGC USAF, 1970—74. Mem.: Lawyers Assn. St. Louis, Boone County Bar Assn. (sec. 1977—79), Am. Legion, Phi Delta Phi. Methodist.

SCHWALB, BRIAN L., lawyer; b. Washington, Sept. 24, 1967; married; 3 children. AB magna cum laude, Duke Univ., 1989; JD cum laude, Harvard Univ., 1992. Bar: Va. 1992, Md. 1993, DC 1998, US Dist. Ct. (ea. dist. Va., DC, Md.), US Ct. Appeals (4th, DC cir.), US Supreme Ct. Law clk. Judge John R. Hargrove, Sr., US Dist. Ct., Md. Dist., 1992—94; atty. U.S. Dept. Justice, tax div., 1994—98, pvt. practice, 1998—2004; ptnr., Comml. Litigation practice Venable LLP, Washington, 2005—. Mem.: ABA, Md. State Bar Assn., Va. State Bar Assn., DC Bar Assn., Phi Beta Kappa. Office: Venable LLP 575 7th St NW Washington DC 20004 Office Phone: 202-344-4356. Office Fax: 202-344-8300. Business E-Mail: blschwalb@venable.com.

SCHWALLER, JOHN FREDERICK, academic administrator, historian, educator; b. Hays, Kans., July 2, 1948; s. Henry and Juliette (Trembly) S.; m. Anne Cardot Taylor, Aug. 15, 1970; children: Robert Clemens, William Henry. AB, Grinnell Coll., Iowa, 1969; MA, U. Kans., 1971; PhD, Ind. U., 1978. Asst. prof. Fort Hays State U., Hays, Kans., 1978-79, Fla. Atlantic U., Boca Raton, 1979-82, assoc. prof., 1982-86, prof. history, 1986—, asst. dean, 1989-90, assoc. dean, 1990-93; dir. Acad. Am. Franciscan History Franciscan Sch. Theology, Berkeley, Calif., 1993—2002; assoc. provost, prof. history U. Mont., Missoula, 1995—2001; vice chancellor academic affairs, dean U. Minn., Morris, 2001—06, prof. history, 2001—06; pres. SUNY, Potsdam, 2006—. Author: Partidos y parrocos bajo la real corona en la Nueva Espana, sigio XVI, 1981, Origins of Church Wealth in Mexico: Ecclesiastical Finances and Church Revenues, 1523-1600, 1985, The Church and Clergy in Sixteenth-Century Mexico, 1987, The Church in Colonial Latin America, 2000, Francis in the Americas, 2005; (with Barry Sell) A Guide to Confession Large and Wmall, 1999; contbr. articles to profl. jours. Grantee Fla. Atlantic U., 1980, 81, 82, 83, 88, Am. Philos. Soc., 1982, NEH, 1989-90; fellow Newberry Library Assocs., 1982, Fulbright-Hays, 1982-83, Tulane U., 1983, Tinker Found., 1984-86. Mem. Am. Hist. Assn., Am. Cath. Hist. Assn., Conf. Latin Am. History, Latin Am. Studies Assn., Fullbright Assn., Hist. of Early Modern Europe, Rocky Mountain Conf. Latin Am. Studies, Phi Alpha Theta, Sigma Delta Pi. Democrat. Episcopalian. Office: SUNY at Potsdam Office of Pres 44 Pierrepont Ave Potsdam NY 13676 Office Phone: 315-267-2100. Office Fax: 315-267-2496. Business E-Mail: schwaljf@potsdam.edu.

SCHWAN, LEROY BERNARD, artist, retired art educator; b. Dec. 8, 1932; s. Joseph L. and Dorothy (Papenfuss) S.; children from previous marriage: David A., Mark J., William R., Catherine L., Maria E. Student, Wis. State U., River Falls, 1951-53, Southeastern Signal Sch., Ga., 1954; BS, U. Minn., 1958, MEd, 1960, postgrad., 1961-64, No. Mich. U., 1965, Tex. Tech. U., 1970, So. Ill. U., 1978, U. Iowa, 1980, EdD (hon.), 1988. Head art dept. Unity Pub. Schs., Milltown, Wis., 1958-61; instr. art Fridley Pub. Schs., Mpls., 1961-64; asst. prof. art No. Mich. U., Marquette, 1964-66, Mankato (Minn.) State Coll., 1966-71, assoc. prof., 1971-74; tchr. off-campus grad. classes Northeast Mo. State U., John Wood Cmty. Coll.; dir. Art Workshop Educultural Ctr., 1968; dir. art edn. Quincy (Ill.) Pub. Schs., 1974-78, art tchr., 1978-88, ret., 1988. Tchr. art to mentally retarded children, Faribault, Minn., Owatonna, Minn., Mankato, Lake Owasso Children's Home, St. Paul; dir. art workshops, Mankato, 1970, St. Paul, 1972, 73, 74, 75; dir. workshops tchrs. mentally retarded Mankato, 1971, Faribault, 1972, Omaha, 1972-73, Quincy, 1974, 79, 82, 84-86, asst. adj. Ill. VA Home, 1980—. Author: Art Curriculum Guide Unity Public Schs., 1961, Portrait of Jean, 1974, Schwan's Art Activities, 1984, Poems of Life, 1995, LeRoy Remembers, 2003; co-author: Bryant-Schwan Design Test, 1971, Bryant-Schwan Art Guide, 1973; contbr. articles to profl. jours., author numerous poems; one-man shows: Estherville Jr. Coll., 1968, Mankato State Coll., 1968, 71, 73, 75, 97, Farmington, Wis., 1970-71, 91, Good Thunder, Minn., 1972, Quincy, 1975, 77, 84, Western Ill. U., 1979, St. Croix River Valley Arts Coun. Gallery, Osceola, Wis., 1993-96, The Northern Ctr. for the Arts, Amery, Wis., 1994, 2001, Borders Books Gallery, Woodbury, Wells Fargo Gallery, Woodbury, Health Ptnrs. Gallery, Woodbury, 2000, Gallery at Fortes Ins., Woodbury, 2001; exhibited in group shows at Pentagon, Washington, 1955, U. Minn., 1958, No. Mich. U., 1965, St. Cloud State Coll., 1967, Moorhead State Coll., 1967, Bemidji (Minn.) State Coll., 1967, MacNider Mus., Mason City, Iowa, 1969, 72-74, Gallery 500, Mankato, Minn., 1970, Rochester, Minn., 1972, Minn. Mus., St. Paul, 1973, Hannibal, Mo., 1976, 77-78, Quincy, Ill., 1976-77, 85, Ill. Art Educators Show, 1984-85, Tchrs. Retirement Art Show, Springfield, Ill., 1987, Phipps Ctr. Arts, Hudson, Wis., 1997-99, 2000-01, 03, 04; prodr. ednl. TV series, 1964-65, also 2 shows Kids Komments, Sta. WGEM, Quincy; mural commd. Gem City Coll., 1977. Webelos leader Twin Valley coun. Boy Scouts Am., 1968-69; bd. dirs. Quincy Soc. Fine Arts, 1975-85, Polk County Hist. Soc., 1993—. With Signal Corps., AUS, 1954-56. Recipient cert. of accomplishment Sec. Army, 1955, Golden Poet award, 1985, 86, 88, 90, 91, Silver Poet award 1989. Mem. Nat. Art Edn. Assn., Ill. Art Edn. Assn., Cath. Order Foresters, Am. Legion, Phi Delta Kappa. Home: 849 County Road H New Richmond WI 54017-6209

SCHWANAUER, FRANCIS, philosopher, educator; b. Zsámbék, Hungary, Jan. 20, 1933; arrived in US, 1959; s. Georg and Maria (Keller) S.; m. Johanna Maria Koelln, Sept. 29, 1957; children: Stephan Michael, Miriam Frances. Maturum, Ulrich von Hutten Gymnasium, Korntal, Germany, 1954; PhD, U. Stuttgart, Germany, 1959. Asst. prof. Lebanon Valley Coll., Annville, Pa., 1960—62, U. Maine, Orono, 1962—65, U. So. Maine, Portland Gorham, 1965—67, assoc. prof., 1967—72, prof., 1972—2006, prof. emeritus, 2006—. Author: Truth is a Neighborhood with Nothing in Between, 1977, Those Fallacies by Slight of Reason, 1978, No Many is not a One (For the Case is Comparison), 1981, The Flesh of Thought is Pleasure or Pain, 1982, To Make Sure is to Cohere, 1982, Philosophical Fact and Paradox, 1987, Fables from the Fox, 1991; contbr. articles to profl. jours. Grantee, John Anson Kittredge Ednl. Fund, 1991, 1993. Mem.: New Eng. Philos. Assn. Democrat. Roman Catholic. Avocation: fishing. Home: 4 Woodmont St Portland ME 04102-2709

SCHWANDA, GRACE ELAINE, music educator; b. Paterson, NJ; d. Cornelius Herbert and Matilda Dunning; m. Tom Schwanda, July 30, 1977; children: Rebecca, Stephen. BA, Montclair State U., 1972, MA, 1977; postgrad., Manhattan Sch. Music, 1977; phys. edn. cert., Calvin Coll., 1992; postgrad., Western Mich. U., 1999. Music educator Bloomingdale (N.J.) Pub. Schs., 1972—78; min. music Wanaque (N.J.) Reformed Ch., 1972—86; music literacy coach St. Cecilia Music Soc., Grand Rapids, Mich., 1987—98; children and youth choral dir. St. Robert Ch., Ada, Mich., 1992—2006; music instr. Grand Rapids CC, 1995—; instr. Wheaton Coll. Sch. Arts, Ill., 2007—. Music workshop presenter Grand Rapids Symphony, 1998, 2005; choir dir. K-2 program Glen Ellyn Children's Choir. Contbr. articles to profl. jour. Vol. nursing home singer St. Cecilia Music Soc., Grand Rapids, 2000—06; knitting workshop presenter Gilda's Club, Grand Rapids, 2003—06; H.S. soccer referee. Recipient Mich. Compac award for svc. learning, 2002, Raider award, Grand Rapids C.C., 2003. Mem.: Orgn. Am. Kodaly Educators, Choristers Guild, Am. Choral Dirs. Assn., Am. Orff Schulwerk Assn. Avocations: knitting, fitness. Home: 1999 Nottingham Ln Wheaton IL 60187

SCHWANDA, TOM, religious studies educator; b. E. Stroudsburg, Pa., Oct. 23, 1950; s. Theodore Frank and Madlyn Betty (Backensto) S.; m. Grace Elaine Dunning, July 30, 1977; children: Rebecca Joy, Stephen Andrew. Student, Worcester Polytechnic Inst., 1968-69; BA in Econ., Moravian Coll., 1969-72; student, Gordon-Conwell Sem., 1972-74; MDiv, New Brunswick Sem., 1975; DMin, Fuller Theol. Sem., 1992. Ordained to ministry Reformed Ch. in Am., 1975. Pastor Wanaque (N.J.) Reformed Ch., 1975-87; pastor congl. care Immanuel Reformed Ch., Grand Rapids, Mich., 1987-92; interim sr. pastor Remembrance Reformed Ch., Grand Rapids, 1992-93; rsch. fellow H. Henry Meeter Ctr. for Calvin Studies Calvin Coll., Grand Rapids, 1993-95; instr. spirituality and worship Bethlehem Ctr. for Spirituality, Grand Rapids, 1993—; dir. Reformed Spirituality Network, Grand Rapids, 1992—; assoc. for spiritual formation Reformed Ch. in Am., 1995-99; prof. spiritual formation Reformed Bible Coll., Grand Rapids, Mich., 1999—2006; assoc. prof. Christian formation and ministry Wheaton Coll., Ill., 2006—. Organizer, convener Gathering Reformed Spirituality, 1993, 94, 95, 97, 99, 2001, 2004; chair spirituality com. Synod of Great Lakes, 1989-2000, mem. Christian discipleship com., 1988-94; mem. ch. life, evangelism, missions com. South Grand Rapids Classics, chair, 1992; mem. commn. on worship Reformed Ch. in Am., 1978-94; mem. care of students com. Passaic Classis, 1975, 87, chair, 1978, 83-86, pres., 1979; adj. prof. spirituality and spiritual direction and worship Fuller Theol. Sem., San Francisco Theol. Sem., No. Bapt. Theol. Sem., Western Theol. Sem., Columbia Theol. Sem., Charlotte, Orlando, Reformed Theol. Sem., Charlotte. Author: Celebrating God's Presence: The Transforming Power of Public Worship, 1995; contbr. articles to religious jours.; author poetry; manuscript reader, evaluator religious pub. co. Established, managed Wanaque Cmty. Food Pantry, 1977-87; vol. Domestic Crisis Ctr., Grand Rapids, 1988—; bd. dirs. Nat. Inst. Rehabilitation Engrng., Hewitt, N.J., 1984—, pres. bd. dirs., 1986—. Recipient Barnabas award Iglesia Cristiana Ebenezer, 1987. Mem. Czechoslovak Soc. Arts and Sci., Czechoslovak Hist. Conf., Soc. for Study of Christian Spirituality, Evangelical Theol. Soc., Calvin Studies Soc. Mem. Reformed Ch. Am. Avocations: running, landscaping, genealogy, amateur radio. Home: 1999 Nottingham Ln Wheaton IL 60187 Office: Wheaton College 501 College Ave Wheaton IL 60187 Office Phone: 616-988-3680.

SCHWANK, JOHANNES WALTER, chemical engineering educator; b. Zams, Tyrol, Austria, July 6, 1950; came to U.S., 1978; s. Friedrich Karl and Johanna (Ruepp) S.; m. Lynne Violet Duguay; children: Alexander Johann, Leonard Friedrich, Hanna Violet, Rosa Joy. Diploma in chemistry, U. Innsbruck, Austria, 1975, PhD, 1978. Mem. faculty U. Mich., Ann Arbor, 1978—, assoc. prof. chem. engring., 1984-90, acting dir. Ctr. for Catalysis and Surface Sci., 1985-90, prof., interim chmn. dept. chem. engring., 1990-91, assoc. dir. Electron Microbeam Analysis Lab., 1990—2000; chmn. dept. chem. engring., 1991-95; prof. chem. engring. U. Mich., Ann Arbor, 1995—. Vis. prof. U. Innsbruck, 1987-88, Tech. U. Vienna, 1988; cons. in field. Contbr. over 125 articles to profl. jours. Fulbright-Hays scholar, 1978. Mem. Am. Chem. Soc., Am. Inst. Chem. Engrs., Mich. Catalysis Soc. (sec.-treas. 1982-83, v.p. 1983-84, pres. 1984-85). Achievements include patents for bimetallic cluster catalysts, hydrodesulfurization catalysts and microelectronic gas sensors. Home: 5633 Meadow Dr Ann Arbor MI 48105-9368 Office: U Mich Dept Chem Engring 2300 Hayward St Ann Arbor MI 48109-2136 E-mail: schwank@umich.edu.

SCHWANTES, BRIANNE CATHERINE, marketing professional; b. Kenosha, Wis., Apr. 9, 1980; d. Terry James and Theresa Gilgenbach Schwantes. Postgrad., George Mason U., Fairfax, Va, 2007—. Notary public Commonwealth of Va., 2006. Comm. specialist Give Kids World Found., Orlando, Fla., 2004—05; comm., mktg. specialist NIH, Bethesda, Md., 2005—07. Patient adv. NIH, 1980—. Editor: (patient newsletter) Little Bones Newsletter, (website) www.brianneschwantes.com. Vol. Heart Am. found., Washington, 1996—2007; vol. relief worker ARC, Des Moines, 1993; vol. Counselor Camp AmeriKids, Carmel, NY, 1998—98; oreganizer book dr. Independant Cmty. Svc. Project, South Milwaukee, Wis., 2004. Recipient Citizens award, South Milw. Lions Club, 1987, Golden Lantern award, Delta Gamma Sorority, 2002, Trailblazer award, Am. U., 2002, Outstanding Leadership award, Am. U. Sch. Pub. Affairs, 2003, Outstanding Young Wis. award, Wis. Jaycees, 2006, Outstanding Contbns. award, Osteogenesis Imperfecta Found., 1990, award, Wis. chpt. Yes I Can Found., 1993, Nat. Yes I Can found., 1993, Leadership award, Pride Industries, 1994, Internat. Caring award, Caring Inst., 1996, Vol. Extraordinaire award, South Milw. Cmty. Ctr., 1997. Liberal. Lutheran. Avocations: quilting, travel, writing, reading, public speaking. Home: 1725 Lakeview Ave South Milwaukee WI 53172 Home Phone: 202-421-5882. Personal E-mail: brianneschwantes@hotmail.com.

SCHWANTES, CARLOS ARNALDO, history professor, consultant; b. Wilmington, NC, Mar. 7, 1945; s. Arnaldo and Frances (Casteen) Schwantes; m. Mary Alice Dassenko, Sept. 4, 1966; children: Benjamin, Matthew. BA, Andrews U., 1967; MA, U. Mich., 1968, PhD, 1976. From instr. to prof. Walla Walla Coll., College Place, Wash., 1969-85; prof. history U. Idaho, Moscow, 1984—2002; St. Louis Merc. Libr. endowed prof. transp. studies U. Mo., St. Louis, 2001, 2002—. Cons. TV History Idaho, 1988. Author: Coxey's Army: An American Odyssey, 1985, The Pacific Northwest: An Interpretive History, 1989, Railroad Signatures Across the Pacific Northwest, 1993, Going Places: Transportation Redefines the Twentieth Century West, 2003; mem. editl. bd.: Pacific NW Quart, 1982—97, Idaho Yesterdays, 1987—2002, Forest and Conservation History, 1988—95, Pacific Hist Rev, 1991—95; contbr. articles to profl. jours. Fellow NEH, 1982—83. Research, Idaho Humanities Coun, 1989—90; grantee, Idaho State Bd Educ, 1990—91. Mem.: Mo. Hist. Soc., Lexington Soc., Mining Hist. Assn. (mem. coun. 1990—94), Western Hist. Assn. (pres Pacific Ct br 1999—2000), Am Hist. Assn. Republican. Seventh Day Adventist. Avocations: photography, travel. Personal E-mail: caschwantes@sbcglobal.net.

SCHWANTES, ROBERT SIDNEY, international relations executive; b. Beetown Township, Wis., July 11, 1922; s. Kurt John and Lillian Ellen (Walker) S.; m. Marion Laura Miles, July 15, 1943; children: Virginia, Janet, Ingrid. AB summa cum laude, Harvard U., 1943; MA, U. Colo.,

1947; PhD, Harvard U., 1950. Instr. in history Harvard U., Cambridge, Mass., 1950-52; Carnegie resch. fellow Coun. on Foreign Rels., NYC, 1952-54; various positions The Asia Found., San Francisco and Tokyo, 1954-66, dir. of programs San Francisco, 1966-69, v.p. for programs, 1969-84, exec. v.p., 1984-88; vis. rsch. scholar Hoover Inst., Stanford, 1988—. Mem. Am. adv. com. Japan Found., Tokyo, 1984-86, vis. History lectr. Harvard U., 1958. Author: Japanese and Americans, 1955, What Did You Do in the War, Daddy?, 1998; contbr. articles to profl. jours. Vestryman St. Paul's Episcopal Ch., Burlingame, Calif., 1993-95. Lt. (j.g.), USNR, 1942-46, PTO. Assn. Asian Studies, Japan Soc. No. Calif. Democrat. Avocations: reading, travel. Home: 1432 Benito Ave Burlingame CA 94010-5550 Personal E-mail: robertschwantes@sbcglobal.net.

SCHWANTNER, JOSEPH, composer, educator; b. Chgo., Mar. 22, 1943; m. Janet Elaine Rossate; 2 children. B.Mus., Chgo. Conservatory Coll.; M.Mus., Northwestern U., 1966, D.Mus., 1968. Teaching fellow Northwestern U., 1966-68; mem. faculty Chgo. Conservatory Coll., 1967-68; asst. prof. Pacific Lutheran U., 1968-69, Ball State U., 1969-70; successively asst. prof., assoc. prof., prof. Eastman Sch. Music, U. Rochester, 1970—, prof. composition, 1970—. Composer-in-residence St. Louis Symphony Orch., 1982-84 Compositions include Aftertones of Infinity (Pulitzer prize for music 1979), Diaphonia Intervallum, Chronicon, Autumn Canticle, Consortium, In Aeternum, Modis Caelestis, Canticle for the Evening Bells, Elixir, Wild Angels of the Open Hills, And the Mountains Rising Nowhere, Sparrows. Recipient Faricy award, 1965, BMI Student award, 1965, 66, 67, Bearns prize Columbia U., 1967; Nat. Inst. Arts and Letters Charles Ives scholar, 1970; N.Y. State Council on Arts Creative Arts Public Service grantee, 1973; NEA grantee; Guggenheim fellow, 1978-79 Mem.: Am. Acad. Arts and Letters (v.p. 2006—). Mailing: c/o Amer Acad Arts and Letters Board of Directors 633 West 155th St New York NY 10032

SCHWARCZ, STEVEN LANCE, lawyer, educator; b. NYC, Nov. 10, 1949; s. Charles and Elinor Schwarcz; m. Susan Beth Kolodny, Aug. 24, 1975; children: Daniel Benjamin, Rebekah Mara. BS summa cum laude in Aero. Engring., NYU, 1971; JD, Columbia U., 1974. Bar: N.Y. 1971, U.S. Dist. Ct. (so. dist.) N.Y. 1975. Assoc. Shearman & Sterling, NYC, 1974-82, ptnr., 1983-89; ptnr., chmn. structured fin. Kaye, Scholer, Fierman, Hays & Handler, 1996—; prof. Duke U. Sch. Law, Durham, NC, 1996—, Stanley A. Star prof., 2004—; spl. counsel Kaye, Scholer, Fierman, Hays & Handler, 1996—2004; faculty dir. Duke Global Capital Markets Ctr.; spl. cons. Kaye Scholer LLP, 2004—. Adj. prof. law Yeshiva U., Benjamin N. Cardozo Sch. Law, N.Y.C., 1983-92; vis. lectr. Yale Law Sch., 1992-96; lectr. Columbia Law Sch., 1992-96. Contbr. articles to profl. jours. Chmn. Friends of the Eldridge St. Synagogue, N.Y.C., 1979-96, Legis. Drafting Rsch. Fund. George Granger Brown scholar, 1971; NSF grantee in Math., 1969. Fellow Am. Coll. Comml. Fin. Lawyers; mem. Am. Law Inst., Assn. of Bar of City of N.Y. (environ. law com. 1975-78, nuc. tech. com. 1979-81, sci. and law com. 1985—, chmn. 1987-90), Am. Law and Econs. Assn., Tau Beta Pi, Sigma Gamma Tau. Jewish. Office: Duke U Sch Law Box 90360 Science Dr & Towerview Rd Durham NC 27708 Office Phone: 919-613-7060. E-mail: schwarcz@law.duke.edu.

SCHWARCZ, VERA, historian, educator, poet; d. Elmer and Katherine Savin; m. Jason Wolfe, July 31, 1983; children: Elie, Esther. BA in French Lit. and Oriental Religions, Vassar Coll., 1969; MA in East Asian Studies, Yale U., 1971; PhD in Chinese History, Stanford U., Calif., 1977. Instr. Stanford U., 1973; lectr. Chinese history Wesleyan U., Middletown, Conn., 1975-77, asst. prof. Chinese history, 1975-83, assoc. prof. history, 1983-87, prof. history, 1987—, chair East Asian studies, 1985-88, 94-96, Mansfield Freeman prof. East Asian Studies, 1987—; dir. Ctr. East Asian Studies, 1998—99. Dir. Mansfield Freeman for East Asian Studies, 1987-88, 94-96, 2007—; exch. scholar Beijing U., 1979-80, vis. scholar, 1983, 86, 89; vis. scholar Ctr. de Documentation sur la Chine Contemporaine, Paris, 1985, DAO Assn., Cluj, Romania, 1993, Miskenot Sha'ananim, Jerusalem, 1991; vis. prof. East Asian studies Hebrew U., Jerusalem, 1996-97; presenter, referee in field. Author: Long Road Home: A China Journal, 1984, Chinese Enlightenment: Intellectuals, and the Legacy of the May Fourth Movement in Modern China, 1986, Zhongguo de qimeng yundong, 1989, Time for Telling Truth is Running Out: Conversations with Zhang Shenfu, 1992, Bridge Across Broken Time: Chinese and Jewish Cultural Memory, 1998, Fresh Words for a Jaded World, 2000, A Scoop of Light: Poems, 2000, Zhonguo Oimeng Yundong, 2000, Zhang Shenfu Fangtan Lu, 2001, In the Garden of Memory, 2004, Truth is Woven, 2005; author numerous poems; co-editor: China: Inside the People's Republic, 1972; mem. editl. bd. History and Theory, 1981-84, 96-99, China Rev. Internat., 1994—; contbr. articles to profl. jours. Fellow Danforth Found., 1971-73, NDFL, 1973-74, NAS, 1979-80, Guggenheim Found. fellow, 1989-90, Great River Arts Inst. poetry fellow, 2000, Founders fellow AAUW, 1988-89, Faculty fellow Ctr. for Humanities Wesleyan U., 1988; grantee AAUW, 1974-75, Am. Philos. Soc., 1985, Am. Coun. Learned Socs., 1978, 96; finalist Nat. Jewish Book award in History, 1999; recipient Wesleyan Writers Conf. Poetry scholarship, 1999; poetry fellow Great River Arts Inst., Mex., 2000; recipient Poetry prize Taproot Lit. Rev., 2002-03. Mem. Assn. for Asian Studies (coun. on confs. 1989—, mem. Levenson prize com. 1991-92, chair 1992-93), New Eng. Assn. for Asian Studies (pres. 1988-89). Home: 42 Seneca Rd West Hartford CT 06117-2245 Office: Wesleyan U History Dept Middletown CT 06459-0001

SCHWARM, HAROLD CHAMBERS, artist; b. Fairmont, W.Va., May 5, 1925; s. Harold Chambers Schwarm and Ethel Eleanor Toothman; m. Claudia Beechum Chapline, Feb. 14, 1989; m. Margaret Elizabeth Collins Schwarm (div.); children: Mark, Eric, Kurt, Kim, Paul, Lisa, Karl, Mary. Student, U. Iowa, 1945—48; BFA, Bradley U., Peoria, Ill., 1951; MA, Bradley U., 1952. Instr. sculpture and drawing Bradley U., Peoria, 1952—55; supr. art svcs. So. Ill. U., Carbondale, 1955—59; asst. prof. graphic arts Calif. State U., Northridge, 1959—75; artist, 1973—. One-man shows include Claudia Chapline Gallery, Stinson Beach, Calif., 1989—2006, Bolinas Mus., Calif., 1998—99, Anagma Arte Contemporaneo, Valencia, Spain, 1994, Palais Maeterlinck, Nice, France, 1994, Represented in permanent collections Galeria del Ayantamienta, Naguera, Spain, Kaiser Hosp., Milpitas, Calif., Shriners Children's Hosp., Sacramento, Bolinas Mus., Calif., commd. paintings for, Ornick, Harrington and Sutcliffe, Kronick, Moskowitz, Tiedmann andGirard, Hyatt Regincy, U. Calif. Med. Ctr., others. Office: Claudia Chapline Gallery PO Box 1117 Stinson Beach CA 94970 Office Phone: 415-868-2308. Business E-Mail: info@cchapline.com.

SCHWARTE, DAVID A., lawyer, travel company executive; b. 1950; BA, U. Ky.; JD, Salmon P. Chase Coll. Law. Atty., legal dept. Am. Airlines, 1979—98; dir. Kelly, Hart & Hallman, Ft. Worth, 1999—2000; exec. v.p., gen. counsel Sabre Holdings, Southlake, Tex., 2000—. Mem.: ABA (past chmn., forum on air and space law), Tex. State Bar Assn. Office: Sabre Holdings Co 3150 Sabre Dr Southlake TX 76092 *

SCHWARTZ, AARON ROBERT, lawyer, former state legislator; b. Galveston, Tex., July 17, 1926; s. Joseph and Clara (Bulbe) S.; m. Marilyn Cohn, July 14, 1951; children: Richard Austin, Robert Allen, John Reed, Thomas Lee. Pre-law student, Tex. A&M U., 1948; JD, U. Tex., 1951. Bar: Tex. 1951. Mem. Tex. Ho. of Reps., 1955-59, Tex. Senate, 1960-81, past chmn. rules, jurisprudence and natural resources coms. Chmn. Tex. Coastal and Marine Coun., U.S. Coastal States Orgn.; adj. prof. legis. and cosatal mgmt. law Bates Law Sch., U. Houston, Tex. A&M U., Corpus Christi. Contbr. articles to profl. jours. Mem. emeritus exec. com. Galveston Bay Fond.; apptd. to Tex. Oil Spill Oversight Commn., 1993. Served with USN, 1944-46, 2d lt. USAFR, 1948-53. Recipient conservation and legis. awards, Outstanding Citizen award Galveston Jr. C. of C., 1981, Man of Yr., People of Vision award Galveston chpt. Soc. for Prevention of Blindness, 1986, Disting. Service award Nat. Hurricane Conf., Tex. Coastal Mgmt. Adv. Com., 1987, Lifetime Coastal Achievement award, 1997. Mem. Tex. State Bar Assn., Galveston County Bar Assn. Democrat. Jewish. Address: 1122 Colorado St Apt 2102 Austin TX 78701-2142 Personal E-mail: ars71726@aol.com.

SCHWARTZ, ALAN DAVID, diversified financial services company executive; b. Bklyn., Mar. 23, 1950; s. Walter and Ruth Ann Schwartz; m. Katherine Sue Frizzell, Feb. 9, 1980; children: Jennifer, Adam, Ryan. BS, Duke U., Durham, NC, 1972. Instl. salesman P.W. Pressprich & Co., NYC, 1972-74, Wertheim & Co., NYC, 1974-76; fin. mgmt. positions Bear Stearns Companies Inc., NYC, 1976—85, exec. v.p., co-head investment banking, 1985—2001, co-pres., co-COO, 2001—07, pres., 2007—. Bd. dirs. DAKA Inc., Wakefield, Mass., Protein Databases Inc., LI, St. Vincent's Home Svcs., Inc., Bklyn., Fuqua Sch. Bus., Durham, NC. Recipient Banker of Yr. award, Investment Dealer's Digest, 2003. Office: Bear Stearns 383 Madison Ave New York NY 10179 *

SCHWARTZ, ALAN EARL, lawyer, director; b. Detroit, Dec. 21, 1925; s. Maurice H. and Sophia (Welkowitz) S.; m. Marianne Shapero, Aug. 24, 1950; children: Marc Alan, Kurt Nathan, Ruth Anne. Student, Western Mich. Coll., 1944-45; BA with distinction, U. Mich., 1947; LLB magna cum laude, Harvard U., Cambridge, Mass., 1950; LLD, Wayne State U., Detroit, 1983, U. Detroit, 1985. Bar: NY 1951, Mich. 1952. Assoc. Kelley, Drye & Warren, NYC, 1950-52; mem. Honigman, Miller, Schwartz & Cohn, Detroit, 1952—. Spl. asst. counsel NY State Crime Commn., 1951; bd. dirs. Pulte Corp. Editor: Harvard Law Rev., 1950. Dir. Detroit Symphony Orch.; v.p., bd. dirs. United Way; bd. dirs. Detroit Renaissance, New Detroit, Jewish Welfare Fedn. Detroit, Wayne State U. Found.; trustee Cmty. Found. for Southeastern Mich.; adv. mem. Arts Commn., City of Detroit; bd. dirs., mem. investment com. Skillman Found., Wayne State U. Found. Served as ensign Supply Corps, USNR, 1945-46. Recipient Mich. Heritage Hall of Fame award, 1984, George W. Romney award for lifetime achievement in volunteerism, 1994, Max M. Fisher Cmty. Svc. award, 1997; named one of Top 200 Collectors, ARTnews, 2004, 2005, 2006. Mem. Mich. Bar Assn., Franklin Hills Country Club, Econ. Club (dir.). Avocation: collecting Old Masters and modern prints. Office: Honigman Miller Schwartz & Cohn 2290 1st National Bldg Detroit MI 48226

SCHWARTZ, ALAN GIFFORD, sport company executive; b. NYC, Nov. 7, 1931; s. Kevie Waldemar and Vera (Isaacs) S.; m. Roslyn Smulian, Sept. 6, 1958; children: Steven, Andrew, Sally, Elizabeth. BS, Yale U., 1952; MBA, Harvard U., 1954. Ptnr. Gifford Investment Co., Chgo., 1954—; CEO Tennis Corp. of Am., Chgo., 1969—, chmn. bd., 1974—. Dir. Firstar Bank Ill., Comtrex Systems, Inc., Mt. Laurel, N.J.; trustee Roosevelt U., 1994—, Inst. European & Asian Studies, 1993—; v.p. U.S. Tennis Assn., 1994—. Contbr. articles to profl. jours.; editorial cons. Club Industry mag., 1985—. Bd. dirs. Grad. Sch. of Bus., Duke U., Durham, N.C., 1977—, McCormick Boys and Girls Club, 1989—. Elected to Club Industry Hall of Fame, 1987. Mem. Standard Club of Chgo., Exec. Club. Chgo. Jewish. Avocations: travel, tennis. Office: Tennis Corp of Am 3611 N Kedzie Ave Chicago IL 60618-4513

SCHWARTZ, ALAN LEIGH, pediatrician, educator; b. NYC, Apr. 25, 1948; s. Robert and Joyce (Goldner) S.; m. Judith Child, June 22, 1974; 1 child, Timothy Child. BA, Case Western Res. U., 1974, PhD in Pharmacology, 1974, MD, 1976. Diplomate Am. Bd. Pediatrics. Intern Children's Hosp., Boston, 1976-77, resident, 1976-78, fellow Dana Farber Cancer Inst., 1978-80; instr. Harvard Med. Sch., Boston, 1980-81, asst. prof., 1981-83, assoc. prof., 1983-86; prof. pediatrics, molecular biology and pharmacology Washington U. Sch. Medicine, St. Louis, 1986—, chmn. dept. pediatrics, 1995—; chmn. faculty practice plan Washington U., 1999—2001. Vis. scientist MIT, Boston, 1979-82; mem. sci. adv. bd. Nat. Inst. Child Health and Human Devel., NIH, Bethesda, Md., 1988-94; investigator Am. Heart Assn. Alumni Endowed Prof. Pediats. Wash. U. Sch. Medicine, 1987-97, Harriet B. Spoehrer Prof. Pediats., 1997—. Mem. Inst. Medicine of NAS. Office: Washington U Sch Medicine Dept Pediatrics Box 8116 One Children's Pl Saint Louis MO 63110-1093 E-mail: schwartz@kids.wustl.edu.

SCHWARTZ, ALAN VICTOR, advertising executive; b. Detroit, July 12, 1948; s. Seymour and Adeline (Goldstein) S.; children: Stacy Ilana, Andrew Robert. BS with honors, Lehigh U., 1970; MBA with highest honors, Cornell U., 1972. CPA, N.Y. Mgr. Price Waterhouse, Huntington, NY, 1972-79; v.p., dir. fin. control Doyle Dane Bernbach, NYC, 1979-81; v.p., CFO, Bernard Hodes Group, NYC, 1981-84, sr. v.p., chief oper. and fin. officer, 1984-87, exec. v.p., COO, 1987—2001, pres., CEO, 2002—; trustee The Healthcare Chaplaincy, 2005—. Bd. mgrs. Evans Tower, treas. 1991-92, pres. 1992-93. Campaign vice chmn. United Way L.I., 1978. Mem. Nat. Assn. Accts. (various directorships, treas.), N.Y. State Soc. CPAs, Lehigh Alumni Assn. (pres. L.I. chpt. 1977-79, treas. 1975-77). Office: Bernard Hodes Group 220 E 42d St New York NY 10017

SCHWARTZ, ALFRED, former dean; b. Chgo., Jan. 8, 1922; s. Isadore and Lena (Ziff) S.; m. Delle Weiss, Aug. 26, 1945; children: Reid Mitchell, Karen Ruth. B.Ed., Chgo. Tchrs. Coll., 1944; MA in Polit. Sci., U. Chgo., 1946, PhD in Ednl. Adminstrn., 1949. Tchr. Chgo. pub. schs., 1944-45; contract officer VA, 1946; instr. U. Chgo. Lab. Sch., 1946-50; assoc. prof. edn. Drake U., 1950-56, U. Del.; also exec. sec. Del. Sch. Study Council, 1956-58; dean (Univ. Coll.); prof. Coll. Edn., Drake U., 1958-85, dean, 1964-79, 80-84, dean emeritus, 1985—; acting v.p. acad. adminstrn. Coll. Edn., Coll. Edn., 1979-80; cons., 1985—. Adviser Iowa Dept. Pub. Instrn.; mem. coordinating bd. Nat. Council Accreditation for Tchr. Edn.; chmn. tchr. edn. and adv. com. Iowa Dept. Pub. Instrn. Author: (with Harlan L. Hagman) Administration in Profile for School Executives, 1954, (with Stuart Tiedeman) Evaluating Student Progress, 1957, (with Willard Fox) Managerial Guide for School Principals, 1965. Mem. Gov.'s Commn. State-Local Relations, pres. condo assn., 1987-97. Mem. World Council on Curriculum and Instrn., Iowa Assn. Colls. for Tchr. Edn. (pres., exec. sec.), Am. Profs. for Peace in Middle East, Am. Ednl. Research Assn., Iowa Edn. Assn., NEA, Phi Delta Kappa, Kappa Delta Pi. Home: 3450 3rd Ave Apt 511 San Diego CA 92103-4939

SCHWARTZ, ALLEN R., lawyer; b. Greeley, Colo., Oct. 13, 1951; s. David L. and Margaret L. Schwartz; m. Beverly S. Stephens, Mar. 23, 1985; 1 child, Christopher; 1 stepchild, Shawn Jensen. BA in Psychology and Sociology, U. Colo., 1973, JD, 1976. Bar: Colo. 1976, US Dist. Ct. Colo. 1976, US Ct. Appeals (10th cir.) 1983. Law clk. Denver Dist. Ct., 1976-77; assoc. Fischer & Wilmarth, Ft. Collins, Colo., 1977-79; ptnr. Dean, Martin, Mitchell & Schwartz, Ft. Collins, 1979-83; mng. ptnr. Nelson & Schwartz, Ft. Collins, 1983-90; ptnr. Nelson, Reid & Schwartz, Ft. Collins, 1990-96; pvt. practice Ft. Collins, 1996—; county ct. magistrate Larimer County, Colo., 2006—. V.p., legal advisor acad. adv. com. Wingshadow Inc., Frontier HS and Frontier Mid. Sch., Ft. Collins, 1994-2005. Asst. scoutmaster Boy Scouts Am., Ft. Collins, 1991-94. Mem. Colo. Bar Assn., Larimer County Bar Assn., Overland Sertoma (pres., chmn. bd., Sertoman of the Yr. 1994-95), High Plains Dist. Sertoma (dist. gov. 1996-98, Cmty. Achievement award 1991-92). Home: 1601 Centennial Rd Fort Collins CO 80525-2418 Office: 315 W Oak St Ste 501 Fort Collins CO 80521-2729 Home Phone: 970-223-2978; Office Phone: 970-493-0456. Business E-Mail: allen@allenschwartz.com.

SCHWARTZ, ALLYSON Y., congresswoman; b. NYC, Oct. 3, 1948; d. Everett and Renee Perl Young; m. David Schwartz, 1970; children: Daniel, Jordan. BA in Sociology, Simmons Coll., Boston, 1970; MSW, Bryn Mawr Coll., Pa., 1972. Founder, exec. dir. Elizabeth Blackwell Health Ctr. for Women, 1975-88; acting commr., 1st dep. commr. Dept. Human Svcs., 1988-90; mem. Pa. State Senate, Harrisburg, 1990—2004, minority chmn. edn. com., 1994—2004; mem. US Congress from 13th Pa. dist., 2005—, mem. ways and means com., mem. budget com. Mem. Pa. State Bd. Edn., Pa. Coun. Higher Edn., 2000, Pa. Hist. and Mus. Commn., Edn. Commn. States, Nat. Dem. Leadership Coun.; v.p. Women's Network; co-chair Pa. New Dem. Coalition; bd. trustees Arcadia U., Chestnut Hill Healthcare; chair Instl. Rev. Bd., Phila. Health Mgmt. Corpn.; bd. dirs. Nat. Jewish Dem. Coun.; adv. bd. Tuition Assistance (TAP) Democrat. Jewish. Office: US House Reps 423 Cannon House Office Bldg Washington DC 20515-3813 Office Phone: 202-225-6111. Office Fax: 202-226-0611. *

SCHWARTZ, ANNA JACOBSON, economist; b. NYC, Nov. 11, 1915; married; 4 children. BA, Barnard Coll., 1934; MA, Columbia U., 1935, PhD, 1964; LittD (hon.), U. Fla., 1987, Emory U., 2000; ArtsD (hon.), Stonehill Coll., 1989; LLD (hon.), Iona Coll., 1992, Rutgers U., 1998; LHD (hon.), CUNY, 2000; LLD (hon.), Williams Coll., 2002; LHD (hon.), Loyola U., Chgo., 2003; ScD (hon.), City U., London, 2006. Rschr. USDA, 1936, Columbia U. Social Sci. Rsch. Coun., 1936-41; sr. rsch. staff Nat. Bur. Econ. Rsch. Inc., NYC, 1941—. Instr. Bklyn. Coll., 1952, Baruch Coll., 1959-60; adj. prof. econs. grad. CCNY, 1967-69, grad. sch. CUNY, 1986—, NYU Grad. Sch. Arts and Sci., 1969-70; hon. vis. prof. City U. Bus. Sch., London, 1984—; hon. fellow Inst. of Econ. Affairs, London, 1998. Mem. editl. bd. Am. Econ. Rev., 1972-78, Jour. Money, Credit and Banking, 1974-75, 84—, Jour. Monetary Econs., 1975—, Jour. Fin. Svcs. Rsch., 1993—; contbr. articles to profl. jours. Disting. fellow Am. Econ. Assn., 1993; hon fellow Inst. Econ. Affairs, London. Fellow Am. Acad. Arts & Scis.; mem. Western Econ. Assn. (pres. 1987-88). Office: Nat Bur Econ Research 365 Fifth Ave 5th Fl New York NY 10016-4309 Business E-Mail: aschwartz@gc.cuny.edu.

SCHWARTZ, ANTHONY, veterinary surgeon, educator; b. Bklyn., July 30, 1940; s. Murray and Miriam Sarah (Wittes) S.; m. Claudia Rosenberg, July 21, 1963; children: Thomas Frederick, Eric Leigh. Student, Mich. State U., 1957—58; DVM, Cornell U., 1963; PhD, Ohio State U., 1972. Diplomate Am. Coll. Vet. Surgeons (bd. of regents 1989-92). Gen. practice vet. medicine, Huntington, NY, 1963—66; resident in surgery Animal Med. Ctr., NYC, 1968—69, Ohio State U., Columbus, 1969—70, asst. prof., head sect. small animal surgery, 1973; asst. prof. then assoc. prof. comparative medicine Yale U. Sch. Medicine, New Haven, 1973—79; assoc. prof. then prof., chmn. dept. surgery, assoc. dean Tufts U. Sch. Vet. Medicine, Boston, 1979—89, assoc. dean clin. edn., 1989—93, prof., chmn. dept. surgery, assoc. dean acad. affairs, 1993—97, assoc. dean for acad. and outreach programs, 1997—2002, assoc. dean for continuing edu. and outreach programs, 2003—04, prof. emeritus, 2005—. Cons. U.S. Surg. Corp., Norwalk, Conn., 1975—; mem. Bd. Tufts Animal Expo LLC, program dir., 1999-2003; mem. vet. adv. bd. PetPlace.com, Intelligent Content Corp., 2000-03; exec. dir., chair bd. dirs. N.E. Vet. Conf., 2003-05, chair program com., 2003-04. Author: (with others) Small Animal Surgery, 1989, Complications in Small Animal Surgery, 1996; editl. bd. Vet. Surgery, 1987-90, Jour. Investigative Surgery, 1987-98; assoc. editor: Textbook of Small Animal Surgery, 1985; contbr. articles to profl. jours. Capt. U.S. Army Vet Corps, 1966-68. Recipient 1st prize N.Y. State Vet. Med. Soc., 1963; Robert Wood Johnson Health Policy fellow, Washington, 1988-89; NIH grantee, 1975-84. Mem.: AVMA (legis. planning com. 1989—92, coun. on govt. affairs 1992—97), Mass. Vet. Med. Assn. (chmn. 1990—91, animal welfare com. 1990—98, Merit award for leadership in pub. rels. and colleague devel. 2002), Nat. Acads. of Practice (emeritus; co-chmn. acad. vet. medicine 2002—03), Assn. Am. Vet. Med. Colls. (treas. and exec. dir. 1992—93, Washington), Phi Kappa Phi, Sigma Xi. Democrat. Jewish. Office: Tufts U Sch Vet Medicine Dept Clin Sci 200 Westboro Rd North Grafton MA 01536-1895 Home Phone: 617-859-3948. Personal E-mail: tonyvet@comcast.net. Business E-Mail: Anthony.Schwartz@tufts.edu.

SCHWARTZ, ARTHUR, playwright, poet; b. NYC, May 20, 1931; s. Harry and Sarah Pearl Schwartz; m. Joan Klenin, June 10, 1956; children: Jessy Ann, Rachel Freyda. Student, Champlain Coll., 1950, student, 1951, student, 1952. Minor league baseball player N.Y. Yankees, 1954—55; stand-up comedian, 1968—80; playwright, poet, 1976—. Prodr.: (plays) An Apple a Day, 1977, The King of Empire Boulevard, 1978, The General and the Jew, 1979, A Choice of Weapons, 1996, If The White House Calls, I'm Out, 2000, The Intruder-The National Pastime, 2001, Naked Batting Practice, 2004, A Song for Chaim Levy, 2004; author poetry. Named one of Best Poets of 1994, Nat. Libr. Poetry, Best Poets of 1995, Best Poets of 1996, Best Poets of 1997; recipient Writers Digest Poetry award, 1995, Outstanding Achievement award, Nat. Libr. Poetry, 1994, 1995, 1996, 1997. Home: 420 Merrick Rd Rockville Centre NY 11570

SCHWARTZ, BARRY FREDRIC, lawyer, diversified holding company executive; b. Phila., Apr. 16, 1949; s. Albert and Evelyn (Strauss) S.; m. Sherry L. Handsman, Mar. 21, 1985; children: Fanny Rose, Abraham David. AB cum laude, Kenyon Coll., 1970; JD, Georgetown U., 1974. Bar: Pa. 1974, Ill. 1974, N.Y. 1992, U.S. Dist. Ct. (ea. dist.) Pa. 1974, U.S. Dist. Ct. (no. dist.) Ill. 1975, U.S. Dist. Ct. (so. dist.) N.Y. 1992, U.S. Ct. Appeals (7th cir.) 1977, U.S. Ct. Appeals (3d cir.) 1978, U.S. Ct. Appeals (4th cir.) 1979, U.S. Ct. Appeals (6th cir.) 1981, U.S. Supreme Ct. 1981, N.Y. 1992. Assoc. Sachnoff, Schrager, Jones & Weaver, Chgo., 1974—76; ptnr. Wolf, Block, Schorr & Solis-Cohen, Phila., 1976—89; exec. v.p. gen. counsel MacAndrews & Forbes Holdings, Inc., NYC, 1989—. Bd. dirs. Sci. Games, 2003, REV Holdings LLC, 2004, Revlon Consumer Products, 2004, Harland Clarke Holdings Corp., 2005—, Pharma Core, Inc., 2006—, Trans Tech Pharma, Inc., 2006—, MacAndrews & Forbes Holdings Inc., 2007—; bd. visitors Georgetown U. Law Ctr., 2005—. Mem. adv. coun. Westchester Holocaust Commn., 2000—; trustee Kenyon Coll., 2000—. Mem.: Assn. Governing Bds. of Univs. and Colls. (bd. dirs. 2004). Office: MacAndrews & Forbes Holdings Inc 35 E 62nd St New York NY 10065

SCHWARTZ, BENJAMIN MICHAEL, gynecologist, oncologist; b. NYC, Mar. 17, 1969; s. Robert Sidney and Diane Carole Schwartz; m. Laura Ann Hendricks, July 20, 2002; children: Abigail Margot, Michael Henry, Andrew Zachary. BA in Govt., Dartmouth U., 1991; MD, George Washington U., DC, 1995. Diplomate Am. Bd. of Ob-gyn., 2004. Resident in ob-gyn. Albert Einstein Coll. of Medicine, Bronx, NY, 1995—99; fellow in gynecologic oncology Cleve. Clinic Found., Cleve., 1999—2002; asst. prof. of gynecol. oncology U. of Pitts., Magee Women's Hosp., Pitts., 2002—03; dir. of gynecol. oncology Nassau U. Med. Ctr., East Meadow, NY, 2003—; med. dir. Schwartz Gynecol. Oncology, PLLC, Babylon, NY. Fellow: Am. Coll. of Ob-gyn.; mem.: Am. Assn. of Gynecol. Laparoscopists, Am. Soc. of Clin. Oncology, Soc. of Gynecolo. Oncologists (assoc.), Internat. Soc. of Gynecol. Oncology, NY Yacht Club. Office: Schwartz Gynecol Oncology PLLC 500 West Main St Ste 209 Babylon NY 11702 Office Phone: 631-376-0055.

SCHWARTZ, BENNETT K., dermatologist; MD, U. Vt., Burlington, 1983. Intern Thomas Jefferson U. Hosp., Phila., 1983—84; resident in dermatology Dartmouth-Hitchcock Med. Ctr., Hanover, NH, 1984—87; pvt. practice Voorhees, NJ, 1987—. Chief dermatology sect. Virtua West Jersey Hosp., Voorhees, 2007. Contbr. articles to profl. jours. Fellow: Am. Acad. Dermatology. Office: 2301 Evesham Rd Ste 403 Voorhees NJ 08043

SCHWARTZ, BERNARD, physician; b. Toronto, Nov. 12, 1927; s. Samuel and Gertrude Schwartz; children: Lawrence Frederick, Karen Lynne, Jennifer Carla, Ariane Samara MD, U. Toronto, 1951; MS, State U. Iowa, 1953, PhD, 1959. Intern U. Hosps., State U. Iowa, 1951-52, resident ophthalmology, 1951-54; research fellow U. Iowa, 1954-58; asst. prof. to assoc. prof. Downstate Med. Center fo State U. N.Y., 1958-68; prof. ophthalmology Tufts U., 1968-93, chmn. dept., 1968-90, prof. emeritus ophthalmology, 1993—. Author: Syphilis and the Eye; editor-in-chief Survey of Ophthalmology, 1968—, Comprehensive Ophthalmology Update, 1998—; contbr. articles to profl. jours. Fellow Am. Acad. Ophthalmology, ACS; mem. Assn. Rsch. in Ophthalmology, New Eng. Ophthalmol. Soc., N.Y. Acad. Medicine, Sigma Xi. Home: 180 Beacon St Boston MA 02116-1408 Office: 7 Kent St Ste 3 Brookline MA 02445 Home Phone: 617-267-9015; Office Phone: 617-232-4442. Business E-Mail: glaucomares@mva.net.

SCHWARTZ, BERNARD JULIAN, lawyer; b. Edmonton, Alberta, Can., July 29, 1960; came to U.S., 1982; s. Sol and Anne (Motkovich) S. BA, U. Alberta, 1981; JD, McGeorge Sch. Law, 1986. Bar: U.S. Supreme Ct. 1991. Atty. Ropers, Majeski, San Francisco, 1987-88, Riverside County Pub. Defenders, Riverside, Calif., 1988-89; pvt. practice Riverside, 1990—. Coach Riverside County H.S. Mock Trial Team, 1990, 96, 97. Mem. Calif. Attys. Criminal Justice, Calif. Pub. Defenders Assn., Riverside County Bar Assn., Criminal Cts. Bar Assn. (pres.). Office: 3877 Twelfth St Riverside CA 92501 *

SCHWARTZ, BERNARD LEON, retired space and communications company executive; b. Dec. 13, 1925; BBA, CCNY, 1948. Ptnr. Schnee, Hover & Schwartz, 1948—62; sr. v.p. APL Corp., Fla., 1962—68; chmn. bd., CEO Leasco Corp., Miami Beach, 1969—72; chmn., CEO Loral Corp., NYC, 1972—96, pres., 1973—81; chmn., CEO, bd. dirs. Loral Space & Comm., 1996—2006; chmn., CEO Globalstar Telecomms. Ltd., 1996—, K&F Industries, Inc. Trustee Mt. Sinai NYU Med. Ctr. and Health Systems. With US Army, 1943—45.

SCHWARTZ, BRIAN MICHAEL, philosopher, think-tank executive; s. Bernard and Aileen Schwartz. BA, Oxford U., Eng., 1971; JD, Yale U., 1975. Law clk. to Hon. Irving R. Kaufman U.S. Ct. Appeals (2d cir.), NYC; famine relief coord. UNICEF, Namalu, Uganda, 1981—2002; treas. Prometheus Soc., 2003—. Author: China Off the Beaten Track, 1983, A World of Villages, 1986. Mem.: Lincoln's Inn, Lewis M. Terman High IQ Soc. (pres. 2007—), Omega Soc. (pres. 2007—), Aleph 3, Oxford Union, Polonia Club.

SCHWARTZ, CARL EDWARD, artist, printmaker; b. Detroit, Sept. 20, 1935; s. Carl and Verna (Steiner) S.; m. Kay Joyce Hofmann, June 18, 1955 (div.); children: Dawn Ellen, Cari Leigh; m. Celeste Borah, Jan. 1, 2007. BFA, Art Inst. Chgo. Sch.-U. Chgo., 1957. Past tchr. art Chgo. North Shore Art League, Suburban Fine Arts Ctr., Deerpath Art League; faculty Fla. Gulf Coast U. One-man shows include, South Bend (Ind.) Art Center, Feingarten Gallery, Chgo., 1960, Bernard Horwich Center, Chgo., Covenant Club, Chgo., Barat Coll., Chgo. Pub. Library, Alverno Coll., 1020 Art Center, Rosenberg Gallery, Peoria (Ill.) Art Guild, 1977, Ill. State Mus., 1977 Ill. Inst. Tech., 1978, Miller Gallery, Chgo., 1979, Union League Club, Chgo., 1982, Art Inst. Rental and Sale Gallery, Chgo., 1982, Horwich Gallery, Chgo., 1983, Lake Forest (Ill.) Coll., 1983, Campanile-Capponi Contemporary Gallery, Chgo., 1987, Nagata Gallery, Ft. Myers, Fla., 1988, Jan Cicero Gallery, Chgo., 1990, Neopolitan Gallery, Naples, Fla., 1996, 97; group shows include 9th Ann. Michigana Exhbt, Detroit (Cloetingh and Deman award 1959), Hyde Park Art Center, Chgo., 1960 (prize), Spectrum Exhbn. '63, Chgo. (1st prize), New Horizons Exhbt, Chgo., 1960 (Joseph Shapiro award), Nat. Design Center, Chgo., 1965 (New Horizons in Painting 1st prize), 3d Ann. Chgo. Arts Competition, 1962 (1st prize), Union League Club, Chgo., 1967 (2d prize), North Shore Art League, Chgo., 1965 (1st prize), Artists Guild Chgo., 1965 (prize), McCormack Pl., Chgo., 1965 (1st prize), Detroit Art Inst., 1965 (Commonwealth prize), Park Forest (Ill.) Art Exhbn, 1969 (Best of Show), 14th Ann. Virginia Beach (Va.) Show, 1969 (Best of Show), Suburban Fine Arts Center, Highland Park, Ill., 1970 (prize), 15th Ann. Virginia Beach Show, 1970 (prize), 32d Ann. Artists Guild, Chgo., 1970 (2d prize), North Shore Art League, 1970 (prize), 16th Ann. Virginia Beach Show, 1971 (2d prize), Ill. State Fair, 1972 (prize), Artists Guild Chgo., 1972 (1st prize), 17th Ann. Virginia Beach Exhbt, 1972 (1st prize), Artists Guild 50th Fine Art Exhbn., Chgo., 1973 (prize), Dickinson State U., 1973 (prize), North Shore Art League, 1973 (prize), Lakehurst Exhbt, 1974 (prize), Union League Art Exhbt, 1974 (1st prize), 1976 (prize), Artists Guild Fine Arts Exhbn., 1974 (best of Show), Bluegrass Painting Exhbn, Louisville, 1975 (award Washington, Art Inst. Chgo., K. Van Ella, Chgo., Gardner-Colby Gallery, Naples, Fla., Cape Coral Arts Studio, Van Liebig Art Ctr., 2005, Art League of Bonita Springs (Best of Show, Art Focus award 2007), Alliance for the Arts (award), 2007. Recipient Logan medal, Art Inst. Chgo., 1958. Home: 5825 Briarcliff Rd Fort Myers FL 33912-4204 Office Phone: 239-590-7249. E-mail: carleschwartz@earthlink.net. *I am a painter of light. I'm intrigued and fascinated with form. To me, there are two worlds-the one we all live in, and the one that I create. Painting is the discipline by which I constantly rediscover both of these worlds.*

SCHWARTZ, CARL R., lawyer; b. Chgo., June 13, 1953; AB, Wash. U., 1975; JD cum laude, Harvard U., 1978; BS Chemical engring. with highest honours, Wash. U., 1975. Bar: Wis. 1978, U.S. Ct. Appeals (7th cir.) 1979, U.S. Patent and Trademark Office. Ptnr. Quarles & Brady, Milw. Spkr. in feilds. Contbr. Recipient Best Lawyers in Am., 1991. Mem. ABA, Am. Intellectual Property Law Assn., State Bar Wis. (pres., dir. intellectual property sect. 1990-91), Wis. Intellectual Property Law Assn., Milw. Bar Assn., Phi Beta Kappa. Office: Quarles & Brady 411 E Wisconsin Ave Milwaukee WI 53202-4497 Office Phone: 414-277-5715. Office Fax: 414-978-8715. Business E-Mail: crs@quarles.com.

SCHWARTZ, CAROL LEVITT, government official; b. Greenville, Miss., Jan. 20, 1944; d. Stanley and Hilda (Simmons) Levitt; m. David H. Schwartz (dec.); children: Stephanie, Hilary, Douglas. BS in Spl. and Elem. Edn., U. Tex., 1965. Mem. transiton team Office of Pres. Elect, 1980-81; con. office presdl. personnel The White House, Washington, 1981; cons. U.S. Dept. Edn., Washington, 1982; pres. sec. U.S. Ho. Reps., Washington, 1982-83; mem.-at-large Coun. of D.C., Washington, 1985-89, 97—; candidate for mayor, Washington, 1986, 1994, 1998, 2002. Vice chmn. Nat. Edn. Commn. on Time and Learning, 1992-94, Nat. Adv. Coun. on Disadvantaged Children, 1974-79; lectr. in field; radio commentator, 1990-91; chair transp., vice-chair planning bd. Coun. Govts. Regional columnist Washington Jewish Week, 1995-97. Mem. D.C. Bd. Edn., 1974-82, v.p., 1977-80; bd. dirs. Met. Police Boys and Girls Club, 1st v.p., 1989-93, pres., 1994-96, chmn. membership com., 1984-93; mem. adv. com. Am. Coun. Young Polit. Leaders, 1982-90; mem. Nat. Coun. Friends Kennedy Ctr., 1984-91; bd. dirs. Whitman-Walker Clinic, 1988-2006, v.p., 1995-96; bd. dirs. St. John's Child Devel. Ctr., 1989-91, Hattie M. Strong Found., 1995—; trustee Kennedy Ctr. Cmty. and Friends Bd., 1991—, chmn. ednl. task force, 1993—; trustee Jewish Coun. on Aging, 1991-93; v.p. adv. bd. Am. Automobile Assn., 1988-06; bd. dirs. Washington Hebrew Congregation, 1995-98. Mem. Cosmos Club. Republican. Jewish.

SCHWARTZ, CHARLES MORRIS, lawyer; b. NYC, Jan. 5, 1948; s. Murray Schwartz and Shirley Phillis (Bomart) Schwartz Dinitz; m. Roberta Sue Dick, June 23, 1968; children: Karen, Jamie. BA, U. Wis., 1969; PhD in Corp. Fin., NYU, 1973; JD cum laude (hon.), Harvard U., 1975. Bar: DC 1975, Tex. 1977. Assoc. Shaw, Pittman, Potts & Trowbridge, Washington, 1975-77; ptnr. Hughes & Luce, Dallas, 1977, head (corp. dept.); ptnr. Gibson, Dunn & Crutcher, Dallas, 1995. Mem. ABA, Dallas Bar Assn., Tex. Bar Assn., DC Bar Assn., North Tex. Commn. Avocation: tennis. Office: Gibson Dunn & Crutcher 2100 McKinney Ave Ste 1100 Dallas TX 75201 Office Phone: 214-698-3224. Office Fax: 214-571-2953. Business E-Mail: cschwartz@gibsondunn.com.

SCHWARTZ, CHARLES WALTER, lawyer; b. Brenham, Tex., Dec. 27, 1953; s. Walter C. and Annie (Kuehn) S. BS, U. Tex., 1975, MA, 1980, JD, 1977; LLM, Harvard U., Cambridge, Mass., 1980. Bar: Tex. 1977; bd. cert. civil appellate law Tex. Bd. Legal Specialization. Law clk. U.S. Ct. Appeals (5th cir.), Austin, Tex., 1977-79; assoc. Vinson & Elkins LLP, Houston, 1980—86, ptnr., 1986—2003, Skadden, Arps, Slate, Meagher & Flom, 2003—. Contbr. articles to law revs. Fellow: Tex. Bar Found. (sustaining life), Houston Bar Found. (sustaining life), Am. Bar Found. (life), Coll. State Bar Tex.; mem.: ABA, Tex. Law Rev. Assn., Am. Law Inst., Bar Assn. of 5th Cir., State Bar Tex. (former chmn. grievance com. 1993—99, bd. dirs. 2000—04, exec. com. 2001—04, chmn. 2002—03, immediate past chmn. 2003—04). Home: 2154 Chilton Rd Houston TX 77019 Office: Skadden Arps Slate Meagher & Flom LLP 1000 Louisiana St Ste 6800 Houston TX 77002 Office Phone: 713-655-5160. Business E-Mail: schwartz@skadden.com.

SCHWARTZ, DANIEL BENNETT, artist; b. NYC, Feb. 16, 1929; s. Bennett Henry and Lillian (Blumenthal) S.; m. Judith Nancy Kass, June 12, 1955 (div. 1980); 1 child, Claudia Bennet. Grad., High Sch. of Music and Art, NYC, 1946; student, Art Students League, 1946, Y. Kuniyoshi; BFA, R.I. Sch. Design, 1949. Instr. pvt. painting class, 1965-81, 90-95, Parsons Sch. Design, 1983. One-man shows include Davis Galleries, NYC, 1955—56, 1958, 1960, Hirschl & Adler Galleries, 1963, Maxwell Galleries, San Francisco, 1964, Babcock Galleries, NYC, 1967, F.A.R. Galleries, 1970, Armstrong Galleries, 1985, 1987, Hammer Galleries, 1994, Hudson River Gallery, Yonkers, NY, 2001, 2007, exhibited in group shows at Albany Inst. History and Art, Am. Fedn. Arts, Butler Inst. Am. Art, Libr. of Congress, Nat. Acad. Design, Pa. Acad. Fine Art, Whitney Mus. Art, Collection Nat. Portrait Gallery, Munson-Williams-Proctor Inst., Bates Coll., Brit. Mus., Century Assn., Smithsonian Nat. Portrait Gallery, 2007, others. Louis C. Tiffany Found. grantee, 1956, 60; recipient Purchase prize Am. Acad. Arts and letters, 1964, 84, 11 Gold medals Soc. Illustrators, N.Y.C., 1960-85, Obrig prize for painting Nat. Acad. Design, 1990, winner 1st Benjamin Altman Figure prize, 1992; named to Soc. of Illustrators Hall of Fame, 2002. Mem. NAD, Century Assn. Avocation: jazz piano. E-mail: dschwartz17@nyc.rr.com.

SCHWARTZ, DANIEL C., lawyer; b. Pa., 1943; AB, Stanford U., 1965; JD, George Washington U., 1969. Bar: D.C. 1969. Asst. to dir. Bur. Competition, FTC, Washington, 1973-75, asst. dir. evaluation, 1975-77, dep. dir., 1977-79; gen. counsel Nat. Security Agy., Washington, 1979-81; ptnr., group leader Corp. Compliance and Defense Bryan Cave LLP, Washington. Mem. ABA. Office: Bryan Cave LLP 700 13th St NW Fl 7 Washington DC 20005-5921 Office Phone: 202-508-6025. Business E-Mail: dcschwartz@bryancave.com.

SCHWARTZ, DAVID A., federal agency administrator; m. Louise Sparks; 3 children. BA in biology, U. Rochester, 1975; MD, U. Calif., San Diego, 1979; MPH in occupational medicine, Harvard U., 1985. Diplomate Nat. Bd. Med. Examiners, 1981, Am. Bd. Internal Medicine, 1984, Am. Bd. Occupational Medicine, 1986, Am. Bd. Internal Medicine Subspecialty Bd. Pulmonary Disease, 1988, lic. NC, Iowa, DC, Tex. Training in tropical medicine Walter Reed Army Inst. Rsch., 1979; Pub. Svc. Sci. Resident NSF, 1979—80; intern then resident Boston City Hosp., 1980—83, chief resident in medicine, 1983—84; rsch. fellow Robert Wood Johnson Clin. Scholars Program U. Wash., Seattle, 1985—87, pulmonary and critical care fellow, 1985—88; asst. prof. Pulmonary Disease Divsn., Dept. Internal Medicine U. Iowa, Iowa City, 1988—92, assoc. prof. Pulmonary Disease, Critical Care, and Occupational Medicine Divsn., Dept. Internal Medicine, 1992—96, prof., 1996—2000, dir. occupational medicine, 1988—2000, assoc. chair program devel. Dept. Internal Medicine, 1996—2000, dir. Ctr. Environ. Lung Disease, 1997—2000, co-PI, assoc. dir. Environ. Health Sciences Rsch. Ctr., 1997—2000, mem. Med. Scientist Training Program, 1999—2000, mem. Genetics Program, 1999—2000; staff physician VA Med. Ctr., Iowa City, 1989—2000; chief Divsn. Pulmonary and Critical Care Medicine Duke U. Med. Ctr., Durham, NC, 2000—05, dir. Ctr. Environ. Genomics, Inst. Genome Sci. and Policy, 2000—05, prof. medicine and genetics, 2000—05, Walter Kempner Prof. Medicine, 2001—05, vice chair. rsch. Dept. Medicine, 2003—05; prof. environ. sciences and policy Nicholas Sch. Environment and Health Sciences, Duke U., 2001—05, adj. prof., 2005—; staff physician VA Med. Ctr., Durham, 2000—04; dir. Nat. Inst. Environ. Health Sciences, NIH, Rsch. Triangle Pk., NC, 2005—, Nat. Toxicology Program, NIH, 2005—. Mem.: APHA, Am. Thoracic Soc. (Sci. Accomplishment Award 2003), Soc. Gen. Internal Medicine, Am. Soc. Human Genetics, Assn. Am. Physicians, Am. Soc. Clin. Investigation, Am. Fedn. Clin. Rsch., Am. Coll. Physicians, Am. Coll. Chest Physicians. Office: Nat Inst Environ Health Sciences PO Box 12233 111 TW Alexander Dr Research Triangle Park NC 27709 Office Phone: 919-541-3201. Office Fax: 919-541-2260. E-mail: david.schwartz@niehs.nih.gov.

SCHWARTZ, DAVID JAY, lawyer; b. Oceanside, NY, June 30, 1967; s. Rand and Sandy Schwartz; m. Amy Roslyn Divak, June 1, 1996; 2 children. BA in economics, Duke U., 1989; JD, U. Pa., 1992; MBA, Columbia U., 1999. Bar: 1992. Corp. ptnr. Anderson, Kill & Olick PC, NYC, 1992—2001; v.p., corp. counsel Toys "R" Us Inc., Wayne, NJ, 2001—02, v.p., dep. gen. counsel, 2002—03, v.p., gen. counsel, 2003—. Office: Toys R Us Inc 1 Geoffrey Way Wayne NJ 07470-2030 Office Phone: 973-617-3500. *

SCHWARTZ, DAVID PETER, curator; b. NYC, Nov. 11, 1960; s. Louis and Stella Schwartz; m. Victoria Grace Weisel, Sept. 16, 1989; children: Caleb Django, Oliver Cameron. BFA, Purchase Coll., NY, 1984. Film programmer Cinema Arts Ctr., Huntington, NY, 1984—85; chief curator Mus. of Moving Image, Astoria, NY, 1985—. Lectr. Purchase Coll., 2004—. Recipient Film Heritage award, Nat. Soc. Film Critics, 2006. Office: Mus Moving Image 35 Avenue at 36 St Astoria NY 11106 Home Phone: 914-631-1778; Office Phone: 718-784-4520.

SCHWARTZ, DIANE N., secondary school educator, researcher; b. NYC, Sept. 3, 1925; d. Charles and Sarah (Noritz) Naroff; m. Morris Joseph Schwartz, Feb. 11, 1951; children: David Martin, Judith Frances. BA in English, Hofstra U., Hempstead, NY, 1964, MA in Humanities, 1968; MA in English, SUNY, Stony Brook, 1978. Bookkeeper Local 1250 Dept. Store Union, NYC, 1948—51; tchr. Hauppauge Sch. Dist., NY, 1965—66, Syosset Sch. Dist., NY, 1966—90; ret., 1990. Editor publ. Huntington Pointe Orgn. Rehab. Tng., Delray Beach, Fla., 1995—; life mem. Huntington Pointe IMA Hadassah, Delray Beach, 2003—. Fellow, Hofstra U., 1964—65; sr. scholar, 1963—64. Mem.: NOW, NY State Ret. Tchrs., Huntington Pointe Cancer Rsch. Assn., Phi Beta Kappa. Avocations: competitive running, writing, reading. Home: 6363 Kings Gate Cir Delray Beach FL 33484

SCHWARTZ, DONALD FRANKLIN, communication scientist; b. Jamestown, ND, 1935; m. Lois Carolyn Schwartz, June 26, 1965; children: Daria, Karin, Marc. BS, ND State U., 1957, MS, 1961; PhD, Mich. State U., 1968. Asst. dir. pub. rels. ND State U., Fargo, 1959-66, chmn. social scis., 1969-71, chmn. comm., 1967-79; instr. comm. Mich. State U., East Lansing, 1966-67; vis. scientist US Dept. Agr., Washington, 1979-80; prof. comm. Cornell U., Ithaca, NY, 1980-98, chmn. dept., 1980-85, dir. undergraduate studies, 1995-98, prof. emeritus, 1998—. Vis. scholar U. N.Mex., 1994. Contbr. articles to profl. jours. Recipient Outstanding Svc. award Future Farmers Am., 1976, Svc. award USDA, 1980, A.D. White Prof. of Yr. award, 1993; named Alumni of Yr., Alpha Gamma Rho, 2005. Mem. AAUP, Internat. Comm. Assn. (sec., pub. rels. interest group 1992-93), Am. Acad. Mgmt., Am. Soc. Pers. Adminstrn. (chpt. pres. 1976-77), Pub. Rels. Soc. Am. (nat. faculty advisor student assn. 1989-90, vice-chair educators sect. 1992, Pres.'s Citation for Leadership 1990, nat. ednl. affairs com. 1993-96). Roman Catholic. Office: Cornell U Dept Communication 331 Kennedy Hall Ithaca NY 14853-4203

SCHWARTZ, DONALD LEE, lawyer; b. Milw., Dec. 8, 1948; s. Bernard L. and Ruth M. (Marshall) S.; m. Susan J. Dunst, June 5, 1971; children: Stephanie Jane, Cheryl Ruth. BA, Macalester Coll., 1971; JD, U. Chgo., 1974. Bar: Ill. 1974. Assoc. Sidley & Austin, Chgo., 1974-80, ptnr., 1980-88, Latham & Watkins, Chgo., 1988—. Chmn. Ill. Conservative Union, 1979-81, bd. dirs. 1977-85. Served with U.S. Army, 1971-77. Mem. ABA (uniform comml. code com., comml. fin. svcs. commn.), Ill. Bar Assn. (sec. coun. banking and bankruptcy sect. 1982-83), Chgo. Bar Assn. (chmn. comml. law com. 1980-81, fin. insts. com. 1982-83), Ivanhoe Country Club, Sea Pines Country Club, Colleton River Country Club, Met. Club. Republican. Episcopalian. Avocation: golf. Home: 191 Park Ave Glencoe IL 60022-1351 Office: Latham & Watkins Ste 5800 Sears Tower Chicago IL 60606 Office Phone: 312-876-7631. Business E-Mail: donald.schwartz@lw.com.

SCHWARTZ, EDWARD ARTHUR, lawyer; b. Boston, Sept. 27, 1937; s. Abe and Sophie (Gottheim) S.; m. Sheila Kauffman, Apr. 5, 1997; children: Eric Allen, Jeffrey Michael. AB, Oberlin Coll., 1959; LLB, Boston Coll., 1962; postgrad., Am. U., 1958—59, Northeastern U., 1970; postgrad. exec. program, Stanford U., 1979. Bar: Conn. 1962, Mass. 1965. Legal intern Office Atty. Gen. Commonwealth of Mass., 1961; assoc. Schatz & Schatz, Hartford, Conn., 1962—65, Cohn, Reimer & Pollack, Boston, 1965—67; v.p., gen. coun., sec. Digital Equipment Corp., Maynard, Mass., 1967—88; pres. New Eng. Legal Found., Boston, 1990—98. Vis. prof. law Boston Coll., 1986, adj. prof., 1987—89; bd. dirs., chmn. SatelLife Corp. Editor Boston Coll. Indsl. and Comml. Law Rev, 1960-62, Ann. Survey Mass. Law, 1960-62. Home: PO Box 25 Duxbury MA 02331

SCHWARTZ, ELEANOR BRANTLEY, academic administrator; b. Kite, Ga., Jan. 1, 1937; d. Jesse Melvin and Hazel (Hill) Brantley; children: John, Cynthia. Student, U. Va., 1955, Ga. Southern Coll., 1956-57; BBA, Ga. State U., 1962, MBA, 1963, DBA, 1969. Adminstrv. asst. Fin. Agy., 1954, Fed. Govt., Va., Pa., Ga., 1956-59; asst. dean admissions Ga. State U., Atlanta, 1961-66, asst. prof., 1966-70; assoc. prof. Cleve. State U., 1970-75, prof. and assoc. dean, 1975-80; dean, Harzfeld prof. U. Mo., Kansas City, 1980-87, vice chancellor acad. affairs, 1987-91, interim chancellor, 1991-92, chancellor, 1992-99; prof. mgmt. U. Mo. Block Sch., Kansas City, 1999—2003, prof. emeritus, 2003—. Disting. vis. prof. Berry Coll., Rome, N.Y. State U. Coll., Fredonia, Mons U., Belgium; cons. pvt. industry U.S., Europe, Can.; bd. dirs. Rsch. Med. Ctr., Waddell & Reed Funds, Inc., Toy and Miniature Mus., Menorah Med. Ctr. Found., NCAA, NCCJ, Econ. Devel. Corp. of Kansas City, Silicon Prairie Tech. Assn. Author: Sex Barriers in Business, 1971, Contemporary Readings in Marketing, 1974; (with Muczyk and Smith) Principles of Supervision, 1984. Chmn., Mayor's Task Force in Govt. Efficiency, Kansas City, Mo., 1984; mem. comm. unity planning and rsch. coun. United Way Kansas City, 1983-85; bd. dirs. Jr. Achievement, 1982-86. Named Jones Store Career Woman of Yr., Kansas City, Mo., 1989, Ctrl. Exch. Woman of Yr., 1995; named one of 60 Women of Achievement, Girl Scouts Coun. Mid Continent, 1983; recipient Disting. Faculty award, Cleve. State U., 1974, Disting. Svc. award, Kans. State U., 1992, YWCA Hearts of Gold award, 2002. Mem.: Alpha Iota Delta, Golden Key, Phi Kappa Phi. Office Phone: 816-942-1840.

SCHWARTZ, ELEANORE ANITA, retired elementary school educator, small business owner; b. Milw., Aug. 24, 1934; d. Arthur Eric Hageleit and Anna Wurth; m. James W. Schwartz, July 28, 1956; children: Ray Eric, Ted William. BA, San Francisco State Coll., 1955. Cert. tchr. Calif., 1966. Elem. sch. tchr. Millbrae Sch. Dist., Calif., 1955—59; substitute tchr. Cupertino Sch. Dist., Calif., 1960—67, elem. sch. tchr. Calif., 1961; substitute tchr. San Jose Unified Sch. Dist., 1967—85; tchr. needle art West Valley C.C., Saratoga, Calif., 1986—92; ret. Gift shop mgr. Good Shepherd Auxiliary, Saratoga, 1989—92. Chmn. bd. dirs. The Lace Mus., Sunnyvale, 1999—. Named Citizen of the Day, Radio KABL, San Francisco, 1983; recipient Cross & Bell award, Good Sheperd Cmtys., 1992. Mem.: DEA, Internat. Old Lacers, Inc., Calif., Nev., Hawaii Dist. Luth. Women's Missionary League (v.p. mission svcs. 1979—81, treas. 1981—85, v.p. conv. planning 1986—90). Christian. Avocations: lacemaking, needlecrafts. Office: The Lace Mus 552 S Murphy Ave Sunnyvale CA 94086

SCHWARTZ, ELI, retired economics professor, writer; b. NYC, Apr. 2, 1921; s. Israel and Tillie (Shapiro) S.; m. Renee S. Kartiganer, Aug. 29, 1948; children: Pamela F., Alan G. BS, Denver U., 1943; MA, U. Conn., 1948; PhD, Brown U., 1952. Instr. U. R.I., Kingston, 1947-48; asst. instr. Brown U., Providence, 1948-51; chief regional economist Office Price Stblzn., Boston, 1951-53; lectr. Mich. State U., East Lansing, 1953-54; asst. prof. econs. Lehigh U., Bethlehem, Pa., 1954-58, assoc. prof., 1958-62, prof., 1962-91, Charles Macfarlane prof. econs., 1978-91, chmn. dept. econs., 1978-84, ret., 1991; cons. econs. and fin., expert witness Schwartz-Aronson Assocs., Bethlehem, 1965—. Author: Corporate Finance, 1962, Trouble in Eden, 1980; editor: Managing Municipal Finance, 1980, 83, 87, 96, 2004, Restructuring the Thrift Industry, 1989, Theory and Application of the Interest Rate, 1993; columnist Allentown Moring Call. With U.S. Army, 1943-46, ETO. Recipient sr. teaching Lehigh U., 1972; Earhart Found. grantee, 1978 Mem. Am. Econs. Assn., Am. Fin. Assn., Nat. Assn. Forensic Econs. (founding mem.). Jewish. Home: 3185 W Cedar St Allentown PA 18104-3441 Office: Lehigh U Dept Econs Rauch Ctr 621 Taylor St Bethlehem PA 18015-3107 Home Phone: 610-398-7008; Office Phone: 610-758-3410. *If I have achieved any success it is because I am interested in the subject matter of my field. I am fortunate to enjoy reading, teaching, consulting and writing.*

SCHWARTZ, ELLIOTT SHELLING, composer, writer, music educator; b. Bklyn., Jan. 19, 1936; s. Nathan and Rose (Shelling) S.; m. Dorothy Rose Feldman, June 26, 1960; children: Nina, Jonathan. AB, Columbia U., 1957, MA, 1958, EdD, 1962. Instr. music U. Mass., Amherst, 1960-64; from asst. prof. music to assoc. prof. Bowdoin Coll., Brunswick, Maine, 1964-75, prof. music, 1975—2006. Vis. prof. music Ohio State U., Columbus, 1988-92; vis. composer Trinity Coll. Music, London, 1967, U. Calif. Coll. Creative Studies, Santa Barbara, 1970, 73, 74; composer, pianist, commentator British Broadcast Corp, London, 1972, 74, 78, 83; vis. research musician Center Music Expt., La Jolla, Calif., 1978-79; disting. vis. prof. Ohio State U., 1985-86; music cons. Holt, Rinehart & Winston, Random House, Oxford Univ. Press, Schirmer Books, NYC, 1977—; vis. fellow Robinson Coll., Cambridge U., UK, 1993-94, 99, 2007. Composer: Island, 1970 (Internat. Gaudeamus prize 1970), Chamber Concertos I-IV, 1977-81, Extended Piano, 1980, Dream Music With Variations, 1983, Four Ohio Portraits, 1986, Memorial in Two Parts, 1989, Elan, 1990, Rows Garden, 1993, Equinox, 1994, Timepiece, 1994, Chiaroscuro, 1995, Reflections, 1995, Rainbow, 1996, Tapestry, 1996, Alto Prisms, 1997, Vienna Dreams, 1998, Kaleidoscope, 1999, Jack O'Lantern, 2000, Mehitabel's Serenade, 2000, Rain Forest with Birds, 2001, Voyager, 2002, Downtown Crossing, 2004, Summer's Journey, 2005, Chamber Concerto VI, 2007, Cambridge Mosaic, 2007; author: Electronic Music: A

Listener's Guide, 1973, Music: Ways of Listening, 1982, (with Daniel Godfrey) Music Since 1945: Issues, Materials and Literature, 1993; editor: (with Barney Childs) Contemporary Composers on Contemporary Music, 1967, rev. edit., 1998; contbr. articles to profl. jours. Nat. Endowment for Arts composition grantee, 1974, 76, 82; Rockefeller Found. residence fellow Bellagio, Italy, 1980, 89; MacDowell Colony resident fellow, 1965, 66; Yaddo residence fellow, 1977; recipient Maine State award Maine Commn. Arts and Humanities, 1970, McKim Commn., 1986 Mem.: Am. Composers Alliance (governing bd. 1994—2000), Am. Soc. Univ. Composers (nat. coun. 1968—72, nat. chmn. 1983—88), Coll. Music Soc. (nat. coun. 1982—88, pres. 1988—90), Am. Music Ctr. (v.p. 1981—87). Home: PO Box 451 South Freeport ME 04078-0451 Office: Bowdoin Coll Dept Music Brunswick ME 04011 Office Phone: 207-725-3320. Office Fax: 207-725-3748. E-mail: eschwart@bowdoin.edu.

SCHWARTZ, ERIC LEE, neuroscientist, educator; b. NYC, Mar. 10, 1947; s. Jacob and Edith Schwartz; m. Helen Sheila Eckstein, June 4, 1967; 1 child, Anna Molly. AB, Columbia Coll., NY, 1967; PhD, Columbia U., NY, 1973. Assoc. prof. NYU, NYC, 1983—92; prof. Boston U., 1992—. Chief scientist Vision Applications, Inc., NYC, 1990—2007. Author: (book) Computational Neuroscience. Achievements include patents for computer vision, robotics. Home: 72 York Terr Brookline MA 02446 Office: Boston Univ 677 Beacon St Boston MA 02215 Home Phone: 617-739-9170; Office Phone: 617-353-6179.

SCHWARTZ, ESTAR ALMA, lawyer; b. Bklyn., June 29, 1950; d. Henry Israel and Elaine Florence (Scheiner) Sutel; m. Lawrence Gerald Schwartz, June 28, 1976 (div. Dec. 1977); 1 child, Joshua (dec.); m. James Frances Edward Stuart, Sept. 25, 1999 (div. Aug. 2001). JD, NYU, 1980. Mgr., ptnr. Scheiner, Scheiner, DeVito & Wytte, NYC, 1966-81; social security fraud specialist U.S. Govt., 1982—83; pensions Todtman, Epstein, et al, 1983—85; office mgr., sec. Sills, Beck, Cummis, 1985—86; office mgr., bookkeeper Philip, Birnbaum & Assoc., 1986—87; office mgr., sec. Stanley Posses, Esq., Queens, 1989—90. Owner Estaris Paralegal Svc., Flushing, N.Y., 1992—, Sutel Creative Mgmt. Agy., Flushing, 1999—. Democrat. Jewish. Avocations: needlepoint, horseback riding, tennis, bowling, writing books and cookbooks. Home and Office: 67-20 Parsons Blvd Apt 2A Flushing NY 11365-2960 Home Phone: 718-820-0432; Office Phone: 718-820-0432. Personal E-mail: sutelmmgmt12345@msn.com. Business E-Mail: sutel@email.com, estaris@email.com.

SCHWARTZ, GERALD, public relations and fundraising agency executive; b. NYC, June 22, 1927; s. George and Martha F. S.; m. Felice P. Schwartz, June 25, 1950; children: Gary R., Gregg R., Wendy L. Student, N.C. State U., 1944-45; AB, U. Miami, Fla., 1949, BS, 1950, postgrad., 1966-67. Staff writer Miami Herald, 1941-44; publicity dir. U.S. Army in Europe, 1946-48; editor Miami Beach Sun, 1950-51; fund raising and pub. rels. counselor Miami, 1952-58; press sec. to Gov. Nebr., 1959—60; exec. v.p. Bar-Ilan U., Ramat Gan, Israel, 1960-61; prin. Gerald Schwartz Agy., Miami, Fla., 1962—. Editor, pub. Jewish Herald Newspaper, 1999-2000; editor, pub. emeritus Jewish Star-Times, 2000-2003. Nat. v.p. Am. Zionist Fedn., 1985—89, 1991—93; pres. Pres.'s coun. Zionist Orgn. Am., 1983—85; nat. chmn. Friends of Pioneer Women/Na'amat, 1984—98; pres. Am. Zionist Fedn. So. Fla., 1970—73, 1986—92; vice chmn. Urban League of Greater Miami, 1983—87, City of Miami Beach Planning Bd., 1953—55; bd. dirs. Greater Miami Symphony, 1982—87, Miami Beach Taxpayers Assn., 1988—89; pres. Civic League Miami Beach, 1985—87; pres. Greater Miami chpt. Assn. Welfare of Soldiers in Israel, 1983—86; chmn. City of Miami Beach Hurricane Def. Com., 1978—86, 1990—97; trustee South Shore Hosp. and Med. Ctr., Miami, 1987—2004, exec. vice-chmn. Miami Beach, 1989—2004; vice chmn. South Shore Med. Ctr. Found., 1989—2004; bd. govs. Barry U., 1985—86; chmn. Econ. Devel. Coun. City of Miami Beach, 1985—91; bd. dirs. Crimestoppers of Dade County, 1991—94; mem. exec. bd. State of Israel Bonds Orgn., 1996—; dep. chmn. Dem. Midwest Conf., 1958—60; bd. dirs. adminstrv. com. Jewish Nat. Fund of Am., 1995—, v.p. Greater Miami region, 1996—97; bd. dirs. Temple Emanu-El of Greater Miami, Papanicolaou Cancer Rsch. Inst., Miami, 1962—80; bd. dirs. Fla. chpt. Boys Town of Jerusalem, 2006—. With US Army, 1944—46. Recipient Jerusalem Peace award State of Israel Bonds, 1978, Jerusalem 3000 award State of Israel, 1996. Mem. Pub. Rels. Soc. Am. (accredited; treas. So. Fla. chpt. 1962-64), Am. Pub. Rels. Assn. (pres. chpt. 1960-61), Am. Assn. Polit. Cons., Nat. Assn. Fund Raising Execs. (pres. chpt. 1977-78), Miami Beach Taxpayers Assn. (bd. dirs. 1994-2000), Miami Internat. Press Club (bd. dirs. 1991-99), Miami Beach C. of C. (v.p. 1978-80, 81-84, 86-87, pres.-elect 1988-90, trustee 1990—), Lead and Ink, Tiger Bay Club (pres. 1986-88), Prime Minister's Club of State of Israel (Greater Miami chmn. 1997—), B'nai B'rith (pres. lodge 1964-66), Theta Omicron Pi, Omicron Delta Kappa, Alpha Delta Sigma (pres. 1965-67), Zeta Beta Tau. Office: Gerald Schwartz Agy 21150 Point Pl Unit 406 Aventura FL 33180-4033 Office Phone: 305-792-9711. Personal E-mail: geraldsch62227@aol.com.

SCHWARTZ, GERALD WILFRED, business executive; b. Winnipeg, Man., Can., Nov. 24, 1941; s. Andrew O. and Lillian Arkin (Leith) S.; m. Heather Reisman, May 15, 1982; children: Carey, Jill, Andrea, Anthony. B in Commerce, U. Man., 1962, LLB, 1966; MBA, Harvard U., 1970. V.p. Estabrook & Co., Inc., NYC, 1970-73, Bear Stearns & Co., NYC, 1973-77; pres., dir., mem. exec. com. CanWest Capital Corp., Winnipeg, 1977-83; chmn., pres., CEO ONEX Corp., Toronto, 1984—. Bd. dirs. Celestica Internat. Holdings Inc., Bank of N.S.; chmn. Can. Friends of Simon Wiesenthal Ctr. Bd. dirs. Can. Coun. Christians and Jews; vice chmn., mem. exec. com. Mt. Sinai Hosp. Toronto; trustee Simon Wiesenthal Ctr.; founder, mem. adv. bd. HSEG; cofounder, vice-chmn. Can. Coun. Israel and Jewish Advocacy. With RCAF, 1958. Decorated Order of Can. Office: Onex Corp 161 Bay St 49th Fl PO Box 700 Toronto ON Canada M5J 2S1

SCHWARTZ, GIL (STANLEY BING), broadcast executive, writer; b. Ill., 1951; children: Nina, Will. BA in Theater Arts and English, Brandeis U., Waltham, Mass. Humor writer Boston Phoenix; theater co. mgr. Boston; pub. affairs assoc. Teleprompter Corp. (Westinghouse Group W HBO forerunner), 1981—84; mgr. pub. rels. Westinghouse Broadcasting, dir. comm. Group W Cable NYC, 1984—87, dir. comm. Group W TV, 1987—89, v.p. comm. Group W TV sta. group, 1989—95, v.p. corp. comm., 1995—96; sr. v.p. comm. CBS Corp., NYC, 1996—2000, 2000—04, exec. v.p. Comm. Group, 2004—05, exec. v.p. corp. comm., 2006—. Author: (plays) Ferocious Kisses, Love As We Know It; columnist (as Stanley Bing) Esquire Mag., 1984—95, Fortune Mag., 1995—; author (as Stanley Bing): (books) Crazy Bosses: Spotting Them, Serving Them, Surviving Them, 1992, Lloyd: What Happened, 1998, What Would Machiavelli Do: The Ends Justify the Meanness, 2000, Throwing the Elephant: Zen and the Art of Managing Up, 2002, You Look Nice Today, 2003, The Big Bing: Black Holes of Time Management, Gaseous Executive Bodies, Exploding Careers, and Other Theories on the Origins of the Business Universe, 2003, Sun Tzu Was A Sissy, 2004, 100 Bullshit Jobs...And How to Get Them, 2006, Rome, Inc.: The Rise and Fall of the First Multinational Corporation, 2006. Office: CBS Corp 51 W 52nd St New York NY 10019-6188 Office Phone: 212-975-4321. *

SCHWARTZ, GLENN MARTIN, archaeologist, educator; b. Balt., May 24, 1954; s. Sidney Bernard and Evelyn Pearl Schwartz. BA, Yale U., New Haven, Conn., 1976, PhD, 1982. Prof. Johns Hopkins U., Balt., 1996—2001, Whiting prof. archaeology, 2001—. Author: (book) The Archaeology of Syria from Complex Hunter-Gatherers to Early Urban Societies (ca. 16, 000-300 BC), A Ceramic Chronology from Tell Leilan; editor: After Collapse: The Regeneration of Complex Societies, Archaeological Views from the Countryside: Village Communities in Early Complex Societies, The Study of the Ancient Near East in the 21st Century. Min. music St. John's United Meth. Ch., Balt., 1995—2007. Fellow, Am. Coun. Learned Socs., 1984—85, Mellon Found., 1986—87; grantee, NSF, 1999—2002, 2002—05, 2007—, Nat. Geog. Soc., 1988, 1990, 1994, 1996, 1999, 2002, 2006, NEH, 1989—90, 1993—96. Mem.: Archaeological Inst. Am. (acad. trustee 2007—), Am. Oriental Soc. (assoc.), Am. Schs. Oriental Rsch. (assoc.), Soc. Am. Archaeology (assoc.). Office: Johns Hopkins U/Gilman 128 3400 North Charles St Baltimore MD 21218 Office Phone: 410-516-8492. Office Fax: 410-516-5218; Home Fax: 410-516-5218. Business E-Mail: schwartz@jhu.edu.

SCHWARTZ, GORDON FRANCIS, surgeon, educator; b. Plainfield, NJ, Apr. 29, 1937; s. Samuel H. and Mary (Adelman) S.; m. Rochelle DeG. Krantz, Sept. 5, 1959; children: Amory Blair, Susan Leslie AB, Princeton U., 1956; MD, Harvard U., 1960; MBA, U. Pa., 1990. Intern N.Y. Hosp.-Cornell Med. Ctr., NYC, 1960-61; resident in surgery Columbia-Presbyterian Med. Ctr., NYC, 1963-68; instr. surgery Columbia U., NYC, 1966-68; assoc. in surgery U. Pa., Phila., 1968-70; dir. clin. services Breast Diagnostic Ctr., Jefferson Med. Coll., Phila., 1973-78, asst. prof. surgery, 1970-71, assoc. prof., 1971-78, prof., 1978—, dir. breast surgery fellowship, 2003—. Practice medicine specializing in surgery and diseases of breast, Phila., 1968—; founder, chmn. acad. com, sec. of Med. bd. Breast Health Inst., 1990—; edtl. bd. The Breast Jour., 1994—. Author: (with R.H. Guthrie, Jr.) Reconstructive and Aesthetic Mammoplasty, 1989, (with Douglas Marchant) Breast Disease: Diagnosis and Treatment, 1981; mem. editl. bd. The Breast-Ofcl. Jour. of the European Soc. of Mastology, 1996—, Cancer, 1997—; co-editor Seminars Breast Disease, 1997; mem. editl. bd. ONE, Oncology Econs., 1999—; contbr. mroe than 200 articles to profl. jours. Mem. Pa. Gov.'s Task Force on Cancer, 1976-82; mem. breast cancer task force Phila. chpt. Am. Cancer Soc.; mem. clin. investigation rev. com. Nat. Cancer Inst., 1992-95. Served to capt. AUS, 1961-63. NIH Cancer Control fellow, 1968-69 Mem. ACS, AMA, AAUP, Assn. for Acad. Surgery, Allen O. Whipple Surg. Assn., Soc. Surg. Oncology, Internat. Cardiovasc. Soc., Soc. for Surgery Alimentary Tract, John Jones Surg. Soc., Am. Soc. Clin. Oncology, Am. Soc. Breast Diseases (pres. 1981-83), Soc. Internat. Senologie (treas. 1982-90, v.p. 1990-92, sci. com. 1992—), Am. Soc. Breast Surgeons, N.Y. Acad. Scis., Am. Soc. Artificial Internal Organs, Am. Radium Soc., Philadelphia County Med. Soc. (chmn. com. on econs. 1999-2000, bd. dirs. 1999-2000), Internat. Sentinel Node Soc. (founding mem. 2003), Italian Soc. Senology (hon.), Greek Surg. Soc. (hon.), The Phila. Club, Union League, Princeton Club Phila. (pres. 1989-91), Princeton Club (N.Y.C.), Princeton Terrace Club, Nassau Club, Phi Beta Kappa, Sigma Xi, Alpha Omega Alpha, Nu Sigma Nu. Republican. Jewish. Office: 1015 Chestnut St Ste 510 Philadelphia PA 19107-4305 Home Phone: 215-732-1836; Office Phone: 215-627-8487.

SCHWARTZ, HEIDI K., science educator; d. Russell and Joyce Sandstrom; m. Shannon D. Schwartz, Sept. 2, 1989; children: Shandi, Wyatt. BA, Idaho State U., Pocatello, 1988; M in Learning and Tech., Western Govs. U., Salt Lake City, 2006. Cert. secondary edn.Level 2 Utah. Sci. tchr. Centerville Jr. High, Utah, 1990—. Sci. dept. chair Centerville Jr. High, 1998—2002. SB 61 Edn. scholar, Utah State Senate, 2002. Mem.: NEA, Nat. Sci. Tchrs. Assn., Davis Edn. Assn. Office: Centerville Jr High 625 S Main Centerville UT 84014 Home Phone: 801-296-8449; Office Phone: 801-402-6100. Office Fax: 801-402-6101.

SCHWARTZ, HERBERT FREDERICK, lawyer; b. Bklyn., Aug. 23, 1935; s. Henry and Blanche Theodora (goldberg) S.; m. Gail Lubets, Jan. 23, 1960; children: Wendy Helene, Karen Anne, Peter Andrew; m. Nan Budde Chequer, Mar. 13, 1987; stepchildren: Elizabeth Guthrie, Anne Hamilton, Laura Dunham. BSEE, MIT, 1957; MA in Applied Econs., U. Pa., 1964, LLB, 1964. Assoc. Fish & Neave, NYC, 1964-70, jr. ptnr., 1970-71, mng. ptnr., 1985-91, ptnr., 1972—2004, Ropes & Gray, 2005—. Lectr. law U. Pa., Phila., 1980-89, adj. prof., 1990—, NYU Law Sch., 2003-. Author: Patent Law and Practice, Federal Judicial Center, 1988, 2d edit., 1995, Bureau of National Affairs, 2d edit., 1996, 5th edit., 2006; co-author: Principles of Patent Law, 1998, 2d edit., 2001; contbr. articles to profl. jours. Vice-chmn. Jr. Yacht Racing Assn. of L.I. Sound, 1985-88. 1st lt. U.S. Army, Signal Corps, 1957-59. Mem. Assn. of Bar of City of N.Y., Am. Intellectual Property Lawyers Assn., N.Y. Intellectual Property Lawyers Assn. (pres. 1999-00), Woods Hole Oceanographic Instn. (mem. corp. 2003-, trustee 2006-), Am. Coll. Trial Lawyers, Am. Bar Found., Am. Law Inst., Order of Coif, N.Y. Yacht Club, Riverside Yacht Club, Cruising Club of Am. Avocation: racing and cruising sailboats. Home: 24 Cherry Tree Ln Riverside CT 06878-2629 Office: Ropes & Gray LLP 1211 Avenue Of The Americas New York NY 10036-8704 Business E-Mail: herbert.schwartz@ropesgray.com.

SCHWARTZ, HOWARD S., lawyer; BA magna cum laude, Brown U., 1988; JD, U. Va., 1992. Bar: Md. 1993, D.C. 1993. Ptnr., co-chmn. Life Sciences practice group DLA Piper Rudnick Gray Cary, Balt. Bd. mem. Balt. City Cmty. Coll. Found.; mem. adv. bd. Torah Inst. Balt. Mem. ABA, DC Bar Assn., Md. State Bar Assn., Phi Beta Kappa. Office: DLA Piper Rudnick Gray Cary 6225 Smith Ave Baltimore MD 21209-3600 Office Phone: 410-580-4251. Office Fax: 410-580-3001. Business E-Mail: howard.schwartz@dlapiper.com.

SCHWARTZ, HOWARD WYN, business and marketing educator, consultant; b. Mpls., June 12, 1951; s. Jerry Schwartz and Geraldine (Berg) Brooks; m. Jeannie Marie Holtzmann, Aug. 2, 1975; children: Abigail Jorene, Rachel Elizabeth. BA cum laude, U. Minn., 1973, MBA, 1982, MEd, 1999. Cert. tchr. Minn. Acct. Med. Sch., U. Minn., 1973-77, bus. mgr. dept. neurology, 1977-79, adminstr. found. edn. dept., 1979-82, assoc. to chmn. dept. radiology, 1982-99; chmn. bus./mktg. edn. dept. Robbindale-Cooper H.S., New Hope, Minn., 1999—. Adj. instr. dept. radiology U. Minn., 1982—; pres. Bus. Mgmt. Svcs., Golden Valley, Minn., 1979—; lectr., author topics in bus./mktg. edn., 2000—. Editor-in-chief: RADWORKS Workload Measurement Manual, 1985-87; editor: Radiology Management, 1985-87, Purchasing the Radiology Information System, 1991, Current Concepts in Radiology Management, 1991; contbr. articles to profl. jours. Active Cystic Fibrosis Found., Minn., 1980—; chmn. Human Rights Commn., Robbinsdale, 1982-84; sec. Coord. Coun. Minority Concerns, 1984-85; chmn. imaging tech. adv. com. U. Hosp. Consortium, 1989-92; dir. U. Hosp. Consortium Svcs. Corp., 1990-92, Nat. Summit on Manpower, 1989-92; treas. Tech. Learning Campus Site Coun., Dist. 281, 1990-91, chmn. Bond Referendum campaign, 1995; pres. Armstrong HS Parent Assn., Dist. 281, 1991-92. Recipient In the Spirit of Youth Role Model award, Cmty. Ahead, 2004, Tchr. of Excellence award, Best Prep, 2004, Carpenter Tchr. of Yr. award, 2007. Fellow: Am. Healthcare Radiology Adminstrn. (regional pres. 1986—87, nat. pres. 1988—89, sec. edn. found. 1990—91, bd. dirs. edn. found. 1993—95, 1997—98, Outstanding Author award 1990, 1993, 1996, Midwest Region Disting. Mem. award 1991, Gold award 1991); mem.: NEA, Assn. Career and Tech. Edn., Assn. for Supervision and Curriculum Devel., Am. Fedn. Tchrs., Nat. Bus. Edn. Assn., Minn. Bus. Educators, Inc., Delta Pi Epsilon, Delta Kappa Epsilon. Home: 7400 Winnetka Heights Dr Golden Valley MN 55427-3549 Office: PO Box 27405 Minneapolis MN 55427-0405 Office Phone: 612-327-4165. Personal E-mail: hwschwartz@comcast.net.

SCHWARTZ, IRWIN H., lawyer; b. Bklyn., Mar. 25, 1948; s. Julius and Sylvia (Holzman) S.; m. Barbara T. Granett, July 3, 1971; 1 child, Matthew Lane. BA, Bklyn. Coll., 1968; JD, Stanford U., 1971. Bar: Calif. 1972, Washington 1972, U.S. Ct. Appeals (9th cir.) 1972, U.S. Supreme Ct. 1977, Internat. Criminal Ct., 2005. Asst. U.S. atty. U.S. Dist. Ct. (we. dist.) Wash., Seattle, 1972-74, exec. asst. U.S. atty., 1974-75, fed. pub. defender, 1975-81; pvt. practice Seattle, 1981—. Fellow: Am. Bd. Criminal Lawyers, Am. Coll. Trial Lawyers; mem.: NACDL (pres. 2001—02), ABA (criminal justice sect. coun. 1991—94, 2002—05), Wash. Athletic Club (Seattle). Avocations: photography, woodworking. Office: 710 Cherry St Seattle WA 98104-1925

SCHWARTZ, JEFFREY BYRON, lawyer; b. Phila., Dec. 3, 1940; s. Carl Sidney and Tessie Claire (Cohen) S.; m. Joan S. Weinman, Aug. 4, 1963; children: Kevin, Jill. BS, Pa. State U., 1962; JD, U. Pa., 1965; MBA, Am. U., 1967. Bar: Pa. 1965, D.C. 1968, La. 1969. Staff acct. Price Waterhouse & Co., Washington, 1962; trial atty. SEC, Washington, 1965-68; sr. atty. New Orleans Legal Assistance, 1968-70; gen. counsel Nat. Tenants Orgn., Washington, 1970-73; litigation atty. Nat. Health and Environ. Law Project, Washington, 1971-74; chief counsel Pa. Dept. Health, Harrisburg, 1974-79; ptnr. Berriman & Schwartz, King of Prussia, Pa., 1979-85; sr. ptnr. Wolf, Block, Schorr & Solis-Cohen, Phila., 1985-92; ptnr. Cohen, Shapiro, Polisher, Shiekman & Cohen, Phila., 1992-95, Fox Rothschild, O'Brien & Frankel, LLP, Phila., 1995-99; sr. legal advisor USAID Assistance Program Bulgarian Securities and Stock Exch. Commn., 1999—; atty. Schwartz Law LLC, 2000—; v.p., gen. counsel Crossover Med. Tech., 2000—. Guest lectr. on welfare and health law U. Pa. Sch. Law, Tulane U. Law Sch., Wayne State U. Law Sch. and Georgetown U. Law Sch.; instr. Catholic U. Am. Law Sch., 1972-73; course planner Pa. Bar Inst., 1980—. Contbr. articles to profl. jours. Reginald Heber Smith fellow, 1968-70. Mem. Am. Soc. Hosp. Attys., Am. Health Lawyers Assn. (dir.), Pa. Soc. Hosp. Attys. (pres. 1983-85, bd. dirs. 1983-89), Hosp. Attys. Southeastern Pa., Am. Pub. Health Assn. (chmn. health law com. 1978-81), Pa. Bar Assn., D.C. Bar Assn. Democrat. Jewish. Home: 10 Radcliff Rd Bala Cynwyd PA 19004-2631

SCHWARTZ, JEFFREY H., distribution facilities executive; BS with honors, Emory Univ., 1981; MBA, Harvard Univ., 1985. CPA. Acct. Arthur Anderson, Atlanta, 1981—83; with Anderson Properties, Atlanta; co-founder, mng. ptnr. Krauss/Schwartz Co.; mgr. global develop. ProLogis, Denver, 1994—96, vice-chmn. internat. ops. Mexico, 1996, Amsterdam, 1997—2000; CEO Vizional Technologies, 2001; pres., COO Asia Pro-Logis, Denver, 2002—05, pres. internat. ops., 2003—05, CEO, 2005—07, chmn., CEO, 2007—. Office: ProLogis 4545 Airport Way Denver CO 80239 *

SCHWARTZ, JONATHAN D., lawyer; b. LI, NY, 1961; BS in Fin. and Polit. Sci. summa cum laude, U. Pa.; JD with honors, Stanford U.; MA in Internat. Rels. with hons., Cambridge U., Eng. Bar: DC, NY. Law clk. to Judge Harry T. Edwards US Ct. Appeals DC Cir.; law clk. to Justice Thurgood Marshall US Supreme Ct., 1988—89; with Jones Day Reavis & Pogue, NYC, 1989—91; fed. prosecutor Office US Atty., Manhattan, NY, 1991—95; sr. positions Dept. Justice, Washington, 1995—2001, prin. assoc. dep. atty. gen., 2000—01; gen. counsel Napster, Inc., 2001—02; sr. v.p., dep. gen. counsel Time Warner Inc., 2002—03; exec. v.p., gen. counsel Cablevision Sys. Corp., Bethpage, NY, 2003—. Named one of Top 40 Lawyers Under Age 40, Washingtonian Mag., 1998; recipient Edmund J. Randolph award, Dept. Justice, 2001; fellow, Harvard U. Inst. Politics, 1999; Fulbright scholar, 1986—87. Office: Cablevision Sys Corp 1111 Stewart Ave Bethpage NY 11714 Office Phone: 516-803-1125. *

SCHWARTZ, JONATHAN IAN, information technology executive; b. Oct. 20, 1965; Student, Carnegie Mellon U., Pitts., 1983—84; BS in Econs. and Math., Wesleyan U., Middletown, Conn., 1986. Cons. McKinsey & Co., Inc., 1987—89; co-founder, CEO Lighthouse Design (acquired by Sun Microsystems, Inc.), 1989—96; dir. investment group, devel. tools & Java product mktg. orgn. Sun Microsystems, Inc., Santa Clara, Calif., v.p. venture & strategic investments, 1999—2000, sr. v.p. corp. strategy & planning, 2000—02, exec. v.p. software group, 2002—04, pres., COO, 2004—06, pres., CEO, 2006—. Bd. dirs. Dorado Corp. Office: Sun Microsystems Inc 4150 Network Cir Santa Clara CA 95054 Office Phone: 650-960-1300, 800-555-9786. Office Fax: 408-276-3804. E-mail: jonathan.schwartz@sun.com. *

SCHWARTZ, JORDAN M., lawyer; b. NYC, Oct. 17, 1957; AB, Stanford Univ., 1978; JD, Univ. Chgo., 1981. Bar: Ill. 1981, NY 1988. V.p., gen. counsel Ticketmaster Corp., Chgo., 1985—86; assoc. Cadwalader Wickersham & Taft LLP, NYC, 1987—91, ptnr., corp. structured fin., 1991—. Mem.: ABA, Mortgage Bankers Assn. (mem. secondary & capital markets com.). Office: Cadwalader Wickersham & Taft 1 World Financial Ctr New York NY 10281 Office Fax: 212-504-6136, 212-504-6666. Business E-Mail: jordan.schwartz@cwt.com.

SCHWARTZ, JUDY ELLEN, thoracic surgeon; b. Mason City, Iowa, Oct. 5, 1946; d. Walter Carl and Alice Nevada (Moore) Schwartz. BS, U. Iowa, Iowa City, 1968, MD, 1971; MPH, Johns Hopkins U., Balt., 1996. Diplomate Am. Bd. Surgery, Am. Bd. Thoracic Surgery, Am. Bd. Med. Mgmt., cert. physician exec. Cert. Commn. Med. Mgt. Intern Nat. Naval Med. Ctr., Bethesda, Md., 1971-72, gen. surgery resident, 1972-76, thoracic surgery resident, 1976-78, staff cardiothoracic surgeon, 1979-82, chief cardiothoracic surgeon, 1982-83; chmn. cardiothoracic surg. dept. Naval Hosp., San Diego, 1983-85, quality assurance program dir., 1985-88. Exec. office Rapidly Deployable Med. Facility Four, 1986—88; asst. prof. surgery Uniformed Svcs. U. Health Sci., Bethesda, 1983—99; sr. policy analyst quality assurance Profl. Affairs and Quality Assurance, 1988—90, dep. dir. quality assurance, 1990; dir. clin. policy Health Svcs. Ops., Washington, 1990—94; head performance evaluation and improvement Nat. Naval Med. Ctr., 1994—99; cardiothoracic splty. cons. to naval med. command USN, Washington, 1983—84; Dept. Def. rep. to task force info. mgmt. Joint Commn. Accreditation Health Care Orgn., 1990—93, chmn., 1991—93, mem. task force IMS Tech., 1993—94; chmn. info. mgmt. workshop Fed. Health Care Study Commn.'s Coord. Fed. Health Care, 1993; corp. med. dir. Medcenter One Health Sys., 1999—2002, trustee, 1999—2003; corp. med. dir. ND Dept. Corrections & Rehab., 1990—2002; v.p. med. affairs Medcenter One, 2002; v.p. Surg. Svc. and Electronic Med. Records Informatics, 2003—05, Surg. Svc., 2005—06; bd. dirs. SCCI; mem. adv. com. Blue Cross Blue Shield Care Mgmt., 1999—2002, v.p. med. affairs, 2002; chmn. rsch. and bioethics com. Instnl. Rev. Bd., 2000—06; mem. exec. adv. bd. Surg. Info. Sys., 2005—; examiner Baldridge award, 2006—07; v.p. med. affairs Knox Cmty. Hosp., 2007—. Contbr. articles to various publs. Mem. nat. physician's leadership coun. VHA, 2000—02; trustee St. Vincent's Nursing Home, 2001—05. Capt. USN, 1969—99, ret. USN, 1999. Decorated Legion of Merit, Commendation Medal Navy and Marine Corps, Meritorious Unit Commendation. Fellow: ACS (mem. com. allied health pers. 1985—91, mem. exec. com. 1987—91, mem. accreditation rev. com. edn. physician asst. 1988—94, treas. accreditation rev. com. 1991—93, sr. mem. com. allied health pers. 1991—94), Am. Coll. Cardiology; mem.: AMA, Am. Coll. Physician Execs., Am. Mgmt. Assn., Am. Med. Women's Assn., Am. Thoracic Soc.

SCHWARTZ, KESSEL, modern language educator; b. Kansas City, Mo., Mar. 19, 1920; s. Henry and Dora (Tennenbaum) S.; m. Barbara Lewin, Apr. 3, 1947; children: Joseph David, Deborah, Edward, Michael. BA, U. Mo., Columbia, 1940, MA, 1941; PhD, Columbia U., NYC, 1953. Asst. instr. U. Mo., 1940-42; dir. cultural ctrs. in Nicaragua, Ecuador, cultural observer in Costa Rica State Dept., 1946-48; instr. Hofstra, Hamilton, Colby colls., 1948-53; asst. prof. U. Vt., 1953-57; assoc. prof., then prof. modern langs., chmn. dept. U. Ark., 1957-62; prof. modern langs. U. Miami, Fla., 1962-90, chmn. dept., 1962-64, 74-83, dir. grad. studies, 1964-65, 83-90, now emeritus prof. Vis. prof. U. N.C., Chapel Hill, 1966-67 Author: The Ecuadorian Novel, 1953, An Introduction to Modern Spanish Literature, 1967, The Meaning of Existence in Contemporary Hispanic Literature, 1969, Vicente Aleixandre, 1970, Juan Goytisolo, 1970,

A New History of Spanish American Fiction, 1972 (named Outstanding Acad. Book of Year, Am. Assn. Coll. and Research Librarians), Studies on Twentieth Century Spanish and Spanish American Literature, 1983; co-author: A New History of Spanish Literature, 1961, rev. edit., 1991, A New Anthology of Spanish Literature, 1968; assoc. editor Hispania, 1965-84; editorial adv. bd.: Anales de la Literatura Española Contemporánea Folio; Fiestas (Goytisolo), notes and introduction, 1964; contbr. numerous articles to profl. jours., chpts. to books, ency. Nat. patronato Letras de Oro Spanish Literary Prizes. Served with AUS, 1942-46. July 14, 1989 declared Kessel Schwartz Day in Coral Gables, Miami and Dade County by mayors' proclamation. Mem. MLA (group sec. 1964, group chmn. 1965, chmn. nominating com. for modern Spanish lit. 1966-68), Am. Assn. Tchrs. Spanish and Portuguese (chmn. Peninsular lit. sect. 1972), Internat. Assn. Hispanists, Phi Beta Kappa (pres. So. Fla. chpt. 1977), Phi Sigma Iota, Sigma Delta Pi (nat. Order of Don Quijote award 1984, Order of Discoverers award 1989), Pi Delta Phi, Delta Phi Alpha, Omicron Delta Kappa. Home: 6400 Maynada St Miami FL 33146-3318 Personal E-mail: edschwar@bellsouth.net. *If men loved one another sufficiently, we might not need our legal systems. Given our imperfect nature as human beings, we must believe in some higher goals to give meaning to our lives but be ever vigilant that in the pursuit of success we do not infringe upon the happiness of others or confuse the means with the end.*

SCHWARTZ, LEON, foreign language educator; b. Boston, Aug. 22, 1922; s. Charles and Celia (Emer) S.; m. Jeanne Gurtat, Mar. 31, 1949; children: Eric Alan, Claire Marie. Student, Providence Coll., 1939-41; BA, UCLA, 1948; certificat de phonetique, U. Paris, 1949; MA, U. So. Cal., 1950, PhD, 1962. Tchr. English, Spanish and Latin Redlands HS, Calif., 1951—54; tchr. Spanish and French Redlands HS, 1954—59; prof. French Calif. State U., LA, 1959—87, chmn. dept. fgn. langs. and lit., 1970—73, prof. emeritus, 1987—; instr. Osher Learning Inst., 2006—. Author: Diderot and the Jews, 1981; co-author: Mortier-Tresson, Dictionnaire de Diderot, 1999. Served as 2d lt. USAAF, 1942-45. Decorated Air medal with 5 oak leaf clusters; recipient Outstanding Prof. award Calif. State U. LA, 1976. Mem. Am. Assn. Tchrs. French, Am. Soc. 18th Century Studies, Calif. State U. LA Emeriti Assn. (pres. 1998-2000), Phi Beta Kappa, Phi Kappa Phi, Pi Delta Phi, Sigma Delta Pi, Alpha Mu Gamma. Business E-Mail: lschwar@calstatela.edu.

SCHWARTZ, LEONARD JAY, retired lawyer; b. San Antonio, Sept. 23, 1943; s. Oscar S. and Ethel (Eastman) S.; m. Sandra E. Eichelbaum, July 4, 1965; 1 child, Michele Fay. BBA, U. Tex., 1965, JD, 1968. Bar: Tex. 1968, Ohio 1971, U.S. Supreme Ct. 1971, U.S. Dist. Ct. (no., ea., wes. and so. dists.) Tex., U.S. Dist. Cts. (no. and so. dists.) Ohio, U.S. Dist. Ct. Nebr., U.S. Ct. Appeals (5th, 6th, 7th and 11th cirs.). Assoc. Roberts & Holland, NYC, 1968-70; ptnr. Rigely, Schwartz & Fagan, San Antonio, 1970-71; staff counsel ACLU of Ohio, Columbus, 1971-74; ptnr. Schwartz & Fishman, Columbus, 1974-79; elections counsel to sec. of state State of Ohio, Columbus, 1979-80; ptnr. Waterman & Schwartz and successor firms, Austin, Tex., 1981-85; mng. dir. Schwartz & Eichelbaum, PC, Austin and other cities, 1985—99, 2000—01, shareholder Austin, various locations, 1985—2001, ret., 2001. Gen. counsel various sch. dists., cities and counties; adj. prof. law U. Tex. Sch. Law, Austin; labor and employment law cons. and sch. law Tex. Assn. Sch. Adminstrs; condr. workshops in field; mem. com. on fed. judiciary rels. Tex. Bar. Contbr. articles to profl. jours. Mem. chancellor's coun. U. Tex. Sys.; mem. U. Tex. Pres.'s Assocs., Littlefield Soc., Sch. of Law Keeton Fellows. Recipient Outstanding Tchg. Quiz Master award, U. Tex. Sch. Law, 1968. Fellow Tex. Bar Found.; mem. ABA, FBA, Tex. Bar Assn., Bar Assn. 5th Cir., Phi Delta Phi. Democrat. Jewish. Personal E-mail: lennyjay@sbcglobal.net.

SCHWARTZ, LILLIAN FELDMAN, artist, filmmaker, critic, nurse, writer; b. Cin., July 13, 1927; d. Jacob and Katie (Green) Feldman; m. Jack James Schwartz, Dec. 22, 1946; children: Jeffrey Hugh, Laurens Robert. BSE, U. Cin., 1947; Dr. honoris causa, Kean Coll., 1988. Nurse Cin. Gen. Hosp., 1947; head supr. premature nursery St. Louis Maternity Hosp., 1947-48; cons. AT&T Bell Labs., Murray Hill, NJ, 1968-97; pres. Computer Creations Corp., Watchung, NJ, 1989—2004; cons. Bell Communications Research, Morristown, NJ, 1984-92, Lucent Technologies/Bell Labs. Innovations, 1996—2001. Artist-in-residence Sta. WNET, N.Y.C., 1972-74; cons. T.J. Watson Rsch. Lab. IBM Corp., Yorktown, N.Y., 1975, 82-84; vis. mem. computer sci. dept. U. Md., College Park, 1974-80; adj. prof. fine arts Kean Coll., Union, N.J., 1980-82, Rutgers U., New Brunswick, N.J., 1982-83; adj. prof. dept. psychology NYU, N.Y.C., 1985-86, assoc. prof. computer sci.; guest lectr. Princeton U., Columbia U., Yale U., Rockefeller U.; mem. grad. faculty Sch. Visual Arts, N.Y.C., 1990-91; dir. team from Rutgers U. to create world's first computer-generated 3-D model of Leaning Tower of Pisa to test structures, 1999; invited com. mem. info. tech. and creativity NAS, 2000-03; invited juror L'Oreal/Color/Internat., 2000-01; film retrospective Leeds, Eng. Lumen-Evolution, 2002, 2003-04. Co-author: Information Technology and Creativity, 2001, The Computer Artist's Handbook; contbd. articles to profl. jours including Scientific Am., 1995; contbr. chpts. to books, also Trans. Am. Philos. Soc., vol. 75, Part 6, 1985; one-woman shows of sculpture and paintings include Columbia U., 1967, 68, Rabin and Krueger Gallery, Newark, 1968, Computer Animation, Amsterdam, 2006, Florence, Italy, 2006, Pacific Film Archive, 20056 films shown at Met. Mus., N.Y.C., Franklin Inst., Phila., 1972, U. Toronto, 1972, am. Embassy, London, 1972, L.A. County Mus., Corcoran Gallery, Washington, 1972, Whitney Mus., N.Y.C., 1973, Grand Palais, Paris, Musee Nat. d'Art Moderne, Paris, IBM, (digital print show) Bklyn. Mus. Art, 2001, Chelsea Mus. Art, N.Y.C., 2004, Computer Animation Retrospective, U.K., U.S., 2005, Holland, Italy, U.S., 2006, others; dir.: Save the Leaning Tower. Recipient numerous art and film awards, Emmy award Mus. Modern Art, 1984, Computer Graphics World Smithsonian awards for virtual reality, art analysis, inventing computer medium for art and animation, 1993; named Outstanding Alumnus, U. Cin., 1987; grantee Nat. Endowment for Arts, 1977, 81, Corp. Pub. Broadcasting, 1979, Nat. Endowment Composers and Librettists, 1981, Arts Coun. Eng., 2003. Fellow World Acad. of Art and Sci.; mem. NATAS, Am. Film Inst., Info. Film Prodrs. Am., Soc. Motion Picture and TV Engrs., Internat. Sculptors Assn., Centro Studi Pierfrancescani (Sansepolcro, Italy, founding mem.). Achievements include discovery using morphing algorithms to determine Leonardo's creative decision-making steps in transforming the Duchess of Aragon into the Mona Lisa using his own features to segue; discovery of reason for position of Christ's right hand and Judas's left hand in Leonardo da Vinci's Last Supper. Personal E-mail: lillianschwartz@lillian.com. *I have always been provoked by and concerned with the mechanical and technological world around me. I enjoy experimenting with traditional media and combining them with technology today. For example, I used computers as an art medium when computers were solely programmed for scientific purposes. By using the computer to understand the creative process I have made clear the intent of the great masters and applied their decision-making steps to my own work. The excitement in creating is to discover and to make a new world. My present success was achieved in part by being able to make new rules and not be hindered by old or obvious solutions.*

SCHWARTZ, LLOYD, music critic, poet; b. NYC, Nov. 29, 1941; s. Sam and Ida (Singer) Schwartz. BA, Queens Coll., NYC, 1962; MA, Harvard U., 1963, PhD, 1976. Classical music editor Boston Phoenix, 1977—; dir. creative writing U. Mass., Boston, 1982—, 1990—2002; classical music critic Fresh Air Nat. Pub. Radio, Phila., 1987—. Prof. English U. Mass., Boston, 1986—. Author (poems): These People, 1981, Goodnight, Gracie, 1992, Cairo Traffic, 2000, Lloyd Schwartz: Greatest Hits 1973-2000, 2003; author: (plays) These People: Voices for the Stage, 1990; editor: Ploughshares, 1979, Elizabeth Bishop and Her Art, 1983; actor: The Spider's Web, 1975—82; dir.: These People: Voices for the Stage, 1990; (Operas) L'Heure Espagnol (Ravel), 1972, Mavra (Stravinsky), 1973. Recipient Pulitzer prize for criticism, 1994; NEA creative writing fellow in poetry, 1990. Mem.: MLA, PEN, Associated Writing Programs, New Eng. Poetry Club, Poetry Soc. Am., PEN Am. Avocations: collecting old recordings, books. Home: 27 Pennsylvania Ave Somerville MA 02145-2217 Office: Boston Phoenix 126 Brookline Ave Boston MA 02215-3920 Business E-Mail: lloyd.schwartz@umb.edu. E-mail: lschwartz@phx.com.

SCHWARTZ, LOUIS WINN, ophthalmologist; b. Pa., Apr. 19, 1942; s. Edward and Sylvia Beatrice (Winn) Schwartz; m. Linda Weinberg, June 14, 1964; children: Joanne Karen, Geoffrey Paul. AB, Bowdoin Coll., 1963; MD, Jefferson Med. Coll., 1967. Diplomate Am. Bd. Ophthalmology. Intern Phila. Gen. Hosp.-U. Pa., 1967-68; resident in ophthalmology Wills Eye Hosp., Phila., 1970-73; ophthalmologist Ophthalmic Assocs., Lansdale, Pa., 1973—; clin. assoc. prof. ophthalmology Jefferson Med. Coll., Phila., 1984—; attending surgeon Glaucoma Svc. Wills Eye Hosp., Phila., 1994—, sec.-treas., 1998-2000, v.p., 2000—02, pres., 2002—04. Chief ophthalmology North Penn Hosp., 1995—2000. Co-author: Laser Therapy of Anterior Segment, 1988, 9 other books; assoc. editor: Contact Lens Assn. Ophthalmology Jour., 1988; contbr. articles to profl. jours. Recipient Honor award, Am. Acad. Ophthalmology, 1988. Mem.: InterCounty Ophthalmol. Soc. (pres. 1985—86), Pa. Acad. Ophthalmology, Am. Glaucoma Soc., Ophthalmic Club Phila. (life; pres. 1985—86, honored life mem. 2006). Office: Ophthalmic Assocs 1000 N Broad St Lansdale PA 19446-1138 Office Phone: 215-368-1646. Personal E-mail: oalandsdale@aol.com.

SCHWARTZ, LYLE HOWARD, materials scientist, science administrator; b. Chgo., Aug. 2, 1936; s. Joseph K. Schwartz and Helen (Shefsky) Bernards; divorced; children: Ara, Justin; m. Celesta Sue Jurkovich, Sept. l, 1973. BS in Sci. Engring., Northwestern U., 1959, PhD in Materials Sci., 1964. Prof. materials sci. Northwestern U., Evanston, Ill., 1964-84, dir. Materials Research Ctr., 1979-84; dir. materials sci. and engr. lab. Nat. Inst. Standards and Tech., Dept. Commerce, Gaithersburg, Md., 1984-97; pres. Associated Univs., Inc., Washington, 1997-98; interim dir. Brookhaven Nat. Lab., Washington, 1997; cons., 1998-99; dir. aerospace and material scis. Air Force Office Sci. Rsch., Arlington, Va., 1999-2001, dir., 2001—. Cons. Argonne Nat. Labs., Ill., 1965-79; vis. scientist Bell Telephone Labs., Murray Hill, N.J., 1971-73 Author: (with J.B. Cohen) Diffraction From Materials, 1977, 2d edit., 1987; also numerous articles and papers NSF fellow, 1962-63; recipient Presdl. Rank Award of Meritorious Exec. for outstanding govt. svc., 1990. Fellow Am. Soc. for Metals; mem. AAAS, AIME, Nat. Acad. Engring., Am. Phys. Soc., Am. Crystallography Assn., Materials Rsch. Soc., Sigma Xi. Personal E-mail: lyle.schwartz2@verizon.net.

SCHWARTZ, MARSHALL ZANE, pediatric surgeon; b. Mpls., Sept. 1, 1945; s. Sidney Shay and Peggy Belle (Lieberman) S.; m. Michele Carroll Walker, Oct. 16, 1971; children: Lisa, Jeffrey. BS, U. Minn., 1968, MD, 1970. Diplomate Am. Bd. Surgery, Am. Bd. Pediatric Surgery. Intern NY Hosp., NYC, 1970—71; resident gen. surgery U. Minn., Mpls., 1971—73, 1975—76, rsch. fellow, 1974—75; jr. resident in pediat. surgery Children's Hosp. Med. Ctr., Harvard Med. Sch., 1973—74, sr. resident in pediat. surgery, 1976—77, chief resident in pediat. surgery, 1977—78; instr. Med. Sch. Harvard U., Boston, 1978—79; asst. surgery Children's Hosp. Med. Ctr., Boston, 1978—79; asst. prof. Med. Br. U. Tex., Galveston, 1979—81, assoc. prof., 1981—83, chief. pediat. surgery, 1980—83; assoc. prof. U. Calif., Davis, 1983—86, prof., 1986—92, chief pediat. surgery, 1983—92, vice chmn. faculty Sch. Medicine, 1990—91, chmn. faculty Sch. Medicine, 1991—92; prof. surgery and pediat. George Washington Sch. Medicine, 1992—96; surgeon-in-chief, chmn. dept. pediat.surgery Children's Nat. Med. Ctr., Washington, 1992—96; assoc. med. dir. Dupont Hosp. for Children, Wilmington, Del., 1996—2001, vice chmn. dept. surgery, 1996—2003; prof. surgery and pediat. Thomas Jefferson U., 1996—, vice chmn. dept. surgery, 1996—2003, sr. scholar dept. health policy, 2005—; mem. staff St. Christopher Hosp. for Children, Phila., 2004—06, surgeon-in-chief, chief divsn. pediat. surgery, 2006—; prof. surgery and pediat. Drexel U. Sch. Medicine, Phila., 2004—; bd. dirs. Phila. Acad. Surgery, 2005—. Bd. dirs. Am. Bd. Surgery, 2003—. Mem. editl. bd. Jour. Pediat. Surgery, 1988—, Jour. ACS, 1999—. Vice chmn. Bd. of Childrens Faculty Assocs., Childrens Nat. Med. Ctr.; bd. dir. Am. Pediat. Surg. Assn., 2001—04; pres. bd. dir. Sacramento Children's Hosp. Found., 1990—92; chmn. bd. dir. Delaware Valley Transplant Program, 2000—02; bd. dirs. Gift of Life, 2005—. Recipient Basil O'Connor Rsch. award March of Dimes Found., 1981, Young Investigator award NIH, 1982, Found. for Children Rsch. award, 1982, James W. McLaughlin award U. Tex., 1983, ASPEN-Rhodes Rsch. award, 1999, Rsch. award Am. Colon and Rectal Surg. Assn., 2000. Fellow: ACS (chmn. adv. coun. pediat. surgery 2004—, chmn. adv. coun. chairs 2005—); mem.: Internat. Soc. Surgery (exec. com. 2004—), Pacific Assn. Pediat. Surgeons (pres. 1997—98), Soc. Surgery Alimentary Tract, Am. Pediat. Surg. Assn. (bd. govs. 2001—04), Soc. Univ. Surgeons, Am. Surg. Assn. Jewish. Avocations: photography, fishing, woodworking. Office: St Christopher Hosp for Children Erie Ave at Front St Philadelphia PA 19134 Office Phone: 215-427-5446. Personal E-mail: mzschwartz@msn.com. Business E-Mail: marshall.schwartz@tenethealth.com.

SCHWARTZ, MARVIN, lawyer; b. Phila., Nov. 3, 1922; s. Abe and Freda (Newman) S.; m. Joyce Ellen Sidner, Sept. 7, 1947; children: Daniel Bruce, Pamela Louise Pier. LL.B., U. Pa., 1949. Bar: Pa. 1950, N.Y. 1951, D.C. 1955. Law sec. to judge U.S. Ct. Appeals, 3d Circuit, Phila., 1949-50; law sec. to Justice Burton U.S. Supreme Ct., Washington, 1950-51; assoc. Sullivan & Cromwell, NYC, 1951-60, ptnr., 1960-92, sr. counsel, 1993—. Mediator U.S. Dist. (so. dist.) N.Y., N.Y. Supreme Ct. Comml. Divsn.; arbitrator Am. Arbitration Assn., N.Y. Stock Exch., Nat. Assn. Securities Dealers. Spl. master appellate divsn. 1st dept. Supreme Ct. N.Y.; chmn. Zoning Bd. of Adjustment, Alpine, N.J., 1966-74; mem. Planning Bd., Alpine, 1966-67; bd. overseers emeritus U. Pa. Law Sch.; bd. dirs. Conn. Cmty. Found. With Signal Corps U.S. Army, 1943-46. Mem. ABA, N.Y. Bar Assn., D.C. Bar Assn., Am. Coll. Trial Lawyers (sec. 1986-88, bd. regents 1981-86, chmn. Downstate N.Y. com. 1976-78), Am. Law Inst. (adviser complex litigation project), Univ. Club (N.Y.C.), Litchfield (Conn.) Country Club. Democrat. Jewish. Office: Sullivan & Cromwell 125 Broad St Fl 28 New York NY 10004-2489 Personal E-mail: mvnsch@aol.com.

SCHWARTZ, MATTHEW BARAHAL, historian; b. Detroit, Mich., Aug. 3, 1945; s. William and Pauline Schwartz; m. Nehama Nussbaum, Nov. 16, 1975; children: Margalit Gottlieb, Avigail, Asher. PhD, Wayne State U., Detroit, 1975; BHL in Rabbinics, Yeshivah Gedolah, Oak Park, Mich., 1977. Adj. Wayne State U., Detroit, Mich., 1976—, Ctrl. Mich. U., Mich., 1998—. Cons. Holocaust Meml. Ctr., Farmington Hills, Mich., 2004—. Author: (history book) Roman Letters:History from a Personal Point of View, 1991, (book) A Psychology of Hope: An Antidote to the Suicidal Pathology of the Western Civilization, 1993; author: (editor) Jewish Approaches to Suicide, Martyrdom and Euthanasia, 1998; author: Biblical Stories For Psychotherapy and Counseling, 2004, The Seven Habits of the Good Life, 2006, Greek and Biblical Families; contbr. articles to profl. jours. Mem.: Assn. for Jewish Studies, Assn. of Ancient Historians. Office: Wayne State Univ Hist Dep't Detroit MI 48202 Personal E-mail: ad7943@wayne.edu.

SCHWARTZ, MAX J., lawyer; b. NYC, 1949; BA, Institut d'Etudes Politiques, Paris, 1970; JD, Univ. Mich., 1973. Bar: NY 1975. Ptnr. exec. compensation and benefits practice group Sullivan & Cromwell, NYC. Editl. adv. bd. Jour. of Pension Planning and Compliance. Mem.: ABA (tax section, former chair, exec. compensation subcom. of employee benefits com.), Practising Law Inst. (employee benefits adv. com.), NY State Bar Assn. (exec. com. of section of taxation). Office: Sullivan & Cromwell LLP 125 Broad St New York NY 10004-2498 Office Phone: 212-558-4000. Office Fax: 212-558-3588.

SCHWARTZ, MICHAEL ROBINSON, management consultant; b. St. Louis, Mar. 18, 1940; s. Henry G. and Edith C. (Robinson) Schwartz; m. Kathleen Nowicki, Dec. 9, 1989; children from previous marriage: Christine, Richard. AB, Dartmouth Coll., 1962; MHA, U. Minn., 1964. Asst. in adminstrn. Shands Tchg. Hosp., Gainesville, Fla., 1966-67, asst. dir., 1967-68, assoc. dir., 1968-73; assoc. adminstr. St. Joseph Mercy Hosp., Pontiac, Mich., 1973-76, pres., 1976-85; exec. v.p. Mercy Health Svcs., Farmington Hills, Mich., 1985-96, COO, 1988-96; exec. v.p. Ea. Mich. region Sisters of Mercy Health Corp., 1991-92; pvt. practice Birmingham, Mich., 1996—2004, 2007—; dir. provider rels. Blue Cross Blue Shield of Mich., 2003—04, v.p. contracting, 2004—05, sr. v.p. network rels. contracting, pharmacy Mich., 2005—07. Non-resident lectr. U. Mich., 1982—93; cons. prof. Oakland U., 1980—88; asst. prof. hosp. adminstrn. U. Fla., 1967—73; pres. Eastern Mich. Regional Bd. Sisters of Mercy Health Corp., 1976—79; v.p. Lourdes Nursing Home, 1981—84, United Way-Pontiac/North Oakland, 1982—84; treas. Oakland Health Edn. Program, 1978—79; bd. dirs. Blue Cross/Blue Shield of Mich., 1982—86, coms., 1978—86, chair hosp. contingent to participating hosp. agreement adv. com., 1989—96; bd. dirs. Vis. Nurse Assn., Inc., 1997—2005, treas., 1998—2004, vice chair, 1999—2000, chair, 2000—02; chmn. bd. dirs., pres. Accord Ins. Co. Ltd., 1983—88; chmn. bd. dirs. Mercy Health Plans, 1986—96, Venzke Svc. Co., 1983—88, pres., 1983—84; chmn. bd. dirs., pres. Venzke Ins. Co. Ltd., 1988—96; mem. audit and fin. com. Am. Healthcare Sys., 1988—92; mem. S.E. Mich. Hosp. Coun., chmn. pub. rels. com., 1983—85; mem. Commonfund Healthcare Coun., 1999—2005, U. Detroit Mercy Health Professions Adv. Bd., 2002—07; trustee Sisters of Mercy Health Corp., 1991—93, sec. bd. trustees, 1993; bd. dirs. Hosp. Fund, 1986—96, Visiting Nurse Svc. Corp., 2007—, DenteMax, 2007—. Mem. charitable trust Sisters of Mercy, Regional Cmty. Detroit, 1999—2004. With US Army, 1964—66. Fellow: Am. Coll. Healthcare Execs. (life; mem. exec. com. higher edn. 1990—93, Mich. Regent's award 1992); mem.: Comprehensive Health Planning Coun. (com. mem. 1976—81), Am. Healthcare Sys. Risk Retention Group (bd. dirs. 1990—91), Mich. Hosp. Assn. (at-large rep. corp. bd. 1990—96, exec. com. 1992—96), Pontiac Urban League (pres. com. 1979). Office Phone: 313-378-8400. Business E-Mail: mschwartzbham@aol.com.

SCHWARTZ, MISCHA, electrical engineering educator; b. NYC, Sept. 21, 1926; s. Isaiah and Bessie (Weinstein) S.; m. Lillian Mitchnick, June 23, 1957 (div.); 1 son, David; m. Charlotte F. Berney, July 12, 1970. B.E.E., Cooper Union, 1947; M.E.E., Poly. Inst. Bklyn., 1949; PhD in Applied Physics (Sperry Gyroscope grad. scholar), Harvard U., 1951. Project engr. Sperry Gyroscope Co., 1947-52; mem. faculty Poly. Inst. Bklyn., 1952-74, prof. elec. engring., 1959-74, head dept., 1961-65; prof. elec. engring. and computer sci. Columbia U., NYC, 1974-88, Charles Batchelor prof. elec. engring., 1988-96, Charles Batchelor prof. emeritus, 1996—, dir. Ctr. for Telecommunications Research, 1985-88. Part-time tchr. Adelphi Coll., 1951-52, CCNY, 1952; cons. radiation physicist Montefiore Hosp., N.Y.C., 1954-56; vis. prof. sys. sci. dept. UCLA, 1964; vis. prof. dept. elec. engring. and computer sci. Columbia U., 1973-74; vis. prof. dept. electronic and elec. engring. U. Coll., London, 1995; vis. prof. dept. elec. and computer engring. U. Calif., San Diego, 1997; chmn. Commn. C, U.S. Nat. Com. Internat. Union Radio Sci., 1977-80; vis. scientist IBM Rsch., 1980, 94, NYNEX Sci. and Tech., 1986; vis. mem. tech. staff AT&T Bell Labs., 1995; cons. in field. Author: Information Transmission, Modulation and Noise, 4th edit., 1990, (with L. Shaw) Signal Processing, 1975, Computer Communication Network Design and Analysis, 1977, Telecommunications Networks, 1987, Broadband Integrated Networks, 1996; editor, contbr.: Communication Systems and Techniques, 1966, reissued, 1995; Mobile Wireless Comm., 2005. Trustee Gt. Neck Libr., 1997-2001, pres., 1998, 99. With US Army, 1944—46, with AUS, 1944—46. NSF sci. faculty fellow, 1965-66; recipient Disting. Vis. award Australian-Am. Ednl. Found., 1975, Vis. Scientist award Nippon Tel. & Tel., 1981, Tchg. award Columbia U., 1984, Gano Dunn award Cooper Union, 1986, Mayor's award for excellence in tech., City of N.Y., 1995; finalist Mayor's Awards for Excellence in Sci. & Tech., City of N.Y., 1992, recipient Okawa award for contbns. comm., computer networks, engring. edn., 2003. Fellow AAAS, IEEE (chmn. adminstrv. com. profl. group info. theory 1964-65, bd. dirs. 1978-79, bd. govs. Comm. Soc. 1973-79, v.p. 1982-83, pres. 1984-85, Edn. medal 1983, IEEE Centennial Hall of Fame 1984, Region 1 award for leadership in mgmt. Ctr. for Telecom. Rsch. 1990, Edwin Armstrong award for contbns. to telecomm. 1994, Millennium medal 2000); mem. NAE, AAUP (chpt. pres. 1970-72), Soc. History Tech., Tau Beta Pi, Eta Kappa Nu (eminent mem. 1999). Home: 66 Maple Dr Great Neck NY 11021-1928 Office: Columbia U Schapiro CEPSR Rm 806 New York NY 10027 Home Phone: 516-466-6076; Office Phone: 212-854-3125. Personal E-mail: mcschw66@aol.com. Business E-Mail: schwartz@ctr.columbia.edu.

SCHWARTZ, NEENA BETTY, endocrinologist, educator; b. Balt., Dec. 10, 1926; d. Paul Howard and Pauline (Shulman) S. AB, Goucher Coll., 1948, DSc (hon.), 1982; MS, Northwestern U., 1950, PhD, 1953. From instr. to prof. U. Ill. Coll. Medicine, Chgo., 1953—72, asst. dean for faculty, 1968—70; prof. physiology Northwestern U. Med. Sch., Chgo., 1973—74; Deering prof. Northwestern U., Evanston, Ill., 1974—99, chmn. dept. biol. scis., 1974-78, acting dean, Coll. Arts and Scis., 1996-97, prof. emeritus, 2000—. Contbr. articles to profl. jours., chapters to books. NIH rsch. grantee, 1955—. Fellow: AAAS (exec. bd. 1998—2002, Lifetime Mentor award 2003); mem.: Soc. for Neurosci., Am. Physiol. Soc., Soc. for Study of Reproduction (dir. 1975—77, exec. v.p. 1976—77, pres. 1977—78, Carl Hartman award 1992), Endocrine Soc. (v.p. 1970—71, mem. coun. 1979—83, pres. 1982—83, Williams award 1985, Disting. Educator award 1998), Am. Acad. Arts and Scis. Home: 1511 Lincoln St Evanston IL 60201-2338 Office Phone: 847-491-5529. Business E-Mail: n-schwartz@northwestern.edu.

SCHWARTZ, NORTON A., career military officer; B in Polit. Sci. and Internat. Affairs, USAF Acad., Colorado, 1973; grad., Squadron Officer Sch., Alabama, 1977; MBA, Cen. Mich. U., 1983; grad., Armed Forces Staff Coll., Virginia, 1984, Nat. War Coll., Washington, DC, 1989; seminar fellow, Mass Inst of Tech, 1994. Commd. 2d lt. USAF, 1973, advanced through grades to gen., 2005, C-130E aircraft comdr. 776th & 21st tactical airlift squadrons Clark AFB, Philippines, 1975—77, C-130E/H flight examiner 61st Tactical Airlift Squadron Little Rock AFB, Ark., 1977—79, intern Air Staff Training Program, Office of the Dep. Chief of Staff for Plans, Ops, & Readiness, USAF Hdqs., 1979—80, MC-130E flight examiner, 8th Spl. ops. Squadron Hurlburt Field, Fla., 1980—83; action officer Directorate of Plans Hdqs. USAF, Office of Dep. Chief of Staff Plans & Ops., Washington, 1984-86; comdr. 36th Tactical Airlift Squadron, McChord AFB, Wash., 1986-88; dir. plans & policy Spl. Ops. Command Europe, Stuttgart-Vaihingen, Germany, 1989-91; dep. comdr. for ops., comdr. 1st Spl. Ops. Group, Hurlburt Field, Fla., 1991-93; dep. dir. ops., dep. dir. forces Office Dep. Chief of Staff for Plans and Ops., Hdqs. USAF, Washington, 1993-95; comdr. 16th Spl. Ops. Wing, Hurlburt Field, Fla., 1995-97, Spl. Ops. Command, Pacific, Camp H.M. Smith, Hawaii, 1997-98; dir. strategic planning Dep. Chief of Staff for Plans & Programs, Hdqs. USAF, Washington, 1998—2000; dep. comdr. in chief US Spl. Ops. Command, USAF, MacDill AFB, Fla., 2000; comdr. Alaskan Command, Alaskan N. Am. Def. Command Region & 11th Air Force, Elmendorf AFB, 2000—02; dir. ops. The Joint Staff, The Pentagon, Washington, 2002—04, dir., 2004—05; comdr. US Transp. Command, Scott AFB, Ill., 2005—. Decorated Def. Superior Svc. medal with oak leaf cluster, Def. Disting. Svc. medal, Disting. Svc. medal, Legion of Merit with two oak leaf clusters, Def. Meritorious Svc. medal, Meritorious Svc. medal with two oak leaf clusters, Air Force Commendation medal with oak leaf cluster, Army Commendation medal; Seminar XXI fellow MIT, 1994. Office: 300 Joint Staff The Pentagon Washington DC 20318 *

SCHWARTZ, PAUL D., lawyer; b. Cleve., Jan. 31, 1951; m. Daphne Bement Petri; children: Natalie Petri, Rebecca Elizabeth. BA magna cum laude, Conn. Coll., 1973; MArch, MIT, 1976; JD magna cum laude, Harvard U., 1978. Bar: Mass. Clk. to Hon. Lewis F. Oberdorfer U.S. Dist. Ct., Washington, 1978; assoc. Ropes & Gray, Boston, 1978-83, Goodwin, Procter & Hoar, Boston, 1983-87, ptnr., 1987, Goodwin, Procter, Boston. Named Am Leading Lawyers for Bus., Chambers USA, The Best Lawyers in Am. Mem.: Greater Boston Chpt. of Real Estate Fin. Assn., MIT Ctr. for Real Estate, Pension Real Estate Assn. Office: Goodwin Procter Exchange Pl 53 State St Boston MA 02109-2803 Office Phone: 617-570-1422. Business E-Mail: pschwartz@goodwinprocter.com.

SCHWARTZ, PEPPER JUDITH, sociologist, educator; b. Chgo., May 11, 1945; d. Julius J. and Gertrude (Puris) Schwartz; m. John A. Strait, June 19, 1971; m. Arthur M. Skolnick, Jan. 9, 1982 (div. 2001); children: Cooper, Ryder. BA, Washington U., St. Louis, 1968, MA, 1970; M in Philosophy, Yale U., 1972, PhD, 1974. Assoc. prof. sociology, adj. assoc. prof., 1972—88; prof. psychiatry and behavioral sci. U. Wash., Seattle, 1988—. Chmn. rev. com. NIMH; bd. dirs. Women's Rsch. Ctr.; frequent guest and host local and network TV shows; appt. to Pres. Reagan's ad hoc adv. roundtable on the family, 1984; expert appearance in NBC Sacred Sexless, 1987, Some Thoughts on Being Single, 1984, ABC After The Sexual Revolution, 1986; relationship expert LifetimeTV.com, 1998—, PerfectMatch.com, 2003—. Author: Women at Yale, 1976; author: (with Judith Laws et al) Sexual Scripts, 1977; author: (with P. Blumstein) American Couples, 1983; author: (with V. Rutter) The Gender of Sexuality, 1995; author: (with D. Cappello) Ten Talks Parents Must Have with their Children About Sex and Character, 2002; author: Everything You Know About Love & Sex is Wrong, 2002, Lifetime Book of Love & Sex Quizzes, 2003, Finding Your Perfect Match, 2006; contbr. numerous articles to mags. and jours.; profiles in Savvy, Ladies Home Jour., Playboy, Cosmopolitan, NY Times, Newsweek, others, articles on work in Time, Redbook, New West, American Baby Mag., others; co-author, editor: A Student's Guide to Sex on Campus, 1971. Guardian Ad-Litem Program; bd. dirs. Empty Space Theater, Seattle, pres., 1980; past mem. Gov.'s Commn. Venereal Disease; mem. Presdl. Adv. Rountable on Family, 1984; bd. dirs. Nat. Abortion Rights Action League, Anti-Defamation League, ACLU; nat. bd. dirs. YWCA, Jewish Family Svc. Named Oustanding Young Woman of the Future, Time-Life mag., 1978; named one of Most Powerful People of the 1980s, Next mag., 1981. Fellow: Internat. Acad. Sex Rsch.; mem.: Lluminari Women's Expert Health Network, Nat. Conf. Family Relations, Am. Sociol. Assn. (chairperson com. on coms., Outstanding Contbn. Pub. Understanding Sociology 2005), Soc. for Sci. Study of Sexuality (pres. 1998—), Pacific Sociol. Assn. (mem. coun., pres. 2004—), Yale Club (N.Y.C.), The Diet Club. Office: Dept Sociology Dk 40 U Seattle WA 98195-0001 Home Phone: 425-888-6273; Office Phone: 206-543-4036. E-mail: pepperschwartz@hotmail.com.

SCHWARTZ, PHILIP, lawyer; b. June 7, 1930; s. Louis and Kate (Brodsky) S.; m. Iris M. Ballin, Nov. 28, 1953 (div. 1979); children: David, Elyse, Donna; m. Monique W. Wagner, July 26, 1982 (div. 1991); m. Carol J. Pruett, Aug. 14, 1992. BA, George Washington U., 1952, JD, 1959; LLM in Taxation, Georgetown U., 1961; postgrad., U. Paris, London Sch. Econs., Harvard U. Bar: Va. 1959, D.C. 1966, U.S. Tax Ct. 1966, U.S. Ct. Appeals (D.C. cir.) 1966, U.S. Ct. Mil. Appeals 1966, U.S. Supreme Ct. 1966, U.S. Ct. Appeals (4th cir.) 1982, U.S. Ct. Internat. Trade 1988, N.Am. Coun. London Ct. Internat. Arbitration 1988; diplomate Am. Coll. Family Law Trial Lawyers; fellow Am. Acad. Matrimonial Lawyers, Internat. Acad. Matrimonial Lawyers. Sr. intelligence analyst Nat. Security Agy., Washington, 1952-54, 56-63; assoc. Varoutsos, Koutoulakos & Arthur, Arlington, Va., 1963—68; ptnr. Schwartz & Ellis, Ltd., Arlington, 1968—2002, Schwartz & Assocs., LLC, 2002—. Instr. No. Va. Life Underwriters Tng. Coun., 1974, No. Va. Paralegal Inst., Arlington, 1976; moot ct. judge George Washington U., Washington, Georgetown U., Washington, Jessup Internat. Law Competition; commr. Chancery Arlington Cir. Ct., judge Pro Tempo; spkr. in field. Contbr. articles to profl. jours. Mem. U.S. Sec. of State Adv. Com. on Pvt. Internat. Law; mem. Arlington County Bd. Zoning Appeals, 1972-85, Arlington County Coun. Human Rels., 1973; del. to Hague Conf. Pvt. Internat. Law; bd. dirs. Jewish Cmty. Ctr. Greater Washington, 1975. With M.I., U.S. Army, 1954-56. Master Barrister Am. Inns of Ct.; Diplomate Am. Coll. of Family Law Trial Lawyers; fellow Internat. Acad. Matrimonial Lawyers (pres. 1996-97), Am. Acad. Matrimonial Lawyers (bd. govs., v.p.); mem. ABA (chmn. family law sect. com. internat. laws 1983-86, chmn. internat. law sect. com. enforcement fgn. judgments), Internat. Bar Assn. (chmn. family law divsn. 1988-92, governing coun. gen. practice sect., liaison officer to IMF, Lifetime Achievement award 2007), Am. Coll. Family Trial Layers (diplomate), Va. Trial Lawyers Assn. (instr. 1984), Assn. Trial Lawyers Am. (vice chmn. internat. practice sect.), Va. State Bar (bd. govs. internat. law sect., liaison to ABA internat. law sect., spl. com. reducing litigation delay and costs, com. on bench/bar rels.), Calif. Bar Assn. (internat. law sect.), NY State Bar Assn. (internat. law, family law sect.), DC Bar (internat. law, family law sect.), Arlington County Bar Assn. (cts. com., legis. com., jud. selection com.), Fairfax County Bar Assn. (family law and internat. law sects.), Brit. Inst. Internat. and Comparative Law, Am. Soc. Internat. Law, Union Internat. des Avocats, Inter-Am. Bar Assn., Internat. Soc. Family Law, Solicitors Family Law Assn. Eng. and Wales, Soc. English and Am. Lawyers, Am. Fgn. Law Assn., Internat. Law Assn., Asia-Pacific Lawyers Assn., Arlington Jaycees, Kiwanis, Phi Epsilon Pi, Delta Phi Epsilon, Phi Delta Phi. Office: Schwartz & Assocs LLC Ste 101 8221 Old Courthouse Rd Vienna VA 22182-3839 Office Phone: 703-883-8035. Business E-Mail: pschwartz@maddoxlawoffice.com.

SCHWARTZ, RENEE GERSTLER, lawyer; b. Bklyn., June 18, 1933; d. Samuel and Lillian (Neulander) Gerstler; m. Alfred L. Schwartz, July 30, 1955; children: Carolyn Susan, Deborah Jane. AB, Bklyn. Coll., 1953; LLB, Columbia U., 1955. Bar: N.Y. 1956, U.S. Dist. Ct. (so. and ea. dists.) N.Y. 1956, U.S. Ct. Appeals (2d cir.) 1956, U.S. Dist. Ct. D.C. 1983, U.S. Supreme Ct. 1986. Assoc. Botein, Hays & Sklar, NYC, 1955-64, ptnr., 1965-89, Cooley Godward Kronish (formerly Kronish, Lieb, Weiner & Hellman), NYC, 1990—. Bd. dirs. New Land Found., N.Y.C., 1965—. Mem. Bar Assn. City of N.Y. Home: 115 Central Park W New York NY 10023-4153 Office: Cooley Godward Kronish 1114 Avenue Of The Americas New York NY 10036-7703 Home Phone: 212-874-6937; Office Phone: 212-479-6040. Business E-Mail: rschwartz@cooley.com.

SCHWARTZ, RICHARD, retired lawyer; b. NYC, Jan. 18, 1933; s. Alexander and Frances (Wexler) S. AB, Harvard U., 1954; JD, Columbia U., 1959. Bar: N.Y. 1959, Pa. 1986, Conn. 1990, U.S. Tax Ct. 1963, U.S. Dist. Ct. (so. and ea. dists.) N.Y. 1976, U.S. Ct. Appeals (2d cir.) 1976. Asst. atty. gen. State of N.Y., NYC, 1960-63; atty. James Talcott, Inc., NYC, 1963-64; sr. atty. GE, NYC, 1964-70; staff v.p. corp. law Sperry Corp., NYC, 1970-86, UNISYS Corp., Blue Bell, Pa., 1986-87; sr. v.p., sec., gen. counsel Financing for Sci. Internat., Inc., Farmington, Conn., 1988-97. Arbitrator Pa. Ct. Common Pleas, Norristown, 1987-88. Editor: Legal Aspects of Doing Business in the EEC, 1978; asst. editor in chief The Internat. Lawyer, 1979-82; author book revs.; contbr. articles to profl. jours. 1st lt. USAF, 1955-57. Mem. Hartford County Bar Assn., Assn. of the Bar of the City N.Y. Avocations: walking, stationary bicycling. Home and Office: 3106 La Mancha Way Henderson NV 89014-3684

SCHWARTZ, RICHARD BRENTON, English language educator, dean, writer; b. Cin., Oct. 5, 1941; s. Jack Jay and Marie Mildred (Schnelle) S.; m. Judith Mary Alexis Lang, Sept. 7, 1963; 1 son, Jonathan Francis. AB cum laude, U. Notre Dame, 1963; AM, U. Ill., 1964, PhD, 1967. Instr. English, U.S. Mil. Acad., 1967-69; asst. prof. U. Wis.-Madison, 1969-72, assoc. prof., 1972-78, prof., 1978-81, assoc. dean Grad. Sch., 1977, 79-81; prof. English, dean Grad. Sch., Georgetown U., Washington, 1981-98, interim exec. v.p. for main campus academic affairs, 1991-92; interim exec. v.p. for the main campus Georgetown U., Washington, 1995-96; dean Coll. Arts and Sci. U. Mo., Columbia, 1998—2006, prof. English, 1998—. Mem. exec. bd. Ctr. Strategic and Internat. Studies, 1981-87. Author: Samuel Johnson and the New Science, 1971 (runner-up Gustave O. Arlt prize), Samuel Johnson and the Problem of Evil, 1975, Boswell's Johnson: A Preface to the Life, 1978, Daily Life in Johnson's London, 1983, Japanese edit., 1990, After the Death of Literature, 1997, Nice and Noir: Contemporary American Crime Fiction, 2002, (novels) Frozen Stare, 1989, The Last Voice You Hear, 2001, After the Fall, 2002, Into the Dark, 2002 (hon. mention genre fiction Writer's Digest); short stories, The Biggest City in America, 1999 (Choice Mag. citation); editor: The Plays of Arthur Murphy, 4 vols., 1979, Theory and Tradition in Eighteenth-Century Studies, 1990; contbr. articles to profl. jours. Served to capt. U.S. Army, 1967-69. Decorated Army Commendation medal; recipient Presdl. medal Georgetown U., 1998; Disting. Svc. award, U. Mo. Columbia, Coll. Arts and Sci., 2007; Nat. Endowment Humanities grantee, 1970, 87; Inst. for Research in Humanities fellow, 1976; Am. Council Learned Socs. fellow, 1978-79; H.I. Romnes fellow, 1978-81. Mem. Mystery Writers Am., Johnson Soc. So. Calif., Johnson Soc. of London, Am. Soc. Eighteenth-Century Studies, Coun. Grad. Schs., N.E. Assn. Grad. Schs. (exec. com. 1986-88), Assn. Grad. Schs. in Cath. Univs. (exec. com. 1984-87), Assn. Literary Scholars and Critics, Nat. Assn. Scholars, N.Am. Conf. Brit. Studies, Jefferson Club, Mosaic Soc., Eliot Soc., Alpha Sigma Nu, Alpha Sigma Lambda. Roman Catholic. Home: 5800 Highlands Pkwy Columbia MO 65203-5125 Office: U Mo Dept English 236 Tate Hall Columbia MO 65211-6080 Home Phone: 573-442-2242; Office Phone: 573-884-7038. Business E-Mail: schwartzrb@missouri.edu.

SCHWARTZ, RICHARD EDWARD DERECKTOR, retired sociologist, educator; b. Newark, Apr. 26, 1925; s. Selig and Tillie (Derecktor) S.; m. Emilie Zane Rosenbaum, June 30, 1946; children: David, Margaret Jane, Deborah. BA, Yale U., 1947, PhD in Sociology, 1952. Rsch. fellow Inst. Human Rels., Yale U., 1951—54, instr., asst. prof. sociology and law, 1953—61; faculty Northwestern U., Evanston, Ill., 1961—71, prof. sociology, 1964—71, prof. sociology and law, 1966—71; dir. Coun. Intersocietal Studies, 1965—70, co-dir. law and social sci. program, 1967—70; dean, provost Faculty of Law and Jurisprudence, SUNY Buffalo, 1971—76; Ernest I. White rsch. prof. law Syracuse U., 1977—2004, Ernest I. White prof. emeritus, 2004—. Mem. com. law enforcement and adminstrn. justice NAS, 1975-85; fellowship referee Russell Sage Found., 1970-77, NEH, 1972-77, NSF, 1978-81; exec. dir. NESCO, 1995-2001; sr. rsch. scholar Yale Law Sch., 2002-04, 2006—. Author: (with others) Society and the Legal Order, 1970, Criminal Law, 1974, Handbook of Regulation and Administrative Law, 1994, Unobtrusive Measures, 2000; founding editor: Law and Soc. Rev., 1966-69. With USNR, 1943—45. Ctr. for Advanced Study in Behavioral Scis. fellow, 1989—90. Fellow AAAS, Am. Acad. Polit. and Social Sci.; mem. Am. Sociol. Assn. (Disting. Career award 2006), Law and Soc. Assn. (pres. 1972-75) Jewish. Home: 40 Beach Ave Milford CT 06460-8154 Home Phone: 203-874-4586; Office Phone: 203-874-4586. Personal E-mail: emnred@aol.com. *I believe that we could create a better way of life if we structured society to encourage-rather than to penalize-altruism. Although I have not yet contributed much toward achieving such a society, the effort to do so has been satisfying.*

SCHWARTZ, RICHARD EVAN, mathematician, educator; b. Aug. 11, 1966; BS in Math., UCLA, 1987; PhD in Math., Princeton U., 1991. Postdoctoral staff CUNY, IHES, MSRI, 1992—93; asst. prof. U. Chgo., 1996; assoc. prof. U. Md., 1997—2000, prof., 2000—04, Ruth Davis Prof., 2004—05; prof. Brown U., 2005—. Contbr. articles to profl. jours. Fellow, John Simon Guggenheim Meml. Found., 2003; grantee, NSF, 1998—; grad. fellow, 1988—90, postdoctoral fellow, 1993—95, Sloan Dissertation fellow, 1990—91, Sloan Rsch. fellow, 1996—99. Office: Dept Math Brown Univ Providence RI 02912

SCHWARTZ, RICHARD HARVEY, pediatrician; b. Bklyn., July 6, 1938; s. Hy and Ruth (Marshak) S.; m. Rose Lynne Hass, May 29, 1960; children: Lisa, Keith, Keira. BA, George Washington U., 1960; MD, Georgetown U., 1965. Diplomate Am. Bd. Pediat., Am. Soc. Addiction Medicine. Intern U.S. Army, 1965-66, resident in pediat., 1969-71; pvt. practice, Vienna, Va., 1972—. Contbr. articles to profl. jours. Maj. U.S. Army, 1965-69. Mem. AMA (Outstanding Contbn. in Adolescent Medicine award 1990), Am. Acad. Pediatrics (rsch. award 1989). Jewish. Avocations: walking, travel. Office: Advanced Pediatrics 100 East St SE Ste 301 Vienna VA 22180

SCHWARTZ, RICHARD JOHN, electrical engineering educator, researcher; b. Waukesha, Wis., Aug. 12, 1935; s. Sylvester John and LaVerne Mary (Lepien) S.; m. Mary Jo Collins, June 29, 1957; children: Richard, Stephen, Susan, Elizabeth, Barbara, Peter, Christopher, Margaret. BSEE, U. Wis., 1957; SM, MIT, 1959, ScD, 1962. Mem. tech. staff Sarnoff Rsch. Labs. RCA, Princeton, NJ, 1957-58; instr. MIT, Cambridge, 1961-62; v.p. Energy Conversions, Inc., Cambridge, 1962-64; assoc. prof. Purdue U., West Lafayette, Ind., 1964-71, prof., 1972—, head dept., 1985-95, dean engring., 1995—2001, dir. Optoelectronic Ctr., 1986-89. Co-dir. Nano Tech. Ctr. Purdue U., W. Lafayette, Ind., 2001—06; cons. solar cells, 1965—. Contbr. chpts. to books, articles to profl. jours. Served to 2nd lt. U.S. Army, 1957-58. Recipient Disting. Svc. medal U. Wis., 1989, Centennial medal, 1991. Fellow: IEEE (William R. Cherry award 1998), Internat. Electronics Con.; mem.: Nat. Elec. Engring. Dept. Heads Assn. (bd. dirs.). Achievements include development of high intensity solar cells, of surface charge transfer device, and of numerical models for solar cells. Office: Purdue U 1285 Electrical Engring West Lafayette IN 47907 Office Phone: 765-494-0619.

SCHWARTZ, ROBERT, finance educator; b. NYC, Feb. 12, 1937; s. Fred J. Schwartz and Shirley Liebowitz; m. Jody Silver Schwartz; 1 child, Emily. BA, NYU, 1959; MBA, Columbia U., NYC, 1962, PhD, 1966. Asst. prof. econs. NYU, 1965—70, assoc. prof. econs., 1970—77, prof. econs., 1977—83, prof. econs. and fin., 1983—91; prof. econs. and fin., Yamaichi Faculty fellow Stern Sch. Bus., NYU, 1991—97; Speiser prof. fin., Univ. Disting. prof. Zicklin Sch. Bus. Baruch Coll., CUNY, 1997—. Chmn. econ. adv. bd. NASDAQ, 1995—97, mem. econ. adv. bd., 1997—99. Author (with Kalman J. Cohen, Steven F. Maier and David K. Whitcomb): The Microstructure of Securities Markets, 1986; author: Equity Markets: Structure, Trading and Performance, 1988, Reshaping the Equity Markets: A Guide for the 1990s, 1991, reissue, 1993; author: (with R. Francioni) Equity Markets in Action, 2004; author: (with R. Francioni and B. Weber) The Equity Trader Course, 2006; editor (with Ernest Bloch): Impending Changes for Securities Markets: What Role for the Exchanges?, 1979; editor: (with Yakov Amihud and Thomas Ho) Market Making and the Changing Structure of the Securities Industry, 1985; editor: (with Henry Lucas) The Challenge of Information Technology for the Securities Markets: Liquidity, Volatility and Global Trading, 1989; editor: Global Equity Markets: Technological, Competetive and Regulatory Challenges, 1995, The Electronic Call Auction: Market Mechanism and Trading, Building a Better Stock Market, 2001; editor: (with Antoinette Colaninno) Regulation of U.S. Equity Markets, 2001; editor: (with John A. Byrne and Antoinette Colaninno) Call Auction Trading: New Answers to Old Questions, 2003; editor: A Trading Desk's View of Market Quality, 2004, Coping with Institutional Order Flow, 2004; editor: (with John A. Byrne and Antoinette Colaninno) Electronic vs. Floor Based Trading, 2006; assoc. editor Jour. Fin., 1983—88, Rev. Quantitative Fin. and Acctg., Rev. Pacific Basin Fin. Markets and Policies, Jour. Entrepreneurial Fin. and Bus. Ventures, mem. adv. bd. Internat. Fin.; contbr. articles to profl. jours. Mem.: Am. Fin. Assn. Office: Baruch Coll CUNY One Bernard Baruch Way Box B10-225 New York NY 10010

SCHWARTZ, ROBERT GEORGE, retired insurance company executive; b. Czechoslovakia, Mar. 27, 1928; came to U.S., 1929, naturalized, 1935; s. George and Frances (Antoni) S.; m. Caroline Bachurski, Oct. 12, 1952; children: Joanne, Tracy, Robert G. BA, Pa. State U., 1949; MBA, NYU, 1956. With Met. Life Ins. Co., NYC, 1949-93, v.p. securities, 1962-70, v.p., 1970-75, sr. v.p., 1975-78, exec. v.p., 1979-80, vice chmn. bd., 1980-83, chmn. investment com., 1980-93, chmn. bd., 1983-93, chmn. bd., pres., chief exec. officer, 1989-93. Bd. dirs., mem. Horatio Alger Assn. Trustee Com. for Econ. Devel. With US Army, 1950—52. Mem.: Alpha Chi Rho. Office: MetLife Bldg 200 Park Ave 32d Fl New York NY 10166-0005

SCHWARTZ, ROBERT M., lawyer; b. LA, 1959; BS, U. Calif., LA, 1981; JD, U. So. Calif., 1984. Bar: Calif. 1984, US Dist. Ct., Ctrl. Dist. Calif. 1984, US Ct. Appeals, 9th Cir., DC 1987, US Dist. Ct., No. Dist. Calif. 2000, US District Ct., Ea. Dist. Calif. 2001. Litig. ptnr. O'Melveny & Myers LLP, LA, co-chair entertainment and media litig. practice group, mem. class action and appellate practice group. Bd. dir., mem. exec. com. Bet Tzedek- The House of Justice, LA. Mem.: Assn. of Bus. Trial Lawyers, ABA (mem. litig. sect.), LA County Bar Assn., Beverly Hills Bar Assn. (co-chair, entertainment law sect. 1998—99, 1999—2000). Office: O'Melveny & Myers LLP 1999 Avenue of the Stars 7th Fl Los Angeles CA 90067-6035 Office Phone: 310-246-6835. Office Fax: 310-246-6779. Business E-Mail: rschwartz@omm.com.

SCHWARTZ, ROBERT P., lawyer; b. NYC, Mar. 10, 1927; s. Charles C. and May Brandt Schwartz; m. Betty Sue Bottoaff, Dec. 19, 1958 (dec. Oct. 1992); children: James Stewart, John Pelham. BA, Colgate U., Hamilton, NY, 1949; LLB, U. Mich., Ann Arbor, 1952. Law ptnr. Schwartz & Schwartz, NYC, 1952—90; of counsel Wims, Howes, NYC, 1990—2002; ret., 2002. Officer, dir. A&R Recording, Inc., NYC, 1958—86, Alnav Aircraft Corp., NYC, 1958—79. Camping chmn. Boy Scouts Am., Westchester County, NY, 1947—56, dist. chmn. Weston, Conn., 1972—82. Comdr. USNR, 1944—75. Home: 1704 S Lakeshore Dr Lake Village AR 71653-1573

SCHWARTZ, ROBERT TERRY, industrial designer, director; b. Irvington, NJ, Sept. 29, 1950; s. Edward Herman and Harriet Selma (Rosenstein) S.; m. Carol Fawn Mullenix, July 27, 1975; children: Zachary Jacob, Allison Lizabeth. BFA, Kansas City Art Inst., 1973; M of Indsl. Design, R.I. Sch. Design, 1975. Red Cross project dir. R.I. Sch. Design, Providence, 1975-76; head indsl. design/architecture Red Cross Nat. Hdqrs., Washington, 1976-88; dir. sci. and tech. Health Industry Mfrs. Assn., Washington, 1988-90; exec. dir., COO Worldesign Found., Great Falls, Va., 1990-96, Indsl. Designers Soc. Am., Great Falls, 1990-99; dir. indsl. design Motorola, Inc., Ft. Lauderdale, Fla., 1999—2003; v.p. new product devel. Levolor Kirsch, High Point, NC, 2003; assoc. dir. global design orgn. Procter and Gamble, 2003—. Provider expert testimony before Congress, 1994, commencement address, Kansas City Art Inst., 1995; official delegate to Nat. Medal of Arts Ceremonies, 1997-98; official state delegate for Md. and Va., Nat. Arts Advocacy Days, 1997-99; sr. tech. advisor to Peoples Republic of China, UN, 1998; appointed to curriculum adv. bd., Coll. Arts, Carnegie Mellon U., 1999-; vis. assoc. prof. design, U. Cin. Contbr. chpts. to books, articles to profl. jours.; presenter in field; holder 5 patents, 1 trademark. Recipient Project of Merit award Indsl. Design Mag., 1985, Cert. of Achievement, ARC, 1988, Louis C. Tiffany award ARC, 1987, Personal Recognition award, Industrial Designers Soc. Am., 2000, numerous others; Nat. Endowment for the Arts grantee, 1984, 92, 94; EPA grantee, 1992. Mem. Indsl. Designers Soc. Am. (Personal Recognition award 2000). Avocations: edison antiquities collecting, sailing. Office: Procter and Gamble One P&G Plz Cincinnati OH 45202

SCHWARTZ, ROBERT WILLIAM, management consultant; b. NYC, Oct. 23, 1944; s. Edward and Bertha R. S.; m. Gail Beth Greenbaum, Mar. 18, 1967; children: Jill, Evan. BS, Cornell U., 1967; postgrad., SUNY, Albany, 1970. Assoc. IBM, 1967-68; cons. Peat, Marwick, Mitchell & Co., Albany, 1970-71; v.p. Security Gen. Svcs., Inc., Rochester, 1971—77; v.p. fin. and adminstrn. Gardenway Mfg. Co., Troy, NY, 1973-77; pres. United Telecommunications Corp., Latham, 1980-82, also bd. dir.; pres., chmn. Winsource, Inc., Albany, 1982-85, Schwartz Heslin Group, Inc., 1985—. Bd. dirs. Docucon, Inc., San Antonio, State Industries for Disabled, Donnkenny, NY, Daias Analytic Corp., State Zone Capital Corp., Albany, NY, chmn., 2007—; adj. prof. Rochester Inst. Tech., 1971—73, U. Albany, SUNY Albany, 1998—, Union U., 2002—. Bd. dirs. United Cerebral Palsy of Capital Dist., 1973—, NY State Industries for Disabled, 2001-, Albany-Colonie Regional C. of C., 1999-; chair Coun. on Econ. Outreach U. Albany Found., 1998-, chair nanotech. com. Ctr. for Econ. Growth, 2001-04; trustee Newman Found., Rensselaer Poly. Inst., 1974-78, Gov. Clinton coun. Boy Scouts Am., SUNY Found. Mem. Am. Mgmt. Assn., Esarco Internat., N.Am. Tel. Assn., Assn. for Systems Mgmt., Ft. Orange Club, Econ. Club, Corenell Club (N.Y.C.). Republican. Home: 2 Myton Ln Albany NY 12204-1310 Office: 8 Airport Park Blvd Latham NY 12110-1441 Office Phone: 518-786-7733. Business E-Mail: rschwartz@shggroup.com.

SCHWARTZ, ROGER ALAN, judge; b. NYC, May 2, 1945; s. George Martin Ronald and Claire Marie (Dorsch) Schwartz; 1 child, Julia Claire. BA, Muhlenberg Coll., 1967; JD, Temple U., 1973, M in Labor Law, 1976, MPA, 1979; disting. grad., U.S. Army Command and Gen. Staff Coll.; MA in History summa cum laude, U. Scranton, 1997; postgrad., Marywood U., 1997—. Bar: Pa. 1973, N.Y. 1982, D.C. 1976, U.S. Dist. Ct. (ea. dist.) Pa. 1973, U.S. Ct. Appeals (3d cir.) 1976, U.S. Mil. Appeals 1981, U.S. Ct. Appeals (Fed cir.) 1986, U.S. Supreme Ct. 1976. Personnel mgmt. specialist CSC, Phila., 1973-74, asst. appeals officer, 1974-78; sr. adminstrv. judge U.S. Merit Systems Protection Bd., Phila., 1979-89; adminstrv. law judge Social Security Adminstrn., Wilkes-Barre, Pa., 1989—. Arbitrator Phila. Ct. Common Pleas, 1973—89; asst. prof. Inst. for Paralegal Tng., Phila., 1976—77; adj. prof. Keystone Coll., La Plume, Pa. With U.S. Army, 1968-70, Vietnam, Persian Gulf War, 1990; col. JAGC Res., ret. Decorated Legion of Merit, Bronze Star, Purple Heart, Nat. Svc. medal with svc. star, Meritorious Svc. medal with one oak leaf cluster, Meritorious Achievement medal with 1 oak leaf cluster, Army Commendation medal with 4 oak leaf clusters. Mem. ABA, Phila. Bar Assn., Am. Judicature Soc., Am. Arbitration Assn., Res. Officers Assn. (Pa. state sec. 1996-97), Assn. Adminstrv. Law Judges (v.p. region III 2000-06), Rotary (bd. dirs. Wilkes Barre chpt. 1999-2000). Avocations: computers, billiards, piano. Office: Social Security Adminstrn Office Disability Adj and Rev 7 N Wilkes Barre Blvd Wilkes Barre PA 18702-5249 Personal E-mail: rogschwartz@aol.com.

SCHWARTZ, SHIRLEY E., retired chemist, researcher; b. Detroit, Aug. 26, 1935; d. Emil Victor and Jessie Grace (Galbraith) Eckwall; m. Ronald Elmer Schwartz, Aug. 25, 1957; children: Steven Dennis, Bradley Allen, George Byron. BS, U. Mich., 1957, Detroit Inst. Tech., 1978; MS, Wayne

State U., 1962, PhD, 1970. Asst. prof. Detroit Inst. Tech., 1973—78, head divsn. math. sci., 1976—78; mem. rsch. staff BASF Wyandotte Corp., Mich., 1978—81, head sect. functional fluids, 1981; sr. staff rsch. scientist GM Rsch., Warren, Mich., 1981—99; materials engr. GM Powertrain, 1999—2003; ret., 2003. Part-time contractor GM Powertrain, 2003—. Contbr. articles to profl. jours. Recipient Gold award Engring. Soc. Detroit, 1989 Fellow Soc. Automotive Engrs. (Excellence in Oral Presentation award 1986, 91, 94, Arch T. Colwell Merit award 1991, Lloyd L. Withrow Disting. Spkr. award 1995), Soc. Tribologists and Lubrication Engrs. (treas. Detroit sect. 1981, vice chmn. 1982, chmn. 1982-83, chmn. wear tech. com. 1987-88, bd. dirs. 1985-91, assoc. editor 1989-90, contbg. editor 1989—2003, Wilbur Deutsch award 1987, P.M. Ku award 1994); mem. Am. Chem. Soc., Soc. In Vitro Biology, Soc. Women Engrs. Life Achievement award 1989), Mich. Women's Hall of Fame (lifetime achievement award 1996), Women of Wayne (headliners award 2000), U.S. Nat. Acad. Engring., Mensa, Classic Guitar Soc. Mich., U.S. Power Squadrons, Detroit Navigators, Sigma Xi. Lutheran. Achievements include development of General Motors system that indicates when the engine oil should be changed; patents in field. *I've spent a number of very pleasant hours trying to make water behave like oil and alcohol behave like gasoline—a quest not much different from that of the ancient alchemists, who also spent their time trying to convert one substance to another.*

SCHWARTZ, SIMA M., music educator; arrived in U.S., 1995; d. Michael Shwartz and Sophia Leshchiner; m. Vladimir A. Shpachenko, June 7, 1975 (div. Oct. 1978); 1 child, Nadia Shpachenko. Grad., Music Sch. for Gifted Youth, Kharkov, 1964; MusM in Tchg. Piano, Accompanist, Performer, State Inst. Arts, Kharkov, 1969. Piano faculty Kharkov Music Schs., 1964—91; accompanist Kharkov State Philharm., 1964—91, Kharkov Inst. Arts, 1964—65; piano faculty Severodonetsk State Music Coll., 1969—72; founder, condr. Jewish Children Orch., Kharkov, 1990—91; piano tchr. Gilloh Dalled Sch., Jerusalem, 1992—95; founder, piano tchr. Sima's Music Club, Cambridge, Mass., 1996—2000; piano faculty The Music Sch., Providence, 1999—2000; founder, piano tchr. Shwartz Piano Sch., Marlborough, Mass., 2000—02; piano faculty Performing Arts Sch., Worcester, Mass., 2003—04. Mem.: Mass. Music Tchrs. Assn. (bd. dirs.), Music Tchrs. Nat. Assn. Avocations: walking, ping pong/table tennis, reading, theater. Office Phone: 774-239-1430.

SCHWARTZ, STEPHEN BLAIR, retired information technology executive; b. Chgo., Oct. 19, 1934; s. Herbert S. and Gertrude Schwartz; m. Nancy Jean Astrof, Dec. 18, 1955; children: Debra Lee Schwartz Zaret, Susan Beth Schwartz Derene. BS in Indsl. Engring., Northwestern U., 1957. With IBM Corp., 1957-92; various mgmt. positions, dir. product programs Harrison, NY, to 1977; v.p. Systems Communications div., 1977-81; v.p. Armonk, NY, 1982-90; v.p. Am. Far East Corp. subs. IBM Corp. Tokyo, 1982-84; pres., CEO Satellite Bus. Systems, McLean, Va., 1984; v.p., asst. group exec. Telecommunications, 1985-86; v.p., pres. Systems Products Div., 1986-88; v.p., gen. mgr. Application Bus. Systems, 1988-90; sr. v.p. market driven quality Stamford, Conn., 1990-92. Bd. dirs. MFRI, Inc. Mem.: PGA Nat. Golf Club (Palm Beach Gardens, Fla.). Republican. Jewish. E-mail: sbsone@aol.com.

SCHWARTZ, STEPHEN GREGORY, ophthalmologist; b. Queens, NY, Nov. 28, 1969; s. Charles F. and Patricia Schwartz; m. Melanie Rebak, June 15, 1996; children: Jessica Hope, Reid Alexander. BS with honors, Cornell U., Ithaca, NY, 1991; MD, NYU, NYC, 1995; student, J.L. Kellogg Sch. Mgmt., Coral Gables, Fla., 2007—. Diplomate Am. Bd. Ophthalmology. Intern Lenox Hill Hosp., NYC, 1995—96; resident NYU Sch. Medicine, NYC, 1996—99; fellow Baylor Coll. Medicine, Houston, 1999—2001; asst. prof. ophthalmology Va. Commonwealth U. Sch. Medicine, Richmond, 2001—04, program dir. ophthalmology, 2002—04; asst. prof. clin. ophthalmology U. Miami (Fla.) Miller Sch. Medicine, 2004—; med. dir., divsn. chief Bascom Palmer Eye Inst., Retina Ctr., Naples, Fla., 2004—. Bd. govs. Prevent Blindness Fla., Tampa, 2006—; bd. dirs. Va. Voice for Print Handicapped, Inc., Richmond, 2002—04. Grantee Investigator award, Prevent Blindness Am., 2005; Nat. Glaucoma Rsch. grantee, Am. Health Assistance Found., 2003. Fellow: Am. Acad. Ophthalmology (Achievement award 2006); mem.: AMA, Collier County Med. Soc., Fla. Soc. Ophthalmology (bd. dirs. 2006, Outstanding Young Ophthalmologist Leadership award 2006), Fla. Med. Assn., Assn. Rsch. in Vision and Ophthalmology (members in tng. com. 2003—06), Am. Soc. Retina Specialists. Office: Bascom Palmer Eye Inst 311 9th St N # 100 Naples FL 34102 Home Phone: 239-592-7353; Office Phone: 239-659-3937. Office Fax: 239-659-3982. Business E-Mail: sschwartz2@med.miami.edu.

SCHWARTZ, STEPHEN LAWRENCE, composer, lyricist; b. NYC, Mar. 6, 1948; s. Stanley Leonard and Sheila Lorna (Siegel) Schwartz; m. Carole Ann Piasecki, June 6, 1969; children: Scott Lawrence, Jessica Lauren. Student, Juilliard Sch. Music, 1960—64; BFA, Carnegie-Mellon U., 1968. Composer (works include): title song for Butterflies Are Free, 1969; composer: (theatre) music and lyrics Godspell, 1971, Pippin, 1972, The Magic Show, 1974, The Baker's Wife, 1976, Children of Eden, 1991, Wicked, 2003, Mit Eventyr (Denmark), 2005, four songs, adaptation and direction Working, 1978; composer: (with Leonard Bernstein) English texts for Leonard Bernstein's Mass, 1971; composer: lyrics Rags, 1986, (films) lyrics Pocahontas, 1995 (Acad. award best original score, 1996, Acad. award best original song, 1996), The Hunchback of Notre Dame, 1996, (music and lyrics) The Prince of Egypt, 1998 (Acad. award best original song, 1999), (TV, music and lyrics) Geppetto, 2000, (juvenile) The Perfect Peach, 1977, Captain Louie, 1983, (recording) Reluctant Pilgrim, 1997, Uncharted Territory, 2001. Recipient Drama Desk awards, 1971, 1978, 2004, Grammy awards, 1971, 1996, 2005, Golden Globe award, 1996. Mem.: ASCAP (bd. dirs.), Am. Motion Picture Arts Soc., Dramatists Guild (coun.). Business E-Mail: schwartz@stephenschwartz.com.

SCHWARTZ, STEVE WENDELIN, physician; b. Bethesda, Md., May 16, 1955; s. Wallace John and Gwynne June (Lingenfelter) S. AB in Chemistry summa cum laude, Duke U., 1977, MD, 1981. Diplomate Am. Bd. Family Practice. Rotating intern Med. U. S.C., Charleston, 1981-82, resident in family practice, 1982-84; emergency rm. physician Coastal Emergency Svc., 1985-86; family physician Carolina Health Care, Myrtle Beach, SC, 1984—; CEO Cactus Internat., Inc. Data processing dir. HMI, 1984—; pres. Unitrends Software Corp., 1989-2003, chief tech officer, 2004-05; rschr. Symbol Theory; programmer langs. Columnist SCO World Mag.; contbr. articles to profl. jours. Del. ann. meeting N.C. Med. Soc., 1980; participant Intramural Soccer, 1977-80; mem. Intramural Track, 1980, Blacknall Meml. Presbyn. Ch., 1977-80; coord. Boy Scouts Phys. Exam. Program, 1983; vol. cmty. health care project for poor East End Cmty. Health Ctr.; tchr. seminars on alcoholism for drug edn. project Holistic Medicine Group, 1980; Bible study coord. Valley of Achor. With USAF. 1973-75. First Place Durham Open Chess Tournament, 1974; recipient Grand Strand Leadership, 1986. Fellow Am. Acad. Family Physicians; mem. AMA (Physicians Recognition award 1986), So. Med. Assn., Horry County Med. Soc., Phi Beta Kappa, Upsilon Pi Epsilon. Avocations: chess, soccer. Office: Carolina Health Care 4605 Hwy 17 Byp S Myrtle Beach SC 29577-6681 Personal E-mail: steves@sc.rr.com.

SCHWARTZ, THEODORE H., neurosurgeon; Degree, Havard Coll., 1987; MD, Harvard Med. Sch., 1993. Internship and residency Columbia Presbyn. Med. Ctr.; dir. brain tumor surgery NY Prebyn. Hosp., NYC, 2001—. Dir. inst. minimally invasive skull base and pituitary surgery NY Presbyn. Hosp. Office: New York Presbyterian Hospital 525 East 68th St Box #99 New York NY 10021 Office Phone: 212-746-5620.

SCHWARTZ, VICTOR ELLIOT, lawyer, educator; b. NYC, July 3, 1940; AB summa cum laude, Boston U., 1962; JD magna cum laude, Columbia U., 1965. Bar: NY 1965, Ohio 1974. Law clk. to judge So. Dist. N.Y., 1965-67; from asst. to assoc. prof. law U. Cin., 1967-72, prof., 1972-79, acting dean, 1973-74; vis. prof. U. Va. Law Sch., 1970-71; dist. vis. scholar U. Cin., 2002—; ptnr. firm Crowell & Moring, Washington, 1980—2001; sr. ptnr. firm Fed. Interagy. task Force on Products Liability, 1976; ptnr., chair firm's pub. policy group Shook Hardy & Bacon, Washington, 2001—. Bd. visitors U. Cin. Sch., 1998—; disting. vis. scholar U. Cin., 2003—; gen. counsel, bd. dirs. Am. Tort Reform Assn.; chmn. Civil Justice Task Force, Am. Legis. Exch. Coun.; chmn. Dept. of Commerce Task Force on Product Liability and Accident Compensation, 1977-80. Author: Comparative Negligence, 1974, 4th edit., 2002; (with Kelly and Partlett) Cases and Materials on Torts, 1976, 11th edit., 2005, How to Prepare for the Multi-State Bar Examination, 1977, Products Liability: Cases and Trends, 1987, Products Liability: Asset Trends, 1988, (with Lee and Kelly) Multistate Legislation, 1985; editor: Columbia Law Rev., 1965; prin. draftsman: Model Uniform Product Liability Act. Recipient Sec. of Commerce award for disting. svc., Burton award for best law rev. writing in U.S., Tort Summit award, Am. Tort Reform Assn., 2002, The Jeffersonian Award, Am. Legis. Exchange Coun.; named One of 100 Most Influential Attys. in U.S., Nat. Law Jour., 1994, 97, 2006, Pvt. Sector Person of Yr., Am. Legis. Exch. Coun., 2003. Mem. ABA (chmn. products liability com. 1979, uniform laws com. 1981, torts and ins. practice sect.), Am. Law Inst. (life, adv. com. Restatement Third of Torts), Phi Beta Kappa. Office: Shook Hardy & Bacon LLP 600 14th St NW Ste 800 Washington DC 20005-2004 Office Phone: 202-783-8400. Business E-Mail: vschwartz@shb.com. *The greatest joys in life are found in one's relationships, be it business, romance or friendship, with other people.*

SCHWARTZ, WALLACE L., lawyer; b. Poughkeepsie, NY, 1952; BA, Harvard U., 1974; JD, Cornell U., 1977. Bar: N.Y. 1978. NY office leader Skadden, Arps, Slate, Meagher & Flom, NYC, real estate practice leader. Office: Skadden Arps Slate Meagher & Flom Four Times Sq New York NY 10036 Office Phone: 212-735-2640. Office Fax: 917-777-2640. Business E-Mail: wschwart@skadden.com.

SCHWARTZ, WILLIAM, lawyer, educator; b. Providence, May 6, 1933; s. Morris Victor and Martha (Glassman) S.; m. Bernice Konigsberg, Jan. 13, 1957; children: Alan Gershon, Robin Libby. AA, Boston U., 1952, JD magna cum laude, 1955, MA, 1960; postgrad., Harvard Law Sch., 1955-56; LHD (hon.), Hebrew Coll., 1996, Yeshiva U., 1998. Bar: DC 1956, Mass. 1962, NY 1989. Prof. law Boston U., 1955-91, Fletcher prof. law, 1968-70, Roscoe Pound prof. law, 1970-73, dean Sch. of Law, 1980-88, dir. Ctr. for Estate Planning, 1988-91; univ. prof. Yeshiva U., NYC, 1991—; of counsel Swartz & Swartz, 1973-80; v.p. for acad. affairs, chief acad. officer Yeshiva U., NYC, 1993-98; counsel Cadwalader, Wickersham and Taft, NYC, Washington, Charlotte, London, Beijing, 1988—; mem. faculty Frances Glessner Lee Inst., Harvard Med. Sch., Nat. Coll. Probate Judges, 1970, 77, 78, 79, 88; gen. dir. Assn. Trial Lawyers Am., 1968-73; reporter New Eng. Trial Judges Conf., 1965-67; participant Nat. Met. Cts. Conf., 1968; dir. Mass. Probate Study, 1976—; chmn. spl. com. on police procedures City of Boston, 1989, 91. Chmn. UST Corp., 1993—94; bd. dirs. Viacom Inc., chmn. governance and nominating com., compensation com.; legal adv. bd. NY Stock Exch. Author: Future Interests and Estate Planning, 1965, 77, 81, 86, Comparative Negligence, 1970, A Products Liability Primer, 1970, Civil Trial Practice Manual, 1972, New Vistas in Litigation, 1973, Massachusetts Pleading and Practice, 7 vols., 1974-80, Estate Planning and Living Trusts, 1990, The Convention Method: The Unused Amending Superhighway, 1995, Jewish Law and Contemporary Dilemmas and Problems, 1997, Does Time Heal All Wrongs?, 1999, Amending Irrevocable Trusts, 2003, The Art of Effectuating a Donor's Wishes, 2005, others; note editor: Boston U. Law Rev., 1954-55; property editor: Annual Survey of Mass. Law, 1960—; contbr. articles to profl. jours. Rep. Office of Pub. Info., UN, 1968—73; chmn. legal adv. panel Nat. Commn. Med. Practice, 1972—73; examiner of titles Commonwealth of Mass., 1964—; spl. counsel Mass. Bay Transp. Authority, 1979; pres. Fifth Ave. Synagogue, NYC, 1997—2001, hon. pres., 2001—; trustee Hebrew Coll., 1975—, Salve Regina U., Yeshiva U. Recipient Homer Albers award Boston U., 1955, John Ordronaux prize, 1955, Disting. Svc. award Religious Zionists Am., 1977; William W. Treat award, William O. Douglas award Fellow Am. Coll. Probate Counsel; mem. ABA, Am. Law Inst., Mass. Bar Assn. (chmn. task force tort liability), NY State Bar Assn., Assn. Bar City NY, Nat. Coll. Probate Judges (hon.), Phi Beta Kappa. Office: Cadwalader Wickersham Taft One World Fin Ctr New York NY 10281 Office Phone: 212-504-6399. Personal E-mail: william.schwartz@cwt.com. *I have been guided by the maxim: "Ideals are like stars. You cannot touch them with your hands, but like the seafaring man, if you choose them as your guide and follow them, you will reach your destiny".*

SCHWARTZBACH, M. GERALD, lawyer; b. Wilkes-Barre, Pa., Oct. 6, 1944; m. Susan Schwartzbach; 1 child, Micah. BA in Hist., Washington and Jefferson Coll., 1966; JD, George Washington U., 1969. Bar: Mich. 1970, US Dist. Ct. (ea. dist. Mich.) 1970, US District Ct. (no. dist. Calif.) 1974, Calif. 1974, US Ct. Appeals (9th cir.) 1980, US Supreme Ct. 1982, US Dist. Ct. (so. dist. Calif.) 1978. Staff atty. Legal Aid and Defenders Office, Detroit, 1970—71, Mich. State Appellate Defender Office, Detroit, 1971, Bayview Hunter's Point Cmty. Defender, San Francisco, 1974—76; pvt. practice Detroit, 1971—72, San Francisco, 1977—87, 1989—96, Mill Valley, Calif., 1999—; assoc. Law Office of Sheldon Otis, San Francisco, 1976—77, Law Offices of Joseph W. Carcione, Jr., Redwood City, Calif., 1996—99; ptnr. Garry, McTernan, Stender, Walsh & Schwartzbach, San Francisco, 1987—89. Lectr. in field. Vol. Svc. To Am., 1969—70; bd. dirs. La Casa de Las Madres, shelter for battered women, 1981—90. Named one of Best Lawyers in Am., Woodward/White, Top 10 Trial Lawyers in Am., Nat. Law Jour., 2005; recipient Outstanding Svc. award, No. Calif. Innocence Project, 2003. Mem.: Bar Assn. San Francisco (chair criminal justice sect. 1988—91, mem. criminal justice adv. coun. 1988—92), Marin County Bar Assn., Nat. Lawyers Guild, No. Calif. Criminal Trial Lawyers Assn. (bd. govs. 1989—95), Nat. Assn. Criminal Def. Lawyers, Calif. Attys. for Criminal Justice (bd. govs. 1986—93, 2002—07, Skip Glen Outstanding Lawyer award 1986), State Bar Calif. Achievements include the successful defense of actor Robert Blake in the 2004-05 murder trial. Office: 655 Redwood Hwy Ste 277 Mill Valley CA 94941 Office Phone: 415-388-2343. Office Fax: 415-388-2353. Business E-Mail: mgs@mgslawyer.com. *

SCHWARTZBERG, ALLAN ZELIG, psychiatrist, educator; b. Cleve., Dec. 5, 1930; s. Joseph and Jeanette (Eisenman) S.; m. Katherine Weiss, June 19, 1955; children: Shana, Robert. BS cum laude, Case Western Res. U., 1951; MD, Ohio State U., 1955. Diplomate Am. Bd. Psychiatry and Neurology, Am. Bd. Forensic Medicine. Intern, resident in psychiatry Johns Hopkins Hosp., Balt., 1955—59; pvt. practice Gaithersburg, Md.; assoc. clin. prof. psychiatry Georgetown U. Sch. Medicine, Washington, 1979—89, clin. prof., 1989—. Vis. prof. faculty seminar in cmty. psychiatry Harvard U. Med. Sch., Boston, 1965-67; cons. Dept. Energy, 2002-. Editor-in-chief Internat. Annals Adolescent Psychiatry, 1988—2000; coeditor Adolescent Psychiatry, Vols. 8-19; contbr. articles to med. jours. Recipient Vicennial medal Georgetown U., 1984. Fellow AMA, Am. Psychiat. Assn. (disting. life), Am. Soc. for Adolescent Psychiatry, Am. Soc. Psychoanalytic Physicians (pres. 1986-87, 2000-01), Am. Coll. Psychiatrists; mem. Am. Group Psychotherapy Assn., B'nai B'rith, Phi Beta Kappa. Republican. Jewish. Home: 6616 Kenhill Rd Bethesda MD 20817-6014 Office: Comprehensive Behavioral Svcs 9021 Shady Grove Ct Gaithersburg MD 20877-1308 Office Phone: 301-590-9000. Personal E-mail: azsmd@aol.com.

SCHWARTZEL, CHARLES BOONE, lawyer; b. Louisville, Jan. 4, 1950; s. Charles Joseph and Rosemary Jane (Redens) S.; m. Rose Marie Carlisi, June 20, 1980; children: Sally Ann, Charles Gerard. BA, Vanderbilt U., 1972; JD, U. Tex., 1975. Bar: Tex. 1975. Atty. Vinson & Elkins L.L.P., Houston, 1975-98, ptnr., 1983-98; pvt. practice Houston, 1998—. Contbr. articles to profl. jours. Councilman City of West University Place, Tex., 1985-89. Fellow Am. Coll. Trust and Estate Counsel; mem. Tex. Bar Assn. Roman Catholic. Office: Attorney at Law 1010 Lamar St Ste 1520 Houston TX 77002-6315 Office Phone: 713-654-1133.

SCHWARTZMAN, ANDREW JAY, lawyer; b. NYC, Oct. 4, 1946; s. Joel Jay and Theresa (Greenhauff) S.; m. Linda Lazarus, June 8, 1986. AB, U. Pa., 1968, JD, 1971. Bar: N.Y. 1972, D.C. 1974, Temporary Emergency Ct. Appeals 1977, U.S. Dist. Ct. D.C. 1978, U.S. Ct. Appeals (D.C. cir.) 1981, U.S. Ct. Appeals (2d cir.) 1987, U.S. Ct. Appeals (3rd, 4th, 7th, 8th, 9th cirs.) 1991, U.S. Supreme Ct. 1980. Staff counsel United Ch. of Christ Office of Comm., NYC, 1971-74; atty. adviser Fed. Energy Office, Washington, 1974-77; sr. atty. adviser U.S. Dept. Energy, Washington, 1977-78; bd. dirs. Safe Energy Comms. Coun., pres. bd. dirs., 1989—2003; dir. Media Access Project, Washington, 1978-96, pres., CEO, 1996—. Mem. adv. panel Study on Comms. Systems for an Info. Age; mem. adv. bd. Ctr. for Democracy and Tech., 1996—; lectr. Fairleigh Dickinson U., 1972-73; instr. Johns Hopkins U., 2003—; mem. comms. coun. forum Aspen Inst. on Comms. and Soc., 1992—; bd. dirs. Min. Media and Telecomms. Coalition, 1994—; mem. adv. bd. Nat. Inst. Entertainment and Media Law, Southwestern U. Sch. Law, 2000—, dist. lectr. in residence Southwestern U. Sch. Law Summer Entertainment and Media Law Program, Fitzwilliam Coll., Cambridge U., 2004; mem. adv. com. on diversity for comms. in the digital age FCC, 2006—. Contbg. author: Les Brown's Dictionary of Television, 3d edit., Ency. of the Consumer Movement, 1997; contbr. articles to legal jours. Recipient Everett Parker award United Ch. of Christ, 1994, Just Media Lifetime Achiev. award, 2004. Mem. ABA, Fed. Comms. Bar Assn., U. Pa. Alumni Assn., Sci. Am. Soc (leader in technology policy 2004). Office: Media Access Project # 1000 1625 K St NW Washington DC 20006-1604 Office Phone: 202-232-4300. E-mail: info@mediaaccess.org.

SCHWARTZMAN, PETER DAVID, environmental scientist, educator; s. Barbara Ann Major and David William Schwartzman; m. Huong Minh Hua, June 27, 1998; children: Camellia Nai, Juniper Rose Nai. BS in Physics, Harvey Mudd Coll., Claremont, Calif., 1991; MS in Sci. and Tech. Studies, Va. Poly. Inst., Blacksburg, Ill., 1993; PhD in Environ. Sci., U. Va., Charlottesville, 1997. Assoc. prof. environ. studies Knox Coll., Galesburg, Ill., 1998—. Exec. bd. mem. Assoc. Coll. of Midwest, Chgo., 2000—04. Author: Small is Powerful, Word Nerd Workbook #1 and #2, 2007, Word Nerd Puzzler, 2007; columnist: The Zephyr, 2001—07; contbr. articles to profl. jours. Bd. dirs. Western Ill. Nature Group, Galesburg, Ill., 2001—; vol. educator Knox County Sch. Dist. 205, Galesburg, Ill., 1998—. Recipient Honorable Mention award for original column, Ill. Press Assn. Mem.: Union of Concerned Scientists (assoc.), Amnesty Internat. (assoc.). Office: Knox Coll 2 E South St Galesburg IL 61401 Home Phone: 309-344-0046; Office Phone: 309-341-7142. Personal E-mail: drearth1@gmail.com.

SCHWARTZSTEIN, ADAM, lawyer; b. NYC, Jan. 4, 1969; BS, Boston U., 1990; JD, Quinnipiac U., 1994. Bar: NY 1995, US Dist. Ct. Ea. Dist. NY, US Dist. Ct. So. Dist. NY. Ptnr. Wilson, Elser, Moskowitz, Edelman & Dicker LLP, NYC. Mem.: Assn. of the Bar of the City of NY. Office: Wilson Elser Moskowitz Edelman & Dicker LLP 150 E 42nd St 23rd Fl New York NY 10017-5639 Office Phone: 212-490-3000 ext. 2778. Office Fax: 212-490-3038. Business E-Mail: schwartzsteina@wemed.com.

SCHWARY, RONALD LOUIS, motion picture producer; b. The Dalles, Oreg., May 23, 1944; s. Mitchell Louis and Lorraine (Ablan) S.; children: Brian L., Neil L. BS, U. So. Calif., 1967. Pres. Red Truck Prodns., Inc., LA, 1985—. Prodr. (motion pictures) Ordinary People, 1980 (Golden Globe award 1981, Acad. award 1981), Absence of Malice, 1981, Tootsie, 1982, A Soldier's Story, 1984, Batteries Not Included, 1987, Havana, 1990, Scent of a Woman, 1992, Cops and Robbersons, 1994, Sabrina, 1995, Mirror Has Two Faces, 1996, Meet Joe Black, 1997, Random Hearts, 1999; (TV series) Tour of Duty, 1987, Now and Again, 1999, Medium, 2004—. Mem. Dirs. Guild Am. Republican. Roman Catholic.

SCHWARZ, BARBARA RUTH BALLOU, elementary school educator; b. East Orange, NJ, Aug. 8, 1930; d. Robert Ingram Ballou and Ruth Edna Sweeney; m. Eugene A. Schwarz, Jr., Dec. 24, 1954 (div. 1977); children: Ruth Ellen, Eugene A. III. BS, Trenton State Coll., 1952. Tchr. West Orange N.J. Schs., 1952-54, Franklin Sch., Ft. Wayne, Ind., 1955-56, Parliament Place Sch., North Babylon, N.Y., 1965-91. Trustee welfare trust fund North Babylon Tchrs. Orgn., N.Y., 1988-91. Vol. Safe Home, Suffolk County Coalition Against Domestic Violence, Bayshore, NY, 1979—90; sec. Victims Info. Bur., Suffolk, 1987—88, v.p., 1989—90, pres. bd. dirs., 1990—94, rep. to Women's Equal Rights Coalition, Suffolk County Human Rights Commn., 1989—94; mem. adv. bd. Suffolk County Women's Svcs., 1990—96, vice-chair, 1991—93; rep. LD 14 Suffolk County Women's Adv. Commn., 2001—06; bd. dirs. Suffolk Abortion Rights Coun., 1992—96; mem. Suffolk-Nassau Abortion Def., 1991—94; pub. affairs com. Planned Parenthood Suffolk County, 1990—92; mem. Long Islanders for Fairness and Equality, 1994—97; mem. subcom. Islip Presbyn. Ch. on Legis. Com. of N.Y. State Coalition Against Domestic Violence, 1999—2001; steering com. Save Our Svcs., Long Island, 1998—2001; mem. coun. on women L.I. Presbytery, 2002—; sec. sr. lunch program Presbyn. Ch. of Islip. Women's History Month Community Svc. honoree Town of Babylon, 1997. Mem. AAUW (mem. v.p. Islip area br. 1982-84, pres. 1984-88, legis. chair 1988-93, mem. com. promoting individual liberties Nassau-Suffolk dist. VI 1989-91, pro-choice coord. N.Y. state 1990-92, rep. to women on job task force 1986-98, chair dist. VI inter-br. 1991-92, chair N.Y. state pub. policy 1992-96, rep. on L.I. and N.Y. State Pro-Choice Coalitions, chair N.Y. state voter edn. campaign, 1995-98, assoc. pub. policy com. 1996-98, L.I. Achievement award 1996), N.Y. State Ret. Tchrs. Assn., Western Suffolk Ret. Tchrs. Assn., Coalition Ret. Tchrs. L.I., North Babylon Tchrs. Orgn. (retirees chpt.). Republican. Avocations: lobbying, reading, handcrafts, gourmet cooking, volunteer activities. Home: 23 Wyandanch Ave Babylon NY 11702-1920 E-mail: bbschwarz@optonline.net.

SCHWARZ, BERTHOLD ERIC, psychiatrist; b. Jersey City, Oct. 20, 1924; s. Berthold Theodore Dominick and I. Thyra W. (Ericson) Schwarz; m. Ardis Marilyn Peterson, Jan. 22, 1955; children: Lisa Thyra, Eric Rolf. AB, Dartmouth Coll., 1945; MD, NYU, 1950; MS, Mayo Grad. Sch. Medicine, 1957. Intern Mary Hitchcock Meml. Hosp., Hanover, NH, 1950-51; psychiatrist, researcher pvt. practice, Montclair, NJ, 1955-82; Mayo Found., Rochester, Minn., 1951-55; psychiatrist, researcher pvt. practice, Vero Beach, Fla., 1982—. Cons. Essex County Hosp. Ctr., Cedar Grove, N.J., 1965-82, Med. Correctional Assn., Ossining, N.Y., 1960-72; exec. dir. Internat. Psychosomatics Inst., Mountain Lakes, N.J., 1995—. Contbr. articles to med. jours. With USNR, 1943-45. Fellow AAAS, Am. Psychiat. Assn., Am. Soc. Psychical Rsch., Am. Geriatric Soc. Republican. Avocations: ufos, parapsychiatry, swimming, walking. Home: 1070 Reef Rd Apt 305 Vero Beach FL 32963-4342 Office: 642 Azalea Ln Vero Beach FL 32963-1832 Office Phone: 772-231-5220. Personal E-mail: ardisps@aol.com.

SCHWARZ, CARL A., JR., lawyer; b. NYC, Apr. 27, 1936; s. Carl A. and Genevieve C. Byrne; m. Maryellen McG., Apr. 30, 1966; children: Peter Thomas, Elizabeth Anne. BS, Fordham U., 1957, JD, 1960. Bar: N.Y. 1960,

U.S. Dist. Ct. (so., ea., we. and D.C. dists.) N.Y. 1960, U.S. Ct. Appeals (2d cir.) 1960, U.S. Supreme Ct. 1965. Ptnr. Schwarz & DeMarco, Garden City, N.Y. Chmn., bd. trustees N.Y. Sch. Interior Design. Trustee Cath. Charities; Capt. USAF, 1961-65. Mem. Manhasset Bay Yacht Club (vice commodore), Order of Malta. Roman Catholic. Office: Schwarz & DeMarco LLP 300 Garden City Plz Ste 404 Garden City NY 11530-3332

SCHWARZ, EGON, language educator, writer, critic; b. Vienna, Aug. 8, 1922; arrived in U.S., 1949, naturalized, 1956; s. Oscar and Erna S.; m. Dorothea K. Klockenbusch, June 8, 1950; children: Rudolf Joachim, Caroline Elisabeth, Gabriela Barbara. PhD, U. Wash., 1954; PhD (hon.), U. Vienna, 1997, U. Örebro, Sweden, 2002. Mem. faculty Harvard U., 1954-61; mem. faculty dept. Germanic langs. and lit. Washington U., St. Louis, 1961—, prof. German, 1963—, Rosa May Disting. Univ. prof. in the Humanities, 1975-93, prof. emeritus, 1993—. Vis. prof. U. Hamburg, Fed. Republic Germany, 1962-63, U. Calif., Berkeley, 1963-65, Middlebury Coll., 1969, U. Calif., Irvine, 1977, U. Tübingen, 1986; William Evans prof. U. Otago, Dunedin, N.Z., 1984; Disting. scholar Ohio State U., Columbus, 1987, U. Graz, Austria, 1989, 93, U. Siegen, 1993-94. Author: Hofmannsthal und Calderon, 1962, Joseph von Eichendorff, 1972, Das verschluckte Schluchzen- Poesie und Politik bei Rainer Maria Rilke, 1972, Keine Zeit für Eichendorff: Chronik unfreiwilliger Wanderjahre; an autobiography, 1979, rev., 1992, Dichtung, Kritik, Geschichte: Essays zur Literatur 1900-1930, 1983, Literatur aus vier Kulturen: Essays und Besprechungen, 1987, Ich bin Kein Freund allgemeiner Urteile über ganze Volker: Essays über österreischische, deutsche und jüdische Literatur, 2000, Die japanische Mauer: Ungewöhnliche Reisegeschichten, 2002, Refuge-Chronicle of a Flight from Hitler, 2002, Unfreiwillige Wanderjahre, 2005, others. Recipient Joseph von Eichendorff medal, 1986, Austrian Medal of Honor for Arts and Scis., 1991, Alexander von Humboldt prize for fgn. scholars, 1995; Guggenheim fellow, 1957-58, Fulbright fellow, 1962-63, sr. fellow NEH, 1970-71, fellow Ctr. for Interdisciplinary Studies, Bielefeld, Germany, 1980-81; grantee Am. Coun. Learned Socs., 1962-63. Mem.: MLA, German Acad. Lang. and Letters, Am. Assn. Tchrs. German, German Acad. Lang. and Lit. (hon.). Home: 1036 Oakland Ave Saint Louis MO 63122-6565 Office: Washington U German Dept Saint Louis MO 63130 Personal E-mail: gabrielas@aol.com. *When I was young, heroic phantasies were closer to my heart than ethical ones, desires of self-fulfillment stronger than the hopes for an equitable world. Today my horizon is broader in that I wish for a society where personal satisfactions are not achieved at the expense of others, where the earth which one generation inherits is not left more depleted to the next, a society which does not coerce other societies.*

SCHWARZ, ERNST RUEDIGER, cardiologist, researcher; s. Ernest Johann Ferdinand and Friedel Elise Schwarz; m. Juana Rocio Angel, Nov. 19, 1999; children: Aubriana d'Iwana Angel, Lujain Vanessa. MD, Philipps U. Marburg, Germany, 1987, U. Vienna, Austria, 1989; PhD, RWTH U. of Tech., Aachen, Germany, 2000. Diplomate in internal medicine German Physicians Chamber, in cardiology German Physicians Chamber, in intensive care medicine German Physicians Chamber. Assoc. prof. RWTH U. Hosp., Aachen, 1998—2000; chmn. cardiology Dr. S. Fakeeh Hosp.-Harvard Med. Internat., Jeddah, Saudi Arabia, 2000—03; prof. medicine U. Tex. Med. Br., Galveston, 2003—06, dir. cardiology clinics, 2005—06; prof. medicine UCLA, 2006—. Co-dir. cardiac transplant Cedars Sinai Med. Ctr., LA, 2006; dir. heart failure and transplantation U. Tex. Med. Br., Galveston, 2003—06, dir. heart failure fellowship program, 2004—06, dir. multidisciplinary clinic for sexual health, 2005—06; spkr. in field. Contbr. articles to profl. jours., chapters to books. Recipient Young Investigator award, Internat. Soc. Nuc. Cardiology, 1995. Fellow: Soc. Coronary Angiography and Interventions, European Soc. Cardiology, Am. Coll. Cardiology; mem.: Saudi Heart Assn., German Cardiac Soc., Heart Failure Soc. Am. Achievements include first to transesophageal echocardiography with IVUS catheters in rodent model; research in intensive invasive hemodynamic work in myocardial bridges; clinical and morphologic work in hibernating myocardium; evaluation, assessment and treatment of sexual dysfunction in patients with severe cardio-vascular diseases. Office: Cedars Sinai Med Ctr 8700 Beverly Blvd 6215 Los Angeles CA 90048 Office Phone: 310-423-1876. Office Fax: 310-423-1498. E-mail: cardiol2096@yahoo.com.

SCHWARZ, FREDERICK A.O., JR., lawyer; b. NYC, Apr. 20, 1935; s. Frederick August Otto and Mary Delafield (DuBois) S.; m. Marian Ladd, June 19, 1959; children: Frederick August Otto III, Adair L., Eliza Ladd; m. Frederica Perera, May 11, 1996. BA in History magna cum laude, Harvard Coll., 1957, LLB magna cum laude, 1960; LLD (hon.), N.Y. Law Sch., 1987, CUNY, 1993. Bar: N.Y. 1961, U.S. Dist. Ct. (so. dist.) N.Y. 1963, U.S. Ct. Appeals (2nd cir.) 1978, U.S. Ct. Appeals (9th cir.) 1972, U.S. Ct. Appeals (10th cir.) 1973, U.S. Supreme Ct. 1973. Law clk. to chief judge J. Edward Lumbard U.S. Ct. of Appeals, 2d Circuit, 1960-61; asst. commr. for law revision Govt. of No. Nigeria, 1961-62; assoc. firm Cravath, Swaine & Moore, NYC, 1963-68, ptnr., 1969—81, 1987—2003, sr. counsel, 2003—; sr. counsel Brennan Ctr. for Justice NYU, 2003—. Chief counsel Senate Select Com. on Intelligence, 1975—76; corp. counsel, NYC, 1982—86; chmn. Charter Revision Commn., NYC, 1989. Author: Nigeria: The Tribes, The Nation, or the Race, 1966; Editor Harvard Law Sch. Law Review. Contbr. articles to profl. jours. Chmn. Fund for the City of N.Y., 1977-81, 87-97; pres. Vera Inst. Justice, 1978-81, chmn. 1987—; mem. bd. overseers Harvard U., 1977-83; mem. Com. to Visit Harvard Coll., N.Y.-N.J. Citizens Commn. on AIDS; trustee Experiment in Internat. Living, 1965-82; bd. dirs. NAACP Legal Def. Fund. Constl. Edn. Found., Manhattan Bowery Corp., 1970-81, Lawyers for the Public Interest, 1976-81, FAO Schwarz, 1970-85; chair leadership N.Y. Adv. Coun., 1989—; trustee Nat. Resources Def. Coun., 1987-92, chmn., 1992—, Legal Action Center, 1973-81, N.Y.C. Criminal Justice Agy., 1977-81, Town Sch., 1972-80, Am. Com. on Africa, 1965-79, Milton Acad., 1960's, NAACP Legal Def. Fund, Constitutional Edn. Found., William Nelson Cromwell Found.; chmn. N.Y.C. Campaign Fin. Bd., 2003—. Recipient Liberty award Lambda Legal Def. and Edn. Fund, 1987, The Louis Lefkowitz award Fordham Urban Law Jour. 1990, Civic Leadership award Citizens Union City of N.Y., 1990, The Whitney North Seymour Pub. Svc. award Fed. Bar Coun., 1991., Lifetime Achievement award The Am. Lawyer, 2004. Fellow N.Y. Bar Found.; mem. ABA, Assn. of Bar of City of N.Y. (mem. exec. com. 1986-90, coun. on criminal justice, chmn. juvenile justice com. 1980-81, chmn. nominating com. 1983, Cardozo lectr. 1991), Am. Law Inst., Harvard Law Sch. Assn. of N.Y.C. (pres. 1983-84), N.Y. State Bar Assn., N.Y.C. Bar Assn. Office: Cravath, Swain & Moore 825 8th Ave Fl 38 New York NY 10019-7475

SCHWARZ, GERARD, conductor, musician, music director; b. Weehawken, NJ, Aug. 19, 1947; m. Jody Greitzer, June 23, 1984; children: Alysandra, Daniel, Gabriella, Julian. BS, MA, Juilliard Sch., 1972; DFA (hon.), Fairleigh Dickinson U., Seattle U.; MusD (hon.), U. Puget Sound. Trumpet player Am. Symphony Orch., 1965—72, Am. Brass Quintet, 1965—73, N.Y. Philharm., 1973—77; trumpet player, guest condr. Aspen Music Festival, 1969—75, bd. dirs., 1973—75; music dir. Erick Hawkins Dance Co., 1967—72, SoHo Ensemble, 1969—75, Eliot Feld Ballet Co., NYC, 1972—78, Music Sch. Princeton (N.J.) U., 1977—2002, N.Y. Chamber Symphony, 1977—, L.A. Chamber Orch., 1978—86, White Mountains (N.H.) Music Festival, 1978—80; music advisor Mostly Mozart Festival, Lincoln Ctr., NYC, 1982—84, music dir., 1984—2001, Music Today at Merkin Concert Hall, NYC, 1988—89. Music advisor Seattle Symphony, 1983—84, prin. condr., 1984—85, music dir., 1985—, Royal Liverpool Philharm. Orch., 2001—06; artistic advisor Tokyu Bunkamura's Orchard Hall, Japan, 1994—98; mem. faculty Juilliard Sch., NYC, 1975—83, Mannes Coll. Music, 1973—79, Montclair (N.J.) State Coll., 1975—80; guest condr. various orchs. including Phila. Orch., L.A. Philharm., St. Louis, Buffalo, Detroit, San Francisco, Atlanta, Houston, Pitts., Minn., Jerusalem Symphonies, Israel Chamber Orch., Moscow Philharm., Moscow Radio Orch., Orch. Nat. de France, Paris, London Symphony Orch., Frankfurt Radio, Stockholm Radio, Helsinki Philharm., Ensemble InterContemporain, Monte Caarlo Philharm., Nat. Orch. Spain, English Chamber Orch., London Symphony, Scottish Chamber Orch., City of Birmingham (Eng.) Symphony, Nouvel Orchestre Philharmonique, Sydney (Australia) Symphony, Melbourne (Australia) Symphony, Orchestre Nat. de Lyon, Orchestre Philharm. de Montpellier, France, Washington Opera, Da Capo Chamber Players, 20th Century Chamber Orch., Chamber Music Soc. Lincoln Ctr., San Francisco Opera, Seattle Opera, Tokyu Bunkamura, Japan, Rseidentie Orch. of The Hague, Netherlands, St. Louis Symphony, London Mozart Players, Kirov Orch., St. Petersburg, Russia, Tokyo Philharm., Royal Liverpool Philharm., Vancouver (Can.) Symphony Orch., City of London Symphonia, Evian Festival in France; artistic adv. Tokyo Philharm., 1994—98; mem. Nat. Coun. on the Arts Nat. Endowment for the Arts, 2005—. Rec. artist Columbia, Nonesuch, Vox, MMO, Desto, Angel, Delos Records, Season 1995. Nominee 10 Grammy awards; named Condr. of Yr., Musical Am. Internat. Directory of Performing Arts, 1994; recipient award for concert artists, Ford Found., 1973, Mumms Ovation award, Record of Yr. awards, Ditson Condrs. award, Columbia U., 1989, Seattle Mayors Arts award, 2006. Mailing: Nat Endowment for Arts 1100 Pennsylvania Ave NW Washington DC 20506 *

SCHWARZ, GLENN VERNON, newspaper editor; b. Chgo., Nov. 24, 1947; s. Vernon Edward and LaVerne Louise (Schuster) S.; m. Cynthia Frances Meisenhoelder, June 17, 1984; 1 child, Chloe. BA, San Francisco State U., 1970. Sports writer San Francisco Examiner, 1970—87, sports editor, 1988—2000, San Francisco Chronicle, 2000—. Fundraiser San Francisco Zoological Soc., 1987—. Mem. AP Sports Editors, Baseball Writers Assn. Am. (bd. dirs. 1986-87). Avocation: nature travel. Office: San Francisco Chronicle 901 Mission St San Francisco CA 94103

SCHWARZ, JOE (JOHN J.H. SCHWARZ), former congressman, physician; b. Battle Creek, Mich., Nov. 15, 1937; s. Frank William and Helen Veronica (Brennan) S.; m. Anne Louise Ennis, Jan. 16, 1971 (dec. Feb. 1990); 1 child, Brennan Louise. BA in History, U. Mich., 1959; MD, Wayne State U., 1964. Operative CIA, 1968—70; physician, surgeon Battle Creek, Mich., 1974—; commr. City of Battle Creek, 1979—85, mayor, 1985-87; mem. Mich. State Senate from 24th dist., Lansing, 1987—2002, pres. pro tempore, 1993—2002; mem. US Congress from 7th Mich. dist., 2005—07, mem. com. agr., com. armed services, com. sci. Trustee Leila Y. Post Montgomery Hosp. (now Battle Creek Health Sys.), Mich., 1980-82, Olivet Coll., 1991—, Wayland Acad., 1992-96, Libr. Mich., 1994-2003; trustee, treas. Am. Legacy Found; bd. directors Artrain, Ann Arbor, Detroit Receiving Hosp., Kellogg Cmty. Coll. Found., Univ. Musical Soc., Ann Arbor, Wayne State U. Found. Lt. Comdr. USN, 1965—67, Vietnam. Fellow ACS; mem. AMA, Am. Soc. for Head and Neck Surgery, Calhoun County Mich. Med. Soc. (pres. 1971), Mich Otolaryngological Soc., Mich State Med. Soc., Soc. Med. Consultants to Armed Forces, U. Mich. Club of Battle Creek. Republican. Roman Catholic.

SCHWARZ, JOHN HENRY, theoretical physicist, educator; b. North Adams, Mass., Nov. 22, 1941; s. George and Madeleine (Haberfeld) S.; m. Patricia Margaret Moyle, July 11, 1986. AB, Harvard U., 1962; PhD, U. Calif., Berkeley, 1966. Instr. physics Princeton (NJ) U., 1966-69, asst. prof., 1969-72; research assoc. Calif. Inst. Tech., Pasadena, 1972-85, Harold Brown prof. theoretical physics, 1985—. Co-author: Superstring Theory, 1987. Trustee Aspen (Colo.) Ctr. for Physics, 1982—. Recipient Dirac medal Internat. Ctr. for Theoretical Physics, 1989; Guggenheim fellow, 1978-79, MacArthur Found. fellow, 1987. Fellow NAS, Am. Acad. Arts & Scis., Am. Phys. Soc., Phi Beta Kappa (vis. scholar 1990-91). Office: Calif Inst Tech # 452 48 Pasadena CA 91125-0001 *

SCHWARZ, LOUIS JAY, financial advisor; s. Milton J. and Anita S.; m. Doris Ethel Schwarz, May 31, 1969; children: Jovialis Ona, Iris Nana, Janis Anna. BA, Gallaudet U., Washington, 1968; postgrad., Ill. Inst. Tech., Chgo., 1968-69, U. Md., College Park, 1970-72. CFP, registered fin. cons., registered investment advisor, qualified fin. planner, chartered fed. employees benefit cons. Tchr. Ill. Sch. for Deaf, Jacksonville, 1969-70; tax preparer Income Tax Svc. for the Deaf, Silver Spring, Md., 1971—; chemist U.S. Geol. Survey, Reston, Va., 1970-85; agt. Nat. Fraternal Soc. of Deaf, Mt. Prospect, Ill., 1975-93; owner, fin. planner Schwarz Fin. Svcs. LLC, Bethseda, Md., 1983—; pres. Schwarz & Giuntoli, Inc., Gaithersburg, Md., 1987—91. Stockbroker Integrated Resources Equity Corp., NYC, 1984—89; cons. instr. Nat. Ctr. for Fin. Edn., San Francisco, 1986—; pres. Met. Washington Telecomm. Directory for the Deaf Inc., Silver Spring, 1988—2003; registered rep. Royal Alliance Assocs., Inc., NYC, 1989—; adj. prof. Gallaudet U. Sch. Mgmt., 1993—94, 1997—2002. Author: (with L. Dunton) About Your Future, 1988; columnist NAD Broadcasters, 1984-95, Silent News, 1984-95, Deaf Nation, 1996-2000, Newswaves, 1996-2000, Deaf Digest, 1999-, Deaf Seniors of Am. New Horizons, 2002—. Active Nat. Assn. of Deaf, 1972—, Md. Assn. of Deaf, 1972—, Montgomery County Assn. Deaf, 1990—; consumer adv. C&P Tel. Co., 1981-84; bd. dirs. Telecomms. for Deaf Inc., 1976-82; commr. Montgomery County Commn. for Handicapped Individuals, 1979-83; adv. coun. Telecomms. Exch. of the Deaf, Inc., 1981-87; rep. Md. Gov.'s Adv. Bd. for Telecomms. Relay, 2004—. Named Top Prodr., Nat. Fraternal Soc. of Deaf, 1979, 83, Outstanding Handicapped Fed. Employee, US Dept. Interior, 1974, 77, Bus. Person of Yr., Gallaudet U. Dept. Bus., 2007; recipient Internat. Yr. of Disabled Persons Honor award US Dept. Interior, 1981, Montgomery County Coun. Bus. Svc. award, 1988-89, Knight of Flying Fingers award Nat. Assn. Deaf, 1990, 92, Disting. Svc. award Md. Assn. Deaf, 1993, Bus. of Yr. award Montgomery County Assn. of Deaf, 1997, Cmty. Svc. award Md. Assn. Deaf, 2001. Mem. Nat. Deaf Bus. Inst., Inc. (bd. dirs. 2001—), Internat. Assn. Registered Fin. Cons., Fin. Planning Assn., Deaf and Hard of Hearing Entrepreneurs Coun. (pres. 1993-96, bd. dirs. 1989-96). Jewish. Avocations: photography, swimming, bicycling, hiking, gardening. Office: Schwarz Fin Svcs LLC 4405 East-West Hwy Ste 502 Bethesda MD 20814-4536 Office Phone: 866-753-0333. Business E-Mail: louis@schwarz-financial.com.

SCHWARZ, M. ROY, physician, administrator; b. American Falls, Idaho, July 30, 1936; s. Frank and Hulda Christina (Rast) S.; m. Thelma Constance Schwarz, June 9, 1957; children: Ryan Merle, Tanna Berit. BS, Pacific Luth. U., 1959; MD, U. Wash., 1963; DS, Mont. State U., 1994, U. Idaho, 1995; LHD (hon.), Pacific Luth. U., 2002. From asst. to full prof. medicine U. Wash., Seattle, 1963-79; dean, prof. U. Colo., Denver, 1979-83; sr. v.p. Am. Med. Assn., Chgo., 1984-96; pres. China Med. Bd., NYC, 1997—2006. Co-author (with C. Everett Koop, Clarence E. Pearson): Critical Issues in global Health, 2001; editor: Proceedings of the VI Leukocyte Culture Conf., 1971; contbr. over 175 articles to profl. jours. Home Phone: 914-598-6984; Office Phone: 212-682-8000. Business E-Mail: tcandmr@adelphia.net.

SCHWARZ, MICHAEL, lawyer; b. Brookline, Mass., Oct. 19, 1952; s. Jules Lewis and Estelle (Kosberg) S.; m. Rebecca Handy; 1 child, Patrick Joshua Charles. BA magna cum laude, U. No. Colo., 1975; postgrad., U. N.Mex., 1977, JD, 1980; reader in Negligence Law, Oxford U., 1978; diploma in Legal Studies, Cambridge U., 1981. Bar: N.Mex. 1980, US Dist. Ct. N.Mex. 1980, US Ct. Appeals (10th, DC and Fed. cirs.) 1982, US Ct. Internat. Trade 1982, US Tax Ct. 1982, NY 1987, US Supreme Ct. 1983, cert.: N.Mex. Supreme Ct. (Employment and Labor Law) 2000. Vol. VISTA, Albuquerque, 1975-77; rsch. fellow N.Mex. Legal Support Project, Albuquerque, 1978-79; supr. law Cambridge (Eng.) U., 1980-81; law clk. to chief justice Supreme Ct. N.Mex., Santa Fe, 1981-82; pvt. practice Santa Fe, 1982—. Spl. pros. City of Santa Fe, 1985, spl. asst. atty. gen., 1986-88; mem. west editl. adv. com. Social Security Reporting Svc., 1983-95; mem. N.Mex. Supreme Ct. Com. Profl. Responsibility, 1990—, chmn., 1998—, domestiv rels. task force com., 2004—06, chmn. legal specialization com., employment and labor law, 2005-. Author: New Mexico Appellate Manual, 1990, 2d edit., 1996; contbr. articles to profl. jours. Vice-dir. Colo. Pub. Interest Rsch. Group, 1974; scoutmaster Gt. S.W. Area coun. Boy Scouts Am., 1977—79; mem. N.Mex. Acupuncture Lic. Bd., 1983; master's coaching level U.S.A. Hockey Assn., dir. N.Mex. coaching edn., 2004—05. Recipient Cert. of Appreciation Cambridge U., 1981, Nathan Burke Meml. award, 1980, N.Mex. Supreme Ct. Cert. Recognition, 1992, 93, 95, N.Mex. Supreme Ct. Cert. Appreciation Outstanding Svc. to Legal Sys., 2001, S.W. Super Lawyer, 2007. Mem.: ATLA, ABA (10th cir. editor 1998, litigation com. on profl. responsibility, mem. Ctr. Profl. Responsibility, litigation com. on pretrial practice and discovery), Am. Law Inst. (mem. restatement employment law), N.Mex. State Bar (chmn. 1990—91, bd. dirs. employment law sect. 1990—96, family law sect. bd. 1999—2001), Bar Assn. U.S. Dist. Ct. Dist. N.Mex. (1st judical dis. bar assoc. pres. 1990—91), USA Hockey, Assn. Coaching Edn. (adm., assoc. coach-in-chief Rocky Mt. dist. 2004—), Santa Fe Trailrunners Hockey Assn. (bd. dirs. 2001—02). Home and Office: PO Box 1656 Santa Fe NM 87504-1656 Office Phone: 505-988-2053. Business E-Mail: barrister@pobox.com.

SCHWARZ, NORBERT, psychology professor; b. Annweiler, Germany, Mar. 28, 1953; Dipl. Sociol., Universität Mannheim, Germany, 1977, D. Phil., Sociol. & Psychol. summa cum laude, 1980; D. Phil. Habil., Universität Heidelberg, Germany, 1986. Lectr. Universität Mannheim, 1978—80; postdoctoral fellow Univ. Ill., 1980—81; fellow Decision Rsch., Universität Mannheim, 1981—83; asst. prof. Universität Heidelberg, 1981—86, privatdozent, 1986—92; sci. dir. Zentrum für Umfragen Methoden & Analysen, Mannheim, 1987—92; prof. psychol. & rsch prof. Univ. Mich., Ann Arbor, 1993—, prof. mktg., 2002—; rsch. prof. Joint Univ. Md. & Univ. Mich. prog. in survey methodology, 1995—. Contbr. articles to profl. jour.; author: Stimmung als Information, 1987, Cognition and Communication, 1996; co-author: Thinking About Answers, 1996. Recipient Heinz Maier-Leibnitz prize, Fed. Republic of Germany, 1986. Fellow: Soc. Personality & Social Psychol., Am. Psychol. Soc., Am. Acad. Arts & Sci.; mem.: World Assn. Public Opinion Rsch., Assn. Consumer Rsch. (France Nicosia award 2004), Am. Assn. Public Opinion Rsch., Soc. Personality & Social Psychol., Soc. Judgement & Decision Making, German Psychol. Soc. (hon. Wilhelm Wundt medal 2004), Soc. Experimental Social Psychol., Soc. Applied Rsch. Memory & Cognition, Midwestern Psychol. Assn., Internat. Soc. Rsch. on Emotion, European Assn. Experimental Social Psychol., Am. Psychol. Assn. Office: Institute for Social Research 426 Thompson St PO Box 1248 Ann Arbor MI 48106-1248 Office Phone: 734-647-3616. Business E-Mail: nschwarz@umich.edu.

SCHWARZ, RICARDO B., research scientist; Doctorate (hon.), Tampere U. Tech., 2002. Lab. fellow Los Alamos Nat. Lab., N.Mex., 1994. Recipient A. von Humboldt Rsch. award for sr. U.S. scientists, 2003. Fellow: Minerals, Metals and Materials Soc., Am. Soc. for Metals; mem.: NAE. Office: Los Alamos Nat Lab Materials Sci & Tech Div MST-8, MS G755 Los Alamos NM 87545 Office Phone: 505-667-8454. Office Fax: 505-667-8021. E-mail: rxzs@lanl.gov.

SCHWARZ, RICHARD HOWARD, obstetrician, gynecologist, educator; b. Easton, Pa., Jan. 10, 1931; s. Howard Eugene and Blanche Elizabeth (Smith) S.; m. Patricia Marie Lewis, Mar. 11, 1978; children by previous marriage: Martha L., Nancy Schwarz Tedesco, Paul H., Mary Katherine Schwarz Murray. MD, Jefferson Med. Coll., 1955; MA (hon.), U. Pa., 1971. Diplomate Am. Bd. Ob-Gyn. (examiner 1977-95), Divsn. Maternal Fetal Medicine 1974. Intern, then resident Phila. Gen. Hosp., 1955-59; prof. U. Pa., Phila., 1963-78; prof., chmn. Downstate Med. Ctr., Bklyn., 1978-90, dean, v.p. acad. affairs, 1983-89, provost, v.p. clin. affairs, 1988-93, interim pres., 1993-94, prof. ob.-gyn., 1990-96, disting. Svc. prof. ob.-gyn. emeritus, 1996; chmn. ob.-gyn. N.Y. Meth. Hosp., Bklyn., 1996—2002; prof. ob.-gyn. Cornell U. Med. Coll., NYC, 1996—2002; vice chair for clin. svc. dept. Ob/GYN Maimonides Med. Ctr., 2002—; prof. ob-gyn. and reproductive sci. Mt. Sinai Sch. Medicine, NY, 2005—. Obstetrical cons. March of Dimes Birth Defects Found., 1995— Author: Septic Abortion, 1968. Editor: Handbook of Obstetric Emergencies, 1984, mem. editorial bd. jour. Ob-Gyn., Milw., 1983-87; contbr. over 200 articles to profl. jours. Bd. dirs. March of Dimes, N.Y.C., 1985-95. Capt. USAF, 1959-63. Recipient Career Achievement award, Infectious Disease Soc. Ob-Gyn., 1999, Founder's award, 2004, Wyeth Ayerest Career Achievement award, 2000. Fellow Royal Coll ObGyn (ad eundem), 1999; mem. ACOG (chmn. dist. 2 1984-87, v.p. 1989-90, pres. elect 1990-91, pres. 1991-92, Lifetime Achievement award dist. II 2005). Republican. Presbyterian. Office: Maimonides Med Ctr 967 48th St Brooklyn NY 11219-3645

SCHWARZ, SIDNEY HOWARD, rabbi; b. NYC, Oct. 8, 1953; s. Allan and Judy (Brand) S.; m. Sandra Perlstein, July 3, 1983; children: David, Joel, Jennifer. BA in Polit. Sci. summa cum laude, U. Md., 1974; MA in Modern Jewish and Am. History, Temple U., Phila., 1977, PhD in History, 1982. Ordained rabbi, 1980. Rabbi Congregatin Beth Israel, Media, Pa., 1976-83; mem. faculty Akiba Hebrew Acad., Merion, Pa., 1981-83, Gratz Coll., Wilmington and Phila., Pa., 1981-83, Reconstructionist Rabinnical Coll., Wyncote, Pa., 1982-84; exec. dir. Jewish Community Coun. of Greater Washington, 1984-87; founding rabbi Adat Shalom Reconstructionist Congregation, Bethesda, Md., 1988; founder, pres. PANIM: Inst. for Jewish Leadership and Values, 1988—. Adj. prof. of Jewish history U. Md., 1986-87; bd. dirs. Jewish Reconstructionist Found., Nat. INst. on Holocaust, Interfaith Conf. Met. Washington; mem. editorial bd. Reconstructionist mag.; mem. Washington Area Community Investment Fund; bd. govs. Reconstructionist Rabbinical Coll.; mem. steering com. Nat. Rabbinic Chevrah. Host. TV talk show Jewish Community Hour. Named one of The Top 50 Rabbis in America, Newsweek Mag., 2007; recipient Covenant award, 2002. Mem. Reconstructionist Rabbinical Assn. (founding editor jour. Raayonot, mem. nat. commn. on intermarriage, mem. long range planning com.). Home: 11707 Farmland Dr Rockville MD 20852-4301 Office: Wash Inst Jewish Leadership Ste 200 6101 Montrose Rd Rockville MD 20852

SCHWARZ, THOMAS J., academic administrator, lawyer; b. NYC, 1945; s. Alexander and Thelma Schwarz; children: Jason, Jessica. BA, Hamilton Coll., Clinton, NY, 1966; JD, Fordham U., NYC, 1969. Bar: NY. Assoc. Skadden, Arps, Slate, Meagher & Flom LLP, NYC, 1969—76, ptnr., 1976—2003, of counsel, 2003—; acting pres. Hamilton Coll., Clinton, 1999; interim pres. SUNY, Purchase, 2002—03, pres., 2003—. Counsel Governor's Judicial Screening Com., First Judicial Dept., 1983—87, 1988—95; spl. counsel NY State Commn. on Govt. Integrity, 1987—90; counsel Governor's Statewide Judicial Screening Com., 1988—95. Author: Federal Regulation of Campaign Finance and Political Activity; contbr. articles to profl. jours. Trustee Citizens Rsch. Found., Berkeley, Calif., 1984—2001; mayor Village, Ocean Beach, NY, 1978—87; trustee Riverside Pk. Fund, NYC, 1998, The Preservation League of N.Y. State, Albany, 1998, Arts Connection, NYC, 1998—2002; spl. counsel NY State Commn. on Govt. Integrity, NYC, 1987—91; commr. Commn. to Promote Pub. Confidence in Jud. Elections, NYC, 2003—04; mem. NY State Commn. on Higher Edn., 2007—, Hamilton Coll. Bd. of Trustees, Clinton, 1987. Recipient Pro Bono award, Legal Aid Soc., 1998. Mem.: ABA (mem. litig. com. 1989—2006), NY State Bar Assn., Assn. Bar City of NY (sec. 1975—78, mem. N.Y. spl. com. on election law 1985—86, mem. com. on fed. legis. 1971—74). Office: Purchase College SUNY 735 Anderson Hill Rd Purchase NY 10577 Office Phone: 914-251-6010. Office Fax: 914-251-6014. Business E-Mail: thomas.schwarz@purchase.edu.

SCHWARZ, WOLFGANG, psychologist; b. Stuttgart, Germany, Oct. 30, 1926; came to U.S., 1934, naturalized, 1940; s. Mole and Edith (Gutstein) S.; m. Cynthia Mae Johnson, Sept. 12, 1949 (div.); children: Amy Maria, Casey Andrew, Darcy Lynn, Priscilla Anne, Lydia Beth, Emily Jane; m. Susan Decker, 1976; children: Jaime Bartholomew, Noah. AB, NYU, 1948, AM, 1949, PhD, 1956. Diplomate Am. Bd. Profl. Psychology. Intern Bellevue Med. Ctr., NYC, 1949-51; chief psychology Rip Van Winkle Med. Found., Hudson, N.Y., 1951-53; dir. psychology Hillcrest Med. Ctr., Tulsa, 1953-56, Hollywood Presbyn. Hosp., LA, 1956-58; cons. psychology Cedars Lebanon Hosp., LA, 1956-58; spl. cons. D.C. Govt., 1959-61, NIH, Bethesda, Md., 1962-64; dir. psychol. rsch. Mass. Dept. Mental Health, Boston and Malden, 1965-68; individual practice clin. psychology Tulsa, 1953-56, Beverly Hills, Calif., 1956-59, Washington, 1959-63, Malden and Concord, Mass., 1963-73, Mt. Kisco, N.Y., 1973—. Lectr. U. Tulsa, 1953-54, L.A. State Coll., 1956-57; asst. prof. Howard U., 1961; assoc. prof. George Washington U., 1961-62; vis. rsch. asst. Harvard Psychiatry Lab., 1966-68; prof. Malden Hosp., 1968-71; cons. No. Westchester Hosp., 1974—, United Hosp., 1975—, Four Winds Hosp., 1975-80; cons. psychology Peace Corps, Mass., 1969—. Author: A Survey of the Mental Health Facilities in the Disctict of Columbia, 1961; contbr. articles to profl. jours. and chpt. to book. Exec. com. Mayor's Model City Program, Malden, 1967-68. With USNR, 1945-46. Recipient Founder's Day award NYU, 1956, Individual award USPHS/NIH, 1960-64 Mem. APA, NY Psychol. Assn., Mass. psychol. Assn., Washington Soc. Hist. Medicine (exec. com. 1963-64), NY Acad. Scis. (honoree 2001), Psi Chi, Beta Lambda Sigma. Home: 249 Martling Ave Tarrytown NY 10591-4707 Office: 191 King St Chappaqua NY 10514 Office Phone: 914-238-0438. Personal E-mail: drwschwarz@aol.com.

SCHWARZENEGGER, ARNOLD ALOIS, governor; b. Thal, Styria, Austria, July 30, 1947; came to U.S., 1968, naturalized, 1983; s. Gustav and Aurelia (Jedrny) S.; m. Maria Owings Shriver, Apr. 26, 1986; children: Katherine Eunice, Christina Aurelia, Patrick, Christopher. BA in Bus. and Internat. Econs., U. Wis., Superior; doctorate (hon.), U. Wis. Superior, 1996, Chapman U., 2002. Owner prodn. co. and real estate; gov. State of Calif., Sacramento, 2003—. Speaker Republican Nat. Convention, NYC, 2004. Actor: (films) Stay Hungry, 1976 (Golden Globe award 1976), Pumping Iron, 1977, The Villain, 1979, Conan, The Barbarian, 1982, Conan, The Destroyer, 1983, The Terminator, 1984, Commando, 1985, Red Sonja, 1985, Raw Deal, 1986, Predator, 1987, Running Man, 1987, Red Heat, 1988, Twins, 1988, Total Recall, 1990, Kindergarten Cop, 1990, Terminator 2: Judgement Day, 1991, True Lies, 1994, Junior, 1994, Terminator 2: 3-D, 1996, Jingle All the Way, 1996, Eraser, 1996, Batman & Robin, 1997, End of Days, 1999, Collateral Damage, 2002, Terminator 3: Rise of the Machines, 2003, Around the World in 80 Days, 2004, The Kid and I, 2005; actor, prodr. The Last Action Hero, 1993, The 6th Day, 2000; (TV spl.) Sinatra: 80 Years My Way, 1995; (TV movies) The Jayne Mansfield Story, 1980; dir. TV movie Christmas in Connecticut, 1992; host A Very Special Christmas Story; dir. The Switch, Tales from the Crypt, HBO, 1990; author: Arnold: The Education of a Bodybuilder, 1977, Arnold's Bodyshaping for Women, 1979, Arnold's Bodybuilding for Men, 1981, Arnold's Encyclopedia of Modern Bodybuilding, 1985, 2d edit. 1998; prodr. bodybuilding video tape; exec. editor Muscle & Fitness Mag., Flex Mag. Nat. weight tng. coach Spl. Olympics; vol. prison rehab. programs; chmn. Pres.'s Coun. on Phys. Fitness and Sports, 1990-93. Bodybldg. champion, 1965-80; named Jr. Mr. Europe, 1965, Best Built Man of Europe, 1966, Mr. Europe, 1966; Internat. Powerlifting Championship, 1966, German Powerlifting Championship, 1968; IFFB (Internat. Fedn. Body Builders) Mr. Internat., 1968, IFFB Mr. Universe (amateur), 1969; NABBA (Nat. Assn. Body Builders) Mr. Universe (amateur), 1967, NABBA Mr. Universe (profl.), 1968, 69, 70; Mr. World, 1970; IFFB Mr. Olympia, 1970, 71, 72, 73, 74, 75, 80; recipient Golden Globe award for Best Newcomer in Films, 1976, Timmie Award The Touchdown Club, 1990, Rave award for Politics, WIRED Mag., 2007; named Video Star Yr. VSDA, 1990; voted Internat. Star of 1984, ShoWest; recipient, Muhammad Ali Humanitarian award; Nat. Leadership award, Simon Wiesenthal Ctr.; Father Flanagan Svc. to Youth award, Boys and Girls Town.; named one of The World's Most Influential People, TIME mag., 2007, 50 Who Matter Now, Business 2.0, 2007. Republican. Roman Catholic. Office: Office of Governor State Capitol Sacramento CA 95814-4906 Office Phone: 916-445-2841. Office Fax: 916-445-4633. *

SCHWARZER, WILLIAM W., federal judge; b. Berlin, Apr. 30, 1925; came to U.S., 1938, naturalized, 1944; s. John F. and Edith M. (Daniel) S.; m. Anne Halbersleben, Feb. 2, 1951; children: Jane Elizabeth, Andrew William. AB cum laude, U. So. Calif., 1948; LLB cum laude, Harvard U., 1951. Bar: Calif. 1953, U.S. Supreme Ct. 1967. Teaching fellow Harvard U. Law Sch., 1951-52; asso. firm McCutchen, Doyle, Brown & Enersen, San Francisco, 1952-60, ptnr., 1960-76; judge U.S. Dist. Ct (no. dist.) Calif., San Francisco, 1976—; dir. Fed. Jud. Ctr., Washington, 1990-95. Sr. counsel Pres.'s Commn. on CIA Activities Within the U.S., 1975; chmn. U.S. Jud. Conf. Com. Fed.-State Jurisdiction, 1987-90; mem. faculty Nat. Inst. Trial Advocacy, Fed. Jud. Ctr., All-ABA, U.S.-Can. Legal Exch., 1987, Anglo-U.S. Jud. Exch., 1994-95, Salzburg Seminar on Am. Studies; ret. disting. prof. Hastings Coll. Law U. Calif., ret. Author: Managing Antitrust and Other Complex Litigation, 1982, Civil Discovery and Mandatory Disclosure, 1994, Federal Civil Procedure Before Trial, 1994; contbr. articles to legal publs., aviation jours. Trustee World Affairs Coun. No. Calif., 1961-88; chmn. bd. trustees Marin Country Day Sch., 1963-66; mem. Marin County Aviation Commn., 1969-76; mem. vis. com. Harvard Law Sch., 1981-86. Served with Intelligence, U.S. Army, 1943-46. Recipient Edward J. Devitt Disting. Svc. to Justice award, 2004. Fellow Am. Coll. Trial Lawyers (S. Gates award 1992), Am. Bar Found.; mem. ABA (Meador Rosenberg award 1995), Am. Law Inst., San Francisco Bar Assn., State Bar Calif., Coun. Fgn. Rels. Office: 450 Golden Gate Ave San Francisco CA 94102-3661 Office Phone: 415-522-4660.

SCHWARZMAN, STEPHEN ALLEN (STEVE SCHWARZMAN), investment banker; b. NYC, Feb. 14, 1947; s. Joseph and Arline (Horelley) Schwarzman; m. Christine Schwarzman; children: Elizabeth, Edward. BA, Yale U., New Haven, 1969; MBA, Harvard U., Cambridge, Mass., 1972. Mng. dir. Lehman Bros., NYC, 1978—84, chmn. mergers & acquisitions com., 1983—84; co-founder, chmn., CEO The Blackstone Grp., NYC, 1985—. Adj. prof. Yale Sch. Mgmt.; mem. nat. adv. com. JP Morgan Chase. Bd. dirs. NYC Ballet, NY Pub. Libr., New Film Society of Lincoln Ctr., NYC Partnership, Frick Collection; chmn. bd. trustees Kennedy Ctr. Performing Arts, Washington, 2004-; mem. vis. com. Harvard Bus. Sch. Named one of Forbes' Richest Ams., 2005—, World's Richest People, Forbes mag., 2006—, The World's Most Influential People, TIME mag., 2007. Mem. Coun. Fgn. Rels, Bus, Coun. Jewish. Office: The Blackstone Grp 345 Park Ave Ste 3101 New York NY 10154-0004 Office Phone: 212-583-5823. E-mail: schwarzman@blackstone.com. *

SCHWARZSCHILD, JANE L., lawyer; b. Richmond, Va., 1949; BA, Smith Coll., 1971; JD, Univ. Va., 1974. Bar: Va. 1974. Ptnr. practice group leader trusts and estates Troutman Sanders LLP, Richmond, Va. Named one of Best Lawyers in Am. Trusts and Estates, 1993—2006; named to Legal Elite in Taxes, Estates, and Trusts, Va. Bus. Mag., 2000—06; recipient Spl. Achievements and Contributions award, Va. Women Attys. Assn., 1986. Mem.: Am. Coll. Trusts and Estate Counsel, Richmond Estate Planning Coun., Va. State Bar, Va. Bar Assn. Home and Office: Troutman Sanders LLP PO Box 1122 Richmond VA 23218 Office Phone: 804-697-1382. Office Fax: 804-698-5183. Business E-Mail: jane.schwarzschild@troutmansanders.com.

SCHWARZTRAUBER, SAYRE ARCHIE, former naval officer, maritime consultant; b. Zion, Ill., June 23, 1929; s. Archie Douglas and Eleanor Miriam (Sayrs) S.; m. Beryl Constance Stewart, June 27, 1953; children: Sayre Archie, Beryl Ann, Heidi, Holly. BS cum laude, Maryville Coll., 1951; MA, Am. U., 1964, PhD, 1970. Commd. ensign USN, 1952, advanced through grades to rear adm., 1976; comdr. River Squadron 5, Vietnam, 1968-69, U.S.S. Decatur guided missile destroyer, 1970-71, Navy Recruiting Area 4, 1974-76; dep. chief staff Supreme Command Atlantic (NATO), 1976-79; co-dir. U.S.-Spanish Combined Staff, Madrid, 1979-81; dir. Inter-Am. Def. Coll., Washington, 1981-83; ret., 1983; apptd. rear adm. U.S. Maritime Svc., 1984; pres. Maine Maritime Acad., 1984—86. Mem. Sec. of Navy Adv. Com., 1986-90; nat. and internat. lectr. strategic naval and maritime matters, 1973—. Author: The Three-Mile Limit of Territorial Seas, 1972, Schwarztrauber, Stewart and Related Families, 1995; editor Mass. Maritime Mag., 1987-90; contbr. articles, essays and revs. to profl. jours. Ruling elder Presbyn. Ch. U.S.A., 1965-86. Decorated Def. Disting. Svc. Medal, Legion of Merit, Cross of Gallantry (Vietnam), Gran Cruz de Merito (Spain); recipient Alfred Thayer Mahan award Navy League, 1974. Mem. SAR (pres. Cape Cod chpt. 1993-95, state reg. and genealogist 1992-2003, state pres. 1998-99, nat. trustee 1999-2000), Gamewardens of Vietnam, Nat. Geneal. Soc., U.S. Naval Inst., Am. Legion, Masons (adjutant Aleppo Temple), VFW, Mil. Order World Wars, Mensa, Travelers' Century Club, Phi Kappa Phi, Pi Gamma Mu, Pi Sigma Alpha, Theta Alpha Phi. Home and Office: PO Box 589 Osterville MA 02655-0589

SCHWASS, GARY L., utilities executive; b. Ludington, Mich., Sept. 30, 1945; s. Philip V. and Greta (Beebe) S.; m. Peggy Ann McElroy, Nov. 29, 1968; children: John P., Jeree A. BS, Western Mich. U., 1968; MBA, Eastern Mich. U., 1971. Tchr. maths. Annapolis High Sch., Dearborn Heights, Mich., 1968-71; corp. systems analyst Consumers Power Co., Jackson, Mich., 1971-73, prin. planning analyst, 1974-78, dir. fin. planning, 1979-80, dir. fin. planning and projects, 1981-83, exec. dir. fin. planning and projects, 1984-85; treas. Duquesne Light Co., Pitts., 1985-88, v.p., 1987—, v.p. finance group, CFO, 1989-94, sr. v.p., chief fin. officer, 1995—. V.p., treas. DQE, Pitts., 1989-94; exec. v.p., pres., chief fin. officer, treas. Montauk, 1990—, Western Pa. Devel. Credit Corp., Pitts., 1985—; chmn. bd. dirs. Custom Coals Internat., 1991-92; bd. dirs. Duquesne Enterprises, Protection Mut. Ins. Co.; steering com. Edison Electric Inst. Fin., 1991-94; exec. v.p., CEO and treas., 1995—. V.p., treas. bd. dirs. Cath. Social Services, Jackson, 1984-85; bd. dirs. Mercy Health Svcs., Altoona, 1992—, Holy Family Inst., Pitts., 1988-92; v.p., treas., bd. dirs. Holy Family Found., Pitts., 1992—. Methodist. Avocations: skiing, reading, woodworking. Office: DQE Inc 411 7th Ave Pittsburgh PA 15219-1919

SCHWEBEL, MILTON, psychologist, educator; b. Troy, NY, May 11, 1914; s. Frank and Sarah (Oxenhandler) S.; m. Bernice Lois Davison, Sept. 3, 1939; children: Andrew I., Robert S. AB, Union Coll., 1934; MA, SUNY, Albany, 1936; PhD, Columbia U., NYC, 1949; Cert. in Psychotherapy, Postgrad. Ctr. Mental Health, NYC, 1958. Lic. psychologist, NY, NJ; diplomate Am. Bd. Examiners Profl. Psychology. Asst. prof. psychology Mohawk Champlain Coll., 1946-49; asst. to prof. edn., dept. chmn., assoc. dean NYU, 1949-67; dean, prof. Grad. Sch. Edn., Rutgers U., New Brunswick, NJ, 1967-77; dean emeritus Grad. Sch. Applied and Profl. Psychology, 1977—, prof., 1977-85, prof. emeritus, 1985—. Vis. prof. U. So. Calif., U. Hawaii; postdoctoral fellow Postgrad. Ctr. Mental Health, NYC, 1954-58, lectr. psychology, 1958-90; cons. NIMH, US, state and city depts. edn., UNESCO, ednl. ministries in Europe, Asia, univs. and pub. schs., UNESCO; pvt. cons. psychologist and psychotherapist, 1953—; disting. cons. & faculty Saybrook Grad. Sch. & Rsch. Ctr., 1999—. Author: A Guide to a Happier Family, 1989, Personal Adjustment and Growth, 1990, Student Teachers Handbook, 3d edit., 1996, Interests of Pharmacists, 1951, Health Counseling, 1953, Who Can Be Educated?, 1968, Remaking America's Three School System: Now Separate and Unequal, 2003; editor: Mental Health Implications of Life in the Nuclear Age, 1986, Facilitating Cognitive Development, 1986, Promoting Cognitive Growth Over the Life Span, 1990, Behavioral Science and Human Survival, 1965, The Impact of Ideology on the I.Q. Controversy, 1975; editor Peace & Conflict: Jour. Peace Psychology, 1993-2000 (vol. 9, no. 4. named Pioneer in Peace Psychology: Milton Schwebel); co-editor Bull. Peace Psychology, 1991-94; mem. editl. bd. Am. Jour. Orthopsychiatry, Readings in Mental Health, Jour. Contemporary Psychotherapy, Jour. Counseling Psychology, Jour. Social Issues, others. Mem. sci. adv. bd. Internat. Ctr. for Enhancement of Learning Potential, 1988—; trustee Edn. Law Ctr., 1973-81, Nat. Com. Employment Youth, Nat. Child Labor Com., 1967-75, Union Exptl. Colls. and Univs., 1976-78; pres. Nat. Orgn. for Migrant Children, 1980-85; pres. Inst. of Arts and Humanities, 1984-95. Served with AUS, 1943-46, ETO. Recipient Disting. Leader in Edn. award, Grad. Sch. Edn. Rutgers U., 2006; Met. Applied Rsch. Coun. fellow, 1970—71. Fellow APA, Am. Psychol. Soc., Am. Orthopsychiatry Assn., Soc. Psychol. Study Social Issues, Jean Piaget Soc. (trustee), Am. Ednl. Rsch. Assn., NY Acad. Scis., Psychologists for Social Responsibility (pres.), Sigma Xi. Home and Office: 431 S Brighton Ln Tucson AZ 85711 Office Phone: 520-745-1725. Business E-Mail: mschwebe@rci.rutgers.edu.

SCHWEBEL, RENATA MANASSE, sculptor; b. Zwickau, Germany, Mar. 6, 1930; came to U.S., 1940, naturalized, 1946; d. George and Anne Marie (Simon) Manasse; m. Jack P. Schwebel, May 10, 1955; children: Judith, Barbara, Diane. BA, Antioch Coll., 1953; MFA, Columbia U., 1961; student, Arts Students League, 1967-69. Cartographer Ecostate Inc., Ridgewood, NJ, 1949; display artist Silvestri Inc., Chgo., 1950-51; asst. Mazzolini Art Foundry, Yellow Springs, Ohio, 1952. One-woman shows include Columbia U., 1961, Greenwich Art Barn, Conn., 1975, Sculpture Ctr., N.Y.C., 1979, Pelham Art Ctr., N.Y., 1981, New Rochelle Libr. Gallery, 1980, Outdoor Installations Katonah Gallery, 1986, 1989, Berman/Daferner Gallery, N.Y.C., 1992—93; artist (group shows) Stamford Mus., Conn., 1967, 1996, Hudson River Mus., Yonkers, N.Y., 1972, 1974, Wadsworth Atheneum, Hartford, 1974, Silvermine Art of the Northwest U.S.A. Anns., 1972, 1976, 1980, 1995, 1998, Silvermine Gallery, 1986, 1991, 2000, 2001, 2002, 2003, New Britain Mus. Am. Art, Conn., 1974, Imprimatur Gallery, St. Paul, 1985, 1986, Bergen County Mus., N.J., 1983, Sculpture Ctr., 1978—88, Katonah Gallery, N.Y., 1986—90, Cast Iron Gallery, N.Y.C., 1991, 1993, Kyoto (Japan) Gallery, 1993; exhibitions include Sculptors Guild Anns., 1974—, traveling show exhibitions, in Am. cultural ctrs. in Egypt and Israel, 1981, 3 Rivers Art Festival, Pitts., 1994, FFS Gallery, N.Y.C., 1994, 1995, Russian Consulate, 1998, Long Beach Island Assn. Arts and Scis., N.J., 1999, Grounds for Sculpture, Hamilton, N.J., 1999, Chesterwood Mus., Stockbridge, Mass., 2000, Troy Arts Ctr., N.Y., 2000—01, Rockland Ctr. for Arts, 2001—02, No. Westchester Arts Coun., 2002, 2003, Westport Arts Ctr., 2003, Ednl. Alliance Gallery, N.Y.C., 2003, Carriage Barn Arts Ctr., New Canaan, Conn., 2005, Pleiades Gallery, N.Y.C., 2006, Iowa Gallery, Iona Coll., New Rochelle, NY, 2007, Represented in permanent collections S.W. Bell, Columbia U., Colt Industries, Am. Airlines, Comcraft Industries, Nairobi, Gruber Haus, Berlin, Mus. Fgn. Art, Sofia, Bulgaria, Housatonic Mus., Jule Collins Smith Mus. Fine Art, Auburn, Ala., Hexcel Corp. Bd. dirs. Fine Arts Fedn., N.Y., 1985-87; trustee Sculpture Ctr., 1980-88, chmn. exhbn. com., 1986-88; adv. bd. Pehlham Art Ctr., 1982. Mem.: N.Y. Artists Equity, Silvermine Guild, Conn. N.Y. Soc. Women Artists, Conn. Acad. Fine Arts, Audubon Artists (Chaim Gross award 1980, Medal of Honor 1982, Rennick award 1986, 1990, 1992, 1995), Nat. Assn. Women Artists (Willis Meml. prize 1974, Medal of Honor 1981, Paley Meml. award 1979), Sculptors Guild (bd. dirs. 1975—94, pres. 1980—83, bd. dirs. 1995—2004), Katonah Gallery (artist mem. 1986—90), Ams. for Peace Now (bd. dirs. 1991—2001), Antioch Coll. Assn. (bd. dirs. 1971—77). Home: 10 Dogwood Hills Pound Ridge NY 10576-1508 Personal E-mail: renata99m@gmail.com.

SCHWEBEL, STEPHEN MYRON, arbitrator, mediator, legal advisor; b. NYC, Mar. 10, 1929; s. Victor and Pauline (Pfeffer) S.; m. Louise Ingrid Nancy Killander, Aug. 2, 1972; children: Jennifer, Anna. BA in Govt. magna cum laude with highest honors in govt., Harvard U., 1950; postgrad., Cambridge U., 1950—51; LLB, Yale U., 1954; LLD (hon.), Bhopal U., 1983, Hofstra U., 1997, U. Miami, 2002. Bar: N.Y. 1955, U.S. Supreme Ct. 1965, D.C. 1976. Dir. UN hdqrs. office World Fedn. UN Assns., 1950—53; lectr. Am. fgn. policy various univs. U.S. Dept. State, India, 1952; rsch., drafting asst. Trygve Lie for writing of In the Cause of Peace, 1953; assoc. White & Case, NYC, 1954—59; asst. prof. law Harvard U., Cambridge, Mass., 1959—61; asst. legal advisor U.S. Dept. State, Washington, 1961—66, dep. legal advisor, 1973—81; exec. dir. Am. Soc. Internat. Law, Washington, 1967—72; Burling prof. internat. law Sch. of Advanced Internat. Studies, Johns Hopkins U., Washington, 1967—81; pres. Adminstrv. Tribunal IMF, Washington, 1994—; judge Internat. Ct. Justice, The Hague, Netherlands, 1981—2000, v.p., 1994—97, pres., 1997—2000; judge adminstrv. tribunal World Bank, Washington, 2007—. Hon. fellow Cambridge U. Ctr. for Rsch. in Internat. Law, 1983—; mem. bd. electors Whewell Professorship in Internat. Law U. Cambridge, 1983—; hon. bencher Gray's Inn, London, 1998—; spl. rep. Micronesian claims U.S. Dept. State, 1966—71; legal adv. U.S. del. 16th-20th and 4th Spl. Gen. Assemblies UN; US assoc. rep. Internat. Ct. Justice, 1962; U.S. assoc. rep. U.S. dep. agt., 1979, U.S. counsel, 1980; U.S. rep., chmn. U.S. del. to 1st session UN Spl. Com. on Principles Internat. Law concerning friendly rels. and coop. among states, Mexico City, 1964; US rep. numerous other UN coms.; pres. So. Blue Fin Tuna Arbitration, 2000; mem. Eritrea-Yemen Arbitration Tribunal, 1998—2000, Eritrea-Ethiopia Boundary Commn., 2001—; pres. Barbados-Trinidad & Tobago Arbitration, 2004—06; mem. panels arbitrators and conciliators Internat. Ctr. Settlement of Investment Disputes World Bank, 2000—06; chmn. or party-apptd. arbitrator 48 internat. comml. arbitrations, 1982—2007; mem. Permanent Ct. of Arbitration, The Hague, 2006—; cons. Ford Found., 1990; chmn. supr. bd. Telders Internat. Law Moot Ct. Competition, The Hague, The Netherlands, 1993—98; chmn. Hauser Scholars Selection Bd., N.Y.U. Law Sch., 1997—2000; bd. dirs. Am. Arbitration Assn., 2006—; vis. lectr. in field. Author: The Secretary-General of the United Nations, 1952, International Arbitration: Three Salient Problems, 1987, Justice in International Law, 1994; editor: The Effectiveness of International Decisions, 1971; mem. editorial bd. Am. Jour. Internat. Law, 1967-81, hon. mem., 1996—; chmn. editorial adv. com. Internat. Legal Materials, 1967-73. Mem. UN Internat. Law Commn., Geneva, 1977—81. Frank Knox fellow Harvard U., 1950-51, Hallows Jud. fellow Marquette U. Law Sch., 2000, Hon. fellow Trinity Coll., Cambridge U., 2005; recipient Gherini prize Yale Law Sch., 1954, medal of Merit, 1997, Pres. medal Johns Hopkins U., 1992, Harold Weill medal NYU, 1992, Wolfgang Friedmann award Columbia U., 1998. Mem. ABA, Am. Soc. Internat. Law (exec. v.p 1967-73, hon. v.p. 1982-95, hon. pres. 1996-2001, Manley O. Hudson medal 2000), Internat. Law Assn., Inst. Droit Internat., Coun. Fgn. Rels., Acad. of Experts (v.p. 1995—), Harvard Club (NYC), Athenaeum (London), Met. Club, Cosmos Club, Phi Beta Kappa. Avocation: music. Office: 1501 K St NW Washington DC 20005 Home Phone: 202-232-3114; Office Phone: 202-736-8328. Personal E-mail: judgeschwebel@aol.com.

SCHWEBLER, STEPHEN, retired chemist; b. Flemington, NJ, Dec. 5, 1928; s. Philip and Elizabeth (Pratscher) S.; m. Marian Finch, May 3, 1953; children: Bradley Stephen, Susan Elizabeth, Nancy Carol. AS, Columbia-Greene C.C., Hudson, NY, 1974; BS, SUNY, Saratoga, 1982. With Marshall's Chrysler-Plymouth, Ravena, N.Y., 1953-56; owner/mgr. Steve's Auto Svc., Coxsackie, N.Y., 1956-58; svc. mgr. Jackson & Boone Chrysler-Plymouth, West Coxsackie, N.Y., 1958-66; sr. lab. technician N.Y. State Dept. Health, Albany, 1966-72, N.Y. State Dept. Environ. Conservation, Albany, 1972-85; phys. chemist N.Y. State Office Gen. Svcs., Albany, 1985-88, specification writer, 1988-90, N.Y. State Thruway Authority, Albany, 1990-94; ret. Deacon New Baltimore Ref. Ch., N.Y., 1985-90; rsch. vol. Greene County Hist. Soc., West Coxsackie, 1996—. Democrat. Reformed Ch. Achievements include developing first confirmatory test for the birth defect, galactosemia, by paper chromatography; research in improved methods of sewage treatment and toxic substance monitoring of all bodies of water in N.Y. state. Home: 3931 Rt 51 Hannacroix NY 12087-9708 E-mail: sschweb@aol.com.

SCHWED, ROGER E., lawyer, rental company executive; b. NYC, Jan. 3, 1958; s. Peter and Antonia Holding Schwed; m. Laura F. Dukess, Feb. 26, 1989; children: Benjamin, Stephen. AB cum laude, Princeton U., 1979; JD, Columbia U., 1986. Bar: NY 1987, US Dist. Ct. (ea. dist.) NY 1987, US Dist. Ct. (so. dist.) NY 1988. Subs. rights assoc. Doubleday & Co., Inc., NYC, 1979—83; mgr. subs. rights Harper & Row, NYC, 1983—83; jud. clk. to Hon. Eugene H. Nickerson US Dist. Ct. (ea. dist.), NYC, 1986—87; assoc. Cleary, Gottlieb, Steen & Hamilton, NYC, 1987—95; counsel Skadden, Arps, Slate, Meagher & Flom, NYC, 1995—96; exec. v.p., gen. counsel Maxcor Fin. Group Inc., NYC, 1996—2005, United Rentals, Inc., 2006—. Bd. dirs. I Challenge Myself, Inc., NYC. Coach West Side Little League, NYC, 1998—2003, 2005—, West Side Soccer League, NYC, 1999—2004. Avocations: bicycling, computers, reading. Office: United Rentals, Inc Five Greenwich Office Park Greenwich CT 06831 Home Phone: 212-864-4695. Business E-Mail: roger@rschwed.com.

SCHWEGLER, NANCY ANN, librarian, writer; b. Bklyn., Jan. 22, 1946; d. Richard Donald Newman and Beatrice Ella Stirba; m. Robert Andrew Schwegler, Apr. 6, 1968; children: Brian Alexander, Christopher Robert, Ashley Marie. BA, Hope Coll., Holland, Mich., 1967; MLIS, U. R.I., 1991. Libr. asst. Art Libr., U. of Chgo., Chgo., 1968—71; children's libr. Watertown (Mass.) Pub. Libr., 1971—72; cataloguer Astronomy Libr., U. Cin., 1972—73; children's libr. East Greenwich (R.I.) Free Libr., 1984—89, Bradley Hosp., Riverside, RI, 1988—. Author: (bibliography) Rhode Island Parents' Paper, Writing in Depth, 2004, Choices: Voices Values and Writing Strategies, 2006; contbr. articles to newspapers and jours. Mem.: ALA, Delta Phi Delta, Beta Phi Mu, Phi Kappa Phi. Reformed Church Of America. Avocations: lighthouse preservation advocacy, international adoption advocacy, watercolour painting. Home: 83 Darling St Warwick RI 02886 Office: Bradley Hospital 1011 Veterans Meml Pkwy Riverside RI 02915 Personal E-mail: nnschweg@aol.com. E-mail: nschwegler@lifespan.org.

SCHWEICKERT, RICHARD JUSTUS, psychologist, educator; b. Madison, Wis., July 19, 1946; s. Carl E. and Marie E. (Dilzer) S.; m. Carolyn M. Jagacinski, Dec. 27, 1980; children: Patrick, Kenneth. BS in Math., U. Santa Clara, 1968; MA in Math., Ind. U., 1972; PhD in Psychology, U. Mich., 1979. Statistician Bellevue Psychiatric Hosp., NYC, 1969-71; asst. prof. Purdue U., West Lafayette, Ind., 1978-83, assoc. prof., 1984-91, prof., 1992—. Adv. panel on human cognition and perception NSF, 1993-96. Author (with others): Handbook of Human Factors; editor Jour. Math. Psychology, 2000—04, mem. editl. bd., 1986—94, 2004—, assoc. editor Psychol. Bull. and Rev., 1993—98, mem. editl. bd. Jour. Exptl. Psychology, Learning, Memory and Cognition, 1985—89, 1991—94; contbr. articles to profl. jours. Grantee NSF, 1981-84, 92-2000, NIMH, 1983-89, Air Force Office Sci. Rsch., 2006—. Fellow AAAS, Am. Psychol. Soc.; mem. Soc. for Math. Psychology (pres. 1990-91, bd. dir.), Psychonomic Soc., Informs. Office: Purdue U Dept Psychol Scis Lafayette IN 47907

SCHWEIKER, MARK S., former governor; b. Bucks County, Pa., Jan. 31, 1953; s. John and Mary S.; m. Katherine Schweiker; children: Brett, Eric, Kara. BS, Bloomsburg U., 1975; MA in Adminstrn., Rider U., 1983. Merrill Lynch; McGraw Hill; supr. Middletown Twp., 1979; commr. Bucks County, Pa., 1987-94; elec. lt. gov., 1994—2001; lt. gov., pres. of the Senate, chmn. of the bd. of pardons Commonwealth of Pa., 1995—2001, gov., 2001—03; former chmn. prime coun., chmn. local govt. adv. coun., chmn. gov.'s exec. coun. recycling devel. & waste reduction, dir. Pa. weed and seed program, gov., 2001—03; pres. & CEO Greater Phila. Chamber of Commerce, 2003—. Former chmn. Dela. Valley Regional Fin. Authority. Former bd. dirs. Bucks County United Way. Recipient Alumnus of Yr. Bloomsburg U., 1990, Outstanding Svc. to Conservation award Nature Conservancy Pa. Branch, 1993, Tech. Advocate of Yr. Tech. Coun. Ctrl. Pa., 1996, Outstanding Achievement award Citizens Against Govt. Waste, 1997, Commitment to Excellence in Local Govt. award Pa. Economy League, 1998. Republican. Office: Greater Phila C of C 200 Broad St Ste 700 Philadelphia PA 19102

SCHWEIKER, RICHARD SCHULTZ, former trade association administrator, former secretary of health & human services, former senator; b. Norristown, Pa., June 1, 1926; s. Malcolm Alderfer and Blanche (Schultz) S.; m. Claire Joan Coleman, Sept. 10, 1955; children: Malcolm C., Lani, Kyle, Richard S. Jr., Lara Kristi. BA, Pa. State U., 1950; D of Pub. Svcs. (hon.), Temple U., 1970; D.Sc. (hon.), Georgetown U., 1981. Bus. exec., 1950-60; mem. 87th-90th congresses from 13th Dist. Pa., mem. house armed services and govt. ops. coms., 1961—69; U.S. senator from Pa., 1969-80; mem. appropriations com., ranking mem. Labor-HEW subcom., ranking mem. health and human resources com., ranking mem. health subcom.; sec. US Dept. Health & Human Services, Washington, 1981—83; pres. Am. Council Life Ins., Washington, 1983-94. Chmn. Partnership for Prevention, 1991—97. Alt. del. Nat. Rep. Conv., 1952, 56, del., 1972, 80; designated v.p. candidate with Reagan for Pres. of U.S., 1976. Served with USNR, World War II. Recipient Disting. Alumnus award Pa. State U., 1970, Dr. Charles H. Best award Am. Diabetes Assn., 1974, Outstanding Alumnus of Yr. award Phi Kappa Sigma, 1982, Gold medal Pa. Assn. Broadcasters, 1982, Nat. Outstanding Svc. award Headstart, 1983, Pub. Svc. Gold medal Surgeon Gen. U.S., 1988, Govt. Achievement award Juvenile Diabetes Found., 1990, Disting. Achievement award Nat. Coun. on Aging, 1991, John Newton Russell award Nat. Assn. Life Underwriters, 1992; named Outstanding Young Man of Yr., Jr. C. of C., 1960. Mem. Phi Beta Kappa.

SCHWEIKERT, EDGAR OSKAR, dentist; b. Heidelberg, Germany, Aug. 30, 1938; came to U.S., 1972; s. Oskar and Priska (Zehr) S.; m. Mary Lou Como, Apr. 7, 1969; 1 child, Marisa. Degree, Hamburg Dental Sch., 1966; Dr. Med. Dentistry, U. Munich, 1969. Lic. dentist, Calif., NY Dentist, U.S. Army, Frankfurt, Fed. Republic Germany, 1969-72; gen. practice dentistry, LA, 1972-73, Bklyn., 1973—; lectr. in field. Author: Multiple Cantilevers in Fixed Prosthesis, 1988, Spanish edit., 1990; contbr. articles to profl. jours. Served as capt. German Air Force, 1967-69. Mem. ADA, German Dental Assn., Second Dist. Dental Assn., Bay Ridge Dental Soc., Guild Dental Craftsmen. Home and Office: 429 77th St Brooklyn NY 11209-3205

SCHWEIKERT, MARY LOU, elementary school educator; b. Bklyn., Aug. 6, 1938; d. Frank Salvatore Como and Angela Licciardi-Como; m. Edgar O. Schweikert, Apr. 7, 1969; 1 child, Marisa. Ba in Journalism, L.I. U., 1962; MSc in Edn., Wagner Coll., 1978. Lic. tchr. N.Y.C., 1965, N.Y., 1965. Tchr. N.Y.C. Bd. Edn., Bklyn., 1962—65, Dept. Def., 1965—72; mgr. dental office Dr. Edgar Schweikert, Bklyn., 1973—. Editor: Multiple Cantilevers in Fixed Prosthesis, 1988, Jour. Prosthetic Dentistry, 1984, Dentistry Today, 1994, 1995, 1999. Mem.: Nat. Assn. Women. Democrat. Roman Catholic. Avocations: tennis, gardening, stock market, travel. Home and Office: Dr Edgar Schweikert Dentistry 429 77th St Brooklyn NY 11209 Office Phone: 718-680-4717. Personal E-mail: mschweik@earthlink.net.

SCHWEIKERT, NORMAN CARL, retired musician; b. LA, Oct. 8, 1937; s. Carl Albert and Hilda (Meade) S.; m. Sally Hardin Haizlip, July 22, 1961; 1 son, Eric Carl. Mus.B. performer's certificate in horn, Eastman Sch. Music, 1961. Teaching assoc. Northwestern U., 1973-75, assoc. prof. (part-time), 1975-98; horn instr. Nat. Music Camp, Interlochen, 1967; curator Leland B. Greenleaf Collection Mus. Instruments, Interlochen, 1970-71 Successively 4th, 2d and 3d horn with, Rochester Philharmonic, Civic and Eastman-Rochester symphonies, 1955-62, 64-66, instr. horn, mem., Interlochen (Mich.) Arts Quintet, Interlochen Arts Acad., 1966-71, 1st horn, Rochester Chamber Orch., 1965-66, Midland (Mich.) Symphony Orch., 1969-71, 1st horn, soloist, Northwestern Mich. Symphony Orch., 1966-71, Chgo. Little Symphony, tours, 1967, 68, asst. 1st horn, soloist, Chgo. Symphony Orch., 1971-75, 2d horn, Chgo. Symphony Orch., 1975-97; appearances with, Eastman Chamber Orch., Rochester Bach Festival, Aspen Festival Orch., Moravian Music Festival, Alaska Festival, Peninsula Music Festival, Rochester Brass Quintet, Canterbury Wind Quintet, Westchester Brass Quintet, Eastman Wind Ensemble, Chgo. Symphony Winds, Quadrangle Chamber Players, Washington Island Music Festival; soloist, New Japan Philharmonic, rec. artist for, Mercury, Columbia, Everest, C.R.I., Capitol. Mark Ednl., London-Decca, DGG, RCA Victor records, Sheffield Lab, Koch; recitals, also lecture demonstrations.; Contbr. articles to profl. jours. Served with AUS, 1962-64. Recipient certificate of merit City Chgo., 1971 Mem. Internat. Horn Soc. (hon., chmn. organizing com., sec.-treas. 1970-72, adv. coun. 1972-76), Am. Mus. Instrument Soc., Phi Mu Alpha Sinfonia (life alumni mem.), Pi Kappa Lambda. Home: 1727 White Trillium Trail Washington Island WI 54246-9026

SCHWEINSBURG, JANE DUBERG, librarian; b. Chgo., Oct. 24, 1946; d. John Edward and Mary Andrews Duberg; m. Richard Lyle Schweinsburg, Sept. 3, 1977. BA in Math., Goucher Coll., Towson, Md., 1967; MLS, SUNY, Albany, 1996. Reference libr. Schenectady County C.C., Schenectady, NY; reference libr., instr. Coll. of St. Rose, Albany, NY, 1996—98; reference libr. Johnson and Wales U., Providence, 1998—99, East Providence Pub. Libr., 1999—2000; asst. dir. Coventry Pub. Libr., Coventry, RI, 2000—. Contbr. articles to encys. and publs. Co-chair Episcopal charities campaign Episcopal Diocese of R.I., Providence, 1999—2000. Recipient Profl. Achievement award, Coll. of St. Rose, 1997. Mem.: R.I. Libr. Assn. (intellectual freedom com.). Episcopalian. Home: 46 Fairway Dr Coventry RI 02816-5775 Office: Coventry Pub Libr 1672 Flat River Rd Coventry RI 02816 Office Phone: 401-822-9104. Business E-Mail: js@coventrylibrary.org.

SCHWEITZER, BRIAN, governor; b. Havre, Mont., Sept. 4, 1955; s. Adam and Kay Schweitzer; m. Nancy Hupp, 1981; children: Ben, Khai, Katrina. BS in Internat. Agronomy, Colo. State U., 1978; MS in Soil Sci., Mont. State U., 1980. Agronomist Kaercherv Agr., Libya, 1980—81; crop supt. Alfa Laval Engring. Co., Saudi Arabia, 1981—84; farm owner, rancher Flathead, Sanders Rosebud and Judith Basin counties, Mont.; mem. Mont. state farm svc. agency com. USDA, 1993—99; gov. State of Mont., Helena, 2005—. Apptd. Mont. Rural Devel. Partnership Bd., 1996, Nat. Drought Task Force. Recipient Award for outreach efforts to Native Americans, U.S. Sec. Agr., 1995. Democrat. Achievements include development of various irrigation systems in Africa, Asia, Europe, and South America; over 28,000 acres of irrigated cropland in Saudi Arabia. Office: Office of the Gov PO Box 200801 Helena MT 59620-0801 Office Phone: 406-444-3111. Office Fax: 406-444-5529. *

SCHWEITZER, CAREN S., social worker; b. NYC, Aug. 1, 1931; d. Robert David and Margaret Lane Steefel; m. Ulrich Schweitzer, Jan. 27, 1984; m. Austin K. Haldenstein, Nov. 26, 1953 (div. June 1970); children: Susan Federspiel, Kenneth Haldenstein. BA, Wellesley Coll., Mass., 1953; MSW, Hunter Sch. Social Work, NYC, 1974. LCSW Acad. Cert. Social Workers, N.Y. Job placement for people with disabilities Just One Break, NYC, 1953—56; job placement Cmty. Action Program, Mamaroneck, NY, 1965—70; asst. to psychologist, 1970—72; program dir. West Assn. for Retarded Citizens, White Plains, NY, 1974—80; supr. group homes Westchester Jewish Cmty. Svcs., White Plains, NY, 1980—85; program coord., Tel. support networks Westchester Self-Help Clearinghouse, Hartsdale, NY, 1985—. Author: (column) Westchester Women's News, 1990—99. Campaign mgr. several Dem. party candidates, Westchester, NY, 1960—69. Phi Beta Kappa, Wellesley Coll., Mass., 1953. Democrat. Jewish. Avocations: tennis, bridge, singing. Home: 214 Dogwood Ln Hartsdale NY 10530 Home Phone: 914-946-2098; Office Phone: 914-761-0600 314. E-mail: ulcare@aol.com.

SCHWEITZER, GEORGE KEENE, chemistry professor; b. Poplar Bluff, Mo., Dec. 5, 1924; s. Francis John and Ruth Elizabeth (Keene) S.; m. Verna Lee Pratt, June 4, 1948; children: Ruth Anne, Deborah Keene, Eric George. BA, Central Coll., 1945, ScD in Philosophy, 1964; MS, U. Ill., 1946, PhD in Chemistry, 1948; MA, Columbia U., 1959; PhD in History, NYU, 1964. Asst. Central Coll., 1943-45; fellow U. Ill., 1946-48; asst. prof. chemistry U. Tenn., 1948-52, assoc. prof., 1952-58, prof., 1960-69, Alumni Distinguished prof., 1970—. Cons. to Monsanto Co., Proctor & Gamble, Internat. Tech., Am. Cyanamid Co., AEC, U.S. Army, Massengill, CTI-Siemens; lectr. colls. and univs.; mem. adv. bd. East Tenn. Hist. Soc. *Achievements include chemical expertise in solvent extraction, ion exchange, lanthanide chemistry, stable isotope concentration, radiochemistry, inductively-coupled plasma mass spectroscopy, the chemical implementation of positron-emission tomography and history and philosophy of science. Genealogical expertise in Revolutionary War, War of 1812, Civil War, Georgia, Kentucky, Illinois, Indiana, Massachusetts, Maryland, Missouri, New Jersey, New York, North Carolina, Ohio, Pennsylvania, South Carolina, Tennessee, Virginia, Germany, Ulster Ireland, migration routes, immigration and emigration records, settlement patterns, and tracing ancestors back across the Atlantic Ocean. Theological expertise in science and religion, religious epistemology, comparative religion, American colonial and frontier religion.* Author: Radioactive Tracer Techniques, 1950, The Doctorate, 1966, Genealogical Source Handbook, 1992, Civil War Genealogy, 1993, Tennessee Genealogical Research, 1981, Kentucky Genealogical Research, 1981, Revolutionary War Genealogy, 1982, Virginia Genealogical Research, 1982, War of 1812 Genealogy, 1983, North Carolina Genealogical Research, 1983, South Carolina Genealogical Research, 1984, Pennsylvania Genealogical Research, 1985, Georgia Genealogical Research, 1987, New York Genealogical Research, 1988, Massachusetts Genealogical Research, 1989, Maryland Genealogical Research, 1991, German Genealogical Research, 1992, Ohio Genealogical Research, 1994, Indiana Genealogical Research, 1996, Illinois Genealogical Research, 1997, Missouri Genealogical Research, 1997; also 170 articles. Faculty fellow Columbia U., 1958-60. Mem. Am. Chem. Soc., Am. Philos. Assn., History Sci. Soc., Soc. Genealogists, Phi Beta Kappa, Sigma Xi. Home: 407 Ascot Ct Knoxville TN 37923-5807

SCHWEITZER, PETER, advertising agency executive; b. Chgo., Aug. 31, 1939; children: Mark, Cynthia, Jenifer, Samantha; m. Elaine Elkin, 1986; children: Dana, Taylor. BA, U. of Mich., 1961; MBA, W. Mich. U., 1967. With Post div. Gen. Foods, 1961-69; v.p. Grey Advt., 1969-76; sr. v.p. J. Walter Thompson, 1976-79; sr. v.p. mktg. Burger King Corp., 1990; sr. v.p., gen. mgr., then exec. v.p., gen. mgr. J. Walter Thompson USA, Inc.-Detroit, 1995; v. chmn. of agency ops. J. Walter Thompson Co., Detroit, 1988-95, pres., 1995—, CEO, 2001—. Pres. Internat. Fedn. Multiple Sclerosis. Office: J Walter Thompson Co 500 Woodward Ave 14th Fl Detroit MI 48226-3416 also: 466 Lexington Ave New York NY 10017-3140

SCHWEITZER, VANESSA GAYL, otorhinolaryngologist; b. Pomona, Calif., Jan. 26, 1952; d. Elford J. Nelson and Patricia Wilma (Sherman) Schweitzer. B.S. in Zoology, U. Mich., 1973; M.D., 1977. Diplomate Am. Bd. Otolaryngology. Intern in gen. surgery U. Mich., 1977-79, resident in otorhinolaryngology, 1979-83; emergency physician Chelsea Community Hosp., Mich., 1979-83, Saline Community Hosp., Mich., 1979-80, Beyer Meml. Hosp. Ypsilanti, Mich., 1980-83; sr. staff physician dept. otolaryngology, head and neck surgery Henry Ford Hosp., Detroit, 1983—; clin. prof. dept. otolaryngology, head and neck surgery U. Mich., Ann Arbor, 1984—. researcher Kresge Hearing Inst., also otology research lab. Henry Ford Hosp. and U. Mich.; lectr. in field; emergency physician Emergency Physicians' Med. Group, Inc., Ann Arbor, 1979-83. Contbr. articles to med. jours. Med. examiner Washtenaw County, Ann Arbor, 1980-84. Angell scholar, 1969-75; recipient Branstrom Freshman award, 1970, Triological Soc Fowler Rsch award, 1996. Fellow ACS; mem. AMA, ASCO, Am. Coll. Emergency Physicians, Am. Acad. Otolaryngology, Am. Acad. Facial Plastic and Reconstructive Surgery, Walter P. Work Soc. (Resident Paper Competitive award 1982), Internat. Photodynamic Therapy Assn., Phi Beta Kappa, Alpha Lambda Delta. Republican. Office: Henry Ford Health Sys 2799 W Grand Blvd Detroit MI 48202-2608 Office Phone: 313-916-3279. Business E-Mail: uschwei1@hfhs.org.

SCHWEIZER, GREGORY PAUL, music educator; b. St. Louis, Jan. 14, 1955; s. Marvin Bernard and Lois Joan Schweizer; m. Diane Marie Stipanovich, June 2, 1978; children: Matthew Gregory, Eric Michael. MusB in Edn., Webster U., St. Louis, 1981. Cert. tchr. K-12 Mo., 1981. Music dir./tchr. St. Dominic Savior Ch., St. Louis, 1978—87, Mary, Queen of Peace Sch., St. Louis, 1979—85; music dir. St. Roch Cath. Ch., St. Louis, 1986—94, St. Lucas United Ch. of Christ, St. Louis, 1994—96, Our Lady of Sorrows Cath. Ch., St. Louis, 1997—; music dir., tchr., dept. chair Visitation Acad., St. Louis, 2000—; music dir. Mo. Athletic Club Apollo Men's Chorus, St. Louis, 1985—. Adj. prof. Webster U., St. Louis, St. Louis Symphony Music Sch.; founder, dir. Camerata Singers. Composer: (composition for tv spot) Variety Club of St. Louis Promo; dir.: (theatrical) Music Director for Shooting Star Productions; condr. (chamber concert series) David & Beatrice Kornblum Concert Series, vocalist nat. comml. Chicken of the Sea Tuna, writer, performer (exercise videos) Martha Rounds; performer: (play with Vikki Carr) I'm Getting My Act Together and Taking It On the Road, G.F. Handel's Saul, St. Louis Bach Soc., St. Louis Symphony Orch.; condr., accompanist, arranger: with Ken Page, accompanist: with Donald O'Conner, Georgia Frontierre, Lou Rawles, Tommy Tune, The Manhattan Rhythm Kings, Rita Moreno, Bernadette Peters, Kathy Rigby, pianist, condr.: VP Ball Orch., pianist: Variety Club Telethon. Mem. Ind. Sch. of St. Louis, 2004—05. Named a Tchr. of Distinction, Ind. Schs. St. Louis, 2006; named an Emerson Tchr. of Excellence, 2006; recipient Outstanding Tchr. of Yr. award, Mo., 2005, 2006, 2007. Mem.: Am. Guild Organists, Nat. Assn. of the Tchrs. of Singing (assoc.), Musicians' Assn. of St. Louis (assoc.). Avocations: photography, carpentry. Home: 5801 Westcliffe Dr Saint Louis MO 63129-4267 Office: Visitation Academy 3020 North Ballas Rd Saint Louis MO 63131 Office Phone: 314-625-9193. Personal E-mail: gregschweizer@hotmail.com. Business E-mail: gschweizer@visitationacademy.org.

SCHWEIZER, KARL WOLFGANG, historian, educator, author; b. Mannheim, Germany, June 30, 1946; came to U.S., 1988; 1 child, Paul. BA in History, Wilfrid Laurier U., Can., 1969; MA, U. Waterloo, Can., 1970; MA, PhD, Cambridge U., 1976. Prof. history Bishop's U., Lenoxville, Que., Canada, 1976-88, chmn. dept., 1978-79, 82-84, 86; prof., chmn. humanities dept. NJ Inst. Tech., Newark, 1988-93, prof. dept. social sci. and policy studies, 1993—, chmn. dept. humanities and social scis., 2000—03, prof. dept. humanities, 2003—07, prof. history dept., 2007—; assoc. Ctr. for Study of Global Change Rutgers U., 1995—, prof. history dept., 2007—. Grad. faculty Rutgers U., 1993—; vis. lectr. U. Guelph, Can., 1978-80; rsch. assoc. Russian Rsch. Ctr., Ill., 1979-80, 99; acad. visitor London Sch. Econs., 1986, 94, vis. scholar, 1986-87, Queens U., Ont., Can., 1986-87; vis. fellow Darwin Coll., Cambridge, 1987, 94, 2003, Princeton U., 1994, Yale U., 1994; vis. prof. dept. polit. sci. Rutgers U., 1997—; sr. rsch. assoc. Peterhouse Coll., Cambridge, 2003. Author: The Art of Diplomacy, 1983, Lord Bute: Essays in Reinterpretation, 1988, England, Prussia and the Seven Years War, 1989, Frederick the Great, William Pitt and Lord Bute, 1991, Lord Chatham, A Bibliography, 1993, François de Callières: Diplomat and Man of Letters, 1995, War, Politics and Diplomacy: The Anglo Prussian Alliance, 1756-1763, 2001, Seeds of Evil: The Gray/Snyder Murder Case, 2001, Statesmen, Diplomats and the Press, 2002, Parliament and the Press 1688-1936, 2006, The International Thought of Herbert Butterfield, 2006, The Seven Years War: A Transatlantic History, 2007; co-author: British Literary Periodicals, 1983, The Origins of War in Early Modern Europe, 1987; co-author: (with J. Osborne) Cobbett in His Times, 1990; co-author: paperback edit., 1993, The War of the Spanish Succession, 1994, British Prime Ministers, 1997, Hanoverian Britain and Empire, 1998, A Global Encyclopedia of Historical Writing, 1998, Multiculturation and the History of International Relation, 1999, International Military Encyclopedia, 1999, 2d edit., 2000, Oxford Dictionary of the Enlightenment, 2003, ScribnersEncyclopedia of Modern European History, 2004, Dictionary of National Biography, 2004, Encyclopedia of Russia and the Soviet Union, 1980, 1983; editor: The Devonshire Political Diary, 1757-1762, 1982, Diplomatic Thought 1648-1815, 1982, Warfare and Tactics in the 18th Century, 1984, Herbert Butterfield: Essays on the History of Science, 1998, rev. paperback edit., 2005, In Defense of Australia's Constitutional Monarchy, 2004, Parliament and the Press, 1688-1936, 2006; co-editor: Essays in European History 1648-1815 in Honour of Ragnhild Hatton, 1985, Politics and the Press in Hanoverian Britain, 1989; gen. editor: Studies in History and Politics, 1980—91, editl. cons.: Scribner's Encyclopedia of Modern European History, Oxford Dictionary of National Biography; editl. cons. Internat. Mil. Ency., Peter Lany Put Nat. Endorsement for the Humanities; contbr. articles to profl. jours. Mem. NJ Gov.'s Adv. Panel on Higher Edn. Restructuring, 1994; chmn. ho. majority trust NJ Rep. Party, 2006—; trustee NJ Literary Hall of Fame, 1988—92, 1989—92. Named Wilfrid Laurier Proficiency scholar, 1966—69, Presdl. honoree, Rep. Inner Cir., 2006—07, hon. chmn., U.S. Ho. of Reps. Trust, 2007; recipient Thesis Def. award, Can. Coun., 1976, travel awards, Peterhouse Coll., 1971—73, Adelle Mellen prize for outstanding contbn. to scholarship, Edwin Mellen Press, 1989, Author's award, NJ Writers' Conf., 1993, Tchg. award, NJ Inst. Tech., 2000, Congl. Order of Merit, 2005, 2007; fellow U. Waterloo, 1969—70, Can. Coun., 1970—75; grantee Inter-Univ. Ctr. for European Studies, 1978, 1981; Grad. Fellow, Province of Ont., 1969—70, rsch. grantee, Bishop's U., 1977, 1978, 1980, 1982, 1983, postdoctoral rsch. grantee, Can. Coun., 1977—78, 1982—83, conf. grantee, S.S.H.R.C., 1985, travel grantee, NEH, 1991, Mellon fellow, Harvard U., 1978. Fellow Royal Hist. Soc.; mem. Internat. Commn. on History of Internat. Rels., Hist. Soc., Cambridge Hist. Soc., N.Am. Conf. on Brit. Studies, Can. Assn. Scottish Studies, Can. Assn. 18th Century Studies, Inst. Hist. Rsch., Rep. Inner Cir. Avocations: music, writing, reading, weapon collecting. Home: 49 S Passaic Ave Apt 24 Chatham NJ 07928 Office: NJ Inst Tech Dept HUmanities Newark NJ 07102 Office Phone: 973-596-3274. Business E-Mail: schweizer@adm.njit.edu.

SCHWEIZER, KENNETH STEVEN, physics professor; b. Phila., Jan. 20, 1953; s. Kenneth Paul and Grace Norma (Fischer) S.; m. Janis Eve Pelletier, Oct. 18, 1986; children: Gregory Michael, Daniel Patrick. BS, Drexel U., 1975; MS, U. Ill., 1976, PhD, 1981. Postdoctoral rsch. assoc. AT&T Bell Labs., Murray Hill, NJ, 1981-83; sr. mem. tech. staff Sandia Nat. Labs., Albuquerque, 1983-91; prof. materials sci. engring. and chemistry U. Ill., Urbana, 1991—, prof. chem. engring., 1998—, G. Ronald and Margaret H. Morris prof. materials sci., 2001—. Contbr. articles to profl. jours. Recipient Sandia award for Excellence, 1990, R&D 100 award, 1992, Award for Scientific Achievement in Materials Chemistry DOE, 1996, Burnett Tchg. award, 1997, Everitt Tchg. award, 2002. Fellow Am. Phys. Soc. (John H. Dillon medal 1991); mem. Am. Chem. Soc., Soc. Rheology, Sigma Xi, Pi Mu Epsilon. Office: U Ill Dept Materials Sci Engring 1304 W Green St Urbana IL 61801-2920 E-mail: kschweiz@uiuc.edu.

SCHWEIZER, PAUL DOUGLAS, museum director; b. Bklyn., Nov. 26, 1946; s. Alvin Charles and Marie Gertrude (Scholtz) S.; m. Jane Kulczycki, June 10, 1978 (div. 2004). BA, Marietta Coll., Ohio, 1968; MA, U. Del., 1975, PhD, 1979; postgrad. Mus. Mgmt. Inst., U. Calif., Berkeley, 1990. Instr. art history St Lawrence U., Canton, NY, 1977-78; asst. prof. St. Lawrence U., Canton, NY, 1978-80; curator St. Lawrence U. (Brush Gallery), Canton, NY, 1977-78; dir. St. Lawrence U., Canton, NY, 1979-80; dir. and chief curator Munson-Williams-Proctor Arts Inst. Mus. Art, Utica, 1980—; adj. prof. art history Pratt at Munson-Williams-Proctor, 2000—. Author exhbn. catalog; contbr. articles to profl. jours. Bd. dirs. Remington Art Mus., Ogdensburg, N.Y., 1979-80; bd. dirs. Williamstown (Mass.) Regional Art Conservation Lab., 1981-92, 2007—, pres., 1988-92. Rsch. grantee Nat. Endowment for Arts, 1978. Mem. Coll. Art Assn., Assn. Art Mus. Dirs., N.Y. State Assn. Art Mus. (trustee 1993-95), Mus. Assn. N.Y. (councilor 1995-2002), Gallery Assn. of N.Y. (bd. dirs. 1996-2002, pres. 1999), Otsego Sailing Club, Alpha Sigma Phi, Omicron Delta Kappa. Office: Munson-Williams-Proctor Arts Inst Mus Art 310 Genesee St Utica NY 13502-4799 Business E-Mail: pschweiz@mwpai.org.

SCHWELB, FRANK ERNEST, judge; b. Prague, Czechoslovakia, June 24, 1932; came to U.S., 1947; s. Egon and Caroline (Redisch) S.; m. Taffy Wurzburg, Apr. 9, 1988. BA, Yale U., 1949-53; LLB, Harvard U., 1958. Bar: N.Y. Ct. Appeals 1958, U.S. Dist. Ct. (so. and ea. dists.) N.Y. 1960, U.S. Ct. Appeals (2d cir.) 1961, U.S. Supreme Ct. 1965, U.S. Ct. Appeals (4th cir.) 1968, D.C., D.C. Ct. Appeals, U.S. Dist. Ct. D.C. 1972. Assoc. Mudge, Stern, Baldwin & Todd, NYC, 1958-62; trial atty. Civil Rights Div. U.S. Dept. Justice, Washington, 1962-79, chief eastern sect., 1969, chief housing sect., 1969-79, spl. counsel for litigation, 1979; spl. counsel rev. panel on new drug regulation HEW, Washington, 1976-77; assoc. judge Superior Ct. D.C., Washington, 1979-88, D.C. Ct. Appeals, Washington, 1988—2006, sr. judge, 2006—. Instr. various legal edn. activities. Contbr. articles to profl. jours. With U.S. Army, 1955-57. Recipient Younger Fed. Lawyer award, Fed. Bar Assn., 1967. Mem. Bar Assn. D.C., World Peace Through Law Ctr., World Assn. Judges, Czechoslovak-Am. Orgns., De Tocqueville Soc., Order of the Battered Boot. Avocations: tennis, ping pong/table tennis, sports, gilbert and sullivan operettas, shakespeare. Office: DC Ct Appeals 500 Indiana Ave NW Washington DC 20001-2138 Office Phone: 202-879-2779. Business E-Mail: fschwelb@dcca.state.dc.us.

SCHWEMM, JOHN BUTLER, printing company executive, lawyer; b. Barrington, Ill., May 18, 1934; s. Earl M. and Eunice (Butler) S.; m. Nancy Lea Prickett, Sept. 7, 1956; children: Catherine Ann, Karen Elizabeth. AB, Amherst Coll., 1956; JD, U. Mich., 1959. Bar: Ill. 1959. With Sidley & Austin, Chgo., 1959-65; with legal dept. R.R. Donnelley & Sons Co., Chgo., 1965-69, gen. counsel, 1969-75, v.p., 1971-75, pres., 1981-87, chmn., 1983-89, dir., 1980-92. Bd. dirs. William Blair Mut. Funds, Inc., Walgreen Co., USG Corp. Life trustee Northwestern U., Chgo. Mem. Law Club Chgo., Order of Coif, Phi Beta Kappa. Clubs: Chgo., Univ., Hinsdale (Ill.) Golf, Old Elm. Home (Summer): 2 Turvey Ln Downers Grove IL 60515-4530 Home and Office: 565 Sanctuary Dr Ste A401 Longboat Key FL 34228

SCHWENDEMAN, PAUL WILLIAM, lawyer; b. Chgo., Apr. 7, 1945; s. Oscar and Edna Dorothy (Ellis) S.; m. Shirley Anne Starke; children: Paul A., John E., Thomas D. BA in Econs., Carleton Coll., 1966; MSJ, Northwestern U., 1967; JD, Duquesne U., 1978. Bar: Pa. 1978. Mgr. divsn. ops. Greater Waterbury (Conn.) C. of C., 1971-75; v.p. Greater Pitts. C. of C., 1975-78; assoc. Kirkpatrick & Lockhart, Pitts., 1978-84, ptnr., 1984—. Lt. USNR, 1971. Office: Kirkpatrick & Lockhart 1500 Oliver Bldg Pittsburgh PA 15222-2312

SCHWENGER, WILBUR JOHN, mathematics educator, mathematics professor; s. John William and Helen Elizabeth Schwenger; m. Barbara Ann Silvis, Aug. 15, 1970; children: Karin Christine, Lauralee Ruth, John Daniel, William James. AA, Palm Beach CC, West Palm Beach, Fla., 1967; BA, U. Fla., Gainesville, 1969, MEd, 1971. Tchr. St. Lucie County Sch. Bd., Fort Pierce, Fla., 1971—. Scoutmaster Boy Scouts Am., Ft. Pierce, 1973—88, cubmaster, 1988—94, scoutmaster, 1995—; jr. civitan advisor Civitan, 1973—90. A1C USAF, 1961—65. Recipient Dist. award of Merit, Boy Scouts Am., Silver Beaver, Civitan, Outstanding Jr. Civitan Advisor Fla. Dist., 2001, Dist. award of Merit, 1976, Silver Beaver award, 1976, Tchr. of Yr. award, St. Lucie County Sch. Bd., 1983, Lamb award, Lutheran Ch. Mem.: Am. Math. Assn., Math. Ass. Ft. Pierce, Nat. Coun. Tchrs. Math. Lutheran. Avocations: hiking, camping, scouting. Home: 5207 Citrus Ave Fort Pierce FL 34982 Personal E-mail: schwenw@netscape.net.

SCHWENK, GORDON CAMERON, ophthalmologist; s. Gordon Hazlett and Ruth Pedley Schwenk; m. Lois Annette Moyer, June 5, 1976; children: Krista Anne, Jenna Leigh, Kimberly Gayle. BS, Pa. State U., University Park, 1974, MS, 1976; MD, Temple U., Phila., 1980. Diplomate Am. Bd. Ophthalmology, 1986. Flexible med./surg. intern St. Luke's Hosp., Bethlehem, Pa., 1980—81; ophthalmology resident Med. U. SC, Charleston, 1981—84; sr. ptnr., pres. Ocala Eye, P.A., Fla., 1984—. Mem., vice chmn., chmn. Ocala Regional Hosp., 1991—94. Fellow: ACS, Am. Acad. Ophthalmology; mem.: AMA, Fla. Soc. Ophthalmology, Fla. Med. Assn., Marion County Med. Soc., Am. Soc. Cataract and Refractive Surgery. Conservative. Methodist. Avocations: travel, photography, sailing, woodworking. Office: Ocala Eye PA 1500 S Magnolia Ext Ste 206 Ocala FL 34471-4461 Home Phone: 352-351-8042; Office Phone: 352-622-5183. Office Fax: 352-629-5026.

SCHWENKE, ROGER DEAN, lawyer; b. Washington, Oct. 18, 1944; s. Clarence Raymond and Virginia Ruth (Gould) S.; m. Carol Lynne Flenniken, Nov. 29, 1980; 1 child: Matthew Robert; stepchildren: Tracy L. Wolf Dickey, Mary M. Wolf. BA, Ohio State U., 1966; JD with honors, U. Fla., 1969. Bar: Fla. 1970. Instr. Coll. Law U. Fla., Gainesville, 1969—70; assoc. Carlton Fields, P.A., Tampa, Fla., 1970—74, ptnr., 1975—; adminstr., dept. head Real Estate, Environ. and Land Use Dept., 1978—99. Adj. prof. Coll. Law, Stetson U., St. Petersburg, Fla., 1979-80; mem. faculty U. Miami Coll. of Law Master of Law's in Real Estate Devel. Program, 1994-96. Author chpt. in Environmental Regulation and Litigation in Florida, 1987, chpt. in Florida Real Property Complex Transactions, 1997, 2000; contbr. articles to profl. jours., chpt. to book. Mem. diocesan coun. Episc. Diocese SW Fla., 1978-86, mem. standing com., 1989-92, chief judge Eccles. Ct., 1996—. Recipient Gertrude Brick Law Rev. prize, U. Fla., 1969. Fellow Am. Coll. Real Estate Lawyers (bd. govs. 1985-88), Am. Law Inst.; mem. ABA (liaison to standong com. on environ. law 1980-87, mem. coun. real property sect. 1988-95), Fla. Bar Assn., Air and Waste Mgmt. Assn., Order of Coif, Greater Tampa C. of C. (chmn. environ. coun. 1980-81), Tampa Club. Democrat. Office: Carlton Fields PO Box 3239 Tampa FL 33601-3239 Office Phone: 813-229-4152. E-mail: rschwenke@carltonfields.com.

SCHWENN, LEE WILLIAM, retired health facility administrator; b. Morrisonville, Wis., Dec. 23, 1925; s. LeRoy William and Vivian Mae (Kramer) S.; m. Glenna Edith Mehne, Jan. 16, 1947; 1 son, William Lee. BS, U. Wis., 1948; M.P.H., U. N.C., 1956. Tchr. pub. schs., Appleton, Wis., 1948-52; teaching cons. Wis. Health Dept., 1952-53; adminstrv. asst. Madison (Wis.) Health Dept., 1953-57; adminstrv. cons. U.S. Children's Bur., Atlanta Regional Office, 1957-58; adminstr. USPHS, Washington, 1958-66; assoc. dir. D.C. Dept. Health, 1966-70, D.C. Dept. Human Resources, 1970-71; exec. v.p. Maimonides Med. Center, Bklyn., 1971-88, pres., 1988-89, spl. cons. Bd. Trustees, 1989-96. Recipient Distinguished Pub. Service award D.C. Govt., 1970 Mem. Delta Omega. Home: 1007 Westminster Dr Greensboro NC 27410-4551

SCHWENTERLY, STANLEY WILLIAM, physicist, researcher; b. Phila., Aug. 18, 1945; s. Stanley William and Ruth Dorothy Schwenterly. BS, Yale U., 1967; PhD, Cornell U., 1972. Sr. rsch. staff Oak Ridge Nat. Lab., Tenn., 1972—. Editor IEEE Transactions on Applied Superconductivity, NYC, 1999—. Contbr. articles to profl. jours. Prin. horn Oak Ridge Symphony Orch., Oak Ridge, Tenn., 1975—. Recipient Tech. Achievement award, Martin Marietta Energy Systems, 1991, UT-Battelle, 2000, Engr. of the Yr.award, 2000. Mem.: IEEE, Cryogenic Soc. Am., Internat. Horn Soc., Knoxville Ski Club. Achievements include research in investigations of cryogenic dielectric materials and development of high voltage components for superconducting utility equipment, superconductor ac loss measurements; cryopumping studies for fusion applications, and development of superconducting motors, transformers, generators, and cables. Avocations: music, skiing, bicycling, sailing. Office: Oak Ridge Nat Lab PO Box 2008 Oak Ridge TN 37831 Home Phone: 865-690-1850; Office Phone: 865-574-1460. Personal E-mail: schwenterly@ieee.org.

SCHWERDTNER, FREDERICK HOWARD, lawyer, retired police commander, real estate broker; b. Chgo., Oct. 13, 1949; s. Fred and Lydia (Tatz) S.; m. Julie Anne Carramusa, Oct. 21, 1990; 1 child, Sarah Elizabeth. BS, Loyola U., Chgo., 1973, JD, 1989; MBA with distinction, DePaul U., 1983. Bar: Ill. 1989, U.S. Ct. Appeals (7th cir.) Ill. 1989. Officer Oak Park (Ill.) Police Dept., 1973-93, commdr., 1989-93; with DuPage County Vets. Assistance Commn., 1995—, pres., 1997—99; lawyer Pvt. Practice, Ill. Contbr. articles to profl. jours. Tutor inner city high sch. students, Chgo., 1988; apptd. local bd. mem. Selective Svc. Sys., police commr. Bd. Police Commr., Village of Glendale Heights, Ill., 1999-, chmn., 2002-. Served USMC, 1965-69, Vietnam, 1967-68. Mem. ABA, Fraternal Order Police, Marine Corps League (Band of Bros. Detachment), VFW, Vietnam Vets of Am., Ill. State Bar Assn., Chgo. Bar Assn., DuPage County Bar Assn., Beta Gamma Sigma. Lutheran. Avocations: hiking, tennis, racquetball, golf. Office Phone: 630-653-3494. Personal E-mail: vet-star@comcast.net.

SCHWERIN, HORACE S., marketing research consultant; b. NYC, Jan. 18, 1914; s. Paul and Rose (Lewis) S.; m. Lorraine Roth, June 14, 1941 (div. Dec. 1969); children: Barbara, Bruce; m. Enid May Highton, Apr. 28, 1973. BS, Lafayette Coll., 1935; MA, London U., 1936; MS, U. Paris, 1937. Gen. mgr., research dir., cons. N.Y. advt. agys., 1936-41; pres. Research Analysts, Inc., 1946; chmn. bd. Schwerin Research Corp., NYC, Toronto, London, Hamburg, to 1968; chmn., pres. Horace Schwerin & Assos., Englewood Cliffs, NJ, 1968-72; dir. marketing devel. Campbell Soup Co., Camden, NJ, 1972—, v.p. market planning Canned Food div., 1977-82, mktg. strategy cons., 1982—; CEO, chmn. Schwerin Murphy, Inc., 1991-98; ret., 1998. Author: (with Henry H. Newell) Persuasion in Marketing, 1981; also articles on market research, nutrition, use of govt. data bases. Served as capt. U.S. Army, 1946. Decorated Legion of Merit with oak leaf cluster; inducted into Market Rsch. Coun. Hall of Fame, 1992. Mem. Am. Mktg. Assn., Market Rsch. Coun., Can. Club (NYC), Penn Club (NYC). Methodist. Home: 5D Toll Gate Of Moorestown 633 E Main St Moorestown NJ 08057-3059 Office: 633 E Main St Moorestown NJ 08057-3059 E-mail: hschwerin@comcast.net.

SCHWERIN, KARL HENRY, anthropology educator, researcher; b. Bertha, Minn., Feb. 21, 1936; s. Henry William and Audrey Merle (Jahn) S.; m. Judith Drewanne Altermatt, Sept. 1, 1958 (div. May 1975); children: Karl Frederic, Marguerite DelValle; m. Partha Louise, Jan. 25, 1979; stepchildren: Tamara, Brent, Taryn. BA, U. Calif., Berkeley, 1958; PhD, UCLA, 1965. Instr. Los Angeles State Coll., 1963; asst. prof. anthropology U. N.Mex., Albuquerque, 1963-68, assoc. prof., 1968-72, prof., 1972-2001, asst. chmn. dept. anthropology, 1983-85, chmn. dept. anthropology, 1987-93, prof. emeritus, 2001—. Prof. invitado Inst. Venezolano de Investigaciones Cientificas, Caracas, 1979. Author: Oil and Steel Processes of Karinya Culture Change, 1966, Antropologia Social, 1969, Winds Across the Atlantic, 1970; editor: Food Energy in Tropical Ecosystems, 1985; contbr. articles to profl. jours. V.p. Parents without Ptnr., Albuquerque, 1976-77. Grantee Cordell Hull Found., Venezuela, 1961-62, N.Y. Zool. Soc., Honduras, 1981; Fulbright scholar Cañar, Ecuador, 1969-70, Paris, 1986; founded Karl H. Schwerin Fellowship in Ethnology. Fellow Am. Anthropol. Assn.; mem. Am. Ethnol. Soc., Am. Soc. Ethnohistory (pres. 1975), Southwestern Anthropol. Assn. (co-editor Southwestern Jour. Anthropology 1972-75), N.Mex. Cactus and Succulent Soc. (v.p. 1970-71), Internat. Congress of Americanists (35th-40th, 43d, 46th, 48th, 49th, 50th), Netherwood Pk. Neighborhood Assn. (pres. 2005-07), Sigma Xi (chpt. pres. 1980-81) Avocations: photography, gardening, hiking, camping, bicycling. Office: U NMex Dept Anthropology MSC01-1040 Albuquerque NM 87131-0001 Office Phone: 505-277-4614. Business E-Mail: schwerin@unm.edu.

SCHWERING, FELIX KARL, electronics executive, researcher; b. Cologne, Nordrhein-Westfalen, Federal Republic of Germany, June 4, 1930; came to U.S., 1964; s. Felix Bernhard and Maria (Heinrichs) S. BS, U. Aachen, Federal Republic of Germany, 1951, Diplom-Ingenieur, 1954, PhD, 1957. Asst. prof. U. Aachen, Federal Republic of Germany, 1956-58; electronic scientist U.S. Army R & D Labs., Fort Monmouth, NJ, 1958-61; project leader AEG-Telefunken, Ulm, Federal Republic of Germany, 1961-64; rsch. scientist U.S. Army Communication Electronics Command (CECOM), Fort Monmouth, NJ, 1964-96, ret., 1996, cons., 1996—. Vis. lab. assoc. U.S. Army Rsch. Office, Rsch. Triangle, N.C., 1984-85; vis. prof. N.J. Inst. Tech., Newark, 1986—, Rutgers U., New Brunswick, N.J., 1973-87, Monmouth U., 1996—. Author: (with others) Millimeter Wave Antennas, 1988; author, editor (with others) Microwave Antennas, 1989; mem. editl. bd. Microwave and Optical Tech. Letters, 1988—; contbr. articles to profl. jours.; patentee in field. Fellow IEEE (Best Paper award Antennas and Propagation Soc. 1961, 82), Internat. Sci. Radio Union, Am. Geophys. Union, Armed Forces Comm. Electronics Assn., Sigma Xi. Roman Catholic. Office: US Army CERDEC Attn AMSRD-CER-ST-WL Fort Monmouth NJ 07703-5203 Office Phone: 732-532-0469. Business E-Mail: felix.schwerin@us.army.mil.

SCHWERT, G(EORGE) WILLIAM, III, finance educator; b. Durham, NC, Jan. 26, 1950; s. George William Jr. and Margaret (Houlton) S.; m. Camille Matthews, Dec. 19, 1970 (div. 1983); 1 child, Lisa Margaret; m. Patricia Michel, Dec. 23, 1983; children: Michael William, Andrew Patrick. AB in Econs. with honors, Trinity Coll., 1971; MBA, U. Chgo., 1973, PhD in Fin., 1975. Asst. prof. Grad. Sch. Bus. U. Chgo., 1975-76; asst. prof. to prof. Simon Sch. Bus. U. Rochester, N.Y., 1976-86, Gleason prof. fin. N.Y., 1986-98, Disting. U. prof. N.Y., 1998—. Chmn. Knollwood Cons. Group, Inc., Rochester, 1987—. Co-editor Jour. Fin. Econs., 1979-86, 89-95, adv. editor, 1986-89, mng. editor 1995—; assoc. editor Jour. of Fin., 1983-2000, Jour. Monetary Econs., 1984—; contbr. articles to econs. jour. Recipient Smith-Breeden Disting. Paper prize Jour. Fin., 1990, Graham and Dodd plaque Fin. Analysts Jour., 1990. Mem. Am. Fin. Assn. (bd. dirs. 1987-89), Am. Econs. Assn., Econometrics Soc., Am. Statis. Assn. (chair bus. econs. sect. 1990-91). Avocations: tennis, boating, fishing, golf, numismatics. Home: 71 Knollwood Dr Rochester NY 14618-3512 Office: U Rochester W E Simon Grad Sch Bus Adminstrn Rochester NY 14627 Office Phone: 585-275-2470. Business E-Mail: schwert@schwert.ssb.rochester.edu.

SCHWERTFEGER, TIMOTHY R., investment company executive; b. Mar. 28, 1949; BA in Econs. and Fin., Northwestern U.; JD, Georgetown U.; student, Harvard Bus. Sch., Stanford U. Nat. dir. health care investment banking svcs. Nuveen Investments, Inc. (div. St. Paul Co., Inc.), 1977—86, head corp. mktg., 1987—89, exec. v.p., 1989—96, chmn. Nuveen Mutual Funds & Exch.-traded Funds, 1996—, chmn., CEO, 1996—2007, non-exec. chmn., 2007—. Pres. Hubbard St. Dance Chgo.; bd. dirs. Better Boys Found., Lyric Opera Chgo., Mus. Contemporary Art, Providence St. Mel Sch. Office: Nuveen Investments Inc 333 W Wacker Dr Chicago IL 60606

SCHWETHELM, OTTO C., oil industry executive; B acctg., Univ. Tex., Austin. CPA. Mgmt. positions Saudi Aramco; mgmt. positions through v.p. Tesoro Corp., San Antonio, 1998—2003, v.p., contr., 2003—06, v.p. fin., treas., 2006—07, v.p., CFO, 2007—. Office: Tesoro Corp 300 Concord Plz San Antonio TX 78216-6999 *

SCHWETZ, BERNARD ANTHONY, toxicologist; b. Cadott, Wis., Nov. 27, 1940; married; 4 children. BS in Biology, U. Wis., Stevens Point, 1962; DVM, U. Minn., 1967; MS in Pharmacology, U. Iowa, 1968, PhD in Pharmacology, 1970. Diplomate Am. Bd. Toxicology. USPHS trainee dept. vet. physiology and pharmacology U. Minn., 1964-66; USPHS trainee dept. pharmacology U. Iowa, 1966-70; toxicologist Dow Chem. U.S.A., Midland, Mich., 1970-78, dir. toxicology rsch. lab., 1978-82; chief sys. toxicity br. divsn. toxicology rsch. and testing NIEHS, Research Triangle Park, N.C., 1982-92, acting dir. environ. toxicology program, 1993; dir. Nat. Ctr. for Toxicol. Rsch., Jefferson, Ark., 1993—2000; assoc. commr. for sci. FDA, Rockville, Md., 1994—, sr. advisor. Adj. prof. U. Ark. for Med. Scis., 1993—, Mich. State U., East Lansing, 1973-82, N.C. State U., Raleigh, 1985-93. Assoc. editor Fundamental and Applied Toxicology, 1983-86, editor, 1986-92; editl. adv. bd. Environ. Health Perspectives, 1984-93, Critical Revs. in Toxicology, 1984—; contbr. numerous articles to profl. publs. Recipient Arnold J. Lehman award Soc. of Toxicology, 1991, Dir.'s award NIH, 1991, Founders award Chem. Industry Inst. of Toxicology, 1994, FDA Commr.'s Spl. citation, 1995. Mem. AVMA, Soc. Toxicology (charter mem. Mich. chpt., councilor 1984-86, pres. N.C. chpt. 1987, pres. reproductive toxicology speciality sect. 1986, pres.-elect south ctrl. chpt. 1997), Teratology Soc. (treas. 1978-82), Behavioral Teratology Soc., Phi Zeta. Avocations: fishing, photography. Office: Nat Ctr Toxicol Rsch HFT-1 3900 Nctr Rd Jefferson AR 72079-9501 Home: 17601 Conoy Rd Barnesville MD 20838-9751

SCHWEYEN, STEPHEN GREGORY, engineering company executive; b. Berthold, ND, Aug. 12, 1951; s. Theodore Francis Schweyen and Elizabeth Mae Smith; m. Lauri Ellen Reed, Dec. 17, 1973; children: Rachel, Leah, Sarah, Rebekah, Stephen, Nicholas, Charles. BA in Zoology, U. Wash., Seattle, 1976. Cert. spl. inspector Wash. Assn. Bldg. Ofcls. Inspector engring. svcs. Profl. Svc. Industries, Pitts. Testing Lab., Pitts., 1976—. Tech. dir. Am. Concrete Inst., Farmington Hills, Mich., 1994—; dist. tng. chmn. Thunderbird, Seattle, 2005—07. Author: Family History, 2000. With US Army, 1971—72. Recipient Scoutmaster of Yr., Boy Scouts Am., Seattle Coun., 2003, Dist. award of merit, 2005. Mem.: U. Wash. Alumni Assn., St. Vincent de Paul Soc., KC, 82nd Airborne Divsn. Assn., Am. Legion. Avocations: collecting rare books, coin collecting/numismatics, hiking, camping. Home: 5514 22nd Ave S Seattle WA 98108 Office: Profl Svc Industries 24413 56th Ave W Mountlake Terrace WA 98043 Personal E-mail: remeor@aol.com.

SCHWIEG, FREDERIC P., lawyer; BA, Case Western Res. U., Cleve., 1981, JD, 1985. Bar: Ohio 1985. Law clk. to Hon. John F. Ray Jr. US Dist. Ct. (no. dist.) Ohio, Cleve., 1985—87; assoc. Kahn Kleinman, Cleve., 1987—95, Anne L. Meyers & Assocs. LLC, Cleve., 1995—97; pvt. practice Cleve., 1997—2005; lawyer Cowden Humphrey, Cleve. Presenter in field. Coord. Cleve. Shambhala Meditation Group, 1998—2007. Mem.: Cleve. Bar Assn. (chair CLE com. 2000—01), Ohio Turnaround Mgmt. Assn. (trustee and sec. 1999—2006), Ohio State Bar Assn. Buddhist. Avocations: skiing, hiking, model building. Office: Cowden Humphrey Nagorney & Lovett 50 Public Square Ste 1414 Cleveland OH 44113 Office Phone: 216-241-2880. Office Fax: 216-241-2881. Business E-Mail: fschwieg@cowdenlaw.com.

SCHWIETZ, ROGER L., archbishop; b. St. Paul, Minn., July 3, 1930; MA in Philosophy, U. Ottawa; MA in Sacred Theology, Loyola U.; STL in Sacred Theology, Gregorian U., Rome; HHD (hon.), Lewis U., 1998. Ordained priest Roman Cath. Ch., 1967, consecrated bishop, 1990. Assoc. pastor St. Thomas Aquinas Parish, International Falls, Minn., 1975—78; dir. Coll. Seminary prog. for Oblates of Mary Immaculate Creighton U., Omaha, 1978—84; pastor Holy Family Parish, Duluth, Minn., 1984—89; bishop Diocese of Duluth, 1989—2000; archbishop Archdiocese of Anchorage, 2001—. Episcopal moderator Teens Encounter Christ (TEC) movement, 1991—. Home and Office: Archdiocese of Anchorage 225 Cordova St Anchorage AK 99501-2409

SCHWIMMER, DAVID, actor; b. Queens, NY, Nov. 12, 1966; BS in Speech/Theater, Northwestern U., 1988. Co-founder The Lookingglass Theater Co., Chgo., 1988. Actor: (films) Flight of the Intruder, 1991, Crossing the Bridge, 1992, The Waiter, 1993, Twenty Bucks, 1993, The Party Favor, 1995, The Pallbearer, 1996, Breast Men, 1997, The Thin Pink Line, 1998, Kissing a Fool (also exec. prodr.), 1998, Six Days Seven Nights, 1998, Apt Pupil, 1998, All the Rage, 1999, Picking Up the Pieces, 2000, Hotel, 2001, Duane Hopwood, 2005, (voice) Madagascar, 2005, (TV films) A Deadly Silence, 1989, Since You've Been Gone, 1998, Uprising, 2001, (TV miniseries) Band of Brothers, 2001, (TV series) The Wonder Years, 1992, Friends, 1994-2004, Monty, 1994, (stage appearances) West, The Odyssey, Of One Blood, In the Eye of the Beholder, The Master and Margarita, Some Girls, 2005; dir. The Jungle, The Serpent, Alice in Wonderland (TV appearances) LA Law, NYPD Blue, 1993, L.A. Law, 1992, 93, ER, 1996, The Single Guy, 1997, Curb Your Enthusiasm, 2004; exec. prodr. Humanoid, 2003, Shoot the Moon, 1996

SCHWIMMER, GEORGE, writer, film producer; b. Hodmezovasarhely, Hungary, Feb. 14, 1931; s. John and Marguerite Roth Schwimmer; m. Veronica Leora Enders, July 9, 1957 (div. Jan. 28, 1982); children: Eric, David Albert, Krista Ann. BA, Washington & Jefferson Coll., Washington, Pa., 1953; MFA, Carnegie Inst. Tech., Pitts., 1959; PhD, Columbia Pacific U., San Rafael, Calif., 1987. Mng. artistic dir. Lubbock Little Theatre, Tex., 1959—60; instr. Pitts. Playhouse, 1960—61; asst. plant mgr. John Schwimmer and Co., NYC, 1961—62; instr. MacMurray Coll., Jacksonville, Ill., 1963—65; assoc. artistic dir. Thompson Theatre, NC State U., Raleigh, 1965—68; mng. artistic dir. Valley Theater, University Center, Mich., 1968; asst. prof., dept. head Saginaw Valley Coll., University Center, 1968—71; mng. artistic dir. Dublin Theatre Workshop, 1971—73; asst. plant mgr. John Schwimmer and Co., Raleigh, NC, 1973—76; founder, instr. NC Theatre Inst., Raleigh, 1977—79; dir., prodr. Alpha Theater Prodns., NYC, 1981—82; artistic dir. The New Theatre Group, NYC, 1982—83; past-life therapist NYC, 1982—86; transformational guide Santa Barbara, Calif., 1986—89; v.p. devel. Late Bloomer Co., Burbank, Calif., 1991—92; writer, prodr. Phoenix 11 Prodns., LA, 1992—2004, Phoenix Shakti Prodns., LA, 2004—. V.p. bd. dirs. Assn. Past Life Rsch. And Therapies, Riverside, Calif., 1987—91, newsletter editor, 1988—91. Author: (non-fiction) The Search for David, 1996, 2d edit., 2004, Adventures in Consciousness, 2006; editor: DAVID: Leaves from the Journal of a Soul, 2006; author: (screenplay) CAYCE, 2007; contbr. numerous articles about metaphysics. Served with US Army, 1953—55. Office: Phoenix Shakti Prodns 1041 S Wooster St Ste 5 Los Angeles CA 90035 Office Phone: 310-652-9706. Personal E-mail: georgesch@earthlink.net.

SCHWIMMER, SIGMUND, food enzymologist; b. Cleve., Sept. 20, 1917; s. Solomon and Sarah (Brown) S.; m. Sylvia Klein, Dec. 18, 1941; children: Susan, Elaine. Student Ohio State U., 1935-36; B.S., George Washington U., 1940; M.S., Georgetown U., 1941, Ph.D., 1943. From lab. asst. to research chemist USDA, Washington and Berkeley, Calif., 1936-62; adj. prof. biology Calif. Inst. Tech., Pasadena, 1963-65; chief research biochemist USDA, Berkeley, 1966-72, collaborator emeritus, 1975-; adj. prof. dept. nutritional scis. U. Calif.-Berkeley, 1985-87; sr. expert biochemistry UN Indsl. Devel. Orgn., Haifa, Israel, 1973-74; cons. food enzymology, Berkeley, 1980-; lectr. dept. biotech. food engring. Israel Inst. Tech., Haifa, 1973; vis. scientist Food Industry Rsch. and Devel. Inst., Hsinchu, Taiwan, 1992. Contbr. articles to profl. jours.; editor, Biochem. Sci. Biotech., Cambridge, Eng., 1983—, Trends in Biochemistry, Trends in Biotechnology, 1983—, Jour. Food Biochemistry, 1977-98; author: Source Book of Food Enzymology, 1982 (Jour. Assn. Coll. and Rsch. Librs. award 1983). John S. Guggenheim fellow; NSF fellow; Carlsberg Biol. Inst. fellow, Copenhagen; recipient Superior Service award USDA, 1949, 59, Lifetime Achievement award, 1993, Agrl. and Food Chemistry Divsn. award Am. Chem. Soc., 1996. Fellow Inst. Food Technologists, inductee USDA's ARS Sci. Hall of Fame, 2005; mem. Am. Soc. Biochemistry Molecular Biology, Sigma Xi. Office: Western Regional Ctr USDA 800 Buchanan St Albany CA 94710-1105 also: U Calif Dept Nutritional Sci Berkeley CA 94720-0001 Office Phone: 510-559-5873. Business E-Mail: sig@pw.usda.gov.

SCHWIND, WILLIAM F., JR., lawyer, oil industry executive; b. Chgo., 1944; BS, JD, Loyola U., Chgo. Bar: Tex. 1969. With Marathon Oil Corp., Findlay, Ohio, 1974—83; comml. contract mgr. Jakarta, Indonesia, 1983—84; gen. atty. Marathon Oil Corp., Houston, 1984—91, gen. counsel, sec., 1992—; sr. v.p. adminstrn., gen. counsel, sec. Dehli Gas Pipeline Corp., Dallas, 1991—92. Mem.: ABA, Am. Petroleum Inst. (chmn. gen. com. law), Am. Corp. Counsel Assn. Office: Marathon Oil Co PO Box 4813 5555 San Felipe Rd Houston TX 77210-4813 *

SCHWINGER, DAVID, lawyer; b. Phila., Nov. 8, 1956; BS summa cum laude, U. Pa., 1977; JD with high honors, George Washington U., 1982. Bar: DC 1982. Mng. ptnr. Katten Muchin Zavis Rosenman, Washington, DC. Mem.: Nat. Reverse Mortgage Lenders Assn., Mortgage Bankers Assn. of Am. Office: Katten Muchin Zavis Rosenman East Lobby, Ste 700 1025 Thomas Jefferson St, NW Washington DC 20007 Office Phone: 202-625-3600. Office Fax: 202-298-7570. E-mail: david.schwinger@kmzr.com.

SCHWINGHAMER, MARY DENISE, veterinarian; b. Jasper, Ind., Aug. 25, 1953; DVM, Auburn U., 1978. Preceptor Brentwood Vet. Clinic, Tenn., 1978—79; staff veterinarian Birmingham Humane Soc., Ala., 1980—81; emergency animal clinician Emergency Animal Clinic, Birmingham, 1980—83; small animal clinic propr. Companion Animal Clinic, Irondale, Ala., 1981—94; tech. writer, 1994—. Contbr. articles to profl. jours. Roman Catholic. Achievements include invention of; research in treatment for canine parvovirus enteritis; treatment for HIV-AIDS and Systemic Viremias in human population with companion animals as in vivo models. Avocations: swimming, dog and horse care and breeding. Home: 7313 Martha Dr Huntsville AL 35802 Office Phone: 256-881-5500.

SCHWISTER, JAY EDWARD, portfolio manager; b. Milw., Apr. 16, 1962; s. Jerome Charles and Carol Christina (Keeler) Schwister; m. Sara M. Schlaudecker; children: Katharine Claire, William Edward. BS in Fin.

cum laude, Marquette U., 1984. Chartered fin. analyst. Sr. investment officer First Wis. Trust Co., Milw., 1984-87; sr. v.p., sr. portfolio mgr. Putnam Investments, Boston, 1987—2002; pres., CIO, Juneau Fund Advisors, 2002—04; sr. portfolio mgr. Baird Advisors, Milw., 2004—. Fin. com. mem. Hills Bd. Trustees, Wayland, Mass., 1990—; pres. coun. Marquette U., Milw., 1990—. Chmn. fund raising com. Marquette U. Alumni Fund, Boston, 1989—. Mem. CFA Inst., Milw. Investment Analysts Soc., Bond Analysts Soc., Inc., Beta Gamma Sigma. Avocations: golf, tennis, travel, woodworking, music. Home: 14655 Juneau Blvd Elm Grove WI 53122-1669 Office: Baird Advisors 777 E Wisconsin Ave Milwaukee WI 53202-5391 Office Phone: 414-298-1038. E-mail: Jschwister@rwbaird.com.

SCHWITTERS, ROY FREDERICK, physicist, researcher; b. Seattle, Wash., June 20, 1944; s. Walter Frederick and Margaret Lois (Boyer) S.; m. Karen Elizabeth Chrystal, June 18, 1965; children: Marc Frederick, Anne Elizabeth, Adam Thomas. S.B., MIT, 1966, PhD, 1971. Research asso. Stanford U. Linear Accelerator Center, 1971-74, asst. prof., then asso. prof., 1974-79; prof. physics Harvard U., 1979-90; scientist Fermi Nat. Accelerator Lab., Batavia, Ill., 1980-88, dir. superconducting supercollider, 1989-93; prof. physics U. Tex., Austin, 1994—. Author papers on high energy physics; asso. editor: Ann. Rev. Nuclear and Particle Sci; div. asso. editor: Phys. Rev. Letters. Recipient Alan T. Waterman award NSF, 1980. W.K.H. Panofsky Prize, Am Physical Soc., 1996, Humboldt Rsch. prize, 1999. Fellow AAAS, Am. Phys. Soc. (W. K. H. Panofsky Prize, 1996), Am. Acad. Arts and Scis. Home: 1115 W 7th St Apt 300 Austin TX 78703-5350 Office: U Tex Dept Physics Austin TX 78712-1081

SCHWITZGEBEL, ERIC, philosopher, educator; PhD, U. Calif., Berkeley, 1997. Assoc. prof. philosophy U. Calif., Riverside, 1997—. Office: Univ Calif Department of Philosophy Riverside CA 92521

SCHYVINCK, CHRISTINE, electronics executive; b. Minn., 1967; BS in mech. engring., U. Wis.; MS in engring. mgmt., Northwestern U. Engr., corp. quality divsn. Shure Inc., Niles, Ill., 1989—97, mgr., process engring. dept., 1997—98, v.p. corp. quality, 1998—2000, v.p. ops., 2000—04, exec. v.p. ops., 2004—06, exec. v.p. global mktg. & sales, 2006—. Named one of 40 Under 40, Crain's Chgo. Bus., 2006. Office: Shure Inc 5800 W Touhy Ave Niles IL 60714-4608 Office Phone: 847-600-2000. Office Fax: 847-600-1212. E-mail: info@shure.com.

SCIAME, JOSEPH, university administrator; b. Bklyn., Sept. 9, 1941; s. Joseph and Sophie (Pintacuda) S. EdB, St. John's U., 1971. Fin. aid officer, asst. to dean of admissions St. John's U., Jamaica, NY, 1967-71, dir. fin. aid, 1971-82, dean fin. aid, 1982, v.p. fin. aid and student svcs., 1982-94, v.p. for govt. and cmty. rels., 1994—2002, v.p. for cmty. rels., 2002—. Mem. Gov. Commn. on Sch. Achievement, 1971—, chairperson, 1993—; pres. N.Y. Assn. Student Fin. Aid Adminstrn., 1980-82, Ea. Assn. Student Fin. Aid Adminstrn., 1986-87. Chmn. bd. ethics Town of North Hempstead, N.Y., 1984—; nat. chmn., bd. dirs. Garibaldi-Meucci Mus., N.Y., 1987-93, 97-99, pres., CEO, 1999-2002; mem. Providence Rest Found., 1995—; bd. dirs. St. John's Prep, 1996—; bd. mem. Queens Symphony Orch., 2000—, Boy Scouts Am., 2000—, v.p. membership, 2001—; bd. mem. Holocaust Resource Ctr., 2002—. Decorated Cavaliere Hfficiale del Merito della Repubblica Italiana, Cavaliere Ufficiale Order Merit House of Savoy; recipient Lifetime Membership award Ea. Assn., 1995, Achievement award N.Y. State Fin. Aid Adminstrs., 1982, Congl. Record award, 1979, 91, 93, 94, 95. Mem. Nat. Assn. Student Fin. Aid Adminstrs. (chmn. 1987-88, Disting. Svc. award 1988, Leadership award 1994), Assn. Equestrian Order Holy Sepulchre (knight grand cross 1991, knight invested 1980), Order Sons of Italy in Am. (lodge pres. 1974-75, state pres. 1993-97, nat. v.p. 1997—2003, nat pres. 2003—), Futures in Edn. Found. (vice chair 1991-93, chair 1994-97), Jamaica C. of C. (bd. dirs.), Queens Symphony Orch. (bd. dirs.), Boy Scouts Am.(v.p. membership com. 2001—), Holocaust Rejourne Ctr. (bd. dirs.). Roman Catholic. Avocations: walking, cooking, gardening, reading, lecturing. Home: 6 Jones St New Hyde Park NY 11040-1616 also: Trout Ln Southampton NY 11968 Office: St John's Univ Off Vp Cmty Rels 8000 Utopia Pky Jamaica NY 11439-0001 Business E-Mail: sciamej@stjohns.edu.

SCIANCE, CARROLL THOMAS, chemical engineer, educator; b. Okemah, Okla., Feb. 16, 1939; s. Carroll Elmer and Winifred (Black) Sciance; m. Anita Ruth Fischer, Jan. 30, 1960; children: Steven, Frederick, Thomas, Erica. BSChemE, U. Okla., 1960, M in Chem. Engring., 1964, PhD, 1966. With E.I. duPont de Nemours & Co., Inc., 1966-95, planning mgr. nylon intermediates divsn., petrochem. dept. Wilmington, Del., 1978-80, tech. mgr., 1980-83, dir engring. rsch., engring. dept., 1983-87, prin. cons. corp. rsch. and devel. planning divsn., 1987-89; mgr. petroleum products R & D divsn. Conoco, Inc., 1989-93; dir. environ. tech. partnerships ctrl. R & D dept. DuPont, 1993-95; pres. Sci. Cons. Svcs., Inc., 1995—. Math. scis. and edn. bd. NRC, 1987—89; adv. bd. chem. sci. and tech. NIST, 1988—94; sr. lectr. U. Tex., Austin, 1996—; mem. Travis County Appraisals Rev. Bd., Tex., 1999—2004; instr. U. Phoenix, Austin, Tex., 2005—. Pres. Hudson Bend Colony Homeowners Assn., 2004—06. Officer USAR, 1961—63. Fellow: AIChE (bd. dirs. material engring. and scis. divsn. 1986—92, chmn. new tech. com. 1990—92, mem. govt. rels. com. 1993—96); mem.: Am. Chem. Soc. (mem. environ. R & D com. 1995—99), Fedn. Materials Soc. (v.p. 1988—92, pres. 1993—94), Sigma Xi. Home: 16658 Forest Way Austin TX 78734-1110 Personal E-mail: scscorp@earthlink.net.

SCIARRA, JOHN J., obstetrician, gynecologist, educator; b. West Haven, Conn., Mar. 4, 1932; s. John and Mary Grace (Sanzone) S.; m. Barbara Crafts Patton, Jan. 9, 1960; chidren: Vanessa Patton, John Crafts, Leonard Chapman. BS, Yale U., 1953; MD, Columbia U., NYC, 1957, PhD, 1963. Asst. prof. Columbia U., NYC, 1964-68; prof., dept. head U. Minn. Med. Sch., Mpls., 1968-74; prof. Northwestern U. Med. Sch., Chgo., 1974—; chmn. ob-gyn Northwestern Meml. Hosp. and Northwestern U. Med. Sch., Chgo., 1974—2003. Guest prof. Peking U., China, 2005. Editor Gyn-Ob Reference Series, 1973—2005, Internat. Jour. Gyn-Ob, 1985—. V.p. med. affairs Chgo. Maternity Ctr., Chgo., 1974—2003; treas. Soc. Family Planning, 2005-. Fellow ACS, Am. Coll. Ob-Gyn. (chmn. internal affairs com. 1985-89), Royal Coll. Ob-Gyn. (ad eundem); Internat. Fedn. Gyn-Ob. (pres. 1991-94, pres. Supporters Assn. 1994-2000); mem. Assn. Profs. Gyn-Ob. (sec. 1976-79, pres. 1980-81, Achievement award 1998, Tchg. award 2003), Am. Assn. Maternal and Neonatal Health (pres. 1980-89), Coun. Resident Edn. in Ob-Gyn., Am. Fertility Soc. (Hartman award 1965, bd. dirs. 1971-73), Assn. Profs. Gyn-Ob. Med. Edn. Found. (sec.-treas. 1987-91, pres. 1991-93), Ctrl. Assn. Ob-Gyn. (trustees 1986-90, pres. 1990-91), Chgo. Gynecol. Soc. (pres. 1990-91), Internat. Soc. Gynecol. Endoscopy (hon. 2005, v.p. 1997-99, pres. 1999-01), Am. Gynecol. Club, Internat. Acad. Human Reprodn., Yale Club N.Y.C., Carleton Club (Chgo.). Avocations: photography, travel. Office: Northwestern U Med Sch Dept Ob-Gyn 680 N Lake Shore Dr Ste 1015 Chicago IL 60611-8702 Office Phone: 312-695-5107. Business E-Mail: jsciarra@northwestern.edu.

SCIBELLI, ANDREW M., academic administrator; BA, St. Anselm Coll.; MEd, Boston State Coll.; EdD, U. Mass. Tchr. Springfield (Mass.) Pub. Schs., 1965-69; prof. biology Springfield Tech. Community Coll., 1969-70, 78-83, registrar, 1970-73, asst. to pres., 1974-78, dir. community rels., 1981-83, pres., 1983—. Bd. dirs. Mfg. Partnership of Western Mass., Springfield Ctrl.; trustee Pioneer Valley Planning Commn.; mem. chancellor's coun. U. Mass.; chmn. New Eng. Tech. Edn. Project New Eng. Bd. Higher Edn., Statewide Collective Bargaining Negotiating Team for Mass. C.Cs.; presenter nat. convs. Alliance for C.C. Innovation, 1991, 94, 95; active Toronto Trade Mission, 1992, Hartford Trade Mission, 1992; corporator Chicopee Savs. Bank. Apptd. commr. MASSJOBS West Commn., mem. Massjobs Coun.; chmn., co-host United Cerebral Palsy Telethon, 1981—, past. pres. bd. dirs. western Mass. chpt.; mem. exec. com., bd. dirs. Pvt. Industry Coun. and Regional Employment Bd.; dir. Italian Cultural Ctr.; pres. Make-A-Wish Found. Western Mass.; chmn. maj. firms unit United Way, 1989; bd. dirs. Springfield Edn. Ptnrship, Corp. Pub. Mgmt.; numerous other civic roles and activities. Mem. Am. Assn. Community and Jr. Colls. (presenter nat. conv.), Nat. Coun. Resource Devel., Nat. Inst. Staff and Organizational Devel. (Outstanding Chief Exec. Officer Mass. 1987), Nat. Coun. Community Svcs. and Continuing Edn. (Regional Person of the Yr. awd, 1993), Am. Assn. Higher Edn., Nat. Coun. Occupational Edn. (rep. New Eng.), Nat. Coalition Advanced Tech. Ctrs., Nat. Coun. Pres., Coop. Colls. Greater Springfield (chmn. 1987-88). Avocations: golf, sailing, bicycling, skiing. Office: Springfield Tech C C Office Pres Armory Sq Springfield MA 01105

SCIFRES, DONALD RAY, finance company executive; m. Carol Scifres. BS, Purdue U., 1968; MS, U. Ill., 1970, PhD, 1972; Doctorate (hon.), Purdue U., 2001. Rsch. and tchg. asst. U. Ill., Urbana, 1968-72; rsch. fellow, area mgr. Xerox Corp., Palo Alto, Calif., 1972-83; founder, pres., CEO SDL, Inc., San Jose, Calif., 1983-2001, dir., 1983-2001, chmn., 1992-2001; co-chmn., chief strategy officer JDS Uniphase Corp., 2001—03; chmn. SDL Capital, LP, 2003—; mng. dir. SDL Ventures, LLC, 2003—. Nat. lectr. IEEE Quantum Electronics Soc., 1979 Bd. editors Jour. Fiber and Integrated Optics, 1978; mem. editorial adv. bd. Photonics Spectra, 1992—; contbr. articles to tech. jours.; patentee in field. Recipient Disting. Engring. Alumni award, Purdue U., 1990, Outstanding Elec. Engr. award, 1992, The Gov. Nobert T. Tiemann award, Beta Sigma Pi, 2002, Engring. Alumni award, U. Ill., 1991, Alumni Honor award, 1993, Distinction in Photonics award, Laurin Pub. Co., 1999, Rank prize, Rank Found., U.K., 2001; fellow U. Ill., 1968, Gen. Telephone and Electronics, 1970—72. Fellow IEEE (Jack Morton award 1985, 3d Millenium award 2000, Robert N. Noyce medal 2003, John Tyndall award 2006), IEEE Lasers and Electro-Optics Soc. (pres. 1992, Engring. Achievement award 1994), Optical Soc. Am. (Edward H. Land medal 1996); mem. Am. Phys. Soc. (George E. Pake prize 1997), Lasers and Electro-Optics Mfg. Assn. (bd. dirs. 1992-, sec. 1994, pres. 1996), Nat. Acad. Engring., Tau Beta Pi, Eta Kappa Nu (Eminent Mem. award 2003), Phi Eta Sigma. Office: One First St Ste 14 Los Altos CA 94022

SCIOLARO, CHARLES MICHAEL, cardiothoracic and vascular surgeon; b. Kansas City, Kans., July 5, 1958; s. Gerald Michael and Charleen Gwen Sciolaro; m. Vicki Lynn Mizell, Sept. 29 BA Biology and Chemistry magna cum laude, Mid Am. Nazarene U., 1980; MD magna cum laude, U. Kans., Kansas City, 1984. Diplomate Am. Bds. Gen. Surgery, Thoracic and Cardiac; lic. Ariz., Calif., La., Fla., Kans., Mo., Penn.; cert. ACLS, Calif. x-ray supr. and operator, transesophageal echocardiography. Intern gen. surgery Tucson hosps. surg. program U. Ariz., 1984—85, resident gen. surgery, 1985—86, 1987—89, chief resident gen. surgery, 1989—90; instr. surgery Loma Linda U. Med. Ctr., Tucson, 1991—93; physician divsn. cardiac, thoracic and vascular surgery MacArthur Surg. Clinic, Alexandria, 1993-96; staff physician Bethany Med. Ctr., 1996—2001, Overland Park Med. Ctr., 2001—. Emergency rm. physician, cons. Nat. Emergency Corp., Tucson, 1986-87; emergency care attendent Vets. Med. Ctr., Tucson, 1985-89, Cigna Urgent Care, 1985-89; staff physician Kanza Multispecialty Clinic, Kansas City, 1996-2003, Rapides Regional Med. Ctr., Alexandria, 1993-96, Providence Med. Ctr., Kansas City, 1996-2007, Bapt.-Luth. Med. Ctr., 2003—; pres. Kans. Heart and Lung Surgery, Chartered, 2003—; rschr., lectr., presenter in field Author: (manuscripts) Aortic Coarctation in Infants, 1991 Mem. First Family Ch. Overland Park, Kans. Named America's Top Surgeons, 2005; recipient Congl. Order of Merit, 2005, Presdl. Bus. Commn., 2005; Biochemistry Rsch. fellow, U. Kans., Kansas City, 1978—79. Mem. ACS, Kans. Med. Soc., Wyandotte Med. Soc., Soc. Thoracic Surgery, Internat. Coll. Surgeons, Kans. Med. Soc., Wyandotte County Med. Soc. Republican. Protestant. Avocations: photography, golf, softball. Office: 8919 Parallel Pky Ste 203 Kansas City KS 66112 also: 10550 Quivira Rd Ste 335 Leawood KS 66211 also: 6650 Troost Ste 205 Kansas City MO 64131 also: 3550 South Fourth Ste 141 Leawood KS 66211 Office Phone: 913-660-0438. Office Fax: 913-676-6059. Business E-Mail: csciol@kc.rr.com.

SCIPIO, L. ALBERT, II, (LOUIS ALBERT SCIPIO II), retired aerospace science engineering educator, historian; b. Juarez, Mex., Aug. 22, 1922; s. Louis Albert and Marie Leona (Richardson) Scipio; m. Katherine Ruth Jones, Aug. 15, 1942; children: Louis Albert, Karen R. BS, Tuskegee Inst., 1943; B.Civil Engring., U. Minn., 1948, MS, 1950, PhD, 1958. Archtl. draftsman McKissack & McKissack, Tuskegee, Ala., 1943; instr. Tuskegee Inst., 1946; designer Long & Thorshov, Mpls., 1948-50; lectr. U. Minn., Mpls., 1950-59; research physicist Hughes Aircraft Co., Culver City, Calif., 1954; Fulbright prof. Cairo U., Giza, Egypt, 1955-56; assoc. prof. mechanics Howard U., Washington, 1959-61; Fulbright prof. Cairo U., Giza, Egypt, 1955-56; dir. grad. studies for engring. and architecture, prof. aerospace engring. Howard U., Washington, 1967-70, Univ. prof. space scis., 1970-87, Disting. Univ. prof. emeritus, 1987—; prof. phys. scis. U. PR, Mayaguez, 1961-63; prof. aerospace engring. U. Pitts., 1963-67; pub. Roman Publs., Silver Springs, Md., 1981—; cons. in field. Author: Compendium of Aircraft Stress Analysis and Design, 1956, Principles on continua with Applications, 1966, Structural Design Concepts, 1967, E. M. Collar Insignia 1907-1926, 1981, Last of the Black Regulars, 1983, With the Red Hand Division, 1985, The 24th Infantry at Fort Benning, 1986, Pre-War Days at Tuskegee, 1987, The Collar Dist Story (1907-1999), 1999. Bd. visitors Air Force Inst. Tech., 1979—83. With US Army, 1943—46. Mem.: NSPE, AAAS, AIAA, Coun. Am. Mil. Past, Co. Mil. Historians, Am. Phys. Soc., Soc. Natural Philosophy, Internat. Assn. Bridge and Structural Engrs., NY Acad. Scis., Sigma Xi, Phi Beta Kappa, Pi Tau Sigma, Sigma Gamma Tau, Sigma Pi Sigma, Pi Mu Epsilon, Alpha Kappa Mu. Home: 12511 Montclair Dr Silver Spring MD 20904-2053

SCIRICA, ANTHONY JOSEPH, federal judge; b. Norristown, Pa., Dec. 16, 1940; BA, Wesleyan U., 1962; JD, U. Mich., 1965; postgrad. Fulbright Scholar, Central U., Caracas, Venezuela, 1966. Bar: Pa. 1966, US Dist. Ct. (ea. dist.) Pa. 1984, US Ct. Appeals (3d cir.) 1987. Ptnr. McGrory, Scirica, Wentz & Fernandez, Norristown, Pa., 1966—80; asst. dist. atty. Montgomery County, Pa., 1967—69; mem. Pa. Ho. of Reps, Harrisburg, 1971—79; judge Montgomery County Ct. Common Pleas, Pa., 1980—84, US Dist. Ct. (ea. dist.) Pa., Phila., 1984—87, US Ct. Appeals (3rd cir.), Phila., 1987—, chief judge, 2003—. Chmn. Pa. Sentencing Commn., 1980—85, com. on rules of practice & procedure, Jud. Conf. of US; prof. Penn State U. Sch. of Law, 2004—; mem. US Jud. Panel on Multidistrict Litig., 2006—. Scholar Fulbright scholar, Ctrl. U., Caracas, Venezuela, 1966. Mem.: ABA, Am. Law Inst., Montgomery Bar Assn., Pa. Bar Assn. Office: 22614 US Courthouse Independence Mall W Philadelphia PA 19106-1715 *

SCISM, DANIEL REED, lawyer; b. Evansville, Ind., Aug. 27, 1936; s. Daniel William and Ardath Josephine (Gibbs) S.; m. Paula Anne Sedgwick, June 21, 1958; children: Darby Claire, Joshua Reed. BA, DePauw U., 1958; JD, Ind. U., 1965. Bar: Ind. 1965, U.S. Dist. Ct. (so. dist.) Ind. 1965, U.S. Ct. Appeals (7th cir.) 1967, U.S. Supreme Ct. 1976. Reporter Dayton (Ohio) Jour.-Herald, 1958-59; editor Mead Johnson & Co., Evansville, 1961; first assoc., then ptnr. Roberts, Ryder, Rogers & Scism and predecessor firms, Indpls., 1965—86; ptnr. Barnes & Thornburg, Indpls., 1987—2002, of counsel, 2003—. Cons. Ind. Pers. Assn., 1984-2002. Treas. Marion County chpt. Myasthenia Gravis Found., Indpls., 1970; v.p. Marion County Mental Health Assn., Indpls., 1970-71; pres. The Suemma Coleman Agy., Indpls., 1973-74; bd. dirs. Ind. Humanities Coun., 1995-00, chmn. bd., 1997-98; trustee Indpls. Mus. Art, 2001—07; bd. dirs. Westminster Village North, Inc., 2003-06; pres. Persimmon Woods Homeowners Assn., 2001-03, sec. 2003-. With US Army, 1959—62. Edwards fellow Ind. U., 1964. Mem. ABA, Ind. Bar Assn., Woodland Country Club (bd. dirs. 1984-88, sec. 1998-99). Methodist. Home: 10909 300 Yard Dr Fishers IN 46037-9306 Office: Barnes & Thornburg 11 S Meridian St Indianapolis IN 46204-3535

SCITOVSKY, ANNE AICKELIN, economist, researcher; b. Ludwigshafen, Germany, Apr. 17, 1915; arrived in U.S., 1931, naturalized, 1938; d. Hans W. and Gertrude Margarete Aickelin; 1 child, Catherine Margaret. Student, Smith Coll., 1933—35; BA, Barnard Coll., 1937; postgrad., London Sch. Econs., 1937—39; MA in Econs., Columbia U., 1941. Mem. staff legis. reference svc. Libr. of Congress, 1941—44; mem. staff Social Security Bd., 1944—46; with Palo Alto (Calif.) Med. Found./Rsch. Inst., 1963—, chief health econs. div., 1973—94, sr. staff scientist, 1994—. Lectr. Inst. Health Policy Studies, U. Calif., San Francisco, 1975—94; mem. Inst. Medicine of NAS, Nat. Acad. Social Ins., Pres.'s Commn. for Study of Ethical Problems in Medicine and Biomed. and Behavioral Rsch., 1979—82, U.S. Nat. Com. on Vital and Health Stats., 1975—78, Health Resources and Svcs. Adminstrn., AIDS adv. com., 1990—94; cons. HHS, Inst. Medicine Coun. on Health Care Tech. Assessment, 1986—90. Home: 161 Erica Way Portola Valley CA 94028-7439 Office: Palo Alto Med Found Rsch Inst Ames Bldg 795 El Camino Real Palo Alto CA 94301-2302 Personal E-mail: ascitovsky@aol.com.

SCIUVA, MARGARET W., counselor; b. Cleve., Dec. 22, 1962; d. Joseph Aloysius and Katharine Elizabeth Williams; m. James Salvatore Sciuva, May 23, 1987; children: James Jr., Anthony, Richelle. BA in Comm. and Psychology, John Carol U.; postgrad. in counseling, John Carroll U.; MA in Counseling, Webster U. Rape crisis counselor Safe Homes Rape Crisis Ctr., Lauren, SC; family preservation therapist Spartanburg Mental Health, HSA, Cayce, SC; founder, exec. dir. SC Mental Health Counselors Assn. Treas. Polk County Mid. Sch. PTA, Tryon, NC, 2000; active Polk County Hist. Soc., Tryon, 2003. Mem.: SC Lic. Profl. Counselors, Nat. Bd. Cert. Counselors, NC Lic. Profl. Counselors. Avocations: reading, travel, gardening. Personal E-mail: mwsciuv@attglobal.net.

SCLAFANI, ANTHONY PAUL, plastic surgeon, educator, biomedical researcher; b. Bklyn., Oct. 3, 1963; BA, Columbia U., 1985; MD, U. Pa., 1989. Diplomate Am. Bd. Otolaryngology, Am. Bd. Facial Plastic and Reconstructive Surgery. Intern in gen. surgery Beth Israel Med. Ctr., NYC, 1989-91; from resident in otolaryngology, head and neck surgery to prof. N.Y. Eye and Ear Infirmary, NYC, 1991—2004, prof., 2004—, dir. facial plastic surgery, 1996—, surgeon dir., 2005—; fellow in facial plastic and reconstructive surgery St. Louis U. Sch. Medicine, 1995-96; pvt. practice NYC, 1996—, Chappaqua, NY, 1998—. Editor-in-chief Facial Plastic Surgery; assoc. editor Facial Plastics Clinics N.Am.; contbr. articles to profl. jours. Fellow ACS, Am. Acad. Facial Plastic and Reconstructive Surgery (Sir Harold Delf Gillies award 1996, Ira Tresley Rsch. award 2002, 04); mem. Am. Acad. Otolaryngology and Head and Neck Surgery, Am. Soc. for Laser Medicine and Surgery. Office: NY EE Infirm/Facial Pl Surg Dept Otolaryng/Head Neck 310 E 14th St 6th Fl New York NY 10003-4201 also: 59 S Greeley Ave Chappaqua NY 10514-3321 also: 990 Fifth Ave New York NY 10021 Office Phone: 914-238-5500. Personal E-mail: docs@nyface.com.

SCLAFANI, CHARLES CARLO, language educator, department chairman; b. Sciacca, Italy, Apr. 13, 1941; arrived in US, 1954; s. Leonardo and Leonarda Sclafani; m. Emilia Sclafani, June 11, 1967; children: Dina, Sandra. BA, CCNY, 1964; MA, Rutgers U., New Brunswick, NJ, 1971. Prof. Italian and Spanish Westchester C.C., Valhalla, NY, 1971—, dir. lang. lab., 1975—99, chair dept. modern langs., 1999—. Office: Westchester CC 75 Grasslands Rd Valhalla NY 10595 Office Phone: 914-606-6794. Business E-Mail: carlo.sclafani@sunywcc.edu.

SCLAFANI, JOSEPH L., diversified financial services company executive; Exec. v.p., contr. J.P. Morgan Chase & Co. Office: JP Morgan Chase & Co 270 Park Ave New York NY 10017-2070

SCLAFANI, KAREN C., lawyer; BA, LeMoyne Coll.; JD, NYU. Corp. assoc. Mudge, Rose, Guthrie and Alexander, NYC; v.p., dep. gen. counsel Avis Budget Group Inc., Parsippany, NJ, sr. v.p., gen. counsel, 1998—2006, exec. v.p., gen. counsel, 2006—. Office: Avis Budget Group, Inc 6 Sylvan Way Parsippany NJ 07054 Office Phone: 973-496-3500. Office Fax: 973-496-3444. *

SCLAFANI, SUSAN K., educational consultant, former federal agency administrator; b. Albany, NY, Sept. 22, 1944; AB in German and Math., Vassar Coll., 1966; MA in German Lang. and Lit., U. Chgo., 1967; ME in Ednl. Adminstrn., U. Tex., Austin, 1985, PhD, 1987. Cert. Tchr.Math. Ill., N.Y., Lifetime Tchr. Math. and German 6-12 Tex., Adminstr., Supt., Supr., Midmgr. Tex. Tchr. Ctrl. YMCA H.S., Chgo., 1971—72, Woodson Jr. H.S. Houston Ind. Sch. Dist., Tex., 1972—74, H.S. for Engring. Professions, Houston Ind. Sch. Dist., Tex., 1975—78; coord. magnet sch. Washington H.S. Houston Ind. Sch. Dist., 1978—83; ctrl. office coord. instrnl. tech. Houston Ind. Sch. Dist., Tex., 1983—84, exec. dir. curriculum devel., 1987—89, asst. supt. constrn. mgmt. and program planning, 1989—92, assoc. supt. dist. adminstrn., 1992—94, chief of staff, 1994—96, chief of staff ednl. svcs., 1996—2001; counselor to sec. US Dept. Edn., Washington, 2001—06, acting sec., vocational & adult edn., 2003—04, asst. sec., vocational & adult edn., 2004—06; mng. dir. Chartwell Education Group LLC, NYC, 2006—. V.p. and gen. mgr. Quantum Access, Inc., 1986—87; adj. prof. dept. curriculum and instrn. U. Houston, Tex., 1988—94, adj prof. dept. ednl. leadership, 1999—2001; presenter to numerous ednl. groups. Co-author (with R. Paige): (Book) Strategies for Reforming Houston's Schools; School Choice or Best Systems, What Improves Education, 2001; contbr. articles to profl. jours. Vol. Star of Hope Women and Family Shelter, Houston, 1988—90; mem. com. Tex. Alliance for Minorities in Engring., Houston, 1975—85; activity vol., conf. spkr. Coun. for Exceptional Children, Houston, 1989—91; com. mem. Tex. Task Force for the Homeless, 1990—92; mem. Hispanic Youth Leadership Forum Steering Com., Houston, 1990—, Pub. Policy, Comty. and Agy. Support, Success by Six Coms., United Way, Houston, 1987—2001; chair Children's Policy Com. United Way, Houston, 1987—2001. Office: Chartwell Education Group LLC Empre State Bldg Ste 7506 New York NY 10118 E-mail: sclafani@chartwelleducation.com. *

SCOBLE, ROBERT, podcast network company executive, blog writer; b. Jan. 18, 1965; m. Maryam Ghaemmaghami; 1 child from previous marriage, Patrick. Degree in Journalism, San Jose State U. Sch. Journalism and Mass Comm., 1993. Dir. mktg. UserLand Software; sales support mgr. NEC Mobile Solutions; technical evangelist Microsoft Corp., 2002—06; v.p. media develop. PodTech.net (PodTech.Network, Inc.), Menlo Park, Calif., 2006—. Author: Naked Conversations: How Blogs are Changing the Way Businesses Talk with Customers, 2006; blog writer Scobleizer.com. Named one of Top 25 Web Celebs, Forbes mag., 2007. Office: PodTech-Network Inc 2735 Sand Hill Rd Menlo Park CA 94025 Office Phone: 950-292-2500. E-mail: robertscoble@hotmail.com. *

SCOBLIC, J. PETER, magazine editor; b. NYC, July 29, 1974; s. Joseph Michael and Barbara Scoblic. BA, Brown U., 1997. Editor-in-chief Brown Jour. World Affairs, Providence, 1994-96; rsch. dir. Hedrick Smith Prodns., Bethesda, Md., 1998-99; editor Arms Control Today, Washington,

1999—2003; mng. editor The New Republic, Washington, 2003—04, exec. editor, 2004—. Vis. scholar Carnegie Endowment Internat. Peace, Washington, 2006—. Office: The New Republic 1331 H St NW Ste 700 Washington DC 20005

SCODARI, JOSEPH C., health products executive; Bd. dirs. Centocor, 1997—, pres., COO; pres. Centocor Johnson & Johnson, 1999—2001, co. grp. chmn. North Am. pharm. bus., mem. pharms. grp. oper. com., 2001, co. grp. chmn. biopharmaceutical businesses, 2003—05, worldwide chmn. Pharms. Grp., mem. exec. com., 2005—. Office: Johnson & Johnson 1 Johnson & Johnson Plz New Brunswick NJ 08933

SCOFIDIO, RICARDO, artist, architect, educator; m. Elizabeth E. Diller. Ptnr. Diller & Scofidio (now Diller Scofidio & Renfro), NYC, 1979—; prof. arch. The Cooper Union for the Advancement of Sci. and Art, NY. Works include Inst. Contemporary Art, Blur Bldg. (Progressive Architecture Design award), designed viewing platform for Ground Zero, NYC, media pavillion for Swiss EXPO 2002, Brasserie Restaurant, NY (James Beard Found. award for Best New Restaurant Design), Slither, Gifu, Japan, Loophole, Mus. Contemporary Art, Chgo., 1992, Apparatus Drawing, Mus. of Modern Art, NY, 1993, Case #00-17164, New Mus., 1993, Dysfunction, Ctr. d'Art Contemporian de Castres, France, 1993, Desiring Eye, I'dentity and Difference, Triennale, Milan, 1994, Pelts, Thaddeus Ropac Gallery, Paris, France, 1997, Non-Place, San Francisco Mus. Modern Art, 1997, Slow House, At the End of the Century: One Hundred Years of Architecture, Mus. Contemporary Art, LA, 1998, The American Lawn: Surface of Everyday Life, Canadian Centre for Architecture, Montreal, 1998, Public Faces/Private Places, Pusan Internat. Arts Festival, Korea, 1998, His/Her Bathroom, Thomas Healy Gallery, NY, 1998, Dress Code, Landesmuseum, Linz, Austria, 1998, (permanent collections) Travelogues, Internat. Arrivals Terminal 4, JFK Airport, NY, (installation) The Desiring Eye: Reviewing the Slow House, Gallery MA, Tokyo, 1992, Master/Slave, Fondation Cartier, Paris, InterClone Hotel, Ataturk Airport for Istanbul Biennial, 1997, (dance collaborations with the Lyon Ballet Opera of France and Charlerol/Danses of Belgium (touring exhbn.) EJM1: Man Walking at Ordinary Speed and EJM2:Inertia, 1998, (web project) Refresh, Dia Art Found., (video installation) Pageant, Johannesburg Biennial & Rotterdam Film Festival, 1997, (permanent installation) X,Y, Kobe, Japan, 1997, (multi-media work for stage in collaboration with Builders Assn.) Jet Lag, 1998 (Obie award for Creative Achievement), (pub. art commn., permanent video marques) Jump Cuts, United Artists Cineplex, San Jose, Calif., (collaborative dance work with Charlerol/Danses) Moving Target, (collaborative theater work with Dumb Type and Hotel Pro Forma) Business Class, Copenhagen Cultural Capital, (interactive video installation) Indigestion, Barbican Art Gallery, London, Walter Phillips Gallery, Banff, Canada, Biennial Nagoya, Japan, 1997, (electronic project) Subtopia, ICC Gallery, Tokyo, 1997, and several others, (installations commissioned by) Mus. of Modern Art, Whitney Mus., New Mus. of Contemporary Art, Walker Art Ctr., Minn., Cartier Found., Palais des Beauz-Arts Brussels, and Gallery Ma Tokyo, (works are in permanent collections of) Mus. of Modern Art, Mus. of Modern Art San Francisco, Fond Nat. d'Art Contemporian, several FRACs in France, Musee de la Mode in Paris, and many private collections, co-pub. with Elizabeth Diller Back to the Front: Tourisms of War, FRAC Basse-Normandie, 1994, Flesh: Architectural Probes, Princeton Architectural Press, 1995, Blur: The Making of Nothing, Abrams, 2002. Recipient Chrysler award for Innovation in Design, 1988—89, MacArthur Found. award, 1999, Brunner prize in Arch., AAAL, 2003, MacDermott award for Creative Achievement, MIT; fellow, N.Y. Found. Arts, 1998—99, Graham Found. Fellowship, 1998—99, Chgo. Inst. for Architecture and Urbanism Fellowship. Office: Diller Scofidio & Renfro 36 Cooper Sq New York NY 10003-7971 Address: The Cooper Union for the Advancement Dept Arch Cooper Sq New York NY 10003-7120 Office Phone: 212-260-7971. *

SCOFIELD, GORDON LLOYD, mechanical engineer, educator; b. Huron, SD, Sept. 29, 1925; s. Perry Lee and Zella (Reese) S.; m. Nancy Lou Cooney, Dec. 27, 1947; children: Cathy Lynn, Terrence Lee. B.M.E., Purdue U., 1946; M.M.E., U. Mo., Rolla, 1949; PhD in M.E, U. Okla., 1968. Instr. mech. engring. S.D. State Coll., Brookings, 1946-47; successively grad. asst., instr., asst. prof., asso. prof., prof. U. Mo., Rolla, 1947-69; prof., head mech. engring.-engring. mechs. dept. Mich. Technol. U., Houghton, 1969—80; disting. prof. mech. engring. S.D. Sch. Mines and Tech., Rapid City, 1981-88, asst. v.p. for acad. affairs, 1981-83, v.p., dean engring., 1984-86; pres. S.D. Sch. Mines and Tech. Found., 1982-90. Cons. U.S. Naval Ordnance Test Sta., China Lake, Calif., 1956-71; bd. dirs. Accreditation Bd. for Engring. and Tech., 1994-2000; cons. to industry. Served with USNR, 1943-46. NSF sci. faculty fellow, 1966-67; recipient alumni achievement award U. Mo., Rolla, 1975 Mem. ASME, Soc. Automotive Engrs. (pres. 1977, Excellence in Engring. Edn. award, 1999), Am. Soc. Engring. Edn., Sigma Xi, Tau Beta Pi, Pi Tau Sigma, Phi Kappa Phi. Home: PO Box 1085 Rapid City SD 57709-1085 *Satisfaction comes from sharing achievements. By acknowledging and sharing the importance of others in our success it is possible to accomplish more that is worth remembering.*

SCOFIELD, LOUIS M., JR., lawyer; b. Brownsville, Tex., Jan. 14, 1952; s. Louis M. and Betsy Lee (Aiken) S.; children: Christopher, Nicholas, Emma. BS in Geology with highest honors and high distinction, U. Mich., 1974; JD with honors, U. Tex., 1977. Bar: Tex. 1977, US Dist. Ct. (ea. and so. dists.) Tex., US Ct. Appeals (5th cir.) 1981, US Supreme Ct. 1984. Ptnr. Mehaffy/Weber, Beaumont, Tex., 1982—. Spkr. CNA Ins., Dallas, Jefferson County Ins. Adjusters, SE Tex. Ind. Ins. Agts., Gulf Ins. Co., Dallas, Employers Casualty Co., Beaumont, Tex. Employment Commn., Jefferson County Young Lawyers Assn., Jefferson County Bar Assn., South Tex. Coll. Law, John Gray Inst., Lamar U., 1991, Tex. Assn. Def. Counsel, 1991, 2007, Mfr.'s Alliance, 2007; cert. arbitrator Nat. Panel Consumer Arbitrators; presenter Forest Park HS, Martin Elem. Sch., St. Anne's Sch. Contbr. columns in newspapers, articles to profl. jours. Patron Beaumont Heritage Soc., John J. French Mus.; bd. dirs. Beaumont Heritage Soc., 1983-84, endowment fund com., 1988; chmn. lawyers divsn. United Appeals Campaign, 1984; grand patron Jr. League of Beaumont, 1989-90. Recipient Tex. Super Lawyer, Tex. Monthly Mag., 2005, 2006. Fellow: Tex. Bar Found. (life); mem.: ABA, Jefferson County Bar Assn. (disaster relief project 1979, outstanding young lawyer's com. 1980, dir. 2005), Def. Rsch. Inst., Tex. Assn. Defense Counsel (dir. at large 1986—87, v.p. 1987—89, program chmn. San Diego 1989, adminstrv. v.p. 1989—90), Assn. Defense Trial Attys. (chmn. Tex. membership com. 1999—, exec. coun. 1999—2002, conv. host 2005), State Bar of Tex. (mentors com. 1995), Beaumont County Country Club, Phi Beta Kappa. Democrat. Episcopalian. Avocations: golf, reading, fishing. Home: 4790 Littlefield St Beaumont TX 77706-7748 Office: Mehaffy & Weber PO Box 16 Beaumont TX 77704-0016 Office Phone: 409-835-5011. Business E-Mail: louscofield@mehaffyweber.com.

SCOFIELD, VIRGINIA LEE, research scientist; b. Lincoln, Nebr., May 14, 1948; d. Louis Morris and Betsy Aiken Scofield. BA, U. Tex., Austin, 1970, PhD, 1977. Asst. prof. UCLA Sch. Medicine, 1984—89; rsch. assoc. prof. U. So. Calif., L.A., 1995—2000; faculty scientist M.D. Anderson Cancer Ctr. Sci. Park, Smithville, Tex., 2000—. Vis. prof. dept. biology Pomona/Claremont Colls., Calif., 1995—97. Mem. editl. bd.: Biol. Bull., 1984—88; mem. editl. bd. Frontiers in Biol. Sci., 2006—; contbr. articles to profl. jours. Fellow, U. Tex., Genetics Found., 1972—77, Stanford U. Sch. Medicine, Calif., 1977—83, NIH, 1978—81; grantee, 1987—90, US CDC, 1987—90, U. Calif. Task Force AIDS, 1985—90, Am. Cancer Soc., 1987—90. Mem.: Am. Soc. Cell Biology, Am. Assn. Immunologists, Sigma Xi, Phi Kappa Phi, Angel Flight (sec. 1969—70), Alpha Phi (pledge class pres. 1967—68). Liberal. Episcopalian. Achievements include patents for sperm as immunogen carriers; genital-mucosal vaccines against HIV and other STDs. Home: 303 Quail Run Smithville TX 78957 Office: MD Anderson Cancer Science Park 1808 Park Road 1-C PO Box 389 Smithville TX 78957 Home Phone: 512-360-3454; Office Phone: 512-237-9344. Office Fax: 512-237-2444; Home Fax: 512-237-2444. Business E-Mail: vscofield@mdanderson.org.

SCOGGINS, BILL See SCOGGINS, M. W.

SCOGGINS, BRENDA CAROL, language educator, department chairman; b. Aug. 19, 1954; BA in Math., Tex. A&M U., College Station, 1976; MA in French, U. Tex., Austin, 1978. Cert. tchr. Tex. Tchg. asst. U. Tex., Austin, 1976—78; tchr., chmn. dept. Westfield HS, Houston, 1978—. Named Most Influential Tchr., Westfield HS, 2004—07, Educator of Distinction, Claes Nobel. Mem.: Tex. Fgn. Lang. Assn., Am. Coun. Tchg. Fgn. Langs. Office: 16713 Ella Blvd Houston TX 77090

SCOGGINS, M. W. (BILL SCOGGINS), academic administrator; Grad., U. Tulsa; M in Petroleum Engring., U. Okla.; PhD in Petroleum Engring., U. Tulsa. With Mobil, 1970—99; mem., exec. com. Mobil Oil; pres. Internat. E & P, Global Exploration; exec. v.p. ExxonMobil Prodn. Co., 1999—2004; pres. Colo. Sch. Mines, 2006—. Mem., exec. com. U. Tulsa Bd. Trustees, 2005, mem., fin., investment, audit com., mem., faculty and curriculum com.; mem., bd. dirs. Questar Corp., Trico Marine Services, Inc., Colo. Renewable Energy Authority. Sec. Bapt. Found. Colo. Named to Coll. Engring. Hall of Fame, 1998. Mem.: Colo. Oil and Gas Assn. Office: Office of Pres Colorado School of Mines 1500 Illinois St Golden CO 80401-1887 *

SCOGIN, TROY POPE, publishing executive, finance company executive; b. Manchester, Ala., Oct. 31, 1932; s. James David and Thelma Katie (Helton) S.; m. Katie Elizabeth Bates, May 26, 1956; children: Norma Kay, Joyce Marie. BA, Howard Coll., 1955; MDiv, So. Baptist Theol. Seminary, Louisville, 1959; MA, Samford U., 1972. Ordained to ministry Baptist Ch., 1956. Pastor West Port (Ky.) Baptist Ch., 1956-58, Providence Baptist Ch., Bellevue, Ohio, 1958-61; chaplain/capt. USAF, Lincoln, Nebr., 1961-64; pastor Sycamore (Ala.) Baptist Ch., 1964-65; sales rep. Houghton Mifflin Co., Boston, 1965-74, regional mgr., 1974-89, spl. asst. to exec. v.p. coll. div., 1989-90, v.p., 1984—, nat. accounts exec., 1990-92; pastor Ross Ave. Bapt. Ch. Intercity Mission, Dallas, 1993-98; prof. Wake Tech. C.C., Raleigh, NC, 1998—. Adv. bd. dirs. Ross Ave. Ctr.; faculty Eastfield Coll., 1992-98. Chmn. bd. deacons Ross Avenue Bapt. Ch., Dallas, 1991; trustee St. Johns Met. Cmty. Ch., Met. Cmty. Ch., Raleigh. Mem. Am. Mgmt. Assn., Am. Soc. Tng. Devel., Nat. Coun. Tchrs. English, Tex. Jr. Coll. Tchrs. Assn., N.C. C.C. Faculty Assn., Phi Kappa Phi, Omicron Delta Kappa (nat. leadership fraternity pres. 1954), Alpha Phi Omega (nat. svc. fraternity pres. 1952). Democrat. Avocations: bowling, swimming, fishing, tennis, golf. Personal E-mail: tpscogin@gmail.com. *Accomplishment of goals requires setting priorities. Anything worth doing is worth doing well. To determine what is worthwhile decide if it is right, if it is needed, and if it is worth the cost.*

SCOGLAND, WILLIAM LEE, lawyer; b. Moline, Ill., 1949; s. Maurice William and Harriet Rebecca S.; m. Victoria Lynn, 1976; 1 child, Thomas. BA magna cum laude, Augustana Coll., 1971; JD cum laude, Harvard U., 1975. Bar: Ill. 1975, U.S. Dist. Ct. (no. dist.) Ill. 1975. From assoc. to ptnr. Jenner & Block, Chgo., 1981—. Lectr. in law U. Chgo. Law Sch., 2000—; bd. dirs. Am. Benefits Coun., 2004—; adv. coun. employee welfare and pension benefit plans US Dept. Labor, 2006—. Author: Fiduciary Duty: What Does It Mean?, 1989; co-author Employee Benefits Law, 1987; contr. Tort and Ins. Law Jour., 1989, and others. Fellow: Am. Coll. Employee Benefits Counsel; mem.: Omicron Delta Kappa, Phi Beta Kappa. Republican. Office: Jenner & Block LLP 330 N Wabash Chicago IL 60611 Office Phone: 312-923-2878. Business E-Mail: wscogland@jenner.com.

SCOGNAMIGLIO PASINI, CARLO, economics and finance professor, senator; b. Varese, Italy, Nov. 27, 1944; s. Luigi and esther (Pasini) S.; m. Cecilia Pirelli, May 28, 1980; children: Filippo, Elisabetta Thea. D.Econs., U. Bocconi, Milan, Italy, 1968; spl. student, London Sch. Econs., 1970-71. Asst. prof. U. Bocconi, 1968-73, prof., 1973-79, U. Rome-Luiss, 1979—, dean and rector, 1984—. Senator Constituency of Milan, 1992—, pres. of senate, acting pres. of Republic, 1994-96, defense minister, 1998-99; pres. Corriere della Sera, 1983, Aspens Inst. Italia, 1995—. Author: The Stock Exchange, 1973, Industrial Crises, 1976, Industrial Economics, 1987, Theory of Finance, 1987, The Liberal Project, 1996. Winner prize for econs. French Acad., 1988. Avocations: golf, sailing, skiing. Office: Senato della Repubblica 00100 Rome Italy Office Fax: 3906 67063825. E-mail: c.scognamiglipasini@senato.it.

SCOLES, CLYDE SHELDON, library director; b. Columbus, Ohio, Apr. 14, 1949; s. Edward L. and Edna M. (Ruddock) S.; m. Diane Francis, July 14, 1976; children: David, Kevin, Karen, Stephen. BS, Ohio State U., 1971; MLS, U. Mich., 1972. Libr. Columbus Pub. Libr., 1972-74; libr. dir. Zanesville Pub. Libr., Ohio, 1974-78; asst. dir. Toledo-Lucas County Pub. Libr., 1978-85, dir., 1985—. Adj. lectr., libr. bldg. cons. U. Mich.; v.p. bd. dirs. Read for Literacy. Mem. ALA, Ohio Libr. Assn., Ohio Libr. Coun., Toledo C. of C., Com. of 100, Maumee Hist. Soc. Clubs: Torch (Toledo). Lodges: Rotary. Office: Toledo-Lucas County Pub Libr 325 N Michigan St Toledo OH 43604 Office Phone: 419-259-5256. Business E-Mail: Clyde.Scoles@toledolibrary.org. *

SCOLES, EUGENE FRANCIS, lawyer, educator; b. Shelby, Iowa, June 12, 1921; s. Sam and Nola E. (Leslie) S.; m. R. Helen Glawson, Sept. 6, 1942; children— Kathleen Elizabeth, Janene Helen. AB, U. Iowa, Iowa City, 1943, JD, 1945; LLM, Harvard U., Cambridge, Mass., 1949; JSD, Columbia U., NYC, 1955. Bar: Iowa 1945, Ill. 1946. Assoc. Seyfarth-Shaw & Fairweather, Chgo., 1945-46; asst. prof. law Northeastern U., 1946-48, assoc. prof., 1948-49, U. Fla., 1949-51, prof., 1951-56, U. Ill., Champaign, 1956-68, Max Rowe prof. law, 1982-89, prof. emeritus, 1989—; vis. prof. McGeorge Law Sch. U. Pacific, Sacramento, 1989-92; prof. U. Oreg., 1968-82, dean Sch. Law, 1968-74, disting. prof. emeritus, 1982—. Vis. prof. Khartoum U., Sudan, 1964-65; reporter Uniform Probate Code Project, 1966-70; mem. joint editorial bd. Uniform Probate Code, 1972—, Uniform Law Com., 1970-82. Author: (with H.F. Goodrich) Conflict of Laws, 4th edit., 1964, (with R.J. Weintraub) Cases and Materials on Conflict of Laws, 2d edit., 1972, (with E.C. Halbach, Jr., P.G. Roberts, H.D. Begleiter) Problems and Materials on Decedents' Estates and Trusts, 7th edit., 2006, Problems and Materials on Future Interests, 1977, (with P. Hay, P.J. Borchers, S.C. Symeonides) Conflict of Laws, 4th edit., 2004; contbr. articles to profl. jours.; notes and legislation editor Iowa Law Rev., 1945. Mem. ABA, Soc. Pub. Tchrs. Law, Am. Law Inst., Ill. Bar Assn., Assn. Am. Law Schs. (pres. 1978), Order of Coif Office: U Oreg Sch Law 1515 Agate St Eugene OR 97403-1221 Office Phone: 541-346-3862.

SCOLES, MARIE Y., elementary school educator; d. Richard and Doris Scheg; m. Thomas E. Scheg, Oct. 26, 1991; children: Ian, Courtney. BS in Secondary Edn. Math., SUNY, 1985, MS in Secondary Edn. in Math., 1991. Cert. secondary education mathematics educator N.Y., 1985. Mid. sch. math. tchr. South Seneca H.S., Ovid, NY, 1985—2003, math. tchr., 1985—. Adivsor Jr. Nat. Honor Soc., Ovid, 1997—98. Mem.: Assn. of N.Y. State Math. Tchrs. (assoc.). Office: South Seneca High School 7263 Main St Ovid NY 14521 Home Phone: 315-568-0023; Office Phone: 607-869-9636. Personal E-mail: courian@aol.com. E-mail: mscoles@southseneca.k12.ny.us.

SCOLESE, CHRISTOPHER, federal agency administrator; BSEE, SUNY, Buffalo, 1978; MSEE, George Washington U. Earth Observing Sys. (EOS) program mgr., dep. dir. flight programs and projects for earth sci. Goddard Space Flight Ctr., Greenbelt, Md., EOS Terra Project mgr., EOS sys. mgr., dep. dir.; dep. assoc. adminstr. Office Space Sci. NASA Hdqs., Washington, chief engr., 2005—07, assoc. adminstr., 2007—; sr. analyst Gen. Rsch. Corp., McLean, Va. Spkr. in field. With USN, 1978—83. Recipient Presdl. Rank award of meritorious exec. Fellow: AIAA (assoc.; mem. astrodynamics com., chmn. nat. capitol sect. guidance navication and control tech. com., Young Engr./Scientist of Yr. award nat. capitol sect.); mem.: IEEE, Tau Beta Pi, Eta Kappa Nu. Office: NASA Hdqrs Mail Code S 300 E St SW Washington DC 20546 Business E-Mail: christopher.j.scolese@nasa.gov. *

SCOLLARD, PATRICK JOHN, hospital executive; b. Chgo., Apr. 20, 1937; s. Patrick J. and Kathleen (Cooney) S.; m. Gloria Ann Carroll, July 1, 1961; children: Kevin, Maureen, Daniel, Thomas, Brian. BS in Econs., Marquette U., 1959; grad. sr. exec. program, MIT, 1976. With Equitable Life Assurance Soc. U.S., NYC, 1962-79, asst. v.p., 1969-71, v.p., personnel dir., 1971-75, v.p. corp. adminstrv. svcs., 1975-79; sr. v.p. Chem. Bank, NYC, 1979-80, exec. v.p., 1980-87, chief adminstrv. officer, 1987-92; pres., CEO St. Francis Hosp., Roslyn, NY, 1992-99; pres. Scollard Assocs. LLC, Garden City, NY, 1999—; pres., CEO Cath. Health Svcs. of L.I., Melville, NY, 2003—04, also bd. dirs. Bd. dirs. Curaspan, Inc. Bd. dirs. Ctr. Productive Longevity, Cath. Health Svcs. L.I., North Fork C.C.; chmn. Scollard Family Found. Inc., 1999—. Office: Scollard Assocs LLP 1461 Franklin Ave Garden City NY 11530-1648 Office Phone: 516-739-5107.

SCOMMEGNA, ANTONIO, obstetrician, gynecologist, educator; b. Barletta, Italy, 1931; came to U.S., 1954, naturalized, 1960; s. Francesco Paola and Antonietta S.; m. Lillian F. Sinkiewicz, May 3, 1958; children: Paola, Frank, Roger. BA, State Lyceum A. Casardi, Barletta, 1947; MD, U. Bari, Italy, 1953. Diplomate: Am. Bd. Obstetrics and Gynecology, also sub-bd. endocrinology and reprodn. Rotating intern New Eng. Hosp., Boston, 1954-55; resident obstetrics and gynecology Michael Reese Hosp. and Med. Center, Chgo., 1956-59, fellow dept. research human reprodn., 1960-61, research asso., 1961; fellow steroid tng. program Worcester Found. Exptl. Biology, also Clark U., Shrewsbury, Mass., 1964-65; asso. prof. obstetrics and gynecology Chgo. Med. Sch., 1965-69; mem. staff Michael Reese Hosp. and Med. Center, 1961—, attending physician obstetrics and gynecology, 1961—, dir. sect. gynecologic endocrinology, 1965-81; dir. ambulatory care obstetrics and gynecology Mandel Clinic, 1968-69, chmn. dept., 1969-89; attending, chief svc. U. Ill. Chgo. Hosp. and Med. Ctr., 1989-98; trustee Mandel Clinic, 1977-80; prof. dept. ob-gyn. Pritzker Sch. Medicine, U. Chgo., 1969-89; prof., head dept. ob-gyn. Coll. Medicine, U. Ill. Chgo., 1989-98, prof. emeritus, 1999—. Contbr. articles to profl. jours. Fulbright fellow, 1954-55 Fellow Am. Coll. Obstetricians and Gynecologists, Endocrine Soc., Chgo. Inst. Medicine, Am. Gynecol. and Obstet. Soc.; mem. AMA, Ill., Chgo. med. socs., Am. Fertility Soc., Chgo. Gynecol. Soc. (sec. 1976-79, pres. 1981-82), Soc. Study Reprodn., AAAS, Soc. for Gynecologic Investigation. Home: 1023 W Vernon Park Pl Apt E Chicago IL 60607-3447 Office Phone: 312-996-0222. Business E-Mail: anmis@uic.edu.

SCOPPETTA, NICHOLAS, fire commissioner; b. NYC, Nov. 6, 1932; m. Susan Scoppetta; children: Andrea, Eric. BS, Bradley U., 1958; JD, Bklyn. Law Sch., 1962. Investigator Soc. Prevention of Cruelty to Children; asst. dist. atty. NY County, 1962—69; asst. U.S. atty. (so. dist.) NY US Dept. Justice, 1969—71; commr. of investigation NYC, 1972—76, dep. mayor for criminal justice, 1976—78; founding ptnr. Scoppetta & Schieff LLP, 1980—96; commr. Adminstrn. for Children's Svcs., NYC, 1996—2001, NYC Fire Dept., 2001—. Assoc. counsel The Knapp Commn. (Commn. to Investigate Alleged Police Corruption), 1971; prof. law, dir. Inst. Jud. Adminstrn. NYU, 1978—; mem. Waterfront Commn. of NY Harbor, 1979; chmn. Commn. to Combat Police Corruption, 1994—96; founder, pres. New Yorkers for Children, 1996—. Past pres., former chmn. bd. trustees Children's Aid Soc. Served in US Army. Recipient Hugo-Morgenthau award, Hugo Morgenthau Associates, 1997. *

SCORNAIENCHI, JOAN WEBB, educational association administrator, consultant; b. Johnstown, Pa. d. Calvin John and Amelia Maystrovich Webb; m. John Joseph Scornaienchi, Apr. 19, 1997. BSc, Ind. U. Pa., 1981, MA, 1982. Specialist drug and alcohol prevention Highland Ctr. of Mercy Hosp., Johnstown, Pa., 1982—83; adminstr. Kent State U., Ohio, 1983—94; bus. and industry liaison officer Cambria County C.C., Johnstown, 1995—96; customer svc. rep. Caterpillar Fin. Svcs., Columbia, Md., 1997—2000; edn. program specialist Md. State Dept. Edn., Balt., 2001—; co-founder, etiquette and protocol cons. Ambassador Protocol, Columbia, 2005—. Presenter in field. Co-author: (article) The Residence Hall Experience, 1985. Mem. Balt./Wash. C. of C., 2005—; vol. Balt. City Teen Ct., 2003—, mem. adv. com., 2003—. Recipient Diversity award, Kent State U., 1991, Orientation Week Creative Program award, 1992, citation, City of Balt. Mayor's Office, 2004, Emerging Leader award, South Atlantic Region Soroptimist Internat., 2006. Mem.: Soroptomist Internat. Howard County (treas. 2004—06, com. chair 2004—06, pres. 2006—), Nat. Assn. Multicultural Edn., Nat. Grants Mgmt. Assn. Avocations: travel, reading, writing, etiquette training, bicycling. Home: 6209 Bird Race Columbia MD 21045 Personal E-mail: joanwebbs@comcast.net.

SCORSESE, MARTIN, film director, film producer; b. Flushing, NY, Nov. 17, 1942; s. Charles and Catherine (Cappa) S.; m. Laraine Marie Brennan, May 15, 1965 (div.), 1 daughter: Catherine Terese Glinora Sophia; m. Julia Cameron, 1975 (div.), 1 daughter: Domenica Elizabeth; m. Isabella Rosellini, Sept. 29, 1979 (div. 1983); m. Barbara DeFina, Feb. 9, 1985 (div.); m. Helen Morris, 1999; 1 child, Francesca Kingsland Scorsese. BS in Film Communications, NYU, 1964, MA in Film Communications, 1966, Doctorate (hon.), Princeton U., Wesleyan U., Bard Coll., Williams Coll., Royal Coll. Art. Faculty asst., then instr. film NYU, NYC, 1963-70; founder World Cinema Found., 2007—. Dir. (films) Who's That Knocking at My Door?, 1968, (also writer, assoc. prodr., actor), Boxcar Bertha, 1972 (also actor), Mean Streets, 1973 (also co-writer, actor), Alice Doesn't Live Here Anymore, 1975, Taxi Driver, 1976 (also actor) (Palme d'Or Cannes Internat. Film Festival), New York, New York, 1977, The Last Waltz, 1978, Raging Bull, 1980, The King of Comedy, 1983, After Hours, 1985, The Color of Money, 1986, The Last Temptation of Christ, 1988, New York Stories (Life Lessons segment), 1989, Goodfellas, 1990 (also co-writer), Cape Fear, 1991, The Age of Innocence, 1993 (also co-writer), Casino, 1995 (also writer), Kundun, 1997, Bringing Out the Dead, 1999, The Gangs of New York, 2002, The Aviator, 2004 (also exec. prodr.), The Departed, 2006 (also prodr.)(Best Dir. NY Film Critics Circle award, 2006, Best Dir. Nat. Bd. Review, 2006, 2006 Critics Choice award, Broadcast Film Critics Assn., 2007, Best Dir., Golden Globe award, Hollywood Fgn. Press Assn., 2007, Outstanding Directorial Achievement in Feature Film for 2006, Directors Guild Am., 2007, Acad. award best directing, 2007); prodr. (films) The Grifters, 1990, Mad Dog and Glory, 1993; (exec. prodr.): Naked in New York, 1994, Clockers, 1995, Grace of My Heart, 1996, You Can Count On Me; documentaries include: (editor): Woodstock, 1970 (also asst. dir.), Elvis on Tour, 1973; (assoc. prodr.): Medicine Ball Caravan, 1971; (dir.): The Big Shave, 1968 (also writer), Street Scenes 1970, 1970, Italianamerican, 1974, American Boy: A Profile of Steven Price, 1979, Made in Milan, 1990; dir., prodr. (documentary) No Direction Home: Bob Dylan (Banff Rockie award, 2006, Columbia-DuPont Journalism award, 2007), 2005; co-dir. A Personal Journey with Martin Scorsese Through American Movies, 1997, Il Mio Viaggio in Italia, 1999, The Blues, 2002; other film appearances include: Cannonball, 1976, Pavlova: A Woman for

All Seasons, 1983, 'Round Midnight, 1986, Akira Kurosawa's Dreams, 1990, Guilty by Suspicion, 1991, Quiz Show, 1994, Search and Destroy, 1995 (also prodr.), The Muse, 1999, (TV films) La Memoire Retrouvee, 1996, (exec. prodr.) Kicked in the Head, 1997, The Hi-Lo Country, 1998. Decorated Legion of Honor (France); recipient Edward L. Kingsley Found. award, 1963-64, 1st prize Screen Prodrs. Guild, 1965, Best Dir. Cannes Film Festival, 1986. Am. Cinematheque award, 1991, Britannia award Brit. Acad. Film and TV Arts, 1993, Golden Lion award Venice Film Festival, 1995, Wexner prize Wexner Ctr. for the Arts, Columbus, Ohio, 1996, Life Achievement award Am. Film Inst., 1997, Lifetime Career award Lincoln Ctr. Film Soc., 1998, Ray of Light award Dalai Lama, 1998, Golden Globe, 2003, Evelyn F. Burkey award Writers Guild Am. East, 2003, Lifetime Achievement award Dirs. Guild Am., 2003, Ellis Island Family Heritage award, 2004, Grammy award for No Direction Home: Bob Dylan, 2006; named one of The World's Most Influential People, TIME mag., 2007 Fellow: Am. Acad. Arts and Sciences; mem.: AAAL (hon.).

SCOTCHMER, SUZANNE ANDERSEN, economics professor; b. Seattle, Jan. 23, 1950; d. Toivo Matthias and Margaret A. BA in Econ., U. Wash., 1970; MA in Stats., U. Calif., Berkeley, 1979, PhD in Econ., 1980. From asst. to assoc. prof. econ. Harvard U., Cambridge, Mass., 1981-86; prof. econs. and pub. policy U. Calif., Berkeley, 1986—. Vis. prof. U. Toronto, 1993, Tel Aviv U., 1994, U. Paris, Sorbonne, 1992, New Sch. of Econs., Moscow, 1993, U. Auckland, 2002; prin. investigator NSF, 1986-2002; lectr. in law Stockholm Sch. Econs., 2006, U. So. Calif., 2007; mem. Toulouse Network on Info. Tech., 2005—. Author: Innovation and Incentive, 2004; mem. editl. bd. Am. Econ. Rev., 1991-95, Jour. Pub. Econ., 1986-01, Jour. Econ. Perspectives, 1994-97, Regional Sci. and Urban Econ., 1991—, Jour. Econ. Lit., 1998-01; contbr. articles to profl. jours. Sloan fellow, 1979, Phi Beta Kappa fellow, 1978, Hoover Nat. fellow Stanford U., 1989, Olin fellow Yale Sch. Law, 1993, and Sch. Law U. So. Calif., 2005; France/Berkeley Fund grantee, 1994-95; Kaufmann Found. grantee, 2005. Office: Univ Calif 2607 Hearst Ave Berkeley CA 94720-7320 Business E-Mail: scotch@berkeley.edu.

SCOTT, A. TIMOTHY, lawyer; b. Natchez, Miss., Feb. 16, 1952; s. John William and Patricia (O'Reilly) S.; m. Nancy E. Howard, June 7, 1976; children: Kevin Howard, Brian Howard. BA in Psychology, Stanford U., 1974, JD, 1977. Bar: Calif. 1977, U.S. Tax Ct. 1978. Assoc. then ptnr. Agnew, Miller & Carlson, LA, 1977-83; assoc. Greenberg, Glusker, Fields, Claman & Machtinger, LA, 1983; ptnr. Sachs & Phelps, LA, 1983-91; mem. Heller, Ehrman White & McAuliffe, LA, 1991-96, of counsel, 1996-99; sr. v.p., tax counsel Pub. Storage, Inc., Glendale, Calif., 1996—. Speaker in field. Note editor Stanford Law Rev., 1976-77; contbr. article to profl. publs., chpt. to book. Mem. ABA, L.A. County Bar Assn. (chmn. real estate taxation com. 1988-91, exec. com., taxation sect. 1989-91), Order of Coif. Democrat. Avocations: volleyball, gardening, art, skiing. Office: Pub Storage Inc 701 Western Ave Glendale CA 91201-2349 Business E-Mail: tscott@publicstorage.com.

SCOTT, ADAM, professional golfer; b. Adelaide, Australia, July 16, 1980; Student, UNLV. Amateur tour golfer, 1996—2000; profl. golfer PGA Tour, 2001—. Mem. Australian Team World Cup, 2002; mem. Internat. Team Pres.'s Cup, 2003, 05. Achievements include winning PGA Tour events including the Deutsche Bank Championship, 2003, PLAYERS Championship, 2004, Booz Allen Classic, 2004, THE TOUR Championship presented by Coca-Cola, 2006, Houston Open, 2007; winner, international events including the Alfred Dunhill PGA Championship, 2001, Qatar Masters, 2002, Gleneagles Scottish PGA Championship, 2002, Scandic Carlsberg Scandinavian Masters, 2003, Singapore Open, 2005, Johnnie Walker Classic, 2005; top ten World Ranking, 2006. Mailing: PGA Tour 112 PGA TOUR Blvd Ponte Vedra Beach FL 32082 *

SCOTT, ANNE BYRD FIROR, history professor; b. Montezuma, Ga., Apr. 24, 1921; d. John William and Mary Valentine (Moss) Firor; m. Andrew Mackay Scott, June 2, 1947; children: Rebecca, David MacKay, Donald MacKay. AB, U. Ga., 1941; MA, Northwestern U., 1944; PhD, Radcliffe Coll., 1958; LHD (hon.), Lindenwood Coll., 1968, Queens Coll., 1985, Northwestern U., 1989, Radcliffe Coll., 1990, U. of the South, 1990, Cornell Coll., 1991; LLD (hon.), Wake Forest U., 2007. Congressional rep., editor LWV of U.S., 1944-53; lectr. history Haverford Coll., 1957-58, U. N.C., Chapel Hill, 1959-60; asst. prof. history Duke U., Durham, N.C., 1961-67, assoc. prof., 1968-70, prof., 1971-80, W.K. Boyd prof., 1980-91, W.K. Boyd prof. emerita, 1992—, chmn. dept., 1981-85; Gastprofessor Universität, Bonn, Germany, 1992-93. Vis. prof. Johns Hopkins U., 1972-73, Stanford U., 1974, Harvard U., 1984, Cornell Coll., 1993, Williams Coll., 1994, U. Miss., 2000; Times-Mirror scholar Huntington Libr., 1995; vice chmn. Nat. Humanities Ctr., 1991-98; mem. adv. com. Schlesinger Libr.; lectr. in field. Author: The Southern Lady, 1970, 1995; author: (with Andrew MacKay Scott) One Half the People, 1974; author: Natural Allies, 1991; editor: Jane Addams, Democracy and Social Ethics, 1964, The American Woman, 1970, Women in American Life, 1970, Women and Men in American Life, 1976, Unheard Voices, 1993, Pauli Murray and Caroline Was, 2006; mem. editl. bd.: Revs. in Am. History, 1976—81, Am. Quar., 1974—78, Jour. So. History, 1978—84; contbr. articles to profl. jours. Chmn. Gov.'s Commn. on Status of Women, 1963-64; mem. Citizens Adv. Council on Status of Women U.S., 1964-68; trustee Carnegie Corp., 1977-85, W.W. Ctr. for Scholars, 1977-84; chmn. bd. dirs. Nat. Cmty. Investment Fund, 1996—2002. AAUW fellow, 1956-57; grantee NEH, 1967-68, 76-77, Nat. Humanities Ctr., 1980-81; grad. medal Radcliffe Coll., 1986, Duke U. medal, 1991, John Caldwell medal N.C. Humanities Coun., 1994; fellow Ctrl. Advanced Study in Behavioral Sci., 1986-87; Fulbright scholar, 1984, 92-93. Fellow Am. Acad. Arts & Sci; mem. Am. Antiquarian Soc., Orgn. Am. Historians (exec. bd. 1973-76, pres. 1983, Disting. Pub. Svc. award 2002), So. Hist. Assn. (exec. bd. 1976-79, pres. 1989), Soc. Am. Historians, Phi Beta Kappa. Democrat. Office: Duke U Dept History Durham NC 27708 E-mail: ascott@email.unc.edu.

SCOTT, BENJAMIN, retired electrical engineer; b. Maringoulin, La., Nov. 30, 1929; s. Harry Scott, Sr. and Sarah (London) Scott; m. Doretha L. Scott, June 27, 1959; children: Benjamin Eric Jr., Daryl Deion. AA, Pasadena City Coll., Calif., 1954; BS, Pacific State U., LA, 1959; M in Mgmt. Sci., UCLA, China Lake, 1969. Project elec. enginrg. Defense Dept., China Lake, 1952—69, dir. Sylmar, Calif., 1964—67, spl. projects electronics Pasadena, Calif., 1969—74; CEO, chief cons. Benjamin Scott & Assocs., Inc., San Francisco, 1977—78, LA, 1978—80, Pasadena, 1981—2001; ret. Author: (manuscript) South Africa, An Emerging Democracy, 1990. Cmty. organizer NAACP, Pasadena and China Lake, Calif., 1952—; internat. organizer for Africa People to People, LA, 1972; bd. mem. ARC, Inglewood and LA, 1997—2003; coord. Pasadena Urban Coalition, 1966—74, Congress Racial Equality, LA, 1962—97; cons. Black and Minority Businesses, LA, 1977—79; contbr. South African Peace Negotiations, 1986—90. Master sgt. US Army, 1945—47, PTO. Decorated Heroism During Korean War award US Army; recipient Recognition award, Civil Rights Field-Time Mag. Feature, 1963, Pres. Richard M. Nixon, 1972, LA City Coun., 1977, Einsenhower Commn., 1998, Superior Achievement award, Def. Dept., 1966, Humanitarian award, William R. Tolbert, Jr. Pres., Liberia, 1972, Humanitarian for Peace award, Vista U., South Africa, 1990. Mem.: Clare Barton Soc., Mystic Shrine, Masons, Am. Disabled Vets., Am. VFW, Am. Legion. Republican. Episcopalian. Avocations: water-skiing, boating, tennis, golf.

SCOTT, BRADFORD, surgeon; BA, U. Tex., Austin, Tex., 1990; MD, U. Tex. S.W. Med. Sch., Dallas, 1994. Diplomate Am. Bd. Surgery, 2001. Asst. prof. Michael E. DeBakey dept. surgery Baylor Coll. Medicine, Houston, 1999—; trauma med. dir. Ben Taub Gen. Hosp., Houston, 2004—. Fellow: ACS (sec. 2006—); mem.: Harris County Dart Assn. (life). Avocations: golf, darts. Office Phone: 713-873-3949.

SCOTT, BRIAN DAVID, lawyer; b. Spokane, Wash., Sept. 30, 1946; s. Dick E. and Helene L. (Johnson) S.; m. Lynita G. Muzzall, Sept. 9, 1972; children: D. Alexander, Rachel E., S. Andrew. BA, U. Wash., 1968; JD, U. Wis., 1972. Bar: Wis. 1972, Wash. 1972, U.S. Dist. Ct. (we. dist.) Wash. 1972, U.S. Dist. Ct. (we. dist.) Wis. 1972. Asst. atty. gen. Wash. State Atty. Gen.'s Office, Seattle, 1972-74; assoc. Jackson, Ulvestad, Goodwin, Grutz, Seattle, 1974-81; ptnr. Goodwin, Grutz & Scott, Seattle, 1981-96, Grutz, Scott & Kinney, Seattle, 1996-99, Grutz, Scott, Kinney & Fjelstad, Seattle, 1999—2004, Scott, Kinney & Fjelstad, Seattle, 2005—. Mem. Am. Assn. Justice, Wash. Trial Lawyers Assn., Wash. Athletic Club. Democrat. Avocations: boating, skiing, travel. Home: 158 Prospect St Seattle WA 98109-3750 Office: Scott Kinney & Fjelstad 600 University St Ste 1928 Seattle WA 98101-4178 Office Phone: 206-622-2200. Business E-Mail: scott@skf-law.com.

SCOTT, BRIAN WALTER, management consultant; b. Melbourne, Victoria, Australia, Apr. 23, 1935; s. Walter and Dorothy Ada (Ransom) S.; m. Dorothy Yvonne Allen, Aug. 15, 1959; children: David, Mark, Jennifer, Susan. B of Econs., Sydney U., Australia, 1955; MBA, Stanford U., 1959; D of Bus. Adminstrn., Harvard U., 1963. Asst. prof. U. So. Calif., Los Angeles, 1961-62; cons. mgmt. W.D. Scott and Co. Pty. Ltd., Sydney, 1963-69, dir., 1969-74, mng. dir., 1974-79, chmn., 1979-85; dep. chmn. A.C.I. Internat. Ltd., Sydney, 1985-86, chmn., 1986-88; dir., mgmt. rev. Edn. Portfolio, New South Wales, 1988-90. Chmn. Mgmt. Frontiers Pty. Ltd., Sydney, 1985—, Found for Devel. Cooperation Ltd., Brisbane, 1990—; bd. dirs. James N. Kirby Found. Ltd. Chmn. Trade Devel. Coun., Canberra, 1984-90, chmn. Australian-Korean Found., 1992-2000; chmn. coun. Knox Grammar Sch., Sydney, 1981-89, Australia-Asean Bus. Coun., Canberra, 1980-82; mem. governing bd. Asian Inst. Mgmt., Manila, 1990—; co-chmn. Australia-Korea Forum, 1989-91. Named Officer, Order of Australia, 1985; recipient Australian Mfrs. Export Coun. award, 1989. Fellow Inst. Dirs. Australia (fed. pres. 1982-86), Internat. Acad. Mgmt., Australian Inst. Mgmt., Inst. Mgmt. Cons.; mem. Trade Policy Rsch. Ctr. (coun. mem. 1985-90), Sydney U. (senate 1990-95), Royal Sydney Yacht Squadron Club, Am. Club (Sydney). Avocations: reading, travel. Home: PO Box 829 Avalon Beach NSW 2109 Australia Office: Mgmt Frontiers Pty Ltd PO Box 494 North Sydney 2059 Australia Business E-Mail: brian.scott@mgtfrontiers.com.au. E-mail: brianwscott@aol.com.

SCOTT, BYRON, professional basketball coach, retired professional basketball player; b. Ogden, Utah, Mar. 28, 1961; m. Anita Scott; children: Thomas, LonDen, DaRon. Student, Ariz. State U., 1979-85. Draft pick San Diego Clippers (now LA Clippers), 1983; player LA Lakers, 1983—93, 1996—97, Ind. Pacers, Indpls., 1993—95, Vancouver Grizzlies, 1995—96, Pananthinaikos, Greece, 1997—98; asst. coach Sacramento Kings, 1998—2000; head coach NJ Nets, East Rutherford, 2000—04, New Orleans Hornets (now New Orleans/Okla. City Hornets), 2004—. Head coach NBA Ea. Conf. All-Star Team, 2002. Achievements include winning NBA Championships as a member of the Lakers, 1985, 87, 88. Office: New Orleans/Okla City Hornets Okla Tower Ste 1850 210 Park Ave Ste 1850 Oklahoma City OK 73102 *

SCOTT, CAMPBELL, actor; b. NYC, July 19, 1961; s. George C. Scott and Colleen Dewhurst; m. Anne Scott, 1991; 1 child. BA, Lawrence U., 1983. Appearences include (theatre) The Queen and the Rebels, 1982, The Real Thing, 1984, Our Town, 1984, Hay Fever, 1985, A Man For All Seasons, 1986, Dalliance, 1986, Copperhead, 1987, Ah, Wilderness!, 1987-88, Long Day's Journey Into Night, 1987-88; (TV series) Six Degrees, 2006; (TV films) The Kennedys of Massachusetts, 1990, The Perfect Tribute, 1991, Would You Kindly Direct Me to Hell?: The Infamous Dorothy Parker, 1994, The Love Letter, 1998, The Tale of Sweeney Todd, 1998, Hamlet, 2000, Follow the Stars Home, 2001, The Pilot's Wife, 2002; (TV miniseries) LIBERTY! The American Revolution, 1997; (films) Five Corners, 1987, From Hollywood to Deadwood, 1988, Longtime Companion, 1989, Ain't No Way Back, 1990, The Sheltering Sky, 1990, Dying Young, 1991, Dead Again, 1991, Singles, 1992, Mrs. Parker and the Vicious Circle, 1994, The Innocent, 1994, Let It Be Me, 1995, Big Night, 1996 (also dir., co-prodr.), The Daytrippers, 1996 (also exec. prodr.), The Spanish Prisoner, 1996, The Imposters, 1998, Hi-Life, 1998, Top of the Food Chain, 1999, Spring Forward, 1999, Lush, 1999, Other Voices, 2000, Delivering Milo, 2000, Roger Dodger, 2002 (also exec. prodr.), The Secret Lives of Dentists, 2002 (also prodr.), Marie and Bruce, 2004, Loverboy, 2004, Duma, 2005, The Exorcism of Emily Rose, 2005, Crashing, 2007, Music and Lyrics, 2007; dir., prodr. (films) Off the Map, 2003; prodr. (films) The Dying Gaul, 2005. *

SCOTT, CARLA ANNE, musician, educator; b. Elmhurst, Ill., Feb. 6, 1951; d. William Frederick and Clara Lou Sommer; m. Kinney Duane Scott, Dec. 22, 1984; 1 child, Joelle Lynn Jewell. BA, Adams State Coll., Alamosa, Colo., 1973; Kodaly level 1, Colo. Coll., 1998; Kodaly Level 2, U. Colo., Boulder, 1999. Asst. libr., music instr. Lamar CC, Colo., 1974—75; tchr. elem. band and gen. music Harrison Sch. Dist. 2, Colorado Springs, 1975—2006; elem. band and orch. tchr. Sch. Dist. 11, Colorado Springs, 2006—. Prin. oboist Pueblo Symphony Orch., 1973—2006, orch. rep., 1988—2006; prin. oboist Pikes Peak Philharm.; 2d oboe and English horn Chamber Orch. of the Springs; free lance musician, Colo.; presenter in field. Pres. Pikes Peak Philharm., Colorado Springs, 2002—. Recipient 25 Yr. award, Colo. Music Educators Assn., 2004. Home: 3031 Fascination Cir Colorado Springs CO 80917 Office: Midland Internat Elem Sch 2110 W Broadway Colorado Springs CO 80904 Office Phone: 719-328-4500. Personal E-mail: casoboe@pcisys.net.

SCOTT, CAROL SEELEY, retired librarian, researcher; b. Phila., Aug. 10, 1921; d. Walter James and Emetta Susan (Weed) Seeley; m. Harley Augustus Scott, Jr., Feb. 2, 1943; children: Michael H., Elisabeth, Sally, David W., John S BA, Duke U., 1941; BS Libr. Sci., U. N.C., 1942; MA Tchg., Winthrop Coll., Rock Hill, SC, 1967. Cert. in Libr. Sci. Libr. Pittsylvania County Pub. Libr., Chatham, Va., 1942—43; jr. profl. asst. D.C. Pub. Libr., Washington, 1943—44; libr. Winthrop Tng. Sch., Rock Hill, 1956—57, Rock Hill H.S., 1959—70, 1973—84, Castle Heights Jr. H.S., Rock Hill, 1970—73; part-time libr. Winthrop Coll. Libr., Rock Hill, 1984—85. Author: William Scott 1732-33 to 1800 of Cabarrus County, North Carolina and Some of His Descendants, 1987, The Rev. Samuel Suther 1722-1788 German Reformed Minister of the Two Carolinas and Some of His Descendants to the Fifth and Sixth Generations, 1993; contbr. articles to geneal. publs Pres. Guild of Mus. York County, S.C., 1988-89; vol. ARC Blood Svcs Mem. AAUW, AARP, DAR, S.C. Libr. Assn. (pres. 1966-70, v.p.), S.C. Assn. Sch. Librs. (bd. dirs., regional network 1980-81), Sierra Club, Phi Beta Kappa, Soc. Mayflower Descendants Democrat.

SCOTT, CATHERINE DOROTHY, librarian, library and information scientist, consultant; b. June 21, 1927; d. Leroy Stearns Scott and Agnes Frances (Meade) Scott Schellenberg. AB in English, Cath. U. Am., 1950, MS in Libr. Sci., 1955. Asst. libr. Export-Import Bank USA, Washington, 1951-55, Nat. Assn. Home Builders, 1955-62, reference libr., 1956-62; founder, chief tech. libr. Bellcomm, Inc., subs. AT&T, 1962-72; chief libr. Nat. Air, Space Mus. Smithsonian Instn., 1972-82, chief libr. Mus. Reference Ctr., 1982-88, sr. reference libr., 1989-95; info. cons., 1995—. Presdl. appointee, mem. Nat. Commn. Librs., Info. Sci., 1971—76; bd. visitors Cath. U. Am. Libr. Sci. Sch., Librs., 1984—93. Editor: International Handbook of Aerospace Awards and Trophies, 1980, 81; guest editor: Aeronautics and Space Flight Collections, 1985, in Spl. Collections, 1984. Vice chmn. DC Rep. Com., Washington, 1960—68; del. Rep. Nat. Conv., San Francisco, 1964; mem. platform com. Rep. Nat. Com., 1968, sec., 1964; del. Rep. Nat. Conv., Miami, Fla., 1968, mem. Inaugural Com., 1969, 1972. Named to Hon. Order Ky. Cols., 1968; recipient Sec.'s Disting. Svc. award Smithsonian Instn., 1976, Alumni Achievement award Cath. U. Am., 1977, Century Circle, 1998—, Disting. Fed. Svc. Nat. Commn. Libr. and Info. Sci. medal, 1985. Mem.: Cath. U. Am. Saint Thomas Aquinas Soc., Am. Soc. Info. Sci., League Rep. Women DC (bd. dirs. 1995—97, nominating com. 1996—97, contbg. 1999—), Nat. Fedn. Rep. Women, Cath. U. Am. Devel. Com., Friends of Cath. U. Librs. (founder, pres. 1984—88, exec. coun. 1984—96, sustaining 1998—), Internat. Fedn. Libr. Assns. (del. 1976, 1983, 1985, 1988—89), Nat. Mus. Women in Arts, Am. Soc. Assn. Execs., Spl. Librs. Assn. (Washington chpt. pres. 1973—74, chair aerospace divsn. 1974—75, cons. com. 1976—91, assn. dir. 1987—90, bd. dirs. 1987—94, award com. 1990—91, pres.-elect 1991—92, bd. dirs. 1991—94, pres. 1992—93, past pres. 1993—94, immediate past pres. 1993—94, chair assn. awards and honors 1994—95, chpt. cons. com. 1994—98, conf. planner 1996—2007, convenor ret. caucus 1997—99, conf. program facilitator 1998—2007, Hall of Fame 1996), Cath. U. Century Club, Spl. Librs. Assn. Legacy Club, Capital Yacht Club. Office Phone: 202-554-3928. Fax: 202-488-9223.

SCOTT, CHARLES DAVID, chemical engineer, consultant; b. Chaffee, Mo., Oct. 24, 1929; s. Charles Perry and Alma Gertrude (Kendall) S.; m. Alice Reba Bardill, Feb. 11, 1956; children: Timothy Charles, Mary Alice, Lisa Ann. BS in Chem. Engring., U. Mo., 1951; MS in Chem. Engring., U. Tenn., 1961, PhD, 1966. Registered profl. engr., Tenn. Devel. engr. Union Carbide Corp., Oak Ridge, 1953-57; rsch. engr. Oak Ridge Nat. Lab., 1957-73, sect. chief, 1973-76, assoc. divsn. dir., 1976-83, rsch. fellow, 1983-86, sr. rsch. fellow, 1987-94; dir. bioprocessing rsch. and devel. ctr., 1991-94; engirng. R&D cons. Oak Ridge, 1994—. Adj. prof. chem. engring. U. Tenn., Knoxville. Contbr. articles to profl. jours.; patentee in field. 1st lt. AUS, 1951-53. Recipient U.S. Dept. Energy E.O. Lawrence award, 1980, U. Tenn. Nathan W. Doughtery award, 1987, U. Mo. Honor award, 1988, David Perlman award Am. Chem. Soc., 1994; Union Carbide Corp. fellow, 1983; Martin Marietta Sr. Corp. fellow, 1987. Mem. Am. Chem. Soc. (chmn. separation sci. subdivsn.), Am. Assn. Clin. Chemistry (chmn. com. advanced analytical concepts, nat. award 1980), Am. Inst. Chem. Engrs. (bd. dirs.), Nat. Acad. Engring., Sigma Xi, Alpha Chi Sigma. Lutheran. Personal E-mail: cdscott1@aol.com.

SCOTT, CHARLES LEWIS, retired photojournalist; b. Grayville, Ill., Aug. 18, 1924; s. Marvin Joseph and Prudence (Blood) S.; m. Jane Turner, Jan. 14, 1945 (dec. 1983); children: Lyntha Ann, Thomas Marvin; m. Martha McDonald, Aug. 23, 1986. BS in Journalism, U. Ill., 1948; MS, Ohio U., 1970. Photographer Champaign-Urbana (Ill.) Courier, 1946-50, chief photographer, 1953-56; photographer Ill. Natural History Survey, 1946-51, Binghamton (N.Y.) Press, 1951-53; asst. picture editor Milw. Jour., 1956-58; picture editor, 1958-66; graphics dir. Chgo. Daily News, 1966-69; instr. Sch. Journalism, Ohio U., Athens, 1969-70, asst. prof., 1971-72, asso. prof., 1972-74, 76-77, prof., 1977—; dir. Sch. Visual Communication, 1978-95, prof. emeritus visual comm., 1995; picture editor Chgo. Tribune, 1974-76; dir. photography Rocky Mountain News, Denver, 1987-88; ret., 1995. Served with U.S. Navy, 1942-45. Decorated D.F.C., Air medal (3); recipient numerous awards in regional and nat. news photo contests; inductee Illini Media Hall of Fame, U. Ill., 2006. Mem. Nat. Press Photographers Assn. (charter mem., Newspaper Photographer of Yr. 1952, Editor of Yr. 1966, Joseph Sprague Meml. award 1975, Robin F. Garland Educator award 1979), Soc. Profl. Journalists, Ohio News Photographers Assn. (Lifetime Achievement award 1995). Presbyterian. Home: 8559 Lavelle Rd Athens OH 45701-9190

SCOTT, CHARNETA CLAUDETTA, psychologist, educator; b. Jacksonville, Fla., May 3, 1963; d. Charles Alexander Scott and Venetia Lemar McLemoure. BS, U. of Fla., 1981—85; MA, Ea. N.Mex U., 1985—86; PhD, Howard U., 1992—2003. Lic. Professional Counselor D.C. Dept. of Health Health and Licensing, 2004. Clin. psychologist D.C. Dept. of Mental Health, 1996—; coord. of ct. services, therapist Francis and Associates, P.C., Washington, 2001—; adj. faculty Trinity U., Washington, 2000—. Assoc. dir. for conf. adminstrn. WBC Learning Conf., Washington, 2005—. Team mem. Capitol Area Crisis Response Team, Washington, 2004. Recipient Dedication to Work with Children, Francis and Associates, 2004, U. of Fla. Hall of Fame, 1984—85; Walter and Theodora Daniel Endowed Ednl. Rsch. Grant, Walter and Theodora Daniel Ednl. Rsch. Fund, 1998. Mem.: APA, Assn. for Play Therapy, Inc., The Am. Acad. of Experts in Traumatic Stress. D-Liberal. Roman Cath. Avocation: dance. Home: 520 U St NW Washington DC 20001 Home Phone: 202-387-3150; Office Phone: 202-409-7100. Personal E-mail: charneta@aol.com.

SCOTT, CHERYL M., foundation administrator, healthcare educator; BA, U. Wash., 1975, MA in Health Adminstrn., 1977. Joined Group Health Coop., Seattle, 1979, regional v.p., exec. v.p., COO, pres., CEO, 1997—2004, pres. emerita, 2004—; COO Bill and Melinda Gates Found., Seattle, 2006—. Clin. assoc. prof. Dept. Health Svcs. U. Wash. Sch. Pub. Health and Cmty. Medicine, 2004—; past bd. mem. Am.'s Health Insurance Plans; past chair Alliance of Cmty. Health Plans and Healthcare Forum; bd. chair Health Tech. Ctr.; mem. Com. on Redesigning Health Insurance Benefits, Payment and Performance Improvement Programs Inst. Medicine. Past chair Alliance for Edn. U. Wash. Health Adminstrn. Program, chair External Adv. Com.; chair King County's Blue Ribbon Com. on Election Reform; trustee Wash. State Life Scis. Discovery Fund. Office: Bill and Melinda Gates Found 1551 Eastlake Ave E Seattle WA 98101 Office Phone: 206-448-6755. Office Fax: 206-448-6464. E-mail: scott.cm@ghc.org.

SCOTT, DALE ALLAN, major league umpire; b. Springfield, Oreg., Aug. 14, 1959; s. Jesse Lee and Betty Ann (Potts) S. AS, Lane C.C., 1979. Radio disc jockey Sta. KBDF, Eugene, Oreg., 1976-81; minor league umpire various orgns., 1981-85; umpire Am. League, 1986-99, Major League Baseball, 2000—. Instr. Golden State Umpire Camp, 1991—99; umpire All Star Game Am. League Baseball, 1993, 2001, umpire World Series, 1998, 2001, 04; crew chief Major League Baseball, 2001—. Mem.: World Umpires Assn. (bd. dirs. 2003—), Lane County Baseball Umpire Assn. (ofcl. 1975—81), Portland Football Ofcls. Assn. (ofcl. H.S. football 1989—96), Lane County Football Ofcls. Assn. (ofcl. 1976—88), Portland Basketball Assn. (86 1996), Lane County Basketball Ofcls. Assn. (ofcl. 1977—85). Democrat. Office: Office of Commr of Baseball 245 Park Ave New York NY 10167-0002

SCOTT, DANIEL J., lawyer; BA, Manhattan Coll., Riverdale, NY, 1999; JD, St. John's U. Sch. Law, Jamaica, NY, 2002. Bar: NY. Assoc. Sullivan & Cromwell LLP, NYC, 2002—05, Withers Bergman LLP, NYC, 2006—. Mem.: ABA, NY State Bar Assn., Phi Beta Kappa. Office: Withers Bergman LLP 430 Park Ave Fl 10 New York NY 10022-3528

SCOTT, DANNY EUGENE, metal products executive, metallurgical engineer; b. Effingham, Ill., Aug. 17, 1947; s. Robert Leonard and Clara Eugena (Welliver) S.; m. Roberta Valenti, June 6, 1970; children: Leanna Marie, Valerie Christine. BSMetE, U. Mo., Rolla, 1970. Registered profl. engr., Tex. Mgr. drill bit devel. Hughes Tool Co., Houston, 1994—, metall. engr., 1970-74, project engr., 1974-77, asst. devel. engr., 1977-81, mgr. mfg. rsch., 1981-85, chief metallurgist, 1985-88, mgr. materials engring., 1988-89, mgr. materials R&D, 1989-91; sr. staff engr., 1992-94. Instr. Metals Engring. Inst., Materials Park, Ohio, 1975-93. Contbr. to profl. pubs.; patentee in field. Officer Dobie Cheerleader Booster Club, Houston, 1988-92. Mem. Soc. Petroleum Engrs. Publs. (ann. internat. conf. program com.), ASTM (B09 com. 1985—), ASM Internat. (exec. com. 1987-91, handbook reviewer 1991), Soc. Automotive Engrs., Am. Petroleum Inst., U. Mo. at Rolla Alumni Assn., Tau Beta Pi. Methodist. Avocations: travel, golf, fishing. Office: Hughes Christensen Co PO Box 2539 Houston TX 77252-2539

SCOTT, DAVID ALBERT, congressman; b. Aynor, SC, June 27, 1945; s. Albert and Mamie (Polite) S.; m. Alfredia Aaron, Oct. 26, 1969; children: Dayna Dorienda, Marcye Michelle. BA, Fla. A&M U., 1967; MBA, U. Pa., 1969. Pres., owner Dayn-Mark Advt., Atlanta; mem. Ga. Ho. of Reps., Atlanta, 1975-82, Ga. Senate, Atlanta, 1983—2002; chmn. edn. com., 1993, chmn. rules com., 1994—2002; mem. US Congress from 13th Ga. dist., 2003—; mem. Agriculture com., Fin. Svcs. Com. Chmn. Atlanta Fulton Senate Del., 1992-94. Creator, prodr., dir. (film) Langston! (4 Emmy awards, best cultural affairs program award NATAS, spl. recognition Congl. Black Caucus, Bronze Jubilee award), (nat. radio program) Inside Black America (spl. cmty. svc. award Mayor of Chgo., James Weldon Johnson journalism award NAACP, spl. citation City of Highland Park, Mich., spl. broadcasting cmty. svc. award Detroit City Coun., spl. tribute Mich. Ho. of Reps.). Mem. exec. bd. dirs. U. Pa. Wharton Sch. Recipient Silver Microphone award, 1986, 1992, 1993, 1994, Amy awards, 1993, Gov.'s award for excellence in edn., Telly award 1994; named one of Most Influential Black Americans, Ebony mag., 2006. Mem. Ga. Bus. Coun., Ga. C. of C. (bd. dirs.), Nat. Assn. Black Elected Ofcls., Black Caucus, NAACP, Alpha Phi Alpha. Democrat. Baptist. Avocations: reading, writing, movies, theater. Office: US Ho Reps 417 Cannon Ho Office Bldg Washington DC 20515-1013 Office Phone: 202-225-2939. Office Fax: 202-225-2939. *

SCOTT, DAVID CLINTON, research scientist; b. Brighton, Colo., Sept. 5, 1960; s. Robert Glenn and Janice Elizabeth (Smith) S.; m. Dana Jungschaffer, Aug. 7, 1988; children: Clinton P., Alexander J., Eric O. BA, U. Colo., 1986; PhD, U. So. Calif., 1993. R & D chemist ICI, Hawthorn, Calif., 1987-88; rsch. asst. chemistry dept. U. So. Calif., LA, 1988-93; rsch. scientist Jet Propulsion Lab, Pasadena, Calif., 1993-2000; sr. mem. tech. staff Atmospheric Scis., Pasadena, Calif., 2000—. Contbr. articles to profl. jours. Mem. AAAS, Am. Geophys. Union, Am. Chem. Soc., Applied Optics, Phi Beta Kappa. Avocations: mountain biking, running, swimming, skiing, hiking. Office: Jet Propulsion Lab M/S 183-401 4800 Oak Grove Dr Pasadena CA 91109

SCOTT, DAVID IRVIN, minister; b. Yakima, Wash., Dec. 5, 1947; s. Jack Phillip and Betty Lucille (Paronto) Scott; m. Jill Louise Baker, June 23, 1982 (div. May 1991). AA, Monterey Peninsula Coll., Calif., 1975. Accredited resident mgr. Inst. Real Estate Mgmt. Courier Gallery Hawaii, Inc., Honolulu, 1981; acting resident mgr. Fairway Gardens, Honolulu, 1981; resident mgr. Waimalu Park, Honolulu, 1981-83, Waikiki Skyliner, Honolulu, 1983-84, Bishop Gardens, Honolulu, 1985-86, Plaza Landmark, Honolulu, 1986-88, Westlake Apts., Honolulu, 1988, Fairway Gardens, Honolulu, 1988-94. Condo mgmt. cons. Mem.: Alpha Gamma Sigma. Avocations: singing, archery, billiards, fishing, community theater. Home and Office: 3601 Fairbanks Ave C-44 Yakima WA 98902-6373 Personal E-mail: chosnstone@msn.com. *Jesus is the way, the truth, and the life: no man comes to the Father, but by Him JN 14:6.*

SCOTT, DAVID J., lawyer, medical products executive; B, St. Lawrence U., Canton, NY; JD, Cornell Law Sch., Ithaca, NY. Pvt. practice lawyer; with RJR Nabisco, Inc., Grand Met. PLC; sr. v.p., gen. counsel Internat. Distillers & Vintners, London, 1996—97; gen. counsel United Distillers & Vintners, London, 1997—99; sr. v.p., gen. counsel Medtronic, Inc., 1999—2004, sec., 2000—04; sr. v.p., gen. counsel, sec., mem. exec. com. Amgen, Inc., Thousand Oaks, Calif., 2004—. Office: Amgen Inc One Amgen Ctr Dr Thousand Oaks CA 91320-1799 Office Phone: 805-447-1000. Office Fax: 805-447-1010. *

SCOTT, DAVID WARREN, statistics educator; b. Oak Park, Ill., July 16, 1950; s. John V. and Nancy (Mellers) S.; m. Jean Charlotte Madera, June 15, 1974; children: Hilary Kathryn, Elizabeth Alison, Warren Robert. BA, Rice U., 1972, MA, PhD, Rice U., 1976. Asst. prof. Baylor Coll. Medicine, Houston, 1976—79, Rice U., Houston, 1979—80, assoc. prof., 1980—85, chmn. stats. dept., 1990—93, Noah Harding prof. stats., 2001—; vis. prof. Stanford U., Palo Alto, Calif., 1985—86. Vis. prof. Dept. Def., Ft. Meade, Md., 1993-94, 99-00, 06-07. Author: Multivariate Density Estimation, 1992; mem. editl. bd. John Wiley & Sons Probability and Stats. Series, 1994—; past editor jour. Computational Stats. and Jour. Statis. Scis.; editor Jour. Computational and Graphical Stats., 2000-03; contbr. articles to profl. jours. Applied and theoretical stats. com. Nat. Rsch. Coun., 2001-05. Grantee NASA, 1982-84, Office Naval Rsch., 1985-93, 2005—, NSF, 1993—; Wilks award U.S. Army, 2004 Fellow Internat. Stats. Inst., Inst. Math. Stats., Am. Statis. Assn. (assoc. editor jour. 1983-94); mem. Inst. Math. Statis. (cons.). Avocations: woodworking, hiking. Home: 4143 Marlowe St Houston TX 77005-1953 Home Phone: 713-664-9208; Office Phone: 713-348-6037.

SCOTT, DEBORAH ELIZABETH, school system administrator, poet; b. Middletown, Conn., July 6, 1969; d. Donald William Troxler, Sr. and Celeste Elizabeth Troxler (Jennings by later remarriage); m. Ashley Van Scott, May 13, 1967; children: Brittney Elizabeth, Ashley Celeste, Destiney Monae'. Cert. Completion Adminstrn. and Typing, Marine Corps Svc. Support Sch., Camp Lejeune, NC, 1988; cert. Tng., Basic Mil. Police Sch., Ft. Jackson, SC, 1995. Adminstrv. clk. USMC, Camp Lejeune, 1988—89; adminstrv. asst. Mayor's Office City Hall, Baker, La., 1991—92; officer mil. police U.S. Army N.G., Sacramento, 1994—97; adminstr. O Happy Day Christian Acad., Yuba City, Calif., 1996—97, Learning Light Acad., Lompoc, Calif., 1998—2002, Victorville, Calif., 2003—. Spl. guest poet/spkr. Buena Vista Elem. Sch., Lompoc, 2001—02; bd. dirs. Learning Light Acad. Author: Debbie ES Poetry Journals, 2002, Debbie ES Poetry, 2005, numerous poems. Mem. /hostess First Assembly of God, Victorville, 2003—05. Lance cpl. USMC, 1988—89. Mem.: Spring Valley Lake Country Club. Democrat. Avocations: poetry, sketch art, swimming, camping. Office: Learning Light Acad 8370 S V L Box Victorville CA 92392-5168

SCOTT, DONALD LAVERN, city manager, librarian, former army officer; b. Hunnewell, Mo., Feb. 8, 1938; s. William Edward and Amanda Beatrice (Dant) S.; m. Betty Jean Forte, Mar. 3, 1962; children: Jeffrey Jerome, Merriell Edward Lavern. BA in Graphic Arts, Lincoln U., 1960; MA in Counseling and Human Devel., Troy State U., 1982. Commd. 2d lt. U.S. Army, 1960, advanced through grades to brig. gen., 1991; bn. comdr. 3d Bn., 47th Inf. Div., Ft. Lewis, Wash., 1978-80; prof. mil. sci. Tuskegee (Ala.) U., 1980-81; dep. insp. gen. U.S. Army Europe, Heidleberg, Fed. Republic Germany, 1982-83; comdr. Hohenfels (Germany) Tng. Ctr., 1983-85; insp. gen. VII U.S. Corps, Stuttgart, Fed. Republic Germany, 1985-86; asst. div. comdr. 1st Cav. Div., Ft. Hood, Tex., 1986-88; chief of staff 2d U.S. Army, Ft. Gillem, Ga., 1988-91; ret. U.S. Army, 1991; chief of staff City of Atlanta, 1991, COO, 1991—; dir., founder AmeriCorps Nat. Civilian Cmty. Corps, 1993—96; mem. Five Star Coun., Vets. History Project, 1996—. Bd. dirs. Atlanta Conv. and Bus. Bur., 1991—; advisor Jimmy Carter's Atlanta Project, 1992; mem. 100 Blackmen, Atlanta, 1992; dep. Libr. of Congress, 1996-; mem. Leg. Br. Coun. Chief Adminstrn. Officers, 1996-. Decorated D.S.M., Legion of Merit, Bronze Star (6), Meritorious Svc. medal. Mem. Assn. U.S. Army, Atlanta C. of C., Kappa Alpha Psi (reporter 1980-82). Avocations: golf, reading, jogging. Office: City of Atlanta Office of Mayor 55 Trinity Ave SW Atlanta GA 30303-3520 Home Phone: 703-698-9799; Office Phone: 202-707-5215. E-mail: dscott@loc.gov.

SCOTT, DONALD MICHAEL, writer, educator; b. LA, Sept. 26, 1943; s. Bernard Hendry and Margherita (Baroni) Scott, Barbara (Lannin) Scott (Stepmother); m. Patricia Ilene Pancoast, Oct. 24, 1964 (div. June 1971); children: William Bernard, Kenneth George. BA, San Francisco State U., 1965, MA, 1968. Cert. tchr. Calif. Tchr. Mercy H.S., San Francisco, 1968-71; pk. ranger Calif. State Pk. Sys., Half Moon Bay, 1968-77; tchr. adult divsn. Jefferson Union HS Dist., Daly City, Calif., 1973-87; dir. NASA-NPS Project Wider Focus, Daly City, 1983-90, also bd. dirs., dir. Geo.S. Spl. Projects, San Francisco, 1990—; nat. pk. ranger, naturalist Grant-Kohrs Ranch Nat. Hist. Site, Deer Lodge, Mont., 1987-88; nat. pk. ranger pub. affairs fire team Yellowstone Nat. Pk., 1988. Rsch. subject NASA, Mountain View, Calif., 1986—90; guest artist Yosemite (Calif.) Nat. Pk., 1986; nat. pk. ranger Golden Gate Nat. Recreation Area Nat. Pk. Svc., San Francisco, 1986, nat. pk. svc. history cons. to Bay Dist., 1988—94; adj. asst. prof. Skyline Coll., 1989—94, Coll. San Mateo, 1992—94; aerospace edn. specialist NASA/OSU/AESP, 1994—2004; state rep. Mont. and Nev. AESP, 1999—2003; cons. Friends Eastern State Penitentiary Project, Phila., 1993; spkr. U. Nev., 2007; extra and actor, 2007—. Author: From Montana to Mars, 2003, From GeoS to Mars, 2004; contbr. articles and photographs to profl. jours., mags., chapters to books. Panelist Cmty. Bds. San Francisco, 1978—87; active CONTACT Orgn., 1991—, bd. dirs., 1995—; mem. edn. working group Case for Mars VI, Boulder, 1996; hon. bd. dirs. T-Rex Discovery Ctr, Canada, 2006—; pres. Youth for Kennedy, Lafayette, Calif., 1960; city chair Yes on A Com., So. San Francisco, San Mateo County, Calif., 1986. Mem.: Friends George R. Stewart, Wider Focus, Yosemite Assn. (life). Avocations: photography, hiking, camping, travel. Home and Office: PO Box 978 Oceano CA 93475 Personal E-mail: dscott943@sbcglobal.net.

SCOTT, DOUGLAS EDWARD, lawyer; b. Evanston, Ill., Jan. 20, 1957; BA in Economics, magna cum laude, U. Ill., 1979, MBA, 1981; JD, UCLA, 1984. Bar: Calif., 1984; U.S. Dist. Ct. (cen. dist.) Calif.; CPA, Ill. Assoc. O'Melveny & Myers, 1984-87; atty. Sci. Applications Internat. Corp., San Diego, 1987—92, corp. v.p., gen. counsel, 1992—97, sr. v.p., gen. counsel, 1997—2003, sr. v.p., sec., gen counsel, 2003—07, exec. v.p., sec., gen. counsel, 2007—. James scholar. Mem. ABA, State Bar of Calif. (sr. v.p., gen. counsel and asst. sec.), Phi Beta Kappa. Office: Sci Applications Internat Corp Mail Stop F 3 10260 Campus Point Dr San Diego CA 92121 *

SCOTT, EDWARD WILLIAM, JR., computer company executive; b. Panama City, Panama, May 25, 1938; s. Edward William and Janice Gertrude (Grimison) S.; m. Cheryl S. Gilliland, apr. 23, 1988; children: Edward William, Heather Yolanda Deirdre, Reece Donald; 1 stepson, Erik Veit. BA, Mich. State U., 1959, MA, 1963; BA, Oxford U., Eng., 1962. Personnel specialist Panama Canal Co., 1962-64, staff asst. to dir. personnel, 1964-66; personnel officer IRS, Detroit, 1966-68; staff personnel mgmt. specialist U.S. Dept. Justice, Washington, 1968-69, chief personnel systems and evaluation sect., 1970-72, dir. Office Mgmt. Programs, 1972-74, assoc. dep. commr. planning and evaluation U.S. Immigration and Naturalization Svc., 1974-75, dep. asst. atty. gen., 1972-75, asst. sec. for adminstrn. Trans. Dept., 1977-80; pres. Office Power, Inc., Washington, 1980-81; dir. mktg. Computer Consoles, Inc., 1981-84; v.p. mktg. Dest Systems, 1984-85; dir. govt. mktg. Sun Microsystems, Mountain View, Calif., 1985-88; exec. v.p. Pyramid Tech., Mountain View, 1988-95; founder, pres. BEA Sys., Inc., San Jose, Calif., 1995—. Founder, chmn. Ctr. for Global Devel., Washington, (with Bill Gates and George Soros) Data-Debt, AIDS, and Trade-Africa; founder, chmn., Friends of the Global Fight, Wash.; founder, pres. escottVentures, Inc.; pres. U.S. Dept. Justice Fed. Credit Union, 1970-73. Recipient Presdl. Mgmt. Improvement certificate, 1971; Spl. Commendation award Dept. Justice, 1973; also Spl. Achievement award, 1976; William A. Jump Meml. award, 1974; presdl. sr. exec. service rank of Disting. Exec., 1980; Mich. State U. scholar, 1957-60. Mem.: Phi Kappa Phi, Phi Eta Sigma. Office: BEA Sys Inc 2315 N 1st St San Jose CA 95131-1010 Business E-Mail: ed@escottventures.com.

SCOTT, EUGENIE CAROL, science foundation director, anthropologist; b. LaCrosse, Wis., Oct. 24, 1945; d. Allen K. and Virginia Meliss (Derr) S.; m. Robert Abner Black, Oct. 18, 1965 (div. 1970); m. Thomas Charles Sager, Dec. 30, 1971; 1 child, Carrie Ellen Sager. BS in Anthropology, U. Wis., Milw., 1967, MS in Anthropology, 1968; PhD in Anthropology, U. Mo., Columbia, 1974; DSc (hon.), McGill U., 2003, Ohio State U., 2005, Mt. Holyoke Coll., 2006, U. Wis., Milw., 2006, Rutgers U., New Brunswick, NJ, 2007. Asst. prof. anthropology U. Ky., Lexington, 1974-82; postdoctoral fellow U. Calif., San Francisco, 1983-84; asst. prof., dept. anthropology U. Colo., Boulder, 1984-86; exec. dir., pub. newsletter NCSE Reports, Nat. Ctr. Sci. Edn., Oakland, Calif., 1987—. Vis. prof., U. Kans., 1976; bd. dirs. Biol. Scis. Curriculum Study, Colorado Springs, Colo., 1993-99; pub. Bookwatch Revs., 1988-92. Author, editor: Biology Textbooks, The New Generation, 1990, Evolution and Creationism: An Introduction, 2004; co-author: Teaching About Evolution and the Nature of Science, 1998; co-editor: Not In Our Classrooms: Why Intelligent Design is Wrong for Our Schools, 2006; prodr.: (videotape series) How Scientists Know About... Mem. nat. adv. bd. Ams. United for Separation of Ch. and State, Washington, 1995—; mem. nat. adv. coun. Am. Civil Liberties Union, 2005-. Recipient Pub. Sci. and Edn. award Com. for Sci. Investigation Claims of Paranormal, 1991, Disting. Alumnus award U. Mo. Arts and Scis., 1993, Isaac Asimov Sci. award Am. Humanist Assn., 1998, James Randi Skeptic of Yr. award Skeptic Soc., 1999, Bruce Alberts award Am. Soc. Cell Biology, 1999, 1st Amendment award Playboy Found., 1999, Outstanding Svc. award, Am. Inst. Biol. Scis, 2002, Pub. Svc. award, Nat. Sci. Bd., 2003, Geol. Soc. Am. Pub. Svc. award, 2001, Margaret Nicholson Dist. Svc. award Calif. Sci. Tchr. Assn., 2002, Ctr. for Inquiry Def. Sci. award, 2003, Anthropology in Media award Anthrop. Assn., 2006, Scientific Freedom and Responsibility award, Am. Assoc Adv. Sci., 2007, Outstanding Educator award, Exploratorium, 2007. Fellow Com. Scientific Investigation, Calif. Acad. Scis. (elected 1994), AAAS; mem. Am. Assn. Phys. Anthropology (bd. dirs., exec. com. 1988-93, sec.-treas. 1993-97, pres. 2001-2003), Am. Anthropol. Assn., Nat. Assn. Biology Tchrs. (hon.), Nat. Sci. Tchrs. Assn., Sigma Xi. Office: Nat Ctr Sci Edn PO Box 9477 Berkeley CA 94709-0477 also: Nat Ctr Sci Edn 420 40th St Ste 2 Oakland CA 94609-2509 Office Phone: 510-601-7203. *

SCOTT, FRAN, adult education educator; b. Gainsville, Fla., July 16, 1971; s. Robert and Rutha Scott; m. Leslie Scott, Mar. 11, 2000; 1 child, Alexis. BS in Health Admin., Albany State U., Ga., 1994. Lic. barber Lively Tech. Inst. Mental health asst. Apalachee Ctr. Human Svcs., Tallahassee, 1996—97, adult edn., 1997—; tchr. basic skills Adult and Cmty. Edn. Ctr. Asst. coach Football Teams, 1996—; bass guitarist; active Big Bros. Big Sisters; minister music True Gospel Mission Ministry. Recipient Glen-Howell Disting. Minority Educator, Adult and Cmty. Edn., 2002, Glen-Howell Disting. Minority Tchr. of Yr. Mem.: NAACP. Democrat. Pentecostal. Avocations: Bible study, chess, fishing, football. Home: 2756 Sandalwood Dr N Tallahassee FL 32305 Office Phone: 850-320-2307. Personal E-mail: fllascott@aol.com.

SCOTT, G. JUDSON, JR., lawyer; b. Phila., Nov. 16, 1945; s. Gerald Judson and Jean Louise S.; m. Ildiko Kalman, Mar. 21, 1971; children: Nathan Emory, Lauren Jean. AA, Foothill Jr. Coll., Los Altos, Calif., 1965; BA, U. Calif., Santa Barbara, 1968; JD cum laude, U. Santa Clara, 1975. Bar: Calif. 1975, U.S. Dist. Ct. (no. dist.) Calif. 1975, U.S. Ct. Appeals (9th cir.) 1975, U.S. Supreme Ct. 1981. Assoc. Feldman, Waldman & Kline, San Francisco, 1975-76, Law Offices John Wynne Herron, 1976-80; of counsel Haines & Walker, Livermore, Calif., 1980; ptnr. Haines Walker & Scott, 1980-84; officer, dir., shareholder Smith, Etnire, Polson and Scott, Pleasanton, 1984-88; pvt. practice, 1988—. Judge pro tem Livermore-Pleasanton Mcpl. Ct., 1981-83; settlement commr. Alameda County Superior Ct., 1994—, judge pro tem, 2001-; lectr. Calif. Continuing Edn. of Bar. Contbg. author: Attorney's Guide to Restitution, 1976; editor: The Bottom Line, 1989-91. Pres. Walnut Creek Open Space Found., Calif., 1981—83. Rear adm. USNR, 1968—2001. Fellow: Nat. Conf. Bar Pres., Am. Bar Found.; mem.: ABA (house dels. 2003—), Alameda-Contra Costa County Trial Lawyers Assn. (bd. dirs. 2005—06, treas. 2006—07), Alameda County Bar Assn. (chmn. law office econs. com. 1986—87, mem. jud. nomination evaluation com. 1996—97, chair task force 1997, bd. dirs. 1997—98, v.p. 1999, pres.-elect. 2000, pres. 2001), Calif. State Bar (mem. standing com. on lawyer referral svcs. 1985—88, mem. exec. com. law practice mgmt. sect. 1988—93, chair 1992—93), Ea. Alameda County Bar Assn. (v.p. 1981—82), Coll. Master Advs. and Barristers (sr. counsel), Consumer Attys. Calif. (reviewer pending legis.), Am. Assn. Justice, Pleasanton C. of C., Livermore C. of C. (past chmn. growth study 1983), Million Dollar Advs. Forum. Republican. Office: 6140 Stoneridge Mall Rd Ste 125 Pleasanton CA 94588-3233 Office Phone: 925-460-0800. Business E-Mail: gjs@scott-law.com.

SCOTT, GARY LEROY, small business owner, photographer; b. Portland, Oreg., May 14, 1954; s. Glenn Howard and Esther Ruth (Robinson) S. Grad., USN Sch. Photography, Pensacola, Fla., 1974; BS, U. Oreg., 1979, MS, 1982. Pres., photographer, filmmaker Scott Cinema and Visual, Inc., various locations, 1969—; computer traffic operator Burlington No. R.R., Portland, 1979-81; instr. U. Oreg., Eugene, 1981-82; S.E. dist. sales mgr. E. Leitz, Inc., 1984-87; mgr. profl. products Fla. divsn. Fuji Photo Film USA, Inc., Lake Mary, Fla., 1987-2000, mgr. profl. products Pacific N.W. divsn. Vancouver, Wash., 2000—05; owner, pres. Scott Cinema and Visual, Inc., Vancouver, Wash., 2005—. Media cons., advt. copywriter, TV and film script writer, 1984—; lectr. in field. Served with USN, 1972-76. U. Oreg. Sch. Journalism research grantee, 1981. Mem. Am. Soc. Media Photographers, Portland Metro. Photographers Assn. Avocations: history, photography, outdoor activities. Home and Office: 8508 NE 15th St Vancouver WA 98664 Personal E-mail: garyl.scott@att.net.

SCOTT, GARY THOMAS, historian; b. Wichita Falls, Tex., Mar. 9, 1944; s. Thomas Clifford, Jr. and Lillian (Hanks) Fecher. BA, Southwestern U., Georgetown, Tex., 1966; MA, U. N.C., Chapel Hill, 1969. History instr. Tusculum Coll., Greeneville, Tenn., 1969-70, Herringswell Manor Sch., Bury St. Edmunds, UK, 1970-71; asst. to clk. of the works Washington Nat. Cathedral, 1971-75; archtl. historian Nat. Park Svc., Washington, 1976-82, regional historian, 1982-95, historian Nat. Capital area, 1995—; chief historian Nat. Capital Region, 1996—. Lectr., tour leader Smithsonian Inst., Washington, 1981—; prin. N.Am. rep. in course on archtl. conservation hist. bldgs. Property Svcs. Agy. and English Heritage of Brit. Govt., West Dean Coll., Chichester, Sussex, Eng., 1982-90. Author: The Kappa Alpha Order-1865-1897, 1994, Aquia and Seneca Stone, White House History, 1998. Rep. Nat. Park Svc., D.C. Bicentennial, Washington, 1991—; mem. Com. of One Hundred, Washington, 1993—, U.S. Capitol Cornerstone Bicentennial, Washington, 1993, Washington Monument Cornerstone Centennial, 1998; active Hist. Soc. Washington, 1977—, So. Hist. Assn., 1980—; mem. Friends Intriguing Summer Sch., N.Y.C., 1981—, Preservation Roundtable, Washington, 1989—; pres. Victorian Soc., Washington, 2002—04. Mem. Masons (33 degree), Scottish Rite, Cosmos Club Washington, Kappa Alpha Order (chief alumnus 1991-95, Disting. Pub. Svc. award 1988, DC Mayor's Hist. Preservation award 2005). Episcopalian. Avocations: book collecting, antiques. Office: Nat Park Svc National Capital Region 1100 Ohio Dr SW Washington DC 20242-0001

SCOTT, GEORGE ALFRED, advertising executive, writer; b. Detroit, Feb. 9, 1925; s. Frederick Harry and Irene Lottie Scott; m. Audrey Jil Scott, Dec. 16, 1950; 1 child, George A. IV; children: Mrs. Michel Princess Martin, James Sellers, Gary Sellers, Monty Sellers. BA, Mich. State Univ., Ea. Lansing, Mich., 1948. Reporter The Marion Star, Marion, Ohio, 1948—50, sports editor, 1952—53; acct. exec. Jay Maish Co., Marion, Ohio, 1953—57; adv. staff Dow Chem. Co., Midland, Mich., 1957—59; v.p. Barnes Chase Adv., San Diego, 1959—65; assoc. creative dir. MacManus, John & Adams, Bloomfield Hills, Mich., 1965—72; v.p., creative dir. D'Ary, MacManus & Masivs, Bloomfield Hills, Mich., 1972—83; sr. v.p., creative dir. D'Ary, Masium, Benton & Bowles, Bloomfield Hills, Mich., 1979—86; pres., owner Encore South, Ft. Myers, Fla., 1986—, Encore North, Lupton, Mich., 1986—. Author: (book) Ribbons & Roses & Rice, 1984, More Ribbons, Roses & Rice, 1994, Secrets of an Ad Pro, 2001, Laughing Your Way Through Life, 2003, (books) 2 books of poetry; co-author: Unlocking the T-Code, 2005. Worker Habitat for Humanity, Ft. Myers, Fla., 1996—2000. 1st Lt. USMC, 1943—46, 1st Lt. USMC, 1950—52. Recipient Aid to Advt., Ed. Award, Am. Advt., Ed., 1984, DMM Ad of the Yr., D'Avery, McManus & Masius, 1982. Avocations: marathons, poetry. Home: 28698 Couzens Ave Madison Heights MI 48071 Office Phone: 248-217-3034. E-mail: adpro29@yahoo.com.

SCOTT, GEORGE COLE, III, investment advisor; b. NYC, July 9, 1937; s. George Cole Scott II and Anne Blair Clark Martindell; m. Leslie Jane Daniels, Apr. 12, 1969; children: Jane Leslie, Anne Blair, John Cole. BA, U. Wash., 1969. Advt. reporter Am. Weekly, London, 1966-68; stockbroker Anderson & Strudwick, Richmond, Va., 1969-73, Scott & Stringfellow, 1973-78, Piper, Jaffray & Hopwood, Seattle, 1978-82, Wheat, First Securities, Inc., Richmond, Va., 1982-87, Anderson & Strudwick, 1988—. Pres. Closed-End Fund Advisors, Richmond, Va., 1996— Co-author: Investing in Closed-End Funds: Finding Value and Building Wealth, 1991; pub., editor: The Scott Letter: Closed-End Fund Report, 1988—; contbr. articles to profl. jours. Founder Seattle-Christchurch, New Zealand Sister City Assn. With USCG, 1960-64. Recipient Disting. Citizen award State of Wash., 1981. Mem. Richmond Soc. Fin. Analysts (assoc.), Soc. Cincinnati, Va. Mus. Fine Arts (mem. bus. coun.), Country Club Va., Wash. Athletic Club (Seattle). Episcopalian. Avocations: freelance writing, travel. Home: 8659 Rio Grande Rd Richmond VA 23229-7822 Office: 707 E Main St Richmond VA 23219-2814 Office Phone: 807-344-3845. E-mail: gscott@cefadvisors.com.

SCOTT, GEORGE GALLMANN, accountant; b. Hattiesburg, Miss., July 8, 1928; s. John Havers and Rebecca Evelyn (Gallmann) S.; m. Patsy T. Womack, June 27, 1953; 1 child, George Gallmann. BS, Millsaps Coll., 1949. Accredited bus. acct., tax advisor, 1992; accredited in acctg. and taxation Nat. Accreditation Coun. for Accountancy. Clk. Spanish Trail Transport, Mobile, Ala., 1949—50, asst. auditor, 1953—55; bookkeeper Met. Engraving & Electrotype Co., Richmond, Va., 1952—53; chief clk. Mobile (Ala.) office Ctrl. Truck Lines of Tampa, Fla., 1955—56; gen. auditor M.R.&R. Trucking Co., Crestview, Fla., 1956—66, sec.-treas., 1967—77; pub. acct. enrolled to represent taxpayers before IRS, 1979—. Mem. data processing adv. com. Okaloosa-Walton Col., Niceville, Fla., 1965- 66, 72-73; mem. Okaloosa County Gen. Advisory Com. for Devel. Vocat. Edn., 1973, 79. Bd. dirs. Okaloosa Cmty. Concert Assn., 1982-87; chmn. Crestview Downtown Devel. Bd., 1988-89; bass-baritone soloist, 1953—, choir dir. Meth. Ch., 1966-83, chmn. ofcl. bd., 1971-73, chmn. fin. com., 1974-75, 79-81, audit com., 1977-86, mem. com. on lay personnel, 1979-87, chmn., 1983-87, 89-90, mem. com. on pastor-parish rels., 1980-86, coun. on ministries, 1985, trustee, 1985-87, treas., 1990-95; mem. Walton Co. C. of C. With U.S. Army, 1950-52. Mem. Nat. Assn. Accts., Nat. Assn. Enrolled Agts., Am. Trucking Assn. (nat. acctg. and fin. coun. 1956-77), Southeastern Acctg. and Fin. Coun. (bd. dirs. 1974-77), Fla. Assn. Enrolled Agts., Crestview Downtown Mchts. Assn. (bd. dirs. 1980-84, treas. 1980-84), Greater Crestview C. of C. (chmn. bus. ethics com. 1973-74, bd. dirs. 1981-83, treas. 1982-83), Fla. Accts. Assn. (bd.

govs. 1979-80, pres. N.W. Fla. chpt. 1979-80), DeFuniak Springs Bus. and Profl. Assn., Kiwanis (past treas., past sec., past pres.), Pi Kappa Alpha. Home: 244 Seminole Trail Crestview FL 32536-2326

SCOTT, GERALD WESLEY, retired American diplomat; b. Oklahoma City, Aug. 7, 1940; s. Charles Wesley and Dorothy Bernadine (Heidlage) S.; m. Frances Helen Gardner-Brown, Aug. 9, 1975; children: Charles Alan, Michael Tacon. BS in Fgn. Svc., Georgetown U., 1962; MA, Johns Hopkins U., 1969, Naval War Coll., 2000. Commd. fgn. svc. officer, 1969; vice consul Am. Consulate Gen., Danang, Viet Nam, 1973-75; polit. officer Am. Embassy, Rome, 1980-83; advisor polit. and security affairs U.S. Mission to UN, NYC, 1983-85; dep. chief of mission Am. Embassy, Mbabane, Swaziland, 1985-88, polit. counselor Kinshasa, Zaire, 1988-92, Nairobi, Kenya, 1992-93, dep. chief of mission Kinshasa, 1993-95; ambassador to The Gambia, Banjul, 1996-98; State Dept. rep. Naval War Coll., Newport, RI, 1998-2000; ret., 2000. Cons. internat. and security affairs, 2000—; sr. advisor US delegation to UN Gen. Assembly, 2001, 02, 03, 04, 05, 06; adv. US delegation to 58th session of UN Commn. Human Rights, 2002. Lt. USNR, 1962-67. Decorated Air medal, Navy Commendation medal. Mem. Am. Fgn. Svc. Assn. (William R. Rivkin award 1992), Sovereign Mil. Order of Malta, SAR, Sons of the Revolution, Lotos Club (NYC), Army and Navy Club (Washington). Roman Catholic. Office: G W Scott PO Box 4915 Buena Vista CO 81211

SCOTT, GLORIA RANDLE, former college president; b. Apr. 14, 1938; d. Freeman and Juanita (Bell) Randle; m. Will Braxton Scott. AB, Ind. U., 1959, MA, 1960, PhD, 1965, LLD, 1977; DHL, Fairleigh Dickinson U., 1978, Westfield State Coll., 1992, Wilson Coll., 1992, Mt. Vernon Coll., Marian Coll., 1999. Rsch. assoc. in genetics Inst. Psychiat. Rsch. Ind. U. Med. Ctr., Indpls., 1961-63; instr. biology Marian Coll., Indpls., 1961-65; dean students Knoxville Coll., Tenn., 1965-67; asst. to pres. N.C. Agrl. and Tech. State U., 1967-68, prof., 1967-76, dir. planning Inst. Rsch., 1973-76; prof. Tex. So. U., 1976-78; v.p., prof. Clark Coll., 1978-86; prof. Grambling State U., 1987; pres. Bennett Coll., Greensboro, NC, 1987-2001, founder Women's Leadership Inst., 1989; owner Scott's Bay Enterprises on Baffin Bay, Riviera, Tex., 1973—. Founding sec. bd. dirs. Africa U., Mutare, Zimbabwe, 1988-97; bd. dirs. Loew Corp.; vice chair Women's Coll. Coalition, 1990-94; bd. dirs. Nat. Assn. Ind. Colls. and Univs., 1992-96, Nat. Assn. Schs. and Colls. of the United Meth. Ch., 1993-95. Del. UN Decade for Women Internat. Forum, Nairobi, Kenya, 1985; chmn. del. UN Decade for Women Conf., Beijing, 1995; chmn. bd. Nat. Scholarship Fund for Negro Students, 1984-85; 1st v.p. Girl Scouts U.S., 1972-75, pres., 1975-78; bd. dirs. Wilson Coll., 1978-83, Nat. Urban League, 1976-85, Neal Marshall Club, Indian U. Alumni; mem bd. visitors Ind. U. Sch. Edn., Bloomington, 1988-94; bd. dirs. United Negro Coll. Fund, 1993-95, chair golden anniversary com., 1992-95; chair edn. adv. com. Delta Sigma Theta, 1989—; mem. adv. bd. James McGregor Leadership Acad., Md., 2000-05; mem. divsn. III pres.'s coun. NCAA, 1998-2001; founder Nat. African Am. Women's Leadership Inst., 1999; mentor Leadership Inst., 1997-98; mem. Internat. Women's Forum; chmn. Coun. Presidents Black Coll. Fund, UMC, 1997-99. Recipient Drum Major for Justice award, 1993, N.C. Gov.'s award for Outstanding N.C. Women, 1991, Achievement award Delta Sigma Theta, 1994. Mem. Rotary (organizing founder East Greensboro 2000-01). Home Phone: 361-297-5233. E-mail: randle@rivnet.com.

SCOTT, GREGORY KELLAM, former state supreme court justice, lawyer; b. San Francisco, July 30, 1943; s. Robert and Althea Delores Scott; m. Carolyn Weatherly, Apr. 10, 1971; children: Joshua Weatherly, Elijah Kellam. BS in Environ. Sci., Rutgers U., 1970, EdM in Urban Studies, 1971; JD cum laude, Ind. U., Indpls., 1977. Asst. dean resident instrn. Cook Coll. Rutgers U., 1972-75; trial atty. U.S. SEC, Denver, 1977-79; gen. counsel Blinder, Robinson & Co., Inc., Denver, 1979-80; asst. prof. coll. law U. Denver, 1980-85, assoc. prof., 1985-93, prof. emeritus, 1993—, chair bus. planning program, 1986-89, 92-93; justice Colo. Supreme Ct., Denver, 1993-2000; gen. counselor Kaiser-Hill Co., Golden, Colo., 2000—; judge trial referee Colo. Supreme Ct., Colo., 2000. Of counsel Moore, Smith & Bryant, Indpls., 1987-90; v.p., gen. counsel Comml. Energies, Inc., 1990-91; presenter in field. Author: (with others) Structuring Mergers and Acquisitions in Colorado, 1985, Airport Law and Regulation, 1991, Racism and Underclass in America, 1991; contbr. articles to profl. jours. Mem. ABA, Nat. Bar Assn., Nat. Assn. Securities Dealers, Inc., Nat. Arbitration Panel (arbitrator), Colo. Bar Found., Sam Cary Bar Assn., Am. Inn Ct. (founding mem. Judge Alfred A. Arraj inn). Avocations: golf, reading, travel. Office: Kaiser Hill Llc 12101 Airport Way Unit B Broomfield CO 80021-2507

SCOTT, GREGORY W., health care company executive; B in Math. Econ., Colgate U.; MS, U. Mich. cert. CLU. Sr. v.p. Prudential Capital Corp.; gen. ptnr. RRY Ptnrs.; v.p. corp. fin. Salomon Brothers, Inc.; exec. v.p., CFO Prudential Securities; pres. no. ctrl. group, healthcare & employee benefits ops. Prudential Ins. Co., v.p., treas., sr. v.p., CFO health care group; COO, CFO Medsite, 1999-01; exec. v.p., CFO PacifiCare Health Sys. Inc., Cypress, Calif., 2001—. Mem. Fin. Exec. Inst. Office: PacifiCare Health Sys 5995 Plaza Dr Cypress CA 90630

SCOTT, HAL S., law educator; b. Chgo., Nov. 25, 1943. AB, Princeton U., 1965; MA, Stanford U., 1967; JD, U. Chgo., 1972. Bar: Mass., 1982. Law clk. to Hon. Harold Leventhal, US Ct. Appeals DC Cir., Washington, 1972-73, to Justice Byron R. White, US Supreme Ct., Washington, 1973-74; acting prof. law U. Calif., Berkeley, 1974-75; asst. prof. law Harvard Law Sch., Cambridge, Mass., 1975-80, prof., 1980-90, Nomura prof. internat. fin. systems, 1990—, dir. program internat. fin. systems, 1986-; bd. dir. Lazard Ltd., 2006-; cons. IBM, NYC, 1977. Contbr. articles to legal journals. Author: Euro: Law and Market Practices, 1999, International Finance: Law and Regulation, 2004; co-author: (with Philip A. Wellons) International Securities Regulation, 2002, International Finance: Transactions, Policy, and Regulation, 2000, 01, 02, 03, 04. Mem.: Internat. Acad. Consumer and Comml. Law (past pres.). Office: Harvard Law Sch 1563 Massachusetts Ave Cambridge MA 02138 Office Phone: 617-495-4590. Office Fax: 617-495-9593. Business E-Mail: hscott@law.harvard.edu.

SCOTT, H(AROLD) LEE, JR., (LEE SCOTT), retail executive; b. Joplin, Mo., Mar. 14, 1949; s. Harold Lee and Avis Viola (Parsons) S.; m. Linda Gale Aldridge, June 7, 1969; children: Eric Sean, Wyatt Parson. BBA, Pitts. State U., Kans., 1971. Br. mgr. Yellow Freight System, Springdale, Ark., 1972-78; mgr. Queen City Warehouse, Springfield, Mo., 1978-79; dir. transp. Wal-Mart Stores, Inc., Bentonville, Ark., 1979-83, v.p. distbn. to sr. v.p. logistics, 1983—93, exec. v.p. logistics, 1993—95, exec. v.p. merchandise and sales, Wal-Mart Stores Divsn., 1995—98, pres., CEO, Wal-Mart Stores Divsn., 1998—99, COO, vice-chmn. Bentonville, Ark., 1999—2000, pres., CEO, 2000—. Bd. dirs. Pvt. Truck Council, Washington, 1985-86. Named one of World's 100 Most Influential People, Time Mag., 2005. Republican. Methodist. Avocations: reading, quail hunting. Office: Wal-Mart Stores Inc 702 SW 8th St Bentonville AR 72716-6299 *

SCOTT, HUGH PATRICK, former surgeon, military officer, medical advisor; b. Phila., Feb. 12, 1938; s. Hugh Patrick and Martha (Papiana) S.; m. Diane Marie Lopatzie, July 1, 1961; children: Karen, Brendan, Catherine. BA, LaSalle Coll., 1960; DO, Phila. Coll. Osteo. Medicine, 1964, LLD (hon.), 1991. Diplomate Am. Osteo. Bd. Ophthalmology and Otolaryngology. Intern Detroit Osteo. Hosp., Highland Park, Mich., 1964-65, resident otorhinolatyngology, 1965-68; lt. med. corps USNR, 1967, advanced through grades to rear adm., 1991; naval med. officer U.S. Naval Dispensary N.O.B., Norfolk, Va., 1968-70, Submarine Squadron 10, Groton, Conn.; Submarine Group 2; naval med. officer Naval Submarine Med. Ctr., New London, Conn., 1975-83; dir. undersea medicine and radiation health Naval Med. Command, Washington, 1983-86; comdg. officer Naval Hosp., Groton, 1986-88, Camp Lejeune, NC, 1988-90; fleet surgeon Comdr. in Chief, U.S. Pacific Fleet, Pearl Harbor, Hawaii, 1990-91; asst. chief for operational medicine and fleet support Bur. Medicine and Surgery, Washington, 1991-92; dir. med. resources, plans and policy Office Chief of Naval Ops., Washington, 1992-94; sr. med. advisor Northrop Grumman Info. Tech. Health Solutions, 2000—. Asst. clin. prof. medicine Mich. State U., Lansing, 1970—75; pvt. practice, Madison Heights, Mich., 1970—75; cons. Am. Coll. Undersea and Hyperbaric Medicine, Washington, 1985—86, 1994—96; sr. program mgr. Data Sys. & Svcs. divsn. Northrop Grumman Co., 1998—99; sr. med. advisor Northrop Grumman Info. Tech.; sr. v.p. Geo-Ctrs. Inc., 2000—01; mem. sr. exec. med. adv. com. for mil. medicine Johns Hopkins U. Applied Physics Lab.; mem. faculty U. So. Calf. Health Scis. Campus for Advanced Biotelecomms. and Bio Informatics. Decorated Legion of Merit, Gold Star (3). Fellow Osteo. Coll. Ophthalmology and Otolaryngology, Am. Acad. Otolaryngology and Head and Neck Surgery; mem. Am. Osteo. Coll. Otolaryngology--Head and Neck Surgery (past pres.), Assn. Mil. Osteopathic Physicians and Surgeons (2nd v.p.). Republican. Roman Catholic. Home: 3707 Merlin Way Annandale VA 22003-1326 Office: Northrop Grumman Info Tech 5113 Leesburg Pike Ste 3090 Falls Church VA 22041 Office Phone: 703-575-5172. Business E-Mail: hugh.scott@ngc.com.

SCOTT, ISADORE MEYER, retired energy executive; b. Wilcoe, W.Va., Nov. 21, 1912; s. David and Libby (Roston) S.; m. Joan Rosenwald, Feb. 14, 1943; children: Betsy Scott Kleeblatt, Peggy, Jonathan D. AB, W.Va. U., 1934, MA, 1938, LLD, 1983; JD, Washington and Lee U., 1937. Bar: Va. 1937. Practiced law, Richmond, Va., 1937-38; v.p. Lee I. Robinson Hosiery Mills., Phila., 1938-42; with Winner Mfg. Co., Inc., Trenton, NJ, 1947-61, v.p., 1947-51, pres., 1951-61; chmn. bd. Tri-Instl. Facilities, Inc., Phila., 1962-78, TOSCO Corp., LA, 1976—83, vice-chmn. bd., 1983—87, chmn. bd. bd. dirs., chmn. Univ. City Assocs., Inc.; founder, mem. U.S. Adv. Bd. Brit.-Am. Project. Bd. dirs. S.E. Pa. chpt. ARC, Univ. City Sci. Ctr., Phila.; mem. adv. com. Urban Affair Partnership; bd. dirs. emeritus, former mem. exec. com., vice-chmn. Phila. Mus. Art; former chmn. World Affairs Coun. Phila.; mem. Phila. Com. Fgn. Rels.; trustee emeritus Washington and Lee U.; emeritus trustee George C. Marshall Found.; former chmn. Christ Ch. Preservation Trust, Phila., Jefferson House Restoration, Phila. With inf. U.S. Army, 1942-46, NATOUSA, ETO. Decorated Legion of Merit, Silver Star, Purple Heart, Bronze Star; Crown of Italy; medal of merit Czechoslovakia; Mentioned-in-dispatches, Eng.; fellow Mus. Am. Jewish History Mem. Va. State Bar, Phila. Club, Gulph Mills Golf, Anglers of Phila., Masons, Phi Beta Kappa, Omicron Delta Kappa, Order of Coif. (hon.). Democrat. Jewish. Office Phone: 610-642-8228.

SCOTT, J. LENNOX, real estate company executive; BBA, U. Washington. Cert. Residential Broker. Pres. John L. Scott Real Estate, 1980—2002, chmn., 2002—, CEO. Author: Next Generation Real Estate, 2002. Mem. John L. Scott Found.; exec. bd. Econ. Develop. Coun. Seattle and King County, Washington Wildlife, Recreation Coalition. Named one of Real Estate's 25 Most Influential Thought Leaders, Realtor Mag., 2006. Mem.: Young President's Alumni Orgn., Nat. Assn. Home Builders, Seattle King County Assn. Realtors (former pres.), Nat. Assn. Realtors (exec. bd.), Rotary Internat. Office: John L Scott 3380 146th Pl SE Ste 450 Bellevue WA 98007 Office Phone: 206-230-7600. Office Fax: 206-230-7650.

SCOTT, JACQUELINE DELMAR PARKER, educational association administrator, consultant; b. LA, May 18, 1947; d. Thomas Aubrey and Daisy Beatrice (Singleton) Parker (div.); children: Tres Mali, Olympia Ranee, Stephen Thomas. AA in Theatre Arts, L.A. City Coll., 1970; BA in Econs., Calif. State U., Dominguez Hills, Carson, 1973; MBA, Golden Gate U., 1979; EdD, Pepperdine U., 1999. Cert. parenting instr., 2000; holder various Microsoft certs. Sales clk. Newberry's Dept. Store, LA, 1963-65; long distance operator Pacific Telephone Co., LA, 1965-66; PBX operator Sears, Roebuck & Co., LA, 1966-68; retail clk. Otey's Grocery Store, Nashville, 1968-69; collector N.Am. Credit, LA, 1970-71; office mgr. Dr. S. Edward Tucker, LA, 1972-74; staff coord. sch. edn. dept. Calif. State U., 1973-74; from bank auditor to corp. loan asst. Security Pacific Bank, LA, 1974-77; from dist. credit analyst to asst. v.p. Crocker Nat. Bank, LA, 1977-80; from capital planning adminstr. to project bus. mgr. TRW, Inc., Redondo Beach, Calif., 1980-87, lab. sr. bus. adminstr., 1984-86, project bus. mgr., 1986-87, div. sr. bus. adminstr., 1987-92; ptnr., co-author, co-facilitator, cons. Diversified Event Planners, Inc., LA, 1990-93; asst. area devel. dir. United Negro Coll. Fund, LA, 1993-96; cons. parenting edn., 1994—. Cmty. coll. instr., dissertation coach, 1999-; cons. in field Co-founder career growth awareness com. TRW Employees Bootstrap, Redondo Beach, Calif., 1980, pres., 1983-84; role model Inglewood High Sch., TRW Youth Motivation Task Force, Redondo Beach, 1981-83, Crozier Jr. High Sch., 1981-83, Monroe Jr. High Sch., Redondo Beach, 1981-83, Frank D. Parent Career Day, TRW Affirmative Action Com., Redondo Beach, 1987, St. Bernard's Career Day, 1991; chairperson community involvement com., 1981, chairperson disaster com., 1989-90; chairperson gen. and local welfare com. TRW Employees Charitable Orgn., 1989-90, disaster com. chair, 1988-89, bd. dirs. 1987-89; pres. Mgmt. Effectiveness Program Alumnae, L.A., 1982-83, TRW Employees Bootstrap Program Alumnae, 1983-84; group leader Jack & Jill of Am., Inc., South L.A., 1980-81, parliamentarian, 1986-87, v.p., 1981-82, chpt. pres., 1984-86, regional dir., 1987-89, nat. program dir., 1992-96, liaison to Young Black Scholars Program, 1986—; bd. dirs. Adolescent Pregnancy Child Watch, 1993—; nat. program dir., bd. dirs. Jack & Jill Am. Found., 1992-96; L.A. mem. Nat. Black Child Devel. Inst., 1994—; vol. ARC, 1994; parenting instr. Am. Red Cross, 1994-96; founder Jack & Jill of Am. Leadership Devel. Program, 1993. Recipient commendation NAACP, 1985, United Negro Coll. Fund, 1986, United Way, 1988, Austistic Children's Telephon, 1980, Inglewood Sch. Dist., 1981, Pres. award Harbor Area Chpt. Links, Inc., 1985, Women of Achievement award City of L.A., Black Pers. Assn., 1994. Mem. Black Women's Forum (sponsor), Phi Delta Kappa, Delta Sigma Theta. Avocations: reading, dance. Personal E-mail: dr.jscott4@gmail.com.

SCOTT, JAMES ARTHUR, radiologist, educator; b. Cleve., Aug. 23, 1950; s. Robert James and Margaret Emma (Hinz) S.; m. Phyllis Virginia Gauthier, Oct. 3, 1981. SB, MIT, 1972; MD, Boston U., 1976. Diplomate Am. Bd. Radiology, Am. Bd. Nuc. Medicine. Resident Harvard U. Med. Sch.-Mass. Gen. Hosp., Boston, 1976-80, fellow, 1980-81, instr., 1982-83, asst. prof., 1984-93, assoc. prof., 1994—. Mem. editl. adv. bd. Jour. Nuc. Medicine, Am. Jour. Roentgen. Recipient New Investigator Rsch. award NIH, 1984-87. Mem. Soc. Sci. Exploration, Sigma Xi, Am. Coll. Radiology, AAAS, Phi Lambda Upsilon, Theta Xi. Lutheran. Avocations: writing, golf, history. Office: Div Nuclear Medicine Mass Gen Hosp Boston MA 02114 Personal E-mail: jas.scott@verizon.net. Business E-Mail: scott@helix.mgh.harvard.edu.

SCOTT, JEAN A., university president; B in History, U. Richmond, 1968; M in History, Harvard U., 1969, PhD in History, 1974. Asst. prof. history Duke U., dir. admission; dean undergrad. admission Case We. Res. U., Ohio; assoc. provost acad. adminstrn., dean admissions Coll. William and Mary, Williamsburg, Va., 1989-94; v.p. enrollment and student svcs. SUNY, Potsdam, 1994—. Office: Potsdam Coll Pierrepont Ave Potsdam NY 13676-2294

SCOTT, JEFFREY RYAN, music educator; b. Pikeville, Ky., Aug. 25, 1964; s. Larry and Peggy Ann Scott; m. Sabrina Salles, May 21, 2006. MusB, U. Ky., 1987; MusM, So. Oreg. U., 2005. Nat. bd. cert. in edn. 2006. Dir. bands John T. Hoggard H.S., Wilmington, NC, 1987—89, Sedgefield Mid. Sch., Goose Creek, SC, 1989—94, Goose Creek (S.C.) H.S.; 1994—2000, Cario Mid. Sch., Mt. Pleasant, SC, 2005—. Clinician, adjudicator in field; guest condr. various univs. and festivals. Mem.: Music Educators Nat. Conf., S.C. Music Educators Assn., Phi Mu. Avocations: travel, hiking, tennis, reading, basketball. Home: 1061 Law Ln Mount Pleasant SC 29464 Office: Cario Middle School 3500 Thomas Cario Blvd Mount Pleasant SC 29466 Office Phone: 843-856-4595.

SCOTT, JILL, poet, musician; b. Phila., 1952; Founder, pres. Blues Babe Found. Singer (with Eric Benet, Will Smith, Roots, Common); musician: (albums) Who is Jill Scott? Words & Sounds, Vol. 1, 2000, Experience: Jill Scott 826+, 2001, Beautifully Human: Words and Sounds, Vol. 2, 2004, The Real Thing, 2007, (songs) God Bless the Child, 2007 (Grammy award for Best Traditional R&B Performance, 2007); co-prodr.(with Dr. Cornel West et. al.): (albums) Never Forget: A Journey of Revelations, 2007; actor: (plays) Rent. Founder Blues Babe Found., Phila. Recipient Grammy Award, 2003. Office: Hidden Beach Recordings 3030 Nebraska Ave Santa Monica CA 90404 *

SCOTT, JIM, radio personality; b. Bridgeport, Conn. m. Donna Scott. With WSAI, Cin., 1968—84; radio host 700 WLW, Cin., 1984—. Active United Way, The Wellness Cmty. Recipient Marconi Radio award for Large Market Personality of Yr., Nat. Assn. Broadcasters, 2002. Avocation: running. Office: WLW 700 AM The Big One 8044 Montgomery Rd Cincinnati OH 45236-2919 Office Phone: 513-241-9597.

SCOTT, JOHN BELDON, art history educator, writer; BA in history, Ind. U., 1968; MA in art history, Rutgers U., 1975, PhD in art history, 1982. Lectr. U. Pa., 1981—82; asst. prof. to prof. art history U. Iowa, Iowa City, 1982—, Elizabeth M. Stanley Prof. of the Arts, 2004—, head art history divsn. Sch. Art and Art History. Vis. mem. Inst. Advanced Study, Princeton, NJ, 1991—92; mem. US Nat. Com. for the History of Art Internat. Congress of the History of Art, 2001—02. Author: Images of Nepotism: The Painted Ceilings of Palazzo Barberini, 1991, Architecture for the Shroud: Relic and Ritual in Turin, 2003 (Charles Rufus Morey Book Award, Coll. Art Assn., 2004), (articles have appeared in) Art Bulletin, Burlington Mag., Memoirs of Am. Acad. Rome, Storia dell'Arte, Jour. of the Warburg and Courtauld Institutes, Jour. of Soc. Archtl. Historians. Served USAF, 1969—73. Samuel H. Kress Found. Rome Prize Fellowship, Am. Acad. Rome, 1979—81, Gladys Krieble Delmas Found. for Venetian Studies Grant, 1979, Andrew W. Mellon Postdoctoral Rsch. Fellow, U. Pa., 1984—85, Rsch. Fellowship for Recent PhD Recipients, Am. Coun. Learned Societies, 1984, Am. Philos. Soc. Rsch. Grant, 1984, 1989, NEH Travel to Collections Grant, 1986, Gladys Krieble Delmas Found. for Venetian Studies Grant, 1986, Nat. Humanities Ctr. Fellow, 1993—94, Trinity Coll. Barbieri Grant in Italian History, Barbieri Endowment for Italian Culture, 1994, Marta Sutton Weeks Fellow, Stanford Humanities Ctr., Stanford U., 1999—2000, Graham Found. for Advanced Studies in the Visual Arts Rsch. Grant, 1999, Am. Philos. Soc. Sabbatical Fellowship, 2000. Mem.: Midwest Art History Soc. (bd. dirs. 1986—89), Coll. Art Assn. (bd. dirs. nominating com. 1998), Soc. Archtl. Historians (bd. dirs. 1997—2000). Office: U Iowa Sch Art and Art History 120 N Riverside Dr #100 Art Bldg Iowa City IA 52242-1706

SCOTT, JOHN BROOKS, retired research and development company executive; b. Morenci, Ariz., Aug. 8, 1931; s. Brooks and Lucile (Slagle) S.; m. Jo Ann Rohrbach, June 5, 1987; children from previous marriage: Janice, Steven, Sarah. BS, U. Ariz., 1957, MA, 1959. Asst. prof. systems engring. U. Ariz., Tucson, 1959—61; mgr. Bell Aerosystems Co., Tucson, 1961—62; sr. v.p. IIT Rsch. Inst., Annapolis, Md., 1963—90, pres. Chgo., 1990-97. Author papers on computer software, electromagnetic compatibility. Past pres. bd. dirs. Md. Hall for Creative Arts, Inc.; past chmn. Md. Hall Found.; past mem. bd. govs. IIT Rsch. Inst.; past trustee Ill. Inst. Tech. Mem. Greater Annapolis C. of C. (pres. 1987); mem. Phi Kappa Phi, Sigma Pi Sigma, Pi Mu Epsilon. Home: Apt 903 3145 S Atlantic Ave Daytona Beach FL 32118-6045 E-mail: jscott2030@cfl.rr.com.

SCOTT, JOHN D., pharmacologist; b. Edinburgh, Apr. 13, 1958; married; 2 children. BSc in Biochemistry with honors, Herriot-Watt U., Edinburgh, 1980; PhD in Biochemistry, U. Aberdeen, 1983. NIH postdoctoral fellow dept. pharmacology U. Wash., Seattle, 1983—86, rsch. asst. prof. dept. biochemistry, 1986—88; asst. prof. dept. physiology and biophysics, dept. biol. chemistry U. Calif., Irvine, 1988—89; asst. scientist Ctr. Rsch. Occupl. & Environ. Toxicology Oreg. Health Scis. U., 1989—90, asst. scientist Vollum Inst. Advanced Biomed. Rsch., dept. biochemistry and molecular biology, 1990—92, scientist, 1993—97, sr. scientist, 1997—; investigator Howard Hughes Med. Ctr. (known as Vollum Inst.), 1997—. Spkr. in field. Mem. editl. bd. Jour. Biol. Chemistry; contbr. articles to profl. jours. Recipient John J. Abel award, Am. Soc. Pharmacology and Exptl. Therapeutics, 1996; scholar Med. Endowments Hon., U. Aberdeen, 1980—83. Fellow: Royal Soc.; mem.: Protein Soc., Biochem. Soc., Am. Soc. Biochemistry and Molecular Biology. Office: Vollum Inst Oreg Health Scis U 3181 SW Sam Jackson Park Rd Portland OR 97239-3011

SCOTT, JOHN EDWARD SMITH, lawyer; b. St. Louis, Aug. 6, 1936; s. Gordon Hatler and Luella Margarite (Smith) S.; m. Beverly Joan Phillips, Dec. 17, 1960; 1 dau., Pamela Anne. AB, Albion Coll., 1958; JD, Wayne State U., 1961. Bar: Mich. 1961, U.S. Dist. Ct. (ea. dist.) Mich. 1962, U.S. Dist. Ct. (we. dist.) Mich. 1970, U.S. Tax. Ct. 1979, U.S. Ct. Appeals (6th cir.) 1964, U.S. Supreme Ct. 1966. Law clk. Supreme Ct. Mich., Lansing, 1961-62; assoc. Dickinson, Wright, Moon, Van Dusen & Freeman, Detroit, 1962-69, ptnr., 1970—. Adj. prof. U. Detroit Law Sch., 1967-71. Supreme Ct. appointee State Bar Rep. Assembly, Detroit, 1972-77; mayor City of Pleasant Ridge, Mich., 1973-81; commr. Mich. Appellate Defender Commn., Detroit, 1979—, chmn., 1992—; hearing referee Mich. Civil Rights Commn., Detroit, 1974-80; chmn. Detroit Legal Aid & Defender Commn., 1972-77; chmn. case flow mgmt. com. Mich. Supreme Ct., 1989-90. Fellow Am. Coll. Trial Lawyers, Internat. Soc. Barristers, Internat. Acad. Trial Lawyers; mem. ABA (chmn. trial evidence com. sect. litigation 1988-91), Am. Bar Found., Mich. Bar Found., Detroit Golf Club, Order of Coif (hon.). Office: Dickinson Wright PLLC 500 Woodward Ave Ste 4000 Detroit MI 48226-3416 Office Phone: 313-223-3622. Business E-Mail: jscott@dickinson.wright.com.

SCOTT, JOHN JOSEPH, lawyer; b. Chgo., Dec. 30, 1950; s. John Joseph and Alice (Pierzhala) S.; m. Maria Crawford, Aug. 17, 1974. BA, Yale U., 1972; JD, U. Chgo., 1975. Bar: Ill. 1975, U.S. Dist. Ct. (no. dist.) Ill. 1976. Assoc. Kirkland & Ellis, Chgo., 1975-82, ptnr., 1982-91; asst. gen. counsel CF Industries Holdings, Inc., Deerfield, Ill., 1991—2006, sr. litig. counsel, 2006—. Mem. ABA, Chgo. Bar Assn., Order of Coif. Roman Catholic. Avocations: reading, swimming, bike riding, playing tennis. Office: CF Industries Holdings Inc 4 Parkway North Ste 400 Deerfield IL 60015-2590

SCOTT, JOHN PAUL, medical educator; b. Kamunting, Malaysia, June 26, 1956; came to U.S., 1991; s. Joseph and Agnes (Beldon) S.; m. Lesley Carol Poole, Dec. 5, 1981; children: Christopher Michael, Elizabeth Mary, David Matthew. MB ChB, Otago U., Dunedin, New Zealand, 1979, MD, 1990; MS, Cambridge U., England, 1992; MS in Econs., U. London, 1999; LLB in Econs. (hon.), U. Wolverhampton, 2000; LLM, U. Glamorgan, 2003, U. Glasgow, 2002; MSc, U. Oxford, England, 2007. Resident Otago

U., Dunedin, New Zealand, 1979-83; assoc. prof. transplantation Mayo Clinic, Rochester, Minn., 1991-96, prof., 1996—. Contbr. articles to profl. jours. Fellow dept. pulmonary medicine Otago U., 1984-85, Cambridge U., 1985-88, sr. fellow, 1988-91. Fellow Royal Coll. Physicians (internat. advisor 2000—, assoc. dir. 2004—), Royal Australian Coll. Physicians, Am. Coll. Physicians, Royal Statis. Soc.; mem. Am. Thoracic Soc. (Minn. rep. 1993-96), Royal Soc. New Zealand, Internat. Soc. Philosophical Enquiry, Mayo Thoracic Soc. (pres. 1996-99). Avocations: philosophy, economics, chess, climbing, travel. Office: Mayo Clinic 200 1st St SW Rochester MN 55905-0002 Business E-Mail: scott.john@mayo.edu.

SCOTT, JOHN ROLAND, business law educator; b. Wichita Falls, Tex, May 13, 1937; s. John and Margaret S.; m. Joan Carol Redding, Sept. 5, 1959; 1 child, John Howard. LLB, Baylor Sch. Law, Waco, Tex., 1962. Bar: Tex. 1962, Alaska 1970, Tex., 1965, U.S. Dist. Ct. (we. dist.), U.S. Dist. Ct. Alaska 1975. Assoc. litigation sect. Lynch & Chappell, Midland, Tex., 1962-65; regional atty. Atlantic Richfield Co., Midland, 1965-79; sr. atty. Anchorage, 1969-77, Dallas, 1977-80; v.p., assoc. gen. counsel Mitchell Energy & Devel. Corp., Houston, 1980-82; asst. gen. counsel Hunt Oil Co., Dallas, 1982-84, v.p., chief counsel, 1984-91, sr. v.p. gen. counsel, 1994-2001; adj. prof. bus. law Dallas Bapt. U., Dallas, 2001—. Bar examiner in Alaska, 1974—77. Mem.: ABA, State Bar Tex. (lectr.), Dallas Bar Assn., Phi Alpha Delta. Republican. Office: 3801 Hanover Ave Dallas TX 75225-7117

SCOTT, JOYCE, writer; d. Charles William and Emma Reardon; m. Edward Dale Scott, Sept. 13, 1971; 1 child, Tonia Louise. Student, Inst. Children's Lit., 1984, student, 1993, Long Ridge Writers Group, 1994. Mem.: The Internat. Women's Writing Guild, Soc. Children's Book Writers and Illustrators.

SCOTT, JOYCE ALAINE, academic administrator; b. Long Beach, Calif., May 21, 1943; d. Emmett Emery Scott and Grace (Evans) Wedum. BA, U. Conn., 1964; MA, U. Va., 1966; PhD, Duke U., 1973. From instr. to assoc. prof. U. Wyo., Laramie, 1971-74, asst. dean, 1974-78, asst. v.p. acad. affairs, 1976-81, assoc. v.p. acad. affairs, 1981-84; provost, v.p. SUNY-Potsdam, 1984-86; exec. v.p. Wichita (Kans.) State U., 1986-90, v.p. on spl. assignment, 1990-91; sr. cons. Am. Assn. State Colls. and Univs., 1991-92, v.p. acad. and internat. programs, 1992-97; dep. commr. Mont. U. Sys., Helena, 1998—2003; provost, v.p. acad. and student affairs Tex. A&M U., Commerce, 2003—06, assoc. prof. dept. ednl. leadership, 2004—. Mem. Commn. on Ednl. Credit and Credentials of Am. Coun. on Edn., Washington, 1982-87; cons. faculty Am. Open U., Lincoln, Nebr., 1981-82. Contbr. articles to profl. jours. Trustee Jones Internat. U. Mem. MLA, Am. Assn. Tchrs. French, Phi Beta Kappa, Phi Kappa Phi, Phi Sigma Iota. Republican. Presbyterian. Office: Dept Educational Leadership PO Box 3011 Commerce TX 75429-3011 Office Phone: 903-886-5503. Business E-Mail: Joyce_Scott@tamu-commerce.edu.

SCOTT, KAMELA KOON, psychologist, educator; b. Carson City, Nev., July 28, 1964; d. Ray Harold and Bert Gardner Koon; m. David Keitt Scott, Feb. 13, 1993; children: Nicolas Keitt, Isaac David. BA, Baylor U., Waco, Tex., 1986; PhD, U. No. Tex., Denton, 1992. Lic. Clin. Psychologist Divsn. Med. Quality Assurance, Fla., 1994. Psychology intern U. Tex. Med. Br. and Shriner's Burns Inst., Galveston, Tex., 1991—92; instr. dept. psychiatry Emory U. Sch. Medicine, Atlanta, 1992—93; asst. prof. dept. of Pediat. U. Fla. Coll. Medicine, Jacksonville, Fla., 1993—96, asst. prof., 1996—2002, assoc. prof. dept. surgery, 2002—. Program dir., psychol. svcs. U. Fla., Dept. Pediat., Dist. Hematology/Sickle Cell Program, Jacksonville, 1993—96, U. Fla. Regional Trauma Sys., Jacksonville, 2001—; chmn. Sexual Harassment Com. U. Fla., Jacksonville, 1997—; mem. Jacksonville Pediat. Injury Control Sys., 1996—; bd. mem. Shands Jacksonville Ethics Com., 1996—, Shands Jacksonville Emergency Preparedness Com., 1998—; adv. bd. mem. Shands Jacksonville Clin. Pastoral Edn. Adv. Bd., 1998—2004; supervising psychologist Shands Jacksonville Trauma Psychology Post-Doctoral Fellowship, 1998—; site reviewer Fla. Brain and Spinal Cord Injury Program, Tallahassee, 1998—; lectr. U. Fla. Risk Mgmt. Ednl. Series, Gainesville, 2002—. Author: (book chapter) Surg. Clinics of North Am., (book chapters (2) Behavioral Aspects of Pediatric Burn Injuries, (jour. article) Current Surgery, Jour. of Trauma, Jacksonville Medicine. Adv. bd. mem. Partnerships for Preventing Violence, Jacksonville, 1998—2003, Serving Child Victims of Traumatic Abuse, Jacksonville, 2002—03; active mem. Compassionate Families, Inc., Jacksonville, 1998—2003. Named Outstanding Alumnae of Yr., U. North Tex., 2005; grantee, City of Jacksonville, Fla., 2001—05, State of Fla. Byrne Grant, 2001-2002, The Blue Found. for a Healthy Fla., 2001—05, The Jacksonville Jaguars Found., 1999-2001, U. of Fla. Dean's Fund, 1997-1998; scholar, Pres. U.S., Washington, D.C., 1982. Mem.: APA. Republican. Baptist. Avocations: scuba diving, skiing, deep sea fishing, camping. Office: U Fla Surgery 655 West 8th St Jacksonville FL 32209 Office Phone: 904-244-3352. Business E-Mail: kamela.scott@jax.ufl.edu.

SCOTT, KAREN ELIZABETH, advocate; b. Buffalo, July 21, 1957; children: James Kenneth-Mark, Alexis Victoria Scott-Davis. BA, Empire State Coll., Buffalo, NY, 2002. Adminstrv. asst. WNY Libr. Resources Coun., Buffalo, 1990—97; rsch. adminstr. U. Buffalo. Civil rights and human rights advocate; bd. dirs. Langston Hughes Inst., Buffalo, 2000. Avocations: interior decorating, fashion design, current affairs.

SCOTT, KATHRYN FENDERSON, lawyer; b. Augusta, Ga., June 6, 1970; d. Robert Thomas Fenderson and Christine (Cunningham) Cormier; m. Charles Dean Scott. BA, Eckerd Coll., St. Petersburg, Fla., 1992; JD, Stetson U., St. Petersburg, 1995. Bar: Fla. 1995, U.S. Dist. Ct. (mid. dist.) Fla. 1995, U.S. Ct. Appeals (11th cir.) 1997. Assoc. Govan, Burns & Jones, St. Petersburg, 1995-97; ptnr. Scott & Fenderson, St. Petersburg, 1997—. Mentor program Stetson U. Coll. Law, St. Petersburg, 1996—. Mem. editl. bd. Paraclete, St. Petersburg Bar Assn., 1996—99. Recipient Am. Jurisprudence award, Lawyer's Coop. Pub., 1992. Mem.: ABA, Clearwater Bar Assn., St. Petersburg Bar Assn., Assn. Fla. Trial Lawyers, Assn. Trial Lawyers Am. Office: Scott and Fenderson 4755 Central Ave Saint Petersburg FL 33713 Office Phone: 727-321-0099. Fax: 727-321-4499. E-mail: fenderlaw@aol.com.

SCOTT, KENNETH ELSNER, mechanical engineering educator; b. Webster, Mass., May 18, 1926; s. Henry Anderson and Amanda (Elsner) S.; m. Elizabeth Ann Oldham, June 21, 1952; children: Kenneth Elsner, Cynthia Lynne, Jeffrey Alan, Donald Leighton. BSMechE, Worcester Poly. Inst., 1948, MS, 1954. Faculty Worcester Poly. Inst., 1948-91, prof. mech. engring., 1966-91, prof. emeritus, 1991—, George I. Alden prof. engring., 1971-75, inst. dir. audio-visual devel., 1971-74, dir. instructional TV, 1974-90, dir. CAD Lab., 1981-93, acting head dept. mech. engring., 1988-89. Active Bd. Health, Holden, Mass., 1963-70. With AUS, 1944-46. Recipient Trustees' award for Outstanding Tchr. of Year, 1971, Tchg. Excellence and Campus Leadership award Sears-Roebuck Found., 1990-91, William R. Grogan award in recognition of support for Mission of Worcester Poly. Inst., 1998. Fellow ASME (exec. com. Worcester sect. 1952-57, sec.-treas. 1955-56, chmn. 1956-57, region I chmn. profl. divns. com. 1957-59, chmn. agenda, audit, budget and nominating com. Worcester 1957-58, chmn. symposium lubrication Worcester sect. 1957-58, chmn. Adm. Earle award com. 1958-59, chmn. devel. com. 1960-61); mem. Am. Soc. Engring. Edn. (sec.-treas. New Eng. chpt., Western Electric Fund award 1972), Sigma Xi, Pi Tau Sigma, Tau Beta Pi. Home: 7054 W Brandywine Cir Fort Myers FL 33919-7317 Personal E-mail: easkes@aol.com.

SCOTT, KENNETH EUGENE, lawyer, educator; b. Western Springs, Ill., Nov. 21, 1928; s. Kenneth L. and Bernice (Albright) S.; m. Viviane H. May, Sept. 22, 1956 (dec. Feb. 1982); children: Clifton, Jeffrey, Linda; m. Priscilla Gay, July 30, 1989; children: Ashley (dec. Apr. 2002), Shaler. BA in Econs., Coll. William and Mary, 1949; MA in Polit. Sci., Princeton U., 1953; LLB, Stanford U., 1956. Bar: N.Y. 1957, Calif. 1957, D.C. 1967. Assoc. Sullivan & Cromwell, NYC, 1956-59, Musick, Peeler & Garrett, LA, 1959-61; chief dep. savs. and loan commr. State of Calif., LA, 1961-63; gen. counsel Fed. Home Loan Bank Bd., Washington, 1963-67; Parsons prof. law and bus. Stanford (Calif.) Law Sch., 1968-95, emeritus, 1995—; sr. rsch. fellow Hoover Instn., 1978-95, emeritus, 1995—; fellow Am. Acad. Berlin, 2001. Mem. Shadow Fin. Regulatory Com., 1986—, Fin. Economists Roundtable, 1991—. Author: (with others) Retail Banking in the Electronic Age, 1977; co-editor: The Economics of Corporation Law and Securities Regulation, 1980. Mem. Calif. Bar Assn., Phi Beta Kappa, Order of Coif, Pi Kappa Alpha, Omicron Delta Kappa. Home: 610 Gerona Rd Stanford CA 94305-8453 Office: Stanford Law Sch Stanford CA 94305-8610 Home Phone: 650-325-0909; Office Phone: 650-723-3070. E-mail: kenscott@stanford.edu.

SCOTT, LEIGHTON REEVES, interior designer, artist, writer; b. Columbus, Ind., Sept. 9, 1942; AB, U. Md., 1968, Knox Coll., 1964. Scientist NASA, Greenbelt, Md., 1968—73; sys. analyst NOAA, Suitland, Md., 1973—76; sr. physicist Johns Hopkins Applied Physics Lab., Laurel, Md., 1976—81; computer software cons. Westinghouse Def. Sys., Linthicum, Md., 1982—84; computer scientist Nat. Security Agy., Ft. George G. Meade, Md., 1984—94; cons., creativity trainer Mt. Airy, Md., 1995—2003. ADA program mgr. Nat. Security Agy., Ft. Meade, 1983—88. Author: (book) The Search for Manhood, 1992, Museum of the Mind, 2002, 2003. Achievements include invention of software blueprints; Vented Bennett Ion Mass Spectrometers orbiting Earth and Venus; design of National Security Agency's first electronic systems support system; U.S. government's first walk-in on-site store for disabled employees. Avocations: art, interior and product design, model building. Office: Pa Design Ctr 594 Shannon Dr N Greencastle PA 17225 Home: 594 Shannon Dr N Greencastle PA 17225 Home Phone: 717-597-3902; Office Phone: 717-597-3902. Business E-Mail: padesign@earthlink.net.

SCOTT, LORI DENISE, music educator, musician; b. Springfield, Mo., May 16, 1958; d. Leo Franklin and Emma June Burrell; m. David Lee Scott, July 5, 1980; children: Christa Denise, Craig Loren. MusB in Edn., Drury U., Springfield, Mo., 1980, BMusArts, 1980; M in Music Edn., U. Kansas, Lawrence, 1987. Lifetime tchg. cert. Music educator Bonner Springs Schs., Kans., 1980—85, State Fair Cmty. Coll., Sedalia, Mo., 1985—87, Benton County R-9 Schs., Warsaw, 1987—2004, Oregon County R-4 Schs., Alton, 2004—. Bd. mem Habitat Humanity, Warsaw, Mo., 2000—04. Named Outstanding Sr. Woman, Drury U., 1980. Mem.: Mo. Choral Dirs. Assn. (mem. state adv. bd. 2002—04), Music Educators Nat. Conf. (pres. West Ctrl. Mo. chpt. 1998—2000). Republican. Methodist. Avocation: gardening. Office: Alton Schs Rt 2 Box 2181 Alton MO 65606 Personal E-mail: scottys@centurytel.net.

SCOTT, LOUIS EDWARD, advertising executive; b. Waterbury, Conn., June 17, 1923; s. Louis Arthur and Ellen (Eckert) S.; m. Phyllis Corrine Denker, Jan. 27, 1942; children: Susan Louise, Eric Richard, Jane Lynn. BS, U. Calif., Berkeley, 1944. Sr. account exec. McCarty Co., LA, 1946-50; from mem. staff to dir. Foote, Cone & Belding, 1950—61; dir. Foote, Cone & Belding/Honig, 1961—98. Bd. dirs. Smart and Final Corp., Casino Internat., True North Comm. Chmn. publicity com. Los Angeles Community Chest, 1960; patron mem. Los Angeles YMCA; mem. Freedoms Found.; chmn. So. Calif. advisory bd. Advt. Council; mem. exec. advisory bd. Art Center Coll. Design. Served with U.S. Maritime Service, also USNR, World War II. Named Western Advt. Man of Year, 1972 Mem. Am. Assn. Advt. Agys. (dir., past chmn. Western region), Rio Verde Country Club, Seattle Yacht Club, Cruising Club Am. Home: 19119 E Tonto Trail Rio Verde AZ 85263 also: PO 682 Imperial Beach CA 91933 Office Phone: 480-390-9890. Personal E-mail: scottlouphyl@aol.com.

SCOTT, MARGARET SIMON, retired mortgage broker; b. Boston, May 12, 1934; d. Frank A. and Margaret Alice (Gotham) Simon; m. Walter Neil Scott, Nov. 21, 1959 (div. June 1997); 1 child, Walter David Kimbley; m. Stephen E. Michelman, Feb. 8, 2003. BA in Physics, Wellesley Coll., Mass., 1956; MA in Polit. Sci., Boston U., 1965; MS in Human Resources Mgmt., U. Utah, Salt Lake City, 1974. Rsch. asst. Bell Tel. Labs., Whippany, N.J., 1956-58; rsch. asst. med. sch. U. Louisville, 1959-60, Harvard U., Boston, 1960-64; instr. polit. sci. Trinity U., San Antonio, 1966-67; cons. info. systems U.S. Dept. Labor, Washington, 1968; dir. manpower planning N.Y.C. Human Resources Adminstrn., 1968-71; asst. v.p. First Nat. City Bank, NYC, 1972-77; v.p. Citibank, N.A., NYC, 1978-86, AMEV Asset Mgmt., Inc., NYC, 1986-88; pres. Mortgage Adv. Svcs., Inc., NYC, 1988-99. Vol. Jr. League, Louisville, 1957; bd. mgr. NY Jr. League, NYC, 1970—74; sec. 1095 Park Ave Corp., NYC, 1977—86; bd. mgrs. McBurney YMCA, NYC, 1995—2000, chmn., 1998—2000; trustee United Adult Ministries, 1998—, mem. exec. com., 1999—, chair, fin. com., 1999—; mem. Affordable Housing Task Force of N.Y. City Cmty. Bd. 4, 2006—; trustee First Presbyn. Ch. in City NY, 1995—98, pres., 1997—98; trustee NY City Presbytery, 1996—98, treas., 1998—2002, chair coun. adminstrn. and support svcs., 2003—05, mem. com. on ministry, 2006—; ruling elder First Presbyn. Ch., 2000—03; mem. steering com. Presbyn. Welcome, 1999—2004, co-moderator, 2001—03; trustee Presbyn. Synod of Northeast, 2002—05; bd. dirs. YWCA, NYC, 1980—85. Named Outstanding Vol. of Yr., Jr. League of City of NY, Inc., 2005. Mem.: Wellesley Club. Democrat. Home: 441 W 24th St New York NY 10011-1253 E-mail: margaretsnyc@mac.com.

SCOTT, MARIAN ALEXIS, journalist; b. Atlanta, Feb. 4, 1949; d. William Alexander and Marian (Willis) Scott; m. Marc Anthony Lewis, Sept. 14, 1968 (div. 1973); m. David Leslie Reeves, Mar. 16, 1974 (div. 1998); children: Cinque Scott, David Leslie Jr. Student, Barnard Coll., 1966-68, Spelman Coll., 1989-90, Regional Leadership Inst., 1992; LHD, Argosy U., 2003. Reporter, asst. city editor, cable TV editor, mgr., video, v.p. cmty. affairs Atlanta Jour. and Constn., 1974-93; dir. diversity Cox Enterprises Inc., 1993-97; pub. Atlanta Daily World, 1997—. Bd. dirs. Atlanta Life Ins. Co.; vis. instr. summer program for minority journalists, Berkeley, Calif., 1980, 81, 84, 85, 87 Grady High Sch., Atlanta, 1982-83; journalist-in-residence Clark Coll., Atlanta, 1983. Rschr., writer: The history of Atlanta NAACP, 1983 (NAACP award 1984). Moderator First Congl. Ch., 1982-92. Named one of 100 Top Black Bus. and Profl. Women, 1986, 20 Women Making a Mark in Atlanta, Atlanta Mag., 1998, Top 25 Women in Bus., The Network Jour., 2004; recipient Disting. Urban Journalism award, Nat. Urban Coalition, 1980, Acad. Achievement award, YWCA, 1989, Media of Yr. award, Ga. Legisl. Black Caucus, 2001, Citizen of Yr. award, Southwest Hosp., 2001, 1st Place Column Writing award, Ga. Press Assn., 2004, Millennium Pacesetter award, Atlanta Bus. League, 2005; Michele Clark fellow, Columbia U. Sch. Journalism, 1974, Grimes fellow, Cox Family Enterprise Ctr., Kennesaw State U. Mem.: Nat. Assn. Black Journalists, Atlanta Assn. Black Journalists (Commentary Print award 1983, Pioneer Black Journalist award 1998), Nat. Assn. Media Women (pres Atlanta chpt. 1985—87, Media Woman of Yr. award 1983, Media Woman of Yr. nat. award 1993), Atlanta Press Club (pres. 2000), Sigma Delta Chi (bd. dirs. 1980—84, treas. 1985—88). Office: Atlanta Daily World 145 Auburn Ave NE Atlanta GA 30303-2503

SCOTT, MARIANNE FLORENCE, retired librarian, educator; b. Toronto, Dec. 4, 1928; d. Merle Redvers and Florence Ethel (Hutton) Scott. BA, McGill U., Montreal, Que., Can., 1949, BLS, 1952; LLD (hon.), York U., 1985, Dalhousie U., 1989; DLitt (hon.), Laurentian U., 1990. Asst. librarian Bank of Montreal, 1952-55; law librarian McGill U., 1955-73, law area librarian, 1973-75, dir. libraries, 1975-84, lectr. legal bibliography faculty of law, 1964-75; nat. librarian Nat. Library of Can., Ottawa, Ont., 1984-99, ret., 1999. Co-founder, editor: Index to Can. Legal Periodical Lit, 1963—; contbr. articles to profl. jours. Decorated officer Order of Can.; recipient Queen Elizabeth II Silver Jubilee medal, 1977, IFLA medal, 1996, Queen Elizabeth II Golden Jubilee medal, 2002. Mem. Internat. Assn. Law Libraries (dir. 1974-77), Am. Assn. Law Libraries, Can. Assn. Law Libraries (pres. 1963-69, exec. bd. 1973-75, honored mem. 1980—), Can. Library Assn. (coun. and dir. 1980-82, 1st v.p. 1980-81, pres. 1981-82), Corp. Profl. Librarians of Que. (v.p. 1975-76), Can. Assn. Rsch. Librs. (pres. 1978-79, past pres. 1979-80, exec. com. 1980-81, sec.-treas. 1983-84), Can. Writers Found. (bd. dirs. 1999—, treas. 2003—), Ctr. for Research Libraries (dir. 1980-83), Internat. Fedn. Library Assns. (honor com. for 1982 conf. 1979-82, chair com. on copyright and other legal matters 1998-2003, hon. fellow 2003), Conf. of Dirs. of Nat. Libraries (chmn. 1988-92). Home: 119 Dorothea Dr Ottawa ON Canada K1V 7C6 E-mail: mfscott@rogers.com.

SCOTT, MARIE CLAUDINE, ceramic artist, writer; b. Pitts., Aug. 9, 1953; d. Walter Phelps and Janine Baptistine (Decruck) Scott; m. David Lovattsmith, Feb. 24, 1984 (div. 1985); m. Jeffrey Lloyd White, Dec. 31, 1990 (div. 1993); children: Trayton, India. Student in interior design, E.S.A.M., Paris, 1975. Self-employed interior decorator, Paris, 1975-76; lyric writer for popular songs E.P.O.C., Paris, 1976-77; pub. rels. cons. Theo Cowan, Ltd., London, 1977-91; art buyer McCann-Erickson, Paris, 1980-89. Contbr. articles to mags. including Lady's Circle, Woman's Circle, South Florida. Mem. Ponte Vedra Inn and Club. Avocations: travel, art history, swimming, ceramics handpainting. Home: 312 Ponte Vedra Blvd Ponte Vedra Beach FL 32082-2407 Mailing: PO Box 2407 Ponte Vedra Beach FL 32004 Personal E-mail: mococoscott@hotmail.com.

SCOTT, MARIETTE A., marketing executive; b. Darien, Conn., July 18, 1953; d. Vincent Charles Arguimbau and Carmen Perez de Guzman de Arguimbau; m. Edward Barton Scott, Sept. 6, 1986. BA cum laude, Skidmore Coll., 1976; MA, Johns Hopkins U., 1980; PhD, NYU, 1985. Instr. Goucher Coll., Towson, Md., 1977, Johns Hopkins U., Balt., 1978—80, NYU, NYC, 1981—83, Princeton U., NJ, 1984—85; dir. Latin Am. Cultural Ctr., NYC, 1980—84; mng. dir. Tucker Capital Corp., Princeton, 1984—85; mktg. mgr. Univision Inc., NYC, 1985—89; pres. Silk Serum Enterprises, Greenwich, Conn., 1986—; ptnr. Arguimbau Co., Greenwich, 1989—. Dir. US-Spain C. of C., NYC, 2002—; trustee Hispanic Soc. Am., NYC, 2000—. Fulbright scholar, 1976. Mem.: Wee Burn Country Club. Republican. Roman Catholic. Avocations: calligraphy, clothing design, sewing, tennis, skiing. Home: 444 E 57th St New York NY 10022 Office: Arguimbau Co 4 Davenport Ave Greenwich CT 06830

SCOTT, MCGREGOR W., prosecutor, lawyer; b. 1962; m. Jennifer Urbanski Scott; 3 children. BA History, Santa Clara Univ.; JD, Hastings Coll. of Law, Univ. of Calif. Dep. dist. atty. Contra Costa County, 1989—97; dist. atty. Shasta County, 1997—2003; US atty. (ea. dist.) Calif. US Dept. Justice, Sacramento, 2003—. Chair Rural Counties Commn., Calif. Dist. Atty. Assn.; bd. dirs. Calif. Dist. Atty. Assn.; mem. US Atty. Gen. Adv. Com. Lt. col. USNG. Avocations: reading, basketball, golf, exercise, college football, hunting. Office: US Attys Office Sacramento Fed Courthouse 501 1 St Ste 10-100 Sacramento CA 95814 *

SCOTT, MELLOUISE JACQUELINE, retired media specialist; b. Sanford, Fla., Mar. 1, 1943; d. Herbert and Mattye (Williams) Cherry; m. Robert Edward Scott, Jr., July 1, 1972; 1 child, Nolan Edward. BA, Talladega Coll., 1965; MLS, Rutgers U., 1974, EdM, 1976, EdS, 1982. Media specialist Seminole County Bd. Edn., Sanford, 1965-72, Edison (N.J.), 1972-98; ret. Edison (N.J.) Bd. Edn., 1999. Mem. ALA, N.J. Ret. Educators Assn., NEA. Baptist. Home: PO Box 1771 Sanford FL 32772-1771

SCOTT, MICHAEL DENNIS, lawyer; b. Mpls., Nov. 6, 1945; s. Frank Walton and Donna Julia (Howard) S.; children: Michael Dennis, Cindal Marie, Derek Walton. BS, MIT, 1967; JD, UCLA, 1974. Bar: Calif. 1974, U.S. Dist. Ct. (no., so. and ctrl. dists.) Calif. 1974, U.S. Patent Office 1974, U.S. Ct. Appeals (9th cir.) 1974, U.S. Supreme Ct. 1978, U.S. Ct. Appeals (fed. cir.) 1989. Systems programmer NASA Electronics Rsch. Lab., Cambridge, Mass., 1967-69, Computer Scis. Corp., El Segundo, Calif., 1969-71, Univac, Valencia, Calif., 1971; from assoc. to ptnr. Smaltz & Neeley, LA, 1974-81; exec. dir. Ctr. for Computer/Law, LA, 1977-94; pvt. practice LA, 1981-86, 88-89; pres. Law and Tech. Press, 1981-94; ptnr. Scott & Roxborough, LA, 1986-88, Graham & James, 1989-93; v.p., gen. counsel Sanctuary Woods Multimedia, Inc., San Mateo, Calif., 1993-94; of counsel Steinhart & Falconer, San Francisco, 1995-97; ptnr. Hosie Wes Sacks & Brelsford, Menlo Park, Calif., 1997-98, Perkins Coie LLP, 1998—2003; prof. law Southwestern U., LA, 2003—. Adj. assoc. prof. law, Southwestern U., LA, 1975-80, 01-03, Loyola U., L.A., 1997-99, 02-04, Pepperdine U., LA, 2001-03; chmn. World Computer Law Congress, LA, 1991, 93; co-chmn. Internat. IT Law Conf., 2005, 2007. Author: (with David S. Yen) Computer Law Bibliography, 1979, Computer Law, 1984, Scott on Computer Law, 1991, Multimedia: Law and Practice, 1993, Scott on Multimedia Law, 1996, (with Warren S. Reid) Year 2000 Computer Crisis: Law Business Technology, 1998, Internet and Technology Law Desk Reference, 1999, Intellectual Property and Licensing Law Desk Reference, 2001, Telecommunications Law Desk Reference, 2003, Scott on Outsourcing Law and Practice, 2006, Scott on Information Technology Law, 2007; editor-in-chief: Computer/Law Jour., 1978-94, Software Protection, 1982-92, Software Law Jour., 1985-94, Internat. Computer Law Adviser, 1986-92, Cyberspace Lawyer, 1996—, E-Commerce Law Report, 1998—. Mem. Computer Law Assn. (bd. dirs. 1994-99), Calif. State Bar Assn.

SCOTT, MIMI KOBLENZ, psychotherapist, actress, journalist, playwright; b. Albany, NY, Dec. 15, 1940; d. Edmund Akiba and Tillie (Paul) Koblenz; m. Barry Stuart Scott, Aug. 13, 1961 (dec. Nov. 1991); children: Karen Scott Zantay, Jeffrey B. BA in Speech and English Edn., Russell Sage Coll., 1962; MA in Speech Edn., SUNY, Albany, 1968; M in Social Welfare, SUNY, 1985; PhD in Psychology, Pacific Western U., Encino, Calif., 1985. Cert. tchr., social worker. Tchr. English, speech Albany Pub. Schs., 1961-63; hostess, producer talkshow Sta. WAST-TV 13, Albany, 1973-75; freelance actress NYC, 1975-77; producer, actress Four Seasons Dinner Theater, Albany, 1978-82; instr. of theatre Albany Jr. Coll., 1981-83; pvt. practice psychotherapy Albany, NY, 1985-92, NYC, 1992—; exec. producer City of Albany Park Playhouse, 1989-92; actor self-employed NYC, 1992—; actor Off Broadway show Grandma Sylvia's Funeral, 1996-98, Split Ends, 2004, Grease, Albany, 2007. Guest psychotherapist Sally Jessy Raphael Show, 1992, 93, Jane Whitney Show, 1994, A Current Affair, 1995, News Talk TV, 1995; founder, producing artistic dir. Manhattan Playwrights Inc., 2001—07. Scriptwriter, dir., actor (TV films) To Liberty and Justice for All, 1985, featured writer Backstage, 1995—96, featured in ind. film Mr. Vincent, Sundance, 1997, book and lyricist (musical) Dressing Room, Soho Playhouse, N.Y.C., 2000; author: Mind Tricks, 2003; dir.: Mind Tricks, 2003; featured on NBC Dateline, 2005, VH1's So Jewtastic, 2006. Event organizer AmFar, 1985; co-chmn. March of Dimes Telethon, 1985-86; fundraiser Leukemia Found., 1987, AIDS Benefit, North Miami Beach, Fla., 1988; elected to SUNY Albany U. Found., 1990. Recipient FDR Nat. Achievement award March of Dimes, 1985, Recognition Cert. Capital Dist. Psychiat. Ctr., 1983-85; named Woman of Yr. YWCA, 1986, Commr. Albany Tricentennial Celebration, 1986; named Mimi Scott Day in her honor Mayor of Albany, 1989. Mem.:

NASW, AFTRA, SAG, AEA, Drama League of N.Y., N.Y. League Profl. Theatre Women. Jewish. Avocations: boating, golf, tennis. Home and Office: 155 W 70th St PH2A New York NY 10023-3767 Home Phone: 212-721-2979; Office Phone: 212-721-2979. Personal E-mail: mscott13@aol.com.

SCOTT, NANCY L., information technology manager, health facility administrator, consultant; b. Berwyn, Ill., Sept. 11, 1962; d. Kenneth N. and Lolita L. Unger; m. Paul A. Scott, Dec. 29, 1990 (div. Sept. 1995). BS, Univ. of Ill., 1983; MBA with hons., U. of Chgo., 1991. Cert. CHE Am. Coll. of Healthcare Execs., Chgo., 2000. Various positions including implementation specialist to fin. product mgr. Enterprise Systems, Inc., Wheeling, Ill., 1993—96; cytogenetics technologist Univ. of Chgo., 1986—88; supr. Reproductive Genetics Inst., Chgo., 1988—90; dist. agt. The Prudential, Des Plaines, Ill., 1992; mgr., sr. cons. Cap Gemini Ernst & Young U.S., Chgo., 1996—2003; acct. exec. AHA Fin. Solutions, Inc., Chgo., 2003—04; payroll project mgr. Hewitt Assocs. LLC, Chgo., 2005—. Home: 3238 Elm Ave Brookfield IL 60513 Office: Hewitt Assocs LLC 120 S Riverside Plz Chicago IL 60606 Office Phone: 312-279-6643. Personal E-mail: NLScott@aol.com.

SCOTT, NATHAN ALEXANDER, JR., minister, literary critic, religious educator; b. Cleve., Apr. 24, 1925; s. Nathan Alexander and Maggie (Martin) S.; m. Charlotte Hanley, Dec. 21, 1946; children: Nathan Alexander III, Leslie K. AB, U. Mich., 1944; BD, Union Theol. Sem., 1946; PhD, Columbia U., 1949; LittD, Ripon Coll., 1965, St. Mary's Coll., Notre Dame, Ind., 1969, Denison U., 1976, Brown U., 1981, Northwestern U., 1982, Elizabethtown Coll., 1989; LHD, Wittenberg U., 1965; DD, Phila. Div. Sch., 1967; STD, Gen. Theol. Sem., 1968; LHD, U. D.C., 1976; DD, The Protestant Episcopal Theological Seminary in Va., 1985; HumD, U. Mich., 1988; LHD, Wesleyan U., 1989, Bates Coll., 1990; STD, Univ of the South, 1992; DD, Kenyon Coll., 1993, Wabash Coll., 1996; Ordained priest Episcopal Ch., 1960; canon theologian Cathedral St. James, Chgo., 1967-76. dean of chapel, Va. Union U., 1946-47; instr. humanities, Howard U., 1948-51, asst. prof., 1951-53, assoc. prof., 1953-55; asst. prof. theology and literature, U. Chgo., 1955-58, assoc. prof., 1958-64, prof., 1964-72, Shailer Mathews prof. of theology and lit., 1972-76, prof. English, 1967-76; Commonwealth prof. religious studies, U. Va., 1976-81, William R. Kenan prof. religious studies, 1981-90, prof. English, 1976-90, prof. emeritus, 1990—. Author: Rehearsals of Discomposure: Alienation and Reconciliation in Modern Literature, 1952, The Tragic Vision and the Christian Faith, 1957, Modern Literature and the Religious Frontier, 1958, Albert Camus, 1962, Reinhold Niebuhr, 1963, The New Orpheus: Essays toward a Christian Poetic, 1964, The Climate of Faith in Modern Literature, 1965, The Broken Center: Studies in the Theological Horizon of Modern Literature, 1966, Ernest Hemingway, 1966, The Modern Vision of Death, 1967, Adversity and Grace: Studies in Recent American Literature, 1968, Negative Capability: Studies in the New Literature and the Religious Situation, 1969, The Unquiet Vision: Mirrors of Man in Existentialism, 1969, The Wild Prayer of Longing: Poetry and the Sacred, 1971, Nathanael West, 1971, Three American Moralists: Mailer, Bellow, Trilling, 1973, The Poetry of Civic Virtue: Eliot, Malraux, Auden, 1976, Mirrors of Man in Existentialism, 1978, The Poetics of Belief: Studies in Coleridge, Arnold, Pater, Santayana, Stevens and Heidegger, 1985, Visions of Presence in Modern American Poetry, 1993; co-editor Jour. Religion, 1963-77, (with Ronald Sharp) Reading George Steiner, 1994; adv. editor Religion and Lit., Literature and Theology, Callaloo. Fellow Am. Acad. of Arts and Scis.; mem. Soc. Arts, Religion and Contemporary Culture, Soc. for Values in Higher Edn. (Kent fellow), MLA., Am. Acad. Religion (pres. 1986), Century Assn. (N.Y.C.), Quadrangle Club, Arts Club (Chgo.), Greencroft Club (Charlottesville, Va.). Office: U Va Dept Religious Studies Charlottesville VA 22903 Personal E-mail: chs5a@ntelos.net.

SCOTT, NORMAN (W. NORMAN SCOTT), orthopedist, sports medicine physician, surgeon; m. Susan Craig Scott; children: Eric, William, Kelly. BA, U. Pa.; MD, Cornell U. Chief implant svcs. Lenox Hill Hosp., NYC, assoc. attending orthopaedic surgeon, 2004—; dir. Insall-Scott-Kelly Inst. for Orthops. and Sports Medicine, chmn. Dept. Orthops. Beth Israel Hosp., Singer Divsn., 1991—2004; clin. prof. orthop. surgery Albert Einstein Coll. Medicine, 1991—2004. Team orthopedist NY Knicks, 1978—; team physician NY Rangers, 1981—87, US Olympic Basketball Team, Barcelona, 1992, US Open, USGA, Springfield, NJ, 1993, PGA Tournament, Mamaroneck, NY, 1997, NY CityHawks, 1997—98; orthop. cons. NY Liberty, WNBA, 1997—; adv. bd. Radius Ventures, LLC. Author: 11 textbooks; assoc. editor-in-chief Jour. Arthroplasty; contbr. articles to med. jours. Mem.: Knee Soc. (founder, past pres.), NBA Physicians Assn. (former pres.), Assn. Profl. Team Physicians (founder, chmn. 1997—). Avocation: golf. Office: 210 E 64th St New York NY 10021 Home: NY Knicks Two Pennsylvania Plaza New York NY 10121 Office Phone: 212-434-4301. *

SCOTT, NORMAN ROSS, electrical engineering educator; b. NYC, May 15, 1918; s. George Norman and Lillias B.H. (Ogg) S.; m. Marjorie M. Fear, Apr. 6, 1950; children: Mari, George, Ian, Charles. BS, MS, MIT, 1941; PhD, U. Ill., 1950. Asst. prof. elec. engring. U. Ill., Urbana, 1946-50; asst. prof. to prof. elec. engring. U. Mich., Ann Arbor, 1951-87, assoc dean Coll. Engring., 1965-68, dean Dearborn Campus, 1968-71, prof. emeritus of elec. engring. and computer sci., 1987—. Cons. Nat. Cash Register Co., Dayton, 1956-65; mem. math. and computer sci. rsch. adv. com. AEC, Washington, 1961-63. Editor-in-chief IEEE Trans. on Computers, N.Y.C., 1961-65; author: Analog and Digital Computer Technology, 1959, Electronic Computer Technology, 1970, Computer Number Systems and Arithmetic, 1985. Maj. U.S. Army, 1941-46. Fellow IEEE. Home: 2260 Gale Rd Ann Arbor MI 48105-9512 Office: U Mich EECS Dept Ann Arbor MI 48109

SCOTT, NORMAN ROY, academic administrator, agricultural engineer, educator; b. Spokane, Wash., Sept. 6, 1936; s. Roy Samuel and Agnes Sarafia (Lilljegren) S.; m. Sharon R. Cogley, June 17, 1961; children: Robin, Nanette, Shirlene. BS in Agrl. Engring., Wash. State U., 1958; PhD, Cornell U., 1962. Mem. faculty agrl. engring dept. Cornell U., Ithaca, NY, 1962—, chmn. agrl. engring. dept., 1978-84, dir. office for rsch. agrl. experimentation sta., 1984-89, v.p. rsch. and advanced studies, 1989-98. Mem. bd. on agriculture NRC, Nat. Acad. Scis., 1993-96. Contbr. articles to profl. jours.; patentee in field. Recipient Alumni Achievement award Wash. State U., 1995. Fellow ASHRAE, Am. Inst. for Med. and Biol. Engring. (founding 1991), Am. Soc. Agrl. Engrs. (tech. v.p. 1989-92, pres. elect 1992-93, pres. 1993-94, Henry Glese award 1989, McCormick-Case Gold Medal award 2002); mem. AAAS, Nat. Acad. Engring., Inst. Biol. Engring. (pres. 2001), Am. Soc. for Engring. Edn., Instrument Soc. Am. (sr.). Democrat. Methodist. Avocations: sailing, golf. Home: 1662 Taughannock Blvd Trumansburg NY 14886-9120 Office: Cornell U 216 Riley Robb Hall Ithaca NY 14853-5701 Office Phone: 607-255-4473. Business E-Mail: nrs5@cornell.edu.

SCOTT, OLOF HENDERSON, JR., priest; b. Phila., May 13, 1942; s. Olof Henderson and Julia Irene (Rutroff) S.; m. Eva Jakowenko, Sept. 13, 1969; children: Lisa Ann, Christopher Olof, Timothy Nicholas. BA in Physics, Franklin and Marshall Coll., 1964; MS in Nuclear Engring., Pa. State U., 1966; postgrad., St. Vladimir's Orthodox Theol. Sem., 1975-76. Ordained deacon Antiochian Orthodox Christian Ch., 1975, priest, 1976, archpriest, 1988. Ops. engr. S3G ops. Knolls Atomic Power Lab., GE Co., Schenectady, N.Y., 1966-68, project engr. S3G ops., 1968-69; lead nuclear engr. Seabrook Nuclear project Pub. Svc. Co. of N.H., Manchester, 1969-70; project engr. VEPCO projects Nuclear Energy Sys. divsn. Westinghouse Elec. Co., Monroeville, Pa., 1970-72, project mgr. VEPCO projects Nuclear Energy Sys. divsn., 1972-74, regional sales mgr. mktg., 1974-75; dean St. George Orthodox Cathedral, Charleston, W.Va., 1976—; dean of clergy Appalachian-Ohio Valley Deanery, 1976—2005, W.Va. Deanery, 2005—. Spiritual advisor NAC-SOYO of Archdiocese, 1977-82, vice-chmn. inter-orthodox and inter-faith rels., 1987-2005, chmn., 2005—; exec. bd. W.Va. Coun. Chs., 1977—; bd. govs. Nat. Coun. Chs., 1977-2005, nominating com., 1979-81, exec. com., 1985-96, membership com., 1988-91, unity and rels., 1989-92, ch. world svc., 1997-2005; active West Va. Ecumenical Coalition on Infant Mortality, 1992-96; rep. Christian Chs. Together in the US, 2006—. Contbr. articles to profl. jours. Bd. dirs. Religious Coalition for Cmty. Renewal in Charleston, 1987-95, Charleston Ch. Recreation Assn., 1998—, Kanawha Home for Children, 1986-89, pres., 1989; long-range planning com. W.Va. State Rep. Exec. Com., 1985-87; adv. bd. Nat. Ctr. for Human Rels., 1997-98, Charleston Area Religious Leaders Assn., 2004—; del. 8th Assembly of WCC, Harare, Zimbabwe, 1998. Named Hon. West Virginian, 2001; Olof H. Scott Day named in his honor, City of Charleston, W.Va., 2001. Mem. Acad. Parish Clergy (pres. W.Va. chpt. 1983-85), Am. Nuclear Soc., St. Vladimir's Theol. Found., Charleston Ministerial Assn., Order of St. John of Jerusalem-Knights Hospitellers (chaplain 1985—), Order of St. Ignatius of Antioch, Soc. for Preservation and Encouragement Barbershop Quartet Singing in Am. Inc. (v.p. 1984-85), Pa. State Club W.Va. (pres. 1984-88), Alden Kindred of Am., Sigma Pi Sigma, Delta Sigma Phi. Avocations: camping, barbershop quartet, motorcycling. Home: 4409 Staunton Ave SE Charleston WV 25304-1743 Office: St George Orthodox Cathedral PO Box 2044 Charleston WV 25327-2044 Personal E-mail: frolof@suddenlink.net. *My thoughts on life are but mere recitations of the Holy Scripture and my feeble attempts at making Those words and Thoughts my own.*

SCOTT, P. MARK, musician, educator; b. Amarillo, Tex., June 16, 1953; s. Peter Mark and Margie Mayfield (Ingham) Scott. MusB in Organ Performance, Tex. Chrstian U., Ft. Worth, 1975, MusB in Sacred Music, 1975; attended, Royal Sch. Ch. Music, Croydon, Eng., 1980, attended, 1985, attended, 1990, Abbey of St. Pierre, Solesmes, France, 2000, Monastery of Christ in Desert, N.Mex., 2000, Ampleforth Abbey, York, Eng., 2000. Min. music, organist St. Stephen Presbyn. Ch., Ft. Worth, 1975—; instr. sacred music U. N. Tex., Denton, 2004—. Arranger: Awake Thou Wintry Earth, 1992, Lord, Let Your Angels Shelter Me, 1992. Dir. spl. series events St. Stephen Presbyn. Ch., Ft. Worth, 1975—. Nordan Fine Arts fellow, Tex. Christian U., 1971—75. Mem.: Tex. Choral Dirs. Assn., Am. Guild Organists (former dean Ft. Worth chpt.), Am. Choral Dirs. Assn. Avocation: history of World War II. Office: Saint Stephen Presbyn Ch 2700 McPherson Ave Fort Worth TX 76109-1450 Office Phone: 817-927-8411. Business E-Mail: muspms@sstephen-pcusa.com.

SCOTT, PETER M., III, utility company executive; married; two children. BS, MBA, U. NC. Prin., ptnr. Theodore Barry & Associates, LA; founder, pres. Scott, Madden & Associates, Inc., 1983-2000; exec. v.p., CFO Progress Energy, Inc., Raleigh, NC, 2000—03, CFO & pres. Progress Energy Svc. Co., 2004—. Bd. mem. Nuclear Elec. Ins. Ltd., RTI Internat. Bd. mem. NC Mus. Art Found., Eckerd Youth Alternatives; mem. bd. vis. Kenan-Flagler Sch. Bus. Univ. NC, Chapel Hill. Office: Progess Energy Inc 410 S Wilmington St Raleigh NC 27601-1748 *

SCOTT, PHILLIP W., financial consultant; BS in Fin., Calif. State U., Chico; M in Internat. Bus., St. Mary's Coll. Cert. fin. mgr. Positions up to wealth mgmt. advisor CFS Group, first v.p. investments Merrill Lynch, Walnut Creek, Calif., 1985—. Named one of Best 100 Brokers, Barron's, 2005—07. Office: CFS Group Merrill Lynch 1331 N California Blvd Ste 130/700 Walnut Creek CA 94596-4534 Office Phone: 925-945-4807. E-mail: phillip_scott@ml.com. *

SCOTT, RACHEL E., lawyer; b. Seattle, Dec. 30, 1976; BA, Univ. Wash., 1998; JD, Univ. Mont. Law Sch., 2001; LLM, Univ. Helsinki Faculty Law, 2002. Bar: Wash. 2001, US Dist. Ct., Western Dist. Wash. 2002. Assoc. atty., personal injury, auto. accidents Scott, Kinney & Fjelstad, Seattle, 2002—. Contbr. articles to numerous profl. jours. Named Wash. Rising Star, SuperLawyer Mag., 2006. Mem.: Wash. State Trial Lawyers Assn., Wash. State Bar Assn., Assn. Trial Lawyers of Am. Office: Scott Kinney & Fjelstad One Union Sq Ste 1928 600 University St Seattle WA 98101-4178

SCOTT, RALPH MASON, retired radiologist, educator; b. Leemont, Va., Nov. 23, 1921; s. Benjamin Thomas and Marion Hazel (Mason) S.; m. Alice Latine Francisco, Dec. 21, 1946; children: Susan Taylor, Ralph Mason, John Thomas. BA, U. Va., 1947; MD, Med. Coll. Va., 1950. Diplomate Am. Bd. Radiology (trustee 1965-76, treas. 1969-70, v.p. 1970-72, pres. 1972-74). Intern Robert Packer Hosp., Sayre, Pa., 1953-54, resident, 1954-57, dir. radiation therapy and nuclear medicine sect., 1957-59; fellow Christie Hosp. and Holt Radium Inst., Manchester, England, 1956-57; asst. prof. radiology U. Chgo. Med. Sch., 1959-60; assoc. prof. radiology, dir. radiation therapy and radioisotopes U. Louisville Med. Sch., 1960-64, prof., dir. radiation therapy, 1964-77; prof. and chmn. dept. rad. oncology U Louisville, 1974-77; prof. radiation therapy U. Louisville Med. Sch., 1981-82; prof. emeritus U. Louisville, 1995; dir. J. Graham Brown Regional Cancer Ctr., Health Scis. Ctr. U. Louisville Med. Sch., 1981-82; dir. dept. radiation medicine Christ Hosp., Cin., 1982-93; ret. Clin. prof. radiology U. Cin. Coll. Medicine, 1982-93; prof., chmn. dept. therapeutic radiology U. Md. Sch. Med., 1977-80; dir. radiation therapy program div. cancer rsch. resources and ctrs., Nat. Cancer Inst. (on leave from U. Louisville), 1976-77. Pres. Ky. divsn. Am. Cancer Soc., 1972-73; bd. dirs. Living Arrangements for the Developmentally Disabled, 1993-95, No. Ky. Assn. for the Retarded, 1993-95, Day Spring Inc., 1993-95, United Health Care, 1994-95, Seven Counties Svcs., Inc., 1997-2003, J. Graham Brown Regional Cancer Ctr. Corp., 1997—. Lt. (j.g.) USNR, 1943-46, PTO. Mem. Am. Roentgen-Ray Soc. (exec. coun. 1968—, chmn. exec. coun. 1972-73), AMA, Am. Coll. Radiology (vice chmn. commn. on cancer 1968-69), Am. Radium Soc., Am. Soc. Therapeutic Radiologists, Assn. U. Radiologists, Radiol. Soc. N.Am., Pi Kappa Alpha, Phi Chi. Home: Treyton Oak Towers 211 W Oak St Apt 922 Louisville KY 40203 Personal E-mail: ramsco1@earthlink.net.

SCOTT, RAYMOND E., manufacturing executive; Pres. GM divsn. Lear Corp., 2000—04, 2005, pres. European Customer Focused Divsn., 2004—05, sr. v.p., pres. North Am. Customer Group, 2005—06, sr. v.p., pres. North Am. Seating Systems, 2006—. Office: Lear Corp 21557 Telegraph Rd PO Box 5008 Southfield MI 48086 Office Phone: 248-447-1500. Office Fax: 248-447-1722. *

SCOTT, RAYMOND PETER WILLIAM, chemistry professor, writer; b. Erith, Eng., June 20, 1924; came to U.S., 1969; s. Ronald and Annie (Hoadley) S.; m. Barbara Winifred Doreen Strange, Apr. 20, 1946; children: Kerry Raymond, Kevin Francis. B.Sc., U. London, 1946, D.Sc., 1958. Lab. leader Burroughs Welcome, Dartford, England, 1946-48; chief chemist APCM, 1948-52; research mgr. Benzole Producers, Watford, England, 1952-60; divisional mgr. Unilever, Sharnbrook and Bedfordshire, England, 1960-69; dir. phys. chemistry Hoffamn La Roche, Nutley, NJ, 1969-80; dir. applied rsch. Perkin-Elmer, Norwalk, Conn., 1980-86; sometime rsch. prof. dept. chemistry Georgetown U., Washington, 1986-2000; writer, cons., 2001—. Rsch. prof. dept. chemistry Birkbeck Coll., London. Author: Liquid Chromatography Detectors, 1977, 3d edit., 1987, Contemporary Liquid Chromatography, 1976, Liquid Chromatography Column Theory, 1991, Silica Gel and Bonded Phases, 1993, Liquid Chromatography for the Analyst, 1994, Chromatography Techniques, 1995, Chromatography Detectors, 1996, Tandem Techniques, 1996, Introduction to Analytical Gas Chromatography, 1997, Chiral Chromatography, 1998, Quantitative Chromatographer Analysis, 2000, Chromatography Theory, 2002; editor: Gas Chromatography, 1960, Small Bore Columns in Liquid Chromatography, 1983. Recipient Tswett medal Am. Internat. Symposia on Chromatography, 1978; recipient Tswett award USSR Tech. Inst. Moscow, 1978, Martin medal in chromatography Chromatography Group Gt. Britain, 1982 Fellow Royal Soc. Chemistry (chartered, Analysis and Instrumentation award 1988), Am. Inst. Chemists (cert.), Am. Chem. Soc. (Chromatography award 1977). Home: Great Sanders House Hurst Ln London TN33 0PE England E-mail: ray_scott@library&science.com.

SCOTT, REBECCA J., law and history educator; AB, Radcliffe Coll.; MPhil in Econ. History, London Sch. Econs.; PhD, Princeton U. Charles Gibson disting. univ. prof. history and law U. Mich. Law Sch., Ann Arbor. Author: Degrees of Freedom: Louisiana and Cuba after Slavery, 2005; contbr. articles to profl. jours. Recipient Frederick Douglass prize, 2006; grantee Guggenheim fellowship, 2004. Mem.: Am. Acad. Arts and Scis. Office: Mich U Law Sch 969 Legal Rsch 625 S State St Ann Arbor MI 48109-1215 Office Phone: 734-615-2082. Office Fax: 734-764-8309. E-mail: rjscott@umich.edu.

SCOTT, RENAY MARIE, academic administrator, educator; d. Douglas and Joan Scott. BA, Calvin Coll., Grand Rapids, Mich., 1984; MA, Mich. State U., Lansing, 1988; PhD, Wayne State U., Detroit, 1995. Cert. in secondary tchg. Mich. Tchr. secondary social studies Freedom Bapt. Acad., Hudsonville, Mich., 1984—89; instr. Grade Sch. of Bible, Grand Rapids, 1990—94; asst. prof. Grace Bible Coll., Wyoming, Mich., 1994—96; assoc. prof. Cornerstone U., Grand Rapids, 1996—98; chairperson Ctrl. Mich. U., Mt. Pleasant, 2003—06, prof., 1998—2006; dean Owens CC, Toledo, 2006—. Adj. faculty Lourdes Coll., 2006—. Editor: Mich. Social Studies Jour., 2001—. Recipient Provost award, Cornerstone U., 1998. Mem.: Organ. of Am. Historians, Nat. Coun. Social Studies (bd. dirs. 2006—07), Mich. Coun. Social Studies (pres. 2001—06, bd. dirs. 2007). Avocations: bicycling, running, travel, reading, photography. Office: Cen Mich U Roran Hall 208 Mount Pleasant MI 48859 Office Phone: 567-661-7545.

SCOTT, RICHARD MALACHI, psychologist; b. Bklyn., Dec. 15, 1968; s. David Malachi and Olive Scott. AA in Gen. Studies, Mira Costa Coll., 1990, AS in Psychology, 1990, AA in Visual Arts, 1990; BA in Psychology, U. Calif., San Diego, 1991; MA in Clin. Psychology, We. Am. U., 1993; MA in Psychology, Saybrook Inst., 1995, PhD in Clin. Psychology, 2000; postgrad., St. Luke Sch. Medicine. Lic. clin. psychologist. Social worker, case worker Salvation Army, Family Svcs. Divsn., San Diego, 1993—2000; social worker Dept. Pub. Social Svcs., Riverside, Calif., 1996—98; psychol. asst. various orgns., Calif., 1997—2000; clin. psychologist Calfi. Dept. Corrections, Chino, Calif., 2000—04; pvt. practice San Diego, 2004—. Project and clin. dir. So. Calif. Alcohol and Drug Program, Inc., Downey, Calif., 2004; clin. psychologist Geriatric Cons., Inc., San Diego, 2003—05, Dept. of Corrections, San Diego, 2005—; landlord multiple home owner, mgr.m bus. investor, Calif. Mem.: Nat. Acad. Sports Medicine, San Diego Psychol. Assn., APA. Avocations: dance, drawing, painting, sculpting, singing. Home: 11672 Ramsdell Ct San Diego CA 92131-3607 Office Phone: 619-661-6500 x6320. Personal E-mail: research2005@hotmail.com.

SCOTT, RICHARD THOMAS, JR., reproductive endocrinologist; b. Selma, Ala., Nov. 28, 1958; s. Richard Thomas and Cynthia Marvin (Coleman) S.; m. Blair MacKerer, June 16, 1979; children: Whitney Blair, Katherine Leigh, Richard Thomas III. BS in Chemistry, Randolph Macon Coll., 1979; MD, U. Va., Charlottesville, 1983. Diplomate Nat. Bd. Med. Examiners, Am. Bd. Ob-Gyn., reproductive endocrinology divsn; bd. cert. high complexity lab dir. embryology, andrology, endocrinology, Am. Bd. Bioanalysts. Commd. 2nd lt. USAF, 1979, advanced through grades to lt. col., 1993; intern Wilford Hall USAF Med. Ctr., San Antonio, 1983-84, resident, 1984-87, chief reproductive endocrinology Lackland AFB, Tex., 1989-93; fellow Jones Inst. for Reproductive Medicine, Ea. Va. Med. Sch., Norfolk, 1987-89; chief reproductive endocrinology Uniformed Svcs. U. Health Scis., Bethesda, Md., 1993—, asst. prof., 1990—, assoc. prof., 1993—. Adj. scientist S.W. Found. Biomed. Rsch., 1990—, dir. Assisted Reproductive Technology, Reproductive Medicine Assocs. of N.J., Morristown, N.J. Ad hoc reviewer Fertility and Sterility, Jour. Clin. Endocrinology and Metabolism, Ob-Gyn., Am. Jour. Ob-Gyn., Contraception, Maturitas, Jour. Pediatric and Adolescent Gynecology, Internat. Jour. Infertility, Jour. In Vitro Fertilization and Embryo Transfer; contbr. articles to profl. jours. and abstracts. Lt Col USAF, 1993—95, Uniformed Services University of the Health Sciences. Grantee Surgeon Gen., Wyeth Rsch., Solvay Pharm. Rsch., Hitachi of Am., Tap Pharms. Fellow Am. Coll. Obstetricians and Gynecologists (chmns. award Armed Forces dist. meeting 1988, Searle award 1989, Prof. of Yr. 1991); mem. Am. Fertility Soc. (Best Poster award 1988), N.Am. Menopausal Soc., Soc. Air Force Clin. Surgeons, Endocrine Soc., Soc. Reproductive Endocrinologists, Phi Beta Kappa, Chi Beta Phi, Omicron Delta Kappa. Achievements include receiving several awards for research. Office: RMA of NJ 111 Madison Ave Ste 100 Morristown NJ 07960-6083 Home: 170 Post Kennel Rd Far Hills NJ 07931-2408

SCOTT, RIDLEY, film director; b. South Shields, Tyne and Wear, Eng., Nov. 30, 1937; m. Felicity Heywood, 1964 (div.); 2 children; m. Sandy Watson, 1979 (div. 1989); 1 child. BA, Royal Coll. Art; grad., London Internat. Film Sch. Dir.: (films) The Duellists, 1977, Alien, 1979, Legend, 1985, Black Rain, 1989; prodr.: The Browning Version, 1994, Clay Pigeons, 1998, Where the Money Is, 2000, Six Bullets from Now, 2002, All the Invisible Children, 2005, In Her Shoes, 2005; exec. prodr.: Monkey Trouble, 1994, The Hire: Hostage, 2002, The Hire: Beat the Devil, 2002, The Hire: Ticker, 2002; (films) Tristan & Isolde, 2006; dir.(and prodr.): Thelma & Louise, 1991, 1492: Conquest of Paradise, 1992, G.I. Jane, 1997, Black Hawk Down, 2001, Matchstick Men, 2003, Kingdom of Heaven, 2005; writer, dir., prodr. Boy on a Bicycle, 1965; dir.(and co-prodr.): Blade Runner, 1982, (and exec. prodr.): Someone to Watch Over Me, 1987, White Squall, 1996, Gladiator, 2000; dir., prodr., exec. music prodr. Hannibal, 2001; dir.: (TV series) Z Cars, 1962, Adam Adamant Lives, 1966, The Informer, 1966; exec. prodr.: The Hunger, 1997, AFP: American Fighter Pilot, 2002, Numb3rs, 2005—; (TV films) RKO 287, 1999, The Last Debate, 2000, The Gathering Storm, 2002 (Emmy award, 2002). Winner Design scholarship, N.Y.; named one of 50 Most Powerful People in Hollywood Premiere mag., 2004, 2005. Address: William Morris Agency One William Morris Pl Beverly Hills CA 90212

SCOTT, ROBERT ALLYN, academic administrator; b. Englewood, NJ, Apr. 16, 1939; s. William D. and Ann. F. (Waterman) S.; children: Ryan Keith, Kira Elizabeth. BA, Bucknell U., 1961; PhD, Cornell U., 1975; LLD, Ramapo Coll., 2000. Mgmt. trainee Procter & Gamble Co., Phila., 1961-63; asst. dir. admissions Bucknell U., Lewisburg, Pa., 1965-67; asst. dean Coll. Arts and Scis. Cornell U., Ithaca, 1967-69, assoc. dean, 1969-79, anthropology faculty, 1978-79; dir. acad. affairs Ind. Commn. for Higher Edn., Indpls., 1979-84, asst. commr., 1984-85; pres. Ramapo (N.J.) Coll., 1985-2000, Adelphi U., 2000—. Cons. Sta. WSKG Pub. TV and Radio, 1977-79, also to various colls. and univs., pubs., 1966—; mem. curriculum adv. com. Ind. Bd. Edn., 1984-87, Lilly Endowment Think Tank, 1984-86; mem. nat. adv. panel Ind. 21st Century Schooling Project, 1990-92; U.S. rep. to creation of U. Mobility Asian-Pacific, 1993—; U.S. rep. to meetings of Coun. European Rectors, 1991—; sr. advisor to U.S. State Dept. on Higher Edn. in Unesco European Region, 1997—; U.S. del. to UNESCO N.Am. and World Confs. on Higher Edn., 1998; sr. cons., chair N.J. Higher Edn. Restructuring Team, 1994. Author books and monographs; editl. bd. Cornell Rev., 1976-79; book rev. editor Coll. and Univ., 1974-78; cons.

editor Change mag., 1979-95, Jour. Higher Edn., 1985-98; exec. editor Saturday Evening Post book div. Curtis Pub. Co., 1982-85; contbr. articles to sociols., ednl. and popular publs. Trustee Bucknell U., 1976-78, First Unitarian Ch., Ithaca, 1970-73, 78-79, chmn., 1971-73, Unitarian Universalist Ch. of Indpls., 1980-85. With USNR, 1963-65. Spencer Found. rsch. grantee, 1977; recipient Sagamore of the Wabash award, 1986, Leader of Yr. award Prudential Found., 1987, Disting. Svc. award West Bergen Mental Health Ctr., 1991, Presdl. medal NYU, 1994, Sci. and Edn. award Boy Scouts Am., 1993, Raoul Wallenberg Humanitarian Leadership award, 2000, Disting. Svc. award ACIT, 2002, Disting. Svc. award Harbor Child Care, 2003, Excellence in Higher Edn. award Huntington Chamber, 2003, Telly award for Excellence in Cable TV Programming, 2003, 07, Cmty. Svc. award Garden City Chamber, 2004, Annual Svc. award Hispanic Counseling Ctr., 2004, Martin Luther King, Jr. Cmty. Svc. award, 2005, Outstanding Paper Excellence award Emerald Group Publishing, Ltd., 2003, 04, Suffolk Child Care Coun. honoree, 2006, David Excellence award Networking Mag., 2007. Fellow Am. Anthrop. Assn.; mem. Am. Sociol. Assn., Am. Assn. Higher Edn., Coun. on Liberal Arts and Scis. (chair 1990-93), Am. Coun. on Edn. Commn. On Internat. Edn. (chair 1991-93), L.I. Assn., Global Kids, Inc., Coun. Fgn. Rels., Regional Plan Assn., Nat. Fgn. Lang. Ctr., Brookings Instn. Study Group, Higher Edn. Colloquium (chmn. 1982-84, 96-98), N.J. Assn. of Coll. and Univs. (chair 1991-92), Bucknell U. Alumni Assn. (bd. dirs. 1971-80, pres. 1976-78, Outstanding Achievement 1991), Indian Trail Club, Century Assn., Phi Kappa Psi, Phi Kappa Phi. Office: Adelphi U Garden City NY 11530 Office Phone: 516-877-3838.

SCOTT, ROBERT CORTEZ, congressman, lawyer; b. Washington, Apr. 30, 1947; s. Charles Waldo and Mae (Hamlin) Scott. BA, Harvard U., Cambridge, Mass., 1969; JD, Boston Coll. Sch. Law, 1973; LLD (hon.), Commonwealth Coll., Hampton, Va., 1988. Lawyer pvt. practice, Newport News, 1973—91; mem. Va. State Ho. Dels., Richmond, 1978—83, Va. State Senate, Richmond, 1983—93, US Congress from 3rd Va. dist., 1993—, mem. edn. and the workforce com., mem. judiciary com., ranking minority mem. crime, terrorism and homeland security subcommittee. Br. pres. NAACP, Newport News, 1974-80; pres. bd. Peninsula Legal Aid Ctr., Hampton, 1977-81; mem. state exec. bd. March of Dimes, Va., 1987—; chmn. 1st dist. Dem. Party Va., 1980-85; bd. dirs. Hampton Roads March of Dimes; adv. com. Peninsula Boy Scouts Am. Served in USAR, 1970—74, served in Mass. N.G., 1974—76. Recipient Brotherhood Citation award Nat. Conf. Christians & Jews, 1985, Child Adv. award Va. Acad. Pediat., 1987, Disting. Svc. award Va. State Fraternal Order Police, 1987, Outstanding Legislator award So. Health Assn., 1989; named one of 100 Most Influential Black Americans, Ebony mag., 2006. Mem. Peninsula C. of C., Alpha Phi Alpha, Sigma Pi Phi. Democrat. Episcopalian. Office: US Ho Reps 1201 Longworth Ho Office Bldg Washington DC 20515 Office Phone: 202-225-8351. *

SCOTT, ROBERT GENE, lawyer; b. Montague, Mass., Aug. 29, 1951; s. Edwin Ray and Barbara Agnes (Painchaud) Scott; m. Laura Beth Williams, May 27, 1978; children: Jason Robert, Amanda Marie, Leah Beth. BS, U. Notre Dame, 1973, MS, 1975, JD, 1980; postgrad., U. Tex., 1975—76. Bar: Ind. 1980, U.S. Dist. Ct. (no. dist.) Ind. 1980, U.S. Patent Office 1980, Mo. 1981, U.S. Dist. Ct. (we. dist.) Mo. 1981, U.S. Ct. Appeals (11th cir.) 1986, U.S. Ct. Appeals (8th cir.) 1987, U.S. Ct. Appeals (10th cir.) 1987, Kans. 1989, U.S. Dist. Ct. Kans. 1989, U.S. Supreme Ct. 1999. Asst. women's basketball coach U. Notre Dame, Ind., 1977-80; assoc. atty. Oltsch, Knoblock & Hall, South Bend, Ind., 1980-81; atty. Swanson, Midgley et al, Kansas City, Mo., 1981-82; exec. adminstr. Coun. of Fleet Specialists, Shawnee Mission, Kans., 1982-83; atty. Levy and Craig, Kansas City, Mo., 1983-89, Turner, Vader & Koch, Chartered, 1989-93; pvt. practice, 1993-95, 98; atty. Neill, Scott, Terrill & Embree, LLC, Lenexa, Kans., 1996-98; pvt. practice, 1998—. Precinct committeeman Johnson County Rep. Party, Kans., 1983—84. Mem. ABA, Ind. Bar Assn., Mo. Bar Assn., Kansas City Bar Assn., Kans. Bar Assn., Johnson County Bar Assn., Nat. Assn. Security Dealers (panel arbitrators, complex litig. panel), Nat. Arbitration Forum (panel of arbitrators), Notre Dame Club of Kansas City (pres. 1985-86), S.W. United Soccer Club of Kans. (pres. 1994-96), Heartland Soccer Assn. (v.p. 1997-2003). Independent. Roman Catholic. Office: 303 E Poplar Olathe KS 66061 Home Phone: 913-888-6103; Office Phone: 913-390-6776. Business E-Mail: bob@rscottlaw.com.

SCOTT, ROBERT HAYWOOD, JR., lawyer; b. Hazelton, Pa., Mar. 1941; s. Robert Haywood and Marjorie Jane Scott; m. Sandra Lou Carroll, June 6, 1966; children: Paige Carroll, Robert Haywood. AB magna cum laude, Kenyon Coll., 1963; JD with distinction, Duke U., 1966. Bar: Mo. 1969, Kans. 1966, Ohio 1972. Assoc. Hoskins King Springer McGannon and Hahn, Kansas City, Mo., 1970-72; operating v.p., sr. counsel Federated Dept. Stores, Cin., 1972-83; ptnr. Roberts Fleischaker & Scott, Joplin, Mo., 1983-88; chief exec. officer W&S Mfg., Inc., Joplin, 1988-92, also chmn. bd. dirs.; CEO Robert Scott Investment Banking, 1988—. Chmn. Deep Sea Archaeology Rsch. Coun., 1994—. Contbr. articles to profl. jours. Capt. USAF, 1966—70. Mem. Mo. Bar Assn., Order of the Coif, Phi Beta Kappa. Home: 1330 Valle Dr Joplin MO 64801-1074

SCOTT, ROBERT LANE, chemist, educator; b. Santa Rosa, Calif., Mar. 20, 1922; s. Horace Albert and Maurine (Lane) S.; m. Elizabeth Sewall Hunter, May 27, 1944; children: Joanna Ingersoll (dec.), Jonathan Armat, David St. Clair, Janet Hamilton. S.B., Harvard U., 1942; MA, Princeton U., 1944, PhD, 1945. Sci. staff Los Alamos Lab., 1945-46; Frank B. Jewett fellow U. Calif., Berkeley, 1946-48; faculty UCLA, 1948—, prof. chemistry, 1960-92, prof. emeritus, 1993—, chmn. dept., 1970-75. Author: (with J.H. Hildebrand) Solubility of Nonelectrolytes, 3d edit, 1950, rev., 1964, Regular Solutions, 1962, Regular and Related Solutions, 1970; Contbr. articles to profl. jours. Guggenheim fellow, 1955; NSF sr. fellow, 1961-62; Fulbright lectr., 1968-69 Fellow AAAS, Am. Phys. Soc.; mem. Am. Chem. Soc. (Joel Henry Hildebrand award 1984), Royal Soc. Chemistry (London), Sigma Xi. Home: 11128 Montana Ave Los Angeles CA 90049-3509 Business E-Mail: scott@chem.ucla.edu.

SCOTT, ROSA MAE, art educator, artist; b. East Hampton, NY, Apr. 12, 1937; d. James Alexander and Victoria (Square) Nicholson; m. Frank Albert Hanna, Apr. 1, 1957 (div. Mar. 1985); 1 child, Frank Albert Hanna III; m. Warner Bruce Scott, Aug. 3, 1985 (dec. Oct. 2002); children: Bernadine, John, Patricia, Charlene, Lawrence. AA, Dabney Lancaster, 1989; BA, Mary Baldwin, 1992. Cosmetologist Rosa's Beauty Shop, East Hampton, 1962-68; sec. Frank Hanna's Cleaning Co., East Hampton, 1962-77; cashier, clk. Brook's Pharmacy, East Hampton, 1992; lead tchr. East Hampton Day Care, 1992-94, 97-98; substitute tchr. Lexington (Va.) Schs., 1994—; lead tchr. Suffolk C.C. Child Care Ctr., River Head, N.Y., 1999; substitute tchr. East Hampton Sch., 2000—03; lead tchr. after sch. program Springs Sch., 2000—02, 2004—05, substitute tchr., 2000—03. Substitute tchr. East Hampton Sch., 1996-97, 2000-04; sec. Lylburn Downing Cmty. Ctr., Inc., Lexington, 1985-92; arts and crafts tutor, supr. East Hampton Town Youth After Sch. Program, 1996—. Pres. Rockbridge Garden Club, Lexington, 1996; co-organizer Va. Co-op. Ex. Garden Clubs, Lexington, 1995; bd. dirs. Rockbridge Area Pres. Homes, 1996, Fine Arts of Rockbridge, 1985-92, Friends of Lime Kiln, Lexington, 1985-92. Mem.: Guild Hall, East End Arts, Montauk Artists Assn. (receptionist 2003—05), Artist Alliance East Hampton, L.I. Black Artists (v.p. 2000—05), Rockbridge Arts Guild (pres. LI Black Artists 2006—). Avocations: collecting emmett kelly clowns, art, reading, theater, tennis. Home: PO Box 1265 East Hampton NY 11937-0708 Personal E-mail: rosahannascott@aol.com.

SCOTT, SAMUEL C., food products executive; B in Engring., Fairleigh Dickinson U., 1966, MBA. V.p. CPC Internat. Inc., 1991; pres. N. Am. corn refining Bestfoods, 1989—97, pres. worldwide corn refining, 1995-97; pres., COO Corn Products Internat., Westchester, Ill., 1997—2001, chmn., pres., CEO, 2001—. Bd. dir. Motorola Inc. Dir. ACCION USA; trustee Chgo. Symphony. Office: Corn Products International 5 Westbrook Corporate Ctr Westchester IL 60154 *

SCOTT, SHERIE RENÉ, actress; m. Kurt Deutsch. Grad., Neighborhood Playhouse Sch. of Theatre. Actress (Broadway plays) The Who's Tommy, 1993, Grease, 1994, Rent, 1996, Aida, 2000, Dirty Rotten Scoundrels, 2005, 2006, (off-Broadway plays) The Last Five Years (Drama League award), Debbie Does Dallas, Landscape of the Body, 2005 (OBIE award, Village Voice, 2006, Lucille Lortel award outstanding featured actress, 2007), (regional plays) Over and Over, Faust, (films) Marci X, (TV films) Vault of Love, My Guys; singer: (albums) Men I've Had. *

SCOTT, SHIRLEY CLAY, dean; PhD, Kent State U., 1973. Dean Grad. Coll. Western Mich. U.; dean Coll. Liberal Arts Southern Ill. U., 1999—, prof. Office: Office of the Dean Coll Liberal Arts So Illinios U Mailcode 4522 Carbondale IL 62901 Office Phone: 618-453-2466. E-mail: scotts@siu.edu.

SCOTT, SIDNEY BUFORD, finance company executive; b. Richmond, Va., Mar. 3, 1933; s. Buford and Mary (Nixon) S.; m. Susan Elder Bailey, Sept. 19, 1959; children: Sidney Buford Jr., Elizabeth Scott Cech, George Reily Bailey. Student, Yale U., 1951-53; BA, U. Va., 1955; LLD (hon.), St. Paul's Coll., 1982. Chmn. Scott & Stringfellow Inc., Richmond, 1974—. Bd. dirs. New Market Corp.; mem. regional firms adv. com. N.Y. Stock Exch., 1982-85; chmn. bd. trustees Securities Industry Found. for Econ. Edn., 1976-86; trustee Va. Retirement Sys., 1984-94; dir. Nat. Coun. Econ. Edn. Bd. dirs. Hollywood Cemetery, Police Benevolent Assn.; trustee, chmn. Elk Hill Farm, Inc.; bd. visitors U. Va., 1987-94; former vice rector, bd. visitors Va. Commonwealth U.; past chmn. United Way Greater Richmond; vestryman, past sr. warden St. Paul's Episcopal Ch.; past pres. Sheltering Arms Hosp; past bd. dirs., v.p. Big Bros. Am.; chmn. Va. Capitol Found.; past bd. dirs., chmn. Big Bros. Richmond, Met. Found., also others. Sgt. U.S. Army, 1956-58. Recipient Outstanding Young Man of Yr. award Richmond Jr. C. of C., 1964, outstanding svc. award Va. Coun. on Econ. Edn., 1976, 80, Brotherhood award NCCJ, 1981, George P. Baker medal Joint Coun. on Econ. Edn., 1986, Bd. Mem. of Yr. award Va. Assn. Children's Homes, 1987. Mem. Securities Industry Assn. (governing coun. 1976-78), Raven Soc., Beta Gamma Sigma. Democrat. Home: 4919 Lockgreen Cir Richmond VA 23226-1748 Office: PO Box 1575 Richmond VA 23218-1575

SCOTT, STANLEY DEFOREST, real estate company executive; b. Hudson County, NJ, Nov. 2, 1926; s. Stanley DeForest and Anne Marie (Volk) Scott; m. Mary Elizabeth Forbes Hazard, Dec. 30, 1953. BA, U. So. Calif., LA, 1950. Gen. mgr. Alfred Scott Pubs., NYC, 1951-56; chmn., pres. S.D. Scott Printing Co., Inc., NYC, 1956-92; gen. ptnr. 145 Hudson St. Assocs. Co-chmn. mus. and art com. Fraunces Tavern Mus., 1973—87, 1998—2007; assoc. J. Carter Brown Libr.; former mem. Mayor's Industry Adv. Com.; former bd. dirs. Bus. Relocation Com. With USNR, 1944—46. Fellow, Frick Collection. Mem.: Friends of Canterbury Cathedral in US, Am. Assocs. Royal Acad. Arts (patron), Am.-Scottish Found., World Monuments Fund (internat. coun.), N.Y. Hist. Soc., Morgan Libr. (patron), Met. Mus. Art, Sir John Soane's Mus. Found. (patron), Am. Friends English Heritage, English-Speaking Union NY (patron), Royal Oak Found., Am. Friends Brit. Mus. (patron), Am. Friends Hermitage Mus., Mus. Modern Art, Am. Mus. Britain (coun. 1986—), Mt. Vernon Ladies Assn. (adv. com.), Am. Trust for the Brit. Libr., NY Philharmonic (patron), Sons of the Revolution (bd. mgrs.), Am. Numismatic Soc. (trustee), Carnegie Hall Soc. (patron), Church Club N.Y., Union Club, Knickerbocker Club, Grolier Club, St. George's Soc., Pilgrims US, Soc. Colonial Wars (mem. coun.), Soc. Mayflower Descs. Republican. Episcopalian. Home: One Sutton Pl South New York NY 10022-2471 Office: 145 Hudson St New York NY 10013-2103

SCOTT, STEPHANIE D., city official; b. 1966; 2 children. Ph.D in Environ. Psychology, CUNY. Researcher Urban Inst., 1998—2003; chief of staff to Councilman Adrian Fenty DC City Coun., 2003—04; chief of staff Adrian Fenty's Re-Election Campaign, 2004; sec. dist. DC Govt., Washington, 2007—. Office: Office Dist Sec John A Wilson Bldg 1350 Pennsylvania Ave Ste 419 Washington DC 20004 E-mail: stephanie.scott@dc.gov. *

SCOTT, STEPHEN BRINSLEY, theater producer; b. Pitts., Aug. 27, 1950; s. Robert Crawford and Lucille (Henrickson) Scott. BS in Edn., U. Kans., 1972; MA, U. Denver, 1973. Artistic dir. Creede (Colo.) Repertory Theatre, 1976-78; chair dept. theatre Baker U., Baldwin, Kans., 1978-80; dir. edn. and cmty. svcs. Goodman Theatre, Chgo., 1980-84, dir. arts in edn., 1986-88, artistic assoc., 1988-94, assoc. producer, 1994—; dir. ednl. programs Chgo. Internat. Theatre Festival, 1985-86. Spl. instr. Loyola U. Chgo., 1987-95; instr. Columbia Coll., Chgo., 1981-85, 92-97, Latin Sch. Chgo., 1984-86, Roosevelt U., 1997—; mem. arts in edn. panel Nat. Endowment for Arts, Washington, 1990-91. Mem. adv. panels Ill. Arts Coun., Chgo., 1984-87; mem. com. League Chgo. Theatres, 1990—; cmty. rep. local sch. coun. Franklin Sch., Chgo., 1990-94. pres. Chgo. Coalition for Arts in Edn., 1983-85. Named Outstanding Lectr., Chgo. Cultural Ctr., 1981, 84, Outstanding Dir., Joseph Jefferson Citation Nominations, 1987, 97, 2005-07, award for outstanding ensemble Joseph Jefferson Award Com., 1999, After Dark award for outstanding dir., 2001. Mem. Ill. Theatre Assn. (exec. com. 1987-97), Soc. Stage Dirs. and Choreographers Ill. Alliance for Arts in Edn., Ill. Arts Alliance, Phi Beta Kappa. Democrat. Home: 124 W Polk St Apt 207 Chicago IL 60605-1766 Office: Goodman Theatre 170 N Dearborn St Chicago IL 60601 Office Phone: 312-443-8478. Business E-Mail: stevescott@goodman-theatre.org.

SCOTT, STEPHEN CARLOS, academic administrator; b. Greenville, SC, Sept. 20, 1949; s. Carlos O'Dell and Christina (Nikitas) S.; m. Patsy Jordan, Apr. 13, 1968; children: Stephanie Christina, Lance Stephen. BA, Clemson U., SC, 1971, MEd, 1975, EdD, 1987. Owner, mgr. Scotty's Inc., restaurant, Clemson, 1967-71; tchr. math. Pickens (S.C.) Sr. High Sch., 1972-74; instr. bus. Tri-County Tech. Coll., Pendleton, SC, 1974-76, head dept., 1976-78, dir. br. campus Easley, SC, 1978-80; dean bus. Greenville Tech. Coll., 1980-85, assoc. v.p., 1985-88; pres. Southeastern C.C., Whiteville, NC, 1988-99; exec. v.p. N.C. C.C. Sys., 1999—2002; pres. Lenoir C.C., Kinston, NC, 2002—. Cons. P.C.E. Fed. Credit Union, Liberty, S.C., 1975-88, Jacobs Mfg. Co., Clemson, 1979-80, Flat Rock Shelter Ctr., Easley, 1980-85; bd. mem. N.C. Rural Ctr. Contbr. articles to profl. jours. and mags. Pres. So. Shelter Ctr., Greenville, 1986—88, Good Shepherd Found., Whiteville, 1990—92; bd. dirs. Good Shepherd, 1988—91; chmn. Columbus County Sch. Bond. Dr., 1989, Am. Heart Fund Drive Columbus County, 1992; co-chmn. Columbus County Long Range Planning Com., 1989—91; vice chmn. Pvt. Industry Coun. Region O, 1992—99; funding dir. Habitat for Humanity Columbus County, 1992; pres. bd. dirs. Columbus County Rural Health Ctr., 1994; bd. dirs. N.C. Rural Ctr., 2000—02. Recipient award for patriotism U.S. Savs. Bonds Program, 1987. Mem. Am. Assn. Cmty. and Jrs. Colls. (Pres.'s Acad.), Greater Kinston C. of C. (exec. bd. 2003—), Rotary (bd. dirs. Whiteville 1990-92, pres. 1992-93). Presbyterian. Avocations: running, chess, coin collecting/numismatics, reading. Home: 1417 Wynncrest Ct Raleigh NC 27603-8770 E-mail: scs320@lenoircc.edu.

SCOTT, STUART, sports anchor; b. Chgo., July 19, 1965; married; 1 child. BA in Speech Comms. and Radio/TV/Film, U. N.C., 1987. News reporter, weekend anchor WPDE-TV, Florence, S.C., 1987-88; news reporter WRAL-TV, Raleigh, N.C., 1988-90; sports reporter, sports anchor WESH-TV, Orlando, Fla., 1990-93; sports anchor, sports reporter ESPN, Bristol, Conn., 1993—, co-host NFL Primetime, 1997—, former anchor SportSmash, 1993. Anchor reporter SportsNight: College Football Edition, 1995—, co-host SportsNight, 1994. Office: ESPN ESPN Plaza Bristol CT 06010

SCOTT, SUSAN CRAIG, plastic surgeon; b. NYC, 1948; m. Norman Scott; children: Eric, William, Kelly. MD, Columbia U., 1974. Diplomate Am. Bd. Plastic Surgery with subspecialty in hand surgery. Intern Roosevelt Hosp., NYC, 1974—75, resident in gen. surgery, 1975—79; resident in plastic surgery NYU Med. Ctr., 1979—81; fellow in hand surgery Roosevelt Hosp., 1981—82; pvt. practice plastic surgery NYC, 1987—. Cons. team physician NY Liberty. Achievements include assisting in the wrist surgery of Patrick Ewing in 1997; has performed surgery on Allan Houston, Latrell Sprewell, John Starks, Charles Oakley and Herb Williams. Office: 150 E 77TH St New York NY 10021-1922 Office Phone: 212-288-9922. Personal E-mail: smcscott@verizon.net. *

SCOTT, T. GORDON, chemistry and math educator, writer; b. Laconia, NH, Nov. 27, 1941; s. William Stafford and Jeanne Richardson Scott; m. Elizabeth Mary Winterberg, Mar. 11, 1995. BA, U. Pa., 1963; BA with honours, Cambridge U., England, 1965, MA, 1970; PhD, U. Ill., 1969. Profl. tchg. cert., Pa.; postgrad. tchg. lic., Va. Tchg. asst. U. Ill., Champaign-Urbana, 1965-66; asst. prof. chemistry Oberlin Coll., Ohio, 1969-70; lectr. biochemistry U. Calif., Santa Barbara, 1971; cons. Sci-Math Cons., Uniontown, Pa., 1972-75; supr. secondary studies Westminster Acad., Carmichaels, Pa., 1975-79; asst. prof. chemistry Alderson-Broaddus Coll., Philippi, W.Va., 1981-84; assoc. prof. chemistry Bryan Coll., Dayton, Tenn., 1984-86, Knoxville Coll., Tenn., 1987-89, Union Coll., Barbourville, Ky., 1989-91, Jarvis Christian Coll., Hawkins, Tex., 1992-98; with Chem. Edn. Cons. USA, Hawkins, Tex., 1998-2000; instr. math. Winona Ind. Sch. Dist., Tex., 1998-99; instr. math, chemistry and astronomy Pittsylvania County Schs., Va.; tchr. Dan River HS, Ringgold, Va., 2000—02; adj. prof. chemistry and natural sci.-biochemistry Danville CC, Va., 1999—2004; adj. instr. pharmacology Nat. Coll., Danville, 2001—03; assoc. prof. chemistry Winston-Salem State U., NC, 2004—. Rsch. assoc. DuPont Chem. Co., Inc., Phila., 1963, EPA, Phila., 1988, Edgewood-Aberdeen Rsch. US Army, Aberdeen Proving Ground, Md., 1993; vis. prof. La. Coll., Pineville, 1992; adj. sci. instr. Hargrave Mil. Acad., Chatham, Va., 2003; undergrad. rsch. mentor NSF, New Orleans, 2004; cons. with Transition State Assocs., Danville, Va. Author: (with others) Synthetic Procedures in Nucleic Acid Chemistry, 1968, Spectroscopic Model Studies of NAD, 1969; contbr. articles to Jour. Am. Chem., Soc., 1967, 1970, 1972, 2003. Musician with Danville Recorder Consort, Danville Area Choral Arts Soc. Thouron fellow to Cambridge U., 1963-65; Thouron scholar Gonville & Caius Coll., Cambridge U.; grantee NSF, 1996-97, Army Rsch. Orgn., 1993-95, Robert A. Welch Found., 1996-98, NSF, 1997-99. Mem. Am. Chem. Soc., Cambridge U. Chem. Soc., Am. Sci. Affiliation (dir. 1998), Rotary Internat. (chmn. internat. edn. com. 1977-81). Achievements include determined the fluorescent lifetime of coenzyme NADH. Avocations: baritone vocal solos, exploring ideas, renaissance music (treble and tenor blockflute), astronomy. Office Phone: 336-750-3179. Business E-Mail: scottg@wssu.edu.

SCOTT, TERRY LEE, communications executive; b. Rockford, Ill., Oct. 21, 1950; s. Wilson C. and Marie G. (Bunger) S.; divorced; children: Andrea, Brady, Tiffany. BS in Acctg. magna cum laude, Bradley U., 1972. CPA Ill., Tex. Audit prin. Arthur Young and Co., Dallas, 1972-82; v.p. fin. and adminstrn., treas. Paging Network Inc., Dallas, 1982-90; sr. v.p. Paging Network, Inc., Dallas, 1990-92, pres., CEO, bd. dirs., 1993-95, Terion Inc., Melbourne, Fla., 1995-97, chmn., CEO, 1997-99, Terry Scott Enterprises, Plano, Tex., 1997—; dir. Chameleon Tech., Inc., Seattle, 2000—03, Metasolv Software, Inc., Dallas, 2003—06; CFO, v.p. Fin. of Chase Med., Inc., 2003—04; pres., CEO, dir. Airimba Wireless, Inc., Plano, Tex., 2004—06. Mem. AICPA, Tex. Soc. CPAs, Phi Kappa Phi, Zeta Pi. Methodist. Home: 5816 Gallant Fox Ln Plano TX 75093-2910 Home Phone: 214-713-7614. Personal E-mail: tscott1704@aol.com.

SCOTT, THEODORE R., retired lawyer; b. Mount Vernon, Ill., Dec. 7, 1924; s. Theodore R. and Beulah (Flannigan) S.; children: Anne Laurence, Sarah Buckland, Daniel, Barbara Gomon. AB, U. Ill., 1947, JD, 1949. Bar: Ill. 1950. Law clk. to judge U.S. Ct. Appeals, 1949-51; pvt. practice Chgo., 1950—2000; assoc. Spaulding Glass, 1951-53, Loftus, Lucas & Hammand, 1953-58, Ooms, McDougall, Williams & Hersh, 1958-60; ptnr. McDougall, Hersh & Scott, Chgo., 1960-87; of counsel Jones, Day, Reavis & Pogue, 1987-97, Rockey, Milnamow & Katz, 1998—2000. 2nd lt. USAAF, 1943-45. Decorated Air medal. Fellow Am. Coll. Trial Lawyers; mem. ABA, Ill. Bar Assn., Chgo. Bar Assn., 7th Cir. Bar Assn. (past pres.), Legal Club Chgo., Law Club Chgo., Patent Law Assn. Chgo. (past pres.), Union League Club, Exmoor Country Club (Highland Park, Ill.), Phi Beta Kappa. Home: 1569 Woodvale Ave Deerfield IL 60015-2350

SCOTT, THOMAS JEFFERSON, JR., lawyer, electrical engineer; b. Montgomery, Ala., Dec. 30, 1943; s. Thomas Jefferson Sr. and Irene (Feagin) S.; m. Betsy Sue Mackta, Apr. 25, 1981; children: Elspeth Watts, Marghuerita Taylor, Thomas Jefferson III. BEE, Yale U., 1966, BA in Econs., 1967; JD, Vanderbilt U., 1974. Bar: Va. 1974, D.C. 1975, N.Y. 1980, U.S. Dist. Ct. D.C. 1986, U.S. Dist. Ct. (ea. dist.) Va. 1993, U.S. Tax Ct. 1981, U.S. Ct. Fed. Claims, 1982, U.S. Ct. Appeals (fed. cir.) 1982, U.S. Ct. Appeals (4th cir.) 1993, U.S. Supreme Ct. 1984. Trial atty. civil div. U.S. Dept. of Justice, Washington, 1974-78; assoc. Cooper & Dunham, NYC, 1978-80, sr. trial counsel civil div., 1980-85; ptnr. Pennie & Edmonds, Washington, 1985—90, Howrey & Simon, Washington, 1990—97, Hunton & Williams, Washington, 1997—2007, Goodwin Procter LLP, Washington, 2007—. Capt. USNR, 1966-71. Decorated D.F.C. Mem. ABA, Am. Intellectual Property Law Assn. Office: Goodwin Procter LLP 901 New York Ave NW Washington DC 20001 Office Phone: 202-346-3442. Business E-Mail: tscott@goodwinprocter.com.

SCOTT, TOM, broadcast executive; BA in Am. Civilization, Brown U. Co-founder, partner Nantucket Nectars, 1989—; founder, chmn. CEO Plum TV, 2002—. Bd. of dir. Do Something, The Shackleton Schools, Nantucket Film Festival. Named one of Inc.'s 500, Inc. Mag; recipient Mercury Award for Advt., Entrepreneur of the Year, Ernst and Young's. Office: Plum TV 419 Lafayette St 7th Fl New York NY 10003 Office Phone: 646-292-4200. Office Fax: 646-292-4201.

SCOTT, TONY, film director; b. Stockton-on-Tees, England, June 21, 1944; m. Donna Wilson; m. Glynis Sanders (div.); m. Donna W. Scott, Nov. 24, 1994; 2 children. Degree in Fine Arts, Sunderland Art School; postgrad., Leeds Coll. Art, 1969; MFA, Royal Coll. Arts, 1972. Film dir. Totem Prodn., LA, 1972—; ptnr. (with Ridley Scott) Scott Free Prodns. Dir. films including One of the Mission (half-hour film, Brit. Film Inst.), Loving Memory (1-hour feature), The Hunger, 1983, Top Gun, 1986, Beverly Hills Cop II, 1987, Revenge, 1990, Days of Thunder, 1990, The Last Boy Scout, 1991, True Romance, 1993, Crimson Tide, 1995, The Fan, 1996, Enemy of the State, 1998, Spy Game, 2001, Agent Orange, 2004, Deja Vu, 2006; dir., exec. prodr.: The Hire: Beat the Devil (short film), 2002, dir., prodr. Man on Fire, 2004, Domino, 2005; exec. prodr.: Clay Pigeons, 1998, Where the Money Is, 2000, Big Time, 2001, The Hire: Hostage, 2002, The Hire: Ticker, 2002, Six Bullets From Now, 2002, In Her Shoes, 2005, Tristan & Isolde, 2006; exec. prodr. (TV movies) RKO

281, 1999, The Last Debate, 2000, The Gathering Storm, 2002, Orpheus, 2006; dir. (TV series episode) The Hunger, 1997; exec. prodr (TV series)The Hunger, 1997-2000, Numb3rs, 2005-. Recipient numerous Clios, Gold and Silver Lions and various other awards. Avocation: mountain climbing. Office: Totem Prodns 8009 Santa Monica Blvd Los Angeles CA 90046-5008 also: Creative Artists Agy 9830 Wilshire Blvd Beverly Hills CA 90212-1804 *

SCOTT, VICKI SUE, school system administrator; b. Pine Bluff, Ark., Feb. 16, 1946; d. John Wesley and Ruby Gray (Whitehead) and Hannah (Lewis) S. BA, Hendrix Coll., 1968; MS in Edn., U. Cen. Ark., 1978, postgrad., 1979-84, U. Ark., 1983-85, Ark. State U., 1993-94. Cert. adminstrn., secondary sch. prin., middle sch., secondary health and phys. edn. Tchr., coach Brinkley (Ark.) Pub. Schs., 1968-76, Lonoke (Ark.) Jr. and Sr. High Schs., 1976-77, S.E. Jr. High Sch., Pine Bluff, 1978-92, asst. prin., 1992-2000, dir. summer sch., 1991, 92; prin. White Hall (Ark.) Jr. H.S., White Hall, Arkansas, 2000—. AIDS educator Arkansas River Edn. Svc. Coop., Pine Bluff, 1989-92. Active Leadership Pine Bluff, 1993-94. Scholar Assn. Women Ednl. Suprs., 1985; named Outstanding Young Women of Am., 1974, Ark. Leadership Acad., 2000. Mem.: DAR, ASCD, Nat. Mid. Sch. Assn., Nat. Assn. Sch. Secondary Prins., Ark. Activities Assn., Ark. Assn. Ednl. Adminstrs., Ark. Assn. Mid. Level Adminstrs. (bd. dirs. 2002—04), Order Ea. Star, Phi Delta Kappa, Delta Kappa Gamma (Epsilon chpt. pres., scholar 1994). Baptist. Avocations: tennis, reading, hiking, travel, golf. Home: 3215 S Cherry St Pine Bluff AR 71603-5983 Office: White Hall Jr HS 8106 Dollarway Rd White Hall AR 71602-6999 Office Phone: 870-247-2711. Personal E-mail: foghorn@cablelynx.com. Business E-Mail: scottv@whjr.arsc.k12.ar.us.

SCOTT, WALTER, JR., telecommunications industry executive; b. May 21, 1931; m. Suzanne Scott. BS, Colo. State U., 1953; LittD, U. Nebr., 1983; LHD, Coll. St. Mary, 1988; D of Commerce, Bellevue U., 1996. With Peter Kiewit Sons, Inc., Omaha, 1953—, engr., project engr., dist. engr., Cleve. dist., 1959—61, asst. dist. mgr., Cleve. dist., 1961—62, dist. mgr. Cleve. dist. Omaha, 1962-64, v.p., 1964, exec. v.p., 1965-79, chmn. bd., 1964, pres., 1979, chmn. bd. dirs., pres., CEO, 1979-97, chmn. emeritus, 1997—; chmn. Level 3 Communications Inc. (former subs. PKS), Broomfield, Colo., 1997—. Bd. trustee Open World Leadership Ctr.; dir. Berkshire Hathaway, Burlington Resources, Commonwealth Telephone Enterprises, MidAmerican Energy Holdings, RCN Corp., Valmont Industries. Served with USAF, 1954-56. Named Philanthropist of Yr., Nat. Soc. Fund-Raising Execs., 1987, Man of Yr., Mid-Am. Coun. Boy Scouts Am., 1988, King Ak-Sar-Ben XCII, Knights of Ak-Sar-Ben, 1988, Disting. Eagle Scout, Boy Scouts Am., 1991, Citizen of Yr., United Way of the Midlands, 1993, Air Force Assn., 1993, Person of Yr., Pmaha Club, 1996; named one of Forbes Richest Americans, 2006; named to Nebr. Bus. Hall Fame, Nebr. C. of C. and Industry, 1995, Omaha Bus. Hall Fame, Greater Omaha C. of C., 1995; recipient Nebr. Builder award, U. Nebr., 1983, Outstanding Achievement in Construction award, The Moles, 1986, Brotherhood award, Nat. Conf. Christians and Jews, 1986, Horatio Alger award, Horatio Alger Assn., 1997, Spirit Youth award, Uta Halee Girls Village, 1988, Perry W. Branch Disting. Svc. award, U. Nebr. Found., 1989, Golden Beaver for Mgmt., The Beavers, 1990, Order of Tower, U. Nebr., Omaha, 1991, Golden Plate award, Am. Acad. Achievement, 1991, Golden Apple award, Met. Cmty. Coll. Found., 1993, Headliner award, Greater Omaha C. of C., 1996, Nebraskalander award, Nebraskaland Found., 1998, Manresa award, Creighton U., 1998, Cmty. Builder award, Greater Omaha C. of C., 1999, Bus. Vol. of Yr., Nat. Alliance Bus., 1999, Midlander of Yr., Omaha World-Herald, 2000. Mem.: Chi Epsilon Soc. (hon.). Office: Peter Kiewit Sons Inc 1000 Kiewit Plz Omaha NE 68131-3302 also: Joslyn Art Mus 2200 Dodge St Omaha NE 68102-1208 Office: Level 3 Communications Inc 1025 Eldorado Blvd Broomfield CO 80021 *

SCOTT, WALTER, JR., business consultant; b. Balt., July 24, 1925; s. Walter and Margaret Catherine (Pfeiffer) S.; m. Barbara Main, July 6, 1946 (dec. 1964); children: Stephen Walter, Susan Marjorie, Cynthia Margaret, Christopher Main; m. Mary Joan Braun, Aug. 5, 1966 (dec. 1986); m. Helene Lyda Burke, May 1, 1987. AB, Duke U., 1945; MBA with distinction, Harvard U., 1949. Advtg. mgr. The Quaker Oats Co., Chgo., 1950-57; v.p. mktg. J.H. Filbert, Inc., Balt., 1957-67, pres., 1968-77; div. gen. mgr. Cen. Soya Co., Ft. Wayne, Ind., 1972-77; exec. v.p. Fairmont Foods Co., Des Plaines, Ill., 1978-81; pres. McKeon, Scott, Woolf & Assocs., Palo Alto, Calif., 1982-84; chmn. bd. Integral Cons. Group, Mill Valley, Calif., 1986-87, Scott, Woolf & Assocs., Palo Alto, 1984—2001, Mulford Moreland & Assocs., San Jose, Calif., 1986-89. Chmn., speaker pres. courses, Am. Mgmt. Assn., N.Y.C., 1970-90; trustee Calif. Inst. Integral Studies, San Francisco, 1983-89; bd. dirs. West Marine, Inc., Watsonville, Calif., 1995-2001. With USNR, 1943-46, PTO. Mem. Phi Beta Kappa. Home and Office: 1450 Redford Dr Palm Springs CA 92264 Home Phone: 760-416-1451; Office Phone: 760-416-0851.

SCOTT, WALTER DILL, management educator; b. Chgo., Oct. 27, 1931; s. John Marcy and Mary Louise (Gent) S.; m. Barbara Ann Stein, Sept. 9, 1961; children: Timothy Walter, David Frederick, Gordon Charles. Student, Williams Coll., Williamstown, Mass., 1949-51; BS, Northwestern U., Evanston, Ill., 1953; MS, Columbia U., NYC, 1958. Cons. Booz, Allen & Hamilton, NYC, 1956—58; assoc. Glore, Forgan & Co., NYC, 1958—63, ptnr. Chgo., 1963-65; pntr. Lehman Bros, Chgo., 1965-72, sr. ptnr., 1972-73, also bd. dirs.; assoc. dir. econs. and govt. Office Mgmt. and Budget, Washington, 1973-75; sr. v.p. internat. and fin. Pillsbury Co., Mpls., 1975-78, exec. v.p., 1978-80, also bd. dirs.; pres., CEO, Investors Diversified Svcs., Inc., Mpls., 1980-84; group mng. dir. Grand Met. PLC, Mpls., 1984-86, also bd. dirs.; chmn. Grand Met USA, Mpls., 1984-86; prof., sr. Austin fellow Kellogg Sch. Mgmt., Northwestern U., Evanston, Ill., 1988—. Bd. dirs. Intermatic, Inc. Mem. adv. bd. dirs. Chgo. Cmtys. in Schs.; bd. dirs. Ctr. Exec. Women. Lt. (j.g.) USN, 1953—56. Home: 55 Meadowview Dr Northfield IL 60093-3547 Office: Northwestern U Kellogg Sch Mgmt 2001 Sheridan Rd Evanston IL 60208-0814 Business E-Mail: wds@kellogg.northwestern.edu.

SCOTT, WILL T., state supreme court justice; b. Ratliff's Creek, Ky., July 20, 1947; s. John H. H. and Betty (Thompson) Scott. Attended, Eastern Ky. U.; BA, Pikeville Coll.; JD, U. Miami, 1974, MS in Taxation, 1975. Bar: Ky., Fla. With trust dept. Pikeville Nat. Bank, 1975—76; atty. priv. practice, 1976—2004; asst. atty. Pike County, 1981—82; judge Pike County Cir. Ct., 1984—88; justice Ky. Supreme Ct., 2005—, dep. chief justice, 2006—. Served to First Lt. US Army, 1966—69. Decorated Bronze Star, Vietnamese Cross of Gallantry, Combat Infantryman's Badge. Mem.: Ky. Circuit Judges' Assn. (second v.p. 1986). Office: Ky Supreme Ct 700 Capital Ave Frankfort KY 40601 Office Phone: 502-564-4168. *

SCOTT, WILLIAM CLEMENT, III, investor; b. NYC, Apr. 25, 1934; s. William Clement and Susan L. (Cameron) S.; m. Cindy L. Taylor, Dec. 5, 1981; children by previous marriage: Katherine Louise, David Campbell. AB, Coll. William and Mary, Williamsburg, Va., 1956. Self-employed, 1956-64; v.p. Booz-Allen & Hamilton, NYC, 1964-69; group v.p. Cordura Corp., Los Angeles, 1969-72; exec. v.p. Western Pacific Industries, NYC, 1972-76, pres., chief operating officer, 1976-87; pvt. investor NYC, 1987-88; chmn., CEO Panavision Inc., NYC, 1988-98. Bd. dirs. Edison Control Corp. Bd. dirs. Opera Orch. of N.Y., pres., 1988-97; bd. dirs. Met. Opera Club N.Y.C., pres., 2002-04. Mem. Met. Opera Club, Racquet and Tennis Club, Knickerbocker Club, Hay Harbor Club, Fishers Island Country Club, Coral Beach Club (Bermuda), Royal Bermuda Yacht Club. Republican. Episcopalian. Office: 445 Park Ave Ste 1905 New York NY 10022 Office Phone: 212-688-4748. E-mail: wcscott@att.net.

SCOTT, WILLIAM FLOYD, accountant; b. Woodland, Miss., Feb. 26, 1936; s. Robert Fulton and Sarah Etta (Watson) S.; m. Carolyn Marie Pierce, Dec. 12, 1958; children: David, Ricky, Stephen, Julie. BS in Bus. Adminstrn., Delta State U., Cleveland, Miss., 1957. Staff acct. Reynolds Elec. & Engring., Las Vegas, Nev., 1957-62, sr. auditor, 1962-65, dir. internal auditing, 1965-70; sr. staff acct. Davis & Mosher, CPAs, Pasadena, Tex., 1970-72; owner Scott & Co., CPAs, Pasadena, 1972—2001; mng. dir. Scott, Forrest, Adams & Co., PLLC, CPAs, Pasadena, 2002—. Chmn. fin. com. Meml. Bapt. Ch., Pasadena, Pasadena, 1974—80, treas., 1974—. Mem. AICPA, Tex. Soc. CPAs, Pasadena Noon Optimist Club (treas. 1973-75), Neighborhood Assn. Three Villas (treas. 2000-). Avocations: reading, gardening, sports. Office: Scott Forrest Adams & Co PLLC CPAs 4620 Fairmont Pky Ste 200 Pasadena TX 77504-3328 Office Phone: 281-487-2501. E-mail: wmfscott@swbell.net.

SCOTT, WILLIAM PROCTOR, III, lawyer; b. Berkeley, Calif., Dec. 1, 1946; s. William Proctor Jr. and Marcia (Wood) S.; children: William Proctor IV, Jennifer Anne Simon. BS, MIT, 1968; JD cum laude, U. Pa., 1975. Assoc. Ballard Spahr Andrews & Ingersoll LLP, Phila., 1975-82, ptnr., 1982-2000, Nixon Peabody LLP, Albany, NY, 2000—. Regional chmn. MIT Ednl. Coun., 1988-2000. Bd. dirs. Cathedral Village, 1998—, vice chair, 2003-07, chair 2007-; Lt. (j.g.) USNR, 1969-72. Office: Nixon Peabody LLP 30 S Pearl St 9th Fl Albany NY 12207-3425 Home Phone: 518-475-1489; Office Phone: 518-427-2700. Business E-Mail: wscott@nixonpeabody.com.

SCOTT, W(ILLIAM) RICHARD, sociology educator; b. Parsons, Kans., Dec. 18, 1932; s. Charles Hogue and Hildegarde (Hewit) S.; m. Joy Lee Whitney, Aug. 14, 1955; children: Jennifer Ann, Elliot Whitney, Sydney Brooke. AA, Parsons Jr. Coll., 1952; AB, U. Kans., 1954, MA, 1955; PhD, U. Chgo., 1961; PhD in Econs. (hon.), Copenhagen Sch. Bus., 2000, Helsinki Sch. Econs., 2001. From asst. prof. to assoc. prof. sociology Stanford (Calif.) U., 1960-69, prof., 1969-99, prof. emeritus, 1999—, chair dept. sociology, 1972-75; sr. scholar John Gardner Ctr./Stanford U., 2002—; sr. rschr. Ctr. Rsch. Global Projects, 2003—. Courtesy prof. Sch. Medicine, Stanford U., 1972—, Sch. Edn., Grad. Sch. Bus., 1977—; fellow Ctr. for Advanced Study in Behavioral Scis., 1989-90; dir. Orgns. Rsch. Tng. Program, Stanford U., 1972-89, Ctr. for Orgns. Rsch., 1988-96; mem. adv. panel Sociology Program NSF, Washington, 1982-84; mem. epidemiol. and svc. rsch. rev. panel NIMH, Washington, 1984-88; mem. Commn. on Behavioral and Social Scis. and Edn., NAS, 1990-96; vis. prof. Kellogg Grad. Sch. Mgmt., Northwestern U., winter 1997, Hong Kong U. Sci. and Tech., fall 2000. Author: (with O.D. Duncan et al) Metropolis and Region, 1960; (with P.M. Blau) Formal Organizations, 1962, 2003, Social Processes and Social Structures, 1970; (with S.M. Dornbusch) Evaluation and the Exercise of Authority, 1975, Organizations: Rational, Natural and Open Systems, 1981, rev. edit., 2003; (with J.W. Meyer) Organizational Environments: Ritual and Rationality, 1983, edit., 1992; (with A.B. Flood) Hospital Structure and Performance, 1987; (with J.W. Meyer), Institutional Environments and Organizations: Structural Complexity and Individualism, 1994, Institutions and Organizations, 1995; (with S. Christensen) The Institutional Construction of Organization, 1995; (with M. Ruef et al) Institutional Change and Healthcare Organizations: From Professional Dominance to Managed Care, 2000, (with G.F. Davis) Organizations and Organizing, 2007; editor Ann. Rev. of Sociology, 1986-91; (with R. Cole) The Quality Movement and Organization Theory, 1999, (with G.F. Davis et al) Social Movements and Organization Theory, 2005. Fellow Woodrow Wilson, 1954-55; mem. Nat. Commn. Nursing, 1980-83; chair Consortium Orgns. Rsch. Ctrs., 1989-91; elder First Presby. Ch., Palo Alto, Calif., 1977-80, 83-86. Named Edmund P. Learned Disting. Prof., Sch. Bus. Adminstrn., U. Kans., 1970—71; recipient Cardinal Citation for Disting. Svc., Labette C.C., Parsons, 1981, Disting. Scholar award, Mgmt. and Orgn. Theory divsn. Acad. Mgmt., 1988, Richard D. Irwin award for scholarly contbns. to mgmt., Acad. Mgmt., 1996; Social Sci. Rsch. Coun. fellow, U. Chgo., 1959, resident fellow, Bellagio Conf. Ctr., 2002. Fellow Acad. Mgmt.; mem. Inst. Medicine, Am. Sociol. Assn. (chmn. sect. on orgns. 1970-71, mem. coun. 1989-92), Sociol. Rsch. Assn. (exec. com. 2003—07, pres. 2006-07), Macro-Organizational Behavior Soc., Phi Beta Kappa. Democrat. Presbyterian. Home: 940 Lathrop Pl Stanford CA 94305-1060 Office: Stanford U Dept Sociology Bldg 120 Stanford CA 94305 Business E-Mail: scottwr@stanford.edu.

SCOTT, YVONNIE MICHELLE, special education educator, diagnostician, paralegal; b. Rochester, NY, Jan. 18, 1963; d. Harry Scott and Mary Jean Crews-Scott; m. Myron E. Miles (div.). BSc, Troy State U., Fort Rucker, Ala., 1987; MEd, Clark Atlanta U., 2002. Cert.: Ga. (paralegal) 2005; edn. specialist Clark Atlanta U., 2003, in ednl. leadership Clark Atlanta U., 2004, tchr. NY, Va., Ga. Kindergarten tchr. Rochester City Schs., 1985—86; tng. instr. Dept. Def., US Army, 1987—91; job coach John Odom Work Ctr., Dothan, Ala., 1992; spl. edn. tchr. asst. Dale County Bd. Edn., Ozark, Ala., 1995—97; spl. edn. tchr., diagnostician Cobb County Bd. Edn., Marietta, Ga., 2000—. Owner Scott's Enterprises, Alexandria, Va., 2001—; mentor, tchrs., students; workshop attendee in field. Named Tchr. of Month, Dept. Def., Fort Rucker, 1988; Academic scholarship, Ozark Hospitality, 1981. Mem.: Coun. Exceptional Children, Nat. Educators Assn., Order of the Eastern Star, Alpha Kappa Alpha (mem. health com. 2004). Democrat. Baptist. Avocations: piano, cooking, travel. Office: South Coff HS 1920 Clay Rd SW Austell GA 30106 Office Phone: 770-355-1531.

SCOTTI, DIEGO, marketing executive; b. Argentina; Head consumer product strategy and devel. for the Latin Am. and Caribbean bus. Am. Express Corp., v.p. global advt. Dir. The Advt. Club. Spkr. in field. Named one of 40 Under 40, Advt. Age, 2007; recipient Effie Award, Financial Services, 2007. Office: Am Express Corp PO Box 297812 Fort Lauderdale FL 33329 *

SCOTT-THOMAS, KRISTIN, actress; b. Redruth, Cornwall, England, United Kingdom, May 24, 1960; m. Francois Olivennes, 3 children, Hannah, Joseph, George. Student, Cen. Sch. Speech and Drama, Ecole Nat. des Arts. Stage debut in Schnitzler's La Lune Déclinante Sur 4 ou 5 Personnes Qui Danse; stage appearances include La Terre Etrangère, Naive Hirondelles, Yes Peut-Etre, Bérénice, 2001, Three Sisters, 2003, As You Desire Me, 2005; appearances on French, German, Australian, U.S. and Brit. TV include L'Ami d'Enfance de Maigret, Blockhaus, Cameleon La Tricheuse, Sentimental Journey, The Tenth Man, Endless Game, Framed, Titmuss Regained, Look at it this Way, Body and Soul; film appearances include Djamel et Juliette, L'Agent Troubé, La Méridienne, Under the Cherry Moon, A Handful of Dust, Force Majeure, Bille en Tete, The Bacheloir, Bitter Moon, Four Weddings and a Funeral (B.A.F.T.A. award), Angels and Insects (Evening Standard Film award), Richard III, 1995, Angels & Insects, 1996, Somebody to Love, 1996, The Pompatus of Love, 1996, Mission: Impossible, 1996, The English Patient, 1996, Amour et confusions, 1997, Souvenir, 1998, The Revenger's Comedies, 1998, The Horse Whisperer, 1998, Up at the Villa, 1999, Random Hearts, 1999, Life as a House, 2001, Gosford Park, 2001. Office: c/o Kevin Huvane & Bryan Lourd Creative Artists Agy 9830 Wilshire Blvd Beverly Hills CA 90212

SCOTT-WILLIAMS, MILDRED P., food service specialist; b. Americus, Ga., Mar. 21, 1928; d. Bouie Lee and Mary (Jackson) Paschal; m. Mar. 10, 1986 (div.); 1 child, Alan Meadows. BS, Fort Valley State Coll., 1949; MA, Antioch U., 1980. Tchr. elem. schs., Ga., 1949-54; asst. dietitian Met. Hosp., Phila., 1954-57, head dietitian, 1957-67; tchr. home econs. Phila. Bd. Edn., 1967-68, food svc. mgr., 1969-71; dietitian Germantown Hosp., Phila., summer 1968; supr. tng. H.E.A.R.T. (Household Employment Assn. Reevaluation Tng.), Phila., 1968-69; tchr. food svc. Camden (N.J.) Bd. Edn., 1971-73, adminstrv. asst., 1973-81, food svc. supr., 1981-99; ret., 1999. Author: Metropolitan Diet Manual, 1965. Cub mother Boy Socuts Am., Phila., 1970-71; block chairperson 5900 Neighborhood Assn., Phila., 1980-89; Dem. committeewoman 17 Ward 28th Divsn.; mem. Phila. Dist. Atty. Panel for Youth. Recipient award The Chapel of Four Chaplains, Phila., 1977, Disting. Svc. Key award LKM Sorority, 2000, Cert. of Appreciation, USDA, 2000, Recognition of Svc. award Camden City Fedn. Sch. Adminstrs., 2000. Mem. Am. Fedn. Sch. Adminstrs. (merit award 1987), Am. Sch. Food Svc. Assn. (cert., Star Club cert. 1999), N.J. Food Svc. Assn. (sec. 1980-82, appreciation award Elizabeth 1987, President's award New Brunswick 1989), Order Ea. Star (sec. 1979-84). Home: 5956 N 21st St Philadelphia PA 19138-2922 Personal E-mail: mscott9837@aol.com.

SCOTT-WILLIAMS, WENDY LEE, library and information scientist; b. Buffalo, Jan. 22; d. Arthur Raymond and June Amelia Schutt; m. Nigel Simon Scott-Williams, Feb. 29, 1980. BA cum laude, SUNY, Buffalo, 1975; MA with honors, Cambridge U., 1979; MLIS with honors, CUNY-Queens Coll., 1987. Applications rep. Barrister, NYC, 1982-83; coord. computer systems Stroock & Stroock & Lavan, NYC, 1983-87; tech. svcs. mgr. Batten, Barton, Durstein & Osborn (BBDO) Worldwide, NYC, 1987-92; adminstr., mgr. info. resources Fairchild Publs., NYC, 1992-96; info. resource mgr. March of Dimes Birth Defects Found., White Plains, NY, 1996—. Active N.Y. Zool. Soc. Mem. Spl. Librs. Assn., Cambridge Union Soc., Oxford-Cambridge Soc., Nature Conservancy, Greenpeace. Presbyterian. Avocations: travel, gardening. Office: March of Dimes Birth Defects Found Nat Hdqs 1275 Mamaroneck Ave White Plains NY 10605-5298

SCOULAR, ROBERT FRANK, lawyer; b. Del Norte, Colo., July 9, 1942; s. Duane William and Marie Josephine (Moloney) Scoular; m. Donna V. Scoular, June 3, 1967; children: Bryan T., Sean D., Bradley R. BS in Aero. Engring., St. Louis U., 1964, JD, 1968. Bar: Mo. 1968, Colo. 1968, ND 1968, US Supreme Ct. 1972, Calif. 1979. Law clk. to chief judge US Ct. Appeals (8th cir.), 1968-69; ptnr. Bryan, Cave, McPheeters & McRoberts, St. Louis, 1969-89, mng. ptnr. LA, 1979—85, exec. com., 1984-85, sect. leader tech., computer and intellectual property law, 1985-89; ptnr. Sonnenschein, Nath, Rosenthal, LA, 1990—, mng. ptnr., 1990—2005. Co-leader intellectual property practice, 1990—98; dir. Mo. Lawyers Credit Union, 1978—79. Contbr. articles to profl. jours. Bd. dirs. St. Louis Bar Found., 1975—76, 1979, bd. dirs., exec. com., pub. counsel, 2004—; bd. dirs., gen. counsel, pres. LA area coun. Boy Scouts Am.; league commr. Am. Youth Soccer Orgn.; mem. alumni coun. St. Louis U., 1979—82, dean's coun. Sch. Law, 2000—; hon. dean Dubourg Soc. Recipient Nat. Disting. Eagle Scout award. Mem.: ABA (nat. dir. young lawyers divsn. 1977—78), Fed. Bar Assn., Mo. Bar Assn. (chmn. young lawyers sect. 1976—77, Disting. Svc. award), Calif. Bar Assn., Assn. Bus. Trial Lawyers (bd. dirs. 2004—), LA County Bar Assn., Bar Assn. Met. St. Louis (chmn. young lawyers sect. 1975—76, v.p. 1978—79, sec. 1979), Calif. Club, Chancery Club. Home: 1505 Lower Paseo La Cresta Palos Verdes Peninsula CA 90274-2066 Office: Sonnenschein Nath & Rosenthal LLP 601 S Figueroa St Ste 1500 Los Angeles CA 90017-5720 Home Phone: 310-378-6349; Office Phone: 213-892-5003. Business E-Mail: rscoular@sonnenschein.com.

SCOUTON, DAVID EARL, lawyer; b. Jan. 17, 1970; BS in Biochemistry, St. Cloud State U., 1994; JD with honors, U. Minn., 2000. Bar: Minn. 2000. Sr. assoc. Foley & Mansfield, P.L.L.P., Mpls. Named Rising Star, Minn. Super Lawyers mag., 2006. Mem.: Def. Rsch. Inst., Hennepin County Bar Assn., Minn. State Bar Assn. Office: Foley & Mansfield PLLP 250 Marquette Ave Ste 1200 Minneapolis MN 55401 Office Phone: 612-349-9846. E-mail: dscouton@foleymansfield.com. *

SCOVANNER, DOUGLAS A., retail executive; BS, Washington and Lee U., 1977; MBA, U. Va., 1979. With Coca-Cola Enterprises and affiliates, Atlanta, 1980-92, v.p., treas., 1989-92; sr. v.p. fin. Fleming Cos., Oklahoma City, 1992-94; sr. v.p. fin., CFO Target Corp., Mpls., 1994—2000, exec. v.p., CFO, 2000—. Trustee Darden Sch. Found. U. Va. Darden Grad. Sch. Bus. Adminstrn.; vice chmn. exec. com. Minn. Orchestral Assn.; bd. mem. Greater Met. Housing Corp. Office: Target Corp 1000 Nicollett Mall Minneapolis MN 55403-2467 *

SCOVEL, CALVIN L., III, federal agency administrator; b. 1952; m. Cathy Scovel; children: Carey, Thomas. BA, U. NC; MA, Naval War Coll.; JD, Duke U. Advanced through grades to brigadier Gen. USMC; legal adv. to sec. USN; first counsel to insp. gen., chief def. counsel USMC; sr. judge USN Marine Corps Ct. Criminal Appeals; insp. gen. US Dept. Transp., Washington, 2006—. Office: US Dept Transp Nassif Bldg 400 Seventh St SW Rm 9210 Washington DC 20590 Office Phone: 202-366-1959. Office Fax: 202-366-3912. *

SCOVILLE, JAMES GRIFFIN, industrial relations professor; b. Amarillo, Tex., Mar. 19, 1940; s. Orlin James and Carol Howe (Griffin) S.; m. Judith Ann Nelson, June 11, 1962; 1 child, Nathan James. BA, Oberlin Coll., 1961; MA, Harvard U., 1963, PhD, 1965. Economist ILO, Geneva, 1965-66; instr. econs. Harvard U., Cambridge, Mass., 1964-65, asst. prof., 1966-69; assoc. prof. econs. and labor and indsl. relations U. Ill.-Urbana, 1969-75, prof., 1975-80; prof. indsl. rels. Indsl. Rels. Ctr., U. Minn., Mpls., 1979—, dir., 1979-82, dir. grad. studies, 1990-97. Cons. ILO, World Bank, U.S. Dept. Labor, Orgn. for Econ. Cooperation and Devel., USAID; labor-mgmt. arbitrator. Author: The Job Content of the US Economy, 1940-70, 1969, Perspectives on Poverty and Income Distribution, 1971, Manpower and Occupational Analysis: Concepts and Measurements, 1972, (with A. Sturmthal) The International Labor Movement in Transition, 1973, Status Influences in 3rd World Labor Markets, 1991, (with H. Buds) The Ethics of Human Resources and Industrial Relations, 2005. Mem. Am. Econ. Assn., Indsl. Rels. Rsch. Assn. (v.p. internat. sect. 1998, pres. 1999), Internat. Indsl. Rels. Assn. Office: U Minn Ind Rels Ctr 3-289 CSOM Minneapolis MN 55455 Office Phone: 612-624-1579. Business E-Mail: jscoville@csom.umn.edu.

SCOWCROFT, BRENT, former national security advisor, retired military officer; b. Ogden, Utah, Mar. 19, 1925; s. James and Lucile (Ballantyne) S.; m. Marian Horner, Sept. 17, 1951 (dec. 1995); 1 dau., Karen. BS, U.S. Mil. Acad., 1947; MA, Columbia U., 1953, PhD, 1967; postgrad., Georgetown U., 1958. Commd. 2d lt. USAF, 1947, advanced through grades to lt. gen., 1974; asst. prof. dept. social sci. U.S. Mil. Acad., 1953-57; asst. air attache Am. Embassy, Belgrade, Yugoslavia, 1959-61; assoc. prof. dept. polit. sci. USAF Acad., Colorado Springs, Colo., 1962-63, prof., head dept., 1963-64; mem. staff long range planning div. Office Dep. Chief Staff Plans and Ops., Washington, 1964-67; assigned Nat. War Coll., 1967-68; staff asst. Western Hemisphere region Office Asst. Sec. Def. Internat. Security Affairs, Washington, 1968-69; dep. asst. dir. plans for nat. security matters office Dep. Chief Staff Plans and Ops., Washington, 1969-70; spl. asst. to dir. Joint Staff, Joint Chiefs of Staff, Washington, 1970-71; mil. asst. to the Pres. The White House, Washington, 1972-73; dep. asst. to the Pres. for nat. security affairs NSC, Washington, 1973-75, asst. to the Pres. for nat. security affairs, 1975-77, 1989-93; mem. Pres.'s Gen. Adv. Com. on Arms Control, Washington, 1977-80; vice chmn. Kissinger Associates., Inc., Washington, 1982-89; pres. Forum for Internat. Policy, Washington, 1993—. Bd. dirs. Nat. Bank Washington, Qualcomm, Inc., Am. Coun. on Germany; chmn. Pres.'s Commn. on Strategic Forces; mem. Pres.'s Commn. on Def. Mgmt., Pres. Spl. Rev. Bd. on Iran/Contra Affair; pres. The Scowcroft Group, 1994—. Bd. dirs. Atlantic Coun. U.S., 1977—; bd. visitors U.S. Air Force Air U., 1977-79; bd. dirs. Internat. Rep. Inst., 1994—; chmn. Pres. Fgn. Intelligence Adv. Bd., 2000-05; chmn. Am.-

Turkish Coun., 2000—, Eisenhower Inst., 2004-05; mem. adv. bd. Georgetown Ctr. for Strategic and Internat. Studies; pres. George Bush Presdl. Libr. Foun.; bd. dirs. Gerald R. Ford Found., Nat. Def. U.; mem. Internat. Rep. Inst. Decorated D.S.M. with two oak leaf clusters, Legion of Merit with oak leaf cluster, Air Force Commendation medal, D.S.M. Dept. Def., Nat. Security medal; recipient Medal of Freedom, 1991; named Hon. Knight Brit. Empire, 1993. Mem. Coun. Fgn. Rels. (bd. dirs.), UN Assn. U.S. (vice chmn.), Am. Polit. Sci. Assn., Acad. Polit. Sci. Mem. Ch. Jesus Christ of Latter-day Saints. Office: # 500 900 17th St NW Ste 500 Washington DC 20006-2507

SCRIBNER, CHARLES, III, art historian, writer; b. Washington, May 24, 1951; s. Charles and Joan (Sunderland) S.; m. Ritchie Harrison Markoe, Aug. 4, 1979; children: Charles IV, Christopher Markoe. AB, Princeton U., 1973, MFA, 1975, PhD, 1977. Editor Charles Scribner's Sons, NYC, 1975—2004, dir. subs. rights, 1978-82, pub. paperback divsn., 1982-83, exec. v.p., 1983-84; v.p. Macmillan Pub. Co., NYC, 1984-94. Instr. dept. art and archaeology Princeton U., 1976-77; mem. adv. coun. Princeton U. Libr., 1981-90; mem. adv. coun. dept. art and archaeology Princeton U., 1983-91, 99-2003, 05—; trustee Princeton U. Press, 1984-90, Homeland Found., 1987—; bd. advisors Wethersfield Inst., 1985—; bd. dirs. Met. Opera Guild, 1990-92; dir. Cath. Edn. Inst., 2004-07. Author: The Triumph of the Eucharist-Tapestries by Rubens, 1982, Rubens, 1989, Bernini, 1991, The Shadow of God, 2006. Trustee St. Paul's Sch., Concord, NH, 1994-2006. Mem. Assn. Princeton U. Press, NYC Racquet and Tennis Club, Ivy Club (Princeton). Roman Catholic. Office: 155 E 72d St #5D New York NY 10021-4371 Office Phone: 917-623-0890. E-mail: cscribner3@yahoo.com.

SCRIGGINS, LARRY PALMER, lawyer, director; b. Englewood, NJ, Nov. 27, 1936; s. Thomas Dalby and M. Patricia (Fowler) S.; m. Victoria Jackola, Feb. 17, 1979; children: Elizabeth J., Thomas P. AB, Middlebury Coll., 1958; JD, U. Chgo., 1961. Bar: Md. 1962. Law clk. to chief judge Md. Ct. Appeals, 1962; assoc. Piper & Marbury, LLP, Balt., 1962-69, ptnr., 1969-98, vice chmn., 1988-93, mem. exec. com., CFO, 1993-98; sr. counsel Piper Rudnick, LLP, Balt., 1999-2001; ptnr. emeritus DLA Piper US LLP, Balt., 2001—. Mem. legal adv. com. N.Y. Stock Exch., 1992-96; bd. dirs. USF & G Corp., 1979-98, Center Stage Assocs., 1979-89, Balt. Choral Arts Soc., 1979-96, Balt. Conv. Bur., 1982-95, YMCA of Greater Balt., 1987-94, Fund for Ednl. Excellence, 1990-98, chmn. bd. trustees, 1993-98; bd. dirs. Nat. Aquarium in Balt., bd. govs. 1987-93; bd. dirs. Balt. Symphony Orchestra, 1996-2001. Contbr. articles to profl. jours. Fellow: Am. Bar Found.; mem.: ABA (sect. on bus. law coun. 1972—76, chmn. law and acctg. com. 1985—88, vice chair and editor-in-chief The Bus. Lawyer 1989—90, chair 1991—92, chmn. com. corp. laws 1996—2000, chmn. ad hoc com. on ethics 2000 1999—2002, sr. advisor 2000—), AICPA (planning com. 1989—92), Fin. Acctg. Stds. Bd., Task Force in Fin. Instruments, Am. Law Inst., Am. Judicature Soc., Md. Bar Assn. (coun. 1976—78, chmn. 1977—78, mem. com. on corp. laws 1981—84). Office: DLA Piper US LLP 6225 Smith Ave Baltimore MD 21209-3600 Office Phone: 410-580-4252. Office Fax: 410-580-3001. Business E-Mail: larry.scriggins@dlapiper.com.

SCRIMGEOUR, GARY JAMES, writer, educator; b. Auckland, New Zealand, Jan. 15, 1934; came to U.S., 1957; s. Colin Graham and Caroline Lenna (Hardie) S. BA with honors, U. Sydney, Australia, 1954; MA in English, Wash. U., 1959; PhD, Princeton U., 1968. Asst. personnel officer Dexion Ltd., London, 1956-57; mem. faculty dept. English Fla. U., Gainesville, 1959-61, Rutgers U., New Brunswick, NJ, 1963-64, Ind. U., Bloomington, 1964-69, Nat. Jud. Coll., 1974—94; editor, writer Benjamin Blom, Inc., NYC, 1969-70; chief social sys. divsn. and head editl. office Sch. Pub. and Environ. Affairs, Ind. U., 1970-74; dir. Profl. Studies Assocs., Bloomington, 1973—; editor Coll. Engring. U. Nev.-Reno, 1992-94, sr. editor Coll. Bus. Adminstrn., 1994—2001; ind. editor for sci./engring. faculty, 2001—. Faculty coord. Nat. Jud. Coll., 1973-93; cons. for rsch. in alcoholism, ct. systems, hwy. safety and design of seminars to various govt. agys., schs. and social orgns., 1970—. Author: A Woman of Her Times, 1982, The Garden Inspector, 1993, The Quilting Women, 1995; contbr. numerous manuals on ct. sys. and alcohol safety to profl. publs. and articles on lit. criticism to lit. jours. Jane E. Procter fellow Princeton U., 1968. Office: 369 Bret Harte Ave Reno NV 89509 Office Phone: 775-786-1442. Business E-Mail: gscrim@unr.nevada.edu.

SCRIMSHAW, NEVIN STEWART, physician, nutritionist, educator; b. Jan. 20, 1918; m. Mary Ware Goodrich, 1941; 5 children. BA with honors, Ohio Wesleyan U., 1938; MA in Biology, Harvard U., 1939, PhD in Physiology, 1941, MPH, 1959; MD with honors, U. Rochester, 1945. Intern Gorgas Hosp., 1945-46; Rockefeller postdoctoral fellow U. Rochester, NY, 1946—47, Merck NRC fellow NY, 1947—49; asst. resident in ob-gyn. Strong Meml. Hosp., Genesee Hosp., NY, 1948—49; dir. Inst. Nutrition C.Am. and Panama, Guatemala, 1949—61, cons. dir., 1961—65, cons., 1965—. Cons. nutrition Pan-Am. San Bur. WHO, 1948—49, regional advisor on nutrition, 1949—53; dir. Clin. Rsch. Ctr. MIT, 1962—66, 1979—83, dir. internat. food and nutrition program, 1976—88, prof. human nutrition, 1961—76, head dept. nutrition and food sci., 1961—79, inst. prof., 1976—87, emeritus, 1988—; vis. prof. Columbia U., NYC, 1976—88, vis. lectr., 1961—66, Harvard U., 1968—85; adj. prof. Tufts U.; mem. govt. adv. com. NIH; chmn. internat. com. NRC; dir. devel. studies divsn. UN U., 1985—86, food nutrition program, 1975—97, sr. advisor, 1998—; mem. adv. com. WHO, Nutrition Found., others. Editor (with others): Amino Acid Fortification of Protein Foods, 1971, Nutrition, National Development and Planning, 1973, The Economics, Marketing and Technology of Fish Protein Concentrate, 1974, Development: Significance and Potential for the Tropics, 1976, Single-Cell Protein: Safety for Animal and Human Feeding, 1979, Nutrition Policy Implementation: Issues and Experience, 1983, Diarrhea and Malnutrition: Interactions, Mechanisms and Interventions, 1983, Chronic Energy Deficiency, 1987, Acceptability of Milk and Milk Products in Populations with Lactose Intolerance, 1988, Nutrition in the Elderly, 1989, Activity, Energy Expenditure and Energy Requirements of Infants and Children, 1990, RAP: Rapid Assessment Procedures: Qualitative Methodologies for Planning and Evaluation of Health Related Programs, 1992, Protein-energy Interactions, 1992, Community-based Longitudinal Nutrition and Health Studies: Classical Examples from Guatemala, Haiti, and Mexico, 1995, The Effects of Improved Nutrition in Early Childhood: The Institute of Nutrition of Central American and Panama Follow-up Study, 1995, The Nutrition and Health Transition of Democratic Costa Rica, 1995, Energy and Protein Requirements, 1996, Causes and Consequences of Intrauterine Growth Retardation, 2000; contbr. articles to profl. jours. Trustee Rockefeller Found., 1971—83, Pan-Am. Health and Edn. Found., 1986—92; pres. Internat. Nutrition Found. for Developing Countries, 1982—. Recipient Osborne and Mendal award, 1960, Internat. award, Inst. Food Technologists, 1969, medal of honor, Fundacion F. Cuenca Villoro, Spain, 1978, Bristol-Myers prize, 1988, Alan Shawn Feinstein award, 1991, World Food prize, 1991, Kellogg award in internat. nutrition, 2002, Lifetime Achievement award, UN, 2004. Fellow: APHA (v.p. 1978, award of excellence in promoting and protecting health of people 1974), AAAS, Am. Soc. Clin. Nutrition, Royal Soc. Health, Am. Soc. Nutritional Scis.; mem.: NAS (chair applied biol. sect. 1973—76, 1988—91), Nat. Inst. Medicine, others, Internat. Epidemiol. Assn., Internat. Union Nutritional Scis. (pres. 1978—81), Am. Epidemiol. Soc., Am. Physiol. Soc., Mass. Med. Soc., New Eng. Pub. Health Assn., Mass. Pub. Health Assn., Am. Bd. Nutrition, Am. Coll. Preventive Medicine, Am. Coll. Nutrition, Am. Acad. Arts and Scis., Inst. Medicine NAS. Home and Office: Sandwich Mountain Farm 115 Sandwich Notch Rd PO Box 330 Campton NH 03223-0330 Office Phone: 603-726-4200. Office Fax: 603-726-4614. Business E-Mail: nscrimshaw@inffoundation.org.

SCRIMSHAW, SUSAN CROSBY, academic administrator; b. Nov. 12, 1945; m. Allan Stern; 1 child from previous marriage, Mary Corey March. AB, Barnard Coll., 1967; MA, Columbia U., 1969, PhD in Anthropology, 1974. Rsch. assoc. Internat. Inst. for Study of Human Reporduction, 1969—75; asst. prof. health adminstrn. Columbia U., 1975; asst. prof. pub. health Div. Population, Family and Internat. Health, Sch. Pub. Health UCLA, 1975—80, assoc. prof. Div. Population and Family Health, 1980—85, assoc. dir. Latin Am. Ctr., 1984—88, prof. pub. health and anthropology, 1985—96, acting chair Dept. Pub. Health, 1988—89, assoc. dean Academic Programs, 1988—94, acting dean, 1991—92, 1992—93; dean, prof. cmty. heath scis. and anthropology U. Ill. Sch. Pub. Health, Chgo., 1995—2006; pres. Simmons Coll., Boston, 2006—. Co-editor: The Handbook of Social Studies in Health & Med. Recipient Margaret Mead award, 1985. Fellow: AAAS; mem.: Nat. Soc. Med. Anthropology (pres. 1985), Soc. Applied Anthropology, Am. Anthropology Assn., Inst. Medicine NAS (coun. mem. 2006—). Office: Simmons Coll Office of Pres 300 The Fenway Boston MA 02115

SCRIPPS, DOUGLAS JERRY, musician, educator, conductor; b. Grand Rapids, Mich., Aug. 25, 1942; s. Kenneth Witvoet and Marguerite F. (Rottier) Scripps; m. Betty Ann Broersma Porter, July 24, 1963 (div. Aug. 1974); children: Elisabeth Ann Scripps Blue, Theodore Jon; m. Merilee Evelyn Collins, Apr. 5, 1975; children: Daniel Collins, Taylor Douglas, Adam Rottier. Student, Eastman Sch. Music, 1961-62; BA, Calvin Coll., 1965; student, U. Music and Dramatic Art, Vienna, 1965—66; MM, U. Mich., 1970. Prin. trumpet player Grand Rapids Symphony Orch., 1961—65, assoc. conductor, 1976—85; dir. music Grand Rapids City Coll., 1967—78; conductor Lake St. Clair Symphony, Detroit, 1970—72, Alma (Mich.) Symphony Orch., 1985—2002; music dir. Grand Rapids Ballet, 1979—99; asst. prof. music Ctrl. Mich. U., Mt. Pleasant, 1981—84; prof. music, dept. chair Alma Coll., 1985—2002, prof. emeritus, 2003—. Guest condr. Interlochen Ctr. Arts, Joffrey Balley, Bay View Music Festival, Blue Lake Fine Arts Camp, Czech Music Camp; vis. prof. Grand Valley State U., Calvin Coll., 1977—81; condr. Ctrl. European Youth Symphony Orch., 2004—05. Recipient Am. Heritage Assn. study abroad lectr., Vienna, 1999. Avocations: reading, travel, sailing. Home: PO Box 476 Northport MI 49670-0476 Business E-Mail: scripps@alma.edu.

SCRIVEN, L. E(DWARD), engineering educator; b. Battle Creek, Mich., Nov. 4, 1931; s. L. Edward and Esther Mabel (Davis) S.; m. Dorene Bates Hayes, June 19, 1952; children: Ellen Dorene, Teresa Ann, Mark Hayes. BS, U. Calif., Berkeley, 1952; PhD, U. Del., 1956. Rsch. engr. Shell Devel. Co., Emeryville, Calif., 1956-59; asst. prof. chem. engring. and fluid mechanics U. Minn., Mpls., 1959-62, assoc. prof., 1962-66, prof., 1966-89, Regents' prof., 1989—, assoc. dept. head, 1975-78, program dir. Ctr. Interfacial Engring., 1988-90. Cons. in fields; advisor to Humboldt Found., Fed. Republic of Germany; vis. com. to chem. engring. MIT, sci. assoc. Jet Propulsion Lab., 1977, 79; tech. expert UN Indsl. Devel. Orgn., Vienna, Austria, 1979-88; exec. com. on chem. engring. frontiers NRC, 1984-87; mem. NRC Bd. on Chem. Scis. and Tech., 1987-92, chmn., 1992; mem. NRC Commn. on Phys. Scis., Math. and Applications, 1994—; sci. adv. com. Packard Found., 1988—. Editor: Physico-chemical Hydrodynamics (V.G. Levich), 1992; assoc. editor Jour. Fluid Mechanics, 1970-75; adv. editor Jour. Coll. Interfluid Sci., Physics of Fluids, L.Am. Jour. Chem. Engring. and Applied Chemistry, Internat. Jour. Numerical Methods in Fluid Mechanics; contbr. numerous articles to sci. jours.; patentee in field. Recipient chem. engring. award Am. Soc. Engring. Edn., 1968, Minn. Achievement award, 1989, Murphree award Am. Chem. Soc., 1990; named Fairchild disting. scholar Calif. Inst. Tech., 1989; Guggenheim fellow, 1969-70, fellow Minn. Supercomputer Inst., 1984—. Mem. NAE, Am. Inst. Chem. Engrs. (mem. nat. program. com. 1964-69, Colburn award 1960, Walker award 1977, Tallmadge award 1992, Founders award 1997), Am. Phys. Soc., Soc. Petroleum Engrs., Gordon Rsch. Confs., Chem. Soc. (Faraday div.), Soc. Indsl. and Applied Math., Soc. Rheology. Achievements include research in capillarity, fluid mechanics and coating processes, porous media, cold-stage electron microscopy, microstructured fluids and interfaces, origins of pattern and form, supercomputer-aided analysis. Office: Univ Minn 151 Amundson Hall 421 Washington Ave SE Minneapolis MN 55455-0373

SCRIVEN, WAYNE MARCUS, lawyer; b. Sumter, SC, Aug. 31, 1953; s. Philip Roosevelt and Sarah Ella (Pringle) S. BA in History Edn. cum laude, Va. Union U., 1975; JD, Golden Gate U. Sch. of Law, 1979. Bar: Va. 1980, U.S. Dist. Ct. (ea. dist.) Va. 1980, U.S. Ct. Appeals (4th cir.) 1980, S.C. 1982, U.S. Dist. Ct. S.C. 1982, U.S. Supreme Ct. 1984, Calif. 1987, U.S. Dist. Ct. (no. dist.) Calif. 1986, U.S. Ct. Appeals (9th cir.) 1986, D.C. 1993, U.S. Dist. Ct. D.C. 1994, U.S. Dist. Ct. Md. 1994, U.S. Ct. Appeals (fed. cir.) 1994, D.C. Directing atty. Petersburg Legal Aid Soc., Va., 1980-81; staff atty. Carolina Regional Legal Svcs. Corp., Florence, SC, 1981-82; pvt. practice Florence, 1982-85, Richmond, Va., 1985-86, San Francisco, 1986-93, Washington, 1993—. Contract atty. Neighborhood Legal Asst. Program, Marion, S.C., 1982-83, pro bonocontract atty., 1983-85, Carolina Regional Legal Svcs. Corp., Florence, 1983-85, Bar Assn. of San Francisco, 1987-93; notary public, S.C., 1981-91, Va., 1986-91. Bd. dirs. Young Men's Christian Assn., Florence, 1982-83, Pee Dee Crisis Ctr., Florence, 1983-84, San Francisco Neighborhood Legal Asst. Program, 1992-93. Named one of Outstanding Young Men of Am., U.S. Jaycees, 1982; recipient Outstanding Lawyer in Pub. Svc., Bar Assn. San Francisco, 1988-91. Mem. ABA, Washington Bar Assn., Assn. Trial Lawyers of Am., U.S. Supreme Ct. Hist. Soc. Baptist. Avocations: fishing, guitar playing, nature trail walking. Office: Ste 900 South Bldg 601 Pennsylvania Ave NW Washington DC 20004 also: 1655 N Fort Meyer Dr Ste 700 Arlington VA 22209 Office Phone: 703-248-2608. Business E-Mail: Wayne-Marcus-Scriven@abanet.org.

SCRIVENER, LOIS DOING, principal, educator; b. Mineola, NY, Oct. 10, 1945; d. Park Atkinson and Mary Houser Doing; m. James W. Scrivener, Jan. 21, 1967; children: Patricia, James Jr., Andrew. BA in English and Edn., St. Bonaventure U., 1967; MA in Theology, Immaculate Conception, 1982; EdS in Ednl. Leadership, U. Ctrl. Fla., 1996; MS in Brain Rsch., Nova Southeastern U., 2006. Cert. tchr. N.Y., tchr. English, ednl. leadership Fla. Substitute tchr. Nassau County, NY, 1970—82; tchr. St. Edward the Confessor, Syosset, NY, 1982—84; tchr., part-time adminstr. Holy Child, Old Westbury, NY, 1984—89; tchr. theology Ctrl. Cath. H.S., Melbourne, Fla., 1989—92; prin. Holy Name of Jesus, Indiatlantic, Fla., 1992—. Adj. prof. Barry U., Miami, Fla., 2000—04; mem. salary scale com. Brevard County Cath. Sch., 1993—2004. Regent NSDAR, Satellite Beach, Fla., 1974—2006; youth min. St. William the Abbot, Seaford, NY, 1975—88. Named Catechist Prin. of Yr., Diocese Orlando, 1996, Nat. Disting. Prin., U.S. Dept. Edn., 2001, Blue Ribbon Sch. Excellence, 2001, U.S. Dept. Edn. No Child Left Behind, 2003; recipient St. Piux X CCD award, 1988, Schs. of Tomorrow Innovations in Tech. award, Today's Cath. Tchr., 1999, Outstanding Sch. Bd. award, NABE, 2000. Mem.: Nat. Cath. Edn. Assn. (Disting. Home and Sch. award 2000, Disting. Prin. 2001, Oustanding Sch. Bd. award 2001). Home: 421 Mallard Ln Indialantic FL 32903

SCRIVER, CHARLES ROBERT, medical researcher, human geneticist, retired medical educator; b. Montreal, Que., Can., Nov. 7, 1930; s. Walter deM. and Jessie (Boyd) S.; m. E.K. Peirce, Sept. 8, 1956; children: Dorothy, Peter, Julie, Paul. BA cum laude, McGill U., Montreal, 1951, MDCM cum laude, 1955; DSc (hon.), U. Man., 1992, U. Glasgow, 1993, U. Montreal, 1993, Utrecht U., 1999, U. B.C., 2002, U. We. Ont., 2007. Intern Royal Victoria Hosp., Montreal, 1955-56; resident Royal Victoria and Montreal Children's Hosps., 1956-57, Children's Med. Ctr., Boston, 1957-58; McLaughlin travelling fellow Univ. Coll., London, 1958-60; chief resident pediat. Montreal Children's Hosp., 1960-61; asst. prof. pediat. McGill U., 1961, prof. biology Faculty of Sci., prof. pediat. Faculty of Medicine, 1969—, Alva prof. human genetics, 1994—2002, prof. emeritus, 2002—. Mem. med. adv. bd. Howard Hughes Med. Inst., 1981-88; dir. Med. Rsch. Coun. Group in Genetics, 1972-94; assoc. dir. Can. Genetic Diseases Network, 1989-98. Co-author: Amino Acid Metabolism and Its Disorders, 1973, Garrod's Inborn Factors in Disease, 1989; sr. online editor Metabolic and Molecular Bases Inherited Disease, 1986—; contbr. more than 550 rsch. publs. in field. Decorated Order of Can., Que., Mont.; named Royal Coll. lectr., 1992, Disting. Scientist, Med. Rsch. Coun., 1995—; named to Can. Med. Hall of Fame, 2001, Can. Sci. Engring. Hall of Fame, 2001; recipient Wood Gold medal, McGill U., 1955, Gairdner Internat. award, Gairdner Found., 1979, Prix Michel-Sarrazin, Club de Rech Clin du Que., 1988, Ross award, Can. Pediatric Soc., 1990, Award of Excellence, Genet Soc. Can., 1992, Prix d'Excellence, Inst. Rsch. Clin. de Montreal, 1993, Prix du Quebec, Wilder Penfield, 1995, Lifetime Achievement award, Montreal Children's Hosp., 1995, Medal of Merit, Can. Med. Assn., 1996, Lifetime Achievement award, March of Dimes Birth Defects Found., 1997, Querci Found. prize, Italy, 2001, Founders award, Can. Coll. Med. Geneticist, 2003; Markle scholar, 1962—67. Fellow: AAAS, Royal Soc. London (Can. Rutherford lectr. 1983), Royal Soc. Can. (McLaughlin medal 1981), Royal Coll. Physicians of Ireland (hon.), Am. Coll. Med. Genetics (hon.); mem.: Am. Acad. Pediat. (Mead Johnson award for rsch. in pediat. 1968), Soc. Francaise de Pediat., Brit. Pediat. Assn. (50th Anniversary lectr. 1978), Assn. Am. Physicians, Am. Soc. Clin. Investigation, Am. Pediat. Soc. (pres. 1994—95), Am. Soc. Human Genetics (dir. 1971—74, pres. 1986—87, William Allan award 1978, Award of Excellence in Human Genetics Edn. 2001), Soc. Pediat. Rsch. (pres. 1975—76), Can. Soc. Clin. Investigation (pres. 1974—75, G. Malcolm Brown Meml. award 1979, Henry Friesen award 2001). Office: McGill Univ-Montreal Childrens Hosp Rsch Inst 2300 Tupper St Montreal PQ Canada H3H 1P3 Business E-Mail: charles.scriver@mcgill.ca.

SCRIVNER, B(ARBARA) E., piano educator; b. Medford, Oreg., May 25, 1931; 4 children. Student (piano student Lawrence Morton), Bob Jones U., 1962-66; corr. student, Inst. Children's Lit., Redding Ridge, Conn., 1974-76. Part time sec., Oreg., 1948-50, 60-62, SC, 1974-76, 80-86, Census Bur., SC, 1980-82; piano tchr. Greenville, SC, 1963—2003. Contbr. column A Life Within, also by-line columns-opinion to Times Examiner, Greenville, 1995-97; writer for monthly newsletter From Whence We Came, 1997—; contbr. articles to local newspapers. Mem. Nat. Presdl. Task Force; active Rep. Nat. Com., S.C. Rep. Party; mem. Nat. Rep. Congl. Com.; coord. hdqs. Greenville County Rep. Party, 1993—94. Office Phone: 864-855-5289.

SCRIVNER, ELLEN M., psychologist; d. John P. O'Shea and Dorothy Mary O'Shea-Hanley; m. Peter C. Scrivner, Aug. 25, 1962; children: Anne Collins (Scrivner) Kuban, Thomas C. BS, St. Louis U., 1961, MS, 1963; PhD in Psychology, Cath. U. Am., 1986. Lic. psychologist Bd. of Examiners, Md. Police psychologist, Fairfax County, Va., Prince Georges County, Md.; dep. dir. COPS Office, U.S. Dept. of Justice, Washington, 2000—02; sr. advisor FBI Office Law Enforcement Coords., 2002—04; dep. supt. bur. of adminstrv. svcs. Chgo. Police Dept., 2004—. Pres. Pub. Safety Innovations, Washington, 2003—04; vis. fellow Nat. Inst. Justice, U.S. Dept. Justice. Author: Law Enforcement Families: Issues and Answers, 1994, Police Psychology Into The 21st Century, 1995. Mem. adv. bd. Local Initiatives Support Corp., NYC, 2003—05. Recipient Women of Courage and Vision award, U.S. Dept. of Justice, 2001, Lifetime Achievement award, 2000. Mem.: APA (life; divsn. pres. 1991—92, Disting. Svc. award 1990). Achievements include research in excessive force/violence, community policing, police psychology. Home: 700 New Hampshire Ave NW Washington DC 20037 Home Phone: 202-625-0644; Office Phone: 312-745-6288. Personal E-mail: ellenscrivner284@msn.com. E-mail: ellen.scrivner@chicagopolice.org.

SCRIVNER, THOMAS WILLIAM, lawyer; b. Madison, Wis., Sept. 10, 1948; s. William H. and Jane (Gehrz) S.; m. Meredith Burke, Aug. 16, 1980; children: Allison, David. AB, Duke U., 1970, MAT, 1972; JD, U. Wis., 1977. Assoc. Michael, Best & Friedrich LLP, Milw., 1978-85, ptnr., 1985—. Mem. ABA, Wis. Bar Assn., Milw. Bar Assn. (labor sect.), Corp. Practice Inst. (pres. 1989-92). Episcopalian. Home: 4626 N Cramer St Milwaukee WI 53211-1203 Office: Michael Best & Friedrich LLP 100 E Wisconsin Ave Ste 3300 Milwaukee WI 53202-4108 Home Phone: 414-332-1377; Office Phone: 414-271-6560. Business E-Mail: twscrivner@michaelbest.com.

SCROGGINS, M. SUZANNE PAONESSA, budget analyst; b. Albany, NY, May 1, 1974; d. Thomas and Mary Laura (Maresca) Paonessa; m. Josh Scroggins. BS in Fin., Siena Coll., 1996. Fin. mgmt. specialist U.S. Dept. Energy, Schenectady (N.Y.) Naval Reactors Office, 1996-99; assoc. dir. fin. aid Siena Coll., 1999-2001; assoc. dir. budget and bus. svcs. U. Maine, Orono, 2001—, instr., Profl. Employees Adv. Coun. (PEAC), chmn., mem. athletic adv. bd., site coord. wellness program. Treas. Schenectady Naval Reactors Office Employee Assn., 1997—98. Vol. YMCA; ch. lector, greeter; co-dir. Siena Coll. Friendly's Fanfest, 1997—98; mem. Siena Coll. Career Adv. Network. Mem.: Nat. Youth Sports Coaches Assn., DOE Women's Golf League (treas. 1998—, named Most Improved Player 1998), Fin. Mgmt. Assn., 21st Century Leaders Soc., Kensho-Do Karate Club (asst. instr. 1998—2000, brown belt), Sigma Beta Delta, Delta Epsilon Sigma, Alpha Kappa Alpha. Roman Catholic. Avocations: golf, softball, dancing. Home: 398 Old County Rd Apt 9 Hampden ME 04444-1936 Personal E-mail: sqboo@yahoo.com.

SCROGGS, LARRY KENNETH, lawyer, state legislator; b. Beebe, Ark., Oct. 8, 1941; s. Kenneth Chalmers and Mildred Lorene (McDonald) S.; m. Mary Patricia Rushing, Aug. 25, 1967; children: Larry Kenneth Jr., James Kevin, Michael Kyle. BA, Harding U., 1963; JD, Vanderbilt U., 1971. Bar: Tenn. 1971, U.S. Dist. Ct. (we. dist.) Tenn. 1971, U.S. Ct. Appeals (8th cir.) 1982, U.S. Ct. Appeals (6th cir.) 1989, U.S. Supreme Ct. 1981. Assoc. Law Firm of Leo Bearman, Memphis, 1971-72, Holt, Batchelor, Spicer, Memphis, 1972-76, ptnr., 1976-80, Less & Scroggs, Memphis, 1980-92; pvt. practice, Germantown, Tenn., 1992-96; ptnr. Scroggs & Rogers, Collierville, Tenn., 1997—2003, Burch, Porter & Johnson, Memphis, 2003—06; chief counsel Juvenile Ct. Memphis and Shelby County, 2006—. Mcpl. ct. judge City of Germantown, 1980-86; atty. for County Trustee, Shelby County, Memphis, 1990—06. Mem. campaign steering com. George Bush for Pres., Memphis, 1987-92, Tenn. Ho. Reps., Nashville, 1996-2002; vol. Ed Bryant for Congress campaign, Memphis, 1994, Don Sundquist for Gov. campaign, Memphis, 1994. Lt. U.S. Navy, 1964-67, Vietnam. Mem. ABA, Tenn. Bar Assn., Memphis Bar Assn. (bd. dirs. 1990-91). Republican. Mem. Ch. of Christ. Avocations: photography, boating, tennis. Office: Juvenile Ct Memphis and Shelby County 616 Adams Ave Memphis TN 38105 Office Phone: 901-405-8543. Business E-Mail: scroggs-l@shelbyjuvenilecourt.com.

SCRUGGS, EARL EUGENE, entertainer; b. Cleveland County, NC, Jan. 6, 1924; s. George Elam and Georgia Lula (Ruppe) Scruggs; m. Anne Louise Certain, Apr. 18, 1948; children: Gary Eugene, Randy Lynn, Steven Earl. HHD in Folk Music (hon.), Gardner-Webb U., 1986; Mus D (hon.), Berklee Sch. Music, Boston, 2005. Recorded album MCA Records released 2001 with guest stars Elton John, Dwight Yoakam, Billy Bob Thornton, Gary Scruggs, Travis Tritt, Melissa Etheridge, Sting, Glen Duncan, Randy Scruggs, Steve Martin, Vince Gill, Marty Stuart, Albert Lee, Paul Shaffer, Jerry Douglas, Leon Russell, Rosanne Cash, John Fogerty, Don Henley and Johnny Cash. Album titled "Earl Scruggs and Friends". Banjo player, 1945—, rec. artist Columbia Records, 1950—, recorded theme song (TV series) The Beverly Hillbillies, 1962; author: Earl Scruggs and the 5-String Banjo, 1968; banjo player formed Earl Scruggs Revue, 1969—, major performances Carnegie Hall, NYC, Wembley Festival, London, Washington Moratorium for Peace, also rock festivals, coll. concerts, 1969—, appearances (TV series) NET-TV Spl. Earl Scruggs: His Family and Friends, 1971; composer (with others): (movie score) Where The Lilies Bloom, 1973; star (films) Banjo Man, 1975, appearances (TV series) Midnight Spl., NBC-Harper Valley U.S.A. Spl., NBC Country Music Awards Show, Phil Donahue Show, Mike Douglas Show, Austin City Limits, 1977, The Grand Ole Opry's 60th Anniversary Show, 1985, The Nashville Network spl. The Am. Music Shop, 1990, The Grand Ole Opry's 65th Anniversary Show, Country Music Assn. Awards Show, 1991, guest appearance (TV films) Return of the Beverly Hillbillies, 1981, appearances (TV series) Country Music Assn. Hall of Fame 25th Anniversary TV show, 1992, The Legend of The Beverly Hillbillies, CBS-TV, 1993, Folk Sound USA-Revlon Revue, The Tonight Show, Les Crane Show, Mac Davis Special, The Johnny Cash Show, The Hootenanny Show, Frank McGee's Here and Now, Ernie Ford Show, Jimmy Dean Show, The Anatomy of Pop, Kraft's Am. Profile, The Roots of Country, CBS-TV, 1994, Red Hot and Country, TNN-TV, A Night at the Ryman, TNN-TV, 1995, An Evening of Country Grt., TNN-TV, CMA 40th Anniversary Celebration, CBS-TV, 1998, albums Nashville Rock, Dueling Banjos, Kans. State, I Saw the Light, Earl Scruggs Revue, Rockin' Cross the Country, Family Portrait, Top of the World, Anniversary Spl. Vol. I and Vol. II, Live! At Austin City Limits, Earl Scruggs: His Family and Friends Soundtrack, Today and Forever, Bold and New, Am.-Made, World-Played, others, guest appearances (TV series) The Beverly Hillbillies, Earl Scruggs Revue rec. music soundtrack for (films) Where The Lilies Bloom; composer: (instrumental) Foggy Mountain Breakdown (used in movie Bonnie and Clyde) (Grammy award, 1968, 2001, Broadcast Music, Inc., 1969, Grammy award, 2003); appearance (radio program) John Boy & Billy, 2001, BBC Radio Network, London, Eng., 2001, (TV show) The Late Show with David Letterman, 2001; appearance: (TV show) The Tonight Show with Jay Leno, 2002. Apptd. hon. mem. Lt. Gov.'s Staff State of Tenn., 1987. Nominee 16 Grammy nominations; named Artist of Yr., Hi-Fi Inst., 1975; named to Gibson Hall of Fame, 1981, Country Music Assn. Hall of Fame, 1985, Internat. Bluegrass Music Assn. Hall of Honor, 1991, Starwalk-Nat. Acad. Recording Arts & Scis., 1997, NC Hall of Fame on Grand Ole Opry, 1999; recipient Country Music award best instrumental group, Billboard Mag., 1975, Best Country and Bluegrass Banjoist, Frets mag, 1980, Cert. of Merit, Internat. Bluegrass Music Assn., 1988, Order of the Long Leaf Pine award, Gov. State of N.C., 1988, cert. appreciation, Tenn. Gov. Ned McWherter, 1990, Nat. Medal of Arts award, Pres. George Bush, 1992, Spl. Citation of achievement recognition of nat. popularity over 1 million broadcasts of Foggy Mountain Breakdown, Broadcast Music, Inc., 1993, NC Folk Heritage award, N.C. Arts Coun. Dept Cultural Resources, others, NC Heritage award, NC Arts Coun. Dept. Cultural Resources, 1996, Grammy award vocal collaboration Same Old Train, 1998, lifetime achievement award, Gibson Guitar Corp., 2002, Star, Hollywood Walk of Fame, 2003; Nat. Heritage fellow NEA, 1989. Achievements include development of Scruggs style of banjo playing; invention of Scruggs Tuning Pegs; honored with a star in Hollywood Walk of Fame, Hollywood, Calif., 2003; 13 Grammy nominations.

SCRUGGS, RICHARD F., lawyer; b. Brookhaven, Miss., May 17, 1946; m. Diane Scruggs. BA, U. Miss., 1969, JD, 1976. Bar: Miss. 1977, US Dist. Ct., So. and No. Dist. Miss., US Dist. Ct., So. Dist. Alaska, US Ct. Appeals, Fifth Circuit. Note editor Miss. Law Jour., 1975—76; editor-in-chief Miss. Lawyer, 1976; ptnr. Scruggs, Millette, Bozeman & Dent, P.A., Scruggs Law Firm, P.A. Mem. Big Brothers Big Sisters Miss. Carrier pilot USN, 1969—74. Named one of 100 Most Influential Lawyers, Nat. Law Jour., 2006. Fellow: Internat. Acad. Trial Lawyers; mem.: Miss. Bar. Assn., Am. Bar Assn., ABA, Phi Delta Phi. Office: Scruggs Law Firm PA 120A Courthouse Sq PO Box 1136 Oxford MS 38655 Office Phone: 662-281-1212. Office Fax: 662-281-1312.

SCRUGGS, SAMUEL D., lawyer, chemicals executive; b. San Francisco, Sept. 6, 1959; BA, U. Utah, Salt Lake City, 1984; JD, Columbia U., NYC, 1987. Bar: NY 1989. Atty. LeBoef, Lamb, Greene & MacRae, NYC, 1987—89, Skadden, Arps, Slate, Meagher & Flom, NYC, 1989—95; v.p., assoc. gen. counsel, then v.p. corp. tax, then exec. v.p. legal tax & corp. devel. Huntsman Cos., 1995—2002, exec. v.p., corp. gen. counsel, mem. office of chmn., 2002—. Office: Huntsman Corp Legal Dept 500 Huntsman Way Salt Lake City UT 84108 Office Phone: 801-584-5700. *

SCUDDER, CHARLES SEELYE KELLGREN, lawyer; b. London, Feb. 20, 1947; arrived in U.S., 1964; s. Evarts Seelye and Henrica Antonina (Kellgren) Scudder; m. Jannette Harris Ericson, June 20, 1970; children: John Whitney, Jocelyn Seelye, Ansley Harris. BA, Yale U., 1968; BA in Law, Oxford U., Eng., 1973, MA (hon.), 1980; JD with honors, U. Conn., 1975. Bar: NY 76, U.S. Dist. Ct. NY 76. Assoc. Winthrop Stimson Putnam & Roberts, NYC, 1975—81; sr. counsel Conoco Inc., E.I. DuPont de Nemours & Co., Wilmington, Del., 1981—87; v.p., assoc. gen. counsel Unisys Corp., Blue Bell, Pa., 1987—91; sr. v.p., gen. counsel Carnaud-Metalbox, Inc., Cin., 1995—96; ptnr. Obermayer Rebmann Maxwell & Hippel, LLP, Phila., 1991—94, 1996—2001; asst. gen. counsel, corp. sec. Akzo Nobel Inc., Dobbs Ferry, NY, 2001—. Editor: Conn. Law Rev., 1974. Mem. George W. Bush Campaign Com., 1997—2004. With military intelligence US Army, 1968—71. Mem.: ABA (subcom. on multinat. corps.), Am. Corp. Counsel Assn., NY State Bar Assn. Republican. Office: 7 Livinstone Ave Dobbs Ferry NY 10522

SCUDDER, THAYER, anthropologist, educator; b. New Haven, Aug. 4, 1930; s. Townsend III and Virginia (Boody) S.; m. Mary Eliza Drinker, Aug. 26, 1950; children: Mary Eliza, Alice Thayer. Grad., Phillips Exeter Acad., 1948; AB, Harvard U., 1952, PhD, 1960; postgrad., Yale U., 1953-54, London Sch. Econs., 1960-61. Rsch. officer Rhodes-Livingstone Inst., No. Rhodesia, 1956-57, sr. rsch. officer, 1962-63; asst. prof. Am. U., Cairo, 1961-62; rsch. fellow Ctr. Middle East Studies, Harvard U., 1963-64; asst. prof. Calif. Inst. Tech., Pasadena, 1964-66, assoc. prof., 1966-69, prof. anthropology, 1969-2000, prof. emeritus, 2000—; dir. Inst. for Devel. Anthropology, Binghamton, NY, 1976—2002; commr. World Commn. on Dams, 1998-2000. Cons. UN Devel. Program, FAO, IBRD, WHO, Ford Found., Navajo Tribal Coun., AID, World Conservation Union, Lesotho Highlands Devel. Authority, South China Electric Power Joint Venture Corp., U.S. Nat. Rsch. Coun., Que.-Hydro, Environ. Def. Fund, Ministry of Industry and Handicrafts, Lao People's Dem. Republic, Nature Conservancy Author: The Ecology of the Gwembe Tonga, 1962, The Future of Large Dams: Dealing with Social, Environmental, Institutional and Political Costs, 2005; co-author: Long-Term Field Research in Social Anthropology, 1979, Secondary Education and the Formation of an Elite: The Impact of Education on Gwembe District, Zambia, 1980, No Place to Go: The Impacts of Forced Relocation on Navajos, 1982, For Prayer and Profit: The Ritual, Economic and Social Importance of Beer in Gwembe District, Zambia, 1950-1982, 1988, The IUCN Review of the So. Okavango Integrated Water Development Project, 1993. Recipient (1st) Lucy Mair medal for applied anthropology, Royal Anthropol. Inst., 1998, John Phillips award, Phillips Exeter Acad, 2005; John Simon Guggenheim Meml. fellow, 1975. Mem. Am. Anthrop. Assn. (1st recipient Solon T. Kimball award for pub. and applied anthropology 1984, Edward J. Lehman award 1991), Soc. Applied Anthropology (Bronislaw Malinowski award 1999). Office: Calif Inst Tech # 228 77 Pasadena CA 91125-0001 Home Phone: 626-791-1120; Office Phone: 626-395-4207. Business E-Mail: tzs@hss.caltech.edu.

SCUDIERE, DEBRA HODGES, lawyer; b. Columbus, Ohio, Sept. 18, 1954; d. L.L. and Anita Lillian (Campbell) Hodges; m. William A. Scudiere, July 16, 1988; 1 child, Rachel Giovanna. BA magna cum laude, W.Va. U., 1976, JD, 1982. Bar: W.Va. 1982, U.S. Dist. Ct. (no. and so. dists.) W.Va. 1982, U.S. Supreme Ct. 1989. With Furbee, Amos, Webb & Critchfield, Morgantown, W.Va., 1982—2001; atty. Kay Casto & Chaney, PLLC, Morgantown, W.Va., 2001—. Mem. W.Va. Law Rev., 1981-82; adj. lectr. trial advocacy W.Va. U., Morgantown, 1991—. Staff mem. W.Va. Law Rev., 1981-82; rsch. editor Jour. Coll. and Univ. Law, 1981-82. Pres., chmn. bd. dirs. North Cen. W.Va. Legal Aid Soc., Morgantown, 1989-95; bd. dirs. W.Va. Sr. Legal Aid, Inc., 1999—. Mem. Def. Rsch. Inst., Def. Trial Counsel W.Va., Marion County Bar Assn., Monongalia County Bar Assn., W.Va. Bar Assn., W.Va. State Bar (mem. bd. govs., v.p., pres.-elect 2004-05, pres. 2005-06), So. Conf. Bar Pres. (pres. 2005-06), Nat. Conf. Bar Pres., Order of Barrister, Pi Delta Phi, Phi Delta Phi. Mem. Lds Ch. Office: 215 Don Knotts Blvd Ste 310 Morgantown WV 26501 Office Phone: 304-296-1100.

SCULCO, THOMAS PETER, surgeon; b. NYC, Feb. 20, 1944; s. Alfred Francis and Mary Jacqueline Sculco; m. Cynthia Davis, June 4, 1966; children: Sarah Jane, Peter. BA in Classics, Brown U., 1965; MD, Coll. of Physicians and Surgeons Columbia U., 1969. Intern in gen. surgery Roosevelt Hosp., NYC, 1969-70, resident in orthopedic surgery, 1970-71; orthop. fellowship London Hosp., 1974—75; asst. attending orthopedic surgery Meml. Hosp., NYC, 1977-83; resident in orthopedic surgery Hosp. for Spl. Surgery, 1971-74, asst. attending orthopedic surgery, 1977-83, assoc. attending orthopedic surgery, 1983-91, attending surgeon in orthopedics, 1991—, Korein-Wilson prof. orthopedic surgery, surgeon-in-chief, med. dir.; asst. attending orthopedic surgery NY Hosp., 1977-83, attending surgeon in orthopedics, 1991—; cons. orthopedic surgeon Mary Manning Walsh Nursing Home, 1978—, Meml. Hosp., 1983—, Bronx Vets. Adminstrn. Hosp., 1987—; from asst. to assoc. prof. clin. surgery Cornell U., 1977-91; dept. chmn., prof. clin. surgery in orthopedics Weill Med. Coll., Cornell U., 1991—. Chief surg. arthritis svc. Hosp. for Spl. Surgery, 1993-2003, dir. orthopedic surgery, 1993-2003, surgeon-in-chief, 2003—; sr. scientist Hosp. for Spl. Surgery, 1996—. Mem. editl. bd. Surg. Blood Mgmt. Forum, 1997. Trustee NY chpt. Arthritis Found., 1997—; mem. Carnegie Hill Assn., St. Bernard's Sch.; bd. dirs. Westerley (RI) Cmty. Chorus, 190-96; sponsor Westerley Pub. Libr., 1996; patron Met. Opera, Carnegie Hall. MC maj. USAF, 1975—77. Recipient Clint Compere award Twentieth Century Orthopedic Assn., 1997, Lifetime Achievement award Arthritis Found., 1999,; recipient numerous grants; named Best Doctors in NY, NY Mag., 2003 Mem. AMA, NY County Med. Soc., Am. Acad. Orthopedic Surgeons (com. on data svcs. chmn. 1981-85, coun. musculoskeletal specialty socs. 1986-90, coord. com. on health policy 1986-89, task force on data chmn. 1987, com. on clin. policies 1991—, patent edn. com. 1999—, liaison to bd. trustees Arthritis Found. 1999—, bd. dirs. 1999-2001), NY Acad. Medicine, NY State Orthopedic Soc., Eastern Orthopedic Soc., Am. Orthopedic Soc., Austrian Orthop. Soc. (hon.), Interurban Orthopedic Assn., Am. Rheumatism Assn., Orthopedic Rsch. and Edn. Found., Knee Soc. (founding mem. 1983, exec. com. 1983-84, program chmn. 1986, membership com. 1986-93, chmn. 1992-93, edn. com. 1990-94, chmn. 1993-94), Assn. VA Orthopedic Surgeons (founder 1986, sec.-treas. 1986-88), Assn. for Arthritis Hip and Knee Surgery, Acad. Orthopedic Soc., Physicians Sci. Soc., Med. Strollers, Internat. Soc. Tech. in Arthroplasty, Am. Austrian Found. (bd. dirs. 2000—), Hip Soc. (membership com. 2000—, Otto Aufranc Rsch. award 1991, Charnley Rsch. award 1995), Austrian Orthop. Assn. (hon.). Office: The Hosp for Spl Surgery 535 E 70th St New York NY 10021 Address: Belaire Bldg 525 East 71st St 2nd Fl between York Ave and East River New York NY 10021 Office Phone: 212-606-1475. Office Fax: 212-734-9572. Business E-Mail: sculcot@hss.edu.

SCULL, ANDREW T., sociologist, educator; b. Edinburgh, May 2, 1947; arrived in US, 1969; s. Allan Edward and Marjorie Therese Scull; m. Nancy Theresa Principi, Aug. 16, 1970; children: Anna, Andrew, Alexander. BA with first class honours, Oxford U., Eng., 1969; MA, Princeton U., 1971, PhD, 1974. Asst. prof. sociology U. Pa., Phila., 1977—78; vis. assoc. prof. Princeton U., Princeton, NJ, 1978—79; assoc. prof., sociology U. Calif., La Jolla, Calif., 1978—82, prof. sociology, 1982—94, disting. prof. sociology and sci. studies, 1994—. Author: Museums of Madness, 1979, Madhouses, Mad-Doctors, and Madmen, 1981, Decarceration, 1984, Social Order/Mental Disorder, 1989, The Most Solitary of Afflictions: Madness and Society in Britain, 1700-1900, 1993, Masters of Bedlam, 1996, Madhouse: A Tragic Tale of Megalomania and Modern Medicine, 2005, The Race of Insanity, 2006, The Insanity of Place/The Place of Insanity, 2006; co-author (with Steven Lukes): Durkheim and the Law, 1983; co-author: (with Jonathan Andrews) Customers and Patrons of the Mad Trade: The Management of Lunacy in Eighteenth Century London, 2003, Undertaker of the Mind: John Monro and Mad-Doctoring in Eighteenth-Century England, 2001; co-editor (with Stanley Cohen): Social Control and the State, 1983. Office: 401 Social Science Bldg U Calif San Diego 9500 Gilman Dr La Jolla CA 92093-0533 Office Phone: 858-534-0492. Business E-Mail: ascull@ucsd.edu.

SCULLEY, PATRICK DAVID, retired army officer, director; b. Jamestown, NY, Sept. 12, 1947; s. Claude Francis and Hildegarde Ruth (Anderson) S.; m. Peggy Ann Carroll, Aug. 26, 1967; children: Patricia, Paul, Perry, Peter. BA, Wash. and Jefferson Coll., Pa., 1969; DDS, SUNY, Buffalo, 1973; MA in Health Svcs. Mgmt., Webster U., St. Louis, 1994. Diplomate Fed. Svcs. Bd. Gen. Dentistry, Am. Bd. Oral Medicine, Am. Bd. Gen. Dentistry; cert. Am. Coll. Health Care Execs., Am. Soc. Assn. Execs. Commd. US Army, advanced through grades to maj. gen., 1999; gen. practice resident Kimbrough Army Hosp., Ft. Meade, Md., 1973-74; gen. dentist US Army MEDDAC, White Sands Missile Range, N.Mex., 1974-76; gen. dentistry resident US Army DENTAC, Ft. Knox, Ky., 1977-79, clinic chief Ft. Riley, Kans., 1979-81; comdr. 576th Med. Detachment, Bad Kreuznach, West Germany, 1982-85; staff officer US Army Health Svcs. Command, Ft. Sam Houston, Tex., 1985-86, asst. inspector gen., 1986-88; dental cons. Dept. Army Surgeon Gen.'s Office, Washington, 1988-90; student US Army War Coll., Carlisle Barracks, Pa., 1990-91; comdr. US Army Dental Activity, Ft. Bragg, NC, 1991-92; dir. dental svcs. Health Svcs. Command US Army, 1992-93, comdr. Dental Command, 1993-95, asst. surgeon gen. pers., 1996, commdg. gen. US Army Ctr. Health Promotion and Preventive Medicine, 1996-99, acting dep. surgeon gen., 1998-99, dep. surg. gen./chief Army Dental Corps, chief of staff US Army Med. Command, 1999—2002, ret., 2002; exec. dir. Sigma Xi, 2002—06; dir. sci. and tech. Ctr. for Applied Tech., Tex. A&M U., San Antonio, 2006—. Instr. oral medicine gen. practice residency, Ft. Riley, 1980-81; mem. bd. examiners Fed. Svcs. Bd. Gen. Dentistry, Washington, 1986-90; mem. bd. examiners Am. Bd. of Gen. Dentistry, 1991-95. Asst. high sch. football coach Bad Kreuznach Am. H.S., 1982-83; basketball coach Vienna Youth Inc., Va., 1988-89, Cath. Youth Orgn., San Antonio, 1985-86; softball coach Girls Recreation Softball League, Manhattan, Kans., 1981; mem. adv. coun. Raleigh-Durham USO, 2004-06; mem. steering com. NC Project Lead the Way, 2004-06. Fellow: Internat. Coll. Dentists; mem.: ADA (alt. del. Ho. Dels. 1999—2000), Assn. Mil. Surgeons US (Fed. Healthcare Adminstr. of Yr. 2001), Am. Bd. Gen. Dentistry, Acad. Gen. Dentistry (chmn. self-assessment com. 1988—91, pres. Army chpt. 1988—91, ho. of dels. 1988—91, examination coun. 1988—92, chmn. reference com. on adminstrn. comm. and constrn. bylaws 1990, long range planning coun. 1997—98, chmn. long range planning coun. 1998—99, chmn. strategic advancement com. 1999—2002, Disting. Svc. award 1999), Am. Coll. Health Care Execs., Triangle Area's Rsch. Dirs. Club (vice chmn. 2004—, chmn. 2005), Sigma Xi, Omicron Kappa Upsilon. Independent. Roman Catholic. Avocation: coaching athletics. Office: Tex Center for Applied Tech Tex A& M Univ Tex Engring Equip Sta PO Box 35399 San Antonio TX 78235-5399 Business E-Mail: patrick-sculley@tamu.edu.

SCULLIN, FREDERICK JAMES, JR., federal judge; b. Syracuse, NY, Nov. 5, 1939; s. Frederick James and Cleora M. (Fellows) S.; m. Veronica Terek, Aug. 31, 1984; children: Mary Margaret, Kathleen Susan, Kellie Anne, Rebecca Rose; 1 stepchild, Angel Jeanette Godleski. BS in Econs., Niagara U., 1961; LLB, Syracuse U., 1964. Bar: NY 1964, Fla. 1976, US Dist. Ct. (no. dist.) NY 1967, US Supreme Ct. 1971. Assoc. Germain & Germain, Syracuse, 1967-68; asst. dist. atty. Onondaga County, Syracuse, 1968-71; asst. atty. gen. NY State Organized Crime Task Force, 1971-78, dir. regional office Albany, 1974-78; chief prosecutor, dir. Gov.'s Coun. on Organized Crime State of Fla., Tallahassee, 1978—; sole practice Syracuse, 1979-82; US atty. for No. Dist. NY, 1982-92; judge US Dist. Ct. (No. Dist.) NY, 1992—2000, chief judge, 2000—05; judge Fgn. Intelligence Surveillance Ct., 2005—, sr. judge, 2006—. With US Army, 1964-67, Vietnam; col. USAR. Decorated Air medal, 2 Bronze Stars; Cross of Gallantry (Vietnam); recipient Meritorious Svc. Cross, Vietnam Svc. medal, Vietnam Campaign medal, 5 stars; Nat. Def. medal, NY State Dist. Svc. medal, various others. Mem. Am. Judicature Soc., Fla. Bar Assn., Fed. Bar Assn., Fed. Bar Coun., Onon City Bar Assn., Fgn. Intelligence Surveillance Ct Office: US Dist Ct US Courthouse 100 S Clinton St Syracuse NY 13261-6100 Office Phone: 315-234-8560.

SCULLION, ANNETTE MURPHY, lawyer, educator; b. Chgo., Apr. 6, 1926; d. Edmund Patrick and Anna (Nugent) Murphy; 1 child, Kevin. BEd, Chgo. Tchrs. Coll., 1960; JD, DePaul U., 1964, MEd, 1966, Loyola U., Chgo., 1970; EdD, No. Ill. U., 1974. Bar: Ill. 1964, U.S. Dist. Ct. (no. dist.) Ill. 1965, U.S. Ct. Appeals (D.C. cir.) 1978. Lectr. Chgo. C.C., 1964-68; pvt. practice Chgo., 1964—; from asst. prof. bus. edn. to prof. Chgo. State U., 1966-98. Founder, adviser Bus. Edn. Students Assn., Chgo. State U., 1976—; sch. law workshop coord. Ill. Divsn. Vocat. and Tech. Edn., 1981, coord. edn. workshops, 1990—. Mem. ABA, Nat. Bus. Edn. Assn., Womens Bar Assn. Ill., Am. Tchr. Edn., Beta Gamma Sigma. Home: 386 Muskegon Ave Calumet City IL 60409-2347

SCULLY, JOHN CARROLL, life insurance marketing research company executive; b. Springfield, Mass., Mar. 16, 1932; s. James and Frances (Carroll) S.; m. Barbara A. Fougere, Sept. 7, 1953; children: Kathleen, Margaret, John, James, Patricia, Mary Ellen, Susan. BA, Holy Cross Coll., 1953; C.L.U., Boston U., 1963; postgrad., Dartmouth Inst., 1977. With John Hancock Mut. Life Ins. Co., 1953-92, gen. agent Indpls., 1966-75, sr. v.p. agency dept. Boston, 1975-80, pres. retail sector, 1980-92; pres. emeritus Life. Ins. Mktg. Rsch. Assoc., Windsor, Conn., 1992-97. Bd. dirs. Greater Boston YMCA, 1975-91; chmn. Mass. campaign Holocaust Meml. Mus., 1985—; div. chmn. United Way, 1985—; bd. dirs. Cath. Charities, 1986—; trustee Springfield Coll., 1986, Suffolk U., 1986, Am. United Life Ins. Co. With U.S. Army, 1954-56. Mem. Am. Coll. Life Underwriters, Nat. Assn. Life Underwriters (v.p. Ind. 1973-75), Life Ins. Mktg. and Rsch. Assn. (past chmn.), Gen. Agts. and Mgrs. Assn. (past pres. Indpls. Nat. Mgmt. award 1973-75), Life Underwriter Tng. Coun. (past chmn.), Greater Boston C. of C. (bd. dirs. 1985—), Wellesley Club, Executives Club (past pres.), Algonquin Club (bd. dirs.), KC. Roman Catholic. Home: Unit 414 4800 N AIA Vero Beach FL 32963 Office: Limra Internat PO Box 208 Hartford CT 06141-0208 Personal E-mail: jscully@limra.com.

SCULLY, JOHN EDWARD, JR., banker; b. Chgo., Jan. 18, 1943; s. John Edward and Ann Berenice (Allenbrand) S.; m. Mary Julia Purvin, June 11, 1966; children: Melissa, Julie, John Edward III. BA, U. Notre Dame, 1964; MA, DePaul U., 1966. Supr., No. Trust Co., Chgo., 1968-69, with personnel dept., 1969-74, personnel officer, 1974-77, bond investment officer, 1977-80; asst. v.p. First Nat. Bank of Chgo., 1980-82, v.p., 1982-87; first v.p. Exch. Nat. Bank, 1987-90; sr. v.p. ABN AMRO, 1990-2005, group sr. v.p., 2005—06, ret., 2006; mem. mgmt. com. LaSalle Bank, Chgo., 1991-2002. Bd. dirs. Chgo. Heart Assn., 1987-98; trustee Village of Riverside, 2001—; chmn. Ill. Employer Support of Guard and Res. Maj. gen., 1964-96; civilian aide to sec. of army, 2006—. Mem. Soc. for Human Resource Management, Mil. Officers Assn., Mil. Order World Wars, Assn. U.S. Army, Am. Legion, VFW, USO of Ill., Riverside Swim Club, Union League Chgo. (dir. 1993-96, 2d v.p., pres. 1999-2000). Roman Catholic. Home: 258 Lawton Rd Riverside IL 60546-2337 Office: LaSalle Bank Corp Chicago IL 60603 Home Phone: 708-447-7531; Office Phone: 708-227-8184. Personal E-mail: john.scully@sbcglobal.net.

SCULLY, JOHN THOMAS, obstetrician, gynecologist, educator; b. NYC, Mar. 11, 1931; s. John Thomas and Mildred Frances (Dunstrop) Scully; m. Kimberly Ann Stamberger; children: John, Helen, Mary, Thomas, Nora, James, Sara, Megan, Devin. BS, Georgetown U., 1952; MD, U. Mex., 1959. Diplomate Am. Bd. Ob-gyn. Intern Nassau Hosp., 1959-60, resident, 1960-63; practice medicine specializing in ob-gyn, 1963—; sr. attending dept. ob-gyn St. Peter's U. Hosp., 1971—75, chmn. dept. ob-gyn., 2003—06. Fellow: ACOG, ACS; mem.: NJ Ob-gyn Soc., Middlesex County Med. Soc., NJ Med. Soc., NJ Right to Life (charter). Republican. Roman Catholic. Office: 215 Union Ave Ste A Bridgewater NJ 08807 Office Phone: 908-722-2900.

SCULLY, MARLAN ORVIL, physics professor; b. Casper, Wyo., Aug. 3, 1939; s. Orvil O. and Thelma G. (Thoms) Scully; m. Judith Bailey, Aug. 16, 1958; children: James, Robert, Steven. AS, Casper Coll., 1959; BS, U. Wyo., 1961; MS, Yale U., 1963, PhD, 1966. Instr. Yale U., New Haven, 1967-69; asst. prof. MIT, Cambridge, 1969-71, assoc. prof., 1971-72; prof. U. Ariz., Tucson, 1972-80; disting. prof. physics U. N.Mex., Albuquerque, 1980—92; prof. physics Tex. A&M U., 1992—96; dir. Ctr. Theoretical Physics, Tex. A&M U., 1995—; Burgess disting. prof. Tex. A&M U., 1996—, prof. elec. engring., 1999—; disting. rsch. chair TEES, 2000—; dir. Inst. Quantum Studies, Tex. A&M U., 2001—. Dir., co-founder Radtech, 1984; mem. Joint coun. on Quantum Electronics, Internat. Commn. on Optics; mem. program com. VIIth and VIIIth Internat. Conf. on Quantum Electronics (co-chmn. program com.); panel mem. Internat. Conf. on Hot Electrons in Semiconductors, North Tex. State U.; co-dir. VIIth Course of NATO Internat. Sch. Quantum Electronics; mem. program com. for OSA sponsored topical meeting on Picosecons Phenomena, Hilton Head, S.C., 1978; invited lectr. U.S.-Japan Coop. Seminar on Laser Spectroscopy, Hakone, Japan, 1977; mem. NRC panel on electron, atomic and molecular physics; advisor to ARO Nat. Acad. Panel, Los Alamos Physics Div. Author: (with others) Laser Physics, 1974; contbr. articles to profl. jours. Recipient Elliott Cresson medal The Franklin Inst., 1990; John S. Guggenheim fellow, 1970, Alfred P. Sloan fellow, 1972. Fellow AAAS, Optical Soc. Am. (dir. at large 1978-80, publs. com. 1972, Ives medal com. 1976, chmn. Wood prize com. 1978, Adolph E. Lomb medal 1970; mem. Max Planck Soc, Nat. Acad. Scis., Academia Europa. Avocations: cattle ranching, inventing.

SCULLY, MARTHA SEEBACH, speech and language pathologist; b. S.I., Nov. 1, 1951; d. Henry F. and Rose Anne (Callahan) Seebach; m. Roger Tehan Scully, Dec. 29, 1979; 1 child, Roger Tehan. BA, Trinity Coll., 1972; MS, George Washington U., 1974; postgrad., Syracuse U., NY, 1976-79. Lic. speech-lang. pathologist, Md. Clin. supr. Syracuse U., 1976-79; speech-lang. pathologist Fairfax (Va.) County Pub. Schs., 1979—. Bd. dirs. Trinity Coll., Washington, Nat. Children's Choir,

1987-91; trustee Davis Meml. Goodwill Industries, 1994-96, bd. dirs. Goodwill Guild, 1990—, chair ball; docent Folger Shakespearean Libr.; chmn. Nat. Challenge Com. of Disabled, 1985; mem. Ear Ball, 1988, 89; mem. Internat. Children's Festival, 1990, 91; co-chmn. Jr. League of Washington Capital Collection, 1990; chmn. Salvation Army Garden Party, 1992, Washington Embassy Tour, 1993; mem. bd. edn. Holy Cross Sch., Garrett Park, Md., 2001-. Recipient First Order Affiliation Order of Franciscans mirror, 1985; named Outstanding Woman in Am., 1987, 88. Mem. Am. Biog. Inst., Am. Speech-Lang.-Hearing Assn., Coun. for Exceptional Children, Montgomery County Assn. for Hearing Impaired Children, Benevolent and Protective Order Elks (mem. Washinton-Rockville lodge, lecturing knight 1999, esteemed loyal knight 2000; chaplain, 2006-07), Christ Child Soc., John Caroll Soc., Chevy Chase Women's Republican Club. Home: 10923 Wickshire Way Rockville MD 20852-3220

SCULLY, ROBERT WILLIAM (BOB SCULLY), diversified financial services company executive; b. Boston; m. Nancy Beth Peretsman, Sept. 17, 1988. AB, Princeton U., 1972; MBA, Harvard Bus. Sch., 1977. Joined Salomon Brothers, 1979, v.p. domestic products capital markets svc. group, mng. dir., 1984—88; co-founder Scully Brothers & Foss, 1988—93; mng. dir. industrials investment banking, mem. investment banking mgmt. com. Lehman Brothers, 1993—96; joined Morgan Stanley, 1996, vice chmn. investment banking, 1999, chmn. global capital markets, 2004, co-pres., 2006—. Bd. dirs. Global Fund for Children. Office: Morgan Stanley 1585 Broadway New York NY 10036 *

SCULLY, ROGER TEHAN, II, lawyer; b. Washington, Jan. 10, 1948; s. James Henry and Marietta (Maguire) S.; m. Martha Anne Seebach, Dec. 29, 1979. BS, U. Md., 1977; JD, Cath. U., 1980. Bar: Md. 1980, D.C. 1981, U.S. Tax Ct. 1982, U.S. Supreme Ct. 1988. V.p. Bogley Related Cos., Rockville, Md., 1971-75; law clk. to presiding justice Superior Ct. of D.C., Washington, 1979-81; assoc. Lerch, Early & Roseman, Bethesda, Md., 1981-82; gen. counsel Laszlo N. Tauber, M.D. & Assocs., Bethesda, 1982-94, Jefferson Meml. Hosp., Alexandria, Va., 1982-94; spl. counsel Venable, Baetjer, Howard & Civiletti, Washington, 1991-96. Cons. in real estate Order of Friar Minor, N.Y.C., 1977—; lectr. Mortgage Bankers Assn., Washington, 1984—; bd. dirs. Nozzoli Constrn. Co., Washington; exec. com., spl. counsel to bd. dirs., bd. dirs. Chromachron Technology Corp., Toronto; bd. dirs. MusicWorks, N.Y.C.; vice chair Sayett Tech., Inc., Rochester, N.Y.; vice chair, bd. dirs., exec. com. MediaShow, Inc., Rochester; mng. dir. Jefferson Meml. LLC, Washington. Author: (with Quarles & Howard) Summary Adjudication Dispositive Motions and Summary Trials, 1991. Mem. pres.'s coun. St. Bonaventure U., Olean, N.Y., 1995—, chmn. pres.'s coun., 1986-96; trustee Belmont Abbey Coll., Charlotte, N.C., 1993-95; bd. trustees Edmund Burke Sch., Washington, 1984-2001, trustees emeritus, 2001-; bd. dirs. Nat. Children's Choir, Washington, 1980-94. Recipient First Order Affiliation Order of Friars Minor, 1985; named one of Outstanding Young Men in Am., 1982. Fellow D.C. Bar Assn.; mem. ABA, ATLA, FBA, Md. Bar Assn. (chmn. corp. counsel sect.), Am. Judicature Soc., Assn. Governing Bd. of Univs. and Colls., Am. Inns of Ct., Irish Legal Soc., Selden Soc., U.S. Jud. Conf. of 4th Cir. (permanent mem.), U.S. Jud. Conf. Fed. Cir. (del.), Jud. Conf. of D.C. (del.). Office: 7712 Greentree Rd West Bethesda MD 20817-1428 Personal E-mail: rts2esq@yahoo.com.

SCULLY, SEAN PATRICK, orthopaedic surgeon, educator; s. Michael A. and Anne Rita Scully; m. Kristi Griffin Scully, Aug. 11, 1979; children: Patrick, Colin. BS in Biochemistry, SUNY, Binghamton, 1978; MD, PhD in Biophysics, U. Rochester, 1986. Cert. Am. Bd. Orthop. Surgery, 1995. Residency Duke U., Durham, NC, 1986—92; intramural rsch. fellowship Nat. Inst. Health, Bethesda, Md., 1989—90; asst. prof. cell biology Duke U. Medical Ctr., 1994—2000, assoc. prof. orthop., 1997—2000; clin. orthop. oncology fellow Mass. Gen. Hosp., Boston, 1992—93; assoc. prof. orthop. Mayo Medical Sch., Rochester, Minn., 2001—03, prof. orthop., 2003—04; prof. orthop., cell biology and cellular molecular pharmacology U. Miami, 2004—. Mem. advisory panel Musculoskeletal Transplant Found., 1994—2001; vice-chmn. Shriners Rsch. Advisory Bd., 1996—; Ad Hoc reviewer, orthop. study section NIH, 1997—, OBM-2, NIH, 2001—; presenter in field. Dep. editor Clinical Orthopaedics and Related Research, 2003—; contbr. articles to prof. jours., chpts. to books. Named one of America's Top Doctors for Cancer, Cantle Connolly's LTD, 2005; recipient William F. Neuman award in biophysics, 1984, George H. Whipple award, 1986, Marshall R. Urist award, 1999; grantee John J. Fahey N.Am. Traveling fellowship, 1993. Mem.: Austriah Swiss German, Nat. Inst. Arthritis, Musculoskeletal and Skin Diseases Nat. Inst. Health (FDA panel on cartilage repair 2005—), Internat. Skeletal Soc., Internat. Soc. Limb Salvage, Soc. Surgical Oncologists, Am. Orthop. Assn. (Howard Hatcher fellowship com. 2000, ASG fellowship com. 2000, Austrian Swiss German Traveling fellowship 2000), Assn. Bone and Joint Surgeons (co-chair symposium on gene therapy in orthop. 2000, awards com. 2002—), Musculoskeletal Tumor Soc. (strategic planning com. 2001, specialty day organizer 2001), Orthop. Rsch. Soc., Am. Acad. Orthop. Surgeons (sub-com. basic sci. evaluation 1995—, program com. 1999—, clinician scientist com. 2001—, fellowship issues task force 2003—, Howard Hatcher pathology fellowship com. 2003—, ASG fellowship exchange com. 2003—). Achievements include research in tumor biology. Office: U Miami 1400 NW 12th Ave Miami FL 33136 Home Phone: 786-457-1694. Fax: 305-325-3928.

SCULLY, THOMAS A., lawyer, former federal agency administrator; b. 1957; BA, U. Va., 1979; JD, Cath. U., 1986. Staff asst. Fed. Election Commn., 1979—81, U.S. Senator Slade Gorton, 1981—85; atty. Akin, Gump, Strauss, Hauer & Feld, LLP, 1986—88; comm. staff Bush-Quayle Campaign, 1988, dep. dir. congl. affairs; assoc. dir. human resources, vets. and labor Office Mgmt. & Budget, Washington, 1989—92, counselor to the dir., 1992—93; pres., CEO Fedn. Am. Hosps., 1995—2001; ptnr. Patton Boggs, LLP, Washington; dep. asst. to the pres. The White House, Washington, 2001—03; CEO, adminstr. Centers. for Medicare and Medicaid Services US Dept. Health & Human Services, Washington, 2001—03; sr. counsel Alston & Bird LLP, Washington, 2003—. Mem.: bd. dirs., SHPS, Inc., 2004-. Republican. Office: Alston & Bird LLP 10th Fl N Bldg 601 Pennsylvania Ave NW Washington DC 20004-3606 Office Phone: 202-756-3459. Business E-Mail: tscully@alston.com.

SCULLY, VINCENT JOSEPH, JR., architectural historian, educator, writer; b. New Haven, 1920; m. Susannah (Nancy) Keith, 1942 (div. 1965); m. Marian La Follette Wohl (div. 1978); m. Catherine Lynn, 1980. Entered Yale U. at age 16; BA in English, Yale U., 1940; MA in art history, Yale U., 1947, PhD in art history, 1949. Mem. faculty art history Yale U., New Haven, 1949—91, prof. art history, 1961-91, Sterling Prof. Emeritus of the History of Art, 1991—, master Morse Coll., 1969—75; disting. vis. prof. Sch. Architecture U. Miami, 1992—. Author: (books) The Shingle Style: Architectural Theory and Design from Richardson to the Origins of Wright, 1955, Frank Lloyd Wright, 1960, Modern Architecture: The Architecture of Democracy, 1961, Louis I Kahn, 1962, The Architectural Heritage of Newport, Rhode Island, 1640-1915, 1967, American Architecture and Urbanism, 1969, Pueblo Architecture of the Southwest, 1971, The Shingle Style and The Stick Style: Architectural Theory and Design from Richardson to the Origins of Wright, 1971, The Shingle Style Today: Or the Historian's Revenge, 1974, Pueblo: Mountain, Village, Dance, 1975, The Earth, the Temple, and the Gods: Greek Sacred Architecture, 1979, Robert Stern, 1981, Studies and Executed Buildings by Frank Lloyd Wright, 1986, The Villas of Palladio, 1986, New World Visions of Household Gods and Sacred Places: American Art and the Metropolitan Museum, 1650-1914, 1988, The Architecture of the American Summer: The Flowering of the Shingle Style, 1989, The Architecture of Robert Venturi, 1989, The Great Dinosaur Mural at Yale: The Age of Reptiles, 1990, Architecture: The Natural and the Man-Made, 1991, French Royal Gardens: The Design of Andre Le Notre, 1992, (book of essays) Modern Architecture and Other Essays, 2003; co-author: (with C. Lynn, E. Vogt, P. Goldberger) Yale in New Haven: Architecture & Urbanism, 2004. Served USMC, 1941—46. Named Jefferson Lectr., NEH, 1995; recipient Wilbur Lucius Cross Medal, Yale Grad. Sch. Alumni Assn., 1994, inaugural Vincent Scully Prize, Nat. Bldg. Mus., Washington, DC, 1999, J.C. Nichols Prize, Urban Land Inst., 2003, Nat. Medal of Arts, 2004; Fulbright Fellow, 1950. Office: Yale U Dept History of Art 56 High St PO Box 208272 New Haven CT 06520

SCURICH, KELLY LEMOS, music director; b. Sharon, Pa., Sept. 21, 1960; d. John and Mildred Novak Lemos; m. Thomas Michael Scurich, Oct. 10, 1987; children: Jenna Christine, Jonathan Frank. MusB, Youngstown State U., Ohio, 1983; MusM, Youngstown State U., 1985. Tchr. St. Mary's Mid. Sch., Warren, Ohio, 1985—86; dir. music Holy Trinity Luth. Ch., Hermitage, Pa., 1983—88; choral music dir. West Branch HS, Beloit, Ohio, 1987—93, Hickory HS, Hermitage, 1993—94, Canfield HS, Ohio, 1994—; dir. music First Covenant Ch., Boardman, Ohio, 1988—94. Named Tchr. of the Yr., Mahoning County Fine Arts Coun., 1992. Mem.: Ohio Choral Dirs. Assn. (show choir chair, bd. dirs. 1988—92), Ohio Music Educators Assn., Am. Choral Dirs. Assn., Nat. Assn. Tchrs. Singing, Music Educators Nat. Conf. Office: Canfield High School 100 Cardinal Dr Canfield OH 44406

SCURLOCK, JO ANN, history professor, researcher; b. Kansas City, Mo., Sept. 22, 1953; d. John Edward and Jean Lorraine Scurlock; m. Richard Henry Beal, May 13, 1978. BA, U. Chgo., 1975; PhD, U. of Chgo., 1988. Prof. of history Elmhurst (Ill.) Coll., 1984—. Author: (scholarly book) Diagnoses in Assyrian and Babylonian Medicine, Magico-Medical Means of Treating Ghost Induced Illnesses in Ancient Mesopotamia; contbr. articles to scholarly jours. Grantee, NEH, 2000—03. Mem.: Chgo. Soc. for Bibl. Rsch., Am. Hist. Assn., Soc. of Bibl. Lit., Am. Oriental Soc. Avocations: travel, architectural and ethnographic photography. Office: Elmhurst Coll 190 Prospect Elmhurst IL 60126 Home Phone: 773-752-2741; Office Phone: 630-617-3569. Home Fax: 773-702-9853.

SCURRY, BRIANA COLLETTE, professional soccer player; b. Mpls., Sept. 7, 1971; BS in Polit. Sci., U. Mass., 1995. Goalkeeper U.S. Women's Nat. Soccer Team, Chgo., 1994—99, 2002—; profl. soccer player Atlanta Beat (WUSA), 2001—03. Mem. U.S. Olympic Soccer Team, Athens, 2004. Named Goalkeeper of Yr., Mo. Athletic Club Sports Found., 1993; recipient Gold medal, Atlanta Olympics, 1996, Athens Olympic games, 2004, World Cup champion, 1999, Silver medal, Sydney Olympic Games, 2000. Office: US Soccer Fedn US Soccer House 1801 S Prairie Ave Chicago IL 60616-1319

SCUSERIA, GUSTAVO ENRIQUE, theoretical chemist; b. San Fernando, Buenos Aires, Argentina, July 30, 1956; arrived in US, 1985, naturalized; s. Eraldo L. and Alicia (Capitanelli) S.; m. Ana Inés Ilvento, Apr. 17, 1982; children: Ignacio, Tomás. BS, MS, U. Buenos Aires, 1979, PhD in Physics, 1983. Grad. asst. U. Buenos Aires, 1979-83, asst. prof., 1983-85; rsch. assoc. U. Calif., Berkeley, 1985-87; sr. rsch. assoc. U. Ga., Athens, 1987-89; asst. prof. Rice U., Houston, 1989-93, assoc. prof., 1993-95, prof., 1995-2000, Robert A. Welch prof. chemistry, 2000—. Recipient IBM Partnership award IBM Corp., 1998-99; Camille and Henry Dreyfus Teacher scholar Camille and Henry Dreyfus Found., 1992; John Simon Guggenheim Meml. Found. fellow, 2003. Fellow AAAS, Am. Phys. Soc.; mem. Am. Chem. Soc., Materials Rsch. Soc. Office: Rice U Dept Chemistry PO Box 1892 Houston TX 77251-1892 E-mail: guscus@rice.edu.

SCZUDLO, WALTER JOSEPH, lawyer; s. Walter and Dolores J. Sczudlo; children: Lauren Hall, Elizabeth Fairbanks, Walter Christopher; m. Rebecca Grey Tucker. AB, Middlebury Coll.; JD, Golden Gate U.; LLM, Georgetown U.; post grad., U. Calif., Santa Barbara, Tulane U., Vt. Law Sch. Bar: Alaska, Calif., DC, US Ct. Appeals (9th cir.), US Ct. Appeals (DC cir.), US Dist. Ct. (no., cen., ea. and so. dists.) Calif., US Dist. Ct. Alaska, US Ct. Claims, US Tax Ct. Law clk. to presiding justice Alaska Supreme Ct.; assoc. atty. Merdes, Schaible, Staley and Delisio, Anchorage; legis. dir., gen. counsel U.S. Senator Murkowski, Washington; sr. tax assoc. Schramm and Raddue, Santa Barbara, Calif.; dir. congl. rels., counsel Natural Gas Supply Assn., Washington; Washington counsel Shell Oil Co.; v.p., Washington counsel Intercontinental Energy Corp.; gen. counsel, exec. v.p. Assn. Fundraising Profls., Washington, 1999—; prin. ptnr. WEBK Broadcasting 105.3 FM, Killington, Vt., 1985—. Dir., exec. com. mem. pub. affairs coun., Washington, 2003-, dir. Pacific & Western Energy, Inc., Fairbanks, Alaska, 1980-, Sun's Edge, Inc., Santa Barbara, 1987—, Natural Gas Roundtable, Washington, 1987—. Author: (with other) Washington Legal Foundation, 1988. Com. chmn. Steve Cowper for Gov., Anchorage, 1982. Recipient Am. Jurisprudence award Bancroft-Whitney Pub. Co. Office Phone: 800-666-3863.

SEABAUGH, WILLIAM F., lawyer; BS magna cum laude, U. Mo., 1978; JD magna cum laude, U. Mich., 1981. Bar: Mo. 1981. Ptnr., group co-leader Transactions Bryan Cave LLP, St. Louis. Office: Bryan Cave LLP One Metropolitan Sq 211 N Broadway, Ste 3600 Saint Louis MO 63102 Office Phone: 314-259-2450. E-mail: wfseabaugh@bryancave.com.

SEABOLD, DANIELLE, educational association administrator; b. Ann Arbor, Dec. 6, 1971; d. Gloria J. and Richard D. Seabold; m. Dirk Bradley, Aug. 21, 2004; 1 child, McKenna H. Bradley. BA, Kalamazoo Coll., Mich., 1994; MA, U. Tex., Austin, 2005. Tchr. physics and math. Kalamazoo Pub. Schs., 1994—2001; program coord. Women in Engring. Program, Austin, 2001—04; sr. program coord. Charles A. Dana Ctr., 2004—. Grantee Nat. Rsch. Grant, Coun. on Undergraduate Rsch., 1993. Mem.: Phi Beta Kappa (assoc.).

SEABOLT, RICHARD L., lawyer; b. Chgo., Aug. 28, 1949; BGS with distinction, U. Mich., 1971; JD, U. Calif., Hastings, 1975. Bar: Calif. 1975. Ptnr. Duane Morris LLP, San Francisco, 1981—. Mem. Calif. Civil Jury Instr. Adv. Com. Author: Matthew Bender Practice Guides, California Pretrial Civil Procedure and Civil Discovery, 2004. Mem.: Assn. Bus. Trial Lawyers (bd. govs.), State Bar Calif. (chair litig. sect. 2006). Office: Duane Morris LLP One Market Spear Tower San Francisco CA 94111 Office Phone: 415-957-3212. Business E-Mail: rlseabolt@duanemorris.com.

SEABOLT, ROBERT D., lawyer; b. Newport News, Va., 1955; BA magna cum laude, Univ. Richmond, 1977; JD, Univ. Va., 1980. Bar: Va. 1980. Adminstrv. ptnr. Troutman Sanders LLP, Richmond, Va., and mem. exec. com. Named one of Virginia's Legal Elite, Civil Litig. Mag., 2003. Mem.: ABA, Va. State Bar, Va. Bar Assn., Richmond Bar Assn. Office Phone: 804-697-1328. Office Fax: 804-698-5100. Business E-Mail: bob.seabolt@troutmansanders.com.

SEABORG, DAVID MICHAEL, evolutionary biologist; b. Berkeley, Calif., Apr. 22, 1949; s. Glenn Theodore and Helen Lucille (Griggs) S.; m. Adele Fong Yee, June 17, 1990. BS, U. Calif., Davis, 1972; MA, U. Calif., Berkeley, 1974. Biology tchr. U. Calif., Berkeley, 1972-73; biol. rschr., photographer Trans Time Labs, Berkeley, 1978; pvt. practice, 1974—; hypnosis and self-hypnosis tchr. Open Edn. Exchange, Oakland, Calif., 1978—81; biol. tchr. Oakland Mus., Calif., 1983-87; rsch. biologist, dept. ecology and evolutionary biology U. Calif., Irvine, 1987; pres. dir. Rsch. Found. for Biol. Conservation and Rsch., Walnut Creek, Calif., 1983—; radio talk show host Sta. KPFA, Berkeley, 1996; biology and life sci tchr. Phillip and Sala Burton Acad. H.S., San Francisco, 1996-97; lab. Chem. Biodynamics U. Calif., Berkeley, 1975; comedian, 1969—. Vol. asst. to curator Smithsonian Instn. 1966-67; lectr. sci, philos., environ. issues, 1974—; Inventor game, Sum-It, 1981; originator, theory of evolution based on organisms as integrated systems; chmn. Com. for Arts and Lectures, U. Calif., Berkeley, 1974-75; chmn. Bastille Day, Lafayette (Calif.)-Langeac Soc., 1982, master of ceremonies, 1982-86, 98-2000. Contbr. articles to profl. sci. jours. Environ. organizer, founder, pres. U Turn Soc., Glenn Seaborg Open Space Fund, World Rainforest Fund, Found. for Biol. Conservation and Rsch.; creator, organizer press conf. on global environ. and social issues 100th Nobel Prize Festivities, Stockholm, 2001. Recipient Meritorius Svc. award Smithsonian Inst., 1967, Animal Photograph award Soc. Photographic Scientists and Engrs., 1967, Best of Show Photo Contest award Klamath Basin Audubon Soc., 1991; award Nat. Libr. Poetry, 1995, 99, 2006, 07. Mem.: UN Assn. of USA (East Bay chpt. bd. dirs. 2006—), Nat. Resources Def. Coun., Earth Island Inst., World Wildlife Fund, Desert Tortoise Preserve Com., Population Connection, Save the Bay Assn., Greenpeace, Rainforest Action Network, Nature Conservancy, Calif. Alumni Assn., Calif. Aggie Alumni Assn., Sierra Club, Club of Rome USA (bd. dirs. 1995—, v.p. 1998—2001). Democrat. Address: 1888 Pomar Way Walnut Creek CA 94598-1424 Office Phone: 925-938-9206. E-mail: davidseaborg@juno.com.

SEABROOK, JOHN MARTIN, retired food products executive, chemical engineer; b. Seabrook, NJ, Apr. 16, 1917; s. Charles Franklin and Norma Dale (Ivins) S.; m. Anne Schlaudecker, Apr. 5, 1939 (div. 1951); children: Carol Ormsby (Mrs. Jacques P. Boulanger), Elizabeth Anne; m. Elizabeth Toomey, 1956; children: John Martin, Bruce Cameron. BS in Chem. Engring, Princeton, 1939; LL.D. (hon.), Gettysburg Coll., 1974. Registered profl. engr., N.J., Del. Engr. Deerfield Packing Corp., 1939-41; v.p. Seabrook Farms Co., 1941-50, exec. v.p., 1950-54, dir., 1941-59, pres., 1954-59, chief exec. officer, 1955-59; dir. Pa. Reading & Seashore Line, 1950-63, N.Y. Ctrl. R.R., 1964-69, Penn Ctrl. R.R., 1968-71; cons. IU Internat. Corp., Wilmington, Del., 1959, v.p., 1960-65, dir., 1963-87, pres., 1965-73, 74-78, chief exec., 1967-80, chmn. bd., 1969-82, chmn. exec. com., 1982-87. Pres., bd. dirs. Cumberland Automobile & Truck Co., 1954-59, Cumberland Warehouse Corp., 1954-59, Salem Farms Corp, N.J., 1948—; chmn. bd. dirs. Frick Co., Waynesboro, Pa., 1959-68; chmn., bd. dirs. S.W. Fabricating & Welding Co., Inc., Houston, 1964-68; chmn. Divcon, Inc., Houston, 1967-69; pres. bd. dirs. Internat. Utilities Overseas Capital Corp., Wilmington, 1966-82, chmn., 1970-80; v.p. Gen. Waterworks Corp., Phila., 1959-66, pres., 1966-68, chmn., 1968-71; chmn. bd. dirs. GWC Inc., Phila., 1971-73; pres. Brown Bros. Contractors, Inc., Phila., 1960, chmn. bd. dirs., 1965-67; pres. Am. Portable Irrigation Co., Eugene, Oreg., 1961, chmn. bd. dirs., 1966-68; chmn. bd. dirs. Gotaas-Larsen Shipping Corp., 1963, chmn., 1979, pres., CEO, 1982-88; chmn. bd. dirs. Amvit Corp., Cleve., 1964-68; bd. dirs. Echo Bay Mines Ltd., South Jersey Gas Co., Folsom, N.J., South Jersey Industries, Inc., Folsom, Bell Atlantic Corp.; dir. emeritus Bell Atlantic-N.J., Inc. Mem. N.J. Migrant Labor Bd., 1945-67, chmn., 1955-67; mem. N.J. Bd. Higher Edn., 1967-70, Pres.' Air Quality Adv. Bd., 1968-70; bd. dirs. Brandywine Conservancy, Inc., 1972-95, pres., 1992-93, hon. dir., 1997—; trustee Eisenhower Exch. Fellowships, 1974-85; trustee Hitchcock Found., 1991-96, chmn., 1993-96. Mem.: Coaching Club (N.Y.C. and U.K.), Wilmington (Del.) Club, Phila. Club, Knickerbocker Club (N.Y.C.), Racquet and Tennis Club (N.Y.C.), Phi Beta Kappa. Home: PO Box 3338 Aiken SC 29802 Office Phone: 856-935-5200, 800-358-5201. E-mail: jmsdrives@snip.net.

SEABROOK, RAYMOND J., corporate financial executive; b. Toronto, Canada, Mar. 1, 1950; married; 2 children. B in Bus., McMaster U., Hamilton, Ontario, 1975. Cert. arch., Humber Coll., Toronto, 1972. With Coopers and Lybrand, Toronto, Canada, 1976—85; v.p. fin. control Onex Packaging and Am. Can Can., 1985—88; sr. v.p., CFO Ball Packaging Products Canada, 1988—92; v.p., treas. Ball Corp., Broomfield, Colo., 1992—96, v.p. planning & control, 1996—98, sr. v.p. fin., 1998—2000, sr. v.p., CFO, 2000—06, exec. v.p., CFO, 2007—. Bd. dir. Andersen Corp., 2004—. Office: Ball 10 Longs Peak Dr Broomfield CO 80021 *

SEACREST, RYAN (RYAN JOHN SEACREST), television and radio personality, entrepreneur; b. Atlanta, Dec. 24, 1976; s. Gary and Connie Seacrest. Attended, U. Ga., 1994—95. DJ WSTR/Star 94, Atlanta, 1992—94, 102.7 KIIS-FM morning show. Launched fashion line, R Line, 2005; part owner at Katana, Sushi Roku and Boa. Host (TV series) Gladiators 2000, 1994, Radical Outdoor Challenge, ESPN, 1995, The New Edge, 1996, The Click, 1997, American Idol, 2002—, American Juniors, 2003, host, exec. prodr. On-Air With Ryan Seacrest, 2004, corr. Extra Weekends, 2002, The Tonight Show, 2005—, host (TV) Wild Animal Games, 1995, (radio) Live from the Lounge, Star 98.7, 1995—2001, Ryan Seacrest for the Ride Home, Star 98.7, L.A., 1995—2004, American Top 40, 2004—, On-Air With Ryan Seacrest, 102.7 KIIS-FM, L.A., 2004—, New Year's Eve: Live From Times Square With Ryan Seacrest, NYC, 2003—; exec. prodr.: New Year's Eve: Live From Times Square With Ryan Seacrest, 2004, New Year's Rockin' Eve 2006, 2005; actor: (TV series) Reality Check, 1995; voice Hey Arnold!, 1999, Robot Chicken, 2005, guest appearances Beverly Hills, 90210, 2000, Mad TV, 2002, 2005, Player$, 2003, guest host Good Day Live, 2003, Larry King Live, 2003, 2004, 2005. Named one of 50 Most Beautiful People, People Mag., 2003, 100 Most Powerful Celebrities, Forbes.com, 2007. Office: William Morris Agy 1 William Morris Pl Beverly Hills CA 90212 Business E-Mail: Ryan@kiisfm.com, ryan@eonline.com. E-mail: Ryan@AT40.com.

SEADEN, GEORGE, civil engineer; b. Cracow, May 26, 1936; s. Simon and Mary (Guttman) S.; m. Linda Helen Mutch, Mar. 18, 1978; children: Amy Elisabeth, Maia Claire. BE, McGill U., Montreal, Que., Can., 1958; MS, Harvard U., 1968; postgrad., Northwestern U., 1992. Engr. Gatineau Power, Hull, Que., 1958-59, Ent. Fougerolle, Paris, 1960-62; mgr. Warnock Hersey Ltd., Montreal, 1959-60; assoc. Cartier, Coté, Piette, Montreal, 1962-67; sr. advisor Ministry Urban Affairs, Ottawa, Ont., Canada, 1969-71; pres. Archer, Seaden & Assoc., Inc., Montreal, 1971-84; dir. gen. Inst. Rsch. in Constrn. Nat. Rsch. Coun., Ottawa, 1985-97, chief Constrn. Tech. Group, 1995-97; exec.-in-residence Faculty Adminstrn. U. Ottawa, 1997—2001. Vis. prof. U. Ottawa, 1968-73; mem. Can. Constrn. Rsch. Bd., 1985-91, Constrn. Industry Devel., Can., 1988-93, Civil Engring. Rsch. Found., 1993—, Rsch. Bd. Am. Pub. Works Assn., 1994-97; dir. Continental Automated Bldg. Assn., 1995-97, Can. Rsch. Mgrs. Assn., CERIU; pres. Conseil Internat. du Batiment, Rotterdam, The Netherlands, 1989-92; vice chair Constrn. for Sustainable Devel. in the Twenty First Century Conf., Washington, 1996; chair INFRA 2000, Montreal; mem. jury to select best Can. Constrn. projects and engring. design; lectr. numerous univs. and rsch. ctrs.; chmn. Internat. Symposium on Innovation, Ottawa, 2001. Contbg. author: Buildings, Culture and Environment, 2003; co-editor: Trends in Building Construction Worldwide, 1989, Innovation in Construction, 2001; mem. editl. bd. Bldg. Rsch. and Practice, Constrn. Bldg. Rev., 1991—; contbr. numerous articles to profl. publs. Chmn. bd. dirs. St. Andrew's Sch., Westmount, Que., 1975-82; dir. SJCC, 2002—Fellow Am. Soc. Civil Engrs. E-mail: george.seaden@rogers.com.

SEADER, JUNIOR DEVERE (BOB SEADER), retired chemical engineering professor; b. San Francisco, Aug. 16, 1927; s. George Joseph and Eva (Burbank) S.; m. Joyce Kocher, Aug. 12, 1950 (div. 1960); m. Sylvia Bowen, Aug. 11, 1961; children: Steven Frederick, Clayton Mitchell, Gregory Randolph, Donald Jeffrey, Suzanne Marie, Robert Clark, Kathleen Michelle, Jennifer Anne. BS, U. Calif., Berkeley, 1949, MS, 1950; PhD, U. Wis., 1952. Instr. chem. engring. U. Wis., Madison, 1951-52; group supr. chem. process design Chevron Rsch. Corp., Richmond, Calif., 1952-57, group supr. engring. rsch., 1957-59; prin. scientist heat transfer and fluid dynamics rsch. Rocketdyne div. N.Am. Aviation, Canoga Park, Calif., 1959-65, sr. tech. specialist, summer 1967; prof. chem. engring. U. Idaho, 1965-66, U. Utah, Salt Lake City, 1966—2003, chmn. dept. chem. engring., 1975-78. Tech. cons.; trustee CACHE Corp., Austin, Tex., 1969—2002. Author 13 books; assoc. editor IEC Rsch. jour., 1986-99; contbr. more than 100 articles to tech. publs. With USNR, 1945—46. Recipient Disting. Tchg. award U. Utah, 1975, Donald L. Katz lectureship, 1990, Dean's Tchg. award U. Utah, 1998, CACHE award for excellence in computing in chem. engring. edn. Am. Soc. Engring. Edn., 2004. Fellow: AIChE (Inst. lectr. 1983, bd. dirs. 1983—85, Computing in Chem. Engring. award 1988, Warren K. Lewis award for chem. engring. edn. 2004). Heat transfer research connected with the development of rocket engines associated with the Apollo and Space Shuttle projects, 1960-65. Home Phone: 801-523-8870. E-mail: j.seader@utah.edu.

SEADLE, MICHAEL STEVEN, data processing executive, writer; b. Detroit, June 16, 1950; s. Peter Stephan Seadle and Ruth Mary (Stevens) Knight; m. Joan Louise Luft, May 18, 1984. BA, Earlham Coll., 1972; MA, U. Chgo., 1973, PhD, 1977. Supr. U. Chgo. Libr., 1976-81; applications programmer Washington Nat. Ins., Evanston, Ill., 1981-83, Bankers Life and Casualty, Chgo., 1983-84; data base adminstr. Am. Dental Assn., Chgo., 1984-87; asst. dir. U. Computing Eastern, Mich. U., Ypsilanti, Mich., 1987-89; systems programmer Network Resources Cornell U., Ithaca, N.Y., 1989-90; online ops. mgr. Cornell U. Libr., Ithaca, N.Y., 1990—. Treas. Midwest Region Am. Friends Svc. Com., Chgo., 1979-85; mem. Allocations Oversight Com., AFSC, Phila., 1985—. Author: Quakers in Nazi Germany, 1979, Automating Mainframe Management, 1991; contbr. articles to profl. jours. Mem. Nat. Systems Programmers Assn., Phi Beta Kappa. Mem. Soc. Of Friends. Avocations: travel, baking. Office: Cornell University 501 Olin Library Ithaca NY 14853-5301

SEAGAL, STEVEN, actor; b. Lansing, Mich., Apr. 10, 1951; m. Miyako Seagal, 1975 (div. 1986); children: Kentaro, Ayako; m. Adrienne La Russa (div.); m. Kelly LeBrock (div. 1994); children: Annaliza, Dominic San Rocco, Arissa, Savannah. Studied martial arts under masters, Japan. Founded Aikido Ten Shin Dojo, LA. Martial arts choreographer The Challenge, 1982; actor, prodr., martial arts choreographer Above the Law, 1988, Marked for Death, 1990, My Giant, 1998; actor, martial arts choreographer Hard to Kill, 1990; actor, prodr. Out for Justice, 1991, Under Siege, 1992, Under Siege 2, 1995, Half Past Dead, 2002, The Foreigner, 2003, Out for a Kill, 2003, Belly of the Beast, 2003; actor, dir., co-prodr. On Deadly Ground, 1994; fight scene choreographer various films; appeared in films The Glimmer Man, 1996, Executive Decision, 1996, Fire Down Below, 1997, The Patriot, 1998, Get Bruce, 1999, Blood on the Moon, 2000, Exit Wounds, 2001, Ticker, 2001, Out of Reach, 2004. Achievements include first non-Asian to open martial arts acad. in Japan; black belt numerous martial arts.

SEAGER, DANIEL ALBERT, university librarian; b. Jacksonville, Fla., Jan. 1, 1920; s. Harry James and Albertina Adeline (Klarer) S.; m. Helen Ruthe Medearis, Mar. 6, 1943; children: Mary Adele, Susan Kathleen, Dana Ruthe. AA, St. John's Coll., Winfield, Kans., 1941; AB, Okla. Bapt. U., 1948; BA in L.S, U. Okla., 1950, MA, 1953; postgrad., Colo. State Coll. (now U. No. Colo.), 1956-59. Head librarian, prof. English Southwest Bapt. U., Bolivar, Mo., 1949-53; head librarian, asst. prof. library sci., chmn. dept. Ouachita U., Arkadelphia, Ark., 1953-56; head librarian, head library sci. edn., assoc. prof. library sci. U. No. Colo., Greeley, 1956-66, dir. library services, 1966-71, coordinator library research and devel., 1971—2006, prof. library sci., 1984—2006, chief bibliographer/editor library publns., cons., instr. ednl. media program, 1968-71, ret., 2006. Libr. cons., 1968—; cons. Ency. Brit. ultramicrofiche project, 1967-69; lectr. in field. Contbr. articles to profl. jours. Mem. book adv. coun. Edn. for Freedom Found.; mem. Com. library standards Colo. pub. schs., 1960-62; mem. exec. bd. Rocky Mountain Bibliog. Ctr. Research, 1959-60, 65-74, sec., 1961-63; sec. Colo. Council Librarians State-Operated Instns., 1966, chmn., 1968-70; mem. exec. bd. Weld County Assn. Mental Health, 1966, mem. library com., 1969; mem. Colo. Civil Service Examining Bd., 1961—; mem. U. N.C. Friends Libr., 1984—; Rep. com. chmn., Weld County, 1985-86; deacon, elder Christian Ch.; mem. The Srs. Coalition, 1995—. With U.S. Army Signal Corps, WWII, 1942-44, ETO, 1944-45, USAR Corps, 1945-48. Recipient several citations of merit profl. orgns. Fellow Intercontinental Biog. Assn.; mem. NEA, AAUP, Am. Library Assn. (library recruitment com. 1957—), Nat., Colo. assns. higher edn., United Profs. for Acad. Order Nat. Hist. Soc., Colo. Assn. Sch. Librarians (cons.), Spl. Libraries Assn., ALA (region recruitment rep. 1958—), Utah Library Assn., Kans. Library Assn., Wyo. Library Assn., Nebr. Library Assn., N.D. Library Assn., S.D. Library Assn., Nev. Library Assn., Mountain Plains Library Assn. (treas. 1959-63, exec. sec. 1963-76, spl. hons. plaque 1968, archivist 1974-84, constitution com. 1979, 83, chmn. nominating com. 1980, awards com. 1984, by-laws and amendments coms. 89-91, Pres.'s and Assn.'s Spl. award 17 Years Service award, Spl. Presdl. award 1994), Colo. Library Assn. (auditor), Tex. Library Assn., Southwestern Library Assn., Ill. Library Assn., Calif. Library Assn., Cath. Library Assn., Mich. Library Assn., Ohio Library Assn., N.Y. Library Assn., Pa. Library Assn., Midcontinent Med. Library Assn., Library Automation Research and Cons. Assn., U N.C. Friends of the Libr., 1984, Intercollegiate Studies Inst., Am. Security Council, Alumni Assn. U. No. Colo., Black Silent Majority Com. (hon.), Colo. Council Higher Edn., Colo. Edn. Assn. (mem. coms., del. to convs.), U. No. Colo. Edn. Assn. (treas. 1980-84, sec.-treas. 1984-85), U. Colo. Safety Com., Assn. Coll. and Reference Libraries, Colo. Hist. Soc., Assn. Research Libraries, Colo. Audiovisual Assn., Air Force Assn., Internat. Platform Assn., Acad. Polit. Sci. Columbia, Nat. Geog. Soc., Weld County Assn. Mental Health (mem. bd., chmn. library com.), Am. Judicature Soc., Emeritus Faculty Assn. U. No. Colo., Am. Numis. Assn., Am. Sci. Affiliation, Council on Consumer Info., Smithsonian Assocs., Chem. Abstracts Service Panel, Colo. Gerontol. Soc., Western Gerontol. Soc., Am. Assn. Retired Persons (vote com.), Am. Legion, Audubon Nature Program, Forest History Soc., Journalism Edn. Assn., Greeley Numis. Club, Greeley C. of C., U. No. Colo. Emeritus Faculty Assn., Nat. Travel Club, Civitan (lt. gov. Mountain Plains dist. 1960-62), Knife and Fork Club, Rep. Club (Washington), Rep. Congl. Club (Washington), Eagles Club, Phi Delta Kappa. Mem. Reformed Christian Ch. Am. Home: 1230 24th Ave Greeley CO 80634-3516

SEAGER, DAUNA GAYLE OLSON-STOKES, speech therapist; b. Logan, Utah, Sept. 22, 1925; d. Helmar Alexander and La Rena Barnes (Jones) Olson; m. Arch Jr. Stokes, Aug. 5, 1943 (dec. Apr.il 1970); children: Jeffrey David, John Phillip, Jeannette; m. Floyd W. Seager, July 7, 1973 (dec. Oct. 1996). AS, Weber State U., Ogden, Utah, 1964; BS, Utah State U., Logan, 1969, MS in Audiology Speech Pathology, 1969. X-ray ech., physician asst. Robins X-Ray, Ogden, Utah, 1946-52; asst. to supt. Lyman Pub. Schs., Wyo., 1952-60; clinic supr. Utah State U., Logan, 1965-69; speech, language, hearing therapist Weber/Davis Sch. District, Ogden, Farmington, Utah, 1969-73, various, Utah, 1970-90; co-founder, coord. Clinic at O.R.M., Ogden, Utah, 1988—. Bd. dirs. Weber County DUP Mus., Ogden. Author: Pioneer Settlers, 1990; contbr. articles to profl. jours. Co-founder Seager Indigent Clinic, Ogden Mission, Utah, 1988—; organized Stroke Club for Families of CVA Support Group, Ogden, 1972-74, Stroke Unit St. Benedict's Hosp., Ogden, 1972-74, Parent Child Tchr. Group, Ogden, 1970-73; mem. Ogden Sesquicentennial Com., OgSesqui, 2000—, Weber County Sesquicentennial, 2000; co-chair Ogden Mayor's Cemetery Enhancement Commn; mem. cmty. rels. com. McKay Dee Hosp., 2000—. Fellow Utah State U., Logan, 1967-68, 68-69; recipient Point of Light award #101 Gov. Utah, 2003. Mem.: DAR, Mus. Action Team, Fedn. Ogden Bus. Profl. Women Internat., Weber County Women's Legis. Coun. and Rep. Women, Weber Far South Ctr. Co., Utah Mus. Assn. (bd. dirs.), Ogden Mayors Project (cemetery com., sesquicentennial com.), Altrusa Internat., Daus. of Utah Pioneers, Child Culture Club, Aglaia Club. Mem. Lds Ch. Avocations: historian/lecturer, writer, golfer, bridge, swimmer, ballroom dance instr. Home and Office: 4046 South 895 East Ogden UT 84403-2416

SEAGER, SARA, astronomer, educator; b. Toronto, Ont., Can., July 21, 1971; m. Michael Isaac Wevrick, 1998; 1 child, Maxwell Solstice. BSc in Math. and Physics, U. Toronto, Ont., 1994; PhD in Astronomy, Harvard U., Cambridge, Mass., 1999. Mem. Inst. Advanced Study, Princeton, NJ, 1999—2001, long-term mem., 2001—02; sr. rsch. staff mem. Carnegie Instn. Wash., Washington, 2002—06; Ellen Swallow Richards assoc. prof. planetary sci. MIT, 2007—. Contbr. articles to sci. jours. Named one of Brilliant 10, Popular Sci. mag., 2006; recipient Bok prize, Harvard U. Astronomy Dept., 2004. Mem.: Can. Astron. Soc., Am. Astron. Soc. (Helen B. Warner prize 2007). Achievements include research in numerous topics related to extrasolar planets. Office: Dept Earth Atmospheric and Planetary Scis MIT 77 Massachusetts Ave Cambridge MA 02139-4307 Office Phone: 617-253-6775. E-mail: seager@mit.edu. *

SEAGLE, EDGAR FRANKLIN, environmental engineer, consultant; b. Lincolnton, NC, June 27, 1924; s. Franklin Craig and Lillie Mae (James) S.; m. Doris Elaine Long, Mar. 23, 1958; children: Rebecca Jane, Mary Elaine, James Craig, William Franklin. AB in Chemistry, U. N.C., 1949, MS in Pub. Health, 1954; BCE, U. Fla., 1961; DPH, U. Tex., 1974. Registered profl. engr., Ala. Sr. sanitarian Health Dept., City of Charlotte, NC, 1950-52, chief indsl. hygiene sect. NC, 1956-59; sanitation cons. N.C. State Bd. Health, Raleigh, 1954-56; engr. dir. USPHS, Rockville, Md., 1961-78; asst. dir. Fellowship Office Nat. Acad. Scis., Washington, 1978-83; pub. health engr. Dept. of Environ., State of Md., Balt., 1985-88; ind. engring. cons. Rockville, 1984-85, 88—. Contbr. articles to profl. publs. With USN, 1943-46, PTO. Mem. ASCE, APHA, Am. Acad. Environ. Engrs. (diplomate). Methodist. Home and Office: 14108 Heathfield Ct Rockville MD 20853-2760 Personal E-mail: edgarseagle@comcast.net.

SEAGLE, J. HAROLD, lawyer; b. Marion, NC, May 9, 1947; s. Rufus James and Alma Rhoda (McMahan) S.; m. Linda Jean Cranford, June 3, 1967; 1 child, James Mark. BA, U. NC, Chapel Hill, 1973, JD, 1977. Bar: N.C. 1977; U.S. Dist. Ct. (ea., middle, we. dists.) N.C. 1977, 88, 92; U.S. Ct Appeals (4th cir.) 1982; U.S. Supreme Ct. 1982. Assoc. atty. Rountree & Newton, Wilmington, NC, 1977-79; ptnr. Rountree & Seagle, L.L.P., Wilmington, 1979—2001. Past pres. Fifth Jud. Dist. Bar. Active Ctrl. United Meth. Ch.; past moderator Wilmington Baptist Assn.; bd. dirs. Rescue Mission of Cape Fear; past adv. Bd. Coastal Bioethics Network; past chmn. annual fund drive Am. Cancer Soc.; past sect. chmn. Cape Fear United Way. Mem.: 28th N.C. Jud. Dist. Bar, N.C. Bar Coun. of Pres. Wilmington Inns of Ct. (exec. com., master), Maritime Law Assn. of U.S. (proctor), Southeastern Admiralty Law Inst. (past chmn., chmn. adv. coun.), N.C. Coll. of Advocacy, N.C. Acad. Trial Lawyers, N.C. State Bar, N.C. Bar Assn., New Hanover County Bar Assn. Avocations: motorcycle racing, guitar. Home and Office: 311 Bradenton Knoll Fletcher NC 28732 Office Phone: 828-545-7777. Personal E-mail: haroldseagle@charter.net.

SEAGREN, ALICE, school system administrator, former state legislator; b. 1947; m. Fred Seagren; 2 children, Christina and Greg. BS in Mktg., SE Mo. State U. Mem. Bloomingdale Sch. Bd., 1989—92; Minn. state repr., Dist. 41A Minn. Ho. of Reps., 1992—2002, chmn. K-12 edn. fin. com., 1999—2004, former mem., Edu. Policy, Local Govt & Met. Affairs & Ways & Means, Transportation Policy Committees; former chair Edu. Com., Nat. Coun. of State Legislatures, Assembly of State Issues; commr. of edn. State of Minn., 2004—. Active Bloomington (Minn.) Sch. Bd., 1989-92; bd. dir. Normandale Cmty. Coll. Found., Fraser Cmty. Services Mem. Bloomington C. of C. (bd. dirs. 1990-92), Phi Gamma Nu, Alpha Chi Omega. Republican. Home: 9730 Palmer Cir Bloomington MN 55437-2017 Office: Minn Dept Children, Famlies, Learning 1500 Highway 36 W Roseville MN 55113-4035 Office Phone: 651-582-8204. E-mail: mde.commissioner@state.mn.us. *

SEAGREN, STEPHEN LINNER, oncologist; b. Mpls., Mar. 13, 1941; s. Morley Raymond and Carol Christine (Linner) S.; m. Jill Garrie; 1 child, Sean Garrie. AB, Harvard U., 1963; MD, Northwestern U., 1967. Diplomate Am. Bd. Internal Medicine, Am. Bd. Med. Oncology, Am. Bd. Radiology. From asst. prof. to assoc. prof. radiology and medicine U. Calif., San Diego, 1977-88, prof., 1988—, chief divsn. radiation oncology. Contbr. over 80 articles to profl. jours. Bd. dirs., chmn. profl. adv. com. Wellness Cmty., San Diego, 1988-2003; chmn. radiol. oncology com. Cancer and Acute Leukemia Group, Chgo., 1986-98; assoc. dir. U. Calif. San Diego Cancer Ctr., 1998-2000. Lt. comdr. USNR, 1971-73. Fellow ACP. Avocations: physical fitness, bridge, skiing, golf, tennis. Office: Moores Cancer Ctr 3855 Health Scis Dr #0843 La Jolla CA 92093-0843 Home Phone: 858-272-2053; Office Phone: 858-822-6040. Business E-Mail: sseagren@ucsd.edu.

SEAL, ROBERT A., library director; b. Canton, Ohio, June 9, 1948; s. Merle E. and Evelyn L. (Baker) S.; m. Adela M. Rosca, July 10, 1996; children: Katherine Anne, Corinne Marie. BA, Northwestern U., 1971; MLS, U. Denver, 1972. From circulation libr. to sci.-tech. circulation libr. U. Va., Charlottesville, 1972-76; head adminstrv. svcs. U. Va. Librs., 1976-81; dir. libr. svcs. U. Okla., Norman, 1981-85; libr. U. Tex., El Paso, 1985-94, Tex. Christian U., Ft. Worth, 1994—2005; dean of libraries Loyola U., Chgo., 2005—. Chmn. bd. trustees Amigos Bibliographic Coun., Dallas, 1993-97; cons. Acad. for Ednl. Devel., Washington, 1996-97, Banco Ctrl. de Nicaragua, 1997-98; bd. trustees Online Computer Libr. Ctr. Author: Guide to the Literature of Astronomy, 1977, Bibliography of Astronomy 1970-79, 1982. Elder First Presbyn. Ch., El Paso, 1990-92. Mem. ALA, Tex. Libr. Assn., Assn. Coll. & Rsch. Librs., Libr. Adminstrn. & Mgmt. Assn., Internat. Rels. Roundtable, Downtown Lions Club (v.p. 1993-94, bd. dirs. 1991-93). Office: Loyola U Chgo Cudahy Libr Rm 105 6525 N Sheridan Rd Chicago IL 60626 Office Phone: 773-508-2657. Office Fax: 773-508-8691. E-mail: rseal@luc.edu.

SEAL, musician; b. London, Jan. 3, 1963; m. Heidi Klum, May 10, 2005. Albums Seal, 1992, 1994, Being Human, 1998, Waiting for You, 2003, Seal IV, 2003, The Acoustic Session, 2003, singles Crazy, Killer, 1991, song Kiss From a Rose, included in Batman Forever, 1995. Recipient Grammy award Song of Yr., 1996, Grammy award Record of Yr., 1996, Grammy award Best Male Pop Vocal Performance, 1996. Office: Warner Bros Records Inc 75 Rockefeller Plz New York NY 10019-6908 also: Warner Bros Records 3300 Warner Blvd Burbank CA 91505-4632

SEALE, JAMES LAWRENCE, JR., agricultural studies educator, trade association administrator, researcher; b. Memphis, Mar. 12, 1949; s. James Lawrence and Mary Helen (Keefe) S.; divorced. BA, U. Miss., 1972; postgrad., U. Chgo., 1978-79; PhD, Mich. State U., 1985. Agrl. vol. Peace Corps, Tondo, Zaire, 1973-75; agrl. advisor Harvard Inst. for Internat. Devel., Abyei, Sudan, 1978; specialist Mich. State U., Fayoum, Arab Republic of Egypt, 1980-83; asst. prof. agrl. econs. U. Fla., Gainesville, 1985-90, assoc. prof. agrl. econs., 1990-95, prof. agrl. econs., 1995—. Vis. prof. U. Leicester (Eng.), 1992, 94, hon. vis. fellow, 95. Author: (with H. Theil and C.F. Chung) International Evidence on Consumption Patterns, 1989; editor: Journal of Agricultural and Applied Economics, 1998-2001, spl. edit., 2002-03; contbr. articles to profl. jours. Vol. Farmer to Farmer, UOCA, Namibia, 1994, Farmer to Farmer, Wenrock Internat., 1994; vol. agrl. bus. svcs. Wenrock Internat., Far Eastern Russia, 1998. NIMH scholar U. Chgo., 1978-79; traveling scholar U. Mich., 1979; rsch. fellow Cairo U., 1980-83; McKethan-Matherly rsch. fellow, 1986-88, McKethan-Matherly sr. rsch. fellow, 1991-94. Mem. Am. Econs. Assn., Am. Agrl. Econs. Assn., Internat. Assn. Agrl. Economists, Econometrics Soc., Caribbean Agro-Econ. Soc., Internat. Agrl. Trade Rsch. Consortium, Gamma Sigma Delta. Episcopalian. Avocations: scuba diving, Karate. Office: U Fla Dept Food and Resource G-125 McCarty PO Box 110240 Gainesville FL 32611-0240 Home: 406 NE 7th Ave Gainesville FL 32601 Office Phone: 352-256-5917. Business E-Mail: jseale@ufl.edu.

SEALE, JAMES MILLARD, retired religious organization administrator, minister; b. Middlesboro, Ky., Oct. 4, 1930; s. Albert Tyler and Edith Josephine (Buchanan) S.; m. Mary Dudley Harrod; children: William Alan, Ann Lynn Seale Hazelrigg. BA, Transylvania U., 1952; BD, Lexington Theol. Sem., 1955, MDiv, 1963, D Ministry, 1981. Ordained to ministry Christian Ch. (Disciples of Christ), 1951. Student pastor various Christian Chs., Ky., 1949-54; pastor 1st Christian Ch., Pikeville, Ky., 1954-58, Erlanger (Ky.) Christian Ch., 1958-61; sr. minister 1st Christian Ch., Mt. Sterling, Ky., 1961-70, Paris, Ky., 1978-82; stewardship sec. Gen. Office Christian Ch., Indpls., 1970-74; adminstr. Christian Ch. Home of Louisville, 1974-78; dir. devel. Christian Ch. Homes Ky., Louisville, 1978; pres. Disciples of Christ Hist. Soc., Nashville, 1983-95, pres. emeritus, 1995. Author: A Century of Faith and Caring, 1983, Forward From The Past, 1991; editor: (jour.) Discipliana, 1983—92. Pres. Kiwanis Club, Pikeville, 1957, Mt. Sterling, 1963, lt. gov., Ctrl. Ky., 1965. Mem. Christian Ch. Avocations: writing, photography, golf, fishing.

SEALE, ROBERT ARTHUR, lawyer; b. Shreveport, La., July 17, 1942; s. Robert Arthur Sr. and Lucille (Frank) S.; m. Chalon Fontaine; children: Robert A. III, John Meyers. BBA, La. State U., 1964, JD, 1967. Bar: La. 1967, Tex. 1969. Mem. La. Law Rev., 1965—67; rsch. asst. La. Law Inst. for La. Mineral Code, Baton Rouge, 1967; law clk. U.S. Dist. Ct. (WD-LA), Shreveport, 1967-68; atty./ptnr. Vinson & Elkins, Houston, 1968—97; ptnr. Phelps Dunbar LLP, Houston, 2002—04; of counsel Liskow & Lewis, Houston, 2005—. Former trustee and gen. counsel Mus. of Fine Arts, Houston, 1981-89, pres., trustee The Lyons Found., Houston, 1986—. Pres. trustee Vivian Smith Found. Neurological Rsch., Houston, 1988—; mem. devel. bd. U. Tex. Health Sci. Ctr., Houston, 1995—; trustee Episcopal H.S., Houston, 1985—88. Named one of Best Lawyers in Am. Fellow: Houston Bar Fedn. (life); mem.: ABA, Tex. Bar (sustaining life fellow), Omicron Delta Kappa. Avocations: civic and charitable activities, golf, travel. Office: Liskow & Lewis First City Tower 1001 Fannin Ste 1800 Houston TX 77002 Office Phone: 713-651-2910. Business E-Mail: raseale@liskow.com.

SEALE, WALTER LOUIS, cardiologist; b. Dec. 25, 1958; MD, Stanford U. Sch. Med., 1985. Cert. Internal Medicine, Clin. Cardiac Electrophysiology, Cardiovascular Disease. Intern Stanford U. Hosp., Palo Alto, Calif., resident, internal medicine, 1985—88; fellow, cardiology Cedars-Sinai Med. Ctr., LA, 1988, fellow, cardiac electrophysiology; hosp. appointments St. Alphonsus Regional Med. Ctr., St. Luke's Regional Med. Ctr.; co-founder, cardiologist Idaho Cardiology Associates, PA, 1994—. Fellow: Am. Coll. Cardiology. Office: Idaho Cardiology Associates PA 6140 W Curtisian Ave Ste 200 Boise ID 83704 Office Phone: 208-322-1680. *

SEALL, STEPHEN ALBERT, lawyer; b. South Bend, Ind., Oct. 24, 1940; s. Stephen Henry and Mildred Rita (MacDonald) S.; m. Barbara Ann Halloran, June 25, 1966; children: John Paul, Edward Andrew, Ann Marie. BA, Purdue U., 1963; postgrad., Cornell U. Grad. Sch. Bus. Adminstrn., 1963; LLB, U. Notre Dame, 1966. Bar: Ind. 1966, U.S. Claims Ct. 1973, U.S. Tax Ct. 1968, U.S. Ct. Appeals (6th cir.) 1980, U.S. Ct. Appeals (7th cir.) 1969, U.S. Supreme Ct. 1973. Assoc. Thornburg, McGill, Deahl, Harman, Carey & Murray, South Bend, 1966-71; ptnr. Barnes & Thornburg LLP and predecessor firm Thornburg, McGill, Deahl, Harman, Carey & Murray, 1972—2005, vice chmn. and mgmt. com., mng. ptnr. South Bend office, 1985—2001. Spkr. in field. (Mem. editl. bd.) Notre Dame Law Rev., 1964—66. Mem. Mayor's Com. on Downtown Devel., South Bend, 1975-77, Mayor's Com. on Utilization of Downtown Bldgs., South Bend, 1988-96; trustee Project Future, South Bend, 1986-2002; exec. com. Meml. Hosp. South Bend, Inc., 1999-2003; dir. Meml. Health Found., 1992-98, Meml. Health Sys., 1997-2003, United Way of St. Joseph County, Inc., 1992-98, Conv. and Tourism Industry Coun., 1994-2000, CASIE Ctr., Inc., 1998-2006, Home Mgmt. Resources, Inc. 2003-06. Fellow Am. Coll. Tax Counsel, Am. Bar Found., Ind. Bar Found.; mem. ABA (taxation sect.), Ind. State Bar Assn. (chmn. taxation sect. 1977-78), Summit Club (chmn. 1976-77), Morris Park Country Club (bd. dirs., sec. 1998-2001). Democrat. Roman Catholic. Avocations: golf, softball, weightlifting. Office: Barnes & Thornburg LLP 600 1st Source Bank Ctr 100 N Michigan St Ste 600 South Bend IN 46601-1632 Home: 245 Martellago Dr North Venice FL 34275-6710 Office Phone: 574-233-1171.

SEALS, DAVID W., lawyer; b. Culver City, Calif., May 22, 1964; s. Wendell D. and Eva L. Seal. BA, Calif. State U., Long Beach, 1990; JD, Western State U., Fullerton, Calif., 1994. Bar: Calif. Assoc. Bridi & Seal, Irvine, Calif., 1994—. Mem.: State Bar Caluf., Am. Mensa. Office: Bridi & Seal 2030 Main St Ste 1300 Irvine CA 92614

SEALS, MARGARET LOUISE CRUMRINE, retired journalist; b. Buckhannon, W.Va., Oct. 27, 1944; d. James Richard and Helen Margaret (Brown) Crumrine; m. Harry Eugene Seals, Jan. 10, 1975. BS in journalism, W. Va. U., 1966; MS in mass. comm., Va. Commonwealth U., 1983. Reporter, copy editor Democrat & Chronicle, Rochester, NY, 1966-67, Dayton (Ohio) Daily News, 1967-68; copy editor Richmond (Va.) Times-Dispatch, 1968-75, copy desk slot editor, 1975-81, exec. news editor, 1981, asst. mng. editor, 1982-92, dep. mng. editor, 1992-93, mng. editor, 1994—2006; ret., 2006. Adj. intr. Va. Commonwealth U. Mass Comm. Sch., 2007. Mem. Leadership Metro Richmond, 1986, seminar days co-chair, 2007—; mem. alumni adv. bd. sch. mass. comm. Va. Commonwealth U., 1988-93, 04-; mem. vis. com. Sch. Journalism, W.Va. U., 1999—. Named Outstanding Woman in Comms. YWCA Met. Richmond, 1989; recipient Perley Isaac Reed award W.Va. U. Journalism Sch. Alumni Assn., 1996; inducted into Va. Comm. Hall of Fame, 2003. Mem.: Va. Press Assn. (dir. 2001—03, treas. 2003—04, sec. 2004—05, v.p. 2005—06), AP Mng. Editors (editor APME News 1993—94, dir. 1993—95, treas. 1996—97, dir. 1998—2001, Disting. Svc. award 2002), Va. Press Women (treas. 1986—88, 2d v.p. 1988—90, pres. 1990—92, Press Woman of Yr. 1986, Communicator of Achievement award 1997), Soc. Profl. Journalists (bd. dirs. Va. profl. chpt. 1998—2003, pres. Va. profl. chpt. 2000—02), Nat. Fedn. Press Women (bd. dirs. 1990—92, Communicator of Achievement award 1997), Phi Kappa Phi. Avocations: history, jazz, hiking. Personal E-mail: louise.seals@comcast.net.

SEAMAN, ALFRED BARRETT, journalist, writer; b. Rockville Center, NY, July 4, 1945; s. Alfred Jarvis and Mary Margaret (Schill) S.; m. Laura Powers Maxwell, Apr. 25, 1970; children: Katherine Maxwell, Margaret Elise, Elizabeth Barrett. BA, Hamilton Coll., 1967; MBA, Columbia U., 1971. Reporter Life mag., NYC, 1971-72, Fortune mag., NYC, 1972; corr. Time mag., NYC, 1973, Chgo., 1973-76, Bonn, Germany, 1976-78, bur. chief Detroit, 1978-81, dep. bur. chief Washington, 1981-83, White House corr., 1984-88, dep. chief corrs. NYC, 1988-91, sr. editor, 1991-94, spl. projects editor, 1994—2001. Co-author: Going for Broke: The Chrysler Story, 1981; author: Binge: Campus Life in an Age of Disconnection and Excess, 2005. Alumni trustee Hamilton Coll., Clinton, N.Y., 1990-93, 94-95, charter trustee, 1997—; trustee Village of Irvington, N.Y., 1992-94.

With USNR, 1969-71. Mem.: U.S. Sr. Golf Assn., Univ. Glee Club N.Y.C., Ardsley County Club. Episcopalian. Avocations: tennis, golf. Home: Ardsley Ave W Ardsley On Hudson NY 10503 Personal E-mail: absea@aol.com.

SEAMAN, ALFRED JARVIS, retired advertising agency executive; b. Hempstead, L.I., NY, Sept. 17, 1912; s. Alfred J. and Ellen (Delaney) S.; m. Mary M. Schill, Sept. 26, 1937 (dec. June 1975); children: Marilyn Hollingsworth, Susan, Barry, Deborah; m. Honor S. Mellor, July 16, 1977. BS, Columbia U., 1935; LittD, L.I. U., 1987. Account exec. Fuller & Smith & Ross, Inc., NYC, 1937-41; partner Knight & Gilbert. Inc., Boston, 1941-43; with Compton Advt., Inc., NYC, 1946-59, exec. v.p., creative dir., dir., 1954-59; vice chmn. bd., chmn. exec. com. SSC & B, Inc., 1959-60, pres., chief exec. officer, 1960-79, chmn., chief exec. officer, 1979-81. Dir., mem. exec. com. Interpublic Group of Cos., Inc. Hon. bd. dirs., adv. council, founding chmn. Advt. Ednl. Found.; bd. dirs., hon. dir. com. Advt. Council.; chmn. planning bd., 1962—, mayor Village Upper Brookville, 1966-98; chmn. emeritus Samuel Waxman Cancer Research Found.; dir. Jupiter Hosp., 1991-2002. Lt. USNR, 1943-46. Named to Advt. Hall of Fame, 1983 Mem.: U.S. Sr. Golf Assn., Creek (Locust Valley, L.I.) (pres.), Piping Rock (Locust Valley, L.I.), Racquet and Tennis (N.Y.C.), Jupiter Island (Fla.), Nat. Golf Links Am. (Southampton, N.Y.), Seminole (Fla.), Hobe Sound Yacht (Fla.). Home: Wolver Hollow Rd Upper Brookville Oyster Bay NY 11771 also: Jupiter Island 126 Gomez Rd Hobe Sound FL 33455-2424 Office: 220 E 42nd St New York NY 10017-5806

SEAMAN, ARLENE ANNA, retired musician; b. Pontiac, Mich., Jan. 21, 1918; d. Roy Russell and Mabel Louise (Heffron) S. BS, life cert., Ea. Mich. U., 1939; MMus, Wayne State U., 1951; postgrad., Colo. Coll., 1951-52, Acad. Music, Zermatt Switzerland, 1954-58, U. Mich. Guest conductor Shepherds and Angels, Symphonic Concertante, 1951; asst. conductor Detroit Women's Symphony, 1960-68; adjudicator Mich. State Band and Orch. Festivals, Solo and Ensemble Festivals, 1950-70, Detroit Fiddler's Band Auditions, 1948-52, Mich. Fedn. Music Clubs, 1948-55; tchr. Ea. Mich. U., 1939-42, Hartland Sch. Music, 1939-42, Pontiac (Mich.) Pub. Schs., 1942-45, Detroit Pub. Schs., 1945-73, pvt. studio, 1973-90. Performer cello South Oakland Symphony, 1958-65, Detroit Women's Symphony, 1951-68, Riviera Theatre Orch., 1959, 60, Masonic Auditorium Opera, Ballet Seasons, 1959-65, Toledo Ohio Symphony, 1963-70, others; performer trumpet Detroit Brass Quartet, 1974-78; piano accompanist various auditions, recitals, solo and ensemble festivals; composer: Let There Be Music, 1949, Fantasy for French Horn and Symphonic Band, 1951. Mem. Quota Internat., Delta Omicron. Home: 6231 N Montebella Rd #347 Tucson AZ 85704

SEAMAN, BARBARA (ANN ROSNER), author; b. NYC, Sept. 11, 1935; d. Henry Jerome and Sophie Blanche (Kimels) Rosner; m. Gideon Seaman, Jan. 13, 1957 (div.); children: Noah Samuel, Elana Felicia, Shira Jean. BA (Ford Found. scholar), Oberlin Coll., 1956, LHD (hon.), 1978; cert. in advanced sci. writing (Sloan-Rockefeller fellow), Columbia U., 1968. Columnist Brides Mag., NYC, 1964-68; columnist, contbg. editor Ladies' Home Jour., NYC, 1965-69; editor child care and edn. Family Cir., NYC, 1970-73; contbg. editor Omni mag., 1978; cons. FYI, ABC-TV, 1979-80; v.p. for devel. David Brooks Prodn., 1990-94; contbg. editor MS Mag., 1993—; columnist Hadassah Mag., 2000—03. Cons. US Senate subcom. on monopoly: Nelson pill hearings, 1970; presented testimony to Senate and Congl. coms., 1970—; lectr. in field; participant TV discussion shows; tchr. Coll. New Rochelle, 1975, Sagaris Inst., 1975, CUNY, 1993; founding mem. NY Women's Forum, 1973-99; co-founder Nat. Women's Health Network, 1975—, Comm. Consultants for Choice, 1985-86, Nat. Task Force Sexual Malpractice, 1985-86, Families Against Sexually Abusive Therapists and Other Profl., 1992—; v.p. Women's Med. Ctr., NYC, 1971-73; mem. ERA Emergency Task Force, 1979; adv. coun. Feminist Press, Old Westbury, NY, 1975; adv. bd. Feminist Ctr. for Human Growth and Devel., 1979, Women's History Libr., Berkeley, Calif., 1973-75; steering com. Women's Forum, 1974; adv. bd. NOW, NY, 1973, Women's Guide to Books, 1974, Jewish Women for Affirmative Action, Evanston, Ill., 1973—, Jour. Women and Health, 1975, Jewish Feminist Orgn., NYC, 1975; chair com. domestic violence Nat. Coun. Women's Health, 1993-98; judge for various journalism awards. Author: The Doctors' Case Against the Pill, 1969, rev. edit., 1980, 25th anniversary edit., 1995, Free and Female, 1972; (with G. Seaman) Women and the Crisis in Sex Hormones, 1977, Lovely Me: The Life of Jacqueline Susann, 1987, anniversary edit., 1996; (with Gary Null) For Women Only: Your Guide to Health Empowerment, 2000; The Greatest Experiment ever Performed on Women: exploding the Estrogen Myth, 2003; contbg. author: foreword to Lunaception, 1975; The Bisexuals, 1974, Career and Motherhood, 1979, The Menopause Industry, 1994; author (play) I Am a Woman, 1972; (movie) Scandalous Me: The Jackie Susann Story, 1998; contbr. (anthologies) Rooms with No View, 1974, Women and Men, 1975, Seizing Our Bodies, 1978, Women's Health Care: A Guide to Alternatives, 1984; Encyclopaedia of Childbirth, 1992, Lawyers Manual on Domestic Violence: Representing the Victim, 1995, The Conversation Begins, 1996, Real Majority Media Minority, 1997, The Reader's Companion to US Women's History, 1997, Jewish Women in America: An Historical Encyclopedia, 1997, Textbook of Women's Health, 1997, Women's Health, 1999, Routledge International Encyclopedia of Women, 2001; George Mag., 250 ways to make Am. Better, 1999; Hands On! 33 More Things Every Girl Should Know, 2001, Sexual Revolution, 2003, Controversies in Science and Technology, 2005, Jewish Women's Archive: Feminism and Jewish Women Web Exhibit; cons. (film) The Pill, 1999; PBS Am. Experience the Pill, 2003; narrator (film) Taking Our Bodies Back, 1974; contbr. articles to newspapers, popular mags.; books and articles translated into Spanish, German, Dutch, Turkish, Japanese, Hebrew, French, Italian; contbr. articles to mags. Alumni cons. women's studies program Oberlin Coll., 1975; motivation com. Am. Cancer Soc., 1973; adv. com. Older Women's Health Project, NYU Med. Ctr., 1980; bd. dir. Safe Transp. of People, NYC, 1975, Women's Health Newsletter, 1983; adv. bd. DES Action, 1977, 7 Stories Press, 1997-; cons. Nat. Task Force on DES, 1978; contraceptive rsch. br. HEW, 1980; v.p., bd. dirs. ARM (Abortion Rights Moblzn.), 1981—2007; hon. bd. dirs. Carcinogen Info. Program, St. Louis, 1981, Am. Friends of Rabin Med. Ctr., 1998—; trustee Nat. Coun. on Women in Medicine, 1989-1991, Nat. Coun. on Women's Health, 1992-2000; chmn. adv. bd. Coalition for Family Justice, 1991-99; co-chair Domestic Violence com. NY Women's Agenda, 1992-93, del. Can.-USA Women's Health Forum, 1996; host com. Womens Health Day, Beijing, Plus-Five UN Reunion, 2000; cons. FDA Patient Labels on Oral Contraceptives, 2000-01; nat. judge Project Censored Award, 1997—; adv. Matilda Joslyn Gage Found., 2005—. Recipient citation for books as first to raise issue of sexism in health care as world-wide issue Libr. of Congress, 1973, citation as author responsible for patient package inserts on prescriptions HEW, 1970, Matrix award, 1978, Pioneer Woman award Resources Divsn. of Am. Assn. Retired Persons, 1986, Athena award Nat. Coun. Women's Health, 1992, Health Advocacy award Health Policy Adv. Ctr., APHA, 1994, Project Censored award, 1996, Postal Service Women's Rights Movement stamp, 2000; Poynter Journalism Fellow, Yale U., 2003; inviting com. Am. Writers Congress. Mem. PEN, Authors Guild, Nat. Assn. Sci. Writers. Address: 110 W End Ave Apt 5D New York NY 10023-6348

SEAMAN, DARYL KENNETH, oil industry executive; b. Rouleau, Sask., Can., Apr. 28, 1922; BSME, U. Sask., 1948, LLD (hon.), 1982, U. Calgary, 1993. Cert. mech. engr. CEO Bow Valley Industries Ltd., Calgary, Alta., Canada, 1962-70, 85-91, chmn., chief exec. officer, 1970-82; chmn. Box Valley Industries Ltd., Calgary, Alta., Canada, 1982-85; pres. Bow Valley Industries Ltd., Calgary, Alta., Canada, 1985-87, chmn., 1991-92. Bd. dirs. Far West Mining Ltd., Pure Techs. Ltd., Bow Valley Energy Ltd.; co-owner Calgary Flames Hockey Club; chmn., pres. Dox Investments, Inc.; hon. regent Athol Murray Coll. of Notre Dame, 2001—. Mem. Royal Commn. Econ. Union and Devel. Prospects for Can., 1982-85; active numerous coms. for fundraising U. Sask.; Served with RCAF, 1941-45, North Africa, Italy. Can. Oilmen's Hall of Fame, 1997, Calgary Bus. Hall of Fame, 2004. Mem. Assn. Profl. Engrs., Geologists and Geophysicists (hon. life, Frank Spragins award, 1985, McGill Mgmt. Achievement award, 1979), Order of Canada 1993, Ranchmen's Club, RAF Club, Earl Grey Golf Club, Calgary Petroleum Club, Calgary Golf and Country Club, U. Calgary Chancellor's Club. Progressive Conservative. Mem. United Ch. Can. Avocations: ranching, golf, hunting. Home and Office: Dox Investments Inc 2320 300-5 Ave SW Calgary AB Canada T2P 3C4 Home Phone: 403-264-2172; Office Phone: 403-290-1884. E-mail: admin@doxinvestments.com.

SEAMAN, DONNA JEAN, editor, writer; b. Seattle, July 5, 1955; d. Harold A. and Elayne S. BFA, Kansas City Art Inst.; MA in English Lit., DePaul U. Assoc. editor, reviewer Booklist, Am. Libr. Assn., Chgo.; host, radio show, Open Books WLUW, Chgo., NW U., Chgo., Columbia Coll., Chgo. Vis. faculty Gloucher Coll., Balt., Sch of the Art Inst. of Chgo.; dir., judge Claudia Ann Seaman Poetry award, 1984—; judge Carl Sandburg Lit. Arts Coun., 1997. Author: In Our Nature, 2000, Writers on the Air, 2005, contbr. essays and revs. to Chgo. Tribune, 1996—; author, host, prodr.: (radio program) Open Books (Ill. Arts Coun. award 1997). Recipient James Friend Meml. award for lit. criticism, Writers Who Make a Difference award, The Writer's Mag. Mem. Nat. Book Critics Cir. Address: Booklist Am Libr Assn 50 E Huron St Chicago IL 60611-5295 Business E-Mail: dseaman@ala.org.

SEAMAN, IRVING, JR., banker; b. Milw., July 14, 1923; s. Irving and Anne (Douglas) S.; m. June Carry, June 24, 1950, (dec. 2001); children: Peter Stewart, Marion Carry, Terry Osborne, Anne Douglas; m. Barbara P. Gardner, May 22, 2002. BA, Yale U., 1944. With Continental Ill. Nat. Bank & Trust Co., Chgo., 1947-61, v.p., 1959-61; pres., chief exec. officer, dir. Nat. Boulevard Bank, Chgo., 1961-65, chmn. exec. com., chief exec. officer, dir., 1966-76; vice chmn. bd., dir. Sears Bank and Trust Co., Chgo., 1976-77, pres., chief operating officer, dir., 1977-82; sr. cons. Burson-Marsteller, Chgo., 1982-94. Chmn. bd. Associated Bank Chgo., 1985-05. Mem. Northwestern U. Assn.; life mem. bd. dirs. Lake Forest Hosp.; bd. dirs. United Way of Chgo., 1975-89, pres., 1979; bd. dirs. United Way/Crusade of Mercy, 1980-89, 94-95, vice chmn., 1980-81; trustee Chgo. Symphony Orch., 1987—. Lt. (j.g.) USNR, WWII. Mem. Commonwealth Club, Econ. Club, Chgo. Club, Comml. Club, Racquet Club, Onwentsia Club, Old Elm Club (Highland Park, Ill.), Shoreacres Club (Lake Bluff, Ill.), Augusta Nat. Golf Club (Ga.), Marsh Landing Club (Fla.), Sawgrass (Fla.) Country Club. Home: 666 N Sheridan Rd Lake Forest IL 60045-1410

SEAMAN, JEFFREY, consumer products company executive; Grad., U. Pa., 1984. Pres. Rooms to Go, Feffner, Fla., 1990—. Office: Rooms to Go 11540 Us Highway 92 E Seffner FL 33584-7346

SEAMAN, NATASHA, art historian, educator; b. Apr. 30, 1969; AB, Bryn Mawr Coll., Pa., 1991; MA, Tufts U., Medford, Mass., 1997; PhD, Boston U., 2006. Adj. asst. prof. Berklee Coll., Boston, 2006—07; lectr. Tufts U., 2007. Organizer and lectr. in field. Fellow, Fulbright Found., 2003—04; Ctr. Advanced Study in Visual Arts, 2005. Mem.: Historians Netherlandish Art, Coll. Art Assn.

SEAMANS, WILLIAM, writer, retired reporter, commentator; b. Providence, July 8, 1925; s. William and Mary Seamans; m. Jane Kingsbury, Sept. 15, 1951; children: Laurie, Jonathan, Adam. AB, Brown U., 1949; MS, Columbia U., 1952. Freelance journalist, 1952-53; journalist CBS News, 1953-63; producer evening news ABC News, 1963-65, European producer London, 1965-70, field producer NYC, 1970-72, corr., bur. chief Tel Aviv, 1972-92; commentator Vt. Pub. Radio, lectr., freelance writer, 1992—. Producer Nightline in Israel Week (including Palestinian-Israeli town meeting) (Emmy award, Dupont award). Served with inf. AUS, 1942-45. Decorated Bronze Star medal; CBS Murrow News fellow Columbia U., 1961-62. Mem. Writers Guild Am., Nat. Acad. TV Arts and Scis. (Emmy award 1961, 89), Overseas Press Club Am. (award for best radio reporting invasion of Cyprus 1974, award for best fgn. affairs documentary Yitzhak Rabin biography 1975), Nat. Press Club (Washington), Fgn. Corrs. Assn. in Israel. E-mail: wmseamans@verizon.net.

SEAN PAUL, (SEAN PAUL HENRIQUES), singer; b. Kingston, Jamaica, Jan. 8, 1973; Grad., U. Tech. Jamaica. Former mem. Jamaican Nat. Water Polo Team. Singer: (albums) Stage One, 2000, Dutty Rock, 2002 (Billboard Top Reggae Album, 2003, 2004, Source award for Dancehall Reggae Album of Yr., 2003, Grammy award for Best Reggae Album, 2004), The Trinity, 2005 (Billboard Top Reggae Album, 2005), (songs) Gimme the Light, 2002, Get Busy, 2003, Like Glue, 2003, We Be Burnin', 2005 (Best Crossover Song, Internat. Reggae & World Music awards, 2006), Temperature, 2006. Named Top Reggae Artist, Billboard, 2003—05; recipient MTV Europe award for Best New Act of Yr., 2003, Bob Marley award for Entertainer of Yr., Internat. Reggae & World Music Awards, 2004, Spl. award for Cmty. Svc., 2005, Top Selling Reggae Artist of Yr., Billboard Music Awards, 2005, Rhythm & Soul Music award, ASCAP, 2005, Favorite Male Artist, Am. Music Awards, 2006. Office: Atlantic Records 28th Fl 1290 Ave of the Americas New York NY 10104 *

SEAPKER, JANET KAY, museum administrator, architectural historian, history consultant; b. Pitts., Nov. 2, 1947; d. Charles Henry and Kathryn Elizabeth (Dany) Seapker; m. Edward F. Turberg, May 24, 1975. BA, U. Pitts., 1969; MA, SUNY, Cooperstown, 1975. Park ranger Nat. Park Svc., summers 1967-69; archtl. historian N.C. Archives and History, Raleigh, 1971—76, hist. preservation adminstr., 1976—77, grant-in-aid adminstr., 1977—78; dir. Cape Fear Mus. (formerly New Hanover County Mus.), Wilmington, NC, 1978—2000, ret.; archtl. historian-preservation/mus. cons.; curator U. N.C. Wilmington's Kenan House, 2003—04. Bd. dirs. Bellamy Mansion Found., Wilmington, 1986-89, 91-97, Lower Cape Fear Hist. Soc., Wilmington, 1985-88; N.C. rep. S.E. Mus. Conf., 1986-90; bd. dirs. Cape Fear Coast Conv. and Vis. Bur., 1997-2001, sec., 2001, Wrightsville Beach Mus., 2004-05; field reviewer Inst. Mus. Svcs., 1982-2001 Contbr. articles to profl. jours. Bd. dirs. Downtown Area Revitalization Effort, Wilmington, 1979-81, Thalian Hall Ctr. for Performing Arts, 1996-98; bd. dirs. Hist. Wilmington Found., 1979-84, pres., 1980-81; mem. Cmty. Appearance Commn., Wilmington, 1984-88, 250th Anniversary Commn., Wilmington, 1986-90; mem. Wilmington Historic Preservation Commn., 2005-; pres. Friends of Oakdale Cemetery, Inc., 2004-. Grad. program fellow SUNY, Cooperstown, 1969-70; recipient Profl. Svc. award N.C. Mus. Coun., 1982, Woman of Achievement award YWCA, 1994. Mem. Am. Assn. Mus. (accreditation vis. com. 1983-2001, reviewer mus. assessment program 1982-2002), Nat. Trust Hist. Preservation, Southeastern Mus. Conf. (N.C. state rep. 1986-90), N.C. Mus. Coun. (sec.-treas. 1978-84, pres. 1984-86; recepient William T. Anderson award 2004), Hist. Preservation Found N.C. (sec. 1976-78). Presbyterian. Home and Office: 307 N 15th St Wilmington NC 28401-3813 Office Phone: 910-762-6301. Personal E-mail: jseapker@ec.rr.com.

SEARBY, RICHARD HENRY, academic administrator, lawyer; b. Melbourne, Victoria, Australia, July 23, 1931; s. Henry and Mary Searby; m. Caroline McAdam, 1962; 3 sons. MA with honors, U. Oxford; LLD (hon.), Deakin U., Geelong, 2005. Bar: London 1956, Victoria, Australia 1957. Assoc. to Chief Justice of Australia Rt. Hon. Sir Owen Dixon, 1956-59; ind. lectr. law relating to executors and trustees U. Melbourne, Australia, 1961-72; bd. dirs. News Corp. Ltd., Australia, 1977-92, chmn., 1981-91; bd. dirs., chmn. Equity Trustees Executors and Agy. Co. Ltd., 1975—2000, S. China Morning Post, 1987—92; bd. dirs. Times Newspapers Holdings Ltd., 1981—, dep. chmn., 1981—92; bd. dirs. Rio Tinto Ltd., 1977—97, Shell Australia Ltd., 1977—98, News Internat. plc, England, 1981-92, Reuters Founders Share Co., Ltd., 1987—93, Tandem Australia Ltd., 1992—98, Amrad Corp. Ltd., 1992—2001, BRL Hardy Ltd., 1992—2003, Rio Tinto plc, 1995—97, Woodside Petroleum Ltd., 1998—2004; chancellor Deakin U., 1997—2005. Bd. dirs. Ansett Transport Industries Ltd, 1979—92; chmn. Bowater Trust, 2006—; Hearing CRC Ltd, 2007—. Chmn. Geelong Grammar Sch., 1983-89; mem. coun. Nat. Libr. Australia, 1992-95, Mus. of Victoria, 1993-98. Decorated Queen's Counsel, Australia, 1971, Order of Australia, 2006. Mem.: Melbourne Club. Avocations: reading, music, tennis, fishing. Office: 25 Flinders Ln Melbourne 3000 Australia also: 23A Hampden Rd Armadale 3143 Victoria Australia

SEARCH-WINTERS, MICHELLE DAWN, corporate financial executive, consultant; b. Bellefonte, Pa., Feb. 16, 1967; d. R. and J. Search; m. Richard Allen Winters, Apr. 19, 2003; 1 child, Alexander Search Winters. BSBA, Boston U., 1989. CPA Colo., 1991. Staff auditor Deloitte, Haskins & Sells, Boston, 1989—91; sr. auditor Coopers & Lybrand, Denver, 1991—94; fin. analyst Cyprus Minerals, Denver, 1994; mgr. fin. reporting Golden Star Resources, Denver, 1994—97; sr. mgr. PricewaterhouseCoopers LLP, Denver, 1997—2004; dir. fin. ops. Jefferson Wells Internat., Denver, 2004—. Bd. mem., fin. dir. Am. Lung Assn. Colo., Denver, 1998—2000. Mem.: AICPA, Colo. Soc. CPAs. Home: 9585 S Flower Way Littleton CO 80127 Office: Jefferson Wells International 1125 17th St Ste 2550 Denver CO 80202 Home Phone: 303-885-9796; Office Phone: 303-297-5405. Personal E-mail: michellesearch@comcast.net. Business E-Mail: michelle.search@jeffersonwells.com.

SEARCY, MARSHALL MAYES, JR., lawyer; b. San Diego, Calif., Oct. 30, 1946; s. Marshall Mayes and Evelyn Williamson Searcy; m. April Annette Thomas Giroir, Dec. 27, 1995; children: Marshall Mayes III, Kyle Eric Giroir, Amy Meredith, Dustin Nils Giroir, Alisa Holland Giroir, Rebecca Merrill, Timofee Wallace. BA with honors, U. Tex., Austin, 1969; JD with honors, U. Tex., 1972. Bar: Tex., US Ct. Appeals (5th cir. and fed. cir.), Tex. (fed. dist. cts.). Ptnr. Rain Harrell Emery, Dallas, 1972—87, Locke Purnell Rain Harrell, Dallas, 1987—93, Kelly Hart & Hallman LLP, Fort Worth, Tex., 1993—. Named one of Best Lawyers in Am. Super Lawyers, Tex. Monthly Mag.; recipient Law Good Scout award, Boy Scouts of Am. Longhorn Coun., 2006. Fellow: Am. Coll. Trial Lawyers; mem.: Fort Worth Bar Found., Tex. Bar Found., Am. Bd. Trial Advocates. Avocation: Russian lang. & hist. Home: 1517 Hillcrest St Fort Worth TX 76107-1575 Office: Kelly Hart & Hallman LLP 201 Main St Ste 2500 Fort Worth TX 76102-3105 Business E-Mail: marshall.searcy@khh.com.

SEARCY, WILLIAM NELSON, lawyer, director; b. Moultire, Ga., June 26, 1942; s. Floyd Hartsfield and Anna (Pidcock) Searcy; m. Camille Heery, June 17, 1967; 1 child, Amelia Ashburn. AB, U. Ga., 1964, JD, 1967; LLM in Taxation, Washington U., St. Louis, 1968. Bar: Ga. 1967, U.S. Dist. Ct. (so. dist.) Ga. 1970, U.S. Ct. Appeals (5th and 11th cirs.) 1976, U.S. Tax Ct. Assoc. Bouhan, Williams & Levy, Savannah, Ga., 1970-73; ptnr. Brannen, Searcy & Smith LLP, Savannah, 1973—. Sec. Am. Fed. Savs. and Loan Assn., 1978—81; mem. adv. bd. Liberty Savs. Bank, 1984—88; chmn. bd. dirs. Citizens Bank, 1991—. Pres. Chatham-Savannah Voluntary Action Ctr., Inc., 1978—80; bd. trustees Mighty Eighth USAF Mus., 2005—, U. Ga. Found., 2006—. Served to maj. gen. Ga. N.G. USAF, 1967—2004, comdr. Ga. N.G. USAF, 2000—04. Mem.: ABA (sec. spl. liaison tax com. S.E. region 1983—85, chmn. 1984—85), Inst. Continuing Legal Edn., Savannah Estate Planning Coun., Am. Judicature Soc., Savannah Bar Assn. (pres. Younger Lawyers sect. 1975—76), State Bar Ga. (mem.-at-large exec. coun. Young Lawyers sect. 1975—78, chmn. conf. with Ga. Soc. CPAs 1979—81, chmn. sect. taxation 1983—84, Ga. commn. continuing lawyer competency 1989—95, vice chmn. 1995), N.G. Assn. U.S. (chmn. air resolution com. 2001—03, bd. dirs. 2002—04, chmn. resolutions com. 2003—05, spl. adv. com. 2005—), Georgian Club, Savannah Golf Club, Oglethorpe Club, Rotary (pres. Savannah West 2004—05). Office: PO Box 8002 Savannah GA 31412-8002

SEARIGHT, KAREN S., language educator; d. Nadya L. and Karl E. Keller; m. Lowell R. Searight, Dec. 19, 1977; children: Maggie L., Randall G. BA in French, Ft. Hays State U., Hays, Kans., 1977, BA in History, 1977. Tchg. cert. Kans. State Bd. Edn., 1977. Spanish educator USD 442, Seneca, Kans., 1984—86, USD 415, Hiawatha, Kans., 1986—. Chmn. dept. fgn. lang. Hiawatha H.S., Kans., 2003—. Pres. Morrill Pub. Libr. Bd. Trustees, Hiawatha, 1988—92. Mem.: Phi Kappa Phi. Avocations: travel, reading, gardening. Home: 401 Green Ct Hiawatha KS 66434 Home Phone: 785-742-2507.

SEARING, SUSAN ELLIS, librarian; b. Lockport, NY, Aug. 5, 1950; d. Samuel Richard and Dorothy Jean (Meeks) S. BA, SUNY, Binghamton, 1972; AMLS, U. Mich., 1976. Reference librarian Yale U., New Haven, 1976-82; women's studies librarian U. Wis., Madison, 1982-91, acting dep. dir. Gen. Library System, 1991, dep. dir., assoc. dir. public services, 1991—97; library & info. sci. librarian U. Ill. Urbana-Champaign, 1997—, head rsch. & planning user services, 1997—99, interim women & gender resources librarian, 2000—02. Lectr. U. Wis. Sch. of Libr. & Info. Studies, Madison, 1988. Author: Introduction to Library Research in Women's Studies, 1985. Mem. ALA (women's studies sect.), Phi Beta Kappa, Beta Phi Mu (dir. at large). Office: U Ill Urbana-Champaign 306 Main Library 1408 W Gregory Dr Urbana IL 61801 *

SEARL, STANFORD JAY, JR., language educator; b. Rutland, Vt., Oct. 27, 1943; s. Stanford Jay Searl, Sr. and Stephonia Kupiec; m. Rebecca Warren Searl, June 21, 2003; children: Julia Searl Rusert, Stephen Andrew Wickham. AB in Music, Syracuse U., 1965; MA, SUNY, Buffalo, 1966—67; PhD, Syracuse U., NY, 1967—69, MBA, 1981. Cert. gerontology Gerontology Ctr., Syracuse U., 1981. Assoc. dir. ctr. human policy Syracuse U., 1980—85; exec. dir. East End Cmty. Svcs., Inc., Southole, NY, 1985—86; core prof. Union Inst. & U., Cin., 1987—; instr. English Instrnl. TV, LA C.C. Dist., Sylmar, Calif., 1999—2006. Author: (nonfiction book) Voices from the Silence, The Meanings of Silence in Quaker Worship. Ministry, counsel Santa Monica Friends Meeting, Calif., 2000—03. Fellow Youth Project, Nat. Endowment Humanities, 1984, Quaker Worship, Faculty Rsch., Union Inst. & Univ., 1998; Regional Resource Ctr. grant, US Dept. Edn., 1981—84. Mem.: Assn. Integrated Studies, Quaker Studies Assn., Friends Assn. Higher Edn., Coll. English Assn., Am. Acad. Religion. Home Phone: 310-204-4225.

SEARLE, PHILIP FORD, banker; b. Kansas City, Mo., July 23, 1924; s. Albert Addison and Edith (Thompson) S.; m. Jean Adair Hanneman, Nov. 22, 1950 (dec. Nov. 1990); 1 child, Charles Randolph; m. Jean Walker, Oct. 4, 1992 (dec. oct. 1993); m. Elizabeth Gordon, Nov. 4, 1994. AB, Cornell U., 1949; grad. in banking, Rutgers U., 1957-64. With Geneva (Ohio) Savs. & Trust Co., 1949-60, pres., 1959-60; pres., sr. trust officer Northeastern Ohio Nat. Bank, Ashtabula, 1960-69; pres., CEO BancOhio Corp., Columbus, 1969-75; chmn., CEO Flagship Banks, Inc., Miami, 1975-84; chmn. bd. Sun Banks, Inc., Orlando, 1984-85, cons., 1986-94. Faculty Sch. Banking, Ohio U., 1959-70, Nat. Trust Sch., Northwestern U., Evanston, Ill., 1965-68; corp. adv. com. Nat. Assn. Securities Dealers, 1981-83; v.p., fed. adv. coun. to bd. govs. FRS, 1983-85; chmn. Nat. Adv. Bd. to Oversight Bd. for Resolution Trust Corp., 1991-92. Co-author: The

Management of a Trust Department, 1967. Past chmn. bd. regents Stonier Grad. Sch. Banking, Rutgers U., 1974-76, past mem. faculty; trustee Fin. Acctg. Found., Norwalk, Conn., 1989-93. Capt. AUS, 1943-46, 51-52, ETO. Decorated Bronze Star; named outstanding citizen in Ashtabula County, 1967. Mem. Am. Bankers Assn. (bd. dirs. 1972-74, governing coun.), Bank Adminstrn. Inst. (nat. chmn. 1987-88, bd. dirs. Chgo. 1985-89), Fla. Bankers Assn. (bd. dirs. 1979-81, coun. 1981), Ohio Bankers Assn. (pres. 1970-71), Assn. Bank Holding Cos. (pres. 1979-81), Fla. C. of C. (bd. dirs. 1978-82), Royal Poinciana Golf Club (Naples, Fla.), Catawba Island Club (Port Clinton, Ohio), Phi Kappa Tau.

SEARLE, ROBERT FERGUSON, minister; b. Auburn, NY, July 13, 1951; s. Loren Rawson and Esther Lucille (Ferguson) Searle; m. Elizabeth Jane Anderson, 1981; children: Joshua Michael Anderson, Nathanael Jeremiah Ferguson. BS, Cornell U., 1973; MDiv, Princeton Theol. Sem., 1977; DMin, Asbury Theol. Sem., 1997; MA, St. John's Coll., 2005. Ordained deacon United Meth. Ch., 1978, ordained elder United Meth. Ch., 1980, cert. in pastoral care 1981, in pastoral edn., bd. cert. chaplain Nat. Assn. Vet. Affairs Chaplains, 2004, Assn. Profl. Chaplains. Pastor of Blodgett Mills Freetown and McGraw (NY) United Meth. Ch., 1978-84; pastor Pennsylvania Ave. United Meth. Ch., Pine City, NY, 1984-98; chaplain U.S. Army Res., 1991—; chaplain resident Duke U. Med. Ctr., 1998-99; pastor Clyde United Meth. Ch., 1999—2003; adj. prof. spiritual formation Northeastern Sem., Rochester, NY, 2000—; contract chaplain Canandaigua and Syracuse VA Hosp., 2000—; mobilized as chaplain Operation Enduring Freedom, 2003; pastor Red Creek Westbury Sterling United Meth. Chs., 2004—. Mem. dist. bd. Ordained Ministry, Syracuse, NY, 1980-84, mem. conf. bd., 1980-85, dist. youth dir., Syracuse, 1981-84; mem. Cortland County Youth Bur., 1980-81; mem. hosp. com. Cortland County Coun. of Chs., 1980-84. Mem. McGraw Bd. Edn., 1981-84; bd. dirs. Meals on Wheels, Elmira, 1985-88, CPC, Elmira, 1985-93; mem. edn. and rsch. instl. rev. bd. Arnot Ogden Hosp., Elmira, 1995-98; mem. cmty. bd. Southport Correctional Facility, 1987-98; spiritual dir. Spiritual Exercises, High Acres, Geneva, NY, 1986-98, 99-2003, spiritual dir. Walk to Emmaus, Rome, NY, 1993; mem. design team Ctrl. Lakes Dist. Acad. Spiritual Devel., 1999-2003. Mem.: Charles Wesley Soc., Masons, KT. Republican. Avocations: reading, exercise, travel, music. Home: 5905 Draper St Wolcott NY 14590-1148 Office Phone: 315-754-8853. E-mail: r0027@aol.com.

SEARLE, RODNEY NEWELL, state legislator, farmer, insurance agent; b. Camden, NJ, July 17, 1920; s. William Albert and Ruby Marie (Barrus) S.; m. Janette Elizabeth Christie, May 17, 1941 (dec.); children: R. Newell Jr., Linda Jennison Grant, Alan John; m. Ruth Anne Bartlett, May 6, 2001. BA, Mankato State U., 1960; DHL, Winona State U., 2001. Prodn. coordinator Johnson & Johnson, New Brunswick, NJ, 1940-47; farmer Waseca, Minn., 1947—; spl. agt. John Hancock Mut. Ins. Co., Waseca, Minn., 1961-84; mem. Minn. Ho. of Reps., St. Paul, 1957-80, speaker, 1979—. Bd. pres. Minn. Legis. Soc., 1996—. Author: Minnesota Standoff-The Politics of Deadlock, 1990. Lay reader St. John's Episcopal Ch., 1952—; chmn. Upper Mississippi River Basin Commn., 1981-82; pres. Minn. State U. Bd., 1981-92; chmn. Minn. Higher Edn. Bd., 1991-92; bd. dirs. Minn. Wellsprings, 1984-90; emeritus mem. adv. bd. Hubert H. Humphrey Inst.; emeritus mem. coun. Minn. Hist. Soc.; bd. dirs. Minn. Agrl. Interpretive Ctr., 1983-02; mem. Waseca County Hist. Bd., 1995—; capt. Minn. Wing of the Civil Air Patrol. Named Minn. State Tree Farmer of Yr., 1978 Mem. Am. Tree Farm Sys., Nat. Conf. State Legislators, Minn. Forestry Assn. (bd. dirs. 1991-01), Masons, Rotary (pres. club 1968). Independent.

SEARLES, EDNA LOWE, artist, illustrator, composer, poet; b. Minden, La., Sept. 10, 1936; m. Thomas D. Searles. AA, Mont. Coll., 1975; BA in Edn., La. Poly., 1958. Tchr. pub. sch., 1958—65. Guest curator Delaplaine Visual Arts Ctr., Frederick, Md., 1995, East Meets West. Illustrator Soy for the 21st Century, 1984, ABC Coloring Book, 1994, Mind Children, 1995, Mind Travel, 1998, About You, 1998, Choose Life, 2002, Animal Alphabet Coloring Book, 2003, Creator and Creativity, 2004, Musical Alphabet Coloring Book, 2006, Art Doors, Columbia Festival of the Arts, Md., 2007, Art Train, Gaithersburg, Md., 2007; one-woman shows include Arnot Art Mus., Elmira, N.Y., 1988, Va. Tech State U. Grad. Ctr., 1989, Gwinnett County Art Gallery, Ga., 1990, VA Honorarium, 1990, Other: Affiliation and Exhibits, Janice Aldridge Gallery (Cat Series), Washington, 1996, Sculpture on the Ground, Md., 1994, 1999, The Artist's Gallery, Frederick, Md., 1997—2002, The Garden Gallery, Carlisle, Pa., 1999—, Nancy Stamm's Galleria, 1999—, Gallery of New Masters, Sandy Spring, Md., 2000—01, Millinneum Exhibit Music for the Eyes, 1999—2000, Musicians and All that Jazz, Frederick, Md., 2000, Gallery of New Masters, Olney, Md., 2000—01, others, exhibited in group shows at Boarman Art Ctr., Martinsburg, W.Va., 2001, Nat. League Am. Pen Women, 2003, Summer Sch. Mus., Washington, 2004, Sandy Spring Mus., Md., 2004, Friendship Gallery, Chevy Chase, 2004, Ratner Mus., 2005, murals, Ambrosia Restaurant, 1991, Still Lake Greenhouse and Florist, 1999, Damascus United Meth. Ch., 2000, The Original Ambrosia Greek Restaurant, 2004, Baronessa Italian Restaurant, 2005, jazz poster for, Mel Brown and Western Oreg. U., 2001. Past pres. Clarksburg (Md.) Cmty. Assn. Recipient Juror's award for painting Montgomery County Art, 1993, Internat. Gold medal painting Accademia Italia, Rome, 1973, 4 grants Crabtown Fund of Balt. Cmty. Found., 2005, others; named Wilson Wims Citizen of Yr., Clarksburg Comm. Assn., 1974. Mem.: DAR (vice regent Pleasant Plains of Damascus chpt. 2001—02), Nat. League Am. Pen Women (pres. Chevy Chase br. 1980—82, 2002—04, Md. state pres. 2004—05, 3d v.p. Chevy Chase br. 2004—, 2005, Poetry award). Methodist. Achievements include invention of music system for the deaf to "see" music as art "Music for the Eyes". Avocations: hammered dulcimer, music, folk singer, harp, piano.

SEARS, DAVID O'KEEFE, psychology professor; b. Urbana, Ill., June 24, 1935; s. Robert R. and Pauline (Snedden) S.; married; children: Juliet, Olivia, Meredith. BA in History, Stanford U., 1957; PhD in Psychology, Yale U., 1962. Asst. prof. to disting. prof. psychology and polit. sci. UCLA, 1961—, dean social scis., 1983-92. Dir. Inst. for Social Sci. Rsch., 1993—. Author: Public Opinion, 1964, Politics of Violence, 1973, Tax Revolt, 1985, Political Cognition, 1986, Social Psychology, 12th edit., 2005, Racialized Politics, 2000, Oxford Handbook of Political Psychology, 2003. Recipient Edward L. Bernays award, Soc. for Psychol. Study of Social Issues, 1979, Warren E. Miller Career award, Am. Polit. Sci. Assn., 2003; fellow, Guggenheim, 1988—89. Fellow Am. Acad. Arts and Scis.; mem. Soc. for Advancement Socio-Econs. (pres. 1991-92), Internat. Soc. Polit. Psychology (pres. 1994-95, Harold D. Lasswell award 1994). Office: UCLA Psychology Dept Los Angeles CA 90095-0001 Office Phone: 310-825-2160. Business E-Mail: sears@psych.ucla.edu.

SEARS, JOHN PATRICK, lawyer; b. Syracuse, NY, July 3, 1940; s. James Louis and Helen Mary (Fitzgerald) Sears; m. Carol Jean Osborne, Aug. 25, 1962; children: James Louis, Ellen Margaret, Amy Elizabeth. BS, Notre Dame U., 1960; LLB, JD, Georgetown U., 1963. Bar: N.Y. 1963. Clk. N.Y. Ct. Appeals, 1963-65; assoc. Nixon, Mudge, Rose, Guthrie, Alexander & Mitchell, 1965-66; mem. staff Richard M. Nixon, 1966-69; dep. counsel to U.S. Pres. Richard Nixon Washington, 1969-70; ptnr. Gadsby & Hannah, Washington, 1970-75, Baskin & Sears, Washington, 1977-84; pvt. practice Washington, 1984—. Polit. analyst NBC Today Show, 1984—89; mem. bd. polit. experts Wall St. Jour., 1984—. Columnist: LA Times, Newsday, 1992—. Mgr. Ronald Reagan's Presdl. Campaign, 1975—76, 1979—80; sr. advisor Jack Kemp for V.P. Campaign, 1996. Fellow, Kennedy Inst. Politics, Harvard U., 1970. Home and Office: 3350 SW 47th Ave Apt 1203 Miami FL 33133

SEARS, JOHN WINTHROP, lawyer; b. Boston, Dec. 18, 1930; s. Richard Dudley and Frederica Fulton (Leser) S.; m. Catherine Coolidge, 1965 (div. 1970). AB magna cum laude, Harvard U., Cambridge, Mass., 1952, JD, 1959; MLitt, Oxford U., Eng., 1957; D Polit. Sci. (hon.), Bridgewater State Coll., Mass., 2006. Bar: Mass. 1959, U.S. Dist. Ct. Mass. 1982. Rep. Brown Bros. Harriman, NYC, 1959-63, Boston, 1963-66; mem. Mass. Ho. Reps., 1965-68; sheriff Suffolk County, Mass., 1968-69; chmn. Boston Fin. Commn., 1969-70, Met. Dist. Commn., 1970-75; councilor-at-large Boston City Coun., 1980-82; trustee Sears Office, Boston, 1975—. Contbr. articles to profl. jours. Apptd. bd. dirs. Fulbright Scholarship, 1991-93; trustee Christ's Ch., Longwood, Brookline, Mass., 1965—, Sears Trusts, Boston, 1975—; hon. trustee J.F. Kennedy Libr., 1991—2003; bd. dirs. Am. Mus. Textile Heritage, 1987-97, Shirley-Eustis Assoc., Environ. League, Mass., 1994-97; Rep. candidate Sec. State, Mass., 1978, Gov. of Mass., 1982; vice chmn. Ward 5 Rep. Com., 1965-69, 75-85; chmn. Rep. State Com., 1975-76, mem., 1980-85; del. Rep. Nat. Conv., 1968, 76, State Conv., 1966-92; mem. U.S. Electoral Coll., 1984; bd. dirs. United South End Settlements, 1966—, chmn., 1977-78. Lt. comdr. USNR, 1952-54, 61-62. Recipient Outstanding Pub. Servant award Mass. Legis. Assn., 1975; Rhodes scholar, 1955 Mem. Mass. Bar Assn., New Eng. Hist. and Geneal. Soc. (bd. dirs., councillor 1977-82), Mass. Hist. Soc., Handel and Haydn Soc. (gov. 1982-87), Signet Soc., Boston Atheneum, Tennis and Racquet Club, Somerset Club, The Country Club (Brookline), St. Botolph Club, Club of Odd Vols., Wednesday Evening Club of 1777, Thursday Evening Club of 1846 (pres. 1999-2004), Spee Club (Cambridge chpt., pres., trustee), Longwood Cricket Club (hon.), Phi Beta Kappa. Republican. Home: 7 Acorn St Boston MA 02108-3501 *As the working years come to an end, some of us look for ways to teach, to help neighbors, especially those in need, to build up the beauty and excellence we may have encountered in our own lives, and do our best to pass them on to others.*

SEARS, LEAH WARD, state supreme court justice; b. June 13, 1955; d. Thomas E. and Onnye J. Sears; married; children: Addison, Brennan. BA, Cornell U., 1976; JD, Emory U., 1980; M in Apellate Jud. Process, U. Va.; JD (hon.), Morehouse Coll., 1993. Judge City Ct. Atlanta; atty. Alston & Bird, Atlanta; trial judge Superior Ct. Fulton County, Atlanta; justice Ga. Supreme Ct., Atlanta, 1992—, former presiding justice, chief justice, 2005—. Contbr. articles to profl. jours. Bd. dirs. Conf. Chief Justices, southeast chpt. UNICEF, Emory Law Sch. Coun., Woodruff Arts Ctr.; mem. Cornell U. Women's Coun., steering com. Ga. Women's History Month, Children's Def. Fund Black Cmty. Crusade Children; founder Battered Women's Project, Columbus, Ga. Recipient Outstanding Young Alumna award Emory U., One of 100 Most Influential Georgians Ga. Trend mag., Excellence in Pub. Svc. award Ga. Coalition Black Women, 1992, Outstanding Woman of Achievement YWCA Greater Atlanta, One of Under Forty & On the Fast Track, 1993, Ga. Woman of Year Ga. Commn. Women, Margaret Brent Women Lawyer of Achievement ABA, Leadership award Atlanta Bar Assn., Trumpet award for Distinction in Law, Woman Power award Nat. Urban League, Drum Maj. Justice award Southern Christian Leadership Conf. Mem. ABA (chair bd. elections), Nat. Assn. Women Judges, Ga. Bar Assn., Women's Forum Ga., Gate City Bar Assn., Atlanta Bar Assn. (past chair jud. sect.), Ga. Assn. Black Women Attys. (founder, pres.), Fourth Tuesday Group, Jack & Jill Am. (Atlanta chpt.), Links Inc. (Atlanta chpt.), Alpha Kappa Alpha. Office: Ga Supreme Ct 244 Washington Street Atlanta GA 30334-9007

SEARS, MARY HELEN, lawyer; b. Syracuse, NY; d. James Louis and Helen Mary (Fitzgerald) Sears. AB, Cornell U., Ithaca, NY, 1950; JD with honors, George Wash. U., Washington, DC, 1960. Bar: Va. 1960, DC 1961, US Supreme Ct. 1963. Chemist Allied Chem. and Dye Corp., Syracuse, 1950-52, Hercules Powder Co., Wilmington, Del., 1952-55; patent examiner US Patent Office, Washington, 1955-60; pvt. practice Washington, 1960-61; assoc. Irons, Birch, Swindler & McKie, Washington, 1961-69; mem. firm Irons and Sears, Washington, 1969-84; chmn. trade regulation practice dept. Memel, Jacobs, Pierno, Gersh & Ellsworth, Washington, 1984-87; ptnr., chmn. intellectual property and unfair competition practice dept. Ginsburg, Feldman & Bress, Washington, 1987-91; ptnr., chmn. intellectual property and telecomm. practice group Reid & Priest, Washington, 1991-94; founder, chmn. M. H. Sears Law Firm, 1994—. Mem. adv. bd. Boardroom Reports, Inc., NYC, 1980-85; mem. Cornell U. Coun., 1981-87, 89-93, life mem., 1995—, mem. adminstrv. bd., 1984-86. Contbr. articles to various publs. Named one of World's Leading Patent Law Experts, Euromoney Publs., PLC, 1995, 1997, 2005, 2007; recipient Outstanding Performance award, US Dept. Commerce, 1957, Belva Lockwood prize, George Wash. U. Law Sch. Assn. for Women, 2007. Mem.: ABA (co-chmn. appellate practice com., litigation sect. 1989—92), DC Bar Assn., Va. State Bar Assn., Am. Soc. Internat. Law, Am. Intellectual Property Law Assn., George Wash. U. Law Alumnae Assn. (bd. dirs. 1995—2001), Order of Coif, Phi Alpha Delta. Republican. Fax: 202-337-1474. E-mail: mhsears@mhsears.com.

SEARS, SANDRA JONES, medical/surgical nurse, consultant; b. Auburn, Mass., 1945; d. Harold Douglas Jones and Margaret Catherine Buckley; m. Raymond R. Johnson (div.); 1 child, Sharon Rae; m. Norman Allen Sears, June 22, 1980; 1 child from previous marriage, Allen Norman. AS with hons., Quinsigamond CC, 1975; BS in Psychology with hons., Worcester State Coll., Mass., 1978; BSN, Fitchburg State Coll., 1981. RN Mass., Ariz., cert. operating room nurse, Ariz., 2004, legal nurse consultant, Ariz., 2002. Registered nurse Meml. Hosp., Worcester, 1975—81; staff nurse John C. Lincoln Hosp., Phoenix, 1982—83, Paradise Valley Hosp., 1983—, charge nurse, 1985—86; owner Horizon Light Legal Nurse Cons., Phoenix. Lectr. in field; prin., owner HorizonLight Legal Nurse Cons. Mem.: Assn. Operating Rm. Nurses, Nat. Alliance Certified Legal Nurse Cons., Am. Assn. Legal Nurse Cons., Assn. Perioperative Nurses. Roman Cath. Avocations: reading, baseball, travel, history of lighthouses, stamp collecting/philately. Personal E-mail: horizonlightlnc@gmail.com.

SEARY, LAWRENCE ANTHONY, cinematographer, television producer; b. NYC, June 13, 1951; m. Phyllis Cole, Oct. 2, 1976; children: Tara Ann, Paul Anthony. BFA, NYU, 1973. News cameraman, assignment desk supr., prodr. NBC, NYC, 1974—. Recipient N.Y. State Broadcast award UPI, 1987. Mem. Nat. TV Acad. (bd. govs. 1996-2000, 03-05, nat. bd. trustees 2003-06, awards com., 9 Emmy award nominations 1978, 82, 94, 95, 2003, 05, Emmy awards 1978, 2 Emmy awards 2003), Mensa, N.Y. Press Club (1st v.p., 2002—, Feature Video award 1994). Democrat. Roman Catholic. Office: NBC 30 Rockefeller Plz Rm 728E New York NY 10112-0002 E-mail: larryseary@aol.com.

SEASE, GENE ELWOOD, communications executive; b. Portage, Pa., June 28, 1931; s. Grover Chauncey and Clara Mae (Over) S.; m. Joanne D. Cherry, July 20, 1952; children: David Gene, Daniel Elwood, Cheryl Joanne. AB, Juniata Coll., 1952; B.D., Pitts. Theol. Sem., 1956, Th.M., 1959; PhD, U. Pitts., 1965, M.Ed., 1958; LL.D., U. Evansville, 1972, Butler U., 1972; Litt.D., Ind. State U., 1974; DD, U. Indpls., 1989. Ordained to ministry United Methodist Ch., 1956; pastor Grace United Meth. Ch., Wilkinsburg, Pitts., 1952-63; conf. dir., supt. Western Pa. Conf. United Meth. Ch., Pitts., 1963-68; lectr. grad. faculty U. Pitts., 1965-68; mem. staff U. Indpls., 1968-89, asst. to pres., 1968-69, pres., 1970-88, chancellor, 1988-89, pres. emeritus, 1989—; chmn. Sease, Gerig & Assocs., Indpls., 1989—. Bd. dirs. Bankers Life Ins. Co. of N.Y. Author: Christian Word Book, 1968; also numerous articles. Pres. Greater Indpls. Progress Com., 1972-75, Marion County Sheriff's Merit Bd.; mem. Ind. Scholarship Commn.; cons. Time Warner; bd. dirs. Indpls. Conv. Bur., Ind. Law Enforcement Tng. Acad., 500 Festival, Crossroads coun. Boy Scouts Am., Community Hosp. Indpls., St. Francis Hosp.; chmn. Ind. State Fair Commn. Mem. Internat. Platform Assn., English Speaking Union, Japan-Am. Soc. Ind., Ind. C. of C. (bd. dirs.), Indpls. C. of C. (bd. dirs.), Ind. Schoolmen's Club, Ind. State Fair Commn. (chmn.), Econ. Club of Indpls. (bd. dirs.), Skyline Club (bd. dirs.), Phi Delta Kappa, Alpha Phi Omega, Alpha Psi Omega. Clubs: Mason (Indpls.) (33 deg., Shriner), Kiwanian. (Indpls.), Columbia (Indpls.). Office Phone: 317-634-1171.

SEASHORE, MARGRETTA REED, physician, educator; b. Red Bank, NJ, June 20, 1939; d. Robert Clark and Lillie Ann (Heaviland) Reed; m. John Seashore, Dec. 26, 1964; children: Robert H., Carl J., Carolyn L. BA, Swarthmore Coll., 1961; MD, Yale U., 1965. Diplomate Am. Bd. Pediatrics, Am. Bd. Med. Genetics, Nat. Bd. Med. Examiners. Intern in pediat. Yale U. Sch. Medicine, New Haven, 1965-66, asst. resident in pediat., 1966-68, postdoctoral fellow in genetics and metabolism, depts. pediat. and medicine, 1968-70, asst. clin. prof. human genetics and pediat., 1974-78, from asst. prof. to assoc. prof., 1978-90, prof. genetics and pediatrics, 1990—; clin. asst. prof. pediat. U. Fla. Coll. Medicine, Gainesville, 1970-71, asst. prof., 1971-73; attending physician Duvall Med. Ctr., U. Hosp. Jacksonville, 1970-73, asst. prof., 1970-71; attending physician Hope Haven Children's Hosp., Jacksonville, Fla., 1970-73, Shands Tchg. Hosp., Gainesville, 1971-73, Danbury (Conn.) Hosp., 1977—, Yale-New Haven Hosp., 1974—, dir. Genetic Consultation Svc., 1977-86, 1989—; cons. physician Bridgeport (Conn.) Hosp., 1974—, Lawrence and Meml. Hosp., New London, Conn., 1979—, Norwalk (Conn.) Hosp., 1981—. Contbr. chapters to books. Fellow: Am. Coll. Med. Genetics (founding fellow), Am. Acad. Pediat. (mem. screening com. Conn. chpt. 1977—, mem. genetics com. 1989—94, chair com. genetics 1990—94); mem.: AAAS, AMA, New Eng. Genetics Group (chmn. outreach com. 1979—89, mem. steering com. 1979—98, chmn. screening com. 1989—93, co-dir. 1992—95), Soc. Study Inborn Errors of Metabolism, Am. Bd. Med. Genetics (bd. dirs. 2004—), Soc. Inherited Metabolic Disorders (bd. dirs. 1989—, sec. 1991—96, pres. 1997), Am. Soc. Human Genetics (mem. genetic svcs. com. 1986—91). Avocations: music, gardening, sewing, computers. Office: Yale U Sch Med Dept Genetics 333 Cedar St New Haven CT 06510-3289 Home Phone: 203-565-6267; Office Phone: 203-785-4938. Business E-Mail: margretta.seashore@yale.edu.

SEATON, EDWARD LEE, editor, publishing executive; b. Manhattan, Kans., Feb. 5, 1943; s. Richard Melvin and Mary (Holton) Seaton; m. Karen Mathisen, Sept. 4, 1965; children: Edward Merrill, John David. AB cum laude, Harvard U., 1965; postgrad., U. Ctr., Quito, Ecuador, 1965-66, U. Mo., 1966—67. Staff writer Courier-Jour., Louisville, 1968—69; editor-in-chief, pub. Manhattan Mercury, 1969—. Bd. dirs., officer 8 newspaper and broadcasting affiliates; mem. Pulitzer Prize Bd., 1992—2001, chmn., 2001; mem. adv. com. Knight Internat. Press Fellowship Program, 1994—2006; mem. Cabot Awards bd. Columbia U., 1995—2003. Contbr. articles to profl. jours. Chmn. Alfred M. Landon lecture patrons Kans. State U.; chmn. Latin Am. Scholarship Program Am. Univs., Cambridge, Mass., 1986—87. Decorated comendador Order Christopher Columbus (Dominican Republic); recipient Cabot prize, Columbia U., 1993; Fulbright scholar, 1965. Mem.: Internat. Press Inst., Internat. Ctr. Journalists (bd. dirs. 1990—2001), Inter-Am. Press Assn. (pres. 1989—90, exec. com. 1976—), Am. Soc. Newspaper Editors (Found. pres. 1994—, pres. 1998—99), Kans. C. of C. and Industry (pres. 1987), Fly Club (Harvard U.). Avocations: tennis, cooking. Office: 318 N 5th St Manhattan KS 66505-0787

SEATON, JAMES EVERETT, humanities educator; s. John Everett and Frances Kopecky Seaton; m. Sandra Cecelia Harris-Browne, Nov. 9, 1966; children: Ann Louish, James Everett Seaton, Jr., Amanda Cecelia Webster, Jeremy Evans Francis. BA, U. Ill., Urbana-Champaign, 1966; MA, PhD, U. Iowa, Iowa City, 1971. Instr. dept. humanities Mich. State U., 1971—76, asst. prof. Dept. Humanities, 1976—81, assoc. prof. Dept. English, 1981—91, prof. Dept. English, 1991—. Mem. academic bd. Nat. Humanities Inst., Washington, 1999—; reviewer NEH, Washington, 2006. Author: A Reading of Vergil's Georgics, 1983, Cultural Conservatism, Political Liberalism, 1996; editor: Beyond Cheering and Bashing: New Perspectives on The Closing of the American Mind, 1992; mem. editl. bd.: Humanitas, 1998—2006; contbr. essays to publications. Recipient Essay prize, Midwest Heritage, 1991, 2006. Mem.: Soc. Study Midwestern Lit. (pres. 2006—07). Office: Michigan State University Dept of English Morrill Hall East Lansing MI 48824 Home Phone: 517-332-6446; Office Phone: 517-355-1730. Office Fax: 517-355-1730; Home Fax: 517-355-1730. Business E-Mail: seaton@msu.edu.

SEATON, ROBERT LAMAR, pharmacist; b. Henderson, Tenn., Nov. 30, 1943; s. Frank Lamar and Vaneida Ladeon Seaton; m. Margaret Nella Ellington, Sept. 30, 1966; children: Jennifer Anniece, Brian Lamar. B in Pharmacy, U. Tenn., Memphis, 1971. Double roll cloth operator Am. Finishing Co., Memphis, 1961—62; receiving clk. Ellis-Boswell Drag Co., Memphis, 1962—63; aviator electric technician USN, Meredian, Miss., 1964—67; rental clk. Nat. Car Rental, Memphis, 1967—68; pharmacy student Alta Vista Drug, Memphis, 1968—71; pharmacist Family Drug, Lexington, Tenn., 1971—73, Walgreen, Jackson, Tenn., 1973—. With USN, 1963—67. Mem.: U. Tenn. Alumni Assn., Tenn. Pharmacist Assn., Am. Pharmacist Assn., Lions Club (pres., treas., bd. mem.). Republican. Home: 279 Rolling Hills Dr Jackson TN 38305 Office: Walgreen 1334 N Highland Jackson TN 38301

SEATON, SHIRLEY SMITH, academic administrator, consultant; b. Cleve. d. Kibble Smith and Cecil Wright; m. J. Lawrence Seaton, Oct. 2, 1965; 1 child, Eric Dean BA, MA in History, Howard U., 1949; MEd, Case We. Res. U., 1956; EdD, U. Akron, 1981; cert. Chinese history and culture, Beijing Normal U. Tchr. Cleve. Dist., 1950—59, dir. social studies, 1976—87; prin. Lafayette, Dike, Cleve., 1959—63, 1965—75; with Stas. WEWS-TV, WVIZ-TV, Cleve., 1963—67; adj. prof. Cleve. State U., 1988—90; adminstr. John Carroll U., University Heights, Ohio, 1990—. Program dir. OEO, Cleve., 1965; peer rev. Ohio Proficiency Test, 1986—2005; cons. Basics and Beyond, Cleve., 1990— Coord. Ctr. Civic Edn., 11th Congress Dist., 1987—; peer interview chair Fulbright tchr. exch. U.S. Dept. State, 1994-99, 2001-05; trustee We. Res. Hist. Soc., Cleve., 1996—, Ret. Vol. Program, Cleve., 1997-2003; commr. City of Cleveland Heights, 1997— Recipient Ohio Humanitarian award Govt. of Ohio, 1992; Fulbright grantee USIA, 1959, 82 Mem. AAUW, Fulbright Assn., Nat. Alliance Black Edn., Coalition 100 Black Women, Phi Delta Kappa, Alpha Kappa Alpha, Phi Beta Delta, Alpha Sigma Nu Episcopalian. Avocation: bridge. Home: 3680 Bendemeer Rd Cleveland Heights OH 44118 Office: John Carroll U 20700 North Pk Blvd University Heights OH 44118 Office Phone: 216-397-1604, 216-320-1911. Personal E-mail: ssseaton@sbcglobal.net. Business E-Mail: sseaton@jcu.edu.

SEATON, VAUGHN ALLEN, retired veterinary pathology educator; b. Abilene, Kans., Oct. 11, 1928; m. Clara I. Bertelrud; children: Gregory S., Jeffrey T. BS, DVM, Kans. State U., 1954; MS, Iowa State U., 1957. Pvt. practice, Janesville, Wis., 1954; instr. pathology Vet. Diagnostic Lab. Iowa State U., Ames, 1954-57, from asst. to assoc. prof. pathology Vet. Diagnostic Lab., 1957-64, prof., head Vet. Diagnostic Lab., 1964-94. Lab. coord. regional emergency animal disease eradication orgn. Animal and Plant Health Inspection Svc. USDA, 1974—; mem. rsch. com. Iowa Beef Industry Coun., 1972-85; mem. adv. bd. Iowa State Water Resources Rsch. Inst., 1973-80; cons. several orgns. Co-author: (monographs) Feasibility Study of College of Veterinary Medicine, 1972, Veterinary Diagnostic Laboratory Facilities-State of New York, 1970; bd. dirs. Iowa State U. Press, 1985-88, mem. manuscript com., 1982-85; contbr. articles to profl. jours. Trustee Ames Pub. Libr., 1979-85; mem. Iowa State Bd. Health, 1971-77, v.p., 1976-77; bd. dirs. Masonic Edn. Found., 1985-88; v.p. Iowa

Scottish Rite Masonic Found. Recipient Disting. Alumnus award, Coll. Vet. Medicine, Kans. State U., 2005. Mem. AVMA, Am. Assn. Vet. Lab. Diagnosticians (bd. govs. 1973-88, pres. 1968, E.P. Pope award 1980), Am. Coll. Vet. Toxicologists, U.S. Animal Health Assn., Iowa Vet. Med. Assn. (pres. 1971), North Ctrl. Assn. Vet. Lab. Diagnosticians, Western Vet. Conf. (exec. bd. 1986-90, v.p. 1994, pres.-elect 1995, pres. 1996), World Assn. Vet. Lab. Diagnosticians (pres. 1980-86), Ames C. of C. (bd. dirs. 1970-73), Phi Kappa Phi, Phi Zeta (pres. 1964), Alpha Zeta, Gamma Sigma Delta. Office: Iowa State U Coll Vet Medicine Vet Diagnostic Lab Ames IA 50011-0001

SEATS, PEGGY CHISOLM, public affairs executive; b. Lisman, Ala., Oct. 12, 1951; d. William H. and Bernice (Berry) Chisolm; m. Melvin Seats (dec.). BA in Communications cum laude, Lewis U., 1974; grad. cert. in event mgmt., George Washington U., 1995; MA in Pub. Comm., Am. U., 1997; grad. cert. in intercultural comm., Vaxjo (Sweden) U., 1997; Master's cert. in Pub. Affairs & Exec. Non-profit mgmt., Georgetown U., 2005. Account exec. Globe Broadcasting, Chgo., 1976-78, Merrill Lynch, Chgo., 1978-79, Transp. Displays, Inc., Chgo., 1979-81; with Reverie, Inc., 1981—; nat. accounts mgr. Soft Sheen Products Co., Chgo., 1981-83; mktg. cons. Reverie, Inc., Chgo., 1983-85; pub. rels., mktg. mgr. Proctor & Gardner Advt., Chgo., 1985-86; dir. pub. rels., mktg. Morris Brown Coll., Atlanta, 1986-87; mgr. mktg. Howard U. Press, Washington, 1989-90; cons. White House Initiative on Historically Black Colls., Univs., 1990-92. State advisor U.S. Congl. Adv. Bd., Ill., 1982. Contbr. numerous articles to newspapers and mags. Founder Benjamin Banneker Meml. Found., Washington, 1996; organizer S.W. Waterfront Initiative, 2000—; facilitator L'Enfant Plaza Revitalization Project, 1997—; bd. dir. Congl. Award Found. Recipient Kizzie award Black Women Hall of Fame, Chgo., 1981, Svc. award Nat. Assn. Women in Media, Chgo., 1982. Mem. Internat. Platform Assn., Internat. Assn. Bus. Communicators, Internat. Spl. Events Soc., Pub. Rels. Soc. Am., Black Pub. Rels. Soc. (founder Atlanta chpt.), Nat. Assn. Market Developers, World Affairs Coun., Comittee of 100, Lewis U. Alumni Assn. (bd. dirs. Ill. 1979), Washington Interdependence Coun. (founder, CEO 1996), Benjamin Banneker Inst. Math. and Sci. (founder). Unitarian Universalist. Avocations: music, art collecting, reading. Home: 2020 Pennsylvania Ave NW Washington DC 20006-1811 Office Phone: 202-387-3380. Business E-Mail: info@bannekermemorial.org.

SEAVER, BARTON, chef; Grad., Culinary Inst. Am., Hyde Park, NY. Cert. Sommelier Sommelier Soc. Am. Cook Tru, The Dining Room; grad. tchr. Culinary Inst. Am.; chef Finch Tavern, NYC, exec. sous chef; chef Jaleo, Washington; exec. chef Café Saint-Ex, Washington, 2005—, Pilar, Washington, 2005—. Official chef embassy of Iceland, 2005—. Named one of Washington DC's Rising Stars, StarChefs.com, 2006. Mem.: Seafood Alliance. Office: Cafe Saint-Ex 1847 14th St NW Washington DC 20009 Office Phone: 202-265-7839. Business E-Mail: barton@saint-ex.com. *

SEAVEY, CHRISTOPHER GORDON, psychotherapist, alcohol/drug abuse services professional; b. Syracuse, NY, Dec. 4, 1942; s. Gordon Crowell and Shirley Edith Seavey; m. Eudene Sawyer, Aug. 8, 1965 (div. Mar. 1983); children: Sandra, Sherry, Gordon; m. Nancy Bowen, 1983. BA in Human Svcs., U. Mass., 1986; MA in Rehab. Counseling, U. South Fla., 1991; PhD in Psychotherapy, Internat. U. Grad. Studies, 2001. Sr. counselor Project Turnabout, Hingham, Mass., 1982—86; counselor Coastal Cmty. Counseling, Braintree, Mass., 1986—87, South Shore Coun. on Alcoholism, Quincy, Mass., 1987; chem. dependency counselor II David Lawrence Ctr., Naples, Fla., 1989—90; cons. vocat. rehab. Intracorp, Naples, 1990—96; acting dir. Addiction Recovery Ctr., Ft. Myers, Fla., 1993—98; clin. dir. Assisted Addiction Recovery, Naples, 1995—2004; dir. Christopher Seavey LMHG PA, 2004—. Mem. adv. bd. Naples Rehab. Inc., 1994-97. Mem. adj. bd. Project Help, Naples, 1996—; chmn. Collier County Depression Coalition, Naples, 1997. Recipient Book award U. Mass., Boston, 1986; U. Calif. San Francisco fellow, 1986; Tobacco Coalition grantee, 1998. Mem. NADAAC, ACA, Internat. Assn. Rehab. Profls., Internat. Coun. on Alcohol and Addictions, Fla. Rehab. Assn. (pres. S.W. Fla. chpt. 1994-95, Svc. award 1999), S.W. Fla. Marriage and Family Counseling Assn., Fla. Mental Health Counselors, Gulf Coast Mental Health Counselors Assn. (past pres.), Phi Kappa Phi. Office: 9853 N Tamiami Trail Ste 213 Naples FL 34108 Office Phone: 239-595-7775. Personal E-mail: chriseavey@earthlink.net.

SEAVEY, WILLIAM ARTHUR, lawyer, vintner; b. LA, Aug. 28, 1930; s. Arthur Jones and Dorothy (Keyes) S.; m. Mary van Beuren, June 25, 1955; children: Dorothy K., Arthur V.B., William G., Frederic A., Charles K. AB, Princeton U., 1952; LLB, Harvard U., 1955; grad. Inst. Internat. Studies, U. Geneva, Switzerland, 1956, D in Polit. Sci., 1970. Bar: Calif. 1957, U.S. Dist. Ct. (so. and no. dist.) Calif. 1957, U.S. Ct. Appeals (9th cir.) 1957. Assoc. Luce, Forward, Kunzel & Scripps, San Diego, 1956-57; asst. U.S. atty. U.S. Dist. Ct. (so. dist.) Calif., 1957-59; with Noon & Seavey, San Diego, 1959-65; lectr. in internat. law and econ., asst. to pres. Mills Coll., Oakland, Calif., 1968-74; ptnr. Richards & Seavey, San Francisco, 1974-76, Davis, Stafford, Kellman & Fenwick, San Francisco, 1976-78; of counsel Friedman, Olive, McCubbin, Spalding, Bilter, Roosevelt etal, San Francisco, 1987—2004. Proprietor Seavey Vineyard, St. Helena, Napa County, 1981—. Author: Dumping Since the War: The Gatt and National Laws, 1970. Councilman City of Coronado, Calif., 1960-62, mayor 1962-64; trustee French-Am. Internat. Sch., San Francisco, 1968-96; pres. English Speaking Union, San Francisco, 1982-85, Alliance Francaise, San Francisco, 1979-81; chair Javits Fellowship Bd., Washington, 1989-92; mem. Columbus Fellowship Found. Bd., Washington, 1993-99; dir. San Francisco Com. on Fgn. Rels., 1995-98, 2001—, chmn., 1998-2001. Mem. ABA, Calif. Bar Assn., Am. Soc. Internat. Law, Pacific Union Club, Cercle de l'Union, Met. Club (Washington). Republican. Avocations: skiing, piano. Home: 90 Hazel Ln Piedmont CA 94611-4033 Home and Office: 1310 Conn Valley Rd Saint Helena CA 94574-9624 Business E-Mail: info@seaveyvineyard.com.

SEAWELL, DONALD RAY, lawyer, performing company executive; b. Jonesboro, NC, Aug. 1, 1912; s. A.A.F. and Bertha (Smith) S.; m. Eugenia Rawls, Apr. 5, 1941; children: Brook Ashley, Donald Brockman. AB, U. N.C., 1933, JD, 1936, DLitt, 1980; LHD, U. No. Colo., 1978. Bar: NC 1936, NY 1947. With SEC, 1939-41, 45-47, Dept. Justice, 1942-43; chmn. bd., dir., pub., pres. Denver Post, 1966-81; chmn. bd., dir. Gravure West, LA, 1966-81; dir. Swan Prodns., London; of counsel firm Bernstein, Seawell, Kove & Maltin, NYC, 1979—; chmn. bd., chief exec. officer Denver Ctr. for Performing Arts, 1972—. Ptnr. Bonfils-Seawell Enterprises, NYC; bd. vis. U. NC Chmn. bd. ANTA, 1965—; theatre panel Nat. Coun. Arts, 1970-74; bd. govs. Royal Shakespeare Theatre, Eng.; trustee Am. Acad. Dramatic Arts, 1967—, Hofstra U., 1968-69, Cen. City Opera Assn., Denver Symphony; bd. dirs., Air Force Acad. Found., Nat. Ints. Outdoor Drama, Walter Hampden Meml. Library, Hammond Mus.; pres. Helen G. Bonfils Found., 1972-97, pres. emeritus, 1997—, chmn. fin. com., 1997—, Denver Opera Found.; Population Crisis Com., 1982-91; bd. dirs. Family Health Internat., Found. for Internat. Family Health; bd. visitors NC Sch. Arts, 1992-98; pres. Frederick G. Bonfils Found., 1972-92; chmn. Civilian Mil. Inst. Named Officer, Most Excellent Order of the Brit. Empire, 2002; recipient Am. Acad. Achievement award, 1980, Tony award for producing, On Your Toes, 1983, Vocie Rsch. and Awareness award, Voice Found., 1983, Arts and Entertainement Cable Network award, 1987, Third Millennium Leadership award, Am. Diabetes Assn., 1996, Colo. Tourism Hall of Fame award, 1999, Thomas Degaetani award, U.S. Inst. for Theatre Tech., 2000, Benjamin F. Stapleton, Jr. award, 2000, Disting. Svc. award, U. Colo., 2000, Downtown Denver award for Tantalus, 2001, AWARE Honoree award, 2001, Donald Seawell Outstanding Achievement in Theatre award, Colo. Festival World Theatre, 2005, Founders award for Outstanding Contbn. to Am. Theater, Theater Hall Fame, NYC, 2005, Theatre Hall Fame, NYC, 2006. Mem. Bucks Club (London), Dutch Treat Club (NYC), Denver Country Club, Denver Club, Cherry Hills Country Club, Mile High Club (Denver), Garden of Gods Club (Colorado Springs, Colo.). Office: Denver Ctr for Performing Arts 1101 13th St Denver CO 80204 E-mail: geary@dcpa.org.

SEAWELL, THOMAS ROBERT, artist, retired art educator; b. Balt., Mar. 17, 1936; s. Robert James and Cynthia Edith (Bass) S.; m. Barbara Louise Frey, Nov. 30, 1985; children: James Bradford, Lee Thomas, Gustin Charles, Jay Turner Frey. B.F.A., Washington U., 1958; M.F.A., Tex. Christian U., 1960. Mem. faculty dept. art SUNY-Oswego, 1963-91, prof., 1973-91; tchg. adj. Tex. A&M, Commerce, 1999—2006. Juror 50th Cooperstown Nat., 1985, Nat. Print Exhbn. Minot State U., ND, 1985, Rochester Print Club Ann. Meml. Art Gallery U., Minn., 1988; vis. artist Ox Bow Print Symposium, 1985, Ann. Matrix Artist U. Dallas, 1989, Midwestern State U., Wichita Falls, 1993, East Tenn. State U., Knoxville, 1997; guest spkr. L.A. Coll., 2004. One-man exhbns. include retrospective U. Md., Baltimore County, 1983, Retrospective Tyler Art Gallery, SUNY, Oswego, 1991, Univ. Gallery, Tex. A&M U., Commerce, 1995, Brazos Gallery, Dallas, 1997, La. Coll., Pineville-Alexandria, 2004; group exhbns. include Contemporary Am. Prints in Leningrad, USSR, 1983-84, The Collagraph, U. Mont., 1987, The Streets Suite, Rochester Meml. Art Gallery, 2005; traveling exhbn. So. Arts Fedn. Traveling Exhbn. "A Sense of Place," 1986—, Columbia Coll., 1996-97, Art in the Metroplex, J.M. Moudy Gallery, Ft. Worth, Tex., 1997, Contemporary Tex. Clay, Dallas Visual Arts Ctr., 1997, To Have and to Hold, Irving (Tex.) Arts Ctr. Main Gallery, 1998, Kennedy-Douglass Ctr. for the Arts Nat. Ceramic Competition, 1999, Woodmere Art Mus., 1999, San Angelo Mus. Fine Arts, 2000, 2004, Ark. State U., 2000, U. Wis., Parkside, 2000, 2003, 2005, Oxford Gallery, Rochester, N.Y., 2000; represented in permanent collections Bklyn. Mus., DeCordova Mus. Art, Rochester Meml. Art Gallery, Pushkin Mus., USSR, Brit. Mus., Munson-Williams-Proctor Inst., Library of Congress, Portland Art Mus., Ark. Arts Ctr., Alexandria Mus. Art, La., Phila. Watercolor Soc., 2005, Roberson Art Mus., Binghamton, NY, 2005, Phila. Water Color Soc., Berman Mus., 2005; commd. print editions: Geldermann Securities Ltd., 1985-92, 8 Stock Exchange Images, The Print Club Albany, N.Y., 2004. Recipient Joseph A. Cain Meml. Purchase award for sculpture Del Mar Coll., 1999, 2d prize 15th Internat. Miniature Print Exhbn. Roberson Art Mus., Binghamton, N.Y., 2005. Mem. Boston Printmakers, Phila. Water Color Soc., Soc. Am. Graphic Artists, Tex. Sculpture Assn. Office Phone: 903-886-3102. Personal E-mail: tseawell@9plus.net.

SEAWRIGHT, JAMES L., JR., sculptor, educator; b. Jackson, Miss., May 22, 1936; s. James L. and Josephine (Power) S.; m. Mabelle M. Garrard, June 22, 1960; 1 child, James Andrew. Student, U. of South, 1953-54, Delta State Coll., 1954-55; BA in English, U. Miss., 1957; postgrad., Art Students League of N.Y., 1961-62. Tech. supr. Columbia-Princeton Electronic Music Center, NYC, 1963-69; tchr. Sch. Visual Arts, 1967-69; dir. visual arts program Princeton U., 1972-2001, prof. coun. of humanities and visual arts, 1992—; prof. visual arts U. Ctr. for Creative and Performing Arts, 2006—. Asst. to choreographer, Henry St. Playhouse, N.Y.C., 1962-63, spl. effects, tech. cons., Mimi Garrard Dance Co., N.Y.C., 1964—; sculptor represented in permanent collections, Mus. Modern Art, N.Y.C., Whitney Mus., N.Y.C., N.J. State Mus., Trenton, Guggenheim Mus., N.Y.C., Wadsworth Atheneum, Hartford, Conn., others; pub. commns. for SEA-TAC Internat. Airport, Seattle, Logan Internat. Airport, Boston; also pvt. collections. Served with USN, 1957-61. Recipient Theodoron award Guggenheim Mus., 1969, Am. Acad. Arts and Letters Art award, 1997, Lifetime Achievement award Miss. Inst. Arts and Letters, 2003, Howard T. Behrman award for disting. accomplishment in humanities Princeton U., 2004; Graham Found. Advanced Study in Arts fellow, 1970. Mem. Am. Abstract Artists, Phi Delta Theta. Democrat. Episcopalian. Office: 185 Nassau St Princeton NJ 08544-2003 Home Phone: 845-386-4883; Office Phone: 609-258-5098. Personal E-mail: james@seawright.net. Business E-Mail: jims@princeton.edu.

SEAY, STEPHANIE, elementary school educator; b. Spartanburg County, SC; B in Early Childhood Edn., Univ. SC-Upstate; M in Early Childhood Edn., Furman Univ. Tchr., 1995—, Wellford (SC) Elem. Sch., 2004—. Adj. prof., mentor, early childhood edn. Presbyn. Coll. Named SC Tchr. of Yr., 2006. Office: Wellford Elem Sch 684 Syphrit Rd Wellford SC 29385 Business E-Mail: seays@spart5.k12.sc.us.

SEBASTIAN, JOAN (JOSÉ MANUEL FIGUEROA), musician; b. Juliantla, Mexico; m. Maribel Guardia (div.); 1 child. Musician: (albums) Rumores, 1985, Oiga, 1987, Ranchero vol. 2, 1987, Mascarada, 1988, Norteno, 1989, Con Banda, 1991, Viva La Vida, 1991, Al Rojo Vivo, 1995, Embustero, 1995, Con Tambora, 1995, Bandido De Amores, 1995, Mis Nuevas Baladas, 1995, Peor de Tus Antojos, 1995, En Vivo en La Arena Mexico, 1995, Tambora Remix, 1995, Me Enamore De Ti, 1995, Con Mariachi, 1995, Tu Y Yo, 1996, Gracias Por Tanto Amor, 1998, Rey del Jaripeo, 1999, Con Norteno, 2000, Secreto de Amor, 2000, Nostalgia y Recuerdos, 2000, Con el Mariachi Vargas de Tecal, 2001, Un Carino Como Tu, 2001, Vivo en el Progreso de Guadalajara, 2001, Lo Dijo el Corazon, 2002 (Grammy award for Best Mexican album, 2002), Afortunado, 2002 (Grammy award for Best Mexican album, 2003), Que Amarren a Cupido, 2004, El Poeta del Pueblo, 2004, Enamorado del Amor, 2004, Frente a Frente: Con Banda, 2004, Mujeres Bonitas, 2004, Inventario, 2005, Rancheras Con Banda, 2005, Canta Para Ti, 2006, Mas Allá del Sol, 2006 (Grammy award for Best Banda Album, 2007), Corridos y Algo Mas, 2007, (songs) Mas Allá del Sol, 2006 (Song of Yr., ASCAP Latin Music awards, 2007, Regional Mex. Album of Yr., Billboard Latin Music awards, 2007); actor: (films) La Sangre de nuestra raza, 1982, Sangre De Rey, 1997; (TV series) Tu y Yo, 1996. Recipient Silver Pen award, ASCAP, 2000, Golden Note award, 2007, Hall of Fame award, Billboard Latin Music Awards, 2006. Office: Balboa Records Co 10900 Washington Blvd Culver City CA 90232-4025 Office Phone: 310-204-3792. E-mail: info@balboarecords.com. *

SEBASTIAN, PETER, political scientist, consultant, retired diplomat; b. June 19, 1926; m. Harvel Huddleston, Dec. 11, 1951; 1 child, Christopher. BA, U. Chgo., 1950; postgrad., U. d'Aix-Marseille, Nice, France, 1949, New Sch. for Social Research, NYC, 1950, Nat. War Coll., 1969-70. Dir., owner cons. co., NYC, 1950-57; U.S. Fgn. Service officer Dept. State, Washington, 1957-76, dep. exec. sec., 1976-77, sr. seminar, 1977-78; U.S. consul gen. Casablanca, Morocco, 1978-80; minister, counselor Am. embassy, Rabat, Morocco, 1980-82; dir. for North Africa Dept. State, Washington, 1982-84; ambassador to Tunisia Tunis, 1984-87; ambassador-in-residence Ctr. for Strategic Internat. Studies, Georgetown U., Washington, 1987-88; cons. in fgn. affairs to the public and pvt. sector, lectr., 1988—. Mem. V.P. Bush's task force on border control, 1988—89. Contbr. poems to Osmose, 1949; author studies for the pvt. sector U.S. Dept. State and other U.S agys. Bd. dirs. Santa Fe Coun. on Internat. Rels., 2005. Sgt. AUS, 1944-46. Decorated Ouissam Alaouite (Morocco), numerous U.S. mil. decorations; recipient Presdl. Meritorious Service award, 1985. Mem. Am. Fgn. Svc. Assn., Nat. Geog. Soc., Mid. East Inst. Episcopalian. Avocations: painting, drawing, photography. Home Phone: 505-820-2780; Office Phone: 505-983-6364. Personal E-mail: Batuta@aol.com.

SEBASTIAN, PHYLIS SUE (INGRAM), real estate broker, antiques, appraiser; b. Childersburg, Ala., Jan. 24, 1945; d. Albert Freeman and Era Mae (McGowin) Ingram; m. Robert Emmett Martin, March 31, 1965 (div. Sept. 1976); children: Connie, Michael, Toni, Steve; m. Thomas Haskell Sebastian III, June 26, 1985; stepchildren: Shellie, Tabatha, Cherie, Thomas IV. Ordained minister Progressive Universal Life Ch., 2002; lic. real estate broker Mo., real estate appraiser Tenn., Mo., PREA, CIMA. Owner, broker Phylis Sebastian Real Estate, Farmington, Mo., 1989—, U.S. Auto Sales, Park Hills, Mo., 1993—96; owner Bus. Legal Svs., Park Hills, Mo., 1993—; ptnr. La Femme Fine Antique Auction Svc., Ironton, Mo., 1997—. Owner Astrology Cons., 1970—; numerous appearances St. Louis TV; hostess radio show, St. Louis. Contbr. articles to newspapers; author: Marriages in Madison County Missouri for 1848-1868, 1998, 1910 Census for Madison County Missouri, 1998, numerous poems. Co-founder Astrological Assn., St. Louis, 1976-77, Mo. Mental Health Consumer Network, 1989-93, Mineral Area chpt. 1989-93; founder, CEO Sho-Me Retreats, Inc. for the Homeless Mentally Ill.; founder, CEO She-Me Retreats Inc. Mem. Nat. Gardening Club, Libr. Congress, Smithsonian, Nat. Hist. soc., Geneal. Assn. Madison County, Mo. (founder, sec., treas., genealogist). Mem. Lds Ch. Avocations: reading, walking, gardening, piano, guitar. Home: 5231 West 72 Highway Fredericktown MO 63645 Office: Arcadia Valley Auction Company Inc and Real Estate 315A W Russell St Ironton MO 63650-1316 Home Phone: 573-915-0868; Office Phone: 573-546-3900, 573-546-7440. Personal E-mail: psrealestate@myway.com. E-mail: avac@myway.com.

SEBASTIANELLI, MARIO JOSEPH, internist, nephrologist, health facility administrator; b. Jessup, Pa., Sept. 14, 1935; s. Carlo and Antonia (Antonelli) S.; m. Alena Marie Drazdauskas, June 26, 1993 (div. July 2004); children: Mario, Alexa, Marco. BS in Biology, U. Scranton, 1958; MD, Jefferson Med. Coll., 1962. Diplomate Am. Bd. Internal Medicine. From sr. instr. to assoc. prof. medicine Hahnemann U., Phila., 1969—87; pvt. practice Scranton, Pa., 1971—; chief nephrology, founding dir. hemodialysis Moses Taylor Hosp., Scranton, 1972—76; founding med. dir. Pa. Regional Tissue Bank, Scranton, 1983—91; founding dir. inpatient hemodialysis svcs. Comty. Med. Ctr., Scranton, 1996—2006; founding med. dir. Fresenius Med. Care Dialysis Svcs. Dunmore, Scranton, 2001—. Mem. senateconfirmed gov. apptd. Govs. Renal Disease Adv. Com., Harrisburg, Pa., 1973-76; creator, owner Comprehensive Health Svcs. Ctr., Dunmore, Pa., 1979—; founding med. dir. Diagnostic Lab., Dunmore, 1981-95. Contbr. articles to profl. jours. Bd. dirs. Scranton Lackawanna Human Devel. Agy., Scranton, 1977-82. Lt. USNR, 1963-65. Fellow: ACP; mem.: KC (4th degree), AMA, Renal Physicians Assn., Internat. Soc. Nephrology, Am. Soc. Nephrology, Alpha Omega Alpha. Republican. Roman Catholic. Avocations: fishing, swimming, travel, sports cars, reading. Office: Comprehensive Health Svcs Ctr 1416 Monroe Ave Ste 206 Dunmore PA 18509-2477 Home Phone: 570-876-2086; Office Phone: 570-347-5212. E-mail: drsebjsj@hcrn.com.

SEBEK, MICHAEL, research scientist, entrepreneur, educator; b. Prague, Czech Republic, Jan. 25, 1954; s. Antonín and Jana (Hanzlová) S.; m. Ivana Ornestová, Nov. 21, 1992; children: Michael, Natalie. Diploma in elec. engring., Czech Tech. U., Prague, 1978; PhD, Czech Acad. Scis., Prague, 1981, DSc, 1995. Scientist Inst. Info. Theory and Automation, Prague, 1981-88, sr. scientist, 1988-90, chief scientist, 1991-98, head control theory dept., 1998—2005; prof. Czech Tech. U., 2000, head control engring. dept., 2003—. Vis. prof. U. Twente, Netherlands, 1990-91, Swiss Fed. Inst. Tech., Zurich, 1994-95; mem. policy com. Internat. Fedn. Automatic Control, 1993—2005, adminstrv. and finance com., 2005—; coord. of EUROPOLY (European Network of Excellence for Indsl. Applications of Polynomial Methods) 1998; co-founder and CEO of PolyX, Ltd. (world-wide producer of software for polynomial methods in systems, signals and control), 1998; mgr. Ctr. applied cyberntics Conrol, Czech Tech. U. Prague, 2000—; lectr. in field. Contbr. numerous articles to profl. jours.; co-author Polynomial Toolbox software, Metlab. Mgr., coach Medicina Baseball Club, Prague, 1985-90. Recipient Czech Nat. prize Czech Parliament, 1989. Mem. IEEE (sr., mem. exec. com. Czech sect. 1996—), IEEE Control Sys. Soc. (mem. conf. editl. bd. 1994-2000, chmn. Czech chpt. 1996-2000), Am. Math. Soc., N.Y. Acad. Scis, Soc. Indsl. and Applied Math. Achievements include invention of 2D and nD polynomial equations with application to 2D and 3D systems; new techniques for robust controller design; research in computational algorithms for polynomials and polynomial matrices; contribution to polynomial methods for systems, signals and control. Avocations: jogging, baseball, photography. Home: Jarní 4 16000 Prague 6 Czech Republic Office: Czech Tech U Prague Technicka 2 166 27 Prague 6 Czech Republic also: Inst Info Theory & Automation 18208 Prague 8 Czech Republic Personal E-mail: m.sebek@polyx.cz. Business E-Mail: m.sebek@c-a-k.cz.

SEBEK, MIKLÓS LÁSZLÓ, sculptor, educator; b. Sóskút, Hungary, Dec. 6, 1941; arrived in U.S., 1970; s. Rudolf Sebek and Mária Zámecsnik; m. Villö Katalin Varga, June 18, 1993. BA in Sculpture, Montclair State U., NJ, 1978; Diploma in Architecture, Budapest Tech. Inst. Architecture, Hungary, 1968. Exhbn. com. chair Audubon Artists, NY, 2003—, Allied Artists of Am., NY, 2006—. Wood sculpture, Origin No. 2, 2004 (Excellence award, 2004), bronze sculpture, Freedom, 2005 (Best in Show, 2005), marble sculpture, Baroque, 2005 (Best Sculpture, 2005). Mem. Southwestern Vt. Arts Ctr., Manchester, 2005—. Recipient Best in Show, West Essex Art Assn., 2005, Best Sculpture, West Essex Art Ann. Exhbn., 2005, Best in Show, State Show. Mem.: So. Vt. Arts Ctr., Allied Artists of Am. Inc., Audubon Artists Inc. Home: 112 Lafayette Ave Passaic NJ 07055 Office Phone: 973-773-7266. E-mail: miklossebek@hotmail.com.

SEBELIUS, KATHLEEN GILLIGAN, governor; b. Cin., May 15, 1948; d. John J. and Mary K. (Dixon) Gilligan; m. Keith Gary Sebelius, 1974; children: Edward Keith, John McCall. BA, Trinity Coll., 1970; MA in Pub. Adminstrn., U. Kans., 1977. Exec. dir. Kans. Trial Lawyers Assn., 1978—86; mem. Kans. Ho. of Reps., 1987-95; ins. commr. State of Kans., 1995—2002, gov., 2003—. Founder Women's Polit. Caucus; precinct committeewoman, 1980-86; mayor, Potwin, 1985-87; appointed Presdl. adv. commn. consumer protection and quality in Health Care, 1997. Mem. Common Cause (state bd., nat. gov. bd. 1975-81), Nat. Assn. Ins. Commrs. (chair). Democrat. Roman Catholic. Office: Office of the Gov State Capitol 2nd Fl Topeka KS 66612-1590 Office Fax: 785-296-7973. *

SEBO, STEPHEN ANDREW, electrical engineer, educator, researcher, consultant; b. Budapest, Hungary, June 10, 1934; s. Emery Sebo and Elizabeth Thieben; m. Eva Agnes Vambery, May 25, 1968. MSEE, Budapest Poly-tech. U., 1957; PhD, Hungarian Acad. Sci., 1966. Engr. Budapest Elec. Co., 1957-61; asst. prof. Budapest Poly. U., 1961-66, assoc. prof., 1966-68, Ohio State U., Columbus, 1968-74, prof., 1974—82, Am. Electric Power prof. in power sys. engring., 1982—2003, Neal A. Smith prof., 1995—2003, prof. emeritus, 2003—. Recipient Power Educator award Edison Elec. Inst., 1981, Tech. Person of Yr. award Columbus Tech. Coun., 1994. Fellow IEEE (Prize Paper award 1981). Office: Ohio State U Elec Engring 2015 Neil Ave Columbus OH 43210-1272 Office Phone: 614-292-7410. Business E-Mail: sebo.1@osu.edu.

SEBOLD, ALICE, writer; b. Madison, Wis., 1963; d. Jane and Russell Sebold; m. Glen David Gold, 2001. BA, Syracuse U., 1984; studied poetry, U. Houston, 1984—85; MFA in fiction, U. Calif., Irvine, 1998. Author: (memoir) Lucky, 1999, (novels) The Lovely Bones, 2002. Office: c/o Steven Barclay Agy 12 Western Ave Petaluma CA 94952

SEBOLD, RUSSELL PERRY, III, Romance languages educator, writer; b. Dayton, Ohio, Aug. 20, 1928; s. Russell Perry and Mary (Kiger) Sebold; m. Jane Norvell Hale, Nov. 24, 1955; children: Mary Norvell, Alice Hale. Student, U. Chgo., 1945—47; BA, Ind. U., 1949; MA (Woodrow Wilson fellow), Princeton U., 1951, PhD, 1953; D.Phil. and Letters (hon.), U. Alicante, Spain, 1984. Instr. Spanish, Duke U., 1955-56; instr. Spanish, U.

Wis., 1956-58, asst. prof., 1958-62, assoc. prof., 1962-66; prof. Spanish, chmn. dept. fgn. langs. and lits. U. Md., 1966-68; prof. Spanish, U. Pa., 1968-88, chmn. dept. Romance langs., 1968-78, Edwin B. and Leonore R. Williams prof. Romance langs., 1988—. Mem. adv. com. Soc. Ibero-Am. Enlightenment, 1968—, treas., 1969—; mem. steering com. Am. Soc. Eighteenth Century Studies, 1970—; corr. academician Royal Spanish Acad., 1993—, Royal Acad. Humane Letters of Barcelona, 1993—. Author: Tomás de Iriarte: poeta de rapto racional, 1961, El rapto de la mente, 1970, 1989, Colonel Don José Cadalso, 1970, Cadalso: el primer romántico europeo de España, 1974, Novela y autobiografía en la Vida de Torres Villarroel, 1975, Trayectoria del romanticismo español, 1983, Descubrimiento y fronteras del neoclasicismo español, 1985, Bécquer en sus narraciones fantásticas, 1989, De Ilustrados y románticos, 1992, La novela romantica en España, 2000, La perduración de la modalidad clásica, 2001, Lírica y poética en España, 1536-1870, 2003, Ensayos de meditacion y critica literaria, 2004, En el principio del del movimiento realista, 2007; author, editor Fray Gerundio de Campazas (José Francisco de Isla), 4 vols., 1960—64, 2d edit., 1992, Visiones y visitas de Torres con don Francisco de Quevedo por la Corte (Diego de Torres Villarroel, 1966, 2d edit., 1991, Numancia destruida (Ignacio López de Ayala, 1971, 2d edit., 2005, Poética (Ignacio de Luzán), 1977, Comedias (Tomás de Iriarte), 1978, 2d edit., 1986, Gustavo Adolfo Bécquer (antologia critica), 1985, Vida (Diego de Torres Villarroel), 1985, Rimas (Gustavo Adolfo Bécquer), 1991, author, editor (with David T. Gies) Ilustración y neoclasicismo, 1992, Noches lúgubres (José de Cadalso), 1993, author, editor (with Jesus Perez Magallon) El hombre practico (Conde de Fernán Nuñez), 1996, Cartas marruecas, Noches lúgubres (Jose de Cadalso), 1999, 5th edit., 2005, gen. editor Hispanic Rev., 1968—97, adv. editor Eighteenth Century Studies, 1983—, Cuadernos para Investigación de la Literatura Hispánica, 1987—, El Gnomo, 1992—, Dieciocho, 1994—, Siglo XIX, 1995—, Salina, 1999—, columnist ABC newspaper, Madrid, 1985—; contbr. articles to profl. jours. Recipient Elio Antonio de Nebrija Internat. prize, U. Salamanca, 2001; grantee, Am. Philos. Soc., 1971, 1976, 1982; Guggenheim fellow, 1962—63, Am. Coun. Learned Socs. fellow, 1979—80. Mem.: Hispanic Soc. Am., Sociedad de Literatura Española del Siglo XIX, Ctr. 18th Century Studies (Oviedo, Spain), Am. Assn. Tchrs. French, Am. Assn. Tchrs. Spanish and Portuguese, Sigma Delta Pi, Phi Gamma Delta, Phi Beta Kappa. Episcopalian. Home: 16 Flintshire Rd Malvern PA 19355-1108 Office: U Pa Dept Romance Langs Philadelphia PA 19104-6305 Personal E-mail: rpsebold@verizon.net.

SEBOLT-GEORGE, ALBERTA, retired museum administrator; b. 1935; married. B in Polit. Sci., U. Mass. Amherst, 1955; M, Springfield Coll. Dir. state grant Old Sturbridge Village, Mass., 1971, exec. v.p., COO, pres., 1992—2002. Reviewer Nat. Endowment for Humanities; mem. Nat. Mus. Svc. Bd., 1996; mem. vis. com. Longwood Gardens, Kennett Square, Pa.; corporator Worcester Art Mus. Mem.: Am. Assn. Museums (mem. bd. dirs. 1987, vice chair bd. dirs., chairperson ethics com., Disting. Svc. award 2002, named to Centennial Honor Roll 2006), New England Mus. Assn. (pres.). Avocation: golf. *

SEBOROVSKI, CAROLE, artist; b. San Diego, June 16, 1960; d. Stanley and Eleanor Ononsko S. BFA, Calif. Coll. Arts and Crafts, 1982; MFA, Hunter Coll., 1987. Artist: solo exhibitions include: Damon Brandt Gallery, N.Y.C., 1986, Hunter Coll. Art Gallery, N.Y.C., 1986, Lorence-Monk Gallery, N.Y.C., 1988, 89, Galerie Karsten Greve, Paris, 1991, 94, 2003, Cologne, 1992, 2004, Milan, 1995, 2001, Angles Gallery, Santa Monica, Calif., 1991, 92, 93, 96, Betsy Senior Contemporary Prints, N.Y.C., 1993, John Weber Gallery, N.Y.C., 1993, 95, John Berggruen Gallery, San Francisco, 1994, Locks Gallery, Phila., 1997, Karsten Greve, Koln, 1997, Galerie Karsten Greve, Milan, Italy, 1997, 2001, John Weber Gallery, N.Y.C., 1998, Cheryl Haines Gallery, San Francisco, 2000, 2002, Mitchell-Innes and Nash Gallery, N.Y.C., Miller Block Gallery, Boston, 2001; group exhbns. at: Willard Gallery, N.Y.C., 1984, Nora Haime Gallery, N.Y.C., 1985, 86, 93, 95, 2002, Manhattan Arts Ctr., N.Y.C., 1985, Hillwood Art Gallery L.I. Univ., Brookville, N.Y., 1985, Damon Brandt Gallery, 1985, 86 (2), 87, Mus. de Arte, La Tertuila, Columbia, 1986, Weatherspoon Gallery, Greensboro, N.C., 1986, Barbara Krakow Gallery, Boston, 1986, 88, 90 (travels to John C. Stoller & Co., Mpls.), Anne Plumb Gallery, N.Y.C., 1987, Am. Acad. and Inst. Arts and Letters, 1987, Bklyn. Mus., 1987, Lorence-Monk Gallery, 1987, 89 (3), 90, 91 (2), Carnegie Mellon U. Art Gallery, Pitts., 1988, Reynolds/ Minor Gallery, Richmond, Va., 1988, John Good Gallery, N.Y.C., 1988, 92, Pamela Auchincloss Gallery, N.Y.C., 1988, Dart Gallery, Chgo., 1988, Angles Gallery, 1989, Persons & Lindell Gallery, Helsinki, Finland, 1989, Anderson Gallery Va. Commonwealth U., Richmond, 1989, Baxter Gallery, Richmond, 1989, Hillwood Art Gallery, Brookville (travels through 1991 to Blum Helman Gallery, N.Y.C., Richard F. Brush Gallery, Canton, N.Y., Contemporary Mus. Art, Caracas, Venezuela), Cheryl Haines Gallery, San Francisco, 1989, 94, 96, 2003, Security Pacific Corp. Gallery, Santa Monica, 1990, Meml. Art Gallery U. Rochester, N.Y., 1990, Hood Mus. Art Dartmouth Coll., Hannover, N.H., 1990, San Francisco Mus. of Art, 1991, Pfizer, Inc. (Mus. Modern Art, N.Y. Collection), 1991, John Berggruen Gallery, 1991, travelling exhbn. to Anthony Ralph Gallery at Earl McGrath, L.A., Mars Gallery, Tokyo, Katonah Mus. Art, N.Y., Ind. U. Fine Arts Gallery, Kerr Gallery, Alberta Coll. of Art, Can., Huntsville Mus. Art, Ala., Worcester Art Mus., Mass., Lamont Gallery N.H., San Diego State U. Gallery, 1992, Barbara Mathes Gallery, N.Y.C., 1993, Transamerica Pyramid Lobby, San Francisco, 1993, travelling exhbn. to The Drawing Ctr., N.Y., Corcoran Gallery Art, Washington, Santa Monica Mus., L.A., The Forum, St. Louis, Am. Ctr., Paris, 1993, Addison Gallery, Andover, Mass., 1994, John Weber Gallery, 1994, 96, Huntington Gallery Mass. Coll. Art, Boston, 1995, Rice U. Art Gallery, Houston, 1995, The Altered Stages, N.Y., 1995, Brooke Alexander Gallery, N.Y.C., 1995, Thread Waxing Space, N.Y., 1996, Duchess County C.C., N.Y., 1996, Gallery 7, Hong Kong, 1996, Century Club, N.Y.C., 1996, Dutchess Coll., N.Y., 1997, Vassar Coll., Poughkeepsie, N.Y., 1997, Mus. Cantonale d'Arte, Lugano, Switzerland, 1997, Kunst-Mus., Ahlen, Germany, 1998, Kunstmus., Winterhur, Switzerland, 1998, Acad. der Kunste, Berlin, 1999, Mitchell-Innes and Nash, N.Y.C., Nohra Haime Gallery, N.Y.C., 2002, Margaret Thatcher Projects, N.Y.C., 1999, 2002, San Francisco Mus. Modern Art, Calif., 2000, Block Mus., Chgo., 2000, Contemporary Mus., Honolulu, 2000, Fogg Art Mus., 2000, Neuberger Mus. Art, Purchase, NY, 2000, Lyman Allyn Mus, Conn., 2000, Yale Art Galley, 2002, Bertha and Karl Leubsdorf Art Gallery, N.Y.C., 2002, Charles Cowles Gallery, N.Y.C., 2002, Humanities Gallery, Ill., 2002, Anthony Grant, Inc., 2003, Cin. Art Mus., 2003, The Workspace, N.Y.C., 2003, others; represented in permanent collections including Whitney Mus. Art, N.Y., Paine Webber, N.Y., Weatherspoon Art Gallery, Greensboro, N.C., J. Walter Thompson, N.Y., Refco Collection, Chgo., Panza Collection, Italy, San Francisco Mus. Modern Art, Mus. Modern Art, N.Y., Mus. Cantonale d'Arte, Lugano, Switzerland, Met. Mus. Art, N.Y., Merril Lynch Inc., N.Y., MIT Visual Ctr., Hood Mus. Art, Hanover, N.H., Fogg Art Mus., Harvard U., Cambridge, Mass., Cleve. Ctr. Contemporary Art, Chase Manhattan Bank, N.Y., Carnegie Mus. Art, Pitts., Bklyn. Mus., Balt. Mus., Anderson Collection, Calif., Addison Gallery, Phillips Acad., Andover, Mass., Bklyn. Mus., Yale U. Art Gallery, Wadsworth Atheneum, Conn., Tel Aviv Mus., Nat. Gallery Art, Washington. Grantee Pollock-Krausner Found., 1986, NEA, 1991, Art Devel. Com., 1997; named Artist in Residence, Villa Monalvo, Saratoga, Calif., 1989, Djerassi Found., Calif., 1990; Agnes Bourne fellow in visual arts, 1990. Home: 171 E 81st St Apt #3A New York NY 10028

SEBRING, MARJORIE MARIE ALLISON, former home furnishings company executive; b. Burnsville, NC, 1926; d. James William and Mary Will (Ramsey) Allison Shockey; 1 child, Patricia Louise Banner Krohn (dec.). Student, Mars Hill Coll., 1943, Home Decorators Sch. Design, NYC, 1948, Wayne State U., 1953; cert. home furnishings rep., U. Va., 1982. Dir. decorating divsn. Robinson Furniture, Detroit, 1949—57; head buyer Tyner Hi-Way House, Ypsilanti, Mich., 1957—63, Town and Country, Dearborn, Mich., 1963—66; instr. Nat. Carpet Inst., 1963—71; owner Adams House, Inc., Plymouth, Mich., 1966—72; exec. v.p. mktg. and sales, regional sales and mktg. mgr. Triangle Industries, LA, 1972—89; co-owner Markham-Sebring, Inc., St. Petersburg, Fla., 1983—89. Co-owner Accessories, Etc., 1985-89, Talamanca Pipeline Ltd., Costa Rica; chmn. bd. dir. U.S. Homes, Heritage Lakes, 1990-1992, 2002-04. Vol. coord. Pasco County Clk. Ct., Suncoast Theatre; adv. bd. Webster Coll.; charter mem. Presdl. Task Force; pres. Presbyn. Ch. Seven Springs; bd. dir. Fla. Presbyn. Homes, Gills Trinity YMCA, 2001—; mem. Tampa Bay Presbytery Rev. and Evaluation; bd. dir. James P. Gills Suncoast YMCA, 2001-05; citizens adv. com. Pasco County, 2001-06. Recipient recognition for work with youth and aged; named to Fla. Finest List, Gov. of Fla., 1994. Mem. Internat. Home Furnishings Assn., Fla. Home Furnishings Rep. Assn. (officer), Am. Security Coun. (coun.), Williamsburg Found., USCG Aux., Nat. Audubon Soc., Internat. Platform Assn. (jouvenile justice coun. 2003-05), Pasco County Planning Com., Heritage Lake Assn. (bd. dir. 2002—, chmn.), II Westminster Assn.(chmn. bd. 1992-95, 97-99, 2001—, pres. 2002—), Pasco Rep. Club (pres. 2002—). Republican. Achievements include contbr. creative display to Better Homes & Gardens, 1957-64. Home: 4902 Cathedral Ct New Port Richey FL 34655-1486 Office Phone: 727-808-7992, 727-376-9533.

SEBRIS, ROBERT, JR., lawyer; b. NYC, May 20, 1950; s. Robert and Ruth (Kagis) Sebris; m. S. Lawson Hollweg, Sept. 8, 1973; children: Jared Matthew, Bryan Taylor. BS in Indsl. Labor Rels., Cornell U., 1972; JD, George Washington U., 1978. Bar: DC 1978, Wash. 1980. Labor rels. specialist Onondaya County Office labor rels., Syracuse, NY, 1973-74, U.S. Dept. Labor, Washington, 1972-75; labor rels. mgr. U.S. Treasury Dept., Washington, 1975-78, employee rels. mgr., 1978-80; assoc. Davis, Wright, Todd, Riese & Jones, Seattle, 1980-84; ptnr. Davis, Wright, Tremain, Bellevue, Wash., 1985-92, Sebris Busto James, Bellevue, 1992—. Expert witness Amendments NLRA US Senate hearing, 1997. Co-author: (book) Employer's Guide to Strike Planning, 1985; contbr. articles to profl. jours. Mem. Bellevue CC Found., 1988—95, pres., 1995—96; chair employment law cert. program U. Wash. Law Sch., 1996—97. Mem.: ABA (health law forum, labo and employment law sect., mem. com. employee rights), Soc. Human Resource Mgmt., Am. Health Lawyers Assn., Pacific Coast Labor Law Conf. (planning com. 1980—93, chmn. 1991—92), Seattle/King County Bar Assn. (chmn. labor law sect. 1991—92), DC Bar Assn., Wash. Bar Assn. Avocation: golf. Home: 16301 Mink Rd NE Woodinville WA 98072-9463 Office: Sebris Busto James Ste 325 14205 SE 36th St Bellevue WA 98006 Office Phone: 425-450-0300. Business E-Mail: rsebris@sebrisbusto.com.

SECCHIA, PETER F., forest products executive, former United States ambassador to Italy; b. Englewood, NJ, Apr. 15, 1937; s. Charles P. and Valerie Margaret (Smith) Secchia; m. Joan Peterson, 1964; children: Mark, Charles, Sandra, Stephanie. BS, Mich. State Univ., 1962; AA (hon.), Grand Rapids Cmty. Coll., 1993; LLD (hon.), Grand Valley State Univ., 1990, Davenport Coll., 1993, Cooley Law Sch., 1993; HHD (hon.), Mich. State Univ., 1997. Positions through v.p. sales Universal Forest Products, Grand Rapids, Mich., 1962—71, dir., 1967—, chmn., pres., CEO, 1971—89, chmn., 1993—2006, chmn. emeritus, 2006; U.S. Amb. to Italy, 1989—93. Chmn. River City Food Co.; mng. ptnr. SIBSCO LLC. Mem. exec. com. Gerald R. Ford Found., past chmn. endowment com.; trustee Bush Presdl. Libr. Found., James A. Baker III Inst. Pub. Policy, Rice Univ, John Cabot Univ., Rome; Mich. del. Rep. Nat. Convention, 1976, 1980, 1984; mem. Rep. Nat. Com., 1980—89, vice chmn. Midwest region, 1984—89; co-chmn. Dole for Pres. Nat. Campaign, 1995—96. Served to sgt. USMC, 1956—59. Named Master Entrepeneur of the Year for Mich., 1994, Businessman of the Year, Econ. Club We. Mich., 1995; recipient Cavaliere di Gran Croce, Govt. of Italy, Disting. Honor award, U.S. Dept. State, 1993, Louis A. Smith Disting. Jurist award, Cooley Law Sch., 1993, Michelangelo D'Oro Children of the World award, 1993, Peace award, Internat. Commn. for Peace. Mem.: Council of Am. Ambassadors. Republican. Methodist. Office: Universal Forest Products 2801 East Beltline NE Grand Rapids MI 49525

SECCHIUTTI, RONALD, electrical engineering designer; b. East Liverpool, Ohio, Aug. 4, 1943; s. Mario Secchiutti and Mary Sialino; m. Karen Chimley, Aug. 20, 1964; children: Lynette, Ronald Jr. Attended, Youngstown U., Ohio, 1970—72. Lineman Duquesne Light Co., Pitts., 1963—70; elec. field engr. Bechtel Corp., Salem, NJ, 1970—75; lead elec. designer Stone & Webster Corp., Cherry Hill, NJ, 1975—82; lead elec. and instrumentation designer Designer Contractor, Newark, Del., 1982—95; lead elec. designer Jacobs Engring., Conshohocken, Pa., 1995—2000, Shaw Group, Trenton, NJ, 2000—. V.p. Parvin State Pk. Appreciation Com., Pittsgrove, NJ, 1991—92; walkathon com. Assn. for Retarded Citizens, Vineland, NJ, 2003—; ofcl. Spl. Olympics, Trenton, 2004—; state exec. com. United We Stand Am., Edison, NJ, 1993—94; state conv. spkr. United We Stand Am. NJ. Chpt., Marilton, 1994. Quartermaster USNR, 1960—63, USS Kidd. Recipient World Weightlifting Record Holder for Powercurl Master Divsn., World Natural Powerlifting Fedn., 2003. Master: Free & Accepted Masons (worshipful master 2007—); mem.: Order Sons Italy in Am., Am. Mensa (life), Highlander Unit at NUR Shriners Ancient Arabic Order Nobles Mystic Shrine (clan chief 1996), Knights Templar, Royal Select Masters, Royal Arch Masons, Clown Unit at NUR Shriners Ancient Arabic Order Nobles Mystic Shrine (unit pres. 2005). Achievements include created map for Parvin State Park use that identified and named the trails. Avocations: hiking, bicycling. Office Phone: 609-584-8900.

SECHRIST, CHALMERS FRANKLIN, JR., electrical engineering educator; b. Glen Rock, Pa., Aug. 23, 1930; s. Chalmers F. and Lottie V. (Smith) S.; m. Lillian Beatrice Myers, June 29, 1957; children: Jonathan A., Jennifer N. BE in Elec. Engring., Johns Hopkins U., 1952; MS, Pa. State U., 1954, PhD in Elect. Engring., 1959. Sr. engr. Bendix Corp., summers 1952, 53, 54; instr. elec. engring. Pa. State U., 1954-55; staff engr. HRB-Singer, Inc., State College, Pa., 1959-65; from asst. prof. to prof. elec. engring. U. Ill., Urbana, 1965-96, assoc. head instructional programs dept. elec. and computer engring., 1984-86, asst. dean engring., 1986-96, prof. Emeritus, 1996—; program dir. divsn. undergrad. edn. NSF, Washington, 1992-96; adj. prof. engring. Fla. Gulf Coast U., 1998—2006; mem. adv. bd. Whitaker Sch. Engring., Fla. Gulf Coast U., 2006—. Acting sci. sec. Sci. Com. on Solar-Terrestrial Physics, 1981; chmn. publs. com. Middle Atmosphere Program, 1980-86, editor handbook, 1981-86; mem. adv. com. on tech. edn. Fla. Dept Edn., 2001-2005 Editor: Proc. Aeronomy Confs, 1965, 69, 72; contbr. articles to profl. jours. Grantee NSF. Fellow: IEEE (edn. activities bd. 1990, tech. activities bd. 1991—92, edn. activities bd. 1992—93, chmn. com. on pre-coll. edn. ednl. activities bd. 1997—99, edn. activities bd. 1997—99, awards and recognition com. edn. activities bd. 2000—01, oversight subcom. Virtual Mus. 2000—02, precoll. edn. coord. com. edn. activities bd. 2000—03, Millennium medal 2000); mem.: Internat. Tech. Edn. Assn., Am. Soc. Engring. Edn., Am. Meteorol. Soc., Am. Geophys. Union, Edn. Soc. of IEEE (v.p. 1989—90, pres. 1991—92, Achievement award 1993). Office Phone: 239-454-0640. Personal E-mail: csechrist@comcast.net.

SECK, MAMADOU MANSOUR, ambassador, military officer; b. Dakar, Senegal, July 3, 1935; children: Ndeye, Safi, Makura, Astou Dior, Sonia Penda. Attended, St. Cyr Milit. Acad., France, Salon Air Force Acad., French Air War Coll., Institut des Hautes Etudes de la Def. Nat. Commanding officer 1st Senegalese Air Force Squad, 1966; comdr. 1st Senegalese Air Force, 1972; dep. chief gen. staff, 1980-84; spl. chief of staff to Pres. of Republic of Senegal, chief of staff of Sene-Gambia Confedn., 1984; gen. chief of staff, gen. chief Confedn., 1988; chmn. Joint Chiefs of Staff of Senegal, 1988-93; amb. to U.S. Govt. of Republic of Senegal, 1993—; amb. to Mex., Argentina, Jamaica, Haiti, Trinidad and Tobago, Barbados, 1993—. Decorated Senegal, France, Gabon, Hollan, Luxembourg. Office: Embassy of Republic of Senegal 2112 Wyoming Ave NW Washington DC 20008-3926

SECKEL, BROOKE RUTLEDGE, plastic surgeon; b. Columbus, Ohio, Oct. 2, 1943; s. Raymond Clyde and Virginia Caine (Rutledge) S.; m. Deborah Anne Johnson, May 8, 1982; children: Laura, Thomas. BS summa cum laude, Ohio U., 1965; MD, Med. Coll. of Va., 1969. Diplomate Am. Bd. Psychiatry and Neurology, Am. Bd. Emergency Medicine, Am. Bd. Plastic Surgery, Nat. Bd. Med. Examiners; lic. physician, Va., Calif., Mass. Internship in surgery Univ. Hosp., San Diego, 1969-70; jr. asst. resident in neurology, jr. resident Boston City Hosp., Harvard Neurol. Unit, 1971-72, 72-73, chief resident in neurology, 1973-74; instr. in neurology Harvard Med. Sch., Cambridge, Mass., 1974-77; jr. resident in surgery, sr. resident New Eng. Med. Ctr., Boston, 1978-79, 79-80; sr. resident plastic/reconstructive surgery, chief resident Brigham and Women's Hosp. and The Children's Hosp., Boston, 1980-81, 81-82; instr. in surgery Harvard Med. Sch., Cambridge, 1982-85, clin. instr. in surgery, 1986-89, asst. prof. surgery, 1990-93; chmn. dept. plastic and reconstructive surgery Lahey Clinic Med. Ctr., Burlington, Mass., 1986—. Courtesy staff The Children's Hosp., Boston, 1982—, New Eng. Deaconess Hosp., Boston, 1986—; assoc. surgeon Brigham and Women's Hosp., Boston, 1982—; dir. Microsurgical Ctr. Lahey Clinic Med. Ctr., 1986—, Plastic Surgery Rsch. Lab., Lahey Clinic Med. Ctr., 1986—, Plastic Surgery Residency Tng. Program, Lahey Clinic Med. Ctr., 1989—. Assoc. editor Jour. of Plastic and Reconstructive Surgery, 1988-94; expert reviewer Jour. of Muscle and Nerve, 1989—; assoc. editor Jour. of Reconstructive Microsurgery, 1990—; author: Plastic Surgery Research Directory, 1990, Facial Danger Zones: Avoiding Nerve Injury in Facial Plastic Surgery, 1993; author of numerous non-print materials including videotapes; contbr. numerous articles to profl. jours. and chpts. to books. Grantee Am. Assn. Plastic Surgeons, 1983, Plastic Surgery Ednl. Found., 1984, Eleanor Naylor Dana Charitable Trust, 1986-90, Donaldson Charitable Trust, 1990, Charles E. Culpeper Found., 1991, 92, The Robert Leet and Clara Guthrie Patterson Trust, 1993, 94. Fellow Am. Coll. Emergency Physicians, Am. Coll. Surgeons; mem. New Eng. Surg. Soc., Soc. Microsurgical Specialists, Assn. Acad. Chmn. Plastic Surgery, Am. Soc. for Aesthetic Plastic Surgery, Am. Assn. Plastic Surgeons, Northeastern Soc. Plastic Surgeons, The Sunderland Soc., Boston Surg. Soc., Plastic Surgery Rsch. Coun., Am. Soc. Plastic and Reconstructive Surgeons, New Eng. Soc. Plastic and Reconstructive Surgeons, Mass. Soc. Plastic Surgery, Mass. Med. Soc., Am. Coll. Emergency Physicians. Achievements include pioneer in the development of the Superpulser CO2 laser for use in aesthetic plastic surgery; research in plastic surgery and biophysiology of nerve regeneration. Home: 39 Cottage Ln Concord MA 01742-2346 Office: Lahey Clin Med Ctr Plastic Surgery 41 Mall Rd Burlington MA 01805-0001

SECKLER, BERNARD DAVID, retired mathematics professor, translator; b. NYC, Feb. 14, 1925; s. Samuel and Anna Seckler; m. Evelyn Aida Mehler, Nov. 25, 1953; children: Judith, Stephen. BA, Bklyn. Coll., 1945; MA, Columbia U., NYC, 1948; PhD, NYU, 1958. Instr. math. Sch. Gen. Studies, Bklyn. Coll., 1947—55, instr., 1957—58, LI U., Bklyn., 1948—54, prof. math. C.W. Post Coll., Brookville, NY, 1964—94, chmn. dept., 1968—72; rschr. math. Courant Inst., NYU, 1954—58; assoc. prof. math. Pratt Inst., Bklyn., 1958—64. Sr. translator Russian SIAM Theory of Probability jour., Phila., 1964—90, co-editor Russian transls., 1986—90. Author: The Programmable Hand Calculator in the Classroom, 1983; editor 8 book transls. from Russian, editor, pres. Jour. Fine Arts Philately, 1995—2006. Vol. Recording Blind and Dyslexic, NYC, 1973—2003. Served with US Army, 1945—46. Mem.: Pi Mu Epsilon. Home: 19 Ramsey Rd Great Neck NY 11023 Personal E-mail: ebs19@optonline.net.

SECREST, GEORGE MCCALL, JR., (MAC SECREST), lawyer; b. Laredo, Tex., Jan. 5, 1952; BA, U. Houston, 1974; JD with distinction, St. Mary's U. Sch. Law, 1977. Admitted: Tex. 1977, US Ct. Appeals, 5th Cir. 1981, US Dist. Ct., No., So., Ea. & We. Dists. Tex. 1982, US Supreme Ct. 1984, US Ct. Appeals, 11th Cir. 1989, US Ct. Appeals 6th Cir. 1990. Briefing atty. Tex. Ct. Criminal Appeals, 1977—78; asst. dist. atty. Harris County, Tex., 1978—81; asst. fed. pub. defender So. Dist. Tex., 1981—83; adj. prof. law So. Tex. Coll. Law, 1984, U. Houston, 1994—2003; ptnr. Bennett & Secrest, LLP, Houston, 2003—. Mem. Gov.'s Ad Hoc Com. to Revise the Tex. Code of Criminal Procedure, 1995—96, Tex. Bd. Legal Specialization Exam Commn., Criminal Law. Named one of Best Lawyers in Am., 1997—2005. Mem.: Nat. Assn. Criminal Def. Lawyers, Tex. Criminal Def. Lawyer's Assn., Harris County Criminal Lawyers Assn. (treas. 1996—97), Houston Bar Assn., State Bar Tex. (Criminal Def. Lawyer of Yr. 1998), Bar Assn. 5th Fed. Cir., John Harlan Soc. Office: Bennett & Secrest LLP 24th Fl Esperson Bldg 808 Travis St Houston TX 77002 Office Phone: 713-757-0679. Office Fax: 713-650-1602. *

SECREST, GLENDA, music educator; MusB, Ariz. State U., 1978, MusM, 1985; DMA, U. of Memphis, 2000. Asst. prof. music Manhattan (Kans.) Christian Coll., 1984—87; instr. music Chandler/Gilbert (Ariz.) C.C., 1989—90, Cameron U., Lawton, Okla., 1990—93; assoc. prof. music Ouachita Bapt. U., Arkadelphia, Ark., 1995—. Contbr. articles NATS Jour.; leading roles: (Operas) Amahl and the Night Visitors; The Barber of Seville; La Bohème; The Tales of Hoffman; Hansel and Gretel; The Turn of the Screw; The Magic Flute; The Marriage of Figaro; appeared with: Phoenix Symphony, Mesa Symphony, Scottsdale Symphony, Nouveau West Orch., Lawton Philharmonic, Lyric Opera of Ariz. State U. Recipient M. May Robertson scholarship, So. Bapt. Found., 1997—2000, doctoral fellowship, U. of Memphis, 1997. Mem.: Nat. Assn. Tchrs. of Singing (pres.-elect 2002—04, chosen to perform and lectr. at nat. conf. 2004), Nat. Assn. of Teachers of Singing (pres. Ark. chpt. 2004—06), Pi Kappa Lambda, Sigma Alpha Iota Alumni Assn. Office Phone: 870-245-5131.

SECREST, GLENN JAMES, artist; b. New Haven, Conn., June 27, 1941; s. James Maxson and Kathryn Adele Secrest; m. Ellen Maddock Breede, Jan. 8, 1966; children: Christopher, Lauren. BS, NY State Maritime Coll., NYC, 1963; MBA, U. RI, Kingston, 1972. Dir. ops. Holland Am. Line, Inc., NYC, 1982—86; pres. DLA Assocs., Inc., Millburn, NJ, 1986—87, MCR Indsl. Distbn., Inc., Newark, 1987—88; sr. v.p. Nat. Car Rental, Inc., Mpls., 1988—91; adj. prof. Bryant Coll., Smithfield, RI, 1991—95; cons. G.J. Secrest Assocs., Inc., Newport, RI, 1995—2001; oil painter Jupiter, Fla., 2001—. Capt. USN, 1963—88. Mem.: Am. Soc. Marine Artists, Naval Submarine League, US Naval Inst. Avocations: photography, computers, fly fishing. Home: 308 St Lucia Dr Jupiter FL 33458 Personal E-mail: secrestfineart@comcast.net.

SECULAR, SIDNEY, actor, writer, fundraiser, business consultant; b. NYC, Dec. 20, 1940; s. Benjamin and Mollie (Stern) Secular; m. Mildred Vance, Oct. 31, 1969. BA, SUNY, Stony Brook, 1962. Cert. HS tchr. Contract asst. U.S. Army, Bklyn., 1962-66; contract specialist USN, Washington, 1966-67, FDA, Washington, 1967-68; contracting officer Dept. Justice, Washington, 1968-81; conf./expo organizer, counselor to small bus. SBA, Washington, 1986-97; govt. mktg. cons. to small bus. Silver Spring, Md., 1997—. Mem. consumer bd. WSSC Water Utility; freelance writer, Silver Spring, Md., 1985—; weathercaster NOWCAST Weather, Bethesda, Md., 1982—91; weather broadcaster Comprehensive Weather Svcs., 1982—85, Verizon Comm., 1991—; total quality mgmt. cons., 1995—. Activist East Sliver Spring Citizens Assn., 1981—; chief election judge Montgomery County, Md., 1998—2006. With US Army, 1963—69. Recipient Performance and Suggestion awards, U.S. DEA and SBA. Mem.: Nat. Active and Retired Fed. Employees Assn. (program dir.), Area Small and Disadvantaged Bus. Coun., Am. Meteorol. Soc., Nat. Contract Mgmt. Assn., Ctr. Hiking Club (trails dir. 1975), Masons. Avocations: weather forecasting, entrepreneurial activities, voiceovers, musical recording restoration, writing history articles. Home: 740 Silver Spring Ave Silver Spring MD 20910-4661 Office Phone: 301-588-7668. E-mail: sidsecular@safe-mail.net.

SECUNDA, EUGENE, marketing professional, educator; b. Bklyn., June 15, 1934; s. Sholom and Betty (Almer) Secunda; m. Shirley Carol Frummer, Sept. 23, 1961; children: Ruthanne, Andrew. Comml. degree, N.Y. Inst. Photography, 1955; BS, NYU Sch. Bus., 1956; MS, Boston U., 1962; PhD, NYU, 1988. News editor Sta.-WBMS, Boston, 1956-57; reporter New London (Conn.) Daily Day, 1958-59; publicist various Broadway shows, 1959-62; sr. publicist 20th Century Fox Film Corp., NYC, 1962-65; with J. Walter Thompson Co., NYC, 1965-73, dir. corp. and pub. affairs, 1974-78, sr. v.p., dir. entertainment group, 1974-80, dir. entertainment divsn., 1978-80; sr. v.p., dir. comm. svcs. N.W. Ayer Internat., NYC, 1980-82; pres. Barnum/Secunda Assocs., NYC, 1982-85, Secunda Mktg. Comm., NYC, 1985—2005. Adj. prof. media studies NYU, NYC, 1972—2003, prof. mktg. and advt. Grad. Sch. Bus., 1985—88, prof. mktg., 1993—96, adj. prof. mktg. and media studies, 1996—; prof. mktg. and advt. Baruch Coll. CUNY, 1988—93; prof. mktg. Adelphi U., Garden City, NY, 1993—96; guest lectr. FBI Acad., Columbia U., UCLA; Fulbright scholar U. Ljubljana, Slovenia, 2006—. Contbr. articles to profl. jours. Mem. Greenwich Village Trust. With USAR, 1957—63. Mem.: NATAS, Am. Mktg. Assn., Mcpl. Arts Soc., Am. Acad. Advt., Internat. Advt. Assn., Internat. Comm. Assn., Greenwich Village Preservation Soc., Soc. of Silorians. Address: 30 5th Ave New York NY 10011-8859

SEDAKA, NEIL, singer, songwriter; b. Mar. 13, 1939; s. Mac and Eleanor (Appel) S.; m. Leba Margaret Strassberg, Sept. 11, 1962; children: Dara Felice, Marc Charles. Grad., Juilliard Sch. Music. Composer numerous popular songs including Breaking Up Is Hard to Do, Stupid Cupid, Calendar Girl, Oh! Carol, Stairway to Heaven, Happy Birthday Sweet Sixteen, Laughter in the Rain, Bad Blood, Love Will Keep Us Together, Solitaire, The Hungry Years, Lonely Night (Angel Face); solo performer worldwide, 1959—; appeared in NBC-TV Special, 1976; recorded numerous albums including In The Pocket, Sedaka's Back, The Hungry Years, Steppin' Out, A Song, All You Need Is the Music, Come See About Me, Greatest Hits, 1988, Oh! Carol and Other Hits, 1990, Timeless, 1992 (Platinum LP), Classically Sedaka, 1995, Tales of Love & Other Passions, 1997, Singer & His Songs, 2000; author: Laughter in the Rain: My Own Story, 1982. Recipient numerous gold records and industry awards, Sammy Cahn Lifetime Achievement award, Nat. Acad. Popular Music, Songwriter Icon award, Nat. Music Pubs.' Assn., 2007; named to Songwriters' Hall of Fame, 1983; received star on Hollywood Walk of Fame. Mem. AGVA, Am. Fedn. Musicians, AFTRA. Office: Neil Sedaka Music Crown Bldg Ste 950 730 5th Ave New York NY 10019 also: c/o Rob Heller William Morris Agy 151 El Camino Dr Beverly Hills CA 90212 Office Fax: 212-593-0526. E-mail: leba@neilsedaka.com, rhe@wma.com. *

SEDARIS, AMY, writer, actress; b. Endicott, NY, Mar. 19, 1961; d. Lou Sedaris. Performer: (TV series) Exit 57, 1995—96; co-writer (TV series) Exit 57, 1995—96, co-creator, 1995—96; performer: (TV series) Strangers With Candy, 1999—2000; co-writer (TV series) Strangers With Candy, 1999—2000, co-creator, 1999—2000; actor(guest appearances): (TV series) Just Shoot Me, Monk, Sex and the City, Ed, Cracking Up,; (films) Commandments, 1997, Bad Bosses Go to Hell, 1997, Six Days Seven Nights, 1998, Jump Tomorrow, 2001, Maid in Manhattan, 2002, The School of Rock, 2003, Elf, 2003, My Baby's Daddy, 2004, Strangers with Candy, 2005, Stay, 2005, Bewitched, 2005, Romance and Cigarettes, 2005, (voice) Chicken Little, 2005, Full Grown Men, 2006; (TV films) Untitled New York Pilot, 2003; (plays) Jamboree, 1993; co-author (with brother David Sedaris): (plays) Jamboree, 1993; actor: (plays) Stump the Host, 1993; co-author (with brother David Sedaris): (plays) Stump the Host, 1993; actor: (plays) One Woman Shoes, 1995; co-author (with brother David Sedaris): (plays) One Woman Shoes, 1995 (Obie award, 1995); actor: (plays) Froggy, The Country Club, 1998—99 (nominated Drama Desk award, 1999), The Most Fabulous Story Ever Told, 1998—99, The Little Freida Mysteries, 1999; co-author (with brother David Sedaris): (plays) The Little Freida Mysteries, 1997; actor: (plays) The Book of Liz; co-author (with brother David Sedaris): (plays) The Book of Liz, 2001; co-author: (book), 2002; actor: (plays) Drama Department, 2001, Wonder of the World, 2001—02 (Lucille Lortel award for outstanding featured actress League of Off-Broadway Theatres and Prodrs., 2002), (short film) Wheels of Fury, 1998; co-writer (short film) Wheels of Fury, 1998; co-author (with brother David Sedaris): (plays) Stitches, Incident at Cobbler's Knob; co-author: (books) Wigfield: The Can-Do Town That Just May Not, 2003; author: I Like You, 2006. Office: c/o Jonathan Bluman Paradigm 10100 Santa Monica Blvd 25th Fl Los Angeles CA 90067

SEDARIS, DAVID RAYMOND, writer; b. Johnson City, NY, Dec. 26, 1956; s. Lou and Sharon Sedaris. Student, Kent State U.; BFA, Art Inst. Chgo., 1987. Tchr. writing Art Inst. Chgo., 1987—90; commentator Nat. Pub. Radio, 1992—. Author: (books) Barrel Fever: Stories and Essays, 1994, Holidays on Ice, 1997, Naked, 1997, Me Talk Pretty One Day, 2000 (Thurber Prize for Am. Humor, 2001), Dress Your Family in Corduroy and Denim, 2004 (Publishers Weekly Bestseller); co-author (with sister Amy under the name The Talent Family): (plays) Stump the Host, Stitches, 1994, One Woman Shoe, 1995 (Obie award, 1995), Incident at Cobbler's Knob, 1997, The Little Freida Mysteries, 1997, The Book of Liz, 2001; writer: (TV series) Exit 57, 1995; contbg. writer Esquire, The New Yorker. Named Humorist of Yr., Time mag., 2001; recipient Lambda Award, 2001.

SEDAS, D(ANNA) MICHELLE, editor; b. Fort Worth, May 20, 1977; d. Gary Don and Barbara Nell Maberry; m. Hebert Ivan Sedas; children: Diego Ryan, Isabella Kate. BBA, Tex. A&M U., College Station, 1999. Editor: Selling It Right, 2005, Leadership Courage, 2005, Positive Discipline: How to Resolve Tough Performance Problems Quickly and Permanently, 2005, Solving Performance Problems: A Leader's Toolkit, 2005, Five Star Teamwork, 2005, Way to Grow, 2005, Peer Today Boss Tomorrow, 2005, Inspiring Passion In Others, 2006, 212 the extra degree Gift Version, 2006, 180 Ways to Spread Contagious Enthusiasm, 2006, Generations Working Together, 2006, How to Lead From a Distance, 2006, We're #1, 2006, Ouch! That Stereotype Hurts, 2006, Three Dimensional Interviewing, 2007, 180 Way to Effective Deal With Change, 2007. Mem.: Toastmasters, Mensa. Republican. Avocations: running, racquetball, photography.

SEDDON, JOHANNA MARGARET, ophthalmologist, epidemiologist; b. Pitts. BS, U. Pitts., 1970. MD, 1974; MS in Epidemiology, Harvard U., 1976. Intern Framingham (Mass.) Union Hosp., 1974-75; resident Tufts New Eng. Med. Ctr., Boston, 1976-80; fellow ophthalmic pathology Mass. Eye and Ear Infirmary, Boston, 1980-81, clin. fellow vitreoretinal Retina Svc., 1981-82; instr. clin. ophthalmology Harvard Med. Sch., Boston, 1982-84, asst. prof., asst. surgeon ophthalmolgy, 1984, assoc. prof., 1989—; assoc. surgeon, dir. ultrasound svc. Mass. Eye and Ear Infirmary, Boston, 1989—, founder, dir. epidemiology rsch. unit, 1984—85, dir. epidemiology unit, 1985—, surgeon in ophthalmology, 1992—2007; assoc. prof. faculty dept. epidemiology Harvard Sch. Pub. Health, Boston, 1992—; founding dir. ophthalmic epidemiology and genetics svc. New Eng. Eye Ctr., Tufts-New Eng. Med. Ctr., 2007—; prof. Tufts U. Sch. Medicine. Mem. com. vision Commn. Behavioral and Social Scis. and Edn., NRC, NAS, Washington, 1984; mem. divsn. rsch. grants NIH, 1987-89, 94—; mem. sci. adv. bd. Found for Fighting Blindness, 1994—, Macular Degeneration Internat., 1994—, adv. panel, Age-Related Macular Degeneration Alliance Internat.; spkr. in field; lectr. in field. Author books and articles in field, especially in field of ocular tumors and macular degeneration; mem. editl. staff ophthalmic jours. Recipient NIH Nat. Svc. Rsch. awards, 1975, 80-81, Lewis R. Wasserman Merit award Rsch. to Prevent Blindness for contbns. to ophthalmic rsch., 1996, 1st Maurice Rabb, Jr. award Prevent Blindness Am. Orgn., 2005; grantee, prin. investigator Nat. Eye Inst., 1984—, Nat. Cancer Inst., 1986; med. sch. scholar, 1970-74, Henry H. Clark Med. Edn. Found. scholar, 1973, voted one of Am.'s top ophthalmologists, Consumer Rsch. Coun. Am., 2004. Mem. AMA (Sr. Honor award 2003), APHA, Am. Acad. Ophthalmology (Honor award 1990, Sr. Honor award 2003), Am. Med. Women's Assn., Assn. Rsch. in Vision and Ophthalmology (elected, chair epidemiology sect. 1990, trustee clin. vision epidemiology sect. 1992-97. v.p. 1996-97, Spl. Recognition award 1997), Soc. Epidemiologic Rsch., New Eng. Ophthal. Soc., Am. Coll. Epidemiology, Retina Soc., Macula Soc. (mem. com. 2006—), Mass. Soc. Eye Physicians and Surgeons (v.p. 2000-02, mem. com. 2006—), Am. Epidemiol. Soc., Am. Soc. Ret. Surgeons (Hon. award 2005). Achievements include first to evaluate association between nutrition, dietary antioxidants, and systemic inflammatory biomarkers and age-related macular degeneration; and genetic markers associated with progression of age-related macular degeneration; identification of novel genetic variants associated with this disease. Home: 4 Louisburg Sq Boston MA 02108-1203 E-mail: jseddon@earthlink.net.

SEDDON, PRISCILLA TINGEY, painter; b. Boston, Apr. 1, 1938; d. Richard Hume and Mildred Gurina (Lundgren) Tingey; m. James Alexander Seddon, Jr., Nov. 28, 1959; children: Amy, Sarah, Carroll, Alice. BFA, Tufts U., 1989; Cert., Sch. of the Mus. of Fine Arts, Boston, 1990, Postgrad. 5th Yr., 1991. Associated with Imagining Angels: World AIDS Day Show, Howard Yezersky Gallery, Boston, 1995, others. Exhbns. include: U. Bridgeport, Conn., 1997, Gallery 84, N.Y.C., 1996, Erector Square Gallery, New Haven, Conn., 1996, Harvard U., Cambridge, Mass., 1996, ArtsWorcester Gallery, Worcester, Mass., 1995, Wellesley Coll., Mass., 1994, Grove Street Gallery, Worcester, 1993, Carvajal Sculpture Gallery, Boston, 1992; works include metal work, paintings and sculptures. Grantee MIT Coun. for Arts, Cambridge, 1988, Firstnight, Inc., Boston, 1991, Hingham Edn. Found., Mass., 1993. Mem. Womens Caucus for Art, Visual AIDS. Avocation: watercolour.

SEDEI RODDEN, PAMELA JEAN, psychologist, director; b. Johnstown, Pa., Jan. 31, 1956; d. Joseph and Betty Ruth (Watkins) Sedei; m. William Eugene Rodden, Dec. 4, 1982; 1 child, Gretchen Jean Rodden. BA, Southwestern Coll., Winfield, Kans., 1977; MS, Pitts. State U., Kans., 1979; PhD, Western Colo. U., 1983. Lic. profl. counselor Colo., diplomate in psychotherapy, cert. cognitive behavior therapist, nat. cert. counselor, domestic violence counselor, criminal justice specialist. Staff psychologist Autumn Manors Inc., Florence, Kans., 1982-83; clin. psychologist Richmond (Tex.) State Hosp., 1984-86; unit psychologist Wheat Ridge (Colo.) Regional Ctr., 1986-89, acting unit dir., 1989; dir. behavioral svcs. Colo. State Divsn. Devel. Disabilities, Denver, 1989-97; dir. Forensic Mental Health Svcs., Boulder, Colo., 1997—2001, Pamela JS Rodden & Assocs., Fort Collins, Colo., 2001—. Dir. Rodden Consultants, Longmont, Colo., 1986—90, Rodden Assocs., 2001—. Co-author: A Model For Interdisciplinary On Site Evaluation of People Who Have Dual Diagnosis, 1991. Fellow: Am. Coll. Forensic Examiners; mem.: ACA. Republican. Roman Catholic. Address: 1420 Blue Spruce Dr Ste G Fort Collins CO 80524 Office Phone: 970-482-8553. E-mail: Pjsrodden@juno.com.

SEDELMAIER, J. J., filmmaker; b. Chgo., Mar. 11, 1956; s. John Josef and Marie S.; m. Patrice Estella Masters, Nov. 4, 1981. Student, Millikin U., 1974-75; BS in Art, U. Wis., 1979. Asst. animator Perpetual Motion Pictures, NYC, 1981-82; asst. animator, animator Buzzco Prodns., NYC, 1982-84, The Ink Tank Corp., NYC, 1984-85, producer, 1985-86, exec. producer, 1986-88, assoc. dir., dir., exec. producer, rep., 1989-91; pres., producer, dir. J. J. Sedelmaier Prodns., White Plains, NY, 1990—. Launched Beavis and Butthead for MTV (Art Dirs. Club gold medal, BDA awards, Comm. awards, Hatch awards, Emmy award nomination 1995); subject of retrospectives: Ottawa Animation Festival, 1997, Cinematique Quebecoise, 1997; acclaimed series of cartoons for "Saturday Night Live", animated peacocks for NBC, Captain Linger series for Cartoon Network; studio created and produced Tek Jansen Series for The Colbert Report; co-creator Ambiguously Gay Duo, X-Presidents, Fun with Real Audio; prodr. (3 episodes) Schoolhouse Rock; vis. artist Sch. Visual Arts, assisted in saving and restoration of Dempster St. terminal, Skokie, Ill., Bar Bldg. White Plains, NY; mem. adv. bd. Mercy Coll., Savannah Coll. Art and Design. Prodr., dir. Saturday TV Funhouse, Captain Linger, Harvey Birdman-Attorney at Law. Recipient Annecy Film Festival, France, NY Festivals, Annie award, Mobius award, medal Multiple NY Festivals, Multiple Worldfest. Mem. Am. Inst. Graphic Artists, Assn. Internat. Film Animation, Art Dirs. Club (2 Gold medals, honored guest San Diego Comic Conv., 2005), Shore Line Interurban Hist. Soc., Chgo. Transit Posters Archtl. Restoration. Achievements include successful in arranging landmark status on National Register of historic places for studio building in White Plains, N.Y. Avocations: collecting illustrations, animation art, animation film cons, architecture. Office: The Bar Bldgs 199 Main St White Plains NY 10601-3200 Office Phone: 914-949-7979. Personal E-mail: sedelmaier@aol.com.

SEDELMAIER, JOHN JOSEF, filmmaker; b. Orrville, Ohio, May 31, 1933; s. Josef Heinrich and Anne Isabel (Baughman) S.; m. Barbara Jean Frank, June 6, 1965; children: John Josef, Nancy Rachel, Adam Frederich. BFA, Art Inst. Chgo. at U. Chgo., 1955. Dir. art Young and Rubicam, Chgo., 1955-61; dir. art, assoc. creative dir. Clinton E. Frank, Chgo., 1961-64; dir. art, producer J. Walter Thompson, Chgo., 1964-67; pres. Sedelmaier Film Prodns., Chgo., 1967—. Spkr. Brit. design and art direction Lectr. Series, London, 1998; spkr. Harvard Bus. Sch., 2003. Exhibitions include Mus. Broadcast Comms., Chgo., 1988, Mus. Broadcasting, LA, 1991, Mus. TV and Radio, NYC, 1992, Represented in permanent collections Acad. TV Arts and Scis. Archive; dir.: (films) OpenMinds, 2003 (Sundance Film Festival Official Selection, 2003). Recipient Golden Ducat award for short film MROFNOC Mannheim Film Festival, 1968, Golden Gate award for short film Because That's Why, San Francisco Film Festival, 1969, 82 Clio awards, 1968-92, numerous Gold, Silver and Bronze Lion awards Cannes Film Festival, 1972-90, Gold Hugo award Chgo. Film Festival, 1976, 91, 2d Ann. IDC Creative award, Chgo., 1980, Internat. Broadcasting award for world's best TV comml., 1980, 86, Clio award for dir. of yr., 1981, London Internat. Advt. awards, 1986-88, numerous awards Internat. Festival of NY, 1984-93, Ann. Achievement award Assn. Ind. Comml. Producers, 1988; named Advt. Person of Yr., Chgo. Advt. Club, 1984, Jewish Communicator of Yr., 1985; named one of 50 Pioneers & Visionaries Who Made TV America's Medium, Advt. Age Mag., 1995; profiled in Communication Arts mag., Mar. 1976, Print mag., Jan. 1982, Fortune mag., June 1983, Newsweek mag., Nov. 1986, numerous others; featured on 60 Minutes, 48 Hours; subject of cover story Esquire mag., Aug. 1983; included in Arts & Entertainment's Top 10 Greatest Commls. of All Time, 1999; inducted The Art Dirs. Hall Fame, 2000; body of work and interview made part of permanent collections Acad. TV Arts and Scis. Archive, 2006. Office Phone: 312-822-0110. Personal E-mail: sedelmaier@hotmail.com.

SEDEÑO, EUGENE RAYMOND, electronics engineer, consultant; b. Honolulu, Aug. 31, 1952; s. Josephine Marie Sedeño Rosa; m. Theresa Ann Contreras, Dec. 28, 1980; children: Roxanne Guadelupe, Raymond Contreras, Darrell Kealoha Albright. ASET, Heald Engring. Coll., 1974; BSEE, Coll. Allied Sci., 1980; MBA, Calif. Coast U., 2002. Field svc. engr. Bausch & Lomb, San Leandro, Calif., 1974—81; project mgr. Tylan Corp., Carson, Calif., 1981—85; field svc. supr. Sci. Atlanta, Santa Fe Springs, Calif., 1985—86; facilities and systems engr. Refractory Composities, Inc., Whittier, Calif., 1986—90, cons., 1985—91; supr. test and integration Thermco Systems, Orange, Calif., 1989—90; field engring. So. Calif. Edison, 1990—. With US Army, 1970—76. Mem. Am. Mgmt. Assn., Mensa. Democrat. Roman Catholic. Avocations: kenpo karate, kobudo, kajukenbo, photography, collecting antique books. Home: 16137 Minnetonka St Victorville CA 92395-9146 Office: So Calif Edison 12353 Hesperia Rd Victorville CA 92395-4797 Office Phone: 760-951-3132. Office Fax: 760-951-3115. Business E-Mail: Eugene.Sedeno@sce.com.

SEDER, SAM, radio personality; b. NYC, Nov. 28, 1966; Co-host Air America Radio's The Majority Report, 2004—05; host The Sam Seder Show, 2005—. Actor: (TV series) All-American Girl, 1994, The Show, 1996; (films) The Big Fall, 1996; actor, producer, writer, dir. (films) Who's the Caboose?, 1997; actor: (TV series) Spin City, 1997; (films) Next Stop Wonderland, 1998; (TV series) Sex and the City, 2000; (films) Happy Accidents, 2000, Endsville, 2000; actor, writer, prodr. (films) Beat Cops, 2001; dir.: (films) I'm with Busey, 2003; actor, dir., writer prodr. (TV series) Pilot Season, 2004; actor: (films) Man About Town, 2005; (TV series) Am. Undercover, 2005; co-author: (novels) F.U.B.A.R.: America's Right-Wing Nightmare, 2006. Office: Air Am Radio 641 Sixth Ave 4th Fl New York NY 10011 *

SEDERBAUM, ARTHUR DAVID, lawyer; b. NYC, Sept. 14, 1944; s. William and Harriet (Warschauer) Sederbaum; m. Francine Haba, Dec. 30, 1967 (div. Aug. 1982); children: Rebecca, David; m. Phyllis Padow, Jan. 18, 1988 (div. Aug. 2002); 1 child, Elizabeth. AB cum laude, Columbia U., 1965, JD, 1968; LLM, NYU, 1972. BAr: N.Y. 1968, Fla. 1980, U.S. Dist. Ct. (so. and ea. dists.) N.Y. 1972. Assoc. Zissu Nelper & Martin, NYC, 1968-70, Berlack, Israels & Liberman, NYC, 1970-72, Rubin Baum Levin Constant & Friedman, NYC, 1972-76; ptnr. Certilman, Haft, Balin, Buckley, Kremer & Hyman, NYC, 1976-88, Olshan, Grundman, Frome, Rosenzweig & Orens, NYC, 1988-92, Patterson, Belknap, Webb & Tyler, L.L.P., NYC, 1992—. Mem. adv. bd. Bur. Nat. Affairs Estates, Gifts and Trusts Jour.; mem. adv. bd. NYU Inst. Fed. Taxation, CCH Fin. and Estate Planning. Author: Setting Up and Executing Trusts, 1988; contbr. articles to Tax Mgmt. Estates, Gifts and Trusts Jour. Recipient J.K. Lasser Tax prize NYU Inst. Fed. Taxation, 1968. Fellow Am. Coll. Trusts and Estates Coun.; mem. ABA, N.Y. State Bar Assn. (vice chmn. com. on estate planning trustes and estates law sect.), Assn. Bar City N.Y. (com. surrogates cts.), Practicing Law Inst. (chmn. income taxatin of estates and trusts program). Office: Patterson Belknap Webb & Tyler LLP Ste 1405 1133 Avenue Of The Americas New York NY 10036-6710 Office Phone: 212-336-2550. E-mail: adsederbaum@pbwt.com.

SEDERBAUM, WILLIAM, marketing professional; b. NYC, Dec. 22, 1914; s. Harry and Sarah (Steingart) S.; m. Harriet Warschauer, Aug. 29, 1940 (dec. Mar. 1980); children: Arthur David, Caroline Joan; m. Pearl Leibowitz, Jan. 11, 2003. BS, NYU, 1936, MA, 1943, PhD. Assoc. Sigmund Pines Co., Pub. Accts., 1935-38; tchr. N.Y.C. pub. schs., 1935-39; restaurant propr., 1939-41; v.p. Schenley Distillers Co., NYC, 1941-61; pres. Distbrs. New Eng., 1956-61, Melrose Distillers Co., 1959-60, Park & Tilford Distillers Co., 1959-61; exec. v.p. Meade & Co., 1961-62; v.p., mktg. dir. J. T. S. Brown Distillers Co., 1962-65; mktg. cons., 1965-67; exec. v.p., gen. mgr. Fulton Distbg. Co., 1967-77; asst. gen. mgr., dir. spl. projects Am. Distbrs. Fla., 1977—. Instr. acctg. Fla. Jr. Coll., 1984-89 Active Eleanor Roosevelt Cancer Com., U.S. Olympic Games Com.; exec. com. Fedn. Jewish Charities, March of Dimes; bd. dirs. Jacksonville Urban League, 1975-87; mem. Com. of 100; bus. cons. Jr. Achievement Project, Jacksonville; chmn. bd. trustees, pres. men's club Reform Cong. of Merrick, L.I. Recipient Arch award NYU; named Chevalier, Confrerie de la Chaine des Rotisseurs, Bailliage de Jacksonville, Fla. Mem. Jacksonville Wholesale Liquor Assn. (pres. 1970-76), Jacksonville Symphony Assn., Jacksonville Civic Music Assn., Jacksonville C. of C. (econ. edn. com., airline svc. com., hon. adm. of flag ship Am. Airlines), Kappa Phi Kappa. Clubs: River, Carriage (N.Y.C.); NYU, Playboy, Key. Office: So Wine and Spirits 6867 Stuart Ln S Jacksonville FL 32254-3438 Home: 3820 La Vista Cir Unit 108 Jacksonville FL 32217 *Live life the way it should be-not the way it is.*

SEDERBURG, WILLIAM ALBERT, academic administrator, former state senator; b. Chadron, Nebr., Aug. 1, 1947; s. Marion E. and Viola A. (Shalender) S.; m. Joyce I. Witte, July 29, 1972; children: Matthew E., Karl A. BA in Edn. and Polit. Sci., Mankato State Coll., 1969; MA in Polit. Sci., Mich. State U., 1972, PhD in Polit. and Pub. Adminstrn., 1974; LLD (hon.), Kalamazoo Coll. Postdoctoral fellow dept. polit. sci. Mich. State U., East Lansing, 1973-75; dir. rsch. and programs, edn. specialist Mich. Ho. Rep. Caucus, Lansing, 1975—77, exec. dir., 1977—78; pres. Survey Rsch. Co., 1974—91; senator, 24th dist. Mich. Senate, Lansing, 1978—91; v.p. pub. policy, dir. Pub. Opinion Rsch. Inst., 1991—94; pres. Ferris State U., Big Rapids, Mich., 1994—2003, Utah Valley State Coll., Orem, Utah, 2003—. Mem. appropriations com., 1983-95, chmn. higher edn. and tech. com., health policy com., 1987-95, Mich. Capitol com., 1989-95. Contbr. articles to profl. jours. Bd. dirs. Luth. Social Svcs. Mich. Recipient Phil Sirotkin award for Higher Edn. Leadership, Pub. Svc. award, Am. Cancer Soc., Am. Lung Assn., award for Contributions to Ind. Higher Edn., Assn. Ind. Colleges and Universities, William P. Faust award, Am. Cancer award, Dir.'s Conf. award, Mich. Dept. Pub. Health, Pub. Svc. award, Mich. Coll. and U. Placement Coun., Outstanding Alumni award, Mich. State U.; NSF fellow, 1970—73. Mem. Phi Beta Kappa, Kappa Delta Pi, Omicron Delta Kappa, Golden Key Soc., Am. Polit. Sci. Assn. Republican. Office: Utah Valley State Coll 800 W Univ Pkwy Orem UT 84058 Business E-Mail: William.Sederburg@uvsc.edu. *

SEDGWICK, ALEXANDER, retired historian, educator; b. Boston, June 8, 1930; s. William Ellery and Sarah (Cabot) S.; m. Charlene Mary Maute, June 24, 1961; children— Catherine Maria, Alexander Cameron BA, Harvard U., 1952, PhD in History, 1963. Asst. prof. history Dartmouth Coll., 1962-63; assoc. prof. U. Va., Charlottesville, 1963-66, 1966-74, prof., 1974—, chmn. history dept., 1979-85, dean Coll. Arts and Scis., 1985-90, dean grad. studies Charlottesville, 1990-95, univ. prof., 1995-97, univ. prof. emeritus, 1997—; ret., 1997. Mem. adv. com. in history Sr. Fulbright Awards Council for Internat. Exchange of Scholars. Author: The Ralliment in French Politics 1890-98, 1965, The Third French Republic, 1870-1914, 1968, Jansenism in Seventeenth Century France, Voices in the Wilderness, 1977, The Travails of Conscience. The Arnauld Family and the Ancien Regime, 1998; co-author: Church, State and Society Under the Bourbon Kings of France, 1982, For Want of a Horse, 1985, That Gentle Strength, 1980, Les Discour sur les Révolutions, 1991, History Today, 1991, Chroniques de Port-Royal, 1993, 95. Served with U.S. Army, 1952-54. Fulbright fellow, 1960-62; recipient Am. Coun. Learned Socs. grant-in-aid, 1967-68, Am. Philos. Soc. grant-in-aid, 1971. Mem. AAUP (nat. council 1976-79), Soc. French Hist. Studies (sec. 1979-83, pres. 1983-84), Am. Hist. Assn., Century Assn. Home: 1409 Rugby Rd Charlottesville VA 22903-1240 E-mail: as6d@virginia.edu.

SEDGWICK, JEFFREY LEIGH, federal agency administrator, political science professor; b. Columbus, Ohio, Dec. 11, 1951; married; 2 children. AB, Kenyon Coll., 1973; MAPA, U. Va., 1975, PhD, 1978. Instr. polit. sci. U. Va., 1975, acting asst. prof., 1977—78; asst. prof. U. Mass., 1978—84, assoc. prof., 1984—2006, grad. program dir., 1987—90, undergrad. program dir., 1997—2001; dep. dir. data analysis Bur. Justice Statistics, US

Dept. Justice, Washington, 1984—85, dir., 2006—. Asst. dean Coll. Arts and Scis., 1991—93; assoc. dean, acting dir. Coll. Arts and Scis. Info. and Advising Ctr., 1993—94; vis. assoc. prof. govt. Smith Coll., 1985, 88, 94. Office: US Dept Justice Bur Justice Statistics 810 Seventh St NW Washington DC 20531

SEDGWICK, KYRA, actress; b. NYC, Aug. 19, 1965; m. Kevin Bacon, Sept. 4, 1988; children: Travis, Sosie. Appeared in off-Broadway prodns. Time Was, 1981, Dakota's Belly Wyoming, 1989; stage appearances in Ah Wilderness!, 1988 (Theatre World award), Maids of Honor, 1990, Oleanna, 1994; Actress (films) War and Love, 1985, Tai-Pan, 1986, Kansas, 1988, Born on the Fourth of July, 1989, Mr. and Mrs. Bridge, 1990, Pyrates, 1991, Singles, 1992, Heart and Souls, 1993, Murder in the First, 1995, Something to Talk About, 1995, Losing Chase, 1996, Phenomenon, 1996, Montana, 1997, Critical Care, 1997, Twelfth Night, 1998, The Red Door, 1999, Labor Pains, 1999, What's Cooking, 2000, Just a Kiss, 2002, Behind the Red Door, 2002, Secondhand Lions, 2003, The Woodsman, 2004, Loverboy, 2005; (TV movies) The Man Who Broke 1,000 Chains, 1987, Women & Men II, 1991, Hallmark Hall of Fame, 1992 (Golden Globe award nomination 1993), The Wide Net, 1997, Door to Door, 2002, Cavedweller, 2004, Something the Lord Made, 2004, (TV series) Another World, 1982-83, Talk to Me, 2000, The Closer, 2005-(Best Performance by an Actress in a TV Series-Drama, Golden Globe award, Hollywood Fgn. Press Assn., 2007); (mini-series) Family Pictures, 1983; (TV appearances) ABC Afternoon Spls., 1985, Am. Playhouse, 1987, 88, Miami Vice, 1985, Amazing Stories, 1986, Ally McBeal, 2002, Queens Supreme, 2003 Address: WMA 151 S El Camino Dr Beverly Hills CA 90212-2704 *

SEDIGHI, ARTIN, application developer, researcher; b. Shiraz, Iran, July 13, 1976; arrived in U.S., 1990; s. Mousa and Flora Sedighi. BSEE, Rensselaer Poly Inst., Troy, NY, 1998, MS, 2004. Software engr. GTE, Waltham, Mass., 1999—2000, Lavastorm.com, Waltham, Mass., 2000—01; cons. Tibco Software, NYC, 2001—03; software arch. SIAC/NYSE, NYC, 2003—04, Tibco Software, NYC, 2004—05, Data-Synapse, NY, 2005—. Contbr. articles to profl. jour., scientific papers to meetings, workshops and confs. Mem.: IEEE, Assn. for Computing Machinery, Eta Kappa Nu, Chi Phi. Republican. Jewish. Avocations: jazz, photography. Home Phone: 917-856-5892; Office Phone: 917-856-5892. Business E-Mail: sediga@alum.rpi.edu.

SEDLACEK, MARTIN, nephrologist; MD, U. Libre, Brussels, 1991. Asst. prof. Darthouth-Hitchcock Med. Ctr., Lebanon, 2003—. Investigator in clin. nephrology. Achievements include research in nephrology. Office: Dartmouth-Hitchcock Med Ctr One Medical Center Dr Lebanon NH 03756-0001 Office Phone: 603-653-3830. Office Fax: 603-650-0924. Business E-Mail: martin.sedlacek@dartmouth.edu.

SEDLAK, JAMES WILLIAM, organization administrator; b. Tarrytown, NY, Nov. 17, 1943; s. Jacob Frank and Catherine Eva (Sedlak) S.; m. G. Michaeleen Bizub, June 17, 1967; children: Frank George, Jeanette Michele Sedlak Veltri, Terri Lynn Rose Sedlak Ferrara. BS in Physics, Manhattan Coll., 1967; MS in Indsl. Adminstrn., Union Coll., Schenectady, 1975. Customer engr. IBM, NYC, 1963-67, semicondr. engr. East Fishkill, NY, 1967-80, sr. engr. Harrison, NY, 1980-92; co-founder, nat. dir. Stop Planned Parenthood, La Grangeville, NY, 1986-93; pres., writer, editor The Ryan Report, STOPP (Stop Planned Parenthood) Internat., La Grangeville, 1994-98; v.p. pub. policy and edn. Am. Life League, Inc., Stafford, Va., 1998—. Former guest lectr. med. ethics Mt. St. Mary's Coll., Newburgh, N.Y.; guest lectr. ethics Vassar Coll., Poughkeepsie, N.Y., 1986-92. Author: Quarterly Dividends, 1975, Parent Power!!, 1990, Deadly Deception, 1996; co-author: Title X: The Six Billion Dollar Scam, 1997; contbr. to pro-life publs. Past pres. PTO; mem. bd. advisors Am. Life League, Inc.; former mem. faculty Apostles of Life Leadership Acad., Human Life Internat.; cons. to nat. and internat. pro-life groups; speaker numerous state-wide pro-life convs. and events, U.S., Can., Mex., Italy, Australia, No. Ireland, Eng. and New Zealand; workshop presenter nat. convs. Concerned Women for Am., Human Life Internat., Am. Life League; numerous appearances on radio and TV. Recipient Dutchess County Right to Life Pro-Lifer of Yr. award, 1984, Expectant Mother Care N.Y. Pro-Life Champion award, 1987, family life award Parent's Roundtable, 1987, Unsung Hero award Am. Life League, 1988, Disting. Svc. to Life award Grand Haven (Mich.) Pro-Lifers, 1993, Svc. to Life award N.W. and Putnam Life Ctr., NY, 2003, also others. Mem. KC (3d degree). Roman Catholic. Office: Am Life League Inc PO Box 1350 Stafford VA 22555-1350 E-mail: jwsedlak@aol.com.

SEDLAK, VALERIE FRANCES, retired English language and literature educator, academic administrator; b. Balt., Mar. 11, 1934; d. Julian Joseph and Eleanor Eva (Pilot) Sedlak; 1 child, Barry. AB in English, Coll. Notre Dame of Md., 1955; MA, U. Hawaii, 1962; PhD, U. Pa., Phila., 1992. Grad. tchg. fellow East-West Cultural Ctr. U. Hawaii, 1959-60; adminstrv. asst. Korean Consul Gen., 1959-60; tchr. Boyertown Sr. H.S., Pa., 1961-63; asst. prof. English U. Balt., 1963-69; assoc. prof. Morgan State U., Balt., 1970-2000, assoc. prof. English emerita, 2001—, asst. dean Coll. Liberal Arts, 1995-2000, sec. to faculty, 1981-83, faculty rsch. scholar, 1982-83, 92-93, comm. officer, 1989-90, dir. writing for TV program, 1990-97; exec. dir. Renaissance Inst. Coll. of Notre Dame of Md., 2000—03, ret., 2003—. Cons. scholar Md. Humanities Coun., 1992—; adj. prof. York Coll., Pa., 2004-05. Author numerous poems and lit. criticism; editor Liberal Arts Rev., 1996-2000; assoc. editor Md. English Jour., 1994-2000; assoc. editor Morgan Jour. Rsch., 1995-2000, CEA mag., 2002-05; mem. editl. bd. CEA Critic, 2003-06; contbr. articles to lit. jours. Coord. Young Reps., Berks County, Pa., 1962-63; chmn. Md. Young Reps., 1964; election judge Baltimore County, Md., 1964-66; regional capt. Am. Cancer Soc., 1978-79; mem. adv. bd. Md. Our Md. Anniversary, 1984, The Living Constitution: Bicentennial of the Fed. Constitution, 1987. Morgan-Penn Faculty fellow, 1977-79, NEH fellow, 1984; named Outstanding Tchg. prof., U. Balt. Coll. Liberal Arts, 1965, Outstanding Tchg. Prof. in English Dept., Morgan State U., 1987. Mem. MLA, South Atlantic MLA, Coll. Lang. Assn., Coll. English Assn. (Mid-Atlantic Group v.p. 1987-90, pres. 1990-92, exec. bd. 1992-2005, nat. bd. dir. 2001-04, nat. liaison officer 1993-2004), Women's Caucus for Modern Langs., Md. Coun. Tchrs. English, Md. Poetry and Lit. Soc., Md. Assn. Depts. English (bd. dir. 1992-2006), Mid. Atlantic Writers' Assn. (founding 1981, exec. assoc. editor Mid. Atlantic Writers' Assn. Rev. 1989-2000), Delta Epsilon Sigma (v.p. 1992-94, pres. 1994-96), Pi Kappa Delta Roman Catholic. Home: 17049 Keeney Mill Rd New Freedom PA 17349 Personal E-mail: vfsedlak@aol.com.

SEDLER, ROBERT ALLEN, law educator; b. Pitts., Sept. 11, 1935; s. Jerome and Esther (Rosenberg) S.; m. Rozanne Friedlander, Jan. 24, 1960; children: Eric, Beth. BA, U. Pitts., 1956, JD, 1959. Bar: D.C. 1959, Ky. 1968, Mich. 1979; U.S. Supreme Ct. 1969. Asst. prof., assoc. prof. law St. Louis U., 1961-65; assoc. prof. law, asst. dean Addis Ababa U., Ethiopia, 1963-66; assoc. prof. to prof. law U. Ky., Lexington, 1966-77; prof. law Wayne State U., Detroit, 1977—; disting. prof. law U. Ky., 2000—; Gibbs chair civil rights and civil liberty Wayne State Acad. Scholars, Detroit, 2000—05, disting. prof. law, 2005—, pres., 2007—. Author: Across State Lines, 1989: Applying the Conflict of Law to Your Practice, 1989, American Constitutional Law, 2005; (with R. Cramton) The Sum and Substance of Conflict of Laws, 1987, Ethiopian Civil Procedure, 1968; contbr. articles to profl. jours. Gen. counsel ACLU Ky., 1971-76. Named Gershenson Disting. Faculty fellow, Wayne State U., 1985—87. Mem. ABA, AAUP, Phi Beta Kappa, Order of the Coif. Democrat. Jewish. Home: 18851 Capitol Dr Southfield MI 48075-2680 Office: Wayne State U 471 W Palmer Detroit MI 48202-3620 Office Phone: 313-577-3968. Personal E-mail: rsedler@aol.com. Business E-Mail: rsedler@wayne.edu.

SEDLER, ROZANNE FRIEDLANDER, social worker, educator; b. Greensburg, Pa., June 16, 1938; d. Ernest and Belle (Marchel) Friedlander; m. Robert Allen Sedler, Jan. 24, 1960; children: Eric Mark, Beth Ellen. BA, U. Pitts., 1960; MSW, St. Louis U., 1962. Social worker Family & Children's Svc., St. Louis, 1962—63; lectr. Sch. Social Work Haile Selassie U., Addis Ababa, Ethiopia, 1963—66; social worker U. Ky. Med. Ctr., Lexington, 1966—68, Renaissance Home Health Care, Detroit, 1984—86; geriatric social worker Jewish Family Svc., Southfield, Mich., 1986—. Bd. dirs. Mich. Citizens for Better Care, 2007—. Mem.: AFSME (chair Jewish Family Svcs. bargaining unit 1998—2006, bd. dir. 2000—06, exec. bd. local 1640 2000—06), ACLU Mich. (chpt. pres. 2001—04, chmn. bd. dir. Oakland County, Mich.). Democrat. Jewish. Home: 18851 Capitol Dr Southfield MI 48075-2680 Office: Jewish Family Svc 24123 Greenfield Rd Southfield MI 48075-3116 Office Phone: 248-592-2348. Personal E-mail: rozsedler@aol.com.

SEDLIN, ELIAS DAVID, orthopedist, educator; b. NYC, Jan. 21, 1932; s. Arnold Boris and Sonia Lipschitz Sedlin; m. Barbara Sue Zidell, July 9, 1960; children: Faith Avril, Adrian. BS in Biology, U. Ala., 1951; MD, Tulane U., 1955; D.Med. Sci., U. Gothenburg, Sweden, 1966. Diplomate: Am. Bd. Orthopedic Surgery. Intern Mobile (Ala.) Gen. Hosp., 1955-56; resident Charity Hosp., New Orleans, 1956-57; chief resident Bronx (N.Y.). Mcpl. Hosp., 1959-60; sr. resident Henry Ford Hosp., Detroit, 1960-61, rsch. assoc., emergency room lectr., 1961-63, NIH fellow, 1963-64; jr. attending physician Detroit Receiving Hosp., 1962-63; spl. NIH fellow dept. orthopedic surgery Sahlgrenska Sjukhuset, Gothenburg, 1964-66; asst. prof. dept. orthopaedic surgery Albert Einstein Coll. Medicine, 1966-69, assoc. prof., 1969-75, prof., 1975—, dir. orthopaedic surgery, 1969-79; prof. orthopaedic surgery Mt. Sinai Sch. Medicine, 1980—. Contbr. to multiple symposia, profl. meetings, also articles to profl. jours. Served to capt. AUS, 1957-59. Fulbright scholar, 1962; NSF postdoctoral fellow, 1964; recipient P.D. McGehee award Mobile Gen. Hosp., 1956; Ludvic Hektoen gold medal AMA, 1963; Nicholas Andry award Assn. Bone and Joint Surgeons, 1964 Fellow ACS, AAAS, Am. Acad. Orthopaedic Surgeons; mem. Orthopaedic Rsch. Soc., Phi Beta Kappa. Office: 133 E 73d St New York NY 10021 Personal E-mail: edsedlin@hotmail.com.

SEDMAK, DANIEL D., academic administrator; b. Columbus, Ohio, Apr. 18, 1952; m. Peggy Sedmak; 5 children. BS in biology, U. Cin.; MD, Ohio State U., 1980. Resident in pathology Cleveland Clinic Found., 1980—84, fellow in immunopathology, 1984—85; joined faculty Ohio State U., 1985; dir. nephropathology and transplant pathology programs Ohio State U. Hosp.; prof. and chair pathology Coll. Medicine and Pub. Health, Ohio State U., 1997, interim dean, sr. assoc. v.p. health sci. and exec. vice dean; exec. dean Georgetown U. Sch. Medicine, 2003—04, exec. v.p. health sci., 2003—04; exec. vice dean, assoc. v.p. health sciences Ohio State Med. Ctr., Columbus, 2003—. Office: Ohio State Univ Med Ctr 200 Meiling Hall 370 West 9th St Columbus OH 43210 Office Phone: 202-687-4600. Business E-Mail: sedmak@georgetown.edu.

SEDO, MANUEL ARTURO, psychologist, researcher; b. Barcelona, Catalonia, Spain, 1932; arrived in US, 1972; s. Manuel Sedo and Manuela Garcia-Tunon; m. Asuncion Sastre, July 10, 1965; children: Silvia Johnson, Natalia C., Arturo. PhD, Boston Coll., Chestnut Hill, 1978; diploma, Inst. Psychology, Sorbonne, 1960. Lic. psychologist, sch. psychologist Commonwealth of Mass. Staff psychologist Children's Hosp. Med. Ctr., Boston, 1975—78; sch. psychologist Boston Pub. Schs., 1980—2000; dir. of test devel. MultiLingual Testing, Natick, Mass., 2000—. Author, rschr.: multicultural multilingual psychol. tests Five Digit Test, Oral Trails, Animal Span, Kiddy Words (Edith Kaplan award, 2004). Recipient Fulbright Fellowships, 1990, 1991; fellow, Harvard Coll., 1972, Harvard U., 1972—73. Mem.: APA (mem. bd.), Mass. Neuropsychol. Soc. Achievements include design of Tests of Minimal Language Load (elementary cognitive units); Neuropsych tests based on school materials (EX-P.RE.S.S.); Language tests based on Sentence Repetition (Spanish sentences with simple and with complex syntax); Kiddy Words: Naming Tests ages 2, 3, 4, 5, 6; Neuropsych tests from school curriculum materials (EXP.RE.S.S.); Naming test ages 2, 3, 4, 5 or 6; Language test: Sentence Repetition, sentences; Neuropsych test from curriculum materials (EX-P.RE.S.S.); Language test, Spanish sentence repetition comparing sentences of equal length and different language complexity. Office: Multi-Lingual Testing 9 Ingleside Rd Natick MA 01760 Office Phone: 508-655-6970. Business E-Mail: manuel@sedo.net.

SEDRA, ADEL SHAFEEK, engineering educator, academic administrator; b. Assuout, Egypt, Nov. 2, 1943; arrived in Can., 1966; s. Chafik and Hélène (Monsour) S.; m. Doris M. Barker, May 5, 1973; children: Paul Douglas, Mark Andrew. BSEE, Cairo U., 1964; MASc in Elec. Engring., U. Toronto, Ont., Can., 1968, PhD in Elec. Engring., 1969; DSc (hon.), Queen's U., 2003; LLD (hon.), U. Toronto, 2005; DSc (hon.), McGill U., Montreal, 2007. Registered profl. engr., Ont. Instr. Cairo U., 1964-66; asst. prof. elec. engring. U. Toronto, 1969-72, assoc. prof., 1972-78, prof., 1978—2003, chmn. dept., 1986-93, v.p., provost, chief acad. officer, 1993—2002; prof. elec. engring., dean faculty of engring. U. Waterloo, Ont., Canada, 2003—. Pres. Elec. Engring. Consociates Ltd., Toronto, 1979-81; bd. dirs. Info. Tech. Rsch. Ctr., Toronto, 1988-93; mem. rsch. coun. Can. Inst. for Advanced Rsch., 1994—; del. Oxford U. Press, 1995—. Co-author: Filter Theory and Design, 1978, Microelectronic Circuits, 1982, 5th edit., 2004 (also Spanish, Korean, Greek, Italian, Portuguese, Chinese, Persian, and Hebrew transls.), SPICE, 1997; contbr. over 120 articles to sci. jours. Operating grantee Nat. Scis. and Engring. Rsch. Coun. Can., 1970—; Ryerson Poly. Inst. fellow, 1988. Fellow IEEE (Darlington best paper award 1984, Edn. medal 1996, Cir. and Sys. Soc. Edn. award 1994, Guillemin Cauer Best Paper award 1987, Golden Jubilee medal 2000, 3d Millennium medal 2000), Can. Acad. Engrs., Royal Soc. Can., Am. Soc. Engring. Edn. (Terman award 1988); mem. Info. Tech. Assn. Can. (Tech. Achievement award 1993), Assn. Profl. Engrs. Ont. (Excellence award 2002). Home: 18 High Park Blvd Toronto ON Canada M6R 1M4 Office: U Waterloo Dean of Faculty of Engring 200 University Ave W Waterloo ON Canada N2L 3G1 Office Phone: 519-888-4567 ext. 33348. Business E-Mail: sedra@uwaterloo.ca.

SEDWAY, LYNN MASSEL, real estate economist; b. Washington, Nov. 26, 1941; d. Mark S. and Jean M. (Magnus) Massel; m. Paul H. Sedway, June 12, 1966; children: Mark, Carolyn, Jan. BA in Econs., U. Mich., 1963; MBA, U. Calif., Berkeley, 1976. Economist San Rafael (Calif.) Redevel. Agy., 1976-78; prin. Sedway Group, San Francisco, 1978—99; exec. mng. dir. CB Richard Ellis, San Francisco, 1999—. Instr. Appraisal Bus. Sch. U. Calif., Berkeley; corporate bd. mem. Hunting Gate Capital, Swig Co., AMB Alliance Fund III Bride Housing. Bridge housing bd., exec. com. trust Public Land Real Estate Coun. 1984-86, Internat. Coun. of Shopping Ctrs.; chmn San Rafael Downtown Retail Com., 1985; former trustee Urban Land Inst., former chmn. retail comml. coun., San Francisco District Council. Fellow, Homer Hoyt. Mem. Counselors of Real Estate, San Francisco Chamber of Commerce (former bd. of dirs.), City Club, Intl. House, Lambda Alpha (past pres., bd. dirs.), Internat. Land Econs. Soc., San Francisco Mayors Mcpl. Fiscal Advisory Com. Avocation: tennis. Home: 765 Market St Apt 26G San Francisco CA 94103-2038 Office Phone: 415-733-5321. Personal E-mail: lynn.sedway@cbre.com.

SEE, CAROLYN, English language educator, writer, book critic; b. Pasadena, Calif., Jan. 13, 1934; d. George Newton Laws and Kate Louise (Sullivan) Daly; m. Richard Edward See, Feb. 18, 1955 (div. June 1959); 1 child, Lisa Lenine; m. Tom Sturak, June 11, 1959; 1 child, Clara Elizabeth Marya. BA, Calif. State U., LA, 1958; PhD, UCLA, 1963. Prof. English Loyola Marymount Coll., LA, 1970-85, UCLA, 1985—; book critic L.A. Times, 1981-93, Washington Post, 1993—. Author: Rhine Maidens, 1980, Golden Days, 1986, Making History, 1991, Dreaming: Hard Luck and Good Times In America, 1995, The Handyman, 1999, Making a Literary Life, 2002, There Will Never Be Another You, 2006 Bd. dirs. Calif. Arts Coun., L.A., 1987-91, Day Break, for homeless, Santa Monica, Calif., 1989—, Friends of English, UCLA, 1990—; buddy for life AIDS Project L.A., AIDS relief, L.A., 1990—. Recipient award Sidney Hillman Found., 1972, Robert Kirsch award L.A. Times, 1994; PEN Ctr. USA West Lifetime Achievement award 1998; grantee Nat. Endowment for Arts, 1980, Guggenheim fellow, 1990-91. Mem. Writers Guild Am., Libr. Found. Calif., PEN Ctr. USA West (pres. 1990-91), Nat. Book Critics Cir. (bd. dirs. 1986-90). Democrat. Avocations: gardening, sailing, dance, brush clearing. Home: 17339 Tramonto Dr Pacific Palisades CA 90272-3124 Office: UCLA Dept English 405 Hilgard Ave Los Angeles CA 90095-9000 Office Phone: 310-454-7724. Business E-Mail: csee@ucla.edu.

SEE, EDMUND M., lawyer; b. Marietta, Ohio, Oct. 9, 1943; s. Edgar Thorpe and Katherine M. (Merriam) S.; m. Ellen Engler, June 5, 1976; children: Kevin, Gregory, Tyler. BA, Wesleyan U., Middletown, Conn., 1965; JD, Harvard U., 1971. Bar: Conn. 1971. Assoc. Day Pitney LLP (formerly Day, Berry & Howard LLP), Hartford, Conn., 1971—77, ptnr., 1978—. Chmn. Mcpl. Fin. Practice Group. Vol. Peace Corps, Gabon, 1965-67, Vista, 1968-69; pres. bd. dirs. Legal Aid Soc., 1977-85, Hartford Arch. Conservancy, 1983-86; trustee St. Joseph Coll., 1991-2003, 2004—; dir. Conn. Bar Found., 1994-; corporator Hartford Sem., 1994-. Mem. ABA, Conn. Bar Assn., Hartford County Bar Assn., Nat. Assn. Bond Lawyers, Conn. Govtl. Fin. Officers Assn., U.S. Govtl. Fin. Officers Assn., Phi Beta Kappa. Office: Day Berry & Howard LLP Cityplace 25th Fl Hartford CT 06103-3499 Office Phone: 860-275-0100. Business E-Mail: emsee@daypitney.com.

SEE, HAROLD FREND, state supreme court justice; b. Chgo., Nov. 7, 1943; s. Harold Frend and Corinne Louise (Rachau) S.; m. Brenda Jane Childs, Dec. 2, 1978; children: Callie Suzanne, Garrett Brittain; children by previous marriage: Mary Elisabeth, Eric Palmer. Student, U. Chgo., 1962-63; BA, Emporia State U., 1966; MS, Iowa State U., 1969; JD, U. Iowa, 1973. Bar: Ill. 1973, U.S. Dist. Ct. (no. dist.) Ill. 1973, Ala. 1981, U.S. Ct. Appeals (fed. cir.) 1991; U.S. Supreme Ct. Instr. econs. Iowa State U., Ames, 1967-69; asst. prof. econs. Ill. State U., Normal, 1969-70; assoc. Sidley & Austin, Chgo., 1973-76; assoc. prof. law U. Ala., Tuscaloosa, 1976-78, prof., 1978-97; justice Supreme Ct. Ala., 1997—. Contbr. to books, also articles and book reviews. Mem. ABA, Ala. Bar Assn., Am. Econ. Assn., Am. Law and Econs. Assn., Soc. Profls. in Dispute Resolution, Am. Law Inst., Ala. Law Inst. Baptist. Office: Supreme Ct Ala 300 Dexter Ave Montgomery AL 36104-3741 *

SEE, SAWTEEN, structural engineer; b. Georgetown, Penang, Malaysia, Mar. 23, 1954; came to US, 1974; d. Hock-Eng and Ewe-See (Lim) S.; m. Leslie Earl Robertson, Aug. 11, 1982; 1 child, Karla Mei. BSCE, Cornell U., 1977, MCE, 1978. Registered profl. engr., NY, Calif., Conn., Fla., Mass., Md., NJ, Ohio, Pa., Wash., Ark., Ill., Tex., NC. Design engr. Leslie E. Robertson Assocs., R.L.L.P., NYC, 1978-81, assoc., 1981-85, ptnr., 1986—, mng. ptnr., 1990—. Cons. M of Engring. class Cornell U., 1994-95, mem. adv. coun. Sch. Civil and Environ. Engring., 1999—; project dir., project mgr. Miho Mus., Kyoto, Japan, West Side HS, NYC, Jr. HS 234, Bklyn., Jewelry Trade Ctr., Bangkok, Bilboa (Spain) Emblematic bldgs., Internat. Trade Ctr., Barcelona, Spain, Seattle Art Mus., San Jose (Calif.) Convention Ctr., San Jose Arena; project dir. Hong Kong Sta. South West & North East Tower Structural Audit, Balt. Conv. Ctr., Rock 'N Roll Hall of Fame and Mus., Cleve., Pontiac Marina Hotel and Retail, Singapore, acad. bldgs. and greenhouse, SUNY, Binghamton, NY; project mgr. Coll. of Law bldg. U. Iowa, Iowa City, Neiman-Marcus store, San Francisco, AT&T Exhbn. bldg., NYC, Bank of China Tower, Hong Kong; ptnr.-in-charge Nat. Constn. Ctr., Phila. Contbr. articles to profl. jours. Named to Those Who Made Marks in the Constrn. Industry in 1988, Engrng. News Record, NYC, 1989, Spl. Recognition award Profl. Women in Constrn., 2002. Fellow ASCE (hon., performance study team World Trade Ctr. with FEMA), N.Y. Acad. Sci.; mem. Archtl. League, Coun. on Tall Bldgs. and Urban Habitat (chair com. on gravity loads and temperature effects 1982-85), Architects, Designers, Planners for Social Responsiblity, N.Y. Assn. Cons. Engrs. (dir. 1989-93, structural codes com. 1991—). Avocations: sailing, skiing, reading, photography. Home: 45 E 89th St Apt 25C New York NY 10128-1230 Office: Leslie E Robertson Assocs RLLP 30 Broad St Fl 47 New York NY 10004-2304 Home Phone: 212-860-4327; Office Phone: 212-750-9000. E-mail: sawteen.see@lera.com.

SEEBACH, LYDIA MARIE, physician; b. Red Wing, Minn., Nov. 9, 1920; d. John Henry and Marie (Gleusen) S.; m. Keith Edward Wentz, Oct. 16, 1959; children: Brooke Marie, Scott. BS, U. Minn., 1942, MB, 1943, MD, 1944, MS in Medicine, 1951. Diplomate Am. Bd. Internal Medicine. Intern Kings County Hosp., Bklyn., 1944; fellow Mayo Found., Rochester, Minn., 1945-51; pvt. practice Oakland, Calif., 1952-60, San Francisco, 1961—. Asst. clin. prof. U. Calif., San Francisco, 1981—; mem., vice chmn. Arthritis Clinic, Presbyn. Hosp., San Francisco, 1961-88, pharmacy com., 1963-78; chief St. Mary's Hosp. Arthritis Clinic, San Francisco, 1968-72; exec. bd. Pacific Med. Ctr., San Francisco, 1974-76. Contbr. articles to med. jours. Fellow ACP; mem. AMA, Am. Med. Womens Assn. (pres. Calif. chpt. 1968-70), Am. Rheumatism Assn., Am. Soc. Internal Medicine, Pan Am. Med. Womens Assn. (treas.), Calif. Acad. Medicine, Calif. Soc. Internal Medicine, Calif. Med. Assn., San Francisco Med. Soc., San Francisco Med. Assn., San Francisco Soc. Internal Medicine, No. Calif. Rheumatism Assn., Internat. Med. Women's Assn., Mayo Alumni (bd. dirs. 1983-89), Iota Sigma Pi. Republican. Lutheran. Avocations: music, cooking, gardening, needlepoint. Office: 490 Post St Ste 939 San Francisco CA 94102-1414 Home Phone: 415-922-0305; Office Phone: 415-397-9571. Personal E-mail: lseebach@sbcglobal.net.

SEEBAUER, EDMUND GERARD, chemical engineer, educator; b. Chgo., May 15, 1961; s. Edmund Joseph and Mary Ann (Herold) S. BS, U. Ill., 1983; PhD, U. Minn., 1986. Postdoctoral assoc. Sandia Nat. Labs., Albuquerque, 1987-88; prof. chem. engring. U. Ill., Urbana, 1988—. Contbr. articles to profl. jours. Named Presdl. Young Investigator NSF, 1988, Sloan Fedn. fellow in chemistry, 1994; recipient Teaching Excellence award Dow Chem. Corp., 1988, Young Faculty award DuPont Corp., 1989. Mem. Am. Inst. Chem. Engrs., Am. Chem. Soc., Am. Phys. Soc., Am. Vacuum Soc. (Varian fellow award 1985), Materials Rsch. Soc. Roman Catholic. Avocations: jogging, model building. Office: U Ill Dept Chem Engring 600 S Mathews Ave Urbana IL 61801-3602

SEEDS, SHARON LYNN, bank processor; d. Don A. and Marguerite Morairty Seeds. BA in Edn., Ariz. State U., 1972. Tchr. gen. and vocal music edn. Paradise Valley Unified Sch. Dist. # 69, Phoenix, 1973—76; advt. coord. Greater Phoenix Jewish News, 1976—83; disbursements/loan rev. processor Merabank, Phoenix, 1984—88; loan processor II Citibank, Scottsdale and Mesa, Ariz., 1989—91; acctg. specialist, ops. processor I and II, store acctg. support, mortgage lending home equity Internet divsn. Wells Fargo & Co., Phoenix, 1992—. Festival adjudicator Ariz. Solo and Ensemble Festival, Phoenix, 1973—; jr. choir dir. Christ Ch. of the Ascension, Paradise Valley, 1983—87; soloist and sect. leader Congregation Ch., Tempe, Presbyn. Ch., Phoenix, Ch. of Divine Sci., Trinity Episcopal Cathedral, St. Barnabas-on-the Desert, 1976—2002. Contbr.ghost editor: textbook Arizona Construction Lending and the Law, 1988; actor: (plays) Mesa Music Theatre, Ariz., 1st United Meth. Ch., Tempe, Ariz., 1st United Meth. Ch., Phoenix, St. Barnabas-on-the-Desert. Vol. libr. catalog and music areas Lillian Valley Sch., Blackfoot, Idaho, 2002, 2004;

neighborhood activist on hist. preservation com. Sunview Estates II, Phoenix, 2002—; vol. press release area Episcopal Ch. Gen. Conv., Phoenix, 1991. Mem.: Am. Choral Dirs. Assn., Music Educators Nat. Conf., Phi Kappa Phi, Kappa Delta Pi, Pi Lambda Theta, Sigma Alpha Iota (local chair/co-chair for nat. bazaar at triennial conv. 1987—, nat. elections chair triennial conv. 2003, Sword of Honor 1972, Rose of Honor 1995, Rose of Dedication 2003). Episcopalian. Avocations: music theater/liturgical drama, needlecrafts, reading.

SEEGAL, JOHN FRANKLIN, lawyer; b. Newton, Mass., May 21, 1946; s. Samuel Melbourne and Martha (Lewenberg) S.; m. Barbara Ellen Wayne, Apr. 2, 1982; children: Sarah Rachel, Laura Rose. BA in econ. summa cum laude, Harvard U., MBA with distinction, 1973, JD magna cum laude, 1973. Bar: Calif. 1973. Assoc. Orrick, Herrington & Sutcliffe, LLP, San Francisco, 1973-78, ptnr., 1979—, practice leader mergers & acquisitions. Co-chmn. Inst. on Securities Regulation, 2001. Author: Bargaining Power, Acquiring or Selling the Privately Held Co., 1999, Private Co. M&A: Deal Structures, Execution & Related Issues, 2001. Mem.: ABA, Practicing Law Inst. (co-chmn. Securities Regulation Inst. 2001), Calif. Bar Assn. Republican. Jewish. Fluent in french. Office: Orrick Herrington & Sutcliffe LLP 405 Howard St San Francisco CA 94105 Office Phone: 415-773-5797. Office Fax: 415-773-5759. Business E-Mail: jseegal@orrick.com.

SEEGER, GUENTER OTTO, chef; b. Loffenau, Baden, Germany, Mar. 23, 1949; s. Otto Emil and Margarete (Temme) S.; m. Marion Boehmlander (div. Aug. 1991); children: Diana, Denise. Student, Cook and Hotel Sch., Lucerne, Switzerland. Apprentice Hotel Funk, Dobel, Germany, 1963-66; cook various locations, Switzerland, 1966-77; owner, operator restaurant Pforz Heim, Germany, 1977-84; exec. chef maifar Regent Hotel, Washington, 1984-85; exec. chef dining rm. Ritz-Carlton Hotel, Atlanta, 1985—. Pres., cons., produce developer Smi, Inc., Atlanta, 1993. Editor calendars, 1982, 83 (award 1982). Named Best Chef of Atlanta, Atlanta Mag., 1993. Mem. Chefs Collaborative 2000 (bd. overseers 1994). Avocation: Kung Fu. Office: The Ritz-Carlton Buckhead 3434 Peachtree Rd NE Atlanta GA 30326-1172

SEEGER, LAUREEN E., lawyer, health products executive; BBA, U. Wis., Eau Claire, 1983; JD, U. Wis., Madison, 1986. Atty. Jones, Day, Reavis & Pogue, 1986—92; ptnr.-in-charge tech. litigation sect. Morris, Manning & Martin, LLP, 1992—2000; v.p., gen. coun. McKesson Provider Technologies, 2000—06; exec. v.p., gen. counsel, sec. McKesson Corp., San Francisco, 2006—. Office: McKesson Corpn 1 Post St San Francisco CA 94104 *

SEEGER, PETE, folk singer, songwriter; b. NYC, May 3, 1919; s. Charles Louis and Constance de Clyver (Edson) Seeger; m. Toshi-Aline Ohta, July 20, 1943; children: Daniel Adams, Mika Salter, Tinya. Student, Harvard U., 1936-38. Co-founding mem. The Weavers, 1948—59. Singer: (songs) (albums/CDs) Am. Indsl. Ballads, 1957, Dangerous Songs, 1966, Abiyoyo, 1967, World of Pete Seeger, 1973, Essential, 1978, Greatest Hits, 1987, Traditional Christmas Carols, 1989, (albums/CDs) Children's Concert at Town Hall, 1990, Folk Music of the World, 1991, Pete Seeger's Family Concert, 1992, Singalong-Live at Sanders Theatre, 1992, Darling Corey/Goofing Off Suit, Live at Newport, Waist Deep in the Big Muddy, 1993, Clearwater Classics, Link in the Chain, 1996, American Favorite Ballads, 1997, Birds, Beasts, Bugs & Fishes, For Kids & Just Plain Folks, God Bless the Grass, If I Had a Hammer-Songs of Hope & Struggle, Pete, 1998, Headlines & Footnotes, 1999, American Folk Game & Activity, Stories & Songs for Little Children, 2000, Song and Play Time, 2001; co-author (with Paul DuBois Jacobs): (children's book) The Deaf Musicians, 2006 (Schneider Family Book award). With US Army, 1942—45. Named to Rock and Roll Hall of Fame, 1996; recipient Nat. Medal of the Arts, 1994, Kennedy Center Honor, 1994, Grammy award, 1996. Subject of book: How Can I Keep from Singing: Pete Seeger, by David King Dunaway, 1981. Office: care Harold Leventhal 250 W 57th St New York NY 10107 *

SEEGERS, HARVEY, retail executive; B, U. Va.; JD, Cath. U.; MBA, Harvard Bus. Sch. With GE, 1991—96; pres., CEO Global Exch. Svcs., 1996; tchr. internet commerce U. Md. Grad. Bus. Sch.; pres. Home Depot Direct Home Depot, 2005—. Faculty adv. internet commerce rsch. U. Md. Served in USMC. Decorated 2 Meritorious Svc. medals. Office: Home Depot 2455 Paces Ferry Rd Atlanta GA 30339

SEEHAUSEN, RICHARD FERDINAND, architect; b. Indpls., Mar. 17, 1925; s. Paul Ferdinand and Melusina Dorothea (Nordmeyer) S.; m. Phyllis Jean Gates, Dec. 22, 1948; children: Lyn, Dirk. Student, DePauw U., 1943, Wabash Coll., 1944, State U. Iowa, USN Pre Flight, 1944; BArch, U. Ill., 1949. Registered profl. arch., 1951. Pilot training Norman Naval Air Base, 1945; ptnr. Johnson, Kile, Seehausen & Assocs., archs., engrs., Rockford, Ill., 1955-82, pres., 1974-82, Richard F. Seehausen-Arch., Inc., Rockford, Ill., 1983—2001. Mem. com. jail planning and constrn. stds. Bur. Detention Facilities, Ill. Dept. Corrections, 1970-73; analyst Dept. Def., 1962-66; analyst Fed. Fall-Out Shelter, 1962—. Prin. works include No. Ill. U. Ctr., Harrison Hall, Lorado Taft, Oreg., Health Svc. Bldg., No. Ill. U. (Renovation) Old Winnebago County Pub. Safety Bldg., Rockford, Ill., St. Mark Luth. Ch., Christ Meth. Ch., Forest Hills Free Ch., Page Park Spl. Edn. Sch., Winnebago County Courthouse, Court Street Meth. Ch., Willows Personal Care Ctr., 1st Presbyn. Ch., Rochelle, Ill., Messiah Luth. Ch., Rock Falls, Ill., Rockford Mut. Ins. Home Office Bldg., Ch. of the Nazarene, Freeport, Ill., Stephenson County Courthouse, LDS Temple, McHenry County Ct. House, Woodstock, Ill., Ogle County Pub. Safety Bldg., Oreg., DeKalb H.S., Freeport YWCA Bldgs., renovation Carroll County Ct. House, DeKalb Area Retirement Ctr., Oak Crest Retirement Ctr., Sycamore/DeKalb, Ill., St. Paul Ch. of Christ, Davis, Ill., Savanna Meth. Ch., Savanna, Ill., others. Bd. dir. Rockford Boys Club, Lincoln Pk. Boys Club, past dir.; trustee Emmanuel Luth. Ch., Rockford, 1989-92; mem. Nat. Trust Hist. Preservation, 2000—. Served with USN, 1943-45, USNR, 1945-47, lt. USAF, 1949-55. Mem. AIA (dir. No. Ill. chpg. 1966-68, 75-77, pres. chpt. 1978-79, nat. design com. 2005—), Ill. Coun. of Am. Inst. Archs., U. Ill. Alumni Assn., Mason (Shriner), Kiwanian, Forest Hills Country Club (gov. 1970-72), Saddle Brooke Country Club, Saddle Brooke Arc. Com., Lambda Chi Alpha. Lutheran. Office: Richard F Seehausen Arch Inc 65297 E Emerald Ridge Dr Tucson AZ 85739-1434

SEEHRA, MOHINDAR SINGH, physics professor, researcher; b. Panjab, Pakistan, Feb. 14, 1940; came to U.S., 1963; s. Bakhshish Singh and Rattan (Kaur) S.; m. Harbhajan Kaur, May 12, 1963; children: Jasmeet, Parveen. BS, Panjab U., 1959; MS, Aligah Muslim U., India, 1962; PhD, U. Rochester, 1969. Instr. chemistry Arya Coll., Nawanshahr, India, 1959-60; lectr. physics Jain Coll., Ambala City, India, 1962-63; asst. prof. physics W.Va. U., Morgantown, 1969-73, assoc. prof., 1973-77, prof., 1977-91, Eberly disting. prof. physics, 1992—. Contbr. more than 225 articles to profl. jours. Rsch. fellow A.P. Sloan Found., 1973-75, ORAU Summer fellow, 1976, 77, 84, 85; recipient Outstanding Rsch. award Coll. Arts and Scis., U. W.Va., 1985. Fellow Am. Phys. Soc., Inst. Physics (Eng.). Office: WVa State U Dept Physics PO Box 6315 Morgantown WV 26506-6315 Home Phone: 304-599-0761; Office Phone: 304-293-3422 ext. 1473. Business E-Mail: mseehra@wvu.edu.

SEELAN, SANTHOSH KUMAR, science educator; b. India; arrived in US, 1998; BS in Geology, Annamalai U., India, 1971; MS in Applied Geology, IIT Bombay, India, 1974; diploma in Groundwater, Hebrew U. Jerusalem, Israel, 1975; PhD, Jawaharlal Nehru Technol. U., India, 1994. Cert. in remote sensing GTZ, Germany, 1978. Sr. rsch. analyst Ops. Rsch. group, Baroda, India, 1975—77; scientist Nat. Remote Sensing Agy., Hyderabad, India, 1977—89, head data ctr. Dept. Space, 1990—95; cons. Terralink, Wellington, New Zealand, 1996—98; rsch. faculty Upper Midwest Aerospace Consortium U. N.D., Grand Forks, ND, 1998—2003, chair Dept. Earth Sys. Sci. and Policy, 2003—05, prof., applied remote sensing Dept. Space Studies, 2005—. Contbr. articles to profl. jours. Recipient Silver medal, Indian Inst. Tech., 1974, Best Spkr. award, Asian Conf. Remote Sensing, 1986; fellow, UNESCO, 1974—75. Mem.: Am. Soc. Photogrammetry and Remote Sensing, Indian Nat. Cartography Assn. (life), Indian Soc. Photointerpretation and Remote Sensing (life). Office: U ND Clifford Hall Rm 516 Grand Forks ND 58202-9008 Office Phone: 701-777-2355. Business E-Mail: seelan@space.edu.

SEELAND, ARTHUR DAVID, bishop; b. Jersey City, Oct. 31, 1931; s. Theodore Arthur and Dorothea Augusta (Thomas) Seeland; m. Mary Ann Hove, Apr. 10, 1954; children: John Robert, Eric David, Tellef Martin, Karen Victoria. BA, Houghton Coll., 1953; MDiv, Temple U., 1958; D Ministry, McCormick Theol. Sem., 1978; grad. with highest distinction, U.S. Naval War Coll., 1981; ThM, Princeton Theol. Sem., 1973. Diplomate Am. Bd. Med. Psychotherapists. Pastor NJ United Meth. Conf., 1953—64; commd. lt. (j.g.) USN, 1963, advanced through grades to comdr., 1975, chaplain, 1964—87; clin. dir. Family and Psychol. Svcs., Cherry Hill, NJ, 1987—90; rector Holy Sacraments Anglican Cath. Ch., King of Prussia, Pa., 1988—93; archdeacon Diocese of the Resurrection, Quakertown, Pa., 1990—93; bishop Diocese of the Pacific and SW of the Anglican Rite Cath. Ch., LA, 1993—. Lectr. med. ethics Med. Sch. Uniformed Services U., Bethesda, Md., 1980—84; lectr. ethics U.S. Nat. War Coll., Washington, 1980—84; asst. prof. Pa. State U., Hershey; pres. Holy Cross Seminary, Hereford, Ariz., 2005—. Contbr. articles to profl. jours. Editl. bd. Jour. of Christian Bioethics, Waco, Tex., 1994—99; pres. Houghton (NY) Coll. Alumni, 1981—83. Master: Mason (life; grand chaplain NJ 1963—, grand chaplain France 1977—); mem.: Assn. of Mil. Surgeons of the U.S. (life), NY Acad. of Scis. (life). Anglican Catholic. Avocations: sailing, travel, hiking, hunting. Home: 764 West Bay Ave Barnegat NJ 08005 Office: Diocese of the Pacific and Southwest 6752 East Ramsey Rd Hereford AZ 85615

SEELENFREUND, ALAN, retired pharmaceutical company executive; b. NYC, Oct. 22, 1936; s. Max and Gertrude (Roth) S.; m. Ellyn Bolt; 1 child, Eric. BME, Cornell U., 1959, M. in Indsl. Engring., 1960; PhD in Mgmt. Sci., Stanford U., 1967. Asst. prof. bus. adminstrn. Grad. Sch. Bus. Stanford U., Palo Alto, Calif., 1966-71; mgmt. cons. Strong, Wishart and Assocs., San Francisco, 1971-75; various mgmt. positions McKesson Corp., San Francisco, 1975-84, v.p., chief fin. officer, 1984-86, exec. v.p., chief fin. officer, 1986-89, chmn., CEO, 1989-97, chmn., 1997-99, also bd. dirs., chmn., 1997—2002; ret., 2002. Mem. Nature Conservancy, St. Francis Yacht Club, Villa Taverna Club, Pacific Union Club, Francisco Yacht Club. Avocations: sailing, skiing, hiking. Office: McKesson Corp 1 Post St Ste 2625 San Francisco CA 94104-5296

SEELER, RUTH ANDREA, pediatrician, educator; b. NYC, June 13, 1936; d. Thomas and Olivia Seeler. BA cum laude, U. Vt., 1959, MD, 1962. Diplomate Am. Bd. Pediat., Am. Bd. Pediatric Hematology/Oncology. Intern Bronx (N.Y.) Mcpl. Hosp., 1962—65; pediats. hematology/oncology fellow U. Ill., 1965—67; dir. pediatric hematology/oncology Cook County Hosp., 1967—84; prof. pediatrics and pediatric edn. Coll. Medicine U. Ill., Chgo., 1984—; assoc. chief pediatrics Michael Reese Hosp., Chgo., 1990—97, acting chief pediatrics, 1997—99; pediatrician St. Anthony's Hosp./U. Ill. Coll. Medicine, 1999—2001. Course coord. pediatrics Nat. Coll. Advanced Med. Edn., Chgo., 1987-96; mem. subboard Pediatric Hematology/Oncology, Chapel Hill, 1990-95; chief Midwest Am. Bd. Pediat., 1990-, Mem. editl. bd. Am. Jour. Pediat. Hematology/Oncology, 1985-95. Founder med. dir. camp for hemophiliacs Ill. Hemophilia Found., 1973—2000, pres. Ill., 1981—85; sec. exec. com. U. Vt. Med. Sch. Alumna Assn.; jr. and sr. warden, treas. Ch. Our Saviour, Chgo., 1970—92. Mem.: U. Vt. Med. Sch. Alumna Assn. (pres.-elect), Phi Beta Kappa, Gamma Phi Beta Found. (trustee 1994—2000, 2002—). Avocations: triathalons, biking, swimming. Office: U Ill Coll Medicine Pediats M/C 856 840 S Wood St Chicago IL 60612-7317 Office Phone: 312-355-1021. Business E-Mail: seeler@uic.edu.

SEELIG, GERARD LEO, management consultant; b. Schluchtern, Germany, June 15, 1926; came to U.S., 1934, naturalized, 1943; s. Herman and Bella (Bach) S.; m. Lorraine Peters, June 28, 1953; children: Tina Lynn, Robert Mark and Carol Ann (twins). BEE, Ohio State U., 1948; MS in Indsl. Mgmt, N.Y. U., 1954. Registered profl. engr., Ohio. Electronics engr. Martin Corp., Balt., 1948-50; sr. engr. Fairchild Aircraft Co., Farmingdale, NY, 1950-54; program mgr. RCA, Moorestown, NJ, 1954-59, Van Nuys, Calif., 1959-61; div. mgr. Missile & Space Co. div. Lockheed Aircraft Corp., Van Nuys, 1961-63; v.p., gen. mgr. Lockheed Aircraft Corp. (Lockheed Electronics div.), Los Angeles, 1963-68; exec. v.p. Lockheed Electronics Co., Inc., Plainfield, NJ, 1968-69, pres., 1969-71; group exec., exec. asst. to office of pres. ITT, NYC, 1971-72, corp. v.p., 1972-79, sr. v.p., 1979-81, exec. v.p., 1981-83; pres. indsl. and tech. sector Allied Corp., exec. v.p. Morristown, NJ, 1983-87. Disting. exec. lectr. Rutgers Grad. Sch. Mgmt.; exec.-in-residence, vis. prof. Columbia U. Grad. Sch. Bus.; bd. dirs. 5 corps.; cons. various investment firms. Served with AUS, 1944-46. Recipient Disting. Alumnus award Ohio State U., 1987. Fellow AIAA (assoc.); mem. IEEE (sr.).

SEELIG, JILL, publishing executive; MBA, Fordham U., NY. Various positions in fin. svcs. industry including mktg. dir. for Mastercard, 1984—89; advt. sales rep. NY Mag., Self Mag., 1993—94, beauty dir., 1994—95; nat. sales mgr. Self Mag., 1996—99; advt. dir. Vanity Fair, 1998—99, O, The Oprah Mag., 1999—2000, pub., 2000—. Office: O, The Oprah Magazine 1700 Broadway New York NY 10019 *

SEELY, DENNIS M., secondary school educator; m. Vivian D. Gaden, July 4, 1996. BA in Speech and Theater, U. LaVerne, La., 1971; postgrad., Ball State U., 1975, U. Okla., Norman, 1987; MS in Comm., Lacross U., Covington, La., 2004, PhD, 2005. Cert. tchr. Ariz. Commd. 2d lt. US Army, 1971, advanced through grades to maj., 1991; congrl. press sec. Rep. Jim Kolbe, Tucson, 1991—92; tchr. Santa Rita HS, Tucson, 1994, Blue Ridge HS, Lakeside, Ariz., 1994—. Mem.: US Inst. Theater Tech., Nat. Coun. Tchrs. English, Alpha Psi Omega. Mailing: PO Box 1445 Lakeside AZ 85929 Office: Blue Ridge HS 1200 W White Mountain Blvd Lakeside AZ 85929

SEELY, JAMES MICHAEL, retired military officer, defense consultant, small business owner; b. LA, Oct. 15, 1932; s. Louis K. and Mary Edith (Gleason) S.; m. Gail Margaret Deverman, July 13, 1957; children: Ted Andrew, Nina Marie. BS, UCLA, 1955; MS, George Washington U., 1976. Commd. ensign USN, 1955, advanced through grades to rear adm.; student pilot, 1955-56; attack pilot, 1957-75; comdg. officer Attack Squadron 165, Naval Air Sta. Whidbey Island, Wash., 1972-73; comdr. Carrier Air Wing 9, Naval Air Sta. Lemoore, Calif., 1974-75; comdg. officer U.S. Naval Air Sta., Whidbey Island, 1977-79; dep. dir. DCNO (Air Warfare, OP-50), Pentagon, Washington, 1979-82; dir. Joint Analysis Directorate, Office Joint Chiefs Staff, Washington, 1982-84; comdr. Medium Attack Tactical Electronic Warfare Wing, Pacific Fleet, Naval Air Sta. Whidbey Island, 1984-86; dir. DCNO (Air Warfare, OP-50), Pentagon, 1986-88; dep. comptr. of Navy, Pentagon, 1988-89; ret., 1989; with RRP Def. Cons. Assocs., Arlington, Va., 1989—2002; owner, pres. JMS Cons., 2002—. Vietnam combat duty with Attack Squadrons 93, 152, 165 flying from aircraft carriers USS Enterprise, Hancock, Bon Homme Richard, Shangri-La and Constellation; 447 combat missions. Decorated Defense Superior Service, Legion of Merit (3), D.F.C. (4), Bronze Star, Air Medal (43), Navy Commendation medal with combat v (7). Mem. Naval Inst., Tailhook Assn., Assn. Naval Aviation, Marine Corps Aviation Assn., Red River Valley Fighter Pilots Assn., Navy League, Assn. Old Crows, Golden Eagles, Sigma Pi. Republican. Roman Catholic. Avocations: sports, automobiles. Home: 15552 Legacy Way Haymarket VA 20169-6117 Home Phone: 703-753-2618; Office Phone: 703-753-2618. E-mail: jimseely@comcast.net.

SEELY, MARIBETH WALSH, elementary school educator; d. William F. and Agnes C. Walsh; m. Thomas P. Seely; children: Timothy Patrick Francis, Keribeth Francis. BS in Elem. Edn., Lowell U., 1966. Cert. reading specialist Mass. Tchr. Town of Methuen, Mass., 1966—71, City of Lawrence, Mass., Sandyston-Walpack Sch., Layton, NJ. Testified to Ho. Reps. Am. Legion and Citizens Flag Alliance, Washington, 1997; testified for Am. flag Senate Judiciary Com., Washington, 1999. Nominee Gov.'s Tchr. Recognition award, State N.J., 1994; named Woman of Distinction, Lenni-Lenape Girl Scouts, 1995, Woman of the 90's, N.J. Herald Newspaper, 1995; recipient Inspiring Tchr. award, Sussex County C.C., 2005, Cert. Appreciations, Vietnam Vets. Am., 2005. Mem.: Sierra Club (assoc.). Roman Catholic. Avocations: hiking, art museums, travel, baseball. Home: 19 Summit Dr Branchville NJ 07826 Office: Sandyston-Walpack School PO Box 128 Layton NJ 07851

SEELY, ROBERT DANIEL, cardiologist, medical association administrator; b. Woodmere, NY, Nov. 4, 1923; s. Harry and Ethel (Weil) S.; m. Marcia Ann Wells, June 19, 1953; children: Ellen Wells, Anne Wells. BS, NYU, 1943; MD, Columbia U., 1946. Intern Mt. Sinai Hosp., NYC, 1946-47, asst. resident in medicine, 1950-51, resident in pathology, 1951-52, chief resident in medicine, 1952-53; Sara Welt fellow in cardiovascular research Presbyn. Hosp., NYC, 1953-54; instr. dept. physiology, cardiovascular research Western Res. U., Cleve., 1947-48; chief rheumatic heart disease clinic Mt. Sinai Hosp., NYC, 1961-70, attending physician medicine and cardiology, 1978—, chief of service dept. medicine, 1979—, clin. prof. medicine, cardiology Sch. Medicine, 1970—; practice medicine specializing in cardiovascular disease NYC, 1953—. Contbr. articles to profl. jours. Served to capt. M.C. AUS, 1948-50. Recipient Solomon Berson Meml. award Mt. Sinai Hosp., 1977 Fellow Am. Coll. Cardiology, ACP; mem. N.Y. Heart Assn., AMA, N.Y. County Med. Soc., Soc. Cert. Internists N.Y., Phi Beta Kappa, Alpha Omega Alpha, Beta Lambda Sigma Office: 49 E 96th St # 11D New York NY 10128-0782 Personal E-mail: billybobseedy@gmail.com.

SEELY, ROBERT EUGENE, management consultant; b. Bangor, Mich., Oct. 23, 1941; s. Leroy W. and Ruth A. Seely. Cert., A&M U., 1961; BBA, West Mich. U., 1969. Officer Am. Nat. Bank, Kalamazoo, 1969—74; v.p. mktg. and fin., gen. mgr. Portage Rapid Cut, 1974—78; CEO Sutliff & Case, Inc., Peoria, Ill., 1978—81, Allied Material Handing Co., Peoria, 1981—83; pres. S.E.R., Inc., Kalamazoo, 1983—86; bus./mgmt. cons. Seely & Assocs., L.L.C., Kalamazoo, 1986—. Mem. adv. com. C & S Plastic Climax, Mich., 1986—88; advisor to bd. dirs. Simpson Enterprises, 1990—2003; bd. dirs. Sunset Shares Coop, Inc., Azon USA, Inc., Maro, Inc., Venureprise, Inc., Portage Rapid Cut, Allied Material Handling, New World Condo Assn., Champion Furnace Pipe, Wonder Makers, Inc., Exhibit House, Portage Dist. Libr. Contbr. articles to profl. publs. First chmn. Kalamazoo Valley Quality Coun., 1993-95; bd. dirs. city of Portage Economic Devel. Fin. Authority, 1998—; mem. City of Portage Devel. Authority. With U.S. Army, 1966-68, Vietnam Recipient Cert. of Appreciation Gov. of Mich., Cert. South Mich. Water Quality Commn., 1978, Cert. of Achievement Entrepreneurship Inst., 1983. Mem. Nat. Assn. Corp. Dirs., Austin Lake Riparian (pres. 1991-93, bd. dirs.), C. of C. (chmn. small bus. week 1990, chmn. small bus. coun. 1991-92, organizer and 1st chmn. mfg. coun. 1992-96, Portage dir. Kalamazoo county), Kal Valley Cmty. Quality Coun. (1st chmn. 1993, 94), Kal County C. of C. (bd. dirs. 1996-99) Avocations: golf, racquetball, skiing. Home: 9930 E Shore Dr Portage MI 49002-5879 Office: PO Box 924 Portage MI 49081-0924

SEEMANN, ROSALIE MARY, international business and foreign policy association executive; b. St. Louis, July 30, 1942; d. Ulysses Sylvester and Helen Maire (Hootselle) Simon; m. Richard Vaughn, Jan. 20, 1968 (dec.); 1 child, Heather Elizabeth. Student, Lindenwood Colls., St. Charles, Mo., 1973-76, Harris Tchrs. Coll., St. Louis, 1961, U. Fla., Gainesville, 1964. Vol. U.S. Peace Corps, Brazil, 1964-66; tech. analyst, group leader Conductron-Mo., St. Charles, 1966-71, bus. mgr., 1971-77; maintenance engr. McDonnell Douglas Astronautics, St. Louis, 1977-78; mgr. supply support Northrop Def. Systems Divsn., Rolling Meadows, Ill., 1978-80; logistics mgmt. cons. Logistic Support Svcs., Spring Grove, Ill., 1980-85; mgr. reliability, maintainability, integrated logistic Recon/Optical, Inc., Barrington, Ill., 1985-90; v.p., exec. dir. Mid-Am. Com. Internat. Bus. & Govt. Coop., Chgo., 1991-97; exec. dir. World Affairs Coun., St. Louis, 1997-99; founder, pres. Mid-West Internat. Exch., 1999—; v.p. global initiatives World Trade Ctr., St. Louis, 1999—2001. Bd. dirs. Libr. Internat. Rels., Chgo.-Kent Coll. Law, Prime Med. Products. Bd. dirs. U. Mo.-St. Louis Chancellor's Coun., internat. affairs com.; bd. dirs. World Affairs Coun. Am.; mem. women's bd. Goodman Theatre, Chgo.; active Girl Scouts U.S.A.; master gardener Mo. Bot. Garden, 2005. Recipient commendation Conductron-Mo., 1967, pres. award Recon-Optical, 1989. Mem. Am. Soc. Assn. Execs. (internat. sect. coun. 1996—), Nat. Coun. Internat. Visitors, Am. Women Internat. Understanding, Soc. Logistics Engrs. (Mem. of Yr. award, sr. mem.), English Speaking Union, Japan Am. Soc., Chgo. Coun. Fgn. Rels. (Chgo. com.), Assn. Old Crows, Coun. Women Leaders, Execs. Club Chgo., Arts & Edn. Coun. Greater St. Louis, Internat. Trade Assn., Senate Constantine Prophyrogenetus Internat. Assn. (Greece, hon. pres.), Inst. Mid. East Studies Al-Mamun, Mo. Botanical Garden (named master gardner 2005) Home Phone: 636-745-8533; Office Phone: 636-745-2352. Office Fax: 636-745-2352.

SEENITH, SIVASUNDARAM, mathematician, educator; s. Sam Seenith and Tham Kanaga; m. Irene M Siva, May 21, 1973; 1 child, Diantha A Siva. PhD, U. Tex., 1987. Prof. Embry-Riddle Aero. U., Daytona Beach, Fla., 1989—. Organizer, gen. chair various profl. confs. Author: Vector Lyapunov Functions and Stability Analysis of Nonlinear Systems, 1991, College Mathematics for Aviation I, 1992, College Mathematics for Aviation II, 1993, Dynamics Systems on Measure Chain, 1996, Advances in Nonlinear Dynamics, 1997, Nonlinear Problems in Aviation and Aerospace, 2000, Advances in Dynamics and Control, 2004; editor-in-chief Jour. Nonlinear Studies; editor-in-chief: Nonlinear Systems in Aviation, Aerospace and Astronautics Book Series; editor-in-chief Nonlinear Systems in Aviation, Aerospace and Astronautics Series; editor: Proceedings of Nonlinear Problems in Aviation Aerospace, Proceedings of Mathematical Problems in Engineering and Aerospace Sciences, Jour. Aerospace Engineering, Global Jour. Mathematical Analysis, Scientific Journal of Actual Problems of Aviation and Aerospace Systems. Mem.: AAUP, Soc. Indsl. and Applied Math., Internat. Fedn. Nonlinear Analysts (charter), Math. Assn. Am. (charter math. for bus., industry and govt. 1999), Acad. Nonlinear Scis., Am. Math. Soc. Avocations: travel, cricket. Office: Embry-Riddle Aero U 600 S Clyde Morris Blvd Daytona Beach FL 32114 Business E-Mail: siva@erau.edu.

SEEP, DOROTHY M., music educator; d. Frederick Henry and Estelle May Muller; m. Ralph Vincent Seep, Nov. 11, 1978; children: Jessica, Jeremy. MusB, Eastman Sch. Music, 1969, MusM, 1972. Music tchr. Taft Elem. Sch., Washingtonville, NY, 1969—71, Wayne Ctrl. Sch., Ontario, NY, 1972—81, Rochester Christian Sch., Penfield, NY, 1987—92; sr. choir dir. Rochester Christian Reformed Ch., Penfield, NY, 1988—91; music tchr. Annapolis Area Christian Sch., 1998—. Founder and dir. children's chorale Annapolis Area Christian Sch., Md., 1998—; founder and dir. adult cmty. choir and orch., 2003. Mem. choir Nat. Presbyn. Ch., Washington, 2004—; music dir. Safe Harbor Presbyn. Ch., 2000—03. Mem.: Music Educators Nat. Conf., Am. Choral Dir. Assn., Phi Kappa Lambda, Sigma Alpha Iota. Presbyterian. Avocations: sewing, gardening, reading, cooking. Office: Annapolis Area Christian Sch 710 Ridgely Ave Annapolis MD 21401 Office Phone: 410-266-8255.

SEETHALER, WILLIAM CHARLES, manufacturing executive; b. NYC, Dec. 4, 1937; s. William Charles and Catherine Frances (Flaherty) Seethaler. Student, Quinnipiac Coll., Conn., 1955-56, Ohio State U., 1956-58; BSBA, U. San Francisco, 1977; MBA in Internat. High Tech., Pepperdine U., 1982; grad. tech. mktg. program, Stanford U., 1990; grad. global enterprise mgmt. program, Oxford U., Eng., 2000. Lic. real estate salesperson Calif. Asst. to v.p. sales T. Sendzimir, Inc., Waterbury, Conn. and Paris, 1960-66; mgr. internat. ops. Dempsey Indsl. Furnace Co., East Longmeadow, Mass., 1966-67; mgr. internat. sales Yoder Co., Cleve., 1967-74; mng. dir., owner Seethaler & Assocs., Palo Alto, Calif., 1974—; owner, chief exec. officer Seethaler Internat. Ltd., Palo Alto, Calif., 1982-92; ptnr. DFS Computer Assocs., San Jose, Calif., 1976-87; v.p. mktg. and sales Telewave Inc., Mountain View, Calif., 1996—2001; area mgr. IMSM, Malmesbury, Wiltshire, England, 2002—; rep. Spacesonic, San Carlos, Calif., 2004—; assoc. prof. Internat. Mktg. Mission Coll., Santa Clara, Calif., 2006—. Bd. dirs. Palo Alto Fund, 1979—93, chmn., 1986—88; cmty. rels. advisor Stanford U., 1986—2003; mem. Friends of Rewley House, Oxford U., 2001—. Mem.: Soc. Mfg. Engrs., Joint Venture: Silicon Valley (bd. dirs. 1992—95), Assn. MBA Execs., Assn. Iron and Steel Engrs. (life), Inst. Indsl. Engrs. (sr.; v.p. profl. rels. Peninsula chpt. 1988—90, bd. dirs. 1988—, del. to Silicon Valley Engring. Coun. 1991—97), Oxford Alumni Assn., Stanford U. Alumni Assn. (life), Palo Alto C. of C. (bd. dirs. 1975—79, v.p. orgn. affairs 1976—77, pres. 1977—78), Ohio State U. Alumni Assn., Pepperdine U. Alumni Assn., U. San Francisco Alumni Assn., Stanford Diamond Club. Office: 345 Stanford Shopping Ctr #144 Palo Alto CA 94304-1412

SEEWALDT, VICTORIA L., medical educator, researcher; b. Jackson Heights, NY, Jan. 9, 1959; d. Alfred and Elizabeth Seewaldt; m. Eric Carl Dietze, Aug. 25, 1993; 1 child, Erin Rebecca Seewaldt-Dietze. BA, Cornell U., Ithaca, NY, 1980; MD, U.Calif., Davis, 1989. Assoc. prof. Duke U. Sch. of Medicine, Durham, NC, 2000—. Dir. breast cancer rsch. Duke U. Sch. of Medicine, Durham, 2002—06. Cons. Susan G. Komen, Dallas, 2000—06. Recipient 3 basic/translational R01 rsch. awards, NIH, 2001—. Democrat. Mem. Soc. Of Friends. Achievements include research in early events in breast cancer. Avocation: gardening. Office: Duke Univ Sch Medicine Box 2628 Rm 221A MSRB Research Drive Durham NC 27710 Office Phone: 919-668-3051. Office Fax: 919-668-2458. Business E-Mail: seewa001@mc.duke.edu.

SEFERIAN, EDWARD G., medical educator; BS, Tufts U., Medford, Mass., 1980—84; MD, Ind. U., Indpls., 1988—92; MS, U. Chgo., 1998—2000. Diplomate Am. Bd. Internal Medicine, 1996, Am. Bd. Pediat., 2004. Chem. engr. W.R. Grace & Co., Lexington, Mass., 1985—88; resident in internal medicine, pediat. U. Chgo. Med. Ctr., Chgo., 1992—96, pediat. critical care fellow, 1996; clin. asst. prof. pediat. Ind. U. Sch. Medicine, Indpls., 1999—2002; asst. prof. pediat. Mayo Med. Sch., Rochester, Minn., 2002—. Mem.: Am. Acad. Pediat., Acad. Health Svcs. Rsch., Am. Thoracic Soc., Soc. Critical Care Medicine. Office: Mayo Clinic 200 First St SW Rochester MN 55905 Business E-Mail: seferian.edward@mayo.edu.

SEFF, JAMES M., lawyer; b. NYC, Jan. 27, 1941; AB with honors, U. Mich., 1963; JD, U. Calif., 1966. Bar: Hawaii 1969, Calif. 1970, US Dist. Ct. (no., ctrl. dist Calif., Hawaii), US Supreme Ct. Mem. Pillsbury Winthrop Shaw Pittman LLP, San Francisco, ptnr., chmn. Wine Beer & Spirits practice, co-chair restaurant, food & beverage group. Lectr. Univ. Calif., Davis; co-chmn. CLE Internat. Seminar on Wine Beer & Spirits Law; mem. adv. com. Columbia Univ. Legis. Drafting Rsch. Fund. Author (contributing): Univ. Calif. / Sotheby Book of California Wine; contbr. articles to profl. jours. Dir. Carmel Bach Festival; counsel Soc. Medical Friends of Wine; dir. Lasallian Edn. Fund; past v.p. Jewish Family & Children's Svc., San Francisco. Capt. USNR. Recipient Disting. Cmty. Svc. award, Jewish Family & Children's Svc. of San Francisco. Fellow: Am. Bar Found.; mem.: ABA (past chmn. alcoholic beverage practice com.), Barristers Club San Francisco (past pres.), San Francisco Bar Found. (past pres.), State Bar Calif. (past v.p., gov., vice chmn. conf. del.), Bar Assn. San Francisco (past pres., Award of Merit), Assn. Internationale des Juristes pour le Droit de la Vigne et du Vin, Am. Soc. Enology & Viticulture. Office: Pillsbury Winthrop Shaw Pittman 50 Fremont St San Francisco CA 94105 Office Phone: 415-983-7441. Office Fax: 415-983-1200. Business E-Mail: james.seff@pillsburylaw.com.

SEFF, KARL, zeolite chemist, chemistry educator; b. Chgo., Jan. 23, 1938; s. Joseph and Rose (Hauser) S. BS, U. Calif., Berkeley, 1959; PhD, MIT, 1964. Asst. rsch. chemist UCLA, 1965—67; asst. prof. chemistry U. Hawaii, Honolulu, 1968—73, assoc. prof. chemistry, 1973—75, prof. chemistry, 1975—2006, emeritus prof. chemistry, 2007—. Cons. Filtrol Corp., L.A., 1966-73, Mitsubishi Heavy Industry, Nagasaki, Japan, 1992-94; vis. scholar Princeton (N.J.) U., 1974-75, Oxford (Eng.) U., 1988, 89, Pusan and Kyungpook Nat. Univs., Korea, 1996; assoc. rschr. U. Mex, 1981-82; vis. prof. U. Leuven, Belgium, 1975, Dartmouth U., 1989; lectr. Tokyo Inst. Tech., 1980, 91, Los Alamos Nat. Lab., 1985, U. Bristol, 1988, ETH, Zurich, Switzerland, 1988, Goethe U., Frankfurt, Germany, 1988, Imperial Coll., London, 1989, Cambridge U., 1989, Kyungpook Nat. U., Korea, 1990, Acad. Sci. Leningrad, 1990, Pusan Nat. U., Korea, 1990, Northwestern U., 1994, others; assoc. chair chemistry dept. U. Hawaii, 2000, chair, 2000-03. Contbr. numerous articles to profl. jours. NATO sr. fellow, NSF, 1975, Rsch. Travel award, 1988-90; grantee Army Rsch. Office, 1969-72, NIH, 1972-75, 75-78, NSF, 1973-76, 75, 77, 78-81, Petroleum Rsch. Fund, 1974-76, 95-98, Gordon Conf., 1976, U.S.-Korea Coop. Rsch., NSF, 1982, 84-86, Mitsubishi Industries, 1992-93. Mem. Am. Chem. Soc. (local sect. pres., award 1983, councilor 1992-94, 2005—), Am. Crystallographic Assn., Vegetarian Soc. Hawaii (exec. com. 1993—), Internat. Zeolite Assn., Sigma Xi. Democrat. Avocations: travel, gardening, cacti. Office: U Hawaii Dept Chemistry 2545 The Mall Honolulu HI 96822-2275 Business E-Mail: seff@hawaii.edu.

SEFF, RICHARD, actor, writer; b. NYC, Sept. 23, 1927; s. Chester and Henrietta (Levy) Siff. BA, NYU, 1947. Agt. MCA, Inc., NYC, 1954-62; sec., treas. Hesseltine, Bookman & Seff, NYC, 1962-69; v.p. Creative Mgmt. Assn., NYC, 1969-74. Staff writer Theater Week Magazine, N.Y.C, 1988—. Author: (musical book) Shine!, 2001; (plays) Paris Is Out, 1969-70, The Whole Ninth Floor starring Alan Alda, 1966; appeared on Broadway in Darkness At Noon, 1950-52, Herzl, 1976, The Seagull, 1982, End of the World, 1984, Musical Comedy Murders of 1940, 1987; off-Broadway in Modigliani, 1979-80, Childe Byron, 1981, Richard II, 1982, Angels Fall, 1984, Only You, 1987, Summer and Smoke, 1988, Established Price, 1990, Countess Mitzi, 1991, Lend Me a Tenor, 1991, The Cocktail Hour, 1992, The Truth Teller, 1995, The Countess, 1999-2000; appeared in films The Onion Field, 1979, Being There, 1979, Where The Buffalo Roam, 1980, A Stranger is Watching, 1982, Quiz Show, 1994, The Hours, 2002. Recipient Carbonell award for best featured actor in play Angels Fall, Carbonell (Fla.) Com., 1984. Avocations: financial planning, theatrical investment, travel.

SEFFRIN, JOHN REESE, health science association administrator, educator; b. Hagerstown, Ind., May 19, 1944; s. Theodore H. and Mary Ellen (Reese) Seffrin; m. Carole Sue Washburn, Apr. 16, 1966; 1 child, Mary. BS in Edn., Ball State U., Muncie, Ind., 1966, DSc (hon.), 1994; MS, U. Ill., Champaign-Urbana, 1967; PhD in Health Edn., Purdue U., West Lafayette, 1970, D (hon.) in Social Sci., 2003. Asst. prof. health edn. Purdue U., West Lafayette, Ind., 1970—76, assoc. prof., 1976—79; prof., chmn. dept. applied health sci. Ind. U., Bloomington, 1979—92; CEO Am. Cancer Soc., Atlanta, 1992—. Trustee Am. Cancer Soc. Found., 1992—; guest lectr. various pub. health orgns. and schs., 1970—; bd. dirs. Healthcare Inc.; mem. subcom. on cessation Dept. HHS, Washington, 2002—03; charter mem., mem. steering com. C-Change (formerly Nat. Dialog on Cancer), 1999. Nat. bd. dirs. Am. Lung Assn., 1980—90; treas. Partnership for Prevention of Premature Death, Disease and Disability, 1991—; mem. Pres.'s Commn. on Improving Econ. Opportunity in Cmtys. Dependent on Tobacco Prodn. While Protecting Pub. Health, 2000—01; trustee Ctr. for Advancement of Health; pres. State Welfare Bd. Ind. Dept. Pub. Welfare, 1979—80, 1982—84; treas. Midwest Nuc. Bd., 1973—75; chmn. cmty. edn. com. Am. Lung Assn., 1981—83, v.p., 1980, pres., 1982; bd. dirs. Nat. Ctr. Tobacco-Free Kids, 1997—2000; chmn. bd. dirs. Nat. Health Coun., 1998—2000; bd. advisors Discovery Health Media, 2000—; bd. dirs. Wabash Ctr. for the Mentally Retarded, 1970—73. Named Commr.-at-large, Nat. Commn. Health Edn. Credentialing, 1995—2000, Sagamore of Wabash, State of Ind., 1980, 1988; recipient Cert. appreciation, Surgeon Gen. Pub. Health Svc., 1992, Outstanding Alumnus award, Ball State U., 1982. Fellow: Am. Sch. Health Assn. (mem. governing coun. 1979—81, 1982—89, pres. 1987—88, Howe award 1991); mem.: NAS (Nat. Cancer Policy Bd. 1997—2002), AMA, Am. Acad. Family Physicians (pub. adv. bd. 1999—), Rsch. Am. (bd. dirs. 1996—), Independent Sector (bd. dirs. 1997—2006), Nat. Interagy. Coun. on Smoking and Health (bd. dirs. 1979—), Internat. Union Against Cancer (ex-officio mem. US nat. com. 2000—, pres. 2002—06), Ind. Assn. for Health, Phys. Edn. and Recreation (pres. 1976, Cert. of Appreciation 1977, Honor award 1982), Am. Cancer Soc. (dir. Ind. Divsn. 1977—90, chmn. Ind. Divsn. 1982—85, dir.-at-large to nat. bd. dirs., chmn. nat. pub. edn. com. 1984—87, nat. v.p. 1986—87, chmn. nat. bd. dirs. 1989—91), Ind. Thoracic Soc. (mem. governing coun. 1977—84), Ind. Family Health Coun. (dir. 1979—81, v.p. 1980—81, pres. 1981), Ind. Assn. Health Educators (pres. 1975—76, chair 1997—2000), Assn. for Advancement Health Edn. (bd. dirs. 1989—92), Nat. Assn. State Bds. of Edn. (commn. on sch. cmty. role in improving adolescent health 1989—90), Eta Sigma Gamma, Phi Delta Kappa. Roman Catholic. Office: Am Cancer Soc 250 Williams St Atlanta GA 30303

SEGA, A. CHRISTOPHER, lawyer; b. Frankfurt, Germany, Oct. 12, 1954; AB, Dartmouth Coll., 1976; MBA, George Washington Univ., 1981; JD with cert. in Comparative & Internat. Law, Catholic Univ. Am., 1991. Bar: Md. 1991, DC 1992, US Tax Ct. 1993. Ptnr., Trusts & Estates, Taxation practices Venable LLP, Washington. Adj. prof. Catholic Univ. Am., 1993—95, Georgetown Univ., 2004—. Contbr. articles to profl. jours. Named a Top Washington Lawyer, Washingtonian Mag., 2004. Fellow: Am. Coll. Trust & Estate Counsel; mem.: ABA (vice chmn. com. fiduciary income tax, chmn. subcom. grantor trusts), DC Bar Assn. Office: Venable LLP 575 7th St NW Washington DC 20004 also: Venable LLP 5th Fl 1 Church St Rockville MD 20850 Office Phone: 202-344-8565, 301-217-5658. Office Fax: 202-344-8300. Business E-Mail: acsega@venable.com.

SEGA, RONALD MICHAEL, civilian military employee, former dean; b. Cleve., Dec. 4, 1952; m. Bonnie Dunbar. BS in Math. and Physics, USAF Acad., 1974; MS in Physics, Ohio State U., 1975; grad., Squadron Officers Sch., 1979; PhD in Elec. Engring., U. Colo., 1982; grad., Air Command and Staff Coll., 1985, Air War Coll., 1991; Ph.D (hon.), Clarkson U., 1993; grad. Mgmt. Inst., Harvard U., 1997; Ph.D (hon.), Bridgewater State Coll., 1998; exec. program in global security, Harvard U., 2001. Commd. 2d lt. USAF, 1974, advanced through grades to maj. gen., 2001, ret., 2005, instr. pilot Williams AFB, Ariz., 1976—79; mem. faculty USAF Acad., 1979—82, asst. prof., 1982—85, assoc. prof., 1985—90, tech. dir. Lasers & Aerospace Mechanics Directorate, Frank J. Seiler Rsch. Lab, 1987—88; astronaut Space Shuttle Discovery, 1990; dir. ops. Gagarin Cosmonaut Training Ctr. NASA, Russia, 1994—95; payload comdr. 3d Shuttle/Mir docking mission Atlantis, 1996; dean Coll. Engring. & Applied Sci. U. Colo., Colorado Springs, 1996—2001; dir. def., rsch. & engring. US Dept Def., Washington, 2001—05, under sec. Dept. Air Force, 2005—. Contbr. articles to tech. publs. Decorated Legion of Merit, Def. Meritorious Svc. medal, Meritorious Svc. medal with oak leaf cluster; named a Air Force rsch. fellow, Air Force Office Sci. Acad., 1980; named to, Ohio Vets. Hall of Fame, 1994; recipient Outstanding Leadership medal, NASA, 1997. Fellow: AIAA (assoc. Achievement award 1996), Inst. for Advancement of Engring.; mem.: IEEE (sr.), Aerospace Edn. Found. (trustee 2000). Office: USAF 1670 Air Force Pentagon Rm 4E886 Washington DC 20330

SEGAL, BERNARD LOUIS, cardiologist, educator; b. Montreal, Feb. 13, 1929; came to U.S., 1961, naturalized, 1966; s. Irving and Fay (Schecter) S.; m. Idajane Fischman, Feb. 17, 1963; 1 dau., Jody Segal Reinbold. BSc cum laude, McGill U., 1950, postgrad., 1950-51, MD, C.M. high standing, 1955. Diplomate Am. Bd. Internal Medicine. Intern Jewish Gen Hosp., Montreal, 1955-56; resident Balt. City Hosp., 1956-57, Beth Israel Hosp., Boston, 1957-58, Georgetown Med. Ctr., Washington, 1958-59, St. George's Hosp., London, 1959-61; pvt. practice internal medicine and cardiology Phila., 1961—; prof. medicine Med. Coll. Pa., Hahnemann U., 1996—; prof. medicine, sr. attending physician Jefferson Med. Coll./Thomas Jefferson U., 1998—. Dir. cardiology Thomas Jefferson U., 1998. Author: Auscultation of the Heart, 1965; Editor: Theory and Practice of Auscultation, 1964, Engineering in the Practice of Medicine, 1966, Your Heart, 1972, Arteriosclerosis and Coronary Heart Disease, 1972; mem. editl. bd. Am. Jour. Cardiology, 1970—, Clin. Echocardiography, 1978; contbr. articles to profl. jour. Fellow ACP, Am. Coll. Cardiology (chmn. scholar-trainee com., trustee 1969-71), Am. Coll. Chest Physicians; mem. NY Acad. Sci., Alpha Omega Alpha. Home: 1156 Red Rose Ln Villanova PA 19085-2121 Office: Jefferson Heart Inst 925 Chestnut St Mezzanine Philadelphia PA 19107-4824 also: 401 E City Line Ave Ste 525 Bala Cynwyd PA 19004-1125 Office Phone: 215-955-8145.

SEGAL, DANIEL ALAN, anthropologist, educator; b. NYC, Aug. 22, 1958; s. Norman and Bernice Segal; m. Laurie Shrage, June 9, 1985; children: Hannah, Nathan Shrage. BA, Cornell U., Ithaca, NY, 1980; PhD, U. Chgo., 1989. Jean M. Pitzer prof. anthropology and hist. studies Pitzer Coll., Claremont, Calif., 1986—. Author: (book) Jane Austen And the FIction of Culture; editor: Cultural Anthropology, 1995—2000; contbr. articles to profl. jours. Fellow: Ctr. Advanced Study Behavioral Scis.; mem.: Am. Hist. Assn. (Gilbert award 2001). Office: Pitzer Coll 1050 N Mills Claremont CA 91711 Office Phone: 909-621-8000. Business E-Mail: dsegal@pitzer.edu.

SEGAL, JACK, mathematics professor; b. Phila., May 9, 1934; s. Morris and Rose (Novin) S.; m. Arlene Stern, Dec. 18, 1955; children: Gregory, Sharon. BS, U. Miami, 1955, MS, 1957; PhD, U. Ga., 1960. Instr. math. U. Wash., Seattle, 1960-61, asst. prof., 1961-65, assoc. prof., 1965-70, prof., 1970-1999, prof. emeritus, 2000—, chmn. dept., 1975-78. Author: Lecture Notes in Mathematics, 1978, Shape Theory, 1982. NSF postdoctoral fellow Inst. Advanced Study, Princeton, N.J., 1963-64; Fulbright fellow U. Zagreb, Croatia, 1969-70, U. Coll. London hon. rsch. fellow, 1988; NAS exch. prof. U. Zagreb, 1979-80. Mem. Am. Math. Soc. Home: 8711 25th Pl NE Seattle WA 98115-3416 Office: U Washington Dept Mathematics Seattle WA 98195-0001 Home Phone: 206-522-4208; Office Phone: 206-543-1914. E-mail: segal@math.washington.edu.

SEGAL, JEFFREY L., gynecologist, obstetrician, researcher; b. Phila., Dec. 26, 1970; s. Sydney L. and Beverly H. Segal; m. Kazne Hiki, Oct. 12, 2003; 1 child, Matthew T. BS in Econs. cum laude, U. Pa., Phila., 1993; MD, Jefferson Med. Coll., Phila., 1997. Clin. instr. dept. ob-gyn. Wright State U. Sch. Medicine, Dayton, Ohio, 2001—04; asst. clin. instr. dept. ob-gyn. and reproductive svcs. Mt. Sinai Sch. Medicine, NYC, 2004—; dir. Ctr. Urogynecology, St. Barnabas Med. Ctr., Livingston, NJ, 2004—. Mem. staff Clara Maass Med. Ctr., Belleville, NJ, 2005—, Newark Beth Israel Med. Ctr., 2005—; lectr. in field. Contbr. articles to profl. jours., chpts. to books. Mem. alumni secondary sch. com. network U. Pa., 2001—03; cert. mohel Merit Milah Program, 2002—. Recipient Ferring Acad. award for outstanding grand rounds presentation; grantee, Johnson & Johnson Consume & Personal Products Worldwide, 2006—. Avocations: tennis, bicycling, hiking, travel. Office: Ctr Urogynecology St Barnabas Med Ctr 94 Old Short Hills Rd Livingston NJ 07039

SEGAL, LORE, writer; b. Vienna, Mar. 8, 1928; came to US, 1951, naturalized, 1956; d. Ignatz and Franzi (Stern) Groszmann; m. David I. Segal, Nov. 3, 1960 (dec.); children: Beatrice Ann, Jacob Paul. BA in English, Bedford Coll., U. London, Eng., 1948. Prof. writing div. Sch. Arts, Columbia U., also Princeton U., Sarah Lawrence Coll., Bennington Coll.; prof. English U. Ill., Chgo., 1978-92, Ohio State U., 1992-97. Author: Other People's Houses, 1964, (children's book) Tell Me A Mitzi, 1970, All the Way Home, 1973, Lucinella, 1976, Tell Me a Trudy, 1977, The Story of Mrs. Brubeck and How She Looked for Trouble and Where She Found Him, 1981, Her First American, 1985, The Story of Mrs. Lovewright and Purrless Her Cat, 1985, Morris the Artist, 2003, Why Mole Shouted and Other Stories, 2004, More Mole Stories and Little Gopher Too, 2005, Shakespeare's Kitchen, 2007; translator: (with W.D. Snodgrass) Gallows Songs, 1968, The Juniper Tree and Other Tales from Grimm, 1973, The Book of Adam to Moses, 1987, The Story of King Saul and King David, 1991; contbr. short stories, articles to N.Y. Times Book Rev., Partisan Rev., New Republic, The New Yorker, others5 Guggenheim fellow, 1965-66; Council Arts and Humanities grantee, 1968-69; Artists Public Service grantee, 1970-71; CAPS grantee, 1975; Nat. Endowment Arts grantee, spring 1982, 1987; NEH grantee, 1983; Acad. Arts and Letters award, 1986. Fellow: Acad. Arts & Scis. Address: 280 Riverside Dr New York NY 10025-9010 Office Phone: 212-663-1524. E-mail: Lore@usa.net.

SEGAL, MARTIN ELI, retired actuarial and consulting company executive; b. Vitebsk, Russia, Aug. 15, 1916; came to U.S., 1921, naturalized, 1928; s. Isidor and Anna (Title) S.; m. Edith Levy, June 17, 1937; children: Susan Segal Rai, Paul. LHD (hon.), Pratt Inst., 1976; MusD (hon.), Mannes Coll. Music, 1976; LHD (hon.), Grad. Ctr. CUNY, 1979, L.I. U., 1986, NYU, 1988, The Julliard Sch., 2006; D in Music (hon.), Manhattan Sch. Music, 1999. Various positions ins. industry, 1935-39; founder The Segal Co., consultants and actuaries, NYC, 1939, pres., CEO, 1939-67, chmn. bd., 1967-91, cons., 1991—. Pres. Wertheim Asset Mgmt. Svcs., Inc., N.Y.C., 1972-75, chmn., bd., 1975-82; ptnr. Wertheim & Co., investment bankers, N.Y.C., 1967-82. Former columnist: Associated Press. Founding chmn. NY Internat. Festival of the Arts, Inc., 1985-02; chmn. bd. Lincoln Ctr. Performing Arts, Inc., 1981-86, chmn. emeritus, 1986—; gen. chmn. Night of 100 Stars (first ever AIDS Benefit), Actors' Fund Am., 1985; organizing co-chmn. Internat. Conf. on Future of Arts Edn., 1999; bd. dirs., founding mem. Pub. Radio Internat., 1981-94, dir. emeritus, 1994-98; counselor at large, 1998—; co-chmn. Conf. on Intellectual Property The Arts and Tech., 1994; chmn. arts and culture com., NY92, NY93, NY94, NY95; nat. bd. dirs. Nat. Urban League, 1961-70, chmn. First Equal Opportunity Day Dinner, 1961, v.p. 1967-70; bd. dirs. Nat. Bldg. Mus., 1983-91; founding mem., bd. advisers Libr. of Am., 1984—, sole hon. mem. bd. dirs., 2005—; trustee Am.-Scandinavian Found., 1986-91, adv. trustee, 1991—; bd. visitors Grad. Sch. and Univ. Ctr., CUNY, 1983-96; bd. trustees Grad. Ctr. Found., Inc., 1996—, vice chmn. bd. trustees, 2003—; bd. dirs. ASCAP Found., 1997-03, S.L.E. Lupus Found., 2000—; adv. com. arts Harvard, 1993-99, coun. mem., 1999—; bd. trustees, chmn. exhbns. com. Mus. Modern Art, 1978-81; trustee Inst. for Advanced Study, Princeton, NJ, 1972-91, trustee emeritus, 1991—; bd. dirs. City Ctr. Music and Drama, 1971-74, trustee NY City Ctr., 1974—; founder, pres. Cultural Assistance Ctr., Inc., 1974-82, chmn., 1982-84, hon. chmn., 1984—; founding pres. Film Soc. of Lincoln Ctr., 1968-78, pres. emeritus, 1978—; adv. com. Tony voter Am. Theater Wing, 2000—; adv. coun. Theatre Devel. Fund, 1992—, Town Hall Found., 1986-; nat. bd. Young Audiences, Inc., 1979—; adv. bd. Concert Artists Guild, 1983-00; founding mem. publs. com. The Pub. Interest, 1965-2002; vis. com. Harvard U. Sch. Pub. Health, 1979-92, dean's coun. Sch. Pub. Health, 1990-2006; adv. bd. Studio in a Sch. Assn., 1988—; bd. dirs. Helena Rubinstein Found., 1972-95; chmn. Mayor's Com. on Cultural Policy, 1974; founding chmn. Commn. for Cultural Affairs City of NY, 1975-77; chmn. pub. svc. awards com. Fund for City of NY, 1978-79, bd. dirs., 1978-87; co-chair China cultural exch. mission, Ctr. US-China Arts Exchange, 1979; bd. dirs. Bd. Hosps. City NY, 1962-70, NY City Health and Hosps. Corp., chmn. fin. com., exec. com. mem., 1970-72; founder Film Guild N.Y., 1940-41. Decorated Royal Swedish Order of Polar Star; named comdr. Order Arts and Letters, Ministry Culture French Govt., 2005; recipient Spl. award, Internat. Film Importers and Distbrs. Am., 1973, Cert. of Merit, Mcpl. Art Soc., 1974, award for Svc. to Music, Third Street Music Sch. Settlement, 1981, award of Honor for Arts and Culture, N.Y.C. Mayor, 1982, Ann. award of Distinction, Mus. City of N.Y., 1982, Concert Artists Guild award, 1983, Edn. Fund award, LWV of NYC, 1984, Disting. Am. Fgn. Birth award, Internat. Ctr. NYC, 1985, John H. Finley medal, Alumni Assn. CCNY, 1985, Annual Arts Leadership award, Alumni and Friends of LaGuardia H.S., 1985, Friend of the Arts award, Town Hall, 1987, Dirs. Emeriti award, Lincoln Ctr. for Performing Arts, Inc., 1987, Patron of the Arts award, Songwriters Hall of Fame, 1988, NY State Gov.'s Arts award, 1989, Presdl. Citation award, Nat. Fedn. Music Clubs, 1989, Pub. Spirit award, Creative Arts Rehab. Ctr., 1989, Pres.'s award, Grad. Sch. and Univ. Ctr. of City Univ. of N.Y., 1990, Honor medal, Nat. Arts Club, 1992, Laureate award, Lincoln Ctr., 1997, Our Town Treasure award, Mus. City of N.Y., 1998, Civic Leadership award, Citizens Union of City of N.Y., 1998, award of Honor, Arts Roundtable, 1998, CUNY Graduate Ctr., Martin E. Segal Theatre Ctr., 2000, Acting Co. Joan Warburg Humanitarian award, 2001, S.L.E. Lupus Found. award, 2001, Honoree, Am.-Scandinavian Found., 2004, Alliance for Arts, 2004, Chamber Music Soc. Lincoln Ctr., 2005, Living Landmark Honoree, NY Landmarks Conservancy, 2005. Mem.: The Pilgrims of the U.S., Century Assn. Democrat. Jewish. Office: 375 Park Ave Ste 2602 New York NY 10152-2699

SEGAL, MINDY, chef; Grad., Kendall Coll. Pastry asst. Ambria, Chgo.; pastry chef Metropolis 1800, Chgo., Charlie Trotter's, Chgo., Gordon, Chgo., Spago, Chgo., Marche, Chgo., MK the Restaurant, Chgo.; owner, exec. pastry chef Hotchocolate, Chgo., 2005—. Developed dessert menus Mia Francesca, Harvest on Huron, Thyme. Named Best Pastry Chef in Chgo., Chgo. Mag., 2005, Rising Star Pastry Chef, StarChefs.com, 2005. Office: Hotchocolate 1747 N Damen Ave Chicago IL 60647 Office Phone: 773-489-1747. Office Fax: 773-489-1777. *

SEGAL, PHYLLIS NICHAMOFF, mediator; b. Apr. 18, 1945; d. Sidney and Theresa Helen (Uroff) Nichamoff; m. Eli J. Segal, June 13, 1965; children: Jonathan, Mora. Student, Brandeis U., 1962-65; BA, U. Mich., 1966; JD, Georgetown U., 1973. Bar: N.Y. 1974, U.S. Dist. Ct. (so. and ea. dists.) N.Y. 1975, Mass. 1983, U.S. Supreme Ct. 1979. Deputy atty. gen. Commonwealth Mass., 1986—88; assoc. Weil, Gotshal and Manges, NYC,

1973-77; legal dir. NOW Legal Def. and Edn. Fund., NYC, 1977-82, gen. counsel, 1986—94; mediator ADR Assoc., L.L.C., Boston, 2001—. Chmn. Fed. Labor Rels. Auth., Washington, 1994-2000; gen. counsel Exec. office Transp. and Constrn., Commonwealth of Mass., 1984-86; adj. asst. prof. law NYU, 1980-82; fellow Bunting Inst. Radcliffe Coll., 1982-83; cons. U.S. Commn. Civil Rights. Contbr. articles to profl. jours. Mem. Commn. on Party Reform Nat. Dem. Party, 1972-73, mem. Compliance Rev. Commn., 1974-76; mem. adv. bd. Mass. Commn. Against Discrimination, 1983—; bd. chmn. Handgun Control Inc./Ctr. to Prevent Handgun Violence; former chairwoman Nat. Labor Rels. Authority. Mem. ABA, Fedn. Women Lawyers Jud. Screening Panel, Mass. Bar Assn.

SEGAL, ROBERT MARTIN, lawyer; b. Atlantic City, Apr. 7, 1935; s. Nathan Albert and Edna (Dutkin) S.; m. Rhoda Sue Luber, June 8, 1958; children: Deborah Ann, William Nathan, Elizabeth Ann Student, Cornell U., 1953-54; BS in Econs., U. Pa., 1957; LLB cum laude, Harvard Law Sch., 1960. Bar: Pa. 1961. Assoc. Wolf, Block, Schorr & Solis-Cohen LLP, Phila., 1960-69, ptnr., 1969—2007, sr. counsel, 2007—, chmn., exec. com., 1978-79, 82-83, 86-87, 89-98. Hon. pres. Jewish Employment and Vocat. Svc.; bd. dirs. Orleans Homebuilders, Inc. Contbr. articles to profl. jours. and mags. Constable of elections Lower Merion Twp., Pa., 1970-72; bd. dirs. Jewish Family and Children's Agy., Am. Jewish Com., Feinstein Ctr. for Am. Jewish History at Temple U., Greater Phila. Urban Affairs Coalition; bd. govs. Rep. Jewish Coalition; past trustee Hahnemann U., Fedn. Jewish Agys., Phila. Rehab. Plan, Inc., Rosenbach Mus. and Libr. Mem. ABA, Pa. Bar Assn., Phila. Bar Assn., Internat. Coun. Shopping Ctrs., Urban Land Inst. (assoc.), Am. Coll. Real Estate Lawyers, Phila. Bar Found. (trustee 1981-87), Am. Law Inst., Harvard Law Sch. Assn. Phila., Federalist Soc., Wharton Club, Chaine des Rotisseurs, Societe Mondiale du Vin, Anglers Club of Absecon Island, Sunday Breakfast Club, La Coquille Club, Harvard Club, Beta Gamma Sigma. Avocations: golf, swimming. Office: Wolf Block Schorr & Solis-Cohen LLP 1650 Arch St Fl 22 Philadelphia PA 19103-2097 Office Phone: 215-977-2230. Personal E-mail: rsegal@wolfblock.com.

SEGAL, SHELDON JEROME, biologist, educator, foundation administrator; b. NYC, Mar. 15, 1926; s. Morris M. and Florence (Bogen) S.; m. Harriet Ellen Feinberg, May 22, 1961; children: Amy Robin, Jennifer Ann, Laura Jane. BA, Dartmouth Coll., 1947; postgrad., U. Geneva, 1947-48; MS, U. Iowa, 1951, PhD, 1952; MD (hon.), U. Tampere, Finland, 1984, U. Upssala, Sweden, 1985; LHD (hon.), Mercy Coll. Rsch. scientist William S. Merrill Co., Cin., 1952-53; rsch. assoc., asst. prof. U. Iowa, 1953-56; asst. med. dir. Population Coun., NYC, 1956-63, med. dir., 1963-78, v.p., 1969-76, sr. v.p., 1976-78; affiliate Rockefeller U., NYC, 1956-76, adj. prof., 1977-87; dir. population scis. Rockefeller Found., 1978-91; disting. scientist Population Coun., NYC, 1991—. Lectr. Columbia U., 1959-61; vis. prof. All-India Inst. Med. Scis., New Delhi, 1962-63, Amir Chand lectr., 1975; mem. Marine Biol. Lab, Woods Hole, Mass.; cons. World Bank, WHO, NIH, Ford Found., Indian Govt., UN Office Sci. and Tech., UN Fund Population Activities; mem. com. on contraceptive tech. NAS, 1977-80, com. on health effects of marijuana Inst. Medicine, 1981-82, NAS com. on demographic impact of contraceptive tech., 1988-89, nat. rsch. con., overview com. for Indo-U.S. sci. initiative, 1985-89; adv. com. on human reproduction FDA; cons. to dir. Nat. Inst. Child Health and Human Devel., 1978-80; plenary lectr. 3d World Congress Endocrinology, 1968, Upjohn lectr. Am. Fertility Soc., 1971, plenary lectr. World Fertility Congress, 1975, Sigma Xi lectr. U. Idaho, 1976, plenary lectr. World Congress on Ob-Gyn., 1976, lectr. Chinese Acad. Scis., 1977, Carl Gemzell lectr. U. Upssala, 1982, Pierre Soupart lectr. Axel Munthe Found., 1988, Alpha Omega Alpha lectr. U. Pa. Coll. Medicine, 1989, plenary lectr. World Congress on Human Reproduction, 1990, 2005; hon. prof. Peking Union Med. Coll., Beijing, 1987, Chinese Acad. Scis., 1988; trustee Marine Biol. Lab., 1985—, chmn. bd. trustees, 1991-2004; pres. 10th World Congress on Human Reproduction, 1999, 2004. Co-editor 8 books; author 3 books; contbr. 300 articles to profl. jours. Trustee Rye Country Day Sch., 1979-85, pres. bd. trustees, 1981-85; trustee Ctr. for Reproductive Law and Policy, 1992—. Lt. (j.g.) USNR, 1943-45. Decorated Order Comdr. of Lion (Finland); recipient Honor award Innsbruck U., Austria, hon. citation Pres. of India, 1978, Clarence J. Gamble award World Acad. Arts and Scis., 1980, Joseph C. Wilson award Rochester Assn. for UN, 1981, UN Population award, 1984, Axel Munthe award in medicine Axel Munthe Found., Italy, 1985, Sci. award Planned Parenthood Fedn. Am., 1990, Dmitirus N. Chorafas award in medicine Swiss Acad. Scis., 1995, Joseph Bolivar DeLee Humanitarian award, U. Chgo. Hosps., 2007. Fellow AAAS, Royal Coll. Obstetricians and Gynecologists (hon.); mem. Am. Reproductive Med. Soc. (hon. v.p. 1975-76, trustee found. 1975-77), Endocrine Soc., Internat. Soc. for Study Reprodn. (pres. 1968-72), Coun. Fgn. Rels., Internat. Acad. Human Reproduction (hon. pres. 2005), Mexican Acad. Medicine (hon.), Inst. Medicine, Dartmouth Club N.Y., Woods Hole Yacht Club. Home: 525 E 72nd St New York NY 10021 Office: Population Coun One Dag Hammarskjold Plz New York NY 10017 E-mail: ssegal@popcouncil.org.

SEGAL, STEVEN E., retired lawyer; b. Norfolk, Va., May 19, 1941; AB, Coll. William & Mary, 1963; MBA, U. Miami, 1965; JD, U. Houston, 1971. Bar: Tex. 1971. Mem. Fulbright & Jaworski L.L.P., Houston, 1971—2001; ret., 2001. Mem. State Bar Tex., Houston Bar Assn., Phi Delta Phi, Omicron Delta Kappa Office: Fulbright & Jaworski LLP 1301 Mckinney St Ste 5100 Houston TX 77010-3031 Office Phone: 713-651-5554. Business E-Mail: ssegal@fulbright.com.

SEGAL, THEODORE D., lawyer; b. Washington, Aug. 7, 1955; BA magna cum laude, Duke U., 1977; JD magna cum laude, Georgetown U., 1984. Bar: Md. 1985, DC 1986. Law clk. Chief Judge William C. Pryor, DC Ct. Appeals, 1984—86; ptnr. DLA Piper, Washington. Mem.: ABA, Am. Health Lawyers Assn. Office: DLA Piper 1200 19th St NW Washington DC 20036-2412 Office Phone: 202-861-3838. Office Fax: 202-223-2085. Business E-Mail: theodore.segal@dlapiper.com.

SEGALL, JAMES ARNOLD, lawyer; b. Columbus, Ohio, Aug. 19, 1956; s. Arthur and Greta Helene (Cohen) S.; m. Janice Faye Wiesen, Mar. 14, 1981; children: Gayle Helene, Aryn Michelle, Craig Lawrence. BA, Coll. of William and Mary, 1978; JD, Washington and Lee U., 1981. Bar: Va. 1981, U.S. Dist. Ct. (ea. dist.) Va. 1981. Assoc. Phelps & King P.C., Newport News, Va., 1981-84, Buxton & Lasris P.C., Yorktown, Va., 1984-85; sole practice Newport News, 1985-89; pres. James A. Segall & Assocs., 1990-91, James A. Segall & Assocs., P.C., 1991-92, Segall & Moody, Newport News, 1992-98; ptnr. Krinick, Segall, Moody & Lewis, Newport News, Va., 1998—2004, Krinick & Segall, 2004—. Lectr. Hampton Roads Regional Acad. Criminal Justice, 1986-89. Bd. dirs. ct.-apptd. Spl. Adv. Program, Newport News, 1986-87, Hamton-Newport News Cmty. Svcs. Bd., 1993-2002, treas., 1995-96, 99-2002, vice-chair, 1996-97, chair 1997-99; participant coop. office edn. program Newport News Pub. Schs., 1987-90; lectr. vol. programs 7th Dist. Ct. Svc. Unit, 1986-89; active City Newport News Cable TV Adv. Commn., 1990-93, Newport News Dem. City Com., 1990-91; bd. dirs. Rodef Sholom Temple, 1992-94, United Jewish Cmty., Va. Peninsula, Inc., 1990—, chmn. spl. activities and fundraising com., 1990-91, chmn. bylaws com., 1992-93, 95-2006, campaign coun., 1995—, cmty. rels. coun., 1995-98, v.p. human svcs., 1998-2000, v.p. fin. and adminstrn., 2002-04, pres. elect, 2004-06, pres. 2006—; Sunday sch. tchr. Rodef Sholom Temple, 2001—04. Mem. Newport News Bar Assn., Va. Trial Lawyers Assn., Va. Assn. Criminal Def. Lawyers, B'nai B'rith (pres. 1989-91), Ruritan (sec. 1985-87). Avocations: computers, history, philosophy. Home: 306 Dogwood Dr Newport News VA 23606-3728 Office: Krinick & Segall 11848 Rock Landing Dr Ste 103 Newport News VA 23606-4427 Home Phone: 757-595-1078; Office Phone: 757-596-1700. E-mail: jsegall@peninsulalaw.com.

SEGALL, PAUL, geologist, educator; BA/MS in Earth Scis., Case Western Reserve U., 1976; PhD in Geology, Stanford U., Calif., 1981. Geologist US Geol. Survey, 1981—83, project chief mechanics of faulting and fracturing, 1983—93; assoc. prof. rsch. Stanford U., Calif., 1989—93, assoc. prof., 1993—98, prof., 1998—. Consulting prof. Stanford U., Calif., 1987—89, assoc. chair geophysics dept., 2003—04; vis. assoc. prof. U. Grenoble, France, 1991; sci. adv. team Long Valley caldera US Geol. Survey, 1994—; vis. prof. Inst. Earth Physics, Paris, 2000; mem. Calif. Earthquake Prediction Evaluation Coun., 2002—; mem. sci. earthquake adv. com. Dept. Interior, 2002—06. Contbr. articles to sci. jours. Fellow: Am. Geophys. Union (pres. tectonophysics sect. 2003—04, J.B. Macelwane medal 1990), Geol. Soc. Am. Office: Stanford U Dept Geophysics Mitchell Bldg 397 Panama Mall Stanford CA 94305-2215 E-mail: segall@pangea.stanford.edu.

SEGALL, ROBERT D., lawyer; b. Chgo., 1946; BA, Vanderbilt U., Nashville, 1968; JD summa cum laude, U. Ala., Tuscaloosa, 1971; LLM, Harvard U., Cambridge. Law clerk Hon. Frank M. Johnson Jr., 1971—72; shareholder Copeland, Franco, Screws & Gill PA, Montgomery, Ala. Mem.: ABA, Am. Coll. Trial Lawyers, Ala. Bar Assn. (pres.-elect 2004—05, pres. 2005—06), U.S. Supreme Ct., 1975, U.S. Ct. of Appeals 11th Cir., U.S. Ct. of Appeals 5th Cir., 1974, U.S. Dist. Ct. Middle Dist. Ala., 1972, Am. Bd. Trial Advocates, Ala. Bd. of Bar Commrs., Montgomery Bar Assn. (pres. 1989), Ala. Law Found. (life). Office: Copeland Franco Screws & Gill PA PO Box 347 Montgomery AL 36101-0347 Office Phone: 334-834-1180. Business E-Mail: segall@copelandfranco.com.

SEGALL, WYNN H., lawyer; b. Phila. AB cum laude, U. Pa., 1983; JD, U. Chgo., 1989; MPhil, Oxford U., 1985. Bar: NY 1990, DC 1991, US Ct. Internat. Trade, US Ct. Appeals, Fed. Cir. Polit. risk analyst Middle East; ptnr. internat. trade Akin Gump Strauss Hauer & Feld LLP, Washington, DC. Contbr. articles to profl. jours. Thouron scholar, 1985. Mem.: ABA (mem. internat. sec.), NY State Bar Assn., DC Bar Assn. Office: Akin Gump Strauss Hauer & Feld LLP Robert S Strauss Bldg 1333 New Hampshire Ave NW Washington DC 20036-4288 Office Phone: 202-887-4573. Office Fax: 202-877-4288. E-mail: wsegall@akingump.com.

SEGALLA, THOMAS FRANCIS, lawyer; b. Lee, Mass., Apr. 7, 1943; s. Stanley John and Ann (Finnegan) S.; m. Mary Louise, Aug. 5, 1967. BBA, U. Miami, Coral Gables, Fla., 1965; JD cum laude, SUNY-Buffalo, 1972. Bar: N.Y. 1973, U.S. Dist. Ct. (we.dist.) N.Y. 1973, U.S. Supreme Ct. 1983. Prodn. mgr. UniRoyal Inc., Naugatuck, Conn., 1966-69; law asst. N.Y. Atty. Gen., Buffalo, 1971; ptnr. Spearance & Day, PC, Buffalo, 1972-2001, Goldberg Segalla, Buffalo, 2001—. Lectr. Erie C.C., Buffalo, 1970-73, Bryant & Stratton Inst., Buffalo, 1975; assoc. prof. SUNY, 1985-90. Editor SUNY Buffalo Law Rev., 1971-72. Mem. ABA, Def. Rsch. Inst., Erie County Bar Assn., Fed. Def. and Corp. Counsel, Internat. Assn. Def. Counsel, Kappa Sigma (pres. Miami 1964-65). Roman Catholic. Home: 25 Westfield Rd Buffalo NY 14226-3492 Office: Goldberg Segalla 665 Main St Ste 400 Buffalo NY 14203 Office Phone: 716-566-5480. Business E-Mail: tsegalla@goldbergsegalla.com.

SEGARS, KELLY SCOTT, SR., physician, banker; b. Red Bay, Ala., Mar. 11, 1930; s. Dock and Ora (Sims) S.; m. Martha Ann Thompson, oct. 3, 1952; children: kelly Scott, Jr., Mark Thompson, Leigh Ann. BS in Pharmacy, Auburn U., 1952; MD, U. Miss.-Jackson, 1959. Diplomate Am. Bd. Fam. Practice. Intern USPHS Hosp., Norfolk, Va., 1959-60; physician Segars Clinic, Iuka, Miss., 1960—. Founder. pres., chmn. First Am. Nat. Bank, Iuka, 1964—; pres. Segars Communications, Iuka, 1970—, S & G Cablevision, Iuka, 1978—; pres. Tri-State Savs. & Loan, 1963-64; chief med. staff Tishomingo County Hosp., Iuka, 1968, 76, 82, dir. coronary care unit, 1970—; chmn. constrn. com. Kelly Segars Field, 1964, Iuka Mcpl. Library, 1971. Exec. coun. Boy Scouts Am., Tupelo, Miss., 1971—. 1st lt. U.S. Army, 1953-55. Decorated Army Commendation medal. Fellow Am. Acad. Family Physicians; mem. AMA, Miss. Med. Assn., Flying Physicians assn., Ole Miss Med. Alumni, Rotary (paul Harris Fellowship). Republican. Methodist. Address: Segars Clinic 1507 W Quitman St Iuka MS 38852-1132 Home Phone: 662-423-3741; Office Phone: 662-423-3656. Personal E-mail: ksegars@fanb.net.

SEGEL, KAREN LYNN JOSEPH, lawyer, tax specialist; b. Youngstown, Ohio, Jan. 15, 1947; d. Samuel Dennis and Helen Anita Joseph; m. Alvin Gerald Segel, June 9, 1968 (div. Sept. 1976); 1 child, Adam James. BA in Soviet and East European Studies, Boston U., 1968; JD, Southwestern U., LA, 1975. Bar: Calif., 1996, US Tax Ct., 1996, US Dist. Ct. (ctrl. dist.) Calif., 1996, US Ct. Appeals (9th cir.), 1997. Adminstrv. asst. Olds Bruel & Co., NYC, 1968-69, US Banknote Corp., NYC, 1969-70; tax acct. S.N. Chilkov & Co. CPA's, Beverly Hills, Calif., 1971-74; intern Calif. Corps. Commr., 1975; tax. sr. Oppenheim Appel & Dixon CPA's, LA, 1978, Fox, Westheimer & Co. CPA's, LA, 1978, Zebrak, Levine & Mepos CPA's, LA, 1979; ind. cons. acctg., taxation specialist Beverly Hills, 1980—. Settlement officer LA County Superior Ct., 2000—; law student mentor Southwestern U., 1996—2007; tax moot ct. judge, 1997. High sch. amb. to Europe People-to-People Orgn., 1963. Mem. Calif. State Bar, Women's Inner Circle of Achievement, So. Calif. Bus. Litig. Inns of Ct., LA County Bar Assn, Beverly Hills Tinseltown Rose Soc. Avocations: collecting seashells, art, travel, music. Personal E-mail: kjslaw@earthlink.net.

SEGELHORST, CINDY MARIE, pre-school educator; b. St. Louis, Oct. 2, 1957; d. Bernard Anthony and Marjorie Ann Engler; children: April Christine Brooks, Kenneth Andrew. BS in Edn., U. Mo., St. Louis, 1994; MA, Lindenwood U., 1998. Cert. early childhood edn. Dept. Elem. and Secondary Edn., Mo., 1994, elem. edn. Dept. Elem. and Secondary Edn., Mo., 1994, middle sch. social studies Dept. Elem. and Secondary Edn., Mo., 1994, early childhood spl. edn. Dept. Elem. and Secondary Edn., Mo., 1998, trainer work sampling sys. assessment. Early childhood educator Francis Howell Sch. Dist., St. Charles, Mo., 1995—; adj. instr. St. Charles C.C., St. Peters, Mo., 2001—. Cooperating tchr. for student teachers Lindenwood U. and U. of Mo. at St. Louis, St. Charles, 1997—; chairperson for cmty. wellness fair Francis Howell Pub. Sch. Dist., St. Charles, 1998—; mentor for new educators Francis Howell Sch. Dist., St. Charles, 1998—, mem. mentor-mentee com., 2003—; contbg. mem. Pub. Sch. Kindergarten Transition Team, St. Charles, 2000—; adv. bd. mem. St. Charles C.C. Child Care and Early Childhood, St. Peters, 2001—; contbg writer for fine arts and math curriculum Francis Howell Sch. Dist., St. Charles, 2001—; adv. bd. mem. for pre-kindergarten math stds. Dept. Elem. and Secondary Edn., Jefferson City, Mo., 2001—; dist. rep. Francis Howell Sch. Dist. Profl. Devel. Com., St. Charles, 2002—; presenter Crucial Early Years Confs., 1998—, Young Years Confs., 1998—. Mem. Citizens for a Healthy Environment, St. Charles, 2001—; vol. Vacation Bible Sch., 2004, 2005. Named Tchr. of Yr., Walmart Stores, 1997—98, Tchr. of Week, St. Charles Jour., 2002; recipient Golden Apple for Early Childhood, St. Peters C. of C., 1996—97, Tchr. of Yr., Francis Howell Sch. Dist., 2004, Bldg. Tchr. of Yr., 2004. Mem.: Mo. C.C. Assn., Nat. Assn. Edn. Young Children (presenter Mo. conf.), Womens Small Group Study. Avocations: remodeling, reading, travel, tennis, gardening. Home: 1312 Presidents Landing Dr O Fallon MO 63366-8480 Office: Francis Howell Sch Dist 2555 Hackmann Rd Saint Charles MO 63303

SEGELMAN, ALVIN BURTON, pharmaceutical executive, educator, research scientist; b. Boston, Sept. 27, 1931; s. Joseph Theodore and Anna (Klein) Segelman; m. Florence Hannah Pettler, Apr. 27, 1972 (dec. Jan. 7, 1994); children: Lauren Beth, Sheera Toba. BS, Mass. Coll. Pharmacy, 1954, MS, 1967; PhD, U. Pitts., 1971. Registered pharmacist Mass., cert. nutritional specialist Am. Coll. Nutrition. Chief pharmacist Kenmore Pharmacy, Boston, 1954—61; pres. Bell Pharmacy, Somerville, Mass., 1961—67; instr. pharmacognosy and microbiology pharmacognosy dept. U. Pitts., 1967—71; asst. prof. pharmacognosy dept. Rutgers U., Piscataway, NJ, 1971—74, assoc. prof., chmn. pharmacognosy dept., 1974—90; v.p. R&D health scis. Nature's Sunshine Products, INc., Provo, Utah, 1990—2000; CEO Pharmacognosy Rsch. Inst., Orem, Utah, 2001—. Prin. investigator rsch. Rutgers Biomed. Rsch. Grants, New Brunswick, 1972—85, U.S. Pub. Health Svc. Grant, Washington, 1973; co-prin. investigator rsch. Am. Cancer Soc., Washington, 1987—88; expert med. cons. U.S. Congress Select Com. on Aging, Washington, 1981—83; vis. prof. Jagellonian U., Cracow, Poland, 1989, Patrice Lamumbe U., Moscow, 1999; cons. in field. Co-author: Antibiotics in Historical Perspective, 1981; contbr. articles to profl. jours.; sci. reviewer: various profl. and sci. jours. Mem. various coms. Acad. Pharm. Scis., Washington, 1976—89; mem. med. adv. com. Planned Parenthood Middlesex County, New Brunswick, NJ, 1979—90. Served to 2d lt. U.S. Army N.G., 1949—59. Avocations: small arms pistol competition, ethnopharmacognosy research and writing, mountain climbing. Home and Office: Pharmacognosy Rsch Inst 54 West 680 South Orem UT 84058 Office Phone: 801-226-2184. Personal E-mail: herbdoctoralvin@aol.com. E-mail: chattiecathe@aol.com.

SEGER, THOMAS M., lawyer; b. Cleve., Oct. 11, 1946; BA magna cu laude (hon.), Miami U., 1968; JD, Harvard U., 1972. Bar: Ohio 1972, US Ct. Appeals (1st cir.) 1972, US ct. Appeals (6th cir.) 1976, US Ct. Appeals (7th cir.) 1987. Law clk. to Hon. Ed McEntree US Ct. Appeals (1st cir.) Ohio, 1972-73; ptnr. Baker & Hostetler, Cleve. Editor-in-chief Baker Hostetler Labor Newsletter. Contbr. articles to profl. jour. Mem.: Cuyahoga County Bar Assn., The Am Ohio, Ohio Coun. Sch. Bd. lawyers. Office: Baker & Hostetler 3200 Nat City Ctr 1900 E 9th St Cleveland OH 44114-3475 Office Phone: 216-861-7413. Office Fax: 216-696-0740. Business E-Mail: tseger@bakerlaw.com.

SEGERSTEN, ROBERT HAGY, lawyer, investment banker; b. Boston, June 24, 1941; s. Wendell C. and Claire H. Segersten; m. Marie E. Makinen, Feb. 13, 1965; children: Amanda Beth, Vanessa Bryce. AB, Bates Coll., 1963; JD, Boston U., 1970. Bar: Mass. 1970. Assoc. Nessen & Csaplar, Boston, 1970-75; v.p. March Co., Boston, 1975-77; pres. March-Eton Corp., Concord, Mass., 1977-82; ptnr. Nessen, Goodwin & Segersten, Concord, 1977-82, Kane & Segersten, Dedham, Mass., 1983-85; pres. Woodbine Optical Corp., Boston, 1990—2006; pres., CEO Solos Endoscopy, Boston, 2006—. Officer, bd. dirs. Friends of Jimmy Fund, Boston. Served to lt. USN, 1963—67. Mem.: ACLU, Mass. Bar Assn. Democrat. Episcopalian. Home: 64 Folsom Ave Hyannis MA 02601-4823 Business E-Mail: rsegersten@solosendoscopy.com.

SEGERSTRALE, ULLICA CHRISTINA, social sciences educator, researcher; d. Curt Olof Segerstrale and Dagny Cecilia Flodin; m. Val Jason Martin, Dec. 6, 1991. MS in Sociology, U. Helsinki, Finland, 1973; MA in Comm., U. Pa., Phila., 1975; PhD, Harvard U., Cambridge Mass., 1983. Vis. asst. prof. Smith Coll., Northampton, Mass., 1984—86; prof. and acting chair Abo Akademi U., Finland, 1986—87; sr. rschr. Acad. of Finland, Helsinki, 1988—91; asst. prof. Ill. Inst. Tech., Chgo., 1988—93, assoc. prof., 1993—2000, chair dept. social sci., 2000—, prof. sociology, 2003—. Adv. bd. Ctr. for the Study of Ethics in the Professions, IIT, Chgo., 1989—; sr. fellow Ctr. on Nanotechnology and Soc., IIT, Chgo., 2005—; assoc. editor Sci. Studies, Helsinki, 1988—; mem. editl. bd. Social Epistemology, Pitts., 2002—, Jour. Biosci., Bangalore, India, 2002—05. Author: Defenders of the Truth: The Battle for Science in the Sociobiology Debate and Beyond, 2000, Nature's Oracle: An Intellectual Biographu of William D. Hamilton, 2007; editor: Nonverbal Communication: Where Nature Meets Culture, 2000, Beyond the Science Wars, 2000. Recipient Julia Beveridge award, Ill. Inst. Tech., 2006, Hon. Fgn. Mem., Finnish Soc. of Sciences and Letters, 2003; fellow, Salzburg Seminar in Am. Studies, 1974, Fulbright Program, 1974, Guggenheim Meml. Found., 2002—03, Am. Philos. Soc., 2002—03, Bellagio Residency, Rockefeller Found., 2003; grantee, Sloan Found., 2004. Mem.: AAAS, Am. Sociol. Assn., Soc. for the Social Studies of Sci., Sigma Xi. Achievements include research in underlying reasons for the sociobiology controversy. Avocations: travel, languages. Office: Ill Inst Tech 3301 S Dearborn Ste 116 Chicago IL 60616 Home Phone: 312-225-2610; Office Phone: 312-567-5128. Office Fax: 312-567-6821. Business E-Mail: segerstrale@iit.edu.

SEGGER, MARTIN JOSEPH, museum director, educator, art historian; b. Felixtowe, Eng., Nov. 22, 1946; s. Gerald Joseph and Lillian Joan (Barker-Emery) S.; m. Angele Cordonier, Oct. 4, 1968; children: Cara Michelle, Marie-Claire, Margaret Ellen. BA, U. Victoria, 1969, diploma in edn., 1970; MPhil, U. London, 1973. Prof. art history U. Victoria, BC, Canada, 1970—74; museologist Royal B.C. Mus., Victoria, 1974—77; dir. Maltwood Art Mus., prof. art history U. Victoria, 1977—, dir. cmty. rels., 2001—. Cons. Nat. Mus. Corp., Ottawa, 1977, UNESCO, O.E.A., Cairo, 1983; bd. dirs. Canadian Cultural Rsch. Network, Victoria Coll. Art, Can. Rsch. Alliance; bd. advisors Greater Victoria Econ. Devel. Commn.; pres. Pacific northwest chpt. Soc. Archtl. Historians, 2002— Author: exhbn. catalogue House Beautiful, 1975, Arts of the Forgotten Pioneers, 1971, Victoria: An Architectural History, 1979, (commendation Am. Assn. State and Local History 1980), This Old House, 1975, This Old Town, 1979, British Columbia Parliament Buildings, 1979, The Heritage of Canada, 1981, Samuel Maclure: In Search of Appropriate Form, 1986 (Hallmark award 1987, 98), (a guide) St. Andrew's Cathedral, 1990, The Development of Gordon Head Campus, 1988, An Introduction to Museum Studies, 1989, An Introduction to Heritage Conservation, 1990, Botswana Live, 1994, Exploring Victoria's Architecture, 1996; contbr., cons. British Columbia Encyclopedia, 2000, Victoria Modern, 2006. Mem. heritage policy rev. com. Govt. Can., 2001—; Canadian Decorative Arts Soc., 2001—; mem. cultural diversity experts com. Govt. Can., 2002—; v.p. Commonwealth Museums Assn., 2003—; bd. govs. Heritage Can. Found., 1979—83; chmn. City of Victoria Heritage Adv. Com., 1975—79; bd. dirs. Downtown Victoria Cmty. Alliance, Heritage Trust, 1977—86, B.C. Touring Coun., Sta. CFUV Radio, B.C. Govt. Ho. Found., Royal B.C. Mus., 1996—99; co-chair B.C. Arts Festival; mem. B.C. Heritage Adv. Bd., 1973—83; councillor City of Victoria, 1987—93; vice-chair Provincial Capital Commn., 1991—2001; pres. Assn. Vancouver Island Municipalities, 1993—94; chmn. B.C. Festival of the Arts, 1999; bd. dirs. Internat. Coun. Mus.-Can., 1999, Victoria Coll. Art, 2001—, Victoria Harbour Authority, 2002—, dir.; bd. chair Queenswood Soc., 2007—. Decorated knight Equestrian Order of Holy Sepulchre of Jerusalem; named Hon. Citizen, City of Victoria, 2000, Arts Citizen of Yr., 2001; recipient award, Heritage Can. Comm., 1976, Heritage Conservation award, Lt. Gov. B.C., 1989, Harley J. McKee award, Assn. Preservation Tech., 1994, Queen's Golden Jubilee medal. Fellow Royal Soc. Arts, Can. Mus. Assn. (counsellor 1975-77); mem. Internat. Coun. Mus. (chair internat. com. for tng. pers. 1995-98), Internat. Coun. Monuments and Sites (bd. dirs. 1980-82), Soc. Study Architecture Can. (bd. dirs. 1979-81), Can Mus. Dirs. Orgn., Commonwealth Assn. Museums (pres. 2005—), Union Club Victoria. Roman Catholic. Avocations: travel, motor mechanics, water color painting. Home Phone: 250-384-3694; Office Phone: 604-721-8298. Business E-Mail: msegger@uvic.ca.

SEGGERMAN, ANNE CRELLIN, foundation executive; b. Los Angeles, May 13, 1931; d. Curtis Vergil and Yvonne (LaGrave) Crellin; m. Harry G.A. Seggerman, Apr. 14, 1951; children: Patricia, Henry, Marianne, Yvonne, Suzanne, John. Studies with Albert Levesque, Paris, 1948-50; Student, Sch. Decorative Arts, Paris, 1950, Sch. of the Louvre, 1950, Albertus Magnus Coll., 1951; D.H.L. (hon.), Sacred Heart U., 1980. French tchr., Beverly Hills, Calif., 1958-60; translator World Affairs Council, Los Angeles, 1958-60; staff mem. West Side Sch. Gifted Children, Beverly Hills, 1958-60; pres. Huxley Inst. for Bio-Social Research, Fairfield, Conn., 1972—, 4th World Found. Interfaith Media Action, Fairfield, 1977—, Steiner Prodns., Fairfield, 1981—; founder The Com. for Guadalupe Research, Fairfield, 1982—. Bd. dirs. Anuk, Inc. Financer with Lee Edwards Kahn (documentaries) The Bronx Frontier, 1985. Co-founder Christian/Jewish Ctr. Understanding Sacred Heart U., Fairfield, Conn.; active Pres. Reagan's Health Task Force Resources Com. on Health Adv. Couns. of U.S. Dept. Health and Human Svcs.; mem. Pres.'s Com. Mental Retardation, 1981-86, Com. Housing Handicapped Families, 1989; mem. Nat. Coun. on Disability, 1992-95; bd. dirs. Easter Seal Rehab. Ctr., Fairfield, Internat. Coll. Applied Nutrition, World Health Med. Group, Cath. League for Religion and Civil Rights. Recipient Am. Assn. Sovereign Mil. Order of Malta, 1991, Cmdr. of Equestrian Order of Holy Sepulchre of Jerusalem, 1991. Mem. Nat. Health Fedn., The Inst. for Study of Human Knowledge, Am. Holistic Med. Inst., Internat. Acad. Preventive Medicine, Calif. Orthomolecular Soc., Am. Phys. Rsch., Fairfield County Organic Gardeners.

SEGLER, CHRISTOPHER PAIGE, surgeon, researcher; s. David Otis and Julia Cate Segler; m. Paige Elizabeth Clem, May 29, 2004. BA in English, U. Houston, 1996; DPM in podiatric medicine, Calif. Coll. Podiatric Medicine, 2003. Rsch. asst. U. Houston, Dept. Chemistry, 1994—97; hospice vol. Hospice at the Tex. Med. Ctr., Inpatient Unit, Houston, 1994—95; psychiat. tech. Sharpstown Gen. Hosp., Houston, 1995—97; psychiat. technician Harris County Psychiat. Ctr., Houston, 1997—98; med. illustrator Calif. Coll. Podiatric Medicine, Dept. Basic Scis., San Francisco, 2000—02; sr. editor Nat. Foot and Ankle Rev., Oakland, Calif., 2002—03; podiatric surg. resident Dept. Veterans Affairs Health Care Sys., Salt Lake City, 2003—; design prin., co-founder Orthovation, LLC, Houston, 2003—; pvt. practice Chattanooga, 2006—. Chief resident U. Utah/VAMC, 2005—06. Contbr. articles to profl. jours., chapters to books. Named 1st place, Outstanding Resident Rsch Abstract Competition, Am. Podiatric Med. Assn., 2006; recipient Excellence in Rsch. award, Calif. Coll. of Podiatric Med., 2003; grantee, Gilkey Meml. Fund, 2000. Mem.: Soc. for Exptl. Biology and Medicine, Am. Podiatric Med. Writers Assn., Utah Podiatric Med. Assn., Am. Podiatric Med. Assn., Am. Coll. Foot and Ankle Surgeons (assoc. 2nd pl. Sci. Rsch. Post Competition, Instnl. Category 2005, 3rd pl. Sci. Rsch. Post Competition, Instnl. Category 2006, others), Omicron Delta Kappa (life), Alpha Epsilon Delta (life), Sigma Tau Delta (life). Achievements include invention of Tarsal Joint Space Distractor, surgical instrument for use in foot and ankle surgery. Avocations: rock climbing, kayaking, writing, painting, running. Office: Ankle & Foot Ctr Chattanooga 5870 Highway 153 Hixson TN 37343 Home Phone: 423-822-7604; Office Phone: 423-877-8870. Home Fax: 801-486-7464. Personal E-mail: chris@orthovation.com. Business E-Mail: drsegler@anklecenter.com.

SEGLIN, JEFFREY L., columnist, educator; b. Plattsburgh, NY, Dec. 26, 1956; s. Lester L. and Beverly K. Seglin; m. Nancy L. Long, Jan. 18, 1986; children: Edward Coleman, Bethany Whitemyer. BA, Bethany Coll., 1978; cert., Radcliffe Pub. Course, Cambridge, Mass., 1978; MTS, Harvard Divinity Sch., 1981. Exec. editor Inc. Mag., Boston, 1989—98; asst. prof. Emerson Coll., Boston, 1999—, dir. grad. writing & pub. program, 2004—. Author: (NY Times Syndicated Column) The Right Thing, 1998—, (books) The Good, the Bad and Your Business, 2000, The Right Thing: Conscience, Profit, & Personal Responsibility in Today's Bus., 2003. Fellow, Ctr. for the Study of Values in Pub. Life at Harvard U., 1998-1999; Poynter Ethics fellow, Poynter Inst. for Media Studies, 2001. Office: Emerson Coll 120 Boylston St Boston MA 02116 also: NY Times Syndication Sales Corp 14th Fl 122 E 42nd St New York NY 10168 E-mail: jseglin@post.harvard.edu, rightthing@nytimes.com.

SEGLUND, BRUCE RICHARD, lawyer; b. Lansing, Mich., June 3, 1950; s. Richard Oswald and Josephine Ann (Kraus) S.; m. Connie Sue Roberts, June 19, 1970; children: Jennifer Lynne, Nicole Marie. BS, Mich. State U., 1973; JD, Thomas M. Cooley Law Sch., 1979. Bar: Mich. 1981, U.S. DIst. Ct. (ea. dist.) Mich. 1981. Assoc. Michael W. Reeds, P.C., Walled Lake, Mich., 1981-82; sole practice Walled Lake, 1982-85; ptnr. Mick and Seglund, Walled Lake, 1985-89, Connelly Groth & Seglund, Walled Lake, 1989—2007, Connelly, Groth, Elowsky, Kelley, Pawlak & Seglund, Walled Lake, 2007—. Mem. Mich. Bar Assn. (mem. character and fitness com. dist. J 1988-2000), Oakland County Bar Assn. (lectr. 1984), Mich. Jaycees (pres. Walled Lake 1982-83, execllence award 1982-83, pres. of yr. 1982-83), Walled Lake C. of C. (bd. dirs. scholarship fund 1985-88). Lodges: KC (adv. 1982-94). Roman Catholic. Home: 8618 Buffalo Dr Commerce Township MI 48382-3408 Office: Connelly Groth Elowsky Kelley Pawlak & Seglund 2410 S Commerce Rd Walled Lake MI 48390-2129 Home Phone: 248-363-4653; Office Phone: 248-624-4505. Business E-Mail: bseglund@ccgs-law.com.

SEGNER, EDMUND PETER, III, natural gas company executive; b. Dallas, Oct. 23, 1953; s. Edmund Peter Jr. and Martha Fairfax (Smith) S.; m. Kathryn Louise Daily, July 10, 1976; children: Peter Michael, Christian James. BSCE, Rice U., 1976; MA in Econs., U. Houston, 1980. CPA, Tex. Acct. Touche Ross & Co., Houston, 1976-78; asst. v.p. planning United Gas Pipe Line Co., Houston, 1978-86; asst. v.p. rsch. Drexel Burnham Lambert, NYC, 1986-88; v.p. pub. and investor rels. Enron Corp., Houston, 1988-90; sr. v.p. pub. and gov. rels., investor Enron Corp, Houston, 1990-92, exec. v.p., chief staff, 1992-98; vice-chmn., chief of staff Enron Oil & Gas Co., 1997-99; pres., chief of staff EOG Resources, Inc., 1999—2007, sr. exec., v.p., chief of staff, 2007—. Prof. civil engring. Rice U., Houston, 1982-84, 97—. Bd. dirs. Zool. Soc. Houston, 1992-95, Greater Houston Partnership for Ednl. Excellence, 1991-93,; treas. Tex. Nature Conservancy, 1992-99, vice-chmn., 1999-2001, chmn., 2001-03; chmn. Cmty. Ptnrs., 1993-95; trustee Houston Mus. Natural Sci., 1999-2004. Mem. Houston City Club, River Oaks Country Club, Briar Club, Lochinvar Golf Club, Coronado Club, Catamount Club. Office: EOG Resources Inc 333 Clay St Ste 4200 Houston TX 77002-4501

SEHILI, MAHMOUD, artist; b. Tunis, July 27, 1931; m. Gabriele Buth, Apr. 11, 1959; children: Thouraya, Lilia, Raouf. Student, Fine Arts Sch., Tunis; diploma supérieur des arts plastiques, Ecole des Beaux-Arts, Paris. Tchr. Inst. Technol. Art, Arch., Urbanisme, Tunis; dir. Irtissem Art Gallery, Tunis, 1977—. Recipient Golden medal, Cagnes sur Mer, 1st prize, Town of Tunis, 1963, others. Avocations: music, playing the luth, composition of arabic music, fishing. Home: 4 Rue Victor Hugo Carthage Tunisia Office Phone: 71-740-515, 00216-98-305-007.

SEHRING, ADOLF, artist, sculptor; came to the U.S., 1949; s. George Henry M. and Clair (Burstin) S.; married, 1992; children: Nina, Marc. Student, Acad. Fine Arts, Germany. Pres. A. Sehring Studio Inc., Orange, Va., 1970—, Am. Artist Portfolio Inc., Orange, 1987—. Lectr. in field. One man shows include Grand Palais, Paris, 1980, Bayley Mus., Va., 1983, Va. Mus., 1984, World Bank, Washington, 1985, Yokohama, Japan, 1989, Newport Beach, Calif., 1993, Palm Desert, Calif., 1994; commd. by the Vatican to paint the ofcl. portrait of Pope John Paul II, Hearst Castle, Calif., to sculpt Pocahontas bronze, Town of Gloucester, Va., bronze in collection of Pres. Bush; represented in permanent collections Chrysler Mus., Am. Embassy, Stockholm, Bayly Mus., Victoria and Albert Mus.; represented in 10 galleries; art is now available at art auctions on Carnival and Princess Cruise Lines worldwide.; www.adolfsehring.com. Recipient Stalin medal for art, Rias award, 1946. Avocations: antiques, gardening, birds. Home: 3 Mandershaw Ln Punta Gorda FL 33982-9617 E-mail: lsregina@msn.com.

SEHRING, HOPE HUTCHISON, library science educator; b. Akron, Ohio; d. Welsey Harold and Jane (Brown) Hutchison; m. Frederick Albert Sehring, July 15, 1978. BS, Slippery Rock U., Pa., 1968; MEd, U. Pitts., Pa., 1973, MLS, 1984; postgrad. studies, Seton Hill U., Greensburg, Pa., 2002. Cert. instrnl. media specialist. Reference libr.-intern Carnegie Mellon U., Pitts., 1981; libr. media specialist Gateway Sch. Dist., Monroeville, Pa., 1968—2003; dir. Jeannette Pub. Libr., 2006—. Mem. pub. rels. com. Westmoreland County Federated Libr. Sys.; assoc. Wal-Mart, Delmont, Pa., 2006. Contbr. articles to profl. jours. Active Pa. Citizens Better Librs., Friends of Monroeville Pub. Libr., Monessen Adv. Coun., Westmoreland Libr. Network; pub. rels. com. Westmoreland County Libr. Network. Recipient Gift of Time Tribute, Am. Family Inst., 1992, 1996; Henry Clay Frick Found. scholar, U. London, 1969, 1973. Mem.: Gateway Edn. Assn., Pa. State Edn. Assn., Sch. Librs. Assn. (treas. 1982—84), Pa. Libr. Assn., Rotary, Alpha Xi Delta. Avocation: culinary arts. Home: 265 Fenneltown Rd New Alexandria PA 15670 Personal E-mail: gg7495@yahoo.com. Business E-Mail: jeannettepl@hotmail.com.

SEIB, BILLIE MCGHEE RUSHING, nursing administrator, consultant; b. Brookport, Ill., Mar. 04; d. Frank and Ila (Paris) McGhee; m. Alfred Rushing, Jan. 2, 1958 (dec.); children: Lisa, Libbi; m. Bob Seib, Mar. 21, 1986 (dec. Mar. 17, 2006) Diploma, DePaul Sch. Nursing, St. Louis, 1947; postgrad. in oper. rm. nursing, Washington U., St. Louis, 1950; BS, U. St. Francis, Joliet, 2002. Cert. geriat. nurse; cert. legal nurse cons., 2005. Dir. oper. rm. Jennie Stuart Med. Ctr., Hopkinsville, Ky.; clin. mgr. oper. rm. Meml. Med. Ctr., Savannah, Ga.; mgr. oper. rm. Meth. Med. Ctr., Oak Ridge, Tenn.; coord. oper. rm. Parkwest Hosp., Knoxville, Tenn.; mem. oper. rm. pool Ft. Sanders Park West Hosp., Knoxville, 1992-93; geriat. supr. Briarcliff Health Care Ctr., Oak Ridge, Tenn., 1993-96, Windwood Health Care Ctr. (now Beverly Health & Rehab. Ctr.), Clinton, Tenn., 1996—, asst. dir. nursing, 1997—2001; pvt. duty Family Med. Leave, 2001—06; with PRN geriatric NSQ multiple facilities, 2007—. Cons. Washington, Fla., Ky., Nev.; mgr. Oak Ridge, Tenn., 1997—. Mem. Assn. Oper. Rm. Nurses (cert., bd. dirs., past pres. East Tenn. chpt.), Am. Gerontol. Nursing Assn. Office Phone: 865-254-5879. E-mail: BJ23P@bellsouth.net.

SEIBEL, CHARLES BURGESS, accountant, educator; b. Annapolis, Md., May 31, 1950; s. John Edward and Amelia Lucille (Tucker) Seibel; m. Teresa Mae McCauley, Sept. 15, 1979; children: Charles Laundle, Daniel Lee. AA in Fin. Acctg., Anne Arundel CC, Arnold, Md., 1975; BS in Acctg., Bowie State U., 1997. Asst. br. acct. Internat. Harvester Co., Tuxedo, Md., 1970—77; chief acct. Am. Gas Assn., Arlington, Va., 1977—84; sr. cost acct. Honeywell, Inc., Annapolis, 1984; accounts receivable supr., credit mgr. Mash's Inc., Landover, Md., 1985—86; comptr. Gateway Ford Tractor, Inc., Upper Marlboro, Md., 1986—87; pvt. practice acct. West River, Md., 1987—95; acct. Alcoholism Recovery, Inc., Crownsville, Md., 1995—99; substitue tchr. Anne Arundel County Pub. Schs., Annapolis, 1999—2002; tchr. Riverdale Bapt. Sch., Upper Marlboro, 2002—. Fellow: Lions (pres. 1988—89, 1989—90, Melvin Jones fellow 2004); mem.: Delta Mu Delta (sec. 1977). Democrat. Methodist. Avocations: golf, umpiring, hunting, farming, singing. Home: 4824 Sudley Rd West River MD 20778 Office: Riverdale Bapt Sch 1133 Largo Rd Upper Marlboro MD 20774 Personal E-mail: cbtmseibel@msn.com.

SEIBER, RICHARD ALLAN, retired minister; b. LA, Nov. 15, 1932; s. Edward Maurice and Dorothy Mildred (Ball) S.; m. Wilma Ellen Shook, Sept. 24, 1955; children: Bruce Wayne, Roger Kent, Dale Eugene, Michael Allan. BA in History, U. Puget Sound, 1958; MDiv, Garrett Bibl. Inst., 1960; grad., Air Command & Staff Coll., 1962, Air War Coll., 1970. Ordained elder United Meth. Ch., 1960. Enlisted USAF, 1950, advanced through grades to lt. col., ret., 1976, chaplain, 1960—76; student pastor Meth. Ch., Algona-Pacific, Wash., 1955—57, Sciota-Friendship, Ill., 1957—60; pastor United Meth. Ch., Spanaway, Wash., 1976—83, Epworth-LeSourd United Meth. Ch., Tacoma, 1983—97; ret. United Meth. Ch., Tacoma, 1997. Mem. editl. bd. Meth. History United Meth. Ch., Madison, NJ, 1982—86, mem. gen. conf. archives and history, 1980—88, mem. jurisdictional conf. archives and history, 1980—, pres. jurisdictional conf. archives and history, 1980—84; chmn. com. on chaplains Pacific N.W. Conf., 1977—88, archivist, 1978—2004. Editor: Memoirs of Puget Sound: David Blaine, 1978 (Wash. Gov.'s Writer's award), Methodist History Index: Oct. 1962-July 1982, 1984, Jour. Henry Bridgeman Brewer, 1839-48, 1986; contbr. Sprague, Lamont, Edwall, WA, 1881-1981, 1982; contbr. Religious Heritage of Washington State, 1988, Illustrated History of Methodism, 1999; co-editor: William Roberts: Circuit Riding Superintendent of the Oregon-California Mission Conference, 1847-1853, 2004. Mem. Tacoma Mayor's Task Force on Vets. Affairs, 1986-91; chmn. Ministry with Service People—Co-NeXion, Tillicum, Wash., 1976-79, 87-90; mem. Wesley Homes Corp., Des Moines, Wash., 1984—; v.p. exploring, exec. com. Mount Rainier Coun., Boy Scouts Am., 1976-81, v.p. rels., 1981-92, mem. nat. coun., rep. Pacific Harbors coun., 1999-2004. Recipient Silver Beaver award Boy Scouts Am., 1977, God and Svc. recognition award Boy Scouts Am., 1988, James E. West fellow, 1997, Ministry of Memory award, United Methodist Ch. Gen. Commn. on Archives and History, 2007. Mem.: SAR (life; chpt. pres. 1989—91), Hist. Soc. The United Meth. Ch. (charter), Air Force Hist. Found., Air War Coll. Alumni Assn. (life), Scouting Heritage Soc. (life; charter), Air Force Assn. (life; chpt. pres. 1980—84, state pres. 1994—98, Exceptional Svc. award 1999, 2005, Presdl. citation 2006), Nat. Eagle Scout Assn. (life), Mil. Officers' Assn. (life), Mil. Chaplains' Assn. (Puget Sound chpt. pres. 1985—93, 2002, chmn. Pacific NW Nat. Security Forum 2006—07, hon. vice comdr. We. Air Def. sector 2007), Sigma Chi. Avocations: stained glass, genealogy, clocks, early northwest church history, collecting royal doulton. Home: 5514 89th Avenue Ct W University Place WA 98467-1532 Home Phone: 253-564-3757; Office Phone: 253-564-3757. Personal E-mail: raseiber@nventure.com.

SEIBERG, NATHAN, physics professor; b. Israel, Sept. 22, 1956; married; two children. BSc with high distinction, Tel-Aviv U., 1977; PhD, Weizmann Inst. Sci., Israel, 1982. Sr. scientist Weizmann Inst., 1985-86, assoc. prof., 1986-89, prof., 1989-91, Rutgers U., 1989-90, prof. II, 1990-97; prof. Inst. Advanced Study, Princeton, NJ, 1997—. Vis. mem. Inst. for Advanced Study, 1994-95. With Israeli Def. Force, 1977-82. Recipient Israel Phys. Soc. prize, 1976, Mifal Hapais prize, 1979, Michael Landau prize, 1981, J.F. Kennedy prize, 1982, N.J. Pride award N.J. Monthly Mag., 1996, Bd. Trustees award Rutgers U. for Excellence in Rsch., 1996, Dannie Heineman prize Am. Inst. of Physics, 1998; named Racah lectr. Weizmann Inst. Sci., 1985, Oskar Klein lectr. and Oskar Klein medal, 1995, Disting. IFT lectr. U. Fla., 1996; Amos de-Shalit Found. scholar, 1976; John D. and Catherine T. MacArthur Found. fellow, 1996. Fellow: Am. Acad. Arts and Scis. Office: Inst for Advanced Study Sch Natural Sci Einstein Dr Princeton NJ 08540 Business E-Mail: seiberg@ias.edu.

SEIBERLING, JOHN FREDERICK, retired congressman, lawyer, educator; b. Akron, Ohio, Sept. 8, 1918; s. J. Frederick and Henrietta (Buckler) S.; m. Elizabeth Pope Behr, June 4, 1949; children: John B., David P., Stephen M. AB, Harvard U., 1941; LLB, Columbia U., 1949. Bar: NY 1950, Ohio 1955. Assoc. mem. firm Donovan, Leisure, Newton, Lumbard & Irvine, NYC, 1949-53; atty. Goodyear Tire & Rubber Co., Akron, 1954-71; mem. 92d-99th Congresses from 14th Ohio Dist.; mem. com. on judiciary, com. on interior and insular affairs, chmn. subcom. on public lands; vis. prof. law U. Akron, 1987, 90, dir. Ctr. for Peace Studies, 1991-96; ptnr. Goldman, Seiberling, Davis & Tsarnas, Akron, 1988-89. Served to maj. AUS, 1942-46. Mem. United Ch. of Christ. Home: 154 Tecumseh Ln Akron OH 44321-2753

SEIBERT, TROY J., lawyer; b. Mankato, Minn., June 11, 1972; m. Cara Seibert; 2 children. BA, U. Minn., Duluth, 1994; JD magna cum laude, William Mitchell Coll. Law, 1998. Bar: Minn. 1998. Ptnr. Zelle, Hofmann, Voelbel, Mason & Gette, L.L.P., Mpls. Named a Rising Star, Minn. Super Lawyers mag., 2006. Mem.: Minn. State Bar Assn., Hennepin County Bar Assn., ABA. Office: Zelle Hofmann Voelbel Mason & Gette LLP 500 Washington Ave South Ste 4000 Minneapolis MN 55415 Office Phone: 612-339-2020. E-mail: tseibert@zelle.com.

SEIBLE, FRIEDER, structural engineer, educator; b. Schwaebisch Gmuend, Germany, 1952; m. Betsy Seible; children: Michael, Daniel, Anika. Dipl. Ing. in civil engring., U. Stuttgart, Germany, 1976; MCE, U. Calgary, Alta., Can., 1978; PhD in civil engring., U. Calif., Berkeley, 1982. Registered profl. engr., 1985. Mem. faculty U. Calif.-San Diego, La Jolla, 1983—, founding chair dept. structural engring., 1995—2001, Eric and Johanna Reissner Prof. Applied Mechanics and Structural Engring., dir. Charles Lee Powell Structural Rsch. Laboratories, prof. Structural Engring., interim dean Irwin & Joan Jacobs Sch. Engring., 2002—03, dean, 2003—. Mem. seismic adv. bd. Calif. Dept. Transp. (Caltrans). Recipient Best paper award Can. Soc. Civil Engring., 1982, K.B. Woods award Transp. Rsch. Bd., 1983, 92, Presdl. Young Investigator award Pres. Reagan, 1986, Japanese Govt. Rsch. award for fgn. rsch. specialists Sci. and Tech. Agy., 1987, Outstanding Paper award N.Am. Masonry Conf. award, 1990, 93, Best Paper award Internat. Conf. on Short and Medium Span Bridges, 1990, Raymond C. Reese Rsch. prize ASCE, 1992, Outstanding Jour. Paper award Masonry Soc., 1993, Shiley Achievement award Chancellor's Assocs., 1994, Outstanding Concrete Project award Am. Concrete Inst., 1994, Orchid award for design of Scripps Crossing pedestrian bridge San Diego Cmty. Awareness Program, 1994, citation for Lighting Design, Internat. Assn. Lighting Designers, 1994, Alan H. Yorkdale award ASTM, 1994, Concrete Bridge award Portland Cement Assn., 1994, Moisseiff award ASCE, 1995, Charles Pankow award for innovation CERF, 1996, Best Paper award ASCE, 1997. Mem.: NAE. Achievements include being one of the world's foremost seismic structural engineers.

SEIBOLD, JAMES RICHARD, physician, educator; b. Washington, Apr. 5, 1950; s. Herman Rudolph and Clara Bond (Taylor) S.; m. Margaret Frances Bennett, Jan. 20, 1968; children: Jon Drew, Zachary Bennett. BS, La. State U., 1972; MD, SUNY, Stony Brook, 1975. Diplomate Am. Bd. Internal Medicine, Am. Bd. Rheumatology. Intern in medicine L.I. Jewish Hosp., New Hyde Park, NY, 1975-76, resident in medicine, 1976-78; fellow in rheumatology U. Pitts., 1978-80; asst. prof. medicine Robert Wood Johnson Med. Sch. U. Medicine and Dentistry N.J., New Brunswick, 1980-86, assoc. prof., 1986-92, prof., 1992—, chief rheumatology, 1986-91, dir. clin. rsch. ctr., 1989-95; prof., dir. scleroderma program U. Mich., Ann Arbor, 2004—. Mem. adv. bd. Ctr. for Advanced Biotech. and Medicine, Piscataway, N.J., 1989-95, dir. Scleroderma program 1995—; W.H. Conzen chair clin. pharmacology Schering-Plough Found., 1989; prof. internal medicine Scleroderma Program U. Mich., 2006, Marvin and Betty Danto rsch. prof., 2006—, dir. Author: (chpt.) Rheumatology, 1988, 91, 94, 95, 99, 2001, 03, 05; contbr. over 300 articles to profl. jours. Bd. dirs. Arthritis Found. Fellow ACP, Am. Coll. Rheumatology (regional coun. 1985), Scleroderma Clin. Trials Consortium (founder 1994, pres. 2004—). Mem. Soc. Of Friends. Home: 1622 Kriss Crossing Brighton MI 48114 Office: U Mich Health Sys 3918 Taubman Ctr 1500 E Medical Center Dr Ann Arbor MI 48109-0358 Office Phone: 734-736-3110. Business E-Mail: jseibold@umich.edu.

SEIDE, PAUL, civil engineering educator; b. NYC, July 22, 1926; s. Julius David and Sylvia (Eiler) S.; m. Joan Cecilia Matalka, Jan. 7, 1951; children: Richard Laurence, Wendy Jane Seide Kielsmeier. B.C.E., CCNY, 1946; M. Aero. Engring, U. Va., 1952; PhD, Stanford U., 1954. Aero. research scientist Nat. Adv. Commn. for Aeros., Langley AFB, Va., 1946-52; research asst. Stanford Calif. U., 1952-53; research engr. Northrop Aircraft Co., Hawthorne, Calif., 1953-55; head methods and theory sect. TRW Inc., Los Angeles, 1955-60; head methods and research sect. Aerospace Corp., El Segundo, Calif., 1960-65; prof. civil engring. U. So. Calif., LA, 1965-91, prof. emeritus, 1991—, assoc. chmn. dept. civil engring., 1971-73, 81-83; Albert Alberman vis. prof. Technion-Israel Inst. Tech., Haifa, 1975; vis. prof. U. Sydney, Australia, 1986, U. Canterbury, N.Z., 1986. Cons. Northrop Inc., 1972-77, Aerospace Corp., 1966-68, Rockwell Inc., El Segundo, 1982-85 Author: Small Elastic Deformations of Thin Shells, 1975; contbr. numerous articles to profl. jours. NSF fellow, 1964-65 Fellow (life) ASME, Am. Acad. Mechanics; mem. ASCE (life), Tau Beta Pi, Sigma Xi. Democrat. Jewish. Home: 300 Via Alcance Palos Verdes Estates CA 90274-1105

SEIDEL, ARTHUR HARRIS, lawyer; b. NYC, May 25, 1923; s. Philip and Pearl (Geller) S.; m. Raquel Eliovich, Aug. 21, 1949; children: Stephen A., Paul B., Mary Beth Sharp. BS, CCNY, 1942; A.M., U. Mich., 1943; JD with honors, George Washington U., 1949. Bar: DC149, Pa. 1956, NY 1957. Atty. patent dept. Gulf Oil Corp., Washington and Pitts., 1947-52; individual practice law, 1952-64; sr. ptnr. firm Seidel & Gonda, 1964-68, Seidel, Gonda & Goldhammer (P.C.), Phila., 1968-72, pres., 1972-84, Seidel, Gonda, Goldhammer & Abbott, P.C., Phila., 1984-88, Seidel, Gonda, Lavorgna & Monaco, Phila., 1988-2001; of counsel Drinker, Biddle & Reath, Phila., 2001—. Lectr. in Intellectual Property Temple U. Law Sch., 1973-86, Am. Law Inst. Editor: George Washington Law Rev, 1949; author: (with others) Trademark Practice, 2 vols, 1963, Monographs on Patent Law and Practice, 5th edit, 1993, Trademarks and Copyrights, 6th edit., 1992, Trade Secrets and Employment Agreements 3d edit, 1995; also articles. Mem. Adv. Com. for Restatement of Law of Unfair Competition. Mem. ABA, Am. Law Inst., Pa. Bar Assn., Phila. Bar Assn., Am. Intellectual Property Law Assn., Phila. Intellectual Property Law Assn., Order of Coif. Home: The Quadrangle C104 3300 Darby Rd Haverford PA 19041-1095 Office: Drinker Biddle & Reath LLP Ste 300 1000 Westlakes Dr Berwyn PA 19312-2409 Office Phone: 610-993-2218. Business E-Mail: arthur.seidel@dbr.com. *My entire professional career has been devoted to the question of innovation, patents for inventions, trademarks for new businesses and copyrights for new writings. I have seen the United States become the world's leader in technology and business.*

SEIDEL, FREDERICK LEWIS, poet; b. St. Louis, Feb. 19, 1936; s. Jerome Jay and Thelma (Cartun) S.; children: Felicity, Samuel. AB, Harvard U., 1957. Occasional lectr., Rutgers U., New Brunswick, 1964—; Paris editor, Paris Review, 1961, advisory editor, 1962. Author: (poetry) Final Solutions, 1963, Sunrise, 1979 (Lamont Poetry prize Acad. Am. Poets 1980, Am. Poetry Rev. prize 1980, Nat. Book Critics Circle award for poetry 1981), Men and Woman: New and Selected Poems, 1984, Poems 1959-1979, 1989, These Days, 1989, My Tokyo, 1993, Going Fast, 1998, The Cosmos Poems, 2000, Life on Earth, 2001, Area Code 212, 2002, The Cosmos Triology, 2003, Barbados, 2004, Ooga-Booga, 2006. Guggenheim Fellow, 1993; recipient Pen/Voelcker award for poetry, 2002, Poetry prize LA Time, 2006.

SEIDEL, GEORGE ELIAS, JR., zoology educator; b. Reading, Pa., July 13, 1943; s. George E. Sr. and Grace Esther (Heinly) S.; m. Sarah Beth Moore, May 28, 1970; 1 child, Andrew. BS, Pa. State U., 1965; MS,

Cornell U., 1968, PhD, 1970; postgrad., Harvard U. Med. Sch., Boston, 1970-71. Asst. prof. physiology Colo. State U., Ft. Collins, 1971-75, assoc. prof., 1975-83, prof., 1983-93, univ. disting. prof., 1993—. Vis. scientist Yale U., 1978-79, MIT, 1986-87; mem. bd. on agr. NRC. Co-editor: New Technologies in Animal Breeding, 1981; contbr. articles to profl. jours. Recipient Alexander Von Humboldt award, N.Y.C., 1983, Animal Breeding Research award Nat. Assn. Animal Breeders, Columbia, Mo., 1983, Clark award Colo. State U., 1982, Upjohn Physiology award, 1986; Gov's. award for Sci. and Tech., Colo., 1986. Mem. AAAS, NAS, Am. Dairy Sci. Assn., Am. Soc. Animal Sci. (Young Animal Scientist award 1983), Soc. for Study of Reprodn., Internat. Embryo Transfer Soc. (pres. 1979, disting. svc. award 2001). Home: 3101 Arrowhead Rd Laporte CO 80535-9374 Office: Colo State U Animal Repro Biotech Lab Fort Collins CO 80523-1683 Office Phone: 970-491-5287. Business E-Mail: gseidel@colostate.edu.

SEIDEL, JAMES P., manufacturing executive; s. Robert A. and Mary Ann Seidel; m. Deborah J. Aziz, Nov. 14, 1998; children: Allison J., Grace C. BS, U. Wis., LaCrosse, 1989. Regional fleet mgr. Bridgestone Corp., Nashville, 1991—2002; nat. sales mgr. Gt. Am. Tire & Auto, Denver, 2002; dir. sales Continental Tire N.Am., Charlotte, NC, 2003—05; v.p., COO Stamford Tires & Wheels, Inc., Charlotte, 2005—, also sec., dir. Avocations: bicycling, running, gardening, antique cars, cooking. Office: Stamford Tires & Wheels Inc 929 Jay St Charlotte NC 28208 Office Phone: 704-409-7300. Business E-Mail: jseidel@stamford-tires.com.

SEIDEL, JOAN BROUDE, securities dealer, investment advisor; b. Chgo., Aug. 16, 1933; d. Ned and Betty (Treiger) Broude; m. Arnold Seidel, Aug. 18, 1957; children: David, Craig. BA, UCLA, 1954; postgrad., N.Y. Inst. Fin. Registered prin., investment advisor Morton Seidel & Co. Inc., LA, 1970-74, v.p., 1974-93; pres., 1993—; also bd. dirs. Morton Seidel & Co. Inc., LA. Instr. UCLA Extension, 1979—84; bd. overseers Hebrew Union Coll. Treas. City of Beverly Hills, Calif., 1990-2001, chmn. rent adjustment bd., 1989-90, mem., 1983-89; investment com. YWCA of greater LA, 1987-2002, treas. 1992-95; bd. dirs. Discovery Fund for Eye Rsch., LA, 1987—, treas., 1999—; corp. bd. dirs. Queen's Care, 1999-2005, fin. com., 1999-2005, audit com., 2004-05; bd. dirs. LA Opera, 2002—; CFO Maple Couns. Ctr., 2002-04; bd. govs. Cedars Sinai Med. Ctr. Named Citizen of Yr. Beverly Hills C. of C., 1993. Fellow Assn. for Investment Mgmt. and Rsch., Israel Inst. Tech. (hon.); mem. Am. Technion Soc. (v.p. 1998-2002, pres. So. Calif. chpt. 2001-04, nat. bd. dirs. 2002—, internat. bd. 2003—, nat. pres. 2006—), Nat. Assn. Security Dealers (dist. bus. conduct com. 2S 1993-95, 98-2000, small firm adv. bd. 1998-2000, chair dist. 2 1999-2000), L.A. Soc. Fin. Analysts, Orgn. Women Execs., Rotary, Phi Sigma Alpha. Avocations: reading, travel. Office: Morton Seidel & Co Inc 8730 Wilshire Blvd Ste 530 Beverly Hills CA 90211-2792 Office Phone: 310-360-7541. Personal E-mail: seidel350@aol.com.

SEIDEL, ROBERT WAYNE, science historian, educator; b. Kansas City, Mo., June 9, 1945; s. Wayne Herman and Harriet Anita (Day) S.; m. Alison Publicover, Aug. 26, 1972 (div. 1989); 1 child, Mary Ruth; m. Christine Ruth Stack, July 1, 1993. BA, Westmar Coll., 1967; MA, U. Calif., Berkeley, 1968, PhD, 1978. Exhibit designer Lawrence Hall Sci., Berkeley, 1970-72; specialist Poland 4-city tour USIA, Warsaw, 1971-72; grad. rsch. and teaching asst. U. Calif., 1972-78; asst. prof. Tex. Tech U., Lubbock, 1978-83, dir. rsch. history of engring. program, 1979-83; rsch. historian U. Calif., Berkeley, 1980-82, Laser History Project, Albany, Calif., 1983-85; adminstr. Bradbury Sci. Mus., Los Alamos, N.Mex., 1985-90, overview project leader, 1990-92; sr. staff mem. Ctr. Nat. Security Studies, Los Alamos, N.Mex., 1992-94; dir. Charles Babbage Inst., U. Minn., Mpls., 1994-99; ERA Land Grant prof. History of Tech. U. Minn., Mpls., 1994-99, prof. chem. engring., 1999—. Author: Lawrence and His Laboratory: A History of the Lawrence Berkeley Laboratory, 1989, Los Alamos and the Making of the Atomic Bomb, 1995. Mem. N.Mex. Sci. Ctr. Commn., 1989-92; bd. dirs. The Bakken Mus., 1994-2004. Woodrow Wilson fellow, l967, U. Calif. Regent's fellow, l968, German Marshall Fund fellow, Grenoble, France, l975, Sr. fellow Dibner Inst., MIT, 2001; recipient Bicentennial Essay prize Nat. Sci. Tchrs. Assn., 1976. Mem. AAUP, History Sci. Soc., Soc. for History Tech. Democrat. Avocation: computer simulations. Home: 5625 Woodlawn Blvd Minneapolis MN 55417-2667 Office: 151 Amundson Hall/U Minn Minneapolis MN 55455 Home Phone: 612-722-7591; Office Phone: 612-624-8003. Business E-Mail: rws@tc.umn.edu.

SEIDEL, SELVYN, lawyer, educator; b. Long Branch, NJ, Nov. 6, 1942; s. Abraham and Anita (Stoller) S.; m. Deborah Lew, June 21, 1970; 1 child, Emily. BA, U. Chgo., 1964; JD, U. Calif., Berkeley, 1967; diploma in law, Oxford U., 1968. Bar: N.Y. 1970, D.C. Ct. Appeals 1982. Ptnr. Latham & Watkins, NYC, 1985—2006; chmn. and CEO Burford Advisors LLC. Adj. prof. Sch. Law, NYU, 1974-84; instr. Practicing Law Inst., 1980-81, 84. Contbr. articles to profl. jours. Bd. dirs. Citizen Scholarship Fund Am., 1995-2000. Mem. ABA, N.Y. County Bar Assn., N.Y.C. Bar Assn. (mem. fed. cts. com. 1982-85, internat. law com. 1989-92, 95-96, art law com. 1997-2000), Boalt Hall Alumni Assn. (bd. dirs. 1980-82). Home Phone: 646-522-6168. Business E-Mail: s.seidel@burfordadvisors.com.

SEIDELMANN, PAUL KENNETH, astronomer, educator; s. Paul Emil and Esther (Momberg) S.; m. Roberta Jane Buck, Aug. 27, 1960; children: Holly Marie Flippen, Alan David. BSEE, U. Cin., 1960, MS, 1962, PhD, 1968. Dir. US. Naval Obs., Washington, 1975—2000; rsch. prof. U. Va., Charlottesville, Va., 2000—. Vis. assoc. prof. U. Md., College Park, 1972-90, vis. prof., 1992-97; pres. Celestial Mechanics Inst., Washington, 1986—. Contbr. over 100 articles to profl. jours. Pres. Emmanuel Luth., Bethesda, Md., 1985-86, chmn. bldg. com., 1986-91. 1st lt. U.S. Army, 1963-65. Recipient Norman P. Hays award I.O.N., 1992; named Disting. Alumni, U. Cin. Engring. Coll., 1975; minor planet 3217 named Seidelmann in his honor. Fellow AAAS (co-recipient 2005 AAAS Internat. Scientific Cooperation award, 2006); mem. AIAA, Internat. Astron. Union (pres. com. 4 1988-91, pres. divsn. I 1997-00), Inst. Navigation (pres. 1979-80), Am. Astron. Assn. (pres. divsn. on dynamical astronomy). Luth. Achievements include co-discovery of Saturn Satellite XIV Calypso; design of star map, Einstein statue, Nat. Acad. Scis. Home: 129 Fontana Ct Charlottesville VA 22911-3531 Office Phone: 434-243-5567.

SEIDEN, HENRY (HANK SEIDEN), advertising executive; b. Bklyn., Sept. 6, 1928; s. Jack S. and Shirley (Berkowitz) S.; m. Helena Ruth Zaldin, Sept. 10, 1949; children: Laurie Ann, Matthew Ian. BA, Bklyn. Coll., 1949; MBA, CCNY, 1954. Trainee Ben Sackheim Advt. Agy., 1949-51; nat. promotion mgr. NY Post Corp., 1951-53; promotion mgr. Crowell-Collier Pub. Co., Inc., 1953-54; copy group head Batten, Barton, Durstine & Osborn, Inc., 1954-60; v.p., creative dir. Keyes, Madden & Jones, 1960-61; sr. v.p., assoc. creative dir. McCann-Marschalk, Inc., 1961-65, chmn. plans bd., 1964-65; creative dir., dir., prin. Hicks & Greist, Inc., NYC, 1965—, sr. v.p., 1965-74, exec. v.p., 1974-83, COO, 1983—, pres., 1986—; CEO Ketchum/Hicks & Greist Inc., 1987-89; chmn., CEO Ketchum Advt., 1989-91; exec. v.p. Ketchum Comm. Inc., also bd. dirs.; vice chmn. Jordan, McGrath, Case & Taylor, Inc., 1992—97; chmn., CEO The Seiden Group, Inc. Bd. dirs. Ketchum Internat. Inc.; guest lectr. Bernard M. Baruch Sch. Bus. and Pub. Adminstrn., CCNY, 1962—, Baruch Coll., 1969—, New Sch. Social Scis., 1968, 72-73, Sch. Visual Arts, 1979—, Lehman Coll., CCNY, 1980—, Ohio U., 1981, Newhouse Grad. Sch., Syracuse U., 1981, NYU, 1983; cons. pub. rels. and comm. to mayor City of New Rochelle, NY, 1959—; cons. mktg. dept. Ohio State U.; cons. to pres. NYC City Coun., 1972-73; cons. Postmaster Gen. US, 1972-74; comm. advisor to commr. NYC Police Dept., 1973—, hon. dept. commr., 1991—, spl. cons. to commr., 1992—; bd. advisors Stillman Sch. Bus., Seton Hall U., 2002; adv. circle, Columbia U., Health Sci. Divsn., 2003. Author: Advertising Pure and Simple, 1976, Advertising Pure and Simple: The New Edition, 1990; contbg. editor: Madison Ave. mag, 1966-, Advt. Age, Mag. Age; guest columnist: NY Times, 1972. Vice commr. Little League of New Rochelle; bd. dirs. Police Res. Assn. NYC, 1973—, pres. exec. com.; bd. dirs. Cancer Rsch. and Treatment Fund, Inc., pres., 1992—; bd. dirs. Am. Heart Assn., 2002, Transmedia Network, Inc.; bd. dirs., chmn. New York's Finest Found., 1975—, pres., 1996, chmn., 2002; bd. dirs., chmn., sr. v.p. Drug Enforcement Agy. Found., 1995—; advisors cir. Columbia Presbyn. Hosp., 2002; assoc. Marine Corps Univ. Found., 2004. Recipient award Four Freedoms Found., 1959, award Printers Ink, 1960, promotion award Editor and Pub., 1955, Am. TV Commls. Festival award, 1963-69, Effie award Am. Mktg. Assn., 1969, 70, award Art Dirs. Club NY, 1963-70, award Am. Inst. Graphic Arts, 1963, Starch award, 1969, spl. award graphic art lodge B'nai B'rith Greater NY, 1971, 87, award of highest honor FBI Nat. Acad., 1994, Commendation, 1995. Mem. NATAS, Am. Inst. Mgmt. (assoc.), Drug Enforcement Agts. Found. (sr. v.p. 1995), Advt. Club NY (exec. judge Andy awards, award 1963-65), Advt. Writers Assn. NY (Gold Key award for best newspaper and mag. advts. 1962-640, Copy Club (co-chmn. awards com., Gold Key award for best TV comml. 1969), Alpha Phi Omega. Home: 1056 5th Ave New York NY 10028-0112 Office: The Seiden Group 708 3rd Ave New York NY 10017-4201 Personal E-mail: hankruthseiden@aol.com. Business E-Mail: handseiden@theseidengroupadv.com. *Be yourself but don't take yourself too seriously.*

SEIDEN, STEVEN ARNOLD, executive search consultant; b. NYC, Feb. 18, 1936; s. Leon and Eleanor (Troy) S.; m. Katherine Cohen, June 8, 1965; children: Lisa Brooke, Hilary Anne. AB, Yale U., New Haven, Conn., 1958. Pres. Seiden Krieger Assocs., 1984—. Mem. NY Stock Exch. Regulatory Adv. Com., 1981-83, policy com. Am. Coun. for Capital Formation, 1982-87. Mem. adv. bd. Registered Rep. Mag., 1982-84. With US Army, 1961—62. Mem.: US C. of C. (small bus. coun. 1985—89), Internat. Assn. Corp. and Profl. Recruiters (editl. bd. 1993—95), NY Biotech. Assn., Turnaround Mgmt. Assn. (program co-chair NY chpt. 1991—92), NY Soc. Security Analysts, Securities Industry Assn. (bd. dirs. 1981—83), Assn. Corp. Growth (asst. v.p. 1987—88, bd. dirs.), Wall St. Tax Assn. (bd. dirs. 1981—83), Bond Club, Century Country Club. Republican. Office: Seiden Krieger Assocs 375 Park Ave New York NY 10152-0002 Business E-Mail: steven@seidenkrieger.com.

SEIDEN, STEVEN JAY, lawyer; b. NYC, June 21, 1960; s. Martin S. and Rita (Glazer) S.; m. Kathryn LaRussa, Sept. 30, 1984; children: Robert B., Daniel M., Michael J. BA, SUNY, Oneonta, 1981; JD, Hofstra U., 1984. Bar: NY 1985, US Dist. Ct. (ea. and so. dists.) NY 1985, US Supreme Ct. 1995, US Ct. Appeals (fed. cir.) 1995, US Ct. Fed. Claims 1995, US Ct. Appeals for the Armed Forces, 1995. Assoc. Shapiro, Baines,Saasto & Shainwald, Mineola, NY, 1984-88; ptnr. Seiden & Kaufman, Carle Place, NY, 1988-93, 95—, Seiden, Kaufman, & Bosek, Carle Place, 1993-95. Mem. ABA, NY State Bar Assn., NY State Trial Lawyers Assn., Assn. Trial Lawyers Am., Nassau County Bar Assn., LI Trial Lawyers Assn. (bd. dirs.), Civil Justice Found. (founding sponsor). Jewish. Office: Seiden & Kaufman 1 Old Country Rd Ste 114 Carle Place NY 11514-1821 Office Phone: 516-747-2433.

SEIDENBERG, IVAN G., telecommunications industry executive; b. NYC, Dec. 10, 1946; s. Howard and Kitty (Zaretsky) S.; m. Phyllis A. Maisel, Dec. 13, 1969; children: Douglas, Lisa. BS in Math., CUNY, 1972; MBA in Mktg. Mgmt., Pace U., 1980. Various engring. positions NY Tel., 1966-74; dist. mgr. transmission design AT&T, Basking Ridge, NJ, 1974-76, dist. mgr. tech. planning, 1976-78, div. mgr. fed. regulatory NYC, 1978-81, asst. v.p. mktg., 1981-83; v.p. fed. relations Nynex Corp., Washington, 1983-86, v.p. external affairs, pres., vice chmn., chmn., CEO, 1995-98, Bell Atlantic Corp, NYC, 1999-2000; pres., co-CEO Verizon Comm., Inc. (formerly Bell Atlantic Corp.), NYC, 2000—02; pres, CEO Verizon Comm. (formerly Bell Atlantic Corp.), NYC, 2002—05, chmn., CEO, 2005—. Bd. dirs. Boston Properties Inc., CVS Corp., Honeywell, Wyeth, Viacom, Inc. Bd. dirs. NY Hall Sci., Nat. Urban League., Pace U., Mus. TV and Radio, Verizon Found. Sgt. US Army, 1966—68, Vietnam. Mem. US Telephone Assn. (bd. dirs. 1985—), Rockland Bus. Council (trustee 1987). Office: Verizon Communications Ste 200b 1095 Avenue of the Americas New York NY 10036-6704 *

SEIDENMAN, NEIL ARNOLD, interpreter; b. Balt., Apr. 3, 1933; s. Louis J. and Bertha Lapidus Seidenman; m. Agnese Fois Seidenman (div.); children: Nathan Louis, Steven Attile, Kenneth Joseph. BS in Langs., Georgetown U., DC, 1955. Sr. staff interpreter US State Dept., DC, 1958—87, asst. chief interpreter working with Spanish, Portuguese and Italian, 1977—87; ret., 1988; freelance interpreter, 1988—. With US Army, 1955—58. Recipient Hall of Fame award, Balt. City Coll., 2005. Mem.: Brazilian Am. Cultural Inst., Am. Assn. Lang. Specialists, Pentagon Ski Club, Ski Club Washington, DC. Democrat. Avocations: languages, travel, piano, tennis, skiing.

SEIDLER, ALAN RICHARD, composer, musician, music company executive; b. NYC, Dec. 4, 1951; s. Jack and Martha (Kahn) Seidler. Student, Juilliard Sch., NYC, 1969—72; MusB, Manhattan Sch. Music, NYC, 1988; student, New Sch. U., NYC, 1972—73, UCLA, 1975. Adj. instuctor musical theatre Inst. for Arts Iona Coll., New Rochelle, NY, 1970—71; chmn., pres. Ook Ook Productions, Inc., NYC, 1974—75; faculty voice and piano N.Y. Schs. Music, NYC, 1978—79; chmn., pres. New Classics Entertainment, NYC, 1995—, Furhoof Enterprises, Ltd., NYC, 2001—, Hoove Ape Records, 2006—. Cons. programming Radio Pacifica WBAI-FM, NYC, 1971—72; musical dir. Roundabout Theatre, NYC, 1967—68. Composer: (films) He Outta Be Committed (Audience Appreciation award Louisville Film Festival, 2000), Alan Seidler: Chamber Music, From The Soul-Sonata for Violin and Piano, 1994, Five English Poems for Voice and Piano, 1977-80, (choral works) Three Profundities for Unison Chorus, 1971-72, Two Sacred Pieces for a capella chorus, 1992, Four Poems of William Blake for capella chorus, 1994, (choral symphony) The Mystic Trumpeter, 1999-2006, (Pulitzer prize nomination), (chamber music) Wind Quintet, 1987, Piano Sonata, 1995, String Quartet #1, 1991-93, Sonata for Violin and Piano, 1994, Quartet for Piano and Strings, 1988-89, (songs and vocal chamber music) Four Preludes on Playthings of the Wind, 1990, rev. 1995, In The Arc of Your Mallet: 4 Love Poems of Jelaluddin Rumi, 1997-99, The Bete Noire Fragments, 2006-; singer, songwriter, pianist: (albums) Alan Seidler: The Duke of Ook, 1975; pianist, singer: Morning Impromptus/Evening Bacchanals, 1974; musician: I'm In Love, 1975, Ragtime Millionaire, 1976. Scholar, Young Artists New Rochelle, N.Y., 1969. Mem.: Soc. Composers, Inc., Chamber Music Am., Am. Music Ctr., Am. Fedn. TV and Radio Artists, Am. Soc. Composers, Authors and Publishers (grantee 1997—2006). Avocations: swimming, ping pong/table tennis. Office: c/o George T Gilbert Esq 100 Fifth Ave Fl 11 New York NY 10011 Office Phone: 877-597-5676. Business E-Mail: aseidler@furhoofenterprises.com.

SEIDLER, B(ERNARD) ALAN, lawyer; b. NYC, Nov. 26, 1946; s. Aaron H. and Ethel T. (Berkowitz) S.; m. Lynne Aubrey, Jan. 21, 1978; children: Jacob A., Morgan H., Lily R. BA, Colgate U., 1968; JD, Seton Hall U., 1972. Bar: NY 1973, US Dist. Ct. (ea., no. and so. dists.) NY 1975, US Ct. Appeals (2d cir.) 1976, US Ct Appeals (3d cir.) 1984, US Ct Appeals (4th cir.) 2004, US Supreme Ct. 1977. Staff atty. NY Legal Aid Soc., NYC, 1972-75; sole practitioner NYC, 1975—. Mem. Snedens Landing Tennis Assn. (Palisades, NY), Palisades Swim Club. Office: 580 Broadway New York NY 10012 Office Phone: 212-334-3131. Personal E-mail: snedens66@aol.com.

SEIDLER, DORIS, artist; b. London, Nov. 26, 1912; m. Bernard Seidler, Sept. 5, 1935; 1 child, David. Exhibited in group shows at Bklyn. Mus. Bi-Ann., Vancouver Internat., Honolulu Acad. Arts, Pa. Acad. Fine Arts, Phila., Soc. Am. Graphic Artists, Assoc. Am. Artists Gallery, Jewish Mus., N.Y.C., Albright-Knox Mus., 1994, Brit. Mus. Recent Acquisitions, 1997, Whitworth Gallery, Manchester, Eng., 2003, Represented in permanent collections Libr. of Congress, Smithsonian Instn., Washington, Phila. Mus. Art, Bklyn. Mus., Seattle Mus. Art, Whitney Mus., Nat. Gallery Art, Nassau County (N.Y.) Mus. Fine Arts, Brit. Mus., London, Victoria and Albert Mus. London, Pallant House Coll., Eng., Portland Mus. Art, Oreg., Birmingham Mus., Eng. Address: 14 Stoner Ave Great Neck NY 11021-2101

SEIDMAN, CHRISTINE E., medical educator; BA, Harvard U.; MD, George Washington U., 1978. Resident in internal medicine Johns Hopkins U., Balt.; resident in cardiology Mass. Gen. Hosp., Boston; staff Brigham and Women's Hosp. Harvard U., Boston, 1987, dir. cardiovasc. genetics svc., prof. Dept. Medicine and Dept. Genetics; assoc. investigator Howard Hughes Med. Inst., 1994, investigator. Recipient Bristol-Myers Squibb award, 2002. Mem.: NAS, Inst. Medicine. Office: Harvard U Med Sch Genetics NRB 256 77 Avenue Louis Pasteur Boston MA 02115 Business E-Mail: cseidman@genetics.med.harvard.edu.

SEIDMAN, DAVID N(ATHANIEL), materials scientist, engineer, educator; s. Charles and Jeanette (Cohen) S.; m. Shoshanah Cohen-Sabban, Oct. 21, 1973; children: Elie, Ariel, Eytan. BS, NYU, 1960, MS, 1962; PhD, U. Ill., Urbana, 1965. Postdoc. assoc. Cornell U., Ithaca, NY, 1964-66, asst. prof. materials sci. and engring., 1966-70, assoc. prof. materials sci. and engring., 1970-76, prof. materials sci. and engring., 1976-85, Northwestern U., Evanston, Ill., 1985-96, Walter P. Murphy prof. materials sci. and engring., 1996—; founding dir. Northwestern U. Ctr. for Atom-Probe Tomography, Evanston, Ill., 2004—. Vis. prof. Technion, Haifa, 1969-70, Tel-Aviv U., Ramat-Aviv, 1972; Lady Davis vis. prof. Hebrew U., Jerusalem, 1978, 80-81, prof. materials sci., 1983-85; vis. scientist C.E. de Grenoble, 1981, C.N.E.T.-Meylan, 1981, C.E. de Scalay, 1989, U. Goettingen, 1989, 92; sci. cons. Argonne Nat. labs., Ill., 1985-94. Editor: Jour. Materials Sci., 2004—06, Materials Rsch. Soc. Bulletin, 2007—; editor-in-chief (jour.) Interface Sci., 2002—04, mem. editl. bd., editor spl. issues, 1993—2001, mem. editl. bd. Materials Sci. Forum, 1996—; contbr. numerous articles to profl. jours. Recipient Max Planck Rsch. prize Max-Planck-Gesellschaft and the A. von Humboldt-Stiftung, 1993; Guggenheim fellow, 1972-73, 80-81, Humboldt fellow, 1989, 92; named chair for phys. metallurgy Gordon Conf., 1982. Fellow Am. Phys. Soc., TMS (mem. fellows award com. 2002-2005, chair, 2006, Hardy Gold medal 1966), Am. Soc. Materials Internat. (Grossman and Howe awards com. 2005-07, Albert Sauveur Achievement award, 2006), AAAS; mem. Materials Rsch. Soc. (editl. bd. 2007—), Microscopy Soc. Am., A. von Humboldt Soc. Am., Internat. Field-Emission Soc. (mem. steering com. 1997-2002, pres. 2000-2002), Böhmische Phys. Soc. Democrat. Jewish. Achievements include research in nanostructural temporal evolution, internal interfaces, atomic-scale imperfections in metals and semiconductors, three-dimensional atom-probe tomography and electron microscopy. Avocations: reading, history, travel. Office: Northwestern U MS&E Dept Cook Hall Evanston IL 60208-3108 Office Phone: 847-491-4391. Business E-Mail: d-seidman@northwestern.edu.

SEIDMAN, ELLEN SHAPIRO, lawyer, government official; b. NYC, Mar. 12, 1948; d. Benjamin Harry Shapiro and Edna (Eysen) Stern; m. Walter Becker Slocombe, June 14, 1981; 1 child, Benjamin William. AB, Radcliffe Coll., 1969; JD, Georgetown U., 1974; MBA, George Washington U., 1988. Bar: D.C., 1975. Law clk. US Ct. of Claims, Washington, 1974-75; assoc. Caplin & Drysdale, Washington, 1975-78; atty., advisor US Dept. Transp., Washington, 1978-79, dep. asst. gen. counsel, 1979-81; assoc. gen. counsel Chrysler Corp Loan Guaranty Bd., Washington, 1981-84; atty., advisor US Dept. of Treasury, Washington, 1981-86, spl. asst. to the Under Sec. Fin., 1986-87; dir. strategic planning Fed. Nat. Mortgage Assn., Washington, 1987-88, v.p., asst. to chmn., 1988-91, sr. v.p. regulation rsch. and econs., 1991-93; spl. asst. to the pres. for econ. policy The White House, Washington, 1993-97; dir. Office Thrift Supervision US Dept. Treasury, Washington, 1997—2001; sr. counsel, Minority Staff, fin. svcs. com. US Ho. of Reps., Washington, 2002; sr. mng. dir. nat. practice Shorebank Adv. Svcs., 2002—05; exec. v.p. Shorebank Corp., 2006—; dir. fin. svcs. and edn. project New Am. Found., 2007—. Office Phone: 202-822-9146. Business E-Mail: ellen_seidman@sbk.com.

SEIDMAN, GLENN ELLIOTT, sales executive, marketing professional, consultant; b. June 18, 1953; m. Charlene Goldberg, 1988; children: Brooke, Michelle. BA, CUNY, 1975; MA, NYU, 1977. Asst. dir. student activities Columbia U., NYC, 1978-83; assoc. dean students Poly. U., Bklyn., 1983-88; territory mgr. Quality Products & Svcs., Reading, Pa., 1988—2000; pres. Oxford Bus. Cons. Group, LLC, Huntington, NY, 2000—. Mem. Queens Coll. Alumni Assn. (pres. 1987-89), Huntington C. of C. E-mail: oxfordbcg@optonline.net.

SEIDMAN, JOEL C., pulmonary physician; b. Detroit, Aug. 15, 1948; s. Jacob M. and Sylvia G. Seidman; m. Susan E. Lane, Nov. 23, 1975; children: Jennifer A., Carl D. MD, U. Mich., Ann Arbor, 1973. Diplomate Am. Bd. Internal Medicine, 1976, pulmonary diseases Am. Bd. Internal Medicine, 1978. Attending physician divsn. pulmonary and critical care medicine William Beaumont Hosp., Royal Oak, Mich., 1978—, chmn. divsn. pulmonary medicine, 1978—90. Clin. asst. prof. internal medicine Wayne State Med. Sch., Detroit, 1990—. Fellow: Am. Coll. Phyisicians, Am. Coll. Chest Physicians; mem.: Mich. Thoracic Soc., Am. Thoracic Soc. Office: William Beaumont Hosp 3535 W 13 Mile Rd Ste 507 Royal Oak MI 48301-3642 Home Phone: 248-855-4292. Office Fax: 248-551-4556; Home Fax: 248-551-4556. Personal E-mail: jcsmd@comcast.net. Business E-Mail: jseidman@beaumont.edu.

SEIDMAN, JONATHAN G., geneticist, educator; m. Christine Edry, 1973; 3 children. BA in Biochemistry, Harvard U., 1971; PhD, U. Wis. Postdoctoral studies Nat. Inst. Child Health and Human Develop.; Henrietta B. and Frederick H. Bugher Prof. Cardiovascular genetics Harvard Med. Sch., Boston; investigator Howard Hughes Med. Inst. Contbr. articles to profl. jours. Recipient (with wife) Bristol-Myers Squibb award for Disting. Achievement in Cardiovascular Rsch., 2002. Mem.: NAS. Avocations: sailing, gardening. Office: Havard Med Sch, Seidman Lab Dept Genetics 77 Avenue Louis Pasteur Boston MA 02115 Business E-Mail: seidman@genetics.med.harvard.edu. *

SEIDMAN, L(EWIS) WILLIAM, television commentator, publisher; b. Grand Rapids, Mich., Apr. 29, 1921; s. Frank E. and Esther (Lubetsky) S.; m. Sarah Berry, Mar. 3, 1944; children: Thomas, Tracy, Sarah, Carrie, Meg, Robin. AB, Dartmouth Coll., 1943; LL.B., Harvard U., 1948; MBA, U. Mich., 1949. Bar: Mich. 1949, D.C. 1977. Spl. asst. fin. affairs to gov. of Mich., 1963-66; nat. mng. partner Seidman & Seidman C.P.A.s, NYC, 1969-74; asst. for econ. affairs to Pres. Gerald R. Ford, 1974-77; dir., chief fin. officer Phelps Dodge Corp., NYC, 1977-82, vice chmn., 1980-82; dean Coll. Bus. Adminstrn. Ariz. State U., Tempe, 1982-85; chmn. RTC FDIC, Washington, 1985—91; chief commentator Sta. CNBC-TV, 1991; pub.-bd. Bank Dir. Mag., 1992. Chmn. Detroit Fed. Res. Bank Chgo., 1970, RTC, 1989-91; co-chair White House Conf. on Productivity, 1983-84. Lt. USNR, 1942-46. Decorated Bronze Star. Mem. D.C. Bar Assn., Chevy Chase Club (Md.), Univ. Club (N.Y.C.), Crystal Downs Club (Mich.), Nantucket Yacht Club (MA). Office: CNBC 8th Flr 1025 Connecticut Ave NW Washington DC 20036-5405 Home Phone: 941-795-8631, 508-325-6305; Office Phone: 202-530-0910. Personal E-mail: lws1025@aol.com.

SEIERSEN, NICHOLAS STEEN, management consultant; b. Geneva, June 23, 1955; s. Ove Steen and Kamini Shoshiela (Bhandari) S.; m. Sylvie Jacqueline Fenouillet, Nov. 7, 1981. BSc with honors, U. Sussex, 1976; MBA, Pacific State U., LA, 1987. Project chief Metra Proudfoot Internat. Mgmt. Cons., Brussels, 1977-81; unit mgr. Auchan Hypermarkets, Paris, 1981-83; internat. controller Pain Jacquet Group, Paris, 1983-85; sr. cons. A.T. Kearney Mgmt. Cons., Paris, 1985-88; European mktg. mgr. Digital Equip. Corp., Paris, 1988-95; dir. sales, mktg., logistics and distbn. European Mfg. Expertise Ctr., Digital Equipment Corp., Paris, 1995-96; prin. KPMG Mgmt. Consulting (now BearingPoint, LP), Toronto, Ont., Canada, 1996—99, sr. mgr., 1999—2005; sr. mgr. adv. svcs. KPMG, Toronto, Canada, 2005—. Sci. bd. Logistique & Mgmt. Jour. (in French); editl. com. Global Supply Chain Forum mgmt. jour., Logistics Quarterly, Editl. adv. bd.: Logistics Quar. Jour., 2001—03, Can. exec. editor:, 2003—; contbr. articles to profl. jours. Mem. U.S. Bus. Logistics Assn. (coun. supply chain mgmt. profls., v.p. 1998-2000, pres. Toronto Roundtable 2000-02), Can. Assn. for Supply Chain and Logistics Mgmt., French Assn. Logistics Mgmt. (bd. dirs. 1994-96, v.p. internat. affairs 1994-96). Office: KPMG Ste 3300 Commerce Ct W 199 Bay St Toronto ON Canada M5L 1B2 Office Phone: 416-777-8391. Business E-Mail: nseiersen@kpmg.ca.

SEIF, MARGARET K., lawyer, electronics executive; BA, Brown U.; JD, U. Mich. V.p., gen. counsel Firefly Network, Inc.; v.p., gen. counsel, sec. RSA Security Inc., 1998—2000, sr. v.p. corp. devel., gen. counsel, sec., 2000—05; v.p., gen. counsel, sec. Analog Devices, Inc., Norwood, Mass., 2006—. Office: Analog Devices, Inc One Technology Way Norwood MA 02062 Office Phone: 781-329-4700. *

SEIFE, HOWARD, lawyer; b. NYC, Apr. 10, 1952; BA cum laude, Union Coll., NY, 1973; JD cum laude, Georgetown U., 1978; LLM, U. London, 1983. Bar: NY 1979, US Dist. Ct. (Ea. Dist.) NY 1980, US Dist. Ct. (So. Dist.) NY 1980, US Ct. Appeals (2nd Cir.) 1982, US Ct. Appeals (9th Cir.) 1990, US Ct. of Claims 1985, US Supreme Ct. 2001. Ptnr. Chadbourne & Parke LLP, NYC, chmn., Fin. Restructuring and Bankruptcy Practice Group. Mediator Bankruptcy Ct. (So. Dist.) NY, 1996—; arbitrator US Dist. Ct. (Ea. Dist.) NY, 1985—. Contbr. articles to profl. jour.; spkr. in field. Mem.: INSOL Internat. (chmn. tech. rsch. com. 2003—). Office: Chadbourne & Parke LLP 30 Rockefeller Plaza New York NY 10112 Office Phone: 212-408-5361. Office Fax: 212-541-5369. Business E-Mail: hseife@chadbourne.com.

SEIFERT, CAROLINE HAMILTON, community health nurse; b. Warren, Ohio, May 28, 1937; d. Oliver L. and Martha (Moran) Hamilton; m. Dale E. Seifert, Sept. 5, 1959; children: Brian Dale, Joan Kimberly. Diploma, Youngstown Hosp., Ohio, 1959; BSN, U. Cin., 1964, MEd, 1979. Cert. sch. nurse, health educator, spl. edn. educator. Caseworker Children's Svcs. div. Dept. Health and Human Svcs., Batavia, Ohio, 1966-68; dir. Happy Days Nursery Sch. Bethel (Ohio) United Meth. Ch., 1970-73; social worker Clermont County Bd. Mental Retardation/Devel. Disabilities, Batavia, 1973-97; sch. nurse, health educator Thomas A. Wildey Sch., Owensville, Ohio, 1973-97; retired, 1997. Instr. Sch. Health Svcs. U. Cin., 1976, preceptor nursing students, 1992-97. Mem. Hamilton/Clermont Sch. Nurses Orgn. (v.p.), S.W. Ohio Sch. Nurses Assn. (program chmn.), Profl. Assn. for Retardation (v.p. nursing div., Nurse of Yr.). Home: 2631 Oldforge Ln Cincinnati OH 45244-2831 Office: Thomas A Wildey Sch PO Box 8 Owensville OH 45160-0008

SEIFERT, FRANK C., thoracic surgeon; b. Chgo., Feb. 27, 1948; MD, U. Chgo. Pritzker Sch. Medicine, 1974. Cert. Thoracic Surgery, Surgical Critical Care. Intern, gen. surgery U. Chgo. Hospitals, 1974—75, resident, cardiothoracic surgery, 1976—80; resident, anatomy Stanford U. Med. Ctr., 1980—83; fellow U. Goteborg, 1977—78; hosp. appt. U. Hosp., Stony Brook, NY; assoc. prof. surgery SUNY-Stony Brook, NY. Named one of Medical Marvels, New York Mag., 2006. Fellow: Am. Coll. Cardiology, Am. Coll. Surgeons. Office: Health Sciences Center T19-080 SUNY Stony Brook Surgery Stony Brook NY 11790 Office Phone: 631-444-1820. Business E-Mail: fseifert@notes.cc.sunysb.edu. *

SEIFERT, JAMES J., lawyer; b. New Ulm, Minn., Nov. 24, 1956; BA, U. Notre Dame, 1979; MS in Manufacturing Systems, U. St. Thomas, 1994; JD, Creighton U. Sch. of Law, 1982. Bar: Minn. 1983, U.S. Dist. Ct., Dist. of Minn. 1983, Wis. 1992. Law clerk Judge Donald J. Porter U.S. Dist. Judge S.D., Pierre, 1982—83; atty. Carlsen, Greiner and Law, Minneapolis, Minn., 1983—85, Am. Hoist and Derrick Co., 1985—90, The Toro Co., 1990—94, asst. gen. counsel, 1994—99; v.p., gen. counsel, sec. Tennant Co., 1999—2002, Bemis Co., Inc., 2002—. Mem. Minn. House of Reps., 1999—2001. Mem.: ABA. Office: Bemis Co Inc 2300 Piper Jaffray Tower 222 S 9th St Minneapolis MN 55402-4099

SEIFERT, JEFFREY W., political scientist, researcher; BA summa cum laude, Towson State U., Md., 1992; MA, Syracuse U., NY, 1995, PhD, 2001. Global programs coord. Syracuse (N.Y.) U., 1999—2000; specialist info. sci. and tech. policy Congl. Rsch. Svc., Washington, 2000—. Vis. instr. Va. Tech. U., Blacksburg, Va., 2001—. Contbg. author: The New International Studies Classroom, 2000, Comparative Perspectives on E-Government, 2006, mem. editl. bd.: Govt. Info. Quar., 2003—, Jour. E-Gov., 2004—06, assoc. editor: Jour. Info. Tech. & Politics, 2007—; contbr. articles to profl. jours. Mem.: Midwest Polit. Sci. Assn., Internat. Studies Assn. (active learning internat. affairs sect. 2000—01, Jr. scholar 1999), Internat. Soc. Polit. Psychology, Assn. Am. Geographers, Am. Polit. Sci. Assn. (bd. dir. info. tech. politics sect. 2002—04, pres. info. tech. politics sect. 2005—06), Gamma Theta Upsilon. Office: Congressional Research Service 101 Independence Avenue SE Stop 7450 Washington DC 20540-7450 Office Phone: 202-707-0781. Office Fax: 202-707-7000.

SEIFERT, KATHI P., manufacturing executive; b. Appleton, Wis., 1949; m. Steve Seifert; children: Erin, Andrew. BA Valparaiso U., 1971. Various mgmt. positions P&G, Beatruce Foods, Fort Howard Paper Co., 1972—78; from product mgr. to mktg. dir. feminine care products Kimberly-Clark, Inc., Neenah, Wis., 1978—92, pres. feminine care sectory, 1992—94, group pres. N. Am. consumer products, 1994—95, group pres. N. Am. personal care products, 1995—98, group pres. personal care products, 1998—99, exec. v.p., group pres. global personal care products, 1999—, ret.; with Pinnacle Perspectives, LLC. Bd. dirs. Eli Lilly and Co. Bd. dirs. U.S. Fund for UNICEF; bd., dirs. Fox Cities Performing Art Ctr., 1999—, chmn. of bd., 2003—; bd, dirs. Theda Health Care Group, Wis. Commn. in Arts Edn. Office: Pinnacle Perspectives LLC Ste 303 330 W College Ave Appleton WI 54911

SEIFERT, RACHEL A., lawyer; b. New Brunswick, NJ, 1959; BA, U. Md., 1981, JD, 1985. Bar: Md. 1985. Atty. priv. practice, Dallas, 1985—92; v.p., assoc. gen. counsel Columbia/HCA, 1992—98; sr. v.p., sec., gen. counsel Cmty. Health Sys. Inc., Brentwood, Tenn., 1998—. Bd. mem. Women Bus. Leaders of U.S. Health Care Industry Found. Mem.: ABA, Federation of Am. Hospitals, Am. Health Lawyers Assn. Office: Cmty Health Sys Inc 155 Franklin Rd Ste 400 Brentwood TN 37027

SEIFERT, SHELLEY ELIZABETH, psychologist; d. Marc Richard Seifert and Rita Mary Seiert. BS, Ohio State U., Columbus, 2000; MEd, Kent State U., Ohio, 2004, EdS, 2006. Lic. sch. psychologist Ohio Dept. Edn. Designer Bridgestone/Firestone, Akron, 2000—03; sch. psychologist Springfield City Schs., Ohio, 2006—. Sunday sch. tchr. Vineyard Ch. Columbus, Westerville, Ohio. Independent. Achievements include patents for tire design. Avocations: bicycling, art. Office: Springfield City Schs 601 Selma Ave Springfield OH 45505

SEIFERT, SHELLEY JANE, bank executive; b. Aug. 12, 1954; BS in Consumer Econs. and Journalism, U. Mo., 1976; MBA with honors in Fin., U. Louisville, 1980. Fin. analyst Nat. City Bank, Ky., 1979-81, compensation analyst, 1981-85, mgr. compensation, 1985-86, mgr. compensation, recruiting and tng., 1986-91; mgr. compensation and devel. Nat. City Corp., Cleve., 1988-91, human resource dir., 1991-94, sr. v.p., 1994—2000, corp. human resource dir., 1994—2004, exec. v.p. corp. svcs., 2000—. Spkr. in field.; bd. dirs., Blair Corp., 2006-. Grad. Leadership Cleve.; vice chair bd. dirs. Bus. Vols. Unlimited, Vis. Nurse Assn. Greater Cleve.; bd. dirs. Arthritis Found.; mem. Cleve. Commn. on Econ. Partnership and Inclusion. Recipient Woman of Distinction award YMCA. Mem. Urban League (bd. dirs., chair employment com., Ohio labor adv. com.). Office: Nat City Corp Nat City Ctr 1900 E 9th St Cleveland OH 44114-3401 Office Phone: 216-222-2000. *

SEIFERT, THOMAS LLOYD, lawyer; b. Boston, June 6, 1940; s. Ralph Frederick and Hazel Bell (Harrington) S.; m. Ann Cecelia Berg, June 19, 1965. BS cum laude, Ind. U., Bloomington, 1962; JD cum laude, Ind. U., 1965. Bar: Ill. 1965, Ind. 1965, N.Y. 1979. Assoc. law firm Keck, Mahin & Cate, Chgo., 1965-67; atty. Essex Group, Inc., Ft. Wayne, Ind., 1967-70, Amoco Corp., Chgo., 1970-73; assoc. gen. counsel, asst. sec. Canteen Corp., Chgo., 1973-75; sec., gen. counsel The Marmon Group, Inc. (and predecessor cos.), Chgo., 1975-78; v.p., gen. counsel, sec. Hanson Industries, Inc., NYC, 1978-82; sr. v.p. law, chief fin. officer Petrie Stores Corp., NYC, 1982-83; mem. Finley, Kumble, Wagner, Heine, Underberg, Manley, Myerson & Casey, NYC, 1983-87, Paul, Weiss, Rifkind, Wharton & Garrison, NYC, 1987-91; gen. counsel, chief legal officer Sterling Grace Capital Mgmt., L.P. and affiliated cos., NYC, 1991—. Note editor Ind. Law Jour., 1964-65. Named to Ind. Track and Cross Country Hall of Fame, 1993. Mem. ABA, N.Y. State Bar Assn., Order of Coif, The Creek, Beta Gamma Sigma. Home: Museum Tower 15 W 53d St Apt 31 E New York NY 10019-5401 Office: Sterling Grace Capital Mgmt 405 Park Ave Ste 1203 New York NY 10022 Home Phone: 212-757-8821; Office Phone: 212-644-5067. Personal E-mail: tlseifert@msn.com.

SEIFF, ERIC A., lawyer; b. Mt. Vernon, NY, Apr. 25, 1933; s. Arthur N. and Mathilde (Cohen) S.; m. Sari Ginsburg, June 26, 1960 (div. Oct. 1983); children: Judith C., E. Kenneth, Dean A.; m. Meredith Feinman, Jan. 15, 1984; children: Abigail, Sarah. BA, Yale U., 1955; LLB, Columbia U., 1958. Bar: N.Y. 1958, U.S. Dist. Ct. (so. dist.) N.Y. 1960, U.S. Dist. Ct. (ea. dist.) N.Y. 1981, U.S. Ct. Appeals (2d cir.) 1965, U.S. Supreme Ct. 1967. Assoc. Bower and O'Connor, NYC, 1959-60, Yellin, Kramer & Levy, NYC, 1961; asst. dist. atty. N.Y. County Dist. Atty.'s Office, 1962-67; asst. counsel Agy. for Internat. Devel., Washington, 1967-70, regional legal advisor Rio de Janeiro, 1970-72; gen. counsel N.Y. State Divsn. Criminal Justice Svcs., 1972-74; dep. chief atty. Legal Aid Soc. Criminal Def., NYC, 1974-75; first dep. commr. N.Y. State Investigation Commn., 1975-77, chmn. NYC, 1977-79; ptnr. Seiff, Kretz & Abercrombie (formerly Scoppetta & Seiff), NYC, 1981—; spl. dist. atty. Bronx County, 1986-89. Spl. asst. atty. gen. State of N.Y., Gov.'s Task Force Investigating Conduct of Attica Prosecutions, 1975. Gen. counsel Friends of Van Cortlandt Pk., 1989—; bd. dirs. Legal Aid Soc., NYC, 1994—2000, Prisoners' Legal Svcs., NYC, 1989—, Lawyers Fund for Client Protection, NY, 1980—. Recipient Frank S. Hogan Meml. award, Frank S. Hogan Assn., 1994. Mem.: N.Y. State Assn. Criminal Def. Lawyers (bd. dirs. 2001—), Bar Assn. City N.Y. (chmn. project on the homeless 1999—2003), N.Y. Criminal Bar Assn. (bd. dirs. 1980—, past pres.). Office: Seiff Kretz & Abercrombie 444 Madison Ave 30th Fl New York NY 10022 Office Phone: 212-371-4500.

SEIFF, STEPHEN S., ophthalmologist; b. LA, Sept. 30, 1925; s. Max and Minnie F. (Feldman) S.; m. Gloria Louise Holtzman, Apr. 16, 1950; children: Stuart R., Sherri Seiff Sloane, Karen Seiff Sacks. AA, UCLA, 1945; AB, U. Calif., Berkeley, 1946; MD, U. Calif., San Francisco, 1949. Diplomate Am. Bd. Ophthalmology. Intern County Gen. Hosp., LA, 1949-50; fellow in anesthesiology Lahey Clinic, Boston, 1950-51; resident in ophthalmology U. Calif., San Francisco, 1952-55; clin. prof. dept. ophthalmology UCLA, 1956—2002, emeritus clin. prof., 2002—; pvt. practice Beverly Hills, Calif., 1955—; clin. chief divsn. ophthalmology Cedars/Sinai Med. Ctr., LA, 1957—; attending ophthalmologist Children's Hosp., LA, 1956-94. Lectr. in field; assoc. examiner Am. Bd. Ophthalmology. Collaborating author: Clinical Anticoagulant Therapy, 1965; contbr. articles to profl. jours. Bd. dirs. That Man May See Inc., San Francisco; former exec. com. mem. UCLA Hosp. Lt. M.C. USNR, 1950-52. Recipient Sr. Honor award UCLA Dept. Ophthalmology, 1994. Fellow ACS, Am. Acad. Ophthalmology; mem. L.A. Soc. Ophthalmology (past pres.), Frederick Cordes Eye Soc. (past nat. pres.), Am. Soc. Cataract and Refractive Surgery (founding mem.). Avocation: sailing. Personal E-mail: sseiff@aol.com.

SEIGEL, JAN KEARNEY, lawyer; b. Bayonne, NJ, Feb. 7, 1947; s. Max and Margaret (Kearney) S.; m. Judy L. Mascuch, Aug. 29, 1971; children: Margaret, Emily, Jonas, Luke. BSBA, Georgetown U., 1968, JD, 1971; LLM in Taxation, NYU, 1974. Bar: N.J. 1971, D.C. 1972, Ga. 1972, U.S. Ct. Appeals (3d cir.) 1979, U.S. Supreme Ct. 1979. Law sec. to Hon. Theodore Rosenberg Superior Ct. of N.J., Paterson, NJ, 1971—72; asst. prosecutor Passaic County Pros.'s Office, Paterson, NJ, 1972—76; prin. Seigel & Assocs., Ridgewood, NJ, 1976—. Mem. faculty William Paterson Coll., 1974-79; lectr. N.J. Inst. for Continuing Edn., 1981—, N.J. State Bar and various county bar assns. Recipient Police Hon. Legion award Police Chiefs Assn. of N.J., 1980. Mem. ABA (rep. of N.J. young lawyers divsn. 1980-82), N.J. State Bar Assn. (Young Lawyer of Yr. award 1983, bd. trustees 1978-79), Passaic County Bar Assn. (bd. trustees 1973-81), Bergen County Bar Assn. Office: Seigel & Assoc 505 Goffle Rd Ridgewood NJ 07450-4027 Office Phone: 201-444-4000.

SEIGEL, JERROLD EDWARD, historian, writer; b. St. Louis, June 9, 1936; s. William and Katherine (Ginsberg) S.; m. Jayn Rosenfeld, Aug. 28, 1966; children: Micol, Jessica. AB, Harvard U., 1958; PhD, Princeton U., 1963. Instr. Princeton (N.J.) U., 1962-65, asst. prof., 1965-68, assoc. prof., 1968-78, prof. history, 1978-88, NYU, NYC, 1988—, Kenan prof., 1994—2006, emeritus, 2006—. Vis. prof. history Maitre d'Etudes, Ecoles des hautes études, Paris, 1988-94; finalist Nat. Book Critics Cir., 1987. Author: Rhetoric and Philosophy, 1968, Marx's Fate, 1978, Bohemian Paris, 1986, Private Worlds of Marcel Duchamp, 1995, The Idea of the Self, 2005. Fulbright fellow Inst. Internat. Edn., 1961-62; NEH fellow, 1979-80, 87-88; resident Am. Acad. Rome, 2000; Guggenheim fellow, 2004-05. Mem. N.Y. Inst. for Humanities, Phi Beta Kappa. Home: 48 Horatio St New York NY 10014-1614 Business E-Mail: jes3@nyu.edu.

SEIGEL, STUART EVAN, lawyer; b. NYC, Mar. 25, 1933; s. Philip Herman and Betty Sarah (Leventhal) S.; m. Joyce Roberta Meyers (div.); children: Charles Meyers, Lee Bennett, Suzanne Marcie; m. Sherry Diane Jackson,Sept. 24, 1989. BS, NYU, 1953, LLB, 1957; LLM in Taxation, Georgetown U., 1960. Bar: N.Y. 1958, D.C. 1958. Atty. Office Chief Counsel, IRS, Washington, 1957—65, Office Tax Legis. Counsel, Dept. Treasury, Washington, 1965—69, assoc. tax legis. counsel, 1968—69; ptnr. Cohen and Uretz, Washington, 1969—77; chief counsel IRS, Washington, 1977—79; ptnr. Williams and Connolly, Washington, 1979—89, Arnold and Porter, NYC, 1989—2002; chmn., CEO Seigel & Assocs., LLC, NYC, 2006—. Lectr. George Washington U. Sch. Law, 1970-73; adj. prof. law Antioch Sch. Law, 1973-76, Georgetown U. Sch. Law, 1981. Mem. ABA, Am. Law Inst., Am. Coll. Tax Counsel, N.Y. State Bar Assn., Met. Club Washington Office: 100 Park Ave 23rd Fl New York NY 10017 Business E-Mail: stuart@seigel-llc.com.

SEIGENTHALER, JOHN MICHAEL, newscaster; b. Nashville, Dec. 21, 1955; s. John Lawrence and Dolores (Watson) S.; m. Kerry Lynn Brock, Jan. 4, 1992. BA in Pub. Policy, Duke U., 1978. Reporter Nashville Tennesean, 1978-79; advance rep. Kennedy for Pres., Washington, 1979-80; writer WDCN-TV, Nashville, 1980; prodr. WNGE-TV, Nashville, 1980-81; reporter, anchor WSMV-TV, Nashville, 1981-90, KOMO-TV, Seattle, 1990—99; weekend anchor, NBC Nightly News WNBC-TV, NYC, 1999—2007. Reporter, producer documentaries: An Eye For An Eye, 1984 (ABA award), Reflections in Black and White, 1986 (Robert F. Kennedy Journalism award), Breaking Down the Barriers, 1990 (Pres.'s Com. on Employment for Disabled award); reporter, producer pub. affairs programs: Prison Riots, 1985 (Am. assn. TV Program Execs. award). Recipient 2 local Emmy awards, 1986. Mem. NATAS, Soc. Profl. Journalists. Roman Catholic. Avocations: tennis, skiing, water-skiing.

SEIGLER, DAVID STANLEY, botanist, educator, chemist; b. Wichita Falls, Tex., Sept. 11, 1940; s. Kenneth R. and Floy M. (Wilkinson) S.; m. Janice Kay Cline, Jan. 20, 1961; children: Dava, Rebecca. BS in Chemistry, Southwestern State Coll., Okla., 1961; PhD in Organic Chemistry, U. Okla., 1967. Postdoctoral assoc. USDA No. Regional Lab., Peoria, Ill., 1967-68; postdoctoral fellow dept. botany U. Tex., Austin, 1968-70; asst. prof. botany U. Ill., Urbana, 1970-76, assoc. prof., 1976-79, prof. botany, 1979—, head dept. plant biology, 1988-93. Curator U. Ill. Herbarium, 1993—. Author: Plant Secondary Metabolism, 1999; editor: Crop Resources, 1977, Phytochemistry and Angiosperm Phylogeny, 1981; contbr. numerous articles to profl. jours. Recipient Fulbright Hays Lecturer award Fulbright Commn., Argentina, 1976, (alternate) Germany, 1995-96, study award Deutsche Akademischer Austauschdienst, Germany, 1995, Rupert Barneby award NY Bot. Garden, 1997. Mem. Phytochem. Soc. N.Am. (pres. 1988-89), Bot. Soc. Am., Am. Chem. Soc., Am. Soc. Plant Taxonomists, Internat. Soc. Chem. Ecology (pres. 1990-91). Mem. Assembly of God Ch. Avocation: genealogy. Home: 510 W Vermont Ave Urbana IL 61801-4931 Office: U Ill Dept Plant Biology 265 Morrill Hall 505 S Goodwin Ave Urbana IL 61801-3707 Home Phone: 217-384-1192; Office Phone: 217-333-7577. Business E-Mail: seigler@life.uiuc.edu.

SEIGLER, MICHAEL EDWARD, lawyer, librarian; b. Tallahassee, Oct. 14, 1948; s. Claude Milo and Roberta Bradford (Whitfield) S.; m. Janet Cummings, Feb. 19, 1971; children: Kelly Elizabeth, Megan Whitfield. AA, Lake Sumter C.C., 1968; BS, Fla. State U., 1970, MS, 1974; JD, Atlanta Law Sch., 1980. Bar: Ga. 1980, U.S. Ct. Appelas (5th cir.) 1980, U.S. Ct. Appeals (11th cir.) 1980, U.S. tax Ct. 1985, U.S. Supreme Ct. 1985, Cert. tchr. Libr., tchr. Sumter Correctional Inst., Bushnell, Fla., 1970—73; asst. libr. dir. Leesburg Pub. Libr., Fla., 1974—75, libr. dir., 1975—77, Atlanta Law Sch., 1979—81; atty. Brooks & Brock, Marietta, Ga., 1981—83; libr. Port Charlotte Pub. Libr., 1983—84; assoc. Brooks & Brock, Marietta, 1985, Brock & Barr, Marietta, 1985—86, Brock & Clay, 1987; judge pro hoc vice State Ct. of Cobb County, 1986; pvt. practice, 1986—. Asst. dir. Pine Mountain Regional Libr., 1988-95; libr. dir. Smyrna Pub. Libr., 1995—; design judge Ben Franklin Awards, 2001, 03, 04. Columnist Smyrna Vinings Living, 2000-02; contbr. articles to jours. Vol. worker ACLU, Atlanta, 1979; mem. Fla. State U. Libr. Com., Tallahassee, 1974, Children's Program Com., Port Charlotte, 1983, Port Charlotte Cultural Ctr. Adv. Com., 1984, Pine Mountain Arts Coun., past bd. dirs.; mem. Cobb County Dem. Exec. Com., 1986-87; exec. com. Cobb Christmas, 1986-87; com. mem. Smyrna Cmty. Culture, 2000-2002; sec. program com. WRFG Cmty. Radio, 2002, bd. dirs., 2003--, chair fin. com., 2003--. Named Tchr. of Yr., Sumter Correctional Inst., 1973. Mem. Nat. Libr. Assn. (com. chmn. 1975-76), Fla. Libr. Assn. (caucus chmn. 1976-77), Ga. Libr. Assn. (mem. com. chmn. 1992—, sec. 1993-94, parliamentarian 1997, 1st v.p. 1999, pres. 2000), Metro Atlanta Libr. Assn. (v.p. 1997, pres. 1998), Southeastern Libr. Assn. (mem. com. 1988—, convention chair 2000, com. chair 2001—), ALA (con. spkr.), Atlanta Law Sch. Alumni Assn. (treas. 1986-90), Fla. State U. Alumni Assn. (life), Ga. Libr. Video Assn. (pres. 1991-92), Mensa (sec. 1987, 89, pres. Ga. chpt. 1988, mediator Ga. chpt. 2000-02, regional vice chmn. 2003-07, trustee Mensa Edn. and Rsch. Found. (v.p. 1993), Ga. Coun. Media Orgn. (chair steering com. 2000), Leadership Meriwether (pres. 1993). Office: 100 Village Green Cir SE Smyrna GA 30080-3478 Home: 192 Katrina Dr Powder Springs GA 30127 Office Phone: 770-431-2860. E-mail: mjseigler@msn.com.

SEIGLER, RUTH QUEEN, college nursing administrator, educator, consultant, nurse; b. Conway, SC, July 31, 1942; d. Charles Isaac and Berneta Mae (Weaks) Queen; m. Rallie Marshall Seigler, Sept. 1, 1963; children: Rallie Marshall Jr., Scot Monroe. ADN, Lander Coll., 1962; BSN, U. S.C., 1964, M of Nursing, 1980. Pub. health nurse Richland County Health Dept., Columbia, SC, 1964—66; dir. nurses Columbia Area Mental Health Ctr., 1966—69; program nurse specialist Midlands Health Dist., 1969—72; discharge planner Richland Meml. Hosp., 1972—73, clin. dir., 1973—75; exec. dir. S.C. State Bd. Nursing, 1976—83; v.p. nursing dept. Self Meml. Hosp., Greenwood, SC, 1983—86; exec. dir. S.C. Commn. on Aging, Columbia, 1986—95; asst. dean Coll. Nursing U. S.C., Columbia, 1995—96, assoc. clin. prof., 1996—. Cons. intergenerational family studies, 1999—; dir. Cockcroft Leadership Program for Nurse Execs., 2002—, Ctr. for Nursing Leadership, 2004-05, sr. cons., 2005—; bd. dirs. Queen Gas Co., Barnwell, S.C.; nurse cons. Creative Nursing Mgmt., Mpls., 1984—. Advisor: The Role of Cmty. Mental Health Nurse, 1971. Moderator Trinity Presbytery, 2003—. Recipient Disting. Alumni award Lander Coll., 1978, Career Woman Recognition award Columbia YWCA, 1980, William S. Hall award S.C. Assn. Residential Care Homes, 1988, U. S.C. Coll. Nursing Disting. Alumni award, 1993, award for excellence S.C. League for Nursing, 1995, Svc. Recognition award S.C. AARP, 1995; named one of Ten Women of Achievement, S.C. March of Dimes, 1987, hon. fellow AVC Leadership, 2002, Excellence in Leadership award, 2004, Ordie P. Taylor Humanitarian award, 2005, Palmetto Gold award Top 100 Nurses in S.C., 2006. Mem. ANA, APHA, S.C. Nurses Assn. (sec. 1965-68, bd. dirs. 1986-88, Excellence award 1984, Recognition award 1984), S.C. Hosp. Assn., S.C. Gerontol. Soc., S.C. Nurses Found., S.C. Healthy People 2000 (vice chair), Partnership for Older South Carolinians (founder, chair bd. dirs.), Columbia Luncheon Club (pres. 1997-98), S.C. Fedn. Older Ams., Evening Mission Action Group, Bd. Nursing Home Examiners, Pilot Club, Inc. (pres. 1988-89, 97-98), Vols. of Am.-Carolinas (bd. dirs., chair, 1998-00, elder, 1999-01), Rotary Internat., Sigma Theta Tau, Beta Sigma Phi (pres. chpt. 1997-98). Presbyterian. Avocations: gardening, travel. Home: 6 Beaver Dam Ct Columbia SC 29223-3100 Office: U SC Coll Nursing Ctr Nursing Leadership Columbia SC 29208-0001

SEIL, FREDRICK JOHN, retired neuroscientist; b. Nove Sove, Yugoslavia, Nov. 9, 1933; s. Joseph and Theresa (Krieger) S.; m. Daryle Faith Wolfers, July 2, 1955; children: Jonathan Fredrick, Joel Philip Timothy. BA, Oberlin Coll., 1956; MD, Stanford U., 1960. Intern Kaiser Found. Hosp., San Francisco, 1960-61; resident in neurology Stanford U., Calif., 1961-64, fellow in neurology, 1964-66; staff neurologist VA Med. Ctr., Palo Alto, Calif., 1969-76, clin. investigator Portland, Oreg., 1976-79, staff neurologist, 1979-81, dir. VA office regeneration research programs, 1981—2001, ret., 2001. Asst. prof. neurology Stanford U., 1969-75, assoc. prof. neurology Oreg. Health and Sci. U., Portland, 1976-78, prof. neurology, 1978-2001, prof. cell and devel. biology, 1990-2001, prof. emeritus neurology, 2001—. Editor: Nerve, Organ and Tissue Regeneration: Research Perspectives, 1983, Neural Regeneration, 1987, 94, Current Issues in Neural Regeneration Rsch., 1988, Neural Regeneration and Transplantation, 1989, Advances in Neural Regeneration Research, 1990, Neural Injury and Regeneration, 1993, Multiple Sclerosis: Current Status of Research and Treatment, 1994, Neural Regeneration, Reorganization, and Repair, 1997, Neural Plasticity and Regeneration, 2000; contbr. articles to profl. jours. Capt. US Army Med. Corps, 1966—68. Grantee VA,

1970-2001, NIH, 1986-95. Mem. Internat. Brain Rsch. Orgn., Internat. Soc. Develop. Neurosci., Am. Neurol. Assn., Am. Assn. Neuropathologists, Soc. Neurosci., Soc. Exptl. Neuropathology. Democrat. Achievements include founding of biennial International Symposium on Neural Regeneration; co-founding of biennial Asia Pacific Symposium on Neural Regeneration. Home: 1 Twain Ave Berkeley CA 94708 Personal E-mail: seilf@comcast.net.

SEILER, CHRISTINE KAY, history professor; BS in Interdisciplinary Social Scis., Fla. State U., Tallahassee, 1995, MS in Interdisciplinary Social Scis., 1997, PhD in History, 2003. Prof. history Hillsborough C.C., Tampa, Fla., 2005—. Office: Hillsborough Cmty Coll Brandon Campus 10414 E Columbus Dr Tampa FL 33619 Home Phone: 305-772-0432; Office Phone: 813-253-7836. Business E-Mail: cseiler@hccfl.edu.

SEILER, FRITZ ARNOLD, physicist; b. Basel, Switzerland, Dec. 20, 1931; came to U.S., 1980; s. Friedrich and Marie (Maibach) S.; m. Mary Catherine Coster, Dec. 22, 1964; children: Monica, Simone, Daniel. BA in Econs., Basel Sch. of Econs., 1951; PhD in Physics, U. Basel, 1962. Rsch. assoc. U. Wis., Madison, 1962-63; scientific assoc. U. Basel, 1963-69, privat dozent, 1969-75, dozent, 1975-80; sr. scientist Lovelace Inhalation Toxicology Inst., Albuquerque, 1980-90; sr. tech. assoc. IT Corp., Albuquerque, 1990-92, disting. tech. assoc., 1992-96; v.p. Inst. Regulatory Sci., Albuquerque, 1996-97; prin. Sigma Five Cons., Los Lunas, N.Mex., 1997—. Cons. Swiss Dept. Def., 1968-74; vis. scientist Lawrence Berkeley Labs., 1974-75. Contbr. numerous articles to profl. jours. With Swiss Army staff, 1964-75. Fellow Am. Phys. Soc., Health Physics Soc., Soc. for Risk Analysis, Fachverband fuer Strahlenschutz, Am. Nat. Stds. Inst. (mgmt. coun. 1987-2002, com. N14 1986-2002), Internat. Hormesis Soc Office: Sigma Five Consulting PO Box 1709 Los Lunas NM 87031-1709 Office Phone: 505-866-5193. Office Fax: 505-866-5197. Business E-Mail: faseiler@nmia.com.

SEILER, JAMES ELMER, judge; b. LaCrosse, Wis., Sept. 2, 1946; s. Elmer Bernard and Margaret Theresa (Mader) Seiler; m. Sonia Gonzales, Feb. 9, 1968; children: Rebecca, Cristina. BA, U. Wis., LaCrosse, 1968; JD, U. Wis., 1973. Bar: Wis. 1973, Minn. 1981, U.S. Supreme Ct. 1985, Mo. 1986. Pvt. practice, Balsam Lake, Wis., 1973-81; in-house counsel Farm Credit Banks, St. Paul, 1981-85; corp. counsel Hussmann Corp., St. Louis, 1985-94; adminstrv. law judge Social Security, Evansville, Ind., 1994-95, Office Hearings and Appeals, Creve Coeur, Mo., 1995—, chief adminstrv. law judge, 1997—. Candidate dist. atty. Polk County, Wis., 1980. With US Army, 1969—71. Avocations: soccer coach, swimming, water-skiing, Senior Olympics. Home: 18 Harbor Point Ct Lake Saint Louis MO 63367-1336 Office: 11475 Olde Cabin Rd Saint Louis MO 63141-7130

SEINFELD, JERRY, comedian, actor, television producer, scriptwriter; b. Bklyn., Apr. 29, 1954; s. Kalman and Betty S.; m. Jessica Sklar, Dec. 25, 1999; children: Sascha, Julian, Shepherd Kellen Grad. with degree in theatre communications, Queens Coll., NY, 1976. Former salesman. Stand-up comedian, 1976—; joke-writer (TV series) Benson, ABC, 1980; actor, co-writer, prod. (TV series) Seinfeld, NBC-TV, 1990-97 (Emmy award Outstanding Comedy Series, 1993, Emmy nomination, Lead Actor - Comedy Series, 1994, Golden Globe winner, 1994, best actor comedy series), (TV movie) The Ratings Game, 1984, I'm Telling You for the Last Time, 1999; (TV specials) The Tommy Chong Roast, 1986, The Seinfeld Chronicles, 1989; (film) Comedian (also exec. prodr.), 2002; writer Jerry Seinfeld-Stand-Up Confidential, 1987; author: Sein Language, 1993; guest appearances The Larry Sanders Show, 1992, News Radio, 1995. Recipient Am. Comedy award funniest male comedy stand-up, 1988, funniest actor in a TV series, 1992, 93; Screen Actors Guild award, Outstanding Performance by an Ensemble in a Comedy Series, 1994, 96, 97; People's Choice award, Favorite TV Comedy Series, 1998. Jewish. Avocations: zen, yoga. *

SEINFELD, JOHN HERSH, chemical engineering professor; b. Elmira, NY, Aug. 3, 1942; s. Ben B. and Minna (Johnson) S. BS, U. Rochester, 1964; PhD, Princeton U., 1967; DSc honoris causa, U. Patras, Greece, 2002, Carnegie Mellon U., 2002. Asst. prof. chem. engring. Calif. Inst. Tech., Pasadena, 1967-70, assoc. prof., 1970-74, prof., 1974—, Louis E. Nohl prof., 1980—, exec. officer for chem. engring., 1973-90, chmn. engring. and applied sci. div., 1990-2000. Allan P. Colburn meml. lectr. U. Del., 1976; Camille and Henry Dreyfus Found. lectr. MIT, 1979; mem. coun. Gordon Rsch. Confs., 1980-83; Donald L. Katz lectr. U. Mich., 1981; Reilly lectr. U. Notre Dame, 1983; Dean's Disting. lectr. U. Rochester, 1985; Katz lectr. CUNY, 1985; McCabe lectr. N.C. State U., 1986; Lewis lectr. MIT, 1986; Union Carbide lectr. SUNY, Buffalo; Van Winkle lectr. U. Tex., 1988; Bicentennial lectr. La. State U., 1988; Ida Beam lectr. U. Iowa, 1989, David Mason lectr. Stanford U., 1989; Julian Smith lectr. Cornell U., 1990; Merck lectr. Rutgers U., 1991; Henske Disting. lectr. Yale U., 1991; lectr. AIChE, 1980; Centennial lectr. U. Pa., 1993; Miles Disting. lectr. U. Pitts., 1994; Kelly lectr. Purdue U., 1996; Disting. rsch. lectr. Carnegie Mellon U., 1998; Berkeley lectr. U. Calif., Berkeley, 1998; Sigma Xi lectr., 1998—, Merck Sharp & Dohme lectr. U. P.R., 1998; Hess lectr. U. Va., 1998; inaugural disting. lectr. U. Toledo, 1999; Priestley lectr. Commonwealth Sci. and Indsl. Rsch. Orgn., 2000; Amundson lectr. U. Houston, 2002, Hottel lectr. MIT, 2002, Lowrie lectr. Ohio State U., 2004; Fingerson/TSI lectr. U. Minn., 2004; Frontiers lectr. U. Conn., 2005; ICI disting. lectr. U. Alta., 2005; Mah lectr. Northwestern U., 2006; Holtz lectr. Johns Hopkins U., 2006. Author: Numerical Solution of Ordinary Differential Equations, 1971, Mathematical Methods in Chemical Engineering, Vol. III, Process Modeling, Estimation and Identification, 1974, Air Pollution: Physical and Chemical Fundamentals, 1975, Lectures in Atmospheric Chemistry, 1980, Atmospheric Chemistry and Physics of Air Pollution, 1986, Fundamentals of Air Pollution Engineering, 1988, Distributed Parameter Systems--Theory and Applications, 1989, Atmospheric Chemistry and Physics, 1998, 2nd edit., 2006; assoc. editor Environ. Sci., Tech., 1981-97; mem. editorial bd. Computers, Chem. Engring, 1974-96, Jour. Colloid and Interface Sci, 1978-95, Advances in Chem. Engring, 1980-03, Revs. in Chem. Engring, 1980—, Aerosol Sci. and Tech., 1981-93; assoc. editor: Atmospheric Environment, 1976—. Recipient Donald P. Eckman award Am. Automatic Control Coun., 1970, Pub. Svc. medal NASA, 1980, Disting. Alumnus award U. Rochester, 1989, Nev. medal Desert Rsch. Inst., 2001, Haagen-Smit Clean Air award Calif. Air Resources Bd., 2003, Haagen-Smit award, Atmos Environ., 2004; Camille and Henry Dreyfus Found. Tchr. Scholar grantee, 1972. Fellow AIChE (bd. dirs. 1988-91, mem. editl. bd. jours. 1985—, Allan P. Colburn award 1976, William H. Walker award 1986, Warren K. Lewis award 2000), NAE, AAAS, Japan Soc. Promotion Sci., Am. Geophysical Union; mem. Am. Soc. Engring. Edn. (Curtis W. McGraw Rsch. award 1976, George Westinghouse award 1987), Assn. Aerosol Rsch. (bd. dirs. 1983—, v.p. 1988-90, pres. 1990-92), Am. Acad. Arts and Scis., Am. Chem. Soc. (Svc. through Chemistry award 1988, Creative Advances in Environ. Sci. and Tech. award 1993), Internat. Aerosol Rsch. Assembly (Fuchs award 1998), Sigma Xi, Tau Beta Pi. Home: 4409 Beulah Dr La Canada CA 91011 Office: Calif Inst Tech Divsn Chem Engring and Applied Sci 210-41 Pasadena CA 91125-0001 E-mail: seinfeld@caltech.edu.

SEINUK, YSRAEL A., architectural engineer; b. Cuba; Grad. in Civil Engring., U. Havana, 1954. Lic. in 15 states, DC, Puerto Rico, United Kingdom. Founder, CEO Ysrael A. Seinuk P.C., NYC, 1977—; co-founder, CEO Cantor Seinuk, NYC; CEO WSP New York, NYC; prof., chmn. structural dept. Irwin S. Chanin Sch. Architecture, Cooper Union, NYC, 1969—. Supv. structural design of Trump World Tower, NYC, Bear Stearns World Headquarters, NYC, Time Warner Centre at Columbus Cir., NYC, Riverside So. apartments, NYC, New York Mercantile Exch., Four Times Sq., NYC, 7 World Trade Ctr., NYC, Trump Tower 5th Ave., NYC, Lipstick Bldg., NYC, Arthur Ashe Tennis Stadium, NYC, Torre Mayor, Mexico City. Named one of 25 Most Influential Hispanics, Time Mag., 2005; recipient Leader of Industry award, Concrete Industry Bd., Urban Visionary award, Cooper Union. Fellow: Inst. Civil Engineers (U.K.), Am. Soc. Civil Engineers, Am. Concrete Inst. Office: Ysrael A Seinuk PC 2d Fl 228 E 45th St New York NY 10017

SEIPEL, MICHAEL, social sciences educator; b. Seoul, Republic of Korea, July 27, 1949; s. Suki and adopted s. Rudolf Seipel; m. Verla Porter, Aug. 13, 1986; children: Benjamin, McKay, Melissa. BS, U. Utah, Salt Lake City, 1974, MSW, 1976; PhD, Cornell, Ithaca, NY, 1982. Cert. social worker Utah, 1976. Social worker Dept. Social Svcs., Salt Lake City, 1976—79; prof. social work Brigham Young U., Provo, Utah, 1982—. Assoc. dir. Brigham Young U. Sch. Social Work, Provo, 2004—, grad. coord.; accreditation reviewer Coun. on Social Work Edn., Alexandria, Va. Contbr. articles to profl. jours. Founder Utah County Tenants United, Provo, 1996; Asian adv. coun. Utah State Govs. Office, Salt Lake City, 1996—2002; mem. Assn. of Asian Pacific Cmty. Health Orgn., Oakland, Calif., 2000—04; pres. Food and Shelter Coalition, Provo, Utah, 1994—95; commr. Martin Luther King Jr. Human Rights Commn., Salt Lake City, 1995—98. Recipient John R. Christiansen Alumni Prof. award, Brigham Young U., Sch. Social Work, 2004. Mem.: NASW, Nat. Assn. Social. Workers (pres. so. br. 1983—86, chair Utah chpt. 2000—03, Social Work Educator Yr. 2000), Coun. Social Work Edn. Office: Brigham Young Univ School of Social Work 2164 JFSB Provo UT 84602 Home Phone: 801-226-3409. Business E-Mail: michael_seipel@byu.edu.

SEIPLE, JOHN W., JR., corporate financial executive; b. July 20, 1958; married; 3 children. BA in Econs., Davidson Coll.; MBA, Tex. Christian U. With Interfirst Bank Dallas, N.A.; ptnr., sr. v.p. Trammell Crow Co.; v.p., market officer Prologis, Houston, 1993—94, sr. v.p., regional dir., 1994—97, mng. dir. S.E. region, 1997—99, COO, 1999, pres., chief investment officer N.Am. Denver, 2004—, chair N.Am. mgmt. com., chair N.Am. investment com., mem. Office of the Chmn.

SEITEL, FRASER PAUL, public relations executive; b. Jersey City, June 6, 1946; s. Robert and Helen (Barmad) S.; m. Rosemary Kierstein, Dec. 20, 1969; children: Raina, David. BJ, U. Mo., 1964; MA, U. ND, 1970; MBA, NYU, 1977. Pub. rels. officer Chase Manhattan Bank, NYC, 1970-73, v.p., 1974-85, sr. v.p., dir. pub. affairs, 1985-92; mng. ptnr. Emerald Ptnrs., Ft. Lee, NJ, 1992—; sr. counselor Burson Marsteller, NYC, 1992—; asst. prof. pub. rels. NYU, 2006—; vis. prof. reputation mgmt. Fla. Internat. U., 2005—; sr. counselor investor rels. and mktg. communications Greater NY Savs. Bank, 1994-97. Pub. rels. con. Hill and Knowlton, NYC, 1973; instr. Profl. Devel. Inst., NYC, Ragan Comms., Chgo., Estes Park Inst., Colo.; columnist US Banker, 1989—94, Odwyerpr.com, 2001—, Profit Mag., 1993—95, Tech Central Station, 2003—; adj. asst. prof. NYU, 2006—. Author: The Practice of Public Relations, 10th edit., 2006; co-author: Idea Wise, 2002; pub., editor: The Public Relations Strategist, 1995—2001, columns editor: PRSA Tactics mag., 1994—95, columnist: odwyerpr.com, 2001—; contbr. ABC Good Morning America, CNN, MSNBC, Fox News Channel, CNBC, Inside Edit. Named among Top 100 Pub. Rels. Profls. of 20th century PR Week. Mem. Pub. Rels. Soc. Am., Bank Mktg. Assn. Avocations: baseball, football, basketball, tai chi, rugby. Office: 177 Main St Ste 215 Fort Lee NJ 07024-6936 Office Phone: 201-784-8880. E-mail: yusake@aol.com.

SEITMAN, JOHN MICHAEL, arbitrator, mediator, lawyer; b. Bloomington, Ill., Feb. 9, 1942; BS, U. Ill., 1964, JD, 1966. Bar: Calif., U.S. Dist. Ct. (so., ctrl., no. and ea. dists.) Calif., U.S. Ct. Appeals (9th cir.). Prin. Lindley, Lazar & Scales, San Diego, 1966-97; full-time neutral affiliated with JAMS, 1997—. Lectr. in continuing legal edn. Bd. dirs. San Diego County Bar Found., 1983-89, treas., 1983-84, pres., 1988-89; del. to 9th Cir. Jud. Conf., 1986, 88. Fellow Am. Bar Found.; mem. ABA, State Bar Calif. (pres. 1991-92), San Diego County Bar Assn. (pres. 1986). Office: PO Box 2156 Del Mar CA 92014-1456 Home Phone: 858-793-4426; Office Phone: 858-793-4555. Personal E-mail: jseitman@pacbell.net.

SEITZ, CAROLE JANE, composer, educator; d. Charles N. Hicks and Ermagene Virginia Hicks, nee Riley; m. Richard John Seitz, Aug. 10, 1991; children: Kimberly Ann Santora, Jeffrey Ward Bean. MusM Edn., MusB Edn., Wichita State U., Wichita, Kansas, 1956—61. Assoc. chair of performing arts Creighton U., Omaha, Nebr., 1976—, assoc. prof. of music. Asst. condr., chorus master Opera Omaha, 1976—89; violinist Omaha Symphony, 1961—75; musical dir. Coun. Bluffs Cmty. Chorus, Council Bluffs, Iowa, 1969—73, Chanticleer Theatre, Council Bluffs; violinist Wichita Symphony, 1958—60, Lincoln Symphony, Nebr., 1972—79, Des Moines Symphony, 1972—79; dir. of music St. John's Luth. Ch., Council Bluffs; jr. choir dir., soprano soloist St. Andrews Episc. Ch., Omaha, 1980—89. Composer: (play) The Devils, (choral compositions) Midwinter Carol Two Wee Girls Christmas Eve Prayer Alleluia He is Risen, (music for indiv. ballet practice, dance compositions) Dances for the Young Ballerina, (dance compositions) Music for Individual Practice, (string orchestra) Little Fugue, (ballet music) Requiem inspired by poem by Desmond Egan. Founder and pres. Coun. Bluffs Arts Coun., 1970—73. Recipient Citizenship award, AAUW. Mem.: Am. Choral Dirs. Assn. (life; iowa bd. mem. 1968—69), Mortar Bd., Mu Phi Epsilon. Episcopalian. Avocations: horseback riding, travel, reading, knitting. Home: 1705 Laguna Drive Fremont NE 68025 Office: Creighton University 2500 California Plaza Omaha NE 68178 Home Phone: 402-753-1875; Office Phone: 402-280-2766. Office Fax: 402-280-2320. Business E-Mail: cseitz@creighton.edu.

SEITZ, FREDERICK, former university administrator; b. San Francisco, July 4, 1911; s. Frederick and Emily Charlotte (Hofman) S.; m. Elizabeth K. Marshall, May 18, 1935. AB, Leland Stanford Jr. U., 1932; PhD, Princeton U., 1934; Doctorate Hon. Causa, U. Ghent, 1957; DSc (hon.), U. Reading, 1960, Rensselaer Poly. Inst., 1961, Marquette U., 1963, Carnegie Inst. Tech., 1963, Case Inst. Tech., 1964, Princeton U., 1964, Northwestern U., 1965, U. Del., 1966, Poly. Inst. Bklyn., 1967, U. Mich., 1967, U. Utah, 1968, Brown U., 1968, Duquesne U., 1968, St. Louis U., 1969, Nebr. Wesleyan U., 1970, U. Ill., 1972, Rockefeller U., 1981; LLD (hon.), Lehigh U., 1966, U. Notre Dame, 1962, Mich. State U., 1965, Ill. Inst. Tech., 1968, N.Y. U., 1969; LHD (hon.), Davis and Elkins Coll., 1970, Rockefeller U., 1981, U. Pa., 1985, U. Miami, 1989. Instr. physics U. Rochester, 1935-36, asst. prof., 1936-37; physicist research labs. Gen. Electric Co., 1937-39; asst. prof. Randal Morgan Lab. Physics, U. Pa., 1939-41, assoc. prof., 1941-42; prof. physics, head dept. Carnegie Inst. Tech., Pitts., 1942-49; prof. physics U. Ill., 1949-57, head dept., 1957-64, dir. control systems lab., 1951-52, dean Grad. Coll., v.p. research, 1964-65; exec. pres. Nat. Acad. Scis., 1962-69; pres. Rockefeller U., NYC, 1968-78; dir. Richard Lounsbery Found., NYC, 1980—, pres., 1995—2002, U. Miami (Fla.), 1989. Trustee Ogden Corp.; 1977—; dir. tng. program Clinton Labs., Oak Ridge, 1946-47; chmn. Naval Rsch. Adv. Com., 1960-62; vice chmn. Def. Sci. Bd., 1961-62, chmn., 1964-68; sci. adviser NATO, 1959-60; mem. nat. adv. com. Marine Biomed. Inst. U. Tex., Galveston, 1975-77; mem. adv. group White House Conf. Anticipated Advances in Sci. and Tech., 1975-76; mem. adv. bd. Desert Rsch. Inst., 1975-79, Ctr. Strategic and Internat. Studies, 1975-81; mem. Nat. Cancer Adv. Bd., 1976-82; dir. Akzona Inc. Author: Modern Theory of Solids, 1940, The Physics of Metals, 1943, Solid State Physics, 1955, The Science Matrix, 1992, On the Frontier: My Life in Science, 1994, Stalin's Captive: Nikolaus Riehl and the Soviet Race for the Bomb, 1995, Electronic Genie: The Tangled History of Silicon. Trustee Rockefeller Found., 1964-77, Princeton U., 1968-72, Lehigh U., 1970-81, Rsch. Corp., 1966-82, Inst. Internat. Edn., 1971-78, Woodrow Wilson Nat. Fellowship Found., 1972-82, Univ. Corp. Atmospheric Rsch., Am. Mus. Natural History, 1975—; trustee John Simon Guggenheim Meml. Found., 1973-83, chmn. bd., 1976-83; mem. Belgian Am. Edn. Found. Decorated Order of the Brilliant Star (Republic of China); recipient Franklin medal Franklin Inst. Phila., 1965, Hoover medal Stanford U., 1968, Nat. Medal Sci., 1973, James Madison award Princeton U., 1978, Edward R. Loveland Meml. award ACP, 1983, Vannevar Bush award Nat. Sci. Bd., 1983, J. Herbert Holloman award Acta Metallurgica, 1993, Von Hippel award Materials Rsch. Soc., 1993, Joseph Henry medal Smithsonian Instn., 1997. Fellow Am. Phys. Soc. (pres. 1961); mem. NAS, Am. Acad. Arts and Scis., AIME, Am. Philos. Soc., Am. Inst. Physics (chmn. governing bd. 1954-59), Inst. for Def. Analysis, Finnish Acad. Sci. and Letters (fgn. mem.), Phi Beta Kappa Assos.; mem. GM Adv. Council, Cancer Rsch. Found. Address: Rockefeller U 1230 York Ave New York NY 10021-6307 Office Phone: 212-327-8423.

SEITZ, HENRY W., information technology manager; b. Ishpeming, Mich., Jan. 9, 1974; s. Henry L. and Barbara J. Seitz. BS in Physics, U. Mich., Ann Arbor, 1996. Info. sys. network adminstr. Gen. Physics, Columbia, Md., 1997—2000; MTS-1 Lucent Techs., Hunt Valley, Md., 2000—02; info. sys. network ops. MCare, Ann Arbor, 2002—. Mem.: Am. Mensa. Home Phone: 734-657-4244; Office Phone: 734-332-2123. Personal E-mail: raistlin303@yahoo.com.

SEITZ, JAMES EUGENE, retired college president, freelance writer; b. Columbia, Pa., July 27, 1927; s. Joseph Stoner and Minnie (Frey) S.; m. Florence Arlene Dutcher, Apr. 6, 1950; children: Diane Louise, Ellen Kay, Linda Marie, Karl Steven. BS, Millersville State Coll., 1950; MEd, Pa. State U., 1952; PhD, So. Ill. U., 1971. Tchr. pub. schs., Pa., 1950-56; lectr. Temple U., Phila., 1956-62; asst. prof. engr. tech. Kans. State U., Pitts., 1962-65; dean Mineral Area Coll., Flat River, Mo., 1965-69, Coll. of Lake County, Gravslake, Ill., 1969-73; founding pres. Edison State Community Coll., Piqua, Ohio, 1973-85; freelance writer Sidney, Ohio, 1985—. Founding sec.-treas. Ohio Tech. and C.C. Assn., Columbus, 1976; speaker in field. Author: Woodcarving: A Designer's Notebook, 1989, Country Creations, 1991, Selling What You Make, 1992, Effective Board Participation, 1993, Substance for the Soul, 1999, Practical Woodcarving Design and Application, 2003, Carved Gifts for All Occasions, 2006; contbr. articles to profl. jours. Founding pres. Exch. Club Grayslake, 1970; pres. Epicurian Soc., Sidney, Ohio, 1978-79; mediator Mcpl. Ct., Sidney, 1992-2003; sr. citizens' steering com. Arbor Day Found.; founding pres. Sr. Ctr. of Sidney-Shelby Co., 1996—, choir, 2001—04; trustee Sidney Meml. Bldg., 2003-; named Outstanding Sr. Citizen, 2001; mem. Ret. Srs. Vol. Program, 2005—. Named to Manor High Sch. Wall of Honor, 2007; recipient Leadership and Svc. award, Pa. State U. Alumni Soc., 1990, Disting. Alumni Svc. award, Millersville U., 2007. Mem. Am. Assn. Ret. Persons (founding chpt. pres. 1990-91), Assn. for Career & Tech. Edn., VFW (charter Post 8757), Am. Legion (scholarship com. and judge Post 217 1996-97, exec. com. 1997—, publicity dir. 1998-2000), Sidney Singing Soldiers (pres., 1998), AmVets, Shelby Woodcarvers Guild (founding pres. 1999), Iota Lambda Sigma. Avocations: woodworking, lecturing. Home: 55 Brown Rd Sidney OH 45365-8949 E-mail: jseitz@netpenny.net.

SEITZ, KARL RAYMOND, editor; b. Corpus Christi, Tex., Sept. 26, 1943; s. Kerlin McCullough and Martha Elisabeth (Tillman) S.; m. Patricia Jean Floyd, June 13, 1970; 1 child, Lee Kerlin. BA, Birmingham So. Coll., 1970. Copy editor Birmingham (Ala.) Post-Herald, 1967-70, asst. news editor, 1970-73, chief editorial writer, 1973-78, editor editorial page, 1978—2005. Dir. Birmingham Post-Birmingham Typographical Union Pension Plan, 1983-90, chmn., 1986-90; v.p. Goodfellow Fund, Inc., Birmingham, 1986—2005. Active exec. in residence Birmingham So. Coll., 1987, Leadership Birmingham, 1986—, mem. mem.'s coun., 1998—2001. With USN, 1961—64. Mem. Nat. Conf. Editl. Writers, Acad. Polit. Sci. Home: 1212 30th Street S Birmingham AL 35205-1910 E-mail: kseitz@earthlink.net.

SEITZ, MARY LEE, mathematics professor; BS in Edn. summa cum laude, SUNY, Buffalo, 1977, MS in Edn., 1982. Cert. secondary tchr., N.Y. Prof. math. Erie C.C.-City Campus, Buffalo, 1982—. Reviewer profl. jours. and coll. textbooks. Vol. Buffalo (N.Y.) Philharmonic Orch. Mem. NY Maths. Assn. Two Yr. Colls., Assn. Maths. Tchrs. NY, NY Assn. Two Yr. Colls., Inc., Buffalo (N.Y.) Philharmonic Orch. Soc., Commerative AF, Pi Mu Epsilon. Avocations: gardening, photography, bird watching. Office: Erie C C-City Campus 121 Ellicott St Buffalo NY 14203-2601 E-mail: seitzm@ecc.edu. *Quotable quote from Alfred Lord Tennyson, "To strive, to seek, to find, and not to yield".*

SEITZ, NICHOLAS JOSEPH, editor, journalist; b. Topeka, Jan. 30, 1939; s. Frank Joseph and Lydia Natalie (Clerico) S.; m. Velma Jean Pfannenstiel, Sept. 12, 1959; children: Bradley Joseph, Gregory Joseph. BA, U. Okla., 1966. Sports editor Manhattan (Kans.) Mercury, 1960-62, Norman (Okla.) Transcript, 1962-64, Okla. Jour., Oklahoma City, 1964-67; staff Golf Digest mag., Norwalk, Conn., 1967—, editor, 1973-82; editorial dir. Golf Digest and Tennis, 1982-90; editorial dir. Sports/Leisure divsn. N.Y. Times Co. Mag. Group, 1991-92, sr. v.p., editor in chief, 1992-98, editor at large, 1999—. Syndicated golf instrn. and commentary CBS Radio Network; commentary ESPN TV Network. Author: Superstars of Golf, 1978; (with Dave Hill) Teed Off, 1977; (with Tom Watson) Getting Up and Down, 1983, Getting Back to Basics, 1991, Tom Watson's Strategic Golf, 1993; contbr. articles to profl. jours.; anthologized in: Best Sports Stories. Named Okla. Sports Writer of Year Nat. Sportswriters and Sportscasters Assn., 1965; winner contests Nat. Basketball Writers Assn.; winner contests Golf Writers Assn.; recipient Lincoln A. Werden award for outstanding contbn. to golf journalism, 1993, Meml. Tournament Golf Journalism award, 2000, PGA Lifetime Achievement in Journalism award, 2002, Major Achievement award The Masters, 2007. Home: 36 Hunt St Norwalk CT 06853-1015 Office: 20 Westport Rd Wilton CT 06897-0850 Personal E-mail: nseitz@optonline.net.

SEITZ, PATRICIA ANN, judge; b. Washington, Sept. 2, 1946; d. Richard J. and Bettie Seitz; m. Alan Graham Greer, Aug. 14, 1981. BA in History cum laude, Kans. State U., 1968; JD, Georgetown U., 1973. Bar: Fla. 1973, D.C. 1975, U.S. Dist. Ct. (no., mid., so. dists., trial bar) Fla., U.S. Ct. Appeals (5th and 11th cirs.), U.S. Supreme Ct. Reporter Dallas Times Herald, Washington, 1970-73; law clk. to Hon. Charles R. Richey U.S. Dist. Ct., Washington, 1973-74; assoc. Steel, Hector & Davis, Miami, Fla., 1974-79, ptnr., 1980-96; dir. office legal counsel Office of Nat. Drug Control Policy, Exec. Office of Pres., Washington, 1996-97; judge U.S. Dist. Ct. (so. dist.) Fla., 1998—. Adj. faculty U. Miami Law Sch., Coral Gables, Fla., 1984-88; faculty Nat. Inst. Trial Advocacy, Boulder, Colo., 1982, 83, 95, Chapel Hill, N.C., 1984, 87. Fla. region, 1989; lectr. in field. Contbr. numerous articles to law jours. Mem. Dade Munroe Mental Health Bd., Miami, 1982-84, United Way of Greater Miami comty. devel. com., 1984-87; chmn. family abuse task force United Way of Greater Miami, 1986; chmn. devel. com. Miami City Ballet, 1986-87, bd. dirs., 1986-90. Fellow Am. Bar Found., Am. Bd. Trial Advocacy, Internat. Soc. Barristers; mem. ABA (chmn. various coms. 1979-85, Ho. Dels. 1992-96), Am. Arbitration Assn. (nat. bd. dirs. 1995-97, complex case panel arbitrator), The Fla. Bar (bd. govs. young lawyer divsn. 1981-82, bd. govs. 1986-92, pres. 1993-94, bd. cert. civil trial), Fla. Assn. Women Lawyers, Dade County Bar Assn. (pub. interest law bank). Roman Catholic. Avocations: travel, art. Office: Fed Courthouse Square 301 N Miami Ave Fl 5 Miami FL 33128-7702

SEIVERS, LANA C., school system administrator; b. Clinton, Tenn, 1951; BEd, Middle Tenn. State U.; MA in Ednl. Adminstrn., U. Tenn., D in Ednl.

Leadership. Speech pathologist Spl Edn. Oak Ridge Sch. System, Tenn.; adminstr. early childhood and edn programs Oak Ridge Sch. System, prin. Linden Elem. Sch.; supt. Clinton City Schs., Tenn., 1989—2003; commr. Tenn. Dept. Edn., Nashville, 2003—. Design cons. Inst. Sch. Leaders; mem. adv. coun. Edn of Childen with Disabilities. Mem.: Assn. Ind. and Mcpl. Schs. (bd. dirs.), Tenn. Orgn. Sch. Supts. (treas.), E. Tenn. Supts. Stidy Coun. (chair), So. Assn. Colls. and Schs. (chair). Office: Tenn Dept Edn 6th Fl Andrew Johnson Twr 710 James Robertson Pkwy Nashville TN 37243-0375 *

SEJNOWSKI, TERRENCE JOSEPH, science educator; b. Cleve., Aug. 13, 1947; s. Joseph Francis and Theresa (Cudnik) Sejnowski; m. Beatrice Alexandra Golomb, Mar. 24, 1990. BS, Case Western Res. U., 1968; PhD, Princeton U., 1978. Rsch. fellow Harvard Med. Sch., Boston, 1979-82; prof. biophysics Johns Hopkins U., Balt., 1982-90; prof. Salk Inst. U. Calif. San Diego, La Jolla, 1988—, dir. computational neurobiology tng. program, 2001—; Francis Crick prof. Salk Inst., 2005—. Investigator Howard Hughes Med. Inst., 1991—; bd. dirs. San Diego McDonnell-Pew Ctr. for Cognitive Neurosci., 1990-98, Inst. for Neural Computation, U. Calif. San Diego., 1990—. Editor-in-chief Neural Computation, 1989—; co-inventor: (with others) the Boltzmann machine and NET talk; mem. editl. bd. Sci. Mag., 1990—. Pres. Neural Info. Processing System Found. Recipient Presdl. Young Investigator award NSF, 1984, Wright prize Harvey Mudd Coll., 1996; Sherman Fairchild Disting. scholar Calif. Inst. Tech., 1993. Fellow IEEE (Neural Network Pioneer award 2002, AAAS; mem. Soc. for Neurosci., Am. Phys. Soc., Internat. Neural Network Soc. (governing bd. 1988-92, Hebb prize 1999), Am. Math. Soc., Assn. Rsch. in Vision and Ophthalmology, Am. Assn. Artificial Intelligence, Biophys. Soc., Optical Soc. Am., Am. Psychol. Soc., Am. Psychol. Assn., N.Y. Acad. Scis., Fedn. Am. Soc. Exptl. Biophysics, Soc. Neuroscience, Internat. Soc. Neuroethology, Soc. Math. Biology, Johns Hopkins U. Soc. of Scholars. Achievements include co-invention of the Boltzmann machine, of NETtalk, a neural network for text-to-speech. Office: Salk Inst PO Box 85800 San Diego CA 92186-5800 Home Phone: 858-587-0423. E-mail: sejnowski@salk.edu.

SEKANINA, ZDENEK, astronomer; b. Mlada Boleslav, Czechoslovakia, June 12, 1936; came to U.S., 1969; s. Frantisek Sekanina and Hedvika Sekaninova; m. Jana Soukupova, Apr. 1, 1966; 1 child, Jason. Diploma, Charles U., Prague, Czechoslovakia, 1959, PhD in Astronomy, 1963. Astronomer Stefanik Obs., Prague, 1959-66, Ctr. for Numerical Math., Charles U., Prague, 1967-68; vis. scientist Inst. d'Astrophysique, Univ. de Liege, Cointe-Ougree, Belgium, 1968-69; physicist Smithsonian Astrophys. Obs., Cambridge, Mass., 1969-80; mem. tech. staff Jet Propulsion Lab., Pasadena, Calif., 1980-81, rsch. scientist, 1981-84, sr. rsch. scientist, 1984—. Assoc. Harvard Coll. Obs., Cambridge, 1969-80; mem. NASA Comet Sci. Working Group, 1977-80; cons. Jet Propulsion Lab., 1977-80; prin. U.S. co-investigator Particulate Impact Analyzer Experiment, Dust Impact Detector Sys. Experiment, European Space Agy.'s Giotto Mission to Comet Halley, 1980-89; mem. NASA-European Spacy Agy. Comet Halley Environ. Working Group, 1980-89; discipline specialist Near Nucleus Studies Network, Internat. Halley Watch, 1982-90; mem. imaging sci. subsys. team Comet Rendezvous Asteroid Flyby Mission, 1986-92; mem. sci. definition team ESA/NASA Comet Nucleus Sample Return Mission, 1988—; co-investigator STARDUST Discovery Mission, 1994—. Editor Comet Halley Archive, 1982-91; mem. editorial bd. Kosmicke Rozhledy, 1963-69. Recipient Exceptional Sci. Achievement medal NASA, 1985, 2005; minor planet named Sekanina, 1976. Mem. Internat. Astron. Union (mem. commns. 15, 20, 22, mem. organizing commn. 22 1976-82, organizing commn. 15 1979-85, mem. working group on comets 1988—, assoc. dir. Ctrl. Bur. for Astron. Telegrams 1970-80), COSPAR (working group 3, panel C, exec. mem. 1980-82), Learned Soc of Czech Republic (hon. 1996—), Czech Astron. Soc. (hon. 2001-, Nušl prize 2006). Roman Catholic. Office: Jet Propulsion Lab 4800 Oak Grove Dr Pasadena CA 91109-8001 Business E-Mail: zs@sek.jpl.nasa.gov.

SEKERKA, ROBERT FLOYD, physics and mathematics professor; b. Wilkinsburg, Pa., Nov. 27, 1937; s. John Jacob and Vivian Mae (Smith) S.; m. Dianne Thompson, Apr. 30, 1960 (div. Apr. 1981); children: Lee Ann, Robert Thompson; m. 2d Carolyn Lee Confer, May 24, 1981. BS in Physics, U. Pitts., 1960; AM, Harvard U., 1961, PhD, 1965; PhD (hon.), U. Timisora, Romania, 1996. Engr. Westinghouse Rsch. Labs., Pitts., 1965-68, mgr. materials growth and properties dept., 1968-69; from lectr. to univ. prof. Carnegie-Mellon U., Pitts., 1967—91, univ. prof., 1991—. Mem. space studies bd. NRC, 1989-91. Assoc. editor Jour. Crystal Growth, 1971-94; Metallurgical Trans., 1970-76; editorial bd. Applied Microgravity Tech., 1987-90. Past bd. dirs. Forbes Health Sys., Pitts., Pitts. Regional Ctr. for Sci. Tchrs.; past vice chmn. bd. dirs. NMR Inst.; past mem. rsch. com. Allegheny Singer Rsch. Inst., Pitts. Recipient A.G. Worthing award U. Pitts., 1959, Philip M. McKenna Meml. award, 1980, Bruce Chalmers award TMS, 1998; Woodrow Wilson fellow, 1960, NSF fellow, 1962-65. Fellow: Am. Phys. Soc., Am. Soc. Metals, Japanese Soc. for Promotion of Sci.; mem.: Internat. Orgn. Crystal Growth (pres. 2001—, Frank prize 1992), Am. Assn. Crystal Growth (mem. exec. com.), Minerals Metals Materials Soc., Edgewood Country Club, Sigma Xi, Phi Beta Kappa, Omicron Delta Kappa. Home: 307 S Dithridge St Atrium 911 Pittsburgh PA 15213-3519 Office: Carnegie Mellon U Dept Physics 6416 Wean Hall Pittsburgh PA 15213-3890 Office Phone: 412-268-2362. Business E-Mail: sekerka@cmu.edu.

SEKOWSKI, CYNTHIA JEAN, health products executive, medical consultant, contact lens specialist; b. Chgo., Feb. 14, 1953; d. John L. and Celia L. (Matusiak) S. PhD in Health Svcs. Adminstrn., Columbia Pacific U., 1984, PhD in Health Scis., 1984; grad., Realtor Inst., 1998. Chief contact lens dept. Lieberman & Kraff, Chgo., 1974—87; pres., CEO Seko Eye Care, Inc., Chgo., 1988—; realtor Country Club Realty Group, Naples, Fla., 1995—2002, John R. Wood, Inc. Realtors, 2002—. Rschr., technologist U. Ill., Chgo., 1976-78. Active Chgo. Zool. Soc., 1984—, Little City Inner Cir., 1991—, Aurora Lakeland Med. Ctr. Found.; sponsor Save the Children Orgn., 1983—; asst. to campaign mgr. Rep. state senatorial candidate, Chgo., 1972; pres. Compass Point Condo Assn., Naples, Fla., 1996-99; budget com. Windstar Country Club Master Homeowner's Assn., Naples, 1996-99; mem. ptnrs. coun. Habitat for Humanity. Fellow: Contact Lens Soc. Am.; mem.: Women's Coun. Realtors, Naples Area Bd. Realtors, Nat. Assn. Realtors, Fla. Assn. Realtors, Nat. Contact Lens Examiners, Better Vision Inst., Opticians Assn. Am., Ill. Soc. Opticianry, Am. Fedn. Police and Concerned Citizens (sustaining mem.), Wis. Hist. Soc., Geneva Lakes Conservancy, The Phoenix Soc. (med. profl.), Columbia Pacific U. Alumnae Assn., U.S. Golf Assn., Nat. Geog. Soc., S.W. Fla. Conservancy, Nat. Wildlife Fedn. (charter mem.), Soc. of the Little Flower, Bear's Paw Country Club (mktg. com. 2002—), Vanderbilt Country Club (residents adv. bd. 1999—2001, vice-chmn. adminstrn. com. 2001—03). Roman Catholic. Avocations: gardening, reading, photography, golf, writing poetry. Office: John R Wood Inc Realtors 3255 Tamiami Trl N Naples FL 34103 Office Phone: 239-269-5000. E-mail: luvfla@mindspring.com.

SEKULA-GIBBS, SHELLEY, former congresswoman, dermatologist; b. Floresville, Tex., June 22, 1953; m. Allen Greenberg (div.); m. Sylvan Rodriguez (dec. 2000); m. Robert W. Gibbs Jr., 2002; 2 children. BS summa cum laude, Our Lady of Lake U., 1975; MD, U. Tex., 1979. Pvt. practice dermatology, Houston; at-large mem. Houston City Coun., 2002—06; mem. US Congress from 22nd Tex. dist., 2006—07. Clin. asst. prof. Baylor Coll. of Medicine, Houston; tchr. Ben Taub Hosp.; mem. Health Care Adv. Com. Houston Partnership. Mem. Friends of Tex. Med. Ctr. Libr.; co-founder Ellington Field Task Force, Tex.; bd. dirs. Bay Area Transp. Partnership. Republican. Roman Catholic.

SEKULARAC, NADEZDA, software architect, researcher; b. Aleksandrovac, Serbia and Montenegro, Mar. 30, 1976; arrived in US, 2004; d. Radomir and Vucica Sekularac. BS in Computer Sci. (hon.), Faculty of Math., Belgrade, Serbia and Montenegro, 2000; M of Info. Sys., Faculty of Orgnl. Scis., Belgrade, Serbia and Montenegro, 2003. Software developer IPConsulting, Frankfurt, Germany, 2000—03; sr. software developer Ilumnis, Toronto, Ont., Canada, 2003—04; sr. software engr. Viking River Cruises, LA, 2004—07; sr. software arch. Internat. Med. Corps, Santa Monica, Calif., 2006—. Cons. UMCOR Serbia, Belgrade, 2002—03; artificial intelligence rschr. Good Old AI, Belgrade, 2000—; Web content mgr. faculty math. Belgrade U., 2000—06. Mem.: Am. Mensa (life). Achievements include discovery of pattern for text search engine based on Bayesian networks. Home: #6 1248 9th St Santa Monica CA 90401 Office: Internat Med Corps 1919 Santa Monica Blvd Ste 300 Santa Monica CA 90404 Home Phone: 310-985-3687. Personal E-mail: nsekularac@yahoo.com.

SEKULER, ROBERT WILLIAM, psychologist, educator; b. Elizabeth, NJ, May 7, 1939; s. Sidney and Mary (Siegel) Sekuler; m. Susan Pamela Nemser, June 25, 1961; children: Stacia, Allison, Erica. AB, Brandeis U., 1960; MSc, Brown U., 1963, PhD, 1964; postgrad. (NIH postdoctoral fellow), MIT, 1964-65. Prof. psychology Northwestern U., Evanston, Ill., 1973-89, prof. ophthalmology Med. Sch., 1978-89, prof. neurobiology and physiology, 1982-89, John Evans prof. neuroscience, 1986-89, chmn. dept., 1975-79, assoc. dean Coll. Arts and Scis., 1985-89; v.p. Optronix, Inc., 1980-82; Louis and Frances Salvage prof. psychology Brandeis U., Waltham, Mass., 1989—, provost, dean faculty, 1989-91, dir. program cognitive scis., 1998—, chair program on neurosci., 2003—; mem. Ctr. Complex Sys., 1990—. Rsch. prof. biomed. engring. Boston U., 1992—, adj. prof. cognitive and neural sys., 1994—2001; vis. prof. psychology U. Toronto, 2000; cons. NWSF, NIH, AAAS, USAF, U. Calif., APA; chmn. vision com. NRC-NAS; chmn. working group on visual function and aging NRC, chmn. working group on aging workers and visual impairment; scientist Rotman Inst. Baycrest Geriatric Ctr., 2000. Author (with D. Kline and K. Dismukes): (book) Aging and Human Visual Function, 1981; author: Star Trek on the Brain, 1998, Star Trek on the Brain, paperback edit., 1999, Star Trek on the Brain, Japanese edit., 2000; author: (with R. Blake) Perception, 1985, Perception, Hungarian edit., 2000, Perception, 5th edit., 2005; editor: Perception & Psychophysics, 1971—86, Jour. Exptl. Psychology, 1973—74, Vision Rsch. Jour., 1974—79, 1980—92, Optics Letters, 1977—79, Am. Jour. Psychology, Ophthalmic and Physiol. Optics, 1986—99, Intelligent Sys., 1986—92, Psychology and Aging, 1987—92; co-author: Oxford Textbook of Geriatric Medicine, 1992, 1999, Ency. Psychology, 1999; contbr. articles to profl. jours. Grantee, Nat. inst. Neurol. Diseases and Stroke, USAF, NSF, Nat. Eye Inst., Nat. Inst. Aging, USN, James McDonnell Found., Alzheimer's Found. Fellow: AAAS, Am. Psychol. Soc., Optical Soc. Am.; mem.: New England Coll. Optometry, Knowles Inst. for Hearing Rsch. (bd. dirs. 1988—90), Psychonomic Soc., Neurosci. Soc., Assn. Rsch. in Vision and Ophthalmology, Sigma Xi. Home: 64 Strawberry Hill Rd Concord MA 01742-5502 Office: Brandeis U Ctr for Complex Systems Waltham MA 02454

SEKULOVICH, MLADEN See MALDEN, KARL

SEKULOW, JAY ALAN, lawyer; b. Bklyn., June 10, 1956; m. Pam Sekulow; 2 children. BA cum laude, Mercer U, JD; PhD in Am. Legal History, Regent U. Bar: Ga. 1980. Mem., lawyer Jews for Jesus; chief counsel Am. Ctr. for Law and Justice, Virginia Beach, 1990—, European Ctr. for Law and Justice, 1998—; host Jay Sekulow Live!. Adj. prof. law Regent U. Author: From Intimidation to Victory, 1990, Knowing Your Rights, 1993, Students Rights and the Public School, And Nothing But The Truth, 1996, Christian Rights in the Workplace, 1997; The Christian, The Court, and The Constitution, 2000 Mem. bd. of trustees Supreme Court Historical Soc., Washington D.C. Named a Mem. of The Pub. Sector 45, American Lawyer magazine, 1997; named one of The 25 Most Influential Evangelicals in America, Time Magazine, 2005, 100 Most Influential Lawyers in America, Nat. Law Journ., 1994, 1997. Office: Am Ctr for Law & Justice 1000 Regent University Dr Virginia Beach VA 23464-5037 *

SELANDER, ROBERT W., finance company executive; BS, Cornell Univ., 1972; MBA, Harvard Univ., 1974. Mgmt. positions through dir. global retail strategy Citicorp., 1974—94; exec. v.p., pres. Europe, Middle East/Africa & Canada regions MasterCard Inc., 1994—97, pres., CEO Purchase, NY, 1997—. Bd. dir. The Hartford, 1998—. Mem. Com. to Encourage Corp. Philanthropy. Office: MasterCard Inc 2000 Purchase St Purchase NY 10577 *

SELANNE, TEEMU, professional hockey player; b. Helsinki, Finland, July 3, 1970; Right wing Winnipeg Jets, 1992—95, Phoenix Coyotes, 1995—97, Anaheim Ducks (formerly Mighty Ducks of Anaheim), 1997—2001, 2005—, San Jose Sharks, 2001—03, Colo. Avalanche, 2004—05. Mem Finnish Nat. Olympic Team, 1992, 98, 2002, Finnish Nat. Team, World Cup of Hockey, 1996, 2004, Finnish Nat. Team, World Championships, 1996, 99; player NHL All-Star game, 1993, 94, 1996—2000, 2002, 03. Named World Championships Tournament MVP, 1999; named to All-Rookie Team, 1993, First All-Star Team, NHL, 1993, 1997; recipient Calder Meml. Trophy, 1993, Maurice Richard Trophy, 1999, Bill Masterton Trophy, 2006. Achievements include being a member of Stanley Cup Champion Anaheim Ducks, 2007. Office: Anaheim Ducks PO Box 61077 2695 E Katella Ave Anaheim CA 92803-6177

SELBY, CECILY CANNAN, dean, science educator, scientist; b. London, Feb. 4, 1927; d. Keith and Catherine Anne Cannan; m. Henry M. Selby, Aug. 11, 1951 (div. 1978); children: Norman, William, Russell; m. James Stacy Coles, Feb. 21, 1981. AB cum laude, Radcliffe Coll., 1946; PhD in Phys. Biology, MIT, 1950. Teaching asst. in biology MIT, 1948-49; adminstrv. head virus study sect. Sloan-Kettering Inst., NYC, 1949-50, asst. mem. instr., 1950-55; instr. microscopic anatomy Cornell U. Med. Coll., 1955-57; tchr. sci. Lenox Sch., NYC, 1957-58, headmistress, 1959-72; nat. exec. dir. Girl Scouts U.S.A., NYC, 1972-75; adv. com. Simmons Coll. Grad. Mgmt. Program, 1977-78; mem. Com. Corp. Support of Pvt. Univs., 1977-83; spl. asst. acad. planning N.C. Sch. Sci. and Math., 1979-80, dean acad. affairs, 1980-81, chmn. bd. advisors, 1981-84; prof. sci. edn. NYU Sch. Edn., 1985—92. Cons. U.S. Dept. Commerce, 1976-77; dir. Avon Products Inc., RCA, NBC, Loehmanns Inc., Nat. Edn. Corp., 1977-83, pres. Am. Energy Ind., 1976; co-chmn. commn. pre-coll. math. and sci. Nat. Sci. Bd., 1982-83; mem. policy steering com. Gov. Cuomo's Conf. on Sci. and Engring., 1989-90; co- chair Nat. Sci. Bd. Commn. on Pre-Coll. Sci., Math. and Tech., 1982-83; chair NY Acad. Sci. Conf. on Women in Sci. and Engring., 1998; affil. scholar Steinhardt Sch. Edn., NYU, 1993-, Radcliffe Inst., Harvard U., 2000-2001; trustee emeritus NY Hall Sci., 2006. Contbr. articles to profl. jours., chapters to books. Founder, chmn. NY Ind. Schs. Opportunity Project, 1968-72; mem. invitational workshops Aspen Inst., 1973, 75, 77, 79;; bd. dir. RCA, NBC, 1973-86; trustee MIT, Bklyn. Law Sch., Radcliffe Coll., Woods Hole Oceanographic Instn., Women's Forum N.Y., NY Hall of Sci., 1982—, vice chmn., 1989—, trustee Girls Inc., 1992—, Nat. Coun. Women in Medicine, 1990-94; bd. dir. Avon Products, 1973-97; mem. Yale U. Peabody Mus. Adv. Coun., 1981-89; v.p. NY Hall Sci., 1986-99; chair NY Hall of Sci. Coun., 1999-; co-chair program in sci., soc. and gender Radcliffe Inst. of Harvard U., 1999-2001. Recipient Woman Scientist of Yr. award, N.Y. chpt. Am. Women in Sci., 1992, Alumnae Achievement award, Radcliffe Coll., 2001. Fellow: Am. Women Sci., NY Acad Scis.; mem.: Century Assn. Club, Woods Hole Golf Club, The Explorers Club, Cosmopolitan Club, Sigma Xi, Phi Delta Kappa. Home and Office: 1 E 66th St New York NY 10021-5854 also: 100 Ransom Rd Falmouth MA 02540-1652 Business E-Mail: selbyc@aol.com.

SELBY, CORA NORWOOD, retired elementary school educator; b. Nassau, Del., July 15, 1920; d. Clarence Paige and Martha Loretta (Maull) Norwood; m. Paul Myron Selby, Sr., May 26, 1945; children: Paul M.N., Clarence P.N., Clyde L.N., Clyde L.N., Adrian L.N., Terence P.N. BS in Elem. Edn., Del. State U., 1940; MS in Edn., U. Del., 1959, degree (hon.), 1987. Tchr. Ross Point 215-C, Laurel, Del., 1941—64, Paul Laurence Dunbar, Laurel, 1964—66, N. Laurel Sch., 1964—68, faculty adv. Head Start, 1968—80; adult educator Laurel Sch. Dist., 1968—2002, migrant specialist, 1980—87; ret., 2002. Mentor Read Aloud N. Laurel, 1998—; tchr. Elem. Start Program Lake Forest, 1993—2002. Bd. trustees Del. State U., Dover, Del., 1997—; pres. Laurel Sr. Ctr., 2000—; mem. Laurel C. of C.; bd. dirs. Laurel Gardens, 1999—. Mem.: Nat. Assn. Equal Opportunity Higher Edn., Retired Educators Assn., Delaware Assn. Adult and Continuing Edn. (life), Exchange Club, Phi Delta Kappa, Alpha Delta Kappa. Home: 34385 Whaleys Rd Laurel DE 19956

SELBY, DIANE RAY MILLER, fraternal organization administrator; b. Lorain, Ohio, Oct. 11, 1940; d. Dale Edward and Mildred (Ray) Miller; m. David Baxter Selby, Apr. 14, 1962; children: Elizabeth, Susan, Sarah. BS in Edn., Ohio State U., 1962. Sec. Kappa Kappa Gamma Frat., Columbus, Ohio, 1962-63, editor, 1972-86; tchr. Hilliard (Ohio) High Sch., 1963-65; exec. dir. Mortar Bd., Inc. Nat. Office, Columbus, Ohio, 1986—. Editor The Key of Kappa Kappa Gamma Frat, 1972-86 (Student Life award, 1983, 84, 85). Founding officer Community Coordinating Bd., Worthington, Ohio, 1983; pres. PTA Coun., Worthington, 1984, Worthington Band Boosters, 1985; sec., treas. Sports and Recreation Facilities Bd., Worthington, 1986-90; mem. sustaining com. Jr. League Columbus, 1991-93, docent Kelton House, 1979—. Mem.: Assn. Coll. Honor Soc. (exec. com. 1999—2001, 2003—04, 2004—, chmn. bylaws com., trustee 2004—, v.p. 2005—06, pres. 2006—), Mortar Bd., Inc., Ladybugs and Buckeyes, Twig 53 Children's Hosp. (assoc.), Kappa Kappa Gamma (House Bd. v.p. 1997—2000). Republican. Lutheran. Home: 6750 Merwin Pl Columbus OH 43235-2838 Office: Mortar Bd Inc 1200 Chambers Rd Ste 201 Columbus OH 43212-1754 Business E-Mail: selby.1@osu.edu.

SELBY, JEROME M., mayor; b. Wheatland, Wyo., Sept. 4, 1948; s. John Franklin and Claudia Meredith (Hudson) S.; m. Gloria Jean Nelson, June 14, 1969; children: Tyan, Cameronn, Kalen. BS in Math., Coll. Idaho, 1969, MA in Ednl. Adminstrn., 1974; MPA, Boise State U., 1978. Assoc. engr. Boeing Co., Seattle, 1969-71; dir. evaluation WICHE Mountain States Regional Med. Program, Boise, 1971-74; dir. rsch., evaluation Mountain States Health Corp., Boise, 1974-76, with health policy analysis and accountability, 1976-78; dir. health Kodiak (Alaska) Area Native Assn., 1978-83; mgr. Kodiak Island Borough, 1984-85, mayor, 1985-98, 2004—, mcpl. and fisheries cons., 1998—; regional dir. planning and devel. Providence Health System, 1998—2003. Propr. Kodiak Tax Svc., 1978—, Registered Guide, Kodiak, 1987—; cons. Nat. Cancer Inst., Washington, 1973-78, others. Contbr. articles to profl. jours. Treas. ARC, Kodiak, 1978-93, bd. dirs., 1978-95, chmn., 1989-90, mem. western ops. hdqrs. adv. bd., 1986-92, mem. group IV and V nat. adv. coj., 1986-89, nat. bd. govs., 1989-95, chmn. chpt. rels. com., 1994-95, mem. Alaska statewide chpt. bd. dirs., 2002—; pres. S.W. Alaska Mcpl. Conf., Anchorage, 1988-89, v.p., 1986-87, treas., 1996-98, bd. dirs., 1986-98; pres. Alaska Mcpl. League Investment Pool, Inc., 1992-98; v.p. Alaska Mcpl. League, 1988-90, pres., 1990-91, bd. dirs., 1988-98, 2004—; bd. dirs. Alaska Mcpl. League Jt. Ins. Assn. Bd., 1995—, v.p., 1996-98, pres., 1998-2000; mem. Coun. on Econ. Policy for Rural Alaska, 2006-; mem. Alaska Resource Devel. Coun., 1987-2001, exec. com., 1989-2000; bd. dirs. Alaska State C. of C., 2000—, exec. com., 2002-06; mem. policy com. of outer continental shelf adv. bd. U.S. Dept. Interior, 1990-2004, vice chair, 1996-98, chair, 1998-2000; chmn. Natural Gas Subcom., 2000-01; co-chair Alaska Task Force, 1995-2004; mem. Com. on Oil Pollution Act, 1995; mem. Nat. Assn. Counties, Cmty. and Econ. Devel. Steering Com., 1990-98, Alaska govtl. roles task force, 1991-92; mem. Alaska state/local govt. task force, 1996-98; chmn. Kodiak Island Exxon Valdez Restoration Com., 1991-95; bd. dirs. Kodiak Health Care Found., 1992—, v.p. 1992—; co-chmn. Arctic Power, 1993-2005; bd. dirs. Western Interstate Region Nat. Assn. Counties, 1993-98; bd. dirs. Alaska Oceans, Seas, Fisheries Rsch. Found., 1998-2005, pres., 1998-2005; mem. environment, energy and land use steering com. Nat. Assn. Counties, 1997-98; mem. grad. med. edn. com. Alaska Family Practice Residency, 2000-01; mem. Koniag Edn. Found., 2002-03; mem. Oiled Regions of Alaska, 2001—, pres., 2002—. Paul Harris fellow, 1987, 88, 91, 92, 96, 2005; recipient Outstanding Contbn. award Alaska Mcpl. League, 1994, Disting. Alumni award Albertson Coll. of Idaho, 1997, Lifetime Achievement award Alaska Mcpl. League, 1998, Mem. Yr., Kodiak C. of C., 2005. Mem. Alaska Conf. Mayors, Nat. Soc. Tax Profls., Acad. Polit. Sci., Alaska Mcpl. Mgrs. Assn., Kodiak C. of C. (dir. 1983-99, Mem. of Yr. 2005), Rotary (bd. dirs. 1989-97, 2004—, treas. 1989-93, v.p. 1993-94, pres.-elect 1994-95, pres. 1995-96). Office: Kodiak Tax Svc 1120 Baranof St Kodiak AK 99615 Home Phone: 907-486-4833; Office Phone: 907-486-4833. E-mail: jselby@ptialaska.net.

SELBY, JOHN BAYNE, SR., retired radiologist, medical educator; b. Cheyenne, Wyo., Feb. 17, 1924; s. John Edwin Selby and Caroline Lansdale Duckett; m. Jane Claire Dentry, June 11, 1950; children: John Bayne Jr., Henry Gordon, Rebecca Jane. BS, U. Tenn., 1948, MD, 1946; MS in Medicine, U. Minn., 1957. Diplomate Am. Bd. Internal Medicine, Am. Bd. Nuc. Medicine. Asst. in pathology Johns Hopkins U., Balt., 1950—51; intern Evanston (Ill.) Hosp., 1947—48; resident Garfield Hosp., Washington, 1948—50; fellow in pathology Johns Hopkins U., Balt., 1950—51, Mayo Clinic, Rochester, Minn., fellow in medicine, 1954—57, asst. staff mem., 1957; assoc. prof. medicine U. Ky., Lexington, 1958—75; chief nuc. medicine VA Hosp., Lexington, 1966—75, Charleston, SC, 1975—89; prof. radiology Med. U. SC, Charleston, 1995—2000, emeritus prof. radiology, 2001—. Mem. editl. bd. Clin. Nuc. Medicine, Phila., 1985—, Jour. SC Med. Assn., Columbia, 2000—06. Author: Self Assessment Nuclear Medicine, 1977, 1981, Mission in Space, 1994. Mem. Med. Discipline Commn., SC, 1985—88; pres. Ky. Diabetes Assn., Lexington, 1968—69; bd. dirs. Sch. Applied Radiol. Sci., Med. U. SC, Charleston, 1984—86. Capt. US Army, 1952—54, Korea, col. USAR, 1956—74. Fellow: ACP; mem.: Soc. Nuc. Medicine, Endocrine Soc., Alpha Omega Alpha. Avocation: tennis. Home: 2602 Atlantic Ave Sullivans Island SC 29482 E-mail: selbysr2@aol.com.

SELBY, LELAND CLAY, lawyer; b. Granite City, Ill., July 4, 1944; s. William Edward and Agnes (Newell) Selby; m. Diane Schryver, Aug. 20, 1966; children: L. Clay, Thomas S., Amanda E. Henry. BA, U. Richmond, 1966; LLB, U. Va., 1969. Bar: Conn. 1969, NY 1989. Assoc. Hirschberg, Pettengill & Strong, Greenwich, Conn., 1969-74; ptnr. Hirschberg, Pettengill, Strong & Nagle, Greenwich, 1974-78, Whitman & Ransom, Greenwich, 1978-93, Whitman Breed Abbott & Morgan, Greenwich, 1993-95; mem. Fogarty Cohen Selby & Nemiroff LLC, Greenwich, 1995—. Chmn. bd. govs. Greenwich Found. for Cmty. Gifts, 1980—90; pres. United Way of Greenwich, 1978—80; co-pres. Greenwich chpt. English-Speaking Union, 2001—06; bd. dirs., v.p. Stamford Ctr. for Arts, Conn., 1989—2003, chmn. adv. coun., 2003—05; bd. dirs. Retirement Sys., Town of Greenwich, 1993—2001, Greenwich Symphony Orch., 1986—95; bd. dirs. exec. com. English-Speaking Union US. Named Greenwich Young Man of Yr., Greenwich Jaycees, 1974. Fellow Am. Coll. Trust and Estate Counsel; mem. ABA, Conn. Bar Assn., NY State Bar

Assn., Greenwich Bar Assn., Preston Mountain Club (sec. 1999-04), Riverside Yacht Club, Indian Harbor Yacht Club, Va. Club NYC, Harpoon Club of Greenwich. Episcopalian. Avocations: fly fishing, sporting clays, hiking, reading, travel. Office: Fogarty Cohen Selby & Nemiroff 88 Field Point Rd Greenwich CT 06836-2508 Home: 303 W Lyon Farm Dr Greenwich CT 06831-4356

SELBY, RONALD M., orthopedic surgeon; b. New Brunswick, NJ, Feb. 24, 1951; s. Raymond V. and Louise Selby; m. Rosemary Selby. AB, Rutgers U., 1973; postgrad., U. Vt., 1974; MD, Autonomous U. Guadalajara, Mex., 1979. Diplomate Am. Bd. Orthop. Surgery, Am. Bd. Forensic Medicine, cert. advanced shoulder arthroscopy. Intern Muhlenberg Hosp., Plainfield, NJ, 1979—80; resident in gen. surgery NY Med. Coll./Westchester County Med. Ctr. and Met. Hosp. Ctr., 1980—81; resident, chief resident in orthop. surgery St. Vincent's Hosp. and Med. Ctr. NY, 1981—84; James A. Dickson fellow in adult reconstructive surgery Cleve. Clinic Found., 1984—85; clin. asst. prof. orthop. surgery N.Y. Med. Coll., Valhalla, 1988—; attending dept. surgery divsn. orthop. surgery St. Peter's U. Hosp., New Brunswick, NJ; attending CARES Ambulatory Surgery Ctr., New Brunswick; attending dept. orthop. surgery Robert Wood Johnson U. Hosp., New Brunswick. Team physician N.Y.C. Marathon, Spl. Olympics World-Wide Games, NC, 1999; orthop. surgery team cons. St. Bartholomew's Pop Warner Football and Cheerleaders, 1992—; orthop. surgery cons. jr. divsn. U.S. Tennis Assn., 1998—; orthop. team cons. New Brunswick (NJ) H.S. Athletics, 1998—; instr. Coll. Medicine Drexel U., Phila., 2005—; orthop. cons. various athletic orgns. and teams.; presenter in field. Assoc. editor Arthroscopy: The Jour. Arthroscopic and Related Surgery, 2003—; contbr. articles to profl. jours. Hon. co-chmn. physician's adv. bd. Nat. Congl. Com. Named Physician of Yr., Nat. Congl. Com.'s Physician's Adv. Bd., 2002; named one of Am.'s Top Surgeons, Consumer's Rsch. Coun. Am., 2002—07, Best Drs., Better Living Mag., 2002—03; named to Best Doctors, Better Living mag., 2002—03; recipient Nat. Leadership award, Physician's Adv. Bd., Nat. Congl. Com., Order of Merit cum laude, Orthop. Rsch. and Edn. Found., Honors, Arthritis Found. Fellow: Royal Soc. Medicine, Am. Acad. Orthop. Surgeons (spkr. mgr. 2004, mem. comms. coun. 2005—, chmn. sports medicine/arthroscopy program subcom. 2005—, mem. ctrl. program subcoms. 2005—, mem. sports medicine evaluation subcom., chmn. subcom. arthroscopy and sports medicine), Am. Coll. Sports Medicine; mem.: Nat. Assn. Sports Physicians, Athletic Trainers' Soc. NJ, Irish Am. Orthop. Assn., Internat. Fedn. Sports Medicine, European Soc. Sports Traumatology, Knee Surgery and Arthroscopy, Nat. Athletic Trainer's Assn., Internat. Cartilage Repair Soc., Am. Med. Soc. Sports Medicine, Osteoarthritis Rsch. Soc. Internat., Internat. Soc. Arthroscopy, Knee Surgery and Orthop. Sports Medicine (mem. program com. 2005—, mem. editl. bd. 2005—, chmn. comms. com. 2005—), Am. Orthop. Soc. for Sports Medicine (mem. subcom. of edn. com.), Arthroscopy Assn. N.Am. (advisor comms. com. 2005—, presenter, bd. dirs., archives com., rsch. com, learning ctr. com., edn. com., Cert. for Dedication and Svc.), St. Vincent's Hosp. and Med. Ctr. NY Alumni Assn., Cleve. Clinic Found. Alumni Assn. Office: 20 W 13th St New York NY 10011 also: 330 Livingston Ave New Brunswick NJ 08901 Office Phone: 212-255-8000, 732-846-4900.

SELDEN, ROBERT WENTWORTH, physicist, consultant; b. Phoenix, Aug. 11, 1936; s. Edward English and Mary Priscilla (Calder) S.; m. Mary Tania Hudd, June 1958 (div. 1976); 1 child, Ian Scott; m. Marjorie Anne Harmon, Feb. 20, 1977; children: Brock, Thane, Shawna, Kirsten. BA in Physics cum laude, Pomona Coll., 1958; MS in Physics, U. Wis., 1960, PhD in Physics, 1964. Rsch. assoc. Lawrence Livermore Nat. Lab., Calif., 1965—67, staff mem. Calif., 1967—73, group leader Calif., 1973—78, asst. assoc. dir., 1978—80; div. leader applied theoretical physics Los Alamos Nat. Lab., N.Mex., 1980—83, dep. assoc. dir. strategic def. rsch. N.Mex., 1983—84, assoc. dir. theoretical and computational physics, 1984—86, dir. Ctr. for Nat. Securities Studies, 1986—88, assoc. dir. for lab. devel., 1991—94; chief scientist USAF, Washington, 1988—91, panel chmn. sci. adv. bd., 1984-88, 91-96, 1991—96, 2002—05, chmn. sci. adv. bd., 1999—2002, mem., 2002—05; cons. Los Alamos, 1994—. Chmn. study group on reactor materials and nuclear explosives U.S. Dept. Energy, 1976-78; mem. ballistic missile def. techs. adv. panel U.S. Congress Office Tech. Assessment, 1984-85, The Pres.'s Defensive Tech. Study Team, Washington, 1983; strat. adv. group U.S. Strat. Command, 1996—, panel chair, 2003-; strat. adv. group jt. adv. com. Sec. Def., Sec. Energy, 1996—. Editor Rsch. Jour. Lawrence Livermore Nat. Lab., 1976-77; contbr. sci. and tech. papers to profl. jours. Pres. Livermore Cultural Arts Coun., 1969-72; chmn. Livermore Sister City Orgn., 1973, Planning Commn. City of Livermore, 1971-76; bd. dirs. Orch. of Santa Fe, 1986-88. Capt. U.S. Army, 1964-67. Grad. fellow Edward John Noble Found., 1958-62; recipient Theodore von Karman award for outstanding contbn. to def. sci., 1989, medal for outstanding pub. svc. U.S. Sec. Def., 1996; decorated for exceptional civilian svc. USAF, 1988, 91, 96, 2005. Mem. AAAS, Am. Phys. Soc., N.Y. Acad. Sci., Air Force Assn. Avocations: tennis, hiking, music. Office: 624 La Bajada Los Alamos NM 87544-3805 E-mail: selden@cybermesa.com.

SELDERS, JEAN E., retired psychology professor; b. La Junta, Colo., Nov. 6, 1942; d. Samuel Allen and Dorothy Jean Selders; m. Paul J. Fraker (div.); m. James R. Powell (div.). BA, U. No. Colo., 1964, MA, 1967; PhD, U. Denver, 1980. Cert. Colo. Dept. Edn., Colo. Soc. Sch. Psychologists, Nat. Assn. Sch. Psychologists, Nat. Cert. Sch. Psychologist. Spl. edn. tchr. Jefferson Co. Pub. Schs., Lakewood, Colo., 1964—65; elem. tchr. Mt. Calm Pub. Schs., Tex., 1965—66; spl. edn. tchr. Dept. Def. Overseas Schs., Tokyo, 1967—70, Cumberland County Schs., Fayetteville, NC, 1970—72; Ednl. diagnostician NC Dept. Pub. Health, 1972—78; sch. psychologist Littleton Pub. Schs., Littleton, Colo., 1980—2004; coll. instr. Arapahoe CC, 1990—2004; ret., 2005. Bd. dirs. Nat. Fragile X Found., Denver, 1988—92; pres., bd. dirs. Arapahoe Assn. Retarded Citizens, Littleton, 1980—88; state sec.,. bd. Colo. Soc. Sch. Psychologists, 1984—89. Vol. Opera Corado, Denver, 1980—, Central City Opera, Central City, 1980—. Recipient State Champion-Toastmistress, NC, 1976, Colo. Sch. Psychologist Yr., Colo. Soc. Sch. Psychologists, 1985. Mem.: APA, Arapahoe/Douglas Mental Health Assn., Colo. Soc. Sch. Psychologists (state bd. sec. 1980—85), Alpha Gamma Delta (rec. sec. 1963—64, panhellenic del. 1982—84). Republican. Lutheran. Avocations: travel, reading, theater, opera.

SELDES, MARIAN, actress; b. NYC; d. Gilbert and Alice (Hall) S.; m. Julian Claman, Nov. 3, 1953 (div.); 1 child, Katharine; m. Garson Kanin, June 19, 1990 (dec. Mar. 1999). Grad., The Dalton Sch., NYC, 1945, Neighborhood Playhouse, 1947; DHL, Emerson Coll., 1979; DFA (hon.), Julliard Sch., 2003. Faculty drama and dance divsn. Juilliard Sch. Lincoln Ctr., NYC, 1969-91; faculty drama dept. Fordham U., 2003, 2005. Appeared with Cambridge (Mass.) Summer Theatre, 1945, Boston Summer Theatre, 1946, St. Michael's Playhouse, Winooski, Vt., 1947-48, Bermudiana Theatre, Hamilton, Bermuda, 1951, Elitch Gardens Theatre, Denver, 1953, The Cretan Woman, Lysistrata, 1955 (actress/artist-in residence Stanford U.), The Flowering Peach, L.A., 1956, Witness for the Prosecution, The Players' Ring, L.A., 1957; Broadway appearances include Medea, 1947, Crime and Punishment, 1948, That Lady, 1949, Tower Beyond Tragedy, 1950, The High Ground, 1951, Come of Age, 1952, Ondine, 1954, The Chalk Garden, 1955, The Wall, 1960, A Gift of Time, 1962, The Milk Train Doesn't Stop Here Any More, 1964, Tiny Alice, 1965, A Delicate Balance, 1967 (Tony award for best supporting actress), Before You Go, 1968, Father's Day, 1971 (Drama Desk award, Tony nomination), Mendicants of Evening (Martha Graham Co.), 1973, Equus, 1974-77, The Merchant, 1977, Deathtrap, 1978 (Tony nomination), Ivanov (Drama Desk nomination), 1997, Ring Round the Moon, 1999 (Tony nomination), 45 Seconds from Broadway, 2001 Dinner At Eight, 2003 (Tony nomination); off-Broadway appearances include Diff'rent, 1961, The Ginger Man, 1963 (Obie award), All Women Are One, 1964, Juana LaLoca, 1965, Three Sisters, 1969, Am. Shakespeare Festival, Stratford, Conn., Mercy Street at Am. Place Theater, N.Y.C., 1969, Isadora Duncan, 1976 (Obie award), Painting Churches, 1983, 84 (Outer Critics Circle award 1984), Other People, Berkshire Theatre Festival, 1969, The Celebration, Hedgerow Theater, Pa., 1971, Richard III, N.Y. Shakespeare Festival, 1983, Remember Me, Lakewood Theatre, Skowhegan, Maine, Gertrude Stein and a Companion, White Barn Theatre, Westport, Conn., 1985, Lucile Lortel Theatre, N.Y.C., 1986, Richard II, N.Y. Shakespeare Festival, 1987, The Milk Train Doesn't Stop Here Anymore, WPA Theatre, N.Y.C., 1987, Happy Ending, Bristol (Pa.) Riverside Theatre, 1988, Annie 2 John F. Kennedy Ctr., Washington, 1989-90, Goodspeed Opera House, Chester, Conn., 1990, A Bright Room Called Day, N.Y. Shakespeare Festival, 1991, Three Tall Women, River Arts, Woodstock, N.Y., 1994, Another Time, Am. Jewish Theatre, 1993, Breaking the Code, Berkshire Theatre Festival, 1993, Three Tall Women, Vineyard Theatre, N.Y.C., 1994, Promenade Theatre, 1994-95, nat. tour, 1995-96, Boys From Syracuse, City Ctr., N.Y.C., 1997, Dead End: Williamstown, 1997, Dear Liar, Irish Repertory Theater, 1999, The Matchmaker: Williamstown, 1998, Tongue of a Bird, Mark Taper Forum, 1998, Sail Away, Carnegie Hall, 1999, Mad About The Boy, Carnegie Hall, 1999, The Torch-Bearers, 2000, Ancestral Voices, 2000, The Skin of our Teeth, 2000, Williamstown, The Play About the Baby, Alley Theatre, Houston, 2000, The Butterfly Collection, Playwrights Horizon, NY, 2000, The Play About the Baby, Helen, NY Shakespeare Festival, 2001, Play Yourself, N.Y. Theater Workshop, 2002, Beckett/Albee, Century Ctr. Theatre, N.Y.C., 2003, The Royal Family Ahmanson Theatre, L.A., 2004, Dedication or the Stuff of Dreams, 2005; nat. tour Three Tall Women, 1995-96, Deuce, 2007; film appearances include The Greatest Story Ever Told, Gertrude Stein and a Companion, 1988, In a Pig's Eye, 1988, The Gun in Betty Lou's Handbag, 1992, Tom and Huck, 1995, Digging to China, 1997, Home Alone 3, 1997, Affliction, 1997, Celebrity, 1998, The Haunting, 1999, Town and Country, 1999, Duets, 1999, Hollywood Ending, 2002, Mona Lisa Smile, 2003, (documentary) Golden Age of Broadway, 2005, (narrator documentary) Ballet Russes, 2005, August Rush, 2006; (TV series) Good and Evil, 1991, Murphy Brown, 1992, Truman, 1995, Cosby, 1996, 98, Trinity, 1998, Remember WENN, 1999, The Others, 2000, If These Walls Could Talk 2, 2000, Nero Wolfe, 2001 (A&E), The Education of Max Bickford, 2002, American Masters PBS "Juillard Documentary, 2003", Hallmark Hall of Fame, 2004, Frasier, 2004, TV: The Book of Daniel, 2005; also appeared on radio CBS Mystery Theater, 1976-81, Theatre Guild on The Air; author: The Bright Lights, 1978, Time Together, 1981; appeared in soap opera One Life to Live, 1998. Bd. dirs. Neighborhood Playhouse, The Acting Co., Nat. Repertory Theatre, Theatre Hall of Fame, 1996; bd. trustees Broadway Cares/Equity Fights Aids. Winner Ovation award Theater L.A. for Three Tall Women, 1996, Conn. Critics award for Three Tall Women, 1996; recipient Madge Kennedy/Sidney Kingsley award Dramatists Guild Fund, 2000, Obie award for sustained achievement, Lucille Lortel award for Sustained Achievement, 2003, Edwin Booth award, Players Club, 2003, Lifetime Mem. award Theatre Libr. Assn., 2003, Breukelein Inst. Gaudium award, 2003, Julliard Sch. medal svc. to arts, 2005, Drama League award sustained achievement, 2006, Dutch Treat Gold medal award, 2006, Rebekah Kohut award Nat. Coun. Jewish Women, 2006. Mem. Players Club, Century Assn. Home: 210 Central Park S Apt 19D New York NY 10019-1426 *

SELDES, RICHARD M., orthopedist, consultant; MD, U. Pa., 1994; BA, Johns Hopkins U., 2000. Diplomate Am. Bd. Orthop. Surgeons, 2003. Dir., orthop. surgery Forest Hills (N.Y.) Hosp., 2003—. Fellow: Am. Acad. Orthop. Surgeons; mem.: N.Y. Med. Soc., Arthroscopy Assn. N.Am. Achievements include development of surgical technique for shoulder surgery. Office: Forest Hills Hosp 102-01 66th Rd Forest Hills NY 11375 Home Phone: 201-767-5556; Office Phone: 718-830-1290.

SELDIN, DAVID C., internist, medical educator; b. Springfield, Mass., Jan. 18, 1957; m. Elizabeth L. Hohmann. MD, Harvard U., Cambridge, Mass., 1986; PhD, MIT, 1986. Diplomate Am. Bd. Internal Medicine, 1994. Prof. sch. medicine Boston U., 1994—. Mem.: Am. Soc. Clin. Investigation, Am. Soc. Hematology. Achievements include research in protein kinase CK2 signaling in cancer and development, pathogenesis and treatment of systemic amyloidosis (protein misfolding).

SELDMAN, NEIL NORMAN, cultural organization administrator; b. Bklyn., Aug. 2, 1945; s. Fred Herman and Sylvia (Flaster) S.; m. Laura Jane Klugherz, Feb. 22, 1968; children: Oliver, Chloe. BS in Indsl. and Labor Rels., Cornell U., 1966; MS in Internat. Communism, George Washington U., 1968, PhD in Internat. Rels., 1974. Asst. to pres. B.H. Krueger Co., Bklyn., 1969-72; assoc. prof., lectr. George Washington U., Washington, 1974-76, asst. dir. exptl. program, 1976-77; founder Inst. for Local Self-Reliance (ILSR), Washington, 1974—, pres., 1980—. Cons. World Bank/UN Environ. Program, Washington, 1980-81, City Coun., Phila., 1984-90. Author: Common Sense Radicalism, 1976, Waste to Wealth: A Guide for Community Enterprise, 1985; co-author: Integrated Resource Recovery-Recycling from Municipal Refuse: A State-of-the-Art Review and Annotated Bibliography, 1985, Proven Profits from Pollution Prevention, 1986, Garbage in Europe: Economics, Technologies, Trends, 1987, Deconstruction, 1999, State of Wasting and Recycling in the U.S., 2000; contbr. article to Ency. of Energy Tech. and the Environment, 1995; contbg. editor International Dialogue on Zero Waste, 2005 Fabrangen Cheder Jewish Community Orgn.; elected chair Neighborhood Planning Coun., Washington, 1976-82; co-founder D.C. Interracial Coalition for Environ. Equity, Washington, 1989, Nat. Recycling Coalition, 1980, Grass Roots Recycling Network, 1996. With NG, 1968-74. Grantee Moriah Fund, 1990-95, Pew Charitable Trusts, 1991, NSF, 1979-80, H. Heinz Endowment, 1995-96, EPA, 1993-98, Turner Found., 1995-98, Ford Found. Environl. Justice Program, 2002-03 Jewish. Avocations: fast pitch softball, nineteenth-century literature, French and Russian revolutions. Home Phone: 202-686-4218; Office Phone: 202-898-1610 x210. Business E-Mail: nseldman@ilsr.com.

SELDNER, BETTY JANE, environmental engineer, consultant, aerospace transportation executive; b. Balt., Dec. 11, 1923; d. David D. and Miriam M. (Mendes) Miller; m. Warren E. Gray, June 20, 1945 (div. 1965); children: Patricia, Deborah; m. Alvin Seldner, Nov. 15, 1965; children: Jack, Barbara. BA in Journalism, Calif. State U., Northridge, 1975, MA in Communications, 1977. Dir. pub. info. United Way, Van Nuys, Calif., 1958-63, dir. edn. Los Angeles, 1963-68; dir. pub. relations, fin. San Fernando Valley Girl Scout Council, Reseda, Calif., 1968-73; asst. dir. pub. info. Calif. State U., Northridge, 1973-75; dir. environ. mgmt. HR Textron Corp., Valencia, Calif., 1975-87; environ. engr. Northrop Aircraft, Hawthorne, Calif., 1987-88, EMCON Assocs., Burbank, Calif., 1988-92, Atkins Environ., 1992-93, Seldner Environ., Valencia, Calif., 1993—; pres. Seldner Environ. Svcs., 1993—. Author non-fiction. Named Woman of Yr., Santa City C. of C. and vol. orgns., 2000. Mem. Santa Clarita Valley Environ. Mgrs. Soc. (chmn. bd. dirs. 1984), San Fernando Valley Round Table (pres. 1971-72), Hazardous Materials Mgrs.' Assn., Zonta Internat., Valencia Indsl. Assn. (environ. chair). Republican. Jewish. Avocation: sailing. Office Phone: 661-255-6427. Personal E-mail: Betty13ix@ca.rr.com.

SELES, MONICA, professional tennis player; b. Novi Sad, Yugoslavia, Dec. 2, 1973; arrived in US, 1996; d. Karolj and Esther Seles. Profl. tennis player, 1989—. Mem. U.S. Fed Cup Team, 1996, 99, 2000, WTA Tour Players' Coun., 1998—99. Author: (novels) From Fear to Victory, 1996. Active Spl. Olympics. Named Sportswoman of Yr., Yugoslavia, 1985, Female Rookie of Yr., TENNIS Mag./Rolex Watch, 1989, Most Improved Player, WTA Tour, 1990, Player of Yr., 1991, Female Athlete of Yr., AP, 1991, 1992, Comeback Player of Yr., TENNIS Mag., 1995, Female Pro Athlete of Yr., Fla. Sports Hall of Fame, 1998, Player Who Makes a Difference, Family Circle Cup, 1999; recipient Ted Tinling Diamond Award, 1990, Rado Topspin Award, 1990, Comeback Player of Yr. Award, WTA Tour, 1995, 1998, Committment to Cmty. Award, Fla. Times-Union, 1999, Flo Hyman Meml. Award, Women's Sports Found., 2000, Sanex Hero of Yr. Award, WTA Tour, 2002. Achievements include 3rd player in the Open-era to capture the Australian and Roland Garros in same calendar year; World #1 ranked player, 1991, 92, 95; youngest #1 ranked player in tennis history for women and men at 17 years, 3 months, 9 days; Winner Grand Slam titles: Roland Garros, 1990, 91, 92, French Open, 1990, 91, 92, U.S. Open, 1991, 92, Australian Open, 1991, 92, 93, 96; Winner 53 Career Singles Titles and 6 Career Doubles Titles, WTA Tour. Office: c/o Internat Mgmt Group 1 Erieview Plz Cleveland OH 44114-1715

SELF, BILL, men's college basketball coach; b. Okmulgee, Okla., Dec. 27, 1962; m. Cindy Self; children: Lauren, Tyler. BSBA, Okla. State U., 1985, M in Athletic Adminstrn., 1989. Asst. coach U. Kans., 1985-86, head coach, 2003—; asst. coach Okla. State U., 1986-93; head coach Oral Roberts U., 1993-97, U. Tulsa, 1997—2000, U. Ill. Champaign-Urbana, 2000—03. Mem. competition com. U.S.A. Men's Basketball, 2005—. Named Don Haskins Coach of Yr., Western Athletic Conf., 2000, John and Nellie Wooden Coach of Yr., Utah Tipoff Club, 2000, Nat. Coach of Yr., The Sporting News, 2000, Big 12 Coach of Yr., 2006. Led Tulsa U. to Western Athletic Conf. titles, 1998-2000 and consecutive trips to the NCAA tournament; has been asst. or head coach of ten teams that reached the playoffs, 8 times to the NCAA Tournament and 3 times to the National Invitational Tournament. Office: U Kans Men's Basketball Allen Fieldhouse 1651 Naismith Dr Lawrence KS 66045 Office Phone: 785-864-7929. *

SELF, MARK EDWARD, communications consultant; b. Tyler, Tex., Dec. 6, 1955; s. Edward and Ruby (Rogers) S.; m. Dianne Logan; children: Patricia Bartlett, Marcile Christine. Student, Tenn. Tech. Sch., 1973-76. Gen. mgr. Gulf Telephone Inc., Beaumont, Tex., 1980-82; gen. sales mgr. CSC Telephone Inc., Tyler, Tex., 1982-83; v.p. sales Teleci Inc., Irving, Tex., 1983-85; cons. Self & Assocs., Inc., Grapevine, Tex., 1985—; pres. S&A Equipment Co., Grapevine, 1990—; v.p. mktg. Hicom, Inc., Euless, Tex., 1994—, MediFACTS, Inc., Euless, Tex., 2003—. Fundraiser Freedom Ride Found., Dallas, 1987. Named Outstanding Young Men of Am., 1985. Mem. Am. Hotel and Motel Assn., Nat. Office Machine Dealer Assn., Nat. Fedn. Ind. Bus., Dallas C. of C., Masons. Avocations: fishing, hunting, woodworking. Office: MediFacts, Inc 1105-B S Airport Cir Euless TX 76040 Business E-Mail: mself@medifacts.net.

SELF, SCOTT W., lawyer; b. Bethesda, Md., 1975; BA cum laude in Polit. Sci., Rhodes Coll., 1997; JD, U. Tex. Sch. Law, 2001. Bar: Tex. 2001, US Dist. Ct. (no. dist. Tex.) 2001, US Dist. Ct. (we. dist. Tex.) 2002. Assoc. Fee, Smith, Sharp & Vitullo, L.L.P., Dallas. Named a Rising Star, Tex. Super Lawyers mag., 2006. Mem.: Tex. Assn. Def. Counsel, Dallas Assn. Young Lawyers, ABA, Dallas Bar Assn. Office: Fee Smith Sharp & Vitullo LLP 3 Galleria Tower 13155 Noel Rd Ste 1000 Dallas TX 75240 Office Phone: 972-934-9100. E-mail: sself@feesmith.com. *

SELFE, EDWARD MILTON, lawyer; b. St. Paul, Sept. 26, 1921; s. Edward Milton and Eleanor (Moen) S.; m. Rena Hill McMurry, July 10, 1950 (div. Oct. 1979); children: Murry, Edward, James; m. Jane Comer Bowron, Dec. 31, 1979. BA, Presbyn. Coll., Clinton, SC, 1943; LLB, U. Va., 1950. Bar: N.Y., Va., Ala. Asst. prof. law Law Sch., U. Va., Charlottesville, 1950-51; assoc. Shearman & Sterling, NYC, 1951-52, Bradley Arant Rose White, Birmingham, Ala., 1952-57, ptnr., 1957-2000, of counsel, 2000—; vice chmn. Secor Bank, Birmingham, 1988-91, gen. counsel, 1991-93. Lectr. Law Sch., U. Ala., Tuscaloosa, 1968—90. Chmn. Birmingham-Jefferson County Transit Authority, 1972-82. Served to capt., inf. U.S. Army, 1943-47, ETO. Decorated Silver Star, Bronze Star (V) with oak leaf cluster, Purple Heart. Fellow Am. Coll. Tax Counsel; mem. ABA, Ala. Bar Assn., Birmingham Bar Assn. Democrat. Avocation: tennis (ranked 2nd nationally by USTA in men's singles-age 85). Home: 84 Arlington Crest 2600 Arlington Ave S Birmingham AL 35205-4167 Office: Bradley Arant Rose & White One Federal Pl 1819 Fifth Ave N Birmingham AL 35203-2104 Office Phone: 205-521-8280. Business E-Mail: eselfe@bradleyarant.com.

SELFRIDGE, GEORGE DEVER, retired dentist, retired military officer; b. Pitman, NJ, Sept. 24, 1924; s. William John and Edith (Gorman) S.; m. Ruth Motisher, 1948; children: Pamela Ruth, Kimberly Dawn, Cheryl Beth. Student, Gettysburg Coll., 1942-43, Muhlenburg Coll., 1943-45; DDS, U. Buffalo, 1947; MA, George Washington U., 1974. Commd. lt. (j.g.) USN, 1948, advanced through grades to rear adm., 1973; intern Naval Dental Sch., Bethesda, Md., 1948-49, Naval Hosp., St. Albans, NY, 1949-50; asst. dental officer U.S.S. Midway, 1949-51; with USN, 1951-64; sr. dental officer U.S.S. Randolph, 1958-60, U.S.S. Cadmus, 1964-65, U.S.S. Vulcan, 1965-66, Svc. Force, 1964-66, Submarine Force, Atlantic Fleet, 1967-69; from asst. dir. grad. edn. to comdg. officer Navy Grad. Dental Sch., Bethesda, 1969-76; exec. officer Norfolk (Va.) Navy Dental Clinic, 1972-73; ret. USN, 1976; dean Dental Sch., Washington U., St. Louis, 1976-86; dir. dental services Barnes Hosp., St. Louis, 1976—87, Children's Hosp., St. Louis, 1976-87; exec. dir. Am. Bd. Orthodontics, 1986-97; ret., 1998. Adv. bd. VA Hosp., St. Louis, 1977-79; mem. exec. coun. Cen. Region Testing Svc., 1976-86; adv. com. St. Louis Jr. Coll. Dist., 1976-86. Contbr. articles to med. jours. Decorated Legion of Merit; recipient commendation medals, Greater St. Louis Gold Medallion award, 1995, Spl. Recognition award Am. Bd. Orthopedics, 1996. Mem. ADA, Am. Coll. Dentists (past pres.), Internat. Coll. Coll. Dentists (dep. registrar, sec. U.S. sect., Spl. Recognition award), Assn. Mil. Surgeons U.S., Omicron Kappa Upsilon. Republican. Home: 14545 Foxham Ct Chesterfield MO 63017-5620

SELI, EMRE UTKU, reproductive endocrinology and infertility specialist, physician researcher; s. Kemal Ali Seli and Ayla Zeliha Hungen; m. Meltem Solak, Dec. 10, 1994; children: Devin Murat, Denis Aydin. MD, Istanbul U., Turkey, 1984—92. Postdoctoral rsch. fellow dept. ob-gyn. Divsn. Reproductive Endocrinology and Infertility, Yale U. Sch. Medicine, New Haven, 1995—97, resident dept. ob-gyn., 1997—2001, instr. and fellow dept. ob-gyn., 2001—04, asst. prof. dept. ob-gyn. Contbr. articles to profl. jours. Recipient Outstanding Laparoendoscopic Surgeon Award, Soc. Laparoendoscopic Surgeons, 2001; grantee, Am. Coll. Obstetrics and Gynecology, 1999, 2000, N.Am. Menopause Soc., 1999, 2000, NIH, 2004—. Achievements include discovery of a mammalian embryonic polyA binding protein that regulates gene expression during mammalian oocyte and embryo development; non-invasive metabolomic embryo assessment; research in gene expression during gamete and embryo development; infertility; and fertility preservation in women with cancer; development of non-invasive metabolic embryo assessment technology for assisted reproductive technologies. Business E-Mail: emre.seli@yale.edu.

SELIG, BUD (ALAN HUBER SELIG), major league baseball commissioner; b. Milw., July 30, 1934; s. Ben and Marie Selig; m. Suzanne Lappin Steinman, Jan. 18, 1977; children: Sari, Wendy. Grad., U. Wis., Madison, 1956; LHD (hon.), Lakeland Coll., 1989. With Selig Ford (became Selig Chevrolet 1982), West Allis, Wis., 1959-90, pres., owner, 1966-90; with Selig Exec. Leasing Co., West Allis, 1959—, pres., owner, 1977—; part owner Milw. Braves, 1963-65; co-founder Teams, Inc., 1964; co-owner, pres., CEO Milw. Brewers Baseball Club, Inc., 1970-98; interim commr. MLB, 1991-98, commr., 1998—. Bd. dirs. Green Bay Packers Profl. Football Team., Marcus Corp., Oil-Dri Corp. Am.; coord. World Baseball Classic, 2006 Co-founder Child Abuse Prevention Fund, 1988. With U.S. Army, 1956-58. Recipient Major League Exec. of Yr. award UPI, 1978, Internat. B'nai B'rith Sportsman of Yr. award 1981, Sportsman of Yr. award U.S. Olympic Com., 1988, August A. Busch, Jr. award for long and meritorious svc. to baseball, 1989, Ellis Island Congl. medal of honor, 1993, Anti-Defamation League's "A World of Difference Award" 1994, Herbert Hoover Humanitarian award Boys and Girls Clubs for Outstanding Svc. to Benefit Am.'s Youth 1998, Sports Leadership Award, March of Dimes NYC Chpt. 2000, Sports Torch of Learning American Friends of Hebrew Univ. 2001, Inducted Wisconsin Athletic Hall of Fame 2001. Office: Office of the Commr Major League Baseball 245 Park Ave New York NY 10167-0002 *

SELIG, KARL-LUDWIG, literature and language professor; b. Wiesbaden, Germany, Aug. 14, 1926; naturalized, 1948; s. Lucian and Erna (Reiss) S. BA, Ohio State U., 1946, MA, 1947; postgrad., U. Rome, Italy, 1949—50; PhD, U. Tex., 1955. Asst. prof. Romance langs. and lit. Johns Hopkins U., Balt., 1954-58; assoc. prof. U. N.C., Chapel Hill, 1958-61, U. Minn., Mpls., 1961-63; vis. prof. U. Tex., Austin, 1963-64, prof. Romance langs. and lit., 1964-65; Hinchliff prof. Spanish lit. Cornell U., Ithaca, NY, 1965-69, dir. grad. studies in Romance lit., 1966-69; prof. Spanish lit. Columbia U., NYC, 1969—. Brown Found. fellow, vis. prof. Spanish and comparative lit. U. of the South, Sewanee, Tenn., 1990; vis. prof. U. Munich, 1963-64, U. Berlin, 1967; vis. prof. U. Greifswald, Germany, 1991-96, hon. prof., 1996—; cons. prof. Ohio State U., Columbus, 1967-69; vis. lectr. U. Zulia, Maracaibo, Venezuela, 1968; dir. summer seminar NEH, 1975, cons., 1975-77; vis. scholar Ga. U. Sys., 1977; vis. rsch. scholar Fondation Hardt, Vandoeuvres, Switzerland, 1959, Herzog August Bibliothek Wolfenbüttel, Fed. Repubic Germany, 1979—; mem. com. grants-in-aid Am. Coun. Learned Soc., 1969-73; chmn. Comparative Lit. Program and Colloquia, Columbia Coll., 1976-88. Author: (books) The Libr. of Vincencio Juan de Lastanosa, Patron of Gracián, Geneva, 1960, Studies on Alciato in Spain, 1990, Studies on Cervantes, 1993, also numerous articles, revs.; editor: (books) (Thomas Blundeville) of Councils and Counselors, 1963; editor: (with A.G. Hatcher) Studia Philologica et Litteraria in Honorem L. Spitzer, 1958; editor: (with J.E. Keller) Essays in Honor of N.B. Adams, 1966; editor: (with R. Brinkmann) Theatrum Europaeum. Festschrift E.M. Szarota, 1982; editor: (with S. Neumeister) Theatrum Mundi Hispanicum, 1986; editor: (with R. Somerville) Florilegium Columbianum: Essays in Honor of Paul Oskar Kristeller, 1987; editor; (with E. Sears) The Verbal and the Visual: Essays in Honor of William Sebastian Heckscher, 1990; editor: Polyanthea Essays on Art and Lit. in Honor of William Sebastian Heckscher, 1993, Mira de Amescua, La hija de Carlos Quinto, 2002; assoc. editor: Modern Lang. Notes, 1955—58, mng. editor: Romance Notes, 1959—61; editor: U. NC Studies in Comparative Lit., 1959—61, Bull. Comediantes, 1959—64; assoc. editor:, 1964—68, mem. editl. bd.:, 1979—88; co-editor: Yearbook of Comparative Lit., vol. IX, 1960; mem. editl. bd.: Colección Támesis, 1962—79, Romanic rev., 1969—89, Yale Italian Studies, 1976—80, Tchg. Lang. Through Lit., 1978—88, Edición Reichenberger, 2002—, assoc. editor: Hispania, 1969—74, Ky. Romance Quar., 1973—85, gen. editor: Revista Hispánica Moderna, mem. nat. adv. bd.: MLA Internat. Bibliography, 1978—88. Recipient Mark Van Doren award Columbia, 1974, spl. citation Columbia Coll. Alumni Assn., 1991, Festschrift, Über Texte, 1997; fellow Fulbright Found., Rome, 1949-50, Newberry Libr., 1958, Folger Shakespeare Libr., 1959, 63, Belgian Am. Ednl. Found., 1961, 62; sr. fellow Mediaeval and Renaissance Inst. Duke U., 1978; Fulbright rsch. scholar Utrecht, The Netherlands, 1958-59; DAAD rsch. grantee, 1979; Karl-Ludwig Selig scholarship named in his honor, Columbia Coll., 2001. Mem. MLA (sec., then chmn. Romance sect. 1965-66, chmn. comparative lit. 1973, James Russell Lowell prize com. 1989-90, chmn. 1990), Internat. Assn. Hispanists, Acad. Lit. Studies, Am. Friends Herzog August Bibliothek (bd. dirs. 1996—), Phi Beta Kappa (hon.). Home: 333 W 86th St Apt 406 New York NY 10024

SELIG, WILLIAM GEORGE, academic administrator; b. Prince Rupert, BC, Can., Sept. 25, 1938; s. George Oliver Selig and Minerva Junuetta (Brand) Goodale; m. Judith Margaret Sprague, June 20, 1964; children: Cheryl, Cynthia. BA, Cen. Washington State Coll., 1961, MA, 1968; CAGS, U. Mass., 1972, EdD, 1973. Tchr. Sharon (Mass.) High Sch., 1963-64, Hydaburg (Alaska) Grade Sch., 1964-65, W. Puyallup (Wash.) Jr. High Sch., 1966-69; dir. spl. edn. Northampton (Mass.) Schs., 1969-73, 1974-76; asst. prof. Westfield (Mass.) State Coll., 1973; dir. pupil svcs. Longmeadow (Mass.) Pub. Schs., 1976-80; prof. Regent U., Virginia Beach, Va., 1980-83, dean, prof., 1984-89, provost, 1989-2000; Disting. prof. ednl. leadership, 2000—. Bd. dirs. Set Net, Virginia Beach; pres. Motivational Teaching Systems, Inc.; spl. edn. adv. bd. dirs. Virginia Beach Pub. Schs.; bd. trustees Klingberg Family Ctrs., New Britain, Conn., 1991—2000. Author: Training for Triumph, 1984, Loving Our Differences, 1989, Handbook of Individualized Strategies for Classroom Discipline, 1995, Handbook of Individualized Strategies for Building Resilience in At Risk Students, 2005; contbr. chpt. to book. Episcopalian. Avocations: skiing, tennis. Office: Regent University 1000 Regent University Dr Virginia Beach VA 23464-9800 Business E-Mail: georsel@regent.edu.

SELIG, WILLIAM PAUL, advocate, cultural organization administrator; b. Ridgewood, NY, Sept. 19, 1949; s. Joseph Lewis and Janet Lucille Selig; m. Donna R. McIntyre, July 1, 1982; 1 child, Hannah Jo He-Young. BA, U. Md., College Park, 1972; MRE, Unification Theol. Sem., Barrytown, NY, 1981. Mgmt. trainee Cambridge Clothing Corp., Cambridge, Md., 1972—75; prin., owner Good Health Food Stores, Washington, 1977—80; dir. office of strategic affairs CAUSA Internat., NYC, 1980—84; sr. v.p. Summit Coun. for World Peace, Washington, 1981—; COO Internat. Security Coun., NYC, 1983—87; adminstrv. dir. Assn. for the Unity of L.Am., NYC, 1984—; gen. mgr. Global Affairs Jour., NYC, 1985—88; adminstrv. dir. Fedn. for World Peace, Washington, 1991—; sr. v.p. World Inst. for Devel. and Peace, Washington, 1996—; dir. dept. cultural affairs Washington Times Found., Washington, 1997—98; v.p. Young Gruppe, Inc., Washington, 1998—; sr. v.p. Universal Cultural Found., Washington, 2005—; dep. dir. internat. office of govt. rels. Universal Peace Fedn., Washington, 2006—. Author: Founding CAUSA Instruction Manual, World Peace, Freedom and Justice; reviewer: films and books The New York City Tribune. Active Rockville Millennium Coun., Md., 1999—2000; vol. Peace Corps, Bogota, Colombia, 1972—75; dep. dir. Lit. Fedn. for World Peace, 1998—99; dir., comm. & logistics World Peace Pilgrimage, Jerusalem, 2003—; dep. sec. gen. N.Am. chpt Interreligious and Internat. Fedn. for World Peace, Washington, 1999—2006; metro chaircouple Blessed Family Assn. 8000, Washington, 1993—95; dist. leader Family Fedn. for World Peace and Internat., Rockville, Md., 1996—2002; elder Montgomery Family Ch., Rockville, 2002—; exec. dir. Montgomery County chpt. Am. Clergy Leadership Conf., Rockville, 1999—; dir. Nat. Won Jeon Shrine of Am., Washington, Md., 2001—. Named Amb. for Peace, Interreligious and Internat. Fedn. for World Peace, 2001; recipient Cheon Il Guk award, CheongPyeong Heaven & Earth Tng. Ctr., 2003. Mem.: World Assn. Non-Govtl Orgns. (assoc.), Nat. Coun. Returned Peace Corp Vols. (assoc.). Republican. Office: Universal Peace Fedn 3600 New York Ave NE Ste 360 Washington DC 20002 Office Phone: 202-269-5337.

SELIGER, CHARLES, artist; b. NYC, June 3, 1926; s. George Zekowski and Hortense S.; m. Ruth Lewin, June 20, 1948 (dec. May 1975); children: Robert, Mark; m. Lenore Klebanow, 1975. Student in pvt. art instrn., WPA Sch., 1940. Robert H. and Clarice Smith Disting. vis. prof. George Washington U., Washington, 1990; lectr. Katonah Art Mus., 1990; panelist Terra Mus. Art, Chgo., 1990, Whitney Mus. Am. Art, N.Y.C., 1990, Michael Rosenfeld Gallery, N.Y.C., 1994. One man shows include Peggy Guggenheim Gallery, N.Y.C., 1945-46, Carlebach Gallery, 1948, DeYoung Meml. Mus., San Francisco, 1949, Whitney Mus. ann., 1949-57, Willard Gallery, N.Y.C., 1951, 53, 55, 57, 61, 62, 66, 68, Seligman Gallery, Seattle, 1955, 58, 65, Nassau Community Coll., N.Y.C., 1965, Wooster Community Art Center, Conn., 1969, Andrew Crispo Gallery, 1973, 75, 76, 78, 80, 81, 83, Mus. Modern Art, Hayden Calhoun Gallery, Dallas, Makler Gallery, Phila., 1979, Miami-Dade Community Coll., 1981, Jacksonville (Fla.) Art Mus., 1981, Gallery Schlesinger-Boisanté, 1985, 86, Guggenheim Mus., 1986, Galerie Lopes, Zurich, Switzerland, 1986, 89, 95, 97, 99, 2003, 2006, Greenville County Mus. Art, S.C., 2003, others; exhibited in Norlyst Gallery, N.Y.C., 1942, 67 Gallery, N.Y.C., 1943, David Porter Gallery, Washington, 1945, Four Arts Club, Palm Beach, Fla., 1946, Va. Mus. Fine Arts, 1946, U. Iowa, 1946, Salon des Realites Nouvelle, Paris, France, 1948, Bklyn. Mus., 1949, Cornell U., 1951, Art Inst. Chgo., 1961, 64, Syracuse Mus. Fine Arts, 1953, Nebr. Art Assn., 1953, Am. Acad. Arts & Letters, 1965, 67, 68, Smithsonian Inst., 1968, Taft Mus., Cin., 1981, Okla. Art Ctr., 1981, Saidenberg Gallery, N.Y.C., 1983, 89, Wight Art Gallery, UCLS, traveling to Nat. Gallery Modern Art, New Delhi, 1987, 88, Frances Wolfson Art Gallery, Miami, Fla., 1987, Guggenheim Mus., traveling to Venice, Italy, 1987, 88, Sid Deutsch Gallery, N.Y.C., 1989, 90, Weatherspoon Gallery, Greensboro, N.C., 1989, Nat. Acad. Mus., NYC, 2005, many others.; exhbn. Abstract Expressionism: Other Dimensions traveling to Lowe Art Mus., Coral Gables, Fla, Terra Art Mus., Chgo. (also panelist), Jane Voorhees Zimmerli Art Mus., Rutgers, New Brunswick, 1990, 92; works in permanent collections Herbert F. Johnson Mus., Cornell U., Ithaca, N.Y., Norton Mus. Art, West Palm Beach, Fla., Addison Gallery, Andover, Mass., Munson Williams Proctor Mus., Utica, N.Y., Guggenheim Mus., Miss. Mus. Art, Whitney Mus., High Mus., Atlanta, Terra Mus. Am. Art, Evanston, Ill., Mus. Modern Art, Chgo. Art Inst., Newark Mus. Art, Iowa State U., Municipal Art Mus., The Hague, Holland, Tel Aviv Mus., Balt. Mus. Art, Hirshhorn Mus. and Sculpture Garden, Met. Mus. Art, N.Y.C., Phillips Collection, Washington, Carnegie Inst., Pitts., Rutgers U., Jane Voorhees Zimmerli Art Mus., New Brunswick, N.J., Worcester (Mass.) Art Mus., Nat. Mus. Am. Art Smithsonian Inst., Washington, Met. Mus. Art, NYC, Peggy Guggenheim Collection, Venice, Italy, others, also numerous pvt. collections; artist, 1960—. Recipient Pollock-Krasner Lifetime Achievement Award. Office: Michael Rosenfeld Gallery 24 W 57th St New York NY 10019-3918

SELIGMAN, BRAD, lawyer; b. Cin., Aug. 25, 1951; s. Selig J. and Muriel (Bienstock) S.; children: Corina Kasten, Mariana Campos, Sofia Maya Campos. BA, Sonoma State U., Calif., 1975; JD, U. Calif., San Francisco, 1978. Bar: Calif. 1978, US Dist. Ct. (no. dist.) Calif. 1978, US Dist. Ct. (ea. dist.) Calif. 1979. Teaching fellow Law Sch. Stanford U., Calif., 1978-79; sr. law clk. to Hon. Lawrence K. Karlton US Dist. Ct. (ea. dist.) Calif., Sacramento, 1979-80; assoc. Farnsworth, Saperstein & Brand, Oakland, Calif., 1981-85; ptnr. Farnsworth, Saperstein & Seligman, Oakland, 1985-89; mng. dir. Saperstein, Seligman & Mayeda, Oakland, 1989-91; of counsel Saperstein, Mayeda, Larkin & Goldstein, Oakland, Calif., 1991-94; exec. dir. The Impact Fund, Berkeley, Calif., 1992—. Advisor Disability Rights Edn. and Def. Fund, Inc., 1992—; trustee Calif. Rural Legal Assistance, San Francisco, 1982-88; bd. dirs. Equal Rights Advisors, San Francisco, 1989-92. Author: (with others) CEO: Wrongful Employment Termination Practice, 1987, Tax Aspects of Litigation and Settlements, 1989. Named one of 100 Most Influential Lawyers, Nat. Law Jour., 2006. Office: The Impact Fund 125 University Ave Berkeley CA 94710 Business E-Mail: bs@impactfund.org.

SELIGMAN, DANIEL, editor; b. NYC, Sept. 25, 1924; s. Irving and Clare (O'Brien) S.; m. Mary Gale Sherburn, May 23, 1953; children: Nora, William Paul. Student, Rutgers U., 1941-42; AB, NYU, 1946. Editl. asst. New Leader, 1946; asst. editor Am. Mercury, 1946-50; assoc. editor Fortune, 1950-59, editl. bd., 1959-66, asst. mng. editor, 1966-69, exec. editor, 1970-77, assoc. mng. editor, 1977-87, contbg. editor, 1988-97, Forbes, 1997—. Sr. staff editor all Time, Inc. (publs.), 1969-70. Author: A Question of Intelligence: The IQ Debate in America, 1992. Home: 190 E 72nd St New York NY 10021-4370 Office Phone: 212-249-5650. Personal E-mail: ad453@aol.com.

SELIGMAN, DELICE, lawyer; b. Worcester, Mass. m. Frederick Seligman. AB, MA, Clark U.; JD, NYU, 1971. Bar: N.Y. 1972, U.S. Dist. Ct. (so. and ea. dists.) N.Y. 1973, U.S. Supreme Ct. 1979. Assoc. Legal Aid Soc. Nassau County, Mineola, NY, 1972-76; ptnr. Seligman, Stein & Abromowitz, Garden City, 1976-86, Seligman & Seligman, NYC, 1986—. Legal counsel Contemporary Sculptors, Roslyn, N.Y., 1987-90, Artists Network Great Neck, N.Y., 1987-90, Woodstock Animal Rights Movement, Legal Action for Animals, Stop Graffiti Now, Inc.; pres. Wildlife Legal Action, Inc. Bd. dirs. For Our Children and Us, Hicksville, N.Y., 1985—; pres. Vol. Lawyers for Animal Rights, 2001—, Animal Advocates, Inc., 1999—. Mem. N.Y. State Bar Assn., Nassau Women's Bar Assn. (pres. 1982-83), Bar Assn. Nassau County (chair arts com. 1984-85), Phi Alpha Delta. Home: Runge Rd Shokan NY 12481 Office: 26 Broadway New York NY 10004-1703 also: Seligman & Seligman 70 Main St Kingston NY 12401-3802 Home Phone: 845-657-2967; Office Phone: 845-338-4100. Personal E-mail: Fredeli@aol.com.

SELIGMAN, FREDERICK, lawyer; b. Bklyn. s. Martin and Florence (Alperin) S.; m. Delice Felice. AB, Clark U., 1957; JD, N.Y. Law Sch., 1972. Bar: N.Y. 1973, U.S. Dist. Ct. (so. and ea. dists.) N.Y. 1974, U.S. Tax Ct. 1974, U.S. Ct. Appeals (2d cir.) 1975, U.S. Supreme Ct. 1979. Atty. N.Y.C. (N.Y.) Police Dept., 1972-73; asst. dist. atty. N.Y. County, NYC, 1973-79; pvt. practice NYC, 1980-85; ptnr. Seligman & Seligman, NYC, 1986—. Mem. N.Y. Criminal Bar Assn., N.Y. State Defenders Assn. Home: Runge Rd Shokan NY 12481 Home Phone: 845-657-2367; Office Phone: 845-338-4100. E-mail: fredeli@aol.com.

SELIGMAN, JOEL, academic administrator; b. NYC, Jan. 11, 1950; s. Selig Jacob and Muriel (Bienstock) Seligman; m. Friederike Felber Seligman, July 30, 1982; children: Andrea, Peter. AB in polit. sci. magna cum laude, UCLA, 1971; JD, Harvard U., 1974. Bar: Calif. 1975. Atty., writer Corp. Accountability Rsch. Group, Washington, 1974-77; prof. law Northeastern U. Law Sch., 1977-83, George Washington U., 1983-86, U. Mich., Ann Arbor, 1987—95; dean law sch. U. Ariz., Tucson, 1995-99, Samuel M. Fegtly prof. law, 1995—99; dean law sch. Washington U., St. Louis, 1999—2005, Ethan A. H. Shepley prof. law, 1999—2005; pres. Rochester U., NY, 2005—. Cons. Fed. Trade Commn., 1979—82, US Dept. Transp., 1983, Office Tech. Assessment, 1988—89; chair adv. com. on mktg. info. SEC, 2000—01; reporter Nat. Conf. of Commrs. on Uniform State Laws, Uniform Securities Act, 2002. Co-author: Constitutionalizing the Corporation: The Case for the Federal Chartering of Giant Corporations, 1976, The High Citadel: The Influence of Harvard Law School, 1978, The Transformation of Wall Street: A History of the Securities and Exchange Commission and Modern Corporate Finance, 1982, The SEC and the Future of Finance, 1985, Securities Regulation, The New Uniform Securities Act, 2002; contbr. articles to profl. jour. Mem.: Am. Law Inst. (adv. com., adv. corp. governance project), State Bar Calif., NASD (bd. govs.), AICPA (profl. ethics exec. com. 2000—02).

SELIGMAN, MARTIN E.P., psychologist, educator; b. Albany, NY, Aug. 12, 1942; s. Adrian and Irene Seligman; m. Mandy M. Seligman; children: Amanda, David, Lara, Nicole, Darryl, Carly, Jenny. AB, Princeton U., NJ, 1964; PhD in Psychology, U. Pa., Phila., 1967; PhD (hon.), Uppsala U., Sweden, 1989, Mass. Coll. Profl. Psychology, 1997, Complutense U., Madrid, 2004, U. East London, 2006. Asst. prof. Cornell U., 1967-70; assoc. prof. psychology U. Pa., 1972-76, prof., 1976—, Fox Leadership prof., 1999—, dir. clin. program, 1980-94. Vis. fellow Maudsley Hosp. Inst. Psychiatry, U. London, 1975; hon. prof. psychology U. Wales, Cardiff. Author: Helplessness, 1975, Learned Optimism, 1991, What You Can Change & What You Can't, 1993, The Optimistic Child, 1995, Authentic Happiness, 2002 (Best Psychology Book 2003), (with Christopher Peterson) Character Strengths and Virtues, 2004; contbr. numerous articles to profl. jours. Recipient MERIT award, 1991, William James fellow award Am. Psychol. Soc., 1992, James McKeen Cattell Fellow award, 1995; NIMH grantee, 1969—; NSF fellow, 1963-64, Woodrow Wilson fellow, 1964-65, Guggenheim fellow, 1974-75, Ctr. Advanced Study in Behavioral Scis. fellow, 1978-79, Theodore Roosevelt fellow, 2002, Am. Acad. Polit. and Social Sci. Fellow AAAS, APA (pres. divsn. clin. psychology 1993-95, pres. 1997-99); mem. Ea. Psychol. Assn. (bd. dirs.), Am. Psychopathol. Assn., Phi Beta Kappa, Sigma Xi. Office: Positive Psychology Ctr 3701 Market St Ste 200 Philadelphia PA 19104 Business E-Mail: seligmaninfo@psych.upenn.edu.

SELIGMAN, NICOLE K., broadcast executive, lawyer; BA magna cum laude, Harvard Coll., Radcliffe, 1978; JD magna cum laude, Harvard Law Sch., 1983. Assoc. editl. page editor The Asian Wall St. Jour., Hong Kong, 1978—80; law clk. to Judge Harry T. Edwards U.S. Ct. of Appeals, Wash., DC, 1983—84; law clk. to Justice Thurgood Marshall U.S. Supreme Ct., 1984—85; ptnr., litig. Williams & Connolly LLP, Wash., DC; exec. v.p., gen. counsel Sony Corp. of Am., 2001—; corp. exec. Sony Corp., Tokyo, 2003—, group deputy gen. counsel, 2003—.

SELIGMANN, WILLIAM ROBERT, lawyer, author; b. Davenport, Iowa, Oct. 10, 1956; s. William Albert and Barbara Joyce (Carmichael) S.; m. Carole Lee Francis; children: D Anna, Matthew. BA, U. Calif., Santa Barbara, 1979; JD, Santa Clara U., 1982. Bar: Calif. 1983, U.S. Dist. Ct. (no. dist.) Calif. 1983. Assoc. Office of J.R. Dempster, Cupertino, Calif., 1983-85; city atty. City of Campbell, Calif., 1985—; ptnr. Dempster, Seligmann & Raineri, Los Gatos, Calif., 1985—2001, pvt. practice, 2001—. Reviewer: California Municipal Law Handbook, 1997—98, 2007, cons.: Continuing Education of the Bar, California Land Use Practice, 2006. Bd. dirs. Los Gatos C. of C. Mem. Santa Clara County Bar Assn. (civil practice com., judiciary com.), State Bar Calif. (exec. bd. pub. law sect. 2001—, chair 2004-05, advisor 2005—), Calif. League Cities (fair polit. practices com., city atty. divsn.). Avocations: cross country skiing, scuba diving, swimming, writing, Aikido. Office: 333 Church St Santa Cruz CA 95060 Home Phone: 831-438-8595; Office Phone: 831-423-8383. Business E-Mail: bill@southbaylaw.com.

SELIGSON, CARL HAROLD, corporate financial executive; b. NYC, Feb. 25, 1935; s. Harold P. and Lilian (Yohalem) Seligson; m. Bonnie Laskin, Mar. 6, 1983; children: Susan S. Pattenaude, Barbara S. Zweig, Nina Priven, Eric M. Drath. AB, Brown U., 1956; postgrad., NYU Grad. Sch. Bus. Adminstrn., 1961—63. Textile salesman Cohn, Hall, Marx Co., Montreal, Canada, 1958—61; security analyst Burnham & Co., NYC, 1961—67, Kuhn, Loeb & Co, NYC, 1967—71; mng. dir. Merrill Lynch, NYC, 1971—87, Kidder, Peabody & Co., NYC, 1987—90; sr. exec. cons. regulated industries Deloitte & Touche, NYC, 1990—92; mng. dir. Prudential Securities, NYC, 1992—95; sr. advisor Andersen Consulting, NYC, 1996—2000; sr. v.p. energyLeader.com, NYC, 2000; sr. advisor Prospect St. Ventures, NYC, 2001, K Rd. Power, NYC, 2002—05; fin. cons. Edison Electric Inst., Washington, 2003—. Contbr. articles to profl. jours. including Pub. Utilities Fortnightly, Telephony, Fin. Exec., The So. Banker, Coal Monthly and Energy News. Chmn. Regulatory Industry Com., Securities Industry Assn., 1985—87; mem. strategic issues com. and adv. coun. Elec. Power Rsch. Inst., Palo Alto, Calif., 1998—2006; mem. adv. coun. Nat. Assn. Registry Utilities Commrs. Edn. & Rsch. Found., 2005—; bd. dirs. Nuc. Energy Inst., Washington, 1988—95. With Counter Intelligence Corps US Army. Fellow Fin. Analysts Fedn.; mem. Univ. Club. NY. Avocations: water sports, travel, theater. Personal E-mail: cseligson@nyc.rr.com.

SELIGSON, FREDERIC LEE, physician, cardiothoracic surgeon; b. Erie, Pa., July 12, 1956; BA, Dartmouth Coll., 1978; MD, U. Pitts., 1982. Diplomate Am. Bd. Thoracic Surgery, Am. Bd. Surgery. Intern, resident in surgery Beth Israel Hosp., Boston, 1982-87; resident in cardiothoracic surgery U. Ill., Chgo., 1987-89; cardiothoracic surgeon Thoracic and Vascular Surgeons, P.C., Prairie Village, Kans., 1989—. Office: Thoracic/Vascular Surgeons 6420 Prospect Ave Ste 301 Kansas City MO 64132-4178 *

SELIGSON, MITCHELL A., political science educator; b. Hempstead, NY, Nov. 12, 1945; m. Susan Berk, June 18, 1967; 1 child, Amber Lara. BA cum laude, Bklyn. Coll., 1967; MA, U. Fla., 1968; PhD, U. Pitts., 1974. Vol. U.S. Peace Corps, Costa Rica, 1968-70; asst. prof./assoc. prof. U. Ariz., Tucson, 1974-85; prof. U. Pitts., 1986-93, Daniel H. Wallace prof. polit. sci., 1994—2004, dir. Latin Am. studies, 1986-92, rsch. prof., 1992—2004; Centennial prof. polit. sci. Vanderbilt U., Nashville, 2004—. Fellow Ctr. Ams.; dir. L.Am. pub. opinion project; cons. to World Bank, UN Devel. Program, US AID, Inter-Am. Devel. Bank, Guatemala, Honduras, Nicaragua, Costa Rica, Colombia, Dominican Republic, Mex., Ecuador, Jamaica, Panama, El Salvador, Peru, Bolivia, Paraguay, 1980—. Author, editor: Peasants of Costa Rica and the Development of Agrarian Capitalism, 1980, The Gap Between Rich and Poor, 1984, Authoritarians and Democrats, 1987, Elections and Democracy in Central America, 1989, rev. edit. 1995, Development and Underdevelopment, 1993, The Political Economy of Global Inequality, 2003. Fulbright fellow, Costa Rica, 1986, Rockefeller Found. fellow, 1985-86; grantee Social Sci. Rsch. Coun., Ford Found., NSF, Mellon Found., Heinz Endowment. Mem. Am. Polit. Sci. Assn., Latin Am. Studies Assn. (chmn. fin. com. 1991). Office: Vanderbilt U Dept Polit Sci Nashville TN 37235 Office Phone: 615-322-6938. Business E-Mail: m.seligson@vanderbilt.edu.

SELIGSON, THEODORE H., architect, interior designer, urban planner; b. Kansas City, Mo., Nov. 10, 1930; s. Harry and Rose (Haith) S.; m. Jacqueline Rose, Dec. 27, 1964 (div. 1976). BArch, Washington U., St. Louis, 1953. Registered architect, Mo., Kans. Intern Marshall & Brown, Kansas City, Mo., 1949-54; designer, head design Kivett & Myers, Kansas City, Mo., 1954-62; prin. Design Assocs., 1955—, Atelier Seligson, Kansas City, Mo., 1962-64; pres. Seligson, Eggen, Inc., Kansas City, 1964-73, Seligson Assocs., Inc., Architects Planners, Kansas City, 1973-97; prin. Foss, Seligson, Lafferty, 1997—. Vis. lectr. adult edn. U. Mo.-Kansas City, 1958-61, vis. prof. arch., 1989—, vis. prof. urban design, 2002—; tchr., critic Kansas City Art Inst., Mo., 1961-64, 71-72, adj. prof., 1986, 89, 91, 92; adj. prof. Kans. State U., 1991-92, 97; vis. prof. Washington U., St. Louis, 1975, 77, 78, 81, 86, 91, U. Kans., Lawrence, 1978, 79, 80, 91, 92; art cons. Design Assocs., Kansas City, Mo., 1955—. Projects pub. in archtl. jours. V.p. Friends of Art Nelson-Atkins Mus. Art, Kansas City, bd. dirs. 1963-67, chmn. selections com., 1981, vis. curator, 1972, 87; chmn. Capitol Fine Arts Commn. Mo., 1983-90, Kansas City Worlds Fair goals and themes subcom., 1985-90; bd. dirs. Westport Tomorrow, Kansas City, 1980-87, Hist. Kansas City Found., 1984-90; pres. Native Sons of Kansas City, 1989, bd. dirs. 1978-94, Westport Cmty. Coun., 1973-75; bd. govs. Truman Med. Ctr., Kansas City, 1998-2002, mem. bd. advisors, 2002—; mem. Kansas City Key to City Commn., 2001-02; bd. dirs. Sacred Structures, 2003—. Recipient Urban Design award Kansas City Mcpl. Art Commn., 1968, 74, 78; Nat. Archtl. award Am. Inst. Steel Constrn., 1970; Nat. award ASID/DuPont Corian, 1989. Fellow AIA (Kansas City chpt. pres. 1983, bd. dirs. 1979-84, Design Excellence award 1966, 68, 70, 74, Ctrl. States Regional award 1974, 78, Honor award for outstanding svc. to chpt. and profession 1982-83); mem. Coun. Archs., Am. Soc. Interior

Designers, Nat. Coun. Archtl. Registration Bds. (task analysis adv. com. 1988-90), Soc. Archtl. Historians (pres. 1973-75, bd. dirs. 1994-97). Jewish. Office: Foss Seligson Lafferty 450 E 4th St Kansas City MO 64106

SELIN, IVAN, entrepreneur; b. NYC, Mar. 11, 1937; s. Saul and Freda (Kuhlman) Selin; m. Nina Kallet, June 8, 1957; children: Douglas, Jessica. BE, Yale U., 1957, ME, 1958, PhD, 1960; DSc, U. Paris, 1962. Rsch. engr. Rand Corp., Santa Monica, Calif., 1960-65; sys. analyst Dept. Def., Washington, 1965-67, dep. asst. sec. def., 1967-69, acting asst. sec. for systems analysis, 1969-70; founder, chmn. bd. Am. Mgmt. Systems, Inc., Arlington, Va., 1970-89; undersec. state Dept. State, Washington, 1989-91; chmn. Nuc. Regulatory Commn., Washington, 1991—95; chmn., CEO Phoenix Internat., Washington, 1995—; chmn. Enumerale Solutions, Inc., 1998—. Lectr. UCLA, 1961-63; chmn. mil. econ. adv. panel to CIA, 1978-89; bd. dirs. BZL Biologics, Inc. Author: Detection Theory, 1964; contbr. articles to profl. jours. Pres. Corp. Against Drug Abuse, 1988-95; bd. dirs., gov. UN Assn. U.S., 1979-89; exec. com. Greater Washington Research Ctr., Fed. City Council; trustee Asia Soc., 1996-98; chmn., bd. dirs. Smithsonian Nat. Mus. of Am. History, 1996—, Yale U. Coun., 2000—. Recipient Disting. Civilian Svc. medal, 1970, Disting. Svc. medal Sec. of State, 1991; Fulbright scholar, 1959-61; Ford Found. grantee, 1952-54. Mem. IEEE (editor Trans. on Info. Theory 1960-65), Coun. Fgn. Rels., Yale Club, Sigma Xi, Tau Beta Pi. Office: Phoenix Internat Inc PO Box 58277 Washington DC 20037-5503 Home: 1455 Ocean Dr Apt 1602 Miami FL 33159 Office Phone: 202-337-2337. Business E-Mail: ixs@phnx-intl.com.

SELIN, LISA K., physician; b. Helsinki, Finland, Apr. 8, 1952; d. Lauri Oscar and Hilma K Selin. BSc, Dalhousie Univ, 1970—74; MD, Dalhousie U., 1974—79, FRCP, 1980—84; PhD, Univ. Man., 1986—93. Med. intern Dalhousie U., Halifax, Canada, 1979—80, resident in internal medicine, 1980—84; fellow in infectious diseases Univ. of Man., Winnipeg, Canada, 1984—86; doctoral student Univ of Man., 1986—91; postdoctoral fellow Univ. Mass. Med. Sch., 1992—95, instr., 1995—96; asst. prof. Univ. Mass. Med Sch., 1996—2001; assoc. prof. Univ. Mass. Med. Sch., 2001—. Contbr. articles to profl. jours. Med. Coun. of Can. Student fellowship, Med. Coun. of Can., 1986—91, Dalhousie Entrance schoarship, Dalhousie Univ, 1970, Izaak Walton Killam scholarship, Izaak Walton Killam Found., 1984—86, Clin. Investigator award, Nat. Inst. of Health, 1996—99, Rsch. grant, NIH- NIAID, 2000—, NIH-NIAID, 2001—, 1999—2003. Mem.: Can. Infectious Disease Soc., Am. Assn. of Immunologists. Achievements include research in T cell-mediated heterologous immunity in viral infections. Avocations: painting, cross country skiing, swimming, gardening, travel. Office: Univ Mass Med Sch 55 Lake Ave North Worcester MA 01655 E-mail: liisa.selin@umassmed.edu.

SELIN, NINA EVVIE, museum director, electric power industry executive, volunteer; b. NYC, Dec. 16, 1935; d. Louis Harry and Ida Kallet; m. Ivan Selin, June 8, 1957; children: Douglas Scott, Jessica Beth. BS, Boston U., 1957. Tchr., Conn., 1957-60; dir. Nat. Consumers League, Washington, 1968-75; propr. Relax-Relocation Cons., Washington, 1975-80; vice chmn. Phoenix Internat. Power Plant Co., Washington, 1995-98; chmn. Nat. Aquarium, Washington, 1986—. Bd. dirs. Am. Cancer Soc., 1972-87, Nat. Geog. Soc., 1995—, Mt. Sinai Hosp. Found., Miami Beach, Fla., 1998-2004, Smithsonian Environ. Rsch. Ctr., 2004—, Nat. Aquarium, Balt., 2003—; chmn. Selin Family Found., Del., 1995; judge Nathan Davis award AMA, Washington, 2001. Recipient Disting. Svc. award, Am. Cancer Soc., 1987, Mt. Sinai Found., 1999. Mem. Internat. Club III, Welcome to Washington Internat. Club. Avocations: exotic travel, scuba diving, reading, public service. Office Phone: 202-337-2337. E-mail: nselin@phnx-intl.com.

SELINGER, JERRY ROBIN, lawyer; b. Peekskill, NY, Nov. 3, 1947; s. Philip R. and Helen D. (Klein) S.; m. Barbara D. Wax, Aug. 2, 1969; children: Elise, Scott. BS in Engring. Sci., SUNY, Buffalo, 1969; MS, Columbia U., 1971; JD, George Washington U., 1975. Bar: Md. 1975, D.C. 1976, U.S. Ct. Appeals (fed. cir.) 1977, U.S. Supreme Ct. 1978, Tex. 1980, U.S. Ct. Appeals (5th cir.) 1981, U.S. Ct. Appeals (3d cir.) 1982. Atty. Arent, Fox, Kintner, Plotkin & Kahn, Washington, 1975-79, Richards, Harris & Medlock, Dallas, 1979-82; mem., dir. Baker, Mills & Glast, Dallas, 1982-90; ptnr. Vinson & Elkins LLP, Dallas, 1990-97; 1997shareholder Jenkens & Gilchrist, Dallas, 1997—2005; ptnr. Morgan Lewis & Bockius LLP, Dallas, 2005—. Contbr. articles to profl. jours. Bd. trustees Dallas Bar Found., 2001—. Fellow Dallas Bar (chair 2007); mem. ABA, Tex. Bar Assn. (chair intellectual property law sect. 1996-97, bd. dirs. 1998-01), Dallas Bar Assn. (bd. dirs. 1995-96), Tex. Young Lawyers Assn. (bd. dirs. 1984-86, Pres. award 1986), Am. Intellectual Property Law Assn. (bd. dirs. 2002-05), Dallas Assn. Young Lawyers (sec. 1983, treas. 1984), Order of Coif, Phi Delta Phi. Home: 10414 Woodford Dr Dallas TX 75229-6317 Office: Morgan Lewis & Bockius LLP 1717 Main St Ste 3200 Dallas TX 75201 Office Phone: 214-466-4109. Business E-Mail: jselinger@morganlewis.com.

SELINGER, PATRICIA GRIFFITHS, computer science professional; b. Cleve., Oct. 15, 1949; d. Fred Robert and Olive Mae (Brewster) Priest; m. James Alan Griffiths, Aug. 29, 1970 (div. 1973); m. Robert David Selinger, July 22, 1978; children: David Robert, Thomas Robert. AB, Harvard U., 1971, MS, 1972, PhD, 1975. Rsch. staff IBM Rsch. Lab, San Jose, Calif., 1975-78, mgr., 1978-83, mgr. computer sci., 1983-86, program dir. Database Technology Inst., 1986, with devel. team, 1997, v.p. Rsch. Area Strategy, Info. and Interaction. Patentee in field; co-author numerous tech. papers. IBM fellow, 1994; recipient YWCA Tribute to Women in Industry award, 1989; named to Hall of Fame, Women in Tech. Internat., 2004. Mem. NAE, Assn. for Computing Machinery (System Software award 1989, former vice-chmn. spl. interest group for mgmt. data). Avocations: cooking, reading. Office: IBM Almaden Rsch Ctr 650 Harry Rd San Jose CA 95120-6099

SELIX, KAREN ELIZABETH, writer, artist, vocalist; b. Alice, Tex., Jan. 10, 1960; d. LeRoy Albert; 3 children. Owner, designer Spark a Link, Inc., 1999—. Author: (children's stories) Rainbow's End, 2000, Black Rainbow, 2003; co-author (with LeRoy Selix): (cassette recording) The Easter Bunny That Wasn't a Rabbit, 1988; musician: (albums) I'll Be There, 2005, Until We Meet Again, 2005. Recipient Gift of Life award, Ben Taub Gen. Hosp., 1973. Roman Catholic. Home: PO Box 711 Malvern AR 72104 Home Phone: 501-609-3138.

SELK, STEPHEN JEFFREY, chemical engineer; b. Toronto, Ont., Can., Dec. 26, 1953; came to U.S., 1992; s. Milan M. and Valeda (Couture) S.; m. Grace Doreen Kobe, Nov. 29, 1980; children: Karen, Susanne. BScChemE, U. Toronto, 1976. Registered profl. engr., Ont. Process engr. Dow Chem. Co., Sarnia, Ont., 1977-80, Gulf Oil Co., Toronto, 1980-86; cons. engr. Selk & Assocs., Toronto, 1986-91; mgr. process engring. Safety-Kleen Can., Breslau, Ont., 1991-92; chief engr. Safety-Kleen Corp., Elgin, Ill., 1992—. Forensic engr. Selk & Assocs., Barrington, Ill. Mem. ASME, AIChE, Can. Soc. Forensic Sci., Soc. Automotive Engrs. Achievements include design of world's largest oil re-refinery, processing 400,000 gallons per day of used crankcase oil; authority in recycling of used automotive fluids. Home: 4226 Kerrigan Ln Fairfax VA 22030-8552

SELKIRK, ALEXANDER MACDONALD, JR., lawyer; b. Jamaica, NY, Oct. 2, 1943; s. Alexander MacDonald and Anne (Roth) S.; m. Joanne Patrician Diskant, July 21, 1974; children: Marianne C., Victoria L. BA in Polit. Sci., St. Johns U., Jamaica, 1965; JD, N.Y. Law Sch., 1970; LLM in Trade Regulation, NYU, 1973. Bar: N.Y. 1971, U.S. Dist. Ct. (so. and ea. dists.) N.Y. 1972, U.S. Ct. Appeals (2d cir.) 1972, U.S. Supreme Ct. 1976, Fla. 1991. Sr. staff atty. Hartford Ins. Co., NYC, 1971-74; assoc. Richard C. Mooney, Esq., Hempstead, NY, 1974-77; sr. trial atty. Home Ins. Co., Huntington Sta., NY, 1978-80; asst. county atty. Suffolk County, Hauppauge, NY, 1980-88; assoc. Garcia & Stallone Esqs., Melville, NY, 1988-90, CIGNA Ins. Co., Woodbury, NY, 1990-95; trial counsel Martin Fallon Mulle, Huntington, NY, 1995—2004; asst. atty. Town of Huntington. Arbitrator Suffolk County Dist. Ct. 10th Jud. Dist., 1982-88; instr. N.Y. State JAG's Sch., 1997—. Feature writer Ronkonkoma Rev., 1986-90; contbr. articles to legal publs. Committeeman Suffolk Country Rep. Com., Ronkonkoma, N.Y., 1977-92; del. 10th Jud. Dist. Conv. Suffolk County, 1981-84; v.p. Holbrook Rep. Club, 1979-81, pres., 1981-83; bd. dirs. Holbrook Youth Devel. Corp., 1985-91; pilot legal officer Nassau sr. squadron CAP, 1978-84; counsel. Com. for A Drug Free Holbrook, 1988-90. Maj. JACG, N.Y. Army N.G., 1983-2003. Mem. Am. Arbitration Assn. (comml. arbitrator), N.Y. State Bar Assn., Internat. Platform Assn., Suffolk Country Bar Assn., NYU Alumni Assn., Holbrook C. of C. (bd. dirs. 1981-92, v.p. 1987-89, pres. 1984-91, 92-93), Gt. Neck (N.Y.) Sportsman's Club (pres. 1998), KC (adv. 1981-84, 87—, trustee 1984-87), Lions (bd. dirs. 1985-86, v.p. 1986-87, pres. 1987-88). Roman Catholic. Home: 12 Glen Summer Rd Holbrook NY 11741-5006 Office: 100 Main St Huntington NY 11743 Office Phone: 631-351-3342. Personal E-mail: flyallaw@hotmail.com.

SELKIRK, JAMES KIRKWOOD, biochemist, researcher; b. NYC, Dec. 3, 1938; s. James Kirkwood and Doris (Schuler) S.; m. Carole Ann Bozzone, Sept. 16, 1961; children: James Kirkwood, David Edward. BS in Biochemistry, Coll. Environ. Sci. and Forestry, Syracuse U., NY, 1964; BS in Environ. Sci., Chemistry, Syracuse U., NY, 1964; PhD in Biochemistry, Syracuse U. Upstate Med. Ctr., Syracuse, 1969. Postdoctoral fellow McArdle Lab. Cancer Rsch., U. Wis., Madison, 1969-72; staff fellow Nat. Cancer Inst., NIH, Bethesda, Md., 1972-74, sr. staff fellow, 1974-75; sr. staff scientist unit leader chem. carcinogenesis biology divsn. Oak Ridge (Tenn.) Nat. Lab., 1975-85; chief carcinogenesis and toxicology evaluation br. nat. toxicology program Nat. Inst. Environ. Health Scis., 1985-89, assoc. dir. divsn. toxicology rsch. and testing, 1989-92, chief carcinogen mechanism group Lab. Molecular Carcinogenesis, 1992—97; spl. asst. to sci. dir. for technology devel. Nat. Inst. Evniron. Health Scis., 1997-2000; deputy dir. Nat. Ctr. Toxicogenomics, 2000—; adj. prof. Oak Ridge Biomed. Grad. Sch., U. Tenn., 1975-85; mem. breast cancer task force NIH, 1979-82; mem. com. on pyrenes and analogs NAS, 1981-83; chmn. Interagy. Testing Commn., 1986-90. Author rsch. articles, chpts. in books; mem. editl. bd. Carcinogenesis Jour., 1984-87, 91-93, Cancer Rsch., 1981-86, Environ. Health Perspectives, 1993-98, contbg. editor, 2003—. Mem. Orange County Planning Bd., 1997—; chmn. Weaver Dairy Precinct, Dem. Party Orange County, 1996-99. With AUS, 1959-61. With chem. corps US Army, 1959—60. Recipient U.S. Interagy. Testing Com. Exemplary Svc. award, 1992. Mem. Am. Cancer Soc. (carcinogenesis study sect. 1975-78, 92-96). Avocations: scuba diving, coin collecting/numismatics, marksmanship. Home: 30119 Settle Dr Chapel Hill NC 27517 Office: Nat Inst Environ Health Scis PO Box 12233 Research Triangle Park NC 27709 Home Phone: 919-967-0017; Office Phone: 919-541-2548. Business E-Mail: selkirk@niehs.nih.gov.

SELKOE, DENNIS JESSE, neurologist, researcher, educator; b. NYC, Sept. 25, 1943; s. Herbert E. and Mary P. (Lille) S.; m. Polly Ann Strasser, June 24, 1967; children: Gregory, Kimberly. BA, Columbia U., 1965; MD, U. Va., 1969. Diplomate Am. Bd. Psychiatry and Neurology, Nat. Bd. Med. Examiners. Intern in medicine Hosp. U. Pa., Phila., 1969-70; rsch. assoc. NIH, Bethesda, Md., 1970-72; resident in neurology Peter Bent Brigham/Children's Hosp., Boston, 1972-74, chief resident in neurology, 1974-75; rsch. assoc. Harvard Med. Sch., Boston, 1975-78, asst. prof. neurology, 1978-82, assoc. prof., 1982-85, assoc. prof. neurology and neurosci., 1985-90, faculty mem. divsn. on aging, 1980—, prof. neurology and neurosci., 1990—, Vincent and Stella Coates prof. neurol. diseases, 2001—; co-dir. Ctr. Neurologic Diseases Brigham and Women's Hosp., Boston, 1985—. Mem. sci. adv. bd. Alzheimer's Disease Assn., Chgo., 1983-89; mem. Gov.'s Commn. on Alzheimer's Disease, Mass., 1985-87; neurosci. adv. com. Howard Hughes Med. Inst., 1996—. Author over 200 articles, book chpts. on biochemistry and molecular biology of Alzheimer's Disease. Recipient Wood-Kalb Found. prize Alzheimers Disease Assn., 1984, Med. Rsch. award Met. Life Found., 1986, LEAD award Nat. Inst. on Aging, 1988, NIH Merit award, 1991—, Arthur Cherkin award UCLA, 1995, Mathilde Solowey award in neurosci. Found. for Advanced Edn. in Scis., NIH, 1998, Rita Hayworth award Alzheimer's Assn., 1995, Boerhaave medal U. Leiden, 1998, Pioneer award Alzheimer's Assn., 1999; grantee Bristol-Myers Squibb Neurosci., 1990. Fellow AAAS, Am. Acad. Neurology (Potamkin prize 1989, Dr. A.H. Heineken prize for Medicine 2002); mem. Am. Neurol. Assn., Soc. for Neurosci., Am. Assn. Neuropathologists, World Fedn. Neurologists, Inst. Medicine NAS. Office: Harvard Med Sch Brigham & Womens Hosp 77 Avenue Louis Pasteur Boston MA 02115-5727

SELKOWITZ, ARTHUR, retired advertising executive; b. NYC, May 26, 1943; s. Harry and Anne (Lichten); m. Betsey Wattenberg, Apr. 15, 1967; children: Adam, Jed. AB, Syracuse U., NY, 1965. Account exec. Dancer Fitzgerald Sample, 1969-71; with Benton & Bowles, Inc., NYC, 1971-82, v.p., account supr., 1972-75, sr. v.p., mgmt. supr., 1975-81, sr. v.p., account dir., 1981-82; founder, pres. Penchina, Selkowitz Inc., NYC, 1982-90; exec. v.p. internat. D'Arcy, Masius, Benton & Bowles, NYC, 1990-94, pres. Asia and Pacific, 1995-96, pres. N.Am., 1996-97, chmn., CEO, 1997-2000; vice chmn., chief client officer BCom3 Group, Inc., NYC, 2001—02, Publicis Groupe, 2002. Lectr. Columbia U., 2003—06; mem. adv. bd. Spot Runner, Inc. Dancer Fitzgerald Sample, N.Y.C., 1966—71. Chmn. Mill River Collaborative, Stamford, Conn.; bd. mem. Stamford Mus. and Nature Ctr., Conn. Mem.: Lotos (N.Y.) Club.

SELL, CLAY (JEFFREY CLAY SELL), federal agency administrator; b. 1967; married; 3 children. BS in Bus. Adminstrn., Tex. Tech. U., 1989; JD, U. Tex. Staff mem. to Congressman Mac Thornberry US Ho. Reps., Washington, 1995—97, adminstrv. asst. to Congressman Mac Thornberry, 1997—99; majority clk. & staff dir. for energy & water sub com. of the Senate Com. on Appropriations US Senate, Washington, 2000—03; spl. asst. to the Pres. for econ. policy The White House, Washington, 2003—04, spl. asst. to Pres. for legis. affairs, 2004—05; dep. sec. US Dept. Energy, Washington, 2005—. Office: US Dept Energy Forrestal Bldg 1000 Independence Ave SW Rm 7B-252 Washington DC 20585 *

SELL, LEELOU, retired elementary school educator; d. Werner William and Lydia Veryl Sell. BA, Long Beach State Coll., Calif., 1960; postgrad., Pepperdine U., Calif. State U., Fullerton, U. Calif., Irvine. Cert. tchr. Calif. Tchr. Anaheim City Sch. Dist., Calif., 1960, 1961—97; chpt. counselor Zeta Tau Alpha, 1960—61; ret., 1997—. Co-author: Math for Kindergartners, 1970. Vol. Braille Inst., Anaheim, 1997—; vol., bd. dirs., mem. com. Pacific Symphony, Orange County, Calif., 1997—; bd. dirs., mem. com. Am. Heart Assn., Orange County, 1998—2001. Named Hon. Life Mem., Jefferson PTA, Anaheim, 1970, Price PTA, Anaheim, 1986. Mem.: AAUW, Calif. Ret. Tchrs. Assn., Zeta Tau Alpha (pres., v.p., sec. membership 1955—60), Delta Kappa Gamma (2d v.p., sec. rec. sec., chmn. various coms. 1985—). Avocations: reading, theater, needlecrafts, herb gardening, travel.

SELL, ROBERT EMERSON, electrical engineer; b. Apr. 23, 1929; s. Cecil Leroy and Ona Arletta (Stevens) S.; m. Ora Lucile Colton, Nov. 7, 1970. BS, U. Nebr., 1962. Registered profl. engr., Nebr., Mo., Ill., Ind., Ohio, W.Va., Ky., Ark., Tex., Oreg., Wash., Calif. Chief draftsman Dempster Mill Mfg. Co., Beatrice, Nebr., 1949-53; designer-engr. U. Nebr., Lincoln, 1955-65; elec. design engr. Kirkham, Michael & Assocs., Omaha, 1965-67, Leo A. Daly Co., Omaha and St. Louis, 1967-69; mech. design engr. Hellmuth, Obata, Kassabaum, St. Louis, 1969-70; chief elec. engr. Biagi-Hannah & Assocs., Inc., Evansville, Ind., 1971-74; elec. project engr. H.L. Yoh Co. under contract to Monsanto Co., Creve Coeur, Mo., 1974-77, Dhillon Engrs., Inc., Portland, Oreg., 1978-85; project coord. Brown-Zammit-Enyeart Engring., Inc., San Diego, 1985-88; elec. engr. Morgen Design, Inc., San Diego, 1988; lead elec. engr. Popov Engrs., Inc., San Diego, 1988-89; mech. and elec. specialist Am. Engring. Labs., Inc. divsn. Profl. Svc. Industries, Inc., San Diego, 1990—. Instr. Basic Inst. Tech., St. Louis, 1971. Mem. ASHRAE, IEEE. Home and Office: PO Box 261578 San Diego CA 92196-1578

SELLECK, TOM, actor; b. Detroit, Jan. 29, 1945; s. Robert D. and Martha S.; m. Jacquelyn Ray, 1970 (div. 1982); 1 stepson, Kevin; m. Jillie Joan Mack, Aug. 7, 1987; 1 child, Hannah Margaret. Ph.D (hon.), Pepperdine U. Actor: (films) Myra Breckinridge, 1970, The Seven Minutes, 1971, Midway, 1976, Coma, 1982, High Road to China, 1983, Lassiter, 1984, Runaway, 1985, Three Men and a Baby, 1987, Her Alibi, 1989, An Innocent Man, 1989, Quigley Down Under, 1990, Three Men and a Little Lady, 1990, Folks!, 1992, Christopher Columbus: The Discovery, 1992, Mr. Baseball, 1992, In and Out, 1997, The Love Letter, 1999, Angus Magillicutty, 2003, (voice) Meet the Robinsons, 2007; (TV films) The Sacketts, 1979, Divorce Wars, 1982, Louis L'Amour's "The Shadow Riders", 1982, Broken Trust, 1995, Ruby Jean and Joe, 1996, Last Stand at Saher River, 1998, Louis l'Amour's Crossfire Trail, 2000, Monte Walsh, Reversible Errors, Ike: Countdown to D Day, 2004, Stone Cold, 2005, Jesse Stone: Night Passage, 2006; (TV series) The Young and the Restless, 1973-74, Magnum P.I. 1980-88, Las Vegas, 2007-; (TV appearances) Lancer, 1969, Bracken's World, 1969, Sarge, 1971, THe F.B.I., 1973, Marcus Welby, M.D., 1974-75, The Streets of San Francisco, 1975, The Rockford Files, 1978-79, Simon & Simon, 1982, Friends, 1996, 2000, Boston Legal, 2006 Bd. mem. Michael Josephson Inst. Ethics. Mem.: NRA. Office: care Esme Chandlee 2967 Hollyridge Dr Los Angeles CA 90068-1949 Office Phone: 323-962-5704. *

SELLER, GREGORY EROL, marketing executive, consultant, writer; b. Denver, Oct. 4, 1953; s. Otto Gustave and Dolores Louise (Crawford) S. BBA, U. Colo., 1975. Account exec. Gt.-West Life, LA, 1975-79, asst. v.p. group devel. Denver, 1980-84; v.p. govt. mkts. and nat. accts. Great-West Life, LA, 1988—; pres., chief exec. officer Benefits Communication Corp., Denver, 1985-87, sr. v.p. govt. mkts., 1991—. Bd. dirs. Benefits Communication Co., Fascorp, Emjoy Corp Editor newsletter Focus on 457, 1988—. Mem. vestry, treas. St. Thomas Episc. Ch., Hollywood, Calif., 1990-93 Mem. Delta Upsilon. Democrat. Office: Great West Life Ste 560 18111 Von Karman Ave Irvine CA 92612-7131

SELLER, ROBERT HERMAN, cardiologist, physician; b. Phila., Mar. 21, 1931; s. David and Elsie (Straussman) S.; m. Maxine Schwartz, June 3, 1956; children: Michael, Douglas, Stuart. AB, U. Pa., 1952, MD, 1956. Intern. Grad. Hosp. of U. Pa., Phila., 1956-57; research asst. dept. pharmacology U. Pa., 1953-55; resident in cardiology, research fellow Am. Heart Assn., Phila. Gen. Hosp., 1957-58; resident in internal medicine Albert Einstein Med. Ctr., Phila., 1958-59, chief resident, 1959-60; instr. medicine Hahnemann Med. Coll. and Hosp., Phila., 1960-64, asst. prof., 1964-69, assoc. prof., 1969-72, dir. Service F, 1962-67, asst. coordinator mil. edn. for nat. def., 1961-64, dir. div. family medicine, 1967-72, acting chmn. dept. family medicine and community health, 1972-74, prof. medicine, family medicine and community health, 1973-74; practice medicine, specializing in cardiology Buffalo, 1974—; prof., chmn. dept. family medicine, prof. medicine SUNY-Buffalo, Deaconess Hosp., 1974-82, chmn. dept. family practice and dir. family practice residency program, 1974-82; prof. medicine and family medicine SUNY-Buffalo, 1974-2000; emeritus prof. medicine and family medicine, 2000—. Author: Differential Diagnosis of Common Complaints, 1986, 5th edit., 2007, Diagnosis of Common Complaints, 2004; contbr. articles to profl. jours. NIH grantee, 1972-75; Deaconess Hosp. family practice resident tng. grantee, 1975-; health professions spl. projects grantee, 1975- Fellow ACP, Am. Coll. Cardiology, Am. Acad. Family Physicians, Phila. Coll. Physicians; mem. AMA, N.Y. Med. Soc., Erie County Med. Soc., Am. Fedn. Clin. Research, Am. Heart Assn., Soc. of Tchrs. of Family Medicine, N.Y. Acad. Sci., N.Y. Acad. Family Physicians. Home: 125 Crestwood Ln Buffalo NY 14221-1462 Office: 1542 Maple Rd Buffalo NY 14221-3625

SELLERS, CLAUDIA LEE, biology professor; b. Stockton, Calif., May 2, 1968; d. William Lee and Shirley Ann Sellers. PhD, U. Calif., Berkeley, 1999. Prof. biology Cerro Coso Coll., Ridgecrest, Calif., 1998—. Office: Cerro Coso Coll 3000 College Heights Blvd Ridgecrest CA 93555 Home Phone: 760-499-6265; Office Phone: 760-384-6308. Business E-Mail: clseller@cerrocoso.edu.

SELLERS, FRED EVANS, accounting educator; b. Lexington, Mo., Feb. 28, 1941; s. James MacBrayer and Rebekah Hall (Evans) S.; m. Katherine Ann Griggs, May 3, 1969; children: Mark Griggs, Rebekah Field. BA in History, Yale U., 1965; MBA, U. Kans., 1976, PhD in Bus., 1984. CPA Tex. Reporter Kansas City Star, Kansas City, Mo., 1965—66, copy editor, 1966—70, Washington Star, 1970—72, asst. nat. editor, 1972—73; asst. prof. U. Tulsa, 1979—87; assoc. prof. Southwestern U., Georgetown, Tex., 1987—. Sec., treas. planning com. U. Tulsa Conf. Accts., 1980—87; chmn. dept. econ. and bus. Southwestern U., Georgetown, Tex., 1994—2004, sec. of faculty, 2004—. Contbr. articles to profl. jours. Trustee Wentworth Mil. Acad., Lexington, Mo., 1986—, pres., 1990-92; trustee Williamson County (Tex.) Literacy Coun., 1989-91; treas., bd. dirs. St. John's Presch., Tulsa, 1984-87; conv. del. Episc. Diocese Okla., 1984, 85; audit com. St. John's Episc. Ch., Tulsa, 1983-87; bishop's com. Grace Episc. Ch., 1989, jr. warden, 1989, bishop's warden, 1990, chmn. audit com., 2004, treas., 2004-05, mem. rector search com., 2004; alt. Tex. State Rep. Conv., 1988; treas. Georgetown Area United Way, 1993-99; mem. Georgetown Ethics Commn., 2004—, vice chair, 2004-06, chair, 2006—. Mem. Inst. Mgmt. Accts. (dir. manuscripts Austin chpt. 1988-96), Am. Acctg. Assn. (membership com. 1980-81), AICPA, Tex. Soc. CPAs (edn1. instns. com. Austin chpt.), Rotary. Avocations: bridge, piano, trombone, singing, jogging. Home: 1610 E 15th St Georgetown TX 78626-7206 Office: Southwestern U Dept Econs and Bus Adminstrn Georgetown TX 78627-0770 Home Phone: 512-863-7720; Office Phone: 512-863-1574. Business E-Mail: sellersf@southwestern.edu.

SELLERS, GREGORY JUDE, physicist; b. Far Rockaway, NY, June 20, 1947; s. Douglas L. and Rita R. (Dieringer) S.; m. Lucia S. Kim, Nov. 26, 1983; 1 child, Kristin Kim. AB in Physics, Cornell U., 1968; MS, U. Ill., 1970, PhD, 1975. Sr. scientist B-K Dynamics, Inc., Rockville, Md., 1974-76; with Allied-Signal Corp., Morristown, NJ, 1976-88, applications physicist, 1977-88; product supr. Amphenol Fiber Optic Products, Naperville, Ill., 1985-88; mgr. Cinch Connectors, Elk Grove, Ill., 1988-91; pres. Forss, Inc., Naperville, 1991-96, Fotron, Inc., Naperville, 1995—. Bd. dirs. Fotron; lectr. Benedictine U., 2004—. Mem. AAAS, IEEE, Am. Phys. Soc. Achievements include development and commercialization of electronic connectors and fiber optic products; development of applications for polymeric materials and glassy metals in the electrical and electronics arena. Co-inventor adhesive bonding metallic glass, electromagnetic shielding, testing of thermal insulation, amorphous antipilferage marker, amorphous spring-shield, multiple fiber positioner for optical fiber connection, raised rib waveguide ribbon for precision optical interconnects. Home and Office: Fotron Inc 7S 515 Oak Trails Dr Naperville IL 60540 Home Phone: 630-983-4146; Office Phone: 630-983-4146. E-mail: fotron1gs@aol.com.

SELLERS, PETER HOADLEY, mathematician, educator; b. Phila., Sept. 12, 1930; s. Lester Hoadley and Therese (Tyler) S.; m. Lucy Bell Newlin, June 21, 1958; children: Mortimer, Therese, Mary, Lucy Bell BA, U. Pa., 1953, MA, 1958, PhD, 1965. Math. tchr. Kangaru Sch., Embu, Kenya, 1961-63; programmer U. Pa., Phila., 1958-61; mem. faculty Rockefeller U., NYC, 1966—. Johnson Found. postdoctoral fellow, 1963-65 Mem. editl. bd. Genomics, 1986-97; author: Combinatorial Complexes, 1979; contbr. articles to profl. jours. Trustee Coll. of the Atlantic, Bar Harbor, Maine, 1985-96; curator Rockefeller Hist. Instrument Collection, 1997—. Lt (j.g.) USNR, 1953-55 Mem. Am. Math. Soc., Math. Assn. Am., Soc. Indsl. and Applied Math. Democrat. Episcopalian. Avocations: boat building, sailing. Home: 413 W Stafford St Philadelphia PA 19144-4407 Office: Rockefeller Univ 1230 York Ave New York NY 10021-6399 Business E-Mail: sellers@rockefeller.edu.

SELLERS, PIERS J., astronaut; b. Crowborough, Sussex, Eng., Apr. 11, 1955; married; 2 children. BS in Ecol. Sci., U. Edinburgh, Scotland, 1976; PhD in Biometeorology, Leeds U., Eng., 1981. Astronaut, mission specialist NASA, Johnson Space Ctr., Houston, 1996—. Mem. flight team STS-112 Atlantis, 2002; crew mem. STS-121 (Discovery), a return-to-flight test mission and assembly flight to the Internat. Space Station, 2006. Recipient Arthur Fleming award, 1995. Fellow: Am. Meteorology Soc. (Houghton award 1997), Am. Geophys. Union. Achievements include research in how the earth's biosphere and atmosphere interact, computer modeling of climate system, satellite remote sensing studies; field work utilizing aircraft, satellites and ground teams in Kansas, Russia, Africa, Canada and Brazil. Office: Astronaut Office/CB NASA Johnson Space Ctr Houston TX 77058

SELLES, ROBERT HENDRIKUS, retired actuary; b. Amsterdam, Nov. 8, 1938; arrived in U.S., 1969; s. Albertus Henrikus and Jansje Suzanna (Cordes) Selles; m. Manuela Ioana Comnene, Aug. 26, 1966 (div. Mar. 1978); 1 child, Melina Joanna. B of Commerce with honors, U. Manitoba, 1961. Actuarial asst. Can. Premier Life Ins. Co., Winnipeg, Man., Canada, 1961-62; asst. actuary Sun Life Assurance Co. Can., Montreal, 1962-69; sr. v.p. Hay/Huggins Co., Inc., Phila., 1969—91, ret., 2004. Fellow: Soc. Actuaries; mem.: Gavel Soc., Western Pension and Benefits Conf., Am. Acad. Actuaries, Conf. Cons. Actuaries, Netherlands Am. Assn. Delaware Valley (bd. dirs. 1993—96), Rainbow River Inc. (pres. 1995—2005), Netherlands Soc. Phila. (bd. dirs. 1991—, pres. 1993—96, 1999—2000), Internat. Benefits Found., Actuaries Club San Francisco. Home: 1420 Locust St Apt 34-A Philadelphia PA 19102-4220 Personal E-mail: rselles@aol.com.

SELLICK, KATHLEEN A., hospital administrator; b. Phoenix; m. Phil Sellick; 1 child, Grace. BS, Ariz. State U.; MBA, U. Chgo. Grad. Sch. Bus., 1984. With Am. Med. Internat., Beverly Hills, Calif., Westgate Med. Ctr., Denton, Tex.; adminstrv. resident Mayo Clinic, Rochester, Minn.; v.p. adminstrn. and dir. outreach devel. Hoag Meml. Hosp. Presbyn., Newport Beach, Calif.; exec. v.p. and COO St. Joseph Hosp., Orange, Calif., 1995—99; assoc. exec. dir. and COO U. Wash. Med. Ctr., Seattle, 1999—2001, acting exec. dir., 2000—01, exec. dir., 2001—. Clin. asst. prof., dept. health services U. Wash. Sch. of Public Health and Community Medicine. Office: U Wash Med Ctr 1959 NE Pacific St Box 356151 Seattle WA 98195-6151 Office Fax: 206-598-6292.

SELLIN, THEODORE, diplomat, consultant; b. Phila., June 17, 1928; s. Thorsten and Amy (Anderson) S.; m. Taru Jarvi, July 10, 1965; 1 child, Derek. Student, U. Uppsala, Sweden, 1946-48; BA, U. Pa., 1951, MA, 1952. Joined Fgn. Svc., Dept. State, 1952; vice consul Copenhagen, 1952-56; rsch. analyst Dept. State, Washington, 1956-58; program officer Office Internat. Confs., 1965-67; acad. tng. staff U. Ind., 1958-59; 2d sec. Am. Embassy, Helsinki, Finland, 1959-64, 1st sec., polit. officer, 1971-73, 1st sec., labor-polit. officer Oslo, 1967-71; polar affairs officer Dept. State, 1975; consul gen. Goteborg, Sweden, 1978-80; fgn. rels. cons. Dept. State, Washington, 1980—. Office: Dept State A/ISS/IPS/CR/IR Washington DC 20520

SELLINGSLOH, HULDA KNIPLING, retired artist; b. Port Lavaca, Tex., Nov. 29, 1912; d. Henry John and Hulda (Rasch) Knipling; m. August Sellingsloh, May 1, 1943 (dec. Apr. 1998); children: Susan Louise, Marian Kay, Ellen Agnes, John August. LLB, Houston Law Sch., 1939. Bar: Tex. 1940. Sec. draftsman Calhoun County Abstract Co., Port Lauaca, 1933—34; sec. to pres. Tex. Luth. Coll., Seguin, 1935—36; legal sec., draftsman Fohs Oil Co., Houston, 1936—43; draftsman, asst. engr. U.S. Coast & Geodetic Survey, Balt., 1943—45; civic leader various civic and religious orgns., Beacon and Fishkill, NY, 1945—72; profl. visual artist NY, N.Mex., and Tex., 1973—99. Leader, pres. various chs., clubs, Beacon and Fishkill, 1950—72; artist Eastside Creative Art Club, 1960—72; pres. Santa Fe chpt. Artists Equity, N.Mex., 1973—78. Author: (life history) Top Crop, 1999—2000. Pres. Houston Women Lawyers, 1943, Santa Fe Artists Assn., 1974—76, St. John's Women's Club, Beacon, 1959—60, 1966—69; pres., leading minister St. Clare Secular Franciscan Fraternity, Crowley, Tex. Recipient numerous awards, various regional art assns., 1960—, Best of Show awards, Santa Fe, N.Y., Tex., 1960—, Editors Choice award, Nat. Libr. Poets, 1998. Mem.: Tex. Bar Assn., Pastel Soc. Am. (juried assoc.), Tarrant County Women's Section, Internat. Soc. Poets. Democrat. Roman Catholic. Home: 5 Oak Dr Hopewell Junction NY 12533

SELLKE, FRANK WILLIAM, cardiothoracic surgeon, researcher; b. Ft. Wayne, Ind., Feb. 5, 1956; s. Erwin A. and Anna Luise (Schumacher) S.; m. Amy Marie Brill, Jan. 31, 1987; children: Michelle, Eric, Nicholas, Amanda. AB summa cum laude, Wabash Coll., 1978; MD, Ind. U., Indpls., 1981. Diplomate Am. Bd. Thoracic Surgery, Am. Bd. Surgery. Intern Ind. U. Hosp., Indpls., 1981-82; emergency physician Culver Union Hosp., Crawfordsville, Ind., 1982-83; resident in surgery Akron (Ohio) City Hosp., 1983-87; postdoctoral fellow cardiac surgery U. Iowa, Iowa City, 1987-90; from instr. to asst. prof. surgery Harvard Med. Sch., Boston, 1990-95, assoc. prof. surgery, 1995—2000, prof. surgery, 2000—; cardiothoracic surgeon Beth Israel Hosp., Boston, 1990—; chief cardiothoracic surgery Beth Israel Deaconess Med. Ctr., Boston, 1999—2006, chief cardiothoracic surgery rsch., 2006—. Chmn. dept. cardiovascular surgery and medicine Landmark Med. Ctr., 2005—. Mem. editl. bd. Jour. Thoracic and Cardiovascular Surgery, Jour. Surg. Rsch., Jour. Cardiac Surgery, Shock; contbr. rsch. articles to profl. jours. Fellow Am. Coll. Cardiology, Am. Coll. Surgeons; mem. AMA, Am. Surg. Assn., Am. Heart Assn., Am. Physiol. Soc., Am. Coll. Chest Physicians, Soc. Univ. Surgeons, Assn. Acad. Surgeons, Am. Assn. for Thoracic Surgery, Soc. Thoracic Surgeons, Phi Beta Kappa. Lutheran. Home: 121 Monadnock Rd Chestnut Hill MA 02467-1136 Office: Beth Israel Deaconess Med Ctr 110 Francis St Boston MA 02215 Home Phone: 617-964-1783; Office Phone: 617-632-8383. Business E-Mail: fsellke@bidmc.harvard.edu.

SELLMANN, MEINOLF, computer science educator; s. Paul and Marianne Elisabeth Sellmann. D summa cum laude, U. Paderborn, Germany, 2002. Postdoctoral assoc. Cornell U., Ithaca, NY, 2003—04; asst. prof. Brown U., Providence, 2004—. Assoc. editor Informs Jour. Computing, 2005—. Fellow German Nat. Merit Found., 1994—98. Achievements include co-invention of several combinatorial methods, including CP-based Lagrangian Relaxation, Streamlining and Symmetry Breaking by Dominance Detection.

SELLMYER, DAVID JULIAN, physicist, researcher; b. Joliet, Ill., Sept. 28, 1938; s. Marcus Leo and Della Louise (Plumhoff) S.; m. Catherine Joyce Zakas, July 16, 1962; children: Rebecca Ann, Julia Maryn, Mark Anthony. BS, U. Ill., 1960; PhD, Mich. State U., 1965. Asst. prof. MIT, Cambridge, 1965-72, assoc. prof., 1972, U. Nebr., Lincoln, 1972-75, prof., 1975—, chmn. dept. physics, 1978-84, George Holmes disting. prof., 1987—, dir. Nebr. Ctr. Materials and Nanosci., 1988—. Contbr. articles, book revs. to refereed jours. Recipient tech. award NASA, 1972; disting. vis. prof. S.D. Sch. Mines and Tech., Rapid City, 1981. Fellow Am. Phys. Soc. Office: U Nebr Lincoln Nebr Ctr Materials and Nanosci 112 Brace Lab Lincoln NE 68588-0111 Business E-Mail: dsellmyer@unl.edu.

SELLS, BOAKE ANTHONY, private investor; b. Ft. Dodge, Iowa, June 24, 1937; s. Lyle M. and Louise (Gadd) S.; m. Marian S. Stephenson, June 20, 1959; children: Damian, Brian, Jean Ann. BSc, U. Iowa, 1959; MBA, Harvard U., 1969. Bus. office mgr. Northwestern Bell Tel., Des Moines, 1959-63; salesman Hydraulic Cos., Ft. Dodge, 1964-67; pres. Cole Nat. Corp., Cleve., 1969-83; vice chmn. Dayton Hudson Corp., Mpls., 1983-84, pres., 1984-87; chmn., pres., chief exec. officer Revco D.S., Inc., Twinsburg, Ohio, 1987-92. Bd. dirs. Promus Cos. (name changed to Harrah's Entertainment, Inc. Trustee Cleve. Play House, Mus. Contemporary Art, Cleve., dir.

SELMAN, RUSSELL BERTRAM, lawyer, department chairman; b. Oceanside, NY, May 31, 1954; s. Leon Daniel and Lorraine Thelma (Leichter) S.; m. Elizabeth Friedgut. BA, New Coll., 1975; MPA, Syracuse U., 1978; JD, Washington U., 1980. Bar: Ill. 1987, D.C. 1981, Mo. 1980. Asst. enforcement counsel U.S. Environ. Protection Agy., Washington, 1980-82, atty., advisor, 1983; atty. McKenna, Conner & Cuneo, Washington, 1983-86, Schiff, Hardin & Waite, Chgo., 1986-88, Bell, Boyd & Lloyd, Chgo., 1988-93; ptnr., chmn. environ. law dept. Katten Muchin Rosenman, Chgo., 1993—. Contbr. Chicago Lawyer mag. Office: Katten Muchin Rosenman 525 W Monroe St Ste 1600 Chicago IL 60661-3693 Office Phone: 312-902-5390. Business E-Mail: russell.selman@kattenlaw.com.

SELOVER, R. EDWIN, lawyer, utilities executive; b. Norman, Okla., Aug. 18, 1945; BA, Union Coll., 1967; JD, U. Minn., 1972. Bar: NJ 1972. Atty. Pub. Svc. Electric & Gas Co. (PSE&G), Newark, 1972-75, asst. gen. counsel, 1975-79, assoc. gen. counsel, 1979-80, gen. counsel, 1980-83, v.p., gen. counsel, 1983-88, sr. v.p., gen. counsel, 1988—; v.p., gen. counsel Pub. Svc. Enterprise Group Inc. (PSEG), Newark, 1988—2002, sr. v.p., gen. counsel, 2002—06, exec. v.p., gen. counsel, 2006—; sr. v.p., gen. counsel PSEG Services Corp., 1999—2006. Bd. trustees NJ Conservation Found., NJ Future, 1998—, Stockton Alliance, NJ; nuc. ind. sector chmn., Infrastructure Adv. Com. NJ Office of Counterterrorism. Served US Army, 1969—71. Mem.: NJ Bar Assn., ABA. Office: Pub Svc Enterprise Group Inc PO Box 570 Newark NJ 07101 Office Phone: 973-430-7000. *

SELTSER, RAYMOND, epidemiologist, educator, oncologist; b. Boston, Dec. 17, 1923; s. Israel and Hannah (Littman) S.; m. Charlotte Frances Gale, Nov. 16, 1946; children: Barry Jay, Andrew David. MD, Boston U., 1947; MPH, Johns Hopkins U., 1957. Diplomate Am. Bd. Preventive Medicine (trustee, sec.-treas. 1974-77), Am. Bd. Med. Specialties (mem. exec. com. 1976-77). Asst. chief med. info. and intelligence br. U.S. Dept. Army, 1953-56; epidemiologist divsn. internal health USPHS, 1956-57; from asst. prof. to prof. epidemiology Johns Hopkins U. Sch. Hygiene and Pub. Health, Balt., 1957-81, assoc. dean, 1967-77, dep. dir. Oncology Ctr., 1977-81; dean U. Pitts. Grad. Sch. Pub. Health, 1981-87, prof. epidemiology, 1981-88, emeritus dean, emeritus prof. epidemiology, 1988—; assoc. dir. USPHS Ctrs. for Disease Control, Rockville, Md., 1988-90; assoc. dir. Ctr. for Gen. Health Svcs. Extramural Rsch. Agy. for Health Care Policy and Rsch., Rockville, 1990-95, sr. advisor spl. population rsch. Ctr. Primary Care Rsch., 1995-98; med. and healthcare advisor Dept. Va Office Inspector Gen. Office Health Care Inspections, Chevy Chase, Md., 1997—2000. Cons. NIMH, 1958-70, also various govtl. health agys., 1958-79; expert cons. Pres.'s Commn. on Three Mile Island, 1979-80; mem. Three Mile Island Adv. Panel Health, Nat. Cancer Inst. Cancer Control Grant Rev. Com., Pa. Dept. Health Preventive Health Service Block Grant Adv. Task Force, Gov.'s VietNam Herbicide Info. Commn. Pa.; chmn. Toxic/Health Effects Adv. Com., 1985-87. Trustee, exec. com., chmn. profl. adv. com. Harmarville Rehab. Ctr., Pitts., 1982-87; bd. dirs. Health Edn. Ctr., Media Info. Svc.; chmn. USPHS Task Force on Improving Med. Criteria for SSA Disability Determination, 1988-92. Capt. AUS, 1951-53, Korea Decorated Bronze Star; recipient Centennial Alumni citation Boston U. Sch. Medicine, 1973; elected to Johns Hopkins Soc. of Scholars, 1986. Fellow AAAS, APHA (mem. governing coun. 1975-77, chmn. EPI sect. coun. 1979-80), Pa. Pub. Health Assn. (bd. dirs. 1985-88, pres.-elect 1986-88), Am. Coll. Preventive Medicine, Am. Heart Assn.; mem. Am. Epidemiol. Assn., Internat. Epidemiol. Assn., Am. Soc. Preventive Oncology, Am. Cancer Soc. (bd. dirs. Pa. divsn. 1985-87, exec. com. 1986-87), Assn. Schs. Pub. Health (sec. 1969-71, exec. com., chmn. edn. com. 1983-87), Soc. Med. Cons. Armed Forces, Soc. Epidemiologic Rsch., Nat. Coun. Radiation Protection and Measurements (consociate), Johns Hopkins Alumni Coun. (exec. com. 1994-97), Sigma Xi, Delta Omega. E-mail: rseltser@comcast.net.

SELTZER, BARRY S., federal judge; b. 1954; BA magna cum laude, Hamilton Coll., 1976; MBA, JD, NYU, 1980, LLM in Taxation, 1984. Atty. Trenam, Simmons, Kemker, Scharf, Barkin, Frye & O'Neill, Tampa, Fla., 1980-82; asst. U.S. atty. So. Dist. Fla., 1984-88; judge Broward County Ct., 1988-91; magistrate judge U.S. Dist. Ct. (so. dist.) Fla., Ft. Lauderdale, 1991—. Comment editor NYU Law Rev. of Law and Social Change. Recipient Spl. Achievement award Dept. Justice, plaques and commendations Drug Enforcement Agy., US Secret Svc., Bur. of Alcohol, Tobacco and Firearms, Postal Inspection Svc., US Customs Svc., USDA. Mem. ABA, Fed. Bar Assn., Fla. Bar, Broward County Bar Assn., Fed. Magistrate Judges Assn., Stephen Booher Inn of Ct. (past pres.), B'nai B'rith Justice Unit (past pres.), Beta Gamma Sigma. Office: 109 US Courthouse 299 E Broward Blvd Fort Lauderdale FL 33301-1944

SELTZER, LEO, cinematographer, educator; b. Montreal, Que., Can., Mar. 13, 1910; came to U.S., 1916; s. Boris and Atalia (Gerowitz) S.; m. Elaine Basil, Apr. 15, 1941 (div. 1950); children: Janzie, John; m. Dicky Ransohoff, 1951 (div. 1963). BA, U. Mass., 1979. Faculty CCNY, 1949-54, New Sch. Social Rsch., 1949-51; pres. Leo Seltzer Assocs., Inc., NYC, 1950-90; faculty Columbia U., 1954-60, Phila. Coll. Art, 1955-56, NYU, NYC, 1966-67; dir. audio-visual therapy program pediatrics ward Univ. Hosp., NYC, 1970-76; instr. film prodn. workshop Sch. Visual Arts, NYC, 1969-84; adj. prof. performing and creative arts Coll. S.I., NY, 1977-78; prof. film Bklyn. Coll., 1978-83, prof. emeritus film, 1983—. Lectr. in U.S. and abroad, including Mus. Modern Art, N.Y.C., Marymount Coll., Ghent U., Belgium, Libr. Congress, others. Prodr., dir. over 60 social documentaries and TV films in 35 countries, including First Steps, UN Divsn. Social Affairs, 1946 (Acad. award for best documentary 1947), Fate of a Child, UN Divsn. Tech. Assistance, 1949, For the Living, City of N.Y., 1952, (with Walter Cronkite) Conquest of Aging, 1958, All the Years, 1959, Jacqueline Kennedy's Asian Journey, 1962, Progress Through Freedom (pres. Kennedy's visit to Mex.), 1962, (with Edward R. Murrow) The American Commitment, USIA, 1963, Report on Acupuncture, 1977, (with John Huston) Let There Be Light; prodr., dir.: Nat. Film Bd. Can., 1941, films include Air-Sea Rescue Techniques; chief cons. visual aids City of N.Y., 1941-42; prodr.: N.Y.C. Mcpl. Film and TV Unit Sta. WNYC, 1949-50; film biographer to White House for Pres. Kennedy, 1962; exec. prodr. Quadrant Comms., Inc., 1973-75 (7 citations Cannes and Edinburgh Film Festivals 1948-63); films are in U.S. Nat. Archives, Libr. of Congress, in collection and distributed by Mus. Modern Art; photographs are in Houston Mus. Fine Arts collection, Nat. Gallery Can., Visual Studies Workshop, Rochester, N.Y., N.Y.C. 5th Ave. Libr.; reconstructed 6 Am. social documentary films of 1930's in 1978 for Mus. Modern Art Film Archives, 1976-77,; edited and filmed much of original footage; subject of TV program by Bill Moyers, A Walk Through the Twentieth Century, Blackside Prodns., CBC, BBC TV; contbr. film footage to Nat. Geographic, History Channel, others. 1st lt. Signal Corps. U.S. Army; directed tng. and information films for U.S. Army and public; officer in charge of Film and Equipment Depot, ETO, 1947. Recipient Acad. award for best documentary, 1948, Silver medals Venice Film Festival, 1949, Freedom's Found. award, 1953, Golden Reel award Scholastic Mag., 1955, Robert Flaherty award CCNY, 1956, Silver medal Atlanta Internat. Film Festival, 1977; honored in tribute Mus. Modern Art, 1990; oral history N.Y. Fifth Ave. Libr. Archives. Mem. Dirs. Guild Am. (charter). Achievements include research on Early American social documentary films. Office Phone: 212-879-0990.

SELTZER, TERRY F., endocrinologist, medical educator; s. Bernard and Jean Seltzer; m. Doryce K. Penn, Aug. 11, 1972; 2 children. BA, SUNY, Binghamton, 1973; JD, Harvard Med. Sch., Boston, 1977. Diplomate Am. Bd. Internal Medicine, Am. Bd. Internal Medicine in Endocrinology and Metabolism. Intern, resident NYU-Bellevue Hosps., NYC, 1977—80, fellow endocrinology, 1980—82; asst. prof. emdicine NYU Sch. Medicine, NYC, 1982—. Avocations: running, fishing, canoeing. Office: 530 1st Ave 4D New York NY 10016

SELTZER, VICKI LYNN, obstetrician, gynecologist; b. June 2, 1949; d. Herbert Melvin and Marian Elaine (Willinger) Seltzer; m. Richard Stephen Brach, Sept. 2, 1973; children: Jessica Lillian Brach, Eric Robert Brach. BS, Rensselaer Poly. Inst., 1969; MD, NYU, 1973. Diplomate Am. Bd. Ob-Gyn. (examiner 1988-2001). Intern Bellevue Hosp., NYC, 1973—74, resident ob-gyn., 1974—77; fellow gynecol. cancer Am. Cancer Soc., NYC, 1977—78, Meml. Sloan Kettering Cancer Ctr., NYC, 1978—79; assoc. dir. gynecol. cancer Albert Einstein Coll. Medicine, NYC, 1979—83, prof. ob-gyn., 1989—. Assoc. prof. ob-gyn SUNY, Stony Brook, 1983—89; Edie and Marvin H. Shur prof. ob-gyn and women's health Albert Einstein Coll. Medicine, NYC, 2003—; dir. ob-gyn. Queens Hosp. Ctr., Jamaica, NY, 1983—93, pres. med. bd., 1986—89; chair ob-gyn L.I. Jewish Med. Ctr., 1993—; v.p. women's health svcs. North Shore-L.I. Jewish Health Sys., 1999—; chair ob-gyn North Shore U. Hosp., 1999—, chair med. bd., 2001—; mem. steering com. N.Y. State Coun. Grad. Med. Edn., 2005—, chair subcom. primary care; mem. U.S. Coun. Grad. Med. Edn., 2006—. Author: Every Woman's Guide to Breast Cancer, 1987; editor: Women's Primary Health Care, 1995, 2000; editor-in-chief: Primary Care Update for the Ob-Gyn, 1993—; mem. editl. bd. Women's Life mag., 1980—82, Jour. Jacobs Inst. Women's Health, 1990—95, Ob-Gyn. Survey, 2005—, Jour. Reproductive Medicine, 2005—, mem. internat. editl. bd. Jour. Soc. Obstreticians and Gynecologists Can., 2000—; contbr. articles to profl. jours.; host (TV series) Weekly Ob-Gyn. program, Lifetime Med. TV. Mem. Mayor Beame's Task Force on Rape, NYC, 1974—76; chair health com. Nat. Coun. Women, NYC, 1979—84; bd. govs. Nat. Coun. Women's Health, 1985—94; chair Coun. Resident Edn. Ob-Gyn., 1987—93. Recipient citation, Nat. Safety Coun., 1978, Achiever award, L.I. Ctr. Bus. and Profl. Women, 1987; Galloway Fund fellow, 1975. Fellow: ACOG (gynecol. practice com. 1981, v.p. 1993—94, pres.-elect 1996—97, pres. 1997—98), N.Y. Obstet. Soc. (pres. 1999—2000); mem.: Am. Hosp. Assn. (governing coun. maternal and child health 2004—, chair-elect 2007), N.Y. Cancer Soc., Am. Med. Women's Assn. (com. chair 1975—79, editl. bd. jour. 1986—2002, citation 1973), Internat. Fedn. Gynecology and Obstetrics (internat. steering com. to reduce maternal mortality 2000—02), Women's Med. Assn. (v.p. N.Y. 1974—79, resident rev. com. ob-gyn 1993—98, Lila Wallis Lifetime Achievement award 2002), NYU Sch. Med. Alumni Assn. (bd. govs. 1979—, v.p. 1987—91, pres. 1992—93), Alpha Omega Alpha. Office: LI Jewish Med Ctr New Hyde Park NY 11040 Office Phone: 718-470-7660. Business E-Mail: vseltzer@lij.edu.

SELTZER, WILLIAM, statistician, social science administrator; b. NYC, Sept. 22, 1934; s. William B. Seltzer and Edith S. (Goldman) Alt.; m. Jane E. Berger, Nov. 20, 1970; children: Benjamin, Ezra. BA, U. Chgo., 1956. Rsch. asst. Health Info. Found., NYC, 1957-60; statistician U.S. Bur. Census, Suitland, Md., 1960-64; advisor Pakistan Inst. Devel., Econs. and Cen. Statis. Office, Karachi, 1964-68; staff assoc. Population Coun., NYC, 1968-74; br. chief UN Statis. Office, NYC, 1974-86, dir., 1986-94; sr. advisor to under-sec.-gen. Dept. Econ. and Social Info. and Policy Analysis, NYC, 1993-94; sr. rsch. schlar Fordham U., NYC, 1995—. Mem. com. on population and demography, chair panel on data collection NAS, Washington, 1977-82, mem. Roundtable on the Demography of Forced Migration, 2001-04; cons. UN Population Fund, 1995, Internat. Criminal Tribunal for Rwanda, 1996, UN Stats. Divsn., 1996-98, Internat. Labor Office, 1997, World Bank, 1997-98; mem. panel of Ind. Experts, Metagora Project Orgn. for Econ. Cooperation and Devel., 2005—. Author: Poems, 1960, Politics and Statistics, 1994; co-author: Population Growth Estimation, 1973; also various UN documents, jour. articles, reports. Fellow Am. Statis. Assn. (chair social stats. sect. 1983-84, chair com. on internat. rels. 1986-87, chair com. on profl. ethics 2000—05), Royal Statis. Soc. (hon.); mem. Population Assn. Am., Internat. Statis. Inst., Internat. Assn. Ofcl. Statisticians. Mem. Soc. Of Friends. Office: Fordham U Dept Sociology and Anthropology 441 E Fordham Rd Bronx NY 10458-5149 Office Phone: 718-817-3868. E-mail: seltzer@fordham.edu.

SELTZNER, RACHEL, curator, science educator; d. Gary Dennis Seltzner and Beth Ann Murray; m. Brian Wayne Meixner, Sept. 28, 2002; 1 child, Carson Annan Meixner. BS in Environ. Edn. and Interpretation, U. Wis., Stevens Point, 2001; post grad. in Natural Health, Clayton Coll. Natural Health, Birmingham, Ala., 2006—. Naturalist Peninsula State Park Wis. Dept. Natural Resources, Fish Creek, 1999, 2001; tchr. Countryside Montessori Sch., Madison, 2001—02; camp dir. Dane County Humane Soc., 2002; mus. coord. Nat. Wild Turkey Fedn., Edgefield, SC, 2002—06; curator Sauk Prairie Area Hist. Soc., Prairie du Sac, Wis., 2007—. Mem. Ctrl. Savannah River Area Environ. Sci. Edn. Coop., Augusta, Ga., 2002—. Vol. tchr. Roots and Shoots Jane Goodall Inst., Stevens Point, 1998—2001; pres. Environ. Coun., 2000—01; coord. Moonlight Delight Festival, Edgefield, SC, 2002—05. Recipient U. Leadership award, U. Wis. Stevens Point, 2001; scholar, Wis. Rural Opportunities Found., 2000—01. Mem.: Am. Assn. Museums, S.C. Fedn. Museums, Nat. Assn. Interpretation. Achievements include development of expansion plan doubling size of Nat. Wild Turkey Fedn. Winchester museum. Avocations: backpacking, canoeing, snowshoeing, camping, travel. Office: 565 Water St Prairie Du Sac WI 53578 Office Phone: 608-644-8444. Personal E-mail: raseltzner@verizon.net.

SELVADURAI, ANTONY PATRICK SINNAPPA, civil engineer, mathematician, educator, consultant; b. Matara, Sri-Lanka, Sept. 23, 1942; arrived in Can., 1975; s. Kanapathiyar Sinnappa and W. Mary Adeline (Fernando) S.; m. Sally Joyce; children: Emily, Paul, Mark, Elizabeth. Diploma in Engring., Brighton Poly., 1964; Diploma, Imperial Coll./London U., 1965; MS, Stanford U., 1967; PhD in Theoretical Mechanics, U. Nottingham, 1971, DSc in Theoretical Mechanics, 1986. Registered profl. engr., Can.; chartered mathematician, UK. Staff rsch. engr. Woodward Clyde Assoc., Oakland, Calif., 1966-67; rsch. assoc. dept.

theoretical mechanics U. Nottingham, 1969-70; lectr. dept. civil engring. U. Aston, Birmingham, England, 1971-75; asst. prof. civil engring. Carleton U., Ottawa, Ont., Canada, 1975-76, assoc. prof., 1976-81, prof., 1982-93, chmn. dept., 1982-90, Davidson Dunton Rsch. lectr., 1987; prof., chmn. dept. civil engring./applied mechanics McGill U., Montreal, Canada, 1993-96, William Scott prof., 2004, James McGill prof., 2005. Vis. rsch. sci. Bechtel Group, Inc., San Francisco, 1981-82; vis. prof. U. Nottingham, 1986, Inst. de Mécanique de Grenoble, France, 1990; cons. Atomic Energy of Can. Ltd., Pinawa, Man., 1983-96—, Ministry of Transp. Ont., Toronto, 1984-97, Fleet Tech., Ottawa, 1988—, Atomic Energy Control Bd., 1987—. Author: Elastic Analysis of Soil Foundation Interaction, 1979, (with R.O. Davis) Elasticity and Geomechanics, 1996, (with R.O. Davis) Plasticity and Geomechanics, 2002; editor: Mechanics of Structured Media, 1981, (with G.Z. Voyiadjis) Mechanics of Material Interfaces, 1986, Developments of Mechanics, 1987, (with M.M. Zaman and C.S. Desai) Recent Accomplishments and Future Trends in Geomechanics in the 21st Century, (with M.J. Boulon) Mechanics of Geomaterial Interfaces, 1995, Mechanics of Poroelastic Media, 1996, Partial Differential Equations in Mechanics, Vol. 1, Fundamentals, Laplace's Equation, Diffusion Equation, Wave Equation, 2000, Vol. 2, The Biharmonic Equation, Poisson's Equation, 2000, (with J.M. Hill) Mathematics and Mechanics of Granular Materials, 2005. King George VI Meml. fellow English Speaking Union of Commonwealth, 1965, Rsch. fellow SRC, UK, 1969, Erskine fellow U. Canterbury, New Zealand, 1992, 98, Killam Rsch. fellow Can. Coun. for Arts, 2000-02; recipient Rsch. award Alexander von Humboldt Found., 1997, Gold medal Can. Congress Applied Mechanics, 2007. Fellow Am. Acad. Mechanics, Can. Soc. Civil Engring. (Leipholz medal 1991), Assoc. Profl. Engrs. Ont. (Engring. medal 1993), Engring. Inst. Can., Inst. Math. and Its Applications, Can. Acad. Engring.; mem. Internat. Assn. for Computer Methods and Advances in Geomechanics (award for significant paper in the category theory computational analytical 1994, paper prize computational and analytical theory category 1997, John Booker medal 2001), Max Planck Soc. (Max Planck Rsch. prize 2003), Can. Coun. for Arts (Killam prize 2007). Roman Catholic. Office: McGill U Dept Civil Engring Montreal PQ Canada H3A 2K6 E-mail: patrick.selvadurai@mcgill.ca.

SELVER, PAUL DARRYL, lawyer; b. NYC, May 28, 1947; s. Rene T. Selver and Marilyn (Steiner) Pomerance; m. Ellen J. Roller, Jan. 22, 1984; children: Adam, Max, Katelyn. BA magna cum laude, Harvard U., 1969, JD, 1972. Bar: N.Y. 1973. Assoc. Hale Russell & Gray, NYC, 1972-74; ptnr. Brown and Wood (formerly Tufo and Zuccotti), NYC, 1974-94, Battle Fowler, NYC, 1994-2000, Paul Hastings Janofsky & Walker, NYC, 2000—05, Kramer Levin Naftalis & Frankel LLP, NYC, 2005—. Lectr. law Columbia U. Law Sch., 1994-97; assoc. adj. prof. Sch. Architecture, Planning and Preservation Columbia U., NYC, 1986-88; chmn. zoning and design com. Real Estate Bd. NY, 2000— Edit. bd. Metropolis Mag., 1983-86; author: (guide book) Real Estate: Land Use Regulations, 1986. Mem. Borough Mountain Lakes Planning Bd., 2005—; mem. adv. bd. Cityland, Ctr. for N.Y.C. Law at N.Y. Law Sch., 2004—; mem. bd. dirs. Citizens Housing and Planning Council, 2005—. Mem.: ABA, Assn. of Bar of City of N.Y. Office: Kramer Levin Naftalis & Frankel LLP 1177 Avenue of the Americas New York NY 10036 Business E-Mail: pselver@kramerlevin.com.

SELVIG, JETTIE PIERCE, lawyer; b. Bee Branch, Ark., Dec. 16, 1932; d. Jefferson Davis Pierce and Ruba Ann Bivens; m. Rolf S. Selvig Sr., Jan. 27, 1962; children: Rolf S. Jr., Erik K., John L. LLB, U. Ark., Little Rock, 1954. Bar: Ark. 1953, Calif. 1961, US Supreme Ct. 1969. Pvt. practice, San Francisco, 1961—99, Mill Valley, Calif., 2000—. Pres. Queen's Bench Found., 1974—76; bd. dirs. San Francisco Neighborhood Legal Assistance Found., 1975. Named Hidden Heroine, San Francisco Bay Girl Scout Coun., 1976; recipient cert. of honor, Bd. Suprs. of City and County of San Francisco, 1969, Countess of Pulaski Proclamation, Quorum Ct. of Pulaski County, 1969, Silver Bowl of Appreciation, Girl Scouts Am. Mem.: Queens Bench Found. (pres. 1974—76), Legal Aid Soc. San Francisco (bd. dirs. 1976), Women's Equity Action League (treas. Calif. divsn. 1970—72, pres. Calif. divsn. 1973), Calif. Applicants' Attys. Assn. (dir. No. Calif. chpt. 1974, v.p. 1975, pres. 1976, 1977, sec. and pres.-elect statewide assn., pres. statewide assn. 1981—82, Lifetime Achievement award 2005), Calif. State Bar (disciplinary com. 1972—74), Lawyer's Club San Francisco (life; del. state bar conv. and various spl. coms.), Queen's Bench Bar Assn. (life; asst. sec.-treas., dir. 1972, treas. 1973, mem. Law Day com., chmn. publicity com. and other spl. coms., v.p. 1974, pres. 1975, Lifetime Achievement award 1995), Nat. Assn. Women Lawyers (life; state del., assembly del., bus. mgr., treas., v.p., pres.-elect, pres. 1969—70, chairperson women in pub. svc. com. 1971—75). Democrat. Home and Office: 469 Molino Ave Mill Valley CA 94941-3380 Home Phone: 415-338-2973; Office Phone: 415-383-9105. Office Fax: 415-383-6605. Personal E-mail: jettiecoleen@msn.com.

SELVY, BARBARA, dance instructor; b. Little Rock, Jan. 20, 1938; d. James Oliver and Irene Balmat Banks; m. Franklin Delano Selvy, Apr. 15, 1959; children: Lisa Selvy Yeargin, Valerie Selvy Miros, Lauren Kroll, Franklin Michael, Madison Banks Selvy. Student, U. Ctrl. Ark., Conway, 1955—57. Founder, dir. Carolina Ballet Theater, Greenville, SC, 1973—; pres. Dance Arts Inc. and Incentives, Inc. Mem. adv. bd. dirs. Met. Arts Coun., and S.C. Govs. Sch., St. Marys Cath. Sch. Appeared in numerous TV commls., on Goodson-Toddman game show Play Your Hunch, 1958-59; toured Far East with TV show Hit Parade, 1958; named Miss Ark., 1956, Mrs. S.C., 1981; dir. and staged Mrs. Va., Mrs. N.C., Mrs. S.C. pageants; choreographed Little Theater prodns., Furman U. Opera. Mem. Nat. Rep. Congl. Com., 2003, Pres. Bush Small Bus. Adv. Coun., 2003. Mem. So. Assn. Dance Masters (ballet adviser, regional dir.), Dance Educators Am., Dance Masters of Am., Profl. Dance Tchrs. Home: 18 Oglethorpe Lane Hilton Head Island SC 29926 Personal E-mail: barbarabselvy@aol.com.

SELWYN, DONALD, engineering administrator, researcher, inventor, educator; b. NYC, Jan. 31, 1936; s. Gerald Selwyn and Ethel (Waxman) Selwyn) Moss; m. Delia Nemec, Mar. 11, 1956 (div. Mar. 1983); children: Laurie, Gerald, Marcia; m. Myra Rowman Markoff, Mar. 17, 1986 BA, Thomas A. Edison Coll. N.J., 1977. Svc. engr. Bendix Aviation, Teterboro, NJ, 1956-59; svc. mgr. Bogue Electric Mfg. Co., Paterson, NJ, 1959; proposal engr. advanced design group Curtiss-Wright Corp., East Paterson, NJ, 1960-64; ind. bioengr., rehab. engring. cons. NYC, 1964-67; pres. bd. trustees, exec. tech. and tng. dir. Nat. Inst. for Rehab. Engring., Hewitt, NJ, 1967—. Cons. N.Y. State Office Vocat. Rehab., 1964—, Pres.'s Com. on Employment of Handicapped, 1966—, bus. and industry and for Am. with Disabilities Act compliance, also numerous state rehab. agys., health depts., vol. groups, agys. for handicapped in fgn. countries; cons., trainer computer applications. Contbr. articles on amateur radio, rehab. of severely and totally disabled to profl., gen. mags. Trustee Nat. Inst. for Rehab. Engring., Rehab. Research Center Trust. Decorated Knight of Malta; recipient Humanitarian award U.S. Ho. of Reps., 1972, Bicentennial Pub. Service award, 1975. Mem. Am. Acad. Consultants, I.E.E.E. (sr.), Soc. Tech. Writers and Pubs. (sr.), Nat. Rehab. Assn., N.Y. Acad. Scis., Mensa. Achievements include being the developer or co-developer field-expander glasses for hemianopsia, tunnel and monocular vision, electronic speech clarifiers, electronically guided wheelchairs, off-road vehicles and cars for quadriplegics, others; patentee indsl., mil. and handicapped rehab. inventions; expert, cons. on handicapped employment, handicapped product safety including design, manufacture, labelling and user instrnl. material, 1990—. Office: Nat Inst Rehab Engring PO Box T Hewitt NJ 07421-1020 Office Phone: 973-853-6585, 800-736-2216. Personal E-mail: dons@warwick.net. E-mail: nire@warwick.net. *As I travel the road of life, it becomes more and more evident to me that people matter most, and technology is useful and good only so long as it serves man, and man is not made to serve technology. From technician I have evolved to humanist, using technology only as a tool. Always think positive. Don't waste your time or emotional energy on people who do not appreciate your good will. Think only about those who do, and you'll achieve more and enjoy life.*

SELYA, BRUCE MARSHALL, federal judge; b. Providence, May 27, 1934; s. Herman C. and Betty (Brier) S.; children: Dawn Meredith Selya Sherman, Lori Ann Selya Young. BA magna cum laude, Harvard U., Cambridge, Mass., 1955, JD magna cum laude, 1958. Bar: DC 1958, RI 1960. Law clk. US Dist. Ct. RI, Providence, 1958-60, judge, 1982-86; assoc. Gunning & LaFazia, Providence, 1960-62; ptnr. Gunning, LaFazia, Gnys & Selya, Providence, 1963-74, Selya & Iannuccillo, Providence, 1974-82; judge US Ct. Appeals (1st cir.), Providence, 1986—2006, sr. judge, 2006—; judge Fgn. Intelligence Surveillance Ct. of Rev., 2005—. Judge Lincoln Probate Ct., RI, 1965-72; mem. RI Jud. Council, 1964-72, sec., 1965-70, chmn., 1971-72; mem. Gov.'s Commn. on Crime and Adminstrn. Justice, 1967-69; del. Nat. Conf. on Revisions to Fed. Appellate Practice, 1968-82; judge Panel on Multi-District Litigation, 1989-2004; mem. various spl. govtl. commns. and adv. groups Chmn. bd. trustees Bryant U., Smithfield, RI, 1986-92,chair emeritus, 1993-; bd. dirs. Lifespan Health Sys., 1993-2000, chair emeritus, 2000-, chmn. bd. dirs., 1994-; mem. bd. trustees RI Hosp. subs. Recipient Louis Dembitz Brandeis medal for disting. legal svc. Brandeis U., 1988, Neil Houston award Justice Assistance of Am., 1992. Mem. ABA, FBA, Fed. Judges Assn., RI Bar Assn. (chmn. various coms.), RI Bar Found., US Jud. Conf. (mem. com. on jud. br.), Am. Arbitration Assn., Am. Judicature Soc. (bd. dirs.). Jewish. Home: 224 George St Providence RI 02906-3115 Office: US Ct Appeals US Courthouse 1 Exchange Terr Rm 316 Providence RI 02903 *

SELYUZHENKOV, ILYA, research scientist; b. Moscow, 1976; s. Vladimir Selyuzhenkov and Irina Selyuzhenkova; m. Veronika Selyuzhenkova, 1998; 1 child, Nadezda Selyuzhenkova. Diploma in engring./physics with honors, Moscow Engring. Physics Inst., 1999, PhD in Physics and Math., 2002. Vis. scientist Rsch. Ctr. Juelich, Germany, 2001—04, European Orgn. Nuc. Rsch., Geneve, 2003; sci. rschr. Inst. Theoret. and Exptl. Physics, Moscow, 1998—2004; rsch. assoc. Wayne State U., Detroit, 2004—. Sys. adminstr. Inst. Theoret. and Exptl. Physics, Moscow, 2000—04. Global Edn. grant, Wayne State U., 2000. Mem.: STAR Collaboration. Office: Wayne State Univ 666 W Hancock Detroit MI 48202 Office Phone: 313-577-5419. Personal E-mail: ilya.selyuzhenkov@gmail.com. Business E-Mail: ilya.selyuzhenkov@wayne.edu.

SELZ, PETER HOWARD, art historian, educator; b. Munich, Mar. 27, 1919; arrived in US, 1936, naturalized, 1942; s. Eugene and Edith S.; m. Thalia Cheronis, June 10, 1948 (div. 1965); children: Tanya Nicole Eugenia, Diana Gabrielle Hamlin; m. Carole Schemmerling, Dec. 18, 1983 Student, Columbia U., U. Paris; MA, U. Chgo., 1949, PhD, 1954; DFA, Calif. Coll. Arts and Crafts, 1967. Instr. U. Chgo., 1951-56; asst. prof. art history, head art edn. dept. Inst. Design, Ill. Inst. Tech., Chgo., 1949-55; chmn. art dept., dir. art gallery Pomona Coll., 1955-58; chief curator dept. painting and sculpture exhbns. Mus. Modern Art, 1958-65; dir. univ. art mus. U. Calif., Berkeley, 1965-73, prof. history of art, 1965—; Zaks prof. Hebrew U., Jerusalem, 1976. Vis. prof. CUNY, 1987; pres.'s coun. on art and architecture Yale U., 1971-76 Author: German Expressionist Painting, 1957, New Images of Man, 1959, Art Nouveau, 1960, Mark Rothko, 1961, Fifteen Polish Painters, 1961, The Art of Jean Dubuffet, 1962, Emil Nolde, 1963, Max Beckmann, 1964, Alberto Giacometti, 1965, Directions in Kinetic Sculpture, 1966, Funk, 1967, Harold Paris, 1972, Ferdinand Holder, 1972, Sam Francis, 1975, The American Presidency in Political Cartoons, 1976, Art in Our Times, 1981, Art in a Turbulent Era, 1985, Chillida, 1986, Twelve Artists from the GDR, 1989, Max Beckmann: The Self Portraits, 1992, William Congdon, 1992, Beckmann, 1996, Gottfried Helnwein, 1997, Beyond the Mainstream, 1997; co-author: Theories and Documents of Contemporary Art, 1996, Beyond the Mainstream, 1998, Barbara Chase-Riboud, 1999, Nathan Oliveira, 2001, The Art of Engagement, 2006; editor: Art in Am., 1967—, Art Quar., 1969-75, Arts, 1981-92, Cross-Currents in Modern Art, 2000; contbr. articles to profl. jours. Trustee Am. Crafts Coun., 1985—89; mem.adv. coun. archives Am. Art, 1971—; mem. acquisitions com. Fine Arts Mus., San Francisco, 1993; pres. Berkeley Art Project, 1988—93; project dir. Christo's Running Fence, 1973—76; commr. Alameda County Art Commn., 1990—95; bd. dirs. Richmond Art Ctr., 1998—2004; chair Berkeley Arts Festival, 1997—2000; trustee Neue Galerie, New York, 2002—, Kala Inst., Berkley, Calif., 2001—. Decorated Order of Merit Fed. Republic Germany; Fulbright grantee Paris, 1949-50; fellow Belgian-Am. Ednl. Found.; Sr. fellow NEH, 1972; resident Rockefeller Found. Study Ctr., Bellagio, 1994. Mem. Coll. Art Assn. Am. (dir. 1959-64, 67-71, Charles Rufus award 2007), AAUP, Internat. Art Critics Assn. Office: U Calif Dept Art History Berkeley CA 94720-0001 Office Phone: 510-524-5402.

SEMAK, MICHAEL WILLIAM, photographer, educator; b. Welland, Ont., Can., Jan. 9, 1934; s. John and Lena (Roketsky) S.; m. Annette Antoniuk, Jan. 30, 1960; children: James, Arlene. Student archtl. tech., Ryerson Poly. Inst., 1956-58. Freelance photographer Toronto-Pickering, 1961—; mem. faculty York U., Toronto, 1971—, assoc. prof. photography, 1977—. Exhibitor one-man shows, Image Gallery, NYC, 1972, Il Diaframma Canon Gallery, Milan, Italy, 1976, Enjay Gallery, Boston, 1977, Ukraina Soc., Kiev, U.S.S.R., 1980, 81, Can. Mus. Contemporary Photography, Ottawa, 2005, Mus. Contemporary Photography, Fed. Govt. Can., Ottawa, Ont., 2005; group shows, Ont. Art Gallery, 1967, Expo '67 Internat. Exhbn., Montreal, 1967, Neikrug Gallery, NYC, 1971; represented in permanent collections, Nat. Film Bd. Can., Ottawa, Nat. Gallery Can., Ottawa, Mus. Modern Art, NYC, UN, Geneva. Recipient Photo Excellence Gold medal Nat. Film Bd., 1969; recipient Excellence award Pravda newspaper, Moscow, 1970, 71, Excellence diploma Fedn. Intenationale de l'art Photographique, Switzerland, 1972 Achievements include first to be included in a speech of the federal government's member of parliament regarding photographs at solo show at The Canadian Museum of Contemporary Photography in Ottowa, 2005. Home: 1796 Spruce Hill Rd Pickering ON Canada L1V 1S4 Office: Dept Photography York U 4700 Keeles St Toronto ON Canada M3J 1P3 *I see many contradictions around us, social realities which I believe rob us of our self-esteem and individuality. Must we continually accept and succumb to the never-ending hot baths for the mind society offers us? I wish my photography and words to disturb the complacent and the sleeper. I offer you cold showers for the mind.*

SEMANS, MARY DUKE BIDDLE TRENT, foundation administrator; b. NY, Feb. 21, 1920; d. Anthony Joseph Drexel and Mary (Duke) B.; m. Josiah Trent; m. James H. Semans. Attended, Hewitt Sch., NYC; AB in History, Duke U.; LLD (hon.), N.C. Cen. U., 1963; HHD (hon.), Elon Coll., 1965; degree (hon.), Davidson Coll., N.C. Wesleyan Coll., 1982, U.N.C. at Chapel Hill, Duke U., 1983; LLD (hon.), Furman U., 1993. Trustee emeritus Duke U., 1961-81; chmn. The Duke Endowment, 1960-2001; various positions N.C. Sch. Arts, 1981—; former trustee Davidson Coll., N.C. Mus. Art, 1961-83, Shaw U., Converse U., Lincoln Hosp.; vice chmn. The Mary Duke Biddle Found., 1960—; chmn. Angier B. Duke Meml., Exec. Mansion Fine Arts Com., 1965—, Friends of Duke U. Library; pres. Durham Homes, Inc., 1968; mem. bd. dirs. Goodwill Industries of the Rsch. Triangle Area, 1964—, First Union Corp., 1980-82, N.C. State Library, 1958-61, Durham Pub. Library; numerous other positions. Mem. Durham City Coun., 1951-55; mayor pro-tem City of Durham, 1953-55; commencement speaker Duke U., 1983. Recipient Merit award Duke U. Health and Hosp. Adminstrn. Alumni Assn., 1989, Giannini medal for meritorious svc. to N.C. Sch. of the Arts, 1990, Alan Keith-Lucas Friend of Children award N.C. Childcare Assn., 1991, Elna Spaulding award Women-in-Action, 1993, Outstanding Philanthropist award Triangle Chpt. Nat. Soc. Fund Raising Execs., 1993, Sam Ragan award St. Andrews Coll., 1993. Mem. LWV, Bus. and Profl. Women's Club, Altrusa Club, Half Century Club, Rotary Club. Democrat. Methodist. Home: 1415 Bivins St Durham NC 27707-1519 Office: The Mary Duke Biddle Found 1044 W Forest Hills Blvd Durham NC 27707-1678

SEMAS, PHILIP WAYNE, editor; b. Gilroy, Calif., Feb. 23, 1946; s. Louis Alexander and Marian (Crapper) S.; m. Robin Lucille Tuttle, Sept. 7, 1967; children: Katherine Lucille, Anna Marian, Ellis Jeremy. Student, U. Oreg., 1963-67. Editor Coll. Press Service, Washington, 1967-68; freelance writer Berkeley, Calif., 1968-69; asst. editor Chronicle of Higher Edn. Inc., Balt. and Washington, 1969-76, 1976-78, mng. editor, 1978-88; editor Chronicle of Philanthropy, Washington, 1988—95; editor, new media Chronicle of Higher Edn. Inc., Washington, 1995—2002, editor in chief, 2002—. Recipient Higher Edn. Writers award, AAUP, 1974 Mem. Am. Soc. Mag. Editors Office: Chronicle of Higher Edn 1255 23rd St NW Ste 700 Washington DC 20037-1125 Home Phone: 301-422-2859; Office Phone: 202-466-1000. *

SEMBLER, MELVIN F., former ambassador, real estate developer; b. St. Joseph, Mo., 1930; m. Betty Schlesinger; children: Steve, Brent, Greg. BS, Northwestern U., 1952. Developer shopping ctrs.; chmn. bd. The Sembler Co., St. Petersburg, Fla., 1962—; US amb. to Australia & Nauru US Dept. State, Canberra, 1989-93, US amb. to Italy Rome, 2001—05. Trustee George Bush Presdl. Libr. Found., Internat. Coun. Shopping Ctrs.; bd. dirs. Am. Momentum Bank, Am. Enterprise Inst., Am.-Australian Edn. Leadership Found., Rep. Jewish Coalition, Moffitt Cancer Ctr.; resident mem. Fla. Coun. of 100. Mem. Internat. Coun. Shopping Ctrs. (pres. 1986-87). Office Phone: 727-384-6000.

SEMEL, GEORGE HERBERT, plastic surgeon; b. NYC, Apr. 20, 1938; s. Louis Bennett and Sara Sonja (Eutis) S. AB, Columbia U., 1959; MD, Boston U., 1963. Diplomate Am. Bd. Plastic Surgery. Intern L.A. County Gen. Hosp., 1963-64; resident gen. surgery Long Beach (Calif.) VA Hosp., 1964-67; residency in plastic surgery Mayo Clinic, Rochester, Minn., 1967-69; chief resident plastic surgery Med. U. S.C., Charleston, 1969-70; pvt. practice LA, 1970—; staff Midway Hosp. Founder L.A. Music Ctr., 1978, Mus. Contemporary Art, 1980. With Calif. NG, 1964-69, USNG, 1969-73. Mem. AMA, Am. Soc. Plastic Surgery, Am. Lipoplasty Soc., L.A. Soc. Plastic Surgeons, Phi Gamma Delta. Office: 450 S Beverly Dr Beverly Hills CA 90212-4402 Office Phone: 310-274-7547. E-mail: drsemel@drsemel.com.

SEMEL, TERRY S., Internet company executive; b. NYC, Feb. 24, 1943; s. Ben and Mildred S.; m. Jane Bovingdon, Aug. 24, 1977; children: Eric Scott, Courtenay Jane, Lily Bovingdon Semel, Kate Bovingdon Semel. BS in Acctg., L.I.U., 1964; postgrad. in market research, CCNY, 1966-67; LHD (hon.), Emerson Coll., 2004. Domestic sales mgr. CBS Cinema Center Films, Studio City, Calif., 1970-72; v.p., gen. mgr. Walt Disney's Buena Vista, Burbank, Calif., 1972-75; pres. W.B. Distbn. Corp., Burbank, 1975-78; exec. v.p., chief operating officer Warner Bros., Inc., Burbank, 1979-80, pres., COO, 1980-94, chmn., co-CEO, 1994-99, Warner Music Group Inc, 1995-99; chmn., CEO Yahoo! Inc., 2001—07, non exec. chmn., 2007—. Bd. dirs. Revlon., Polo Ralph Lauren Corp. Vice chmn. Pres.'s Com. for the Arts and Humanities; vice chair San Diego Host Com. for 1996 Rep. Nat. Conv.; bd. trustee Solomon R. Guggenheim Mus., Edn. First, Cedars Sinai Med. Ctr., Environ. Media Assn., Emerson Coll.; bd. dir. Mus. TV and Radio, LA County Mus. Art. Named Pioneer of the Year, 1990, Found. of Motion Pictures Pioneers; recipient UCLA medal, 2005, Yale Legends in Leadership award, 2005. Office: Yahoo! Inc 701 First Ave Sunnyvale CA 94089 *

SEMERJIAN, HRATCH GREGORY, federal agency administrator; b. Istanbul, Turkey, Oct. 22, 1943; came to U.S., 1966; s. Krikor and Diruhi (Semerciyan) S.; m. Sona Kohar Kurkciyan, July 12, 1969 (dec. 1983); children: Tamar, Ara; m. Ayda Karabal, Feb. 8, 1986 (div. 1994). BSME, Robert Coll., Istanbul, 1966; MSc in Engring., Brown U., 1968, PhD in Engring., 1972. Rsch. asst. div. engring. Brown U., Providence, 1966-70; lectr. chemistry U. Toronto, Ont., Can., 1971-73; rsch. engr. Pratt & Whitney Aircraft United Technologies Corp., East Hartford, Conn., 1973-77; group leader Ctr. for Chem. Tech. Nat. Bur. Standards (now Nat. Inst. Standards and Tech.), Gaithersburg, Md., 1977-87, divsn. chief Chem. Sci. and Tech. Lab., 1987-92, dir. Chem. Sci. and Tech. Lab., 1992—2003, dep. dir. Gaitherburg, 2003—, acting dir. Gaithersburg, Md., 2004—05. Organizer tech. sessions, confs. and symposiums for various profl. orgns., 1978—. Contbr. rsch. articles to profl. publs.; editor numerous conf. procs. Mem. parish coun. St. George Armenian Apostolic Ch., Hartford, Conn., 1975-77; chmn. parish coun., dir. choir St. Mary Armenian Apostolic Ch., Washington, 1977—; coach youth soccer Montgomery Soccer Inc., Rockville, Md., 1978-81; mem. Ani Armenian Choral Group, Washington, 1988—. Hagopian scholar Robert Coll., 1961-64, A.M.&F. corp. fellow, 1965, C.B. Keen fellow Brown U., 1969; recipient Silver medal Dept. Commerce, Washington, 1984, Gold medal US Dept. Commerce, Washington, 1995, Brown Engring. Alumni medal, 1997; named Fed. Engr. of Yr., NSPE, Washington, 1991. Fellow ASME; mem. AAAS, AIAA, AIChE, Am. Chem. Soc., Combustion Inst., NAE. Avocations: soccer, singing, boating. Office: Nat Inst Standards and Tech 100 Bur Dr Gaithersburg MD 20899-0001

SEMINARA, LYNDA ANNE, editor; b. Needham, Mass., Jan. 17, 1961; d. Donald Cecil Garaventi and Lois Ann Pichulo Garaventi; children: Daniel Joseph, Robert James. BA cum laude, U. Pa., 1985. Writer, editor, tour coord. Cultural Heritage Alliance, Phila., 1985—88; from prodn. editor to sr. ops. mgr. W.B. Saunders Co., Phila., 1988—93; self-employed editor and writer, 1993—; pres. and owner The WordShop, Cherry Hill, NJ, 1993—; sr. editor OCC N.Am., NYC, 2003—. Game creator Senior Sez trivia games, 2002—. Vol. sr. citizens and children, 1996—2001; sponsor Children Internat., 2003—; music ministry, 1974—. Mem.: Internat. Scleroderma Network (sr. editor 2004—), Soc. Children's Book Writers and Illustrators. Roman Catholic. Avocations: volunteer work, writing, guitar, languages.

SEMKE-FOX, SUZANNE MARIE, retired middle school educator; d. Leon and Pearl Semke; m. Dickson David Fox, July 24, 1976; 1 child, Christopher Fox. BA, U. Wash., Seattle, 1964; MEd. in Literacy, Lesley U., 2007. Cert. Tchr. K-12 Wash. Dept. Edn., 1964. Elem. educator Tigard Sch. Dist., Oreg., 1964—66, 1967—68, Burlington Sch. Dist., Ont., Canada, 1966—67; elem./secondary educator Washougal Sch. Dist., Wash., 1968—2007. Pres. Washougal Assn. Educators, 1984—88; bldg. rep. District-Wide Writing Comm., Washougal, 2003—04; charter mem. Wash. Assn. Mid.-Level Educators, Washougal. Advisor literacy mag.: Jemtegaard Mid. Sch., 2003—07. Founder Karen Jundt Found., Washougal, 2004—05. Recipient Poetic Achievement - Student Lit. Mag., Creative Comm., 2003—06; grantee, Washougal Schools Found., 2002—03, Dr. Seuss Lit. Grant, Wash. Assn. Educators. Mem.: Internat. Reading Assoc. (assoc.), Washougal Assn. Educators (assoc.; pres. 1984—88). Avocations: gardening, reading, poetry, travel. Home: PO Box 205 Washougal WA 98671 Home Phone: 360-835-1140. Personal E-mail: chrisfox10@aol.com.

SEMLER, WILLIAM LUDWIG, retired obstetrician, retired gynecologist; b. Racine, Wis., Dec. 21, 1922; s. Rudolph and Ida Frederica (Schmidt) Semler; m. Ellen Natalie Poulson, July 8, 1956; children: David William, Karen Lorraine, Barbara Jean. BS, U. Wis., Madison, 1944, MD, 1949. Lic. Wis., 1952. Intern Jersey City Med. Ctr., 1949—50; resident, ob-gyn. Mt. Sinai Hosp., Milw., 1952—54, St. Lukes Hosp., Milw., 0195—4195; pvt. practice ob-gyn. Miw., 1955—99; ret., 1999. Mem. exec. com. St. Michael's Hosp., Milw., 1976—88, chmn. credentials com., 1976—84, chmn. dept. ob-gyn., 1980—84, chmn. quality assurance com., 1980—84, chmn. exec. com., 1984—86, pres. med. staff, 1984—86, chmn. quality assurance com., 1986—95, chmn. family practice residency adv. com., 1988—99; staff St. Lukes Hosp., Milw., St. Joseph's Hosp., Milw., Mt. Sinai Hosp., Milw., Good Samaritan Med. Ctr., Milw., Columbia Hosp., Milw., Family Hosp., Milw; clin. instr. Med. Coll. Wis., 1990—2003; ret. tchg., 2004. Contbr. articles to profl. jours. With med. corp US Army, 1943—46, flight surgeon USAF, 1950—52. Mem.: AMA, Am. Coll. Physician Execs., Am. Menopause Soc., Soc. Laparoscopic Surgeons, Can.-Am. Med.-Dental Assn., Milw. Soc. Ob-gyn., Wis. Soc. Ob-gyn., Am. Coll. Physicians, Sports Car Club Am. Lutheran. Avocations: golf, photography, jewelry, travel, stained glass.

SEMLIES, LORI R., lawyer; b. LI, NY, 1969; BA, SUNY, Albany, 1991; JD magna cum laude, Touro Coll., 1994. Bar: NY 1995, NJ 1995, US Dist. Ct. Ea. Dist. NY, US Dist. Ct. So. Dist. NY. Ptnr. Wilson, Elser, Moskowitz, Edelman & Dicker LLP, NYC. Mem.: NY State Bar Assn. Office: Wilson Elser Moskowitz Edelman & Dicker LLP 150 E 42nd St 23rd Fl New York NY 10027-5639 Office Phone: 212-490-3000 ext. 2390. Office Fax: 212-490-3038. Business E-Mail: semliesl@wemed.com.

SEMMEL, BERNARD, historian, educator; b. NYC, July 23, 1928; s. Samuel and Tillie (Beer) S.; m. Maxine Loraine Guse, Mar. 19, 1955; 1 child, Stuart Mill. BA, CCNY, 1947; MA, Columbia U., NYC, 1951; PhD, Columbia U., 1955; postgrad., London Sch. Econs., 1959—60. With Nat. Citizens Commn. for Pub. Schs. and Coun. for Fin. Aid to Edn., NYC, 1951-55; asst. prof. history Park Coll., Parkville, Mo., 1956-60; mem. faculty SUNY, Stony Brook, 1960-91, prof. history, 1964-91, chmn. dept., 1966-69; Disting. prof. Grad. Sch. CUNY, 1991-96. Vis. prof. Columbia U., 1966-67. Author: Imperialism and Social Reform, 1960, Jamaican Blood and Victorian Conscience, 1963, The Rise of Free Trade Imperialism, 1970, reprinted, 2004, The Methodist Revolution, 1973, John Stuart Mill and the Pursuit of Virtue, 1984, Liberalism and Naval Strategy, 1986, The Liberal Ideal and The Demons of Empire, 1993, George Eliot and the Politics of National Inheritance, 1994; editor: Occasional Papers of T.R. Malthus, 1963; editor, translator: Halévy's The Birth of Methodism in England, 1971; editor Jour. Brit. Studies, 1969-74, Marxism and the Science of War, 1981. Rockefeller Found. grantee, 1959-60; Am. Council Learned Socs. fellow, 1964-65; Guggenheim fellow, 1967-68, 74-75; Nat. Humanities Ctr. fellow, 1986-87 Fellow Royal Hist. Soc.; mem. Am. Hist. Assn. (profl. divsn. 1984-86), Conf. Brit. Studies, Cosmos Club, Phi Beta Kappa. Home: PO Box 1162 Stony Brook NY 11790-0749

SEMMEL, STUART, history professor; s. Bernard and Maxine Semmel; m. Tina Lu. AB, Harvard Coll., 1988; AM, Harvard U., 1988, PhD, 1997. Asst. dir. history and lit. Harvard U., Cambridge, Mass., 1995—98; fellow Penn Humanities Forum, Phila., 1999—2000; vis. asst. prof. dept. history Am. U., Washington, 2000—01; asst. prof. dept. history U. Del., Newark, Del., 2001—06, assoc. prof., 2006—. Author: Napoleon and the British, 2004. Fellow, Nat. Humanties Ctr., 2005—06. Mem.: Am. Hist. Assn., North Am. Conf. Brit. Studies. Office: University of Delaware Dept of History Newark DE 19716 Home Phone: 610-328-1010; Office Phone: 302-831-0794. Personal E-mail: semmel@udel.edu.

SEMMLER, CARL D., lawyer; b. New Bern, NC, Feb. 2, 1958; s. Henry C. and Gene P. Semmler; m. Diane K. Kett, Aug. 25, 1990; children: Sean A., Nathan D. BA, U. N.C., Chapel Hill, 1980; JD, Wake Forest U., Winston-Salem, NC, 1987. CLU The Am. Coll., 2001. Intern Friends Com. on Nat. Legislation, Washington, 1980—81; ho. parent Presbyn. Children's Home of Highlands, Wytheville, Va., 1983—84; law clk. White & Crumpler, Winston-Salem, 1986—87; asst. v.p., assoc. counsel Lincoln Fin. Group, Greensboro, NC, 1987—. Mem. electronic commerce com. Am. Coun. Life Insurers, Washington, 2003—04, mem. privacy com., 2003—. Vice chair Lincoln Nat. Fed. Credit Union, Greensboro, 1991—98; bd. dirs. Quaker Lake Camp, Greensboro, 2001—06; chmn. admissions com. Friends Homes, Inc., Greensboro, 2002—. Fellow: Life Mgmt. Inst. Avocations: reading, gardening. Office: Lincoln Fin Group 100 N Greene St Greensboro NC 27401 Office Phone: 336-691-3369.

SEMON, WARREN LLOYD, information scientist, educator; b. Boise, Idaho, Jan. 17, 1921; s. August and Viola Lorreta (Eastman) S.; m. Ruth Valerie Swift, Dec. 1, 1945; children— Warren Lloyd, Nolan David, Jonathan Richard, Sue Anne. Student, Hobart Coll., 1940-43; S.B., U. Chgo., 1944; MA, Harvard, 1949, PhD, 1954. Instr. math. Hobart Coll., 1946-47; lectr. applied math. Harvard U., Cambridge, Mass., 1956-61, asst. dir. computation lab., 1954-61; head applied math. dept. Sperry Rand Research Ctr., Sudbury, Mass., 1961-64; mgr. computation and analysis lab. Burroughs Research Ctr., Paoli, Pa., 1964-67; prof. computer sci. Syracuse (N.Y.) U., 1967-84, prof. emeritus, 1984—, dir. system and information sci., 1968-76, dean Sch. Computer and Info. Sci., 1976-84. Cons. USAF, 1957, NSA, 1957, Lockheed Electronics Corp., 1967, Monsanto Co., 1972. Contbr. articles to profl. jours. Served to 1st lt. USAAF, 1943-46, MTO. Fellow IEEE; mem. Assn. Computing Machinery, Math. Assn. Am., IEEE Computer Soc. (chmn. publs. com. 1972-74, bd. govs. 1973-74, editor-in-chief 1975-76), Sigma Xi. Home: 1035 Scott Drive Apt 224 Prescott AZ 86301

SEMONIN, RICHARD GERARD, retired state official; b. Akron, Ohio, June 25, 1930; s. Charles Julius and Catherine Cecelia (Schooley) S.; m. Lennie Stuker, Feb. 3, 1951; children: Cecelia C., Richard G. Jr. (dec.), James R., Patricia R. BS, U. Wash., 1955. With Ill. State Water Survey, Champaign, 1955-91, chief, 1986-91, chief emeritus, 1991—; co-chmn. Ill. Water Rsch. & Land Use Planning Task Force, 1992-94. Adj. prof. U. Ill., 1975-91; chmn. Ill. Low-Level Radioactive Waste Task Group, 1994-96. Contbr. chpts. to books and articles to profl. jours.; co-editor: Atmospheric Deposition, 1983. Staff sgt. USAF, 1948-52. Grantee, NSF, 1957—76, US Dept. Energy, 1965—90. Fellow: AAAS, Am. Meteorol. Soc. (councilor 1983—86); mem.: Ill. Acad. Scis., Weather Modification Assn., Nat. Weather Assn. (councilor 1978—81), Sigma Xi. Roman Catholic. Avocations: civil war, golf, fishing, genealogy. Home: 1002 Devonshire Dr Champaign IL 61821-6620 Office: Ill State Water Survey 2204 Griffith Dr Champaign IL 61820-7495 E-mail: semonin@uiuc.edu.

SEMPLE, CECIL SNOWDON, retired manufacturing executive; b. Assam, India, Aug. 12, 1917; arrived in U.S., 1927, naturalized, 1948; s. Fordyce B. and Anne (Munro) Semple. BA, Colgate U., 1939. Buyer R.H. Macy & Co., 1939-42, 46-48; buyer, div. supt. Montgomery Ward, 1948-50; v.p. Nachman Corp., Chgo., 1950-55; sales mgr. radio receiver dept. GE, Bridgeport, Conn., 1955-60, mktg. cons. merchandising NYC, 1966-67, gen. mgr. audio products dept., 1967-68, dep. divsn. gen. mgr. housewares divsn., 1968-69, gen. mgr. housewares divsn., 1969, v.p., 1969-71, v.p. corp. customer rels., 1971-85; v.p. Rich's Inc., Atlanta, 1960-62, sr. v.p., dir., 1962-66, ret., 1985. Trustee Peoples Bank, 1975—89, trustee emeritus. Bd. dirs. Nat. Jr. Achievements Inc., Bridgeport Area Found., 1970—91, dir. emeritus, 1991—; bd. dirs. Bridgeport Hosp., 1970—93, chmn., 1983—89, dir. emeritus, 1993—; trustee Colgate U., 1970—84, vice chmn., 1978—84; trustee emeritus, past pres., bd. dirs. Alumni Corp.; chmn. So. Conn. Health Svc. Inc., 1990—93. Serrved to maj. USAAF, 1942—46. Mem.: Fairfield Country Club, Brooklawn Country Club (Fairfield, Conn.), St. Andrews Soc. State of N.Y. (chmn. bd. mgrs. 1968—70), Delta Kappa Epsilon. Home: 25 Cartright St Bridgeport CT 06604-2047

SEMPLE, JAMES WILLIAM, lawyer; s. Calvin James and Marie (Robinson; m. Ellen Burns; children: Megan Semple Greenberg, Luke Robinson. AB, St. Josephs U., Phila., 1965; JD, Villanova U., 1974. Bar: Del. 1974, U.S. Dist. Ct. Del. 1974, D.C. 1975, U.S. Ct. Appeals (3d cir.) 1982, U.S. Tax Ct. 1996. Ptnr. Morris, James, Hitchens & Williams, Wilmington, 1983—. Lectr. numerous seminars; mediator Superior Ct. Voluntary Mediation Program. Mem.: ABA, Fedn. Defense and Corp. Counsel, Am. Bd. Trial Advs. Office: Morris James Hitchens & Williams, LLP PO Box 2306 Wilmington DE 19899-2306 Office Phone: 302-888-6800. Business E-Mail: jsemple@morrisjames.com.

SEMPLE, JANE FRANCES, health facility director; b. Lakewood, Ohio, Feb. 14, 1951; d. Frank Joseph and Margaret Eleanor (Carpenter) Semple; m. Nick N. Morana, June 24, 1977 (div. Sept. 1981). AAB, Cuyahoga CC, Cleve., 1977; BA, Baldwin-Wallace Coll., 1980; MBA, Case Western Res. U., 1984; ND, Trinity Coll. Natural Health, 1999. Diplomate Am. Bd. Naturopaths. Adminstrv. asst. DeVilbiss Co., Cleve., 1969—77; project dir. Nat. Survey Rsch. Ctr., Cleve., 1977—80; market rsch. mgr. Sherwin-Williams Co., Cleve., 1980—85; instr. Cuyahoga CC, Cleve., 1986—92, Baldwin-Wallace Coll., Berea, Ohio, 1992—93; dir. Alternative Healing Inst., 1989—. Author: Influenza, 2006, Parkinson Disease, 2006, HPV and Cervical Displasia, 2006, Fertility, 2006. Mem. S. B. Anthony Soc. Womenspace, Cleve., 1980—88. Mem.: Coalition for Natural Health, Am. Botanic Coun., Am. Assn. Nutritional Cons., Am. Naturopathic Med. Assn. Democrat. Home: 26969 Greenbrooke Dr Olmsted Falls OH 44138 Office: Alternative Healing Inst 4965 Doven Ctr Rd North Olmsted OH 44070 Office Phone: 440-777-2665. Personal E-mail: drjane@bright.net.

SEMPLE, ROBERT BAYLOR, JR., editor, journalist; b. St. Louis, Aug. 12, 1936; s. Robert B. and Isabelle Ashby (Neer) S.; m. Susan Riker Kirk, Aug. 19, 1961 (div. Feb. 1980); children: Robert Baylor III, Elizabeth, William, Mary; m. Lisa Pulling, Jan. 10, 1981. Grad., Phillips Acad., 1954; BA, Yale U., 1959; MA, U. Calif., Berkeley, 1961. Reporter Nat. Observer, 1961-63; corr. NY Times, 1963-68, White House corr., 1968-72, dep. nat. editor, 1973-75, London bur. chief, 1975-77, fgn. editor NYC, 1977-82, op-ed page editor, 1982-88, assoc. editor editl. page, 1988—, and editl. bd. mem. Recipient Pulitzer prize for editl. writing on environ. issues, 1996; Carnegie fellow, 1959-60; Woodrow Wilson fellow, 1960-61. Mem. Century Assn. (NYC), Yale Club (NYC). Episcopalian. Office: NY Times 229 W 43rd St New York NY 10036-3913 E-mail: semple@nytimes.com.

SEMPLE, SUSAN, early childhood educator; b. Phila., Aug. 1, 1946; d. Calvin James and Marie Dolores Semple. BS in Elem. Edn., Gwynedd Mercy, Pa., 1975. Tchr. Arch Diocese Phila., 1964—70, Pre Sch. Learning Ctr., Westminster, Pa., 1970—76, St. Hilary Sch., Rydal, Pa., 1992—. Dir. outreach ministries St. Hilary Sch., Rydal, 1992—. Mem.: NCE.

SEMROD, T. JOSEPH, banker; b. Oklahoma City, Dec. 13, 1936; s. L.J. and Theda Jo (Hummel) S.; m. Janice Lee Wood, June 1, 1968 (div. 1988); children: Ronald, Catherine, Christopher, Elizabeth; m. Jaye Patricia Hewitt, May 27, 1989; 1 child, Kelsey. BA in Polit. Sci., U. Okla., 1958, LLB, 1963. Bar: Okla. 1963. With Liberty Nat. Bank, Oklahoma City, 1963-81, v.p., 1967-69, sr. v.p., 1969-71, exec. v.p., 1971-73, pres., 1973-81, Liberty Nat. Corp., Oklahoma City, 1976-81; chmn. bd., pres., CEO United Jersey Banks (now UJB Fin. Corp.), Princeton, N.J., 1981-96; chmn., CEO Summit Bancorp. (merged with UJB Fin. Corp.), Princeton, 1996—; chmn., bd. dirs., CEO Summit Bank, Princeton, N.J., 1981—; vice chmn. Fleet Boston Fin., 2001—; chmn. Fleet Bank, N.J., 2001—. Bd. dirs. Fed. Res. Bank N.Y., Internat. Fin. Conf., chmn., 1994. Trustee, mem. exec. com. Nat. Urban League, 1963-95; mem. bd. advisors Outward Bound, Inc., 1984-2000, Ind. Coll. Fund NJ, 1986-90; commr. Citizens Commn. on Aids, 1988-90; chmn. bd. regents Stonier Grad. Sch. Banking, Rutgers U., 1983; mem. NJ Transp. Trust Fund Authority, 1985-87; chmn. The Partnership for NJ, 1999-01, trustee; chmn. banking industry US Savs. Bonds campaign, 1992-93. 1st lt. U.S. Army, 1958-60. Mem. Am. Bankers Assn., NJ Bankers Assn., NJ Bar Assn., Okla. Bar Assn., Bankers Roundtable (bd. dirs. 1995-97), Regional Plan Assn. (bd. dirs. 1989-91), Youn Pres. Orgn., Am. Running and Fitness Assn. (bd. dirs. 1983-86), NJ C. of C. (bd. dirs., chmn. 1998-99, chair prosperity NJ 1998-00, chmn. 1999-00), Drumthwacket Found. (chmn. 1990-94), Bedens Brook Club (Skillman, NJ), River Club (NYC), Jasna Polana TPC (Princeton), Coral Beach Club (Bermuda), Nassau Club, Tournament Players Club, Adirondack League Club (Old Forge, NY), The Port Royal Club (Naples, Fla.). Democrat. Roman Catholic.

SEN, AMARTYA KUMAR, economist, educator; b. Santiniketan, India, Nov. 3, 1933; s. Ashutosh and Amita Sen. BA, Calcutta U., 1953, Cambridge U., Eng., 1955; PhD, 1959; DLitt (hon.), U. Sask., 1979, Visva-Bharati U., 1983, U. Essex, 1984, Georgetown U., 1989, Jødavpur U., 1990, Kalyani U., 1990, Athens U. Econs. and Bus., 1991, Williams Coll., 1991, London Guildhall U., 1991, New Sch. Social Rsch., 1992, Calcutta U., 1992, Oberlin Coll., 1993, Syracuse U., 1994, Wesleyan U., 1995, Oxford, 1996; DSc (hon.), U. Bath, 1984, U. Edinburgh, 1995; D (hon.), U. Caden, 1987, U. Caen, 1987, Louvain, 1989, U. Valencia, 1994, U. Zurich, 1994, U. Antwerp, 1995, U. Stockholm, 1996, Bard Coll., 1997, Kiel U., 1997; dottore ad honorem, U. Bologna, 1988; LLD (hon.), U. Tulane, 1990, Queen's U., 1993. Prof. econs. Jadavpur U., Calcutta, 1956-58; fellow Trinity Coll., Cambridge U., 1957-63; prof. econs. Delhi U., 1963-71, London Sch. Econs., 1971-77, Oxford (Eng.) U., 1977-80, Drummond prof. polit. economy, 1980-88; prof. econs. and philosophy Harvard U., Cambridge, Mass., 1987-98, Lamont univ. prof., 1988-98, vis. prof., 1968-69; master Trinity Coll., Cambridge U., 1998—. Vis. prof. U. Calif., Berkeley, 1964-65; Andrew D. White prof.-at-large Cornell U., Ithaca, N.Y., 1978-84; chmn. expert group role advanced skill and tech. UN, 1967; hon. fellow Trintiy Coll., Cambridge Inst. Social Studies, The Hague, Inst. Devel. Studies, U. Sussex, London Sch. Econs., U. London. Author: Choice of Techniques, 1960, Collective Choice and Social Welfare, 1970, Growth Economics, 1970, Guidelines for Project Evaluation, 1972, On Economic Inequality, 1973, Employment, Technology and Development, 1975, Poverty and Famines: An Essay on Entitlement and Deprivation, 1981, Utilitarianism and Beyond, 1982, Choice, Welfare and Measurement, 1982, Resources, Values and Development, 1984, Commodities and Capabilities, 1985, On Ethics and Economics, 9187, The Standard of Living, 1987, Hunger and Public Action, 1989, The Political Economy of Hunger, 1990, Inequality Reexamined, 1992, Quality of Life, 1993, India: Economic Development and Social Opportunity, 1995, Indian Development: Selected Regional Perspectives, 1997, On Economic Inequality, 1997; contbr. articles to profl. jours. Recipient Adam Smith Prize, Cambridge U., 1954, Stevenson Prize, 1956, Mahalanobis award, 1976, Rank E. Seidman Disting. award in Polit. Economy, 1986, Agnelli Internat. prize, 1990, Alan Shawn Feinstein World Hunger award, 1990, Jean Mayer Global Citizenship award, 1993, Indira Gandhi Gold Medal award, Asiatic Soc., 1994, Edinburgh Medal, 1997, 9th Catalonia Internat. prize, 1997, Nobel prize in econ. scis., 1998; co-recipient Wassily Leontief prize for advancing frontiers econ. thought Tufts Global Inst. for Environ. and Devel., 2000; grantee Wrenbury Scholarship, Cambridge U., 1956. Fellow Brit. Acad., Econometric Soc. (past pres.); mem. AAAS (fgn. hon.), Am. Econ. Assn. (past pres.), Indian Econ. Assn. (past pres.), Royal Econ. Soc. (v.p.), Indian Econometric Conf., Devel. Studies Assn. (past pres.), Internat. Econ. Assn. (pres. 1986-89, hon. pres.), Accademia Nazionale dei Lincei, Am. Philosophical Assn. Office: Lamont U Prof Dept Econs Harvard U Cambridge MA 02138 *

SEN, AYUSMAN, chemistry professor; b. Calcutta, India, Jan. 5, 1951; came to U.S., 1973; s. Amiya Kumar and Geeti (Datta) S.; m. Suchismita Roomjhoom Gupta, July 29, 1979; 1 child, Deepa Amrita. BSc with honors, U. Calcutta, India, 1970; MS, Indian Inst. Tech., Kanpur, India, 1973; PhD, U. Chgo., 1978. Rsch. fellow Calif. Inst. Tech., Pasadena, 1978-79; asst. prof. Pa. State Univ, University Park, Pa., 1979-84; assoc. prof. Pa. State Univ., University Park, Pa., 1984-89, prof., 1989—, chem. dept. chmn. Imperial Oil disting. lectr. Univ. Toronto, 1993; Iberdrola vis. prof. Univ. Valladolid, Spain, 1999—2000; Gerhard Closs lectr. Univ. Chgo., 2002. Contbr. numerous articles to profl. jours. Recipient Nat. Sci. Talent Search scholarship Govt. of India, 1967-74, Young Investigator award Chevron Rsch. Co., 1982-84, Paul J. Flory Sabbatical award IBM, 1987-88; Alfred P. Sloan Rsch. fellow, 1984-88. Mem. Am. Chem. Soc. Office: Pa State Univ Chemistry Dept 104 Chemistry Bldg University Park PA 16802

SENA, CHARALENA, dental office executive; d. Charles Howard Huntley and Linda Gayle Helms; m. Bartholomew Sena; children: David Wayne Williams, Sena Rhyan Joshua children: Ricky Darrell Williams. BA in Bus., Appalachian State U., NC, 1981, MBA, 1981; PhD in Math., Camborne U., Eng., 1984, PhD in Arts, 1986; BA in Pub. Rels., Weybridge U., Del., 2002; MBA in Criminal Justice, Felton U., New Castle, Del., 2004; D Clin. Psychology, Williamstown U., Wilmingston, Del., 2006; PhD in Clin. Psychology and Behavioral Sci., Williamstown U., Wilmingtonm Del., 2006. Office mgr., fin. mgr. Office of Dr. Jeffrey F. West, Charlotte, NC, 1989—94; bus. mgr. Lee & Associates, Charlotte, 1996—2001; bus. cons./fin. mgr. Charles Payet, DDS, Charlotte, 2000—01; CFO Viken Incorporation, Bound Brook, NJ, 2001—05, R&S Mgmt. Corp. (formerly Viken, Inc.), Flushing, NY, 2005—06; CEO CS Exec. Cons., Raritan, NJ, 1988—. Contbr. articles to profl. publs. Mem.: AADOM (cons. 2003—07), CPMM. Republican. Home Phone: 908-526-0044; Office Phone: 908-698-3520. Business E-Mail: charalena2006@yahoo.com.

SENATOR, RONALD PAUL, composer, writer, retired music educator; b. London, Apr. 17, 1926; arrived in US, 1981; m. Dita Branicky (dec.); m. Miriam Brickman, Aug. 15, 1986. BMus, Oxford U., England, 1949; PhD, London U., England, 1950. Sr. lectr. London U., 1958—75; profl. Guildhall Sch. Music, London, 1976—82; vis. prof. MIT, USC, 1980—85; ret., 1985. Composer: Holocaust Requiem, 1986; author: Gaia of Music, 1980, Requiem Letters, 1988. Nominee Pulitzer Prize, 1991; recipient Rsch. Program award, Social Sci. Rsch. Coun., 1970—76. Mem.: ASCAP, Montserrat Sacred Music Assn. (founding mem.). Home: 81 Hillcrest Ave Yonkers NY 10705-1509 Office Phone: 914-476-1962. E-mail: ronaldsenator@hotmail.com.

SENCIÓN, FELIX, publishing executive; Sales exec. NY Daily News; founder & CEO Mundial Group, 2002—; pub. Fútbol Mudial, 2002—, Beisbol Mundial, 2005—, Fútbol Mundial USA. Named one of 40 Under 40, Crain's NY Bus., 2007; Nat. Hispanic Corp. Achiever, 1992. Office: Fútbol Mundial 11th Fl 9 E 38th St New York NY 10016 Office Phone: 212-213-1400. *

SENCZUK, ANNA MARIA, cell biologist, researcher; b. Czestochowa, Poland, Nov. 3, 1965; d. Janusz and Halina Senczuk; m. Miroslaw Josef Studzinski, Dec. 29, 1990; children: Tom Studzinski, Lukas Studzinski. MS, U. Calgary, Alta., Can., 1999. Assoc. U. Calgary, 1999—2000; assoc. scientist Amgen, Seattle, 2000—. Presenter in field. Contbr. articles to profl. jours. Mentor Sci. Expo, Seattle, 2002—07. Mem.: Sigma Xi. Achievements include patents for HIC dual salt. Home: 19110 Stone Ave N Shoreline WA 98133 Office: Amgen 1201 Amgen Ct West AW2D2177 Seattle WA 98119 Home Phone: 206-533-8683; Office Phone: 206-265-8338. Personal E-mail: senczukowa@hotmail.com. Business E-Mail: senczuka@amgen.com.

SENDAK, MAURICE BERNARD, writer, illustrator; b. Bklyn., June 10, 1928; s. Philip and Sadie (Schindler) S. Student, Art Students League, NYC, 1949-51; LHD, Boston U., 1977; degree (hon.), U. So. Miss., 1981, Keene State Coll., 1986. Window display artist Timely Svc., NYC, 1946; display artist FAO Schwartz, NYC, 1948-51; co-founder, artistic dir. The Night Kitchen, 1990—. One-man shows include Gallery Sch. Visual Arts, N.Y.C., 1964, Rosenbach Found., Phila., 1970, 75, Trinity Coll., 1972, Galerie Daniel Keel, Zurich, 1974, Ashmolean Mus., Oxford, 1975, Am. Cultural Center, Paris, 1978, Pierpont Morgan Library, N.Y.C., 1981; author, illustrator: Kenny's Window, 1956 (Spring Book Fesitval honor book 1956), Very Far Away, 1957, The Acrobat, 1959, The Sign on Rosie's Door, 1960, The Nutshell Library (contains Chicken Soup with Rice, One Was Johnny, Alligators All Around, Pierre: A Cautionary Tale), 1962, Where The Wild Things Are, 1963 (N.Y. Times Best Illustrated Book award 1963, Caldecott medal 1964, Lewis Carroll Shelf award 1964, Internat. Bd. on Books for Young People award 1966, Art Books for Children award 1973, 74, 75, Best Young Picture Books Paperback award Redbook Mag. 1984, Children's Choice award 1985), Hector Protector and As I Went Over the Water: Two Nursery Rhymes, 1965, Higglety, Pigglety, Pop!; or, There Must Be More to Life, 1967 (Am. Book award nomination 1980), In the Night Kitchen, 1970 (N.Y. Times Best Illustrated Book award 1970, Caldecott medal nomination 1971, Art Books for Children award 1973, 74, 75, Redbook Mag. award 1985), Ten Little Rabbits: A Counting Book with Mino the Magician, 1970, Pictures by Maurice Sendak, 1971, Maurice Sendak's Really Rosie, 1975, Some Swell Pup; or, Are You Sure You Want A Dog, 1976, Seven Little Monsters, 1977, Outside Over There, 1981 (N.Y. Times Best Illustrated Book award 1981, Boston Globe/Horn Book award 1981, Caldecott medal nomination 1982, Am. Book award 1982), We Are All in the Dumps with Jack and Guy, 1993, Tsippi, 1994, Moishe, 1994, Max, 1994; illustrator: Atomics for the Millions, 1947, Good Shabbos, Everybody!, 1951, The Wonderful Farm, 1951, A Hole is to Dig, 1952 (N.Y. Times Best Illustrated Book award 1952), Maggie Rose: Her Birthday Christmas, 1952, The Giant Story, 1953, Hurry Home Candy, 1953, Shadrach, 1953, A Very Special House, 1953 (Caldecott medal nomination 1954), I'll Be You and You Be Me, 1954 (N.Y. Times Best Illustrated Book award 1954), Happy Hanukkah, Everybody, 1954, The Tin Fiddle, 1954, Magic Pictures, 1954, Mrs. Piggle-Wiggle's Farm, 1954, The Wheel on the School, 1954, Charlotte and the White Horse, 1955, The Little Cow and the Turtle, 1955, Singing Family of the Cumberlands, 1955, What Can You Do With a Shoe?, 1955, Happy Rain, 1956, The House of Sixty Fathers, 1956, I Want to Paint My Bathroom Blue, 1956 (N.Y. Times Best Illustrated Book award 1956), Birthday Party, 1957 (N.Y. Times Best Illustrated Book award 1957), Circus Girl, 1957, You Can't Get There From Here, 1957, Little Bear, 1957, Along Came a Dog, 1958, No Fighting, No Biting!, 1958, Somebody Else's Nut Tree, 1958, What Do You Say, Dear?, 1958 (N.Y. Times Best Illustrated Book award 1958, Caldecott medal nomination 1959), The Moon Jumpers, 1959 (Caldecott medal nomination 1960), Father Bear Comes Home, 1959 (N.Y. Times Best Illustrated Book award 1959), Seven Tales, 1959, Dwarf Long-Nose, 1960, Little Bear's Friend, 1960, Open House for Butterflies, 1960 (N.Y. Times Best Illustrated Book award 1960), Let's Be Enemies, 1961, The Tale of Gockel, Hinkel and Gackeliah, 1961, What Do You Do, Dear?, 1961, Little Bear's Visit, 1961 (Caldecott medal nomination 1962), Schoolmaster Whackwell's Wonderful Sons, 1962, Mr. Rabbit and the Lovely Present, 1962 (Caldecott medal nomination 1963), The Singing Hill, 1962 (N.Y. Times Best Illustrated Book award 1962), Nikolenka's

Childhood, 1963, She Loves Me, She Loves Me Not, 1963, The Bat-Poet, 1964 (N.Y. Times Best Illustrated Book award 1964), How Little Lori Visited Times Square, 1964, Pleasant Fieldmouse, 1964, Lullabies and Night Songs, 1965, The Animal Family, 1965 (N.Y. Times Best Illustrated Book award 1965), Zlateh the Goat, 1966 (N.Y. Times Best Illustrated Book award 1966), The Golden Key, 1967, Poems from William Blake's Songs of Innocence, 1967, The Big Green Book, 1968, Griffin and the Minor Canon, 1968, A Kiss for Little Bear, 1968 (N.Y. Times Best Illustrated Book award 1968), The Light Princess, 1969 (N.Y. Times Best Illustrated Book award 1969), The Bee-Man of Orn, 1971, Sarah's Room, 1971, The Juniper Tree and Other Tales from Grimm, 1973 (N.Y. Times Best Illustrated Book award 1973), Fortunia: A Tale by Mme. D'Aulnoy, 1974, Fly by Night, 1976 (N.Y. Times Best Illustrated Book award 1976), King Grisly-Beard: A Tale from the Brothers Grimm, 1978, The Nutcracker, 1984 (N.Y. Times Best Illustrated Book award 1984), In Grandpa's House, 1985, The Children's Books of Randall Jarrell, 1988, Dear Mili: An Old Tale by Wilhelm Grimm, 1988, I Saw Esau, 1992, The Ubiquitous Pig, 1992; author: Fantasy Sketches, 1970, Collection of Books, Posters, and Original Drawings, 1984, The Love for Three Oranges: The Glyndebourne Version, 1984, Posters, 1986, Caldecott & Co.: Notes on Books and Pictures, 1988, Maurice Sendak Book and Poster Package: Wild Things, 1991, Bears, 2005 (Publishers Weekly children's picture book bestseller list); editor: Maxfield Parrish Poster Book, 1974, The Disney Poster Book, 1977; contbr.: The Publishing Archive of Lothar Meggendorfer, 1975, Babar's Anniversary Album, 1981, Masterworks of Children's Literature, Vol. 7, 1984, Victorian Color Picture Books, 1985, Winsor McCay: His Life and Art, 1987, Mickey Mouse Movie Stories, 1988; dir., lyricist: Really Rosie, 1975; lyricist, set designer: Really Rosie, 1978; lyricist, set designer, costume designer: Where the Wild Things Are, 1980, Higglety, Pigglety, Pop!, 1984; set designer, costume designer: The Magic Flute, 1980, The Cunning Little Vixen, 1981, Love for Three Oranges, 1982, The Goose of Cairo, 1984, Idomeneo, 1988, L'Enfant et les Sortileges, 1989, L'Heure Espagnol, 1989, It's Alive!, 1994, So, Sue Me, 1994; photographer: The Cunning Little Vixen, 1985; set designer: The Nutcracker, 1983, Hansel and Gretel, 1998, Brundibar, 2004; designer: (film) The Nutcracker, 1986. Recipient Chandler Book Talk Reward of Merit, 1967, Hans Christian Andersen Internat. medal, 1970, Laura Ingalls Wilder award Assn. Libr. Svc. to Children, 1983, Nat. Medal Arts, 1997, Lindgren award, 2003, Pell Lifetime Achievement award, 2003, Lifetime Achievement award Child mag., 2004. Office: Harper Collins Childrens Divsn 1350 Ave of the Americas New York NY 10019

SENDAX, VICTOR IRVEN, dentist, educator, dental implant researcher; b. NYC, Sept. 14, 1930; s. Maurice and Molly R. S.; m. Deborah deLand Cobb, Dec. 17, 1969 (div. June 1976); 1 child, Jennifer Reiland; m. Marcia Ayer Pearson, Dec. 13, 1986; children: Anneliese Chase, Cordelia Ayer. Grad., Tanglewood Music Ctr., 1953; BA, NYU, 1951, DDS, 1955; postgrad., Harvard U. Sch. Dental Medicine, Cambridge, Mass., 1969-72. Diplomate Am. Bd. Oral Implantology/Implant Dentistry (pres. 1996, dir.). Commr. N.Y. State Dental Svc. Corp., 1969-73; pres., dir. BioDental Rsch. Found., Inc., NYC, 1975—; pres. Victor I. Sendax, D.D.S., P.C., NYC, 1972—, Sendax Mini Dental Implant Ctrs. Mgmt., Inc., 1985—; assoc. attending implantologist mini-dental implant program St. Lukes-Roosevelt Hosp., NYC, 1979—. Adj. assoc. prof. implant prosthodontics Columbia U. Sch. Dental and Oral Surgery, N.Y.C., 1974-92; vis. lectr. dept. implant dentistry NYU Coll. Dentistry; faculty N.Y. County Dental Soc. Sch. for Continuing Dental Edn.; mem. dental implant rsch. programs adv. com. Nat. Inst. Dental Rsch., HHS; cons. Julliard Sch. Voice and Drama, N.Y.C., 1972—, Vocal Dynamics Lab. Dept. Otolaryngology, Lenox Hill Hosp., N.Y.C., 1970-90; founder Sendax Seminars; 1st dir. implant prosthodontics resident program Columbia U. Sch. Dental and Oral Surgery and Columbia Presbyn. Hosp. Editor: Dental Clinics of North America: HA-Coated Dental Implants, 1992; mem. editl. bd. Oral Implantology, 1979-98; patentee in mini-implants, oral implant magnetics, implant abutments and sinus graft implant stabilizers; co-developer IMTEC/SENDAX mini-dental implant system. Bd. dirs. City Ctr. Music and Drama, Inc. divsn. Lincoln Ctr. Performing Arts, N.Y.C., 1966-75; mem. adv. bd. Amagansett (N.Y.) Hist. Assn., 1969-89; trustee Leukemia Soc. Am., N.Y.C., 1967; bd. dirs. Schola Cantorum, 1980-90, Soc. Asian Music, 1965-76. Capt. Dental Corps USAF, 1955-57. Recipient Cert. of Honor, Brit. Dental Implant Assn., 1988., Aaron Gershkoff Meml. award for Outstanding Contbns. and Dedication to Oral Implantology Am. Acad. of Implant Dentistry, 1996. Fellow: Royal Soc. Medicine Gt. Britain, Am. Acad. Implant Dentistry (nat. pres. 1981), Internat. Coll. Dentists, Am. Coll. Dentists; mem.: ADA (ho. of dels. 1969), Japan Soc., N.Y. Acad. Scis., Internat. Assn. Dental Rsch., Am. Assn. Dental Rsch. (implant group), Fedn. Dentaire Internat., Am. Analgesia Soc., Acad. of Osseointegration, Am. Dental Edn. Assn. (former chmn. spl. interest group on dental implant edn.), Century Assn. Home: 70 E 77th St Apt 6A New York NY 10021-1811 Office: Mini Dental Implant Ctr 30 Central Park S Ste 14B New York NY 10019-1628 Office Phone: 212-753-2775. Business E-Mail: vis@sendax-minidentimpl.com. *I stand in awe of mankinds' eternal need to innovate and push back the frontiers of knowledge, while tempering the harsher realities of existence with a perspective born of our cultural heritage.*

SENDER, ADAM D., investment company executive, art collector; Gen. ptnr. Exis Capital Mgmt., NYC, 1998—. Named one of Top 200 Collectors, ARTnews Mag., 2004, 2005, 2006. Avocation: Collector of Contemporary Art. Office: Exis Capital Mgmt 33rd Fl 767 Third Ave New York NY 10017

SENDER, JAMES LEROY, retired military officer, retired federal agency administrator; b. Chgo., Sept. 4, 1924; s. Andrew Frank and Estelle Elizabeth Sender; m. Genevieve Fern Pierce (dec.); m. Arline Nola Kesner (dec.); m. Marion Francis Hicks, Nov. 19, 1991; children: Gregory, Melanie, Timothy, Gloria. BA, U. Wash., Seattle, 1951. Lt. col. US Army, 1943—73; agt. US Treasury Dept., Sarasota, Fla., 1974—84. Mem. vis. com. Meth. Ch. Mem.: Order Ea. Star (worthy patron), Shriners, Freemasons (lodge master 1970—), Alpha Kappa Delta, Phi Sigma Kappa. Avocations: gardening, reading, dance, church activities. Home: 5 Foliage Way NE Rome GA 30165-9646

SENDO, TAKESHI, mechanical engineering educator, researcher, writer; b. Ena City, Japan, Aug. 5, 1917; s. Shigeyoshi and Michie (Yamamoto) S.; m. Hide Okamoto, Apr. 16, 1945; children: Mitsuyoshi, Sachiko, Kazuyasu. B of Engring., Tokyo U., 1941. Prof. mech. engring. Meijo U., Nagoya City, Japan, 1959-90, hon. prof., 1990—. Curator libr. Meijo U., Nagoya City, 1975-80. Author: Treatise of High Speed Deformation of Metal, 1993, 2nd edit., 1994, Experiment: Behavior of Al Column by Drop Hammer Test, 1959-90; contbr. over 60 articles to profl. jours. Mem. cmty. activity com. Local Self-Governing Orgn., Moriyama City, Japan, 1990, 91. Served to lt. comdr. Japanese Navy, 1941-45. Fellow Japan Soc. Mech. Engring., Japan Soc. Precision Engring. Avocations: composing haiku and tanka, trying essay, jogging. Home: 21-8 Choei Moriyama-ku Nagoya 463 Japan

SENECHAL, ALICE R., federal magistrate judge, lawyer; b. Rugby, ND, June 25, 1955; d. Marvin William and Dora Emma (Erdman) S. BS, N.D. State U., 1977; JD, U. Minn., 1984. Bar: Minn. 1984, U.S. Dist. Ct. Minn. 1984, N.D. 1986, U.S. Ct. Appeals (8th cir.) 1987. Law clk. U.S. Dist. Judge Bruce M. Van Sickle, Bismarck, ND, 1984-86; with Robert Vogel Law Office, Grand Forks, ND, 1986—. U.S. magistrate judge, 1990—.

SENEKER, CARL JAMES, II, (KIM), lawyer; b. San Jose, Calif., Oct. 12, 1942; s. Carl James and Beth D. (Hearn) S.; m. Julie Marie Pardee, June 17, 1967; children: Mark Gwynn, Todd Christian. AB, Stanford U., 1964; JD, U. Calif., Berkeley, 1967. Bar: Calif. 1969, U.S. Dist. Ct. (no. dist.) Calif. 1973. Law clk. to Hon. William O. Douglas U.S. Supreme Ct., Washington, 1967-68; ptnr. Morrison & Foerster, San Francisco, 1971-84, 96—, LA, 1984—96. Adj. prof. law, lectr. law sch. Stanford U., Palo Alto, Calif., 1982-83. Co-editor: California Real Estate Law and Practice, Vols. 12 & 13, 1983-96; contbr. articles to profl. jours. Bd. dirs. L.A. Hdqs. City Assn., 1988-93. Capt. USAF, 1968-71. Mem. Am. Coll. Real Estate Lawyers (bd. govs. 1989-97, pres.-elect 1996-97, pres. 1997-98), State Bar Calif. (real property law sect., vice-chair exec. com. 1987-90), Am. Coll. Mortgage Attys., Anglo-Am. Real Property Inst., Lambda Alpha Internat. Roman Catholic. Avocations: golf, travel, music. Office: Morrison & Foerster 425 Market St Fl 32 San Francisco CA 94105-2467 Home Phone: 925-377-8420; Office Phone: 415-268-6619. Office Fax: 415-268-7522. Business E-Mail: cseneker@mofo.com.

SENER, STEPHEN FRANCIS, oncologist, surgeon; b. Chgo., Jan. 30, 1950; m. Sherri Abbott, June 21, 1971; children: Matthew Charles, Michael Stephen. BA in Chemistry, Northwestern U., Evanston, Illinois, 1972; MD, Northwestern U., Chgo., 1977. Lic. surgeon Am. Bd. Surgery, 1983, surg. oncologist Soc. of Surg. Oncology, 1988. Asst. prof. surgery Northwestern U., Chgo., 1987—92, assoc. prof. surgery, 1992—98; prof. of surgery Northwestern U. Dept. of Surgery, 1998—; head, divsn. gen. surgery Evanston Northwestern Healthcare, 1996—2001, attending surgeon, 1984—, vice-chairman, dept. surgery, 1999—. Recipient Departmental Honors award, Northwestern U. Dept. Chemistry, 1972, Faculty Tchr. Yr., Northwestern U. Dept. Surgery, 1998. Fellow: Soc. Surg. Oncology; mem.: Am. Surg. Assn., Midwest Surg. Assn. (mem. exec. com. 2003—), Am. Cancer Soc. (Ill. pres. 1992—94, nat. bd. dirs. 1992—2006, nat. pres. 2004—05, pres. 2004—05, immediate past pres. 2005—06, St. George medal 1998), Chgo. Surg. Soc. (sec. 1999—2003), Am. Soc. Clin. Oncology, Ctrl. Surg. Assn. Achievements include first to organize and lead six surgical teams from Evanston Northwestern Healthcare on humanitarian surgical missions to Moscow State University, Latvia Cancer Inst., and Peking University. Office: Evanston Northwestern Healthcare 2650 Ridge Walgreen Bldg Rm 2507 Evanston IL 60201 Office Phone: 847-570-1328.

SENEY, ROBERT WILLIAM, retired education educator; s. A. Paul and I. Idell Seney. BA, U. Mo., Columbia, 1960; MDiv, Nashotah Ho., Wis., 1965; EdD, U. Houston, Tex., 1987. Adj. instr. U. Houston, 1985—87; coord. gifted programs Spring Branch Ind. Sch. Dist., Houston, 1987—92; asst. prof., chair gifted edn. La Mar U., Beaumont, Tex., 1992—93; prof. Miss. U. Women, Columbus, Miss., 1993—2006, prof. emeritus, 2006—. Dir. Miss. Gov.'s Sch., Columbus, 1996—2006; sec. Nat. Conf. Gov.'s Schs., Washington, 1997—2004; chmn. World Conf. for Gifted and Talented Children, New Orleans, 2002—05; coord. grad. programs Miss. U. Women, 2000—06. Contbr. articles to profl. jours. Bd. dirs. Columbus Arts Coun., 1997—2006. Capt. USAR, 1960—62. Mem.: Nat. Assn. Gifted Children (bd. dirs. 2002—05, Bd. Members Appreciation award 2005), Nat. Conf. Gov.'s Schs. (life; sec. 1997—2005, The Jim Bray and Lillian Press Lifetime Contribution to Gifted Edn. award 2005). Episcopalian. Avocations: skiing, travel, cooking, reading, hiking. Home: 892 West Second Ave Mancos CO 81328 Home Phone: 970-533-9104.

SENFT, MASON GEORGE, musician; b. Bklyn., Nov. 1, 1942; s. Arthur and Ann (Nagel) S. BA cum laude, Adelphi U., 1964. Pvt. practice accompanist/vocal coach, Roslyn Heights, NY, 1964—. Tchr. Adelphi U., Garden City, NY, 1964-73; dir. Nat. Scholastic Aptitude Tng. Inst., Garden City, 1966-69; musical dir. Tibbits Opera House, Coldwater, Mich., 1972-73, Canal Fulton Playhouse, Ohio, 1974-84, Island Lyric Opera, Garden City, 1980—, A Small Co. in America, Glen Cove, NY, 1984—; cons. Island Chamber Symphony Orch., Glen Head, NY, 1985—, Nat. Grand Opera, Tilles Ctr., Greenvale, NY, 1988—, PBS TV spl. Christmas with Flicka, 1988, Dark Summer debut by Christine Berl, Lincoln Ctr. Chamber Soc., Alice Tully Hall, NY, 1989, Glimmerglass Opera, 1992—; accompanist to Frederica von Stade 350th Convocation Celebration, Harvard U., Cambridge, Mass., 1986; accompanist ARC benefit concert In Concert, Carnegie Hall, 1989, Met. Opera Gala, NYC, 1994; music coach The Aspern Papers, Dallas Opera, debut 1988; cons. NY Virtuoso Chamber Symphony, 1989—; music coach DiCapo Opera Co., 1975-90; accompanist in concert in honor of Queen Margrethe II of Sweden, The White House, 1991, hist. gala concert at Steinway Hall, NY, 1991, gala concert for Met. Opera Four Seasons Hotel, 1993. Author: Chimera, 1997, Elusive Thought, 1998, Windows, 1998; orchestrator: (films) Liberty Heights, 1998; prodr.: (CD) A Memorial Tribute-To the Fallen Heroes of September 11, 2001, Three Tenors-Home for the Holidays, 2004; musician (with violinist Jeremy Cushman): (TV broadcast) Madison Sq. Garden, NYC, 2003. Apptd. to the Rep. Presdl. Task Force, 2001. Recipient citation for lifetime achievement NY State Assembly, 1994. Mem. Musicians Union Local 802, LI Singers Soc. (accompanist 1985-96), Mensa. Avocations: travel, writing, metaphysics. Home: 18 Osborne Ln Greenvale NY 11548 Personal E-mail: msenft@optonline.net.

SENG, COLEEN JOY, mayor; b. Council Bluffs, Iowa, Feb. 8, 1936; d. Otis A. and Helen V. (Anderson) McElwain; m. Darrel E. Seng, Oct. 22, 1960 (dec. 1993); children: Marcee Lee, Christopher Charles, Phillip Scott. BA, Nebr. Wesleyan U., 1958. Dist. dir. Girl Scouts U.S.A., Saginaw, Mich., 1958-60, Lincoln, Nebr., 1960-62; cmty. ministry 1st United Meth. Ch., Lincoln, 1977-97; mem. Lincoln City Coun., 1987—2003; mayor City of Lincoln, 2003—07. Mem. Mayor's first multi-cultural task force, co-chair of Gov. Nelson's urban adv. team, chmn. railroad transp. safety dist. Lincoln/Lancaster county joint budget com., mem. Lincoln/Lancaster county homeless coalition; active U. Place Cmty. Orgn. N.E. Family Resource Ctr.; past chair Lincoln/Lancaster county family resource ctr. bd.; past pres. Lincoln Fellowship of Chs.; mem. Lincoln Interfaith Coun.; mem Lincoln Urban Ministries com.; past pres. Homestead Girl Scouts Coun. Democrat. United Methodist. Avocations: reading, movies, gardening. Home: 6101 Walker Ave Lincoln NE 68507-2467 Office: County City Bldg 555 S 10th St Lincoln NE 68508-2810 Office Phone: 402-441-7511.

SENGER, JEFFREY M., lawyer; b. 1962; AB magna cum laude, Harvard U.; JD cum laude, Harvard Law Sch. Law clerk for Hon. Earl B. Gilliam U.S. Dist. Ct., So. Dist. Calif.; dir. training civil and appellate dept. lawyers U.S. Dept. Justice; sr. trial atty.; spl. asst. U.S. atty. U.S. Dept. Justice, asst. U.S. atty., sr. coun. Office Dispute Resolution, sr. coun., office assoc. atty. gen.; dep. chief coun. US FDA. Fed. mediator U.S. Dist. Ct.; civil, family, and criminal misdemeanor mediator Superior Ct., Washington, DC; arbitrator Better Bus. Bur., DC Bar Assn.; tchr. negotiations Harvard Law Sch.; tchr. trial techniques Nat. Inst. Trial Advocacy, Harvard Law Sch. Author: Federal Dispute Resolution: Using ADR with the United States Government; contbr. chapters to books, articles to law jours. Fellow: Am. Bar Found.; mem.: Am. Law Inst. Office: FDA 5600 Fishers Ln Rockville MD 20857

SENGERS, JOHANNA M. H. LEVELT, physicist; b. Amsterdam, The Netherlands, Mar. 4, 1929; arrived in US, 1963, naturalized, 1977; m. Jan V., 1963; 4 children. Drs, U. Amsterdam, 1954, PhD in Physics, 1958; PhD (hon.), Delft U. Tech., 1992. Rsch. assoc. U. Amsterdam, Van der Waals Lab. 1954-58, 59-63, U. Wis., Inst. Theoretical Chemistry, Madison, 1958-59; physicist heat divsn. Inst. Basic Stds., Nat. Bur. Stds., Gaithersburg, Md., 1963-78; group leader thermophysics divsn. Nat. Engring. Lab., 1978-87; sr. fellow thermophysics divsn. Nat. Inst. Standards and Tech., 1983-95, fellow emeritus, 1995—. Lectr Cath. U., Louvain, Belgium, 1971; rsch. assoc. Inst. Theoretical Physics, U. Amsterdam, 1974—75; regent's prof. chemistry U. Calif., LA, 1982; Alexander von Humboldt rschr. Ruhr U., Bochum, 1991; co-chair inter acad. coun. adv. panel Women for Sci., 2005—06. Author: How Fluid Unmix: Discoveries by the School of Van der Waals and Kamerlingh Onnes, 2002. Chair working group A Internat. Assn. Properties Steam, 1985-90; pres. Internat. Assn. Properties Water and Steam, 1991-92. Recipient Silver medal U.S. Dept. Commerce, 1972, Gold medal, 1978, Wise award Interagy. Com. Women in Sci. and Engring., 1985, Alexander von Humboldt Rsch. award Alexander von Humboldt-Stiftung, Bonn, Germany, 1991, L'Oreal-UNESCO Women in Sci. award, 2003. Fellow: AAAS, ASME (Yeram S. Touloukian award 2006), Am. Phys. Soc., Internat. Assn. Properties Water and Steam (hon.); mem.: AIChE, Assn. Women in Sci., Royal Holland Soc. of Scis. and Humanities, Dutch Phys. Soc., Netherlands Royal Acad. Arts and Sci. (corr.), European Phys. Soc., Nat. Acad. Engring., Nat. Acad. Sci., Cosmos Club. Democrat. Unitarian Universalist. Office: Phys & Chem Properties Div Nat Inst Stds & Tech 100 Bureau Dr Stop 8380 Gaithersburg MD 20899-8380 Home Phone: 301-424-8089; Office Phone: 301-975-2463. Business E-Mail: johanna.sengers@nist.gov.

SENGPIEHL, PAUL MARVIN, lawyer, former state official; b. Stuart, Nebr., Oct. 10, 1937; s. Arthur Paul and Anne Marie (Andersen) S.; B.A., Wheaton (Ill.) Coll., 1959; M.A. in Pub. Adminstrn., Mich. State U., 1961; J.D., Ill. Inst. Tech.-Chgo. Kent Coll. Law, 1970; m. June S. Cline, June 29, 1963; children— Jeffrey D., Chrystal M. Bar: Ill. 1971, U.S. Supreme Ct. 1982. Adminstrv. asst. Chgo. Dept. Urban Renewal, 1962-65; supr. Ill. Municipal Retirement Fund, Chgo., 1966-71; mgmt. officer Ill. Dept. Local Govt. Affairs, Springfield, 1971-72, legal counsel, Chgo., 1972-73; spl. asst. atty. gen. Ill. Dept. Labor, Chgo., 1973-76; asst. atty. gen. Ct. of Claims div. Atty. Gen. of Ill., 1976-83; hearing referee Bd. Rev., Ill. Dept. Labor, 1983-84; local govt. law columnist Chgo. Daily Law Bull., 1975-84; instr. polit. sci. Judson Coll., Elgin, Ill., 1963. Republican candidate for Cook County Recorder of Deeds, 1984; dep. committeeman Oak Park Twp Rep. Orgn.; elected alt. del., served del. Rep. Nat. Conv., 1992; People's Choice candidate pres. Oak Park Village, 1993; Rep. alt. state ctrl. committeeman 7th Congl. Dist., Oak Park Twp., 1994-98; elected del. Rep. Nat. Convention, 1996; co-chmn. Cook County Jail Ministry Bd., chmn. 2003—; treas. Cook County Correctional Chaplaincy Coun., 2003-06, chmn., 2006-. Mem. Ill. Bar Assn. (local govt. law sect. council 1973-79, vice chmn. 1976-77, co-editor local govt. newsletter 1976-77, chmn. 1977-78, editor newsletter 1977-78, state tax sect. council 1979-82, 84-85), Chgo. Bar Assn. (local govt. com., chmn. legis. subcom. 1978-79, sec. 1979-80, vice chmn. 1980-81, chmn. 1981-82, state and mcpl. tax com.), John Ericsson Rep. League Ill. (state sec. 1983-85, 95—, hon. past pres. Cook County 1982-97, pres. 1997—), Oak Park-River Forest C. of C. (small bus. coun. 1991-00). Baptist (vice chmn. deacons 1973-76, 79-80, moderator 1983-86, supt. Sunday sch. 1986-93). Home and Office: 727 N Ridgeland Ave Oak Park IL 60302-1735 Office Phone: 708-383-8859. Business E-Mail: sengpiehllaw@aol.com.

SENGUPTA, ABHIJIT, molecular and optical physicist; PhD, Stanford U., 1995. Rsch. asst. Stanford U., Calif., 1989—95; NSF postdoctoral fellow Mass. Inst. Tech., Cambridge, Mass., 1995—97; rsch. scientist Eastman Kodak Co., Rochester, NY, 1997—99; asst. prof., rsch. Jefferson Lab. Consortium, Old Dominion U., Norfolk, Va., 1999—2001; sr. scientist, project leader Bell Labs., Lucent Tech., Norcross, Ga., 2001—02, OFS, Norcross, Ga., 2002—03; prin. rsch. scientist SYSTIMAX Solutions, Richardson, Tex., 2004—; founder, pres. FEMTONIX, Alpharetta, Ga., 2003—. Vis. scientist Inst. Optics, U. Rochester, 1998—99; adj. asst. prof., physics Old Dominion U., 1999—2003, adj. asst. prof., elec. computer engring., 1999—2001; cons. SOLAREX, Toano, Va., 1999—2000, Laser Ctr. Va., Ctr. Anti-Aging Rsch., Va. Beach., 2000—01; panel reviewer NSF, Arlington, Va., 1999—2000; peer reviewer Internat. Sci. Tech. Ctr., Wash., DC, 2000—. One-man shows include Stanford U. Tressidor Union Gallery; co-author: Laser Techniques in Chemistry, 1995. Recipient Innovation award, Va. Ctr. Innovative Tech., 2000, US Patent award in Optical Comms. Mem.: AAAS, OSA, IEEE. Office Phone: 678-528-5109. E-mail: asengupta@femtonix.com.

SENGUPTA, ARUP KUMAR, engineering educator, researcher; b. Calcutta, Bengal, India, June 11, 1951; came to US, 1980; s. Ajay K. and Ranu S.; m. Susmita Chanda, Jan. 19, 1983; 1 child, Neal. BSChemE, Jadavpur U., Calcutta, 1973; MS in Environ. Engring., U. Houston, 1982, PhD in Environ. Engring., 1984. Registered profl. engr., Pa. Process devel. engr. Kuljian Corp., Phila. and Calcutta, 1973-80; grad. rsch. asst. U. Houston, 1980-84; asst. prof. Lehigh U., Bethlehem, Pa., 1985—90, assoc. prof., 1990—94, prof., 1994—, chair dept. civil and environ. engring., 1998—2005. Contbr. articles to profl. jours. Co-recipient Grainger Challenge Silver award, NAE, 2007; recipient Indsl. Ecology Fellowship award, NSF and Lucent Technologies, 1999, Profl. Rsch. award, Pa. Water Environment Assn., 2001, Frontier Rsch. award, Assn. Environ. Engring. and Sci. Profs. and Malcolm Pirnie, 2001, Internat. Ion Exch. award in Cambridge U., Soc. Chem. Industry (Separation Sci. and Tech. Divsn.), UK, 2004, Mondialogo Sustainable Engring. award, Daimler-Chyrsler and UNESCO, 2005; grantee, NSF, 1985, 1986, EPA, 1988, 1990. Mem. NSPE, ASCE (Rudolph Hering medal 1994), AIChE, Am. Chem. Soc., Pa. Soc. Profl. Engrs., Assn. Environ. Engring. and Sci. Profs., Sigma Xi. Avocations: playing tennis, reading history. Office: Dept Civil and Environ Engring Lehigh U 13 E Packer Ave Bethlehem PA 18015 Office Phone: 610-758-3534. E-mail: arup.sengupta@lehigh.edu. *

SENGUPTA, CHAITALI, computer engineer; BS in Tech., Indian Inst. Tech., Kharagpur, 1992; MS in Elec. and Computer Engring., Rice U., 1995, PhD in Elec. and Computer Engring., 1999. Sr. mem. tech. staff Texas Instruments, Inc. Contbr. articles to profl. jours. Named one of Top 100 Young Innovators, MIT Tech. Review, 2004. Office: Texas Insuments Inc MS8723 12500 Texas Instruments Blvd Dallas TX 75243-4136

SENHAUSER, JOHN CRATER, architect; b. New Philadelphia, Ohio, Apr. 7, 1947; s. Edwin Crater and Margaret Jean (Huffman) S.; m. Teri A. Schleyer, June 25, 1988. BS in Architecture, U. Cin., 1971. Registered architect, Ohio, Ky., Fla. Designer Jones, Peacock, Garn & Ptnrs., Cin., 1971-72; project architect Smith Stevens Architects, Cin., 1972-76; project mgr. Herrlinger Enterprises, Cin., 1976-79; prin., owner John C. Senhauser, Architect, Cin., 1979—. Adj. assoc. prof. Sch. Architecture and Interior Design, U. Cin., 1992-98 Exhibited in group shows at Toni Birckhead Gallery, 1990, Contemporary Arts Ctr., Cin., 1993, 98, Canton (Ohio) Art Inst., 1993; prin. works include residences. Mem. historic conservation bd. City of Cin., 1986-98, chmn. 1998—; mem. urban design rev. bd., 1998—; mem. dean's adv. coun. Coll. Design Architecture Art and Planning U. Cin., 1990; mem. design rev. com. U. Cin., 1997—. Recipient Merit award Builder mag., 1985, 88, 94, 96, 99, Grand award, 1990, Grand Best in Region award Profl. Builder, 1988, 90, Grand award for Best Overall Design, Custom Home Mag., 1996, 97, Merit award, 1990, 94, other awards. Fellow AIA (pres. 1991, Honor award Cin. chpt. 1983, 85, 90-96, 2000, 04, Merit award 1990, 93-94); mem. AIA Ohio (bd. dirs., sec. 1997-98, v.p. 1999, pres. 2000, regional dir. nat. bd. dirs. 2001—03, Inst. sec. 2005-06, Honor award 1985, 90-91, 93-94, 99, 2003-04) Office: John Senhauser Architects 1118 Saint Gregory St Cincinnati OH 45202-1724

SENIA, GRACE MELANIE, language and music educator; d. Gibson Kenyon Davis and Gertrude Mae Cook; m. Anthony Joseph Senia, June 26, 1971; children: Carmella Grace Bullick, Filene Marie Travis. BA, U. Buffalo, 1965; MS in Reading summa cum laude, Marywood U., 2001; postgrad., SUNY, Binghamton. Cert. tchr. Latin and English NY, 1974, tchr. Latin Pa., 1980, English Pa., 1990, instr. reading NY, 2001, tchr. Latin NJ, 2001. Tchr. Latin and English Greene Ctrl. Sch., NY, 1964—68; tchr. English East HS, Rochester, NY, 1970—71, Hancock Ctrl. Sch., NY, 1971—87; tchr. Latin and English Scranton HS, Pa., 1993—94, Honesdale HS, Pa., 1999; adj. tchr. SUNY, Binghamton, 2001; instr. Latin Binghamton City HS, 2005—. Tchr. after sch. program Hancock Cmty. Edn. Found.,

2003—06. Past conf. del. Emory United Meth. Ch. Mem.: Internat. Honor Soc. in Edn., Nat. Scholar's Honor Soc., Kappa Delta Pi. Avocations: piano, golf. Home: 257 E Main St Hancock NY 13783 Office: Binghamton City Sch Dist 31 Main St Hancock NY 13783 Home Phone: 607-637-2695; Office Phone: 607-762-8200.

SENIOR, DONALD PAUL, religious organization administrator; b. Phila., Jan. 1, 1940; s. Vincent Edward and Margaret (Tiernan) S. BA in Philosophy, Passionist Sem. Coll., Chgo., 1963; Licentiate in Sacred Theology, U. Louvain, Belgium, 1970, STD, 1972. Prof. New Testament Cath. Theol. Union, Chgo., 1972—, dir. Israel program, 1980-88, acting dean, 1986-87, acting pres., 1988, pres., 1988—. Author books and articles on New Testament; assoc. editor The Bible Today, New Theology Rev., New Testament Message (22 vols.); gen. editor The Cath. Study Bible; writer, commentator, host radio and TV programs, Chgo. Mem. Cath. Bibl. Soc. Am., Soc. Bibl. Lit., Soc. for New Testament Studies, Cath. Theol. Soc. Am., Chgo. Soc. Bibl. Rsch. Democrat. Home and Office: 5401 S Cornell Ave Chicago IL 60615-5664

SENIOR, ENRIQUE FRANCISCO, investment banker; b. Havana, Cuba, Aug. 3, 1943; came to U.S., 1960; s. Frank and Dolores (Hernandez) Senior; m. Robin Suffern Gimbel, Sept. 7, 1977; children: Tailer, Heather, Fern, Seanna. BA in Architecture, Yale U., 1964, BS in Elec. Engring., 1967; MBA, Harvard U., 1969. Corp. fin. exec. White, Weld & Co., NYC, 1969-73; v.p. Allen & Co., Inc., NYC, 1973-80, exec. v.p., mng. dir., 1980—. Bd. dirs. Allen & Co., Inc., Televisa S.A. de CV, Coca Cola Femsa, Cinemark Inc. Mem. The Brook Club, Piping Rock Club, Sailfish Club, The Beach Club, Phi Beta Kappa, Tau Beta Pi. Avocations: flying, fishing, hunting, skiing, woodworking. Office: Allen & Co Inc 711 5th Ave Fl 8 New York NY 10022-3111

SENIOR, RICHARD JOHN LANE, linen and uniform services executive; b. Datchet, Eng., July 6, 1940; arrived in U.S., 1972, naturalized, 1977; s. Harold Dennis Senior and Jane Lane Dorothy (Chadwick) Senior Rigg; m. Diana Morgan, Dec. 19, 1966; children: Alden, Alicia, Amanda. BA, Oxford U., 1962, MA, 1966; MIA, Yale U., 1964. Jr. mgr. Tate & Lyle, London, 1964—66; mgmt. cons. McKinsey & Co., Inc., London, Chgo., 1967-74; pres., CEO Morgan Svcs., Inc., Chgo., 1974—2004, chair, CEO, 2004—. Bd. dir. Northwestern Meml. Healthcare, 1992-2001, Chgo. Crime Commn., 1994-99, Ball Hort. Co., 1996-, Near South Planning Bd., 2001-2003, Northwestern Meml. Found., 2001-; regional adv. bd. Kemper Ins. Cos., 1994-96. Pres. bd. trustees Latin Sch., Chgo., 1979-83. Hon. scholar Christ Ch., Oxford U., 1960-1962; Fulbright travel fellow, Yale U., 1962-64. Mem. Uniform and Textile Svc. Assn. (bd. dirs. 1996-99, exec. com. 2001-06, chmn. 2002-04), Textile Rental Svcs. Assn. Am. (pres. 1983-85, dir., exec. com. 1978-86), Northwestern U. Assocs., Racquet Club (bd. govs. 1983-91, 2006—), Chgo. Club, Glen View Club, Casino (bd. govs. 1991-96, treas. 1993-94), Econ. Club, Yale Club Chgo. (bd. dirs. 1991-95, AYA del. 1992-95, chmn. grad. sch. task force 1990-95). Home: 1550 N Lake Shore Dr Chicago IL 60610-6657 Office: Morgan Svcs Inc 323 N Michigan Ave Chicago IL 60601-3798 Office Phone: 312-346-3184. Business E-Mail: senior@morganservices.com.

SENIOR, ROBERT THOMAS, retired military officer; b. Phila., June 18, 1944; s. Matthew John and Julia Mary Senior. Cert. in bus., Pierce Jr. Coll., Phila., 1963; AS, SUNY, Albany, 1980; BA, Widener U., Chester, Pa., 1993, postgrad., 1994. Clk. Phila. Electric, 1963—64; chief hosp. corps USN, 1964—89; combat medic 2d Marine Divsn., Camp LeJeune, NC, 1966, 2d Marine Air Wing, Beaufort, SC, 1966—67, 3d Batallion 1st MAR, Vietnam, 1967—68, USS Coranado, 1977—78, USS Independence, 1979—80, USS Sylvania, 1981—82, 1st Platoon Truck Co., Connellsville, Pa., 1982—85; ret., 1989. EMT, Chgo. Jr. Coll., 1981; ind. med. technician Portsmouth VA Hosp., 1969—85. Vol. USO Phila. Airport. Decorated Combat Action Ribbon, Marine Combat Insignia, 3 Presdl. Unit Citations, 1 Navy Unit Citation, Surface Warfare Pin, Fleet Marine Force Pin. Mem.: KC (4th degree), VFW (Americanism recorder 1991—), DAV (life), Naval Inst., Navy League, Marine Corps League, Am. Vets. (life). Avocations: reading, exercise, volunteer work, music. Home: 201 President Ave Rutledge PA 19070 Personal E-mail: rts0200mail@widener.edu.

SENIOR, THOMAS BRYAN A., electrical engineering educator, researcher, consultant; b. Menston, Yorkshire, Eng., June 26, 1928; arrived in U.S., 1957; s. Thomas Harold and Emily Dorothy (Matthews) Senior; m. Heather Margaret Golby, May 4, 1957; children: Margaret, David, Hazel, Peter. B.Sc., Manchester U., 1949, M.Sc., 1950; PhD, Cambridge U., 1954. Sr. sci. officer Royal Radar Establishment, Malvern, Eng., 1952-57; rsch. scientist U. Mich., Ann Arbor, 1957-69, prof. elec. engring., 1969-84, prof. elec. and computer sci., 1984-98, Arthur F. Thurnau prof., 1990-98, prof. emeritus, 1998—, dir. radiation lab., 1975-87, assoc. chmn. elect. engring. & computer sci. dept., 1984-90, acting chmn., 1987-88, assoc. chmn. acad. affairs, 1991-98. Cons. in field. Author: (with Bowman and Uslenghi) Electromagnetic and Acoustical Scattering by Simple Shapes, 1969; Mathematical Methods in Electrical Engineering, 1986; (with Volakis) Approximate Boundary Conditions in Electromagnetics, 1995; contbr. articles to profl. jours. Fellow IEEE (3d Millennium medal, AP-S Disting. Achievement award 2000); mem. Internat. Sci. Radio Union (chmn. U.S. nat. com. 1982-84, vice chmn. Com. B. 1985-87, chmn. 1988-90, pres. 1996-99, Van der Pol Gold medal 1993). Home: 1919 Ivywood Dr Ann Arbor MI 48103-4527 Office: U Mich Dept Elec Engring Comp S Ann Arbor MI 48109 E-mail: senior@eecs.umich.edu.

SENIORS, PAULA MARIE, history professor, researcher; b. Cleve., Mar. 29, 1963; d. Audrey Proctor and Clarence Henry Seniors. BFA Dance, CCNY, 1985; MA Music, NYU, 1996; MA, PhD Ethnic Studies, U. Calif., San Diego, 2003. Tchg. asst. U. Calif., San Diego, 1998—2003; asst. prof. African Am. studies Coll. NJ, 2005—. Bd. mem. African and African-Am. Studies Rsch. project, San Diego; mem. book award com. Assn. Black Women Historians, Lansing, Mich., 2004—; rschr. Bldg. Curriculum Focused on S.Am. and the Caribbean: United Negro Coll. Fund Spl. Programs, Fla. Meml. Coll., Washington, 2004—; com. mem., rschr. creation history maj. Fla. Meml. Coll., Miami, 2004—; rschr. San Diego Urban League; presenter at confs. Contbr. book manuscripts for profl. seminars. Facilitator, organizer Themes in African Am., U.S. History, and Contemporary Soc. Student Conf. Fla. Meml. Coll., Miami, 2003—. Thelma Hill Meml. Dance scholar, CCNY, 1982, fellow, Dept. Ethnic Studies, U. Calif. San Diego, 1998—2002. Mem.: Nat. Coun. for Black Studies, Am. Studies Assn., Assn. Black Women Historians (book award com. 2004—), Assn. Study African Am. Life, Am. Hist. Assn. Avocation: rollerblading. Home Phone: 609-882-6837. Personal E-mail: pseniors@comcast.net. E-mail: seniors@tcnj.edu.

SENKLER, ROBERT L., insurance company executive; BA in Math. and Stats., Minn. Duluth Coll., 1974. Began Minn. Life Ins. Co., 1974—, v.p. Individual Ins. Divsn., 1987-94; pres. Securian Fin. Group (Minn. Life Ins. Co.), 1994—2007, CEO, 1994—, chmn., 1995—. Past chmn. Ins. Fed. Minn.; pres. Minn. Bus. Prtnrshp., 2003; chmn. Cap. City Partnership. Recipient Univ. Minn.-Duluth Acad. Sci. Engring., 2003. Fellow Soc. Actuaries. Office: Securian Fin Group 400 Robert St N Saint Paul MN 55101-2015 *

SENNEMA, DAVID CARL, arts consultant; b. Grand Rapids, Mich., July 6, 1934; s. Carl Edward and Alice Bertha (Bieri) S.; m. Martha Amanda Dixon, Feb. 22, 1958; children: Daniel Ross, Julia Kathryn, Alice Dixon. BA, Albion Coll., 1956. Mgr. Columbia Music Festival Assn., 1964-67; exec. dir. S.C. Arts Commn., Columbia, 1967-70; assoc. dir. Fed.-State Partnership and Spl. Projects program Nat. Endowment for the Arts, Washington, 1971-73; prof. arts adminstrn., dir. cmty. arts mgmt. program Sangamon State U., Springfield, Ill., 1973-76; dir. SC State Mus., Columbia, 1976-85; bus. mgr. Palmetto Mastersingers, 1986—2004. Cons. in field. Co-author: Columbia, S.C. A Postcard History, 1997. Mem. adv. panel Nat. Endowment for the Arts Music, 1968-70; chmn. Springfield Arts Commn., 1975-76. Served with U.S. Army, 1957-58. Named to Order of Palmetto, SC, 1986; recipient Verner Lifetime Achievement award, 2006. Mem. Rotary. Avocation: singing. Office Phone: 803-782-3581. Personal E-mail: dsennema@sc.rr.com.

SENNET, CHARLES JOSEPH, lawyer; b. Buffalo, Aug. 7, 1952; s. Saunders M. and Muriel S. (Rotenberg) S. AB magna cum laude, Cornell U., 1974; JD with high honors, George Washington U., 1979. Bar: Ill. 1979, U.S. Dist. Ct. (no. dist.) Ill. 1979, U.S. Ct. Appeals (7th cir.) 1982, U.S. Ct. Appeals (D.C. cir.) 1993. Assoc. Reuben & Proctor, Chgo., 1979-83; assoc. counsel Tribune Co., Chgo., 1984-91, sr. counsel, 1991—. Adj. faculty Medill Sch. Journalism, Northwestern U., 1991-94, 2004—; chmn. Television Music Lic. Com., 1995—. Contbr. articles to profl. jours. Chmn. cable royalty distbn. com. Nat. Assn. Broadcasters, 2005—. Mem. ABA (spkr. 1984-88, 91-97, 2000—, mem. gov. bd. Forum on Comms. Law 1995-98), NATAS, Ill. Bar Assn. (chmn. media law com. 1989-91), Chgo. Bar Assn., Fed. Comms. Bar Assn. Office: Tribune Co 435 N Michigan Ave Chicago IL 60611-4066 E-mail: csennet@tribune.com.

SENNETT, JOHN O., lawyer; b. Broken Bow, Nebr., Apr. 10, 1948; BS, Univ. Nebr., 1970, JD, 1972. Bar: Nebr. 1972, US Dist. Ct. (Dist. Nebr.) 1972, US Supreme Ct. 1975, US Ct. Appeals (8th Cir.) 1976. Ptnr. Sennett Duncan Borders & Jenkins PC, LLO, Broken Bow, Nebr. Mem.: ABA, Assn. of Trial Lawyers of Am., Nebr. Trial Lawyers Assn., Custer County Bar Assn., Nebr. State Bar Assn. (Ho. of Del. 1986—92, chmn. 1991—92, bd. trustees 1992—98, pres. 2004—05). Office: Sennett Duncan Borders & Jenkins PC LLO 425 S 7th St Broken Bow NE 68822 Office Phone: 308-872-6868. Office Fax: 308-872-2191. Business E-Mail: jsennett@adb-law.com. *

SENNETT, MICHAEL, lawyer; b. Chgo., Oct. 24, 1951; BA with honors, Quincy U., 1973; JD cum laude, Loyola U., 1977. Bar: Ill. 1977, (US Supreme Ct.) 1984. Assoc. Bell, Boyd & Lloyd, Chgo., 1977—83, ptnr., 1984—; chair antitrust and trade regulation Bell, Boyd & Lloyd, LLP, Chgo., 1996—. Exec. editor Loyola U. Chgo. Law Jour., 1976—77; adj. law faculty Loyola U., 1996—; bd. advisors Inst. for Consumer Antitrust Law Studies, Chgo., 1998—. Contbr. chpt. to book. Trustee Children's Home and Aid Soc. of Ill., Inc., Chgo., 2004—, Quincy U., Ill., 2006—. Mem.: Internat. Bar Assn., Chgo. Bar Assn. (chair, antitrust law com. 1996—97), ABA, Lawyers Club Chgo. Office: Bell Boyd & Lloyd LLP 70 W Madison St Ste 3100 Chicago IL 60602 Home Phone: 847-920-0231; Office Phone: 312-807-4243. Office Fax: 312-827-8161. E-mail: msennett@bellboyd.com.

SENNETT, NANCY J., lawyer; b. Milw., Nov. 26, 1951; BS in English & comm. arts with honors, U. Wis., 1973; JD cum laude, Northwestern U., 1979. Bar: Wis. 1979. With Foley & Lardner LLP, Milw., 1979—, chair securities litig. practice group, mng. ptnr. Milw. office. Chair merit selection com. reappointment magistrate judges Ea. Dist. Wis. Notes and comments editor Northwestern U. Law Rev., 1978-79. Active Jr. Achievement. Mem.: ABA (securities litig. com.), Securities Industry Assn. (compliance & legal divsn.), State Wis. Bar Assn., Milw. Bar Assn. (Lawyer Year 2003), ABCD, Inc. (bd. dirs.), Betty Brinn Children's Mus. (founding bd. dirs.), Greater Milw. Com., Tempo & Rotary, U. Wis. Alumni Assn. (bd. dirs., Distinguished Alumni Award 2003). Office: Foley & Lardner LLP US Bank Ctr 777 E Wisconsin Ave Milwaukee WI 53202-5367 Office Phone: 414-297-5522. Business E-Mail: nsennett@foley.com.

SENSENBRENNER, F(RANK) JAMES, JR., congressman; b. Chgo., June 14, 1943; s. F. James and Margaret Sensenbrenner; m. Cheryl Warren, Mar. 26, 1977; children: F. James III, Robert Alan. AB in Polit. Sci., Stanford U., 1965; JD, U. Wis., Madison, 1968. Bar: Wis. 1968, US Supreme Ct. 1972. State rep. Wis. State Assembly, Madison, 1969-75; mem. Wis. State Senate, Madison, 1975-79, asst. minority leader, 1976-79; mem. US Congress from 5th Wis. dist., 1979—, chmn. sci. com., 1997—2001, chmn. judiciary com., 2001—07. Mem. Friends of Milw. Mus., Riveredge Nature Ctr. Mem. Am. Philatelic Soc., Chenequa Country Club, Capitol Hill Club. Republican. Office: US Ho Reps 2449 Rayburn Ho Office Bldg Washington DC 20515-4905 Office Phone: 202-225-5101.

SENSENIG, DAVID MARTIN, retired surgeon; b. May 4, 1921; s. Wayne and Elizabeth Long (Crawford) S.; m. Constance Campbell, June 6, 1947; children: Philip Campbell, David Martin, Andrew Wilson, Thomas O'Brien; m. Bernice Evans, Dec. 20, 1975. BS, Haverford Coll., 1942; postgrad., U. Pa., 1942-43; MD, Harvard U., 1945; JD, Temple U., 1998. Diplomate Am. Bd. Surgery, Am. Bd. Thoracic Surgery. Rotating intern Allentown (Pa.) Hosp., 1945-46; surg. ho. officer, jr. asst. resident Peter Bent Brigham Hosp., Boston, 1948-50; sr. asst. resident, resident surgeon New Eng. Ctr. Hosp., Boston, 1950-52; surg. resident Westfield (Mass.) State Sanatorium, 1952-53; asst. chief surg. svc., dir. surg. rsch. lab. VA Med. Tchg. Group Hosp., Memphis, 1953-55; asst. chief surg. svc. VA Hosp., Albany, N.Y., 1955-57; resident in thoracic and cardiac surgery Univ. Hosp. State U. Iowa, Iowa City, 1957-59, instr. in surgery, 1957-58, assoc. in surgery, 1958-59, from asst. prof. to assoc. prof., 1960-62; chief thoracic surgery sect. VA Hosp., Phila., 1959-60, asst. chief surg. svc., 1963-66; cardiothoracic surgeon Pa. Hosp., Phila., 1962-63; asst. prof. surgery U. Pa., Phila., 1962-66, supr. Animal Rsch. Lab., 1963-66; pvt. practice medicine specializing in surgery Bangor, Maine, 1966-88; attending surgeon Ea. Maine Med. Ctr., Bangor, 1966-88, St. Joseph Hosp., Bangor, 1966-88, chief surg. svc., 1974-79, VA Hosp., Togus, Maine, 1988-95, ret., 1995. Contbr. articles to profl. jours. Capt. US Army, 1943—48. Mem. ACS (gov. at large 1985-91), Am. Thoracic Soc., Internat. Cardiovasc. Soc., Am. Geriatric Soc., Am. Coll. Chest Physicians, New Eng. Surg. Soc., New Eng. Soc. Vascular Surgery v.p. 1991), Maine Vascular Soc. (pres. 1978), Iowa Acad. Surgery, Pa. Assn. Thoracic Surgery, N. Am. Soc. Pacing and Electrophysiology, Penobscot County Med. Soc. (pres. 1974), Phila. Acad. Surgery, Bangor Med. Club (pres. 1970). Republican. Lutheran. Home: 101 Sunset Dr Lansdale PA 19446-1706 Personal E-mail: daverski@aol.com.

SENSIPER, SAMUEL, electrical engineer; b. Elmira, NY, Apr. 26, 1919; s. Louis and Molly (Pedolsky) S.; m. Elaine Marie Zwick, Sept. 10, 1950; children: Martin, Sylvia, David. BSEE, MIT, 1939, ScD, 1951; EE, Stanford U., 1941. Asst. project engr. to sr. project engr., cons. Sperry Gyroscope, Garden City, Great Neck, NY, 1941-51; sect. head and sr. staff cons. Hughes Aircraft, Culver City, Malibu, Calif., 1951-60; lab. divsn. mgr. Space Gen. Corp., Glendale, Azuza, L.A., 1960—67; lab. mgr. TRW, Redondo Beach, Calif., 1967—70; cons. elec. engr. LA, 1970—73; dir. engring. Transco Products, Venice, Calif., 1973—75; cons. elec. engr. in pvt. practice LA, 1975—95; cons., 1995—. Faculty U. So. Calif., L.A., 1955-56, 79-80. Contbr. articles to profl. jours.; patentee in field. Recipient Cert. of Commendation U.S. Navy, 1946; indsl. electronics fellow MIT, 1947-48. Fellow IEEE, AAAS; mem. Calif. Soc. Profl. Engrs., MIT Alumni Assn., Stanford Alumni Assn., Electromagnetics Acad., Sigma Xi, Eta Kappa Nu. Home and Office: 215 Moreton Bay Ln # 2 Goleta CA 93117-2206 Office Phone: 805-967-9264. Personal E-mail: sensiper1@ieee.org.

SENTELLE, DAVID BRYAN, federal judge; b. Canton, NC, Feb. 12, 1943; s. Horace Richard Jr. and Maude (Ray) Sentelle; m. Jane LaRue Oldham, June 19, 1965; children: Sharon Lewis, Regan Herman, Rebecca Acheson. BA, U. NC, 1965, JD with honors, 1968. Bar: NC 1968, NC (US Dist. Ct. (we. dist.)) 1969, (US Ct. Appeals (4th cir.)) 1970. Assoc. Uzzell & Dumont, Asheville, NC, 1968—70; asst. US atty. (we. dist.) NC US Dept. Justice, 1970—74; dist. judge City of Charlotte, NC, 1974—77; ptnr. Tucker, Hicks, Sentelle, Moon & Hodge, P.A., Charlotte, 1977—85; judge US Dist. Ct. (we. dist.) NC, Charlotte, 1985—87, US Ct. Appeals (DC cir.), 1987—. Adj. prof UNC, 1991—92; adj. prof. Fla. State U. Coll. Law, 1993; presiding judge Spl. Divsn. for Appointment of Ind. Counsels, 1992—; Disting. adj. prof. Geroge Mason U. Sch. Law. Contbr. articles to profl. jours. Chmn. Mecklenburg County Rep. Com., 1978—80, NC State Rep. Conv., 1979—80. Fellow, Dameron Found., 1967. Mem.: Mecklenburg County Bar Assn., Shriners, Masons (Scottish Rite), Am. Inn of Ct. Found. (bd. dir.), Edward Bennett Williams Inn of Ct. (pres.). Baptist. Office: US Court of Appeals 333 Constitution Ave NW Washington DC 20001-2866 *

SENTENNE, JUSTINE, corporate ombudsman consultant; b. Montreal, Que., Can. d. Paul Emile and Irene Genevieve (Laliberte) Sentenne. MBA, U. Que., Montreal, 1993; postgrad., McGill U., Ecole Nat. d'Adminstrn. Publique, 1989—91. Fin. analyst, assoc. mgr. portfolio Bush Assocs., Montreal, 1970-82; city councillor, mem. exec. com. City of Montreal and Montreal Urban Com., 1978-82; adminstrv. asst. Montreal Conv. Ctr., 1983; dir. sponsorship Ctrl. Com. for Montreal Papal Visit, 1984; dir. pub. rels. Coopers & Lybrand, Montreal, 1985-87; exec. dir. Que. Heart Found., 1987-89; corp. ombudsman Hydro-Que, Montreal, 1991—. Tchr. DSA program Concordia U.; mem. jury John Labatt Ltd., London, 1982—86. V.p., bd. dirs. Armand Frappier Found., Canada, Chateau Dufresne Mus. Decorative Arts, Montreal, 1985—90; chmn. bd. dirs. Wilfrid Pelletier Found., Montreal, 1986—91; bd. govs. Youth and Music Can., Montreal, 1981—86; chmn. bd. dirs. Women's Ctr., Montreal, 1986—88, Vol. Bur. Montreal, 1986—87; bd. dirs. Palais des Congres de Montreal, 1981—89, Port of Montreal, 1983—84, Can. Ctr. Ecumenism, Montreal, 1968—85, 2006—, Montreal Diet Dispensary, 1989—2001, treas., 1996; bd. mgmt. Saidye Bronfman Ctr. Arts, 1994—99; Notre Dame de Grace v.p. riding assn. Liberal Party of Can., chairperson women's commn., 2000—; mem. exec. com. Ville Marie Liberl Party of Can.; bd. dirs. Pathways to Faith, 1990—2000. Named Career Woman of the Yr., Sullivan Bus. Coll., 1979; recipient Silver medal, ville de Paris, 1981, Women's Kansas City Assn. Internat. Rels. and Trade medal, 1982. Fellow: Montreal Soc. Investment Analysts, Inst. Fin. Analysts, Fin. Analysts Fedn. N.Y.; mem.: Health and Welfare Svcs. Ctr. Cavendish (chair, bd. dirs. 2004—06), Internat. Ombudsman Assn. (bd. dirs. 1996—99, 2000—03, founding mem. Forum of Can. Ombudsmen, bd. dirs. 2001—, sec.). Roman Catholic.

SENTER, LYONEL THOMAS, JR., federal judge; b. Fulton, Miss., July 30, 1933; s. L. T. and Eva Lee (Jetton) S. BS, U. So. Miss., Hattiesburg, 1956; LLB, U. Miss., Oxford, 1959. Bar: Miss. 1959. Pros. atty. Aberdeen County, 1960—64; U.S. commr. US Dist. Ct. (no. dist.) Miss., 1966—68; judge Miss. Cir. Ct. First jud. Dist., 1968—80, US Dist. Ct. (no. dist.) Miss., 1980—82, chief judge, 1982—98, sr. judge, 1998—. Mem. Miss. State Bar Office: 2012 15th St Ste 514 Gulfport MS 39501 Office Phone: 228-563-1755. Business E-Mail: lt_senter@mssd.uscourts.gov.

SENTHIL NATHAN, SELVARAJ, internist, geriatrician; b. Madras, India, July 11, 1957; s. Selvaraj and Duraichi Chellappa. MBBS, Madras U., 1981, MD, 1984, DM, 1989. Diplomate Am. Bd. Internal Medicine, Am. Bd. Geriatrics., Am. Bd. Hospice and Palliative Medicine; cert. med. rev. officer; bd. cert. in hospice and palliative medicine. Resident in internal medicine Stanley Med. Coll., Madras, 1981-84; fellow in pathology Madras Med. Coll., 1985-87; fellow in oncology Cancer Inst., Madras, 1987-89; resident in internal medicine Eng., Ireland, 1990-93; resident in interneral medicine U. Medicine and Dentistry of N.J., 1993-95; fellow in internal medicine/geriatrics U. Tex. Med. Br., Galveston, 1995-96; physician internal medicine and geriatrics Cmty. Action Orgn. of Lawrence County, 1996-97; med. dir. Holzer Sr. Care Ctr., Bidwell, Ohio, 1997—. Cons. internal medicine and geriat. Holzer Med. Ctr., Gallipolis, Ohio; clin. asst. prof. dept. family and cmty. health Marshall U. Sch. Medicine, Huntington, W.V. Fellow Acad. Medicine of N.J.; mem. ACP. Avocations: surfing, computers, alternative medicine research. Office: 90 Jackson Pike Gallipolis OH 45631-1560

SENTY, JAMES A., energy executive; BS metallurgical and mining engring., Univ. Wis. Chmn. bd. Western Gas Resources, Inc., 2003—. Chmn. State Wis. Investment Bd.; chmn. bd., pres. Midwest Bottle Gas Co.; chmn. Park Bark, Madison, Wis.

SENZEL, MARTIN LEE, lawyer; b. Rochester, NY, June 21, 1944; s. Albert Benjamin and Besse (Lipson) S.; m. Dagni Maren Belgum, Feb. 17, 1979; 1 child, Whitney. BA, Yale U., 1966, LLB, 1969. Bar: N.Y. 1971, U.S. Dist. Ct. (so. dist.) N.Y., U.S. Ct. Appeals (2nd cir.) 1973. Assoc. Cravath, Swaine & Moore LLP, NYC, 1969—77, ptnr., 1977—2000. Bd. dir. Medinol Ltd. Mem.: ABA, N.Y. State Bar Assn., Assn. Bar City N.Y. Home: Apt 4-E 101 Central Park W New York NY 10023-4204 Office: Cravath Swaine & Moore LLP Worldwide Plz 825 8th Ave Fl 38 New York NY 10019-7475 Office Phone: 212-474-1520. E-mail: msenzel@cravath.com.

SEOK, JAEWOOK, materials scientist, polymer scientist; s. Jong Ku Seok and Qyu Sun Song; m. Su Jin Kim, Oct. 10, 1974; 1 child, Yeon Seo. BEng in Polymer Sci., Kyungpook Nat. U., Taegu, Republic of Korea, 1997, MEng in Polymer Sci., 1999; MEng in Materials Sci. and Engring., Cornell U., Ithaca, NY, 2006; postgrad., NC State U., Raleigh, 2004—. Rsch. engr. Anam Semiconductor, Seoul, 1999—2000; sr. rschr. Amkor Tech. CZ, Ariz., 2000—04. Contbr. scientific papers to profl. jours. Nat. rschr. Korean Army, 1999—2004, Seoul. Mem.: Semiconductor Equipment and Materials Internat., Internat. Microelectronics and Packaging Soc., Polymer Soc. Korea. Democrat. Roman Catholic. Achievements include patents for innovative fabrication method of organic substrates for semiconductor micro-system-packaging to have enhanced reliability performance; high molecular weight polymeric photoinitiator for flat panel liquid display application. Avocations: tennis, classical music, painting. Home: 202-603 Bosung Apt Bummul dong Susung gu Taegu 706-100 Republic of Korea Business E-Mail: jseok@ncsu.edu, js554@cornell.edu.

SEOL, DAI-WU, geneticist, educator; PhD, U. Pitts., Pitts., Pa., 1998. Asst. prof. U. Pitts., 2000—. Cons. Genenmed Inc., Seoul, Republic of Korea, 2000—. Dir. Sunday Sch. Korean Ctrl. Ch. Pitts., 2003. Achievements include patents for cancer gene therapy using a secretable trimeric TRAIL. Office: University of Pittsburgh 200 Lothrop Street Pittsburgh PA 15261 Office Phone: 412-624-6704. Office Fax: 412-624-1172. Business E-Mail: seold@pitt.edu.

SEON, YVONNE, cultural educator, minister; d. George Raymond and Beatrice M. Reed; 3 children. BA, Allegheny Coll., 1959; MA, Am. U., 1960; PhD, Union Inst., 1974; MDiv, Howard U., 1981. Exec. dir. High Commn. Inga Dam Project, Kinshasa, Democratic Republic of Congo, 1961—63; program officer Office Internat. Confs., US Dept. State, Washington, 1964—67; dir. student life programs Wilberforce U., Ohio, 1967—71; dir. Bolinga Black Cultural Resources Ctr. Wright State U., 1971—73; student svcs. program coord. Prince Georges CC, Largo, Md., 1993—96, prof. African Am. studies, 1996—2006. Sec. del. US Del. 14th Gen. Assembly UNESCO, Paris, 1966; disting. vis. dir. Bolinga Black Cultural Resources Ctr., 2005—06, dir., 2007—. Pres. Capitol Hill Group

Ministries, Washington, 1987—89; ordained min. Unitarian Universalist Assn., Boston, 1981—; bd. dirs. Africare, DC, 1977—2000, vice-chair, 2002—04; bd. dirs. Prince George's County So. Christian Leadership Conf., Largo, 1994—; mem. Bretton Woods Com., Washington, 2000—. Office: Wright State U 3640 Colonel Glenn Hwy Dayton OH 45435 Business E-Mail: yvonne.seon@wright.edu.

SEONG, BYEONGCHAN, mathematics professor; PhD, Seoul Nat. U., Korea, 2004. Fellow, assoc. rschr. mgmt. and ops. Wash. State U., Pullman, 2004—05; vis. prof. math. Pohang U. Sci. and Tech., Kyeongbuk, Republic of Korea, 2006—07; asst. prof. stats. Chung-Ang U., Seoul, 2007—. Contbr. articles to profl. jours. Office: Dept Stats Chung-Ang Univ 221 Heukseok-dong Dongjak-gu Seoul Seoul 156756 Republic of Korea Home Phone: 82-2-877-0516; Office Phone: 82-17-331-0805.

SEONG, YOUNHO, engineering educator; arrived in US, 1994; s. Younghyeon Seong and Sanhyung Lee; m. Youngme Choo, Mar. 24, 1991; children: Danielle, Matthew. BS, Inha U., Incheon, 1991, MS, 1993; PhD, SUNY, Buffalo, 2002. Quality mgr. Hanjin Mfg. Co., Incheon, 1991; rsch. asst. Inha U., 1991—93, U. Mich., Ann Arbor, 1994—95, SUNY, Buffalo, 1996—2002; asst. prof. NC A&T State U., Greensboro, 2002—, rsch. assoc. Ctr. Human-Machine Studies, 2002—. Lectr. in field. Contbr. articles to profl. jours., chpt. to book. Vol. meal delivery Sr. Resource Guilford, Greensboro, 2004—. With Republic of Korea Army, 1987—88. Grantee, NSF, 2002, AF Rsch. Lab., Wright-Patterson, Ohio, 2005—06, Army Rsch. Lab., 2006. Mem.: Ergonomics Soc. Korea, Inst. Indsl. Engrs. (chpt. sr. v.p. 2005—), Human Factors and Ergonomics Soc. Avocation: photography. Office: NC A&T State U 1601 E Market St Greensboro NC 27411

SEPULVEDA, SONJA MARIAN ATKINSON, choral director, accompanist; b. Lancaster, SC, May 15, 1952; d. Leo Laten and Mary Lou Hatfield Atkinson; m. Juan Pablo Sepulveda, June 10, 1972; children: Dru Adrian, Brys Kristofer. MusB in Edn., Winthrop U., Rock Hill, SC, 1974; MusM in Choral Conducting, Winthrop U., 1975; D in Mus. Arts, U. S.C. Cert. tchr. music edn., choral edn. S.C., 1975. Choral dir. Wilder Fine Arts and Elem. Sch., Sumter, SC, 1975—81, Sumter H.S., SC, 1981—99, Clarendon Sch. Dist. 1, Summerton, SC, 2000—02, DuBose Mid. Sch., Summerville, SC, 2002—; condr. Carolina Alive and Renaissance Singers of U. S.C., 2005—. Choral dir. Palmetto Choirs, Sumter, 2000—; choral dir. and organist St. John Meth. Ch., Sumter, 2002—; dance tchr. Freed Spirits Dance Co., Sumter, 1979—89; piano tchr., Sumter, 1975—81; music edn. tchr. U. S.C., Sumter, 1979—83; choral dir. First Presbyn. Ch., Sumter, 1985—2001, Shaw Heights Bapt. Ch., Sumter, SC, 1978—81, Crosswell Bapt. Ch., Sumter, 1965—78. Composer: (musical) Robin Hood. Named SC. Outstanding Educator of the Yr., Jaycees, 1987, Tchr. of the Yr., Wilder Elem. Sch., 1981; recipient Ivey Reuben Edn. award, NAACP, 1990, Paul Harris fellow, Rotary Internat., 1992. Mem.: PTA (life), Music Educators Nat. Conf. (chmn. S.C. all state com. 1994—98), Am. Choral Dirs. Assn. (jazz choir chmn. S.C. 1995—96), Delta Kappa Gamma (music chmn. 1991—2002). R-Consevative. Presbyterian. Achievements include Choral Director for mini seriesNorth and South; Singer in the Robert Shaw Festival Chorus, 1991-1997; Solo performance at the Lincoln Center; Montreat Chamber Singer, 1988-2001; Singer in the National American Choral Directors Multicultural Choir, 2001; Solo performance for the National Television in Mexico. Avocations: travel, bicycling. Home: 618 Antlers Dr Sumter SC 29150 Office: U SC Sch Music Columbia SC 29208 Personal E-mail: sonjasepulveda@hotmail.com.

SEPÚLVEDA AMOR, JAIME, public health service officer; b. Mexico City, 1954; married; 2 children. MD, Nat. Autonomous U. Mex., 1978; MPH, Harvard Sch. Pub. Health, 1980, MS, 1981, PhD, 1985. Dir. gen. epidemiology, Mexico, 1985—91; vice-min. health, 1991—94; dir. Nat. Pub. Health Inst., Cuernavaca, Mexico, 1995—2003; dean Nat. Sch. Pub. Health, Mexico, 1995—2003; dir. NIH, Mexico, 2003—. Founder Nat. AIDS Coun., 1986, Nat. Immunization Coun.; chair adv. bd. epidemiology in Mex., 1988—91, AIDS & Reproductive Health Networks; founding pres. Coun. Health Rsch. for Devel., 1993—96; mem. bd. Internat. Network Clin. Epidemiology, 1997—; mem. Harvard Bd. Overseers, 2002—; mem. adv. coun. NIH Fogarty Internat. Ctr. Recipient Red Cross award, 1989. Mem.: Inst. Medicine (fgn. assoc.). Office: Institutos Nacionales de Salud Periférico 4118 Edif Zafiro 1 1er piso Col Jardines del Pedregal Deleg 01900 Alvaro Obregon Mexico Office Phone: (55)5135-2229 5568-0754. Office Fax: (55)5135-1980 ext 298. E-mail: jsepulveda@salud.gob.mx.

SEQUEIRA, LEON R., federal agency administrator; b. June 7, 1968; Legal counsel Com. on Rules and Adminstrn. US Senate, Washington, legal counsel to US Senator Mitch McConnell, 2003—05; dep. asst. sec. for policy US Dept. Labor, Washington, asst. sec. for policy, 2007—. Office: US Dept Labor Rm S2006 200 Constitution Ave NW Washington DC 20210 Office Phone: 202-693-6151. Office Fax: 202-693-5960. *

SÉQUIN, CARLO H., computer science educator; b. Winterthur, Switzerland, Oct. 30, 1941; arrived in US, 1970, naturalized, 1974; s. Carl R. and Margrit (Schaeppi) S.; m. Margareta Frey, Oct. 5, 1968; children: Eveline, André. BS, U. Basel, Switzerland, 1965, PhD, 1969. Mem. tech. staff Bell Labs., Murray Hill, NJ, 1970-76; vis. Mackay lectr. U. Calif.-Berkeley, 1976-77, prof. elec. engring. computer scis., 1977—, assoc. chmn. computer sci., 1980-83, assoc. dean capital projects, 2001—. Author: First Book on Charge-Coupled Devices, Charge Transfer Devices, 1975; sculpture designer: Pax Mundi II; H&R Block Headquarters, Kansas City, 2007; contbr. articles to profl. jours. Fellow IEEE (Tech. Achievement award 2003), Assn. Computing Machinery, Swiss Acad. Engring. Scis. Achievements include patents for integrated circuits. Office: U Calif Dept EECS Computer Scis Divsn Soda Hall Berkeley CA 94720-1776 Office Phone: 510-642-5103. Business E-Mail: sequin@cs.berkeley.edu.

SERAFIN, DONALD, plastic surgeon, educator; b. NYC, Jan. 18, 1938; s. Stephen Michael and Julia (Sopko) S.; m. Patricia Serafin; children: Allison Elizabeth, Christina Julia, Donald Stephen, Lara Leigh. AB, Duke U., 1960, MD, 1964. Diplomate Am. Bd. Surgery, Am. Bd. Plastic Surgery. Surg. intern Grady Meml. Hosp., Atlanta, 1964-65; resident in surgery Emory U. Hosp., Atlanta, 1965-69; asst. resident in plastic and reconstructive surgery Duke U. Med. Ctr., Durham, NC, 1971-73, chief resident, 1973-74; Christine Kleinert fellow in hand surgery U. Louisville Hosp., 1972-73; practice medicine specializing in plastic surgery, Durham. Mem. staff N.C. Splty. Hosp., Durham Regional Hosp., Maria Parham Hosp.; attending faculty Durham VA Med. Ctr.; asst. prof. plastic, reconstructive and maxillofacial surgery Duke U., 1974-77, assoc. prof., 1977-81, prof., 1981-2000, prof. emeritus, 2000—, chief divsn. plastic reconstructive and maxillofacial and oral surgery, 1985-95, chmn. Plastic Surgery Rsch. Coun., 1983. Assoc. editor Jour. Reconstructive Microsurgery; contbr. articles to profl. jours. Served to col. Marine Corp. USAR, 1971—2004, served to maj. Marine Corp. USAF, 1969—71, ret., 2004. Decorated Air Force Commendation medal, Army Commendation medal, Army Achievement medal, Army Meritorious Svc. medal. Fellow ACS; mem. AMA, Internat. Soc. Reconstructive Microsurgery, Am. Soc. Plastic Surgeons, Am. Assn. Plastic Surgeons, Am. Soc. Aesthetic Plastic Surgery, Am. Soc. Surgery Hand, Am. Assn. Hand Surgery, Am. Burn Assn., Plastic Surgery Rshc. Coun., N.C. Soc. Plastic, Maxillofacial and Reconstructive Surgeons, Southeastern Soc. Plastic and Reconstructive Surgeons. Office: 511 Ruin Creek Rd Ste 104B Henderson NC 28350 Office Phone: 252-438-8252, 919-220-7711. Personal E-mail: seradonald@aol.com.

SERAFIN, ROBERT JOSEPH, science center administrator, electrical engineer; b. Chgo., Apr. 22, 1936; s. Joseph Albert and Antoinette (Gazda) S.; m. Betsy Furgerson, Mar. 4, 1961; children: Katherine, Jenifer, Robert Joseph Jr., Elizabeth. BSEE, U. Notre Dame, 1958; MSEE, Northwestern U., 1961; PhDEE, Ill. Inst. Tech., 1972. Engr. Hazeltine Rsch. Corp. Ill. Inst. Tech. Rsch. Inst., 1960-62; assoc. engr., rsch. engr., sr. rsch. engr. Nat. Ctr. for Atmospheric Rsch., Boulder, Colo., 1962-73, mgr. field observing facility, 1973-80, dir. atmospheric tech. div. Bouulder, Colo., 1981-89, dir. ctr., 1989-2000. Chair Nat. Weather Svc. Modernization Com. Author: Revised Radar Handbook, 1989; contbr. numerous articles to profl. jours.; editl. bd./com. Acta Meteorologica Sinica; editl. founder Jour. Atmospheric and Oceanic Tech.; patentee in field. Speaker various civic groups in U.S. and internationally. Fellow IEEE, Am. Meteorol. Soc. (pres.); mem. NAE, NAS (human rights com.), Boulder C. of C., Sigma Xi. Avocations: golf, fishing, skiing. Office: Nat Ctr Atmospheric Rsch 1850 Table Mesa Dr PO Box 3000 Boulder CO 80307-3000

SERAFINE, MARY LOUISE, psychologist, educator, lawyer; b. Rochester, NY, July 2, 1948; BA in Music with honors, Rutgers U., 1970; PhD, U. Fla., 1975; JD, Yale U., 1991. Bar: Calif. 1992, DC 1993, US Tax Ct. 1995, NY 1999, Tex. 2005. Tchg. and rsch. fellow U. Fla., Gainesville, 1970-76; vis. asst. prof. U. Tex., San Antonio, 1976-77, asst. prof. Austin, 1977-79; postdoctoral fellow dept. psychology Yale U., New Haven, 1979-83, lectr., 1981-83; asst. prof. dept. psychology Vassar Coll., Poughkeepsie, N.Y., 1983-88; with O'Melveny & Myers, LA, 1991-96, Chadbourne & Parke, LA, 1996-97, Fried, Frank, Harris, Shriver & Jacobson, LA, 1997-99; pvt. practice, 1999—. Author: Music as Cognition: The Development of Thought in Sound, 1988; editl. reviewer Child Devel., Devel. Psychology, Am. Scientist, Jour. Exptl. Child Psychology, Jour. Applied Developmental Psychology, Yale Law Jour.; contbr. articles to profl. jours. Grantee State of Fla., 1974-75, U. Tex.-Austin, 1977, Spencer Found., 1979-85. Office: PO Box 4342 Austin TX 78765 Office Phone: 512-220-5452. Business E-Mail: serapen@earthlink.net.

SERBAROLI, FRANCIS J., lawyer, educator, writer; b. NYC, Feb. 8, 1952; AB, Fordham U., 1973, JD, 1977. Bar: NY 1978, US Dist. Ct. (ea. and so. dists.) NY 1978, US Ct. Appeals (2d and DC cirs.) 1979, US Supreme Ct. 1983. Asst. atty. gen. NY State Dept. Law, 1978-80; ptnr. Cadwalader Wickersham & Taft, NYC, 1995—. Vice chmn. NY State Pub. Health Coun., 1995—; health law columnist The NY Law Jour. Author: The Corporate Practice of Medicine Prohibition in the Modern Era of Health Care, 1999. Chmn. bd. trustees Loyola Sch., NYC, 1999—2006; mem. bd. trustees Cath. Healthcare Sys., Archdiocese of NY. Fellow NY Acad. Medicine; mem. Am. Health Lawyers' Assn., NY State Bar Assn., Assn. Bar City NY Office: Cadwalader Wickersham Taft LLP One World Fin Ctr New York NY 10281

SERCHUK, IVAN, lawyer; b. NYC, Oct. 13, 1935; s. Israel and Freda (Davis) S.; children: Camille, Bruce Mead, Vance Foster. BA, Columbia U., 1957, LLB, 1960. Bar: N.Y. 1961, U.S. Dist. Ct. (so. dist.) N.Y. 1963, U.S. Ct. Appeals (2d cir.) 1964, U.S. Tax Ct. 1966. Law clk. to judge U.S. Dist. Ct. (so. dist.) N.Y., NY, 1961-63; assoc. Kaye, Scholer, Fierman, Hays & Handler, 1963-68; dep. supt., counsel N.Y. State Banking Dept., NYC, Albany, 1968-71; ptnr. Berle & Berle, 1972—73; spl. counsel N.Y. State Senate Banks Com., 1972; ptnr. Serchuk & Zelermyer LLP, White Plains, NY, 1976—2003; mem. Todtman, Nachamie, Spizz & Johns, PC, NYC, 2003—. Lectr. Practising Law Inst., 1968-71. Mem. N.Y. State Bar Assn., Assn. of Bar of City of N.Y. Office: Todtman Nachamie Spizz & Johns PC 425 Park Ave New York NY 10022 Home: 100 United Nations Plaza New York NY 10017 Office Phone: 212-754-9400. Business E-Mail: iserchuk@tnsj-law.com.

SERDAHELY, DOUGLAS J., lawyer, former state judge; b. Rhinelander, Wis., June 1, 1946; AB with highest honors, Northwestern Univ., 1968; JD, Harvard Univ., 1972. Bar: Alaska 1972, US Dist. Ct. (Alaska dist.) 1972, US Ct. Appeals (9th & DC cir.) 1973, US Supreme Ct. 1994. Law clk. Chief Justice Jay A. Rabinowitz, Alaska Supreme Ct., 1972—73; judge Alaska Superior Ct., 1981—89, presiding judge, 1985—89; pro tem panelist Alaska Ct. Appeals, Alaska Supreme Ct., 1981—89; former ptnr. Bogle & Gates, Anchorage; ptnr., Litigation & Dispute resolution, Environ. Health & Safety, Antitrust practices, mem. mgmt. com., office mng. ptnr. Patton Boggs LLP, Anchorage. Instr. Nat. Inst. Trial Advocacy, 1981, Hastings Coll. Trial Advocacy, 1985; adj. prof. Puget Sound Law Sch., 1987. Mem.: ABA, Alaska Bar Assn., Phi Beta Kappa. Office: Patton Boggs LLP Ste 700 601 W Fifth Ave Anchorage AK 99501-2226 Office Phone: 907-263-6310. Office Fax: 907-263-6345. Business E-Mail: dserdahely@pattonboggs.com.

SERDARI, THOMAÏ, architect, historian; b. Athens, Greece, May 5, 1970; d. Vasilis Serdaris and Despina Serdari. MA in Architecture, Nat. Tech. U. of Athens, 1994; MA in Media studies, New Sch. for Social Rsch., NYC, 1997; MA in Art History, NYU, 2001, PhD in Art History, 2005, postgrad. in Bus. Cert. archtl. engr., Hellenic Republic Tech. Chamber of Greece. Arch., Lamia, Greece, 1994—95; art and architecture libr. Dept. Fine Arts NYU, 1999—; prin., owner Novel May Properties LLC, NYC, 2006—. Founder, editor-in-chief (jour.) POLIS. Scholar, Pratt Inst., Bklyn., 1999—2000; Bogardus scholar, 1999—2000. Mem.: Art Librs. Soc. N.Am., Soc. Archtl. Historians, Documentation and Conservation of Bldgs., Sites and Neighborhoods of Modern Movement.

SEREBRIER, JOSÉ, musician, composer, conductor; b. Montevideo, Uruguay, Dec. 3, 1938; came to U.S., 1956; s. David and Frida (Wasser) S.; m. Carole Farley, Mar. 29, 1969; 1 child, Lara Adriana Francesca. Diploma, Nat. Conservatory, Montevideo, 1956, Curtis Inst. Music, 1958; BA, U. Minn., 1960; studied with Aaron Copland, Anatal Dorati, Pierre Monteux. Ind. composer, condr., 1955—. Apprentice condr. Minn. Orch., 1958-60; assoc. condr. Am. Symphony Orch., N.Y.C., 1962-66; music dir. Am. Shakespeare Festival, 1966; composer-in-residence Cleve. Orch., 1968-71; artistic dir. Internat. Festival of Ams., Miami, 1984—, Festival Miami, 1985—; guest condr. numerous orchs. including London Symphony, London Philharm., Paris Radio, Cleve. Symphony Orch., Phila. Symphony Orch., Pitts. Symphony Orch.; founder, artistic dir. Festival Miami (internat. arts festival), 1984. Composer: (for orch.) Variations on a Theme from Childhood, (for chamber) Symphony for Percussion, Concerto for Violin and Orch. (recorded by Royal Phila. Orch. on ASV), (concerto for harp and orch.) Colores Magicos, 1970, Symphonie Mystique, 2003 (5 Grammy nominations including best new composition 2004), Symphony No. 3 (Grammy nomination for best new competition 2004), also works for chorus, voice, keyboard; recs. for RCA, CRI, ASV, KEM, Disc, Trax Classique, EMI, Tioch, Chandos, Varese-Sarabande Decca, IMG, Pickwick, BMG, BIS Records, Vox, Dinemec, Conifer Classics, Decca, Warner Classics, Naxos, with various orchs.; condr. for many recs. including Sibelius Symphony No. 1, Holst's The Planets, Carmen, Poulenc's opera La Voix Humaine, Shostakovich Film Suites vol. 1, 2 and 3(Deutsche Schallplatten award 1988), Carole Farley Sings French Songs (Deutsche Schallplaten award 1988), (home video) Kultur, Prokoviev's Alexander Nevsky, Beethoven's Eroica and Tchaikovsky Symphony No. 1 with Sydney and Melbourne Symphony Orch., Mendelssohn Symphonies, Beethoven Symphonies, Bloch's Violin Concerto and Serebrier's Poema Elegiaco CD, 1992, Le Orchestral Music of Tchaikovsky (several vols.), Laserdisc of Operas The Telephone by Menotti and La Voix Humaine by Poulenc with Scottish Chamber Orch., 1992, Royal Philharm. Orch., 1992, Dvŏrak Symphonies with Czech State Philharm. for Conifer/BMG, Music of Janacek and Chadwick (4 CDs) for R.R., Hindemith CD with Philharmonia Orch. for ASV; (first complete recording) Partita, Ned Rorem For Naxos; (world-premiere recordings) Winterreise, Fantasia; solo-violin sonata with London Philharm. Orch.; Gershwin CD with Royal Scottish Nat. Orch. for Dinemic; Delius songs and orch. works, Grieg songs, London Philharmonic Orch. recording for Dinemic; conductor Grammy Awards, 2003; recordings: music by William Schuman (2 Grammy nominations), Ives Symphony No. 4 (Grammy nomination), Carmen Symphony (Latin Grammy for best classical album 2004). Recipient Ford Found. Condr.'s award, Alice M. Ditson award, 1976, commn. award Nat. Endowment Arts, 1978, Deutsche Schall Platten Critics award, Music Retailers Assn. award for Best Symphony Rec., 1991, 2002; Guggenheim fellow, 1958-60; Rockefeller Found. grantee, 1968-70. Mem. Am. Symphony Orch. League, Am. Music Ctr., Am. Fedn. Musicians. Home: 270 Riverside Dr New York NY 10025-5209 E-mail: caspi123@aol.com. *A composer has the duty to communicate with his audience. The academic-intellectual composer of the 50's has become obsolete. Writing just for one's colleagues has fortunately been proven a dead-end.*

SERENBETZ, ROBERT, manufacturing executive, financial planner; b. Rockville Centre, NY, Apr. 18, 1944; s. Raymond Robert Serenbetz and Mildred (Egner) Clapp; m. Karen Jeanne Jackson, Dec. 30, 1967; children: Todd, Gregg, Kathryn. AB, Dartmouth Coll., 1966; MBA, Harvard U., 1968. Cert. fin. planner. Mktg. staff asst. to group product mgr. Colgate-Palmolive Co., NYC, 1968-75; dir. mktg. Colgate-Palmolive Colombia, Cali, Colombia, 1975-77; v.p. mktg. Colgate-Palmolive Canada, Toronto, Ont., Canada, 1977-81; v.p. mktg. western hemisphere Warner-Lambert Co., Morris Plains, NJ, 1981; pres. Warner-Lambert Can., Toronto, 1981-85; pres. Latin Am., Asia, Australia Warner-Lambert Co., Morris Plains, 1986-89; pres. Am. Chicle, Morris Plains, 1989-91; pres., COO DNA Plant Tech. Corp., Cinnaminson, NJ, 1991-92, pres., CEO Oakland, Calif., 1992-94, chmn., CEO, 1994-96; COO DNAP Holding Corp., Oakland, Calif., 1996-98; pvt. practice CFP, 2003—. Mem. adv. bd. Coun. Ams., N.Y.C., 1987-89; mem. steering com. Pharm. Mfrs. Assn., Washington, 1987-89; bd. dirs. Caribbean/Cen. Am. Com., Washington, 1989; mem. adv. bd. Coun. for Internat. Unity, N.Y.C., 1987-89; alumni coun. Dartmouth Coll., 2002-05, student life com. chmn., 2004-05. Bd. dirs. Notch Brook Resort Gen. Ptnrs. Condominium Assn., Stowe, Vt., 1988-94; pres. bd. dirs. Seaside Homeowners Assn., Isle of Palms, S.C., 1997—; mem. U.S. Postal Svc. Mktg. Adv. Bd., 1990-2004, vice chmn., 1998-2004. Mem. Nat. Candy Wholesalers Assn. (bd. dirs. 1989-91), Morris County C. of C. (bd. dirs. 1989-91), Leadership Inc. (bd. dirs. Phila. br. 1993-94), Fin. Planning Assn., Wild Dunes Club (Isle of Palms, SC), Trillium Links and Lake Club (Cashiers, NC). Republican. Episcopalian. Avocations: golf, stamp collecting/philately, photography, tennis. E-mail: bobserenbetz@prodigy.net.

SERENSON, LYNN ANN, mathematics educator; d. Roy William and Marie Elizabeth Eden; m. Peter Martin Serenson, Aug. 3, 1975; children: Traci Lynn, Heather Lisa. BSc, Ctrl. Mich. U., Mt. Pleasant, 1974; M in Curriculum Edn., Oakland U., Rochester, Mich., 1979. Tchr. math. Novi Cmty. Schs., Mich., 1974—. Recipient Edith Slyth award, Am. Math. Coun., 2006. Mem.: Mich. Assn. Mid. Sch. Educations, Detroit Area Coun. Tchrs. Math. (v.p. 1992—94), Mich. Coun. Tchrs. Math. (h.s. proficiency test bd.), Nat. Coun. Tchrs. Math. Catholic. Avocations: reading, travel, swimming, racquetball, jet ski. Home: 3572 Loon Lake Rd Wixom MI 48393 Office: Novi Middle Sch 49000 11 Mile Novi MI 48374 Home Phone: 248-624-9220; Office Phone: 248-449-1600.

SERFATY, DANIEL, human systems engineer; b. Fes, Morocco, Oct. 31, 1954; came to U.S., 1981; s. Jacques and Viviane; m. Irene Mizrahi, July 9, 1980; children: Nastasha, Gabriel. DUES in Math. and Physics, U. de Paris, 1973; BS, Technion, IIT, Haifa, Israel, 1977, MS in Aero. Engring., 1981; MBA in Internat. Mgmt., U. Conn., 1985. Lectr. elec. engring. U. Conn., Storrs, 1985-86; group leader human-machine and decision systems Alphatech, Inc., Burlington, Mass., 1986—95; prin. founder, pres. Aptima, Inc., Woburn, Mass., Wash., 1995—. Educator computer literacy The Learning Clin., Brooklyn, Conn., 1982-85; bd. dirs. New Eng. Tax Svcs., Inc., Malden, Mass., Net Train Solutions, Newton, Global Wisdom, Inc., Wash., Qualtech Sys. Inc., Conn. Author: (with others) Teams: Their Training and Performance, 1991, Command and Control, 1988, guide to computer literacy for gifted children, 1985; contbr. over 100 articles chpts. to profl. jours. and books. With Internat. Sephardic Edn. Found., NYC, 1981—. Recipient Wohl award Alphatech, 1989. Mem. AIAA, IEEE (gen. coord. internat. conf. on SMC, 1989), Judgment and Decision Making Soc., Human Factors and Ergonomics Soc. (Cognitive Engring. and Decision Making Tech. Group), Eta Kappa Nu, Sigma Chi (chair 2004-06). Office: Aptima Inc 12 Gill St Ste 1400 Woburn MA 01801 Office Phone: 781-496-2411. E-mail: serfaty@aptima.com.

SERGENT, JOHN STANLEY, rheumatologist, educator; m. Carole Sergent; children: Ellen, Katie. MD, Vanderbilt U., 1966. Chief rheumatology Vanderbilt U., 1975—79; pvt. practice, 1979—88; chair dept. medicine St. Thomas Hosp., Nashville, 1988—95; mem. faculty Vanderbilt U., Nashville, 1975—88, prof. medicine, 1988—; chief med. officer Vanderbilt U. Hosp. and Clinic, Nashville, 1995—2003; vice chmn. for edn. Vanderbilt U. Sch. of Medicine, Nashville, 2003—, prog. dir. resident tng., dept. medicine, 2003—. Columnist: The Nashville Tennessean, 1992—. Master: Am. Coll. Physicians; mem.: Am. Coll. Rheumatology (pres. 1992—). Office: Vanderbilt U 1161 21st Ave S D 3100 MCN Nashville TN 37232-2358 Office Phone: 615-343-0339. E-mail: john.sergent@vanderbilt.edu.

SERGEY, JOHN MICHAEL, JR., investment company executive, consultant; b. Chgo., Nov. 17, 1942; m. Sharon Lee Ourada (div. 1982); children: John Michael III, Elisabeth Ann, Mark William, Tanya Ruth; m. Pamela Lynne Murphy, Aug. 8, 1987; children: Brian M., Sarah L. BA in Bus., Northwestern U., 1968; MBA, U. Chgo., 1976. Mgr. rolled products A. M. Castle, Chgo.; v.p. Dietzgen Corp., Chgo.; dir. sales and mktg. Avery Label, Azusa, Calif., 1978-80; v.p., gen. mgr. Fasson Roll div. Avery, Painesville, Ohio, 1980-84; group v.p. Soabar Products Group div. Avery, Phila., 1984-87, Materials Group div. Avery, Painesville, 1987-89; pres., CEO GAF Materials Corp., Wayne, N.J., 1989-96; CEO Strategic Distbn., Inc., Bensalem, Pa., 1997—2001; chmn. Sergey Enterprises, 2002—. Office: Sergey Enterprises 517 Falcon Point Dr New Hope PA 18938

SERGI, VINCENT A.F., lawyer; Grad., Beloit Coll.; JD with honors, Northwestern U. With fin. and reorganization dept. Katten Muchin Zavis Rosenman, 1974, dept. head, nat. mng. ptnr., 1996—, mem. bd. dirs., mem. exec. and operating com., chmn. compensation com. Bd. dirs. Goodman Theatre, Joffrey Ballet, Providence-St. Mel Sch. Office: 525 W Monroe St Chicago IL 60661-3693 Office Phone: 312-902-5255. Business E-Mail: vincent.sergi@kmzr.com.

SERIDO, JOYCE, psychologist, researcher; b. Plainfield, NJ, May 13, 1953; d. Mary Ann Gibriano and John Carmen Serido; m. Barry Edward Runyon, Jan. 1, 1985; 1 child, Evan Tyler Runyon. BA, Rutgers U., 1971—75; MBA, Seton Hall U., 1976—81; MS, U. Ariz., 1999—2001, PhD, 2001—03. Programmer First Nat. State Bank, Newark, 1975—76; programmer/analyst A T & T, Piscataway, NJ, 1976—83; sr. ptnr. CSC Cons., Roseland, 1983—91; mng. ptnr. Egal Inc., Milford, 1991—94; pres. Methods & Solutions, Tucson, Ariz., 1994—98; project mgr. Sunquest Info. Sys., Tucson, 1998—2000; post-doctoral assoc. Cornell U., Ithaca, NY, 2004—05; rsch. scientist U. Ariz., 2005—. Author: (jour. article) Chronic Stressors and Daily Hassles: Unique and Interactive Relationships with Psychological Distress. Recipient Tribute to Women and Industry, YWCA, 1990; grantee Paolucci Rsch. grant, Kappa Omicron Nu / W. K. Kellogg Found., 2002; scholar Travel scholarship, APA, 2001, Ruth R. Cowden scholarship, U. Ariz., 2003. Mem.: AAUW (assoc.), Gerontol.

Soc. Am. (assoc.), Am. Psychol. Assn. (assoc.), Nat. Coun. Family Rels. (assoc.). Avocations: hiking, travel, dance. Office: Univ Arizona PO Box 210033 Tucson AZ 85712-0033 Home Phone: 520-529-4931; Office Phone: 520-621-7127. Office Fax: 520-621-3401. Personal E-mail: jserido@email.arizona.edu, joyceserido@hotmail.com.

SERKES, JEFFREY D., former energy executive; b. Dec. 24, 1950; BBA in Acctg., George Washington U.; MBA in Fin., Rutgers U. With RJR Nabisco; from v.p. fin, sales and distbn. to v.p., treas. IBM, 1995—2002; pres. JDS Opportunities, LLC, 2002—03; sr. v.p., CFO Allegheny Energy, Inc., Hagerstown, Md., 2003—06. Bd. adv. Rutgers U.; dir., chmn., audit com., compensation com. REFAC.

SERLET, BERTRAND, information technology executive; PhD in computer sci., U. Orsay, France. Rsch. engr. Xerox PARC, 1985—89; engring./managerial positions NeXT, 1989—97; sr. v.p. software engring. Apple Computer Inc., Cupertino, Calif., 1997—. Achievements include key player in the definition, development and creation of Mac OS X, the world's most advanced operating system. Office: Apple Computer Inc 1 Infinite Loop Cupertino CA 95014 Office Fax: 408-996-1010.

SERLETIS, APOSTOLOS, finance educator; s. Dimitrios and Anna Serletis; m. Aglaia Serletis, Feb. 26, 1978; children: Demitre, Anna. PhD, McMaster U., 1984. Prof. econs. and fin. U. Calgary, Alberta, Canada, 1991—2006, prof., 2006—. Pres. ICC Econ. Rsch. Ltd., Calgary, 1990—2006. Mem.: Can. Economics Assn., Am. Econ. Assn. Home: 5011 Valiant Dr NW Calgary AB Canada T3A 0Y6 Office: U Calgary 2500 University Dr NW Calgary AB Canada T2N 1N4 Office Phone: 403-220-4092. Business E-Mail: serletis@ucalgary.ca.

SERLING, JOEL MARTIN, educational psychologist; b. Seneca Falls, NY, Feb. 8, 1936; s. Philip and Cecil Serling; children: Meredith Anne, Rebecca Lynne, Heather Lee. AA, U. Buffalo, 1957; BS in Edn., Ohio No. U., 1959; MA, Columbia U., 1960. Instr. psychology West Liberty (W.Va.) State Coll., 1961-63; vocat. psychologist, div. child welfare, Cleve., 1963-64; sch. psychologist Steuben County Bd. Coop. Ednl. Svcs., Bath, NY, 1964-65, Chenango County Bd. Coop. Ednl. Services, Norwich, NY, 1965-67, Delaware County Bd. Coop. Ednl. Services, Walton, NY, 1967-68; sch. psychologist Vestal Ctrl.Sch., NY, 1968-70, Whitesboro Ctrl. Sch., NY, 1970-92; adj. prof. psychology Utica Coll., Syracuse U., 1971-75, 86—, SUNY Coll. Tech., Utica-Rome, 1975—, Mohawk Valley CC, 1971-91, CC of So. Nevada, 1995—; cons., mentor Empire Coll., SUNY, 1975—; instr. psychology Am. Inst. Banking, 1971—. Bd. edn., bd. dirs. Hillel Day Sch., Utica-Rome, 1971-75; bd. profl. advs. Mohawk Valley Learning Disabilities Assn., 1972-76. Recipient cert. of recognition Mohawk Valley Learning Disabilities Assn., 1973; cert. sch. psychologist, NY State, NC Mem. Am. Psychol. Assn., Nat. Assn. Sch. Psychologists (charter), NY Assn. Sch. Psychologists (cert. of recognition, 1977), Sch. Psychologists of Upper NY, Central NY Psychol. Assn., United Univ. Professions, NY State United Tchrs. Assn., Whitesboro Tchrs. Assn., Phi Delta Kappa. Jewish. Clubs: Odd Fellows, Zeta Beta Tau. Co-author, co-developer; Early Identification Screening Index, 1971; contbr. articles to profl. publs., presenter in field E-mail: jssp@cox.net.

SERNA, PATRICIO, state supreme court justice; b. Reserve, N.Mex., Aug. 26, 1939; m. Eloise Serna; children: Elena Patricia, Anna Alicia 1 stepchild, John Herrera. BSBA with honors, U. Albuquerque, 1962; JD, U. Denver, 1970; LLM, Harvard U., 1971; postgrad., Nat. Jud. Coll., 1985, postgrad., 1990, postgrad., 1992, postgrad., 1994; LLD (hon.), U. Denver, 2002. Bar: N.Mex. 1970, Colo. 1971, U.S. Dist. Ct. N.Mex. 1970. Probation and parole officer State of N.Mex., Santa Fe, Las Cruces, 1966—67; spl. asst. to commn. mem. Equal Opportunity Commn., Washington, 1971—75; asst. atty. gen. State of N.Mex., Santa Fe, 1975—79; pvt. practice Santa Fe, 1979—85; dist. judge First Jud. Dist., Santa Fe, 1985—96; justice N.Mex. Supreme Ct., Santa Fe, 1996—, chief justice, 2001—02. Adj. prof. law Georgetown U., Washington, 1973, Cath. U., Washington, 1974—75; faculty advisor Nat. Jud. Coll., Reno, 1987. Bd. dirs. Santa Fe Group Homes Inc. With US Army, 1963—65. Mem.: Santa Fe Bar Assn., No. N.Mex. Am. Inns of Ct., Nat. Hispanic Bar Assn. (Judge of Yr. award 2002, Judge of Yr. 2002), N.Mex. Hispanic Bar Assn., N.Mex. Bar Assn., Elks, Phi Alpha Delta. Avocations: hiking, fishing, Ping Pong, chess, painting. Office: NMex Supreme Ct PO Box 848 Santa Fe NM 87504-0848 Office Phone: 505-827-4886. Business E-Mail: suppms@nmcourts.com. *

SERNA, PHILLIP WOODROW, music educator, musician; b. Houston, Aug. 12, 1976; s. Fred Louis and Kathleen Louise Serna; m. Magdalena Ewa Serna, July 17, 2005. MusB, San Francisco Conservatory of Music, 1998; MusM, Northwestern U., Evanston, Ill., 2001, DMus, 2007. Prin. double bass Northbrook (Ill.) Symphony Orch., 2003; sect. double bass Ill. Philharm. Orch., Park Forest, 2002; music faculty Sherwood Conservatory of Music, Chicago, 2002—04. Pvt. music tchr. Willowbrook H.S., Villa Park, Ill., 2003; adj. pvt. music tchr. Neuqua Valley H.S. Music Dept., Naperville, Ill., 2003; pvt. music tchr. Glenbard East H.S., Lombard, Ill., 2004, Glenbard South H.S., Glen Ellyn, Ill., 2004, Carl Sandburg H.S., Orland Park, Ill., 2004. Edn. com. Early Music Chgo., 2005; outreach adv. Northbrook Symphony, 2003. Mem.: Viola da Gamba Soc. Gt. Britain (assoc.), Internat. Soc. Bassists (assoc.), Early Music Am. (assoc.), Viola da Gamba Soc. Am. (assoc.), Chgo. Fedn. Musicians (assoc.), Early Music Chgo. (assoc.), Ill. Music Educators Assn. (assoc.), Am. String Tchrs. Assn. (assoc.). Home: 22041 W Petoskey Ct Plainfield IL 60544 Office Phone: 847-722-2093. Personal E-mail: phillip@phillipwserna.com.

SERNETT, RICHARD PATRICK, lawyer; b. Mason City, Iowa, Sept. 8, 1938; s. Edward Frank and Loretta M. (Cavanaugh) S.; m. Janet Ellen Ward, Apr. 20, 1963; children: Susan Ellen, Thomas Ward, Stephen Edward, Katherine Anne. BBA, U. Iowa, 1960, JD, 1963. Bar: Iowa 1963, Ill. 1965, U.S. Dist. Ct. (no. dist.) Ill. 1965, U.S. Supreme Ct. 1971. House counsel, asst. sec. Scott, Foresman & Co., Glenview, Ill., 1963-70, sec., legal officer, 1970-80; v.p., law sec. SFN Cos., Inc., Glenview, 1980-83, sr. v.p., sec., gen. counsel, 1983-85, exec. v.p., gen. counsel, 1985-87; pvt. practice Northbrook, Ill., 1988-90; v.p., sec., gen. counsel Macmillan/McGraw-Hill Sch. Pub. Co., 1990-92; ptnr. Sernett & Blake, Northfield, Ill., 1993-95; ret., 1995. Mem. U.S. Dept. State Adv. Panel on Internat. Copyright, 1972-75. Chmn. bd. dirs. Iowa State U., Broadcasting Co., 1987-94. Mem. ABA (chmn. copyright divsn. 1972-73, com. on copyright legis. 1967-70, com. on copyright office affairs 1966-67, 79-81, com. on program for revision copyright law 1971-72), Am. Intellectual Property Law Assn., Am. Soc. Corp. Secs., Ill. Bar Assn. (chmn. copyright com. 1971-72), Chgo. Bar Assn., Patent Law Assn. Chgo. (bd. mgrs. 1979-82, chmn. copyright law com. 1972-73, 77-78), Copyright Soc. U.S.A. (trustee 1972-75, 77-80), Wyndemere Country Club, Naples, Fla., Mission Hills Country Club, Northbrook, Ill. Home: 3741 Mission Hills Rd #409 Northbrook IL 60062

SEROKA, JAMES HENRY, social studies educator, academic administrator; b. Detroit, Mar. 5, 1950; s. Henry S. and Mary (Wyoral) S.; m. Carolyn Marie White, June 27, 1970; children: Mihail, Maritsa. BA, U. Mich., 1970; MA, Mich. State U., 1972, PhD, 1976. Labor mkt. analyst U.S. Dept. of Labor, Washington, 1970-71; asst. prof. U. N.C., Greensboro, 1976-77, Appalachian State U., Boone, N.C., 1977-79, So. Ill. U., Carbondale, 1979-81, assoc. prof., 1981-87, prof., dir., 1987-88; prof., head div. humanities and social scis. Pa. State U., Erie, 1988-90; prof. U. North Fla., Jacksonville, 1990-98; dir. Ctr. for Pub. Leadership, Jacksonville, 1991-98; vis. prof. internat. security studies U.S. Air War Coll., Maxwell AFB, Ala., 1997-98, 2005—; prof. Auburn (Ala.) U., 1998—; dir. Ctr. for Govtl. Svcs., Auburn, 1998—2005. Dir. Master of Pub. Affairs Program Soc. Ill. U., 1987-88, Rural and Small Town Adminstrn. Project, 1980-85; asst. dir. Appalachian Regional Bur. Govts., Boone, N.C., 1977-79; manpower planning analyst U.S. Dept. Labor, Washington, 1970-71; exchange prof. Fakultet Politickih Nauka, Univerzitet u Beogradu, Yugoslavia, 1986; vis. prof. Air War Coll., Montgomery, Ala.; sr. researcher Coun. for the Internat. Exchange Scholars Yugoslavia, 1980; mem. state adv. com. Gov.'s Rural Affairs Coun. for State of Ill., 1988; dir. Ctr. Govt Svcs., Auburn, 1998—. Co-author: Political Organizations in Social Yugoslavia, 1986 (Choice award 1987); editor Rural Public Adminstration, 1986; co-editor: Developed Socialism, 1982, Comparative Political Systems, 1990, Yugoslavia: The Failure of Democratic Transformation, 1992; contbr. numerous articles to profl. jours. Recipient Akademischer Austausch Dienst Lang. scholar Fed. Republic of Germany, 1988 and numerous other grants, traveling fellows. Mem. Am. Soc. Pub. Adminstrn., Am. Polit. Sci. Assn., Internat. Polit. Sci. Assn., Midwest Polit. Sci. Assn., So. Polit. Sci. Assn., Southwestern Polit. Sci. Assn., Western Polit. Sci. Assn., Policy Studies Orgn., Acad. Polit. Sci., Internat. Studies Assn., Am. Assn. Advancement of Slavic Studies, Western Social Sci. Assn., Cmty. Devel. Soc., Hon. Order of Ky. Colonels. Office: Auburn Univ Dept Political Sci 7080 Haley Ctr Auburn AL 36849 Business E-Mail: jseroka@auburn.edu.

SEROTA, JAMES IAN, lawyer; b. Chgo., Oct. 20, 1946; s. Louis Henry and Phyllis Estelle (Horner) S.; m. Susan Perlstadt, May 7, 1972; children: Daniel Louis, Jonathan Mark. AB, Washington U., St. Louis, 1968; JD cum laude, Northwestern U., 1971. Bar: Ill. 1971, US Dist. Ct. (no. dist.) Ill. 1972, DC 1978, US Supreme Ct. 1978, US Ct. Appeals (DC cir.) 1978, U.S. Dist. Ct. (DC dist.), US Ct. Claims 1980, NY 1981, US Dist. Ct. (so. and ea. dists.) NY, 1981, US Dist. Ct. (no dist.) NY, 2003, US Ct. Appeals (2d cir.) 1983. Trial atty. Antitrust div. US Dept. Justice, Washington, 1971—77; assoc. Bell, Boyd & Lloyd, Washington, 1977—81; ptnr. Werner, Kennedy & French, NYC, 1982—85, Levitsky & Serota, 1985-86, Huber, Lawrence & Abell, NYC, 1987—98, Vinson & Elkins, NYC, 1998—2002; shareholder Greenberg Traurig, NYC, 2003—. Contbr. articles to profl. jours.; editor Law Rev.; ed bd., antitrust columnist CCH Power and Telecom Law jour. Mem. law bd. Northwestern U. Law Sch. Recipient Spl. Achievement award U.S. Dept. Justice, 1976. Mem. ABA (chmn. ins. industry com. 1987-90, vice chair program com. 1990-91, chair annual mtg. program 1991-94, chair fuel & energy com. 1994-97, coun. 1997-2000), N.Y. State Bar Assn., Assn. of Bar of City of N.Y. (antitrust and trade regulation com. 1988-91), Fed. Bar Council. Office: Greenberg Traurig LLP 15th Fl 200 Park Ave Met Life Bldg New York NY 10166 Office Phone: 212-801-2277. Business E-Mail: serotaj@gtlaw.com.

SEROTA, SUSAN PERLSTADT, lawyer, educator; b. Chgo., Sept. 10, 1945; d. Sidney Morris and Mildred (Penn) Perlstadt; m. James Ian Serota, May 7, 1972; children: Daniel Louis, Jonathan Mark. AB, U. Mich., 1967; JD, NYU, 1971. Bar: Ill. 1971, DC 1972, NY 1981, US Dist. Ct. (no. dist.) Ill. 1971, US Dist. Ct. (so. dist.) NY 1981, US Dist. Ct. (ea. dist.) NY 1985, US Ct. Claims 1972, US Tax Ct. 1972, US Ct. Appeals (DC cir.) 1972. Ptnr. Pillsbury Winthrop Shaw Pittman LLP, NYC, 1982—, ptnr., chmn. Exec. Compensation & Benefits practice, 2001—. Adj. prof. Sch. Law, Georgetown U., Washington, 1974-75; mem. faculty Practicing Law Inst., NYC, 1983—. Editor: ERISA Fiduciary Law, 1995, 2006; assoc. editor Exec. Compensation Jour., 1973—75, dep. editor Tax Mgmt., Estate and Gift Taxation and Exec. Compensation, 1973—75, mem. editl. adv. bd. Benefits Law Jour., 1973—, Tax Mgmt. Compensation Jour., 1993—, mem. bd. editors ERISA and Benefits Law Jour., 1992—; contbr. articles to profl. jours. Fellow: Am. Coll. of Employee Benefits Counsel (pres. 2004—05, dir., charter fellow), Am. Coll. Tax Counsel (regent 1999—2005); mem.: ABA (chmn. joint com. employee benefits 1987—88, chmn. com. employee benefits 1991—92, vice-chair taxation sect. 1999—2001, chair taxation sect. 2006—07), Am. Bar Retirement Assn. (dir. 1994—2004, pres. 1999—2000), NY State Bar Assn. (exec. com. tax sect. 1988—92), Internat. Pension and Employee Benefit Lawyers Assn. (co-chair 1993—95). Democrat. Office: Pillsbury Winthrop Shaw Pittman 1540 Broadway New York NY 10036 Office Fax: 212-858-1500. Business E-Mail: susan.serota@pillsburylaw.com.

SERRA, MATTHEW D., consumer products company executive; b. 1945; With R.H. Macy & Co., 1962—69, Bloomingdale's, 1969—76; divisional merchandising mgr. men's wear Lord & Taylor, 1976; v.p. & divisional merchandise mgr. Saks Fifth Ave, NYC, 1976—78, assoc. gen. merchandise mgr, men's and boys' wear, 1978—79, sr. v.p. & gen. merchandise mgr. men's and boys' wear, 1979—83; pres. Gimbels NY divsn., 1983, Gimbels East, 1983—86, CEO, 1985—86; pres. Sibleys, Rochester, NY, 1986—90, CEO, 1987—90; pres. CEO Seaman's Furniture Co., NY, 1991—92; chmn., CEO Sterns divsn. of Federated Dept. Stores Inc., 1993-98; pres., CEO Foot Locker Worldwide, 1998—2000; COO Foot Locker Inc. (formerly Venator Group Inc.), 2000—01, pres., 2000—, CEO, 2001—, chmn., 2004—. Office: Foot Locker Inc 112 W 34th St New York NY 10120 *

SERRA, RICHARD, sculptor; b. San Francisco, Nov. 2, 1939; m. Clara Weyergraf-Serra. BA in English Lit., U. Calif., 1961; BFA, MFA, Yale U., 1964; DFA (hon.), Calif. Coll. Arts and Crafts, 1994. One-man shows include Galleria La Salita, Rome, 1966, Kunsthalle Tübingen, Germany, 1978, Richard Hines Gallery, Seattle, 1979, Venice Biennale, 1981, Pace Gallery, Leo Castelli Gallery, 1987, Musée Nat. d'art Moderne, Paris, 1984, Mus. Haus Lange, Krefeld, Germany, 1985, Mus. Modern Art, NYC, 1986, Bonnefantenmuseum, Maastricht, 1990, Pace Gallery, 1992; exhbns. include Stedelijk Mus., Amsterdam, 1969, Kunsthalle, Bern, Switzerland, 1969, Solomon R. Guggenheim Mus., NYC, 1969, Pasadena Art Mus., Calif., 1970, Leo Castelli Gallery, NYC, 1970, 72, 74, 82, 84, ACE Gallery, LA, 1970, 72, 74, Whitney Mus. Am. Art, NYC, 1973, Akira Ikeda Gallery, Nagoya, Japan, 1982, Margo Levin Gallery, 1984, Visual Arts Mus., 1985, Mus. Modern Art, NYC, 1986; group shows include Tony Shafrazi Gallery, 1991-92, Pace Gallery, 1992, Dia Ctr. for Arts, NYC, Whitney Biennial: Day for Night, Whitney Mus. Am. Art, 2006; represented in permanent collections: Mus. Modern Art, NYC, Whitney Mus. Am. Art, NYC, Guggenheim Mus., NYC, Pasadena Mus. Art, LA County Mus. Art, Art Gallery Ont., Toronto, Stedelijk Mus.; also filmmaker. Recipient Praemium Imperiale, Japan Art Assn., 1994, Gold Medal for Sculpture, Am. Acads. Arts and Letters, 2001, Internat. Art award, Cristóbal Gabarrón Found., 2005. Fellow: Am. Acad. Arts and Sciences. Office: 173 Duane St Fl 5 New York NY 10013-3334

SERRANO, JOSÉ ENRIQUE, congressman; b. Mayagüez, PR, Oct. 24, 1943; arrived in US, 1950; s. Jose E. and Hipolita (Soto) Serrano; m. Mary Staucet; children: Lisa Marie, Jose Marco, Justine, Jonathan, Benjamin. Student, CUNY Lehman Coll., 1961. With Mfrs. Hanover Trust Co., 1961-69; mem. Bd. Edn., NYC, 1969-74, NY State Assembly, 1975—90, US Congress from 16th (formerly 18th) NY dist., 1990—, mem. appropriations com., 1993—95, 1996—, chmn. subcommittee on fin. svcs. and gen. govt., mem. Congl. Hispanic Caucus. With 172nd Support Bn. Med. Corps US Army, 1964—66. Recipient Congl. Recognition award, Nat. Coun. La Raza, 1993, Evelina Lopez Antonetty award, Disting. Pub. and Cmty. Svc., Hunter Coll. Ctr. Puerto Rican Studies, 2003, Man of Yr. award, Bronx Puerto Rican Day Parade, 2003, Friend of the Nat. Pks. award, Nat. Pks. Conservation Assn., 2005. Democrat. Roman Catholic. Office: US House Reps 2227 Rayburn House Office Bldg Washington DC 20515-3216 Office Phone: 202-225-4361. Office Fax: 202-225-6001. *

SERRANO, JUSTIN FORBES, education executive; b. 1973; BA, Cornell U.; MBA, Harvard Bus. Sch., 2001. Tchr., student adv. Kaplan, Inc., 1995, mgr., dir., tchr. recruitment and devel.; v.p., graduate programs Kaplan Test Prep and Admissions; pres. SCORE! Ednl. Ctrs., Chgo., 2006—. Office: SCORE! Educational Centers 10 S Wacker Dr Ste 3425 Chicago IL 60606 *

SERRE, JEAN-PIERRE, mathematician, scholar; b. Bages, France, Sept. 15, 1926; s. Jean and Adèle (Diet) S.; m. Josiane Heulot, Aug. 10, 1948; 1 child, Claudine. Baccalauréat, Lycée de Nîmes, France, 1944; agrégation, Ecole Normale Supérieure, France, 1948; PhD, Sorbonne, 1951; PhD (hon.), Cambridge U., Eng., 1978, U. Stockholm, 1980, U. Glasgow, Scotland, 1983, U. Athens, 1996, Harvard U., 1998, Durham U., 2000, London U., 2001, U. Oslo, 2002, U. Oxford, 2003, Acad. Bucharest, 2004, U. Barcelona, 2004, U. Madrid, 2006. With Centre Nat. de la Recherche Scientifique, Paris, 1948—54, U. Nancy, 1954—56; prof. Coll. de France, Paris, 1956—94, prof. emeritus. Author: Groupes algébriques et corps de classes, 1959, Corps Locaux, 1962, Lie Algebras and Lie Groups, 1965, Représentations linéaires des groupes finis, 1968, Cours d'arithmétique, 1970, Trees, 1980, Galois Cohomology, 1997, Local Algebra, 2000, Collected Papers, 1986, 2000. Recipient Fields medal, 1954, prix Balzan, 1985, Leroy P. Steele prize Am. Math. Soc., 1995, Wolf prize in math., Israel, 2000, Abel prize, 2003. Mem. Acad. Sci. Paris, Royal Soc. London (hon. fellow), London Math. Soc. (hon.), Nat. Acad. Sci. U.S. (fgn.), Nederland Acad. Sci. (fgn.), Acad. Sci. Stockholm (fgn.), Russian Acad. Sci. (fgn.). Home: 6 Ave de Montespan 75116 Paris France Office: Coll de France 75005 Paris France Business E-Mail: serre@dma.ens.fr.

SERRELL, BEVERLY, museum consultant; BA, Antioch Coll., Ohio, 1965; MA in Sci. Tchg., Governors State U., Ill., 1977. Tchr. biology, Chgo., 1968—69; curator of edn. John G. Shedd Aquarium, 1970—78; dir. Serrell & Associates, Chgo., 1979—. Author: Exhibit Labels: An Interpretive Approach, 1996, Judging Exhibitions: A Framework for Assessing Excellence, 2006. Named to Centennial Honor Roll, Am. Assn. Museums, 2006. Avocations: Sea Kayaking, cross country skiing, West African Dance and Drumming, rock-and-roll music. Home: 5203 S Kenwood Ave Chicago IL 60615 Personal E-mail: bserrell@aol.com. *

SERRIE, HENDRICK, retired anthropology and international business educator; b. Jersey City, July 2, 1937; s. Hendrick and Elois (Edge) S.; m. Gretchen Tipler Ihde, Sept. 3, 1959; children: Karim Jonathan, Keir Ethan. BA with honors, U. Wis., 1960; MA, Cornell U., 1964; PhD with distinction, Northwestern U., 1976. Dir. Solar Energy Field Project, Oaxaca, Mex., 1961-62; instr. U. Aleppo, Syria, 1963-64; asst. prof. Beloit (Wis.) Coll., 1964-69, Calif. State U., Northridge, 1969-70, Purdue U., West Lafayette, Ind., 1970-72, New Coll./U. South Fla., Sarasota, 1972-77; tchr. Pine View Sch., Sarasota, 1978; prof. anthropology, internat. bus. Eckerd Coll., St. Petersburg, Fla., 1978—2002, dir. internat. bus. overseas programs, 1981—2002; ret., 2002. Sr. rsch. assoc., Human Resources Inst., St. Petersburg, 1988—. Author, editor: Family, Kinship, and Ethnic Identity Among the Overseas Chinese, 1985, Anthropology and International Business, 1986, What Can Multinationals Do for Peasants, 1994, The Overseas Chinese: Ethnicity in National Context, 1998; writer, dir. films: Technological Innovation, 1962, Something New Under the Sun, 1963; contbr. articles to Wall Street Jour. and Wall Street Jour. Europe. Tchr. Sunday sch., North United Methodist Ch., Sarasota, 1977—. Exxon scholar, So. Ctr. for Internat. Issues, Atlanta, 1980-81; Presdl. fellow Am. Grad. Sch. Internat. Mgmt., 1991; recipient Leavy award, Freedoms Found., Valley Forge, Pa., 1989. Fellow Am. Anthropol. Assn., Soc. Applied Anthropology; mem. So. Ctr. Internat. Issues, Acad. Internat. Bus., Tampa Bay Internat. Trade Coun., Internat. Soc. Intercultural Edn., Tng. and Rsch. Republican. Avocations: singing, drawing, beach walking, bicycling, sailing. E-mail: serrieh@eckerd.edu.

SERRIN, JAMES BURTON, mathematics professor; b. Chgo., Nov. 1, 1926; s. James B. and Helen Elizabeth (Wingate) S.; m. Barbara West, Sept. 6, 1952; children: Martha Helen Stack, Elizabeth Ruth, Janet Louise Sucha. Student, Northwestern U., 1944-46; BA, Western Mich. U., 1947; MA, Ind. U., PhD, 1951; DSc, U. Sussex, 1972; DSc in Engring., U. Ferrara, Italy, 1992; DSc in Math., U. Padova, Italy, 1992; DSc, U. Tours, France, 2004. With MIT, Cambridge, 1952-54; mem. faculty U. Minn., Mpls., 1955—, prof. math., 1959-95, Regents prof., 1968—, head Sch. Math., 1964-65; emeritus, 1995. Vis. prof. U. Chgo., 1964, 75, Johns Hopkins U., 1966, U. Sussex, 1967-68, 72, 76, U. Naples, 1979, U. Modena, 1988, Ga. Inst. Tech., 1990. Author: Mathematical Principles of Classical Fluid Mechanics, 1957. Mem. Met. Airport Sound Abatement Council, Mpls., 1969—. Recipient Disting. Alumni award Ind. U., 1979 Fellow AAAS; mem. NAS, Am. Math. Soc. (G.D. Birkhoff prize 1973), Math. Assn. Am., Soc. for Natural Philosophy (pres. 1969-70), Finnish Acad. Sci. and Letters. Home: 4422 Dupont Ave S Minneapolis MN 55419-4739

SERRITELLA, WILLIAM DAVID, lawyer; b. Chgo., May 16, 1946; s. William V. and Josephine Dolores (Scalise) S. JD, U. Ill., Champaign, 1971. Bar: Ill. 1971, US Dist. Ct. (no. and cen. dists.) Ill. 1972, US Dist. Ct. (ea. and we. dists.) Wis. 1995, US Ct. Appeals (7th cir.) 1974, US Supreme Ct. 1979, US Dist. Ct. (so. dist.) Ind. 1997. Law clk. U.S. Dist. Ct., Danville, Ill., 1971-72; ptnr. Ross & Hardies, Chgo., 1972—2003, McGuire Woods, Chgo., 2003—07, Johnson & Bell, Ltd., Chgo., 2007—. Arbitrator Am. Arbitration Assn. Named to Leading Lawyers Network, Ill. Super Lawyers, Top Best Lawyers Network. Fellow Am. Bar Found.; mem. ABA, Ill. Bar Assn., Chgo. Bar Assn., Internat. Assn. Def. Counsel, Soc. Trial Lawyers, Defense Rsch. Inst., Trial Lawyers Club (Chgo.), Lawyers Club Chgo. Office: Johnson & Bell Ltd 33 W Monroe St Ste 2700 Chicago IL 60603 Business E-Mail: serritellaw@jbltd.com.

SERRY, CYRUS, medical educator; MD, Tehran Med. U., Iran, 1962. Bd. cert. cardio thoracic surgery and vascular surgery. Sr. attending, assoc. prof. Rush U., 1972—; chief sect. cardiac surgery Elmhurst Hosp., Ill., 1988—98; chief divsn. thoracic surgery Cook County Hosp., Chgo., 1993—98. Mem.: ACS, Chgo. Surg. Soc., Soc. Thoracic Surgeons. Office: 1725 W Harrison St Ste 1156 Chicago IL 60612

SERTICH, KELLI ANN, land use planner; b. Riverside, Calif., Nov. 9, 1959; d. Robert Sr. and Lillian Patricia (Hale) S. AAS in Constrn. Drafting, Glendale C.C., 1981; BS in Design Urban Planning, Ariz. State U., 1983; MPA, Western Internat. U., 2002. Draftsman, facilities planner Washington Elem. Sch. Dist., Phoenix, 1980-83; planner various pvt. sector planning & archtl. firms, Phoenix, 1983-88; dir. planning and econ. devel. Town of Buckeye, 1988-93; dir. tourism and econ. devel. City of Williams, 1993-95; dir. cmty. devel., interim city mgr. City of Bisbee, 1995-98; sr. planner Cmty. Scis. Corp., Phoenix, 1998; sr. planner policy analyst Maricopa County Dept. Transp., 1998-2000; regional area planning mgr. Flood Control Dist. Maricopa County, 2000—07; mgr. regulatory divsn.Flood Control Dist. Maricopa County, 2007—. Pres. Bisbee Christmas in April, 1997; chmn. Ariz. Cmty. Found. Cochise Project Team, Bisbee, 1997; chmn. Buckeye Clean and Beautiful, 1989-93. Mem. Am. Planning Assn. (bd. dirs. region 5 2006—), Ariz. Planning Assn. (dir.-at-large 1993-2001, sec. 1994-99, pres. 2003-04). Roman Catholic. Avocations: sewing, horseback riding, travel, gardening. Office: Maricopa County Flood Control 2801 W Durango St Phoenix AZ 85009-6357

SERVAAS, BEURT RICHARD, manufacturing executive; b. Indpls., May 7, 1919; s. Beurt Hans and Lela Etta (Neff) S.; m. Cory Jane Synhorst, Jan. 7, 1950; children: Eric, Kristin, Joan, Paul, Amy. Student, U. Mex.,

Mexico City, 1938-39; AB, Ind. U., 1940, MD, 1970; postgrad., Purdue U., 1941; D Bus. Mgmt., Ind. Inst. Tech.; LHD (hon.), Butler U. Agt. CIA, China, 1946; v.p. constrn. Vestar Corp., NYC, 1948; founder, chief exec. officer, chmn. bd. No. Vernon Forge, Inc. Rev. Pub. Co., SerVaas Labs., Indpls., 1949—. Chmn. bd. SerVaas, Inc., Indpls. and affiliated cos. Curtis Pub. Co., Forge Mexicana, Edgerton Tool, Dependable Engring., SerVaas Mgmt., SerVaas Rubber, Premier, Indpls. Rubber Co., Bridgeport Brass Co.; bd. dirs. Bank One Ind. Pres. City-County Coun., Indpls.; chmn. Ind. State Commn. Higher Edn., Kirksville Coll. Osteo. Medicine; bd. dirs. Coll. Univ. Corp., Ind. Pub. Health Found., Robert Schuller Ministries; past chmn. bd. dirs. Ind. State Bd. Health, Nat. Fgn. Rels. Commn. With USNR, 1941—45. Decorated Bronze Star, Army Commendation medal; recipient Horatio Alger award, 1980. Mem. NAM, Am. Acad. Achievement (Golden Plate award 1973), Assn. Am. Med. Colls., Ind. C. of C., Indpls. C. of C., Marion County Hist. Soc., Ind. Hist. Soc., Newcomen Soc. N.Am., U.S. Naval Res. Assn., World Future Soc., Am. Legion, Columbia Club, Econ. Club, Indpls. Athletic Club, Indpls. Press Club, Meridian Hills Country Club, Phi Delta Kappa. Presbyterian. Home: 2525 W 44th St Indianapolis IN 46228-3249 Office: Office of the City County Coun 241 City-County Bldg 200 E Washington St Indianapolis IN 46204-3307 also: SerVaas Inc 1000 Waterway Blvd Indianapolis IN 46202-2155

SERVAAS, CORY, editor-in-chief; AB in Journalism, Univ. Iowa; MD, Ind. Univ.; PhD (hon.), Vincennes Univ. Chmn., pres., CEO Curtis Pub. Co., 1975—82; former chmn. Country Gentleman Pub. Co.; founder, pres., CEO Benjamin Franklin Literary and Med. Soc., 1976—; also editorial dir. Children's Better Health Inst., Indpls.; and editor Saturday Evening Post, Indpls., editor-in-chief, 2004—. Mem. Pres. Coun. on Phys. Fitness and Sports, 1990—94. Named to Univ. Iowa Journalism Hall of Fame; recipient Ind. Woman of Achievement award, Nat. Fedn. of Press Women, Kappa Tau Alpha award for outstanding svc., Nat. Journalism Scholarship Soc., Outstanding Bus. Leader award, Northwood Inst. Mem.: Nat. Women's Coalition, Women in Comm. Inc., Indianapolis Arthritis Guild, Am. Med. Women's Assn., Ind. State Med. Assn., AMA, Education CHOICE Charitable Trust, Epsilon Sigma Alpha. Office: Saturday Evening Post 1100 Waterway Blvd Indianapolis IN 46202-2174

SERVIEN, LOUIS-MARC (COMTE DE BOISDAUPHIN, LORD OF QUENDON), finance company, import/export company executive; b. Yverdon-les-Bains, Switzerland, Jan. 8, 1934; Doctorate, Acad. Tiberina, Rome. Pres., mng. dir. Soc. de Financement SA, Geneva, Compagnie des Grands Crus SA. Pres., mng. dir., Cmte. European Excellence. Author: Mutual Funds, Why Not? A Survey of International Investment Funds, 1968; "Gibraltar: Tax on the Rock" (Revue Premier Monte Carlo, Monaco, No. 17, 1985-86); several publications in German, French, Italian & Spanish; contbr. articles to profl. publs., journalist. Named hon. col. Confederate Air Force, Midland, Tex., Commendatore of the Concordia Order, Brazil, 1974, Commedador of Imperial Orden Hispanica de Carlos V, Spain, 1992; recipient cert. recognition. Mem. Manorial Soc. Gt. Britain, Com. European Excellence, Diplomat Club Geneva, Chow Chow Club Paris.

SERVODIDIO, PAT ANTHONY, broadcast executive; b. Yonkers, NY, Nov. 9, 1937; s. Pasquale and Catherine (Verdisco) S.; children: Christian, Alexa. BS, Fordham U., 1959; postgrad., St. John's U., NYC, 1960-63. Asst. to bus. mgr. Sta. WCBS-TV, NYC, 1960-64; account exec. Sta. WTNH-TV, New Haven, 1964-66; account exec., N.Y. sales mgr. RKO TV Reps., NYC, 1967-74; v.p., N.Y. sales mgr. Sta. WOR-TV, NYC, 1974-79, v.p., gen. sales mgr., 1979-81; v.p., gen. mgr. Sta. WHDN-TV, Boston, 1981—82; pres. RKO TV, NYC, 1982-87, RKO Gen., Inc., NYC, 1987—91, also bd. dirs.; v.p., gen. mgr. Sta. WKYC-TV, Cleve., 1991-92; pres. Multimedia Broadcasting Co., Cin., 1992-94; broadcast cons., 1995—. Bd. regents St. Peter's Coll., 1983-99; mem. com. future financing Rutgers U., New Brunswick, N.J., 1983-85; dir. TV bur. Advt. Bd., 1993-94; bd. dirs. Internat. Radio and TV Found., 1983-93, Assn. for Maximum Svc. TV, Inc., 1993-95. With U.S. Army, 1959-62. Office: 380 Lexington Ave Ste 1700 New York NY 10168-0002

SERWATKA, JUDY ANN, computer and information systems educator; d. Carl Daniel and Mary Ellen Penovich; m. Conrad Mitchell Serwatka, Oct. 4, 1997. BS in Computer Tech., Purdue U. Calumet, Hammond, Ind.l, 1978, MS in Mgmt., 1983; EdD in Bus. Edn., No. Ill. U., 1993. Sys. engr. Bethlehem Steel Corp., Burns Harbor, Ind., 1979—85; assoc. prof. info. sys. and computer programming Purdue U. Calumet, Hammond, 1985—2002; assoc. prof. computer and info. tech. Purdue U. North Ctrl., Westville, Ind., 2002—06, prof. computer and info. tech., 2006—, dir. MBA program, 2006, chair dept. computer and info. tech., 2007—. Author: Business Data Communications: Introductory Concepts and Techniques, 2004; contbr. articles to profl. jours. Recipient cert. recognition, Ind. Partnership for Statewide Edn., 2002, 2004, Merlot Vol. of the Yr. award, Project Merlot, 2005. Mem.: Assn. Computing Machinery, Internat. Assn. Computer Info. Sys., Network and Sys. Profls. Assn. (dir. 2002—04), Sigma Xi. Office: Purdue U North Ctrl 1401 S US 421 Westville IN 46391 E-mail: jserwatka@pnc.edu.

SERWER, ALAN MICHAEL, lawyer; b. Detroit, Aug. 31, 1944; s. Bernard Jacob and Marian (Borin) S.; m. Laurel Kathryn Robbert, June 6, 1968; children: David Matthew, Karen Anne. BA in Econs., U. Mich., 1966; JD, Northwestern U., 1969. Bar: Ill. 1969, D.C. 1980, U.S. Dist. Ct. (no. dist.) Ill. 1970, U.S. Ct. Appeals (7th cir.) 1979, U.S. Supreme Ct. 1979, U.S. Ct. Appeals (6th cir.) 1982, U.S. Ct. Appeals (5th cir.) 1983, U.S. Ct. Appeals (9th cir.) 1986. Trial atty. U.S. Dept. Labor, Chgo., 1969-78, counsel safety and health, 1978-79; assoc. Haley, Bader & Potts, Chgo., 1979-82, ptnr., 1983-87; mem. Bell, Boyd & Lloyd, Chgo., 1987—. Ill. Bar Assn., Chgo. Bar Assn. Home: 233 Woodland Rd Highland Park IL 60035-5052 Office: Bell Boyd & Lloyd 70 W Madison St Ste 3200 Chicago IL 60602-4244 Home Phone: 847-432-7338; Office Phone: 312-372-1121. Business E-Mail: aserwer@bellboyd.com.

SERWER, ANDY (ANDREW E. SERWER), editor, journalist; b. Sept. 16, 1959; BA in History, Bowdoin Coll., 1981; MBA, Emory U., 1984; M in Journalism, Columbia U. Reporter Fortune, NYC, 1984, assoc. editor, sr. writer, 1995—98, editor-at-large, 1998—2006, mng. editor, 2006—. Contbg. writer Money mag. Host (TV series) CNN's American Morning, CNN's In the Money. Named Bus. Journalist of Yr., TJFR, 2000. Office: Fortune Time & Life Bldg Rockefeller Ctr New York NY 10020-1393 also: CNN In the Money 1 CNN Ctr Atlanta GA 30303 *

SESHADRI, SRIVATSAN, optics scientist; b. Chennai, Tamil Nadu, India, July 26, 1969; s. Indira Seshadri and Seshadri S. PhD, U. So. Calif., 1998. Optical scientist Osmic Inc., Auburn Hills, Mich., 1998—2004; staff scientist Xradia, Inc., 2005—. Presenter: in field; contbr. articles to profl. jours. Recipient Disting. Scholar award, Microbeam Analysis Soc., U.S. Dept. of Commerce, 1995; Rsch. assistanship, Dept. of Materials Sci. and Engring., U. So. Calif., 1993-1998. Mem.: IEEE, Microbeam Analysis Soc., Soc. Photo-optical Instrumentation Engrs. Achievements include patents for Protective Layers for Multilayers Exposed to X-rays; Protective Layers for Multilayers exposed to hard X-rays. Office: Xradia Inc 4075A Sprig Dr Concord CA 94520 E-mail: Srivatsan_Seshadri@yahoo.com.

SESHADRI, SUDHA, neurologist, educator; b. Bangalore, India, Apr. 3, 1961; d. Gangaikondan Swami Iyer and Chitra Seshadri; m. Vasan S. Ramachandran, July 10, 1987; 1 child, Aditi Vasan. MBBS, Vellore and Madras Med. Coll., Madras, India, 1984; MD in Internal Medicine, All India Inst. Med. Scis., New Delhi, 1988, DM in Neurology, 1992. Diplomate Am. Bd. Neurology and Psychiatry, 2006. Fellow in neurobiology of aging U. Mass. Med. Ctr., Worcester, 1993—96; asst. prof. dept. neurology All India Inst. Med. Scis., New Delhi, 1996—98; asst. prof. dept. neurology Sch. Medicine Boston U., 2001—. Investigator Framingham Heart Study, Mass., 1998—; spkr. in field. Co-author: Textbook of Internal Medicine, 1998 (Selected by Nat. Book Trust of India for subsidized publ., 1998); contbr. articles to profl. jours.; reviewer: in field. Recipient Thomas Dina prize for physiology, Christian Med. Coll., Vellore, 1961, Cmty. Orientation Program prize, 1979, Dhananjay Abhyankar Meml. award for best undergraduate rsch. essays in physiology, 1981, George Chacko Meml. award for excellence in preclinical scis., 1981, Dr. A. Venogopal medal and prize in urology, Madras Med. Coll., 1983, E.Merck Gold medal in neurology and allied scis., Neurol. Soc. India, 1991, Resident award for excellence in tchg., dept. neurology Sch. Medicine Boston U., 2006; Nat. Sci. Talent scholar, Nat. Coun. Ednl. Rsch. and Tng., 1977. Mem.: World Fedn. Neurology, Mass. Med. Soc., Am. Stroke Assn. (mem. sci. coun.), Am. Acad. Neurology, Alzheimer and Related Disorders Soc. India, Indian Epilepsy Soc. (life), Indian Acad. Neurology (life), Neurol. Soc. India (life), Alpha Omega Alpha. Hindu. Achievements include research in some of the genes underlying brain aging in the Framingham study cohort; design of a dementia clinic at the All India Institute of Medical Sciences, New Delhi, India; research in clinical care for patients with Alzheimers and various neurological problems and teaching of residents. Avocations: poetry, trekking. Office: Boston Univ Sch Medicine 715 Albany St B602 Boston MA 02118 Home Phone: 978-838-0253; Office Phone: 617-414-1337. Business E-Mail: suseshad@bu.edu.

SESONSKE, ALEXANDER, nuclear and chemical engineer; b. Gloversville, NY, June 20, 1921; s. Abraham and Esther (Kreitzer) S.; m. Marjorie Ann Mach, Apr. 17, 1952 (dec. Jan. 1995); children: Michael Jan, Jana Louise. B.Chem. Engring., Rensselaer Poly. Inst., 1942; MS, U. Rochester, 1947; PhD, U. Del., 1950. Engr. Chem. Constrn. Corp., NYC, 1942; chem. engr. Manhattan Project, 1943-45, Columbia Chem. Corp., 1945-46; staff Los Alamos Sci. Lab., 1950-54, 60-61, cons., 1961-63; faculty Purdue U., Lafayette, Ind., 1954, prof. nuclear and chem. engring., 1959-86, prof. emeritus, 1986—, asst. chmn. dept. nuclear engring., 1966-73. Cons. Oak Ridge Nat. Lab., 1963-67, Electric Power Reserach Inst., 1974; mem. rev. com. Argonne (Ill.) Nat. Lab., 1965-67, 75-81; ind. cons. 1986—. Author: (with Samuel Glasstone) Nuclear Reactor Engineering, 1963, 4th edit., 1994, Nuclear Power Plant Design Analysis, 1973; mem. editorial bd. Advances in Nuclear Sci. and Tech., 1972—; contbr. numerous articles to profl. jours. Recipient Wall of Fame award U. Del., 1988. Fellow Am. Nuclear Soc. (Arthur H. Compton award 1987); mem. Am. Inst. Chem. Engrs., Am. Soc. Engring. Edn., Sigma Xi, Omega Chi Epsilon. Achievements include research on nuclear fuel mgmt., liquid metal heat transfer and nuclear reactor engring. Home and Office: 700 Black Lake Blvd SW Apt 109 Olympia WA 98502 Office Phone: 360-943-5467.

SESSIONS, JEFF (JEFFERSON BEAUREGARD SESSIONS III), senator, former state attorney general; b. Hybart, Ala., Dec. 24, 1946; s. Jefferson Beauregard and Abbie (Powe) S.; m. Mary Montgomery Blackshear, Aug. 9, 1969; children: Mary Abigail, Ruth Blackshear, Samuel Turner BA, Huntingdon Coll., Montgomery, Ala., 1969; JD, U. Ala., 1973. Bar: Ala. 1973. Assoc. Guin, Bouldin & Porch, Russellville, Ala., 1973-75; asst. U.S. atty. (so. dist.) Ala. US Dept. Justice, Mobile, Ala., 1975-77, US atty., 1981-93; assoc. then ptnr. Stockman & Bedsole Attys., Mobile, Ala., 1977-81; ptnr. Stockman, Bedsole & Sessions, Mobile, 1993-94; atty. gen. State of Ala., Montgomery, 1995—97; U.S. Senator from Ala., 1997—; mem. armed services com., budget com., health, edn., labor & pension com. Mem. U.S. Atty. Gen's. adv. com., 1987-89, vice-chmn. 1989 Presdl. elector State of Ala., 1972; trustee, mem. exec. com. Mobile Bay Area Partnership for Youth, 1981-95; chmn. adminstrv. bd. Ashland Pl. United Meth. Ch., Mobile, 1982; 1st v.p. Mobile Lions Club, 1993-94. Capt. USAR, 1975-85 Recipient U.S. Atty. Gen's. award for significant achievements in the war against drug trafficking, US Dept. Justice, 1992, George (Buck) Gillespie Congl. award, Blinded Americans Veterans Found., 2000, Nat. Leadership award, Civil War Preservation Trust, 2004, Disting. Eagle Scout award, Guardian of Small Bus. award, Minuteman of the Yr. award, Reserve Officers Assn., Svc. to Agrl. award, AL Farmers Fedn., Teddy Roosevelt Environ. award, Watchdog of the Treasury award Mem. ABA, Ala. Bar Assn., Mobile Bar Assn. Republican. Methodist. Office: 335 Senate Russell Office Bldg Washington DC 20510-0001 E-mail: senator@sessions.senate.gov. *

SESSIONS, JOAN T., director, educator; d. David Pyper and Rose Smith Thomas; children: Linda Ann Hadley, Gina Louise. BS in Edn., Kent State U., 1962; postgrad., U. Akron, 1970; MA in Edn., Ohio State U., 1966; PhD in Edn., Kent State U., 1975; postgrad., U. Chgo., 1996, St. Michael's Coll., Burlington, Vt., 1998. Cert. elem. tchr., elem. prin. Ohio. Rsch. asst. Ohio State U., 1965—66; tchr. pub. schs., Wooster, Ohio, 1962—64, Elyria City Schs., 1966—67; dir. of info. systems, planning quality assurance Ctr. for Human Services, Cleve., 1974—91; program specialist UN Volunteers, Beijing, 1991—96; tutoring program dir. U. Chgo., 1998—; Headstart dir. Elyria City Schs., 1967—70, elem. prin. Ohio, 1970—72; tchg. fellow Ohio State U., 1972—73; rsch. assoc. Bur. Ednl. Rsch., 1973—74; dir. evaluation Ctr. for Human Svcs., Cleve., 1974—91; instr. John Carroll U., 1985—90; vol. UN, Beijing; lang. evaluation cons. Beijing Diplomatic Svc. Grad. sch. lectr. John Carroll U., Cleve., 1987—89; grad. tchg. fellow Kent State U., 1972—74; cons. and lectr. in field; tutor program dir., mgr. VISTA and AmeriCorps, 1999—2005; primary literacy tutoring cons. City Yr. Chgo., 2001—05; USI primary literacy tutor program tng. materials evaluation methodology Dept. Neighborhood Schs., U. Chgo., 2006—; adj. prof. Loyola Chgo., 2006. Pres. Ohio City Redevelopment Assn., Cleve., 1986—91; treas., pres., deacon, trustee and elder Fairmont Presbyn. Ch.; bd. dirs. 5000 S Cornell Condominium Assn., 2001—, Literacy Vols. of Ill. Recipient Deacons award, Fairmont Presbyn. Ch., 1984, award, Luth. Med. Ctr. Women's Bd., 1988, Cmty. Svc. award, Mayor George Voinovich, City of Cleve., 1991, Moccasin award for cmty. svc., City Yr. Chgo., 2004; grantee, Cleve. Found., United Way of Cuyahoga County, Gund Found., Luth. Med. Ctr. Found., 1989, BP Am. Found., numerous others. Mem.: Wooster Edn. Assn., Ohio Fedn. Women, Wooster Jr. Women's Club. Avocations: collecting art, studying Chinese language and culture. Home: 5000 S Cornell #3A Chicago IL 60615 Home Phone: 773-643-1176; Office Phone: 773-834-3286. Personal E-mail: joansessions@comcast.net.

SESSIONS, JUDITH ANN, dean, university librarian; b. Lubbock, Tex., Dec. 16, 1947; d. Earl Alva and Anna (Mayer) S. BA cum laude, Cen. Fla. U., 1970; MLS, Fla. State U., 1971; postgrad., Am. U., 1980, George Washington U., 1983. Head libr. U. S.C., Salkehatchie, 1974-77; dir. Libr. and Learning Resources Ctr. Mt. Vernon Coll., Washington, 1977-82; planning and systems libr. George Washington U., Washington, 1981-82, asst. univ. libr. for adminstrn. svcs., acting head tech. svcs., 1982-84; univ. libr. Calif. State U., Chico, 1984-88; univ. libr., dean of libr. Miami U., Oxford, Ohio, 1988—. Cons. Space Planning, SC, 1976, DataPhase Implementation, Bowling Green U., 1982, TV News Study Ctr., George Washington U., 1981; asst. prof. dept. child devel. Mt. Vernon Coll., 1978—81; mem., lectr. U.S.-China Libr. Exch. Del., 1986, 91; lectr., presenter in field; mem. coord. com. OhioLink Adv. Coun., 1995—2003, v.p., 1996—97, chair, 1998—2000; mem. gov. bd. OhioLink, exec. com., 1998—2001; mem. OCLC Users Coun., 1998—2001; convenor Pub. Acad. Libr. Group, 1999—2000; mem. OCLC Preservation Resources Interest Group, 1999—2001, chmn., 2001. Contbr. articles, book revs. to profl. jours. Trustee Christ Hosp., Cin., 1990-94, Deaconess Gamble Rsch. Ctr., Cin., 1990-94, OhioNet, 1990-94, treas. 1993; bd. dirs. Hamilton (Ohio) YWCA, 1994-98, pres., 1995-96, v.p., 1996-97, 97-98; mem. OCLC user's coun., 1998—; mem. steering com. Tri City Reading Initiative, 2002-03. Recipient award for outstanding contbn. D.C. Libr. Assn., 1979; rsch. grantee Mt. Vernon Coll., 1980; recipient Fulbright-Hayes Summer Travel fellowship to Czechoslovakia, 1991. Mem. ALA (Olofson award 1978, councillor-at-large policy making group 1981-94, coun. com. on coms. 1983-84, intellectual freedom com. 1984-88, directions and program rev. com. 1989-91, fin. and audit subcom. 1989-90, mem. exec. bd. 1989-94, mem. del. to Zimbabwe Internat. Book Fair 1997), Assn. Coll. and Rsch. Librs. (editorial bd. Coll. and Rsch. Librs. jour. 1979-84, nominations and appointments com. 1983-85, faculty status com. 1984-86), Libr. and Info. Tech. Assn. (chair legis. and regulation com. 1980-81), Libr. Adminstrn. and Mgmt. Assn. (bd. dirs. libr. orgn. and mgmt. sect. 1985-87), Calif. Inst. Librs. (v.p., pres. elect 1987-88), Mid-Atlantic Regional Libr. Fedn. (mem. exec. bd. 1982-84), Jr. Mems. Round Table (pres. 1981-82), Intellectual Freedom Round Table (sec. 1984-85), Freedom to Read Found. (trustee 1984-88, v.p. 1985-86, treas. 1986-87, pres. 1987-88), Rotary, Beta Phi Mu. Office: Miami U Edgar W King Oxford OH 45056 Office Phone: 513-529-2800. E-mail: judith@lib.muohio.edu.

SESSIONS, PETE, congressman; b. Waco, Tex., Mar. 22, 1955; m. Juanita Diaz, 1984; children: Bill, Alex. BS in Polit. Sci., Southwestern U., Georgetown, Tex., 1978. Dist. mgr. mktg. Southwestern Bell Tel. Co., 1978—94; v.p. pub. policy Nat. Ctr. Policy Analysis, Dallas, 1994—95; mem. US Congress from 32nd (formerly 5th) Tex. dist., 1997—, mem. rules com., mem. budget com., chair Results Caucus. Bd. mem. YMCA; mem. exec. bd. Circle Ten Coun. of Boy Scouts Am.; active United Meth. Ch. Recipient Nat. Disting. Eagle Scout award, 1999. Mem. Rotary Club. Republican. Methodist. Avocations: hiking, mountain climbing, running. Office: US Ho Reps 1514 Longworth Ho Office Bldg Washington DC 20515-4305 Office Phone: 202-225-2231. *

SESSIONS, ROY BRUMBY, otolaryngologist, educator; b. Houston, July 28, 1937; s. Roy Brumby and Elizabeth (Compton) S.; m. Mary Cousart, Aug. 28, 1976: children: Kate, Elizabeth, Abigail, Matthew. BS, La. State U., Baton Rouge, 1958; MD, La. State U., New Orleans, 1962. Resident gen. surgery and otolaryngology Washington U. Sch. Medicine, St. Louis, 1965-69; asst. prof. Baylor Coll. Medicine, Houston, 1969-73, assoc. prof., 1973-83; prof. head and neck surgery Meml. Sloan Kettering Cancer Ctr., NYC, 1983-89; prof., chmn. dept. otolaryngology, head and neck surgery Med. Sch. Georgetown U., Washington, 1989-97; chmn. dept. otolaryngology, head and neck surgery Beth Israel Med. Ctr., NYC, 1998—, assoc. dir. Cancer Ctr., co-dir. Inst. Head and Neck Surgery, 1998—. Contbr. articles to profl. jours., chpts. to books; author one textbook. Lt. comdr. USN, 1962-65. Roman Catholic. Home: 411 Forest St Rye NY 10580 Office: Beth Israel Med Ctr 10 Union Sq E Ste 4J New York NY 10003-3314

SESSIONS, WILLIAM K., III, federal judge; b. Hartford, Conn., 1947; BA, Middlebury Coll., 1969; JD, George Washington U., 1972. Bar: 1973; Ct. of Appeals, DC, 1973; Ct. of Appeals (2nd cir.) 1975; US Dist. Ct., Vt., 1973; US Supreme Ct., 1992. Law clk. Hon. Hilton Dier, Jr. Addison (Vt.) Dist. Ct., 1973; exec. dir. Addison County Youth Svcs. Bur., 1973-74; staff Addison County Pub. Defender, 1974-78; pvt. practice Middlebury, Vt., 1978-80; ptnr. Sessions, Keiner, Dumont & Barnes, P.C., Middlebury, Vt., 1980-95; judge US Dist. Ct., Burlington, 1995—, chief judge, 2002—. Adj. prof. law Vt. Law Sch., 1978-95; vice chmn. US Sentencing Commn., 1999—; chair Vt. State com. of selection for Rhodes Scholarship Trust, 2000; trustee Vt. Law Sch., 1999-2001. 1st Lt. US Army, 1972—77. Mem.: Friends Children's Art Exch. Office: US Dist Ct PO Box 928 Burlington VT 05402-0928 *

SESSIONS, WILLIAM STEELE, lawyer, former FBI director; b. Ft. Smith, Ark., May 27, 1930; s. Will Anderson and Edith A. (Steele) S.; m. Alice Lewis, Oct. 5, 1952; children: William Lewis, Mark Gregory, Peter Anderson, Sara Anne. BA, Baylor U., 1956, LLB, 1958; degree (hon.), John C. Marshall Law Sch., St. Mary's U., 1989; LLD (hon.), Dickinson Coll., 1988, Flager Coll., 1990, Davis & Elkins Coll., 1992, McMurry U., 1997. Bar: Tex. 1959; U.S. Dist Ct. (Western Dist.) Tex.; Ct. Appeals (5th Cir.). Ptnr. McGregor & Sessions, Waco, Tex., 1959-61; assoc. Tirey, McLaughlin, Gorin & Tirey, Waco, 1961-63; ptnr. Haley, Fulbright, Winniford, Sessions & Bice, Waco, 1963-69; sect. chief, govt. ops sect. criminal divsn. U.S. Dept. Justice, Washington, 1969-71; U.S. atty. (we. dist.) Tex. U.S. Dept Justice, San Antonio, 1971-74; judge U.S. Dist. Ct. (we. dist.) Tex., San Antonio, 1974-87, chief judge, 1980-87; dir. FBI, Washington, 1987-93; ptnr. Sessions & Sessions, San Antonio and Washington, 1995-2000, Holland & Knight, LLP, San Antonio and Washington, 2000—. Bd. dirs., chmn. book com. Fed. Jud. Ctr., Washington, 1981—; mem. Tex. Commn. on Judicial Efficiency, 1995, Tex. Commn. on a Representative Student Body, 1998, Gov.'s Task Force on Homeland Security, Gov.'s Anti-Crime Commn., Tex., 2002, ABA Standing Com. on the 21st Century Judiciary, ABA Standing Com. on the Libr. of Congress; mem. steering com. of coastal Tex.; mem. George W. Bush presdl. lib. steering com. Baylor U.; served on initiatives of Constitution Project; served as signatory The Ctr. for Study of Presidency; served as commr. Commn. on Safety & Abuse in America's Prisons. Contbr. articles to profl. jours. Active Dr. Martin Luther King Jr. Fed. Holiday Commn., 1991-96, hon. bd. dirs., 1993-94; bd. trustees Nat. Environ. Edn. & Tng. Found., Inc., 2001—. Lt. USAF, 1951-55; capt. USAFR. Recipient Rosewood Gavel award St. Mary's U. Sch. Law, San Antonio, 1982, Disting. Alumni award Baylor U., Golden Plate award Am. Acad. Achievement, 1988, Law Enforcement Leadership award Assn. Fed. Investigators, 1989, medal of honor DAR, 1989, Disting. Eagle Scout award Boy Scouts Am., 1990, Person of Yr. award Am. Soc. for Indsl. Security, 1990, Magna Charta award Baronial Order of Magna Charta, 1990, Price Daniel Disting. Pub. Svc. award Baylor U., 2002; named Lawyer of Yr., Baylor Law Sch., 1988, Father of Yr., Nat. Fathers Day Com., 1988, Ellis Island Congl. Medal of Honor, 1992; inducted into Eagle Scout Hall of Fame, 1998. Fellow ABA (chmn. spl. com. on judicial independence 1997—, Nat. Law Day chmn. 2000-02, hon. co chmn., pres. commn. on the 21st Century Judiciary, 2002-, mem. commn. on civic edn. and separation of powers); mem. Jud. Conf. U.S. (com. on ct. adminstrn., chmn. jud. improvements subcom. 1983-85, ad hoc com. on automation to subcom. 1984-87, mem. ad hoc ct. reporter com. 1984-87), San Antonio Bar Assn. (bd. dirs. 1973-74), Fed. Bar Assn. (pres. San Antonio sect. 1974), Am. Judicature Soc. (exec. com. 1982-84), Dist. Judges Assn. of 5th Cir. (pres. 1982-83), State Bar of Tex. (chmn. com. to develop procedures for cert. state law questions to Supreme Ct. by Fed. Cts. 1983-85), Waco McLennan County Bar Assn. (pres. 1968), San Antonio Inns of Ct. (pres. 1986), William S. Sessions Inns of Ct. Republican. Methodist. Avocations: hiking, climbing, canoeing. Office: Holland & Knight LLP Ste 100 2099 Pennsylvania Ave NW Washington DC 20006 Office Phone: 202-955-3000. Office Fax: 202-955-5564. Business E-Mail: wsessions@hklaw.com, william.sessions@hklaw.com.

SESSLE, BARRY JOHN, adult education educator, researcher; b. Sydney, NSW, Australia, May 28, 1941; arrived in Can., 1971; s. Frederick George and Sadie Isobel (Lawson) S.; m. Mary Baldwin; children from previous marriage: Erica Jane, Claire Marie. BDS, Sydney U., New South Wales, 1963, MDS, MSc, Sydney U., New South Wales, 1965; PhD, U. New South Wales, 1969, DSc (hon.), 2000. Scholar Dental Found. Sydney U., 1963-64; tchg. fellow U. New South Wales, 1965-68; vis. assoc. U.S. Nat. Inst. Dental Rsch., Bethesda, Md., 1968-70; assoc. prof. U. Toronto Dental Sch., Ont., Canada, 1971-76, prof., 1976-85, chmn. divsn. biol. scis., 1978-84, assoc. dean rsch., 1985-90, dean, 1990-2001. Mem. com. on dental scis. Can. Med. Rsch. Coun., Ottawa, 1979-82, 1990, 1992, 1994, 2002-03, 2006—; mem. com. grants rev. U.S. NIH, Bethesda, 1976-. Author: The Neural Basis of Oral and Facial Function, 1978; editor:

Mastication and Swallowing, 1976, Oro-facial Pain and Neuromuscular Dysfunction, 1985, Effects of Injury of Trigeminal and Spinal Somatosensory Systems, 1987, Trigeminal Neuralgia: Current Concepts Regarding Pathogenesis and Treatment, 1991, Temporomandibular Joint and Masticatory Muscle Disorders, 1994, Temporomandibular Disorders and Related Pain Conditions, 1995, Neurobiology of Mastication, 1999, Orofacial Pain, 2001, Sleep and Pain, 2007; mem. editl. bd. Arch. Oral Biol. Jour., 1988—, Pain Jour., 1986-90, Jour. Dental Rsch., 2003-05, Dysphagia Jour., 1990—, Pain Rsch. and Mgmt. Jour., 1995—, Oral Bioscis. and Medicine, 2003-2005, Jour. of Oral Rehab., 2003—; editor-in-chief Jour. Orofacial Pain, 1997—. Can. rsch. chair, 2001—. Recipient Tchr. award Can. Fund for Dental Edn., 1977, Disting. Career award Can. Pain Soc., 1999, Nat. Recognition award Am. Acad. Orofacial Pain, 2004; grantee Med. Rsch. Coun., 1971—, NIH, 1974—, Inst. Musculoskeletal Health and Arthritis Quality Life award Can. Inst. Health Rsch., 2005. Fellow Royal Soc. Can., Can. Acad. Sci., Internat. Coll. Dentists, Can. Acad. Health Scis.; mem. Internat. Assn. Study Pain (hon., sec. Can. chpt. 1982-87, mem. coun. 1993-96, pres.-elect 1997-99, pres. 1999-2002, chmn. orofacial pain group 2002-05), Soc. Neurosci. (pres. South Ont. chpt. 1982-83), Internat. Assn. Dental Rsch. (pres. Can. divsn. 1977-78, sec.-treas. 1976-79, chmn. neurosci. group 1985-86, pres. 1994-95, Oral Sci. award 1976, Pindborg Oral Biol. prize 1994), Internat. Union Physiol. Sci. (sec. oral physiology commn. 1983-90). Office: Faculty Dentistry U Toronto 124 Edward St Toronto ON Canada M5G 1G6

SESSLER, ANDREW MARIENHOFF, physicist; b. Bklyn., Dec. 11, 1928; s. David and Mary (Baron) S.; m. Gladys Lerner, Sept. 23, 1951 (div. Dec. 1994); children: Daniel Ira, Jonathan Lawrence, Ruth. BA in Math. cum laude, Harvard U., 1949; MA in Theoretical Physics, Columbia U., 1951, PhD in Theoretical Physics, 1953. NSF fellow Cornell U., Ithaca, NY, 1953—54; asst. prof. Ohio State U., Columbus, 1954, assoc. prof., 1960; on leave Midwestern Univs. Rsch., 1955—56; vis. physicist Lawrence Radiation Lab., 1959—60; vis. physicist, summer Niels Bohr Inst., Copenhagen, 1961; rschr. theoretical physics Lawrence Berkeley Lab. U. Calif., Berkeley, 1961—73, rschr. energy and environment Lawrence Berkeley Lab., 1971—73, dir. Lawrence Berkeley Lab., 1973—80, sr. scientist plasma physics Lawrence Berkeley Lab., 1980—94, disting. sr. staff scientist Lawrence Berkeley Lab., 1994—2001, disting. vis. scientist Lawrence Berkeley Lab., 2001—02, disting. scientist Lawrence Berkeley Lab., 2002—, dir. emeritus, 2002—. U.S. advisor Panjab U. Physics Inst., Chandigarh, India; mem. U.S.-India Coop. Program for Improvement Sci. Edn. in India, 1966, high energy physics adv. panel to U.S. AEC, 1969-72, adv. com. Lawrence Hall Sci., 1974-78; chmn. Stanford Synchrotron Radiation Project Sci. Policy Bd., 1974-77, EPRI Advanced Fuels Adv. Com., 1978-81, BNL External Adv. Com. on Isabelle, 1980-82; mem. sci. pol. bd. Stanford Synchrotron Radiation Lab., 1991-92; L.J. Haworth dist. scientist Brookhaven Nat. Lab., 1991-92; spokesperson Neutrino Factory and Muon Collider Collaboration, 1999-2002, assoc. spokesperson 2002—. Mem. editl. bd. Nuc. Instruments and Methods, 1969—2000, correspondent Comments on Modern Physics, 1969—71; contbr. articles to profl. jours. Mem. Superconducting Super Collider Sci. Policy Com., 1991—93; mem. radiation effects rsch. bd. Nat. Rsch. Coun., 2001—04, mem. nuclear radiation studies bd., 2005—. Recipient E.O. Lawrence award US Atomic Energy Commn., 1970, US Particle Accelerator Sch. prize, 1988, Nicholson Medal for Humanitarian Svc., 1994, Robert R. Wilson prize 1997; fellow Japan Soc. for Promotion Sci. at KEK, 1985. Fellow AAAS (nominating com. 1984-87), Am. Phys. Soc. (chmn. com. internat. freedom scientist 1982, study of directed energy weapons panel 1985-87, chmn. panel pub. affairs 1988, chmn. divsn. physics of beams 1990, chmn. com. applications of physics 1993, councilor for divsn. physics of beams 1994-97, pres.-elect 1997, pres. 1998, past pres. 1999, vice-chmn. forum on physics and soc. 2001, chmn.-elect 2002, chmn. 2003), N.Y. Acad. Sci.; mem. NAS (bd. on radiation effects rsch. 2002-05, nuclear radiation studies bd., 2005-), IEEE (sr.), Fedn. Am. Scientists Coun. (vice chmn. 1987-88, chmn. 1988-92), Assoc. Univ. Inc. (bd. dirs. 1991-98), Sigma Xi. Avocations: skiing, hiking, jogging, exercise, flute. Office: Lawrence Berkeley Lab Univ Calif MS 71R0259 1 Cyclotron Rd Bldg Berkeley CA 94720-8211 Office Phone: 510-486-4992. Business E-Mail: AMSessler@lbl.gov.

SESSLER, JONATHAN LAWRENCE, chemistry professor; b. Urbana, Ill., May 20, 1956; s. Andrew M. and Gladys Sessler; m. Carol Ann Rubel, Jan. 13, 1963; children: Jordan Elija, Chanan David. BS, U. Calif., Berkeley, 1973—77; PhD, Stanford U., Calif., 1977—82. Asst. prof. U. Tex., Austin, 1984—89, assoc. prof., 1989—92, prof., 1992—2001, Roland K. Pettit Centennial prof., 2001—. Co-founder and cons. Pharmacyclics, Inc., Sunnyvale, Calif., 1991—; editor Supramolecular Chemistry, Reading, 2000—; co-founder Anionics, Inc., Oakland, Calif., 2003—; standing mem., msfa study sect. NIH, Bethesda, Md., 2005—; assoc. editor ChemComm, Cambridge, England, 2005—; vis. prof. U. Southampton, England, 2006—; adj. prof. U. Calif., Santa Barbara, 2006—. Contbr. over 400 papers to profl. jours. and pubs. Mem. Temple Beth Shalom, Austin, Tex., 2002—06. Recipient Dreyfus Tchr. Scholar award, 1988, Cope Scholar award, Am. Chem. Soc., 1991, Sr. Scientist award, Alexander von Humboldt Found., 1992, Japanese Soc. for Promotion of Sci., 1992, 2004; fellow, AAAS, 1999; Sloan fellow, 1989. Jewish. Achievements include patents for Texaphyrin, Sapphyrin, Calixpyrrole And Related Inventions (75 Total). Avocation: languages. Office: Univ Texas 1 University Sta A5300 Austin TX 78712-0165 Home Phone: 512 419 1861; Office Phone: 512-471-5009. Office Fax: 512-471-7550; Home Fax: 512 471 7550. Business E-Mail: sessler@mail.utexas.edu.

SESSOMS, ALLEN LEE, academic administrator, physicist, educator, retired diplomat; b. NYC, Nov. 17, 1946; s. Albert Earl and Lottie Beatrice (Leff) Sessoms; m. Karley Allison Sessoms; children: Manon Elizabeth, Stephanie Csilla, Avery Danielle. BS in Physics with hon., Union Coll., Schenectady, NY, 1968; MS in Physics, U. Wash., Seattle, 1969; PhD in Physics, Yale U., 1972; DSc (hon.), Union Coll., 1998; PhD (hon.), Soka U., Japan, 2000. Sci. assoc. CERN, Geneva, 1973-78; asst. prof. physics Harvard U., Cambridge, Mass., 1974-81; sr. tech. advisor OES, State Dept., Washington, 1980-82; dir. Office Nuclear Tech. & Safeguards, State Dept., Washington, 1982-87; counselor for sci. and tech. U.S. Embassy, Paris, 1987-89, polit. minister, counselor Mexico City, 1989-91, dep. chief of mission, 1991-93; exec. v.p., v.p. for acad. affairs U. Mass. Sys., Boston, 1993-95; pres. CUNY Queens Coll., Flushing, NY, 1995-2000; lectr., fellow Belfer Ctr. for Sci. and Internat. Affairs, JFK Sch. Govt., Harvard U., Cambridge, Mass., 2000—03; pres. Del. State U., 2003—. Adv. com. U.S. Sec. Energy, 1995-2002; mem. NCAA Pres. Coun., 1996-2000; nuc. energy rsch. adv. com. U.S. Dept. Energy. Contbr. articles to profl. jours. Bd. dirs. Milestone Capital, Drawing Ctr.; mem. Del. Arts Coun.; mem. adv. coun. Toda Internat.; mem. bd. trustees Chapman U. Travel/study grant Ford Found., 1973-74; Alfred P. Sloan Found. fellow, 1977-81; recipient Wilbur Cross medal Yale Grad. Sch. Alumni, 1999, Medal of Highest Honor, Soka U., Japan, 1999; officer dans l'Ordre des Palmes Académiques, France, 1999. Mem. AAAS, Am. Phys. Soc., N.Y. Acad. Sci., Cosmos Club. Office: Office of the Pres Del State Univ 1200 N Dupont Hwy Dover DE 19901 Home Phone: 302-857-6090; Office Phone: 302-857-6001. Personal E-mail: allensessoms@aol.com. Business E-Mail: asessoms@desu.edu.

SESTAK, JOE (JOSEPH A. SESTAK JR.), congressman, retired military officer; b. Springfield, Pa., Dec. 12, 1951; m. Susan L. Clark; 1 child, Alexandra. BS, US Naval Acad., 1974; MPA, Harvard U., PhD in Polit. Economy and Govt. Advanced through ranks to vice adm. USN, 2005, ret., 2005, served six sea tours Atlantic and Pacific Fleets, comdr. Cruiser Destroyer Group 2 Arabian Gulf and MTO, comdr. George Washington Battle Group, joint staff Force Structure Resources and Assessment Directorate, dir. Strategy and Policy Divsn. on staff of Chief of Naval Ops., dir. Navy Quadrennial Def. Rev., dir. Navy Ops. Group, dir. Assessment Divsn./Capability Analysis Group, dep. chief. naval ops. for warfare requirements & programs., comdr. USS Samuel B. Roberts, 1991—93, head Strategy and Concepts Br. on staff of Chief of Naval Ops., 1993—94; dir. def. policy NSC, 1994—97; comdr. Destroyer Squadron 14 USN, 1997; mem. US Congress from 7th Pa. dist., 2007—, mem. armed services com., edn. & labor com., small bus. com. Decorated Def. Disting. Svc. medal, Legion of Merit with Gold Star, Meritorious Svc. medal with Gold Star, Navy Commendation medal with two Gold Stars, Def. Superior Svc. medal, Joint Svc. Commendation medal, Navy Achievement medal. Democrat. Roman Catholic. Achievements include being the highest ranking military officer to ever serve in the US Congress. Office: 600 N Jackson St Ste 203 Media PA 19063 also: 1022 Longworth House Office Bldg Washington DC 20515 Office Phone: 610-891-8956, 610-892-8623, 202-225-2011. Office Fax: 610-892-8628. *

SESTRIC, ANTHONY JAMES, lawyer; b. St. Louis, June 27, 1940; s. Anton and Marie (Gasparovic) Sestric; m. Carol F. Bowman, Nov. 24, 1966; children: Laura Antonette, Holly Nicole, Michael Anthony. Student, Georgetown U., Washington, DC, 1958-62; JD, Mo. U., 1965. Bar: Mo. 1965, Minn. 1996, US Ct. Appeals (8th cir.) 1965, US Ct. Appeals (7th cir.) 1984, US Dist. Ct. Mo. 1966, US Dist. Ct. (no dist.) Tex. 1985, US Dist. Ct. Ill. 1994, US Tax Ct. 1969, US Supreme Ct. 1970, US Claims Ct. 1986. Law clk. US Dist. Ct., St. Louis, 1965-66; ptnr. Sestric, McGhee & Miller, St. Louis, 1966-77, Fordyce and Mayne, 1977-78, Sestric & Garvey, 1978-96, Sestric Law Firm, St. Louis, 1996—: Spl. asst. to Mo. atty. gen., St. Louis, 1968; spl. asst. cir. atty., 2001—; mem. Fed. Jud. Selection Commn., 1993, US Jud. Selection Commn., 1993—94, US Magistrate Merit Selection Commn., 2005; gen. chmn. 22d jud. cir. bar com., 1995; mem. Region XI disciplinary com., 2001—. Contbr. articles to profl. jours. Hearing officer St. Louis Met. Police Dept.; active St. Louis Air Pollution Bd. Appeals and Varience Rev., 1966-73, chmn., 1968-73; active St. Louis Airport Commn., 1975-76; dist. vice-chmn. Boy Scouts Am., 1970-76; bd. dirs. Full Achievement, Inc., 1970-77, Legal Aid Soc. St. Louis, 1976-77, Law Libr. Assn. St. Louis, 1976-78, Thomas Dunn Memls., 1995-98, Marquette Learning Ctr., 1995-98; v.p. bd. St. Elizabeth Acad., 1985-86 Mem. ABA (state chmn. judiciary com. 1973-75, cir. chmn. com. condemnation, zoning and property use 1975-77, standing com. bar activities 1982-88), Nat. Conf. Bar Pres.'s (exec. coun. 1987-90), Mo. Bar Assn. (vice-chmn. young lawyers sect. 1973-76, bd. govs. 1974-77, chmn. law practice mgmt. com. 1997-99), Bar Assn. Met. St. Louis (chmn. young lawyers sect. 1974-75, exec. com. 1974-83, 94-95, pres. 1981-82, bd. govs. 1995-98, chmn. survey com. 1999). Home: 3967 Holly Hills Blvd Saint Louis MO 63116-3135 Office Phone: 314-351-2512. Personal E-mail: ajsestric@juno.com.

SETEAR, JOHN K., law educator; BA, Williams Coll., 1981; JD, Yale U., 1984. Law clerk U.S. Ct. Appeals D.C. cir., Sandra Day O'Connor, U.S. Supreme Ct.; policy analyst RAND Corp.; prof. Univ Calif. Los Angeles, 1991—97; vis. prof. Univ. Va. Sch. Law, 1997—98, prof., 1998—, now Thomas F. Bergin prof. Dir. Internat. Environmental Cooperation Project, Ctr. Internat. Rel., Univ. Calif. Los Angeles. Editor (in chief): Yale Law Journal, 1984. Fellow Woodrow Wilson Internat. Ctr. Scholars, 1995—96. Office: Univ Va Law Sch 580 Massie Rd Charlottesville VA 22903

SETHI, RAJAT, cardiologist, educator; b. New Delhi, Sept. 2, 1964; arrived in US, 2005; s. Prabhu Dayal Sethi; m. Manjit Dhalla, Aug. 25, 1990; children: Vishal, Akshay. Pharm D, U. Delhi, India, 1985, MSc, 1987; PhD, U. Man., Winnipeg, Canada, 1994. Registered pharmacist Delhi. Asst. rsch. officer NRC, Canada, 1994—96; dir. preclin. rsch. Medicure Inc., Canada, 1996—2000; sr. scientist U. Manitoba, Canada, 2000—05; mem. faculty Tex. A&M Health Sci. Ctr., Irma Lerma Rangel Coll. Pharmacy, Kingsville, 2005—. Co-author: book; contbr. chapters to books, more than 150 articles to profl. jours. Recipient Best Rsch. Trainee award, Heart and Stroke Found. Can., 1991—92, Prize for excellence in rsch., Man. Med. Svc. Found., 1993; scholar, U. Delhi, 1985—87, Man. Health Rsch. Coun., 1990—91, Heart and Stroke Found. Can., 1990—94; Rsch. Ctr. scholar, St. Boniface Gen. Hosp., 1989—90. Mem.: Can. Pharmacy Assn., Internat. Soc. Heart Rsch., Am. Assn. Colls. of Pharmacy. Achievements include beneficial effect of distiller's grain in cardiovascular disease; treatment of cardiovascular and related pathologies; adenine based inhibitors of adenylyl cyclase. pharmaceutical compositions and other methods of use; treatment of cerebrovascular disease; treatment of cardiovascular and related pathologies; treatment of diabetes and related pathologies; treatment of iatronic and age-related hypertension and pharmaceutical compositions. Office: Tex A&M Health Sci Ctr Irma Lerma Rangel Coll Pharmacy MSC 131 Kingsville TX 78363 Office Phone: 361-593-4275. Business E-Mail: rsethi@pharmacy.tamhsc.edu.

SETHI, SHYAM SUNDER, management consultant; b. Rawalpindi, Pakistan, July 11, 1942; s. Balraj and Shakuntala (Sawhney) Sethi; m. Kiran Nair, Oct. 17, 1972; children: Seema, Shana. B.E. in Mech. Engring., Birla Inst. Tech., Ranchi, India, 1964; MSI.E., U. Wis., 1970. Cert. mgmt. cons. V.p. Drake Sheahan/Stewart Dougall, NYC, 1970-80; pres., ptnr. Distbn. Mgmt. Assocs., Inc., Princeton, NJ, 1980-96; exec. dir. Dechert-Hampe & Co./DMA, 1996-2000; pres. Distbn. Mgmt. Assocs., Inc., 2001—. Cons. in supply chain, logistics, inventory mgmt., ops. for maj. consumer goods, indsl. and retail cos., Europe, S.Am. and US; spkr. internat. logistics conf. Contbr. articles to profl. jours. Pres. NJ chpt. Coun. Logistics Mgmt., 1987-88, NJ chpt. Inst. Mgmt. Consultants, 1987-88. Mem. Yacht Assn. India. Hindu. Avocations: tennis, sailing. Home: 4 Haelig Ct Bridgewater NJ 08807-2377 Office: DMA Inc PO Box 6843 Bridgewater NJ 08807-0843 Office Phone: 732-469-1885. Personal E-mail: sethinj@optonline.net.

SETHNA, BEHERUZ NARIMAN, academic administrator, educator, management consultant; b. Bombay, July 31, 1948; came to U.S., 1973; s. Nariman Dhanjishaw and Mithu Nariman (Mistry) S.; m. Madhavi Kaji, May 25, 1974; children: Anita B., Shaun B. B in Tech. with honors, Indian Inst. Tech., Bombay, 1971; MBA, Indian Inst. Mgmt., Ahmedabad, 1973; MPhil, Columbia U., 1975, PhD in Bus., 1976; student, Ind. U., 1986, Harvard U., 1991. Cert. computing profl. Inst. for Cert. Computing Profls. Engring. and mgmt. trainee various corps., Bombay, 1968-69, 70-72; case writer, trainee Clarion Advt., Bombay, 1973; project mgr., cons. Lever Bros. Co., NYC, 1974-76; prof., chair mktg. and mgmt. info. systems Clarkson U., Potsdam, NY, 1976-89, dir. grad. programs, 1978-80; mktg., rsch. and strategic planning mgr. Procter & Gamble (India)/Richardson Hindustan (Vicks), Bombay and Westport, Conn., 1980-81; interim exec. v.p. acad. and student affairs; dean Coll. of Bus., chief acad. officer Lamar (Tex.) U., 1989-94, Gulf States Utilities prof. bus., 1991-94; pres. West Ga. Coll., Carrollton, 1994—96, State U. West Ga., 1996—2005, U. West Ga., 2005—; interim sr. vice chancellor Univ. Sys. Ga., 1999—2000, interim exec. vice chancellor, chief acad. officer, 2006—07; pres. Ga. Assn. Colls., Carrollton, 2000—01. Mem. adv. coun. SUNY-Canton (N.Y.) Coll., 1975-89; cons. in field. Author: Research Methods in Marketing, 1984; contbr. articles to profl. jours. Scoutmaster Boy Scouts Am., Potsdam, 1987—89, pack com. chair, den leader, 1987—89, mem. dist. bd., 1991—94, mem. exec. bd. Atlanta Area coun., 1997—2003, Pres.'s Scout Gold Cord, 1966; leader Girl Scouts U.S., Beaumont, 1989—94. Named one of 100 Most Influential Georgians, Ga. Trend, 2003, 2006; recipient Minority Achiever's award, Role Model award, 1991, Dean's Leadership award, Acad. Bus. Adminstrn., 1993, Nat. Svc. award, 1996, Alumnus award (hon.), 1999, Disting. Alumnus award, Indian Inst. Tech., Bombay, 2000, Carroll County Citizen of Yr., 1999, rated 1st among Carroll County's Movers, Shakers and Newsmakers, 2002, Resolution of Commendation, State Senate, 2003, Instructional Innovation award (hon.), 1984—89, 2004, Empowerment award, Ctr. Student Leadership, 2007; grantee, US Dept. Energy, 1980, IBM Corp., 1984, AT&T, 1985; Fulbright scholar, U.S. Info. Agy., 1986—87, Paul Harris fellow, Rotary Internat., 1997. Mem. Rotary (polio plus edn. chair). Avocation: scouting. Home: 107 Windsong Ct Carrollton GA 30117-8978 Office: U W Ga Office Pres Carrollton GA 30118-0001 Office Phone: 678-839-6442. Business E-Mail: bsethna@westga.edu.

SETLIN, ALAN JOHN, entrepreneur; b. NYC, Oct. 27, 1933; s. Samuel and Alyce (Inginito) S.; children: Susan Marie, Peggy Ann, Gina Marie, Alycia Ruth, Alana Jean; m. Deborah Ann Kozlowski, Oct. 14, 1986. Student, U. Miami. CLU. V.p. Figurette, Ltd., Miami, Fla., 1956-60; ptnr. Robins & Clarke, NYC, 1960-63; leading agt. Equitable Life Ins. Co., NYC, 1963; gen. agt. Madison Life Ins. Co., NYC, 1963-66, Beneficial Nat. Life Ins. Co., NYC, 1967-72; pres., chief exec. officer Alliance Assoc., Inc., Beverly Hills, Calif., 1972—; ptnr. McMutry & Bell, Inc., Beverly Hills, 1982—; chief exec. officer Emergency Help, Inc., Beverly Hills, 1989-91; COO, dir. Clinica Medica Familiar, LA, 1993-96; COB, CEO Futurenet On-Line, Inc., Valencia, Calif., 1996—. Bd. dirs. Six Million Dollar Forum, 1979-80. Mem. Rep. Senatorial Inner Circle, 1988-90. Sgt. AUS, 1952-54. Mem. Nat. Assn. Life Underwriters (fed. legis. chmn. Western States div. 1980-81, pres. L.A. chpt. 1979-80), CLU Assn. (pres. county chpt. 1979-80), Million Dollar Round Table (life), Golden Key (nat. com.). Roman Catholic. Avocations: weightlifting, boxing, skiing, white water rafting, motorcycling. Office: Futurenet On-Line Inc 12711 Ventura Blvd Ste 480 Studio City CA 91604-2456

SETLOW, JANE KELLOCK, biophysicist; b. NYC, Dec. 17, 1919; d. Harold A. and Alberta (Thompson) Kellock; m. Richard Setlow, June 6, 1941; children: Peter, Michael, Katherine, Charles. BA, Swarthmore Coll., 1940; PhD in Biophysics, Yale U., 1959. With dept. radiology Yale U., 1959-60; with biology div. Oak Ridge Nat. Lab., 1960-74; biophysicist Brookhaven Nat. Lab., Upton, N.Y., 1974—. Mem. recombinant DNA molecule program adv. com. NIH, chmn., 1978-2005. Editor: Genetic Engineering, Principles and Methods; mem. editl. bd. various jours.:; contbr. articles to profl. jours. Predoctoral fellow USPHS, 1957-59; postdoctoral fellow, 1960-62 Mem. Biophys. Soc. (pres. 1977-78), Am. Soc. Microbiology. Democrat. Home: 57 Valentine Rd Shoreham NY 11786-1243 Office: Biology Dept Brookhaven Nat Lab Upton NY 11973 Office Phone: 631-344-3420.

SETLOW, RICHARD BURTON, biophysicist, researcher; b. NYC, Jan. 19, 1921; s. Charles Meyer and Elsie Setlow; children: Peter, Michael, Katherine, Charles; m. Neva Delihas, Mar. 3, 1989. AB, Swarthmore Coll., 1941; PhD, Yale U., 1947; DSc, U. Toronto, 1985; MD, U. Essen, 1993. Assoc. prof. Yale U., 1956-61; biophysicist Oak Ridge (Tenn.) Nat. Lab., 1961-74, sci. dir. biophysics and cell physiology, 1969-74; dir. U. Tenn.-Oak Ridge Grad. Sch. Biomed. Scis., 1972-74; sr. biophysicist Brookhaven Nat. Lab., Upton, NY, 1974—2006, chmn. biology dept., 1979-87, assoc. dir. life scis., 1985-98, assoc. lab. dir., 1998, sr. biophysicist emeritus, 2007—. Prof. biomed. scis. U. Tenn., 1967-74; adj. prof. biochemistry SUNY, Stony Brook, 1975—. Author: (with E.C. Pollard) Molecular Biophysics, 1962; editor: (with P.C. Hanawalt) Molecular Mechanisms for Repair of DNA, 1975; contr. books to chap. Recipient Finsen medal Internat. Assn. Photobiology, 1980, Enrico Fermi award U.S. Dept. Energy, 1988, Environ. Mutagen Soc. award, 2002. Mem. NAS, Am. Acad. Arts and Scis., Biophys. Soc. (pres. 1969-70), Internat. Com. Photobiology (pres. 1972-76), Radiation Rsch. Soc., Am. Soc. Photobiology, Am. Assn. Biochemistry and Molecular Biology, Am. Soc. Cancer Rsch., Environ. Mutagen Soc., 11th Internat. Congress on Photobiology (hon. pres. 1992), Phi Beta Kappa. Home: 4 Beachland Ave East Quogue NY 11942-4941 Office: Brookhaven Nat Lab Dept Biology Upton NY 11973 Office Phone: 631-344-3391. Personal E-mail: setlow@optonline.net. Business E-Mail: setlow@bnl.gov.

SETO, THEODORE PAUL, lawyer, educator; b. Kermanshah, Iran, Feb. 18, 1951; came to U.S., 1951; s. Paul Susumu and Genevieve (Reynolds) S.; m. Lenore T. Rothman, Aug. 2, 1980 (div. 1999); 1 child, Kira Rothman Seto; m. Sande Lynn Buhai, July 8, 2000; children: Samantha Elizabeth, Genevieve Danielle. BA, Harvard U., 1973, JD, 1976. Bar: Mass. 1977, U.S. Dist. Ct. Mass. 1978, U.S. Dist. Ct. (ea. dist.) Pa. 1983, U.S. Tax Ct. 1985, U.S. Ct. Appeals (1st cir.) 1983, U.S. Ct. Appeals (3d cir.) 1990, U.S. Supreme Ct. 1983, U.S. Claims Ct. 1990. Law clk. to Hon. Judge Mansfield U.S. Ct. Appeals (2nd cir.), NYC, 1976-77; assoc. Foley, Hoag & Eliot, Boston, 1977-83, Drinker Biddle & Reath, Phila., 1983-86, ptnr., 1986-91; assoc. prof. Loyola Law Sch., LA, 1991-97, prof., 1997—. Vis. prof. U. Paris X, 1998, Cornell Law Sch., 2005. Author: A Uniform System of Citation, 12th edit. 1976; contbr. articles to profl. jours. Democrat. Office: Loyola Law Sch 919 Albany St Los Angeles CA 90015-1211 Home Phone: 323-255-6195; Office Phone: 213-736-1154. Business E-Mail: tseto@lls.edu.

SETRAKIAN, BERGE, lawyer; b. Beirut, Apr. 14, 1949; came to U.S. 1976; s. Hemayak and Arminee S.; m. Vera L. Nazarian, Nov. 22, 1975; children: Ani, Lara. Diplome d'Etudes de Doctorat, U. Lyons, France, 1973; Diplome d'Etudes de Doctorat Droit Compare, F.I.E.D.C., Strasbourg, France, 1974; Licence en Droit Francais, U. St. Joseph, Beirut, 1972, Licence en Droit Libanais, 1972. Bar: Beirut 1972, N.Y. 1983. Assoc. Tyan & Setrakian, Beirut, 1972-76; ptnr. Whitman & Ransom, NYC, 1976-93, Whitman, Breed, Abbott & Morgan, NYC, 1993-2000, Winston & Strawn, NYC, 2000—05, LeBoeuf, Lamb, Greene & MacRae, 2005—. Bd. dirs. Cedars Bank, Calif., 1987—, Interaudi Bank, NY, 1991; fgn. law cons., NY, 78. Pres. Armenian Gen. Benevolent Union, N.Y.C., 2002-; bd. dirs. Armenian Assn. of Am., Washington, 1978-87; bd. dirs. Am. Task Force for Lebanon, 1988—; bd. dirs. Am. U. Armenia, 1992—. Mem. ABA, N.Y. Bar Assn., Beirut Bar Assn., Am. Fgn. Law Assn., Englewood Field Club. Office: LeBoeuf, Lamb, Greene & MacRae 125 W 55th St New York NY 10019

SETSER, CAROLE SUE, food scientist, educator; b. Warrenton, Mo., Aug. 26, 1940; d. Wesley August and Mary Elizabeth (Meine) Schulze; m. Donald Wayne Setser, June 2, 1969; children: Bradley Wayne, Kirk Wesley, Brett Donald. BS, U. Mo., 1962; MS, Cornell U., 1964; PhD, Kans. State U., 1971. Grad. asst. Cornell U., Ithaca, NY, 1962-64; instr. Kans. State U., Manhattan, 1964-72, asst. prof., 1974-81, assoc. prof., 1981-86, prof., 1986-2001, prof. emeritus, 2001—. Vis. prof. Bogazici U., Istanbul, Turkey, 2000—01. Recipient Rsch. Excellence award, Coll. of Human Ecology, Manhattan, 1990. Mem.: Inst. Food Techs. (chmn. sensory evaluation divsn. edn. com. 1989—92, continuing edn. com. 1992—95, sec. product devel. divsn. 1997—99, also other offices), Am. Assn. Cereal Chemists (assoc. editor 1989—93), Kappa Omicron Nu (Excellence for Rsch. award 1987), Sigma Xi, Phi Tau Sigma (Outstanding Food Scientist 1998), Gamma Sigma Delta, Phi Upsilon Omicron, Phi Kappa Phi (Scholar award 1998). Home Phone: 785-537-9449. Business E-Mail: setser@ksu.edu.

SETSER, CHRISTIE ELAINE, auditor; d. James David and Helen Emma Setser; m. Norman Bodenstein (div.). BA in History, Pittsburg State U., Kans., 1977, MS in Sociology, 1979. Social worker Mo. Dept. Social Svcs., St. Louis, 1979—97; tax auditor Mo. Dept. Labor, St. Louis, 1999—. Adj. prof. Columbia Coll., Mo., 1980. Mem.: Internat. Assn. Workforce Profls. (zone sec. 2000—), Mensa, Daus. Union Vets. (past state pres.). Avocations: reading, writing, genealogy, mathematics. Office: Mo Dept Labor 505 Washington Ave Saint Louis MO 63101

SETSER, PATRICIA A., music educator; b. Kansas City, Mo., June 29, 1951; d. Flo Daulton and George Sterling Waugh; m. Michael W. Setser, Sept. 9, 1972. MusB Edn., Ctrl. Mo. State U., 1973, MA in Music Edn., 1978. Cert. tchr., life - music coord. K-12, history K-8 Mo., 1973. Coord. music North Kansas City Sch. Dist., 1996—; band dir. Winnetonka HS, Kansas City, 1983—. Guest condr., adjudicator Heart of Am. Wind Symphony, Mo., 1978—, musician, Mo., 2001—; musician, guest conductor Kansas City Wind Symphony, Shawnee Mission, Kans., 2002—. Condr. (music contest) St. Louis Music Festival (Grand Champions, 2001, 2005), Nat. Adjudicators Nat. Festival, Va. (Grand Champions, 2002), Chgo. Music Festival (Grand Champions, 2000); instr. (tchg.) Tchg. (Excellence in Tchg. Award, 1994); condr. (orch. condr.) State Contest (First Pl. Ratings), band condr. (conducting) State Music Contests (First Pl. Ratings - all years); composer: (entry level jazz for young band students) Musical composition. Bd. mem. Warrensburg Cmty. Band, Mo., 2001—. Named Disting. Music Alumnus, Ctrl. Mo. State U., 2005—06. Mem.: Mo. Music Educators Assn. (assoc.), Music Educators Nat. Conf. (assoc.), Am. Quarter Horse Assn. (assoc.), Epsilon Omega - Sigma Alpha Iota (assoc.; pres., v.p, sec. 1970—73, Sword of Honor - Leadership 1974). Avocations: antique automobiles, gardening, genealogy. Office: North Kansas City Sch Dist 1950 NE 46th St Kansas City MO 64116 E-mail: psetser@nkcsd.k12.mo.us.

SETTERHOLM, JEFFREY MILES, systems engineer; b. Rochester, NY, May 8, 1946; s. Vernon Miles and Grace Lorraine (Bogema) S.; m. Donna Jean Stollenwerk, July 6, 1974; children: Gregory Todd, Vincent Michael. BS in Engring., Applied Sci. cum laude, Yale U., 1968; MS in Sys. Sci. and Math., Washington U., 1976. Electronic engr. McDonnell Douglas Aircraft Divsn., St. Louis, 1974, sr. engr. flight simulation, 1976-78; prin. devel. engr. mil. avionics divsn. Honeywell Inc., Mpls., 1978-84; prin. engr. aerospace divsn. Rosemount, Inc., Burnsville, Minn., 1984-92; ind. software tech. cons. Lakeville, Minn., 1992-94; geodetic scientist Geospan Corp., Maple Grove, Minn., 1994—2003, contract engr., 2006—, Alliant Techsys., Plymouth, Minn., 2005—06. Author: The Philosophy Works Manual, 1993, Learning Together in a Diverse World, 2004. Capt. USAF, 1969-73. Decorated DFC. Mem. AIAA, Soc. Automotive Engrs. Lutheran. Achievements include patents in field; origination of the computer configurable six-axis hand controller concept; invention of surveying from non-coplanar images; research in virtual cockpit concepts. Home: 8095 230th St E Lakeville MN 55044-8287 Personal E-mail: jeff@setterholm.com.

SETTIS, SALVATORE, archaeologist, art historian; b. Rosarno, Italy, June 11, 1941; s. Rocco and Carmela (Megna) Settis; m. Chiara Frugoni, Dec. 9, 1965 (div. 1982); children: Silvano, Andrea, Marta; m. Maria Michela Sassi, Jan. 4, 1984; children: Bruno, Nicola. Degree, U. Pisa, Italy, 1963; PhD, Scuola Normale Superiore, Pisa, 1965. Asst. prof. U. Pisa, 1965—69, lectr., 1969—75, prof., 1976—84, dean Faculty Letters and Philosophy, 1978—81; prof. Scuola Normale Superiore, Pisa, 1984—, dean Faculty Letters and Philosophy, 1986—91, dir., 1999—, Getty Rsch. Inst. for History Art and Humanities, Santa Monica, Calif., 1994—99. Author: La Tempesta Interpretata, 1978, La Colonna Traiana, 1988, I Greci, 5 vols., 1996—2001, Laocoonte Fama e Stile, 1999, Italia SpA L'assalto al patrimonio culturale, 2002, Futuro del "Classico", 2004, Battaglie senza eroi, 2005. Office: Scuola Normale Superiore Piazza dei Cavalieri 7 56125 Pisa Italy Office Phone: +39050509215. E-mail: direttore@sns.it.

SETTLE, BENJAMIN HALE, federal judge; b. Olympia, Wash., 1947; BA, Claremont McKenna Coll., 1969; JD, Willamette U. Coll. Law, 1972. Bar: Washington DC 1972. Assoc. Don Miles Attorneys, 1972; judge adv., gen. corps US Army, 1973—76; assoc. Don Miles Attorneys, 1976—77; ptnr. Settle & Johnson, P.L.L.C., 1977—2007; judge US Dist. Ct. (we. dist.), Wash., 2007—. Capt., active duty USAR, 1973—75. Office: 3100 US Courthouse 1717 Pacific Ave Tacoma WA 98402-3234 Office Phone: 253-882-3800. *

SETTLE, MARK, information technology executive; BS Earth and Planetary Sci., MS Earth and Planetary Sci., MIT; PhD Geol. Sci., Brown U. CIO Occidental Petroleum, 1997—99; exec. v.p., systems and processing Visa Internat., 1999—2001; v.p., CIO Arrow Electronics, Inc., Melville, NY, 2001—. Retired USAF. Office: Arrow Electronics Inc 50 Marcus Dr Melville NY 11747-4210

SETTLES, F. STAN, JR., engineering educator, manufacturing executive; b. Denver, Oct. 3, 1938; s. Frank S. and Dorothy Marie (Johnson) S.; m. Evelyn Brown, June 10, 1961; children: Frank S. III, Richard, Charles, Michael. BS in Prodn. Tech., Indsl. Engring., LeTourneau Coll., Longview, Tex., 1962; MS in Indsl. Engring., Ariz. State U., Tempe, 1967, PhD in Indsl. Engring., 1969. Sr. systems analyst AiResearch Mfg. Co., Phoenix, 1968-70, project mgr., 1970-74, mgr. operational planning, 1974-80; mgr. indsl. engrs. Garrett Pneumatic Systems, Phoenix, 1980-83; mgr. indsl. mfg. engring. Garrett Turbine Engring. Co., Phoenix, 1983-85; v.p. mfg. ops. AiResearch Mfg. Co., Torrance, Calif., 1985-87; dir. indusl. mfg. engring. The Garrett Corp., Phoenix, 1987-88; dir. planning Garrett Engine Div., Phoenix, 1988-92; asst. dir. White House Office of Sci. and Tech. Policy, 1992-93; program dir. NSF, 1992-94; prof., chmn. indsl. and systems engring. dept. U. So. Calif., LA, 1994—2003, IBM prof. engring. mgmt., dir. sys. arch. & engring. program, 2003—. Faculty assoc. Ariz. State U., Tempe, 1974-85, 90-92, rsch. prof., 1992-94. Mem. sch. bd. Tempe Elem. Sch. Dist., 1976-80; mem. YMCA Indian Guides, nat. chief, 1978-79. Fellow Inst. Indsl. Engrs. (pres. 1987-88, Ops. Rsch. award 1980), Inst. Ops. Rsch. and Mgmt. Sci., Nat. Acad. Engrs., Soc. Mfg. Engrs. (sr.), IEEE Engring. Mgmt. Soc., Am. Soc. Quality Control, Am. Soc. Engring. Edn. Republican. Presbyterian. Home: 1310 E Ocean Blvd Unit 1602 Long Beach CA 90802-6917 Office: U So Calif Dept Indsl Sys Engring Los Angeles CA 90089-0193 Office Phone: 213-740-0263. Business E-Mail: settles@usc.edu.

SETZER, ARLENE J., state representative, retired secondary school educator; b. Dayton, Ohio, Mar. 2, 1944; BS in Bus. Adminstrn., U. Dayton, 1966; MEd, Wright State U., 1973, postgrad. Tchr. bus. and computer applications Vandalia-Butler HS, 1967—2000; rep. Ohio State Ho. Reps., Columbus, 2000—. Mem. agr. and natural resources com. Ohio State Ho. Reps., chmn. edn. com., mem. ins. com. Mem. ins. rev. com. and state govt. com. City of Vandalia, 1998—2000; chair Vandalia-Butler Food Pantry Bldg. Fund; pres. Pres.'s Club of Vandalia, 1997—99; mem. Ednl. Trust Project, Advocates for People with Devel. Disabilities, Montgomery County Ednl. Advancement Dialogue; precinct capt. Montgomery County Rep. Party, mem. ctrl. com., exec. com.; mem. Vandalia City Coun., 1982—2000, vice-mayor, 1986—88, 1995—2000. Named Rep. Woman of Yr., 1997, 2001, 2003; recipient Clara Weisenborn award, 1999, Horace M. Huffman Jr. Svc. to Bicyclists award, Ohio Bicycle Fedn., 2001, Appreciation award, S.W. Ohio Hemophilia Found. and W. Ctrl. Ohio Hemophilia Ctr., 2002, Rep. of Yr. award, Ohio Coll. Rep. Fedn., 2003; Martha Holden Jennings scholar, 1983—84. Mem.: Sister Cities of Vandalia, Montgomery County Farm Bur., Inc., Montgomery County Cattlemen's Assn., Montgomery Agrl. Soc., Sr. Citizens of Vandalia-Butler, Miami Valley Mil. Affairs Assn., Vandalia-Butler (Ohio) Hist. Soc. (v.p. 2000), Rotary (hon.; Dist. 6670 dir. 1992—96, pres. 1994—95, Dist. 6670 scholarship com. 1997, Dist. 6670 bd. dirs., asst. dist. gov. 1998—2000, named to Hall of Fame). Republican. Office: Ohio State Ho of Reps 77 S High St 13th Fl Columbus OH 43215-6111

SETZLER, EDWARD ALLAN, lawyer; b. Kansas City, Mo., Nov. 3, 1933; s. Edward A. and Margaret (Parshall) S.; m. Helga E. Friedemann, May 20, 1972; children: Christina, Ingrid, Kirstin. BA, U. Kans., 1955; JD, U. Wis., 1962. Bar: Mo. 1962, US Tax Ct. 1962. Assoc. Spencer, Fane, Britt & Browne, Kansas City, 1962-67, ptnr., 1968-2000, mng. ptnr., 1974-77, 78-82, chmn. trust and estate sect., 1974-2000; ptnr. Husch & Eppenberger, LLC, 2000—06, Lathrop & Gage, 2006—. Co-author: Missouri Estate Administration, 1984, supplements, 1987—2004; contbg. editor: Understanding Living Trusts, 1990—2004; co-author: Missouri Estate Planning, 1986; co-author supplements, 1988—2004; contbg. editor: A Will is Not the Way--The Living Trust Alternative, 1988; bd. editors: Wis. Law Rev., 1961—62. Bd. govs., bd. dirs., chmn. found. com. Am. Royal, 1982—2006; mem. planning giving com. Nelson Atkins Mus. Art, 1984—95; mem. deferred giving com. Children's Mercy Hosp., 1991—; mem. Kansas City Estate Planning Symposium Com., 1984—92, chmn., 1991; mem. adv. com. Greater Kansas City Cmty. Found., 2000—; trustee Zoo Learning Fund, 2002—; mem. adv. bd. Children's Svc. League, 2003—06. Fellow: Am. Coll. Trust and Estate Counsel (state chmn. 1992—97, mem. state membership com. 1986—2001); mem.: Assn. Conflict Resolutions, Estate Planning Soc. Kansas City (co-founder 1965, pres. 1983—84, dir. 1984—85, mem. social com. 1968—), Kansas City Met. Bar Assn. (lectr., chmn. probate and trust 1979, 1992, vice chmn. 1983—85, 1991, legis. rev. com. 1991—95), Mo. Bar Assn. (lectr., vice chmn. probate and estate planning com. 1994—97), Sigma Xi, Order of the Coif, Phi Delta Phi. Office: 2345 Grand Ste 2400 Kansas City MO 64108 Home Phone: 816-753-4855; Office Phone: 816-460-5412. Fax: 816-292-2001. Business E-Mail: esetzler@lathropgage.com.

SETZLER, WILLIAM EDWARD, retired chemicals executive; b. Bklyn., Dec. 20, 1926; s. William Edward and Gertrude A. (Seyer) S.; m. Dorothy C. Kress, Dec. 2, 1950 (dec. Mar. 1987); children: William John, Heather A.; m. Lenore Kelly, July 13, 1991. B of Chem. Engring., Cooper Union, 1950; MS in Liberal Studies, Columbia U., 1993. V.p. ops. Argus Chem. Corp., NYC, 1950-66; v.p. engring., then group v.p. Witco Chem. Corp. (now Crompton Corp.), NYC, 1966-75, exec. v.p., 1975-90, ret., 1990, also bd. dirs.; chmn. and CEO Faimount Chem. Inc., 1993-97. Author and patentee in field. Served with USAAF, 1945-46. Mem. Am. Inst. Chem. Engrs., Soap and Detergent Assn. (bd. dirs.), The Dorothy Setzler Fund (pres. 1991—). Home: 3921 Lincoln St Seaford NY 11783-2115 Personal E-mail: billchair@att.net.

SEUBERT, LORI A., elementary school educator; d. Harry Marx Seubert Jr. and Ruth Janice Seubert. BA in English and Elem. Edn. cum laude, U. Toledo, 1981, MEd in Sci. and Early Childhood cum laude, 1990. Tchr. Franklin Sch., Toledo, 1985—90; NSF-funded Toledo Area Partnership in Edn: Support Tchrs. as Resources to Improve Elem. Sci. sci. support tchr. Toledo City Schs., U. Toledo, Bowling Green State U., 1998—2002; TAPESTRIES summer inst. educator Bowling Green State U., Ohio, 2000, U. Toledo, 1999—2002; tchr. Toledo City Schs., 2002—04; tchr., grade 5 Reynolds Sch., Toledo, 1990—. Young exptl. scientist tchr. intern Columbus's Ctr. Sci. and Industry, Ohio Coun. for Elem. Sch. Sci., 1989, workshop coord., 1990—93; edn. cons., Toledo, 1996—; Full Option Sci. Sys. cons. Delta Edn., Nashua, NH, 1999—. Author: (book) A Unit on Physics of Flight for Third Graders, 1990; co-author, editor: guide TAPESTRIES's K-6 Science Curriculum Alignment to Ohio Outcomes for Toledo City Schools, 2001. Recipient Outstanding K-3 Tchr. award, Toledo Assn. for Edn. of Young Children, 2004, Impact II award, Ameritech Ohio Dept. Edn., 1995, 1996, Bd. Trustees award, U. Toledo, 1989—91; Award grant, Ohio Space Grant Consortium, 2000, 2 Ohio's BEST Practice Award grants, NSF-funded TAPESTRIES, 2002. Mem.: DAR, NSTA, Ohio Coun. Elem. Sch. Sci. (bd. dirs. 1992—95, pres.-elect to pres. 1994—96), Nat. Assn. for Edn. of Young Children, Assn. Supervision and Curriculum Devel., Kappa Delta Pi, Delta Delta Delta. Avocations: photography, hiking, reading, art and antique collecting, travel. Office: Toledo City Schs 420 E Manhattan Blvd Toledo OH 43608 Home Phone: 419-537-9769. Business E-Mail: lori.seubert@tps.org.

SEUNG, THOMAS KAEHAO, philosophy educator; b. Jungju, Korea, Sept. 20, 1930; m. Kwihwan Hahn, May 29, 1965; children: Hyunjune Sebastian, Kwonjune Justin, Haesue Florence. BA, Yale U., 1958, MA, 1961, PhD, 1965. Instr. Yale U., 1963-65; asst. prof. Fordham U., 1965-66; mem. faculty dept. philosophy U. Tex., Austin, 1966—, prof. in philosophy, 1972—, prof. in govt., 1985—, prof. in law, 1993—, Jesse H. Jones prof. liberal arts, 1987—. Author: The Fragile Leaves of the Sybil, 1962, Kant's Transcendental Logic, 1969, Cultural Thematics, 1976, Structuralism and Hermeneutics, 1982, Semiotics and Thematics, 1982, Intuition and Construction, 1993, Kant's Platonic Revolution, 1994, Plato Rediscovered, 1996, Nietzche's Epic of the Soul, 2005, Goethe, Nietzsche, and Wagner, 2006, Kant, 2007. Served as officer Korean Army, 1950-53. Recipient Wilbur Lucius Cross medal Yale Grad. Sch. Alumni Assn., 1988; Soc. Religion in Higher Edn. fellow, 1969-70; Am. Council Learned Soc. fellow, 1970-71; NEH fellow, 1977-78 Office: U Tex Dept Philosophy Austin TX 78712 Mailing: PO Box 28055 Austin TX 78755 Business E-Mail: t.k.seung@mail.utexas.edu.

SEURKAMP, MARY PAT, college president; b. Pitts., Sept. 6, 1946; d. Frank H. and Loretta (Husic) Reuwer; m. Robert W. Seurkamp, Aug. 6, 1983; children: Kris, Robert, Brooke. BA, Webster U., 1968; MA, Washington U., 1969; PhD, SUNY, Buffalo. Counselor to dir. student living Gannon U., Erie, Pa., 1969-76; assoc. v.p. St. John Fisher Coll., Rochester, N.Y., 1976-92, adj. asst. prof. dept. psychology, 1992—, acting v.p. academic affairs, dean, 1992-98; pres. Coll. of Notre Dame of Md., Balt., 1998—. Mem. planning team Monroe County Ednl. Outcomes Conf.; bd. dirs. Bishop Kennedy High Sch.; cons. Women's Career Ctr., Rochester, N.Y., 1987—. Com. mem. various parish coms., Pittsford, N.Y., 1983—, Diocesan Com. Devel. of Mins. and Employees, Rochester, 1986-89, Internat. Alliance Leadership Conf., 1991; mentor Career Beginnings Program; vol. Career Connections Mentoring Program, 1988-90. Mem. AAUP, Am. Assn. High Edn., Nat. U. Continuing Edn. Assn., Rochester Women's Network. Republican. Roman Catholic. Home: 5502 Lombardy Pl Baltimore MD 21210-1420 Office: Office of the President Coll Notre Dame Md 4701 N Charles St Baltimore MD 21210-2404

SEVART, DANIEL JOSEPH, lawyer; b. Oswego, Kans., June 25, 1944; s. Vernon Joseph and Alma Bridget (Carland) S.; m. Shoko Kato, Apr. 17, 1968; 1 child, Eric J. AA, Parsons Jr. Coll., 1964; BA, Washburn U., 1973, JD with honors, 1975. Bar: Kans. 1976, U.S. Dist. Ct. Kans. 1976, U.S. Ct. Appeals (10th cir.) 1976. Assoc. Render & Kamas, Wichita, Kans., 1976-78, ptnr., 1978-82, Schartz & Sevart, Wichita, 1982-83, Sevart & Sevart, Wichita, 1983—. Bd. dirs. Wichita Symphony Soc., Inc., 1989—. Served to staff sgt. USAF, 1965-72. Mem. Assn. Trial Lawyers Am., Kans. Bar Assn. (bd. govs. 1995-98, 2000-01, sec.-treas. 1998-99, v.p. 2001-02, pres.-elect 2002-03, pres. 2003-04, Kans. Trial Lawyers Assn. (bd. govs. 1989—), Wichita Bar Assn. (bd. govs. 1988-90, sec.-treas. 1990-91, v.p. 1991-92, pres.-elect 1992-93, pres. 1993-94), Wichita C. of C. Democrat. Roman Catholic. Avocations: classical music, gardening, fishing, camping, travel. Office: Sevart & Sevart Ste 400 100 S Main St Wichita KS 67202-3208 also: 1900 L St NW Ste 500 Washington DC 20036-5031

SEVCENKO, IHOR, history and literature professor; b. Radosc, Poland, Feb. 10, 1922; came to U.S., 1949, naturalized, 1957; s. Ivan and Maria (Cherniatynska) S.; m. Oksana Draj-Xmara, Apr., 1945 (div. 1953); m. Margaret M. Bentley, July 16, 1953 (div. 1966); m. Nancy Patterson, June 18, 1966 (div. 1995); children: Catherine, Elisabeth. Dr.Phil., Charles U., Prague, 1945; Doct. en Phil. et Lettres, U. Louvain, Belgium, 1949; PhD (hon.), U. Cologne, Germany, 1994; D in Hist. Scis. (hon.), U. Warsaw, Poland, 2001; D in Liberal Arts (hon.), Cath. U., Lublin, Poland, 2005. Fellow in Byzantinology Dumbarton Oaks, 1949-50, dir. studies, 1966, prof. Byzantine history and lit., 1965-75, sr. research assoc., 1975—; lectr. Byzantine and ancient history U. Calif., Berkeley, 1950-51; fellow Byzantinology and Slavic lit., research program USSR, 1951-52; instr., then asst. prof. Slavic langs. and lit. U. Mich., 1953-57; mem. faculty Columbia U., 1957-72, prof., 1962-65, adj. prof., 1965-72; vis. prof. Harvard U., 1973-74, prof., 1974-92, emeritus, 1992. Vis. fellow All Souls Coll., Oxford U., 1979—80, Wolfson Coll., Oxford U., 1987, 93, Onassis Found., Athens, 2002; vis. mem. Princeton Inst. for Advanced Study, 1956; vis. prof. Munich U., 1969, Coll. de France, 1985, Cologne U., 1992, 96, Ctrl. European U., Budapest, 1995, 97; treas., acting treas., bd. dirs. Am. Rsch. Inst. in Turkey, 1964—66, 1967, 1975—; assoc. dir. Harvard Ukrainian Rsch. Inst., 1973—89, acting dir., 1977, 1985—86; chmn. US Nat. Com. Byzantine Studies, 1966—77; mem. Internat. Com. for Greek Paleography, 1983—; hon. pres. Byzantine studies Ukrainian Nat. Com., 1993—; guest of the rector Collegium Budapest, 1998. Author: Etudes sur la polémique entre Théodore Métochite et Nicéphore Choumnos, 1962, Society and Intellectual Life in Late Byzantium, 1981, Ideology, Letters and Culture in the Byzantine World, 1982, Byzantium and the Slavs in Letters and Culture, 1991, Ukraine Between East and West, 1996; co-author: Der Serbische Psalter, 1978, Life of St. Nicholas of Sion, 1984; contbr. articles to profl. jours. Recipient Hruševs'kyj medal, Sci. Ševcenko Soc., 1996, Antonovych Lit. prize, Kiev, 2000; Guggenheim fellow, 1963, Humboldt-Forschungspreistraeger, 1985. Fellow Mediaeval Acad. Am., Brit. Acad. (corr.); mem. Am. Philos. Soc., Am. Acad. Arts and Scis., Ukrainian Acad. Arts and Scis. US (hon. pres. 2003-), Sci. Sevcenko Soc., Société des Bollandistes Belgium (adj.), Accademia di Palermo (fgn.), Accademia Nazionale dei Lincei (fgn.), Internat. Assn. Byzantine Studies (v.p. 1976-86, pres. 1986-96, hon. pres. 1996—), Christian Archeol. Soc. Athens (hon.), Austrian Acad. Sci. (corr.), Accademia Pontaniana Naples (fgn.), Acad. Humanities Rsch. (Moscow), Polish Acad. Arts and Scis. (fgn.), Cosmos Club (Washington), Harvard Club (NYC), Signet Soc., Phi Beta Kappa (hon.) Office: Harvard Univ 204 Boylston Hall Cambridge MA 02138 Office Phone: 617-495-4027. Office Fax: 617-496-6720. Business E-Mail: sevcenko@fas.harvard.edu.

SEVENING, DIANE KAY, alcohol/drug abuse studies educator, researcher; b. Platte, SD, July 27, 1951; d. James Clayton (Stepfather) and Florence June Rommen; m. Douglas Lee Sevening, Aug. 15, 1981; children: Rodney Justin, Ryan Lee. D of edn., U. SD, 1998—99. Instr. U. SD Arts & Sciences Alcohol & Drug Abuse Studies Dept., Vermillion, 1984—89, 1989—99, asst. prof. Internat. pres. Internat. Coalition for Addiction Studies Edn. (INCASE), Vermillion, SD, 2000—02. Contbr. articles to profl. jours.; co-author: A Comparison of Traditional Teaching Methods and Problem-Based Learning in Addictions Studies Class, 2002. Sec. U. SD Student Affairs Com., 2001—03; mem. U. SD Academic Integrity Task Force, 2002—03; presenter Internat. Coalition for Addiction Studies Edn. (INCASE) Conf., Portland, Oreg., 2003, Nat. Drug and Alcohol Recovery Month, Sioux Falls, SD, 2003, Vol. Am., Sioux Falls, SD, 2003—03. Mem.: Internat. Coalition for Addiction Studies Educators (assoc.; immediate past pres. 2002—03), Gamma Sigma Delta (assoc.), Phi Delta Kappa (assoc.). Home: 602 W Dartmouth St Vermillion SD 57069 Office: Univ SD 414 E Clark St Vermillion SD 57069 Office Phone: 605-677-5519. Business E-Mail: dsevenin@usd.edu.

SEVER, JOHN LOUIS, medical researcher, educator; b. Chgo., Apr. 11, 1932; s. John Louis and Harriet (Link) Sever; m. Gerane Werle, Mar. 3, 1956; children: Kimberly, Beverly, Valerie. BA, U. Chgo., 1952; BS, MD, MS, PhD, Northwestern U., 1957. Head sect. infectious diseases NINDS, NIH, Bethesda, Md., 1960—71, chief infectious diseases, 1971—88; chmn. pediat. Children's Nat. Med. Ctr., Washington, 1988—90, prof. pediat., ob-gyn., immunology, microbiology and tropical medicine, 1988—. Cons. Rotary Internat., Evanston, Ill., 1964—, NIH, Bethesda, 1988—, WHO, Geneva, 1991—. Editor: 11 med. books; contbr. more than 600 articles to profl. jours. Capt. USPHS, 1960—88. Recipient Kimbel award, Am. Soc. for Microbiology, 1979, Wellcome Diagnostics award, Pan Am. Med. Virology, 1989, Meritorious Alumni award, Northwestern U., 1989, Pasteur award, Microbiology Soc., 1987, Abbott award, 1996, Soc. for Biomolecular Screening award, 2001. Mem.: Pan Am. Soc. Rapid Viral Diagnosis (pres. 1995—96), Assn. Med. Lab. Immunologists (pres. 1994—95, Erwin Niter award 1997), Teratology Soc. (pres. 1976—77), Assn. Med. Clin. and Lab. Immunologists (pres. 1992—94), Infectious Disease Soc. of Ob-gyn. (pres. 1994—96, Ortho-McNeill award 1998), Country Glen Club, Potomac Rotary Club. Avocation: gardening.

SEVERANCE, DIANA LYNN, curator; b. Wharton, Tex., Mar. 22, 1948; d. Arthur Walter Walzel and Dorothy Mae Kucera; m. Gordon Barker Severance, June 8, 1991. BA, Rice U., Houston, 1970, MA, 1972, PhD, 1974. Cert. secondary tchr. Tex. Tchr., dept. chair Klein Ind. Sch. Dist., Tex., 1976—93, mus. curator, 1995—2003; writer, hist. cons. Christian History Inst., Worcester, Pa., 1993—95; curator Dunham Bible Mus. Houston Bapt. U., 2003—. Hist. cons. Christian History Inst., Worcester, 1990—; adj. faculty, history curriculum writer LeTourneau U., 1994—2003. Author: Deep Roots, Strong Branches, 1999, Against the Gates of Hell: The Life and Times of Henry Perry, Christian Missionary in a Moslem World, 2003, A Cord of 3 Strands: Three Centuries of Christian Love Letters, 2004; contbr.: Faith in God and Generals, 2003; editl. advisor Christian History & Biography, Christianity Today, 1991—. Named Outstanding Tchr. for State of Tex., DAR, 1982; recipient Leadership in Edn. award, Tex. State Hist. Assn., 1997. Mem.: Internat. Soc. Bible Collectors (sec.), Conf. on Faith and History, Am. Soc. Ch. History, The History Soc., Am. Hist. Assn. Evangelical. Office: Houston Bapt U 7502 Fondren Houston TX 77074 Business E-Mail: dseverance@hbu.edu.

SEVERDIA, ANTHONY GEORGE, chemistry researcher; b. Sharon, Pa., Sept. 20, 1946; s. George Anthony and Angela Mary (Tomich) S. BS, Pa. State U., U. Park, 1968; MS, Case Western Res. U., Cleve., 1971, PhD, 1974. Rsch., teaching assoc. Rensselaer Poly. Inst., Troy, NY, 1975-77; chemist NYU, 1977-79, 82-83, Columbia U., NYC, 1979-82; analytical chemist Mallinckrodt Group, Terre Haute, Ind., 1983-92; sr. chemist analytical sci. Sanofi-Aventis Rsch., Gt. Valley, Pa., 1992—. Presenter in field. Contbr. articles to profl. jours. Summer fellow NSF, Cleve., 1971. Mem. Am. Chem. Soc. (exec. com., treas. Terre Haute sect. 1991-92), Soc. Applied Spectroscopy, The Internat. Soc. for Optical Engring. Home: 301 Pritchard Ln Wallingford PA 19086-6104 Home Phone: 610-627-1601; Office Phone: 610-889-6103. Personal E-mail: aseverdia@comcast.net.

SEVERIN, CHRISTINA, public health service officer; BS in Polit. Econ., Univ. Mass. Amherst; MS in Publ. Health Svcs., Boston Univ. Sch. Publ. Health. Dir. community health ctr. svcs. Boston Univ. Hospital; dir., managed care, practice mgmt. Health Svcs. Partnership, Boston; practice mgr. Codman Sq. Health Care, Dorchester, Mass.; dir. quality Network Health, COO, v.p., mng. dir., now exec. dir. Instr., health care admin. Tufts Health Care Inst. Office: Network Health Ste 23 432 Columbia St Cambridge MA 02141

SEVERINO, ELIZABETH FORREST, consulting company executive, animal communicator, spiritual healer; b. Bryn Mawr, Pa., Dec. 29, 1945; d. John Joseph and Elizabeth (Patton) Girard-diCarlo; m. Joseph Domenic Severino, Oct. 20, 1973 (div. Oct. 1983); 1 child, Nicole Marie. AB, Vassar Coll., 1967; MS in Computer Sci., Syracuse U., 1969; DD, Universal Life Ch., 1977; D of Religious Studies, U. Global Religious Studies, 2000. Ordained spiritual healer; cert. biofeedback therapist. Systems programmer IBM Corp., Poughkeepsie, N.Y., 1967-71, competitive analyst Phila., 1977-79; systems analyst Fidelity Bank, Phila., 1971-72; mng. editor Auerbach Pubs., Phila., 1972-77; v.p. editorial and technology McGraw-Hill Pubs., Delran, N.J., 1979-81; v.p. Symcro Systems, Pennsauken, N.J.,

1981-82; pres. The PC Group, Inc., Turnersville, NJ, 1982—, also bd. dirs.; pres. The Healing Connection, Cherry Hill, 1996—. Bd. dirs. Tech E-Writers, Cherry Hill, Simple Solutions, Inc., Cherry Hill. Author: Guide to International Computer Systems Architecture, 1976, Do-It-Yourself Vibrant Mind/Body/Spirit Health, 1995, Reiki: The Healer's Touch, 1995, Diet to Raise Your Spiritual Level, 1996, The Animals' Viewpoint on Dying, Death, and Euthanasia, 2001; (poetry) Garden of Life, 1995, 100 Breaths, 1998; Guided Full Energy Breathwork Session, 1998; Prayers and Meditations for Animal Well-Being, 2007; Animal Reincarnation: Stories of Undying Love, 2007, (CD) Breathing for Energy, 2007, Trauma to Triumph, 2007, Animal Communication Stories, vol. 1, 2007, Wake Up!...Live the Life You Love: Stories of Transformation, 2007; contbr. over 200 articles to profl. jours.; choreographer Faust, Der Vampyr, Sound of Music. Vol. exec. dir. Nat. Reiki Assn., 1995—. Recipient Editors Choice award Nat. Libr. Poetry, 1995. Mem. Assn. Personal Computers Cons. (bd. dirs. Phila. chpt., pres. 1987-90), NAFE, Phila. Area Computer Soc., Inst. Noetic Scis., U.S. Amateur Ballroom Dancers Assn. (Phila. chpt. bd. dirs.), South Jersey Holistic Health Assn. (treas.). Republican. Episcopalian. Avocations: meditation, gardening, dog training, reading. Personal E-mail: spirit1@beyond1.com.

SEVERINO, ROBERTO, language educator, academic administration executive; b. Catania, Italy, July 19, 1940; s. Giuseppe and Alba (Scroppo) S. Student U. Catania, Italy, 1960-62; BA, Columbia Union Coll., 1967; MA, U. Ill., 1969, PhD, 1973. Head acct., pers. dir. Industria Nazionale Apparecchiature Scientifiche, Milan, 1961-63; teaching asst., lang. lab. supv. Columbia Union Coll., Takoma Park, Md., 1965-67; grad. teaching asst. U. Ill., Urbana, 1967-70, coord. Corr. Sch., 1970-71; instr. dept. French and Italian U. Mass., Amherst, 1971-73; prof. dept. Italian Georgetown U., Washington, 1973—, acting chmn., 1987, chmn. dept., 1988—93; pres., co-founder Nat. Inst. Contemporary Italian Studies, 1986—; co-founder Associazione Internazionale del Diritto e dell'Arte, 1994—; pres. emeritus Am. U. of Rome, 1990-93, chair. Lit. dir. Georgetown U. Elec. Text Repository, Italian Archive, 1988-91, Ultramarina, 1992-96; mem. adv. bd. Nat. Italian Am. Found. Nat. Christopher Columbus 1992 Celebration; mem. U.S. delegation to 1st Conf. on Italian lang. and culture in U.S., 1987; founder Georgetown Poetry Series; pres. Coun. Promotion of Italian Lang. in Am. Schs., 1999—; hon. pres. U.S. Assn. Internat. Antonietta Labisi, 2000—; pres. Italian Muse Found., Washington, 2003—; inst. dir. NEH "The Art of Tchg. Italian Through Italian Art", 2004; elected mem. exec. com. Lista Unitalia Com. of Italians Residing Abroad; mem. selecting com. Washington Post Ednl. Found.; lectr., spkr. in field Author: Le soluzioni immaginarie, 1985, The Signs and Sounds of Italian, 1985, A carte scoperte, 1990, Presente imperfetto ed altri tempi, 1992, The Battle for Humanism, 1994, A Dumas: Mariano Stabile Sindaco di Palermo, 1994, My Dream-The Paintings of Gaetano N. Musto, 2002, Uga Martinotti, Io sono un pittore, 2005, Campania, Land of Myth and History, 2005; co-author: Periscopio, 1986, International Nuclear Agreements Multilingual Glossary, 1988, United Nations Organization Multilingual Glossary, 1988, Regularizing the Irregular Italian Verb, 1990, Preserving and Promoting Italian language and Culture in North America, 1997, Napoleon: One Image, Ten Mirrors, 2002; translator; The Next 6000 Days by Saverio Avveduto, 1987; editor: (serials) Segni, 1985-88, Hispano-Italic Studies, 1976, 79; mem. editorial bd. Educazione Comparata, 1993—; contbr. articles to profl. jours.; translator: Angelo Scandurra: The Hot-Tempered Musician and Other Poems, 1996, M. Rotelli's E. Sanguineti, If, For Me, You Write a Poem, 1999, Francesco Battiato: Amnesia of the Blue, 2000; editor: Giuseppe Severino: Ricordi di Castelnuovo primi '900. Scene di vita paesana, 1992; co-founder, U.S. editor: Colophon, An Internat. Jour. Arts and Letters, 1997-2003 Trustee Joel Nafuma Refugee Ctr., Rome, 1993—; chmn. Strega Lit. Prize, Washington D.C. Jury, 1997-2001; mem. jury Prima Parete in Concerto, Lion's Internat. Art Prize, Catania, 1998—, Spoleto Poetry Prize, 1999—. Rsch. grantee Interuniversity Ctr. European Studies, 1977; recipient Accademia Internazionale di Lettere, Scienze, Arti medal, 1983, Internat. Poetry prize, 1986, Gold Cross Cavaliere dell'Ordine al Merito della Repubblica Italiana, 1983, Gold medal Italian Ministries of Univs. and Sci. Rsch., 1988, Marranzano d'Argento prize, 1989, Gold Commander class Cross al Merito della Repubblica Italiana, 1990, Georgetown U. Vicennial Disting. Svc. medal, 1994, Telamone prize, 1995, Top Sprint: Siciliani nel Mondo award, 2000, Premio Internazionale "Castello di Pietrarossa" Caltanissetta, 2001, Gold Comdr. Cross Order "Stella della Solidarieta Italiana" by decree of Pres. of Italy, 2004 Mem. MLA, So. Atlantic Modern Lang. Assn., Nat. Assn. Secondary Sch. Prins. (mem. sch. partnerships internat. Italian adv. coun. 1988—), Italian Am. Cultural Found., Italian Cultural Soc. (pres. 1979-81, 83-85, Outstanding Svc. award 1983, chmn. acad. policy com. 1981—), Assn. Internationale Critiques Literaires and Associazione Italiana Critici Letterari, Greater Washington Assn. Tchrs. Fgn. Langs. (mem. award selection com. 1983-85), Manuscript Soc., Renaissance Soc. Am., Circolo Culturale Italiano (hon.), Am. Club (Rome), Touring Club Italiano (hon.), Gamma Kappa Alpha (v.p. 1990—, sec.-treas. and chpt. advisor 1985-90), World Jurist Assn. Ctr. Assocs. (U.S. pres. 1993—, chmn. program devel. and fin. com. 2000—), Associazione Internazionale del Diritto e dell'Arte (v.p. 1994—), Nat. Italian Am. Found. Coun. of 1,000, Napoleonic Soc. Am., Soc. di Studi Valdesi, Istituto Internazionale di Epistemologia la Magna Grecia, Unione Nazionale per la lotta contro l'Analfabetismo, Sons of Italy. Home: 4949 Quebec St NW Washington DC 20016-3230 Office: Georgetown U Dept Italian 37th And O Sts NW ICC 307 Washington DC 20057-0001 E-mail: Severiro@georgetown.edu.

SEVERINSEN, DOC (CARL H. SEVERINSEN), conductor, musician; b. Arlington, Oreg., July 7, 1927; m. Emily Marshall; children: Nancy, Judy, Cindy, Robin, Allen. Ptnr. Severinsen-Akwright Co.; pops condr. The Phoenix (Ariz.) Symphony Orchestra; prin. pops condr. Minn. Orch., Milw. Symphony Orch., Phoenix Symphony Orch. Mem. Ted Fio Rito Band, 1945, Charlie Barnet Band, 1947—49, Tommy Dorsey Band, Benny Goodman Band, Vaughn Monroe Band, soloist network band Steve Allen Show NBC-TV, 1954—55, mem. orch. Tonight Show, 1962—67, music dir. Tonight Show, 1967—92, host Midnight Spl., rec. artist Brass Roots album RCA Records, 1971, rec. artist Facets album, 1988, rec. artist The Tonight Show Band, Night Journey album. Address: Minn Orch 1111 Nicollet Mall Minneapolis MN 55403-2406 also: c/o William Morris Agency 151 S El Camino Dr Beverly Hills CA 90212-2704 also: c/o The Phoenix Symphony Orch 455 N 3rd St Ste 390 Phoenix AZ 85004-3942 *

SEVERO, RICHARD, writer; b. Newburgh, NY, Nov. 22, 1932; s. Thomas and Mary Theresa (Farina) S.; m. Emöke Edith de Papp, Apr. 7, 1961. BA, Colgate U., 1954; postgrad., NYU Inst. Fine Arts, 1955-56, Columbia U. Sch. Architecture and Urban Planning, 1964-65. News asst. CBS, NYC, 1954-55; reporter Poughkeepsie New Yorker, NY, 1956-57, A.P., Newark, 1957-61, NY Herald Tribune, 1961-63; writer TV news CBS, NYC, 1963-66; reporter Washington Post, 1966—68; reporter, fgn. correspondent, feature writer, feature obituary reporter, sci. and environ. reporter NY Times, 1968—2006. Assoc. Seminar on the City, Columbia U., 1966-69; vis. lectr. Am. culture Vassar Coll., 1985-99; bd. dirs. Hudson Valley Philharm., 1998-99, Colgate U. Alumni Corp., 1988-92. Author: Lisa H., 1985; (with Lewis Milford) The Wages of War, 1989 (Am. Legion Nat. Comdr.'s award 1990); contbr. articles to mags. Established Thomas and Mary Severo Scholarship funds for majors in music and Italian Vassar Coll., 2002. Poynter fellow-in-residence Vassar Coll., 1974-75; CBS News fellow, 1964-65; Recipient Front Page award Washington-Balt. Newspaper Guild, 1967; Journalistic award H.A.V.E.N., 1969; Schaeffer Gold Typewriter award NY Newspaper Reporters Assn., 1969; Page One award Newspaper Guild of N.Y., 1970; hon. mention Mike Berger award Columbia U., 1970; Leone di San Marco award Italian Heritage and Culture Com., 1982; George Polk Meml. award L.I. U. Sch. Journalism, 1975; Hudson River Fisherman's Assn. award, 1976; Mike Berger award Columbia U., 1976; James Wright Brown award Deadline Club, Sigma Delta Chi, NYC, 1976; Feature award NY Press Club, 1977; Page One award Newspaper Guild NY, 1977, 82; Media award Am. Cancer Soc., 1977; hon. mention Heywood Broun Meml. award Am. Newspaper Guild, 1977; Penney-Mo. Newspaper award U. Mo. Sch. Journalism, 1978; Media award Agt. Orange Victims Internat., 1982; Page One award NY Newspaper Guild, 1982; Gift of Life award NY Blood Ctr., 1991, Spl. Writing award Soc. of the Silurians, 1992. Avocations: music, cello. Personal E-mail: richard.severo2@verizon.net.

SEVERS, CHARLES A., III, lawyer; b. NYC, Sept. 16, 1942; s. Charles A. and Gertrude (O'Neill) S.; m. Regina Ferrone, Sept. 4, 1965; children: Charles A. IV, Cornelius Forsythe, Rudyard Pierrepont, Olivia Consuelo Poor. BA, Georgetown U., 1964, JD, 1967. Bar: N.Y. 1968, D.C. 1985. Ptnr. Dewey Ballantine, NYC, 1967-96; gen. counsel, exec. v.p. Nat. Madison Group, NYC, 1996—2007. Lectr. various continuing legal edn. programs. Contbr. articles to profl. jours. Dir., trustee various orgns. Fellow Am. Coll. Trust and Estate Counsel; mem. ABA, N.Y. State Bar Assn., Assn. of Bar of City of N.Y., D.C. Bar Assn., Union Club. Address: High Meadow Old Chatham NY 12136

SEVERS, WALTER BRUCE, pharmacology educator, researcher; b. Pitts., June 10, 1938; s. Walter Bruce and Pauline Marie (Sever) S.; m. Anne Elizabeth Daniels, Apr. 25, 1970; children: Mary, Jane, Steven, William, Katherine. BS, U. Pitts., 1960, MS, 1963, PhD, 1965. Postdoctoral fellow NIH, Bethesda, Md., 1966-68; asst. prof. pharmacology Coll. Medicine, Pa. State U., Hershey, 1968-71, assoc. prof., 1971-77, prof., 1977-99, prof. emeritus, 1999—. Cons. pharmacology/toxicology, 1999—; v.p. for sci. affairs Ednl. Horizons, Inc., Lemoyne, Pa., 1998—; ad hoc grant cons. NIH, U.S. Army, NSF; vis. prof. physiology U. Belgrade Med. Sch., 1994—. Mem. editl. Bd. Am. Jour. Physiology, 1978-98; assoc. editor Pharmacology, 1998-2000; contbr. numerous articles, chpts., revs. to profl. publs. Recipient Disting. Alumnus award U. Pitts., 1978, I.M. Setchenov medal Acad. Med. Sci. USSR, 1983, Blue medal for sci. Acad. Med. Sci., Bulgaria, medal for sci. U. Belgrade; NASA grantee, 1976-98. Fellow Am. Coll. Clin. Pharmacology; mem. Am. Physiol. Soc., Am. Soc. Pharmacology and Exptl. Therapeutics, Soc. for Neurosci., Soc. for Exptl. Biology and Medicine, Sigma Xi (pres. Pa. State U. chpt. 1981-82), Kiwanis (pres. Hershey area 1980, bd. dirs.). Republican. Roman Catholic. Avocations: reading, camping, hiking. Home: 1011 Grubb Rd Palmyra PA 17078-3510 Office: Pa State U Coll Medicine Dept Pharm Mail Code H78 500 University Dr Hershey PA 17033-2360 Office Phone: 717-531-8291. Business E-Mail: wbs2@psu.edu.

SEVERS, WILLIAM FLOYD, actor; b. Britton, Okla., Jan. 8, 1932; s. Harry Lysander Fletcher and Katherine Lucinda (McAuliffe) S.; m. Mary Anne Proctor, Jan. 18, 1964 (div. 1971); 1 child, Pilar; m. Barbara Alice Schonger, Sept. 9, 1978; children: Katherine Meghan, Erin Christine. AA, Pasadena Playhouse Coll., 1956. Appeared on Broadway in Cut of the Axe, 1959-60, The Moon Is Blue, 1962, On Borrowed Time, 1991-92, nat. tour Look Homeward, Angel, 1960; co-star nat. tour Spoon River, 1964; actor Secret Storm, All My Children, One Life to Live, Guiding Light, Texas, Search for Tomorrow, Another World, Loving, 1963-93; other TV appearances include Armstrong Circle Theatre, 1963, The Defenders, 1964, World War II, A GI Diary, 1978, Nurse, 1980, Muggable Mary, 1986, Law and Order, recurring role as Hon. Henry Fillmore, 1990-2004, Hallmark Hall of Fame, Grace and Glorie, 1998, Law and Order: Criminal Intent, 2000, The Sopranos, 2007; appeared in films including Funny Farm, 1988, Regarding Henry, 1991, Meet the Parents, 2000, Revolution #9, 2000, 13 Conversations About 1 Thing, 2001, The Departed, 2005; actor European tour West Side Story, 1990-91, 94, Asian tour West Side Story, 1999; actor, voice artist numerous commls., 1964— Staff sgt. USAF, 1946-53. Mem. SAG, AFTRA, Actors Equity Assn., Pasadena Playhouse Alumni Assn. Democrat. Avocations: reading, golf. Home: 10 Waterside Plz Apt 6F New York NY 10010-2610 Office: Hartig/Hilefo Agy Ltd 54 W 21st St New York NY 10010-7002 Personal E-mail: wfsevers@gmail.com.

SEVERSON, ROGER ALLAN, bank executive; b. Thief River Falls, Minn., Sept. 2, 1932; s. Alfred Gerhard and Esther Olga (Landro) S.; m. Beverly Diane Hays, Aug. 30, 1953; children: Eric Hays, Holle Diane. BS, U. Minn., 1954. Group v.p. First Nat. Bank, Mpls., 1952-73; pres. FBS Fin., Inc., Mpls., 1974-77; exec. v.p. F&M Savs. Bank, Mpls., 1977-82; sr. v.p. First Nat. Bank, St. Paul, 1983-85; exec. v.p. Shelard Nat. Bank, Mpls., 1985-86, TCF Bank Savs., Mpls., 1986-92; ret., 1992. Mem. Robert Morris Assocs., 1980-92; trustee Heitman Mortgage Investors, Chgo., 1970-71, Mass. Mut. Mortgage Realty Investors, Springfield, 1972-85. Vice chmn. bd. of trustees The Am. Luth. Ch. Synod, Mpls., 1976-81; trustee Children's Health Ctr., Mpls., 1971-72; bd. dirs. Goodwill Industries, Mpls., 1967-70. Fellow Versterheim Mus.; mem. Ethics in Pub. Policy Ctr., Ctr. for Am. Experiment. Home: 8321 Essex Rd Chanhassen MN 55317-8705

SEVIGNY, CHLOË, actress; b. Darien, Conn., Nov. 18, 1974; d. Paul Sevigny. Actor: (films) Kids, 1995, Trees Lounge, 1996, Gummo, 1997, Palmetto, 1998, The Last Days of Disco, 1998, Boys Don't Cry, 1999, Julien Donkey-Boy, 1999, A Map of the World, 1999, American Psycho, 2000, Ten Minutes Older: The Trumpet, 2002, Demonlover, 2002, Party Monster, 2003, Death of a Dynasty, 2003, Dogville, 2003, The Brown Bunny, 2003, Shattered Glass, 2003, Melinda and Melinda, 2004, Manderlay, 2005, Broken Flowers, 2005, 3 Needles, 2005, Lying, 2006, Sisters, 2006, Zodiac, 2007; (TV films) Mrs. Harris, 2005, If These Walls Could Talk 2, 2000; (TV series) Big Love, 2006—, (TV appearances) Will & Grace, 2004. Office: Endeavor Talent Agy 9601 Wilshire Blvd 10th Fl Beverly Hills CA 90212 *

SEVIK, MAURICE, acoustical engineer, researcher; b. Istanbul, Turkey, Mar. 19, 1923; s. Benjamin and Esther (Barzilai) S.; m. Jacqueline Delannoy, June 2, 1953; children: Michele, Martine. DIC, Imperial Coll. Sci. Tech., London, 1946; PhD, Pa. State U., 1963. Registered profl. engr., Ont. With Bristol Aircraft Corp., U.K., 1946-51; sr. structures engr. Avro Aircraft Ltd., Can., 1952-59; prof. aerospace engring., dir. Garfield Thomas Water Tunnel, Pa. State U., University Park, 1959-72; mem. assoc. tech. dir. ship signatures directorate David Taylor Rsch. Ctr., Bethesda, Md., 1972-96, sr. rsch. scientist, 1996-99; ret., 1999. Vis. prof. Cambridge (Eng.) U., 1970; cons. USAF Office Sci. Rsch. 1965; cons. applied physics lab. U. Wash., Seattle, 1999—. Contbr. articles to profl. jours. Overseas fellow Churchill Coll., Cambridge U., 1970; recipient Gold Medal award The Am. Soc. of Naval Engrs., 1990, Disting. Alumni award Central Pa. chpt. Acoustical Soc. of Am., Charles B. Martell Tech. Excellence award Nat. Security Indsl. Assn., 1992, Robert Dexter Conrad award Office Naval Rsch., 1996, French decoration Ordre Nat du Mérite, 1997; Dr. M. M. Sevik Acoustic Data Analysis Ctr. Bldg. named in his honor. Fellow ASME (Rayleigh lectr. 1995, Per Bruel Gold medal for noise control and acoustics 1996), Acoustical Soc. Am., Sigma Xi; mem. Nat. Acad. Engring. Home: 2 Spruce Ct Hilton Head Island SC 29928 Office: David Taylor Model Basin 9500 Macarthur Blvd West Bethesda MD 20817-5700 Office Phone: 843-341-7994. Personal E-mail: msevik@aol.com.

SEVILLA, STANLEY, lawyer; b. Cin., Apr. 3, 1920; s. Isadore and Dienna (Levy) S.; m. Lois A. Howell, July 25, 1948; children: Stanley, Susan, Donald, Carol, Elizabeth. BA in Econs. with high honors, U. Cin., 1942; JD, Harvard U., 1948. Bar: Calif. 1949. Since practiced in, Los Angeles; assoc. Williamson, Hoge & Curry, 1948-50; mem. firm Axelrod, Sevilla and Ross, 1950-75, Stanley Sevilla (P.C.), 1975—. Gen. counsel La.-Pacific Resources, Inc., 1970-90. Bd. dirs. Caesars World, Inc., 1989-95. With USAAF, 1942-46. Mem. Beverly Hills Bar Assn., Phi Beta Kappa, Tau Kappa Alpha. Home: 16606 Merrivale Ln Pacific Palisades CA 90272-2236 Office: PO Box 308 Pacific Palisades CA 90272-0308 Office Phone: 310-459-8116.

SEVILLA-SACASA, FRANCES ALDRICH, bank executive; BA in Langs., U. Miami, 1977; MA in Internat. Mgmt., Am. Grad. Sch. Internat. Mgmt., 1978. Joined Bankers Trust, 1983; mng. dir. L.Am. pvt. banking Bankers Trust Internat. Pvt. Banking Group, Miami, Fla.; sr. v.p. pvt. client svcs. Lehman Bros., Miami, 1997—98; mng. dir. L.Am. pvt. bank divsn. Deutsche Bank; pres. Bankers Trust Internat. Pvt. Banking Corp., 1998—2000; mng. dir., S.E. region head Citibank Pvt. Bank, 2000—01; mng. dir., head L.Am. Citigroup, NYC, 2001—05, head Europe Citigroup Pvt. Bank, 2003—04, CEO Latin Am. Citigroup Private Bank, 2004—05; pres. US Trust Corp. Charles Schwab Corp., NYC, 2005—, exec. v.p. Office: US Trust Corp 114 W 47th St New York NY 10036 Office Phone: 415-627-7000. Office Fax: 212-852-1140.

SEVIN, DIETER HERMANN, literature and language professor; b. Mühlanger, Germany, Nov. 5, 1938; arrived in US, 1958; s. Wolf-Dieterich and Erna (Brockmann) Sevin; m. Ingrid Antje Dirks, June 15, 1963; children: Sonja, Karen. BA, San Jose State U., 1963; MA, U. Wash., Seattle, 1964, PhD, 1967. Asst. prof. Pacific Lutheran U., Tacoma, 1967-68, Vanderbilt U., Nashville, 1968-73, assoc. prof., 1973-82, prof., 1982—, chair dept., 2002—. Author: Individuum und Staat, 1972, Zur Diskussion: A Modern Approach to German Conversation, 3d edit., 1987, The Resonance of Exile. Successful and Unsuccessful Reception Of German Exile, 1992, Text Strategies in GDR Prose Fiction Between the Building and Fall of the Berlin Wall, 1994, Christa Wolf: Divided Heaven/The Quest for Christa T. Interpretations, 4th rev. edit., 2000; author: (with Ingrid Sevin) Wie Geht's? An Introductory German Course, 8th edit., 2007; editor: Georg Büchner: New Perspectives On His International Reception, 2007; co-editor (with Richard E. Schade): Practicing Progress: The Promise and Limitations of Enlightenment, 2007; contbr. articles to profl. jours. Fellow: German Acad. Exch. Svc. (grantee 1980), Am. Coun. Learned Socs. (grantee 1981—82), Am. Philos. Soc. (grantee 1991). Avocations: travel, reading, music. Office: Vanderbilt U Dept Germanic And Slav Nashville TN 37235 Office Phone: 615-322-2611. Business E-Mail: dieter.h.sevin@vanderbilt.edu.

SEWARD, GEORGE CHESTER, lawyer; b. Omaha, Aug. 4, 1910; s. George Francis and Ada Leona (Rugh) S.; m. Carroll Frances McKay, Dec. 12, 1936 (dec. 1991); children: Gordon Day, Patricia McKay (Mrs. Dryden G. Liddle), James Pickett, Deborah Carroll (Mrs. R. Thomas Coleman). BA, U. Va., 1933, LLB, 1936. Bar: Va. 1935, NY, Ky., DC, US Supreme Ct. With Shearman & Sterling, NYC, 1936-53, Seward & Kissel LLP, NYC, 1953—. Dir. Witherbee Sherman Corp., 1952-66, pres. 1964-66, Howmet Corp., 1955-75, Chas. P. Young Co., 1965-72, Howmedica Inc., 1970-72, Benson Mines, Inc., 1980-85; trustee Benson Iron Ore Trust, 1969-80. Author: Basic Corporate Practice, 1977, Seward and Related Families, 1994; co-author: Model Business Corporation Act Annotated, 1960, We Remember Carroll, 1992. Trustee Arts and Scis. Coun. U. Va., 1983-93, pres., 1991-93; trustee Edwin Gould Found. for Children, 1955-96, Nature Conservancy of Ea. L.I., 1969-80, N.Y. Geneal. and Biog. Soc., 1991-2006. Named to Louisville Male H.S. Alumni Assn. Hall of Fame, 1991; commd. Ky. Col., 1993. Fellow: N.Y. State Bar Found., Am. Bar Found.; mem.: ABA (chmn. sect. com. corp. laws 1952—58, chmn. bus. law sect. 1958—59, ho. of dels. 1959—60, chmn. sect. banking com. 1960—61, ho. of dels. 1963—74, joint com. with Am. Law Inst. on continuing legal edn. 1965—74), Internat. Bar Assn. (hon. life pres., lectr. series by heads of state named in his honor, New Delhi 1988, Lisbon 1992, Budapest 1993, Geneva 1994), Downtown Assn. (N.Y.C.), Athenaeum Lit. Assn. (Louisville), Greencroft Club (Charlottesville, Va.), Univ. Club (Chgo.), Met. Club (Washington), Bohemian Club (San Francisco), Gardiner's Bay Country Club (Shelter Island, N.Y.), N.Y. Yacht Club, Knickerbocker Club, Delta Sigma Rho, Theta Chi, Phi Beta Kappa, Phi Beta Kappa Fellows (pres. 1969—75), Order of Coif, Raven Soc., Cum Laude Soc. Home: 48 Greenacres Ave Scarsdale NY 10583-1436 Office: Seward & Kissel LLP One Battery Park Plz New York NY 10004 also: Internat Bar Assn 1 Stephen St London W1T 1AT England

SEWARD, NATHAN WILLIAM, biologist, researcher; b. Xenia, Ohio, May 10, 1975; s. William Arthur and Diana Lynn Seward; m. Kathleen Ann MacCarthy, Dec. 30, 2006; 1 child, Reilly Alice. BS in Natural Resources, Ohio State U., Columbus, 2000; MS in Forestry, U. Ky., Lexington, 2003. Resource mgmt. intern Columbus and Franklin County Met. Pk. Dist., Columbus, Ohio, 1998—98; biol. sci. technician USDA Forest Svc., Gunnison, Colo., 1999; rsch. asst. U. Ky., Lexington, 2000—03; biol. sci. technician USDI Nat. Pk. Svc., Gunnison, 2003, USDA Nat. Wildlife Rsch. Ctr., Fort Collins, Colo., 2003—. Contbr. articles to profl. jours. Com. mem. Rocky Mountain Elk Found., Fort Collins, 2004. Recipient Merit award, USDA Nat. Wildlife Rsch. Ctr., 2006. Mem.: Wildlife Soc. (assoc.; cert.). Independent. Methodist. Avocations: hunting, fly fishing, hiking, wildlife. Office: USDA Nat Wildlife Rsch Ctr 4101 LaPorte Ave Fort Collins CO 80521 Office Phone: 970-266-6174. Office Fax: 970-266-6183. Personal E-mail: nathanseward@hotmail.com. Business E-Mail: nathan.w.seward@aphis.usda.gov.

SEWELL, D. BRUCE (BRUCE SEWELL, DURWARD BRUCE SEWELL), lawyer; b. 1958; B, U. Lancaster, UK, 1979; JD, George Washington U., 1986. Bar: Calif. 1986, DC 1987, US Ct. Appeals, Fed. cir. Assoc. Schnader Harrison Segal & Lewis; ptnr. Brown & Bain PC; sr. atty. Intel Corp., Santa Clara, Calif., 1995—2001, v.p. legal & govt. affairs, dep. gen. counsel, 2001—04, v.p., gen. counsel, 2004—05, sr. v.p., gen. counsel, 2005—. Office: Intel Corp 2200 Mission College Blvd Santa Clara CA 95052 *

SEWELL, JOHN WILLIAMSON, research association executive; b. Cleve., Dec. 19, 1935; s. William and Hilda F. (Gaunt) S.; m. Maryann Strauss, July 19, 1958; children: Gregory J., Michael P. BA, U. Rochester, 1957; MA, NYU, 1967. Fgn. service officer Dept. State, 1961-68; asst. to dir. Bur. Intelligence Research, Dept. State, Washington, 1968-70; asst. to pres. Brookings Inst., Washington, 1970-71; v.p. Overseas Devel. Council, Washington, 1971-77, exec. v.p., 1977-79, pres., 1980-2000; sr. scholar Woodrow Wilson Internat. Ctr., 2001—. Mem. Bretton Woods Com.; former vice-chair Internat. Ctr. for Rsch. on Women; vice chair New Rules for Global Fin.; mem. Internat. Adv. Group for 1995 World Summit for Social Devel.; spl. advisor to the adminstrn. UNDP, 1988-99; chair Working Group on Devel. of Role of IMF; advisor UN Assn. USA. Author: U.S. Foreign Policy and the Third World Agenda, 1985-86, Growth, Exports, & Jobs in a Changing World Economy: Agenda 1988, The Real Politik of Poverty: An Action Plan for American Foreign Policy, 2005; co-editor: United States Budget for a New World Order, FY, 1992, Challenges and Priorities in the 1990s: An Alternative U.S. International Affairs Budget, FY, 1993; contbr. articles to jours. Pres. Nat. Choral Found., 1969-75. With U.S. Army, 1958-60. Mem. Coun. on Fgn. Rels.

SEWELL, MICHAEL E., music educator, musician; b. Hancock, Mich., Dec. 14, 1976; s. William Clyde and Jeanine Delores Sewell. MusB in Music Edn., U. Wis., Stevens Point, 2001. Lic. educator Wis. Dept. Pub. Instrn. Dir. bands Newman Cath. Schs., Wausau, Wis., 2002—. Named Tchr. of Distinction, U. Wis., Oshkosh.

SEWELL, RICHARD HERBERT, retired historian, retired educator; b. Ann Arbor, Mich., Apr. 11, 1931; s. Herbert Mathieu and Anna Louise (Broene) Sewell; m. Natalie Paperno, Jan. 13, 1971; 1 child, Rebecca Elizabeth. AB, U. Mich., 1953; MA, Harvard U., 1954, PhD, 1962. Asst. prof. No. Ill. U., DeKalb, 1962-64, U. Wis., Madison, 1965-67, assoc. prof., 1967-74, prof, 1974-95, prof. emeritus, 1995—; ret., 1995. Vis. lectr. U. Mich., Ann Arbor, 1964—65; adv. bd. Lincoln and Soldiers Inst. Gettysburg Coll., Pa., 1990—. Author: (book) John P. Hale and the Politics of Abolition, 1965, Ballots for Freedom, 1976, A House Divided, 1988; contbr. articles to profl. jours. Lt. (j.g.) USNR, 1954—57. Fellow: Wis. Hist. Soc. (hon.); mem.: Orgn. of Am. Historians, So. Hist. Assn., Soc. Civil War Historians, Phi Beta Kappa, Phi Kappa Phi. Home: 2206 Van Hise Ave Madison WI 53726 Business E-Mail: rhsewell@wisc.edu.

SEWELL, RUFUS, actor; b. Twickenham, England, Oct. 29, 1967; s. William and Jo Sewell; m. Yasmin Abdallah, Mar. 24, 1999 (div. Mar. 2000); m. Amy Gardner, Feb. 2004; 1 child, William Douglas. Student, Ctrl. Sch. Speech & Drama, London. Actor theatrical debut As You Like It, Shefield's Crucible Theatre, Rock 'n Roll, 2006 (Evening Standard Best Actor award, 2006, Olivier award best actor, 2007); (miniseries) Middlemarch, 1994, Arabian Nights, 1999; (films) Twenty-One, 1991, Dirty Weekend, 1993, Victory, 1995, Carrington, 1995, Hamlet, 1996, The Woodlanders, 1997, Dangerous Beauty, 1998, Dark City, 1998, Martha, Meet Frank, Daniel, and Laurence, 1998, Illuminata, 1998, In Sachem Farm, 1998, In a Savage Land, 1999, Bless the Child, 2000, A Knight's Tale, 2001, Extreme Oops, 2002, Victoria Station, 2003, The Legend of Zorro, 2005, The Illusionist, 2006, Tristan & Isolde, 2006, Paris, I Love You, 2006, Amazing Grace, 2006, The Holiday, 2006; (TV films) Cold Comfort Farm, 1995, King Henry IV, 1995, Arabian Nights, 2000, Mermaid Chronicles Part 1: She Creature, 2001, Helen of Troy, 2003, The Taming of the Shrew, 2005. Office: UTA 9560 Wilshire Blvd Ste 500 Beverly Hills CA 90212-2427 *

SEWELL, WILLIAM GEORGE, III, electronics engineer, writer; b. Roanoke, Va., Dec. 14, 1950; s. William George Jr. and Elizabeth Marie (Morrison) S.; m. Verna Landry, Aug. 25, 1970 (div. 1974); children: Ronald Allen, Bryan Joseph; m. Colleen Rose Gaynor, May 15, 1981 (div. 2005); m. Nancy A. Levy, Dec. 31, 2005. BS in Engring., U. Ill., Chgo., 1980; PhD, Calif. U., Modesto, 1983. Electronic technician 928 Airlift Group, Chgo., 1972-74; with FAA, Chgo., 1974-85, staff engr. Wheeling, Ill., 1980-82, regional nav. and landing systems engr. Chgo., 1982-85, nat. program mgr., 1985—87; with Jerry Thompson & Assocs., Kensington, Md., 1987-88; v.p. Navcom Systems, Inc., 1988-89, B2 Software, Inc., 1988-89; v.p., CEO The Thinkk Corp., 1988-89; founder, CEO Software Coalition, 1989—99. Dir. comm. and info. systems group SEMA, Inc., 1990—93; dir. comm. solutions Jacobs Facilities, Inc., 1993—2000; Sverdrup fellow, 1998; v.p. Holmes & Narver, Inc., 2000—01; sr. v.p. DMJM Holmes & Narver, Inc., 2001—; pres. GEOLINC, 2002—04; cons. engr. W.G. Sewell & Assocs., Internat., Niles, Ill., 1981—88; chair TIA Indsl. Telecoms Standards Body, 1999—2001; sr. v.p. DMJM Tech., 2003—, gen. mgr., 2003—; mem. joint venture bd. Lawa Assoc. Contbr. articles to profl. jours., chapters to books. Mem. Chgo. Coun. Fgn. Rels., 1976-80. Served with USAF, 1970-72, Vietnam. Recipient 1st prize, Am. Soc. Electro-Surgery, 1982. Mem. IEEE Soc. Automotive Engrs., Aircraft Owners and Pilots Assn. Achievements include invention of high speed turn control for land vehicles, 1980; co-inventor child's hidden identification and location device, 1990. Office: 515 S Flower St Los Angeles CA 90071 Office Phone: 213-593-8487. E-mail: bill.sewell@dmjm.com.

SEWELL, WILLIAM HAMILTON, JR., historian; b. Stillwater, Okla., May 15, 1940; s. William Hamilton and Elizabeth Lucille (Shogren) S.; m. Ellen Martha Wheeler, June 16, 1962 (dec. July 2001); children: Jessica Ellen, Adrienne Felicity; m. Jan Goldstein, Dec. 2004. BA, U. Wis., 1962; MA, U. Calif., 1963, PhD, 1971. Instr. history U. Chgo., 1968-71, asst. prof. history, 1971-75; assoc. prof. history U. Ariz., Tucson, 1980-83, prof. history, 1983-85; dir. d'etudes associe Ecole de Hautes Etudes en Scis. Sociales, Paris, 1984, 88; prof. history and sociology U. Mich., Ann Arbor, 1985-90; prof. polit. sci. and history U. Chgo., 1990—, Max Palevsky prof., 1996—2004, Frank P. Hixon disting. svc. prof., 2004—07, emeritus prof., 2007; fellow Ctr. for Advanced Study in Behavioral Scis., 1990-91, Nat. Humanities Ctr., 2006—07. Mem. bd. editors Jour. Modern History, 1984-86, French Hist. Studies, 1985-88, Sociol. Theory, 2004—07; mem., bd. dirs. Social Sci. Rsch. Coun., N.Y.C., 1986-92; dir. Program in Comparative Study of Social Transformations, U. Mich., Ann Arbor, 1987-90, Ctr. for Rsch. Social Orgn., 1988-90; dir. Wilder House Ctr. for Politics, History and Culture, U. Chgo., 1999-2004; mem. Sch. Social Sci. Inst. Advanced Study, Princeton, NJ, 1971-72, 75-80, 2002-03. Author: Work and Revolution in France, 1980, Structure and Mobility, 1985, A Rhetoric of Bourgeois Revolution, 1994, Logics of History, 2005. Recipient Herbert Baxter Adams prize Am. Hist. Assn., 1981, William Koren Jr. prize Soc. French hist. studies, 1982; grantee Nat. Sci. Found., 1972-75; Guggenheim fellow, 1990-91, Nat. Humanities Ctr., 2006-. Fellow Am. Acad. Arts and Sci.; mem. Am. Hist. Assn., Soc. French Hist. Studies, Am. Sociol. Assn. (Best Article prize comparitive hist. sociology sect. 1991, culture sect. 1993, theory sect. 1997), Social Sci. History Assn., Coun. European Studies, Am. Polit. Sci. Assn. Office: U Chgo Dept Polit Sci 5828 S University Ave Chicago IL 60637-1515 E-mail: wsewell@uchicago.edu.

SEWRIGHT, CHARLES WILLIAM, JR., mortgage banking advisory services company executive; b. Great Lakes, Ill., Feb. 22, 1946; s. Charles William Sewright Sr. and Selma Joy Kester; m. Bonnie Joyce Knight, July 2, 1967; children: Kimberly Ann, Traci Lynn, Megan Paige. BS in Acctg., Calif. State U., Long Beach, 1969, MBA, 1974. Fin. analyst aeronautic div. Philco-Ford Corp., Newport Beach, Calif., 1969-73; sr. acctg. analyst Calif. Computer Products, Anaheim, 1973-74; product line controller McGaw Labs. div. Am. Hosp. Supply Corp., Irvine, Calif., 1974-75, div. acctg. mgr., 1975-76, fin. planning dir., 1976-80; v.p., controller critical care div. McGaw Park, Ill., 1980-85; v.p., controller EZ Painter Corp., Milw., 1985-86; v.p. dept. mgr. automotive fin. services secondary mkts. Marine Midland Bank, Buffalo, N.Y., 1986-87; pres., chief exec. officer Marine Midland Mortgage Corp., Buffalo, 1987-91, Anchor Mortgage Svcs., Inc., Wayne, NJ, 1991-95; exec. v.p., COO Avondale Fed. Savs. Bank, Chgo., 1997—2000; founder, chmn., CEO Quest Advisors, Inc., Northbrook, Ill., 1995—. Chair credit com. Am. Employees Fed. Credit Union, McGaw Park, Ill., 1980-85; vice chmn. Bd. Am. Employees Fed. Credit Union, 1981-85; mem. Fannie Mae Adv. Bd., 1990-92; speaker in field; mem. bd. trustees Medaille Coll., 1989-92; dir. Avondale Fed. Savs. Bank. Mem. Nat. Assn. Accts., Inst. of Cert. Mgmt. Accts. (cert.), Mortgage Bankers Assn. Am. (legis. com. 1990—), Mortgage Bankers Assn. Am. (bd. govs. 1990-98), Beta Gamma Sigma, Phi Kappa Phi. Avocation: golf. Office: Quest Advisors Inc 3710 Commercial Ave Ste 5 Northbrook IL 60062 Business E-Mail: csewright@questadvisors.com.

SEXSON, WILLIAM ROBERT, pediatrician, educator; b. Washington, Dec. 3, 1945; children: Sara Kristen, Ryan William. BS, USAF Acad., 1967; MD, U. Miss., 1971. Diplomate Am. Bd. Pediatrics, Am. Bd. Neonatal-Perinatal Medicine; cert. in extra corporeal membrane oxygenation. Pediat. resident Wilford Hall USAF Med. Ctr., 1994; fellow in neonatology Vanderbilt U., Nashville, 1976; staff neurologist Crawford Long Hosp., Atlanta, 1984—, Egleston's Children's Hosp., Atlanta, 1984—; dir. nurseries Grady Meml. Hosp., Atlanta, 1987-94; vice-chair dept. pediatrics, assoc. prof. Emory U. Sch. Medicine, Atlanta, 1994—, interim assoc. dean clin. affairs, 1998-2000, assoc. dean clin. affairs, 2000—; chief pediatrics Grady Health Sys., Atlanta, 1994—2000. Contbr. articles to profl. jours. Active Ga. Policy Coun. for Children and Families, 1995-2000; co-chair Children's Health Com., 1998—, Ga. Dept. Med. Assts.; child health adv com., physicians adv. coun. Ga. Medicaid, 2001—; chmn. health and safety com. Boy Scouts Am. Atlanta Area Coun., 1998—. Col. USAFR. Named Outstanding Citizen of Ga., 1990, 2004. Fellow WHO (collaborating ctr. 2003—, asst. dir. collaborating ctr. 2005—); mem. Am. Acad. Pediatrics (v.p. Ga. chpt. 1990-92, pres. 1993-96, exec. com. 1996—, chair com. on bioethics for Ga., chair hosp. ethics com. 1987—, co-chair legis. com. 2000—), Coun. on Maternal and Infant Health (chair 1993-95), Ga. Perinatal Assn. Home: 804 Springdale Rd NE Atlanta GA 30306-4618 Office: Grady Health Sys 49 Jesse Hill Dr SE Atlanta GA 30303-3040 E-mail: wsexson@emory.edu.

SEXTON, CAROL BURKE, finance company executive, consultant; b. Chgo., Apr. 20, 1939; d. William Patrick and Katharine Marie (Nolan) Burke; m. Thomas W. Sexton Jr., June 30, 1962 (div. June 1976); children: Thomas W., J. Patrick, M. Elizabeth. BA, Barat Coll., 1961; cert. legal, Mallinckrodt Coll., 1974. Tchr. Roosevelt High Sch., Chgo., 1961-63, St. Joseph's Sch., Wilmette, Ill., 1975-80; dir. Jane Byrne Polit. Com., Chgo., 1980-81; mgr. Chgo. Merc. Exch., 1981-84, sr. dir. govt. and civic affairs, 1984-87, v.p. pub. affairs, 1987-94, exec. v.p. corp. rels., 1995-2001. Mem. internat. trade an investment subcom. Chgo. Econ. Devel. Commn., 1989, 90. Bd. dirs. Chgo. Sister Cities, 1992—2000, Ill. Ambs., 1991—98, pres., 1994—98; bd. dirs., sec. Internat. Press Ctr., 1992—97, chmn. bd., 1994. Mem. Chgo. Conv. and Tourism Bur. (sec. 1989-90, exec. com. 1987-2000, chmn.-elect 1990, chmn. 1991-92). Roman Catholic. Avocations: books, gardening, travel.

SEXTON, DAVID FARRINGTON, lawyer, bank executive; b. Montclair, NJ, Aug. 20, 1943; s. Dorrance and Marjorie (McComb) S.; m. Ann Hemelright, Feb. 27, 1971; children: James, Ashley, Christopher. AB cum laude, Princeton U., 1966; JD cum laude, U. Pa., 1972. Bar: N.Y. 1972. Assoc. Sullivan & Cromwell, NYC, 1972-77; with First Boston Corp., NYC, 1977-90, v.p., gen. counsel, 1980-83, mng. dir., gen. counsel, 1983-86; mng. dir., pres. First Boston Internat. Ltd., 1986-90; sr. exec. v.p., dir. Yamaichi Internat. (America), Inc., NYC, 1990-95, vice-chmn., 1995-98; pres., CEO The Farrington Group, LLC, Greenwich, Conn., 1998—. Global Alliance assoc. for N.Am. IBS Securities Co., Ltd., Tokyo; adj. prof. law Fordham U., 1985—86; mem. U.S.-Japan Friendship Commn., Washington, 1990—94; adv. bd. mem. Manifold Products, LLC; sr. advisor Milbank Roy & Co., NYC. Lt. USNR, 1966—69. Mem. Assn. Bar City N.Y., Racquet and Tennis Club, N.Y. Yacht Club, Ivy Club, Bucks Harbor Yacht Club (bd. govs. 1991-, commodore 2003-05), The Nat. Assn. of Japan Am. Socs. (bd. dirs. 1998-, dir. exec. com. 1997-). Republican. Presbyterian. Office: The Farrington Group 186 Field Point Rd Ste 1B Greenwich CT 06830

SEXTON, DONALD LEE, retired business administration educator; b. New Boston, Ohio, June 14, 1932; s. Benjamin Franklin and Virgie Marie (Jordan) S.; m. Levonne Bradley, June, 1954 (div. June 1964); 1 child, Rhonda Jane; m. Carol Ann Schwaller, Dec. 18, 1965; children: David Lee, Douglas Edward BS in Math. and Physics, Wilmington Coll., 1959; MBA, Ohio State U., 1966, PhD in Mgmt., 1972. Indsl. engr. Detroit Steel Corp., Portsmouth, Ohio, 1959-61; sr. rsch. engr. Rockwell Internat., Columbus, Ohio, 1961-68; v.p. merchandising R.G. Barry Corp., Columbus, 1968-74; v.p., gen. mgr. Henri Fayette, Inc., Chgo., 1976; gen. mgr. M.H. Mfg. Co., Jackson, Miss., 1976-77; assoc. prof. Sangamon State U., Springfield, Ill., 1977-79; Caruth prof. entrepreneurship Baylor U., Waco, Tex., 1979-86; Davis prof. entrepreneurship Ohio State U., Columbus, 1986-94, prof. emeritus, 1994—; dir. Nat. Ctr. for Entrepreneurial Rsch. Kauffman Found., Kansas City, Mo., 1994-97, scholar-in-residence, 1997-2000. Adj. faculty Nova Southeastern U., Ft. Lauderdale, Fla., 1997-99; mem. adv. bd. SBA, Columbus, 1986-94; rsch. adv. bd. U. So. Calif., L.A., 1986-90 Co-author: Entrepreneurship Education, 1981, Experiences in Small Business, 1982, Starting A Business in Texas, 1983; co-editor: Encyclopedia of Entrepreneurship, 1981, Art and Science of Entrepreneurship, 1986, Women Owned Business, 1989, Entrepreneurship: Creativity and Growth, 1990, The State of the Art of Entrepreneurship, 1991, Leadership and Entrepreneurship, 1996, Entrepreneurship: 2000, 1996, The Handbook of Entrepreneurship, 1999, Strategic Entrepreneurship, 2002 Served to staff sgt. USAF, 1951-55 Recipient Leavy Free Enterprise award Freedoms Found. Valley Forge, 1985, Cert. Appreciation SBA, Washington, 1984, 85, Outstanding Contbn. to Entrepreneurship Edn. award Assn. Coll. Entrepreneurs, 1991, Disting. Alumni award Wilmington Coll., 1993, Entrepreneurship Adv. of the Yr., 1997; named Adv. of Yr.-Innovation SBA, Dallas, 1982, 83, 84 Mem. Internat. Coun. for Small Bus. (sr. v.p. 1986), U.S. Assn. for Small Bus. (v.p. pub. rels. 1987), Acad. Mgmt. (chmn. entrepreneurship com. 1981, mem. adv. bd. 1984-85), Masons, Shriners, Eagles, Am. Legion, Alpha Tau Omega Republican. Baptist. Avocation: golf. Home: 2940 West Bay Dr 303 Belleair Bluffs FL 33770 Personal E-mail: dlsexton@aol.com.

SEXTON, J. STAN, lawyer; b. Hays, Kans., 1948; BA, Univ. Kans., 1970, JD, 1977. Bar: Kans. 1977, Mo. 2001. Ptnr. complex litigation, toxic tort, insurance practices Shook Hardy & Bacon LLP, Kans. City, Mo. Editor (assoc., note & comment): Kans. Law Rev. Served to Lt. USN, 1970—74. Mem.: Am. Coll. Trial Lawyers, ABA, Def. Rsch. Inst., Kans. Inst. Trial Advocacy, Kans. Assn. Def. Counsel, Kans. Bar Assn., Mo. Bar. Office: Shook Hardy & Bacon LLP 2555 Grand Blvd Kansas City MO 64108 Home Phone: 816-531-7472; Office Phone: 816-474-6550. Office Fax: 816-421-5547. Business E-Mail: jsexton@shb.com.

SEXTON, JOE, editor; Dep. met. editor NY Times. Office: NY Times 229 West 43rd St New York NY 10036 Office Phone: 212-556-7371. Office Fax: 212-556-3690.

SEXTON, JOHN EDWARD, academic administrator, law educator; b. Bklyn., Sept. 29, 1942; s. John Edward and Catherine (Humann) S.; m. Lisa Ellen Goldberg; children: Jed, Katherine. BA in History, Fordham U., 1963, MA in Comparative Religion, 1965, PhD in History of Am. Religion, 1978; JD magna cum laude, Harvard U., 1979; Ph.D (hon.), Fordham U., 2005; degree (hon.), St. Francis Coll., Katholieke Universiteit, Leuven. Bar: NY 1981, US Supreme Ct. 1984. Prof. religion St. Francis Coll., Bklyn., 1966—75, religion dept. chair, 1970—75; law clk. to Hon. Harold Leventhal and Hon. David L. Bazelon US Ct. Appeals DC Cir., Wash., 1979—80; law clk. to Chief Justice Warren E. Burger US Supreme Ct., Wash., DC, 1980-81; assoc. prof. law NYU Sch. Law, NYC, 1981—84, prof., 1984—, Warren E. Burger prof. constl. law, 1994—2001, Benjamin F. Butler prof. law, 2001—, dean, 1988—2002, dean emeritus, 2002—; pres. NYU, 2002—. Dir. Washington Sq. Legal Services, NYC, 1983-2002, Pub. Interest Law Found., NYC, 1983-85, dep. chmn., Fed. Res. Bank NY, 2002-04, chmn., 2004-; past founding chmn. NASD Dispute Resolution; mem. exec. com. Consortium Ind. Colleges and Universities. Author: Modern Federal Jury Instructions-Civil, 1985, How Free Are We: A Non-Lawyer's Guide to the Constitution, 1986, Redefining the Supreme Court's Role: A Theory of Managing the Federal Court System, 1986, Civil Procedure, Cases and Materials, 1988. Dir. Root-Tilden Scholarship Program, 1984-88. Named one of NY Influentials, NY Mag., 2006; recipient Golden Plate award, Acad. Achievement, 2005. Fellow Am. Acad Arts & Sciences; mem. Assn. Am. Law Schs. (pres. 1997-98), Assn. Am. Univ. Presidents, Coun. Fgn. Rels. Office: NYU Sch Law Vanderbilt Hall Rm 316 40 Washington Sq S New York NY 10012-1099 Office Phone: 212-998-2345. E-mail: john.sexton@nyu.edu. *

SEXTON, JOHN JOSEPH, oral and maxillofacial surgeon, educator; b. Boston, Dec. 4, 1947; s. Bernard Thomas and Margaret Theresa (Carrigg) S.; m. Judith Whelden, Aug. 21, 1971; 1 child, Benjamin. BS, Boston Coll., 1970; DMD, Tufts U., 1975; MScD, Boston U., 1978, CAGS, 1979. Diplomate Am. Bd. Oral and Maxillofacial Surgery. Orthognathic fellow Boston U. Inst. for Correction of Facial Deformities, 1976-77; intern, jr. resident, chief resident Boston U./Tufts U., 1975-79; asst. prof. Goldman Sch. Dental Medicine, Boston U., 1979-81; chief oral and maxillofacial surgery Beth Israel Hosp., Boston, 1981—2001, dir. maxillofacial trauma svc., 1990—2001, dir. mucosal disorders unit, 1990—2001; chief oral and maxillofacial surgery Lahey Clinic Med. Ctr., Burlington, Mass., 2001—04; dir. Maxillofacial Trauma Svc. Beth Israel Deaconess Med. Ctr., 2004—, chief oral and maxillofacial surgery emeritus, 2005—. Cons. dermatology Beth Israel Hosp.; asst. prof. oral and maxillofacial surgery Harvard Med. Sch., Boston, 1999-2006. Contbr. numerous articles to profl. jours. Avocations: philosophy, physics, history, travel. Office: 372 Washington St Ste 2500 Wellesley MA 02481-6202 Office Phone: 781-235-4554. Business E-Mail: jsexton@bidmc.harvard.edu.

SEXTON, RANDALL C., art educator; b. East Hampton, Conn., Apr. 27, 1958; m. Carol Frances Neilson, Mar. 17, 2007; m. Arlene Kimberly Frohsin (div.); 1 child, Lesah. BFA in Painting, U. Conn., Storrs, 1980. Instr. Acad. of Arts U., San Francisco, 1995—2004; tchr. Pixar, Emeryville, Calif., 2005—. Artist John Pence Gallery, San Francisco, 1995—; tchr. Tippet Studios, Berkeley, Calif., 1999—2000; workshop instr., 2003—; curator Bolinas Mus, Calif., 2001. Contbr. articles to profl. jours.; exhibitions include Monterey Mus Art, Calif., 2000, Triton Mus. Art, Santa Clara, 2002—05, Hearst Mus. Gallery, St. Mary's Coll., Moraga, Calif., 2005, book catalogue, Havana and Back, 2004. Recipient Purchase award, So. Utah U., 1994, Best of Show, Carmel Art Festival, Calif., 2003, Maui Plain Air Invitational, Lahaina, Haiwaii, 2006, Artist's Choice award, 2006, Best of Show, Sedona Plein Air Invitational, Ariz., 2006, Merit award, 68th Ann. Crocker Kingsley Exhib., Crocker Mus, Sacramento, 1993. Mem.: Lagune Plein Air Painters Assn., The Outsiders, Calif. Art Club. Office: 1400 Pomona Crockett CA 94525

SEXTON, ROBERT FENIMORE, educational organization executive; b. Cin., Jan. 13, 1942; s. Claude Fenimore and Jane (Wisenall) S.; m. Pam Peyton Papka, Sept. 15, 1985; children: Rebecca, Robert B., Ouita Papka, Paige Papka, Perry Papka. BA, Yale U., 1964; MA in History, U. Wash., Seattle, 1968, PhD in History, 1970; DHL (hon.), Berea Coll., 1990, Georgetown Coll., Ky., 1993, Eastern Ky. U., 2000. Asst. prof. history Murray (Ky.) State U., 1968-70; dir. Office Acad. Programs, Commonwealth of Ky., Frankfort, 1970-73; assoc. dean, exec. dir. Office Exptl. Edn. U. Ky., Lexington, 1973-80; dep. exec. dir. Ky. Coun. Higher Edn., Frankfort, 1980-83; exec. dir. Prichard Com. for Acad. Excellence, Lexington, 1983—; founder, pres. Ky. Ctr. Pub. Issues, Lexington, 1988—94. Vis. scholar Harvard U., Cambridge, Mass., 1992, 94; chair Nat. Ctr. for Internships, Washington, 1973-80, Coalition for Alternatives in Post-Secondary Edn., Washington, 1977-80; bd. dirs. Editl. Projects in Edn., Consortium Policy Rsch. in Edn., Ky. Long Term Policy Rsch. Ctr., Edn. Trust, Trust for Early Edn., 1992-94. Pub. The Ky. Jour., 1988-2001; editor book series: Public Papers of Governors of Kentucky, 1973-86, Mobilizing Citizens for Better Schools, 5 books, 2004; contbr. articles to profl. jours. Co-chmn. Carnegie Ctr. for Literacy, Lexington, 1990-93; mem. Gov.'s Task Force on Health Care, Frankfort, 1992-99; bd. dirs. Ky. Inst. Edn. Rsch. Fund for Improvement in Postsecondary Edn., 1993-2000; chair Bluegrass Edn. Work Coun., Lexington, 1978-80; founder, steering com. Gov.'s Scholars Program, Frankfort, 1983-85. Recipient Charles A. Dana award for pioneering achievement, 1994. Mem. Am. Assn. Higher Edn. (bd. dirs. 1979-83). Democrat. Avocations: fishing, travel. Office: Prichard Com Acad Excell 167 W Main St Ste 310 Lexington KY 40507-1702

SEXTON, RONALD P., academic administrator; b. Greybull, Wyo. Grad., Ea. Mont. Coll.; PhD. Tchr. Mont. State U. (formerly Ea. Mont. Coll.), Billings, 1979, chancellor, 1995—. Chmn. Big Sky Econ. Devel. Authority. Office: Mont State U Office of the Chancellor 1500 University Dr Billings MT 59101-0298 Office Phone: 406-657-2300. E-mail: rsexton@msubillings.edu. *

SEXTON, SCOTTY EUGENE, music educator, gifted and talented educator; b. Somerset, Ky., Apr. 19, 1973; s. Isaac Roy and Verna Gussie (Hunley) Sexton. BA of Music Edn. summa cum laude, Cumberland Coll., 1996; MA in Edn., Ea. Ky. U., 1999. Dir. band, tchr. music Hart County Schs., Munfordville, Ky., 1996—98; dir. band, gifted & talented resource specialist Wayne County Schs., Monticello, 1998—. Chmn. adv. bd. Family Pl. Resource Ctr., Monticello, 2002—. Founder, dir. Cardinal Chorus, Monticello, 1998—, Cardinal Drama Club, 1998—; coach Turner Intermediate Sch. Acad. Team, 1998—. Mem.: NEA, Nat. Band Assn., Ky. Music Educatos Assn. (chair elem./mid. sch. band 2004—), Hon. Order Ky. Cols. Democrat. Nazarene. Avocations: music, scrapbooks, reading, exercise. Home: 130 Golden Pond Rd Monticello KY 42633 Office: Wayne County Schs 534 Albany Rd Monticello KY 42633 Business E-Mail: scott.sexton@wayne.kyschools.us.

SEYBERT, JOANNA, federal judge; b. Bklyn., Sept. 18, 1946; BA, U. Cin., 1967; JD, St. John's U., 1971. Bar: N.Y. 1972, U.S. Dist. Ct. (ea. and so. dists.) N.Y. 1973. Trial staff atty. Legal Aid Soc., NYC, 1971-73, sr. staff atty. Mineola, N.Y., 1976-80; sr. trial atty. Fed. Defender Svc., Bklyn., 1973-75; bur. chief Nassau County Atty's Office, Mineola, 1980-87; judge Nassau County Dist. Ct., Hempstead, N.Y., 1987-92, Nassau County Ct., Mineola, 1992-94, U.S. Dist. Ct. (ea. dist.) N.Y., Uniondale, 1994—. Mem.: Nassau Lawyers Assn. (past pres.), Fed. Judges Assn. (v.p.), Theodore Roosevelt A. Inns of Ct. (past pres.), Suffolk County Bar Assn., Internat. Assn. Judges (del.). Office: 100 Federal Plz Central Islip NY 11722

SEYDEL, RUTHERFORD (JOHN), (II), professional sports team owner, lawyer; b. Dallas, Apr. 4, 1963; m. Laura Turner Seydel; children: John, Laura Elizabeth, Vasser. BA in Polit. Sci., U. Ga., 1986; JD, Walter F. George-Mercer Law Sch., Macon, Ga., 1989. Bar: Ga. 1989. Ptnr. Lawson, Davis, Pickren & Seydel; prin. Atlanta Spirit, LLC (parent co. of NBA Atlanta Hawks and NHL Atlanta Thrashers). Dir., vice chmn. The Conservation Fund; co-founder, CEO Upper Chattahoochee RiverKeeper Fund Inc.; mem. Ga. State Properties Commn.; bd. dirs. So. Environ. Law Ctr., Emory U. Sch. Law Turner Environ. Law Clinic, Metro Atlanta C. of C., Atlanta Sports Coun. Mem.: Internat. Coun. Shopping Ctrs., Atlanta Coun. Young Lawyers, ABA (mem. real property, corp., entertainment & environ. law practice sects), Atlanta Bar Assn. Office: Lawson Davis Pickren & Seydel Ste 2300 285 Peachtree Center Ave Atlanta GA 30303 E-mail: rseydel@ldpslaw.com. *

SEYFERTH, DIETMAR, chemist, educator; b. Chemnitz, Germany, Jan. 11, 1929; arrived in U.S., 1933; s. Herbert C. and Elisabeth (Schuchardt) S.; m. Helena A. McCoy, Aug. 25, 1956; children: Eric Steven, Karl Dietmar, Elisabeth Mary. BA summa cum laude, U. Buffalo, 1951, MA, 1953; PhD, Harvard, 1955; D honoris causa, U. Aix-Marseille, 1979, Paul Sabatier Univ., Toulouse, France, 1992, Tech. U. Chemnitz, Germany, 2007. Fulbright scholar Tech. Hochschule, Munich, Germany, 1954-55; postdoctoral fellow Harvard U., 1956-57; faculty MIT, 1957—, prof. chemistry, 1965-2000, prof. emeritus, 2000—, Robert T. Haslam and Bradley Dewey prof., 1983-99. Cons. to industry, 1957—. Author: Annual Surveys of Organometallic Chemistry, 3 vols, 1965, 66, 67; regional editor: Jour. Organometallic Chemistry, 1963-81; coordinating editor revs. and survey sects., 1964-81; editor: Organometallics, 1981—; contbr. research papers and articles to profl. lit. Recipient Disting. Alumnus award U. Buffalo, 1964, Alexander von Humboldt Found. sr. award, 1984, Clifford C. Furnas Meml. award SUNY-Buffalo, 1987; Guggenheim fellow, 1968. Fellow AAAS, Am. Inst. Chemists, Inst. Materials, Am. Acad. Arts and

Scis.; mem. NAS, Am. Chem. Soc. (Frederic Stanley Kipping award in organosilicon chemistry 1972, disting. svc. award advancement inorganic chemistry 1981, award in organometallic chemistry, 1996, Arthur C. Cope Sr. Scholar award 2003), Materials Rsch. Soc., Am. Ceramic Soc., Royal Soc. Chemistry, Gesellschaft Deutscher Chemiker, German Acad. Scientists-Leopoldina, Phi Beta Kappa, Sigma Xi. Office: MIT 77 Massachusetts Ave Rm 4-382 Cambridge MA 02139-4307 Office Phone: 617-253-1861. Business E-Mail: seyferth@mit.edu.

SEYHUN, HASAN NEJAT, finance educator, department chairman; b. Ankara, Turkey, May 19, 1954; came to U.S., 1972; s. Niyazi and Serife (Sayilgan) S.; m. Tamara Z. Cleland, Aug. 10, 1992; children: Kent E., Jon C. and Evan G. BEE, Northwestern U., 1976; MA in Econs., U. Rochester, 1981, PhD in Fin., 1984. Elec. engr. Sungurlar, Istanbul, 1976-77; asst. prof. fin. U. Mich., Ann Arbor, 1983-91, assoc. prof., 1991-93, prof., 1993—, Jerome B. and Eilene M. York prof. bus. adminstrn., 1998—, chmn. fin. dept., 1994-95, 97-00. Vis. prof. Koc U., Istanbul, 2000-01, vis. assoc. prof. U. Chgo., 1988-89, 92, Wissenschaftliche Hochschule für Unternehmens führung, Koblenz, Germany, 1994; co-dir. banking and fin. svcs. program, cons. Citibank, Zurich, Switzerland, 1991; cons. Tweedy Brown, N.Y.C., 1993—, Towneley Capital, N.Y.C., 1994—. Mem. Am. Fin. Assn., Western Fin. Assn., European Fin. Assn., Beta Gamma Sigma. Avocations: volleyball, running. Office: U Mich 701 Tappan Ave Ann Arbor MI 48109-1217 E-mail: nseyhun@umiu.edu.

SEYMOUR, BARBARA LAVERNE, lawyer; b. Columbia, SC, July 9, 1953; d. Leroy Semon and Barbara Lucile (Youngblood) Seymour. BS, SC State Coll., 1975; JD, Georgetown U., Washington, DC, 1979; MBA, Harvard U., Cambridge, Mass., 1985. Bar: SC 1979, Tex. 1984, US Dist. Ct. (ea. dist.) Tex. 1983, US Dist. Ct. (so. dist.) Tex. 1985, US Tax Ct. 1986, US Claims Ct. 1991. Tax atty. Texaco Inc., White Plains, NY, 1979-80, Houston, 1980-98; asst. Office of the CFO-Gen. Counsel, Equilon Enterprises LLC, Houston, 1998-99, asst. sec., counsel, 1999—2003; pvt. practice Houston, 2004—. Mem. IRS Commr.'s Adv. Group, 1995-97; mem. Simplified Tax and Wage Reporting Sys. Working Group, 1994-97; loaned exec. for task force to audit Tex. Employment Commn. by Gov. of Tex., 1987-88. Troop leader Girl Scouts US, White Plains, 1979-80, asst. troop leader, Houston, 1981-82; bd. dirs. Sickle Cell Assn. of the Tex. Gulf Coast, Houston, 1986-92, treas., 1986-88, pres., 1988-90, chair 25th ann. gala, 1996; vol. allocation panel United Way of the Tex. Gulf Coast; bd. dirs. Found. for Main St., Assistance Fund, v.p., 2002-05; bd. dirs. Sandra Organ Dance Co., v.p., 2000-03; mem. Black Exec. Exch. program Nat. Urban League 1980-03; bd. dirs., exec. com. Houston Area Urban League, 1995-01, 02—, 3d v.p., 1998-00, 01—, treas. 2002-, 1st v.p., 2000-01, chair 1997 Equal Opportunity Day Dinner, co-chair Host Com., Nat. Urban League Conf., 1999; bd. dirs., asst. treas. Sheila Jackson Lee for Congress, 1995-97; mem. Houston Bd. Pub. Trust, 2003—, v.p., 2006-. Named one of 50 Outstanding Young Leaders of the Future, Ebony Mag., 1983, One of Ten Women of Distinctive Style, Onyxstyle Mag., 2004; recipient Disting. Bus. Alumnus award S.C. State Coll., 1991, Eagle award Nat. Eagle Leadership Inst., 1995; selected for Leadership Houston, Leadership Am., 1990; finalist Five Outstanding Young Houstonians award Jaycees, 1988, one of 10 Foremost Fashionables in Houston, Alpha Kappa Alpha, 1994; named one of 2001's ABC channel 13 Women of Distinction, one of Best Dressed. Houston Chronicle, 2005. Mem. ABA (employment tax com.), Houston Black Women Lawyers Assn. (sec. 1981-82, treas. 1982-83), Houston Bus. Forum (bd. dirs. 1983, 87-90, treas. 1988-89, sec. 1989-90), Nat. Bar Assn. (com. chmn. 1982-83), SC Bar Assn., Tex. Bar Assn., Harvard U. Bus. Sch. Black Alumni Assn. (historian 1985-86), Black Law Alumni Coun. of Georgetown U. Law Ctr., W.J. Durham Soc., The Links, Inc. (v.p. Houston chpt. 1996-2000, pres. 2000-2004, chair 1995 Cotillion), Alpha Kappa Alpha. Democrat. Roman Catholic. Home Phone: 713-961-3138; Office Phone: 713-807-1032. Personal E-mail: blseymour@att.net.

SEYMOUR, CHARLENA, academic administrator; m. Harry Seymour. BA, Howard U., 1965; MA, Ohio State U., 1967, PhD in Speech and Hearing Sci., 1981. Asst. prof. U. Mass., Amherst, 1971—78, assoc. prof., 1978—89, chair dept. comm. disorders, 1984—92, dean Grad. Sch., 1994—2001, provost, 2001—. Chair Coun. Grad. Schs. Adv. Com. on Minorities in Grad. Edn. Creative editor: Communication Disorders Textbook Series. Recipient Disting. Alumni award, Sch. Intercultural and Race Rels., Harvard Found., Harvard U., 1997. Fellow: Am. Speech-Lang. Hearing Assn.; mem.: N.E. Assn. Grad. Schs. (pres.-elect). Office: U Mass Office of the Provost 362 Whitmore Bldg 181 Presidents Dr Amherst MA 01003 *

SEYMOUR, CLAUDIA HULTGREN, painter; b. St. Paul, Feb. 2, 1948; d. John Bradford and Ruth Conley Hultgren; m. S. Mark Seymour, 1970; 1 child, P. Griffith. BA with honors, Duke U., Durham, NC, 1970; MA, NYU, NYC, 1979. One-woman shows include Hoorn-Ashby Gallery, NYC, 2006, exhibited in group shows at Oil Painters Am., 2003—, Allied Artists Am., 2003, Pastel Soc. Am., 2003—, Hudson Valley Art Assn., 2003, Salmagundi Club, 2003—. V.p. Artists' Fellowship, NYC. Fellow: Am. Artists Profl. League (Bernhard Gold medal 2006); mem.: Pastel Painters Soc. Cape Cod, Pastel Soc. Conn. (signature status), Hudson Valley Art Assn., Oil Painters Am. (assoc.), Allied Artists Am. (editor newsletter), Academic Artists Assn., Salmagundi Club (v.p. 2004—), Catharine Lorillard Wolfe Art Club.

SEYMOUR, DOROTHY Z. See MILLS, DOROTHY

SEYMOUR, EVERETT HEDDEN, JR., lawyer; b. Tuxedo Park, Apr. 16, 1958; s. Everett Hedden and Deborah (Robinson) S. BA, Yale U., 1980; JD, U. Va., 1986. Bar: N.Y. 1988, U.S. Dist. Ct. (so. and ea. dists.) N.Y. 1988, Conn. 1988, U.S. Dist. Ct. Conn. 1988. Law clk. to justice U.S. Dist. Ct., New Haven, 1986-87; assoc. Davis Polk & Wardwell, NYC, 1987-97; mng. dir., assoc. gen. counsel J.P. Morgan Chase & Co., NYC, 1997—. Articles rev. editor U. Va. Law Rev., 1984-86. Office: JP Morgan Chase & Co 270 Park Ave 40th Fl New York NY 10017-2014

SEYMOUR, JANE, actress; b. Hillingdon, Middlesex, Eng., Feb. 15, 1951; came to U.S., 1976; d. John Benjamin and Mieke Frankenberg; m. David Flynn, July 18, 1981 (div. 1991); 2 children; m. James Keach, May 15, 1993; 2 children (twins). Student, Arts Ednl. Sch., London. Advisor Eons, Inc., Boston, 2006—. Appeared in films Oh What A Lovely War, 1968, The Only Way, 1968, Young Winston, 1969, Live and Let Die, 1971, Sinbad and the Eye of the Tiger, 1973, Somewhere in Time, 1979, Oh Heavenly Dog, 1979, Lassiter, 1984, Head Office, Scarlet Pimpernel, Haunting Passion, Dark Mirror, Obsessed with a Married Woman, Killer on Board, The Tunnel, 1988, The French Revolution, Touching Wild Horses, 2002, Wedding Crashers, 2005, The Beach Party at the Threshold of Hell, 2006, After Sex, 2007; TV films include Frankenstein, The True Story, 1972, Captains and The Kings, 1976 (Emmy nomination), 7th Avenue, 1976, The Awakening Land, 1977, The Four Feathers, 1977, Battlestar Galactica, Dallas Cowboy Cheerleaders, 1979, Our Mutual Friend, PBS, Eng., 1975, Jamaica Inn, 1982, Sun Also Rises, 1984, Crossings, 1986, Keys to Freedom, Angel of Death, 1990, Praying Mantis, 1993, A Passion for Justice: The Hazel Brannon Smith Story, 1994, The Absolute Truth, 1997, A Marriage of Convenience, 1998, A Memory in My Heart, 1999, Dr. Quinn, Medicine Women (The Movie), 1999, Murder in the Mirror, 2000, Enslavement: The True Life Story of Fanny Kemble, 2000, Blackout, 2000, Yesterday's Children,2000, Dr. Quinn, Medicine Women: The Heart Within, 2001, Heart of a Stranger, 2002; Broadway appearances include Amadeus, 1980-81, I Remember You, 1992, Matters of the Heart, 1991, Sunstroke, 1992, Praying Mantis, 1993, Heidi, 1993; TV mini-series include East of Eden, 1980, The Richest Man in the World, 1988 (Emmy award), The Woman He Loved, 1988, Jack the Ripper, 1988, War and Remembrance, 1988, 89; host PBS documentary, Japan, 1988; TV series: Dr. Quinn: Medicine Woman, 1993-98 (Emmy nomination, Lead Actress - Drama, 1994, 98, Golden Globe award 1996); guest appearances Law & Order: Special Victims Unit, 2004, Smallville (6 episodes), 2004-2005, Modern Man (7 episodes) 2006, "How I Met Your Mother", 2006, Justice, 2006, In Case of Emergency, 2007, Marple: Ordeal by Innocence, 2007; author: Jane Seymour's Guide to Romantic Living, 1986, Two at a Time, 2001; co-author: Yum, Splat, 1998, Boing, 1999; performer Dancing With the Stars, 2007. Decorated Order Brit. Empire; recipient OBE award, 2000; named Hon. Citizen of Ill., Gov. Thompson, 1977. Mem. Screen Actors Guild, AFTRA, Actors Equity, Brit. Equity. Office: Guttman Assocs 118 S Beverly Dr Ste 201 Beverly Hills CA 90212-3016 *

SEYMOUR, JEFFREY ALAN, governmental relations consultant; b. LA, Aug. 31, 1950; s. Daniel and Evelyn (Schwartz) S.; m. Valerie Joan Parker, Dec. 2, 1973; 1 child, Jessica Lynn. AA in Social Sci., Santa Monica Coll., 1971; BA in Polit. Sci., UCLA, 1973; MPA, 1977. Councilman aide L.A. City Coun., 1972-74; county supr.'s sr. dep. L.A. Bd. Suprs., 1974-82; v.p. Bank of L.A., 1982-83; prin. Jeffrey Seymour & Assocs., LA, 1983-84; ptnr. Morey/Seymour & Assocs., LA, 1984—2002, Seymour Consulting Group, 2002—. Mem. comml. panel Am. Arbitration Assn., 1984—90. Chmn. West Hollywood Parking Adv. Com., L.A., 1983-84; chmn. social action com. Temple Emanuel of Beverly Hills, 1986-89, bd. dirs. 1988-93, v.p. 1990-93; v.p. Congregation N'Vay Shalom, 1994-95; mem. Pan Pacific Park Citizens Adv. Com., L.A., 1982-85; bd. dirs. William O'Douglas Outdoor Classroom, LA, 1981-88; mem. bd. regents U. Calif., 2001-02; pres. Alumni Assns. U. Calif., 2000-02; chair UCLA Fund, 2002-04; friend com. LA Free Clin., 2005—; mem. govtl. affairs com. Venice Family Clin., 2005—; mem., bd. dirs. UCLA Found., 2007—. Recipient plaques for svcs. rendered Beverlywood Cheviot Hills Dem. Club, L.A., 1981, Jewish Fedn. Coun. Greater L.A., 1983, certs. of appreciation, L.A. Olympic Organizing Com., 1984, County of L.A., 1984, City of L.A., 1987, Santa Monica Mountains Conservancy, 1999, UCLA Alumni Assn., 2002, others; commendatory resolutions, rules com. Calif. State Senate, 1987, Calif. State Assembly, 1987, 96, County of L.A., 1987, City of L.A., 1987; mem. bd. Regents of U. Calif., 2000-2002. Mem. ASPA, UCLA Alumni Assn. (mem. govtl. steering com. 1983-97, bd. dirs. 1995—, chair govtl. rels. steering com. 1995-97, pres. 1998-2000); exec. sect. Calif. Fedn. Young Dems., 1971; mem. Calif. Dem. Cen. Com., 1979-82; pres. Beverlywood-Cheviot Hills Dem. Club, L.A., 1978-81; co-chmn. Westside Chancellor's Assocs. UCLA, 1986-88; mem. L.A. Olympic Citizens Adv. Com.; mem. liaison adv. commn. with city and county govt. for 1984 Olympics, 1984; v.p. comty. rels. metro region, Jewish Fedn. Coun. of L.A., 1985-87, co-chmn. urban affairs commn., 1987-89, vice chmn., 1989-90, subcom. chmn. local govt. law and legislation commn., 1990, chmn. campus outreach task force, 1994; mem. adv. bd. Nat. Jewish Ctr. for Immunology & Respiratory Medicine, 1991-93; bd. dirs. Hillel Coun. of L.A., 1991; mem. platform on world peace and internat. rels. Calif. Dems., 1983; pres. 43d Assembly Dist. Dem. Coun., 1975-79; arbitrator BBB, 1984; trustee UCLA Found., 1989-97; pres. UCLA Jewish Alumni, 1992-95; mem. Santa Monica Mountains Conservancy adv. com., 1996-99; mem. cabinet Jewish Cmty. Rels. Com. Greater L.A., 1994, chair campus outreach task force, 1994-95, govtl. rels. commn., 1995-96, v. chair Jewish Cmty. Rels. com. Jewish Fedn. Coun. Greater L.A., 1998; mem. bd. dirs., Century City C of C, 1998-2000, adv. bd. L.A. Peace Now, UCLA Fund (chair 2002-04), Alumni Assn. of U. Calif. (pres. 2001-2002, chmn. 2002-2004, bd. govs. 2004—, mem. adv. com. 2004—). Office: 2815 Townsgate Rd Ste 140 Westlake Village CA 91361 Office Phone: 818-905-0283. Business E-Mail: jeff@jseymourgroup.com.

SEYMOUR, JOHN, former senator; b. Chgo., Dec. 3, 1937; M. Judy Thacker, 1972; children: John III, Lisa, Jeffery, Shad, Sarena, Barrett. BS in Fin. and Real Estate, UCLA, 1962. Pres., CEO Seymour Realty and Investment Co., 1964—82; mem. Anaheim City Coun., 1974-78; mayor Anaheim, 1978; state sen. Calif., 1982, 84, 88; sen. U.S. Senate, Washington, 1991—93; dir. Calif. Housing Fin. Agy., 1992—94. Chmn. Calif. Senate Rep. Caucus, 1983-87; mem. Agr., Nutrition and Forestry Com., Energy and Natural Resources Com., Govtl. Affairs Com., Small Bus. Com.; bd. dir. Inco Homes 1995-2001, Indymac Bank, 2000-, Indymac, 2004-, LA Fed. Savings Bank, Irvine Apt. Communities, Countrywide Financial Services; bd. dir., cons. Orange Coast Title Ins., 1995-. Sgt. USMC, 1955-59. Child Care Adv. Am. award, Dayle McIntosh Ctr. for Disabled award, Golden Pineapple award, Leukemia Soc. Am., 1984, 1985, N Anaheim Pony League award; The Founders award, No. & So. Calif Head Injury Assn., 1988, Legis. Yr., Calif. Sch. Bd. Assn., 1988; Transp. Partnership award, Orange County Transp. Comm., 1988; Senator of Yr., Univ Calif Student Assn., 1989. Mem. Anaheim C. of C. (pres. 1973), Rotary Internat., Nat. Assn. Realtors, Calif. Assn. Realtors (pres., 1980) Republican. Office: Orange Coast Title Co 640 N Tustin Santa Ana CA 92705 *

SEYMOUR, KAREN PATTON, lawyer, former prosecutor; b. Big Springs, Tex. m. Samuel Seymour; 2 children. BA, So. Methodist U., 1983; BS, So. Meth. U., 1986; JD, U. Tex., 1986; LLM, U. London, 1987. Bar: NY 1988. Fed. prosecutor US Attys. Office, So. Dist. NY, 1990—96, Asst. US Atty., Criminal Div. Chief, 2002—04; ptnr. Sullivan & Cromwell, NY, NY, 1987—90, 1996—2002, 2004—. Office: Sullivan & Cromwell 125 Broad St New York NY 10004-2498

SEYMOUR, MARY FRANCES, lawyer; b. Durand, Wis., Oct. 20, 1948; d. Marshall Willard and Alice Roberta (Smith) Thompson; m. Marshall Warren Seymour, June 6, 1970; 1 foster child, Nghia Pham. BS, U. Wis., LaCrosse, 1970; JD, William Mitchell Coll., 1979. Bar: Minn. 1979, Wis. 2003, US Dist. Ct. Minn. 1979, US Ct. Appeals (8th cir.) 1979, US Supreme Ct. 1986. With Cochrane and Bresnahan, P.A., St. Paul, 1979-94, Loper & Seymour, P.A., 1994—2003; pvt. practice Pepin, Wis., 2003—, Mary F. Seymour Atty. At Law, 2003—. Mem.: ABA, Tri-County Bar Assn., Wis. Bar Assn., Wabasha County Bar Assn., Minn. Bar Assn. Office: PO Box 146 511 2nd St Pepin WI 54759 Office Phone: 715-442-2615. Personal E-mail: maryfseymour@msn.com.

SEYMOUR, MCNEIL VERNAM, lawyer; b. St. Paul, Dec. 21, 1934; s. McNeil Vernam and Katherine Grace (Klein) S.; children: Margaret, McNeil Vernam, James, Benjamin; m. Mary Katherine Velner, May 15, 1993. AB, Princeton U., 1957; JD, U. Chgo., 1960. Bar: Minn. 1960, U.S. Dist. Ct. Minn. 1960. Mem. Seymour & Seymour, St. Paul, 1960-71; mem. firm Briggs & Morgan, St. Paul, 1971—, ptnr., 1976—2005, of counsel, 2005—. Pres. Thomas Irvine Dodge Nature Ctr.; sec., bd. dirs. Ramsey County Law Libr., 1972—76; pres. White Bear Unitarian Ch., treas.; trustee Oakland Cemetery Assn., 2006—. With US Army, 1960—62. Mem. Minn. Bar Assn., Ramsey County Bar Assn., Somerset Country Club. Republican. Unitarian Universalist. Home: 886 S Highview Cir Mendota Heights MN 55118-3686 Office: Briggs & Morgan W-2200 1st Nat Bank Bldg Saint Paul MN 55101 Office Phone: 651-808-6601. E-mail: MSeymour@Briggs.com.

SEYMOUR, RICHARD DEMING, technology educator; b. Shelby, Ohio, Oct. 3, 1955; s. G. Deming and Elizabeth (Peterson) S.; m. Vicki Stebleton; 1 child, Ryan. BS in Edn., Ohio State U., 1978; MA, Ball State U., 1982; EdD, W.Va. U., 1990. Tchr. Crestview Sr. High Sch., Ashland, Ohio, 1978-81; from instr. to assoc. prof. Ball State U., Muncie, Ind., 1982—. Vis. instr. W.Va. U., Morgantown, 1985, Oreg. State U., 1990-91. Co-author: Exploring Communications, 1987, rev. edit., 2000; co-editor: Manufacturing in Technology Education, 1993. Advisor 4-H Clubs, Richland County, Ohio, 1978-81; dir. tech. in-svc. workshops Ind. Dept. Edn., Indpls., 1988-2000. Named technology tchr. educator of yr. Coun. on Technology Tchr. Edn., 1998. Mem.: Tech. Edn. Collegiate Assn. (internat. advisor 1990—92, nat. contest coord. 1992—), Am. Soc. Engring. Edn., Tech. Educators Ind. (pres. 1995—96), Ind. Math., Sci., Tech. Alliance (bd. dirs. 1994—), Coun. on Tech. Tchr. Edn. (v.p. 2003—05, pres. 2007—), Soc. Mfg. Engrs., Internat. Tech. Edn. Assn. (bd. dirs. 1992—94, chmn. internat. conf. 1999, award of distinction 1999), Phi Delta Kappa, Epsilon Pi Tau. Methodist. Avocations: model railroads, sports, travel. Office: Ball State Univ Dept Tech Muncie IN 47306-0255 E-mail: rseymour@bsu.edu.

SEYMOUR, SAMUEL WHITNEY, lawyer; b. Hanover, NH, 1957; AB, Dartmouth Coll., 1979; JD, Columbia U., 1982. Bar: NY 1983. Asst. US Atty. US Dist. Ct. (so. dist.) NY, 1988-91; ptnr. Sullivan & Cromwell, NYC, 1991—, and coord. criminal def. and investigations practice area. Bd. dir. Fund for Modern Courts, First Dept. Assigned Counsel Corp.; adj. lectr. trial advocacy Columbia Law Sch., NYC. Mem.: NY Coun. Def. Lawyers, Assn. of Bar City of NY (past v.p. and chair, exec. com.). Office: Sullivan & Cromwell 125 Broad St Fl 28 New York NY 10004-2489 Office Phone: 212-558-4000. Office Fax: 212-558-3588. Business E-Mail: seymours@sullcrom.com.

SEYMOUR, STEPHANIE KULP, federal judge; b. Battle Creek, Mich., Oct. 16, 1940; d. Francis Bruce and Frances Cecelia (Bria) Kulp; m. R. Thomas Seymour, June 10, 1972; children: Bart, Bria, Sara, Anna. BA magna cum laude, Smith Coll., 1962; JD, Harvard U., 1965. Bar: Okla. 1965. Practice, Boston, 1965—66, Tulsa, 1966—67, Houston, 1968—69; assoc. Doerner, Stuart, Saunders, Daniel & Anderson, Tulsa, 1971—75, ptnr., 1975—79; judge US Ct. Appeals (10th cir.), Tulsa, Okla., 1979—, chief judge, 1994—2000, sr. judge, 2006—. Mem. US Jud. Conf., 1994—, com. defender svcs., 1985—90, chmn., 1987—90, com. to review cir. council conduct and disability, 1996—; joint fed. tribal rels. com. 9th and 10th cirs., 1993—; mem. Okla. State Fed. Tribal Judicial Coun., 1993—94. Task force Tulsa Human Rights Commn., 1972—76; legal adv. panel Tulsa Task Force Battered Women, 1971—77; trustee Tulsa County Law Libr., 1977—78. Mem.: ABA, Am. Inns of Ct. (Council Oak chpt.), Nat. Assn. Women Judges, Fed. Judges Assn., Tulsa County Bar Assn., Okla. Bar Assn. (assoc. bar examiner 1973—79), Phi Beta Kappa. Office: US Courthouse 333 W 4th St Ste 4-562 Tulsa OK 74103-3819

SEYMOUR, THADDEUS, language educator; b. NYC, June 29, 1928; s. Whitney North and Lola Virginia (Vickers) S.; m. Polly Gnagy, Nov. 20, 1948; children: Elizabeth Halsey, Thaddeus, Samuel Whitney, Mary Duffie, Abigail Comfort AB, U. Calif., 1950; MA, U. N.C., 1951, PhD, 1955; D.H.L. (hon.), Wilkes Coll., 1968; LL.D. (hon.), Butler U., 1971, Ind. State U., 1976; LLD (hon.), Wabash Coll., 1984, U. Cen. Fla., 1990, Stetson U., 1990; DHL (hon.), Rollins Coll., 1990. Mem. faculty Dartmouth Coll., 1954-69, prof. English, dean coll., 1959-69; pres. Wabash Coll., Crawfordsville, Ind., 1969-78, Rollins Coll., Winter Park, Fla., 1978-90, prof. English, 1978—. Pres. Ind. Conf. Higher Edn., 1977; v.p. Assoc. Colls. Ind., 1978; vice-chmn. Fla. Ind. Colls. Fund Past mem. Ind. Bicentennial Commn.; trustee Park-Tudor Sch., 1970-78, Bach Festival Soc., Winter Park Pub. Libr., 1998—2004; chmn. Fla. selection com. Rhodes Scholarship Trust, 1983-88; chmn. Habitat for Humanity of Winter Park, 1994—; sec.-treas. Winter Park Health Found., 1998—2005. Mem. Cmty. Found. Ctrl. Fla. (bd. dirs.), Ring 219 (charter), Internat. Brotherhood Magicians, Century Assn., Rotary, Omicron Delta Kappa. Home: 1804 Summerfield Rd Winter Park FL 32792 Office Phone: 407-646-1985. Business E-Mail: tseymour@rollins.edu.

SEZNEC, JEAN-FRANCOIS, international trade and investment manager; b. Laval, France, Oct. 18, 1945; came to U.S., 1962; s. Louis Corentin and Denise Marie (Josse) S.; m. Thackray Weems Dodds; children: Gwenann, Corentin, Yann-Loic. BA, Washington Coll., Chestertown, Md., 1970; M Internat. Affairs, Columbia U., 1973; MA, Yale U., 1993, PhD, 1994. Project mgr., regional rep., Saudi mktg. mgr., others Chase Manhattan Bank, NY, Bahrain, Jordan, Saudi Arabia, 1973-78; sr. v.p., gen. mgr. Saudi European Bank, Bahrain, 1978-84, NYC, 1985, Bahrain Middle East Bank, NYC, 1986-91; adj. prof. Columbia U., NYC, 1984—; pres. Lafayette Group Inc., Greenwich, Conn., 1991—. Mem. bd. advisors Human Rights Watch, Mid. East, 1997, Washington Coll., 1994; adj. prof. sch. internat. & pub. affairs Columbia U., 1989—. Author: The Financial Markets of the Arabian Gulf, 1987; contbr. articles to profl. jours. 2nd lt. French Navy, 1970-71. Mem. Am. Field Svc., Am. Bahraini Friendship Soc. Democrat. Congregationalist. Office: Lafayette Group LLC 301 4th St Annapolis MD 21403 E-mail: jfseznec@thelafayettegroup.com.

SFEKAS, STEPHEN JAMES, lawyer, educator; b. Balt., Feb. 12, 1947; s. James Stephen and Lee (Mesologites) S.; m. Joanne Lorraine Murphy, May 27, 1973; children: James Stephen, Andrew Edward Stephen, Christina Marie; m. Elizabeth Ruff, Nov. 1, 1997. BS in Fgn. Svc., Georgetown U., 1968, JD, 1973; MA, Yale U., 1972. Bar: Md. 1973, U.S. Dist. Ct. Md. 1974, U.S. Ct. Appeals (4th cir.) 1974. Law clk. U.S. Dist. Ct., Balt., 1973-74; assoc. firm Frank, Bernstein, Conaway & Goldman, Balt., 1974-75; asst. atty. gen. State of Md., Balt., 1975-81; assoc. firm Tydings & Rosenberg, Balt., 1981-82, ptnr., 1983-86; with firm Miles & Stockbridge, Balt., 1986-90; ptnr. Weinberg & Green, Balt., 1991-98, Saul, Ewing, LLP, Balt., 1998—2001; counsel Cook & Di Franco, LLC, 2001—05; sole practice Balt., 2005—. Instr. legal writing C.C. Balt., 1976-79; instr. legal ethics Goucher Coll., Balt., 1979; adj. prof. adminstrv. law U. Md., Balt., 1981-93, health, 1993—, law sch. U. Balt., 1993—. Editor Georgetown Law Jour., 1972-73; contbr. articles to legal publs. Bd. dirs. Md. region NCCJ, 1981-89, co-chmn. Md. region, 1986-89, Orthodox Christian Laity, 1990—98, Ctrl. Md. Ecumenical Coun., 1991—93, ARC of Balt. Vol. for Med. Engring., 2001-; mem. Piraeus Sister City Com., City of Balt., 1983-89; mem. parish coun. Greek Orthodox Cathedral of Annunciation, Balt., 1981-84; mem. internat. com. Balt. region ARC, 1984-85; mem. adv. com. on bread for the world Dept. Ch. and Soc., Greek Orthodox Archdiocese North and S.Am., 1984—; pres. Greek Orthodox Counseling and Social Svcs. of Balt., 1984-88; mem. bylaw com. Girl Scouts Ctrl. Md., 1989-91, Md. Leadership Program, 1997; mem. pres.'s adv. coun. U. Md., Baltimore County; mem. human rights com. ARC of the U.S., 2002—. Danforth fellow, Woodrow Wilson fellow, WHO fellow, London, 1979. Fellow: Md. Bar Found., Soc. for Values in Higher Edn. (bd. dir. 2002—); mem.: ABA (forum com. on health law, Grant Morris fellow 1979), Am. Health Lawyers Assn., Bar Assn. Balt. City, Md. Bar Assn. Democrat. Home Phone: 410-448-0548; Office Phone: 410-385-5322. Business E-Mail: stephen@sfekaslaw.com.

SFIKAS, PETER MICHAEL, lawyer, educator; s. Michael E. and Helen (Thureanos) S.; m. Freida Platon, Apr. 24, 1966; children: Ellen M., Pamela C., Sandra N. BS, Ind. U., 1959; JD, Northwestern U., 1962. Bar: Ill. 1962, U.S. Dist. Ct. (no. dist.) Ill. 1963, U.S. Ct. Appeals (7th cir.) 1963, U.S. Supreme Ct. 1970, U.S. Ct. Appeals (9th cir.) 1976, U.S. Ct. Appeals (3d cir.) 1981, U.S. Ct. Appeals (D.C. cir.) 1984, U.S. Ct. Appeals (8th cir.) 1995, U.S. Dist. Ct. (cen. dist.) Ill. 1988. Atty. Legal Aid Bur., United Charities Chgo., 1962-63; sr. ptnr. Peterson & Ross, Chgo., 1970-95; chief counsel, assoc. exec. dir. divsn. legal affairs ADA, Chgo., 1995—2006; ptnr. Bell, Boyd & Lloyd, Chgo., 1996—. Prosecutor Village of LaGrange Park, Ill., 1969-74; mem. rules com. Ill. Supreme Ct., 1975-95, mem. spl. joint com. on discovery rules, 1995; arbitrator Nat. Panel Arbitrators, 1972—; adj. prof. Loyola U. Sch. Law, 1978—; guest lectr. U. Ill. Coll. Dentistry, 1988-95; lectr. corp. counsel inst. Northwestern U. Sch. Law, 1984, lectr. Ray Garret Jr. Corp. and Securities Law Inst., 1996. Co-author: Antitrust and Unfair Competition Practice Handbook, 1996; contbr. articles to profl. jours. Mem. Ill. steering com. Ct. Watching Project, LWV,

1975-77; pres. Holy Apostles Greek Orthodox Ch. Parish Coun., 1987-89; co-pres. Oak Sch. PTO, 1989-90; mem. com. to select sch. supr., dist. 86, DuPage County, Ill., 1993-94. Named Super Lawyer, Chgo. Mag., 2005, 2006, 2007, Leading Lawyer, 2005, 2006, 2007; recipient Maurice Weigle award, Chgo. Bar Found., 1973, Fones award, Conn. Dental Assn., 1998. Fellow Am. Bar Found., Am. Coll. Trial Lawyers, Chgo. Bar Found. (life); mem. ABA (editor in chief Forum Law Jour. sect. ins., negligence and compensation law 1972-76), Ill. Bar Found. (bd. dirs. 1975-77), Northwestern U. Law Alumni Assn. (1st v.p. 1985-86, pres. 1986-87, Svc. award 1990), Ill. State Bar Assn. (bd. govs. 1970-76, chmn. antitrust law sect. coun. 1986-87), Chgo. Bar Assn. (editl. bd. Chgo. Bar Record 1973-84), Bar Assn. 7th Fed. Cir. (chmn. com. on meetings 1973-75), Ill. Inst. Continuing Legal Edn. (chmn. profl. antitrust problems program 1976, author program on counseling corps., antitrust and trade regulation), Am. Nat. Standards Inst. (mem. copyright ad hoc group 2004-), Legal Club Chgo. (sec.-treas, 1984-86, v.p. 1989-90, pres. 1990-91). Office: Bell Boyd & Lloyd 70 W Madison St Ste 3300 Chicago IL 60602-4284 Home Phone: 630-323-6848; Office Phone: 312-807-4348. Personal E-mail: petersfi@comcast.net. Business E-Mail: psfikas@bellboyd.com.

SFIROUDIS, GLORIA TIDES, library and information scientist, educator; d. George and Mary Despotides; m. Harry Sfiroudis, June 30, 1957; children: Steven, Christina. BA in Geography and Geology, Hunter Coll., 1954, MS in Edn., 1957; Profl. Diploma in Adminstrn. and Supervision, Queens Coll., 1981. Cert. tchr. effectiveness instrn. N.Y. Tchr. North Babylon Sch., LI, NY, 1954—55, P.S. 123, Bklyn., 1955—61; tchr. 2nd and 3rd grade P.S. 229, Queens, NY, 1970—72, tchr., libr., 1972—74, corrective reading tchr., 1974—82, talented and gifted tchr., 1982—89, acting asst. prin., 1989—90, ednl. enrichment specialist, 1991—2000, tchrs. coll. literacy coach, 2000—04, libr./rsch. tchr., 2004—. Chairperson sch. bd. William Spyropolous Sch. of St. Nicholas, Flushing, NY, 1982—2000; mem., participant Law in a Free Soc., Albany, NY, 1985—89. Co-author: (handbook) The Opera, 1990. Vol. Hosp. Audiences, Inc., NYC, 1975—; active fundraiser Reading Olympics, March of Dimes, UNICEF, Am. Cancer Soc.; mem. exec. bd. St. Nicholas Shrine Ch., Flushing, 1995—. Recipient Vol. Cmty. Action award, Hosp. Audiences, Inc., award, Audubon Soc., 1995; CVS Innovations Charitable Trust Inc. grant, TPI Philanthropic Initiative, 2002—05, Greenwich Conn. fellow, Korean Summer Inst. Yale U. fellow, 1997. Mem.: St. Nicholas Ladies Philoptochos Soc. (sec. 1999—, Pastor's award 2002). Avocations: piano, swimming. Office: Emanuel Kaplan Sch PS 229 67-25 51st Rd Woodside Woodside NY 11377 Office Phone: 718-446-2120.

SFORZINI, RICHARD HENRY, aerospace engineer, educator; b. Rochester, NY, July 25, 1924; m. Corinne Lorenz, 1947; children: Richard Jr., Suzanne Simonelli, Deborah Pugh, Michael, Stephen, Andrew, Mark. Degree of Mech. Engr., MIT, 1954; BS, U.S. Mil. Acad., 1947. Instr. ordnance U.S. Mil. Acad., 1954-56, asst. prof., 1956-57; project dir. anti-tank missile sys. R&D Army Rocket and Guided Missile Agy., Redstone Arsenal, Ala., 1958-59; engr. Huntsville divsn. Thiokol Chem. Corp., Ala., 1959-62, mgr. engring. dept. Ala., 1962-64, dir. engring. space booster divsn. Brunswick, Ga., 1964-66; vis. prof. Auburn (Ala.) U., 1966-67, prof., 1967-85, prof. emeritus aerospace engring., 1985—. Home and Office: 912 Cherokee Rd Auburn AL 36830-2723

SGARRO, DOUGLAS A., pharmaceutical executive, lawyer; b. NY, 1959; m. Breda Sgarro; 3 children. Grad, Hamilton Coll., 1981; law degree, Univ. of Va. Sch. of Law, 1984. Assoc. Brown & Wood LLP, New York, NY, 1984—93, ptnr., 1993—97; sr. v.p. and chief legal officer CVS Pharmacy, Woonsocket, RI, 1997—2004; pres. CVS Realty Co., Woonsocket, RI, 1999—; sr. v.p. and chief legal officer CVS Corp., Woonsocket, RI, 2000—04; exec. v.p. strategy, chief legal officer CVS Corp., CVS Pharmacy, Woonsocket, RI, 2004—07; exec. v.p., chief legal officer, pres. CVS Realty CVS Caremark Corp., Woonsocket, RI, 2007—. Dir. Providence Children's Mus., United Way, Rye, NY. Mem.: Am. Bar Assoc. Bus. Law Sect., Internat. Assoc. of Atty. Exec. in Corp. Real Estate. Avocations: reading, exercise. Office: CVS Caremark Corp One CVS Dr Woonsocket RI 02895 *

SGRO, JOSEPH ANTHONY, retired psychologist, educator; b. New Haven, Nov. 22, 1937; s. Fred and Tullia (Francesconi) S.; m. Beverly Ann Huston, Feb. 1, 1964; children: Anthony, Jennifer. BA, Trinity Coll., 1959; MS, Lehigh U., 1961; PhD, Tex. Christian U., 1966. Asst. prof. Old Dominion U., Norfolk, Va., 1965-67, Va. Poly. Inst. & State U., Blacksburg, 1967-71, assoc. prof., 1971-79, prof., 1979-99; prof. emeritus, 1999—; dept. head psychology Va. Poly. Inst. & State U., Blacksburg, 1982-96, mem. exec. bd., sec.-treas. coun. grad. dept. psychology, 1990-92, chmn., 1992-93; adj. prof. Warren Wilson Coll., 2000, U. NC Asheville, 2004. Vice-chmn. Va. Bd. Psychologists Examiners, Richmond, 1970-75. Editor: Virginia Tech Symposium on Applied Behavioral Science, 1980. Mem. APA, Southeastern Psychol. Assn. (chmn. assn. heads depts. psychology 1987-89), Ea. Psychol. Assn., Va. Psychol. Assn. (pres. 1974-76), Soc. Indsl. and Orgnl. Psychology, Omicron Delta Kappa, Psi Chi, Sigma Xi. Avocations: golf, cooking, yoga, Italian studies. Home: 22 Hilltop Rd Biltmore Forest NC 28803 E-mail: jsgro@charter.net.

SHA, WILLIAM T., nuclear scientist, consultant; Grad. in Mech. Engring., Poly. U., 1958; D, Columbia U., NYC, 1964. Mech. engr. Combustion Engring. Inc.; fellow scientist Westinghouse Atomic Power Divsn.; positions including dir. Analytic Thermal Hydraulic Rsch. prog., dir. Multiphase Flow Rsch. Inst. and spl. cons. to lab. dir. Argonne Nat. Lab., Ill., 1968—97; pres. Sha and Assocs., Inc. Tchr. Tsinghua U., Xian Jiaotong U.; cons. Heat Transfer Rsch. Facility, Columbia U., Lungmen Nuc. Power Plant Project of Taiwan Power Co., China Guangdong Nuc. Power Holding Co. Contbr. articles to sci. jours.; mem. editl. bd.: Internat. Jour. Nuc. Engring. and Design. Recipient Outstanding Asian Am. award, Asian Am. Heritage Coun., 1982. Fellow: Am. Nuc. Soc. (Thermal Hydraulics Divsn. Tech. Achievement award 2005, Seaborg medal 2006). Achievements include patents in field. *

SHABANOWITZ, HARRY, electronics engineer, educator; b. Brooklyn, NY, Nov. 11, 1918; s. Abraham and Ida Shabanowitz; m. Sophie Mackoff Shabanowitz, May 8, 1943; children: Judith, Robert B. BS, Coll. City NY, New York, NY, 1949; MA, Columbia U., New York, NY, 1950; PhD, Syracuse U., Syracuse, NY, 1974. Sr. design and devel. engr. Westinghouse Elec. Corp., Elmira, NY, 1951—65, GE, Syracuse, NY, 1965—66; prof. math. Elmira Coll., Elmira, NY, 1966—84, prof. emeritus, math., 1985—. Contbr. articles to profl. jours. Maj. U.S. Army. Mem.: Am. Assn. U. Professors, The NY Acad. Sciences, Alpha Sigma Lambda. Achievements include research and development of photoemissive and photoconductive electronic imaging tubes; tech. mgr., Westinghouse Lunar Television Camera Tube project for the NASA Apollo video transmission of man's first excursion on the surface of the moon, 1969. Home: 205 Scenic Dr Horseheads NY 14845

SHABAZ, JOHN C., judge; b. West Allis, Wis., June 25, 1931; s. Cyrus D. and Harriet T. Shabaz; children: Scott J., Jeffrey J., Emily D., John D. LLB, Marquette U., 1957; BS in Polit. Sci., U. Wis., 1999. Comd. 2d. lt. US Army, 1953, assigned to inactive reserves as capt., 1964; pvt. practice law West Allis, Wis., 1957—82; mem. Wis. Assembly, 1965—81; judge US Dist. Ct. (we. dist.) Wis., 1982—96, chief judge, 1996—2001. Office: US Dist Ct PO Box 591 Madison WI 53701-0591

SHABESTARI, KHOSROW TOUTOUNCHI (T. SHABESTARI), research scientist; arrived in US, 2003; s. Javad Shabestari; m. Azam Akhtari, Sept. 19, 1973; 1 child, Neda. BSc, Istanbul Tech. U., Dept. of Geophysics, Istanbul, 1989; MS, Istanbul Tech. U., Istanbul, 1993; PhD, U. Tokyo, Tokyo, 1999. Geophysical, Istanbul Tech. U./Istanbul, 1989. Rsch. assistance Istanbul Tech. U., Turkey, 1990—91; rsch. assoc. Internat. Inst. of Earthquake Engring. and Seismology, Tehran, Iran, 1993—96; post doctoral fellowship U. Tokyo, 1999—2000; rsch. scientist Earthquake Disaster Mitigation Rsch. Ctr., EDM, NIED, Kobe, 2000—03, Air Worldwide, Boston, 2003—. Referee Earthquake Engring. Rsch. Inst., Oackland, Calif., 2003—, Seismology Soc. of Am., Los Alamos, N.Mex., 2004—. Contbr. scientific papers pub. to profl. jour. Scholar (monbusho) rsch. scholarship, Japanese govtl., 1996—99. Mem.: Seismol. Soc. of Japan (assoc.), Japan Assn. for Earthquake Engring. (assoc.), Japan Soc. of Civil Engring. (assoc.), Seismol. Soc. of Am. (assoc.), Earthquake Engring. Reseach Inst. (assoc.). Achievements include first to time develop JMA intesity attenuation equation for Japan site application for entire Japans rapid generation of GM maps. Office: Air Worldwide Corp 131 Dartmouth st Boston MA 02116-5134 Office Phone: 617-267-6645. Office Fax: 617-267-8284. Business E-Mail: kshabestari@air-worldwide.com.

SHABICA, CHARLES WRIGHT, geologist, earth science educator; b. Elizabeth, NJ, Jan. 2, 1943; s. Anthony Charles and Eleanor (Wright) S.; m. Susan Ewing, Dec. 30, 1967; children: Jonathan, Andrew, Dana. BA in Geology, Brown U., 1965; PhD, U. Chgo., 1971. Prof. earth sci. Northeastern Ill. U., Chgo., 1971—; disting. prof., 1991; pres. Shabica & Assocs. Coastal Cons., Inc., Northfield, Ill., 1985—. Chmn. bd. dirs. Aesti Corp., 1991-96; rsch. collaborator Nat. Park Svc., 1978-82, 89—; adj. prof. Coll. V.I., St. Thomas, 1980, adj. prof. environ. sci. Northwestern U., Evanston, 1999-2003; Kellogg fellow Northeastern Ill. U., 1979—; chmn. Task Force on Lake Michigan, Chgo., 1986-89; mem. Chgo. Shoreline Protection Commn., 1987-88; cons. Shedd Aquarium, Chgo., 1991; mem. Ft. Sheridan Commn., 1989-90; bd. dirs. Winnetka (Ill.) Hist. Soc. Editor: (with Andrew A. Hay) Richardson's Guide to the Fossil Fauna of Mazon Creek, 1997. Commr., packmaster Boy Scouts Am., Winnetka, Ill., 1984-88. Coop. Inst. for Limnology and Ecosystems Rsch. Lab. fellow. Mem. ASCE, Internat. Assn. for Great Lakes Rsch., Am. Shore and Beach Preservation Assn. (bd. dirs., pres. Great Lakes chpt.), Sigma Xi. Home: 326 Ridge Ave Winnetka IL 60093-3842 Office: 550 W Frontage Rd Ste 3735 Northfield IL 60093-1246 Office Phone: 847-446-1436. Personal E-mail: charles@shabica.com.

SHABOT, MYRON MICHAEL, critical care educator; b. Houston, Aug. 5, 1945; s. Sam and Mona Doris (Stalarow) S.; 1 child, Samuel Laib. Student, Tulane U., 1963-64; BA, U. Tex., Austin, 1966; MD, U. Tex., Dallas, 1970. Intern Parkland Meml. Hosp., Dallas, 1970—71; resident Harbor Gen. Hosp., Torrance, Calif., 1973—78; lectr. surgery UCLA Sch. Medicine, 1977-78, asst. prof., 1978-82, clin. assoc. prof. surgery and anesthesiology, 1983-97, prof. surgery, 1997—; dir. surg. ICU, LA County Harbor Med. Ctr.-UCLA Sch. Medicine, 1980-82; med. dir. Enterprise Info. Svcs. Cedars-Sinai Med. Ctr., LA, dir. surg. ICU, 1982—, vice chief of staff, 2000—01, chief of staff, 2002—03, also bd. dirs. Sec. Cedars-Sinai Med. Ctr. Attending Staff, 1999-2000; bd. dirs. eHealth Initiative and Found., 2006—; adj. prof. U. Tex. Health Scis. Ctr., Houston; v.p., chief quality officer Meml. Hermann Healthcare Sys., Houston, 2007—. Contbr. articles to profl. jours. Served to lt. comdr. USPHS, 1971-73. Fellow ACS (So. Calif. chpt. bd. dirs. 1988—, pres. 1992-93, gov., 1992—), Am. Coll. Critical Care Medicine, Am. Coll. Med. Informatics; mem. Western Surg. Assn., Pacific Coast Surg. Assn., Soc. Critical Care Medicine, Am. Assn. Surgery of Trauma, Soc. Computers in Critical Care and Pulmonary Medicine (bd. dirs. 1988—, treas. 1989—, pres., 1993-94), Soc. Clin. Data Mgmt. Systems (pres. 1985-86), L.A. Surg. Soc. (pres. 1997-98), Phi Eta Sigma. Jewish. Home Phone: 713-647-9894. Business E-Mail: michael.shabot@memorialhermann.org.

SHABTO, URI, vitreo-retinal surgeon; m. Beth Scharfman-Shabto. MD, Harvard U., Boston, 1986. Diplomate Am. Bd. Ophthalmology, 1991. Attending surgeon NY Eye and Ear Infirmary, NYC, 1992; attending retinal surgeon. Office: Retina Cons NY 310 East 14th St New York NY 10003 Office Phone: 212-677-2000. Office Fax: 212-353-5754.

SHACHAR, AVISHAI, lawyer; b. Bklyn., Oct. 29, 1953; s. Zeev and Natasha (Kisler) S. m. Orly Eylan, Sept. 6, 1977; children: Carmel, Tal, Abigail. LLB magna cum laude, Tel-Aviv U., 1980; SJD, Harvard U., 1984. Bar: Israel 1983, N.Y. 1984. With Prof. Yuval Levi Law Offices, Tel-Aviv, 1979-80, Herzog, Fox, Neeman & Co., Tel-Aviv, 1980-81; assoc. Davis, Polk & Wardwell, NYC, 1984-86, ptnr., 1987—, head tax practice group. Recipient acad. award Yad Avi Ha-Yeshuv, Israel, 1982. Mem. ABA, Internat. Fiscal Assn., Israeli Bar Assn. Office: Davis Polk & Wardwell 450 Lexington Ave New York NY 10017 Office Phone: 212-450-4638. Office Fax: 212-450-3638. Business E-Mail: avishai.shachar@dpw.com.

SHACK, R. (ROBERT) BRUCE, plastic surgeon, department chairman; b. Vernon, Tex., Oct. 7, 1947; s. Nathan Lee and Patsy Lee (Holliday) S.; m. Sharon Summers Frazier, Aug. 16, 1969 (div. 1982); children: Robert David, Nathan Andrew; m. Wanda Kaye, Nov. 11, 1984; children: Jerion Elizabeth, Austin Ryan. BS, Midwestern U., Wichita Falls, Tex., 1969; MD, U. Tex., Galveston, 1973. Diplomate Am. Bd. Surgery, Am. Bd. Plastic Surgery with added qualifications in surgery of the hand. Extern St. Paul's Hosp., Dallas, 1971, St. Bartholomew's Hosp., London, 1971; intern surgery Vanderbilt U. Med. Ctr., Nashville, 1973—74, asst. resident surgery, 1974—77, chief resident surgery, 1977—78, resident plastic surgery, 1978—79, chief resident plastic surgery, 1979—80, asst. prof. plastic surgery, 1982—87, assoc. prof. plastic surgery, 1987—96, interim chmn., assoc. prof. dept. plastic surgery, 1996, chmn. and prof. dept. plastic surgery, 1997—; asst. prof. plastic surgery Johns Hopkins Hosp., Balt., 1980—82, U. Med. Sch. Medicine, Balt., 1981—82. Attending surgeon Children's Hosp. and Ctr. for Reconstructive Surgery, Balt., 1980—82; attending surgeon plastic surgery Md. Inst. for Emergency Medicine, 1980—82, Ch. Hosps., Balt., 1980—82, Vanderbilt U. Med. Ctr., Nashville, 1982—; cons. head and neck surgery VA Hosp., 1982—; mem. instrnl. course com. Plastic Surgery Ednl. Found., 1985—86, 1986—87, 1987—88, mem. in svc. exam com., 1985—86, 1987—88, chmn. breast/aesthetic subcom. in-svc. exam. com. plastic surgery, 1988—94, chmn. in-svc. exam com., 1994—97, assoc. vis. prof., 1996; mem. adv. bd. Tenn. chpt. Neurofibromatosis Found., 1990—; sr. guest examiner Am. Bd. Plastic Surgery, 1999—2002, CAQSH exam cons., 1999—2002; mem. carrier adv. com. Tenn. Medicare Part B, 2004—; vis. prof. plastic surgery Scott-White Clinic, Tex. A&M, Temple, 1996; vis. prof. dept. plastic surgery U. Miss., Jackson, 1997; XV Marzoni lectr. and vis. prof. U. Ala., Birmingham, 2000; IX Ann. Coleman lectr. and vis. prof. U. Va., 2001; vis. prof. plastic surgery So. Ill. Sch. Medicine, 2003, Baylor Coll. Medicine, 2003; presenter and lectr. in field. Contbr. chapters to books, articles to profl. jours. Named one of Outstanding Young Men in Am., 1969; recipient Disting. Alumnus award, Midwestern State U. Divsn. Scis., 1998; grantee, LPG, Inc., 1998—99, Aesthetic Surgery Edn. and Rsch. Found., 1998, 1999, Southeastern Soc. for Plastic Surgeons, 2002—03. Fellow: ACS (mem. Tenn. dist. 2 com. on applicants 1990—2000); mem.: AMA, Am. Soc. Plastic and Reconstructive Surgeons (treas. practice rels. commn. 1983—84, mem. fin. com. 1983—84, treas. practice rels. commn. 1984—85, mem. fin. com. 1984—85, 1985—86, socioeconomic com. 1985—86, mem. fin. com. 1986—87, socioeconomic com. 1986—87, 1987—88, v.p. associated mgmt. svcs. 1988—90, chmn. fin. com. 1988—90, mem.-at-large bd. dirs. 1991—93, chmn. profl. liability ins. com. 1991—94, pres. associated mgmt. svcs. 1991—98, chmn. mktg. com. 1995—97, asst. sect. 1997), Tenn. Soc. Plastic and Reconstructive Surgery (pres. 2002—), Tenn. Med. Assn., So. Surg. Assn., So. Med. Assn. (asst. sec. plastic surgery sect. 1984—85, sec. plastic surgery sect. 1986—88, assoc. councilor State of Tenn. 1986—, chmn. elect plastic surgery sect. 1989, chmn. plastic surgery sect. 1990, councilor 2004—), Southeastern Soc. Plastic and Reconstructive Surgeons (resident and rsch. com. 1984—85, chmn. So. Med. Assn. liaison com. 1986—90, chmn. resident and rsch. com. 1993—95, trustee bd. dirs. 1995—, chmn. spl. edn. com. 1998, 2001—02, pres. 2006—, grantee 1998—99), Nashville Surg. Soc. (sec.-treas. 1993—96, pres.-elect 1996, pres. 1996—97), Nashville Acad. Medicine, John Staige Davis Soc. Plastic Surgeons Md., John B. Lynch Soc. (v.p. 1984—85, pres. 1985—), H. William Scott, Jr. Soc. (sec. 1993—97, pres.-elect 1999, pres. 2000—01), Am. Soc. for Aesthetic Plastic Surgery (grantee 1997—98), Am. Soc. for Reconstructive Microsurgery, Am. Soc. Plastic Surgeons (sec. 1998—2001, alt. del. AMA 2000—02, practice commr. 2000—, v.p. 2001—01, chmn. by-laws com. 2001—), Am. Soc. Maxillofacial Surgeons (mem. fin. com. 1993—98), Am. Cancer Soc., Am. Burn Assn., Am. Assn. Plastic Surgeons, Sigma Xi, Mu Delta, Beta Beta Beta. Republican. Methodist. Avocations: golf, shooting. Office: Vanderbilt U Med Ctr Dept Plastic Surgery 1161 21st Ave S D-4207 MCN Nashville TN 37232-2345 Office Phone: 615-936-0169. Business E-Mail: bruce.shack@vanderbilt.edu.

SHACKELFORD, JAMES FLOYD, materials science educator, researcher; b. Springfield, Mo., Sept. 1, 1944; s. Amos Franklin and Opal Leona Shackelford; m. Penelope Lea Openshaw, Dec. 11, 1971; 1 child, Scott. BS, U. Wash., Seattle, 1966, MS, 1967; PhD, U. Calif., Berkeley, 1971. Postdoctoral fellow U. Calif., Berkeley, 1971, McMaster U., Hamilton, Ont., Canada, 1972—73; asst. prof. U. Calif., Davis, 1973—79, assoc. prof., 1979—84, prof., 1984—, assoc. dean, 1984—2001, dir. integrated studies honors program, 2001—. Author: Introduction to Materials Science for Engineers, 1984, 6th edit., 2005, (book) Bioceramics, 1999; editor: CRC Handbook of Materials Science and Engineering, 1992, CRC Practical Handbook of Materials Selection, 1995, CRC Materials Science and Engineering Handbook, 2nd Edition, 1994, Bioceramics - Applications of Ceramic and Glass Materials in Medicine, 1999, CRC Handbook of Materials Science and Engineering, 3rd Edition, 2001. Fellow: Am. Ceramic Soc. (Outstanding Educator 1996); mem.: ASM Internat. Office: U Calif Dept Chem Engring and Materials Sci Davis CA 95616 Business E-Mail: jfshackelford@ucdavis.edu.

SHACKELFORD, SCOTT ADDISON, air force officer, chemist; b. Long Beach, Calif., Aug. 11, 1944; s. Richard Walter and Phyllis Marian (Pearson) S.; m. Alpha Marilyn Coon, Aug. 23, 1969; children: Laura DeAnna, Vicki LeAnna. Student Colo. State U., 1962-64; BA, Simpson Coll., 1964-66; MA, No. Ariz. U., 1968; PhD, Ariz. State U., 1973. Second lt. US Air Force, 1972, advanced through grades to major, 1999; rsch. chemist F.J. Seiler Rsch. Lab., U.S. Air Force Acad., Colo., 1972-74, rsch. group chief, 1974-77,instr., asst. prof. dept. chemistry and biol. scis., 1977-78; lang. student Nat. Def. Lang. Inst., Monterey, Calif., 1978; exchange scientist DFVLR-Institut fuer Chemische Antriebe und Verfahrenstechnik, Hardthausen A.K., Fed. Republic Germany, 1978-80; rsch. sect. chief Air Force Rocket Propulsion Lab., Edwards AFB, Calif., 1980-84; rsch. liaison officer European Office Aerospace Rsch. and Devel., London, 1984-87; dir. Aerospace Rsch. Liaison, 1986-88; sr. scientist F.J. Seiler Rsch. Lab. USAF Acad., Colo., 1987—92, rsch. fellow, Alliance Pharm. Corp., San Diego, 1992-1994, prin. scientist, 1994-1996, adj. assoc. prof., dept. chemistry Point Loma Nazarene U., 1997, sr. scientist I and II Pfizer Inc., La Jolla, Calif., 1998-2003, sr. rsch. chemist, rsch. advisor propellant chemistry Air Force Rsch. Lab., Edwards AFB, Calif., 2003—; sec. Tri-Svcs. Joint Tech. Coordinating Group/Munitions Devel./Working Party for Explosives, Washington, 1975-77; lab. rsch. task mgr. to Air Force Office Sci. Research, Washington, 1981-84, 88-1992; nat. propellant survey cons., 1981-82; mem. sci. adv. com. Simpson Coll., Indianola, Iowa, 1983-87; chmn. Jannaf combustion sub-com. panel Chem. Combustion Kinetics, 1990-1991; chemistry cons. Technica Inc., Orlando, Fla., 1997-1998; vp. USAF Acad. Jr. Officer Coun, 1974-1975; lectr. in field. Contbr. articles to profl. publs. Patentee in field. Co-mgr. Tee Ball Youth Baseball Team, Fort Collins, Colo., 1964; asst. coach Am. Legion Summer Baseball Team, Pacifica, Calif., 1967, 68; Sunday school tchr. Village Christian Ch., Colorado Springs, Colo., 1975-77; adult bible study tchr. Warton Barracks Base Chapel, Heilbronn, Germany, 1979-1980; adult class leader Base Protestant Chapel, Edwards, Calif., 1984, chmn. community christian ch. permanent relocation com, 1989—; deacon Torrey Pines Christian Ch., La Jolla, 1995-1997, elder, 1997-2003; Recipient Tech. Achievement award, Air Force Sys. Command, 1977, R&D award USAF Chief-of-Staff, 1982, Alumni Achievement award Simpson Coll. Alumni Assn., 1985; Rsch. grant, Office Naval Rsch., 2005—. Mem. NRC (mentor), Am. Chemical Soc. (fluorine divsn., chair San Diego sect. 1998-99). Mem. Disciples of Christ. Ch. Current work: In-situ mechanistic studies of thermochemical decomposition and combustion processes with deuterium isotope effects, energetic material sensitivity, anhydrous nitration reactions, iconic solid salt synthesis. Subspecialties: Organic chemistry; Condensed Phase Reaction Mechanisms. Office Phone: 661-275-5847, 661-275-5847. Personal E-mail: scottshack@adelphia.net.

SHACKLETON, ROBERT JAMES, finance company executive; b. Louisville, Aug. 21, 1936; s. Robert James and Annelle (Barrett) Shackleton; m. Mary Randall, Dec. 21, 1963; children: Scott Randall, David Eric, Nancy Lynne. BSc, U. Louisville, 1958; MBA, U. So. Calif., 1969. 100 ton masters lic. USCG, 2000. Acct. audit dept. KPMG Peat Marwick, LA, 1961-69, audit ptnr., 1969, ptnr. in charge San Fernando Valley, 1970-71, mem. profl. practice review com., 1974-76, SEC reviewing ptnr., 1976-97, ptnr. in charge audit dept. Orange County, Calif., 1976-88, ptnr. in charge profl. practice, 1988-97; mng. ptnr. Shackleton & Co., Orange County, 1998—. Co-author: Audits of Airlines, 1981. Dir. LA Master Chorale So. Calif. Choral Music Assn., 1968—69; pres. Arts Found., 1970—71, trustee, 1970—75; treas. Jr. Achievement So. Calif., 1972—74, bd. dirs., 1972—80, treas. Orange County chpt., 1989—93; exec. bd. dirs. Orange County coun. Boy Scouts Am., 1981—99, chmn. Scout-O-Rama, 1982, chmn. camp promotion, 1986, dist. chmn. Rancho Del Mar, 1984—85, advisor Order of Arrow, 1984—86; assoc. mem. Calif. Rep. State Ctrl. Com.; chmn. LA Jr. C. of C., 1967—68, dir., 1968—70; bd. dirs. Newport Harbor Area C. of C., Calif., 1979—91, CFO Calif., 1983—84, pres. orgnl. affairs divsn. Calif., 1988, vice chmn. bd. dirs. Calif., 1989, chmn. bd. dirs. Calif., 1990; mem. Calif. State Bd. Accountancy, 1992, chmn. profl. conduct com., bd. liaison to qualifications com., 1992—94, mem. enforcement program mgmt. com., 1993—95, mem. article 9 task force, 1993—94, v.p., 1995, pres., 1996—97. Lt. USN, 1958—61. Recipient cert. of Merit for rescuing 7 persons from burning boat, USCG, 1990. Mem.: AICPA (mem. fed. govt. panel advisors 1973—80), Calif. Soc. CPA (chmn. aerospace and electronics industry com. LA chpt. 1972—74, mem. state savs. and loan com. 1980—92, chmn. savs. and loan conf. 1985, cert. estate planning 1998), Nat. Assn. State Bds. Accountancy (mem. rels. govt. agys. com. 1992—95, mem. legal liability task force 1992—95, mem. CPA adv. panel 1995—96, mem. audit com. 1995—98, mem. future licensing, litig. and legis. com. 1995—98, bd. dirs. 1997—98), Nat. Assn. Accts. (bd. dirs. San Fernando Valley chpt. 1971—72), Fin. Mgrs. Soc. Savs. Insts. (assoc.), Balboa Yacht Club, St. Francis Yacht Club, Newport Harbor Yacht Club (bd. dirs. 1989—90, treas. 1990), Am. Legion. Presbyterian. Avocations: boating, collecting nautical artifacts, collecting presidential memorabilia. Office: Shackleton & Co 87 Ocean Vista Newport Beach CA 92660-6207 Business E-Mail: bob@shack.com.

SHACKLEY, DOUGLAS JOHN, fire alarm company executive; b. Oakland, Calif., Sept. 21, 1938; s. Floyd H. and Margret I. Shackley; m. Chloe Jeanne Olson, Sept. 11, 1965; children: Derek Todd, Darren James, Daniel John, Christina Louise. Student, San Jose State U., 1957, Chabot Coll., 1962-63; diploma in bus. mgmt., LaSalle Extension U., 1972. Officer mgr. service dept. Am. Dist. Telegraph Co., Oakland, 1961-67; office mgr. Pacific Aux. Fire Alarm Co., San Francisco, 1967-69, mgr., 1969-73, gen. mgr.; 1974—2004, pres., CEO, 2004—, also bd. dirs. Mem. task force improved fire protection Gov. of Calif., 1989; contbg. mem. Alarm Industry Telecom. Com.; pres. Dad's Club Chabot Sch., 1969—70, pres. Paren'ts Club, 1971—72; mem. Eden area YMCA, San Francisco YMCA, Boy Scouts Am.; sustaining mem. Calif. Rep. Com.; mem. Rep. Presdl. Task Force, 1994—95; moderator Eden United Ch. of Christ, 1980—81, vice moderator, 1987—88. With USMC, 1957—61. Mem.: Calif. Automatic Fire Alarm Assn. (bd. dirs. 1986—87, v.p. No. Calif. 1987—88, pres. 1988—89, bd. dirs. 1994—95, v.p. No. Calif. 1996—2000, pres. 2003, 2003—, v.p. No. Calif. 2004—, Art Kane Meml. award 2000), Nat. Automatic Fire Alarm Assn. (bd. dirs. 2003—), Nat. Fire Prevention Assn., San Francisco C. of C. (mem. code com.), Lake Mont Pine Home Owners Assn. (bd. dirs. 1988—89), Rotary. Home: 1380 Carlton Pl Livermore CA 94550-6400 Office: Pacific Aux Fire Alarm Co 95 Boutwell St San Francisco CA 94124-1903 Office Phone: 415-467-9393. Business E-Mail: doug@pafa.com.

SHACKOULS, BOBBY S., oil and gas industry executive; b. Dec. 29, 1950; BSChemE, Miss. State U. Various mgmt. positions in oil and gas industry; sr. mgmt. positions Torch Energy Advisors affil. Torchmark Corp., Plains Resources, Houston Oil & Minerals; exec. v.p., COO Burlington Resources, 1993-95, exec. v.p Meridian Oil subs., pres., CEO oil & gas subs., 1994, pres., CEO, 1995—97, chmn., pres., CEO, 1997—2005. Bd. dir. Conoco Phillips, 2006—, Kroger Co.; treas. Am. Petroleum Inst. Vice chmn. Tex. Heart Inst.; mem. nat. bd., mem. exec. bd. Houston area council Boy Scouts Am. Mailing: Conoco Phillips Bd Directors PO Box 2197 Houston TX 77252-2197

SHACTER, DAVID MERVYN, lawyer; b. Toronto, Ont., Can., Jan. 17, 1941; s. Nathan and Tillie Anne (Schwartz) S. BA, U. Toronto, 1963; JD, Southwestern U., 1967. Bar: Calif. 1968, US Ct. Appeals (9th cir.) 1969, US Supreme Ct. 1982. Law clk., staff atty. Legal Aid Found., Long Beach, Calif., 1967-70; asst. city atty. City of Beverly Hills, Calif., 1970; ptnr. Shacter & Berg, Beverly Hills, 1971-83, Selwyn, Capalbo, Lowenthal & Shacter Profl. Law Corp., 1984-99; pvt. practice, 1999—. Del. State Bar Conf. Dels., 1976-2000; lectr. Calif. Continuing Edn. of Bar, 1977, 82-83, 86; judge pro tem LA and Beverly Hills mcpl. cts.; arbitrator LA Superior Ct., 1983—, judge pro tem; disciplinary examiner Calif. State Bar, 1986. Bd. dirs. and pres. Los Angeles Soc. Prevention Cruelty to Animals, 1979-89. Mem.: City of Hope Med. Ctr. Aux., Am. Arbitration Assn. (nat. panel arbitrators, neutral arbitrator, panel chmn.), Beverly Hills Bar Found. (pres. 1995—97, bd. govs. 1998—2001), Beverly Hills Bar Assn. (bd. govs. 1985—90, sec. 1987—88, treas. 1988—89, v.p. 1989—90, pres.-elect 1990—91, pres. 1991—92, editor-in-chief jour.), Nat. Assn. Securities Dealers (arbitrator 1998—), West LA C. of C. Office: 10801 National Blvd Ste 608 Los Angeles CA 90064 Office Phone: 310-474-4115. Business E-Mail: david@shacterlaw.com.

SHADDOCK, CARROLL SIDNEY, lawyer; b. Beaumont, Tex., July 7, 1940; s. Carroll Bitting Jr. and Hulda Martha (Gaertner) S.; m. Dorothea Schulze, Nov. 30, 1963; children: Carroll Christian, Peter Eric, Matthew Nolan. BA, Rice U., 1962; JD, Yale U., 1965. Ptnr. Locke Liddell & Sapp LLP, Houston, 1967—. Chmn. Scenic Am., Washington, 1985-92, Scenic Tex., 1992—, Trees for Houston, 1982—, Billboards Limited, Houston, 1982-92. Republican. Lutheran. Avocations: music, golf, travel. Home: 1715 South Blvd Houston TX 77098-5419 Office: Locke Liddell & Sapp LLP JP Morgan Chase Tower 600 Travis St Ste 3400 Houston TX 77002-3095 E-mail: cshaddock@lockeliddell.com.

SHADE, GEORGE HENRY, JR., obstetrician, gynecologist, educator; b. Detroit, Jan. 4, 1949; s. George Henry Shade, Sr. and Julia M. Ballard-Shade; m. Carlotta Ann Johnson, July 24, 1976; children: Carla Nicole, Ryan McNeal. BS in Psychology, Wayne State U., Detroit, 1971, MD, 1974. Diplomate Am. Bd. Ob-gyn., 1980. Resident physician dept ob-gyn. Wayne State U., 1974—78; ptnr. Vincent, Combs, Massé & Shade, MD, PC, Detroit, 1978—2000; chmn. physicians adv. coun. St. John Health, 2000—02; chief dept. ob-gyn. Sinai-Grace Hosp. Detroit Med. Ctr., 2002—07, v.p. med. affairs Sinai-Grace Hosp., 2005—. Clin. instr. Wayne State U., 1978—82, asst. prof., 1982—2002, assoc. prof., 2002—; asst. prof. Mich. State U., 1982—2002, assoc. prof., 2002—; nat. spkrs. bureau Wyeth Pharm. Corp., 2000—; vice chmn. bd. medicine State Mich., Lansing, 2006—. Contbr. articles to profl. jours. Bd. dirs. Omnicare Health Plans, Detroit, 2001—03. Recipient Psi Chi Nat. honor Soc., Dept. of Psychology-Wayne State U., 1971. Mem.: Sigma Pi Phi, Kappa Alpha Psi (life). Democrat. Baptist. Achievements include research in pelvic endometriosis in the Africian American female. Avocations: horseback riding, music, photography, art, sports cars and auto racing. Office: Sinai Grace Hosp Wayne State U 6071 W Outer Dr Ste M541 Detroit MI 48235 Office Phone: 313-966-3246. Office Fax: 313-966-4296. Business E-Mail: gshade@dmc.org.

SHADE, JOSEPH, law educator; b. Riga, Latvia, Oct. 9, 1935; s. Louis and Ethel Shade; m. Denise Lee Alper, Dec. 26, 1964; children: Ronald, Randi, Brian. BBA, U. Tex., Austin, 1958, JD, 1960. Assoc. Turner Atwood Meer & Francis, Dallas, 1960—62; staff atty. SEC, Washington, 1962—65; assoc. Pope Ballard Kennedy Stepond & Fowler, Chgo., 1965—70; asst. gen. counsel LTV Corp., Dallas, 1970—76; assoc. gen. counsel Houston Oil and Minerals Corp., 1977—79; owner, prin. Joseph Shade and Assocs., P.C., Dallas, 1979—90; prof. law Tex. Wesleyan U. Sch. Law, Ft. Worth, 1990—. Pres. energy sect. Dallas Bar Assn., 2001. Author: Primer on Texas Law of Oil & Gas, 3rd edit., 2004, Business Associations in a Nutshell, 2nd edit., 2005; contbr. articles to profl. jours. Capt. US Army, 1958, capt. USAR, 1958—66. Named Outstanding Prof., Tex. Wesleyan U. Law Sch. Student Bar Assn., 1992—93, 1994—95. Republican. Jewish. Avocations: golf, reading. Home: 5905 Club Oaks Dr Dallas TX 75248 Office: Tex Wesleyan Sch Law 1515 Commerce Fort Worth TX 76102

SHADEGG, JOHN BARDEN, congressman; b. Phoenix, Oct. 22, 1949; s. Stephen and Eugenia Shadegg; m. Shirley Shadegg; children: Courtney, Stephen. BA, U. Ariz., 1972, JD, 1975. Advisor U.S. Sentencing Commn.; spl. asst. atty. gen. State of Ariz., 1983-90; spl. counsel Ariz. State Ho. Rep. Caucus, 1991-92; pvt. practice; mem. U.S. Congress from 4th Ariz. dist., 1995—, asst. whip, mem. commerce com., fin. svcs. com., homeland sec. com. Mem. Victims Bill of Rights Task Force, 1989-90; mem. Fiscal Accountability and Reform Efforts Com., 1991-92; counsel Arizonian's for Wildlife Conservation, 1992; chmn. Proposition 108-Two-Thirds Tax Limitation Initiative, 1992. Rep. Party Ballot Security chmn., 1982; active Corbin for Atty. Gen., 1982-86; Rep. Precinct committeeman; chmn. Ariz. Rep. Caucus, 1985-87; chmn. Ariz. Lawyers for Bush-Quayle, 1988; mem. steering com., surrogate spkr. Jon Kyl for Congress, 1988-92; former pres. Crime Victim Found.; founding dir. Goldwater Inst. Pub. Policy; chmn. Ariz. Juvenile Justice Adv. Coun.; mem. adv. bd. Salvation Army; mem. vestry Christ Ch. of Ascension, 1989-91; mem. class II Valley Leadership; bd. dirs. Ariz. State U. Law Soc. Republican. Episcopalian. Office: US Ho Reps 306 Cannon Ho Office Bldg Washington DC 20515-0001 *

SHADER, RICHARD IRWIN, psychiatrist, pharmacologist, educator; b. Mt. Vernon, NY, May 27, 1935; s. Myer and Beatrice (Epstein) Shader; m. Aline Brown, Sept. 21, 1958 (dec. Aug. 10, 2002); children: Laurel Beth, Jennifer Robin, Robert Andrew; m. Cynthia H. Livingston, Dec. 6, 2003. Student, Harvard U., Cambridge, Mass., 1952-56; MD, NYU, 1960; grad., Boston Psychoanalytic Inst., 1970. Diplomate Am. Bd. Psychiatry and Neurology (dir. 1977-84, treas. 1982-83, pres. 1984). Intern Greenwich Hosp., Conn., 1960-61; resident in psychiatry Mass. Mental Health Ctr., Boston, 1961-62, 64-65, NIMH, Bethesda, Md., 1962-64; assoc. prof. psychiatry Harvard Med. Sch., 1970-79; psychiatrist in chief New Eng. Med. Ctr. Hosp., Boston, 1979-91; prof. dept. psychiatry Tufts U. Med. Sch., Boston, 1979—2007, prof. emeritus, 2007—, chmn. dept., 1979-91, prof. pharmacology, 1989—2007, prof. emeritus, 2007—, chmn. dept. pharmacology and exptl. therapeutics, 1991-93, dir. grad. program dept. pharmacology and exptl. therapeutics, 1999—, sr. rsch. fellow, med. cons. Ctr. for the Study of Drug Devel., 2007—. Author (with A. DiMascio): Psychotropic Drug Sides Effects, 1970; author: (with D. J. Greenblatt) Benzodiazepines in Clinical Practice, 1974; author: Manual of Psychiatric Therapeutics, 1975; editor: Psychiatric Complications of Medical Drugs, 1972; editor: (with A. DiMascio) Clinical Handbook of Psychopharmacology, 1970, Butyrophenones in Psychiatry, 1972; editor: (with D. J. Greenblatt) Pharmacokinetics in Clinical Practice, 1985, MAOI Therapy, 1988; editor: (with J. P. Tupin and D. S. Harnett) Handbook of Clinical Psychopharmacology, 1988; editor: (with D.A. Ciraulo) Pharmacotherapy of Depression, 2004; editor: 2d edit., 2007; editor: (with others) Drug Interactions in Psychiatry, 1989, 3d edit., 2005; editor: Clinical Manual of Chemical Dependence, 1991; editor-in-chief Jour. Clin. Psychopharmacology, 1980—. Bd. dirs. Med. Found., Inc., 1980—87. With USPHS, 1962—64. Recipient Seymor Vestermark award, Am. Psychiat. Assn., 1988, 1990; fellow, Ctr. Advanced Study Behavioral Scis., Stanford, Calif., 1990—91; Joseph J. Michaels Merit scholar, 1968—69. Fellow: Am. Coll. Neuropsychopharmacology (v.p. 1984, pres. 1990, emeritus 2005, life emeritus); mem.: AMA (emeritus), Am. Soc. Pharmacology and Exptl. Therapeutics, Am. Soc. Clin. Pharmacology and Therapeutics (emeritus), Mass. Med. Soc. (emeritus,). Democrat. Jewish.

SHADLEY, ROBERT D., retired army officer; b. Circleville, Ohio, Aug. 5, 1942; BS in Indsl. Engring., MS in Indsl. Engring., Purdue U.; M of Mil. Arts and Scis., Army Command/Gen. Staff Coll. Commd. 2d lt. U.S. Army, 1965, advanced through grades to maj. gen., 1997; served in Vietnam and Desert Shield/Desert Storm; exec.officer to the comdg. gen. U.S. Army Materiel Command, 1992-94; dir. for logistics U.S. Atlantic Command, 1994-95; chief of ordnance, comdg. gen. U.S. Army Ordnance Ctrs. and Schs., 1995-97; dep. comdg. gen. for ordnance U.S. Army Combined Arms Support Command, Aberdeen Proving Ground, Md.; dep. chief of staff for logistics Hdqrs. U.S. Army Forces Command, Ft. McPherson, Ga., 1997-2000. Decorated Disting. Svc. medal, Legion of Merit with 2 oak leaf clusters, Bronze Star medal with oak leaf cluster, others. Address: Alliant Techsystems MN07-ME10 4700 Nathan Ln North Plymouth MN 55442-2512

SHADOAN, WILLIAM LEWIS, retired judge; b. Galesburg, Ill., July 12, 1931; s. William Parker and Hortense (Lewis) S.; m. Katherine E. Thomson, 1961; children: Ann-Wayne Harlan, Kate, Tom. BS, U. Ky., 1955; JD, U. Louisville, 1961. Bar: Ky. 1961, U.S. Dist. Ct. (we. dist.) Ky. 1961. City atty., Wickliffe, Ky., 1963; county atty. Ballard County, Ky., 1963-76; chief regional judge 1st cir. Wickliffe, Ky., 1983—2006; ret., 2006. Chmn. Ballard County Dem. Party, 1963; trustee Meth. Ch., Wickliffe, 1961-84; advisor Selective Svc., Peducah, Ky., 1968; chmn. Wickliffe C. of C., 1967-71; mem. exec. com. Ky. Hist. Soc., Frankfort; vice chmn. Ky. Cert. of Need and Lic. Bd., 1973-84; named assoc. justice Ky. Surpeme Ct., 1984. Capt. U.S. Army, 1955-59. Mem. ABA, Ky. Health Systems Assn. (vice chmn. 1976-82), Ky. Bar Assn. (Outstanding Judge 1997), Assn. Trial Lawyers Am., Ky. County Ofcls. Bd. (chmn. 1976-80), Miss. River Commn. (chmn. 1976-83), Ky. County Attys. Assn. (pres. 1966-77), First Dist. Bar Assn. (pres.), Masons (Wickliffe, 32 degree), Shriners (Madisonville, Ky.), Orer Ea Star, Elks. Home: RR 2 Wickliffe KY 42087-9804

SHADPOUR, HAMED, research assistant; BS, Guilan U., Rasht, Iran, 1997; MS, Tehran Poly. (Amirkabir U. Tech.), Iran, 2000; PhD, La. State U., Baton Rouge, 2006. Rsch. asst. La. State U., 2002—06; post doc. fellow U. Calif., Irvine, 2007—. Office: Univ Calif D340 Med Sci 1 Irvine CA 92697

SHADUR, MILTON IRVING, judge; b. St. Paul, June 25, 1924; s. Harris and Mary Shadur; m. Eleanor Pilka, Mar. 30, 1946; children: Robert, Karen, Beth. BS, U. Chgo., 1943, JD cum laude, 1949. Bar: Ill. 1949, U.S. Supreme Ct. 1957. Pvt. practice, Chgo., 1949-80; assoc. Goldberg, Devoe & Brussell, 1949-51; ptnr. Shadur, Krupp & Miller and predecessor firms, 1951-80; judge U.S. Dist. Ct. (no. dist.) Ill., Chgo., 1980-92, sr. judge, 1992—. Commr. Ill. Supreme Ct. Character and Fitness, 1961-72, chmn., 1971; gen. counsel Ill. Jud. Inquiry Bd., 1975-80; chmn. adv. com. on evidence rules to Jud. Conf. of U.S., 1999-2002, mem. adv. com., 1992-99. Editor-in-chief: U. Chgo. Law Rev., 1948-49. Chmn. visiting com. U. Chgo. Law Sch., 1971-76, mem. vis. com., 1989-92, 99-2002; bd. dirs. Legal Assistance Found. Chgo., 1972-78; trustee Village of Glencoe, 1969-74, Ravinia Festival Assn., 1976-93, exec. com. 1983-93, vice chmn. 1989-93, life trustee, 1994—. Lt. (j.g.) USNR, 1943-46. Fellow Am. Bar Found.; mem. ABA (spl. com. on youth edn. for citizenship 1975-79), Ill. State Bar Assn. (joint com. on rules of jud. conduct 1974), Chgo. Bar Assn. (chmn. legis. com. 1963-65, jud. com. 1970-71, profl. ethics com. 1975-76, sec. 1967-69), Chgo. Council Lawyers, Order of Coif Office: US Dist Ct 219 S Dearborn St Ste 2388 Chicago IL 60604-1800 Office Phone: 312-435-5766.

SHADYAC, THOMAS, film director, producer; b. Falls Church, Va., 1960; m. Richard Shadyac. Grad., U. Va.; MA in Film, UCLA, 1989. Stand-up comedian Improv, L.A. Motion pictures include: (dir.) Ace Ventura: Pet Detective, 1994, The Nutty Professor, 1996, Liar, Liar, 1997; (dir., prodr.) Patch Adams, 1998, Dragonfly, 2002, Bruce Almighty, 2003; (prodr.) Nutty Professor II: the Klumps, 2000, Accepted, 2006; TV movies: (dir.) Frankenstein: The College Years, 1991. TV series: (exec. prodr.) 8 Simple Rules for Dating My Teenage Daughter, 2002-05. Office: United Talent Agy care Dan Aloni 9560 Wilshire Blvd Fl 5 Beverly Hills CA 90212-2400

SHAEFFER, JOHN NEES, historian, educator; b. Wapato, Wash., Dec. 7, 1929; s. John Nees Shaeffer and Helen May Kerns. BA, Wash. State U., 1953; AM, Harvard U., 1957; PhD, U. Wis., 1968. Instr. history Columbia Basin Coll., Pasco, Wash., 1957—63; prof. history Calif. State U., Northridge, 1968—92, prof. emeritus, 1992—. Contbr. articles to profl. jours. 1st lt. USAF, 1953—57, Korea. Mem.: Orgn. Am. Historians (life), Am. Hist. Assn. (life), Phi Kappa Phi (life).

SHAEVITZ, GEOFF, film company executive; b. Apr. 8, 1974; Student in Hist., Stanford U., Calif.; student, Harvard Bus. Sch. Intern Radar Pictures; v.p. prodn. Warner Premiere. Achievements include acting as a studio executive on the films The Lake House, 2006 and Poseidon, 2006, and the upcoming films Mama's Boy, 2007 and 300, 2007. Avocation: cooking. *

SHAEVSKY, MARK, lawyer; b. Harbin, Manchuria, China, Dec. 2, 1935; came to U.S., 1938, naturalized, 1944; s. Tolio and Rae (Weinstein) S.; m. Lois Ann Levi, Aug. 2, 1964; children: Thomas Lyle, Lawrence Keith. Student, Wayne State U., Detroit, 1952—53; BA with highest distinction, U. Mich., Ann Arbor, 1956; JD with highest distinction, U. Mich., 1959. Bar: Mich. 1959. Law clerk to presiding judge US Dist. Ct., Detroit, 1960-61; assoc. Honigman, Miller, Schwartz & Cohn, Detroit, 1961-64, ptnr., 1965-69, sr. ptnr., 1969—2001, of counsel, 2001—05; prin., owner Mark Shaevsky & Assocs., LLC, Farmington Hills, 2006—. Instr. law Wayne State U. Law Sch., Detroit, 1961-64; comml. arbitrator Am. Arbitration Assn., Detroit; bd. dir. Charter One Fin. Inc., Charter One Bank, H.W. Kaufman Fin. Group, Inc., Freya Fanning Mgmt., LLC, USF Ins. Co. Contbr. Wayne State U. Law Rev., U. Mich. Law Rev., 1957-59, asst. editor, 1958-59. Dir. Detroit Mens Orgn. of Rehab. through Tng., 1969—79; trustee William Beaumont Hosp., 1997—, Beaumont Found., 1997—2005, Jewish Vocat. Svcs., 1973—76; mem. exec. bd. Am. Jewish Com., 1965—74; sec., dir. Am. Friends Hebrew U., 1976—84; mem. capital needs com. Jewish Welfare Fedn., 1986—97; bd. dir. William Beaumont Hosp., 2002—, Shaevsky Family Found., 2000—. With US Army, 1959—60. Burton Abstract fellow, 1959. Mem. ABA, Mich. Bar Assn., Franklin Hills Country Club, Detroit Athletic Club, Order of the Coif, Phi Beta Kappa. Home: The Hills of Lone Pine 4750 N Chipping Gln Bloomfield Hills MI 48302-2390 Office: 30883 Northwestern Hwy Ste 200 Farmington MI 48334 Office Phone: 248-737-0808. Business E-Mail: advisors@mshaevsky.com.

SHAFER, BYRON EDWIN, American government educator; b. Hanover, Pa., Jan. 8, 1947; s. Byron Henry and Doris Marguerite (von Bergen) S.; m. Wanda Kathleen McErn, Aug. 22, 1981. BA, Yale U., 1968; PhD, U. Calif., Berkeley, 1979; MA, Oxford U., 1985. Andrew W. Mellon prof. Am. govt. Oxford (Eng.) U., 1985-2001; Hawkins prof. polit. sci. U. Wis., Madison, 2001—. Author: Presidential Politics, 1983, Quiet Revolution, 1983, Bifurcated Politics, 1988, Is America Different?, 1991, The End of Realignment?, 1991, The Two Majorities, 1995, Postwar Politics in the G-7, 1996, Present Discontents, 1996, Partisan Approaches to American Politics, 1998, Contesting Democracy, 2001, The State of American Politics, 2002, The Two Majorities and the Puzzle of Modern American Politics, 2003, The End of Southern Exceptionalism, 2005. Resident scholar Russell Sage Found., N.Y.C., 1977-85; recipient Schattschneider prize Am. Polit. Sci. Assn., 1980, Burdette prize, 1990, Party Politics prize, 2001, 2003. Mem.: Phi Beta Kappa. Lutheran. Avocations: gardening, livestock management, furniture restoration. Home: Nether Blenheim 10621 W Blue Mounds Rd Blue Mounds WI 53517 Office: U Wis Dept Polit Sci Madison WI 53706-1389 Office Phone: 608-263-1909. Business E-Mail: bshafer@polisci.wisc.edu.

SHAFER, ERIC CHRISTOPHER, minister; b. Hanover, Pa., Apr. 10, 1950; s. B. Henry and Doris M. (Von Bergen) S.; m. Kristi L. Owens, Nov. 24, 1973. BA, Muhlenberg Coll., 1972; MDiv, Hamma Sch. Theology, 1976. Ordained to ministry Luth. Ch. Am., 1976. Pastor Holy Trinity Meml. Luth. Ch., Catasauqua, Pa., 1976-83; asst. to Bishop Northeastern Pa. Synod, Wescosville, Pa., 1983-92; staff commn. for fin. support Evang. Luth. Ch. in Am., Chgo., 1988-92, asst. dir. dept. for comm., 1992-93, dir. dept. for comm., 1993—. Contbg. editor The Lutheran mag., 1989-92. Trustee Muhlenberg Coll., Allentown, Pa., 1972-83; bd. dirs. Luth. Film Assn., 1993—; chmn. comm. commn. Nat. Coun. Chs. in USA, 1996—2003, mem. exec. bd., 1996—2003. Democrat. Lutheran. Avocations: running, computers, photography, travel. Office: Evang Luth Ch in Am 8765 W Higgins Rd Chicago IL 60631-4178 Office Phone: 773-380-2960. Business E-Mail: eric.shafer@elca.org.

SHAFER, JOHN MILTON, hydrologist, consultant, data processing executive; b. Findlay, Ohio, Mar. 18, 1951; s. Paul Eugene and Mary Ethel (Schwyn) S.; m. Elise Ann Dunne, Apr. 11, 1980; children: Paul Emery, Jessica Elise, Elise Ann. BS in Earth Sci., Pa. State U., 1973; MS in Resource Devel., Mich. State U., 1975; PhD in Civil Engring., Colo. State U., 1979. Cert. hydrologist #218. Asst. rsch. prof. Colo. State U., Fort Collins, 1979-80; rsch. engr. Battelle Meml. Inst., Richland, Wash., 1980-83, sr. rsch. engr., 1983-84; hydrologist Ill. State Water Survey, Champaign, 1984-85, asst. head ground water sect., 1985-90, prin. hydrologist, 1988-91, head hydrology div., 1990-92; assoc. dir., rsch. prof. Earth Scis. and Resources Inst., U. S.C., Columbia, 1992-95, dir., 1995—. Cons. pvt. cos., 1984—; owner GWPATH, Columbia, S.C., 1992; v.p. Environ. and Archtl. Signage, Findlay, Ohio; prin. hydrologist, co-owner Applied Hydrogeologic Rsch., Inc., Seattle, 1995-00. Developer software, 1987; contbr. articles to profl. jours. Recipient John C. Frye Meml. award in geology, 1991, Ill. Groundwater Sci. Achievement award, 1993. Mem. Intergovt. Coord. Com. Groundwater, Am. Geophys. Union, Am. Inst. Hydrology (pres. Ill. sect. 1985-92), Nat. Ground Water Assn., Ill. Groundwater Assn., Sigma Xi. Presbyterian. Avocations: tennis, handball, woodworking, model building. Home: 321 Lake Front Dr Columbia SC 29212-2426 Office: Earth Scis Resouces Inst U SC 901 Sumter St Columbia SC 29201-3961 Office Phone: 803-777-6484. Business E-Mail: jshafer@sc.rr.com.

SHAFER, L. M., writer; b. New Albany, Ind., Apr. 23, 1961; d. Arlin Cleo and Edith Marie Shafer; m. John Franklin Stepp, Dec. 17, 1984. AAS, Ky. Coll. Tech., Louisville, 1981. Novelist/freelance writer, English, Ind., 1989—. Mem., contbr. Plan USA, Warwick, RI, 1999—2007; active Ind. chpt. Neruofibromatosis Network, Ferdinand, 2007. Democrat. Pentecostal. Avocation: gospel singing.

SHAFER, ROBERT TINSLEY, JR., judge; b. Cin., Sept. 11, 1929; s. Robert Tinsley and Grace Elizabeth (Welsh) S.; m. Barbara Jean Hough, Dec. 27, 1950; children: Richard Hough, Janet Lee Shafer Davis, Charles Welsh. BA, Coll. of Wooster, 1951; JD, U. Cin., 1956. Bar: Fla. 1956, U.S. Ct. Appeals (5th cir.) 1963, U.S. Dist. Ct. (so. dist.) Fla. 1961, U.S. Supreme Ct. 1965. Asst. trust officer 1st Nat. Bank, Ft. Myers, Fla., 1956-57; ptnr. Henderson, Franklin, Starnes & Holt, P.A., Ft. Myers, 1957-77; cir. judge 20th Jud. Cir. State of Fla., Ft. Myers, 1977-92, chief cir. judge, 1985-89, sr. judge, 1992—2004. Former mem. com. for ret. and sr. judges Nat. Conf. State Trial Judges. Contbr. article to Corp. Law, 1955-56 (Goldsmith Corp. Law prize, 1956). Elder Covenant Presbyn. Ch., 1982-85; mem. jud. commn. Fla. Presbyn. Synod, 1960-63; chmn. Lee County chpt. Red Cross, Ft. Myers, 1963; chair Permanent Judicial Commn., Peace River Presbytery, Presbyn. Ch. U.S.A., 2001-05, mem. Permanent Judicial Commn., South Atlantic Synod., Presbyn. Ch. U.S.A., 2005-, pres. S.W. Fla. Hist. Soc. 2003-2005. 2nd lt. USMCR, 1951-53, PTO, Korea. Mem. ABA, Fla. Conf. Cir. Judges (exec. com. 1986-88), Fla. Bar Assn. (bd. govs. Jr. Bar sect. 1961-64), Lee County Bar Assn. (pres. 1968), Am. Judicature Soc., Nat. Conf. Met. Cts. Calusa Inn of Ct. Republican. Avocations: bicycling, travel, reading, walking. Home: 5879 Key Lime Way Fort Myers FL 33919

SHAFF, KAREN E., lawyer, insurance company executive; BA, Northwestern U., Evanston, Ill.; JD, Drake U., Des Moines. Atty. Austin and Gaudineer, Des Moines, 1979—82, Principal Fin. Group, 1982—83, asst. counsel, 1983—86, assoc. counsel, 1986—90, sr. v.p., gen. counsel, 1999—2004, exec. v.p., 2004—, gen. counsel, 2004—. Bd. dir. Sargasso Mut. Ins. Co., GuideOne Mut. Ins. Co., GuideOne Specialty Mut. Ins. Co. Bd. mem. Hospice of Ctrl. Iowa Found., Sci. Ctr. of Iowa; trustee Grinnell Coll.; mem. Greater Des Moines Partnership. Mem.: ABA, Assn. Life Ins. Counsel (bd. mem., pres. elect), Am. Corp. Counsel Assn., Polk County Bar Assn., Iowa State Bar Assn. (mem. bd. gov. 1989—95). Office: Principal Fin Group 711 High St Des Moines IA 50392 *

SHAFFER, ANITA MOHRLAND, counselor, educator; b. Racine, Wis., Apr. 5, 1939; d. Milton Arthur and Gudrun Amanda Stoffel. BS magna cum laude, U. Wis., 1961; MEd, U. Wash., 1966; postgrad., Ariz. State U., 1971-76. Cert. in elem. edn., social sci. secondary edn., spl. edn., Tex.; lic. profl. counselor, Tex. Tchr. Racine Unified Dist. 1, 1961-63, Edmonds Sch. Dist. 15, Lynnwood, Wash., 1963-70, Ariz. Dept. Corrections, Phoenix, 1971-77; tchr. spl. edn. Pasadena (Tex.) Ind. Sch. Dist., 1977-78, spl. edn.

counselor, 1978-90, elem. counselor, 1990-98; univ. supr. U. Houston, 1998—. Ednl. cons., 1998—. Mem. Tex. Counseling Assn., Houston Counseling Assn., Mus. Fine Arts Houston (patron), Houston Lic. Profl. Counselors Assn., Pi Lambda Theta. Home: 5905 Woodway Place Ct Houston TX 77057-2005

SHAFFER, BERNARD WILLIAM, mechanical and aerospace engineering educator; b. NYC, Aug. 7, 1924; s. Abraham and Eva (Ellinsky) S.; m. Florence Solow, Feb. 23, 1947 (dec. Oct. 29, 1986); children: Janet Ilene, Roberta Franceen. BME, CCNY, 1944; MSME, Case Inst. Tech. (now Case W. Res. U.), 1947; PhD, Brown U., 1951. Registered profl. engr., N.Y., R.I. Aero. rsch. scientist flight propulsion rsch. lab. NACA (now NASA), Cleve., 1944-47; spl. lectr. applied mechanics Case Inst. Tech. (now Case Western Reserve Univ.), Cleve., 1946-47; rsch. assoc., grad. div. applied math. and engring. instr. Brown U., Providence, 1947-50; asst. prof. mech. engring. NYU, NYC, 1950-53, assoc. prof., 1953-58, prof., project dir. rsch. divsn., 1958-73; prof. dept. mech. and aerospace engring. Poly. U., Bklyn. and Farmingdale, NY, 1973-93, prof. emeritus, 1993—. Cons. in field; mem. adv. coun. Coll. Aeros., N.Y.C., 1982—; vis. rsch. prof. mech. engring. Fla. Atlantic U., Boca Raton, 1992, Disting. vis. rsch. prof., 1993-95, 97—. Contbr. articles to profl. jours. Bd. dirs. Harbor Hills Civic Assn., Great Neck, N.Y., 1968-71. With USAAF, 1944-47. Recipient various govt. grants. Fellow ASME (Richards Meml. award 1968); mem. AIAA (assoc. fellow), Sigma Xi, Tau Beta Pi, Pi Tau Sigma. Avocations: golf, swimming.

SHAFFER, DAVID JAMES, lawyer; b. Springfield, Ohio, July 30, 1958; s. Frank James Shaffer and Martha Isabelle (Hardman) Matthews; children: Brynn Danielle, Jedediah Clay. BA, Wittenberg U., 1980; JD, Stanford U., 1983. Bar: Calif. 1984, U.S. Dist. Ct. (no. and ea. dists.) Calif. 1984, U.S. Ct. Appeals (9th cir.) 1984, U.S. Dist. Ct. (so. dist.) Calif. 1985, U.S. Dist. Ct. (we. dist.) Wash. 1986, D.C. 1988, U.S. Dist. Ct. D.C. 1988, U.S. Ct. Appeals (D.C. cir.) 1988, U.S. Dist. Ct. (no. dist.) Tex. 1991, U.S. Supreme Ct. 1993, Md. 1994, U.S. Dist. Ct. Md. 1997. Supr. field ops. U.S. Census Bur., Columbus, Ohio, 1980; legal intern Natural Resources Def. Coun., Inc., San Francisco, 1982-83; assoc. Gibson, Dunn & Crutcher, San Jose, Calif., 1983; law clk. to Judge Betty B. Fletcher, U.S. Ct. Appeals for 9th Cir., Seattle, 1983-84; assoc. Gibson, Dunn & Crutcher, San Jose, 1984-87, Arnold & Porter, Washington, 1987-92; ptnr. Semmes, Bowen & Semmes, Washington, 1992-94, Arter & Hadden, Washington, 1995-99, Thelen Reid & Priest LLP, Washington, 1999—. Contbr. articles to profl. and legal jours. Campaign mgr. Clark County Dem. Party, Springfield, 1978-80; organizer Citizens for Sensible County Planning, Fairfax, Va., 1989-94. Alumni scholar Wittenberg U., 1976. Mem. ABA, FBA (chmn. EEO com. 1992-94, individual rights and responsibilities 1994-95, co-chmn. alt. dispute resolution 1995-96, mem. governing bd. labor law and labor rels. sect., editor newsletter Labouring Oar, Outstanding Svc. award 1992), D.C. Bar Assn., Calif. Bar Assn., Order of Coif. Avocations: music, hiking, nature study. Office: Thelen Reid & Priest LLP 701 Pennsylvania Ave NW Washington DC 20004-2608 E-mail: dshaffer@thelenreid.com.

SHAFFER, DENNY RICHARD, small business owner; b. Altoona, Pa., Feb. 13, 1931; s. Melvin Anson and Mildred Catherine Shaffer; m. Kim Martin, May 6, 1984; 1 child, Francesca Martin; m. Betty Blair (dec. Dec. 1972); children: Robert Daniel, David Richard. BBA, U. Pitts., 1952; student, Inst. for Advanced Pastorial Studies, Bloomsfield Hill, Mich., 1968. Mgr. One Hour Koretizing / One Hour Martinizing, Fayetteville, NC, 1954—66, Burlington, 1954—66, Durham, 1954—66, Rocky Mount, 1954—66, Charleston, SC, 1954—66; v.p. One Hour Koretizing, Lynchburg, NC, 1962—66; field mgr. One Hour Valet, Miami, Fla., 1963—65; pres. Kore-O-Mat of Fayetteville, 1965—2003, One Hour Koretizing, Fayetteville, 1966—99, Shaffer Mgmt. Co., Fayetteville, 1966—99; ptnr. Scots Hills Floral Nursery, Cameron, NC, 1968—75. Author: (oral history forward) Ted Synder, 1984, Brock Evans, 1987, (book forward) Images of Wilderness, 1993. Mem. Fayetteville City Coun., 1967—71; del. Sierra Club Coun., San Francisco, 1972—77; lobbyist Easter Wilderness Bill, Washington, 1974, chmn. nat. membership com., 1976—79; nat. bd. dirs. Sierra Club, Washington, 1977—84, bd. dirs., 1985—91, 1994—97; pres. Nat. Sierra Club, 1982—84, treas., CFO, 1978—82, 1985—86, 1994—95, sec., 1997, v.p. for planning, v.p. for electorial politics, 1982—85, 1987—94; mem. bd. trustees The Sierra Club Found., 1979—86, 1991—94; founding mem. Sierra Club of Fayetteville, NC Group, 1970; chmn. NC Conservation, 1972—74; exec. com. mem Sierra Club Coun., 1974—77; founding dir. Hillsboro St. Sch., 1958, Spainhour Sch., 1967—84, The People's Clinic, 1968—72. Recipient Gov.'s award, 1983, Realtor's Cup, Fayetteville C. of C., 1967, William Colby award, Sierra Club, 1996, Disting. Environ. Series, Bancroft Libr., 2003, U. Calif., Berkley, 2003, Order of the Long Leaf Pine, State of N.C., 2003. Democrat. Presbyterian. Avocations: golf, hiking. Home: 2910 Skye Dr Fayetteville NC 28303-5925

SHAFFER, LEIGH S., psychology professor; d. Edward Wesley and Ruth D. Shaffer; m. Barbara Anne Benskin, Aug. 14, 1971; 1 child, Victoria Anne. BA, Wichita State U., 1969, MA, 1971; DPhil, Pa. State U., 1974. Asst. prof. psychology Pa. State U., McKeesport, 1974—77, Nebr. Wesleyan U., Lincoln, 1977—80, West Chester U., Pa., 1980—. Acting assoc. provost West Chester U., 2002. Co-author: Voices From the Pagan Census, 2003; contbr. articles to profl. jours. Avocation: golf. Office: West Chester U 407 Old Libr Bldg West Chester PA 19383

SHAFFER, MARGARET MINOR, retired library director; b. New Orleans, Sept. 20, 1940; d. Milhado Lee and Margaret Minor (Krumbhaar) S. BS, Nicholls State U., Thibodaux, La., 1962; MLS, La. State U., 1965. Asst. dir. Terrebonne Parish Pub. Libr., Houma, La., 1965-72, dir., 1973-95; ret., 1995. Named Woman of Yr., Houma Bus. and Profl. Women's Club, 1981. Mem. ALA, La. Libr. Assn. (chmn. pub. libr. com. 1986-87), Southeastern Libr. Assn. Democrat. Episcopalian. Avocations: crafts, travel. Home: 2678 Highway 311 Schriever LA 70395-3240

SHAFFER, PEGGY S., music educator; b. South Bend, Ind., Dec. 25, 1951; d. Phyllis L. White. MusM, Ind. State U., 1970—76; M in Guidance, Purdue U.-Calumet, 1994—97. Music Ind. Dept. Edn., 1976. Tchr. Crown Point Schs., Ind., 1977—. Musician: (free-lance performer) drummer. Bd. mem. Ind. Music Educator's Assn., Crown Point, 1986—88. Mem.: Music Educators Nat. Conf., Nat. Band Assn., Ind. Bandmasters Assn., Ind. State Teachers Assn. Home: 702 W Sigler Hebron IN 46341 Office: Crown Point HS 1500 S Main St Crown Point IN 46307 Home Phone: 219-996-3048; Office Phone: 219-663-4885. Office Fax: 219-662-5661. Personal E-mail: pshaffer@cps.k12.in.us.

SHAFFER, PETER (SIR PETER SHAFFER), playwright; b. Liverpool, Eng., May 15, 1926; s. Jack and Reka (Fredman) S. BA, Cambridge U., Eng., 1950. Conscript coal mines, Eng., 1944-47; with N.Y. Pub. Libr., NYC, 1951-54, Boosey & Hawkes, London, 1954-55; lit. critic Truth, 1956-57; music critic Time and Tide, 1961-62; freelance playwright, 1957—. Vis. prof. contemporary drama Oxford (Eng.) U., 1994-95. Author: (plays) Five Finger Exercise, 1958 (Evening Standard Drama award 1958, N.Y. Drama Critics Cir. award 1960), The Private Ear, 1962, The Public Eye, 1962, It's About Cinderella, 1963, The Royal Hunt of the Sun, 1964, Black Comedy, 1965, The White Liars, 1967, The Battle of Shrivings, 1970, Equus, 1973 (Best Play Tony award 1975, Outer Critics Cir. Best Play award 1975), Amadeus, 1979 (Evening Standard Drama award 1979, London Drama Critics award 1979, Best Play Tony award 1980, Plays and Players Best Play award 1980), Yonadab, 1985, Lettice and Lovage, 1987 (Evening Standard Drama award 1988), The Gift of the Gorgon, 1992, Whom Do I Have the Honor of Addressing?, Chichester Festival Theatre, 1996, (screenplays) Follow Me!, 1971, Equus, 1977 (Acad. award nomination for best screenplay adaptation 1977), Amadeus, 1984 (Acad. award for best screenplay adaptation 1984), (TV plays) The Salt Land, 1955, Balance of Terror, 1957, (radio plays) The Prodigal Father, 1955, Whom Do I Have the Honor of Addressing?, 1989, (novels) The Woman in the Wardrobe, 1951, (novels, with Anthony Shaffer), How Doth the Little Crocodile?, 1952, Withered Murder, 1955. Created knight, 2001; decorated comdr. Order Brit. Empire, 1987; recipient Hamburg Shakespeare prize, 1987, William Inge award for disting. achievement in Am. theatre, 1992; hon. fellow St. Andrews U., Scotland, emeritus fellow St. Catherine's Coll., Oxford, Eng. Fellow Royal Soc. Lt. (London chpt.). Address: 173 Riverside Dr New York NY 10024

SHAFFER, RICHARD JAMES, lawyer, retired manufacturing executive; b. Pe Ell, Wash., Jan. 26, 1931; s. Richard Humphrys and Laura Rose (Faas) S.; m. Donna M. Smith, May 13, 1956; children: Leslie Lauren Shaffer Litsinger, Stephanie Jane Athenton. BA, U. Wash.; LL.B., Southwestern U. Bar: Calif. Various positions in mfg. and contracts adminstrn. depts. N. Am. Aviation Inc./Rockwell Corp.; western regional counsel The Bendix Corp., 1968—73; v.p., gen. counsel Norris Industries Inc., Long Beach, Calif., 1974—81; v.p., gen. counsel, sec. NI Inc., Long Beach, Calif., 1981—89; gen. counsel Masco Bldg. Products Corp., 1985—89; pvt. practice, 1989—98; internat. ops. officer Newport Fin. Group, 2003; CFO Dreamquest Entertainment Ltd., 2004; cons., 2005—. Chmn. Calif. State Senate Ltd. Liability Co. Act drafting com., mem. task force Calif. State Bar, 1992-94; lectr. in field. Co-author: Practicing Under the Limited Liability Company Act. Trustee Ocean View Sch. Dist., 1965-73, pres., 1966, 73; mem. fin. adv. com. Orange Coast Coll., 1966; mem. Long Beach Local Devel. Corp., 1978-89, Calif. Senate Commn. on Corp. Governance, Shareholders' Rights and Securities Transactions, 1986-97, chmn. drafting com. ltd. liability co. act for senate com., 1991-93; mem. Pers. Commn. City of Huntington Beach, 1996-98; mem. Huntington Beach clean water subcom. Huntington Harbour; bd. dirs. Huntington Beach Libr. Patrons, 1996-98. Ensign and lt. j.g. USN, 1954—57. Mem. ABA, Am. Arbitration Assn.(bd. arbitrators), Calif. Bar Assn. (exec. com. corp. law dept. com. bus. sect. 1981-88), Orange County Bar Assn., Trinidad Island Homeowners Assn. (pres.), Huntington Harbour Yacht Club, Catalina Island Yacht Club, Wanderlust Skiers of Huntington Harbour. Avocations: skiing, yachting.

SHAFFER, RICHARD PAUL, financial planner, real estate company executive, military officer; b. Ft. Worth, Oct. 12, 1949; AA in Bus., Coll. of the Mainland, 1975; BBA in Bus., Sam Houston State U., Huntsville, Tex., 1975, MBA in Bus., 1976. Pers. technician U.S. Govt., Houston, 1968-75; pers. recruiter M.D. Anderson Cancer Hosp., Houston, 1976-79; acctg. auditor State of Tex., Galveston, 1979-82; owner, fin. planner Co. Benefits, Galveston, 1982—; owner Shaffer & Assocs. Real Estate, Galveston, 1982—. Master sgt. USAFR, 1967—87. Mem.: N.G. Assn. Tex., Modern Woodmen Am. (No. 2 Agt. Calif. 2004, No. 7 Agt. Annuity Sales 2004, No. 10 Agt. Pres.' Cabinet 2004, Million Dollar Round Table). Republican. Methodist. Avocations: pilot, swimming, fishing, dance, reading. Home: 743 Marlin Bayou Vista Hitchcock TX 77563-2611 Office: Co Benefits 743 Marlin St Hitchcock TX 77563-2611 Office Phone: 409-938-1265. E-mail: richard.p.shaffer@mwareg.org.

SHAFFER, RICHARD STANLEY, mechanical engineer, researcher; b. Hudson, Mich., May 21, 1957; s. Richard Keith and Carolynn Emma Shaffer; m. Bonnie Jean Krauss, July 29, 1978; children: Jessica Ann, David Stanley, Michelle Jean, Michael Richardson. AS with honors, Jackson C.C., Mich., 1993; BS in Mech. Engring. with honors, Tri-State U., Angola, Ind., 1996. EIT Ind. Profl. Licensing Agy., 1996. Pre-engring. instr. Jackson Area Career Ctr., 2000—03; rsch. asst. U. Toledo, 2006—. On site energy specialist, engr. Consumers Energy, Jackson, 2001. Mem. Hillsdale County 4-H Coun., Mich., 1999—2005. Named Pittsford Area Sch. Disting. Citizen, Pittsford Edn. Assn., 1991; recipient Excellence in Learning award, Jackson C.C., 1992, 1994, 4—H Award of the Gold Clover, Hillsdale County 4-H Coun., 2000, Friend of 4-H award, Hillsdale County 4-H Program, 2003; Tomas Furth Academic scholar, Tri-State U., 1995. Mem.: Mid—Mich. Mensa, Am. Mensa, Ltd., Tau Beta Pi (life), Order of the Engr. (life), Pi Tau Sigma (life). Achievements include research in hydraulic hybrid vehicle. Avocations: camping, alternative energy applications, travel, home improvement. Home: 9511 Culbert Rd Pittsford MI 49271-9618 Home Phone: 517-523-3147; Office Phone: 419-530-8180. Personal E-mail: esquire777@hotmail.com.

SHAFFER, ROBERT M.M., lawyer; b. Cin., June 6, 1968; BA, Yale U., 1990; JD, U. Cin., 1996. Bar: Ohio 1996. Atty. Warren County Prosecutor's Office, Ohio; assoc. Vorys, Sater, Seymour and Pease LLP, Cin. Named one of Ohio's Rising Stars, Super Lawyers, 2006. Mem.: Ohio State Bar Assn., Cin. Bar Assn. Office: Vorys, Sater, Seymour and Pease LLP Atrium Two Ste 2000 221 E Fourth St PO Box 0236 Cincinnati OH 45202-0236 Office Phone: 513-723-4085. Office Fax: 513-852-7815.

SHAFFER, SHERRILL LYNN, economist; b. Tyler, Tex., Aug. 1, 1952; s. Douglas Marsene and Ethel Elizabeth (Green) S.; m. Margaret Jane Ahrens, Jun 20, 1987; 1 child, David Carsten. BA, Rice U., Houston, 1974; MA, Stanford U., Calif., 1978, PhD, 1981. Rsch. asst. Stanford U., Calif., 1976—79, instr., 1979—80; from economist to chief Fed. Res. Bank NY, NYC, 1980—88; from rsch. officer, economist to asst. v.p./discount officer Fed. Res. Bank Phila., 1988—97; John A. Guthrie disting. prof. banking and fin. svcs. U. Wyo., Laramie, 1997—. Vis. scholar Stanford U., 2004; chmn. tenure and promotion com., grad. coun., 2000-02, MBA adv. com., grad. admissions com., 1999-2000, grad. program rev. com., 2000-02; violinist solo and with orchs., Calif., NY, 1976-88; cons. asst. Rosse & Olszewski, Palo Alto, Calif., 1978-80; cons. in field. Contbr. articles to profl. jours.; assoc. editor to editor Jour. Econs. and Bus., 1993—, mem. editl. bd. Jour. Regulatory Econs., 2002—. Sec. bd. dirs. NY Arts Group, NYC, 1982—83; mem. program com. So. Fin. Assn., 1996; exec. adv. coun. mem. dept. fin. Temple U., 1996—97; bd. advisors cultural programs series U. Wyo., 1999—; mem. fin. com. St. Matthew's Cathedral, Laramie, Wyo., 1998—2004, mem. vestry, 1999—2002; bd. dirs. artist selection com. Tri-County Concerts Assn., 1996—. Recipient Messier cert. Astron. League, 1993, U. Wyo. Coll. Bus. Sr. Rsch. award, 2006—07, Outstanding Sr. Rsch. award, U. Wyo. Coll. Bus., 2006—07; vis. scholar, Stanford Univ., 2004. Mem. AAAS, Am. Econ. Assn., Am. Math. Soc., Math. Assn. Am., N.Am. Econs. and Fin. Assn., Indsl. Orgn. Soc., NY Acad. Scis., Fin. Mgmt. Assn. (program com. 1991, 01, 03, 04, 05, 07, nat. awards com. 2000, 01), So. Fin. Assn. (program com. 1996), Del. Valley Amateur Astronomers (observing chmn. 1993, publicity chmn. 1994-96), Chamber Music Am. Episcopalian. Avocations: hiking, astronomy, computer programming, theology, number theory. Home: 30 Silver Spur Rd Laramie WY 82072-9563 Office: U Wyo Dept Econs and Fin PO Box 3985 Laramie WY 82071-3985 Business E-Mail: shaffer@uwyo.edu.

SHAFFER, THOMAS LINDSAY, lawyer, educator; b. Billings, Mont., Apr. 4, 1934; s. Cecil Burdette and Margaret Jeanne (Parker) S.; m. Nancy Jane Lehr, Mar. 19, 1954; children: Thomas, Francis, Joseph, Daniel, Brian, Mary, Andrew, Edward. BA, U. Albuquerque, 1958; JD, U. Notre Dame, 1961; LLD, St. Mary's U., 1983. Bar: Ind. 1961. Assoc. Barnes, Hickam, Pantzer, & Boyd, Indpls., 1961-63; prof. law U. Notre Dame, Ind., 1963-80, assoc. dean, 1969-71, dean, 1971-75, Robert and Marion Short prof., 1988-97; Robert and Marion Short prof. emeritus, 1997—; supervising atty. Notre Dame Legal Aid Clinic, 1991—; prof. law Washington and Lee U., 1980-87, Robert E.R. Huntley prof. law, 1987-88. Vis. prof. UCLA, 1970-71, U. Va., 1975-76, U. Maine, 1982, 87, 98, Boston Coll., 1992; mem. Ind. Constl. Revision Commn., 1969-70, Ind. Trust Code Study Commn., 1968-71; reporter Ind. Jud. Conf., 1963, 67. Author: Death, Property, and Lawyers, 1970, The Planning and Drafting of Wills and Trusts, 1972, 5th edit., 2007, On Being a Christian and a Lawyer, 1981, American Legal Ethics, 1985, Faith and the Professions, 1987, Moral Memoranda From John Howard Yoder, 2002; co-author: Lawyers, Law Students, and People, 1977, Cases in Legal Interviewing and Counseling, 1980, American Lawyers and Their Communities, 1991, Property Cases, Materials and Problems, 1992, 3rd edit., 2006, Lawyers, Clients, and Moral Responsibility, 1994, Legal Interviewing and Counseling, 1976, 4th edit., 2004; co-editor: The Mentally Retarded Citizen and the Law, 1976; contbr. articles to profl. jours. Served with USAF, 1953-57. Frances Lewis scholar Washington and Lee U., 1979; recipient Emil Brown Found. Preventive Law prize, 1966, Presdl. citation U. Notre Dame, 1975, St. Thomas More award St. Mary's U., 1983, Law medal Gonzaga U., 1991, Reinhold Niebuhr award U. Notre Dame, 1991, Jour. Law and Religion award, 1993. Mem. Ind. State Bar Assn., Jewish Law Assn. Roman Catholic. Home: 1865 Champlain Dr Niles MI 49120-8935 Office: Notre Dame Legal Aid Clinic 725 Howard St South Bend IN 46617-1529 Office Phone: 574-631-7250. Personal E-mail: shaffer@nd.edu.

SHAFFER, WAYNE EUGENE, lawyer; b. Wauseon, Ohio, June 25, 1922; s. Chalmer L. and Leva Louella (Rashley) Shaffer; m. Georgia Grace Frey, June 4, 1949; children: Julie Anne, Wayne Daniel(dec.). BA, Ohio No. U, Ada, 1946; JD, Ohio No. U., 1949. Bar: Ohio 1949. Ptnr. Newcomer, Shaffer, Spangler & Breininger, Bryan, Ohio, 1949—. Founding mem., pres. Nat. Assn. State Bds. Edn., Washington, 1963; mem. Ohio State Bd. Edn., Columbus, 1955—92, pres.; founding mem., pres. Bryan Area Found., 1974. Lt. (j.g.) USN, 1942—46, ETO, PTO. Named 3 time winner, Capt. Budd Carr Sailfish Tournament; recipient Good Citizenship award, Bryan C. of C., 2005. Fellow: Ohio State Bar Assn. (life; chmn. legal edn. com. 1965); mem.: ABA, Ohio Cmty. Sch. Assn., Ohio Supts. Assn. (Ohio Educator of Yr.). Republican. Home: 604 Circle Dr Bryan OH 43506 Office: Newcomer Shaffer Spangler & Breininger 117 W Maple St Bryan OH 43506

SHAFFERT, KURT, retired lawyer, chemical engineer; b. Vienna, July 20, 1929; s. Rudolph nee Schafranik and Irma (Altar) S.; m. Judith Pytel, June 12, 1955; children: Elona Ruth, Robin Laurette. BChemE, CCNY, 1951; LLB cum laude, NYU, 1963. Bar: N.Y. 1963, D.C. 1965, U.S. Supreme Ct. 1967, U.S. Patent and Trademark Office 1964. Chem. engr. Diamond Alkali Co., Newark, 1951-54; process devel. engr. Am. Cyanamid Co., Stamford, Conn., 1957-59; patent liaison engr. Uniroyal Inc., 1959-63; assoc. Arthur, Dry & Kalish, NYC, 1963-66, Office of Robert F. Conrad, Washington, 1966-69; sr. ptnr. Shaffert, Miller & Browne, Washington, 1970-74; sr. trial atty. intellectual property sect. Antitrust divsn. Dept. of Justice, Washington, 1974-85, professions and intellectual property sect., 1985-94, intellectual property guidelines task force, 1994, civil task force, 1994-2000; ret., 2000. Mem. Bethesda-Chevy Chase Jewish Comm. Group, 1965, pres., 1973-74, v.p. 1972-73, treas. 1971-72; mem. Jewish Comm. Ctr. of Greater Wash., 1970-78, bd. dirs., 1973-78; provided tape recorded Holocaust recollections for Stephen Spielberg Holocaust Archive Survivors of the Shoa Visual History Found., 1998. With U.S. Army, 1955-56. Mem. ABA (antitrust sect., patent, trademark and copyright sect.), Profl. Assn. Antitrust Divsn. Dept. of Justice (pres. 1978-79), Bar Assn. D.C. (council del. 1972-74), D.C. Bar Assn.

SHAFFNER, PATRICK NOEL, retired architectural engineering executive; b. Burlington, NC, Nov. 1, 1939; s. Samuel Hubert and Martha Jane (Noel) Shaffner; m. Patricia Anne Anders, June 12, 1961; children: Scott Anders, Kimberly Page, Melissa Hope. BS, Va. Poly. and State U., 1961. Registered profl. engr., Va. Structural engr. Hayes, Seay, Mattern & Mattern, Roanoke, Va., 1963-68; sr. structural engr. Sherertz & Franklin, Roanoke, 1968-72; ptnr. Sherertz, Franklin, Crawford, Shaffner, Roanoke, 1972-87; chmn., CEO Sherertz, Franklin, Crawford, Shaffner, Inc., Roanoke, 1988-98. Bd. dirs. Mill Mountain Theatre; mem. adv. bd. Va. Tech. Coll. Engring. Com. 100; v.p. Roanoke Found. for Downtown, Inc.; trustee Va. Bapt. Children's Home and Family Svcs.; interim exec. dir. Downtown Roanoke, Inc., 2005-06. Capt. C.E., U.S. Army, 1961-63. Paul Harris fellow. Fellow ASCE; mem. AIA (assoc.), Roanoke Regional C. of C. (Small Bus. Person of Yr. 1991), Rotary (pres. Roanoke club 1986). Lodges: Rotary (Roanoke) (pres. 1986). Republican. Baptist. Home: 2635 Turnberry Rd Salem VA 24153-7483 E-mail: shaffner@adelphia.net.

SHAFFNER, RANDOLPH PRESTON, shop owner, educator, writer, publisher; b. Winston-Salem, NC, Jan. 17, 1940; s. Emil Nathaniel and Anna Jackson (Preston) S.; m. Margaret Farmer Rhodes; children: Eric Randolph, Edward David, Joseph Andrew, Thomas Matthew, Jackson Rhodes. Student, Davidson Coll., NC, 1958-60; BA in English with honors in writing, U. NC, Chapel Hill, 1962, MA in Comparative Lit., 1969, PhD, 1973. Surveyor's lineman Joyce Mapping Co., Winston-Salem, 1955-58, 62; counselor, scoutmaster Camp Sequoyah, Weaverville, NC, 1959; track repairman Alaska R.R., Anchorage, 1960; case handler Emard Packing Co., Anchorage, 1960, AYR Canneries, Seldovia, Alaska, 1961; tchr. US Peace Corps., Chiengrai, Thailand, 1963-65, St. Christopher's Sch., Richmond, Va., 1969-71; instr. U. NC, 1968-69, 71-73; asst. prof. Fairfield U., Conn., 1973-78, Western Carolina U., 1984, 87, Continuing Edn. program World Masterpieces, Highlands, NC, 1987—89; moderator Highlands lecture series Western Carolina U., 1989-92. Instr. Carolina environ. program U. NC, Chapel Hill, 2003; editor John F. Blair Pub., Winston-Salem, 1966-68; bookseller, owner Cyrano's Bookshop, Highlands, NC, 1978-05; founder, pub. Faraway Pub., 2001; asst. to dean Sch. Libr. Scis. U. NC, Chapel Hill, 1973-74; literary mag. adv., various subcoms. Dept. Eng. Fairfield U., 1973-78. Author: Apprenticeship Novel, 1984, Tree Ordinance for Town of Highlands, 1987, Good Reading Material, Mostly Bound and New: The Hudson Library 1884-1994, 1994, Heart of the Blue Ridge: Highlands, North Carolina, 2001, 2d edit., 2004, Highlands Heritage Trail: A Walking Tour of Many Highlands Historical Buildings and Landmarks, 2003; (with others) Nineteenth Century Literature Criticism, Vol. 21, 1989; contbr. poetry to NC Poetry Soc. anthology Here's to the Land, 1992; contbr. short stories to mags; contbr. Heritage of Macon Co., NC, Vol. 2, 1999. Lectr. with Alexander, String Quartet, Words & Music, 1989, 92, 94, for Western Carolina U., Highlands lectr. series, 1991-93, 2000; inaugural lectr. Chattooga Watershed Cultural Heritage Series, 2005; instr. Ctr. for Life Enrichment, 2000, 06, 07; chmn. ARC Disaster Svcs., Fairfield, 1974-78, Zoning Bd. of Adjustment, Highlands, 1981-83, 85-90; pres., bd. trustees Hudson Libr., Inc., Highlands, 1987-90, 99-2001, chmn. libr. com., 1995-99; trustee Hudson Libr. Bascom-Louise Art Gallery, 1987-90, 95-99, Highlands Land Trust, Inc., 1995-96; bd. dirs. ARC, Fairfield, 1974-78, Highlands Cultural Art Ctr., 1987; fundraising com. Highlands Permanent Endowment Scholarships, 1987-89; Town of Highlands Millennium Com., 1999; historian Highlands Hist. Soc., Inc., 1999—, adv. com., 2001—, archivist, 2005—; v.p. Highlands Plateau Greenway, Inc., 2005-, mem. Macon County Hist. Preservation Commn. Task Force, 2006, Macon County Heritage Coun., 2006—; bd. dirs. Friends Mtn. Hist., 2006—, editor Mtn. Hist. Museums-in-Partnership Newsletter, 2007-; vice-chmn. bd. missions Greenfield Hill Congl. Ch., Fairfield, Conn., 1977, chmn. scholarship co., 1975-77; chaperon Am. Inst. for Fgn. Study, Grenoble, France, 1970. Recipient God and Country award, 1955, Outstanding Pres. and Trustee award Hudson Libr. and Bascom-Louise Gallery, 1990, Daniel Boone Coun. Boy Scouts Am. Disting. Citizen award, 2002, Gertrude and Dolly Harbison award, Hudson Libr., 2004; Goethe Inst. scholar German Embassy, Munich, Fed. Rep. Germany, 1965, Univ. Besançon, France, 1965. Mem.: NC Writers' Network, Writer's Workshop, Am. Assn. for State and Local History (ann. award for Heart of the Blue Ridge 2005), Highlands Biol. Found. (trustee 1981—2006, fund raising com. 1986, environ. protection com. 1986—88, exec. com. 1986—2004, treas.

1990—2004, adv. com. on Nature Ctr. 1992, hon. trustee 2006—), Highlands Mchts. Assn. (chmn. fin. com., treas. 1984—87, chmn. tree com. and beautification com. 1984—89, greenways com. 2004—), Am. Acad. Poets, NC Poetry Soc., Writers' Workshop, Am. Comparative Lit. Assn., Internat. Comparative Lit. Assn., Soc. NC Archivists, Highlands-Cashiers Land Trust, Nat. Peace Corps Assn., Highlands Hist. Soc., Highlands C. of C., Clan Morrison Soc., NC Soc. Historians (History Book award 2002), Trail Hikers Am., Rotary (Outstanding Vol. award 1989), Lambda Iota Tau (faculty moderator Delta Omicron Ch. 1975—80, founder). Democrat. Moravian. Avocations: construction, reading, travel, hiking, writing. Office: Highlands Hist Soc 524 N 4th St Highlands NC 28741-0670 Home: PO Box 765 189 Cowee Gap Ln Highlands NC 28741-0765 Office Phone: 828-787-1050. Business E-Mail: highlandshistory@nctv.com.

SHAFIEI-SARARODI, MAJOUD, language educator; b. Isfahan, Iran, Mar. 28, 1962; arrived in US, 1991; s. Mostafa Shafiei-Sararodi and Fatemeh Bagherian; m. Alice Shafiei-Sararodi, Jan. 24, 1997; children: Cyrus Shafiei, Kaveh Shafiei. BA in Applied English Linguistics, U. Isfahan, 1984; MA in Applied English Linguistics, U. Houston, 1994; EdD in Instnl. Tech., U. Houston, 05; cert. CELTA, Cambridge U., Eng. Instr. U. Houston, 1994—99; prof. North Harris Coll., Houston, 1999—2001, Kingwood Coll., Houston, 2001—. Bd. dirs. ESL exit test Tex. Edn. Agy., Austin, 2002—03. Author: (book series) New Vistas, 1999—2000, Effective Academic Writing 1. Cofounder Multicultural Families, Houston, 2003—. Recipient writing award, North Harris Montgomery Coll., Houston, 1997; grantee, 1999—2007. Mem.: TESOL (bd. dirs. region IV 1997—99, pres. 1999—2000). Avocations: reading, public speaking, travel, camping. Office: Kingwood Coll 20000 Kingwood Dr Houston TX 77339

SHAFIPOUR, POUYA, physician, dermatologist; s. Hamid Reza Shafipour and Fereshteh Amin; m. Pantea Tahouri, May 18, 2003. BA, U. Calif., Berkeley, 1998; MS, Georgetown U., Washington, 1999; MD, Loma Linda U., Calif., 2003. Lic. physician Calif., 2004. Resident physician U. Calif. Irvine, Orange, Calif., 2003—04, Kaiser Permanente, LA, 2005—. Fellow: Am. Acad. Family Physicians; mem.: AMA, Calif. Med. Assn., Am. Soc. Laser Medicine and Surgery (assoc.), Am. Acad. Cosmetic Surgery (assoc.), Am. Soc. Bariatric Physicians. Home Phone: 323-848-6929; Office Phone: 800-954-8000. Home Fax: 319-937-0206. Personal E-mail: pshafipourmd@gmail.com.

SHAFIR, ROBERT S., finance company executive; BA, Lafayette Coll.; MBA, Columbia U. With Morgan Stanley & Co., 1985—90; sr. mgmt. positions Lehman Brothers Holdings Inc., 1990—2000, co-head, global equities, 2000—05; CEO Americas Credit Suisse, 2007—. Mem. exec. com. Lehman Brothers Holdings Inc. Office: Credit Suisse 11 Madison Ave New York NY 10010 *

SHAFRIR, DOREE, editor, journalist; b. 1977; BA, U. Pa., Phila., 1999; MA, Columbia U. Grad. Sch. Journalism, 2006. Intern Slate mag.; editor Go mag., Phila., CampusPhilly.org, Phila.; arts & entertainment editor Phila. Weekly, 2003—05; co-founder & editor Crier lit. mag., Bklyn., 2005—; assoc. editor Gawker.com, NYC, 2006—07; with NY Observer, NYC, 2007—. Office: NY Observer LLC 9th Fl 915 Broadway New York NY 10010 Office Phone: 212-655-9524. *

SHAFRITZ, DAVID ANDREW, physician, research scientist; b. Phila., Oct. 5, 1940; s. Saul and Ethel (Kohn) S.; m. Sharon C. Klemow, Aug. 16, 1964; children: Gregory S., Adam B., Keith M. AB in Chemistry with honors, U. Pa., 1962, MD, 1966. Diplomate Nat. Bd. Med. Examiners, Am. Bd. Internal Medicine. Intern, then asst. resident U. Md. Hosp., Balt., 1966-68; rsch. assoc. NIH, Bethesda, Md., 1968-71; clin. and rsch. fellow Mass. Gen. Hosp., Boston, 1971-73; instr. Harvard Med. Sch., Boston, 1971-73, asst. prof. medicine, 1973; asst. prof. medicine and cell biology Albert Einstein Coll. Medicine, Yeshiva U., Bronx, NY, 1973-76, assoc. prof., 1976-81, prof. medicine and cell biology, 1981—, dir. Marion Bessin Liver Rsch. Ctr., 1985—, Herman Lapota prof. liver disease rsch. (endowed chair), 1992—. Cons. integrated Genetics, Inc., Framingham, Mass., 1981-86, Immuno, Vienna, Austria, 1986-91, Innovir, Inc., N.Y.C., 1991-98, Eugenetech Internat., Inc., Ramsey, N.J., 1991-93, Ctrs. for Med. Innovation, 1997-2001; temp. advisor WHO, Geneva, 1983; mem. Nat. Com. for Clin. Lab. Stds., Villanova Pa., 1983—, Renaissance Techs., 1996—, Affymetrix, Inc., 1997—; sci. adv. bd. com. liver cancer program Inst. for Cancer Rsch., Fox Chase and Phila., 1987—, mem. rev. panel C. study sect. Nat. Inst. Diabetes and Digestive and Kidney Diseases, 1988-92, chmn., 1991-92; mem. cen. coord. com. Liver Tissue Procurement and Distbn. Sys., 1986-95, Nat. Inst. Health Metabolic Pathology Study sect., 1995-99; mem. Nat. Bd. Med. Examiners and U.S. Med. Exam. Com., 1996-98. Co-author: The Liver: Biology and Pathobiology, 1982, 4th edit., 2001, Hepatobiliary Diseases, 1991; assoc. editor Hepatology, 1981-86; mem. editl. bd. Jour. Med. Virology, 1982-93, Hepatology, 1990-96, Jour. Virology, 1992-98; contbr. numerous rsch. articles and revs. to profl. publs.; contbr. chpts. to books; patentee in field. Trustee Westchester Jewish Ctr., Mamaroneck, N.Y., 1980-86. Lt. comdr. USPHS, 1968-71. Recipient Merck award U. Pa., 1962, Morton McCutcheon Meml. Rsch. prize Sch. Medicine, 1966, Career Scientist award Irma T. Hirschl Trust, N.Y.C., 1974-79, NIH Merit award, 1994, Disting. Rsch. Achievement award Am. Liver Found., 2000; European Molecular Biology Orgn. fellow, 1978; recipient Rsch. Career Devel. award NIH, 1975-80, spl. rsch. fellow, 1971-73, rsch. grantee, 1974—. Mem. Am. Assn. for Study of Liver Diseases, Internat. Assn. for Study of Liver, Am. Gastroenterol. Assn. (Mentors award 2007), Am. Soc. Biochemistry and Molecular Biology, Am. Soc. Investigative Pathology, Am. Soc. Clin. Investigation, Assn. Am. Physicians, N.Y. Acad. Scis., Harvey Soc., Interurban Clin. Club (sec./treas. 1996-99, pres. 1999-2000). Democrat. Jewish. Avocations: jogging, tennis. Home: 4 Pheasant Run Larchmont NY 10538-3423 Office: Yeshiva U Albert Einstein Coll Med Marion Bessin Liver Rsch Ctr 1300 Morris Park Ave Bronx NY 10461-1926 Office Phone: 718-430-2098. Business E-Mail: shafritz@aecom.yu.edu.

SHAFRITZ, KEITH MICHAEL, psychology professor; b. Boston, Dec. 29, 1972; s. David A. and Sharon K. Shafritz; m. Donna J. Lutz, May 30, 1999; 1 child, Matthew. BA, Haverford Coll., 1995; MPhil, Yale U., 1999, PhD, 2002. Rsch. asst. Albert Einstein Coll. Medicine, Bronx, NY, 1996—97; grad. rsch. fellow Yale U., New Haven, 1997—2002, grad. tchg. fellow, 1998—2000, postdoctoral rsch. fellow, 2002—03; rsch. assoc. Duke U., Durham, NC, 2003—05; asst. prof. Drew U., Madison, NJ, 2005—06, Hofstra U., Hempstead, NY, 2006—. Adj. prof. Quinnipiac U., Hamden, Conn., 2002; sci. reveiwer various profl. jours.; rsch. affiliate Yale U., Conn., 2007—. Contbr. articles to profl. jours. Recipient Rsch. Travel award, Yale U., 1997—99, Nat. Rsch. Svc. award, NIMH, 2002—03, Rsch. Travel award, Drew U., 2005, Hofstra U., 2007; fellow, Yale U., 1997—2002, 2000, Duke U., 2003—05. Mem.: AAAS, Cognitive Neurosci. Soc., Soc. Neurosci., Sigma Xi. Democrat. Office: Hofstra Univ Dept Psychology Hempstead NY 11549 Office Phone: 516-463-4856. Office Fax: 516-463-6052. Business E-Mail: keith.shafritz@aya.yale.edu.

SHAFTEL, MATTHEW ROBERT, music educator, tenor, conductor; b. Tucson, Ariz., Sept. 10, 1973; s. Timothy L. Shaftel and Cassie L. Wesselius; m. Pascale R. Rodrigue, Aug. 16, 1994; children: Veronique, Alexandre, Genevieve. BA, Yale U., New Haven, Conn., 1991—95, MPhil, 1995—97, PhD, 1995—2000. Cert. music tchr. Conn., 1995. Dir. of music Good Shepherd Cath. Ch., Tallahassee, 2001—; music theory prof. Fla. State U., Tallahassee, 2001—. Treas. Music Theory SE, Tallahassee, 2004—. Author, editor (non-fiction book and edition) Anton Webern's Early Vocal Music, 2004; contbr. articles to profl. music jours. Recipient U. Tchg. award, Fla. State U., 2005. Mem.: Coll. Music Soc. (music theory adv. bd. 2004—), Soc. for Music Theory (com. on the status of women 2003—). Roman Catholic. Avocations: travel, cooking, basketball. Office: Fla State Univ Sch Music Tallahassee FL 32306-1180 Office Phone: 850-644-6271. Business E-Mail: mshaftel@fsu.edu.

SHAGAM, MARVIN HÜCKEL-BERRI, private school educator; b. Monongalia, W.Va. s. Lewis and Clara (Shagam) S. AB magna cum laude, Washington and Jefferson Coll., 1947; postgrad., Harvard Law Sch., 1947—48, Oxford U., 1948—51. Tchr. Mount House Sch., Tavistock, England, 1951—53, Williston Jr. Sch., Easthampton, Mass., 1953—55, Westtown Sch., Pa., 1955—58, Thacher Sch., Ojai, Calif., 1958—; head English dept. Kurasini Internat. Edn. Centre, Dar-es-Salaam, Tanzania, 1966—67; head dept. Nkumbi Internat. Coll., Kabwe, Zambia, 1967—68. Vol. visitor Prisons in Calif., 1980-95, Calif. Youth Authority, 1983-93; sr. youth crisis counsellor InterFace, 1984-94. With U.S. Army, 1942-46, 1st lt. M.I. res.,1946-57. Danforth Found. fellow, 1942; Coun. for the Humanities fellow, Tufts U., 1983. Mem. We. Assn. Schs. and Colls. (accreditation com.), Great Tchg. (Cooke chair 1977—), Phi Beta Kappa, Delta Sigma Rho, Cum Laude Soc. Republican. Avocations: hiking, camping, travel. Home: 5025 Thacher Rd Ojai CA 93023-8304 Office: The Thacher Sch 5025 Thacher Rd Ojai CA 93023-9001 Home Phone: 805-646-7400; Office Phone: 805-646-4377. Fax: 805-646-4377. E-mail: mshagam@thacher.org.

SHAGAN, STEVE, scriptwriter, film producer; b. NYC, Oct. 25, 1927; m. Elizabeth Florance, Nov. 1956. Film technician Consol. Film, Inc., NYC, 1952-56, RCA, Cape Canaveral, Fla., 1956-59; asst. to publicity dir. Paramount Pictures, Hollywood, Calif., 1962-63. Prodr.: (TV series) Tarzan, 1966; prodr., writer movies for TV, Universal and CBS, Hollywood, Calif., 1968-70; writer original screenplay: Save the Tiger, 1972 (Writers Guild award, Acad. award nominee 1973); prodr. film, author screenplay: City of Angels (produced as movie Hustle), 1975, novel, screenplay The Formula, 1979, screenplay Voyage of the Damned, 1976 (Acad. award nominee); writer, prodr. film The Formula, 1980; author: (novels) Save the Tiger, 1972, City of Angels, 1975, The Formula, 1979, The Circle, 1982, The Discovery, 1985, Vendetta, 1986, Pillars of Fire, 1989, A Cast of Thousands, 1993, (screenplays) Primal Fear, 1996, Gotti, 1996 (Emmy nominee Best Screenplay). Served with USCG, 1944-46. Mem. Writers Guild Am. (bd. dirs. West chpt. 1978-82).

SHAGGY, See BURRELL, ORVILLE

SHAH, AASHIT K., neurologist; b. Baroda, India, Feb. 19, 1964; m. Jigna Shah; children: Aashka, Ananya. MBBS, N.H.L. Mcpl. Med. Coll., Gujarat, India, 1987. Diplomate Am. Bd. Neurology. Intern Interfaith Med. Ctr., Bklyn., 1988-89; res. Wayne State U. Detroit Med. Ctr., 1989-92, fellowship, 1992-93; staff neurologist Hutzel Hosp., Detroit, 1993, Harper Hosp., Detroit, 1993, Detroit Rec. Hops., 1993. Assoc. prof. Wayne State U., 1993. Office: 8A-UHC/Dept Neur 4201 Saint Antoine St Detroit MI 48201-2153 Home Phone: 248-641-9889; Office Phone: 313-745-4275. Business E-Mail: ashah@med.wayne.edu.

SHAH, BHUPEN, consumer electronics company executive; MS in Computer Sci. and Elec. Engring., U. Mich., Ann Arbor. V.p. software Dazzle (acquired by SCM Microsystems); v.p., products and tech. Real-Chip Communications, Sunnyvale, Calif.; co-founded, COO, exec. v.p. enging. to chief tech. officer, v.p. mktg. Emuzed, Inc. (acquired by Flextronics Internat. Ltd.), San Jose, Calif., 1999—2004; founder DiTango (acquired by Sling Media, Inc.), 2004; co-founder, COO, v.p. engring. Sling Media, Inc., San Mateo, Calif., 2004—. Former chmn. USB video and imaging device working group. Achievements include with other members of Slingbox Media, Inc., created Slingbox, a device that allows a person to watch their own TV from a laptop anywhere in the world; Slingbox Player named one of PC World Innovations in 2006, Business Week Best Products of 2005, Time Best Inventions of 2005, Popular Science Best of What's New 2005 & Laptop Best of CES 2005; Slingbox Player has won awards including Mobile Trax Mobility award-Accessories in 2006 and International Consumer Electronics Show Innovations 2006 Design and Engineering Finalist; Sling Media Inc. was chosen by Fortune as one of the 25 Breakout Companies of 2005 and 2006 ACE award Finalist-Start-up Company of Year. Office: Sling Media Inc 901 Mariners Island Blvd Ste 300 San Mateo CA 94404 Office Phone: 650-293-8000. Office Fax: 650-378-4422.

SHAH, BIPIN CHANDRA, banker; b. Bombay, July 23, 1938; s. Manilal and Keshar Shah; m. Fay Shah, 1962 (div. 1985); m. Ellen T. Dever, Sept. 20, 1985 (div. 1992); children: Nelie, Sarah Lynn, Genevieve. BA, Baldwin-Wallace Coll., 1962; MA, U. Pa., 1965. Pres. Vertex Systems, Inc., King of Prussia, Pa., 1970-74; sr. v.p. Fed. Res. Bank, Phila., 1974-78, Am. Express, NYC, 1979-80; exec. v.p. Phila. Nat. Bank, 1980-84, CoreStates Fin. Corp., Phila., 1984-86, vice chmn., 1986-89, COO, 1990-91; pres., CEO Gensar Holdings, Inc., Ft. Washington, Pa., 1992-96; CEO, pres. Genpass, Inc. (formerly Shahdill, Inc.), Fort Washington, Pa., 1996—2005. Bd. dirs. VISA, USA, San Matteo, Calif., Franklin Inst., Phila., Phila. Internat. Bank, N.Y.C., U.S. Pro Indoor Tennis, Phila.; chmn. bd. dirs. CoreStates Bank Del., Wilmington. Fund raiser Phila. Indoor Tennis, 1985-88. Mem. Union League. Republican. Avocations: reading, golf, tennis, fishing.

SHAH, HARESH CHANDULAL, civil engineering educator; b. Godhra, Gujarat, India, Aug. 7, 1937; s. Chandulal M. and Rama Shah; m. Mary-Joan Dersjant, Dec. 27, 1965; children: Hemant, Mihir. BEngring., U. Poona, 1959; MSCE, Stanford U., 1960, PhD, 1963. From instr. to assoc. prof. U. Pa., Phila., 1962-68; assoc. prof. civil engring. Stanford (Calif.) U., 1968-73, prof., 1973—, chmn. dept. civil engring., 1985-94, John A. Blume prof. engring., 1988-91, Obayashi prof. engring., 1991-97, dir. Stanford Ctr. for Risk Analysis, 1987-94, Obayashi prof. engring. emeritus, 1998—. Trustee Geohazards Internat.; bd. dir. OYO-RMS, Inc., Japan, ERS, R.M. Software Ltd., India, Risk Mgmt. Solutions, Inc., World Seismic Safety Initiative, Buildfolio, Inc.; cons. in field; pres. World Seismic Safety Initiative, 1994—. Author 1 book; contbr. over 250 articles to profl. jours. Mem. ASCE, Am. Concrete Inst., Earthquake Engring. Rsch. Inst., Seismol. Soc. Am., Sigma Xi, Tau Beta Pi. Avocations: hiking, climbing, travel. Office: Risk Mgmt Solutions Inc 7015 Gateway Bldg Newark CA 94560 E-mail: hshah@stanford.edu, haresh.shah@rms.com.

SHAH, JAMES M., actuary; b. Amadhara, India, Feb. 4, 1943; arrived in US, 1980; s. Manekchand Keshrichand and Kamuben Manekchand Shah; m. Urmila Jashwantlal Shah, May 16, 1966; children: Meeta, Keena, Jatin. BS, Gujarat U., India, 1965; MS, Gujarat U., 1969; MA, Georgetown U., 1983; MS, U. Nebr., 1986. Sr. rsch. asst. Nat. Inst. Rural Devel., Hyderabad, India, 1972-74; rsch. officer Population Ctr. World Bank Population Project, Bangalore, India, 1974-77; actuarial analyst Shelby Ins. Co., Ohio, 1987-90; actuary ins. dept. State of ND, Bismarck, ND, 1990-91; pres. A S D Consulting Svc., Mansfield, Ohio, 1991—2005; asst. actuary Blue Cross Blue Shield Utica, Utica, NY, 2000; ret., 2005. Contbr. articles to profl. jours. UN fellow Ministry of Fgn. Affairs, 1978; recipient Outstanding Young Person award Garden City Jaycees, 1977, 7th Summer Seminar award U. Hawaii, 1976. Mem. Internat. Actuarial Assn. (cert. 1996), Internat. Union for Sci. Study of Population, Soc. Actuaries (cert. 1994), Am. Acad. Actuaries (cert. 1994). Avocations: travel, reading, ping pong/table tennis. Home: 91 S Ireland Blvd Mansfield OH 44906-2220 Office: ASD Cons Svc 91 S Ireland Blvd Mansfield OH 44906 Personal E-mail: shahjames@hotmail.com.

SHAH, JATIN PREMANAND, head and neck surgeon, educator; b. Visnagar, Gujarat, India, Dec. 31, 1940; came to U.S., 1967; s. Premanand C. and Sarla P. (Mehta) S.; m. Bharti N. Gandhi, May 11, 1967; 1 child, Mili MD, Baroda Med. Coll., India, 1964, MS in Surgery, 1967; PhD (hon.), U. Athens. Diplomate Am. Bd. Surgery. Attending surgeon Meml. Sloan Kettering Cancer Ctr., NYC, 1974—, chief head and neck svc., 1992—, E.W. Strong chair in head and neck oncology; prof. surgery Cornell U. Med. Coll., NYC, 1987—. Vis. prof. Royal Soc. Medicine, London, 1997. Author: Head and Neck Surgery, 1996 (prize Royal Soc. Medicine 1996), rev. edit., 1997 (1st prize Brit. Med. Assn. 1997), 3d edit., 2003 (George D. Howells prize U. London 2003). Hon. fellow in dental surgery Royal Coll. Surgeons Eng. Fellow ACS, Royal Coll. Surgeons Edinburgh (hon.), Royal Australian Coll. Surgeons (hon.); mem. Soc. Head and Neck Surgeons (pres. 1991), Internat. Fedn. Head and Neck Oncological Socs. (bd. dirs. 2002), NY Cancer Soc. (pres. 1984), NY Head and Neck Soc. (pres. 1985), North Am. Skull Base Soc. (pres. 2003), Internat. Acad. Oraloncology (pres. 2005) Office: Meml Sloan Kettering Cancer Ctr 1275 York Ave New York NY 10021-6094

SHAH, NANDLAL CHIMANLAL, retired physiatrist; b. Sadra, Gujarat, India, July 3, 1933; came to U.S., 1969; s. Chimanial D. and Dahiben C. (Shah) Shah; m. Indira N. Shah, May 15, 1960; children: Sandip N., Tushar N. Student, M.G. Sci. Inst., Ahmedabad, India, 1952; MB, BS, B.J. Med. Coll., Ahmedabad, India, 1957. Diplomate Am. Bd. Phys. Medicine and Rehab., Am. Bd. Quality Assurance and Utilization Review Physicians. Intern Yonkers (N.Y.) Gen. Hosp., 1970; resident in internal medicine St. Barnabas Hosp., Bronx, NY, 1971; resident in phys. medicine and rehab. Albert Einstein Coll. Medicine, Bronx, 1971-74; staff physiatrist, dir. med. svcs. Inst. Phys. Medicine and Rehab., Peoria, Ill., 1974-79; med. dir. Thomas Rehab. Hosp., Asheville, NC, 1979-81; staff physiatrist phys. medicine and rehab. Charlotte (N.C.) Inst. Rehab. (formerly Charlotte Rehab. Hosp.), 1981; pvt. practice Carolina Rehab. Clinic, Charlotte, 1981-99, ret., 2001. Mem. Greater Charlotte (N.C.) Assn. Physicians Indian Origin (chartered), N.C. Assn. Physicians Indian Origin (past pres.), Masons. Hindu. Avocations: Indian classical music, cultural and religious programs.

SHAH, RAHUL K., surgeon, researcher; b. Jackson, Mich., Feb. 14, 1975; s. Kanaiyalal R. and Dakshaben K. Shah; m. Banu Abbas Karimi, June 3, 2000; 1 child, Nishrin R. BA, Boston U., MD, 2000. Diplomate Am. Bd. Otolaryngology, 2006. Surg. intern St. Elizabeth Med. Ctr., Boston, 2000—01; otolaryngology resident Tufts-NEMC, Boston, 2001—05, adminstrv. chief resident, 2004—05; fellow in pediatric otolaryngology Children Hosp., Boston, 2005—06; asst. prof. otolaryngology/pediat. Children Nat. Med. Ctr., Washington, 2006—. Mem. task force preoperation Children's Nat. Med. Ctr., Washington, 2007—; others; cons. in field. Contbr. articles to profl. jours. Fellow: Am. Acad. Pediat., Am. Acad. Otolaryngology; mem.: Triologic Soc., Phi Beta Kappa, Alpha Omega Alpha. Office: Childrens Nat Med Ctr Divsn Otolaryngology 111 Michigan Ave NW Washington DC 20010 Office Phone: 202-884-3852.

SHAH, SAURABH B., surgeon; b. Hartlepool, Eng., Feb. 6, 1970; s. Bharat and Sudha Shah; m. Resham Shah, Jan. 6, 2001; children: Amani Devi, Ayanna Kumari. BA in Biology, Stanford U., Palo Alto, Calif., 1991; MD, U. Calif., San Francisco, 1995. Lic. dr. Calif., 1995, Faaoa Am. Acad. Otolaryngic Allergy, 2002. Clin. faculty U. Calif., 2000—03; attending surgeon Granger Med. Clinic, Salt Lake City, 2000—. Fellow: Am. Acad. of Otolaryngology-Head and Neck Surgery (young physician rep. 2002—05). Hindu. Avocations: tennis, skiing, golf, travel. Office: Granger Med Clinic 3725 W 4100 South West Valley City UT 84120 Office Fax: 801-965-3542.

SHAH, SHIRISH KALYANBHAI, computer science, chemistry and environmental science educator; b. Ahmedabad, India, May 24, 1942; came to U.S., 1962, naturalized, 1974; s. Kayyanbhai T. and Sushilaben K. S.; m. Kathleen Long, June 28, 1973; 1 son, Lawrence. BS in Chemistry and Physics, St. Xavier's Coll. Gujarat U., 1962; PhD in Phys. Chemistry, U. Del., 1968; cert. in bus. mgmt., U. Va., 1986; PhD in Cultural Edn. (hon.), World U. West, 1986. Asst. prof. Washington Coll., Chestertown, Md., 1967-68; dir. quality control Vita Foods, Chestertown, Md., 1968-72; asst. prof., assoc. prof. sci., adminstr. food, marine sci. and voc. programs Chesapeake Coll., Wye Mills, Md., 1968-76; rsch. grant Food Tech. Program, 1973—75; assoc. prof., prof. sci., chmn. dept. tech. studies CC Balt., 1976—91; assoc. prof. chemistry Coll. Notre Dame Md., 1991—2002. Cons. joint apprentice com. Balt. City Govt., 1980-91; chmn. computer sys. and engring. techs. CC Balt., 1979-89, project facilitator telecom. curriculum and lab., 1985-89, coord. tech. studies, 1989-91; mem. Balt. City Adult Edn. Adv. Com., 1982-89, Distance Learning Task Force, 1996-97, chmn. Coll. wide computer user com., 1985-91; higher edn. eval. team Mid. Atlantic States Assn., 1987-2006; adj. prof. Phys. Sci. Coppin State Coll., 1996-98; coun. mem. Faculty R&D, 1994-97; reviewer AAAS, 1996-2005, NIH Edn. grant, 2000-02; adj. prof. chemistry Villa Julie Coll., 2002-05; lectr., prof. chemistry Towson U., 1998—, Morgan State U., 1999—. Contbr. numerous sci. projects, articles to profl. jours. Permanent mem. Rep. Senatorial Com.; charter mem. Rep. Presdl. Task Force; mem. Congl. Adv. Com., 1983—; tchr., developer prison programs Patuxent Inst., Jessup, Md., 1982-91; developer joint program for computer aided design between Coll. and HS, 1989-91; adviser Young Reps., 1992-2002. Comm. grant, Mayor's Manpower Office for release of prisoners, 1980—81, Md. Dept. Transp. grant, 1981—82. Fellow Am. Inst. Chemists (co-chair internat. com. 2002); mem. IEEE, APHA, NSTA, Am. Lung Assn. (chair environ. affairs com., 1976-80), Am. Lung Assn. Md. (bd. dir. 1971-80), Am. Chem. Soc. (chmn.-elect Md. sect. 1995-96, chmn. 1996-98, chair kids and chemistry program Md. sect. 1996-99, sec. Mid-Atlantic regional conf., 2002-04, chmn. com. govt. rels. Md. sect. 1998-, chair pub. rels. com. 2000-, pres.-elect Chesapeake sect. 2002-03, co-coord. chemagination program 2005, Phoenix award 1996-97, Pub. Rels. award, 1996, Sci. Policy award, 2000, Salute to Excellence award, 2004, Outstanding Coord. Chemagination, 2005), Indsl. Hygiene Assn. (pres. Chesapeake sect. 2003-04), Nat. Environ. Tng. Assn., Nat. Assn. Indsl. Tech. (dir. local region, bd. dir. 1989-95), Md. Pub. Health Assn. (bd. dir., chair pub. health nursing edn. 2005), Am. Vocat. Assn., Am. Tech. Edn. Assn., Am. Fedn. Tchrs., Md. State Tchrs. Assn., Md. Assn. Cmty. and Jr. Colls. (v.p. 1977-78, pres. 1978-97), Sigma Xi, Epsilon Pi Tau, Iota Lambda Sigma Nu. Roman Catholic. Home: 5605 Purlington Way Baltimore MD 21212-2950 Office: Chemistry Dept Towson University Towson MD 21252-Office Phone: 410-704-2720. Personal E-mail: dr.shah@juno.com. Business E-Mail: sshah@towson.edu.

SHAH, SURENDRA POONAMCHAND, engineering educator; b. Bombay, Aug. 30, 1936; s. Poonamchand C. and Maniben (Modi) S.; m. Dorothie Crispell, June 9, 1962; children: Daniel S., Byron C. BE, B.V.M. Coll. Engring., India, 1959; MS, Lehigh U., 1960; PhD, Cornell U., 1965. Asst. prof. U. Ill., Chgo., 1966-69, assoc. prof., 1969-73, prof., 1973-81; prof. civil engring Northwestern U., Evanston, Ill., 1981—, dir. Ctr. for Advanced Cement Based Materials, 1989—, prof. civil engring., 1989—, Walter P. Murphy prof. of engring., 1992—. Cons. govt. agys. and industry, U.S.A., UN, France, Switzerland, People's Republic China, Denmark, The Netherlands; vis. prof. MIT, 1969, Delft U., The Netherlands, 1976, Denmark Tech. U., 1984, LCPC, Paris, 1986, U. Sidney, Australia, 1987; NATO vis. sci. Turkey, 1992; disting. vis. prof. Nat. Singapore U., 1999, vis. chair prof. Denmark Tech. U., 2002; hon. prof. Hongkong Poly. U, 2003-. Co-author: Fiber Reinforced Cement Composites, 1992, High Performance Concrete and Applications, 1994, Fracture Mechanics of Concrete, 1995; contbr. more than 400 articles to profl. jours.; editor 20 books; mem. editorial bds. 2 internat. jours.; editor-in-chief Jour. Materials and Structures, 2001-05. Recipient Thompson award ASTM, Phila., 1983, Disting. US Vis. Scientist award Alexander von Humboldt Found., 1989, Swedish Concrete award, Stockholm, 1993, Engring. News Record award of Newsmaker, 1995, Charles Perkow award, 1997, Fulbright Lectureship award, India, 2007, Della Roy Lecture, Am. Ceramic Soc., Detroit, 2007; named one of 10 Most Influential Persons, Concrete Constrn., 2006. Fellow Am. Concrete Inst. (chmn. tech. com., Anderson award 1989, 99, Henry Crown award 2000, Symposium in his honor 2002, Robert Philbo award 2006), Internat. Union Testing and Rsch. Labs. Materials and Structures (chmn. tech. com. 1989—, mgmt. adv. bd. 1996—, Gold medal 1980, symposium in his honor 2004); mem. NAE, ASCE (past chmn. tech. com., mem. exec. com., mem. adv. bd., Richard J. Caroll Meml. Lectr. 2001). Achievements include dedicated in his honor RILEM 7th international conference on fiber reinforced concrete and was given a special award, Italy, 2004; symposium in his honor during the 13th European fracture conference in Greece, 2006. Home: 921 Isabella St Evanston IL 60201-1773 Office: Northwestern U Tech Inst Rm A130 2145 Sheridan Rd Evanston IL 60208-0834 Home Phone: 847-475-6858; Office Phone: 847-491-3858. Business E-Mail: s-shah@northwestern.edu.

SHAH, UDAYAN KANAIYALAL, surgeon; b. Lexington, Va., Mar. 6, 1968; s. Kanaiyala Ramanlal and Daksha Kanaiyalal Shah; life ptnr. Barbara Ziv; children: Henry S.U., Silas L.U. MD, Boston U. Sch. Medicine, 1992. Cert. Am. Bd. Otolaryngology-Head & Neck Surgery, 1998. Attending surgeon Children's Hosp. Phila. & U. Pa. Sch. Medicine, 1998—2007, Alfred I duPont Hosp. for Children & Thomas Jefferson U. Sch. Medicine, Wilmington, Del., 2007—. Author: sci. papers in field. Treas. Soc. Ear, Nose and Throat Advances in Children, 2004—. Fellow: ACS, Am. Soc. Pediatric Otolaryngology (mem. program com. 2005—). Office: Alfred I duPont Hosp for Children Divsn Otolaryngology 1600 Rockland Rd Wilmington DE 19803 Home Phone: 215-753-9484; Office Phone: 302-651-5829. Personal E-mail: udayankshah@msn.com. Business E-Mail: ushah@nemours.org.

SHAH, VIVEK, publishing executive; BA, Tufts Univ. Former gen. mgr. dr. fin. exec. group The Fortune Group (now The Fortune/Money Group), also former gen. mgr. Fortune Americas; sr. v.p. CNNMoney.com; pres. digital publ. group The Fortune/Money Group, 2005—07, pres., 2007—. Named one of 40 Under 40, Crain's NY Bus. Mag., 2006; recipient three Fortune awards, Time Inc. Consumer Mktg. Achievement award, two Time Inc. Pres. awards. Office: Fortune/Money Group One Time Warner Ctr New York NY 10019-8016 *

SHAH, Y. T., academic administrator; BSChemE, U. Mich.; MS, ChE, DSc, MIT. Prof. chem. engring. U. Pitts., 1969—87; dean engring. and sci. U. Tulsa, 1987—91; disting. prof., dean Coll. Engring. Drexel U., Phila., 1991—97; sr. vice provost for rsch. and grad. studies, chief rsch. scientist Clemon U., 1997; provost U. Mo., Rolla, 2002—. Mem.: AIChE, Am. Chem. Soc., Am. Soc. Elec. Engring. *

SHAHANI, SUDHIN, entrepreneur, Internet company executive; b. India, 1983; BSBA, Babson Coll., Wellesley, Mass. Founder, mng. ptnr. Ready To Go? Animate, Kolkata, India; founder MyMPO. Ptnr. Animaction India. Named one of Best Entrepreneurs Under 25, BusinessWeek mag., 2006. Achievements include creation of the Musicane service, which allows artists to sell audio, video or ringtones online. Office: MyMPO Ste 1003b 201 Ocean Ave Santa Monica CA 90402 *

SHAHDA GERACI, CAROLE ANNE, retired elementary school educator; d. Isaac Shahda and Mary LeGerda; children: Lorri Lee Geraci, Steven V. Geraci, Christopher B. Geraci. BA, Bklyn Coll., 1956; MS, Addelphi U., 1975. Tchr. art P.S. 145, Bklyn., 1956—63; tchr. elem. sch. Oceanside Sch. Dist., 1965—80, tchr. program gifted children, 1980—88; dir. Oceanside Tchr. Ctr., 1980—90. Pres. Oceanside Fedn. Tchrs., 1988—91. Editor: (newsletters) LWV Beacon, Long Beach Hist. Soc. Heritage. Pres. LWV Nassau County, NY, 2001—04, Long Beach Hist. & Preservation Soc., 2004—, trustee. Named Trailblazer of Millenium, Nassau County Legis., 2002, Citizen of Yr., Kiwanis Club, Long Beach, 2003. Avocations: history, museum house restoration, travel. Home: 410 East Broadway Long Beach NY 11561 Home Phone: 516-889-5347.

SHAHEEN, BILL (WILLIAM HENRY), lawyer; b. Dover, NH, Dec. 30, 1943; s. William Nickolas and Josephine (Skiep) S.; m. Jeanne Shaheen; children: Stefany, Stacey, Molly. BA in History, U. N.H., 1965; JD with honors, U. Miss., 1973; grad. trial atty's. program, Atty. Gen's. Trial Advocacy Inst., 1977. Bar: N.H., Miss., U.S. Dist. Ct. Miss., U.S. Dist. Ct. N.H., U.S. Ct. Appeals (1st cir.), U.S. Supreme Ct. High sch. tchr., Milton, N.H., 1969-70; co-owner Bill and Bob's, York Beach, Maine, 1969-76; assoc. Ovila J. Gregoire, Dover, N.H., 1973-76; city atty. City of Somersworth, N.H., 1974-77; ptnr. Keefe, Dunnington & Shaheen, Dover, 1976-77; US atty. Dist. NH US Dept. Justice, 1977-81; ptnr. Shaheen & Gordon, P.A. (formerly Shaheen, Cappiello, Stein & Gordon, P.A.), Manchester, Dover, Concord, Portsmouth, NH, 1981—; judge Durham (N.H.) Dist. Ct., 1981—96. Mem. U.S. Judge Nomination Panel for 1st Cir. Ct., 1977; bd. govs. Dist. Ct. Judges State of N.H., 1988—; mem. controlled substances conspiracy conf. US Dept. Justice, L.A., 1979; co-chair, Senator Hillary Clinton's New Hampshire Campaign, 2007-Mem. editorial bd. Miss. Law Jour., 1972. Chmn. N.H. Heart Fund Campaign, 1978-79. Capt. U.S. Army, 1965-71. Recipient Annual Award for Excellence in Field of Narcotic and Drug Prosecution, 1980. Mem. Order of Coif, Omega Delta Kappa. Democrat. Roman Catholic. Office: Shaheen & Gordon PA 848 Elm St Ste 303 Manchester NH 03101 E-mail: wshaheen@shaheengordon.com.

SHAHEEN, CHRISTOPHER T., lawyer; b. 1962; BA in Internat. Rels. magna cum laude, Bucknell Univ., 1984; JD cum laude, Harvard Univ., 1987. Bar: Pa. 1989, Minn. 1994. Assoc. Bustamante & Crespo, Ecuador, 1987; law clerk, Hon. Samuel Conti US Dist Ct, No. Dist., Calif., 1988—89; trial atty. US Dept. Justice, civil rights divsn., 1989—94; assoc., litig. dept. Dorsey & Whitney LLP, Mpls., 1994—97, ptnr., trial dept., 1998—, and co-chair, tax, trust, estate litig. group. Bd. dir. Project for Pride in Living, Inc.; chmn. Kenwood Isles Area Assn. Grantee Humphrey Inst. Policy Fellow, Univ. Minn., 1999—2000. Mem.: ABA, Hennepin County Bar Assn., Minn. State Bar Assn. Office: Dorsey & Whitney LLP Ste 1500 50 S Sixth St Minneapolis MN 55402-1498 Office Phone: 612-340-2886. Office Fax: 612-340-2807. Business E-Mail: shaheen.christopher@dorsey.com.

SHAHEEN, GEORGE T., software company executive; b. 1944; BS in Mktg., Bradley U., MBA. With Andersen Worldwide Orgn., 1967—89, mng. ptnr.-cons. for N.Am., 1977—89; mng. ptnr., CEO Andersen Cons. (now Accenture), Chgo., 1989-99; chmn., CEO Webvan Group, Inc., Foster City, Calif., 1999—2001; CEO Siebel Systems, Inc., San Mateo, Calif., 2005—. Bd. dirs. Memec, Siebel Systems, Inc., 1996—; mem. adv. bd. Marcus & Millichap Co. Mem. bd. advisors Northwestern Univ. J.L. Kellogg Grad. Sch. Bus.

SHAHEEN, GERALD L., manufacturing executive; B in Mktg., Bradley U., 1966, M, 1968. With Caterpillar Inc., Peoria, Ill., 1967—, mng. dir. Geneva, Switzerland, 1995, v.p. engring. products divsn. Peoria, 1995, group pres., 1998—. Chmn. bd. dirs. US C. of C.; bd. dir. UtiliCorp United, National City Corp. Office: Caterpillar Inc 100 NE Adams St Peoria IL 61629-0002 Office Phone: 309-692-0822. *

SHAHEEN, JEANNE, political scientist, former governor; b. St. Charles, Mo., Jan. 28, 1947; d. Ivan and Belle Bowers; m. William H. Shaheen; children: Stefany, Stacey, Molly. BA, Shippensburg U., 1969; M of Social Sci. in Polit. Sci., U. Miss., 1973. Campaign mgr. Pres. Jimmy Carter, NH, 1980, Gary Hart, 1984, Gov. Paul McEachon, 1986, 1988; mem. N.H. Senate, 1991-96; gov State of N.H., Concord, 1997—2003; vice chair Democratic Nat. Convention Com., 2004; nat. chair John Kerry Presidl. Campaign, 2004; dir. Inst. Politics Harvard U., Cambridge, Mass., 2005—. Chair Edn. Commn. States, 2000—01. Democrat. Protestant. Office: Inst Politics Kennedy Sch Govt Mailbox 63 75 JFK St Cambridge MA 02138 Office Phone: 617-495-1363. E-mail: jeanne_shaheen@ksg.harvard.edui.

SHAHEEN, SHAHEEN AZEEZ, minister, textiles executive; b. Chgo., Jan. 23, 1928; s. Azeez and Saleemeh (Balluteen) S.; m. Pierina Barbaglia, June 30, 1951; children: John A., David M. BS, Ill. Inst. Tech., 1949. Regional sales Katherine Rug, Dalton, Ga., 1949-53; chmn., pres., founder World Carpets, Inc., Dalton, Ga., 1954-92. Author: World Carpets-The First Thirty Years, 1984; mineral exhbn. Dalton State Coll., Ga., 2000-. Min. Jehovah's Witnesses, 1942--; helped establish Fed. Housing Authority carpet standards, Washington, 1970-75; mem. stay-in-sch. task force Dalwhichcom Found., Dalton, 1984-90; participant, bd. dirs. Harvest Outreach Rehab. Ctrs. for the Homeless, Dalton, 1990-2000; pres., treas. Dalton Land Co., 1982—. Named Permanent Carpet Industry Elected Mem. of World Floor Covering Hall of Fame, World Floor Covering Assn., Anaheim, Calif. Developed modern carpet production and technology with methods and techniques for carpet production in areas of manufacturing, equipment development and innovation, quality assurance, continuous dyeing, product flow, distribution, marketing, merchandising, personell incentives and programs, profit sharing, direct private trucking.

SHAHIDULLAH, MOHAMMAD, medical researcher, medical educator; b. Village Ruhuli, Bangladesh, Nov. 1, 1959; s. Akkel Ali Mondal and Saleha Khatun; m. Sadequn Nahar, Aug. 19, 1988; children: Asif, Archie. PhD, U. Glasgow, 1994; DVM, Bangladesh Agrl. U., 1982. Lectr. pharmacology Bangladesh Agrl. U., Mymensingh, 1983—87, asst. prof., 1987—94, U. Ariz., 2005—, U. Louisville, 2005—06; postdoctoral rsch. fellow U. Glasgow, 1994—2001; rsch. fellow, lectr. Hong Kong Poly. U., Kowloon, 2001—05. Contbr. articles to profl. jours. Recipient U. Prize, Bangladesh Agrl. U., 1985, Rsch. Louisville award, 2005; Merit scholar, Dhaka Edn. Bd., Bangladesh, 1975, Bangladesh Agrl. U., 1977—83, Commonwealth scholar, Assn. Commonwealth Univs. UK, 1990. Mem.: Internat. Soc. Eye Rsch., Fedn. U. Tchrs. Bangladesh, Assn. U. Tchrs. UK, Assn. for Rsch. in Vision and Ophthalmology. Achievements include development of isolated eye preparation as an experiemtal model for diverse ocular research; in vitro eye model to study retinal physiology using multifocal electroretinogram; discovery of link between intracellular calcium movement and aqueous humor formation; first to show in the isolated whole eye preparation that chloride ion is involved in the secretion of eye's aqueous humor; development of novel method of isolating and culturing ocular nonpigmented ciliary epithelial cells. Office: U Ariz Dept Physiology Tucson AZ 85724 Office Phone: 520-626-7351. Office Fax: 620-626-2382. Business E-Mail: shahidua@email.arizona.edu.

SHAHIED, ISHAK I., science educator; BA, Ea. Nazarene Coll., 1959; MS, U. Tenn., 1964; PhD, Colo. State U., 1973. Sr. rsch. chemist Aerospace Med. Rsch. Lab. USAF, Dayton, 1973—74; prof., dept. chmn. St. George's Med. Coll., Grenada, 1977—86; prof. Cleveland Coll., Kansas City, Mo., 1986—89; prof., head biochemist Life U., Marietta, Ga., 1989—94; prof. St. Matthew's Med. Coll., Belize, 1997—98, Ctrl. Bapt. Coll., Conway, Ark., 2001—02; prof., dean basic scis. St. James Sch. Medicine, Bonaire, Netherlands Antilles, 2002—. Tchr. Cleve. Coll., Kansas City, Mo., 1976-77, 86-89. Author: Biochemistry of Foods and the Biocatalysts, 1977, (textbook) Physiology, 1980. Named Hon. fellow Truman Libr. Inst.; recipient Best Instr. award, 1984. Mem. N.Y. Acad. Sci. Avocations: writing, swimming. Home Phone: 011-599-786-1986; Office Phone: 011-599-717-2150. Personal E-mail: shahiedishak@hotmail.com.

SHAICH, RONALD M., food service executive; b. Newark, Dec. 30, 1953; s. Joseph and Pearl (Kalfus) S. AB in Govt., Clark U., 1976; MBA, Harvard U., 1978. Ea. regional mgr. Cole Nat. Corp., Cleve., 1978-80; pres. Targeting Systems, Inc., Washington, 1980-81; owner, pres. The Cookie Jar, Boston, 1981-82; co-founder, co-chmn., co-CEO Au Bon Pain Co., Inc., Boston, 1982—98; co-founder, chmn.; CEO Panera Bread Co. (formerly Saint Louis Bread Co.), Richmond Heights, Mo., 1998—. Bd. dirs. Store 24, Inc., Boston. Trustee Clark U., Worcester, Mass., 1989—; incorporator Mt. Auburn Hosp., Cambridge, Mass.; treas. Mass. Dem. Party, Boston, 1990—. Recipient Golden Plate award, Internat. Foodservice Mfrs. Assn., 2005. Jewish. Avocation: swimming. Office: Panera Bread Co 6710 Clayton Rd Richmond Heights MO 63117

SHAIKH, BAHU SULTAN, physician, educator; b. Karachi, Sind, Pakistan, 1945; came to US, 1969; s. Noor Mohammad and Shahkhatoon Shaikh.; m. Yasmeen Khamisani, 1972 (div. Nov. 1995); children: Maheen, Sasha Ghulam Mohammad; m. Mona Sayed, July 1996; 1 child: Aneesa. Student, St. Patrick's Coll., Karachi, Pakistan, 1963; MBBS, Dow Med. Coll., Karachi, 1968. Intern Ellis Hosp., Schenectady, NY, 1969; resident in internal medicine Thomas Jefferson U., Phila., 1970-72, rsch. fellow, 1972-74; asst. prof. coll. medicine Penn State U., Hershey, Pa., 1974-80; assoc. prof. Med. Coll. Ohio, Toledo, 1980-87, clin. assoc. prof., 1987—99, clin. prof., 1999—. Cons. Toledo Clinic, Ohio, 1987—. Contbr. several chpts. in books related to cancer and AIDS, 1983-87, numerous articles to prof. jours. Recipient Key to the Golden Door award, Internat. Inst. Greater Toledo, 1999. Fellow. ACP, Pakistan Acad. Med. Scis.; mem. Am. Soc. Clin. Oncology, Am. Soc. Hematology, Assn. Internat. Physicians of NW Ohio,, Assn. Pakistani Physicians N.Am. Office: Toledo Clinic 4235 Secor Rd Toledo OH 43623-4299 Office Phone: 419-479-5605.

SHAIKUN, MICHAEL GARY, lawyer; b. Ky., Mar. 17, 1942; s. Leon J. and Cleo (Taub) S.; m. Phyllis Miriam Cohen, Aug. 21, 1964; children: Benjamin, Stephanie, Alissa. BS in Econs. with highest honors, U. Pa., 1963; JD, Harvard U., 1966. Bar: Ky. 1966, U.S. Dist. Ct. (we. dist.) Ky. 1966. Assoc. Greenebaum Doll & McDonald PLLC, Louisville, 1966-69, mem., 1970—. Contbr. articles to profl. jours. Bd. dirs. Jewish Cmty. Fedn. Louisville, 1971—, past pres., YMCA Safe Place Svcs., 1995—; past chmn. Found. for Planned Giving, Jewish Cmty. Fedn., Louisville. Mem. ABA, Ky. Bar Assn., Louisville Bar Assn. Democrat. Jewish. Avocation: computers. Home: 5907 Burlington Ave Louisville KY 40222-6118 Office: Greenebaum Doll & McDonald PLLC 3500 National City Tower Louisville KY 40202 Home Phone: 502-425-3326; Office Phone: 502-587-3540. Business E-Mail: MGS@gdm.com.

SHAIMAN, MARC, composer, arranger, orchestrator; b. Newark, Oct. 22, 1959; s. William Robert and Claire (Goldfein) Shaiman; life ptnr. Scott Wittman. Vocal arranger for Bette Midler, musical dir. & co-prodr. Arranger, musical dir.: (Broadway concerts/revues) Peter Allen: Up in One, 1979, Bette! Divine Madness, 1979, Andre De Shield's Harlem Nocturne, 1984, An Evening with Harry Connick Jr. & His Orchestra, 1990, Patti LuPone on Broadway, 1995, (Broadway plays) Leader of the Pack, 1985, composer & lyricist: Hairspray, 2002 (Drama Desk awards for Outstanding Music & Lyrics, 2003, Tony award for Best Original Score, 2003, Grammy award for Best Musical Show Album, 2003), Martin Short: Fame Becomes Me, 2006, composer: The Odd Couple, 2005; Arranger (films) Beaches, 1988, When Harry Met Sally, 1989 (ASCAP award, 1990), composer: Misery, 1990, Scenes from a Mall, 1991, City Slickers, 1991 (ASCAP award, 1992), The Addams Family, 1991 (ASCAP award, 1992), Sister Act, 1992 (ASCAP award, 1993), Mr. Saturday Night, 1992, A Few Good Men, 1992 (ASCAP award, 1993), Sleepless in Seattle, 1993 (Acad. award nominee), Heart & Souls, 1993, Addams Family Values, 1993, City Slickers II: The Legend of Curly's Gold, 1994, North, 1994, Speechless, 1994, Stuart Saves His Family, 1995, Forget Paris, 1995, The American President, 1995 (Acad. award nominee), Bogus, 1996, Mother, 1996, The First Wives Club, 1996 (ASCAP award, 1996, Acad. award nominee), Ghosts of Mississippi, 1996, George of the Jungle, 1997 (ASCAP award, 1997), In & Out, 1997, My Giant, 1998, Simon Birch, 1998, Patch Adams, 1998 (ASCAP award, 1998, Acad. award nominee), The Out-of-Towners, 1999, South Park: Bigger, Longer & Uncut, 1999 (Acad. award nominee, LA Film Critics Assn. award for Best Music, 1999, Chgo. Film Critics Assn. award for Best Original Score, 2000, Online Film Critics Soc. Award for Best Original Score, 2000), The Story of Us, 1999, The Kid, 2000, One Night at McCool's, 2001, Down with Love, 2003, Alex & Emma, 2003, Rumor Has It, 2005, Hairspray, 2007, (TV series) What's Alan Watching?, 1989, (TV miniseries) From the Earth to the Moon, 1998, (TV movies) Jackie's Back!, 1999, 61*, 2001; Assoc. prodr. (films) Sister Act 2: Back in the Habit, 1993, exec. prodr.: Hairspray, 2007; Actor: (TV series) Saturday Night Live, 1986-89, (films) Broadcast News, 1987, Beaches, 1988, Scenes from a Mall, 1991, Hot Shots!, 1991,The Addams Family, 1991, Mr. Saturday Night, 1992, Heart & Souls, 1993, North, 1994, The Wedding Planner, 2001, Down with Love, 2003; Albums include: (with Bette Midler) Thighs & Whispers, 1979, Mud Will Be Flung Tonight, 1985, Some People's Lives, 1990, For the Boys, 1991, Experience the Divine, 1993, Bathhouse Betty, 1998, 3 for One, 2000, Bette, 2000, (with Harry Connick, Jr.) We Are in Love, 1990, It Had to be You, 1999, Come by Me, 2000. Recipient Emmy award for Outstanding Individual Achievement in Writing a Variety or Music Program, 1992, Hollywood Film award for Outstanding Achievement in Music in Film, Hollywood Film Festival, 2002, Harry Mancini Career Achievement award, ASCAP, 2007. Address: Kelly Bush Pub Rels 2047 Glencoe Way Los Angeles CA 90068-3129 also: The Kraft-Benjamin Agency 345 N Maple Dr Ste 385 Beverly Hills CA 90210-3869 *

SHAIN, IRVING, retired chemicals executive, academic administrator; b. Seattle, Jan. 2, 1926; s. Samuel and Selma (Blockoff) S.; m. Mildred Ruth Udell, Aug. 31, 1947; children: Kathryn A., Steven T., John R., Paul S. BS in Chemistry, U. Wash., 1949, PhD in Chemistry, 1952. From instr. to prof. U. Wis., Madison, 1952-75, vice chancellor, 1970-75, chancellor, 1977-86; provost, v.p. acad. affairs U. Wash., Seattle, 1975-77; v.p. Olin Corp., Stamford, Conn., 1987-92, ret., 1992, also bd. dirs. Mem. tech. adv. bd. Johnson Controls, Inc., Milw., 1980-2003; trustee Univ. Rsch. Park, Inc., Madison, pres., 1984-86, v.p., 1987—; mem. Nat. Commn. on Superconductivity, 1989-90. Contbr. articles on electroanalytical chemistry to profl. jours. Bd. dirs. Madison Gen. Hosp., 1972-75; v.p. Madison Cmty. Found., 1984-86; mem. CEO adv. bd. Kamehameha Schs./Bishop Estates, 2002-04; mem. bd. dirs. Madison Symphony Orch., 2006-. With U.S. Army, 1943-46, PTO. Fellow AAAS, Wis. Acad. Scis., Arts and Letters; mem. Am. Chem. Soc., Electrochem. Soc., Conn. Acad. Sci. and Engring., Phi Beta Kappa, Sigma Xi, Phi Kappa Phi, Alpha Chi Sigma (Chemistry Hall of Fame 2006-). Home: 2820 Marshall Ct # 8 Madison WI 53705-2270 Office Phone: 608-441-8000. E-mail: i.shain@att.net.

SHAIN, KENNETH STEPHEN, management consultant, executive, writer; b. Bridgeport, Conn., Sept. 24, 1952; s. Albert Benjamin and Gladys Ann (Lustig) S.; m. Nancie Ann Taylor, Apr. 1983 (div. Dec. 2002); children: Ian Alexander, Kevin Mitchell, Andrew Thomas. BA, U. Mass., 1978. Prin. Shain Assocs., Atlanta, 1982—87, 1993—; chmn., pres. Geovision, Inc., Norcross, Ga., 1985—93, cons.; pres. Cyco Internat., Inc., Atlanta, 1995—98; CEO MENSI, Inc., Atlanta, 1999—2001; pres. XOBOX Corp., 2001—, cons.; v.p. sales, mktg. and bus. devel. Synaps, Inc., Atlanta, 2002—03; pres. SMB Automation, Inc., 2004—05; COO OrthoCure, Inc., 2006—. Chmn. mech. engring. curriculum com. Gov.'s High-Tech Adv. Coun., State of Ga., 1984. Recipient Cert. Appreciation Gov.'s Office of Ga., 1985, Arthur Andersen Best Bus. Practices award, 1998. Mem. Soc. Mfg. Engrs. (sr., chmn. 1983-84), Computer and Automated Sys. Assn. (sr.), Nat. Info. Stds. Orgn., Southeastern Software Assn., ACM Siggraph. Office Phone: 770-841-0700. E-mail: kenshain@comcast.net.

SHAINWALD, SYBIL, lawyer; b. NYC, Apr. 27, 1928; d. Samuel and Anne; m. Sidney Shainwald; children: Robert, Louise, Laurie, Marsha. BA, Coll. William and Mary, 1948; MA, Columbia U., 1972; JD, N.Y. Law Sch., 1976, LLD (hon.), 2000. Bar: N.Y. 1976. Pvt. practice, NYC, 2005—. Legal advisor Am. Found. for Maternal Child and Health; adj. prof. dept. law Baruch Coll., 1981—82. Co-editor: Jour. Women and Health; contbr. articles to profl. jours. Active Abortion Rights Action; co-founder, bd. mem. Trial Lawyers for Pub. Justice, 1982—88; bd. mem. Hysterectomy Edn. Resources and Svcs., 1985—, Dalkon Shield INfo. Network, Nat. Network to Prevent Birth Defects, No. Ariz. Sch. Midwifery, 1989—; bd. advisors Med. Legal Aspects of Breast Implants; bd. dirs. Consumer Interest Rsch. Inst.; fellow Roscoe Pound Inst., Morgan Libr.; trustee Civil Justice Found., 1998—99; bd. dirs. Am. Friends of Tel Aviv Mus., 2000, Friends of Tel Aviv Mus., 2000-; trustee N.Y. Law Sch., 2000—; adv. bd. Southampton The Hamptons Shakespeare Festival, 2000—; co-chair Take Home a Nude N.Y. Acad. Art, 2001; active Sybil Shainwald Charitable Found., N.Y.C. Comptrs. Health Task Force. Recipient Susan B. Anthony award, NOW; grantee, Nat. Endowment for the Humanities, Rockefeller Found., Gov. W. Averell Harriman; scholar Pres. Bryan scholar, Coll. of William and Mary, Edward Coles scholar. Mem.: ATLA (chair environ. and toxic tort sect. 1988—89, co-chair breast implant litigation group 1992—2000, mem. Dalkon shield litigation group 1995, mem. contraceptive implant litigation group 1995, co-chair DES litigation group, environ. law adv. com.), N.Y. State Trial Lawyers (bd. govs.), Assn. of the Bar of the City of N.Y. (judge nat. moot ct. competition 1988—2003), Soc. Med. Jurisprudence, Health Action Internat.-U.S. (co-founder, mem. steering com.), Lawyers Com. for Human Rights, Am. Soc. Law, Medicine and Ethics, Nat. Women's Health Alliance (pres.), Nat. Women's Health Network (bd. mem. 1980—86, chair litigation svc. 1980—86, chair health law and regulation 1981—88, chmn. bd. dirs. 1982—86, chair N.Y. state affiliate), Phi Beta Kappa. Avocations: art, music. Home: 955 5th Ave 15B New York NY 10021 Office: Law Offices of Sybil Shainwald 111 Broadway 4th Fl New York NY 10006 Business E-Mail: shainwaldlaw@aol.com.

SHAKEEL, ARIF, computer company executive; BSME, Memphis State U., 1977; MBA, Pepperdine U., 1982. From product mgr. to v.p. positions in various areas Western Digital Corp., Lake Forest, Calif., 1985—2001, pres., 2002—, COO, 2003—05, CEO, 2005—07, bd. dir., 2004—, spl. adv. to CEO, 2007—. Bd. dir. Share Our Selves, Calif. Office: Western Digital Corp 20511 Lake Forest Dr Lake Forest CA 92630-7741

SHAKELY, JOHN BOWER (JACK SHAKELY), foundation executive; b. Hays, Kans., Jan. 9, 1940; s. John B. and Martha Jean (Gaston) S.; 1 child, Benton. BA, U. Okla., 1962. Vol. Peace Corps., Costa Rica, 1963-64; editor publs. Dept. Def., 1967-68; dir. devel. U. Okla., 1968-70, Resthaven Mental Health Ctr., LA, 1970-74; pres. Jack Shakely Assocs., LA, 1974-75; sr. adv. Grantsmanship Ctr., LA, 1975-79, Coun. on Founds., Washington, 1979; pres. Calif. Community Found., LA, 1980—. Lectr. in field. Bd. dirs. Emergency Loan and Assistance Fund, 1985—, chair bd. dirs., 1988-93; mem., vice chair L.A. Am. Indian Commn.; bd. dirs. So. Calif. Assn. Philanthropy, 1980—, Comic Relief, 1987—; chmn. bd. dirs. Nonprofit Channel. Served to 1st lt. U.S. Army, 1965-68. Decorated Army Commendation medal; named Nat. Philanthropy Day Outstanding Exec., L.A. Com. Nat. Philanthropy Day, 1989. Office: 445 S Figueroa St Ste 3400 Los Angeles CA 90071-1638

SHAKER, WILLIAM HAYGOOD, marketing professional, public policy reformer; b. Downey, Calif., Apr. 22, 1938; s. Elmer S. and Marylee Shaker; m. Joanna Drummond, Jan. 28, 1966; children: Catherine Patricia, Marylee, Marcus, Matthew. *Children include: Catherine Patricia (Shaker) Scanlon (SA, NVCC), Marylee (Shaker) Verdi (BA, GMU; BSN, Gerogetown University), twin sons, Marcus Shaker (BS, JMU; MD, University of Virginia) and Matthew Shaker (BS, JMU; MS George Washington University). Biographies of William's great-grandfather, Bishop Atticus Haygood (b. 1839), great-aunt, Laura Haygood (b. 1845), and wife, Joanna's great-great-great-grandfather, George Taylor, are published in Marquis' Who Was Who in America.* BS in Engring., U. So. Calif., 1964; MS in Engring., U. Mich., 1969. Registered profl. engr., Calif. Exec. Dow Chem. Co., Midland, Mich., 1966-78; v.p. Nat. Legal Ctr. for the Pub. Interest, Washington, 1979; exec. v.p. Nat. Tax Limitation Com., Washington, 1980-86; pres. Am. Coun. for Health Care Reform, Arlington, Va., 1982—, Heart to Heart Found., Arlington, 1982—; CEO Washington Mktg. Group, Arlington, 1987—, The List Store, Arlington; pres. Health PAC, Arlington, 1994—. Pres. RepublicanPac.com, 2000—, Rule of Law Com., 2001—. Author: Health Care Reform, 1994, also legis. and govt. publs.; editor: Electric Power Reform, 1979; editor, pub. millennium edit. The Man of Galilee, 2001; contbr. articles to profl. jours. Founder, chmn. Taxpayers United, Mich., 1972-84. Mem. Govtl. Rsch. Assn. (most effective presentation of govtl. rsch. award 1973), Direct Mktg. Assn. (Echo award 1982-97, Maxi award 1987-2006), Pub. Rels. Soc. (Silver Anvil 1979), Am. Conservative Union (Health Care Reform award 1995), Am. Assn. Polit. Consultants (Silver and Bronze Pollie awards 2007). Republican. Lutheran. Home Phone: 703-241-8422; Office Phone: 703-534-9331. E-mail: william.shaker@twmg.com.

SHAKESPEARE, FRANK, ambassador; b. NYC, Apr. 9, 1925; s. Francis Joseph and Frances (Hughes) S.; m. Deborah Anne Spaeth, Oct. 9, 1954; children: Mark, Andrea, Fredricka. BS, Holy Cross Coll., 1945; D.Eng. (hon.), Colo. Sch. Mines, 1975; DCS (hon.), Pace U., 1979; LLD (hon.), Del. Law Sch., 1980, Sacred Heart U., 1985, U. Dallas, 1987, Pepperdine U., 1990, Nichols Coll., 1991, Marquette U., 1993; D of Pub. Svc. (hon.), Hillsdale Coll., 1996. Formerly pres. CBS-TV Services; exec. v.p. CBS-TV Stas.; dir. USIA, 1969-73; exec. v.p. Westinghouse Electric Corp., 1973-75; pres. RKO Gen. Inc., NYC, 1975-85, vice chmn., 1983-85; U.S. ambassador to Portugal Lisbon, 1985-87; U.S. ambassador to The Holy See Vatican City, 1987-89. Chmn. Heritage Found., 1975-85, dir., 1989—; chmn. Radio Free Europe/Radio Liberty, Inc., 1976-85; dir. Bradley Founhd., 1989—. Served to lt. (j.g.) USNR, 1945-46. Mem.: Union League. Home: 303 Coast Blvd La Jolla CA 92037-4630

SHAKESPEARE, VALERIE MONROE, curator, director, art gallery owner; b. Kalamazoo, Mar. 30, 1947; d. Monroe Shakespeare and Martha Ellen Wright; m. R. Tery Fugate-Wilcox, Nov. 1, 1963. Student, Ariz. State U., Tempe, 1961—63. Owner Little Rm. Gallery, Galesburg, Mich., 1964—68, Fvlcrvm Gallery, SoHo, NY, 1993—97, Shakespeare's Fvlcrvm, SoHo, 1997—2001, Trbeca, NY, 2001—05; dir./curator Candlewood Lake Art Ctr., New Fairfield, Conn., 2005—. Chmn. ann. arts festival Kalamazoo C. of C., 1965; jr. com. Guggenheim Mus., New York, 1978—89; guest curator Gallery of City of NY, 1987; pres. New Art Found., New York, 1990—; bd. dirs., moderator Artists Talk on Art, New York, 1990—99. Contbr. articles to profl. jours. Vol. aux. policewoman NYPD, 1979—97; benefit com. Mothers for More Halfway Houses, New York, 1980—85, Night of 100 Trees, New York, 1985—90, Vols. for Schs., New York, 1983—89, South St. Seaport for Muscular Dystrophy, New York, 1986—86. Fellow: Mus. Modern Art (patron 1978—), Whitney Mus.; mem.: Aldrich Mus., Guggenheim Mus. (assoc.; patron 1979—). Avocations: cooking, sewing, horseback riding. Office: Actual Art Found 48 1/2 East 7th St Ste 7 New York NY 10003 Office Phone: 212-966-6848. Personal E-mail: fvlcrvm@aol.com.

SHAKIR, FAIZ, writer, political blogger; BA in Govt., Harvard Univ.; JD, Georgetown Univ. Comm. aide White House Office Nat. Drug. Control Policy; legis. aide, Senate Veterans Affairs Com. Senaor Bob Graham; rsch. assoc. Dem. Nat. Com.; rsch. dir. Ctr. for Am. Progress, Washington, and editor, ThinkProgress.org, also, asst. editor to editor, The Progress Report. Contbr. articles to Jerusalem Post, Fla. Today, and Salon. Office: Think Progress Ctr Am Progress Action Fund 1333 H St NW 10th Fl Washington DC 20005 Office Phone: 202-682-1611. Business E-Mail: faiz@thinkprogress.org. *

SHAKIRA, (SHAKIRA ISABEL MEBARAK RIPOLL), musician; b. Barranquilla, Colombia, Feb. 2, 1977; Actor: (TV series) El Oasis, 1996; musician: (albums) Magia, 1991, Peligro, 1994, Pies descalzos, 1995, The Remixes, 1995, Dónde Están Los Ladrones?, 1998, MTV Unplugged, 2000, Laundry Service, 2001, Grandes éxitos, 2002, Live & Off the Record, 2004, Fijación Oral Vol. 1, 2005 (Latin Pop Album of Yr., Billboard Music Awards, 2005, Grammy Award for Best Lation Rock/Alternative Album, 2006, Spanish Album of Yr., Nat. Coun. La Raza ALMA award (Am. Latin Media Arts), 2006, Latin Pop Album of Yr., Billboard Latin Music Awards, 2006, Latin Grammy award album of yr., 2006, Latin Grammy award best female pop vocal album, 2006), Oral Fixation Vol. 2, 2005, (songs) La Tortura (Latin Song of Yr., Billboard Music Awards, 2005, 4 Billboard Latin Music awards: Hot Latin Song, Hot Latin Vocal Duet, Latin Pop Airplay Song for Duo, Latin Ringtone, 2006, Latin Grammy award record of yr., 2006, Latin Grammy award song of yr., 2006), Hips Don't Lie (MTV Video Music award for Best Choreography, 2006, Billboard Latin Music award for Hot Latin Duet of Yr., 2007). Global Goodwill Amb. UNICEF, 2003—; founder Pies Descalzos, 1996, 3 elementary schools, Colombia. Named Latin Pop Album Artist of Yr., Billboard Music Awards, 2005, Outstanding Female Musical Performer, Nat. Coun. La Raza ALMA award (Am. Latin Media Arts), 2006; recipient Eres award, pop singer of yr., 1997, Casandra award, best Latin female singer, 1997, Best Latin Artist, World Music Awards, 1998, Best Latin Female Artist, 2003, Best Female Pop Artist, Billboard Latin Music Awards, 1999, Spirit of Hope award, 2006, Gardel award, 2000, Nickelodeon Kids Choice award, 2000, Echo award, best female pop artist, 2003, Luna award, best Latin pop artist, 2003, Favorite Latin Music Artist, Am. Music Awards, 2005, Best Female award, MTV Europe Awards, 2005, Best Latin Entertainer, Internat. Reggae & World Music Awards, 2006, Favorite Latin Music Artist, Am. Music Awards, 2006, Favorite Pop Song-Hips Don't Lie, People's Choice Awards, 2007. Office: c/o Sony Music Entertainment 10 Great Marlborough St London W1F 7LP England Office Phone: 212-833-8000. *

SHAKLEY, ELAINE M., organist, department chairman; b. Boswell, Pa., Dec. 23, 1922; d. John Henry and Pearl Beatrice Morrison; m. Glenn Huling Shakley; children: Susan, Bonnie, Pam. MusB, Heidelberg Coll., Tiffin, Ohio, 1944; MA, Case Western Res. U., Cleve., 1965. Music supr. K-1 Northfield Pub. Schs., Ohio, 1944—45, music supr. K-12, 1959—74; music tchr. Roosevelt Jr. HS, Cleveland Heights, Ohio, 1944—46; music cons. Cleveland Heights, 1959—74; adj. prof. Cleve. State U., 1961—99; music tchr. Chagrin Falls Pub. Schs., Ohio, 1974—83; tchr. WVIZ-TV, Cleve., 1965—66; organist Fed. Ch. Chagrin Falls, Ohio, 1965—93, Chagrin Falls United Meth. Ch., 1993—2004; music dir. First English Luth. Ch., Cleveland Heights, 1959—63; bell choir dir. Federated Ch., Chagrin Falls, Ohio, 1974—93. Chmn. Chagrin Valley Nat. Piano Auditions, Cleve., 1998—2007. Composer: (songs) April, 1944, Mass in Pentatonic, 1970; prodr., writer script for songs; author: various music courses of study. Chmn. Musical Club Jr. Divsn., Cleve., 1996—2006, Fortnightly Chagrin Valley Jr. Divsn., Cleve., 1998—2007. Recipient Alumni Excellence award, Heidelberg Coll., 2002; grantee, Martha Holden Jennings Found., 1966. Achievements include restarting string education in Chagrin Falls school system. Avocations: knitting, swimming, walking. Home and Office: 7662 Birchmont Dr Chagrin Falls OH 44022 Office Phone: 440-247-6223. Personal E-mail: eshakley@aol.com.

SHAKNO, ROBERT JULIAN, hospital and social services administrator; b. Amsterdam, Holland, Aug. 15, 1937; came to U.S., 1939, naturalized, 1944; s. Rudy C. and Gertrude S.; m. Linda, June 10, 1962; children: Steven Lee, Deborah Sue. BBA (scholar 1955), So. Methodist U., 1959; M.H.A., Washington U., St. Louis, 1961. Adminstrv. asst. Mt. Sinai Hosp., Chgo., 1961—63; asso. adminstr. Tex. Inst. Rehab. and Research, Houston, 1963—65; asst. adminstr. Michael Reese Hosp., Chgo., 1965—70, v.p., hosp. dir., 1970—73; asso. exec. dir. Cook County Hosp., Chgo., 1973—75; pres. Hackensack Med. Center, NJ, 1975—85, Mt. Sinai Med. Ctr., Cleve., 1985—96; dir. nat. strategy practice KPMG Peat Marwick, 1996-98; v.p. med. affairs, vice dean sch. of medicine Case Western Res. U., 1998—2002; pres., CEO Jewish Family Svc., Cleve., 2002—05; ptnr. Tatum Ptnrs., LLC, Deerfield, Ill., 2005—. Bd. dirs. Ohio Hosp. Inc. Co. Mem. editorial bd. Mgmt. Series, Am. Coll. Healthcare Execs. Mem. Leadership Cleve.; bd. dirs. Premier Hosp. Alliance, chmn., 1994-96; bd. dirs. The New Cleve. Inc., Univ. Circle Inc., Cleve., Cleve. Sight Ctr.; trustee Hope Lodge, Cleve. chpt. Am. Cancer Soc.; chmn. elect, bd. dirs. Jewish Family Svcs.; chmn. social svcs. divsn. United Jewish Appeal, Cleve., 1987-88, chmn. health cabinet, 1990, gen. co-chmn., 1990—; chmn. Hosp. Pacesetter campaign United Way, chmn. health svcs. portfolio, 1988-89, oversight commn., 1992-93; bd. trustees Mount Sinai Health Sys., Chgo., 2006-. Served to 1st lt. USAR, 1960-66. Named Young Adminstr. of Yr., Washington U., 1968 Fellow Am. Coll. Hosp. Adminstrs.; mem. Am. Hosp. Assn. (coun. urban hosps., del. coun. on met. hosps., rep. regional policy bd.), Washington U. Alumni Assn. (past pres.), Greater Cleve. Hosp. Assn. (bd. dirs.), Ohio Hosp. Assn. (bd. dirs.), Cleve. Sight Ctr. (trustee, bd. dirs.), Sigma Alpha Mu (past pres.). Home: 908 Island Ct Deerfield IL 60015 Office Phone: 312-909-2022. Personal E-mail: lbs1shak@sbcglobal.net.

SHAKOW, ALEXANDER, economist, government official; b. Apr. 12, 1937; s. David and Sophie (Harap) S.; m. Patricia Connell, Dec. 26, 1967; children: John, Peter, Thomas. BA with honors, Swarthmore Coll., 1958; PhD in Internat. Rels./Econ. Devel., London Sch. Econs., 1962. Assoc., dep., then dir. Indonesia program U.S. Peace Corps, Washington and Jakarta, Indonesia, 1963-65, asst., dep. then dir. Office Vol. Tng. Washington, 1965-67; dir. Office Indonesia Affairs-Office Asia Devel. Planning, US AID, Washington, 1968-74, dep. asst. adminstr., then asst. adminstr. program-policy, 1974-81; spl. policy advisor, chief policy unit, sr. advisor internat. econ. affairs World Bank, Washington, 1981-85, chief internat. econ. affairs, 1985-87, dir. strategic planning and rev., dir. external affairs, 1987-94, exec. sec. World Bank/IMF devel. com., 1995—2002; dep. sec. World Bank group World Bank/IMF, 1997—2002, acting v.p., sec., 2001—02; ind. cons., 2002—. Chmn. bd. sci. and tech. for internat. devel. NAS, Washington, 1989-95; bd. Enterprise Works/VITA, 2003—. Bd. trustees Inst. Devel. Studies, Sussex, Eng., 1991-2002, hon. gov., 2002—. Recipient William A. Jump Meritorious award for outstanding pub. svc. William A. Jump Meml. Found., 1967. Mem. Am. Friends London Sch. Econs. (founding). Avocations: carpentry, gardening, reading. Fax: 301-933-3218. E-mail: ashakow@comcast.net.

SHAKOW, DAVID JOSEPH, lawyer, educator; b. NYC, May 26, 1945; s. Jacob and Rae (Levine) S.; m. Kineret Piltch, Aug. 3, 1980; children: Rachel Esther, Chava Leah, Yaakov, Tuvia Simcha, Rivka Sara, Chana Miriam. BA, Harvard U., 1967, JD, 1970; LLM, NYU, 1976. Bar: NY 1971. Law clk. to Hon. William H. Hastie, Phila., 1970-71; assoc. Davis Polk & Wardwell, NYC, 1971-77; atty., adviser Office Tax Legis. Counsel US Treasury, Washington, 1977-79, assoc. tax legis counsel, 1979-80, dep. tax legis. counsel, 1980-81; assoc. prof. U. Pa., Phila., 1981-87, prof. law, 1987-2000, prof. law emeritus, 2000—; of counsel King & Spalding, Washington, 1998-99; dir. KPMG, Washington, 2000—05; of counsel McKee Nelson LLP, NYC, 2005—. Author: The Taxation of Corporations, Partnerships, and Their Owners, 2d edit., 1997; co-reporter Taxation of Pass-through Entities, Am. Law Inst. Fed. Income Tax Project, 1994-99. Office: McKee Nelson LLP One Battery Park Plz New York NY 10004 Business E-Mail: dshakow@mckeenelson.com.

SHALALA, DONNA EDNA, academic administrator, former secretary of health and human services; b. Cleve., Feb. 14, 1941; d. James Abraham and Edna (Smith) S. AB, Western Coll., 1962; MSSC, Syracuse U., 1968, PhD, 1970; 39 hon. degrees, 1981-91. Vol. Peace Corps, Iran, 1962-64; asst. prof. polit. sci. CUNY, 1970-72; assoc. prof. politics and edn. Tchrs. Coll. Columbia U., 1972-79; asst. sec. for policy devel. & rsch. US Dept. Housing & Urban Devel., Washington, 1977-80; prof. polit. sci., pres. Hunter Coll., CUNY, 1980-87; prof. polit. sci., chancellor U. Wis., Madison, 1987-93; sec. US Dept. Health & Human Services, Washington, 1993-2001; pres. U. Miami, 2001—. Dir., treas. Mcpl. Assistance Corp. NYC, 1975—77; co-chair Pres. Commn. on Care for Am. Returning Wounded Warriors, 2007—. Author: Neighborhood Governance, 1971, The City and the Constitution, 1972, The Property Tax and the Voters, 1973, The Decentralization Approach, 1974. Mem. Trilateral Commn., 1988—92, Knight Commn. on Intercollegiate Sports, 1989—91; bd. govs. Am. Stock Exch., 1981—87; trustee TIAA, 1985—89, Com. Econ. Devel., 1982—92, Brookings Inst., 1989—92; bd. dirs. Children's Def. Fund, 1980—93, Am. Ditchley Found., 1981—93, Spencer Found., 1988—92, M&I Bank of Madison, 1991—92, NCAA Found., 1991, Inst. Internat. Econs., 1981—, Gannett Co., Inc., McLean, Va., United Health Group, Mpls., Lennar Corp., Miami; trustee emeritus Kennedy Ctr. Bd. of Trustees, Washington. Ohio Newspaper Women's scholar, 1958, Western Coll. Trustee scholar, 1958-62; Carnegie fellow, 1966-68; Guggenheim fellow, 1975-76; recipient Disting. Svc. medal Columbia U. Tchrs. Coll., 1989. Mem. ASPA, Am. Polit. Sci. Assn., Nat. Acad. Arts and Scis., Nat. Acad. Pub. Adminstrn., Coun. Fgn. Rels., Nat. Acad. Edn. (Spencer fellow 1972-73), Inst. Medicine (coun. mem. 2006-). Office: U Miami Office Pres 230 Ashe Bldg Coral Gables FL 33146 E-mail: dshalala@miami.edu. *

SHALHOUB, TONY, actor, television producer; b. Green Bay, Wis., Oct. 9, 1953; m. Brooke Adams, 1992; 1 child, Sophie 1 stepchild, Josie. Grad., U. So. Maine, 1977; attended, Yale U. Actor: (Broadway plays) The Odd Couple, 1985, The Heidi Chronicles; (plays) Waiting for Godot, For Dear Life, Zero Positive, Rameau's Nephew, 1988, Conversations with My Father, 1992, The Scene, 2007; (films) Longtime Companion, 1990, Quick Change, 1990, Barton Fink, 1991, Honeymoon in Vegas, 1992, Searching for Bobby Fischer, 1993, Addams Family Values, 1993, I.Q., 1994, Big Night, 1996 (Nat. Soc. Film Critics award best supporting actor, 1996), Men in Black, 1997, Gattaca, 1997, A Life Less Ordinary, 1997, Primary Colors, 1998, Paulie, 1998, The Siege, 1998, The Impostors, 1998, A Civil Action, 1998, The Tic Code, 1998, The Man Who Wasn't There, 2001, Spy Kids, 2001, Thir13en Ghosts, 2001, Men in Black II, 2002, Life or Something Like It, 2002, Impostor, 2002, Something More, 2003, Against the Ropes, 2003, Spy Kids 3-D: Game Over, 2003, T for Terrorist, 2003, The Great New Wonderful, 2005, (voice) Cars, 2006, Maybe It's in the Water, 2006, Careless, 2007; actor, dir.: (films) Made-Up, 2002; actor: (TV films) Alone in the Neon Jungle, 1988, Money, Power, Murder, 1989, Day One, 1989, Gypsy, 1993, Radiant City, 1996, That Championship Season, 1999, The Heart Department, 2001, (video game) Fallout: A Post-Nuclear Role-Playing Game, 1997; (TV series) Wings, 1991—97, Stark Raving Mad, 1999—2000, Monk, 2002— (Golden Globe award, 2002, Emmy award best actor in a comedy, 2003, Screen Actors Guild Award for best actor in a comedy series, 2004, Screen Actors Guild award, outstanding performance by male actor in comedy series, 2005, Emmy award for outstanding lead actor in a comedy series, 2005, Emmy award for Outstanding Lead Actor in a Comedy Series, 2006), (TV guest appearances) Late Late Show with Craig Kilborne, Ally McBeal, Frasier, Almost Perfect, The X Files, many others. Office: UTA 9560 Wilshire Blvd # 500 Beverly Hills CA 90921 *

SHALIKASHVILI, JOHN MALCHASE, former Chairman of the Joint Chiefs of Staff; b. Warsaw, June 27, 1936; s. Dimitri and Maria (Ruediger) S.; m. Joan E. Zimpelman, Dec. 27, 1966; 1 child, Brant. BSME, Bradley U., 1958; attended, Naval War Coll., 1969—70, U.S. Army War Coll., 1977—78; MA in Internat. Affairs, George Washington U., 1970; LLD (hon.), U. Md., 1993, Bradley U., 1994. Joined U.S. Army, 1958, advanced through grades to gen., 1992, ret., 1997, various troop and staff assignments Alaska, U.S., Fed. Republic of Germany, Vietnam, Korea, Italy, Belgium, 1959-75, commdr. 1st bn. 84th field arty. Ft. Lewis, Wash., 1975-77; dep. chief of staff ops. So. European Task Froce U.S. Army, Vicenza, Italy, 1978-79; comdr. div. arty., 1st Armored Div. U.S. Army, Nuernberg, Fed. Republic of Germany, 1979-81, chief., politico-mil div., later dep. dir. ODCSOPS Washington, 1981-84, asst. div. comdr. 1st. Armored div. Nuernberg, Fed. Republic of Germany, 1984-86, dir. strategy, plans, policy ODCSOPS Washington, 1986-87; comdg. gen. 9th inf. div. Ft. Lewis, Wash., 1987-89; dep. comdr.-in-chief Hdqrs. USAREUR and 7th Army, Heidelberg, Fed. Republic of Germany, 1989-91; asst. to chmn. Joint Chiefs of Staff, Washington, 1991-92; Supreme Allied Comdr. Europe, Comdr.-in-Chief NATO, Brussels, 1992-93; chmn. Joint Chiefs of Staff, US Dept. Def., Washington, 1993-97. Vis. prof. Ctr. Internat. Security and Cooperation, Stanford U.; bd. dirs. Boeing Co., 2000—, Frank Russell Trust Co., L-3 Comm. Holdings, Inc., Plug Power Inc. Bd. trustees Bradley U.; mem. Buffalo Soldier Meml. Hon. Com. Decorated Def. D.S.M. with 3 oak leaf clusters, D.S.M. (Army) with oak leaf cluster), D.S.M. (Navy), D.S.M. (Air Force), D.S.M. (Dept. Trans.), Legion of Merit with 2 oak leaf clusters, Bronze Star medal with V device, Meritorious Svc. medal with 3 oak leaf clusters, Air medal, Joint Svc. Commendation medal, Army Commendation medal, Nat. Def. Svc. medal with bronze svc. star, Armed Forced Expeditionary medal, Republic of Vietnam Svc. medal with silver service star, S.W. Asia Svc. medal with bronze svc. star, Humanitarian Svc. medal, Army Svc. Ribbon, Overseas Svc. Ribbon with bronze Arabic numeral 5, Inter-Am. Def. Bd. medal, Kuwait Liberation medal, Order of Combat Infantryman badge, Parachutist badge, Joint Chiefs of Staff Identification badge, Army Staff Identification badge, Brazilian Order of Mil. Merit with 1st and 2d award, French Grand Officer of Nat. Merit, Belgian Grand Cordon of Order of Leopold, German Order of Merit with star and sash, Japanese Order of Rising Sun, Argentine Order of May in Grade of Gt. Cross for Mil. Merit, Korean Order of Nat. Security Merit, Tong-IL medal, Bintang Yudha Dharama Utama Hon. Decoration (Indonesia), Kuwait Def. medal, Grand Cross of Royal Norwegian Order of Merit, Grand Cross of Mil. Merit medal of Portuguese Republic, Republic of Vietnam Gallantry Cross with 2 silver and 1 bronze star, Republic of Vietnam Armed Forces Honor medal 1st class, Republic of Vietnam Armed Forces Honor medal 1st class, Republic of Vietnam Campaign medal, Republic of Vietnam Chung My medal 2d class, Tng. Svc. medal 1st class, Netherlands Comdr. Order Orange Nassau with swords, Mexican U.S. Mil. Merit 1st class, Great Cross Repub. Poland; recipient Chilean Bernardo Higgins award, Dwight D. Eisenhower Dist. Svc. award Vets. Fgn. Wars, Dist. Alumni Achievement award George Washington U., Presdl. Medal of Freedom award, 1997

SHALITA, ALAN REMI, dermatologist; b. Bklyn., Mar. 22, 1936; s. Harry and Celia; m. Simone Lea Baum, Sept. 4, 1960; children: Deborah (dec.) and Judith (twins). AB, Brown U., 1957; BS, U. Brussels, 1960; MD, Bowman Gray Sch. Medicine, 1964; DSc (hon.), L.I. U., 1990. Intern Beth Israel Hosp., NYC, 1964-65; resident dept. dermatology NYU Med. Ctr., 1967-68, NIH tng. grant fellow dept. dermatology, 1968-70, instr. dermatology, 1970-71; asst. prof. NYU, 1971-73, Columbia U., 1973-75; assoc. prof. medicine, head divsn. dermatology SUNY Downstate Med. Ctr., Bklyn., 1975-79, prof., 1979—, head divsn. dermatology, 1979-80, chmn. dept. dermatology, 1980—, asst. dean, 1977-83, acting dean Queens campus, 1983-84; assoc. dean clin. affairs SUNY Health Sci. Ctr., Bklyn., 1989-92, assoc. provost for clin. affairs, 1992-93, assoc. v.p. clin. affairs, 1993—2005, assoc. dean grad. med. edn., 1999—2006. Disting. tchg. prof. SUNY Health Sci. Ctr., Bklyn., 1996—; asst. attending in dermatology U. Hosp., NYC, 1970-73, Bellevue Hosp. Ctr., 1970-73, Manhattan VA Hosp., 1971-73, Presbyn. Hosp., 1973-75; bd. dirs. Kings County Hosp. Ctr.; cons. dermatology Bklyn. VA Hosp., 1975—; chief dermatology U. Hosp. Bklyn., 1975—, Brookdale Med. Ctr., 1977-90, Kings County Hosp. Ctr., Bklyn., 1975—, acting med. dir., 1989-92; med. dir. U. Hosp. Bklyn., 1992-96. Pres. Temple Shaaray Tefila, N.Y.C., 1982-86, chmn. bd. trustees, 1987-95. Lt. M.C. USNR, 1965-67. Recipient Torch of Liberty award Anti-Defamation League, 1987, Surg. and Pediat. awards Beth Israel Hosp., NYC, 1965, Leah Dickstein Man of Good Conscience award Women's Med. Assn. NY, 1999, Leadership in Urban Med. Edn. award Arthur Ashe Inst. for Urban Health, 1999; Spl. fellow NIH, 1970-73. Mem.: AMA, Venezuelan Dermatology Soc., Argentina Dermatology Soc., Brit. Assn. Dermatologists, N.Y. Dermatol. Soc. (pres. 1989—90), Dermatol. Soc. Greater N.Y. (pres. 1980—81), N.Y. State Dermatol. Soc., N.Y. Acad. Medicine, N.Y. State Med. Soc., N.Y. Acad. Scis., Internat. Soc. Dermatology, Assn. Profs. Dermatology (sec.-treas. 1988—94, pres. 1996—98), Am. Soc. Dermatol. Surgery (past bd. dirs.), Am. Dermatol. Assn. (sec.-treas. 1996—2001, pres. 2001—02), Dermatology Found. (past trustee), Soc. Investigative Dermatology, Am. Acad. Dermatology (bd. dirs. 1983—87, v.p. 1995—96), Polish Dermatology Soc. (hon.), Soc. Francaise de Dermatology (hon.), Alpha Omega Alpha. Republican. Home: 70 E 77th St New York NY 10021-1811 Office: 450 Clarkson Ave Brooklyn NY 11203-2056 Office Phone: 718-270-1229. Business E-Mail: ashalita@downstate.edu. *Treat others with compassion, dignity and respect, add a little humor to everyone's life. Speak up for what you truly believe, be charitable.*

SHALLCROSS, DORIS JANE, education educator; b. Cranford, NJ, Feb. 28, 1933; d. John William and Ethel Belle (Ruth) S. BA, Montclair State Coll., NJ, 1955; MA, Wesleyan U., Middletown, Conn., 1962; EdD, U. Mass., Amherst, 1973. Tchr. Hunterdon Ctrl. H.S., Flemington, NJ, 1955-61, Roosevelt Jr. H.S., Cleveland Heights, Ohio, 1961-65, Cleveland Heights H.S., 1965-67; adminstr. Cleveland Heights Pub. Schs., 1967-69; dir. humanistic edn. Montague Pub. Schs., Mass., 1972-75; program devel. specialist Tchr. Corps., SUNY, Oneonta, NY, 1976-78; asst. prof. edn. divsn. home econs. U. Mass., Amherst, 1978-82, prof., dir. grad. studies in creativity, 1982-95; pres. Shallcross Creativity Inst., Haydenville, Mass., 1995—. Pres. bd. trustees Creative Edn. Found., Buffalo, 1988-94, trustee emerita, 2006; co-dir. Global Odyssey, 1992—; bd. dir. Ctr. for Critical and Creative Thinking, Hartford, Conn., 1989-92, 95—; prof. internat. grad. program in creativity U. Santiago, Santiago de Compostela, Spain, 1999. Author: Teaching Creative Behavior, 1981; co-author: The Growing Person, 1985, Leadership: Making Things Happen, 1987, Intuition: An Inner Way of Knowing, 1989, Celebrating the Soul of CPSI, 2004; cons. editor Jour. Creative Behavior, 1967—; contbr. articles to profl. jours. Mem. Planning Bd., Town of Williamsburg, 1981-89; v.p. bd. dirs. Pioneer Valley Performing Arts H.S., 1995-98, pres., 1998—; chair edn. com. Arts in Edn. Ctr., 1997—, pres. 2002—; bd. dirs. Mass. Charter Schs. Assn., 2001-, v.p., 2007—, Enchanted Cir. Theater, 2007-; mem. Creative Problem Solving Inst. Coun., co-chair, 2004-05. Recipient Disting. Leader award Creative Edn. Found., 1986; named to Creative Problem Solving Inst. Hall of Fame, 2004, named Trustee Emeritus Creative Edn. Found.; grantee, NSF, 1987-89, U. Mass., Amherst, 1987-89. Mem. NEA, Mass. Soc. Profs., Inst. for Noetic Scis., Am. Creativity Assn. (bd. dirs. 1990-93). Avocations: music, golf, reading, gardening. Home: 26 S Main St Haydenville MA 01039-9735 E-mail: dshallx@highstream.net.

SHALLENBERGER, GARVIN F., retired lawyer; b. Beloit, Wis., Jan. 7, 1921; s. Garvin D. and Grace (Hubbell) S.; m. Mary L., May 5, 1945; children: Diane, Dennis Clark. BA in Pre-law, U. Mont., 1942; JD, U. Calif., Berkeley, 1949; LLD (hon.), Western State U., Fullerton, Calif., 1988. Bar: Calif. 1949, U.S. Dist. Ct. (cent. dist.) Calif. 1949, U.S. Ct. Appeals (9th cir.) 1949, U.S. Supreme Ct. 1961, U.S. Dist. Ct. (no. and so. dists.) Calif. 1963. Of counsel Rutan & Tucker, Costa Mesa, Calif.; ret., 1996. Chmn. spl. adv. com. state bar legal svcs. program, 1979-89, pub. law ctr Orange County, 1979-90. Recipient distinguished svc. award Boalt Hall (U. Calif. Berkeley), Judge Learned Hand Human Rel. award Nat. Jewish Com., 1990, Outstanding Alumnus award, U. Mont., 1999. Fellow Am. Coll. Trial Lawyers; mem. Am. Bd. Trial Advs. (a founder and 1st sec.),Calif. Bar Assn. (bd. govs. 1975-76, pres. 1977-78; mem. com. on jud. nominees 1978-79, pres. 1980), mem. Orange County Bar Assn. (bd. dirs. 1970-71, pres. 1972, Franklin West award 1979). Democrat. Avocations: tennis, writing. Office: Rutan & Tucker PO Box 1950 Costa Mesa CA 92628-1950 E-mail: woojj@aol.com, woojjy@hotmail.com.

SHALOM, GALIT, psychologist; b. Béer-Sheva, Israel, Dec. 26, 1969; arrived in US, 1992; d. Emil and Nourit Assor; m. Moshe Shalom, July 7, 1996; children: Nathan, Brit. BA in Edn. & Behavioral Scis., Ben-Gurion U. Negev, 1995; MA in Clinical Psychology, Forest Inst. Profl. Psychology, 1998, PsyD in Clinical Psychology, 2000. Lic. psychologist Fla., 2002. Evening news anchor ICS, Beer-Sheva, 1991—92; psychologist-in-tng. Forest Human Svcs. Ctr., Springfield, Mo., 1997—99, Neuropsychological & Assocs. SW Mo., 1999; intern Forest Inst. Profl. Psychology, Springfield, Mo., 1999—2000, tchg. asst., 1999—2000, clinical supr., 1999—2000; clinical psychologist Greene County Jail, Springfield, 2000; adj. prof. psychology Fla. Internat. U., Miami, 2001—02, post-doctorate residence, 2001—02; postdoctoral resident Fla. Internat. U. Counseling and Psychol. Svcs. Ctr., Miami, 2001—02; licensed clinical psychologist S. Fla. State Hosp., Atlantic Shores Healthcare, Inc., Pembroke Pines, Fla., 2003, pvt. practice, Boca Raton, Fla., 2003—, Jewish Family Svc., Inc. Broward County, Plantation, Fla., 2004—. Guest spkr. various seminars & presentations, 1999—2001. With Israeli mil., comdr. naval divsn. Israeli Defence Force, 1988—90. Recipient Outstanding Psychological Trainee of Month, The Resident Com., Forest Human Svcs. Ctr., 1998. Mem.: APA, Soc. for Psychology of Women. Jewish. Avocation: reading. Office: 370 W Camino Gardens Blvd Ste 204 Boca Raton FL 33432 E-mail: drshalom@bellsouth.net.

SHALOWITZ, ERWIN EMMANUEL, civil engineer; b. Washington, Feb. 13, 1924; s. Aaron Louis and Pearl (Myer) S.; m. Elaine Mildred Langerman, June 29, 1952; children: Ann Janet, Aliza Beth, Jonathan Avram. Student, U. Pa., U. Notre Dame, 1944-45; BCE, George Washington U., 1947, postgrad., 1948-49; grad. soil mechanics, Cath. U., 1951; MA in Pub. Adminstrn. (fellow U.S. Civil Service Commn.), Am. U., 1954. Registered profl. engr., Washington. Engr. Klemitt Engrng. Co., NYC, 1947; with cons. firm Whitman, Requardt & Assos., Balt., 1947-48; chief structural rsch. engr., head def. rsch. sect., project officer and tech. adviser for atomic tests Bur. Yards and Docks, Dept. Navy, Washington, 1948-59; supervisory gen. engr. spl. asst. for protective constrn. programs, project mgr. for bldg. systems, chief rsch. br., chief mgmt. info, chief contracting procedures and support, chief contract evaluation and analysis, team leader/project mgr. acquisition sys., acquisition/procurement exec., Pub. Bldg. Svc., Gen. Svcs. Adminstrn., Washington, 1959—98; mgr. edнl. svc. for individual improvement Silver Spring, Md., 1998—. Chmn. fed. exec. tng. program U.S. Civil Service Commn., 1950; fallout shelter analyst Dept. Def.; chmn. GSA Fire Safety Com., GSA Fallout Protection Com., GSA Bldg. Evaluation Com.; mem. Interagy Com. on Housing Rsch. and Bldg. Tech.; mem. Nat. Evaluation Bd. Architect-Engr. Selections; mem. standing com. on procurement policy Nat. Acad. Sci. Bldg. Research Adv. Bd. and Interagency Com. on Procurement Curriculum Rev.; coordinator pub. bldgs. design and constrn. Small Bus. Program and Minority Enterprise and Minority Subcontracting Programs. Contbr. articles profl. jours. Served to engrng. and cmdg. officer USNR, 1944-46. Recipient Commendable Svc. award GSA, 1968, Outstanding Performance recognition, 1976, 77, 79, 83, 87, 93-96, Superior Accomplishment award, 1995, others; Engr. Alumni Achievement award George Washington U., 1985. Fellow ASCE, Am. Biog. Inst.; mem. Soc. Advancement Mgmt., Am. Biog. Inst. (nat. bd. advisors), Soc. Am. Mil. Engrs., Sigma Tau, Pi Sigma Alpha. Jewish. Avocations: Bible study, ping pong/table tennis. Home: 3122 Gracefield Rd Apt 108 Silver Spring MD 20904-5801 Personal E-mail: eshalowitz@aol.com. *PRINCIPLES: Look beyond the material for lasting values and meaning, optimize managerial effectiveness by creating an objective and challenging climate in an organization, delve into the underlying causes of problem areas for meaningful solutions, and persevere in spite of obstacles. IDEAS: Cultural pluralism; the intrinsic potential of each individual; and love, appreciation, and support of one's family as indispensable for real accomplishment. GOALS: To attain the highest level of professional accomplishment within my capabilities and to continue to have a rich, happy, and fulfilling family life. STANDARDS OF CONDUCT: To be fair, consistent, and straightforward; and to avoid over-reacting.*

SHAM, LU JEU, physics professor, physicist; b. Hong Kong, Apr. 28, 1938; s. T. S. and Cecilia Maria (Siu) Shen; m. Georgina Bien, Apr. 25, 1965; children: Kevin Shen, Alisa Shen. GCE, Portsmouth Coll., Eng., 1957; BS, Imperial Coll., London U., Eng., 1960; PhD in Physics, Cambridge U., Eng., 1963. Asst. rsch. physicist U. Calif., San Diego, 1963-66, assoc. prof., 1968-75, prof., 1975—, chair dept. physics, 1995-98, dean div. natural scis., 1985-89, Disting. physics prof., 2005—, asst. prof. physics Irvine, 1966-67; rsch. physicist IBM Corp., Yorktown Heights, NY, 1974-75. Reader Queen Mary Coll., U. London, 1967—68. Assoc. editor: Physics Letters A, 1992—; contbr. articles to profl. jours. Recipient Churchill Coll. studentship, Eng., 1960—63, U.S. Scientist award, Humboldt Found., 1978, Faculty Rsch. Letter award, 2000, Lamb medal, 2004, Chancellor Assocs. award for Excellence in Rsch., 1995; fellow, Guggenheim Found., 1984. Fellow: Am. Phys. Soc.; mem.: NAS, AAAS, Optical Soc. Am., Acad. Sinica Republic of China. Democrat. Avocations: tennis, folk dancing. Office: U Calif San Diego Dept Physics 0319 La Jolla CA 92093-0319 Office Phone: 619-534-3269. E-mail: lsham@ucsd.edu.

SHAMAMIAN, OSCAR, architect; BA, Columbia Coll., 1981; MArch, Columbia U., 1985. With Office of Robert A.M. Stern, Parish-Hadley, 1985; co-founder, ptnr. Ferguson & Shamamian Archs., LLP, 1988—. Rsch. asst.: New York 1900. Recipient Arthur Ross award for Architecture, Inst. Classical Architecture & Classical Am., 2003. Office: Ferguson & Shamamian Archs LLP 270 Lafayette St Ste 300 New York NY 10012 Office Phone: 212-941-8088. E-mail: oshamamian@fergusonshamamian.com. *

SHAMASH, YACOV, dean, electrical engineering educator; b. Iraq, Jan. 12, 1950; BSEE, Imperial Coll., London, 1970; PhD in Control Systems, Imperial Coll., 1973. Postdoctoral fellowin elec. engring. Tel-Aviv U., 1973-75, from lectr. elec. engrng. to sr. lectr. elec. engrng., 1975-78; prof. elec. engrng. Fla. Atlantic U., Boca Raton, 1977-85; prof., chair dept. elec. engrng. dept. Wash. State U., Pullman, 1985-92; dean engrng. SUNY, Stony Brook, 1992—. Bd. dirs. KeyTronics, Spokane, Wash., 1990—; vis. asst. prof. U. Pa., Phila., 1976-77. Contbr. over 100 articles to profl. jours., book chpts. Fellow IEEE (sr.). Office: SUNY Coll Engrng & Applied Sci Stony Brook NY 11794-2200

SHAMASK, RONALDUS, fashion designer; b. Amsterdam, The Netherlands, Nov. 24, 1945; Window display artist, Melbourne, Australia, 1963-66; fashion illustrator The Times and The Observer, London, 1967-68; freelance stage set, costume designer for ballet, opera, Company of Man Buffalo, 1968-71; freelance interior and clothing designer NYC, 1971-77; founder, ptnr. Moss Shamask Fashion Co., NYC, 1978—; founder Moss Boutique, NYC, 1979—. Contbr. design packing Revlon Cosmetics and Fragrances, 1993; launched cosmetic line, Fire & Ice Fragrance, Revlon, 1993—. Exhibit at MIT, 1982. Recipient Coty Fashion award, 1981; Fil d'Or award Conf. Internat. du Lin, 1982. Office: c/o Revlon 625 Madison Ave New York NY 10022

SHAMATAVA, IRMA, physicist, researcher; arrived in U.S., 2000; d. Iuri and Tsiuri Shamatava; m. Fridon Shubitidze, July 20, 1993; children: Tornike Shubitidze, Salome Shubitidze. MS, Sukhumi br. Tbilisi State U., Tbilisi, Georgia, 1993. Physicist (radio physics), Dept. Edn. of Ga. Tchr. Sukhumi U., Tbilisi, 1997—98; rsch. engr. Dartmouth Coll., Hanover, NH, 2001—. Cons. Cold Regions Rsch. and Engrng. Lab., NH, 2005—. Contbr. scientific papers to profl. jours. Achievements include development of User friendly computer programs; research in unexploded ordnances detection and discrimination. Office Phone: 603-646-2685.

SHAMBAUGH, DAVID LEIGH, political scientist, educator, writer; b. Chgo., Jan. 18, 1953; s. George E. Shambaugh, Jr. and Genevieve (Krum) Shambaugh; m. Ingrid Cecile Larsen, Aug. 7, 1982; children: Christopher Leigh, Alexander George. BA in East Asian Studies, George Washington U., 1977; MA in Internat. Affairs, Johns Hopkins U., 1980; PhD in Polit. Sci., U. Mich., 1989. Prof. U. London, 1988—96, George Washington U., Washington, 1996—; sr. fellow Brookings Instn., 1998—. Cons. in field. Editor China Quar., 1991—96, mem. editl. bd., 1989—, Studies on Contemporary China, 1991—, Internat. Security, 2003—, China Perspectives, 1998—, Current History, 1999—; author: The Making of a Premier: Zhao Ziyang's Provincial Career, 1984, Beautiful Imperialist: China Perceives America, 1991, China and Europe, 1996, Modernizing China's Military Progress, Problems, and Prospects, 2002, The Odyssey of China's Imperial Art Treasures, 2005; editor, contbr. American Studies of Contemporary China, 1993, Greater China: The Next Superpower?, 1995, Deng Xiaoping: Portrait of a Chinese Statesman, 1995, China's Military in Transition, 1997, Contemporary Taiwan, 1998, The Modern Chinese State, 2000, Is China Unstable?, 2000, co-editor Chinese Foreign Policy: Theory and Practice, 1994, co-editor, contbr. China's Military Faces the Future, 1999, The China Reader: The Reform Era, 1999, Making China Policy: Lessons from the Bush and Clinton Administrations, 2001, Power Shift: China and Asia's New Dynamics, 2005, China Watching, 2006. Fellow, Smith Richardson Found., 2005—06; grantee, Brit. Acad./Econ. & Social Rsch. Coun. China Exch. Program, 1990, 1994, Chiang Ching-kuo Found., 1998—2000; Rsch. fellow, Pacific Cultural Found., 1998—2000, Woodrow Wilson fellow, 2002—03, others. Mem.: Pacific Coun. on Internat. Policy, Coun. on Fgn. Rels., Asia Soc., Internat. Studies Assn., Assn. for Asian Studies, Coun. on Security Coop. in the Asia Pacific, Nat. Com. U.S.-China Rels., Internat. Inst. Strategic Studies, World Econ. Forum. Avocations: travel, basketball, tennis, canoeing, bluegrass music. Office: George Washington Univ Elliott Sch Internat Affairs 1957 E St NW Ste 503 Washington DC 20052 Office Phone: 202-994-5887. Business E-Mail: shambaug@gwu.edu.

SHAMBAUGH, IRVIN CALVIN, JR., aptitude test firm executive; b. Harrisburg, Pa., June 7, 1943; s. Irvin Calvin and Viola Mary (Deibler) Shambaugh; m. Amy Wilcox Shambaugh, Jan. 3, 1975. BS in Geol. Sci., Pa. State U., 1964; postgrad., MIT, Cambridge, Mass., 1964—65, Tex. Christian U., Ft. Worth, 1974—76, East Tex. State U., 1976—77. Rsch. coord. Johnson O'Connor Rsch. Found., Ft. Worth, 1965—76; pres., chief scientist Aptitude Inventory Measurement Svc., Dallas, 1976—. Centennial fellow Coll. Earth and Min. Scis., Pa. State U., 1996. Author: The Test-Taker's Guide to Career Literature, 1982, Test Manual for Selected AIMS Worksamples, 1986, Books About Careers, 1986, Career Facts: Where to Find Them and How to Use Them, 1992, The AIMS Guide to Career Facts, 1997; co-author: AIMS Information About Aptitudes, 1979, The Aptitude Handbook: A Guide to the AIMS Program, 1996, 2004, Career Facts: In Print and on the World Wide Web, 2003; co-prodr.: (e-pub.) AIMS Information Disk, 2004; editor: You and Your Aptitudes, 1983; developer Activity Preference Questionnaire, 1994, psychometric instrument lll Interest Inventory, 1996; contbr. articles to profl. jours.; developer AIMS test battery, 1976—, digital version, 2005—, AIMS Measure of Color Perception, 2005—, AIMS Reasoning Measure, 2006, 3-D Mental Gymnastics Worksample, 2006. With USMC, 1966—68. Mem.: AAAS, ACA, APA (assoc.), Nat. Assn. Test Dirs., Nat. Assn. Coll. Admissions Counselors, Nat. Coun. Measurement in Edn., Am. Psychol. Soc., Assn. Assessment in Counseling and Edn. Achievements include development of psychometric instruments. Home: 934 Westbrook Dr Garland TX 75043-5243 Office: Aptitude Inventory Measurement Svc 12160 Abrams Rd Ste 314 Dallas TX 75243-4525

SHAMBAUGH, STEPHEN WARD, lawyer; b. South Bend, Ind., Aug. 4, 1920; s. Marion Clyde and Anna Violet (Stephens) S.; m. Marilyn Louise Pyle (dec. 1993); children: Susan Wynne Shambaugh Hinkle (dec. 1998), Kathleen Louise Shambaugh Thompson. Student, San Jose State Tchrs. Coll., 1938-40, U. Ark., 1951; LLB, U. Tulsa, 1954. Bar: Okla. 1954, Colo. 1964. Mem. staff Reading & Bates, Inc., Tulsa, 1951-54; v.p., gen. mgr., legal counsel Reading & Bates Drilling Co. Ltd., Calgary, Alta., Canada, 1954-61; sr. ptnr. Bowman, Shambaugh, Geissinger & Wright, Denver, 1964-81; sole practice Denver, 1981-97; now ret. Dir., fin. counsel various corps. Col. USAF ret. Mem. Colo. Bar Assn., Okla. Bar Assn., P-51 Mustang Pilots Assn., Mil. Officers Assn. Am. (life), Am. Legion, Masons, Elks, Phi Alpha Delta.

SHAMBERG, MICHAEL, film producer; m. Carla Santos, 1996; 1 child. Grad., Washington U. Films produced include Heart Beat, 1980, Modern Problems, 1981, The Big Chill, 1983, Club Paradise, 1986, Salvation!, 1987, A Fish Called Wanda, 1988, How I Got Into College, 1989, 8 Seconds, 1994, (with Danny DeVito) Reality Bites, 1994, (with Danny DeVito and Stacey Sher) Pulp Fiction, 1994, Get Shorty, 1995, Sunset Park, 1996, Matilda, 1996, Feeling Minnesota, 1996, Fierce Creatures, 1997, Gattaca, 1997, Out of Sight, 1998, Living Out Loud, 1998, Drowning Mona, 2000, Erin Brockovich, 2000, The Caveman's Valentine, 2001, Ghost World, 2001, How High, 2001, Camp, 2003, Along Came Polly, 2004, Garden State, 2004, Be Cool, 2005, The Skeleton Key, 2005, World Trade Center, 2006, Freedom Writers, 2007, Reno 911!: Miami, 2007, (TV films) The Pentagon Wars, 1998, The Funkhousers, 2002, Other People's Business, 2003, (TV series) UC: Undercover, 2001-02, The American Embassy, 2002, Karen Sisco, 2003-04. *

SHAMBROOM, PAUL, artist, photographer; b. Teaneck, NJ, 1956; BFA, Mpls. Coll. Art Design, 1978. One-man shows include Film in the Cities, St. Paul, 1979, Minn. Hist. Soc., 1984, Bockley Gallery, Mpls., 1990, CEOA Gallery and Medaillel Coll., Buffalo, 1995, Walker Art Ctr., Mpls., 1995, Tanya Bonakdar Gallery, N.Y.C., 1997—98, Franklin Artworks, Mpls., 2001, Julie Saul Gallery, NYC, 2002, 2004, 2006, Le Mois de la Photo a Montreal, 2003, Mus. Contemporary Photography, Chgo., 2003, Arles Recontres de la Photographie, France, 2004, Nederlands Fotomuseum, Rotterdam, 2005, Howard Yezerski Gallery, Boston, 2005, Atomic Testing Mus., Las Vegas, 2005, Rocket Gallery, London, 2005, exhibited in group shows at Camerawork Gallery, San Francisco, 1979, Northlight Gallery, Tempe, Ariz., 1981, Forecast Pub. Artspace Prodns., Mpls., 1981, Univ. Gallery, U. Minn., 1986, Minn. Coll. Art Design, 1988, Film in the Cities, St. Paul, 1990, Mpls. Inst. Arts, 1990, 1996, Bockley Gallery, Mpls., 1991, Mus. Modern Art, N.Y.C., 1996, Whitney Mus. Am. Art, 1997, Madison Art Ctr., Wis., 2001, Ludwig Mus., Budapest, 2002—03, Univ. Art Mus., Santa Barbara, Calif., 2003—04, Ronald Feldman Fine Arts, NYC, 2003, Milw. Art Mus., 2004, Weinstein Gallery, Mpls., 2005, N.C. Mus. Art, 2005, Represented in permanent collections Whitney Mus. Am. Art, N.Y.C., San Francisco Mus. Modern Art, L.A. County Mus. Art, Mus. Modern Art, N.Y.C., Walker Art Ctr., Mpls., Mpls. Inst. Arts, Mus. Fine Arts, Houston. Fellow Photography fellow, McKnight Found., Mpls., 1985, 1989, 1995, Visual Arts fellow, Jerome Found., St. Paul, 1987, Artist Assistance fellow, Minn. State Arts Bd., 1988, 1993, Artist fellow, Bush Found., St. Paul, 1992; Dayton Hudson Found. grantee, Mpls., 1979, Jerome Found. grantee, St. Paul, 1996. Office: c/o Julie Saul Gallery 535 W 22nd St New York NY 10011 E-mail: paul@paulshambroomart.com.

SHAMBUREK, ROLAND HOWARD, physician; b. Adell, Wis., June 7, 1928; s. William and Catherine (Illig) Shamburek; m. Gladys Irene Gibbons, June 21, 1952; children: Steven J., Robert D., Daniel J. BS, U. Wis., 1950, MD, 1953; MPH, Harvard U., 1960; grad., U.S. Army War Coll., Carlisle Barracks, Pa., 1972. Diplomate Am. Bd. Preventive Medicine. Commd. 1st lt. M.C., U.S. Army, 1953, advanced through grades to col., 1968; intern St. Joseph's Hosp., Marshfield, Wis., 1953-54; grad. U.S. Naval Sch. of Aviation Medicine, Pensacola, Fla., 1957; resident in preventive (aerospace) medicine USAF Sch. Aerospace Medicine, Brooks AFB, 1960-63; service in 216th Field Artillery (Atomic) Battalion, 1954—56, 1966, Office of Army Surgeon Gen., Washington, 1966—70, 1972—75; comdr. 67th EVAC Hosp., Vietnam, 1970-71, U.S. Army Med. Pers. Support Agy., 1975-77; ret. U.S. Army, 1977; exec. v.p. Aerospace Med. Assn., 1977-79; clin. practice Pentagon Health Clinic, Washington, 1981-85; med. researcher Office of Army Surgeon Gen., 1985-87. Med. monitor Canary Island Tracking Sta. for Gemini missions NASA, 1965—66. Contbr. scientific papers in field. Decorated Legion of Merit with oak leaf cluster, Army Commendation medal, Meritorious Svc. medal; recipient Gold Palm Eagle Scout award, Boy Scouts Am., 1945. Mem.: AMA (del. 1978), Internat. Acad. Aviation and Space Medicine, Soc. NASA Flight Surgeons, U.S. Army Flight Surgeons, Soc. Med. Cons. Armed Forces, Aerospace Med. Assn. (v.p. 1968—69), Am. Coll. Preventive Medicine (v.p. 1968—69), Assn. Mil. Surgeons (John Shaw Billings award 1968). Address: 3700 Moss Dr Annandale VA 22003-1915

SHAMIM, MAH TALAT, chemist; b. Karachi, Pakistan, Sept. 7, 1952; came to U.S., 1976; d. Syed Hasan and Askaribi (Nuzhat) Akhtar; m. A. Najm Shamim, Dec. 20, 1975. BS in Chemistry, Karachi U., 1972, MS in Chemistry, 1973, Howard U., 1981, PhD in Chemistry, 1983. Postdoctoral fellow NIH, Bethesda, Md., 1983-89, sr. staff fellow, 1989-91; chemist EPA, Washington, 1991-93, sect. chief environ. fate and effects divsn., 1993-97, chief environ. risk br. environ fate and effects divsn., 1997—. Panelist U.S. Merit Sys. Protection Adv. Bd., Washington, 1996—; mem. internat. environ. fate workgroups. Co-author: Rejection Rate Analysis: Environmental Fate Guidelines, 1995; contbr. articles to profl. jours. Mem. Am. Chem. Soc., Assn. Asian-Pacific Ams. Avocations: gardening, sewing, painting, writing. Office: Environmental Protection Agency 1200 Pennsylvania Ave Nw Washington DC 20004-2403 E-mail: shamim.mah@epa.gov.

SHAMIR, ADI, computer scientist; b. Tel Aviv, 1952; BSc, Tel Aviv U., 1973; MSc, Weitzmann Inst. Sci., 1975, PhD, 1977; postgrad., MIT, 1980. With faculty Weitzman Inst. Sci., Israel, 1980—84, prof., 1984—, Paul and Marlene Borman prof. applied math. Dir. Cyota Corp. Recipient Kanellakis award, Erdös award, Israel Math. Soc., W.R.G. Baker Prize, IEEE, Koji Kobayashi Computers and Comm. award, UAP Sci. Prize, Pius XI Gold Medal, Turning award, 2002. Mem.: NAS (fgn. assoc.). Achievements include co-invention of the RSA security algorithm; cryptography expert. Office: Weitzmann Inst Sci Faculty Math and Computer Sci POB 26 76100 Rehovot Israel

SHAMIS, EDWARD ANTHONY, JR., lawyer; b. Pensacola, Fla., Dec. 12, 1949; s. Edward Anthony Sr. and Mona Kathryn (McLaughlin) S.; m. Elizabeth Handley, Jan. 24, 1971. BS, La. State U., 1972, JD, 1974. Bar: La. 1974, US Dist. Ct. (ea. dist.) La. 1975, US Tax Ct. 1981, US Ct. Appeals (5th cir.) 1982, US Supreme Ct. 1983. Pvt. practice, Slidell, La., 1974—. Spl. counsel to Slidell City Coun., 1984. Bd. dirs. Pope John H.S., Slidell, 1988-90, Children's Wish Endowment Fund, Inc. (formerly Northshore Children's Endowment Fund) 1991—; mem., pres. St. Tammany Assn. for Children with Learning Disabilities, Slidell, 1976-81; chmn. Slidell Bd. Zoning Adjustments, 1976-81; past mem. Boys Club; past mem. and chmn. St. Tammany Parish Ethics Commn. Mem. ATLA, La. Bar Assn. (hos. of dels. 1985-86, 88-89, 89-90, 94-97), Slidell Bar Assn. (pres. 1978-79), La. Trial Lawyers Assn. (pres.'s adv. coun. 1980-81, 84-85, 89-90, 95-96, bd. govs. 2003-04). Republican. Office: 486 Brownswitch Rd Slidell LA 70458-1102 Office Phone: 985-641-5570.

SHAMMAS, NAZIH KHEIRALLAH, environmental engineer, consultant, engineering educator; b. Homs, Syria, Feb. 18, 1939; arrived in US, 1991; s. Kheirallah Hanna and Nazha Murad (Hamwi) Shammas; m. Norma Massouh, July 28, 1968; children: Sarmed Erick, Samer Sam. Degree in engrng. with distinction, Am. U., Beirut, 1962; MS in Sanitary Engrng., U. NC, Chapel Hill, 1965; PhD in Civil Engrng., U. Mich., Ann Arbor, 1971. Instr. civil engrng. Am. U., Beirut, 1965-68; tchg. fellow U. Mich., Ann Arbor, 1968-71; asst. prof. civil engrng. Am. U., Beirut, 1972-76, King Saud U., Riyadh, Saudi Arabia, 1976-78, assoc. prof., 1978-91; prof. environ. engrng. Lenox Inst. Water Tech., Mass., 1991-2001, dean edn., 1992-93. Cons., ptnr. Cons. and Rsch. Engrs., Beirut, 1973—76; cons. Ar-Riyadh Devel. Authority, 1977—93, Riyadh Water and Sanitary Drainage Authority, 1979—83, Assoc. Cons. Engrng. Team, 1994—99, Vikakis Internat., 1995—2002; adj. prof. environ. sci. Berkshire CC, 1995—; planning assoc. Berkshire Regional Planning Commn., 1999—2003. Co-author: Environmental Sanitation, 1988, Wastewater Engineering, 1988, Physicochemical Treatment Processes, 2005, Advanced Physicochemical Treatment Processes, 2006, Advanced Physiochemical Treatment Technologies, 2007, Biosolids Treatment Processes, 2007; contbr. articles to profl. jours. and confs. Recipient Excellence in Tchg. award, King Saud U., 1981, 1984; Block grantee, U. Mich., 1968—70. Mem.: ASCE, Assn. Environ. Engrng. and Sci. Profs., Internat. Water Assn., New Eng. Water Works Assn., New Eng. Water Environ. Assn., Am. Water Works Assn., Water Environ. Fedn. Achievements include research in biological and physiochemcial remediation processes; mathematical modeling of nitrification process; water and wastewater management in developing countries; water conservation; wastewater treatment and reuse; appropriate technology for developing countries; multidisciplinary studies in environmental management and planning. Home: 35 Flintstone Dr Pittsfield MA 01201 Personal E-mail: nazihshammas@aol.com.

SHAMMAS, NICOLAS WAHIB, internist, cardiologist; b. Amyoun, El-Koura, Lebanon, Jan. 31, 1963; arrived in U.S., 1988; s. Wahib Nicolas and Vera Yousuf (El-Helou) Shammas; m. Gail Ann Hanson, Feb. 22, 1991; children: Waheeb John, Andrew Nicolas, Anna Elizabeth. BSc with distinction, Am. U. Beirut, 1983, MD, 1987, MSc in Physiology, 1987, Diploma in Computer Programming, 1985. Diplomate Am. Bd. Internal Medicine, Am. Bd. Cardiology and Interventional Cardiology. Postdoctoral rsch. fellow Am. U. Beirut, 1987-88; resident in internal medicine U. Iowa Hosps., Iowa City, 1988-91; instr. medicine, clin. fellow cardiology U. Rochester (N.Y.) Med. Ctr., 1991-94; fellow assoc. in cardiology U. Iowa Hosps., Iowa City, 1994—95; mem. staff Genesis Med. Ctr., Davenport, Iowa, 1995—; clin. asst. prof. U. Iowa. Founder Mastermind Pub., 1995, Phenix Realty Co., 1997; founder, pres. Midwest Cardiovasc. Rsch. Found., 2002. Author (with others): Flavors of Lebanon, 1995, Learn About Your Heart.Made Simple, 2004, Cardiovascular Interventions and Practice Guidelines, 2004, Live Longer, Live Healthier: The Secrets of Graceful Aging, 2007; contbr. articles to profl. jours. Am. U. Beirut U.

Rsch. Bd. award, 1986-87, John C. Sable Meml. Heart award J.C. Sable Fund, 1993, Trainee Investigator award, Balt., 1994, Extra-mile award Am. Heart Assn. 2002, First Poster award Internat. Congress of Angiology, 2003 Fellow: ACP, Acad. Transcatheter Therapeutics, Am. Coll. Chest Physicians, Internat. Coll. Angiology, Am. Coll. Cardiology, Soc. Cardiac Angiography and Interventions; mem.: AMA, Am. Soc. Echocardiography, Am. Soc. Nuclear Cardiology, Iowa Med. Soc., Am. Soc. Internal Medicine, Am. Fedn. Clin. Rsch. Achievements include research in basic cardiology: prostacyclin and transmembrane calcium movements; adrenergic binding sites; hypertension; myocardial ischemia and coronary flow reserve; inflammation and thrombosis. Avocations: writing, skiing, golf, travel. Office: Cardiovasc Medicine PC 1236 E Rusholme St Ste 300 Davenport IA 52803-2400 Office Phone: 563-324-2992. Business E-Mail: shammas@mchsi.com.

SHAMOO, ADIL ELIAS, biochemist, educator; b. Baghdad, Iraq, Aug. 1, 1941; came to U.S., 1964, naturalized, 1973; s. Elias M. and Mariam T. (Mansour) S.; m. Joan Hutchison, Dec. 16, 1967 (div. Dec. 1997); children: Abraheem, Zachary, Jessica. B.Sc. in Physics, U. Baghdad, 1962; MS in Physics (grad. fellow), U. Louisville, 1966; PhD in Biophysics, CUNY, 1970. Instr. engring. physics Speed Sch., U. Louisville, 1965-68; asst. prof. physiology City U. N.Y., 1971-73; guest worker Lab. Biophysics and Neurochemistry, NIH, Bethesda, Md., 1972-73; asst. prof. radiation biology and biophysics U. Rochester, 1973-75; guest prof. Max-Planck Inst. Biophysics, Frankfurt, West Germany, 1977-78; assoc. prof. radiation biology and biophysics U. Rochester, 1975-79; prof., chmn. dept. biol. chemistry U. Md., Balt., 1979-82, prof. biochemistry and molecular biology, 1982—, prof. epidemiology and preventive medicine, 2003—, head membrane biochemistry research lab., 1982-90. Cons. div. biol. scis. Kodak Co., Rochester, 1976-77; NIH tng. fellow U. Louisville, 1967; investigator Am. Heart Assn., 1976-79; Neurosci. Rsch. Program fellow, Boulder, Colo., summer 1977; chmn. symposia, various coms. in field; mem. organizing coms. workshops in field; adj. profl. dept. physics East Carolina U., Greenville, N.C., 1996-2000; bd. dirs. Friends Rsch. Inst., 1994-2001; ethics cons. Armed Forces Epidemiol. Bd.; chair ethics adv. group GlaxoSmithKline Co., 2003. Editor (with M.W. Miller) Membrane Toxicity, 1977, Carriers and Channels in Biological Systems, 1975, Carriers and Channels in Biological Systems-Transport Proteins, 1980, Regulation of Calcium Transport Across Muscle Membranes, 1985, Principles of Research Data Audit, (with R. Verna) Biotechnology Today, 1995, Ethics in Neurobiological Research with Human Subjects, 1997; editor in chief Membrane Biochemistry, 1977-93, Accountability in Research: Policies and Quality Assurance, 1988—; mem. editl. bd. Molecular and Cellular Biochemistry, 1987-94, Quality Assurance: Good Practice Regulation and Law, 1991—; contbr. articles and abstracts to profl. jours., chpts. to books. Bd. dirs. Alliance for Mentally Ill of Md., 1990-93, Friends Rsch. Inst. Inc., 1994-2002; mem. rsch. monitoring com. Nat. Alliance for Mentally Ill, bd. dirs. 1994-97; pres. faculty senate U. Md., Balt., 1993-94; mem. coun. univ. systems U. Md., 1994-97; mem. adv. com. Vantage Pl., 1995-97; bd. dirs. Howard County Mental Health Authority, 1997-00, pres., 1997-2000; bd. dirs. Citizens for Responsible Care and Rsch., 1998—, v.p., 1998—; mem. Nat. Human Rsch. Protections Adv. Com., 2000-02; mem. Def. Health Bd., 2006—. Recipient Advocacy award Mental Health Assn. Md., 1994, Disting. Svc. award Alliance for Mentally Ill of Md., 1994, Howard County Mental Health Auth., 1999. Mem. AAAS, AAUP (chpt. sec. 1971-72), Basic Sci. Council of Am. Heart Assn., Am. Soc. Biol. Chemists and Mol. Biol., Am. Coll. Sports Medicine, Am. Assn. Physics Tchrs., Am. Soc. Bioethics and Human Values, Am. Physiol. Soc., Biophys. Soc. (Cole Membrane Award Com. 1983-84, chmn. biophysics subgroup 1982-83, council 1986-89), Membrane Biophys. Group (chmn. 1982-83, sec.-treas. 1983-85, co-chmn. U.S. bioenergetics group 1979-80), Md. Acad. Scis. (chmn. com. programs and exhbns. 1986-87, sci. council 1985-89), N.Y. Acad. Scis., Coun. of Biology (editor 1989—), Soc. Quality Assurance. Achievements include patents for liquid scintillators. Office: 108 N Greene St Baltimore MD 21201-1503 E-mail: ashamoo@umaryland.edu.

SHAMOUN, JOHN MILAM, plastic surgeon; b. Greenville, Miss., Apr. 1, 1960; s. Joseph David Shamoun and Phyllis Ann Joseph. BS, U. Miss., 1982, MD, 1986. Bd. cert. Am. Bd. Surgery, Am. Bd. Plastic and Reconstructive Surgery, Am. Bd. Facial Plastic and Reconstructive Surgery, Am. Bd. Forensic Examiners. Gen. surgeon U. South Ala., Mobile, 1986-91; plastic surgeon U. Tex., Dallas, 1991-93, Mt. Sinai Hosp., Miami Beach, Fla., 1993-94, Plastic Surgery Ctr. of the Pacific, Honolulu, 1994-95, Atlanta Plastic Surgery, 1994-95, Newport Inst. Plastic Surgery, Newport Beach, Calif., 1995; solo practice Beverly Hills, Palm Springs, Newport Beach, Calif. Legal cons. Law Firm of Charles G. Shamoun, Dallas, 1995—. Author: (books) Aesthetic Surgery, 1996, Microvascular Atlas, 1997; contbr. articles to profl. jours. Fellow ACS; diplomate Am. Bd. Plastic Surgery; mem. Am. Soc. Plastic and Reconstructive Surgery, Calif. Soc. Plastic Surgery, Anti Aging Soc., Alpha Omega Alpha. Roman Catholic. performed plastic surgery (facelift and forehead lift) on female celebrity, Christopher Templeton, live on the Internet, June 7, 1999; featured in NY Post, Dallas (Tex.) Morning News, London Times, Sunday Mirror (UK), LA bus. Jour., People mag., and Women's Jour. mag. Office: 360 San Miguel Dr Ste 406 Newport Beach CA 92660-7822 *

SHAMPO, MARC ANTHONY, retired editor; b. Green Bay, Wis., Oct. 20, 1924; s. Norman Joseph Shampo and Antoinette Rondou; m. Norma Eileen Beyea, Oct. 23, 1945 (div. Oct. 1965); 1 child, Teresa; m. Lila Irene Mayhew, July 29, 1967; children: Barbara, Charles, Nancy, Scott. BS, U. Wis., 1948, MS, 1949; PhD, U. Wis., Madison, Wis., 1960. H.S. tchr., Pewaukee, Wis., 1949—51, Racine, Wis., 1951—58; prof. Duquesne U., Pitts., 1958—62; med. editor Mayo Clinic, Rochester, Minn., 1962—89; ret., 1989. Contbr. articles to profl. jours., chpts. to books. With US Army, 1943—46, ETO. Decorated Combat Inf. Badge, Purple Heart, Bronze star. Mem.: Phi Delta Kappa, Phi Eta Sigma. Home: 211 2d St NW Rochester MN 55901

SHAMSHAM, FADI MICHEL, cardiologist; b. Beirut, Nov. 28, 1968; arrived in U.S., 1994; s. Michel Salim Shamsham and Marie Assi Gemayel. BS, Am. U. of Beirut, 1989, MD, 1993. Diplomate Am. Bd. Internal Medicine, Am. Bd. Internal Medicine with subspecialities in cardiovascular diseases and interventional cardiology. Resident in internal medicine S.I. U. Hosp., SI, NY, 1994—97; fellow in cardiovascular diseases SUNY, Bklyn., 1997—2000; fellow in interventional cardiology Kaiser Permanente Found. Hosp., LA, 2000—01; fellow in vascular medicine Charleston Area Med. Ctr., W.Va., 2001—02; cardiologist Med. Group of North Fla., Tallahassee, 2002—06, Heart and Vascular Ctr., Venice, Fla., 2006—; med. staff Tallahassee Meml. Hosp., Fla., 2002—06, Capital Regional Med. Ctr., 2002—06, Venice Regional Med. Ctr., 2006—, Sarasota Meml. Hosp., 2007—. Clin. inst. SUNY, Bklyn., 1997—2000. Contbr. articles to profl. jours. Fellow: Soc. Cardiac Angiography and Interventions, Am. Coll. Cardiology; mem.: AMA, ACP. Office: 1287 US 41 Bypass South Venice FL 34285 Home Phone: 941-918-8098. Personal E-mail: fshamsham@aol.com.

SHAMSUZZOHA, M. D., research scientist, chemical engineer; b. Begusarai, Bihar, India, Jan. 1, 1978; s. M.D. Kalim Uddin and Nasima Khatoun. BS in Chem. Engring., Amu Aligarh U., India, 1999; PhD with honors, Sch. Chem. Engring. and Tech., Republic of Korea, 2006. R&D rschr. dept. petroleum studies Amu Aligarh U., India, 1999—2003; scientist Program Sys. Design and Control, Dae-Dong Kyongsan, Republic of Korea, 2003—. Rsch. group head Petroleum Studies, India, 2001—03. Contbr. scientific papers. Head Poor Devel. Soc., Begusarai, India, 1990—. Recipient Best student award, Amu Aligrah U., 2001. Mem.: Korea Instn. Chem. Engrs. (life). Achievements include research in effect of submergence in thermosiphon reboiler; process design and control; heat transfer and adsorption. Home: Vill Qusba Po Hussaina PS Ballia Distt Begusarai Bihar 851211 India Office: Process Sys Design and Control Lab Sch Chem Engring Yeungnam Univ 214-1 Dae-Dong Kyongsan Gyeongsan 712-749 Republic of Korea Office Phone: 82-10-8697-6528. Office Fax: 82-053-811-3262. Personal E-mail: smzoha2002@hotmail.com.

SHAN, KESAVAN, cardiologist, researcher; b. Jaffna, Sri Lanka, Dec. 6, 1965; s. Krishnambal and Shanmuganathan; m. Girija Shan, Nov. 28, 1992; children: Tamara, Devan, Evan. BSc with honors, U. London, 1987, MBBS MD with honors, 1990. Diplomate Am. Bd. Internal Medicine, 1996, Nat. Bd. Echocardiography, 1999, cardiovas. diseases Am. Bd. Internal Medicine, 2000, cert. nuc. cardiology Am. Bd. Nuc. Medicine, 2001. Clin. instr. medicine Baylor Coll. Of Medicine, Houston, 1998—2000; cardiologist Tex. Heart Inst., Houston, 1999—2001, Cardiology Of Houston, 2001; clin. asst. prof. medicine U. Tex., Houston, 2001—. Med. edn. com. S.W. Meml. Hosp., Affiliate U. Tex., Houston. Contbr. articles to profl. jours.; author: (multiple pubs. in peer-rev. jours. including) The Lancet, Circulation, Jour. Am. Coll. Cardiology, Annals Internal Medicine, Am. Jour. Cardiology. Fellow: Am. Coll. Cardiology (fellow, Merck award and Young Clin. Investigator award finalist 1999); mem.: Royal Coll. Physcians. Achievements include research in cardiovascular MRI echocardiography; discovery of tissue doppler changes and diastolic dysfunction in hibernating myocardium; cardiovascular MRI and nuclear cardiology. Office: Cardiology Of Houston 7737 SW Freeway Ste 780 Houston TX 77074 Office Phone: 713-988-9512. E-mail: shankg@att.net.

SHANAHAN, BETTY, professional society administrator; BSEE, Mich. State. U.; M of Software Engring., Wang Inst. of Grad. Studies; MBA in Strategic Mgmt., U. Chgo. Grad. Sch. of Bus. Various positions in devel., engring. mgmt. and mktg. Data Gen., Alliant Computer Sys., 1978—90; mktg. mgmt., including v.p., prod. mgmt. and mktg., software components divsn. Stellent, Inc., 1990—2002; exec. dir. Soc. of Women Engr., Chgo., 2002—. Bd. dir. Women in Engring. Programs and Adv. Network. Fellow: Soc. Women Engr. (life); mem.: IEEE, Am. Soc. of Assn. Execs., Assn. for Computing Machinery. Office: Exec Dir Soc of Women Engr 230 E Ohio St Chicago IL 60611

SHANAHAN, BRENDAN FREDERICK, professional hockey player; b. Mimico, Ont., Can., Jan. 23, 1969; Left wing NJ Devils, 1987—91, St. Louis Blues, 1991—95, Hartford Whalers, 1995—97, Detroit Red Wings, 1997—2006, NY Rangers, 2006—. Player NHL All-Star Game, 1994, 1996—2000, 2002. Named to First All-Star Team, NHL, 1994, 2000, Second All-Star Team, 2002; recipient King Clancy Meml. Trophy, 2003, Mark Messier Leadership Award, 2006. Achievements include being a member of Stanley Cup Champion Detroit Red Wings, 1997, 1998, 2002; being a member of gold medal Canadian Hockey team, Salt Lake City Olympic Games, 2002. Office: NY Rangers Hockey Club 2 Pennsylvania Plaza New York NY 10121

SHANAHAN, EDWARD J., headmaster; b. NYC; m. Sandra Podesta Shanahan; children: Tom, Nell, Kate. BA in Philosophy, St. Joseph's Coll., Yonkers, NY, 1965; MA in Eng. Lit., Fordham U., Bronx, NY, 1968; PhD in Eng. Lit., U. Wis., Madison, 1982. Prof. Eng. Fordham U., Bronx, 1970—71; hall adv. U. Wis., Madison, 1971—72; dir. housing Wesleyan U., Middletown, Conn., 1972—73, assoc. dean, 1973—77, dean of students, 1977—82; dean Dartmouth Coll., Hanover, NH, 1982—91; pres. & headmaster Choate Rosemary Hall, 1991—. Bd. mem. Conn. Assn. of Independent Schools, 1993—97, 2003—; bd. dirs. United Educators Inc., 1989—2004, chair, 1998—2004; chmn. commn. on institutions of higher ed. New England Assn. of Schools and Colleges, 1990. Mem.: NEASC (pres. 1992). Office: Choate Rosemary Hall 333 Christian St Wallingford CT 06492 *

SHANAHAN, LAURI M., lawyer, retail executive; b. 1962; BS in Fin., U. Colo., Boulder; JD, UCLA. Bar: Calif. 1987. Assoc. Thelen, Reid & Priest, San Francisco, 1987—92; dir. legal dept. Gap Inc., San Francisco, 1992—98, sr. v.p., gen. counsel, 1998—2004, corp. sec., 2000—04, chief compliance officer, 2001—04, exec. v.p., chief compliance officer, gen. counsel, corp. sec., 2004—06, chief legal and adminstrv. officer, 2006—. Co-chmn. Lawyers Com. for Civil Rights. Office: Gap Inc 2 Folsom St San Francisco CA 94105 Office Phone: 650-952-4400. *

SHANAHAN, MICHAEL FRANCIS, retired manufacturing executive, former hockey team executive; b. St. Louis, Oct. 29, 1939; m. Mary Ann Barrett; children: Megan Elizabeth, Michael Francis Jr., Maureen Patricia. BS in Commerce, St. Louis U.; postgrad., Washington U., St. Louis; LHD (hon.), St. Louis Rabbinical Coll., 1987; PhD (hon.), St. Louis U., 2002. With McDonnell Douglas Automation Co., St. Louis, 1962-73, sales mgr., 1969-71, br. mgr., 1971-72, mktg. dir. cen. region, 1972-73; mktg. v.p. Numerical Control Inc., St. Louis, 1973-74, pres., 1974-79; v.p. Cleve. Pneumatic Co. (formerly Numerical Control Inc.), St. Louis, 1979-82; chmn., chief exec. officer Engineered Air Systems Inc., St. Louis, 1982—; former chmn., ceo St. Louis Blues Hockey Team. Bd. dirs. Engineered Air Systems Inc. (chmn.), St. Louis Blues Hockey Inc. (chmn.); adv. com. Nat. Hockey League; mem. U.S. Senatorial Bus. Adv. Bd.; bd. dirs. Capital Bank and Trust of Clayton, The Graphic Arts Ctr. Inc., Kilo Rsch. Found. (vice chmn.). Bd. dirs. Am. Heart Assn., St. Louis Ambassadors, Catholic Charities of St. Louis, Galway Sister City Com., The Backstoppers, Christmas in St. Louis Found.; nat. bd. dirs. Boys Hope; bd. trustees, pres. coun. St. Louis U.; adv. bd. Safe Kids; hon. bd. Paraquad; hon. chmn. Small Bus. Week in St. Louis, 1989; hon. co-chmn. Veteran's Day Observance and Parade, 1989; co-chairperson AMC Cancer Rsch. Ctr. Community Svc. award. Named St. Louis Ambassador of Yr., 1986, Olivette Businessman of Yr., 1987, St. Louis Bus. Leader of Yr. Coll. Bus. Adminstrn., So. Ill. U. at Carbondale, 1987,Outstanding Philanthropist St. Louis chpt., Nat. Soc. Fund Raising Execs., 1987; recipient Spirit of Life award City of Hope Labor Mgmt., 1987, St. Louis U. Alumni Merit award, 1987, Meritorious Svc. to Sports award MS Soc., 1987, Presdl. Sports award Maryville Coll., 1987, Sales Exec. of Yr. award Sales and Mktg. Execs. of Met. St. Louis, 1988, St. Louis Port Coun.'s Mgmt. Man of the Yr. award Greater St. Louis Area and Vicinity Port Council, Maritime Trades Dept., AFL-CIO,, 1989. Mem. Alzeimer's Disease and Related Disorders Assn. (hon.), St. Louis Counts, Hawthorn Found., St. Louis Club, Mo. Athletic Club, Old Warson Country Club, Boone Valley Country Club. Home: 10 Trent Dr Saint Louis MO 63124-1033 Office: Engineered Air Systems Inc 201 Evans Ln Saint Louis MO 63121-1126

SHANAHAN, MIKE, professional football coach; b. Oak Park, Ill., Aug. 24, 1952; m. Peggy, children: Kyle, Krystal. BS Phys. Edn., Eastern Illinois U., Charleston, 1974; MS Phys. Edn., 1975. Student coach Eastern Illinois U.; asst. coach U. Oklahoma, 1975-76; offensive coord. No. Ariz. U., 1976—77, Ea. Ill. U., 1977—78, U. Minn., 1979—80, U. Fla., Gainesville, 1980—84, asst. head coach, 1983—84; receivers coach Denver Broncos, 1984-87; head coach LA Raiders, 1988-89; asst. coach Denver Broncos, 1989-91; offensive coord. San Francisco 49ers, 1992-94; head coach Denver Broncos, 1995—. Achievements include coaching the Super Bowl Champion Denver Bronco's, 1997, 1998. Avocations: golf, travel. Office: Denver Broncos 13655 Broncos Pkwy Englewood CO 80112-4150

SHANAHAN, REBECCA M., lawyer; b. 1953; BA magna cum laude, Ind. U., 1974; JD cum laude, 1977. Bar: Ind. 1977, Ill. 1997, Fla. 2003. Of counsel RCA Consumer Electronics, 1980—86; v.p., gen. counsel Cmty. Hosps. Ind., Inc., 1986—91; sr. v.p. Methodist Health Group, 1991—96; v.p. managed care and bus. devel. U. Chgo. Hosps. and Health Systems, 1997—2002; exec. v.p. adminstrn., gen. counsel, sec. Priority Healthcare Corp., Lake Mary, Fla., 2002—05; gen. mgr. Aetna Specialty Pharmacy, Orlando, Fla., 2006—. Cons. The Shanahan Group, 1996—97; bd. dirs. SinusPharma, Priority Healthcare Corp., Sanovia. Office: Aetna Specialty Pharmacy 503 Sunport Ln Orlando FL 32809 Office Phone: 407-513-6440. Personal E-mail: rorysh@aol.com.

SHANAHAN, SHEILA ANN, pediatrician, educator; m. Justin Laurence Cashman Jr., Sept. 14, 1968; children: Justin III, Gillis. BA, Trinity Coll., 1963; MD cum laude, Med. Coll. Pa., 1969. Diplomate Nat. Bd. Med. Examiners, Am. Bd. Pediats. Intern Presbyn. Hosp., NYC, 1969-70, resident in pediats., 1970-72, asst. in clin. pediats., 1972-75, assoc. clin. pediats., 1975-78; pvt. practice specializing in pediats. Greenwich, Conn., 1972-78; asst. attending Greenwich Hosp., 1972-73, assoc. attending, 1973-78; from instr. to assoc. Columbia Coll. Physicians and Surgeons, NYC, 1972-78; asst. prof. pediats. George Washington U. Sch. Medicine, Washington, 1980—, Georgetown U. Sch. Medicine, Washington, 1984—; pvt. practice specializing in pediats. Washington, 1984—. Attending dept. ambulatory medicine Children's Hosp. Nat. Med. Ctr., Washington, 1980—84; courtesy staff Georgetown U. Hosp., Washington, 1984—, Sibley Meml. Hosp., Washington, 1984—, Children's Hosp. Nat. Med. Ctr., 1984—. Fellow Am. Acad. Pediats.; mem. Am. Women's Med. Assn. Office: 4900 Massachusetts Ave NW Washington DC 20016-4358

SHANAHAN, THOMAS M., judge; b. Omaha, May 5, 1934; m. Jane Estelle Lodge, Aug. 4, 1956; children: Catherine, Thomas M. II, Mary Elizabeth, Timothy F. AB magna cum laude, U. Notre Dame, 1956; JD, Georgetown U., 1959. Bar: Nebr., Wyo. Mem. McGinley, Lane, Mueller, Shanahan, O'Donnell & Merritt, Ogallala, Nebr.; assoc. justice Nebr. Supreme Ct., Lincoln, 1983-93; judge U.S. Dist. Ct. Nebr., Omaha, 1993—. Office: US Dist Ct 111 S 18th Plz Ste 3141 Omaha NE 68102

SHANAHAN, WILLIAM STEPHEN, consumer products company executive; b. Cin., Apr. 15, 1940; s. William Stephen and Dorothea (Murken) S.; children: Kimberly, Michael Erika, Alejandra. BA, Dartmouth Coll., 1962; postgrad., U. Calif.-Berkeley, 1962-63, Internat. Christian U., Tokyo, 1963-64, U. Philippines-Manila, 1964-65. Joined Colgate-Palmolive Co., 1965, pres., gen. mgr. Sao Paulo, Brazil, 1972-76, v.p. mktg. services div. Colgate U.S.A. NYC, 1976-78; pres., CEO Helena Rubinstein, NYC, 1978-80; v.p. western hemisphere, group v.p. Colgate-Palmolive Co., NYC, sr. exec. v.p. ops., until 1989, chief oper. officer, 1989-2000, pres., 2000—. Office: Colgate-Palmolive Co 300 Park Ave New York NY 10022-7402

SHANE, JEFFREY NEIL, federal agency administrator, lawyer; b. NYC, Mar. 27, 1941; s. Albert and Ann (Semanoff) S.; m. Jean Wu, June 27, 1992; 1 child Ann Wu. AB, Princeton U., 1962; LLB, Columbia U., NYC, 1965. Bar: D.C. 1966. Trial atty. FPC, Washington, 1966-68, Dept. Transp., Washington, 1968-70, spl. asst. to gen. counsel, 1970-72; traveled in Africa, Europe, 1972-73; researcher Environ. Law Inst., Washington, 1974-75; mem. UN Task Force on Human Environ., Bangkok, 1975-77; atty., cons. environ. law in developing countries, Washington, 1978-79; asst. gen. counsel internat. law Dept. Transp., Washington, 1979-83, dep. asst. sec. policy and internat. affairs, 1983-85, asst. sec. policy and internat. affairs, 1989—93, assoc. dep. sec., 2002—03, under sec. for policy, 2003—; dep. asst. sec. transp. affairs Dept. of State, Washington, 1985-89; counsel Wilmer, Cutler & Pickering, Washington, 1993-96, ptnr., 1997-2000, Hogan & Hartson, Washington, 2000—02. Adj. prof. law Georgetown U., Washington, 1985-89; mem. Archl. and Transp. Barriers Compliance Bd., 1989-93, 2005-06, vice-chmn., 1992-93; vice chmn. Adv. Com. on Confs. in Ocean Shipping, 1990-91; chmn. commn. on air transport Internat. C. of C., Paris, 1994-2001, chmn. mil. airlift com. Nat. Defense Transport Assn.; mem, Air Transp. Stabilization Bd., 2004-. Co-author: Developing Economies and the Environment, 1978; co-author-editor: NEPA in Action: The Impact of the National Environmental Policy Act on Federal Decision-Making, 1975, Environmental and Natural Resource Management in Developing Countries, 1979. With USAR, 1965—71. Named Transportation Person of Yr., U. Md. Sch. Bus., 2006; recipient Presdl. Meritorious Rank award, Dept. of State, 1988, L. Welch Pogue award for Lifetime Achievement in Aviation, 2006. Mem.: ABA (chmn. forum on air and space law 2001), Cosmos Club (Wash.), Met. Club, Columbia Country Club (Chevy Chase, Md.), Wings Club (N.Y.C. bd. govs. 1995—98), Internat. Aviation Club (Washington pres. 1999—2000), Aero Club (Washington bd. govs. 1984—86). Jewish. Home: 5015 Rockwood Pkwy NW Washington DC 20016-1913 Office: Dept Transp West Bldg 1200 New Jersey Ave SE Washington DC 20590 Home Phone: 202-244-5279; Office Phone: 202-366-1815. Business E-Mail: jeff.shane@dot.gov.

SHANE, JOHN MARDER, endocrinologist; b. Kansas City, Mo., Oct. 5, 1942; s. Henry Kamsler and Ruth (Marder) S.; m. Eileen Goodart, June 18, 1967; children: Robert M., Edward G. BS, U. Okla., 1964, MD, 1967. Diplomate Am. Bd. Ob-Gyn., Am. Bd. Reproductive Endocrinology; cert. master gardener. Resident Harvard Med. Sch., Boston, 1970-73, fellowship, 1973-75, instr., 1970-75, asst. prof., 1975-78; pvt. practice Tulsa, 1978-99. Lectr., cons. Tutorial Svcs. Internat., England, 1984—; bd. dirs. St. Francies G.I.F.T. Lab., Tulsa; cons. to preimplantation genetics project Chapman Genetics Inst., Children's Med. Ctr., Tulsa. Author: CIBA Symposium Infertility: Diagnosis and Treatment; contbr. articles to profl. jours. and publs.; exhibitions include Okla. Woodturners, The Philbrook Mus. Active Tulsa Garden Ctr., 1988—; bd. dirs. Temple Israel, Tulsa, 1985-86, Up With Trees Found., 2000—, Tulsa, master gardener. Capt. USAF, 1967-69. Recipient Annual award Boston Obstet. Soc., 1977; named one of Best Doctor's in Am., Tulsa's Best Doctors, Tulsa People Mag. Mem. ACS, Tulsa Gynecol. Soc. (past pres. 1986-87), Soc. Reproductive Endocrinologists, Tulsa bonsai Soc. (bd. dirs. 1988—), Am. Coll. Ob-Gyn. (v.p. 1971-92, pres. New England Jr. divsn. 1972-73), Am. Bonsai Soc. (nat. bd. dirs.), Chanie des Rotisseurs (l'Ordre Mondial, Tulsa v.p., advisor to bd., Bronze Star 2001), Southside Rotary of Tulsa (bd. dirs., pres. 1997-98, Nat. Arboretum Bonsai Pavillion (nat. bd. dirs.), Rotary Club Tulsa (past pres. Southside club). Republican. Jewish. Avocations: gardening, cooking, bonsai, collector Oriental arts, woodturning.

SHANE, KEVIN, apparel executive, entrepreneur; b. 1981; B in Entrepreneurial Studies and Fin., Babson Coll., Wellesley, Coll., 2003. Owner, pres. K.O. Stogie Innovations, LLC (Telmé Clothing), Mantoloking, NJ, 2003—. Named one of Best Entrepreneurs Under 25, BusinessWeek mag., 2006. Roman Catholic. Avocations: kayaking, skiing, soccer, history. Office: KO Stogie Innovations LLC Ste 4101 438 Hwy 35 N Mantoloking NJ 08738 Office Phone: 732-546-4669. Office Fax: 609-883-2352. E-mail: info@kostogie.com. *

SHANE, PENNY, lawyer; b. NYC, 1963; BA, Barnard Coll., 1985; JD, NYU, 1988. Bar: NY 1989, US Ct. of Appeal (2nd cir.) and (DC cir.), US Dist. Courts (so., ea., we. districts) NY, NY State Courts. Law clk. Judge Richard Owen US Dist. Ct. (so. dist.) NY, 1988—90; ptnr. and mem. litig. group, fin. institutions group, criminal def. and investigations group Sullivan & Cromwell, NYC. Office: Sullivan & Cromwell 125 Broad St New York NY 10004-2498 Office Phone: 212-558-4000. Office Fax: 212-558-3588. Business E-Mail: shanep@sullcrom.com.

SHANE, PETER MILO, law educator; b. Oceanside, NY, July 12, 1952; s. Albert and Ann (Semanoff) S.; m. Martha Elisabeth Chamallas, June 27, 1981; 1 child: Elisabeth Ann. AB, Harvard U., 1974; JD, Yale U., 1977. Bar: N.Y. 1978, U.S. Ct. Appeals (5th cir.) 1978, D.C. 1979, U.S. Ct. Appeals (8th cir.) 1983, U.S. Supreme Ct. 1984, Pa. 1995. Law clk. to judge U.S. Ct. Appeals (5th cir.), New Orleans, 1977-78; atty., advisor office of legal counsel U.S. Dept. Justice, Washington, 1978-81; asst. gen. counsel Office of Mgmt. and Budget, Washington, 1981; assoc. prof. law U. Iowa, Iowa City, 1981-85, prof., 1985-94; dean U. Pitts., 1994-98, prof., 1994—2001; Disting. Service prof. law & pub. policy, dir. Inst. for Study of Info. Tech. and Soc., Carnegie Mellon U., 2001—03, Disting. Service prof. law & pub. policy (adj.), 2003—, chair adv. bd., 2003—06; Joseph S. Platt-Porter, Wright, Morris and Arthur prof law, dir. Ctr. Interdisciplinary Law & Policy Studies, Ohio State U., 2003—07; Jacob E. Davis and Jacob E. Davis II chair in law Ohio State U., 2007—, dir. project law and democratic devel., 2007—. Adj. lectr. Am. U., Washington, D.C., 1979-80; vis. prof. law Duke U., Durham, N.C., 1986, Boston Coll., Newton, Mass., 1999, Villanova (Pa.) U., 1999, Carnegie Mellon U., 2000-01; cons. U.S. Dept. Edn., Washington, D.C., 1980, MacArthur Justice Found., Chgo., 1987; active Adminstrv. Conf. U.S., 1991, pub. mem., 1995; cons. Nat. Commn. Jud. Discipline and Removal, 1992-93; cooperating atty. Iowa Civil Liberties Union, Des Moines, 1982-94, bd. dirs., 1987-89; active Coun. on Legal Edn. Opportunity, 1996-2004; reporter Civil Justice Adv. Group, U.S. Dist. Ct. (we. dist.) Pa. Author: (with H.H. Bruff) The Law of Presidential Power: Cases and Materials, 1988, (with H.H. Bruff) Separation of Powers Law, 1996, 2005, (with J. Mashaw and R. Merrill) Administrative Law: The American Public Law System, 2003, Democracy Online: The Prospects for Political Renewal Through the Internet, 2004, (with John Podesta and Richard C. Leone) A Little Knowledge: Security, Privacy and Public Information After September 11, 2004. Mem. Dem. cen. com. Johnson County, Iowa, 1982-88. Recipient citation for outstanding svc. Pa. House of Reps., 1998, Cleo Disting. Svc. award, 2004; named Young Leader of Higher Edn., Am. Assn. Higher Edn., 1998; Old Gold Summer fellow U. Iowa, 1981-84, Mellon Found. fellow, 1982. Mem. ABA (coun. sect. adminstrv. law and regulatory practice 1993-96, chmn. com. on govt. orgn. and separation of powers 1987-91), Assn. Am. Law Schs. (chair adminstrv. law 1990, chair remedies 1992, chair law sch. deans 1997), Am. Law Inst. Jewish. Office: Ohio State U Moritz Coll Law 55 W 12th Ave Columbus OH 43210 Office Phone: 614-688-3014. Business E-Mail: shane.29@osu.edu.

SHANE, WILLIAM WHITNEY, astronomer; b. Berkeley, Calif., June 3, 1928; s. Charles Donald and Mary Lea (Heger) S.; BA, U. Calif., Berkeley, 1951, postgrad., 1953-58; ScD, Leiden U., The Netherlands, 1971; m. Clasina van der Molen, Apr. 22, 1964; children: Johan Jacob, Charles Donald. rsch. assoc. Leiden U., 1961-71, sr. scientist, 1971-79; prof. astronomy, dir. Astron. Inst., Cath. U. Nijmegen, The Netherlands, 1979-88; guest prof. astronomy Leiden U., 1988-93; C.H. Adams fellow Monterey Inst. Rsch. Astronomy, Calif., 1994—. With USN, 1951-53. Fellow AAAS; mem. Internat. Astron. Union (commns. 33, 34), Am. Astron. Soc., Astron. Soc. Netherlands, Astron. Soc. of the Pacific, Phi Beta Kappa. Achievements include rsch. on structure and dynamics of galaxies, observational astronomy. Home: 9095 Coker Rd Prunedale CA 93907-1401 Office: Monterey Inst Rsch Astronomy 200 8th St Marina CA 93933-6002 Office Phone: 831-883-1000.

SHANG, CHARLES YULIN, medical physicist; b. Shanghai, June 1957; came to U.S., 1987; s. Jian and Ming Shang; m. Monica M. Shang, Aug. 1, 1985; children: Stephen, Michael. MD, 2nd Med. U., Shanghai, China, 1983; postdoctoral cert., Chgo. Med. Sch., North Chgo., Ill., 1988; MS in Radiation Health/Med. Physics, U. Pitts., 1990. Diplomate in Radiological Physics, Am. Bd. Radiology. Resident 301 Gen. Hosp., Beijing, 1983-85, radiologist, 1985-87; vis. radiologist Evanston (Ill.) Univ. Hosp., 1988, Allegheny Gen. Hosp., Pitts., 1988-89; grad. student rschr. Presbyn. Univ. Hosp., Pitts., 1989-90; med. physicist St. Mary's Hosp., Waterbury, Conn., 1991-93; sr. med. physicist Boca Raton (Fla.) Comty. Hosp., 1993-97; med. physicist, radiation safety officer N. Broward Med. Ctr., Pompano Beach, Fla., 1998—2001; dir. med. physics Boca Raton Cmty. Hosp., 2001—. Contbr. articles to profl. jours. including Radiology, Neurosurgery, Annals N.Y. Acad. Scis., IEEE Transactions on Biomed. Engring. Recipient grad. scholarship U. Pitts., 1989-90. Mem. Am. Assn. Physicists in Medicine, Am. Coll. Radiology. Achievements include patents on a handheld body stereotactic guider for interventional radiology, China and U.S. Home and Office: 8643 Yellow Rose Ct Boynton Beach FL 33437

SHANG, YI, computer scientist, educator; b. Taiyuan, Shanxi, China, Sept. 25, 1967; came to U.S., 1991; s. Zhixiang Shang; m. Lei Zhu, July 3, 1970. PhD, U. Ill., 1997. Rsch. asst. U. Ill., Champaign-Urbana, 1991-97; asst. prof. U. Mo., Columbia, 1997—2004, assoc. prof., 2004—; rsch. scientist Xerox Palo Alto (Calif.) Rsch. Ctr., 2000—02, Palo Alto (Calif.) Rsch. Ctr., 2002—03. Grantee U. Mo., 1998—, NSF, 1998—, DARPA, 2001-04. Mem. IEEE, ASEE, AAAI, ACM. Office: U Mo-Columbia Dept Computer Sci 201 EBW Columbia MO 65211 Office Phone: 573-884-7794. E-mail: shangy@missouri.edu.

SHANGRAW, ROBERT EDWARD, medical educator, researcher; b. Troy, NY, Mar. 16, 1954; s. Robert Dixon and M. Janice (Bonacker) S.; m. Patricia Mary Ford, May 25, 1985; children: Kirsten Celanire, Sarah Elizabeth, Kathleen Ford. BS, Rensselaer Poly. Inst., 1976; PhD, Albany Med. Coll., NY, 1981, MD, 1985. Resident in surgery U. Wash., Seattle, 1985-86; rsch. assoc. U. Tex. Med. Br., Galveston, 1986-87; resident in anesthesia Hosp. U. Pa., Phila., 1987-90; asst. prof. anesthesiology Oreg. Health and Sci. U., Portland, 1990—96, assoc. prof., 1996—2001, prof., 2001—. Cons. NIH Study Sects., 1998—. Contbr. articles on biomedicine to profl. jours. Fellow NIH, 1977-80, 82, 83. Mem. AMA, Am. Physiol. Soc., Am. Soc. Anesthesiologists, Internat. Anesthesia Rsch. Soc., Biochem. Soc., Assn. Univ. Anesthesiologists, Sigma Xi, Alpha Omega Alpha. Roman Catholic. Avocations: skiing, sailing, hiking, kayaking, swimming. Home: 5776 SW Calusa Loop Tualatin OR 97062-9757 Office: Oreg Health and Sci U Dept Anesthesiology and Periop Medicine 3181 SW Sam Jackson Park Rd Portland OR 97239-3098 Office Phone: 503-494-7641. Business E-Mail: shangraw@ohsu.edu.

SHANINE, GEORGE, sales executive, information technology executive; b. Peoria, Ill., 1974; Grad., U. Ill., Chgo. With IBM Corp., 1995—, head of Midwest brand sales divsn. Named one of 40 Under 40, Crain's Chgo. Bus. Home: 3803 Looking Post Ct Naperville IL 60564-5928

SHANK, CHARLES VERNON, science administrator, educator, physicist; b. Mt. Holly, NJ, July 12, 1943; s. Augustus Jacob and Lillian (Peterson) S.; m. Brenda Buckhold, June 16, 1969. BS, U. Calif., Berkeley, 1965, MS, PhD, 1969. Mem. tech. staff AT&T Bell Labs., Holmdel, NJ, 1969-76, head quantum physics and electronics dept., 1976-83, dir. Electronics Rsch. Lab., 1983-89; dir. Lawrence Berkeley Lab., prof. chemistry, physics, elec. engring. and computer scis. U. Calif., Berkeley, 1989—2004. Co-author over 200 sci. pubs. Recipient E. Longstreth medal Franklin Inst., Phila., 1982, Morris E. Leeds award IEEE, 1982, David Sarnoff award IEEE, 1989, Edgerton award Optical Soc. Engring., John Scott award, Edward P. Longstreth award Franklin Soc. Fellow AAAS, IEEE, Am. Phys. Soc. (George E. Pake prize 1996, Arthur L. Schawlow prize 1997), Optical Soc. Am. (R. W. Wood prize 1981); mem. NAS, NAE, Am. Acad. Arts and Scis. Numerous patents in field. Home: 118 S Kalaheo Ave Kailua HI 96734-2932

SHANK, FRED ROSS, food scientist; b. Harrisonburg, Va., Oct. 11, 1940; m. Peggy Anne Westbrook, June 1967; children: Virginia Anne, Fred Ross III. BS in Agriculture, U. Ky., 1962, MS in Nutrition, 1964; PhD, U. Md., 1969. Dep. dir. Office Nutrition and Food Sci. FDA, Washington, 1979-86, dir. Office Phys. Sci., 1986-87, dep. dir. Ctr. for Food SAfety and Applied Nutrition, 1987-89, dir., 1989-98, sr. advisor to FDA commr., 1998-99; sr. v.p. sci. Chocolate Mfrs. Assn., McLean, Va., 1999—2000; v.p. Sci. Inst. Food Tech., Washington, 2000. Fellow Inst. Food Technologists; mem. Am. Assn. Cereal Chemists, Am. Soc. for Nutrition. Home: 2621 Steeplechase Dr Reston VA 20191-2130 Home Phone: 703-620-3133; Office Phone: 202-466-5980. E-mail: fred_shank001@comcast.net.

SHANK, J. WILLIAM, art conservator; Studied art history and art conservation, Villa Schifanoia, Florence, Italy; grad. studies, NYU Inst. Fine Arts; advanced tng. in art conservation, Harvard U. With We. Ctr. for the Conservation of Fine Arts; mem. staff San Francisco Mus. Modern Art, 1985—2000, chief conservator, 1991—2000; now with Conservation Resources Mgmt. Founder Rescue Pub. Murals (in cooperation with Heritage Preservation). Curator (conservation based exhbn.) A Hidden Picasso, Guggenheim Mus., Bilbao, Spain, 2004. Booth Family Rome Prize Fellowship for Historic Preservation and Conservation, Am. Acad. in Rome, 2004—05. Address: P O Box 410266 San Francisco CA 94141-0266

SHANK, MARK A., lawyer; b. Quincy, Ill., Sept. 22, 1954; BS cum laude, S.W. Mo. State U., 1976; JD, Mo. U., 1979; LLM, So. Meth. U., Dallas, 1984. Bar: Mo. 1979, Tex. 1981. Ptnr. Hughes & Luce, LLP, Dallas. Mem. editl. bd. adv. Employment Law Counselor newsletter. Mem. Target Kids in Ct. Steering Com., East Dallas C. of C., Leadership Dallas, 1994; bd. dir. Tex. Gen. Counsel Forum, Profl. Bank. Named Most Outstanding Mem., East Dallas C. of C., 1998; named one of Best Lawyers in Dallas, D Mag., 2001, 2005; named to The World's Leading Lawyers, Chambers and Ptnrs., London; recipient Dallas Vol. Project Pro Bono Svc. award, 2001. Fellow: ABA, Tex. Bar Found.; mem.: Dallas Bar Assn. (chair labor and employment law sect. 1994, pres. 2001, v.p and chair), Am. Bd. Trial Advs. (bd. dirs.), Ctr. Am. Internat. Law Rsch. (fellows and planning com.), Coll. State Bar Tex., Fedn. Def. Corp. Counsel, Dallas Bar Found. (trustee), Dallas Assn. Young Lawyers (pres. 1996), Tex. Young Lawyers Assn. (chair, v.p. and sec. 1989—90), State Bar Tex. (chair labor and employment law sect. 1998—99, dir. 2002—, Pres.'s Citation Merit 2003), Phi Kappa Phi, Phi Delta Phi. Office: Hughes & Luce LLP 1717 Main St Ste 2800 Dallas TX 75201 Office Phone: 214-939-5420. Office Fax: 214-939-5849. E-mail: mark.shank@hughesluce.com. *

SHANK, MAURICE EDWIN, aerospace engineer, consultant; b. NYC, Apr. 22, 1921; s. Edwin A. and Viola (Lewis) S.; m. Virginia Lee King, Sept. 25, 1948; children: Christopher K., Hilary L. Shank-Kuhl, Diana L. Shank. BS in Mech. Engring., Carnegie-Mellon U., 1942; D.Sc., MIT, 1949. Registered profl. engr., Mass. Assoc. prof. mech. engring. MIT, Cambridge, 1949-60; dir. advanced materials R&D Pratt & Whitney, East Hartford, Conn., 1960-70; mgr. materials engring. and rsch., 1971-72; dir. engring. tech., 1972-80; dir. engine design and structures engring. Pratt & Whitney, East Hartford, Conn., 1980-81, dir. engring. tech., 1981-85, dir. engring. tech. assessment, 1985-86; v.p. Pratt Whitney of China, Inc., East Hartford, 1986-87; pvt. exec. cons. to industry and govt., 1987—. Cons. editor McGraw-Hill Book Co., N.Y.C., 1960-80; adv. com. to mechanics div. Nat. Bur. Standards, Washington, 1964-69; vis. com. dept. mech. engring. Carnegie-Mellon U., Pitts., 1968-78; corp. vis. coms. depts. materials sci. and engring., dept. aeros. and astronautics MIT, 1968-74, 79-92; mem. rsch. and tech. adv. coun. com. on aero. propulsion NASA, Washington, 1973-77, mem. aero. adv. com., 1978-86; mem. aero. and space engring. bd. NRC, 1989-92; lectr. in field. Contbr. articles to profl. jours. Served to maj. U.S. Army Corps. of Engrs., Ordnance Corps, 1942-46, Middle East/North Africa. Fellow AIAA, ASME, AIME, Am. Soc. Metals; mem. Nat. Acad. Engring., Conn. Acad. Sci. and Engring. Clubs: Cosmos. Episcopalian. Avocations: boating, fishing.

SHANK, RON, publishing executive; m. Gwen Shank; 2 children. Grad., So. Ill. Univ. Joined Libr. Jour., Sch. Libr. Jour., 1988, advt. dir., 1995—98, assoc. pub., 1998—2006, pub., 2006—. Mem.: Nat. Assn. of Media & Tech. Centers. Office: Library Journal 360 Park Ave S New York NY 10010 Office Phone: 615-377-1332. Business E-Mail: rshank@reedbusiness.com.

SHANK, RUSSELL, librarian, educator; b. Spokane, Wash., Sept. 2, 1925; s. Harry and Sadie S.; m. Doris Louise Hempfer, Nov. 9, 1951 (div.); children: Susan Marie, Peter Michael, Judith Louise. BS, U. Wash., 1946, BA, 1949; MBA, U. Wis., 1952; DrLS, Columbia U., 1966. Reference libr. U. Wash., Seattle, 1949; asst. engring. libr. U. Wis.-Madison, 1949-52; chief pers. Milw. Pub. Libr., 1952; engring.-phys. scis. libr. Columbia U., NYC, 1953-59, sr. lectr., 1964-66, assoc. prof., 1966-67; asst. univ. libr. U. Calif.-Berkeley, 1959-64; dir. sci. libr. N.Y. Met. Reference and Rsch., 1966-68; dir. librs. Smithsonian Instn., Washington, 1967-77; univ. libr. prof. UCLA, 1977-89, asst. vice chancellor for libr. and info. svcs. planning, 1989-91, univ. libr., prof. emeritus, 1991—. Cons. Indonesian Inst. Sci., 1970; bd. cons. Pahlavi Nat. Library, Iran, 1975-76; pres. U.S. Book Exchange, 1975; bd. trustees Freedom to Read Found., 1989—. Trustee OCLC, Inc., 1978-84, 87, chmn., 1984; mem. library del. People's Republic of China, 1979; bd. dirs. Am. Council on Edn., 1980-81. Served with USNR, 1943-46. Recipient Disting. Alumnus award U. Wash. Sch. Librarianship, 1968, Role of Honor award Freedom to Read Found., 1990, Disting. Alumnus award Columbia U. Sch. Libr. Sci., 1992; fellow Coun. on Libr. Resources, 1973-74. Fellow AAAS; mem. ALA (pres. 1978-79, coun. 1961-65, 74-82, exec. bd. 1975-80, chmn. internat. rels. com. 1980-83, pres. info. sci. and automation div. 1968-69), Assn. Coll. and Rsch. Librs. (pres. 1972-73, Hugh Atkinson award 1990), Assn. Rsch. Librs. (bd. dirs. 1974-77), Beta Phi Mu. Home: 12919 Montana Ave Apt 101 Los Angeles CA 90049-4843 Business E-Mail: rshank@ucla.edu. *Intellectual freedom is the paramount human right. It is the American's premier heritage. Without it the claim to democracy is a sham. Should the principles of our society fade or perish, the survival of this freedom alone would justify the nation's experience. The freedom to think, to read, and to speak will be our enduring monument. Their diffusion throughout the world must be our unending crusade.*

SHANK, SUZANNE ADAMS, lawyer; b. Kansas City, Mo., Nov. 13, 1946; d. Howard Howe and Bettie Ann (Winkler) Hettick; m. Martin Smoler, May 18, 1991. BJ, U. Mo., 1972; MPA in Health Adminstrn., U. Mo., Kansas City, 1982, JD, 1982. Bar: Mo. 1982, U.S. Dist. Ct. (we. dist.) Mo. 1982. Journalist U. Kans. Med. Ctr., Kansas City, 1972-73; asst. editor Am. Family Physician, Kansas City, Mo., 1973-75; exec. dir. Lambert Med. Clinic, Kansas City, Mo., 1975-80; assoc. Shughart, Thomson & Kilroy, Kansas City, 1982-85; v.p. GE/Employers Reins. Corp., Overland Park, Kans., 1985-2000; sr. v.p. Attys. Liability Assurance Soc., Chgo., 2000—. Mem. Friends of Zoo, Kansas City, Mo., 1981—, Menorah Med. Ctr. Aux., Kansas City, 1982—, Women's Vision Internat., Kansas City, Mo., 1999—; mem. Internat. Rels. Coun., 1999—; bd. dirs. Friends Conservatory Music, Kansas City, 2002—, Found. on Aging, Kansas City, 2003—. Mem. ABA, Mo. Bar Assn., Kansas City Bar Assn. (chmn. ins. law com.), Soc. Profl. Journalists, Soc. CPCU (rsch. com.), Com. to Protect Journalists, Kappa Tau alpha. Home: 2703 W 66th Ter Shawnee Mission KS 66208-1810 Office: Attorneys Liability Assurance Soc 311 S Wacker 5700 Chicago IL 60606

SHANK, WILLIAM O., lawyer; b. Hamilton, Ohio, Jan. 11, 1924; s. Horace Cooper and Bonnie (Winn) S.; m. Shirleen Allison, June 25, 1949; children— Allison Kay, Kristin Elizabeth. BA, Miami U., Oxford, Ohio, 1947; JD, Yale, 1950. Bar: (Ohio), (Ill.), (US Supreme Ct.). Pvt. practice, Hamilton, Ohio, 1951-55, Chgo., 1955—; mem. firm Shank, Briede & Spoerl, Hamilton, Ohio, 1951-55; assoc. Lord, Bissell & Brook, Chgo., 1955-58; atty. Chemetron Corp., 1958-60, sr. atty., 1960-61, gen. atty., asst. sec., 1961-71, sec., gen. counsel, 1971-78; v.p., gen. counsel, sec. Walgreen Co., Deerfield, Ill., 1978-89; ptnr. Burditt & Radzius, Chartered, Chgo., 1989-98; exec. v.p. Internat. Bus. Resources, Inc., Chgo., 1993—2000; ptnr. Williams Montgomery & John Ltd., Chgo., 1998—2003; of counsel Hinshaw & Culbertson, Crystal Lake, Ill., 2003—. Mem. bus. adv. coun. Miami U., Oxford, Ohio, 1975—; arbitrator 19th and 22d Jud. Cir., Ill., 1995—; adv. bd. eLawForum, Washington, 1999—. Bd. dirs. Coun. for Cmty. Svcs. Met. Chgo., 1973-77; trustee Libr. Internat. Rels., 1971-78; bd. dirs. Chgo. Civic Fedn., 1984-89, Walgreen Drug Stores Hist. Found., 1990—; mem. Chgo. Crime Commn., 1985-89. 1st lt., pilot 8th Air Force, USAAF, World War II, ETO. Fellow Am. Bar Found. (life); mem. ABA (com. corp. gen. counsel), Soc. Corp. Secs. and Governance Profls. (pres. Chgo. regional group 1983-84, nat. bd. dirs. 1984-87), Ill. State Bar Assn., Chgo. Bar Assn. (chmn. com. on corp. law depts. 1971-72, 89-90), Yale U. Law Sch. Assn. (past pres. Ill. Alumni, exec. com. New Haven), Walgreen Alumni Assn. (pres. 1992-94), Legal Club (pres. 1979-80), Law Club, Lawyers Club (Chgo.), Univ. Club, Econ. Club, Yale Club of Chgo., Am. Air Mus. in Britain (sustaining mem. 2004-), Omicron Delta Kappa, Phi Delta Phi, Sigma Chi. Home: 755 S Shore Dr Crystal Lake IL 60014-5530 Office: Hinshaw & Culbertson 500 Coventry Ln Crystal Lake IL 60014 Office Phone: 815-459-5123. E-mail: wshank@hinshawlaw.com.

SHANKAR, MAYA, research scientist; d. Ramamurt and Uma S. BS, Yale Univ., New Haven, 2007; MSc. stud. in experimental psychology, Oxford Univ., 2007—. Co-founder, co-editor-in-chief (mag.) Five Mag. Founder, dir. Downtown Devel. Vol. Prog., New Haven. Named one of Top 10 Coll. Women, Glamour Mag., 2006; Rhodes Scholar, 2007. Achievements include founding a publicaion for social justice and human rights; doing rsch. in Australia, Germany and Puerto Rico on subjects relating to psychology, language, visual perception and cognition; being a pvt. violin student of Itzhak Perlman through Juillard precoll. prog., performing at Carnegie Hall. Avocation: bhangra dancer. *

SHANKAR, RAVI, composer, musician; b. Apr. 7, 1920; m. Sukanya Rajan; children: Shubho, Geetali, Anoushka. Studied under, Ustad Allauddin Khan of Maihar; trained in Guru-Shishya tradition, pupil of Ustad Allauddin Khan, 1938. Solo sitar player; former dir. music All India Radio, also founder Nat. Orch.; founder, dir. Kinnara Sch. Music, Bombay, 1962, Kinnara Sch. Music, L.A., 1967; many recordings of traditional and exptl. variety in India, U.K., U.S., including Tana Mana, 1987; concert tours in Europe, U.S., The East; vis. lectr. U. Calif., 1965; appeared in film Raga, 1974; fellow Sangeet Natak Akademi, 1976; responsible for music and choreography for ASIAD, 1982; film scores: Pather Panchali, The Flute and the Arrow, Nava Rasa Ranga, Charly, Gandhi, and many musical compositions including Concerto for Sitar No. 1, 1971, No. 2, 1981, Ghanashyam, 1989, and numerous ragas and talas; author: My Music, My Life, 1969, Rag Anurag (Bengali), (autobiography) Raga Mala, 1997. Recipient Deshikottam award, 1982; Silver Bear of Berlin; award of Indian Nat. Acad. Music, Dance and Drama, 1962; award of Padma Bhushan, 1967, Padma Vibushan, 1981, Internat. Music Coun. UNESCO award, 1975; elected to the Rajya Sabha, India, 1986; recipient 16 hon. doctorates around the world; recipient Grand prize Fukuoka Asian Cultural Prizes, Japan, 1991, Ramon Magsaysay award, The Philippines, 1992, Bharatiya Vidya Bhavan Mahatma Gandhi award, 1992, U.K. Ho. of Commons Shield, 1995, Crystal award, Switzerland, 1995, Premium Imperial Arts award, Japan, 1997, Light of Asia award, U.S., 1997, Juliet Hollister award, U.S., 1998, The Polar Music prize, Sweden, 1998, Bharat Ratna, India, 1999, Hon. KBE, 2000; named Commdr. of Legion of Honour, France, 2000. Address: care Sulivan Sweetland 28 Albion St London W2 2AX England

SHANKEL, DELBERT MERRILL, microbiologist, biologist, educator; b. Plainview, Nebr., Aug. 4, 1927; s. Cecil Wilfred and Gladys Dalton (Dodd) Shankel; m. Carol Jo Mulford, Sept. 10, 1962; children: Merrill, Jill, Kelley. BA, Walla Walla Coll., 1950; PhD, U. Tex., 1959. Tchr. Walla Walla Coll. Acad., College Place, Wash., 1950-51; instr. San Antonio Coll., 1954-55; asst. prof., assoc. prof. microbiology and biology U. Kans., Lawrence, 1959-68, prof., 1968—, asst. dean, assoc. dean arts and sci., 1966-72, acting dean, 1973, exec. vice chancellor, 1974-80, 86, 90-92, acting chancellor, 1980-81, chancellor, 1994-95, chancellor emeritus, 1996. Commr. N. Ctrl. Assn. Colls. and Schs., Chgo., 1991—95, cons., evaluator, 1969—96, NW Comm. Coll., 1997—. Editor: Artimutagenesis and Anti-carcinogenesis: Mechanisms vols. I-III, 1986, 1988, 1993; assoc. editor: Mutation Rsch., 1992—95. Active numerous civic orgns. With US Army, 1952—54. Named Disting. Alumnus of the Yr., Walla Walla Coll., 1989; recipient Outstanding Educator award, Mortar Bd., U. Kans., 1982, 1985, 1990; numerous rsch. grantee. Fellow: Am. Acad. Microbiology; mem.: Radiation Rsch. Soc., Soc. Gen. Microbiology (Eng.), Genetics Soc. Am., Environ. Mutagen Soc. (chmn. pub. policy com. 1991—93, mem. nat. coun. 1994—97), Am. Soc. Microbiology (past chmn. edn. com., chmn. numerous coms.), U. Kans. Alumni Assn. (interim pres., CEO 2004), Sigma Xi (pres. U. Kans. chpt. 1967). Republican. Unitarian Universalist. Avocations: sports, music, theater, reading. Office: U Kans 1002 Haworth Hl Lawrence KS 66045-0001 Office Phone: 785-864-3150. Business E-Mail: shankel@ku.edu.

SHANKLIN, CAROL W., dietician, educator; BS in Home Econs. Edn., U. Tenn., Martin, 1973; MS in Food Sys. Adminstrn., U. Tenn., Knoxville, 1974, PhD in Food Sys. Adminstrn., 1976. Asst. prof. foods and nutrition Tex. Tech. U., 1977—78; asst. food svc. dir. Highland Hosp., Lubbock, Tex., 1978; asst. prof. food sys. mgmt. Tex. Women's U., 1978—82, assoc. prof. food sys. mgmt., 1982—88, assoc. prof., chair dept. nutrition and food scis., 1985—87, prof., chair dept. nutrition and food scis., 1987—90; tech. advisor, cons. Miss. Inst. Higher Learning, 1988—89; grad. program dir., prof. dept. hotel, restaurant, instn. mgmt. and dietetics Kans. State U., Manhattan, 1990—2001, asst. dean. Grad. Sch., prof. dept. hotel, restaurant, instn. mgmt. and dietetics, 2001—04, assoc. dean. Grad. Sch., prof. dept. hotel, restaurant, instn. mgmt. and dietetics, 2004—. Contbr. articles to profl. jours. Recipient Michael Olsen Rsch. Achievement award, U. Del. Mem.: Am. Dietetic Assn. (Medallion award 2001). Achievements include research on environmental issues in the food service and hospitality industry; dietetics and hospitality education; quality service in food service operations; research in food service management, food safety and nutrition in food service operations. Office: Kansas State U Graduate Sch 103 Fairchild Manhattan KS 66502-1404 Office Phone: 785-532-7927. Business E-Mail: shanklin@k-state.edu.

SHANKLIN, KENNETH DALE, plastic surgeon; b. Toluca, Ill., Dec. 21, 1931; s. Walter Arthur and Elsie Ida Josephine (Holz) S.; m. Doris Gay Minton, July 24, 1955 (div. Jan. 21, 1971); 1 child, Steven Dale; m. Colleen Jean Wheeler, July 30, 1978. BS, U. Ill., 1954; MD, U. Utah, 1967. Diplomate Am. Bd. Med. Specialists in gen. surgery, plastic surgery; lic. Calif. Commd. 2d lt. USAF, 1954, advanced through grades to lt. col., ret., 1977; intern Wilford Hall USAF Med. Ctr., San Antonio, 1967-68, resident in plastic surgery, 1972-74, resident in gen. surgery Travis AFB, Calif., 1968-72; assoc. clin. prof. plastic surgery U. Tex., San Antonio, 1974-77; asst. clin prof. plastic surgery U. Calif., Davis, 1977-84, assoc. clin. prof. plastic surgery San Francisco, 1984—2004; pvt. practice plastic surgery Fresno, Calif., 1977-93; acting chief med. officer Mil. Entrance Processing Sta., Sacramento, 1994—2001. Bd. dirs., pres. Valley Children's Hosp. Med. Staff, Fresno; bd. dirs. Liga Flying Physicians, Fresno, 1995-98. Prodr., dir. films sci. meetings (Outstanding award 1976). Mem. Am. Soc. Plastic Surgeons, Internat. Congress Plastic and Reconstructive Surgeons (bd. dirs. 1983-91), Am. Med. Soc. Vienna, Mil. Order of the World Wars (dept. N. Calif. comdr. 1996-97, region 14 comdr. 1998-99, nat. surgeon gen. 2004—, Disting. Chpt. Comdr. 1997, Silver Patrick Henry Patriotism award, 1997), Am. Legion (dist. vice comdr. 1998-99, dist. comdr. 1999-2000, vice comdr. Calif. 2001-02), Rotarian. Avocations: teaching, flying. Home and Office: Mil Order World Wars 5100 John D Ryan Blvd 2211 San Antonio TX 78245-3513 Personal E-mail: shanklinken@aol.com.

SHANKS, DAVID, publishing executive; Grad, Holy Cross Coll., 1968. V.p., dir. of sales Berkley Pub. Co. (now known as Penguin Putnam Pub. Co.), 1979—82, sr. v.p., dir. of planning ops., 1982—85, sr. v.p., 1985—91, pres. NYC, 1991—97, COO, 1997—2001; CEO Penguin Putnam Pub. Co., 2001—. Office: Penguin Group USA Inc 375 Hudson St New York NY 10014

SHANKS, ERIC, communications executive; b. 1972; Broadcast assoc. CBS Sports, 1993; broadcast assoc., NFL prodn. crew Fox Sports, 1994—95, broadcast assoc., NHL prodn. crew, 1995—96, graphics prodr., 1997—2004; v.p., Enhanced Programming Fox TV Network, 1999—2004; sr. v.p., Adv. Services and Content DirecTV, 2004—. Named one of 40 Executives Under 40, Multichannel News, 2006. Office: DirecTV Group Inc 2230 E Imperial Hwy El Segundo CA 90245

SHANKS, EUGENE BAYLIS, JR., banker; BA, Vanderbilt U., 1969; MA, PhD, Stanford U., 1974. With Bankers Trust Co., NYC, 1973—78, 1980—95, pres., dir., 1992-95; pres. NetRisk, Inc., Greenwich, Conn., 1997—2002. Treas. Tenn. Valley Bancorp, 1978—80, Commerce Union Bank, 1978—80. Trustee Vanderbilt U.; bd. dir. Posse Found, IFL, Ltd., New Power, Inc. Office: IFL Ste 450 630 Fifth Ave New York NY 10111 Office Phone: 212-209-2134. Business E-Mail: ebshanks@optonline.net.

SHANKS, HERSHEL, editor, writer; b. Sharon, Pa., Mar. 8, 1930; s. Martin and Mildred (Freedman) S.; m. Judith Alexander Weil, Feb. 20, 1966; children: Elizabeth Jean, Julia Emily. BA, Haverford Coll., Pa., 1952; MA, Columbia, 1953; LLB, Harvard, 1956. Bar: D.C. 1956. Trial atty. Dept. Justice, 1956-59; pvt. practice Washington, 1959-88; ptnr. Glassie, Pewett, Beebe & Shanks, 1964-88; editor Bibl. Archaeology Rev., Washington, 1975—. Pres. Bibl. Archaeology Soc., 1974—2004, Jewish Ednl. Ventures Inc., 1987—. Author: The Art and Craft of Judging, 1968, The City of David, 1973, Judaism in Stone, 1979, Jerusalem--An Archaeological Biography, 1995, The Mystery and Meaning of the Dead Sea Scolls, 1998, also articles; co-author: (with Ben Witherington III) The Brother of Jesus, 2003; co-editor: Recent Archaeology in the Land of Israel, 1984; editor: Ancient Israel, A Short History, 1988, revised edit., 1999, Christianity and Rabbinic Judaism, 1992, Understanding the Dead Sea Scrolls, 1992; editor Bible Rev., 1985—2004, Moment mag., 1987—2004, Archaeology Odyssey, 1998—2004; contbr. articles to profl. jours. Fellow Royal Asiatic Soc.; mem. ABA, D.C. Bar Assn., Am. Schs. Oriental Rsch., Soc. Bibl. Lit., Cosmos Club, Phi Beta Kappa. Home: 5208 38th St NW Washington DC 20015-1812 Office: Bibl Archaeology Soc 4710 41st St NW Washington DC 20016-1706 Office Phone: 202-966-9888. E-mail: hshanks@bib-arch.org. *I try to take time to identify what is important in my life, to focus on that and ignore the rest when it conflicts. It takes conscious effort not to dissipate energy on activities and attitudes that don't matter in the big picture of my priorities. Free to concentrate on what I value most, I try to accomplish something each day in a regular, habitual way.*

SHANKS, PATRICIA L., lawyer; b. Salt Lake City, Apr. 3, 1940; BA in Microbiology with honors, Stanford U., 1962; JD, U. Colo., 1978. Bar: Calif. 1978. Mng. ptnr. McCutchen, Doyle, Brown & Enersen, LA, 1990-94, ptnr., 1985—. Trustee L.A. County Bar Found., 2001-04. Recipient West Publishing award; Stork scholar. Mem. Order of the Coif, Practice in Environ. Law. Office: Bingham McCutchen 355 S Grand Ave Ste 4400 Los Angeles CA 90071-3106

SHANLEY, JOHN DAVID, epidemiologist; b. LA, June 13, 1945; s. John Edward Shanley and Harriet Carolee Myers; m. Linda L. Dobrowolsky, Feb. 18, 1994; children: John Allen, Erin Beth, Kristen L. Dickison, Lisa M. Dickison. BS, UCLA, 1967, MD, 1971. Cert. internal medicine ACP, 1976, infectious diseases ACP, 1978. Asst. prof. U. Iowa, 1978—82; assoc. prof. U. Conn. Health Ctr., Farmington, 1982—89, prof., 1989—, dir., divsn. infectious diseases, 1989—. Ct. state chair infectious diseases U. Conn. Health Ctr., Farmington, 1989—. Contbr. over 80 sci. papers to profl. jours. Full surgeon 04 Pub. Health Svc., 1973—75, Honolulu. Rsch. grants, NIH, 1978—2005. Fellow: Infectious Diseases Soc. Am.; mem.: Conn. Infectious Diseases Soc. Independent. Achievements include research in virology. Avocations: scuba diving, photography. Office: Univ Conn Health Ctr 263 Farmington Ave Farmington CT 06030-3212 Home Phone: 860-675-1618; Office Phone: 860-679-4700. Office Fax: 860-679-4701. Business E-Mail: jshanley@nso1.uchc.edu.

SHANLEY, JOHN PATRICK, playwright, screenwriter; b. NYC, 1950; s. Nicholas and Frances Shanley; m. Jayne Haynes (div.); adopted children: Nick, Frank. Grad., NYU. Disting. artist-in-residence The New Sch. for Drama, NYC, 2006—. Writer (plays) Rockaway, 1982, Welcome to the Moon, 1982, Danny and the Deep Blue Sea, 1984, Savage in Limbo, 1985, the dreamer examines his pillow, 1985, Women of Manhattan, 1986, All for Charity, 1987, Italian-American Reconciliation, 1988, The Big Funk, 1990, Beggars in the House of Plenty, 1991, Four Dogs and a Bone, 1993, Psychopathia Sexualis, 1996, Missing/Kissing, 1997, Cellini, 1998, Where's My Money, 2001, Dirty Story, 2003, Doubt, 2004 (Pulitzer Prize for drama, 2005, Tony Award for best play, 2005), Sailor's Song, 2004, Defiance, 2006, Down and Out, The Red Coat, Let Us Go Out Into the Starry Night, Out West, A Lonely Impulse of Delight, (screen adaptations) Alive, 1993, Congo, 1995, (teleplay) Live From Baghdad, 2002, (screenplays) Moonstruck, 1987 (Acad. Award for best writing- screenplay written directly for the screen, 1988), January Man, 1989, We're Back! A Dinosaur's Story, 1993, writer, assoc. prodr. Five Corners, 1987, writer, dir. Joe Versus the Volcano, 1990, Chain of Command, 2005, Appeared in film Crossing Delancey, 1988. Served USMC. Fellow: Am. Acad. Arts & Scis. Office: c/o William Morris Agy 151 S El Camino Dr Beverly Hills CA 90212-2704 *

SHANMAN, JAMES ALAN, lawyer; b. Cin., Aug. 1, 1942; s. Jerome D. and Mildred Louise (Bloch) S.; m. Marilyn Louise Glassman, June 11, 1972; 1 child, Ellen Joan. BS, U. Pa., 1963; JD, Yale U., 1966. Bar: NY 1967, Conn. 2004, US Ct. Appeals for the Armed Forces, 1971, US Supreme Ct. 1971, US Ct. Appeals (2d cir.) 1972, US Dist. Ct. (so. and ea. dists.) NY 1972, US Ct. Internat. Trade 1976, US Ct. Appeals (fed. cir.) 1987, US Dist. Ct. (ea. dist.) Mich. 1989, US Ct. Appeals (7th cir.) 1999, US Dist. Ct. Conn. 2006. Assoc. Cahill Gordon & Reindel, NYC, 1971-74, Freeman, Meade, Wasserman, Sharfman & Schneider, NYC, 1974-76; mem. firm Sharfman, Shanman, Poret & Siviglia, P.C., NYC, 1976-95; ptnr. Camhy Karlinsky & Stein LLP, NYC, 1995-96; mem. firm Sharfman, Siviglia, Poret, Kook, Ross & Shanman, P.C., NYC, 1996-98; ptnr. Edwards, Angell, Palmer & Dodge LLP (formerly Edwards & Angell LLP), NYC and Stamford, 1998—. Speaker on reins. law topics. Contbr. articles to profl. jours. Capt. USAF, 1966-71. Mem.: ABA, ARIAS.US (cert. arbitrator), Am. Arbitration Assn. (comml. panel arbitrators 1980—), Assn. of Bar of City of N.Y. (com. ins. law 1985—88, 1990—92, 1998—2001, com. profl. liability ins. 1988—92, com. on assn. ins. plans 1989—), N.Y. State Bar Assn. Office: Edwards Angell Palmer & Dodge LLP Three Stamford Plz 301 Tresser Blvd Stamford CT 06901 Office Phone: 203-975-7505. Business E-Mail: jshanman@eapdlaw.com.

SHANMUGAM, GANAPATHY, geologist, researcher; b. Sirkali, Tamilnadu, India, Apr. 23, 1944; came to U.S., 1970; s. Ganapathy Mudaliar and Sambooranam; m. Jean Marie Barham, Aug. 21, 1976. BSc in Geology and Chemistry, Annamalai U., South India, 1965; MSc in Applied Geology, Indian Inst. Tech., Bombay, 1968; MS in geology, Ohio U., 1972; PhD in Geology, U. Tenn., 1978. Rsch. geologist Mobil Exploration & Product Tech. Ctr., Dallas, 1978-82, sr. rsch. geologist, 1982-84, assoc., 1984-85, rsch. assoc., 1985-89, sr. rsch. assoc., 1989-93, assoc. geol. rsch. advisor, 1993-96, geol. scientist, 1996-2000; adj. prof. geology U. Tex., Arlington, 2000—. Conf. chmn. Geol. Soc. London, 1996; debate panelist Am. Assn. Petroleum Geologists, Dallas, 1997. Author: Deep-Water Processes and Facies Models: Implications for Sandstone Petroleum Reservoirs, 2006; contbr. over 120 articles to profl. jours. Geology adv. bd. U. Tenn., Knoxville, 1985-89. Recipient Silver medal Indian Inst. Tech., 1968; Penrose grantee Geol. Soc. Am., 1976-78; recipient best Paper award Nigerian Assn. Petroleum Explorationists, 1995. Achievements include questioning of the deep-water turbidite paradigm and advocation of sandy debris flows in forming deep-water petroleum reservoirs. Avocation: photography. Office: U Tex Arlington Dept Earth and Environ Scis PO Box 19049 Arlington TX 76019 E-mail: shanshanmugam@aol.com.

SHANMUGASUNDARAM, ANANTHARAMAN, geologist, consultant; b. Pulavanur, Tamil Nadu, India, Mar. 11, 1944; s. Anantha Pillai and Sethu Ammal Shanmugasundaram; m. Kalyani Sivasankaran, June 17, 1970; children: Senthilkumar Anantharaman, Saravanan Anantharamamn. BS in Geology, Annamalai U., Chidambaram, Tamil Nadu, India, 1964; MS in Geology, Annamalai U., Chidambaram, Tamilnadu, India, 1966; postgrad., Indian Inst. Tech., Kharagpur, India, 1973. Tng. in ground water techniques Neyveli Lignite Corp., 1965, tng. in seismic field ops. and seismic interpretations Oil and Natural Gas Commn., India, 1966, cert. ground water techniques Directorate of Groundwater, TamilNadu, 1973, orientation for geologists in mapping, mineral exploration, geotechnic Geol. Survey India, Tng. Inst., 1976, aerial photo interpretation and remote sensing Geol. Survey India, Tng. Inst., 1980, new concepts and methods in stratigraphy Indian Inst. Tech., Kharagpur, 1983, preparation, molding and casting of micromammal teeth U. Calif., Mus. Paleontology, 2004. Rsch. scholar geology dept. Annamalai U., Chidambaram, 1966—71; geol. asst. UNDP Groundwater Investigation Project, Thanjavur, Tamil Nadu, India, 1971, Directorate of Ground Water, Tamil Nadu, 1971—75; asst. geologist Geol. Survey India, 1976—83, geologist jr., 1983—2001, geologist sr. Hyderabad, India, 2001—04; pvt. practice cons. Hyderabad, 2005—. Contbr. articles to profl. jours. Sec. Tipirneni Colony Welfare Soc., Hyderabad, Andhra Pradesh, India, 1992. Grantee Doris and Samuel P. Welles Fund, U. Calif., Berkeley, 2004, Nat. Sci. Mus., Tokyo, 2004. Hindu. Achievements include discovery of collection of several late Cretaceous mammalian (micro) fauna from the inter and infra trappean sediments in Andhra Pradesh and Karnataka States of India which includes several new species; first record of Haramiyida from India and the first mammalian record in Infra trappeans of India; recorded a new species of Quaternary Hippopotamid in Bhima valley in India. Avocations: travel, reading. Home: 7-51 JS Nagar St No 8 Habsiguda Hyderabad 500 007 India Home Phone: 91 40 27173293. Personal E-mail: gsi_sa@hotmail.com.

SHANNAHAN, WILLIAM PAUL, lawyer; b. Detroit, Nov. 21, 1934; s. William and Jean (Boyle) S.; children: MeglynAnne, Michael-Padraic. AB, U. Detroit, 1956; JD, Georgetown U., 1958. Bar: D.C. 1958, Mich. 1958, Calif. 1962. Ptnr. Higgs, Fletcher & Mack, La Jolla, Calif., 1967-81, Aylward, Kintz, et al, La Jolla, Calif., 1981-87, pvt. practice, La Jolla, Calif., 1987—. With U.S. Army, 1959-60. Democrat. Roman Catholic. Office: 1200 Prospect St Ste 425 La Jolla CA 92037-3660 Home Phone: 858-457-0057; Office Phone: 858-454-4424.

SHANNON, CAREEN BRETT, lawyer, writer, law educator; b. Oakland, Calif., Dec. 11, 1958; d. Larry Richard and Janet Loretta Shannon; life ptnr. William Considine; 1 child, Rachel Vineberg Shannon-Solomon. BA, Oberlin Coll., 1981; JD, CUNY, 1989. Bar: N.J. 1989, U.S. Dist. Ct. N.J. 1989, N.Y. 1990, U.S. Dist. Ct. (so. dist.) N.Y. 1990. Motions law clk. U.S. Ct. Appeals (2nd cir.), NYC, 1989—90, pro se law clk., 1990—91; staff atty. The Legal Aid Soc., NYC, 1991—92; assoc. Whitman, Breed, Abbott & Morgan, NYC, 1994—95, Satterlee, Stephens, Burke & Burke, NYC, 1992—94, Reid & Priest, NYC, 1995—96; legal editor Matthew Bender & Co., NYC, 1996—98; counsel Fragomen, Del Rey, Bernsen & Lowey, P.C., NYC, 1998—. Adj. prof. law Benjamin N. Cardozo Sch. Law, NYC, 1991—92; spkr. in field. Author (and co-author): handbooks; contbr. chapters to books, articles to profl. jours. Pro bono atty. N.Y. Lawyers for the Pub. Interest, NYC, 2002—04. Recipient Oberlin Study Abroad Program in France, Oberlin Coll., 1980; scholar Yr. Abroad Program in Denmark, Am. Field Svc., 1976—77; Grad. fellow in Japan, Oberlin Shansi Meml. Assn., 1981—83, Grad. fellow at Oberlin Coll., 1984, Robert Masur fellow in Civil Liberties, The Nation Inst., 1988—99. Mem.: ABA (mem. steering com. internat. law sect. ann. conf. 2002—03), Am. Immigration Lawyers Assn. Avocations: fly fishing, rock climbing, skydiving, weightlifting, skiing. Office: Fragomen Del Rey Bernsen & Loewy LLP 515 Madison Ave New York NY 10022 Home Phone: 718-399-0310; Office Phone: 212-891-7517. Business E-Mail: cshannon@fragomen.com.

SHANNON, DAVID M., lawyer; b. Gardena, Calif., July 22, 1955; s. William R. Shannon and Delores Ann (Nettleton) DeBenedictis; m. Maureen Michelle Green, Feb. 18, 1978; 1 child, Ryan Edward. BA, Pepperdine U., 1976, JD cum laude, 1985. Law clk. Office of Dist. Atty. County of Ventura, Calif., 1984-85; assoc. Gibson, Dunn & Crutcher, LA, 1985-87, San Francisco & San Jose, Calif., 1987—93; v.p., asst. gen. counsel Intel Corp., Santa Clara, Calif., 1993—2002; v.p., gen. counsel NVIDIA Corp., Santa Clara, Calif., 2002—. Mem. ABA, Calif. Bar Assn., L.A. County Bar Assn. Avocations: swimming, basketball. Office: NVIDIA Corp 2701 San Tomas Expressway Santa Clara CA 95050 Office Phone: 408-486-2000. Office Fax: 408-486-2200. *

SHANNON, DONALD HAWKINS, retired editor; b. Auburn, Wash., Feb. 1, 1923; s. Ernest Victor and Fern (McConville) S.; m. Sally van Deurs, June 13, 1952; children— John McConville, Susanna Shepard. BA, Stanford, 1944; postgrad., Law Sch., 1946-47. Reporter Brazil Herald, Rio de Janeiro, 1947-48; Reporter UPI, London, 1949-51, Western Reporters, Washington, 1951-53; mem. staff L.A. Times, 1954-92, bur. chief Paris Paris, 1962-65, bur. chief Africa, 1965-66, bur. chief Tokyo Tokyo, 1966-71; bur. chief UN, NYC, 1971—75, Washington, 1975—92; sr. editor Georgetown and Country, Washington, 1996-99; ret., 1999. Served with AUS, 1944-46, PTO. Mem. Nat. Press Club, City Tavern Club, Overseas Press Club (NYC), Phi Gamma Delta. Address: 1068 30th St NW Washington DC 20007-3822 Personal E-mail: toodad@verizon.net.

SHANNON, GEORGE RAYMOND, gerontologist, educator; b. Chgo., Dec. 30, 1939; m. Ellen Levine, Dec. 31, 1978; m. Elizabeth Mary Elkin, Oct. 31, 1959 (div. Aug. 25, 1965); children: Mary Ellen Shannon-Amenda, Elizabeth Mary Shannon-Reedy, Margaret Mary, Catherine Mary. BA, Antioch U., LA, 1997; M in Gerontology, U. So. Calif., 1999, PhD in Gerontology, 2004. Post-doctoral fellow VA Ctr. Excellence, Sepulveda, Calif., 2004—06; rsch. assoc. Ptnrs. in Care Found., San Fernando, Calif., 2006—. Lectr. in field. Contbr. articles to profl. jours. Recipient Poster of Yr. award, Am. Acad. Home Care Physicians, 2006; Mary Pickford scholarship, Davis Sch. Gerontology U. So. Calif., 1997—99. Mem.: AFTRA, SAG, Am. Geriat. Soc. (Presdl. Poster of Yr. award 2006), Am. Soc. Aging, Gerontol. Soc. Am., Actors Equity Assn., Sigma Phi Omega, Phi Kappa Phi. Liberal. Avocations: reading, exercise, travel, acting. Office: Ptnrs in Care Found 732 Mott St Ste150 San Fernando CA 91340 Office Phone: 323-850-5229. Office Fax: 562-622-3892; Home Fax: 323-850-8809. Personal E-mail: gshannon@usc.edu, georgershannon@aol.com.

SHANNON, HOLDEN E., air transportation executive; Grad., Rice U., Houston, 1985. V.p. corp. real estate and environ. affairs Continental Airlines, Inc., Houston, 1995—2004, sr. v.p. global real estate & security, 2004—. Office: Continental Airlines Inc PO Box 4607 Houston TX 77210 Office Phone: 713-324-5000. Office Fax: 713-324-2637. *

SHANNON, IRIS REED, health facility administrator, consultant; b. Chgo. d. Ira Paul and Iola Sophia Reed. BS in Nursing, Fisk U.-Meharry Med. Coll., 1948; MA, U. Chgo., 1954; PhD, U. Ill., Chgo., 1987; D in Pub. Svc. (hon.), Elmhurst Coll., 1993. Staff nurse Chgo. Bd. Health, 1948-50; instr. pub. health nursing Meharry Med. Coll., Nashville, 1951-56; tchr.-nurse, health coordinator child devel. Head Start, Chgo. Bd. Edn., 1957-66; dir. community nursing Mile Sq. Neighborhood Health Center, Presbyn.-St. Luke's Hosp., Chgo., 1966-69; co-dir. nurse assoc. programs Rush Presbyn.-St. Luke's Hosp., 1971-76; chairperson community nursing Rush U., Chgo., 1972-77, acting chairperson, 1988-90; asst. prof. pub. health nursing U. Ill., 1971-74; assoc. prof. cmty. nursing Rush U., 1974-97, health sys. mgr., 1988—, health cons., 1974—. Adj. faculty Sch. Pub. Health, U. N.C., 1977—85; mem. profl. adv. bd. Vis. Nurse Assn. Chgo., 1973—75; cons. Video Nursing, Inc.; mem. profl. adv. com. Mile Sq. Home Health Unit, Chgo., 1975—77; mem. nat. adv. coun. on nurse tng. HEW, 1978—81; mem. Nat. Task Force on Credentialing in Nursing, 1979—82; mem. Chgo. regional com. Ill. White House Conf. on Children, 1979—80; v.p. Chgo. Bd. Health, 1989—99. Named Prin. for a Day, Brownell Elem. Sch., Mayor's Office, City of Chgo., 1998—99, Englewood Tech. Prep. Acad., 2000—01; recipient award of merit, Ill. Pub. Health Assn., 1979, 1989—2000, Outstanding Achievement award, YWCA of Met. Chgo., 1988, Disting. Svc. award, Chgo. chpt. Meharry Alumni, 1989, Lowenberg Chair of Excellence in Nursing, Memphis State U., 1993, Bd. Trustees' Svc. medal, Rush-Presby. St. Luke's Med. Ctr., 1996, Lifeline award, Cmty. Mental Health Coun., 2002. Fellow: APHA (chmn. pub. health nursing sect. 1977—79, governing coun. 1980—82, exec. bd. 1985—87, pres. 1988—89, governing coun. 1989—99), Am. Acad. Nursing, Royal Soc. Health (hon. 1989); mem.: ANA (Pearl McIver Pub. Health Nurse award 1998), Inst. of Medicine of NAS, Delta Sigma Theta, Sigma Theta Tau. Home: 3100 S King Dr Chicago IL 60616-3634 Office Phone: 312-842-6164. E-mail: irisshannon@aol.com.

SHANNON, JERRY WAYNE, mathematician, educator; b. Hixson, Tenn., June 29, 1946; s. Milton Eugene and Ila Agnes Shannon; m. Donna Lively, June 22, 1982; 1 child, Daniel Ray. MEd, Trevecca Nazarene Coll., Nashville, 1990. Tchr. math. Red Bank HS, Chattanooga, 1980—2000, Girls Prep. Sch., Chattanooga, 2001—. Mem.: PTA (life), Nat. Coun. Tchrs. Math. Home: 928 Fairway Ln Soddy Daisy TN 37379-4520 Office: Girls Prep Sch 205 Island Ave Chattanooga TN 37405 Home Phone: 423-332-9048; Office Phone: 423-634-7602. Office Fax: 423-634-7651. Personal E-mail: jws928@comcast.net. Business E-Mail: jerrys@gps.edu.

SHANNON, JOE, art critic, painter; b. Lares, Puerto Rico, 1933; Exhbn. technician Smithsonian Mus. Nat. History; former curator Hirshhorn Mus. & Sculpture Garden; prof. Corcoran Sch. Art, Md. Inst. Coll. Arts (MICA), Baltimore. Exhibitions include Studies Monuments & Variations, Haslem Gallery, 1983, Shoe Salesman, Corcoran Gallery, 1969; reviews art shows Art in America, writer (art related articles) Washington Times. Office: Md Inst Coll Arts (MICA) 1300 Mount Royal Ave Baltimore MD 21217

SHANNON, JOE, JR., lawyer; b. Nov. 9, 1940; s. Joe and Juanita Elizabeth (Milliorn) S.; children: Kelley Jane, Joseph Patrick, Shelley Carol. BA, U. Tex., 1962, LLB, 1963. Bar: Tex. 1963, U.S. Dist. Ct. (no. dist.) Tex. 1970, U.S. Supreme Ct. 1977, U.S. Ct. Appeals (5th cir.) 1977, U.S. Dist. Ct. (we. dist.) 1998, cert.: Am. Acad. (matrimonial arbitrator). Ptnr. Shannon & Shannon, Ft. Worth, 1963-72; adminstrv. asst. to spkr. Tex. Ho. of Reps., Austin, 1970; chief criminal div. Tarrant County Dist. Atty., Ft. Worth, 1972-78; pvt. practice Ft. Worth, 1978-99; ptnr. Snakard & Gambill, Ft. Worth, 1986-90; chief econ. crimes Tarrant County Dist. Atty., 1999—. Adj. prof. Tex. Wesleyan Sch. Law; dir. State Bar Tex. Mem. Tex. Ho. of Reps., 1964-70. Fellow Tex. Bar Found. (life); mem. State Bar of Tex. (adv. com. family law, state bd. legal specialization 1985-99, dist. grievance com. 1973-76, chmn. 1975-76, 95-97, sec. 2d ct. appeals adv. com. 1995—), Tarrant County Family Law Bar Assn. (pres. 1998), Tarrant County Bar Assn. (dir. 1999-01, sec. treas. 2002, 2d v.p. 2003, pres.-elect, 2003, pres. 2004), Phi Alpha Delta, Masons, Shriners. Office: 401 W Belknap Fort Worth TX 76196 Office Phone: 817-884-1661. E-mail: jshannon@tarrantcounty.com. *Notable cases include: State vs. Cullen Davis, 1977, richest man to be tried for murder; State vs. Mutscher, bribery conspiracy trial of Tex. House Speaker and assocs.*

SHANNON, JOHN SANFORD, lawyer, retired rail transportation executive; b. Tampa, Fla., Feb. 8, 1931; s. George Thomas and Ruth Evangeline (Garrett) S.; m. Elizabeth Howe, Sept. 22, 1962; children: Scott Howe, Elizabeth Garrett, Sandra Denison. AB, Roanoke Coll., 1952; JD, U. Va., 1955. Bar: Va. 1955. Assoc. Hunton Williams Gay Powell & Gibson, Richmond, Va., 1955-56; solicitor Norfolk & Western Ry., Roanoke, Va., 1956-60, asst. gen. solicitor, 1960-64, gen. atty., 1964-65, gen. solicitor, 1965-68, asst. gen. counsel, 1968-69, v.p. law, 1969-80, sr. v.p. law, 1980-82; exec. v.p. law Norfolk (Va.) So. Corp., 1982-96, ret., 1996. Bd. dirs. Norfolk So. Ry. Co., Pocahontas Land Corp., Va. Holding Corp., Norfolk and Western Ry. Co. Editor-in-chief: Va. Law Rev, 1954-55. Chancellor Episcopal Diocese Southwestern Va., 1974-82; pres. bd. trustees North Cross Sch., Roanoke, 1973-82; trustee, past chmn. exec. com. Roanoke Coll., Salem, Va., 1974-2005; bd. dirs. Legal Aid Soc., Roanoke Valley, 1969-80, pres., 1970-79; trustee Chrysler Mus., Norfolk, 1982-94, Norfolk Acad., 1987-99. Mem. Va. Bar Assn., Norfolk and Portsmouth Bar Assn., Shenandoah Club, Roanoke Country Club, Norfolk Yacht and Country Club, Order of Coif, Sigma Xi, Omicron Delta Kappa, Phi Delta Phi. Home: 7633 Argyle Ave Norfolk VA 23505-1701

SHANNON, MARGARET ANNE, lawyer; b. Detroit, July 6, 1945; d. Johannes Jacob and Vera Marie (Spade) Van De Graaf; m. Robert Selby Shannon, Feb. 4, 1967. Student, Brown U., 1963-65; BA in History, Wayne State U., 1966, JD, 1973. Bar: Mich. 1973. Housing aide City of Detroit, 1967-68; employment supr. Sinai Hosp., Detroit, 1968-69; assoc. gen. counsel regulatory affairs Blue Cross Blue Shield Mich., Detroit, 1969-80; ptnr. Honigman Miller Schwartz and Cohn, Detroit, 1980-95, of counsel, 1996—. Nat. Merit scholar, 1963-66. Mem. Mich. State Bar (chmn. health care com. 1991, 92, co-chmn. payor subcom. health law sect.). Home: 1111 Orinoco Way Palm Beach Gardens FL 33410 Office: Honigman Miller Schwartz and Cohn 2290 First National Bldg Detroit MI 48226-3583 Office Phone: 313-465-7552. E-mail: mshannon@honigman.com.

SHANNON, MARGARET BARRETT, lawyer; b. 1949; BA, Baylor U., 1971; JD, Southern Methodist U., 1976. Bar: 1976. Ptnr. Andrews Kurth LLP, 1984—94; v.p., gen. counsel BJ Services Co., Houston, 1994—. Mem. United Way Women's Initiative of Alexis de Tocqueville Soc., 2003—04; mem. bd. dirs. St. Luke's Episcopal Health Charities, Houston. Mem.: ABA. Office: BJ Services Co 4601 Westway Park Blvd Houston TX 77041

SHANNON, MARY LOU, adult health nursing educator; b. Memphis, Apr. 4, 1938; d. Sidney Richmond Shannon and Lucille (Gwaltney) Cloud. BSN, U. Tenn., 1959; MA, Columbia U., 1963, MEd, 1964, EdD, 1972. Staff nurse City of Memphis Hosps., 1959—60, instr. Sch. Nursing, 1960—62; asst. prof. U. Tenn., Memphis, 1964—70, assoc. prof., 1970—73, prof., 1973—89; prof., chair adult health dept. Sch. Nursing U. Tex., Galveston, 1989—98, prof., 1989—2000, prof. emeritus, 2000—. Bd. dirs. Nat. Pressure Ulcer Adv. Panel, Buffalo, 1987-96; vis. prof. U. Alta., Edmonton, Can., 1982, Union U., Memphis, 2001, Bapt. Coll. Health Scis., 2003, U. Tex., Galveston, 2004; mem. project adv. bd. RAND, Santa Monica, Calif., 1994. Contbr. chpts. to books in field and to periodicals; mem. editl. bd. Advances in Wound Care, 1987-2000. Trustee Nurses Edn. Funds, N.Y.C., 1972-86. Mem. AAAS, ANA, Nat. League Nursing (bd. of rev. 1983-86), Orthopedic Nurses Assn., So. Nursing Rsch. Soc., Am. Assn. for History of Nursing, Sigma Xi, Sigma Theta Tau, Phi Kappa Phi. Avocations: travel, reading.

SHANNON, RANDY LANNARD, college football coach; b. Miami, Feb. 24, 1966; s. Dorleatha Johnson; children: Ty, Xavier, Randy Jr., Steven. BS, U. Miami, 1989. Linebacker Dallas Cowboys, 1989—91; grad. asst. U. Miami, 1991, defensive line, 1992, linebackers coach, 1993—97, 2000, defensive asst., 1998—99, defensive coord., 2001—06, head football coach, 2006—. Recipient Christopher Plumer award for Most Inspirational Player, 1988, Frank Broyles award for Nat. Asst. Coach of Yr., 2001. Achievements include being mem. of coaching staff in 10 Bowl Games. Office: U Miami Dept Athletics 5821 San Amaro Dr Miami FL 33146 *

SHANNON, STEPHEN CURTIS, medical association administrator, occupational health physician; b. Frederick, Md., Dec. 9, 1948; s. James Lee and Mary Catherine (Fry) S.; m. Barbara Jean Winterson, Jul. 31, 1971; children: Joyce Megan Shannon-Winterson, Sally Catherine Shannon-Winterson. BA in hist., U. Md., 1971, MA in Am. hist., 1975; DO, U. New Eng. Coll. Osteopathic Medicine, 1986; MPH, Harvard U., 1990. Diplomate Am. Bd. Preventive Medicine and Family Practice. Program mgr. WESM-FM Radio, Prince Frederick, Md., 1971-73; instr. Am. hist. U. Md., College Park, 1973-79; congl. rels. analyst U.S. Dept. Energy, Washington, 1979-80; family practice resident Brighton Medical Ctr., Portland, Maine, 1986-88; preventive medicine resident U. Mass. Medical Ctr., Worcester, Mass., 1988-90; medical epidemiologist Mass. Dept. Pub. Health, Boston, 1990-92; asst. prof. U. New Eng. Coll. Osteopathic Medicine, Biddeford, Maine, 1990-95; medical dir. Ctr. Health Promotion Brighton Medical Ctr., 1991-95; dir. occupational health Maine Bureau of Health, Augusta, 1990-95; acting dean U. New Eng. Coll. Osteo. Medicine, 1995, dean & v.p. health services, 1995—2005; pres. Am. Assn. Colleges of Osteopathic Medicine, 2005—. Med. epidemiologist cons. Maine Bur. Health, 1990—91; chmn. occupational health sect. Brighton Med. Ctr., 1994; former pres. Maine Biomedical Rsch. Coalition, Maine Ctr. for Pub. Health. Editor: The Maryland Historian, 1976-78; contbr. articles to profl. jours. Exec. com. York County Health Services Bd., Saco, Maine; bd. dirs. Maine Inst. Occupational Health Edn., Waterville, Maine, 1993, Brighton Consortium, 1991. Recipient Dan Hanley Meml. Trust award, 2003, Disting. Svc. award in field of higher edn. Fin. Authority of Maine, 2002, New Eng. Found. Osteopathic Medicine award, 1986, U.S. Sec. Health & Human Svcs. award for Health Promotion, 1984, Ciby-Geigy award for Outstanding Comm. Svc., 1984, fellow William Randolph Hearst, U. Md., 1979. Mem. Am. Pub. Health Assn., Maine Pub. Health Assn. (bd. dirs. 1993), Am. Osteopathic Assn., Maine Osteopathic, Physicians for Nat. Health Program, Am. Coll. Occupational & Environ. Medicine. Democrat. Avocations: canoeing, hiking, camping, writing, reading. Office: American Assn Colleges Osteopathic Medicine Ste 310 5550 Friendship Blvd Chevy Chase MD 20815-7231

SHANNON, THOMAS A., JR., federal agency administrator; BA, Coll. William and Mary; M in Politics, Oxford U., doctorate. Consular/polit. rotational officer U.S. Embassy, Guatemala City, Guatemala, 1984—86; country officer Cameroon, Gabon, Sao Tome, Principe, 1987—89; spl. asst. to amb. U.S. Embassy, Brasilia, Brazil, 1989—92; regional labor attache U.S. Consulate General, Johannesburg, 1992—96; polit. counselor U.S. Embassy, Caracas, Venezuela, 1996—99; dir. Inter-Am. affairs Nat. Security Coun., 1999—2000; U.S. dep. permanent rep. OAS, 2000—01; dir. Andean affairs US Dept. State, 2001—02, dep. asst. sec. we. hemisphere affairs, 2002—03, asst. sec. for we. hemisphere affairs, 2005—; sr. dir. we. hemisphere affairs Nat. Security Coun., 2003—05; spl. asst. to Pres. The White House, 2003—05. Career mem. Sr. Fgn. Svc. Office: US Dept State 2201 C St NW Washington DC 20520

SHANNON, THOMAS ALFRED, retired educational association administrator emeritus; b. Milw., Jan. 2, 1932; s. John Elwood and Eleanor Ann (Mitchell) S.; m. Barbara Ann Weidner, June 26, 1954; children: Thomas Alfred, Paul J., Suzanne L., Terrence D. BS, U. Wis, 1954; JD, U. Minn., 1961. Bar: Minn. 1961, Calif. 1963, U.S. Supreme Ct. 1965, D.C. 1977, Va. 1984; Life cert. as sch. adminstr., Calif.; cert. assoc. exec. Am. Soc. Assn. Execs. Pvt. practice law, Mpls., 1961-62; schs. atty. San Diego City Schs., 1962-73; dept. supt., gen. counsel, 1973-77; exec. dir. Nat. Sch. Bds. Assn., Washington, 1977-97, ret., 1997. Adj. prof. law and edn. U. San Diego; vis. prof. edn. U. Va.; adv. mem. Edn. Commn. of States; prof. Nat. Acad. Sch. Execs., 1971-77; legal counsel Am. Assn. Sch. Adminstrs., 1973-77; adj. prof. ednl. adminstrn. George Washington U., 1996-97. Exec. pub. The Am. Sch. Bd. Jour., 1977-96, Exec. Educator, 1978-96, Sch. Bd. News, 1981-96. Chmn. San Diego County Juvenile Justice Commn., 1973-74; mem. nat. coun. Boy Scouts Am., 1979-97; bd. dirs. Found. for Teaching Econ., San Francisco, 1993-2003. With USN, 1954—59. Mem. VFW (life), Am. Bar Assn. (chmn. com. public edn. 1978-82), Nat. Orgn. on Legal Problems of Edn. (pres. 1973), Nat. Sch. Bds. Assn. (chmn. council sch. attys. 1967-69) Home: 3811 26th St N Arlington VA 22207-5241 Office Phone: 703-525-8577. Personal E-mail: tombar2@juno.com.

SHANNON, THOMAS FREDERIC, German language educator; b. Cambridge, Mass., Mar. 16, 1948; m. Christine D. Höner. BA in German summa cum laude, Boston Coll., 1969; MA in German Lit., SUNY, Albany, 1973; MA in Theoretical Linguistics, Ind. U., 1975, PhD in Germanic Linguistics, 1982. Instr. in German Boston Coll., 1969-70; tchg. fellow in German SUNY, Albany, 1971-73; univ. fellow Ind. U., Bloomington, 1973-74, assoc. instr., 1974-76, 79-80; acting asst. prof. in Germanic linguistics U. Calif., Berkeley, 1980-82, asst. prof., 1982-87, assoc. prof., 1987-94, prof., 1994—, dir. lang. lab., 1989-92, assoc. dir. Berkeley Lang. Ctr., 1994-95, dir. abroad study ctr. Germany, 2000—02. Co-organizer Berkeley Confs. on Dutch Lang. and Lit., 1987, 89, 91, 93, 95, 97, 2005, 10th Interdisciplinary Conf. Netherlandic Studies, 2000; econs. presenter and spkr. in field. Mem. editl. adv. bd. Jour. Germanic Linguistics, 1998—; contbr. articles to profl. jours. With USAR, 1970-76. Grantee Fulbright Found., 1976-78, U. Calif. Berkeley, 1983-84, 94-95, ACLS, 1987, Internat. Assn. Netherlandic Studies, 1988, 91, 94, 97, 06, German Acad. Exch. Svc., summer 1996; NDEA fellow, 1969; Fulbright rsch./lectr. grantee Rijksuniversiteit Groningen, Netherlands, 1992-93; Inst. fuer deutsche Sprache summer rsch. grantee, Mannheim, Germany, 1997. Mem. MLA (exec. com. discussion group in Germanic philology 1989-94, discussion group for Netherlandic Studies 1995-99, divsn. on lang. change 1995-99), Am. Assn. Netherlandic Studies (exec. com. 1988—, editor newsletter 1989-95, series editor publs. 1994-2006), Am. Assn. Tchrs. German, Internat. Assn. Netherlandic Studies, Linguistic Soc. Am., Pacific Ancient and Modern Lang. Assn., European Linguistic Soc., Soc. Germanic Philology (v.p. 1991-92, 95-99), Internat. Cognitive Linguistics Soc., Alpha Sigma Nu. Home: 770 Rose Dr Benicia CA 94510-3709 Office: U Calif Dept German 5319 Dwinelle Hall Berkeley CA 94720-3243 Home Phone: 701-748-1493; Office Phone: 510-642-2004. E-mail: tshannon@berkeley.edu.

SHANNON, THOMAS O., plastic surgeon; b. Pottstown, Pa., Aug. 25, 1962; s. John H. and Rosemary E. Shannon; m. Kelly R. Shannon, Nov. 4, 1995; children: Sydney, Mitchell. BA in Chemistry, U. Rochester, 1984; MD, Pa. State U., 1988. Diplomate Am. Bd. Surgery, lic. physician Tex., Pa. Surg. resident Lankenau Hosp. and Med. Rsch. Ctr., Phila., 1993; resident in plastic surgery U. Tex. Med. Br., Galveston, 1996; plastic surgeon Keystone Plastic Surgery, Conroe, Tex., 1996—, Woodlands, Tex., 1996—. Med. dir. Woodlands Meml. Woundcare Ctr., 1998—2001; med. dir. wound care Triumph N.W. Hosp., 2002; med. dir. woundcare Nexus Hosp., 2006—; presenter in field. Contbr. articles to profl. jours. Capt. US Army, 1986—2004. Ames Rsch. Lab. fellow, 1983, Std. Oil Rsch. Profl. Program trainee, 1984, summer fellow, NIH, 1985. Mem.: AMA, Tex. Med. Assn., Montgomery County Med. Soc., Am. Chem. Soc., Blocker-Lewis Plastic Surg. Soc., Singleton Surg. Soc., Galveston Hist. Found., Mixed Volleyball League, The Woodlands Mixed Bowling League. Republican. Presbyterian. Avocations: tennis, skiing, volleyball, bowling, choir. Home: 75 Pleasant Bend Pl The Woodlands TX 77382 Office: Keystone Plastic and Reconstructive Surgery LLC 3115 College Park Dr Bldg 101 The Woodlands TX 77384 also: 13628 Michael Rd Tomball TX 77375 also: 18955 Memorial N Ste 590 Humble TX 77338 Office Phone: 936-321-4345. E-mail: tshannon@keystoneplasticsurgery.com.

SHANNON, W. PATRICK, telecommunications industry executive; BSBA, U. Ga. CPA. With Arthur Andersen, Atlanta, 1983—91; dir. fin. planning, analysis, dir. investor rels., dir. tech. acctg. US West, Inc., 1991—94, v.p. corp. devel., 1994; v.p., chief fin. officer MediaOne, Inc., 1994—97, CFO domestic ops., contr., 1997—2004, sr. v.p. fin., 2004—05, CFO, 2006—.

SHANNON, WILLIAM NORMAN, III, finance educator, food service executive; b. Chgo., Nov. 20, 1937; s. William Norman Jr. and Lee (Lewis) S.; m. Bernice Urbanowicz, July 14, 1962; children: Kathleen Kelly, Colleen Patricia, Kerrie Ann. BS in Indsl. Mgmt., Carnegie Inst. Tech., 1959; MBA in Mktg. Mgmt., U. Toledo, 1963. Sales engr. Westinghouse Electric Co., Detroit, 1959-64; regional mgr. Toledo Scale, Chgo., 1964-70; v.p. J. Lloyd Johnson Assoc., Northbrook, Ill., 1970-72; mgr. spl. projects Hobart Mfg., Troy, Ohio, 1972-74; corp. v.p. mktg. Berkel, Inc., La Porte, Ind., 1974-79; gen. mgr. Berkel Products, Ltd., Toronto, Canada, 1975-78; chmn. Avant Industries, Inc., Wheeling, Ill., 1979-81; chmn., pres. Hacienda Mexican Restaurants, South Bend, Ind., 1978—95; chmn. Ziker Shannon Corp., South Bend, 1982-88, Hacienda Franchising Group, Inc., South Bend, Ind., 1987—92. Assoc. prof. mktg. and internat. bus. St. Mary's Coll., Notre Dame, Ind., 1982—; chmn. Hacienda Franchise Group, Inc., 1987-96, Hacienda Mex. Restaurants Mgmt., Inc., 1994-96; sr. chmn. Hacienda Mex. Restaurants, 1996-2004; mem. London program faculty, 1986, 89, 92, 94, coord. internat. bus. curriculum, 1989—, mktg. curriculum, 1983; advisor Coun. Internat. Bus. Devel., Notre Dame, 1991-2005; mng. dir. Alden & Torch Lake Railway, 1995—. Co-author: Laboratory Computers, 1971; columnist Bus. Digest mag., 1988-1994; mem. editl. bd. Jour. Bus. and Indsl. Mktg., 1986-1992, South Bend Tribune Business Weekly, 1990-1994; contbr. articles to profl. jours. V.p. mktg. Jr. Achievement, South Bend, Ind., 1987-90; pres. Small Bus. Devel. Coun., South Bend., 1987-90; bd. dirs. Ind. Small Bus. Coun., Indpls., 1986—, Mental Health Assn., South Bend, 1987-90, Michiana World Trade Orgn., Internat. Bus. Edn., 1989-91, Entrepreneurs Alliance Ind., 1988-92, Nat. Small Bus. United, Washington, 1989-92, Women's Bus. Initiative, 1986-90, dir. ednl. confs., 1986-90; chmn. bd. trustees, Holy Cross Coll., Notre Dame, Ind., 1987-1993, chmn. edn. com., 1993-1993; chmn. St. Joseph County Higher Edn. Coun., 1988-91, Nat. Coun. Small Bus., Washington, 1988-1994; Midwest region adv. coun. U.S. SBA, 1988-91; at-large mem. U.S. Govt. Adv. Coun. on Small Bus., Washington, 1988-90, 1994-1996, chmn. Bus. and Econ. Devel. Com., 1988-90, 1994-1996; vice chmn. Internat. Trade Com., 1994-1996; nat. adv. coun. Women's Network for Entrepreneur Tng., 1991-1994; vice chmn. State of Ind. Enterprise Zone Bd., 1991-1994; elected del. White House Conf. Small Bus., Washington, 1986; bd. dirs. Ind. Small Bus. Devel. Ctrs. Adv. Bd.; co-pres. Helena Twp. Downtown Devel. Authority, 2002—. Named Small Bus. Person of the Yr., City of South Bend, 1987, Small Bus. Advocate of the Yr., State of Ind., 1987, Ind. Entrepreneur Advocate of the Yr., 1988. Mem. Am. Mktg. Assn. (chmn. Mich./Ind. chpt., pres. 1985-86), U.S. Assn. Small Bus. and Entrepreneurship (nat. v.p. for entrepreneurship edn. 1991-92, nat. v.p. entrepreneurship devel. 1992-1996), Ind. Inst. New Bus. Ventures (mktg. faculty 1987-91), Michiana Investment Network (vice chmn. 1988-91), SBA (adminstrn. adv. coun. 1988-1992, contbg. editor Our Town Michiana mag. 1988-91), U.S. C. of C., Nat. Coun. Small Bus. (Washington), South Bend C. of C. (bd. dirs. 1987-1996, vice chmn. membership 1993-1996), Assn. for Bus. Communications (co-chmn. Internat. Conf. 1986), Univ. Club Notre Dame (vice chmn.), Shamrock Club Notre Dame (exec. dir., trustee 1993-1996), Rotary. Roman Catholic. Office: Saint Mary's Coll Dept Bus Adminstrn Eco Notre Dame IN 46556 Office Phone: 574-284-4508. *Enjoy good fortune resulting from LUCK, an acronym for (L) Learning how to (U)Use your talents with genuine (C) Concern on how your (K) Knowlege can benefit others.*

SHANOR, DONALD READ, journalism educator, writer; b. Ann Arbor, Mich., July 11, 1927; s. William Wilson and Katherine Creamer (Read) S.; m. Constance May Collier, 1951; children: Rebecca, Donald (dec.), Elizabeth BS, Northwestern U., 1951; MA, Columbia U., NYC, 1964. Corr. Am. Forces Network, Frankfurt, Fed. Republic Germany, 1952-54; corr. UPI, Frankfurt and London, 1954-59, Chgo. Daily News, Vienna and Bonn, 1967-71; editor UPI, NYC, 1959-65; lectr. Columbia U., NYC, 1965-67, prof. Grad. Sch. Journalism, 1971—92, Godfrey Lowell Cabot prof. emeritus, 1992—, prof. Sch. Internat. and Pub. Affairs, 1979-92, prof. Harriman Inst., 1985-92, prof. Inst. on East Cen. Europe, 1991—92. Vis. prof. Chinese Acad. Social Scis., Beijing, 1984-85, Charles U., Prague, 1992-93; online writing instr. U. Phoenix, 2002-. Author: Soviet Europe, 1975, The Soviet Triangle, 1980, Behind the Lines/The Private War Against Soviet Censorship, 1985, News From Abroad, 2003; co-author: News From Abroad, 1981, China Today, 1993, After the Russians, 2004; advisor Journalists in Europe, Paris, 1973—92; contbg. editor World Press Rev., 1974-93; mem. adv. panel Himal mag., 1988—92. Trustee Arthur F. Burns Internat. Fellowship Program, 1990—2004. Served with USNR, 1945-46 Recipient Fed. Republic of Germany Friendship award, 2005; U.S. Inst. Peace grantee, 1988-89. Mem. Soc. Profl. Journalists, Am. Council on Germany Democrat. Home: 13 Pierce Ln Edgartown MA 02539 Office: Columbia U New York NY 10027 Personal E-mail: dcshanor@earthlink.net.

SHANSBY, JOHN GARY, investor; b. Seattle, Aug. 25, 1937; s. John Jay and Jule E. (Boyer) S.; m. Joyce Ann Dunsmore, June 21, 1959 (div.); children: Sheri Lee, Kimberly Ann, Jay Thomas; m. Barbara Anderson De Meo, Jan. 1, 1983 (div.); m. Jane Robinson Dettner, May 1, 1990. BA, U. Wash., 1959. Mktg. exec. Colgate-Palmolive Co., NYC, 1959-67; subs. pres. Am. Home Products Corp., NYC, 1968-71; v.p. Clorox Co., Oakland, Calif., 1972-73; ptnr. Booz, Allen & Hamilton, San Francisco, 1974-75; chmn. bd., chief exec. officer, dir. Shaklee Corp., San Francisco, 1975-86; co-founder, chmn. TSG Consumer Ptnrs., San Francisco, 1986—. Former chmn. Calif. State Commn. for Rev. of Master Plan Higher Edn.; founder J. Gary Shansby chair mktg. strategy U. Calif., Berkeley, U. Wash., Seattle; trustee Calif. State U. Mem. San Francisco C. of C. (past pres.), Villa Traverna Club, Pennask Lake Fishing Club (B.C.), Sigma Nu Republican. Office: TSG Consumer Ptnrs 600 Montgomery St Ste 2900 San Francisco CA 94111 Personal E-mail: jgshansby@tsgconsumer.com.

SHAO, OTIS HUNG-I, retired political science professor; b. Shanghai, July 18, 1923; came to U.S., 1949, naturalized, 1956; s. Ming Sun and Hannah (Chen) S.; m. Marie Sheng, Apr. 2, 1955. BA, St. John's U., 1946; MA, U. Colo., 1950; PhD, Brown U., 1957. From instr. to prof. polit. sci. Moravian Coll., Bethlehem, Pa., 1954-62; assoc. prof., then prof. polit. sci. Fla. Presbyn. Coll., St. Petersburg, 1962-68; prof. internat. politics, dean (Grad. Sch., U. Pacific), 1968-74; dir. Pub. Affairs Inst., 1969-74; provost Callison Coll., 1974-76; dean faculty, v.p. Occidental Coll., 1976-78; asso. exec. dir. sr. commn. Western Assn. Schs. and Colls., 1978-80; v.p., dean Hawaii Loa Coll., 1980-85; pres. Sheng Shao Enterprises Calif., 1985-92; CEO, chmn. D.S. Capital Internat., Calif., 1993-94. Mem. grad. students relations com. Council Grad. Schs. U.S., 1970-73; mem. exec. council undergrad. assessment program Ednl. Testing Service, 1978-80. Contbr. articles to profl. jours. Chmn. bd. dirs. Fgn. Policy Assn. Lehigh Valley, 1961-62; bd. dirs. World Affairs Council, San Joaquin County, 1969-77; trustee Inst. Med. Scis., Pacific Med. Center, San Francisco, 1968-72, optical scis. group of Profl. and Pub. Service Found., 1969-72; Resident fellow Harkness House, Brown U., 1953-54, Danforth Asso., 1958-85. Recipient Distinguished Service award Fgn. Policy Assn. Lehigh Valley, 1962 Mem. AAUP (pres. Fla. Presbyn. Coll. chpt. 1965-66), Am. Assn. Higher Edn., Rho Psi, Tau Kappa Epsilon. Democrat. Presbyterian. Home: 1784 Curtner Ave San Jose CA 95124

SHAO, WEI, writer, educator; BA, China; MA, NYU, 1998. Author: (nonfiction, poetry) Pulling A Dragon's Teeth (Agnes Lynch Starrett Poetry award, 2002). Recipient Rona Jaffe Found. Writers' award, 1999; N.Y. Found. Fellowship For Arts, 2001. Home: Apt 3LL 601 W 110st New York NY 10025 Personal E-mail: wendyshao7@yahoo.com.

SHAO, ZHENHUA, electrical engineer, consultant; arrived in U.S., 1989; s. Jinrui Shao and Rujing Hua. Diploma in elec. engring., Shanghai Jiao Tong U., 1983, MSME, 1989; MSEE, Wichita State U., 1991; PhD Elec. Engring., U. Kans., 1994. Registered profl. engr., Calif. Elec. engr. Shanghai Jiao Tong U., 1983—86; rsch. asst. Nat. Inst. Aviation Rsch., Wichita, 1990—92; tchg. asst. U. Kans., Lawrence, 1993—94; elec. design engr. Eastman Kodak, Kansas City, 1995; chief engr. NGK Insulators Inc., Torrance, Calif., 1996—2002; circuit design mgr. L.A. divsn. Ibiden USA Inc., Torrance, Calif., 2003—. Cons. Lawrence Paper Co., 1994—95; cons. engring., San Gabriel, Calif., 1997—; reviewer IEEE and Inst. Elec. Engring. Contbr. articles to profl. jours. Named Outstanding Rschr., Shanghai Jiao Tong U., 1985; named one of Top 50 Pairs in Open Pair Game, N.Am. Bridge Championships U.S., Am. Contract Bridge League, 1998, Top 50 Pairs in Open Pair Game, N.Am. Bridge Championships Can., 1999. Achievements include patents in field; design of high frequency integrated circuits. Home: PO Box 1083 San Gabriel CA 91778 Home Phone: 626-374-0837. E-mail: zshao2001@yahoo.com.

SHAPER, C. PARK, energy executive; BA, BS, Stanford Univ.; MBA, Northwestern Univ. Cons. Boston Consulting Group, 1995—97; v.p., CFO First Data Corp., 1997—99; pres., bd. dir. Altair Corp., 1999; v.p., CFO Kinder Morgan Inc., Kinder Morgan Energy Partners LP, Kinder Morgan Mgmt. LLC, Houston, 2000—04, exec. v.p., CFO, 2004—05, pres., 2005—. Bd. dir., treas. Children's Fund, Houston. Office: Kinder Morgan Inc Ste 1000 500 Dallas St Houston TX 77002 *

SHAPER, CHRISTOPHER THORNE, sales executive; b. Columbus, Ohio, Sept. 6, 1955; s. Charles R. and M. Caroline (Garringer) Shaper. BA, Wake Forest U., 1977; MA in Mgmt., Coll. of Notre Dame, 1992. Sales rep. Intex Products Inc., Winston-Salem, NC, 1978; tech. sales rep. Am. Can Co., Oak Brook, Ill., 1979-81, J.T. Baker Chem. Co., Atlanta, 1981-83; corp. accts. rep. Erachem Comilog, Inc., Balt., 1983-84, industry sales mgr., 1984-92, dir. mktg. and sales, 1992—2000, dir. sales, 2000—03, v.p. global manganese sales, 2003—, v.p. sales, 2005; pres. South Mountain Assocs., LLC, 2006—. Mem.: Am. Feed Industries Assn., Am. Chem. Soc. Republican. Roman Catholic. Avocations: sports, reading. Office: Southmountain Assoc LLC PO Box 1524 Hagerstown MD 21741 Office Phone: 301-665-1177. Business E-Mail: cshaper@myactv.net.

SHAPERE, DUDLEY, philosophy educator; b. Harlingen, Tex., May 27, 1928; s. Dudley and Corinne (Pupkin) S.; m. Hannah Hardgrave; children: Hannah Elizabeth, Christine Ann; children by previous marriage: Alfred Dudley, Catherine Lucretia. BA, Harvard U., 1949, MA, 1955, PhD, 1957. Instr. philosophy Ohio State U., 1957-60; asst. prof. U. Chgo., 1960-65, assoc. prof., 1965-67, prof., 1967-72, mem. com. on evolutionary biology, 1969-72, chmn. undergrad. program in history and philosophy of sci., 1966-72, chmn. com. on conceptual founds. sci., 1970-72; prof. U. Ill., Urbana, 1972-75, chmn. program in history and philosophy of sci., 1972-75; prof. U. Md., College Park, 1975-84; Z. Smith Reynolds prof. philosophy and history of sci. Wake Forest U., 1984—2002; ret., 2002. Mem. com. on history and philosophy of sci. U. Md., 1975-84, chmn. program in history and philosophy of sci., 1983-84.; vis. prof. Rockefeller U., 1965-66, Harvard U., 1968; mem. Inst. Advanced Study, Princeton, N.J., 1978-79, 81, 89, Otto Neugebauer fellow, 2001; spl. cons. (program dir.) program in history and philosophy of sci. NSF, 1966-75; Sigma Xi nat. bicentennial lectr., 1974-77. Author: Philosophical Problems of Natural Science, 1965, Galileo: A Philosophical Study, 1974, Reason and the Search for Knowledge, 1984; editorial bd.: Philosophy of Sci., Studies in History and Philosophy of Sci.; rev. bd.: Philosophy Research Archives; contbr. articles to profl. jours. Served with AUS, 1950-52. Recipient Quantrell award for excellence in undergrad. tchg. U. Chgo., 1968; Disting. Scholar-Tchr. award U. Md., 1979-80. Fellow AAAS (sec. sec. 1972); mem. APA, Philosophy of Sci. Assn., History of Sci. Soc., Am. Philos. Assn., Acad. Internat. de Philosophie des Scis. Home: 3125 Turkey Hill Ct Winston Salem NC 27106-4951 E-mail: shapere@wfu.edu.

SHAPERO, DONALD CAMPBELL, physicist, government official; b. Detroit, Apr. 17, 1942; s. Donald Mayer and Lillian Emily (Campbell) S.; m. Diana B. Berner, Dec. 17, 1969 (div.); 1 child, Stephen B.; m. Linda J. Ravdin, Sept. 8, 1985; child, Daniel R. BS, MIT, 1964, PhD, 1970. Thomas J. Watson fellow IBM Corp., Yorktown Heights, N.Y., 1970-72; asst. prof. physics Am. U., Washington, 1972-73, Cath. U., Washington, 1973-75; exec. dir. energy rsch. adv. bd. U.S. Dept. Energy, Washington, 1978-79; sr. staff officer Nat. Acad. Scis., Washington, 1975-78, spl. asst. for program coord., 1979-82, dir. bd. physics and astronomy, 1982—. Exec. sec. com. effects on multiple nuclear weapon detonations Nat. Acad. Scis.-NRC, Washington, 1975-76, exec. sec. geophys. data panel, 1976, exec. sec. panel to assess nat. need for facilities dedicated to prodn. synchrotron radiation, 1976, sr. staff officer geophys. study com., 1976-78; dir. com. sci. and pub. policy nuclear risk survey Nat. Acad. Sci., 1976-78, sr. staff officer for five yr. outlook sci. and tech., 1979-82, sr. staff officer workshop sci. instrumentation, 1982; staff dir. physics survey Physics Through the 1990's, 1982-86, Materials Sci. and Engring. study for the 1990's, 1985-89. Contbr. sci. articles to profl. publs. V.p. Jewish Congregation, 1983-84, pres., 1984-85; sec. James Clark Maxwell Found., 1992—. NSF fellow, 1964-68; rsch. grantee Cottrell, 1975. Mem. Am. Phys. Soc., Am. Astronomical Soc., Internat. Astronomical Union, Am. Geophys. Union. Home: 7537 Heatherton Ln Rockville MD 20854-3232 Office: Nat Acad Scis KECK 956 500 5th St Washington DC 20001

SHAPIRA, DAVID S., food products and retail grocery executive; b. 1942; married. BA, Oberlin Coll., 1964; MA, Stanford U., 1966. V.p. Giant Eagle, Inc. (formerly Giant Eagle Markets, Inc.), Pitts., 1974—81, pres., 1981—94, CEO, also bd. dirs.; chmn. & CEO Giant Eagle, Youngstown; now chmn. bd. Phar-Mor Inc., Youngstown. Mem. bd. Allegheny Conf. Community Devel. *

SHAPIRO, AMIR, mechanical engineer, researcher; b. Haifa, Israel, Oct. 24, 1971; s. David Shapiro and Sylvie Shapira; m. Haya Edelstein, Oct. 4, 1994; children: Elad Moshe, Avichay Eliezer, Uriel Shlomo, Hila. BS-MechE (hon.), Israel Inst. of Tech., Haifa, 1997, MSMechE, 2000, PhD, 2004. Tchg. asst. Israel Inst. Tech., 1997—2004; post doctoral fellow Ben Gurion U. of Negev, Beer-Sheva, Israel, 2004—05, lectr., 2005—; rsch. scholar Carnegie Mellon U., Pitts., 2005—06. Reviewer Israel Ministry Sci. and Tech., 2004—; cons. in field. Contbr. articles to profl. jours. Sgt., 1990—93, Israeli Army. Recipient Excellence in Tchg. award, Ben Gurion U., 2005; grantee, Asher Peled Found., Technion., 2003—05; scholar, Technion-Israel Inst. Tech., 1997—2004, Salim and Rachel Benin Found., 2003; Gutwirth scholar, Technion-Israel Inst. Tech., 1999, Excellence in Study scholar, Israel Ministry Edn., Rsch. grantee, Ministry Def., State of Israel, 2005. Mem.: IEEE (assoc.; reviewer Trans. on Robotics and Automation 2001—04). Achievements include research in spider-like robot for motion in planar tunnel environments; wall climbing robot; climbing of a snake like robot; invention of dual tracked mobile robot for motion in rough terrain; research in stability of second-order asymmetric linear systems with application to robot grasping; force closure set of linearly controlled grasps; design and motion planning of a semi-passive mobile platform for locomotion on slippery surfaces.

SHAPIRO, BURTON LEONARD, dentist, geneticist, educator; b. NYC, Mar. 29, 1934; s. Nat Lazarus and Fay Rebecca (Gartenhouse) S.; m. Eileen Roman, Aug. 11, 1958; children: Norah Leah, Anne Rachael, Carla Faye. Student, Tufts U., Medford, Mass., 1951-54; DDS, NYU, 1958; MS, U. Minn., 1962, PhD, 1966. Faculty U. Minn. Sch. Dentistry, Mpls., 1962—, assoc. prof. div. oral pathology, 1966-70, prof., chmn. div. oral biology, 1970-79, prof., chmn. dept. oral biology, 1979-88, prof. dept. oral pathology and genetics, 1979-88, dir. grad. studies, mem. grad. faculty genetics, 1966—, prof. dept. oral sci., 1988—2006, mem. grad. faculty pathobiology, 1979; prof. dept. lab. medicine and pathology U. Minn. Sch. Medicine, 1985—; prof. emeritus U. Minn. Sch. Dentistry, 2006; mem. Human Genetics Inst. U. Minn. Sch. Medicine, 1988—, univ. senator, 1968-72, 88-93; also mem. med. staff U. Minn. Health Scis. Center; exec. com. Grad. Sch. U. Minn., chmn. health scis. policy rev. council, chmn. univ. faculty consultative com., 1988-92; chmn. univ. fin. and planning com. Grad. Sch. U. Minn., 1988. Hon. research fellow Galton Lab. dept. human genetics Univ. Coll., London, 1974; spl. vis. prof. Japanese Ministry Edn., Sci. and Culture, 1983 Mem. adv. editorial bd.: Jour. Dental Research, 1971—; Contbr. articles to profl. jours. Served to lt. USNR, 1958-60. Am. Cancer Soc. postdoctoral fellow, 1960-62; advanced fellow, 1965-68; named Century Club Prof. of Yr., 1988. Fellow Am. Acad. Oral Pathology, AAAS; mem. Internat. Assn. Dental Research (councilor 1969), Am. Soc. Human Genetics, Craniofacial Biology Soc. (pres. 1972), Sigma Xi, Omicron Kappa Upsilon. Home: 148 Nina St # 2 Saint Paul MN 55102-2160 Office: U Minn Sch Dentistry Dept Oral Sci Minneapolis MN 55455 Office Phone: 612-624-3991. Business E-Mail: burt@umn.edu.

SHAPIRO, DAVID L., lawyer; b. Corsicana, Tex., May 19, 1936; s. Harry and Alice (Laibovitz) S. BA, U. Tex., Austin, 1967; JD, St. Mary's U., 1970. Bar: Tex. 1970, U.S. Dist. Ct. (we. dist.) Tex. 1972, U.S. Supreme Ct. 1975, U.S. Ct. Appeals (5th cir.) 1981. Assoc. Law Office Jim S. Phelps, Houston, 1971; pvt. practice, Austin, 1972—. Spl. counsel com. human resources Tex. Ho. Reps., Austin, 1973-74; counsel subcom. health svcs. Tex. Senate, Austin, 1983-87. With U.S. Army, 1959-61. Mem.: Am. Legion, Austin Criminal Def. Lawyers Assn., Coll. of State Bar of Tex., State Bar Tex. (chmn. lawyer referral svc. com. 1980—82, contbr. Media Law Handbook supplement 1986, adminstrn. of justice com. 1990—93, jury svc. com. 1998—2001). Democrat. Avocations: automobiles, football. Office: 500 W 16th St Ste 101 Austin TX 78701-1536 Office Phone: 512-322-5255. Personal E-mail: daveinaustintexas@yahoo.com.

SHAPIRO, DAVID LOUIS, law educator; b. NYC, Oct. 12, 1932; s. Louis and Sara (Grabelsky) Shapiro; m. Jane Wilkins Bennett, June 19, 1954; 1 child: Lynn Mayson. Grad., Horace Mann Sch., 1950; AB magna cum laude, Harvard U., 1954, LLB summa cum laude, 1957. Bar: DC 1957, Mass. 1964. Assoc. Covington & Burling, Washington, 1957-62; law clk. to Justice John M. Harlan US Supreme Ct., 1962-63; asst. prof. law Harvard Law Sch., Cambridge, Mass., 1963—66, prof., 1966—84, William Nelson Cromwell prof. law, 1984—2006, emeritus, 2006—, assoc. dean, 1971-76; dep. solicitor gen. US Dept. Justice, Washington, 1989—91. Vis. prof. NYU, 2003, U. Ariz., 2004. Author: Federalism: A Dialogue, 1995, Civil Procedure: Preclusion in Civil Actions, 2001; co-author: The Federal Courts and the Federal System, 1973, 88, 96, 2003; editor: The Evolution of a Judicial Philosophy: Selected Opinions of Justice John M. Harlan, 1969, The Judicial Code and the Rules of Procedure in the Federal Courts, annually 1988-2000. Mem.: Am. Law Inst. Office: Harvard Law Sch 1563 Massachusetts Ave Cambridge MA 02138 Office Fax: 617-496-4880. Business E-Mail: dshapiro@law.harvard.edu.

SHAPIRO, DAVID W., prosecutor; BA in English Lit. and Creative Writing, SUNY, Binghamton; JD, SUNY, Buffalo. Bar: Calif., NY, Ariz., admitted to practice: US Dist. Cts. (So. and Eastern Dists. NY, Dist. Ariz., No. and Ctrl. Dists. Calif.), US Ct. Appeals (2nd and 9th Cirs.). Fed. Prosecutor Eastern Dist., NY, 1986—92, chief organized crime unit NY; Fed. Prosecutor Dist. of Ariz., 1992—94; chief Appellate Div. Northern Dist., Calif., 1994—2001, chief Criminal Div. Calif., 1994—2001, U.S. Atty. Calif., 2001—02; adminstrv. ptnr. Boies, Schiller & Flexner, Oakland, Calif., 2002—. Spkr. in field. Mng. editor Buffalo Law Review. Office: Boies, Schiller & Flexner 1999 Harrison Street Ste 900 Oakland CA 94612

SHAPIRO, DONALD P., retired otolaryngologist; b. NYC, Nov. 5, 1946; s. Irvin and Sonia Shapiro; m. Karlyn Weinberg, July 1, 1969; children: Stacey Crout, Adam. BA, Columbia U., NYC, 1967; MD, Tufts U. Sch. Medicine, Boston, 1971; MPH, Univ. Medicine and Dentistry of New Jersey, 1997, Rutgers U., Piscataway, NJ, 1997. Diplomate Nat. Bd. Med. Examiners, 1972, cert. Am. Bd. Otolaryngology-Head and Neck Surgery, 1976. Surg. internship, residency U. Rochester Sch. Medicine, NY, 1971—73; resident otolaryngology Harvard Med. Sch., Boston, 1973—76; sec., treas. Kenneth S. Rosen, M.D., and Donald P. Shapiro, M.D., P.A., Woodbury, NJ, 1979—93; ret., 1993. Chief, otolaryngology David Grant USAF Med. Ctr., Fairfield, Calif., 1976—78; clincal instr. in otolaryngology and maxillofacial surgery U. Calif. Sch. Medicine, Sacramento, 1976—78; clin. asst. prof. surgery UMDNJ, Stratford, NJ, 1980—93. Maj. USAF, 1976—78. Home Phone: 856-751-6380.

SHAPIRO, EDWARD MURAY, dermatologist; b. Denver, Oct. 6, 1924; s. Isador Benjamin and Sara (Berezin) Shapiro; m. Ruth Young, Oct. 14, 1944; children: Adrian Michael, Stefanie Ann; m. Dorothy Rosmarin, July 22, 1990. Studied, U. Colo., 1941—43; AB with honors, U. Tex., 1948, MD, 1952. Diplomate Am. Bd. Dermatology. Intern Jefferson Coll. Medicine Hosp., Phila., 1952—53; resident in dermatology U. Tex. Med. Br., Galveston, 1953—55, Henry Ford Hosp., Detroit, 1955—56, assoc. in dermatology divsn., 1956—57; clin. instr., dermatology Baylor U. Coll. Medicine, Houston, 1957—68, assoc. clin. prof., 1968—; staff mem. Ben Taub Gen. Hosp., Houston, 1958—; active staff mem. Columbia Bayshore Hosp., 1962—, Meml. Hosp. S.E., Houston, 2000. Contbr. articles to profl. jours. With USAAF, 1943—46. Grantee, Henry J.N. Taub, 1958—60. Fellow: Am. Acad. Dermatology; mem.: AMA, Am. Physicians Art Assn., Am. Physicians Art Assn. (v.p. 1993, pres. 2003—04, 2003—04, 2004—05), Houston Dermatology Assn., Harris County Med. Assn. (pres., S.E. br. 1968—69), South Ctrl. Dermatol. Assn. (bd. dirs. 1987—88), Tex. Dermatol. Soc. (pres.-elect 1988, pres. 1989—90), Tex. Med. Assn., Rotary Internat. (Paul Harris fellow 1995, 1997), B'nai B'rith. Republican. Jewish. Avocations: painting, sports. Office: 1020 Pasadena Blvd Pasadena TX 77506-4700 Home Phone: 713-785-1200; Office Phone: 713-477-8183.

SHAPIRO, EDWARD ROBERT, psychiatrist, educator, health facility administrator, psychotherapist; b. Boston, Sept. 13, 1941; s. Jacob and Ruth (Yankelovich) S.; m. Donna Elmendorf; 1 child, Joshua Jackson; 1 child from previous marriage, Jacob Matthew; 1 stepchild, Zachary Andrew Robbins. BA magna cum laude, Yale U., 1962; MA in Anthropology, Stanford U., 1966; MD, Harvard U., 1968. Diplomate Am. Bd. Psychiatry and Neurology. Intern in medicine Beth Israel Hosp., Boston, 1968-69; resident in psychiatry Mass. Mental Health Ctr., Boston, 1969-72, chief resident in psychiatry, 1971-72; clin. assoc. NIMH, Bethesda, Md., 1972-74; dir. Adolescent and Family Treatment and Study Ctr. McLean Hosp., Belmont, Mass., 1974-89, dir. Psychosocial Tng. and Consultation, 1989-91; bd. dirs. Ctr. for Study of Groups and Social Systems, Boston, 1983-90, A.K. Rice Inst., Washington, 1983-90, dir. Nat. Group Rels. Conf., 1989-91; faculty mem. Boston Psychoanalytic Inst., 1978—; assoc. clin. prof. psychiatry Harvard Med. Sch., Boston, 1982—; med. dir., CEO The Austen Riggs Ctr., Stockbridge, Mass., 1991—; tng. and supr. analyst Psychoanalytical Inst. of the Berkshires, 2003—. Dir. The Erik H. Erikson Inst. for Edn. and Rsch., 1994-2000. Co-author: (with A.W. Carr) Lost in Familiar Places: Creating New Connections Between the Individual and Society, 1991; editor: The Inner World in the Outer World: Psychoanalytic Perspectives, 1997; mem. editorial bd. Jour. Adolescence, 1977-82, Psychiatry, 1988—; assoc. editor Jour. Adolescence, 1982-84; contbr. articles to profl. jours. Mem. Yale Russian Chorus. With USPHS, 1972-74. Recipient Isenberg Teaching award McLean Hosp., 1980, Rsch. prize Soc. for Family Therapy and Rsch., 1984, Felix and Helen Deutsch Sci. prize Boston Psychoanalytic Inst., 1980, Outstanding Psychiatrist for Advancement of the Profession award Mass. Psychiat. Assn., 2007. Fellow Am. Psychiat. Assn. (disting. life), Am. Coll. Psychoanalysis, A.K. Rice Inst.; mem. Am. Psychoanalytic Assn. Achievements include helping develop the Erik H. Erikson Inst. for Edn. and Rsch. as a vehicle for applying the clinical insights developed at Riggs to larger social issues. Avocation: music. Office: The Austen Riggs Ctr PO Box 962 25 Main St Stockbridge MA 01262-0962

SHAPIRO, EDWIN STANLEY, lawyer, judge; b. Bklyn., Jan. 14, 1931; s. Harry I. and Ann (Safanie) S.; m. Sandra I. Bernstein, Sept. 15, 1957; children: James A., Sarah E. BA, Trinity Coll., Hartford, Conn., 1952; LLB, JD, Harvard Law Sch., Cambraidge, Mass., 1955. Bar: NY 1956, US Dist. Ct. (so. and ea. dist.) NY 1956, US Ct. Appeals 1957. Atty. Levin & Weintraub, NYC, 1956—57; pvt. practice NYC, 1957-59; ptnr. Smith, Shapiro & Scheier, NYC, 1959—62; pvt. practice NYC, 1962—69; ptnr. Basch, Seits & Shapiro, NYC, 1970—74, Seits & Shapiro, NYC, 1974—81; town justice Ossining, NY, 1980—; pvt. practice NYC, 1981—95, Briarcliff Manor, NY, 1996—. Lawyer Staten Island Open Lands Found., 1965-67. Mem. Assn. of Bar of City of NY (environ. law com. 1970-73, com. on state cts. 1982-83, corrections com. 1996-98), Ossining Area Bar Assn. (pres. 2003). Home Phone: 914-762-3810; Office Phone: 914-941-2606. E-mail: shaplaw1@optonline.net.

SHAPIRO, ELI, business consultant, educator, economist; b. Bklyn., June 13, 1916; s. Samuel and Pauline (Kushel) S.; m. Beatrice Ferbend, Jan. 18, 1946 (dec. July 1999); 1 child, Laura J. AB, Bklyn. Coll., 1936; A.M., Columbia U., 1937, PhD, 1939. Instr. Bklyn. Coll., 1936-41; rsch. assoc. Nat. Bur. Econ. Rsch., 1938-39, cons., 1939-42, mem. rsch. staff, 1955-62; asst. prof. fin. U. Chgo., 1946-47, asso. prof., 1948-52, prof., 1952; prof. fin. Mass. Inst. Tech., 1952-61; assoc. dean Mass. Inst. Tech. (Sch. Indsl. Mgmt.), 1954-58, Alfred P. Sloan prof. mgmt., 1976-84, Alfred P. Sloan prof. emeritus, 1984—; prof. fin. Harvard Bus. Sch., 1962-72, Sylvan C. Coleman prof. fin. mgmt., 1968-72; chmn. fin. com., dir. Travelers Ins. Cos., Hartford, Conn., 1971-78, vice chmn. bd., dir., 1976-78; chmn. bd. Mass. Co., 1971-72; pres. Nat. Bur. Econ. Research, 1982-84. Chmn. bd. Fed. Home Loan Bank Boston, 1970-89; econ. analyst div. monetary rsch. US Dept. Treasury, 1941-42; economist rsch. div. OPA, 1941-42; staff cons. Com. Econ. Devel., 1950-51, mem. rsch. adv. com., 1961-64, 69—, project dir., 1966-69; cons. sec. treasury; mem. enforcement commn. WSB, 1952-53; cons. Inst. Def. Analyses; dep. dir. Rsch. Com. Money Credit, 1959-61. Author: (with others) Personal Finance Industry and Its Credit Standards, 1939, (with Steiner) Money and Banking, 1941, Development of Wisconsin Credit Union Movement, 1947, Money and Banking, 1953, (with others), 1958, (with D. Meiselman) Measurement of Corporate Sources and Uses of Funds, 1964, (with others) Money and Banking, 1969, (with Wolf) The Role of Private Placement in Corporate Finance, 1972; Editor: (with W.L. White) Capital for Productivity and Growth, 1977. Served from ensign to lt. USNR, 1942-46. Recipient Econ. Dept. award Bklyn. Coll., 1936, Honors Day award distinguished alumni, 1949 Fellow Am. Acad. Arts and Scis.; mem. Nat. Bur. Econ. Research (pres.), Am. Econ. Assn., Council Fgn. Relations, Am. Fin. Assn. Home and Office: 180 Beacon St Boston MA 02116-1408 Office Phone: 617-266-5512.

SHAPIRO, EUGENE DAVID, pediatrician, epidemiologist, educator; s. Jonah R. and Rita R. Shapiro; m. Susan K. Bowers; children: Lauren R., Amy E., Daniel J. BA, Yale Coll., New Haven, Conn., 1970; MD, U. Calif., San Francisco, 1976. Resident Children's Hosp. Pitts., 1976—79; asst. prof. pediat. Yale Sch. Medicine, New Haven, 1983—89, assoc. prof. pediat., 1989—93, prof. pediat., 1993—. Fellow, Children's Hosp. Pitts., 1979—81; grantee, NIH, 1983—; Robert Wood Johnson scholar, Yale Sch. Medicine, 1981—83. Fellow: Am. Acad. Pediat.; mem.: Am. Epidemiologic Assn., Pediatric Infectious Disease Soc., Infectious Disease Soc. Am., Soc. Pediatric Rsch., Am. Pediatric Soc., Am. Bd. Pediatrics-Infectious Diseases. Achievements include research in assessment of clinical effectiveness of vaccines. Office: Yale U Dept Pediatrics 333 Cedar St PO Box 208064 New Haven CT 06520-8064

SHAPIRO, FLORENCE, state legislator, advertising and public relations executive; b. NYC, May 2, 1948; d. Martin Nmi and Ann (Spiesman) D.; m. Howard Nmi Shapiro, Dec. 28, 1969; children: Lisa, Todd, Staci. BS, U. Tex., 1970. Tchr. Richardson High Sch., Tex., 1970-72; advt., pub. rels. Shapiro & Co., Plano, Tex., 1982—; formerly mayor and mem. city coun. City of Plano, Tex.; now mem. Tex. Senate, 1992—, chmn. edn. com., mem. fin. com., adminstrn. com. and transp. and homelend security coms. Bd. dirs. Plano C. of C., Presbyn. and Children's Healthcare Ctr., Plano Econ. Devel. Bd., U. Tex. at Dallas Adv. Coun., The North Tex. Commn., The Dallas Regional Mobility Coalition; mem. nat. bd. dirs. Susan B. Komen Breast Cancer Found.; mem. adv. bd. Children's Edn. Fund Dallas, Dallas County Domestic Violence Task Force, Family Violence Prevention Coun. Injury Prevention Ctr. Greater Dallas. Recipient Plano Vol. of Yr. award, 1983, Plano Citizen of Yr. award, 1985, Athena award Plano C. of C. for Businesswoman of Yr., 1990, Child Advocate award Dallas Children's Advocacy Ctr., 1995, Legislator of Yr. award Tex. Mcpl. League, 1995, 97, Nat. Rep. Legislators Assn., 1997, Tex. Ct. Apptd. Spl. Advs., 1997; Outstanding Legislator of Yr. award Tex. Police Chiefs Assn., 1995, Legislator of Yr. award, 1997, Friend of the Taxpayer award Citizens for a Sound Economy, 1999, Centennial Hero award Plano Ind. Sch. Dist., 1999, Voice of Children award, Ct. Apptd. Spl. Advs. of Collin County, 2001, others; Outstanding Legislator award Tex. Assn. Dist. and County Attys., 1997, Leader of Excellence award Free Market Com., 1997, Senate Statesman award Lonestar Found., 1997, Polit. Courage award John Ben Sheppard Pub. Leadership Forum, 1997; named One of 10 Best Legislators family law session State Bar Tex., 1997, One of 3 State Senators on YCT Honor Roll, 1997, Legis. Star, Tex. Classroom Tchrs. Assn., 1997, Guardian of Free Enterprise, Nat. Fedn. Ind. Bus., 1999, Woman of Yr., Les Femmes du Monde, 2002, Woman of Yr., Women's Transp. Seminar Dallas-Ft. Worth, 2002, others; honored by Texans for Lawsuit Reform, 1997, Assn. Ob-Gyn. and Southwestern Med. Sch., 1997. Mem. Rotary (Paul Harris fellow 1990), Alpha Epsilon Phi (Nat. Outstanding Young Alumnae award). Republican. Jewish. Office: Tex Senate PO Box 12068 Austin TX 78711-2068 Home: 1500 Eastwick Ln Plano TX 75093-2443

SHAPIRO, FRED DAVID, lawyer; b. Cleve., Nov. 10, 1926; s. Isadore R. and Lottie (Turetsky) S.; m. Helen Solomon, Sept. 5, 1948; children—Gary N., Ira R., Diane S. BA cum laude, Ohio State U., 1949; LL.B., Harvard U., 1954. Bar: Ohio 1954. Since practiced in, Cleve.; sr. ptnr. Shapiro and Lodwick, Co., L.P.A, 1994—. Served with USNR, 1945-46. Mem. Ohio Bar Assn., Greater Cleve. Bar Assn., Cuyahoga County Bar Assn., The Rowfant Club, Phi Beta Kappa. Jewish. Home: 29226 S Woodland Rd Cleveland OH 44124-5737 Office Phone: 216-378-9730. Personal E-mail: fshapo@aol.com.

SHAPIRO, GARY EVAN, newspaper journalist; b. Lewiston, Maine, Feb. 5, 1964; s. Sherman George and Charlotte (Cominsky) S. AB, Harvard U., 1986; JD, Columbia U., 1993. Assoc. Skadden Arps Slate Meagher & Flom, NYC, 1993-94; writer, event prodr. NYC, 1994-99; journalist Forward newspaper, NYC, 1999—. Contbg. editor Am. Scholar, 2000—; note editor Columbia Jour. Environ. Law, 1993; contbr. numerous articles to profl. jours.; prodr. numerous programs on diplomacy, history, arch., bus., arts and lit., politics and econs., sci., edn., philosophy. Recipient Charles William Eliot medal for Citizenship, 1986, Cox Medal, Phillips Exeter, 1982; John Finley Traveling fellow, 1986. Mem. Overseas Press Club, Nat. Arts Club (lit. com. 1997—), Harvard Club (program com. 1995-2000). Avocation: book collecting. Home: 27 W 44th St # 50 New York NY 10036-6613 Office: Forward Newspaper 45 E 33rd St New York NY 10016-5336

SHAPIRO, GEORGE HOWARD, retired lawyer; b. St. Louis, Nov. 10, 1936; s. Isadore T. and Alice (Schucart) S.; m. Mary Kenney Leonard, 1977 (div. 1994); m. Ray Ann Kremer, 1999; 1 child, Ellen. BA, Harvard U., 1958, LLB, 1961; postgrad., London Sch. Econs., 1961-62. Bar: Ga. 1960, D.C. 1963. Atty. U.S. Dept. Labor, Washington, 1962-63; assoc. Arent Fox Kintner Plotkin & Kahn, Washington, 1963-69, ptnr., 1970-99; ret., 2000. Co-author: 'Cable Speech' The Case for First Amendment Protection, 1983; editor: New Program Opportunities in the Electronic Media, 1983, Current Developments in CATV, 1981. With USAR, 1962-68. Frank Knox Meml. fellow Harvard U., 1961-62. Mem. D.C. Bar Assn., Fed. Communications Bar Assn. Democrat. Jewish. Avocation: skiing. Home: Apt 906 3180 Mathieson Dr NE Atlanta GA 30305-1871 E-mail: GHSinATL@aol.com.

SHAPIRO, HAROLD TAFLER, economics professor, former academic administrator; b. Montreal, Que., Can., June 8, 1935; s. Maxwell and Mary (Tafler) Shapiro; m. Vivian Bernice Rapoport, May 19, 1957; children: Anne, Marilyn, Janet, Karen. BComm, McGill U., Montreal, 1956; PhD in Econs. (Harold Helm fellow, Harold Dodds sr. fellow), Princeton U., NJ, 1964. From asst. prof. to assoc. prof. econ. U. Mich., Ann Arbor, 1964—70, prof., 1970—76, prof. econ. and pub. affairs, 1977, chmn. dept. econ., 1974—77, v.p. acad. affairs, 1977—79, pres., 1980—87; rsch. adv. Bank Can., 1965-72; pres. Princeton U., 1988—2001, pres. emeritus, prof. econ. and pub. affairs Woodrow Wilson Sch., 2001—. Mem. exec. com. Assn. of Am. Universities, 1985—89; trustee NJ Commn. Sci. and Tech., 1988—91; mem. Pres.'s Coun. Advisors Sci. and Tech., 1990—92, Stem Cell Inst. of NJ Joint Bd. Mgrs., 2005—; chmn. com. employer-based health benefits Inst. Medicine, 1991; bd. overseers Robert Wood Johnson Med. Sch., 2000—; bd. dir. DeVry Inst., The Hastings Ctr., Reading is Fundamental, Knight Found. Comm. on Intercollegiate Athletics, Merck Vaccine Adv. Bd., Princeton Healthcare Sys.; bd. trustees U. Medicine & Dentistry NJ, 2006—; trustee tech. Israel Inst. Tech., 2002—; chmn. Orgn. NIH Nat. Sci., 2000—03; mem. adv. com. Human Embryonic Stem Cell Rsch. NRC, 2006—. Author: A Larger Sense of Purpose: Higher Education and Society, 2005; editor (with William G. Bowen): Universities and Their Leadership, 1998; editor: (with James F. Childress & Eric M. Meslin) Belmont Revisited: Ethical Principles for Research With Human Subjects, 2005. Chair Nat. Bioethics Adv. Commn., 1996—2001; chmn. spl. Presdl. com. Rsch. Librs. Group, 1980—89; mem. Gov.'s High Tech. Task Force, Mich., 1980—87, Gov.'s Commn. Jobs and Econ. Devel., Mich., 1983—87, Carnegie Commn. Coll. Retirement, 1984—86; dir. Am. Coun. Edn., 1989—91; mem. Pres. Bush Coun. Advisors Sci. and Tech., 1990—93; trustee Alfred P. Sloan Found., 1980—, Interlochen Ctr. Arts, 1988—95, U. Pa. Med. Ctr., 1992—, Univ. Corp. Advanced Internet Devel., 2000, Am. Jewish Com., 2002—, Ednl. Testing Svc., 1994—2000. Recipient Lt. Gov.'s medal in commerce, McGill U., 1956, William D. Carey Lectureship award Leadership in Sci. Policy, 2006. Fellow: AAAS, Mich. Soc. Fellows (sr.); mem.: Am. Philos. Soc., Inst. Medicine of NAS/NRC, Univs. Rsch. Assn. (trustee 1988—2001). Office: Princeton U Woodrow Wilson School 355 Wallace Hall Princeton NJ 08544 Office Phone: 609-258-6184. Business E-Mail: hts@princeton.edu.

SHAPIRO, HARRY DEAN, lawyer; b. Louisville, June 21, 1940; s. Herman Shapiro and Toby (Spector) Levy; m. Linda Siegel, Dec. 19, 1970; 1 child, Deborah Anne. BS, U. Louisville, 1962, JD, 1964. Bar: Ky. 1964, D.C. 1968, Md. 1970. Trial and appellate atty. U.S. Dept. Justice, Washington, 1964-70; assoc. Venable, Baetjer & Howard, Balt., 1970-74, ptnr., 1975-87; sr. ptnr., head of tax practice Weinberg & Green, Balt., 1987—98, chmn. corp. dept., 1993-95; transaction group coord., 1995-98; head tax practice Saul Ewing LLP (formerly Saul, Ewing, Remick & Saul LLP), 1998-99; chmn. tax group Saul Ewing LLP (formerly Saul, Ewing, Remick & Saul LLP), 1999—. Author: Federal Tax Liens, 1981, The Successful Practice, 2005; contbr. articles to profl. jours. Mem. Md. State Bd. Edn., 1990-97; v.p. Assoc. Jewish Charities of Balt., Inc. 1991-94; vice chmn. The Assoc. Jewish Cmty. Fedn. Balt. 1987-89, asst. treas., 1989-91, mem. exec. com., 1993-97; trustee Sinai Hosp., Balt., 1987-90; counsel Balt. Mus. Art, 1984-97, trustee, 1984-96, sec., 1985-92, v.p., sec., 1992-94, v.p., 1994-96; dir., 1989-96; chmn. Joint Budgeting Coun., 1993-96, Coun. Jewish Fedns.; trustee Acad. Art Mus., Easton, 1998-2005. Capt. USAR, 1967-70. Recipient Disting. Alumni award Brandeis Sch. of Law, 1996, Chmn.'s award Balt. Mus. Art, 1996. Mem. ABA (tax sect.), Md. State Bar Assn., Ky. Bar Assn., D.C. Bar Assn., Md. Club, Center Club. Home: 717 S President St Unit 602 Baltimore MD 21202 Office: Saul Ewing LLP Lockwood Pl 500 E Pratt St Baltimore MD 21202-3133 Office Phone: 410-332-8658. Business E-Mail: hshapiro@saul.com. *Our country is at a crossroads in its history, and it is becoming clear that a sea change is necessary. Basic reforms must occur in our governmental and educational structures. The question is whether we have the intelligence to reject the cries for bigger government and more taxes to solve these problems when fundamental action is required.*

SHAPIRO, HARVEY, poet; b. Chgo., Jan. 27, 1924; s. Jacob J. and Dorothy (Cohen) S.; m. Edna Lewis Kaufman, July 23, 1953 (div.); children: Saul, Dan. BA, Yale U., 1947; MA, Columbia U., 1948. Instr. English Cornell U., 1949-50, 51-52; creative writing fellow Bard Coll., 1950-51; mem. editl. staff Commentary, New Yorker, 1955-57, N.Y. Times Mag., NYC, 1957, asst. editor, 1964-75; editor N.Y. Times Book Rev., 1975-83; dep. editor N.Y. Times Mag., 1983-96, consulting editor, 1996—2002. Author: The Eye, 1953, The Book and Other Poems, 1955,

Mountain, Fire Thornbush, 1961, Battle Report, 1966, This World, 1971, Lauds, 1975, Nightsounds, 1978, The Light Holds, 1984, National Cold Storage Company, 1988, A Day's Portion, 1994, Selected Poems, 1997, How Charlie Shaver Died and Other Poems, 2001; editor: Poets of World War II, 2003, The Sights Along the Harbor: New and Collected Poems, 2006. With USAAF, World War II. Decorated D.F.C., Air medal with 3 oak leaf clusters.; Rockefeller Found. grantee in poetry, 1967 Club: Elizabethan (New Haven), Century (N.Y.).

SHAPIRO, HOWARD M., lawyer, former prosecutor; b. May 8, 1960; BA magna cum laude, Williams Coll., 1982; JD, Yale Univ., 1985. Bar: NY 1986, DC 1997. Law clk. Judge Pierre N. Leval, US Dist. Ct. (so. NY dist.), 1985—87; asst. U.S. atty. U.S. Dept. Justice, so. NY dist., 1987—92; gen. counsel FBI, Washington, 1993—97; ptnr., co-chmn. Litigation dept., co-chmn. investigations & criminal litigation group Wilmer Cutler Pickering Hale & Dorr, Washington. Assoc. prof. Cornell Law Sch. Contbr. articles to newspapers. Named one of Top DC Lawyers, Washingtonian mag., 2002, 2004, DC Go-to Litigators, Legal Times, 2003; recipient Nat. Intelligence Disting. Svc. medal, dir. of Ctrl. Intelligence, 1997. Office: Wilmer Cutler Pickering Hale & Dorr 1875 Pennsylvania Ave NW Washington DC 20006 Office Phone: 202-663-6606. Office Fax: 202-663-6363. Business E-Mail: howard.shapiro@wilmerhale.com.

SHAPIRO, IRWIN IRA, physicist, researcher; b. NYC, Oct. 10, 1929; s. Samuel and Esther (Feinberg) S.; m. Marian Helen Kaplun, Dec. 20, 1959; children: Steven, Nancy. AB, Cornell U., 1950; A.M., Harvard U., 1951, PhD, 1955. Mem. staff Lincoln Lab. MIT, Lexington, 1954-70; Sherman Fairchild Distinguished scholar Calif. Inst. Tech., 1974; Morris Loeb lectr. physics Harvard, 1975; prof. geophysics and physics MIT, 1967-80, Schlumberger prof., 1980-84; Paine prof. practical astronomy, prof. physics Harvard U., 1982-97; sr. scientist Smithsonian Astrophys. Obs., 1982—; dir. Harvard-Smithsonian Ctr. for Astrophysics, 1983—2004; prof. Harvard U./Timken, 1997—. Cons. NSF, NASA. Contbr. articles to profl. jours. Recipient Albert A. Michelson medal Franklin Inst., 1975, award in phys. and math. scis. N.Y. Acad. Scis., 1982, Einstein medal Einstein Soc. Bern, 1994, Joseph Henry medal Smithsonian Instn., 2004; Guggenheim fellow, 1982. Fellow AAAS, Am. Geophys. Union (Charles A. Whitten medal 1991, William Bowie medal 1993), Am. Phys. Soc.; mem. AAAS, NAS (Benjamin Apthorp Gould prize 1979), Am. Astron. Soc. (Dannie Heineman award 1983, Dirk Brouwer award 1987, Gerard Kuiper award 1997), Am. Philos. Soc., Internat. Astron. Union, Phi Beta Kappa, Sigma Xi, Phi Kappa Phi. Home: 17 Lantern Ln Lexington MA 02421-6029 Office: Harvard-Smithsonian Ctr Astrophysics 60 Garden St Cambridge MA 02138-1516 Business E-Mail: ishapiro@cfa.harvard.edu.

SHAPIRO, ISAAC, lawyer; b. Tokyo, Jan. 5, 1931; arrived in U.S., 1946, naturalized, 1951; s. Constantine and Lydia (Chernetzky) S.; m. Jacqueline M. Weiss, Sept. 16, 1956; children: Tobias, Alexandra, Natasha. AB, Columbia U., 1954, LLB, 1956; postgrad., U. Paris, 1956—57. Bar: N.Y. 1957, U.S. Supreme Ct. 1971, Paris 1991. Assoc. Milbank, Tweed, Hadley & McCloy, NYC, 1956-65, ptnr., 1966-86, resident ptnr. Tokyo, 1977-79; ptnr. Skadden Arps Slate Meagher & Flom LLP, NYC, 1986—2001; resident ptnr. Skadden Arps Slate Meagher & Flom, Hong Kong, 1989-90, Paris, 1990—2001; of counsel Skadden Arps Slate Meagher & Flom LLP, NYC, 2001—; ptnr. Skadden Arps Slate Meagher & Flom (Europe) LLP, 2006—; tchg. fellow comparative law NYU, 1959-61. Lectr. Soviet law, 1961-67; adj. asst. prof. NYU, 1967-69, adj. assoc. prof., 1969-71, 74-75; adj. prof., dir. Russian legal studies Columbia Law Sch., 1999-2000. Author: (with Hazard and Maggs) The Soviet Legal System, 1969; author: Japan: The Risen Sun (in Japanese), 1982; editor: The Middle East Crisis-Prospects for Peace, 1969; contbr. articles to profl. jours. Mem. Joint Com. US-Japan Cultural and Ednl. Cooperation, Washington, 1972—78, Japan-US Friendship Commn., 1976—78; mem. svcs. policy adv. com. to US Trade Rep., 1982—91; trustee Nat. Humanities Ctr., Triangle Park, NC, 1978—89, Bank of Tokyo Mitsubishi Found., 1986—; trustee, v.p. Chamber Music Soc. Lincoln Ctr., 1980—86; pres. Japan Soc., NYC, 1970—77; trustee Isamu Noguchi Zaidan, Japan, 1999—, Isamu Noguchi Found., NY, 1985—, pres., 1985—2005; trustee, chmn. Isa Cultural Found., 1984—90; bd. advisors Trust for Mutual Understanding, NYC, 1985—; dir. Bank of Tokyo-Mitsubishi Trust Co., NY, 1975—77, 1980—2001, Japan Soc., 1969—77, 1979—80; bd. dirs. Bus. Coun. for Internat. Understanding, 1989—95, Nat. Com. US-China Rels., 1989—95, Asian Cultural Coun., 1980—. With US Army, 1950—52. Fulbright scholar, 1956-57; decorated Order of the Rising Sun with gold rays and neck ribbon Emperor Japan, 2006. Mem.: ABA, N.Y. State Bar Assn., Coun. Fgn. Rels., Japan Soc. N.Y. (trustee 1969—77, 1979—80), Century Assn. (N.Y.C.), Cercle de l'Union Interalliee (Paris), Royal Automobile Club (London). Office: Skadden Arps Slate Meagher & Flom LLP 4 Times Sq New York NY 10036-6522 Office Phone: 212-735-3480. Business E-Mail: ishapiro@skadden.com.

SHAPIRO, JAMES EDWARD, judge; b. Chgo., May 28, 1930; BS, U. Wis., 1951; JD, Harvard U., 1954. Bar: Wis. 1956, U.S. Dist. Ct. (ea. dist.) Wis. 1956, U.S. Ct. Appeals (7th cir.) 1962, U.S. Supreme Ct. 1971. Sole practice, Milw., 1956-57; resident house counsel Nat. Presto Industries, Eau Claire, Wis., 1957-60; ptnr. Bratt & Shapiro, Milw., 1960-64; sole practice Milw., 1964-74; ptnr. Frank, Hiller & Shapiro, Milw., 1974-82; judge U.S. Bankruptcy Ct., Milw., 1982—, chief judge, 1996-2000. Mem. Bayside Bd. Appeals, Wis., 1969-77; Milwaukee County Ct. commr., 1969-78; dir. Milw. Legal Aid Soc., 1969-77. Served to 1st lt. U.S. Army, 1954-56. Jewish. Office: US Courthouse 140 Fed Bldg 517 E Wisconsin Ave Milwaukee WI 53202-4500 Office Phone: 414-297-3291 ext. 3201. Business E-Mail: james_e_shapiro@wieb.uscourts.gov.

SHAPIRO, JAMES STEPHEN, English professor; b. NYC, Sept. 11, 1955; s. Herbert and Lorraine (Ackerman) S. BA, Columbia U., 1977; PhD, U. Chgo., 1982. Asst. prof. Columbia U., NYC, 1985, Larry Miller Prof. of English and Comparative Lit. Co-dir. NEH Summer Shakespeare Insts., 1989-91. Author: Rival Playwrights Marlowe, Shakespear, Jonson, 1991, Shakespeare and the Jews, 1996, A Year in the Life of William Shakespeare: 1599, 2005; contbr. Theater Week, 1989—; assoc. editor: Medieval and Renaissance Drama in England, 1989. Recipient Rsch. stipend NEH, NY 1988, Huntington Libr., San Marion Calif. 1988; grantee NEH, NY, 1989. Office: Eng Comp Lit MC 4954 606B Phil Columbia Univ 1150 Amsterdam New York NY 10027

SHAPIRO, JERALD STEVEN, chemist, bank executive; b. Dec. 3, 1943; s. Isadore and Mae (Hirsch) S. BS, UCLA, 1964, student, 1970. Lic. real estate broker, Calif.; cert. review appraiser, real estate broker, mortgage banker, escrow officer, investment broker, investment specialist; registered mortgage underwriter. Mgr. process engring., quality control Aerospace Chem. Sys., Inc., Gardena, Calif., 1963-66; chem. engr. HITCO, Gardena, Calif., 1966-67; materials and process engr. McDonnell Douglas Corp., Long Beach, Calif., 1967-70; chemist L.A. county Sanitation Dist., 1971-74; staff scientist TRW Def. and Space Sys. Group, Redondo Beach, Calif., 1975—86. Cons. Century 21 Beverlywood Realty, Inc., L.A., 1977-; pres. Nationwide Mortgage Corp., L.A., 1983-, Heritage Realty Group, L.A.; adv. bd. 1st Women's Bank of Calif., 1977-78; JSK Capital Group, Inc. Beverly Hills, 1990-94; trustee, prof. Internat. Coll. of Calif., Irvine, 1991-93; bd. dirs. Western Advanced Tech. Systems, Inc., Environ. Protection Polymers, Inc. Author: Aware and Beware Guide to Intelligent Home Buying, 1974; co-inventor particle discriminator, 1964. Bd. dirs. Internat. Wellness Inst., Beverly Hills, 1992-93. Mem. Nat. Assn. Mortgage Bankers, Nat. Assn. Rev. Appraisers and Mortgage Underwriters, Chem. Soc., Century 21 Investment Soc. (charter), Mortgage Bankers Assn., Calif. Escrow Assn., Calif. Assn. Realtors, L.A. Bd. Realtors, Alpha chi Sigma. Office: 2800 S Robertson Blvd Los Angeles CA 90034-2406

SHAPIRO, JOAN ISABELLE, lab administrator, medical/surgical nurse; b. Aug. 26, 1943; d. Macy James and Frieda Lockhart; m. Ivan Lee Shapiro, Dec. 28, 1968; children: Audrey, Michael. Diploma, Peoria Meth. Sch. Nursing, 1964. RN. Nurse Nurse Grant Hosp., Columbus, Ohio, 1975—76, Cardiac Thoracic and Vascular Surgeons Ltd., Geneva, Ill., 1977—, mgr. non-ivasive lab., 1979—. Owner operator Shapiro's Mastiff's 1976-82; sec.-treas. Sounds Svcs., 1976—, Mainstream Sounds Inc., 1980-84; co-founder Cardio-Phone Inc., 1982-99, Edgewater Vascular Inst., 1987-89, Associated Profls., 1989-92; v.p. Computer Specialists Inc., 1986-89; founder, pres. Vein Ctr., Edema Ctr. Ltd. Mem. DAR (sec. Katahdin Valley-Lydia Putman chpt. 2004—), Soc. Non-invasive Technologists, Soc. Peripheral Vascular Nursing (cmty. awareness com. 1984-2004), Kane County Med. Soc. Aux. (pres. 1983-84, adviser, 1984-85), Katahdin Valley Putnam Cpt. of DAR (sec. 2004-). Lutheran. Home: Cardiac Thoracic/Vas Surg PO Box 325 Fort Fairfield ME 04742-0325 Business E-Mail: joan@ivanshapiro.com.

SHAPIRO, JOEL ELIAS, artist; b. NYC, Sept. 27, 1941; s. Joseph and Anna (Lewis) S.; m. Ellen Phelan; 1 dau., Ivy Bess. BA, NYU, 1964, MA, 1969. One-man shows include Paula Cooper Gallery, NYC, 14 shows, 1970—90, The Clocktower Gall., Inst. Art and Urban Resources, NYC, 1973, Mus. Contemporary Art, Chgo., 1976, Albright-Knox Art Gallery, Buffalo, 1977, Gallery M. Bochum, W. Germany, 1978, Galerie Mukai, Tokyo, 1980, 1981, 1988, 1991, Asher/Faure, LA, 1980, 1989, 1991, Whitechapel Gallery, London, 1980, Haus Lange, Krefeld, W.Germany, 1980, Moderna Museet, Stockholm, 1980, Brown U., 1980, Ackland Art Mus., Chapel Hill, NC, 1981, Contemporary Arts Ctr., Cin., 1981, Israel Mus., Jerusalem, 1981, Portland Ctr. Visual Arts, Oreg., 1982, Whitney Mus. Am. Art, NYC, 1982, Galerie Aronowitsch, Stockholm, 1984, Delahunty Gallery, Dallas, 1980, Donald Young Gallery, Chgo., 1987, Stedelijk Mus., Amsterdam, 1985, Kunstmuseum, Dusseldorf, 1985, Staatliche Kunsthalle, Baden-Baden, 1986, Seattle Art Mus., 1986, Galerie Daniel Templon, Paris, 1986, 1988, The John and Mable Ringling Mus., Sarasota, 1986, John Berggruen Gallery, San Francisco, 1987, Hirshhorn Mus. and Sculpture Garden, Washington, 1987, Hans Strelow, Dusseldorf, Germany, 1988, Toledo Mus. Art, 1989, Waddington Gallery, London, 1989, Museet I Varberg, Sweden, 1990, Balt. Art Mus., 1990, Des Moines Art Ctr., 1990, Ctr. for Fine Arts, Miami, 1991, IVAM Centre Julio Gonazlez, Valencia, Spain, 1990, John Berggruen Gallery, San Francisco, 1991, Pace Gallery, 1993, Galerie Karsten Greve, Cologne, Germany, 1993, Gallery Seomi, Seoul, 1994, 1996, Galerie Aronowitsch, Stockholm, 1995, Karsten Greve, Paris, 1995, Walker Art Ctr./Mpls. Sculpture Garden, 1995, Nelson-Atkins Mus. Art/Kansas City Sculpture Park, 1996, Pace Wildenstein Gallery, NY, 1995, 1996, 1998, 2001, 2002, 2003, 2005, Galerie Biedermann, Munich, Germany, 1997, Addison Gallery, Andover, Mass., 1997, Haus der Kunst, Munich, 1997, Barlach Halle K, Hamburg, 1998, Galerie Jamileh Weber, Zurich, Switzerland, 1997, Pace Wildenstein, LA, 1999, Am. Acad. in Rome, 1999, Boston Mus. Fine Arts, 1999, New Art Ctr., Salisbury, Eng., 1999, Yorkshire Sculpture Park, Wakefield, Eng., 1999—2000, Nat. Gallery Can., 1999—2000, John Berggruen Gallery, San Francisco, 2000, Timothy Taylor Gallery, London, 2000, Spoleto Festival USA, Charleston, SC, 2000, McNay Art Mus., San Antonio, 2000—01, Denver Art Mus., 2001, Galerie Daniel Templon, Paris, 2001, 2004, Met. Mus. Art, NY, 2001, Gerald B. Cantor Rooftop Galleries, 2001, L.A. Louver Gallery, 2004, Musee d'Orsay, Paris, 2005, numerous group exhibits, Represented in permanent collections Mus. Modern Art, NYC, Whitney Mus. Art, Walker Art Ctr., Mpls., Met. Mus. Art, NYC, Albright Knox Art Gallery, Buffalo, Detroit Inst. Art, Stedelijk Mus., Amsterdam, Moderna Museet, Stockholm, Dallas Mus. Art, Centre Pompidou, Paris, Nat. Gallery Art, Washington, Brit. Mus., London, Bklyn. Mus., Cocoran Gallery, Washington, Fogg Art Mus. at Harvard U., Cambridge, Mass., High Mus. Art, Atlanta, Hirshhorn Mus. and Sculpture Garden at Smithsonian Instn., Washington, Israel Mus., Jerusalem, Kunsthaus Zürich, Switzerland, Mus. Contemporary Art, LA, Mus. Fine Arts, Boston, Mus. Modern Art, Friuli, Italy, Parrish Art Mus., Southampton, NY, Phila. Mus. Art, Tate Gallery, London, Cleve. Mus. Art, NC Mus. Art, Raleigh, Des Moines Art Ctr., commns. include, Cigna Corp., Phila., 1983—84, Fukuoka (Japan) Sogo Bank, 1988, Creative Artists Agy., LA, 1988—89, Kawamura Meml. Mus. Art, Chiba, Japan, 1988—89, Govt. Svc. Adminstrn., LA, 1988—90, Hood Mus. Art at Dartmouth Coll., Hanover, N.H., 1989—90, U.S. Holocaust Meml. Mus., Washington, 1993, Sony Music Entertainment, NYC, 1994—95, Friedrichstadt Passagen, Berlin, 1994—95, Kansas City (Mo.) Internat. Airport, 1995—96, Embassy of U.S.A., Ottawa, 1999, Koln Skulpture Park, 1999, The Principal Riverwalk, Des Moines, 2005. Recipient Nat. Endowment for Arts award, 1975, Brandeis award, 1984, Skowhegan medal, 1986. Mem. Am. Acad. and Inst. Arts and Letters (Merit award 1990), Am. Acad. Arts and Letters, Swedish Royal Acad. Art. Office: care Pace Idenstein 32 E 57th St New York NY 10022-2513

SHAPIRO, JUDITH R., academic administrator, anthropology educator; b. NYC, Jan. 24, 1942; Student, Ecole des Haute Etudes Inst. d'Etudes Politiques, Paris, 1961—62; BA, Brandeis U., 1963; PhD, Columbia U., 1972. Asst. prof. U. Chgo., 1970—75; fellow U. Calif., Berkeley, 1974—75; Rosalyn R. Schwartz lectr., asst. prof. anthropology Bryn Mawr Coll., Pa., 1975—78, assoc. prof. Pa., 1978—85, prof. Pa., 1985—94; pres. Barnard Coll., 1994—. Chmn. dept. Bryn Mawr Coll., 1982—85, acting dean undergrad coll., 1985—86, provost, 1986—94; bd. dir. Fund for City of NY; ptnr. NYC Partnership and C. of C.; exec. com. NY Bldg. Congress. Contbr. articles to profl. jours. Nat. adv. com. Woodrow Wilson Nat. Fellowship Found.; chair bd. dirs. Consortium on Financing Higher Edn.; bd. dirs. Fund for the City of N.Y.; chair bd. dirs. Women's Coll. Coalition. Recipient Gold Medal, Nat. Inst. of Social Sciences, 2002; fellow, Woodrow Wilson Found., 1963—64, Columbia U., 1964—65, Younger Humanist fellow, NEH, 1974—75, Am. Coun. Learned Socs., 1981—82, Ctr. for Advanced Study in the Behavioral Scis., 1989; grantee Summer Field Tng. grant, NSF, 1965, Ford Found., 1966, NIMH, 1974—75, Social Sci. Rsch. Coun., 1974—75. Fellow: Am. Acad. Arts & Scis.; mem.: NY State Leadership Coun. (devel. of World's Mus., NYC), Am. Philos. Soc., Social Sci. Rsch. Coun. (com. social sci personnel 1977—80), Am. Anthrop. Assn. (ethics com. 1976—79, bd. dirs. 1984—86, exec. com. 1985—86), Am. Ethnol. Soc. (nominations com. 1983—84, pres. elect 1984—85, pres. 1985—86), Phila. Anthrop. Soc. (pres. 1983), Morningside Area Alliance (pres. 2003—04), adv. com, Save the Children, Women's Forum, Sigma Xi, Phi Beta Kappa. Office: Barnard Coll Office of Pres 109 Milbank Hall New York NY 10027 Office Phone: 212-854-2021. *

SHAPIRO, KEITH J., lawyer; b. Chgo., Nov. 14, 1958; BS, Univ. Ill., 1980; JD, Emory Univ., 1983. Bar: Ill. 1983. Former chmn., pres. Am. Bankruptcy Inst.; co-mng. shareholder, co-chair nat. bus. reorganization and bankruptcy practice Greenberg Traurig LLP, Chgo. Fellow: Am. Coll. Bankruptcy; mem.: Am. Bankruptcy Bd. of Certification (founder, first chmn. 1992—95), R3, London, Chgo. Bar Assn. (chair, bankruptcy and reorganization com. 1999—2000), Am. Bankruptcy Inst. (pres. 2000—01, chmn.bd. 2002—03). Office: Greenberg Traurig Ste 2500 77 W Wacker Dr Chicago IL 60601 Office Phone: 312-456-8405. Office Fax: 312-456-8435. Business E-Mail: shapirok@gtlaw.com.

SHAPIRO, LARRY J., pediatrician, educator, scientist, dean; b. July 6, 1946; s. Philip and Phyllis Shapiro; m. Carol-Ann Uetake; children: Jennifer, Jessica, Brian. AB, Washington U., St. Louis, 1968, MD, 1971. Diplomate Am. Bd. Pediat., Am. Bd. Med. Examiners, Am. Bd. Med. Genetics. Intern St. Louis Children's Hosp., 1971—72, resident, 1971—73; rsch. assoc. NIH, Bethesda, Md., 1973—75; asst. prof. Sch. Medicine UCLA, 1975—79, assoc. prof., 1979—83, prof. pediat. and biol. chemistry, 1983—91; investigator Howard Hughes Med. Inst., 1987—91, investigator, W.H. and Marie Wattis Disting. prof.; prof., chmn. dept. pediat. U. Calif.-San Francisco Sch. Medicine, 1991—2003; chief pediat. svcs. U. Calif.-San Francisco Med. Ctr., 1991—2003; Spencer T. and Ann W. Olin Disting. prof., exec. vice chancellor for med. affairs, dean Washington U. Sch. Medicine, St. Louis, 2003—. Contbr. numerous articles to profl. publs. Served to lt. comdr. USPHS, 1973—75. Fellow: AAAS, Am. Acad. Pediat. (E. Mead Johnson award in rsch. 1982); mem.: Am. Acad. Arts and Scis., Am. Pediatric Soc. (coun. mem. 1999—2001, pres. 2003—04), Am. Soc. Clin. Investigation, Am. Soc. Human Genetics (coun. 1985—88, pres.-elect 1995, pres. 1997), Assn. Am. Physicians, Soc. for Inherited Metabolic Disease (coun. 1983—88, pres. 1986—87), Western Soc. for Pediatric Rsch. (coun. 1983—87, pres. 1989—90, Ross award in rsch. 1981), Soc. Pediatric Rsch. (coun. 1984—87, pres. 1991—92), Inst. Medicine of NAS. Office: Wash U 660 S Euclid campus box 8106 Saint Louis MO 63110

SHAPIRO, LEO J., social researcher; b. NYC, July 8, 1921; m. Virginia L. Johnson, Feb. 9, 1952; children: David, Erik, Owen, Amy. BA, U. Chgo., 1942, PhD, 1952. Survey specialist Fed. Govt. Agy., Washington, 1941-45, Sci. Rsch. Assn., Chgo., 1948-52; prin., founder Leo J. Shapiro and Assocs., Chgo., 1952-91; pres. Greenhouse, Inc., 1991—2001, SAGE LLC Survival & Growth Enterprise, Chgo., 2002—. Bd. dirs. Field of Flowers. Fellow U. Chgo., 1949. Fellow Social Sci. Rsch. Coun.; mem. Am. Sociol. Assn., Phi Beta Kappa.

SHAPIRO, LUCY, molecular biology educator; b. NYC, July 16, 1940; d. Philip and Yetta (Stein) Cohen; m. Roy Shapiro, Jan. 23, 1960 (div. 1977); 1 child, Peter; m. Harley H. McAdams, July 28, 1978; stepchildren: Paul, Heather. BA, Bklyn. Coll., 1962; PhD, Albert Einstein Coll. Medicine, 1966. Asst. prof. Albert Einstein Coll. Medicine, NYC, 1967-72, assoc. prof., 1972-77, Kramer prof., chmn. dept. molecular biology, 1977-86, dir. biol. scis. divsn., 1981-86; Eugene Higgins prof., chmn. dept. microbiology, Coll. Physicians and Surgeons Columbia U., NYC, 1986-89; Joseph D. Grant prof. devel. biology Stanford (Calif.) U. Sch. Medicine, 1989-97, chmn. dept. devel. biology, 1989-97, Virginia and D.K. Ludwig prof. cancer rsch., dept. devel. biology, 1998—; dir. Beckman Ctr. Molecular and Genetic Medicine, Stanford U., 2001—. Mem. bd. sci. counselors NIH, Washington, 1980—84; mem. bd. sci. advisors G.D. Searle Co., Skokie, Ill., 1984—86; trustee Scientists Inst. for Pub. Info., 1990—94; mem. sci. adv. bd. SmithKline Beecham, 1993—2000, Anacor Pharms., Inc., 2001—, PathoGenesis, 1995—2000, Ludwig Found., 2000—, Glaxo Smith Kline, 2001—; mem. adv. bd. Biodesign Inst., Ariz. State U., 2006—, Singapore Inst. Molecular and Cell Biology, 2006—, Lawrence Berkeley Nat. Labs., 2006—; bd. dirs. Anacor Pharms. Inc., 2001—. Editor: Microbiol. Devel., 1984; mem. editl. bd. Jour. Bacteriology, 1978-86, Trends in Genetics, 1987—, Genes and Development, 1987-91, Cell Regulation, 1990-92, Molecular Biology of the Cell, 1992-98, Molecular Microbiology, 1991-96, Current Opinion on Genetics and Devel., 1991—; contbr. articles to profl. jours. Mem. sci. bd. Helen Hay Witney Found., N.Y.C., 1986-94, Biozentrum, Basel, 1999-2001, Hutchinson Cancer Ctr., Seattle, 1999; mem. grants adv. bd. Beckman Found., 1999—; co-chmn. adv. bd. NSF Biology Directorate, 1988-89; vis. com., bd. overseers Harvard U., Cambridge, Mass., 1987-90; mem. sci. bd. Whitehead Inst., MIT, Boston, 1988-93; mem. sci. rev. bd. Howard Hughes Med. Inst., 1990-94, Cancer Ctr. of Mass. Gen. Hosp., Boston, 1994; mem. Presidio Coun. City of San Francisco, 1991-94; mem. pres. coun. U. Calif., 1991-97. Recipient Hirschl Career Scientist award, 1976, Spirit of Achievement award, 1978, Alumna award of honor Bklyn. Coll., 1983, Excellence in Sci. award Fedn. Am. Soc. Exptl. Biology, 1994; Jane Coffin Child fellow, 1966; resident scholar Rockefeller Found., Bellagio, Italy, 1996. Fellow AAAS, Am. Acad. Arts and Scis., Am. Acad. Microbiology, Calif. Coun. on Sci. and Tech.; mem. NAS (Selman A. Waksman award 2005), Inst. Medicine of NAS, Am. Philos. Soc., Am. Soc. Biochemistry and Molecular Biology (nominating com. 1982, 87, coun. 1990-93), Am. Heart Assn. (sci. adv. bd. 1984-87). Avocation: watercolor painting. Office: Stanford U Sch Medicine Beckman Ctr Dept Devel Biology Stanford CA 94305 Office Phone: 650-725-7678.

SHAPIRO, MARC ROBERT, retail executive; b. North Hollywood, Calif., Apr. 1, 1959; s. Mel and Sally Shapiro; children: Julie Joseph Jack, Shapiro Shapiro. AA in Bus. Adminstrn., LA Harbor Coll., Wilmington, Calif., 1987; BSBA, U. Phoenix, 2006. Ops. mgr. Name Bears, Inc., Victorville, Calif., 1989—92; exec. v.p. Retail Project Mgrs., LLC, Irvine, Calif., 1992—. Mem.: Am. Numis. Assn. (life). Jewish. Avocations: travel, languages, home remodeling. Home Phone: 949-422-1493; Office Phone: 949-420-2500 ext 1106.

SHAPIRO, MARJORIE, accountant; d. Lee and Elaine Spellman; m. Marc Spellman, May 15, 1999. BA in Comm., SUNY, Albany, 1996; BS in Acctg., SUNY, Old Westbury, 2006. Acctg. analyist Stepic Med. Distbn. Co., Hicksville, NY, 2002—06; forensic acct. Forensic Accts., Inc., Jericho, NY, 2006—. Mem.: ACFE (assoc.), NYSSCPA (assoc.). Office: Forensic Accs Inc PO Box 745 Jericho NY 11753 Home Phone: 516-625-0952; Office Phone: 516-681-2772.

SHAPIRO, MARK, professional sports team executive; b. Baltimore, Md., Apr. 3, 1967; s. Ronald M. Shapiro. BA, Princeton Univ. Former real estate devel.; asst. player devel. Cleve. Indians, 1992, mgr., minor league ops., 1993, dir., minor leagues ops., 1994—98, v.p. baseball ops., asst. gen. mgr., 1999—2001, exec. v.p., gen. mgr., 2002—. Named Exec. Yr., MLB, 2005; named one of 40 Under 40, Sports Bus. Jour., 2006. Office: Cleveland Indians Jacobs Field 2401 Ontario St Cleveland OH 44115-4003 *

SHAPIRO, MARK HOWARD, physicist, educator, dean; b. Boston, Apr. 18, 1940; s. Louis and Sara Ann (Diamond) S.; m. Anita Rae Lavine, June 8, 1961; children: David Gregory, Diane Elaine, Lisa Michelle. AB with honors, U. Calif., Berkeley, 1962; MS (NSF coop. fellow), U. Pa., 1963, PhD, 1966. Research fellow Kellogg Radiation Lab., Calif. Inst. Tech., Pasadena, 1966-68; vis. assoc. divsn. math., physics and astronomy Calif. Inst. Tech., 1976—; research assoc. Nuclear Structure Research Lab. U. Rochester (N.Y.), 1968-70; mem. faculty Calif. State U., Fullerton, 1970—2002, prof. physics, 1978—2002, acting assoc. dean Sch. Math., Sci. and Engring., 1985-86, acting dir. Office Faculty Research and Devel., 1986-87, chmn. physics dept., 1989-96, 98-01, prof. physics emeritus, 2002—; dir. tchr. enhancement program NSF, Washington, 1987-88. Tour speaker Am. Chem. Soc., 1983-85 Editor, publisher: The Irascible Professor, 1999; contbr. over 125 articles to profl. jours. Pres. Pasadena Young Democrats, 1967-68; mem. pub. info. and edn. com. Calif. Task Force on Earthquake Preparedness, 1981-85; bd. dirs. Calif. State U. Fullerton Found., 1982-85. Grantee Research Corp., 1971-74, Calif. Inst. Tech., 1977-78, U.S. Geol. Survey, 1978-85, Digital Equipment Corp., 1982, NSF, 1985-87, 90—. Fellow Am. Phys. Soc., Materials Rsch. Soc., Coun. on Undergrad. Rsch. (physics/astronomy councillor 1993-2002). Achievements include research in experimental nuclear physics, experimental nuclear astrophysics, geophysics and atomic collisions in solids. Office: Calif State Univ Physics Dept Fullerton CA 92834-6866 Business E-Mail: mshapiro2@adelphia.net.

SHAPIRO, MARK JEFFREY, lawyer; s. Raymond Shapiro; m. Maura Faye Smotrich, May 3, 1987. BA magna cum laude, Hobart Coll., Geneva, NY; JD, Columbia Law Sch., NYC. Assoc. Shearman & Sterling, ptnr., 1995—, co-head bankruptcy and restructuring grp.; mng. dir., co-head global restructuring grp. Lehman Bros., 2002—. Named one of Top 12 US Lawyers in Restructuring Field Under 40, Turnarounds & Workouts mag., 1999. Mem.: NYC Bar Assn. (mem. bankruptcy com.). Office: Lehman Bros 745 7th Ave New York NY 10019 Office Phone: 212-526-5937. Business E-Mail: mark.shapiro@lehman.com.

SHAPIRO, MARTIN, law educator; b. 1933; BA, UCLA, 1955; PhD, Harvard U., 1961. Instr. polit. sci. Harvard U., Cambridge, Mass., 1960-62, prof., 1971-74; asst. prof. Stanford U., Calif., 1962-65; assoc. prof. U. Calif., Irvine, 1965-70, prof. Berkeley, 1970, prof. law, 1977—, prof. San Diego, 1974-77. Author: Law and Politics in the Supreme Court, 1964, Freedom of Speech, The Supreme Court and Judicial Review, 1966, Supreme Court and Administrative Agencies, 1968, Courts, 1981, Who Guards the Guardians, 1987, Law, Politics and Judicialization, 2002. Mem. Law and Soc. Assn. (trustee 1992-95), Western Polit. Sci. Assn. (pres. 1978), Am. Acad. Arts and Scis., Am. Polit. Sci. Assn. (v.p. 1988). Office: U Calif Law Sch 886 Simon Hl Berkeley CA 94720-0001 Home Phone: 510-482-1206; Office Phone: 510-642-7190.

SHAPIRO, MARVIN LINCOLN, communications company executive; b. Erie, Pa., Feb. 12, 1923; s. Hyman and Flora (Burstein) S.; m. B. Gertrude Berkman, Oct. 25, 1946; children: Susan Jo, Barbara Ann, Jonathan David. BS, Syracuse U., 1948; postgrad., Williams Coll., 1966, Columbia U., 1975. Account exec. WSYR, Syracuse, 1948-50; account exec. sta. WCAU-TV, Phila., 1950-55, nat. sales mgr., 1956-58; account exec. CBS TV Spot Sales, Chgo., 1955-56, NYC, 1958-60; with TV Advt. Reps., Inc., NYC, 1961-66, exec. v.p., 1965-66, pres., 1968-69, dir., vice chmn., 1969-77, chmn., 1978; pres. Radio Advt. Reps., Inc., NYC, 1966-68, dir., vice chmn., 1969-77; exec. v.p., COO, pres. sta. group Westinghouse Broadcasting Co., Inc., NYC, 1969-77, sr. v.p., 1978-83, also dir., 1969-83; pres., dir. Foxwood Comm. Inc., NYC, 1983—; mng. dir. Veronis Suhler Stevenson, NYC, 1983—; dir. Queen City Broadcasting, 1986—95; pres., dir. Farragut Comm., Inc., NYC, 1992-99, Columbia Empire Broadcasting Corp., Yakima, Wash., 1992-96. Dir. Broadcasting Ptnrs. Holdings, L.P., 1996-00, VS&A Spectrum, Inc., 1997-2000, dir. Riviera Broadcasting Group, LLC, 2005-, ITN Networks, LLC, 2006-; chmn. bd. Micro-Relay, Inc., 1974-83; chmn. bd. dirs., pres. CATV Enterprises, Inc., 1970-83. Boxing official Pa. Athletic Commn., 1952-55; Bd. dirs. TV Bur. Advt., 1974-81, chmn., 1977-79; bd. dirs. Radio Advt. Bur., 1970-77; With USAAF, 1942-45. Decorated Air medal with 9 oak leaf clusters.; recipient Communications Alumni award Syracuse U., 1960 Mem. Internat. Radio and TV Soc., DAV, Alpha Epsilon Rho (hon.). Clubs: Long Ridge (Stamford). Home: 26 Foxwood Rd Stamford CT 06903-2207 Office: Veronis Suhler Stevenson 350 Park Ave New York NY 10022-6022

SHAPIRO, MATTHEW DAVID, economist, educator; b. Mpls., Apr. 11, 1958; s. Irving and Janet (Reinstein) S.; m. Susan L. Garetz, Oct. 21, 1989; children: Benjamin Avigdor, Molly Kendall. BA summa cum laude, Yale U., 1979, MA, 1979; PhD, MIT, 1984. Jr. staff economist Coun. Econ. Advisers, Washington, 1979-80, sr. economist, 1993-94; asst. prof. Yale U., New Haven, 1984-89; assoc. prof. U. Mich., Ann Arbor, 1989-95, prof., 1995—, L.R. Klein Collegiate prof., 2004—, sr. rsch. scientist, 2000—, chair, 2003—07. Rschr. Nat. Bur. Econ. Rsch., Cambridge, Mass., 1986—; mem. acad. adv. coun. Fed. Res. Bank Chgo., 1995-; mem. com. on nat. stats. NAS, 1999-2002; mem. Fed. Econ. Stats. Adv. Com., 2000—, chmn., 2006—. Bd. editors Am. Econ. Rev., 1993-96, 2000-02, co-editor, 1997-2002; contbr. articles to profl. jours. Recipient Paul A. Samuelson Cert. of Excellence, TIAA-CREF, 1997; Olin fellow Nat. Bur. Econ. Rsch., Cambridge, 1986-87, Alfred P. Sloan fellow Sloan Found., 1991-93. Mem. Am. Econ. Assn., Econometric Soc., Phi Beta Kappa. Office: U Mich Dept Econs 611 Tappan Ave Ann Arbor MI 48109-1220

SHAPIRO, MAURICE MANDEL, nuclear astrophysicist; b. Jerusalem, Nov. 13, 1915; came to U.S., 1921; s. Asher and Miriam R. (Grunbaum) S.; m. Inez Weinfield, Feb. 8, 1942 (dec. Oct. 1964); children: Joel Nevin, Elana Shapiro Ashley Naktin, Raquel Tamar Shapiro Kislinger; m. Ruth Auslander, Nov. 30, 2002. BS, U. Chgo., 1936, MS, 1940, PhD, 1942. Instr. physics and math. Chgo. City Colls., 1937-41; chmn. dept. phys. and biol. scis. Austin Coll., 1938-41; instr. math. Gary Coll., 1942; physicist Dept. Navy, 1942-44; lectr. physics and math. George Washington U., 1943-44; group leader, mem. coordinating council of lab. Los Alamos Sci. Lab., U. Calif., 1944-46; sr. physicist, lectr. nucleonics tng. sch. Oak Ridge Nat. Lab., Union Carbon and Carbide Corp., 1946-49. Cons. div. nuc. energy for propulsion aircraft Fairchild Engine & Aircraft Corp., 1948-49; head cosmic ray br. nucleonics div. U.S. Naval Research Lab., Washington, 1949-65, supt. nucleonics div., 1953-65, founder, chief scientist Lab for Cosmic Physics, 1949-82, apptd. to chair of cosmic ray physics, 1966-82, chief scientist emeritus, 1982—; lectr. U. Md., 1949-50, 1952—, assoc. prof., 1950-51, vis. prof. physics and astronomy, 1986—; vis. prof. physics and astronomy U. Iowa, 1981-84; vis. prof. astrophysics U. Bonn, 1982-84; vis. scientist Max Planck Inst. für Astrophysik, W. Ger., 1984-85; cons. Argonne Nat. Lab., 1949; cons. panel on cosmic rays U.S. nat. com. IGY; lectr. physics and engring. Nuclear Products-Erco div. ACF Industries, Inc., 1956-58; lectr. E. Fermi Internat. Sch. Physics, Varenna, Italy, 1962; vis. prof. Weizmann Inst. Sci., Rehovoth, Israel, 1962-63, Inst. Math. Scis., Madras, India, 1971; Inst. Astronomy and Geophysics Nat. U. Mex., 1976; vis. prof. physics and astronomy Northwestern U., Evanston, Ill., 1978, exec. dir. Astrophysics Assoc. 1995—; cons. space rsch. in astronomy Space Sci. Bd., Nat. Acad. Scis., 1965; cons. Office Space Scis., NASA, 1965-66, 89; prin. investigator Gemini S-9 Cosmic Ray Expts., NASA, 1964-69, Skylab, 1967-76, Long Duration Exposure Facility, 1977—; mem. Groupe de Travail de Biologie Spatiale, Council of Europe, 1970—; mem. steering com. DUMAND Consortium, 1976—, mem. exec. com., 1979-82, mem. sci. adv. com., 1982—; lectr. Summer Space Inst., Deutsche Physikalische Gesellschaft, 1972; founder, dir. Internat. Sch. Cosmic-Ray Astrophysics, Ettore Majorana Centre Sci. Culture, Erice, Italy, 1977—; chmn. U.S. IGY com. on interdisciplinary research, mem. nuclear emulsion panel space sci. bd.; Nat. Acad. Scis., 1959—; chief U.S. rep., steering com. Internat. Coop. Emulsion Flights Cosmic Ray Rsch.; cons. CREI Atomics, 1959—; vis. com. Bartol Rsch. Found., Franklin Inst., 1967-74; mem. U.S. organizing com. 13th and 19th Internat. Confs. on Cosmic Rays; mem. sci. adv. com. Internat. Confs. on Nuclear Photography and Solid State Detectors, 1966—; mem. Com. of Honor for Einstein Centennial, Acad. Naz. Lincei, 1977; mem. Internat. Organizing com. Tex. Symposia on Relativistic Astrophysics, 1976—; Regents lectr. U. Calif. Riverside, 1985; Edison lectr. Naval Rsch. Lab award, 1990; plenary lectr. Oppenheimer Centennial, Gamow Centennial, 2004. Mem. editorial bd. Astrophysics and Space Sci., 1968-75; assoc. editor: Phys. Rev. Letters, 1977-84; editor (NATO) ASI Series on Cosmic-Ray Astrophysics; contbr. to Am. Inst. Handbook of Physics, various encys. Mem. exec. bd. Cong. Beth Chai, Washington, 1987—; trustee Nat. Capital Astronomers, Washington, 1989—; mem. internat. panel Chernobyl World Lab., 1988. Recipient Disting. Civilian Svc. award Dept. Navy, 1967, medal of honor Soc. for Encouragement au Progrés, 1978, Sr. U.S. Scientist award Alexander von Humboldt Found., 1982, Profl. Achievement citation U. Chgo., 1992; Guggenheim fellow, 1962-63. Fellow Am. Phys. Soc. (chmn. organizing com. div. cosmic physics, chmn. 1971-72, com. on publs. 1977-79), AAAS, Washington Acad. Scis. (past com. chmn., Disting. Career in Scis. award, 1993); mem. Am. Astron. Soc. (exec. com. div. high-energy astrophysics 1978—, chmn., 1982), Philos. Soc. Washington (past pres.), Am. Technion Soc. (Washington bd.), Alexander von Humboldt Assn. of Am. (pres. Washington area chpt. 2000—), Assn. Los Alamos Scientists (past chmn.), Assn. Oak Ridge Engrs. and Scientists (past chmn.), Fedn. Am. Scientists (past mem. exec. com., nat. council), Internat. Astron. Union (organizing com. commn. on high-energy astrophysics), Internat. Conf. on Cosmic Rays (Victor Hess Meml. lectr., Rome, 1995), Phi Beta Kappa, Sigma Xi (Edison lectr. 1990). Clubs: Cosmos (Washington). Achievements include patents in field; discovery of first definitive evidence for production of cosmic ray secondaries in the interstellar medium; first determination of the source composition of cosmic rays; prediction of isotopic composition of "arriving" cosmic rays, co-discovery of the sigma hyperon; research in cosmic radiation, composition, origin, propagation, and nuclear transformations, high-energy astrophysics, particles and fields, nuclear physics, neutron physics and fission reactors, hydrodynamics and piezoelectricity, gamma-ray and neutrino astronomy; design of a low-enrichment nuclear reactor for submarines used at Shippingport and in various naval ships; identification of the fissile fuel in the first Soviet atomic explosion as plutonium. Address: 5809 Nicholson Ln # 801 Rockville MD 20852 Personal E-mail: mmshapiro@mailaps.org. *In scientific achievement, good judgement (e.g., in choice of research problems)is sometimes more important than brilliance.*

SHAPIRO, MEL, playwright, educator, theater director; b. Bklyn., Dec. 16, 1935; s. Benjamin Shapiro and Lillian (Lazarus) Bestul; m. Jeanne Elizabeth Shapiro, Feb. 23, 1963; children: Joshua, Benjamin. BFA, MFA, Carnegie-Mellon U., 1961. Resident dir. Arena Stage, Washington, 1963-65; producing dir. Tyrone Guthrie Theater, Mpls., 1968-70; master tchr. drama NYU, NYC, 1970-80; guest dir. Lincoln Ctr. Repertory, NYC, 1970; dir. N.Y. Shakespeare Festival, NYC, 1971-77; prof. Carnegie Mellon U., Pitts., 1980-90, head. dept., 1980-87. Disting. prof. theater UCLA Sch. Theater, Film and TV, 1990—. Dir. N.Y.C. prodns. The House of Blue Leaves, 1970, Bosoms and Neglect, 1978, Marco Polo Sings a Solo, 1998, Taming of the Shrew, 1999, Big Love (L.A.), 2002; co-adaptor mus. Two Gentlemen of Verona, 1971 (Tony award); author: (plays) The Price of Admissions, 1984 (Drama-Logue mag. award), The Lay of the Land (Joseph Kesselring award 1990), A Life of Crime, 1993; (books) An Actor Performs, 1996, The Director's Companion, 1998. With U.S. Army, 1955-57. Recipient N.Y. Drama Critics award, 1971, 72, Obie award Village Voice, 1972, Drama Desk award, 1973, Drama-logue award, 1993. Mem. Soc. Stage Dirs. and Choreographers (founder, editor The Jour. 1978). Office: UCLA Sch Theatre Film & TV 405 Hilgard Ave Los Angeles CA 90095-9000 Business E-Mail: mshapiro@ucla.edu.

SHAPIRO, MERYL, lawyer; d. Robert M. and Thelma Shapiro. JD, NY Law Sch., 1978. Atty. Guggenheimer & Untermyer, NYC, 1978—79, Law Offices of Henry R. Simon, NYC, 1979—81, Toberoff & Tessler, NYC, 1981—86, Katz, Katz & Brand, NYC, 1986—87, Law Offices of Henry R. Simon, White Plains, NY, 1988—91, Wiesen, Gurfein & Jenkins, NYC, 1991—93, Weinstein, Chase, Messinger & Peters, P.C., Bklyn., 1995—2005; founder Meryl Shapiro, Atty.-at-Law, NYC, 2005—. Supporter Sylvia Rivera LAw Project, NYC, Soka U. of Am., Aliso Viejo, Calif.; com. mem. Dem. Party County Com., 74th Asssembly Dist., NYC; NE zone legal divsn. chair, women's divsn. chpt. leader Soka Gakkai Internat.-USA, NYC. Mem.: Nat. Lesbian and Gay Law Assn., Bars of the So. and Ea. Dists. of NY, NY State Trial Lawyers' Assn., NY State Bar Assn. (com. on women in the law 2006—), Assn. of Bar of City of NY (civil rights com. 2001—03). Buddhist. Office: Meryl Shapiro Atty at Law Ste 7F 305 East 24th St New York NY 10010 Office Phone: 212-213-9252. Business E-Mail: mshapiro@merylshapiro.com.

SHAPIRO, MICHAEL, lawyer; b. NYC, Jan. 21, 1950; s. Howard H. and Rita (Pearlman) S.; m. Marica J. Cardarelli, July 7, 1979; 1 child, Rebecca. BA cum laude, CCNY, 1970; JD, NYU, 1973. Bar: NY 1974, US Dist. Ct. (so. and ea. dists.) NY 1975, US Supreme Ct. 1980, US Ct. Appeals (2d cir.) 1986, US Ct. Appeals (11th cir) 1989, US Dist. Ct. (ea. dist) Mich. 2006, US Ct. Appeals (6th cir.) 2006. Asst. dist. atty. Queens County Dist. Atty. Office, Queens, NY, 1973-75; spl. asst. atty. gen. Health and Social Svcs., NYC, 1975-77, Compensation Dept., NYC, 1977-85; assoc. Slotnick & Baker, NYC, 1985-88, ptnr., 1989, Buchanan Ingersoll & Rooney, Pitts., Carter Ledyard & Milburn, NYC, 2007—; legal analyst In Depth with Chris Matthews, 1994—95; faculty mem. intensive advocacy trial prog. Benjamin N. Cardozo Sch. Law, 2000—. Mem. Nat. Assn. Criminal Def. Lawyers, NY State Bar Assn., NY Criminal Bar Assn., NY County Lawyers Assn., Westchester Bar Assn. Avocations: tennis, skiing, foreign travel. Office: Carter Ledyard & Milburn 2 Wall St New York NY 10005 Office Phone: 212-238-8676. Office Fax: 212-732-3232. Business E-Mail: mshapiro@clm.com. *

SHAPIRO, MICHAEL EDWARD, museum director; b. NYC, Nov. 15, 1949; s. Edward Aaron and Sylvia (Fishman) S.; m. Elizabeth Harvey, 1977; 2 children. BA, Hamilton Coll., 1972; MA, Williams Coll., 1976, Harvard U., 1978, PhD, 1980. Asst. prof. dept. art history Duke U., Durham, NC, 1980-84; curator 19th-20th century art St. Louis Art Mus., 1984-92, chief curator, 1987-92; dir. Los Angeles County Mus. Art, 1992-93; dir. mus. programs, chief curator High Mus. Art, Atlanta, 1994-95, dep. dir., chief curator, 1996-99, dir., 2000—. Author: Bronze Casting and American Sculpture, 1985; contbg. author: Frederic Remington: The Masterworks, 1988, George Caleb Bingham, 1990; mng. curator, editor Rings: Five Passions in World Art, 1996; co-curator Impressionism: Paintings Collected by European Museums, 1998, mng. curator, 1999. Office: High Museum Art 1280 Peachtree St NE Atlanta GA 30309

SHAPIRO, NEAL, broadcast executive, television producer; s. Sumner and Mildred Shapiro; m. JuJu Chang, Dec. 2, 1995; 1 child. BA in History and Polit. Sci., Tufts U., 1980. With ABC News, 1980—93; spl. segment prodr. World News Tonight, 1986—89; broadcast prodr. PrimeTime Live, 1989—93; exec. prodr. NBC News, Dateline, NYC, 1993—2001; pres. NBC News, NYC, 2001—05, Sta. WNET Channel 13, 2007—. Recipient George Polk award, 1992, 2000, 2 Emmy awards, Investigate Reporter and Editor award. Office: Thirteen/WNET 450 W 33rd St New York NY 10001 *

SHAPIRO, NELLA IRENE, surgeon, educator; b. NYC, Nov. 13, 1947; d. Eugene and Ethel (Pearl) Shapiro; m. Jack Schwartz, Oct. 16, 1977; children: Max Schwartz, Molly Schwartz. BA, Barnard Coll., 1968; MD, Albert Einstein Coll., 1972. Resident in gen. surgery Montefiore Hosp., NYC, 1972-76; mem. staff N. Ctrl. Hosp., Bronx, NY, 1976-77, Bronx Mcpl. Hosp., 1977-87, chief gen. surgery, 1983-87; mem. staff gen. surgery Albert Einstein Coll. Hosp., Bronx, 1977-93, chief gen. surgery, 1991-93; atty. Lear Surg. Assocs., 1993-94; pvt. practice Bronx, 1994—; dir. breast surgery Eastchester Ctr. Cancer Care, Bronx, 2004—. Asst. prof. surgery Albert Einstein Coll., Bronx, 1980—; assoc. dir. gen. surgery Weller Hosp., Bronx, 1991—93; co-founder Whaecom Breast Ctr., Bronx, 1991—. Fellow: ACS. Avocations: travel, opera. Office: Eastchester Ctr Cancer Care 2330 Eastchester Rd Bronx NY 10469 Home Phone: 914-238-3544; Office Phone: 718-405-0400, 718-732-4000.

SHAPIRO, NELSON HIRSH, lawyer; b. Feb. 3, 1928; s. Arthur and Anna (Zenitz) S.; m. Helen Lenora Sykes, June 27, 1948; children: Ronald Evan, Mitchell Wayne, Jeffrey Mark, Julie Beth. BEE, Johns Hopkins U., 1948; JD, George Washington U., 1952. Bar: D.C. 1952, Va. 1981. Patent examiner U.S. Patent Office, 1948-50; patent advisor U.S. Signal Corps, 1950-52; mem. Shapiro & Shapiro, Arlington, Va., 1952-98, Vorys, Sater, Seymour and Pease LLP, Washington, 1998-2001, Miles & Stockbridge, McLean, Va., 2001—. Patentee; contbr. articles to legal publs. and Ency. of Patent Practice and Invention Mgmt., 1964. Mem. ABA, Am. Patent Law Assn., Bar Assn. DC, Order of Coif, Tau Beta Pi. Home: 7001 Old Cabin Ln Rockville MD 20852-4531 Office: 1751 Pinnacle Dr Ste 500 Mc Lean VA 22102-3833 Home Phone: 301-881-0841; Office Phone: 703-610-8687. E-mail: nshapiro@milesstockbridge.com.

SHAPIRO, NORMA SONDRA LEVY, federal judge; b. Phila., July 27, 1928; d. Bert and Jane (Kotkin) Levy; m. Bernard Shapiro, Aug. 21, 1949; children: Finley, Neil, Aaron. BA in Polit. Theory with honors, U. Mich., 1948; JD magna cum laude, U. Pa., 1951. Bar: Pa. 1952, U.S. Supreme Ct. 1978. Law clk. to presiding justice Pa. Supreme Ct., 1951-52; instr. U. Pa. Law Sch., 1951-52, 55-56; assoc. Dechert Price & Rhoads, Phila., 1956-58, 67-73, ptnr., 1973-78; judge U.S. Dist. Ct. 3rd circuit (ea. dist.) Pa., 1978—98, sr. judge, 1998—. Assoc. trustee U. Pa. Law Sch., 1978-93; former trustee Women's Law Project, Albert Einstein Med. Ctr.; v.p. Jewish Pub. Soc.; trustee Fedn. Jewish Agys., 1980-83; mem. lawyers adv. panel Pa. Gov.'s Commn. on Status of Women, 1974; legal adv. regional Coun. Child Psychiatry, bd. dirs. Women Judges' Fund for Justice. Guest editor: Shingle, 1972. Mem. Lower Merion County (Pa.) Bd. Sch. Dirs., 1968-77, pres., 1977, v.p., 1976; v.p. Jewish Community Relations Council of Greater Phila., 1975-77; chmn. legal affairs com., 1978; pres. Belmont Hills Home and Sch. Assn., Lower Merion Twp.; legis. chmn. Lower Merion Sch. Dist. Intersch. Council; mem. Task Force on Mental Health of Children and Youth of Pa.; treas., chmn. edn. com. Human Relations Council, Lower Merion; v.p., parliamentarian Nes Ami Penn Valley Congregation, Lower Merion Twp. Named Woman of Yr., Oxford Circle Jewish Community Center, 1979, Woman of Distinction, Golden Slipper Club, 1979; Gowen fellow, 1954-55; recipient Hannah G. Solomon award Nat. Coun. Jewish Women, 1992; Mem. Daughter of Pa.; Liberty Bell award, Berks County Bar Assn. Mem. Am. Law Inst., Am. Bar Found., ABA (ho. dels. 1990-96, coun./chmn. conf. fed. judges 1986-87, chmn. jud. divsn. 1996-97, Margaret Brent Women Lawyers Achievement award 1999, bd. gov. 2003-), Pa. Bar Assn. (ho. of dels. 1979-81), Phila. Bar Assn. (chmn. com. women's rights 1972, 74-75, chmn. bd. govs. 1977-78, chmn. pub. rels. com. 1978, Sandra Day O'Connor award), Fed. Bar Assn. (Bill of Rights award 1991), Nat. Assn. Women Lawyers, Phila. Trial Lawyers Assn., Am. Judicature Soc., Phila., Nat. Assn. Women Judges (exec. comm. bd. dir.), Fellowship Commn., Order of Coif (chpt. pres. 1973-75), Tau Epsilon Rho. Office: US Dist Courthouse Independence Mall West 601 Market St Rm 10614 Philadelphia PA 19106-1714 *

SHAPIRO, NORMAN RICHARD, literature and language professor; b. Boston, Nov. 1, 1930; s. Harry Alexander and Eva (Goldberg) Shapiro. BA, Harvard U., 1951, MA, 1952, PhD, 1958; diplôme in French lang. and lit., U. d'Aix-Marseille, 1956; MA (hon.), Wesleyan U., 1972. Instr. French Amherst Coll., 1958-60; asst. prof. romance langs. and lits. Wesleyan U., Middletown, Conn., 1960-65, assoc. prof., 1965-71, prof., 1971—. Writer-in-residence Adams House, Harvard U., 2003—. Editor: Echos, 1965, Palabres, 1973; translator, editor: Négritude, 1971; translator: Four Farces (Georges Feydeau), 1970 (nominated for Nat. Book award), Comedy of Eros, 1971, Kamouraska (Anne Hébert), 1973, Virginie, or the Dawning of the World (Joseph Majault), 1974, The Camp of the Saints (Jean Raspall), 1975, Feydeau, First to Last, 1982, Fables from Old French: Aesop's Beasts and Bumpkins, 1983, A Fitting Confusion (Georges Feydeau), 1985, The Pregnant Pause, or Love's Labor Lost (Georges Feydeau), 1987, The Brazilian (Henry Melhac and Ludovic Halévy), 1987, A Slap in the Farce (Eugène Labiche), 1988, A Matter of Wife and Death (Eugène Labiche), 1988, Fifty Fables of La Fontaine, 1988, The Fabulists French: Verse Fables of Nine Centuries, 1992, La Fontaine's Bawdy: Of Liberties, Louts and Lechers, 1992, A Flea in Her Rear, or Ants in Her Pants, and Other Vintage French Farces, 1994, Fifty More Fables of La Fontaine, 1998, Selected Poems from Les Fleurs du Mal, 1998, One Hundred and One Poems of Paul Verlaine, 1999 (MLA Scaglione award), All Gall: Malicious Monologues and Ruthless Recitations, 1999, Once Again (La Fontaine), 2001, Take Her, She's Yours, or Till Divorce do Them Part (Georges Feydeau), 2001, The Jew of Seville (Victor Sèjour), 2002, The Fortune Teller (Victor Sèjour), 2002, Lyrics of the French Renaissance: Marot, Du Bellay and Ronsard, 2002, revised edit., 2006, Creole Echoes: Francophone Poetry of 19th Century Louisiana, 2003; composer: Three Songs, 1961; mem. editl. bd. Tex. Rev.; contbr. articles, transls. and revs. to profl. jours. Mem.: Acad. Am. Poets, Poetry Soc. Am., Beast Fable Soc. (mem. editl. bd. Bestia), Dramatist Guild, Am. Translators Assn., Am. Lit. Transl. Assn. (Disting. Transl. award 1992), Signet Soc. Harvard, Delta Kappa Epsilon. Jewish. Office: Wesleyan U Dept Romance Langs & Lit 300 High St Middletown CT 06459-3233 Home Phone: 617-876-5334; Office Phone: 860-685-3089. Business E-Mail: nshapiro@wesleyan.edu.

SHAPIRO, PAULA, retired maternal/women's health nurse; b. Pitts., Nov. 16, 1927; d. Ben and Esther (Halpert) Cohn; m. Bernard Shapiro, July 17, 1982; children: Eugene Hershorin, Abby Hershorin, Marc Hershorin, Jay Hershorin, Ellen Fenerty, Kenneth, Fred, Stacy Pierce. RN, Montefiore Hosp. Sch. Nursing, 1948; BS, Phila. U., 1987. RN, Pa. Nursing care coord. Thomas Jefferson U. Hosp., Phila.; asst. supr. operating rm. Wakefield (R.I.) Gen. Hosp.; staff RN operating rm. Jefferson Hosp., Phila., ret., 1993. Contbr. articles to profl. jours. Vol. Thomas Jefferson U. Hosp., gift shop Nat. Mus. Am. Jewish History; vol. o.r. nurse Tel Aviv, Israel, 1977; election judge. Home: 1500 Locust St Apt 2216 Philadelphia PA 19102-4317 Personal E-mail: paulashapiro@hotmail.com.

SHAPIRO, PHILIP ALAN, lawyer; b. Chgo., May 14, 1940; s. Joe and Nettie (Costin) Shapiro; m. Joyce Barbara Chapnick, May 29, 1966 (dec. Feb. 2006); children: David Ian, Russell Scott, Mindi Jennifer. AA, Wilson Coll., 1960; BS in Fin., So. Ill. U., 1965; MBA, Nat. Univ., San Diego, Calif., 1975; MBA in Mktg. with distinction, San Diego State U., San Diego, 1977; JD, Western State U., 1985. Bar: Calif. 1988. Spl. agt. U.S. Secret Svc., Washington, 1965-67, Chgo., 1967-77; mgr. divsn. sales Roche Labs. divsn. Hoffman-La Roche, Inc., Chgo.; account exec. Cellular Comm., Inc., San Diego, 1985; with Complete Comm., San Diego, 1983—; assoc. Law Office Jeffrey S. Schwartz, 1988-91; pvt. practice, 1991—. Chair gen. and solo practice sect. State Bar of Calif. Editor (law rev.): We. State U. Coll. Law. Mem. adv. bd. Spreckes Elem. Sch., San Diego, 1976—77; mem. Univ. City Town Coun., San Diego, 1977; pres. Congregation Beth El, La Jolla, Calif., 1976—79. With USMC, 1958—60. Named Alum of Yr., Thomas Jefferson Sch. Law, 2006—07; recipient Merit award, U.S. Treasury Dept., 1965, Israel Solidarity award, 1977, U. Judaism award, 1978. Mem.: ABA (vice chmn. gen. practice sect.), Assn. Former Agts. of U.S. Secret Svc., San Diego Bus. Referrals (pres. 1998—99), San Diego County Bar Assn., State Bar Calif. (exec. com. gen. practice sect. chair, Wiley W. Manuel award 1990—91), Calif. Trial Lawyers Assn., Thomas Jefferson Sch. of Law Alumni Assn. (pres. 2004—, bd. dirs.). Office: The Law Offices of Shapiro and Clamon 1010 2d Ave Ste 1000 San Diego CA 92101 Office Phone: 619-239-1511. Office Fax: 619-239-1007. Business E-Mail: shapiroclamon@gmail.com.

SHAPIRO, PHILIP EDWIN, dermatologist, dermatopathologist, educator; b. New Hyde Park, NY, Mar. 30, 1959; s. Lewis and Suzanne Marie (Bassewitz) Shapiro; m. Kimberly Ann Bouchard, Oct. 4, 1998; m. Jacklyn Marie Trimble (div.); children: Adam Henry, David Alexander. BS magna cum laude, Rensselaer Polytech. Inst., Troy, NY, 1982; MD, Albany Med. Coll., NY, 1982. Diplomate Am. Bd. Dermatology, 1986, Am. Bd. Dermatology and Pathology (Dermatopathology), 1988, lic. physician Conn., NY, Fla. Intern Albany Med. Ctr. Hosp., 1982—83; resident in dermatology Columbia-Presbyn. Hosp., NYC, 1983—86; postdoctoral fellow dermatology Yale U. Sch. Medicine, New Haven, 1986—87; fellow dermatopathology NYU Med. Ctr., 1987—88; asst. prof. dermatology, dir. dermatopathology lab. Yale U. Sch. Medicine, 1988—91, asst. prof. dermatology and pathology, dir. dermatopathology fellow tng. program, 1991—95, assoc. clin. prof. dermatology, 1996—. Dir. Dermatopathology Lab. New Eng., Meriden, Conn., 1995—; attending physician Yale-New Haven Hosp., New Haven, 1988—; asst. attending physician St. Francis Hosp., Hartford, Conn., 1995—; lectr., presenter in field. Contbr. articles to profl. jours., chapters to books. State chmn. Conn. Dermatology Foun.,

Evanston, Ill., 2004—. Fellow: Am. Soc. Dermatopathology, Am. Acad. Dermatology; mem.: AMA, Am. Soc. Clin. Pathologists, New Eng. Dermatol. Soc., US and Can. Acad. Pathology, New Haven County Med. Assn., Conn. State Med. Soc., Internat. Soc. Dermatopathology. Achievements include research in melanocytic neoplasia, delineating new entities or diagnostic criteria through clinicopathologic correlation. Avocations: tennis, cello, boating. Office: Dermapathology Lab New England 140 Green Rd Meriden CT 06450

SHAPIRO, RICHARD CHARLES, publishing executive, sales executive, marketing professional; b. Bklyn., May 28, 1936; s. Isidore and Sylvia (Rappaport) Shapiro; m. Marilyn Joyce Baily, Feb. 17, 1957 (div. 1974); children: Joseph, Scott; m. Francine L. Shaw, Sept. 19, 1975. BS in Edn., Golden State U., 1978, MBA, 1981; PhD in Bus. Adminstrn. and Mktg., Honolulu U., 1987. Lic. real estate broker Ill. Sales mgr. Coca Cola Bottling Co. of N.Y., 1955-62; affiliate Effective Motivation Assocs./Success Motivation inst., Bethpage, N.Y., 1965-68; v.p. sales, dir. Field Enterprises, Chgo., 1962-78; pres., CEO Snack-In, Inc., Detroit, 1978-82; sr. ptnr. Directions Growth and Strategy Cons., Chgo., 1982-95; v.p. domestic & internat. mktg. & sales, oper. officer Ency. Brit.-Compton's Learning Co., 1991-93, specialist network mktg. & relationship mktg., CEO, pres., bd. dirs.; CEO Am.'s Home Detailing Corp., 1995—, CEO, chmn. bd., 2001—; pres., COO Am.'s Deep Clean Divsn., Deerfield, Ill., 1995—2000; CEO, chmn. emeritus Am.'s Home Detailing Corp., Deerfield, Ill.; instr. grad. studies mktg. mgmt., instr. human resources mgmt. Robert Morris Coll., Chgo., 2001—; owner, operator PennyPincherDepot.com, 2005—. Instr. planning Life Underwriter Tng. Coun., LI, 1965—66; assoc. editor Media Technics Pub. Assn., Lake Forest, 1988; bd. dirs. Master Deep Clean Co., Nat. Video Libr.; spkr. on mktg., sales and leadership; cons. in field; liaison Chgo. Daily News, Chgo. Sun Times, Sta. WFLD-TV; founder Discovery Toy Divsn.; tennis pro, instr. Frank Sacks Tennis Camps, Chgo., 2001—; profl. tennis registry tennis instr., 2002—; asst. e-bay Auction Svcs., Deerfield, Ill., 2001—; continuing edn. instr. Gen. Contracting, Highland Pk., Ill., 2005—; founder Pennyincberdepot.com, 2005—. Pub.: Real Estate Property Marketing News; author: self-improvement cassettes; contbr. articles to profl. jours. Active Explorers, high schs., youth clubs, 1965—74; founder, pres. Abundance and Goodwill Soc., 1968—. With USAF, 1957—60. Named Sales/Mktg. Execs. Leadership Recruiter/Trainer of Decade award, Profl. Tennis Assocs. Singles champion, 1957, 1958, 1960; recipient Leadership award, Am. Sales Masters, 1968, 1999—2000, POPAI-OMA Best Industry Point of Purchase Display and Mktg. award, 1992. Mem.: Chgo. Computer Soc., Effective Motivation Assocs., Salesman with a Purpose, Deercreek Tennis Club (tchr., mem. rels. 2000—). Avocations: white-water rafting, canoeing, camping, tennis, writing. Home Phone: 847-459-0122; Office Phone: 847-459-3435. Personal E-mail: ahd10@yahoo.com, leadership_01@yahoo.com. E-mail: richard@pennypincherdepot.com, richard@tennis2win.com.

SHAPIRO, RICHARD GERALD, retail executive, consultant; b. NYC, Apr. 24, 1924; s. David and Sophie (Hayflich) S.; m. Lila Eig, July 27, 1951; children: Judith, Amy, Donald. BA, U. Mich., 1946; MBA, Harvard, 1948. With Lord & Taylor, NYC, 1948-64, v.p., 1959-63, sr. v.p., 1963-64; also mem. adv. bd.; pres. Wm. Filene's Sons Co., Boston, 1965-68, chief exec. officer, chmn. bd., 1968-73; pres. Gimbel Bros. Corp., NYC, 1973-76; v.p. W.R. Grace & Co., pres. sporting goods div., 1977-79, pres. splty. store div., 1979-84; pres. Richard Shapiro Assocs., 1979—; sr. v.p. Montgomery Ward, Inc., 1986-88. Bd. dirs. Assoc. Merchandising Corp., Nitrotec Corp., Capital Market Fund; retail chmn. Greater N.Y. Fund, 1963; chmn. merc. div. Mass. Bay United Fund, 1967 Mem. corp. Simmons Coll., Boston Mus. Fine Arts (permanent); bd. dirs. Mass. Mchts.; bd. dirs Family Counseling and Guidance Centers, 1969-72, v.p., 1970; trustee Brandeis U. Served with AUS, 1942-46. Mem.: Harvard Bus. Sch. Assn. (gov.). Home: 10019 Gable Manor Ct Potomac MD 20854-5000 Personal E-mail: rgsle@webtv.net.

SHAPIRO, RICHARD MICHAEL, lawyer; b. New Haven, Feb. 7, 1951; s. Robert and Pearl Edith (Glassman) S. BA, U. South Fla., 1978; JD, Southwestern U., 1980. Bar: Conn. 1981, Fla. 1981, U.S. Dist. Ct. (mid. dist.) Fla. 1982. Jud. intern to presiding judge U.S. Dist. Ct. for Conn., 1979; assoc. Mitzel, Mitzel and Feegel, Tampa, Fla., 1981; asst. pub. defender State of Fla., Bradenton, 1981; pres. and prin. Shapiro Law Group, Bradenton, 1981—. Fellow Roscoe Pound Found., 1994—; lectr. in field. Mem. FBA, ABA, ATLA (sustaining mem., bd. govs. 1997—, med. quality assurance com. 1994—, co-chmn. spkrs. bur./people's law sch. com. 1999-2000, stalwarts/endowment com. 1999-2000, key persons com. 1999-2000), Am. Judicature Soc., Fla. Bar Assn. (jud. selection, nomination and tenure com. 1989—, exec. coun. trial lawyers sect. 1997-2000), Acad. Fla. Trial Lawyers (Eagle founder 2000-01, F.L.A.G. trustee 1995—, co-chmn. med. malpractice taskforce 1996-97, pres. 2003-2004, Jon E. Krupnick award for perseverance 2001), Conn. Bar Assn., Hillsborough County Bar Assn., Tampa Bay Trial Lawyers Assn. (founder, bd. dirs. 2000—), So. Trial Lawyers Assn. (bd. govs. 1996—, pres. 2003-04), Trial Lawyers for Pub. Justice (Fla. state coord. 1992-97). Democrat. Jewish. Avocations: tennis, volleyball, scuba diving, boating. Office: Shapiro Law Group 1732 Manatee Ave W Bradenton FL 34205-5925 Business E-Mail: rshapiro@shapirolawgroup.com.

SHAPIRO, RICHARD STANLEY, physician; b. Moline, Ill., June 11, 1925; s. Herbert and Esther Dian (Grant) S.; m. Arlene Blum, June 12, 1949; children: Michele Pamela, Bruce Grant, Gary Lawrence; m. Mary Lou Coook, Oct. 11, 1971. BS in Pharmacy, U. Iowa, 1951, MS in Preventive Medicine & Environ., 1951, MD, 1957. Diplomate Am. Bd. Allergy and Immunology. Pharmacist, Rock Island, Ill., 1951-53; rsch. asst. U. Iowa Coll. Medicine, Iowa City, 1950-51, 53-57; practice medicine specializing in allergy Beverly Hills, Calif., 1958-62, Lynwood, Calif., 1962—. Attending physician Good Hope Found. Allergy Clinic, Los Angeles, 1958-62, Cedars of Lebanon Hosp., Hollywood, Calif., 1959-68, U. So. Calif.-Los Angeles County Med. Center, 1962—; physician St. Francis Hosp., Lynwood, 1962—; assoc. clin. prof. medicine U. So. Calif., 1978-84, emeritus, 1984—. Contbr. articles to profl. jours. Bd. dirs. Westside Jewish Cmty. Ctr., 1961—65, Camp JCA, 1964—65. With USNR, 1943—46. Fellow Am. Geriatric Soc., Am. Coll. Allergy, Am. Assn. Clin. Immunology & Allergy; mem. AMA, AAAS, Am. Soc. Tropical Medicine and Hygiene, Am. Acad. Allergy, Am. Soc. Internal Medicine, Am. Heart Assn., West Coast Allergy Soc., Calif. Med. Assn., Calif. Soc. Internal Medicine, Calif. Soc. Allergy, L.A. County Med. Assn., L.A. Allergy Soc., Sierra Club, B'nai B'rith, Masons, Sigma Xi. Jewish. Office: 8301 Florence Ave Ste 104 Downey CA 90240-3946 Office Phone: 562-862-1991.

SHAPIRO, ROBERT, lawyer; b. Plainfield, NJ, Sept. 2, 1942; BS in Fin., UCLA, 1965; JD, Loyola U., LA, 1968. Bar: Calif. 1969, U.S. Ct. Appeals (9th cir.) 1972, U.S. Dist. Ct. (ctrl., no. and so. dists.) Calif. 1982. Dep. dist. atty. Office of Dist. Atty., LA, 1969-72; sole practice LA, 1972—87; of counsel Bushkin, Gaims, Gaines, Jonas, LA, 1987-88, Christensen, Miller, Fink & Jacobs, LA, 1988-95; ptnr. Christensen, Miller, Fink, Jacobs, Glaser, Weil & Shapiro (formerly known as Christensen, Glaser, Fink, Jacobs, Weil & Shapiro), LA, 1995—. Founder legalzoom.com. Author: Search for Justice, 1996, Misconception, 2001. Recipient Am. Jurisprudence award Bancroft Whitney, 1969. Mem. Nat. Assn. Criminal Def. Lawyers, Calif. Attys. for Criminal Justice, Trial Lawyers for Pub. Justice (founder 1982), Century City Bar Assn. (Best Criminal Def. Atty. 1993). Office: 10250 Constellation Blvd Fl 19 Los Angeles CA 90067 Office Phone: 310-553-3000, 310-556-7886. Business E-Mail: rs@chrisglase.com. *

SHAPIRO, ROBERT FRANK, investment company executive; b. St. Louis, Dec. 19, 1934; s. Eugene J. and Clara (Katz) S.; m. Anna Marie Susman, Dec. 21, 1960; children: Albert Andrew, Robert Jr., Jeanne Savitt. Grad., St. Louis Country Day Sch., 1952; BA, Yale U., 1956. Assoc. Lehman Bros., NYC, 1956-67, ptnr., 1967-73, dir., sr. mng. dir., 1970-73; ptnr. Wertheim & Co., 1974; exec. v.p. Wertheim & Co., Inc., NYC, 1974-75, pres., 1975-86; co-chmn. Wertheim Schroder & Co., Inc., 1986-87; chmn. RFS and Assocs., Inc., NYC, 1988—2004, New Street Capital Corp., 1992-94; vice-chmn. Klingenstein, Fields & Co., L.P., NYC, 1997—. Bd. dirs. TJX Cos., Inc., Genaera Corp., The Burnham Fund, chmn. nominating com. N.Y. Stock Exch., 1980, mem. regulatory adv. com., 1988—, surveillance com., 1989—; bd. govs. Am. Stock Exch., 1970-76. Trustee Lenox Hill Hosp., Skowhegan; mem. gov. bd. Yale U. Art Gallery, New Haven, 1993—; trustee Louis Comfort Tiffany Found. Named one of Top 200 Collectors, ARTnews Mag., 2004. Mem. Securities Industry Assn. (chmn. 1985, Bond Club N.Y. (pres. 1987-88, Yale Club, Century Country Club, Knickerbocker Club. Avocation: Collector of Contemporary Art, especially American. Office: Klingenstein Fields & Co LLC 787 7th Ave New York NY 10019-6018 Office Phone: 212-492-6143.

SHAPIRO, ROBERT N., lawyer; b. June 18, 1950; AB cum laude, Harvard Univ., 1972; postgraduate, Trinity Coll., Cambridge Univ., England; JD cum laude, Harvard Univ., 1978. Bar: Mass. 1978. Law clk. US Dist. Ct. (Conn.), Judge Jon O. Newman, US Ct. Appeals 2d cir.; assoc. Ropes & Gray, Boston, 1979—87, ptnr., 1987—, head private client dept. Pres. Harvard Law Sch. Assn.; past pres. Harvard Alumni Assn.; chmn. Friends of Philip Exeter Acad. Libr.; trustee Noble & Greenough Sch., Dedham, Mass., Peabody Essex Mus., Salem, Mass.; overseer Handel & Haydn Soc., Boston. Fiske scholar. Office: Ropes & Gray 1 International Pl Boston MA 02110-2624 Office Phone: 617-951-7217. Office Fax: 617-951-7050. Business E-Mail: robert.shapiro@ropesgray.com.

SHAPIRO, ROBYN SUE, lawyer, educator; b. Mpls., July 19, 1952; d. Walter David and Judith Rae (Sweet) S.; m. Charles Howard Barr, June 27, 1976; children: Tania Shapiro-Barr, Jeremy Shapiro-Barr, Michael Shapiro-Barr. BA summa cum laude, U. Mich., 1974; JD, Harvard U., 1977. Bar: D.C. 1977, Wis. 1979, U.S. Supreme Ct. 1990. Assoc. Foley & Lardner, Washington, 1977-79; ptnr. Barr & Shapiro, Menomonee Falls, Wis., 1980-87; assoc. Quarles & Brady, Milw., 1987-92; ptnr. Michael Best & Friedrich, Milw., 1992—2005, chair health law practice, 2003—05; ptnr. Gardner Carton & Douglas LLP, Milw., 2005—06, Drinker Biddle Gardner Carton, Milw., 2006—. Adj. asst. prof. law Marquette U., Milw., 1979-83; assoc. dir. bioethics ctr. Med. Coll. Wis., Milw., 1982-85, dir., 1985—; asst. prof. bioethics Med. Coll. Wis., 1984-89, assoc. prof. bioethics, 1989-97, prof. bioethics, 1997—, Ursula Von der Ruhr prof. bioethics, 2000—; dir. Wis. Ethics Com. Network, 1987-98, Midwest Ethics Com. Network, 1998-2004, Med. Ethics Com. Network, 2004—; bd. dirs. Wis. Health Decisions, 1990-93; drug safety and risk mgmt. adv. com. FDA, 2003—; mem. data and safety monitoring bd. Med. Coll. Wis., 2003-2007; mem. recombinant DNA adv. com. NIH, 2005—. Mem. editl. bd. Cambridge Quar., 1991—, HEC Forum, 1988—91, Human Rights, 1998—2007; contbr. articles to profl. jours. Mem. ethics com. St. Luke's Med. Ctr., Milw., 1983—, Elmbrook Meml. Hosp., Milw., 1983-86, Cmty. Meml. Hosp., Menomonee Falls, 1984—, Aurora Sinai Med.Ctr., Milw., 1986—, Milw. County Mental Health Complex, 1984—, Froedtert Meml. Luth. Hosp., 1985—; mem. subcom. organ transplantation Wis. Health Policy Coun., Madison, 1984, bioethics com., 1986-89; mem. com. study on bioethics Wis. Legis. Coun., Madison, 1984-85; bd. dirs. Jewish Home and Care Ctr., 1994-2005, chair ethics com., 1994—; chair Bayside Ethics Bd., 1994—; bd. dirs. Milw. area chpt. Girl Scouts U.S., Am. Bioethics Assn., 1995-97, Wis. Perinatal Found., 1996-99, Am. Soc. Bioethics and Humanities, 1997-00, Manor Park Found., 2002—; mem. sec.'s adv. com. on xenotransplantation U.S. Dept. Health and Human Svcs., 2001-05; mem. sci. adv. com. Alzheimer's Assn. Southeastern Wis., 1997—; mem. data and safety monitoring bd. GlaxoWellcome, 1995-03; mem. med. and cmty. adv. bd. After Breast Cancer Diagnosis, 1999—. James B. Angell scholar, 1971—72. Fellow: Am. Bar Found.; mem.: ACLU, ABA (health law sec., coordinating com. on bioethics and law 1993—, individual rights and responsibilities sect., health rights com. chair 1994—99, vice chair clin. ethics group 1998—2001, coun. 1999—, working group on health info. privacy 2000—02, misuse of genetic info. study group 2002—, AIDS coordinating com. 2003—, sec. individual rights and responsibilites vice chair 2005—06, chair-elect individual rights and responsibilities sect. 2006—, adv. nat. conf. of commrs. on uniform state laws), Profl. Dimensions (Golden Compass award 1994), Internat. Bioethics Assn. (chair task force on ethics coms.), Am. Soc. Transplant Surgeons (ethics com. 1999—), Milw. AIDS Coalition (steering com. 1988—91), Milw. Acad. Medicine (coun. 1992—98, chair bioethics com. 1992—98), Am. Soc. Law, Medicine and Ethics, Assn. Post-Doctoral Programs in Clin. Neurophysiology (bd. dirs.), Wis. Found. (Atty. of Yr. 1988), Assn. Women Lawyers, Wis. Bar Assn. (individual rights sect. coun. 1987—90, chair Wis. health law sect. 1988—89), Am. Hosp. Assn. (spl. com. HIV practitioners 1991—93, bioethics tech. panel 1991—94), Am. Health Lawyers Assn., Susan G. Komen Breast Cancer Found., Phi Beta Kappa (Wis. chpt. scholarship com. chair 1990—93). Home: 9474 N Broadmoor Rd Milwaukee WI 53217-1309 Office: Med Coll Wis Bioethics Ctr 8701 Watertown Plank Rd Milwaukee WI 53226-3548 Office Phone: 414-221-6040. Business E-Mail: rshapiro@mcw.edu, robyn.shapiro@dbr.com.

SHAPIRO, RONALD GARY, psychologist; b. Providence, Oct. 10, 1953; s. Nathan and Raquel (Rebe) S. BA, U. Rochester, 1975; MA, Ohio State U., 1977, PhD, 1981. Cert. human factors profl. Teaching, rsch. assoc. Ohio State U., Columbus, 1975-81; asst. prof. Denison U., Granville, Ohio, 1981-82; prin. assoc. Dunlap and Assocs. Inc., Norwalk, Conn., 1982-85; sr. engring. mgr. IBM, Poughkeepsie, N.Y., 1985-96, cons. human resources profl., 1996—, mgr. enterprise-wide tech. and strategic learning curricula, US external edn. univ. programs, 2002—, mgr. new employee orientation, career counseling, 2006—. Evening faculty U. Conn., Stamford, 1983-85, Dutchess C.C., Poughkeepsie, 1986-94; bd. cert. Profl. Ergonomics Recert. Com. Contbr. articles to Psychol. Rev., Jour. Exptl. Psychology and other profl. jours. Recipient Grad. Sch. Leadership award Ohio State U., 1979; recipient Sr. Engring. Mgr. promotion IBM, 1993. Fellow Human Factors and Ergonomics Soc. (nat. program com. 1994-97, tech. program com. 1997-2000, chair computer sys. tech. group 1999-2000, chair coun. tech. groups 2001-02, vol. chair 2003-05, chair nat. ergonomics month 2003-05, chair spkrs. bur., 2004-05, exec. coun. 2006—), Human Factors and Ergonomics Soc. (Oliver Keith Hansen Outreach award 2005); mem. APA (pres. divsn. 21 applied exptl. and engring. psychology 2005-06), Soc. Indsl. Orgnl. Psychologists, SHARE, Inc. (IBM rep. 1987-91), Sigma Xi, Phi Kappa Phi. Achievements include design of computer products and learning deliverables; corporate learning programs. Home and Office: 17 Brookway Rd Providence RI 02906 Office Phone: 401-272-4664. Personal E-mail: drronshapiro1981@sigmaxi.net. E-mail: rshapiro@us.ibm.com.

SHAPIRO, SANDER WOLF, retired lawyer; b. St. Louis, Sept. 24, 1929; s. Robert and Bess (Fisher) S.; m. Lottie F. Frankel, Aug. 14, 1955; children: Julie A. Shapiro Schechter, Susan B. Shapiro Schmitz. BA, Rice U., 1951; postgrad., Columbia U., 1951-52; JD, U. Tex., 1954. Atty. tax div. Dept. Justice, Washington, 1955-57; atty. advisor U.S. Tax Ct., Washington, 1957-58; ptnr. Clark, Thomas, Winters & Shapiro, Austin, Tex., 1958-84; sr. prtnr. Shapiro, Edens & Cook, Austin, 1984-91; of counsel Jenkens & Gilchrist, P.C., Austin, 1991-2000; ret. Adj. prof. law U. Tex., 1975-2000; lectr. in tax field. Author, editor Tex. Franchise Earned Surplus and Tax, 1985, Family Solutions to Family Concerns, 1991, A Walk Through Form 706, 1991; co-editor Tex. Tax Svc., 1986-94. Bd. dirs. Austin Symphony Orch. Soc., 1974-97, dir. emeritus, 1997—, fin. v.p., 1980-95; bd. dirs. U. Tex. Coll. Fine Arts Adv. Coun., 1987-95, hon. bd. dirs., 1995—, pres., 1991-94; bd. dirs. Capital of Tex. Pub. Telecomm. Coun., 1988-97, pres., 1994-95; bd. dirs. Ronald McDonald House of Ctrl. Tex., Austin, 1990-98, pres., 1994-95; bd. dirs. Capital Met. Transit Authority, 1988-91, chair, 1990; bd. dirs. Austin Cmty. Found., 1985-92, pres., 1991; adv. coun. U. Tex. Press, 1998—, vice chmn. 1999, chmn. 2000. Sander W. Shapiro Presdl. Scholarship in Law at U. Tex. endowed in his honor by Jenkens & Gilchrist, 1992; recipient Disting. Lawyer award Travis County, 1999. Fellow Am. Bar Found. (life), Am. Coll. Tax Counsel, Tex. Bar Found. (sustaining life); mem. ABA, State Bar of Tex., Am. Law Inst., Nat. Assn. State Bar Tax Sects. (bd. dirs., chair 1997, dir. emeritus 2002—), Tex. Law Rev. Assn. (pres. 1992-93). Avocations: reading, music, golf. E-mail: sws@austin.rr.com.

SHAPIRO, SANDOR SOLOMON, hematologist; b. Bklyn., July 26, 1933; BA, Harvard U., 1954, MD, 1957. Intern Harvard med. svc. Boston City Hosp., 1957-58, asst. resident, 1960-61; asst. surgeon divsn. biol. std. NIH, USPHS, 1958-60; NIH spl. fellow MIT, 1961-64; from instr. to assoc. prof. Cardeza Found. Jefferson Med. Coll., Phila., 1964-72, prof. medicine, 1972—2003, assoc. dir., 1978-85, dir., 1985-2000, prof. biochem. and molecular pharmacology, 1987—, rsch. prof. physiology and biophysics, 2003—. Mem. hematology study sect. NIH, 1972-76, 78-79; mem. med. adv. coun. Nat. Hemophilia Found., 1973-75; chmn. Pa. State Hemophilia Adv. Com., 1974-76. Fellow AAAS; mem. Am. Soc. Clin. Investigation, Am. Soc. Hematology, Am. Assn. Immunologists, Assn. Am. Physicians, Internat. Soc. Thrombosis and Hemostasis. Achievements include research in hemostasis and thrombosis, prothrombin metabolism, hemophilia, lupus anticoagulants, endothelial cells, filamins. Office: Thomas Jefferson U Dept Physiology 1020 Locust St Philadelphia PA 19107-5005

SHAPIRO, SANDRA, lawyer; b. Providence, Oct. 17, 1944; d. Emil and Sarah (Cohen) S. AB magna cum laude, Bryn Mawr Coll., Pa., 1966; LLB magna cum laude, U. Pa., 1969. Bar: Mass. 1970, U.S. Dist. Ct. Mass. 1971, U.S. Ct. Appeals (1st cir.) 1972, U.S. Supreme Ct. 1980. Law clk. U.S. Ct. Appeals (1st cir.), Boston, 1969-70; assoc. Foley, Hoag & Eliot LLP, Boston, 1970-75, ptnr., 1976—. Mem. bd. bar overseers Mass. Supreme Judicial Ct., 1988-92, mem. gender bias study com., 1986-89; dir. Mass. Govt. Land Bank, 1994-96; dir. Lex Mundi, 2004—. Contbr. articles to profl. jours. Bd. dirs. Patriots' Trail coun. Girl Scouts U.S., 1994—97; mem. bd. overseers Boston Lyric Opera, 1993—99, New Eng. Conservatory of Music, 1995—2001, Celebrity Series of Boston, 1997—, chair, 2003—. Woodrow Wilson fellow, 1966. Mem.: ABA (ethics, profl. and pub. edn. com. 1994—), U. Pa. Law Sch. Alumni Assn. (bd. mgrs. 1990—94), Boston Bar Assn. (mem. coun.), Mass. Bar Assn. (chmn. real property sect. coun., com. on profl. ethics), Nat. Women's Law Ctr. Network, New Eng. Women in Real Estate, Women's Bar Assn. Mass. (pres. 1985—86), Boston Club, Order of Coif. Office: Foley Hoag LLP 155 Seaport Blvd Boston MA 02210-2600 Office Phone: 617-832-1156. Business E-Mail: sshapiro@foleyhoag.com.

SHAPIRO, SELMA, retired museum director; Exec. dir. libr. mus. Jefferson Jr. H.S., 1973; exec. dir. Oak Ridge Children's Mus., retired, 2004, vol., 2004—. Named to Centennial Honor Roll, Am. Assn. Museums, 2006; recipient Gordon Holl award for Outstanding Arts Adminstr., Tenn. Arts Commn., 1982, Grandest Grandparent award, Beck Cultural Ctr., Knoxville; Inst. Mus. Services grant, 1990. Mem.: Assn. Children's Mus. (pres. 1987). Mailing: c/o Oak Ridge Children's Library 461 W Outer Dr Oak Ridge TN 37830 *

SHAPIRO, STEPHEN MICHAEL, lawyer; b. Chgo., May 3, 1946; s. Samuel H. and Dorothy A. (D'Andrea) S.; m. Joan H. Gately, Oct. 30, 1982; children: Dorothy Henderson, Michael Clifford. BA magna cum laude, Yale U., 1968, JD, 1971. Bar: Ill. 1971, Calif. 1972, DC 1991, US Dist. Ct. (no. dist. trial bar Ill.) 1992, US Ct. Appeals (all cirs.), US Supreme Ct. 1975. Law clk. US Ct. Appeals (9th cir.), San Francisco, 1971—72; with Mayer, Brown & Platt, Chgo., 1972—78; asst. to solicitor gen. US Dept. Justice, Washington, 1978-80, dep. solicitor gen., 1981—83; sr. mem. Supreme Ct. and Appellate Ct. practice Mayer, Brown, Rowe & Maw, LLP, Chgo., 1983—, ptnr., 1983—. Trustee Product Liability Adv. Found. Co-author: Supreme Ct. Practice, 2002; contbr. articles to profl. jours. Mem. ABA, Am. Law Inst. (life), Am. Acad. Appellate Lawyers, 7th Cir. Bar Assn., Inst. Jud. Adminstrn. (bd. dirs.), Phi Beta Kappa. Republican. Jewish. Office: Mayer Brown Rowe & Maw LLP 71 S Wacker Dr Ste 4430 Chicago IL 60606 Office Phone: 312-701-7327. Office Fax: 312-706-8684. E-mail: sshapiro@mayerbrownrowe.com. *

SHAPIRO, STEVEN A., lawyer; b. Chgo., Oct. 22, 1950; BS, U. Ill., 1971; JD, Ill. Inst. Tech., 1975. Bar: Ill. 1975, Fla. 1983. Ptnr. Katten Muchin Zavis Rosenman, Chgo. Mem.: ABA. Office: Katten Muchin Zavis Rosenman 525 W Monroe St Chicago IL 60661 Office Phone: 312-902-5545. Office Fax: 312-577-8881. E-mail: steven.shapiro@kmzr.com.

SHAPIRO, STEVEN R., legal association administrator; JD, Harvard U., 1975. Law clk. to Hon. J. Edward Lumbard US Ct. Appeals 2nd Cir., 1975—76; with ACLU, 1976—, staff counsel Children's Rights Project, gen. staff counsel, assoc. legal dir., 1987—93, legal dir., 1993—. Adj. prof constl. law Columbia U.; bd. dirs. Human Rights First (previously Lawyers Com. for Human Rights); mem. Asia Adv. Com. Human Rights Watch, mem. policy com. Named Civil Rights Lawyer of Yr., Am. Lawyer, 1981. Office: ACLU 125 Broad St 18th Fl New York NY 10004 *

SHAPIRO, STUART CHARLES, computer scientist, educator; b. NYC, Dec. 30, 1944; s. Louis M. and Bertha (Rubinstein) S.; m. Caren Dee Knight, July 16, 1972. BS, MIT, 1966; MS, U. Wis., 1968, PhD, 1971. Lectr. computer scis. dept. U. Wis., Madison, 1971; vis. asst. prof. Ind. U., Bloomington, 1971-72, asst. prof., 1972-77, assoc. prof., 1977-78; asst. prof. SUNY, Buffalo, 1977-78, assoc. prof., 1978-83, prof., 1983—, chmn., 1984-90, 96-99, dir. Ctr. for Cognitive Sci., 2004—. Pres. Principles of Knowledge Representation and Reasoning, Inc., 1998-2000; rsch. scientist Nat. Ctr. for Geographic Info. and Analysis, 1989—. Author: Techniques of Artificial Intelligence, 1979, LISP: An Interactive Approach, 1986, Common Lisp: An Interactive Approach, 1992; editor: Encyclopedia of Artificial Intelligence, 1987, paperback edit., 1990, 2d edit., 1992, (with Lucja Iwanska) Natural Language Processing and Knowledge Representation: Language for Knowledge and Knowledge for Language, 2000; contbr. articles to profl. jours. Grantee NSF, 1971—; recipient numerous grants for computer sci. research, 1971—. Fellow Am. Assn. Artificial Intelligence; mem. IEEE (sr.), Assn. Computing Machinery (chmn. spl. interest group on artificial intelligence 1991-95, Disting. Scientist 2006—), Assn. Computational Linguistics, Cognitive Sci. Soc., Assn. Computing Machinery Disting. Scientist, Sigma Xi. Home: 142 Viscount Dr Buffalo NY 14221-1770 Office: Univ at Buffalo Dept of Comp Sci & Engring 201 Bell Hall Buffalo NY 14260-2000 Home Phone: 716-636-0816; Office Phone: 716-645-3180 ext. 125. Personal E-mail: shapiro@roadrunner.com. Business E-Mail: shapiro@cse.buffalo.edu.

SHAPIRO, SUSAN STOBBART, lawyer; b. Stone Harbor, NJ, July 19, 1969; BA, Washington Coll., 1991; JD, Villanova U., 1994. Bar: Pa. 1994, Md. 1995, NJ 1995, US Dist. Ct. (dist. Md.) 1998, DC 2000, US Dist. Ct. (DC dist.) 2002, US Ct. Appeals (4th cir.) 2003. Dir. Council, Baradel, Kosmerl & Nolan, P.A., Annapolis, Md. Pres. alumni coun. Washington Coll., 2000—02; bd. dirs. Marine Trades Assn. Md., 2000—02; mem. Annapolis & Anne Arundel County C. of C.; spkr. in field. Mem. editl. adv. bd.: The Daily Record, 2004—; contbr. articles to profl. jours. Named one of Top Lawyers, Balt. Mag., 2003. Mem.: ABA, Anne Arundel County Bar Assn., Md. State Bar Assn. Office: Council Baradel Kosmerl & Nolan PA 125 West St 4th Fl PO Box 2289 Annapolis MD 21404-2289 Office Phone: 410-268-6600 ext. 3413. Business E-Mail: shapiro@cbknlaw.com. *

SHAPIRO, THEODORE, psychiatrist, educator; b. NYC, Feb. 26, 1932; s. Herman Alexander and Nettie (Rosenblatt) S.; m. Joan May Itkin, June 26, 1955; children: Susan, Alexander Herman. BA, Wesleyan U., 1953; MD, Cornell U., 1957. Diplomate Am. Bd. Psychiatry and Neurology, Am. Bd. Child Psychiatry, Am. Psychoanalytic Assn. Intern Montefiore Hosp., NYC, 1957—58; resident in psychiatry NYU-Bellevue Hosp., 1958—61; instr. to prof. NYU Sch. Medicine, 1960—76; rsch. assoc. child psychiatry NYU-Bellevue Hosp., 1961—65; asst. lectr. N.Y. Psychoanalytic Inst., NYC, 1970—86; prof. psychiatry and pediatrics Cornell U. Med. Coll., NYC, 1976—2002; tng. and supervising analyst N.Y. Psychoanalytic Inst., NYC, 1986—; vice chair for child and adolescent psychiatry, 1995—2002; emeritus prof. Cornell U. Med. Coll., NYC, 2002—. Cons. alcohol, drug abuse and mental health adminstrn. WHO, Washington, Geneva and Copenhagen, 1980—82; chair com. on stewardship Task Force Future, 1980—82, acad. sec., 1981—83, chair work group on sci. issues, 1988—89, chair com. editorship and stewarship of jour., 1984—86, 1990—92; participant APA bilateral exch. in Ea. Europe, 1992; mem. reviewer child psychopathology and treatment rev. com. NIMH, 1994—98; lectr. in field; spkr. in field. Author: Clinical Psycholinguistics, 1979; co-editor: Infant Psychiatry, 1976; editor: Psychoanalysis and Contemporary Science, 1976, Structure in Psychoanalysis, 1991, Affect: Psychoanalytic Perspectives, 1992; co-author: Manual of Panic-Focused Psychodynamic Psychotherapy, 1996, Psychodynamic Treatment of Depression, 2004, Psychodynamic Approaches to the Adolscent with Panic Disorder, 2004; editor Jour. Am. Psychoanalytic Assn., 1984-93; book rev. editor Internat. Jour. Psychoanalysis, 1993-2002; co-editor Research in Psychoanalysis, 1995; contbr. articles to profl. jours. Keynote lectr. Am. Psychoanalytic Assn., Boston, 2003, H. Hartmann Meml. NY Psychoanalytic Inst., 2004. Recipient Wilfred C. Hulse award, N.Y. Coun. Child Psychiatry, 1982, Harry Bakwin Meml. award, NYU, 1982, Heinz Hartmann award, N.Y. Psychoanalytic Inst., 2004; grantee, NIMH, 1976—86. Fellow Am. Acad. Child Psychiatry (sec. 1981-83), Am. Psychiat. Assn.; mem. Internat. Acad. Child/Adolescent Psychiatry (chmn. com. 2006), Soc. Profs. Child Psychiatry (chmn. com. on edn. 1982-90), Group for Advancement of Psychiatry (chmn. com. on child psychiatry 1985-90), Am. Bd. Psychiatry & Neurology (com. on child and adolescent psychiatry 1987-93, chmn. 1992-93), N.Y. Psychoanalytic Soc. Jewish. Office: Weill Med Coll Cornell U Payne Whitney Clinic PO Box 140 New York NY 10021-0012 Office Phone: 212-746-5713. E-mail: tshapiro@med.cornell.edu.

SHAPIRO, TODD D., lawyer; b. Plano, Tex., Nov. 22, 1974; s. Howard Shapiro; married. BA in Govt., U. Tex., Austin, 1997, JD, 2000. Bar: Tex. 2000. Asst. dist. atty. Dallas County, 2000—03; ptnr. Shapiro Law Firm, Plano, Tex. Named a Rising Star, Tex. Super Lawyers mag., 2006. Mem.: Dallas Criminal Def. Lawyers Assn., Collin County Bar Assn., Dallas Bar Assn., Tex. Bar Assn. Office: Shapiro Law Firm PO Box 861720 Plano TX 75086 Office Phone: 972-423-0033. E-mail: todd@shapiro-law.net. *

SHAPIRO, VICTOR LENARD, mathematics professor; b. Chgo., Oct. 16, 1924; s. Joseph E. and Anna (Grossman) S.; m. Florence Gilman, Mar. 21, 1948; children: Pamela Sue Shapiro Baer, Laura Fern Shapiro Young, Charles R., Arthur G. BS, U. Chgo., 1947, MS, 1949, PhD, 1952. Mem. faculty Rutgers U., 1952-60, prof. math., 1959-60; mem. Inst. Advanced Studies, Princeton, N.J., 1953-55, 58-59; mem. faculty U. Oreg., Eugene, 1960-64; prof. math. U. Calif., Riverside, 1964—, faculty research lectr., 1978. Author: Topics in Fourier and Geometric Analysis, 1961, Contemporary Mathematics, Vol. 208, 1997, Singular Quasilinearity and Higher Eigen Values, 2001; contbr. articles to profl. jours. and publs. Served with AUS, 1943-46. NSF postdoctoral fellow, 1954-55 Fellow AAAS; mem. Am. Math. Soc., Math. Assn. Am., Am. Soc. Indsl. and Applied Math. Office: U Calif Math Dept Riverside CA 92521-0001 Office Phone: 951-827-3113. Business E-Mail: shapiro@math.ucr.edu.

SHAPIRO, WALTER ELLIOT, columnist; b. NYC, Feb. 16, 1947; s. Salem Seeley and Edith Geraldine (Herwitz) S.; m. Meryl Gordon, Aug. 24, 1980. BA, U. Mich., 1970, postgrad., 1970-71. Reporter Congl. Quarterly, Washington, 1969-70; editor Washington Monthly, 1972-76; spl. asst. U.S. Sec. Labor, Washington, 1977-78; Presdl. speechwriter The White House, Washington, 1979; reporter Washington Post, 1979-83; gen. editor Newsweek, NYC, 1983-87; sr. writer Time Mag., NYC, 1987-93; White House corr. Esquire mag., 1993-97; polit. columnist USA Today, 1995—2004; fellow Joan Shorenstein Ctr. on the Press, Politics and Pub. Policy Kennedy Sch. Govt. Harvard U., Boston, 2005; chief Washington bur. Salon.com, 2006—. Contbg. editor Washington Monthly, 1976—. Author: (book) One-Car Canavan: On the Road with the 2004 Democrats Before America Tunes In", 2003. Leadership fellow Japan Soc., U.S.-Japan, 1991. Mem.: White House Correspondents Assn., Judson Welliver Soc., Author's Guild. Jewish. Avocations: standup comedy, rotisserie baseball. Office: Salon Media Group 3417 1/2 M St NW Washington DC 20007 Home Phone: 212-580-0928; Office Phone: 202-333-5695. Business E-Mail: wshapiro@salon.com.

SHAPIRO, ZALMAN MORDECAI, chemist, consultant; b. Canton, Ohio, May 12, 1920; s. Abraham and Minnie (Pinck) S.; m. Evelyn Greenberg, June 24, 1945; children: Joshua, Ezra David, Deborah Esther. BA, Johns Hopkins U., 1942, MA, 1945, PhD, 1948. Rsch. assoc. Johns Hopkins for Nat. Rsch. Coun., Balt., 1942—45; instr. chemistry Johns Hopkins U., 1946—48; sr. engr. Westinghouse Electric Corp., Pitts., 1948; mgr. phys. chemistry, mgr. chem. metallurgy AEC Bettis Naval Nuc. Power Lab., Westinghouse, West Mifflin, Pa., 1949—56, asst. divsn. mgr. pressurized water reactor divsn., 1956—57; pres., chmn. bd. Nuc. Materials and Equipment Corp., Apollo, Pa., 1957—70, Numec Instruments and Controls Corp., Apollo, 1960—70, Numec Decontamination Corp., Apollo, 1961—70, Isotope & Radiation Enterprises, Israel, 1964—70; pres. Assoc. Tech. and Bus. Consultants, Pitts., 1970—. V.p. Arco Chem. Co., Phila., 1967-70. Contbr. 2 chpts. to books; patentee in field. Mem. Govs. Sci. and Tech. Coun., Harrisburg, 1963-64; cons. Pa. Subcom. on Atomic Energy, Harrisburg, 1970-71; founder, vice-chmn., Ams. for Energy Independence, Washington, 1975—; organizer Project Pacesetter, Allegheny County, 1976. Named hon. fellow Technion Israel Inst. Tech., Haifa, 1988, Disting. Alumnus, Johns Hopkins U., 2002. Fellow Am. Nuc. Soc. (citation of merit); mem. AAAS, Am. Soc. Metals, Am. Chem. Soc., Phi Beta Kappa, Sigma Xi. Avocations: sailing, wood working.

SHAPIRO-MATHES, ANGELA, broadcast executive; BA, St. Peter's Coll. Co-owner Brookville Mktg/Greybark Advt.; owner, oper. several businesses; co-founder, pub. Soap Opera Digest, 1975, Soap Opera Update, 1988; co-prodr. Soap Opera Awards; sr. v.p. mkg. and promotion ABC Daytime, 1995, pres., 1998, Buena Vista Prodns., 2000; pres. ABC Family Channel Walt Disney Co., Burbank, Calif., 2002—03; pres. Fox TV Studios, 2004—. Named one of 100 Most Powerful Women in Entertainment, Hollywood Reporter, 2006. Office: Fox Television Studios Po Box 900 Beverly Hills CA 90213 *

SHAPIROV, SALIZHAN SHAKIROVICH, cosmonaut; b. Uzgen, Kirghizia, Aug. 24, 1964; s. Shakirzhan Sharipov; m. Nadezhda Mavlyanovna Sharipova; 2 children. Grad., Air Force Pilot Sch., 1987; degree in cartography, Moscow State U., 1994. Pilot/instr. Russian Air Force, 1987—90; cosmonaut candidate Y.A. Gagarin Cosmonaut Tng. Ctr., Russia, 1990—92, cosmonaut, 1992—, mission specialist STS-89 8th Shuttle-Mir docking mission, 1998. Office: NASA/Johnson Space Ctr c/o Astronaut Office Houston TX 77058

SHAPO, HELENE S., law educator; b. NYC, June 5, 1938; d. Benjamin Martin and Gertrude (Kahaner) Seidner; m. Marshall S. Shapo, June 21, 1959; children: Benjamin Mitchell, Nathaniel Saul. BA, Smith Coll., 1959; MA in Teaching, Harvard U., 1960; JD, U. Va., 1976. Bar: Va. 1976, U.S. Dist. Ct. (we. dist.) Va. 1977, Ill. 1993. Tchr. Dade County, Miami, Fla., 1960-64; assoc. Robert Musselman & Assocs., Charlottesville, Va., 1976-77; law clk. to presiding justice U.S. Dist. Ct. Va., Charlottesville, 1977-78; asst. prof. law Northwestern U., Chgo., 1978-81, assoc. prof. law, 1981-83, prof. law, 1983—, Perkins-Bauer prof., 1987. Instr. Sweet Briar Coll., Va., 1976-77, U. Va., Charlottesville, 1976-78; vis. fellow Wolfson Coll., Cambridge U., 2001, vis. scholar, 1992; mem. com. law sch. admissions coun./testing and devel., 1983—; cons. in field. Author (with Walter and Fajans): Writing and Analysis in the Law, 1989, 4th edit., 2003; author: (with Marshall Shapo) Law School Without Fear, 1996, 2d edit., 2003; author: Writing for Law Practice, 2004; contbr. articles to legal jours. Recipient award, sect. on legal writing, Assn. Am. Law Schs., 2002, award for disting. achievement, Assn. Legal Writing Dirs., 2005. Mem. ABA, Va. Bar Assn., Assn. of Am. Law Schs. (sect. chairperson 1985—), Women's Bar Assn. Chgo. Office: Northwestern U Sch Law 357 E Chicago Ave Chicago IL 60611-3059 E-mail: h-shapo@law.northwestern.edu.

SHAPO, MARSHALL SCHAMBELAN, lawyer, educator; b. Phila., Oct. 1, 1936; s. Mitchell and Norma (Schambelan) S.; m. Helene Shirley Seidner, June 21, 1959; children: Benjamin, Nathaniel. AB summa cum laude, U. Miami, 1958, JD magna cum laude, 1964; AM, Harvard U., Cambridge, Mass., 1961, SJD, 1974. Bar: Fla. 1964, Va. 1977, Ill. 1993. Copy editor, writer Miami News, Fla., 1958-59; instr. history U. Miami, 1960-61; asst. prof. law U. Tex., 1965-67, asso. prof., 1967-69, prof., 1969-70; prof. law U. Va., 1970-78, Joseph M. Hartfield prof., 1976-78; Frederic P. Vose prof. Northwestern U. Sch. Law, Chgo., 1978—; of counsel Sonnenschein, Nath & Rosenthal, Chgo., 1991-2001. Vis. prof. Juristisches Seminar U. Gottingen (Fed. Republic Germany), 1976; cons. on med. malpractice and tort law reform U.S. Dept. Justice, 1978-79; mem. panel on food safety Inst. Medicine, NAS, 1978-79; vis. fellow Centre for Socio-legal Studies, Wolfson Coll., Oxford, vis. fellow of Coll., 1975, Wolfson Coll., Cambridge, 1992, 2001; mem. Ctr. for Advanced Studies, U. Va., 1976-77; cons. Pres.'s Commn. for Study of Ethical Problems in Medicine and Biomed. and Behavioral Rsch., 1980-81; reporter Spl. Com. on Tort Liability System Am. Bar Assn., 1980-84; del. leader People to People Citizen Amb. program delegation to East Asia Tort and Ins. Law, 1986; lectr. appellate judges' seminars ABA, 1977, 83, 90; reporter symposium on legal and sci. perspectives on causation, 1990; advisor Restatement of the Law, Third, Torts: Products Liability, 1992-97. Author: Towards a Jurisprudence of Injury, 1984, Tort and Compensation Law, 1976, The Duty to Act: Tort Law, Power and Public Policy, 1978, A Nation of Guinea Pigs, 1979, Products Liability, 1980, Public Regulation of Dangerous Products, 1980, The Law of Products Liability, 1987, Tort and Injury Law, 1990, (with Richard Peltz) 3d edit., 2006, The Law of Products Liability, 2 vols., 2d edit., 1990, 4th edit., 2001, supplements, 1991, 92, 93, 95, 96, 97, 98, 99, 2002, 03, 04, 05, 06, Products Liability and the Search for Justice, 1993, (with Helene Shapo) Law School Without Fear, 1996, 2d edit., 2002, Basic Principles of Tort Law, 1999, 2d edit., 2003, Tort Law and Culture, 2003, Compensation for Victims or Terror, 2005; (with Page Keeton) Products and the Consumer: Deceptive Practices, 1972, Products and the Consumer: Defective and Dangerous Products, 1970, (with D. Jacobson & A.N. Weber) International e-Commerce: Business & Legal Issues, 2001, (with G. Hernandez & others) eBusiness & Insurance, 2001, Concise Hornbook on Tort Law, 2003; mem. editl. bd. Jour. Consumer Policy, 1980-88, Products Liability Law Jour.; author: A Representational Theory of Consumer Protection: Doctrine, Function and Legal Liability for Product Disappointment, 1975; mem. adv. bd. Loyola Consumer Law Reporter; contbr. articles to legal and med. jours. Recipient Andrew J. Hecker award Fedn. Ins. and Corp. Counsel, 2001, Robert B. McKay Prof. award Am. Bar Assn., 2005, Disting. Alumnus award U. Miami Sch. Law, 2005; NEH sr. fellow, 1974-75 Mem. Am. Law Inst., Am. Assn. Law Schs. (chmn. torts compensation systems sect. 1983-84, torts round table coun. 1970). Home: 1910 Orrington Ave Evanston IL 60201-2910 Office: Northwestern U Sch Law 357 E Chicago Ave Chicago IL 60611-3059 E-mail: m-shapo@law.northwestern.edu.

SHAPPERT, GRETCHEN C(ECILIA) F(RANCES), prosecutor, lawyer; b. 1956; AB, Duke U.; JD, Washington & Lee U. Bar: 1980. Assoc. Maupin, Taylor, & Ellis, P.A., Raleigh, 1980—81, Tucker, Hicks, Sentelle, Moon, & Hodge, P.A., Charlotte, 1981—83; asst. pub. defender Mecklenburg County, NC, 1983—88, asst. dist. atty., 1988—90; asst. US atty. (we. dist.) NC US Dept. Justice, 1990—2004, acting US atty., 2004—05, US atty. (we. dist.) NC, 2005—. Republican. Office: US Attys Office 227 West Trade St Ste 1650 Charlotte NC 28202 Office Phone: 704-344-6222. *

SHARANSKY, NATAN (ANATOLY SHARANSKY), human rights activist, former Israeli government official; b. Donetsk, Ukraine, Jan. 20, 1948; s. Boris and Ida (Milgrom) Sharansky; m. Avital Stieglitz; children: Rachel, Hana. Grad. in cybernetics, Moscow Phys. Tech. Inst. Computer programmer Moscow Rsch. Inst. for Oil and Gas; assoc. editor The Jerusalem Report, 1990-95; mem. Knesset (Israeli Parliament), 1996—; min. industry & trade Govt. Israel, 1997-99, min. interior, 1999-2000, min. housing and constrn., 2001—03, dep. prime min., 2001—03, min. Jerusalem and Diaspora affairs, 2003—05; chmn. The Israeli Forum for Countering Antisemitism. Founder, chmn., Yisrael B'Aliyavis, 1996-; prof. Brandeis U., Waltham, Mass. Author: Fear No Evil: The Classic Memoir of One Man's Triumph Over a Police State, 1988, The Case for Democracy: The Power of Freedom to Overcome Tyranny & Terror, 2004. Co-founder Moscow Helsinki Watch, 1976; pres. Soviet Jewry Zionist Forum, 1988-96, co-founder, chmn. One Jerusalem, bd. mem. Peace Watch. Named one of 100 Most Influential People of 2005, Time mag.; recipient Congl. Gold Medal of Freedom, US Pres. Ronald Reagan, 1989, Presdl. Medal of Freedom, 2006. Polit. prisoner, USSR, 1977-86. *

SHARAPOVA, MARIA, professional tennis player; b. Nyagan, Russia, Apr. 19, 1987; d. Yuri and Yelena Sharapova. Trained, Bollettieri's Acad., 1996. Prof. tennis player WTA Tour, 2001—; model IMG Modeling Agy., 2003—; winner Wimbledon, 2004. Nominee Laureus World Newcomer Yr., 2004; named Sports-Choice Athlete (Female), Teen Choice Awards, 2006, Acad. Female Athlete of Yr., US Sports Acad., 2006, Whirlpool 6th sense Player of Yr., 2006; recipient Sports-Choice Athlete (Female), Teen Choice Awards, 2007. Achievements include 15 career singles WTA championships; 3 career doubles championships; 4 career ITF Women's Circuit singles titles; first Russian woman to win at Wimbledon, 2004; signed endorsement deals with Parlux Fragrances Inc and Motorola. Avocations: singing, reading, stamp collecting/philately, fashion, Russian music. Mailing: WTA Tour One Progress Plz Ste 1500 Saint Petersburg FL 33701 *

SHARBAUGH, THOMAS J., lawyer; b. June 18, 1947; BS, Pa. State U., 1973; JD, U. Mich., 1976. Bar: Pa. 1976. Ptnr., mem. firm mgmt. com. (ops.) Morgan, Lewis & Bockius LLP, Phila. Mem.: Pa. Bar Assn., ABA (bus. law sect.).

SHARBEL, JEAN M., editor; b. Lansford, Pa. d. Joseph and Star S. BA in Journalism, Hunter Coll. Editl. dir., v.p. Dauntless Books, NYC, 1962-75; editor romance mags., True Confessions mag. Macfadden Holdings, Inc., NYC, 1976-92; freelance editor fiction and non-fiction books, NYC, 1989—. Home: 165 E 66th St New York NY 10021-6132

SHARE, RICHARD HUDSON, lawyer; b. Mpls., Sept. 6, 1938; s. Jerome and Millicent Share; m. Carolee Martin, 1970; children: Mark Lowell, Gregory Martin, Jennifer Share Frolik, Ashley Share Jakubowsky. BS, UCLA, 1960; JD, U. So. Calif., 1963. Bar: Calif. Sup. Ct. 1964, U.S. Dist. Ct. (cen. and so. dists.) Calif., U.S. Supreme Ct. 1974. Field agt. IRS, 1960—63; mem. law divsn., asst. sec. Avco Fin. Svcs., 1963—72; founder Frandzel and Share, A Law Corp., LA, 1972—99, Richard Hudson Share & Assocs., 1999—. Lectr. Nat. Bus. Inst., Creditor's Rights; adj. prof. Loloya Law Sch., 1999. Office: PO Box 1003 Pacific Palisades CA 90272-1003 also: 150 N Santa Anita Ave Ste 530 Arcadia CA 91006-3127 Office Phone: 800-771-0104. E-mail: sharelaw@aol.com.

SHARER, JOHN DANIEL, lawyer; b. Bklyn., Sept. 19, 1950; s. Albert Robert and Alda Loretta (Tapiro) S.; m. Kathleen Gail Donaldson, Feb. 14, 1981; 1 child, Stephanie Erin. AB, Dartmouth Coll., Hanover, NH, 1972; JD, U. Pa., 1975. Bar: Pa. 1975, NJ 1975, DC 1976, NY 1989, Va. 1994. Law clk. Superior Ct. Pa., Hon. Edmund B. Spaeth, Jr., Phila., 1975-76; assoc. Sutherland, Asbill & Brennan, Washington, 1976-82, ptnr., 1982-94; counsel Christian & Barton, L.L.P., Richmond, Va., 1994-95, ptnr., 1996-99; sr. counsel Dominion Resources Svcs. Inc., Richmond, 1999—2001, mng. counsel electric delivery, 2001—06, asst. gen. counsel, 2006—. Faculty Va. State Bar Professionalism Course, 2001—04; mem. Third Dist. Disciplinary Comm. Sect. III, 2003—06; grader Va. State Bar Examination, 2003—; mem. Va. State Bar Coun., 2005—. Bd. dirs. Wakefield Sch., Marshall, Va., 1990-94; pres. Dartmouth Club of Cen. Va., 1997-2003. Fellow Va. Law Found.; mem. Phi Beta Kappa. Republican. Avocations: classical music, judicial biographies, computers, Norfolk and Skye Terriers. Home: 12317 Northlake Ct Richmond VA 23233-6635 Office: 120 Tredegar St PO Box 26532 Richmond VA 23261-6532 Office Phone: 804-819-2271. Business E-Mail: john.d.sharer@dom.com.

SHARER, KEVIN W., medical products executive; b. Clinton, Iowa, Mar. 2, 1948; m. Faye M. Sharer (div.); children: Heather, Keith; m. Carol Sharer. BS in Aero. Engring., US Naval Acad., 1970; MS in Aero. Engring., US Naval Postgraduate Sch., 1971; MBA, U. Pitts., 1982. Commd. lt. to lt. comdr. USN, 1970—78; with AT&T, 1978-82; cons. McKinsey & Co., 1982-84; pres., chief exec. officer GE, Princeton, NJ, 1984-89; exec. v.p., pres. bus. markets divsn. MCI Comm., Washington, 1989—92; pres., COO, bd. dirs. Amgen Inc., Thousand Oaks, Calif., 1992-2000, pres., CEO, 2000—, chmn., 2001—. Bd. dirs. UNOCAL, 3M, Northrup Grumman Corpn., 2003—, US Naval Acad. Found. Chmn. bd. trustees LA County Mus. Natural Hist. Office: Amgen Inc 1 Amgen Ctr Dr Thousand Oaks CA 91320-1799 Office Phone: 805-447-1000. Office Fax: 805-447-1010. *

SHARER, ROBERT JAMES, archaeologist; BA, Mich. State Univ.; PhD, Univ. Pa., 1968. Sally & Alvin V. Shoemaker prof. Univ. Pa., 1972—, curator Am. sect., Mus. Archaeology & Anthropology. Author: Prehistory of Chalchuapa, El Salvador, 1978, Fundamentals of Archaeology, 1979, Quiriqua: A Classic Maya Center and Its Sculptures, 1990, Daily Life in Maya Civilization, 1996; co-author: Archaeological Investigations in the Northern Maya Highlands, Guatemala, 1987, The Ancient Maya, 1994, Discovering Our Past: A Brief Introduction to Archaeology, 1995, Archaeology: Discovering Our Past, 2002, Understanding Early Classic Copan, 2003; co-editor: Olmec and the Development of Formative Mesoamerican Civilization, 1989, River of Gold: Precolumbian Treasures from Sitio Conte, 1992, New Theories on the Ancient Maya, 1992. Fellow: Am. Acad. Arts & Sci. Office: Department of Anthropology University Museum Room 323 3260 South St Philadelphia PA 19104-6398 Office Phone: 215-898-7461. Business E-Mail: rsharer@sas.upenn.edu.

SHARF, STEPHAN, automotive executive; b. Berlin, Dec. 30, 1920; came to U.S., 1947; s. Wilhelm and Martha (Schwartz) S.; m. Rita Schantzer, June 17, 1951. Degree in Mech. Engring., Tech. U., Berlin, Fed. Republic Germany, 1947. Tool and die maker Buerk Tool & Die Co., Buffalo, 1947-50; foreman Ford Motor Co., 1950-53, gen. foreman Chgo., 1953-58; with Chrysler Corp., Detroit, 1958-86, master mechanic Twinsburg stamping plant, 1958-63, mfg. engring. mgr., 1963-66, mrg. prodn. Twinsburg stamping plant, 1966-68, plant mgr. Warren stamping plant, 1968-70, plant mgr. Sterling stamping plant, 1970-72, gen. plants mgr. stamping, 1972-78, v.p. Engine and Casting div., 1978-80, v.p. Power Train div., 1980-81, exec. v.p., mfg., dir., 1981-85, exec. v.p. internat., 1985-86, also bd. dirs.; pres. SICA Corp., Bloomfield Hills, Mich., 1986—. Columnist Ward's Auto World Common Sense mag., 1987—. Bd. dirs. Jr. Achievement, Detroit council Boy Scouts Am.; trustee, v.p. Oakland U. Mem. Soc. Auto Engrs., Detroit Engring. Soc. Clubs: Wabeek Country. Home: 966 Adams Castle Dr Bloomfield Hills MI 48304-3713 Office: SICA Corp President 725 Adams Rd Ste 230 Birmingham MI 48009 Personal E-mail: sharfsteve@yahoo.com.

SHARFSTEIN, HOWARD F., lawyer; b. NYC, Oct. 2, 1945; AB cum laude, Dartmouth Coll., 1967; JD, Harvard U., 1970. Bar: N.Y. 1971, Fla. 1977. Law clk. to Hon. William H. Timbers U.S. Ct. Appeals (2nd cir.), 1970-71; ptnr. Schulte, Roth & Zabel, NYC. Bd. dirs., pres. Mental Health Assn. N.Y. and Bronx Counties, Inc., 1981—; bd. dirs. Met. Jewish Geriatric Ctr., 1989—, pres., trustee and mem. of exec. com., ctrl. Â Â Synagogue NYC, trustee Healthcare Chaplaincy NYC, mem. Dartmouth Coll. Alumni coun., chmn. Dartmouth coll. 35th Reunion Alumni Fund Campaign Bequests & trusts chmn. Dartmouth coll. Class 1967. Mem. ABA, Fla. Bar, NY State Bar Assn. (com. law office econs. and mgmt. 1983—), Assn. Bar City NY (com. law firm mgmt.), Phi Beta Kappa. Office: Schulte Roth & Zabel 900 3rd Ave Fl 19 New York NY 10022-4774 Office Phone: 212-756-2315. Office Fax: 212-593-5955. Business E-Mail: howard.sharfstein@srz.com.

SHARFSTEIN, JOSHUA M., city health department administrator, pediatrician; s. Steven Sharfstein and Margaret Shiling; m. Yngvild Olsen; 2 children. Grad., Harvard, 1991; MD, Harvard Med. Sch., 1996. Pediatrician Children's Nat. Med. Ctr., Mt. Wash. Pediatric Hosp.; sr. public health aide for Rep. Henry A. Waxman Calif.; commr. Balt. Health Dept., 2005—. Office: Balt Health Dept 210 Guilford Ave Baltimore MD 21202

SHARGEL, GERALD L., lawyer; b. New Brunswick, NJ, Oct. 5, 1944; BA, Rutgers U., 1966; JD, Bklyn. Law Sch., 1969. Bar: NY 1969, US Dist. Ct. (ea. and so. dists.) NY 1969, US Ct. Appeals (2nd, 3rd, 5th and 9th cirs.) 1969. Pvt. practice, NYC, 1970—. Faculty mem. Practising Law Inst., 1976—77; adj. assoc. prof. law NYU, 1977—82; mem. adv. bd. NYU Sch. Law, Ctr. for Rsch. in Crime and Justice, 1984—88; practitioner in residence Bklyn. Law Sch. Mem.: ABA, Fed. Bar Coun., NY State Trial Lawyers Assn., NY County Lawyers Assn., Assn. Bar City NY, NY State Bar Assn., Criminal Bar Assn. Office: 570 Lexington Ave 45th Fl New York NY 10022 Office Phone: 212-446-2323. *

SHARICK, MERLE DAYTON, JR., sales executive; b. Bloomington, Ill., May 5, 1946; s. Merle Dayton and Joyce Madeline (Reed) Sharick; m. Cheryl Jean Easterday, Dec. 28, 1966; children: Amber Dawn, Cami Nicole. BA, Southwestern Coll., Winfield, Kans., 1968; MS in Edn., U. Kans., 1970. Tchr., coach Kans. High Schs., Lawrence, Hutchinson, 1968-73, asst. prin., prin. Buhler, Inman, Leoti, 1973-77; auctioneer, real estate salesman R.E.I.B., Inc., Hutchinson, 1977-78; acct. exec. Mortgage Guaranty Ins. Co., Hutchinson, 1978-81, regional sales mgr. Shawnee Mission, Kans., 1981-83, Houston, 1983-86, divsn. risk mgr. Atlanta, 1986-90, regional dir. Charlotte, NC, 1990-93; v.p., mgr. risk mgmt.

Republic Mortgage Ins. Co., Winston-Salem, NC, 1993-99; mgr. S.E. divsn. Sheldon Good & Co. Auctions, Charlotte, 1999-2001; sr. v.p. Infinity Info. Solutions and Gen. Info. Svcs., Chapin, SC, 2001—03; v.p., dir. sales Mortgage Asset Rsch. Inst., Prosperity, SC, 2003—. Sports editor Winfield (Kans.) Daily Couier, 1966—68; owner, operator Riverside Home Style Laundry, South Hutchison, 1975—79; founder, owner Sport Shack, Hutchison, 1977—79; mem. UNBOG adv. group Freddie Mac, 1995—; spkr. in field. Active Rep. support groups, Houston, Atlanta, 1983—. Fellow: Inst. Devel. Ednl. Adminstrs.; mem.: Charlotte Region Comml. Bd. Realtors, Nat. Auctioneers Assn., Nat. Assn. Realtors, Housing Roundtable, Charlotte Mortgage Bankers, Tex. Mortgage Bankers, Fla. Mortgage Bankers, S.C. League Savs. Instns., N.C. Alliance Cmty. Fin. Instns., N.C. Bankers Assn., Mortgage Bankers Carolinas, Ga. Mortgage Bankers, Mortgage Bankers Am., Nat. Assn. Rev. Appraisers and Mortgage Underwriters, Charlotte Touchdown Club, Town Club. Methodist. Office Phone: 803-364-9048. Personal E-mail: msharick@mari-inc.com.

SHARIF, MASOUD, electrical engineer, researcher; b. Tehran, Iran, June 14, 1977; s. Khalilollah Sharif and Azam Hoseini; m. Eram Dadvar, Aug. 4, 2004. BSc, Sharif U., Tehran, 1999—99, MSc, 2001; PhD in Elec. Engring., Calif. Inst. Tech., 2005. Rsch. asst. Calif. Inst. of Tech., Pasadena, 2002—. Cole fellow, Calif. Inst. of Tech., 2001—02. Mem.: IEEE. Achievements include research in wireless communications. Office: MC 136-93 Calif Inst Tech 1200 E California Blvd Pasadena CA 91125 Home Phone: 626-644-6480; Office Phone: 626-644-6480. Office Fax: 626-564-9307. Personal E-mail: masoud@systems.caltech.edu.

SHARIFI, AZALEA A., orthodontist and general dentist; b. Hays, Kans., Mar. 2, 1967; d. Iraj Alagha Sharifi and Sara D. Salehian; m. Ramin Farmand; 1 child, Shayan-Daniel Farmand. DDS, Westfalian U., Muenster, Germany, 1995, MSc in Orthodontics and Dentofacial Orthopedics, 2001; PhD, U. Muenster, 1997; DMD, U. Pa., Phila., 2004. Cert. orthodontics. Orthodontics fellow Clinic for Orthodontics, Osnabrueck, Germany, 1996—98; pvt. practice Collegeville, 2004—. Interdisciplinary cons. dentofacial anomalies and clefts dept. maxillo-facial surgery U. Muenster Dental Sch., 1998—2001, instr., 1998—2001; instr. restorative dentistry dept. U. Pa., 2004—. Translator dentistry articles in internat. jours. Mem.: ADA, Acad. Gen. Dentistry, Montgomery-Bucks (Pa.) Dental Assn., Pa. Dental Assn., German Dental Assn. Avocations: travel, arts, skiing. Office: Market Place at Collegeville 201 S 2nd Ave Collegeville PA 19426 Office Phone: 610-454-7991. Personal E-mail: azaleasharifi@yahoo.com.

SHARIFI, NIMA, oncologist, researcher; s. Mohammad and Roghieh Sharifi. BS, Va. Tech., Blacksburg, 1992—95; MD, U. Pitts., Pa., 1996—2001. Res. Cleve. Clinic Found., Cleve., 1998—99; res., internal medicine Yale New Haven Hosp., Conn., 2001—03. Grantee fellowship, Howard Hughes Med. Inst., 1998, Med. Oncology fellowship, NIH, 2006. Mem.: AAAS, Am. Assn. Cancer Rsch., Am. Soc. Clin. Oncology. Home: 13215 Dairymaid Dr Unit 201 Germantown MD 20874 Office: Nat Cancer Inst Bldg 560 Rm 21-81 Frederick MD 21702

SHARIFOV, ROVSHAN CHINGIZ, lawyer; b. July 19, 1974; BA in Polit. Sci., NYU, NYC, 1997, JD, 2002. Legal aide NY State Atty. Gen.'s Office, NYC, 2001—02; asst. dist. atty. Dist. Atty.'s Office Nassau County, Mineola, NY, 2002—06; mng. ptnr. Sharifov & Russell, LLP, Hempstead, NY, 2006—. Pub. Svc. fellow, NYU, 2001. Mem.: Nassau County Former Asst. Dist. Atty.'s Assn., NY State Trial Lawyers Assn., NY State Bar Assn. Office: Sharifov and Russell LLP 50 Main St Hempstead NY 11550

SHARIFY, NASSER, librarian, educator, writer; b. Tehran, Iran, Sept. 23, 1925; came to U.S., 1953, naturalized, 1972; s. Ebrahim and Eshrat (Saghafy) S.; m. Homayoun Taslimy, June 14, 1950 (div. 1978); children: Sharareh, Shahab. Licencie es Lettres, U. Tehran, 1947; MS, Columbia U., 1954, Dr. L.S., 1958. Editorial staff Teheran jours. Rah-e Now, Jahan-e Now, Saba, Jonb va Jush, 1943-51; translator, announcer All India Radio, 1948-49; librarian, dep. dir. Library of Parliament Iran, Tehran, 1949-53; cataloger Library of Congress, 1954-55; program asst. libraries devel. sect. UNESCO, Paris, 1959-61; acting chief servicing sect. Dept. Edn., 1962-63; dir. gen. Ministry Edn., Tehran, 1961-62; asst. prof. library and info. scis. and internat. edn. U. Pitts., 1963-66; founder, dir. Internat. Library Info. Center, 1964-66; vis. lectr. SUNY Albany Sch. Library Sci., summer, 1966; dir. internat. librarianship and documentation, internat studies and world affairs SUNY, Oyster Bay, 1966-68; dean, prof. grad. sch. library and info sci. Pratt Inst., Bklyn., 1968-87, chmn. inst. research council, 1971-89, disting. prof., dean emeritus sch. computer, info. and library scis., 1987—; pres. B.E.L.T., Inc., internat. planning cons., 1981—. Dir. Grad. Library Tng. Program, UNESCO Mission, Nat. Tchrs. Coll., Tehran, 1960; Iran's Ofcl. del. to UNESCO Conf. Ednl. Pubs., Geneva, 1961, SE Asia Edn. Secs. Conf., Murree, Pakistan, 1961, Internation Conf., on Cataloging Prins., Paris, 1961, CENTO Libr. Devel. Conf., Ankara, Turkey, 1962; chmn. standing com. for preparation reading materials for new literates UNESCO, Tehran, 1961-62; mem. U.S. AID Mission, Turkey, Iran, Pakistan, 1966; dir. Conf. on Internat. Responsibility Coll. and Univ. Librarians, Oyster Bay, 1967; U.S. del. 33d Conf. and Internat. Congress on Documentation, Tokyo, 1967; ALA del. UN Conf. on Non-Govtl. Orgn., 1969; cons. U.S. AID, Conf. on Book Devel., 1967; mem. adv. bd. Ency. Libr. and Info. Scis., 1969—; chmn. Pre-Am. Library Assn. Conf. Inst. on Internat. Libr. Manpower, Edn. and Placement in N.Am., Detroit, 1970; mem. Am. del. Internat. Fedn. Libr. Assn. Conf., Liverpool, Eng., 1971, Budapest, 1972, Grenoble, France, 1973, Washington, 1974, Brussels, 1977, Montreal, 1982, Chgo., 1985, Barcelona, 1992; organzier USAID sponsored Global Info. Village Conf., Rabat, Morocco, Bklyn., N.Y., 1997, spkr., 1997; bldg. cons. Learning Resources Center, Nat. Tchrs. Coll., Iran, 1972-73, cons. campus planning, 1972-73; UNESCO cons. missions to plan and evaluate Nat. Sch. Info. Sci., Morocco, 1973-74, 79-81, 89, 96-; cons. U.S. Info. Agy., Morocco, 1991, 92, 95; chmn. Conf. on Orgn. and Control of Info for Islamic Research, 1982; chmn. bd. cons. to Nat. U. Iran, 1974-75, Pahlavi Nat. Library of Iran, 1975-77; speaker Symposium Internat. sur l' information Economique, Casablanca, Morocco, 1990; inaugural speaker Ctr. Documentation et D'Information Multimedia, Rabat, Morocco, 1995. Author: cataloging of Persian works Including Rules for Transliteration Entry and Description, 1959, Book Production, Importation and Distribution in Iran, Pakistan and Turkey, 1966; Beyond the National Frontiers: The International Dimension of Changing Library Education for a Changing World, 1973; The Pahlavi National Library of the Future, 17 vols., 1976, other books; contbr. to Ency. of Library and Info. Sci., 1969, ALA World Ency. Library and Info. Services, 1980, 86, library jours., 1973—, Bookmark, 1972, Library Education in the Middle East, 1991, Remembering Rangathan: A Sentimental Reflection, 1992; contbr. poetry to various jours. and anthologies, 1947-51, 67, 91-93 lyrics to Iranian motion pictures and recs., 1948-52; works on display at Archieves of Hoover Inst. on War Revolution and Peace, Stanford U.; Contbr. to: film script for motion picture Morad, 1951-52. Trustee Bklyn. Public Library, 1970-82; pres. Maurice F. Tauber Found., 1981—. Recipient Taj (crown) medal and citation for disting. svc. Mohammad Reza Shah Pahlavi, Shah of Iran, 1978, Kaula Gold medal and citation for disting. svc. to internat. librarianship, 1985; named for Annual Nasser Sharify Lecture Series, Sch. of Computer Info. and Libr. Scis., Pratt Inst., 1988—; writings by and about Nasser Sharify are preserved at Archives of Hoover Instn. on wars, revolutions and peace., Stanford U., Stanford, Calif. Mem. ALA (chmn. com. equivalencies and reciprocity 1966-71, mem. UNESCO panel, mem. nominating com. 1970-71, chmn. Pakistan, Iran, Turkey, Morocco, and Middle East Resource panels, internat. libr. edn. com. 1973—, mem. com. internat. libr. schs. div. libr. edn. 1968-72, coord. country resources panels, internat. libr. edn. com. libr. edn. div. 1973-78, Citiation extraordinary and exemplary svc. internat. librarianship 1999, John Ames Humphry OCLC Forest Press award 2004), NY Libr. Assn. (dir. library edn. sect. 1969-72), Pub. Libr. Assn. (task force on internat. relations 1981-86), Am. Assn. Libr. Schs. (chmn. govtl. relations com., 1984-88), Am. Soc. Info. Sci., Spl. Libr. Assn., Internat. Fedn. Libr. Assns. (adv. group libr. edn. 1971-73, v.p. libr. schs. sect. 1973-77). Home: 252 Jericho Tpke Westbury NY 11590-1213 Office: Pratt Inst Sch Info and Libr Sci 200 Willoughby Ave # 4 Brooklyn NY 11205-3899 Office Phone: 212-647-7682. Personal E-mail: nsharify@aol.com. *If I am asked to wash a car, I try to make it spotless. If I am to write a book, I try to make it faultless. But it seems that I always find spots on the shining surface of the car, and faults in many well-written pages of the book. This gives me another reason to live for another day.*

SHARKEY, CATHERINE MOIRA, law educator; b. Balt., May 1, 1970; BA in Economics, summa cum laude, Yale U., 1992; JD, Yale U., 1997; MS in Economics for Devel., Oxford U., 1994. Bar: Md. 1998, DC 2000, NY 2000. Law clk. to Hon. Guido Calabresi US Ct. Appeals (2nd Cir.), New Haven, 1997—98; law clk. to Hon. David H. Souter US Supreme Ct., Washington, 1998—99; Supreme Ct. & appellate litig. assoc. Mayer, Brown Rowe & Maw, NYC, 2000—02, cons., 2002; assoc. prof. law Columbia U., NYC, 2003—07, NYU Sch. Law, 2007—. Rhodes Scholar, 1992—94. Office: NYU Sch Law 40 Washington Sq S New York NY 10012 *

SHARKEY, LEONARD ARTHUR, automobile company executive; b. Detroit, May 21, 1946; s. Percy and Lillian (Peros) S.; m. Irene Johnson, Aug. 9, 1969 (div. Nov. 1991); children: Michelle, Wesley Tucker (step-son). Cert. pvt. pilot. Tool and diemaker Ford Motor Co., Dearborn, Mich., 1965-85, indsl. hazardous substance educator, 1985-86, indsl. health, safety and energy control educator, 1987-88, tool and diemaker leader, 1989—2006; non-fiction author Individual Initiative, Brighton, Mich., 1989—. Author: Journey Into Fear (reprinted title Split Decision, 1997), 1995, Hidden Shadows - An Opening to the Windows of the Mind, 1996. Mem. Nat. Geog. Soc., Nat. Rifle Assn., Boat U.S., Drummond Island Sportsman's Club, Mich. United Conservation Clubs. Avocations: boating, shooting sports, political awareness studies, biblical prophetic studies, theater.

SHARKEY, (JOHN) MICK, biology educator; BS in Biology, Boise State Univ., 1989. Formerly in retail grocery industry; biology tchr. Parma (Idaho) H.S., 1989—. Finalist GenzymeInvitrogen Biotech Educator award, 2007; named Idaho Tchr. of Yr., 2006; named one of nation's top 5 percent of biology tchrs., Dolan DNA Learning Ctr., 2002; recipient John 'Mick' Sharkey Day in Idaho, Feb. 27, 2006, Idaho Gov.; grantee summer fellowship, Cold Spring Harbor Lab., NY. Office: Parma High Sch 908 N 8th Parma ID 83660 Business E-Mail: jsharkey@parmaschools.org. *

SHARKEY, ROBERT EMMETT, lawyer; b. Chgo., Oct. 21, 1942; s. Edward Francis and Catherine Christine (Grundhoefer) S.; m. Phoebe Dadakis, July 28, 1963 (div.); children: Siobhan, Edward, Catherine, James. BA, Georgetown U., 1964, JD, 1967. Bar: Md. 1967, D.C. 1995, U.S. Dist. Ct. Md. 1967, U.S. Ct. Appeals (4th cir.) 1972, U.S. Ct. Appeals (2nd cir.) 1973, U.S. U.S. Supreme Ct. 1973, U.S. Ct. Appeals (fed. cir.) 1986, U.S. Ct. Fed. Claims 1986, D.C. 1995, D.C. Ct. Appeals 1995, U.S. Dist. Ct. D.C. 1996. Mem. staff subcom. fed., state, local rels. Commn. for Re-orgn. Exec. Branch Md. Govt., College Park, 1967; law clerk for Chief Judge Edward S. Northrop U.S. Dist. Ct. Md., Balt., 1967-68; assoc. Gordon, Feinblatt, Rothman, Hoffberger & Hollander, Balt., 1968-74, ptnr., 1974—. Mem. counsel Balt. Hist. Soc., 2000. Mem. Md. Bar Assn. (profl. ethics 1987—, vice chmn. com. profl. ethics 1991-93, chmn. com. profl. ethics 1993), Bar Assn. Balt. City (com. profl. ethics 1984-86), St. Thomas More Soc. Md. (pres. 1982-83), Georgetown U. Alumni Assn. (law alumni rep. 1992), Ice Club Balt. (v.p. 1981-83), Phi Delta Phi. Avocation: figure skating. E-mail: rsharkey@gfrlaw.com.

SHARKEY, THOMAS DAVID, botanist, educator; b. Detroit, Jan. 28, 1953; s. Robert Hugh and Patricia June (Elliott) S.; m. Paulette Marie Bochnig June 21, 1974; 1 child, Jessa Sung. BS in Biology with honors, Mich. State U., 1974, PhD in Botany and Plant Pathology, 1980. Postdoctoral fellow Australian Nat. U., Canberra, 1980-82; assoc. rsch. prof. Desert Rsch. Inst., Reno, Nev., 1982-87; asst. prof. U. Wis., Madison, 1987-88, assoc. prof., 1988-91, prof., 1991—. Assoc. dir. Biolog. Scis. Ctr., Reno, Nev., 1983-87; chmn. dept. botany U. Wis., Madison, 1992-94; dir. Inst. Cross-Coll. Biology Edn. Editor: Trace Gas Emissions from Plants, 1991, Photosynthesis: Physiology and Metabolism, 2000; contbr. more than 160 articles to profl. peer-reviewed jours. Mem.: AAAS, Internat. Soc. Photosynthesis Rsch., Am. Soc. Plant Biologists. Home: 5901 S Highlands Ave Madison WI 53705-1108 Office: Univ Wis Dept Botany 430 Lincoln Dr Madison WI 53706-1313 Office Phone: 608-262-6802. Business E-Mail: tsharkey@wisc.edu.

SHARKEY, VINCENT JOSEPH, finance company executive; b. Newport, RI, May 25, 1944; s. Vincent Joseph and Dorothy (Auvil) S.; m. Joyce Toomey, Dec. 27, 1969; children: Alison Greeley, Christina Geist, John, Julia. BA in Econs., Yale U., 1966; JD, U. Va., 1971. Bar: N.J. 1971, U.S. Ct. Appeals (3d cir.) 1985. Asst. prosecutor Bergen County Prosecutor's Office, Hackensack, NJ, 1971-72; pvt. practice, Bergen County, 1972-75; ptnr. Riker, Danzig, Scherer, Hyland & Perretti, Morristown, NJ, 1979—2006; sr. v.p. Fidelity Nat. Fin., 2007—. Lt. U.S. Army, 1966-68. Mem. Yale U. Alumni Assn. (pres. Bergen County chpt. 1986-88). Business E-Mail: vincent.sharkey@fnf.com.

SHARLACH, JEFFREY, public relations executive; b. Conn., June 11, 1953; BA, Northwestern U., 1974; JD, NYU, 1977. V.p., client svc. mgr. Burson-Marsteller, NYC, 1982-85; v.p., dir. creative svcs. Carl Byoir & Assocs., NYC, 1986-88; exec. v.p. internat. ops. Rowland Worldwide, NYC, 1988-93; chair, CEO Jeffrey Group, Miami Beach, Fla., 1993—. Mem. Pub. Rels. Soc. Am. Office: Jeffrey Group 1111 Lincoln Rd Ste 800 Miami Beach FL 33139-2451

SHARMA, ANAND, manufacturing executive; BS in Mech. Engring., Roorkee U., India; MS in Bus. Adminstrn., Boston U.; grad. in Adv. Mgmt. Studies, Wharton Sch. Mgmt. With Am. Standard, Inc., v.p. ops.; exec. v.p. Productivity Inc.; co-founder, pres., CEO TBM Consulting Group, Durham, NC, 1991—. Spkr. AME Annual Conf. Author: The Perfect Engine: How to Win in the New Demand Economy by Building to Order With Fewer Resources, 2001; monthly columnist The Manufacturer. Recipient Hero of U.S. Mfg., Fortune, 2001, Donald Burnham Mfg. Mgmt. Award, Soc. Mfg. Engrs., 2002. Office: TBM Consulting Group 4400 Ben Franklin Blvd Durham NC 27704

SHARMA, ARJUN DUTTA, cardiologist; b. Bombay, June 2, 1953; came to U.S., 1981; s. Hari D. and Gudrun (Axelsson) S.; m. Carolyn D. Burleigh, May 9, 1981; chldren: Allira, Eric, Harrison. BSc, U. Waterloo, Ont., Can., 1972; MD, U. Toronto, Ont., 1976. Intern Toronto Gen. Hosp., 1976-77, resident in medicine, 1978-80, St. Michael's Hosp., Toronto, 1980-81; residency medicine Toronto Gen. Hosp., 1977-78; Rsch. assoc. Washington U., St. Louis, 1981-83; asst. prof. pharmacy and toxicology U. Western Ont., London, 1985-89, asst. prof. medicine, 1983-89, assoc. prof. medicine, 1989-90; dir. interventional electrophysiology Sutter Meml. Hosp., Sacramento, 1990-95. Assoc. clin. prof. U. Calif., Davis, 1990—96, clin. prof. medicine, 1997—2002; new product adv. bd. Medtronic, Inc., 2007; mem. rsch. com. Sutter Inst. Med. Rsch., 1991—2007; mem. exec. com. Sutter Heart Inst., 1992; faculty ann. sci. sessions N.Am. Soc. Pacing and Electrophysiology, 1993—97, Heart Rhythm Soc., 2005, Am. Coll. Cardiology, 2005; program dir. Update in Tachyarhythmia Mgmt., Palm Springs, 1996, Pacing Defibrillation and Electrophysiology, Squaw Valley, Calif., 1997; resynchronization co-chair Am. Heart Ann., 2003; mem. atrial fibrillation adv. bd. Guidant Inc.; mem. steering com. David I, II and Rethin Q Clin. Trials; reviewer profl. jours. in field; sci. adv. bd. Cardiomind, 2007; West Coast Physician adv. bd. Boston Sci., 2007—; cons. in field. Reviewer profl. jours., including Circulation, Am. Jour. Cardiology; contbr. articles to profl. publs. Recipient John Melady award, 1972, Dr. C.S. Wainwright award, 1973-75, Rsch. prize Toronto Gen. Hosp., 1979, 80, Ont. Career Scientist award Ont. Ministry of Health, 1983-89; Med. Rsch. Coun. Can. fellow, 1981-83. Fellow ACP, Am. Coll. Cardiology; mem. Am. Fedn. Clin. Rsch., Canadian Cardiovasc. Soc., N.Y. Acad. Scis., Sacramento Eldorado Med. Soc. Avocations: skiing, tennis, stamp collecting/philately, oenology, photography. Office: 3941 J St Ste 260 Sacramento CA 95819-3633 Office Phone: 916-736-2323. E-mail: asharma@rcamd.com.

SHARMA, AVANTI, physician; d. Anil K. and Sunita Sharma. BS in Psychology, Miss. State U., Starkville, 2003; postgrad., St. Matthew's U. Sch. of Medicine, Chgo., 2007—. Physician's asst. North Ctrl. Miss. Regional Cancer Ctr., Greenwood, 2001—03; parenting class instr. Haymarket Ctr., Chgo., 2006; founder, pres., CEO The Anokhi Found., Chgo., 2006—07. Editor, photographer, columnist Vision Newspaper. Named Design Contest Winner, Psi Chi, Miss. State Chpt., 2002—03; named to Shackouls Honors Coll., Miss. State U., 2000—03; recipient Emergent Leader Workshop award, 2001, Academic Achievement award, 2002, 2003; scholar, Nat. Indian Am. Scholarship, 1999; Miss. Eminent Scholars grantee, Miss. State U., 2000—03. Mem.: AMA (life), Psi Chi (life). Home Phone: 662-455-2310. Business E-Mail: info@anokhifoundation.org.

SHARMA, BRAHAMA D., chemistry professor; b. Sampla, Punjab, India, June 5, 1931; naturalized Am. citizen; s. Des Raj and Kesara Devi (Pathak) S.; m. Millicent M. Hewitt, Dec. 22, 1956 (div. 1996); children: Nalanda V. Sharma Bowman, Renuka D; m. Katharine A. McAfee, June 17, 2001. BS with honors, U. Delhi, India, 1949, MS, 1951; PhD, U. So. Calif., 1961. Chemist Govt. Opium Factory, Ghazipur, India, 1951-52; lab. assoc., sci. asst. Nat. Chem. Lab., Poona, India, 1952-55; lab. assoc. U. So. Calif., LA, 1955-61; research fellow Calif. Inst. Tech., Pasadena, 1961-65; asst. prof. chemistry U. Nev., Reno, 1963-64, Oreg. State U., Corvallis, 1965-70, Calif. State U., Northridge, 1973-75, assoc. prof., 1975-76; prof. L.A. Pierce Coll., Woodland Hills, Calif., 1976-96. Part-time assoc. prof. chemistry Calif. State U., L.A., 1973-85, prof., 1985—; vis. assoc. Calif. Inst. Tech., 1979, 82; pres. L.A. Pierce Coll. Senate, 1981-82, chmn. profl. and acad. stds., 1989-92. Contbr. articles to profl. jours. Key leader sci. and tech. 4-H U. Calif., San Luis Obispo County. Grantee E.I. duPont de Nemours, L.A., 1961, NSF, 1967-69. Mem. Am. Chem. Soc. (chmn. edn. com. So. Calif. chpt. 1981-82, rsch. grantee 1965-69), Royal Soc. Chemistry (chartered chemist), Am. Inst. Parliamentarians (sec., adminstr., lt. gov. region VII, exec. lt. gov.), Nat. Assn. Parliamentarians (registered parliamentarian, life), Calif. Assn. Parliamentarians (pub. rels. chmn., statewide edn. chmn. So. area, pres. Calif. Sigma unit), San Luis Obispo Gem and Mineral Club Inc. (pres. 1998, sec. 1999, v.p. 2000). Avocations: playing bridge, reading, history, classical music, crystal models. Office: LA Pierce Coll Chem Dept Woodland Hills CA 91371-0001 E-mail: mercury610@aol.com.

SHARMA, DEVEN, financial information company executive; b. Oct. 20, 1955; BS, Birla Inst. Tech., India; MS, U. Wis.; D in Bus. Adminstrn., Ohio State U. With Anderson Strathclyde, Dresser Industries; ptnr. Booz-Allen & Hamilton, 1988—2002; exec. v.p., global strategy The McGraw-Hill Companies, Inc., 2002—07; exec. v.p., investment svc. & global sales Standard & Poor's, NYC, 2007, pres., 2007—. Bd. dirs. 800-Flowers Inc., CRISIL, The US-China Bus. Coun., Asia Soc. Bus. Coun. Office: Standard & Poor's 55 Water St New York NY 10041 *

SHARMA, DINESH KUMAR, management science educator; arrived in U.S., 1988; s. Phool W. Sharma; m. Preeti R. Rani; children: Amit K., Rajat K. BS in Math., M.D. U., Rohtak, India, 1985; PhD, Chaudhary Charan Singh U., India, 1999. Asst. prof. U. Md. Ea. Shore, Princess Anne, 1999—2002, assoc. prof., 2002—. Contbr. articles to profl. publs. (Received 6 Best Paper awards). Mem.: N.E. Decision Scis. Inst., S.E. Decision Scis. Inst., Decision Sciences Inst., Operational Rsch. Soc. India (life), Acta Ciencia Indica (life), Sigma Beta Delta (hon.; chpt. pres.). Office: U Md Ea Shore Dept Bus Mgmt and Acctg Princess Anne MD 21853 Office Phone: 410-861-6523.

SHARMA, GAURAV, imaging scientist, electrical engineer; b. Dehradun, India, Oct. 12, 1968; came to U.S., 1992; s. Sohan Lal and Santosh Sharma. B Engring., Indian Inst. Tech., Roorkee, India, 1990; M Engring., Indian Inst. Sci., Bangalore, 1990; MS in Applied Math., NC State U., Raleigh, 1995, PhD in Elec. Emgring., 1996. Rsch. engr. Ctr. for Devel. Telematics, Bangalore, 1992; rsch. asst. NC State U., Raleigh, 1992—96, tchg. asst., 1995; summer rsch. intern Webster Rsch. Ctr. Xerox Corp, NY, 1993, 94, 95, mem. rsch. staff, Ditigal Imaging Tech. Ctr. Webster, 1996—2003; assoc. prof. U. Rochester, 2003—. Editor Digital Color Imaging Handbook, 2003; contbr. articles to profl. jours. Mem. IEEE (sr.; referee trans. on signal/image processing/coms. 1995—; chair Rochester sect., 2007), Soc. Imaging Sci. and Tech., Sigma Xi, Phi Kappa Phi, Pi Mu Epsilon. Achievements include 26 patents on digital imaging and image processing; over 20 patents pending. Office: ECE Dept U Rochester PO Box 270126 Rochester NY 14627-0126 Office Phone: 585-275-7313. Business E-Mail: gaurav.sharma@rochester.edu.

SHARMA, MANU, risk management consultant, researcher; s. Sarvesh and Meeta Sharma. BTech. in Mfg. Sci. and Engring., Indian Inst. Tech., New Delhi, 1997; MS in Indsl. Engring., Ga. Inst. Tech., Atlanta, 2002, PhD in Indsl. and Systems Engring., 2004. Exec. engr. Maruti Udyog Ltd., Gurgaon, India, 1997—2000; sr. risk analyst JPMorgan Chase, Columbus, Ohio, 2005—06, risk mgr., 2007—. Contbr. articles to profl. jours. Recipient Inst. Silver medal, Indian Inst. of Tech., Delhi, 1997. Mem.: INFORMS. Avocations: tennis, cricket, fencing. Home: 5431 Bermuda Bay Dr Apt 1A Columbus OH 43235 Office: JPMorgan Chase 1111 Polaris Pky Mail Code OH1-0250 Columbus OH 43240 Home Phone: 404-542-4526; Office Phone: 614-213-6667. Personal E-mail: manu_sharma50@yahoo.com.

SHARMA, MARTHA BRIDGES, geography educator; b. Balt., Feb. 2, 1945; d. Gail and S. Evelyn Bridges; m. Narendra P. Sharma, Aug. 16, 1968; 1 child, Stephanie. BA in Geography, Internat. Studies, U. N.C., 1967; postgrad., U. Hawaii, 1967—68, George Washington U., 1986. Tchr. geography Washington Internat. Sch., 1976—80; dir. records/accounts Washington Internat. Sch., 1981—82, adminstrv. dean, 1983—84; tchr. geography Nat. Cathedral Sch., Washington, 1984—2004. Mem. AP Human Geography Test Devel. Com., 1996—2005; geography cons.; lectr. in field. Joint author: 7-12 Geography: Themes, Key Ideas, and Learning Opportunities, 1989; co-author: The National Council for Geographic Education: The First Seventy-Five Years and Beyond, 1990, Using Internet Primary Sources to Teach Critical Thinking Skills in Geography, 2000; contbg. author: Revisiting the Americas: Teaching and Learning the Geography of the Western Hemisphere, 1992; author: (online) Making Population Real, 2005; contbr. articles to profl. jours. Mem. Nat. Coun. Geographic Edn. (Region VIII awards com. 1988-90, dir. spl. pub.s 1989-92, gender/ethnicity project task force 1991-92, v.p. curriculum and instrn. 2002-04, pres. 2005), Assn. Am. Geographers, Soc. Woman Geographers. Avocations: reading, music, needlecrafts, travel. E-mail: geogsharma@yahoo.com.

SHARMA, PADMANEE, immunologist, oncologist; b. Georgetown, Guyana, June 26, 1970; MD, PhD, Pa. State U., Hershey. Asst. prof. medicine, genitourinary med. oncology and immunology M. D. Anderson Cancer Ctr., Houston, 2004—. Office Phone: 713-792-2830.

SHARMA, RAJ, financial consultant; m. Nalini Sharma; 4 children. Grad. in Commerce, Nizam Coll., India; MBA, Osmania U., Hyderabad, India; MA in Comm., Emerson Coll., Boston, 1983. Cert. investment mgmt. analyzer Inst. Investment Mgmt. Consultants. Film prodr. WGBH; pvt. wealth advisor Sharma Group, sr. v.p. investments Merrill Lynch, Boston. Mem. Am. India Found.; co-chmn. Island Alliance; bd. overseers Boston Mus. Sci. Named one of Am.'s Top Brokers, Registered Rep, 2002—03, Top 100 Brokers, Barron's, 2005—07, Best Fin. Advisors, Boston Mag., 2006. Office: Merrill Lynch One Federal St Fl 24 Boston MA 02110 Office Phone: 617-946-8030. E-mail: raj_sharma@ml.com. *

SHARMA, RAVI IVAN, lawyer; b. Kingston, Ontario, Canada, Dec. 17, 1965; s. Shashi Nath Sharma and Jeanne Alexandra Heintzelman-Sharma. BS in Neurobiology, McGill U., Montreal, 1986; JD, Northeastern U. Sch. Law, Boston, 1990. Bar: NY 1991, Calif. 1991, Mass. 1990, Supreme Ct. USA 1998. Atty., counselor Ravi Ivan Sharma Law Offices, N.Y.C., 1994—. Office: Ravi Ivan Sharma Law Offices 404 Park Ave S 14th Fl New York NY 10016 Office Phone: 212-686-3434 212. Office Fax: 212-202-4598. Business E-Mail: ravi@sharmalaw.com.

SHARMA, SANJIV, cardiologist; s. Sohan Lal and Inder Mohini Sharma; m. Geetanjali Sharma, May 2, 1994; children: Rohan, Rhea. Degree in Premed., Multani Mal Modi Coll., Punjabi U., 1983; MBBS, All India Inst. Med. Scis., New Delhi, India, 1988, MD, 1993. Diplomate Am. Bd. Internal Medicine, 1996, Am. Bd. Cardiovasc. Disease, 1999, Am. Bd. Interventional Cardiology, 2000. Jr. resident All India Inst. Med. Scis., New Delhi, 1989—91, sr. resident, 1992—93; resident Mass. Gen. Hosp., Harvard Med. Sch., Boston, 1993—94, Boston U. Sch. Med., 1994—96; cardiology fellowship West LA VA Med. Ctr., 1996—99; interventional cardiology fellowship Cedars Sinai Med. Ctr., LA, 1999—2000; interventional cardiologist Bakersfield Heart Hosp., Calif., 2000—. Dir. rsch. and edn., chmn. health edn. and CME com. Bakersfield Heart Hosp., Calif., 2000—; instr. clinical medicine UCLA, 2000—. Fellow: Am. Coll. Cardiology, Soc. Cardiac Angiography and Intervention. Achievements include invention of guiding catheter for coronary intervention-patent pending; research in novel strategy for preventing the complication of slow-flow and no-reflow phenomena in saphenous vein graft interventions; first to use of drug eluting stent and filter-wire in vertebral artery percutaneous intervention; research in status paper advocating the use of intracoronary administration of abciximab in percutaneous coronary interventions; intragraft administration of abciximab and verapamil prevents slow-flow and no-reflow phenomena during saphenous vein graft percutaneous coronary interventions. Office: Ctrl Cardiology Medicine Clinic 2901 Sillect Ave Ste 100 Bakersfield CA 93308 Home Phone: 661-665-9973; Office Phone: 661-323-8384. Personal E-mail: sanjiv1122@yahoo.com.

SHARMA, SURENDRA PRASAD, aerospace engineer, scientist; b. Gorakhpur, India, Feb. 3, 1943; came to U.S., 1971; s. Suresh Dutt and Dhanpati (Devi) S.; m. Prabha Durgapal; 1 child, Seema. BS, U. Gorakhpur, 1962; MS in Engring., Peoples' Friendship U., Moscow, USSR, 1968; PhD, MIT, 1978. Scientist Scientists' Pool, Coun. of Sci. and Indsl. Rsch., New Delhi, 1968-70; lectr., Dept. of Aeronautics Indian Inst. Tech., Bombay, India, 1970-71; rsch. asst. MIT, Cambridge, Mass., 1972-78; adj. rsch. prof. aeronautics Naval Postgrad. Sch., Monterey, Calif., 1979; rsch. engr. U. Tenn. Space Inst., Tullahoma, Tenn., 1979-81; sr. engr. Brown & Root, Inc., Houston, 1981-82, Sii Drilco, Smith Internat., Houston, 1982-85; rsch. scientist NASA Ames Rsch. Ctr., Moffett Field, Calif., 1986—. Contbr. articles profl. jours. Mem. PTA, Cupertino, Calif. Assoc. fellow Am. Inst. Aeronautics and Astronautics; mem. Soc. Petroleum Engrs., IEEE, Sigma Xi (MIT chpt.). Avocations: gardening, classical music. Home: 20309 Silverado Ave Cupertino CA 95014-4437 Office: MS 269-2 NASA Ames Rsch Ctr Moffett Field CA 94035-1000 Home Phone: 408-996-2036; Office Phone: 415-604-3432. E-mail: spsharma@pacbell.net.

SHARMA, SUSHIL K., medical educator; b. Bharmar, India, Dec. 2, 1952; arrived in Can., 1988, naturalized, 2000; s. Shri Ram and Ram Piari Sharma; m. Kusum Sharma, June 27, 1983; 1 child, Aditya. BSc with honors in biophysics, Panjab U., India, 1974; MSc with honors in biophysics, Panjab U., 1976; PhD in neuroscience, All India Inst. of Med. Scis., India, 1986; postgraduate diploma in med. radio tech. (hon.), Bhabha Atomic Rsch Ctr., India, 1978. Rsch. officer All India Med. Inst., New Delhi, 1979—88; rsch. assoc. U. Manitoba, Winnipeg, 1988—93; sr. scientist U. Montreal, Montreal, Canada, 1993—97; deputy dir. Defence Inst. Physiology, New Delhi, 1997; rsch. scientist U. Manitoba, Winnipeg, 1997—2000; assoc. prof. U. ND Sch. Medicine, Grand Forks, ND, 2000—; dir. Cyclotron /microPET Labs. Author: (med. rsch. operation) Reputed Internat. Jours. of Med. Rsch. Certified, 1978. Mem.: Soc. of Neuroscience. Home: 715 N 4oth St 204J Grand Forks ND 58203 Office: Positron Imaging Rsch Lab 501 N Columbia Rd Grand Forks ND 58203 Office Phone: 701-777-6295. Business E-Mail: skumar@medicine.nodak.edu.

SHARMA, TINA, lawyer; b. New Delhi, Sept. 25, 1968; BS, Georgetown U., 1990; JD, Fordham U., 1993. Bar: NY 1994, NJ 1994, Md. 1996, US Dist. Ct. Dist. Md. 1996, US Ct. Appeals 4th Cir. 1996, DC 2005. Shareholder, immigration practice group Jenkens & Gilchrist, P.C., Washington, mng. shareholder Washington DC office. Mem.: ABA, Assn. Am. Lawyers from the Indian Subcontinent, NY State Bar Assn., Md. State Bar Assn., Network of Indian Professionals, Am. Immigration Lawyers Assn. Office: Jenkens & Gilchrist PC Ste 900 901 15th St NW Washington DC 20005-2301 Office Phone: 202-326-1516. Office Fax: 202-326-1555. Business E-Mail: tsharma@jenkens.com.

SHARMAN, RICHARD LEE, telecommunications executive, consultant; b. Warren, Pa., Oct. 23, 1932; s. Scott Albert Sr. and Viola Lena Marie (Kittner) S.; m. Diane Lee Van Patten, Nov. 3, 1973; children: Daria Lee, Deedra Lee; children by previous marriage: Suzanne Annette, Cynthia Lee. BS in Engring. Physics, U. Toledo, 1959; MSEE, Cornell U., 1961. Project engr. advanced electronics ctr. GE, Ithaca, NY, 1959—64, Syracuse, N.Y., 1965-68, mgr. infrared and optics, electronics lab., 1965-68, mgr. info. networks, info. sys. divsn. Bethesda, Md., 1968-73; mgr. comml. analysis Xerox Corp., Rochester, N.Y., 1973-78, mgr. mktg. sys., 1978-80; v.p. bus. sector GTE Corp., Stamford, Conn., 1980-84; v.p. mktg. GTE Mobilnet Inc., Houston, 1984-87, gen. mgr. Tex. region, 1987-90; v.p. ops. GTE Mobilnet Inc. Hdqrs., Houston, 1990-92; pres., owner Mgmt. Consulting Svcs. Co., The Woodlands, Tex., 1993—. Adj. faculty Montgomery Coll., Conroe, Tex., 1997—; mem. Svc. Corps of Ret. Execs., 1998-2003 Contbr. articles to profl. jours. With USCG, 1951-54. Mem. Am. Mktg. Assn. (exec.), Cornell Alumni Assn. (admissions amb.), Tau Beta Pi. Republican. Episcopalian. Avocation: photography. Home and Office: 26 Fernglen Dr The Woodlands TX 77380-3955 Personal E-mail: rshar@sbcglobal.net.

SHARMAN, WILLIAM, professional basketball team executive; b. Abilene, Tex., May 25, 1926; m. Joyce Sharman; children from previous marriage: Jerry, Nancy, Janice, Tom. Student, U. So. Calif. Basketball player Washington Capitols, 1950-51, Boston Celtics, 1951-61; coach LA/Utah Stars, 1968-71, LA Lakers, 1971-76, gen. mgr., 1976-82, pres., 1982-88, spl. cons., 1991—. Author: Sharman on Basketball Shooting, 1965. Named to All Star 1st Team, NBA, 1956-59, 2nd Team, 1953, 55 (game MVP), 60, All League Team, 7 times, named Coach of Yr., 1972, One of Top Players in NBA History, league 50th anniversary, 1997, league leader free-throw percentage, 7 times; named to Basketball Hall of Fame, 1976, Naismith Basketball Hall of Fame (as player), 2004, as coach (3d man ever as both player and coach), 2004; named All-Am., twice; inductee U. So. Calif. Hall of Fame, 1994; Porterville H.S. gymnasium renamed in his honor, 1997; recipient John Wooden All-Time All-Am. award, 2003.

SHAROFF, LEIGHSA, nursing educator, researcher; d. Burton and Geraldine Sharoff; 1 child, Brody. BSN, Adelphi U., NY, 1983; MSN, Hunter Coll., NY, 1995; EdD, Columbia U., NYC, 2004. RN NY State Licensing, 1983, cert. psychiatric nurse practitioner, NY State Licensing, 1996, advanced cert. holistic nurse, Am. Holistic Nurses Assn., 2004. With Columbia U. Med. Ctr., NYC, 1983—84, Cedars Sinai Med. Ctr., LA, 1984—85, NY Hosp. Med. Ctr., NYC, 1985—91, Rockefeller U. Hosp., NYC, 1991—92; prof. nursing LI U., Bklyn., 1999—2004, Hunter Coll., NYC, 2004—. Contbr. articles to jour. Grantee Holistic Nurses Experience with Modalities, PSC-CUNY, 2005, Creative Expression of Holistic Nursing, 2005, Use of PDA's in the Clin. Setting, CUNY, 2005, Increasing PDA use in Nursing Practice, 2007; scholar Academic Fed. Grant Scholarship, CUNY/Hunter Coll., 1993-1995. Mem.: Am. Holistic Nurses Assn. (chair edn. approval com. 2004, Charlotte McGuire Scholarship 1994), Sigma Theta Tau. Office: Hunter Coll 425 E 25th St New York NY 10010 Home Phone: 917-842-7902.

SHARON, YITZHAK YAAKOV, physicist, educator; b. Tel Aviv, Feb. 29, 1936; came to U.S., 1948; s. Abraham Sharon-Schwadron and Dina Freidenberg; m. Sandra Brook, Jan. 13, 1991; 1 child, Dina Avrahama Jennie. AB with highest honors, Columbia U., 1958; MA in Physics, Princeton U., 1960, PhD in Physics, 1966. Asst. Inst. for Advanced Study, Princeton, NJ, 1965-66; asst. prof. Northeastern U., Boston, 1966-72; assoc. prof. Richard Stockton Coll., Pomona, NJ, 1972-75, prof. physics, 1975—, trustee fellow in scis., 2000-01. Cons. Ednl. Svcs., Inc. Phys. Sci. Study Commn., 1962-63; vis. prof. Temple U., Phila., 1970-71, U. Montreal, 1970; vis. fellow Princeton U., 1980-82, 91-92; summer physicist Nat. Bur. Standards, Washington, 1971, Oak Ridge (Tenn.) Nat. Lab., 1969, Lawrence Radiation Lab., Berkeley, Calif., 1968; vis., cons. Rutgers U., 1995—. Contbr. articles to profl. jours. Grantee NSF, N.J. Dept. Higher Edn., Ctr. for Theology and Natural Scis. Mem. Am. Phys. Soc., Am. Assn. Physics Tchrs. (NJ exec. bd., NJ Lifetime Contbn. Physics Edn. award 2005), Sigma Xi, Phi Beta Kappa. Jewish. Home: 19 James Ave Kendall Park NJ 08824-1620 Office: Richard Stockton Coll NJ Dept Physics Pomona NJ 08240 Office Phone: 609-652-4500. Business E-Mail: sharon@physics.rutgers.edu.

SHARP, ALLEN, federal judge; b. Washington, Feb. 11, 1932; s. Robert Lee and Frances Louise (Williams) S.; children: Crystal Catholyn Sharp Bauer, Scarlet Frances Thomas. Student, Ind. State U., 1950-53; AB, George Washington U., 1954; JD, Ind. U., 1957; MA, Butler U., 1986. Bar: Ind. 1957. Practiced in, Williamsport, 1957-68; judge Ct. of Appeals Ind., 1969-73, U.S. Dist. Ct. (no. dist.) Ind., South Bend, 1973—. Served to JAG USAF, Res. Mem.: Ind. Judges Assn., Phi Delta Kappa, Tau Kappa Alpha, Pi Gamma Mu, Blue Key. Republican. Mem. Christian Ch. Club: Mason. Office: US Dist Ct 124 Fed Bldg 204 S Main St South Bend IN 46601-2122

SHARP, ANNE CATHERINE, artist, educator; b. Red Bank, NJ, Nov. 1, 1943; d. Elmer Eugene and Ethel Violet (Hunter) S. BFA, Pratt Inst., Bklyn., 1965; MFA, Bklyn. Coll., CUNY, 1973. Tchr. art Sch. Visual Arts, 1978-89, NYU, 1978, SUNY, Purchase, 1983, Pratt Manhattan Ctr., N.Y.C., 1982-84, Parsons Sch. Design, N.Y.C., 1984-90, Visual Arts Ctr. of Alaska, Anchorage, 1991, Anchorage Mus. Hist. and Art, 1991, 93, 94, 95, U. Alaska, Anchorage, 1994-96, Fashion Inst. Tech., SUNY, 1997-98; lectr. AAAS, The 46th Arctic Divsn. Sci. Conf., U. Alaska, Fairbanks, 1995, Cmty. Ch., Ho-Ho-Ku, N.J., 2005. One-person shows Pace Editions, N.Y.C., Ten/Downtown, N.Y.C., Katonah (N.Y.) Gallery, 1974, Contemporary Gallery, Dallas, 1975, Art in a Public Space, N.Y.C., 1979, Eatontown Hist. Mus., N.J., 1980, N.Y. Pub. Library Epiphany Br., 1988, Books and Co., N.Y., 1989, The Kendall Gallery, N.Y.C., 1990, Alaska Pacific U., Carr-Gottstein Gallery, Anchorage, 1993, Internat. Gallery Contemporary Art, Anchorage, 1993, Art Think Tank Gallery, N.Y.C., 1994, U.S. Geol. Survey, Reston, Va., 1994, Stonington Gallery, Anchorage, 1994, on TV Ltd. Benefit, N.Y.C., 1998-2000; group shows include Arnot Art Mus., Elmira, N.Y., 1975, Bronx Mus., 1975, Mus. Modern Art, N.Y.C., 1975-76, Nat. Arts Club, N.Y.C., 1979, Calif. Mus. Photography, Riverside, 1983-92, Jack Tilton Gallery, N.Y.C., 1983, Lincoln Ctr., N.Y.C., 1983, Cabo Frio Print Biennale, Brazil, 1983, Pratt Graphic Ctr., N.Y.C., 1984, State Mus. N.Y., Albany, 1984, Kenkeleba Gallery, N.Y.C., 1985, Hempstead Harbor Art Assn., Glen Cove, N.Y., 1985, Mus. Mod. Art, Weddel, Fed. Republic of Germany, 1985, Kenkeleba Gallery, N.Y.C., 1985, Paper Art Exhbn. Internat. Mus. Contemporary Art, Bahia, Brazil, 1986, Mus. Salon-de-Provence, France, 1987, Mus. Contemporary Art, Sao Paulo, Brazil, 1985-86, Salon de Provence, France, 1987, Adirondack Lakes Ctr. for Arts, Blue Mountain Lake, N.Y., 1987, Kendall Gallery, N.Y.C., 1988, Exhibition Ctr. Parsons Sch. Design, N.Y.C., 1989, F.M.K. Gallery, Budapest, Hungary, 1989, Galerie des Kulturbundes Schwarzenberg, German Dem. Republic, Q Sen Do Gallery, Kobe, Japan, 1989, Anchorage Mus. History and Art, 1990-91, 94, U. Alaska, Anchorage, 1990, 91, Coos Art Mus., Coos Bay, Oreg., 1990, Spaceship Earth, Mus. Internat. de Neu Art, Vancouver, Can., 1990, Councourse Gallery, Emily Carr Coll. Art and Design, 1990, Nat. Mus. Women in the Arts, Washington, 1991, Visual Arts Ctr. Alaska, 1991, 92, Nomad Mus., Lisbon, Portugal, 1991, Mus. Ostdeutsche Gallery, Regensberg, Germany, 1991, Mcpl. Mus. Cesley Krumlov (So. Bohemia) CSFK, Czechoslovakia, 1991, Böltmiche Dörter Exhbn. Hochstrass 8, Munich, 1992, BBC-TV, Great Britain, U.K., Sta. WXXI-TV, Rochester, N.Y., 1992-93, Site 250 Gallery Contemporary Art., Fairbanks, 1993, Santa Barbara (Calif.) Mus. Art, 1993, The Rochester (N.Y.) Mus. and Sci. Ctr., 1990-94, Space Arc: The Archives of Mankind, Time Capsule in Earth Orbit, Hughes Comm., Divec TV Satellite Launch, 1994, Stonington Gallery, Anchorage, 1994, 95, UAA Art Galley U. Alaska, 1995, Arctic Trading Post, Nome, Alaska, 1995, Allan P. Kikbuarts Ctr. Gallery at the Lawrenceville (N.J.) Sch., 1996, Blue Mountain Gallery, N.Y., 1998, The Book Room, Jersey City, 2000, 01, A.I.R. Gallery, 2002, 03, 04, 05, 06-, others; represented in permanent collections Smithsonian Instn., Nat. Air and Space Mus., Washington, Albright Knox Gallery, Buffalo, St. Vincent's Hosp, N.Y.C., N.Y. Pub. Libr., N.Y.C., U.S. Geol. Survey, Reston, Va., White House (Reagan, Bush adminstrns.), Site 250 Gallery Contemporary Art, Fairbanks, Alaska, Anchorage Mus. History and Art, others; Moon Shot series to commemorate moon landing, 1970-76, Cloud Structures of the Universe Painting series, 1980-86, Am. Landscape series, 1987-89, Thoughtlines, fall 1986, Swimming in the Mainstream with Her, U. Va., Charlottesville; author: Artist's Book - Travel Dreams U.S.A., 1989, Artworld-Welt Der Kunst, Synchronicity, 1989—, Art Think Tank: Projects in Art and Ecology, 1990—, The Alaska Series, 1990—, Portraits in the Wilderness, 1990—, Family History Project J. Lindemann, 2004—; columnist: Anchorage Press, 1995. Sponsor Iditorod Trail Com., Libby Riddles. Tchg. fellow Bklyn. Coll., 1972; Artist-in-residence grantee Va. Ctr. for Creative Arts, 1974, Artpark, Lewiston, N.Y., 1980, Vt. Studio Colony, 1989; recipient Pippin award Our Town, N.Y.C., 1984, certificate of Appreciation Art in Embassy program U.S. Dept. State, 1996. Mem. Mus. Women in Arts, Pratt Inst. Alumni Assn., Internat. Assn. Near-Death Studies. *As an active painter I explore the mysteries of the 21st century space adventure in my American landscapes, painted directly from nature and in planetary landscapes, fantastic pictures of the cosmos. I believe it is in the reconciliation between inner and outer experience, through a personal sense of humor and use of universal symbols that a mystical or cosmic harmony can be expressed in art.*

SHARP, BARRY J., school system administrator; BBA, Coll. William and Mary, 1981. CPA. Dir. fin. and adminstrn. The AES Corp., Arlington, Va., 1986—87, v.p., CFO, 1987—2006, sr. v.p., 1998, exec. v.p., 2001—06, COO, 2002, cons., 2006—; bd. dirs. Imagine Schools, Arlington, Va., 2005—, CFO, 2006—. Bd. mem. Coll. William and Mary Bus. Found. Office: Imagine Schools 1005 N Glebe Rd Ste 610 Arlington VA 22201 Office Phone: 703-527-2600. Office Fax: 703-527-0038.

SHARP, CHRISTINA KRIEGER, retired nursing educator; b. Ft. Montgomery, NY, Aug. 4, 1928; d. Joseph Lewis and Mary Agnes Krieger; m. Andrew Asa Sharp, Jr., Feb. 3, 1957 (dec. Jan. 31, 1969); children: Shawn Patrick, Sharon Paula Zegers. RN, cadet nurse, St. Lukes Hosp., Newburgh, NY, 1948; BS, Coll. William and Mary, 1955; MA, NYU, 1974. RN N.Y. Staff nurse Vets. Hosp., Richmond, Va., 1948—53, Army Hosp., West Point, NY, 1954—56; instr. nursing Orange County CC, Middletown, NY, 1956—57, Santa Rosa (Calif.) Jr. Coll., 1961—62; supr. nursing Vocat. Edn. and Extension Bd., New City, NY, 1957—60; coord. practical nursing program Newburgh Sch. Dist., 1963—83. Cons. N.Y. State Edn. Dept. Nursing, Albany, 1983—84. Mem.: VFW, AAUW (sec. 1999—2001), Am. Fedn. Labor and Congress of Indsl. Orgn., Fla. Educators Assn., N.Y. State United Tchrs. (Cmty. Svc. award 1998), Fla. Alliance Ret. Ams. (bd. mem. 2002—, sec. ctrl. Fla. chpt. 2004—), Fla. Soc. RNs Ret., Inc. (Orlando dist. pres. 1994—97, editor yearbooks 1997—, state pres. 1998—2002, Fla. state coun. 43 pres. 2001—), Widow and Widowers Soc. Ctrl. Fla. (pres. 1999—2002), Orange County Ret. Educators Assn., Tchr. Retirees Fla., Golden Rod Civic Club (bd. dirs. 2001—), Am. Legion Aux. Avocations: travel, opera, ballet, Broadway shows, ice shows. Home: 2735 Mystic Cove Dr Orlando FL 32812-5344 E-mail: tisharp@aol.com.

SHARP, DAN STEVEN, epidemiologist; s. Darrell Dean Sharp and Stella Louise Morrison-Sharp; m. Carol Lee Thomas, Dec. 26, 1996; m. Caroline Stanley Johnson, June 20, 1970 (div. Apr. 16, 1996); children: Sarah Elizabeth, David Henry. BS in Chemistry, U. Redlands, Calif., 1972; MD, U. Calif., Irvine, 1975; MPH, U. Calif., Berkeley, 1984; PhD in Epidemiology, U. Calif., 1987. Board Certified in Public Health and General Preventive Medicine Am. Bd. of Preventive Medicine, 1990, diplomate Nat. Bd. of Med. Examiners, 1977, Physician's and Surgeon's Certificate Bd. of Med. Quality Assurance, State of Calif., 1977, Certificate of Registration as a Visiting Overseas Doctor Gen. Med. Coun., UK, 1989. Flight surgeon US Army, Natick, Mass., 1977—80; sr. med. epidemiologist Med. Rsch. Coun., Cardiff, Wales, 1988—90; dir., Honolulu heart program Nat. Heart, Lung and Blood Inst., 1992—97; assoc. dir. sci. Health Effects Lab., Nat. Inst. for Occupl. Safety and Health, Morgantown, W.Va., 2000—. Contbr. scientific papers. Capt. US Army, 1977—80, Natick, Massachusetts. Mem.: Soc. for Epidemiologic Rsch. Achievements include research in cardiovascular disease in populations. Office Phone: 304-285-6260.

SHARP, DAVID HOWLAND, physicist; b. Buffalo, Oct. 14, 1938; s. Russel Howland and Margaret (Dorries) E.; m. Gloria Evanitsky, Jan. 9, 1982; children: Lisa E., Michelle L.; stepchildren: Brian P. Riepe, Michael A. Riepe. AB, Princeton U., 1960; PhD, Calif. Inst. Tech., 1964. Mem. staff Los Alamos Nat. Lab., N.Mex., 1974—84, fellow, 1984—, group leader complex systems group, theoretical divsn., 2002—04, sr. sci. advisor applied physics divsn., 2002—04, dep. chief sci. officer, 2004—06, chief scientist, 2006—. Vis. fellow Ctr. Theoretical Neurosci., Salk Inst., 1995—98; mem. indsl. adv. bd. Inst. Math. and Its Applications, 2002—, mem. bd. gov., 2007—; mem. N. Mex. Rsch. Coun., 2005—, Coun. on Rsch. U. Calif., 2006—, Nat. Lab. Rsch. Adv. Bd. U. Calif., 2007—. Mem. editl. bd.: Jour. Math. Physics, 1985—87. Recipient def. programs award of excellence, U.S. Dept. Energy, 2001; Postdoctoral fellow, NSF, 1963—64. Fellow AAAS, Am. Phys. Soc.; mem. Am. Math Soc. (mem. editl. bd. Jour. Procs. 1992-2003), Internat. Assn. Math. Physicists, Internat. Soc. for Gen. Relativity and Gravitation, N.Y. Acad. Scis., Soc. Indsl. and Applied Math., Soc. Petroleum Engrs., N.Mex. Acad. Scis. Home: 174 Laguna St Los Alamos NM 87544-2603 Office Phone: 505-667-5266. Personal E-mail: davidandglory@msn.com. Business E-Mail: dcso@lanl.gov.

SHARP, ELAINE CECILE, obstetrician, gynecologist; b. Hoven, SD, Feb. 19, 1952; d. Lewis Ralph and Bernadette Teresa (Bastien) Arbach; m. Walton H. Sharp, Oct. 26, 1979 (div.); m. Shane Daigle, Nov. 1991; 1 child, Sean Patrick Daigle. BA, No. State U., 1974, BS, 1976; MD, U. Tex., Houston, 1985. Diplomate Am. Bd. Ob-Gyn. Pvt. practice, Pensacola, Fla., 1989—. Speaker, chmn. Body Talk, Milton, Fla., 1989—. Mem. Am. Med. Women's Assn., Am. Diabetes Assn., Am. Bus. Women's Assn., Am. Coll. Ob-Gyn, Soc. Laparoendoscopic Surgeons, Fla. Ob-Gyn Soc., Exec. Club (asst. chmn. cancer com.), Flying Physicians Assn., Am. Yankee Assn. Republic. Roman Catholic. Avocations: biking, running, swimming, boating, racquetball. Office: PO Box 70 Jerseyville IL 62052 Office Phone: 618-639-2006. Office Fax: 618-639-0149.

SHARP, J(AMES) FRANKLIN, finance educator, portfolio manager; b. Johnson County, Ill., Sept. 29, 1936; s. James Albert and Edna Mae (Slack) S. BS in Indsl. Engring., U. Ill., 1960; MS, Purdue U., 1962, PhD, 1966, cert. mgmt. acctg., 1979. Chartered fin. analyst, 1980; cert. in fin. mgmt., 1997. Asst. prof. engring., econs. Rutgers U., New Brunswick, NJ, 1966-70; assoc. prof. NYU Grad. Sch. Bus., NYC, 1970-74; supr. bus. research AT&T, NYC, 1974-77, dist. mgr. corp. planning, 1977-81, dist. mgr. fin. mgmt. and planning, 1981-85; prof. fin. Grad. Sch. Bus. Pace U., NYC, 1975-91; chmn. Sharp CFA Rev. & Inst. for Investment Edn., 1987-96, Sharp Seminars, 1996—. Speaker, moderator meetings, 1965—; cons. Sharp Investment Mgmt., 1967—. Contbr. numerous articles to profl. publs.; corr.: Interfaces, 1975-78; fin. editor: Planning Rev., 1975-78. Mem. N.Am. Soc. Corp. Planning (treas. 1976-77, bd. dirs. at large 1977-78), Inst. Mgmt. Sci. (chpt. v.p. acad. 1972-74, chpt. v.p. program 1974-75, chpt. v.p. membership 1975-76, chpt. pres. 1976-77), Internat. Affiliation Planning Socs. (coun. 1978-84), N.Y. Soc. Security Analysts (CFA Rev. 1985-87), Ops. Rsch. Soc. Am. (pres. corp. planning group 1976-82), AAUP (v.p. Pace U. chpt. 1988-90), Theta Xi. Republican. Office: 315 E 86th St Apt 7H New York NY 10028-4740

SHARP, JULIE ERVIN, communications educator; PhD, Vanderbilt U., Nashville, 1987. Prof. English and reading Vol. State C.C., Gallatin, Tenn., 1976—88; assoc. prof. tech. comm. Vanderbilt U., Nashville, 1988—. Comm. cons. Julie Sharp, The Wordsmith, Nashville, 1980—. Contbr. chapters to books, articles to profl. jours. Recipient Tchr. of Month, Vanderbilt Chpt. of Alpha Delta Pi. Mem.: Nat. Coun. Tchrs. of English, Assn. Profl. Comm. Cons., Am. Soc. Engring. Edn., Soc. Tech. Comm. (sr.; pres. mid. Tenn. chpt. 1990—91), Phi Delta Kappa. Office: Vanderbilt Univ VU Station B Box 351604 24th & Garland Nashville TN 37235-1604 Office Phone: 615-322-3700.

SHARP, LEWIS INMAN, museum director, curator; b. NYC, Dec. 22, 1941; BA, Lewis & Clark Coll., 1965; MA, U. Del., 1968, PhD. Asst. curator paintings & sculpture Met. Mus. Art, NYC, 1972—75, assoc. curator, 1975—82, curator, adminstr. Am. Wing, 1982—89; dir. Denver Art Mus., 1989—. Office: Denver Art Mus 100 W 14th Ave Pkwy Denver CO 80204-2749

SHARP, PAUL DAVID, institute administrator; b. Youngstown, Ohio, Nov. 3, 1940; s. Robert Henderson and Kathryn (Tadsen)S.; m. Carole G. Graff, Sept. 16, 1967; children: David Allen, Kathryn Sharp Snyder. BA cum laude, Kenyon Coll., Gambier, Ohio, 1962; MPA, Auburn U., 1974. Commd. 2d lt. USAF, 1962, advanced through grades to col., 1983, comdr. Detachment 1, 7450th Intelligence Squadron Neubruecke, Germany, 1980-83, comdr. 480th Reconnaissance Tech. Group Langley AFB, Va., 1983-85, dir. intelligence systems HQ Tactical Air Command, 1985-86, dep. chief intelligence Tactical Air Command, 1986-88; mgr. operational intelligence group Battelle Meml. Inst., Columbus, Ohio, 1988-89, mgr. fgn. tech. assessment group, 1989-91, mgr. intelligence projects/programs, 1991-92, v.p. bus. devel. fgn. sci. and tech., 1992-95, dir. fgn. sci. and tech. programs, 1995-98; dir. Air Force spl. programs Batelle Meml. Inst., Columbus, Ohio, 1998-99, mgr. spl. programs office, 1999-2000; mgr. Internat. Tech. Assessments Product Line, 2000—. Student career coun. Kenyon Coll., Columbus, 1992—. Trustee Brandywine Assn., Yorktown, Va., 1987, Chase Assn., Powell, Ohio, 1991. Decorated Legion of Merit. Mem. Nat. Mil. Intelligence Assn., Armed Forces Communications and Electronics Assn., Air Force Assn., Retired Officers Assn., Sigma Pi (pres. Lambda chpt. 1961-62). Republican. Episcopalian. Avocations: golf, woodworking, photography, music. Office: Battelle Meml Inst 505 King Ave Columbus OH 43201-2681 Personal E-mail: sharppd@aol.com.

SHARP, PAUL FREDERICK, retired academic administrator, educational consultant; b. Kirksville, Mo., Jan. 19, 1918; s. Frederick J. and L. Blanche (Phares) S.; m. Rosella Ann Anderson, June 19, 1939; children: William, Kathryn, Paul Trevor. AB, Phillips U., 1939; PhD, U. Minn., 1947; LLD (hon.), Tex. Christian U., 1961, Austin Coll., 1978, Drake U., 1980; LHD (hon.), Buena Vista Coll., 1967, U. Nev., Towson State U., 1980, Oklahoma City U., 1996, U. Okla., 1997; LittD (hon.), Limestone Coll., 1971; HHD, Okla. Christian U. Sci. & Arts, 1992. Instr. U. Minn., 1942, 46-47, vis. lectr., 1948; asso. prof. Am. history Iowa State U., 1947-54; prof. Am. history, chmn. Am. Instns. program U. Wis., 1954-57, vis. lectr., 1953, San Francisco State Coll., 1950, U. Oreg., 1955; Fulbright lectr. Am. Instns., univs. Melbourne, Sydney, 1952; pres. Hiram Coll., 1957-64; chancellor U. N.C., Chapel Hill, 1964-66; pres. Drake U., Des Moines, 1966-71, U. Okla., Norman, 1971-78, pres. emeritus, Regents' prof., 1978-88, pres. emeritus, Regents' prof. emeritus, 1988—; disting. prof. history U. Sci. and Arts, Okla., 1990—96. Dir. Am. Coun. on Edn. Insts. for Coll. and Univ. Presidents, 1977-79; vis. lectr. Harvard U. Bus. Sch. summer session, 1970-72. Author: Agrarian Revolt in Western Canada, 1948, Old Orchard Farm, Story of an Iowa Boyhood, 1952, Whoop-Up Country, Canadian American West, 1955; cons. author: Heritage of Midwest, 1958; editor: Documents of Freedom, 1957; contbr. articles to profl. jours. Pres. Norman Cmty. Found., 1995-97, Okla. State Coun. Aging, 1997-99. USN liaison officer His Majesty's Australian Ship, Hobart, 1943-46. With USNR, 1943-47. Recipient Iowa State U. Alumni Fund award, 1952, award of merit Am. Assn. State and Local History, 1955, Silver Spur award Western Writers Am., 1955, Fulbright award to Australia, 1952; named to Okla. Higher Edn. Hall of Fame, 1995; Minn. Hist. Soc. grantee, 1947, 48, Social Sci. Rsch. Coun. grantee, 1949, 51; Ford Faculty fellow, 1954, Guggenheim fellow, 1957. Mem. Phi Beta Kappa, Phi Kappa Phi, Phi Delta Kappa, Pi Gamma Mu, Phi Alpha Theta. Mem. Christian Ch. (Disciples Of Christ). Home: 701 Mockingbird Ln Norman OK 73071-4829

SHARP, PHILLIP ALLEN, biologist, educator; b. Ky., June 6, 1944; s. Joseph Walter and Katherin (Colvin) S.; m. Ann Christine Holcombe, Aug. 29, 1964; children: Christine Alynn, Sarah Katherin, Helena Holcombe. BA, Union Coll., Barbourville, Ky., 1966; PhD, U. Ill., 1969; LHD (hon.), Union Coll., Barbourville, Ky., 1991; DSc (hon.), U. Ky., 1994, Bowdoin Coll., 1995, U. Tel Aviv, Israel, 1996, Albright Coll., 1996; degree (hon.), U. Glasgow, 1998, U. Uppsala, 1999, Thomas Moore Coll., 1999, U. Buenos Aires, 1999, No. Ky. U., 1999, PhD (hon.), 2001. NIH postdoctoral fellow Calif. Inst. Tech., 1969—71; sr. research investigator Cold Spring Harbor (N.Y.) Lab., 1972—74; assoc. prof. MIT, Cambridge, 1974—79, prof. biology, 1979—99, dir. Ctr. Cancer Rsch., 1985—91, head dept. biology, 1991—99, inst. prof., 1999—. Co-founder, bd. dirs. BIOGEN IDEC, 1978—, chmn. sci. bd., 1987—2002, pres. adv. coun. sci. and tech., 1991—97; chmn. GM Cancer Rsch. Found. Awards Assembly, 1994—2007; mem. presdl. appt. Nat.Cancer Adv. Bd. NIH, 1996—2000; mem. sci. bd. Ludwig Inst., 1998—; mem. bd. sci. govs. Scripps Rsch. Inst., 1999—; trustee Mass. Gen. Hosp., 2001—; co-founder, chair of sci. bd. and mem. of bd. dirs. Alnylan Pharm. Inc., 2002—; bd. advisors Polaris Venture Ptnrs., 2002; mem. Corp. Ptnrs. HealthCare Systems, Inc., 2003—; sci. adv. bd. Fidelity Bioscis. Group, 2004—; dir. sci. bd. Sirtris Pharm. Inc., 2005—; co-founder, dir. sci. bd. Magen Pharmaceuticals Inc., 2006—. Mem. editl. bd.: Cell, 1974—95, Jour. Virology, 1974—86, Molecular and Cellular Biology, 1974—85, RNA, 1995—. Trustee Alfred P. Sloan Found., 1995—2004. Co-recipient Nobel Prize in Physiology or Medicine, 1993; named Class of '41 chair, MIT, 1986—87, John D. MacArthur chair, 1987—92, Salvador E. Luria chair, 1992—99; recipient award, Am. Cancer Soc., 1974—79, Eli Lilly, 1980, NAS/US Steel Found., 1980, Howard Ricketts award, U.Chgo., 1985, Alfred P. Sloan Jr. prize, Gen. Motors Rsch. Found., 1986, award, Gairdner Found. Internat., 1986, NY Acad.Scis., 1986, Louisa Horwitz prize, 1988, Albert Lasker Basic Med. Rsch. award, 1988, Dickson prize, U. Pitts., 1990, Fourth Ann. Biotech. Heritage award, 2002, Alumni Achievement award, U. Ill., 2003, Nat. Sci. medal in Biol. Scis., 2004, Winthrop-Sears award, Chemists' Club NY, 2007. Fellow: AAAS, Royal Soc. Edinburgh (hon.); mem.: NAS (councilor 1986, Nat. Medal of Sci. 2004, Double Helix medal 2006), Alfred P. Sloan Mgmt. Soc. of MIT, Corp. Ptnrs. HealthCare Systems, Inc., Inst. Medicine of NAS (elected mem.), Am. Philos. Soc. (elected mem., The Benjamin Franklin medal 1999), European Molecular Biology Orgn. (assoc.), Am. Soc. Biochemistry and Molecular Biology (elected mem. coun.), Am. Acad. Arts and Scis., Am. Soc. Microbiology, NAS Republic of Korea (hon.). Office: MIT Rm E17529B Ctr for Cancer Rsch 40 Ames St Cambridge MA 02139-4307 Business E-Mail: sharppa@mit.edu.

SHARP, RON, secondary school educator; b. Shawnee, Okla., May 15, 1952; s. Halbert K. and Virginia Pauline Sharp; m. Debbie Marie Buckmaster (div.); 1 child, Kara Meli. BA in Social Studies, Southeastern Okla. State U., Durant, 1974; MEd in Polit. Sci., U. Ctrl. Okla., Edmond, 1979; PhD in Polit. Sci., Kensington U., Glendale, Calif., 1988. Cert. tchr. Okla. Instr. social scis. Shawnee (Okla.) Pub. Schs., 1974—. Instr. U.S. Profl. Tennis Assn., Shawnee, 1978—; mem. adv. bd. Pottawatomie County Jail Trust, Shawnee, 2002—06. Author: Clarisa Leflore/Choctaw Princess, 2004. Adv. Nat. Youth Leadership Forum, Washington, 2005; parliamentarian Rep. Party, Pattawatomie, Okla., 1996—99, chmn. precinct, 1996—2004. Named Tennis Coach of Yr., Okla. State Tennis Coaches Assn., 1976, 1977, 1979, 1984, 1996, Nat. Tennis Coach of Yr., Nat. H.S. Athletic Coaches Assn., 1987, All-American Tennis Coach of Yr., 1987, Tchr. of Yr., Shawnee (Okla.) H.S., 1996, 1997, 1998, Masonic Lodge, 1998; recipient Pres.'s award, U.S. Interpreunmenal and Interagency Affairs, 2001, Leadership award, Heritage Found., 2002, Am. Medal Hon., 2002. Mem.: Nat. Coun. Social Studies, Okla. States Tennis Coaches Assn. (pres. 1977—82), U.S. Profl. Tennis Assn. (mentor 1983—), Shawnee Assn. Classroom Tchrs. (legis. liaison 1996—2004). Republican. Bapt. Avocations: tennis, genealogy, politics. Home: 1835 N Oklahoma Shawnee OK 74804 Office: Shawnee High School 1001 N Kennedy Shawnee OK 74801 Office Phone: 405-275-3084.

SHARP, RONALD ALAN, language educator, writer, dean; b. Cleve., Oct. 19, 1945; s. Jack Trier and Florence (Tenenbaum) S.; m. Inese Brutans, June 22, 1968; children: Andrew Janis, James Michael. BA, Kalamazoo Coll., 1967; MA, U. Mich., 1968; PhD, U. Va., 1974. Instr. in English Western Mich. U., Kalamazoo, 1968-70; from instr. to prof. English Kenyon Coll., Gambier, Ohio, 1970—2002, assoc. provost, provost, acting pres., 1998—2003; prof. English, dean of faculty Vassar Coll., Poughkeepsie, NY, 2003—. Dir. Keats Bicentennial Conf., Harvard U., 1995. Author: Keats, Skepticism and the Religion of Beauty, 1979, Friendship and Literature: Spirit and Form. 1986; translator: Teatro Breve (Garcia Lorca), 1979, editor (with Eudora Welty) The Norton Book of Friendship, 1991, (with Nathan Scott) Reading George Steiner, 1994, (with Robert Ryan) The Persistence of Poetry: Bicentennial Essays on John Keats, 1998, Selected Poems of Michael Harper, 2002; co-editor Kenyon Rev., 78-82; contbr. articles to profl. jours. Recipient award for editl. excellence Ohioana Assn., 1980; fellow Nat. Humanities Ctr., 1981, 86, NEH, 1981, 84-87, 93, 94, 96, 98, Ford Found., 1971, Mellon Found., 1980, Danforth Found., 1971, English Speaking Union, 1973, Am. Coun. Learned Socs., 1986. Mem. MLA, NEH (chmn's. adv. group humanities edn. 1987), Wordsworth-Coleridge Assn., Keats-Shelley Assn. Jewish. Office: Dean of Faculty Vassar Coll Box 4 Poughkeepsie NY 12604 Home Phone: 845-471-7435; Office Phone: 845-437-5300. Business E-Mail: sharp@vassar.edu.

SHARP, WALTER L. (GARY SHARP), career military officer; Grad., US Mil. Acad., 1974; MS in Ops. Analysis and Engring., Rensselaer Poly. Inst., 1981; grad., Command and Gen. Staff Coll., 1986, Army War Coll. Advanced through grades to lt. gen. US Army, 2003, platoon leader A Company, later exec. officer, B Company, later S-3 (Air), 1st Bn., 67th Armor, 2d Armored Divsn. Fort Hood, Tex., 1975—77; armor co. comdr. 1st Bn., 67th Armor, 2nd Armored Divsn., Fort Hood, Tex., 1978—80; combat devel. analysis officer Office of Dir. Combat Developments US Army Armor Sch., Fort Knox, Ky., 1981—84; combat devel. officer, Deep Attach Programs Office, Office Dep. Chief of Staff for Ops. & Plans US Army, 1984—85; exec. officer, 2nd Squadron, 11th Armored Cavalry Regiment US Army Europe/Seventh Army, Germany, 1986—88; combat devel. analysis officer, A3 Task Force, Office Chief of Staff US Army, Washington, 1988—89, dir. analysis, Force Devel. Divsn, Office Dep. Chief of Staff for Ops. & Plans., 1989—90; comdr., 7th Cavalry Squadron, 1st Cavalry divsn., Desert Shield/Storm, 1990—93; dir., models & simulations directorate US Army Combined Arms Command, Nat. Simulations Ctr., Fort Leavenworth, 1993—94; comdr., 2d Armored Cavalry Regiment Operation Uphold Democracy, Haiti, 1994—96; exec. officer to comdr.-in-chief UN Combined Forces Command/US Forces Korea, Republic of Korea, 1996—97; asst. divsn. comdr. for maneuver 2nd Infantry Divsn., Camp Red Cloud, Republic of Korea, 1997—98; comdr. 3rd Infantry Divsn. (Mechanized), Fort Stewart, 1999—2001; dep. dir. for Global/Multilateral Issues/Internat. Am. Affairs (J-5) The Joint Staff, Washington, 1998—99, vice dir. for force structure, resources & assessment (J-8), 2001—03, dir. strategic plans and policy (J-5), 2003—05, dir., 2005—. Decorated DSM, Defense Superior Svc. Medal with Oak Leaf Clusters, Bronze Star, Legion of Merit with Oak Leaf Cluster, Meritorious Svc. Medal with 5 Oak Leaf Clusters, Army Commendation Medal, Army Achievement Medal. Office: The Pentagon 300 Joint Staff Washington DC 20318 *

SHARP, WAYNE DAVID, retired military officer; b. Alexandria, Va., Apr. 12, 1968; s. Wilbur Deon and Shirlane Marie Sharp, Margarette C Shelton (Stepmother); m. Elaine Beth Boring, May 15, 1993; 1 child, Jessica LeighAnn. BS, Touro U., Cypress, 2007. Lic. airframe and powerplant FAA/TN, 1991. First sgt. US Army 200th Material Mgmt. Ctr., Kaiserslautern, Germany, 1998—2000; aviation prodn. control ncoic US Army 615th Aviation Support Bn., Fort Hood, Tex., 2000—05; ops. sgt. maj. US Army Sergeants Maj. Acad., Fort Bliss, Tex., 2005—07. Shift leader Woodlawn Fire Dept., Tenn., 1991—95. Sgt. maj. US Army, 1986—2007, Fort Bliss TX. Decorated Legion of Merit Dept. of Army, Bronze Star, US Army Gold Recruiter Badge, Meritorious Svc. medal, Master Aviation Crewmember Badge, Bronze Star, Combat Action Badge 1st Cav. Divsn., Air Assault Badge 101st ABN Divsn. Mem.: Am. Assn. Army Aviation, VFW. Home: PO Box 252 Woodstock VA 22664 Home Phone: 540-477-2303.

SHARP, WILLIAM THOMAS, information technology executive; b. Balt., Sept. 2, 1952; s. George Lewis and Emily Louise Sharp; m. Maryann Sharkey, Mar. 30, 1985; 1 child, Brian William. BA, Pa. State U., University Park, 1975, MS, 1978—2008. Mktg. rep., bus. analyst Hartford Ins. Group, Conn., 1978—81; dist. mgr. IVAC Corp., San Diego, 1982—84; sales rep. Baxter Internat., Sci. Products Divsn., Bedford, Mass., 1984—87, region sales mgr. Edison, NJ, 1987—88, region mgr., 1988—90; v.p., sales and mktg. Heraeus Instruments, Inc., South Plainfield, NJ, 1990—93; gen. mgr., gen. products group Terumo Med. Corp., Somerset, NJ, 1993—94; worldwide dir., molecular biology bus. Life Techs., Inc., Rockville, Md., 1994—98, dir., new bus., 1998—2001; sr. v.p., bus. devel. MWG Biotech AG, Ebersberg, Germany, 2001; v.p., bus. devel. Gentra Sys., Inc., Mpls., 2002—04, Cellomics, Inc., Pitts., 2004—06; sr. v.p., comml. ops. BioProcessors Corp., Woburn, Mass., 2006—. Democrat. Avocations: golf, reading, travel. Office: BioProcessors Corp 12 Cabot Rd Woburn MA 01801 Home Phone: 781-985-2997; Office Phone: 781-305-8872.

SHARPE, CONSTANTINE, engineer, consultant, mathematics professor; b. Bacau, Romania, Aug. 27, 1941; s. Constantin and Elisabeta; m. Antonina Casam-Sharpe, Nov. 10, 1971; children: Christian Tiberius, Patricia Sorina. MSEE in Math., Polytech. U., Bucharest, 1967; MS in Econ., Acad. Econ. Studies, Bucharest, 1974; PhD in Energy Conservation Engring., Acad. Econ. Studies, 1978. Sr. rschr., devel. engr. scientist Ctrl. Rsch. and Design Inst. for Electrotechnics, Bucharest, 1978—89; cons. engr. Engring. Design, Costa Mesa, Calif., 1991—95; h.s. math tchr. Tustin and Santa Ana Unified Sch. Dist., Calif., 1996—99; math. prof. Irvine (Calif) Valley Coll., 1999—2005. Assoc. prof. Polytech. U., 1975—79, Acad. Econ. Studies, 1979—88; math. instr. Nat. U., San Diego, 1997—99; founder Math Master, Costa Mesa, Calif., 1997—. Author: (novels) Running Hope, 1999, Unfamiliar Ground, 2004, Energy Conservation Engineering, vol. I and vol.II; contbr. over 60 articles to profl. jours. Mem.: Mathematical Assn. Am., Internat. Assn. Conservation of Natural Resources and Energy, Assn. Profl. Engrs. and Scientist. Republican. Greek Orthodox. Avocations: writing, politics, history, physics. Address: 170 E 17th St # 207 Costa Mesa CA 92627 Office Phone: 949-515-4710. Personal E-mail: casoumsharpe@adelphia.net.

SHARPE, JAMES SHELBY, lawyer; b. Ft. Worth, Sept. 11, 1940; s. James Henry and Wanzel (Vanderbilt) S.; m. Martha Moudy Holland, June 9, 1962; children: Marthanne Freeman, Caren Sharp, Stephen. BA, U. Tex., 1962, JD, 1965. Bar: Tex. 1965, U.S. Dist. Ct. (no. dist.) Tex. 1966, U.S. Dist. Ct. (ea. dist.) Tex. 1993, U.S. Dist. Ct. (ea. and we. dists.) Ark. 1997, U.S. Ct. Appeals (5th and 6th cirs.) 1982, U.S. Ct. Appeals (fed. cir.) 1983, U.S. Ct. Appeals (10th cir.) 1992, U.S. Supreme Ct. 1972. Briefing atty. for chief justice Supreme Ct. of Tex., Austin, 1965-66; ptnr. Brown, Herman, Scott, Dean & Miles, Ft. Worth, 1966-84, Gandy Michener Swindle Whitaker & Pratt, Ft. Worth, 1984-87; shareholder Sharpe Tillman & Melton, Ft. Worth, 1988—. Adj. prof. polit. sci. Tex. Christian U., Ft. Worth, 1969-79, Dallas Bapt. U., 1987, 1992-94; gen. counsel U.S.A. Radio Network, Internat. Christian Media, Denton Pub. Co. Pres. Ft. Worth-Tarrant County Jr. Bar, 1969-70, bd. dirs., sec., 1968, v.p., 1968-69; head marshal USA-USSR Track and Field Championships, Ft. Worth, USA-USSR Jr. Track and Field Championships, Austin, Tex., Relays, Austin, 1963—, NCAA Nat. Track and Field Championships, 1976, 80, 85, 92, 95, S.W. Conf. Indoor Track and Field Championships, 1987-96, Olympic Festival, San Antonio, 1993, Colorado Springs, 1995; 12 time head marshal S.W. Conf. Track and Field Championships, Big 12 Outdoor Conf. Track and Field Championship, 1997-99, 2001-03, head marshall Olympic Trials in Track and Field, 2000, 04. USA/Mobil Track Championship, 1994, 95; USA Nat. Jr. Track Championship, 1994, 95, 98, 99, USA Track and Field Track Championship, 1997, 2001-03, Master's Nat. Track and Field Nat. Championship, 1996, 98, 2002. Mem. ABA, State Bar of Tex. (dist. 7-A grievance com. 1983-85, com. adminstrn. of justice 1985-92, com. on ct. rules 1992-2003, chmn. 1992-93, 93-94). Baptist. Office: Sharpe & Tillman 6100 Western Pl Ste 1000 Fort Worth TX 76107-4679 Home Phone: 817-731-8511; Office Phone: 817-338-4900. Personal E-mail: utlawman@aol.com.

SHARPE, KATHRYN MOYE, retired psychologist; b. Barnesville, Ga., Nov. 27, 1922; d. Herbert Johnston and Henri Lucile (Winter) Moye; m. William Herschel Sharpe, Mar. 2, 1946; children: William Herschel Jr., Mark Stephens. AB, Piedmont Coll., Demorest, Ga., 1942; MA, U. N.C., 1947; PhD, U. S.C., 1975. Tchr., guidance counselor Charleston (S.C.) Pub. Schs., 1947-66; prof. sociology, chmn. dept. Bapt. Coll. at Charleston (now Charleston So. U.), 1966-88, prof. emeritus, 1988—; ret., 2005. Pvt. practice psychology, Charleston, SC, 1975—2005. Named One of Twelve Outstanding Women in Greater Charleston by The Ctr. for Women; Kathryn Moye Sharpe scholarship given in her honor Bapt. Coll. at Charleston, 1988. Fellow Am. Assn. for Marriage and Family Therapy (approved supr., pres. S.C. div. 1975-77, disting. svc. award S.C. chpt. 1999). Congregationalist. Home and Office: 6 Cavalier Ave Charleston SC 29407-7702

SHARPE, KEITH YOUNT, retired lawyer, writer; b. Hiddenite, NC, July 11, 1930; s. Ruel Yount and Eileen Lois (Lackey) S.; m. Margaret Joyce Land, Aug. 27, 1955 (div.); children: Jonathan, Matthew, Leonora, Felicia. AB, Duke U., 1952; JD, Wake Forest U., 1957, MBA, 1982; MLA, U. NC, Asheville, 2001. Bar: NC 1957. Pvt. practice law, Winston-Salem, NC, 1957-62, 82-94; asst. solicitor Mcpl. Ct. of Winston-Salem, 1958-60; with Pilot Freight Carriers Inc., Winston-Salem, 1962-82, sr. v.p., 1967-76, exec. v.p., 1976—82, also dir.; v.p., dir. Comml. Automotive Co., 1967-76, Terminal Warehouse Corp., 1967-82. Bd. govs. So. Motor Carriers Rate Conf., 1977-81. Served with inf. U.S. Army, 1952-54. Mem. Assn. Transp. Practitioners, Phi Alpha Delta, Theta Chi. Democrat. Episcopalian. Home: 5932 Fox Ridge Ln Winston Salem NC 27104

SHARPE, ROBERT FRANCIS, JR., lawyer, food products executive; b. Long Branch, NJ, Mar. 9, 1952; s. Robert Francis and Audrey Carolyn (Rembe) Sharpe; m. Maria Renna, Sept. 9, 2000; 1 child, Robert Francis III. BA, DePauw U., Greencastle, Ind., 1974; JD, Wake Forest U., Winston-Salem, NC. Bar: NC 1978. V.p. Tyco Internat. Ltd.; with RJR Nabisco Holdings Corp., sr. v.p., gen. counsel; sr. v.p. pub. affairs, gen. counsel, sec. Pepsico Inc., Purchase, NY, 1998—2002; ptnr. Brunswick Group, LLP, 2002—05; exec. v.p. legal & external affairs ConAgra Foods, Inc., Omaha, 2005—. Bd. dirs. Ameriprise Fin. Mem.: ABA, Am. Corp. Counsel Assn., NC Bar Assn. Republican. Episcopalian. Avocations: golf, fishing. Office: ConAgra Foods Inc 1 ConAgra Dr Omaha NE 68102 Office Phone: 402-595-4000. *

SHARPE, ROBERT KENT, writer, director, producer, photographer; b. Chgo., Nov. 17, 1930; s. Byron C. and Helen Lee Sharpe; m. Mary Kahn, 1955 (div. 1971); m. T. Tina Ditta, Apr. 26, 1980; children: Steven W., Sharon E., Jonathan K., Julia A. BA in English, Brown U., 1953. Writer, dir. Ford Found., NYC, 1956-57, CBS, NYC, 1957-58, NBC Spl. Projects Dept., NYC, 1959-61, freelance dir., 1962-63; pres. RKS Devel. Corp., Ardsley, 1963-75, Robert K. Sharpe Prodns., Inc., Ardsley, NY, 1965—, Hastings on Hudson, NY, 1965—. Prodr., writer, dir.: (documentary) Before the Mountain Was Moved, 1969 (awards 1969-70); writer, dir.: (shorts) Night in a Pet Ship, 1959 (awards 1959-60), prodr., writer, dir. (shorts) Pancho, 1966-67 (awards 1966-67), Joe, 1965 (awards 1965), Face of Excellence, 1962, The Forgotten, 1958 (awards 1958-59); screenwriter: (films) WFAT, 1982, The Long Night, 1962, Barbero, 1983, A Dead Issue, 1963, Computer, 1965, A Letter Home, 1965, Squaw Gap Speaking, 1976; dir.: (TV) The Twentieth Century Series, 1962-63, Keep It Cool, Rhodes Scholar, The Jazz of Dave Brubeck, The Songs of Harold Arlen, Fire Brand on Ice - Stan Mikita, Here is New York, Buildings for Business and Government, Call it Courage, Equestrianism, others; staff writer, dir.: (TV) Wisdom Series, 1959-61, The Ordeal of Woodrow Wilson as Told by President Herbert Hoover, The Seven Lively Arts Series, Omibus Series, 1956-57; prodr., dir. (films) The Great Debate, 1963; writer, dir. (films) Light as You Like It, 1958; photographic series Assisi, 1953, Spanish Patterns, 1990, Interplay, 1998, The Unseen, 1999, Changes, 2003, Portugal, 2003, Glimpses of the Gates, 2005, Silent City, 2005. Mem. Am. Soc. Media Photographers, Dirs. Guild Am., Photographic Adminstrs., Inc., Phi Beta Kappa. Democrat. Jewish. Avocations: amateur radio, hi-fi & electronics, wood working. Home and Office: 765 N Broadway Apt 15E Hastings On Hudson NY 10706 Office Phone: 914-478-3434. Personal E-mail: rksharpe@optonline.net.

SHARPE, ROLAND LEONARD, structural engineer, consultant; b. Shakopee, Minn., Dec. 18, 1923; s. Alfred Leonard and Ruth Helen Sharpe; m. Jane Esther Steele, Dec. 28, 1946; children: Douglas Rolfe, Deborah Lynn, Sheryl Anne. BSCE, U. Mich., 1947, MSE, 1949. Registered civil engr., structural engr. Designer Cummins & Barnard, Inc., Ann Arbor, Mich., 1947-48; instr. engring. U. Mich., 1948-50; exec. v.p. John A. Blume & Assocs., engrs., San Francisco, 1950-73; chmn., founder Engring. Decision Analysis Co., Inc., Cupertino, Calif., 1974-87; cons. earthquake engr. Sharpe Structural Engrs., Los Altos, Calif., 1987—. Mng. dir. EDAC, GmbH, Frankfurt, Germany, 1974—82; pres. Calif. Devel. & Engring. Co., Inc., Las Vegas, Nev., 1973—81; mem. nat. earthquake hazard reduction program adv. com. overviewing Fed. Emergency Mgmt. Agy., U.S. Geol. Survey, NSF and Nat. Inst. Stds. and Tech., 1990—93. Author (with J. Blume, E. G. Kost): (book) Earthquake Engineering for Nuclear Facilities, 1971; co-author: DOE Seismic Safety Manual, 1996; contbr. articles to profl. jours. Mem. Planning Commn., Palo Alto, 1955—60; mng. dir. Applied Tech. Coun., Palo Alto, 1973—83; dir. Earthquake Engring. Rsch. Inst., 1972—75, mem.; project dir., editor Tentative Provision Devel. Seismic Regulations Bldgs., 1978; tech. mgr., contbr., editor Data Processing Facilities: Guidelines Earthquake Hazard Mitigation, 1987. With USMC, 1942—46. Recipient citation for contbn. to constrn. industry, Engring. News Record, 1978—79, 1986—87, chmn. U.S. Joint Com. Earthquake Engring., 1982—88, citation for devel. of improvements in structural design and constrn. practices, Applied Tech. Coun., Japan Structural Cons. Assn., 1990. Mem.: ASCE (hon.; chmn. dynamic effects com. 1978—80, exec. com. structural divsn. 1980—84, chmn. 1983, exec. com. structural divsn. 1989—93, mgmt. group B 1989—93, Earnest E. Howard award 1994), Structural Engrs. World Congress (pres. 1995—, chair 1998), Structural Engrs. Assn. Calif. (coll. of fellows dir. 1971—73, chmn. seismology com. 1972—74), Earthquake Engring. Rsch. Inst. (hon.; dir. 1972—75), Structural Engrs. No. Calif. (hon.; dir. 1969—71), Japan Structural Cons. Assn. (hon.), Am. Concrete Inst. (life). Avocations: gardening, hiking, fly fishing. Home: 10320 Rolly Rd Los Altos CA 94024-6568 Office: Sharpe Struct Engrs 10320 Rolly Rd Ste 1 Los Altos CA 94024-6568 Office Phone: 650-948-9095. Personal E-mail: rsharpe3@mindspring.com. *Personal philosophy: One's conduct should be beyond reproach both morally and ethically and I should serve each of my clients to the best of my ability.*

SHARPE, SHANNON, commentator, retired professional football player; b. Chgo., June 26, 1968; Student, Savannah State U. Tight end Denver Broncos, 1990—99, Balt. Ravens, 2000—02, Denver Broncos, 2002—04; commentator NFL Today, CBS, 2004—. Named to Pro Bowl Team, 1992—98, 2001. Achievements include being ranked first in NFL history in recieving yards, receptions, and touchdowns for a tight end; being a member of Superbowl Championship Team, Denver Bronco's, 1997, 1998, Baltimore Ravens, 2000. Office: NFL Today 51 W 52nd St New York NY 10019

SHARPE, WILLIAM FORSYTH, economics professor; b. Cambridge, Mass., June 16, 1934; s. Russell Thornley Sharpe and Evelyn Forsyth (Jillson) Maloy; m. Roberta Ruth Branton, July 2, 1954 (div. Feb. 1986); children: Deborah Ann, Jonathan Forsyth; m. Kathryn Dorothy Peck, Apr. 5, 1986. AB, UCLA, 1955, MA, 1956, PhD, 1961; DHL (hon.), DePaul U., 1997; D (hon.), U Alicante, Spain, 2003, U. Vienna, Austria, 2004. Economist Rand Corp., 1957—61; asst. prof. econs. U. Wash., 1961—63, assoc. prof., 1963—67, prof., 1967—68, U. Calif., Irvine, 1968—70; Timken prof. fin. Stanford (Calif.) U., 1970—89, Timken prof. emeritus, 1989—92, prof. fin., 1993—95, STANCO 25 prof. fin., 1995—99, prof. emeritus, 1999; prin. William F. Sharpe Assocs., 1986—92; chmn. Fin. Engines, Inc., 1996—2003. Author: The Economics of Computers, 1969, Portfolio Theory and Capital Markets, 1970; co-author: Fundamentals of Investments, 1989, 3d edit., 2000, Investments, 6th edit., 1999. With US Army, 1956—57. Recipient Graham and Dodd award, Fin. Analysts' Fedn., 1972, 1973, 1986—88, Nicholas Molodovsky award, 1989, Nobel prize in econ. scis., 1990, UCLA medal, 1998. Mem.: Am. Econ. Assn., Ea. Fin. Assn. (Disting. Scholar award 1991), Western Fin. Assn. (Enduring Contbn. award 1989), Am. Fin. Assn. (v.p. 1979, pres. 1980), Phi Beta Kappa. *

SHARPES, DONALD KENNETH, graduate program educator; b. Yakima, Wash., Nov. 16, 1934; m. Linda Bamberg; June 27, 1964; children: Michael, Mary. AB, Gonzaga U., 1959, MA, 1961, Stanford U., 1967; PhD, Ariz. State U., 1968. Research asst. Stanford U., Palo Alto, Calif., 1966-67; faculty assoc. Ariz. State U., Tempe, 1967-68; sr. program officer U.S. Office Edn., Washington, 1968-73; assoc. prof., dir. Ctr. for Internat. Edn. Va. Poly. Inst. and State U., Blacksburg, 1973-78, Weber State U., Ogden, Utah, 1978—, Utah State U., Ogden, 1978—. Vis. fellow U. Sussex, Lewes, Eng., 1984-85. Author: (with F. English) Strategies for Differentiated Staffing, 1972, An Asian Enquiry, 1986, Education and the US Government, Curriculum Traditions and Practices, International Perspectives on Teacher Education; contbr. articles to profl. jours. Chmn. bd. dirs. Rocky Mountain Symphony Orch., Ogden, 1980-83. Sr. Fulbright scholar, Cyprus, 1985-86, Malaysia, 1976-77, Washington, 1976, 85. Mem.: Exchange (Ogden) (bd. dirs. 1982-84). Avocations: tennis, private pilot. Office: Utah State U Sch Edn Ogden UT 84408-0001

SHARPLES, RUTH LISSAK, communications executive; b. NYC, Feb. 3, 1952; d. Saul and Nettie (Field) Lissak; m. Winston Sharples, June 26, 1981; stepchildren: Hadley, John, Gillian. BA, CUNY, 1973; MFA, Columbia U., 1975. Rschr. Am. Film Inst./Motion Picture Divsn. of Libr. of Congress, Washington, 1977-79; mgr. audio-visual programs Am. Soc. Microbiology, Washington, 1979-82; mgr. video tech. Am. Gas Assn., Arlington, Va., 1982-96; dir. comm. Am. Gas Cooling Ctr., 1996—; exec. asst., gen. counsel Quaker Fabric Corp., Fall River, Mass., 2005—06; exec. office dir. chancellor U. Mass., Dartmouth, 2006—. V.p., corp. sec. Cantab Motors, Ltd., Purcellville, Va., 1988—; corp. sec. Am. Gas Cooling Ctr., Arlington, 1996—. Editor Cool Times Newsletter, 1996-98. Mem. Nat. Trust Historic Preservation, Nature Conservancy, Mass. Audubon Soc., English Heritage, Nat. Trust, Internat. TV Assn. Avocations: hiking, archaeology.

SHARPLES, WINSTON SINGLETON, automobile importer and distributor; b. Springfield, Mass., Oct. 24, 1932; s. Winston Singleton and Carmela (Parrino) S.; m. Jeanette Williams, July 196l (div. Apr. 198l); children: John, Hadley, Gillian; m. Ruth Emily Lissak, June 26, 198l. BA, Harvard Coll., 1953; postgrad. drama, Yale U., 1956-57; MFA, Carnegie Mellon U., 1959; postgrad., Univ. Md., 1978-80. Freelance writer, 1959—; producer, dir. Mon. Valley Playhouse, Charleroi, Pa., 1959, Robin Hood Theater, Arden, Del., 1960-61; pres., film and music editor Synchro-Sound Inc., NYC, 1961-71; prof. CUNY, NYC, 1969-74, Temple Univ., Phila., 1974-76, U. Md., College Park, 1978-79; adminstr. film preservation and documentation Am. Film Inst., Washington, 1976-78; prof. Howard Univ., Washington, 1978-80; pres. Cantab Motors, Ltd., Purcellville, Va., 1984—. Author: (with others) A Primer for Film-Making, 197l—; supr. Am. Film Inst. Catalog of Feature Films, 1960-69, 77; editor, music editor films and cartoons; contbr. articles to profl. jours. and mags. With U.S. Army, 1953-56. Nat. Endowment for the Humanities grantee, 1977. Mem. ASCAP, Archeol. Soc. Va., Am. Studies Assn., Univ. Film Assn. (v.p. l975-76), Soc. for Cinema Studies, Soc. Automotive Engrs., Washington Automotive Press Assn., Morgan Car Club, Land Rover Owners Assn. Va., British Automobile Mfrs. Assn., Harvard Club (N.Y.C.). Democrat. Avocations: forestry, archeology. Office: Cantab Motors Ltd Valley Indsl Park 37251 E Richardson Ln Purcellville VA 20132-3505 Home: 15 Gerrish Rd Rochester MA 02770-1815

SHARPLESS, JOSEPH BENJAMIN, retired county official; b. Takoma Park, Md., Feb. 4, 1933; s. William Raiford and Julia Maude (Rouse) Sharpless; m. Nancy Kathleen Steffen, July 28, 1962 (dec. Feb. 1988); 1 child, Carole Marie. BA, Earlham Coll., 1955; MS, Pa. State U., 1960. Instr. recreation Montgomery County Recreation Dept., Rockville, Md., 1957—58; from program supr. to dir. Recreation and Parks Dept., Livingston, NJ, 1959—70; chief recreation svc. Md.-Nat. Capital Park and Planning Commn. Prince George's County, Riverdale, Md., 1970—77, parks and recreation div. chief, 1977—95; ret., 1995. Mem. bd. regents, instr. Sch. Sports Mgmt. N.C. State U., 1989—92. Contbr. articles to profl. jours. Dir. volleyball Spl. Olympics Inc., 1994—; tech. del. Spl. Olympics World Summer Games, 1995, 1999, 2003, Spl. Olympics World Summer Nat. Games, 2006; trustee U.S. Volleyball Edn. Found., 1976—2005, sec., 1996—2005; nat. volleyball chmn. AAU, 1966—69, 1972; nat. commr. U.S. Volleyball, 1976—81; mem. volleyball games staff 1996 Olympic Games, Atlanta; staff World Volleyball Congress, Atlanta, 1996; v.p. Montpelier Cmty. Assn., South Laurel, Md., 1983—84, pres., 1985; mem. Md. Sports Adv. Com., 1988—92, Md. State Games Commr., 1986—91; volleyball chmn. N.J. assn., 1961—70, Potomac Valley Assn., 1971—73; pres. NJAAU, 1968—70. Named to, Earlham Coll. Athletic Hall of Fame, 2005; recipient Pioneer award, AAU, 1998, Breitkeutz Leadership award, 1972. Fellow: Nat. Recreation Pks. Assn. (life Berman Profl. Citation award Mid-Atlantic Regional Coun. 1995, Disting. Svc. award 1995, Disting. Fellow award 1996); mem.: N.J. Soccer Ofcls. Assn. (sec., treas. 1966—70), Nat. Capitol Area Bd. Volleyball Ofcls. (sec. 1985—89), Sch. and Coll. Soccer Ofcls. Assn. (sec., treas. 1965—70, del. Mid-Atlantic NRPA regional coun. 1969—79), Md. Recreation and Pk. Assn. (v.p. 1975—77, pres. 1977—78, Mem. of the Yr. 1975, citation 1985), N.J. Recreation and Pks. Assn. (sec. 1965, v.p. 1966, pres. 1967), Am. Pk. and Recreation Soc. (bd. dirs. 1977—80, nat. coun., coun. affiliate pres.), Nat. Intercollegiate Soccer Ofcls. Assn. (sec. 1966—68, treas. 1968—70), U.S. Volleyball Assn. (regional commr. 1965—78, nat. ofcl. 1967—96, v.p. 1973—90, bd. dirs. 1973—, exec. com. 1976—80, 1985—89, exec. cons. 1989—2004, exec. com. 1992—96, corp. sec. 1992—96, mng. editor pubs. 1994—98, v.p. 1996—2004, regional commr., referee, scorekeeper emeritus 2000, v.p. 1996—2004, numerous awards). Independent. Mem. Soc. Of Friends. Home: 26205 S Cedarcrest Dr Sun Lakes AZ 85248-7206 Personal E-mail: chessycrab@aol.com.

SHARPLESS, K. BARRY, chemist, educator; b. Phila., Apr. 28, 1941; m. Jan Dueser, Apr. 28, 1965; children: Hannah, William, Isaac. BA, Dartmouth Coll., 1963; PhD, Stanford U., 1968; doctorate (hon.), Dartmouth Coll., 1995, Swedish Royal Inst. Tech., 1995, Tech. U. Munich, 1995, Cath. U. Louvain, Belgium, 1996. Postdoctoral assoc. Harvard U., Stanford U., to 1970, faculty dept. chemistry, 1977-80; faculty MIT, Cambridge, 1970-77, 1980-90; W. M. Keck prof. chemistry Scripps Rsch. Inst. and Skaggs Inst. of Chem. Biology, La Jolla, Calif., 1990—. Recipient Pual Janssen prize for Creativity in Organic Synthesis, Chem. Pioneer award, Am. Inst. Chemists, 1988, Prelog medal, Swiss Fed. Inst. Tech., Zurich, 1988, Scheele medal and prize, Swedish Acad. Pharm. Scis., Tetrahedron prize for Creativity in Organic Chemistry, 1993, King Faisal Internat. prize for sci., 1995, Microbial medal, Kitasato Inst., Tokyo, 1997, Harvey medal, Technion-Israel Inst. Tech., 1998, Carothers award, 1999, John Scott Medal, City of Phila, 2001, Benjamin Franklin medal in chemistry, 2001, Wolf prize in chemistry, Wolf Found., Israel, 2001, Nobel prize in Chemistry, 2001; fellow A. P. Sloan, 1987—88, Guggenheim, 1987—88; scholar Camille and Henry Dreyfus Tchr. Fellow: AAAS, Am. Acad. Arts and Scis., Royal Soc. Chemistry (hon.); mem.: NAS (Award in Chemical Sciences 2000), Am. Chem. Soc. (Creative Work in Synthetic Organic Chemistry award 1983, Harrison Howe award Rochester chpt. 1987, Remsen award Md. sect. 1989, Arthur C. Cope award 1992, Roger Adams award 1997, Richards medal Northeastern sect. 1998, Top 75 Contbrs. to Chem. Enterprise 1998). Office: Scripps Rsch Inst BCC 315 10550 N Torrey Pines Rd La Jolla CA 92037-1000

SHARPNACK, JOHN TRENT, judge; b. Columbus, Ind., May 7, 1933; s. Lew G. Sharpnack and Mary Harvey (Lingle) Moody; m. Helen E. Carroll, Dec. 26, 1960; children: Rosanne, Christopher. BA, U. Cin., 1955, LLB, 1960. Bar: Ohio 1960, Ind. 1963, U.S. Dist. Ct. (so. dist.) Ind. 1963. Atty. antitrust div. U.S. Dept. Justice, Washington, 1960-63; ptnr. Sharpnack, Bigley, David & Rumple, Columbus, 1963-90; judge Ind. Ct. Appeals, Indpls., 1991—, chief judge, 1992—2001. Mem. com. rules of practice and procedure Ind. Supreme Ct., 1986-92. With U.S. Army, 1955-57. Fellow Am. Coll. Trial Lawyers, Am. Bar Found.; mem. Ind. Bar Assn. (chmn. trial sect. 1983-84, chmn. ho. of dels. 1986-87). Home: 9682 W Harrison Ct Columbus IN 47201-4741

SHARPTON, ALFRED CHARLES, JR., minister, political activist; b. Bklyn., Oct. 3, 1954; m. Kathy Lee Jordan, 1980; children: Dominique, Ashley. Student, Bklyn.Coll., 1973—75. Cert. ordained a Rev. 1964. Youth dir. Operation BreadBasket, 1969; founder Nat. Youth Movement, 1971—; road mgr. James Brown concert tours, 1973—80; founder, pres., CEO Nat. Action Network, Inc., Bklyn., 1991—. Candidate NY State Senate, 1978, US Senate, 1988, 92, 94, NYC mayor, 1997, Pres., 2004. Co-author (with Anthony Walton): Go Tell the Pharaoh: The Autobiography of Reverend Al Sharpton, 1996; co-author: (with Karen Hunter) Al on America, 2002. Named one of 100 Most Influential Black Americans, Ebony mag., 2006. Pentecostal. E-mail: info@sharpton2004.org.

SHARPTON, THOMAS, physician; b. Augusta, Ga., July 15, 1949; s. Thomas and Elizabeth (Dozier) S. BA, Northwestern U., 1971; MS, Stanford U., 1973, MD, 1977. Intern Martinez (Calif.) VAMC, 1977-78, resident, 1978-80; mem. staff Kaiser Permanente Med. Group, Oakland, Calif., 1980—; asst. clin. prof. medicine U. Calif., San Francisco, 1994—. Cons. Berkeley (Calif.) Free Clinic, 1977—; chmn. peer review Kaiser Permanente Med. Group, Oakland, 1985-86; clin. mem. faculty U. Calif., San Francisco, 1992, asst. clin. prof., 1994; chair AIDS therapeutics com. No. Calif. Kaiser Hosps., 1996-2000. Mem. Rep. Nat. Com., 1996—, Alameda County Profl. Adv. Com., Oakland, 1984-88, Alameda County AIDS Task Force, Oakland, 1985-88, Alameda County Pub. Health Adv. Com., 2000-. Fellow ACP; mem. Calif. Med. Assn., Alameda-Contra Costa Med. Assn., Am. Soc. Microbiology, Mensa, Sigma Pi Sigma, Phi Beta Kappa. Clubs: Phi Beta Kappa of No. Calif. Republican. Avocation: classical piano. Office: Kaiser Permanente 280 W Macarthur Blvd Oakland CA 94611-5642 Business E-Mail: thomas.sharpton@kp.org.

SHARROCK (WRENTMORE), ANITA KAY, management and program analyst; b. Logan, Ohio, Dec. 3, 1955; d. Lloyd Earl and Gayle Irene (Daubenmier) W. BS, Ohio U., Lancaster, 1978; MS, Ohio U., Athens, 1979; postgrad., Ohio State U., Columbus, 1985, Ctrl. Ohio Tech. Coll., Newark, 1987. Cert. tchr. Vis. lectr. Denison U., Granville, Ohio, 1980; lectr. Ohio State U., Newark, 1980-83; instr. Cen. Ohio Tech. Coll., Newark, 1983-86; substitute tchr. Newark City Schs., 1986-87, Northfork Sch. Dist., Utica, Ohio, 1987, Lakewood Sch. Dist., Hebron, Ohio, 1987; with Kelly Services, Reynoldsburg, Ohio, 1986-87; computer specialist Def. Constrn. Supply Ctr., Columbus, Ohio, 1987—92, DLA Sys. Automation Ctr., 1992—2000, DLA Sys. Integration Office, 2000—04, DLA Info. Ops., Columbus, 2004—06, mgmt. and program analyst, 2006—. Mem. exec. bd. Newark-Licking County Coun. Tchrs. Math., Newark, 1985-88. Mem. Nat. Coun. Tchrs. Math., Ohio Coun. Tchrs. Math., Am. Math. Soc., Assn. for Computing Machinery, Phi Kappa Phi, Kappa Delta Pi. Independent. Methodist. Avocations: swimming, dance, hiking, tv, reading. Home: 103 Ramona Ave Newark OH 43055-1334 Office Phone: 614-692-8347. Business E-Mail: anita.sharrock@dla.mil.

SHARROW, MARILYN JANE, library administrator; b. Oakland, Calif. d. Charles L. and H.Evelyn Sharrow; m. Larry J. Davis. BS in Design, U. Mich., 1967, MALS, 1969. Libr. Detroit Pub. Libr., 1968-70; head fine arts dept. Syracuse U. Librs., NY, 1970-73; dir. libr. Roseville Pub. Libr., Mich., 1973-75; asst. dir. librs. U. Wash., Seattle, 1975-77, assoc. dir. librs., 1978-79; dir. librs. U. Man., Winnipeg, Canada, 1979-82; chief libr. U. Toronto, Canada, 1982-85; univ. libr. U. Calif., Davis, 1985—. Chair bd. North Regional Libr. Facility, 1999—2001; bd. dirs. Press U. Calif., 2005—. Recipient Woman of Yr. in Mgmt. award Winnipeg YWCA, 1982; named Woman of Distinction, U. Calif. Faculty Women's Rsch. Group, 1985. Mem. ALA, Assn. Rsch. Librs. (bd. dirs., v.p., pres.-elect 1989-90, pres. 1990-91, chair sci. tech. work group 1994-98, rsch. collections com. 1993-95, 2000-2002, preservation com. 1997-99, 2003-05, ARL leadership devel. task force 2006-07, chair membership com. 2007—), OCLC-Rsch. Librs. Adv. Com. (vice-chair 1992-93, chair 1993-94), Calif. State Network Resources Libr. Com., Can. Assn. Rsch. Libr. (pres. 1984-85). Office: U Calif Shields Libr 100 NW Quad Davis CA 95616-5292 Office Phone: 530-752-2110. E-mail: mjsharrow@ucdavis.edu. *

SHARRY, JANICE VYN, lawyer; b. Toledo, Aug. 1, 1951; d. John Cameron and Patricia Mae (Hammontree) Vyn; m. Michael Sharry, Aug. 14, 1976; children: Jessica, Greg, Melanie. Grad. cum laude, Knox Coll., 1973; JD magna cum laude, So. Meth. U., 1977. Atty. Haynes & Boone, L.L.P., Dallas, 1977—, head corp. fin. sect., 1989—, ptnr., corp. fin., bd. dir. Rsch. editor Southwester Law Jour. Bd. dirs. Dallas Children's Theatre, 1989-93; edn. com. Greenhill Sch., Dallas, 1990; active Dallas Summer Mus. Guild, 1989—, Dallas Dem. Forum, 1993. Named a Texas Super Lawyer, Tex. Monthly Mag., 2003; named one of Best Lawyers in Dallas, D Magazine, 2003. Mem. ABA (mem. ad hoc com. on form of model simplified indenture, bus. law sect., com. on devels. in bus. fin. 1991—), Tex. Bar Assn.(bus. law sect.), Tex. Bus. Law Found. (bd. trustees 1990—), Dallas Bar Assn., Dallas C. of C. (chair, Executive Women's Roundtable), Phi Beta Kappa, Order of Coif. Presbyterian. Avocations: reading, sports, politics. Office: Haynes and Boone LLP 901 Main St Ste 3100 Dallas TX 75202-3789 Office Phone: 214-651-5562. Office Fax: 214-200-0620. Business E-Mail: janice.sharry@haynesboone.com.

SHARTLE, STANLEY MUSGRAVE, engineering executive, consultant, surveyor; b. Brazil, Ind., Sept. 27, 1922; s. Arthur Tinder and Mildred C. (Musgrave) Shartle; m. Anna Lee Mantle, Apr. 7, 1948; 1 child, Randy. Student, Purdue U., 1947—50. Registered profl. engr., land surveyor. Ind. chief dep. surveyor Hendricks County, Danville, Ind., 1941—42, dep. county surveyor, 1944—50, county engr., surveyor, 1950—54, county hwy. engr., 1975—77; asst. hydrographer Fourteenth Naval Dist., Pearl Harbor, Hawaii, 1942—44; staff engr. Ind. Toll Rd. Commn., Indpls., 1954—61; chief right of way engring. Ind. State Hwy. Commn., Indpls., 1961—75; owner, civil engr. Shartle Engring., Indpls., 1977—89; prin. Parsons Cunningham & Shartle Engrs., Inc., Indpls., 1990—. Right of way engring. cons. Gannett Fleming Transp. Engrs., Inc., Indpls., 1983—88; part-time lectr. Purdue U. Ind. State Hwy. Commn., 1965—67. Author: Shartle Genealogy, 1955, 2d edit., 2005, Musgrave Family History, 1961, 2d edit., 1995, Right of Way Engineering Manual, 1975, (novel) Her Word of Honor, 2001; contbr. articles to profl. jours. Ex-officio mem., charter mem. exec. sec. Hendricks County Planning Commn., 1951—54; mem. citizen adv. com. Hendricks County Subdivision Control Ordinance, 1988—. Named Stanley Shartle Day, Hendricks County, 1997; recipient Outstanding Contbn. award, Henricks County Soil and Water Conservation Dist., 1976. Mem.: Geog. and Land Info. Soc., Internat. Right of Way Assn. (founder chpt. 10), Ind. Toll Rd. Employees Assn. (pres. 1959—60), Nat. Soc. Profl. Surveyors, Ind. Soc. Profl. Land Surveyors (life; bd. dirs. 1979), Am. Congress Surveying and Mapping (life). Avocations: astronomy, genealogy, geodesy.

SHASSIAN, DONALD R., telecommunications company executive; b. Sept. 2, 1955; m. Pamela; children: Brian, Daniel. BSBA, Bucknell U., 1977. Ptnr.-in-charge Arthur Anderson & Co., 1977-93; sr. v.p., CFO So. New England Telecomms. Corp., New Haven, 1993—98; exec. v.p., CFO RSL Communications, Ltd., 1998—2000, COO, 2000—01; ind. cons., 2001—05; CFO Health Net of the Northeast, Inc., Shelton, Conn., 2005—06, Citizens Communications Co., Stamford, Conn., 2006—. Office: Citizens Communications Co Three HIgh Ridge Pk Stamford CT 06905

SHASTEEN, DONALD EUGENE, retired government official, small business consultant; b. Englewood, Colo., Dec. 3, 1928; s. George Donald and Frances True (Meyers) S.; m. Shirley Mae Johnson, Aug. 8, 1954; children: Jon Randolph, Ron Winston, Sherilyn Sue Kosman. BA in Journalism, U. Colo., 1950. Reporter Omaha World-Herald, Des Moines, 1954-58, Lincoln, Nebr., 1958-66; exec. asst. to Senator Carl T. Curtis of Nebr., Washington, 1966-73, adminstrv. asst., 1973-78, to Sen. Gordon J. Humphrey, 1979-80; with transition group Senate Republican Conf., 1980; dep. under sec. for legislation and intergovtl. rels. Dept. Labor, 1981-83, dep. asst. sec. for vets. employment, 1983-85, asst. sec. for vets. employment and tng., 1985-89; small bus. cons. pvt. practice, 1989—. Pres. Shasteen Assocs. Rep. nominee for U.S. Senate Nebr., 1978. Served with U.S. Army, 1951-52. Mem. Am. Legion, VFW, Am. Vets., Disabled Am. Vets., Phi Delta Theta. Republican. Lutheran. Office Phone: 301-983-0264. E-mail: shasteens@juno.com, shasteen@msn.com.

SHASTRY, SURESH, research scientist; s. Shrinivas and Kusum Shastry; m. Sheela Colluray, Feb. 6, 2003. PhD, Ctrl. Food Tech. Rsch. Inst., India, 2000. Post-doctoral fellow U. Tex. S. W. Med. Ctr., Dallas, 2004—06; scientist-1 U. Miss. Med. Ctr., Jackson, Miss., 2006—. Doctoral fellow Coun. Sci. and Indsl. Rsch., 1995—2000; vis. fellow TATA Inst. Fundamental Rsch., Mumbai, India, 2001—02. Contbr. articles to profl. jours. Home Phone: 601-936-4607. Personal E-mail: shastrysuresh@hotmail.com.

SHATILA, AHMAD HUSSAIN, surgeon, oncologist; arrived in U.S., 1970; s. Hussain Ahmad and Yisir Omar Shatila; m. Bonnye Lynn Oliver, June 24, 1972; children: Suzanne, Sarah, David. BS in Biology, Am. U. Beirut, 1965, MD, 1970. Diplomate Am. Bd. Surgery. Resident surgery U. Louisville, 1970—72, SUNY, Syracuse, 1972—75; fellow surg. oncology Luth. Med. Ctr., Cleve., 1975—76, Cleve. Met. Health Med. Ctr., Case We. Res. U., 1976—78; pvt. practice Cleve., 1976—. Asst. clin. prof. surgery Case Western Res. U., Cleve., 1984—; chmn. dept. surgery S.W. Gen. Health Ctr., Middleburg Heights, Ohio, 1989—91, chief surg. oncology, 1990—, co-founder cancer program; pres. med. staff S.W. Med. Corp., 1986—94, 2000—; dir., founder Cleve. Breast Clinic, Middleburg Heights; presenter in field. Contbr. articles to profl. jours. Com. mem. S.W. Cmty. Health Found., Middleburg Heights, 1990—. Fellow: ACS, U.S. Soc. Surg. Oncology; mem.: Ea. Coop. Oncology Group (investigator 1976—2005, mem. breast steering com. 1980—86, vice chair toxicity com. 1983—88, mem. surgery steering com. 1984—87), Ohio State Med. Assn., Am. Cancer Soc. (med. adv. com.), Am. Soc. Clin. Oncology. Muslim. Avocations: golf, photography, boating. Office: Cleve Breast Clinic 18660 E Bagley Rd Cleveland OH 44130 Office Phone: 440-234-2988.

SHATIN, JUDITH, composer, educator; b. Boston, Nov. 11, 1949; d. Leo and Harriet Evelyn (Sommer) S.; m. Michael Kubovy, June 28, 1992. AB, Douglass Coll., 1971; MM, Julliard Sch., 1974; PhD, Princeton U., 1979. Asst. prof. U. Va., Charlottesville, 1979-85, assoc. prof., 1985-92, prof., 1992—, chmn. McIntire dept. music, 1995—2002, William R. Kenan, Jr. prof., 1999—. Dir. Va. Ctr. Computer Music, 1988—. Composer: (orch.) Aura, 1981, (piano concerto) Passion of St. Cecilia, 1985, (flute concerto) Ruah, 1985, (piano trio) View from Mt. Nebo (commd. by Garth Newel Chamber Players), 1985, (piano trio) Ignoto Numine (commd. Monticello Trio), 1986, (flute, clarinet, violin, cello) Secret Ground (commd. by Roxbury Chamber Players), 1990, (soprano and tape) Three Summers Heat, 1989 (Barlow Found. Commn.), (orch.) Piping the Earth (commd. by Women's Philharm.), 1990, (flute and piano) Gabriel's Wing (commd. by Julia Bogorad and the Upper Midwest Flute Assn.), 1990, (flute and electronics) Kairos (Commd. Va. Commn. for the Arts), 1991, (chorus, brass quintet, tympani) We Hold These Truths (commd. U. Va., for Thomas Jefferson's 250th birthday), 1992, (string orch.) Stringing the Bow (commd. Va. Chamber Orch.), 1992, COAL (commd. as part of 2-yr. retrospective of work, sponsored by Lila Wallace- Readers Digest Arts Ptnrs. Program), 1994, (piano and percussion) 1492 (commd. Arioso Ensemble), 1992, (piano) Chai Variations on Eliahu HaNavi, 1995, (flute and guitar) Dreamtigers (commd. Ekko!), 1996, (chorus) Adonai Roi, 1995, (string quartet) Janus Quartet (commd. for the Arcata Quartet), 1994, (string quartet and electronic playback) Elijah's Chariot (commd. Kronos Quartet), 1995, (amplified clarinet with PVC extensions effects processor, foot pedals and playback sys.) Sea of Reeds (commd. F. Gerard Errante), 1997, (chorus and piano) Songs of War and Peace, 1998, (brass quintet) Fantasia sobre el Flamenco, 1998, (piano, cello, percussion) Houdini: Memories of a Conjurer, 1999 (commd. Core Ensemble), (wind quintet and piano) Ockeghem Variations (commd. Hexagon Ensemble), 2000, Run (piano quartet) (commd. Currents) 2001, (SATB chorus) Alleluia, 2001, Singing the Blue Ridge (commd. Wintergreen Performing Arts through Ams. for the Arts), 2002, Animating Democracy Project, Tree Music (commd. U. Va. Art Mus., interactive electronics), 2003, Penelope's Song (viola and electronics), 2003, Amulet (commd. N.Y. Treble Singers, SSA Chorus), 2005, Civil War Memories (commd. Jane Franklin Dance, electronics), 2005, Clave (commd. New Ear, flute, clarinet, saxophone, violin, viola, piano, percussion), 2006, Jabberwocky, 2006 (commd. Va. Glee Club), (amplified cello and electronics) For the Birds, 2006, Why the Caged Bird Sings, 2007. Nat. Endowment for Arts Composer fellow, 1980, 85, 89, 92; recipient award Va. Commn. for the Arts, 1989, 02. Mem. Am. Music Ctr., Am. Women Composers (pres. 1989-93), Am. Composers Alliance (bd. dirs. 1993-98), Internat. Alliance for Women in Music (chair nominating com. 1996-98, adv. bd. 1999-). Business E-Mail: shatin@virginia.edu, asst@judithshatin.com.

SHATKIN, JESS PARKER, psychiatrist; s. Eugene Parker and Joyce Cooper Shatkin; m. Alice Jankell; 2 children. BA in History, U. Calif., Berkeley, 1985; MPH, U. NC, Chapel Hill, 1988; MD, SUNY, Bklyn., 1996. Lic. AM. Bd. Psychiatry and Neurology, 2001. Staff psychiatrist Western Ark. Counseling and Guidance Ctr., Fort Smith, Ark., 2001—03;

med. dir. child psychiatry U. Pitts., Western Psychiat. Inst. and Clinic, 2003—05; dir. edn. and tng. NYU Child Study Ctr., NYC, 2005—. Office: NYU Child Study Ctr 577 First Av New York NY 10016 Office Phone: 212-263-4769.

SHATNER, WILLIAM, actor; b. Montreal, Que., Can., Mar. 22, 1931; s. Joseph and Anne S.; m. Gloria Rosenberg, Aug. 12, 1956 (div. Mar. 1969); three children; m. Marcy Lafferty, Oct. 20, 1973 (div. 1996); m. Nerine Kidd, Nov. 15, 1997 (dec. Aug. 1999); m. Elizabeth Anderson, Feb. 2001. BA, McGill U., 1952. Stage debut, 1952; appeared Montreal Playhouse, summers 1952, 53; played juvenile roles Canadian Repertory Theatre, Ottawa, 1952-53, 53-54; appeared Stratford Shakespeare Festival, Ont., 1954-56; Broadway appearances include Tamburlaine the Great, 1956, The World of Suzie Wong, 1958, A Shot in the Dark, 1961; films include The Brothers Karamazov, 1958, The Explosive Generation, 1961, Judgement at Nuremburg, 1961, The Intruder, 1962, The Outrage, 1964, Dead of Night, 1974, The Devil's Rain, 1975, Star Trek: The Motion Picture, 1979, The Kidnapping of the President, 1979, Star Trek: The Wrath of Khan, 1982, Airplane II: The Sequel, 1982, Star Trek III: The Search for Spock, 1984, Star Trek IV: The Voyage Home, 1986, (dir.) Star Trek V: The Final Frontier, 1989, Star Trek VI: The Undiscovered Country, 1991, National Lampoon's Loaded Weapon, 1992, Star Trek: Generations, 1994, Trekkies, 1997, Free Enterprise, 1998, Shoot or be Shot, 2000, Groom Lake, 2000, Miss Congeniality, 2000, American Psycho II, 2001, Osmosis Jones, 2001, Dodgeball: A True Underdog Story, 2004, Miss Congeniality 2: Armed and Fabulous, 2005, The Wild, 2006, Over the Hedge (voice), 2006, Gonzo Ballet, 2007; also TV movies and appearances on The Andersonville Trial, The Bastard, 1978, Disaster on the Coastliner, 1979, Secrets of a Married Man, 1984, North Beach and Rawhide, 1985, Columbo, 1993; TV series Star Trek, 1966-69, animated series, 1973-75, Barbary Coast, 1975-76, The Babysitter, 1979, T.J. Hooker, 1982-86; host (TV series) Rescue 911, CBS, 1989—96, Third Rock From the Sun, 1996, The Practice, 2004 (Emmy award for Outstanding Guest Actor in a Drama Series 2004), Boston Legal (Golden Globe award for best supporting actor series, miniseries or TV movie, 2005, Emmy award for outstanding supporting actor in a drama series, 2005), 2004-, (TV spls.) Invasion Iowa, 2005, How William Shatner Changed the World, 2006, William Shatner in Concert, 2006, The Comedy Central Roast of William Shatner, 2006; dir. TV movie TekWar; author: (novels) TekWar, 1989, TekLords, 1991, TekLab, 1991, Tek Vengeance, 1992, Tek Secret, 1993, (memoirs) Star Trek Memories, 1993, Star Trek Movie Memories, 1994, Tek Power, 1994, Tek Money, 1995, The Ashes of Eden, 1995, Man O' War, 1996, Tek Kill, 1996, The Return, 1996, Avenger, 1997, Delta Search: Quest for Tomorrow, 1997, Delta Search: In Alien Hands, 1998, Delta Search: Step Into Chaos, 1999, Get A Life, 1999, I'm Working on That, 2002, Captain's Glory, 2006, (book) Star Trek Academy Collision Course, 2007; albums: Transformed Man, 1968, Has Been, 2004, Exodus, 2007. Recipient Tyrone Guthrie award, 1956, Theatre World award, 1958; named to Acad. TV Arts & Sciences Hall of Fame, 2006 Mem.: AFTRA, SAG, Dirs. Guild, Actors Equity Assn. Office: care Melis Prodns Ste 500 8383 Wilshire Blvd Beverly Hills CA 90211

SHATTER, SUSAN LOUISE, artist; b. NYC, Jan. 17, 1943; d. Aubrey and Florence (Breines) S.; m. Paul Brown (div. June 1975); 1 child, Scott Brown. Student, Skowhegan Sch. Sculpture, Maine, 1964; BFA, Pratt Inst., 1965; MFA, Boston U., 1972. Artist in residence Skowhegan (Maine) Sch Painting and Sculpture, 1977, 79; art instr. Sch. Visual Arts, NYC, 1980-84, Tyler Sch. of Art, Phila., 1985, San Francisco Art Inst., 1989, Vt. Studio Ctr., Johnson, 1989, Bklyn. Coll., 1991-95. Vis. critic, U. Pa., 1974-85, acting co-chair, 1983-84; bd. govs. Skowhegan Sch. Painting and Sculpture, 1979—, chair, 1988-91. One-woman shows include Catalogue by D. Kuspit, SUNY Fine Arts Ctr., 2003, Fischbach Gallery, N.Y.C., 1973-97, Harcus Gallery, Boston, 1975-87, Mattingly Baker Gallery, Dallas, 1981, John Berggruen Gallery, San Francisco, 1986, Heath Gallery, Atlanta, 1987, SECCA, Winston-Salem, NC, 2001, Lyons Wier Gallery, N.Y.C., 2002, Staller Ctr. Arts, 2003, Lyonswier Gallery, 2005, Ancocisco Gallery, Portland, Maine, 2006, DFN Gallery, NYC Catalogue by David Cohen, 2006; works reproduced in America '76: A Bicentennial Exhibition, 1976, Boston Watercolor Today, 1976, Realist Drawings and Watercolors: Contemporary Works on Paper, 1980, Contemporary Realism Since 1960, 1981, Perspectives on Contemporary American Realism: Works of Art on Paper from the Collection of Jalane and Richard Davidson, 1983, Eireland, McMullen Mus. of Art, Boston Coll., 2003, New Vistas: Contemporary American Landscapes, 1984, American Realism: Twentieth Century Drawings and Watercolors from the Glenn C. Janss Collection, 1984, A Graphic Muse: Prints by American Women, 1987, Spirit of Place: Contemporary Landscape Painting & the American Tradition, 1989, Twentieth Century Watercolors, 1990, American Realism and Figurative Art: 1952-1991, 1991, (catalogue) Meridian Shift, 12 yrs. of paintings by Susan Shatter, U. Tex., San Antonio, 1998; represented in permanent collections Art Inst. Chgo., Mus. Fine Arts, Boston, MIT, Cambridge, Currier Gallery of Art, Manchester, N.H., Hood Art Mus., Dartmouth Coll., Hanover, N.H., Phila. Mus. Art, Utah Mus. Fine Art, Salt Lake City, Farnesworth Mus., Maine, Buffalo Bill Hist. Soc., Cody, Wyo., U. Tex., San Antonio, Nat. Mus. Am. Art, Washington, Yale U. Art Gallery, Boise (Idaho) Mus., Colby Mus., Maine, Walker Art Mus., Brunswick, Maine, Nat. Acad. Mus., NYC, U. Maine, Bangor. Recipient grants Mass. Creative Artists Humanities, Radcliff Inst., Ingram-Merrill Found., NEA, N.Y. State Found. for the Arts, Yaddo Corp., Ballinglen Artists Fellowship, Ireland, 1999, Pollock-Krasner Found, 2004-05; Brittany fellow Rochefort-en-Terre, 2002; recipient Childe Hassam Purchase award, Am. Acad. Arts and Letters, 2003; Yaddo resident, Saratoga Springs, NY, 2001, 02. Mem. NAD (W. Paten Prize 2003, treas. 1998-05, pres. 2005-), The Century Club. Office: DFN Gallery 176 Franklin St New York NY 10013-2806 E-mail: sshatter@mindspring.com.

SHATTUCK, CATHIE ANN, lawyer, former government official; b. Salt Lake City, July 18, 1945; d. Robert Ashley S. and Lillian Culp (Shattuck). BA, U. Nebr., 1967, JD, 1970. Bar: Nebr. 1970, U.S. Dist. Ct. Nebr. 1970, Colo. 1971, U.S. Dist. Ct. Colo. 1971, U.S. Supreme Ct. 1974, U.S. Ct. Appeals (10th cir.) 1977, U.S. Dist. Ct. D.C. 1984, U.S. Ct. Appeals (D.C. cir.) 1984. V.p., gen. mgr. Shattuck Farms, Hastings, Nebr., 1967-70; asst. project dir. atty. Colo. Civil Rights Commn., Denver, 1970-72; trial atty. EEOC, Denver, 1973-77, vice chmn. Washington, 1982-84; pvt. practice law Denver, 1977-81; mem. Fgn. Svc. Bd., Washington, 1982-84, Presdl. Pers. Task Force, Washington, 1982-84; ptnr. Epstein, Becker & Green, L.A. and Washington, 1984—. Lectr. Colo. Continuing Legal Edn. Author: Employer's Guide to Controlling Sexual Harrassment, 1992; co-editor Nat. Employment Law Insider, 2004-; mem. editl. bd. The Practical Litigator, 1988-2003. Bd. dirs. KGNU Pub. Radio, Boulder, Colo., 1979, Denver Exch., 1980-81, YWCA Met. Denver, 1979-81. Named Nebr. Young Career Woman, Bus. and Profl. Women, 1967, Outstanding Nebraskan, Daily Nebraskan, Lincoln, 1967. Fellow Am. Coll. of Labor and Employment Lawyers; mem. ABA (mgmt. chair labor and employment law sect. com. on immigration law 1988-90, mgmt. chair com. on legis. devels. 1990-93), Nebr. Bar Assn., Colo. Bar Assn., Colo. Women's Bar Assn., D.C. Bar Assn., Nat. Women's Coalition, Delta Sigma Rho, Tau Kappa Alpha, Pi Sigma Alpha, Alpha Xi Delta, Denver Club. Office Phone: 202-861-0900. Business E-Mail: cshattuck@ebglaw.com.

SHATTUCK, GARY G., lawyer; b. Nashua, NH, 1950; m. Katherine H. Catlin, 1972. BA, U. Colo., 1972; JD magna cum laude, Vt. Law Sch., 1987. Bar: Vt. 1987, U.S. Dist. Ct. Vt. 1987, U.S. Ct. Appeals (2d cir.) 1992. Dep. sheriff Boulder County Sheriff's Dept., Boulder, Colo., 1973-75; patrol comdr. Vt. State Police, Waterbury, 1975-87; litigation assoc. Reiber, Kenlan, Schweibert & Hall, P.C., Rutland, Vt., 1987-89; asst. atty. gen. Office of Atty. Gen., Montpelier, Vt., 1989-91; supervising atty. Vt. Drug Task Force, Montpelier, 1989-91; asst. U.S. atty. Organized Crime Drug Enforcement Task Force, U.S. Dept. Justice, Burlington, Vt., 1991—. Adj. prof. Castleton (Vt.) State Coll., 1997-98; U.S. Dept. Justice legal advisor to UN Mission in Kosovo, Pristina, 2000, Sarajevo, Bosnia-Herzegovina, 2001, coalition provisional authority, Baghdad, Iraq, 2003; anti-terrorism coord. Dist. Vt., 2002—03; appointee Gov.'s Homeland Security Adv. Coun., 2003. Bd. dirs. Rutland Mental Health, 1991; citizen's adv. com. Rutland Solid Waste Dist., 1987; del. Nat. Assn. Asst. U.S. Attys., 1994-99; bd. dirs. Vt. Archeol. Soc., 1998-99 Office: Office of US Atty PO Box 570 Burlington VT 05402-0570

SHATTUCK, GEORGE CLEMENT, retired lawyer; b. Syracuse, NY, Sept. 2, 1927; s. Frank M. and Geneveive Mary (Hannon) S.; m. Sheila Eagan, Sept. 21, 1957 (div. 1985); children: Edward, George, Frank, Mark, Patrick; m. Carla A. Amussen, June 16, 1987; 1 dau., Morgan. BS in Mgmt., Syracuse U., 1950, JD, 1953. Bar: N.Y. 1954, U.S. Supreme Ct. 1973. Retired ptnr., estate planning splty. practice group Bond, Schoeneck & King Law Firm, Syracuse, 1954—94. Author: Oneida Land Claims, 1991. Mem. Syracuse Bd. Edn., 1968-75. Roman Catholic. Avocations: writing, reading, fishing. Home: 5158 W Lake Rd Cazenovia NY 13035-9616

SHATTUCK, JOHN, diplomat, civil rights lawyer, educator; b. Pasadena, Calif., Sept. 22, 1943; s. H. Francis Jr. and Ruth (Murphy) S.; m. Petra Tölle, May 17, 1970 (dec. Mar. 1988); m. Ellen Hume, Feb. 14, 1991; children: Jessica, Rebecca, Peter, Susannah. BA magna cum laude, Yale U., 1965, JD, 1970; MA with 1st class hon. in internat. law, Cambridge U., Eng., 1967; doctorate (hon.), CUNY, 1995, Kenyon Coll., 2001, U. R.I., 2002, U. Western Bohemia, Czech. Rep., 2002. Law clk. to Hon. Edward Weinfeld U.S. Dist. Ct. (so. dist.) N.Y., 1970-71; nat. counsel ACLU, 1971-77, dir. Washington office, 1977-84; v.p. govt., community and pub. affairs Harvard U., 1984-93, sr. assoc. sci. tech. and pub. policy program John F. Kennedy sch. govt., 1984-93; asst. sec. of state bur. democracy, human rights and labor Dept. of State, Washington, 1993-98; U.S. amb. Czech Republic, 1998-2000; CEO John F. Kennedy Presdl. Libr. Found., 2001—. Lectr. Harvard Law Sch., 1986—93. Author: Freedom on Fire: Human Rights Wars and America's Response, 2003; contbr. articles to profl. jours. Bd. dir. The Petra Fedn., Am. Friends of Czech Republic, ABA Ctrl. & E. Law Inst., Common Cause. Recipient UN Assn. Human Rights award 1998, Am. Bar Assn. Ambassador award 2000, H.L. Mencken award Free Press Assn. 1988, Pub. Svc. award Yale U. Law Sch. 1988, Roger Baldwin medal 1984, Global Leadership award Tufts U., 2003. Fellow Am. Acad. Arts & Scis. Office: John F Kennedy Presdl Libr & Mus Columbia Point Boston MA 02125 Home Phone: 617-332-6002. Personal E-mail: john.shattuck@jfklfoundation.org.

SHATTUCK, MAYO ADAMS, III, utilities executive; b. Boston, Oct. 7, 1954; s. Mayo Adams Jr. and Jane (Bergwall) S.; m. Molly Anne George, Sept. 29, 1997; children: Mayo Adams IV, Kathleen Elizabeth, Spencer George, Wyatt Augustus, Lillian Jessie. BA, Williams Coll., 1976; MBA, Stanford U., 1980. Analyst Morgan Guaranty Trust Co., NYC, 1976-78; mgr. Bain & Co., Menlo Park, Calif., 1980-83; v.p. to mng. dir. and head of corp. fin. Alex Brown & Sons, San Francisco, 1985-91, pres. and COO Balt., 1991-97; co-chmn., CEO BT Alex Brown Inc., from 1997; vice chmn. Bankers Trust N.Y., from 1997; co-chmn., co-CEO, Deutsche Banc Alex Brown Inc., Balt., 1999—2001; pres., CEO, chmn. bd. Constellation Energy Group, Balt., 2001—02, chmn., pres., CEO, 2002—. Bd. dir. Constellation Energy, Gap Inc., Edison Electric Inst., Capital One Fin.; bd dir., mem. exec. com. Nuclear Energy Inst. Trustee Noble & Greenough Sch.; adv. dir. U. Md. Balt. County, Johns Hopkins Medicine. Avocations: tennis, golf. Office: Constellation Energy Group 750 E Pratt St 18th Floor Baltimore MD 21202

SHATZ, CARLA J., biology professor, researcher; b. NYC; BA in Chemistry, Radcliffe Coll., 1969; MPhil, Univ. Coll., London, 1971; PhD, Harvard U., 1976, postdoc., 1976—78. Assoc. prof. neurobiology Sch. Medicine Stanford U., Palo Alto, Calif., 1985—89, prof. neurobiology, 1989—92; investigator Howard Hughes Med. Inst., 1994—2000; Class of 1943 prof. neurobiology U. Calif., Berkeley, 1992—2000; prof., chair dept. neurobiology Harvard Med. Sch., Boston, 2000—07, Nathan Marsh Pusey prof. neurobiology; head Bio-X program, prof. biological scis. and neurobiology Stanford U., 2007—. Mem. commn. on life scis. NRC, 1990—96; nat. adv. NIH, 1996—99; mem. coun. NAS, 1998—2001. Fellow: Inst. Medicine, Am. Philos. Soc., NAS, AAAS. Office: Stanford U Bio-X Program 3rd Fl S, Rm S356 Stanford CA 94305 E-mail: cshatz@stanford.edu.

SHATZ, PHILLIP, lawyer; b. White Plains, NY, Sept. 1, 1926; s. Hyman and Ruth (Futoran) S.; m. Bettie Dorsey, Oct. 18, 1957 (dec.); children: Phillip Dorsey, Sallie Dean; m. Natalie Marshall, May 27, 1988. BS, Syracuse U., 1948; LLB, Columbia U., 1954. Bar: N.Y. 1954, U.S. Dist. Ct. (so. dist.) N.Y. 1955, U.S. Supreme Ct. 1960. Pres., chmn. bd. Rich, Shatz and Duncan, Inc., Mahopac, N.Y., 1948-75; v.p. Putnam County Fed. Savs. and Loan Assn., 1953-63, pres., chmn. bd., CEO, 1963—78; sole practice Mahopac, 1954-70; ptnr. Shatz & Braatz, Mahopac, 1970-74, Shatz & Thomsen, Mahopac, 1974-77, Shatz, Thomsen & Mace, Mahopac, 1977-80; sr. ptnr. McCabe & Mack, Poughkeepsie, NY, 1980—2000, of counsel, 2000—. Spl. prosecutor Putnam County; dir. Mid-Hudson Legal Svcs. Chmn. Putnam County Young Republicans. With USNR, 1943-46. Mem. ABA, N.Y. State Bar Assn., Dutchess County Bar Assn., Assn. Bar City of N.Y., Univ. Club (N.Y.C.). Home: 157 Skidmore Rd Pleasant Valley NY 12569-5001 Office: McCabe & Mack LLP 63 Washington St Poughkeepsie NY 12601-2313 Office Phone: 845-486-6880. E-mail: pshatz@mccm.com.

SHAUGHNESSY, ALLEN F., pharmacist, educator; b. Plainfield, NJ, Jan. 11, 1959; s. Francis Henry and Dorothy Suzanne (Allen) S.; m. Rebecca Joan Clark, July 26, 1980; children: Christopher, Joshua. Student, Gettysburg Coll., 1977-79; BS in Pharmacy, Temple U., 1982; PharmD, Med. U. of S.C., 1984. Registered pharmacist; bd. cert. pharmacotherapy specialist. Cons. pharmacist Sandlapper Cons. Pharmacists, Lexington, S.C., 1984-85; poison info. Med. U. of S.C., Charleston, 1983-84, asst. prof., 1987-89; clin. pharmacist Lexington Family Practice-Irmo, Columbia, S.C., 1984-87; asst. prof. U. S.C., Columbia, 1985-87; dir. pharmacologic edn. St. Margaret Meml. Hosp., Pitts., 1989-92; asst. prof. U. Pitts. Coll. Pharmacy, 1990—; dir. rsch./assoc. dir. ed. Harrisburg (Pa.) Family Practice Residency, 1992—; clin. assoc. prof. Med. Coll. Pa./Hahnemann U., 1995—. Fellow Am. Coll. Clin. Pharmacy; mem. Soc. Tchrs. Family Medicine, Rho Chi. Republican. Presbyterian.

SHAUGHNESSY, EDWARD LOUIS, language educator; b. Sewickley, Pa., July 29, 1952; s. James Francis and Marie Rosalia (Kraus) S.; m. Gina Lynn Look, May 15, 1976 (div. Sept. 1992); m. Elena Valussi, Sept. 6, 1997; children Guilia, Maria. BA, U. Notre Dame, 1974; MA, Stanford U., 1980, PhD, 1983. Asst. prof. U. Chgo., 1985-90, assoc. prof., 1990-96, prof., 1996—, Lorraine J. and Herrlee G. Creel prof. of early China, disting svc. prof., 2006—. Assoc. editor: Early China, 1985-88, editor, 1988-96; editor: New Sources of Early Chinese History: An Introduction to the Reading of Inscriptions and Manuscripts, 1997, (with Michael Loewe) The Cambridge History of Ancient China: From the Origins of Civilization to 221 B.C., 1999, China Empire and Civilization, 2000; author: Sources of Western Zhou History: Inscribed Bronze Vessels, 1991, I Ching, The Classic of Changes: The First English Translation of the Newly Discovered Second-Century B.C. Mawangdui Manuscripts, 1996, Before Confucius: Studies in the Creation of the Chinese Classics, 1997, Ancient China: Life, Myth and Art, 2005, Rewriting Early Chinese Texts, 2006, (with Robert Poor and Harrie A. Vanderstappen) Ritual and Reverence: Chinese Art at the University of Chicago, 1989, (with Cai Fangpei and James F. Shaughnessy) A Concordance of the Xiaotun Nandi Oracle-Bone Inscriptions, 1988; contbr. essays to books. Andrew W. Mellon fellow for Chinese studies, 1984-85; Divsn. of Humanities jr. faculty fellow U. Chgo., 1986; J. William Fulbright fellow in China, 2003-04, Nat. Endowment for Humanities, 2007-. Office: U Chgo East Asian Langs/Civilizat 1050 E 59th St Chicago IL 60637-1559 Home: 1050 E 59th St Chicago IL 60637-1559 Business E-Mail: e-shaughnessy@uchicago.edu.

SHAUGHNESSY, MARIE KANEKO, artist; b. Detroit, Sept. 14, 1924; d. Eishiro and Kiyo (Yoshida) Kaneko; m. John Thomas Shaughnessy, Sept. 23, 1959. Assocs. in Liberal Arts, Keisen U., Tokyo, 1944. Ops. mgr. Webco Alaska, Inc., Anchorage, 1970-88; ptnr. Webco Partnership, Anchorage, 1983-98, also bd. dirs. Faculty Art League Sch., Alexandria, Va., Fairfax County Pub. Sch. Adult Continuing and Cmty. Edn. Paintings, Lilacs, 1984, Blooms, 1985, The Fence, 1986 (Purchase award, 1986). Bd. dirs. Alaska Artists Guild, 1971—87; commr. Mcpl. Anchorage Fine Arts Commn., 1983—87; organizing com. Japanese Soc. Alaska, 1987. Recipient Art Affiliate award, Anchorage C. of C., 1975, 1978, 1984, Univ. Artists award, Alaska Pacific U., 1986, Am. Juror's Choice award, Sumi-E Soc. Am., 1994, Ikebana Internat. award, 1994, Dorothy Klein Meml. award, 1995, Yasutomo Calligraphy award, 1997, 1998, Oriental Calligraphy award, 1997, 1998, Sarasota Chpt Painting award, 1999, Paul Schwartz Meml. award, 2001, Sm. Works Exhibit 1st Pl. award, Wash. Watercolor Assn., 2001, Wang Chi Yuan award, 2000. Mem.: Washington Water Color Assn. (1st place award Strathmore Mansion summer exhbn. 2005), Nat. League Am. Penwomen (Grumbacher Gold medal award excellence 1993), Vienna Art Soc. (bd. dir. 1995—96), Sumi-E Soc. Am. (past pres. 1992—94, bd. dir., Nat. Capital Area chpt. past pres. awards 1990, Nat. Capital Area chpt. award 1990—92, Purchase award 1993, Nat. Capital Area chpt. award 1994), Va. Watercolor Soc. (pres. 1993, co-chmn. 2004 All State Juried Show), Potomac Valley Watercolorists (exhibits chair 1989—93, bd. dir. 1989—99, newsletter editor 1993—96, v.p., workshop chair 1996—2001, historian 2003, awards 1989, 1991, Spl. award 1995), Alaska Watercolor Soc. (life; charter, Grumbacher Silver medal 1989), McLean Art Soc. (pres. 2006—, 1st pl. award 1991). Republican. Roman Catholic. Personal E-mail: markaneko@aol.com.

SHAUGHNESSY, MEGHANN, professional tennis player; b. Richmond, Apr. 13, 1979; d. Bill and Joy. Profl. tennis player, 1996—. Recipient WTA Tour Doubles Title, Quebec City, 2000, German Open, 2001, Gold Coast, 2002, Moscow, 2003, WTA Tour Singles Title, Shanghai, 2000, Quebec City, 2001, Canberra, 2003, Grand Prix SAR, 2006, Forest Hills Women's Tennis Classic, 2006, Barcelona KIA, 2007, Ranked #17, WTA, Ranked #6 Among U.S. Players, Highest Season Ending Single's Ranking #12, 2001, Resident Pro, Scottsdale Hyatt Gainey Ranch Resort, 6 Internat. Women's Circuit Singles Titles. Mem.: U.S. Fedn. Cup Team. Office: WTA Tour Corporate Headquarters One Progress Plz Ste 1500 Saint Petersburg FL 33701 *

SHAUGHNESSY, THOMAS WILLIAM, retired librarian; b. Pitts., May 3, 1938; s. Martin T. and LaVerne (O'Brien) Shaughnessy; m. Marlene D. Reuben, Aug. 11, 1968; 1 child, Mark Andrew. AB, St. Vincent Coll., 1961; MLS, U. Pitts., 1964; PhD, Rutgers U., 1970. Asst. dean Rutgers U., New Brunswick, NJ, 1969-71, libr. dir. Newark, 1971-74; assoc. dean U. So. Calif., LA, 1974-78; asst. libr. dir. U. Houston, 1978-82; libr. dir. U. Mo., Columbia, 1982-89; univ. libr., dir. U. Minn., Mpls.-St. Paul, 1989—2002; dir. Metronet, St. Paul, 2005—. Rsch. dir. Chgo. Pub. Libr. Survey, 1968—69; cons. U. Tulsa Libr., 1982—83; mem. faculty exch. USIA, Poland, 1998; trustee OCLC, Inc., 1997—2004. Author (with Lowell A. Martin): (book) Library Response to Urban Change, 1969, Developing Leadership Skills: A Source Book for Librarians, 1990. Recipient Hugh C. Atkinson Meml. award, 1996; fellow, Coun. Libr. Resources, 1973; U.S. Office Edn. grantee, Rutgers U., 1971, Sr. fellow, Coun. Libr. Resources, 1985. Mem.: ALA, Minn. Libr. Assn. (Disting. Achievement award 2002), Assn. Rsch. Librs. (cons. tng. fellow 1981, bd. dirs. 1989—92), Assn. Coll. and Rsch. Librs. Home: 5705 Wycliffe Rd Minneapolis MN 55436-2264 E-mail: tws@umn.edu.

SHAUL, DAVID LEEDOM, linguist, archivist; b. Cheyenne, Wyo., May 18, 1952; s. Jack Leedom and Rosa Grams. BA, U. Ariz., Tucson, 1973, MusB, 1974, MA, 1978; PhD, U. Calif., Berkeley, 1982. Libr., archivist Tohono O'odham Nation, Sells, Ariz.; instr. Pima CC, Tucson; prof. Ind. U. -Purdue U. Fort Wayne. Pro bono archivist Summer Inst. Linguistics Mex. br., Catalina, Ariz. Composer: (symphonies) Symphony in F, 1982, Symphony Monegasque, 2006, (Operas) Hamlet, 1998, musician folk harp. Artistic dir. Camerata Tucson, 1995—2000, Altar Valley Chamber Orch., Robles Junction, Ariz., 1999—; founder Friends of Tohono O'odham Librs., Sells, Ariz., 1999—. Mem.: Linguistics Soc. Am., Am. Anthropol. Assn., Soc. Study of Indigenous Langs. Ams. Avocations: gardening, cooking. Office: Dave Shaul Prodns 15980 W Killarney Ave Tucson AZ 85736-1408

SHAVELL, STEVEN M., law educator; b. Wash., May 29, 1946; AB in Math. and Economics, U. Mich., 1968; PhD in Economics, MIT, 1973. Lt. j.g. US Pub. Health Svc. Centers for Disease Control, 1968—70; asst. prof. economics Boston Coll., 1973—74, Harvard U., Cambridge, Mass., 1974—79, assoc. prof., 1979—80; asst. prof. law and economics Harvard Law Sch., 1980—82, prof., 1982—, Samuel R. Rosenthal prof., 2000—, dir. John M. Olin Ctr. for Law, Economics, and Bus., 1985—. Vis. prof. U. Chgo. Law Sch., 1984—85, NYU Law Sch., 1999; assoc. editor Geneva Risk and Ins. Rev., 1990—; bd. editors Internat. Rev. Law and Economics, 1987—, Jour. Law, Economics, and Orgn., 1989—, Rsch. in Law and Economics, 1990—, Am. Law and Economics Rev., 1999—, Ency. Law and Economics, 1999—; bd. advisors Ctr. for Law, Economics, and Fin. Institutions, Copenhagen Bus. Sch., 2001—; bd. faculty advisors Jour. Law, Economics, and Policy, 2003—. Author: Economic Analysis of Accident Law, 1987, Foundations of Economic Analysis of Law, 2004; co-author: Fairness versus Welfare, 2002, Analytical Methods for Lawyers, 2003. NSF Grad. Fellowship, 1968, NSF Nat. Needs Postdoctoral Rsch. Fellowship, 1977—78, Harvard Law Sch. Liberal Arts Fellow, 1977, Liberty Fund Summer Fellow in Law and Economics, 1979, Guggenheim Meml. Found. Fellowship, 1983—84. Fellow: Econometric Soc.; mem.: Am. Law and Economics Assn. (bd. dirs. 1990—94, pres. 2001—02), Am. Acad. Arts and Sciences. Office: Harvard Law Sch 1563 Massachusetts Ave Cambridge MA 02138 Office Phone: 617-495-3668. Office Fax: 617-496-2256. Business E-Mail: shavell@law.harvard.edu.

SHAVENDER, MARILYN FAYE, retired elementary school educator; b. Washington, Feb. 22, 1938; d. Redden Hudnell and Alice Gray Shavender; 1 child, Annette Byrd (dec.). BS in Elem. Edn., East Carolina U., 1959. 2d grade tchr. Virginia Beach Sch. Sys., Va., 1959—, lang. arts com., 1988—2003; ret., 2003. Author: (book) Poetry by Grammy, 2000, Marsh Winds...A Sentimental Journey. Mem.: DAR, Virginia Beach Edn. Assn. Republican. Mem. Church Of Christ. Avocations: piano, writing, antiques, gardening. E-mail: Twingrand@aol.com.

SHAVER, JAMES PORTER, retired education educator, dean; b. Wadena, Minn., Oct. 19, 1933; BA magna cum laude, U. Wash., Seattle, 1955; MAT, Harvard U., Cambridge, Mass., 1957, EdD, 1961. Instr. Grad. Sch. Edn., Harvard U., 1961-62; asst. prof., dir. Social Studies Curriculum Ctr., Ohio State U., Columbus, 1964-65; assoc. prof. Utah State U. Coll. Edn., Logan, 1962-64, prof., 1965—, chmn. Bur. Rsch. Svcs., 1965-93, assoc. dean rsch., 1978-93, acting dean Sch. Grad. Studies, 1990-91, 92-93, dean, 1993-99, prof. emeritus secondary edn., 1999—. Mem. Commn. Youth Edn. for Citizenship, ABA, 1975-81; mem. edn. task force Am. Hist.

Assn.-Am. Polit. Sci. Assn. Project '87, 1981-84; tech. advisor Nat. Ctr. on Effective Secondary Schs., 1988-91; mem. adv. bd. program in civic and moral edn. Inst. for Philosophy and Pub. Policy, U. Md., 1992—; mem. steering com. Nat. Assessment Ednl. Progress Civics Consensus Project, 1995-96. Co-author: Teaching Public Issues in the High School, 1966, 2d edit., 1974, Facing Value Decisions: Rationale-building For Teachers, 1976, 2d edit., 1982; editor: Building Rationales for Citizenship Education, 1977, Handbook of Research on Social Studies Teaching and Learning, 1991; co-editor: Democracy, Pluralism, and the Social Studies, 1968; also others. Recipient Outstanding Svc. and Tchg. award, Utah Coun. for the Social Studies, 1975, 1978, Lifetime Achievement award, 1998. Mem. AAAS, AAUP, Nat. Coun. Social Studies (pres. 1976, Exemplary Rsch. award 1977, Exemplary Rsch. Editor award 1991), Am. Ednl. Rsch. Assn., Phi Beta Kappa, Phi Kappa Phi. Home: PO Box 176 Hyrum UT 84319-0176 Office: Utah State U 2800 Old Main Hill Logan UT 84322-2800 Office Phone: 435-797-1469. Business E-Mail: jim.shaver@usu.edu.

SHAVER, JOAN LOUISE FOWLER, dean, women's health nurse; BS in Nursing, U. Alberta, Can., 1966; M in Nursing, U. Wash., 1968-70, PhD in Physiology and Biophysics, 1976. Nursing instr. chair med. surgical prog. Holy Cross Hosp. Sch. Nursing, Calgary, Canada, 1966-68; staff nurse Virginia Mason Hosp., Seattle, 1970-71; asst. prof. Sch. Nursing U. Ariz., Tucson, 1976-77; assoc. prof. U. Calgary, Canada, 1977-80; asst. prof. Dept. Physiological Nursing U. Wash., Seattle, 1980-85, rsch. affil. Regl. Primate Rsch. Ctr., 1983-86, assoc. prof., 1985-89, chair Dept. Physiological Nusring, 1988-95, prof., 1989-95, prof., chair Dept. Biobehavioral Nursing & Health Systems, 1995-96, co-dir. Ctr. Women's Health Rsch., 1989-96; prof., dean Coll. Nursing U. Ill., Chgo., 1996—, co-dir. Rsch. Core Nat. Ctr. Excellence in Women's Health, 1997—. Mem. editl. bd. Health Care for Women Internat., 1984—, Heart and Lung: The Jour. of Critical Care, 1988-90, Jour. of Applied Nursing Rsch., 1988-91, IMAGE: Jour. Nursing Scholarship, editl. adv. bd. Nursing Rsch., 1997—, Biol. Rsch. for Nursing, 1999—, Jour. Nursing Scholarship, 2000—; contbr. artilces to profl. jours. Abe Miller Meml. scholar Alberta Assn. Registered Nurses, 1968-69; Kathryn McLaggen Meml. fellow Can. Nurses Found., fellow Am. Acad. Nursing Am. Nurses Assn., 1988—. Office: U Ill Coll Nursing 845 S Damen Ave Mc802 Chicago IL 60612-7350

SHAVERS, CHERYL L., technology and business consultant; married; 3 children. BS in Chemistry, Ariz. State U., PhD in Solid State Chemistry; degree in engring. mgmt. (hon.), Calif. Poly. State U., 1996. Practicing registered patent agent Patent and Trademark Office of Dept. of Commerce. Prod. engr. Motorola; process devel. engr. Hewlett-Packard, patent agent, tech. legal dept.; microelectronics sect. mgr. Wiltron Co.; engring. mgr., thin films devel. lab. Varian Associates; sector mgr. microprocessor div., corp. bus. devel. div. Intel Corp.; under sec. commerce for tech. U.S. Dept Commerce, 1999—2001; chmn., CEO Global Smarts, Inc., Santa Clara, Calif., 2001—. Spkr., workshop leader in field; non-exec. chmn. BitArts Ltd., 2001—03; bd. dirs. Rockwell Collins, Inc., 2002—. Weekly columnist San Jose Mercury News Bus. Sect.; contbr. articles to profl. publs.; featured in articles, books and Web sites; TV appearances include documentary Wizards and Alchemists, 1995, Real Science Program, Sta. KTEH-TV, NBC New Media News, Women in Technology, 1997 Active numerous outreach programs, including Real Sci., Wizards and Alchemists, KTEH Silicon Valley Report, KRON New Media News programs; bd. dirs. San Jose Tech Mus. of Innovation, 1996—; former bd. dirs. Internat. Network Women in Tech., 1995-96, ARC, 1995-96. Recipient Janet Gray Hayes award, award Phi Lambda Upsilon, Outstanding Presenter of Yr., San Francisco Bay Area chpt. Nat. Assn. of Black MBAs, 1998; Henry Crown fellow Aspen Inst.'s Crown Felloship Program; inductee Internat. Women in Tech. Hall of Fame, Coll. Liberal Arts and Scis. Hall of Fame, Ariz. State U., 1997, Internat. Network of Women in Tech. Hall of Fame, 1996. Mem. Libr. of Congress (assoc.). Office: Global Smarts Inc 3333 Bowers Ave Ste 130 Santa Clara CA 95050

SHAW, ADAM, broadcast executive; b. 1972; BA magna cum laude, Yale Univ., New Haven, Conn. Former sr. v.p., bus. ops., fin. FX Networks; v.p. affiliate sales Fox Cable Networks; sr. v.p., distbn. NFL Networks, 2003—. Named one of 40 Under 40, Sports Bus. Jour., 2006. Office: NFL Network 280 Park Ave New York NY 10017

SHAW, ALAN, lawyer; b. Long Branch, NJ, July 23, 1930; m. Margaret Knight, Oct. 15, 1959; children: Andrew Macbeth, Adriane Macbeth. AB, U. Mich., 1952; LLB, Harvard U., 1955. Bar: Mass. 1955, N.Y. 1958. Atty. Skadden, Arps, Slate, Meagher & Flom, NYC, 1958-65; v.p., gen. counsel, sec. Athlone Industries Inc., Parsippany, NJ, 1966-93, also bd. dirs. Adj. prof. law Fordham U.; arbitrator Am. Arbitration Assn., NASD Dispute Resolution, N.Y. Stock Exch.; panelist Contract Dispute Resolution Bd., N.Y.C. Mem. co-chair fundraising Jefferson Soc. Morristown Meml. Hosp. With U.S. Army, 1955-57. Mem. ABA (sect. on corps., litig., alt. dispute resolution sect.), NJ Gen. Counsel Group, Assn. Bar City NY, Soc. Profls. Dispute Resolution, Morristown (NJ) Club, Washington Assn. Morristown (trustee, 2d v.p.), Morris County Golf Club, Harvard Club, Churchill Ctr. (charter mem.), Alexander Hamilton Hist. Soc. Home: 490 S Maple Ave Basking Ridge NJ 07920-1327 Office: 1812 Front St Scotch Plains NJ 07076

SHAW, ALAN BOSWORTH, geologist, retired paleontologist; b. Englewood, NJ, Mar. 28, 1922; s. Carroll Harper and Natalie Frederique (Howe) S.; m. Helen Louise Wilson, Nov. 2, 1945 (div. Apr. 1952); m. Marian Tavenner Stoll, Mar. 11, 1954 (dec. Apr. 1981); children: Nancy Jeanne, Sally Ann; m. Mary Elizabeth Merrem, Sept. 3, 1982. AB magna cum laude, Harvard Coll., 1946; AM, PhD, Harvard U., 1949. Asst. prof. geology U. Wyo., Laramie, 1949-55; paleontologist Shell Oil Co., Denver, 1955-60; owner Nat. Elec. Svc., NYC, 1960-61; freelance cons. geologist Denver, 1961; supr. Pan Am. Rsch. (now BP), Tulsa, Okla., 1961-68; various positions Pan Am. Petroleum, Denver, 1968-76; chief paleontologist Amoco Prodn., Chgo., 1976-77, chief geologist, 1977-81; geol. rsch. cons. Amoco Rsch., Tulsa, 1981-85; ret., 1985. Oil industry rep. NRC Com. on Paleontology, Washington, 1963-69; mem. Com. on Paleontology and Stratigraphy Deep Sea Drilling Program, 1973-75. Author: Time in Stratigraphy, 1964; contbr. numerous articles to profl. jours. Served to 1st lt., USAAF, 1943-45. Recipient Moore Paleontology medal Soc. Sedimentary Geology, 1996. Achievements include invention of graphic correlation system for use of fossils in making time correlations of sedimentary rocks. Home: 210 Kamira Kerrville TX 78028 Personal E-mail: shaw99@ktc.com.

SHAW, ALAN ROGER, finance educator, retired company executive; b. Bklyn., July 7, 1938; s. Sewall S. and Vera (Dimmick) S.; children: Stephen S., Todd J., Bradley C.; m. Mary Elizabeth Hogg, May 30, 1987. Student, Susquehanna U., 1957, Adelphi U., 1963-66; LLD (hon.), Susquehanna U., 1999. Analyst Harris Upham & Co., NYC, 1958-71, asst. v.p., 1971-73, v.p., 1973-75; 1st v.p. Smith, Barney, Harris, Upham & Co., NYC, 1975-80; sr. v.p., mng. dir. Smith Barney, NYC, 1980—2004. Tchr. N.Y. Inst. Fin., 1966— Mem. Market Technicians Assn. (pres. 1974), N.Y. Soc. Security Analysts, Securities Industry Assn. Inst. (trustee 1986-92), Unqua Corinthian Yacht Club (commodore 1988-90). Home: PO Box 322 79 N Midway Rd Shelter Island NY 11964 E-mail: almed@optonline.net.

SHAW, ANGELYNN RENEE, protective services official; b. Vallejo, Calif., Oct. 27, 1972; d. Robert J. and Lita M. Moore; m. Brian Romeyn Shaw, Sept. 23, 2006. BS in Forensic Sci., Calif. State U., Sacramento, 1997. Forensic toxicologist Valley Toxicology Svc., West Sacramento, Calif., 1997—99; sr. criminalist Calif. Dept Justice, Jan Bashinski DNA Lab., Richmond, 1999—. Mem.: Calif. Assn. Criminalists (treas. 2005), Am. Acad. Forensic Scis. (assoc.). Office: CA Dept of Justice Jan Bashinski DNA Lab 1001 W Cutting Blvd Ste 110 Richmond CA 94804 Home Phone: 916-923-6217; Office Phone: 510-620-3311. E-mail: angel.shaw@doj.ca.gov.

SHAW, ANNITA LOUISE, art educator; b. Scottsbluff, Nebr., Feb. 13, 1941; d. Harold Kenneth and Velma Loraine Shaw; m. Max Le Roy Shaw, June 29, 1968; 1 child, Justin Owen. BS in Elem. Edn., Chadron State Coll., Nebr., 1963; MA in Art Supervision and Direction, NYU, 1969. Tchr. 2d grade Bridgeport Sch. Dist., Nebr., 1961—64; tchr. 3rd grade Geneva Sch. Dist., Nebr., 1964—66; elem. art specialist Omaha Sch. Dist., 1966—68; tchr. jr. high sci. New London Sch. Dist., Conn., 1968—70; tchr. jr. and sr. high visual arts and visual arts curriculum specialist Ctrl. Kitsap Sch. Dist., Silverdale, Wash., 1974—2003; owner A.Shaw Originals. Mem. adv. com. Wash. State Commn. on Student Learning, Olympia, 1993—95; mem. assessment cert. team Nat. Bd. Profl. Tchg. Stds., San Francisco, 1996; mem. People to People Am. Program Art Edn. Delegation to Russia, 2006; presenter in field. Prodr.: (video) Whistle Wisdom, 1993, Perspective: More than Converging Line, 1999, Roll, Pinch, Shake and Rattle, 2001; contbr. articles to mags. and profl. jours. Mem.: Nat. Art Edn. Assn. (mem. dels. assembly 1994, pres. Wash. chpt., treas. Wash. chpt., historian and ret. rep. Wash. chpt., Pacific Region Elem. Art Educator 1988, Christa McAliffe Excellence in Edn. 1990, Pacific Region Mid. Level Art Educator 2001, Wash. Art Educator of Yr. 2000, Nat. Mid. Level Art Educator of the Yr. 2002), Women in the Arts (charter mem.). Avocations: sculpting, designing pins and medallions, writing. Home: PO Box 737 Silverdale WA 98383-0737 Personal E-mail: mashaw@mindspring.com.

SHAW, ANTHONY, pediatric surgeon, retired educator; b. Shanghai, Oct. 31, 1929; s. Bruno and Regina (Hyman) S.; m. Iris Violet Azian, Mar. 12, 1955; children: Brian Anthony, Diana Shaw Clark, Daniel Aram. BA cum laude, Harvard Coll., 1950; MD, NYU, 1954. Diplomate Am. Bd. Surgery; cert. spl. competence pediat. surgery. Intern and resident in surgery Columbia-Presbyn. Med. Ctr., NYC, 1954-56, 58-62; resident in pediat. surgery Babies Hosp., NYC, 1962; asst. prof. surgery Columbia U. Coll. Physicians and Surgeons, NYC, 1965-70; chief pediat. surgery St. Vincent's Hosp., NYC, 1963-70, Harlem Hosp. Ctr., NYC, 1965-70; prof. surgery U. Va., Charlottesville, 1970-81, chief pediat. surgery Med. Ctr., 1970-81; prof. surgery UCLA, 1981-2001, emeritus prof. surgery, 2001—; chief pediat. surgery Olive View-UCLA Med. Ctr., Sylmar, 1986-2001, cons. surgeon, 2003—. Expert witness on child abuse L.A. Superior Ct., 1986—; chmn. gov.'s adv. com. child abuse and neglect Commonwealth of Va., 1975-80; vis. prof. pediat. surgery People's Republic of China, 1985. Contbr. more than 220 articles to profl. jours. Mem. Gov.'s Task Force on Child Abuse Va., 1973-74. Capt. U.S. Army, 1956-58. Recipient Commrs. award Va. Dept. Social Svcs., 1980, award Gov.'s Adv. Bd., Cert. of Recognition HEW, 1978. Fellow Am. Pediat. Surg. Assn. (sec. 1982-85), ACS (v.p. 1987-89); mem. AMA, Pacific Coast Surg. Assn. (v.p. 1989-90), Am. Soc. Law, Medicine, and Ethics, Am. Profl. Soc. on Abuse of Children, Alpha Omega Alpha. Avocation: writing humor. Home and Office: One S Orange Grove Blvd # 9 Pasadena CA 91105 Home Phone: 626-796-8588; Office Phone: 626-796-8588. Personal E-mail: shawpas@pacbell.net.

SHAW, ANTHONY RAYMOND, JR., research company executive; b. NYC, Dec. 26, 1942; s. Anthony Raymond and Isabelle Leone (Bisson) S.; m. Diane Lynn Tomason, Nov. 1986; children: Amy, Anthony Raymond III (dec.), Danielle, Devon Young. BA cum laude, St. John's Sem. Coll., Boston, 1964; postgrad. Loyola U., Chgo., 1970-71, Rutgers U., 1975, Brookings Instn., 1987-88. Positions in personnel, purchasing and service ops. AT&T Bell Labs., Chgo., Denver and NJ, 1969-77, head adminstrn. network planning div., Holmdel, NJ, 1977-81, mgr. adminstrn. pers. svcs., 1981-85, dir. R&D security and spl. projects, Whippany, NJ, 1986-96, dir. info. svcs, ret.; prin., bus. ops., GeoPartners Rsch., Cambridge, Mass.; dir. labs., co-dir. grad. studies dept. chemistry Harvard U., Cambridge, 2001—. Sgt. Westfield Spl. Police Force, NJ, 1980-99. Capt. USMC, 1965-69. Decorated Purple Heart. Mem. South Coastal Hockey League. Republican. Roman Catholic. Author: Low/High Altitude Instrument Approach Procedures, 1969. Office: Harvard U Dept Chemistry 12 Oxford St Cambridge MA 02138 Home Phone: 781-829-6936; Office Phone: 617-495-4283. Business E-Mail: shaw@chemistry.harvard.edu.

SHAW, BRAD, communications executive; b. Apr. 10, 1966; B in Journalism, Washington and Lee U., Lexington, Va. Account mgr. Doremus Pub. Rels., NYC; sr. account mgr. Ketchum Pub. Rels., NYC; sr. mgr. comm. N.Am. Pepsi-Cola Co., Puchase, NY, dir. worldwide comm. Purchase, NY; v.p. corp. comm. Gateway, Inc., Poway, Calif., 1999, sr. v.p. corp. comm.; sr. v.p. corp. comm. and external affairs Home Depot, Inc., Atlanta, 2004—. Chair coordinating com. Bus. Roundtable Partnership for Disaster Response Task Force. Bd. mem. Hands On Network; bd. dirs. San Diego Regional C. of C.; bd. mem. Homer Fund, KABOOM!. Mem.: Arthur W. Page Soc. Office: Home Depot Inc 2455 Paces Ferry Rd Atlanta GA 30339

SHAW, CAROLE, editor, publisher; b. Bklyn., Jan. 22, 1936; d. Sam and Betty (Neckin) Bergenthal; m. Ray Shaw, Dec. 27, 1957; children: Lori Eve Cohen, Victoria Shaw Locknar. BA, Hunter Coll., 1962. Singer Capitol Records, Hilton Records, Rama Records, Verve Records, 1952-65; TV appearances Ed Sullivan, Steve Allen, Jack Paar, George Gobel Show, 1957; owner The People's Choice, LA, 1975-79; founder, editor-in-chief Big Beautiful Woman mag., Beverly Hills, Calif., 1979—. Creator Carole Shaw and BBW label clothing line for large-size women. Author: Come Out, Come Out Wherever You Are, 1982. Avocations: piano, painting, swimming, travel. Office: BBW Mag 6666 Brookmont Ter Ste 412 Nashville TN 37205-4622 Personal E-mail: bibewa@comcast.net.

SHAW, CECELIA, retired chef; b. Mankato, Minn., Feb. 18, 1959; d. Maxine Adele and Robert Cyril Shaw; m. Steve Schept, Sept. 15, 1990. Degree in Culinary Arts, Mankato Tech. Coll., Minn., 1984. Owner, head chef Soupstone, Mankato, 1980—81; pvt. practice Mankato, 1981—83; salad and prep cook Maggies Cafe, Mankato, 1983; asst. kitchen mgr. Phoenix Restaurant, Mankato, 1983—84; 1st commis chaud Hotel Sofitel, Bloomington, Minn., 1984—86; supr., chef Ebenezer Soc., Mpls., 1986—87; dietary mgr. Mar. Ho., Mpls., 1987—90; kitchen mgr. Table of Contents, St. Paul, 1990—91; line chef Azur Restaurant, Mpls., 1991—92; sous chef Blue Point Restaurant, Wayzata, Minn., 1992—94; prep chef D'Amico Cucina, Mpls., 1994—96; ret., 1996. Vol. Hope Now, Arlington Heights, Ill., 2002—04. Avocations: languages, travel, gardening, cooking. Home Phone: 952-736-8492. Personal E-mail: ceceliasrd2@earthlink.net.

SHAW, CHARLES ALDEN, engineering executive; b. Detroit, June 8, 1925; s. Fred Alden and Amy (Ellis) S.; m. Barbara Loveland, Mar. 9, 1963 (div. 1979); children: Amy Elizabeth, Polly Nicole; m. Jeanne Steves Partridge, Apr. 22, 1989. BS, Harvard U., 1945; MSEE, Syracuse U., 1958. Test and design engr. G.E., Syracuse-Schenectady, NY, 1947-51; chief engr. electronics divsn. Onondaga Pottery Co., Syracuse, 1951-60; mgr. semiconductor div. G.E., Syracuse-Schenectady, 1960-66; cons. to gen. dir. Bull-G.E., Paris, 1966-69; mgr. CAD sect. integrated cir. product dept. G.E., Syracuse, 1969-71, mgr. CAD ctr. solid state applied ops., 1971-78, mgr. computer support solid state applied ops., 1978-81; dir. CAD G.E. Intersil, Cupertino, Calif., 1981-88; cons. in field Cupertino, 1988-89; mgr. tech. program Cadence Design Systems, Santa Clara, Calif., 1989—. Trustee Hidden Villa, Los Altos Hills, Calif., 1986—92; bd. dirs. Unitarian Universalist Ch., Livermore, 1999—2002. With USN, 1942—45, PTO. Mem. IEEE (officer 2003—, bd. govs. 2005—), Assn. Computing Machinery (chmn. spl. interest group SIGDA 1986-91), Design Automation Conf. (exec. bd. 1985-95), Harvard Club of Silicon Valley. Democrat. Unitarian Universalist. Home and Office: 4925 Monaco Dr Pleasanton CA 94566-7671 Personal E-mail: shawcha@comcast.net.

SHAW, CHARLES ALEXANDER, judge; b. Jackson, Tenn., Dec. 31, 1944; s. Alvis and Sarah S.; m. Kathleen Ingram, Aug. 17, 1969; 1 child, Bryan Ingram. BA, Harris Stowe State U., 1966; MBA, U. Mo., 1971; JD, Cath. U. Am., 1974. Bar: D.C. 1975, Mo. 1975, U.S. Ct. Appeals (8th and D.C. cirs.) 1975, U.S. Dist. Ct. (ea. dist.) Mo. 1976, U.S. Ct. Appeals (6th and 7th cirs.) 1976. Tchr. St. Louis Pub. Schs., 1966-69, D.C. Pub. Schs., Washington, 1969-71; law clk. U.S. Dept. Justice, Washington, 1972-73, NLRB, Washington, 1973-74, atty., 1974-76; assoc. Lashly, Caruthers, Theis, Rava & Hamel, St. Louis, 1976-80, asst. U.S. atty., 1980-87; judge Mo. Cir. Ct., St. Louis, 1987-94, asst. presiding judge, 1993-94; judge U.S. Dist. Ct., St. Louis, 1994—. Hearing officer Office of the Mayor, Washington, 1973-74; instr. U. Mo., St. Louis, 1980-81. State bd. dirs. United Negro Coll. Fund, St. Louis, 1979-83; trustee St. Louis Art Mus., 1979-82, 89-96; bd. dirs. Arts and Edn. Coun., 1992-96, Metro Golf Assn., 1993-2000, Landmarks Assn., St. Louis, 1980-82. Recipient Silver Gavel award Fed. Def. Bar, 2005; named Disting. Alumnus, Cath. U., 2001; fellow Danforth Found., 1978-79; scholar Cath. U. Am., 1971-74. Mem. D.C. Bar Assn., Mo. Bar Assn., Mound City Bar Assn., Bar Assn. Met. St. Louis, Harris-Stowe State Coll. Alumni Assn. (Disting. Alumni 1988), Nat. Assn. Guardsmen (sec. St. Louis chpt. 1999-2001), Phi Alpha Delta (svc. award 1973-74), Sigma Pi Phi (pres. St. Louis chpt. 1999-2001). Avocation: golf. Office: 111 S 10th St Saint Louis MO 63102 Office Phone: 314-244-7480.

SHAW, CHARLES RAYMOND, journalist; b. Phila., Feb. 2, 1951; s. Charles Raymond Sr. and Dorothy Blanche (Buckman) S.; m. Francine Ruth Pennock, Jan. 14, 1983. BS in Journalism, Temple U., 1972; MS in Journalism, Columbia U., 1973. Staff writer Intelligencer Jour., Lancaster, Pa., 1973-83, asst. news editor, 1983-88, news editor, 1989-97, editor, 1997—. Mem. Pa. Soc. of Newspaper Editors, Am. Soc. Newspaper Editors, Pa. Assoc. Press (bd. dirs.). Office: Lancaster Newspaper PO Box 1328 Lancaster PA 17608-1328 Office Phone: 717-291-8650. E-mail: rshaw@lnpnews.com.

SHAW, CHARLES RUSANDA, retired government investigator; b. Detroit, Aug. 17, 1914; s. Leonard George and Harriet (Kratzer) S.; m. Sally Madeline Jock, May 3, 1947 (dec. June 1996); children: Patrick R., Sandra L. Keding (dec.), Janice L., Lisa Keding. Cert., Wicker Sch. of Fine Arts, 1936, Mich. Acad. Advt. Art, 1937; student, Intelligence Corps Sch., 1947. Freelance artist, Detroit, 1936-39; spl. agt. U.S. Army Counter Intelligence Corps, Washington, 1947-48, Office Spl. Investigations, USAF, Washington, 1948-66; pvt. investigator Charles Shaw Assocs., Mt. Clemens, Mich., 1966-84; contract investigator USAF & U.S. Customs Svc., Washington, 1984-94; prin. C.R. Shaw Assocs., New Haven, Mich., 1994—. Author: Immaculate Misconception, 1999. Master sgt. U.S. Army, 1939-45, PTO, ETO. Mem. Assn. Former OSI Spl. Agts. (chartered), VFW, Pearl Harbor Survivors Assn. Democrat. Roman Catholic. Achievements include invention of neoteric products; patents pending for. Avocations: fine arts, photography, gardening. Home and Office: 59295 Bates Rd Lenox MI 48048-1728 Home Phone: 586-749-9223; Office Phone: 586-749-9223.

SHAW, (EUGENE) CLAY, (JR.), former congressman; b. Miami, Fla., Apr. 19, 1939; s. E. Clay and Rita (Walker) S.; m. Emilie Costar, Aug. 22, 1960; children: Emilie, Jennifer, E. Clay, John C. BS, Stetson U., 1961, JD, 1966; MBA, U. Ala., 1963. Bar: Fla. 1967; CPA, Fla. Asst. city atty. City of Ft. Lauderdale, 1968, chief city pros., 1968-69, assoc. mcpl. judge, 1969-71, city commr., 1971-73, vice mayor, 1973—75, mayor, 1975-80; mem. US Congress from 22nd (formerly 15th) Fla. dist., 1981—2007; mem. ways and means com.; chmn. subcom. on human resources, 1995-98; chmn. social security subcom., 1999—2007. U.S. spl. ambassador to Papua New Guinea Independence; pres. U.S. Conf. Republican Mayors; mem. adv. and exec. bd. U.S. Conf. Mayors.; former chmn. mcpl. div. Ft. Lauderdale United Fund Campaign, 1971; former Young Rep. Club Broward County, Ft. Lauderdale Rep. Exec. Com.; past mem. exec. com. Rep. Nat. Com.; former mem. house select com. narcotics abuse and control; past bd. dirs. Broward County Traffic Assn.; mem judiciary com. Pub. Works and Transp. Bd. overseers Stetson Coll. Law. Republican. Roman Catholic.

SHAW, CURTIS S., lawyer, chemicals executive; b. 1948; BA in Econs. with honors, Trinity Coll., 1970; JD, Columbia U., 1973. Corp. lawyer, 1973—; atty. Shearman & Sterling, Mudge, Rose, Guthrie & Alexander; assoc. gen. counsel Occidental Chem. Corp., 1983—88; v.p., gen. counsel divsn. of Occidental Chem. Corp.; corp. counsel NYNEX, 1988—96; sr. v.p., gen. counsel, sec. Charter Investments, 1997—2003; exec. v.p., gen. counsel, sec. Charter Comm., 2003—05; exec. v.p., gen. counsel, corp. sec. Celanese Corp., Dallas, 2005—. Office: Celanese Corp 1601 W LBJ Fwy Dallas TX 75234 *

SHAW, DAVID ELLIOT, financial executive; b. Chgo., Mar. 29, 1951; s. Charles B. Jr. and Marilyn (Baron) Shaw. BA, U. Calif., San Diego, 1972; MS, Stanford U., 1975, PhD, 1980. Pres. Stanford Systems Corp., Palo Alto, Calif., 1976-79; assoc. prof. Columbia U., NYC, 1980-86; v.p. Morgan Stanley & Co., NYC, 1986-88; chmn. D.E. Shaw & Co., Inc. and Juno Online Svcs., Inc., NYC, 1988—, Schrödinger, Inc., NYC, 1988—. Contbr. articles to profl. jours. Chmn. NYC Mayor's Panel on Tech. and Fin., 1987; mem. NYC Partnership Subcommittee on Tech. and Fin., 1987; apptd. to Pres. Clinton's Com. of Advs. on Sci. and Tech., 1994; chmn. Pres. Clinton's Panel on Ednl. Tech., 1995. Named one of 400 Richest Ams., Forbes mag., 2006. Fellow Am. Acad. Arts & Scis.; mem. AAAS (bd. dirs. 1999), NY Acad. Scis. (bd. govs. 1993-95), Coun. on Competitiveness (exec. com. 1998—). Democrat. Jewish. Office: DE Shaw and Co 39th Fl Tower 45 120 W 45th St New York NY 10036-4041 *

SHAW, DAVID ROBERT, secondary school educator, theater director; b. Greenfield, Mass., May 16, 1950; s. Robert E. and Marion L. (Briggs) S. BA, Parsons Coll., 1973; MEd, Nat. Coll. Edn., 1996; grad., Inst. Children's Lit.; postgrad., No. Ill. U. Tchr. Bolingbrook (Ill.) H.S., 1973—. Asst. dir. Ill. High Sch. Theater Assn. All State Prodn., 1993, 96. Editor yearbook; writer and pub. children's lit.; asst. dir. All State H.S. Theater Prodn., 1996. Bd. dirs. Child Sexual Abuse Treatment Tng. Ctr., H.S. Theater Festival; vol. Big Bros., Youth Groups, Chgo.; artistic dir., bd. dirs. Chgo. Theater Ensemble; mem. DuPage Homeless Placement Coun.; bd. dirs. Outstanding Young Woman Pageant; mentor Kirk 4 Kids, 2006. Recipient Disting. Svc. award Bolingbrook Jaycees, 1991, 92, 98. Mem. Internat. Tchrs. Assn., Am. Fedn. Tchrs., Internat. Assn. Tchrs. English, Ill. All State Theater Assn. (bd. dirs.), Phi Delta Kappa, Alpha Psi Omega, Kappa Pi, Chi Beta Phi. Office Phone: 630-759-6400.

SHAW, DAVID TAI-KO, electrical and computer engineering educator, academic administrator; b. China, Mar. 13, 1938; came to U.S., 1960, naturalized, 1972; m. Katharine Lin-Yee Yang; children: Albert, Stanley. BSM.E., Nat. Taiwan U., Taipei, 1959; MS in Nuclear Engring., Purdue U., 1961, PhD, 1964. Asst. prof. div. interdisciplinary studies and research Sch. Engring., SUNY-Buffalo, 1964-67, assoc. prof. faculty engring. and applied scis., 1967-74, prof. elec. engring. and nuclear engring., aerospace and engring. sci., 1974-77, prof. elec. engring., 1974—, dir. lab. for power and environ. studies, 1978—90. Exec. dir. State Inst. on Superconductivity, 1987-97; vis. prof. U. Paris, 1976-77; vis. scientist Centre d'Etudes Nucleairs de Fontenay-aux-Roses (France) Commissariat a L'Energie

Atomique, 1976-77; vis. assoc. dept. environ. health engring. Calif. Inst. Tech., 1970-71; mem. U.S. del. French Commissariat a L'energie Atomique, 1974, U.S. del. Joint Nuclear Energy Agy. IAEA Internat. Liaison Group on Thermionic Elec. Power Generation, Paris, 1974; mem. U.S. vis. team USSR Acad. Scis. Editor: Fundamentals of Aerosol Science, 1978, Recent Developments in Aerosol Science, 1978, Assessment of Airborne Radioactivity, 1978; editor-in-chief: Jour. Aerosol Sci. and Tech., 1982-93; contbr. articles to profl. jours. Mem. IEEE, ASME, AAAS, Am. Assn. Aerosol Rsch. (pres. 1982-85, Assn. award 1984, Internat. Aerosol Fellow award 1994), Sigma Xi, Sigma Pi Sigma. Office: SUNY-Buffalo Materials Rsch Lab/Ctr for Innovation Engring 330 Bonner Hall Buffalo NY 14260-1900 E-mail: dshaw@buffalo.edu.

SHAW, DENNIS FREDERICK, former library director, chartered physicist, consultant; b. Teddington, Middlesex, Eng., Apr. 20, 1924; s. Albert and Lily Florence (Hill) S.; m. Joan Irene Chandler, June 25, 1949; children: Peter James, Margaret Denise, Katherine Joan, Deborah Mary. BA in Physics, U. Oxford, 1945, MA, 1950, DPhil in Nuc. Physics, 1950. Sr. rsch. officer Oxford (Eng.) U., 1950-75; tutor in physics Keble Coll., 1956-75, professorial fellow, 1977—, keeper of sci. books, 1975-91, emeritus, 1991. Vis. scientist CERN, Geneva, 1961-62; vis. prof. U. South Tenn., 1974; chmn. IFLA Sci. and Tech. Librs., 1987-91, hon. treas. spl. librs. div., 1991-93, cons., 1993—; mem. Home Office Sci. Adv. Coun., London, 1966-78; mem. Home Def. Sci. Adv. Com., London, 1978-95; mem. Hebdomadal Coun., Oxford U., 1980-89; mem Com. for the Internat. Coun. of Sci. Unions Press, 1991-96, mng. editor electronic pub., 1997-2002. Author: Introduction to Electronics, 1962, 70, Information Sources in Physics, 1985, 95; editor: Proceedings of ICSU/UNESCO Internat. Conferences on Electronic Publishing in Sci., 1996, 2001, Guidelines for Scientific Publishing, 1999; contbr. articles to profl. jours. Gov. Christ's Hosp., London, Almoner, 1980-98, chmn. edn. com., 1993-96; mem. Oxford City Coun., 1963-67; freeman City of London, 1998. Decorated Comdr. Brit. Empire, 1974. Fellow Inst. Physics, Zool. Soc.; mem. Am. Inst. Physics (sr.), Internat. Assn. Tech. Univs. Librs. (hon., sec. 1983-85, pres. 1986-90, chmn. pub. bd. 1991-93), N.Y. Acad. Sci., Oxford and Cambridge Club. Anglican. Home: 29 Davenant Rd Oxford OX2 8BU England Office: Keble Coll Parks Rd Oxford OX1 3PG England Business E-Mail: dennis.shaw@keb.ox.ac.uk.

SHAW, DONALD HARDY, lawyer; b. Oelwein, Iowa, June 1, 1922; s. John Hardy and Minnie (Brown) S.; m. Elizabeth Jean Orr, Aug. 16, 1946; children: Elizabeth Ann, Andrew Hardy, Anthony Orr. BS cum laude, Harvard U., 1942; JD with high distinction, U. Iowa, 1948. Bar: Ill. 1949, Iowa 1948, cert. fin. planner 1983. With firm Sidley & Austin, Chgo., 1948-55; with Iowa-Ill. Gas & Electric Co., Davenport, Iowa, 1956-87, treas., 1960-72, v.p. finance, 1973-87, also dir.; of counsel Walton, Creen, Curry and Robertson, Davenport, Iowa, 1987-88, Newpor, Bell, Leon & Martinez, Davenport, 1989-98. Author: As We Were, 2006. Mem. Iowa State Bd. Regents, 1969-81, Iowa State TV-Radio Com., 1976-81; trustee St. Luke's Hosp., Davenport, 1966-91. Served to capt. USAAF, 1942-45. Recipient Philo Sherman Bennett award, 1942 Mem.: Order of Coif, Delta Theta Phi. Congregationalist. Home: Vantage House #P11 Columbia MD 21044

SHAW, DONALD LESLIE, Spanish language educator; b. Feb. 11, 1930; s. Stephen Leslie and Lily (Hughes) S.; m. Maria Concetta Cristini, June 30, 1958; children: Andrew Leslie, Sylvia Maria Pierina. BA, U. Manchester, Eng., 1952, MA, 1953; PhD, U. Dublin, Ireland, 1960. Asst. lectr. U. Dublin, 1955-57, U. Glasgow, Scotland, 1957-64, U. Edinburgh, Scotland, 1964-69, sr. lectr., 1969-72, reader, prof. spanish, 1972-86; prof. spanish U. Va., Charlottsville, 1986—. Vis. prof. Brown U., Providence, 1967, U. Va., Charlottsville, 1983. Author: Historia de la Literatura Española, Siglo XIX, 1973, La Generación del 98, 1977, Nueva Narrativa Hispanoamericana, 1981, Alejo Carpentier, 1985, Borges' Narrative Strategies, 1992, Antonio Skármeta and the Post-Boom, 1994, The Post-Boom in Spanish American Fiction, 1998, A Companion to Spanish American Fiction, 2001. Served with RAF, 1953-55. Avocation: cycling. E-mail: dls6h@vriginia.edu. Office: U Va 115 Wilson Hall Charlottesville VA 22903-3238 Home: 102 Shamrock Rd #16 Charlottesville VA 22903 Office Phone: 434-924-4658. Business E-Mail: dls6h@virginia.edu.

SHAW, DORIS BEAUMAR, film and video producer, executive recruiter, management consultant; b. Pitts., July 13, 1934; d. Emerson C. and Doris Llorene (Rees) Beaumar; m. Robert Newton Shaw, July 6, 1957. BA summa cum laude, Lindenwood Coll., St. Charles, Mo., 1955. Writer, asst. to pres. Baker Prodns., Benton Harbor, Mich., 1955; asst. prodn. mgr. Condor Films, Inc., St. Louis, 1955-57; chief editor, asst. to v.p. Frederick F. Watson Inc., NYC, 1957-58; v.p. Gen. Pictures Corp., Cleve., 1958-71; dir., editor, unit mgr. Cinecraft Inc., Cleve., 1971-72; mgr. audio-visual dept. Am. Greetings Corp., Cleve., 1972-73; proprietor Script to Screen Svcs., Chagrin Falls, Ohio, 1973-76; pres. D & B Shaw, Inc., Chardon, Ohio, 1976-87, Hudson, Ohio, 1987—, Execusearch, Inc., Hudson, 1987—, Infosearch Inc., Hudson, 1994—, Cybersearch, Inc., Hudson, 1995—, Wellness Unltd. N.A., Inc., Peninsula, 2003—, The Write Stuff, Peninsula, 2005—. Film festival judge, tchr. Martha Holden Jennings Found./Hawken Sch., Gates Mills, Ohio, 1970-85; advisor teenage film contests, seminars Cleve. Bd. Edn., 1970-88; contest judge/film and video WVIZ-TV, Channel 25, Parma, Ohio, 1971—; guest lectr. Lindenwood Coll., 1973-80; adj. prof. U. Akron, 1990—; writer, cons. to bus. and industry regarding sales, mktg., bus. mgmt., info. and rsch. svcs., computer multimedia prodn., web page design and devel. Writer, dir., editor, prodr. hundreds of film, video, multi-image, multi-media, audio/visual prodns., radio, TV commls. and programs; contbr. articles to profl. jours. Bd. trustees Ohio Boys Town, Cleve., 1957-68; mem. alumnae coun. Lindenwood Coll., 1973-77; publicity chmn. Geauga County Preservation Soc., 1984-91; active various charitable orgns. Named Outstanding Young Woman of Am., Fedn. of Women's Clubs, 1965, Alumna of Yr. Merit award Lindenwood Coll., 1971; recipient numerous awards and grants for film, video projects including Gold Camera Best Documentary award, 1979. Mem. Soc. Motion Picture and TV Engrs., Info. Film Prodrs. Am., Assn. for Multi Image (charter), Detroit Prodrs. Assn., Internat. TV and Video Assn. (charter), Internat. Comm. Industries Assn., Internat. Tech. Assn., Coyahoga Valley Nat. Pk. Photographical Soc., Alpha Epsilon Rho. Republican. Avocations: science, travel, physical fitness, environmental issues, organic horticulture. Office: The Write Stuff PO Box 116 Peninsula OH 44264-0116 Business E-Mail: thewritestuff@windstream.net.

SHAW, ELEANOR JANE, newspaper editor; b. Columbus, Ohio, Mar. 23, 1949; d. Joseph Cannon and Wanda Jane (Campbell) S. BA, U. Del., 1971. With News-Jour. newspapers, Wilmington, Del., 1970-82, editor HEW desk, asst. met. editor, 1977-80, bus. editor, 1980-82; topics editor USA Today, 1982-83; asst. city editor The Miami Herald, 1983-85; projects editor The Sacramento Bee, 1985-87, news editor, 1987-91, exec. bus. editor, 1991-93, editor capitol bur. news, 1993-95, state editor, 1995-99; mgr. employee comm. The McClatchy Co., Sacramento, 1999—2004; associate TMT Worldwide, 2004—. Bd. dirs. Del. 4-H Found., 1978-83. Safety Ctr., Inc., Sacramento, 2003—, chair, 2005—. Mem. Calif. Soc. Newspaper Editors (bd. dirs. 1990-96), No. Calif. Wine Soc. (v.p. 1987-93, pres. 1993-2002). Office: 11682 Gold Country Blvd Gold River CA 95670 Office Phone: 800-732-1722. Personal E-mail: ellieshaw@sbcglobal.net. Business E-Mail: ellie@tmtww.com.

SHAW, ELIZABETH ORR, retired lawyer; b. Monona, Iowa, Oct. 2, 1923; d. Harold Topliff and Hazel (Kean) Orr; m. Donald Hardy Shaw, Aug. 16, 1946; children: Elizabeth Ann, Andrew Hardy, Anthony Orr. AB, Drake U., 1945; postgrad., U. Minn., 1945—46; JD, U. Iowa, 1948. Bar: Ill. 1949, Iowa 1956. Assoc. Lord Bissell & Brook, Chgo., 1949-52; pvt. practice Arlington Heights, Ill., 1952-56; ptnr. Wood & Shaw, Davenport, Iowa, 1968-72; mem. Iowa Ho. of Reps., Des Moines, 1967-72, Iowa Senate, Des Moines, 1972-77; county atty. Scott County, Davenport, 1977-78; corp. atty. Deere & Co., Moline, Ill., 1979-89; pvt. practice Davenport, 1990-98; ret., 1999. Mem. Scott County Bar Assn. (com. chmn. 1970-72), Iowa State Bar Assn. (chmn. family law com. 1970-76), Order of Coif, Phi Beta Kappa, Kappa Kappa Gamma, PEO. Republican. Mem. United Ch. of Christ.

SHAW, HAROLD, retired performing arts association administrator; b. Hebron, NY, June 11, 1923; Student, Ithaca Coll., 1942, Columbia, 1944, N.Y. U. Extension, 1948. Former assoc. Hurok Concerts, Inc., NYC; chmn., owner Shaw Concerts, Inc., NYC, 1969-99; ret., 1999; performing arts dir. Seattle World's Fair, 1961-62. Former concert mgr. Nathan Milstein, Vladimir Horowitz, Dame Janet Baker, Jessye Norman, Helen Donath, Jacqueline duPre, Wolfgang Holzmair, Jard van Nes, Mitsuko Uchida, Garrick Ohlsson, Shura Cherkassky, Horacio Gutiérrez, Julian Bream, John Williams, Elmar Oliveira, Kyoko Takezawa, Robert Shaw, Andrew Davis, and over 100 artists and attractions; exec. dir. President's Shakespeare Ann. Com., 1964. Dir. exec. staff, mem. performing arts com. Cultural Commn., N.Y.C., 1966; nat. chmn. Performing Arts Energy Commn., 1974; chmn. bd. trustees Am. Shakespeare Theatre, Straftord, Conn., 1974. With USAAF, 1942-43. Mem.: Am. Summer Stock Mgrs. Assn. (co-founder), Actors Equity Assn., Assn. Coll., Univ. and Cmty. Arts Adminstrs., Am. Symphony Orch. League, Internat. Performing Arts Adminstrs., Athletic Club, Phi Mu Alpha Sinfonia. E-mail: hshaw611@msn.com.

SHAW, HELEN LESTER ANDERSON, nutrition educator, researcher, retired dean; b. Lexington, Ky., Oct. 18, 1936; d. Walter Southall and Elizabeth (Guyn) Anderson; m. Charles Van Shaw, Mar. 14, 1988. BS, U. Ky., Lexington, 1958; MS, U. Wis., Madison, 1965, PhD, 1969. Registered dietitian. Dietitian Roanoke (Va.) Meml. Hosp., 1959-60, Santa Barbara (Calif.) Cottage Hosp., 1960-61; dietitian, unit mgr. U. Calif., Santa Barbara, 1961-63; rsch. asst., NIH fellow U. Wis., Madison, 1963-68; from asst. prof. to prof. U. Mo., Columbia, 1969-88, assoc. dean, prof., 1977-84; prof., chair dept. food and nutrition U. N.C., Greensboro, 1989-94, dean Sch. Human Environ. Scis., 1994-2000; ret., 2000. Cluster leader Food for 21st Century rsch. program U. Mo., 1985-88. Contbr. articles to rsch. publs. Elder First Prebsbyn. Ch., Columbia, Mo., 1974—89, Greensboro, NC, 1992—. Recipient Teaching award Home Econ. Alumni Assn., 1981, Gamma Sigma Delta, 1984, Centennial Legacy medallion U. Ky., 2007; rsch. grantee Nutrition Found., 1971-73, NIH, 1972-75, NSF, 1980-83. Mem. Am. Soc. for Nutrition, Am. Bd. Nutrition, Am. Soc. for Clin. Nutrition, Am. Dietetic Assn., Sigma Xi, Phi Upsilon Omicron, Kappa Omicron Nu. Democrat. Avocations: tennis, singing, volunteering, watercolor painting. Personal E-mail: shaw713helen@aol.com.

SHAW, JACK ALLEN, communications company executive; b. Auburn, Ind., Jan. 1, 1939; s. Marvin Dale and Vera Lucille (Harter) S.; m. Martha Sue Collins, Aug. 24, 1963; 1 child, Mark Allen. BSEE, Purdue U., 1962; DSc (hon.), Capitol Coll., 1994, DSc (hon.), 1995; D in Engring. (hon.), Purdue U., 1998. Project engr. Hughes Aircraft Co., El Segundo, Calif., 1962-69; dir. program mgmt. ITT Space Comms., Ramsey, NJ, 1969-74; v.p., corp. devel. Digital Comms. Corp., Gaithersburg, Md., 1974-78, exec. v.p., COO Germantown, Md., 1978-81, pres., CEO, 1981-84, M/A-com Telecom divsn., Germantown, Md., 1984-87; chmn., CEO Hughes Network Sys., Inc., 1988—, chmn., also bd. dirs., 1978—, Germantown, 1987-2000, corp. sr. exec. v.p. enterprise sector, 2000—; pres., CEO Hughes Elecs., 2001. Bd. dirs. XM Satellite Radio, Guidant Corp.; exec. v.p. Hughes Electronics, 1999. Mem.: IEEE (sr.), Radio Club Am. (hon.). Republican. Personal E-mail: jackbrasshat@aol.com.

SHAW, JEANNE OSBORNE, editor, poet; b. Stone Mountain, Ga., June 1, 1920; d. Virgil Waite and Daisy Hampton (Scruggs) Osborne; m. Harry B. Shaw, Dec. 10, 1982; children from previous marriage: Robert Allan Gibbs, Marilyn Osborne Gibbs Barry. BA, Agnes Scott Coll., Atlanta/Decatur, 1942. Editl. staff Atlanta Constitution, 1942; feature writer New London Day, Conn., 1943; book reviewer Atlanta Constitution, 1940—42, Atlanta Jour., 1945—48; poetry Banner Press Emory U., Atlanta, 1957—59; book editor Georgia Mag., Decatur, 1957—73. Author: The Other Side of the Water, 1970 (author of yr. in poetry award Dixie Coun. Authors and Journalists), From Cowslip to Cobalt, 1971, Unravelling Yarn, 1979, Faithbuilders, 1982—84, Third Millennium Christmas, 2001, The First Easter Parade, 2003; co-author: Noel: Poems of Christmas, 1979, They Continued Steadfastly, History of Druid Hills Baptist Church, 1987; contbr. poems, pen and ink sketches to mags.; author: Serious Poem, 2005. Mem. nat. arts and humanities com. Learning Life Boy Scouts Am., 2000—; pres. Newton class Druid Hills Bapt. Ch., 1973—74, dir. ch. tng., 1978—79, ch. clk., 1995—2001. Recipient Internat. Narrative Poem award, Poets and Patrons, Inc., 1992, Robert Martin, Burke, Otto in Praise of Poetry award, N.Y. Poetry Forum, 1973, 1979, 1981, Westbrook award, Ky. Poetry Soc., 1976, Ariz. award, 1981, Ind. State Fedn. Poetry Clubs award, Ala. State Poetry Soc. award, 1990, Rev. Earl M. Smith Meml. award, 1997, Joseph V. Hickey Meml. award, Nat. Fedn. State Poetry Socs., 1998. Mem.: Ga. Poetry Soc. (artistic dir. 2000, judge Nat. River of Words Contest 2002—05, 2007, Traditional award 1984, Cole and Ledford award 1986, Goreau award 1987, Melissa Henry award 1989, Charles and Virginia Dickson award 1990, Jo Ann Yeager Adkins award 1991, Poem About Atlanta award 1992, Goreau award 1993, Free Verse award 1993, My Very Best Poem award 1995, Traditional award 1997, Jabberwocky award 1997, Annette Peery award 1998, 1999, Charles Bruehler award 2000, Annette Peery award 2001, 22d Anniversary award 2002, Mikki Morris award 2002, Reece award 2002, Poems in Reach of Song award 2004—06), Atlanta Writers Club (pres. 1949—50, Aurelia Austin Writer of Yr. in poetry 1971, Wyatt award 1986, Light Verse award 1989, 1990, Daniel Whitehead Hicky award 1991, F. Levering Neely award 1991, Poet Laureate's award 1993, Wyatt award 1995, Daniel Whitehead Hicky award 1995, Gerry Crocker award 1995, Villanelle award 1997, 1998, Virginia Cole Veal award 1999, Light Verse award 2001, 2005, Serious Poetry award 2005, Formal Verse award 2006, Ben Willingham award), Poetry Soc. Ga. (John Clare prize 1955, Katharine H. Strong prize 1975, Eunice Thomson prize 1976, Jimmy Williamson prize 1977, Capt. Frank Spencer prize 1985, Conrad Aiken prize 1987, 1988, Capt. Frank Spencer prize 1988, Sarah Cunningham prize 1989, Soc. prize 1989, Lucy McEntire prize 1990, Grace Schley Knight prize 1991, Gerald Chan Sieg prize 1991, Eunice Thomson prize 1992, Grace Schley Knight prize 1993, Sarah Cunningham prize 1994, Harriet Ross Colquitt prize 1994, Lucy McEntire prize 1994, Gerald Chan Sieg prize 1995, Harriet Ross Colquitt prize 1995, Eva Tennyson Forbes Meml. prize 1996, Sarah Cunningham prize 1997, About Holes prize 1998, Soc. prize 2001, Formal prize 2005, Grace Schley Knight prize 2005, Monday prize 2005, Conrad Aiken prize 2006, Critics' Com. prize 2006, Conrad Aiken prize 2007, Lucy McEntire prize 2007), Ga. Writers Assn. (Lit. Achievement award 1971, Ga. Sr. Poet Laureate award 2006), Phi Beta Kappa. Home: 809 Pinetree Dr Decatur GA 30030-2332

SHAW, JEFFREY WILLIAM, gas industry executive; b. Salt Lake City, Nov. 9, 1958; s. William R. Jr. and Janet (Engar) S.; m. Cynthia Roberts, July 3, 1984; children: Morgan, Lauren, Catherine, Michael. BA in Acctg., U. Utah, 1983. CPA, Nev. With audit div. Arthur Andersen & Co., Dallas, 1983-85, Las Vegas, Nev., 1985-88; dir. internal audit SW Gas Corp., Las Vegas, Nev., 1988—91, controller, chief acctg. officer, 1991—93, v.p., controller, chief acctg. officer, 1993—94, v.p., treas., 1994—2000, sr. v.p. fin., treas., 2000—02, sr. v.p. gas resources & pricing, 2002—03, pres., 2003—04, CEO, 2004—. Active Boy Scouts Am., Dallas, 1985, Las Vegas, 1987—. Mem. AICPA, Am. Law Assn. (bd. dirs.), Nev. Soc. CPAs., U. Nev. Las Vegas Found. (bd. trustees). Republican. Mem. Lds Ch. Avocations: writing, guitar, composing music, golf, basketball. Office: SW Gas Corp PO Box 98510 Las Vegas NV 89193-8510 *

SHAW, JOHN FREDERICK, retired naval officer; b. Dallas, Oct. 14, 1938; s. John Frederick and Sarah E. (Crouch) S.; m. Janice Muren, July 14, 1962; children: Elizabeth Lee, Suzanne Michele. BS, U.S. Naval Acad., 1960; MS in Mgmt. with distinction, Naval Postgrad. Sch., Monterey, Calif., 1970; grad., Armed Forces Staff Coll., 1971. Commd. ensign USN, 1960, advanced through grades to rear adm., 1983; exec. officer USS Long Beach (CGN 9), 1978-79; comdg. officer USS Bainbridge (CGN 25), 1980-83; dir. guided missile destroyer 51, Arleigh Burke program Comdr. Naval Sea Systems Command, Washington, 1983-85, mgr. AEGIS shipbldg. program, 1985-87; comdr. Cruiser-Destroyer Group One, San Diego, 1987-88; dep. chief staff plans and policy Supreme Allied Comdr., Atlantic, Norfolk, Va., 1988-89, chief staff, 1989-91; ret., 1991; prof. joint mil. ops. Coll. Continuing Edn., Naval War Coll., San Diego, 1992-94. Bd. advisors United Svc. Benefit Assn., Kansas City, Kans., 1987-93; mem. cmty. bd. advisors Sam and Rose Stein Inst. for Rsch. on Aging, 1998-2004; membership chmn., 1999-2000, sec.-treas., 2000-2004, mem. bd. mem., 2006—; tax. cons. for elderly, AARP, 2000—. Trustee Coronado Libr., 1998—, exec. sec., 2001—02, pres., 2002—04. Decorated Def. D.S.M., Legion of Merit with two gold stars, Meritorious Svc. medal with gold star, Navy Commendation medal with gold star, Meritorious Unit Commendation (civilian) USN. Mem. AARP, U.S. Naval Inst. (life), U.S. Naval Acad. Alumni Assn. (life, pres. Washington chpt. 1986, bd. govs. San Diego/Coronado chpt. 1996-99), Surface Navy Assn. (life), San Diego Navy League (dir. 1997-2002), Coronado Men's Golf Club. Avocations: golf, reading, economics, travel. Personal E-mail: jshaw14@aol.com.

SHAW, JOHN W., lawyer; b. Mo., 1951; m. Cynthia Shaw; children: Sarah Ann, Katherine Kennan, Amy Elizabeth. BA, MA, U. Mo., 1973, JD, 1977. Bar: Mo. 1977. Ptnr. Lathrop & Norquist, 1983-92, Bryan Cave LLP, 1992-98, Berkowitz Oliver Williams Shaw & Eisenbrandt LLP (formerly Berkowitz Stanton Brandt Williams and Shaw LLP), Kansas City, 1998—. Bd. advisors, dept. personal fin. planning U. Mo.-Columbia, bd. advisors, Coll. Arts and Sci. Named Commencement Keynote Spkr., Coll. Arts and Sci., U. Mo.-Columbia, 2003, Best of the Bar, Kansas City Bus. Jour., 2003; named one of Mo. Super Lawyers, Law and Politics, 2006, Best Lawyers in Am., 2007; recipient Disting. Alumni award, Coll. Arts and Sci., U. Mo.-Columbia, 2005. Mem. ABA, Securities Industry Assn. (legal and compliance group), Mo. Bar, Def. Rsch. Inst. (chmn. firearms litigation subcom.), Order of Coif. Office: Berkowitz Oliver Williams Shaw & Eisenbrandt LLP 2600 Grand Blvd Ste 1200 Kansas City MO 64108 Home Phone: 913-491-9332; Office Phone: 816-561-7007. Business E-Mail: jshaw@bowse-law.com.

SHAW, JOSEPH THOMAS, Slavic languages educator; b. Ashland City, Tenn., May 13, 1919; s. George Washington and Ruby Mae (Pace) S.; m. Betty Lee Ray, Oct. 30, 1942 (dec. Sept. 2002); children: David Matthew, Joseph Thomas (dec. Dec. 2005), James William (dec. Jan. 1999). AB, U. Tenn., 1940, AM, 1941, Harvard, 1947, PhD, 1950. Asst. prof. Slavic langs. Ind. U., 1949-55, assoc. prof., 1955-61; prof. Slavic langs. U. Wis., 1961-89, prof. emeritus, 1989—, chmn. dept. Slavic langs., 1962-68, 77-86, chmn. div. humanities, 1964-65, 72-73, assoc. dean Grad. Sch., 1965-68. Author: The Letters of Alexander Pushkin, 1963, Pushkin's Rhymes: A Dictionary, 1974, Baratynskii: A Dictionary of the Rhymes and a Concordance to the Poetry, 1975, Batiushkov: A Dictionary of the Rhymes and a Concordance to the Poetry, 1975, Pushkin: A Concordance to the Poetry, 1985, American Association Teachers Slavic and East European Languages: The First Fifty Years 1941-91, 1991, Pushkin's Poetry of the Unexpected: The Nonrhymed Lines in the Rhymed Poetry and the Rhymed Lines in the Nonrhymed Poetry, 1994, Pushkin, Poet and Man of Letters, and His Prose (collected works, vol. 1), 1995, Pushkin Poems and Other Studies (collected works vol. 2), 1996, The Letters of Alexander Pushkin (collected works vols. 3-5), 3d edit., 1997, Konkordans k stikham Pushkina, 2000, Pushkin's Rhymes: A Dictionary (collected works, vol. 6-7), 2d edit., 2001, Batiushkov: A Dictionary of the Rhymes & A Concordance to the Poetry (collected works, vol. 8), 2d edit., 2001, Baratynskii: A Dictionary of the Rhymes & A Concordance to the Poetry (collected works, vol. 9), 2d edit., 2001, Poeziia neozhidannogo u Pushkina, 2002, Studies in Pushkin's Rhyming: Theory from Practice (collected works, vol. 10), 2002, The Letters of Alexander Pushkin(vol. 10-12 in The Complete Works of Alexander Pushkin 15 vols.1999-2003) 4th edit.; editor: The Slavic and East European Jour., 1957-70; contbr. articles to profl. jours. Served to capt. USNR, 1942-46, 51-53. Mem. Am. Assn. Tchrs. Slavic and East European Langs. (mem. exec. council 1953-70, 73-80, pres. 1973-74) Personal E-mail: jtshaw@wisc.edu.

SHAW, KATHLEEN M. TROUTNER, retired librarian; b. Waverly, Iowa, May 17, 1935; d. Bert Clifton and Kathleen Marjorie Troutner; m. Robert Einar Shaw (div.); children: Robert Belden(dec.), Ellen Katherine Shaw Karnes. BA in Edn., Western Wash. U., Bellingham, 1970; MS in Ednl. Media, Western Oregon State U., Monmouth, 1978. Tchr. Corvallis Sch. Dist., Oreg., 1970—73, resource tchr., 1973—76; media specialist Salem Sch. Dist., Oreg., 1978—82; libr. Saudi-Aramco Schs., Dhahran, Saudi Arabia, 1982—92; ret., 1992. Pres. Oak Harbor Libr. Bd., Wash., 1999—; bd. dirs. Sr. Svcs. Island County, Island County, Wash., 2004—. Mem.: AAUW (pres. Whidbey Island, Wash. br. 1997—98, named gift honoree 1998). Avocations: singing, reading, knitting.

SHAW, KENDALL (GEORGE), artist, educator; b. New Orleans, Mar. 30, 1924; s. George Kendall and Florence Gladys (Worner) S.; m. Frances (Glenn) Fort, Oct. 31, 1955. Student, Ga. Inst. Tech., 1944-46; BS in Chemistry, Tulane U., 1949, MFA, 1959; postgrad., La. State U., 1950, Fashion Inst. Tech., NYC, 1981—86. Instr. Columbia U., 1961-66, Hunter Coll., 1966-68, Parsons Sch. Design, N.Y.C., 1966-86, Lehman Coll., 1968-70, Bklyn. Mus. Art Sch., 1970-76, Bklyn. Coll., 2007—; US del. to UNESCO Conf., London, 1965. One-man shows include Orleans Gallery, New Orleans, 1960, 61, 63, Columbia U., 1962, 65, Bienville Gallery, New Orleans, 1968, Tibor de Nagy Gallery, N.Y.C., 1964, 65, 67, 68, Southampton Coll., 1969, John Bernard Myers Gallery, 1972, Alessandra Gallery, 1976, Lerner Heller Gallery, N.Y.C., 1979, 81, 82, Nature Morte, N.Y.C., 1983, Bernice Steinbaum Gallery, N.Y.C., 1991, Artists Space, N.Y.C., 1992, The Gallery of South Orange, NJ, 1997, U. Richmond, Va., 1999, Tulane U., 2001, Ogden Mus. So. Art, New Orleans, 2007, Ruskin Gallery, Cambridge U., Eng., 2007; group shows include Downtown Gallery, New Orleans, 1959, Orleans Gallery, 1959, 60, 61, Mus. Contemporary Art, Nagaoka, Japan, 1965, Alessandra Gallery, N.Y.C., 1976, Gallerie Simonne Stern, New Orleans, 1968, Albright-Knox Gallery, Buffalo, 1970, P.S.I., N.Y.C., 1977, curator Rice U., Houston, 1977, Gladstone Villani Gallery, N.Y.C., 1978, Galerie Habermann, Cologne, 1979, Modern Art Gallery, Vienna, 1980, Ill. Wesleyan U., Bloomington, 1980, Contemporary Art Ctr., New Orleans, 2002, Jacksonville Art Mus., Fla., 1983, The Ogden Mus. So. Art, New Orleans, 2001-04, Leslie/ Lohman Gallery, NYC, 2007, others; represented in permanent collections Sammlung Ludwig, Aachen, Bklyn. Mus., Mus. Contemporary Art, Nagaoka, Japan, Everson Mus., Syracuse, Chase Bank, N.Y.C., NYU, Polk Mus. Art, Lakeland, Fla., Orlando Mus. Art, Weatherspoon Art Gallery, Greensboro, NC, Marsh Art Gallery, Richmond, Va., Tulane U., New Orleans, New Orleans Mus. Art, Miss. Mus. Art, The Ogden Mus. So. Art, New Orleans. Served in USN, 1943—46. Named Disting. Alumnus, Tulane Coll., 2001. Mem.: NY Artists Equity Assn., Coll. Art Assn. Address: 916 President St Brooklyn NY 11215-1604 Personal E-mail: kendallshaw@aol.com.

SHAW, L. EDWARD, JR., lawyer; b. Elmira, NY, July 30, 1944; s. L. Edward and Virginia Anne (O'Leary) S.; m. Irene Ryan; children: Christopher, Hope, Hillary, Julia, Rory BA in Econs., Georgetown U., Washington, 1966; JD, Yale U., New Haven, 1969. Bar: N.Y. 1969. Assoc. Milbank, Tweed, Hadley & McCloy, NYC, 1969—76, ptnr., 1976—82; sr. v.p., gen. counsel Chase Manhattan Corp., NYC, 1982—85, exec. v.p., gen. counsel, 1985-96; vice chmn., gen. counsel Natwest Markets, NYC, 1996-97, pres., 1997-99; exec. v.p. and gen. counsel Aetna Inc., 1999—2004; of counsel Gibson Dunn & Crutcher LLP, 2004—. Bd. dirs. HealthSouth Corp., Birmingham, Ala., 2005—. Mem.: Am. Law Inst., Phi Beta Kappa. Roman Catholic. Office Phone: 212-351-3846. Business E-Mail: eshaw@Gibsondunn.com.

SHAW, LEONARD GLAZER, retired electrical engineering educator, consultant; b. Toledo, Aug. 15, 1934; s. A. Daniel and Mary (Glazer) S.; m. Susan Gail Weil, Dec. 24, 1961; children: Howard Benjamin, Mitchell Bruce, Jenny Louise. BSEE, U. Pa., 1956; MSEE, Stanford U., 1957, PhD, 1961. From asst. to assoc. prof. Polytech. U. N.Y., Bklyn., 1960-75, prof., 1975—99, prof. emeritus, 1999—, head dept. elec. engring. and computer sci., 1982-90, dean Sch. Elec. Engring. and Computer Sci., 1990-94, vice provost for undergrad. studies, 1995-96. Vis. prof. Tech. U., Eindhoven, Netherlands, 1970, Ecole Nationale Superieure de Mecanique, Nantes, France, 1977, U. Sussex, Brighton, Eng., 1998; cons. Sperry Systems Mgmt. Div., Great Neck, N.Y.; mem. grant rev. panels NSF, 1986-98. Co-author: Signal Processing, 1975; contbr. articles to profl. jours. Rsch. grantee NSF, 1973, 81. Fellow: IEEE (mem. pub. bd. 1961—92, mem. various coms., editor-in-chief IEEE Press 1988—91, gen. chmn. Conf. of Decision and Control 1989, chmn. Tech. Field Award Coun. 1995—97), Control Sys. Soc. of IEEE (fin. v.p. 1992—93, 2000, pres.-elect 2001, pres. 2002). Office: Polytech U 6 Metrotech Ctr Brooklyn NY 11201-3840 Business E-Mail: lpshaw@poly.edu.

SHAW, MELVIN PHILLIP, physicist, engineering educator, psychologist; b. Bklyn., Aug. 16, 1936; s. Harry and Yetta (Stutsky) S.; m. Carol Joan Phillips, Sept. 5, 1959 (div. Feb. 1987); children: Adam, Evan; m. Bernetta Berger, May 16, 1987. BS, Bklyn. Coll., 1959; MS, Case Western Res. U., 1963, PhD, 1965; MA, Ctr. for Humanistic Studies, 1988. Research scientist United Techs. Research Labs., E. Hartford, Conn., 1964-68, scientist-in-charge, 1966-70; prof. Wayne State U., Detroit, 1970-96, prof. emeritus, 1997—; adminstrv. dir. Assocs. of Birmingham/Kingswood Hosp., 1991-93. Cons. Energy Conversion Devices, Troy, Mich., 1970-92. Co-author: The Gunn-Hilsum Effect, 1979, The Physics and Applications of Amorphous Semiconductors, 1988, The Physics of Instabilities in Solid State Electron Devices, 1992, Creativity and Affect, 1994. Fellow Am. Phys. Soc.; mem. IEEE (sr.), Am. Psychol. Assn. (assoc.). Avocations: cooking, walking, exercise, travel. Office Phone: 248-644-8330. E-mail: bunny3336@talkamerica.net.

SHAW, MICHAEL, biologist, educator; b. Barbados, W.I., Feb. 11, 1924; s. Anthony and Myra (Perkins) S.; m. Jean Norah Berkinshaw, Oct. 16, 1948; children: Christopher A., Rosemary E., Nicholas R., Andrew L. BSc, McGill U., 1946, MSc, 1947, PhD, 1949, DSc (hon.), 1975, U. B.C., 2003. NRC Can. postdoctoral fellow Botany Sch., Cambridge U., 1949-50; assoc. prof. biology U. Sask., Canada, 1950-54, prof., 1954-67, prof., head dept. biology, 1961-67; dean faculty agrl. scis. U. B.C., Canada, 1967-75, v.p. acad. devel., 1975-81, acad. v.p., provost, 1981-83, univ. prof., 1983-89, univ. prof. emeritus, 1989—. Mem. Sci. Coun. Can., 1976-82, Natural Scis. and Engring. Rsch. Coun. Can., 1978-80. Contbr. articles to profl. jours. Recipient Queen's Silver Jubilee medal, 1977, Gold medal Biol. Coun. Can., 1983. Fellow Royal Soc. Can. (Flavelle medal 1976), Can. Phytopath. Soc., Am. Phytopath. Soc.; mem. AAAS, Can. Bot. Assn., Can. Soc. Plant Physiologists (Gold medal 1971), Am. Soc. Plant Biologists. Home: 1792 Western Pky Vancouver BC Canada V6T 1V3

SHAW, MONTGOMERY THROOP, chemical engineering professor; b. Ithaca, NY, Sept. 11, 1943; s. Robert William and Charlotte (Throop) S.; m. Stephanie Habel, Sept. 5, 1966 (dec. 1989); 1 child, Steven Robert; m. Maripaz Nespral, June 25, 1994. BChemE, MS, Cornell U., 1966, Princeton U., NJ, 1968, PhD, 1970. Engr., project scientist Union Carbide Corp., Bound Brook, N.J., 1970-76; assoc. prof. Dept. Chem. Engring., U. Conn., Storrs, 1977-83, prof., 1983—; sabbatical prof. Sandia Nat. Labs., Albuquerque, 1983-84. Vis. scientist E.I. Dupont de Nemours and Co., Experimental Station, Wilmington, Del., 1991-92; adv. bd. Jour. of Applied Polymer Sci., 1984-89. Co-author: Polymer-Polymer Miscibility, 1977, Computer Programs for Rheologists, 1994, Introduction to Polymer Viscoelasticity, 2005. Grantee Alcoa Found., 1985, Exxon Edn. Found., 1986. Mem. IEEE (sr. mem., assoc. editor transactions on dielectrics and elec. insulation), Soc. Rheology (sec. 1977-81, treas. 1997—), Am. Chem. Soc., Am. Phys. Soc. Achievements include patents on rheological measurement method and apparatus and low density microcellular foams. Office: U Conn IMS 97 N Eagleville Rd Storrs Mansfield CT 06269-3136 Business E-Mail: montgomery.shaw@uconn.edu.

SHAW, NINA L., lawyer; b. NYC; BA, Barnard Coll., 1976; JD, Columbia U., 1979. Bar: Calif. 1981. Founding ptnr., entertainment law Del, Shaw, Moonves, Tanaka, Finkelstein & Lezcano, Santa Monica, Calif. Bd. dirs. The Montel Williams MS Found.; mem. Barbara A. Black Professorship Com. Named one of 100 Most Powerful Women in Entertainment, Hollywood Reporter, 2003, 2004, 2006, 100 Most Influential Blacks in America; recipient Disting. Alumna/us Award, Columbia Black Law Students Assn., 2002, Women in Film Crystal award, 2005. Mem.: State Bar Calif., LA County Bar Assn., Kernochan Ctr. Law, Media and Arts (West Coast adv. bd.), Black Women Lawyers Assn. *

SHAW, RICHARD EUGENE, cardiovascular researcher; b. Springfield, Ohio, Jan. 20, 1950; s. Eugene Russell and Marjorie Caroline Shaw; m. Nov. 26, 1976; 2 children. BA, Duquesne U., 1972; MA, U.S. Internat. U., San Diego, 1977; PhD, U. Calif., San Francisco, 1984. Cert. nuc. med. technologist. Nuclear Medicine Tech. Cert. Bd. Staff nuc. med. technologist Scripps Meml. Hosp., La Jolla, Calif., 1975-79; rsch. asst. U. Calif. San Francisco Sch. Medicine, 1980-85; mgr. rsch. programs San Francisco Heart Inst., Daly City, Calif., 1985-87, dir. rsch., 1988-90, dir. rsch. and ops., 1991—2003; dir. rsch., quality and edn. Sutter Pacific Heart Ctrs., 2003—. Sr. advisor steering com. for databases Daus. of Charity Nat. Health Sys., St. Louis, 1993-96. Editor-in-chief Jour. Invasive Cardiology, 1989—; contbr. articles to profl. jours; chpts. to books. Coach Am. Youth Soccer Orgn. and Youth Baseball Assn., bd. dirs., Burlingame, Calif., 1990-94; pres. Burlingame H.S. Athletic Boosters, 2000—. Fellow Am. Coll. Cardiology (nat. cardiac database com., outcomes assessment subcom. 1998—, NCDR task force 2001—, publs. subcom. 2001—), Am. Coll. Angiology; mem. Am. Heart Assn., Soc. for Clin. Trials, N.Y. Acad. Scis., Am. Statis. Assn., Am. Med. Informatics Assn., Soc. Behavioral Medicine. Avocation: music. Office: Sutter Pacific Heart Ctr CPMC 2200 Webster # 303 San Francisco CA 94115 Home Phone: 650-678-2375. Business E-Mail: shawr@sutterhealth.org.

SHAW, RICHARD H., dean; m. Delphine Red Shirt; children: Justin, Megan, Kirsten. BA, Dartmouth Coll.; MA in Coll. Student Personnel, Guidance and Counseling, U. Colo., Boulder. With U. Colo., Boulder, 1972—81; assoc. dir. admissions and records U. Calif., Berkeley, 1983—88; dir. admissions U. Mich., 1988—93; dean undergraduate admissions and fin. aid Yale U., 1993—2005; dean admissions and fin. aid Stanford U., 2005—. Mem.: Nat. Assn. Admissions Councelors, Consortium on Financing Higher Edn. Office: Stanford U Dean Undergrad Admission 355 Galvez Stanford CA 94305 Office Phone: 650-725-3770. Office Fax: 650-725-2846. E-mail: richard.shaw@stanford.edu. *

SHAW, RICHARD THOMAS, humanitarian, retired federal agent, retired military officer; b. Manchester, NH, Nov. 22, 1943; s. Elwood Barton and Carmella (DiGennaro) Shaw; m. Carla Ann Harnden, July 14, 2003; children: Steven S., Michael J. BBA, MPA, Nat. Coll. Arts and Sci., Tulsa, Okla., 1980; PhD, Sussex Coll. Tech., Eng., 1984. Sr. sgt. mil. pers. US Army, 1961—67; sr. claims adjudicator US HHS, 1967—74; mil. pers. officer USAR, 1968—2003; ret. US Army, 2003. Motivational spkr. Mem. Internat. Platform Assn. Pub. Spkrs.; nat. chmn. Pride in Am. Found. Decorated Army Commendation medal, cert. appreciation US Army Reserve, cert. of recognition Sec. of Defense; named life fellow, Sussex Coll. Tech., Eng., 1991, elected, Orgn. Amazing Men, 2003. Mem.: Nat. Assn. Ret. Fed. Employees (life), Am. Legion (life; past chmn., prisoner of war, missing in action), Veterans of Fgn. Wars (life), Jaycees (life, past state pres. Maine Jaycees, 1974-75, attained Number 1 status, US Jaycees Parade of States, 1974-75, received Clayton Frost award, elected nat. v.p. US JCI Senate 1979, received Number 1 US JCI Senator award 1980), Lions Club Internat. (life mem.; past zone chmn., past regional chmn., Outstanding Zone Chmn. award Dist. 41L, 1996, Outstanding Regional Chmn. award Dist. 41L, 1997, conferred Melvin Jones fellow 2006). Democrat. Roman Catholic. Avocations: travel, golf, reading, antiques.

SHAW, ROBERT GILBERT, retired state legislator, food service executive; b. Erwin, NC, Nov. 22, 1924; s. Robert Gilbert B. and Annie Elizabeth (Byrd) S.; m. Grace Lee Wilson, Jan. 29, 1951 (div. 1976); children: Ann Karlen, Barbara Jean; m. Linda Owens, May 27, 1982. AA, Campbell U., 1948; postgrad., U. N.C., 1948-50. Restaurateur, 1951—. County commr. County of Guilford, Greensboro, N.C., 1968-76; chair N.C. Rep. Party, Raleigh, 1975-77; minority leader N.C. Senate, Raleigh, 1984-2002; chair Guilford County Rep. Party, 1973-75; mem. Rep. Nat. Com., Washington, 1975-77. With USAAC, 1943-46. Named Legislator of Yr. Nat. Fedn. Wildlife, 1990. Mem. Elks (life, bd. govs. 1953—). Presbyterian. Avocations: fishing, hunting, politics. Home: 5105 Bennington Dr Greensboro NC 27410 Home Phone: 336-855-7533. Personal E-mail: RGB112224@aol.com.

SHAW, ROBERT WILLIAM, JR., management consultant, venture capitalist; b. Ithaca, NY, Aug. 10, 1941; s. Robert William and Charlotte G. (Throop) Shaw; m. Anne P. Meads, Aug. 29, 1964; children: Mark Andrew, Christopher Matthew. B of Engring. Physics, Cornell U., 1964, MSEE, 1964; PhD, Stanford U., 1968; MPA, Am. U., 1981. Postdoctoral fellow Cavendish Lab., Cambridge, England, 1968-69; mem. tech. staff Bell Tel. Labs., Murray Hill, NJ, 1969-72; with Booz Allen Hamilton, Bethesda, Md., 1972-83, sr. v.p. energy and environ. divsn., 1979-83, mem. oper. coun., 1981-83, also bd. dirs.; pres. Arete Ventures, Inc., 1983-97, Utech Venture Capital Corp., 1985—2003, Utech, LLC, 2003—05; gen. ptnr. Utech Venture Capital Corp. Fund I, 1985—2000, Utech Venture Capital Corp. Fund II, 1988—2003, Utech Venture Capital Corp. I Parallel Fund L.P., 1988—2001, Utech Venture Capital Corp. II Parallel Fund, L.P., 1991—2003, Utech Climate Challenge Fund, LLC, Bethesda, 1995—2005; v.p. Can. Energy and Environment Ventures, Inc., 1993-95; pres. Arete Corp., Center Harbor, NH, 1997—; ptnr. Atrium Capital/Honda Ventures, 2004—. Spl. ltd. ptnr. Nth Power Techs. Fund II; mem. investment com. Sustainable Asset Mgmt. Pvt. Equity Fund, Commons Capital LLC; mng. ptnr. Micro-Generation Tech. Fund, LLC, 1997—; mng. mem. SC Green Tech Ventures, LLC, 2007; mem. bd. energy and environ. sys. Nat. Rsch. Coun., 1998—2004; mem. energy com. Aspen Inst. Humanistic Studies, Investor's Cir., Solar Cir.; bd. councillors China-US Ctr. Sustainable Devel.; chmn. bd. dirs. CTP Hydrogen Corp., Distributed Energy Systems, 1996—2007, Evergreen Solar, 1994—2005; bd. dirs. H2Gen Innovations, Inc.; mem. adv. coun. Cornell U. Engring. Coll., 2005—; mem. hydrogen tech. adv. com. The US Dept. Energy, 2006—. Contbr. articles to profl. jours. Named NASA trainee; Office Sci. Rsch. fellow, USAF, 1968—69. Mem.: AAAS, Social Venture Network, Inst. Noetic Scis., Assn. Humanistic Psychology, Orgnl. Devel. Network, Nat. Venture Capital Assn., Am. Phys. Soc., Tau Beta Pi, Sigma Xi, Kappa Delta Rho, Pi Alpha Alpha, Phi Kappa Phi. Home: PO Box 1664 Center Harbor NH 03226-1664 Office: PO Box 1299 Center Harbor NH 03226-1299 Office Phone: 603-253-9797. Business E-Mail: aretecorp@adelphia.net.

SHAW, RONALD AHREND, physician, educator; b. Toledo, July 20, 1946; s. Harold Michael and Eve Helen (Ganch) S.; m. Carol Ann Rapp, June 13, 1970; children: Robert, Benjamin, Daniel. BS, U. Toledo, 1968; MD, Washington U., 1972. Diplomate Am. Bd. Emergency Medicine. Intern, then resident in surgery St. Luke's Hosp., St. Louis, 1972-73, resident in surgery, 1973; mem. staff Bapt. Med. Ctr.-Montclair, Birmingham, Ala., 1976-81, chief emergency svc., 1979-81; assoc. dir. lifesaver flight ops. Caraway Meth. Med. Ctr., Birmingham, 1981-85; dir. emergency svc. sch. medicine U. Ala., 1985-89; asst. dir. emergency svc. R.I. Hosp., Providence, 1989-95; attending physician emergency dept. Bapt. Med. Ctr., Montgomery, Ala., 1996—; med. dir. emergency dept. Jackson Hosp., 2000—01; sec.-treas., med. staff Bapt. Med. Ctr., 2001—03. Cons. U. Tex., Houston, 1986, Bell Helicopter, Ft. Worth, 1986, Mut. Assurance, Birmingham, 1986-89, NYU, 1988-89, R.I. State Med. Examiners Office, 1991-96, Fla. Dept. Health, EMS Office, 1991—, Joint Underwriters Assocs. of R.I., 1991-96; chmn. adv. bd. emergency svc. Ala. Dept. Pub. Health, 1986-89; med. dir. Emergency Med. Svcs. div. R.I. Dept. Health, 1990-95; med. dir. Health Care Rev., Inc., 1995-96. Bd. dirs. MADD, Ala., 1986, Univ. Emergency Medicine Found., 1995-96; mem. planning com. Youth Baseball, Vestavia Hills, ala., 1986, 87; mem. disaster com. City of Birmingham, 1984-89; mem. 911 Commn., State of R.I., 1991-96. Recipient Disting. Achievement award Birmingham Emergency Med. Svc., 1988. Fellow Am. Coll. Emergency Physicians (bd. dirs. Ala. chpt. 1984-89, steering com. EMS sect. 1991-94, sec.-treas. R.I. chpt. 1995-96); mem. AAAS, ACS (state com. on trauma R.I. chpt. 1990-96), N.Y. Acad. Sci., Med. Assn. Ala. (mem. coun. med. svc. 1985-86). Republican. Avocations: hunting, stamp collecting and computer programming. Office Phone: 334-272-1050. Personal E-mail: kd1hp@msn.com.

SHAW, RUSSELL BURNHAM, writer, journalist; b. Washington, May 19, 1935; s. Charles Burnham and Mary (Russell) S.; m. Carmen Hilda Carbon, July 19, 1958; children: Mary Hilda, Emily Anne, Janet, Charles, Elizabeth. BA, Georgetown U., 1956, MA, 1960. Staff writer Cath. Standard, Washington, 1956-57; reporter Nat. Cath. News Svc., 1957-66; dir. publs., pub. info. Nat. Cath. Ednl. Assn., 1966-69; dir. Nat. Cath. Office for Info., 1969-73; assoc. sec. for communication U.S. Cath. Conf., 1973-74, sec. for pub. affairs Nat. Conf. Cath. Bishops, 1975-87; dir. pub. info. KC, 1987-97; assoc. prof. Pontifical Univ. of the Holy Cross, 1996—, Cath. Distance U., 2006—. Consultor Pontifical Coun. for Social Comms., 1984—89, 2001—; editor The Pope Speaks, 1998—2005. Author: The Dark Disciple, 1961, Abortion on Trial, 1968, Church and State, 1979, Choosing Well, 1982, Why We Need Confession, 1986, Renewal, 1986, Signs of the Times, 1986, Does Suffering Make Sense?, 1987, To Hunt, To Shoot, To Entertain, 1993, Understanding Your Rights, 1994, Papal Primacy in the Third Millennium, 2000, Ministry or Apostolate—What Should the Catholic Laity Be Doing?, 2002, Catholic Laity in the Mission of the Church, 2005; co-author: S.O.S. for Catholic Schools, 1970, Beyond the New Morality, 3d edit., 1988, Fulfillment in Christ, 1991, Personal Vocation, 2003, Good News, Bad News, 2007, others; editor Ency. of Cath. Doctrine, 1997; columnist Washington Report, 1966-2006,Cath. Herald, 1999—; contbg. editor Crisis Mag., 2002—, Columbia Mag., 2002-06, Our Sunday Visitor, 2006—. Mem. Equestrian Order of Holy Sepulchre of Jerusalem, Phi Beta Kappa. Roman Catholic. Home and Office: 2928 44th Pl NW Washington DC 20016-3555 Home Phone: 202-363-9566; Office Phone: 202-363-9566. Personal E-mail: rshaw10290@aol.com.

SHAW, RUTH G., energy company executive; b. Feb. 19, 1948; m. Colin Stuart Shaw; 2 children. BA in English magna cum laude, East Carolina U.; PhD, U. Tex. Pres. El Centro Coll., Dallas, 1984—86, Central Piedmont Cmty. Coll., 1986—92; v.p. corp. comms. Duke Energy Corp., Charlotte, NC, 1992-94, sr. v.p. corp. resources, 1994-97, exec. v.p., chief adminstrv. officer, 1997—2003, pres. Duke Power Co., 2003—06, group exec. pub. policy, pres. Duke Nuclear, 2006, exec. adv. to chmn. & CEO, 2006—, pres. Duke Energy Found., 1994—2003. Bd. dirs. Wachovia Corp., 1990—, MedCath Corp., 2003—, The Dow Chemical Co., 2005—, DTE Energy, 2007—, Edison Electric Inst., Nuclear Energy Inst., S. E. Electric Exchange; chair Charlotte Rsch. Inst.; mem. Palmetto Bus. Forum. Mem. Order of the Long Leaf Pine; trustee U. N.C., Charlotte; bd. dirs. Rsch. Triangle Found. of N.C.; mem. Conf. Bd. Chief Adminstrv. Officer's Coun.; chmn. Found. for the Carolinas; elder 1st Presbyn. Ch., Charlotte; active United Way, Arts and Scis. Coun., YMCA, Boy Scouts Am. Named Outstanding Alumni, East Carolina U., disting. grad. U. Tex., Charlotte Woman of Yr., 1992, Businesswoman of Yr., 1995; recipient award for comms. excellence, 1997. Office: Duke Energy Corp 526 S Church St Charlotte NC 28202-1802 *

SHAW, SONIA, retired lawyer; b. Nov. 3, 1928; BA, Hunter Coll., NYC, 1949; JD, U. Mich., Ann Arbor, 1952. Rsch. asst. U. Mich. Law Sch., Ann Arbor, 1952—53; pvt. practice Ann Arbor, 1968—92; ret., 1992. Mem.: State Bar Mich. (editor, bulletin negligence sect. 1968—90). Home: 2576 Devonshire Rd Ann Arbor MI 48104-2708

SHAW, STANLEY MINER, pharmacist, educator; b. Parkston, SD, July 4, 1935; s. George Henry and Jensina (Thompson) S.; m. Excellda J. Watke, Aug. 13, 1961; children: Kimberly Kay, Renee Denise, Elena Aimee. BS, S.D. State U., 1957, MS, 1959; PhD, Purdue U., 1962. Instr. S.D. State U., 1960-62; asst. prof. bionucleonics Purdue U., West Lafayette, Ind., 1962-66, assoc. prof., 1966-71, prof. nuclear pharmacy, 1971—2005, prof. emeritus nuclear pharmacy, 2005—, head. divsn. nuclear pharmacy, 1990—2004, acting head Sch. Health Scis., 1990-93. Bd. pharm. spltys. Splty. Council Nuclear Pharmacy, 1978-82. Contbr. articles to profl. jours. Recipient Lederle Pharmacy faculty award, 1962, 1965, Parenteral Drug Assn. Rsch. award, 1970, Henry Heine Outstanding Tchr. award, Sch. Pharmacy Purdue U., 1989, 1993, 1999, Disting. Alumnus award, S.D. State U., 1991, Coll. Pharmacy Disting. Alumnus award, 2006, Disting. Pharmacy Educator award, Am. Assn. Colls. Pharmacy, 1994. Fellow Acad. Pharmacy Practice (chmn. sect. nuclear pharmacy 1979-80, historian 1981-85, mem.-at-large 1993-95, chmn.-elect 1995-96, chmn. 1996-97, Disting. Achievement award 1998), Am. Soc. Hosp. Pharmacy, Am. Pharm. Assn. (ho. of dels. 1977, 79, 86, 92, Founder's award, Daniel B. Smith Practice Excellence award 2000); mem. Health Physics Soc., Sigma Xi, Phi Lambda Upsilon, Phi Lambda Sigma, Rho Chi. Home: 7208 W Greenview Dr Battle Ground IN 47920-9732 Office: Purdue U Sch Pharmacy West Lafayette IN 47907-1336 Business E-Mail: sshaw@pharmacy.purdue.edu.

SHAW, STEVEN A., information technology executive; BBA, MBA, Univ. So. Calif. Mgmt. positions with Volt Info. Sciences Inc., NYC, 1995—97, pres. ProcureStaff subs., 1997—2005, bd. dir., 1998—, sr. v.p., 2000—05, exec. v.p., COO, 2005, co-CEO, 2005—06, pres., CEO, 2006—. Office: Volt Info Sciences 560 Lexington Ave New York NY 10022 *

SHAW, SUE ANN, medical transcriptionist; b. Van Nuys, Calif., Oct. 7, 1938; d. Harry Herbert and Elizabeth (Allison) Nesbit; m. Gerald Cargile Shaw (dec.); children: Deanna Christine Rushing, Jody Ray Rushing(dec.), John Paul Rushing. Cert. med. transcriptionist Am. Assn. Med. Transcription. Med. transcriptionist Meth. Hosps. of Dallas, 1975—2005. Vol. Meals on Wheels, Waxahachie, Tex., 2003, Charlton Meth. Hosp., Dallas, 2005—. Mem.: Am. Assn. Med. Transcription (founding officer, corr. sec. Greater Dallas chpt. 1979—82, com. mem. 1989—92). Republican. Baptist. Avocations: embroidery, stained glass, quilting, painting, gardening. Home: 110 Sunglow Loop Red Oak TX 75154

SHAW, THEODORE MICHAEL, legal association administrator; b. NYC, Nov. 24, 1954; s. Theodore and Jean Audrey (Churchill) Shaw; m. Cynthia E. Muldrow; children: T. Winston, Zora Jean. BA with honors, Wesleyan U., 1976; JD, Columbia U., 1979. Bar: Calif., NY. Trial atty. Civil Rights Divsn. US Dept. Justice, 1979—82; dir. ednl. docket NAACP Legal Def. and Ednl. Fund, 1982—87, assoc. dir.-counsel NYC, 1993—2004, pres., dir.-counsel, 2004—; founder, counsel Legal Def. and Edn. Fund's Western Regional Office, 1987—90. Asst. prof. law U. Mich. Law Sch., 1990—93; adj. prof. Columbia U. Sch. Law, 1993—. Named one of Most Influential Black Ams., Ebony mag., 2006; recipient Lawrence A. Wein prize for social justice, Columbia U., Baldwin medal, Wesleyan U. Mem.: ABA, Langston Bar Assn., LA County Bar Assn., Nat. Bar Assn. (A. Leon Higginbotham Jr. Meml. award Young Lawyers Divsn.). Office: NAACP Legal Def and Ednl Fund Inc Ste 1600 99 Hudson St New York NY 10013 Office Phone: 212-965-2200.

SHAW, THOMAS, conductor, director; b. Whichita Falls, Tex., May 25, 1930; s. Lloyd L. Shaw and Flora Mabry; m. Joan H. Shaw, June 26, 1957; children: Thomas Jr., Kenneth Mark, Sara Lynn. MusB in Edn., Midwestern State U., Tex., 1951; MusM in Edn., U. North Tex., 1952, D of Edn., 1971. Choral dir. Wichita Falls H.S, Tex., 1957—65; asst. prof. music Okla. Coll. of Liberal Arts, Chickasha, 1966—69; assoc. prof. music Fla. So. Coll., Lakeland, 1972—76; choral dir. Whichita Falls H.S., 1976—78; supr. of music, dir. fine arts Wichita Falls Ind. Sch. Dist., 1978—91; retired. Ch. choir dir., Wichita Falls, Tex., Chickasha, Lakeland, Fla.; pvt. voice lessions tchr. E-4 USAF, 1952—52, San Antonio and Japan. Republican. Presbyterian. Avocations: woodworking, stained glass.

SHAW, TIMOTHY MILTON, political science professor; b. Frimley, Surrey, Eng., Jan. 27, 1945; came to Can., 1971; s. Arnold J. and Margaret E. (Milton) S.; m. Jane L. Parpart, Sept. 2, 1983; children: Laura, Lee Parpart; m. Susan M. Sturt, July 8, 1967 (div. 1980); children: Benjamin, Amanda. BA, Sussex U., 1967; MA, East Africa U., 1969, Princeton U., 1971, PhD, 1975. Prof. polit. sci. Dalhousie U., Halifax, Canada, 1971—2002; dir. Ctr. African Studies, Halifax, 1983—89, Ctr. for Fgn. Policy Studies, Halifax, 1993—2000, Internat. Devel. Studies Program, 1986—89, dir. BA and MA program, 1998—2000; dir. Pearson Inst., Halifax, 1985—87, Can. Internat. Devel. Agy., 1994—95. Vis. faculty Makerere U., Kampala, 1968-70, U. Zambia, Lusaka, 1973-74, Carleton U., Ottawa, Ont., Can., 1978-79, U. Ife, Nigeria, 1979-80, U. Zimbabwe, 1989, Rhodes U., South Africa, 1993, 2002-03, Warwick U., U.K., 1997, U. Western Cape & Stellenbosch U., South Africa, 1998—, Mbarara U. Sci. and Tech., 1998—, Aalborg U., 2000-01, Bus. Sch., Makerere U., 2006-; cons. UN Econ. Commn. for Africa, Addis Ababa, Ethiopia, 1983-88. Editor: Palgrave Macmillan Internat. Polit. Economy Series, 1984—, Ashgate Publishing Series on the International Political Economy of New Regionalisms, 2001—; author: Reformism and Revisionism in Africa's Political Economy in the 1990s, 1993; author: (with Julius Ihonvbere) Illusions of Power: Nigeria in Transition, 1998; co-editor (with Julius Nyangoro): Beyond Structural Adjustment in Africa, 1992; co-editor: Corporatism in Africa, 1988; co-editor: (with Kevin Dunn) Africa's Challenge to International Relations Theory, 2001; co-editor: (with Sandra Maclean & John Harker) Advancing Human Security & Development in Africa, 2002; co-editor: (with Fredrik Soderbaum) Theories of New Regionalism: A Palgrave Reader, 2003; co-editor: (with Natalie Mychajlyszyn) Twisting Arms & Flexing Muscles: Humanitarian Intervention & Peacebuilding in Perspective, 2005; co-editor: (with Morten Boas & Marianne Marchand) The Political Economy of Regions & Regionalisms,

2005; co-editor: (with Sandra Maclean and David Black) A Decade of Human Security, 2006; co-editor: others. Mem. New Dem. Party, Halifax, 1984—. Grantee, Social Sci. & Humanities Rsch. Coun. Can., Africa, 1981—2006, Ford Found., 1999—2001. Mem. Internat. Polit. Soc. Assn. (chair rsch. com. #40 on New World Orders, 1997-2003), Can. Assn. Devel. Studies (pres. 1993-94), European Assn. Devel. Inst. (co-chmn. working group on new regionalisms), Can. Assn. African Studies (pres. 1984-85), Internat. Studies Assn. (pres. global devel. sect. 1995-96), Waegwoltic Club (Halifax). Avocations: jogging, cooking, building, travel. Home: 1701-751 Fairfield Rd Victoria BC V8W 4A4 Canada Office: Royal Roads Univ Victoria BC V9B 5Y2 Canada Office Phone: 250-391-2600 ext. 4786. Office Fax: 250-391-2500. Business E-Mail: tim.shaw@royalroads.ca.

SHAW, WILLIAM FREDERICK, statistician; b. Bklyn., Feb. 24, 1920; s. Charles Peter and Josephine Veronica (Seusing) S.; m. Josephine Cannington Kerbey, Jan. 18, 1947; children: William Frederick, Teresa Anne. BBA, U. Miami, 1949; MA, George Washington U., 1953; postgrad. studies in econometrics, math. and computer scis., U.S. Dept. Agr. Grad. Sch., 1964-74; PhD (fellow), Walden U., 1977. Rsch. asst. U. Miami, 1948—49; with Rsch. and Stats. divsn. FHA, Washington, 1950—73, chief statistician Rsch. and Stats. divsn., 1969—; chief statistician, dir. Advanced Statis. Analysis and Computer Applications Staff HUD, 1974—82, chief statistician, dir. housing stats. divsn., 1982—89, chief statistician, dir. info. sys. divsn., 1990—91, chief statistician, dir. Office of Evaluation, 1991—. Pres. Kerbey-Shaw Assos. Served with F.A. AUS, 1943-45. Decorated Bronze Star; recipient Superior Performance award HUD, 1977; named by Info. Resources Adminstrn. Coun. as Fed. Office Sys. Profl. of Yr., 1983. Mem. AAAS, Am. Statis. Assn., Am. Risk and Ins. Assn., Am. Real Estate and Urban Econ. Assn., Am. Econ. Assn., Am. Fin. Assn., N.Y. Acad. Scis., Nat. Assn. Rev. Appraisers and Mortgage Underwriters, Soc. Cost Estimating and Analysis, Res. Offcers Assn. U.S., 101st Airborne Divsn. Assn., Air Force Assn., Alpha Kappa Psi. Roman Catholic. Home: 6527 Byrnes Dr Mc Lean VA 22101-5227 Office: HUD 7th and D Sts SW Washington DC 20411-0001

SHAW, WILLIAM J., hotel facility executive; b. Arlington, Va., Oct. 3, 1945; married; 3 children. BBA, U. Notre Dame, 1967; MBA, Washington U., 1972. With Arthur Andersen & Co., 1972-74, Marriott, 1974-79, corp. controller, 1979-82, corp. v.p., 1982-85, sr. v.p. fin., head dept. tax and risk mgmt., 1985-88, treas., 1986, CFO, exec. v.p., 1988-92; pres. Marriott's Svc. Group, 1992-97; pres., COO Marriott Internat., Inc., Washington, 1997—; chmn. bd. Host Marriott Svcs. Corp., Bethesda, Md., 1995-99, Sodexho Marriott Svcs., Gaithersburg, Md., 1998. Bd. trustees Suburban Hosp. Found., U. Notre Dame, South Bend, Ind.; mem. NCAA Leadership Adv. Bd.; bd. dirs. Wolf Trap Found. for Performing Arts. Office: Marriot Internat Marriot Dr Washington DC 20058-0001 *

SHAW, WILLIAM J., religious organization administrator; BA in Philosophy and Religion summa cum laude, Bishop Coll.; MDiv, Union Theol. Seminary; DMin, Colgate Rochester Div. Sch. Supply pastor New Bethel Baptist Church, Marshall, Tex.; pastor White Rock Baptist Church, 1956—; pres. Nat. Baptist Conv. USA, Inc., 1999—. Chmn. bd. dir. Jr. Achievement Del. Valley, Inc., Cmty. Legal Svcs. Phila., Med. Ctr. Univ. Penn., Phila. Airport Adv. Bd. Named one of 100 Most Influential Black Americans, Ebony mag., 2006. Mem.: Baptist Min. Conf. Phila. (pres.), Greater Phila. Urban Affairs Coalition. Office: White Rock Baptist Church Office 5240 Chestnut St Philadelphia PA 19139 Office Phone: 215-474-5785. Office Fax: 215-474-3332. E-mail: president@nationalbaptist.com.

SHAWN, WALLACE, playwright, actor; b. NYC, Nov. 12, 1943; s. William and Cecille (Lyon) S; m. Twink Caplan. BA, Harvard U., 1965; BA, Oxford U., Eng., 1968, MA, 1975. Instr. English Indore Christian Coll., Madhya Pradesh, India, 1965-66; tchr. English, Latin, drama Ch. of Heavenly Rest Day Sch., NYC, 1968-70; shipping clk. Laurie Love Ltd., NYC, 1974-75; machine operator Hamilton Copy Ctr., NYC, 1975-76. Author: (plays) Our Late Night, 1975 (Obie award for disting. playwriting 1975), Summer Evening, 1976, The Youth Hostel, 1976, Mr. Frivolous, 1976, (libretto) In the Dark, 1976, (trans.) The Mandrake, 1977, Marie and Bruce, 1980, The Hotel Play, 1981, Aunt Dan and Lemon, 1985, The Music Teacher, 2006; (monologue) The Fever, 1990 (Obie award for best play 1991); (screenplay) My Dinner with Andre, 1981; actor: (theatre) The Mandrake, 1977, The Master and Margarita, 1978, Chinchilla, 1979, The First Time, 1983, Ode to Napoleon Bonaparte, 1984, Aunt Dan and Lemon, 1985, The Fever, 1991; (films) Manhattan, 1979, Starting Over, 1979, All That Jazz, 1979, Simon, 1980, Atlantic City, 1981, My Dinner with Andre, 1981, A Little Sex, 1982, The First Time, 1983, Deal of the Century, 1983, Lovesick, 1983, Strange Invaders, 1983, Saigon-Year of the Cat, 1983, Crackers, 1984, The Hotel New Hampshire, 1984, The Bostonians, 1984, Micki and Maude, 1984, Heaven Help Us, 1985, Head Office, 1986, Radio Days, 1987, The Bedroom Window, 1987, Nice Girls Don't Explode, 1987, Prick Up Your Ears, 1987, The Princess Bride, 1987, The Moderns, 1988, She's Out of Control, 1989, Scenes From the Class Struggle in Beverly Hills, 1989, We're No Angels, 1989, Shadows and Fog, 1992, Mom and Dad Save the World, 1992, Nickel and Dime, 1992, The Cemetary Club, 1993, Un-Becoming Age, 1993, The Meteor Man, 1993, Vanya on 42nd Street, 1994, Mrs. Parker and the Vicious Circle, 1994, Canadian Bacon, 1995, Clueless, 1995, (voice) Toy Story, 1995, All Dogs Go to Heaven 2, 1996, House Arrest, 1996, Vegas Vacation, 1997, Critical Care, 1997, My Favorite Martian, 1999, (voice) Toy Story 2, 1999, The Prime Gig, 2000, The Curse of the Jade Scorpion, 2001, Love Thy Neighbor, 2002, Duplex, 2003, The Haunted Mansion, 2003, Melinda and Melinda, 2004, (voice) The Incredibles, 2004, Chicken Little, 2005, Southland Tales, 2006, (voice) Happily N'Ever After, 2007; (TV films) How to Be Perfect In Three Days, 1983, Saigon: Year of the Cat, 1983, Just Like Dad, 1995, Blind Men, 1998, Noah, 1998, Mr. St. Nick, 2002, Monte Walsh, 2003, Karroll's Christmas, 2004, (TV series) One Life to Live, 1992, Clueless, 1996-97, (voice) The Lionhearts, 1998. Fulbright scholar, India, 1956-66, PEN/Laura Pels Found. award for drama, 2005. Mem.: Am. Acad. Arts and Letters. Office: care Rosenstone/Wender 3 E 48th St New York NY 10017-1027 *

SHAY, ALBERT W., lawyer; b. Cherry Hill, NJ, May 17, 1959; BA, U. Md., 1982; MHA, St. Louis U., 1987, JD magna cum laude, 1987. Bar: Va. 1987, DC 1988. Ptnr., health care practice group Sonnenschein Nath & Rosenthal LLP, Washington. Mem.: Am. Health Lawyers Assn. Office: Sonnenschein Nath & Rosenthal LLP Ste 600, E Tower 1301 K St NW Washington DC 20015 Office Phone: 202-408-6401. Office Fax: 202-408-6399. Business E-Mail: ashay@sonnenschein.com.

SHAY, ANTHONY VICTOR, choreographer, dance historian; b. LA, Oct. 31, 1936; s. Jack Wendell Shay and Margaret Martha Read. MLS, UCLA, LA, 1963; MA anthropology, Calif. State Univ., LA, 1970; MA, UCLA, 1971; PhD dance hist. and theory, Univ. Calif. Riverside, Riverside, Calif., 1997. Artistic dir. Aman Folk Ens., LA, 1960—77, Avaz Internat. Dance Theatre, LA, 1977—. Author: Choreographic Politics, 2002 (Outstanding dance svc., 2002), Chorephobia, 1999, Choreographing Identities, 2006; choreographer over 250 works (Calif. Arts Coun. Lifetime Acheivement award, 2001); author, co-editor: Belly Dance, 2005; editor: Balkan Dance, 2007. James Irvine Choreographic fellow, 1998, Soc. Sci. Rsch. Coun. fellow, 2000, NEH fellow, 2003, APSIH Disting. scholar. Home: 3756 Aloha St Los Angeles CA 90027

SHAY, KATHLEEN M., lawyer; b. Drexel Hill, Pa., Feb. 21, 1952; AB, Villanova U., 1974, JD, 1977. Bar: Pa. 1977, US Ct. Appeals 3rd Cir., US Dist. Ct. Ea. Dist. Pa., Supreme Ct. Pa. Ptnr. Duane Morris LLP, Phila., chair firm corp. practice group, 1998—. Bd. consultors Villanova U. Sch. Law, 1992—, vice chair, 2001—04, chair, 2004—; bd. trustees Acad. Notre Dame de Namur, 1995—2001, 2004—, chair, 1998—2001. Mem.: ABA (bus. law sect.), Phila. Bar Assn. (exec. com. bus. sect. 2001—, sec. 2002, treas. 2003, vice chair 2004, chair 2005), Pa. Biotech. Assn., Pa. Bar Assn. (corp., banking & bus. law sect.), Tech. Coun. Ea. Pa., Women's Investment Network (bd. dir. 2000—06), Greater Phila. Venture Group, Assn. Corp. Growth (bd. dir. Phila. chpt. 2004—), Order of Coif. Office: Duane Morris LLP 30 S 17th St Philadelphia PA 19103-4196 Office Phone: 215-979-1210. Office Fax: 215-979-1020. Business E-Mail: kmshay@duanemorris.com.

SHAY-BYRNE, OLIVIA, lawyer; b. Trenton, NJ, Aug. 14, 1957; d. Stewart and Elizabeth (Sherrill) B. Student, Vanderbilt U., 1975-76; BA, Bowdoin Coll., 1979; JD, U. Toledo, 1982; LLM in Taxation, Georgetown U., 1987. Bar: Tex. 1982, Ohio 1984, Md. 1985. Assoc. Whiteford, Taylor & Preston, Balt., 1984-87, Linowes & Blocher, Silver Spring, Md., 1987-90; ptnr. Sutherland Asbill & Brenna LLP, Washington, 1996—2000, ReedSmith LLP, Washington, 2000—. Bd. dir. D.C. Mktg. Ctr., mem. exec. com., 2004. Author: The At-Risk Rules Under the Tax Reform Act of 1986, The Door Closes on Tax Motivated Investments, IRS Issues New Guidelines for Management Contracts Used for Facilities Financed with Tax Exempt Bonds, 1993, RRA '93 Loosens Real Estate Rules for Exempt Organizations, 1993; editor Nat. Mcpl. Fin. Jour.; contbr. articles to profl. jours. Mem. Tax Coun. for State of Md., Leadership Montgomery, 1996; bd. dirs. Bethesda Acad. Performing Arts, Inc.; chair GULC Nat. Tax Exempt Bond Conf., 1997. Mem. ABA (exempt orgn. com. taxation sect. 1991—), Md. Bar Assn. (coun. taxation sect.), Balt. City Bar Assn. (chmn. speakers bur. young lawyers sect.), Lawyers for Arts Washington, Comml. Real Estate Woman (bd. dirs., pres.), Profls. for Strathmore Hall (co-chmn.), D.C. Bowdoin Coll. Alumni Assn. (pres. 1992—), Howard County C. of C. (legis. com. 1989), Rotary. Home: 1083 Mill Field Ct Great Falls VA 22066

SHAYE, ROBERT KENNETH, film company executive; s. Max and Dorothy S.; m. Eva G., 1970; children: Katja, Juno. BBA, U. Mich., 1960; postgrad., Sorbonne U., 1961; JD, Columbia U., 1964. Bar: N.Y. 1967. Founder, chmn., CEO New Line Cinema, NYC, 1967—. Trustee Am. Film Inst. Recipient 1st prize Rosenthal competition Soc. Cinematologists, 1964, cert. of merit Inst. Copyrights and Patents, U. Stockholm, 1966, award ASCAP/Nathan Burkan Meml. competition, 1964; Fulbright scholar, 1964-66. Mem. Motion Picture Pioneers (bd. dirs.). Office: New Line Cinema 116 N Robertson Blvd West Hollywood CA 90048-3103 also: New Line Cinema Corp 888 7th Ave Fl 19 New York NY 10106-2599 Office Phone: 310-854-5811, 212-649-4900. *Life is a lot tougher than television watching in the '50's led me to believe.*

SHAYMAN, JAMES ALAN, nephrologist, educator; b. Chgo., June 14, 1954; s. Benjamin and Chernie (Abrams) S.; children: Rebecca Lynn, David Aaron. AB, Cornell U., 1976; MD, Washington U., St. Louis, 1980. Intern and resident Barnes Hosp., St. Louis, 1980-83; instr. Washington U., St. Louis, 1985-86; asst. prof. U. Mich., Ann Arbor, 1986-92, assoc. prof., 1992-97; prof. internal medicine and pharmacology, 1997—; assoc. chair rsch. programs dept. internal medicine U. Mich., Ann Arbor, 1997—. Mem. Am. Soc. Nephrology, Internat. Soc. Nephrology, Am. Diabetes Assn., Am. Soc. Clin. Investigation, Am. Physiol. Soc., Phi Beta Kappa, Phi Kappa Phi, Alpha Omega Alpha. Achievements include research in renal inositol phosphate metabolism and renal glycolipid metabolism.

SHAYS, CHRISTOPHER, congressman; b. Darien, Conn., Oct. 18, 1945; m. Betsi deRaismes, 1968; 1 child: Jeramy Alice. BA, Principia Coll., 1968; MBA, NYU, 1974, MPA, 1978. Vol. US Peace Corps, 1968-70; state rep. State of Conn. (Dist. 147), Stamford, 1974—87; mem. US Congress from 4th Conn. dist., Washington, 1987—, mem. fin. svcs. com., vice chmn. govt. reform com., vice chmn. budget com., mem. select com. on homeland security chmn. subcom. on nat. security. Republican. Office: US Ho Reps 1126 Longworth Ho Office Bldg Washington DC 20515-0704 also: Bridgeport Dist Office 11th Fl 10 Middle St Bridgeport CT 06604 also: Government Center 888 Washington Blvd Stamford CT 06901 *

SHAYWITZ, BENNETT ARTHUR, medical educator; MD, Yale U., 1963. Prof. pediats. and neurology Sch. Medicine Yale U., 1972—; co-founder, co-director National Inst. Child Health & Human Development-Yale Ctr. for the Study of Learning and Attention. Mem.: Inst. Medicine. Office: Yale New Haven Hosp LMP 3089 20 York St New Haven CT 06504-8900

SHCHERBAKOVA, ESTELLA, chemist, mathematician, educator; b. Dnepropetrovsk, Ukraine, Oct. 15, 1938; arrived in Russia, 1951, arrived in U.S., 1994; d. Stepan and Fira (Poltorak) Masko; m. Stanislav Shcherbakov; 1 child, Yuriy Shcherbakov. MA math and drawing, State Pedagogical Inst., Moscow, Russia, 1956—61; PhD chem. sci., Post grad. Sch. of L. Karpov Rsch. Physical Chem. Inst., Moscow, Russia, 1968—74. Math tchr. HS #79, Moscow, 1961—62; engr. State Inst. of Caouchouc, Moscow, 1962—64; sci. worker from jr. to maj. L. Karpov Rsch. Phys. Chem. Inst., Moscow, 1964—94. Cons. and joint rsch. Inst. of Thin Chem. Tech., Moscow, 1971—89, State External Polytech. Inst., Moscow, 1978—90. Co-author: 113 articles, SU Jour. Miscellaneous reports, 1961—91, (book, monograph) Math Matters of Investigation of Chem. Equilib., 1978, (3 inventions) SU Bull. of Inventions, 1985, 1992—93. Recipient Semicentennial, L. Karpov Inst./ Moscow, Russia, 1988. Finding common math technology for investigation of the multiple equilibriums in solutions and applying it to various chemical systems, including solutions of bromine and iodine that brought to inventions of industrial modus of their deriving from a leach. Finding the method for nonlinear optimizations, as to apply non-equilibrium thermodynamics to processes of polymerizations. Home: 2820 W 32nd St Apt 3E Brooklyn NY 11224 E-mail: shchest@aol.com. *She evacuated in Kuybishev (Samara) Russia, 1941-1945; resided in Moscow from 1951 because of father's job in aerospace engineering.*

SHE, CHIAO-YAO, physics professor, researcher; s. Young-Chi She and I-Jung Fang; m. Lucia Shumai Yein, Feb. 8, 1964; children: Colleen Suelie Kirtland, Fannie Camille. BS, Taiwan U., 1957; MS, N.D. State U., 1961; PhD, Stanford U., 1964. Asst. prof. elec. engring. U. Minn., Mpls., 1964—68; from asst. to prof. physics Colo. State U., Fort Collins, 1968—. Editor: (book) Selected Papers on Laser Applications in Remote Sensing, SPIE Milestone Series, MS 141 (1997); contbr. articles to profl. jours. Recipient, Fulbright scholarship, 2000, Lecture prize, NSF/Coupling, Energetics and Dynamics of Atmospheric Regions Sci. Steering Com., 2003. Fellow: Optical Soc. of Am.; mem.: Am. Phys. Soc., Am. Geophys. Union. Achievements include invention of Two high-spectral-resolution atmospheric lidars. Office: Colo State U Dept Physics 200 W Lake St Fort Collins CO 80523-1875 Home Phone: 970-223-2977; Office Phone: 970-491-6261. Office Fax: 970-491-7947.

SHEA, BERNARD CHARLES, retired pharmaceutical executive; b. Bradford, Pa., Aug. 7, 1929; s. Bernard and Edna Catherine (Green) S.; m. Marilyn Rishell, Apr. 12, 1952; children: David Charles, Melissa Leone. BS in Biology, Holy Cross Coll., Worcester, Mass. Dir. mktg. Upjohn Co., Kalamazoo, 1954-80; pres. pharm. div. Pennwalt Corp., Rochester, NY, 1980-86, v.p. health div. Phila., 1986, sr. v.p. health div., 1987-88, sr. v.p. chemicals, 1988-89; group pres. Atochem N.Am., Inc., Phila., 1989-90, pharm. cons., 1990-93. Served to lt. (j.g.) USN, 1951-54, Korea Personal E-mail: Berniemari@comcast.com. E-mail: berniemari@msn.com.

SHEA, BRENT MACK, social sciences educator; b. Oneida, NY, June 3, 1946; s. Mack Evered and Alice May (Meeker) Shea. BA, SUNY, Binghamton, 1968, MA, 1972, PhD, 1977. Vis. instr. Harpur Coll. SUNY, Binghamton, 1975-76, resident dir. Coll.-in-the-Woods, 1976-78, rsch. assoc., 1977-78; from asst. prof. to prof. Sweet Briar Coll., Va., 1978—92, chmn. dept. anthropology and sociology, 1986—90, 1996—99, 2005—06, prof., 1992—. Vis. fellow Yale U., New Haven, 1984—85, postdoctoral fellow, 1985—86; sci. collaborator Centro studi per l'Evoluzione Umana, Rome, 1990—; vis. scholar Summer Inst. Survey Rsch. U. Mich., 1991; presenter, rschr. in field. Co-editor, contbg. author: Social Psychiatry across Cultures, 1995; editor: conf. procs. Work and Mental Health, 1996; mem. editl. bd. Internat. Scope Rev., 1999—; co-editor: Internat. Scope Rev., 2000—01; contbr. articles to profl. jour., chapters to books. Regents scholar, Harpur Coll. SUNY, 1964—68, Faculty Rsch. fellow, Sweet Briar Coll., 1984—85, 1992—93, NIMH Postdoctoral Rsch. fellow, Instn. Social and Policy Studies, Yale U., 1985—86. Mem.: AAUP (chpt. pres. 1996—99, chair state com. on coll. and univ. governance 1998—2001, state exec. com. 1998—2001), Va. Sociol. Assn. (mem. exec. com. 1980—81, pres., co-chmn. conf. program), Ea. Ednl. Rsch. Assn. (dir. rsch. ethics 1979—83, bd. dirs. 1979—85, gen. sec. 1983—85), Ius Primi Viri Internat. Assn., Rome (v.p. bd. govs. 1994—), Internat. Sociol. Assn. (v.p. exec. bd. 1994—98, mental health and illness rsch. com.), Am. Sociol. Assn. (task force on internat. focus of Am. sociology 1999—2003), Soc. Automotive Historians. Avocations: classical piano, classic cars. Home: PO Box 1 Sweet Briar VA 24595-0001 Office: Sweet Briar Coll Dept Anthropology & Sociology Sweet Briar VA 24595 Office Phone: 434-381-6193.

SHEA, DION WARREN JOSEPH, academic administrator, fundraiser; b. New London, Conn, June 10, 1937; s. Frank Steven and Violette Marie (Dion) S.; m. Elizabeth M. Siaba, Dec. 31, 1986; children from previous marriage: Dion Warren Joseph, Nancy Wallace. AB, ScB in Physics, Brown U., 1959; MA in Physics, Boston U., 1962; PhD in Physics, U. Colo., 1968. Mem. tech. staff RCA, 1959-62; asst. prof. physics Creighton U., 1967-68; NRC/Environ. Sci. Svc. Adminstrn. fellow, rsch. assoc. Environ. Sci. Svc. Adminstrn., Boulder, Colo., 1968-70; exec. dir. Soc. Physics Students, Am. Inst. Physics, 1970-87, mgr. edn. div., 1972-87; cons. ednl. and computer sytems, 1988—; dir. alumni affairs US Mcht. Marine Acad., Kings Point, NY, 1989-93; asst. dir. devel. CUNY Grad. Sch., 1993-99. Contbr. scientific papers to profl. jours. Fellow AAAS; mem. Am. Phys. Soc., Am. Assn. Physics Tchr., Assn. Coll. Honor Soc. (exec. com. 1984-86), Am. Soc. Assn. Exec., Assn. Fundraising Profl., Coun. Advancement and Support Edn., Sigma Xi, Sigma Pi Sigma, Sigma Chi, Huntington Bicycle Club (treas. 2000-01), Colo. Mountain Club, Port Dive Club (treas. 1980-83). Home: 11821 Lionel Ln Golden CO 80403 Home Phone: 303-642-0699; Office Phone: 303-642-0699. Personal E-mail: dion_shea@yahoo.com.

SHEA, EDWARD EMMETT, lawyer, educator, writer; b. Detroit, May 29, 1932; s. Edward Francis and Margaret Kathleen (Downey) S.; m. Ann Marie Conley, Aug. 28, 1957; children: Michael, Maura, Ellen. AB, U. Detroit, 1954; JD, U. Mich., 1957. Bar: Mich. 1957, Fla. 1959, N.Y. 1961. Assoc. Simpson Thacher & Bartlett, NYC, 1960-63, Dykema, Wheat, Spencer, Detroit, 1963-69, Cadwalader Wickersham & Taft, NYC, 1969-71; v.p., gen. counsel, chmn. Reichhold Chems., White Plains, NY, 1971-81; adj. prof. Pace U. Grad. Sch. Bus., NYC, 1982—; counsel, ptnr. Windels, Marx, Davies & Ives, NYC, 1982-84; ptnr. Windels, Marx, Lane & Mittendorf, NYC, 1986—; sr. v.p., gen. counsel GAF Corp., 1984-86. Sec. Peridot Chems., 1988-97; lectr. N.Y. Inst. Fin., 1995—. Author: An Introduction to the U.S. Environmental Laws, 1995, The Lead Regulation Handbook, 1996, 2d edit., 2007, The McGraw-Hill Guidebook to Acquiring and Divesting Businesses, 1998, Environmental Law and Compliance Methods, 2002; editor: The Acquisitions Yearbook, 1991-93; contbr. articles to profl. jours. Mem. adv. bd. N.Y. State Small Bus. Ctr. Program, 1988-93. lst lt. JAGC, USAF, 1957-60. Mem. N.Y. Athletic Club. Office: Windels Marx Lane & Mittendorf 156 W 56th St Fl 23 New York NY 10019-3867 Office Phone: 212-237-1140. Business E-Mail: eshea@windelsmarx.com.

SHEA, JAMES L., lawyer; b. Balt., June 19, 1952; Ab cum laude, Princeton U., 1974; JD, U. Va., 1977. Bar: Md. 1977, DC 1998. Law clk. to Hon. Joseph H. Young US Dist. Ct. Md., 1977-78; asst. atty. gen. State of Md., 1981-83; mng. ptnr. Venable LLP, Washington, 1994—2006, chmn., 2006—. Chmn. bd. Empower Balt. Mgmt. Corp., Downtown Partnership of Balt., Downtown Mgmt. Authority; bd. mem. Greater Balt. Com., Mercantile Safe-Deposit and Trust Co.; trustee U. Md., College Park. Named Power 50: The Men and Women Who Rule award, Balt. Mag., 2003, 2006; recipient Leadership in Law Award, The Daily Record. Fellow Am. Coll. Trial Lawyers; mem. ABA, Md. State Bar Assn., Bar Assn. Balt. City, Defense Rsch. Inst., Md. Assn. of Defense Trial Counsel, Order of Coif. Address: Venable LLP 1800 Mercantile Bank & Trust Bldg 2 Hopkins Plz Baltimore MD 21201-2930 Office Phone: 410-244-7734. Office Fax: 410-244-7742. E-mail: jshea@venable.com.

SHEA, JAMES WILLIAM, lawyer; b. NYC, July 10, 1936; s. William P. and Mildred E. (McCaffrey) S.; m. Ann Marie Byrne, June 6, 1964; children: James T., Kathleen A., Tracy A. BS, St. Peters Coll., 1957; JD, Fordham U., 1962; LLM in Taxation, NYU, 1965. Bar: N.Y. 1962, U.S. Dist. Ct. (so. and ea. dists.) N.Y. 1966, U.S. Supreme Ct. 1967. Revenue agt. U.S. Treasury Dept., NYC, 1961-63; tax atty. Kennecott Copper Corp., NYC, 1963-67; tax counsel CBS Inc., NYC, 1968-71; ptnr. Hunton & Williams and predecessor firm Conboy, Hewitt, O'Brien & Boardman, NYC, 1971—2001, sr. counsel, 2001—. Rep. committeeman, S.I., N.Y., 1980; mem. adv. com. tax and fin. N.Y. State Charter Commn. City of S.I. Served to 1st lt. U.S. Army, 1957-61, to capt. USAR, 1962-72. Mem. N.Y. State Bar Assn., Richmond County Country Club S.I. (sec. 1993-96, v.p. 1996-98, pres. 1998-2000, bd. dirs. 1993-2004). Republican. Roman Catholic. Home: 399 Tysens Ln Staten Island NY 10306-2844 Office: Hunton & Williams 200 Park Ave Rm 4300 New York NY 10166-0091 Office Phone: 718-987-9798. E-mail: jws@si.rr.com.

SHEA, JIM, Olympic athlete; b. Hartford, Conn., June 10, 1968; Mem. U.S. Skeleton Team. Vol. fireman, Lake Placid, NY. Named Athlete of Month, USA Today, 1995, Rookie of Yr., 1995; recipient Gold medal, Nat. Championships, Lake Placid, 1996, 1st pl., Push Championships, 1995, 1997, 1998, Gold medal, Skeleton World Cup, 1998, Stubai Cup, 1999, 1st pl., Skeleton World Championship, Winterberg, Germany, 1999, Gold medal, Winter Goodwill Games, Lake Placid, 2000; mem., US Nat. Team and World Cup Team, 9502, 1st American to win World Cup, 10 World Cup medals worldwide. Address: PO Box 681367 Park City UT 84068 Office Phone: 435-602-6786. E-mail: dkeletonwc@aol.com.

SHEA, JOHN JOSEPH, electrical engineer; b. Buffalo, Aug. 18, 1962; s. John Anthony and Julia Anne (Browne) S.; m. Lisa Anne Hahne, Nov. 4, 1989. PhD in Elec. Engring., SUNY, Buffalo, 1989. Sr. engr. Westinghouse Sci. and Tech. Ctr., Pitts., 1988—94; consulting engr. Eaton Elec., Pitts., 1994—. Contbr. over 27 articles to profl. jours. Recipient Erle Shobert Prize paper, 2002; Hughes Aircraft fellow, 1985. Mem. IEEE (sr. mem.), Tau Beta Pi, Eta Kappa Nu. Achievements include 15 patents in arc interruption and conductive current limiting polymers; created plasma physics lab. at Eaton Electrical. Office: Eaton Elec RIDC Park W 170 Industry Dr Pittsburgh PA 15275-1014

SHEA, KENNETH J., chemistry professor; BS, Univ. Toledo, 1968; PhD, Pa. State Univ., 1973; postdoctoral studies, Calif. Inst. Tech. Prof., chemistry dept. chair Univ. Calif., Irvine. Grantee Winston Churchill Coll.

Overseas Fellowship, Cambridge Univ., NIH Sr. Internat. Fellow. Fellow: AAAS; mem.: Am. Chem. Soc. (Arthur C. Cope Scholar award 2007). Achievements include holder of three patents. Office: 5042D Frederick Reines Hall Dept Chemistry Univ Calif Irvine CA 92697 Office Phone: 949-824-5844. Office Fax: 949-824-2210. Business E-Mail: kjshea@uci.edu. *

SHEA, KEVIN MICHAEL, lawyer; b. Indpls., Dec. 23, 1951; s. James Louis and Elizabeth (Walker) S.; children: Brendan Alkire, Maura Kathryn. BS, U. Colo., 1973; JD, U. Detroit, 1976. Bar: Colo. 1976, U.S. Dist. Ct. D.C. 1976, U.S. Ct. Appeals (10th cir. 1980), U.S. Supreme Ct. 1982. Dep. dist. atty., Boulder, Colo., 1976—79; shareholder, dir., assoc. Roath & Brega P.C., Denver, 1980—84; spl. counsel, ptnr. Holme Roberts & Owen, Denver, 1984—94; ptnr. Ballard, Sphar, Andrews & Ingersoll, Denver, 1995—. Named in Best Lawyers in Am., Leading Lawyers Bus. Chambers USA. Fellow Am. Coll. Trial Lawyers; mem. ABA (vice chair environ. crime sect. 1991—), Colo. Bar Assn. (chair criminal law sect. 1990-91), Denver Country Club (bd. dirs.). Democrat. Avocation: fishing. Office: Ballard Sphar Andrews Inger 1225 17th St Ste 2300 Denver CO 80202-5596 Office Phone: 303-299-7337. Business E-Mail: shea@ballardspahr.com.

SHEA, MARTIN M., broadcast executive; BS, U. Hartford, West Hartford, Conn. Various positions up to v.p. investor rels. Paramount Comm. Inc. (formerly Gulf & Western), 1977—94; sr. v.p. corp. comm. Triarc Cos., Inc., 1994—95, 1995—97; mng. dir. Edelman Worldwide, 1995; sr. v.p. investor relations Viacom, Inc., 1998—2004, exec. v.p. investor relations, 2004—05; exec. v.p. investor rels. CBS Corp., 2005—. Named Number One Investor Rels. Office in Media Industry, Instl. Investor, 2003, Number One Investor Rels. Officer Across All Industries, Investor Rels. Mag., 2003. Mem.: Nat. Inst. Investor Relations (past pres. NY chpt.). Office: CBS Corp 51 W 52nd St New York NY 10019-6188 Office Phone: 212-975-4321. *

SHEA, MARY FRANCES, retired elementary school educator; b. Spring Valley, Ill., Nov. 23, 1949; d. Joseph Charles and Jean Violet (Stevenson) Mertel; m. Patrick Dennis Shea, Dec. 15, 1973; children: Megan, Patrick. AA, Ill. Valley C.C., Oglesby, 1969; BS in Edn. magna cum laude, No. Ill. U., 1971. Cert. elem. sch. educator K-9. Second grade educator Ladd (Ill.) Cmty. Consolidated Sch., 1971-77, chpt. 1 educator, 1978-80, chpt. 1 educator, gifted educator, 1980-85, kindergarten educator, chpt. 1 educator, gifted educator, 1985-93, kindergarten educator, computer educator, 1993-96, tech. cons., kindergarten educator, 1992—2005; ret., 2005. Named Tchr. of Yr., Wal-Mart, 2004. Mem. Phi Theta Kappa. Roman Catholic. Avocation: collecting longaberger baskets. Home: 3105 E 5th Rd La Salle IL 61301-9759 Office: Ladd Cmty Consolidated Sch 232 E Cleveland St Ladd IL 61329-9741 Home Phone: 815-224-2139. Personal E-mail: ladd_marys@hotmail.com.

SHEA, THOMAS CHARLES, physician, educator; b. Phila., Sept. 17, 1952; s. Thomas M. and Grace V. (Taylor) S.; m. Katharine Marie Dressler Shea, June 27, 1981; children: Margaret, Joseph. BA in Psychology, U. N.C., 1974, MD, 1978. Internship U. N.C., Chapel Hill; residency Beth Israel Hosp., fellow/instr. in medicine Boston, 1982-88, Dana-Farber Cancer Inst., Boston, 1982-88, Harvard Med. Sch., Boston, 1982-88; asst. prof. medicine U. Calif., San Diego, 1988-92; assoc. prof. medicine U. N.C., Chapel Hill, 1992-97, prof. medicine, 1997—; and assoc. chief, divsn. med. oncology Univ. NC Lineberger Comprehensive Cancer Ctr., Chapel Hill. Exec. Com. N. Am. and Internat. Bone Marrow Transplant Registry. Named one of NC's Best Doctors, Bus. NC mag., 2004, 2006. Office: Divsn Med Oncology Univ NC Cb 7305 104 MacNider Bldg Chapel Hill NC 27599-0001 *

SHEA, WILLIAM J., former insurance company executive; With Coopers & Lybrand, 1974—93; vice chmn., CFO BankBoston Corp., Boston, 1993—98; CEO View Tech, Camarillo, Calif., 1999—2000; pres., CEO Conseco, 2001—04; chmn. Demoulas Supermarkets, Tewksbury, Mass., 1998—99. Office: Demoulas 875 East St Tewksbury MA 01876

SHEA, WILLIAM RENE, historian, history and philosophy professor; b. Gracefield, Que., Can., May 16, 1937; s. Herbert Clement and Jeanne (Lafreniere) S.; m. Evelyn Fischer, May 2, 1970; children: Herbert, Joan-Emma, Louisa, Cecilia, Michael. BA, U. Ottawa, 1958; LPh, Gregorian U., Rome, 1959; LTh, Gregorian U., 1963; PhD, Cambridge U., Eng., 1968. Assoc. prof. U. Ottawa, 1968-73; fellow Harvard U., Cambridge, Mass., 1973-74; prof. history and philosophy of sci. McGill U., Montreal, 1974—; dir. d'etudes Ecole des Hautes Etudes, Paris, 1981-82. Sec.-gen. Internat. Union of History and Philosophy of Sci., 1981-89, pres., 1990-93; mem. gen. com. Internat. Coun. of Sci. Union, Paris, 1983-89; cons. Killam Found., Ottawa, Ont., 1983-85; mem. McGill Centre for Medicine, Ethics and Law, 1990-95; Hydro Que. prof. environ. ethics, 1992—; vis. prof. U. Rome, 1992; dir. Inst. History of Sci. U. Louis Pasteur, Strasbourg, 1995-2003; Galileo chair history of sci. U. Padua, 2003—. Author: Galileo Intellectual Revolution, 1972, The Magic of Numbers and Motion, 1991, Copernico, 2001, Designing Experiments and Games of Chance, 2003; co-author: Galileo Florentine Residences, 1979, Galileo in Rome, 2003, Galileo Observed: The Politics of Belief, 2006; editor: Nature Mathematized, 1983, Otto Hahn and the Rise of Nuclear Physics, 1983, Revolutions in Science, 1988, Creativity in the Arts and Science, 1990, Persuading Science: The Art of Scientific Rhetoric, 1991, Interpreting the World, Science and Society, 1991, Energy Needs in the Year 2000: Ethical and Environmental Perspectives, 1994, Science and the Visual Image in the Enlightenment, 2000, Campanus of Novara's Theorica Planetarum, 2007. Recipient The Alexandre Koyre medal, Internat. Acad. of History of Sci., 1993, Knight of the Order of Malta, 1993; Can. Coun. fellow, 1965—68, Can. Cultural Inst. fellow, Rome, 1973, Social Scis. and Humanities Rsch. Coun. Can., 1980—81, Inst. of Advanced Studies in Berlin fellow, 1988—89. Fellow Royal Soc. Can.; mem. Royal Swedish Acad. Scis. (fgn.), Acadmie D'Alsace, Academia Europaea (mem. coun., 2003-07), History of Sci. Soc. (coun. 1973-76), European Sci. Found. (standing com. for humanities 1989-95, chmn. 1999-2003), Can. Nat. Com. of History and Philosophy of Sci. (coun. 1982-93), Can. Philos. Assn., Internat. Acad. History of Sci. (pres. 1997-2001), Rotary. Home: 35 Via Guglielmo Marconi 35122 Padua Italy Office Phone: 39-049-827-5073. Fax: 39-049-827-5068. E-mail: william.shea@unipd.it.

SHEAFFER, RICHARD ALLEN, electrical engineer; b. Bronxville, NY, May 30, 1950; BSEE, Pa. State U., 1972; MSEE, U. So. Calif., 1975; MBA, Pepperdine U., 1996. Registered profl. engr., Calif., Fla. Elec. engr. So. Calif. Edison Co., Rosemead, 1973-79, 80-90, Harris Controls divsn., Melbourne, Fla., 1979-80; cons. San Diego Gas & Elec., 1990-91, sr. transmission planner, 1991-2000, prin. engr., 2004—; rep. for decommissioning San Onofre Nuc. Generating Sta. Unit 1, 2000—; rep. for steam generator replacement project Units 2 and 3, 2005—. Project leader nomogram study for Pacific and S.W. transfer subcom. Western Systems Coordinating Coun., 1988, 91; project leader Ariz.-Calif. 7550 NW Path Rating, 1994-97. Author: 1984 West-of-the-River Operating Study, 1985, December 22, 1982 Disturbance Study, 1983. Mem. IEEE (Power Engring. Soc., Engring. Mgmt. Soc.), Am. Nuc. Soc., Phi Eta Sigma.

SHEAHAN, JOHN BERNARD, economist, educator; b. Toledo, Sept. 11, 1923; s. Bernard William and Florence (Sheahan) S.; m. Denise Eugénie Morlino, Nov. 29, 1946; children: Yvette Marie, Bernard Eugene. BA, Stanford U., Calif., 1948; PhD, Harvard U., Cambridge, Mass., 1954. Econ. analyst Office Spl. Rep. in Europe, ECA, Paris, France, 1951-54; mem. faculty Williams Coll., 1954-94, prof. econs. Williamstown, Mass., 1966-94, prof. emeritus. Mem. devel. adv. service Colombia adv. group Harvard, 1963-65; nat. research prof. Brookings Instn., 1959-60; vis. prof. El Colegio de México, Mexico City, 1970-71; Fulbright research scholar Institut de recherche économique et de planification, Université de Grenoble, France, 1974-75; vis. scholar Inst. Devel. Studies, U. Sussex, 1981-82; vis. fellow Ctr. for U.S.-Mexican Studies, U. Calif. at San Diego, 1991. Author: Promotion and Control of Industry in Postwar France, 1963, The Wage-Price Guideposts, 1967, An Introduction to the French Economy, 1969, Patterns of Development in Latin America, 1987, Conflict and Change in Mexican Economic Strategy, 1992, Searching for a Better Society: The Peruvian Economy from 1950, 1999. Mem. Presdl. Price Adv. Com., 1979-80 Mem. Latin Am. Studies Assn., New England Coun. Latin Am. Studies (pres. 1989-90), Phi Beta Kappa. Home: PO Box 751 Williamstown MA 01267

SHEAHAN, ROBERT EMMETT, lawyer, consultant; b. Chgo., May 20, 1942; s. Robert Emmett and Lola Jean (Moore) S.; m. Pati Smith, Mar. 20, 1991. BA, Ill. Wesleyan U., 1964; JD, Duke U., 1967; MBA, U. Chgo., 1970. Bar: Ill. 1967, La. 1975, N.C. 1978. Vol. VISTA, NYC, 1967-68; trial atty. NLRB, Milw., New Orleans, 1970-75; ptnr. Jones, Walker, Waechter, Poitevent, Carrere & Denegre, New Orleans, 1975-78; pvt. practice High Point, NC, 1978—. Bd. dirs. Inst. for Effective Mgmt., Bus. Publs. Inst. Author: Employees and Drug Abuse: An Employer's Handbook, 1994, The Encyclopedia of Drugs in the Workplace, Labor and Employment Law in North Carolina, 1991, Personnel and Employment Law in North Carolina, 1992, Desk Book of Labor and Employment Law for Healthcare Employers' Desk Manual, 1995, North Carolina Lawyers' Desk Book; contbg. author: The Developing Labor Law, 1975—; editor: The World of Personnel; contbg. editor: Employee Testing and the Law; contbr. periodic supplements N.C. Gen. Practice Deskbook, 1992—. Bd. dirs. High Point United Way, 1979-83; mem. congl. action com. High Point C. of C., chmn., 1991—, bd. dirs., 1996—. Mem. ABA, N.C. Bar Assn., High Point Bar Assn., Ill. Bar Assn., La. Bar Assn., Sedgefield (N.C.) Country Club, String and Splinter Club, Bald Head Island Club. Republican. Roman Catholic. Home: 101 Bellwood Ct Jamestown NC 27282 Office: Robert E Sheahan & Assocs 603 Eastchester Dr Ste B High Point NC 27262-7647 Office Phone: 336-889-2711.

SHEAKS, BARCLAY, artist; b. Oct. 22, 1928; s. Earl Leroy and Jeanie Rice Sheaks; m. Deborah Mae Joyner; 1 child, Owen James. BFA, Va. Commonwealth U., 1948; LHD (hon.), Christopher Newport U., 1997. Disting. resident artist Va. Wesleyan Coll., Norfolk, 1990—2005. Author: (poetry book) Stretching the Eyes Distance, 1980, (book) The Acrylics Book, 1995; Represented in permanent collections Va. Mus. Fine Arts, Chrysler Mus., Butler Inst. Am. Art, Valentine Mus., Mobile Mus., Med. Coll. Va., Christopher Newport U., others. Mem.: Peninsula Fine Arts Ctr. Avocation: boating. Home: 51 Hopkins St Newport News VA 23601

SHEAN, TIMOTHY JOSEPH, manufacturing executive; b. Norfolk, Va., Sept. 19, 1945; s. Hobart Philip S.; m. Adriana Bergo, July 12, 1970; children: Jonathan Michael, Arianne Marie. BSME, U. Notre Dame, 1967; postgrad., U. Va., 1991. Sales engr. Shean Equipment Co., Syracuse, NY, 1967-69; application engr. Gen. Electric Co., Schenectady, 1970-71, prodn. control supr., 1972-75, process devel. engr., 1975-78, project mgr., 1978-80, mgr. facilities and engring., 1980-83; plant mgr. Hughes Tool Co., Bristol, Va., 1983-85; mgr. mfg. Sandvik Rock Tools, Inc., Bristol, 1985-89, gen. mgr., 1989-92, v.p., 1992-2000; pres. Sandvik Mineral Tools USA, Bristol, 2000—02, Sandvik CPD-MTD Prodn. Co., Bristol; pres., CEO R.P. Abrasives and Machine, Inc., Milton, NH, 2002—. Sr. patrolman Nat. Ski Patrol Sys., Wilminton, Vt., 1970-80; instr., trainer first aid ARC, Schenectady, 1975-78, vice-chmn. disaster svcs., 1976-77; mem. sch. bd. Schalmont Ctrl. Sch. Dist., Schenectady, 1979-82; cmty. involvement com. Bristol Sch. Dist., 1990; chmn. Literacy Acad. Bristol, 1991-92; chmn. fin. coun. St. Anne's Cath. Ch., 1992-96; mem. Va. Atty. Gens. Commn., 1995-96, Commn. on Future S.W. Va., 1995-97; bd. fellows Va. Intermont Coll., 1996-99; mem. pres.'s adv. bd. King Coll., 1997-2002; bd. dirs. Mfg. Tech. Ctr. S.W. Va., 1998-2002, Va. Mfg. Assn., 1999-2000. Named one of Outstanding Young Men of Am., U.S. Jaycees, 1979. Mem. Soc. Mfg. Engrs., Nat. Mining Assn. (chmn. resins group 1989-95, tech. com. 1990-96), Va. Coal Coun. (bd. dirs. 1993-2002), Bristol C. of C. (bd. dirs. 1994-2000, chmn. 1999-2000). Roman Catholic. Avocation: skiing. Office: R P Abrasives & Machine Inc 61 Old Wakefield Rd Milton NH 03851 Office Phone: 603-335-2132. Business E-Mail: joe@rpabrasives.com.

SHEA-PORTER, CAROL, congresswoman, social worker; b. NYC, Dec. 2, 1952; d. William and Peggy Shea; m. Gene Porter; 2 children. BS in Social Services, U. NH, 1975, MPA, 1979. Instr. The Charter House, 1987—2001; history instr. Prince George's C.C., 1987—89; dir. The Shepard's Ctr., Multi-Purpose Sr. Ctr.; mem. Mayor's Taskforce on sr. housing, Washington, US Congress from 1st NH dist., 2007—, mem. armed svcs. com. and edn. & labor com. NH regional coord. Wesley Clark for Presdl. Campaign. Democrat. Roman Catholic. First Congresswoman elected from NH. Office: 1508 Longworth House Office Bldg Washington DC 20515 also: 104 Washington St Dover NH 03820 *

SHEAR, NATALIE PICKUS, conference and event management executive; b. NYC, Oct. 18, 1940; d. Sam and Mildred (Shulman) Pickus; m. Daniel H. Shear, Dec. 14, 1968 (dec. Apr. 1989); children: Adam Brian, Tamara Beth; m. Henry D. Lewis, Jan. 10, 1999. BA in Journalism, Fairleigh Dickinson U., 1962. Editl. asst. Show Bus. Newspaper, NYC, 1962-64, Jewish News, Newark, 1964-66; dir. Manhattan women's divsn., program asst. Am. Jewish Congress, NYC, 1966-68; mng. editor Jewish Week, Washington, 1968-71; dir. pub. rels. United Jewish Appeal, Washington, 1973-74; pub. affairs dir. Leadership Conf. Civil Rights, Washington, 1977-83; pres. Natalie P. Shear Assocs., Inc., Washington, 1983—. Editor: (newspaper) Books Alive, 1973—74; editor, pub.: newsletter Trends, Inc., 1989—94. V.p. Nat. Child Rsch. Ctr., Washington, 1974—76; bd. dirs. Urban Philharm. Soc., 1998—99; vol., bd. dirs. Nat. Jewish Dem. Coun., Washington, 1996—; vol. nat. bd. Ams. Dem. Action, 2001—; pres. Ohr Kodesh Sisterhood, Chevy Chase, Md., 1980—82; chairperson women's task force Am. Jewish Congress, Washington, 1984—86. Mem.: Nat. Press Club. Avocation: needlecrafts. Home: 4701 Willard Ave Chevy Chase MD 20815-4643 Office: 1730 M St NW Ste 801 Washington DC 20036 Home Phone: 301-986-0421; Office Phone: 202-833-4456. Business E-Mail: natalie@natalieshear.com.

SHEAR, THEODORE LESLIE, JR., archaeologist, educator; b. Athens, Greece, May 1, 1938; s. Theodore Leslie and Josephine (Platner) S.; m. Ione Doris Mylonas, June 24, 1959; children: Julia Louise, Alexandra. AB summa cum laude, Princeton U., NJ, 1959, MA, 1963, PhD, 1966. Instr. Greek and Latin Bryn Mawr Coll., Pa., 1964-66, asst. prof., 1966-67; asst. prof. art and archaeology Princeton U., 1967-70, assoc. prof., 1970-79, chmn. program in classical archaeology, 1970-85, assoc. chmn. dept. art and archaeology, 1976-78, 82-83, prof. classical archaeology, 1979—; prof. archaeology Am. Sch. Classical Studies, Athens, 1988-94. Mem. mng. com. Am. Sch. Classical Studies, Athens, 1972—; mem. archaeol. expdns. to Greece and Italy, including Mycenae, 1953-54, 1958, 1962-63, 1965-66, Eleusis, 1956, Perati, 1956, Corinth, 1960, Morgantina, Sicily, 1962; mem. Ancient Agora of Athens, 1955, 1967, field dir., 1968-94; trustee William Alexander Procter Found., 1982-89, Princeton Jr. Sch., 1983-2006, pres., 1994-2006. Author: Kallias of Sphettos and the Revolt of Athens in 286 B.C., 1978; contbr. articles to profl. jours. White fellow Am. Sch. Classical Studies, 1959-60. Mem. Archaeol. Inst. Am., Am. Philol. Assn., Coll. Art Assn., Archaeol. Soc. Athens (hon.), Century Assn. Club (NYC); Nassau Club (Princeton), Princeton Club (NYC), Hellenic Yacht Club (Piraeus, Greece), Phi Beta Kappa. Republican. Episcopalian. Home: 87 Library Pl Princeton NJ 08540-3015 also: 30 Deinokratous St Athens Greece

SHEARD, CHARLES, III, dermatologist; b. Toronto, Ont., Can., Nov. 22, 1914; came to U.S., 1945; s. Charles Jr. and Alice Elizabeth (Ramsay) S.; m. Katherine Patricia Murphy, Nov. 19, 1937; children: Joan Virginia Sheard Cumming (dec.), Pamela Carol Sheard McGuiness, Wendy Alice Sheard Geyer. Matriculation, Upper Can. Coll., Toronto, 1933; MD, U. Toronto, 1939. Diplomate Am. Bd. Dermatology. Intern Toronto Gen. Hosp., 1939-40; instr. physiology, anatomy U. Toronto Med. Faculty, 1940-41; surgical asst. resident Hosp. for Sick Children, Toronto, 1945; from resident to chief resident dermatologist Columbia Presbyn. Hosp., NYC, 1945-49; assoc. prof. medicine Cornell U. Med. Coll., NYC, 1950-94, assoc. prof. emeritus, 1994—. Author: (textbook) Treatment in Dermatology, 1978; contbr. articles to profl. jours. Flight lt. RCAF, 1941-45. Fellow ACP, Royal Coll. Physicians (Can.); mem. Metro-Manhattan Dermatol. Soc. NYC (sec. 1970-80), Royal Can. Yacht Club, Muskoka Lakes Golf and Country Club. Republican. Episcopalian. Avocations: sailing, fishing, golf.: 10 Merry Meeting Ln Lloyd Harbor NY 11743

SHEARER, CHARLES LIVINGSTON, academic administrator; b. Louisville, Nov. 23, 1942; s. Guy Cooper and Kathryn (Aufenkamp) S.; m. Susan Pulling Shearer, Nov. 30, 1968; children: Todd A., Mark G., Scott B. BS, U. Ky., 1964, MA, 1967, Mich. State U., 1973, PhD, 1981. Instr. Henderson CC, Ky., 1967-69; asst. prof. Ferris State Coll., Big Rapids, Mich., 1969-71; grad. asst. Mich. State U., East Lansing, 1971-73; dir. mgmt. program Albion Coll., Mich., 1973-75, dir. ops. Mich., 1975-79; v.p. fin. Transylvania U., Lexington, Ky., 1979-83, pres., 1983—. Bd. dirs. Lexington Philharm. Soc., 1983-89; mem. adv. bd. Salvation Army, Lexington, 1983-87; mem. Henry Clay Meml. Found., Lexington, 1983-89. Capt. U.S. Army Nat. Guard, 1966-76. Named One of Outstanding Young Men in Am., 1978. Mem. Am. Econs. Assn., Lexington C. of C. (bd. dirs. 1985—), Rotary. Mem. Disciples Of Christ Ch. Office Phone: 606-233-8111. *

SHEARER, DAVID A., JR., lawyer; b. Lexington, Ky., Apr. 20, 1968; married; 2 children. BA, Vanderbilt U., 1990; JD, U. Ky., 1993. Bar: Ky. 1993, US Dist. Ct. Eastern Dist. Ky. 1993, US Ct. of Appeals Sixth Cir. 1993, Ohio 1999. Ptnr. Freund, Freeze & Arnold, Cin. Named one of Ohio's Rising Stars, Super Lawyers, 2006. Mem.: Ohio Assn. Civil Trial Attorneys, ABA, Ohio State Bar Assn., Ky. Bar Assn., Northern Ky. Bar Assn., Cin. Bar Assn. Avocations: skiing, hunting, fishing, golf. Office: Freund Freeze & Arnold Fourth and Walnut Ctr 105 E Fourth St Ste 1400 Cincinnati OH 45202-4035 Office Phone: 513-665-3500. Office Fax: 513-665-3503.

SHEARER, DEREK NOCROSS, political science professor, diplomat, academic administrator; b. LA, Dec. 5, 1946; s. Lloyd and Marva (Peterson) S.; m. Sue Toigo; 1 child, Casey (dec.); stepchildren: Anthony, Julie. BA, Yale U., 1968; PhD, Union Grad. Sch., Yellow Springs, Ohio, 1977. Lectr. U. Calif., LA, 1979-81; dir. internat. and pub. affairs ctr., prof. of pub. policy Occidental Coll., LA, 1981-94, 98—; dep. undersec. U.S. Dept. Commerce, Washington, 1993; U.S. amb. to Finland U.S. Dept. State, Washington, 1994-97; prof. internat. affairs Occidental Coll., LA, 1997—; internat. advisor Ziff Bros. Investments, 1998—. Fellow Econ. Strategy Inst., Washington, 1993; policy adv. to Presidential Candidate Bill Clinton, 1990-92; adv. on NATO peace keeping USN, 1997—; pub. policy fellow Woodrow Wilson Internat. Scholars Ctr., 1999-2000; dir. global affairs Occidental Coll., 2001—, Chevalier prof. diplomacy and world affairs, 2002—; founder Pacific Coun. Internat. Policy, 1994—; sr. fellow USC Inst. Public Diplomacy. Contbr. articles to profl. pubIs. Planning commr. City of Santa Monica (Calif.), 1984; bd. mem. Nat. Consumer Bank, Washington, 1991. Fellow Guggenheim Found., 1984, U.S.-Japan Leadership fellow Japan Soc., 1991. Democrat. Avocations: basketball, tennis, travel, mysteries. Office: Global Affairs Occidental Coll Los Angeles CA 90041 Office Phone: 323-259-1459. Business E-Mail: dshearer@oxy.edu.

SHEARER, HARRY JULIUS, scriptwriter, actor, television director; b. LA, Dec. 23, 1943; s. Mack Shearer and Dora (Kohn) Warren; m. Penelope Joyce Nichols, June 12, 1974 (div. 1977); m. Judith Owen, March 28, 1993. BA in polit. sci., UCLA, 1964; postgrad. in urban govt., Harvard U., 1964-65. Cert. secondary tchr., Calif. Reporter Newsweek mag., LA, Boston, 1964-65; legis. intern Calif. State Assembly, Sacramento, 1965-66; tchr. Compton (Calif.) Unified Sch. Dist., 1966-68; writer, actor, producer The Credibility Gap, LA, 1968-76; creator nat. pub. radio show Sta. KCRW, Santa Monica, Calif., 1983—. Co-creator, co-producer (recs.) A Great Gift Idea, 1974, A Star is Bought, 1975; author: (weekly column) Man Bites Town, 1990—; actor: (films) Cracking Up, 1977, American Raspberry, 1977, Fish That Saved Pittsburgh, 1979, Loose Shoes, 1980, The Right Stuff, 1983, Plain Clothes, 1988, Oscar, 1991, Pure Luck, 1991, Blood and Concrete, 1991, The Fisher King, 1991, A League of Their Own, 1992, Wayne's World 2, 1993, I'll Do Anything, 1994, Little Giants, 1994, Speechless, 1994, My Best Friend's Wedding, 1997, Godzilla, 1998, Almost Heroes, 1998, The Truman Show, 1998, Edtv, 1999, Dick, 1999, Haiku Tunnel, 2001, Out There, 2001, Marilyn Hotchkiss Ballroom Dancing & Charm School, 2005, For Your Consideration, 2006, (voice) Animalympics, 1980, Flicks, 1987, My Stepmother is an Alien, 1988, Small Soldiers, 1988, Encounter in the Third Dimension, 1999, Ghost Dog: The Way of the Samurai, 1999, Edwurd Fudwupper Fibbed Big, 2000, Haunted Castle, 2001, Chicken Little, 2005, The Simpsons Movie, 2007; actor, writer, composer: This is Spinal Tap, 1984; actor, dir. Portrait of a White Marriage, 1988; actor, writer, dir., exec. prodr. Teddy Bears' Picnic, 2002; actor, composer A Mighty Wind, 2003; actor: (TV films) Serpico: The Deadly Game, 1976, Million Dollar Infield, 1982, Hometown By Makes Good, 1990, (voice) Spitting Image: Down and Out in the White House, 1986, Spitting Image: The Ronnie and Nancy Show, 1987; actor, writer, composer, prodr. (TV films) The T.V. Show, 1979; actor, dir.: (TV films) The History of White People in America, 1985; The History of White People in America: Volume II, 1996; actor: (TV series) The Simpsons, 1989—, Sunday Best, 1991, The News Hole, 1995, State of the Union Undressed, 1996; actor, writer (TV series) Saturday Night Live, 1979—80 (Emmy award nomination for Outstanding Writing Variety or Music Program, 1980), 1984—85, Likely Stories, Vol. 1, 1981; actor(voice): (TV specials) The Simpsons Christmas Special, 1989; actor, writer, composer: videos Spinal Tap: Break Like the Wind - The Videos, 1992; actor: (numerous TV guest appearances); writer, composer, prodr.: (TV films) A Spinal Tap Reunion: The 25th Anniversary London Sell-Out, 1992; composer: (films) Waiting for Guffman, 1996; writer (TV films) Disco Beaver from Outer Space, 1978, Real Life, 1979, (TV series) America 2-Night, 1978 (Emmy award nomination for Outstanding Writing Comedy-Variety or Music Series, 1978); author: (novels) Not Enough Indians, 2006. Recipient Cable ACE award for Best Game Show Series or Special, 1995. Mailing: Author Mail Justin Charles & Co 236 Huntington Ave Boston MA 02115 *

SHEARER, LINDA RAE, English educator; b. Connellsville, Pa., Aug. 3, 1954; d. Randall Wilbur and Gertrude Elizabeth Shearer. BA, Alderson-Broaddus Coll., Philippi, WV, 1976; MEd, Calif. U., California, Pa., 1980. Tchr. Connellsville Area Sch. Dist., Pa., 1978—. Advisor Nat. Honor Soc. Connellsville Area H.S., 1988—98; activities dir. Connellsville Area Sr. H.S., 1988—98, founder and sponsor Patriots, 2003—. Decorated Army Commendation Medal; named Fayette County Tchr. of the Yr., Fayette County C. of C., 1998, 2007; recipient Elks Disting. Citizen award,

Connellsville Elks # 503, 2006, Individual Award for Vol. Svc., Connellsville C. of C., 2006, Citation from Senate of Pa., Senators Jane Orie and Richard Kasunic, 2003, Disting. Alumni award, Alderson Broaddus Coll., 2005. Mem.: NEA, Connellsville Area Edn. Assn., Pa. State Edn. Assn. Baptist. Home: 304 Stadium Rd Connellsville PA 15425-1964 Office: Connellsville Area Senior High School 201 Falcon Dr Connellsville PA 15425 Home Phone: 724-628-9745; Office Phone: 724-628-1350. Personal E-mail: teddy@cvzoom.net. E-mail: lshearer@casdfalcons.org.

SHEARER, PAUL SCOTT, federal agency and trade association administrator; b. Clinton, Ill., Feb. 27, 1948; s. Lloyd Jr. and Pauline Lucille (Glosser) S.; m. Barbara Boston, July 3, 1981; children: Jason J. Brunk, Carrie K. Premo. BS, U. Ill., 1970, MS, 1975. Asst. dir. cash mgmt. State Treas. Ill., Springfield, 1973-74, asst. CFO, 1974-77, chief fiscal officer, 1977-78; dir. vehicle svc. State of Ill., Springfield, 1978-81; legis. asst. Senator Dixon U.S. Senate, Washington, 1981-84; exec. dir. Nat. Corn Growers Assn., St. Louis, 1984-90; dir. govt. rels. Halfpenny, Hahn, Roche & Marchese, 1990-93; dep. asst. sec. congl. rels. USDA, 1993-96; dir. nat. rels. Farmland Industries, Inc., Washington, 1996—2003; v.p. Bockorny Group, 2003—. Mem. adv. com. Ill. Atty.'s Gen. Agr. Law, State of Ill., 1985-91; dean Coll. Agr., U. Ill., 1989-90, U. Ill. Dept. Agrl. Econs., 1986-89; mem. agrl. tech. com. for trade in animals and animal products USDA/U.S. Trade Rep., 1998-2002; U.S. del. to WTO Ministerial Conf., 1999; food security adv. com. USAID, 1998-2002. Del. Dem. Nat. Conv., 1978, Mo. Dem. State conv., 1988, Va. Dem. State Conv., 1992, 93, 94, 96, 97, 2000; mem. Police Bd. Commrs., Chesterfield, Mo., 1988-90; pres. Mo. River Dem. Club, 1987-89. Named to Hon. Order of Ky. Cols., 1990, Alpha Gamma Sigma nat. merit award, 1991; named to Villa Grove (Ill.) HS Alumni Hall of Fame. Mem. St. Louis Agr.-Bus. Club (sec.-treas. 1987-88, 2d v.p. 1988-89, v.p. 1989-90, pres. 1990), U. Ill. Alumni Assn., U. Ill. Coll. Agr. Alumni Assn. (dir. at large 1990), Ill. Group (chmn. 1993, 04-05), Ill. State Soc. (bd. dirs. 1996-2007, pres. 2002-03), Mo.-Kans. Forum (chmn. 1998-2000), Alpha Zeta (Honor Roll), Nat. Democrat Club. Methodist. Home: 2744 Clarkes Landing Dr Oakton VA 22124-1120 Office: Bockorny Group 1101 16th St NW Ste 500 Washington DC 20036 E-mail: sshearer@bockornygroup.com.

SHEARER, ROBERT K., apparel executive; BA, Catawba Coll. Asst. contr. VF Corp., Greensboro, NC, 1986—89, contr., 1989—94, v.p., contr., 1994—98, v.p. fin., CFO, 1998—2003, v.p. fin. & global processes, CFO, 2003—05, sr. v.p., CFO, 2005—. Office: VF Corp 105 Corporate Ctr Blvd Greensboro NC 27408 *

SHEARER, RONALD ALEXANDER, economics professor; b. Trail, BC, Can., June 15, 1932; s. James Boyd and Mary Ann (Smith) S.; m. Renate Elizabeth Selig, Dec. 20, 1956 (dec.); children: Carl, Bruce. BA, U. B.C., 1954; MA, Ohio State U., 1955, PhD, 1959. Asst. prof. econs. U. Mich., 1958-62; economist Royal Commn. Banking and Fin., Toronto, Canada, 1962-63; mem. faculty U. B.C., Vancouver, 1963—, prof. econs., 1970-98, emeritus prof., 1998—, head dept., 1972-76. Co-author: Money and Banking, 1975, The Economics of the Canadian Financial System, 1994; editor: Trade Liberalization and a Regional Economy, 1971. Mem. Can. Econs. Assn. Office: U BC Dept Econs Vancouver BC Canada Home Phone: 604-266-2852. Business E-Mail: rshearer@interchange.ubc.ca.

SHEARER, WILLIAM THOMAS, pediatrician, educator; b. Detroit, Aug. 23, 1937; BS, U. Detroit, 1960; PhD, Wayne State U., 1966; MD, Washington U., St. Louis, 1970. Diplomate Am. Bd. Pediat., Am. Bd. Allergy and Immunology (chmn. 1994-95, dir. 1990-95, chair nominations com., clin. immunology soc.), Nat. Bd. Med. Examiners, cert. in diagnostic lab. immunology. Post-doctoral fellow in biochemistry dept. chem. Indiana U., Bloomington, 1966—67; intern in pediat. St. Louis Children's Hosp., 1970—71, resident in immunology in pediat., 1971—72, dir. divsn. allergy and immunology, 1974—78; fellow in immunology in pediat. Barnes Hosp., Washington U., St. Louis, 1972—74; spl. USPHA sci. rsch. fellow in medicine dept. medicine Washington U., 1972—74, assoc. prof., 1978, prof., 1978; prof. pediat., microbiology, immunology Baylor Coll. Medicine, Houston, 1989—, dir. AIDS rsch. ctr., 1991—; head sect. allergy & immunology Tex. Children's Hosp., Houston, 1978—, med. dir. AIDS ctr. Mem. ACTU Cmty. Adv. Bd. Tex. Children's Hosp., Houston, 1991—; chmn. pediat. core com. pediat. AIDS clin. trial group Nat. Inst. Allergy and Infectious Diseases, NIH, Bethesda, Md., 1989—, ad hoc reviewer, 1991, mem. therapeutics subcom. AIDS rsch. adv. com., 1993—, chmn. pediat. AIDS clin. trial group immunology com., 1994—, mem. pediat. AIDS clin. trials group exec. Com., 1991—95, mem. spl. rev. com. persons affected by chronic granulomatous disease, 1992; site visitor Gen. Clin. Rsch. Ctr. NIH, Bethesda, Md., 1993, vice chmn. pediat. AIDS clin. trials group exec. com., 1996—; chmn. study populatoin/patient mgmt. com. Clin. Ctrs. for the Study of Pediat. Lung and Heart Complications of HIV Infection, Nat. Heart, Lung and Blood Inst., NIH, Bethesda, Md., 1989—, mem. AIDS ad hoc work group, 1991; dir. Pediat. HIV/AIDS Clin. Rsch. Ctr., Houston, 1988—; chmn. exec. com. clin. trial intravenous gammaglobulin in HIV infected children Nat. Inst. Child Health and Human Devel., Bethesda, 1989—; dir. Am. Bd. Allergy and Immunology, 1990—95, chair, 1994—95; vice-chair exec. com. Pediat. AIDS Clin. Trials Group, 1996—2001. Editor: Pediatric Asthma, Allergy, and Immunology, 1989; editl. bd. Jour. Allergy and Clin. Immunology, 1993—, Clin. and Diagnostic Lab. Immunology, 1994—, editor Pediatric Allergy and Immunology, 1995—, Allergy and Immunology Tng. Program Dir.; assoc. editor: Jour. Allergy and Clin. Immunology, 2003—; guest editor Seminar Pediatric Infectious Disease, 1990, contbr. intro. Allergy: Princples and Practice, 1992, contbr. articles to profl. jours. including New Eng. Jour. Medicine. AIDS cons. Houston Ind. Sch. Dist., 1986—; med. adv. Spring Br. Ind. Sch. Dist., Houston, 1987—; chmn. cmty. HIV/AIDS adv. group Tex. Med. Ctr., 1991—. Recipient faculty rsch. award, Am. Cancer Soc., 1977—79, Myrtle Wreath award, Hadassah, 1985, spl. recognition award, Am. Acad. Allergy and Immunology, 1994; grantee NIH, 1988—; scholar rsch., Cystic Fibrosis Found., 1974—77. Mem.: Clin. Immunology Soc. (chair Am. Bd. Allergy and Immunology nominations com. 1994—96, pres. 2001—02), Am. Acad. Allergy, Asthma and Immunology (assoc. chmn. for planning of 1997-98 internat. meetings, profl. ednl. coun.), Am. Acad. Allergy and Immunology (chmn. clin. and lab. immunology com. 1994—96, chmn. tng. program dirs. nat. issues subcom. 1994—96), Tex. Allergy and Immunology Soc. (chmn. nat. issues com. 1992—96, pres. 1994—96), Tex. Allergy Soc. (exec. com. 1990—), Am. Acad. Pediat. (exec. com. sect. allergy and immunology 1991—), Am. Soc. Clin. Investigation. Achievements include research in half-matched T-cell-depleted bone marrow transplants; membrane signal pathway of human B lymphcytes. Office: Baylor Coll Med Allergy/Immun Clinic 6621 Fannin MC FC 330 01 Houston TX 77030-2600 E-mail: wshearer@bcm.tmc.edu.

SHEARING, MIRIAM, retired state supreme court chief justice; b. Waverly, NY, Feb. 24, 1935; BA, Cornell U., 1956; JD, Boston Coll., 1964. Bar: Calif. 1965, Nev. 1969. Justice of peace Las Vegas Justice Ct., 1977-81; judge Nev. Dist. Ct., 1983-92, chief judge, 1986; justice Nevada Supreme Ct., Carson City, 1993—2005, chief justice, 1997, 2004, sr. justice, 2005—. Mem. ABA, Am. Judicature Soc. (chair 2001-03), Nev. Judges Assn. (sec. 1978), Nev. Dist. Ct. Judges Assn. (sec. 1984-85, pres. 1986-87), State Bar Nev., State Bar Calif., Clark County Bar Assn. Democrat. Personal E-mail: shearing@nvcourts.state.nv.us.

SHEARMUR, ALLI, broadcast executive; married. V.p. prodn. Walt Disney Co., 1994—97; exec. v.p. prodn. Universal Pictures, Paramount Pictures, co-pres. prodn., 2005—. Named one of 100 Most Powerful Women in Entertainment, Hollywood Reporter, 2006. Office: Paramount Pictures 5555 Melrose Hwy West Hollywood CA 90038 Office Phone: 323-956-5000. *

SHEA-STONUM, MARILYN, federal bankruptcy judge; b. 1947; AB, U. Calif., Santa Cruz, 1969; JD, Case Western Res. U., 1975. Law clk. to Hon. Frank J. Battisti, Cleve., 1975-76; ptnr. Jones, Day, Reavis & Pogue, Cleve., 1984—94; bankruptcy judge U.S. Dist. Ct. (no. dist.) Ohio, Akron, 1994—. Editor-in-chief Am. Bankruptcy Law Jour., Nat. Conf. Bankruptcy Judges. Mem. Order of Coif. Office: US Bankruptcy Ct No Dist Ohio 240 Fed Bldg 2 S Main St Akron OH 44308-1813 Office Phone: 330-252-6130.

SHEATH, ROBERT GORDON, botanist, educator; b. Toronto, Can., Dec. 26, 1950; arrived in U.S., 1978; s. Harry Gordon and Shirley Irene (Rose) Sheath. BSc, U. Toronto, 1973, PhD, 1977. Nat. Rsch. Coun. Can. postdoctoral fellow U. B.C., 1977-78; asst. prof. aquatic biology U. RI, Kingston, 1978-82, assoc. prof., 1982-86, chmn. dept. botany, 1986-90, prof., 1987-91; head dept. biology Meml. U., St. Johns, Canada, 1991-95; dean coll. biol. sci. U. Guelph, Ont., 1995-2001; provost Calif. State U. San Marcos, 2001—. Mem. evolution and ecology grant selection com. NSERC, 1994—97, chair, 1996—97, selection com. life scis., 1996, chair maj. facilities access life scis. subcom., 2001; mem. Can. Rsch. Chairs Coll. of Reviewers, 2000—01. Editor (with M. M. Harlin): Freshwater and Marine Plants of RI, 1988; editor: (with K. M. Cole) Biology of the Red Algae, 1990; editor: (with J.D. Wehr) Classification and Ecology of Freshwater Algae of North America, 2003; contbr. 131 articles to profl. jours. Recipient G. A. Cox Gold medal, U. Toronto, 1973, Darbaker prize, Bot. Soc. Am., 1997, T. Christensen prize panel, 2000; grantee, NSF, 1980—91, 2001—05, NSERC, 1991—2002. Mem.: Japanese Phycological Soc. (editl. bd. 2000—05), Brit. Phycological Soc. (freshwater flora com. 1993—2002, overseas v.p. 1997—99, assoc. editor 1999—2001), Arctic Inst. N.Am., Phycological Soc. Am. (editl. bd. 1983—86, assoc. editor 1984—89, pres. 1991—92, editl. bd. 1996—2000, publs. com. chair 2001—, bd. trustees 2001—, Bold award 1976), Internat. Phycological Soc. (editl. bd. 1993—95, T. Christensen prize panel 2000, nominating com. 2000—01). Office: Calif State U San Marcos Office of Provost San Marcos CA 92096-0001 Office Phone: 760-750-4050. E-mail: rsheath@csusm.edu.

SHECTER, HOWARD L., lawyer; b. Boston, May 13, 1943; AB, Harvard U., 1965; JD, U. Pa., 1968. Bar: Pa. 1968, N.Y. 1996. Assoc. Morgan, Lewis & Bockius LLP, Phila., 1968-73, ptnr. NYC, 1973—, bus. and fin. practice group leader, firm mng. ptnr., 1979—84, chmn., 1985—86. Founder & former chmn. seminar series, Acquiring or Selling the Privately Held Company, Practicing Law Inst. Office: Morgan Lewis & Bockius LLP 101 Park Ave New York NY 10178-0060 Office Phone: 212-309-6384. Office Fax: 212-309-7044. Business E-Mail: hshecter@morganlewis.com.

SHEDD, DENNIS W., federal judge; b. Cordova, SC, Jan. 28, 1953; BA, Wofford Coll., 1975; JD, U. SC, 1978; LLM, Georgetown U., 1980. Bar: SC. Law clerk Harry Dent & Assoc., 1977—78; admin. asst. US Senator Strom Thurmond, 1978—88; chief counsel US Senate Jud. Com., Washington, 1985-86; of counsel Bethea, Jordan & Griffin, Columbia, S.C., 1988-90; pvt. practice, 1989-90; judge US Dist. Ct. SC, Greenville, 1990—2002, US Ct. Appeals (4th cir.), 2002—. Adj. prof. U. SC, 1989-92. Mem. SC Bar Assn., Richland County Bar Assn., Phi Beta Kappa. Office: US Courthouse 1100 Laurel St Columbia SC 29201-2431 *

SHEDD, DONALD POMROY, surgeon; b. New Haven, Aug. 4, 1922; s. Gale and Marion (Young) S.; m. Charlotte Newsom, Mar. 17, 1946; children: Carolyn, David, Ann, Laura BS, Yale U., New Haven, Conn., 1944, MD, 1946. Diplomate Am. Bd. Surgery. Intern Yale New Haven Hosp., 1946-47, asst. resident, resident, 1949-53; instr. surgery Yale U. Med Sch., New Haven, 1953-54, asst. prof., 1954-56, assoc. prof., 1956-67; chief dept. head and neck surgery Roswell Park Cancer Inst., Buffalo, 1967-96, prof. emeritus, 1996—; rsch. prof. emeritus SUNY at Buffalo, 1996—. Co-editor: Surgical and Prosthetic Speech Rehabilitation, 1980, Head and Neck Cancer, 1985, (with Prof. Abel Fink) The Early History of Hospice Buffalo, 2003; author: Historical Landmarks in Head and Neck Cancer Surgery, 2000; contbr. numerous articles to profl. jours. Founding bd. dirs. Hospice Buffalo, Inc., 1973—83. Capt. US Army, 1947—49. Mem. Am. Head and Neck Soc., Soc. Univ. Surgeons, Soc. Surg. Oncology, New Eng. Surg. Soc., Soc. Head and Neck Surgeons (pres. 1976-77). Avocations: sailing, windsurfing, tennis, history of medicine. Home: 671 Lafayette Ave Buffalo NY 14222-1435

SHEDLARZ, DAVID L., pharmaceutical executive; b. NYC, 1948; m. Patricia Shedlarz; 1 child, Danielle. BS in Econs. and Math., Mich. State U., 1970; MBA in Fin. and Acctg., NYU, 1975. Various position including sr. fin. analyst, Pharmaceutical divsn., fin. mgr. & controller mktg./sales/prodn., Diagnostics divsn. Pfizer Inc., NYC, 1976-79, prodn. contr. U.S. pharms. divsn., 1979-81, asst. group contr. U.S. Pharms. divsn., 1981-84, group contr., 1984-89, v.p. fin. U.S. pharms. group, 1989-92, corp. officer, v.p. fin. parent co., 1992-95, CFO, 1995—2005, sr. v.p., 1997—99, exec. v.p., 1999—2005, vice chmn., 2005—. Bd. dirs. Pitney Bowes Inc., 2001—, Nat. Multiple Sclerosis Bd.; mem. NYU Stern Sch. Bd. Overseers, J.P. Morgan Chase & Co. Nat. Adv. Bd., Nat. Assn. Mfrs. Bd., Internat. Acctg. Standards Bd., Standing Adv. Group, Pub. Acctg. Oversight Bd. Mem. Nat. Jr. Achievement Bd.; chmn. Nat. Jr. Achievement NY. Office: Pfizer Inc 235 E 42d St New York NY 10017-5755 *

SHEDLIN, GARY STEPHEN, investment banker; b. Nov. 8, 1963; s. Victor and Susan S.; m. Deborah Rae Winograd, Mar. 23, 1991. Grad. summa cum laude, Colgate Univ.; MBA, Harvard Univ. Assoc. to ptnr. Lazard Freres & Co. LLC, NYC, mng. dir., 1997—2004, Citigroup, NYC, 2004—. Recipient Rainmaker prize, fin. sector, Dealmaker mag., 2006. Mem.: Phi Beta Kappa. Office: Citigroup 399 Park Ave New York NY 10043 Office Phone: 212-559-1000. Office Fax: 212-793-3946. *

SHEDRINSKY, ALEXANDER MIKCHAIL, chemistry professor, conservator, consultant; b. Leningrad, USSR, Mar. 27, 1943; arrived in USA, 1980. s. Mikchail Alexander Shedrinsky and Mussa A. (Gordon) Tsipkina; m. Raissa A. (Bekker), Oct. 16, 1965 (div. Apr. 1975); one child, Mikchail Alexander; m. Maria G. (Kurbatova), June 30, 1982; one child, Maria Antonia. MS in Chemistry, Leningrad U., 1965; MS in Organic Chemistry, N.Y. Univ., 1983, PhD in Organic Chemistry, 1986. Rsch. asst. State Sci. Rsch. Inst. Pulp and Paper, Leningrad, 1971—72; asst. prof. chemistry Leningrad N.W. Poly. Tech., 1972—75, LI Univ., Bklyn., 1988—92; lectr. in organic chemistry Leningrad Pharm. Sch., 1976—79; tchg. fellow NY Univ., NYC, 1981—83, postdoctoral fellow Conservation Ctr. Inst. Fine Arts, 1986—88; assoc. prof. chemistry LI Univ., Bklyn., 1992—97; adj. assoc. prof. Conservation Ctr. Inst. Fine Arts NY Univ., NYC, 1993—97; cons. Met. Mus. Art, NYC, 1994—; prof. chemistry LI Univ., Bklyn., 1997—; adj. prof. Conservation Ctr. Inst. Fine Arts NY Univ., NYC, 1998—99; cons. internat. coun. Mus. Modern Art, 2001—. Vis. scientist Am. Mus. Natural History, NYC, 1995—; vis. prof. Forchheimer, 1997, Hebrew U. Jerusalem; Fulbright prof. USIA, St. Petersburg (Russia) Acad. Art, 1995, 2001-02. Contbr. chpt. to book, articles to internat. scientific journals; reviewer, Jour. Analytical and Applied Pyrolysis, Curator, Archeometry, 1989—. Andrew W. Mellon Fellow Met. Mus. Art, Dept. Object Conservation, 1988-90, Charles and Francis Atkins Fellow Met. Mus. Art, Dept. Paintings Conservation, 1984-86. Mem. Am. Chem. Soc. (tour spkr.) Washington,1992-, Internat. Inst. Conservation, NY Acad. Sci. Achievements include synthesis of new synthetic varnish for the purpose of painting conservation; introducing analytical pyrolysis in the field of art conservation (first rev. on the subject in 1989); devel. of new analytical approach (Py-GC and Py-GC-MS) to analysis of different ambers. Office: LIU 1 Univ Plz Brooklyn NY 11201-5301 Office Phone: 718-488-1208.

SHEDROFF, SHARON D., psychologist, researcher, anthropologist, consultant; b. Middletown, Conn., Feb. 7, 1952; d. Leon and Sylvia Shedroff. BA summa cum laude, Syracuse U., NYC, 1974; MA, Calif. Sch. Profl. Psychology, San Diego, 1979. Lic. marriage, family and child counselor Calif., 1981. Psychology intern T.R.I. Cmty. Svcs., San Diego, 1978—81, marriage, family & child counselor, 1981—82; rsch. psychologist Grid Rsch., San Diego, 1983—85; founder, ptnr. Edwards Assocs., San Diego, 1985—, Strategic Vision Inc., San Diego, 1989—, Inst. for Value-Centered Life, San Diego, 1999—. Author: (novels) Dakota Dreams, 2003; contbr. articles to profl. jours. Mem.: Am. Morgan Horse Assn., U.S.A. Equestrian. Avocations: skiing, competitive horseback riding. Home: PO Box 420036 San Diego CA 92142 Office: The Edwards Assocs PO Box 420429 San Diego CA 92142 Office Phone: 858-576-7141.

SHEEDER, ROBERT ELWOOD, lawyer; b. Ind., Pa., Apr. 8, 1951; s. Elwood B. and Alice (Poole) Sheeder; m. Martha Ann Painter. BA with high honors, U. Va., 1973; JD cum laude, U. Mich., 1976. Bar: Tex. 1976, Pa. 1978, US Dist. Ct. We. Dist. Pa. 1980, US Ct. Appeals 3rd Cir. 1981, US Dist. Ct. No. Dist. Tex. 1985, US Dist. Ct. Ea. Dist. Tex. 1986, US Ct. Appeals 5th Cir. 1988, US Dist. Ct. So. Dist. Tex. 1989, US Dist. Ct. We. Dist. Tex. 1991, US Supreme Ct. 1996. Assoc. Reed, Smith, Shaw & McClay, Pitts., 1977-84; ptnr. Winstead, McGuire, Sechrest & Minick, Dallas, 1984-92; shareholder Jenkens & Gilchrist, P.C., Dallas, 1992—2007, Bracewell & Guiliani, Dallas, 2007—. Lectr. labor law So. Meth. U., 1988-90. Editor-in-chief: Tex. Labor Letter, 1994-01. Fellow: Coll. Labor and Employment Lawyers; mem.: ABA, Dallas Bar Assn., Tex. State Bar Assn. (governing coun. labor & employment law sect. 2002—04, Best Lawyers in Am. 2001—), Chambers USA. Republican. Presbyterian. Office Phone: 214-758-1643. Business E-Mail: roebrt.sheeder@bgllp.com.

SHEEDY, JOHN THOMAS (JACK), writer; b. Boston, Sept. 4, 1962; s. John James Sheedy and Sandra Jean Rappoli; m. Adriana Maria Rockwell, May 31, 1986; children: Melissa Catherine, Gregory John. B in Mktg., Stonehill Coll., 1984. Mktg. officer Sentry Bank, Hyannis, Mass., 1984—91; prodn. mgr. Internat. Fund for Animal Welfare, Yarmouthport, Mass., 1992—2002; owner, book pub. Harvest Home Books, Dennis, Mass., 1995—2004; mktg. writer CCBT Fin. Cos., 2002—04; ref. libr. Dennis Pub. Libr., 2005—. Author: Insider's Guide to Cape Cod, 1997; author, editor: Cape Cod Companion, 1999, Cape Cod Voyage, 2001, Cape Cod Harvest, 2007, mng. editor, contbr.: Summerscape Mag., 1999 (winner first place editl. excellence New Eng. Press Assn.); contbr. articles to newspapers; co-host Ghostly Homes of Cape Cod, 2001. Roman Catholic. Avocations: astronomy, tennis, drawing.

SHEEDY, WILLIAM M., finance company executive; BS, W. Va. Univ.; MBA, Univ. Notre Dame. Mgmt. positions First Nationwide Bank, 1990—93; positions through exec. v.p. interchange fee strategy Visa USA, San Francisco, 1993—. Mailing: Visa USA PO Box 194607 San Francisco CA 94119-4607 *

SHEEHAN, CHARLES VINCENT, investment banker; b. London, Dec. 19, 1930; came to U.S., 1931; s. Charles Vincent and Mary Margaret (Stokes) S.; m. Susan Ellen Rosar, May 5, 1962. BS, Georgetown U., 1952. Chief fin. officer Gen. Electric Co., Tokyo, Sydney, Australia and Sao Paulo, Brazil, 1962-64, 64-66, 67-71, staff exec. Fairfield, Conn., 1972-83, v.p. corp. exec. office, 1983-87; sr. v.p., chief fin., adminstrn. officer Kidder, Peabody Group, Inc., NYC, 1987-90. Bd. dirs. Fleet Trust Co., Highlands-Cashiers Hosp.; chmn. bd. dirs. Indian River Meml. Hosp. Chmn. Non-partisan Polit. Action Com. for Gen. Electric Co. employees, Fairfield, 1982-83. Served to lt. USN, 1952-54. Mem. Johns Island Club (Vero Beach, Fla.), Quail Valley Golf Club (Vero Beach, Fla.), Wildcat Cliffs Country Club (Highlands, N.C.) (pres. 1998-99). Republican. Roman Catholic. Avocations: golf, boating. Home (Winter): 884 Indian Lane Vero Beach FL 32963-1131 E-mail: gecharlie@earthlink.net.

SHEEHAN, D'EANE, biology professor; M, La. Tech. U., Ruston. Biology instr. La. Tech U., Ruston, 1989—. Office Phone: 318-257-4573. Business E-Mail: dsheehan@latech.edu.

SHEEHAN, GREGORY D., lawyer; AB magna cum laude, Harvard U., 1977; JD, U. Calif., Berkeley, 1980. Bar: Mass. 1980, Calif. 1981. Law clk. Judge Walter J. Skinner, US Dist Ct. (Mass.), 1980—81; ptnr. corp. dept. & chmn. investment mgmt. practice group Ropes & Gray, Boston. Editor (exec.): Calif. Law Rev. Pres. French-Am. C. of C. of New England, 1993—95. Mem.: Phi Beta Kappa, Order of the Coif. Office: Ropes & Gray 1 International Pl Boston MA 02110-2624 Office Phone: 617-951-7621. Office Fax: 617-951-7050. Business E-Mail: gsheehan@ropesgray.com.

SHEEHAN, JAMES JOHN, historian, educator; b. San Francisco, May 31, 1937; s. James B. and Sally W. (Walsh) S.; m. 1960; 1 child, Michael L.; m. Margaret L. Anderson, Sept. 2, 1989. BA, Stanford U., 1958; MA, U. Calif., Berkeley, 1959, PhD, 1964. From asst. to assoc. prof. Northwestern U., Evanston, Ill., 1964-79; prof. Stanford (Calif.) U., 1979-86, chmn. dept., 1982-89, Dickason prof. in humanities, 1986—. Author: Lujo Brentano, 1966, German Liberalism, 1978, German History 1770-1866, 1989, Der Ausklang des alten Reiches, 1994, Museums in German Artworld, 2000; editor: The Boundaries of Humanity, 1991; contbr. articles to profl. jours. Decorated officer's cross Order of Merit; fellow Am. Coun. Learned Socs., 1981-82, NEH, 1985-86, Wissenschaftskolleg Berlin; Guggenheim fellow, 2000—. Fellow AAAS (Humboldt Rsch. prize 1995), Am. Acad. Berlin; mem. Royal Hist. Soc. (corr.), Am. Hist. Assn. (nominating com. 1979-81, chmn. conf. group on Ctrl. European history 1985-86, pres. 2005), Am. Philos. Soc. (Orden pour le Mérite). Office: Stanford U Dept History Stanford CA 94305 Home Phone: 510-649-8910. Business E-Mail: sheehan@stanford.edu.

SHEEHAN, JAMES PATRICK, printing company executive, former media company executive; b. Jersey City, June 6, 1942; s. John Patrick and Helen Teresa (Woods) S.; m. Mary Ellen Finnell, July 1, 1967; children: James, Christopher. BS, Seton Hall U., 1965; MBA, Wayne State U., 1973. Contr. Otis Elevator Co. N.Am., Farmington, Conn., 1976-78, dir. mfg. Yonkers, N.Y., 1978-80; v.p., contr., Pratt & Whitney Aircraft, East Hartford, Conn., 1980-82; sr. v.p. A. H. Belo Corp., Dallas, 1982-84; CFO, A.H. Belo Corp., Dallas, 1984-86, pres., COO, 1987-93, CEO, 1993-99; pres., CEO, chmn. Goss Graphic Systems, Westmont, Ill., 1999—. Mem. devel. bd. U. Tex.-Dallas, 1985—; bd. dirs. United Way, The Dallas Partnership, The Dallas Morning News Charities; trustee St. Paul Med. Ctr. Found. Served to Lt. (j.g.) USN, 1967-69, Vietnam. Mem. Am. Newspaper Pubs. Assn., So. Newspaper Pubs. Assn. Roman Catholic. Avocations: tennis, racquetball, golf, running. Office: Goss International 3 Territorial Ct Bolingbrook IL 60440-3557

SHEEHAN, JASON, neurosurgeon; s. James and Jacqueline Sheehan; m. Diane Kimball, May 30, 1998; children: Kimball, Darrah. BS, MS, PhD, U. Va., Charlottesville, MD, 1998. Neurol. surgeon U. Va., 1998—. Dir. Lars Leksell Gamma Knife Ctr., Charlottesville, 2004—. Mem.: Am. Assn.

Neurol. Surgeons. Achievements include research in intracranial and spinal radiosurgery. Office: U Va Box 800-212 Health Sciences Center Charlottesville VA 22908 Office Phone: 434-982-1454. Office Fax: 434-982-0543.

SHEEHAN, KEVIN EDWARD, venture capitalist; b. Deerfield, Mass., June 17, 1945; s. Walter Francis and Lillian (Fontaine) S.; m. Barbara Ann Frank, July 6, 1974; children: Timothy John, James Frank. BA, Williams Coll., 1966; MBA, Harvard U., 1971. Traffic mgr. New England Tel., Boston, 1966-69; foreman H Block Line Cummins Engine Co., Columbus, Ind., 1971, employee rels. mgr., 1972-75, dir. employee rels., 1975-77, mgr. engine plant, 1977-80, v.p. mgmt. systems, 1980-83, v.p. parts, 1984, v.p. parts and distbn., 1984-86, v.p. components group, 1986; gen. ptnr. CID Equity Partners, 1994—. Bd. dirs. One Call Comm., Hetsco, Inc., SPS Commerce; bd. observer SmartSignal, Emerald BioAgr.; non-exec. chmn. Flowserve Corp. Pres., bd. dirs. Quinco Mental Health Ctr., Columbus, 1976-80, St. Agnes Parish, Nashville, Ind., 1980-84. Mem. Country of Brown County Club (Nashville, Ind., pres., bd. dirs. 1984-88). Avocations: golf, reading, nature study. Office: CID Capital 1 American Sq Ste 2850 Indianapolis IN 46282 Office Phone: 317-269-2350. Business E-Mail: kevins@cidcap.com.

SHEEHAN, LAWRENCE JAMES, lawyer; b. San Francisco, July 23, 1932; AB, Stanford U., 1957, LLB, 1959. Bar: Calif. 1960. Law clk. to chief judge U.S. Ct. Appeals 2d Cir., NYC, 1959-60; assoc. O'Melveny & Myers, LA, 1960-68, ptnr., 1969-94, of counsel, 1995—2004. D. dirs. FPA Mut. Funds, Source Capital, Inc. Mem. ABA, Los Angeles County Bar Assn., Calif. Bar Assn., Order of Coif. Office: O Melveny & Myers 1999 Avenue Of The Stars Los Angeles CA 90067-6035 also: 400 S Hope St Los Angeles CA 90071-2801 Office Phone: 310-246-6895. Business E-Mail: lsheehan@omm.com.

SHEEHAN, MICHAEL ANDREW, former protective services official, former federal agency administrator; b. Red Bank, NJ, Feb. 10, 1955; s. John M. and Janet M. (Purcell) S.; m. Sita Sheehan; children: Alexandra, Michael BS, US Mil. Acad., 1977; MS in Fgn. Svc., Georgetown U., 1988. Commd. 2d lt. U.S. Army, 1977-97, advanced through grades to lt. col., ret., 1997; intelligence analyst The White House, Washington, 1989-91; dir. internat. programs NSC, Washington, 1992-93, dir. global issues, 1995-97; dir. POLMIL affairs U.S. Mission to UN, NYC, 1993-95; dept. asst. sec. for internat. org. affairs US Dept. State, Washington, 1997-98, coord. for counter terrorism, 1998-2000; asst. sec. gen. Dept. Peacekeeping Ops. UN, NYC, 2001—03; dep. commr. counter-terrorism NY Police Dept., NYC, 2003—06; Disting. Fellow, Ctr. for Law & Security NYU Sch. Law, NYC, 2006—. Mem.: Coun. on Fgn. Rels., Spl. Forces Assn. Roman Catholic. Office: NYU Sch Law 110 W 3rd St Ste 224/5 New York NY 10012

SHEEHAN, MICHAEL JARBOE, archbishop; b. Wichita, Kans., July 9, 1939; s. John Edward and Mildred (Jarboe) Sheehan. MST, Gregorian U., Rome, 1965; D of Canon Law, Lateran U., Rome, 1971. Ordained priest Roman Cath. Ch., 1964. Asst. gen. sec. Nat. Coun. Cath. Bishops, Washington, 1971—76; rector Holy Trinity Sem., Dallas, 1976—82; pastor Immaculate Conception Ch., Grand Prairie, Tex., 1982—83; bishop Diocese of Lubbock, Tex., 1983—93; archbishop Archdiocese of Santa Fe, Albuquerqe, N.Mex., 1993—. Bd. dirs. Tex. Conf. of Chs.; past chmn. Am. Bd. Cath. Missions, 1989—91. Contbr. articles to profl. jours. Trustee St. Mary Hosp., Lubbock, Tex., 1983—89, Cath. Relief Svcs., 1992—. Mem.: Serra Club (chaplain 1983—93, chmn. NCCB com. on Evangelization 1996—99, NCCB adminstrv. com. Washington). Avocations: skiing, racquetball. Office: Archdiocese Santa Fe 4000 Saint Josephs Pl NW Albuquerque NM 87120-1714

SHEEHAN, MIKE, advertising executive; m. Maureen Sheehan. Student, U.S. Naval Acad.; BA in English, St. Anselm Coll. With Leo Burnett, Chgo., Clarke Goward and Ingalls Quinn & Johnson, Boston; exec. creative dir. Hill Holliday, Connors, Cosmopulos Interpub. Group, Boston, DDB, Chgo., Hill Holliday, Connors, Cosmopulos Interpub. Group, NYC, 2000—02, pres., 2002—, CEO, 2003—. Vice chmn., bd. trustees St. Anselm Coll. Named Nat. Creative Dir. of Yr., Adweek, 1998; recipient Grand Clio award, One Show Gold award, Cannes Lions award, Best of Show award, Hatch, Conmunication Arts award. Office: Hill Holliday Franfurt Balkind 622 3RD Ave #15 New York NY 10017-6710

SHEEHAN, NEIL, reporter, writer; b. Holyoke, Mass., Oct. 27, 1936; s. Cornelius Joseph and Mary (O'Shea) Sheehan; m. Susan Margulies, Mar. 30, 1965; children: Maria Gregory, Catherine Fair. AB cum laude, Harvard, 1958; LittD (hon.), Columbia Coll., Chgo., 1972; LHD (hon.), Am. Internat. Coll., 1990, U. Lowell, 1991. Vietnam bur. chief UPI, Saigon, 1962—64; reporter N.Y. Times, NYC, Djakarta, Saigon, Washington, 1964—72. Author: The Arnheiter Affair, 1972, A Bright Shining Lie: John Paul Vann and America in Vietnam, 1988 (Nat. Book award, 1988, Pulitzer Prize for gen. non-fiction, 1989, Robert F. Kennedy Book award, 1989, Vetty award Vietnam Vets. Ensemble Theatre Co., 1989, Spl. Achievement award Vietnam Vets. Am., 1989, Outstanding Investigative Reporting award Investigative Reporters and Editors Inc. of U. Mo. Sch. Journalism, 1989, Amb. award English Speaking Union, 1989, John F. Kennedy award Holyoke, Mass., 1989, selected by Modern Libr. as one of the 100 best works of non-fiction of the 20th century 1999), After the War Was Over: Hanoi and Saigon, 1992; contbr. articles and book revs. for popular mags., The Pentagon Papers, 1971. With US Army, 1959—62. Recipient Louis M. Lyons award for conscience and integrity in journalism, 1964, Silver medal, Poor Richard Club, Phila., 1964, Cert. of Appreciation for best article on Asia, Overseas Press Club Am., 1967, 1st Ann. Drew Pearson prize for excellence in investigative reporting, 1971, Columbia Journalism award, 1972, 1989, Sidney Hillman Found. awards, 1972, 1988, Page One award, Newspaper Guild N.Y., 1972, Disting. Svc. award and Bronze medallion, Sigma Delta Chi, 1972, Citation of Excellence, Overseas Press Club, 1972, Lit. Lion award, N.Y. Pub. Libr., 1992; Guggenheim fellow, 1973—74, Adlai Stevenson fellow, 1973—75, Lehrman Inst. fellow, 1975—76, Rockefeller Found. fellow in humanities, 1976—77, Woodrow Wilson Internat. Ctr. for Scholars fellow, 1979—80. Mem.: Am. Acad. Achievement, Soc. Am. Historians, Lansdowne Club (London). Achievements include obtaining Pentagon Papers, 1971. Home and Office: 4505 Klingle St NW Washington DC 20016-3580

SHEEHAN, PATTY, professional golfer; b. Middlebury, Vt., Oct. 27, 1956; 4th ranked woman LPGA Tour, 1992; winner U.S. Women's Open, 1992, 94, McDonald's LPGA Championship, 1983-84, 93. Inductee LPGA Hall of Fame, 1993, Sports Illustrated Sportsman of the Yr., 1987. Achievements include being the winner for 31 LPGA Tournaments including Mazda Japan Classic, 1981, 88, Inamori Classic, 1982-83; 86, Orlando Lady Classic, 1982, Safeco Classic, 1982, 90, 95, LPGA Corning Classic, 1983, LPGA Championship, 1983-84, 93, Henredon Classic, 1983-84, Elizabeth Arden Classic, 1984, McDonald's Kids Classic, 1984, 90, Sarasota Classic, 1985-86, 88, J&B Scotch Pro AM, 1985, Konica San Jose Classic, 1986, Rochester Internat., 1989-90, 92, 95, Jamaica Classic, 1990, Ping-Cellular One Championship, 1990, Orix Hawaiian Ladies Open, 1991, Jamie Farr Toledo Classic, 1992, Weetabix Women's Brit. Open, 1992, U.S. Women's Open, 1992, 94, Mazda LPGA Championship, 1993, The Nabisco Championship, 1996; in 17 tournaments earning $179,453, 1997, 16 tounaments earning $342,391, 1996, 35th victory, Nabisco Dinah Shore earning 6th major champ. title, crossed $5 million mark in career earnings, 1996, winner Michelob Light Front Runner Awd. for leading most rounds in season, 1996. Office: LPGA 100 International Golf Dr Daytona Beach FL 32124-1092

SHEEHAN, ROBERT C., lawyer; b. NYC, Oct. 12, 1944; s. John Edward and Mary Elizabeth (Trede) Sheehan; m. Elizabeth Mary Mammen, Aug. 17, 1968; children: Elizabeth, Robert, William. BA, Boston Coll., 1966; LLB, Univ. Pa., Phila., 1969. Bar: NY 1970. Joined Skadden, Arps, Slate, Meagher & Flom LLP, 1969, ptnr. NYC, 1978—94, exec. ptnr., 1994—. Head, founder, Financial Institutions Merger & Acquisition Group Skadden, Arps, Slate, Meagher & Flom LLP; counsel for fin. institutions in connection with their rels. with various state and fed. banking regulatory authorities; bd. dir. Lawyers' Com. for Civil Rights Under Law; co-chair, Law Firm Pro Bono Project Pro Bono Inst. Mem. bd. overseers U. Pa. Law Sch.; bd. dir. Harlem RBI. Mem.: Assn. of the Bar of City of NY. Office: Skadden Arps Slate Meagher Flom LLP 4 Times Sq New York NY 10036-6595 Office Phone: 212-735-3350. Office Fax: 212-735-2000, 917-777-3350. Business E-Mail: rsheehan@skadden.com.

SHEEHAN, ROBERT JAMES, II, management and market research consultant; b. Pitts., May 13, 1937; s. Regis James and Helen Lillian (O'Leary) S.; m. Marie Elizabeth Yoskovich, Apr. 24, 1964; children: Stephanie Ann, Robert James III. AB in Econs., U. Pitts., 1967, MA, 1970; postgrad., Am. U. Cert. mgmt. cons. Rsch. analyst Action Housing Inc., Pitts., 1960-63; from project rep. to dir. rehab. Urban Redevel. Authority Pitts., 1963-73; assoc. chief economist, dir. econ. rsch. Nat. Assn. Homebuilders, Washington, 1973-82, v.p econ. policy analysis, 1982-83; v.p. Regis J. Sheehan & Assocs., McLean, Va., 1983-96, pres., 1997—. Founding dir. Georgetown Cons., Inc., 1993—; vice-chmn. Fairfax County Housing and Redevel. Authority, 1988-92, chmn. 1993-95. cons. in field. Author: The Basics of Land Acquisition, 1985; co-pub., prin. contbr. Mgmt./Econs. & Constrn. Real Estate newsletters; contbr. articles to profl. jours. Pres. bd. dirs. Touchstone Theatre Co., 1984-2003; pres. Caths. for Housing, 1998-2003; founding mem. Superior Bus. Roundtable. Mem. Nat. Economists Club, Inst. Mgmt. Cons. (pres. Washington chpt. 1989-96), Nat. Assn. Bus. Econs., KC. Roman Catholic. Avocations: walking, jogging, reading. Personal E-mail: rjscmc@comcast.net.

SHEEHAN, SAMANTHA, gymnast; b. Cin., May 20, 1986; d. Kevin and Cindy Sheehan. Gymnast Cincinnati Gymnastics/U.S. Natl. Team, 2002—. Achievements include Level 10 National Bar Champion; Level 10 State Champion; Qualified to 2001, 02 U.S. Gymnastics Championships, World Championships, 2002; Bronze Medal Floor Exercise, World Championships, 2002; 1st place All Around, USA-Belgium dual competition, 2003. Office: 3635 Woodbridge Blvd Fairfield OH 45014

SHEEHAN, SUSAN, writer; b. Vienna, Aug. 24, 1937; arrived in U.S., 1941, naturalized, 1946; d. Charles and Kitty C. (Herrmann) Sachsel; m. Neil Sheehan, Mar. 30, 1965; children: Maria Gregory, Catherine Fair. BA, Wellesley Coll., Mass., 1958; DHL (hon.), U. Lowell, Mass., 1991. Editl. rschr. Esquire-Coronet, NYC, 1959-60; freelance writer NYC, 1960-61; staff writer New Yorker mag., NYC, 1961—; contbg. writer Archtl. Digest, 1997—. Writer-in-residence, lectr. Georgetown U., 1999. Author: Ten Vietnamese, 1967, A Welfare Mother, 1976, A Prison and a Prisoner, 1978, Is There No Place on Earth for Me?, 1982, Kate Quinton's Days, 1984, A Missing Plane, 1986, Life For Me Ain't Been No Crystal Stair, 1993, The Banana Sculptor, the Purple Lady, and the All-Night Swimmer, 2002; contbr. articles to various mags., including N.Y. Times Sunday Mag., Washington Post Sunday Mag., Harper's, Atlantic, New Republic, McCall's, Holiday, Boston Globe Sunday Mag., Life. Judge Robert F. Kennedy Journalism awards, 1980, 84; mem. lit. panel DC Commn. on Arts and Humanities, 1979-84; mem. pub. info. and edn. com. Nat. Mental Health Assn., 1982-83; mem. adv. com. on employment and crime Vera Inst. Justice, 1978-86; chair Pulitzer Prize nominating jury in gen. non-fiction for 1988, 1994, mem., 1991; bd. dirs. Brides Against Breast Cancer, 2006—. Recipient Sidney Hillman Found. award, 1976, Gavel award ABA, 1978, Individual Reporting award Nat. Mental Health Assn., 1981, Pulitzer prize for gen. non-fiction, 1983, Feature Writing award NY Press Club, 1984, NY Pub. Libr. Lit. award, 1992, Alumnae Assn. Achievement award Wellesley Coll., 1984, Carroll Kowal Journalism award NASW, 1993, Disting. Grad. award Hunter Coll. H.S., 1995, Pub. Awareness award Nat. Alliance for Mentally Ill, 1995, Casey medal for meritorious journalism, 1997; Durant scholar Wellesley Coll., 1958; fellow Guggenheim Found., 1975-76, Woodrow Wilson Internat. Ctr. for Scholars, 1981, Open Soc. Inst., 1998-99. Mem.: Soc. Am. Historians, Authors Guild, Lansdowne Club (London), Phi Beta Kappa. Home: 4505 Klingle St NW Washington DC 20016-3580 Office: New Yorker Mag 4 Times Sq New York NY 10036-7441

SHEEHAN, TIMOTHY J., lawyer; b. Beacon, NY, Apr. 28, 1959; BA magna cum laude, SUNY, Buffalo, 1981; JD, U. Buffalo, 1984. Bar: NY 1985, US Dist. Ct. Ea. Dist. NY, US Dist. Ct. So. Dist. NY. Ptnr. Wilson, Elser, Moskowitz, Edelman & Dicker LLP, White Plains, NYC. Mem.: NY State Med. Malpractice Def. Bar, NY State Bar Assn., Westchester County Bar Assn. Office: Wilson Elser Moskowitz Edelman & Dicker LLP 3 Gannett Dr White Plains NY 10604 Office Phone: 914-323-7000 ext. 4243. Office Fax: 914-323-7001. Business E-Mail: sheehant@wemed.com.

SHEEHEY, PATRICIA ANN, secondary school educator; b. Des Moines, Sept. 25, 1946; d. James Michael Sheehey and Elizabeth Ann Markunas; m. William Elwin McConnell, June 24, 1978 (dec. Aug. 1999). BA English, Marycrest Coll., Davenport, Iowa, 1968; MA English, We. Ill. U., 1970; postgrad., U. Iowa, 1971—2000, U. London, 1971. Instr. West H.S., Davenport, 1969—, head dept. lang. arts, 1998—. Mem. alumni bd. Marycrest Coll., Davenport, 1980—84. Recipient Golden Apple Outstanding Tchr. award, Scott County, 1980. Mem.: NEA, Iowa State Edn. Assn., Davenport Edn. Assn., Nat. Coun. Tchrs. English (regional judge), Alpha Delta Kappa (sec., treas., pres. 1978—82, scholarship chair 1983—86, state bylaws chair 2004—, internat. bylaws com. 2006—). Roman Catholic. Avocations: writing, antiques, reading. Home: 5 Birchwood Dr Blue Grass IA 52726 Office: West High Sch 3505 W Locust Davenport IA 52804 Personal E-mail: sheeheyp@aol.com.

SHEEHY, BETTY JO, real estate company executive, investment advisor; b. Baileysville, W.Va., Oct. 1, 1936; d. Virgil and Virginia Graham Lester; m. John D. Sheehy, Sept. 21, 1963 (div. 1976); children: John, Peter, Barbara. Student, Marshall U., 1956; lic. in real estate, Southampton Coll., 2002. Fin. cons. Merrill Lynch, Short Hills, NJ, 1984—90; fin. adv., assoc. v.p. Morgan Stanley, Southampton, NY, 1991—2002; owner, broker Betty Jo Sheehy Real Estate, Southampton, 2002—06; v.p. investments Newbridge Securities, West Palm Beach, Fla., 2006—. Chpt. pres. NJ Symphony Women League, Short Hills, 1977—81; vol. Red Cross of the Oranges, NJ, 1970; benefactor Parish Art Mus., Southampton, 1999—. Named Bus. Woman of Yr., Nat. Congressional Com., 2006; recipient Leadership Devel. award, Merrill Lynch, 1985—86. Avocations: golf, music, reading, running. Home: 422 N Lakeside Dr Lake Worth FL 33460 Office Phone: 800-497-7318.

SHEEHY, JEROME JOSEPH, electrical engineer; b. Hartford, Conn., Dec. 3, 1935; s. Jeremiah and Anna (Foley) S.; m. Jean Ann Baldassari, Oct. 13, 1962; children: Caroline, Jerome, Daniel, Carlene. BSEE, U. Conn., Storrs, 1962, MSEE, 1967. Electronic engr. USN Underwater Sound Lab., New London, Conn., 1962-69; mem. tech. staff Rockwell Internat., Anaheim, Calif., 1969-74; staff engr. Hughes Aircraft Co., Fullerton, Calif., 1974-83; systems engr. Norden Systems, Santa Ana, Calif., 1983-89; advanced engrng. specialist Lockheed Martin Aircraft Svc., Ontario, Calif., 1990-97. Contbr. articles to Jour. Acoustical Soc. Am. With USAF, 1954-57. Mem. Tau Beta Pi, Eta Kappa Nu Achievements include research in detection and estimation theory for non-gaussian noise, non-normal statistics. Home: 8 Sagitta Way Coto De Caza CA 92679-5102 Personal E-mail: jerome_sheehy@cox.net.

SHEEHY, RICK, lieutenant governor, former mayor; b. Hastings, Nebr., Oct. 3, 1959; m. Connie Sheehy; children: Maggie, Joel. Attended, Ctrl. CC, U. Nebr.-Lincoln. City coun. mem. City of Hastings, Nebr., 1994—2005, mayor, 2000—05; lt. gov. State of Nebr., Lincoln, 2005—. Market gen. mgr., paramedic Rural/Metro Ambulance, 1982—. Exec. com. mem. Cottonwood Festival; mem. Nebr. State Trauma Adv. Bd., Mary Lanning Hosp. Found. Bd., Crane Meadows Bd. Dirs., Nebr. Rural Health Assn. Mem.: Hastings C. of C. (former chair), Hastings Noon Rotary, Hastings Sertoma Club (past pres.). Republican. Office: Lt Gov State Capitol, Rm 2315 PO Box 94863 Lincoln NE 68509-4863 Office Phone: 402-471-2256. Office Fax: 402-471-6031.

SHEEHY, ROBERT J., insurance company executive; V.p., gen. mgr. Lincoln Nat. Corp.; with UnitedHealthcare, UnitedHealth Grp., Minnetonka, Minn., 1992—, CEO, UnitedHealthcare Ohio, 1994—98, pres. UnitedHealthcare, 1998—2000, CEO UnitedHealthcare, 2000—. Office: UnitedHealth Grp 9900 Bren Rd E Minnetonka MN 55343

SHEELER, JIM, journalist; b. Tex., 1969; m. Annick Sheeler; 1 child, James. BA, Colo. State U., 1990. With Boulder (Colo.) Daily Camera, 1991—96; sr. staff writer Boulder Planet, 1996—2000; freelance writer Denver Post, 1999—2003; staff writer Rocky Mountain News, Denver, 2004—. Contbr. (books) Life On the Death Beat, 2005. Recipient Pulitzer Prize for feature writing, 2006. Office: Rocky Mountain News 100 Gene Amole Way Denver CO 80204 Office Phone: 303-892-2561. Office Fax: 303-892-2841. E-mail: sheelerj@rockymountainnews.com.

SHEEN, CHARLIE (CARLOS IRWIN ESTEVEZ), actor; b. NYC, Sept. 3, 1965; s. Ramon (Martin Sheen) and Janet Estevez; m. Donna Peele, Sept. 3, 1995 (div. Nov. 19, 1996); m. Denise Richards, June 15, 2002 (div. Nov. 17, 2006); children: Sam, Lola Rose; 1 child, Cassandra. Actor (films) Grizzly II: The Predator, 1984, Red Dawn, 1984, The Boys Next Door, 1985, Ferris Bueller's Day Off, 1986, Lucas, 1986, Platoon, 1986, Wisdom, 1986, The Wraith, 1986, A Life in the Day, 1986, Wall Street, 1987, No Man's Land, 1987, Three for the Road, 1987, Eight Men Out, 1988, Young Guns, 1988, Major League, 1989, Never on Tuesday, 1989, Comicitis, 1989, Courage Mountain, 1990, Navy SEALS, 1990, Backtrack, 1990, Hot Shots!, 1990, Men At Work, 1990, The Rookie, 1990, Cadence, 1991, Beyond the Law (aka Fixing the Shadow), 1992, Hot Shots, Part Deux, 1993, The Three Musketeers, 1993, Loaded Weapon I, 1993, Deadfall, 1993, Major League 2, 1994, Terminal Velocity, 1994, The Shadow Conspiracy, 1995, Shockwave, 1995, Loose Women, 1996, (voice only) All Dogs Go to Heaven 2, 1996, The Arrival, 1996, Postmortem, 1997, Bad Day On the Block, 1997, Money Talks, 1997, Mission to Mars, 1997, Free Money, 1998, Letter From Death Row, 1998, Five Acres, 1999, Being John Malkovich, 1999, Rated X, 2000, Famous, 2000, Good Advice, 2001, Scary Movie 3, 2003, Deeper Than Deep, 2003, The Big Bounce, 2004, Scary Movie 4, 2006; actor, exec. prodr. (films) The Chase, 1994, No Code of Conduct, 1998; actor (TV movies) Execution of Private Slovik, 1974, Silence of the Heart, 1984, The Fourth Wise Man, 1985, Out of the Darkness, 1985; (TV series) Sugar Hill, 1999, Spin City, 2000-02 (Golden Globe award bext actor, 2001), Two and a Half Men, 2003-. *

SHEEN, MARTIN (RAMON ESTEVEZ), actor; b. Dayton, Ohio, Aug. 3, 1940; s. Francisco and Mary Ann (Phelan) Estevez; m. Janet Sheen, Dec. 23, 1961; children: Emilio, Ramon, Carlos, Renee. Grad. high sch. Made NY stage debut as mem. Living Theatre in The Connection, 1959; Broadway debut in Never Live Over a Pretzel Factory, 1964; other stage appearances include The Subject Was Roses, 1964-66, The Wicked Crooks, 1967, Hamlet, 1967, Romeo and Juliet, 1968, Hello and Goodbye, 1969, The Happiness Cage, 1970, Death of a Salesman, 1975, Julius Caesar, 1988; film appearances include The Incident, 1967, The Subject Was Roses, 1968, Catch-22, 1970, No Drums, No Bugles, 1971, Rage, 1972, Badlands, 1973, The Legend of Earl Durand, 1974, The Cassandra Crossing, 1976, The Little Girl Who Lives Down the Lane, 1977, Apocalypse Now, 1979, The Final Countdown, 1980, Gandhi, 1982, That Championship Season, 1982, The King of Prussia, 1982, No Place to Hide, 1983, The Dead Zone, 1983, Man, Woman, and Child, 1983, Enigma, 1983, Eagle's Wing, 1983, Firestarter, 1984, The Believers, 1987, Wall Street, 1987, Siesta, 1987, Judgement in Berlin, 1988, Walking After Midnight, 1988, Da, 1988 (exec. producer, dir.), Beverly Hills Brats, 1989, Cadence, 1991 (dir.), JFK, 1991 (narrator), Hot Shots, Part Deux!, 1993 (cameo), Hear No Evil, 1993, Gettysburg, 1993, The Break, 1995, The American President, 1995, The War At Home, 1996, Truth or Consequences, 1997, Spawn, 1997, Letter From Death Row, 1998, Stranger in the Kingdom, 1998, Storm, 1998, Monument Avenue, 1998, Free Money, 1998, Catch Me If You Can, 2002, The Departed, 2006, Bobby, 2006; TV series include As the World Turns, The Edge of Night, The West Wing, 1999-2006 (Golden Globe award, 2001, SAG award, 2001, 2002); TV movies and miniseries include Then Came Bronson, 1969, The Subject Was Roses, 1969, Mongo's Back in Town, 1971, Welcome Home, Johnny Bristol, 1972, That Certain Summer, 1972, Catholics, 1973, The Execution of Private Slovik, 1974, The California Kid, 1974, The Story of Pretty Boy Floyd, 1974, The Missiles of October, 1974, Sweet Hostage, 1975, The Last Survivors, 1975, Blind Ambition, 1979, Taxi!!, 1978, The Long Road Home, 1980, Fly Away Home, 1981, Kennedy, 1982, Choices of the Heart, 1983, The Atlanta Child Murders, 1985, Consenting Adult, 1985, Out of Darkness, 1985, Shattered Spirits, 1986, Samaritan, 1986, News at Eleven, 1986, Babies Having Babies (dir.), 1986, Conspiracy: The Trial of the Chicago 8, 1987, No Means No (exec. producer), Night Breaker, 1989, Project Alf, 1996, Marlon Brandon: The Wild One, 1996, D.R.E.A.M. Team, 1999; TV appearances include Mannix, 1967, The Streets of San Francisco, 1972, Murphy Brown, 1988 (Emmy award, Guest Actor - Comedy Series, 1994), The Simpsons (voice), 1989, The Great War, 1996, The Elevator, 1996, Entertaining Angels, 1996, Spin City, 1996, Medussa's Child, 1997, 187 Documented, 1997, Titanic: Anatomy of a Disaster (narrator), 1997, Tudjman (narrator), 1997 Babylon 5: The River of Souls, 1998, Letter From Death Row, 1998, Ambrose Chapel, 1998, Gunfighter, 1998, No Code of Conduct, 1998, Shadrach (voice), 1998, Stranger in the Kingdom, 1998, Talk of the Town, 1998, Voyage of Terror, 1998, Celebrity Poker Showdown, 2003. Named Favorite Actor in a New Series, TV Guide Awards; recipient Lifetime Achievement award, Imagen Found., 1998. Roman Catholic.

SHEEN, MICHAEL, actor; b. Feb. 5, 1969; one child, Lily (with Kate Beckinsale) Grad., Royal Acad. Dramatic Art. Actor: (TV films) Gallowglass, 1993, Lost In France, 1998, Dirty Filthy Love, 2004, Essential Poems for Christmas, 2004, Kenneth Williams: Fantabulosa!, 2006; (films) Othello, 1995, Mary Reilly, 1996, Wilde, 1997, Heartlands, 2002, The Four Feathers, 2002, Bright Young Things, 2003, Underworld, 2003, The Deal, 2003, Timeline, 2003, Laws of Attraction, 2004, The Banker, 2004, Dead Long Enough, 2005, Kingdom of Heaven, 2005, The League of Gentlemen's Apocalypse, 2005, Underworld: Evolution, 2006, The Queen, 2006 (Award for Best Supporting Actor, LA Film Critics Assn., 2006), HG Wells: War with the World, 2006, Blood Diamond, 2006; voice (TV films) Beowulf, 1998, Doomwatch: Winter Angel, 1999; actor: (TV miniseries) The Battle for Rome, 2006; guest appearance Ancient Rome: The Rise and Fall of an Empire, 2006; performer: (songs) (theatre) When She Danced, 1991, Le Livre de Spencer, 1994, The Dresser, 1995, 1999, The Seagull, 1995, The Ends of the Earth, 1996, The Home Coming, 1996, Look Back in Anger, 1999 (nominee for Laurence Olivier Theatre award for Best Actor, 2000), Amadeus, 1999 (nominee for 1999 Laurence Olivier Theatre award for Best Supporting Performance of 1998), (Broadway plays), 2000, Frost/Nixon, 2007, (theatre) Caligula (nominee for 2004 Laurence Olivier Theatre award for Best Actor of 2003, 2003 London Critics Circle Theatre award for Best Actor), Charley's Aunt, Peer Gynt. Mem.: Royal Acad. Dramatic Art (assoc.). *

SHEERAN, MICHAEL JOHN LEO, priest, academic administrator; b. NYC, Jan. 24, 1940; s. Leo John and Glenna Marie (Wright) Sheeran. AB, St. Louis U., 1963, PhL, 1964, AM in Polit. Sci., 1967, AM in Theology, 1971, STL, 1971; PhD, Princeton U., 1977. Joined Soc. of Jesus, 1957, ordained priest Roman Cath. Ch., 1970. Exec. editor Catholic Mind, NYC, 1971-72; assoc. editor Am. Mag., NYC, 1971-72; assoc. chaplain Aquinas Inst., Princeton, NJ, 1972-75; asst. dean Regis U., Denver, 1975-77, dean, 1977-82; v.p. acad. affairs Regis Coll., Denver, 1982-92, acting pres., 1987-88, pres., 1993—. Retreat dir., cons. governance religious cmtys., 1970—. Author: Beyond Majority Rule, 1984; contbr. articles and editls. to publs. Trustee Regis Jesuit HS, 1999—2005; chmn. Mile High United Way, Denver, 1999—2000; nat. bd. dirs. Campus Compact, 2002—06; trustee Rockhurst Coll., Kansas City, Mo., 1982—91, Creighton U., Omaha, 1985—95, U. San Francisco, 1985—94, 2001—, Loyola U., New Orleans, 1994—96, Rocky Mountain Coll. Art and Design, Denver, 1994—99; mem. adv. bd. Cmty. Coll. Aurora, Colo., 2001—; bd. dirs. Colo. Inst. Tech., 2001—. Ford Found. scholar, 1963. Democrat. Roman Catholic. Home: 3333 Regis Blvd Denver CO 80221-1099 Office: Regis U 3333 Regis Blvd Denver CO 80221-1099 Office Phone: 303-458-4190. Business E-Mail: president@regis.edu.

SHEERAN, ROBERT T. (MONSIGNOR), academic administrator; b. Troy, NY; BA in Classical Languages, Seton Hall U., 1967; postgrad., U.S. Sem., N.Am. Coll., Rome; theology licentiate degree, Gregorian U., Rome, 1971; MA in Theology, Princeton U.; D in Theology, Angelicum U., 1979; mgmt. devel. program, Harvard U., 1989. Ordained priest, 1970. Rector St. Andrew's Coll. Sem. Seton Hall U., South Orange, NJ, 1980, asst. provost, 1987—91, assoc. provost, 1991—93, exec. vice chancellor, 1993-95, pres., 1995—. Participant Priests-in-Residence program Seton Hall U.; dir. advising program N.Am. Coll., Rome, 1974-79. Fellow: Am. Coun. on Edn. (mem. Commn. on Women in Higher Edn.); mem.: NJ Pres. Coun. (exec. bd.), US Conf. Cath. Bishops (Bishops & Pres. com.), Assn. Cath. Colleges & Universities (bd. dirs. 2003—). Office: Seton Hall U 400 S Orange Ave South Orange NJ 07079-2697 E-mail: president@shu.edu. *

SHEERAN, TIMOTHY J., lawyer; b. Cin., 1948; BA, Ohio State U., 1971; JD, Harvard U., 1975. Bar: Ohio 1975, US Dist. Ct.(no. dist.) Ohio 1976, US Ct. of Appeals (6th cir.) 1985. Lawyer Squire, Sanders & Dempsey, Cleve., ptnr. Co-author Baldwin's Ohio School Law, 1991—. Named Am's. Leading Bus. Lawyers, by Chambers USA, 2006, Best Lawyers Am., 2006, 2007. Mem. ABA (labor & employment law sect.), Nat. Coun. Sch. Attys., Nat. Orgn. Legal Problems in Edn., Ohio State Bar Assn. (labor & employment law sect.), Cleve. Bar Assn.(labor & employment com.), Ohio Coun. Sch. Attys. & Edn. Law Assn. Office: Squire Sanders & Dempsey 4900 Key Tower 127 Public Sq Cleveland OH 44114-1304 Office Phone: 216-479-8605. Office Fax: 216-479-8780. Business E-Mail: tsheeran@ssd.com.

SHEESLEY, MARY FRANK, art educator; b. Redwood Falls, Minn., Aug. 1, 1947; d. Wencel and Lois (Dooner) Frank; m. Gary James Sheesley, Apr. 30, 1966 (div. Mar. 25, 1985); children: Jason, John. AA summa cum laude, Chipola Jr. Coll., 1984; BS magna cum laude, Troy State U., 1986; MS, Fla. State U., Panama City, 1991; PhD, Fla. State U., 2000. Child devel. assoc. credential Washington, 1976. Co-owner Qurly-Q Pork Farm, Buffalo Lake, Minn., 1969—79, Bonifay, Fla., 1979—84; editor Nat. Drillers Buyers Guide, Bonifay, Fla., 1982; art educator Bay Dist. Schs., Panama City, 1986—2003, 2005—; tchg. asst. Fla. State U., Tallahassee, 1991—92; adj. prof. U. West Fla., Ft. Walton Beach, 1992; art educator Frankfurt Internat. Sch., Oberursel, Germany, 1995—96; adj. prof. Gulf Coast C.C., Panama City, 2002; asst. prof. U. West Ga., Carrollton, 2003—05. Mem. adv. bd. Region 6E Head Start, Willmar, Minn., 1975—79; chair Fla. State Art Textbook Adoption Com., Tallahassee, 1993—94; founder Global Art Exch. Program, 1994—; mem. tchr. edn. adv. coun. com. U. West Ga., 2003—05, mem. tchr. edn. field experience evaluation com., 2003—05, mem. assessment adv. com., 2003—05; presenter of various workshops and numerous inservice sessions, 1993—. V.p. Minn. Porkettes, 1978—79; treas. V.F.W. Auxiliary, Hutchinson, Minn., 1973—78; sch. restructuring task force com. Bay Dist. Sch. Sys., Panama City, Fla., 1989—91; chairperson Cath. Charities, Hector, Minn., 1977—79; mem. ch. coun., lector Blessed Trinity Cath. Ch., Bonifay, 1982—84; euchristic minister Our Lady of Perpetual Help, Carrollton, Ga., 2005; mem. sch. bd. St. John's Cath. Sch., Panama City, 2002—03; bd. dirs. Panhandle Alcoholism Coun., Panama City, 1980—84. Recipient Arrowmont Scholarship, 1987; grantee Fulbright Meml. Tchr. Scholarship, Tokyo, 1997; Art scholar, Chipola Jr. Coll., 1982, Returning Woman scholar, Marianna Jr. Women's Club, 1981, Acad. scholar, Troy State U., 1984—86, scholar, Fla. Ctr. for Tchrs., 1993, 2002, Ednl. grant, Truth About Tobacco, 1997. Mem.: Fla. Art Edn. Assn., Fla. League Art Tchrs. (charter mem.), Bay County Art Tchrs. Assn. (pres. 1996—2001), Nat. Art Edn. Assn., Internat. Soc. for Edn. through Art, Garnet Key Honor Soc., Gamma Beta Phi, Phi Theta Kappa. Independent. Roman Catholic. Avocations: travel, painting, reading, gardening, scuba diving. Office Phone: 850-872-7540 ext. 4829. Business E-Mail: sheesmf@bay.k12.fl.us.

SHEETS, BEN M., professional baseball player; b. Baton Rouge, July 18, 1978; m. Julie Sheets; 1 child, Seaver. Student, NE La. State U. Draft pick Milw. Brewers, 1999, pitcher, 2001—. Mem. US Olympic Team. Named a First Team All-Am., Collegiate Baseball, 1999, Baseball Am., 1999; named La. Player of Yr., Southland Conf. Player of Yr., 1999, Player of Yr., USA Baseball, 2000; named to Nat. League All-Star Team, Maj. League Baseball, 2001, 2004, 2007. Achievements include winning a Gold Medal at the 2000 Olympics in Sydney, Australia. Mailing: Milw Brewers One Brewers Way Milwaukee WI 53214-3652 *

SHEETS, FREDRICK SIDNEY, retired military officer, auditor; b. Greenville, SC, Aug. 16, 1946; s. Sidney Wesley Sheets and Mabel Eve (Whitfield) Becht; m. Mary Cahterine White, July 14, 1973; children: Brenda Justine, Valerie Claire, Brian Arthur. BA, Ohio U., 1969; BBA, U. Tex., El Paso, 1986, M in Accountancy, 1988. CPA, Fla.; cert. acquisition profl. Dept. Def. Commd. 2d lt. U.S. Army, 1969, advanced through grades to lt. col., 1991, served in Korea, Germany, Vietnam, Md., Tex., Wash., to 1997; sr. auditor Def. Contract Audit Agy., Palm Bay, Fla., 1988—. Counselor, Vol. Income Tax Assistance, Melbourne, Fla., 1993—. Decorated Bronze Star. Mem. Inst. Mgmt. Accts., Am. Inst. CPA, Assn. Govt. Accts. (cert. govt. fin. mgr., pres-elect, sec.-treas., chpt. pres. 1989—, Mem. of Yr. 1994, 98, Superior Performance award 1995), Assn. Cert. Fraud Examiners, Brevard Fla. Inst. CPA (pvt. practice chair 1994—), Am. Volkssport Assn. (dir. S.E. region 1996—, Disting. Achievement award 1995), Fla. Volkssport Assn. (treas., pres. 1991—). Republican. Avocation: walking. Home: 378 Godfrey Rd SE Palm Bay FL 32909-8841 Office: PO Box 61419 Palm Bay FL 32906-1419

SHEETS, THOMAS R., lawyer, gas industry executive; BA, Ashland U., 1973; JD, U. Toledo, 1975. Bar: Ohio 1975, Nev. 1982, Tex. 1986. Sr. atty. Tex. Eastern Corp., 1985—87; litig. atty. Southwest Gas Corp., Las Vegas, 1987—89, assoc. gen. counsel, 1989—90, dir. regulatory affairs, 1990—94, asst. gen. counsel, 1994—96, v.p., gen. counsel, 1996—98, sr. v.p., gen. counsel, 1998—. Mem. Nev. Tax Commn., chair; former mem. Nev. Standing Com. Jud. Ethics. Mem.: ABA, Am. Arbitration Assn., Energy Bar Assn., Am. Gas Assn., Clark County Bar Assn. (pres. 1995). Office: Southwest Gas Corp 5241 Spring Mountain Rd Las Vegas NV 89193-8510 Business E-Mail: thom.sheets@swgas.com.

SHEETZ, STANTON R., grocery retail executive; b. May 26, 1955; BS, Bentley Coll.; MBA, Pace U., NY. With Colt Industries, 1977-81; exec. v.p., dir. Sheetz Inc., Altoona, Pa., 1981—95, pres., CEO, 1995—, dir. Dir. Omega Bank, 1994—, Hollidaysburg Trust, 1996—, PBS. Mem.: Nat. Assn. Convenience Stores (vice chmn. 2000—). Office: Sheetz Inc 5700 6th Ave Altoona PA 16602

SHEFF, RONALD B., lawyer; b. Balt., Apr. 18, 1949; BA, Cornell U., 1970; AM, Harvard U., 1972, JD magna cum laude, 1975. Bar: Md. 1975. Lawyer Piper & Marbury, Balt.; mem. Adelman, Sheff & Smith, LLC, Annapolis, Md. Mem.: ABA, Am. Health Lawyers Assn., Md. State. Office: Adelman Sheff & Smith LLC 180 Admiral Cochrane Dr Ste 370 Annapolis MD 21401 Office Phone: 410-224-3000 ext 228. Office Fax: 301-294-6406. Business E-Mail: rsheff@hospitallaw.com.

SHEFFER, JAMES THOMAS, music educator; b. Phila., May 27, 1970; s. James F. and Antoinette Patricia Sheffer; m. Terri Lynn Huffman, June 25, 1994; children: Victoria Lynn, Jamie Lynn. BS in Music Edn., West Chester U., 1992; MA in Edn. Adminstrn. and Supervision, U. Phoenix, 2004, MA in Edn. Curriculum and Instrn., 2005. Cert. music tchr. grades K-12 State of NJ., 1992, Commonwealth of Pa., 1992. Tchr. music, band dir. Medford Lakes Neeta Sch., NJ, 2001—04; dir. instrumental music Medford Meml. Mid. Sch./Haines 6th Grade Ctr., 2004—. Dir. instrumental music Manchester Twp. H.S., Lakehurst, NJ, 1996—2001. Dir.: (marching band director) Salute to the 50s and 60s (US Scholastic Band Assn. Group I Champions, 2001). Grantee Excellence in Edn., Medford Lakes Edn. Found., 2003. Mem.: ASCD, NAESP, N.J. Music Educators Assn., Music Educators Nat. Conf., Olympic Conf. Band Dirs. Assn., Internat. Assn. Jazz Edn., South Jersey Band and Orch. Dirs. Assn. (treas. 1996—2000). Roman Catholic. Achievements include development of Scales, Chorales, and Arpeggios for Band Warm-up. Avocations: music, fishing, swimming, travel. Home: 218 Kihade Trail Medford Lakes NJ 08055 Office: Medford Township Memorial Middle Sch 55 Mill St Medford NJ 08055 Home Phone: 609-953-8283; Office Phone: 609-654-7707 8231. Home Fax: 609-953-6929. Personal E-mail: jimsheffer@aol.com. E-mail: jsheffer@medford.k12.nj.us.

SHEFFEY, RUTHE T., language educator; m. Vernon R. Sheffey, Dec. 29, 1950; children: Illona Sheffey Rawlings, Renata Sheffey Strong. BA, Morgan State U., Balt., 1947; MA, Howard U., 1949; PhD, U. Pa., 1959. Prof. English Morgan State U., Balt., 1949—, chair dept. English, 1970-76. Author: Impressions in Asphalt, 1969, Trajectory (My Collected Essays), 1989; editor Zora Neale Hurston Forum, 1986—. Named Md. Outstanding Faculty Mem. of Yr., 1994, Disting. Scholar in African-Am. Studies for Yr., Towson State U., 2002, Sheroe as Honor, Women for Responsive Govt., Inc., 2003; named to Morgan State U. Hall of Fame, 2000. Mem. Nat. Coun. Tchrs. English (past mem. coll. bd.), Coll. English Assn. (past pres. Mid. Atlantic Group), Zora Neale Hurston Soc. (founder, 1984, pres.), Langston Hughes Soc. (past pres.), other lit. socs., Alpha Kappa Alpha (Golden mem.). Mem. United Ch. of Christ. Avocations: reading, theatregoing, dance.

SHEFFI, YOSSI, engineering educator, researcher; b. Jerusalem, 1948; BSc, Technion, 1975; MS, Mass. Inst. Tech., 1976, PhD, 1978. Prof. civil and environ. engring., dir. ctr. transp. and logistics Mass. Inst. Tech., Cambridge, Mass., founder Master of Engring. Logistics Program, 1997. Co-founder Logicorp, 1988, co-owner, 1991—94; co-founder Princeton Transp. Consulting Group, 1987, owner. chmn., cons., 1992—96; co-founder Syncra, 1997, e-Chemicals, 1997, Home Preview Channel; founder, CEO Logistics.com, 1999—2000, chmn. bd., 2000—; spkr. in field. Author: Urban Transportation Networks: Equilibrium Analysis with Mathematical Programming Methods, 1995, The Resilient Enterprise: Overcoming Vulnerability for Competitive Advantage, 2005; contbr. articles to profl. jours. Capt. Israeli Air Force, 1966—71. Recipient Disting. Svc. award, Coun. Logistics Mgmt., 1997. Achievements include development of computerized decision support systems for LTL and TL motor carrier operations, rail car distribution, vehicle routing and scheduling, and other various carrier problems; decision support systems used by shippers. Office: Mass Inst Tech 77 Massachusetts Ave Rm E40-275 Cambridge MA 02139-4307 Office Phone: 617-253-5316. Business E-Mail: sheffi@mit.edu.

SHEFFIELD, GARY ANTONIAN, professional baseball player; b. Tampa, Fla., Nov. 18, 1968; m. DeLeon Sheffield, Feb. 5, 1999; children: Ebony, Carissa, Gary Jr. Outfielder Milw. Brewers, 1986-92; third baseman San Diego Padres, 1992-93; outfielder Fla. Marlins, 1993-98, L.A. Dodgers, 1999—2001, Atlanta Braves, 2002—03; outfielder, designated hitter NY Yankees, 2004—06, Detroit Tigers, 2006—. Founder Gary Sheffield Found., 1995—. Co-author (with David Ritz): Inside Power, 2007. Named to Nat. League All-Star Team, 1992-93, 96, 98-2000, 2003, Am. League All-Star Team, 2004-05; Sporting News Player of the Year, 1992; Nat. League Comeback Player of Yr., Sporting News, 1992; Silver Slugger award, Major League Baseball, 1992, 1996, 2003-05. Nat. Batting League Champion, 1992. Office: Detroit Tigers Comerica Park 2100 Woodward Ave Detroit MI 48201 *

SHEFFIELD, GREG, media blogger; Co-founder RatherBiased.com, 2000; editor, NewsBusters.org Media Rsch. Ctr., 2005, now contbr. editor, NewsBusters.org. Work has been featured by CNN, MSNBC, Fox News Channel, NY T. Office: Media Rsch Ctr 325 S Patrick St Alexandria VA 22314 E-mail: gsheffield@mediaresearch.org. *

SHEFFIELD, JEFFREY T., lawyer; b. Oct. 1954; BA phi beta kappa, U. Chgo., 1976; JD, Harvard Law Sch., 1979. Bar: Ill. 1980. Law clk. Mass. Supreme Jud. Ct., Mass., 1979—80; ptnr., mem. firm mgmt. com. Kirkland & Ellis LLP, Chgo. Former adj. prof. IIT/ Chgo. Kent Coll. Law; former lecturer U. Chgo. Sch. Law. Contbr. articles to profl. jours. Office: Kirkland & Ellis LLP 200 E Randolph Dr Chicago IL 60601 Home: 125 Laurel Ave Wilmette IL 60091-2830 Home Phone: 847-251-1270; Office Phone: 312-861-2454. Office Fax: 312-861-2200. Business E-Mail: jsheffield@kirkland.com.

SHEFFIELD, MATTHEW, media blogger; Co-founder RatherBiased.com, 2000; pres. Dialog Media; media and tech. cons., exec. editor, NewsBusters.org Media Rsch. Ctr., 2005—. Lectr. in field. Work has been featured in NY Times, Washington Post, BBC, Fox News Channel, CNN, MSNBC and the New Yorker, maintains personal blog site matthewsheffield.blogspot.com. Mem. Lds Ch. Office: Media Rsch Ctr 325 S Patrick St Alexandria VA 22314 *

SHEFFIELD, NANCY, city agency administrator; b. Mpls. BA in Sociology and Psychology, U. Minn., 1969; postgrad., U. Wis., 1992. Participant City of Aurora (Colo.) Supervisory Cert. Series Program, 1988-90. Social worker LeSueur County Human Svcs., Le Centre, Minn., 1969-71; quality control reviewer Minn. Dept. Human Svcs., St. Paul, 1971-74, quality control supr., 1974-75; neighborhood planner City of Aurora, 1987, neighborhood support supr., 1987-94, acting mgr. Original Aurora Renewal, 1994-95, acting mgr. neighborhood support divsn., 1995, dir. neighborhood svcs., 1996—. Mem. PTO, vol. elem. sch. media ctr., 1980-86. Office: City Aurora Dept Neighborhood Svcs 15151 E Alameda Pkwy Aurora CO 80012 Office Phone: 303-739-7280. Business E-Mail: nsheffie@auroragov.org.

SHEFFIELD, SCOTT D., oil industry executive; BS in Petroleum Engring., U. Tex. Prodn. and reservoir engr. Amoco Prodn. Co.; petroleum engr. Parker & Parsley Devel. Co., 1979—85, v.p. engring., 1981—85, pres., bd. dirs., 1985—89, chmn., CEO, 1989; pres., bd. dirs. Parker & Parsley Petroleum Co., 1990—97, chmn., CEO, 1990—97; pres., CEO Pioneer Natural Resources, Irving, Tex., 1997—99, chmn., pres., CEO, 1999—2004, chmn., CEO, 2004—. Office: Pioneer Natural Resources 5205 N O'Connor Blvd Irving TX 75039 *

SHEFFIELD, VAL C., medical geneticist; MD, PhD, U. Chgo. Pediat. resident U. Calif. San Francisco, med. genetics fellow; with U. Iowa, 1990—; prof. pediatrics U. Iowa Roy J. & Lucille A. Carver Coll. Medicine, Iowa City, dir. med. genetics div.; investigator Howard Hughes Med. Inst., 1998—. Mem.: Inst. Medicine. Office: U Iowa Hosp Med Genetics Div 200 Hawkins Dr Iowa City IA 52242 Office Phone: 319-356-2674. Office Fax: 319-356-3347. E-mail: val-sheffield@uiowa.edu.

SHEFTEL, ROGER TERRY, merchant banker; b. Denver, Sept. 10, 1941; s. Edward and Dorothy (Barnett) S.; m. Phoebe A. Sherman, Sept. 7, 1968; children: Tisha B., Ryan B. BS in Econs., U. Pa., 1963. Comml. lending officer Provident Nat. Bank, Phila., 1963-65; asst. to pres. Continental Fin. Corp., Denver, 1965-68; v.p. Eastern Indsl. Leasing Corp., Phila., 1968-71, exec. v.p., dir., 1971-73, HBE Leasing Corp., Phila., 1971-73; dir. Kooly Kupp, Inc., Boyertown, Pa., 1974-77, pres., dir., 1977; prin. Trivest, Phila., 1973-77, pres., 1977-78, 1670 Corp., 1978-82, Am. Cons. Group, Inc., 1982-83; exec. v.p., dir. Argus Rsch. Labs., Inc., 1982-83; pres. Leasing Concepts, Inc., 1983-87, Brice Capital Corp., 1987-92, Rhodes Fin., Inc., 1992—. Dir. strategic planning Wharton Sch., U. Pa., 1999; pres. AttendByWeb, Inc., 1999—, AssignByWeb, Inc., 1999—; CEO, chmn. FlyOff, Inc., 1998—. Mem.: Friars Club. Home: 414 Barclay Rd Bryn Mawr PA 19010-1218 Office: Rhodes Fin Inc PO Box 7338 Saint Davids PA 19087-7338 E-mail: rtsheftel@comcast.net.

SHEFTZ, STEPHEN WALTER ROBERT, music educator, director, conductor; b. Chester, Pa., Feb. 23, 1961; s. Stephen Adelbert Walter and June Barbara Sheftz; life ptnr. BA in Music and Drama, Allegheny Coll., Meadville, Pa., 1983; MusM, U. NC, Greensboro, 1985; D in Musical Arts, U. Cin. Coll. Condr. High Point Cmty. Theatre, 1985—93; choral dir. T. Wingate Andrews HS, High Point, 1988—93; dir. music Guilford Coll. United Meth. Ch., Greensboro, 1990—93; choral dir. High Point U., 1991—93; chorus master Minn. Opera, Mpls., 1995—97; dir. music Westminster Presbyn. Ch., Mpls., 1995—99, First Presbyn. Ch./Theatre, Ft. Wayne, Ind., 2000—06; assoc. faculty Ind. U., Purdue U., Ft. Wayne, 2001—06; vis. asst. prof. U. Wis., Stevens Point, 2006—; interim dir. Wausau Lyric Choir, Wausau. Conductor, musical dir. (over 55 musicals/operas), conductor (over 35 choral/orchestral works), (over 25 orchestral works/ballet), choral preparation (over 20 operas, choral symphonic works). Adv. Voce Magna, Mpls., 1995—97; adjudicator Ind. Arts Commn., Indpls., 2001—02; exec. com. Am. Guild Organists, Ft. Wayne, Ind., 2000—03, dean, 2001—03. Recipient Outstanding Performance, Am. Choral Dirs. Assn. Minn., 1995. Mem.: NCAE, NCMEA, Chorus Am., MENC (assoc.), Nat. Guild Cmty. Schs. for the Arts (assoc.), Presbyn. Assn. Musicians (assoc.; regional resource rep. 1995—99), Am. Choral Dirs. Assn. (life; north ctrl. divsn. chair nat. choral repertoire & stds. 1996—99). Avocations: art, gardening, travel. Home: 3019 Bush St Stevens Point WI 54481 Office: U Wis 1800 Portage St Stevens Point WI 54481 Home Phone: 715-544-0702; Office Phone: 715-346-3979. Personal E-mail: swrsheftz@aol.com.

SHEHAN, GERALDEAN HARRISON, ESL educator; b. Dallas, Sept. 4, 1950; d. Jerrold Harrison and Violet Elizabeth Herndon; m. Thomas Nelson Shehan, Dec. 13, 1986; children: David Harrison Hardy, Daniel Patrick Hardy. BS in edn., Stephen F. Austin State U., 1973; MEd, North Tex. State U., 1984. Cert. Elem. Tchr. Self Contained grades 1-8 Tex. Edn. Agy., 1973, ESL grades 1-8 Tex. Edn. Agy., 1996, Reading Recovery Tex. Woman's U., 1998. Educator reading and ESL specialist Irving Ind. Sch. Dist., Tex., 1973—2003; testing diagnostician Knowledge Point Tutoring, Colleyville, Tex., 2004—; educator reading specialist NW Ind. Sch. Dist., Fort Worth, Tex., 2005—. Chairperson Elliott Campus Improvement Com., Irving, Tex., 1997—2002; adv. mem. IISD Dist. Improvement Com., Irving, Tex., 1999—2003; pres. elect Alpha Delta Kappa Tex. Beta Omicron Chpt., Irving, Tex., 1998—; mentor and grade level chair Irving ISD, Tex., 1990—2003. Mem. PTA; tchr. First United Meth. Ch., Irving, Tex., 1984—98. Recipient Irving Dist. Elem. Tchr. of the Yr., Irving Ind. Sch. Dist., 1999—2000, Outstanding Grad., 1990; grant, Irving Schools Found., 1988, 1988, 1995, 1997. Mem.: Internat. Reading Assn., Tex. Teachers of English to Speakers of Other Languages, Reading Recovery Coun. of N.Am., Parent Tchr. Assn. (life; bd. mem. 1990—2000), Kappa Delta Pi, Alpha Chi, Tex. Beta Omicron Chpt. of Alpha Delta Kappa (pres. elect 2004—). R-Conservative. Methodist. Avocations: outdoor activities, reading, travel, farming. Home: 1812 Krokus Dr Keller TX 76248 Office: Northwest Ind Sch Dist PO Box 77070 Fort Worth TX 76177-0070 Home Phone: 817-379-0669. Personal E-mail: gshehan@verizon.net.

SHEIK, DUNCAN, singer, songwriter; b. Montclair, NJ, Nov. 18, 1969; Degree in semiotics, Brown U., New Providence, RI, 1992. Performed with bands His Boy Elroy, 1993, Liz and Lisa. Singer, musican, co-prodr. (albums) Duncan Sheik, 1996; singer, musician, co-prodr.: albums Humming, 1998, Phantom Moon, 2001, Daylight, 2002, White Limousine, 2006, songs "Wishful Thinking", 1998; TV Appearances: Boston Public, 2003, American Dreams, 2003; composer: (plays) (musical score) The Nightingale, 2006, Nero (Another Golden Rome), 2006, Spring Awakening, 2006 (Drama Desk award outstanding music, 2007, Tony award best original score written for the theatre, 2007, Tony award best orchestrations, 2007). Office: c/o Gold Mountain Entertainment Ste 212 2 Music South Nashville TN 37203 *

SHEIKH, AAMER, accounting educator; b. Rawalpindi, Punjab, Pakistan, July 21, 1971; arrived in US, 1990; s. Arif Anwar Sheikh and Parveen Rozina. BBA, Coll. William and Mary, Williamsburg, Va., 1994; M of Acctg. Sci., U. Ill., Urbana-Champaign, 1996; PhD, U. Ga., Athens, 2001. CPA Va., 1995, accredited bus. advisor, Nat. Soc. Accts., 2005; cert. bus. mgmt. Assn. Profls. in Bus. Mgmt., 2002. Asst. prof. acctg. Coll. William and Mary, Williamsburg, 2001—06, Quinnipiac U., Hamden, Conn., 2006—. Office: Quinnipiac U Sch Bus 275 Mount Carmel Ave Hamden CT 06518-1908 Office Phone: 203-582-8261. Business E-Mail: aamer.sheikh@quinnipiac.edu.

SHEIKH, AATIF MANZOOR, military officer, pharmacist; b. Lahore, Punjab, Pakistan, Dec. 6, 1972; s. Manzoor Ilahi and Wasima Manzoor Sheikh. PharmD, U. Md., Balt., 1998; postgrad., Army Baylor Program Health and Bus. Adminstrn., San Antonio, 2006—. Cert. Md. Bd. Pharmacy, 1998. Commd. 2d lt. US Army, 1998, advanced through grades to maj.; chief outpatient pharmacy Walter Reed Army Med. Ctr., Washington, 1998—99, pharmacy practice resident, 1998—99, chief pharmacy informatics Washington DC, DC, 2000—01; chief, ancillary services Med. Element: Joint Task Force Bravo, Sato Cano Air BAse, Honduras, 1999—2000; chief pharmacy Kimbrough Ambulatory Care Ctr., Fort Meade, Md., 2001—05; support ops. officer 16th Med. Logistics Bn., Camp Carroll, Republic of Korea, 2005—06. Contbr. articles to profl. jours. Decorated Army Commendation medal for Outstanding Performance, Army Commendation medal for Outstanding Svc., Army Svc. Ribbon, Govt. War on Terrorism medal, Army Commendation medal for Outstanding Performance, Army Commendation medal for Meritorious Achievement, Joint Svc. Achievement medal, Nat. Def. Svc. medal, Army

Commendation medal for Meritorious Svc., Meritorious Svc. medal, Govt. War on Terrorism Expeditionary medal, Korean Def. Svc. medal. Mem.: Am. Soc. Cons. Pharmacists, Assn. Mil. Surgeons US, Md. Pharmacists Assn. (Harry D. Kaufman award for svc. to profession 1997), Am. Soc. Health Sys. Pharmacists, Am. Pharmacists Assn. (UMAB chpt. Outstanding Sr. award 1998). Islam. Avocations: computers, basketball, reading. Home Phone: 210-846-2375. Home Fax: 703-783-0249.

SHEIKH, FAZAL, photographer, writer; b. NYC, 1965; BA, Princeton U., 1987. Author: (books) A Sense of Common Ground, 1996, The Victor Weeps, 1998, A Camel for the Son, 2001, Ramadan Moon, 2001, Moksha, 2005; photographer (exhibitions) Art Inst. Chgo., Seattle Art Mus., Internat. Ctr. Photography, NYC, Corcoran Gallery of Art, Washington, Tate Modern, London, Fondátion Cartíer-Bresson, Paris, Mus. Fine Arts, Orleans, France, Mus. Contemporary Art, Moscow, UN, NYC. Named MacArthur fellow, John D. and Catherine T. MacArthur Found., 2005; recipient Ruttenberg Award, The Friends of Photography, 1995, Ferguson Award, 1995, Mother Jones Internat. Documentary Award, 1995, Infinity Award, Internat. Ctr. of Photography, 1995, Leica Medal of Excellence, 1995, Volkart Found. Grant, 2000, Recontres d'Arles, Le Prix Dialogue de l'Humanité, 2003, Henri Cartier-Bresson Internat. Grand Prize, 2005; grantee Fulbright Fellowship, 1992, Fellowship in Photography, NEA, 1994, NJ State Coun. on Arts Fellowship, 1994.

SHEILS, DENIS FRANCIS, lawyer; b. Ridgewood, NJ, Apr. 7, 1961; s. Denis Francis and Anna Marie (Clifford) Sheils; m. Harriet A. Bonawitz, Sept. 17, 1988; children: Denis F., Dylan I., Matthew D. BA, La Salle Coll., 1983; JD, Fordham U., 1986. Bar: NY 1987, Pa. 1987, US Dist. Ct. (ea. dist.) Pa. 1987, US Ct. Appeals (3d cir.) 1987, US Dist. Ct. (so. and ea. dists.) NY 1992, US Supreme Ct. 1994, US Dist. Ct. (no. dist.) NY 1997, US Ct. Appeals (2d cir.) 1999, Nev. 2003, US Dist. Ct. Nev. 2003. Assoc. Kohn, Swift & Graf, PC, Phila., 1987—97, shareholder, 1997—. Mem.: ABA, Phila. Bar Assn. Roman Catholic. Office: Kohn Swift & Graf PC 21st Fl One South Broad St Philadelphia PA 19107 Home: The Dorchester Unit Number 1613 226 W Rittenhouse Sq Philadelphia PA 19103 Office Phone: 215-238-1700. Business E-Mail: dsheils@kohnswift.com.

SHEILS, PAUL T., lawyer; b. NYC, Aug. 17, 1954; s. James Henry and Margaret (Lambert) S.; m. Theresa V. Sheils; children: Erin Margaret, James Henry II. BA, Williams Coll.; JD, Fordham U. Assoc. Patterson, Belknap, Webb & Tyler, NYC, 1980-84; counsel Dow Jones & Co., Inc., Princeton, NJ, 1984, exec. dir., 1993—94, v.p. interactive publishing, 1994—98; CEO, pres., dir. Medscape, Inc. (negotiated merger into MedicaLogic, Inc.), 1998—2000; chmn. Medscape / MedicaLogic, Inc.; CEO Mayo Health Ventures; CEO, pres., dir. InterCure, Inc., 2001; pres., CEO Aetna Health Info. Solutions Aetna Inc., 2005—. Mem. ABA, N.Y. State Bar Assn., N.Y. County Lawyers Assn. Achievements include led the team that launched The Wall Street Journal Online in 1996 which has over 700,000 subscribers and is among the most successful subscription-based publications on the Web.

SHEIMAN, RONALD LEE, lawyer; b. Bridgeport, Conn., Apr. 26, 1948; s. Samuel Charles and Rita Doris Sheiman; m. Deborah Joy Lovitky, Oct. 16, 1971; children: Jill, Laura. BA, U. Mich., 1970; JD, U. Conn., 1973; LLM in Taxation, NYU, 1974. Bar: Conn. 1973, US Ct. Appeals (2d cir.) 1975, US Supreme Ct. 1977, DC 1978, NY 1981. Tax atty. Office Regional Counsel IRS, Phila., 1974-78; pvt. practice Westport, Conn., 1978—. Mem.: ABA, Conn. Bar Assn., Fed. Bar Assn. Home: 128 Random Rd Fairfield CT 06432-1408 Office: 1804 Post Rd E Westport CT 06880-5607 Home Phone: 203-371-4941.

SHEINDLIN, JUDITH (JUDGE JUDY), television personality, judge; b. Bklyn., Oct. 21, 1942; d. Murray and Ethel Blum; m. Ronald Levy, 1964 (div. 1976); children: Jamie, Adam; m. Gerald Sheindlin, 1977 (div. 1990); stepchildren: Greg, Jonathan, Nicole; m. Gerald Sheindlin, 1991. BA, Am. U., Wash., DC, 1963; JD, NY Law Sch., 1965; LLD (hon.), Elizabethtown Coll. Pros. atty. Family Ct., NYC, 1978—82, judge Bronx, 1982—86; supervising judge Manhattan, NYC, 1986—96. Appeared as herself (TV films) ChiPs '99, 1998, (TV series) Judge Judy, 1996— (nominee Daytime Emmy for outstanding special class series, 1999, 2000, 2001, 2002, 2003); author: Don't Pee on My Leg and Tell Me It's Raining: America's Toughest Family Court Judge Speaks Out, 1996, Beauty Fades, Dumb is Forever: The Making of a Happy Woman, 1999, Keep It Simple, Stupid: You're Smarter Than You Look: Uncomplicating Families in Complicated Times, 2000, Judge Judy Sheindlin's Win or Lose by How You Choose, 2000, You're Smarter Than You Look: Uncomplicating Relationships in Complicated Times, 2001, Judge Judy Sheindlin's You Can't Judge a Book By Its Cover: Cool Rules for School, 2001. Named one of 100 Most Powerful Celebrities, Forbes.com, 2007. *

SHEINFELD, MYRON M., lawyer, educator; b. Mass., Mar. 18, 1930; s. Robert and Sadye (Rosenberg) S.; m. Christina Trzcinski, Mar. 30, 1985; children: Scott, Tom. BA, Tulane U., New Orleans, 1951; JD, U. Mich., 1954. Bar: Mich. 1954, Tex. 1956. Rschr. Legis. Rsch. Inst., U. Mich., 1954; asst. US atty. So. Dist. Tex., 1958-60; law clk. US Dist. Judge, 1960-61; ptnr. Strickland, Gordon & Sheinfeld, Houston, 1961-68; shareholder, of counsel Sheinfeld, Maley & Kay, PC, Houston, 1968-96, counsel to firm, 1996—2001; sr. counsel Akin, Gump, Strauss, Hauer & Feld LLP, Houston, 2001—06; of counsel King & Spalding LLP, Houston, 2007—. Past adj. prof. law U. Tex.; mem. Nat. Bankruptcy Conf.; past chmn. Tex. Bankruptcy Adv. Commn.; bd. dirs. Nabors Industries, Ltd.; chmn. ABA Standing Com. on Specialization. Bd. editors Collier On Bankruptcy (15th edit.); contbr. articles to profl. jours. With JAG US Army, 1955-58. Fellow: Am. Coll. Bankruptcy Found. (bd. dirs.); mem.: Nat. Assn. Corp. Dirs. (bd. dirs. and former pres. Houston chpt. 2003—), State Bar Tex. (past chmn. bus. law sect.), State Bar Mich., Downtown Club at Houston Ctr. (bd. govs. 1995—), Phi Sigma Alpha, Phi Beta Kappa. Office: King & Spalding LLP 1100 Lousiana St Houston TX 77002 Office Phone: 713-751-3252. Business E-Mail: msheinfeld@kslaw.com.

SHEINGOLD, DANIEL H., electrical engineer; b. Boston, Sept. 26, 1928; s. Louis S. and Elsie Sheingold; m. Ann Silverman, Aug. 2, 1953 (dec. Feb. 1995); children: Mark J., Laura S. Duffy. BSEE with distinction, Worcester Poly. Inst., 1948; MSEE, Columbia U., 1949. Engr. George A. Philbrick Rschs. Inc., Boston, 1949-55, application engring. mgr., 1957-63; v.p. George A. Philbrick Researches, Inc., Dedham, Mass., 1964-67; staff cons. Teledyne Philbrick, Dedham, 1967-68; tech. mktg. mgr. Analog Devices, Inc., Norwood, Mass., 1969—. Editor: Analog-Digital Conversion Handbook, 1972, 3d edit., 1986, Nonlinear Circuits Handbook, 1974, Transducer Interfacing Handbook, 1980; editor Analog Dialogue jour., 1969—, others. Vol. reader Rec. for Blind and Dyslexic, 2003—. With AUS, 1955-57. Fellow IEEE; mem. IEEE Instrumentation and Measurement Soc. (sec.-treas. 1976, v.p. 1977, pres. 1978), AAAS. Jewish. Avocations: music, walking, reading. Office: Analog Devices Inc PO Box 9106 3 Technology Way Norwood MA 02062-9106 Office Phone: 781-461-3294. Business E-Mail: dan.sheingold@analog.com.

SHEININ, ROSE, biochemist, educator; b. Toronto, Ont., May 18, 1930; d. Harry and Anne (Szyber) Shuber; m. Joseph Sheinin, July 15, 1951; children: David Matthew Khazanov, Lisa Basya Judith, Rachel Sarah Rebecca. BA, U. Toronto, 1951, MA (scholar), 1953, PhD in Biochemistry, 1956, LHD, 1985; DHL (hon.), Mt. St. Vincent U., 1985; DSc (hon.), Acadia U., 1987, U. Guelph, 1991. Demonstrator in biochemistry U. Toronto, Ont., Canada, 1951-53, asst. prof. microbiology Ont., 1964-75, asst. prof. med. biophysics Ont., 1967-75, prof. microbiology Ont., 1975-90, assoc. prof. med. biophysics Ont., 1975-78, prof. med. biophysics Ont., 1978-90, chmn. microbiology and parasitology Ont., 1975-82, vice dean Sch. Grad. Studies Ont., 1984-89; vice-rector acad. Concordia U., Montreal, Que., Canada, 1989-94, prof. dept. biology, 1989-2000. Mem. Health Scis. Com.; vis. rsch. assoc. chem. microbiology Cambridge U., 1956-57, Nat. Inst. Med. Rsch., London, 1975-58; rsch. assoc. fellow divsn. biol. rsch. Ont. Caner Inst., 1958-67; sci. officer cancer grants panel Med. Rsch. Coun. Can.; mem. Can. Sci. Del. to People's Republic of China, 1973; mem. adv. com. Provincial Lottery Health Rsch. Awards; mem. adv. com. on biotech. NRC Can., 1984-87; mem. Sci. Coun. Can., 1984-87; adv. com. on sci. and tech. CBC, 1980-85; mem. bd. dirs. Can. Bacterial Disease Network, 1989-94; vis. prof. biochemistry U. Alta., 1971. Assoc. editor Can. Jour. Biochemistry, 1968-71, Virology, 1969-72, Intervirology, 1974-85; editl. bd. Microbiol. Revs., 1977-80; author, co-author various publs. Nat. Cancer Inst. Can. fellow, 1953-56, 58-61; Brit. Empire Cancer Campaign fellow, 1956-58; recipient Queen's Silver Jubilee medal, 1978, Woman of Distinction award Health and Edn., YWCA, 1988, Josiah Macy Jr. faculty scholar, 1981-82; fellow Ligue Contre le Cancer, France, 1981-82, Massey Coll., U. Toronto, 1981—, continuing sr. fellow, 1994—; hon. fellow Ryerson Polytech. U., 1993. Fellow Am. Acad. Microbiology, Royal Soc. Can. (chair women in scholarship com. 1990-93); mem. Can. Biochem. Soc. (pres. 1974-75), Can. Soc. Cell Biology (pres. 1975-76), Am. Soc. Virology, Am. Soc. Microbiologists, Can. Assn. Women in Sci., Internat. Assn. Women Bioscientists, Sigma Xi Rsch. Soc., Scitech. Soc. Complex Carbohydrates, Toronto Biochem. and Biophys. Soc. (pres. 1960-70, coun. 1970-74). E-mail: rosesheinin@sympatico.ca.

SHEINMAN, MORT, editor, consultant, writer, photographer; b. NYC, Oct. 7, 1933; s. Irving and Molly (Feigenblatt) S.; m. Claire Rosenfeld, Aug. 27, 1967 (div.). BA in English, CCNY, 1954. Sports tabulator New York Daily News, 1956-58; reporter Women's Wear Daily, NYC, 1960-69, news editor, 1970-71, mng. editor, 1971-2000, W Mag., NYC, 1972-82, assoc. editor, 1982-2000; editl. dir. Publicis Dialog N.Y., NYC, 2000-01; journalism instr. Fashion Inst. Tech., 2001—; spl. projects Flatiron-23d St. Partnership, NYC, 2006—. Cons., writer ATT Summer Olympics Exhibit, LA, 1984, Pru Ctr. Obs., Boston, 1995. Co-author Fashion Retailing and a Bygone Era: Inside Women's Wear Daily, 2005; contbr. articles and photographs to various publs. including Ency. Judaica, 2005. With U.S. Army, 1954-56. Mem.: CCNY Comm. Alumni (Hall of Fame 2003), Soc. of the Silurians. Home: 60 Gramercy Park N New York NY 10010-5423 E-mail: mortone@aol.com.

SHEKAR, SAM S., federal agency administrator; MD, MPH, U. Mich. Asst. surgeon gen., rear admiral USPHS Commd. Corps.; assoc. adminstr. field ops. Bur. Health Professionals Health Resources and Services Adminstrn., HHS, 1998—2000, assoc. adminstr. health professions, 2000—02, assoc. adminstr Bur. Primary Health Care, 2002—05, dir. Ctr. for Quality, HIV/AIDS Bur., 2005—. Fellow: Am. Coll. Preventive Medicine. Office: US HHS Health Resources and Services Adminstrn 5600 Fishers Ln Rockville MD 20857 Office Phone: 301-443-0458.

SHEKHAR, STEPHEN S., obstetrician, gynecologist; b. New Delhi, Jan. 13, 1944; arrived in U.S., 1972; s. S.P. Jain and Shakuntala Mithal; m. Claudette Dorita, Jan. 6, 1978; children: Sasha, Stephen. MBBS, Punjabi U., Patiala, India, 1966. Surgeon Nat. Health Svc. U.K., 1966-72; intern Roosevelt Hosp.-Columbia Coll. Physicians and Surgeons, NYC, 1972-73; resident in ob-gyn. St. Clare's Hosp., N.Y. Med. Coll., NYC, 1973-76, Harlem Hosp.-Columbia U., NYC, 1976-77; pvt. practice Studio City, Calif., 1977—. Mem. staff L.A. County-U. So. Calif. Med. Sch.; clin. prof. ob-gyn. and family medicine U. So. Calif. Sch. Medicine, Oreg. Health Scis. U. Sch. Medicine. Fellow ACS, Am. Coll. Ob-Gyn., L.A. Soc. Ob-Gyn.; mem. AMA, Calif. Med. Assn., L.A. County Med. Assn., Oreg. Med. Assn., Jackson County Med. Assn. Home and Office: PO Box 1742 Medford OR 97501-0136 Office Phone: 541-608-6199. Personal E-mail: drsshekhar@yahoo.com.

SHELANSKI, MICHAEL L., cell biologist, educator; b. Phila., Oct. 5, 1941; s. Herman Alder and Bessie B.; m. Vivien Brodkin, June 9, 1963; children: Howard, Samuel, Noah. Student, Oberlin Coll., 1959-61; MD (Life Ins. Med. Research Fund fellow), U. Chgo., 1966, PhD, 1967. Intern in pathology Albert Einstein Coll. Medicine, NYC, 1967-68, fellow in neuropathology, 1968-70, asst. prof. pathology, 1969-74; staff scientist NIH, Bethesda, Md., 1971-73; vis. scientist Inst. Pasteur, Paris, 1973-74; assoc. prof. neuropathology Harvard U., Cambridge, Mass., 1974-78; sr. research assoc., asst. neuropathologist Children's Hosp. Med. Center, Boston, 1974-78; prof., chmn. dept. pharmacology N.Y. U. Med. Center, NYC, 1978-86; Delafield Prof., chmn. dept. pathology Coll. Physicians and Surgeons, Columbia U., NYC, 1987—; dir. pathology services Presbyn. Hosp., NYC, 1987—; co-dir. Taub Inst. for Rsch. on Alzheimer's Disease and the Aging Brain, NYC, 1998—. Mem. Neurology A study sect. NIH, 1974-78; Pharmacological Scis. study sect., 1986-90; mem. sci. and med. adv. bd. Alzheimer's Disease and Related Disorders Assn., 1985-92, sec., 1987-92, mem. Zenith award panel, 1993-95; chmn. overhead powerline adv. panel State of N.Y., 1981-87; dir. Alzheimer's disease rsch. ctr. Columbia U., 1989—; mem. Am. Cancer Soc. IRG Panel, 1989-93, sci. adv. bd. Dystonia Assn., Amyotrophic Lateral Sclerosis Assn; elected mem., Inst. of Medicine, 1999. Mem. editl. bd. Jour. Neurochemistry, 1982-90, Jour. Neuropathology and Exptl. Neurology, 1983-85, Neuroscis., 1985—, Neurobiology of Aging, 1988-95, Lab. Investigation, 1989—, Brain Pathology, 1990-93. Served as sr. asst. surgeon USPHS, 1971-73. Guggenheim fellow, 1973-74 Mem. Am. Soc. Cell Biology, Inst. Medicine NAS, Am. Assn. Neuropathologists, Assn. Med. Coll. Pharmacologists, Am. Soc. Neurochemistry, Am. Assn. Physicians. Achievements include research on fibrous proteins of brain, aging of human brain, devel. neurobiology. Office: Columbia U Coll Physicians and Surgeons Dept Pathology 630 W 168th St New York NY 10032-3702

SHELAT, AMIT MAHESH, neurologist; b. Baroda, Gujarat, India, Dec. 25, 1974; s. Mahesh Narharilal and Urmila Mahesh Shelat; m. Shreya Bhavan Dave; 1 child, Khushie Amit. BA in Psychology hons., NYU, 1997, BA in Chemistry cum laude, 1997, MPA in Health Policy and Mgmt., 2002; D in Osteo Medicine, NY Coll. Osteo. Medicine, Old Westbury, 2002. Lic. Medicine and Surgery NY Edn. Dept., 2006. Resident physician osteo. medicine North Shore U. Hosp., Plainview, NY, 2002—03, resident physician internal medicine Forest Hills, NY, 2003—04, resident physician neurology dept. neurology Manhasset, NY, 2004—. Alumnus interviewer com. on admissions NY Coll. Osteo. Medicine, Old Westbury, 2005—. Bd. dirs. Found. Rsch. on Sexually Transmitted Diseases, NYC, 2005. Recipient Neurology Resident's award, Angioma Alliance, 2006, First Pl. in Clin. Rsch., North Shore LI Jewish Health Sys., 2006. Mem.: Assn. Indian Neurologists in Am., Am. Assn. Physicians Indian Origin, Am. Osteo. Assn., Am. Acad. Neurology, Am. Mensa, Ltd., Phi Beta Kappa, Psi Chi Nat. Honor Soc. in Psychology (life; v.p. 1996—97). Independent. Hindu. Office: North Shore University Hospital 300 Community Drive 9 Tower Manhasset NY 11030

SHELBURNE, JOHN DANIEL, pathologist; b. Washington, Aug. 27, 1943; s. Clarence Daniel and Edith (McDanel) S.; m. Katherine Howard Parrish, June 17, 1966; children: Mark, Kerri. BA, U. N.C., 1966; PhD, Duke U., 1971, MD, 1972. Intern, then resident Duke U. Med. Ctr., Durham, NC, 1972-76; asst. prof. Duke U., Durham, 1973-78, assoc. prof., 1978-85, prof. pathology, 1985—; dir. electron microscopy lab. VA Med. Ctr., Durham, 1976-92, chief lab. svc., 1983-99, chief of staff, 1999—. Adv. WHO, Manila, 1990; panel mem. VA Program, Washington, 1987—; participant Nordrhein/Westfalen Exchange, Germany, 1988. Editor: Basic Methods in Biological X-Ray Microprobe, 1983; author, editor: Microprobe Analysis in Medicine, 1989, Biomedical Applications of Microprobe Analysis, 1999. Mem. Appalachian Trail Conf., Harpers Ferry, West, Va., 1970—; bd. dirs. Cen. Carolina Youth Soccer, Durham, 1987-90; founding mem. N.C. Soc. for Electron Microscopy and Microprobe, Research Triangle Park, N.C., 1980—. Recipient Morehead scholarship, 1961-66, AOA Med. Honorary Duke Med. Sch., 1970; named Med. Scientist Tng. Program participant NIH, 1966-72, Shelley Meml. lectr., 1985, Florey Meml. lectr., 1988. Fellow Coll. Am. Pathologists; mem. Am. Assn. Pathologists, Microscopy Soc. Am., Microbeam Analysis Soc. Democrat. Episcopalian. Home: 4302 Malvern Rd Durham NC 27707-5451 Office: Duke U Dept Pathology PO Box 3712 Durham NC 27710-3712 Business E-Mail: john.shelburne@med.va.gov.

SHELBY, JAMES STANFORD, surgeon, researcher; b. Ringgold, La., June 15, 1934; s. Jesse Audrey and Mable (Martin) S.; m. Susan Rainey, July 15, 1967; children: Bryan Christian, Christopher Linden. BS in Liberal Arts, La. Tech. U., 1956; MD, La. State U., 1958. Diplomate Am. Bd. Surgery, Am. Bd. Thoracic Surgery. Intern Charity Hosp. La., New Orleans, 1958-59, resident in surgery and thoracic surgery, 1959-65; fellow in cardiovasc. surgery Baylor U. Coll. Medicine, Houston, 1965-66; practice medicine specializing in cardiovasc. surgery Shreveport, La., 1967—2004; ret., 2004. Mem. staff Schumpert Med. Ctr., Highland Hosp., Willis-Knighton Med. Ctr.; assoc. prof. surgery La. State U. Sch. Medicine, Shreveport, 1967—; pres. Shelby Oil and Gas. With M.C., AUS, 1961-62. Recipient Medallion award La. Tech. U., 1982. Mem. AMA, Am. Coll. Cardiology, Soc. Thoracic Surgeons, Am. Heart Assn., Southeastern Surg. Congress, So. Thoracic Surgery Assn. Home: 6003 E Ridge Dr Shreveport LA 71106-2425 Office: 2751 Albert Bicknell Dr Ste 5C Shreveport LA 71103-3970 Office Phone: 318-632-9438. Personal E-mail: jshelby@worldnet.att.net.

SHELBY, NINA CLAIRE, special education educator; b. Weatherford, Tex., Oct. 23, 1949; d. Bill Hudson and Roselle (Price) S.; m. Richard Dean Powell, May 29, 1971 (div. 1973); 1 child, Stoney Hudson. BA in English, Sul Ross State U., 1974, MEd, 1984; MA in English, U. Tex., 1995. Jr. high lang. arts educator Liberty Hill, Tex., 1974-75; H.S. resource educator Georgetown (Tex.) I. S. D., 1976-77; intermediate resource educator Raymondille (Tex.) I. S. D., 1977-81; educator of severe profound Napper Elem. Pharr (Tex.) San Juan Alamo Ind. Sch. Dist., 1981-90; H. S. life skills educator Pharr (Tex.) San Juan Alamo ISD North H.S., 1990-93; intermediate inclusion educator Carman Elem. Pharr (Tex.) San Juan Alamo Ind. Sch. Dist., 1993—2000, chair dept. spl. edn. Carman Elem., 1998—2000; primary resource/inclusion educator Elgin (Tex.) Elem. Sch., 2000—, chair dept. spl. edn., 2002—. Coach asst. Tex. Spl. Olympics, Pharr, 1981-2000, sponsor vocat. adj. club, 1990-93, adaptive asst. device team, Edinburg, Tex., 1993-95; spl. edn. rep. to Elgin Primary Campus Performance Adv. Coun., 2000— Asst. cub scout leader Boy Scouts Am., 1994-95, sec. parental com. bd. rev., 1997—; parent vol. boy's and girl's Club McAllen, 1992-96. Mem. DAR, Daus. Republic of Tex., Assn. Tex. Profl. Educators, Alpha Delta Kappa. Democrat. Mem. Ch. Of Christ. Avocations: reading, horticulture, piano, opera. Home: PO Box 426 Elgin TX 78621-0426 Office: Elgin Elem Sch Elgin ISD 1001 W 2d St Elgin TX 78621 Office Phone: 512-281-3457. Business E-Mail: nshelby@elginisd.net.

SHELBY, RICHARD CRAIG, senator, former congressman; b. Birmingham, Ala., May 6, 1934; s. O.H. and Alice L. (Skinner) S.; m. Annette Nevin, June 11, 1960; children: Richard Craig, Claude Nevin. AB, U. Ala., 1957, LLB, 1963. Bar: Ala. 1961, DC 1979. Law clk. Supreme Ct. of Ala., 1961-62; practice law Tuscaloosa, Ala., 1963—78; prosecutor City of Tuscaloosa, 1963—71; spl. asst. atty. gen. State of Ala., 1968—71; U.S. magistrate No. Dist. of Ala., 1966—70; mem. Ala. State Senate, 1971—78, 96th-99th Congresses from 7th Ala. dist., 1979-87; mem. energy and commerce com.; mem. vets. affairs com.; US Senator from Ala., 1987—. Mem. com. appropriations US Senate, chmn. com. banking, housing, and urban affairs, spl. com. aging. Active Boy Scouts Am.; pres. Tuscaloosa County Mental Health Assn., 1969-70; bd. govs. Nat. Legis. Conf., 1975-78. Recipient Taxpayer's Friend award, Nat. Taxpayers Union, 1998, Congressional Leadership award, Airports Coun. Internat.-N.Am., 2003. Mem. ABA, Ala. Bar Assn., Tuscaloosa County Bar Assn., DC Bar Assn., Am. Judiciary Soc., Exch. Club, Tuscaloosa County Mental Heatgh Assn.(former pres.) Republican. Presbyterian. Office: US Senate 110 Hart Senate Bldg Washington DC 20510-0001 also: Federal Bldg Ste 240 1118 Greensboro Ave Tuscaloosa AL 35401-2816 Office Phone: 202-224-5744, 205-759-5047. Office Fax: 202-224-3416, 205-759-5067. *

SHELBY, ROSELLE PRICE, writer, retired special education educator; b. Granbury, Tex., Sept. 6, 1929; d. Ernest Blanton and Alice Parthenia (Merrill) Price; m. Billy Hudson Shelby, May 5, 1948; 1 child, Nina Claire. AA, Weatherford Coll., 1948; BA, Tex. Wesleyan U., Ft. Worth, 1960; NDEA diploma, U. Minn., 1963; MEd, Sul Ross State U., Alpine, Tex., 1974. Cert. tchr., Tex. Tchr. Waka Ind. Sch., Tex., 1956-57, 60-65, 69-72, Hart Ind. Sch., Tex., 1957-60, Eagar Ind. Sch., Ariz., 1966-67, New Waverly Ind. Sch., Tex., 1967-68, Willis Ind. Sch., Tex., 1968-69, Georgetown Ind. Sch., Tex., 1972-87. Author: Frogs in the Milk, 1967; editor: Quick and Easy Way to Riches, 1980. Active local Democratic Party, 1968—, precinct chair, Georgetown, 1980-90, election judge, 1991-2000; mem. sch. bd., Alpine, Ariz. Fulbright scholar U. Costa Rica, 1964; Reynolds fellow U. NC, 1971. Mem. AAUW (br. pres. Perryton 1971-72, state bd. dirs. 1971-73, 75-77, br. pres. Georgetown 1975-77), DAR, Daughters of Republic of Tex. (charter mem. Brazos River Chpt.), Am. Assn. Ret. Persons, Beta Sigma Phi, Delta Kappa Gamma (v.p. 1979-81). Mem. Ch. of Christ. Avocations: bible study, reading, cooking, travel. Home: 2006 Terry Ln Georgetown TX 78628-3338

SHELDON, ELEANOR HARRIET BERNERT, sociologist, writer; b. Hartford, Conn., Mar. 19, 1920; d. M.G. and Fannie (Myers) Bernert; m. James Sheldon, Mar. 19, 1950 (div. 1960); children: James, John Anthony. AA, Colby Jr. Coll., 1940; AB, U. N.C., 1942; PhD, U. Chgo., 1949. Asst. demographer Office Population Rsch., Washington, 1942-43; social scientist USDA, Washington, 1943-45; assoc. dir. Chgo. Community Inventory, U. Chgo., 1947-50; social scientist Social Sci. Rsch. Coun., NYC, 1950-51, rsch. grantee, 1953-55, pres., 1972-79; rsch. assoc. Bur. Applied Social Rsch. Columbia U., 1950-51, lectr. sociology, 1951-52, vis. prof., 1969-71; social scientist UN, NYC, 1951-52; rsch. assoc., lectr. sociology UCLA, 1955-61; assoc. rsch. sociologist, lectr. Sch. Nursing U. Calif., 1957-61; sociologist, exec. assoc. Russell Sage Found., NYC, 1961—72; vis. prof. U. Calif., Santa Barbara, 1971. Author: (with L. Wirth) Chicago Community Fact Book, 1949, America's Children, 1958, (with R.A. Glazier) Pupils and Schools in N.Y.C, 1965; editor: (with W.E. Moore) Indicators of Social Change, Concepts and Measurements, 1968, Family Economic Behavior, 1973; contbr. articles to profl. jours. Bd. dirs. Colby-Sawyer Coll., 1979-85, UN Rsch. Inst. for Social Devel., 1973-79; trustee Rockefeller Found., 1978-85, Nat. Opinion Rsch. Ctr., 1980-87, Inst. East-West Security Studies, 1984-88, Am. assembly, 1976-95. William Rainey Harper fellow, U. Chgo., 1945—47. Fellow AAAS, Am. Acad. Arts and Scis., Am. Sociol. Assn., Am. Statis. Assn.; mem. U. Chgo. Alumni Assn. (Profl. Achievement award), Sociol. Rsch. Assn. (pres. 1971-72), Coun. on Fgn. Rels., Am. Assn. Pub. Opinion Rsch., Ea. Sociol. Soc., Internat. Sociol. Assn., Internat. Union Sci. Study of Population, Population Assn. Am. (2d v.p. 1970-71), Inst. of Medicine (chmn. program com. 1976-77), Cosmopolitan Club. Home and Office: 630 Park Ave New York NY 10021-6544 E-mail: ehbsheldon@aol.com.

SHELDON, GEORGE FRANK, medical educator; b. Dec. 20, 1934; s. Richard Robert and Helen Irene (Zerzan) S.; m. Ruth Guy, Aug. 28, 1959; children: Anne Anderson, Elizabeth, Julia. BA, U. Kans., Lawrence, 1957, MD, 1961; postgrad., Mayo Clinic Grad. Sch., 1965. Asst. instr. we. civilization U. Kans., 1955—57; intern Kans. U. Med. Ctr.; resident in surgery U. Calif., San Francisco, 1965-69; fellow in surg. biology Harvard Med. Sch. of Peter Bent Brigham Hosp., 1969-71; from asst. to prof. U. Calif., 1971-82; Dr. Zack D. Owens Disting. prof. surgery, dept. chmn. U. NC, Chapel Hill, 1984—2001. Chmn. residency rev. com. accreditation Coun. Grad. Med. Edn.; mem. Coun. Grad. Med. Edn. of Health and Human Svcs., 1986, chmn. 1998; mem. adminstrv. bd. Coun. Acad. Socs., chair, 1998-99; chmn. Merit Rev. Bd. Surgery Va., AAMC, 2000, 01; pres. vis. bd. UN Formed Svcs. U. Health Scis., 2002-03; mem. Coun. on Physician and Nurse Shortage Wharton Sch. Bus. U. Penn. Author: (with J.B. Runnell) Pictorial History of Kansas Medicine, 1961; (with Jill Ridky) Managing in Academics, 1993; editor: (with J.B. Davis) Clinical Surgery, 1995; editor-in-chief: E-Facs.org. With USPHS, 1962-64. Recipient Surgeon's Dist. award for Svc. to Safety, Nat. Safety Coun., 1993, Douglass Stubbs award Nat. Med. Assn., 1991, Disting. Faculty award Med. Alumni Assn. U. N.C., 2001; named Disting. Med. Alumnus, Kans. U., 2000. Fellow Royal Coll. Surgeons of Edinburgh (hon.), Royal Coll. Surgeons Eng., European Surg. Assn., Assn. of Surgeons of Gt. Britain and Ireland, Phila. Acad. Surgeons (Hunterian Orator 2001); mem. ACS (sec. bd. govs., regent 1984-93, pres. 1998, editor-in-chief e.facs.org web portal 2004—, Surgeon of Yr. 2001, Fitts Orator, 1987, Scudder Orator Honored Surgeon, editor E facs.org web ponta 2004-), Am. Bd. Surgery (chmn. 1989-90), Nat. Bd. Med. Examiners (test com. 1981-84), Am. Assn. Surgery of Trauma (pres. 1984, Fitts medal), Am. Surg. Assn. (sec. 1989-94, pres. 1994-95), Assn. Am. Med. Colls. (exec. com., chair elect 1999, chair 2000-01, disting. svc. mem.), Soc. Surg. Chmn. (pres.), Coun. Acad. Socs. (chmn. 1998—, com. on gender equity and com. on health workforce), Inst. Medicine (sec. com. on employer based health ins. and tech. assessment edn. bds., Fluid Resuscitation com. on Nation's Physician Workforce 1996, Reviewer Poison Ctrs), Hunter Soc. (172nd Hunterian Orator). Achievements include being recognized as the leading authority on surgical workforce. Office: U NC at Chapel Hill Dept Surgery Campus Bx 7050 136 Burnett-Womack Bldg Chapel Hill NC 27599-7228 Office Phone: 919-966-4052. Business E-Mail: gsheldon@med.unc.edu.

SHELDON, GILBERT IGNATIUS, clergyman; b. Cleve., Sept. 20, 1926; s. Ignatius Peter and Stephanie Josephine (Olszewski) S. Student, John Carroll U.; M.Div., St. Theol. Sem., 1970; D.Min., St. Mary Sem. and Ohio Consortium of Sems., 1974; HHD, Jesuit U. of Wheeling, 1993; STD, Franciscan U., Steubenville, 1994. Ordained priest Roman Cath. Ch., 1953, bishop, 1976. Assoc. pastor Cleve. Diocese, 1953-64, diocesan dir. propagation of faith, 1964-74; pastor, Episcopal vicar Lorain County, Ohio, 1974-76; aux. bishop Cleve., 1976—; vicar for Summit County, 1979-80, So. Region, 1980-92; bishop Steubenville, 1992—. Bd. dirs. Soc. Propagation of Faith, 1968-74, Diocesan Presbyteral Coun.; instr. theology St. John Coll.; clergy adv. bd. econ. edn. Akron U.; mem. Bishop's Com. Latin Am.; adv. bd., Franciscan U.; bd. trustees St. Mary Seminary, Diocesan Health Ins. Adv. Bd., Cath. Charities Corp.; former mem. bd. trustees Borromeo Coll.; mem. acad. bd. St, Mary Seminary; bd. dirs. Bishops' Com. Latin Am., adminstrv. com. Nat. Conf. Cath. Bishops/USCC, Nat. Adv. Coun., Bishops' Com. for Missions, Nat. Bd. Soc. for Propagation of Faith; bd. trustees Pontifical Coll. Josephinum, Bishop Emeritus of Steubenville, 2002, Adj. Faculty, Franciscan U. of Steubenville, 2003. Goals for Greater Akron. With USAF, 1944—45. Mem. Nat. Conf. Cath. Bishops (adminstrv. bd. 1985—), Am. Legion, Cath. War Vets., Knights of Columbus, Order of Alhambra., Rotary Club Akron and Steubenville. Clubs: K.C. Lodges: Rotary (Akron). Roman Catholic. Avocations: golf, astronomy, photography, history, travel. Home: 609 N 7th St Steubenville OH 43952-1748 Home Phone: 740-283-9608. Business E-Mail: lnichols@diosteub.org.

SHELDON, INGRID KRISTINA, retired mayor, controller; b. Ann Arbor, Mich., Jan. 30, 1945; d. Henry Ragnvald and Virginia Schmidt Blom; m. Clifford George Sheldon, June 18, 1966; children: Amy Elizabeth, William David. BS, Eastern Mich. U., 1966; MA, U. Mich., 1970; doctorate (hon.), Cleary U., 2001. Cert. tchr., Mich. Tchr. Livonia (Mich.) Pub. Schs., 1966-67, Ann Arbor Pub. Schs., 1967-68; bookkeeper Huron Valley Tennis Club, Ann Arbor, 1978—; acct. F.A. Black Co., Ann Arbor, 1984-88; coun. mem. Ward II City of Ann Arbor, 1988-92, mayor, 1993-2000. Commr. Housing Bd. Appeals, Ann Arbor, 1988—91; vice chmn. fin. and budget com. S.E. Mich. Coun.Govts.; treas. Huron Valley Child Guidance Clinic, Ann Arbor, 1984—, Ann Arbor Hist. Found., 1985—, Parks Adv. Commn., 1987—92, Ann Arbor Planning Commn., 1988—89; excellence com. Ann Arbor Pub. Schs. reorgn., 1985; treas. SOS Cmty. Crisis Ctr., Ypsilanti, Mich., 1987—93; chair United Meth. Retirement Cmty., Ann Arbor, 2003—06; trustee Cmty. Found., 2001—05; chair Ann Arbor Summer Festival, 2005; treas. Dixboro United Meth. Ch., 2006—. Recipient Cmty. Svc. award Ann Arbor Jaycees, 1980, DAR Cmty. Svc. award, 1997; AAUW fellow, 1982. Mem.: Mich. Mcpl. League (life; del. 1989—97, hon. life mem. 1994, trustee 1997—2000, pres. 1999—2000), Ann Arbor Rotary (pres.-elect 2006—, pres. 2006—07), Ann Arbor Women's City Club (fin. com. 1987—90, chair endowment com. 1989—90, treas. 2003), Alpha Omicron Pi, Kappa Delta Pi. Republican. Methodist. Avocation: musical theatre. Home: 1416 Folkstone Ct Ann Arbor MI 48105-2848 Personal E-mail: aasheldon@aol.com.

SHELDON, J. MICHAEL, lawyer, educator; b. Mt. Carmel, Pa., Sept. 01; s. Lloyd Loomis and Helen Roberta (Sosnowski) S. AA, Harrisburg CC, Pa., 1978; BS, Pa. State U., 1980; M in Journalism, Temple U., 1991; JD, Widener U. Sch. Law, 1996. Bar: U.S. Ct. Appeals 2004, U.S. Surpeme Ct. 2006. News announcer Sta. WNUE-AM, Ft. Walton Beach, Fla., 1974-76, Sta. WFEC-AM, Harrisburg, 1977-78; announcer Sta. WCMB-AM, Wormleysburg, Pa., 1979-80; writer newspaper Pa. Beacon, Harrisburg, 1982-85; media specialist Commonwealth Media Svcs., Harrisburg, 1982-86; dir. communications Pa. Poultry Fedn., Harrisburg, 1986-89; news anchor Sta. WGAL-TV, Lancaster, Pa., 1989-90; dir. pub. rels. Profl. Ins. Agts. - Pa., Md., Del., Mechanicsburg, Pa., 1990-92; v.p. comm. and mktg. United Way of the Capital Region, Harrisburg, Pa., 1992-93, Widener U. Sch. of Law, 1994-96; pres. Open Mike Comm., Harrisburg, 1994—. Mem. adj. faculty dept. journalism Temple U., 1992; mem. faculty dept. humanities Pa. State U., 1995-97, 99-04. Contbg. author: Pa. 12th Annual Civil Litigation Update, Spoliation of Evidence: Why You Can't Have Your Cake and Eat it Too, 1999; contbg. editor: A Practical Guidebook to Massachusetts Aviation Law, 1999; Contbr. articles to profl. jours. Pub. rels. advisor Cen. Pa. Leukemia Soc., Harrisburg, 1989-90; media advisor Polit. Campaign, Hershey, Pa., 1990. With USAF, 1969-73. Mem. Pa. Bar Assn., Pa. Criminal Def. Lawyers Assn., Dauphin County Bar (bd. dirs. 2006—), VFW (life), Am. Legion (life), Loyal Order of Moose, Chi Gamma Iota, Delta Tau Kappa. Republican. Roman Catholic. Avocations: motorcycles, music, electronics, martial arts. Office: 6059 Allentown Blvd Harrisburg PA 17112-2672

SHELDON, MARK, assistant dean; b. Camp Blanding, Fla., Dec. 17, 1944; s. Marvin and Georgianna Sheldon; children: Ivan, Noah. AB, Shimer Coll., Ill., 1968; PhD, Brandeis U., Mass., 1975; Sachar Fellow, Wadham Coll., Oxford U., Eng., 1973. Prof. philosophy Ind. U., Gary, Ill., 1982—2002; sr. policy analyst AMA, Chgo.; asst. dean, sr. lectr. Northwestern U., Evanston, Ill., 2002—. Med. ethics cons. Rush U. Med. Ctr., Chgo., 1986—. Contbr. articles various profl. jours., chapters to books, Adv., program on genetics Ill. Humanities Coun., Chgo., 2005—. 2nd lt US Army, 1967—69. Recipient Sachar award, Brandeis U., 1972-73. Mem.: Am. Philos. Assn. (co-editor, newsletter on philosophy and medicine 2000). D-Liberal. Jewish. Avocations: reading, music. Home: 611 Sheridan Rd Evanston IL 60202 Office: Northwestern U 1922 Sheridan Rd Evanston IL 60208 Home Phone: 847-328-2739; Office Phone: 847-491-8918. Business E-Mail: sheldon@northwestern.edu.

SHELDON, ROBERT, composer; b. Chester, Pennsylvania, Feb. 3, 1954; s. Robert and June (Burnett) Sheldon; 1 child, Marie. MusB in edn., U. Miami, Coral Gables, Fla., 1975; MFA, U. Fla., Gainesville, 1980. Cert. tchr. secondary music Ill. Dir. instrumental music N. Shore H. S., W. Palm Beach, Fla., 1975—79; condr. Alachua County Youth Orch., Gainesville, Fla., 1979—83; dir. of bands P. K. Yonge Lab. Sch., Gainesville, Fla., 1980—83; dir. instrumental music South East H.S., Bradenton, Fla., 1983—89; asst. prof. music Fla. State U., Tallahassee, 1989—91; dir. of bands East Peoria Cmty. H.S., Ill., 1991—. Composer C. L. Barnhouse Co., Oskaloosa, Iowa, 1980—; dir. Marching Chiefs Fla. State U., Tallahassee, 1989—91; composer, concert band editor Alfred Pub. Co., Van Nuys, Calif., 1997—; composer F.J. H. Music, Ft. Lauderdale, Fla., 2002—03. Author: (text book) The Complete Woodwind Instr., 1996; composer: (for concert band) Divertimento, 1976 (Am. Sch. Band Dirs. Assn. Volkwein Composition award, 1976), Fall River Overture, 1981, Intrada for Winds, 1983, (concert band) A Bayside Portrait, 1984, Mark of Triumph, 1985, Manatee Lyric Overture, 1986, Sandcastle Sketches, 1987, Southwest Saga, 1987, Bristol Bay Legend, 1988, Fanfare and Intermezzo, 1988, Crest of Nobility, 1989, Danse Celestiale, 1989, Ocean Ridge Rhapsody, 1989, Eagle Mountain Overture, 1990, Visions of Flight, 1990, The Corsair's Landing, 1991, Lindbergh Variations, 1991, Spirit Lake Overture, 1991, Silver Spring Soliloquy, 1992, A Symphonic Narrative, 1992, Willow Grove, 1992, Four Winds Overture, 1993, Pevensey Castle, 1993, West Highlands Sojourn, 1993, Images, 1994, Lost Colony, 1994, Red Rock Canyon, 1994, Appalachian Legacy, 1995, Voices from the Battlefield, 1995, Cold Water Creek, 1996, In the Shining of the Stars, 1996, Legend of Starved Rock, 1996, Prairiescape, 1996, Cape Fear Chronicles, 1997, Of Kindred Spirit, 1997, Century Point, 1998, A Lantern in the Window, 1998, A Longford Legend, 1998, Storybrook Mountain, 1999, Beyond the Higher Skies, 1999, The Crossings, 1999, N. W. Rising, 1999, Spoon River, 1999, Chanteys, 2000, Let Evening Come, 2000, The Pioneer's Passage, 2000, Prelude on an Old English Hymn, 2000, Garden of the Black Rose, 2001, Gently Touch the Sky, 2001, Ghost Fleet, 2001, Hill Country Holiday, 2001, Infinite Horizons, 2001, Ritmico, 2001, A Simple Celebration, 2001, Winds of Morocco, 2001, Barrier Reef, 2002, Brule River Celebration, 2002, Chiaroscuro: Symphonic Dances in Shades of Darkness and Light, 2002, Christmastimes Three, 2002, A Joyful Journey, 2002, (concert band) Quixotic Episode, 2002, Rock Island Trail, 2002, In This Quiet Pl., 2003, Phrygian Phantasy, 2003, Blaze of Glory, 2003, others. Named Outstanding Internat. Bandmaster, Phi Beta Mu, 1990; recipient Stanbury award for the outstanding young band dir., Am. Sch. Band Dir. Assn., 1985. Mem.: Am. Soc. Composers, Authors, and Pub. (Std. Award of Excellence in Composition 1988—2004), Music Educators Nat. Conf., Phi Mu Alpha Sinfonia. Avocations: travel, music, art. Office Phone: 309-454-6628. Personal E-mail: robertsheldon@hotmail.com.

SHELDON, ROY ALBERT, literature and language professor; b. Elyria, Ohio, Mar. 1, 1948; s. Floyd Carl Sheldon and Elsie Emma Rehg; 1 child, Emily Rose. BA summa cum laude, Kent State U., Ohio, 1974; MA, Bowling Green U., Ohio, 1976; PhD, Purdue U., West Lafayette, Ind., 1982. Grad. tchg. asst. Bowling Green U., 1974—76, Purdue U., 1976—81, instr., 1981—82; asst. prof. English Franklin Coll., Ind., 1982—83, Washburn U., Topeka, 1983—89, assoc. prof. English, 1989—. Bus. writing cons., Topeka, 1984—. Editor: Business Writing Samples, 1993, Business Writing Guidelines, 1995, Grammar and Writing Exercises, 1998. Named Outstanding Undergrad. Alumnus, Kent State U., 2005; recipient Scholarship Recognition award, Washburn U. Student Assn., 1990—91. Mem.: Popular Culture Assn., Am. Mensa Ltd. (proctor 1993—), Phi Kappa Phi. Avocations: genealogy, coin collecting/numismatics. Office: Washburn U 1700 SW College Topeka KS 66621

SHELDON, STEPHEN, pediatric sleep medicine educator, researcher; b. Miami Beach, Fla., Nov. 4, 1947; s. Murray M. and Sally (Lee) Sheldon; m. Rebecca Sheldon, May 17, 1996; children: David Patrick, Susan Victoria, Mara Elyn, Amy Michel. BS, U. Fla., 1969; DO, Chgo. Coll. Osteo. Medicine, 1975. Diplomate Am. Bd. Physicians and Surgeons, Am. Bd. Sleep Medicine, Am. Bd. Pediat. Resident in pediatrics Rush-Presbyn.-St. Luke's Med. Ctr., Chgo., 1975-78, chief pediatric resident, 1977-78, coord. pediatric residency, 1978-80, dir. pediatric residency, 1980-83; dir. pediatric research Mt. Sinai Hosp. Med. Ctr., Chgo., 1983-85; chmn. dept. pediatrics Chgo. Coll. Osteo. Medicine, 1985—. Cons. pediatrician Rush-Presbyn.-St. Lukes Med. Ctr., 1983—; prof. pediat. Feinberg Sch. Medicine Northwestern U., 2006—; assoc. dept. neurology U. Chgo., 1986—. Author: Pediatric Differential Diagnosis, 1979, 1986, Manual of Practical Pediatrics, 1981, Diagnosis and Management of the Hospitalized Child, 1984, Pediatric Sleep Medicine, 1992, Atlas of Sleep Medicine in Infants and Children, 1999, Evaluating Sleep in Infants and Children, 1996; sr. editor: Principles and Practice of Pediatric Sleep Medicine. Fellow: Am. Acad. Pediat. (cert. merit 1985); mem.: AMA, Ambulatory Pediatric Assn., Am. Acad. Sleep Medicine. Avocations: painting, ship building, cabinetry, writing, photography. Business E-Mail: ssheldon@northwestern.edu.

SHELDON, TERRY EDWIN, lawyer, investment advisor; b. Sacramento, June 22, 1945; s. Earl M. and Christine M. S.; m. Jan L. Winters, Aug. 26, 1966; children: Jeffrey, Tiffini, Melissa. BS magna cum laude, Abilene Christian U., 1967; JD, So. Meth. U., 1970. Bar: Calif. 1970. Assoc. Bronson, Bronson & McKinnon, San Francisco, 1970-74; gen. counsel, also dir. Consol. Capital Cos., Emeryville, Calif., 1974-83, exec. v.p., chief oper. officer, 1984-85, cons., advisor, 1986-87; pres., trustee Consol. Capital Spl. Trust, 1980-85; exec. v.p., trustee Consol. Capital Realty Investors, 1975-85, Consol. Capital Income Trust, 1978-85, Consol. Capital Income Opportunity Trust, 1983-85, Consol. Capital Income Opportunity Trust 2, 1985; chmn. Nat. Syndication Forum (a div. of RESSI), 1981-82; real estate securities specialist RESSI. V.p., prin. Alpha Venture Corp., Walnut Creek, Calif., 1987; bus. cons., 1988—. Chmn. bd. visitors adv. com. Coll. of Bus. Adminstrn. Abilene Christian U., 1990. Mem. ABA, Calif. Bar Assn., Nat. Assn. Securities Dealers (direct participation programs com., real estate com., standing adv. com. to bd. govs. 1980-83), Nat. Syndication Forum. Republican. Mem. Ch. of Christ.

SHELDON-MORRIS, TIFFINI ANNE, clinical psychologist, consultative examiner; b. Berkeley, Calif., Apr. 20, 1976; d. Terry E. and Jan L. Sheldon; m. John Christopher Morris, Aug. 6, 2000. BS in Psychology, Abilene Christian U., 1997; MS in Psychology, Fla. Inst. Tech., 2001, D of Psychology, 2001. Licensed Clinical Psychologist Tex., 2004. Postdoctoral fellow Houston Veterans Affairs Med. Ctr., Houston, 2001—02; team leader and counselor Sr. Connections, Houston, 2003—04; clin. psychologist VeriCare, 2004—. Consultative examiner Dept. of Assistive and Rehabilitative Svcs., Austin, Tex., 2004—. Active mem. Monterey Ch. Christ, Lubbock, Tex., 2004—. Scholar Grad. Student Tchg. Assistantship, Fla. Inst. of Tech., 1998-2000. Mem.: APA, Alpha Kappa Delta Internat. Hon. Soc., Alpha Chi Nat. Honor Soc., Girls Aiming Toward Achievement. Avocations: travel, reading, swimming, music, theater. Home: 6508 89th St Lubbock TX 79424 Office: VeriCare 4715 Viewridge Ave Ste 230 San Diego CA 92123 Home Phone: 806-577-3050; Office Phone: 806-577-3050. Office Fax: 800-819-1655; Home Fax: 806-698-8994. Personal E-mail: drtiffini@yahoo.com.

SHELITE, LESLIE MICHELLE, middle school educator; d. Joyce Merle Oakes and Chester Henry Shelite; children: Chandra Dawn Murrow, Cynthea Diane Baker, Caleb Tip Murrow. BS, Northwestern Okla. State U., 1993; MS, US Sports Acad., 1994. Cert. tchr. Okla. State Dept. Edn., 1993. Vocat. svc. mgr. Arrowhead West, Inc., Medicine Lodge, Kans., 1994—97; case mgr. Okla. Dept. Corrections, 1997—98; tchr. South Barber Pubic Schs., Kiowa, Kans., 1998—99, Okla. City Pub. Schs., 1999—2000, Putnam City Pub. Schs., 2000—. Named Nat. Honor Soc. Tchr., 2006; recipient Tchr. of Yr., Mayfield Mid. Sch., 2005, Mayfield Tchr. of Yr., 2006; grantee Schools for Healthy Lifestyles, Okla. Med. Assn., Schools for Healthy Lifestyles, 2000—01. Mem.: Okla. Sci. Tchr.'s Assn., Okla. Secondary Schools Activities Assn., PCACT (bldg. rep. 2005—07), NEA, OEA. D-Conservative. Christian. Avocation: walking. Home: 1200 Glenwood Dr Yukon OK 73099 Office: Mayfield Mid Sch 1600 N Purdue Oklahoma City OK 73127 Home Phone: 405-354-1152; Office Phone: 405-947-8693.

SHELKROT, ELLIOT L., library director; b. Pitts., June 24, 1943; m. Evelyn Minick; children: Benjamin, Max, Daniel. BA, Oberlin Coll., 1965; MLS, U. Pitts., 1966. Trainee Pa. State Libr., 1965-66; branch head, young adult svcs. librarian Free Libr. Phila., 1966-69, pres., dir., 1987—; specialist cmty. svcs. divsn. libr. devel. Md. State Dept. Edn., 1969-76; chief pub. svcs. support Balt County Pub. Libr., 1976-80; state librarian Commonwealth Pa., 1980-87. Mayor's commn. literacy, 1987-99; bd. dirs. Ctr. Literacy, trustee, 1987-00. Mem. Mayor's Cultural Adv. Coun., 1987-92, Ben Franklin Pkwy. Coun., 1997—, chair, 2000; mem. Phila. Citizens Children and Youth, 1997—, Greater Phila. Urban Affairs Coun., 1998—, Greater Phila. Cultural Alliance, 1999—; bd. dirs. Fellowship Commn., 1989-92, Nat. Conf. Christians & Jews, 1991-94. Mem. ALA (coun. 1972-78, 83-91, intellectual freedom com. 1975-79, nat. libr. week com. 1983-85, councilor at large 1988-91, legis. com. 1989-91), Urban Libr. Coun. (bd. dirs. 1997—, pres. 2000—), Pub. Libr. Assn. (goals, guidelines and stds. task force com. 1979-83, dir.-at-large, new stds. task force 1983-86, v.p., rsch. com. 1983-84, pres. 1991-93), Assn. Specialized Coop. Libr. Agys. (legis. com. 1982-85, chair 1984-85, bd. dirs. 1985-91), Chief Officers State Libr. Agys. (chair com. liaison Nat. Commn. Libr. Info. Sci. 1981-85, bd. dirs. 1983-84), Pa. Libr. Assn. Avocations: clarinet, biking, reading, skiing. Office: Free Libr Phila 1901 Vine St Philadelphia PA 19103-1189 Office Phone: 215-686-5300. E-mail: shelkrote@library.phila.gov. *

SHELL, ART (ARTHUR SHELL JR.), former professional football coach; b. Charleston, SC, Nov. 26, 1946; m. Janice Shell; children: Arthur III, Christopher. BS in Industrial Arts, Md. State Coll., 1968. Offensive lineman Oakland Raiders, 1968—81, L.A. Raiders, 1982, asst. coach, 1983-89, head coach, 1989-94; offensive line coach Kans. City Chiefs, 1995-96, Atlanta Falcons, 1997—2000; appeals officer NFL, 2001—04, sr. v.p. football ops. & devel., 2004—06; head coach Oakland Raiders, 2006. Inducted into Pro Football Hall of Fame, 1989; recipient, Jackie Robinson Award for Athletics (Ebony mag.), 1990; named All-Pro, 1973, 1974, 1976, 1977; named to Pro Bowl, 1972-78, 1980; named NFL Coach of Yr., 1991 member of two Super Bowl Champion teams with Oakland Raiders, 1977, 1981; the first African-American to become an NFL head coach, 1989.

SHELL, OWEN G., JR., retired bank executive; b. Greenville, SC, June 19, 1936; s. Owen and Katherine S.; m. Mary Ruth Trammell, Aug. 9, 1980; children: Katherine Sloan, Mary Carroll, Robert Owen, James Walker. BS, U. S.C., 1960; postgrad., Stonier Grad. Sch. Banking, 1971; grad., Advanced Mgmt. Program, Harvard U., 1979. V.p. Citizens & So. Nat. Bank S.C., Columbia, 1968-71, sr. v.p., 1971-74, exec. v.p., 1974-79; pres., dir., chief exec. officer First Am. Nat. Bank, Nashville, 1979-86; vice chmn. bd., dir. First Am. Corp., 1979-86; chmn., pres., chief exec. officer Sovran Bank/Tenn., Nashville, 1986-91; pres. Nations Bank of Tenn. (formerly Sovran Bank), Nashville, 1992-96; pres. asset mgmt. group NationsBank Corp., St. Louis, 1997-99; pres. Asset Mgmt. Bank of Am., Charlotte, 1997—2002; ret., 2002. Bd. dirs. Nashville br. Fed. Res. Bank, Atlanta, Ctrl. Parkine, Inc., chmn. bd., Lifepoint Hosp. Inc. Chmn. Leadership Nashville, Tenn. Performing Arts Found., Mid. Tenn. coun. Boy Scouts Am., Vanderbilt U. Owen Grad. Sch. Mgmt.; trustee Met. Nashville Pub. Edn. Found.; chmn. bd. INROADS/Nashville; bd. dirs. Tenn. Bus. Roundtable, Tenn. Tomorrow. Mem.: Assn. Res. City Bankers, Old Warson Country Club (St. Louis), Harvard Club N.Y.C., Belle Meade Country Club (Nashville), Kappa Alpha. Presbyterian. Home: 4412 Chickering Ln Nashville TN 37215-4915 also: 114 Tern Dr Anna Maria FL 34216

SHELL, ROBERT EDWARD LEE, photographer, writer; b. Roanoke, Va., Dec. 3, 1946; s. James Ralph and Mary (Terry) S.; m. Darlene Bridget. Student, Va. Poly. Inst. and State U., 1965—68, Elkins Inst., 1972, Nat. Camera Inst., 1973. Staff Smithsonian Inst., Washington, 1968—72; photographer Sta. WBRA-Pub. TV, Roanoke, 1972—74; owner Camera, Inc., Salem, Va., 1974—76; photographer, technician Gentry Studios, Blacksburg, Va., 1976—81; tech. editor Shutterbug Mag., Patch Comm., Radford, Va., 1984—91, editor Titusville, Fla., 1991—98, Primedia Spl. Interest Mags., 1998—; U.S. corr. Asahi Camera, Tokyo, 1986—, Color Foto, Munich, 1989—, Photo Answers, England; pub. PIC Mag., England, 1994—96. Tech. photographic cons. Eastman Kodak Co., 1997—, Nat. Geog. Soc., 1999—. Author: Photography with Canon EOS System, 1990, Hasselblad Camera System Guide, 1991, Mamiya Camera System Guide, 1992, Photo Business Careers, 1992, Canon Compendium, 1994, Metz Flash System Handbook, 1994, Olympus IS System Handbook, 1994, Canon Rebel Handbook, 1994, Canon EOS-3 Handbook, 1999, Canon Rebel 2000 Handbook, 1999, The Hand Exposure Meter Book, 1999, Mamiya Camera System Guide, 2000, Canon EOS-3, 2000, Canon Flash System Guide, 2000, Canon EOS-1V, 2000, Canon Compendium, 2d edit., 2004, The Complete Idiot's Guide to Digital Photography Like a Pro, 2005, Complete Idiot's Guide to Massage Illustrated, 2006, 18 other books on photography, 1994-99; tech. editor numerous publs; contbr. articles to profl. jours. Smithsonian Inst. grantee, Washington, 1968. Mem. Photo Mktg. Assn. Internat., German Photographers Soc., Megapress, Profl. Photographers of Am. Avocations: painting, drawing, classic automobiles. Home and Office: Bob Shell Photography 1601 Grove Ave Radford VA 24141-1624 E-mail: bob@bobshell.com.

SHELL, ROBERT J., construction executive; b. Honolulu, Oct. 16, 1930; s. Roscoe and Gladys Rose (Callahan) Shell; m. Virginia Louise Brooks, Apr. 7, 1973; children: Linda Shell Squires, Vickie Doss, Scott, Cathy Gammill, Allison Nelson. Grad. high sch., Little Rock, 1947. Project mgmt. acct. The Baldwin Co., Little Rock, 1950-61, sec., treas., 1961-76, exec. v.p., 1976-83, pres., 1983—, also bd. dirs.; pres. Baldwin & Shell Constrn., Little Rock, 1980—. Chmn. Little Rock Censor Bd., 1969, Little Rock Bd. Adjustment, 1979; pres. Pulaski Acad., Little Rock, 1984—85, Ark. Arthritis Assn., 1991—; treas. Metro YMCA; bd. dirs., pres. Bapt. Med. Sys. Found.; pres. 50 for the Future, 2000; charter mem. Ark. Constrn. Hall of Fame, 2000; chmn. found. bd. U. Ark., Little Rock, 2004; bd. dirs. Twin City Bank. Mem.: Associated Gen. Contractors Am. (nat. bd. dirs. 1982—, Disting. Svc. award 1984, Ark. Bus. Exec. of the Yr. 1991), Am. Inst. Constructors, Am. Arbitration Assn., Alzheimer Ark. (bd. dirs. 1999—), Pleasant Valley Country Club (Little Rock) (sec. 1985—86). Baptist. Home: 4 Bretagne Cir Little Rock AR 72223-9136 Office: Baldwin & Shell Constrn 523 Ringo PO Box 1750 Little Rock AR 72203-1750 Office Phone: 501-374-8677.

SHELLER, JOHN WILLARD, lawyer; b. LA, Oct. 29, 1950; s. Willard and Barbara S.; m. Mary Elizabeth Hodor, Aug. 9, 1975; children: Matthew John, James Henry. BA, Stanford U., 1972; JD, Loyola U., LA, 1975. Bar: Calif. 1975. Ptnr. in charge Hinshaw & Culbertson, LA. Mem. Am. Bd.

Trial Advs. Contbr. articles to profl. jours. Mem. Calif. State Bar Assn., LA County Bar Assn., LA Country Club. Avocation: golf. Office: Hinshaw & Culbertson 11601 Wilshire Blvd Ste 800 Los Angeles CA 90025 Home: 16 Park Ave Venice CA 90291-3222 Home Phone: 310-392-3700; Office Phone: 310-909-8000. Business E-Mail: jsheller@hinshawlaw.com.

SHELLEY, BONNIE J., retired voice educator; b. Sullivan, Mo., Nov. 15, 1926; d. Earl William Sperry and Erma Laura Trout; m. Peter Lipkan (dec.); children: Kathleen, Michael, Christopher, Charissa, Brian; m. Clark C. Shelley (dec.); m. Dean F. Hollister, Nov. 15, 1990. MusB, U. Ariz., Tucson, 1965; MA in Music, Calif. State U., Fullerton, 1976. Adj. prof. voice Yavapai Coll., Prescott, Ariz., 1986—93, 1998—2007, No. Ariz. U., Flagstaff, 1989—93; ret., 2007. Youth choir dir. St. Francis Episcopal Ch., Palos Verdes, Calif., 1982—85; choir dir., bell dir. 1st Congl. Ch./St. Lukes Episcopal, Prescott, 1989—93, Prescott, 1994—96; choir dir. United Meth. Ch., Prescott Valley, 2000—05, Mingus View Presbyn. Ch., 2005—. Mem.: Nat. Assn. Tchrs. Singing. Home: 5325 N Bremont Way Prescott Valley AZ 86314

SHELLEY, CAROLE, actress; b. London, Aug. 16, 1939; arrived in U.S., 1964; d. Curtis and Deborah (Bloomstein) Shelley; m. Albert G. Woods, July 26, 1967 (dec.). Student, Arts Ednl. Sch., 1943-56, Prepatory Acad. Royal Acad. Dramatic Art, 1956-57; studies with Iris Warren and Eileen Thorndike. Trustee Am. Shakespeare Theatre, 1974—82. Actor: (plays) The Odd Couple, 1965, Absurd Person Singular, 1973, The Norman Conquests (L.A. Drama Critics Cir. award, 1975), As You Like It, King Lear, She Stoops to Conquer, 1972, The Country Wife, 1973, A Doll's House, Man and Superman, 1977, Misalliance, 1980, Grand Hunt, 1980, The Play's the Thing, 1978, Lion in Winter, 1987, The Elephant Man (Outer Critics Cir. award, 1979, Tony award for Best Actress, 1979), What the Butler Saw, 1989, Broadway Bound, 1987—88, Lettice and Lovage, 1989—90, The Miser, 1990, Cabaret Verboten, 1991, The Destiny of Me, 1992—93, Later Life, 1993 (Outer Critics nominee), Richard II, 1994, London Suite, 1995, Show Boat, 1995—96, 1998, The Film Society, 1997, The Last Night of Ballyhoo, 1997—98, Cabaret, 1999—2002, Wicked, 2002—04, 2005—, The Importance of Being Earnest, 2005—, Ring Round the Moon, 2006; (films) The Boston Strangler, The Odd Couple, 1968, The Super, 1990, Devlin, 1991, Quiz Show, 1993, The Road to Wellville, 1993, Bewitched, 2005, others; (TV series) The Odd Couple, 1965, Robin Phillips Grand Theatre Co., 1983—84, Nat. Co. The Royal Family (L.A. Drama Critics Cir. award, 1977); (Broadway plays) Noises Off, 1985, Stepping Out, 1986 (Tony nominee, 1986), Waltz of the Toreadors, 1986, Oh Coward, 1986—87, Broadway Bound, 1987—88; voice actor: (films) Robin Hood; The Aristocats; Hercules. Recipient Obie award for Twelve Dreams, N.Y. Shakespeare Festival, 1982. Jewish. Office: Robert Duva 277 W 10th St New York NY 10014 Office Phone: 212-807-8344.

SHELLEY, CLYDE BURTON, artist; b. Murphy, Tex., Mar. 21, 1922; s. Jesse Dewey and Florrie Elizabeth (Eldridge) S.; m. Freddie Lavern Mitchell, Aug. 31, 1946 (dec. Aug. 1978); m. Grace Rosamond Muder, Dec. 24, 1979. Student, Ohio Weslayan U., 1944-45, Art Ctr. Sch., LA, 1957-58. Artist Interstate Theatres, Inc., Dallas, 1941-42, Oakite Products, NYC, 1946-47; cartoonist Reddy Kilowatt, Inc., NYC, 1947-50; freelance cartoonist, comml. artist NYC, 1950-52, Dallas, 1952-55, LA, 1955-56, Las Vegas, 1970-75; comml. artist Northrup Corp., Hawthorne, Calif., 1956-59; indsl. illustrator Douglas Aircraft Corp., Long Beac, El Segondo, Calif., 1959-62; comml. artist Nortronics, Palos Verdes, Calif., 1962-64; sr. illustrator Holmes & Narver, Inc., Honolulu, 1964-70, Las Vegas, 1964-70; sr. artist Houston Post Newspaper, 1975-87. One man shows at First City Nat. Bank, 1985, 87; exhibited in group shows at Clampitt Paper Co., Houston, 1985, Sportsman's Gallery, Galleria, Houston, 1986, Marriott Hotel, Houston, 1990, Lone Star Restaurant, Houston, 1991-92, CMR Gallery, Corpus Christi, Tex., 1994, 96; contbr. cartoons Am. Mag., Bluebook Mag., King Features Syndicate, AT&T, Las Vegas Sun, Las Vegas Rev./Jour., others; caricaturist Mem. Houston World Affairs Coun., 1996—. With U.S. Navy, 1942-46. Mem. Houston Mus. Fine Arts, Braeburn Valley West Civic Club, Am. Legion. Avocations: running, physical fitness, reading, politics, world affairs. Home and Office: 9443 Portal Dr Houston TX 77031-2212

SHELLEY, HERBERT CARL, lawyer; b. Stamford, Tex., Jan. 28, 1947; s. Carl B. and Lourena A. (Whitley) S.; m. Jerilyn S. Ray, Aug. 9, 1969; children: Megan, Caitlyn, Daniel. BA, Columbia Coll., 1969; JD, Vanderbilt U., 1972; LLM in Internat. and Comparative Law magna cum laude, Vrije U. Brussels, 1973. Bar: D.C. 1973, Md. 1985, U.S. Ct. Appeals (fed. cir.) 1981, U.S. Ct. Internat. Trade 1982, U.S. Supreme Ct. 1987. Atty./adv. U.S. Tariff Commn., Washington, 1973-74; Internat. trade specialist, asst. Office dir. Office Tariff Affairs U.S. Dept. Treasury, Washington, 1974-76; internat. trade negotiator Office Spl. Trade Reps., Geneva, Switzerland, 1976-79; ptnr. Plaia & Schaumberg, Washington, 1979-86, Howrey & Simon, Washington, 1986-99, Steptoe & Johnson LLP, Washington, 1999—. Mem. ABA, D.C. Bar Assn., Md. Bar Assn. Avocations: skiing, golf, cooking, travel. Office: 1330 Connecticut Ave NW Washington DC 20036-1704 Home Phone: 301-299-1832; Office Phone: 202-429-8146. Business E-Mail: hshelley@steptoe.com.

SHELLEY, KEVIN FRANCIS, former state official; b. Washington, Nov. 16, 1955; s. John Francis and Thelma (Smith) Shelley; m. Dominique Shelley; 1 child, Jack. BA in Polit. Sci., U. Calif., Davis, 1978; JD, Hastings Coll. Law, 1983. Asst. to U.S. Congressman Phil Burton US Ho. Reps., 1978—87; mem. bd. suprs., pres. bd. San Francisco Bd. Suprs., 1990—96; mem., majority leader Calif. State Assembly, 1996—2002; sec. state State of Calif., 2003—05; atty. Calif., 2005—. Mem.: Calif. State Bar.

SHELLEY, WALTER BROWN, dermatologist, educator; b. St. Paul, Feb. 6, 1917; s. Patrick K. and Alfaretta (Brown) S.; m. Marguerite H. Weber, 1942 (dec.); children: Peter B., Anne E. Kiselewich, Barbara A. (dec.); m. E. Dorinda Loeffel, 1980; children: Thomas R., Katharine D., William L. BS, U. Minn., 1940, PhD, 1941, MD, 1943; MA honoris causa, U. Pa., 1971; MD honoris causa, U. Uppsala, Sweden, 1977; DSc (hon.), Med. U. Ohio, 2006. Diplomate: Am. Bd. Dermatology (pres. 1968-69, dir. 1960-69). Instr. physiology U. Pa., Phila., 1946-47, asst. instr. dermatology and syphilology, 1947-49, asst. prof. dermatology, 1950-53, assoc. prof., 1953-57, prof., 1957-80, chmn. dept., 1965-80; prof. dermatology U. Ill. Peoria Sch. Medicine, 1980-83; prof. medicine (dermatology) Med. Coll. Ohio, 1983-97, emeritus prof. medicine, 1997—. Instr. dermatology Dartmouth Coll., 1949-50; Regional cons. dermatology VA, 1955-59; mem. com. on cutaneous system NRC, 1955-59, Commn. Cutaneous Diseases, Armed Forces Epidemiological Bd., 1958-61, dep. dir., 1959-61; cons. dermatology Surgeon Gen. USAF, 1958-61, U.S. Army, 1958-61; mem. NRC, 1961-64 Author (with Crissey): Classics in Clinical Dermatology, 1953, 2003; author: (with Pillsbury, Kligman) Dermatology, 1956; author: Cutaneous Medicine, 1961; author: (with Hurley) The Human Apocrine Sweat Gland in Health and Disease, 1960; author: (with Botelho and Brooks) The Endocrine Glands, 1969; author: Consultations in Dermatology with Walter B. Shelley, 1972, 2006, Consultations II, 1974; author: (with Shelley) Advanced Dermatologic Therapy, 1987; author: Advanced Dermatologic Diagnosis, 1992, A Century of International Dermatological Congresses, 1992, Advanced Dermatogical Therapy II, 2001, Shelley's 77 Skins, 2001, Consultations in Dermatology, 2006; mem. editl. bd. Jour. Investigative Dermatology, 1961—64, Archives of Dermatology, 1961—62, Skin and Allergy News, 1970—93, Excerpta Medica Dermatologica, 1960—, Cutis, 1972—, Jour. Geriatric Dermatol, 1993; assoc. editor: Jour. Cutaneous Pathology, 1972—81; editl. cons. Medcom, 1972—. Served as capt. M.C. AUS, 1944-46. Recipient Spl. award Soc. Cosmetic Chemists, 1955, Hellerstrom medal, 1971, Am. Med. Writers Assn. Best Med. Book award, 1973, Dohi medal, 1981, Rothman medal Soc. for Investigative Dermatology, 1987, Rose Hirschler award, 1990, Humane Dermatologist award, 2005. Master ACP; fellow Assn. Am. Physicians, St. John's Dermatol. Soc. London (hon.); mem. AMA (chmn. residency rev. com. for dermatology 1963-67, chmn. sect. dermatology 1969-71), Assn. Profs. Dermatology (pres. 1972-73), Pacific Dermatol. Assn. (hon.), Am. Dermatol. Assn. (hon., dir., pres. 1975-76), Soc. Investigative Dermatology (hon. pres. 1961-62), Am. Physiol. Soc., Phila. Physiol. Soc., Brit. Dermatol. Soc. (hon.), Phila. Dermatol. Soc. (pres. 1960-61), Mich. Dermatol. Soc., Ohio Dermatol. Soc. (hon.), Am. Acad. Dermatology (Gold medal 1992, hon. pres. 1971-72), Pa. Acad. Dermatology (pres. 1972-73), Am. Soc. Dermatologic Surgery, N.Am. Clin. Dermatol. Soc. (hon.), Noah Worcester Dermatol. Soc., Royal Soc. Medicine; corr. mem. Nederlandse Vereniging Van Dermatologen, Israeli Dermatol. Assn., Finnish Soc. Dermatology, Swedish Dermatol. Soc., French Dermatologic Soc.; fgn. hon. mem. Danish Dermatol. Assn., Japanese Dermatol. Assn., Dermatol. Soc. S.Africa, Austrian Dermatol. Soc. Home: 21171 W River Rd Grand Rapids OH 43522-9703 Office: U Toledo Coll Medicine 3000 Arlington Ave Toledo OH 43614 Home Phone: 419-832-0648; Office Phone: 419-383-3720. Business E-Mail: walter.shelley@utoledo.edu.

SHELLMAN-LUCAS, ELIZABETH C., special education educator, researcher; b. Thomas County, Ga., Feb. 5, 1937; d. Herbert and Juanita (Coleman) Smith; m. John Lee Lucas, Jr. (dec.); 1 child, Sandie Juanita Lucas Boyce; m. Eddie Joseph Shellman; 1 child, Eddie Joseph Shellman, Jr. MS in Edn., CUNY, 1990. Cert. tchr. NY. Pvt. practice cosmetologist, NYC, 1959—; tchr. N.Y.C. Bd. of Edn. High Sch. Dist., 1984—. Vol. various cmty. orgns.; citizen amb. del. People to People Internat., 1994; ch. sch. tchr., supt. Canaan Bapt. Ch., Harlem, 1990-2002. Mem. Coun. for Exceptional Children. Avocations: reading, music, dance, jogging, languages.

SHELLY, NICHOLAS J., military officer, international relations scholar; s. Dave and Pat S. BA in Computer Sci., US Air Force Acad., Colo., 2007; student, German Air Force Acad.; MS student in Internat. Rels., Oxford Univ., 2007—. Rhodes Scholar. Achievements include presenting rsch. at nat. computer sci. conference. *

SHELOV, STEVEN PATRICK, pediatrician, educator; b. Honolulu, Nov. 19, 1944; s. Sidney M. and Faith R. S.; m. Marsha Liberman, Aug. 30, 1968; children: Joshua, Danielle, Eric. BS, Yale, 1966; MD, Med. Coll. Wisc., 1971; MS in Med. Admin., U. Wisc., 1995. Diplomate Am. Bd. Pediatrics. Intern, then resident Montefiore Med. Ctr., Bronx, 1971-74, chief resident, 1974-75; asst. dir. amb. pediat. Albert Einstein Coll. Med., Bronx, NY, 1977-79; dir. pediat. edn. Montefiore Med. Ctr., Bronx, 1980—, prof. and vice chmn. pediat., 1989-97; chmn. pediat. Infants and Children's Hosp. of Bklyn., Maimonides Med. Ctr., Bklyn., 1997—; prof. Mt. Sinai Sch. Medicine. Editor: Caring for Your Baby and Young Child: Birth to 5, 1991, 1996, 2004, Pediatrics for Medical Students, 2003, Guide to Your Child's Symptoms, 1997, The First Year of Life, 2004. Recipient Geo. Armstrong award Ambulatory Pediat. Assn., 1996, Lifetime Achievement in Edn. award Am. Acad. Pediat., 2002. Mem.: Am. Acad. Pediats. (Holroyd-Sherry award 2004). Office: Maimonides Med Ctr 4802 10th Ave Brooklyn NY 11219-2844 Home Phone: 914-472-2714; Office Phone: 718-283-6150. Business E-Mail: sshelov@maimonidesmed.org.

SHELTON, CAROLYN JOHNSON, professional society administrator; d. Ernest Gustav Johnson and Anne Mabel Nemergut; m. Philo Sherwood Shelton, June 27, 1962; children: Philo Sherwood, Anne F. Mele. AS (hon.), U. Bridgeport, 1962. Dir. membership Conn. Audubon Soc., Fairfield, 1984—. V.p. Fairfield Women's Club, Conn., 1980—82. Recipient 10 Yr. Award for Volunteerism on the Four Seasons Ball Com. to raise money for the mentally challenged, The Kenndey Ctr., 10. Mem.: Greenfield Hill Garden Club. R-Consevative. Catholic. Achievements include design of Designed the pussy willow stencils and applied the stencils for a suite in a National Historic Restoration inn called the Inn at National Hall located in Westport, Conn. Home and Office: Conn Audubon Soc 2325 Burr St Fairfield CT 06824 Business E-Mail: cshelton@ctaudubon.org.

SHELTON, CRAIG, food service executive; b. Rye, NH; naturalized, U.S., naturalized, France; Trained with Joel Rubochon, trained with Ferran Adriá, trained with Paul Haeberlin. Chef Ma Maison, LA, Rainbow Rm., Le Chantilly, Le Bernardin, Bouley; chef, owner Ryland Inn, Whitehouse, NJ, 1991—. Named Relais Gourmand, Relais & Chateaux, 1999; recipient Best award Excellence, Wine Spectator's, 1994—, James Bears award, 2000. Mem.: N.J. Restaurant Assn. (bd. dirs.), Internat. Assn. Culinary Profls. Office: Ryland Inn Rt 22 W Whitehouse NJ 08888

SHELTON, DARLENE, psychologist, consultant; d. Harvey Clinton and Opal Lyles Shelton; m. David Weinberg, Oct. 10, 2003. BA in Psychology, So. Ill. U., 1979, MA in Psychology, 1986, PhD in Behavioral Medicine and Psychology, 1990. Lic. clin. psychologist State of Ky., State of Conn. Dir., coord. psychol. svcs. Econ. Opportunity Family Health Ctr., Miami, 1991—94; rsch. asst. prof. dept. psychiatry U. Miami Sch. Medicine, 1993—94; assoc. prof., dir. diversity and minority affairs Spalding U. Sch. Profl. Psychology, Louisville, 1995—2003; assoc. rsch. scientist dept. psychiatry Yale U. Sch. of Medicine, New Haven, 2003—04; CEO Ctr. for Humanitarian Initiatives, Guilford, Conn., 2004—; sr. fellow Garrison Inst., NY, 2005—; assoc. of the Chaplain's Office, Yale U., New Haven, 2006—. Rsch. cons. U.S. HHS, Pub. Health Svc., Health Resources and Svcs. Adminstrn., Bur. Health Resources Devel., Washington, 1991—93; forensic psychology cons. Thematix Group, Guilford, Conn., 2001—; program cons. Garrison Inst., Garrison, 2004—; rsch. cons. Ctr. for Women Policy Studies, Washington, 1993; mem. adv. com. Pediat. AIDS Health Care Demonstration Project of U. Miami/Jackson Meml. Hosp., 1992—94; grant reviewer Women's Initiative for HIV Care and Reduction of Perinatal HIV Transmission, Maternal and Child Health Bur., Health Resources and Svcs. Adminstrn., Rockville, Md., 1995; mem. Ky. HIV Prevention Cmty. Planning Group, State of Ky. Dept. of HIV Prevention, Frankfort, 1996—98; mem. African-Am. adv. com. Ky. HIV Prevention Cmty. Planning Group, State of Ky., Dept. HIV Prevention, Frankfort, 1996—98, advisor, 1998—99; psychol. cons. State of Fla. Dept. Juvenile Justice Dist. XI, Miami, 1994—95; rsch. cons. R.E.A.C.H., Louisville, 1995—96, Coun. on Prevention and Edn.: Substances, Inc. (COPES) Family Connection Demonstration Project, Louisville, 1996—2000; psychologist U. Louisville Sch. Medicine WINGS (HIV/AIDS) Clinic Aux. Support Team, Louisville, 1996—2000; co-process evaluator Ky. Incentives for Prevention, Louisville, 1997—2000; psychologist site supr. Americana Cmty. Ctr., Louisville, 1999—2003; adj. asst. prof. dept. psychology Barry U., Miami Shores, Fla., 1995; presenter, lectr., spkr. in field. Author: (nonfiction book) Babies Mamas, (booklet) Health Care Utilization and Medical Adherence Issues Among Prenatal HIV Seropositive African American Women in Miami: The Role of The Family and The Extended Kinship Networks.; panelist (television program) KENTUCKY TONIGHT: Coping Emotionally with the Aftermath of September 11th; author: (public service television script) Make Your Next Move Count, (public service TV script) Child Abuse: Sticks and Stones and Words Can Hurt; contbr. articles to scholarly jours. Mem. planning com. Ann. Nat. Conf. on the Black Family in Am., Louisville, 2001—03; judge panelist ABA Regional Client Counseling Competition, Louisville, 2002; facilitator One Louisville, 2001—02; bd. dirs. Ctr. for Haitian Studies, Miami, 1993—95. Named Outstanding Leader and Mentor, Spalding U. Black Student Assn., 1997, Nat. Inst. of Drug Abuse Sponsored Jr. Minority Investigator, APHA, 1992; recipient White Ho. Briefing Honoring World AIDS Day invitation, 2005, NIMH Postdoctoral fellowship in psychoimmunology, Ctr. for the Biopsychosocial Study of AIDS, Dept. Psychiatry, U. Miami Sch. of Medicine, 1990—91, Cert. Appreciation for Contbns. in Devel. of Creative AIDS Edn. Programs, U.S. Dept. VA, 1990, Ill. Minority Grad. Incentive Program fellowship, State of Ill., 1986—90, So. Ill. U. Grad. Dean's fellowship, 1984—85, Cert. of Appreciation, Omega Psi Phi, 1997, 1998, 1999, 2000; grantee Ongoing Program of Stress Mgmt. for Spl. Immunology Unit Staff., U.S. Dept. VA, Office Acad. Affairs, and Regional Med. Edn. Ctr., 1989, Five-year Plan for Ethnic Minority Recruitment, Retention and Tng. in Psychology, APA, 2002, Qualitative studies addressing the sexual behaviors and biopsychosocial issues of patients in the Women's HIV/AIDS Clinic at the U. of Miami, U. Miami Sch. of Medicine Ctr. for Comprehensive Study of HIV/AIDS, 1990—92; scholar Non-Traditional Student Scholarship award, Delta Sigma Theta, Carbondale Alumnae Chpt., 1989. Mem.: APA, Inst. Noetic Scis., Kentuckiana Assn. of Black Psychologists (pres. 2002—03), Ky. Psychol. Assn., Conn. Psychol. Assn. (ethnic diversity task force 2004, co-chair 2005—), Nature Conservancy. Achievements include research in Ethnographic Study of Miami-area HIV Positive Expectant Mothers with Previous Children. Office: Ctr for Humanitarian Initiatives Deep River Center 3 Taliar Ridge Rd Guilford CT 06437 Office Phone: 203-458-3244. E-mail: darlene.shelton@chiglobal.org.

SHELTON, DAVID HOWARD, economics professor; b. Winona, Miss., Nov. 30, 1928; s. Tuttle M. and Kate (Moss) S.; m. Margaret Murff, Feb. 4, 1951; children: David Keith, Sarah Katherine, Susan Esther. BA, Millsaps Coll., 1951; MA, Ohio State U., 1952, PhD, 1958. Instr. Ohio State U., 1958; asst. prof. U. Del., 1958-63, assoc. prof., 1963-65; prof. U. N.C., Greensboro, 1965—93, head dept. econs., bus. adminstrn., 1967-70, dean Sch. Bus. and Econs., 1970-83, head dept. econs., 1988-93, prof. emeritus, 1993—. Cons. Joint Coun. on Econ. Edn., 1969-72, N.C. Dept. Pub. Instrn., 1970-73. Trustee N.C. Coun. on Econ. Edn., 1971-96, chmn., 1971-75, pres., 1975-85. Served with USN, 1946-48. M.D. Lincoln fellow, 1956-57; H.L. and Grace Doherty fellow, 1957. Mem. Beta Gamma Sigma, Omicron Delta Kappa, Kappa Sigma. Episcopalian. Home: 3609 Dogwood Dr Greensboro NC 27403-1010 Office: UNC 462 Bryan Bldg Greensboro NC 27412-0001

SHELTON, DOROTHY DIEHL REES, lawyer; d. William Walter John and Hedwig Diehl; m. Charles W. Rees, Jr., June 15; children: Jane Rees Stebbins, John B. Rees, Anne Rees Slack, David C. Rees; m. Thomas C. Shelton, Mar. 4. BA in Music, Stanford Univ.; JD, Western State Univ. Coll. Law. Bar: Calif. U.S. Dist. Ct. (so. dist.). Pvt. practice, San Diego, 1977—. Mem.: ABA, Calif. State Bar, San Diego County Bar Assn., Consumer Attys. San Diego, Stanford U. Alumni Assn., Jr. League San Diego, Dachshund Club Am., Gt. Pyrenees Club Am., Nu Beta Epsilon. Avocations: gardening, reading, great pyrenees dogs. Office: 110 W C St Ste 711 San Diego CA 92101-3906

SHELTON, HILARY O., civil rights organization administration; b. St. Louis; m. Paula Young Shelton; 3 children. Grad. in Polit. Sci., Howard U., Washington; grad. in Comm., U. Mo., St. Louis; grad. in Legal Studies, Northeastern U., Boston. Fed. policy prog. dir. The Gen. Bd. of Ch. & Soc.; fed. liaison, asst. dir. to govt. affairs dept. of Coll. Fund United Negro Coll. Fund, Washington; dir. Washington bur. NAACP. Bd. dirs. Leadership Conf. Civil Rights, Ctr. Dem. Renewal, Coalition to Stop Gun Violence, Congl. Black Caucus Inst.; commr. Commn. on Safety and Abuse in Am.'s Prisons. Recipient Medgar W. Evers award for Excellence, Nat. NAACP, Civil Rights Leadership award, Israeli Embassy and Religious Action Ctr. of Reform Judaism, 2005, Congl. Black Caucus' Chmn.'s award. Office: NAACP 1156 15th St NW Ste 915 Washington DC 20005 Office Phone: 202-463-2940. Office Fax: 202-463-2953. *

SHELTON, HUGH (HENRY HUGH SHELTON), former Chairman of the Joint Chiefs of Staff; b. Tarboro, NC, Jan. 2, 1942; m. Carolyn L. Johnson; children: Jon, Jeff, Mark. BS, N.C. State U.; MS, Auburn U.; grad., Air Command and Staff Coll., Nat. War Coll. Commd. 2d lt. US Army, 1963, advanced through grades to gen., 1996, ret., 2001; with 5th Spl. Forces Group, Vietnam, 173d Airborn Brigade, Vietnam; comdr. 3d Bn., 60th Infantry, 9th Infantry Divsn., Ft. Lewis, asst. chief of staff for ops.; comdr. 1st Brigade, 82d Airborne Divsn., Ft. Bragg, N.C.; chief of staff 10th Mountain Divsn., Ft. Drum, N.Y.; with ops. directorate Joint Staff, Washington, 1987—89; asst. divsn. comdr. for ops., 101st Airborne Divsn., Joint Staff, The Pentagon, 1989-91; comdr. 82d Airborne Divsn., Ft. Bragg, N.C., XVIIIth Airborne Corps., 1993, US Spl. Ops. Command, 1996—97; chmn. Joint Chiefs of Staff, US Dept. Def., Washington, 1997—2001; pres., internat. ops. M.I.C. Industries, 2002—06. Bd. dirs. Anheuser-Busch Companies Inc., 2001—, Anteon Internat. Corp., 2002—06, Red Hat, Inc., 2003—, CACI Internat. Inc., 2007—. Decorated Def. D.S.M. with two oak clusters, D.S.M., Bronze Star with V device with three oak clusters, Purple Heart, Legion of Merit with oak leaf cluster. *

SHELTON, JAMES D. (DENNY SHELTON), hospital management company executive; BA in Polit. Sci. and History, La. State U.; MS in Pub. Adminstrn., U. Mo. Hosp. adminstr. La., Iowa, NC, Ga., Ill., Mo.; exec. dir. Westbank Hosp. Ops. Nat. Med. Enterprises (now Tenet Healthcare Corp.), New Orleans, 1984—86, v.p. ops., 1986—90, sr. v.p. ops., 1990—93, exec. v.p. ctrl. divsn., 1993—94; pres Ctrl. Group Columbia/HCA, 1994—98, pres. Pacific Group, 1998—99; chmn., CEO Triad Hosps. Inc., 1999—. Chmn. Fedn. Am. Hosps., 1999, mem. bd. govs., 1999—2002; bd. dirs. Am. Hosp. Assn. Office: Triad Hosp Inc 5800 Tennyson Pwy Plano TX 75024-3548 *

SHELTON, JAMES DOUGLAS, banker; b. Boynton Beach, Fla., Feb. 28, 1939; s. Clarence Wilton and Lou Anna (Ward) S.; m. Claudia Ellen Marshall, Oct. 20, 1973; children: Christopher John, Ryan Marshall. BA, Duke U., 1961; MDiv, Union Sem., 1965; STM, Boston U., 1966; SEP, Stanford U., 1975. Adj. prof. NY Sem., NYC, 1966-68; asst. treas. Bankers Trust Co., NYC, 1968-71; v.p. Chase Manhattan Bank, NYC, 1971-84; sr. v.p. Conn. Bank & Trust, Hartford, Conn., 1984-88; chmn., pres., chief exec. officer First Fed. Savs., East Hartford, Conn., 1988-2001. Bd. dirs. Conn. On-Line Computer Ctr., Avon, chmn., 1989-2001; bd. dirs. Cmty. Bank League of New Eng., Boston, chmn., 1989-96; mem. Conn. Legislature Interstate Banking Task Force, Hartford, 1989-90. Bd. dirs. Jr. Achievement North Ctrl. Conn., Windsor, 1986-90, Sci. Ctr. Conn., West Hartford, 1988-94, Riverfront Recapture, Inc., Hartford, 1994-98, Charter Oak State Coll. Found., New Britain, Conn., 2004—; corporator Am. Sch. for the Deaf, West Hartford, 1986-2001; trustee Noah Webster House, West Hartford Hist. Soc., 2005— Mem. Am. Cmty. Bankers Assn. (bd. dirs. 1995-2001), New Eng. Automated Clearing House Assn. (bd. dir. 1983-98), The Country Club of Farmington, Old Guard of West Hartford.

SHELTON, KATHRYN H., librarian; d. Bruce Whittington and Edna Poyas (Hall) Martin; m. L. Jev Shelton, Aug. 27, 1970; children: Kirsten Anna, Martin Harold, Andrew Olaf. BA in English, Randolph-Macon Woman's Coll., 1963; MS in Libr. Sci., Simmons Coll., 1966; MA in Am. Studies, U. Minn., 1969; postgrad., U. Alaska SE; cert., Modern Archives Inst., 1986. Profl. libr. asst. Boston Pub. Libr., 1965-67; substitute libr. Mpls. Pub. Libr., 1967-68; teaching assoc. Gen. Coll. U. Minn., Mpls., 1968-69; asst. libr., reader svcs. libr. Carleton Coll., Northfield, Minn., 1969-70; part-time libr. III Dept. Environ. Conservationand Dept. Edn. Alaska State Libr., Juneau, 1975-76; assoc. prof. libr. sci., head libr. U. Alaska, Juneau, 1970-75, 76-78; libr. II. State Legislature, Juneau, 1979—85; archivist I Alaska State Archives Dept. Administrn., Juneau, 1985-86; libr. III head pub. svcs. sect. Dept. Edn. Alaska State Libr., 1986-87, libr. III head Hist. Libr. Dept. Edn., 1987—2005, Alaska state libr., dir. divsn. librs., archives and museums, 2005—. Spkr. in field. Editor:

Alaskana Books, 1993, Some Books About Alaska Received in..., 1988—2001; contbr. articles to profl. jours. Project dir. Alaska Newspaper Project, 1991-98; mem. Gold Rush Centennial Task Force, 1993-2003, Alaska Geographic Names Bd., 1987-93, Alaska Gov.'s Adv. Coun. on Libr., 1973-74. Recipient Kudo award Office of Ombudsman State of Alaska, 1985. Mem. ALA, Alaska Libr. Assn. (pres. 1973-74, v.p. program chmn. annual conf. 1973, continuing edn. com. 1984, Alaska collection devel. com. 1986-88, Alaskana subcom. 1987-95, chair 1987-93), Alaska Hist. Soc. (pres. 2000-2002), Gastineau Channel Hist. Soc. (sec. 1991, Cert. Appreciation 1989), Soc. Am. Archivists, Acad. Cert. Archivists (cert. 1991), Polar Librs. Colloquy (co-editor Polar Librs. Bull. 1989-98). Office: Alaska State Libr PO Box 110571 Juneau AK 99811-0571 Office Phone: 907-465-2911.

SHELTON, KENNETH R., JR., real estate company executive, artist; b. Galveston, Tex., Aug. 29, 1946; Pres. Moore Climatic Inc., 1984—87; gen. ptnr. Various Real Estate Ltd. Partnerships, 1978—, Moore-Shelton, LP, 1984—; pres. Polybus, Inc., 1989—; gen. ptnr. Video Lane Ltd., 1983—. Exhibited in group shows at Rosenberg Gallery, Galveston, 1982, one-man shows include Galveston Art Ctr., 1991, exhibited in group shows at Island Inspired, Galveston Art Ctr., 1992. Mem. Galveston Bd. Realtors, 1983—; pres. Galveston County Apt. Assn., 1984—85; chmn. Cancer Crusade, 1983—84; pres. Galveston Acad. Excellence Booster Club, 2000—03, v.p., 1999—2000, 2003—; founding pres. Galveston Fencing Club, 1999—2001, Knights of Momus, 1984—85. Mem.: Galveston Fencing Club (dir.). Episcopalian. Avocations: painting, fencing, furniture making. Office: 2002 45th St Ste 103 Galveston TX 77550 Mailing: PO Box 3123 Galveston TX 77552 Office Phone: 404-765-5600. Personal E-mail: krskrs@swbell.net.

SHELTON, MICHAEL PATRICK, principal; b. Seymour, Ind., July 16, 1972; s. John Michael Shelton and Paula Michelle Kemp, William Newt Kemp (Stepfather); m. Stacy Leigh Conway, Aug. 12, 1995; children: Brendan Patrick, Kelsey Rae, Katelyn Grace. MusB, Culver-Stockton Coll., 1994—94; MS in Edn., So. Ill. U., Edwardsville, 2002. Dir. of vocal music Staunton (Ill.) Cmty. Unit Sch. Dist., 1994—2002; prin. Wood River (Ill.) -Hartford Elem. Sch. Dist., 2002—. Pres. St. Paul United Ch. of Christ, Staunton, 2001—02. Mem.: ASCD, Nat. Assn. of Elem. Sch. Prin., Ill. Alliance Adminstrs. Spl. Edn., Internat. Reading Assn., Ill. Music Educators Assn., Ill. Principals Assn., Staunton Optimist Club (pres. 2000—02), Delta Upsilon (vice-president 1993—94). Avocations: golf, music, travel. Home: 610 Stone Creek Dr Staunton IL 62088 Office: Lewis and Clark Elem Sch 501 E Lorena Ave Wood River IL 62095 Office Phone: 618-254-9814. Business E-Mail: pshelton@madison.k12.il.us.

SHELTON, ROBERT ARTHUR, lawyer; b. Atlanta, July 15, 1941; s. James Hill and Julia Elizabeth (Gemmill) S. AB, Oberlin Coll., 1963; LLB, Harvard U., 1966. Bar: Md. 1966. Law clk. to judge U.S. Dist. Ct. Md., 1966-67; assoc. Venable LLP, Balt. & Washington, 1967—72, ptnr., Health Care, Nonprofit Organizations, Pub. Fin. practices, 1973—. Perm. mem. Judicial Conf., US Ct. Appeals (4th cir.); assoc. spl. counsel impeachment inquiry staff, com. on judiciary, Ho. of Reps., Washington, 1974; counsel to RI Ho. Reps. in impeachment of State Chief Justice; bd. dirs. Dome Corp., Balt. Mem. Revenue Bond Adv. Bd., Md. Dept. Housing & Cmty. Devel.; past chmn. & trustee Md. Inst. Coll. Art, Balt. Episcopalian. Office: Venable LLP 1800 Merc Bank & Trust Bldg 2 Hopkins Plz Ste 2100 Baltimore MD 21201 also: Venable LLP 575 7th St NW Washington DC 20004 Office Phone: 410-244-7660, 202-344-4973. Office Fax: 410-244-7742. Business E-Mail: rashelton@venable.com.

SHELTON, ROBERT NEAL, academic administrator, physics professor, researcher; b. Phoenix, Oct. 5, 1948; s. Clark B. and Grace M. (McLaughlin) S.; m. Adrian Ann Millar, Aug. 30, 1969; children: Christian, Cameron, Stephanie. BS, Stanford U., 1970; MS, U. Calif., San Diego, 1973, PhD, 1975. Postdoctoral researcher U. Calif.-San Diego, La Jolla, 1975-76, asst. rsch. physicist, 1976-78; asst. prof. Iowa State U., Ames, 1978-81, assoc. prof., 1981-84, prof. physics, 1984-87; prof. physics, chmn. dept. U. Calif.-Davis, 1987-90, vice chancellor for rsch., 1990-96, vice provost for rsch., 1996-2001; exec. vice chancellor, provost U. N.C., Chapel Hill, 2001—06; pres. U. Ariz., Tucson, 2006—. Contbr. over 200 articles to profl. jours. Fellow Am. Phys. Soc., Calif. Coun. on Sci. and Tech.; mem. AAAS, Materials Rsch. Soc., Sigma Xi, Phi Beta Kappa. Office: Univ Ariz Adminstrn Bldg Rm 712 PO Box 210066 Tucson AZ 85721-0066

SHELTON, ROBERT WARREN, marketing professional; b. Albuquerque, Apr. 26, 1943; s. Eugene and Rusty M. (Jentsch) S.; children: Elise Straus, Samantha; m. Ginger Lee Rapp, Feb. 14, 1984. BBA in Mktg., St. Mary's U., San Antonio, 1969; postgrad., Ga. State U., 1972-73, postgrad. in fin. and internat. bus., 1973. Field mgr. Ford Motor Co., Atlanta, 1969-78; dir. fleet ops. Rollins, Inc., Atlanta, 1978-81; v.p. sales and ops. Lease Plan U.S.A., Atlanta, 1981-85; v.p. mktg. Spencer Services, Inc., Roswell, Ga., 1985-87; v.p. FX-10 Corp., 1987-88; pres. Shiloh Capital Corp., 1989—, USA Calling, Inc. and Canada Calling, Ltd., 1992—95, Innovators.Com, Inc., 2000—. Pres. Victory Svcs., Inc., 1989—. Mem. Lost Forest Civic Assn. (pres. 1980-81). Mem. Nat. Assn. Fleet Adminstrs., Am. Fleet and Leasing Assn., NRA. Republican. Christian. Avocations: golf, racquetball, tennis, shooting. E-mail: rshelton@innovators.com.

SHELTON, STEPHANI, broadcast journalist, consultant; b. Boston; d. Phil and Babette (Belloff) Saltman; m. Frank Herold. BS, Boston U. Corr. CBS News, NYC, 1973—84; news corr. WWOR-TV, NYC, 1984—88; corr., anchor Fin. News Network, NYC, 1989—91. Freelance reporter Sta. WPIX-TV, 1991-95, Sta. WNBC-TV, 1993-96, WWOR-TV, 1999-02; writer, prodr., radio anchor CNBC, 2003—; cons. trainer Ctrl. and Eastern Europe broadcast journalists, 1998—; med. health prodr.-reporter PBS, The Learning Channel, 1997-99; owner The Fred Group Ltd., video/internet prodn. co., 1998—; freelance radio documentary writer Westinghouse Group W Broadcasting, NYC, 1970-73. Recipient Peabody award, 1972, N.J. Best Spot News award AP, 1987, 88, N.J. Working Press award, 1993-94; Emmy nominee, 1995, 96, 99, 2000. Mem. Soc. Profl. Journalists (award 1999), Radio and TV News Dirs. Assn., N.Y.C. Press Club, Investigative Reporters and Editors, Com. to Protect Journalists. E-mail: backbay38@aol.com, fred@fredgroupltd.com. *Guiding principles: a questioning mind, a refusal to take no for an answer and the memory of 28 marathons. If you don't ask "why", you are not a journalist.*

SHELY, JOHN B., lawyer; b. Detroit, 1958; BA magna cum laude, Albion Coll., 1980; JD, U. Houston, 1986. Bar: Tex. 1986, admitted to practice: US Dist. Ct. (No. Dist.) Tex., US Dist. Ct. (So. Dist.) Tex., US Dist. Ct. (Ea. Dist.) Tex., US Dist. Ct. (We. Dist.) Tex., US Ct. Appeals (5th Cir.), US Ct. Appeals (9th Cir.), US Supreme Ct. Ptnr., Litig. Andrews Kurth LLP, Houston, mem. mgmt. com. Mem. Houston Law Rev., 1985—86. Mem.: Fed. Bar Assn. (dir. South Tex. Chpt.), State Bar Tex., Houston Bar Assn., Order of Coif, Phi Delta Phi, Phi Beta Kappa, Phi Eta Sigma. Office: Andrews Kurth LLP 600 Travis St Ste 4200 Houston TX 77002-3090 Office Phone: 713-220-4105. Office Fax: 713-238-7228. Business E-Mail: jshely@andrewskurth.com.

SHEMIN, BARRY L., actuary; b. Bklyn., Dec. 17, 1942; AB magna cum laude, Brown U., 1963; MA, U. Mich., 1964. With John Hancock Life Ins. Co., Boston, 1968—2003, sr. v.p., corp. actuary; cons actuary. Chmn. bd. dirs. ARC of Mass. Bay; bd. dirs. Harvard Pilgrim Health Care Fellow: Soc. Actuaries (bd. govs.); mem.: Am. Acad. Actuaries, Sigma Xi, Phi Beta Kappa. Office: PO Box 111 Boston MA 02117-0111

SHEMMERI, THAFUR, pediatric dentist; m. Nida Kazzaz, July 17, 1977; children: Ealaf, Esel, Aws. BDS, Baghdad U., 1977; DMD, Boston U., 1991, MSc in Dentistry, 1990, DSc in Dentistry, 1991. Cert. in pediatric dentistry Boston U., 1988. Pvt. practice, Baghdad, Iraq, 1977—86; pvt. practice in pediatric dentistry Mass., 1992—. Mem.: Mass. Dental Soc., Am. Orthodontic Soc., Am. Acad. Pediatric Dentistry, ADA, Am. Acad. Pediat. (assoc.). Office: Wachusett Pediatric Dentistry 100 Whalon St Fitchburg MA 01420 Office Phone: 978-342-3004. Office Fax: 978-343-5979. Business E-Mail: thafurshemmeri@hotmail.com.

SHEMONSKY, NATALIE KAPLIN, physician, lawyer, army officer; b. Bridgeport, Conn., June 5, 1934; d. Harry C. and Clara (Dronkow) Kaplin; m. Sidney Shemonsky, Aug. 26, 1954 (div. 1974); children— Kim R. Shemonsky Fischel, Sherri E. Shemonksy Paulsen, Caryn L. Shemonsky Bart. B.A., Western Conn. State Coll., 1967; M.D., Med. Coll. Pa., 1971; J.D., U. S.D., 1984. Intern, Med. Coll. Pa. Hosp., Phila., 1971-72, resident, 1972-75; clin. dir. USPHS Hosp., Rosebud, S.D., 1975-76; practice medicine specializing in internal medicine, Vermillion, S.D., 1977-81; legal-med. lectr. U. S.D. Sch. Law, Vermillion, 1981-84; commd. maj. U.S. Army, 1984; lt. col. 1986; col. 1992; staff physician-lawyer, Armed Forces Inst. Pathology, Washington, 1984-86; cons. dept. legal medicine, Armed Forces Inst. Pathology, 1986—; pathology resident, Walter Reed Army Med. Ctr., Washington, 1986-90; forensic pathology fellow, Armed Forces Inst. of Pathology, 1990-91; assoc. med. examiner, Office of the Armed Forces Med. Examiner Armed Forces Inst. of Pathology (AFIP), 1991-92; chief deputy med. examiner, 1993—. Assoc. editor Legal Aspects of Med. Practice, 1985—; contbr. articles to med.-legal profl. jours. and chpts. in med. legal textbooks. Fellow ACP, Am. Coll. Legal Medicine; mem. Am. Soc. Law and Medicine, Pitts. Soc. Legal Medicine, Health Lawyers Am., Trial Lawyers Assn. Am.

SHEMWELL, ROBERT H., federal judge; b. 1941; BA, La. State U., 1963, JD, 1967. Assoc. Seale, Smith, Baine & Phelps, 1967-70; asst. U.S. atty. U.S. Dist. Ct. (we. dist.) La., 1970-75, clk. of ct., 1975—, part-time magistrate judge Shreveport, 1984—; acting clk. of ct. U.S. Bankruptcy Ct., 1986-87. Office: US Dist Ct We Dist 1167 US Courthouse 300 Fannin St Shreveport LA 71101-3141 Fax: 318-676-3966.

SHEN, ALFRED C., neurosurgeon; b. Ithaca, NY, Oct. 5, 1964; s. C. C. and Helen H. Shen; m. Kim Nguyen, Feb. 12, 2000; children: Eric Y., Erin Y. BSEE, Rice U., Houston, 1987; MD, U. Tex., Dallas, 1991. Diplomate Am. Bd. Neurol. Surgery, 2004. Spine fellow U. Tenn., 1999; neurosurgeon Desert Spine and Neurosurg. Inst., Rancho Mirage, Calif., 2002—. Mem.: AMA, Congress Neurol. Surgeons, Am. Assn. Neurol. Surgeons. Office: 39000 Bob Hope Dr W410 Rancho Mirage CA 92270

SHEN, BENJAMIN SHIH-PING, physicist, educator; b. Hangzhou, China, Sept. 14, 1931; s. Nai-cheng and Chen-chiu (Sun) S.; m. Lucia Elisabeth Simpson, 1971; children: William, Juliet. AB, Assumption Coll., Mass., 1954, ScD (hon.), 1972; AM in Physics, Clark U., 1956; DSc d'Etat in Physics, U. Paris, 1964; MA (hon.), U. Pa., 1971. Tchr. Assumption Prep Sch., Mass., 1954-56; asst. prof. physics SUNY, Albany, 1956-59; assoc. prof. space sci., dept. aeros. and astronautics NYU, 1964-66; assoc. prof. astronomy and astrophysics U. Pa., Phila., 1966-68, prof., 1968-72, Reese W. Flower prof. astronomy and astrophysics, 1972-96, Reese Flower prof. emeritus, 1996—, chmn. coun. grad. deans, 1979-81, assoc. provost, 1979-80, provost, 1980-81, chmn. dept. astronomy and astrophysics, 1973-79, dir. Flower and Cook Obs., 1973-79, mem. Ctr. for Energy and Environment, 1976-93, chmn. roundtable on sci., industry and policy, 1976-96, hon. prof. Sch. Engring. and Applied Sci., 1980-85; ret., 1996. Mem. U.S. Nat. Sci. Bd., 1990-94, chmn. U.S. sci. and engring. indicators, 1990-92, chmn. Task Force on Sci. Literacy, 1992-94; mem. Nat. Coun. on Sci. and Tech. Edn., 1996-2001; cons. GE, 1961-68, Office Tech. Assessment, U.S. Congress, 1977-78; sci. and tech. adviser U.S. Senate Budget Com., 1976-77; guest staff Brookhaven Nat. Lab., 1963-64, 65-70; chmn. Commn. on Pub. Understanding of Sci., N.Y. Acad. Scis., 1972-75; mem. adv. com. Mt. John Obs., New Zealand, 1978-84. Author: Nuclear Problems in Radiation Shielding in Space, 1963, Passage des Protons dans des Milieux Condenses, 1964; co-editor, co-author: High-Energy Nuclear Reactions in Astrophysics, 1967; Spallation Nuclear Reactions and Their Applications, 1976, Research in the Age of the Steady-state University, 1982; mem. editorial bd. Earth and Extraterrestrial Scis., 1974-78, assoc. editor, 1978-79; assoc. editor: Comments on Astrophysics, 1979-85; contbr. articles to profl. jours. Mem. Hayden Planetarium com. of bd. trustees Am. Mus. Natural History, 1978—; mem. sci. adv. bd. Children's TV Workshop, N.Y.C., 1977, 79-00; mem. ABA-AAAS Nat. Conf. Bd. Lawyers and Scientists, 1986-92; former trustee or bd. dirs. NSF, N.Y. Acad. Scis., Pa. Ballet Co., Assumption Coll., University City Sci. Ctr., Phila., U. Pa. Rsch. Found., Morris Arboretum, Phila., Univ. Mus., Phila. Decorated Ordre des Palmes Academiques (France); recipient Vermeil medal for sci. Soc. d'Encouragement au Progres, France, 1978. Fellow emeritus AAAS, Am. Phys. Soc., Royal Astron. Soc. (U.K.); mem. Internat. Astron. Union, Penn Assn. Emeritus and Sr. Faculty (pres. 2005-06). Office: U Pa Dept Physics & Astronomy Philadelphia PA 19104-6396 Business E-Mail: bshen@sas.upenn.edu.

SHEN, MICHAEL, lawyer; b. Nanking, Jiangsu, Peoples Republic of China, Aug. 15, 1948; came to U.S., 1951; s. James Cheng Yee and Grace (Pai) S.; m. Marina Manese (div.); m. Pamela Nan Bradford, Aug. 12, 1983; 1 child, Jessica Li. BA, U. Chgo., 1969; MA, U. Pa., 1970; JD, Rutgers U., 1979. Bar: U.S. Dist. Ct. N.J. 1979, N.Y. 1980, U.S. Dist. Ct. (so., no. and ea. dists.) N.Y. 1980, N.J. 1981, U.S. Ct. Appeals (2d cir.) 1987, U.S. Supreme Ct. 1988, U.S. Ct. Appeals (3rd cir.) 1996. Staff atty. Bedford Stuyvesant Legal Svcs., Bklyn., 1979-80, Com. for Interns and Residents, NYC, 1980-81; ptnr. Michael Shen & Assocs., PC, NYC, 1981—. Bd. dirs. Asian Am. Legal Def. and Edn. Fund, NYC; pres. bd. dirs. Anti-Discrimination Ctr. Metro New York. Pres. bd. dirs. Nat. Employment Law Project; past bd. dirs. N.Y. Civil Liberties Union, N.Y.C., Nat. Asian Pacific Am. Legal Consortium. Mem. Internat. Platform Assn., Nat. Employees Lawyers Assn., N.Y. State Bar Assn., N.Y. County Bar Assn., Nat. Lawyers Guild. Avocations: arts, reading. Office: 225 Broadway Ste 2515 New York NY 10007 Home Phone: 917-359-8035; Office Phone: 212-227-0300. E-mail: mslaw@alumni.uchicago.edu.

SHEN, MICHAEL YUE-HUA, cardiologist; b. Harbin, China, Apr. 25, 1958; arrived in US, 1987; s. Ho-Fu Shen and Hong-Yun Liu; m. Jennifer Fang-Yin Lin, 2001; children: Alexander David, Annabelle Ellian. MD, Jiamusi Med. Coll., Jiamusi, Heilongjiang, China, 1982; MS in Exercise Physiology, Beijing Inst. Phys. Edn., 1987. Diplomate Cardiovascular Disease Am. Bd. of Internal Medicine, 1999, Internal Medicine Am. Bd. of Internal Medicine, 1996, Certification Bd. of Nuc. Cardiology, 1997. Dir., nuc. cardiology and dir., ctr. for cardiovasc. informatics UMDNJ - Robert Wood Johnson Med. Sch. South Campus, Camden, NJ, 1999—2003; head, sect. of cardiac imaging Cleve. Clinic Fla., Ft Lauderdale/Weston, Fla., 2003—. Bd. dirs. Am. Soc. of Nuc. Cardiology, Bethesda, Md., 2005—; coding and reimbursement com. Am. Coll. of Cardiology, Bethesda, Md., 2005—; epiccare steering com. Cleve. Clinic Found., Cleveland, Ohio, 2003—. Contbr. scientific papers pub. to profl. jour. Grantee Referral Analysis on Cardiac Imaging, Fujisawa Healthcare, 2003, Effect trial, IVIVI Technologies, 2005, 5A Trial, Astellas, 2005; FACC, Am. Coll. of Cardiology, 2001. Mem.: Healthcare Info. Mgmt. Sys. Soc. Achievements include patents for Healthcare informatics. Office: Cleve Clin Fla 2950 Cleve Clin Blvd Fort Lauderdale FL 33331 Home Phone: 954-434-6779; Office Phone: 954-659-5317. Office Fax: 954-659-5291; Home Fax: 954-434-7789. Personal E-mail: drmikeshen@aol.com. Business E-Mail: shenm@ccf.org.

SHEN, QING, urban planning educator, researcher, associate dean; b. Jinyun, Zhejiang, China, Apr. 5, 1962; s. Xianxing and Aili (Cheng) S.; m. Yongmei Zhu, Aug. 25, 1989; 1 child, Sophie. BS, Zhejiang U., 1982; MA in Urban Planning, U. of B.C., Canada, 1986; PhD in Urban Planning, U. Calif., Berkeley, 1993. Asst. prof. urban studies and planning MIT, Cambridge, 1993-99, assoc. prof. urban studies and planning, 1999—2001, U. Md., College Park, 2001—06, prof. urban studies and planning, 2006—, assoc. dean Sch. Architecture, Planning and Preservation, 2007—. Affiliate faculty Ctr. Trans. Studies MIT, 1996—; affiliate faculty Nat. Ctr. Smart Growth Rsch. and Edn. U. Md., 2001—, affiliate faculty Md. Transp. Initiative, 2003—; mem. jour. adv. bds.; Siyuan chair prof. Nanjing U., Nanjing, 2006—. Contbr. articles to profl. jours. Emerging Scholar Paper award Assn. Am. Geographers, 1999; Horwood Critique prize Urban and Regional Info. Sys. Assn, 1998. Mem. Assn. Collegiate Schs. Planning, Assn. Am. Geographers, Transp. Rsch. Bd. Avocations: poetry, tennis. Office: Univ Maryland 1215 Sch Architecture College Park MD 20742-1411 Business E-Mail: qshen@umd.edu.

SHEN, RONGER, artist, educator; b. Shanghai, Nov. 11, 1942; came to U.S., 1984; d. Jianping and Huijun (Peng) S.; m. Yi Wu, Dec. 31, 1965; 1 child, Yan Wu. BA, Nat. Nanjing Acad. Arts, 1965. Dir. arts and crafts dept. Jiangsu Light Industry Bur., Nanjing, 1965-79; dir. Jiangsu Acad. Arts and Crafts, 1982—. Profl. painter Jiangsu Acad. Traditional Chinese Painting, 1979—; pres. Qigong Ctr., Inc., N.Y., 1989—; Qigong cons. to dept. orthopedics Mt. Sinai Sch. Medicine, N.Y.C., 1991—, N.J. Med. Ctr. Pain Mgmt. Ctr., Newark, 1991; NIH approved rsch. project on Life Info. Pictures, Life Info. Rhythm and Qigong, 1993; dir. Assn. Modern Chinese Arts Inc., 1994—. Mem. Artists Assn. China (Jiangsu br.), Acad. Arts and Crafts China, Eastern Am. Qigong U.S. (chmn. 1991—). Home: 32-05 146th St Flushing NY 11354-3151

SHEN, SIN-YAN, physicist, acoustical engineer, musicologist; b. Singapore, Nov. 12, 1949; came to the U.S., 1969, naturalized, 1984; s. Shao-Quan and Tien-Siu (Chen) S.; m. Yuan-Yuan Lee, Aug. 4, 1973; children: Jia, Jian. BSc, U. Singapore, 1969; MS, Ohio State U., 1970, PhD, 1973. Concert recitalist on Erhu Chinese fiddle, 1963—; instr. math. U. Singapore, 1969; asst. prof. physics Northwestern U., Evanston, Ill., 1974-77, assoc. prof., 1977-81; faculty assoc. Argonne (Ill.) Nat. Lab., 1974-77, scientist, 1977-83, sr. rsch. leader, 1983—. Dir. rsch. divsn. natural resource mgmt. SUPCON Internat., 1988—; prof. Harvard U., 1989—; meeting series reviewer NSF, Washington, 1981—; coord. Tech. Rev., Argonne, Atlanta, Phoenix, Portland, Oreg., 1983—; dir. Global Warming Internat. Ctr., 1991—, chmn. Internat. Conf. Chgo., 1990-93, San Francisco, 1994-95, Vienna, 1996, Columbia U., N.Y.C., 1997, Hong Kong U. Sci. and Tech., 1998, Yamanashi Inst. Environ. Scis., 1999, Harvard U., 2000, Cambridge U., 2001, Max Planck Inst., 2002, Mass. Inst. Tech., 2003; Chinese Music Internat. Conf., 1991, 94, 2002; advisor Internat. Energy Agy., 1986—, Gas Rsch. Inst., 1984—, SUPCON Internat., 1986—, Nat. Geog., 1986—, Internat. Boreal Forest Rsch. Assn., 1991—, Electric Power Rsch. Inst., 1992—, World Climate Rsch. Programme WMO, 1993—, UN Devel. Program, 1993—, World Bank, 1994—, US Dept. Energy and US EPA, 1995—; prof. Chinese Acad. Forestry, 1986—; panel on biol. diversity Nat. Acad. Scis., Smithsonian Instn., 1986; chmn. internat. program com. Austrian Acad. Scis., 1995-96, Columbia U., 1996-97, Japan Environ. Agy., 1998-99, Intergovt. Panel on Climate Change, 1999—; music dir. Orch. Chinese Music Soc. N.Am., 1976—, Silk & Bamboo Ensemble, 1981—; adv. Ctrl. Traditional Orch., 1984—; del. leader, UN Conf. Environ. and Devel., Rio, 1992; del. chmn. Third All China Arts Festival, Kunmin, 1992, panelist Nat. Endowment for Arts, 1981—, New Eng. Found. for Arts, 1987—, Arts Midwest, 1985—, Ill. Arts Coun., 1982—, Chgo. City Arts, 1990—, Ill. Art's Alliance Found., adv. coun., 1992—, adv. coun. Mid-Am. Arts Alliance, 1992—, bd. dirs.; tech. adv. Shanghai Nat. Musical Instrument Co., 1985—; adv. West Lake Qin Soc., Hangzhou, China, 1991—. Author: Superfluidity, 1982, Acoustics of Ancient Chinese Bells, 1987, Chinese Music and Orchestration: A Primer om Principles and Practice, 1991, Global Warming Science and Policy, 1992, The Boreal Forests and Global Change, 1993, Global Warming Eludidated, 1994, Chinese Musical Instruments, 1999, Global Warming and Public Health, 1999, China: A Journey through Its Musical Art, 1999, Chinese Music in the 20th Century, 2001; editor-in-chief Chinese Music Internat. Jour., 1978—; mem. internat. editl. bd. World Resource Rev., 1989—, Internat. Boreal Forest Rsch., 1992—, Ency. of Life Support Sys., 1994—; adv. Ency. Brit., 1983—; contbr. over 300 articles to profl. jours.; patentee molten liquids, 1974, 80. Recipient Mich. Heritage award, 1992; Fulbright scholar U.S. State Dept., 1969; merit scholar Govt. Singapore, 1967; named Artistic Treasure Gov. Jim Edgar of Ill., 1998. Mem. AAAS, Am. Phys. Soc., Ops. Rsch. Soc. Am., Acoustical Soc. Am., Chinese Music Soc. N.Am. Achievements include rsch. in renewable energy and materials techs.; global change and global warming; extreme event index; indsl. sonic techs.; energy policy, planning and economics; acoustics; cultural acoustics. also: SUPCON Internat PO Box 5275 Woodridge IL 60517-0275 Office Phone: 630-910-1551.

SHEN, WEI-CHIANG, medical educator; b. Wenzhou, Zhejiang, China, May 3, 1942; s. Tze-Ping and Yi-Ching Shen; m. Daisy Hsia, Jan. 13, 1968; children: Howard, Jerry. PhD, Boston U., 1972; BS, Tunghai U., 1965. Assoc. prof. Boston U. Sch. Medicine, 1983—87; prof. pharm. scis. U. So. Calif. Sch. Pharmacy, LA, 1987—. Contbr. scientific papers to profl. jours. Recipient Eurand award for Outstanding Novel Rsch. in Oral Drug Delivery, Controlled Release Soc., 2002. Fellow: Am. Assn. Pharm. Scientists; mem.: AAAS, Am. Soc. for Biochemistry and Molecular Biology, Am. Soc. for Pharmacology and Exptl. Therapeutics, Am. Soc. for Cell Biology, Controlled Release Soc., Chinese-American Faculty Assn. So. Calif. (pres. 2004—05). Achievements include research in protein and peptide drug delivery; patents in field. Office: U So Calif 1985 Zonal Ave PSC 404B Los Angeles CA 90033 Office Phone: 1-323-442-1902. Office Fax: 1-323-442-2263. Business E-Mail: weishen@usc.edu.

SHEN, WEIXING, meteorologist; arrived in USA, 1991, naturalized, 2005; m. Grace Furonghe Howe; children: Emily, Kimberly. BS in Meteorology, Hangzhou U., China, 1984; MS in Atmospheric Dynamics, Chinese Acad. Sci., Beijing, 1987; PhD, SUNY, 1995. Rsch. asst. Stony Brook U., NY, 1991—95; from postdoctoral rschr. to asst. marine scientist U. RI, Kingston, 1996—2001; vis. scientist U. Corp. Atmospheric Rsch., Camp Springs, Md., 2001—05; vis. rsch. scientist U. Md., College Park, 2005—. Named Environ. Hero, NOAA, 2002. Mem.: Am. Geophy. Union (assoc.), Am. Meteorol. Soc. (assoc.). Achievements include development of a simple physical model for hurricane intensity research and prediction; discovery of environmental circulation-associated zonal variability of transient atmospherics waves in the tropics; nonlinear responses of stratospheric Quasi-Biennial Oscillation to sea surface temperature changes; modeling of standing surface water's effects on landfall hurricanes. Home: 10627 Alison Dr Burke VA 22015 Home Phone: 301-250-1628; Office Phone: 301-405-8245. Personal E-mail: wshenhz@yahoo.com. E-mail: wshen@essic.umd.edu.

SHEN, XIAOPING, geography educator; b. China; 1 child, Jane An. BS, Beijing Normal U., China, 1983, MS; PhD, U. Ottawa, Canada, 1995. Lectr. Beijing Normal U., Beijing, 1986—89; prof. Ctrl. Conn. State U., New Britain, 1995—. Adj. prof. grad. Sch. Chinese Acad. Scis., Beijing, 2003—06. Contbr. articles various profl. jours., chapters to books. Activity coord. Conn. Chinese Culture Ctr., Hartford, 2000—03. Faculty Rsch. grantee, Conn. State U., 2000—. Mem.: Assn. Am. Geographers (chair, china splty. group 2002—03), Gamma Theta Upsilon Internat. Geog. Honor Soc. (regional councilor for New Eng. - St. Lawrence Valley 2000—06). Office: Ctrl Conn State U 1615 Stanley St New Britain CT 06050 Office Phone: 860-832-2794.

SHEN, YU-CHU, economics professor; b. Kaohsiung, Taiwan, Jan. 25, 1974; MA, Harvard U., PhD, 2001. Asst. prof. econs. Naval Postgrad. Sch., Monterey, Calif., 2004—. Faculty rsch. fellow Nat. Bur. Econ. Rsch., Cambridge, Mass., 2004—.

SHENDEROV, KEVIN, immunologist; b. Ukraine, 1987; arrived in US, 1990; s. Peter and Faina S. BS in Biochemistry, NYU, 2007; PhD student in Immunology, Oxford Univ., 2007—. Rhodes Scholar. Achievements include being instrumental in est. the Global Health Rev., and organizing a world health conference; conducting rsch. at Memorial Sloan-Kettering in cancer immunology.

SHENEFELT, PHILIP DAVID, dermatologist; b. Colfax, Wash., July 31, 1943; s. Roy David and Florence Vanita (Cagle) S.; m. Debrah A. Levenson; children: Elizabeth, Sara, Shaina. BS with honors, U. Wis. Madison, 1966, MD, 1970, MS in Adminstrv. Medicine, 1984. Diplomate Am. Bd. Dermatology, Am. Bd. Med. Hypnosis. Intern U.S. Naval Hosp., Bethesda, Md., 1970-71; gen. practice Oreg. (Wis.) Clinic, 1975; resident in dermatology U. Wis. Hosp., Madison, 1975-78, mem. staff, 1978-87; asst. prof. dermatology U. South Fla., Tampa, 1987—97, assoc. prof., 1997—. Chief dermatology sect. VA Hosp., Bay Pines, Fla., 1987—89, asst. chief, Tampa, 1988—2002, chief, 2002—07; dermatologist Univ. Health Svc. U. Wis., Madison, 1978—87, VA Hosp., Madison, 1982—85. Served to lt. comdr. USN, 1969-74; capt. USNR (ret.). Kellogg fellow, 1980-82. Mem.: AMA, Fla. Med. Assn., Soc. Clin. Exptl. Hypnosis, Noah Worcester Dermatol. Soc., Fla. West Coast Dermatol. Soc., Fla. Dermatol. Soc., Am. Soc. Clin. Hypnosis, Am. Coll. Physician Execs., Am. Acad. Dermatology. Home: 15919 Notting Hill Dr Lutz FL 33548-6147 Office: U South Fla Dermatol # 79 12901 Bruce Downs Blvd Tampa FL 33612-4742 Office Phone: 813-974-2188. Business E-Mail: pshenefe@health.usf.edu.

SHENG, MORGAN HWA-TZE, neuroscientist, educator; b. Taipei, Taiwan, Feb. 23, 1958; came to US, 1986. s. Jans Ceen and Nancy Cheng-Feng (Niue) S.; m. Lida Wen, May 18, 1991. BA with honors, U. Oxford, Eng., 1979; MA, U. Oxford, 1984; MB, BS, London U., 1982; PhD in Molecular Genetics, Harvard U., 1990. Resident London Tchg. Hosps., 1982-86; rsch. asst. Harvard Med. Sch., Boston, 1986-90; rsch. assoc. Howard Hughes Med. Inst./U. Calif., San Francisco, 1990-94; asst. investigator, asst. prof. Mass. Gen. Hosp./Harvard Med. Sch., Boston, 1994; Menicon prof. neuroscience MIT, Cambridge. Contbr. articles to profl. jours. Nat. Multiple Sclerosis Soc. fellow, 1990-91. Fellow Royal Soc. UK; mem. AAAS, Royal Coll. Physicians, UK, Soc. Neuroscience. Office: Dept Biology MIT 77 Massachusetts Ave 46-4303 Cambridge MA 02139 Office Phone: 617-452-3716. E-mail: msheng@mit.edu. *

SHENG, QIN, mathematics professor; s. Re and Sh Sheng; m. Helen Huang, Jan. 1, 1962; children: Andy, Danny. BS, U. Nanjing, China, 1982, MS, 1985; PhD, U. Cambridge, England, 1990. Prof. U. Dayton, Ohio, 2001—04, Baylor U., Waco, Tex., 2004—. Rsch. fellow, USAF, 2005—07. Mem.: Am. Math Soc. Achievements include research in applied mathematics and computer simulation. Avocations: music, paintings, sightseeing, mountain walks. Office: Dept Math Baylor Univ One Bear Pl Waco TX 76798-7328 Home Phone: 254-214-7764; Office Phone: 254-710-1241. Office Fax: 254-710-3569. Business E-Mail: qin_sheng@baylor.edu.

SHENK, GEORGE H., lawyer; b. NYC, Sept. 10, 1943; BA, Princeton U., 1965; M in Internat. Affairs, Columbia U., 1967; JD, Yale U., 1970. Bar: N.Y. 1971, Calif. 1985. Assoc. Coudert Bros., Paris, 1970, NYC, 1970-73, Hong Kong, 1973-75, Tokyo, 1975-78, ptnr. NYC, 1978-91, San Francisco, 1991-94, Heller Ehrman LLP, 1994—. Exec. dir. San Francisco Com. on Fgn. Rels. Contbr. articles to publs. Mem. Bar Assn. City of N.Y., Calif. State Bar Assn., Coun. Fgn. Rels., Pacific Coun. on Internat. Policy. Office: Heller Ehrman LLP 333 Bush St San Francisco CA 94104-2806

SHENK, LOIS ELAINE LANDIS, writer; b. Ephrata, Pa., May 30, 1944; BA in English, Eastern Mennonite Coll., 1966; MSc in Edn., Temple U., Phila., 1984. English mistress Githumu Secondary Sch., Thika, Kenya, 1966-68; English tchr. Kraybill's Jr. High, Mount Joy, Pa., 1976-77; freelance writer, 1978—; religious news corr. Gospel Herald, Scottdale, Pa., 1978-82. Observer, corr. The US Senate, Washington, 1987-2001, 2006—. Author: Out of Mighty Waters, 1982 (R.I.M. excellence award 1983), The Story of Ephrata Mennonite School, 1996; (one act play) A House for David in (anthology) Swords into Plowshares, 1983; (study guide for Christian edn.) Hebrews, 1988; contbr. poems, stories & features to jours.; editl. work Mennonite Ctrl. Com., Akron, Pa., 1977. Cmty. living advisor Friendship Cmty., Lititz, Pa., 1997-99; Sunday sch. tchr. Ephrata Mennonite Ch., 1997-99; tutor English as a Second Lang., 2004. Recipient Rep. Senatorial Medal of Freedom, Lifetime Achievement award, Internat. Biog. Ctr., Eng., 2007, Global Fellowship cert., World Forum, Washington, 2007, Ambassadorship of US cert., 2007. Avocations: reading, cooking, music. Home and Office: 821 Hershey Ave Lancaster PA 17603 E-mail: lshenk@verizon.net.

SHENK, THOMAS EUGENE, molecular biology educator, academic administrator; b. Bklyn., Jan. 1, 1947; s. Eugene Richard and Helen Marie (Deffenbaugh) S.; m. Susan Mary Hillman, July 4, 1979; children—Christopher Thomas, Gregory Thomas BS in Biology, U. Detroit, 1969; PhD in Microbiology, Rutgers U., 1973. Postdoctoral fellow, molecular biology Stanford Med. Ctr.; asst. prof. molecular biology U. Conn., Farmington, 1975-80; prof. molecular biology SUNY, Stony Brook, 1980-84; Elkins prof., dept. molecular biology Princeton U., 1984—, Am. Cancer Soc. prof., 1996—, chmn. dept. molecular biology, 1996—. Bd. dirs. Merck & Co., Inc., 2001—, CV Therapeutics, Inc., Palo Alto, Calif., 2001—, Cell Genesys, Inc., 2001—, mem. scientific adv. bd., 1997—, Novalon Pharm. Corp.; investigator Howard Hughes Inst.; mem. pres. adv. group Fox Chase Cancer Ctr.; chair Sloan General Motors prize Selection Com.; spkr. in field; chair NIH Virology Study Sect.; bd. trustee Cold Spring Harbor Lab. Co-editor: Enhancers and Eukaryotic Gene Expression, 1983; contbr. articles to profl. jours.editor, Journal of Virology, 1984-94. Recipient NIH Rowe award. Mem. Am. Soc. Microbiology (Eli Lilly award 1982, pres.), NAS, Inst. Medicine,, Am. Soc. for Virology (past pres.); fellow Am. Acad. Arts and Sciences., Am. Acad. Microbiology. Achievements include patents in field. Office: Princeton U Dept Molecular Biology Lewis Thomas Lab 203 Princeton NJ 08544-0001 *

SHENKER, JOSEPH C., lawyer; b. NYC, Nov. 6, 1956; BS in Acctg., CUNY, 1977; JD, Columbia U., 1980. Bar: NY 1981, US Dist. Ct. (ea. and so. dists.) NY 1981, US Claims Ct. 1982, US Tax Ct. 1982, US Supreme Ct. 1988. Assoc. Sullivan & Cromwell, NYC, 1980-86, ptnr., 1986—, also mem. mgmt. com. and coord. comml. real estate practice area, vice chmn., 2006—. Contbr. articles to profl. jours. Pres. Met. Coun. on Jewish Poverty, bd. dir. Jewish Cmty. Rels. Coun. Fellow Am. Bar Found.; mem. ABA, NY State Bar Assn., Assn. Bar City NY Office: Sullivan & Cromwell 125 Broad St Fl 33 New York NY 10004-2400 Office Phone: 212-558-3768. Office Fax: 212-558-3588. E-mail: shenkerj@sullcrom.com.

SHENKER, STEPHEN, physics professor; BA, Harvard U., 1975; PhD, Cornell U., 1980. Faculty U. Chgo., 1981—89; prof. Rutgers U., 1989—98; prof. and dir. Stanford Inst. Theoretical Physics, 1998—; Richard Herschel Weiland prof. Sch. Humanities Stanford U., 2004—. Recipient Young Investigator award, Nat. Sci. Found., 1985; fellow Sloan Found., 1983, MacArthur Found., 1987. Fellow: Am. Acad. Arts and Sciences, Am. Physical Soc. Office: Dept of Physics Stanford U Stanford CA 94306 Office Phone: 650-723-4615. Business E-Mail: sshenker@stanford.edu.

SHENKIR, WILLIAM GARY, business educator; b. Three Rivers, Tex., June 27, 1938; s. William and Lydia (Jancik) S.; m. Missy Smith, Jan 1, 1973. BBA, Tex. A & M U., 1960; postgrad. (Rockefeller Bros. Theol. fellow), Drew U. Sem., 1960-61; MBA, U. Tex., 1962, PhD, 1964. Asst. prof. McIntire Sch. Commerce, U. Va., Charlottesville, 1967-69, assoc. prof., 1969-72, prof., 1972—75, dean, 1977-92, Paul Goodloe McIntire prof. Charlottesville, 1977—82; William Stamps Farish prof. McIntire Sch. Commerce U. Va., 1982—2007, William Stamps Farish prof. emeritus, 2007—. Project dir. Fin. Acctg. Stds. Bd., Stamford, Conn., 1973—76; vis. prof. NYU Grad. Sch. Bus., NYC, 1976—77; bd. dirs. ComSonics Corp., Harrisburg, Va. Editor: Carman Blough: His Professional Career and Accounting Thought, 1978; co-author: The University of Virginia's McIntire School of Commerce: The First 75 Years, 1921-96, 1996, Open-Book Management: Creating an Ownership Culture, 1998, Making Enterprise Risk Management Pay Off, 2001, Making Enterprise Risk Management Pay Off: How Leading Companies Implement Risk Management, 2002, Enterprise Risk Management: Pulling It All Together, 2002, Enterprise Risk Management, 2007; contbr. articles to profl. jours. Capt. USAF, 1964—67. Mem. AICPA, Am. Acctg. Assn. (former v.p.), Acctg. Edn. Change Commn. (former vice chmn.), Assn. Advance Collegiate Schs. of Bus. (former bd. dirs., pres. 1990-91), Fin. Execs. Inst., Va. Soc. CPAs, Raven Soc., Landfall Club, Farmington Country Club, Phi Delta Kappa, Beta Gamma Sigma, Phi Kappa Phi. Presbyterian. Home: 420 Rookwood Dr Charlottesville VA 22903-4732 E-mail: wgs2Z@virginia.edu.

SHENKMAN, MARK RONALD, investment and finance executive; b. Providence, Aug. 17, 1943; s. George and Florence (Littman) S.; children: Andrew Harris, Gregory Alexander; m. Rosalind Schmidt, Aug. 10, 1997; 1 stepson, Justin Warren Slatky. BA, U. Conn., Storrs, 1965; MBA, George Wash. U., Washington, DC, 1967; LHD (hon.), U Conn., Storrs, 2007. Security analyst New Eng. Mchts. Bank, Boston, 1969-71; fin. analyst Stone & Webster Securities Corp., Boston, 1971-73; rsch. analyst, portfolio mgr. Fidelity Mgmt. & Research Co., Boston, 1973-79; v.p. Lehman Bros. Kuhn Loeb, NYC, 1979-83; pres. First Investors Asset Mgmt. Co., NYC, 1983-85; pres., chief exec. officer Shenkman Capital Mgmt. Inc., NYC, 1985—. Bd. dirs. Mason sch. bus. found. Coll. William & Mary. Vice chmn. bd. trustees Wilbraham, Mass. and Monson Acad.; bd. visitors, trustee George Washington U. Sch. Bus.; bd. govs. Hillel Found. 1st lt. US Army, 1967-69. Mem. Am. Bankruptcy Inst., NY Soc. Security Analysts, Boston Security Analysts Soc., Am. Statis. Assn., CFA Inst. Home: Gaston Farm Rd Greenwich CT 06831 Office: 461 Fifth Ave New York NY 10017-6234 also: 462 Harbor Dr Stamford CT 06902 Office Phone: 212-867-9090.

SHENOI, RANEE MELANIE, physiatrist; b. Bombay, May 16, 1964; d. Arthur Desilva and Elyn Mary Shenoi; m. Norse Rey Bear, June 1, 1991; children: Christina Bear, Eric Bear. MD, U. Tex., Houston, 1991. Diplomate Am. Bd. Phys. Medicine and Rehab., 1996. Staff physiatrist Panorama Orthop. Clinic, Colo., 1997—2001; pvt. physiatrist Lakewood, Colo., 2001—07. Asst clin. prof. U. Colo. Health Sci. Ctr., Denver, 1995—96. Contbr. articles to profl. jours. Teagle Found. scholar, Exxon, 1987—91. Fellow: Am. Assn. Phys. Medicine and Rehab. Office: Ranee Shenoi Md Llc 255 Union Blvd Ste 380 Lakewood CO 80228 Home Phone: 303-949-2053; Office Phone: 303-989-0256. Office Fax: 303-989-0166.

SHENON, PHILIP, journalist; b. San Francisco, June 26, 1959; s. Peter and Philippa (Richards) Shenon. BA in English Lit., Brown U., 1981. Reporter N.Y. Times, NYC, 1983—85, corr. Washington, 1985—90, S.E. Asia corr. Bangkok, 1991—95, def. corr. Washington, 1996—97, diplomatic corr., 1997—99, investigative corr., 2000—. Office: NY Times Washington Bur 1627 I St NW Washington DC 20006-4007

SHEON, AARON, art historian, educator; b. Toledo, Oct. 7, 1937; s. Benjamin William and Katherine (Rappoport) S.; m. Martine Bruel, Jan. 26, 1963 (div. 1986); children: Sandrine, Nicolas; m. Jill Belasco, Nov. 11, 2000. BA, U. Mich., 1959, MA, 1960; M.F.A. (Wilson fellow), Princeton U., 1962, PhD, 1966; postgrad., U. Paris, 1962-63. Staff officer, dir. gen.'s cabinet UNESCO, Paris, 1963-66; asst. prof. U. Pitts., 1966-69, asso. prof., 1969-78, acting chmn. dept. fine arts, 1969, 79-80, dir. univ. program Rouen, France, 1974-75, prof. art history, 1979—2003, prof. emeritus, 2004; vis. prof. Carnegie-Mellon U., 1981, 2002—03. Vis. exhbn. curator Mus. Art, Carnegie Inst., Pitts., 1977-81; program cons. Nat. Endowment Arts and Humanities, 1978-85; visual arts cons. Pa. Arts Council, 1981; vis. mem. Inst. for Advanced Study, Princeton, 1984-85 Author: The Gosman Collection, 1969, Monticelli, His Contemporaries, His Influence, 1978, Organic Vision, The Architecture of Peter Berndtson, 1980, Monticelli, 1986, Paul Guigou, 1987. Recipient Charles E. Merrill faculty award, 1968; Chancellor Bowman award, 1976; Honor award Pa. Soc. Architects, 1982, Innovation award in tchg. Art History Course for Blind Students U. Pitts., 2001, Bellet Teaching award, 2002, Innovation in Tchg. award, 2003; grantee Ford Found., 1967, NEH, 1979, European Union grantee, 2006; Gould Arts Found. fellow, 1986 Mem. Coll. Art Assn., Société de l'histoire de l'art français, Am. Assn. of Mus. Office: U Pitts Dept History Arts & Arch Pittsburgh PA 15260 Office Phone: 412-648-2400. Business E-Mail: ash2@pitt.edu.

SHEPARD, BEATRICE L., retired microbiologist, historian; b. Hillsdale, Mich., May 15, 1919; d. James Wesley Shepard and Ona Ola Kinney. AB in Zoolog., U. Calif., Berkeley, 1940. Regional lab. dir. L.A. County Health Dept., LA, 1945-46; sr. biologist, sr. chemist S.E. Regional Lab., Juneau, Alaska, 1946-67; acting chief of labs. Alaska Dept. Health & Social Svcs., Juneau, 1967-70; microbiologist in charge S.E. Regional Lab., Alaska Dept. Health and Social Svcs., 1967—77; ret., 1977. Chemist L.A. County Health Dept., 1944-45, L.A. County Gen. Hosp., 1943-44; dir. pub. health lab. Health Dept. Riverside (Calif.) County, 1942-43. Author: Praise the Lord and Pass the Penicillin, 1979; co-author: Have Gospel Tent, Will Travel, History of 100 Years of Alaskan Methodism, 1986; editor: (newsletter) Western Cir. Rider, 1998—2005, Eagle River United Meth. Camp, 1998—; contbr. articles to profl. jours., chapters to books. Docent Alaska State Mus., 1992—2004; mem. Juneau Borough Commn. on Aging, 1997—; curator Alaska State Mus., 2003; mem. gen. commn. archives and history United Meth. Ch. Archives Ctr., Madison, NJ, 1988—96; historian Alaska Meth. Ch., Alaska Missionary Conf., Anchorage, 1980—; bd. dirs., advocacy chair Mus. Alaska, 1992—2005; sec. bd. dirs. Eagle River Meth. Camp, 1955—2005; bd. dirs. Western Jurisdictional Commn. on Archives and History, 1984—2005; chair Alaska Missionary Conf. Commn. on Archives and History, 1980—2004. Named Outstanding Lay Person of Yr. award Alaska Missionary Conf. of United Meth. Ch., 1986; recipient Meritorious Health Svc. award Alaska Pub. Health Assn., 1990. Mem.: Friends of Alaska State Mus. (hon.; life), Museums Alaska (hon.; life). Avocation: photography. Home: 12585 Glacier Hwy Juneau AK 99801 E-mail: BShep98308@aol.com.

SHEPARD, CHRISTY J., special education educator; d. William E. and Shirley M. Shepard. BS in Spl. Edn., U. Houston, 1974, MS in Occupl. Edn., 1989. Salesperson/customer svc. Sears, Roebuck & Co., Houston, 1968—93; sec. Preston Exterminating Co., Houston, 1971—74; tchr. Aldine Ind. Sch. Dist., Houston, 1974—76; tchr. of students with visual impairments Cypress-Fairbanks Ind. Sch. Dist., Houston, 1976—. Facilitator Region IV Edn. Svc. Ctr., Houston, 1999—. V.p. Harris County MUD #23, asst. sec./treas., 1989—. Mem.: Assn. Tex. Profl. Educators, Assn. Edn. and Rehab. Blind and Visually Impaired (treas. 2000—, Outstanding Mem. award 2007). Avocations: reading, travel, cross stitch. Home Phone: 713-896-0789; Office Phone: 281-897-6490.

SHEPARD, DAVID HASPEL, film restoration specialist; b. NYC, Oct. 22, 1940; s. Bertram David Shepard and Marjorie (Haspel) Markley; m. Kimberly Fetter, Mar. 26, 1977 (div.); 1 child, Benjamin Baker. AB, Hamilton Coll., 1962; MA, U. Pa., 1963. Asst. prof. theatre Pa. State U., State College, 1965-68; film acquisitions mgr., programmer Am. Film Inst., Washington, 1968-73; v.p. Blackhawk Films, Inc., Davenport, Iowa, 1973-76; spl. projects officer Dirs. Guild Am., Hollywood, Calif., 1976-87; adj. prof. cinema-TV U. So. Calif., LA, 1982—2002; owner Film Preservation Assocs., Hat Creek, Calif., 1989-2000; managing dir. Film Preservation Assocs., Inc., 2000—. Trustee Internat. Film Seminars, NYC, 1972-82; adv. bd. Hollywood (Calif.) Entertainment Mus., 1984—, San Francisco Silent Film Festival, 1998—. Prodr. (video series) Chaplin: A Legacy of Laughter, 1992-93, Masterworks of D.W. Griffith, 1992/2007, Landmarks of Early Soviet Cinema, 1992—, Great British Documentary Movement, 1993-2003, Golden Age of German Cinema, 1994—, Art of Buster Keaton, 1995, Douglas Fairbanks: King of Hollywood, 1996, Cecil B. De Mille: The Visionary Years, 1997-2005, Slapstick Encyclopedia, 1998, Les Vampires (1915 serial), 1998, Lon Chaney: Behind the Masks, 1997-2003, Valentino Lives!, 2002, Unseen Cinema: American Avant-Garde Films 1894-1941, 2005, Georges Melies: First Wizard of the Cinema, 2007. Recipient Preservation award Soc. Cinephiles, 1970, 95, 2 Emmy awards Acad. TV Arts & Scis., 1973, Scholarship and Preservation award Internat. Documentary Assn., 1989, Prix Jean Mitry, Giornate des Cinema Muto, Pordenone, Italy, 1993, Saturn award Acad. Sci. Fiction, Horror and Fantasy Films, 1999, Mel Novikoff award San Francisco Internat. Film Festival, 2000, Preservation award Anthology Film Archives, 2005, Heritage award Nat. Soc. Film Critics, 2006, Hubbard award Niles Essanay Film Mus., 2006, Silver Light Lifetime Achievement award, Assn. Moving Image Archivists, 2007. Mem.: Soc. Cinema and Media Studies (hon. life), Acad. Motion Picture Arts and Scis. Home: PO Box 71 Hat Creek CA 96040-0071 Office Phone: 530-335-7420. Personal E-mail: dshepfilm@aol.com.

SHEPARD, DONALD SLOANE, public policy research educator; b. NYC, Sept. 15, 1947; s. Bertram David Shepard and Marjorie (Haspel) Markley; m. Emily A. Maitin, Aug. 17, 1980; children: Melissa R. Maitin-Shepard, Jeremy B. Maitin-Shepard. BA (magna cum laude) with highest honors, Harvard U., 1969, M in Pub. Policy, 1973, PhD, 1976. Lectr. U. Nairobi, Kenya, 1970—71; sr. economist Mass. Dept. Pub. Health, Boston, 1977—79; dir. econ. rsch. VA, West Roxbury, Mass., 1979—85; lectr. Harvard U., Cambridge, Mass., 1977—80, assoc. prof., 1980—91; prof. Brandeis U., Waltham, Mass., 1991—. Co-developer QALY (Quality Adjusted Life Year), 1976; mem. pub. policy adv. com. Am. Found. AIDS Rsch., Washington, 1991-95; vis. lectr. Harvard U., 1992-99; adj. faculty Boston U., 1986-2004; affiliated faculty Brown U., Providence, 1995—; dir. cost and value work group Schneider Inst. Health Policy Brandeis U., 2000-; health svcs. rsch. study sects. Nat. Inst. Alcohol Abuse and Alcoholism, 1998-2002, Nat. Inst. Drug Abuse, 2004-06, other NIH ad hoc rev. coms. Author: Assessing Costs for Cost-Effectiveness Analysis, 1988, Analysis of Hospital Costs: A Manual for Managers, 2000; guest editor Adminstrn. and Policy in Mental Health, 2005; contbr. more than 100 articles to profl. jours. Bd. sci. advisors Sabin Vaccine Inst., Washington DC, 1994—; bd. councilors Pediat. Dengue Vaccine Initiative, 2002—2005; mem. alumni coun. Phillips Acad. Grad. fellow NSF, 1971; prin. investigator Nat. Inst. on Drug Abuse and Nat. Inst. on Alcohol Abuse and Alcoholism, 1993—, Ctrs. Medicine & Medicaid Svcs., 2000—, Pediat. Dengue Vaccine Initiative, 2003-. Mem. APHA, Mass. Pub. Health Assn., Acad. Health, Internat. Health Econs. Assn., Phi Beta Kappa. Avocations: cross country skiing, swimming. Home: 16 Cranmore Rd Wellesley MA 02481-1329 Office: Brandeis U Heller Sch 415 South St Waltham MA 02454-9110 Office Phone: 781-736-3975. Business E-Mail: shepard@brandeis.edu.

SHEPARD, GEOFFREY CARROLL, insurance company executive; b. Santa Barbara, Calif., Nov. 7, 1944; s. James J. and Barbara (Hoose) S.; m. Saundra Gayle Carlton, Jan. 10, 1973; children: Jonathan Pettus, William Dabney. BA, Whittier Coll., 1966; JD, Harvard U., 1969. Bar: D.C. 1972, Pa. 1977, U.S. Supreme Ct. 1973. White House fellow, 1969-70; staff asst. to Pres. White House, 1970-72, assoc. dir. domestic coun., 1972-75; sr. assoc. Steptoe & Johnson, Washington, 1975-77; sr. v.p., assoc. gen. counsel CIGNA Corp., Phila., 1977-91; sr. v.p., gen. counsel, corp. sec. Reliance Ins. Group, Phila., 1991-94; pres. corp. divsn. Karr Barth Assocs., Phila., 1994—. Trustee Whittier Coll., 2002—. Office: Karr Barth Assocs Inc 40 Monument Rd Bala Cynwyd PA 19004-1797

SHEPARD, JEAN HECK, retired publishing consultant; b. NYC, Feb. 2, 1930; d. Chester Reed and Anna S. (Charig) Heck; m. Lawrence Vaeth Hastings, Mar. 29, 1950 (div. 1953); 1 child, Lance Clifford Hastings; m. Daniel A. Shepard, July 26, 1954 (div. 1981); 1 child, Bradley Reed. BA, Barnard Coll., 1950; postgrad., Columbia U., 1952. Mem. sch. and libr. svc. Viking Press, NYC, 1956-57; asst. dir. sch. and libr. promotion E.P. Dutton, NYC, 1957-58; dir. advt. publicity and promotion Thomas Y. Crowell Co., NYC, 1958-62; dir. advt. and promotion Charles Scribner's Sons, NYC, 1962-67; cons. Stephen Greene Press, Brattleboro, Vt., 1970-73; mktg. mgr. A&W Publishers, NYC, 1979-80, Franklin Watts Publ., NYC, 1980-82; pub. 2 mags., divsn. advt. & promotion mgr. McGraw Hill Book Co., NYC, 1983-85; cons. Monitor Publ. Co., NYC, 1988-2000. Author: Simple Family Favorites, 1971, Herb and Spice Sampler, 1972, Cook With Wine!, 1973, Earth Watch: Notes on a Restless Planet, 1973, Harvest Home Steak Cookbook, 1974, Fresh Fruits and Vegetables, 1974, Yankee Magazine, 1972, Let Them be Sea Captains. Mem.: Authors Guild, Am. Libr. Assn., Women's Nat. Book Assn., Pub. Ad Club. Methodist. Avocations: reading, writing, travel, music, dance. Home: 73 Kingswood Dr Bethel CT 06801-1834 Office Fax: 203-798-2924. E-mail: shepardagcy@mindspring.com.

SHEPARD, JEAN M., city health department administrator; b. San Diego; BA in Sociology, San Diego U. Employee San Diego County, 1976—, adminstrv. dept. Auditor, Contr., 1978—85, asst. chief adminstrv. officer, 1985—89, various positions Dept. Social Services, 1989—95, asst. dir. health, 1995—98, COO health and human services agy., 1998; dir. County of San Diego Health and Human Services Agy. Office: Health and Human Services Agy 1700 Pacific Hwy Rm 207 San Diego CA 92101

SHEPARD, JUDITH BETHEA, librarian; b. Tuscaloosa, Ala., Apr. 12, 1947; d. Odis Hamner Reynolds and Audrea Earle Thomas; m. James Crenshaw Shepard, Feb. 19, 1978; children: Angela Elaine Ashcraft, Penelope Lea Taylor. BA, Ala. Coll., 1969; MLS, U. Ala., 1974. Tchr., libr. Decatur City Schs., Ala., 1969—71; libr. Gadsden Pub. Libr., Ala., 1974—76; libr., head of info. svcs. Ala. Pub. Libr. Svc., Montgomery, 1976—. Contbr. articles to profl. jours. Mem. Montgomery Mus. Fine Arts, Ala., 1999—, Montgomery Zool. Soc., Ala., 2002—; St. Peter's Parish Coun. Mem.: Ala. Libr. Assn. (moderator ref. and adult svcs. roundtable 2000—03), Capital City Artists Group. Republican. Roman Catholic. Achievements include development of State of Ala. Resource Sharing Sys. Avocations: painting, travel, reading. Home: 30 Tecumseh Dr Montgomery AL 36117 Office: Ala Pub Libr Svc 6030 Monticello Dr Montgomery AL 36130

SHEPARD, JULIAN LEIGH, lawyer, humanitarian; b. St. Paul, Feb. 17, 1957; s. Frank and Beatrice (Getsug) S. BS, Ind. U., 1980, JD, 1983; postgrad., Am. U., 1995-98. Bar: Pa. 1985, Ind. 1984, DC 1987; US Ct. Appeals (DC cir.) 1984; US Dist. Ct. (so. dist.) Ind. 1984. Atty. Nat. Assn. Broadcasters, Washington, 1984-86, asst. gen. counsel, 1986-87; counselor at law Heron, Burchette, Ruckert & Rothwell, Washington, 1987-88; sr. policy adv. mass media Nat. Telecommunications & Info. Adminstrn./U.S. Dept. Comm., Washington, 1988-90; v.p., gen. counsel Assn. for Maximum Svc. TV, Inc., Washington, 1990-95; atty., shareholder Verner, Liipfert, Bernhard, McPherson & Hand, Washington, 1995—2001; ptnr. Venable, Baetjer, Howard and Civiletti, L.L.P., 2001—03; ptnr., comm. practice chmn. Williams Mullen Profl. Corp., Washington, 2003—. Mem. fed. spectrum planning and policy adv. com., US Dept. Commerce, Washington, 1992—2002. Co-chmn. editorial adv. bd. Fed. Comms. Law Jour., Washington, 1992-94; contbr. articles to profl. jour. Bd. vis. Georgetown U. Inst. on Comparative Polit. and Econ. Systems, 1984-95; prin. Coun. for Excellence in Govt., Washington, 1990-02. Paul Harris fellow, Rotary Internat. Found. Bd. Regents Fund for Am. Studies, Washington, 1999—; mem. ABA (law practice mgmt. sect. leadership activities bd. 1995-96), Fed. Comms. Bar Assn. (law jour. com. 1992-95), Minority Media and Telecomm. Coun. (life), Phi Delta Phi (Nat. Balfour scholar 1983), Rotary Club (charter). Avocations: visual arts, scuba diving, photography. Home: PO Box 6643 Mc Lean VA 22106-6643 Office: Williams Mullen 1666 K St NW Ste 1200 Washington DC 20006

SHEPARD, LANCE HASTINGS, marketing professional, consultant, newscaster; b. NYC, Dec. 11, 1950; s. Lawrence Vaeth Hastings and Jean Heck Hastings Shepard. Student, Boston U., 1969—70; BS in Psychology, Franklin Pierce Coll., Rindge, NH, 1973. Cert. radio operator NY. Mgmt. tng. Waltham Savs. Bank, Mass., 1974—75; news and sports anchor Ch. 10 Cable TV, Danbury, Conn., 1975—76; guest rels. reception Plaza Hotel, Waldorf Astoria, NYC, 1978—80; owner DJ-on-Call, NYC, 1981—88; v.p., dir. fin. Shepard Agy., Brewster, NY, 1988—2000, exec. v.p., treas. Bethel, Conn., 2000—. Umpire Nat. Assn. Baseball Umpires, NH, 1970, Babe Ruth Baseball, Conn., 1978, Little League, Conn., 1978; referee Accredited NH Basketball Ofcls., 1973. Mem.: Princeton Club. Avocations: French horn, trumpet, reading, sports, films. Home: 73 Kingswood Dr Bethel CT 06801 Office: Shepard Agy M&T Bank Bldg Brewster NY 10509 Office Phone: 845-279-2900. Office Fax: 203-798-2924. Personal E-mail: shepardagcy@mindspring.com.

SHEPARD, MICHAEL J., prosecutor; Atty. U.S. Dept. Justice, Chgo., 1993—, asst. atty.

SHEPARD, RANDALL TERRY, state supreme court chief justice; b. Lafayette, Ind., Dec. 24, 1946; s. Richard Schilling and Dorothy Ione (Donlen) S.; m. Amy Wynne MacDonell, May 7, 1988; one child, Martha MacDonell. AB cum laude, Princeton U., 1969; JD, Yale U., 1972; LLM, U. Va., 1995; LLD (hon.), U. So. Ind., 1995, U. S.C., 1996. Bar: Ind. 1972, U.S. Dist. Ct. (so. dist.) Ind. 1972. Spl. asst. to under sec. U.S. Dept. Transp., Washington, 1972-74; exec. asst. to mayor City of Evansville, Ind., 1974-79; judge Vanderburgh Superior Ct., Evansville, 1980-85; assoc. justice Ind. Supreme Ct., Indpls., 1985-87, chief justice, 1987—. Instr. U. Evansville, 1975-78, Indiana U., 1995, 99; pres. Nat. Conference of Chief Justices, 2005—. Author: Preservation Rules and Regulations, 1980, Indiana Legal History, 2005; contbr. articles to profl. publs. Bd. advisors Nat. Trust for Hist. Preservation, 1980-87, chmn. bd. advisors, 1983-85, trustee, 1987-96; dir. Hist. Landmarks Found. Ind., 1983—, chmn., 1989-92, hon. chmn., 1992—, chmn. State Student Assistance Commn. Ind., 1981-85; chmn. Ind. Commn. on Bicentennial of U.S. Constn., 1986-91; vice chmn. Vanderburgh County Rep. Ctrl. Com., 1977-80. Recipient Disting. Svc. award Evansville Jaycees, 1982, Herbert Harley award Am. Judicature Soc., 1992, Wickler award Nat. Assn. Women Judges, 2004. Mem. ABA (coun. mem. sect. on legal edn. 1991—, chair sect. on legal edn. 1997-98, chair appellate judges conf. 1996-97), Ind. Bar Assn., Ind. Judges Assn., Princeton Club (N.Y.), Capitol Hill Club (Washington), Columbia Club (Indpls.), Woodstock Club (Indpls.). Republican. Methodist. Home: 3644 Totem Ln Indianapolis IN 46208-4171 Office: Ind Supreme Ct 315 State House Indianapolis IN 46204-2213 Office Phone: 317-232-2550. *

SHEPARD, RICAHRD, film director, producer, writer; b. NYC; m. Carolyn Horwitz, July 6, 2002. Dir., writer (films) Cool Blue, 1988, The Linguini Incident, 1991, The Matador, 2005; dir.: (TV films) The Royale, 1996, Class Warfare, 2001; (TV series) Remember WENN, 1996, Criminal Minds, 2005, Ugly Betty, 2006 (Outstanding Directorial Achievement in Comedy Series, Dirs. Guild Am., 2007); prodr., dir., writer (films) Mercy, 1995, Oxygen, 1999, Mexico City, 2000; prodr.: (films) Scotland, Pa., 2001. Office: c/o Abandon Entertainment 711 Route 302 Pine Bush NY 12566 E-mail: SaltyShep@aol.com. *

SHEPARD, RICHARD BLOUNT, surgeon, educator; b. Birmingham, Ala., May 9, 1926; m. Winyss Renee Acton, Mar. 26, 1955; children: Winyss Elizabeth, Kathryn Bouchelle, Richard Kesniel, Karen Acton. BS in Physics, Pa. State U., 1949; MD, U. Pa., 1953. Intern, resident in surgery U. Pa. Hosp., Phila., 1953-59; instr., rsch. assoc. in physiology U. Pa., Phila., 1954-56; chief resident Fitkin Hosp. Hahnemann Med. Coll., Neptune, NJ, 1959-60; from instr. to prof. surgery U. Ala., Birmingham, 1960-98, prof. surgery, emeritus, 1998—. Engr. Victoreen Instrument Co., Cleve., 1946; engr. Haller, Raymond & Brown, State College, Pa., 1948; cons. for device implant mfrs. and electronics mfr., 1960-2004; chmn. USRA-NASA biomed. com. for studies selection, shuttle orbital flight tests, 1981-83. Contbr. articles to profl. jours. and chpts. to books. With US Army, 1943—46, spl. engr. detatchment Manhattan Project US Army, 1945—46. Grantee Heart Assn. S.E. Pa., NIH. Fellow ACS, Am. Coll. Cardiology, Soc. for Vascular Surgery (disting.); mem. IEEE (life), Heart Rhythm Soc., Soc. Thoracic Surgeons. Achievements include research in blood flow and energy characteristics, especially as related to cardiopulmonary bypass operations and underlying physiology; one of the first to implant cardiac pacemakers and investigational defibrillators; application of physics and tissue biology to clinical and laboratory implantable device development, teaching and problem solutions. Office Phone: 205-934-4672. Business E-Mail: RShepard@uab.edu.

SHEPARD, ROBERT M., lawyer, investment banker, engineer; b. Amityville, NY, Feb. 15, 1932; s. Sidney M. and Undine L. (Lehmann) Shapiro; m. Barbara S. Stannard, June 25, 1955 (div. 1980); children: Karen Michele Shepard Sweer, Daniel Robert; m. Joanne E. Devlin, May 16, 1981 (div. 1993); m. Martha Kothe, Nov. 24, 1999. B.C.E., Cornell U., 1954; MBA, Hofstra Coll., 1960; LL.B., Yale U., 1963; LLM, NYU, 1988. Bar: N.Y. 1964; registered profl. engr., N.Y., Conn. Project engr. Lockwood Kessler & Bartlett, Syosset, NY, 1956-60; assoc. atty. Cravath, Swaine & Moore, NYC and Paris, 1963-70; gen. ptnr. Kuhn, Loeb & Co., NYC, 1970-77; sr. v.p. Donaldson, Lufkin & Jenrette, NYC, 1977-83; gen. ptnr. Donovan Leisure Newton & Irvine, NYC, 1983-89, Adler & Shepard, NYC, 1989-91, Shepard & van Essche, NYC, 1991, Ballon Stoll Bader & Nadler, P.C., NYC, 1992—. Note and comment editor: Yale Law Jour., 1962-63. Bd. dirs. N.Y. Grand Opera; bd. govs. Regency Whist Club. Recipient Fuertes Medal Cornell U., 1953 Mem. ABA, Am. N.Y. State Bar Assn., Pub. Power Assn., Nat. Assn. Bond Lawyers, Order of Coif, Union League Club (bd. govs.), Regency Whist Club, Inc., Tau Beta Pi, Chi Epsilon. Home: 750 Park Ave Apt 2C New York NY 10021-4252 Office: Ballon Stoll Bader & Nadler 1450 Broadway New York NY 10018-2201 Office Phone: 212-575-7900 x248.

SHEPARD, SAM (SAMUEL SHEPARD ROGERS), playwright, actor; b. Ft. Sheridan, Ill., Nov. 5, 1943; s. Samuel Shepard and Jane Elaine (Schook) Rogers; m. O-Lan Johnson Dark, Nov. 9, 1969 (div. 1984); 1 child, Jesse Mojo; life ptnr. Jessica Lange; children: Hannah Jane, Samuel Walker. Student, Mt. San Antonio Jr. Coll., Walnut, Calif., 1961-62. Playwright-in-residence Magic Theatre, San Francisco. Author: (plays) Cowboys, The Rock Garden, 1964, 4-H Club, Up to Thursday, Dog, Rocking Chair, 1965, Chicago, 1965 (Obie award, 1966), Icarus's Mother, 1965 (Obie award, 1966), Fourteen Hundred Thousand, 1966, Red Cross, 1966 (Obie award, 1966), Melodrama Play, 1966 (Obie award, 1968), La Turista, 1967 (Obie award, 1967), Cowboys #2, 1967, Forensic and the Navigators, 1967 (Obie award, 1968), The Holy Ghostly, The Unseen Hand, 1969, Operation Sidewinder, Shaved Splits, 1970, Mad Dog Blues, Terminal, (with Patti Smith) Cowboy Mouth, Black Bog Beast Bait, 1971, The Tooth of Crime, 1972 (Obie award, 1973), Blue Bitch, (with Megan Terry and Jean-Claude van Itallie) Nightwalk, 1973, Geography of a Horse Dreamer, Little Ocean, Killer's Head, 1974, Action, 1974 (Obie award, 1975), Starving Class, 1977, Buried Child, 1978 (Obie award, 1977, Pulitzer Prize in drama, 1979, Obie award, 1979), Tongues, Savage/Love, Seduced, 1979, True West, 1981, Fool for Love, 1983 (Obie award, 1984), Superstitions, The Sad Lament of Pecos Bill on the Eve of Killing his Wife, 1983, A Lie of the Mind, 1985 (New York Drama Critics' Circle award, 1986), States of Shock, 1991, Simpatico, 1993, The Late Henry Moss, 2000, (collections of plays) Five Plays by Sam Shepard, 1967, The Unseen Hand and Other Plays, 1971, 1986, Mad Dog Blues and Other Plays, 1972, The Tooth of Crime and Geography of a Horse Dreamer, 1974, Angel City, Curse of the Starving Class and Other Plays, 1976, Buried Child, Seduced, Suicide in B-Flat, 1979, (collection of plays) Four Two-Act Plays by Sam Shepard, 1980, Chicago and Other Plays, Seven Plays, 1981, Fool for Love and The Sad Lament of Pecos Bill on the Eve of Killing His Wife, 1983, Fool For Love and Other Plays, 1984, 1986, contbr. to Oh! Calcutta, 1976, (with Bob Dylan) Renaldo and Clara, 1978, (collection of plays) Paris, Texas, 1984, (other writings) Rolling Thunder Logbook, 1977, Hawk Moon: A Book of Short Stories, Poems and Monologues, 1981, Motel Chronicles, 1982; dir.(writer): (plays) Fool for Love, 1983, A Lie of the Mind, 1985; (screenplays) Far North, 1988, Silent Tongue, 1993; actor: (plays) A Number, 2004—05; (films) Renaldo and Clara, Days of Heaven, 1978, Resurrection, 1980, Raggedy Man, 1981, Frances, 1982, The Right Stuff, 1983 (Academy award nomination best supporting actor, 1984), Country, 1984, Fool for Love, 1985, Crimes of the Heart, 1986, Baby Boom, 1987, Steel Magnolias, 1989, Hot Spot, 1990, Bright Angel, Defenseless, 1991, Thunderheart, 1992, The Pelican Brief, 1993, Safe Passage, 1994, The Good Old Boys, 1995, Curtain Call, The Only Thrill, 1997, All the Pretty Horses, 2000, The Pledge, 2001, Swordfish, 2001, Black Hawk Down, 2001, Leo, 2002, Blind Horizon, 2003, The Notebook, 2004, Don't Come Knocking, 2005, Stealth, 2005; (TV films, performance) Streets of Laredo, 1995, Lily Dale, 1996, Purgatory, Dash & Lilly, 1999, Hamlet, 2000 (nominated for Golden Globe, Best Actor). Named to Theater Hall of Fame, 1994; recipient Nat. Inst. and Am. Acad. Arts and Letters award for lit., 1974, Creative Arts award Brandeis U., 1975; grantee Rockefeller Found., 1967, Guggenheim Found., 1968, 1971; Fellow, U. Minn., 1966, Yale U., 1967. Mem.: Am. Acad. and Inst. of Arts and Letters.

SHEPARD, SARA LYNETTE, elementary school educator; b. Rochester, NY, Oct. 15, 1982; d. Robert C. and LaVaughn M. Shepard; life ptnr. Benjamin Rawleigh. BS in Edn., Keuka Coll., Keuka Park, NY, 2004; MS in Edn., Alfred U., NY, 2005. Lic. tchr. elem. edn. NY State Dept. Edn., 2004, tchr. children with disabilities grades 1-6 NY State Dept. Edn., 2004, cert. literacy tchr. birth through grade 6 NY State Dept. Edn., 2005, lic. elem. tchr. Commonwealth Va. Dept. Edn., 2005. First grade tchr. Culpeper County Schools - A.G. Richardson Elem. Sch., Culpeper, Va., 2005—06; reading specialist grade K-5 Whitesville Ctrl. Sch., Whitesville, NY, 2006—. Mem.: NY State Tchrs. Union. Avocations: travel, reading, scrapbooks.

SHEPARD, STEPHEN BENJAMIN, journalist, educator, retired editor; b. NYC, July 20, 1939; s. William and Ruth Shepard; m. Lynn Povich, Sept. 16, 1979; children: Sarah, Ned. BS, CCNY, 1961; MS, Columbia U., 1964. Reporter, editor, writer Bus. Week, NYC, 1966—75; asst. prof., dir. Walter Bagehot fellowship program econs. and bus. journalism Columbia U., NYC, 1975—76; sr. editor Newsweek, NYC, 1976—81; editor Saturday Rev., NYC, 1981—82; exec. editor Bus. Week mag., NYC, 1982—84, editor in chief, 1984—2005; dean Grad. Sch. Journalism CUNY, NYC, 2005—. Adj. prof. Columbia Grad. Sch. Journalism, 1971—75. Bd. visitors Columbia Grad. Sch. Journalism. Recipient Lifetime Achievement award, Gerald Loeb Found., 1999, Henry Johnson Fisher award, Mag. Publs. Am., 2000, President's award, Overseas Press Club, 2003. Mem.: Coun. Fgn. Rls., Am. Soc. Mag. Editors (v.p. 1990—92, pres. 1992—94, Hall of Fame 1999), Century Assn. Office: CUNY Grad Sch Journalism 230 West 41st St New York NY 10036 Business E-Mail: steve.shepard@journalism.cuny.edu.

SHEPARD, WILLIAM SETH, diplomat, writer; b. Boston, June 7, 1935; s. Robinson and Myra Ellen (Foster) S.; m. Lois Rosalie Burke, June 25, 1960; children: Stephanie Lee, Cynthia Robin, Warren Burke (dec.) AB cum laude, Wesleyan U., Middletown, Conn., 1957; JD, Harvard U., Cambridge, Mass., 1961. Bar: NH 1961, US Ct. Mil. Appeals 1962 US Supreme Ct., 1970. Aide to ambs. Henry Cabot Lodge and Ellsworth Bunker, Am. embassy, Saigon, Vietnam, 1966-67; staff officer Exec. Secretariat Dept. of State, Washington, 1967-69; consul, polit. officer Am. Embassy, Budapest, Hungary, 1970-73; desk officer Hungarian affairs Dept. State, Washington, 1973-75; desk officer Singapore and Malaysian affairs Dept. of State, Washington, 1975-77; dep. polit. counselor Am. embassy, Athens, Greece, 1978-80; consul gen. Am. Consulate Gen., Bordeaux, France, 1983-85; dir. Office Congl. Affairs, ACDA, Washington, 1987-89; cons. to gen. counsel USDA, Washington, 1991-92. Lectr. internat. law U. Singapore, 1965—66; lectr. Chesapeake Coll., 2006—; CEO The Shepard Internat. Group, Inc., 1994—. Author: Consular Tales, 2001, Murder on the Danube, 2001, Vintage Murder, 2002, Foreign Service Tales, 2002, Shepard's Guide to Mastering French Wines, 2003, Murder in Dordogne, 2005, Diplomatic Tales, 2006; wine editor: Bonjour Paris, 2002—. Candidate for Rep. nomination 8th Md. Congl. Dist., 1985—86; Rep. nominee for Gov. of Md., 1990; Rep. candidate for Gov. of Md., 1994; del. Rep. Nat. Conv., 1992; Md. co-chmn. Dole Presdl. Campaign, 1996; apptd. mem. citizens adv. com. Chesapeake Exec. Coun., by Gov. of Md., 2004—07. Recipient Pro Libertate Hungariae Commemorative medallion, 1981, Pub. Svc. Leadership award U.S.-Baltic Found., 1996, George L. Plimpton Pub. Svc. award Tilton Sch., 2003; French Govt. teaching asst. and Fulbright travel grantee, 1957-58; Congl. fellow Am. Polit. Sci. Assn. and fgn. policy legis. asst. to Senator Robert Dole, 1982-83. Mem. Soc. Mayflower Desc., Gov. Bradford Compact, Soc. Desc. Colonial Govs. (chancellor gen. 1993-95), Soc. Desc. Colonial Wars, Montesquieu Acad. France (corr.), City Tavern Club (Washington), Flagon and Trencher (Trencher award 2003), Les Chevaliers de Bretvin, Ordre des Compagnons de Bordeaux, Connetablie de Guyenne, La Jurade de St. Emilion, Bontemps Medoc et des Graves, Tred Avon Players. Republican. Unitarian Universalist. Avocations: reading, vintage Bordeaux wines, gastronomy, cruise lecturing. Home: 28800 Outram St Easton MD 21601 *I remember Himalayan peaks, Asian sunsets, Greek islands and Bordeaux vineyards. Along the way, hard work in a principled cause is its own reward. In the end, family life and friends, a foyer, pets, a book worth reading, and a glass of wine matter most.*

SHEPHARD, BRUCE DENNIS, obstetrician, educator, medical writer; b. San Francisco, Apr. 21, 1944; s. Richard G. and Madelyn (Rogers) S.; children: Christopher, Carleton, Elizabeth. BA in History, U. Calif., Berkeley, 1966; MD, U. Calif., San Francisco, 1970. Diplomate Am. Bd. Ob-Gyn. Intern Jackson Meml. Hosp.-U. Miami (Fla.), 1970-71, resident in ob-gyn., 1971-74; pvt. practice Tampa, 1976—; clin. assoc. prof. obstetrics U. So. Fla. Sch. Medicine, Tampa, 1976—. Bd. dirs. Ctr. of Excellence, Humana Women's Hosp., Tampa, Fla., 1983-90, Gulf Coast Health Systems Agy., 1980-83; mem. midwifery adv. com. Fla. Dept. Health and Human Resources, Tallahassee, 1982-86. Prin. author: The Complete Guide to Women's Health, 1982, 3d rev. edit., 1997; prin., writer, spokesperson (series of TV commls.) The Healthy Woman (Gold Link award 1987); mem. med. adv. bd. Baby Talk mag., 1992—; bd. dirs. PBS affiliate WEDU, 1998-2005; contbr. articles to profl. jours. and women's mags. Lectr. Continuing Edn., Inc., 2002—; mem. Agy. Health Care Adminstrn., Dept. Health and Rehab. Svcs., Fla., cert. med. expert Fla., 2001—; mem. Healthier Fla. Provider Adv. Bd., 2007—; med. adv. bd. Welcare HMO, 1996—; pres. coun. AVMED HMO, 1999—2002; bd. dirs. Mus. Sci. and Industry, Tampa, 2007—. Served as maj. USAF, 1974—76. Mem. AMA, Am. Coll. Ob-Gyn. (patient edn. com. 1984-86, John McCain fellow 1981), Hillsborough County Med. Assn. (v.p. 2003-04, pres. 2006—), Phi Beta Kappa. Democrat. Lutheran. Avocations: tennis, photography, golf, antique glass collecting, running. Home: 14516 Nettle Creek Rd Tampa FL 33624 Office: 4302 N Habana Ave Ste 300 Tampa FL 33607

SHEPHARD, MARK SCOTT, civil and mechanical engineering educator; b. Buffalo, Oct. 27, 1951; s. William N. and Beatrice (Hass) S.; m. Sharon L. Nirschel, Nov. 25, 1972; children: Steven W., Kari L. BS, Clarkson U., 1974; PhD, Cornell U., 1979. Asst. prof. civil engring. and mech. engring. Rensselaer Poly. Inst., Troy, N.Y., 1979-84, assoc. prof., 1984-87, prof., 1988—, dir. Sci. Computation Rsch. Ctr., 1990—, Samuel A. and Elisabeth C. Johnson Jr. prof. engring., 1993—; assoc. dir. Rensselaer Design Rsch. Ctr., Troy, N.Y., 1980-90. Vis. rsch. fellow GE Corp., R & D Schenectady, 1985, cons., 1984-87; cons. GM Rsch. Lab., Detroit, 1980—, others; tech. adv. bd. Aries Tech., Lowell, Mass., 1987-89. Editor: Engring. with Computers; mem. editl. bd. Internat. Jour. Numerical Methods Engring., Computer Methods in Applied Mechanics and Engring., Engring. Applications of Artificial Intelligence, Internat. Jour. Engring. Analysis and Design, Computational Mechanics; contbr. articles to profl. jours., chpts. to books. Fellow ASME, AIAA (assoc.), U.S. Assn. for Computational Mechanics (past pres.), Internat. Assn. for Computational Mechanics (exec. bd.); mem. Am. Soc. Engring. Edn., Am. Acad. Mechanics, Sigma Xi, Tau Beta Pi, Phi Kappa Phi. Home: 305 Algonquin Beach Rd Averill Park NY 12018-6007 Office: Rensselaer Poly Inst 110 8th St Troy NY 12180-3522 Home Phone: 516-674-3619; Office Phone: 518-276-8044. Business E-Mail: shephard@scorec.rpi.edu.

SHEPHERD, ALAN J., construction executive, management consultant; b. Bklyn., Jan. 15, 1942; s. Morris Elijah and Jean (Birnbaum) Shapiro; children: Robin Elyse, Kevin Peter BS in Mech. Engring., Mich. State U.; MS in Indsl. Engring., Wayne State U., 1966. Mgmt. trainee Chrysler Corp., Detroit, 1964-65, product engr., 1965-66; exec. v.p. Bruce Erts & Assocs., Southfield, Mich., 1966-70; pres. Creative Mgmt. Group, Inc., Southfield, Mich., 1970-76, chmn. bd., 1976, pvt. cons., 1976-79. Dir. planning and coordination Mgmt. Support Assocs., Tel Aviv, Israel, 1979-81, gen. mgr., 1981-82; mgmt. cons. MSA Consortium, Washington, 1982-83; regional mktg. dir. Hill Internat., Washington, 1983-84; mng. v.p. spl. projects CRS Sirrine, Inc., Washington, 1984-85; dir. advanced mgmt. program BDM Corp., McLean, Va., 1986-89; v.p. Hill Internat., Inc., Willingboro, N.J., 1989-90; v.p. mktg. and bus. devel. AWD Techs., Inc., Rockville, Md., 1990-94; dir. bus. devel. and cons. Brown & Root, Inc., Washington, 1994-98; v.p. Montgomery Watson, Washington, 1998—. Mem. Am. Inst. Indsl. Engrs., Project Mgmt. Inst., Soc. Am. Mil. Engrs. Office: Montgomery Watson Harza 1133 21st St NE Ste 710 Washington DC 20036-3390

SHEPHERD, BOBBY E., federal judge; b. Arkadelphia, Ark., Nov. 18, 1951; BA, Ouachita Bapt. U., 1973; JD, U. Ark., 1976. Ptnr. Spencer & Spencer, El Dorado, Ark., 1976—81, Spencer, Spencer & Shepherd, 1981—84, Landers & Shepherd, 1987—90; pvt. law practive, 1984—87; circuit-chancery judge Ark. 13th Jud. Dist., 1991-93; magistrate judge US Dist. Ct. (we. dist.) Ark., El Dorado, Ark., 1993—2006; judge US Ct. Appeals (8th cir.), Little Rock, 2006—. Served with US Army Res., 1976-81. *

SHEPHERD, BRUCE P., lawyer; BA, Harvard U., 1979; MBA, JD, U. Calif., Berkeley, 1983. Bar: Calif. 1984. Mng. ptnr. Latham & Watkins LLP, San Diego, and mem. fin. and real estate dept. Bd. dir. San Diego County Big Brothers and Big Sisters, Coronado Schools Found.; elected sch. bd. mem. (pres. 2001-02) Coronado Sch. Dist., 1998—2002. Mem.: ABA. Office: Latham & Watkins LLP Ste 1800 600 W Broadway San Diego CA 92101-3375 also: Latham And Watkins Llp 12636 High Bluff Dr Ste 400 San Diego CA 92130-2071

SHEPHERD, CRAIG ALLEN, environmental services administrator; b. Wichita, Kans., Mar. 14, 1955; s. Joe Glen and Leila Grace Shepherd; m. Amy Lee Todd; children: Elizabeth Elaine, Jeffrey Allen, Ryan Andrew. BS, U. Md., Coll. Pk., 1978; MPH, U. NC, Chapel Hill, 1990. Registered environ. health specialist Md., 2005. Consumer safety officer FDA, Falls Church, Va., 1980—84; staff environ. health specialist Indian Health Svc., Rockville, Md., 1984—88, dist. environ. health officer Atmore, Ala., 1988—92, chief environ. health svcs. br. Nashville, 1992—. Chief environ. health officer USPHS, Atlanta, 2005—; sr. environ. health officer Ctr. Disease Control and Prevention, Atlanta, 2003—; environ. health specialist Alcohol Drug Abuse and Mental Health Adminstrn., Washington. Capt. USPHS, 1979—2007. Decorated Spl. Assignment award USPHS, citation, Achievement medal, Outstanding Svc. medal, Commendation medal, Crisis Response Svc. award, Field Med. Readiness Badge, Bicentennial Unit commendation, Unit commendation, Commd. Corps Tng. ribbon, Nat. Emergency Preparedness award, Outstanding Unit citation, Hazardous Duty award; recipient Commrs. Spl. citation, FDA, 1983, Area Dir.'s Exceptional Performance award, Indian Health Svc., 1991, 1992, Area Dir.'s Outstanding Group Performance award, 1993, Area Dir.'s Managerial Excellence award, 1993, Area Dir.'s Superior Mgmt. award, 1994, Mid. Tenn. Fed. Employee award, Mid. Tenn., 1994, Outstanding Non-Scientific Profl. Employee award, 1997, Telly award, 2002, Nat. Partnership for Reinventing Govt. award, Al Gore, 2002, Virgil Peavy Workforce Devel. Group award, Ctrs. Diseas Control, 2004, The Cumming award, Soc. Am. Engrs., 2005, The John G. Todd award, USPHS, 2005. Mem.: Am. Acad. Sanitarians, Commd. Officers Assn., Mil. Officers Assn. of Am., Uniformed Svcs. Environ. Health Assn. (mem. exec. coun. 2005—07), Nat. Environ. Health Assn. Avocations: woodworking, gardening, travel. Home: 5407 Cabot Creek Dr Sugar Hill GA 30518 Office: Ctrs Disease Control 4770 Buford Hwy NE F 28 Atlanta GA 30341 Home Phone: 678-714-4908; Office Phone: 770-488-7026. Office Fax: 770-488-7310. Business E-Mail: cfs4@cdc.gov.

SHEPHERD, CYBILL LYNNE, actress, singer; b. Memphis, Feb. 18, 1950; d. William Jennings and Patty Shobe (Micci) S.; m. David Ford, Nov. 19, 1978 (div., 1982); 1 child, Clementine; m. Bruce Oppenheim, March 1, 1987 (div., 1990); children: Molly Ariel and Cyrus Zachariah (twins) Student, Hunter Coll., 1969, Coll. of New Rochelle, 1970, Washington Sq. Coll., NYU, 1971, U. So. Calif., 1972, NYU, 1973. Actor: (films) Last Picture Show, 1971, The Heartbreak Kid, 1973, Daisy Miller, 1974, At Long Last Love, 1975, Taxi Driver, 1976, Special Delivery, 1976, Silver Bears, 1977, The Lady Vanishes, 1978, Earthright, 1980, The Return, 1986, Chances Are, 1988, Texasville, 1990, Alice, 1990, Married to It, 1991, Once Upon a Crime, 1992, The Last Word, 1995, The Muse, 1999, Marine

Life, 2000, Open Window, 2006, (TV series) The Yellow Rose, 1983-84, Moonlighting, 1985-89, Cybill, 1994-98 (also prodr.), The L Word, 2007-, (TV films) A Guide for the Married Woman, 1978, Secrets of a Married Man, 1984, Seduced, 1985, The Long Hot Summer, 1985, Which Way Home, 1991, Memphis, 1992 (also co-writer, co-exec. prodr.), Stormy Weathers, 1992, Telling Secrets, 1993, There Was a Little Boy, 1993, Journey of the Heart, 1997, Due East, 2002, Martha, Inc.: The Story of Martha Stewart, 2003, Martha Behind Bars, 2005; record albums include Cybill Does It To Cole Porter, 1974, Cybill and Stan Getz, 1977, Vanilla with Phineas Newborn, Jr, 1978; appeared in stage plays A Shot in the Dark, 1977, Picnic, 1980, Vanities, 1981, The Muse, 1999, Marine Life, 2000; co-author Cybill Disobedience, 2000. *

SHEPHERD, DONNA LOU, interior designer; b. Uvalde, Tex., Sept. 25, 1948; d. Herbert Quarrels Jr. and Wanna Lou (Ray) Haile; m. Richard Ray Shepherd, June 2003; children from previous marriage: Laura Anne Howell, Christopher J. Huffman. BS, U. Houston, 1969, MEd, 1973. Owner Rainbow Design LLC, Greenwood Village, Colo., 1975—. Ptnr. Health By Design; spkr. in field. Designer Parade of Homes, 1989, Jr. Symphony Guild Showhome, 1996, designs featured in Colo. Homes and Lifestyles, Denver Post. Founder, pres. Prime Time Today, Littleton. Republican. Baptist. Avocations: water fitness, fly fishing, white-water rafting. Office: PO Box 3285 Littleton CO 80161-3285

SHEPHERD, DOUGLAS, hospital administrator; b. Aug. 1, 1944; married; three children. BA in Zoology, Miami U., 1966, postgrad., 1966-68; MHA, U. Mich., 1970. Grad. rsch. asst. in zoology Miami U., Oxford, Ohio, 1967-68; resident Ohio State U. Hosp., Columbus, 1969; asst. to adminstrv. officer Nat. Naval Med. Ctr., Bethesda, Md., 1970-73, hosp. project officer, 1973-79; assoc. adminstr. for clin. affairs Washington Hosp. Ctr., Washington, 1979-84; COO, sr. v.p. Nat. Rehab. Hosp., Washington, 1984—2004; with Laurel Regional Hosp., 2005—. Bd. trustees Commn. on Accreditation of Rehab. Facilities; faculty George Washington U., Washington, Ithaca Coll., N.Y. Cons. editor: Hospital Topics mag.; editl. adv. bd. Aspen Publishers, Inc., Jour. of Rehab. Adminstrn. Lt. comdr USN, 1970. Fellow Am. Coll. of Healthcare Execs. (bd. govs., regent-at large dist. 2, 1993-2002); mem. Am. Hosp. Assn. (governing coun. sect. of rehab. hosps. and programs 1986, chmn. 1991, former house of dels.), D.C. Hosp. Assn. (past chmn.), Md. Hosp. Assn. (past pres.), Va. Hosp. Assn. (past pres.), Am. Congress Rehab. Medicine, Assn. Health Care Adminstrs. of Nat. Capital Area (pres. 1978-79), others. Home Phone: 301-407-0201; Office Phone: 301-497-7978. E-mail: douglas.shepherd@dimensionshealth.org.

SHEPHERD, GAAL, artist; b. Gainesville, Fla., Jan. 25, 1951; d. Charles Claypoole and Ruby Frances (Grogan) S.; m. John Allen Crowl. Student, Stella Adler Theater Studio, 1968-73, U. Tampa, 1974-75, Corcoran Sch. Art, 1985-88. Artist, Atlanta, Tampa, Ga., Fla., 1973-76; graphic designer Art Prodn., Inc., Washington, 1976-79; art dir., illustrations editor Chronicle Higher Edn., Washington, 1979-88; painter, sculptor North Pomfret, Vt., 1988—; dir. Cooler Gallery, White River Junction, Vt., 2006—. Exhbn. agt. The Carving Studio, West Rutland, Vt., 1996—. One-woman shows include Pierre Antoine Gallery, Washington, 1987, 1989, Beside Myself Gallery, Arlington, Vt., 1993, Bromfield Gallery, Boston, 1993, Colby-Sawyer Coll., New London, NH, 1993, Lyndon State Coll., Lyndonville, Ct., 1993, Chaffee Art Ctr., Rutland, Vt., 1994, 1997, 1998, 2002, Vt. Coun. on Arts, Montpelier, 1995, Clarke Galleries, Stowe, Vt., 1995, Between the Muse Gallery, Rockland, Maine, 1996, No B.I.A.S. Gallery, Bennington, Vt., 1997, Steinway Gallery, Chapel Hill,NC, 1998, Red Mill Gallery, Johnson, Vt., AVA Gallery, Lebanon, N.H., 2003, Vt. Supreme Ct., Montpelier, 2003, Cooler Gallery, White River, Vt., 2004, exhibited in group shows at Middletown (NY) Arts Ctr., 1994, Vt. State Craft Ctr. at Frog Hollow, Middlebury, 1994, Attleboro (Mass.) Mus., 1996, Helen Day Art Ctr., Stowe, 1996, Vt. Coun. on Arts, West Rutland, 1996, AVA Gallery, Lebanon, NH, 1996, Harvard U., Cambridge, Mass., 1996, Ashuah-Irving Gallery, Boston, 1996, Ctr. for Contemporary Arts, Santa Fe, N.Mex., 1997, Guadalupe Fine Arts, Santa Fe, 1997, State Capitol Rotunda, 1997, Vt. Inst. Natural Sci., Woodstock, 1997, Beside Myself Gallery, Arlington, Vt., 1998, Maine Coast Artists, Rockport, 1999, Shelburne Farms, Vt., 2001, N.Mex. State Capitol, Santa Fe, 2002, two-person shows, Colby-Sawyer Coll., New London, NH, 1997, Milton Acad., Mass., 1998, The Munson Gallery, Chatham, Mass., 2001, exhibited in group shows at N.Mex. State Capital, Santa Fe, 2002, Rosewood Gallery, Sunapee, N.H., 2002, Munson Gallery, Chatham, Mass., 2002, Woodstock (Vt.) Folk Art, 2002, Elements Gallery, Rockland, Maine, 2002, Alliance for Visual Arts, Lebanon, N.H., 2003; author: Tranquil Vermont, 2000. Democrat. Avocations: mycology, gardening. Home: Thistle Hill Rd PO Box 307 North Pomfret VT 05053-0307 E-mail: coolergallery@together.net.

SHEPHERD, GILLIAN MARY, physician; b. Mar. 12, 1948; d. John Thompson and Helen (Johnston) S.; m. Eduardo Goar Mestre, Aug. 4, 1973; children: Laura Elena, Cristina Alicia, Eduardo Goar. BA, Wheaton Coll., Norton, Mass., 1970; postgrad., Tufts U., 1970-73; MD, N.Y. Med. Coll., 1976. Diplomate Am. Bd. Internal Medicine, Am. Bd. Allergy and Immunology. Intern, resident Lenox Hill Hosp., NYC, 1976-79; fellow in allergy and immunology N.Y. Hosp./Cornell Med. Sch., NYC, 1979-81; assoc. prof. medicine Cornell U. Med. Coll., NYC, 1988—, clin. assoc. prof. medicine, 1995—. Assoc. attending physician N.Y. Hosp., N.Y.C.; cons. allergy and immunology dept. medicine Meml. Sloan-Kettering Cancer Ctr., N.Y.C., 1982—. Contbr. articles in field to profl. jours. Fellow ACP, Am. Acad. Asthma, Allergy and Immunology (chair Edn. and Rsch. Trust 1999-2001, bd. dirs. 2000-2003); mem. AAAS, Am. Fedn. for Clin. Rsch., Joint Coun. Allergy and Immunology, N.Y. Allergy Soc. (exec. com. 1982-94, pres. 1991-92), N.Y. County Med. Soc. Office: 235 E 67th St Rm 203 New York NY 10021-6040 Office Phone: 212-288-9300.

SHEPHERD, GORDON GREELEY, space physics educator, researcher; b. Senate, Sask., Can., June 19, 1931; s. George Fredrick and Irene Eleanor (Thompson) S.; m. Marian Margaret Morgenroth, Aug. 15, 1953; children: Theodore Gordon, David Michael, Paul Ronald; m. Marianna Genova Gerdjikova, Dec. 19. 1987. BSc in Engring. Physics, U. Sask., 1952, MSc in Physics, 1953; PhD in Physics, U. Toronto, 1956. Asst. prof. physics U. Sask., 1957-64, assoc. prof., 1964-69; prof. York U., Toronto, 1969—, dir. Ctr. for Rsch. in Earth and Space Sci., 1994—. Author: Spectral Imaging of the Atmosphere, 2002. Recipient John H. Chapman award of excellence, Canadian Space Agy., 2003. Fellow Royal Soc. Can., Can. Aeronautics and Space Inst. (Alouette award 2004), Am. Geophys. Union; mem. Can. Assn. Physicists. Mem. United Ch. of Can. Avocations: travel, swimming, skiing. Home: 14 E Humber Dr King City ON Canada L7B 1B6 Office: York Univ/Ctr Rsch E/S Sci 4700 Keele St Toronto ON Canada M3J 1P3 E-mail: gordon@yorku.ca.

SHEPHERD, GORDON MURRAY, neuroscientist, educator; Faculty mem. med. sch. Yale U., 1967—, prof. neurobiology, prof. emeritus. Editor-in-chief Jour. Neurophysiology, Jour. Neuroscience; mem. adv. com. for cyberinfrastructure Nat. Sci. Found. Fellow: Am. Acad. Arts and Sciences. Office: Dept Neurobiology Yale Sch Med PO Box 208001 333 Cedar St SHM C303 New Haven CT 06520-8001 Office Phone: 203-785-4323. E-mail: gordon.shepherd@yale.edu.

SHEPHERD, JOHN FREDERIC, lawyer; b. Oak Park, Ill., May 22, 1954; s. James Frederic Shepherd and Margaret Joanne (Crotchett) Woollen; m. Jane Lowell Montgomery; children: Eliza Marion, Justine Catherine, Austin Frederic, Jack Lowell. AB magna cum laude, Dartmouth Coll., Hanover, NH, 1976; JD, U. Denver, 1979. Bar: Colo. 1979, US Dist. Ct. Colo. 1979, DC 1981, Okla. 2005, US Dist. Ct. DC 1981, US Ct. Appeals (10th cir.) 1981, US Ct. Appeals (DC cir.) 1982, US Supreme Ct. 1984, US Ct. Appeals (9th cir.) 1990. Assoc. Holland & Hart, Denver, 1979-81, Washington, 1981-85, ptnr., 1985-87, Denver, 1987—; natural resources disting. practitioner in residence U. Denver Coll. Law, 1998. Reporter Mineral Law Newsletter, 1985-92. Mem. 50 for Colo., Denver, 1989. Mem. ABA (chmn. pub. lands and land use com. 1991-93, mem. coun. sect. of natural resources energy and environ. law 1993-96), Rocky Mountain Mineral Law Found. (mem. long-range planning com. 1988—, trustee 1993-95), Inst. Energy Law (exec. com. 2006-), Dartmouth Alumni Club (pres. Washington chpt. 1985-86, trustee Rocky Mt. chpt., 1998-2001), Denver Athletic Club. Avocations: fly fishing, basketball, running. Home: 320 Clermont St Pky Denver CO 80220-5642 Office: Holland & Hart 555 17th St Ste 3200 Denver CO 80202-3950 Office Phone: 303-295-8309. Business E-Mail: jshepherd@hollandhart.com.

SHEPHERD, JON GLEN, lawyer; b. Des Moines, May 22, 1968; s. Jerry Wayne and Vicki Jean (Clark) S.; m. Stacy Kenna York, May 23, 1992. BA, U. No. Iowa, 1990; JD magna cum laude, U. Mich., 1992. Bar: Tex. 1993, U.S. Ct. Appeals (5th cir.) 1994, U.S. Dist. Ct. (no. dist.) Tex. 1994, U.S. Dist. Ct. (ea. dist.) Tex. 1995. Jud. clk. U.S. Ct. Appeals (5th cir.), San Antonio, 1993-94; assoc. Gibson, Dunn & Crutcher LLP, Dallas, 1994—2003, ptnr., 2003—05. Mem. bd. dirs. Sequoia, Inc., 2005—, v.p., 2006—; adj. prof., exec. MBA prog. Tex. Woman's U., 2006—07. Exec editor U. Mich. Law Rev., 1992; sr. editor ABA Antitrust Sec. Antitrust Law Jour., 1997—2006. Mem. Tex. Bar Assn., Dallas Bar Assn., Order of Coif. Avocation: sports. Office: Crews Shepherd & McCarty LLP 2200 Ross Ave Ste 4650W Dallas TX 75201 Office Phone: 214-432-7766. Office Fax: 214-432-7771. Business E-Mail: jshepherd@csm-lawyers.com.

SHEPHERD, KAREN, retired congresswoman; b. Silver City, N.Mex., July 5, 1940; m. Vincent P. Shepherd. BA, U. Utah, 1962; MA, Brigham Young U., 1963. Former instr. Brigham Young U., Am. U., Cairo; former pres. Webster Pub. Co.; former adminstr. David Eccles Sch. Bus., U. Utah; former dir. Salt Lake County Social Svcs., Utah; former dir. continuing edn. Westminster Coll.; former mem. Utah Senate; mem. 103d Congress from 2d Utah dist., Washington, 1993—94; exec. dir., U.S. rep. European Bank for Reconstruction Devel., London, 1996—2002; mem. exec. com., chair East West Trade and Investment Forum Am. C. of C., England, 1998—2002; dir. EMILY's List, 2002. Mem. nat. governing bd. Common Cause, Washington, 1995—96, Internat. Del. to Monitor Elections in West Bank and Gaza, Israel, Nat. Planned Parenthood Action Fund, 2004—; founder Karen Shepherd Fund; founding mem. Utah Women's Polit. Caucus, Project 2000; mem. trustee KeyBank Victory Funds; bd. dirs. UBS Bank, USA, O.C. Tanner; fellow Inst. Politics, Harvard U., 1995. Former mem. United Way, Pvt. Industry Coun.; former mem. adv. bd. U.S. West Grad. Sch. Social Work; trustee Westminster Coll.; bd. dirs. Utah Red Cross, 2003-06; chair Grad. Sch. Social Work, U. Utah, 1986-88, David Essler Sch. Bus., 1996—. Recipient Women in Bus. award, US Small Bus. Assn., Woman of Achievement award, Pathfinder award, Leadership award, YWCA, 1st pl. award, Nat. Assn. Journalists, Disting. Alumni award, U. Utah Coll. Humanities, Eleanor Roosevelt award, Utah Dem. Party, 2002, Merit of Honor award, U. Utah, 2004. Fellow Inst. Politics Kennedy Sch. Govt., Internat. Women's Forum, Salt Lake Area C. of C. (pub. rels. com.), Coun. on Fgn. Rels. Home: PO Box 1049 Salt Lake City UT 84110-1049

SHEPHERD, KAREN SCHILLER, biology educator; BS, MEd, N. Tex. State Univ. (now Univ. N. Tex), Denton. Biology tchr. Vines H.S., 1984—96, Plano (Tex.) H.S., 1996—, and sci. dept. chair, 2004—. Named Region 10 Secondary Tchr. of Yr., 2005, Tex. Tchr. of Yr., 2006; recipient Edison Soc. award for promoting rsch., 1994, USAF, US Army Awards for promoting student rsch., 1998—2003, Outstanding H.S. Sci. Tchr., Tex. Jr. Sci., Engring., Humanities Symposium, 1998, 2000. Office: Plano Senior High Sch 2200 Independence Pkwy Plano TX 75075 Business E-Mail: kshephe@pisd.edu.

SHEPHERD, KEVIN L., lawyer; b. Wichita, Kans., Aug. 4, 1957; BA magna cum laude, Frostburg State Coll., 1979; JD magna cum laude, Univ. Balt., 1984. Bar: Md. 1985, DC 1985. Law clk. Judge Harry A. Cole, Md. Ct. Appeals, 1984—85; ptnr., co-chmn. Real Estate practice group Venable LLP, Baltimore & Washington. Editor (in chief): Balt. Law Rev., Probate & Property; contbr. articles to profl. jours. Recipient Am. Jurisprudence awards. Mem.: Am. Coll. Mortgage Attys., ABA (vice chmn. real property divsn., chair real property, probate and trust law sects.), Anglo-Am. Real Property Inst., Am. Coll. Real Estate Lawyers (bd. gov.), Md. State Bar Assn., Bar Assn. Balt. City, DC Bar Assn., Phi Alpha Theta, Pi Sigma Alpha, Heuslier Honor Soc. Office: Venable LLP 1800 Mercantile Bank & Trust Bldg 2 Hopkins Plz Baltimore MD 21201 also: Venable LLP 575 7th St NW Washington DC 20004 Office Phone: 410-244-7772, 202-344-4881. Office Fax: 410-244-7742. Business E-Mail: klshepherd@venable.com.

SHEPHERD, LESLIE L., architect; BArch, Tex. Tech U., Lubbock, 1983. Pvt. practice arch., Albuquerque; with Gen. Svcs. Adminstrn., 1989—, dir. Nat. Fed. Bldgs. and Modernizations Prog. Washington, 1996, dep. chief arch., acting chief arch., 2005—06, chief arch., 2006—. Mem.: AIA. Office: Gen Svcs Adminstrn 1800 F St NW Washington DC 20405-0001 Office Phone: 202-501-1888. E-mail: les.shepherd@gsa.gov. *

SHEPHERD, MARK, JR., retired electronics company executive; b. Dallas, Jan. 18, 1923; s. Mark and Louisa Florence (Daniell) S.; m. Mary Alice Murchland, Dec. 21, 1945; children: Debra Aline Shepherd Robinson, MaryKay Theresa, Marc Blaine. BSEE, So. Meth. U., 1942; MSEE, U. Ill., at Urbana, 1947. Registered profl. engr., Tex. With GE, 1942-43, Farnsworth TV and Radio Corp., 1947-48, Tex. Instruments, Dallas, 1948-88, v.p., gen. mgr. semicondr.-components div., 1955—61, exec. v.p., COO, 1961—66, pres., COO, 1967—69, pres., CEO, 1969—76, chmn. bd. dirs., CEO, 1976—84, chmn. bd. dirs., chief corp. officer, 1984—85, chmn., 1985—88; ret., 1988. Hon. trustee Com. for Econ. Devel.; councillor conf. Bd.; mem. Bus. Coun. Lt. (j.g.) USNR, 1943-46. Fellow IEEE; mem. NAE, Sigma Xi, Eta Kappa Nu.

SHEPHERD, MILDRED ROOF, retired secondary school educator, art restorer; d. Charles Kiel Roof and Sarah Fields Finter; m. John Tyler Shepherd, Aug. 5, 1945; children: James Scott, Janet Anne. BA, San Francisco State U., 1936; MA in Music Edn., MA in Tchg. Music, Stanford U., 1942. Cert. tchr. Calif., lic. Internat. Soc. Appraisers. Tchr. All-Chinese Sch., San Francisco, 1938—39; tchr. music and drama Everett Jr. High, San Francisco, 1939—41; tchr. Sunset Elem., San Francisco, 1942—44; tchr. music Ruffner HS, Norfolk, Va., 1947—48, Glen Burnie (Md.) High, 1948—49; tchr. English Japanese Officers' Sch., Yokosuka, Japan, 1964—65; proprietor, resident artist Shepherd Studio, Arlington, Va. Chief appraiser St. John's Thrift Shop, Bethesda, Md., 1970—2001. Organizer, dir. girls' choir Hollywood Meth. Ch., Md. Lt. j.g. USNR, 1944—45. Mem.: Am. Inst. Conservation. Home: 5527 3d St S Arlington VA 22204 Office Phone: 703-671-1789. E-mail: johnmilshep@aol.com.

SHEPHERD, NICK P., film rental company executive; b. United Kingdom; BS in Hospitality and Bus. Mgmt., Sheffield City Polytechnic, UK. Various positions Grand Metropolitan Plc, Allied Lyons Plc, Kingfisher Plc; joined Blockbuster Inc., 1995—, sr. v.p. internat. bus., 1998—2001, chief concept officer, 2001—03, exec. v.p., chief mktg. and merchandising officer, 2003—04, exec. v.p., pres. U.S. stores, 2004—05, v.p. and mng. dir. UK bus., exec. v.p., pres. N. Am., 2005—07, former exec. v.p., pres. worldwide stores, 2007, COO, sr. exec. v.p., 2007—. Office: Blockbuster Inc 1201 Elm St Dallas TX 75270 *

SHEPHERD, TERRY L., health facility administrator; BS, Purdue U.; MBA, Ind. U. V.p., CFO Cardiac Pacemakers, Inc.; dir. bus. devel. med. devices and diagnostics divsn., CFO Lilly Industries, Ltd., U.K.; pres. Hybritech Eli Lilly and Co.; pres. heart valve divsn. St. Jude Med. Inc., St. Paul, 1994, mgr. internat. ops., 1996, pres., CEO, 1999—, chmn., 2002—. Office: St Jude Med Inc 1 Lillehei Plz Saint Paul MN 55117-9983

SHEPHERD, TERRY LYNN, special education educator; b. Knox, Ind., Feb. 22, 1958; s. A.B. Shepherd and Verona Darlene Preston; m. Melanie Ann Mullet; children: Jared, Samuel; m. Penny Kaye Price (div. Feb. 12, 1985); children: Shaun, William. EdD, Ball State U., Muncie, Ind., 1998. Social studies tchr. Houston Ind. Sch. Dist., Houston, 1982—85; tchr. Family and Children's Ctr., Mishawaka, Ind., 1985—90; spl. edn. tchr. Joint Svcs. for Spl. Edn., Plymouth, Ind., 1990—98; assoc. prof. spl. edn. Tex. A&M Internat. U., Laredo, Tex., 1998—2007; dept. head spl. edn. Ind. U., South Bend, 2007—, assoc. prof., 2007—. Contbr. articles to profl. jours. Grantee McCay Sch. of Edn. Rsch. Funds, U. Utah, 2000, Regents' Initiative Collaborative Rsch. Grant, State of Tex., 2001; scholar, Tex. A&M Internat. U., 2003—04; Regents' Initiative Fellowship Grant, State of Tex., 2001. Mem.: Coun. for Exceptional Children, Phi Kappa Phi, Pi Lambda Theta. Republican. Baptist. Achievements include research in over representation of Limited English Proficient students in special education; working conditions of special education teachers in Texas. Avocations: music, genealogy, model building. Office: Ind Univ South Bend Greenlawn Hall 129 1700 Mishawaka Ave South Bend IN 46634-7111 Home: 201 Taylors Way North Liberty IN 46554-9226 Office Phone: 574-520-4867. Office Fax: 574-520-4550. Personal E-mail: terrys2956@aol.com. Business E-Mail: tersheph@iusb.edu.

SHEPHERD, WILLIAM MICHAEL, music educator, musician; b. Ft. Knox, Ky., Mar. 26, 1949; s. Elisha and Zella Shepherd; m. Shelley Alice Jaffe, Feb. 10, 1985; children: Kevin, Marc. Student, Vallejo Jr. Coll., Calif., 1968—70; B in Music Edn., Ea. Ky. U., 1975; postgrad., U. Calif., Davis, 1986; MusM, U. Oreg., 1987. Music tchr. Dayton (Ohio) City Schs., 1975—77; profl. musician Stan Kenton, Les Brown, 1977—80; music tchr. Vallejo Unified Schs., 1980—83, Ukiah (Calif.) Unified Schs., 1983—94, Brookings (Oreg.)-Harbor Schs., 1994—. Dir. Curry Big Band, Brookings; leader Banana Belt Brass Quintet, Brookings. Mem.: Internat. Assn. Jazz Educators, Internat. Trumpet Guild, Phi Mu Alpha. Avocations: shooting, sports, fishing, model aviation. Home: 337 Mill Beach Rd Brookings OR 97415 Office Phone: 541-469-2108. Personal E-mail: shepherd@nwtec.com. Business E-Mail: shepherd@harborside.com.

SHEPLEY, HUGH, architect; b. Boston, Mar. 17, 1928; s. Henry Richardson and Anna Lowell (Gardiner) S.; m. Mary Waters Niles, Dec. 27, 1950; children: Hamilton Niles, Philip Foster. BA, Harvard U., 1951; BArch., Boston Archtl. Ctr., 1958; postgrad., Mass. Inst. Tech., 1958-59. Mem. archtl. firm Shepley, Bulfinch, Richardson & Abbott, Boston, 1955-63, ptnr., 1963-91. Bd. dirs. Greater Boston Red Cross, 1967-73, mem. exec. com., 1968-69; bd. dirs. Cmty. Music Ctr., Boston, 1968-72, Boston Ctr. for Blind Children, 1979-87; trustee New Eng. Conservatory Music, 1978-83, overseer, 1983—; trustee Univ. Hosp., 1980-96, mem. exec. com., 1981-92, vice chmn. bd. dirs., 1985-89, chmn. bd. dirs., 1989-92; trustee Am. Coll. of Greece, 1983-92, treas., 1986-88; trustee, sec. Rotch Travelling Scholarship, 1987-93, v.p., 1993-2006; mem. adv. coun. Boston U. Med. Ctr., 1990-96, Corp. Old South Assn., 1993-2002; bd. dirs. Manchester (Mass.) Hist. Soc., 1994-2002; overseer Spaulding Rehab. Hosp., 2003—. Fellow AIA; mem. Mass. Assn. Architects (pres. 1972), Boston Soc. Architects (pres. 1974, Medal Honor award 2007), Boston Archtl. Ctr. (pres. 1969-71), Tavern Club (Boston), Manchester Yacht Club (commodore 1985-87), Essex County Club. Independent. Episcopalian. Home: 8 Andover Ct Bedford MA 01730 E-mail: hshepley@verizon.net.

SHEPLEY, MARDELLE MCCUSKEY, architect, educator; b. Bethesda, Md., June 28, 1949; d. E. Scott McCuskey (father) & James R. and Yvonne Hudson S.; m. Laurence Berger, 1974 (div. 1978); m. Michael Curtis Blair, 1981 (div., 2004); children: Colin, Ian, Teal. BA, Columbia U., 1971, MArch, 1974; MA, U. Mich., 1979, DArch, 1981. Registered architect Calif. Urban designer NYC Dept. City Planning, 1972—74; planner Min. Planning & Econ. policy, Panama, Panama, 1975—77; lectr., teaching asst. U. Mich., Ann Arbor, 1977—81; assoc. Tai Assocs. Architects, San Francisco, 1981—85, The Design Partnership, San Francisco, 1985—93; asst. prof. Tex. A&M U., College Station, 1993—97, assoc. prof., 1997—2003, prof., 2003—, coord. PhD program, 1999-2001, assoc. dean for students, 2001—05, interim head dept. architecture, 2005—06. Rsch. com. Ctr. Health Design, Martinez, Calif., 1993—; assoc. dir. Ctr. Health Sys. and Design, 1995—2004, interim dir., 2004—05, dir., 2005—, prin. art and sci., 2006—; dir. design rsch. Shepley Bulfinch Archs., 2006—. Co-author: Healthcare Environments for Children and Their Families, 1998. Bd. dirs. Assn. for Care of Children's Health, Mt. Royal, NJ, 1998-2000; mem. parent bd. Oakland Montessori Sch., Calif., 1991-93. Recipient Health Facilities Rsch. award AIA, 1992; Tex. A&M U. scholar, 1998; Tex. A&M U. faculty fellow, 2001-, William Pena Endowed Prof., 2003-. Office: Tex A&M U Dept Architecture College Station TX 77843-3137 Business E-Mail: mardelle@tamu.edu.

SHEPP, BRYAN EUGENE, psychologist, educator; b. Cumberland, Md, Sept. 13, 1932; s. Bryan Evert and Dorothy Lorene (Stell) S.; m. June Lee Langeluttig, Jan. 31, 1953; children: Karen Suzanne, David Bryan. BS, U. Md., 1954, MS, 1956, PhD, 1960; MS with honors, Brown U., 1966. Rsch. prof. U. Conn., 1961-63; asst. prof. psychology George Peabody Coll., Nashville, 1963-64, Brown U., Providence, 1964-66, assoc. prof., 1966-69, prof., 1969-98, prof. emeritus, 1998—, chmn. dept. Providence, 1983-88, assoc. dean faculty, 1988-91, dean faculty, 1991-96. Cons. in field; vis. scientist Oxford (Eng.) U., 1970 Contbr. numerous articles to profl. publ.; ad hoc editor for several psychol. jour. Served with USN, 1955-59. Decorated letter of commendation Sec. of Navy; USPHS postdoctoral fellow, 1959-61; Nat. Inst. Child Health and Human Devel. grantee, 1965—82. Fellow APA, Am. Psychol. Soc. (founding fellow); mem. AAAS, AAUP, Psychonomic Soc., Univ. Club. Home Phone: 207-633-4703. Personal E-mail: beshepp@yahoo.com.

SHEPPARD, BEN H., JR., lawyer; b. Amarillo, Tex., Jan. 18, 1943; BA, U. North Tex., 1965; LLB, U. Tex., 1968. Bar: Tex. 1968. Mem. Vinson & Elkins L.L.P., Houston. Adj. prof. U. Houston Law Ctr. Editor-in-chief: Internat. Arbitration News. Adv. bd. Inst. Transnat. Arbitration. Mem. Chancellors, Order of Coif, Phi Delta Phi. Office: Vinson & Elkins 3300 First City Tower 1001 Fannin St Ste 3300 Houston TX 77002-6706

SHEPPARD, BERTON SCOTT, lawyer; b. Zanesville, Ohio, Aug. 6, 1936; s. Isaac and Ruth (Scott) S.; m. Regina Polka, Oct. 6, 1962; children: Kristina M., Cynthia A. BS in Agr. Engring., Mich. State U., 1958; JD, Northwestern U., 1961. Bar: Ill. 1962, U.S. Dist. Ct. (no. dist.) Ill. 1962, U.S. Dist. Ct. Md. 1965, U.S. Ct. Appeals (4th cir.) 1970, U.S. Ct. Appeals (7th cir.) 1974, U.S. Ct. Appeals (fed. cir.) 1982, U.S. Ct. Customs and Patent Appeals 1976, U.S. Supreme Ct. 1976. With Leydig, Voit & Mayer, Ltd. and predecessor firms, Chgo., 1959-62, assoc., 1962-70, ptnr., 1971-2000, of counsel, 2001—. Mem. editl. bd. Northwestern Law Rev., 1960-61. With USAR, 1961. Mich. State U. scholar, 1954-58, Hardy scholar Northwestern U., 1958-61. Mem. ABA, Am. Intellectual Property Law Assn., Fed. Cir. Bar Assn., Fed. Bar Assn., Intellectual Property Law Assn. Chgo., Lawyers Club Chgo. Republican. Office: Leydig Voit & Mayer 2 Prudential Plz Ste 4900 Chicago IL 60601 E-mail: bertons202@earthlink.net.

SHEPPARD, BLAIR H., dean, finance company executive, educator; m. Martha Putallaz; children: Philip, Christopher. BA, MA, U. Western Ont.; PhD, U. Ill., 1980. Asst. prof. orgn. behavior Fuqua Sch. Bus., Duke U., 1981—86, assoc. prof., 1986—93, prof. mgmt., assoc. dean, dir. exec. edn., 1993—97, sr. assoc. dean academic programs, 1997—2000, dean, 2007—; CEO Duke Corp. Edn., 2000—07, chmn., 2007—. Recipient NC Nations-Bank Outstanding Faculty Award, Outstanding Book Award, Internat. Assn. for Conflict Mgmt.; Can. Coun. Doctoral Fellowship. Office: Duke U Fuqua Sch Bus 1 Towerview Dr Durham NC 27708 Office Phone: 919-660-8020. Office Fax: 919-660-8742. *

SHEPPARD, DEAN, medical educator; b. Bronx, N.Y., June 13, 1949; s. Harold J. and Samona Sheppard; m. Margaret Grace Payne, Sept. 23, 1977; children: Jacob Colin, Maya Payne. BA, Harvard Coll., Cambridge, Mass, 1972; MD, SUNY, Stony Brook, 1975. Lic. Calif., 1978, diplomate Am. Bd. Internal Medicine, 1978. Asst. prof. medicine U. Calif., San Francisco, 1981—86, assoc. prof. medicine, 1986—92, dir. lung biology ctr., 1986—, prof. medicine, 1992—, assoc. chair rsch., dept. medicine, 1997—. Chair program project rev. com. NHLBI, Bethesda, Md., 2000—02; chair LIRR study sect. NIH, Bethesda, Md., 2006—. Grantee, NHLBI, 2000—, 2003—, 2005—, 2006—; Asthma SCOR grant, 1996—2006. Mem.: Am. Thoracic Soc., Am. Soc. Cell Biology, Assn. Am. Physicians (life), Am. Soc. Clin. Investigation (life). Achievements include patents for treatment of pulmonary fibrosis, acute lung injury and cancer metastasis by blocking alphavbeta6 integrin. Office: Univ Calif San Francisco Box 2922 San Francisco CA 94143-2922 Home Phone: 415-514-4269; Office Phone: 514-415-4269. Office Fax: 415-514-4278. Business E-Mail: dean.sheppard@ucsf.edu.

SHEPPARD, GAYLE TERESA, software executive; m. Michael T. Sheppard. Grad., U. South Fla., Tampa. V.p., sales and mktg. J.D. Edwards Asia Pacific Ltd.; pres. J.D. Edwards Japan KK; v.p., worldwide sales J.D. Edwards and Co.; pres., CEO Ketera Technologies; v.p., mng. dir., Western USA PeopleSoft, v.p., BPO Strategy. Bd. dir. NetCustomer, Inc., 2005—, Saffron Tech., NC, 2006—; mem. adv. bd. KeyMedia, Inc.; industry fellow Kenan Inst. of Private Enterprise, U. NC Kenan Flagler Bus. Sch.

SHEPPARD, JENNIFER MODLIN, retired genealogist; d. Herbert Raleigh Sheppard and Cleo Virginia Price. Grad. H.S., Newport News, Va. Cert. genealogy, profl. option Brigham Young U., Provo, Utah, 1996. Property record clk. Naval Air Systems Command, Naval Plant Rep. Office, Burbank, Calif., 1973—75, indsl. property clearance specialist, 1975—81; indsl. property mgmt. specialist Naval Air Systems Command, Arlington, 1981—85, Def. Logistics Agy., Alexandria, Va., 1985—88; ret., 1988. Fed. women's program coord. Naval Air Systems Command, Naval Plant Rep. Office, Burbank, Calif., 1974—80. Author: (books) Price Family (History Book award from NC Soc. Historians, Many); contbr. articles to newspapers and profl. publs. Recipient Hist. Article award, NC Soc. Historians, 1994, Family History Book award, 1995, Robert Bruce Cooke Family History Book award, 1997, Joe M. McLauren Newsletter award, 1997, D. T. Smithwick Newspaper & Mag. Article award, 1997, D. T. Smithwick Newspaper/Mag. Article award, 2004, D. T. Smithwick Newspaper/Mag. Article award, 2005, 2005, 2006, Robert Bruce Cooke Family History Book award, 1998, Willie Parker Peace History Book award, 1999, Paul Green Multimedia award, 2000. Mem.: Friends of Oll Martin County Courthouse (life; grant writer 2004—05), Lost Colony Ctr. for Sci. and Rsch. (bd. mem. 2006, sr. advisor, geneal. rsch. 2006), Nat. Soc. DAR, UDC (Manassas, Va. chpt. 175) (life; treas. 1987—88), Martin County Geneal. Soc. (life; v.p. 1993—95, pres. 1995—97, newsletter editor 1995—97, exec. com. mem. 1997), UDC (Theodore Hassell chpt. 437) (life; pres. 1996—2000, registrar 1997—2000), Martin County Hist. Soc. (life). Home Phone: 252-792-5472; Office Phone: 252-792-3440. Business E-Mail: shepjr@coastalnet.com.

SHEPPARD, JOHN WILBUR, computer research scientist; b. Pitts., Aug. 21, 1961; s. Harry Reid and Mary Jane (Amon) S.; m. Justina Anne Pape, Oct. 29, 1988; children: Jesse Carl, Jeannette Alida. BS, So. Meth. U., 1983; MS, Johns Hopkins U., 1989, PhD, 1996. Systems analyst Sheppard Internat., Inc., Hermitage, Pa., 1979-86; fellow ARINC Inc., Annapolis, Md., 1986—; lectr. Johns Hopkins U., 1994—2005, asst. rsch. prof., 2005—. Co-author: System Test and Diagnosis, 1994; author, editor: Research Perspectives and Case Studies in System Test and Diagnosis; contbr. articles to profl. jours. Mem. YMCA, Hermitage, 1979-85, Md. Hall for the Creative Arts, Annapolis, 1988-90; pres. Univ. Chapel Campus Ministry, Dallas, 1982-83. Fellow. IEEE (sr.), mem. Mensa, Kappa Mu Epsilon. Republican. Lutheran. Achievements include development of explanation-based learning approach for fault diagnosis; multi-agent learning approaches for solving Markov games; Bayesian approach to system diagnosis and prognosis; patents for methods and apparatus for diagnostic testing. Personal E-mail: jws@cablespeed.com. Business E-Mail: jsheppa2@jhu.edu.

SHEPPARD, LUVON, art educator; b. Aug. 15, 1940; BFA, Rochester Inst. Tech., NY, 1969, MST, 1970. Cert. tchr. NY. Ednl. curator Meml. Art Gallery U. Rochester, NY, 1970—76; prof. art Rochester Inst. Tech., 1972—; adj. prof. SUNY, Geneseo, 1993—. One-man shows include Skoto Gallery, NYC, 2003; author: My Visual Song, 1995. Recipient Eisenhart Outstanding Tchg. award, Rochester Inst. Tech., 1986, Joseph M. O'Brien Excellence in Tchg. award, SUNY Geneseo, 2003. Mem.: NY State Tchrs. Assn., Restoration Art Guild (founder, dir. 2002—). Office: Rochester Inst Tech 90 Lomb Meml Dr Rochester NY 14623-5604 Home: 551 Genesee St Rochester NY 14611

SHEPPARD, SCOTT S., astronomer; b. Buffalo, Feb. 19, 1976; s. Fred and Margaret Sheppard. PhD, U. Hawaii, 2004. Rschr. U. Hawaii, Honolulu, 1998—2004, Carnegie Inst. Wash., Washington, 2004—. Achievements include discovery of over 70 new moons of Jupiter, Saturn, Uranus and Neptune. Office: Carnegie Institution of Washington 2541 Broad Branch Rd NW Washington DC 20015 Office Phone: 202-478-8854.

SHEPPARD, WILLIAM J., lawyer; b. Portland, Oreg., Nov. 4, 1941; BS, Fla. State U., 1963; JD, U. Fla., 1967. Bar: Fla. 1968, U.S. Dist. Ct. Fla. (Middle and No. Dist.) 1968, U.S. Ct. Appeals (5th cir.) 1971, U.S. Supreme Ct. 1973, U.S. Ct. Appeals (11th cir.) 1981, U.S. Ct. Appeals (4th cir.) 1982, U.S. Ct. Appeals (7th cir.) 1991, U.S. Ct. Appeals (Fed. cir.) 1995, U.S. Tax Ct. 1999, bd. cert. criminal trial lawyer: Fla. Bar Bd. Legal and Specialization Edn. Ptnr. Sheppard, White & Thomas, P.A., Jacksonville, Fla. Mem. Gov.'s Adv. Com. on Corrections, 1982—86; chmn. Jud. Nom. Commn. Fourth Jud. Cir., 1992—96; mem. civil justice reform act commn. Middle Dist. Fla., 1996—98. Exec. editor: U. Fla. Law Rev., 1966—67; contbr. articles to profl. jours. 1st lt. U.S. Army, 1963—65. Decorated Commendation Medal U.S. Army; recipient Disting. Svc. award, Nat. Fedn. Blind Fla., 1978, Nelson Poynter Civil Liberties award, 1982, Tobias Simon Pro Bono Svc. award, Fla. Supreme Ct., 1985, Civil and Human Rights award, Internat. Assn. Official Human Rights Agencies, 1990, Nelson Poynter Civil Liberties award, 2000. Mem.: NACDL, Chester Bedell Inn of Ct. (master of the bench), Am. Coll. Trial Lawyers, Fla. Assn. Criminal Def. Lawyers (Steven M. Goldstein Criminal Justice award 2001), Fla Bar. Assn. (mem. criminal law cert. com. 1986—88, Pres. Pro Bono Svc. award 1984, Selig I. Golden Meml. award 1993), Jacksonville Bar Assn. (mem. 4th jud. cir. professionalism com. 1999—2000), Fla. Bar Found. (life Medal of Honor award 2004), Phi Delta Phi. Office: Sheppard White & Thomas PA 215 Washington St Jacksonville FL 32202 Home Phone: 904-727-7191; Office Phone: 904-356-9661. Office Fax: 904-356-9667. Business E-Mail: sheplaw@att.net. *

SHEPPE, JOSEPH ANDREW, surgeon; b. Huntington, W.Va., Sept. 24, 1953; m. Kathy Chapman; children: Sheree Nicole, Natalee Marie, Brittany Lee. BS summa cum laude in Chemistry and Zoology, Marshall U., 1975; MD, W.Va. U., 1979. Diplomate Am. Bd. Surgery, Am. Bd. Colon and Rectal Surgery. Intern in gen. surgery Charleston (W.Va.) Area Med. Ctr., 1979-84; fellow in colon and rectal surgery William Beaumont Army Med. Ctr., Royal Oak, Mich., 1984-85; pvt. practice Columbia, SC, 1985—. Physician Bapt. Med. Ctr., Columbia, Providence Hosp., Columbia, Richland Meml. Hosp., Columbia, Lexington Med. Ctr., West Columbia, S.C.; clin. instr. in gen./colorectal surgery U. S.C. Med. Sch. Fellow ACS, Am. Soc. Colon and Rectal Surgery; mem. S.C. Med. Soc., Columbia Med. Soc. Home: 204 Leaning Tree Rd Columbia SC 29223-3009 Office: 1333 Taylor St Ste 4-a Columbia SC 29201-2949 Office Phone: 803-779-5600.

SHEPPERD, THOMAS EUGENE, accountant; b. Pekin, Ill., Aug. 19, 1941; s. William Thomas and Marguerite Louise (Meisinger) S.; m. Susan Abbott Belville, Oct. 7, 1960; children: Scott Thomas, Allison Marie Shepperd-Henry, Michele Lea. BS in Acctg., U. Ill., 1964. CPA, Ill., Mo., Iowa, Ind. From jr. acct. to mgr. Haskins & Sells, St. Louis, 1964-74, mgr. Washington, 1974-75, ptnr., 1975-77, Deloitte Haskins & Sells (formerly Haskins & Sells), St. Louis, 1977-89, Deloitte & Touche (merger Deloitte Haskins & Sells and Touche Ross & Co.), St. Louis, 1989—. Treas. Shepley concert com. Christ Ch. Cathedral, St. Louis, 1989; bd. dirs., treas. Care & Counseling, Inc., Howard Park Early Childhood Ctr.; trustee, chmn. bd. Diocesian of Mo. Investment Trust. Mem. AICPA (various coms., mem. exec. coun. 2003--), Mo. Soc. CPAs (adminstrv. v.p., bd. dirs. 1988-92, treas. 1992-95, v.p. 1996-97, pres.-elect 1997-98, pres., 1998-99, chair long range fin. planning com. and the office location com., terms on the tech. standards peer review exec., profl. ethics coms., legislation com., acctg. and auditing procedures com., bd. dirs. 2003--), U. Ill. Press. Coun., David Kinley Assn., Noonday Club (treas., bd. dirs. 1977-81), Glen Echo Country Club. Republican. Episcopalian. Avocations: golf, travel, sports. Home: 15977 Chamfers Farm Rd Chesterfield MO 63005-4717 Office: Deloitte Touche 100 S 4th St Ste 200 Saint Louis MO 63102-1821

SHEPRO, RICHARD W., lawyer; b. Berwyn, Ill., May 9, 1953; s. Justice Warren and Inez Marjorie (McKillip); m. Lindsay Ellen Roberts, Sept. 5, 1981; children: Claire Willoughby, Warren Boyd. AB magna cum laude, Harvard U., 1975, JD. cum laude, 1979; MSc, London Sch. Econs., Eng., 1976. Bar: Ill. 1979, Calif. 1981, US Ct. Appeals (9th cir.) 1981, US Dist. Ct. (no. dist.) Ill. 1981, US Supreme Ct. 1993. Teaching fellow Harvard U., Cambridge, Mass., 1979; law clk. to chief judge U.S. Ct. Appeals (9th cir.), San Francisco, 1979-81; assoc. Mayer, Brown & Platt, Chgo., 1981-85, ptnr., 1986—, Mayer, Brown, Rowe & Maw, Chgo., 1981—. Lectr. law U. Chgo., 1992—; staff mem. U.S. Senate Judiciary Com., 1979; spl. asst. atty. gen., Ill., 1981-82; corr. on bus. law The Fin. Times, London, 1986—. Co-author: Bidders & Targets: Mergers and Acquisitions in the U.S., 1990; editor: (Supreme Ct. notes) Harvard Law Review, 1979; contbr. numerous articles to profl. jours. Del. nat. conv. NOW, Ind., 1982; bd. govs. Kohl Children's Mus.; vestryman St. Chrysostom's Ch., Chgo.; staff mem. US Senate Judiciary Com. 1978-79; spl. asst. atty. gen. State of Ill. 1981-82; bd. dirs. Lyric Opera Ctr. Am. Artists, 2003-, French-Am. C. of C., 2005-, Chgo. Ensemble, 1993-2001. Recipient US Presdl. scholar Pres. US, Wash., 1971, Greenman prize Harvard U., 1975; World's Leading Lawyers for Bus., Chambers Global, 1999-2006, Am.'s Leading Lawyers for Bus., Chambers USA, 2003-2006, Leading Lawyers Network, 2006, Best Lawyers Am. 2006, World's Leading Ins. & Reinsurance Lawyers, 2006. Fellow Chgo. Bar Found.; mem. ABA, Chgo. Coun. Lawyers (bd. govs. 1986-89, chmn. election law com. 1987-94), Chgo. Coun. Fgn. Rels., The Chgo. Ensemble (dir. and v.p.), Chgo. Club, LaSalle Club (dir. and mem. exec. com.), Am. Law Inst. Office: Mayer Brown Rowe & Maw 71 S Wacker Dr Chicago IL 60606 Office Phone: 312-701-7007. Office Fax: 312-706-8203. Business E-Mail: rshepro@mayerbrown.com.

SHER, SIR ANTONY, actor, author; b. Cape Town, South Africa, June 14, 1949; LittD (hon.), U. Liverpool, U. Exeter. Performer (plays): Cloud Nine, Goosepimples, Torch Song Trilogy (Laurence Olivier Best Actor award), assoc. artist Royal Shakespeare Co., King Lear, Moliere, Tartuffe, Maydays, Red Noses, Richard III (London Critics Cir. Theatre award, best actor, 1984, London Evening Standard Theatre award, best actor. 1985), The Merchant of Venice, The Revenger's Tragedy, Hello and Goodbye, Singer, Tambulaine the Great, Travesties, Cyrano de Bergerac, The Winter's Tale, Macbeth, The Roman Actor, The Malcontent, Othello; (nat. theater) True West, The Trial, The Resistible Rise of Arturo Ui, Uncle Vanya, Titus Andronicus (TMA Best Actor award), Stanley (Laurence Olivier Best Actor award, 1997, Theatre World award, Tony award nominee 1997), Primo (Outer Critics' Cir. award, outstanding solo performance, 2006, Drama Desk award, outstanding solo performance, 2006); (TV movie) History Man, Mark Gertler, Moliere, Tartuffe, Collision Course, The Land of Dreams, Genghis Cohen, Macbeth, The Moonstone, Home; (film) Shadey, Erik the Viking, The Wind in the Willows, Alive and Kicking, Nrs. Brown, Churchill The Hollywood Years; author: Year of the King, Middlepost, Characters; The Indoor Boy, Cheap Lives; (with Gregory Doran) Woza Shakespeare!, The Feast, Beside Myself, I.D., Primo, Primo Time. Achievements include knighted for acting and writing. Mailing: c/o Paul Lyon-Maris ICM Oxford House 76 Oxford St London WIN OAX England

SHER, BARTLETT, theater director; b. 1959; Grad., Holy Cross Coll., Worcester, MA. Tchr. Freehold Studio/Theatre Lab; resident dir. Guthrie Theater, Mpls.; assoc. dir. Ahmanson Theater; assoc. artistic dir. Hartford Stage Co.; artistic dir. Intiman Theatre, Seattle. Bd. mem. CityClub, Seattle. Dir.: (plays) A Man's a Man, Waste, 2000 (Best Play, Obie award, 2000), Don Juan, Pericles, Cymbeline, 2002 (Callaway award, 2002), Three Sisters, Our Town, Singing Forest, Nickel and Dimed, Il Barbiere di Siviglia, 2006; (Broadway plays) The Light in the Piazza, 2005, Awake and Sing!, 2006; (Operas) Mourning Becomes Electra. Office: Intiman Theatre PO Box 19760 Seattle WA 98109 *

SHER, GEORGE ALLEN, philosophy educator; b. NYC, Nov. 10, 1942; s. Daniel and Clara (Landesberg) S.; m. Emily Fox Gordon, July 10, 1972; 1 child, Sarah Landesberg. BA, Brandeis U., 1964; PhD, Columbia U., 1972. Instr. philosophy Fairleigh Dickinson U., Teaneck, NJ, 1966—72, asst. prof. philosophy, 1972—74; assoc. prof. philosophy U. Vt., Burlington, 1974-80, prof., 1980-91; Herbert S. Autrey prof. philosophy Rice U., Houston, 1991—, chmn. dept. philosophy, 1993-2000. Mem. Inst. for Advanced Study, Princeton, N.J., 1987-88. Author: Desert, 1987, Beyond Neutrality: Perfectionism and Politics, 1997, Approximate Justice: Studies in Non-Ideal Theory, 1997, In Praise of Blame, 2005; editor: Moral Philosophy: Selected Readings, 1989, 2d edit., 1996; contbr. articles to profl. jours. Named fellow Nat. Humanities Ctr., Rsch. Triangle Park, N.C., 1980-81. Mem. Am. Philos. Assn. Home: 2425 Dryden Rd Houston TX 77030-1001 Office: Rice U Dept Philosophy MS 14 6100 Main St Houston TX 77251-1892 Office Phone: 713-348-2723. Business E-Mail: gsher@rice.edu.

SHER, LEO, psychiatrist; b. Kiev, Ukraine, June 13, 1961; s. Alexander and Ivetta (Iokhved) Sher. MD summa cum laude (hon.), Ukrainian Nat. Med. U., Kiev, 1985. Sr. staff fellow NIMH, Bethesda, Md., 1997—2000; asst. clin. prof. psychiatry and behavioral scis. George Washington U., Washington, 2000—02; rsch. psychiatrist NY State Psychiat. Inst., Columbia U. Med. Ctr., NYC, 2000—; asst. clin. prof. psychiatry Columbia U. Coll. Physicians and Surgeons, NYC, 2001—06, assoc. clin. prof. psychiatry, 2006—; asst. attending physician NY Presbyn. Hosp., Columbia U. Med. Ctr., NYC, 2001—. Contbr. articles to profl. jours., chapters to books. Recipient Charlotte Marker Zitrin, M.D. award, Albert Einstein Coll. of Medicine Psychiatry Residency Program at L.I. Jewish Med. Ctr., 1997, Internat. award for Excellence in Pub. Clin. Rsch. in Jour. Clin. Endocrinology and Metabolism, Endocrine Soc. and Pfizer, 2004. Mem.: Soc. Biol. Psychiatry. Jewish. Achievements include patents in field. Personal E-mail: drleosher@aol.com.

SHERBELL-NA, RHODA, artist, sculptor; b. Bklyn. d. Alexander and Syd (Steinberg) S.; m. Mervin Honig, Apr. 28, 1956 (dec.); 1 child, Susan Honig. Student, Art Students League, 1950—53, Bklyn. Mus. Art Sch., 1959—61; pvt. study art, Italy, France, Eng., 1956. Cons., coun. mem. Emily Lowe Gallery, Hofstra U., Hempstead, NY, 1978, pres., 1989-81, instr., 1991—, life mem. bd. friends, pres. bd. trustees; tchr. instr. Mus. Modern Art, NYC, 1959, NAD Art Sch., NYC, 1985—, Art Students League, NYC, 1980—; Nat. Portrait Gallery Mus. rep. to 150th anniversary Smithsonian Instn., Washington, 1996lectr. Nat. Arts Club, NYC. One-woman shows include Hunting Hardford Mus., NYC, 1965, Art in Embassy Program, Prague, 2002-03, Country Art Gallery, Locust Valley, NY, Bklyn. Mus. Art Sch., 1961, Adelphi Coll., A.C.A. Galleries, NYC, 1960, Capricorn Galleries, Rehn Gallery, Washington, 1968, Huntington Hartford Mus., NYC, 1969, NY Cultural Ctr., 1970, Smithsonian Am. Art Mus., Smithsonian Instn., Washington (formerly Nat. Arts Collection), 1970, Montclair Mus. of Art, 1976, Nat. Art Mus. Sport, 1977, Jewish Mus. NYC, 1980, Morris Mus. Arts and Scis., NJ, 1980, Black History Mus., 1981, Queens Mus., 1981-82, Nat. Portrait Gallery, Smithsonian Inst., Washington, 1981-82, Bergen Mus. Arts and Scis., NJ, 1984, William Benton Mus., Conn., 1985, Palace Theatre of the Arts, Stamford, Conn., Bronx Mus. Arts, 1986, Hofstra Mus. Art, LI, NY, 1989-90, 97-98, County Art Gallery, NYC, 1990, Heckscher Mus., LI, 2000, Bronx Mus., NY, Bklyn. Mus., Mus. Modern Art, NYC, Country Art Gallery, 1990, Port Washington Libr., Nat. Mus. Am. Art, Smithsonian Instn., 1982, NAD, NYC, 1984, 89, Castle Gallery Mus., NYC, 1987, Emily Lowe Mus., NYC, 1987, Heckshire Mus., NYC, 1989, Islip Art Mus., NYC, 1989, Gallery Emanuel, NY, 1993, Sundance Gallery, Bridgehampton, NY, 1995, Artist Equity Exhbn., SoHo, 1995, NAD Exhbn., 1995, Main St. Petile Gallery, 2003, Huntington Arts Coun., 2003, 04, Huntington Twp. Art League, 2002-03, The Art Students League Instructors Exhbn., Salandes O'Reilly Gallery, NYC, 2003; 2 person exhbn. Works on Paper, Hofstra Mus., Hofstra U., 1997-98, pastel exhbn., 2006, 2007; exhibited in numerous group shows including Portrait in bronze of Senator Norman J. Levy for Merrick Train Station, 2000, Aaron Copland's America, Heckscher Mus. Art, 2000, Nat. Art Mus., 2002-, Huntington Arts Coun. Inc., 2003, Petite Gallery, Baseball Hall of Fame & Mus., Cooperstown, NY, 2004, Queens Mus., NY, 2004, Allied Arts of Am., 2003-04 (New Foundry award, 2004), Nat. TiesClub Show, 2004, Nat. Burlington Soc. Art Exhibn., 2004, Salamander OReily Gallery, NY, The Art Students League, 2004, Nat. Acad. Design Exhibitors, 2005, Nat. Portrait Gallery, 2005, 06; represented permanent collections, Stony Brook Hall of Fame, William Benton Mus. Art, Colby Coll. Mus., Oklahoma City Mus., Montclair Mus., NJ, Schonberg Libr. Black Studies, NYC, Albany State Mus., Hofstra U., Bklyn. Mus., Colby Coll. Mus., Nat. Arts Collection, Nat. Portrait Gallery, Smithsonian Instn., Baseball Hall of Fame Cooperstown, NY, Nassau C.C., Hofstra U. Emily Lowe Gallery, Art Students League, Jewish Mus., "The Subway Series: The New York Mets Our National Pastime," Queens Mus., Black History Mus., Nassau County Mus., Stamford Mus. Art and Nature Ctr., Jericho Pub. Libr., NY, African-Am. Mus., Hempstead, NY, Stamford Mus. Art and Scis., Conn., (Monument Work) The Am. Baseball Family Story, The Sea Dogs, 2006, MTA, Pub. Monument for Senator Norman J. Levy Merrik R.R. Sta., NY, Yogi Berra Portrait, Nat. Gallery Smithsonian Inst., Mose Soyer painting, Smithsonian Am. Art Mus., Raphare Soyer Portrait, Dept. State, The Embassy Program, Prague, Czech Republic, 2002-04, Nat. Acad., 2005-06, 07, Nat. Art Club, 2005-06, Nat. Portrait Gallery, 2006, Hofstra Mus., 2006-07; also pvt. collections, TV shows, ABC, 1968, 81; ednl. TV spl. Rhoda Sherbell-Woman in Bronze, 1977; prin. works include Seated Ballerina, portraits of Aaron Copland (Bruce Stevenson Meml. Best Portrait award Nat. Arts Club 1989), Eleanor Roosevelt, Variations on a Theme (36 works of collaged sculpture), 1982-86, Portland Sea Dogs Monument, Lareg Monument, American Baseball Family Group, 2007; appeared several TV shows; guest various radio programs; contbr. articles to newspapers, popular mags. and art jours.; mem. Conservation Art Group Coun. City of NY, 1994-97; exhbns. include: Petite Gallery, Huntington, NY, 2003, The Nat. Acad. Mus., 2003-04, Disegno Exhbn., NAD, 2005—, Nat. Sculpture Soc., 2005—, Nat. Art Club, 2005— (Merit award 2005), Brookgreen Gardens,2005-06, Nat. Portrait Gallery, Smithsonian Inst., 2006. Trustee Nat. Art Mus. of Sport, 1959-; coun. mem. Nassau County Mus., 1978, trustee, 1st v.p. coun.; cons., cmty. liaison WNET Channel 13, cultural coord., 1975-83; host radio show Not for Artists Only, 1978-79; commr. Women's Boxing Fedn., 1978; mem. The Art Commn. The City of NY, 1993; chmn. bd. Hofstra Mus., 1978-89. Recipient Gold medal Allied Artists Am., 1989, Alfred G. B. Steel Meml. award Pa. Acad. Fine Arts, 1963-64; Jersey City Mus. prize for sculpture, 1961, 1st prize sculpture Locust Valley Art Show, 1966, 67, Ann. Sculpture prize Jersey City Mus., Bank for Savs. 1st prize in sculpture, 1950, Ford Found. purchase award, 1964, 2 top sculpture awards Mainstreams 77, Cert. of Merit Salmagundi Club, 1978, prize for sculpture, 1980, 81, award for sculpture Knickerbocker Artists, 1980, 81, top prize for sculpture Hudson Valley Art Assn., 1981, Sawyer award NAD, 1985, Gold medal of honor Audubon Artists, 1985, Silvermine Exhbn. award, Gold medal Allied Artists Am., 1990, medal of honor for Bronze Queen Catherine, Nat. Arts Club, 2004, Pres.' award Nat Arts Club NYC, The Charlotte Danuddie award for Sculpture Nat. Acad. Design, 2003; MacDowell Colony fellow, 1976, AAAL and Am. Inst. Arts and Letters grantee, 1960, Louis Comfort Tiffany Found. grantee, 1962, Ford Found. grantee, 1964, 67, also award, New Foundry award, Allied Artists Am., 2004; named one of top 5 finalist to do Monument of Queen Catherine of England, 1991; named to represent Nat. Portrait Gallery at Smithsonian Mus., 1996, sculpture selected to represent Nat. Portrait Gallery Mus., 1997; guest at Dept. of State Embassy Program, Prague, Czech Republic, 2003-04; Queen Catherine Bronze, Hofstra Mus. Sculpture Gardens, 1985-. Fellow Nat. Sculpture Soc.; mem. NAD (Helen F. Barnett prize 1965, Leila Gordon Sawyer prize 1989, The Dessle Green prize 1993, Charlotte Deenevidde award 2003, award for Am. baseball founding group, 2003, award 2003), Sculpture Guild (dir.), Nat. Assn. Women Artists (Jeffery Childs Willis Meml. prize 1978), Allied Artists Soc. (dir., Gold medal 1990, The Pietro and Alfrieda Montana Meml. award 2000, award 2001), Audubon Artists (dir., Greta Kempton Walker prize 1965, Chaim Gross award, award disting. contbr. to orgn. 1979, 80, Louis Weskeem award), Woman's Caucus Art, Coll. Art Assn., Am. Inst. Conservation Hist. and Artistic Works, NY Soc. Women Artists, Artists Equity Assn. NY, Nat. Sculpture Soc. (E.N. Richard Meml. prize 1989), Internat. Platform Assn., Profl. Artists Guild LI, Painters and Sculptors Soc. NJ (Bertrum R. Hulmes Meml. award), Am. Watercolor Soc. (award for disting. contbn. to orgn.), Catharine Lorillard Wolfe Club (hon. mention 1968), Nat. Arts Club (NYC, Stevenson Meml. award 1989, Pres. award 1992, Robert Sayford award 2000, Bruce Stevenson Meml. award for Portrait 2000, Siegfort award 2000, award for sculpture 2004, award 2005). Personal E-mail: RhodaSherbell@mac.com.

SHERBIN, DAVID M., lawyer; b. Detroit, Sept. 6, 1959; m. Abbe H. Sherbin. BA with honors, Oberlin College, 1981; JD, Cornell Law Sch., 1987. Assoc. Katten Muchin & Zavis, Chgo., 1987—91; sr. counsel Heller Fin. Inc., 1992—97; assoc. gen. counsel Fed. Mogul Corp., Southfield, Mich., 1997—2001, sec., 1999—, v.p., dep. gen. counsel, sec., 2001—04, sr. v.p., gen. counsel, sec., 2004—05; v.p., gen. counsel, sec. Pulte Homes, Inc., Bloomfield Hills, Mich., 2005; v.p., gen. counsel, chief compliance officer Delphi Corp., Troy, Mich., 2005—. Mem.: Chgo. Bar Assn., ABA. Office: Delphi Corp 5725 Delphi Dr Troy MI 48098-2815 Office Phone: 248-813-3009. Office Fax: 248-813-2491.

SHERBINSKI, LINDA ANNE, nurse anesthetist, nursing educator; b. Rochester, NY, Jan. 17, 1956; d. Edward Marion and Helen Marie (Kindzera) S. Student, Genesee Hosp. Sch. Nursing, Rochester, NY, 1977; BSN, Alfred U., 1978; grad. in anesthesia, Univ. Health Ctr. Pitts., 1987; MSN, Duqusne U., 1991. RN, Pa. Leader day team CCU The Genesee Hosp., 1978-84, staff nurse operating rm., 1984-85; staff nurse ICU Forbes Met. Hosp., Pitts., 1985-87; staff anesthetist Presbyn. Univ. Hosp., Pitts., 1987-92, preceptor anesthetist, 1991-92; instr. Univ. Health Ctr. Pitts. Sch. Anesthesia, 1987-90, U. Pitts. Grad. Anesthesia Program, 1990-92; staff anesthetist Meml. Med. Ctr., Springfield, Ill., 1992-94; anesthetist Rochester (N.Y.) Gen. Hosp., Highland Hosp., Genesee Hosp., NY, 1994-98, Emory U. Hosp., Atlanta, 1998—. Item writer Acad. Item Writers AANA, Chgo., 1991—. Contbr. articles to profl. jours., chpt. to book. Med. vol. Pitts. Marathon, 1990, 91. Mem. Am. Assn. Nurse Anesthetists (cert. nurse anesthetist, program dir. internship grant 1990), Nat. League Nursing, Sigma Theta Tau (sec. Delta Sigma chpt. 1978-80, Rsch. scholar Epsilon Phi chpt. 1991). Roman Catholic. Office: Emory U Hosp 1364 Clifton Rd NE Atlanta GA 30322-1061

SHERBORNE, ROBERT, editor; b. Fairborn, Ohio, Mar. 26, 1950; s. Henry Hall and Lauramay (Rider) S.; m. Pamela Saunders, Apr. 16, 1988; children: Laura, Sophie. BS in Comms., U. Tenn., 1976. Reporter Clarksville (Tenn.) Leaf Chronicle, 1976, Tullahoma (Tenn.) News, 1976-77, The Tennessean, Nashville, 1977-92, regional editor, 1993-94, spl. project editor, 1995—. Recipient Nat. Gold Mass Media award Nat. Conf. Christians & Jews, 1983; spl. citation Nat. Headliners award Press Club of Atlantic City, N.J., 1983. Office: The Tennessean 1100 Broadway Nashville TN 37203-3134 Home Phone: 615-221-5149. E-mail: sherborne@comcast.net.

SHERBY, KATHLEEN REILLY, lawyer; b. St. Louis, Apr. 5, 1947; d. John Victor and Florian Sylvia (Frederick) Reilly; m. James Wilson Sherby, May 17, 1975; children: Michael R.R., William J.R., David J.R. AB magna cum laude, St. Louis U., 1969, JD magna cum laude, 1976. Bar: Mo. 1976. Assoc. Bryan Cave, St. Louis, 1976-85; ptnr. Bryan Cave LLP, St. Louis, 1985—. Contbr. articles to profl. jours. Bd. dirs Jr. League, St. Louis, 1989-90, St. Louis Forum, 1992-99, pres., 1995-97; chmn. Bequest and Gift Coun. of St. Louis U., 1997-99; jr. warden Ch. of St. Michael and St. George, 1998-2000; bd. dirs. Bistate chpt. ARC, 2000-06, v.p. fin.; bd. trustees St. Louis Sci. Ctr., 2000—; officer Clayton Edn. Found., 2003—. Fellow Am. Coll. Trust and Estate Coun. (regent 1997-2004), Estate Planning Coun. of St. Louis (pres. 1986-87), Bar Assn. Met. St. Louis (chmn. probate sect. 1986-87), Mo. Bar Assn. (chmn. probate and trust com. 1996-98, chmn. probate law revision subcom. 1988-96); Phi Beta Kappa. Episcopalian. Home: 47 Crestwood Dr Saint Louis MO 63105-3032 Office: Bryan Cave LLP 1 Metropolitan Sq Ste 3600 Saint Louis MO 63102-2733 Home Phone: 314-727-0523; Office Phone: 314-259-2224. Business E-Mail: krsherby@bryancave.com.

SHERE, DENNIS, lawyer, writer, retired publishing executive; b. Cleve., Nov. 29, 1940; s. William and Susan (Luskay) S.; m. Maureen Jones, Sept. 4, 1965 (div. Aug. 23, 2005); children: Rebecca Lynn, David Matthew, Stephen Andrew. BS in Journalism, Ohio U., 1963, MS in Journalism, 1964; JD, DePaul U., 2003. Staff writer Dayton (Ohio) Daily News, 1966-69; asst. prof. Sch. Journalism Bowling Green (Ohio) State U., 1969-70; fin. editor Detroit News, 1970-72, city editor, 1973-75; editor Dayton Jour. Herald, 1975-80; pub. Springfield (Ohio) Newspapers Inc., 1980-83, Dayton Newspapers, Inc., 1983-88; gen. mgr. Media Group Moody Bible Inst., 1989—2001; with death penalty trial assistance divsn. Il. State Appellate Defender's Office, 2004—05; asst. pub. defender Kane County Pub. Defender's Office, Ill., 2005—07. Author: Cain's Redemption - A Story of Hope & Transformation in America's Bloodiest Prison, 2005. Served with AUS, 1964-66. Mem. Sigma Alpha Epsilon, Omicron Delta Kappa. Business E-Mail: Dennis.Shere@moody.edu.

SHERER, JEFFREY TODD, pharmacist, educator; b. Warren, Ohio, Jan. 10, 1971; s. Larry Clinton and Marilyn James Sherer; m. Teresa Annette Allison, Mar. 20, 2004. BS in Pharmacy, Ohio State U., Columbus, 1994; PharmD, Med. U. SC., Charleston, 1996; MPH, U. Tex. Sch. Pub. Health, Houston, 2006. Registered pharmacist Tex., 1999, bd. cert. pharmacoterapy specialist Bd. Pharm. Specialties, cert. geriatric pharmacist Commn. Cert. Geriatric Pharmacy. Clin. asst. prof. U. SC., Columbia, 1997—99; clin. specialist Meth. Hosp., Houston, 1999—2003; clin. asst. prof. U. Houston, 2003—. Recipient Outstanding Blood Donor Yr., Meth. Hosp., Houston, 2000, Favorite Prof. award, U. Houston, 2006. Mem.: Am. Assn. Colls. Pharmacy, Am. Heart Assn., Am. Soc. Health-Sys. Pharmacists, Am. Coll. Clin. Pharmacy. Achievements include research in outcomes of patients with metastatic prostate cancer after treatment with bisphosphonate therapy. Office: Univ Houston Coll Pharmacy 1441 Moursund St Houston TX 77030 Home Phone: 713-527-8969; Office Phone: 713-795-8307. Business E-Mail: jtsherer@uh.edu.

SHERER, SAMUEL AYERS, lawyer, urban planner, consultant; b. Warwick, NY, June 17, 1944; s. Ernest Thompson and Helen (Ayers) S.; m. Dewi Sudewinahidah, June 28, 1980 (dec. Dec. 2000). AB magna cum laude, Oberlin Coll., 1966; JD, Harvard U., 1970; M in City Planning, MIT, 1970. Bar: DC 1972, U.S. Supreme Ct. 1979. Atty., advisor HUD, Boston, 1970; sr. cons. McClaughry Assoc., Washington, 1970-71, 74-76; cons. Urban Inst., Washington, 1971-72; atty., urban planner IBRD Jakarta Urban Devel. Study, Indonesia, 1972-74; atty., advisor Office Minority Bus. U.S. Dept. Commerce, Washington, 1976-77; ptnr. Topping & Sherer, Washington, 1977-90; pres. Sherer-Axelrod-Monacelli, Inc., Cambridge, Mass., 1978-99; prin. The Washington Team, Inc., 1991—2000, Richardson & Sherer, LLC, 2000—04. Bd. dirs. The Urban Agr. Network; rep. Internat. Devel. Law Inst., Washington, 1983-90; sr. fellow Climate Inst., 1988—; cons. in field. Co-author: Urban Land Use in Egypt, 1977; editor: Important Laws and Regulations Regarding Land, Housing and Urban Development in the Arab Republic of Egypt, 1977, Important Laws and Regulations Regarding Land, Housing and Urban Development in the Hashemite Kingdom of Jordan, 1981. Bd. dirs. MIT Enterprise Forum of Washington-Balt., 1980-82; mem. DC Rep. Ctrl. Com., 1984-88; nat. governing bd. Ripon Soc., Washington, 1977-83. Urban Studies fellow HUD, 1969-70. Mem. DC Bar Assn., Phi Beta Kappa. Avocations: tennis, reading. Home and Office: 3801 Connecticut Ave NW Apt 607 Washington DC 20008-4563 Personal E-mail: samuel.sherer@gmail.com.

SHERESKY, NORMAN M., lawyer; b. Detroit, June 22, 1928; s. Harry and Rose (Lieberman) S.; m. Elaine B. Lewis, Oct. 30, 1977; 1 child, from previous marriage, Brooke Hillary. BA, Syracuse U., 1950; LLB, Harvard U., 1953. Bar: NY 1953. Assoc. Gold & Pollack, NYC, 1954-60; sole practice, NYC, 1960-72; ptnr. Sheresky & Kalman, NYC, 1972-77; ptnr. Colton, Hartnick, Yamin & Sheresky, NYC, 1977-93; ptnr. Baer, Marks & Upham, NYC, 1993-95; ptnr. Sheresky, Aronson & Mayefsky, 1995—. adj. prof. matrimonial litigation NY Law Sch., 1979-86; mem. judiciary com. NYC Bar Assn.; founding mem. Am. Coll. Family Trial Lawyers. Mem. Internat. Acad. Matrimonial Lawyers (past treas., gov. NY chpt.), Am. Acad. Matrimonial Lawyers (gov., past pres. NY chpt., pres. elect.), NY State Bar Assn., Assn. Trial Lawyers Am., Met. Trial Lawyers Assn., Internat. Acad. Matrimonial Lawyers (bd. govs. 1986-, com. to examine lawyer conduct in matrimonial actions 1992-95). Author: (with Marya Mannes) Uncoupling, 1972; On Trial, 1977; contbr. editor: Fairshare mag. Office: Sheresky Aronson & Mayefsky LLP 750 Lexington Ave New York NY 10022-1200 Office Phone: 212-521-3501. Business E-Mail: sheresky@samllp.com.

SHERIDAN, CHRISTOPHER FREDERICK, financial consultant, human resources executive; b. Syracuse, NY, June 7, 1953; s. Frederick John and Patricia Ann S.; m. Diane Marie Harman, Dec. 31, 1977; children: Ryan, Kelly. BS in Indsl. Relations, LeMoyne Coll., 1975. Employee rels. trainee Anaconda Co., Buffalo, 1975-76, employee rels. rep. LA, 1976-78; pers. mgr. HITCO, Gardena, Calif., 1978-80; labor rels. rep. Miller Brewing Co., Fulton, NY, 1980-82, labor rels. mgr. LA, 1982-90; employee rels. mgr. Ryder Distbn. Resources, Anaheim, Calif., 1990-91; dir. human resources Alta-Dena Cert. Dairy Inc., City of Industry, Calif., 1991-99; regional human resources dir. west/southwest Dean Foods Co., 1999—2004; regional human resources dir. Mission Foods, 2004—05; fin. cons. Am. Nat. Fin. Svcs. Corp., Upland, Calif., 2006—. Mem. Soc. Human Resources Mgmt. Roman Catholic. Avocations: golf, basketball, reading, music. Office: 1425 W Foothill Blvd Upland CA 91786 Personal E-mail: sheridan.cf@gmail.com.

SHERIDAN, DONALD CHARLES, orthopedist, hand surgeon; b. Dec. 23, 1962; BA in Chemistry, Ariz. State U., Tempe, Ariz., 1986; MD, U. Ariz., 1990. Cert. Am. Bd. Orthop. Surgeons, Am. Acad. Orthop. Surgeons-Surgery of the Hand. Resident, orthop. Mayo Clinic, Rochester, Minn., 1990—95, hand fellowship, 1995—96; instr., orthop. Mayo med. Sch., 1995; chmn., dept. orthop. Scottsdale Healthcare-Shea Hosp., 1998—2001. Hand surgery cons. Ariz. Diamondbacks Baseball Team, Ariz. State U. Athletic Program, Oakland Athletics, Milw. Brewers, San Francisco Giants, Tex. Rangers. Named one of Top Doctors, Phoenix Monthly. Fellow: Am. Acad. Orthop. Surgeons; mem.: Am. Soc. for Surgery of the Hand, State Orthop. Soc., State Med. Soc. Office: 12013 B 92nd St Ste 101 Scottsdale AZ 85258 Office Phone: 480-860-6005. Office Fax: 480-860-1882. *

SHERIDAN, JAMES EDWARD, history professor; b. Wilmington, Del., July 15, 1922; s. Phillip Lambert and Ida Alverna (Green) S.; m. Sonia Landy, Sept. 27, 1947; 1 son, Jamy. BS, U. Ill., 1949, MA, 1950; PhD, U. Calif., Berkeley, 1961. Lectr. Chinese history Stanford U., 1960; mem. faculty Northwestern U., 1961—, prof. history, 1968—, chmn. dept., 1969-74, assoc. dean Coll. Arts and Scis., 1985-89, prof. emeritus, 1992—. Author: Chinese Warlord: The Career of Feng Yu-hsiang, 1966, China: A Culture Area in Perspective, 1970, China in Disintegration: The Republican Era in Chinese History, 1912-1949, 1975, A Community of Caring: An Introduction to Kendal at Hanover, 1998; editor: The Transformation of Modern China series, 1975—. Served to ensign USN, 1941-46. Fulbright fellow, France, 1950-51; Ford Found. fellow, 1958-60; grantee Am. Coun. Learned Socs.-Social Sci. Rsch. Coun., 1966-67, 71-72 Home: 80 Lyme Rd Apt 438 Hanover NH 03755-1236 Office: Northwestern Univ Dept History Evanston IL 60201 E-mail: james.e.sheridan@valley.net.

SHERIDAN, JIM, film director, screenwriter; b. Dublin, 1949; Student, Univ. Coll., Dublin. Artistic dir. Project Arts Theatre, 1976—80, N.Y. Irish Arts Ctr., 1982—87; founder Children's Theatre Co., Dublin. Screenwriter: Into the West, 1993; dir.: My Left Foot, 1989, The Field, 1990, In the Name of the Father, 1993, The Boxer, 1997, In America, 2001, Get Rich or Die Tryin, 2005; prodr., exec. prodr. Some Mother's Son, 1996, Agnes Browne, 1999, On the Edge, 2000, Borstal Boy, 2000, Bloody Sunday, 2001. Office: Hells Kitchen Ltd 21 Mespil Rd Dublin 4 Ireland also: Creative Artists Agy 9830 Wilshire Blvd Beverly Hills CA 90212-1804 E-mail: hellskit@iol.ie.

SHERIDAN, JOHN J., musician, music educator; s. John J. and Martha S. Sheridan; m. Colleen M. Smith, May 5, 1989; children: Erin Colleen, Kelly Ann. AA, Bucks County C.C., 1985; MusB, Temple U., 1989; MA, NYU, 2000. Freelance performer, Langhorne, Pa., 1985—2003; adj. faculty jazz studies Bucks County C.C., Newtown, 1994—2003, assoc. prof. music, 2003—. Arts tech. com. Bucks County C.C., Newtown, Pa., 2002—03, music tech. coord., 1996—2003. Composer, studio musician: songs Another View Point, studio musician: rec. Purity, Is You Is. Office: Bucks County C C 275 Swamp Rd Newtown PA 18940-4106 Office Phone: 215-968-8126. Business E-Mail: sheridaj@bucks.edu.

SHERIDAN, MARK WILLIAM, mechanical engineer, financial planner; b. Bryn Mawr, Pa., July 9, 1959; s. Phillip Frederick and Shirley Frazer Sheridan; m. Deborah Sazdanoff Sheridan, Aug. 14, 1999; children: Kristina, Katrina, Marlena. BSME, Lafayette Coll., 1981; MBA, Cornell U., 1987, M. Engring. (Mech.), 1988. Registered profl. engr., Ohio. Project engr. Internat. Paper Co., Mobile, Ala., 1981-83, sr. process engr., 1983-85; assoc. Booz-Allen & Hamilton, Cleve., 1988-90; coord. long range planning appliance motor divsn. Emerson Electric Co., St. Louis, 1990-93, resident engr. Paragould Plant, 1993-96; dir. mfg. Thermodisc, Mansfield, Ohio, 1996—2002, dir. ops. devel., 2002—. Summer intern Saturn Corp., Troy, Mich., 1986, 87. Patentee in field. Bd. dirs. ABC Condominium Assn., St. Louis, 1992-94; chmn. JGSM Student Faculty Com./Quality of Life Com., Ithaca, N.Y., 1985-87; pres. Mobile Soap Box Derby, 1983-85; v.p. ways and means, bd. dirs. Mobile Jaycees, 1984-85; mem. Leadership Unltd., 2003-04; active YMCA; treas. First Presbyn. Ch. of Mansfield, 1998-03. Lester B. Knight scholar Cornell U., 1986-88, J. Stanford Smith scholar Cornell U., 1985-87; named Outstanding Young Man of Am., 1984, 85, 87. Mem. ASME, Inst. Indsl. Engrs., The Planning Forum, Soc. Indsl. Archaeology, World Future Soc., St. Louis Jaycees (bd. dirs. 1992-94), Am. Mensa. Republican. Avocations: golf, reading, computing, weightlifting. Home: 2403 Ranchwood Dr Mansfield OH 44903-9044 Office: Thermodisc 1320 S Main St Mansfield OH 44907-5500 Office Phone: 419-525-8295. Personal E-mail: sheridanmark@excite.com.

SHERIDAN, NICOLLETTE, actress; b. Worthing, Sussex, Eng., Nov. 21, 1963; d. Sally Sheridan; m. Harry Hamlin, Sept. 7, 1991 (div. 1993). Actor: (films) The Sure Thing, 1985, Noises Off, 1992, Spy Hard, 1996, Beverly Hills Ninja, 1997, I Woke Up Early the Date I Died, 1998, Raw Nerve, 1999, .com for Murder, 2002, Lost Treasure, 2003, Code Name: The Cleaner, 2007; (TV series) Knots Landing, 1986—93 (Soap Opera Digest award, 1990, 1991), Paper Dolls, 1984, Desperate Housewives, 2004— (co-recipient, Outstanding Performance by an Ensemble in a Comedy Series, Screen Actors Guild award, 2005, 2006); (TV films) Dead Man's Folly, 1986, Deceptions, 1990, Somebody's Daughter, 1992, A Time to Heal, 1994, Indictment: The McMartin Trial, 1995, Silver Strand, 1995, The People Next Door, 1996, Murder in My Mind, 1997, Dead Husbands, 1998, The Spiral Staircase, 2000, Haven't We Met Before?, 2002, Deadly Betrayal, 2003, Deadly Visions, 2004; (TV miniseries) Lucky/Chances, 1990, Knots Landing: Back to the Cul-de-Sac, 1997; TV appearances include Paradise, 1991, Will & Grace, 2003, Becker, 2003. Office: Desperate Housewives Touchtone Television 100 Universal City Plaza Bldg 212B Ste G Universal City CA 91608 *

SHERIDAN, PATRICK MICHAEL, retired finance company executive; b. Grosse Pointe, Mich., Apr. 13, 1940; s. Paul Phillip and Frances Mary (Rohan) S.; m. Diane Lorraine Tressler, Nov. 14, 1986; children: Mary, Patrick, Kelly, Kevin, James. BBA, U. Notre Dame, 1962; MBA, U. Detroit, 1975. Acct. Peat, Marwick, Mitchell & Co., Detroit, 1962-72, audit mgr., 1969-72; exec. v.p. fin. Alexander Hamilton Life Ins. Co., Farmington, Mich., 1973-76; sr. v.p. ops. Sun Life Ins. Co. Am., Balt., 1976-78, exec. v.p., 1978-79; pres. Sun Ins. Services, Inc., 1979-81; pres., chief exec. officer Am. Health & Life Ins. Co., Balt., 1981-85; chief exec. officer Gulf Ins. Co., 1985-86; sr. v.p., chief fin. officer Comml. Credit Co., 1985-86, sr. v.p. audit, 1987; exec. v.p., chief fin. officer Anthem, Inc., Indpls., 1987-99, ret., 1999. Rep. candidate for U.S. Congress, 1972; past pres. Charlesbrooke Cmty. Assn.; past v.p. Jr. Achievement of Met. Balt., 1984-85; bd. dirs. Goodwill Industries of Balt., 1986, bd. govs. 1994; bd. dirs. Family Svcs. Assn., 1994, Goodwill Industries of Indpls., 1994; mem. adv. coun. Clowes Meml. Hall. Capt. AUS, 1963-65. Recipient various Jaycee awards. Fellow Life Mgmt. Inst.; mem. Am. Mgmt. Assn. (pres.'s assn.), AICPAs, Mich. Assn. CPAs, Md. Assn. CPAs, Am. Soc. CLUs, U.S. Jaycees (treas. 1973-74), Mich. Jaycees (pres. 1971-72), Detroit Jaycees (pres. 1968-69), Balt. C. of C. (bd. dirs.), Mensa, Notre Dame Club, Skyline Club.

SHERIDAN, PETER GERARD, federal judge, lawyer; b. Cambridge, Mass., Apr. 21, 1950; s. John Patrick and Rita Theresa (Brown) S.; m. Barbara Alworth, July 20, 1974; children: Peter, Thomas, Katherine. BS, St. Peter's Coll., Jersey City, 1972; JD, Seton Hall U. Sch. Law, Newark, 1977. Bar: NJ 1977, NY 1980. Law sec. to Hon. James J. Petrella Superior Ct., Hackensack, NJ, 1977-78; staff atty. Port Authority NY & NJ, NYC, 1978-81; v.p., gen. counsel Casino Assn., Atlantic City, 1983-86; dir. authorities unit Gov. Kean, Trenton, NJ, 1986-89; of counsel Cohen, Shapiro, Polisher, Lawrenceville, NJ, 1990-93; ptnr. Cullen & Dykman, Newark, 1993-95, Graham, Curtin & Sheridan, Trenton, 1995—; judge US Dist. Ct. NJ, Newark, 2006—. Contbr. articles to profl. jours. Gen. counsel NJ Rep. State Commn., Trenton, 1994—, exec. dir., 1993-94; pres. St. Peter's Coll. Alumni Bd., 1994-96; mem. NJ Commn. on Capital Planning and Budgeting, 1991-93. Mem. NJ Bar Assn. Office: Graham Curtin Sheridan 50 W State St Ste 1008 Trenton NJ 08608-1220 also: Martin Luther King Jr Fed Bldg & US Courthouse 50 Walnut St Newark NJ 07101 Office Phone: 973-645-2580.

SHERIDAN, SONIA LANDY, artist, retired educator; b. Newark, Ohio, Apr. 10, 1925; d. Avrom Mendel and Goldie Cornelia (Hanon) Landy; m. James Edward Sheridan, Sept. 27, 1947; 1 child, Jamy. AB, Hunter Coll., 1945; postgrad., Columbia U., 1946-48; MFA with high honors, Calif. Coll. Arts and Crafts, 1961. Tchr. art public high schs., Calif., 1951-57; chmn. dept. art Taipei (Taiwan) Am. Sch., 1957-59; instr. Calif. Coll. Arts and Crafts, 1960-61; asst. prof. art Sch. Art Inst. Chgo., 1961-67, assoc. prof., 1968-75, prof., 1976-80, prof. emeritus, 1980—, founder, head generative sys. program, 1970-80. Artist-in-residence 3M Corp., 1970, 76, Xerox Corp., 1981; cons. French Ministry of Culture, 1986; lectr. univs., mus., art schs., workshops, Hungarian Acad. Scis. Symposium Collected Essays & Exhbn., Budapest, 1989, Internat. Soc. Electronic Arts, Liverpool, England; presenter in field. One-woman shows include Rosenberg Gallery, Chgo., 1966, Visual Studies Workshop, Rochester, N.Y., 1973, Iowa Mus. Art, Iowa City, 1976, Mus. Sci. Industry, Chgo., 1978, exhibited in group shows at Print Ann., Boston Mus., 1963, Software, Jewish Mus., N.Y.C., 1969—70, Photography into Art, London, 1972—73, Photokino, Cologne, Germany, 1974, Mus. Modern Art, N.Y.C., 1974, San Francisco Mus. Modern Art, 1975, 2006, U. Mich. Mus. Art, 1978, Toledo Mus. Art, 1982—83, Mus. Modern Art, Paris, 1983, Siggraph, 1982, 1983, Reina Sofia Mus., Madrid, 1986, Smithsonian Instn., 1990, Tokyo Met. Mus. Photography, 1991, Madrid City Cultural Ctr., 1992, Karl Ernst Osthaus Mus., Hagen, Germany, 1992, Circulo des Belles Artes, Madrid, 1992, Yale U. Art Gallery, 1995, Tokyo Intercom. Ctr., 1995, U. Montreal, 1995, Internat. Soc. Electronic Arts, Liverpool, 1996, Hungarian Art Mus., 1996, Scirpton Mus., The Netherlands, 1997, Video Gallery, Hungary, 2000—02, Mus. Kommunikation, Frankfurt, Germany, 2001, 2d Biennial Museo Nacional de Belles Artes, Buenos Aires, 2002, Represented in permanent collections Hood Mus. Art, Dartmouth, Langlois Found., Montreal, Art Inst. Chgo., San Francisco Mus. Art, Mus. Sci. and Industry, Chgo., U. Iowa Mus. Art, Nat. Gallery Art, Ottawa, Can., Visual Studios Workshop, Rochester, Tokyo Met. Mus. Photography, Fundacion Arte y Technologia, Madrid, Tweed Mus., U. Minn., Scrypton Mus., Tilburg, The Netherlands; author: Energized Artscience: Sonia Landy Sheridan, 1978; co-editor: Leonardo jour.; hon. editor:, 2000; contbr. articles, essays to profl. jours. Recipient citation, Nat. Assn. Schs. Art and Design, 2006; fellow, Guggenheim Found., 1973, Andrew Mellon Found., 2005—06; grantee, NEA, 1974, 1976, 1981, Union Ind. Colls., 1975. Mem.: Internat. Soc. Electronic Arts, Internat. Soc. Interdisciplinary Study Symmetry, Coll. Art Assn. Personal E-mail: sonia.sheridan@valley.net.

SHERIDAN, THOMAS BROWN, mechanical engineering and applied psychology educator, researcher, consultant; b. Cin., Dec. 23, 1929; s. Mahlon Brinsley and Esther Anna (Brown) S.; m Rachel Briggs Rice, Aug. 1, 1953; children: Paul Rice, Richard Rice, David Rice, Margaret Lenore. BS, Purdue U., 1951; MS, UCLA, 1954; ScD, MIT, 1959; Dr. (hon.), Delft U. Tech., The Netherlands, 1991. Registered profl. engr., Mass. Asst. prof. mech. engring. MIT, Cambridge, 1959-65, assoc. prof., 1965-70, prof., 1970-78, prof. engring. and applied psychology, 1978—, prof. aeronautics and astronautics, 1994—, Ford prof., 1995—. Lectr. U. Calif., Berkeley, Stanford U., 1968; vis. prof. U. Delft, The Netherlands, 1972, Stanford U., 1989, Ben Gurion U., Israel, 1995; chmn. com. human factors, mem. com. aircrew-vehicle interaction, com. on commercially developed space facility, com. on human factors in air traffic control, mem. com. on nat. automated hwy. sys., com. on setting and enforceing speed limits, com. on intelligent vehicle initiative; chmn. com. on NASA aviation safety; mem. com. on electronic voting NRC; mem. adv. com. on applied phys., math. and biol. scis. NSF; mem. life scis. adv. com., study group on robotics, oversight com. flight telerobotic servicer NASA; mem. task force on appropriate tech. U.S. Congress Office Tech. Assessment; mem. study sect. accident prevention and injury control NIH; mem. Def. Sci. Bd. Task Force on Computers, Tng. and Gaming, Nuclear Regulatory Commn. on Nuclear Safety Rsch. Rev. Com. Author: Telerobotics, Automation and Human Supervisory Control, 1992, Humans and Automation, 2002; co-author: Man Machine Systems, 1974; editor: (with others) Monitoring Behavior and Supervisory Control, 1976, Perspectives on the Human Controller, 1997; assoc. editor Automatica, 1982-94; mem. edtl. adv. bd. Tech. Forecasting and Social Change, Computer Aided Design, Advanced Robotics, Robotics and Computer Integrated Mfg.; sr. editor Presence: Telerobots and Virtual Environments, 1991—. Served to 1st lt. USAF, 1951-53. Recipient Nat. Engring. award Am. Assn. Engring. Socs., 1997, Rufus Oldenburger medal ASME, 1997. Fellow IEEE (pres. Systems, Man and Cybernetics Soc. 1974-76, Centennial medal 1984, Norbert Wiener award 1993, Joseph G. Wohl award 1995, Millenium medal 2000), Human Factors Soc. (Paul M. Fitts award 1977, Arnold Small award 2000, pres. 1990-91, Pres. Disting. Svc. award 2000), Nat. Acad. Engring. Democrat. Mem. United Ch. of Christ. Home: 32 Sewall St Newton MA 02465 Personal E-mail: sheridan@mit.edu.

SHERIF, S. A., engineering educator; b. Alexandria, Egypt, June 25, 1952; came to US, 1978; s. Ahmed and Ietedal H. (Monib) S.; m. Azza A. Shamseldin, Feb. 6, 1977 (div.); children: Ahmed S., Mohammad S.; m. Vitrell Lynn McNair, May 30, 2003. BSME (hon.), Alexandria U., 1975, MSME, 1978; PhD in Mech. Engring., Iowa State U., 1985. Tchg. asst. mech. engring. Alexandria U., 1975-78; tchg. assoc. mech. and environtl. engring. U. Calif., Santa Barbara, 1978-79; rsch. asst. mech. engring. Iowa State U., Ames, 1979-84; asst. prof. No. Ill. U., Dekalb, 1984-87, U. Miami, Coral Gables, Fla., 1987—91; assoc. prof. mech. engring. U. Fla., Gainesville, 1991-2001, prof. mech. and aerospace engring., 2001—, mem. doctoral rsch. faculty, 1992—, founding dir. Wayne K. and Lyla L. Masur HVAC Lab., 1995—, asst. dir. Indsl. Assessment Ctr., 2001—, minority mentor, 2004—. ABET coord. for mech. engring., 1997—; coord. for mech. engring. So. Assn. Colls. and Schs., 2001—; affiliate Inst. for Sci. and Health Policy U. Fla., 2001—; cons. Solar Reactor Techs., Inc., Miami, 1988-91, Dade Power Corp., Miami, 1988-91, Ind. Energy Sys., Miami, 1988-91, Carey Dwyer Eckhart Mason Spring Beckham, P.A. Law Offices, Miami, 1988-89, Michael G. Widoff, P.A., Attys. at Law, Ft. Lauderdale, Fla., 1989-93, Law Offices Pomeroy and Betts, Ft. Lauderdale, 1991-92, Ctr. for Indoor Air Rsch., 1994-2000; cons. Fla. Power and Light Co., 1996-98; external examiner U. Roorkee, 1994-95, 98—, Indian Inst. Tech., Delhi, 2002-, Alexandria U., Egypt, 2000-; adj. faculty cons. Kennedy Western U., Thousand Oaks, Calif., 1994-97; resident assoc. Argonne (Ill.) Nat. Lab., Tech. Transfer Ctr., summer 1992; faculty fellow NASA Kennedy Space Ctr., Cape Canaveral, Fla., summer 1993; rsch. assoc. summer faculty rsch. program USAF Office Sci. Rsch., Arnold Engring. Devel. Ctr., Arnold AFB, Tenn., 1994; faculty fellow NASA Marshall Space Flight Ctr., Huntsville, Ala., 1996, 97; ABET coord. for aerospace engring., 2002-; coord. for aerospace engring., So. Assn. Colls. and Schs., 2002-. Co-editor: Industrial and Agricultural Applications of Fluid Mechanics, 1989, The Heuristics of Thermal Anemometry, 1990, Heat and Mass Transfer in Frost and Ice, Packed Beds, and Environmental Discharges, 1990, Industrial Applications of Fluid Mechanics, 1990, rev. edit., 1991, Mixed Convection and Environmental Flows, 1990, Measurement and Modeling of Environmental Flows, 1992, Industrial and Environment Applications of Fluid Mechanics, 1992, rev. edit., 1998, Thermal Anemometry-1993, 1993, Developments in Electrorheological Flows and Measurement Uncertainty-1994, 1994, Heat, Mass and Momentum Transfer in Environmental Flows, 1995, Thermal Anemometry, 1996, Fluid Measurement Uncertainty Applications, 1996, Devices for Flow Measurement and Analysis, 1997, Heat and Mass Transfer in Environmental Flows, 1998, Industrial and Environmental Applications of Fluid Mechanics, 1999, rev. edit., 2001, Measurement and Modeling of Environmental Flows, 2002, Industrial and Environmental Applications of Fluid Mechanics, 2003, Fluid Measurement Uncertainty Applications, 2003; reviewer more than 45 internat. jours., more than 200 conf. procs.; mem. editl. com. SECTAM XXI, 2001-2002; book rev. editor ASME Applied Mech. Revs., 2001—; assoc. tech. editor Solar Energy jour., 2002—; guest editor Solar Energy Jour. Spl. Issue on Hydrogen Prodn., 2003-05; contbr. to 16 book chapters and numerous articles to profl. jours. NASA ambassador, 1996-98, lab. host student sci. tng. program Ctr. for Precollegiate Edn. and Tng., 1997—; mem. environ. awareness adv. com., Dade County Pub. Schs., 1989-91, lab. dir. cmty. lab. rsch. program, 1989-91, also faculty liaison design svcs. dept.; active Com. for Nat. Inst. for Environ., 1992—; mem. senate U. Fla., 1994-95, mem. OUTREACH Spkrs. program, 1996-98. Recipient cert. recognition for rsch. contributions, NASA, 1993, 1996, 1997, E.K. Campbell award of Merit for Outstanding Svc. and Achievement in Tchg., ASHRAE, 1997, Kuwait prize for applied scis., 2002. Fellow ASME (mem. energy resources bd. 2001-03, chmn steering com. internat. energy conversion engring. conf., 2002-03, coord. group fluid measurements, fluids engring. divsn. 1987-03, vice chmn. 1990-92, chmn. 1992-94, fluid measurements and instrumentation tech. com., 2003—, fluids engring. divsn. adv. bd. 1994—, fed. honors and awards com. 1995-01, mem. fluid mechs. tech. com. 1990—, fluid mech. com. 1987-90, K-19 com. on environ. heat transfer 1987—, fluid measurements and instrumentation tech. com., 2003-, chmn. 2003—, mem. K-6 com. on heat transfer in energy systems, 2001—, mem. fluid applications and systems tech. com. 1990—, systems analysis tech. com. advanced energy sys. divsn. 1989—, newsletter editor advanced energy sys. divsn. 1995-98, exec. com., 1999—, mem.-at-large honors awards 1999-00, sec., treas. 2000-01, vice chmn., 2001-02, chmn., 2002-03, sr. mem. and past chmn., 2003-04, fundamentals and theory tech. com. solar energy divsn. 1990-97, chmn. CGFM nominating com. 1992-94, mem. 1994-98, chmn. profl. devel. com. Rock River Valley sect. 1987, tech. activities operating com. Gator sect. 1994-96, MEFCC subcom. 1 on uncertainties in flow measurements 1995-00, certificate of appreciation, 1994, 97. 99, 03), ASHRAE (mem. heat transfer fluid flow com. 1988-92, 93-97, corr. mem. 1992-93, 97—, mem. thermodynamics and psychrometrics com. 1988-92, 96-04, corr. mem. 1992-96, vice chmn. 1990-92, mem. liquid to refrigerant heat exchs. com. 1989-93, 96-97, sec. 1990-92, corr. mem. 1993-96, 97-01, corr. mem. air-to-refrigerant heat transfer com., 2000—, chmn. stds. project com. on measurement of moist air properties 1989-95, corr. mem. refrigeration load calculations com., 1999—, mem. tech. activities com. 2004—, head refrigeration sect., 2004-, E.K. Campbell award of merit for Outstanding Svc. and Achievement in Tchg., 1997, Disting. Svc. award, 2003, certificate of appreciation, 1995), AIAA (assoc., mem. terrestrial energy sys. tech. com. 2001—, certificate of appreciation, 2003); mem. AIChE, Internat. Assn. Hydrogen Energy, Internat. Solar Energy Soc., Am. Soc. for Engring. Edn., Internat. Energy Soc. (mem. sci. coun.), European Assn. Laser Anemometry (ASME/FED rep., mem. steering com.), Internat. Inst. Refrigeration (US nat. com., mem. commn. B1 on thermodynamics and transfer processes), Sigma Xi. Muslim. Achievements include co-inventor two US patents. Avocations: reading, soccer, basketball, history, astronomy. Office: U Fla Dept Mech and Aerospace Engring 232 MAE B 720 Bldg PO Box 116300 Gainesville FL 32611-6300 Home: 3440 NE 41st Pl Ocala FL 34479 Home Phone: 352-629-7410; Office Phone: 352-392-7821. Office Fax: 352-392-1071. Business E-Mail: sasherif@ufl.edu.

SHERIFF, SEYMOUR, retired lawyer; b. Rye, NY, Aug. 22, 1917; s. Michael and Anna (Rosenfeld) S.; m. Selene Gloria Wolf, Oct. 15, 1950; children: Steven, Susan, Ellen, Carol. BSS cum laude, CCNY, 1935; JD cum laude, Yale U., 1938. Bar: D.C. 1938, N.Y. 1938, Md. 1957. Pvt. practice, Washington, 1938-58; sr. ptnr. Gardner, Morrison, Sheriff & Beddow, Washington, 1958-2000, ret., 2000. With AUS, 1942—45. Decorated Legion of Merit. Mem.: Phi Beta Kappa, Order of Coif.

SHERIN, EDWIN, theater director, film director, television director, actor; b. Danville, Pa., Jan. 15, 1930; s. Joseph and Ruth (Berger) S.; m. Jane Alexander, Mar. 29, 1975; children: Anthony J., Geoffrey B. (dec.), Jonathan E.; 1 stepchild, Jason E. AB in History and Polit. Sci., Brown U., 1952. Acting tchr. Am. Theatre Wing, NYC, 1962-64; acting tchr. Am. Theatre Tng. Inst. Southeastern Mass. U., South Dartmouth, 1974; Lucille Lortel Disting. guest artist U. Bridgeport (Conn.), 1980; dir. Sch. Theatre Arts Boston U., 1981; acting tchr. Okla. Summer Arts Inst., 1985-86, One on One, LA, 1989, 90; exec. v.p. Altion Prodns., LA, 1985-93; pres. Pumpkin House Prodns., 1993—. Mem. nat. adv. for Mus. Am. Theatre; instr. Okla. Summer Arts Inst., guest dir. Calif. Inst. Arts; prof. dept. drama Fla. State U. Film Sch., Bennington Coll., Columbia U., Sarah Lawrence Coll. Actor with Houseman's troupe Phoenix Theatre, N.Y.C., 1957-58, N.Y. Shakespeare Festival, 1956-60; appeared as: Octavius Caesar in, Anthony and Cleopatra, 1958; appeared in Broadway plays Come Blow Your Horn, 1960, Desert Incident, 1961, Romulus, 1962, Face of a Hero, 1963; TV films Playhouse 90, 1956-58, Studio One, 1956-58, Omnibus, 1957-60, East Side/West Side, 1960; dir. Broadway plays including The Great White Hope, 1968, Glory Hallelujah, 1969, 6 RMS RIV VU, 1973, Find Your Way Home, Of Mice and Men, 1974, Red Devil Battery Sign, 1975, Sweet Bird of Youth, 1976, Eccentricities of a Nightingale, 1976, The First Monday in October, 1978, Goodbye Fidel, 1980, The Visit, 1992; assoc. producing dir. Washington's Arena Stage, 1964-68; dir. Cosi Fan Tutte, N.Y. City Opera Co., 1972, A Streetcar Named Desire, Piccadilly Theatre, London, 1973, Semmelweiss, Studio Arena Theatre, Buffalo, N.Y., 1978, Outrage, Kennedy Ctr., Washington, 1982; films including Valdez is Coming, 1970, My Old Man's Place, 1971; producing artistic dir. Showdown at Adobe Hotel, Semmelweiss, Hedda Gabler, Night Must Fall, A Streetcar Named Desire, Hartman Theatre, Stamford, Conn., 1980-85; dir. Chelsea Walls, Naked Angels, N.Y.C., 1990, Karla, Long Wharf Theater, 2002, Ghosts, Shakespeare Theatre, Washington, 2002, Prymate, B'Way, 2004, TV programs Hill Street Blues, Moonlighting, WIOU, L.A. Law, Tour of Duty, MEN, Medium, The Black Donnellys; co-exec. prodr. Law and Order, 1993-94, exec. prodr., 1994-00, (TV films) The Father Clements Story, Lena, My 100 Children, Daughter of the Streets, Getting Even, A Marriage: Georgia O'Keeffe and Alfred Stieglitz, 1991. With USN, 1952-56, Korea. Recipient Outer Circle award, 1969; New Eng. Theatre award, 1969, N.Y. Drama Critics award, 1969, Drama Desk award, 1969, L.A. Drama Cir. award, 1971, Recipient Tony nomination, 1974, London Evening Std. citation, 1973, Joseph Jefferson award, 1976, Buffalo drama award, 1978, Emmy award, 1997; New Eng. Theatre Conf. award; Ford Found. grantee, 1965-66; Am. Theatre fellow Coll. of Am. Theatre. Mem. AFTRA, SAG, Actors Equity Assn., Dirs. Guild Am. (nat. v.p. 1997—), Dramatists Guild, Soc. Stage Dirs. and Choreographers (v.p. 1970-80), Lincoln Soc., Phi Gamma Delta. Personal E-mail: edsherin@gmail.com.

SHERIN, KEITH S., corporate financial executive; BA, U. Notre Dame, 1981; MBA, Columbia U., 1991. With fin. mgmt. program GE, 1981-84, mem. corp. audit staff, 1984, exec. audit mgr., mgr. programs and planning; mgr. fin. comml. engine ops. GE Aircraft Engines, 1992-93; dir. fin. GE Plastics Europe, Bergen op Zoom, Netherlands, 1993-95; mgr. global fin. and fin. svcs. GE Med. Systems, 1995-96, v.p. fin. and fin. svcs. operation, 1996-98; sr. v.p. fin., CFO GE, Fairfield, Conn., 1998—2007, vice-chmn., CFO, 2007—. Office: GE 3135 Easton Tpke Fairfield CT 06431-0002 *

SHERK, GEORGE WILLIAM, lawyer, educator; b. Washington, Mo., June 23, 1949; s. George William and Lorraine Martha (Meyer) Sherk; m. Patricia F. Sherk, Oct. 27, 2001. AA, St. Louis C.C., 1970; BA, Colo. State U., 1972, MA, 1974; JD, U. Denver, 1978; DSc, George Washington U., 2002. Bar: Am. Samoa 1978, Colo. 1979, U.S. Dist. Ct. Colo. 1979, U.S. Ct. Claims 1984, U.S. Supreme Ct. 1985. Cons. office of legis. counsel Govt. of Am. Samoa, Pago Pago, 1978-79; atty. advisor western area power adminstrn. U.S. Dept. Energy, Colo., 1979—80; pvt. practice law Denver, 1980-82; staff assoc. Nat. Conf. State Legis., Denver, 1980-82; spl. asst. office of water policy U.S. Dept. Interior, Washington, 1982-83; atty. land and natural resources div. U.S. Dept. Justice, Washington, 1984-90; of counsel Will & Muys, Washington, 1990-93; pvt. practice, 1993—. Vis. scholar U. Wyo. Coll. Law, 1993; vis. prof. Ga. State U. Coll. Law, 1994-95, Ga. State U. Policy Rsch. Ctr., 1995-96; assoc. professorial lectr. George Washington U. Sch. Engring. and Applied Sci., Washington, 1997-2002; adj. prof. U. Denver Coll. Law, 2004—; assoc. rsch. prof. Colo. Sch. Mines, 2005—; hon. assoc. Internat. Water Law Rsch. Inst., U. Dundee, Scotland, 1998—; lectr. various colls. and univs.; mem. assoc. faculty Va. Inst. Marine Sci., Coll. of William and Mary, Gloucester Pt., Va., 1989-94; dep. dir. Ctr. Risk Sci. and Pub. Health Sch. Pub. Health and Health Svcs. George Washington U., 2000-01. Author, co-author or editor numerous books and articles on water law and alternative energy law; book review editor Rivers: Studies in the Science, Environmental Policy and Law of Instream Flow, 1989-2000. Mem. ABA, ASCE, State Bar Colo. Avocations: automobile racing and rallying, sports, reading, outdoor activites, sailing. Home and Office: 12472 Home Farm Ct Westminster CO 80234 E-mail: gwsherk@H2Olaw.com.

SHERK, KENNETH JOHN, lawyer; b. Ida Grove, Iowa, Feb. 27, 1933; s. John and Dorothy (Myers) Sherk; children: Karin Fulton, Katrina, Keith, Kyle. BSc, U. Iowa, 1955; JD, George Washington U., 1961. Bar: Ariz. 1962, U.S. Dist. Ct. Ariz. 1962, U.S. Ct. Appeals (9th cir.) 1966, U.S. Supreme Ct. 1974. Assoc. Moore & Romley, Phoenix, 1962-67, ptnr., 1967-79, Romley & Sherk, Phoenix, 1979-85; dir. Fennemore Craig, Phoenix, 1985—. 1st lt. U.S. Army, 1955-58, Korea. Recipient Profl. Achievement Svcs. award George Washington Law Assn., 1986, Ariz. Judges Assn., 1989, Disting. Svc. award Phoenix Assn. Def. Counsel, 1990; named Mem. of Yr. State Bar of Ariz., 1994. Fellow Am. Coll. Trial Lawyers, Am. Acad. Appellate Lawyers, Am. Bar Found., Ariz. Bar Found. (Walter E. Craig award 1999); mem. ABA (ho. of dels. 1990-93), Ariz. Bar Assn. (pres. 1985-86), Maricopa County Bar Assn. (pres. 1978-79). Republican. Congregationalist. Avocations: fishing, hiking, bicycling. Home: 1554 W Las Palmaritas Dr Phoenix AZ 85021-5429 Office: Fennemore Craig 3003 N Central Ave Ste 2600 Phoenix AZ 85012-2913 Office Phone: 602-916-5383. Business E-Mail: ksherk@fclaw.com. E-mail: ksherk@cox.net.

SHERLING, FRED W., lawyer; b. Dec. 22, 1933; s. Weaver V. and Ruth M. (Bowen) S.; m. Camille Margaret Brochetto, Nov. 29, 1969; children: Charlotte, Sharon, Cheryl. BSChE, U. Tenn., 1957; LLB, George Washington U., 1961. Bar: U.S. Ct. Appeals (D.C. cir.) 1963, U.S. Ct. Customs and Patent Appeals 1963, U.S. Ct. Appeals (fed. cir.), 1982, U.S. Supreme Ct. 1982. Patent examiner U.S. Patent Office, Washington, 1957—63; assoc. solicitor, 1963—86; sole practice, 1986—. Mem. Patent Office Soc. Baptist. Office Phone: 703-370-2445. Personal E-mail: fredsherling@hotmail.com, sherlicc@aol.com, fredsherl@yahoo.com.

SHERLOCK, PHYLLIS KRAFFT, psychologist; b. Chgo., Dec. 22, 1936; d. Lee M. and Beatrice Elliott Krafft; m. Hugh Paul Sherlock, June 4, 1960 (dec. Oct. 1991); children: William, John, James BA in Philosophy and Religious Studies, U. N.C., 1958; postgrad., Boston U., 1959—60; PhD in Clin. Psychology, Pacific Grad. Sch. Psychology, 1980. Lic. Psychologist, Marriage, Family and Child Counselor. Social work trainee ARC, Chgo., 1959—60; child welfare worker Santa Clara County Social Svcs., San Jose, Calif., 1961—62; counselor Diabesis, San Francisco, 1973—75; counselor chaplaincy svc. Stanford U. Med. Ctr., Calif., 1977—79; intern North County Cmty. Mental Health Clinic, Palo Alto, Calif., 1977—78; postdoctoral intern counseling and psychol. svcs. Cowell Health Svcs., Stanford U., 1980—81; faculty Pacific Grad. Sch. Psychology, 1989—92; pvt. practice, 1979—; supr., clin. dir. The Transitional Program, 1990—2001. Co-founder Pacific Grad. Sch. Psychology, Palo Alto, 1975-76; group facilitator Grad. Sch. Bus., Stanford U., 1980-82; supr. psychol. assts., 1988-2005, clin. dir. The Transitional Program, 1995-2002; adj. clin. faculty Sch. Edn., U. San Francisco, 1990-97 Author: The Feminine Q Set - Research on Wolf's Feminine Image and Theories, 1980; contbr. articles to profl. jours. Vol. Agnew State Hosp., 1971. Mem. Assn. Psychol. Type, Santa Clara County Psychol. Assn. Democrat. Avocations: reading, gardening, art, travel. Office: 1275 Dana Ave Palo Alto CA 94301-3112 Home Phone: 650-325-1962; Office Phone: 650-325-8131. Personal E-mail: phyllisdec22@earthlink.net.

SHERMAN, ALAN ROBERT, retired psychologist, educator; b. NYC, Nov. 18, 1942; s. David R. and Goldie (Wax) S.; m. Llana Helene Tobias, Aug. 14, 1966 (div. 1989); children: Jonathan Colbert, Relissa Anne; m. Ann Marie Redington, Aug. 22, 2002. BA, Columbia U., 1964; MS, Yale U., 1966, PhD, 1969. Lic. psychologist, Calif. Faculty psychology U. Calif., Santa Barbara, 1969—2007; clin. psychologist in pvt. practice Santa Barbara, 1981—2002. Cons. in field. Author: Behavior Modification, 1973; contbr. articles to profl. jours. and chpts. in books. Pres. Santa Barbara Mental Health Assn., 1978, 84-85, 91, Mountain View Sch. Site Coun., Santa Barbara, 1978-84. Recipient Vol. of Yr. award Santa Barbara Mental Health Assn., 1979, Tchg. Excellence awards Delta Delta Delta, Alpha Chi Omega, Gamma Phi Beta, Santa Barbara; NIMH predoctoral rsch. fellow, 1964-69; grantee in field. Fellow Behavior Therapy and Rsch. Soc.; mem. APA, AAUP (chpt. pres. 1978-79), Calif. Psychol. Assn., Assn. for Advancement of Behavior Therapy, Santa Barbara County Psychol. Assn. (pres. 1985), Phi Beta Kappa (chpt. pres. 1977-78), Sigma Xi, Psi Chi (chpt. faculty advisor, 1979-2005). Office: Univ Calif Dept Psychology Santa Barbara CA 93106-9660 Office Phone: 805-893-3534. E-mail: sherman@psych.ucsb.edu. *Pursuing a creative profession which allows one to help improve the condition of others, provides intrinsic rewards that make the work process satisfying in itself. I am fortunate to be involved in two such professions, college teaching and psychotherapy. When you genuinely enjoy what you are doing, you are likely to be successful at it.*

SHERMAN, ANDREW LAWRENCE, physiatrist, educator; s. Norman Paul and Susan Ruth Sherman; m. Deidre Kelly Sherman, Feb. 3, 2001; children: Samuel, Ryan. BS, Cornell U., Ithaca, NY, 1989; MD, SUNY, Buffalo, 1993. Resident U. Wash., Seattle, 1997; fellow spine & sports Beth Israel Hosp., NYC, 1997—98; attending physician Mt. Sinai Hosp., NYC, 1998—99; assoc. prof. rehab. medicine Sch. Medicine U. Miami, Fla., 1999—. Mem. adv. bd. Allergan Pharm., Irving, Calif.; lectr. Pfizer Pharm., NYC. Advisor Johnson Scholarship Found., Palm Beach, Fla., 2004. Mem.: AMA, Acad. Assn. Physiatrists, Am. Assn. Phys. Medicine and Rehab. Office: U Miami Dept Rehab 1611 NW 12th Ave L105 Miami FL 33136

SHERMAN, ARTHUR, theater educator, writer, actor, composer, sculptor; b. Dec. 5, 1920; s. Herman and Fay (Epstein) S.; m. Margery Frost Sherman, Apr. 15, 1974 (div. Sept. 1989); children: Claudia, Andrew Jay. MusB, Juilliard Sch. Music, NYC, 1955; M in Music Edn., Manhattan Sch. Music, 1957; Doctoral Equivalency, CUNY, 1969. Dir. performing arts N.Y.C. (N.Y.) Tech. Coll., 1964-72; prof. speech and theatre John Jay Coll., NYC, 1990—, Borough Man C.C., NYC, 1990—. Judge Film Award Com., Australia, 1972-89, Acad. Awards, 1990; cons. Min. for Edn., Tasmania, Australia, 1977; presenter in field. Author: (screenplays) Thistle and Thorn, 1982, Same Difference, 1983, (book and lyrics) Lenore and the Wonder House, 1964, Prisms in the Looking Glass, 1993, Once Upon a Crime, We the Common Earth; (short stories) Max the Messiah and Noah's Arc, 2005; (book) Paradise Lagoon, 1989, Picture Book for Young Adults Paintings, Music and Lyrics, 1998, Songwriting Is Easy and Fun, 1996, also short stories; (comedy theater) But Its Not Chekhov, 1999; (comic screenplay) Weaning, 1999; (7-book novel) The Pleiades, Burning in Heaven, Freezing in Hell, Bloody Mooring, Scoring in Limbo, Chasing the Phoenix, The Pleiades and Beyond, Betrayal of Self; (with Edward Mapp) The Road to Mainstream, 1999, Red Herrings No Fishing Allowed, 2005; (play) To Hell with Buffalo Wings-Anyone for Eagle Wings?, 1999, Warsaw Ghetto Uprising, 2001; (music drama) Prisms in the Looking Glass, Paul Robeson Theatre, 2006; actor, dir. films, TV, theater in U.S. and Australia; actor: (films) The Punisher, 1979, Death of a Soldier, 1985, Les Patterson Saves the World, 1988, The Last Bastion, 1987; sculptures displayed YWCA, Hamilton, Ont., Can., 1967, Lincoln Ctr., N.Y.C., 1969, State Bank, Sydney, Australia, 1974; bust of Louis Armstron Meml. Mus. and House, Dame Judith Anderson Australian Consulate N.Y.; contbr. design WTC 9/11 Meml., 2003. Pres. United Fedn. Coll. Tchrs., NYC, 1971. With USN, 1943—46. Grantee, Australian Film Commn., 1981. Mem. ASCAP, Australasian Performing Rights Assn., Actors' Equity U.S. and Australia. Office: John Jay Coll 58th St 10th Ave New York NY 10019 Office Phone: 212-237-8353.

SHERMAN, BEATRICE ETTINGER, hotel executive; b. NYC, May 29, 1919; d. Max and Stella (Schrager) Ettinger; m. Herbert Jacob Howard, Feb. 15, 1942 (dec. 1971); children: Robert David Howard, Carolyn Howard Smith; m. Ernest John Sherman, Dec. 29, 1974 (dec. Oct. 2000). Student, Gulf Park Jr. Coll., Gulfport, Miss., 1934—35, Shimer Jr. Coll., Mt. Carroll, Ill., 1936—38; BA, U. Miami, 1940; postgrad., Harvard U., 1940, Paris-Am. Acad., 1972, Alliance Française, Paris, 1973. Corp. sec., dir. Save Electric Corp., Toledo, 1940—67, Verd-A-Ray Corp., Toledo, 1944—67, Penetray Corp., Toledo, 1962—67; ptnr. Stella Assocs., Newark, 1960—80, BHS Ptnrs., Miami, 1983—; pres. Besman Inc., Miami, 1976—, All Am. Mobile Tel. Co., Coral Gables, 1986—2000; pres., bus. exec. hotelier Besman Hospitality, Gainesville, Fla., 1997—. Vol. worker Jewish Welfare Fedn., Toledo, 1942-69; vol. nurse's aid ARC, 1942-45; nat. spkr. United Jewish Appeal; mem. womens divsn. Greater Miami Jewish Fedn., 1969—, trustee, 1986-95; adv. bd. Miami Bell South; active Miami advertiser adv. bd. Bell South Advt. and Pub. Co.; vol. Nat. Coun. Jewish Women, Toledo, 1946-67, v.p., 1964-67, v.p., Miami, 1970-73; active Toledo chpt. Hadassah, 1943-67. Recipient Lion of Judah award Greater Miami Jewish Fedn., 1986. Mem. Assn. Telemessaging Svcs. Internat., Pioneers of Miami Beach. Home: 5108 SW 72d Ave Miami FL 33155-5530 Office: PO Box 558446 Miami FL 33255

SHERMAN, BRADLEY JAMES, congressman; b. LA, Oct. 24, 1954; s. Maurice H. and Lane (Moss) S. BA summa cum laude, UCLA, 1974; JD magna cum laude, Harvard U., 1979. Bar: Calif. 1979; CPA, Calif. Pvt. practice, LA, 1980-91; chmn. Calif. Bd. Equalization, Sacramento, 1991-95; mem. US Congress from 27th Calif. dist., 1997—; mem. banking and fin. svcs. com., internat. rels. com. Lectr. on tax law and policy; mem. Calif. Franchise Tax Bd., 1991-95. Contbr. articles to legal jours. Bd. dirs., rep. on tax issues Calif. Common Cause, 1984-89; mem. exec. com. Calif. Dem. Com., 1991—. Mem. Calif. State Bar. Democrat. Jewish. Office: US Ho Reps 1030 Longworth HOB Washington DC 20515-0527 E-mail: brad.sherman@mail.house.gov.

SHERMAN, CARY HOWARD, lawyer; b. NYC, Apr. 10, 1948; AB, Cornell U., 1968; JD cum laude, Harvard U., 1971. Bar: DC 1971. Ptnr. Arnold & Porter, Wash.; pres. Rec. Industry Assn. Am., Wash., DC. Bd. editors The Computer Lawyer, 1986—; adv. bd. BNA Patent, Trademark & Copyright Jour., 1987—. Bd. dirs. Washington Area Lawyers for the Arts, 1987—, Libr. Theater, 1987-94. Mem. Computer Law Assn. (bd. dirs. 1986-94). Office: Rec Industry Assn Am 1330 Connecticut Ave NW Ste 300 Washington DC 20036 Office Phone: 202-857-9632. Office Fax: 202-293-0447. Business E-Mail: csherman@riaa.com.

SHERMAN, DANIEL JAMES, history professor, director; b. Ann Arbor, Mich., May 20, 1958; s. Stanley Morton and Claire Richter Sherman; life ptnr. Eduardo deJesus Douglas. AB, MA, Harvard U., 1980, Yale U., 1981, MPhil, 1982, PhD, 1985. Lectr. history, lit., social studies Harvard U., Cambridge, Mass., 1985—88; vis. asst. prof. Cath. U. Am., Washington, 1989; vis. asst. prof. history U. Rochester, NY, 1989—90; asst. prof. French studies and history Rice U., Houston, 1990—94, assoc. prof. French studies and history, 1994—99, prof. French studies and history, 1999—2001; prof. history U. Wis., Milw., 2001—, dir. Ctr. 21st Century Studies, 2001—. Author: Worthy Monuments: Art Museums and the Politics of Culture in Nineteenth-Century France, 1989, The Constuction of Memory in Interwar France, 1999; editor: Museums and Difference, 2007; co-editor: Museum Culture: Histories, Discourses, Spectacles, 1994, Terror Culture, Politics: Rethinking 9/11, 2006; contbr. articles to profl. jours. Recipient History and Lit. Jr. prize, Harvard Coll., 1978, Laurence Wylie prize, 2000, award, Assn. American Publishers, 2000; fellow, NEH, 1988, 1990—91, Inst. Advanced Study, 1993—94, John Simon Guggenheim Meml. Found., 2001—02; grantee, Am. Coun. Learned Socs., 1988; Florence Gould Found. fellowship, Nat. Humanities Ctr., 1999—2000, Paul Mellon fellow, Ctr. Advanced Study Visual Arts, Nat. Gallery Art, 2006—07. Mem.: Soc. French Hist. Studies (mem., editl. bd. 1998—2001), Am. Hist. Assn. (J. Russell Major prize 2000), Coll. Art Assn. (assoc.). Jewish. Avocations: travel, photography, cooking. Office: University of Wisconsin-Milwaukee Center for 21st Century Studies Milwaukee WI 53201-0413 Home Phone: 414-967-7833; Office Phone: 414-229-4141. Office Fax: 414-229-5964.

SHERMAN, DEMING ELIOT, lawyer; b. Providence, July 22, 1943; s. Edwin Fisk and Martha Amy (Parkhurst) S.; m. Jane Catherine Bauer, Dec. 20, 1966; children: Melissa Jane, Nicholas Deming. BA, Amherst Coll., Mass., 1965; JD, U. Chgo., 1968. Bar: R.I. 1968, U.S. Dist. Ct. R.I. 1970, U.S. Supreme Ct. 1974, Mass. 1985, U.S. Dist. Ct. Mass. 1985. Mng. ptnr. Edwards Angell Palmer & Dodge LLP, Providence, 1986—94, ptnr.,

1969—, gen. counsel, 2005—. Trustee First Night Providence, 1988-93, 2001-04, pres., 1991-93; bd. dirs. R.I. Philharm. Orch., 1985-2003, 04—, pres., 1993-95; trustee Providence Preservation Soc., 1990-2004, pres. 1996-99; trustee Providence Athenaeum, 2004—, v.p., 2006—; mem. R.I. Com. on Jud. Tenure and Discipline, 1992-2000; bd. dirs. Providence YMCA, 1975-85, Blackstone Park Improvement Assn., 1979—, Nope's Island Conservation Assn., 1992-98, New Eng. Legal Found., 1994—, R.I. Legal Edn. Partnership, 2000-03, Grow Smart RI, 1998—, sec., 1998—, pres., 2006—; corporator R.I. Hosp., 1989—; bd. dirs. Friends of Blackstone Park and Blvd., 2001—, pres., 2001-06; trustee Festival Ballet Providence, 2002—, v.p., 2003-05, pres., 2005-07. Fellow R.I. Bar Found.; mem. ABA, R.I. Bar Assn., Amherst Alumni Assn. R.I. (pres. 1980-91), Greater Providence C. of C. (bd. dirs. 1991-94). Home: 254 Irving Ave Providence RI 02906-5544 Office: Edwards Angell Palmer & Dodge LLP 2800 Financial Plz Providence RI 02903 Home Phone: 401-861-3313; Office Phone: 401-274-9200. Business E-Mail: dsherman@eapdlaw.com.

SHERMAN, EDWARD FRANCIS, dean, law educator; b. El Paso, Tex., July 5, 1937; s. Raphael Eugene and Mary (Stedmond) S.; m. Alice Theresa Hammer, Feb. 23, 1963; children: Edward F. Jr., Paul. BA, Georgetown U., 1959; MA, U. Tex., El Paso, 1962-67; LLB, Harvard U., 1962, SJD, 1981. Bar: Tex. 1962, Ind. 1976. Aide to gov. Nev., state govt. fellow, Carson City, 1962; law clk. judge U.S. Dist. Ct. (we. dist.), El Paso, Tex., 1963; ptnr. Mayfield, Broaddus & Perrenot, El Paso, 1963-65; tchg. fellow Law Sch. Harvard U., Cambridge, Mass., 1967-69; prof. Sch. Law Ind. U., Bloomington, 1969-77; Edward Clark Centennial prof. U. Tex., Austin, 1977-96; prof., dean Tulane U. Law Sch., 1996—2001, prof., 2001—. Fulbright prof. Trinity Coll., Dublin, 1973-74; vis. prof. Stanford Law Sch., 1977, U. London, 1989, Sch. Pub. Adminstrn., Warsaw, Poland, 1995, Chuo U., Tokyo, 1995, U. New South Wales, Australia, 2002; counsel Tex. County Jail Litigation, 1980-85; bd. dirs., officer Travis County Dispute Resolution, 1993-96; mem. arbitrtor panel, course dir. Internat. Ctrs. Arbitration.; mem. STAR Vietnam Project (USAID) on new code of civil pro., 2003-04 Co-author: The Military in American Society, 1979, Complex Litigation, 1985, 4th edit., 2004, Processes of Dispute Resolution, 1989, 4th edit., 2006, Civil Procedure: A Modern Approach, 1989, 4th edit., 2005, Rau, Sherman & Shannon's Texas ADR and Arbitration Statutes, 1994, 4th edit., 2006. Capt. U.S. Army, 1965-67, lt. col. Res., 1970-90. Fellow Tex. Bar Found.; mem. ABA (reporter civil justice improvements project 1993, offer of judgment task force 1995, com. pro bono and pub. svc. 1997-99, chmn. task force on class action legis. 2002-03, reporter ABA Task Force on Asbestos 2003-2005, Robert McKay award for advancement of justice by law prof. 2004), Am. Arbitration Assn. (arbitrator panel), AAUP (gen. counsel 1986-88), Am. Law Inst., Tex. State Bar Assn. (alternative dispute resolution com. 1985-96, chair pattern jury charge com. 1983-94, Evans Tex. Bar award for excellence in dispute resolution 1998), Tex. Civil Liberties Union (gen. counsel 1985-91), La. Law Inst., La. State Bar (bd. govs. 1997-99, com. codes of lawyer and jud. conduct 1999-2001, com. on multi-juris. practice 2000—); La. Bar Found. (jud. liason com. 1999-2001), Assn. Am. Law Schs. (chmn. Sect. Litigation 1999, chmn. Sect. ADR 1995, com. on clin. legal edn. 1999-2002) Home: 21 Newcomb Blvd New Orleans LA 70118 Office: Tulane Law School 6329 Freret St New Orleans LA 70118 Office Phone: 504-865-5979. Business E-Mail: esherman@law.tulane.edu.

SHERMAN, ERIC, communications executive; b. 1967; B in History, Emory U., Atlanta, 1988. Affiliate sales MTV Networks, Atlanta, 1987—90, NYC, 1990—98; dir., Ops. MTV Digital Ste., 1998; v.p., gen. mgr. VH1 Classic, sr. v.p., gen. mgr., 2004—; v.p. MTV/VH1 Digital TV; sr. v.p., gen. mgr. VH1 Digital TV, 2004—; gen. mgr. Music High-Definition Channel, 2006—. Named one of 40 Executives Under 40, Multichannel News, 2006. Office: VH1 1515 Broadway New York NY 10036 Office Phone: 212-846-6000.

SHERMAN, ETHAN, contractor, publisher; b. NYC, June 23, 1941; s. Frank Issac and Jean (Abel) S.; m. Irene Linder, Oct. 31, 1965; children: Adam Howard, Rachael Suzanne. BS, Rider U., 1963. With Style-Master, Poughkeepsie, NY, 1971—, pres., 1979—. Author, pub.: How I Straightened My Spine, 1991. Trustee The Ethan Sherman Found., Poughkeepsie, NY, 1995—. With USAF, 1969-71. Mem. Knights of Pythias (chancellor comdr. 1989, 2000), Mensa. Avocations: sailing, camping, gardening. Home: 37 Hornbeck Rd Poughkeepsie NY 12603-1121 Office: Style-Master Home Products Inc 37 Hornbeck Rd Poughkeepsie NY 12603 Home Phone: 845-452-5322; Office Phone: 845-452-5322. Personal E-mail: sherm621@verizon.net.

SHERMAN, EUGENE JAY, retired marketing professional, economist; b. NYC, Jan. 10, 1935; s. Samuel and Sarah (Lavinsky) S.; m. Mary Eileen Van, Apr. 22, 1966; 1 child, Rebecca. BA, CCNY, 1956; MBA, NYU, 1959, postgrad., 1959-63. Economist Fed. Res. Bank N.Y., 1959-62, Chase Manhattan Bank, NYC, 1962-65; v.p. Bank of N.Y., NYC, 1965-72; sr. v.p., exec. dir., dir. rsch. Merrill Lynch and Co., NYC, 1972-78; v.p., chief economist, mgr.internat. investment Internat. Gold Corp., NYC, 1980-86; sr. v.p., chief economist Fed. Home Loan Bank N.Y., 1986-93; sr. v.p., dir. rsch. M.A. Schapiro & Co., Inc., NYC, 1993-96. Gold cons., N.Y.C., 1986—; adj. prof. Touro Coll., N.Y.C., 1997-98; exec.-in-residence, adj. prof. Baruch Coll., N.Y.C., 1997—, mem. faculty senate, fellow Weissman Ctr. for Internat. Bus. Author: Gold Investment: Theory and Application, 1986; contbr. articles to profl. jours. Recipient Tchg. Excellence award, Zicklin Sch., 2003. Mem. Money Marketeers (pres. 1971-72, honored fellow 1987), Downtown Economist Club (chmn. 1988-89), Forecasters (winner 1986, 95), Treasury Securities Luncheon (pres. 1995-96), N.Y. Assn. Bus. Econs. Avocations: outdoor activities, performing arts. Home: 115 E 9th St New York NY 10003-5414

SHERMAN, FLOYD F., construction executive; b. Kerhonkson, NY; B, NY State Coll. Forestry, Syracuse Univ.; MBA, Ga. State Univ. Chmn., CEO Triangle Pacific, 1992—2001; pres., CEO, dir. Builders FirstSource, Dallas, 2001—06, CEO, dir., 2006—. Served US Army. Office: Builders FirstSource Ste 1666 2001 Bryan St Dallas TX 75201 *

SHERMAN, FRED, biochemist, educator; b. Mpls., May 21, 1932; s. Harry and Ann (Kaufman) Sherman; m. Revina Freeman, July 25, 1958 (div.); children: Aaron, Mark, Rhea; m. Elena Rustchenko Bulgac, May 5, 2001. BA, U. Minn., Mpls., 1953; PhD, U. Calif., Berkeley, 1958; PhD (hon.), U. Minn., 2002. Postdoctoral fellow U. Wash., Seattle, 1959—60; 60postdoctoral fellow 61Lab. Genetique Physiol., Gif-sur-Yvette, France, 1960-61; sr. instr. U. Rochester, NY, 1961—62, asst. prof. NY, 1962—66, assoc. prof. NY, 1966—71, prof. dept. biochemistry Sch. Medicine & Dentistry NY, 1971—, chmn. dept. biochemistry NY, 1982—99. Instr. Cold Spring Harbor Lab., NY, 1970—87; Wander Meml. lectr., 1975; Wilson prof. U. Rochester, 1982. Co-author: Cold Spring Harbor Manual on Yeast Genetics and Molecular Biology, 1970—87; assoc. editor: Genetics, 1975—82, Molecular Cell Biology, 1979—88. Fellow NIH, 1959—61; grantee, 1963. Mem.: Am. Soc. Microbiology, Genetic Soc. Am. (bd. dirs. 1983—85), NAS (chmn. genet. sec. 2000—03), AAAS. Home: 69 Westminster Rd Rochester NY 14607-2223 Business E-Mail: fred_sherman@URMC.Rochester.edu.

SHERMAN, FREDERICK HOOD, lawyer; b. Deming, N.Mex., Aug. 9, 1947; s. Benjamin and Helen (Hood) Sherman; children: Jerah Elizabeth, Frederick Jakub. BBA, Southern Meth. U., 1970, JD, 1972. Bar: Tex. 1972, N.Mex 1973, US Dist. Ct. N.Mex 1973, US Dist. Ct. (we. dist.) Tex. 1974, US Supreme Ct. 1979, cert.: (mediator). Assoc. Sherman & Sherman, Deming, 1973-74, ptnr., 1974-78, prin., 1978—, owner, 1998—. Mem. specialization com. N.Mex Supreme Ct., 1986—94; liaison N.Mex Supreme Ct. and Workers Compensation Bd., 1991—94; apptd. guardian Assets State Fiscal Acctg. State N.Mex., 1992—; state coord. Nat. Bd. Trial Advs. Bd. Cert. Trial Specialist, 1994—98; mem. jud. selection com. 6th Jud. Selection, 2003. Contbr. articles to profl. jours. Chmn. Luna County Planning Commn., Deming, 1976—78; treas., bd. dirs. Luna County Econ. Devel. PSS, 1987—88; bd. dirs. Deming Pub. Sch., 1991—94, pres., 1991—92, 1991—95; chmn. bd. dirs. Luna County Charitable Found., 1991—; hon. dir. Deming Art Coun., 1989—; pres. Luna County Sch. Bd., 1991—92; pres., chmn. bd. dirs. Sherman Family Charitable Found., 1991—; mem. N.Mex HS Task Force, 1993—94; bd. visitors U. N.Mex Law Sch., 1983—87; bd. dirs. Luna County Hosp., 1991—94. Recipient Svc. award, N.Mex Bd. Legal Specialization, 1994, cert. Advocacy, Nat. Coll. Advocacy, 2001. Fellow: Nat. Coll. Advocacy (Achievement Recognition program 2005—); mem.: ATLA (state del. 2000—, pub. edn. com. 2001—, sec. to state del. 2004, vice chair state dels. 2005), Am. Assn. Justice State Dels. (pres.), Acad. Catastrophically Injured, Supreme Ct. Com. Professionalism, Col. Albert Fountain Inns of Ct. (charter), Coll. State Bar Tex. (pro bono 1995—), Am. Inns of Ct. (master atty. 1995—2002, officer 1997—), 6th Jud. Bar Assn., Tex. Bar Assn., State Bar N.Mex. (commr. 1978—86, alternative dispute resolution com. 1980—91, jud. selection com. 1985—88, mem. jud. selection com. 1985—88, co-chair 1986—87, legal retreat com. 1986—89, med. rev. com. 2000, arbitration com. 2000, Outstanding Svc. award 1986, Dedication award 1986), N.Mex. Bar Assn., N.Mex. Trial Lawyers Assn. (bd. dirs. 1986—, sec. 1989, 1997, officer 1997—98, designated mentor in personal injury/auto and social security 1998—, Notably Large award 1983, 1984, 1985, Amicus Curiae award 1991). Democrat. Roman Catholic. Avocations: skiing, investments, camping, farming, wine making. Office: Sherman & Sherman 210 S Silver Ave Deming NM 88030-3716 Home Phone: 505-546-4303; Office Phone: 505-546-8846. E-mail: fsherman@zianet.com.

SHERMAN, FREDERICK SCOTT, pediatric cardiologist; b. Cambridge, Mass., Feb. 7, 1949; s. Henry Sherman and Doris Gimpelson; m. Kathryn Rich; children: Alexis, Nathaniel. AB, Harvard U., 1971; MD, Yale U., 1975; MBA, U. Pitts., 2002. Resident in pediatrics U. Va., Charlottesville, 1975-78; asst. surgeon U.S. Pub. Health Svc., New Canton, Va., 1978-80; fellow in cardiology Children's Hosp., Boston, 1981-84; asst. prof. in pediatrics U. Calif., San Diego, Calif., 1984-88; prof. of pediatrics U. Pitts., 1988—. Dir. perinatal cardiology Magee Women's Hosp., Pitts., 1988—. Bd. dirs. Children's Home, Pitts., 1990—, Opera Theater of Pitts., 1995—. Fellow Am. Coll. Cardiology, Am. Acad. Pediatrics; mem. The Pitts. Golf Club, Am. Heart Assn., Am. Soc. Echocardiography. Avocations: golf, squash, opera. Office: Magee Womens Hosp 300 Halket St Pittsburgh PA 15213-3180

SHERMAN, GEORGE M., former food products executive; b. NYC, Aug. 6, 1941; s. Joseph B. and Fredericka (Hand) S.; m. Betsy Rae Bicknell, Nov. 26, 1966; children: Jonathan, David, Michael, Matthew. BS, L.I. U., 1963; MBA, U. Louisville, 1971. Product gen. mgr. Gen. Electric Co., Bridgeport, Conn., 1966-79; pres. Weed Eater div. Emersen Electric Co., Houston, 1979-80; pres. Skil Corp. div. Emerson Electric Co., Chgo., 1980-82; group v.p. U.S. power tools group Black & Decker Corp., Balt., 1985, sr. v.p., pres. power tools divsn., 1986—89, exec. v.p., pres. power tools & home improvement divsn., 1989—90; CEO Danaher Corp, Washington, 1990—2001; chmn. Campbell Soup Co., Camden, NJ, 2001—04. Mem. adv. bd. Nat. Home Ctr. Show, Chgo., 1987; bd. dirs. D.I.Y. Research Inst., Lincolnshire, Ill., 1988. Bd. dirs. Ctr. Stage, Balt., 1988. Served with U.S. Army, 1964-66. Mem. Am. Mgmt. Assn. (mem. gen. mgmt. council 1988). Clubs: Center (Balt.); Hillendale Country (Phoenix, Md.). Avocations: flying, skiing, scuba diving, racquetball, golf.

SHERMAN, GERALD HOWARD, lawyer, educator; b. NYC, Aug. 29, 1932; s. Abraham and Jean (Rose) S.; m. Lola Barbara Kay, Mar. 19, 1961; children: Jonathan, Ann. BBA, CCNY, 1953; LLB, Harvard U., 1958. Bar: NY 1959, DC 1960. Mem. firm Cooper & Silverstein, Washington, 1958-61; ptnr. Silverstein & Mullens, Washington, 1961-99; shareholder Buchanan Ingersoll, P.C., Washington, 2000—06, Buchanan Ingersoll and Rooney PC, Washington, 2006—; gen. counsel Assn. Advanced Life Underwriting, 1970—. Dep. tech. dir., adv. bd. Tax Mgmt. Portfolios, 1960—; adv. bd. BNA Pension Reporter, 1975—81; adj. prof. Georgetown U. Law Ctr., Washington, 1974—87. Bd. dirs., v.p. Jewish Found. Group Homes, 1982—90; bd. dirs. Am. Digestive Disease Soc., 1983—87, Washington Conservatory Music, 1995—2001. Mem.: ABA, Bar Assn. DC. Home: 3804 Klingle Pl NW Washington DC 20016-5433 Office: 1700 K St NW Washington DC 20006-2304

SHERMAN, HOWARD D., financial consultant; b. Tuscon, May 25, 1961; s. Donald J. and Elaine (Schwartz) S. BA, George Washington U., 1982; MBA, U. Pa., 1986. Rsch. asst. Fed. Res. Bd., Washington, 1982—84; sr. analyst Investor Responsibility Rsch. Ctr., Washington, 1986—88; sr. v.p., dir. Inst. Shareholder Svcs., Washington, 1988—97, pres., CEO, 1997—99; pres. Thomson Fin. Investor Rels., NYC, 1999—2000; COO Governance Metrics Internat. Inc., 2001—06, pres., CEO, 2007—. Spkr. in field. Contbr. articles to profl. jours. Mem. Phi Beta Kappa.

SHERMAN, IAN MATTHEW, lawyer; b. Chgo., Apr. 30, 1953; s. George and Vivian K. (Soffran) S.; m. Barbara Jan Smiley, Aug. 6, 1978; children: Wendy Joyce, Wesley Jacob, David Scott. AB, U. Ill., 1975; JD, Boston U., 1978. Bar: Ill. 1978, U.S. Dist. Ct. (no. dist.) Ill. 1978, U.S. Dist. Ct. (ea. dist.) Wis. 1995, U.S. Dist. Ct. (no. dist.) Ind. 2000, U.S. Ct. Appeals (7th cir.) 1984. Ptnr. Dykema Gossett PLLC (formerly Rooks, Pitts & Poust), Chgo., 1978—. Lectr. in field. Contbr. articles to profl. jours. Participant Youth Motivation Program Chgo. Pub. H.S., 1982; pro bono Am. Jewish Congress, Chgo., 1992—; vol. Chgo. (Ill.) Vol. Legal Svcs. Inst., 1982—; commr. Winnetka (Ill.) Park Dist., 2001—, v.p., 2002—03, 2007—; bd. dirs. The Vol. Ctr., 1986—90, chmn. fin. com., 1986—87, sec., 1987—88, pres., 1988—89. Named Ill. Super Lawyer, Law and Politics, 2005—07, Leading Lawyer, Law Bull. Pub. Co., 2005—07; recipient Disting. Svc. award, Chgo. (Ill.) Vol. Legal Svcs. Inst., 2003. Mem.: Am. Bd. Trial Advocates, Chgo. Bar Assn. (chmn. med.-legal rels. com. 2001—02, cert. appreciation 1983, 2003), Ill. State Bar Assn., Ill. Assn. Healthcare Attys., Ill. Soc. Trial Lawyers, Phi Kappa Phi, Phi Beta Kappa. Home: 923 Oak St Winnetka IL 60093-2440 Office: Dykema Gossett PLLC 10 S Wacker Dr Ste 2300 Chicago IL 60606-7407 Home Phone: 847-501-4829; Office Phone: 312-876-1700. Business E-Mail: isherman@dykema.com.

SHERMAN, IRWIN WILLIAM, biological sciences educator, academic administrator; b. NYC, Feb. 12, 1933; s. Morris and Anna (Ezaak) S.; m. Vilia Gay Turner, Aug. 25, 1966; children: Jonathan Turner, Alexa Joy. BS, CCNY, 1954; MS, Northwestern U., Evanston, Ill., 1959, PhD, 1960. Asst. prof. U. Calif., Riverside, 1962-67, assoc. prof., 1967-70, prof. biology, 1970—2005, chmn. biology dept., 1974-79, dean Coll. Natural and Agrl. Scis., dir. agrl. expt. sta., 1981-88, exec. vice chancellor, 1993-94, emeritus prof., 2006—; vis. scientist Scripps Rsch. Inst., 2006—. Instr. marine biol. lab., Woods Hole, Mass., 1963-68; mem. study sect. tropical medicine NIH, 1970-73; cons. Agy. Internat. Devel., 1978-90; mem. ad hoc study group U.S. Army, 1975-78. Author: The Invertebrates: Function and Form, 1976, Biology: A Human Approach, 1989, Malaria: Parasite Biology, Pathogenesis, Protection, 1998, Molecular Approaches to Malaria, 2005, The Power of Plagues, 2006. Steering com. World Health Orgn., 1978-87. With U.S. Army, 1954-56. USPHS fellow Rockefeller Inst., 1960-62, Guggenheim fellow, 1967, NIH/Nat. Inst. Med. Rsch. fellow 1973-74, Walter and Eliza Hall Inst. for Med. Rsch. fellow, 1986; Wellcome Trust lectr. Brit. Soc. Parasitology, 1987, Scripps Rsch. Inst. fellow 1991, 2003-05. Mem. AAAS, Am. Soc. Tropical Medicine and Hygiene, Soc. Protozoology, Soc. Parasitology, Sigma Xi. Democrat. Jewish. Avocations: painting, reading. Office: Scripps Research Inst Dept Cell Biology ICND 202 10550 N Torrey Pines La Jolla CA 92037 Office Phone: 858-784-2302. E-mail: isherman@scripps.edu.

SHERMAN, JEFFREY BARRY, retail executive; b. Passaic, NJ, June 25, 1948; s. Maxwell and Elinor (Richman) S.; m. Karin Lynn Swann, May 1, 1971; children— Erik, Brett, Peter, Kristin BS in Econs., CCNY, 1971; MBA, NYU, 1975. With Bloomingdale's, NYC, 1971—, v.p. merchandising, 1982-83, sr. v.p., 1983-85, exec. v.p., 1985—, now pres. Avocations: skiing, sailing. Office: Bloomingdale's 59th St & Lexington New York NY 10022

SHERMAN, JEFFREY SCOTT, lawyer; b. Bklyn., Oct. 26, 1955; s. Martin and Beatrice (Matrick) S.; m. Susan Ellen Ganz, Aug. 13, 1981; children: Elisabeth Faye, Andrew Harris. BA cum laude, SUNY, Albany, 1976; JD magna cum laude, Bklyn. Law Sch., 1980. Bar: NY 1980. Assoc. Proskauer, Rose et al, NYC, 1980-83, Shereff, Friedman, Hoffman & Goodman, NYC, 1983-87, ptnr., 1988—90; with Wyeth, 1990—2003, v.p., assoc. gen. counsel, 2001—03; v.p., gen. counsel Becton, Dickinson & Co., Franklin Lakes, NJ, 2004—06, sr. v.p., gen. counsel, 2006—. Mem. ABA, Assn. of the Bar of the City of NY (young lawyers com. 1983-86). Office: Becton Dickinson 1 Becton Dr Franklin Lakes NJ 07417-1880 Office Phone: 201-847-3223. Office Fax: 201-848-9228. *

SHERMAN, JEREMY P., lawyer; b. Chgo., Mar. 8, 1951; BA magna cum laude, Am. U., 1973; JD with honors, George Washington U., 1976. Bar: Ill. 1976. Mem. Seyfarth Shaw LLP, Chgo., 1976, ptnr. Nat. chairperson Labor and Employment Practice Group, Ill. Office: Seyfarth Shaw LLP Ste 2400 131 S Dearborn St Chicago IL 60603 Office Phone: 312-460-5901. Business E-Mail: jsherman@seyfarth.com.

SHERMAN, JIMMIE LEE, mathematician, educator; b. LA, Feb. 15, 1944; s. Harold and Lillie Lee (White) Sherman. Student, Compton Jr. Coll. Bus. mgr., reporter Watts (Calif.) Star Rev. Newspaper, 1965—66; publicity dir. Watts Happening Coffee House, 1965—67; screen writer Universal Studios, Universal City, Calif., 1967—68; creative dir., tchr. Watts Writers Workshop, 1987; cons., tchr. Compton (Calif.) Unified Sch. Dist., 1988—90, Nat. Coun. Negro Women, Pomona, Calif., 1997—98; tchr. math. Motivational Inst., LA, 2002—. Publ. Lesson Book Libr. Publ. Co., LA, 1979—; tchr., tutor Jimmie Shermans Literacy Campaign, LA, 1999—; cons. in field. Author: numerous poems, Principles of Immortality, 2003. With US Army, 1961—64. Named Worlds' Best Tchr. award, God's Little Angels Pvt. Sch., 2000, Poet of Yr., Famous Poets Soc., 2003; named to Wall of Tolerance, by Rosa Parks and Morris Dees, Nat. Campaign for Tolerance, 2005; recipient Quality of Life award, Sigma Gamma Rho, 1994, Breaking Barriers award, KJLH and LA Dodgers, 1997, Shakespeare Trophy of Excellence award, Famous Poets Soc., 2003. Mem.: Shermans Future Tchrs. Assn. (hon.). Avocations: painting, poetry, writing, reading. Home Phone: 323-294-3465; Office Phone: 323-294-3465. E-mail: jimmysherman2003@yahoo.com.

SHERMAN, JOHN ERIC, plastic surgeon; b. NYC, 1951; m. Emily Sherman; 2 children. MD, NY Med. Coll., 1975. Internship & residency Montefiore Hospital Med. Ctr., NYC, 1975—78; chief resident plastic surgery Cornell Med. Ctr., 1978—80; fellowship reconstructive plastic surgery Memorial Sloan Kettering Cancer Ctr., 1979—80; plastic surgeon priv. practice, NYC, 1980—; attending plastic surgeon NY Hospital, Lenox Hill Hospital; clinical assist. prof. surgery Cornell U. Med. Coll. Author: Surgery of Facial Bone Fractures, 1987. Fellow: Am. Coll. of Surgeons; mem.: Am. Soc. of Maxillofacial Surgeons, Am. Soc. of Aesthetic Plastic Surgeons, Am. Soc. of Plastic & Reconstructive Surgeons. Avocation: golf. Office: 1016 5th Ave New York NY 10028

SHERMAN, JOHN FOORD, biomedical consultant; b. Oneonta, NY, Sept. 4, 1919; s. Henry C. and Ruth (Foord) Sherman; m. Betsy Deane Murray, Feb. 8, 1944 (dec.); children: Betsy Deane, Mary Ann. BS, Union U., 1949, DSc, 1970; PhD, Yale U., 1953. With NIH, 1953—74; assoc. dir. extramural programs Nat. Inst. Neurol. Diseases and Blindness, 1961—62, Nat. Inst. Arthritis and Metabolic Disease, 1962—63; assoc. dir. for extramural programs Office Dir. NIH, 1964—68, dep. dir., 1968—74; v.p. Assn. Am. Med. Colls., Washington, 1974—91, exec. v.p., 1987—91, spl. cons., 1991—94. Bd. advisors Am. Bd. Internal Medicine, 1991—98; sr. advisor Rsch!Am., 1994—. Asst. surgeon gen. USPHS, 1964—68; spl. rsch. chemotherapy and neuropharmacology; panel on data and studies NRC, 1976—87; biomed. libr. rev. com. NIH, 1981—98; bd. dirs. Spinal Cord Injury Edn. and Tng. Found., 1986—92, Musculoskeletal Transplant Found., 1987—2003. With US Army, 1941—46. Decorated Bronze Star; recipient Meritorious Svc. award, USPHS, 1965, Disting. Svc. award, HEW, 1971, Sec.'s Spl. Citation award, 1973, Nat. Civil Svc. League award, 1973, Disting. Alumnus award, Union U.-Pharmacy Coll. Coun., 1974, Lifetime Achievement award, Nat. Assn. for Biomed. Rsch., 1990, Spl. Recognition award, Assn. Am. Med. Colls., 1996. Fellow: AAAS; mem.: Inst. Medicine NAS, Cosmos Club, Sigma Xi. Congregationalist. Personal E-mail: johnfsherman@msn.com.

SHERMAN, JONATHAN HENRY, lawyer; b. Washington, Jan. 4, 1963; s. Gerald Howard and Lola (Kay) Sherman; m. Catherine Sara Foot, Nov. 4, 2000; children: Benjamin Ashton, Julia Jean. BA in History magna cum laude, U. Rochester, 1984; MA in History, Yale U., 1989; JD, Stanford U., 1991. Bar: NY 1992, US Dist. Ct. (so. dist.) NY 1992, US Supreme Ct. 1995, US Dist. Ct. (ea. dist.) NY 1996, US Ct. Appeals (11th cir.) 1996, US Dist. Ct. (we. dist.) NY 1998, DC 2000, US Ct. Appeals (3d cir.) 2006. Assoc. Cahill Gordon & Reindel, NYC, 1991-2000; ptnr. Boies, Schiller & Flexner LLP, Washington, 2001—. Lectr. Stanford U., Palo Alto, Calif., 1991, Yale Coll., New Haven, 1993; adj. assoc. prof. law Fordham Law Sch., N.Y.C., 1998-2001. Sponsor, mentor Student-Sponsor Partnership, N.Y.C., 1992-96; contbr. The Cornerstone Sch., Jersey City, 1994; bd. dirs. Greater D.C. chpt. Crohn's and Colitis Found. Am., 2004—. Mem. ABA, N.Y. State Bar Assn. (media law com. 1997-99), Phi Beta Kappa. Office: Boies Schiller & Flexner LLP Ste 800 5301 Wisconsin Ave NW Washington DC 20015-2061 Home Phone: 301-320-5134; Office Phone: 202-237-9605. E-mail: jsherman@bsfllp.com.

SHERMAN, JOSEPH OWEN, pediatric surgeon; b. Chgo., Aug. 15, 1936; s. Joseph Owen and Mary Elizabeth (Kelly) Sherman; m. June Marie Martin, Mar. 16, 1963; children: Brian William, Lee Ann. Student, U. Ill., 1955—58; BS, Northwestern U., 1959, MD, 1962. Diplomate Am. Bd. Surgery, Am. Bd. Pediatric Surgery, lic. physician Ill. Rotating intern Passavant Meml. Hosp., Chgo., 1963-64; resident in gen. surgery VA Rsch. Hosp., Chgo., 1964-65, 67-68; Am. Cancer Soc. clin. fellow Northwestern U. Med. Sch., Chgo., 1965-66, from instr. to assoc. prof. surgery, 1967—86, prof. clin. surgery, 1986—; resident in pediatric surgery Children's Meml. Hosp., Chgo., 1966, 68-69; resident in thoracic surgery Mcpl. Tb San., Chgo., 1967. Emeritus staff dept. surgery Children's Meml. Hosp., 1995—, Evanston (Ill.) Hosp., 1995—. Contbr. articles to profl. jours. With Ill. Army N.G., 1953—57, with Ill. Air N.G., 1966—67. Fellow: ACS; mem.: AMA, Ill. State Med. Soc., Ill. Pediat. Surg. Assn., Chgo. Surg. Soc., Chgo. Med. Soc., Assn. Acad. Surgery, Am. Pediat. Surg. Assn. Avocations: photography, computer programing, indoor and outdoor gardening. Personal E-mail: j.o.sherman@att.net.

SHERMAN, JUDITH DOROTHY, theater producer, engineer, recording industry executive; b. Cleve., Nov. 12, 1942; d. William Paul and Laverne (Sperke) Luekens; m. Kenneth Sherman, Aug. 1, 1964 ldiv. Aug. 1972); m. Max Wilcox, Jan. 1, 1981 (div. Jan. 1988); m. Curtis Macomber, Apr. 29, 1988. BA, Valparaiso U., 1964; MFA, SUNY, Buffalo, 1971. Rec. engr. Edward at the Moog, NYC, 1971-72; producer-music dir. WBAI-FM, NYC, 1972-76; owner-producer Judith Sherman Prodns., NYC, 1976—. Rec. engr. Marlboro (Vt.) Music Festival, 1976-94; adminstrv. dir. La Musica di Asolo, Sarasota, Fla., 1986-88; vocalist Steve Reich and Musicians, 1971-72. Recipient Corp. Pub. Broadcasting award, 1976, two Grammy award nominations, 1991, Grammy award, Classical Prodr. of Yr., 1993, Grammy award nominations, 1994, 95, 97, 98. Mem. NAFE, Chamber Music Am. (bd. dirs. 2000—), NARAS. Democrat. Home and Office: 645 W 239th St Apt 2A Bronx NY 10463-1236

SHERMAN, LAWRENCE JAY, lawyer; b. Pitts., May 20, 1942; s. Ben E. and Leonora C. (Weill) S.; m. Iris Shapiro, Aug. 19, 1967; children: Rachel L., Jessica S. BA in Polit. Sci. with honors, U. Pitts., 1963; JD, U. Mich., 1966. Bar: D.C. 1967, Calif. 1967, Md. 1984, U.S. Dist. Ct. D.C., U.S. Dist. Ct. Md., U.S. Claims Ct., U.S. Ct. Appeals (D.C., 1st, 3rd, 4th, 5th, 6th cir. and fed. cir.). Appellate atty. NLRB, Washington, 1966-69; assoc. Cohen & Berfield, Washington, 1969-70; exec. dir. Migrant Legal Action Program, Washington, 1970-75; assoc. Lichtman, Abeles, Anker & Nagle, P.C., Washington, 1975-77; pvt. practice Washington, 1977-81; ptnr. Sherman & Lapidus, Washington, 1981-86; counsel Deso, Thomas, Spevack, Weitzman & Rost PC, Washington, 1991-2000; ptnr. Brown & Sherman, LLP, Washington, 2001—02; pvt. practice Washington, 2002—06; of counsel Slevin & Hart, P.C., 2005—. Adj. prof. George Meany Ctr. for Labor Studies, Silver Spring, Md. 1988-2000; prin. Mng. Human Resources For 21st Century, Washington, 1990-99. Contbr. articles to profl. jours. Fellow Am. Bd. Trial Advocates; mem. D.C. Bar (labor and employment law sect., litig. sect., co-chmn. steering com., 1981-85, labor law sect. 1978-84, co-chmn. labor law sect. 1983-84, lawyers coord. com.). Democrat. Avocations: tennis, racquetball, photography, travel, reading. Office: Slevin & Hart PC Ste 450 1625 Massachusetts Ave NW Washington DC 20036 Office Phone: 202-785-0384. Business E-Mail: ljs@slevinhart.com, lsherman@slevinhart.com.

SHERMAN, LAWRENCE WILLIAM, criminologist; b. Schenectady, Oct. 25, 1949; s. Donald Lester and Margaret (Heckman) Sherman; m. Eva Fass Fass; children: Eliot, Katharine. BA, Denison U., Granville, Ohio, 1970; MA, U. Chgo., 1970; Diploma in Criminology, Cambridge U., Eng., 1973; PhD, Yale U., 1976; MA, U. Pa., 1999. Program rsch. analyst N.Y.C. Police Dept., 1971—72; asst. to assoc. prof. criminal justice SUNY, Albany, 1976—82; dir. rsch., v.p. Police Found., Washington, 1979—85; pres. Crime Control Ins., Washington, 1985—95; assoc. prof. to Disting. univ. prof and chair dept. criminology and criminal justice U. Md., College Park, Md., 1982—99; Albert M. Greenfield prof. human relations, dept. sociology, dir. Jerry Lee Ctr. of Criminology and dir. Fels Inst. of Govt. U. Pa., Phila., 1999—, chmn. dept. criminology, 2003—. Pres. Crime Control Rsch. Corp., Phila., 1981—; mem. panel on rsch. policies NRC-NAS, Washington, 2000—; lectr. FBI Acad., Quantico, 1980—2000; adj. prof. law and sci. dir. reintegrative shaming experiments Rsch. Sch. Social Scis., Australian Nat. U., Canberra, ACT, Australia, 1993—; dir. Justice Rsch. Consortium, Oxford, 2000—. Editor: (Book) Police Corruption: A Sociological Perspective, 1974; author: (book) Scandal and Reform: Controlling Police Corruption, 1978, Policing Domestic Violence: Experiments and Dilemmas, 1992 (Am.Sociological Assn. Disting. Scholarship award in Crime, Law and Deviance, 1973); co-author: Evidence Based Crime Prevention, 2002; contbr. articles to profl. jours. Recipient Bruce Smith award for disting. contbn. to criminal justice, Acad. of Criminal Justice Scis., 1994; fellow N.Y.C. Urban fellow, Alfred P. Sloan Foun., 1970—71. Fellow: Am. Soc. Criminology (pres. 2001—02, E.H. Sutherland Award for Disting. Contbn. to Criminology 1999); mem.: Acad. of Exptl. Criminology (pres. 1999—2001), Internat. Soc. Criminology (pres. sci. commn. 1995—99, pres. 2000—05), Am. Acad. Polit. and Social Sci. (pres. 2001—05). Home: 3507 Baring St Philadelphia PA 19104 Office: University of Pennsylvania 3809 Walnut St Philadelphia PA 19104 Business E-Mail: lws@sas.upenn.edu.

SHERMAN, LOUIS ALLEN, biology professor, department chairman; b. Chgo., Dec. 16, 1943; s. Stanley E. and Sarah R. Sherman; m. Debra Meddoff, June 15, 1969; children: Daniel, Jeff. BS in Physics, U. Chgo., 1965, PhD in Biophysics, 1970. Postdoctoral fellow Cornell U., Ithaca, NY, 1970-72; asst. prof. U. Mo., Columbia, 1972-78, assoc. prof., 1978-83, prof., 1983-88, dir. biol. scis., 1985-88; prof., head dept. biol. scis. Purdue U., West Lafayette, Ind., 1989-2000, prof. biol. scis., 1989—. Vis. scholar Hebrew U., Jerusalem, 2004—05. Contbr. articles to profl. jours. NIH fellow, 1965-72; Fulbright Hayes scholar, The Netherlands, 1979-80; NSF travel grantee, Fed. Republic Germany, Japan; grantee NIH, USDA, Dept. Energy. Fellow: AAAS, Am. Acad. Microbiology; mem.: AAUP, Plant Molecular Biology Soc., Biophys. Soc., Am. Soc. Plant Biologists, Am. Soc. Microbiology. Office: Purdue U Dept Biol Scis Lilly Hall West Lafayette IN 47907

SHERMAN, MARY ANGUS, public library administrator; b. Lawton, Okla., Jan. 3, 1937; d. Donald Adelbert and Mabel (Felkner) Angus; m. Donald Neil Sherman, Feb. 8, 1958; children: Elizabeth, Donald Neil II. BS in Home Econs., U. Okla., 1958, MLS, 1969. Br. head Pioneer Libr. System, Purcell, Okla., 1966-76, regional libr. Norman, Okla., 1976-78, asst. dir., 1978—87, dir., 1987—. Bd. dirs. McClain Bank, chair audit com., 1997—. Mem. bd. visitors Coll. Arts and Scis. U. Okla., 1998—2005, mem. internat. programs bd. visitors, 2003—; bd. dirs. U. Okla. Found., 2004—; Women's Resource Ctr., Norman, 1998—2003, pres., 2002. Named one of Disting. Alumni, Sch. Home Econs. U. Okla., 1980; recipient award of merit, U. Okla. Sch. Libr. and Info. Sci., 2000. Mem.: AAUW (pres. Okla. chpt. 1975—77, SW Ctrl. region dir. 1983—85, nat. bd. dirs. 1983—87, v.p. nat. membership 1985—87, Woman of Yr. Purcell chpt. 1982), ALA (councilor 1988—96, internat. rels. round table 1989—, planning and budget assembly 1990—91, internat. rels. com. 1992—96, orientation com. 1998—99, membership com. 1999—2000, chair sister libr. com. 2000—02, exec. bd. 2000—02, internat. rels. com. 2001—05), Okla. Libr. Assn. (pres. 1982—83, interlibr. cooperation com. 1993—95, chair 1994—95, legis. com. 1998—, Disting. Svc. award 1986), Internat. Fedn. Libr. Assns. (standing com. on pub. librs. 1999—), Tech. in Pub. Librs. Com., Pub. Libr. Assn. (divsn. of ALA, pres. pub. policy for pub. librs. sect. 1995—96, chmn. internat. rels. com. 2002—04), Norman Sister City Com., Norman C. of C. (bd. dirs. 1988—96, pres. 1994—95), Norman Soc. Internat. Affairs (v.p. 1998—99, pres. 1999—2001), Norman Assistance League Club (cmty. assoc.), Rotary (program chair 1991—92, bd. dirs. 1993—97, pres. 1995—96, group study exch. leader to Iceland 1996, dist. literacy chair 1998—2000, dist. group study exch. chair 2001—06, dist. gov. nominee 2005—06, dist. gov.-elect 2006—, Paul Harris fellow), Phi Beta Kappa, Beta Phi Mu, Kappa Alpha Theta (pres. Alpha Omicron House Corp. 1984—87, nat. dir. ho. corps. 1987—88), Delta Gamma Mothers (pres. 1978—79). Democrat. Methodist. Office: Pioneer Libr System 225 N Webster Ave Norman OK 73069-7133 Office Phone: 405-701-2642. Business E-Mail: mary@pls.lib.ok.us.

SHERMAN, MICKEY (MICHAEL SHERMAN), lawyer; b. 1946; m. Lis Wiehl, June 23, 2006. AB, U. Conn., JD, 1971. Bar: Conn. 1971. Asst. pub. def. Stamford Superior Ct., 1971—72, asst. pros., 1972—76; asst. town atty. Town of Greenwich, 1976—77; ptnr. Sherman & Richichi, Stamford, Conn., 1977—. Legal analyst CBS News. Mem.: ATLA, Conn. Trial Lawyers Assn., Nat. Assn. Criminal Def. Lawyers, Conn. Criminal Def. Lawyers Assn. (founding mem., bd. mem., lectr., past pres.). Office: Sherman Richichi & Hickley LLC 27 5th St Stamford CT 06905 *

SHERMAN, MIKE (MICHAEL FRANCIS SHERMAN), professional football coach; b. Norwood, Mass., Dec. 19, 1954; m. Karen Sherman; children: Sarah, Emily, Matthew, Benjamin. Student, Ctrl. Conn. State U., 1974, 76-77. Part-time coach U. Pitts. Panthers, 1981-82; offensive line coach Tulane U. Green Wave, New Orleans, 1983-84; offensive coord. Coll. Holy Cross Crusaders, Worcester, Mass., 1985-88; offensive line coord. Tex. A&M Aggies, College Station, 1989-93, 95-96, UCLA Bruins, 1994; offensive coord., tight ends coach Seattle Seahawks, 1999; tight ends/asst. offensive line Green Bay Packers, 1997-98, head coach, 2000—05, exec. v.p., 2001—05, gen. mgr., 2001—04; asst. head coach/offense Houston Texans, 2006—07, asst. head coach, offensive coord., 2007—. Office: The Houston Texans Two Reliant Pk Houston TX 77054

SHERMAN, NORMAN MARK, advertising agency executive; b. NYC, June 19, 1948; s. Sol and Rhoda (Kaplan) S.; m. Michelle Petnov, Jan. 8, 1978; 1 child, Michael Isaac. BA, U. Buffalo, 1970; MBA, Columbia U., 1972. Cert. tchr., N.Y. Product mgr. RCA Records, NYC, 1972-73; dir. mktg. Shelter Records, NYC, 1973-74; account exec. Rosenfeld Sirowitz & Lawson, NYC, 1974-76, Benton & Bowles, NYC, 1976-78, v.p. account supr., 1978-81, sr. v.p., mgmt. supr., 1981-84; exec. v.p., dir. account mgmt. Avrett, Free & Ginsberg, NYC, 1984-85; sr. v.p., group account dir. D'arcy, Masius, Benton & Bowles, 1985-93, mng. dir., bd. dirs., 1993-96, corp. exec. v.p., 1996-98; mng. dir. The Sr. Network, Stamford, Conn., 1998-99; pres. N.Am. Gundersen Ptnrs. LLC, NYC, 1999—2001; exec. v.p., dir. healthcare Hill, Holliday, Connors, Cosmopulos, 2002—05; ptnr. Troyanos Group, Irvington, NY, 2006—. Home: 330 W 72nd St New York NY 10023-2641 Office: Troyanos Group 106 N Broadway Irvington NY 10533 Office Phone: 914-479-1802. Business E-Mail: norman@troyanosgroup.com.

SHERMAN, PATSY O'CONNELL, retired manufacturing executive, chemist; b. Mpls., Sept. 15, 1930; d. James Patrick and Edna Fern (Stitzel) O'Connell m. Hubert Townsend Sherman, Aug. 15, 1953; children: Sharilyn Kay Sherman Loushin, Wendy Jane Sherman Heil. BA, Gustavus Adolphus Coll., 1952. Chemist 3M, St. Paul, 1952-67, rsch. specialist, 1967-73, tech. mgr., 1973-82, mgr. tech. devel., 1982—92; ret., 1992. Trustee GMI Engring. and Mgmt. Inst., Flint, Mich., 1986-92; bd. dirs., owner Advanced Optics Inc., Mpls.; dir. Nat. Inventors Hall of Fame Found., 1996-99, 2002—. Contbr. numerous articles to profl. jours.; patentee in field. Trustee Gustavus Adolphus Coll., 1989-92. Recipient Disting. Alumni award Gustavus Adolphus Coll., 1975, Spurgeon award Boy Scouts Am., 1980; named to Minn. Inventors Hall of Fame, 1989, Nat. Inventors Hall of Fame, 2001. Mem. Am. Chem. Soc., Am. Soc. Tng. and Devel., Am. Soc. Engring. Edn. (dir. continuing profl. devel. div. 1986-89, chair 1989-90). Achievements include invention of Scotchgard (with Samuel Smith) in 1956. Personal E-mail: patsherman@aol.com.

SHERMAN, RANDOLPH, plastic and reconstructive surgeon, educator; b. St. Louis, May 27, 1951; s. Leon and Pearl (Lichtenfeld) S.; 1 child, Max Lassen. BA, U. Rochester, 1973; MD, U. Mo., 1977. Diplomate Am. Bd. Surgery, Am. Bd. Plastic Surgery (cert. added qualification in hand surgery). Intern in gen. medicine U. Wis., Madison, 1978; intern in surgery U. Calif., San Francisco, 1978-79, resident in surgery, 1979-81, SUNY, Syracuse, 1981-83; fellow in plastic and reconstructive surgery U. So. Calif., 1983-85, asst. prof. surgery and orthopedics LA, 1985-91, assoc. prof. clin. surgery and orthopaedics, 1991-92, assoc. prof. clin. surgery, orthopaedics and neurol. surgery, 1992-96, chmn. divsn. plastic and reconstructive surgery, 1994—, prof. clin. surgery, orthopaedics and neurol. surgery, 1996—. Mem. cons. staff City of Hope Nat. Med. Ctr., Duarte, Calif., 1985-91, 94—, St. John's Hosp., Santa Monica, 1989—, USC Univ. Hosp., 1997—; mem. staff, med. dir. Microsurg. Ctr. Hosp. Good Samaritan, L.A., 1985-93; mem. plastic and reconstructive surgery staff Kenneth Norris Jr. Cancer Hosp., L.A., 1985—, L.A. County/U. So. Calif. Med. Ctr., L.A., 1985—; mem. staff St. Vincent Med. Ctr., L.A., 1986-92, Orthop. Hosp., L.A., 1986—; Shriner's Hosp. for Crippled Children, L.A., 1987-92, Children's Hosp. L.A., 1987—, Cedars Sinai Med. Ctr., L.A., 1987—, Estelle Doheny Eye Hosp., L.A., 1994—, numerous others; chief plastic and reconstructive surgery divsn. U. So. Calif. U. Hosp., L.A., 1991—, mem. active staff; dir. Am. Bd. Plastic Surgery 2000—, Am. Bd. Surgery, 2004—; vice-chair dept. surgery Keck Sch. Medicine, 2004-; assoc. med. dir. surg. svcs. L.A. County/U. So. Calif. Med. Ctr., 2005; mem plastic reconstructive surgery staff U. So. Calif. Hosp., 1991—; vice chair dept. surgery Keck Sch. Medicine, U. So. Calif. lectr., 2005; rschr. in field. Editor: Orthopedic Clinics, 1993; assoc. editor Surg. Rounds, 1989—, Jour. Hand Surgery, 1992-96, Am. Jour. Reconstructive Microsurgery, 1995—; sect. editor PRS 2005—; contbr. articles to profl. jours., chpts. to books. Founder L.A. chpt. Operation Smile Internat., 1993—. Recipient L.A. Humanitarian award Calif. Hosp., 1994; Microsurg. Devel. grantee Hosp. Good Samaritan, 1987-92, U. So. Calif. U. Hosp., 1992—; grantee Searle R&D, 1995-97, Cohesion Corp., 1997. Fellow ACS, Am. Assn. Plastic Surgeons, Am. Assn. Hand Surgeons (bd. dirs. 1991-95), Am. Soc. Hand Surgery, Am. Soc. Reconstructive Microsurgery (past pres.), Calif. Soc. Plastic Surgery; mem. Am. Soc. Plastic and Reconstructive Surgery, Am. Soc. Peripheral Nerve, Internat. Soc. Reconstructive Microsurgery, Calif. Med. Assn., Calif. Soc. Plastic Surgery, Assn. Acad. Chmn. Plastic Surgery, Plastic Surgery Rsch. Coun., Musculoskeletal Infection Soc., Undersea Med. Soc., Flying Physicians Assn., Wound Healing Soc. Avocations: flying, mountain climbing, scuba diving, jazz piano, gardening. Office: 1450 San Pablo St Ste 2000 Los Angeles CA 90089-0106 Office Phone: 323-442-6470. Business E-Mail: rsherman@surgery.usc.edu.

SHERMAN, RICHARD ALLEN, SR., lawyer; b. Atlanta, Mar. 16, 1946; s. Robert Hiram and Olivia Mae (Latham) S.; m. Mary Margaret Sawyer, June 23, 1973 (div. June 1994); children: Richard A. Jr., Jill Mary, James Warren. BA, Tulane U., 1968, JD, 1972. Bar: Fla. 1974, La. 1973, U.S. Ct. Appeals (5th cir.) 1978, U.S. Ct. Appeals (11th cir.) 1981, U.S. Supreme Ct. 1981. Ptnr., head appellate divsn. Wicker, Smith, Blomqvist, Davant, Tutan, O'Hara, McCoy et al, Miami, 1973-83; pvt. practice Ft. Lauderdale, Fla., 1983—; practice limited to handling appeals in Fla. Mem. ABA (vice-chmn. U.S. Ct. Appeals 5th cir. com. 1981), Fla. Bar Assn. (appellate rules com. 1979-81), Dade County Bar Assn. (chmn. appellate cts. com. 1982-83), Mensa, Pres. Club, Lauderdale Yacht Club, Upper Keys Sailing Club (bd. dirs.). Avocations: yacht racing, boating, scuba diving, travel, theater. Office: 1777 S Andrews Ave Ste 302 Fort Lauderdale FL 33316-2517

SHERMAN, RICHARD BEATTY, historian, educator; b. Somerville, Mass., Nov. 16, 1929; s. James Beatty and Hilda Louise (Ford) S.; m. Hanni Fey, June 13, 1952; children: Linda Caroline, Alan Theodore. AB, Harvard U., 1951, PhD, 1959; MA, U. Pa., 1952. Instr. history Pa. State U., State College, 1957-60; asst. prof. Coll. of William and Mary, Williamsburg, Va., 1960-65, assoc. prof., 1965-70, prof., 1970-87, chancellor prof., 1987-92, Pullen prof., 1992-94, prof. emeritus, 1994—. Fulbright prof. Am. history U. Stockholm, 1966-67. Author: The Negro and the City, 1970, The Republican Party and Black America, 1973, The Case of Odell Waller, 1992; co-author: The College of William and Mary: A History, 1993; contbr. articles to profl. jours. Served with U.S. Army, 1952-54. Am. Philos. Soc. grantee, 1964, 66, faculty rsch. grantee Coll. William and Mary, 1962, 63, 65, 80, 87. Mem. ACLU, Phi Beta Kappa. Democrat. Home: 205 Matoaka Ct Williamsburg VA 23185-2810 Office: Coll William and Mary Dept History Williamsburg VA 23185 E-mail: richardsherman@cox.net.

SHERMAN, ROBERT ALAN, lawyer; b. Boston, Nov. 10, 1953; s. Samuel and Rose C. (Cutler) S.; children: Matthew, Stephanie. BA, U. Rochester, 1975; JD, Boston U., 1978. Bar: Mass. 1978, U.S. Dist. Ct. Mass. 1979, U.S. Ct. Appeals (1st cir.) 1979. Assoc. Featherston & Griffin, Boston, 1978-81; from assoc. to ptnr. Gaffin & Krattenmaker, Boston, 1981-91; chief consumer protection divsn. Office of Atty. Gen., Boston, 1991-93, spl. counsel for A.G., 1993; spl. counsel Eckert, Seamans, Cherin & Mellott, Boston, 1994-96, ptnr., 1996—; now co-mng. shareholder Greenberg Traurig LLP, Boston. Legal analyst Fox TV, Newton, Mass., 1994-95, New Eng. Cable News, Newton, 1994—, Ct. TV, 1997—, CNBC, 1997—. Contbr. articles to profl. jours. Bd. dirs. Greater Boston Legal Svcs., 1991-93, Jewish Cmty. Ctr., 1994—; trustee Cambridge Ctr. Behavioral Studies, 1989-94; bd. overseers Beth Israel Deconess Med. Ctr. Recipient Humanitarian award Assn. Behavior Analysis, 1987. Avocations: running, scuba diving, reading, travel, music. Office: Greenberg Traurig LLP Third Fl One International Pl Boston MA 02110 Office Phone: 617-310-6015. Office Fax: 617-310-6001. Business E-Mail: shermanr@gtlaw.com.

SHERMAN, ROGER TALBOT, surgeon, educator; b. Chgo., Sept. 30, 1923; s. Joseph Bright and Alice Elizabeth (Baur) S.; m. Ruth Kathryn Thieman, Aug. 23, 1952, (dec. 2002); children: Nann, Alice, Nina, John, Julie; m. Mary Ellen Hulsey, July 12, 2003. AB, Kenyon Coll., 1946; MD, U. Cin., 1948. Diplomate Am. Bd. Surgery (mem.). Intern, fellow in pathology St. Luke's Hosp., Chgo., 1948-50; resident in surgery Cin. Gen. Hosp., 1950-56; chief dept. exptl. surgery Walter Reed Army Med. Ctr., 1956-59; asst. prof. to prof. surgery U. Tenn., Memphis, 1959-72; prof., chmn. dept. surgery U. South Fla., Tampa, 1972-82; prof. surgery Emory U. Sch. Medicine, Atlanta, 1983-93; chief surgery Grady Meml. Hosp., Atlanta, 1983-92; Whitaker prof. surgery Emory U. Sch. Medicine, Atlanta, 1993-97, prof. emeritus, 1997—; dir. surg. edn. Piedmont Hosp., Atlanta, 1993-97. Mem. editorial bd. Am. Surgeon, 1970-91, Jour. Trauma, 1970-93; contbr. articles to profl. jour., chpt. to books. Served to maj. M.C. AUS, 1956-59. Recipient Golden Apple Tchr. of the Yr. award, 1972, Williams Disting. Tchg. award Emory U., 1984, Curtis P. Artz award, 1988. Fellow ACS (gov.); mem. Am. Assn. Surgery of Trauma (pres. 1979), Am. Surg. Assn., So. Surg. Assn., Southeastern Surg. Congress (pres. 1985), Internat. Surg. Soc., Soc. Surgery of Alimentary Tract, Am. Burn Assn., Shock Soc., Am. Trauma Soc., Ga. Surg. Soc. (pres. 1997), Sigma Xi, Psi Upsilon, Alpha Omega Alpha. *Surgery. The opening, exploration and repair of the living human body is an awesome responsibility afforded to only a few. To be privileged to be counted among those is a high honor, surpassed only by being trusted to teach others this demanding, and marvelous craft.*

SHERMAN, RUTH TODD, counseling administrator, educator; b. Memphis, July 3, 1924; d. Robbie M. and Lillie M. (Shreve) Todd. BS, Memphis State U., 1972, MEd, 1975; MA, Western Mich. U., 1986; PhD, Ohio State U., 2001. Cert. tchr., counselor. Youth leader Assembly of God Ch., Memphis, 1962-64, youth dir., 1964-66; counselor Teen Challenge, Memphis, 1973-74; marriage and family therapist Memphis, 1976-77; govt. tng. advisor Def. Logistics Agy., Battle Creek, Mich., 1982-87, advisor Alexandria, Va., 1987-94, ret., 1994; tchr. computer graphics Ohio State U., Columbus, 1998—2001; instrnl. devel. specialist Global U., Springfield, Mo., 2004—. Agy. to Mil. Svc. cons. Def. Logistics Agy., Oklahoma City, 1990-94. Author: Federal Catalog Training Books/Videos, 1987 (Sustained Superior Performance award 1987). Mem. Internat. Assn. Marriage and Family Counselors, Nat. Employment Counseling Assn., Am. Mental Health Counseling Assn. Avocations: drawing, creating computer animations, photography. Home: Apt 217B 1644 Marion Springfield MO 65807

SHERMAN, SANDRA BROWN, lawyer; b. Galesburg, Ill., May 14, 1953; d. Charles Lewis and Lois Maria (Nelson) Brown; m. Robert Sherman, June 10, 1979; children: Michael Wesley, Stephen Averill, Alexander Joseph. B of Music Edn., Ind. U., 1975; JD, U. Ill., 1979, LLM, 1981. Bar: Ill. 1979, Tex. 1982, N.J. 1984, U.S. Tax Ct. 1988, N.Y. 1997. Instr. law U. Ill., Champaign, 1979-81; assoc. Law Offices of William E. Remy, San Antonio, 1984, Gutkin Miller Shapiro & Selesner, Millburn, NJ, 1985-88, ptnr., 1989-91; counsel Riker Danzig Scherer Hyland & Perretti LLP, Morristown, NJ, 1991-95; ptnr. Riker Danzig Scherer Hyland & Perretti, LLP, Morristown, NJ, 1996—. Contbr. articles to profl. jours. Trustee, sec. Found. U. Medicine and Dentistry N.J., 1998—. Scholar Ind. U., 1971-75, U. Ill., 1977-79. Mem. ABA (probate and trust law divsn.), N.J. Bar Assn., Estate Planning Coun. No. N.J., Estate Planning Coun. N.Y.C., Park Ave. Club. Avocation: music. Office: Riker Danzig Scherer Hyland & Perretti LLP Headquarters Plz 1 Speedwell Ave Morristown NJ 07961-1981 Office Phone: 973-538-0800. Business E-Mail: ssherman@riker.com.

SHERMAN, SARAI, sculptor, painter; b. Phila., 1922; BFA, Temple Univ., BS in Edn.; student, Barnes Found.; MFA, Univ. Iowa. Exhibitions include Palazzo Acad., Tod, Italy, 1983, Forum Gallery, NYC, 1986, exhibitions include Idiomi della Scuttura Contemporary, Verona, Italy, 1989, Il Bisonte, Florence, Italy, 1997, exhibitions include Premio Suzzara, Italy, 1998, Premio Biella, 1999, Whitney Am. Mus., 2006. Recipient Award for Painting, Nat. Inst. Arts & Letters, 1964, European Cmty. prize, Premio Marzotto, 1967, Ann. Painting award, Republic of San Marino, 1975, Proctor prize, NAD, 1976. Mem.: NAD (academician 1999—). Subject of "Camera Picta: Sarai Sherman" by Rolando Bellini, 1995. Office: Forum Gallery 745 Fifth Ave New York NY 10151

SHERMAN, SPENCER E., ophthalmologist; AB cum laude, Princeton U., Sigma XI, 1958; MD, Columbia Coll. Physicians & Surgeons, 1962. Diplomate Am. Bd. Ophthalmology. Intern Mt. Sinai Hosp., NYC, 1962-63, attending ophthalmologist, 1968—, resident in ophthalmology, 1965-68; asst. clin. prof. ophthalmology NYU Sch. Medicine, NYC; staff Mt. Sinai Hosp., 1998—. Attending ophthalmologist Manhattan Eye & Ear Hosp., NYC, 1968—, Lenox Hill Hosp., NYC, 1968—, NY Eye and Ear Infirmary, Mt. Sinai Hosp., 1970—. Capt. USAMC, 1963-65. Named one of Best Drs. in NY, Castle Connolly Group, 1980—, Top Drs. in US, Ctr. for Study of Svc. Fellow ACS, Internat. Coll. of Surgeons, Am. Acad. of Ophthalmology (Honor and Svc. award); mem. AMA, Nat. Soc. Prevention Blindness, Found. Children with Learning Disabilities, Am. Soc. Refractive Surgeons, NY Acad. Medicine, NY Ophthalmologic Soc., Internat. Soc. Refractive Surgery, Am. Soc. Cataract & Refractive Surgery, Harmonie Club, Sunningdale Country Club, Maidstone Gun Club, Peconic Sportsman Club, East Hampton Tennis Club. Office: 166 E 63rd St New York NY 10021-7636 Office Phone: 212-753-8300. Fax: (212) 752-4285. E-mail: sesmdpc@aol.com.

SHERMAN, VICTOR, lawyer; b. Indpls., Aug. 28, 1941; s. Marshall and Sara Lee Sherman; m. Claudia Ann Cron, Oct. 8, 1988; children: Mark, Daniel, Miles, Oliver, Luke. BS, UCLA, 1962; LLB, U. Calif., Berkeley, 1965. Bar: Calif. 1966, Conn. 1996, U.S. Ct. Appeals (9th cir.) 1971, U.S. Supreme Ct. 1996, Washington D.C. 2000, N.Y. 2001. Ptnr. Nasatir, Sherman & Hirsch, LA, 1970-83, Main St. Law Bldg., Santa Monica, Calif., 1984—; mng. ptnr. Sherman & Sherman, Santa Monica, 1984—. Speaker, founder Advanced Criminal Law Seminar, Aspen, Colo., 1981—. Pvt. 1st class U.S. Army, 1960-67. Mem. Nat. Assn. Criminal Def. Lawyers (life), Am. Bd. Criminal Lawyers. Office: Sherman & Sherman 2115 Main St Santa Monica CA 90405-2215

SHERMAN, WILLIAM FARRAR, lawyer, former state legislator; b. Little Rock, Sept. 12, 1937; s. Lincoln Farrar and Nancy (Lowe) S.; m. Carole Lynn Williams, Sept. 2, 1967; children: John, Anna, Lucy. BA in History, U. Ark., 1960; LLB, U. Va., 1964. Bar: Ark. 1964, U.S. Supreme Ct. 1970. Assoc. Smith, Williams, Friday & Bowen, Little Rock, 1964-66; asst. U.S. atty. Ea. Dist. Ark., Little Rock, 1966-69, Ark. Securities Commr., Little Rock, 1969-71; ptnr. Jacoway, Sherman & Pence, Little Rock, 1971—2004; pvt. practice William F. Sherman Law Office, Little Rock, 2005—. Legal counsel Voice of the Retarded, 1991-2006; mem. Ark. Ho. of Reps., 1974-84; spl. assoc. justice Supreme Ct., 1991; del. Constnl. Conv. Ark., 1979. With U.S. Army, 1960-61, now brig. gen. U.S. Army ret. Mem. ABA, Ark. Bar Assn., Pulaski County Bar Assn., Ark. Bar Found. Methodist. Office: 809 North Palm St Little Rock AR 72205 Home Phone: 501-661-1963; Office Phone: 501-372-3148. Personal E-mail: wfsherman@sbcglobal.net.

SHERMAN, ZACHARY, civil engineer, aerospace engineer, consultant; b. NYC, Oct. 26, 1922; s. Harry and Minnie (Schulsinger) Sherman; m. Bertha Leikin, Mar. 23, 1947; children: Gene Victor, Carol Beth. BCE, CCNY, 1943; MCE, Polytech. U. N.Y., Bklyn., 1953, PhD in Civil Engring. & Mechanics, 1969; MME, Stevens Inst. Tech., 1968. Registered profl. engr., N.Y., N.J. Stress analyst Gen. Dynamics, San Diego, 1943-45; sr. stress analyst Republic Aviation, Farmingdale, NY, 1945-47, 59-62; prof. civil engring. U. Miss., Oxford, 1954-59; lectr. Stevens Inst. Tech., Hoboken, NJ, 1962-67, CUNY, 1967-69; assoc. prof. aerospace engring. Pa. State U., State College, 1969-73; prin. Dr. Zachary Sherman Cons. Engrs., Santa Monica, Calif., 1973—; aerospace engr. FAA, NYC, 1980-86. Designated cons. engr. rep. FAA, 1986—. Contr.: articles to profl. jours. including Jour. of Aircraft AIAA. NSF grantee, 1972. Fellow: ASCE; mem.: AIAA (v.p. Western Conn. chpt. 1977—78), N.Y. Acad. Scis., Sigma Xi. Achievements include development of beam/beam-column deck suspension bridge; solutions to pothole problems; prestressed aircraft wing. Home and Office: 2021 California Ave Apt 7 Santa Monica CA 90403-4531 Office Phone: 310-264-5990. Fax: 310-264-5990. Personal E-mail: aerozach@earthlink.net.

SHERN, DAVID LEN, mental health services professional, former dean; b. Pueblo, Colo., Feb. 23, 1951; s. Lennox Lyle and Louise Marie Shern; m. Karen Sue Westerman, Nov. 5, 1977 (div.). BA in Psychology, U. Colo., 1973, MA in Social Psychology, 1977, PhD in Social Psychology, 1980; cert. in advanced epidemiologic methods, NIMH Staff Coll., 1980. Asst. dir. research and evaluation sect. Denver Dept. Health and Hosps. Mental Health Programs, 1981-82; research assoc. evaluation services sect. Colo. div. Mental Health, Denver, 1982-84, mgr. sponsored research program, 1984-88; project dir., investigator estimating residential services for chronically mentally ill Colo. divsn. Mental Health, Denver, 1983-87; investigator validation models for estimating mental health need U. Denver, 1983-88; dir. bur. evaluation and svcs. rsch. N.Y. Office of Mental Health, Albany, 1988-95; dean, prof. Louis de la Parte Fla. Mental Health Inst., U. South Fla., Tampa, 1995—2006; pres., CEO Mental Health Am., Alexandria, Va., 2006—. Cons. several health facilities, Denver, 1976—88; chmn. Fla. Commn. Mental Health and Substance Abuse, 1999—2000; prin. investigator Treatment Outcome Study, 1988; prin. investigator rsch. grants NIMH Substance Abuse and Mental Health Svcs. Adminstrn., 1988—2000; dir. NIMH Ctr. for Sudy Issues in Pub. Mental Health, 1993—95; mem. Govs. Suicide Prevention Task Force, 2003—06. Contbr. articles to profl. jours. Bd. dirs. Travelers Aid of Denver, 1981-83, Karis Cmty., 1986-88, pres. 1988; founding mem. Albany County Land Conservancy, 1992-95, pres., 1992-95; treas. USF Charter Sch., 1998-2006;active Crisis Ctr. of Tampa Bay, 2004-06. Mem. APA, APHA (chair mental health sect. 1992-93, governing coun. 1995-97), Orgn. for Program Evaluation in Colo. (pres. 1982-83, assoc. editor bull.), Am. Evaluation Assn., Sigma Xi. Independent. Avocations: hiking, gardening, travel. Office: Mental Health Am 2000 N Beauregard St 6th Fl Alexandria VA 22311

SHERN, STEPHANIE MARIE, investment company executive, accountant; b. Taylor, Pa., Jan. 7, 1948; d. Joseph and Stephanie (Malodovitch) Andrews; m. George Emil Shern, Sept. 25, 1971. AA, Keystone Jr. Coll., 1967; BS, Pa. State U., 1969. CPA, NY. Staff acct. to ptnr., nat. dir. consumer products industry Ernst & Young, NYC, 1969—2001, ptnr., vice chmn., global and US dir. R&CP markets. Bd. mem. Gamestop Corp., 2003-, Embarq Corp, 2006-. Contbr. articles to profl. jours. Named Keystonian of Yr., Keystone Jr. Coll., 1984. Mem. AICPA, NY State Soc. CPAs (bd. dirs. 1985-87), Beta Alpha Psi (mem. adv. forum 1984-86). Republican. Ukrainian Orthodox. Home: 11 Green Briar Rd Little Falls NJ 07424-2307 Office Phone: 973-785-3271. Personal E-mail: stephanieshern@aol.com.

SHERNOFF, DAVID JORDAN, psychology professor; b. Pomona, Calif., July 9, 1967; s. William Martin and JoAnn Shernoff; m. Elisa Steele, June 28, 1997; 1 child, Spencer Laurence. BS, Cornell U., 1989; EdM, Harvard Grad. Sch. Edn., 1991; PhD, U. Chgo., 2001. Asst. prof. No. Ill. U., DeKalb, 2003—. Domestic and internat. rsch. cons.; reviewer jour. articles and conf. papers; presenter in field. Author: (book) The Individual-Maker; contbr. jour. articles and chapters to books. Recipient Susan Colver-Rosenberger Meritorious Achievement award, U. Chgo., Dept. Edn., 1997—98, Role Motivation Dem. Life award, John G. Nichols Trust, Motivation Edn. Spl. Interest Group, Am. Ednl. Rsch. Assn., 2000—01; fellow, U. Wis., Madison, 2001—03. Mem.: Soc. Rsch. Child Devel., Soc. Rsch. Adolescence, Am. Ednl. Rsch. Assn. Liberal. Jewish. Avocations: water-skiing, racquetball, bicycling. Home: 315 Bridgeview Cir Geneva IL 60134 Office: No Ill U LEPF Graham Hall Coll Edn Dekalb IL 60115-2854 Home Phone: 630-845-0634; Office Phone: 815-753-8435. Business E-Mail: dshernoff@niu.edu.

SHERO, RAY (REJEAN SHERO), professional sports team executive; b. St. Paul, Minn., July 28, 1962; s. Fred and Mariette Shero; m. Karen Shero; children: Christopher, Kyle. Grad., St. Lawrence U., 1984. Player agent NHL; sr. ptnr. Sports Consulting Group, 1986—93; asst. gen. mgr. Ottawa Senators, 1993—98, Nashville Predators, 1998—2006; gen. mgr. Pitts. Penguins, 2006—. Office: Pitts Penguins Mellon Arena 66 Mario Lemieux Dr Pittsburgh PA 15219

SHERPA, DONNA M., history educator; m. Phurba Gelzen, Apr. 20, 1989 (div.). B, Shippensburg U., Pa., 1968, M, 1997. Tchr. Town and Country Day Sch., Harrisburg, Pa., 1969, Harrisburg City Sch. Dist., 1969—70; chmn. history dept. Dauphin County Tech. Sch., Harrisburg, 1970—80; tchr. Tyrone Sch. Dist., Pa., 1981—86; owner Hobby Shop, Pa., 1986—89; with Sci. Mus., Pa., 1990—91; substitute tchr. Harrisburg, Pa., 1991—93; with Bur. Workers Compensation, Harrisburg, 1993—97; chmn. history dept. James F. Byrnes Acad., Florence, SC, 1997—99; tchr. Sanford Sch., Hockessin, Del., 1999—. Author: Living in the Middle: Sherpas of the Mid-Range Himalayas, 1994. Mem.: Nat. Coun. Social Studies. Avocations: reading, cross stitch, gardening, walking.

SHERPA, FRAN MAGRUDER, geography educator; b. Midland, Tex., Aug. 20, 1952; d. Edwin Howard Magruder and Barbara June Cowden; m. Ang Kazi Sherpa; children: Sarah, Susie, Sonia, Tsowang. BS in Geography, Tex. State U., San Marcos, 1995, M in Applied Geography, 1998. Registered massage therapist. Owner, operator Himalayan Excursions, Kathmandu, Nepal, 1983—85; investor, mgr. office Nepal Internat. Clinic, Kathmandu, Nepal, 1989—91; instr. geography U. Tex. Permian Basin, Odessa, Tex., 2000—. Mem.: Tex. Photographic Soc., Am. Assn. Geographers. Avocations: photography, travel. Home: 2201 Neely Midland TX 79705 Personal E-mail: fransherpa@hotmail.com.

SHERR, BRIAN J., lawyer; b. Apr. 19, 1944; BA, Rutgers U., NJ, 1967; JD, Boston U., 1970. Bar: Fla., US Supreme Ct. With Greenberg Traurig, Ft. Lauderdale, Fla., 1991—95, shareholder, 1995—. Founder, chmn. First So. Bank, Boca Raton, Fla., 1987—, bd. dirs.; lectr. in field. Contbr. articles to profl. jours. Bd. govs. Mus. Art, Ft. Lauderdale; mem. adv. bd. Aish Hatorah Jerusalem; past mem. adv. com. U.U. Miami Law Ctr. Inst. Condo. and Cluster Devel.; past pres. Jewish Fedn. Greater Ft. Lauderdale, Fla.; bd. dirs. Daniel D. Cantor Sr. Ctr.; former bd. dirs. Fla. Atlantic U. Found.; past bd. dirs. Broward Ctr. Performing Arts; bd. dirs. Nat. Ben Gamla Charter Sch. Found. Inc., Hallandale, Fla. Named one of South Florida's Heavy Hitters in Real Estate, Bus. Jour., 2004; recipient Tree of Life award, Jewish Nat. Fund., 2006; Brian J. Sherr Appreciation Day proclaimed, Broward County Commn., 2006. Mem.: Broward County Bar Assn., Fla. Bar Assn. (co-chmn. condo. and planned devel. com., mem. exec. coun. real property, probate and trust law sect.). Office: 401 E Los Olas Blvd Ste 2000 Fort Lauderdale FL 33301 Office Phone: 954-768-8247. Business E-Mail: sherrb@gtlaw.com.

SHERR, CHARLES J., immunologist, researcher; m. Martine Roussel; 3 children. BS in Biology and Chemistry, Oberlin Coll., 1966; MD, PhD in Immunology, NYU, 1972. Pathology resident Bellevue Hosp. Ctr., NYC; postdoctoral tng., leader rsch. group Nat. Cancer Inst., 1973, senior staff fellow, 1975, chief viral pathology section, 1977; mem. dept. genetics and tumor cell biology St. Jude Children's Rsch. Hosp., 1983—. Investigator Howard Hughes Med. Inst., Chevy Chase, Md.; adj. prof. molecular scis. U. Tenn. Coll. Medicine, Memphis. Recipient Pezcoller Found. Internat.l award for Cancer Rsch., Am. Assn. Cancer Rsch., 2000, Kirk A. Landon prize for Basic Cancer Rsch., 2003, Charles S. Mott prize, GM Cancer Rsch. Found., 2004. Mem.: NAS, Inst. Medicine. Office: St Jude Children Rsch Hosp 332 N Lauderdale Memphis TN 38105-2794

SHERR, ELLIOTT HAROLD, neurologist, researcher; s. Walter R. and Karen Sherr; m. Linda M. Rubinstein, July 2, 1989; children: Rachel J., David A., Jessica J. BAS in Biology and Philosophy, Stanford U., Calif., 1984; MD, PhD, Columbia U., NYC, 1995. Diplomate Am. Bd. of Psychiatry and Neurology. Vis. scientist La Catolica U., Santiago, Chile, 1995—96; resident in pediats. U. Calif., San Francisco, 1996—2000, instr. neurology and pediats., 2000—02, asst. prof., 2002—. Mem. exec. com. Nat. Orgn. Dosirders of Corpus Callosum, Calif., 2003—06. Recipient Sci. Award, Child Neurology Found., 2004—06, Philip Dodge Young Investigator award, Child Neurology Soc., 2006. Mem.: Am. Acad. Neurology. Independent. Avocations: travel, cooking, cycling. Office: U Calif San Francisco Dept Neurology 350 Parnassus Ave San Francisco CA 94143-0137 Office Phone: 415-353-2525.

SHERR, RICHARD, retail executive; Buyer TJX Cos., Inc., Framingham, Mass., 1992, sr. v.p. merchandising Marmaxx Group, 2001—04, exec. v.p. merchandising Marmaxx Group, 2004—05, exec. v.p., chief merchandising officer Marmaxx Group, 2005—07, sr. exec. v.p., COO Marmaxx Group, 2007—. Office: TJX Cos Inc 770 Cochituate Rd Framingham MA 01701 Office Phone: 508-390-1000. Office Fax: 508-390-2091. *

SHERRATT, HOLLY, art appraiser; BA in Art History, UCLA; MA in Visual Studies, U. Calif., Irvine. Trainee Laguna Art Mus., Laguna Beach, Calif.; intern Nat. Mus. Am. Art., Smithsonian Inst., Washington; curatorial staff Huntington Beach Fine Art Ctr., Calif.; modern, contemporary and Latin Am. art specialist Bonhams & Butterfields, San Francisco, 2000—, and cataloguer, prints and photographs dept. Exec. bd. San Francisco Mus. Modern Art contemporary ext. Lectr. in field. Mem.: Phi Beta Kappa. Office: Bonhams & Butterfields 220 San Bruno Ave San Francisco CA 94103 Office Phone: 415-503-3311. Office Fax: 415-503-3274. Business E-Mail: holly.sherratt@bonhams.com.

SHERRELL, JOHN BRADFORD, lawyer; b. Indpls., Jan. 27, 1951; s. Carl and Mary Jean (Bell) S.; m. Sherry Naomi Calhoun, Apr. 28, 1974; children: David Alan, Corinne Elizabeth. BA, Yale U., 1973; JD, U. Mich., 1977. Bar: Calif. 1977. Ptnr. Latham & Watkins, Los Angeles, 1977—. Dep. gen. counsel to Ind. Commn. on L.A. Police Dept. Named an Am.'s Top Black Lawyers, Black Enterprise Mag., 2003. Mem. ABA, Calif. Bar Assn. (co-chair real estate fin. subsect. of real property sec. 1990-92), L.A. County Bar Assn. (barrister's exec. com. 1978-80, bd. trustees 1991-93). Office: Latham & Watkins 633 W 5th St Ste 4000 Los Angeles CA 90071-2005 Office Phone: 213-891-8174. E-mail: john.sherrell@lw.com.

SHERRELL-LEO, CINDY, retired museum administrator; Acting dir. and bus. mgr. Laguna Gloria Art Mus.; dir. Mus. Services Dept. Tex. Hist. Commn.; spl. projects dir. Southwest Mus. Services. Bd. mem. Galveston Hist. Found.; chair Dickens on the Strand Festival. Mem.: Am. Assn. Museums (coun. mem., named to Centennial Honor Roll 2006). *

SHERREN, ANNE TERRY, chemistry professor; b. Atlanta, July 1, 1936; d. Edward Allison and Annie Ayres (Lewis) Terry; m. William Samuel Sherren, Aug. 13, 1966. BA, Agnes Scott Coll., 1957; PhD, U. Fla., Gainesville, 1961. Grad. tchg. asst. U. Fla., Gainesville, 1957-61; from instr. to asst. prof. Tex. Womans U., Denton, 1961-66; rsch. participant Argonne Nat. Lab., 1973-80, 93-94; assoc. prof. chemistry North Cen. Coll., Naperville, Ill., 1966-76, prof., 1976-2001, prof. emeritus, 2001—. Contbr. articles to profl. jours. Ruling elder Knox Presbyn. Ch., 1971—, clk. of session, 1976-94. Mem. Am. Chem. Soc., Am. Inst. Chemists, Sigma Xi, Delta Kappa Gamma (chpt. pres. 2002-2004), Iota Sigma Pi (nat. pres. 1978-81, nat. dir. 1972-78, nat. historian 1989—). Presbyterian. Office: North Ctrl Coll Dept Chemistry Naperville IL 60566 Business E-Mail: atsherren@noctrl.edu.

SHERRER, CHARLES DAVID, dean, clergyman; b. Marion, Ohio, Sept. 21, 1935; s. Harold D. and Catherine E. (Fye) S. AB, U. Notre Dame, 1958, MA, 1965; S.T.L., Gregorian U., 1962; PhD, U. N.C., 1969; HHD, King's Coll., 1997. Ordained priest Roman Cath. Ch., 1961. Instr. English U. Portland, Oreg., 1963-64, asst. prof. Oreg., 1969-74, prof. Oreg., 1990—2005, prof. emeritus Oreg., 2005—, chmn. dept. Oreg., 1970-74, dean Grad. Sch. Oreg., 1982-87, mem. Bd. Regents Oreg., 1986-87, acad. v.p. Oreg., 1987-96; pres. King's Coll., Wilkes Barre, Pa., 1974-81. Bd. trustees Stonehill Coll., 1992-98; dir. studies Holy Cross Fathers, Ind. Province, 1979-88. Office Phone: 503-943-7596. Business E-Mail: sherrer@up.edu.

SHERRICK, DANIEL NOAH, real estate broker; b. Greenup, Ill., Mar. 28, 1929; s. Conrad Donovan and Helen Lorene (Neeley) S.; m. Dora Ann Moore, Aug. 11, 1957; children: Renata Ann Sherrick McBride, Sherrie Dee Sherrick Sierra BS in Edn., Ea. Ill. U., Charleston, 1956. Owner Midwest Ins. Agy., Greenup, 1956—60; supt. agys. Midwest Life Ins. Co., Lincoln, Nebr., 1960—62; asst. v.p. Gulf Life Ins. Co., Jacksonville, Fla., 1962—71; pres. Bank of Carbondale, Ill., 1971—74, Prescription Learning Corp., Springfield, Ill., 1974—76; exec. v.p. Imperial Industries, Inc., Miami Lakes, Fla., 1976—88, pres., CEO, 1988—90; broker, salesman Coldwell Banker Residential Real Estate, 1990—91, 1993—; pres., bd. dirs. Palmer State Bank, Taylorville, Ill., 1991—93; broker-salesman Coldwell Banker Highlands Properties, 1993—. Pres. Alderman Park Civic Assn., Jacksonville, Ill., 1968, Heritage Hills Home Owners Assn., Carbondale, 1973. With USAF, 1948—52. Mem.: VFW, Greater Sebring C. of C., Am. Legion, Elks, Masons. Presbyterian. Home: 6228 Aquavista Dr Sebring FL 33876 Office: Coldwell Banker Highlands Properties 2521 US Hwy 27 S Sebring FL 33870-2127 Office Phone: 863-382-3157. Personal E-mail: dandora@strato.net.

SHERRICK, DANIEL WILLIAM, lawyer; b. Rochester, Minn., Jan. 24, 1958; s. Donald William and Jean Karol (Loudon) S.; m. Ellen Moss, Mar. 6, 1989. BA, Yale U., 1980; JD, U. Mich., 1984. Bar: Mich. 1984, US Ct. Appeals (6th cir.) 1985, US Ct. Appeals (11th cir.) 1985, US Supreme Ct. 1991. Assoc. gen. counsel Internat. Union UAW, Detroit, 1984—98, gen. counsel, 1998—. Office: UAW Legal Dept 8000 E Jefferson Ave Detroit MI 48214-3963 Office Phone: 313-926-5216. *

SHERRILL, GREGG M., automotive executive; BSME, Tex. A&M; MBA, Ind. U. Plant mgr. Ford Motor Com., Dearborn, Mich., dir., supplier tech. assistance; with Johnson Controls, Inc., 1998—2007, v.p., gen. mgr., North Am. automotive ops., 2000—01, grp. v.p., mng. dir., Europe, South Africa, South Am., automotive systems grp., 2001—03, grp. v.p., mng. dir., Japan and Asia Pacific, grp. v.p., gen. mgr., battery ops., automotive systems grp., 2003—07, v.p., pres., power solutions; chmn., CEO Tenneco Inc., Lake Forest, Ill., 2007—. Office: Tenneco Inc 500 N Field Drive Lake Forest IL 60045 Office Phone: 847-482-5000. Office Fax: 847-482-5940. *

SHERRILL, MILTON LEWIS, sculptor, painter; b. NYC, May 30, 1949; s. Ruth M. Sherrill. Student, Cooper Union, 1971; BA, SUNY, Old Westbury, 1974; MFA, Pratt Inst., 1976. Fine artist M.L. Sherrill Creative Concepts, Ltd., Mt. Vernon, NY, 1976—. Works commissioned by, Lcor Inc., NYC, Westchester County, NY, City of Mt. Vernon; contbr. art to newspapers, mags., jours; designer Florence Griffith Joyner Sports Award, Harriet Tubman The Freedom Condr. sculpture. Grantee, Westchester Arts Coun., Adolph & Ester Gottlieb Found.; Westchester Arts Alive grantee, 2000, 2001, 2002. Mem.: NY Artist Equity Assn., Nat. Sculpture Gallery, Internat. Sculpture Ctr. Avocation: antiques. Office: ML Sherrill Creative Concepts Ltd PO Box 2421 Mount Vernon NY 10551-2421 Office Phone: 800-650-6394. E-mail: mlsherrill30@yahoo.com.

SHERRILL, THOMAS BOYKIN, III, retired newspaper publishing executive; b. Tampa, Fla., Nov. 19, 1930; s. Thomas Boykin Jr. and Mary Emma (Addison) S.; m. Sandra Louise Evans, Dec. 27, 1969; children: Thomas Glenn, Stephen Addison. Circulation dir. Tampa (Fla.) Tribune, 1962—67, Sarasota (Fla.) Herald-Tribune, 1967—75; v.p. circulation The Dispatch Printing Co., Columbus, Ohio, 1975—78, v.p. mktg., 1978—97, bd. dirs., 1977—97; v.p., bd. dirs. Ohio Mag., Inc., Columbus, 1979—97; ret., 1997. Bd. dirs., past chmn. bd. dirs. Salvation Army; trustee, past chmn. bd. dirs. Better Bus. Bur. Ctrl. Ohio, Inc.; bd. dirs. Ctrl. Ohio Ctr. Econ. Edn.; v.p., trustee Columbus Dispatch Charities; past pres. Wesley Glen United Meth. Retirement Ctr.; pres.'s adv. bd. Meth. Theol. Sch. With USN, 1951-56. Recipient Disting. Svc. award Editor and Pub. Mag., 1978; named hon. pres. Troy State U., 1979, hon. Ky. Col., 1980, hon. lt. col. aide-to-camp to Gov. State of Ala., 1984. Mem. Internat. Newspaper Mktg. Assn., Ohio Newspaper Assn. (bd. dirs. 1984-97, pres. 1986-88, Pres.'s award 1990), So. Circulation Mgrs. Assn. (life; pres. 1967-68, sec. and treas., 1968-75, C.W. Bevinger Meml. award 1972), Audit Bur. Circulations (bd. dirs. 1980-90), Am. Advt. Fedn., Navy League, Ohio Newspapers Found., Ohio Circulation Mgrs. Assn (life; Pres.' award 1989), Columbus Area C. of C., SAR, Internat. Platform Assn., Athletic Club of Columbus, Muirfield Village Country Club, Kiwanis Club of Columbus (life, pres. 1982, George F. Hixon fellow). Republican. Home: 5215 Hampton Ln Columbus OH 43220-2270

SHERRIS, DAVID ALLAN, surgeon, researcher, educator; b. Buffalo, Feb. 1, 1961; s. Donald Allan Sherris and Doris Mary Jones; m. Lisa Ellen Dubiel, Apr. 11, 1993; children: David Jr., Matthew, Lara. BA, Middlebury Coll., 1984; MD, U. Rochester, 1988. Diplomate Am. Bd. Otolaryngology, Am. Bd. Facial Plastic and Reconstructive Surgery. Resident otolaryngology U. Rochester, NY, 1989—93; fellow facial plastic surgery, clin. instr. U. Wash., Seattle, 1993—94; asst. prof. otolaryngology Mayo Med. Sch., Rochester, Minn., 1994—2000, assoc. prof., 2000—03; cons. surgeon Mayo Clinic, Rochester, 1994—2003, chair facial plastic surgery, 2002—03; chair otolaryngology SUNY, Buffalo, 2003—; chief of svc. otolaryngology Kaleida Health, 2003—; prof. otolaryngology U. Buffalo, 2005—. Author: Basic Surgical Skills, 1999, Essential Surgical Skills, 2004; author, editor: The Principles of Facial Reconstruction, 1995, reviewer: Archives of Facial Plastic Surgery, 2000—, mem. editl. bd.: Rhinology Jour., 2002—; contbr. 70 articles to profl. jours. Fellow: Am. Rhinologic Soc., Am. Acad. Otolaryngology Head and Neck Surgery (home study course faculty 2001—), Am. Acad. Facial Plastic and Reconstructive Surgery (active surgeon Face to Face Domestic Violence Program 1994—, Sir Harold Delf Gilles award 1994); mem.: Am. Bd. Otolaryngology (examiner 1999—). Avocations: running, skiing. Office Phone: 716-884-5104. E-mail: dsherris@buffalo.edu.

SHERROD, DANNY TROY, writer, educator; b. North Richland Hills, Tex., Apr. 27, 1963; s. Yvonne Boatman and Dan Sherrod. AA and Sci., El Centro Coll., 1983—86; B of Humanities, So. Meth. U., 1997—2002. Caseworker Tex. Dept. of Human Services, Dallas, 1991—95; libr. specialist So. Meth. U., 1996—2003; tchr. writing, history L.P. Cowart Sch., 2003—06; tchr. L.V. Stockard Middle Sch., 2006—. Author: (short story) Div. When it Rains - pub. in Primavera; editor: (newsletter) Theatre Hist. Soc. of Am.; contbr. jour. Legacies. Mem.: NEA, Am. Fedn. Tchrs., Nat. Coun. Tchrs. of English, US Humane Soc., Tex. SPCA, People for the Ethical Treatment of Animals, Golden Key Nat. Honor Soc. (life). Democrat. Home: 1119 Newport Ave Dallas TX 75224-1248 Personal E-mail: troy39@swbell.net.

SHERROD, LLOYD BRUCE, retired nutritionist; b. Goodland, Kans., Mar. 5, 1931; s. Charles and Helen S.; m. Judith Harms Sherrod, Dec. 21, 1963; children: Donna J., Barbara E. BS, S.D. State U., Brookings, 1958; MS, U. Ark., Fayetteville, 1960; PhD, Okla. State U., Stillwater, 1964. Rsch. assoc. Okla. State U., Stillwater, 1963; asst. prof. U. Hawaii, Hilo, 1964-67; from assoc. prof to prof. Tex. Tech. U. Ctr., Pantex, 1967-79; nutrition-chemistry instr. Frank Phillips Coll., Borger, Tex., 1979-88; part-time nutrition instr. Amarillo (Tex.) Coll., 1989-95; ret., 1995. Rschr. in field. Contbr. articles to sci. jours. Served with U.S. Army, 1951-53. Mem. AAAS, Am. Soc. Animal Science, Am. Dairy Science Assn., Am. Soc. Agronomy, Am. Inst. Biol. Scis., Tex. Jr. Coll. Tchrs. Assn., Am. Men and Women of Sci., Plains Nutrition Coun., Sigma Xi., Phi Kappa Phi, Gamma Sigma Delta. Home and Office: PO Box 1017 Panhandle TX 79068-1017

SHERROD, PHILIP LAWRENCE, artist, composer, painter, poet; b. Pauls Valley, Okla., Oct. 12, 1935; s. Jesse Lawrence and Edrie Mae (Shumate) S.; m. Peggy Anne Elledge, Jan. 19, 1959 (div. 1959); m. Helena Alicia Decastro, Nov. 18, 1961 (div.); 1 child, Sandro Arentino Mateos. BS, Okla. State U., 1957, BA, 1959; postgrad., Art Students League, NYC, 1961-63, Jacques Seligman Coll., 1968, Carroll Reese Mus., 1968. Tchr. Morristown Art Assn., NJ, 1973-74, NJ Ctr. for Visual Arts, 1977—2003, Art Students League, NYC, 1984—2007, Nat. Acad. Design Sch. of Fine Arts, 1994, 1996, 1998, 2005; master tchr. Bd. Cmty. Ctr., South Orange, NJ, 2004—07. Founding mem. Street Painters, NYC, 1977—. One-man shows include Leonard Hutton Hutschnecker Galleries, 1966, Gallery 9, Chatham, NJ, 1967, Jacques Seligmann Gallery, 1968, Selected Artists Gallery, 1968, East Rockaway Art Exhibition, 1969, Allan Strong Gallery, 1969, 1971, 1973, 1975, 1981, 1996-1997, Sonraed Gallery, 1971, Artemis East Gallery, 1972, Pace U., NYC, 1972, The Humanist Ctr., 1973, 74, Grace Gallery, 1973, Allan Stone Gallery, 1973, 75, 76, 83, 96-97, Tower Art Gallery, Highland Falls, NY, 1975, Gallery 100, Princeton, NJ, 1975, Monique Knowlton Gallery, 1976, Cone Gallery, 1976, Bridgeport U., Conn., 1976 Bayonne Jewish Cmty. Ctr., NJ, 1977, 47 Bond St. Gallery, NYC, 1979, Art Awareness Gallery, Lexington, NY, 1980, Artists Choice Mus., NYC, 1983; exhibited in group shows at Allan Frumkin Gallery,

1973, 75, Boston U. Gallery, 1979, SUNY, 1979, Cork Gallery, Lincoln Ctr., NYC, 1984-2000, Nat. Acad. of Design, NYC, 1966, 75, 76, 78, 82, 88-90, 93-95, 97-99, 2001—, NJ Ctr. for the Arts, 1977-2003, Mus. and Sculpture Garden, Smithsonian Inst., Washington, 1989, New England Fine Arts Inst., Boston, 1993, Rita Dean Gallery, Dan Diego, 1993, Gallerie des Hamptons, Westhampton Beach, 1994, Fordham U., 1996; represented in permanent collections Tulane U. Mus., New Orleans, Mus. of Fine Art, Springfield, Mass., Everhart Mus., Scranton, Pa., Rose Art Mus., Brandeis U., Waltham, Mass., Almsford House, Fine Arts Ctr., Anderson, Ind., Mus. City NY, Hirshorn Mus. & Sculpture Garden, Smithsonian Inst. Mus.& Sculpture Garden, The Phillips Exeter Acad., NH, Worcester Fine Arts Mus., Herbert Johnson Mus., Ithica, NY, RI Sch. Design/Newark Mus., NJ, Nat. Acad. Mus., NYC, Am. Broadcasting Corp., Paramount Pictures Prodns., INA Corp., Montgomery Securities, San Francisco, Boston, NYC, Allan Stone, Steven Paine, Richard Brown Baker, Tom and Mary Paxton, Bill Paxton, others; author: (poems) 30 Mental-Talia, 1980, Black Truck, 1981, Mr. Wigley Cums, 1983, Images Below the Belt, 1984, Sex (I) Con, 1985. Grantee Creative Artists Pub. Svc., 1980, Adolphe/Esther Gottlieb Found., 1981, 88, 96, 06, NEA, 1982, Am. Acad. in Rome, 1985-86, The Pollack-Krasner Found., Inc., 1989; recipient Purchase award Am. Acad. Arts and Letters, 1967, 69, 74, Childe Hassam Purchase award Prixe de Roma, 1985-86. Fellow Am. Acad. in Rome. Home: 41 W 24th St New York NY 10010-3210 Office Phone: 212-989-3174. Personal E-mail: bigdaddiehots@gmail.com.

SHERRY, GEORGE LEON, political science professor; b. Lodz, Poland, Jan. 5, 1924; came to US, 1939, naturalized 1945; s. Leon G. and Henrietta (Mess) S.; m. Doris H. Harf, Mar. 6, 1947; 1 child, Vivien Gail Sherry Greenberg. BA summa cum laude, CCNY, 1944; MA, Columbia U., 1951, MA, cert. Russian Inst., 1955, PhM, 1959; DHL (hon.), Occidental Coll., LA, 2005. Reporter, radio news writer The NY Times, NYC, 1944-46; editor, interpreter, then sr. interpreter UN, NYC, 1946-59, from polit. officer to dir. and dep. to under sec.-gen. for spl. polit. affairs, 1959-84; polit. advisor to missions Congo, Cyprus, India and Pakistan, 1962-66; asst. sec.-gen. for spl. polit. affairs UN (office in charge peacekeeping forces which won Nobel Peace Prize, 1988), NYC, 1984-85; Stuart Chevalier prof. diplomacy and world affairs Occidental Coll., LA, 1985—2004. Dir. Occidental at-the-UN program, NYC, 1986-2002; US del. staff Dartmouth Soviet-Am. confs., 1961-94; assoc. seminar on problem of peace Columbia U., NYC; cons. UN dept. peacekeeping ops., 1992, 93; UN envoy to follow Russian elections, 1993; cons. Internat. Peace Acad., 1993-97. Author: The United Nations Reborn: Conflict Control in the Post-Cold War World, 1990; editorial adv. bd. Polit. Sci. Quar., NYC, 1973-89; contbr. articles and revs. to profl. jours. Recipient Townsend Harris medal CCNY, 1993; UN Inst. for Tng. and Rsch. sr. fellow, 1985-93. Mem. Coun. on Fgn. Rels., UN Assn.-USA. Democrat. Avocations: piano playing, skiing, sailing.

SHERRY, JOHN SEBASTIAN, lawyer; b. Homestead, Pa., Apr. 18, 1946; s. Sebastian John and Margaret Josephine (Coyne) Sherry; m. Joan Carol Paulsen, Aug. 9, 1969; children: Brendan P., Michael S., Conor J. BA, U. Dayton, 1968; JD, Duquesne U., 1971. Bar: Pa. 1971, U.S. Dist. Ct. (we. dist.) Pa. 1971, U.S. Supreme Ct. 1975, U.S. Ct. Appeals (3d cir.) 1976, U.S. Claims Ct. 1977, U.S. Ct. Internat. Trade 1977, U.S. Tax Ct. 1977, U.S. Ct. Mil. Appeals 1977. Pvt. practice, Pitts., 1971—; mng. atty. Travlers Ins. Co., Pitts., 1972-78; mng. trial atty. CNA Ins. Cos., Pitts., 1978-88, sr. mgr. staff counsel, 1988-94, mng. trial atty., 1994-96, asst. v.p. claims litigation, 1996-98; pvt. practice John S. Sherry & Assocs., Pitts., 1999—; prin. Sherry Dispute Resolution Svcs., Pitts., 2001—. Lectr. Trial Advocacy Found., Pitts., 1984, Nat. Inst. Trial Advocacy, 1997, 98. Assoc. opinion editor: Pitts. Legal Jour., 1977—78; editor: YLS newsletter, 1980. Chmn. bd. auditors, South Park, Pa., 1977—85. Fellow: Acad. Trial Lawyers Allegheny County (bd. govs. 1997—98); mem.: ABA, Washington County Bar Assn., Western Pa. Trial Lawyers Assn., Pa. Bar Assn. (jud. adminstrn. com. 1992—, ADR com. 2001—), Pa. Trial Lawyers Assn., Allegheny County Bar Assn. (CLE com. 1978—, coun. civil litigation sect. 1985—87, treas. 1988—2001, vice chmn. 1989, chmn. civil litigation sect. 1990, civil procedure rules com. 1999—, ADR com. 2001—), South Park C. of C. (past pres.), Pine Lake Trout Club, Rivers Club, Lions. Democrat. Roman Catholic. Avocations: fishing, hunting, literature. Home and Office: 113 Stonegate Dr Mc Murray PA 15317-2766 Office Phone: 412-418-8935. Personal E-mail: jsherryesq@msn.com.

SHERRY, PAUL HENRY, minister, religious organization administrator; b. Tamaqua, Pa., Dec. 25, 1933; s. Paul Edward and Mary Elizabeth (Stein) Sherry; m. Mary Louise Thornburg, June 4, 1957; children: Mary Elizabeth, Paul David. BA, Franklin and Marshall Coll., 1955; ThM, Union Theol. Sem., NYC, 1958, PhD, 1969; D (hon.), Ursinus Coll., 1981, Elmhurst Coll., 1990, Defiance Coll., 1991, Lakeland Coll., Sheboygan, Wis., 1991, Reformed Theological Acad., Debrecen, Hungary, 1994, United Theol. Sem. Twin Cities, 1995, Eden Theol. Sem., St. Louis, 2000, Chgo. Theol. Sem., 2000. Ordained to ministry United Ch. Christ, 1958. Pastor St. Matthew United Ch. of Christ, Kenhorst, Pa., 1958—61, Community United Ch. of Christ, Hasbrouck Heights, NJ, 1961—65; mem. staff United Ch. Bd. Homeland Ministry, NYC, 1965—82; exec. dir. Community Renewal Soc., Chgo., 1983—89; pres. United Ch. of Christ, Cleve., 1989—99, pub. policy cons., 2000—02. Mem. gen. bd. Nat. Coun. Chs., NYC, 1989—99, coord. anti-poverty program; cons. Ctr. for Cmty. Change, 2001—; mem. ctrl. com. World Coun. Chs., 1990—99; del. 8th Assembly, Harare, Zimbabwe, 1998, 7th Assembly, Canberra, Australia, 1991. Co-author: A Just Minimum Wage; editor: The Riverside Preachers, Jour. Current Social Issues, 1968—80; contbr. articles to religious jours.; host (weekly programs local sta.), 1974—78, 1984—85, 1993—97. Bd. dirs. Nat. Interfaith Com. Worker Justice, 2000—; coord. anti-poverty program Nat. Coun. Chs., 2002—. Democrat. Mem. United Ch. Of Christ. Avocations: reading, hiking, cultural events. Home: 12700 Lake Ave # 1612 Lakewood OH 44107 Office: United Ch of Christ 700 Prospect Ave Cleveland OH 44115 Office Phone: 216-221-9722. Personal E-mail: psher973@aol.com.

SHERTZER, BRUCE ELDON, education educator; b. Bloomfield, Ind., Jan. 11, 1928; s. Edwin Franklin and Lois Belle S.; m. Carol Mae Rice, Nov. 24, 1948; children: Sarah Ann, Mark Eldon. BS, Ind. U., 1952, MS, 1953, EdD, 1958. Tchr., counselor Martinsville H.S., Ind., 1952-56; dir. div. guidance Ind. Dept. Pub. Instrn., 1956-58; assoc. dir. project guidance of superior students North Ctrl. Assn. Coll. and Secondary Sch., 1958-60; asst. prof. Purdue U., 1960—, assoc. prof., 1962-65, prof., 1965-95, head dept. ednl. studies, 1989-95, prof. emeritus of counseling, 1995—. Vis. prof. ednl. psychology U. Hawaii, 1967; Fulbright sr. lectr., Reading, Eng., 1967-68; vis. prof. U. So. Calif. Overseas Grad. Program, 1975, 82; chmn. Nat. Adv. Council for Career Edn., 1976 Author: Career Exploration and Planning 1973, 2d edit., 1976, Fundamentals of Counseling, 3d edit., 1980, Fundamentals of Guidance, 4th edit., 1981, Individual Appraisal, 1979, Career Planning, 3d edit., 1985, also articles. Chmn. bd. trustees Found. Am. Assn. of Counseling and Devel., 1986-87. With AUS, 1946-47. Mem. Am. Counseling Assn. (pres. 1973-74, Disting. Profl. Svc. award 1986). Home: 1620 Western Dr West Lafayette IN 47906-2236 Office: Beering Hall Purdue University West Lafayette IN 47907

SHERVA, DENNIS G., retired investment company executive; b. Mpls., Dec. 3, 1942; s. Garfield Theodore and Dorothy Genevive (Oberlander) S.; m. Cathleen Marybeth Tischer, Oct. 15, 1965 (dec. July 31, 2004). BA, U. Minn., 1964; MA, Wayne State U., 1965. Chartered fin. analyst. Fin. analyst 1st Nat. Bank, Mpls., 1965-67; fin. analyst Honeywell, Inc., Mpls., 1967; v.p. Smith, Barney & Co., NYC, 1967-71, Baker, Weeks & Co., NYC, 1971-77; mng. dir. Morgan Stanley & Co., Inc., NYC, 1977—2000. Bd. dirs. Morgan Stanley Ventures, San Francisco, Morgan Stanley Venture Capital, N.Y.C., Morgan Stanley Asset Mgmt. Inc., N.Y.C. Recipient All-Am. Research Team 1st place award Instl. Investor Mag., 1979, 81, 83, 84, 85, 87 Mem.: Nat. Assn. Securities Dealers (instl. com. 1985—90), PGA West Club, Torrington Country Club. Home: 42 Old South Rd PO Box 30 Litchfield CT 06759-0030 Home (Winter): 80715 Weiskopf Way La Quinta CA 92253

SHERWIN, JAMES TERRY, lawyer; b. NYC, Oct. 25, 1933; s. Oscar and Stella (Zins) S.; m. Judith Johnson, June 21, 1955 (div. Apr. 1984); children: Miranda, Alison, Galen; m. Hiroko Inouye, June 15, 1985. BA, Columbia U., 1953, LLB (Stone scholar), 1956. Bar: N.Y. 1956, U.S. Supreme Ct. 1963. Assoc. Kaye, Scholer, Fierman, Hays & Handler, NYC, 1957-60; with GAF Corp., NYC, 1960-83, 84-90, assoc. counsel, gen. mgr. European ops., 1969-71, group v.p. photography, 1971-74, exec. v.p. fin. and adminstrn., legal and investment svcs., 1974-83, vice chmn., chief adminstrv. officer Wayne, NJ, 1984-90; exec. v.p., CFO Triangle Industries, Inc., 1983-84, Hunter-Douglas N.V., 1991—99, bd. dirs., 1999—. Bd. dirs. Internat. Rescue Com., chmn. exec. com., v.p. to 1990-; mem. coun. U. Bath, 2001-07. Lt. comdr. USCGR, 1956-57. U.S. intercollegiate chess champion, 1951-53, N.Y. State champion, 1951, U.S. speed champion, 1956-57, 59-60, internat. master., 2001. Am. Chess Found. (pres., bd. dirs. to 1990), Marshall (NY) Chess Club (pres. 1967-69, gov. to 1990), Phi Beta Kappa. Home: The Chase Winsley Nr Bradford-on-Avon Wiltshire BA15 2LX England Office Phone: 44 1225 722113. Business E-Mail: jamestsherwin@btconnect.com.

SHERWIN, MARTIN J., history professor; married. AB, Dartmouth Coll., 1959; PhD, UCLA, 1971. Walter S. Dickson prof. English and Am. History Tufts Univ. Founding dir. Nuclear Age History and Humanities Ctr., Tufts Univ. Author: A World Destroyed: Hiroshima and Its Legacies, 2003 (Stuart L. Bernath prize, Am. History Book prize); co-author (with Kai Bird): American Prometheus: The Triumph and Tragedy of J. Robert Oppenheimer, 2005 (Nat. Book Critics Cir. award for biography, 2005, Pulitzer Prize for biography, 2006); adv. (documentaries) The Day After Trinity, A History of Nuclear Strategy, War and Peace in the Nuclear Age, PBS, gen. editor Stanford Nuclear Age Series. Fellow: Am. Acad. Arts & Scis. Office: History Dept Tufts Univ Medford MA 02155 Office Phone: 617-627-5583. Business E-Mail: martin.sherwin@tufts.edu. *

SHERWOOD, ALLEN JOSEPH, retired lawyer; b. Salt Lake City, Sept. 26, 1909; s. Charles Samuel and Sarah (Abramson) Shapiro; m. Edith Ziff, Jan. 19, 1941; children: Mary (Mrs. John Marshall), Arthur Lawrence Student, UCLA, 1927-30; AB, LLB, U. So. Calif., 1933. Bar: Calif. 1933, U.S. Supreme Ct. 1944. Pvt. practice law, LA, 1933-54, Beverly Hills, 1954-95; ret. Legal counsel Internat. Family Planning Rsch. Assn., Inc., 1970-76; bd. dirs. Family Planning Ctrs. Greater L.A., Inc., 1968-84, pres., 1973-76 Mem. editorial bd. So. Calif. Law Rev., 1932-33. Contbr. articles to profl. jours. Mem. Calif. Atty. Gen.'s Vol. Adv. Coun. and its legis. subcom., 1972-78 Mem. Med.-Legal Soc. So. Calif. (bd. dirs. 1966-74), ABA, L.A. County Bar Assn., Beverly Hills Bar Assn., State Bar of Calif., Am. Arbitration Assn. (nat. panel arbitrators 1965—), Order of Coif, Tau Delta Phi, Brentwood Country Club (L.A.), Masons. Home: 575 Moreno Ave Los Angeles CA 90049-4840

SHERWOOD, ANDREW, management consultant; m. Diane K. Wells; children: Whitney, Kristen. BBA with honors, Nichols Coll., Dudbury, Mass., 1964; MBA program, Fairleigh Dickinson U., Rutherford and Madison, NJ, 1967; postgrad., Harvard U., Boston, 2000—03. Cert. mgmt. cons. Inst. Mgmt. Cons., 1995. Founder, chmn., CEO Goodrich & Sherwood Assocs., Inc., NYC, 1970—95; mng. dir. Stanton Chase Internat., NYC, 1995—. Congl. advisor Reagan and Bush White House; head bus. task force, NY; chmn. Goodrich Capital Internat., 1997—; lectr. in field. Author: Breakpoints, 1986; contbr. numerous articles to profl. jours. Sr. mem. Nat. Ski Patrol; bd. trustees, exec. com. Think First Found., 2004—07; bd. trustees Nichols Coll. Recipient Ronald Reagan Gold medal, Nat. Rep. Congl. Com., 2004. Mem.: Mashomack Field and Game Club, Chief Exec. Orgn., World Pres.'s Orgn., Young Pres.' Orgn. (bd. dirs., chpt. chmn. elect), Safari Club Internat. (bd. dirs.), Madison Ave. Sports Car Driving Club, The Greenwich Polo Club, Explorers Club, Univ. Club, The Econ. Club NY. Avocations: gardening, physical fitness, hunting, riding, antiques. Office: Stanton Chase Internat 52 Vanderbilt Ave New York NY 10017

SHERWOOD, ARTHUR LAWRENCE, lawyer; b. LA, Jan. 25, 1943; s. Allen Joseph and Edith S. Sherwood; m. Frances Merele, May 1, 1970; children: David, Chet. BA magna cum laude, U. Calif., Berkeley, 1964; MS, U. Chgo., 1965; JD cum laude, Harvard U., 1968. Bar: Calif. 1969, U.S. Dist. Ct. (cen. dist.) Calif. 1968, U.S. Dist. Ct. (no. dist.) Calif. 1971, Calif. 1971, U.S. Dist. Ct. (so. and ea. dists.) Calif. 1973, U.S. Ct. Appeals (9th cir.) 1973, U.S. Ct. Appeals (D.C. cir.) 1991, U.S. Supreme Ct. 1980. Instr. UCLA Law Sch., 1968—69; assoc. Gibson, Dunn & Crutcher, LA, 1968—75, ptnr., 1975—98, of counsel, 1998—. Judge pro tem L.A. Mcpl. and Superior Ct., 1980—98; instr. law UCLA, 1968—69; arbitrator N.Y. Stock Exch., Nat. Futures Assn. Co-author: Civil Procedure During Trial, 1995, Civil Procedure Before Trial, 1990; contbr. articles to profl. jours. Chmn. East Asian Art Coun., L.A. County Mus. Art, 1992—97, 2005—06. NASA fellow, U. Chgo., 1964—65. Mem.: Calif. Bar Assn., Phi Beta Kappa. Republican. Avocations: art, history. Office: 11828 Hunting Ridge Ct Potomac MD 20854

SHERWOOD, DONALD LEWIS, former congressman; b. Nicholson, Pa., Mar. 5, 1941; s. Walter A. and Doris (Williams) Sherwood; m. Carol Evans, 1973; children: Jesse, Dana, Maria. BA in Econs., Dartmouth Coll., Hanover, NH, 1963. Founder, pres. Sherwood Chevrolet, Tunkhannock, Pa., 1967—; mem. US Congress from 10th Pa. dist., 1999—2007, mem. appropriations com., vice chmn. fgn. ops. subcommittee, 2005—07. Ptnr. Sun Auto Grp., Clarks Summit, Sun Buick/Pontiac/GMC, Moosic. Appointed to Tunkhannock Area Sch. Bd., 1975-98, pres., 1992-98; pres. Wyo. County Indsl. Found., Wyo. County United Fund; bd. dirs. Triton Hose Fire Co. Fireman's Relief Assn., Wyo. County C. of C. With US Army, 1963—66. Mem. Pa. Chevrolet Dealers Area Mktg. Grp. (dir.), Pa. Hardwood Lumber Mfrs. Assn., Pa. Farmers Assn.; v.p. N.E. Pa. Chevrolet Dealers Assn. Republican. Avocation: raises and shows belgian horses. Mailing: Sherwood Chevrolet 153 E Tioga St Tunkhannock PA 18657 *

SHERWOOD, GLORIA N., graphics designer, genealogist, small business owner; b. Winfield, Kans. d. Edwin E. Schroeder and Anna Y. McClure; stepmother Vivian J. Schroeder; children: Christina Knueven, J.E. Jurey, Jeannette Thornhill. B CMT cert., foster parent cert. Pvt. home health care nurse, Eufaula, Okla., 1996—2006; ret.; bus. owner Angelic Prints, Inc. Author: The Poetic Works of Gloria Sherwood Book 1 vol. 1, 2000, Poetic Work Book 1, vol. 2, 2002, Just Be 2000, Remember Me, 1999, Spiritual Wings, 2001, Awaited Healing, 2001; visual artist: New Trails, 1998, Deep Is the Soul, 2000, Out of Bondage, 2001. Recipient Award of Excellence in Christian Web sites Joyful Mom's Web site. Mem. NAFE, Nat. Home Gardening Club, Nat. Arbor Day Found., Angelwings, Nat. Audubon Soc., Nat. Wildlife Fedn., World Wildlife Fedn., Enfaula Arts Coun. Democrat. Avocations: performing arts, gardening, playing guitar, writing music, crafts.

SHERWOOD, JAMES WEBSTER, III, writer; b. Hollywood, Calif., May 18, 1936; s. James Webster Sherwood Jr. and Vesta Graybeal Hughes; m. Valdi Hiesinger, Apr. 17, 1964 (div. 1972); m. Marylou Coddington Lemke, July 4, 1972 (div. 1989); m. Karyn Virginia Lindig, Mar. 18, 1990; children: Veronica E.C. Sherwood, Alexandra C.E. Sherwood Patterson, Roxanna Z.S.R., Christopher Michael De Santis, James Webster IV, George Marshall De Santis. Student, Choate Sch., U. Chgo., 1954—55; BL, U. Paris, 1963. Reporter, columnist San Mateo (Calif.) Times, Burlingame Advance, 1951-52; mng. editor Chgo. Rev. Mag., 1954-55; prodr. Myers-Sherwood Pictures, Inc., Chgo., 1955; editor Trans World Pictures, Inc., Chgo., 1955; editor, columnist Westchester News-Advertiser, LA, 1956-57; prodn. asst. Cecil B. DeMille-Paramount Pictures, Hollywood, 1957-59; v.p., gen. mgr. Smith Limousine, NYC, 1977-85; pres., owner Sherwood Justice & Barton Limousine Corp., NYC, 1985—2005; dir. Hamilton Mfg. Corp., Holland, Ohio. Prodr., dir. Sherwood Films, Hollywood, 1958-60; cons. on Tom Jones, 1961; adaptor The Sicilian Clan, 1966; producer After Laughter, 1968, others; founder, pub. Opus Books. Author: Dining on Thorns, 1996, Some Sonnets of Flame & Flower, 1998; syndicated columnist 11 western states for Christian Sci. Monitor, Hungry Horse (Mont.) News, Hellenic Rev., 1956-58; editor Popular Libr., 1970-72; biographic researcher Holt, Rinehart & Winston, 1970-72; journalist Ladies Home Jour., Village Voice, N.Y., 1972-73; author: (verse play) The Wooed Wife, 1957; author: 101 Sonnets of Sex, God, The Circus and Love, 2d edit., 1959, (novels) Stradella, 1961, Shakespeare's Ghost, 2001, Sun of Another Sky, 2003. Pres. Shakespeare Oxford Soc., 2004—05. Recipient Nat. Book award for best translation preface to (with Ralph Manheim) Castle to Castle, 1970, John Dos Passos award for Creative Writing, 1987. Republican. Episcopalian. Avocation: walking. Home and Office: 18 Central Five Central Dr Plandome NY 11030-1408 Office Phone: 516-365-8890. E-mail: jazsherwood@aol.com.

SHERWOOD, KEHELA (KAREN KEHELA SHERWOOD), broadcast executive; Grad., UCLA. Asst. prodr. to Brian Grazer Imagine Entertainment, 1986—87, story editor, 1987, dir. devel., v.p., sr. v.p., pres. prodn., co-chair Imagine Films, 1997—. Named one of 100 Most Powerful Women in Entertainment, Hollywood Reporter, 2006. Mailing: Imagine Entertainment 7th Floor 9465 Wilshire Blvd Beverly Hills CA 90212 *

SHERWOOD, MIDGE, author; b. Ironton, Ohio; d. Roy and Addie (Brace) Winters; m. Jack E. Sherwood, Jan. 19, 1946; children: Margaret Sherwood Simms, Melanie Sherwood. BJ, U. Mo., 1938. Women's editor Ironton Daily Tribune, 1933-38; city editor Ironton Daily News, 1938-40; asst. mgr. West coast news bur. TWA, Los Angeles, 1940-42; pub. relations dir. Western Air Lines, 1942-45; aviation columnist, corr. Skyways, So. Flight, 1945-48; owner, operator Midge Winters Agy., 1945-48; assoc. editor Matrix Mag., Women in Communications, 1950-55; book reviewer LA Times, 1963, Western Hist. Quarterly; free-lance writer, 1958—; columnist Pasadena Star-News, Calif., 1987; lectr. on Gen. George Smith Patton and pioneers of Western frontier. Author: And How it Grew, 1965; San Marino Ranch to City, 1977; Days of Vintage, Years of Vision, Vol. 1, 1982, Vol. II, 1987, Fremont: Eagle of the West, 2002, Days of Vintage, Years of Vision, vol. III, 2006, Western Journal Collection (1900-1995), Western Journal Collection (1995-2000); author (plays): Peace at Last; editor Western Jour.; contbr. columns newspapers. Chmn. Hertrich Meml., 1967; Paul Harris fellow Rotary; recipient Commendation award Gov. Pete Wilson, Calif., 1996. Mem. Soc. Fellows of Huntington Library, 1967; founder, archivist San Marino Hist. Soc. Recipient double award Conf. Calif. Hist. Socs., 1987; named Outstanding Citizen of San Marino, 1988. chmn. Annual Fremont's Day, 2005. Mem. Huntington Westerners (founder), Live Poet's Soc. Huntington Libr. (founder), Westerners Internat. (bd. dirs.), Phi Mu. Home: PO Box 80241 San Marino CA 91118

SHERWOOD, ROBERT PETERSEN, retired social sciences educator; b. Black Diamond, Wash., May 17, 1932; s. James Brazier and Zina (Petersen) S.; m. Merlene Burningham, Nov. 21, 1951; children: Robert Lawrence, Richard William, Rolene, RaNae. BS, U. Utah, 1956, MS, 1957; EdD, U. Calif., Berkeley, 1965. Tchr. Arden-Carmichael Sch. Dist., Carmichael, Calif., 1957-59, vice prin. jr. high, 1960-61, prin. jr. high, 1962-65; v.p., prin. San Juan Unified Sch. Dist., Sacramento, 1966-70; assoc. prof. Calif. State U., Sacramento, 1966-71; dir. outreach progs. Am. River Coll., Sacramento, 1971-73, acting assoc. dean of instrn., 1973-74, prof. sociology, 1970-92, chmn. sociology/anthropology dept., 1980-86; ret., 1992. Pres. acad. senate Am. River Coll., 1990-91. With USN, 1953-55. Recipient Merit Recognition award, Boy Scouts Am., 1989. Mem. NEA, Calif. Tchrs. Assn., Faculty Assn. Calif. Community Colls., Western Assn. Schs. and Colls., Calif. Fedn. Coll. Profs., Phi Delta Kappa (life). Mem. Lds Ch. Avocations: reading, writing, woodworking, travel. Home: 4053 Esperanza Dr Sacramento CA 95864-3069

SHERWOOD, ROD(ERICK), III, computer company executive; BA with hons. in Econs., Stanford U.; MBA, Harvard U. With Chrysler Corp., 1981—95; from corp. v.p., treas. to pres. Spaceway Broadband Svcs. Hughes Electronics, 1995—98, pres. Spaceway Broadband Svcs., 1998—99; sr. v.p., CFO BroadStream Corp., 1999—2000, Loudcloud Inc., 2000—02, Gateway Inc., Poway, Calif., 2002—03, exec. v.p., CFO, 2003—. Office: Gateway Inc 7565 Irvine Ctr Dr Irvine CA 92618-2930

SHERZER, HARVEY GERALD, lawyer; b. Phila., May 19, 1944; s. Leon and Rose (Levin) S.; m. Susan Bell, Mar. 28, 1971; children: Sheri Ann, David Lloyd. BA, Temple U., 1965; JD with honors, George Washington U., 1968. Bar: DC 1970, U.S. Ct. Appeals (DC cir.) 1970, U.S. Ct. Fed. Claims 1970, U.S. Ct. Appeals (fed. cir.) 1970, U.S. Supreme Ct. 1974. Law clk. to trial judges U.S. Ct. Fed. Claims, Washington, 1968-69; law clk. to chief judge U.S. Ct. Appeals for Fed. Cir., Washington, 1969-70; assoc. Sellers, Conner & Cuneo, Washington, 1970-75, ptnr., 1975-80, McKenna, Conner & Cuneo, Washington, 1980-82, Pettit & Martin, Washington, 1982-85, Howrey & Simon, Washington, 1985-2000, Howrey Simon Arnold & White, Washington, 2000—01, Greenberg Traurig, McLean, Va., 2001—03, Dickstein Shapiro LLP, Washington, 2003—. Adv. bd. The Govt. Contractor, 1996-99. Author: (with others) A Complete Guide to the Department of Defense Voluntary Disclosure Program, 1996; contbr. articles to profl. jours. Office: Dickstein Shapiro 1825 Eye St NW Washington DC 20006 Home Phone: 301-469-5464; Office Phone: 202-420-4745. Business E-Mail: sherzerh@dicksteinshapiro.com.

SHESKEY, SUSAN E., computer company executive; b. Oct. 13, 1947; Grad., Miami U., Oxford, Ohio. With Ameritech, Ohio Bell, Dell, Inc., Round Rock, Tex., 1993—, v.p. for global sales, svcs., mfg. and fulfillment IT, interim chief info. officer, 2005, v.p., chief info. officer, 2005—. Office: Dell Inc One Dell Way Round Rock TX 78682

SHESTACK, ALAN, museum administrator; b. NYC, June 23, 1938; s. David and Sylvia P. (Saffran) S.; m. Nancy Jane Davidson, Sept. 24, 1967. BA, Wesleyan U., 1961, DFA (hon.), 1978; MA, Harvard U., 1963. Mus. curator graphic art Nat. Gallery Art, Washington, 1965-67; assoc. curator prints and drawings Yale Art Gallery, New Haven, 1967-68, curator prints and drawings, 1968-71, dir., 1971-85; adj. prof. history of art Yale U., 1971-85; dir. Mpls. Inst. Art, 1985-87, Boston Mus. Fine Arts, 1987-93; dep. dir. Nat. Gallery of Art, Washington, 1994—. Mem. adv. com. Art Mus., Princeton, 1972-75; mem. com. prints and illustrated books Mus. Modern Art, NYC, 1972-2007; mem. mus. panel Nat. Endowment for the Arts, 1974-77; mem. Fed. Arts and Artifacts Indemnification Panel, 1979-83; mem. vis. com. Harvard U. Art Mus., 1990-95, Davis Mus. Wellesley Coll., 1997—. Author: Fifteenth Century Engravings of Northern Europe, 1967, The Engravings of Martin Schongauer, 1968, Master LCZ and Master WB, 1971, Exhibitions Organized and Catalogued: Master E.S, 1967, The Danube School, 1969, Hans Baldung Grien, Prints and Drawings, 1981, (exhbn. catalog) Art for the Nation, 2000; contbr. articles to profl. jours. Woodrow Wilson fellow Harvard U., 1963, David E. Finley fellow, 1963-65. Mem. Print Coun. Am. (bd. dirs., v.p. 1970-71), Coll. Art

Assn. (bd. dirs. 1972-76), Am. Assn. Mus., Am. Fedn. Arts (trustee 1981-94), Alpha Delta Phi, Phi Beta Kappa. Office: Nat Gallery Art 2000-B S Club Dr Hyattsville MD 20785 Office Phone: 202-842-6012. Business E-Mail: A_Shestack@nga.gov.

SHESTACK, JEROME JOSEPH, lawyer; b. Atlantic City, Feb. 11, 1925; s. Isidore and Olga (Shankman) Shestack; m. Marciarose Schleifer, Jan. 28, 1951; children: Jonathan Michael, Jennifer. AB, U. Pa., 1944; LLB, Harvard U., 1949; LLD (hon.), Dickinson Coll. Law, 1997, Stetson Sch. of Law, 1998, Whittier Coll. Law, 1998. Bar: Ill. 1950, Pa. 1952. Tchg. fellow Northwestern U. Law Sch., Chgo., 1949—50; asst. prof. law, faculty editor La. State Law Sch., Baton Rouge, 1950—52; dep. city solicitor City of Phila., 1952, 1st dep. solicitor, 1952—55; ptnr. Schnader, Harrison, Segal & Lewis, Phila. and Washington, 1956—91, Wolf, Block, Schorr & Solis-Cohen, Phila., 1991—. Adj. prof. law U. Pa., 1956; U.S. amb. to UN Human Rights Commn., 1979—80; U.S. del. to ECOSOC, UN, 1980; sr. U.S. del. to Helsinki Accords Conf., 1979—80; mem. U.S. Commn. on Improving Effectiveness of UN, 1989—; chmn. Internat. League Human Rights, 1973—94, hon. chmn., 1994—; U.S. del. to CSCE Conf., Moscow, 1991; founder, chmn. Lawyers Com. Internat. Human Rights, 1978—80, Jacob Blaustein Inst. Human Rights, 1988—92; mem. nat. adv. com. legal svcs. OEO, 1965—72; bd. dirs., exec. com. Lawyers Com. Civil Rights; mem. coun. Holocaust Mus., 1999—2004, exec. com., chair com. on conscience. Editor (with others): (monographs) Rights of Americans, 1971, Human Rights, 1979, International Human Rights, 1985, Bill of Rights: A Bicentennial View, 1991, Understanding Human Rights, 1992, Thomas Jefferson: Lawyer, 1993, Francis Scott Key, 1994, Abraham Lincoln, Circuit Lawyer, 1994, The Holocaust, 1997, Moral Foundations of Human Rights, 1997, The Philosophy of Human Rights, 1997, W.B. Yeats, Poet of Passionate Intensity, 1997, Corporate Social Responsibility, 2004. Mem. exec. com. Nat. Legal Aid and Defender Assn., 1970—80; trustee Eleanor and Franklin Roosevelt Inst., 1986—; bd. govs. Tel Aviv U., 1983—, Hebrew U., 1969—; chmn. bd. dirs. Am. Poetry Ctr., 1976—91; trustee Free Libr. Phila., vice chmn., 1989—96; v.p. Am. Jewish Com., 1984—89. With USNR, 1943—46. Fellow, U. Pa. Law Sch., 1980; Rubin fellow, Columbia U. Law Sch., 1984. Mem.: ABA (ho. of dels. 1971—73, 1977—, jud. com. 1985—90, bd. govs. 1992—95, exec. com. 1994—95, pres.-elect 1996, pres. 1997—98, pres. Am. Law Inst.-ABA 1997—98, bd. dirs. 1999—2003, chair Ctr. Human Rights 2003—05), Nat. Conf. Bar Found. (bd. dirs. 1998—, pres. 2004), Internat. Assn. Jewish Lawyers and Jurists (Am. Soc. pres. 2000—02), Am. Acad. Appellate Lawyers, Am. Coll. Trial Lawyers, Am. Arbitration Assn. (highest medal 2006), Am. Law Inst., Am. Soc. Internat. Law (exec. com. 1993—, internat. com. jurists exec. com. 1998—2001, commr. 1999—), Internat. Acad. Trial Lawyers, Internat. Bar Assn. (chmn. com. on human rights 1990—94, chmn. com. profl. ethics 2000—04), Order of Coif. Home: Parkway House 2201 Pennsylvania Ave Philadelphia PA 19130-3513 Office: Wolf Block Schorr & Solis-Cohen 1650 Arch St Fl 25 Philadelphia PA 19103-2029 Office Phone: 215-977-2290. Business E-Mail: jshestack@wolfblock.com.

SHETLAR, JAMES FRANCIS, physician; b. Wichita, Dec. 26, 1944; MD, U. Kans., 1970. Resident in family practice Saginaw Cooperative Hosp., 1970-72; staff Covenant Hosp.; asst. clin. prof. Mich. State U. Mem. AMA, Am. Acad. Family Physicians, Mich. Acad. Family Physicians. Office: 163 Churchgrove Rd Frankenmuth MI 48734-1025 Home Phone: 989-652-0098; Office Phone: 989-652-9969.

SHETTY, GUNAPALA, biologist, researcher, educator; m. Shilpa Shetty, June 19, 1997. PhD, U. Mysore, India, 1993. Rsch. assoc. Indian Inst. Sci., Bangalore, Karnataka, India, 1993—96; post doctoral fellow U. Tex. MD Anderson Cancer Ctr., Houston, 1997—2002, instr., 2002—06, asst. prof., 2006—. Contbr. articles to profl. jours. Recipient Rodney Withers Lecture award, U. Tex. MD Anderson Cancer Ctr., 2002; Sr. Rsch. fellow, Coun. Sci. and Indsl. Rsch., India, 1984—87, Postdoctoral fellow, Lalor Found., Inc., 2000—02, Instl. Rsch. grantee, U. Tex. MD Anderson Cancer Ctr., 2004—05. Mem.: Endocrine Soc., Am. Soc. Andrology, Soc. Study Reproduction. Achievements include the discovery that testosterone, the male hormone, can inhibit the early stage of spermatogenesis in pathological situations. Office: Univ Texas MD Anderson Cancer 1515 Holcombe Blvd Box 66 Houston TX 77030

SHETTY, KAUP RAJMOHAN, endocrinologist, educator; came to U.S., 1966; s. Muddanna and Girija M. Shetty; m. Vasanthi R. Shetty; children: Sandeep, Suparna. MB BChir, Mysore Med. Coll., Karnataka, 1965. Diplomate Am. Bd. Internal Medicine, cert. in internal medicine, endocrinology and metabolism, geriatric medicine. Resident in internal medicine VA Med. Ctr., Chgo. and Milw., 1967-70; fellow in endocrinology and metabolism Med. Coll. Wis. and Affiliated Hosps., Milw., 1970-72, attending physician in endocrinology and metabolism, 1972—; attending physician in geriatrics and gerontology VA Med. Coll., Milw., 1991—; assoc. prof. medicine Med. Coll. Wis., Milw., 1991-95, prof. medicine, 1995-2000, prof. medicine emeritus, 2000—. Contbr. articles to profl. jours., chapters to books. Fellow ACP, Royal Coll. Physicians Can., Am. Coll. Endocrinology; mem. Endocrine Soc., Am. Geriatric Soc., N.Y. Acad. Scis. Achievements include research in hormones and aging, post-polio syndrome, metabolic accompaniments of inactivity. Avocation: tennis. Office: VA Med Ctr 5000 W National Ave Milwaukee WI 53295-0001

SHETTY, MULKI RADHAKRISHNA, retired oncologist; b. Hiriadka, Karnataka, India, July 10, 1940; arrived in U.S., 1974; s. Sunderram and Kusumavati Shetty. MBBS, Stanley Med. Coll., Madras, 1964; DTM, U. Liverpool, Eng., 1968; LMCC, Med. Coun., Can., 1975. House surgeon and physician Bombay Hosp., 1965-66; sr. house officer Manor Pk. Hosp., Bristol, Eng., 1966-67, Torbay Hosp., 1967-68, St. Lukes Hosp., Huddersfield, 1969-70; sr. resident Gen. Hosp. Meml. U., New Foundland, 1971-72; intern Ottawa Gen. Hosp., 1972-73; fellow in chemotherapy Ont. Cancer Found., Ottawa, Can., 1973-74; fellow in clin. oncology U. Fla., Gainesville, 1974-75; attending oncologist N.W. Community Hosp., Arlington Heights, Ill., 1975-2000; ret., 2000. Cons. N.W. Cmty. Hosp., Arlington Heights, Ill., 1975—2000. Author: (book) Lung Cancer, 1980, Recent Advances in Chemotherapy, 1985, Wildlife Adventures, 1997, Chicago, 1997, Quotes and Notes, 2003, The Itinerant Indian, 2005, Encyclopaedia of Quotable Couplets, 2005; contbr. chapters to books, articles to profl. jours.; coined new word calcifectomy. Recipient Cert. for Oustanding Svc., Am. Cancer Soc., 1982. Hindu. Achievements include Reached the North Pole by icebreaker YAMAL, Aug. 5, 2001.

SHEVITZ, MARK H., sales promotion and marketing executive; b. Dioles, France, July 10, 1955; came to U.S., 1956; s. Arthur E. and Marilyn (Sigoloff) S. Student, U. Mo., 1973-75, Rockhurst Coll., 1983-84; MBA, Washington U., St. Louis, 1988. Program dir. KFMZ-FM, Columbia, Mo., 1974-81; mgmt. supr. Bernstein-Rein Advt., Kansas City, Mo., 1981-84; account supr. The Hermann Group, St. Louis, 1984-86; dir. promotions, food svc. products divsn. Seven-Up Co., St. Louis, 1986-87; pres. Landing Assocs., St. Louis, 1987-88, SJI, Inc., St. Louis, 1988-98, SJI Fulfillment, Inc., St. Louis, 1991—; CEO SJI Inc., St. Louis. Lectr. Washington U., St. Louis, 1988—, Bowling Green (Ohio) State U., 1977-89, Stephens Coll., Columbia, Mo., 1976-89, U. Mo., Columbia, 1975-81. Contbr. articles to profl. jours. Chpt. chmn. March of Dimes, mid.-Mo., 1978-81; mem. devel. bd. Cardinal Glennon Children's Hosp., St. Louis, 1984-88; event chmn. March of Dimes, St. Louis, 1990. Named Entrepreneur of Yr. St. Louis region, 1993. Mem. Assn. Promotion Mktg. Agys. Worldwide (sec./treas. 1998-2000), Porsche Club Am. (pres. St. Louis region 1986).

SHEWARD, RICHARD S., judge; b. Jackson, Ohio, May 21, 1944; s. D.J. and M.A. (Rapp) S.; children: Carrin E., Alison M. BBA, Ohio U., 1967; JD, Capital U., 1974. Bar: Ohio 1974, U.S. Dist. Ct. (so. dist.) Ohio 1975, U.S. Supreme Ct. 1978. Asst. pros. atty. Franklin County (Ohio), 1974-76; ptnr. Sheward & Weiner, Columbus, Ohio, 1976-87; judge Franklin County Mcpl. Ct., 1987-91, Franklin County Ct. Common Pleas, 1991—, presiding judge, 1993—; instr. real estate law Columbus Tech. Inst., 1977-80. Mem. Upper Arlington (Ohio) Civic Assn.; mem. Franklin County Republican Central Com., 1978-87; bd. dirs. Easter Seal Soc. Columbus, 1990-93. Served with U.S. Army, 1968-71. Decorated Bronze Star, Air medal. Mem. ABA, Ohio Bar Assn., Columbus Bar Assn. (common pleas ct., chmn. criminal law com. 1985-86, 86-87), Franklin County Trial Lawyers Assn. (pres. 1984-85), Am. Arbitration Assn. (labor panel), Franklin County Pros. Atty. Alumni Assn. (chmn. 1979-87), Buckeye Rep. Club (pres. 1981), Touchdown Club, Agonis Club, Charity Newsies, Am. Inns Ct. (pres. Robert Duncan chpt. 1994-95), Masons (32 deg.). Office: Franklin County Common Pleas Ct 369 S High St Fl 9-c Columbus OH 43215-4516 Home: 7540 James River Close New Albany OH 43054-9026 Office Phone: 614-462-3770. E-mail: richard_sheward@fccents.org.

SHEWMAKER, KENNETH EARL, history professor; b. LA, June 26, 1936; s. James Virgil and Jeanette M. (Greenberg) Shewmaker; m. Elisabeth L. Spalteholz, June 12, 1960; children: Richard Glenn, Nancy Jeanette. BS, Concordia Tchrs. Coll., 1960; MA, U. Calif., Berkeley, 1961; PhD, Northwestern U., 1966. Instr. Northwestern U., Evanston, Ill., 1965-66; asst. prof. Coll. William and Mary, Williamsburg, Va., 1966-67; from asst. prof. to assoc. prof. Dartmouth Coll., Hanover, NH, 1967-78, prof. history, 1978—2005, acting chair dept. history, 1985-86, chmn. dept. history, 1986-89, prof. emeritus, 2005—. Author: Americans and Chinese Communists, 1927-45: A Persuading Encounter, 1971 (Stuart L. Bernath prize, 1972); editor: Papers of Daniel Webster, Diplomatic Papers, Vol. 1, 1841-1843, 1983, Vol. 2, 1850-1852, 1987, Daniel Webster, The Completest Man, 1990; contbr. articles to profl. jours. Recipient Disting. Tchg. awards, Dartmouth Coll., 1986, 1996, 2004. Mem.: Soc. Historians Am. Fgn. Rels., Orgn. Am. Historians, N.H. Hist. Soc. Lutheran. Avocations: fly fishing, fly tying. Office: Dept History Dartmouth Coll Hanover NH 03755 Business E-Mail: shewmaker@dartmouth.edu.

SHI, DAVID E., academic administrator, historian; s. Joseph and Evelyn Shi; m. Susan Thomson, June 1974; children: Jason, Jessica. BA magna cum laude, Furman U., 1973; MA, U. Va., 1975, PhD, 1976; HHD (hon.), Ctr. Coll., 2002. From asst. prof. to Frontis W. Johnston prof., chmn. history dept. Davidson Coll., 1976—93; v.p. acad. affairs Furman U., Greenville, SC, 1993—94, pres., 1994—. Bd. dirs. Nat. Comerce Fin. Corp., Memphis. Author: Facing Facts: Realism in American Thought and Culture 1850-1920, 1995, In Search of the Simple Life: American Voices, Past and Present, 1986, The Simple Life: Plain Living and High Thinking in American Culture, 1985 (Editors Choice award), Matthew Josephson, Bourgeois Bohemian, 1981; author: (with George Tindall) America: A Narrative History, 4th edit., 1996; contbr. articles to profl. jours. Bd. dirs. Urban League, Greenville. Capt. USAR. Recipient Presdl. Leadership award, James L. Knight Found., 1998, Presdl. award, John Templeton Found., 1999; fellow, Nat. Humanities Ctr., 1982—83, NEH, 1982—83, 1991—92, Huntington Libr., 1986—87; grantee, NEH, 1980, 1986; Andrew Mellon Faculty fellow, 1978, Travel grant, NEH, 1988. Mem.: Greenville C. of C. (bd. dirs.), Commerce Club (bd. dirs.), Omicron Delta Kappa, Phi Beta Kappa. Home: 1209 Roe Ford Rd Greenville SC 29617 Office: Furman U 3300 Poinsett Hwy Greenville SC 29613 Office Phone: 864-294-2100. Office Fax: 864-294-3939. E-mail: david.shi@furman.edu. *

SHI, JIAQI, medical educator; MD, Hunan Med. U., China, 1995, PhD, 1999. Rsch. asst. prof. U. Ariz., Tucson, 2003—. Mem.: AACR (Bristol-Myers Squibb Oncology Scholar-in-Tng. award 2003).

SHI, QIN, lawyer, technologist; m. Richard Bone. BSc in Biochemistry, Wuhan U., China, 1989; MSc in Math. and Computer Scis., Loyola U., Chgo., 1997; PhD in Molecular and Cellular Biology, Loyola U., Maywood, Ill., 1997; JD, Georgetown U. Law Ctr., Washington, 2002. Bar: Calif. 2003, D.C. 2004, U.S. Ct. Appeals (9th cir.), U.S. Ct. Appeals (D.C. circ.). Biotech. engr. Wuhan Biotech R&D Ctr., China; bioinformatics specialist Gene Logic, Montgomery County, Md., Foley & Lardner LLP, Washington; informatics sci. advisor Heller Ehrman LLP; attorney Fenwick & West LLP, Mountain View, Calif., Latham & Watkins LLP, Menlo Park, Howrey LLP, Palo Alto. Spkr. ann. meetings Intelligent Sys. Molecular Biology, 2000, 01; spkr. Congress Internat. Drug Discovery Sci. and Tech., China, 2006. Contbr. legal and bus. analysis, articles to profl. jours. and law revs. Mem.: IEEE, AAAS, ABA, Endocrine Soc., Internat. Soc. Computational Biology, Am. Intellectual Property Law Assn. (spkr. winter conf. 2006). Avocations: hiking, bicycling, running, travel. Office: Howrey LLP 1950 Univ Ave Palo Alto CA 94303 Office Phone: 650-798-3522. Business E-Mail: shiq@howrey.com.

SHI, STONE D.H., research scientist; permanent resident, US; s. Ji-Liang Shi and San-Chun Jiang; m. Cathie D. Xiang, May 5, 1995; children: Constance K. X., Alan K. W. BS, Tsinghua U., Beijing, 1992, MS, 1995; PhD, Fla. State U., Tallahassee, 1999. Prin. scientist GlaxoSmithKline, King of Prussia, Pa., 1999—2003, Pfizer Global R&D, San Diego, 2003—. Recipient First award, Chinese Nat. Chemistry Olympic, 1987, Student award, Soc. Applied Spectroscopy, 1998. Mem.: Am. Soc. Mass Spectrometry. Achievements include first to apply electron capture dissociation to phosphopeptide mapping. Avocation: photography. Personal E-mail: stone.shi@homemail.com.

SHI, WEISONG, computer scientist, educator; arrived in US, 2000; m. Wei Wang, Feb. 22, 2000; 1 child, Ivy W. B in Computer Sci., Xidian U., 1995; PhD, Chinese Acad. Scis., 2000. Assoc. rsch. scientist NYU, NY, 2000—02; asst. prof. Wayne State U., Detroit, 2002—. Guest editor Jour. Parallel and Distributed Computing. Recipient Pres. Outstanding Honor award, Chinese Acad. Scis., 2000, 100 Outstanding PhD Rsch. China award, China Ministry Edn., 2002, Best Paper award, ICWE, 2004, Career award, NSF, 2007; fellow, Microsoft, 1999; grantee, Wayne State U., 2004. Mem.: IEEE (Best Paper award 2005), Assn. Computing Machinery. Achievements include research in software distributed shared memory system; an infrastructure for composable adaptive network services; dynamic application-layer protocol adaptation, fractal project; dynamic web content caching and delivery; resource sharing in collaborative high-end computing; data quality mangement and resilient wireless sensor networks; security and privacy in vehicular networks. Office: Wayne State Univ 5143 Cass Ave 420 State Hall Detroit MI 48202 Home Phone: 248-273-0224; Office Phone: 313-577-3186. Business E-Mail: weisong@cs.wayne.edu.

SHIAO, SHYANG-YUN PAMELA K., nursing educator, researcher; d. Fan-Mo Kung and Kuang-Mei Kung-Sun; m. Jeansong Gene Shiao, Dec. 17, 1986; 1 child, Jacqueline Nina. PhD, Case Western Res. U., 1993. RN Bd. Nursing Tex., 1999. Regional RN, U. Ala. Hosp., Birmingham, 1987—88; staff devel. instr. MetroHealth Med. Ctr., Cleve., 1988—90; project dir. Case Western Res. U., Cleve., 1991—93, asst. prof., 1993—98; assoc. prof. Oreg. Health Sci. U., Portland, 1998—99, U. Tex. Health Scis. Ctr., Houston, 1999—2006; prof. U. Houston, Sugarland, 2006—; exec. assoc. chief nurse rsch. VA Med. Ctr., Houston, 2007—. ANCC magnet fellow-appraiser for nursing excellence ANA, Washington, 2006. Leader: rsch. Meta-analysis of acupressure (Shannon Dir.'s award NIH, 1997), prin. program investigator: rsch. Oxygen Saturation Monitoring in Neonates, Vagal tone and Validation of Oxygen Saturation Monitoring in Neonates, Validation of Oxygen Saturation Measurements in Neonates (Rsch. award Am. Assn. Critical Care Nurses, 1995). Mem. award com. Am. Assn. Colls. Nursing, Calif., 2005—06; rsch. award com. Sigma Theta Tau, Ind., 2002—. Fellow: Am. Acad. Nursing (life). Office: MEDVAMC 2002 Holcombe Blvd Houston TX 77030 Personal E-mail: pshiao@msn.com.

SHIARI, BEHROUZ, mechanical engineer, researcher; s. Bahman Shiari and Mahvash N. Sharif; m. Flora Gilanpour; 1 child, Aryan. BSc, AmirKabir U. Tech., Tehran, Iran, 1986, MSc, 1988, PhD, 1999. Cert. profl. engr., Ont., Can. Instr. U. Guilan, Rasht, 1988—2000; rsch. assoc. Queen's U., Kingston, Ont., Canada, 2000—02, Carleton U., Ottawa, Ont., Canada, 2002—04, NRC of Can., Ottawa, 2004—. Head mech. engring. dept. Guilan U., Rasht, 1993—95, asst. dean grad. office faculty engring., 1998—2000. Author: Analytical Dynamics of Discrete Systems Vol.1; contbr. articles to profl. jours. Rsch. fellow, NSERC, 2004. Achievements include patents for Polyfiber Refiner Sensor. Home: 6886 Edgar Brault St Ottawa ON Canada K1C 1L7 Office: Nat Rsch Coun Can 100 Sussex Ottawa ON Canada K1A 0R6 Home Phone: 613 841 9966; Office Phone: 613 990 0981. Office Fax: 613 947 2838. Personal E-mail: shiari@yahoo.ca. Business E-Mail: behrouz.shiari@nrc-cnrc.gc.ca.

SHIBA, WENDY C., lawyer; BA, Mich. State U., 1973; JD cum laude, Temple U. Sch. of Law, 1979. Atty. corp. and securities law O'Melveny & Myers, Los Angeles & NYC; corp. chair Phila. Law Dept., Phila.; v.p., sec., asst. gen. counsel Bowater, Inc., Greenville, SC, 1993—2000; gen. counsel PolyOne Corp., Avon Lake, Ohio, 2000—01, v.p., chief legal officer, sec., 2001—. Former bd. mem. Legal Services Agency of Western Carolina, S.C. Bd. of Accountancy, Greenville Little Theater, Palmetto Soc. of United Way of Greenville County; former mem. United Way of Greenville County Campaign Cabinet, Palmetto Soc. Women's Leadership Council, Greenville Professional Women's Forum. Office: PolyOne Corp 33587 Walker Rd Avon Lake OH 44012

SHIBASAKI, YOSHIO, chemistry professor, researcher; b. Gyoda, Japan, Mar. 21, 1934; s. Reiji and Shige (Kobayashi) S.; m. Teiko Ishizuka Shibasaki, Apr. 15, 1967; children: Hideaki, Miki. BS, Saitama U., Japan, 1959; DSc, U. Tokyo, 1980. Tech. official U. Tokyo, Japan, 1960-63, asst., 1963-67; lectr. Saitama U., Urawa, Japan, 1967-70, assoc. prof., 1970-92, prof., 1992-99, ret., 1999. Inventor: Kobunshi Kagaku, 1964, J. Polymer Science, 1967, 80, 98, 99. Internat. Conf. Thermal Analysis & Calorimetry, Japan Soc. Calorimetry & Thermal Analysis. Mem. AAAS, Am. Chem. Soc., N.Y. Acad. Sci. Avocation: photography. Home: 1642 Tsutsumine Gyoda 361-0035 Japan

SHICK, RICHARD ARLON, finance educator; b. DuBois, Pa., July 17, 1943; s. Arlon Elmer and Melva Elizabeth (Bartell) S.; m. Linda B. Shick; children: Richard Arlon, Charles, Elizabeth. BS, SUNY, Buffalo, 1966, MBA, 1968, PhD, 1972. Asst. prof. banking and fin. U. Ga., Athens, 1970-75; assoc. prof. fin. St. Bonaventure (N.Y.) U., 1975-78, chmn. fin. dept., 1975-78, acting chmn. mktg. dept., 1976-99; assoc. prof. fin. Canisius Coll., Buffalo, 1978-99, prof. fin., 1999—, dean Richard J. Wehle Sch. Bus., 1979—2002. Bd. dirs. Better Bus. Bur., 1990-95, Statler Culinary program Emerson H.S., buffalo, 1992-98; sec., treas., bd. dirs. Chautauqua Brick Co., 1995—. Mem. editl. bd. Jour. Bus. Rsch., 1973-76, Jour. Fin. Rsch., 1977-81, Jour. Econs. and Bus., 1984-88, Fin. Rev., 1976-87, editor, 1981-82; contbr. articles to profl. jours. Chmn. mayor's rev. com. Buffalo Bd. Edn., 1982-83; bd. dirs. Buffalo Alliance Edn., Old Ft. Niagara, 1994-95 chmn. bd. dirs.; chmn. devel. com., bd. dirs. Buffalo Philharm. Orch., 1995-97, treas., 1996-97; mem. NY State Com. to Promote Pub. Trust and Confidence in Legal Sys., 1999; bd. dirs. Studio Arena Theatre, 2001-05, v.p. bd., pres., chmn. NDEA fellow, 1966-68; U.S. Savs. and Loan League grantee, 1974, St. Bonaventure U. grantee, 1976, US Govt. Title III grantee, 1999 Mem. Am. Fin. Assn., Jesuit Colls. and Univs. Deans of Bus. Schs. (treas. 1983-84, v.p. 1985-89, pres. 1987-88), Middle Atlantic Assn. Colls. and Schs. Bus. Adminstrn. (v.p. 1985-86, pres. 1986-87), Automobile Club Western N.Y. (bd. dirs. 1995-99, exec. com. 1998-99, 2001), Moon Brook Country Club, Town Club Jamestown, Beta Gamma Sigma, Alpha Kappa Psi, Di Gamma, Alpha Sigma Lambda, Alpha Signa Nu. Republican. Home: 157 Crestwood Ln Buffalo NY 14221-1508 Office: Canisius Coll 2001 Main St Buffalo NY 14208-1035 Office Phone: 716-888-2660. E-mail: shick@canisius.edu.

SHIDELER, ROSS PATRICK, literature and language educator, writer, translator, poet; b. Denver, Apr. 12, 1936; BA, San Francisco State U., 1958; MA, U. Stockholm, 1963; PhD, U. Calif., Berkeley, 1968. Instr. in comparative lit. U. Calif., Berkeley, 1967-68; asst. prof. English Hunter Coll., NYC, 1968-69; asst. prof. Scandinavian lang. and comparative lit. UCLA, 1969-73, assoc. prof., 1973-79, prof., 1979—, chmn. program in comparative lit., 1979-86, 92-96, assoc. dean Grad. Divsn., 2003—. Author: (monograph) Voices Under the Ground: Themes and Images in the Poetry of Gunnar Ekelof, 1973, Per Olov Enquist-A Critical Study, 1984, Questioning the Father: From Darwin to Zola, Ibsen, Strindberg and Hardy, 1999; translator: (plays) The Night of the Tribades (Per Olov Enquist), 1977, The Hour of the Lynx (Per Olov Enquist), 1990; co-editor (with Kathleen L. Komar): Lyrical Symbols and Narrative Transformations, Essays in Honor of Ralph Freedman, 1998; U.S. assoc. editor Swedish Book Rev., 1984—. Fellow, Nat. Defense Fgn. Language, 1964—65; Fulbright-Hays fellow, 1966—67. Mem. MLA (exec. com. divsn. Scandinavian Langs. and Lits. 1993-97), Soc. Advancement Scandinavian Study (exec. coun. 1985-89, v.p. 1997-99, pres. 1999-2001), Internat. Comparative Lit. Assn. (treas. 2004-). Office: UCLA Dept Comparative Lit Los Angeles CA 90095

SHIEH, ERIC Y., music educator; b. St. Louis, June 26, 1981; s. Huey-Sheng and Min-Tsung Shieh. B in Music Edn., U. Mich., Ann Arbor, 2004, BA in English, 2004. Lic. tchr. Mo., 1999. Cmty. coord. Miniwanca Outdoor Leadership Camp, Shelby, Mich., 2004; orch. dir. Hazelwood Sch. Dist., St. Louis, 2004—. Art tchr. St. Louis Prison Arts. Assoc. Prison Creative Arts Project, Ann Arbor, Mich., 2002; asst. concert master St. Louis Philharmonic Orch. Named Rookie of Yr. award, Hazelwood Sch. Dist., 2005; recipient Earl V. Moore award, U. Mich., Sch. Music, 2004, Arthur Miller award, U. Mich., Honors Coll., 2004. Mem.: St. Louis Suburban Music Educators Assn. (v.p.).

SHIEKMAN, LAURENCE ZEID, lawyer; b. Phila., Feb. 13, 1947; s. Morton and Roberta (Zeid) S.; m. Marjorie Kershbaum, Dec. 25, 1970; children: Wendy K., Thomas K. BS in Econs., U. Pa., 1968, JD, 1971. Bar: Pa. 1971. Law clk. to Hon. A. Leon Higginbotham, Jr. U.S. Dist. Ct. (ea. dist.) Pa., 1971-73; asst. prof. Fla. State U. Coll. Law, Tallahassee, 1973-75; assoc. Pepper, Hamilton & Scheetz, Phila., 1975-78, ptnr., 1978—. Mem. ABA, Pa. Bar Assn., Phila. Bar Assn. Office: Pepper Hamilton LLP 3000 Two Logan Sq 18th & Arch Sts Philadelphia PA 19103-2799 Office Phone: 215-981-4347. Business E-Mail: shiekmanl@pepperlaw.com.

SHIELD, GENE, health products executive; BSBA, The Citadel; MS in Sys. Mgmt., U. So. Calif.; M in Health Care Adminstrn., Med. Coll. Va.; grad., USAF Squadron Officers Sch., Indsl. Coll. of the Armed Forces. Former chief managed care divsn. Office of Air Force Surgeon Gen.; former cons. to Surgeon Gen. on managed care, advisor for legis. and CHAMPUS benefits and policy issues; pres., CEO Humana Mil. Healthcare Svcs. Humana Inc., Louisville, 1994—2000, sr. v.p. govt. programs, pres./CEO Emphesys, 2000—. Office: Humana Inc 500 W Main St Louisville KY 40202

SHIELD, JULIE MARIE KARST, artist, educator; b. St. Louis, Mar. 28, 1933; d. Lansing Peter and Margaret Mary Shield. A, Briarcliff Jr. Coll., NY, 1953; studied at, Nat. Acad. Design, NYC, Art Students League. Oil painting art tchr. Buckingham Coun. Arts, 1995—96, tchr. oil painting, 1999; owner Wooden Boat Art Gallery, River John, NS, Canada, 1997—99; tchr. oil Longwood Ctr. Visual Arts, 1997-1998, 2000—01; tchr. multi-media art Holly Manor Nursing Home, Farmville, 2001—04. Mem. coun. Longwood Ctr. for Visual Arts, Farmville, Va., 2001—07; tchr. art workshops. Set designer: (plays) Ring Around the Moon, 1981; (films) Illegally Yours, 1987; one-woman shows include First Nat. Bank of Palm Beach, Fla., 1984—85, Buckingham Coun. Arts, 1996, 1998, Cumberland Court House, Va., 1999, Cheese & Co., Farmville, Va., 2000, Cafe Zelia, Farmville, 2002, 2005, Va. Southside C.C., Keysville, Va., 2002, exhibited in group shows at Va. Mus. Fine Arts, Warrenton, 1988, Hampden Sydney Music Festival, 1998—2007, Longwood Ctr. Visual Arts Gala, Farmville, 2005, 2007, Buckingham Arts Coun., 1995—2007 (Best of Show), Represented in permanent collections ARC, Palm Beach County. V.p. ctrl. Va. arts affiliate Va. Mus. Fine Arts, Richmond, 2004—05, pres., 2006—. Mem.: DAR (bd. mem., corr. sec. 1971—75), Buckingham Artists Guild (planning com. 1995—2007), Curdsville Cmty. Ctr. (sec. 2006—), English Speaking Union, Friends of the Libr., Hist. Buckingham Inc., Audubon Artists Inc. (assoc.), Art Students League N.Y.C. (life; corr. sec. 1964—67), Buckingham-Dillwyn Garden Club (sec. 1996—). Episcopalian. Avocations: museums, gardening, miniature horse. Home: 843 Simpson Rd Prospect VA 23960

SHIELDS, ALLAN EDWIN, writer, photographer; b. Columbus, Ohio, July 3, 1919; s. Richard Edwin and Eloessa (Smith) S.; m. Bernice Clark, Aug. 2, 1941; children: Allan Oakley, Richard Minter, Larry Michael, Catherine Marie AB, U. Calif.-Berkeley, 1941; MA, U. So. Calif., 1947, PhD, 1951. Prof. philosophy San Diego State U., 1949-68, 70-78; emeritus prof. San Diego State Coll., 1978—; dean Coll. Humanities and Fine Arts U. No. Iowa, 1968-70; owner, pub. Jerseydale Ranch Press, 1992-98. Seasonal ranger naturalist Nat. Park Service, Yosemite Nat. Park, 1955-60; freelance writer, photographer, 1978—; violinist-violist, frequent recitalist; mem., sometime concertmaster Merced Symphony Orch., Calif., 1979-91; founder, with wife, Jerseydale Ranch Press, 1992. Author: Guide to Tuolumne Meadows Trails, 1960, rev. edit., 1973, (with Herbert Searles) A Bibliography of the Works of F.C.S. Schiller, 1969, (with Richard Shields) Tuolumne Profile: Yosemite, 1967, (novella) The Tragedy of Tenaya, 1974, new version 1992, A Bibliography of Bibliographies in Aesthetics, 1974, (poetry) A Horse in the House, 1985, Mariposa Now and Then, 1993, Tuffy, an Angel Hid in a Cloud, 1994, What Animals Taught Me, 1995, (with Bernice Shields) Into the Valley: A Brief History of Jerseydale Ranch, 1995, (with John Sharsmith) Climb Every Mountain: A Portrait of Carl Sharsmith, 1996, The Spirit of Rin-Tin-Tin, 2001, also numerous poems and articles; editor: A Yosemite Adventure in 1863, 1992, Wild Bill Neely and the Pagan Brothers' Golden Goat Winery, 1993, The Song of Sonora, 1993, O.S.S.: One Sad Sack—Pvt. Neely Disciplines the Military, 1994, A Yosemite Naturalist's Odyssey, 1994, Wilderness Treks by Foot, Canoe, and Adobe Rocket, and Father's Far-Flung Fables, 1995, Dream Temple and Other Visions, 1997; pub. various profl. jours. Bd. dirs. San Diego Symphony. Served with USAAF, 1942-45 Mudd fellow in philosophy U. So. Calif., 1948-49 Mem. Am. Soc. for Aesthetics (trustee), Phi Beta Kappa, Phi Kappa Phi, Phi Mu Alpha Sinfonia (hon.). Home: 2444 Beverly Ave Clovis CA 93611-5927 Personal E-mail: ashields@csufresno.edu. *My greatest satisfactions have come with tasks completed to the best of my abilities. Whether raising children, building a building, nurturing a marriage, learning the violin, or writing, all have inherent standards demanding recognition. Though there is always joy in the process of doing, joy can be transformed into satisfaction only in completion evaluated against the standards of worth for that kind of undertaking.*

SHIELDS, ANDREA LYN, psychologist, coach, educator; b. Montgomery, Ala., Aug. 19, 1947; d. Theodore and Alma Lea Shields. BA, U. Ariz., 1969; MA in Psychology, U. of the Pacific, 1971; PhD in Clin. Psychology, Fielding Inst., Santa Barbara, Calif., 1977. Trainer So. Ariz. Mental Health Ctr., Tucson, 1968-69; rsch. asst. Stockton (Calif.) State Hosp., 1970; instr. psychology Modesto (Calif.) Jr. Coll., 1970-71, San Bernardino (Calif.) Valley Coll., 1971-72; instr. for Army recruiters Columbia (Mo.) Coll., 1974; instr., head psychology dept. Crafton Hills Coll., Yucaipa, Calif., 1972-88; adminstrv. dir. U. San Francisco, 1980-82; pvt. practice, Rancho Cucamonga, Calif., 1981—; fellow Prescribing Psychologists Register, 1997—. Presenter in field. Pres. inland unit Am. Cancer Soc., 1993-96. Mem. Rotary (bd. dirs. 1993-96, 2002-, pres. 2005-06). Avocation: hiking. Office: 9045 Haven Ave Ste 107 Rancho Cucamonga CA 91730-5427 Home Phone: 909-867-3873; Office Phone: 909-980-7736.

SHIELDS, CHRISTOPHER ANDREW, website director; b. Oneonta, NY, Aug. 8, 1968; s. Alexander J. Shields and Grace Marie Kathmann. BS, SUNY, New Paltz, 1991; MS, U. Md., Adelphi, 1997. Dir. nasdaq.com The Nasdaq Stock Market, Inc., Rockville, Md., 1996—. Prodr.(on-air personality): (podcast) cIndyCenter.com. Home: 282 M St SW Washington DC 20024 Home Phone: 202-332-2534; Office Phone: 301-978-5286. Personal E-mail: ifwagba@hotmail.com.

SHIELDS, CRAIG M., lawyer; b. Oceanside, NY, Nov. 28, 1941; s. John Anderson and Lillian Ethel (Hagen) S.; m. Candia Atwater Shields, July 13, 1963 (div. 1985); children: Mark, Christopher, Evan; m. Norma Magor Peters, Apr. 25, 1998. BA in History, Lafayette Coll., 1963; LLB, Fordham U., 1966. Bar: N.Y. 1967, U.S. Dist. Ct. (so. and ea. dists.) N.Y. 1967, U.S. Ct. Appeals (2d cir.) 1967, U.S. Supreme Ct. 1976. Assoc. Clark, Carr & Ellis, NYC, 1966—69; ptnr. Borden & Ball, NYC, 1969—76, Sage, Gray, Todd & Sims, NYC, 1976—80; counsel Conboy, Hewitt, O'Brien & Boardman, NYC, 1980—83; ptnr. Collier, Cohen, Shields & Bock, NYC, 1983—92, Quinn & Suhr, White Plains, NY, 1992—95; v.p., gen. counsel United Vanguard Homes, Inc., Glen Cove, NY, 1992—2003; pvt. practice NYC, 2003—. Contbr. articles to profl. jours. Bd. dirs. Group House of Port Washington (N.Y.) Inc., 1973-85, Children's House, Inc., Mineola, N.Y., 1985-89, Resources for Program Devel., Inc., Port Washington, 1982—; pres. Port Washington Community Action Coun., 1968-69; committeeman Dem. Party, Port Washington, 1967-71. Mem. Assn. of Bar City of NY. Democrat. Methodist. Home and Office: 103 E 86th St Apt 7A New York NY 10028-1058 Home Phone: 212-876-4234; Office Phone: 212-876-4234. Personal E-mail: craig.shields@nyc.rr.com.

SHIELDS, CYNTHIA ROSE, college administrator; b. Monterey, Calif., June 1, 1954; d. William Lawrence and Rose Virdell Jackson; m. Franklin Shields, Sept. 19, 1981; 1 child, Brett. AA, San Francisco City Coll., 1980; BS, U. San Francisco, 1986; MPA, Golden Gate U., 1988; MS, Nat. U., 1994; EdD in Ednl. Leadership, U. Calif., Davis, 1997; cert. in conflict mgmt., U. Calif., Irvine, 2003. Cert. community coll. instr., supr., Calif. Acct. exec. KFSN-TV, Fresno, Calif., 1982-85; instr. Merced County Schs., Calif., 1985-89; gen. mgr., owner Ad Line Advt., Merced, 1986-96; instr. Merced Coll., 1989-90; youth outreach specialist, 1990-91; re-entry coord., 1991-98; counselor Long Beach City Coll., Calif., 2000—03, dir. outreach and pub. rels., 2003—. Sr. assoc. Sch. Leadership Ctr., Calif. Sch. Leadership Acad., 1989-92; ednl. cons. 1998-. Author curriculum materials. Bd. dirs. Merced Cmty. Med. Ctr. Found., 1991, MUHSD Found., 1992-94; mem. citizens adv. bd. Merced City Sch. Dist., 1985-87; chmn. Merced Conv. and Vis. Bur., 1991; coord. Merced Cmty. Housing Resource Bd., 1988-90; mem. Leaders program Nat. Inst. for Leadership Devel., 1996. Mem. AAUW, Merced City C. of C. (bd. dirs. 1991-93, v.p. fin. and ops. 1993-94), Phi Delta Kappa. Democrat. Avocations: community volunteer, reading, golf, bicycling.

SHIELDS, GERALD W., insurance company executive; BBA in Acctg., Baylor U., Waco, Tex., B in Computer Sci. Chief tech. officer, dir. info. svcs. LifeWay Christian Resources, Nashville; sr. info. tech. positions Electronic Data Systems; v.p. info. tech.-enterprises svcs. AFLAC Inc., 2002, sr. v.p., chief info. officer, info. tech., 2005—. Mem. inaugural governing body Atlanta Chief Info. Officers Exec. Summit. Bd. trustees Brewton-Parker Coll., Mt. Vernon, Ga.; bd. trustees Cmty. Tech. Adv. Coun. Muscogee County Sch. Dist. Named one of 100 Premier Chief Info. Officers, Computerworld, 2006, 100 Premier Info. Tech. Leaders, 2007. Mem.: Life Mgmt. Inst. Office: AFLAC Inc 1932 Wynnton Rd Columbus GA 31999 Office Phone: 706-323-3431. *

SHIELDS, JAMES JOSEPH, academic administrator, educator, writer; b. Phila., Feb. 11, 1935; s. James Joseph and Lena Josephine (Dyer) Shields. BS in Polit. Sci., St. Joseph's U., Phila., 1956; EdM, Temple U., Phila., 1959; EdD, Columbia U., NYC, 1963. Asst. dir. internat. studies Tchrs. Coll., Columbia U., NYC, 1961, field rschr., Tchrs. East Africa Program NYC, Kampala, Uganda, 1961-62; asst. prof. history and philosophy edn. SUNY, New Paltz, 1962-64; asst. prof. comparative and internat. edn. CUNY, NYC, 1964-69, assoc. prof., 1969-75, prof., 1975-98, prof. emeritus, 1999, head Sch. Adminstrn. Program, 1983-85, dir. Japan Initiative, 1986—98, chair dept. social and psychol. founds., 1988-90; dir. projects Ctr. Edn. Outreach and Innovation Tchrs. Coll. Columbia U., 1998—2004. Vis. prof. Tchrs. Coll. Columbia U., NYC, 1965—69, 1998—2004, Yale U., New Haven, 1997; cons. Inst. Ednl. Devel., NYC, 1968—71, Equitable Life Ins. Co., NYC, 1981, NYC Bd. Edn. Dist. 4, 1996—97, Time Mag., NYC, 1998, Inst. Internat. Edn., NYC, 1998—99; evaluation bd. Nat. Coun. Accreditation Tchr. Edn., Washington, 1970—75; vis. rsch. prof. Tokyo Met. U., 1986—95; assoc. univ. seminar modern Japan Columbia U., 1987—2004, chair, 1990—91. Author: Education in Community Development: Its Function in Technical Assistance, 1967, Problems and Prospects in International Education, 1968, Foundations of Education: Dissenting Views, 1974, Japanese Schooling: Patterns of Socialization Equality and Political Control, 1989, rev. edit., 1993; contbr. chapters to books, articles to profl. jours. Mem. task force reconstructed ednl. sys. Pub. Edn. Assn., NYC, 1977—78, mem. task force tchr. selection, 1981; mem. NY Urban Coalition, 1982—84; mem. lifelong learning adv. com. Tchrs. Coll., Columbia U., 2005—; mem. culture quest adv. bd. CCNY, 2005—; mem. alumni coun. Tchrs. Coll., Columbia U., 1993—98, 1999—2006. With USAR, 1959—65. Recipient Youth Coun. award, Wyo. Gov., 1974, Higher Edn. award, Holy Family Coll., Phila., 1990, Ann. Gertrude Langsam Ednl. Reconstrn. award, Adelphi U., 1992; grantee, N.Y. State Edn. Dept., 1969—72, Japan-U.S. Friendship Commn., 1986—88, Japan Found. Ctr. Global Partnership, 1994, U.S.-Japan Found., 1994—96, Tokyo Found., 1998—2000; Rsch. Found. grantee, SUNY, 1964, Fulbright Travel grantee, 1964, Rsch. Found. grantee, CUNY, 1980—81, City Coll. Provost Fund grantee, 1988—90, postdoctoral fellow, Yale U., 1967—68. Fellow: Comparative and Internat. Edn. Soc. (hon.; N.E. region conf. coord. 1984, bd. dirs. 1992—95); mem.: Soc. Ednl. Reconstruction (exec. com. 1973—), Carnegie Coun. Ethics and Internat. Affairs (trustee 1998—2003, vice-chmn. 2001—03), Am. Ednl. Studies Assn. (exec. coun. 1970—75, pres. 1973—74, founder), Beaux Arts Alliance, Japan Soc. NY, NY Athletic Club (NYC). Avocations: collecting long island painters (1850-1950), travel, gardening. Address: Trump Pl 200 Riverside Blvd Apt 11N New York NY 10069-0911 also: 42 Old Town Xing Southampton NY 11968-5015 Office Phone: 212-787-3326. Personal E-mail: jshields11@juno.com.

SHIELDS, JOHN CHARLES, literature educator; b. Phoenix, Oct. 29, 1944; s. Granville Blaine and Elizabeth Merle (Hartgraves) S. BA, U. Tenn., Knoxville, 1967, MA in Coll. Teaching, 1969, PhD, 1978; EdS, George Peabody Coll., 1975. Tchr. English Sevier County High Sch., Sevierville, Tenn., 1967-68; head dept. English Battle Ground Acad., Franklin, Tenn., 1969-71; dir. academics Brentwood Acad., Nashville, 1971-73, Columbia (Tenn.) Mil. Acad., 1973-74; instr. U. Tenn., Knoxville, 1978-79; asst. prof. Ill. State U., Normal, 1979-86, assoc. prof. English, 1986-93, prof. English, 1993—2005, disting. prof. African Am. Brit. and comparative lit., 2005—, dir., 2007—. Cons. Ency. Britannica, Oxford Companion to African Am. Lit., Norton Anthology African Am. Lit., others; project dir. conf. on Phillis Wheatley NEH, 1983-85; faculty advisor Native Am. Student Soc. Ill. State U., 1990; Coll. of Arts and Sci. Lectr., Ill. State U., 2003—; mem. doctoral dissertation com. Assoc. editor Style, DeKalb, Ill., 1988-90, guest editor, 1990—; editor: The Collected Works of Phillis Wheatley, 1988, paperback, 1989; selected to be a mem. of the Adv. Bd. of The Greenwood Ency. of Am. Poetry, (7 vol.) contbr., adv. editor, contbr. Oxford Companion to African Am. Lit., 1997—, Am. Nat. Biography, 24 vol., 1994—; contbr. Oxford Dictionary of Nat. Biography, Great Britain, 1995—; author: The Am. Aeneas: Classical Origins of the American Self, Univ. of Tenn. Press, 2001 (Winner Outstanding Acad. Book Choice Mag., 2002, Hon. mention Harry Levin prize Am. Comparative Lit. Assn.); contbr. articles to lit. jour. and chpt. to books; manuscript reviewer various presses and jour. Spokesperson for Native Am. citizens, 1990—. Ford Found. fellow, 1968-69, Soc. for Humanities fellow Cornell U., 1984-85, NEH fellow, 1983, 84, 89, 93, John. C. Hodges Teaching Excellence award, 1969. Mem. MLA, Soc. Early Americanists, Internat. Soc. for 18th-Century Studies, Am. Studies Assn., Melville Soc., Coll. Lang. Assn., Phi Mu Alpha Sinfonia, Alpha Phi Omega, Sigma Nu. Unitarian Universalist. Avocations: piano, singing, native american culture, archaeology, rare book collecting. Home: 1412 Donegal Dr Normal IL 61761-5416

SHIELDS, LAWRENCE THORNTON, orthopaedic surgeon, educator; b. Boston, Oct. 2, 1935; s. George Leo and Catherine Elizabeth (Thornton) S.; m. Karen S. Kraus, Sept. 21, 1968; children: Elizabeth Coulter, Laura Thornton, Sarah Daley, Michael Lawrence. AB, Harvard U., 1957; MD, Johns Hopkins U., 1961. Diplomate Am. Bd. Orthop. Surgery. Intern Barnes Hosp., Washington U., St. Louis, 1961—62, resident, 1962—63; resident orthop. surgeon Children's Hosp. Med. Ctr., Boston, 1966—67, Mass. Gen. Hosp., Boston, 1967—68, Peter Bent Brigham, Robert Breck Brigham Hosps., Boston, 1968—69, Harvard Med. Sch., Boston, 1965—69, instr., 1969—; orthop. surgeon Peter Bent Brigham & Women's Hosp., Children's hosps., 1969—, Waltham (Mass.)-Weston Hosp. and Med. Ctr., 1969—, also chief orthop. surgery, pres. med. staff. Mem. Waltham-Weston Orthop. Assocs.; proprietor Boston Athenaeum; mem. staff Hahnemann Hosp., Boston, Newton-Wellesley (Mass.) Hosp.; cons. orthop. surgeon VA Hosp., Boston; mem. faculty Harvard Med. Sch.; vis. scholar Trinity Hall Cambridge U., 1985; hon. prof. New Eng. Coll., Henniker, NH, Sussex, England, 1995; bd. dirs. Wal-West Health Sys., 1986—; pres. Mass. Bay Investment Trust; dir. Waltham Investment Group. Contbr. articles to med. jours. Bd. dirs. Mass. Acad. Emergency Med. Technicians, Waltham Boys' Club; bd. of overseers Boston Lyric Opera, 1993—; trustee, exec. com. Waltham-Weston Hosp. and Med. Ctr. Lt. M.C. USNR, 1963-65. Fellow: ACS, Mass. Hist. Soc. Libr., Am. Acad. Orthop. Surgeons, Mass. Hist. Soc., Olser Club London (corr.); mem.: Thomas B. Quigley Sports Medicine Soc. (v.p., pres. 2001—), R. Austen Freeman Soc. (v.p.), Mass. Med. Soc. (v.p. 1982—83, councillor), Mass. Orthop. Assn. (sec. 1986—, bd. dirs.), Royal Soc. Medicine, N.Y. Acad. Scis., Cox & Co., Boston Lyric Opera (bd. overseers 1993), St. Crisplin's Soc. Boston (pres. 1991—, founding mem.), L'Ordre Mondial (elected 1999), Les Amis d'Escoffier Soc., Handel and Hayden Soc. (bd. overseers), Emerson Soc., Internat. Consular Corps (hon.), Charles River Dist. (pres. 1982—83, treas., exec. com.), Titanic Hist. Soc., Boston Opera Assn. (bd. dirs.), Harvard Mus. Assn., Thoreau Soc., Trollope Soc. (founding mem., bd. dirs., London), Waltham Hist. Soc., Confrerie de La Chaine des Rotisseurs (elected 1996), Academie Brillat-Savarin, English Speaking Union (bd. dirs.), USS Wasp CV-19 Assn., Theodore Roosevelt Assn. New Eng. (founding), Osler Club London, New Eng. Orthop. Club, Boston Orthop. Club, St. Botolph Club (Boston), Harvard Club, Algonquin Club Boston (pres. 1990—, bd. dirs.), East India, Devonshire Sports and Pub. Schs. Club (London), Rotary, Bull Dog Terries, Union Club Boston, Clover Club Boston, 33 Touchdown Club/Found. (founding), Pi Eta (Harvard). Home: 9 Beverly Rd Newton MA 02461-1112 Office: 721 Huntington Ave Boston MA 02115-6010 also: 20 Hope Ave Ste 314 Waltham MA 02453-2717 Business E-mail: ltshields@mcb.harvard.edu.

SHIELDS, PATRICIA ALLENE, retail executive; b. Westminster, Md., June 29, 1968; d. Richard Dean and Joan Elizabeth Munroe Schnably; m. Aidan Hugh Shields, Mar. 20, 2004. BA, Wake Forest U., Winston Salem, NC, 1990. Mgr. divisional mdse. Gap, San Francisco, 2001—05; exec. v.p. Charlotte Russe, San Diego, 2005—. Alumni admissions vol. Wake Forest U., San Diego, 2001—06. Mem.: Delta Delta Delta (life; collegiate dist. officer 2003—06). Office: Charlotte Russe 4645 Morena Blvd San Diego CA 92117 Home Phone: 858-454-5904; Office Phone: 858-490-5912. Personal E-mail: pshields@san.rr.com.

SHIELDS, PORTIA HOLMES, former academic administrator; m. William H. Lewis. BS in Edn., D.C. Tchrs. Coll.; MA in Edn., George Washington U.; PhD in Early Childhood and Elem. Edn., U. Md. Various tchg. positions primary and secondary edn.; dir. med. and biomed. comm. Howard U. Coll. Medicine, Washington, 1989-93, dean Sch. of Edn., 1993-96; pres. Albany State U., Ga., 1996—2005. Presenter and cons. in field. Active Albany Mus. Art, Albany Tomorrow, Inc., Albany/Dougherty Cmty. Partnership for Edn. and Dougherty, 2000; chair steering com. Am. Reads Program; mem. bd. regents U. Sys. Ga., 1997; bd. dirs. Cmtys. in Schs. Mem.: Albany C. of C. (bd. dirs.), Nat. Coun. for Accreditation Tchr. Edn. (bd. dirs.), Am. Coun. on Edn. (bd. dirs., mem. appeals com.), Orgn. Instnl. Affiliates (bd. dirs.), Am. Assn. Colls. for Tchr. Edn. (bd. dirs.), Am. Assn. State Colls. and Univs. (com. on cultural diversity and social change). E-mail: pshields@asurams.edu.

SHIELDS, ROBERT EMMET, merchant banker, lawyer; b. Ridley Park, Pa., May 18, 1942; s. Joseph Leonard and Kathryn J. (Walsh) S.; m. Mary Katherine Reid, July 22, 1967; children: Christopher D., David R., Kevin M., Kathleen. AB, Coll. Holy Cross, 1964; LLB cum laude, NYU, 1967. Bar: Pa. 1968. Mem. faculty Boalt Hall Sch. Law U. Calif., Berkeley, 1967-68; assoc. Drinker Biddle & Reath, Phila., 1968-74, ptnr., 1974-94, mng. ptnr., 1979-83, 85-94, head corp. and securities group, 1983-93, CFO, 1993-94; mng. dir., prin., ptnr., COO Questor Gen. Ptnr., L.P., 1995—2003, Questor Ptnrs. Funds, L.P. and Questor Mgmt. Co., 1995—2003; vice chmn. AlixPartners Holdings, Inc., Southfield, Mich., 2003—07, Questor Ptnrs. Holdings, Inc., Southfield, 2003—, TK Aluminum, Ltd., Hamilton, Bermuda, 2003—; pres., CEO Lakeview Capital, Inc., Southfield, 2007—. Sec. Wallquest Inc.; bd. dirs. Plainfield Direct, Inc.; mem. bd. trustees Archmere Acad. Author: (with Eliot B. Thomas) Federal Securities Act Handbook, 4th edit, 1977; (with Robert H. Strouse) Securities Practice Handbook, 1987. Mem.: ABA, Turnaround Mgmt. Assn., Phila. Bar Assn., Pa. Bar Assn., Am. Law Inst. (life), Skyline Club (Southfield, Mich.). Office: Lakeview Capital Inc 2000 Town Ctr Ste 2400 Southfield MI 48075-1406 Office Phone: 248-213-2200. E-mail: rshields@alixpartners.com.

SHIELDS, THOMAS CHARLES, lawyer; b. Evergreen Park, Ill., Apr. 26, 1941; s. Thomas James and Adelaide (McElligott) Shields; m. Nicoline M. Murphy, Sept. 14, 1974; children: Thomas James II, Nicoline M. E., Suzanne Adelaide, Kerry Anne. AB, Georgetown U., 1963; JD cum laude, Northwestern U., 1966. Bar: Ill. 1966, U.S. Dist. Ct. (no. dist.) Ill. 1966, U.S. Ct. Appeals (7th cir.) 1966, U.S. Tax Ct. 1968, U.S. Supreme Ct. 1977. Assoc. Hopkins & Sutter, Chgo., 1966-73, ptnr., 1973-93; mem., chair health law dept. Bell, Boyd & Lloyd, Chgo., 1994—; chief counsel Cath. Health Assn. U.S., St. Louis, 1994—2005. Lectr. Ill. Inst. Continuing Legal Edn., 1973; mem. adv. bd. Health Law Inst. Loyola U. Sch. Law, Chgo., 1984—89, Health Law Inst. DePaul U. Sch. Law, Chgo., 1985—96. Contbr. articles to profl. jours. Trustee Village of Riverside, Ill., 2001—; mem. Ill. Health Facilities Authority, 2000—03; governing mem. Chgo. Zool. Soc., Chgo., Cath. Charities Chgo.; bd. dirs. Cancer Rsch. Found., Chgo., 1987—, Brother Louie and Fannie Roncoli Found., 1994—2006. Mem.: Chgo. Bar Assn., Ill. Assn. Healthcare Attys. (bd. dir. 1983—89, pres. 1987—88), Ill. Bar Assn., Am. Hosp. Assn. (tax adv. group 1987—90), Am. Health Lawyers Assn. (bd. dir. 1983—91, pres. 1989—90), Chgo. Power Squadron, U.S. Power Squadron (legal officer 2005—06), Mid-Am. Club Chgo. (bd. govs. 2001—, sec. 2004—), Order of Coif. Avocations: skiing, bicycling, golf, boating. Office: Bell Boyd & Lloyd 3 First Nat Plz 70 W Madison St Ste 3100 Chicago IL 60602 Office Phone: 312-807-4232. Business E-Mail: tshields@bellboyd.com.

SHIELDS, THOMAS WILLIAM, surgeon, educator; b. Ambridge, Pa., Aug. 17, 1922; s. John Jr. and Elizabeth (Flanagan) S.; m. Dorothea Ann Thomas, June 12, 1948; children: Thomas William, John Leland, Carol Ann. BA, Kenyon Coll., Gambier, Ohio, 1943, DSc (hon.), 1978; MD, Temple U., Phila., 1947. Resident surgery Northwestern U. Med. Sch., Chgo., 1949-55, prof. surgery, 1968-92, prof. Emeritus of surgery, 1992—; practice medicine specializing in surgery Chgo., 1956—; chief of surgery VA Lakeside Hosp., Chgo., 1968-87; chief thoracic surgery VA Lakeside Med. Ctr., Chgo., 1987-90. Editor: General Thoracic Surgery, 1972, 5th edit., 2000, 6th edit 2004, Bronchial Carcinoma, 1974, Mediastinal Surgery, 1991; assoc. editor Surgery, Gynecology and Obstetrics, Annals of Thoracic Surgery, 1993-2002; mem. editl. bd. Annals of Thoracic Surgery, Lung Cancer; contbr. articles to profl. jours. Served with U.S. Army, 1951-53. Mem. ACS, AMA, Am. Assn. for Thoracic Surgery, Soc. Thoracic Surgery, Central, Western Surg. Assns., Société Internationale de Chirurgie, Soc. for Surgery of Alimentary Tract, Internat. Assn. for Study Lung Cancer, Japanese Assn. Thoracic Surgery (hon.), Pa. Assn. Thoracic Surgery (hon.), Pan Pacific Surg. Assn., Phi Beta Kappa, Sigma Xi, Alpha Omega Alpha. Home: 10513 E Cinnabar Ave Scottsdale AZ 85258-4908 Office: Northwestern U Feinberg Sch Medicine Galter 3-150 201 E Huron St Chicago IL 60611 Office Phone: 480-451-8296. Personal E-mail: twshields@comcast.net.

SHIELDS, WILL HERTHIE, professional football player; b. Fort Riley, Kans., Sept. 15, 1971; m. Senia Shields; 2 children. Degree in comm., U. Nebr. Guard Kansas City Chiefs, 1993—. Named to Pro Bowl, 1996-1999, 2001-2005 Office: Kansas City Chiefs 1 Arrowhead Dr Kansas City MO 64129-1651

SHIELDS, WILLIAM DONALD, physician, educator; b. Salt Lake City, Oct. 29, 1941; s. F. Alburn and Ruth (Clawson) Shields; m. Virginia Mary Howell, May 19, 1970; children: Stephen Christopher, Justin Michael, Christine Rebecca. BA in chemistry, U. Utah, 1967; MD, U. Utah Sch. Medicine, Salt Lake City, 1967—71. Cert. in neurology with special competence in child neurology Am. Bd. Psychiatry and Neurology, 1977, diplomate Am. Bd. Pediat., 1978. Resident U. So. Calif., LA, 1971—73; fellow U. Utah, Salt Lake City, 1973—76; asst. prof. UCLA Sch. Medicine, 1976—83, assoc. prof., 1983—90, prof., 1990—, Rubin Brown prof., 1999. Chief, divsn. pediatric neurology UCLA Sch. Medicine, 1980—2005. Contbr. chapters to books, articles to profl. jours. Pres., bd. mem. Epilepsy Found. L.A., 1981—88; mem. profl. adv. bd. Epilepsy Found. Am., Landover, Md. Named a Top Dr., Am.'s Top Doctors, 2001—07; recipient Maxwell J. Schleifer Disting. Svc. Award, Exceptional Parent Found., 2004; grantee, Milken Family Found., 1986—2004, NIH, 1992—98. Fellow: Am. Acad. Pediat.; mem.: Nat. Inst. Neurologic Disease and Stroke, L.A. County Epilepsy Soc. (chmn. profl. adv. bd. 1981—86, pres. 1986—89), Am. Acad. Neurology, Profs. Child Neurology, Am.

Epilepsy Soc. (Svc. Award 1996), Child Neurology Soc. (counselor 1994—96). Office: David Geffen Sch Medicine UCLA 10833 LeConte Ave Los Angeles CA 90095-1752 Home Phone: 818-991-0969; Office Phone: 310-825-6196. Office Fax: 310-825-5834. Business E-Mail: wshields@mednet.ucla.edu.

SHIELY, JOHN STEPHEN, manufacturing executive, lawyer; b. June 19, 1952; s. Vincent Robert and Mary Elizabeth (Hope) Shiely; m. Helen Jane Pauly, Aug. 29, 1981; children: Michael, Erin, Megan. BBA, U. Notre Dame, 1974; JD, Marquette U., 1977; M in Mgmt., Northwestern U., 1990. With Arthur Andersen & Co., Milw., 1977-79, Hughes Hubbard & Reed, Milw., 1979-83, Allen-Bradley Co., Milw., 1983-86, Rockwell Internat. Corp., Milw., 1985-86, Briggs & Stratton Corp., Milw., 1986—, gen. counsel, 1986-90, v.p., gen. counsel, 1990-91, pres., COO, 1994-2001, pres., CEO, 2001—03, chmn., pres., CEO, 2003—. Bd. dirs. Briggs & Stratton Corp., Quad/Graphics, Inc., Pewaukee, Wis., Marshall & Ilsley Corp., Milw., Scotts Miracle-Gro Co. Mem. Greater Milw. Com., 2000—; chmn. bd. Children's Hosp. and Health Sys., 2005—; mem. bd. regents Milw. Sch. Engring., 1995—; trustee Med. Coll. Wis., 2003—; mem. corp. bd. dirs. Rock and Roll Hall of Fame and Mus.; bd. dirs. Outdoor Power Equipment Inst. Mem.: Assn. Corp. Growth (past pres. Wis. chpt. 1988—). Office: Briggs & Stratton Corp PO Box 702 Milwaukee WI 53201-0702

SHIEMBOB, MARK S., lawyer; b. Hartford, Conn., 1956; BA with distinction, Univ. Va., 1978, JD, 1982. Bar: Va. 1982. Ptnr., sect. chief, fin. Troutman Sanders LLP, Richmond, Va., mem. exec. com. Mem.: Va. Bar Assn., Am. Coll. Real Estate Lawyers, Mortgage Bankers Assn. Am. Office: Troutman Sanders LLP PO Box 1122 Richmond VA 23218-1122 also: Troutman Sanders LLP Troutman Sanders Bldg 1001 Haxall Point Richmond VA 23219 Office Fax: 804-697-1455, 804-698-6004. Business E-Mail: mark.shiembob@troutmansanders.com.

SHIENTAG, FLORENCE PERLOW, lawyer; b. NYC; d. David and Ester (Germane) Perlow; m. Bernard L. Shientag, June 8, 1938. BS, NYU, 1940, LLB, 1933, JD, 1940. Bar: Fla. 1976, N.Y. Law aide Thomas E. Dewey, 1937; law sec. Mayor La Guardia, 1939-42; justice Domestic Relations Ct., 1941-42; mem. Tchrs. Retirement Bd., NYC, 1942-46; asst. U.S. atty. So. dist. NY, 1943-53; cir. ct. mediator Fla. Supreme Ct., 1992; pvt. practice NYC, 1960—, Palm Beach, Fla., 1976—. Lectr. on internat. divorce; mem. Nat. Commn. on Wiretapping and Electronic Surveillance, 1973—, Task Force on Women in Cts., 1985-86. Contbr. articles to profl. jours. Candidate NY State Senate, 1954; bd. dirs. UN Devel. Corp., 1972-95, Franklin and Eleanor Roosevelt Inst., 1985—; bd. dirs., assoc. treas. YM and YWHA; hon. commr. commerce, NYC. Mem. ABA, Fed. Bar Assn. (exec. com.), Internat. Bar Assn., NY Women's Bar Assn. (pres., dir., Life Time Achievement award 1994, special award 2002), NY State Bar Assn., NYC Bar Assn. (chmn. law and art sect.), NY County Lawyers Assn. (dir.), Nat. Assn. Women LAwyers (sec.). Home: 737 Park Ave New York NY 10021-4256 Address: 44 Cocoanut Row Palm Beach FL 33480 Office Phone: 212-861-8800. *Success is a product of self respect and hard work at what you do well.*

SHIER, GLORIA BULAN, mathematics professor; b. The Philippines; came to U.S., 1966. d. Melecio Cauilan and Florentina (Cumagun) Bulan; m. Wayne Thomas Shier; children: John Thomas, Marie Teresita, Anna Christina. BS, U. Santo Tomas; MA, U. Ill., 1968; PhD, U. Minn., 1986. Tchr. Cagayan Valley Coll., Cagayan, Philippines, St. Paul Coll., Manila, Manila Div. City Schs.; asst. prof. U. of East, Manila; rsch. asst. U. Ill., Urbana, 1968—69; instr. Miramar C.C., San Diego, 1974—75, Mesa C.C., San Diego, 1975—80, Lakewood C.C., St. Paul, 1984, U. Minn., Mpls., 1986—87, North Hennepin C.C., Brooklyn Park, Minn., 1987—. Cons. PWS Kent Pub. Co., Boston, 1989—. Chairperson Filipino Am. Edn. Assn., San Diego, 1978-79. Fulbright scholar U.S. State Dept., U. Ill., 1966-70; fellow Nat. Sci. Found., Oberlin Coll., 1967; recipient Excellence in Teaching award UN Ednl. Scientific Cultural Organ., U. Philippines, Cert. Commendation award The Gov. of Minn., 1990, Outstanding Filipino in the Midwest Edn. Cat. award 1992, Cavite Assn., 1998, Gintong Pamana Found.; Outstanding Filipino-Am. in Edn. Mem.: Am. Statis. Assn., Minn. Math. Assn. of Two Yr. Colls., Minn. Coun. Tchrs. Math., Internat. Group for Psychology of Math. Edn., Am. Math. Assn. for Two Yr. Colls., Nat. Coun. Tchrs. Math., Philippine-Am. Acad. Sci. and Engring., Math. Assn. Am., Am. Math. Soc., Fil-Minnesotan Assn. (bd. dirs. 1991—2004, v.p. 2004—), Cultural Soc. Filipino-Ams. (pres. 2001—), Sigma Xi, Phi Kappa Phi. Roman Catholic. Avocation: piano. Office Phone: 763-424-0834. Business E-Mail: mail@bogason.dk.

SHIER, JULIET MARIE, social studies educator; b. Seattle, Jan. 23, 1967; d. James E. and Martha L. Hall; m. Peter M. Shier, Nov. 29, 1991; children: Katherine L., Emily A., Mary E. MS in Edn., Western Oreg. U., Monmouth, 2000. Cert. tchr. K-8 Alaska, 1991. Tchr. 2d and 6th Cath. Schs. of Fairbanks, Alaska, 1991—95; reading tchr. Hunter Elem., Fairbanks, 1996—97; kindergarten tchr. Anderson Elem., Eielson AFB, Alaska, 1997—99; tchr. 2d grade Pearl Creek Elem., Fairbanks, 1999; tchr. English and lit. North Pole Mid. Sch., Fairbanks, 2000—03; tchr. English and social studies Tanana Mid. Sch., Fairbanks, 2003—. Mentor tchr. U. Alaska, Fairbanks, 2004—. Religious edn. and youth group Cath. D. of Fairbanks, 2002—. Mem.: NEA (assoc.). Catholic. Avocations: travel, reading, kayaking, theater, skiing. Home: P O Box 84615 Fairbanks AK 99708 Office: Fairbanks North Star Borough School Dist 520 5th Ave Fairbanks AK 99701 Home Phone: 907-474-3021; Office Phone: 907-452-8145 9166. Business E-Mail: jshier@northstar.k12.ak.us.

SHIER, SHELLEY M., production company executive; b. Toronto, Mar. 15, 1957; d. Harry Shier and Rosaline (Cutler) Sonshine; m. Hank O'Neal, May 14, 1985. Student, H.B. Studio, NYC, 1975—76, Stella Adler Conservatory, 1976—80. Company mem., actor Soho Artists Theater, NYC, 1976-81; casting dir. Lawrence Price Prodns., NYC, 1981-82; pres. Hoss, Inc., NYC, 1983—; v.p. Chiaroscuro Records, NYC, 1987—; pres. Broadway Bound, Inc., NYC, 1998—. Cons. Peter Martin Assocs., NYC, 1983, Norwegian Cruise Line, Miami, Fla., 1983-98, Floating Jazz Festival, 1983—,Oslo (Norway) Jazz Festival, 1986—, New Sch. Social Rsch., NYC, 1989—, Big Bands Sea, Rhythm & Blues Cruise, Dixieland Sea, 1991—, Blues Cruise, 1991—, Beacons Jazz Awards Ceremony, Tribute Music Bob Wills Texas Playboys, Mardi Gras Sea. Talent acquisition agt. Save Children, NYC, 1986, Tomorrow's Children, NYC, 1990, Barcelona Olympics, NBC, 1992, Royal Caribbean Internat., Miami, 1994-96, Ultimate Caribbean Jazz Spectacular, Country Music Festival Caribbean, CUNARD NYC, 1994—, Broadway Sea, 1996, Millennium Sea, 1999—, Broadway Bound, 1999—, others. Avocations: Karate, photography, riding, fishing, weightlifting. Office: HOSS Inc 830 Broadway New York NY 10003-4827 Home Phone: 212-598-4325; Office Phone: 212-674-8631, 212-674-8631. Personal E-mail: shelleymshier@aol.com. Business E-Mail: broadwayboundinc@aol.com.

SHIER, SUSAN LYNNE, music educator; d. Elmer C. and Clara M. Werning; m. Robert L. Shier, June 4, 1982; children: Robert Matthew, Blake M. MusB in Edn., Ctrl. Mo. State U., Warrensburg, 1977, MA in Edn., 1985. Cert. instrumental and vocal music tchr. K-12 Mo., 1977. Band and vocal tchr. King City Sch. Dist., Mo., 1977—81, Platte County R-III Sch. Dist., Platte City, 1981—. V.p. North Ctrl. Mo. Bandmasters, Chillicothe, Mo., 1988—89; bldg. planning com. Platte County R-III Sch. Dist., Platte City, 1988—89, 2004—, new tchr. mentor, 1992—; corr. sec. Platte County Educator Assn., 2005—. Mem. Pk. Hill South Band Parents, Riverside, Mo., PTA, Kansas City, 1981—2005; vol. local recycling ctr.; den mother Cub Scouts, Parkville, 1994—96. Nominee Excellence in Edn., Northland C. of C., 2006. Mem.: NEA, Mo. Music Educators, Mo. Bandmasters Assn., Platte County Edn. Assn. (corr. sec. 2005—06), Mo. Edn. Assn., Kappa Delta Pi, Pi Kappa Lambda, Sigma Alpha Iota (v.p. 1979—80). Democrat. Achievements include directing high school band selected to perform at Missouri Music Educators Conference; directing bands earning I ratings at District and State festivals; directing band selected to play for U.S. president during visit to Kansas City. Avocations: gardening, reading, travel. Office: Platte County R III Sch Dist PO Box 1400 Platte City MO 64079 Home Phone: 816-587-4049; Office Phone: 816-436-9623. Business E-Mail: shiers@periii.k12.mo.us.

SHIFFER, JAMES DAVID, retired utilities executive; b. San Diego, Mar. 24, 1938; s. Kenneth Frederick and Thelma Lucille (Good) S.; m. Margaret Edith Rightmyer, Sept. 5, 1959 (div. July 1986); children: James II, Elizabeth, Russell; m. Esther Zamora, Sept. 13, 1986; stepchildren: Bryan Boots, Jeremy Hellier, Marisol Loughead. BS in Chem. Engring., Stanford U., 1960, MS in Chem. Engring., 1962. Registered profl. engr., Calif. Nuc. engr. Pacific Gas & Electric Co., Humboldt Bay Power Plant, Eureka, Calif., 1961-71; tech. mgr. Pacific Gas & Electric. Co., Diablo Canyon Power Plant, Avila Beach, Calif., 1971-80; mgr. nuc. ops. Pacific Gas & Electric Co., San Francisco, 1980-84, v.p. nuc. power generation, 1984-90, sr. v.p., gen. mgr. nuc. power generation bus. unit, 1990-91; exec. v.p. Pacific Gas & Electric, San Francisco, 1991-97; ret., 1997; pres., CEO PG&E Enterprises, San Francisco, 1994-95, also bd. dirs. Bd. dirs. Math., Engring., Sci. Achievement, 1992-2002. Mem. AIChE, Am. Nuc. Soc., Commonwealth Club of Calif. (bd. govs. 1992-97). Republican. Episcopalian. Avocations: golf, music. Home: 2550 Royal Oaks Dr Alamo CA 94507-2227 E-mail: jshiffer@msn.com.

SHIFFMAN, BERNARD, mathematician, educator; b. NYC, 1942; s. Max and Bella S.; m. Doris Judith Yaffe, July 11, 1965; children: Jonathan, Daniel. BS, MIT, 1964; PhD, U. Calif., Berkeley, 1968. C.L.E. Moore instr. MIT, 1968-70; asst. prof. math. Yale U., 1970-73; assoc. prof. Johns Hopkins U., Balt., 1973-77, prof., 1977—, chair dept. math., 1990-93. Mem. Inst. Advanced Study, Princeton, NJ, 1975, Math. Scis. Rsch. Inst., Berkeley, Calif., 1996, 99; series lectr. U. Kaiserslautern, West Germany, 1977, Inst. Math., Academia Sinica, Beijing, 1978, U. Paris VI, 1979, Nordic Summer Sch., Joensuu, Finland, 1981, U. Tokyo, 2000; mem. Inst. des Hautes Etudes Scientifiques, Bures-sur-Yvette, France, 1979; vis. prof. U. Paris VI, 1981, 85, U. Grenoble, 1992, 95, 2001, 03. Editor Forum Mathematicum, 1989-95; assoc. editor Am. Jour. Math., 1990-92, 2005—, editor, 1992-93, editor-in-chief, 1993-2005; rschr. publs. in complex analysis. Hon. Woodrow Wilson fellow, 1964, NSF fellow, 1965-68, Alfred P. Sloan rsch. fellow, 1973-75; recipient Woodrow Wilson Faculty Devel. award, 1979. Mem. Am. Math. Soc. Office: Johns Hopkins U Dept Math Baltimore MD 21218

SHIFFMAN, MICHAEL A., lawyer; b. Newark, July 23, 1941; LLB magna cum laude, Lincoln U., 1973. Bar: Calif. 1973, U.S. Dist. Ct. (no. dist.) Calif. 1973; lic. real estate broker. Atty. Lanahan & Reilley, San Francisco, EVP and GC-New City N. Am. Editor: Lincoln U. Law Rev., 1972-73. Mem. ABA, Internat. Bar Assn., State Bar Calif. Office: New City N Am 575 Market No 3050 San Francisco CA 94105 Business E-Mail: shifflaw@aol.com.

SHIFFRIN, NANCY, writer, educator; d. Martin and Minna Shiffrin. BA, Calif. State U., 1972; PhD, Union Inst., 1994. Adj. prof. LA Cmty. Coll. Dist., 1990—. Editl. and manuscript cons. Author: What She Could Not Name, 1987, The Holy Letters, 2000, My Jewish Name, 2002. Recipient 1st prize, Acad. Am. Poets Coll. Competition, 1972. Jewish. Avocations: yoga, hiking, Jewish culture. Office: PO Box 1506 Santa Monica CA 90406-1506 Home Phone: 310-463-6722; Office Phone: 310-302-1107. Personal E-mail: nshiffrin@earthlink.net.

SHIFRIN, DONALD LEE, pediatrician; b. Portland, Oreg., Jan. 10, 1949; m. Barbara Sue Chamberlin, Nov. 3, 2002; children: Max Burton, Alexis Chamberlin. MD, Georgetown U., Washington, 1970. Cert. Am. Bd. Pediatics, 1981. Physician Pediatric Assocs., Bellevue, Wash., 1978—. Clin. prof. pediat. U. Wash. Sch. Medicine, Seattle; nat. adv. bd. Civitas. Chair Maimonides Soc. Jewish Fedn. Greater Seattle, 2000—. Fellow: Am. Acad. Pediat. Office: Pedatric Associates 2700 Northup Way Bellevue WA 98004 Office Phone: 425-827-4600. Office Fax: 425-828-2256; Home Fax: 206-275-3244. Business E-Mail: dshifrin@peds-associates.com.

SHIFRIN, HARRIS DAVID, physician; b. Washington, June 4, 1936; s. William and Rose (Wein) S.; children: Arthur, Roger, Renee. BS in Chemistry, George Washington U., 1958, MD, 1962. Intern Montefiore Hosp., Bronx, NY, 1962-63; internal medicine resident U. N.C., Chapel Hill, 1965-67; gastrointestinal fellow Jackson Meml. Hosp., Miami, Fla., 1967—69, gastroenterologist Hollywood, Fla., 1969—2004, attending physician, 2004—. Author: Gastrointestinal Endoscopy, 1972, Gastroenterology, 1995; contbr. articles to profl. jours. Capt. USAF, 1963-65. Fellow ACP, Am. Coll. Gastroenterology; mem. Am. Gastrointestinal Assn. Republican. Jewish. Avocation: collecting watches. Office Phone: 305-585-6827. Personal E-mail: spioman@comcast.net.

SHIGEMASA, TERESA, mental health services professional, educator; d. Kermin Joseph Guidry and Melva Gene Bell; m. Greg Uichi Shigemasa, June 29, 1996; children: Emily Guidry-Nguyen, Skye. BFA, So. Meth. U., Dallas, 1977; MSCP, Chaminade U., Honolulu, 2000. Cert. LMHC #1, DCCA Hawaii, 2005, RPT-S, S-874 Assn. Play Therapy, 2006, registered play therapist, supr. play therapist candidates Assn. Play Therapy, 2006. Instr. domestic violence Child & Family Svc., Honolulu, 1998—2001; behavioral specialist Dept. Edn.-Sunset Beach Elem. Sch., Haleiwa, Hawaii, 2001—. Dancer, singer, actress profl. summer stock prodns., Dallas, Brunswick, Maine. Vol. local schs. various musical prodns. Mem.: Hawaii Assn. Play Therapy (pub. rels. 2005—06), Assn. Play Therapy, Hawaii Counseling Assn., Psi Chi Honor Soc., Alpha Lambda Delta. Avocations: dance, music. Office: Dept Edn Sunset Beach Elem Sch 59-360 Kamehameha Hwy Haleiwa HI 96712 Personal E-mail: tshigema21@yahoo.com.

SHIGEMITSU, TOSHIRO, ophthalmologist, researcher; b. Kyoto, Feb. 7, 1953; s. Yoshito and Eiko (Yoshioka) S.; m. Kumiko Nakahori, Oct. 27, 1990. MD, Fujita Health U., Toyoake, Japan, 1982, DMS, 1987. Asst. prof. ophthalmology Fujita Health U., Toyoake, 1988-91, assoc. prof. ophthalmology, 1991—2001, vis. assoc. prof. ophthalmology, 2002—. Dir. ophthalmology Hojinkai Med. Found., Kawade Hosp., Toyota, 1984—99. Patentee in field; contbr. articles to profl. jours. Mem. judging com. Fund Med. Security Sys., Aichi, 1996—2002. Recipient Japan Soc. Clin. Ophthalmology poster prize, 1998, Silver medal, Japan Ophthalmol. Soc., 1990; grantee Eye Bank Assn. Aichi, 1993, 94, 95. Mem.: Am. Acad. Opthalmology, Toikai Med. Assn. (bd. dirs. 1999—2005), Japanese Soc. Pathology (sci. councillor 2001—), Toukai Soc. Glaucoma (bd. dirs. 1998—2002), Asia Pacific Intraocular Implant Assn. (faculty 1997—98), Japanese Ophthalmic Pathology Soc. (councillor 1997—), Am. Aging Assn., European Soc. Cataract and Refractive Surgeons, Am. Soc. Cataract and Refractive Surgery. Avocations: travel, movies, golf, art. Office: Shigemitsu Eye Clin & Rsch Fdn Inc 3-6-23 Kuzuha-Asahi Hirakata 573-1111 Japan Office Phone: 81 72 866 2238.

SHIH, FRANKLIN, physician; s. Cheng and Helen Shih. MD, U. Calif., Davis, 1984—88. Lic. dr. Am. Bd. PMR, 1993, AANEM, 1996. Physician Rehab. Assoc. Co., Thornton, 1992—, pres., 2002—. Office: Rehab Assocs Co 8515 Pearl St Ste 100 Thornton CO 80229

SHIH-CARDUCCI, JOAN CHIA-MO, food service executive, educator, medical technologist, writer, biochemist; b. Rukuan, Chunghua, Taiwan, Dec. 21, 1933; came to U.S., 1955; d. Luke Chiang-hsi and Lien-chin Shih; m. Kenneth M. Carducci, Sept. 30, 1960 (dec. July 1988); children: Suzanne R., Elizabeth M. BS in Chemistry, St. Mary Coll., Xavier, Kans., 1959; intern in med. tech., St. Mary's Hosp., Rochester, NY, 1960. Med. rschr. Strong Meml. Hosp. U. Rochester, 1960-61; pharm. chemist quality control Strasenburgh Labs., Rochester, 1961-62; cooking tchr. adult edn. Montgomery County Pub. Schs., Rockville, Md., 1973-79; tchr. The Chinese Cookery Inc., Rockville, 1975-86, Silver Spring, Md., 1986—, pres., bd. dirs., 1975—; chemist NIH, Bethesda, 1987-2000; analytical chemist NIH/WRAIR, Rockville, Md., 1994-96. Author: The Chinese Cookery, 1981, Hunan Cuisine, 1984, Vegetarian Cuisine, 2000, The Art of The Chinese Cookery, 2001 (Pinnacle Book award 2005). Mem. Am. Chem. Soc., Internat. Assn. Cooking Profls. (Woman of Yr. 1994-2004). Republican. Roman Catholic. Avocations: piano, music, dance, gardening. Home and Office: The Chinese Cookery Inc 14209 Sturtevant Rd Silver Spring MD 20905-4448 Office Phone: 301-236-5311.

SHIKLER, AARON A., artist; b. Bklyn., Mar. 18, 1922; s. Frank and Annie (Blai) S.; m. Barbara Lurie, Oct. 4, 1947; children: Cathy M., Clifford M. B.F.A., BS in Edn.; M.F.A., Tyler Sch. Fine Arts, Temple U., 1948; student, Barnes Found., Merion, Pa., 1941-43, Hans Hoffmann Sch., NYC, 1949-51. One man shows, Davis Galleries, N.Y.C., 1953, 54, 56, 58, 60, 62, 64, 67, 71, 83, 84, Bklyn. Museum, 1971, Palace of Legion of Honor, San Francisco, 1971, Long Gallery, Houston, 1972, 76, 82, 85, Davis & Long Co., 1975, 79, Temple U., 1985, Claude Bernard Gallery, Paris, 1988, Davis & Langdale Co., 1987, 90, 93, 2000, 03, Kunsthaus Bühler, Stuttgart, Germany, 2002; represented in permanent collections, Montclair (N.J.) Mus., Hofstra Mus. Art, L.I., Carnegie Inst., Pitts., Met. Mus. Art, Mint Mus. Art, Charlotte, N.C., Parrish Mus. Art, Southampton, L.I., N.A.D., Bklyn. Mus., Hirshorn Mus., Washington, Nat. Art Gallery, Wellington, N.Z., Nat. Gallery, Singapore, New Britain Mus. Am. Art, Sun Rise Mus., Charleston, W.Va., Sheldon Meml. Art Gallery, Lincoln, Nebr., Pa. State U. Gallery, Davis Galleries, 1987, Lyme Acad., 1986; executed: portraits Pres. and Mrs. John F. Kennedy for White House, Robert Lehman Pavilion at Met. Mus. Art, Henry F. duPont for Winterthur (Del.) Mus., Robert F. Kennedy for Dept. Justice, Washington, Sec. Carla Hills for HUD, Sec. Carla Hills for Yale Law Sch., Mrs. Lyndon B. Johnson for Johnson Library, Austin, Tex., Senator Mike Mansfield for U.S. Senate, Washington, Dr. Michael DeBakey for Baylor U., Pres.-Elect Ronald Reagan as Man of Yr. for Time mag., James M. Walton for Carnegie Inst., Pitts., Pres. Ronald Reagan and Mrs. Reagan for The White House, Andrew Heiskell for N.Y. Pub. Libr., William S. Paley for Mus. Broadcasting, Dr. Vartan Gregorian, N.Y. Pub. Libr., Dr. Manuel Koehane, Wesley Coll., Mass., Hillary R. Clinton for Time mag., 1999. Served with inf. AUS, 1943-46. Recipient Tiffany award, 1958; Dept. State grantee S.E. Asia and South Pacific, 1976; Temple U. Centennial fellow, 1985. Mem. NAD (Ranger award 1959, Proctor prize 1959, 60, Clarke prize 1961, Altman prize 1976). Clubs: Century Assn.

SHIKUMA, EUGENE YUJIN, travel company executive; b. Tokyo, Nov. 18, 1948; arrived in U.S., 1957; s. Mitsuo and Yukiko (Kanaoka) Shikuma. BSEE, U. Hawaii at Manoa, Honolulu, 1971, MS in Computer Sci., 1975. Lab. test engr. and scientist McDonnell Douglas Astronautics, Inc., 1971-72; systems engr. Lear Siegler Astronics, 1972-73; jr. coord. Japan Travel Bur. Hawaii, Inc., Honolulu, 1978-83, sr. coord., 1983-84, supr., 1984-89, mgr., 1989—. Bd. dir. Maui United Way, Kahului, Hawaii, 1988—89, Maui Hui Malama, Waiulku, 1989—90; mem. Maui County Visitor Task Force, 1995—; adv. bd. mem. Maui Acad. Travel and Tourism; bd. dir. Maui Visitors Bur., 2003—; mem. Maui Sister Cities Internat. Festival Com., 2005; com. mem. Maui County Sister Cities Festival, 2005, Maui Tourism Strategic Plan Com., 2005—; hon. chmn. bus. adv. coun. Hawaii Nat. Rep. Congl. Com., 2003; bd. dir., sec. Kamoa Views Apt. Owners Assn., 1991—96. Named Businessman of Yr., Nat. Rep. Congl. Com., 2004, Rep. of Yr., 2006; recipient Ronald Reagan Rep. Hawaii Gold medal, 2004, 2005, Congl. medal of distinction, 2006, Congl. Order Merit, 2006, 2007. Mem.: Maui Japanese C. of C., Maui C. of C. Avocations: swimming, coin collecting/numismatics, art, antique prints. Office Phone: 808-871-6600. Business E-Mail: eshikuma@jtb-hawaii.com.

SHILEPSKY, NANCY SUE, lawyer; b. Westport, Conn., Apr. 25, 1952; d. Morris Jacob and Rose (Pfeffer) S. BA magna cum laude, Tufts U., 1974; JD, Boston U., 1978. Bar: Mass. 1978, U.S. Dist. Ct. Mass. 1978. Dir. Legal Info. Ctr. Bklyn. Coll., 1978-79; staff atty. Western Mass. Legal Svcs., Springfield, 1980-81; ptnr. Northampton (Mass.) Law Collective, 1982-84; assoc. Schreiber & Assocs., Boston, 1984-87, McDonald, Noonan & Kaplan, Newton, Mass., 1987-88; ptnr. Rudavsky & Shilepsky, Boston, 1988, Shilepsky, Messing & Rudavsky, Boston, 1988—2005, Perkins Smith& Cohen, Boston, Shilepsky O'Connell, Boston, 2005—. Speaker Mass. Continuing Legal Edn., Inc., Boston, 1988—. Named one of top Boston lawyers, Boston Mag., 2004. Mem.: Boston Bar Assn. (treas. 2004—05), Mass. Bar Assn.-Labor & Employment Law Sect. (chmn. employee rights & responsibilities com. 1990—91, 1993—94, sect. coun. 1993—96), Boston Bar Assn.-Labor & Employment Law Sect. (co-chmn. 1996—99, sect. coun. 1996—). Office: Shilepsky O'Connell 225 Franklin St Boston MA 02110 Home Phone: 617-484-1779; Office Phone: 617-854-4275, 617-447-2806. Office Fax: 617-854-4040. Business E-Mail: nshilepsky@sholaw.com.

SHILLER, ROBERT JAMES, economist, educator; b. Detroit, Mar. 29, 1946; s. Benjamin P. and Ruth R. (Radzville) S.; m. Virginia M. Faulstich, June 13, 1976; 2 sons. BA, U. Mich., 1967; SM, MIT, 1968, PhD, 1972. Asst. prof. U. Minn., 1972-74; rsch. fellow Nat. Bur. Econ. Rsch., Cambridge, Mass., 1974-75; vis. scholar dept. econs. MIT, Cambridge, 1974-75, vis. prof., 1981-82; assoc. prof. dept. econs. U. Pa., Phila., 1974-81, prof. econs., 1981-82; prof. fin. Wharton Sch., 1981-82; prof. econs. Yale U., New Haven, 1982—. Co-founder Case, Shiller, Weiss Inc., MacroMarkets, LLC; vis. scholar dept. econs. Harvard U., 1980. Fgn. editor Rev. Econ. Studies, 1981-84; assoc. editor Jour. Econometrics, 1980-83; author: Market Volatility, 1989, Macro Markets, 1993, Irrational Exuberance, 2000, 2d edit., 2005, New Financial Order, 2003. Grantee NSF, 1976—; Guggenheim fellow. Fellow Econometric Soc., Am. Acad. Arts and Scis., Am. Philos. Soc., Am. Econ. Assn. (v.p. 2005), Ea. Econ. Assn. (pres. 2006-07). Office: Yale U Cowles Found New Haven CT 06520-8281 Office Phone: 203-432-3708. Business E-Mail: robert.shiller@yale.edu.

SHILLESTAD, JOHN GARDNER, diversified financial services company executive; b. Oak Park, Ill., Oct. 31, 1934; s. John Nelson and Isabel Blanche (Gardner) Shillestad; m. Astri Cedervall; children: Christine C, Annette. BBA, Northwestern U., 1964, MBA, 1967. CLU, CPCU; ChFC. Mktg. dir. spl. plans CNA Ins., Chgo., 1958-66; asst. v.p. Montgomery Ward Life, Chgo., 1966-69; pres., CEO Fort Dearborn Life Ins. Co., Chgo., 1969-79; sr. v.p. Hartford Life Cos., Conn., 1979-85, also bd. dirs. Conn., 1985-87; pres. JGS Fin. Svcs., Inc., 1987—2007, Columbian Mut. Life Ins. Co., Binghamton, NY, 1987—2007. Chmn. Columbian Life Ins Co, Washington Nat. Life NY; with Golden Eagles Sales Corp., 1997—2007; bd. dirs. Reassure Am, Valley Forge Life Ins. Co., 2004. Mem Bd Educ, Dist 30, Northbrook, Ill., 1976—79; mem adv bd SUNY Sch Mgt, Binghamton, Kellogg Sch Bus, Northwestern Univ; bd dirs Salvation Army, Binghamton, Partnership 2000, Southern Tier Equity Fund. With US Army, 1954—56. Mem.: Broome County CofC (bd dirs), Pelican Marsh

Golf Club (Naples, Fla), Sunset Ridge Club (Northfield, Ill). Republican. Congregationalist. Home: 3 Regentwood Rd Northfield IL 60093-2728 also: Unit 304 1600 Clermont Dr Naples FL 34109 E-mail: sjackshil@aol.com.

SHILLING, A. GARY, economist, consultant; b. Fremont, Ohio, May 25, 1937; s. A. Vaughn and Lettie E. (O'Harrow) S.; m. Margaret E. Bloete, Dec. 22, 1962; children: Geoffrey B., Andrew J., Stephen E., Jennifer E. AB in Physics magna cum laude, Amherst Coll., Mass., 1960; MA in Econs., Stanford U., Calif., 1962, PhD in Econs., 1965; LLD (hon.), Tiffin U., 1999; DHL (hon.), Ch. Divinity Sch. Pacific, 2006. Economist Standard Oil Co. (N.J.), NYC, 1963-67; chief economist Merrill Lynch, Pierce, Fenner & Smith, NYC, 1967-71; rsch. dir. Estabrook & Co., NYC, 1971-72; sr. v.p., chief economist White, Weld & Co., NYC, 1972-78; chmn., pres., dir. A. Gary Shilling & Co., Inc., Springfield, NJ, 1978—; pres. Lakeview Econ. Svcs., Inc., Springfield, 1979—; owner Lakeview Svcs., Inc., Springfield, 1993—. Bd. dirs. Nat. Life Vt., Montpelier, 1989, Palm Harbor Homes, Am. Productivity and Quality Ctr., Houston; adv. dir. Austin (Tex.) Trust Co., 1988—, Nat. Life Vt., Montpelier, 1989-2007; informal econ. advisor Former Pres. George Bush, 1978—; mem. Nat. Com. on Jobs and Small Bus., 1986-87. Author: Is Inflation Ending? Are You Ready?, 1983, The World Has Definitely Changed: New Economic Forces and Their Implications for the Next Decade, 1986, After the Crash: Recession or Depression? Investment and Business Strategies for a Deflationary World, 1988, Deflation: Why it's coming, whether it's good or bad, and how it will affect your investments, business, and personal affairs, 1998, Korean and Chinese edits., 2000, Deflation: How to Survive and Thrive in the Coming Wave of Deflation, 1999, Chinese edit., 2000, Letting Off Steam, 2003; creator bd. game The Deflation Game, 1989; columnist Forbes, 1983—, Nihon Keizai Shimbun Jour. Bd. dirs. Aim Packaging Inc., 1986-89, Episcopal Ch. Found., N.Y.C., N.Y., 1989-97; chmn. Episcopal Preaching Found., Springfield, N.J., 1988—; trustee Bates Coll., Lewiston, Maine, 1988-91, Kent Pl. Sch., Summit, N.J., 1983-89, Henry J. Kessler Found., 1987-95; bd. dirs. The Gen. Theol. Episcopal Sem., N.Y.C., 1988-2001, treas., 1994-2001; chmn. N.J. State Revenue Forecasting Adv. Commn., 1995-2005; bd. dirs. Am. Rep. Ins. Co. N.Y., 1978-81, N.J. Shakespeare Festival, 1987-96, chmn., 1994-96. Named Wall St. Top Econs., Instl. Investor Mag., 1975, 76, Top Commodity Trading Advisor, Futures Mag., 1993, Third best Stockmarket Forecaster in the World, Money Sense Mag., 2003. Mem. Nat. Assn. Bus. Economics, N.Y. Soc. Security Analysts, Short Hills Club, Phi Beta Kappa, Sigma Xi. Republican. Episcopalian. Avocations: tennis, travel, gardening, hunting, fishing. Home: 33 Lakeview Ave Short Hills NJ 07078-2264 Office: A Gary Shilling & Co Inc 500 Morris Ave Springfield NJ 07081-1020 Office Phone: 973-467-0070. Business E-Mail: gary@agaryshilling.com.

SHILLING, KAY MARLENE, psychiatrist; b. July 1, 1953; d. Harrison Gene and Rose Marie (Allen) Herber. BS, U. Nebr., Lincoln, 1976; MD, U. Nebr., Omaha, 1980. Diplomate Nat. Bd. Med. Examiners. Resident in psychiatry U. Nebr. Med. Ctr., Omaha, 1981-84; pvt. practice Omaha, 1984—; med. dir., chief of staff La Plaza (Nebr.) Cmty. Health Ctr., 1999—, also bd. dirs. Encore chair Omaha Symphony Guild, 2000—04, v.p. adminstrn., 2003—04, mem. nominating com., 2002, chair Spring Fundraiser, 2004, exec. bd., 2003—04; mem. Henry Doorly Zoo Guild; mem. bd. Opera Omaha Guild, 2003—, chair Holiday meeting, 2004, chair ann. meetings, 2003—04, 2006—07; mem. Fontenelle Nature assn. Guild, 1999—, Omaha Bot. Gardens Guild, 2001—; chair spring fundraiser Omaha Symphony Music Cir., 2004—, chmn. ann. meeting, 2004—05; bd. trustees faculty com. Grace U.; bd. dirs. Indian Chicano Health Ctr., 1983—92, Opera Omaha, 2004—, Omaha Symphony Guild, 1999—2000, Museo Latino Feria, 2004—05; mem. guild bd. Western Heritage Mus. Durham Soc., 2005—06; co-chair 1st Lady Luncheon Durham Soc., 2006. Mem. AMA, Royal Soc. Medicine, Ctrl. Neuro Psychiat. Assn. (bd. dirs., pres. 1996-97), Am. Med. Women's Assn. (pres. Omaha chpt. 1986-88, Nebr. State dir. 1988-94, regional gov. 1993-95, bd. dirs. 1993-95, book reviewer for JAMWA, Outstanding Physician award 1989, 90-93, nat. cmty. svc. award 1990), Am. Psychiat. Assn., Met. Omaha Med. Soc., Nebr. Med. Assn., Durham Soc., Kiwanis Internat., Alpha Xi Delta. Avocations: gardening, travel, gourmet cooking, interior decorating, house renovation. Home: 1103 S 80th St Omaha NE 68124-1419 Office: 7602 Pacific St Ste 302 Omaha NE 68114-5405

SHILLING, ROY BRYANT, JR., academic administrator; s. Roy Bryant and Lila M. (Prestage) S.; m. Margaret Riddle, Oct. 16, 1952; children: Roy Bryant III, Nancy Gale. BA, McMurry U., 1951, HHD, 1982; BD, So. Meth. U., 1957; MS, Ind. U., 1966, PhD, 1967. Presdl. asst. McMurry U., Abilene, Tex., 1959-61; asst. to pres. Tenn. Wesleyan Coll., 1961-64; asst. in devel. Ball State U., 1964-65; rsch. assoc. Ind. U., 1965-67; dir. planning and rsch. Baldwin Wallace Coll., 1967-68; exec. v.p. Southwestern U., 1968-69, pres., 1981-2000, pres. emeritus, 2000—; pres. Hendrix Coll., 1969-81; interim pres. McMurry Univ., 2002. Mem. Nat. Commn. on United Meth. Higher Edn., 1975-77. Mem. Ark. Arts and Humanities Coun., 1970-76, chmn., 1974-75; bd. dirs. Ark. Children's Hosp., 1981; mem. bd. higher edn. and ministry United Meth. Ch., 1972-80, mem. univ. senate, 1980-88, v.p. 1983-84, pres., 1984-88; chmn. Gulf dist. Rhodes Scholarship Selection Com., 1992, Ark. chmn., 1973-74, Tex. chmn., 1985-91; mem. Young Pres. Orgn., 1975-81; mem. bd. visitors Air U., 1991-94. With U.S. Army, 1952-54. Recipient Disting. Alumnus award McMurry U., 1980, Perkins Disting. Alumnus award So. Meth. U., 1987, Owen B. Sherrill award for leadership in econ. devel. Georgetown, 1988; named one of Top 100 Most Effective Coll. Pres. in Nation, Bowling Green State U./Exxon Edn. Found., 1986. Mem. North Ctrl. Assn. Colls. and Schs. (vice chmn., chmn. elect 1980-81), Nat. Assn Schs. and Colls. of United Meth. Ch. (v.p. 1975-76, pres. 1976-77), Nat. Coun. Ind. Colls. and Univs. (bd. dirs. 1984-88), So. U. Conf. (exec. com. 1974-78), 79-86, sec.-treas. 1979-86, v.p. 1991-92, pres. 1992-93), Am. Coun. Edn. (bd. dirs. 1989-91; mem. commn. on govt. and pub. rels. 1999-2000, spl. counselor to the pres. 2000-01), Inst. for Humanities (bd. dirs. Salado, Tex. chpt. 1985-91, mem. internat. coun. advs. 1994), NCAA Divsn. III Pres.'s Coun., 1998-2000, Philos Soc. Tex., Rotary, Masons, Alpha Chi, Phi Delta Kappa. Office: 1405 Mesa Ridge Ln Austin TX 78735-1639 E-mail: shilling@southwestern.edu.

SHILLINGBURG, HERBERT THOMPSON, JR., dental educator; b. Mar. 21, 1938; s. Herbert Thompson and Stefi Marie (Schuster) Shillingburg; m. Constance Joanne Murphy, June 11, 1960; children: Lisa Grace, Leslie Susan, Lara Stephanie. Student, U. N.Mex., 1955-58, 65-66; DDS, U. So. Calif., 1962; Dr (hon.), U. Medicine and Pharmacy Targu Mures, Romania, 2006. Gen. practice dentistry, Albuquerque, 1964-67; asst. prof. fixed prosthodontics sect. UCLA Sch. Dentistry, 1967-70, chmn., 1970-72; chmn. dept. fixed prosthodontics U. Okla. Coll. Dentistry, Okla. City, 1972—2003, David Ross Boyd Disting. prof., 1983, prof. emeritus, 2003—. Cons. VA Hosp., Muskogee, Okla., 1975—84, Oklahoma City, 1977—93, U.S. Army Dental Activity, Ft. Knox, Ky., 1980—94. Author: (also in Japanese, German, Greek, Spanish, Italian, French, Portuguese, Polish, Korean, Chinese and Russian) Preparations for Cast Gold Restorations, 1974, Fundamentals of Fixed Prosthodontics, 1976, 3d edit., 1997, Guide to Occlusal Waxing, 1979, 3d edit., 2000, Restoration of the Endodontically Treated Tooth, 1984, Fundamentals of Tooth Preparations for Cast Metal and Porcelain Restorations, 1987; co-editor: Quintessence of Dental Technology, 1984—88; sect. editor: Quintessence Internat., 1988—2001, mem. editl. coun.: Jour. Prosthetic Dentistry, 1996—99. Capt. US Army, 1962—64. Named Disting. Lectr., O U Assoc., 1989; recipient Award for tchg. excellence, UCLA Sch. Dentistry, 1969, 1972, 1973, Okla. Coll. Dentistry, 1976, 1978, 1982, 1987, 1993, 1994, 1997, 1st prize, Am. Med. Writers Assn., 1988, La Médaille de la Ville de Paris (échelon Argent), 1990, Outstanding Profl. Achievement award, O U Coll. Dentristy, 2003, Prof. of Hon., U. Medicine and Pharmacy Targu-Mures, 2004, Herbert T. Shillingburg Endowed Professorship in FIXED Prosthodontics, Coll. Dentistry, 2006, Doctorem Honoris Causa, U. Medicine and Pharmacy Targu Mures, 2006. Fellow: Am. Coll. Dentists; mem.: ADA, Okla. State Dental Assn., Internat. Assn. Dental Rsch., Am. Coll. Prosthodontists (hon.), Am. Acad. Restorative Dentistry, Am. Acad. Fixed Prosthodontics (George H. Moulton award 1998), Acad. Operative Dentistry, Phi Kappa Phi, Omicron Kappa Upsilon (Stephen H. Leeper award for Tchg. Excellence Supreme Ch. 2000). Independent. Episcopalian. Avocations: travel, photography. Home: 1312 Brixton Rd Edmond OK 73034-3314 Office: U Okla Coll Dentistry PO Box 26901 Oklahoma City OK 73190-0001

SHILLINGLAW, GORDON, retired finance educator; b. Albany, NY, July 26, 1925; s. James McCombe and Margaret Blanche (Stephens) Shillinglaw; m. Barbara Ann Cross, June 24, 1950; children: James McCombe, Laura Cross. AB magna cum laude, Brown U., 1945; MS, U. Rochester, 1948; PhD, Harvard U., 1952. Asst. prof. Hamilton Coll., Clinton, NY, 1951-52; cons. assoc. Joel Dean Assocs., Yonkers, NY, 1952-55; asst. prof. MIT, Cambridge, 1955-61; assoc. prof. Columbia U., NYC, 1961-66, prof. acctg., 1966-90, prof. emeritus, 1991—. Vis. prof. Mgmt. Devel. Inst., Lausanne, Switzerland, 1964—65, Lausanne, 1967—69; mem. U.S. Cost Acctg. Stds. Bd., 1978—80, U.S. R.R. Acctg. Prin. Bd., 1985—87; dir., trustee Scudder Funds, AARP Investment Program Funds, 1979—2000; cons. in field. Author: Managerial Cost Accounting, 1961, 5th edit., 1982, Accounting: A Management Approach, 1964, 9th edit., 1993, Financial Accounting: Concepts and Applications, 1989; contbr. articles to profl. jours. Bd. dirs., treas. Feris Found. Am., Stamford, Conn., 1970—94; mem. bd. advisors Fund Directions, 1990—96. With USN, 1943—46. Recipient Disting. Tchr. award, Columbia U., 1970, Lifetime Achievement award, Instnl. Investor Newsletter, 2002. Mem.: Am. Acctg. Assn. (v.p. 1966—67), Beta Gamma Sigma, Phi Beta Kappa. Avocations: golf, genealogy. Home: 1150 8th Ave SW Apt 401 Largo FL 33770-3175 Personal E-mail: gshillinglaw@tampabay.rr.com.

SHILLINGSBURG, MIRIAM JONES, literature educator, academic administrator; b. Balt., Oct. 5, 1943; d. W. Elvin and Miriam R. Jones; m. Peter L. Shillingsburg, Nov. 21, 1967; children: Robert, George, John, Alice, Anne Carol. BA, Mars Hill Coll., 1964; MA, U. S.C., 1966, PhD, 1969; BGS, Miss. State U., 1994. Asst. prof. Limestone Coll., Gaffney, SC, 1969, Miss. State U., 1970—75, assoc. prof., 1975—80, prof. English, 1980—96, assoc. v.p. for acad. affairs, 1988—96, dir. summer sch., 1990—96, dir. undergrad. studies, 1994—96; dean arts and scis. Lamar U., Tex., 1996—99; dean liberal arts and scis. Ind. U., South Bend, 2000—04, dean sch. edn., 2005—06. Disting. acad. visitor Mark Twain Ctr., 1993, 2001; Simms rsch. prof. U. S.C., 1998; vis. fellow Australian Def. Force Acad., 1989; Fulbright lectr. U. New South Wales, Duntroon, Australia, 1984-85. NEH fellow in residence, Columbia U., 1976-77. Author: Mark Twain in Australasia, 1988; editor: Conquest of Granada, 1988, The Cub of the Panther, 1997, Confession, 2005; mem. editl. bd. Works of W.M. Thackeray, Miss. Quar., So. Quar.; contbr. articles to profl. jours. and mags. Mem. South Ctrl. 18th Century Soc., Am. Lit. Assn., Pop Culture Assn., Sigma Tau Delta, Phi Kappa Phi, Simms Soc. (pres. 1996-97). Business E-Mail: mshillin@iusb.edu.

SHILOH, ALLEN, writer; b. Bastrop, La., May 24, 1947; s. Al and Rosia B (Davis) S.; children: Datoya Moneake Penn. Grad. high sch., Bastrop; student in Illustration, Cal/Arts, 1966—68, student in Illustration, 2007—. Mail handler U.S. Postal Svc., Bell, Calif., 1972—. Author: (novels) The Brotherhood, Terror, 1973, Bayou Girl, 1990, (paperback) The Real First United States President, 1983, (short stories pub.) New Cosmic Star, 1968. Sgt. USAF, 1968-72, Vietnam. Avocations: photography, drawing. Home: 305 S Essey Ave Compton CA 90221-3417 Home Phone: 310-638-4234; Office Phone: 323-729-4121.

SHILS, MAURICE EDWARD, physician, educator, research scientist; b. Atlantic City, Dec. 31, 1914; s. Samuel L. and Sarah (Harris) S.; m. Cylia Finkiel, Feb. 19, 1939 (dec. Sept. 1987); children: Loraine J., Jonathan R.; m. Betty Ann Bell, Sept. 24, 1988. BA, Johns Hopkins U., 1937, ScD, 1940; MD, NYU, 1958. Intern joint program Cornell divsn. Bellevue Hosp. and Meml. Hosp., NYC, 1958-59; fellow in physiology Meml. Hosp., 1959-60; instr., asst. prof. nutrition Sch. Pub. Health Columbia U., NYC, 1946-54; instr. biochemistry Sch. Hygiene Johns Hopkins U., Balt., 1940-42; head Ctrl. Metabolic Lab. Sloan Kettering Inst., NYC, 1960-72; from asst. to assoc. attending physician Meml. Hosp., NYC, 1962-72, attending physician, 1972-85; asst. prof. biochem. Sloan-Kettering divsn. Med. Coll. Cornell U., NYC, 1959-62, from asst. prof. to prof. medicine Med. Coll., 1962-85, prof. emeritus, 1985—. Adj. prof. nutrition dept. pub. health scis. Wake Forest U. Sch. Medicine, Winston-Salem, N.C., 1989-94, cons., 1994-97. Author, sr. editor: Modern Nutrition in Health and Disease, 10th edit., 2005; contbr. more than 200 rsch. and review articles to profl. jours. Fellow Am. Coll. Physicians, N.Y. Acad. Medicine (Acad. Plaque award 1987), Soc. Nutritional Scis.; mem. AMA (chmn. nutrition adv. group 1974-77, Goldberger award 1983), Am. Soc. Clin. Nutrition (pres. 1985-86, Excellence in Med. Sch. award 1994), Am. Bd. Physician Nutrition Specialists, Phi Beta Kappa, Alpha Omega Alpha. E-mail: mshils@triad.rr.com.

SHILSON, WAYNE, artist, educator; b. Apr. 14, 1943; BS in Art Edn., U. Minn., 1971, MFA, 1972. Artist, illustrator, Mpls., 1974—96; art tchr. Pine Point Native Am. Pub. Sch., Ponsford, Minn., 1997—98, Remer-Longville Schs., Minn., 1998—99, Pine River HS and Elem. Sch., Minn., 1999—. One-man shows include Sky Gallery, St. Paul, 1976, 1977, Mpls. Inst. Arts, 1979, 1980, Minn. Artists Gallery, Mpls., 1983, Normandale Ctr. Gallery, Bloom, Minn., 1987, 1989, Arthurs Internat., Honolulu, 1987—90, Las Vegas, Nev., 1991—, N. Country Mus. Arts, Pine River, 1993—, Stable Art Gallery, Gull Lake, Minn., 2001, Paul Bunyan Art Gallery, Bemidji, Minn., 2001, others, exhibited in group shows at Mpls. Inst. Arts, 1979, Art Ctr. Minn., Minnetonka, 1980, Parks Fine Arts, Chgo., 1986—88, Jem-Alexander Gallery, Westchester, Ill., 1989, Artbanque Gallery, Mpls., N. Country Mus. Arts, Pine River, 2006, others, Represented in permanent collections Normandale Coll., Bloom, N. Country Mus. Arts, Pine River, Bemidji Cmty. Arts Ctr.; contbr. articles to profl. jours. Recipient 1st. pl., STC, 1984, 1991, award of Excellence, 1992, award of Achievement, 1992; grantee, Paris, 1999—2000. Home and Studio: 17767 Emerald Island Cir Park Rapids MN 56470-2083

SHIM, ELISABETH K., dermatologist; b. Chgo. BS, Northwestern U., 1990, MD, 1994. Assoc. clin. prof. U. So. Calif. Med. Ctr., LA; CEO, founder Verdure Lifestyles, Inc. Fellow: Am. Soc. for Dermatologic Surgery, Am. Coll. Mohs Micrographic Surgery, Am. Acad. Dermatology. Office: Ste 570 1301 20th St Santa Monica CA 90404

SHIM, SANG KOO, mental health services professional; b. Tokyo, Oct. 1, 1942; arrived in U.S., 1968; s. Sang Taek and Kum Ryon (Bae) Shim; m. Jae Hee Lee, July 12, 1972; children: Tammy, David. BS, Seoul Nat. U., Republic of Korea, 1967; MBA, No. Ill. U., 1970; MS, U. Wis., Madison, 1975. CPA Ill., cert. valuation analyst. Acct. Vaughn Mfg. Co., Chgo., 1970-72, Stewart-Warner Corp., Chgo., 1972-73; fin. cons. Cen. Acctg. Assn., New Baden, Ill., 1977-79; auditor Ill. Dept. Mental Health, Springfield, 1980-82, CFO, 1983-97; chief bur. gen. acctg. Ill. Dept. Human Svcs., Springfield, 1997—2002. Bd. dirs. Metro City Bank, Doraville, Ga. Treas. Korean Assn. Greater St. Louis, 1982. Mem.: Nat. Assn. Cert. Valuation Analysts, Assn. Govt. Accts. (cert. govt. fin. mgr.), Ill. CPA Soc., Korean-Am. C. of C. (v.p. Greater St. Louis chpt. 1994—95). Office: Shim & Co CPA 1630 Lebanon Ave Ste 102 Belleville IL 62221 Home: 1157 Stonewolf Trl Fairview Heights IL 62208-4187 Office Phone: 618-257-1788. Personal E-mail: skshim@aol.com.

SHIMADA, KATSUNORI, retired electrical engineer; b. Tokyo, Mar. 12, 1922; arrived in U.S., 1950; s. Katsujiro and Mume Shimada; m. Ikuko Ueno, Oct. 30, 1975; m. Kazuko Matsumoto; children: Karl, Keiko Shimada Stearns. BSEE, U. Tokyo, 1945; MSEE, U. Minn., 1954, PhD, 1958. Engr. Toshiba Japan, Kawasaki, Japan, 1945—50; instr. U. Minn., Mpls., 1950—58; asst. prof. engring. U. Wash., Seattle, 1958—64; supr. JPL, G&C Rsch. Group, Pasadena, Calif., 1964—80; mgr., Field Ctr. Integration JPL, Pasadena, 1980—85, supr. Celestrial Sensors, 1985—89; ret., 1989. Cons. Boeing Co., Seattle, 1960—63, NASDA of Japan, LA, 1987—91; invited prof. engring. U. Tokyo, 1973; invited lectr. NEDO of Japan, Tokyo, 1983. Contbr. articles to profl. jours., tech. reports and memoranda. Com. mem. Nat. Parents Day Coalition, LA, 1996—99, RSVP of Pasadena, 1993—95, Assoc. Retirees of Caltech/JPL, Pasadena, 1989. Resident rsch. fellow, JPL, 1963—64. Mem.: AIAA, IEEE (sr.), Sigma Xi, Eta Kappa Nu. Achievements include patents for cavity emitter for thermionics; thermionic diode switch; solid state power converter. Avocations: photography, computers, golf, travel. Home: 3840 Edgeview Dr Pasadena CA 91107 Personal E-mail: kshimmitzy@aol.com.

SHIMCHICK, MARIE, music educator; d. John George and Mary Shimchick. MusB magna cum laude, Ithaca Coll., 1981—85; M in reading, U. of Hartford, 1989—90. Teaching Cert., Music K-12 Conn., Teaching Cert., Reading Cons. K-12 CT, Coaching Cert. Conn., Conn. Writing Project Conn., 1996. Music tchr. New Lebanon Elem. Sch., Byram, Conn., 1985—89, Western and Ctrl. Jr. High Schools, Greenwich, Conn., 1985—87, Ea. Mid. Sch., Riverside, Conn., 1987—2003, Greenwich H.S., Conn., 2003—. Softball coach Western Jr. H.S., Greenwich, Conn., 1986—87, Ea. Jr. H.S., Riverside, Conn., 1988—89; asst. varsity softball coach Greenwich HS, 1992—94, varsity girls' golf coach, 2005—; softball coach Ea. Mid. Sch., Riverside, Conn., 1997—2004. Conductor, artistic director (choral) Eastmen; singer: Greenwich Choral Soc. Recipient Tchr. of the Yr., Phi Delta Kappa, 1999. Mem.: Internat. Reading Assn., Orgn. of Am. Kodaly Educators, Am. Orff-Schulwerk Assn., Nat. Assn. of Teachers of English, Music Educators Nat. Conf., Am. Choral Directors Assn. (life), U.S. Golf Tchrs. Fed. (level II instr.), Phi Delta Kappa, Sigma Alpha Iota (v.p. 1983—85, Scholastic Honor award 1985). Liberal. Eastern Orthodox Christian. Avocations: skiing, racquet sports, fine dining and wines, golf. Office: Greenwich H S 10 Hillside Rd Greenwich CT 06830 Home Phone: 203-847-6159. Personal E-mail: riechick@hotmail.com. Business E-Mail: marie_shimchick@greenwich.k12.ct.us.

SHIMER, DANIEL LEWIS, finance company executive; b. San Angelo, Tex., July 30, 1944; s. Lewis V. and Mary A. (Slick) S.; married. BS in Acctg. and Mktg., Ind. U., 1972; postgrad., Loyola U., New Orleans, 1977. CPA. Sr. acct. Peat, Marwick, Mitchell & Co., Indpls., 1973—75; asst. treas. LTV Corp., Dallas, 1975—79; v.p. fin. Stoller Chem. Co., Houston, 1979—81; v.p., CFO Petro-Silver, Inc., Denver, 1981—83; v.p., treas. FoxMeyer Corp., Denver, 1983—86; v.p., treas., sec. CoastAmerica Corp., Denver, 1986—88; exec. v.p. Bard & Co., Denver, 1989—90; pres. nat accounts divsn. I Can't Believe It's Yogurt/ Brice Foods, Inc., Dallas, 1991—93; exec. v.p., CFO COREStaff Inc., Houston, 1994—96; venture ptnr. Austin Ventures, Dallas, 1996—2004; pres. Shimer Capital Ptnrs., Inc., Dallas, 1996—2004; gen. ptnr. Teakwood Capital, 2005—. Methodist. Avocations: carpentry, fishing. Home: 7436 Glenshannon Cir Dallas TX 75225-2048

SHIMIZU, KAZUHIKO, education educator; b. Akeno, Japan, Jan. 20, 1952; s. Kazuyoshi and Toyoko S.; m. Tsurumi Tamagawa, March 30, 1979; children: Kazutaka, Kazuma, Kazuki. BA, Tokyo U. Edn., 1974, MA, 1976; PhD, U. Tsukuba, Japan, 1997. Rsch. fellow Japan Soc. for the Promotion of Sci., Tokyo, 1980-81; asst. prof. Seisen Women's Jr. Coll., Nagano, Japan, 1983-86, assoc. prof., 1986-88; asst. prof. U. Tsukuba, 1988-91, assoc. prof., 1991-99, prof., 1999—, asst. pres., 2004—06, vice provost grad. sch., 2004—06, chmn. faculty edn., 2006—07, provost grad. sch., 2007—. Vis. assoc. prof. U. Hiroshima, 1992-96; vis. scholar U. Pa., Phila., 1995-96, U. Minn., Mpls., 2002, U. Mo., 2005; spl. lectr. Yonsei U., Seoul, Korea, 1996; guest lectr. Nat. Edn. Commn., Beijing, 1998, East China Normal U., Shanghai, 2001, Beijing Normal U., 2005. Author: Comparative and Hist. Study of Univ. Credit Sys. Between USA and Japan, 1998, Univ. Reform in Japan, 1999; author and editor: Development of University Evaluation, 2004, A Databook of Edn. Statistics, 2006. Mem. Coun. for Univ. Chartering and Sch. Judicial Person (Monbusho), 2000-02; mem. Japanese Univ. Accreditation Assn., 1994-2000, 2004—; trustee Assn. for the Advancement of Colls. in Japan, 1994—; mem. Inter-Univ. Seminar House, Tokyo, 1997-2002. Recipient rsch. fund, Assn. Internat. Edn., Japan, 1990; grantee-in-aid for sci. rsch., Ministry of Edn., Sci., Sport and Culture (Monbusho), Tokyo, 1998, 2000, 2001, 2003—07. Mem.: Japanese Assn. Higher Edn. Rsch. (editor 2000—02, trustee 2003—06), Japan Soc. Ednl. Sys. and Orgn. (office dir. 1999—), Japan Assn. Lifelong Edn. (office dir. 1998—2000), Comparative and Internat. Edn. Soc. Avocation: gardening. Home: 3-709-1 Takezono Tsukuba Japan Office: Faculty of Edn U Tsukuba 1-1-1 Tennodai 305-8572 Tsukuba Japan Business E-Mail: shimizuk@human.tsukuba.ac.jp.

SHIMIZU, MASATO, chef; b. Japan; Chef Benten, LI, Kisso, New Hyde Park, Jewel Bako, NYC, 2001; sushi chef 15 East, NYC. Named one of NYC's Rising Stars, StarChefs.com, 2007. Office: 15 East 15 E 15th St New York NY 10003 Office Phone: 212-647-0015. *

SHIMIZU, YOSHIAKI, art historian, department chairman; b. Tokyo, Feb. 27, 1936; came to U.S., 1953, naturalized, 1999; s. Mamoru and Michiko (Hayasaka) S.; children: Karen Akiko Marie, Kenneth Cuyler Norio, Katherine Kimie, Kei Robert. BA, Harvard U., 1963; MA, U. Kans., 1968; MFA, Princeton U., 1971, PhD, 1974. Asst. prof. dept. art and archaeology Princeton (N.J.) U., 1973-75, prof., 1984—, chmn. dept. art and archaeology, 1990-92, Marquand prof. art and archaeology, 1992—, dir. program in Asian art and archaeology, 1992—; asst. prof. U. Calif., Berkeley, 1975-78, assoc. prof., 1978-79; curator Japanese art Freer Gallery, Smithsonian Instn., Washington, 1979-84; guest curator Nat. Gallery Art, Washington, 1982-89; guest prof. U. Heidelberg, 1993. Guest prof. Ritsumeikan U., 1996; vis. fellow dept. art history U. Tokyo, 1996; mem. art adv. com. Japan Soc. Gallery, 1984—, adv. com. Asia Soc. Galleries, N.Y.C., 1992—, chmn. adv. com., 1999—; vis. fellow dept. comparative culture Sophia U., Tokyo, 1993; sr. cons. for exhbn. Japan Soc. Galleries, 2006, 07. Author: (with John M. Rosenfield) Masters of Japanese Calligraphy, 1984; editor: (with Carolyn Wheelwright) Japanese Ink Paintings, 1976; author, editor: Japan: The Shaping of Daimyo Culture 1185-1858, 1988; mem. editorial bd. Archives of Asian Art, 1979-89. Adv. bd. Asian Art, Smithsonian Inst., 1985-93; mem. vis. com. Arthur M. Sackler Gallery, Washington, 1984-94. Smithsonian Inst. fellow, 1967, Social Sci. Rsch. Coun./Am. Coun. Learned Socs. fellow, 1977-78, Asian Cultural Coun. fellow, 1995; J.D. Rockefeller III fellow, 1969-70. Mem. Coll. Art Assn. (bd. dirs. 1987-91), Japan Art History Assn., Japan Soc. N.Y., Ctr. for the Study of Japanese Woodblock Prints (mem. internat. adv. bd. 1983—) Home: 2 College Rd Princeton NJ 08540-5108 Office: Princeton U Dept Art and Archaeology Princeton NJ 08540 Business E-Mail: shimizu@princeton.edu.

SHIMKUS, JOHN MONDY, congressman; b. Collinsville, Ill., Feb. 21, 1958; s. Gene Louis and Kathleen (Mondy) S.; m. Karen Kay Muth; children: David, Joshua, Daniel. BS, U.S. Mil. Acad., 1980; MBA, So. Ill. U., Edwardsville, 1997. Advanced through grades to capt. U.S. Army,

1980-86; stationed at U.S. Army Base, Columbus, Ga., 1980-81, 85, served at Bamberg, Germany, 1981-84, stationed at Monterey, Calif. 1985-86; tchr. Metro East Luth. H.S., Edwardsville, Ill., 1986-90; treas. Madison County, Edwardsville, 1990-96; mem. U.S. Congress from 19th Ill. dist., 1997—, mem. energy and commerce com. Liaison officer U.S. Mil. Acad., 1987-96; treas. So. Ill. Law Enforcement Commn., 1990-96. Bd. dirs. Sr. Citizen Companion Program, Belleville, Ill., 1991; trustee Collinsville Twp., Ill., 1989-93; Rep. precinct committeeman, Collinsville, 1988—. Lt. col. USAR, 1985—. Mem. Nat. Assn. County Treas. and Fin. Officers (bd. dirs.), Ill. County Treas. Assn., Am. Legion Post 365. Republican. Lutheran. Home: 504 Sumner Blvd Collinsville IL 62234-1934 Office: US Ho Reps 513 Cannon Ho Office Bldg Washington DC 20515-1319 also: Springfield Dist Office Ste C 3130 Chatham Rd Springfield IL 62704 *

SHIMMIN, MARGARET ANN, retired women's health nurse; b. Forbes, ND, Oct. 26, 1941; d. George and Reba S. Diploma in Nursing, St. Luke's Hosp. Sch. Nursing, Fargo, ND, 1962; BSW, U. West Fla., Pensacola, 1978; cert. ob-gyn nurse practitioner, U. Ala., Birmingham, 1983, MPH, 1986. Lic. nurse, Fla., ND, Ala. Head nurse, emergency room St. Luke's Hosps., Fargo, 1962-67; charge nurse, labor and delivery, perinatal nurse educator Sacred Heart Hosp., Pensacola, Fla., 1970-82; ARNP Escambia County Pub. Health Unit, 1983-89; cmty. health nursing cons. Dist. 1 Health and Rehab. Svcs., 1989-96; sr. cmty. health nursing supr. Escambia County Health Dept., 1996—2002, nurse program specialist OSHA staff tng. and quality assurance, 2002—05, nurse program specialist diabetes intervention program, 2005—07; ret., 2007. Capt. nurse corps U.S. Army, 1967-70, Japan. Mem. NAACOG (cert. maternal-gynecol.-neonatal nursing, ob-gyn nurse practitioner), Fla. Nurses' Assn., ANA, N.W. Fla. ARNP (past sec./treas.), Fla. Perinatal Assn., Nat. Perinatal Assn., Healthy Mothers/Healthy Babies Coalition, Fla. Pub. Health Assn., U. West Fla. Alumni Assn., U. Ala. at Birmingham Sch. of Public Health Alumni Assn., Phi Alpha. Republican. Presbyterian. Avocations: cooking, music, travel, photography, reading. Home: 8570 Olympia Rd Pensacola FL 32514-8029

SHIMODA, JERRY YASUTAKA, retired national historic park manager; b. Haleiwa, Hawaii, Mar. 21, 1930; s. Tamotsu and Sasai Shimoda; m. Clara H. Segawa, Aug. 7, 1954; children: Karen Marie K., Randall T., Shaun T., Teri Ellen H., Jacqueline Y., David Y. BA in Govt., U. Hawaii, 1952, MA in Far Ea. Area Studies, 1957; postgrad., St. Louis U., 1957-59; PhD in Pub. Adminstrn., Kennedy-Western U., 2004. Historian Jefferson Nat. Expansion Meml. Nat. Hist. Site, St. Louis, 1957-60; chief historian, in charge hist. rsch. and visitor svcs. Saratoga Nat. Hist. Park, Stillwater, NY, 1960-66; chief historian Home of Franklin D. Roosevelt Nat. Hist. Site and, Frederick Vanderbilt Nat. Hist. Site, Hyde Park, NY, 1966-69; instr. Nat. Park Svc. Stephen T. Mather Tng. Ctr., Harpers Ferry, W.Va., 1969-72; supt. Pu'uhonua o Honaunau (Hawaii) Nat. Hist. Park, 1972-96, Puukohola Heiau Nat. Hist. Site, Kawaihae, 1972-96; ret., 1996. Lectr. environ. edn. Pa. State U., U. W.Va., Shepard Coll., 1969—72; acting supr. Kaloko-Honokohau Nat. Hist. Pk., 1988—90; instr. environ. edn., interpretive and basic instructing techniques U. Hawaii, Hilo, Kapiolani C.C.; instr. Japanese culture U. Hawaii, Hilo, 1994; U.S. del. and translator U.S.-Japan Panel on Nat. Parks and Equivalent Res., 1968—97, World Conf. on Marine Parks, Tokyo, 1975; mem. internat. bd. dirs. Heritage Interpretation Internat., 1989—98; cons., presenter in field. Contbr. articles to profl. jours., popular mags., local newspapers. Bd. dirs. Volcano Art Ctr.; adv. com. Wailoa State Ctr.; active Hawaii Gov.'s Task Force on Ocean and Recreation; chmn. restoration com. St. Benedict's Ch., Honaunau, 1982-95; chmn. bd. dirs. Kahua Na'au 'Ao, 1996-97; vol. training cons. Nat. Pk. Svc., 1996-2005. Recipient Spl. Achievement award Nat. Park Svc., 1964, 68, 70, resolution W.Va. Senate, 1971, Hawaii Ho. of Reps., 1982, sec.'s cert. Dept. Interior, 1971, Exec. of Yr. award West Hawaii chpt. Profl. Secs. Internat., 1981, cert. Govt. of Japan, 1981, staff plaque Pu'uhonua o Honaunau Nat. Hist. Park, Puukohola Heiau Nat. Hist. Site and Kaloko-Honokohau Nat. Hist. Park, 1988, cert. Japan Nat. Parks Assn., 1989, cert. of appreciation South Kona Aloha Lions Club, 1990, Meritorious Svc. award Sec. Interior, 1996, others. Mem. Hawaii Mus. Assn. (bd. dirs. 1988-92), Polynesian Voyaging Soc. (life, hon.), Kona Hist. Soc. (bd. dirs. 1988-92), Big Island Ocean Recreation and Tourism Assn. (exec. com.), Hawaii Natural History Assn. (bd. dirs.), Kona Judo Club (pres. 1977-96), Rotary (pres. Kona Mauka 1978-79, co-founder Volcano chpt. 2001, Paul Harris fellow 1991, Disting. Svc. award 1992). Avocations: writing, reading, travel, teaching.

SHIMOJIMA, CHRIS, retail executive; BA in Internat. Economics, U. Colo.; MBA in Finance and Mktg., U. Chgo. Sr. mktg. and brand positions Nestle Foods; dir. brand strategy PepsiCo, 1992—94; v.p. nat. retention mktg. AT&T, 1994—98; v.p., gen. mgr. 10-10-345 Lucky Dog bus., 1998—2000; chief mktg. officer Kozmo.com, 2000; sr. v.p., chief mktg. officer E-Business Group Prudential, 2000; v.p. mktg. merchandising customer direct Sears, 2002—05; v.p., gen. mgr. Sears-Kmart Customer Direct Sears Holding Corp., 2005—06; v.p. global e-commerce Nike Inc., Beaverton, Oreg., 2006—. Office: Nike Inc One Bowerman Dr Beaverton OR 97005-6453 *

SHIMPOCK, KATHY ELIZABETH, lawyer, writer; b. Mooresville, NC, July 20, 1952; d. Charles Walter and Minna Ethel (McLean) S.; m. David Edward Vieweg, Sept. 3, 1983 (div. Mar. 1997); children: Jessica Kim Vieweg, Jayme Elise Kyung Vieweg. BA, Colo. Coll., 1973; JD, U. Wyo., 1977; MLL, U. Denver, 1979; MBA, Ariz. State U., 1992. Bar: Ariz. 1977. Asst. librarian Stanford (Calif.) U. Coll. Law, 1979—82; law librarian, asst. prof. law U. Bridgeport (Conn.) Coll. Law, 1982—83; dir. Law Libr. Adminstrv. Svcs., Mountain View, Calif., 1983—85; exec. asst. to dean Ariz. State U. Coll. Law, Tempe, 1985—87; dir. Law Libr. Adminstrv. Svcs., Mesa, Ariz., 1987—95; dir. libr. svcs. Jennings, Strouss & Salmon, Phoenix, 1988—89; dir. rsch. svcs. O'Connor, Cavanagh et al, Phoenix, 1989—95; pres. Juris Rsch., Mesa, 1998—; counsel Muchmore & Wallwork, Phoenix, 1995—98; pres. Juris Rsch., Tempe, 1998—; rsch. and legal info. mgr. Bryan Cave LLP, 2000—. Adv. bd. West Pub. Co., St. Paul, 1991-94; bd. dir. Dillon S.W., Scottsdale, Ariz.; mediator Alternative Dispute Resolution Program, Maricopa County, Ariz. Author: Business Research Handbook: Methods and Sources for Lawyers and Business Professionals, 1996—; co-author: Arizona Legal Research Guide, 1992; contbr. chpts. to books, articles to profl. jours.; bi-monthly columnist AzALL News, 1996-97, Legal Assistant Today, 1993-96; contbr. book revs. to Libr. Jour., Legal Info. Alert, 1993-98; editor Southwest Assn. Law Librs. Bull., 1990, Ariz. State U. Coll. Law Law Forum, 1986, Juris Rsch. E-line, 1999-2004. Rsch. atty. Comml. Law Project for Ukraine, Phoenix, 1995-96; v.p. Dillon S.W., 2002-. Mem. ABA (co-chair law practice mgmt. environ. divsn. 1994-95), Am. Assn. Law Librs. (chair 1994-95), Ariz. Assn. Law Librs. (pres. 1996-97, pres.'s award 1997, Disting. Mem. award 1998), State Bar of Ariz. (chair 1996-98, Cont. Legal Edn. award 1998), Ariz. Women Lawyers Assn. (steering com. 1998-2000). Democrat. United Meth. Avocations: reading, yoga, painting, drawing. E-mail: kshimpock@jurisresearch.com.

SHIN, DONG-HEE, communication technology educator; b. Seoul, Republic of Korea, Oct. 30, 1970; arrived in US, 1997, permanent resident; s. Hong-Sik Shin and Young-Ja Seo; m. Youn Joo Shin, Jan. 7, 2003. BA in Comm., Sung Kun Kwan U., Seoul, 1997; MA in Telecomm., So. Ill. U., 1998; MS in Info. Mgmt., PhD in Telecomm., Syracuse U., 2004. Rschr. Korea Info. Soc. Rsch., Seoul, 1997; reporter Korea Ctrl. Daily, LA, 1999; lectr. Syracuse (NY) U., 2002—04; asst. prof. Pa. State U., Reading, 2004—. Cons. SK Club, Seoul, 2000; rschr. SK Telecomm., Seoul, 2001; project mgr. Verizon and NY State, Syracuse, NY, 2000—03; spkr. in field. Activist Assn. for Cmty. Networking, Chgo., 2002; advisor NY State Pub. Svc. Commn., Albany, 2003; adv. cons. Consortium of Seoul Digital City, 2004. Recipient Outstanding Rschr. award, Pa. State U., 2007; fellow, Syracuse U., 2002; scholar, So. Ill. U., 1997; rsch. grantee, Pa. State U., 2004. Mem.: Am. Info. Sci. Assn., Internat. Comm. Assn., Internat. Telecomm. Soc. Presbyterian. Avocations: tennis, fishing, touring. Office: Pa State U Tulpehocken Rd PO Box 7009 Reading PA 19610 Home: 114 Bainbridge Cir Reading PA 19608 Office Fax: 610-396-6024. Personal E-mail: dhshin1030@yahoo.com.

SHIN, ERNEST EUN-HO, physicist, educator, researcher; b. Chin-do, Republic of Korea, Dec. 31, 1935; came to U.S., 1953; s. Hyung Sik and Ok Bin (Lim) S.; m. Shin-Ai Park, July 27, 1963; children: Irene, Juliet, Mariette, Michelle. BS in Physics, Carnegie Inst. Tech., 1957; AM in Physics, Harvard U., 1959, PhD in Physics, 1961. Rsch. fellow Cyclotron Lab., Harvard U., Cambridge, Mass., 1957-58, tchg. fellow physics dept., 1958-59; rsch. assoc. Arthur D. Little, Inc., Cambridge, 1960-62; rsch. assoc. Francis Bitter Nat. Magnet Lab., MIT, Cambridge, 1962-66; prof. physics U. Miami, Coral Gables, Fla., 1966-72, founder, dir. Solid State Physics Lab., 1969-72; dir. Nieman Inst., Dallas, 1972-73; vis. scientist Korea Atomic Energy Rsch. Inst., Seoul, 1973-74; chmn., chief exec. officer Yulsan Am., Inc., San Francisco, 1974-89; dir. Chestnut Hill Inst., Napa, Calif., 1984—. Co-founder Yulsan Group Cos., Seoul, 1974; prof. Intercultural Inst. Calif., San Francisco, 1996—; chmn. Shinergy, LLC, San Francisco, 2001—. Contbr. over 100 articles on biophysics, math. physics and elem. particle physics, superconduuctivity, optical properties of metals to profl. jours.; patentee in field. Woodrow Wilson fellow Harvard U., 1959. Mem. AAAS, Am. Phys. Soc. (life), N.Y. Acad. Scis. Achievements include patent for bouyancy-driven electric power generator, 2005; development of space-time theory of fundamental particles, 2005. Avocations: ranching, gardening, painting, fishing. Office: Chestnut Hill Inst PO Box 3510 Napa CA 94558-0350 Home: 31 Skipping Rock Way Napa CA 94558-7006 Personal E-mail: eunho@aol.com. Business E-Mail: ernestshin@shinergyusa.com.

SHIN, EUI-CHEOL, medical researcher; b. Seoul, Republic Of Korea, Aug. 29, 1971; s. Hyun-Po Shin and Young-Ja Park; m. Sue Haksoo Kim, June 7, 2003. MD, Yonsei U. Sch. Medicine, Seoul, Republic of Korea, 1996; PhD, Yonsei U., Seoul, Republic of Korea, 2001. Lic. doctor Korean Med. Assn., 1996. Chief med. scientist Armed Forces Rsch. Inst. Medicine, Daejon, Republic of Korea, 1999—2002; rsch. fellow Nat. Inst. Diabetes and Digestive and Kidney Diseases, NIH, Bethesda, Md., 2002—. Home: 239 Winter Walk Dr Gaithersburg MD 20878 Office: NIDDK NIH Bldg 10 Rm 9B11 10 Center Dr Bethesda MD 20892 Home Phone: 301-527-0077; Office Phone: 301-402-6930. Office Fax: 301-402-0491. Personal E-mail: ecshin@hotmail.com. Business E-Mail: euicheols@mail.nih.gov.

SHIN, HYUN JOON, industrial engineering professor; b. Seoul, Republic of Korea, Oct. 3, 1971; arrived in US, 2002; s. Seung Kyun Shin and Chung Mi Chang; m. Ji Yoon Jung, Jan. 9, 1999; 1 child, Mina J. BS in indsl. engring., Korea U., Republic of Korea, 1995; MS in indsl. engring., Korea U., 1999; PhD, Korea U., Seoul, 2002. Postdoctoral rschr. Tex. A&M U., College Station, 2002—04; sr. engr. Samsung Electronics Co., Ltd., Asan, Choongnam, Republic of Korea, 2004—05; asst. prof. dept. indsl. info. and sys. engring. Sangmyung U., 2005—. Sr. rschr. Korea U., Seoul, 1997—2002. Fellow, Korea Sci. and Engring. Found., 2003. Home: Dujeongdong Daelim Apt 101-1101 Choongnam Cheonan 330-210 Republic of Korea Office: Sangmyung Univ Anseodong 98-20 Choongnam Cheonan 330-720 Republic of Korea Home Phone: 82-10-7148-6786; Office Phone: 82-41-550-5374. Fax: 82-41-550-5185. Personal E-mail: hjshin@smu.ac.kr.

SHIN, MYUNG-KI, computer scientist, researcher; b. Seoul, Republic of Korea, Feb. 27, 1970; s. Jung-Hwan Shin and Hee-Hyoung Kim; m. Hyun-Joo Park, Mar. 24, 1996; children: Ah-Young Judy, Tai-Yon Tony. BS in Computer Sci., Hongik U., Seoul, 1992, MS in Computer Sci., 1994; PhD in Computer Engring., Chungnam Nat. U., Daejeon, Republic of Korea, 2003. Rschr. Electronics and Telecom. Rsch. Inst., Deajeon, Republic of Korea, 1994—2000, sr. rschr., 2000—03; guest rschr. Nat. Inst. Stds. and Tech., Gaithersburg, Md., 2004—. Chmn. tech. group Open Sys. Interconnection Association, Seoul, 1997—2000; rapporteur Asia—Pacific Telecommunity Standardization Program, Bangkok, 1999; working group chair IPv6 Forum Korea, Daejeon, 2000—03; program com. Global IPv6 Summit, Luxembourg, 2001—03; editor Internet Engring. Task Force, Reston, 2003—. Author: (internat. std.) Dual Stack Hosts Using Bump-in-the-API (Min. Award of Info. and Communication (South Korea), 2003); editor: Application Aspects of IPv6 Transition; author: (book) Next-Generation Protocol. Named This Year's Netizen, Nat. Computerization Agy., 1996; recipient Superior Rschr. award, Electronics and Telecom. Rsch. Inst., 2001. Mem.: Inst. Electronics, Info. and Comm. Engrs. Achievements include development of eXplicit Multicast Extension (Xcast+); IPv6 network and application deployment. Avocations: travel, golf, movies. Office: Elec and Telecomm Rsch Inst 161 Gajeong-dong Yuseong-gu Daejeon 305 700 Republic of Korea

SHIN, SUNGJAE, nutritionist; b. Busan, South Korea, Dec. 15, 1968; s. Yonggoo Shin and Boonnam Lee; m. Kyungil Choi, Mar. 9, 1996; children: Minsuk children: Chewon, Cheyoung. Doctorate, Tokyo U. Fisheries, 1998. Cert. food processing Korea Certifying Orgn. Investigator Nat. Inst. Health and Nutrition, Tokyo, 2001—03; rsch. scholar U. Pitts., Pitts., 2003—. Contbr. scientific papers to profl. publs. Recipient Japanese Inviting Ednl. scholarship, Ministry Edn. In Japan, 1994—98, univ. scholarship, Pukyong U., 1987—94, rsch. grant, Jst Co., 2001. Mem.: JSBBA (assoc.). Achievements include research in Influence of the origin and level of dietary protein on TBI-induced oxidative damage in mice; Different onsets of oxidative damage to DNA and lipids in bone marrow and liver in rats given total body irradiation; Prostaglandin E2 reinforces the activation of Ras signal pathway in lung adenocarcinoma cells via EP3; Relation between oxidative damage and dietary protein: marginal protein level which modulates oxidative damage in mice with total body irradiation; Adequate intakes of vitamin E and protein prevent increases of oxidative damage to DNA, lipids, and protein induced by total body irradiation in mice; Vitamin E modulates radiation-induced oxidative damage in mice fed a high-lipid diet; Severe DNA damage in K-ras gene patterns of PCR products in mice fed a 1% protein diet and exposed to a high dose of radiation; High levels of apoptosis induced by total body irradiation in mice fed a low protein-low vitamin E diet; High levels of apoptosis induced by total body irradiation in mice fed a low protein-low vitamin E diet; High oleic acid oil suppresses lung tumorigenesis in mice through the modulation of extracellular signal-regulated kinase cascade; Induction of apoptosis in a human breast cancer cell overexpressing ErbB-2 receptor by alpha-tocopheryloxybutyric acid; Enhanced oxidative damage induced by total body irradiation in mice fed a low protein diet. Office: U Pitts Pittsburgh PA 15219 Home: 6 Resident Dr Apt C Killeen TX 76549-4136 Home Phone: 412-848-3447. Personal E-mail: ssjkfrihan@hanmail.net.

SHIN, SUNNY HYUCKSUN, social worker, educator; arrived in US, 1993; s. Jae-yeol Shin and Eu-Ja Chung; m. Eunice Eunkyung Lee. BA, Soongsil U., Seoul, 1996; MSW, U. Wis., Madison, 1998; PhD, U. Ill., Urbana-Champaign, 2002. Lic. sch. social worker Wis., 1998. Asst. prof. Boston U. Sch. Social Work, 2002—. Consulting editor Families in Soc. Alliance for Children and Families, Washington, 2003—; consulting editor Children and Sch. NASW, Washington. Co-dir. Fishes and Loaves, Cambridge, Mass., 2002—05. Grantee Youth Alcohol Prevention Rsch., Nat. Inst. Alcohol Abuse and Alcoholism, 2006—; Child Intervention, Prevention, and Svcs. fellow, NIMH, 2005. Office: Boston University School Social Work 264 Bay State Rd Boston MA 02215 Home Phone: 781-237-2145; Office Phone: 617-353-7912. Business E-Mail: hshin@bu.edu.

SHIN, YONGSOON, research scientist; b. Checheon, Chungcheong buk-do, Republic of Korea, Mar. 1, 1965; s. Hyeonpill Shin and Hwawall Jeong; m. Sookyoung Kim, Dec. 24, 1994; children: Mickey K., Michelle K. PhD, U. Tenn., Knoxville, 1999. Postdoctoral Pacific NW Nat. Lab., Richland, Wash., 1999—2001, sr. rsch. scientist, 2002—. Contbr. scientific papers to profl. publs. Recipient Korean Leadership scholarship, 1985—88, Rsch. Merit award, U. Tenn., 1998, Outstanding Performance awards, Pacific NW Nat. Lab., 2002—06. Mem.: Materials Rsch. Soc. (life), Am. Chem. Soc. (life). Achievements include discovery of 5 synthesis of SiC ceramics by the carbothermal reduction of mineralized wood with silica; research in; patents pending for. Home: 1043 Sunstone Court Richland WA 99352 Office: Pacific Northwest Nat Lab 902 Battelle Blvd POBox 999 MSIN K2-44 Richland WA 99354 Office Phone: 509-375-2693. Office Fax: 509-375-2186. Business E-Mail: yongsoon.shin@pnl.gov.

SHINAGEL, MICHAEL, dean, English literature educator; b. Vienna, Apr. 21, 1934; came to U.S., 1941; s. Emanuel and Lilly (Hillel) S.; m. Ann Birdsey Mitchell, Sept. 1, 1956 (div. 1970); children: Mark Mitchell, Victoria Stuart; m. Rosa Joanne Bonanno, Dec. 6, 1973 (div. 1993); m. Marjorie Lee North, May 26, 1995. AB, Oberlin Coll., 1957; AM, Harvard U., 1959, PhD, 1964; Doctorate (hon.), Internat. U. Ecuador, 1997; Doctorate (hon.), U. Argentina Empresa, 2003. Teaching fellow Harvard U., Cambridge, Mass., 1958-59, tutor in English, 1962-64, assoc. dir. career office, 1959-64, dean continuing edn., 1975—, lectr. extension, 1976—, sr. lectr. English, 1983—, master Quincy House, 1986—2001, univ. dean of continuing edn.; asst. prof. English, Cornell U., Ithaca, NY, 1964-67; prof., chmn. dept. English, Union Coll., Schenectady, NY, 1967-75. Bd. dirs. Harvard Coop. Soc., publ. Harvard Rev.; pres. bd. dirs. Ednl. Exch. Boston, 1982-87; editor Continuing Higher Edn. Rev., 1997—. Author: Defoe and Middle-Class Gentility, 1968; co-author: (handbook) Summer Institutes in English, 1965; editor: Concordance to Poems of Swift, 1972, Critical Edition of Robinson Crusoe, 1975 (revised 1993); co-editor: Harvard Scholars in English (1890-1990), 1991. With US Army, 1952—54, Korea. Woodrow Wilson fellow, 1957; NEH grantee, 1965 Mem. Univ. Continuing Edn. Assn., Assn. Continuing Higher Edn., Mass. Hist. Soc., Old South Meeting House, The Johnsonians, The Saturday Club, Harvard Faculty Club (pres. 1985-87), Phi Beta Kappa. Avocations: reading, cooking, music, tennis. Home: 22 Grozier Rd Cambridge MA 02138 Office: Harvard U Divsn Continuing Edn 51 Brattle St Cambridge MA 02138-3701 Office Phone: 617-495-2930. Business E-Mail: michael_shinagel@harvard.edu.

SHINDER, MARCELLA MARIE, marketing executive; b. Indpls., Jan. 4, 1967; d. Anthony S. and Bernice (Duffy) Lazar; m. Richard Shinder, June 29, 1991; 1 child. BEd, Gonzaga U., 1989; MA, Villanova U., 1992. Joined Am. Express, NYC, 1993, with B2B Corp. Svcs., v.p. strategic planning Global Fin. Svcs., v.p. global mktg. Am. Express Bus. Travel, 2003; v.p. brand mktg. and strategy OPEN from Am. Express, NYC. Polit. analyst NY for Guiliani, 1993. Mem.: Women Pres.'s Orgn. (bd. dirs., adv. coun.). Republican. Roman Catholic. Avocation: running. Office: Am Express 200 Vesey St 50th Fl New York NY 10285 *

SHINDLE, WILLIAM RICHARD, retired musicologist, educator; b. Van Orin, Ill., Nov. 2, 1930; s. Ira William Shindle and Elsie Virginia Showalter. MusB, Ill. Wesleyan U., Bloomington, 1959; MusM in Musicology, Ind. U., Bloomington, 1963, PhD in Musicology, 1970. Sch. tchr. Calvert County HS, Prince Frederick, Md., 1959—60; instr., libr. Harpur Coll., Binghamton, 1964—65; prof. musicology Kent State U., Ohio, 1966—91, prof. emeritus, 1991—. Contbr. articles to Grove Dictionary of Music and Musicians, 2nd edit., Ercole Pasquini: Collected Keyboard Works, Girolamo Frescobaldi: Keyboard Compositions Preserved in Manuscripts, 3 Vol., Jean de Macque: Sieben Madrigale zu 5 und 6 Stimmen, and various profl. jours. 2nd class petty officer USN, 1951—55. Fellow, Ind. U., 1965—66; Summer Rsch. fellow, Kent State U., 1974, 1980, 1983. Mem.: Am. Musicological Soc., Pa. German Soc. Avocation: genealogy.

SHINDLER, DANIEL, cardiologist; MD, U. Seville, Spain, 1979. Prof. Robert Wood Johnson Med Sch., New Brunswick, NJ, dir. echocardiography; chair pharmacy & therapeutics Robert Wood Johnson U. Hosp. Editor: (internet e-chocardiography jour.) www2.umdnj.edu/shindler. Recipient Top Dr. award, Castle Connolly, 2000—06. Office: Robert Wood Johnson Med Sch 125 Paterson St New Brunswick NJ 08901 Home Phone: 732-235-7854.

SHINDLER, DONALD A., lawyer; b. New Orleans, Oct. 15, 1946; s. Alan and Isolene (Levy) S.; m. Laura Epstein, 1969; children: Jay, Susan. BSBA, Washington U., St. Louis, 1968; JD, Tulane U., 1971. Bar: La. 1971, U.S. Dist. Ct. (ea. dist.) La. 1971, U.S. Tax Ct. 1974, Ill. 1975, U.S. Dist. Ct. (no. dist.) Ill. 1975; CPA, La.; lic. real estate broker, Ill. Assoc. Pope, Ballard, Shepard & Fowle, Chgo., 1975-78, Rudnick & Wolfe, Chgo., 1978-81, ptnr., 1981-99; gen. counsel America's Second Harvest Nat. Food Bank Network, 1998-2000; ptnr. Piper Marbury Rudnick & Wolfe, Chgo., 1999—2002, Piper Rudnick LLP, Chgo., 2002—05, DLA Piper Rudnick Gray Cary US LLP, Chgo., 2005—. Lectr. in field. Contbr. articles on real estate to legal jours. Trustee Glencoe (Ill.) Pub. Libr., 1981-87, pres., 1986-87; alumni bd. govs. Washington U., 1992-93; mem. Glencoe Zoning Commn./Bd. Appeals, 1994-2000; Glencoe Plan Commn, 1986-87. Lt. JAGC, USNR, 1971-75. Fellow Am. Coll. Mortgage Attys.; mem. ABA, Ill. Leading Lawyers, La. State Bar Assn., Chgo. Bar Assn. (com. chmn. 1979-80, 83-84, 90-94, 96-99, editor land trust seminars 1984-96), Ill. Super Lawyers, Urban Land Inst. (mem. steering com. Chgo. dist. coun.), Ill. Super Lawyers (R/E), CoreNet Global (pres. Chgo. chpt. 1997-98, dir. 1991-2003), Internat. Assn. Attys. and Execs. in Corp. Real Estate (fall forum co-chair 2002, spring conf. co-chair, 2003, bd. dirs. 2003—), Union League Club (chair real estate group 1993-96), Order of Coif, Beta Gamma Sigma, Omicron Delta Kappa. Office: DLA Piper Rudnick Gray Cary US LLP Ste 1900 203 N La Salle St Chicago IL 60601-1210 Office Phone: 312-368-2175. Business E-Mail: donald.shindler@dlapiper.com.

SHINDLER, STEVEN M., telecommunications industry executive; m. Mary Kay Shindler; 3 children. BA, Univ. Mich.; MBA, Cornell Univ. Positions through mng. dir. comm. fin. group Toronto Dominion Bank, 1987—96; exec. v.p., CFO Nextel Comm., 1996—2000; CEO Nextel Comm. (now NII Holdings Inc.), 2000—02; chmn., CEO NII Holdings Inc., Reston, Va., 2002—. Named Greater Washington area Entrepreneur of the Yr., Ernst & Young; recipient Bravo Bus. award as Internat. CEO of the Yr., Latin Trade mag. Office: NII Holdings Inc Ste 600 10700 Parkridge Blvd Reston VA 20191 *

SHINDO, CHARLES J., historian, director; b. LA, Calif., Aug. 4, 1959; s. George and May Shindo. BA, U. So. Calif., LA, 1984; MA, Calif. State U., Fullerton, 1987; PhD, U. Rochester, NY, 1992. Asst. prof. history La. State U., Baton Rouge, 1992—97, assoc. prof. history, 1997—. Office: La State Univ Department of History Baton Rouge LA 70803

SHINE, KATINA LYNNIECE WILBON, neuropsychologist, consultant; d. Alma Armstead. Diploma in practical nursing, Bapt. Sch. Nursing, Little Rock, 1991; ASN, AA, U. Ark., Little Rock, 1996; BS in Liberal Arts,

SUNY, Albany, 1998; MS in Counseling Psychology, U. Ctl. Tex., 1999; PhD in Psychology, U. Louisville, 2002. RN Mo.; lic. psychologist Mo. Staff nurse Ark. Easter Seal Soc., Little Rock, 1993—96; primary care nurse, mgr. Hospice of Ctrl. Ark., North Little Rock, 1996—97; intake coord., psychiat. nurse Metroplex Health Sys., Killeen, Tex., 1997—99; grad. asst., neuropsychology trainee U. Louisville, 2000—01; psychology intern St. Louis VA Med. Ctr., 2001—02, clin. psychologist, neuropsychology clin. mgr., 2002—. Rschr., lectr. in field. Contbr. articles to profl. jours. Vol. ARC Disaster Mental Health Team, St. Louis, 2004, Mental Health Assn. of St. Louis, 2004. Recipient Grad. Dean's citation, U. Louisville, 2002; fellow Acad. fellow, 1999—2001; scholar Edn. Alumni Assn. scholar, 1999—2000, Marie Erma Fust Fund scholar, Truman L. Scott scholar, U. Ark.-Little Rock, 1995, L.A. Horn Meml. scholar, 1995. Mem.: APA (divsn. clin. neuropsychology, divsn. of psychologists in pub. svc.), Nat. Register of Health Svc. Providers, Mo. Psychol. Assn. Office: #1 Jefferson Barracks Dr 116A/JB Saint Louis MO 63026

SHINEFIELD, HENRY ROBERT, pediatrician; b. Paterson, NJ, Oct. 11, 1925; s. Louis and Sarah (Kaplan) Shinefield; m. Jacqueline Marilyn Walker; children: Jill, Michael, Kimberley Putzer, Melissa Strome. BA, Columbia U., 1945, MD, 1948. Diplomate Diplomate: Am. Bd. Pediat. (examiner, 1975—, bd. dirs., 1979-84, v.p., 1981-84). 1949Rotating intern Mt. Sinai Hosp., NYC, 1948; pediatric intern Duke Hosp., Durham, NC, 1949-50; asst. resident pediatrician N.Y. Hosp. (Cornell), 1950-51, pediatrician to outpatients, 1953-59, instr. in pediatrics, 1959-60, asst. prof., 1960-64, asso. prof., 1964-65, asst. attending pediatrician, 1959-63, asso. attending pediatrician, 1963-65; pediatrician to outpatients Children's Hosp., Oakland, Calif., 1951-53; chief of pediatrics Kaiser-Permanente Med. Center, San Francisco, 1965-89, chief emeritus, 1989—; co-dir. Kaiser-Permanente Vaccine Study Ctr., San Francisco, 1984—2005; assoc. clin. prof. pediatrics Sch. Medicine U. Calif., 1966-68, clin. prof. pediatrics, 1968—, clin. prof. dermatology, 1970—; asso. attending pediatrician Paterson (N.J.) Gen. Hosp., 1955-59; chief of pediatrics Kaiser Found. Hosp., San Francisco, 1965-86; attending Moffitt Hosp., San Francisco, 1967-88; practice medicine specializing in pediatrics Paterson, 1953-59. Cons. San Francisco Gen. Hosp., 1967—88, Children's Hosp., San Francisco, 1970—88, Mt. Zion Hosp., San Francisco, 1970—88; mem. rsch. grants rev. br. NIH, HEW, 1970—74; med. dir. USPHSR, 1969—; bd. dirs. San Francisco Peer Rev. Orgn., 1975—81, sec., exec. com., 1976—81; chmn. Calif. State Child Health Disability Bd., 1973—82; mem. Inst. Medicine NAS, 1980—; cons. Bur. Drugs FDA, 1970, NIH, HEW, 1974—85. Editl. bd. We. Jour. Medicine, 1968—80, Am. Jour. Diseases of Children, 1970—82; contbr. articles to profl. publs. Chmn. San Francisco Med. Adv. Com. Nat. Found. March of Dimes, 1969—80. Served USPHS, 1951—53. Fellow: Am. Acad. Pediat. (com. fetus and newborn 1969—76, com. on drugs 1978—82); mem.: AMA, Am. Pediatric Soc., We. Soc. Clin. Rsch., We. Pediatric Soc., Infectious Diseases Soc. Am., Soc. Pediatric Rsch., Phi Beta Kappa. Home: 2240 Hyde St 2 San Francisco CA 94109-1509 Office Phone: 415-519-8613. Personal E-mail: henryshinefield@aol.com.

SHINEMAN, EDWARD WILLIAM, JR., retired pharmaceutical executive; b. Canajoharie, NY, Apr. 9, 1915; s. Edward W. and Bertelle H. (Shubert) S.; m. H. Doris Thompson, Apr. 15, 1939; children: Edward T., Alan B. AB, Cornell U., 1937. With apparatus dept., acctg. dept. Gen. Electric Co., 1938-46, line auditor, 1942-46; with Beech-Nut, Inc. and predecessor cos., 1946-68, asst. treas., 1948-63, contr., 1959-63, treas., 1963-68; asst. sec.-treas. Squibb Corp., 1968-81. Bd. dirs. Taconic Farms, Inc. Trustee Arkell Hall Found.; mem. emeritus coun. Cornell U. Mem. Fin. Execs. Inst., Inst. Mgmt. Accts. Republican. Home: 455 N End Ave Apt 411 New York NY 10282 Personal E-mail: eshineman@aol.com.

SHINER, JOSETTE SHEERAN (JOSETTE SHEERAN), international organization official, former federal agency administrator; b. Orange, NJ, June 12, 1954; d. James Joseph and Sarah Ann (Gallagher) Sheeran; children: Nicole Munier, Daniel John, Gabrielle. BA, U. Colo., 1976. Nat. desk editor N.Y. News World, 1976-77, Washington bur. chief, 1977-80; corr. The White House, 1980-82; Capital Life and mag. editor Washington Times, 1982-84, asst. mng. editor, 1984-85, dep. mng. editor, 1985-92, mng. editor, 1992-97; pres., CEO Empower Am., 1997-2000; mng. dir. Starpoint Solutions, Reston, Va., 2000—01; assoc. U.S. Trade Rep. Exec. Office of the Pres., Washington, 2001—03, dep. U.S. Trade Rep., 2003—05; under sec. for econ. bus. & agrl. affairs US Dept. State, Washington, 2005—06, US alt. gov. to The World Bank, Inter-Am. Bank, African Devel. Bank, Asian Devel. Bank, European Bank for Reconstruction & Devel., 2005—06; exec. dir., World Food Programme UN, Rome, 2007—. Mem. Leadership Washington Alumni Assn., 1987-88, v.p., 1988-89, alumni chmn., 1989-90. Recipient Atrium award U. Ga., 1984, 100 Most Powerful Women in Washington award Washington Mag., 1998. Mem. White House Corrs. Assn., Am. News Womens Club, Nat. Press Club (newsmaker chmn. 1980-82, Meritorious Svc. award 1981, Vivian award 1981), Am. Soc. Newspaper Editors, Coun. Fgn. Rels. (Washington adv. bd. 1999-2001), Sigma Delta Chi. Episcopalian. Office: UN World Food Programme Via CG Viola 68 00148 Rome Italy *

SHINKEL, BERNIE (BERNARD ALBERT SHINKEL), investment advisor; b. 1947; M in Taxation, Walsh Coll. Accountancy and Bus.; M in Mgmt., Purdue U., PhD in Fin. Sr. portfolio mgr., v.p. Huntington Nat. Bank, 1997, portfolio mgr. New Economy Fund, 2001—, lead portfolio mgr. Growth Fund, 2007—. Avocation: skiing. Office: Huntington Nat Bank 7 Easton Oval Columbus OH 43219 Office Phone: 614-331-9452. Office Fax: 614-331-9394. E-mail: bernard.shinkel@huntington.com. *

SHINKLE, JOHN THOMAS, lawyer; b. Albany, NY, May 9, 1946; s. Robert Thomas and Margery Joan (Kneip) S.; m. Csilla Elizabeth Bekasy, Sept. 2, 1967; children: Reka, Ildiko. BA, Yale U., 1967; JD, Harvard U., 1970. Bar: D.C. 1971, N.Y. 1983, U.S. Supreme Ct. 1974. Law clk. U.S. Ct. Appeals for D.C. Cir., Washington, 1970—71; assoc. Caplin & Drysdale, Washington, 1971—77, ptnr., 1977—80; assoc. dir. divsn. corp. fin. SEC, Washington, 1980—81, dep. gen. counsel, 1981—82; gen. counsel Salomon Bros. Inc., NY, 1982—94, v.p., 1982—87, dir., 1988—94, head Asia Pacific legal and compliance, 1995—2003; mng. dir. Salomon Bros. Hong Kong, 1996—97, Salomon Smith Barney Hong Kong, 1998—2003; v.p., dep. gen. counsel Bristol-Myers Squibb Co., NY, 2003—04; gen. counsel global transaction svcs. Citigroup, Inc., NYC, 2003, mng. dir., sr. dep. gen. counsel, global corp. & investment bank, 2004—07, mng. dir., gen. counsel Citi pvt. bank, 2007—. Contbr. articles to profl. jours. Mem. ABA, Assn. Bar City N.Y., Securities Industry Assn. (chmn. fed. regulation com. 1989-91), Futures Industry Assn. (dir. 1989-97). Home: 220 Riverside Blvd Apt 30-G New York NY 10069 Office: Citigroup 787 7th Ave 15th Fl New York NY 10019

SHINN, CLINTON WESLEY, lawyer; b. Haworth, Okla., Mar. 7, 1947; s. Clinton Elmo and Mary Lucille (Dowdy) Shinn; m. Catherine Borne; children: Laura Kathryn, Clinton Wesley, Timothy Daniel. BS, McNeese State U., 1969; JD, Tulane U., 1972; LLM, Harvard U., 1973. Bar: La. 1972, U.S. Dist. Ct. (ea. dist.) La. 1975, U.S. Dist. Ct. (we. dist.) La. 1980, U.S. Ct. Appeals (5th cir.) 1981, U.S. Ct. Appeals (11th cir.) 1982, U.S. Tax Ct. 1982. Asst. prof. law Tulane U., New Orleans, 1973—75; assoc. Stone, Pigman et al, New Orleans, 1975—78, ptnr., 1979—97, Gill & Shinn, LLC, Covington, La., 1998—2000, of counsel, 2000—; assoc. prof. law Appalachian Sch. Law, Grundy, Va., 1999—2002, prof. law, 2006—, dean, COO, 2007—; assoc. prof. law Miss. Coll. Sch. Law, Jackson, 2002—05. Co-founder, bd. dirs. Childhood Ctr. Families Network, 1987—90; co-founder Camp Challenge, 1988; team leader Campaign for Caring, Children's Hosp., New Orleans, 1989—91; bd. dirs. Greater New Orleans YMCA, 1989—98, 1999—2000, exec. com., 1991—98, asst. sec., 1994—95, sec., 1996—98, mem. fin. com., 1994—98, exec. dir. search com., 1996, 2d vice-chair, 1998; mem. Leadership Coun., 1997—98; active Indian Guides/Princesses; bd. dirs. West ST. Tammany YMCA, 1987—95, exec. com., 1988—95, chmn. bd. dirs., 1989—90, 1992—93; bd. dirs. La. Air & Waste Mgmt. Assn., 1993—99, chmn. corp. rels. com., 1992—93, vice chmn., 1996—97, chair, 1997—98, past chair, 1998—99; bd. dirs. Christ Episcopal Sch., Covington, 1988—91, chmn. long-range planning, 1990—91, mem. exec. com., 1989—91, chmn. legal com., 1989—91, chmn. admissions/recruitment com., 1988—90, mem. headmaster search com., 1993; bd. dirs. Christwood, 1992—2001, v.p. bd. dirs., 1997—99; bd. dirs. St. Catherine's Village Found., 2004—. Co-recipient Pals of the Yr. award, Greater New Orleans YMCA Indian Guides/Princesses, 1987—88; named Vol. of the Yr., West St. Tammany YMCA, 1990, 1992. Fellow: La. Bar Found., Am. Coll. Trust and Estate Counsel; mem.: ABA, Air and Waste Mgmt. Assn., New Orleans Estate Planning Coun., Nat. Wildlife Fedn. (life), La. Forestry Assn., La. Bar Assn., Nat. Assn. Securities Dealers (bd. arbitrators), Charles Clark Inn of Ct., Order Coif. Avocations: backpacking, gardening. Home: 101 Aspen Dr Madison MS 39110 Office: Appalachian Sch Law One Slate Creek Rd Grundy VA 24614 *In all things be firm but fair.*

SHINN, DAVID HAMILTON, former diplomat, educator, writer; b. Yakima, Wash., June 9, 1940; s. Guy Wilson and Ada Louise (Gelvin) S.; m. Judy Karen Rolfe, Sept. 9, 1961; children: Steven Hamilton, Christopher Rolfe. AA, Yakima Valley Coll., 1960; BA, George Washington U., 1963, MA, 1964, PhD, 1980; cert. African studies, Northwestern U., Evanston, Ill., 1969. With U.S. State Dept., 1964-2000; rotational officer U.S. Embassy, Beirut, Lebanon, 1964-66; polit. officer Nairobi, Kenya, 1967-68; desk officer East African affairs Washington, 1969-72; polit. officer Dar es Salaam, Tanzania, 1972-74; dep. chief of mission Nouakchott, Mauritania, 1974-76, Office of Mayor, City of Seattle, 1977-78; dep. coord. state and local govt. U.S. Dept. State, Washington, 1978-81; dep. chief of mission Yaounde, Cameroon, 1981-83, Khartoum, Sudan, 1983-86; U.S. ambassador Ouagadougou, Burkina Faso, 1987-90; diplomat-in-residence Southern U., Baton Rouge, La., 1990-91; diplomat State Dept., Washington, 1991-96; U.S. Amb. Addis Ababa, Ethiopia, 1996-99; diplomat-in-residence UCLA, 1999-2000. Adj. prof. George Washington U., 2001—. Co-author: Historical Dictionary of Ethiopia, 2004. Pres. Am. Friends for Inst. Ethiopian Studies; trustee forum internat. Ethiopians Living in Diaspara; adv. People to People, Inc.; bd. dirs. Horn Relief, Ethiopian Christian Relief and Devel. Assn.; bd. dirs. African Ctr. Health and Human Security George Washington U. Recipient Superior Honor award State Dept., 1980, 85, 94, Alumnus of Yr. award Am. Assn. Cmty. Colls., 1994, Phi Theta Kappa, 1995. Mem. Internat. Studies Assn., Ethiopian Studies Assn., Am. Fgn. Svc. Assn., Sudan Studies Assn., Mid. East Inst., African Studies Assn., Am. Philatelic Soc., Rotary Internat. Methodist. Avocations: philately, skiing, physical fitness, antiques. Address: 23 8th St SE Washington DC 20003 Personal E-mail: dhshinn@earthlink.net.

SHINN, GEORGE, professional sports team owner; b. Kannapolis, NC, May 11, 1941; m. Denise Shinn, Mar. 8, 2003; children: Susan, Chad; 1 child, Chris. Student, Evans Bus. Coll., Concord, NC. Ptnr. Evans Bus. Coll.; owner Rutland Edn. Systems, New Orleans/Okla. City (formerly Charlotte) Hornets, 1988—. Author: Miracle of Motivation, The Am. Dream Still Works, You Gotta Believe! The Story of the Charlotte Hornets, Introduction to Professional Selling, Leadership Development. Co-chair fundraising com. Tulane U.; bd. mem. Boy Scouts Am., Nat. D-Day Mus., New Orleans Metrovision Exec. Com., Loyola U. Mem.: Horatio Alger Assn. of Disting. Ams. (Horatio Alger award 1975). Office: New Orleans/Okla City Hornets 1615 Poydras St Fl 20 New Orleans LA 70112 *

SHINN, GEORGE LATIMER, investment banker, consultant, finance educator; b. Newark, Ohio, Mar. 12, 1923; s. Leon Powell and Bertha Florence (Latimer) S.; m. Clara LeBaron Sampson, May 21, 1949; children: Deborah, Amy, Martha, Sarah, Andrew. AB, Amherst Coll., 1948; LLD (hon.), Denison U., 1975, Amherst Coll., 1982; MA, Drew U., 1990, PhD, 1992. Trainee Merrill Lynch, Pierce, Fenner & Beane, 1948-49; various exec. positions, 1949-75; pres. Merrill Lynch & Co., Inc., 1973-75; chmn. bd., chief exec. officer 1st Boston Corp., 1975-83; investment banking cons., 1983—2002. Adj. prof. history Drew U., Madison, N.J., 1992—2002; mem. exec. com. President's Pvt. Sector Survey on Cost Control, 1982-84; exec.-in-residence Columbia U. Grad. Sch. Bus., 1983-85; bd. govs. Am. Stock Exch., 1970-74; bd. dirs., trustee Colonial Group Mut. Funds, 1983-98; bd. dirs. Kelso & Co., 1992—, N.Y. Stock Exch., 1975-83, vice chmn., 1979-83; bd. dirs. N.Y. Times Co., 1978-99, Phelps, Dodge Corp., 1983-95, N.Y. Life Ins. Co., 1983-94, Lehigh Press, 1983-91, Superior Oil Co., 1984-87, Congoleum Corp. Gen. chmn. United Hosp. Fund, N.Y.C., 1973-74; trustee Kent Pl. Sch., Summit, N.J., 1966-73, Carnegie Found. for Advancement Teaching, 1976-85, Pingry Sch., 1977-79, Lucille P. Markey Charitable Trust, 1985-97, Rockefeller Family Office Trust, 1989-97, N.J. Coun. for the Humanities, 1994-2000, Arts Coun. Morris Area, 1978-91, Philharmonic Symphony Soc. N.Y., 1983-91, Nat. Humanities Ctr., 1988-94; trustee emeritus Amherst Coll., 1968-82, chmn. bd. trustees, 1973-80; bd. dirs. Rsch. Corp., 1975-86. Capt. USMCR, 1943-52. Fellow Am. Acad. Arts and Scis., N.Y. Acad. Medicine, River Club, Century Assn. Personal E-mail: gshinn1059@aol.com.

SHINNAR, REUEL, engineering educator, consultant; b. Vienna, Sept. 15, 1923; came to US, 1962; s. Abraham Emil and Rosa (Storch) Bardfeld; m. Miryam Halpern, June 22, 1948; children: Shlomo, Meir Diploma in Chem. Engring., Technion, Haifa, Israel, 1945, M.Sc. in Chem. Engring., 1954; Dr. Engring. Sci., Columbia U., 1957. Various position in chem. engring., Israel, 1945-58; adj. assoc. prof. Technion, Haifa, Israel, 1958-62; visiting research fellow Guggenheim Labs., Princeton (N.J.) U., 1962-64; prof. chem. engring. CCNY, 1964—, disting. prof., 1979—. Pinhas Naor lectr. Technion U., 1974; Wilhelm Meml. lectr. Princeton U., 1985, Kelly lectr. Purdue U., 1991; cons. to various oil and chem. cos. Contbr. numerous articles to profl. jours.; patentee in field. Fellow AICE (Founders award 1992, Alpha Chi Sigma award 1979), N.Y. Acad. Scis.; mem. AIAA, Am. Chem. Soc., Nat. Acad. Engring. Office: City Coll NY Dept Chem Engring 140th St and Convent Ave New York NY 10031 Office Phone: 212-650-6679. Business E-mail: shinnar@ccny.cuny.edu.

SHINNERS, STANLEY MARVIN, electrical engineer; b. NYC, May 9, 1933; s. Earl and Molly (Planter) Shinners; m. Doris Shinners, Aug. 4, 1956; children: Sharon Rose Cooper, Walter Jay, Daniel Lawrence. BEE, CCNY, 1954; MSEE, Columbia U., 1959. Equipment engr. Western Electric Co., NYC, 1953-54; staff engr. electronics divsn. Otis Elevator Co., Bklyn., 1954-56; project engr. Consol. Avionics Corp., Westbury, NY, 1956-58; program mgr., fed. sys. Lockheed Martin Corp. (formerly Loral Corp., Unisys Corp.), Mitchel Field, NY, 1958-99. Adj. prof. engring. The Cooper Union, NYC, 1966—, NY Inst. Tech., Old Westbury, NY, 1972-92, Poly. Inst. Bklyn., 1959-72. Author: Control System Design, 1964, Techniques of Systems Engineering, 1967, A Guide to Systems Engineering and Management, 1976, Modern Control System Theory and Application, 1978, Modern Control System Theory and Design, 1992, 2d edit., 1998, Advanced Modern Control System Theory and Design, 1998. Recipient Career Achievement medal, CCNY Alumni Assn., 1980. Fellow IEEE (life); mem. Am. Soc. for Engring. Edn., Eta Kappa Nu, Tau Beta Pi. Home: 28 Sagamore Way N Jericho NY 11753-2358 Personal E-mail: shinnerssm@optonline.net. *I was very poor financially as a child, but I received an abundance of love and encouragement from parents and family. I have always tried to succeed and to help others succeed. Above all, I have always tried to do what is right whether the decision had to be made in the business world or in private and family matters.*

SHINOHARA, KATSUTO, medical educator; b. Nagano, Japan, Apr. 26, 1954; s. Mitsuo and Fukue Shinohara; m. Beni Shinohara, Jan. 22, 1983; children: Yuma S., Reina M. MD, Yokohama City U., Japan, 1979. Prof. U. Calif., San Francisco, 2004—. Mem.: Japanese Urological Assn., Am. Urological Assn. Office: University of California San Francisco 1600 Divisadero St San Francisco CA 94143-1695 Office Phone: 415-353-7101.

SHINOLT, EILEEN THELMA, artist; b. Washington, May 18, 1919; d. Edward Lee and Blanche Addie (Marsh) Bennett; m. John Francis Shinolt, June 14, 1956 (dec. Aug. 1969). Student, Hans Hoffman Sch Art, 1949, Pa. Acad. Arts, 1950, Corcoran Sch. Art, 1945-51, Am. U., 1973-77. Sect. chief Dept. Army, Washington, 1940-73, retired, 1973. One-woman shows include various locations, 1982, 83, 85, 90, 94, 96; group shows include Perlmutter & Co., 1981, Fitch Fox and Brown, 1986, Foundry Gallery, 1987, Ann. Add Arts, 1986, Westminster Gallery, London, 1995; represented in permanent collections Women's Nat. Mus., Washington, Cameo Gallery, Columbia, S.C., Strathmore Hall Arts Ctr., North Bethesda, Md., 1997, 98, 99, 2000, 01, 02, 03, 04. Mem. Woman's Nat. Dem. Club, Washington, 1980—. Mem. Am. Art League (editor newsletter 1985-86, 1st pl. 1987, 2d pl. 1986), Arts Club Washington (exhbn. com. 1985—, admissions com. 1987-88), Miniature Painters, Sculptors & Gravers Soc. (historian 1989-2003, editor newsletter 1986-89), Fine Arts in Miniature. Roman Catholic. Avocations: reading, studying art periodicals, art galleries.

SHINOZAKI, TAMOTSU, retired physician, retired anesthesiologist; b. Dairen, Japan, Mar. 18, 1934; s. Yuichi and Shizue Shniozaki; m. Kazuko Sakanaka Shinozaki, Feb. 14, 1940; children: Aritomo, Yuji, Emiko. MD, Okayama U., 1958, D in Med. Scis., 1963. Diplomate Am. Bd. Anesthesiology; cert. spl. qualifications in critical care medicine. Intern St. Luke's Internat. Hosp., Tokyo, 1958—59; resident in anesthesiology Mary Fletcher Hosp., 1964—67; attending anesthesiologist Med. Ctr. Hosp. of Vt., Burlington, 1967—99; asst. prof. Med. Sch. U. Vt., Burlington, 1967—72, assoc. prof., 1972—90, clin. prof., 1990—99, med. co-dir. surg. ICU, 1985—99, prof. emeritus, 2000—; adminstrv. dir. surg. ICU Fletcher Allen Healthcare, Burlington, 1997—99, attending emeritus, 2000—. Cons. med. divsn. Hewlett Packard Co., Waltham, Mass., 1972-77, Intelligent Med. Sys., Carlsbad, Calif., 1987. Recipient Quality Cup award, Excellence in the Quality Movement, 1994. Fellow Am. Coll. Critical Care Medicine; mem. Sigma Xi. Home: 335 Dorset Hts South Burlington VT 05403 Business E-Mail: tshinoza@zoo.uvm.edu.

SHINSEKI, ERIC KEN, retired military officer; b. Lihue, Hawaii, Nov. 28, 1942; BS, U.S. Mil. Acad., 1965; MA in English, Duke U., 1976; student, U.S. Army Armor Sch., Ft. Knox, Ky., 1968-69, Army Command and Staff Coll., Ft. Leavenworth, Kans., 1978-79, Nat. War Coll., Ft. Lesley McNair, Washington, 1985-86. Commd. 2d lt. U.S. Army, 1965, advanced through grades to gen., 1997, ret., 2003; forward observer B battery 2d battalion, 9th artillery, 3d brigade, 25th Infantry Divsn., U.S. Army, Vietnam, 1965-66; asst. S1 (pers.) base defense command XXIV Corps U.S. Army, Vietnam, 1969-70; comdr. A Troop, 3d squadron, 5th cavalry, 9th infantry divsn attached to 1st brigade, 5th infantry divsn. U.S. Army, Vietnam, 1970; pers. staff officer U.S. Army Pacific, Fort Shafter, Hawaii, 1971-74; instr. dept. English U.S. Mil. Acad., West Point, N.Y., 1976-78; comdr. 3d squadron 7th cavalry, 3d infantry divsn. then asst chief of staff, G-3, U.S. Army Europe and 7th Army, Germany, 1982-85; comdr. 2d brigade, 3d infantry divsn., to asst chief staff G3 VII Corps, U.S. Army Europe and 7th Army, 1987-90; dep. chief of staff adminstrn./logistics Allied Land Forces So. Europe, Germany, 1990-92; asst. divsn. comdr., 3d infantry divsn. U.S. Army and 7th Army Europe, Germany, 1992-93; commanding gen. 1st Cav. Divsn., Ft. Hood, Tex., 1994-95; asst. dep. chief of staff (ops. and plans) to dep. chief of staff U.S. Army, Washington, 1995-97, comdr. in chief, comdr. Stblzn. Force, U.S. Army Europe and 7th Army Bosnia-Herzegovina, 1997-98, vice chief of staff Washington, 1998-99, chief of staff, 1999—2003. Decorated Defense Disting. Svc. medal, Disting. Svc. medal, Legion of Merit with oak leaf cluster, Bronze Star medal with V device with 3 oak leaf clusters, Purple Heart with oak leaf cluster, Meritorious Svc. medal with 2 oak leaf clusters, Air medal, Army Commendation medal with oak leaf cluster, Army Achievement medal. *

SHIONOIRI, HIDEO, computer technologist; b. Urawa, Saitama, Japan, July 15; arrived in U.S., 1996; m. Kimiko Sekine; 1 child, Yayoi. MSc in MIS, LaSalle U., La., 1998. Sys. designer Kawasaki Steel Corp., Japan, 1966—68; project mgr. CAC, Tokyo, 1968—71; project leader CSG, Canada, 1971—77; mgr. info. tech. Permanent Trust, Toronto, Ont., Canada, 1977—83; v.p. info. sys. Barclays Bank of Can., Toronto, 1983—96; sr. tech. advisor, ptnr. CGI-AMS, NYC, 1996—. Achievements include research in international and wholesale banking systems software development and integration. Office: CGI-AMS 1 Chase Plz New York NY 10005 Home: 6306 City Pl Edgewater NJ 07020 Business E-Mail: hideo.shionoiri@cgi.com.

SHIPE, DALE ALLEN, music educator; b. Chicago Heights, Ill., Nov. 12, 1955; s. Howard Earl and Clara Jean Shipe; m. Nancee Ann Rieke, Apr. 12, 1957; children: Valerie Louise, Elizabeth Lynn, Kurt Allen. BS in Music Edn., U. Ill., Champaign, 1977, MS in Music Edn., 1979. Cert. tchr. Wis., 1989. Band dir. Cerro Gordo Pub. Schs., Ill., 1977—79; grad. asst. U. Ill., Urbana-Champaign, 1979—80; band dir. Herrin HS, 1980—82, Reavis HS, Burbank, 1982—88; band dir., music instr. U. No. Iowa, Cedar Falls, 1988—89; band dir. Theisen Jr. HS, Fond du Lac, Wis., 1989—2001, Fond du Lac HS, 2001—. Assoc. condr. Fond du Lac Symphonic Band, Wis., 2001—. Named Tchr. of Yr., Fond du Lac HS, 2006—07; Herb Kohl Tchg. fellow, 2007. Mem.: Wis. Sch. Music Assn., Music Educators Nat. Conf., Wis. Bandmasters Assn. (exec. bd. mem. 1999—2006), Internat. Assn. Jazz Educators, Phi Delta Kappa. Lutheran. Avocations: woodworking, travel. Home: 582 Taylor Ct Fond Du Lac WI 54935 Office: Fond du Lac HS 801 Campus Dr Fond Du Lac WI 54935 Home Phone: 920-921-7041; Office Phone: 920-906-6700 3335. Personal E-mail: shipe@charter.net.

SHIPKO, JANET M., program director; b. Schenectady, NY, Nov. 3, 1953; d. Frederick J. and Elizabeth Shipko. MSC in Health Care Mgmt., U. Md., 1996. Asst. chief of staff, res. affairs Tripler Army Med. Ctr., Honolulu, 2003—06; chief res. policy Office of Surgeon Gen., Falls Church, Va., 2006—; program dir. res. affairs Office of Sec. of Def., 2007—. Col. USAR, 1982. Decorated Meritorious Svc. medal (4), Army Commendation medal (3), Army Superior Unit award (1), Armed Forces Res. medal (2), Army Achievement medal (3), Nat. Def. Svc. medal (3), Global War on Terrorism medal (1). Home: 3709 S George Mason Drive Apt 1705E Falls Church VA 22041 Office Phone: 703-578-8520. Business E-Mail: janet.m.shipko@us.army.mil.

SHIPLER, DAVID KARR, journalist, writer; b. Orange, NJ, Dec. 3, 1942; s. Guy Emery Jr. and Eleanor (Karr) Shipler; m. Deborah S. Isaacs, Sept. 17, 1966; children: Jonathan Robert, Laura Karr, Michael Edmund. AB, Dartmouth Coll., 1964; LittD (hon.), Middlebury Coll., 1988, Glassboro State Coll., NJ, 1988; AM (hon.), Dartmouth Coll., 1994; JD (hon.), Birmingham Southern Coll., 2006. News clk. N.Y. Times, 1966—67, news summary writer, 1968, reporter met. staff, 1968—73, fgn. corr. Saigon bur., 1973—75, fgn. corr. Moscow Bur., 1975—, bur. chief Moscow bur., 1977—79, chief Jerusalem bur., 1979—84, corr. Washington bur.,

1985—87, chief diplomatic corr., 1987—88; sr. assoc. Carnegie Endowment for Internat. Peace, Washington, 1988—90. Guest scholar Brookings Instn., 1984—85; adj. prof. Am. U. Sch. Internat. Svc., Washington, 1990; Ferris prof. journalism and pub. affairs Princeton U., 1990—91; Woodrow Wilson vis. fellow, 1990—; writer-in-residence U. So. Calif., 1998; Montgomery fellow, vis. prof. gov. Dartmouth Coll., 2003. Author: Russia: Broken Idols, Solemn Dreams, 1983 (Overseas Press Club award), revised, 1989, Arab and Jew: Wounded Spirits in a Promised Land, 1986 (Pulitzer prize for Gen. Nonfiction, 1987), revised, 2002, A Country of Strangers: Blacks and Whites in America, 1997, The Working Poor: Invisible in America, 2004 (Myers Outstanding Book award Simmons Coll., finalist Nat. Book Critics Cir. award, finalist Helen Bernstein N.Y. Pub. Lib. award); exec. prodr.: (documentaries) from Arab and Jew: Wounded Spirits in a Promised Land, 1989 (Alfred DuPont-Columbia U. award for Broadcast Journalism, 1990), Arab and Jew: Return to the Promised Land, 2002; contbr. articles to nat. mags. Trustee Dartmouth Coll., 1993—2003. With USNR, 1964—66. Co-recipient George Polk award, 1982; recipient award for disting. reporting, Soc. Silurians, 1971, award for disting. pub. affairs reporting, Am. Polit. Sci. Assn., 1971, award, N.Y. chpt. Sigma Delta Chi, 1973, Vento award, Nat. Law Ctr. on Homelessness and Poverty, 2004, Martin Luther King, Jr. Social Justice award, Dartmouth Coll., 2005, Labor Communicator of Yr. award, NY Labor Comms. Coun., 2005, award, DC Employment Justice Ctr., 2005. Office: 4005 Thornapple St Chevy Chase MD 20815-5037 *I have been governed professionally by the conviction that an open society needs open examination of itself to survive. Defining problems, inspecting blemishes, probing wounds, and exposing injustice are the required pastimes of a free people. Nothing intelligent can come from ignorance. If information does not guarantee wisdom, it is at least a prerequisite, for the only wise course is through knowledge. To write about current affairs, then, is to play a small role in a great endeavor. It is to measure one's own performance continually against the highest standards of honesty, fairness, thoroughness, intelligence, to search every day for a bit of truth, then share it. These are the ingredients of happiness, for such a job involves a life of constant learning, perpetual self-education. It keeps a man whole.*

SHIPLEY, ANDREW G., psychology scholar; BA summa cum laude in Psychology, Polit. Sci., Univ. Oreg., 2006; MSc. student in Experimental Psychology, Oxford Univ., 2007—. Founder Springfield Creative Comty. Project. Fulbright Scholar, New Zealand, 2006—07, Rhodes Scholar. Achievements include conducting rsch. on issues of social identity in Ghana, the French West Indies and Ecuador. Avocations: tennis, triathalons. *

SHIPLEY, DAVID ELLIOTT, lawyer, educator; b. Urbana, Ill., Oct. 3, 1950; s. James Ross and Dorothy Jean (Elliott) S.; m. Virginia Florence Coleman, May 24, 1980; 1 child, Shannon C. BA, Oberlin Coll., 1972; JD, U. Chgo., 1975. Bar: R.I. 1975. Assoc. Tillinghast, Collins & Graham, Providence, 1975-77; asst. prof. U. S.C. Sch. Law, Columbia, 1977-81, assoc. prof., 1981-85, prof., 1985-90, assoc. dean, 1989-90; dean U. Miss. Sch. Law, University, 1990-93, U. Ky. Coll. Law, Lexington, 1993-98; prof., dean Sch. Law U. Ga., Athens, 1998—2003, Thomas R. R. Cobb prof., 2003—. Vis. prof. Coll. William and Mary, Williamsburg, Va., 1983-84, Ohio State U. Coll. Law, Columbus, 1986-87. Author: South Carolina Administrative Law, 1983, 2d edit., 1989; co-author Copyright Law, 1992. Pres. Shandon Neighborhood Assn., Columbia, 1988-90, Athens Justice Project, Ga., 2003-05, minority affairs com. law sch. admissions coun., 2001-05, fin. and legal affairs coll., 2005—. Named Prof. of Yr., U. SC Sch. Law, 1990, faculty scholar, 1989-90, O'Byrne award for Student Faculty Rels. U. Ga., 2003-04, 04-05. Mem. ABA, R.I. Bar Assn., S.C. Bar Assn. (assoc.), Ga. Bar Assn. (assoc.). Methodist. Avocations: running, golf, yardwork, gardening, reading. Home: 475 River Bottom Rd Athens GA 30606-6430 Office: U Ga Sch Law 323 Rusk Hall Athens GA 30602-6012 Home Phone: 706-613-0647; Office Phone: 706-542-5184. Business E-Mail: shipley@uga.edu.

SHIPLEY, SAMUEL LYNN, advertising and public relations executive; b. Marlborough, Mass., Nov. 14, 1929; s. Clifford Lynn and Esther (Jacobs) S.; m. Sue Finucan, Sept. 5, 1955; children: Jeffrey Lynn, Beth Ann, Amy. Student, Charles Morris Price Sch. Advt. and Journalism, U. N.H., 1948-50. Exec. dir. Democratic Party N.H., 1953-56; pres., chmn. Shipley Assos., Inc., Wilmington, Del., 1962—; pres. Cable TV Advt. Inc., 1982—. Dir. Del. Devel. Dept., Dover, 1965-69; mem. bd. overseers Del. Coll. Art and Design. Nominee for U.S. Congress, 1976; pub. relations dir. Del. Democratic Com., 1964-68; chmn. Del. Dem. Com., 1982-90; bd. dirs. Blood Bank of Del., Jobs for Del. Grads., For Children; mem. Del. Heritage Commn.; trustee Grand Opera House; former chair Dem. State Com. With U.S. Army, 1951-53. Recipient Freedoms Found. Honor medal, 1966, Outstanding Grad. award Charles Morris Price Sch., 1974 Mem. Am. Advt. Fedn., Nat. Press Club, Wilmington Advt. Club, Masons. Home: 1196 Paper Mill Rd Newark DE 19711-2924 Office: 1300 Pennsylvania Ave Wilmington DE 19806-4311 Business E-Mail: samshipley@comcast.net. *The ingredients for success are good health, average intelligence, a giving spirit, positive thinking, good imagination, self-discipline, hard work, and persistence.*

SHIPLEY, TONY L(EE), software company executive; b. Elizabethton, Tenn., July 19, 1946; s. James A. and Edith J. (Crowder) S.; m. Lynda Anne Jenkins, Nov. 19, 1971; children: Blake Alan, Sarah Robyn. BS in Indsl. Engring., U. Tenn., 1969; MBA, U. Cin., 1975. Indsl. engr. Monsanto Co., Pensacola, Fla., 1969—72; mktg. mgr. SDRC, Cin., 1972—76; v.p. sales and mktg. Anatrol Corp., Cin., 1977—81; pres. Entek Sci. Corp., Cin., 1981—96; pres., CEO Entek IRD Internat. Corp., 1996—2000; founding mem. Queen City Angels. Bd. dirs. Ohio IT Alliance, chmn., CHMack; bd. dirs. The Circuit, U. Cin. E-Ctr., RhinoCyte, Forte Industries. Named Small Bus. Person of Yr., Greater Cin. C. of C., 1994, Entrepreneur of Yr. in Cin., No. Ky. Region, 1996; recipient Entrepreneurial Excellence award U. Cin., 2001, C.H. Lindner Outstanding Bus. Achievement award U. Cin., 2004; Hamilton County Bus. Ctr., Larry Albice Entrpreneurship award, 2006. Mem. ASME, Soc. Automotive Engrs., Greater Cin. Software Assn. (pres. 1996-97, chmn. 1997-99, bd. dirs.), Greater Cin. C. of C., Leadership Class XVIII, Terrace Park (Ohio) Country Club (past pres.). Republican. Avocations: golf, fishing. Home: 7825 Calderwood Ln Cincinnati OH 45243-1319 Personal E-mail: tshipley@fuse.net.

SHIPLEY, WALTER VINCENT, retired bank executive; b. Newark, Nov. 2, 1935; s. L. Parks and Emily (Herzog) S.; m. Judith Ann Lyman, Sept. 14, 1957; children: Barbara, Allison, Pamela, Dorothy, John. Student, Williams Coll., 1954-56; BS, NYU, 1961. With Chem. Bank, NYC, 1956-96; chmn., CEO, chmn. bd. dirs. Chase Manhattan Corp., NYC, 1996-99; ret., 1999. Bd. dirs. Exxon Mobil Corp., Verizon Comms., Wyeth. Mem. Coun. Fgn. Rels., Augusta Nat. Golf Club, Baltusrol Golf Club (Springfield, N.J.). Office: JPMorgan Chase & Co 270 Park Ave New York NY 10017-2070

SHIPMAN, JEAN PUGH, medical librarian; b. Chambersburg, Pa., Aug. 6, 1957; d. Andrew Richard and Sara Elizabeth (Bert) Pugh; m. Mark James Shipman, Oct. 8, 1988. BA, Gettysburg Coll., 1979; MSLS, Case Western Res. U., 1980. Reference libr. Johns Hopkins Sch. Medicine, Balt., 1980-81, sr. reference libr., 1981-82, access libr., 1982-84, psychiatry-neuroscis. librarian, 1984-88; mgr. libr. and audiovisual svcs. Greater Balt. Med. Ctr., 1988-90, NN/LM southeastern/atlantic regional coord., 1990—93; outreach info. svcs. libr. Health Scis. Libr., U. Wash., 1993—95, acting head access svcs., 1993—95, assoc. dir. info. resources mgmt., 1995—2000; dir. Tompkins-McCaw Libr. for Health Scis., assoc. Univ. Libr. Va. Commonwealth Univ. Librs., Richmond, Va., 2000—. Contbr. articles to profl. jours. Mem. Med. Libr. Assn. (bd. dirs. 1999-2002, sec. 2000-02, pres.-elect 2005-06, pres. 2006-2007, immediate past pres., 2007—), Beta Phi Mu, Beta Beta Beta. Republican. Lutheran. Avocations: tennis, reading, cooking. Office: Tompkins-McCaw Libr for Health Scis 509 N 12th St PO Box 980582 Richmond VA 23298-0582 Business E-Mail: jpshipma@vcu.edu.

SHIPP, DAN SHACKELFORD, lawyer; b. Yazoo City, Miss., Jan. 6, 1946; m. Carolyn Julie Perry, Nov. 30, 1974; children: Perry Lee, Clay Alexander. AA, Holmes Jr. Coll., 1966; BA, Miss. State U., 1968; JD, U. Miss., 1971. Bar: Miss. 1971, U.S. Dist. Ct. (no. dist.) Miss. 1971, U.S. Dist. Ct. (so. dist.) Miss. 1976, U.S. Ct. Appeals (5th cir.) 1982, Colo. 1986, U.S. Ct. Appeals (10th cir.) 1986, U.S. Dist. Ct. Colo. 1986. Pvt. practice, Yazoo City, 1974-83, Aspen, 1986—2001, Basalt, Colo., 2002—. Spkr. in field. Recipient Master Adv. Cert. award, Nat. Inst. Trial Advocacy Notre Dame Law Sch., 1993. Mem.: ABA, ATLA, Nat. Coll. DUI Def., Colo. Trial Lawyers Assn. (bd. dirs. 1986—88), Colo. Bar Assn., Toastmasters Internat. Avocations: hunting, archery, travel. Home: 0300 Vagneur Ln Basalt CO 81621-9103 Office Phone: 888-326-7447, 888-326-7447. Personal E-mail: danshipplaw@comcast.net.

SHIPPEN, MARGARET ELLEN, special education educator; b. Bloomington, Ind., Aug. 25, 1967; d. Samuel Joseph and Dorothy Mae Shippen; life ptnr. Jennifer Denise Mathis, May 21, 1990. PhD, Auburn U., Ala., 2001. Spl. edn. tchr. Montgomery Pub. Sch., Ala., 1990—97, spl. edn. adminstr., 1997—2001; asst. prof. spl. edn. Ga. State U., Atlanta, 2002—05, Auburn U., 2005—07. Grantee, U.S. Dept. Edn., 2003—05. Mem.: Coun. Exceptional Children. Achievements include research in literacy for individuals at risk. Office: Auburn Univ Coll Edn 1228 Haley Ctr Auburn AL 36849 Home Phone: 334-265-3424; Office Phone: 334-844-5943. Office Fax: 334-844-2080. Business E-Mail: shippme@auburn.edu.

SHIPPEY, SANDRA LEE, lawyer; b. Casper, Wyo., June 24, 1957; d. Virgil Carr and Doris Louise (Conklin) McClintock; m. Ojars Herberts Ozols, Sept. 2, 1978 (div.); children: Michael Ojars, Sara Ann, Brian Christopher; m. James Robert Shippey, Jan. 13, 1991; 1 child, Matthew James. BA with distinction, U. Colo., 1978; JD magna cum laude, Boston U., 1982. Bar: Colo. 1982, U.S. Dist. Ct. Colo. 1985. Assoc. Cohen, Brame & Smith, Denver, 1983-84, Parcel, Meyer, Schwartz, Ruttum & Mauro, Denver, 1984-85, Mayer, Brown & Platt, Denver, 1985-87; counsel western ops. GE Capital Corp., San Diego, 1987-94; assoc. Page, Polin, Busch & Boatwright, San Diego, 1994-95; v.p., gen. counsel First Comml. Corp., San Diego, 1995-96; legal counsel NextWave Telecom Inc., San Diego, 1996-98; ptnr. Procopio, Cory, Hargreaves and Savitch, LLP, 1998—, mgmt. com. Spkr. in field. Contbr. articles to profl. jours. Active Pop Warner football and cheerleading; bd. dirs. Southwestern Christian Schs., Inc., 2002—, San Diego Christian Found., 2001—05. Mem. Calif. State Bar (co-chair uniform comml. code com.), Phi Beta Kappa, Phi Delta Phi. Republican. Mem. Ch. of Christ. Avocations: tennis, golf, photography. Home: 15839 Big Springs Way San Diego CA 92127-2034 Office: Procopio Cory Et Al 530 B St Ste 2100 San Diego CA 92101-4496 Home Phone: 858-722-6072; Office Phone: 619-515-3226. Business E-Mail: sls@procopio.com.

SHIRAI, SHUN, law educator, lawyer; b. Tokyo, June 18, 1942; s. Kyo and Tomi Shirai; m. Junko Matsushita, Apr. 10, 1969; children: Akiko, Yuko, Jin. LLB, Hitotsubashi U., Tokyo, 1966, LLM, 1969. Asst. prof. criminal law Kokugakuin U., Tokyo, 1974-81, prof., 1981—, dean Grad. Sch., 1999-2001. Atty. Tokyo 2nd Bar Assn., 1992—. Author: Phenomenology of Crime, 1984, rev. edit., 1998, Thought on Criminal Law of Ancient India, 1985, Legal History on Criminal Law of Ancient India, 1990, Philosophy of Criminal Law in Ancient India, 1995, Phenomenology and Indian Philosophy for the Study on Ancient Indian Criminal Law, 1997, Prof. Shirai's Lectures on the Law of Criminal Procedure, 1998, Philosophy of Criminal Law in Bhagavad-gītā at Ancient India, 1998, Crime and Sorrowness of Human Being, 1999, Defence Lawyer's Statements in Criminal Court, 2000, Thoughts on Death Penalty in Ancient India, 2000, The Sanskrit, as a Legal Language, appearing in Judicial Documents of British India and Non-Violent Theory of Punishment, originated in Ancient India, 2000, Thought on Righteousness in Criminal Law, handed down by Tradition from Ancient India, 2002, On Basic Principles of Hindu Criminology, derived from Ancient Indian Criminal Law, 2002, Introduction to Study on Practice of Japanese Criminal Jurisdiction, 2003, Philosophy of Crime of Contemporary Indian Thought on Human Being, 2003, Peculiarity in Research Method on Hindu Criminology, 2004, On the Legal Meaning of Yājñavalkyasmṛti, Ancient Indian Legal Script, Book II, Section 1, 2005, Phenomenological Criminology and Transcendental Intersubjectivity, 2006, Thoughts on Sin, Observed in Undercurrent of Indian Legal History and Peculiarity of Method on Treatment for Sinner, 2006, Victimology Without Sense of Victim's Revenge, A Criminological Research to the Dhammapada, 2007; contbr. chpts. to books. Mem. Indian History Congress. Buddhist. Home: 703 Kinsen Bldg 2-16-1 Hanakawado Taito-ku Tokyo 111-0033 Japan Office: Kokugakuin U 4-10-28 Higashi Shibuya-Ku Tokyo 150-8440 Japan Office Phone: 03-5466-0111.

SHIRAZI, ARASH, research scientist; b. Shiraz, Fars, Iran, Sept. 13, 1966; s. Abe Shirazi and Shariat Barghianzadeh; m. Shima Shirazi, Jan. 15, 2002. BS in Gen. Sci., King's Coll., Wilkes Barre, Pa., 1995. Tutor Coll., Nanticoke, Pa., 1989—91; med. technologist Hosp., Dallas, 1998—2001. Translator YMCA and UNHCR. Pub. Cmty. Awareness, Shiraz, 1980—84. Mem.: Am. Assn. Sci. (assoc.). Muslim. Home: 29 Columbus Ave Wilkes Barre PA 18702 Office: Sanofipasteur Inc 01 Discovery Dr Swiftwater PA 18370 Home Phone: 570-262-7927; Office Phone: 570-895-3527. Business E-Mail: arash_g_s@yahoo.com.

SHIRAZI, EMAN ALI, dentist; b. Shiraz, Iran, Sept. 21, 1975; arrived in US, 1983; s. Mohammad Shirazi and Parvin Asadzadeh; m. Marissa Guzman, Sept. 30, 2006. BA in Biology, U. Iowa, Iowa City, 1996; DDS, NY U., NYC, 2001. Dentist Smile Ctr., Chgo., 2001—04, Brighton Pk. Dental, Chgo., 2002—06, Water Tower Family Dental, Lake in the Hills, Ill., 2005—. Mem.: ADA (presiding chair 2007), Chgo. Dental Soc. (chairperson 2006—). Avocations: travel, golf, reading, movies. Office: Water Tower Family Dental 2250 W Algonqoin Rd Ste 101 Lake In The Hills IL 60156

SHIRE, DAVID LEE, composer; b. Buffalo, July 3, 1937; s. Irving Daniel and Esther Miriam (Sheinberg) S.; m. Talia Rose Coppola, Mar. 29, 1970 (div.); 1 child, Matthew Orlando; m. Didi Conn, Feb. 11, 1984; 1 child, Daniel Joshua. BA, Yale U., 1959. Film scores include The Conversation, 1974, The Taking of Pelham 1-2-3, 1974, Farewell, My Lovely, 1975, The Hindenburg, 1975, All the President's Men, 1977, Saturday Night Fever (adaptation and additional music), 1977, Norma Rae, 1979 (Acad. award for best original song It Goes Like It Goes), Only When I Laugh, 1981, The World According to Garp, 1982, Max Dugan Returns, 1983, 2010, 1984, Return to Oz, 1985, Short Circuit, 1986, 'Night, Mother, 1986, Vice Versa, 1988, Monkey Shines, 1988, Paris Trout, 1991, Bed and Breakfast, 1992, The Journey Inside (IMAX), 1993, One Night Stand, 1994, Ash Wednesday, 2002, The Tollbooth, 2004, Zodiac, 2007; TV scores include Raid on Entebbe, 1977 (Emmy nomination), The Defection of Simas Kudirka, 1978 (Emmy nomination), Do You Remember Love?, 1985 (Emmy nomination), Promise, 1986, Echoes in the Darkness, 1987, The Women of Brewster Place, 1989, The Kennedys of Massachusetts, 1990 (Emmy nomination), Common Ground, 1990, Sarah Plain & Tall, 1991, Last Wish, 1992, Broadway Bound, 1992, Skylark, 1993, Remember, 1993, The Companion, 1994, My Brother's Keeper, 1995, Serving in Silence, 1995, The Heidi Chronicles, 1995, My Antonia, 1995, The Streets of Laredo, 1995, Last Stand at Saber River, 1997, Rear Window, 1998 (Emmy nomination), Double Platinum, 1999, Small Vices, 1999, These Old Broads, 2001, Two Against Time, 2001; theatre scores include The Sap of Life, 1961, Graham Crackers, 1962, The Unknown Soldier and His Wife, 1967, How Do You Do, I Love You, 1968, Love Match, 1970, Starting Here, Starting Now, 1977, Baby, 1983 (Tony nominee best mus. and best original score), Urban Blight, 1988, Closer Than Ever, 1989 (Outer Critics Circle award best off-Broadway musical and best score), Big, 1996 (Tony nominee best score), Time for Love, 2006, Take Flight, 2007; composer Sonata for Cocktail Piano, 1965, (symphonic suite for doubles and orch.) Shades of Blue, 2007; recorded songs include Autumn, 1959, Starting Here, Starting Now, 1965, What About Today?, 1969, Manhattan Skyline, 1977, The Promise, 1978 (Acad. award nomination), It Goes Like It Goes, 1979 (Acad. award), With You I'm Born Again, 1979; albums include Saturday Night Fever, 1977 (Grammy award 1978), Starting Here, Starting Now, 1977 (Grammy nomination 1977), Baby, 1984, Return to Oz, 1985, Closer Than Ever, 1990, David Shire at The Movies, 1991, Big, 1996. With Army N.G., 1960-66. Mem. Composers and Lyricists Guild Am., Am. Fedn. Musicians, Broadcast Music Inc., Acad. Motion Picture Arts and Scis., Nat. Acad. Rec. Arts and Scis., Nat. Acad. TV Arts and Scis., Dramatists Guild Am. (coun. mem.). Jewish. Office: Ste 304 16501 Ventura Blvd Encino CA 91436-2067 Office Phone: 818-971-7300. Personal E-mail: dshire@aol.com.

SHIRE, DONALD THOMAS, retired chemicals executive, lawyer; b. Boston, Jan. 13, 1930; s. Thomas J. and Nellie M. S.; m. Anne Court Bither, Nov 21, 1953; children: Jennifer Anne, Andrew Carter, Daniel Orchard. BS in Bus. Adminstrn, Boston U., 1951, LL.B., 1953; postgrad., Harvard Bus. Sch., 1985; LLD (hon.), Muhlenberg Coll., 1997. Atty. Air Products and Chems., Inc., 1957-64, atty., 1964-75, sec., asst. gen. counsel, 1975-78, v.p. energy and materials, 1978-85, v.p. human resources, 1986-90, sr. v.p. human resources and adminstrn., 1990-91, sr. v.p. adminstrn., 1991-93; ret., 1993; also bd. dirs. Air Products and Chems., Inc. Chmn. Air Products Found., 1991-93; bd. dirs. Lehigh Valley Bus./Edn. Partnership. Trustee Muhlenberg Coll. (life), 1976-95, Lehigh Valley Health Network., 1983-99, Lt. USNR, 1954-57. Mem. Am. Arbitration Assn. Home: 27 Drake Ln Scarborough ME 04074

SHIRE, TALIA ROSE (TALIA ROSE COPPOLA), actress; b. Jamaica, NY, Apr. 25, 1946; d. Carmine and Italia (Pennino) Coppola; m. David Lee Shire, Mar. 29, 1970 (div.); 1 son, Matthew Orlando; m. Jack Schwartzman, Aug. 23, 1979; children: Jason Francesco, Robert Carmine Coppola. Films include The Wild Racers, 1968, The Dunwich Horrors, 1970, Gas-s-s-s, 1971, The Christian Licorice State, 1971, Godfather, 1972, The Outside Man, 1972, Godfather II, 1974 (Oscar nominee for Best Supporting Actress), Rocky, 1976 (Oscar nominee for best actress, N.Y. Film Critics award for Best Supporting Actress), Old Boyfriends, 1979, Rocky II, 1979, Prophecy, 1979, Windows, 1980, Rocky III, 1982, Rocky IV, 1985, Rad, 1986, New York Stories, 1989, Cold Heaven, 1991, Godfather Part III, 1990, Rocky V, 1990, Bed and Breakfast, 1992, Deadfall, 1993, (Disney channel movie) Mark Twain, 1990, (HBO movie) Getting There, 1991, A River Made to Drown In, 1997, Divorce: A Contemporary Western, 1998, Can I Play?, 1998, Palmer's Pick Up, 1999, Caminho dos Sonhos, 1999, Lured Innocence, 1999, The Visit, 2000, The Whole Shebang, 2001, Kiss the Bride, 2002, Family Tree, 2003, Dunsmore, 2003, I Heart Huckabees, 2004, Pomegranate, 2005, Rocky Balboa, 2006, Homo Erectus, 2006; TV appearances include Foster & Laurie, 1975, (TV mini series) Rich Man, Poor Man, 1976, Kill Me If You Can, 1977, Daddy, I Don't Like It Like This, 1978, Blood Vows: The Story of a Mafia Wife, 1987, Murderer's Keep, 1988, Mark Twain and Me, 1991, For Richer, For Poorer, 1992, Please, God, I'm Only Seventeen, 1992, Chatilly Lace, 1993, Born into Exile, 1997; prodr. Hyper Sapien: People from Another Star, 1986, Lionheart, 1987; assoc. prodr.: The Landlady, 1998; dir. One Night Stand, 1995.

SHIREK, JOHN RICHARD, retired savings and loan executive; b. Bismarck, ND, Feb. 5, 1926; s. James Max and Anna Agatha (Lala) S.; m. Ruth Martha Lietz, Sept. 22, 1950; children: Barbara Jo (Mrs. James A. Fowler), Jon Richard, Kenneth Edward. Student, U. Minn., 1944-46; BS with honors, Rollins Coll., 1978. Sports editor Bismarck Tribune, ND, 1943-44; with Gate City Savs. and Loan Assn., Fargo, ND, 1947-65, v.p., dir., 1960-65; exec. v.p., dir. 1st Fed. Savs. and Loan Assn., Melbourne, Fla., 1966-70; pres., dir. 1st Fed. Savs. and Loan Assn., Cocoa, Fla., 1970-82; exec. v.p., dir. The First F.A. (formerly 1st Fed. Savs. and Loan Assn. of Orlando), 1982-91. Interim pres. Freedom Savs. and Loan Assn., Tampa, Fla., 1987-88; trustee Savs. & Loan Found., Inc., 1980-84; dir. Fin. Trans. Syss., Inc., Magnolia Svcs. Corp., 1st Cocoa Corp., Magnolia Realty Co., 1982-91. Chmn., dir. United Fund, Fargo, N.D., 1962-65; dir., exec. bd. mem. Boy Scouts Am., 1960-70, mem. adv. bd. cen. Fla. coun., 1983-85, 91-95, exec. bd., 1985-91, v.p. long-range planning, 1989-91; bd. assocs. Fla. Inst. Tech., founding pres., 1968; moderator St. Johns Presbytery, 1979, chmn. adv. coun., 1980-81; chair local arrangements com. 1993 Gen. Assembly Presbyn. Ch.; moderator Synod of Fla., 1983, Ctrl. Fla. Presbytery, 1991, coordinating coun., 1992; coun. mem. Synod of South Atlantic, 2002-2003; mem. adv. bd. Brevard Art Ctr. and Mus., 1980-82; bd. dirs., founding chmn. devel. coun. Holmes Regional Med. Ctr., Melbourne, 1981-84; bd. dirs. Orlando Regional Med. Ctr. Found., 1982-85, Jr. Achievement Cen. Fla., 1989-91; mem. fin. com. Mayor's Task Force on Housing, 1983-84; chmn. spl. com. on Nat. Coun. Chs./World Coun. Chs. rels. Presbyn. Ch. in U.S.A., 1983-86; pres. Ecumenical Ctr. Inc., Orlando, 1985-91, bd. dirs., 2001—; chmn. Fla. adv. com. Ctr. Theol. Studies Columbia Theol. Sem., 1991-95. Lt. (j.g.) USNR, World War II. Mem. Fla. Savs. and Loan League (past dir.), Fla. Savs. and Loan Svcs. (past dir.), Savs. and Loan Found. (state membership chmn. 1976), Fla. Savs. and Loan Polit. Action Com. (dir. 1976-82), U.S. Savs. and Loan League (chmn. advt. and pub. rels. com. 1969-70, dir. S.E. conf. 1975-80), Downtown Melbourne Assn. (past pres.), Cocoa Rotary (pres. 1979), Masons, Shriners, Elks, Beta Theta Pi, Omicron Delta Epsilon. Republican. Home: PO Box 568831 Orlando FL 32856-8831

SHIREMAN, JOAN FOSTER, social work educator; b. Cleve., Oct. 28, 1933; d. Louis Omar and Genevieve (Duguid) Foster; m. Charles Howard Shireman, Mar. 18, 1967; 1 child, David Louis. BA, Radcliffe Coll., 1956; MA, U. Chgo., 1959, PhD, 1968. Caseworker N.H. Children's Aid Soc., Manchester, 1959-61; dir. research Chgo. Child Care Soc., 1968-72; assoc. prof. U. Ill., Chgo., 1972-85; prof. Portland State U., Oreg., 1985—2003, dir. PhD program, 1992-99; interim exec. dir. Partnership for Rsch., Tng. and Grad. Edn. in Child Welfare, 1994; prof. emerita Portland State U., Oreg., 2003—. Research cons. child welfare orgns., Ill., 1968-85, Oreg. 1985—; lectr. U. Chgo., 1968-72. Author: Critical Issues in Child Welfare, 2003; co-author: Care and Commitment: Foster Parent Adoption Decisions, 1985, Adoption: Theory, Policy and Practice, 1997; mem. editl. bd. Jour. Sch. Social Work, 1978-81, Social Work Rsch. and Abstracts, 1990-93, Children and Youth Svcs. Rev., 1990—, Jour. Social Work Edn., 1990-95; contbr. articles to profl. jours., chpts. to books. Bd. dirs. Oreg. chpt. Nat. Assn. for Prevention Child Abuse, 1985-87, Friendly House, Portland, 1991-97, 2002-03, Camp Fire U.S.A. Portland Metro Coun., 2002-04; mem. adv. com. Children's Svcs. divsn. State of Oreg., 1985-95. Grantee HEW, 1980-82, Chgo. Community Trust, 1982-86, Oreg. Children's Trust Fund, 1991-96. Mem. NASW, AAUP, Acad. Cert. Social Workers, Coun. on Social Work Edn., Phi Beta Kappa. Home: 13584 SW Snowfire Dr Portland OR 97236 Office: Portland State U Grad Sch Social Work PO Box 751 Portland OR 97207-0751 Office Phone: 503-725-5005. Business E-Mail: shiremanj@pdx.edu.

SHIRES, GEORGE THOMAS, surgeon, educator; b. Waco, Tex., Nov. 22, 1925; s. George Thomas and Donna Mae (Smith) S.; m. Robbie Jo Martin, Nov. 27, 1948; children: Donna Blain, George Thomas III, Jo Ellen. MD, U. Tex., Dallas, 1948. Intern Mass. Meml. Hosp., Boston, 1948—49; resident in surgery Parkland Meml. Hosp., Dallas, 1950—53; faculty U. Tex. Southwestern Med. Sch., Dallas, 1953—60, assoc. prof. surgery, acting chmn. dept., 1960—61, prof., chmn. dept., 1961—74; surgeon in chief surg. svcs. Parkland Meml. Hosp., 1960—74; prof., chmn. dept. surgery U. Wash. Sch. Medicine, Seattle, 1974—75; chief of svc. Harborview Med. Ctr., Seattle, Univ. Hosp., Seattle, 1974—75; chmn. dept. surgery N.Y. Hosp.-Cornell U. Med. Coll., 1975—91; dean, provost for med. affairs Cornell U. Med. Coll., 1987—91, prof. emeritus, 1996—; prof., chmn. surgery Tex. Tech. U., Lubbock, 1991—95, Canizaro disting. prof. surgery, 1995—97; prof. surgery U. Nev. Sch. Medicine, Las Vegas, 1997—. Cons. Surgeon Gen., U.S. Army, 1965—75, Jamaica Hosp., 1978—91, Inst. Medicine NAS, 1975—; metabolism and trauma com. NAS-NRC, 1964—71, com. trauma, 1964—71; rsch. program evaluation com., reviewer clin. investigation applications career devel. program VA, 1972—76; gen. med. rsch. program projects com. NIH NIH, 1965—69; mem. Surgery A study sect., 1970—74, chmn., 1976—78; mem. Nat. Adv. Gen. Med. Scis. Coun., 1980—84; cons. editl. bd. Jour. Trauma, 1968—88. Mem. editl. bd.: Year Book Med. Publs., 1970—92, Annals of Surgery, 1972—, Surg. Techniques Illustrated: An International Comparative Text, 1974—75, Am. Jour. Surgery, 1968—, Contemporary Surgery, 1973—89, assoc. editor-in-chief: Infections in Surgery, 1981, mem. editl. bd.: Jour. Clin. Surgery, 1980—82; editor: Surgery, Gynecology and Obstetrics, 1982—93. Lt. M.C. USNR, 1949—50, Lt. M.C. USNR, 1953—55. Fellow: Coll. Medicine South Africa (hon.); mem.: AMA, ACS (bd. regents 1971—82, chmn. bd. regents 1978—80, pres. 1981—82), James IV Assn. Surgeons (bd. dirs. 1980—81, sec. 1981—87, pres. 1987—91), Allen O. Whipple Surg. Soc., Western Surg. Assn., N.Y. Surg. Soc. (pres. 1981—82), So. Surg. Assn., Soc. Univ. Surgeons (chmn. publs. com. 1969—71), Soc. Surg. Chairmen (pres. 1972—74), Soc. Clin. Surgery, Soc. Surgery Alimentary Tract, Pan Pacific Surg. Assn., Pan-Am. Med. Assn. (surgery coun. 1971), Am. Burn Assn., Internat. Surg. Soc. (sec. 1978—81, v.p. 1982—83, pres. U.S. chpt. 1984—85), Internat. Soc. Burn Injuries, Halsted Soc., Digestive Disease Found. (founding mem.), Am. Surg. Assn. (sec. 1969—74, pres. 1980), Am. Burn Assn., Am. Assn. Surgery Trauma, Dallas Soc. Gen. Surgeons (pres. 1972—74, pres.-elect), Am. Bd. Surgery (dir. 1968—74, chmn. 1972—74, diplomate), Surg. Biology Club (sec. 1968—70), Phi Beta Pi, Alpha Pi Alpha, Alpha Omega Alpha. Office: U Nev Sch Medicine 2040 W Charleston Blvd Ste 501 Las Vegas NV 89102-2207 Home Phone: 702-450-6280; Office Phone: 702-671-2297. Business E-Mail: gtshires@nvtrauma.com.

SHIRI-GARAKANI, MOHSEN, physicist, educator; s. Mohammad-Taghi Shiri-Garakani and Sedigheh Gharib-Garakani. PhD, Ga. Inst. Tech., Atlanta, 2004. Physics prof. Pace U., Pleasantville, NY, 2005—. Dir. physics and engring. program Pace U., 2005—; vis. fellow Harvard U., Cambridge, Mass., 2006—. Aast. editor: Internat. Jour. Theoretical Physics, 2002—. Grad. scholar, U. Akron, Ohio, 1995—97, Ga. Inst. Tech., Atlanta, 1997—2004, Summer Sch. fellow, Kira Inst., 1998, 1999, 2002, Vis. fellow, Harvard U./Pace U., 2006—07. Mem.: AAAS, Am. Phys. Soc. Achievements include research in quantum theory for spacetime. Home: 10 Riverview Ct Apt B Ossining NY 10562 Office: Pace University 861 Bedford Rd Pleasantville NY 10570 Home Phone: 914-773-3430; Office Phone: 914-773-3430. Business E-Mail: mshirigarakani@pace.edu.

SHIRILAU, MARK STEVEN, utilities executive; b. Long Beach, Calif., Dec. 13, 1955; s. Kenneth Eugene and Marrjorie Irene (Thorvick) Shirey; m. Jeffery Michael Lau, Nov. 25, 1984 (dec. Aug. 9, 1993). BSEE, U. Calif., Irvine, 1977; MS in Bus. Adminstrn., 1980, PhD, 1988; M in Engring., Calif. Poly. State U., 1978; diploma in theology, Episc. Theol. Sch., Claremont, Calif., 1984; MA in Religion, Sch. Theology at Claremont, 1985. Ordained priest Ecumenical Cath. Ch., 1987, consecrated bishop, 1991; registered profl. engr., Calif., N.Y., Tex.; lic. contractor, Calif. Grad. asst. Electric Power Inst., 1977-78; pres., CEO M.S.E., Santa Ana, Calif., 1977-87; adminstrv. mgr. EECO Inc., Santa Ana, 1979-83; fin. engr. So. Calif. Edison Co., Rosemead, 1983-84, conservation engr., 1984-85, conservation supr., 1985-89; exec. v.p. Aloha Sys., Inc., Villa Grande, Calif., 1989-93, pres., 1993—, also bd. dirs.; lectr. engring. Citrus Coll., Glendora, Calif., 2000—. Bd. dirs. Ewing Consol. Corp., Outrider Trucking, Inc.; part-time instr. Santa Ana Coll., 1982-84, Citrus Coll., Glendora, Calif., 2000-; lectr. engring. West Coast U., Orange, Calif., 1984-91; bd. dirs. Am. Electronics Assn. Credit Union, Sweetwater Springs Water Dist., Heat Pump Coun. So. Calif., AIDS Interfaith Network Sonoma County, Stampede Svcs. Inc., Ewmark Corp. Author: Triune Love: An Insight into God, Creation, and Humanity, 1983, Salvation, Scripture and Sexuality, 1992, History and Overview of the Ecumenical Catholic Church, 1993, Power 101, A Basic Introduction to Electric Utility Power, 1998, The Five Fatal Fears, 2002, (screenplay) Blackout!, 2005. Archbishop, primate Ecumenical Cath. Ch.; chief chaplain svcs. Nolanville (Tex.) Police Dept., 1998-2000; chaplain Jonestown (Tex.) Police Dept., 2001—. Mem. IEEE (sr.), ASHRAE, Internat. Assn. Chiefs Police, Assn. Energy Mgrs. (sr.), Assn. Profl. Energy Mgrs. (bd. dirs.), Am. Soc. Nondestructive Testing, Assn. Energy Svcs. Profls. (bd. dirs., charter mem., exec. v.p.), Am. Soc. Safety Engrs., Nat. Assn. Chiefs Police, Pacific Bears Club (v.p.), Dignity Integrity (life), Eta Kappa Nu. Democrat. Office: 14801 Comet St Irvine CA 92604-2464 Office Phone: 949-851-2221. E-mail: archbishop@ecchurch.org, MarkS@alohasys.com.

SHIRLEY, BONNIE J., retired elementary school educator; d. John R. and Catherine G. Bartholomew; m. Alan D. Shirley, Nov. 26, 1966 (dec. Jan. 2003); 1 child, Scott A. BS in Sci., SUNY, Brockport, 1969, postgrad., 1974. Cert. tchr. N.Y. Tchr. Rochester (N.Y.) City Sch. Dist., 1967—2003, lead tchr., mentor, 1991—2003; tchr. Greece (N.Y.) Continuing Edn.; cons. Renaissance Learning, Madison, 2003—; asst. prof. Roberts Wesleyan Coll., Rochester, 1995—97. Mem. adv. bd. dept. edn. and human devel. SUNY, Brockport. Named Sector 3 Tchr. of Yr., Rochester, N.Y., 1999. Avocation: freelance writing. Home: 87 Ayer St Rochester NY 14615 Personal E-mail: bshirle1@rochester.rr.com.

SHIRLEY, BRYAN DOUGLAS, lawyer; b. Sacramento, Sept. 12, 1972; BA, U. Wis., Madison; JD cum laude, Hamline U., 2001. Bar: Minn. 2001. Assoc. Kennedy & Graven, Chartered, Mpls. Bd. dirs. Rakhma Homes, Inc. Named a Rising Star, Minn. Super Lawyers mag., 2006. Mem.: Minn. State Bar Assn. *

SHIRLEY, DAVID ARTHUR, chemistry professor, science administrator; b. North Conway, NH, Mar. 30, 1934; m. Virginia Schultz, June 23, 1956 (dec. Mar. 1995); children: David N., Diane, Michael, Eric, Gail; m. Barbara Cerny, Dec. 26, 1995. BS, U. Maine, 1955, ScD (hon.), 1978; PhD in Chemistry, U. Calif.-Berkeley, 1858; D honoris causa, Free U. Berlin, 1987. With Lawrence Radiation Lab. (now Lawrence Berkeley Lab.), U. Calif., Berkeley, 1958-92, assoc. dir., head materials and molecular research div., 1975-80, dir., 1980-89, lectr. chemistry, 1959-60, asst. prof., 1960-64, assoc. prof., 1964-67, prof., 1967-92, vice chmn. dept. chemistry, 1968-71, chmn. dept. chemistry, 1971-75; sr. v.p. rsch., dean grad. sch. Pa. State U., University Park, 1992-96; dir. emeritus Lawrence Berkeley Nat. Lab., 1997—. Chair bd. overseers Fermilab. Contbr. over 400 rsch. articles. NSF fellow, 1955-58, 66-67, 70; recipient Ernest O. Lawrence award AEC, 1972, Humboldt award (sr. U.S. scientist); listed by Sci. Citation Index as one of the world's 300 most cited scientists for work published during 1965-78. Fellow Am. Phys. Soc.; mem. Nat. Acad. Scis., Am. Chem. Soc., AAAS, Am. Acad. Arts and Scis., Bohemian Club, Explorers Club, Sigma Xi, Tau Beta Pi, Sigma Pi Sigma, Phi Kappa Phi.

SHIRLEY, JON ANTHONY, software company executive; b. San Diego, Apr. 12, 1938; s. Joseph Roy and Mercedes (Miller) S.; m. Gail Grieg (div. June 1964); 1 child, Erickson; m. E. Mary L. Johanson, July 7, 1964; children: Peter, Mary. Grad., Hill. High Sch., Pottstown, Pa., 1956; student, MIT, 1956-57. Several Radio Shack div. Tandy Corp., Ft. Worth, 1963-72, v.p., 1972-83; pres., chief operating officer Microsoft Corp., Redmond, Wash., 1983—90, bd. dir., 1983—. Dir. Manzanita Capital, Seattle. Chmn. bd. trustees Seattle Art Mus.; trustee Mus. Flight, Seattle, Hill Sch., Pottstown, Pa.; mem. chmn. council Mus. Modern Art, NYC. Named one of Top 200 Collectors, ARTnews Mag., 2004, 2005, 2006. Mem. Assn. Data Processing Service Orgns. (bd. dirs. 1986—). Clubs: Seattle Yacht. Democrat. Avocations: Collector of Modern & Contemporary Art, Collecting, restoring, showing and racing of Vintage Ferrari Motor Cars. Office: Microsoft Corp One Microsoft Way Redmond WA 98052

SHIRLEY-QUIRK, JOHN, singer, educator; b. Liverpool, Eng., Aug. 28, 1931; arrived in US, 1990, naturalized, 2002; s. Joseph Stanley and Amelia (Griffiths) S.-Q.; m. Patricia May Hastie, July 1955 (dec. Feb. 1981); children: Kate, Peter; m. Sara Van Horn Watkins, Dec. 29, 1981 (dec. Dec. 1997); children: Benjamin, Emily (dec.), Julia. BSc, Liverpool U., 1953, MusD (hon.), 1977; D Univ., Brunel U., 1981. Asst. lectr. Acton Tech. Coll., London, 1956-60; vicar choral St. Paul's Cathedral, London, 1960-61; profl. singer, 1960—; joint artistic dir. Aldeburgh Festival, 1981-84. Mem. voice faculty Peabody Conservatory, Balt., 1991—; vis. artist Carnegie-Mellon U., Pitts., 1994-98. Numerous recs. and 1st performances, especially works of Benjamin Britten. Mem. ct. Brunel U., 1977-81. Flying officer RAF, 1952-55. Decorated comdr. Order of Brit. Empire. Mem. Royal Acad. Music (hon.), Royal Philharmonic Soc. Personal E-mail: jssq@peabody.jhu.edu.

SHIRTLIFF, BRYAN, retail executive; m. Eve Shirtliff; 4 children. B, U. Mont. Asst. store mgr. to sr. mktg. mgr. health and beauty Am. Stores Co., 1983—96; v.p. health and beauty care and gen. mdse. Bruno's Inc.; dir. health care Rite Aid Corp., Camp Hill, Pa., 1998—99, dir. health care and seasonal, 1999—2000, v.p. seasonal and hardlines, 2000—03, sr. v.p. category mgmt., 2003—. Home: Rite Aid Corp 30 Hunter Ln Camp Hill PA 17011 Office Phone: 717-761-2633. *

SHIRTUM, EARL EDWARD, retired civil engineer; b. Montague, Mich., Feb. 20, 1927; s. Earl Willard and Elizabeth Caroline (Boelke) S.; m. Martha Louise Wright, June 19, 1953. BS in Civil Engring., Ind. Tech. Coll., Ft. Wayne, 1950. Bridge design squad leader Mich. Dept. Transp., Lansing, 1952-63, transp. planning engr., 1963-96. Mem. Bridge Replacement and Rehab. Com., Lansing, 1967-94. With U.S. Army, 1945-46, ETO. Mem. Mich. Profl. Engring. Soc. (rep. engr. in govt. 1974-77), Lansing Engr. Club (bd. mem. 1980-84). Republican. Methodist. Avocations: fishing, bridge. Home: 1617 Victor Ave Lansing MI 48910-6511

SHIRVANI, SIR HAMID, architect, educator, philosopher, writer, university president; b. Tehran, Iran, Oct. 20, 1950; arrived in US, 1974, naturalized, 1986; s. Majid and Taji (Granpisheh) Shirvani; m. Fatemeh Shokrollahi, Oct. 4, 2002. Diploma in architecture, Poly. of Cen. London, 1974; MArch, Pratt Inst., 1975; MS, Rensselaer Poly. Inst., 1977; MLA, Harvard U., 1978; MA, Princeton U., 1979, PhD, 1980; LHD (hon.), Soka U., Japan, 2003. Project designer London Borough of Barnet, 1973-74; asst. prof. architecture Pa. State U., 1979-82; prof., dir. grad. studies SUNY, Syracuse, 1982-85; prof., dir. Sch. Urban Planning and Devel., U. Louisville, 1985-86; prof. architecture and urban design U. Colo., Denver, 1986-92, dean Sch. of Architecture and Planning, 1986-91; prof. philosophy, dean Coll. Arts and Scis. U. Mass., Lowell, 1992-95; v.p. grad. studies and rsch., prof. urban studies CUNY Queens Coll., Flushing, 1995-2000; provost, exec. v.p., Martha Masters prof. art/architecture Chapman U., Orange, Calif., 2000—05; pres., prof. art and architecture Calif. State U., Stanislaus, 2005—. Vis. faculty So. Calif. Inst. Architecutre, U. So. Calif.; lectr. in field, including U. Tex., San Antonio, Lehigh U., U. Waterloo (Can.), U. Sydney (Australia), Mo. State U., Columbia U., NYC, Amsterdam Acad. Art, U. Venice (Italy), Chinese U. Hong Kong, So. China Inst. U., U. Calif., Irvine, Villanova U., Rutgers U., Ariz. State U., Duke U., U. Pa., Yale U., U. Colo., U. NC Author: Urban Design: A Comprehensive Reference, 1981, Urban Design Review, 1981, Urban Design Process, 1985, Beyond Public Architecture, 1990; editor Urban Design Rev., 1982-85, Urban Design and Preservation Quar., 1985-88; mem. editorial bd. Jour. Archtl. Edn., 1988-94, Avant Garde, 1988-93, Jour. Planning Edn. and Rsch., 1987-93, Art and Architecture, 1974-78, Jour. Am. Planning Assn., 1982-88. Recipient Gold medal in Architecture and Urbanism, 1988, Faculty Honor award, 1990, Acad. Leadership award, Faculty Rsch. award, Commendation award AIA, 2003, Justice award SGI, 2003, Pres. of Yr. award, Calif. State U. Student Assn., 2007; Knight of Holy Sepulchre, 2004. Fellow World Acad. Arts and Scis., Am. Soc. Landscape Archs. (recognition award), Royal Geog. Soc., Royal Soc. Arts, World Acad. Arts and Scis.; mem. Am. Inst. Cert. Planners, Am. Planning Assn. (chmn. urban design divsn. 1987-89, Disting. award 1984, Urban Design award 1985), Sigma Xi, Omicron Delta Epsilon, Tau Sigma Delta (Silver medal in archtl. edn. 1988), Tau Beta Pi, Sigma Lambda Alpha. Office: Calif State U 801 W Monte Vista Ave Turlock CA 95382 Office Phone: 209-667-3201. Office Fax: 209-667-3206. E-mail: president@csustan.edu.

SHIRVINSKI, ADAM JOHN, management consultant; b. Mahanoy, Pa., Oct. 25, 1939; s. Adam F. and Louise Shirvinski; m. Jean Shirvinski, June 25, 1966; children: Adam Albert, Lisa Ellen, Lara Jean. BS in Engring., USCG Acad., 1961; MS in Quantitative Analysis, U.S. Naval Postgrad. Sch., Monterey, Calif., 1970; MS in Fin., Am. U, 1987. Group mgr.-product assurance EER Systems, Chantilly, Va., 1988—95; quality assurance mgr., air and space divsn. Sentel Corp., Alexandria, Va., 1995—98; sr. quality assurance specialist EDS Corp., Herndon, Va., 1998—2001; quality assurance mgr. Intelli Dyne, LLC, Falls Church, Va., 1995—. Pres., CEO Adams' Quality, Inc., Potomac, Md. Capt. U.S. Coast Guard, 1961—88. Mem.: AFCEA (assoc.), IEEE (assoc.), Informs (assoc.), US Naval Inst. (assoc.), Am. Soc. for Quality (sr.), Army Navy Club (assoc.). Republican. Roman Catholic. Avocations: tennis, hunting, fishing. Home: L26-B3-S2 Lake Shore Dr HC88 Box 386 Pocono Lake PA 18347 Office: Adams' Quality, Inc 1897 Milboro Dr Potomac MD 20854 Office Phone: 301-279-7336.

SHIRWAN, HAVAL, immunologist, educator; s. Mecit and Siddika Ulker; m. Esma Yolcu, 2000; children: Rojin, Aras. BS with highest honors, Hacettepe U., Ankara, Turkey, 1979; PhD, U. Calif., Santa Barbara, 1987. Prof. U. Louisville, 2004—. Chief sci. officer ApoImmune, Inc., Louisville, 2001—; grant reviewer NIH, Bethesda, Md., 1999—2007, Am. Heart Assn., 2003—07. Recipient Ortho award, Am. Soc. Transplant Physicians, 1992, Young Investigator award, Cedars-Sinai Med. Ctr., LA, 1994, Faculty Excellence awards, U. Louisville, 2002, 2003, First Pl. award in faculty category for innovation in biotechnology rsch., Louisville Med. Ctr., 2006, Ptnrs. in Health Care award, Bus. First, 2006; PhD scholar, NATO, 1982—87, Univ. Scholar, U. Louisville, 2002. Mem.: AAAS, Am. Assn. Immunologists, Am. Soc. Transplantation, Transplantation Soc., Internat. Xenotransplantation Assn., Am. Assn. Cancer Rsch., European Soc. Cancer Immunology and Immunotherapy. Achievements include patents in field. Office: Univ Louisville Baxter I Ste 404 570 S Preston St Louisville KY 40245 Office Phone: 502-852-2066. Business E-Mail: haval.shirwan@louisville.edu.

SHIRZAD, FARYAR, federal official; married; 1 child. BS summa cum laude, U. Md.; JD, U. Va.; M in Pub. Policy, Harvard U. With Robins, Kaplan, Miller & Ciresi, Washington; internat. trade atty. Skadden, Arps, Slate Meagher & Flom, Washington; internat. trade counsel Senate Com. on Fin., 1997—2001; lead internat. trade policy coord. Bush-Cheney Transition Offices; asst. sec. for import adminstrn. U.S. Dept. Commerce, Washington, 2001—03; asst. to the Pres. for internat. econ. affairs The White House, Washington, 2004—; dep. nat. security adv. NSC, Washington, 2005—. Office: The White House 1600 Pennsylvania Ave Washington DC 20500

SHISLER, ARDEN L., insurance and transportation company executive; b. Massillon, Ohio, 1941; COO K&B Transport, Dalton, Ohio, 1986—92, pres., CEO, 1992—2003; chmn. Nationwide Mut. Ins. Co., Columbus, Ohio, 2003—. Mem. Wayne County Farm Bureau; bd. mem. Ohio 4-H Found.; v.p. Ohio Farm Bur., 1974-84; pres. Ohio Agriculture Mktg. Assn., 1982-84. Office: Nationwide Mut Ins Co 1 Nationwide Plz Columbus OH 43215-2220 *

SHIUE, CHYNG-YANN, research director, educator; b. Kaohsiung, Taiwan, Dec. 15, 1941; came to U.S., 1966; s. Tao and Chen (Su) S.; m. Grace Guo, July 22, 1967; children: Peter, Linda. BS, Taiwan Normal U., 1965; PhD, Brown U., 1970. Post-doc U. Ky., Lexington, 1970—72; rsch. assoc. Brown U., Providence, 1972-74, instr., 1974-76; sr. rsch. assoc. Brookhaven Nat. Lab., Upton, NY, 1976-79, asst. chemist, 1979-81, assoc. chemist, 1981-83, chemist, 1983-89; dir. Ctr. Metabolic Imaging Creighton U., Omaha, 1989—93; prof. and dir. U. Pa., Phila., 1993—. Vis. prof. Inst. Nuclear Medicine, Shanghai, China, 1986, Nat. Def. Med. Coll., Taiwan, 2000-04; advisor Inst. Atomic Energy, Beijing, China, 1989-93. Contbr. 140 articles to profl. jours. Lt. Republic of China Air Force, 1965-66, Taiwan. Mem. Am. Chem. Soc., Soc. Nuclear Medicine, The N.Y. Acad. Scis., AAAS, Sigma Xi. Achievements include patents for 18F-4 Fluoroantipyrine, for 11C-D Glucose and Related Compounds, for Process for Production of 18F-2-Deoxy-2-Fluoro-D-Glucose, for No-Carrier Added 18F-N-Fluoroalkylspiroperidols, and for Nitroaromatic Compounds for Detection of Hypoxia. Office Phone: 215-662-7797. Business E-Mail: shiue@rad.upenn.edu.

SHIVCHARRAN, JAIGOBIN, secondary school educator, consultant; b. Rose Hall, Guyana, Apr. 23, 1941; arrived in U.S., 1980; s. Moochoon and Yawa Shivcharran; m. Kawa Sakhichand-Bracelly (div.); children: Sharmila, Rajesh, Ormila; m. Ruby Singh, July 11, 1983. BA in Humanities, Thomas Edison State Coll., 1989; MA in ESL, CUNY, NYC, 1993; BS in Psychology and Sociology, Regents Coll., 1996; PhD in Linguistics, Summit U., 1998. Cert. tchr. N.Y., 1997. Tchr. Dept. Edn., Guyana, 1961—80, 1995—; figure clk. Feature Enterprise, NYC, 1981—89; case mgr. Dept. Social Svcs., NYC, 1989—95. Instr. Coll. St. Rose, NYC, Albany, 2000—, Adelphi U., Garden City, NY, 2001—; staff developer United Fedn. TRS, NYC, 2000—; cons. NY State United Tchrs., NYC, 2000—; trainer of student peer mediator in conflict resolution NYC Dept. Edn. Author: Native Language Transfer in Second Language Learning, 1997, Anthology of Short Stories, 2005. Mem.: Am. Soc. Notaries, Nat. Coun. Social Studies, Nat. Coun. Tchrs. Eng., Acad. Polit. Sci., Nat. Assn. Scholars, NY State Assn. Scholars. Avocations: reading, walking, dance, writing. Home: 132 Freeman St #2D Brooklyn NY 11222-5853 Office: Automotive High Sch 50 Bedford Ave Brooklyn NY 11222 Personal E-mail: jayshivcharran@aol.com.

SHIVE, RICHARD BYRON, architect; b. Cleve., Jan. 16, 1933; s. Roy Allen and Mary Elizabeth (Thompson) S.; m. Patricia Butler, Aug. 28, 1954; children: Lisa Ann, Laura Mary, John Thompson, Nancy Butler. BS, Rensselaer Poly. Inst., Troy, NY, 1954; postgrad., NJ Inst. Tech., 1957, Rutgers U., 1960-63. Registered N.J., N.Y., Pa., Vt.; lic. profl. planner N.J. Field engr. Wigton-Abbott Corp., Plainfield, NJ, 1954-55, The Glenwal Co., Rochelle Park, NJ, 1955; asst. supt. Wigton-Abbott Corp., Plainfield, 1955-57; archtl. draftsman Raymond B. Flatt, Architect, Bloomfield, NJ, 1957-58, chief draftsman, 1958-60; project architect Scrimenti/Swackhamer/Perantoni Architects, Somerville, NJ, 1960-66, assoc., 1966-69; ptnr. Scrimenti, Shive, Spinelli, Perantoni Architects, Somerville, 1969-86, Shive/Spinelli/Perantoni & Assocs., Architects & Planners, Somerville, 1986-97; prin. emeritus SSP Archtl. Group, 1998—2002; pvt. practice Richard B. Shive, AIA, Architect, 2003—. Adv. com. First Fidelity Bank, Bound Brook, N.J., 1989-91; chmn. bd. Somerset Health Care Corp., 1987-91. Contbr. articles to profl. jours. Bd. dirs., exec. com. N.J. Hosp. Assn., Princeton, 1986-92, 93-95; chmn. bd. trustees Somerset Med. Ctr., Somerville, 1973-96; mem. Nat. Trust for Hist. Preservation; bd. dirs. Ctr. for Health Affairs, Inc., 1992-93; mem. Borough of Bound Brook Planning Bd., 2000—; chmn. Borough of Bound Brook Redevel. Adv. Com., 2000—; mem. Somerset County Econ. Devel. Incentive Adv. Com., 1997—. Recipient award James F. Lincoln Arc Welding Found., 1973, Pres. award Rolling Hills coun. Girl Scouts U.S.A., 1988, Trustee of Yr. award NJ Hosp. Assn., 1993, Outstanding Citizen of Yr. award Somerset County C. of C., 1993, Spirit of Somerset award, 2000, Honor award Bound Brook-Middlesex Rotary Club and Bound Brook Area C. of C. Ball, 2007; Paul Harris fellow Bound Brook-Middlesex Rotary Club, 1993. Mem. AIA, ASTM, ASHRAE, ACI (chpt. bd. dirs. 1978-83), N.J. Soc. Architects, Illuminating Engring. Soc., Nat. Fire Protection Assn., Greater Somerset County C. of C. (v.p. 1985-86, 92-93, Outstanding Citizen of Yr. award 1993), Rotary (pres. 1969-70, Paul Harris fellow 1993), Wash. Campground Assn. (pres. 1975-76, v.p. 1977-78, sec. 1978-97), Chi Phi (sec. 1973). Republican. Congregationalist. Avocations: fishing, photography, skiing, canoeing, backpacking. Home and Office: 1786 Middlebrook Rd Bound Brook NJ 08805-1432 Office Phone: 732-469-2682. Personal E-mail: rshive@verizon.net.

SHIVELY, DANIEL JEROME, retired transportation executive; b. Akron, Ohio, Sept. 2, 1924; s. Richard Miles and Josephine (Pellicer) S.; m. Pamela Marion Kurfess, July 31, 1954; children: Jennifer, Laurie, Thomas. Grad., U.S. Mcht. Marine Acad., King's Point, NY, 1945. Chief officer (tanker) Trinidad Corp., NYC, 1946-51; co-owner, mgr. Shively Bros. Jersey Farm, Quaker City, Ohio, 1952-54; staff asst. Gulf Oil Corp., Phila., 1955-57; distbn. coord. Standard Oil Co., Cleve., 1957-73; budget coord. BP Oil Co., Wilmington, Del., 1973-79; mgr. mktg. budget and planning Standard Oil Co., Cleve., 1979-85; owner, mgr. Shively & Assocs., Cleve., 1985-88. Served to lt. (j.g.) USNR, 1945-61. Mem. Transp. Practitioners Assn. (exec. com. 1984-90, pres. local chpt. 1984-85), King's Point Club (treas. N.E. Ohio chpt. 1989-94, sec. 1999-2003), KC (chancellor 1986, dep. grand knight 1987-91). Republican. Roman Catholic. Avocations: farming, sailing. Home: 21347 Erie Rd Rocky River OH 44116-2133

SHIVELY, JOHN D., lawyer; b. Lafayette, Ind., 1947; AB cum laude, Harvard U., 1969, JD, 1972. Bar: Minn. 1972, Colo. 1984, US Ct. of Appeals (8th & 10 th cirs.), US Dist. Ct. Colo. Sr. staff atty. Federal Trade Comm., 1979—82; mem. Faegre & Benson, Denver; mem Faegre & Benson LLP, Mpls; mem. Faegre & Benson, Colo., 1984; ptnr. Faegre & Benson LLP, Denver. Mem. Downtown Denver Partnership (transportation coun.), Ally" for Women's Vision Found. Judge adv. USMC, spl. ct.-martial judge USMC. Named Who's Who in Law, Denver Bus. Jour., Am. Leading Lawyers for Bus., Chambers USA, 2005—06, Super Lawyers, 2006. Mem.: Colo, ABA (litig. and antitrust sects.). Office: Faegre & Benson LLP 1700 Lincoln St 3200 Wells Fargo Center Denver CO 80203 Office Phone: 303-607-3616. Office Fax: 303-607-3600. Business E-Mail: jshively@faegre.com.

SHIVELY, JOHN TERRY, cruise line executive; b. Middletown, NY, July 1, 1943; s. Marvin Rathfelder and Esther (Manning) Westervelt; adopted child, Harold Eugene Shively. BA, U. N.C., 1965. Vol. worker VISTA, Bethel and Fairbanks, Alaska, 1965-68; health planner Greater Anchorage Area Cmty. Action Agy., 1968-69; health cons. Alaska Fed.

Natives, Anchorage, 1969; dep. dir. Rural Alaska Cmty. Action Program, Anchorage, 1971-72; exec. v.p. Alaska Fedn. Natives, Anchorage, 1972-75; v.p. ops. NANA Regional Corp., Kotzebue, Alaska, 1975-77, NANA Devel. Corp., Anchorage, 1977-82; sr. v.p. NANA Regional Corp. Inc., 1986-92; pres. NANA Devel. Corp., 1992-94; commr. DNR, 1995-2000; chmn., CEO United Bar Corp., United Bank Alaska, 1987-88; sr. ptnr. Jade North, 2000—02; v.p. govt. and cmty. rels. Holland Am., 2002—. Dir. Unicorp. Inc., United Bank of Alaska, Resource Devel. Coun., exec. com., 2001—, pres, 2003—; dir. Alaska State C. of C., exec. com., 2003—. Mem. Greater Anchorage Area Comprehensive Health Plan Coun., 1969-75, chmn., 1969-75; founding mem. bd. dirs. Alaska Pub. Interest Rsch. Group, 1974-75, 86-90, chmn. 1987-90; mem. Gov.'s Rural Affairs Coun., 1971-76, Gov.'s Manpower Commn., 1971, Greater Anchorage Health Bd., 1969-75, Alaska Pipeline Edn. Com., 1973-74; bd. regents U. Alaska, 1979-83; bd. trustees Alaska Permanent Fund Bd., 1999-2000. Democrat. Episcopalian. Home and Office: 2301 Loren Cir Anchorage AK 99516 Personal E-mail: jtshively@att.net.

SHIVELY, JUDITH CAROLYN (JUDY SHIVELY), administrative assistant; b. Wilkinsburg, Pa., Jan. 30, 1962; d. John Allen and Edith (Crowell) S. BA in English, U. Nev., Las Vegas, 1984. Circulation aide Charleston Heights Libr., Las Vegas, 1979—86; asst. food editor Las Vegas Sun Newspaper, 1985—88, asst. horse racing editor, 1985—90, features writer, page editor, 1988—89, editor youth activities sect., 1989—90; racebook ticket writer, cashier Palace Sta. Hotel Racebook, Las Vegas, 1989—92; contract adminstr. nat. accts. Loomis, Fargo & Co., Las Vegas, 1992—2000; propr. Creative Computing, Las Vegas, 1996—; content prodn. Preference Techs., Inc., Las Vegas, 2000; data rsch. and processing PurchasePro.com, Las Vegas, 2000; adminstrv. asst. Uinta Bus. Systems, Las Vegas, 2001—02, Law Office of Frank Sorrentino, Las Vegas, 2003—07; legal asst. Lee A. Drizin, 2006, Crosby & Assocs., 2006—; tech. word processor II Red, Inc. Comms., 2007. Horse racing historian, rschr., Las Vegas, 1985—; vol. rsch. asst. Dictionary of Gambling and Gaming, 1982-84; clk. Hometown News, Las Vegas, 1994-96. Staff writer horse race handicaps, columns, articles, feature stories Las Vegas Sun Newspaper, 1985-90; freelance writer for monthly horse racing publ. Inside Track, 1992-94. Mem. Phi Beta Kappa. Republican. Avocations: collecting horse racing books, clippings, materials for personal library of horse racing, computers, historical research. Home: PO Box 26426 Las Vegas NV 89126-0426 Personal E-mail: racehors1@aol.com.

SHIVELY, SARAH ELIZABETH, actress; b. Iowa City, Jan. 23, 1970; d. Philip Lee and Nancy Kay Shively; life ptnr. Marilys Ernst, July 11, 2003. B in Arts and Scis., Oberlin Coll., 1992; MFA, U. N.C., 1998. Tchr. Baruch Coll., NYC, 1999—2000; actress Pa. Renaissance Faire, Lebanon, Pa., 2001—02; writer, prodr., actress Contemplating Emily, SI, NY, 2003—05; tchr. Hunter Coll., NYC, 2005—. Fellow, MacDowell Colony, 2005. Mem.: SAG, Actors Equity Assn. Avocations: running, tap dancing, travel, reading, yoga. Home: 222 Castleton Ave Staten Island NY 10301 E-mail: sarahshively@verizon.net.

SHIVELY, WILLIAM PHILLIPS, political scientist, educator; b. Altoona, Pa., Mar. 31, 1942; s. Arthur and Ruth Shively; m. Barbara Louise Shank, Aug. 29, 1964; children: Helen, David. BA, Franklin and Marshall Coll., 1963; PhD, U. N.C., 1968. Mem. faculty U. Oreg., Eugene, 1967-68, Yale U., 1968-71; mem. faculty U. Minn., Mpls., 1971—, prof. polit. sci., 1979—, provost arts, scis. & engring., 1995-97. Author: Craft of Political Research, 1974, 6th edit., 2004, Research Process in Political Science, 1985, Power and Choice, 1986, rev. edit., 1989, 10th edit., 2006, Comparative Governance, 1995, (with Christopher Achen) Cross-Level Inference, 1995; editor Am. Jour. Polit. Sci., 1977-79; contbr. articles on elections and voting to profl. jours. Home: 1572 Northrop St Saint Paul MN 55108-1322 Office: U Minn Dept Polit Sci 1414 Social Scis Tower Minneapolis MN 55455 Office Phone: 612-624-4395. Business E-Mail: shively@umn.edu.

SHIVERS, MITCHELL EVERETT, diplomat; b. NY, Nov. 19, 1947; s. Carl Everett and Mary Allison (Young) S.; m. Nancy Jane Shorsher; children: Mitchell Jr and Jane B. BS, Monmouth U., 1970; postgrad., New York U., 1975-77. Mgmt. exec. Merrill Lynch, NYC, Singapore, 1973—81; exec. dir. Samuel Montagu & Co., London, 1981—84; pvt. practice, 1984—85, 1992—93, Bay Head, NJ, 2003—; pres. Kleinwort Benson Inc., NYC, 1985—89, Fuji Securities, NYC, Chgo., 1989—92; mng. dir. Merrill Lynch, NYC, 1993—2001; ret., 2002; diplomat, sr. advisor, econ. sector chief Afghanistan Reconstrn. Group, U.S. State Dept., Kabul, 2004—05; bus. cons., 2001—; cons. Dept. Def., 2006—07, sr. advisor, ctrl. Asia, 2007—, dep. asst. sec. of def. for ctrl. Asia, office of sec. of def. Vice-chmn. Cultural Trust of NJ; founder, chmn. Barnegat Bay Charities Inc., 2001—04. Recipient Anniversary Cup, Am.'s Cup Jubilee, 2001, N.J. Disting. Svc. medal, State of N.J., 2002, Outstanding Pub. Svc. medal, Sec. Def., 2006. Mem.: Internat. Guild Bankers, Internat. Securities Markets Assn. (bd. dirs. 2000—). Avocations: competitive sailing, jogging, skiing, travel. Personal E-mail: mitchell_shivers@hotmail.com. E-mail: shiversm@gmail.com.

SHIVERY, CHARLES W., utilities executive; BA, BS, Johns Hopkins U.; MBA, U. Balt. With Balt. Gas & Electric Co., 1972—80, asst. treas., 1980—88, treas., asst. sec., 1988—89, v.p. corp. fin., 1989—93, v.p., CFO, 1993—97; chmn., pres., CEO Constellation Power Source, Inc., 1997—2002; CEO, pres. Constellation Enterprises, Inc., 1998—2002; pres., CEO Constellation Power Source Holdings, Inc., 2000—02; co-pres. Constellation Energy Group, Inc., 2000—02, 2000—02; pres., CEO NU Enterprises, Inc., 2002—04; interim pres. N.E. Utilities, Berlin, Conn., 2004, chmn., pres., CEO, 2004—. Office: Northeast Utilities PO Box 270 Hartford CT 06141-0270 *

SHIVES, PAULA J., lawyer; b. Monongahela, Pa., Sept. 28, 1950; m. William Sutton. BA, Western Ky. U., Bowling Green, 1973; JD, U. Ky., Lexington, 1979. Bar: Ky. 1979. Assoc. gen. counsel Long John Silver Restaurants, Inc., Lexington, Ky., 1985—95, sr. v.p., gen. counsel, sec., 1995—99, Darden Restaurants, Inc., Orlando, Fla., 1999—. Mem.: ABA, Ky. Bar Assn., Fayette County Bar Assn. Office: 5900 Lake Ellenor Dr Orlando FL 32809 Home: 2011 Via Tuscany Winter Park FL 32789-1557 Office Phone: 407-245-6566. Business E-Mail: pshives@darden.com.

SHIVJI, KHUSHNOODA AMIN, hospital administrator; b. Mombasa, Kenya, Apr. 18, 1968; d. Haji Valimohamed and Gulshan Valimohamed Bhimji; m. Amin Sadrudin Shivji, July 26, 1986; children: Sharlina, Alysia. BA, U. Nairobi, 1983; MBA, York U., Toronto, Can., 1985. Personal asst. to dir. Freight Forwarders Kenya Ltd., Mombasa, 1982—83; dep. adminstr. Aga Khan Hosp., Mombasa, 1985—96, acting CEO, 1997—98, dir. ops., 1998—2001; dir. diagnostic imaging, mgr. staffing and scheduling Trillium Health Ctr., Canada, 2002—. Chair Quality Coun., rep. at Nat. Quality Steering Com. Aga Khan Health Svc. Kenya, 1997—; leader of cost containment Aga Khan Hosp., 1999—, mem. project implementation com., 1990—2001. Mem.: Mombasa Sports Club. Home: 50 Fennell St Brampton ON Canada L6S 4X6 Office: Trillium Health Ctr 100 Queensway W Mississauga ON L5B 1B8 Canada

SHKLAR, GERALD, pathologist, periodontist, educator; b. Montreal, Que., Can., Dec. 2, 1924; came to U.S., 1950, naturalized, 1955; s. Louis and Ann (Schleifstein) S.; m. Judith Nisse, June 16, 1948 (dec. Sept. 18, 1992); children: David, Michael, Ruth; m. Se-Kyung Oh, July 13, 1997. BS, McGill U., 1947, DDS, 1949; MS, Tufts U., 1952; MA (hon.), Harvard U., 1971; D (hon.), U. Athens. Diplomate Am. Bd. Oral Pathology, Am. Bd. Periodontology. Asst. prof. oral pathology Sch. Dental Medicine Tufts U., Boston, 1953—59, assoc. prof. Sch. Dental Medicine, 1960—61, rsch. prof. peridontology Sch. Dental Medicine, 1961—71, lectr. oral pathology Sch. Dental Medicine, 1971—. Head dept. oral medicine and oral pathology Sch. Dental Medicine Harvard U., Boston, 1971-93, Charles A. Brackett prof. oral pathology, 1971-2000, Charles A. Brackett prof. oral pathology emeritus, 2000—; sr. clin. invesigator Forsyth Inst., Boston, 1994—; cons. oral pathology Children's Hosp. Med. Ctr., Brigham and Women's Hosp., Mass. Gen. Hosp. Author: Oral Cancer, 1984; co-author (with Edmund Cataldo and Henry Goldman): Oral Pathology: An Atlas of Microscopic Pathology, 1975; co-author: (with Philip L. McCarthy) The Oral Manifestations of Systemic Disease, 1976, Diseases of the Oral Mucosa, 2d edit., 1982; co-author: (with David Chernin) Libellus De Dentibus, 1563, of Bartholomaei Eustachii, 1999, A Sourcebook of Dental Medicine, 2002; co-author: (with Fermin Carranza) History of Periodontology, 2003; contbr. over 350 articles to profl. jours., chapters to books. Fellow AAAS, Am. Acad. Dental Sci., Am. Acad. Oral Medicine, Am. Acad. Oral Pathology, Am. Coll. Dentists, Internat. Coll. Dentists; mem. ADA, Internat. Assn. Dental Rsch., Am. Acad. Periodontology, Am. Cancer Soc., Am. Assn. Cancer Rsch., Am. Assn. Cancer Edn., Am. Acad. History Dentistry, History of Sci. Soc., Sigma Xi, Omicron Kappa Upsilon. Avocations: harpsichord, flute. Home: 154 Evelyn Rd Waban MA 02468-1042

SHLADOVER, STEVEN ELLIOT, transportation research professional; b. NYC, Feb. 15, 1950; s. Joel and Ida Shladover. SB, MIT, Cambridge, 1972, SM, 1974, ScD, 1978. Research asst. MIT, Cambridge, Mass., 1976-78, lectr., 1978; staff engr. Systems Control, Inc., Palo Alto, Calif., 1978-81; sr. engr. Systems Control Tech., Inc., Palo Alto, 1981-84, program mgr., 1984-86, dir. CAE systems, 1986-89, mgr., transp. systems engr., 1987-89; tech. dir. PATH Program, dep. dir. U. Calif., Berkeley, 1989—. US Expert to Internat. Standards Orgn. (tech. com. 204, working group 14). Assoc. editor Jour. of Dynamic Systems, Measurement and Control, 1980-85; contbr. articles to profl. jours. Nat. mem. Met. Opera Guild, NYC, 1973—; mem. San Francisco Opera Guild, 1979—, Mus. Soc., San Francisco, 1979—, Common Cause, Washington, 1983—. Named one of the Outstanding Young Men of Am., US Jaycees, 1983; fellow NSF, 1972-75. Mem. SAE (ITS divsn. 1992-2004), Intelligent Transp. Soc. Am. (chmn. AVCS com. 1990-97), ASME (assoc. editor 1980-85, program chmn. dynamic systems and control div. 1986, honors com. 1988-91, sec. 1989-92, exec. com. 1992-97, chmn. 1996), Transp. Rsch. Bd. (com. new transp. systems and tech. 1988, com. on study advanced vehicle and hwy. techs. 1990-91, com. intelligent transp. systems 1992—, chmn., 2004—, com. on vehicle hwy. automation 1997—), MIT Alumni Assn., Calif. Alliance for Adv. Transp. Sys. (bd. dirs. 1994-2005). Democrat. Avocations: opera critic, tennis, international travel. Office: U Calif PATH Program 1301 S 46th St Bldg 452 Richmond CA 94804-4600 Business E-Mail: steve@path.berkeley.edu.

SHLANTA, PAUL R., lawyer; BA in Polit. Economy, Williams Coll., 1979; JD, Emory U., 1983. V.p., gen. counsel AGL Resources, Inc., Atlanta, 1998—2005, now mng. v.p., gen. counsel, chief ethics and compliance officer, 2005—. Mng. editor Emory Law Jour. Mem. ABA, Ga. Bar Assn., Atlanta Bar Assn., Ga. Bankers Assn. (bd. dirs. bank counsel sect., chmn. bd. legal affairs subcom.). Office: AGL Resources Inc 817 Peachtree St NE Atlanta GA 30308-1220 Fax: 404-584-3714.

SHLAUDEMAN, HARRY WALTER, retired diplomat; b. LA, May 17, 1926; s. Karl Whitman and Florence (Pixley) S.; m. Carol Jean Dickey, Aug. 7, 1948; children: Karl Frederick, Katherine Estelle, Harry Richard. BA, Stanford U., 1952. Joined U.S. Fgn. Svc., 1955; vice consul Barranquilla, Colombia, 1955-56; polit. officer Bogotá, Colombia, 1956-58; assigned lang. tng. Washington, 1958-59; consul Sofia, Bulgaria, 1960-62; chief polit. sect. Santo Domingo, Dominican Republic, 1962-64; officer charge Dominican Affairs State Dept., 1964-66; asst. dir. Office Caribbean Affairs, 1965-66; sr. seminar fgn. policy State Dept., 1966-67, spl. asst. to sec. state, 1967-69; dep. chief of mission Santiago, Chile, 1969-73; dep. asst. sec. state for Inter-Am. affairs Washington, 1973-75; amb. to Venezuela, 1975-76; asst. sec. state for Inter-Am. affairs, 1976-77; amb. to Peru, 1977-80; amb. to Argentina, 1980-83; exec. dir. Nat. Bipartisan Commn. on Central Am., 1983-84; spl. amb. to Cen. Am., 1984-86; amb. to Brazil Brasilia, 1986-89; amb. to Nicaragua, 1990-92; ret., 1992. Served with USMCR, 1944-46. Recipient Disting. Honor award Dept. State, 1966, Pres. Disting. Svc. award, 1988, Brazil's Order of Cruzeiro Benementium, 1989, Pres. Medal Freedom, 1992. Mem. Am. Acad. Diplomacy, San Luis Obispo Golf and Country Club, Phi Gamma Delta. Home: 7006 Pebble Beach Way San Luis Obispo CA 93401-8916 Office Phone: 805-544-7539. Personal E-mail: harrywal@aol.com.

SHLAY, JUDITH CAROL, physician; d. Howard Shlay and Doreen Gloria Drew; m. William Martinez; children: Erica Martinez, Laura Martinez. BS, U. Ill., Urbana, 1979; MD, Rush Med. Coll., Chgo., 1983; MSPH, U. Colo., Denver, 1999. Diplomate Am. Bd. Family Medicine, 1986, Am. Bd. Geriatric Medicine, 1992. Resident in family medicine Cook County Hosp., Chgo., 1983—86; family physician Denver Cmty. Health Svcs., 1989—, team leader La Mariposa Family Health Ctr., 2000—06; attending physician ID/AIDs Clinic, attending physician Denver Metro Health Clinic/STD Clinic Denver Pub. Health, 1989—, dir. family planning svcs. Denver Metro Health Clinic, 2000—, dir. Immunization and Travel Clinic, 2006—. Mem. adv. coun. adolescent health Colo. Dept. Pub. Health and Environment, 1995—2007. Recipient 9th Ann. Faculty Scholarship Achievement award, Denver Health and Hosp. Authority Med. Staff, 1999, Model Practice Initiative award, Nat. Assn. City and County Health Ofcls., 2004, Betsy Bernard Emerging Leader award, Women's Vision Found., 2005; grantee, Nat. Inst. Child Health and Human Devel., NIH, 1996—2001, Colo. Dept. Pub. Health and Environment, 2001—, CDC, 2001—05, CDPHE, Cancer, CVD, and COPD, Early Detection and Treatment Program, 2006—. Fellow: Am. Acad. Family Physicians; mem.: Colo. Pub. Health Assn., Am. Venereal Disease Assn., Colo. Acad. Family Physicians. Achievements include research in women health, family planning, acupuncture, metabolic complications of HIV infection, and STD infections. Office: Denver Pub Health 605 Bannock St Denver CO 80204 Home Phone: 303-377-8329; Office Phone: 303-436-7337. Office Fax: 303-436-7211. Business E-Mail: jshlay@dhha.org.

SHLOSBERG, STUART R., prosthodontist; 3 children. BS, U. Manchester; M, U. Ind. Founder Beverly Hills Aesthetic Dentistry. Former prof. Harvard U., U. So. Calif. Mem.: Calif. Dental Assn., Am. Dental Assn., Am. Coll. Prosthodontists. Office: 414 Camden Dr #925 Beverly Hills CA 90210 Office Phone: 310-278-6630.

SHMAVONIAN, GERALD S., political organization administrator; b. LA, June 26, 1945; s. Sergius Neshan and Berje-Lucia (der Hareutunyan) Shmavonian. Student, U. Calif., Berkeley, 1964-70. Leader archaeol. excavation team, Guatemala, Turkey, 1970-75; pub. City Mags., 1975-80; spl. advisor Bicentennial Commission, Washington, D.C., 1975; chmn. Am. Nationalities Coun., Stanford U., 1983-86; pres. Am. Talent, 1986—2000; ptnr. Assembly Plant Ptnrs., 2001—. Founder Tommorw Party, 2000—. Recipient Intercollegiate Boxing Championship, 1965. Fellow Am. Documentary Film Acad.; mem. Calif. Scholarship Fedn. (life, pres. 1963), Nat. Forensic League (pres. 1963, degree of honor). Avocation: art. Home: 6219 N Prospect Ave Fresno CA 93711-1658

SHMUGER, MARC, film company executive; Grad., Wesleyan U. Sr. v.p. creative advt. Columbia Pictures, Sony Pictures Entertainment, 1991—92, v.p., creative dir., 1992—94, exec. v.p. worldwide mktg. Columbia TriStar, 1994—2000; pres. mktg. Universal Pictures, Universal City, Calif., 1998—2000, vice chmn., 2000—06, chmn., 2006—. Founder Art of War Prodn. Co., 1996. Prodr., writer (films) Dead of Winter, 1987. Named Entertainment Marketer of Yr., Advt. Age, 1999, 2000; named one of 50 Most Powerful People in Mktg., 1999, 2000, 50 Most Powerful People in Hollywood, Premiere mag., 2006. Mem.: Phi Beta Kappa. Office: Universal Pictures 100 Universal City Plz Universal City CA 91608

SHMUNES, EDWARD, dermatologist; b. Jacksonville, Fla., July 24, 1940; s. Nathan and Anne Lillian (Berg) S.; m. Sue Shmunes, Apr. 17, 1996; children: Stephanie, Marjorie, Jenifer. MD, U. Fla., 1965. Diplomate Am. Bd. Dermatology. Intern U.S. Pub. Health Hosp., New Orleans, 1965-66; epidemic intelligence officer svc. Ctr. for Disease Control, Atlanta, 1966-68; resident in dermatology U. Pa., Phila., 1968-71; ptnr. Columbia (S.C.) Skin Clinic, 1973—, pres., 1991—2000. Grantee NIH, 2 yrs., U. S.C., 1985. Mem. Greek Orthodox Ch. Office: Columbia Skin Clinic 3 Medical Park Rd Ste 500 Columbia SC 29203-6873 Office Phone: 803-779-7316. Personal E-mail: edart777@aol.com.

SHNAYERSON, ROBERT BEAHAN, editor, consultant; b. NYC, Dec. 8, 1925; s. Charles and Madalene (Griffin) Beahan; m. Lydia Conde Todd, Dec. 23, 1950 (dec. Sept. 1973); children: Michael, Kate; m. Laurie Platt Winfrey, June 9, 1980; children: Maggie, Bonnie. AB, Dartmouth, 1950. Reporter N.Y. Daily News, 1946; reporter Life mag., NYC, 1950-54; corr. Time-Life News Svc., 1954-56; contbg. editor Time mag., 1957-59, edn. editor, 1959-64, law editor, 1964-67, sr. editor, 1967-71; editor-in-chief Harper's Mag., NYC, 1971-76; editor, pub. Quest mag., NYC, 1976-81, Technology mag., NYC, 1981-82; editorial dir. Sci. Digest mag., 1986-87. Editl. cons. Lear's mag., 1987-90; cons. in mag. field; sr. advisor Travel Holiday mag., 1989-95. Author: Illustrated History of the Supreme Court, 1986; author, editor: Wordworks, 1995—; contbr. articles to various mags. With USNR, 1943-46. Home: 118 Riverside Dr New York NY 10024-3708 Office Phone: 212-787-4590. E-mail: shnay@aol.com.

SHNEIDMAN, EDWIN S., psychologist, thanatologist; b. York, Pa., May 13, 1918; s. Louis and Manya (Zukin) S.; m. Jeanne E. Keplinger, Oct. 1, 1944; children: David William, Jonathan Aaron, Paul Samuel, Robert James. AB, UCLA, 1938, MA, 1940; MS, U. So. Calif., 1947, PhD, 1948. Diplomate: Am. Bd. Examiners Profl. Psychology (past v.p.). Clin. psychologist VA Center, Los Angeles, 1947-50, chief research, 1950-53; co-dir. Central Research Unit for Study Unpredicted Deaths, 1953-58; co.-dir. Suicide Prevention Center, Los Angeles, 1958-66; chief Center Studies Suicide Prevention NIMH, Bethesda, Md., 1966-69; vis. prof. Harvard U., 1969; fellow Ctr. Advanced Study in Behavioral Scis., 1969-70; clin. assoc. Mass. Gen. Hosp., 1969, Karolinska Hosp., Stockholm, 1978; prof. med. psychology UCLA, 1970-75, prof. thanatology, 1975-88, emeritus, 1988—. Vis. prof. Ben Gurion U. of Negev, Beersheva, 1983 Author: Deaths of Man, 1973, Voices of Death, 1980; Definition of Suicide, 1985, Suicide as Psychache, 1993, The Suicidal Mind, 1996, Comprehending Suicide, 2001, Autopsy of a Suicidal Mind, 2004; editor: Thematic Test Analysis, 1951; editor: (with N.L. Farberow) Clues to Suicide, 1957, The Cry for Help, 1961, Essays in Self-Destruction, 1967, (with M. Ortega) Aspects of Depression, 1969, On the Nature of Suicide, 1969, (with N.L. Farberow, L.E. Litman) Psychology of Suicide, 1970, Death and the College Student, 1972, Death: Current Perspectives, 1976, 80, 84, Suicidology: Contemporary Developments, 1976, Endeavors in Psychology: Selections From The Personology of Henry A. Murray, 1981, Suicide Thoughts and Reflections, 1981 Served to capt. USAAF, 1942-45. Recipient Harold M. Hildreth award Psychologists in Pub. Service, 1966; Louis I. Dublin award Am. Assn. Suicidology, 1969. Mem. Am. Assn. Suicidology (founder, past pres.), Am. Psychol. Assn. (past div. pres., Disting. Profl. Contbn. to Pub. Svc. award 1987, Henry A. Murray award 1997), Melville Soc. Address: 11431 Kingsland St Los Angeles CA 90066-1329 Home Phone: 310-397-5640; Office Phone: 310-397-5640.

SHNEIDMAN, J. LEE, historian, educator; b. NYC, June 20, 1929; s. Bernard Wolf and Fannia Abramova (Raskin) S.; m. Conalee Levine, Sept. 3, 1961 (dec.); children: Philip, Jack. BA, NYU, 1951, MA, 1952; PhD, U. Wis., 1957. Lectr. CCNY, 1956-57, U. Md. Overseas, 1957-58; asst. prof. Fairleigh Dickinson U., 1958-62; prof. history Adelphi U., 1963—2001, emeritus prof., 2001—. Chmn. seminar on hist., legal, and polit. thought Columbia U., 1985-2002. Author: Rise of the Aragonese-Catalan Empire, 2 vols, 1970, Spain and Franco, 1949-59, 1973, John F. Kennedy, 1974. Dem. N.Y. County committeeman, 1970—. Mem. Am. Hist. Assn., Medieval Acad. Am., Am. Philatel. Soc., Internat. Psychohist. Assn., Rossica Soc., China Soc. Jewish. Home: 161 W 86th St New York NY 10024-3411 *Only by understanding from where we came can we understand where we are and where we are going.*

SHNEOUR, ELIE ALEXIS, biophysicist, researcher, historian; b. Neuilly-sur-Seine, France, Dec. 11, 1925; came to U.S., 1941, naturalized, 1944; s. Zalman and Salomea (Landau) S.; m. Polly M. Henderson, Sept. 7, 1990; children from previous marriage: Mark Zalman, Alan Brewster. BA, Columbia U., 1947; DSc (hon.), Bard Coll., 1969; MA, U. Calif., Berkeley, 1955; PhD, UCLA, 1958. Tchr. and rsch. fellow U. Calif., Berkeley, 1953-55, Am. Heart Assn. rsch. fellow, 1958-62, tchg. and rsch. fellow LA, 1958; rsch. fellow Nat. Cancer Inst., 1956-57; Am. Heart Assn. rsch. fellow NYU, 1958-59; rsch. assoc. genetics Stanford U., 1962-65; assoc. prof. biology and neuroscis. U. Utah, 1965-69; rsch. neurochemist City of Hope Nat. Med. Ctr., Duarte, Calif., 1969-71. Dir. rsch. Calbiochem., 1971-75; pres. Biosystems Insts., Inc., 1975—; dir. Biosystems Rsch. Inst., 1979; steering com. Nat. Acad. Sci. Study Group on Biology and the Exploration of Mars, 1964; chmn. Western Regional coun. Rsch. in Basic Bioscis. for Manned Orbiting Missions, Am. Inst. Biol. Scis., NASA, 1966-69; fellow Com. Skeptical Inquiry, 1996—; mem. editl. bd. Skeptic Mag., 1992—. Author: Extraterrestrial Life, 1965, (with Eric A. Ottesen) National Academy of Sciences, National Rsch. Coun., 1966, (with S. Moffat) Life Beyond the Earth, 1966, The Malnourished Mind, 1974; contbr. articles to profl. jours. Chmn. citizens adv. coun. San Diego Pub. Schs., 1971-72; adv. coun. Cousteau Soc., 1977-98; bd. dir. Lunar Power System Coalition, 1993-2002; internat. v.p. Transinnova S.A. France, 1990—; chmn. sci. adv. bd. County of San Diego, 1995-2002, 2006—, mem., 2002-06. With U.S. Army, 1944-45. Recipient William Lockwood prize, Bard Coll. of Columbia U., 1947. Mem. IEEE, AAAS (chmn. So. Calif. Skeptics soc. Pacific divsn. 1988-90), Am. Chem. Soc., N.Y. Acad. Scis., Am. Inst. Biol. Scis., Am. Soc. for Biochemistry and Molecular Biology (chmn. sci. advisors program 1973-75, mem. com. on pub. policy 1974-76, congl. liaison 1992—), Am. Soc. Neurochemistry (mem. coun. 1971-73), Soc. Neurosci., Internat. Soc. Neurochemistry, U.S. C. of C. (bd. dirs. 1993-98), La Jolla Chamber Music Soc. (bd. dirs. 1994-97), Internat. Coun. for Global Health Progress (N.Am. adv. bd. 1996—), Sigma Xi, Phi Sigma. Office: Biosystems Rsch Inst 700 Front St M/S CDM 608 San Diego CA 92101-6085

SHNIDER, BRUCE JAY, lawyer; b. Lansing, Mich., Oct. 16, 1950; s. Harold A. and Raynor (Seidner) Shnider; m. Patricia Lynn Strandness, Dec. 28, 1973; 1 child, Ruth Strandness. AB magna cum laude, Dartmouth Coll., 1972; MPP, JD magna cum laude, Harvard U., 1977. Bar: Minn. 1977, US Dist. Ct. Minn. 1977, US Tax Ct. 1978, US Ct. Appeals (8th cir.) 1980, US Supreme Ct. 1981. Asst. to dir. Mich. Dept. Commerce, Lansing, 1972-73; law clk. United Mineworkers Am. Health/Retirement Funds, 1975; summer assoc. Robins, Davis & Lyon, Mpls., 1976; assoc. Dorsey & Whitney, Mpls., 1977-82, ptnr., 1983—2006, chmn. diversity com., 1990-93, chmn. tax practice group, 1994-98, of counsel, 2007—. Vis. disting. prof. Law. Sch., U. Minn., 2006—. Bd. dirs. Minn. Justice Found., Mpls., 1989—91; v.p. Emergency Food Shelf Network, 2003—05, pres., 2005—. Mem.:

ABA, Hennepin County Bar Assn., Minn. State Bar Assn. Home: 1908 James Ave S Minneapolis MN 55403-2831 Office: Dorsey & Whitney 50 S 6th St Ste 1500 Minneapolis MN 55402-1498 Office Phone: 612-340-2862. Business E-Mail: shnider.bruce@dorsey.com.

SHOAF, FORREST, lawyer; BA, West Point Acad.; JD, Harvard U. Ptnr. Bass, Berry & Sims, Nashville; mng. dir. Corp. Fin. Dept. JC Bradford, 1996—2000; mng. dir. Investment Banking Group Morgan Keegan, 2000—02, head Nashville Corp. Fin. Office, 2000—02; mng. dir. Investment Banking Dept. Avondale Partners LLC, Nashville; sec., gen. counsel CBRL Group Inc, 2005—. Infantry officer US Army, served to major US Army. Office: CBRL Group Inc PO Box 787 Lebanon TN 37088-0787 Office Phone: 615-443-9869. Office Fax: 615-443-9818. E-mail: forrest.shoaf@cbrlgroup.com.

SHOAF, R. WAYNE, librarian; b. Boulder, Colo., Oct. 24, 1955; s. John Henry and Sue Chestnut Shoaf; m. Melinda Kay Hayes, July 13, 1991. BA, Oberlin Coll., Ohio, 1979; MusB, Oberlin Conservatory, Ohio, 1979; MS, Columbia U., NYC, 1984. Tchg. asst. U. Colo., Engring. Ctr., Boulder, 1981—83; grad. asst. Columbia U., Serials Cataloging, Butler Libr., NYC, 1983—84; libr. NY Pub. Libr., Rodgers and Hammerstein Archives of Recorded Sound, Lincoln Ctr., 1984—85, cataloger, 1984—85; asst. archivist Arnold Schoenberg Inst., LA, 1985—86, acting archivist, 1986—87, archivist, 1987—98; mitarbeiter Arnold Schönberg Ctr., Vienna, 1998—98; co-team leader, music cataloging team and digital resources cataloging team, tech. svcs. U. So. Calif., LA, 1999—2004, metadata specialist, digital info. mgmt., 1999—2005, dir. tech. svcs., imaging, 2005—. Author: (book) The Horn at the University of Colorado at Boulder: A Retrospective With an Emphasis on Recorded History. Boulder, CO, 1983; author: (with K. Glennan and J. McBride) Preliminary Catalog of the Archives of the Arnold Schoenberg Inst., 1986; author: (discography) The Schoenberg Discography, 1987, The Schoenberg Discography, 2nd ed., 1994; contbr. articles to profl. jours. Mem.: Soc. Calif. Archivists, Music Libr. Assn., Assn. For Recorded Sound Collections, Am. Soc. for Info. Scientists, Hist. Brass Soc., Internat. Horn Soc. Avocations: horn playing, book collecting, comic book historian. Office: U So Calif 651 West 35th St Los Angeles CA 90089-2571 Home Phone: 323-343-8772; Office Phone: 213-740-4090. Office Fax: 213-821-1617. E-mail: shoaf@usc.edu.

SHOAFF, THOMAS MITCHELL, lawyer; b. Ft. Wayne, Ind., Aug. 21, 1941; s. John D. and Agnes H. (Hanna) S.; m. Eunice Swedberg, Feb. 7, 1970; children: Andrew, Nathaniel, Matthew-John. BA, Williams Coll., 1964; JD, Vanderbilt U., 1967. Bar: Ind. 1968. Assoc. Isham, Lincoln & Beale, Chgo., 1967-68; ptnr. Baker & Daniels, Ft. Wayne, Ind., 1968—. Bd. dirs. Weaver Popcorn Co., Inc., Ft. Wayne, Dreibelbiss Title Co., Inc., Ft. Wayne, Am. Steel Investment Corp., Ft. Wayne. Bd. dirs. McMillen Found., Ft. Wayne, Wilson Found., Ft. Wayne. Mem. ABA, Allen County Bar Assn., Ind. State Bar Assn. Presbyterian. Avocations: golf, sailing. Office: Baker & Daniels 111 E Wayne St Ste 800 Fort Wayne IN 46802-2603 Office Phone: 260-460-1618. Business E-Mail: thomas.shoaff@bakerd.com.

SHOBE, DAVID SOREN, librarian, director; b. Kansas City, Mo., Mar. 27, 1967; AB, Washington U., St. Louis, 1989; MS, U. Ill., 1999; PhD, Yale U., 1994. Lic. patent agent: U.S. Patent & Trademark Office 2005. Postdoc. rsch. assoc. Wayne State U., 1994—95, U. Nebr., Lincoln, 1996—97; dir. Sud-Chemie Corp. Libr., Louisville, 1999—. Mem.: Am. Intellectual Property Law Assn., Am. Chem. Soc., Phi Beta Kappa. Home: 425 S Hubbards Lane 59 Louisville KY 40207 Office: Sud-Chemie Inc 1600 W Hill St Louisville KY 40210 Home Phone: 502-897-1831; Office Phone: 502-634-7409.

SHOBE, FRANKLIN DALE, mathematician, educator; b. Great Bend, Kans., Jan. 16, 1942; s. Chester Leslie and Dorothy Minerva Shobe; m. Carolyn Jean Caine, June 8, 1996; children: David, Martin, Nora. BA in Math., U. Kansas, Lawrence, 1964, MBA in Bus., 1977; MA in Math., U. Mo., Kansas City, 1967; PhD in Math. Scis., Clemson U., SC, 1997. Environ. analyst Franklin Assocs., Ltd., Prairie Village, Kans., 1977—79; assoc. environ. analyst Midwest Rsch. Inst., Kansas City, 1979—84; asst. prof. Tarkio Coll., Mo., 1984—85, St. Andrew's Pres. Coll., Laurinburg, NC, 1985—89; instr. math Ind. Acad., Muncie, 1995—, chair, math. and computer sci. divsn., 2005—. Capt. USAF, 1967—75. Mem.: Nat. Coun. Tchrs. Math., Soc. Indsl. and Applied Math., Am. Math. Soc., Math. Assn. Am., Ind. Assn. for Gifted, Nat. Assn. Gifted Children. Office: Ind Acad Ball State Univ Muncie IN 47306

SHOBER, AMY, education educator; d. Lynn E. Murphy and Philip E. Shober. BA, BS, Va. Poly. Inst. and State U., Blacksburg, 1998; MS, Pa. State U., 2002; PhD, U. Del., Newark, 2006. Lab. assessor Am. Assn. of State Hwy. and Transp. Officials, Gaithersburg, Md., 1998—99; grad. rsch. asst. Pa. State U., University Park, 1999—2002; grad. rsch. fellow U. Del., Newark, 2002—06; asst. prof. U. Fla., Wimauma, 2006—. Recipient Hazel Burgett Endowed PEO Scholar award, P.E.O., 2005; Grad. Rsch. Fellowship, Inst. of Soil and Environ. Quality at U. Del., 2002—06, J. Fielding Reed PPI Fellowship, Potash and Phosphate Inst., 2005. Mem.: Am. Soc. Agronomy, Soil Sci. Soc. of Am., Golden Key Nat. Honor Soc., Alpha Zeta, Phi Beta Kappa. Avocations: swimming, weightlifting, crocheting. Office: Univ of Fla Gulf Coast REC 14625 Cr 672 Wimauma FL 33598 Office Phone: 813-634-0000. Office Fax: 813-634-0001. Personal E-mail: ashober@gmail.com.

SHOCHAT, STEPHEN JAY, pediatrician, surgeon; b. Balt., Dec. 17, 1938; s. Albert J. and Rose (Blechman) S.; m. Sheila Floam, July 1960 (div. July 1979); children: Francine Lynne, Alisa Joy; m. Carla Ann Centi, Jan. 26, 1980; children: David Robert, Sarah Elizabeth. BS, Randolph Mason Coll., 1959; MD, Med. Coll. Va., 1963. Surg. resident Washington U. Med. Ctr., St. Louis, 1963-68; pediatric surg. resident Boston Children's Hosp., 1968-70; thoracic surg. resident Queen Elizabeth Hosp., Birmingham, Eng., 1970, George Washington Hosp., Washington, 1972; chief pediatric surgery Hershey (Pa.) Med. Ctr., 1973-77, Stanford (Calif.) Med. Ctr., 1977-94; sr. surgeon Children's Hosp. Phila., 1994-96; surgeon-in-chief, chmn. dept. surgery St. Jude Children Rsch. Hosp., Memphis, 1996—; prof. pediats. and surgery U. Tenn., Memphis, 1996-98. Lt. col. USAF, 1970-72. Office: St Jude Children Rsch Hosp Dept Surgery Memphis TN 38105 Office Phone: 901-495-2911. Business E-Mail: stephen.shochat@stjude.org.

SHOCHET, MELVYN JAY, physicist; b. Phila., Oct. 31, 1944; s. Abraham and Dorothy (Kaminsky) S.; m. Sheila Eileen MAzer, July 4, 1967; children: Stephen, Tara. BA, U. Pa., 1966; MA, PhD, Princeton U., 1972. Rsch. assoc. U. Chgo., 1972-73, instr., 1973-74, asst. prof., 1974-79, assoc. prof., 1979-85, prof., 1985—; Elaine M. and Samuel D. Kersten Jr. Disting. Svc. prof. phys. scis. U. Chgo. and Enrico Fermi Inst., 1995—. Co-spokesman collider detector collaboration Fermilab, Batavia, Ill., 1988. Sloan Found. fellow, 1975-79. Fellow Am. Physical Soc.; mem. AAAS, NAS.

SHOCKEY, GARY LEE, lawyer; b. Casper, Wyo., Sept. 25, 1950; s. Bernis L. and Shirley E. (Diehl) Shockey; m. Dona K. Galles, June 1, 1979; children: Amber, Jeremy, Kimberly. AB in Polit. Sci. and Sociology, Yale U., New Haven, Conn., 1973; JD, U. Wyo., 1976. Bar: Wyo. 1976, U.S. Dist. Ct. Wyo. 1976, U.S. Ct. Appeals (10th cir.) 1984, U.S. Ct. Appeals (9th cir.) 1988, U.S. Claims Ct. 1989, U.S. Supreme Ct. 1989, U.S. Ct. Appeals (fed. cir.) 1993, U.S. Dist. Ct. Ariz. 1994. Pub. defender State of Wyo. and City of Casper, 1976-78; pvt. practice Casper, 1976-79; assoc. Spence, Moriarity & Schuster, Casper and Jackson, Wyo., 1978—82, ptnr. Jackson, 1982—2005; pvt. practice Gary L. Shockey PC, Jackson, Wyo., 2005—. Mem.: ATLA, ABA, Wyo. Trial Lawyers Assn. (bd. dirs. 1984—90), Wyo. State Bar (continuing legal edn. com. 1984—85, law and legis. reform com. 1986—88). Office: Gary L Shockey PC Box 10773 Jackson WY 83002 Office Phone: 307-733-5974. Business E-Mail: gary@garyshockeylaw.com.

SHOCKEY, GEORGE R., JR., lawyer; b. St. Louis, Apr. 10, 1947; AB magna cum laude, Washington U., 1969; M in Philosophy, Yale U., 1972, JD, 1976. Bar: NY 1977. Mem. Stroock & Stroock & Lavan, NYC; ptnr. Stroock, NYC. Recipient Woodrow Wilson fellow. Mem.: Phi Beta Kappa. Office: Stroock 180 Maiden Ln New York NY 10038 Office Phone: 212-806-5848. Office Fax: 212-806-6006. Business E-Mail: gshockey@stroock.com.

SHOCKEY, JEREMY CHARLES, professional football player; b. Ada, OK, Aug. 18, 1980; s. Lucinda. Student, Northeast Oklahoma A&M Jr. College, 1999, Univ. of Miami, 2000—02. Tight end New York Giants, 2002—. Vol. United Way Found. Named NFL Rookie of the Yr., 2002; named to NFC Pro-Bowl team, 2002—03, 2005. Achievements include being a member of NCAA Champion Miami Hurricanes, 2001. Office: c/o New York Giants Giants Stadium East Rutherford NJ 07073

SHOCKLEY, ALONZO HILTON, JR., school system administrator; b. Milford, Del., Sept. 30, 1920; s. Alonzo Hilton Sr. and Elizabeth (Hilton) S.; m. Kay Marilyn Falke, Aug. 13, 1979; children: Novella Lela Shockley Randolph, Cheryl Emmelyn Shockley Durant, Alonzo Hilton III. BS, Del. State Coll., 1943; MA, Mich. State U., 1947; cert., NYU, 1956, postgrad., 1980, Queens Coll., 1961-62, U. Maine, 1963. Cert. tchr., N.Y., Pa., Del. Tchr. sci. Brooks HS, Prince Frederick, Md., 1948; prin. elem., jr. high schs. dept. public instrn., Dover, Del., 1948-58; rsch. assoc. Del. State Coll., Dover, 1958-60; elem. sch. tchr. Cen. Sch. Dist. 4, Plainview, NY, 1960-62; asst. elem. prin. Union Free Sch. Dist., Wyandanch, NY, 1962-64; assoc. adminstrn. official NY State Edn. Dept., Albany, 1964-65; edn. coord. Nassau County Commn. Econ. Opportunity, Garden City, LI, NY, 1965-66; dir. state and fed. programs Freeport Pub. Schs., NY, 1966-85; coord. state and fed. programs Amityville Pub. Schs., LI, NY, 1985-91, ednl. cons., 1988—. V.p. Internat. Rotary, Ronkonkoma, N.Y., 1997; v.p. Phi Delta Kappa of L.I. #1020. Contbr. articles in field of ednl. adminstrn. to profl. jours. Pres. mid L.I. chpt. UN Assn. of U.S., bd. dir. so. N.Y. divsn., mem. coun. pres. steeringcom., pres. Suffolk County chpt., 1995—; organizer of 1997 Mcpl. Elections Bill contbg. to the implementation of the Dayton Peace Accord, 1987; 6 time supr. for Bosnia/Herzegovia elections. Served with U.S. Army, 1942-45, NATOUSA; mem. NYU Alumni Chorus, 1980—, Huntington Men's Chorus, L.I., 1985—. Recipient Cert. of Merit for supervising registration in Bosnia and Herzegovia, Ctrl. Bosnia Canton 6, 1997. Mem. Am. Assn. Sch. Adminstrs., NEA, N.Y. State Tchrs. Edn., Assn. Childhood Edn. Internat., Assn. Supervision and Curriculum Devel., Nat. Assn. Elem. Prins., Amityville Sch. Dist. Adminstrs., Am. Acad. Polit. and Social Sci., NYU Alumni Assn. (bd. dirs., v.p.), Sch. Health, Edn. and Nursing Arts Professionals (pres.), Rotary (pres. Ronkonkomas, L.I.), Phi Delta (v.p. Long Island N.Y. chpt. 1994—). Home: 49 Gaymore Rd Port Jefferson Station NY 11776-1354

SHOCKLEY, ANN ALLEN, librarian, writer; b. Louisville, June 21, 1927; d. Henry and Bessie (Lucas) Allen; children: W. Leslie Shockley Jr., Tamara Ann Shockley. BA, Fisk U., 1948; MSL.S., Case Western Reserve U., 1959. Asst. librarian Del. State Coll., Dover, 1959-60; asst. librarian U. Md. Eastern Shore, Princess Anne, 1960-66, assoc. librarian, 1966-69, Fisk U., Nashville, 1969-98. Author: (novels) Loving Her, 1974, Say Jesus and Come to Me, 1982, Celebrating Hotchclaw, 2005,(short stories) The Black & White of It, 1980, (with E. J. Josey) Handbook of Black Librarianship, 1977, (with Sue P. Chandler) Living Black American Authors, 1973; editor: (anthology) Afro-American Women Writers 1746-1933, 1988 (Susan Koppelman Award 1989). Recipient Hatshepsut Award for Lit., N.Y., 1981, Martin Luther King Jr. Black Author award, Nashville, 1982. Mem. Authors Guild (Tenn. archivists), ALA (Black Caucus, Black Caucus award for editing caucus newsletter 1975, Black Caucus award for Extraordinary Achievement in Profl. Activities, 1992). Home: 5975 Post Rd Nashville TN 37205-3232

SHOCKLEY, EDWARD JULIAN, retired air transportation executive; b. Augusta, Ga., Oct. 31, 1924; s. Julian P. and Margaret (Epps) S.; m. Dorothy Elizabeth Holley, Nov. 24, 1945; children: Edward J., Steven Holley. B.Aero. Engring., Ga. Inst. Tech., 1950; postgrad. (Sloan fellow), Stanford U. Grad. Sch. Bus., 1962-63. Flight test engr. Douglas Aircraft Co., 1950-53; with Lockheed-Ga. Co., 1953-80, dir. quality and safety, 1965-74, dir. mktg., 1974-78, v.p., 1978-80; pres. Lockheed Aircraft Service Co. div. Lockheed Corp., Burbank, Calif., 1980-86, sr. advisor to pres., 1986-87, ret., 1987; pres. Millimeter Wave Tech., Inc., Marietta, Ga., 1988-90, vice chmn. bd. dirs., 1991-92; ret., 1992. Dir. Aerosurge Mgmt. Cons., 1991-92; pres. Lockheed-Ga. Fed. Credit Union, 1971-74 Mem. bus. adv. coun. Ga. So. U.; mem. adv. coun. Sch. Bus. and Econs., Coll. of Charleston. Served with USN, 1941-46. Mem. Cherokee Town and Country Club. Republican. Methodist. Personal E-mail: eshock@charter.net.

SHOCKLEY-ZALABAK, PAMELA SUE, academic administrator; b. May 25, 1944; d. James William and Leatha Pearl (Cartwright) Shockley; m. Charles Zalabak, Dec. 30, 1975. BA in Comm., Okla. State U., 1965, MA in Comm., 1972; PhD in Orgnl. Comm., U. Colo., 1980. Instr. comm. Coll. Letters, Arts and Scis. U. Colo., 1976, from asst. to full prof., 1992, prof. comm. Colorado Springs, 1992—, dir., net and media ctr., 1992, spl. asst. to chancellor, 1994, vice chancellor for student success Colorado Springs, 1998—2001, interim chancellor, 2001—02, chancellor, 2002—. Cons. in field. Author six books; prodr.: (six video documentaries); contbr. articles to profl. jours. Recipient Disting. Svc. award, Colo. Speech Comm. Assn., Telly award; Lew Wentz Tri Delt scholar, 1961—65. Mem.: Internat. Comm. Assn., Speech Comm. Assn., Phi Kappa Phi. Democrat. Avocations: skiing, hiking, fly fishing. Office: Univ Colorado Chancellor's Office 1420 Austin Bluffs Pkwy Colorado Springs CO 80918 *

SHOEMAKER, ALLEN LESLIE, psychology professor, consultant; b. Grand Rapids, Mich., Dec. 26, 1952; s. Leslie and Geraldine Shoemaker; children: James, Benjamin, Rebecca. BS, Calvin Coll., 1976; MS, U. Ill., Champaign-Urbana, 1978, PhD, 1980. Prof. psychology Calvin Coll., Grand Rapids, Mich., 1980—. Cons. in field. Contbr. articles to profl. jours. Mentor Kids Hope USA, Grand Rapids. Office: Calvin Coll 3201 Burton St SE Grand Rapids MI 49546 Business E-Mail: shoe@calvin.edu.

SHOEMAKER, BOBBY JEAN (B.J. FOSTER), writer; d. Farris Lee and Grace Helen Foster; m. Leonard Wiley Shoemaker, June 1, 1958; children: Sharon Dawn, Walker. BA, Va. Intermont Coll., 1981. Cert. paralegal Nat. Ctr. for Paralegal Tng., Atlanta, 1985. Exec. v.p. Leonard W. Shoemaker & Assoc. Consulting Engrs., Houston, 1970—90; author Houston, 1990—. Author: Bayou Shadows, 2000 (named Book of Yr., High Country Writers, 2001). Mem.: Elk River Club. Presbyterian. Avocations: horseback riding, golf, skiing, tennis, hiking.

SHOEMAKER, CAROLYN SPELLMAN, planetary astronomer; b. Gallup, N.Mex., June 24, 1929; d. Leonard Robert and Hazel Adele (Arthur) Spellmann; m. Eugene Merle Shoemaker, Aug. 18, 1951 (dec. July 1997); children: Christine Shoemaker Abanto, Patrick Gene, Linda Shoemaker Salazar. BA cum laude, Chico State Coll., 1949, MA, 1950; ScD, No. Ariz. U., 1990, St. Mary's U., NS, Can., 2003. Vis. scientist Br. astrogeology U.S. Geol. Survey, Flagstaff, Ariz., 1980—; rsch. asst. Calif. Inst. Tech., Pasadena, 1981-85; rsch. prof. astronomy No. Ariz. U., Flagstaff, 1989—; mem. staff Lowell Obs., Flagstaff, 1993—. Guest observer Palomar Obs., Palomar Mountain, Calif., 1982-94; Ruth Northcott Meml. lectr. R.A.S.C., 1995; co-McGovern lectr. Cosmos Club Found., 1995. Co-recipient Rittenhouse medal Rittenhouse Astron. Soc., 1988, Scientist of Yr. award ARCS Found., 1995, James C. Watson medal NAS, 1998; recipient Woman of Distinction award Soroptimists, 1994, 20th Anniversary Internat. Women's Yr. award Zonta and 99s, 1995, NASA Exceptional Scientific Achievement medal, 1996, Woman of Distinction award Nat. Assn. Women in Edn., 1996, Shoemaker award Am. Inst. Profl. Geologists, 1997, plaque Internat. Forest Friendship, Atchison, Kans., 1997, Robert Burnham Jr. award Western Regional Astron. League, 2000, Ariz. Woman of Distinction award Alpha Delta Kappa, 2004; named Disting. Alumna of the Calif. State U., Chico, 1996. Fellow AAAS, Am. Acad. Arts and Scis., Am. Geophys. Union; mem. Meteoritical Soc., Sigma Xi. Achievements include discovery of 32 comets including Periodic Comet Shoemaker-Levy 9 which impacted Jupiter in July 1994, more than 500 asteroids including 44 Earth approachers and approximately 68 Mars crossers, meteorites at Veevers Crater, Australia and impactites at Wolfe Creek Crater, Australia. Home: 5231 Hidden Hollow Rd Flagstaff AZ 86001-3821 Office: Lowell Obs 1400 W Mars Hill Rd Flagstaff AZ 86001-4499 Business E-Mail: cshoemaker@usgs.gov.

SHOEMAKER, ELIZABETH ELLEN, retired military officer; b. Chgo., Feb. 24, 1952; d. Herman Louis Kretschmer, Jr. and Eugenia May Kretschmer; m. Keith A. Wheelwright (div.); m. William Kent Shoemaker, Oct. 30, 1990; children: Robert Louis, Elijah Kent. Grad. H.S., Taos, N.Mex., 1970. Enlisted USN, 1973, submarine repairman Submarine Base Pearl Harbour, Hawaii, 1973—76, submarine repair/ships supt. Submarine Base, 1978—84, tugboat engr. Naval Dist. Washington, 1976—78, advanced through grades to lt. j.g., 1984—86, chief engr. submarine floating drydock Norfolk, Va., 1986—89, dispatcher shore patrol Hampton Roads Shore Patrol, 1989—90, chief engr. YTB 752 Naval Weapons Sta. Yorktown, Va., 1989—90; ret., 1990. Sec. Iroquis Lagoon Yacht Club, Ewa Beach, Hawaii, 1982—83; flutist, v.p. Piedmont Prime Time Cmty. Band, 2005—. Decorated Navy Achievement medal Sec. of the Navy, 2nd Navy Achievement medal.

SHOEMAKER, FRANK CRAWFORD, retired physicist; b. Ogden, Utah, Mar. 26, 1922; s. Roy Hopkins and Sarah Parker (Anderson) Shoemaker; m. Ruth Elizabeth Nelson, July 11, 1944; children: Barbara Elaine, Mary Frances. AB, Whitman Coll., 1943, DSc (hon.), 1978; PhD, U. Wis., 1949. Staff mem. Radiation Lab. MIT, 1943-45; instr. physics U. Wis., 1949-50; mem. faculty Princeton (N.J.) U., 1950-89, prof. physics, 1962—89, prof. emeritus, 1989—, dir. undergrad. physics dept., 1981—89; assoc. dir. Princeton U. Pa. Accelerator, 1962-66; ret., 1989. Vis. scientist Rutherford High Energy Lab., 1965—66; main accelerator sect. head Nat. Accelerator Lab., 1968—69; prin. investigator Dept. of Energy High Energy Physics Contract, 1972—85. Fellow: Am. Phys. Soc.; mem.: Sigma Xi, Phi Beta Kappa. Home: 49 Meadow Lakes 03 East Windsor NJ 08520-3351 Office Phone: 609-258-6602. Business E-Mail: frankcs@princeton.edu.

SHOEMAKER, HAROLD LLOYD, information scientist; b. Danville, Ky., Jan. 3, 1923; s. Eugene Clay and Amy (Wilson) S.; m. Dorothy M. Maddox, May 11, 1947 (dec. Feb. 1991). AB, Berea Coll., 1944; postgrad., State U. Ia., 1943-44, George Washington U., 1949-50, NYU, 1950-52. Rsch. physicist State U. Iowa, 1944-45, Frankford Arsenal, Pa., 1945-47; rsch. engr. N.Am. Aviation, LA, 1947-49, Jacobs Instrument Co., Bethesda, 1949-50; assoc. head systems devel. group The Teleregister Corp., NYC, 1950-53; mgr. electronic equipment devel. sect., head planning Hughes Aircraft Co., LA, 1953-58; dir. command and control systems lab. Bunker-Ramo Corp., LA, 1958-68; v.p. Data Systems, 1968-69, corp. dir. data processing, 1969-75; tech. staff R & D Assocs., Marina Del Rey, Calif., 1975-85; info. systems cons., 1985—. Patentee elec. digital computer. Served with AUS, 1945-46. Mem. IEEE, Ky. Cols. Home: PO Box 3385 Granada Hills CA 91394-0385 E-mail: haroldshoe@cs.com.

SHOEMAKER, HELEN E. MARTIN ACHOR, civic worker; b. Houston, Mar. 24, 1915; d. Earl L. and Blanche L. (Williams) Martin; m. Harold E. Achor, Oct. 11, 1935; children: Dianne Achor Johnston, Lana Achor Rainville; m. Robert N. Shoemaker, May 19, 1972. AB, Anderson Coll., Ind., 1960, LLD, 1978. Resident dir. Anderson Coll., 1967-69, dir. alumni svcs., 1969-72; legis. counsel Ind. Colls. and Univ. Ind., 1970-72; spl. asst. Ctr. Pub. Svc., Anderson, 1973-77, spl. asst. to dean for acad. devel., 1977-78. Sec.-treas. Ind. State Libr. and Hist. Bldg. Expansion Commn., 1973-78; mem. com. region VII, Girl Scouts U.S.A., 1958-66; adv. coun. fin. aid to students Office Edn. HEW, 1976-78; mem. Ind. Ho. of Reps. from Madison County, 1968-70; v.p. Ind. Fedn. Women's Rep. Clubs, 1945-46; treas. Nat. Fedn. Women's Rep. Clubs, 1947-51; Rep. precinct vice chmn. Madison County, 1946-68, vice chmn., Anderson, 1967-68; bd. dirs. Urban League Madison County, 1969-76; adv. com. Georgetown U. Grad. Sch. Acad. in Pub. Svc., 1976-83; adv. com. on sex discrimination Ind. Civil Rights Commn., 1978-83; bd. dirs. Anderson Symphony Womens Guild, Anderson Symphony Orch. Women's Guild, 1987, hon. mem.; trustee Anderson Coll., 1978-85; bd. dirs. Opportunities Industrialization Ctr., Inc., Madison County, 1980-84, Ind. Acad. Pub. Svc., 1981-83, Women's Alternatives Inc., Anderson, 1982-93 (Elizabeth Howard McMahan award 1987); exec. com. devel. bd. St. John's Med. Ctr., Anderson, 1981-92; bd. dirs. life enrichment Park Place Ch. God, 1989-94 Recipient William B. Harper award Urban League Madison County, 1975; named Sagamore of Wabash, State of Ind., 1979. Mem. LWV (dir. Madison County 1973-76, 78-84, 87), Anderson Coun. Women, Anderson Fine Arts Ctr. (treas.). Mem. Ch. Of God. Home: 5801 W Bethel Ave Muncie IN 47304-9549

SHOEMAKER, INNIS HOWE, art museum curator; b. Reading, Pa. d. William Erety and Jean (Miller) S. AB, Vassar Coll., 1964; MA, Columbia U., 1968, PhD, 1975. Curator Vassar Coll. Art. Gallery, Poughkeepsie, NY, 1965-68, 73-76; asst. dir. Ackland Art Mus., U. N.C., Chapel Hill, 1976-82, dir., 1983-86; Audrey and William H. Helfand sr. curator prints, drawings and photographs Phila. Mus. Art, 1986—; adj. prof. U. Pa., 2001—. Fellow in art history Am. Acad. in Rome, 1971-73; adj. prof. U. N.C., Chapel Hill, 1983-86. Author: Mad for Modernism: Earl Horter and His Collection, 1999, Jacques Villon and his Cubist Prints, 2001; co-author: The Engravings of Marcantonio Raimondi, 1981, Paul Cézanne: Two Sketchbooks, 1989, Mexico and Modern Printmaking: A Revolution in the Graphic Arts, 2006. Mem. vis. com. Lehman Loeb Art Ctr., Vassar Coll., 1993-. Mem. Coll. Art Assn. Am., Am. Assn. Mus., Print Coun. Am. (bd. dirs. 1986-89). Office: Phila Mus Art PO Box 7646 Philadelphia PA 19101-7646

SHOEMAKER, ROBERT MORIN, retired military officer, commissioner; b. Almont, Mich., Feb. 18, 1924; s. Uriah Beebe and Pomala (Morin) S.; m. Mary Alice Rickard, July 17, 1948. BS, U.S. Mil. Acad., 1946; postgrad., U.S. Army Command and Gen. Staff Coll., 1959, Army War Coll., 1967. Commd. 2d lt. U.S. Army, 1946, advanced through grades to gen., 1978, platoon leader, bn. staff officer, co. comdr. 18th Inf., Fed. Republic Germany, 1947-50, co. comdr., regtl. S2, S3, 23d Inf. Republic of Korea, 1953-54, staff officer inf. br. DA, 1954-56, student, faculty officer U.S. Army Aviation Sch. Ft. Rucker, Ala., 1959-62, project officer Army Concept Team Vietnam, 1962-63, bn. comdr., asst. chief of staff, G-3, 11th Air Assault Div. Ft. Benning, Ga., 1963-65, bn. cmdr., squadron comdr. 1st Cav. Div., Vietnam, 1965-66, chief plans and programs Army Aviation DA, 1967-69, chief of staff, asst. div. comdr. 1st Cav. Vietnam, 1969-70, dep.

comdr., chief. of staff III Corps and Ft. Hood, Tex., 1970, dept. comdr. MASSTER Ft. Hood, Tex., 1971-72, comdr. 1st Cav., 1973-75, comdr. III Corps Ft. Hood, 1975-77, dep. comdr. FORSCOM Ft. McPherson, Ga., 1977-78; comdr. U.S. Army Forces Command, 1978-82; ret., 1982; county commr. Bell County, Tex., 1987-94. Decorated D.S.M., Silver Star medal with oak leaf cluster, Legion of Merit, D.F.C., Bronze Star, Air medal with 48 oak leaf clusters, Army Commendation medal with oak leaf cluster, Croix de Guerre (France), Gallantry Cross with palm (Republic of Vietnam), RVN Honor medal 1st class; Robert M. Shoemaker H.S., Killeen, Tex. named in his honor, Aug. 2001; named Disting. Grad., West Point, 2004. Home: 111 Bluff Ln Belton TX 76513-9804 E-mail: bshoe5@earthlink.net.

SHOEMAKER, TROY, hazardous materials response team coordinator, fire captain; b. Alliance, Nebr., July 12, 1971; s. Freddie and Virginia Shoemaker; children: Keaton, Kadin. Cert. firefighter I 1992, apprentice fire protection specialist 1992, fire officer I 1995, airport firefighter 1995, hazardous materials technician 1997, advanced hazardous materials technician 1997, registered nat. emergency med. basic technician 2002. Damage controlman, firefighter USN, San Diego, 1989—94; sr. fire capt. Antarctic Support Assoc., Englewood, Colo., 1994—96; hazmat coord., fire capt. Scottsbluff Fire Dept., Nebr., 1996—. Mem. Scotts Bluff County Local Emergency Planning Com., Nebr., 2002—, Nebr. Hazardous Materials Adv. Coun., Lincoln, 2000—; founding chairperson Nebr. Hazardous Materials Assn., 2005. Contbr. articles to profl. jours. With USN, 1989—94. Mem.: Internat. Assn. Firefighters, Mo. Valley Assn. Fire Chiefs, Internat. Assn. Fire Chiefs. Office: Scottsbluff Fire Dept 1818 Ave A Scottsbluff NE 69361-1779 Office Phone: 308-630-6231.

SHOEMAKER, WILLIAM C., journalist; b. Simpson County, Miss., Nov. 19, 1931; s. William Ezra and Saleta (Roach) S.; m. Nell Slade, Apr. 12, 1957. Grad. high sch., Miss. Reporter Jackson (Miss.) Daily News, 1949-51, 54-65; editor, pub. The Star-Herald, Koscivsko, Miss., 1965-89; pres. Shoemaker Offset Inc., Koscivsko, Miss., 1989—, Scott County Times, Miss., 1983-89, Simpson County News, 1983-87, Pontotoc Progress, 1985-89, Bulldog Pubs., 1983-90. Bd. dirs. Merchants and Farmers Bank. Chmn. Miss. Econ. Coun., 1996-97; chmn. Miss. svc. delivery area U.S. Job Tng. Partnership Act, 1983-95. With U.S. Army, 1951-54. Mem. Rotary. Independent.

SHOEMAKER, WILLIAM EDWARD, corporate financial executive; b. Charleston, W.Va., Sept. 17, 1945; s. Robert Edward and Janet Elizabeth (Hoglund) S.; 1 child, Marcus. BBA, U. Notre Dame, 1967. Assoc. buyer Proctor & Gamble, Cin., 1971; gen. mgr. Eastwind Inc., Anchorage, 1972-73; pres., operator Golden Horn Lodge, Inc., Bristol Bay, Alaska, 1973-79; treas. Hawley Resource Group, Inc., Anchorage, 1979-88; treas., chief fin. officer Golden Zone Resources, Inc., Campbell, Calif., 1988-90; ptnr. Resort Mgmt. Corp., Anchorage, 1987-90; pres. Discovery Holdings, Inc., Ft. Lauderdale, Fla., 1991—2005; pres., CEO Foresight Digital Co., 2005—. Bd. dirs. Pacific Art & Design Cons., Inc. Bd. dirs. Anchorage Econ. Devel. Corp., 1988-90, 4 Children's Sake, 1997—; mem. exec. com. Broward Child Welfare Initiative, 2002—; dir. Lovewell Inst. for Creative Arts, 2004-. Served to lt. USN, 1967—71. Republican. Avocations: boating, skiing, fishing. Office: Discovery Holdings Inc Ste 120 2400 E Las Olas Blvd Fort Lauderdale FL 33301-1529 Home: 1733 NE 8TH St Fort Lauderdale FL 33304-3474 Office Phone: 954-761-9111. Personal E-mail: weshoemaker@bellsouth.net.

SHOEN, EDWARD JOSEPH, transportation and insurance companies executive; s. Leonard and Anna (Carty) S. BA, Coll. Holy Cross, 1971; MBA, Harvard U., 1973; JD, Ariz. State Univ., 1981. With Amerco Corp, 1971—; pres. U-Haul Internat., Inc., 1990—; pres., chmn. Amerco Corp., Reno, 1986—. Office: Amerco 1325 Airmotive Way Reno NV 89502 *

SHOFFNER, MARTHA ANN, state official; b. July 10, 1944; Attended, U. Memphis, Ark. State U. Lic. real estate agent. With Sink Realty, Newport, Ark.; asst. auditor State of Ark., Little Rock; mem. Ark. Ho. of Reps. from Dist. 79, Little Rock, 1997—2003; treas. State of Ark., Little Rock, 2006—. Chmn. State Agencies and Govt. Affairs Com.; mem. Joint Budget Com., Joint Com. on Retirement and Soc. Security. Named Jackson County Woman of Yr., 1996. Mem.: Newport C. of C., Jackson County Humane Soc., Bus. & Profl. Women's Club, DAR. Office: Ark State Treas 220 State Capitol Little Rock AR 72201 *

SHOGAN, ROBERT, news correspondent; b. NYC, Sept. 12, 1930; s. Albert and Millie (Jacobs) S.; m. Ellen Shrewsbury, May 26, 1959; children: Cynthia Diane, Amelia Ford. BA, Syracuse U., 1951; postgrad., U. Mich. Inst. Pub. Adminstrn., 1951, Columbia U., 1952. Reporter Detroit Free Press, 1956-59; telegraph editor Miami (Fla.) News, 1959-61; asst. editor Wall St. Jour., NYC, 1961-65; evaluation officer Peace Corps, Washington, 1965-66; corr. Newsweek, Washington, 1966-73; nation polit. corr. Los Angeles Times, Washington, 1973-99. Profl.-in-residence Annenberg Sch. Communication, U. Pa., 1993; adj. prof. Johns Hopkins U., Ctr. for Study of Am. Govt., Washington, 1999—. Author: Question of Judgement, 1972, Promises to Keep, 1977, None of the Above, 1982, The Riddle of Power, 1991, Hard Bargain, 1995, Fate of the Union, 1998, The Double-Edged Sword, 1998, Bad News, 2001, War Without End, 2002, The Battle of Blair Mountain, 2004, Backlash, 2006; co-author: (with Tom Craig) The Detroit Race Riot, 1964. Served with U.S. Army, 1952-54. Recipient 1st prize Feature Writing, Mich. AP, 1959, Disting. Reporting Pub. Affairs award Am. Polit. Sci. Assn., 1969, Scribes Book award, 1972; rsch. grantee Harry S Truman Presdl. Libr., 1989, Lyndon B. Johnson Presdl. Libr., 1989, Gerald R. Ford Presdl. Libr., 1989; McCormick fellow Hoover Presdl. Libr., 1993; fellow Media Studies Ctr., 1998. Mem. Phi Beta Kappa Home: 3513 Raymond St Chevy Chase MD 20815-3227

SHOHET, JUDA LEON, electrical and computer engineering educator, researcher, information technology executive; b. Chgo., June 26, 1937; s. Allan Sollman and Frannye Ina (Turner) S.; m. Amy Lenore Scherz, Sept. 5, 1969; children: Aaron, Lena, William. BS, Purdue U., 1958; MS, Carnegie Mellon U., 1960, PhD, 1961. Registered profl. engr., Wis. Asst. prof. Johns Hopkins U., Balt., 1961-66; assoc. prof. U. Wis., Madison, 1966-71, prof., 1971—, chmn. dept. elec. and computer engring., 1986-90, dir. Torsatron/Stellarator Lab., 1974—99, dir. Engring. Rsch. Ctr. for Plasma-Aided Mfg., 1986—97; dir. Plasma Processing and Tech. Lab., 1999—. Pres. Omicron Tech., Inc., Madison, 1985—; cons., presenter in field. Author: The Plasma State, 1979, Flux Coordinates and Magnetic Field Structure, 1991; contbr. over 150 articles to profl. jours. Recipient Frederick Emmons Terman award Am. Soc. for Engring. Edn., 1978, John Yarborough Meml. medal British Vacuum Coun., 1993. Fellow IEEE (Centennial medal 1984, Richard F. Shea Disting. Mem. award 1992), Am. Phys. Soc.; mem. IEEE Nuclear and Plasma Scis. Soc. (pres. 1980-82, Merit award 1978, Plasma Sci. and Applications prize 1990). Achievements include patents in field. Avocations: skiing, sailing, hiking. Home: 1937 Arlington Pl Madison WI 53726-4001 Office: U Wis Dept Elec & Computer Engring 1445 Engring Hall Madison WI 53706 Office Phone: 608-262-1191. Business E-Mail: shohet@engr.wisc.edu.

SHOHET, STEPHEN BYRON, medical educator; b. Boston, Nov. 29, 1934; s. Harmon Abraham and Grace (Cohen) S.; m. Geraldine Poplack, July 22, 1956; children: Ralph, Grace, Jason, Juliet. BA, Harvard U., 1956, MD, 1960. Diplomate: Am. Bd. Internal Medicine. Intern, resident in medicine Beth Israel Hosp., Boston, 1960—62; clin. assoc. NIH, 1962—64, sr. staff assoc., 1965; fellow in hematology, instr. medicine Peter Bent Brigham Hosp., 1965—69; asst. prof. Harvard U., 1969—71; assoc. prof. U. Calif., San Francisco, 1971—76, prof. medicine and lab. medicine, 1976—2003, prof. emeritus, 2003—, chief hematology, 1974—84, dir. Cancer Rsch. Inst., 1974—80, dir. MacMillan-Cargill Hematology Rsch. Lab., 1980—2003. Contbr. articles to med. jours., also chpts. on hematology and biology of blood cell membranes to books. Recipient various research and tng. grants NIH. Mem. Am. Soc. Clin. Investigation, Am. Soc. Hematology, Biophys. Soc., Am. Assn. Physicians, Red Cell Club, Western Assn. Physicians. Office Phone: 415-922-3070. E-mail: sbshohet@aol.com.

SHOKET, ANN E., editor-in-chief; b. June 16, 1972; BA cum laude, NYU. Cert. in Media The New Sch. With The Am. Lawyer; editor React mag.; various positions CosmoGIRL!, 1999—2003, exec. editor, 2003—07; web editorial dir. Cosmogirl.com, 2000; editor-in-chief Seventeen mag., 2007—. Office: Seventeen Magazine 300 W 57Th St New York NY 10019-3741 *

SHOL, KIM DURAND, accountant, computer scientist; b. Fergus Falls, Minn., Oct. 19, 1955; s. Robert Walter and Doris Ruby (Wahl) S.; m. Cheryl Renee Casmey, Sept. 18, 1992 (div. Aug. 2003); children: Heidi Renee and Heather Kay (twins). AAS in Bus. Computer Sys., U. Minn., 1988. Program asst. Northwestern Apts., Crookston, Minn., 1982—86; jr. programmer U. Minn., Crookston, 1988—90; acctg. technician Northwestern Mental Health Ctr., Inc., Crookston, 1991—. Mem. computer adv. com. U. Minn., Crookston, 1989-90. Mem. ch. coun. Trinity Luth. Ch., Crookston, Minn., 2007—. Mpls. Tribune scholar, 1970. Lutheran. Avocations: studying history and religion, painting still life and landscapes, collecting music. Office: Northwestern Mental Health Ctr 603 Bruce St Crookston MN 56716-0603 E-mail: kshol@hotmail.com.

SHONK, ALBERT DAVENPORT, JR., advertising executive; b. LA, May 23, 1932; s. Albert Davenport and Jean Spence (Stannard) S. BS in Bus. Adminstrn., U. So. Calif., 1954. Field rep. mktg. divsn. LA Examiner, 1954-55, asst. mgr. mktg. and field supr. mktg. divsn., 1955-56, mgr. mktg. divsn., 1956-57; account exec. Hearst Advt. Svc., LA, 1957-59; account exec., mgr. Keith H. Evans & Assocs., San Francisco and Los Angeles, 1959-65; owner, pres. Albert D. Shonk Co., LA, 1965-97; gen. ptnr. Shonk Land Co. Ltd., Charleston, W.Va., 1989-00; dir. Shonk, LLC, Del., 2001—. Pres. Signet Cir. Corp., Inc., 1977-81, dir., 1962-81, hon. life dir., 1981—, treas., 1989-2002, pres., 2002—. Founding chmn. Crittenton Assocs.; bd. dirs. Balboa Island Improvement Assn., 2000—, pres., 2005—; bd. dirs. Balboa Island Mus. & Hist. Soc., 1999—, treas.; co-chair Centennial com. Florence Crittenton Ctr., 1992, bd. dirs., sec., 1978, 1st v.p., 1978—79, exec. v.p., 1979—81, pres., 1981—83, chmn. bd., 1983—85, hon. life dir., 1986—, treas., 1997, pres., 1997—2001, chmn. bd. dirs., 2002—03, pres., 2004—05, pres. emeritus, 2006—. Recipient Medallion of Merit Phi Sigma Kappa, 1976, Founders award, 1961, NIC Interfraternal award, 1989. Mem.: Jr. Advt. Club LA (hon. life, dir., treas., 1st v.p.), Nat. Assn. Pubs. Reps. (past v.p. West Coast 1981—83), Pubs. Rep. Assn. of So. Calif., Advt. Club LA, Town Hall, U. So. Calif. Alumni Assn. (bd. govs. 2000—03), U. So. Calif. Marshall Sch. Bus. Alumni Assn. (nat. bd. 1991—99, treas. 1995—99), World Affairs Coun., U. So. Calif. Assocs., Marshall Assocs. (bd. dirs. 1999—), U. So. Calif. Half Century Trojans (co-chair 50 yr. reunion 2004, bd. dirs. 2004—, pres.-elect 2006—), Rotary (bd. dirs., sec. LA Rotary Found. 2006—, Paul Harris fellow), Trojan Club, Skull and Dagger, U. So. Calif. Cardinal and Gold, Alpha Kappa Psi, Phi Sigma Kappa (dir. grand coun. 1962—70, 1977—79, grand pres. 1979—83, v.p. meml. found. 1979—84, chancellor 1983—87, pres. meml. found. 1984, found. trustee pres. 1984—95, chancellor 1990—91, recorder 1995—, found. trustee emeritus 1995—), Inter-Greek Soc. (v.p. 1976—79, pres. 1984—86, co-founder, hon. life, dir.). Home and Office: 225 Sapphire Ave Newport Beach CA 92662-1148 E-mail: adshonk@msn.com.

SHONROCK, DIANA DONNER, science and technology librarian, consultant, Library Association Executive; b. Osage, Iowa, May 6, 1947; d. Robert Thomas and Marie Ginder Donner; m. William H. Shonrock Jr., May 31, 1969; children: Kelley Lee Seyller, Derek Michael, Sara Noel, Margaret Augusta. BS, Iowa State U., Ames, 1969, MS, 1975; MLS, U. Iowa, Iowa City, 1992. Libr. instrn. faculty Iowa State U., Ames, 1969—92, coord. gen. reference, 1992—97, assoc. prof., 1996, scitech. libr., 1998—. Mem. editl. bd. Pub. Svcs. Quar., Reference Book Bull. Editor: Evaluating Library Instruction, 1996. Mem. St. Cecilia Sch. Bd., Ames. Mem.: ALA (sec. 1996—98, mem. Libr. Instrn. Roundtable), Reference and User Services Assn. (pres.-elect, pres. 2005—07), Kappa Omicron Nu, Beta Phi Mu. Avocations: swimming, cooking, travel. Office: Iowa State U 152 Parks Library Iowa State Ames IA 50011-2140 Home Phone: 515-292-6177; Office Phone: 515-294-7866. Business E-Mail: shonrock@iastate.edu.

SHONS, ALAN RANCE, plastic surgeon, surgical oncologist, educator; b. Freeport, Ill., Jan. 10, 1938; s. Ferral Caldwell and Margaret (Zimmerman) S.; children: Lesley, Susan. AB, Dartmouth Coll., 1960; MD, Case Western Res. U., 1965; PhD in Surgery, U. Minn., 1976. Diplomate Am. Bd. Surgery, Am. Bd. Plastic Surgery. Intern U. Hosp., Cleve., 1965-66, resident in surgery, 1966-67; rsch. fellow transplantation immunology U. Minn., Mpls., 1969-72, asst. prof. plastic surgery, 1976-79, assoc. prof., 1979-84, prof., 1984; resident in surgery U. Minn. Hosp., 1972-74; resident plastic surgery NYU, 1974-76; dir. divsn. plastic and reconstructive surgery U. Minn. Hosp., St. Paul Ramsey Hosp., Mpls. VA Hosp., 1976-84; cons. plastic surgery St. Louis Park Med. Ctr., 1980-84; prof. surgery Case Western Res. U., Cleve., 1984-93, dir. divsn. plastic and reconstructive surgery, 1984-92; prof. surgery, assoc. dir. comprehensive breast program, H. Lee Moffitt Cancer Ctr. and Rsch. Inst. U. South Fla., Tampa, 1992—2003; surgeon pvt. practice, Great Neck, NY, 2004—. Examiner Am. Bd. Plastic Surgery, 1987-2000; dir. divsn. plastic surgery Glen Cove Hosp., NY, 2006-. Author: (with G.L. Adams and D. McQuarrie) Head and Neck Cancer, 1986; (with R. Jensen) Plastic Surgery Review, 1993. Capt. USAF, 1967-69. Fellow ACS (chmn. Minn. com. on trauma 1978-84); mem. AMA, Am. Soc. Plastic and Reconstructive Surgeons, Am. Assn. Plastic Surgeons, Minn. Acad. Plastic Surgeons (pres. 1981-82), Soc. Head and Neck Surgeons, Transplantation Soc., Plastic Surgery Rsch. Coun., Am. Soc. Aesthetic Plastic Surgery, Am. Soc. Maxillofacial Surgeons, Am. Assn. Immunologists, Soc. Exptl. Pathology, Am. Cleft Palate Assn., Am. Soc. Craniofacial Surg. Assn., Fla. Soc. Plastic and Reconstructive Surgeons, Sigma Xi. Office: 935 Northern Blvd Great Neck NY 11021 Office Phone: 516-482-6893.

SHOOK, JOHN ROBERT, philosopher; b. Buffalo, June 16, 1966; s. Robert Harold and Joan Shook; m. Karen Kazmierczak, Aug. 13, 1994; children: Adrienne, Eliza. BA in Philosophy, Case Western Res. U., Cleve., 1988; MA in Philosophy, U. Fla., Gainesville, 1990; PhD in Philosophy, U. Buffalo, 1994. Asst. prof. of philosophy Corning C.C., NY, 1995—99, assoc. prof. of philosophy, 1999—2000; asst. prof. of philosophy Okla. State U., Stillwater, 2000—03, assoc. prof. of philosophy, 2003—06; v.p. for rsch., and sr. rsch. fellow Ctr. for Inquiry Transnational, Amherst, NY, 2006—. Author: (book) Pragmatism: An Annotated Bibliography, 1898-1940, Dewey's Empirical Theory of Knowledge and Reality; editor: Dictionary of Modern American Philosophers, Blackwell Companion to Pragmatism, (acad. jours.) Contemporary Pragmatism. Mem.: Soc. for the Advancement of Am. Philosophy (exec. com. 2006—), Am. Philos. Assn. Office: Center for Inquiry Transnational 3965 Rensch Rd Amherst NY 14228 Office Phone: 716-636-4869. Office Fax: 716-636-1733. Business E-Mail: jshook@centerforinquiry.net.

SHOOP, GLENN POWELL, investment consultant; b. Gracemont, Okla., Sept. 1, 1920; s. Roy Alonzo and Myrtle Nancy (Goodfellow) S.; m. Louise Wilhelmina Vollmer, Mar. 19, 1943; children: Merilou Love, Paul, Nancy Jeffery Student, U. Okla., 1938—42. Pilot Braniff Internat. Airways, Dallas, 1946—80. Cons. bd. dirs. Braniff Inc., 1984—88. Bd. dirs. 1st Bapt. Ch. Dallas, 1950-2000. Maj. USAF, 1942-46, WWII Republican. Achievements include first US pilot to fly Concorde in US scheduled service.

SHOOTER, ERIC MANVERS, retired neurobiology professor, consultant; b. Mansfield, Eng., Apr. 18, 1924; arrived in U.S., 1964; s. Fred and Pattie (Johnson) Shooter; m. Elaine Staley Arnold, May 28, 1949; 1 child, Annette Elizabeth. BA, Cambridge U., Eng., 1945, MA, 1949, PhD, 1950, ScD, 1986; DSc, U. London, 1964. Sr. scientist biochemistry Brewing Industry Rsch. Found., 1950—53; biochemistry lectr. Univ. Coll., London, 1953—63; assoc. prof. genetics Stanford U., 1963—68, prof. genetics and biochemistry, 1968—75, prof., chmn. neurobiology dept., 1975—87, prof. neurobiology, 1987—2004, prof. neurobiology emeritus, 2004—, chmn. Neurosci. PhD Program, 1972—82. Assoc. Neurosci. Rsch. Program, NYC, 1979—89; mem. tchg. staff Internat. Sch. Neurosci., Praglia, Italy, 1987—93; sr. cons. Markey Charitable Trust, Miami, Fla., 1985—97; bd. dirs. Regeneron Pharm., Inc., Tarrytown, NY. Assoc. editor (book series) Ann. Rev. Neuroscis., 1984—2001; contbr. articles to profl. jours. Recipient Wakeman award, Duke U., 1988, Award for Disting. Achievement in Neurosci. Rsch., Bristol-Myers-Squibb, 1997; scholar, Josiah Macy Jr. Found., N.Y.C., 1974—75. Fellow: AAAS, Am. Acad. Arts and Scis., Royal Soc. (London); mem.: NAS, Am. Philos. Soc., Internat. Brain Rsch. Orgn., Internat. Soc. Neurochemistry, Am. Soc. Neurochemistry, Am. Assn. Biol. Chemists, Soc. for Neurosci. (Ralph W. Gerard prize 1995), Inst. Medicine of NAS, Alpha Omega Alpha (hon.). Avocation: travel. Home: 370 Golden Oak Dr Portola Valley CA 94028-7757 Office: Stanford U Sch Medicine Dept Neurobiology 299 Campus Dr Stanford CA 94305-5125 Office Phone: 650-723-7559. Business E-Mail: eshooter@stanford.edu.

SHOPTAUGH, TERRY LEE, historian, archivist; b. St. Louis, Feb. 9, 1952; s. Don C. and Virgalee Shoptaugh; m. Deborah K. Janzen, May 13, 1952; 1 child, Amelia J. BA, Ctrl. Meth. Coll., 1974; PhD in Am. History, U. NH, 1984. Archivist S.E. Mo. State U., Cape Girardeau, 1982—86; prof. history, archivist Minn. State U., Moorhead, 1986—. Author: Roots of Success, 1997 (Red River Valley Heritage award, 1997), Moorhead: Images of America, 2004, Nowhere to Turn: Herman Stern and the German-Jewish Crisis, 2007. Mem.: Soc. Am. Archivists (life; cert. archivist). Office: Minn State Univ 1104 S Seventh Ave Moorhead MN 56563 Home Phone: 218-236-6068; Office Phone: 218-477-2343. Office Fax: 218-477-5924. Business E-Mail: shoptaug@mnstate.edu.

SHOR, GEORGE G., JR., geophysicist, oceanographic administrator, engineer; b. NYC, June 8, 1923; s. George Gershon and Dorothy (Williston); m. Elizabeth Louise Noble, June 11, 1950; children: Alexander Noble, Carolyn Elizabeth, Donald Williston. BS, Calif. Inst. Tech., 1944, MS, 1948, PhD, 1954. Joined Seismic Explorations, Inc., Houston, 1948, party chief, 1949-50; asst. research geophysicist to research geophysicist Scripps Inst. Oceanography, La Jolla, Calif., 1953-69, prof. marine geophysics, 1969-90, prof. emeritus, 1990—, assoc. dir., 1968-91; mgr. Calif. Sea Grant program, 1969-73. Mem. NAS-NRC panel on Mohole site selection, 1959; com. on underwater telecommunications, 1968, USN Marine Geophys. Survey Liaison Council, 1965-67; spl. adv. to Com. for Coordination of Joint Prospecting for Mineral Resources in Asian Offshore Areas, 1976-91; chmn. ship scheduling panel Univ. Nat. Oceanographic Lab. Systems, 1987-89; sci. leader oceanographic expdns. to various parts of Pacific and Indian oceans, 1955-82. Served to lt. (j.g.) USNR, 1943-46; now comdr. USNR Ret. Fellow Geol. Soc. Am., Am. Geophys. Union, Am. Bamboo Soc. (pres. 1994-96); mem. Soc. Exploration Geophysicists, Scholia Club Home: 2655 Ellentown Rd La Jolla CA 92037-1147

SHORE, BILL, nonprofit organization executive; b. Pitts., Feb. 3, 1955; 3 children. BA, U. Pa.; JD, George Washington U. With senatorial and presdl. campaign staff to Sen. Gary Hart, 1978—87; chief of staff to Sen. Robert Kerrey US Senate, 1988—91; founder, exec. dir. Share Our Strength, Washington, 1987—; founder, chmn. Cmty. Wealth Ventures, Inc., 1997—. Bd. dirs. Timberland Co., 2001—; adj. prof. NYU; guest lectr. Harvard U., Stanford U. Author: (books) Revolution of the Heart, 1995, The Cathedral Within, 1999, The Light of Conscience, 2004. Office: Share Our Strength 1730 M St NW Ste 700 Washington DC 20036 Office Phone: 800-969-4767.

SHORE, ELEANOR GOSSARD, retired medical school dean; b. Ottawa, Ill., Aug. 11, 1930; d. Arthur Paul and Mary Catherine (Lineberger) Gossard; m. Miles Frederick Shore, July 4, 1953; children: Miles Paul, Rebecca Shore Lewin, Susanna Shore LeBoutillier. BA magna cum laude, Radcliffe Coll., 1951; MD, Harvard U., 1955, MPH, 1970. Diplomate Am. Bd. Preventive Medicine. Med. intern New Eng. Med. Ctr. Hosp., Boston, 1955-56; resident in occup. medicine Harvard U. Health Svcs., Cambridge, Mass., 1966-68; Macy scholar Radcliffe Inst., Radcliffe Coll., Cambridge, 1966-68; resident in preventive medicine Harvard Sch. Pub. Health, Boston, 1970-71; asst. physician Radcliffe Coll., 1959-61, Harvard U. Health Svcs., 1961-73; rsch. assoc. dept. microbiology Harvard U. Sch. Pub. Health, 1971-76; asst. to pres. Harvard U., 1972-81; assoc. dean for faculty affairs Harvard Med. Sch., 1978-89, mem. faculty, 1978—2004, dean for faculty affairs, 1989—2004, sr. cons. to office acad. and clin. programs, 2005—. Mem. editl. bd. Harvard Med. Alumni Bull., 1976—. Bd. dirs. Mass.-Ukraine Citizens Bridge, Brockton, Mass., 1989-94, pres., 1991-92; bd. dirs. Needham (Mass.) Found. for Pub. Sch. Edn., 1990-94; bd. dirs. Mass. Health Rsch. Inst., Inc., 1990-99, sec., 1995-99; overseer Boston Mus. Sci., 1981—; trustee Schepens Eye Rsch. Inst., Boston, 1993—; mem. acad. coun. Real Colegio Complutense, Harvard U., 1995—; dep. dir. Harvard Med. Sch. Ctr. for Excellence in Women's Health, 1998-2004. Recipient Pres.'s Recognition award Am. Med. Women's Assn., 1996. Fellow Am. Acad. Preventive Medicine; mem. AAAS, APHA, Mass. Pub. Health Assn., Assn. Am. Med. Colls., Mass. Med. Soc., Aesculapian Club (treas. 1986-89, pres. 1990-91), E-mail: eleanor_shore@hms.harvard.edu.

SHORE, ERIC EUGENE, internist, consultant, lawyer; b. Phila., Feb. 12, 1948; s. Reuben and Mary (Osinoff) S.; m. Mona Diane Cherry, Oct. 23, 1977 (div. Dec. 1991); children: Brett Ian, Matthew Adam. Student, Temple U., 1965—67; BS in Biology, Chemistry, Widener U., 1969; DO, Phila. Coll. Osteo. Med., 1973; MBA in Med., Healthcare Mgmt., St. Joseph's U., 1997; postgrad in law, Widener U., 1999—2000; JD, Rutgers U., 2003. Med. diplomate Nat. Bd. Examiners, diplomate Am. Bd. Utilization Rev. and Quality Assurance. Intern Botsford Gen. Hosp., Farmington, Mich., 1973-74; resident Phila. Gen. Hosp., 1974—75; instr. in medicine Hahnemann Med. Coll., Phila., 1975-78; treas. med. staff West Park Hosp., Phila., 1986-87, chief of geriatrics, 1986-88; sec. of med. staff Jefferson Park Hosp., Phila., 1987-91, chief of family medicine, 1988-96; pres. Gen. Medicine Assocs., Ltd., Phila., 1987—, Bala Clin. Assocs., P.C., Phila., 1989; asst. prof. medicine Phila. Coll. Osteopathic Medicine, Phila., 1987—; clin. asst. prof. medicine Med. Coll. Pa., Phila., 1991—2001, Drexel Coll. Medicine, Phila., 2002—; mng. ptnr. Shore Law Offices, Phila., 2003—, Shore and Dicks, LLC, Phila., 2005—06; of counsel Schrom & Sholk, PC, Phila., 2004—. Med. dir. Fairmount Geriatric Ctr., Phila., 1985-88, Bala Nursing & Retirement Ctr., Phila., 1990-95; chmn. bd. UniMed Systems, Inc., Phila., 1989—, Am. Medigroup, Inc., 1997—; CEO, Am. MediGroup, Inc., 1996—; cons. medicine and geriatrics Phila. Psychiat. Ctr., Phila., 1987—. Author: (novel) The Nostradamus Conspiracy, 2000. Med. officer Civil Air Patrol, Phila., 1976-78. Recipient Legion of Honor, Chapel of Four Chaplains, Phila., 1981. Fellow: Am. Coll. Legal Medicine, Am. Coll. Utilization Rev. Physicians, Am. Acad.

Family Physicians; mem.: ATLA, AMA (physician's recognition award 1990, 1994, 1997, 1999, 2003), ABA, AAAS, Pa. Bar Assn. (Mont. chpt.), N.Y. Acad. Scis., Am. Coll. Physician Execs., Am. Health Lawyers Assn., Am. Geriatrics Soc., Royal Soc. Medicine. Avocations: music, flying, computers, sculpting, tennis. Office: Shore Law Offices 2 Bula Plz Ste 300 PO Box 2771 Bala Cynwyd PA 19004 Office Phone: 610-410-0086. Business E-Mail: eshore@shoremedlaw.com.

SHORE, H. ALLAN, lawyer; BS in Acctg., Bklyn. Coll., 1968; JD, U. Miami, 1971, LLM in Taxation, 1972. CPA; bar: Fla. 1971, cert.: Fla. Bar Bd. Legal Specialization and Edn. (tax law), bar: US Tax Ct. Shareholder Akerman Senterfitt, Miami, Fla. Adj. prof. U. Miami Sch. Law. Contbr. articles to profl. publs. Bd. dirs. United Way of Miami-Dade. Named one of Top 100 Attys., Worth mag., 2005. Mem.: Am. Assn. Atty.-CPA. Office: Akerman Senterfitt 1 Southeast Third Ave 28th Fl Miami FL 33131-1714 Office Phone: 305-982-5588. Office Fax: 305-374-5095. E-mail: allan.shore@akerman.com. *

SHORE, HOWARD LESLIE, composer; b. Toronto, Ontario, Canada, Oct. 18, 1946; s. Mac and Bernice (Ash) S.; m. Elizabeth Ann Cotnoir, Aug. 3, 1990; 1 child, Mae. Student, Berklee Sch. Music, 1965-67, Forest Hill Collegiate, Toronto, Ont., Can., 1961-64. Composer The Gorfaine/Schwartz Agy., Sherman Oaks, Calif. Composer film scores including I Miss You, Hugs and Kisses, 1978, The Brood, 1979, Scanners, 1981, Videodrome, 1983, Nothing Lasts Forever, 1984, After Hours, 1985, Belizaire the Cajun, 1987, Fire with Fire, 1986, The Fly, 1986, Nadine, 1987, The Local Stigmatic, 1987, Heaven, 1987, Moving, 1988, Dead Ringers, 1988 (Genie award), Big, 1988 (ASCAP award), She-Devil, 1989, An Innocent Man, 1989, Signs of Life, 1989, The Silence of the Lambs, 1991 (ASCAP award), A Kiss Before Dying, 1989, Naked Lunch, 1990, Prelude to a Kiss, 1992, Single White Female, 1992, (TV score) Scales of Justice, 1990, Guilty as Sin, 1993, Sliver, 1993, M. Butterfly, 1993, Mrs. Doubtfire, 1993 (ASCAP award), Philadelphia, 1993 (ASCAP award), The Client, 1994 (ASCAP award), Ed Wood, 1994, Nobody's Fool, 1994, Moonlight and Valentino, 1995, White Man's Burden, 1995, Se7en, 1995 (ASCAP award), Before and After, 1996, The Truth About Cats and Dogs, 1996, Looking for Richard, 1996, Crash, 1996, Looking For Richard, 1996, That Thing You Do, 1996, The Game, 1997, Cop Land, 1997, Last Night, 1998, Silver, 1998, Analyze This, 1999 (ASCAP award), Dogma, 1999, High Fidelity, 2000, The Yards, 2000, The Cell, 2000, The Score, 2001, Jay and Silent Bob Strike Back, 2001, The Lord of the Rings: The Fellowship of the Ring, 2001 (ASCAP award, Acad. award for Best Original Score, 2002, Broadcast Film Critics Assn. award for Best Composer, 2002, Grammy award for Best Score Soundtrack Album, 2003), Panic Room, 2002 (ASCAP award), Spider, 2002, The Lord of the Rings: The Two Towers, 2002 (ASCAP award, Grammy award for Best Score Soundtrack Album, 2004), Gangs of New York, 2002, The Lord of the Rings: the Return of the King, 2003 (ASCAP award, Acad. awards for Best Original Score & Best Original Song, 2004, Golden Globe awards for Best Original Score & Best Original Song, 2004, Grammy award for Best Score Soundtrack Album & Best Song, 2005, Broadcast Film Critics Assn. award for Best Composer, 2005), The Aviator, 2004 (Broadcast Film Critics Assn. award for Best Composer, 2005, Golden Globe award for Best Original Score 2005), A History of Violence, 2005, The Departed, 2006 (ASCAP award), The Last Mimzy, others; music supr. Places in the Heart, 1984, Postcards From the Edge, 1990; music dir. The Hart & Lorne Terrific Hour, 1970, Saturday Night Live, 1975-80, 85-86. Recipient Most Performed Theme(s) award, ASCAP, 2000—05, Henry Mancini award, 2004, Hollywood Film award for Outstanding Achievement in Music in Film, Hollywood Film Festival, 2003, Career Achievement award for Film Music Composition, Nat. Bd. Review, 2005. Mem. ASCAP, Lighthouse (founding mem.). Home: Wee Wah Lodge Tuxedo Park NY 10987 Office: The Gorfaine Schwartz Agency Inc 4111 W Alameda Ave Ste 509 Burbank CA 91505-4171 *

SHORE, JAMES H(ENRY), psychiatrist; b. Winston-Salem, NC, Apr. 6, 1940; s. James Henry and Ellen Elizabeth (Hayes) S.; m. Christine Lowenbach, Aug. 24, 1963; children— Ellen Ottilie, James Henry. MD, Duke U., 1965. Diplomate Am. Bd. Psychiatry and Neurology. Intern U. Utah Med. Ctr., 1965-66; resident in psychiatry U. Wash., 1966-69; chief mental health office Portland Area Indian Health Svc., Oreg., 1969-73; assoc. prof. psychiatry, dir. cmty. psychiatry tng. program U. Oreg. Health Sci. Ctr., 1973-75, prof., chmn. dept. psychiatry, 1975-85; from chmn. dept. psychiatry Health Sci. Ctr. to chancellor U. Colo., Aurora, 1985—2004, chancellor Health Scis. Ctr., 2004—05, chancellor emeritus Health Scis. Ctr., 2006—. Mem. exptl. and spl. edn. com. NIMH-Internal Rev. Group, 1976-80; dir. Colo. Psychiatry Hosp., 1985-99; interim dir. U. Colo. Hosp., Denver, 1987-88, interim exec. vice chancellor, 1995-97, chancellor, 1998-2005; cons. in field. Contbr. numerous articles to profl. jours. Mem. Various community bds. Served with USPHS, 1969-73. Decorated USPHS Commendation medal; various grants. Fellow Am. Psychiat. Assn., Am. Coll. Psychiatry (pres. 2003-04); mem. Am. Assn. Chmn. Depts. Psychiatry (pres. 1989), Am. Bd. Psychiatry and Neurology (dir. 1987—, pres. 1994), Residency Rev. Com. for Psychiatry (chmn. 1991-92). Office: U Colo Health Scis Ctr Mail Stop F800 PO Box 6508 Aurora CO 80045

SHORE, MARCI, historian; b. Upper Darby, Pa., Feb. 2, 1972; d. Stephen and Sharon (Collins) Shore; m. Timothy Snyder, June 11, 2005. BA, Stanford U., Calif., 1994, PhD, 2001; MA, U. Toronto, Can., 1996. Asst. prof. history Ind. U., Bloomington, 2002—06; vis. asst. prof. judaic studies Yale U., New Haven, 2006—07, asst. prof. history, 2007—. Translator: The Black Seasons; author: Caviar and Ashes: A Warsaw Generation's Life and Death in Marxism, 1918-1968 (Fraenkel prize, Heldt prize, Nat. Jewish Book award, 2006, Book prize Polish Studies Assn., 2006). Fellow, Columbia U., Harriman Inst., 2001—02; grantee, Inst. Internat. Edn. Fulbright, 1997, Fulbright-Hays Doctoral Dissertation award, Dept. of Edn., 1999—2000; Rsch. grant, Internat. Rsch. and Exch. Bd., 1999—2000, Rsch. fellow, Kulturwissenschaftliches Inst., 2003. Office: Yale Univ Dept History PO Box 208324 New Haven CT 06520-8324 Office Phone: 203-432-4872. Office Fax: 203-432-7587. Business E-Mail: marci.shore@yale.edu.

SHORE, MILES FREDERICK, psychiatrist, educator; b. Chgo., May 26, 1929; s. Miles Victor and Margaret Elizabeth S.; m. Eleanor M. Gossard, July 4, 1953; children: Miles Paul, Rebecca M. Lewin, Susanna G. LeBoutillier. BA, U. Chgo., 1948; AB, Harvard U., 1950, MD, 1954. Intern U. Ill. Research and Edn. Hosp., Chgo., 1954-55; resident in psychiatry Mass. Mental Health Center, Beth Israel Hosp., Boston, 1956-61; asst. prof. psychiatry Tufts U. Sch. Medicine, Boston, 1964-68, assoc. prof., 1968-71, prof., 1971-75, prof. community health, 1972-75; founder, dir. Tufts Community Mental Health Center, 1968-74, asso. dean community affairs, 1972-75; mem. faculty Boston Psychoanalytic Inst., 1973—; Bullard prof. psychiatry Harvard Med. Sch., Boston, 1975—; supt. Mass. Mental Health Ctr., 1975-93; vis. scholar John F. Kennedy Sch. Govt. Harvard U., 1993—; cons. exec. edn. Harvard Med. Internat., 1999—, sr. cons., 2000—. Dir. program for chronic mental illness Robert Wood Johnson Found., 1985-92. Editl. bd. Psychat. Svcs. Jour., 1990; bd. editors Jour. Interdisciplinary History, 1975, Psycho History Rev., 1978; column editor Harvard Rev. Psychiatry, 1993; contbr. articles to profl. jours. Bd. dirs. Federated Dorchester Neighborhood Houses, Boston, 1975-78, tr. House, Boston, 1995—; bd. dirs. Med. Found., Boston, 1987—, chmn., 1999-2001; mem. Blue Ribbon Commn., Mass. Dept. Mental Health, 1979-80. Capt. U.S. Army, 1956-58. Community Mental Health Center grantee, 1964-75. Fellow Am. Psychiat. Assn. (life, joint commn. on pub. affairs, adminstrv. psychiatry award 1987), Am. Coll. Psychiatrists (chmn. fin. com. 1983-89, bd. regents 1988-90, 1st v.p. 1994, pres. 1996-97, Bowis award for svc. 1990, Arthur P. Noyes award 1994); mem. Assn. Am. Med. Colls. (coun. acad. socs. 1992—), Boston Psychoanalytic Soc. and Inst. (chmn. bd. trustees 1970-73), Mass. Psychiat. Soc. (pres. 1970-71), Mass. Hosp. Assn. (trustee 1980-85), Am. Hosp. Assn. (chmn. governing coun. for psychiat. and substance abuse svcs. 1992-93, ho. of dels. 1996—02, region I policy bd. 1997—2000), Roxbury Clinic Record Club, Aesculapian Club, Mass. Hist. Soc. Office: Harvard Med Internat Ste 902 1135 Tremont St Boston MA 02120 Business E-Mail: miles_shore@harvard.edu.

SHORE, RICHARD ARNOLD, mathematics professor; b. Boston, Aug. 18, 1946; s. Philip M. and Miriam (Krensky) S.; m. Naomi J. Spiller, Aug. 3, 1969; children: Deena A., Aviva R. B in Jewish Edn., Hebrew Coll., 1966; AB, Harvard U., 1968; PhD, MIT, 1972. Instr. U. Chgo., 1972-74; asst. prof. Cornell U., Ithaca, NY, 1974-78, assoc. prof., 1978-83; asst. prof. U. Ill.-Chgo., 1977; prof. math. Cornell U., Ithaca, 1983—. Organizing com. Logic Yr. at MSRI, 1989-90, other internat. meetings. Author: (with A. Nerode) Logic for Applications; editor North-Holland, Studies in Logic and the Foundations of Mathematics, 1996—; cons. editor Jour. Symbolic Logic, 1980-83, editor, 1984-93, coord. editor, 1989-91; mng. editor: Bull. Symbolic Logic, 1993-2000; contbr. articles to profl. jours. V.p. for edn. Hillel Acad. Broome County, Binghamton, N.Y., 1985-89; treas. Beth David Synagogue, 1993-96; pres. Jewish Fedn. of Broome County, 1998-2000; bd. dirs. Project Euclid, 2002—. Grantee, NSF, 1973—; vis. scholar, MIT, 1997, Harvard U., 1997, 2002. Mem. Am. Math. Soc., Spl. Interest Group in Algorithms and Computation Theory, Assn. for Computing Machinery, Assn. for Symbolic Logic (coun. 1984—, pres. 2001-2004. Jewish. Home: 14 Kenwood Ave Newton MA 02459 Office: Cornell U Dept Math Malott Hall Ithaca NY 14853 Office Phone: 607-255-4081. Business E-Mail: shore@math.cornell.edu.

SHORE, SHELDON G., chemist, educator; With Ohio State Univ., 1957—, prof. chemistry, Charles H. Kimberly Chair Chemistry. Recipient award in inorganic chemistry, Am. Chem. Soc., 2007. Achievements include patents in field. Office: Ohio State U 2042 Evans Laboratory 88 W 18th Ave Columbus OH 43210 Office Phone: 614-292-6000. Business E-Mail: shore.1@osu.edu.

SHORE, STEPHEN, photographer; b. NYC, Oct. 8, 1947; m. Ginger Cramer Seippel, 1980; 1 child, Nicholas; 1 stepchild, Alex Seippel. Student, Minor White, Workshop, 1970. Photographer, 1953—. One-man shows, Met. Mus. Art, N.Y.C., 1971, Light Gallery, N.Y.C., 1972, 73, 75, 77, 78, 80, Phoenix Gallery, San Francisco, 1975, Mus. Modern Art, N.Y.C., 1976, Kunshalle, Dusseldorf, Germany, 1976, U. Akron, Ohio, 1978, Vision Gallery, Boston, 1978, La Photogaleria, Madrid, 1979, Ewing Gallery, Washington, 1979, Catskill Ctr. Photography, Woodstock, N.Y., 1980, Fraenkel Gallery, San Francisco, 1982, Mus. Arts and Scis., Daytona Beach, Fla., 1981, Polk Pub. Mus., 1982, ARCO Ctr. Visual Arts, L.A., 1982, N. Mex. State U. Art Gallery, Las Cruces, 1982, Art Inst. Chgo., 1984, Pace Wildenstein MacGill, N.Y.C., 1989, 95, Sprengel Mus., Hannover, 1995, Württ. Kunstverein, Stuttgart, 1995, Amerika Haus, Berlin, 1995, George Eastman House, Rochester, N.Y., 1996, Skstiftung Kultur, Koln, Germany, 1999, Spazio Oberdan, Milan, Italy, 1999, 303 Gallery, N.Y.C., 2000, 03, 06, Galerie Conrads, Düsseldorf, 2001, 02, Sprueth Magers Lee, London, 2003, Jeu de Paume, Paris, 2005, Hammer Mus., L.A., 2005, Photoespaña, Madrid, 2005, P.S. 1, N.Y.C., 2005, Henry Art Gallery, Seattle, 2006, Internat. Ctr. Photography, 2007; group shows include: Met. Mus. Art, N.Y.C., 1973, 82, 97, Internat. Mus. Photography, George Eastman House, 1975, Documenta 6, Kassel, W. Ger., 1977, Art Inst. Chgo., 1977, 79, 89, Mus. Modern Art, N.Y.C., 1978, 91, 2000, Corcoran Gallery, Washington, 1979, Kunsthaus, Zurich, Switzerland, 1980, U. Ariz. Mus. Art, Tucson, 1981, Nat. Gallery, Washington, 1989, Getty Mus., 1992, 97, Whitney Mus., N.Y.C., 1999, P.S. 1, N.Y.C., 1999, Victoria & Albert Mus., London, 1999, Sprenger Mus., Hannover, Germany, Uffizi Gallery, Florence, 2000, Tate Modern, London, 2003, Mus. Ludwig, Cologne, 2003; represented in permanent collections, Met. Mus. Art, N.Y.C., Mus. Modern Art, N.Y.C., Internat. Mus. Photography, George Eastman House, Rochester, N.Y., Mus. Fine Arts, Boston, Library of Congress, Washington, Art Inst. Chgo., Ctr. Creative Photography, U. Ariz., Tucson, Stedelijk Mus., Amsterdam, Netherlands, Neue Sammlung, Munich, W.Ger., Australian Nat. Gallery, Canberra; author: Andy Warhol, 1968, Uncommon Places, 1982, The Gardens at Giverny, 1983, Stephen Shore: Luzzara, 1993, Stephen Shore: Photographs 1973-1993, 1995, The Velvet Years, 1995, The Nature of Photographs, 1998, American Surfaces, 1999, Essex County, 2003, Uncommon Places: 50 Unpublished Photographs, 1973-1978, 2003, Uncommon Places: The Complete Work, 2004, American Surfaces Phaidon, 2005, Witness No. 1, JGS Found., 2006, The Nature of Photographs, Phaidon, 2007; portfolio 12 Photographs, 1976; contbr. articles to profl. jours. Nat. Endowment Arts grantee, 1974, 79; Guggenheim fellow, 1975, Am. Acad. (Rome) Spl. fellow, 1980, MacDowell Colony fellow, 1993, Aperture award, 2005. Mem. Century Assn.

SHORE, THOMAS SPENCER, JR., retired lawyer; b. Akron, Ohio, Jan. 1, 1939; s. T. Spencer and Harriet G. (Delicate) S.; m. Margaret F. Kudzma, Aug. 12, 1961; children— Thomas Spencer III, John Christopher, Daniel Andrew, Mary Margaret. BA, Brown U., 1961; JD, Northwestern U., 1964. Bar: Ohio 1964. Assoc. Taft, Stettinius and Hollister, Cin., 1964-69, Rendigs, Fry, Kiely & Dennis, Cin., 1969-71, ptnr., 1972—2003; ret., 2003. Adj. asst. prof. Chase Law Sch., U. No. Ky. Bd. dirs. United Cerebral Palsy of Cin., 1978—; bd. dirs., sec. Boys Club Am., Cin.; trustee emeritus Family Svc. of Cin. Area; past pres. Vis. Nurse Assn. of Cin., hon. trustee; mem. Kennebunkport Zoning Bd. Appeals. Mem. Ohio Bar Assn., Cin. Country Club, Queen City Club, Webhanet Club, Edgcomb Tennis Club. Office: 900 4th and Vine Tower 1 W 4th St Cincinnati OH 45202 Home: PO Box 629 Kennebunkport ME 04046 E-mail: t.shore@rendigs.com.

SHORENSTEIN, DOUGLAS W., corporate executive; BA, U. Calif., Berkeley; JD, Hastings Coll. Atty. Real Estate Group Shearman & Sterling LLP, NY, 1980—83; joined Shorestein Properties LLC, San Francisco, 1983, chmn., CEO, 1995—. Chair United Way of the Bay Area, 1998—. Office: Shorenstein 555 California St Ste 4900 San Francisco CA 94104 *

SHORENSTEIN, ROSALIND GREENBERG, internist; b. NYC, Jan. 14, 1947; d. Albert Samuel and Natalie Miriam (Sherman) Greenberg; m. Michael Lewis Shorenstein, June 18, 1967; children: Anna Irene, Claire Beth. BA in Chemistry, Wellesley Coll., 1968; MA in Biochemistry and Molecular Biology, Harvard U., 1970, PhD in Biochemistry and Molecular Biology, 1973; MD, Stanford U., 1976. Diplomate Am. Bd. Internal Medicine. Resident in internal medicine UCLA Med. Ctr., 1976-79; pvt. practice internal medicine Santa Cruz, Calif., 1979—. Mem. dept. internal medicine Dominican Hosp., Santa Cruz, 1979—; co-dir. med. svcs. Health Enhancement & Lifestyle Planning Systems, Santa Cruz, 1983—. Contbr. articles to profl. journals. Dir. Santa Cruz Chamber Players, 1993-94, pres., bd. dirs., 1994—. Recipient Charlie Parkhurst award Santa Cruz Women's Commn., 1989; NSF fellow, 1968-72, Sarah Perry Wood Med. fellow Wellesley Coll., 1972-76. Mem. Am. Soc. Internal Medicine (del. 1994, 95), Calif. Soc. Internal Medicine (trustee 1994—, sec.-treas. 1996-2000), Am. Med. Women's Assn. (Outstanding Svc. award 1987, br. #59 pres. 1986—), Calif. Med. Assn. (com. on women 1987-93), Santa Cruz County Med. Soc. (mem. bd. govs. 1993—, sec. 1997-99, pres. 2000-01, sec. 2002-), Phi Beta Kappa, Sigma Xi. Jewish. Office: 700 Frederick St Ste 103 Santa Cruz CA 95062-2239 Office Phone: 831-458-1002.

SHORENSTEIN, WALTER HERBERT, commercial real estate development company executive; b. Glen Cove, NY, Feb. 23, 1915; m. Phyllis J. Finley, Aug. 8, 1945 (dec.); children: Joan (Dec.), Carole, Douglas. Student, Pa. State U., 1933-34, U. Pa., 1934-36; D in Econs. (hon.), HanYang U., Seoul, Republic of Korea, 1988. With property sales mgmt. depts. Milton Meyer & Co., San Francisco, 1946-51, ptnr., 1951-60, owner, chmn. bd. dirs., 1960—, Shorenstein Group, San Francisco, Shorenstein Co., San Francisco, 1960—. Appt. by Pres. Johnson adv. del. UN Econ. Commn. for Asia and Far East, 1967, Pub. Advisory Com. U.S. Trade Policy; apptd. Pres. Carter Com. for Preservation fo White House; appt. by Pres. Clinton bd. dirs. Corp. Nat. Svc., 1994-96, adv.com. U.S. Commerce Dept. Industry, 1995-96. Past chmn. bd. trustees Hastings Law Ctr., U. Calif., San Francisco; founding mem. exec. adv. com. Hubert H. Humphrey Inst. Pub. Affairs, U. Minn.; bd. visitors; past pres., hon. life bd. dirs. San Francisco Park and Recreation Commn.; chmn. Vietnam Orphans Airlift; bd. dirs. San Francisco Performing Arts Ctr.; trustee Asia Found.; fin. chmn. Dem. Nat. Conv., 1984; founder Joan Shorenstein Ctr. on Press, Politics and Public Policy, Harvard U., 1986; apptd. by Pres. Clinton to Nat. Svc. Commn., 1994, Bd. of Americorp, founding mem. WWII Nat. Monument com., Nat. Endowment Arts, White House Endowment Fund; apptd. by Pres. Carter chair White House Preservation Fund; apptd. by Mayor Frank Jordon chair Save the San Francisco Giants com.; personal advisor Pres. Johnson, Carter, Clinton; chmn. Pacific Rim Econ. Coun., San Francisco; bd. visitors Internat. Studies Bd. Stanford U.; co-founder Orpheum, Curran and Golden Gate Theatres, San Francisco; founder Johnson Presdl. Libr., Carter Ctr.; chmn. San Francisco U. N50 nat. com., 1995, also numerous polit. activities. Maj. USAF, 1940-45. Named Leader of Tomorrow, Time mag., 1953, Calif. Dem. of Yr., 1985; recipient Nat. Brotherhood award NCCJ, 1982, Disting. Svc. award Dem. Nat. Com., 1983, Golden Plate award Am. Acad. Achievement, 1991, Svc. to Youth award Cath. Youth Orgn., 1994, Lifetime Achievement award Dem. Party, 1997; inducted Real Estate Legends Hall of Fame, 1997, Bay Area Coun. Bay Area Bus. Hall of Fame, 1998; Shorenstein award named in his honor Dem. Nat. Com., 1999. Mem. Calif. C. of C. (past bd. dirs.), San Francisco C. of C. (past chmn. bd. dirs., life bd. dirs.). Office: Shorenstein Co 555 California St Ste 4900 San Francisco CA 94104-1714

SHORRIS, ANTHONY ERNEST, state agency administrator; b. NYC, Mar. 7, 1957; s. Earl and Sylvia (Sasson) S.; married, 1 child BA with honors, Harvard U., 1977; MA in Pub. Affairs, Princeton U., 1979. Analyst NYC Dept. Gen. Services, 1979-80, dir. mgmt. planning, 1980-82; dep. asst. dir. NYC Office Mgmt. & Budget, 1982-84, asst. dir., 1984-86, dep. dir., 1986-88; commr. NYC Dept. Fin., 1989—91; mem. faculty, dir. Policy Rsch. Inst. Woodrow Wilson Sch. Pub. & Internat. Affairs, Princeton U., 1995—2001; dep. chancellor ops. & policy NYC Dept. Edn., 2001—03; dep. exec. dir. The Port Authority of NY & NJ, 1991—95, exec. dir., 2007—. Cons. Dem. Nat. Com., Washington, D.C., 1978—. Officer Community Planning Bd., N.Y.C., 1979-82; mem. N.Y. Dem. County Com., N.Y.C., 1980-82. Mem. Am. Council Young Political Leaders. Clubs: Harvard. Jewish. Office: The Port Authority of NY & NJ 225 Park Ave S New York NY 10003 *

SHORS, CLAYTON MARION, retired cardiologist; b. Beemer, Nebr., June 10, 1925; s. Joseph Albert and Morva Edith (Clayton) S.; m. Arlene Towle, June 6, 1948; children: Susan Debra, Clayton Robert, Scott Towle BS, U. Nebr., 1950, MD, 1952. Diplomate Am. Bd. Internal Medicine (subspecialty cardiovascular disease). Intern Detroit Receiving Hosp., 1952-53, resident, 1953-56; practice medicine specializing in cardiology Detroit; chief cardiology St. John Hosp., Detroit; ret., 2005. Bd. dirs. Sedona Acad.; mem. Sedona 30. Served with U.S. Army, 1943-46 Fellow Am. Coll. Cardiology, Internat. Coll. Angiology, Am. Heart Assn. Council on Clin. Cardiology; mem. Alpha Omega Alpha Home and Office: 6562 E Crested Saguaro Ln Scottsdale AZ 85266-7373

SHORS, JOHN DENNIS, lawyer; b. Ft. Dodge, Iowa, July 21, 1937; s. George A. and Catherine (Shaw) S.; m. Patricia Ann Percival, Oct. 7, 1967; children: John, Tom, Matt, Luke. BSEE, Iowa State U., 1959; JD, U. Iowa, 1964. Bar: Iowa, U.S. Supreme Ct. Assoc. then shareholder Davis, Brown, Koehn, Shors & Roberts, P.C., Des Moines, 1964—. Co-author: Closely Held Corporations in Business and Estate Planning, 1982. Pres. Mercy Hosp. Found., Des Moines, 1981-84; chair Iowa State U. Found., Ames, 1989-92; bd. dirs. Mercy Housing, Denver, 1992—. Cpl. U.S. Army, 1960-61. Recipient Iowa State U. Alumni medal, YLS Merit award Iowa State Bar Assn. Mem. Iowa State Bar Assn. (pres. 1992) Iowa Women Profl. Corp. (Good Guy award 1987), Iowa Rsch. Coun. (bd. dirs. 1994—), Am. Judicature Soc. (bd. dirs. 1974-79), Polk County Bar Assn. (pres. 1986), Rotary (Des Moines chpt.), DM Club. Republican. Roman Catholic. Office: Davis Brown Koehn Shors & Roberts PC 666 Walnut St Ste 2500 Des Moines IA 50309-3904 Business E-Mail: johnshors@lawiowa.com.

SHORT, ALEXANDER CAMPBELL, lawyer; b. Washington, July 26, 1940; s. Joseph Hudson and Beth (Campbell) S.; m. Patricia Graves Thompson, Aug. 24, 1968; children: Joseph Graves, Ashley Campbell, Justin Owen. BA, Amherst Coll., 1963; MA, U. Pa., 1968; JD, U. Va., 1972. Bar: Conn. 1972, Md. 1973. Field and site rep. U.S. Dept. of HUD, Phila., 1963-69; assoc. Reid & Riege P.C., Hartford, Conn., 1972-73, Piper & Marbury, Balt., 1973-79, Miles & Stockbridge, Balt., 1979-81, ptnr., 1981-94; pvt. practice Balt., 1994-95; ptnr. Hooper, Kiefer & Cornell, LLP, Balt., 1995-96, Eastman & Short, LLP, Balt., 1996-2000; asst. atty. gen. State of Md., 2000—. Pres. Handel Soc. adv. bd. to Handel Choir, Balt., 1983-87; bd. dirs. Handel Choir, Balt., 1987-88, 2002-03, pres., 1987-88. Pres. North Balt. Neighborhood Coalition, 1996—2000; bd. dirs. Homeland Assn., Balt., 1984—85, Kernewood Assn., Balt., 1995—, Greater Homewood Cmty. Corp., 1997—2001; mem. bd. mgrs. Camp Dudley YMCA, 1991—96, 1998—2001, 2004—. Mem. Md. Bar Assn. (real property planning and zoning sect., 2004-, coun. 1981-88, 96-98, sec. 1982-84, chmn. elect 1984-86, chmn. 1986-88), Balt. Rotary Found. (bd. dirs. 2004-), Rotary Club Balt. (bd. dirs. 2004-). Democrat. Presbyterian. Avocations: choral singing, gardening. Office: Office of Atty Gen Ednl Affairs Divsn 200 St Paul Pl Baltimore MD 21202 Home Phone: 410-323-6519; Office Phone: 410-576-6967. E-mail: ashort@oag.state.md.us.

SHORT, DEAN CHILTON, II, lawyer; b. Akron, Ohio, Mar. 16, 1948; s. Dean C. and Mildred I. (Hahn) S.; m. Carolyn Kay Smith, Jan. 1, 1982; children: Matthew, Emily, Molly, Sadie. BSBA magna cum laude, U. Ariz., 1969; JD cum laude, Harvard U., 1972. Bar: Calif. 1972, U.S. Dist. Ct. (so. dist.) Calif. 1972, Ariz. 1974, U.S. Dist. Ct. Ariz. 1974, U.S. Tax Ct. 1974, U.S. Supreme Ct. 1977. Assoc. Higgs, Fletcher & Mack, San Diego, 1972-74; ptnr. Evans, Kitchel & Jenckes, Phoenix, 1974-85, Jones, Jury, Short & Mast, Phoenix, 1985-88, Gallagher & Kennedy, Phoenix, 1988, also bd. dirs., shareholder. Adj. faculty Ariz. State U. Coll. of Law, 1974—76. Contbr. articles to profl. jours. Pres. Ariz. Friends of Foster Children Found., Phoenix, 1984-85. Recipient Best Lawyers Am., by Woodward/White, Inc., 2007. Mem. Ariz. State Bar (cert. specialist in tax law), Phoenix Country Club, Forest Highlands Country Club, State Bar Calif., Whisper Rock Golf Club, Harvard Club Ariz., Sports Lawyers Assn. Avocations: golf, tennis. Home: 3800 E Lincoln Dr Phoenix AZ 85018-1011 Office: Gallagher & Kennedy PA 2575 E Camelback Rd Ste 1100 Phoenix AZ 85016 Office Phone: 602-530-8308. Office Fax: 602-530-8500. Business E-Mail: dcs@gknet.com.

SHORT, EDMUND COEN, retired education educator; b. Washington, Ind., Nov. 5, 1931; s. Heber Lee Sr. Short and Mary Marguerite Coen. BS, Purdue U., West Lafayette, Ind., 1953; MEd, Tex. Christian U., Fort Worth, 1957; EdD, Teachers Coll. Columbia U., NYC, 1965. Tchr. jr. HS English Warsaw Pub. Schs., Ind., 1953—54; tchr. HS English Richmond Pub. Schs., Ind., 1957—59; tchr. English Niskayuna Pub. Schs., NY, 1960; tchr. HS English Teaneck Pub. Schs., NJ, 1961—62; asst. prof. edn. Ball State

U., Muncie, Ind., 1963—66; assoc. prof. edn. U. Toledo, 1966—72, Pa. State U., University Park, 1972—89, prof. edn., 1989—95, prof. edn. emeritus, 1995—. Prof. edn. Ga. So. U., Stateboro, Ga., 1995—99; part-time faculty assoc. U. Ctrl. Fla., Orlando, Fla., 1999—. Author: Encyclopedia of Educational Research, 5th edit., 1982, International Encyclopedia of Education, 1988, Forms of Curriculum Inquiry, 1991, International Encyclopedia of Education, 1994, Sage Handbook of Curriculum and Instruction, 2007; author: (and editor) Competence: Inquiries into Its Meaning and Acquisition in Educational Settings, 1984; editor (with George Marconnit): Contemporary Thought on Public School Curriculum, 1968; editor: Jour. Curriculum and Supervision, 1985—93; compiler (online searchable annotated bibliograhy) Curriculum Inquiry and Related Studies (CIRS), 2005—. 1st lt. Transp. Corps US Army, 1954—56. Home: P O Box 5060 Winter Park FL 32793 Home Phone: 407-657-1412.

SHORT, ELIZABETH M., internist, educator, retired federal agency administrator; b. Boston, June 2, 1942; d. James Edward and Arlene Elizabeth (Mitchell) Meehan; m. Michael Allen Friedman, June 21, 1976; children: Lia Gabrielle, Hannah Ariel, Eleanor Elana. BA in Philosophy magna cum laude, Mt. Holyoke Coll., 1963; MD cum laude, Yale U., 1968. Diplomate Am. Bd. Internal Medicine, Am. Bd. Med. Genetics. Resident in internal medicine Yale New Haven Hosp., 1968-70; postdoctoral fellow in human genetics Yale Med. Sch., 1970-72; resident U. Calif., San Francisco, 1972-73; sr. chief resident Stanford (Calif.) Med. Sch., 1973-75, asst. prof. medicine, 1975-83, assoc. dean student affairs, med. edn., 1978-83; dep. dir. acad. affairs, dir. biomed. rsch. Assn. Am. Med. Colls., Washington, 1983-88; dep. assoc. chief med. dir. for acad. affairs VA, Washington, 1988-92, assoc. chief med. dir. for acad. affairs, 1992-96; health policy cons. HHS, 1996—2001; emerita prof. clin. medicine Georgetown U. Sch. Medicine; ret., 2001. Vis. prof. human biology Stanford U., 1983-86; mem. Accreditation Coun. Grad. Med. Edn., 1988-97; mem. White House Task Force on Health Care Reform, 1993. Assoc. editor Clin. Rsch. Jour., 1976-79, editor 1980-84; contbr. articles to profl. jours. Mem. Nat. Child Health Adv. Coun., NIH, 1991-97; com. edn. and tng. Office Sci. and Tech. Policy, White House, Washington, 1991-96, Calif. Philharm., 2003-07; exec. com., bd. dirs., treas. Hillsides Home for Children, 2003—, chair program com., exec. com., 2003—; mem. exec. com., chair quality assurance Hillsides. Recipient Maclean Zoology award; Munger scholar, Markle scholar, Sara Williston scholar Mt. Holyoke Coll., 1959-63, Yale Men in Medicine scholar, 1964-68; Bardwell Meml. Med. fellow, 1963. Mem. AAAS, Am. Soc. Human Genetics (pub. policy com. 1984-95, chmn. 1986-94), Am. Fedn. Clin. Rsch. (bd. dirs. 1973-83, co-chmn. com. status women 1975-77, editor Clin. Rsch. Jour., 1978-83, nat. coun., exec. com., pub. policy com. 1977-87), Western Soc. Clin. Investigation, Calif. Acad. Medicine, Phi Beta Kappa, Alpha Omega Alpha. Home and Office: 3535 Ranch Top Rd Pasadena CA 91107 Personal E-mail: elizshort@aol.com.

SHORT, JAMES F., investment company executive; b. Norfolk, Va., Feb. 23, 1968; s. Richard Turner IV and Florence King (Timolat) S.; m. Heather Short; children: Brock, Luke, Jack, Kate. Grad., Woodberry Forest Sch., 1986; BA, Coll. William and Mary, Williamsburg, Va., 1990; MBA, U. Ga., Athens, 1996. CFA, CFP, CIMA, CIMC, ChFC. V.p., sr. portfolio mgr. Kempner Capital Mgmt., Galveston, Tex., 1998-2001; v.p., portfolio mgr. Bank of Am., 2001—02; chief investment officer Waypoint Advisors, Norfolk, Va., 2002—03; v.p. inst. Eagle Asset Mgmt., St. Petersburg, Fla., 2004—07, sr. v.p., dir. inst., 2007—. Arbitrator NASD, 2003—. Mem. Gubernatorial Adv. Com., 1992-93; vol. Am. Health Assn., Am. Cancer Soc., Westminster Canterbury Retirement Home, Surfrider Found.; bd. dirs. Bridgers-Short Found.; mem. endowment com. All Saints' Episcopal Ch.; del. to congl. and state convs. Mem. CFA Inst., Fin. Planning Assn. (former Hampton Rdoads chpt. bd. dirs.), Investment Mgmt. Cons. Assn., CFA Tampa Bay, Princess Anne Country Club, The Revelers (former bd. govs., v.p.), Theta Delta Chi, Sigma Iota Epsilon. Republican. Episcopalian. Avocations: collecting sports cards, surfing, baseball, volunteering, travel, politics. Office: Eagle Asset Mgmt PO Box 10520 Saint Petersburg FL 33733-0520 Home (Summer): 507 W Holly Rd Virginia Beach VA 23451-2829 Home: 2218 Cypress Hollow Ct Safety Harbor FL 34695-5517 Office Phone: 727-567-1059. Personal E-mail: brockturnershort@aol.com. Business E-Mail: jas.short@eagleasset.com.

SHORT, JAY MILTON, biotechnology company executive; b. Lebanon, Ind., Mar. 5, 1958; s. Roy Milton and Patricia Ann (Brewer) S.; m. Heidi Patrice Messinger, July 26, 1980; children: Ryan Milton, Cole Evan. BA in Chemistry with honors, Taylor U., Upland, Ind., 1980; PhD in Biochemistry, Case Western Res. U., 1985. Tchg. asst. Taylor U., 1978-80, Kent (Ohio) State U., 1981, Case Western Res. U., Cleve., 1981-85; staff scientist R & D, Stratagene Cloning Systems, La Jolla, Calif., 1985-88, sr. staff scientist, 1988-89, v.p. long term rsch. and biol. ops., 1989-92, v.p. long term rsch. and ops., 1992-94; pres. Stratcyte, Inc., La Jolla, 1992-94, Diversa Corp., San Diego, 1994—, CEO, 1994—, chief tech. officer, 1994—, bd. dir. Bd. dirs. Stressgen, Inc., Invitrogen, Synomyx, Chem. Engring. News, BioCom, Innovase, Zymetrics; reviewer human genome project and patenting DNA sequences U.S. Congl. Office Tech. Assessment; chmn., ofcl. Instnl. Animal Care and Use Com.; mem. peer rev. com. Nat. Inst. Environ. Health Scis., Molecular Biology, Microbiology, NAS, Genetic Analysis Techniques, Analytical Biochemistry, Nucleic Acids Rsch.; cons. on transgenic toxicology testing EEC, 1991-94; lectr. in field; mem. adj. faculty U. Calif., San Diego, 1991; lectr. Ctr. for Drug Evaluation and Rsch., FDA, 1992, others. Editor Mutation Rsch.; contbr. numerous articles and abstracts to sci. jours Recipient 1st place award for innovation and entrepreneurship in biotech. U. Calif., 1990, 91; named Entrepreneur of Yr., Ernst and Young, 2001; numerous grants including Nat. Inst. Environ. Health Scis., 1989-94, NIH, 1990-94, Nat. Cancer Inst., 1992-95. Mem. AAAS, Am. Soc. Biochemistry and Molecular Biology, Am. Soc. Microbiology, Environ. Mutagenesis Soc., Soc. Toxicology (chmn. conf. discussion group 1993), Japanese Environ. Mutagen Soc., N.Y. Acad. Scis. Achievements include patents in field. Avocations: flying, photography, collecting fossils, scuba diving. Office: Recombinant BioCatalysis Inc 10665 Sorrento Valley Rd San Diego CA 92121-1609

SHORT, MARIANNE DOLORES, lawyer; b. Mpls., Mar. 12, 1951; d. Robert Earl and Marion (McCann) S.; m. Raymond Louis Skowyra Jr., Nov. 1, 1980; 2 children, R. Louis Skowyra III & Nicholas Skowyra. BA in Philos. and Polit. Sci., Newton Coll. of Sacred Heart, 1973; JD, Boston Coll. Law Sch., 1976. Bar: Minn. 1976, Mass. 1977, US Dist. Ct. Minn. 1976, US Dist. Ct. Mass. 1980, US Dist. Ct. ND 2000, US Ct. Appeals (8th cir.) 1980, US Supreme Ct. 1988; civil trial specialist, Minn. State Bar Assn. Spl. asst. atty. gen., St. Paul, 1976-77; assoc. Dorsey & Whitney LLP, Mpls., 1977-82, ptnr., litig. practice, 1983—88, mem. policy com., 1987—88, 2000—, mem. profl. pers. com., 2000—02, mem. capital contbn. com., 2001—03, mem. ptnr. compensation com., 2002—03, mng. ptnr, 2007—; judge Minn. Ct. Appeals, 1988—2000. Chmn. recruiting com. Dorsey & Whitney, Mpls., 1985-87. Trustee Boston Coll., 1985—, Visitation Convent, St. Paul, 1985-91, St. Thomas Acad., 2000—; bd. overseers Boston Coll. Law Sch., 1998—, U. Minn. Law Sch., 2001—. Named Minn. Super Lawyer, Minn. Law & Politics Mag., 2000—06, Women to Watch, Bus. Jour., 2005, Atty. of Yr., Minn. Lawyer, 2005; named one of 15 Top Attys. in Minn., Minn. Lawyers, 2005; recipient Corp. Woman of Achievement award, Nat. Assn. Women Bus. Owners, 2004. Mem. ABA, Mass. Bar Assn., Minn. Bar Assn., Hennepin County Bar Assn. (ethics com.), Ramsey County Bar Assn., Am. Arbitration Assn. (arbitrator), Acad. Cert. Trial Lawyers Minn. Clubs: Town and Country (St. Paul), Mpls. Club (bd. govs.) Avocations: running, skiing. Office: Dorsey & Whitney LLP Ste 1500 50 S Sixth St Minneapolis MN 55402-1498 Home Phone: 651-645-9015; Office Phone: 612-340-2833. Office Fax: 612-340-2807. Business E-Mail: short.marianne@dorsey.com. *

SHORT, MARION PRISCILLA, neurogenetics educator; b. Milford, Del., June 12, 1951; d. Raymond Calistus and Barbara Anne (Ferguson) S.; m. Michael Peter Klein; 1 child, Asher Calistus Klein. BA, Bryn Mawr Coll., 1973; diploma, U. Edinburgh, Scotland, 1975; MD, Med. Coll. Pa., 1978. Diplomate Am. Bd. Psychiatry and Neurology, Am. Bd. Internal Medicine. Intern in internal medicine Hahnemann Med. Coll. Hosp., Phila., 1978-79; med. resident in internal medicine St. Lukes-Roosevelt Hosp., NYC, 1979-81; neurology resident U. Pitts. Health Ctr., 1981-84; fellow in med. genetics Mt. Sinai Med. Ctr., NYC, 1984-86; fellow in neurology Mass. Gen. Hosp., Boston, 1986-90, asst. neurologist, 1990-95; asst. prof. dept. neurology Harvard Med. Sch., Boston, 1990-95; asst. prof. dept. neurology, pediat. and pathology U. Chgo., 1995—2000, clin. assoc. pediat. neurosurgery, 2000—, fellow McLean Ctr. for Clin. Med. Ethics, 2002—03, sr. fellow McLean Ctr. for Clin. Med. Ethics, 2003—04; program dir. genetics, transplantation and clin. rsch. AMA, Chgo., 1997—2002. Recipient Clin. Investigator Devel. award, NIH, 1988—93; fellow, Inst. Medicine, Chgo., 1999. Mem. AMA, Am. Acad. Neurology, Am. Soc. for Human Genetics, Am. Coll. Med. Genetics. Office: Pediat Neurosurgery U Chgo MC 4066 5481 S Maryland Ave Chicago IL 60637-4325 Office Phone: 773-702-2475. Business E-Mail: mpshort@surgery.bsd.uchicago.edu.

SHORT, MARTIN, actor, comedian, film critic; b. Hamilton, Ont, Canada, Mar. 26, 1950; s. Charles Patrick and Olive Short; m. Nancy Dolman, 1980; children: Katherine, Oliver, Henry. Degree in social work, McMaster U., 1972. Actor: (films) Three Amigos, 1986, Innerspace, 1987, Cross My Heart, 1987, Three Fugitives, 1989, The Big Picture, 1989, Pure Luck, 1991, Father of the Bride, 1991, Captain Ron, 1992, (voice) We're Back! A Dinosaur's Story, 1993, Clifford, 1994, (voice) The Pebble and the Penguin, 1995, Father of the Bride 2, 1995, Mars Attacks!, 1996, Jungle 2 Jungle, 1997, The Fairy Godmother, 1997, A Simple Wish, 1997, Mumford, 1998, Akbar's Adventure Tours, 1998, (voice) Prince of Egypt, 1998, Get Over It, 2001, (voice) Jimmy Neutron: Boy Genius, 2001, (voice) Treasure Planet, 2001, Cinemagique, 2002, (voice) Treasure Planet, 2002, The Santa Clause 3: The Escape Clause, 2006; (TV series) The Associates, 1979, I'm a Big Girl Now, 1980-81, SCTV Network 90, 1982-84 (Emmy award for Outstanding Writing 1983), Saturday Night Live, 1985-86, (voice) The Completely Mental Misadventures of Ed Grimley, 1988-89, The Martin Short Show, 1994, (miniseries) Merlin, 1998; (TV films) The Family Man, 1979, Sunset Limousine, 1983, Alice in Wonderland, 1999, Prince Charming, 2001; writer (TV films) Martin Short's Concert for the North Americas, 1985, I, Martin Short Goes Hollywood, 1989, (TV series) Second City TV, 1981, SCTV Network 90, 1981-82, SCTV Channel, 1983, Saturday Night Live, 1984-85; exec. prodr. (TV series) The Martin Short Show, 1994, 99, Primetime Glick, 2001-03; writer, prodr. (TV films) Martin Short Shorts, 2003; dir. (TV films) Friends of Gilda, 1993; actor, writer, prodr. (films) Jiminy Glick in La La Wood, 2004; also numerous revues and cabaret appearances with Second City comedy troupe; 1977-78, Broadway appearances include The Goodbye Girl, 1993, Little Me, 1999 (Tony award for Best Actor in a Musical); stage appearances Martin Short: Fame Becomes Me, 2006. Office: William Morris Agency care Ames Cushing 1 William Morris Pl Beverly Hills CA 90212-2775 *

SHORT, MICHAEL J., automotive executive; Grad., US Naval Acad., Annapolis, Md., 1982; MBA, Columbia U., NYC, 1991. Helicopter pilot, tactics instr. USN, Norfolk, Va.; various fin. positions Univeral Orlando, Joseph E. Seagram & Sons, Inc. and IBM Corp., 1992—2000; exec. v.p., CFO Universal City Devel. Ptnrs., Ltd., 2000—07, AutoNation, Inc., Ft. Lauderdale, Fla., 2007—. Office: AutoNation Inc 110 SE 6th St Fort Lauderdale FL 33301 Office Phone: 954-769-7000. *

SHORT, RAY EVERETT, minister, sociologist, educator, writer; b. Coffeyville, Kans., Jan. 5, 1919; s. Franklin Marion and Jennie (Messersmith) S.; m. Jeannette Louise Stephens, June 12, 1954 (dec. Jan. 2000); children: Glenn Alan, Linda Louise, Kenneth Ray, Timothy Wesley, Karen Amy; 1 stepdau., Mary Jennings. AB, Willamette U., 1944; postgrad., U. Chgo., 1946; BD, Duke U., 1948, PhD, 1961; postgrad., U. Idaho, 1950—51. Ordained to ministry Meth. Ch., 1946. Dir. Westminster Found., Duke, 1944-46; co-pastor Interracial Meth. Ch., Durham, NC, 1947; asst. prof. religion, dir. chapel programs Fla. So. Coll., Lakeland, 1947-48; exec. dir. Fla. br. United World Federalists, 1948-51; dir. Intermountain Region, 1953-54, Wesley Found., U. Idaho, 1950-51; exec. dir. Student YMCA-YWCA, U. Denver, 1951-53; pastor Fairmont Meth. Ch., Lockport, Ill., 1954-56; grad. asst. sociology Duke, 1956-57; assoc. prof. religion, head divsn. religion and philosophy, chaplain Tenn. Wesleyan Coll., 1957-60; assoc. prof. sociology and religion, head dept. sociology U. Dubuque, Iowa, 1960-65, acting chmn. div. social sci. Iowa, 1962-65; assoc. prof. sociology, head dept. sociology and anthropology U. Wis., Platteville, 1965-70, prof. sociology, 1966-87, prof. emeritus, 1987—; prof. sociology and anthropology Copenhagen Study Ctr. U. Wis., spring 1974, nat. lectr., 1975—. Chmn. Peace and World Order divsn. North Iowa Meth. Conf., 1963-69; rep. U.S. Jr. C. of C. in testimony before U.S. Senate Com. on Fgn. Rels., 1950, Advocating Ltd., Dem. Fed. World Govt.; Midwest region rep. Nat. Coun. World Federalist Assn., 1964-73, pres. Midwest region, 1967-69, chmn. nat. coun., 1971-72, nat. v.p., 1991—; (with wife) WFA dels. to NGO Forum and 4th UN Conf. on Women, Beijing, 1995; D.C. hdqrs. WFA property named Ray and Jeannette Short Peacemakers Bldg., 1997 (Presdl. WFA award 1998, Nat. World Federalist of Month, June 2004); co-chmn. Grenville Clark Club; mem. spl. Wis. Conf. called with Pres.'s Comn. for Observance of 25th Anniversary of UN, 1970-87; mem. Wis. U. Meth. Bd. on Ch. and Soc., 1973-80, chmn. World Peace divsn., mem. exec. com., 1975-80. Author: Sex, Love or Infatuation: How Can I Really Know?, 1978, on videocassette, 1987, 2d edit. (Augsburg Bestseller), 11 fgn. edits., Sex, Dating and Love: Questions Most Often Asked, 1984, 2d edit., 1994, Sex, Love or Romance: You Can't Really Trust Your Heart?, 2004; contbr. articles to profl. jours. Nat. bd. Am. Freedom Assn.; nat. v.p. Campaign for UN Reform, 1983—87, 1st v.p., 1989—2004, exec. com., 1997—; bd. dirs. Dubuque Salvation Army, 1961—65; dir., founder Wis. Ann. World Peace Study Program, 1975—; Dem. candidate for Wis. 3d Dist. Congl. Seat, 1970, 1972; del. Dist. and State Convs., 1969—87, state platform com., 1975—87. Recipient Pick a Profl. award, 2003; NSF grantee Anthropology Inst., Fairmont State Coll., W.Va., 1962 Fellow Am. Sociol. Assn.; mem. AAUP, Nat. Coun. on Family Rels., Fedn. Am. Scientists, Nat. United Meth. Men (mem. peace adv. task force 1990—). Home Phone: 303-666-5025; Office Phone: 303-666-5025. Personal E-mail: rayjshort@aol.com. *Nuclear and chemical weapons, crises of environments. While my life has largely been spent helping others have a better future, I now know we have to help assure that they have a future at all by establishing limited democratic enforcible world law.*

SHORT, WILLIAM FREDERICK, gynecologist; b. Colo., Feb. 14, 1935; s. Frederick William Short and Ella Frances Macartney; m. Laura Jean Buck, July 3, 1954; children: Letia J., Melissa Williamson, Mark. BS, Colo. Coll., Colorado Springs, 1957; MD, U. Colo., Denver, 1961. Intern Gorgas Hosp., Canal Zone, Panama, 1961—62, resident, 1962—65; staff physician Penrose Hosp., Colorado Springs, 1965—2000; gynecologist OE-GYN LLC, Colorado Springs, 1965—82; clin. prof. U. Colo. Med. Sch., Denver, 1970—75; prof. biology U. Colo., Colorado Springs, 1975—95; gynecologist Gynecology Ltd., Colorado Springs, 1982—99, pvt. practice, Colorado Springs, 1999—2001; with Sarasota Meml. Hosp., Fla., 2000—. Cons. Penrose Cancer Hosp., Colorado Springs, 1966—85. Lt. col. USAF, 1961. Fellow: Am. Coll. Surgeons, Am. Coll. Ob-gyn.; mem.: Garden of Gods, Field Club. Republican. Episcopalian. Avocations: tennis, golf, kayaking.

SHORTAL, TERENCE MICHAEL, systems company executive; b. St. Louis, Oct. 13, 1937; s. Harold Leo and Catherine Margaret S.; m. Linda Margaret Elias, May 29, 1965; children: Jennifer, Bradley Alexander. BSEE, U. Mo., 1961; MS, U.S. Naval Postgrad. Sch., 1966; grad. program execs., Carnegie Mellon U., 1979. Commd. ensign USN, 1961, advanced through grades to capt., 1980, asst. officer in charge Engring. Duty Officer Sch. Vallejo, Calif., 1974-77, ship engring. mgr. AEGIS shipbldg. project Naval Ea. Sys. Command Washington, 1977-79, tech. dir. DDGX project, 1979-81, ret., 1981; sr. v.p., dir. Kastle Sys., LLC, 1981—2006. Trustee Cathedral Choral Soc., Washington, 1983-95, 97—, pres., 1986-88, 2000-2002; mem. vestry St. John's Episcopal Ch., McLean, Va., 1982-85; bd. dirs. Langley Sch., McLean, 1984-94, pres. 1986-88. Decorated Meritorious Svc. medal (2), Navy Commendation medal (2); recipient award of merit Cathedral Choral Soc., 1996. Mem. IEEE (br. award 1961), Am. Soc. Naval Engrs. (Flagship Sect. award 1979), Nat. Press Club (Washington), City Club, Gridiron Club (Washington), Sigma Xi, Phi Kappa Theta. Home: 858 Canal Dr Mc Lean VA 22102-1408 Personal E-mail: mshortal@cox.net.

SHORTELL, STEPHEN MICHAEL, dean, health services researcher; b. New London, Wis., Nov. 9, 1944; BBA, U. Notre Dame, 1966; MPH, UCLA, 1968; MBA, U. Chgo., 1970, PhD in Behavioral Sci., 1972. Rsch. asst. Nat. Opinion Rsch. Ctr., 1969; instr., rsch. assoc. Ctr. Health Adminstrv. Studies, 1970—72; acting dir. grad. program hosp. adminstrn. U. Chgo., 1973—74, from asst. prof. to assoc. prof., 1974—79; prof. dept. health svc. Sch. Pub. Health and Cmty. Medicine, U. Wash., 1979—82; A.C. Buehler Disting. prof. health svc. mgmt. Northwestern U., Evanston, Ill., 1982—98; Blue Cross disting. prof. health policy and mgmt. Sch. Pub. Health, U. Calif., Berkeley, 1998—; dean Sch. Pub. Health, U. Calif, Berkeley, 2002—. Cons. VA, Robert Wood Found., Henry Kaiser Found.; asst. prof. Health Svcs. Orgn. U. Chgo., 1972—74; adj. asst. prof. dept. sociology U. Wash., 1975—76, dir. doctoral program dept. health svcs. Sch. Pub. Health and Cmty. Medicine, 1976—78; prof. sociology dept. sociology Northwestern U., 1982, prof. preventive medicine Sch. Medicine. Contbr. numerous articles to profl. jours. Recipient Baxter prize, Baxter-Allegiance Found., 1995, Honorary AHA Lifetime Mem. award, Gold Medal award, Amer. Coll. of Healthcare Exec., 1998, Dist. Investigator award, Assoc. for Health Services Research, 1998, Best Paper award, Acad. of Mgmnt., 1996, George R. Terry Book of the Year award, 1990. Fellow: Am. Coll. Healthcare Execs. (Gold medal 1998); mem.: Inst. Med.-NAS. Office: Univ Calif Berkeley Sch Pub Health 407 Warren Hl Berkeley CA 94720-0001

SHORTER, JAMES RUSSELL, JR., lawyer; b. NYC, June 10, 1946; s. James Russell and Helen (Ibert) S. AB, Columbia Coll., 1968; JD, Harvard U., 1975; LLM in Taxation, NYU, 1979. Bar: NY 1976, US Dist. Ct. (so. and ea. dists.) NY 1976, US Tax Ct. 1987. Assoc. Thacher Proffitt & Wood, NYC, 1975-84, ptnr., 1984—. Capt. USNR, 1968-98. Mem. ABA (tax, bus. law sect.), N.Y. State Bar Assn. (internat. law and practice sect.), Assn. Bar City N.Y., Internat. Fiscal Assn., Harvard Club (N.Y.C.), Down Town Assn. (N.Y.C.). Republican. Office: Thacher Proffitt & Wood LLP Two World Financial Ctr 28th Fl New York NY 10281 Home Phone: 212-628-4206; Office Phone: 212-912-7628. Business E-Mail: jshorter@tpwlaw.com.

SHORTER, NICHOLAS ANDREW, pediatric surgeon; b. London, Oct. 14, 1953; came to the U.S., 1961; s. Roy Gerrard and Rhiannon (Morris) S.; m. Sally Jo Trued, Aug. 28, 1982; children: Timothy Anders, Brittain David, Jaime Elizabeth Rhiannon. AB, AM, Harvard U., 1975; MD, Johns Hopkins U., 1979. Diplomate in gen. surgery and pediat. surgery Am. Bd. Surgery. Intern The Johns Hopkins Hosp., Balt., 1979-80, jr. asst. resident in surgery, 1980-81, sr. asst. resident in surgery, 1981-82, 83-84, chief resident in surgery, 1984-85; rsch. fellow in surgery The Children's Hosp. Med. Ctr., Boston, 1982-83; asst. chief resident in pediatric surgery The Children's Hosp., Phila., 1985-86, chief resident in pediatric surgery, 1986-87; hosp. staff Duke U. Med. Ctr., Durham, NC, 1987-91; chief pediatric surgery Children's Hosp. at Dartmouth, Dartmouth-Hitchcock Med. Ctr., 1991-99, exec. com., 1991-99; assoc. attending surgeon Meml. Hosp., NYC, 1999—2002; attending surgeon SUNY-Downstate Med. Ctr., Bklyn., 2002—, chief divsn. pediat. surgery, 2002—. Tchg. fellow biology Harvard U., Cambridge, Mass., 1974-75; asst. instr. pediatric surgery U. Pa., Phila., 1985-87, Duke U., Durham, 1987-91, asst. prof. pediat. surgery and pediat.; asst. prof. pediat. Dartmouth Med. Sch., Hanover, N.H., 1991-94, asst. prof. surgery, 1991-94, assoc. prof. pediat., 1994-99, assoc. prof. surgery, 1994-99; hosp. staff The Children's Hosp., Phila., 1986-87, Dartmouth-Hitchcock Med. Ctr., Lebanon, N.H., 1991-99, Duke U. Med. Ctr., Durham, 1987-91, Meml. Hosp., N.Y., 1999-2002; dir. Kiwanis Affiliated Pediatric Trauma Ctr., Children's Hosp. at Dartmouth, Lebanon, 1993-99; mem. hosp. staff SUNY Downstate Med. Ctr., Bklyn., 2002—; assoc. prof. surgery Cornell U., N.Y.C., 2001-2002; vis. prof. surgery, SUNY, Bklyn., 2002-03, prof. clin. surgery, 2003—, prof. clin. pediat., 2003—. Referee Jour. Pediatric Surgery; contbr. chpts. to books and articles to profl. jours. Regular Clin. fellow Am. Cancer Soc., 1985-86. Fellow ACS, Am. Acad. Pediat., Southeastern Surg. Congress, Royal Soc. Medicine, Soc. Surg. Oncology; mem. Am. Pediatric Surg. Assn., Brit. Assn. Pediat. Surgeons, Internat. Soc. Pediat. Oncology, Internat. Pediatric Surg. Oncology, Am. Assn. for Cancer Rsch., Assn. for Acad. Surgery, N.Y. Acad. Scis., Royal Soc. Medicine, Cum Laude Soc., Phi Beta Kappa, Alpha Omega Alpha. Republican. Episcopalian. Avocation: collecting political memorabilia. Home Phone: 914-478-1907; Office Phone: 718-270-1986. Business E-Mail: nicholas.shorter@downstate.edu.

SHORTESS, EDWIN STEEVIN, marketing consultant; b. Cedar Rapids, Iowa, Oct. 31, 1920; s. Edwin Stephen and Rita (Clemente) S.; m. Jane Elizibeth Gallagher, Dec. 27, 1941 (div. Apr. 1970); children: E. Stephen, Richard J., Mark Andrew, Cathy Shortess Pool; m. Mary Francis Kerns, May 28, 1970; children: Dana Menshing, Emil Bartsche, Roger Bartsche, Lisa Bartsche Coccia, Vincent Bartsche, Kirsten Bartsche Chirico. Student, North Iowa U., 1938-39; BSEE, Chgo. Tech. Coll., 1942. Engring. rsch. analyst Douglas Aircraft Corp., El segundo, Calif., 1942-44; liaison engr. Martin Aircraft Corp., Omaha, 1944-45; chief engr., dir. Burlington (Iowa) Instrument co., 1945-53; adminstrv. engr., dir. Hickok Elec. Instrument Co., Cleve., 1953-59, ea. sales mgr. Paramus, N.J., 1960-65; v.p., gen. mgr., dir. Wacline, Dayton, Ohio, 1959-60; v.p., gen. mgr. Colo. Hickok, Grand Junction, 1965-69; pres. Shortess Rawson & Assocs., Kenilworth, N.J., 1969-86, mktg. cons. Allenwood, NJ, 1986—2004. Bd. dirs. Federated Purchasers Inc., Kenelworth, NJ. Author: Design and Application of Electrical Industrial Instruments, 1964. Mem.: Instrument Soc. Engrs. (sr.). Republican. Methodist. Avocations: golf, bridge. Home and Office: 123 Everest Dr S Brick NJ 08724-2027 Office Phone: 732-458-3266.

SHORTLIFFE, EDWARD HANCE, internist, medical educator, computer scientist; b. Edmonton, Alta., Can., Aug. 28, 1947; s. Ernest Carl and Elizabeth Joan Shortliffe. AB, Harvard U., 1970; PhD, Stanford U., 1975, MD, 1976. Diplomate Am. Bd. Internal Medicine. Trainee NIH, 1971—76; intern Mass. Gen. Hosp., Boston, 1976—77; resident Stanford Hosp., Palo Alto, Calif., 1977—79; asst. prof. medicine Stanford U. Sch. Medicine, Palo Alto, 1979—85, assoc. prof., 1985—90, chief divsn. gen. internal medicine, 1988—95, prof., 1990—2000; assoc. chair medicine Primary Care, 1993—95; assoc. dean info. resources and tech. Stanford U. Sch. Medicine, 1995—2000; prof., chair dept. biomed. informatics Columbia U. Coll. Physicians and Surgeons, NYC, 2000—07, Rolf H. Scholdager prof. biomed. informatics, 2005—07; deputy v.p. Info. Tech., Health Scis., Columbia U., NYC, 2002—07; founding dean U. Ariz. Coll. Medicine, Phoenix, 2007—, prof. basic med. scis., prof. medicine, 2007—; prof. biomed. informatics Ariz. State U., 2007—. Advisor Nat. Bd. Med. Examiners, Phila., 1987—93; pres. Symposium on Computer Applications in Med. Care, Washington, 1988—89; mem. Nat. Fed. Networking Adv. Coun., NSF, 1991—93; mem. computer sci. and telecomm. bd. NRC, 1991—96; bd. regents ACP-Am. Soc. Internal Medicine, 1996—2002; mem. Pres.'s Info. Tech. Adv. Com., 1997—2002; chmn. com. on healthcare and next generation internet NRC, 1998—2000; mem. Nat. Com. on Vital Health Stats., 2000—03; trustee N.Y. Acad. Medicine, 2005—; bd. dirs. Medco Health Solutions, Inc. Editor: Rule-Based Expert Systems, 1984, Readings in Medical Artificial Intelligence, 1984, Medical Informatics: Computer Applications in Health Care, 1990, Medical Informatics: Computer Applications in Health Care and Biomedicine, 2d edit., 2000, Biomedical Informatics, 2006. Com. sci. engring. and pub. policy NAS, 2001—03, 2005—07. Recipient Grace M. Hopper award, Assn. Computing Machinery, 1976, Young Investigator award, Western Soc. Clin. Investigation, 1987, Rsch. Career award, Nat. Libr. of Medicine, 1979—84; scholar, Kaiser Family Found., 1983—88. Fellow: Am. Coll. Med. Informatics (pres. 1992—94), Am. Assn. Artificial Intelligence; mem.: Am. Clin. and Climatol. Assn., Assn. Am. Physicians, Am. Med. Informatics Assn., Am. Soc. for Clin. Investigation, Inst. Medicine (mem. coun. 2000—03, 2005—07), Soc. for Med. Decisionmaking (pres. 1989—90). Achievements include development of several medical computer programs including MYCIN and ONCOCIN. Avocations: skiing, jazz. Office: Univ Ariz Coll Medicine 550 E Van Buren St Phoenix AZ 85004-2230 Home Phone: 602-956-5778; Office Phone: 602-827-2010. E-mail: ted@shortliffe.net.

SHORT-MAYFIELD, PATRICIA AHLENE, business owner; b. Ft. Benning, Ga., Oct. 12, 1955; d. William Pressley and Ilse Marie (Hofmann) Short; m. Thomas Hicks Fort, June 2, 1973 (div. Jan. 1981); m. Michael Patrick Mayfield, Aug. 11, 1984; 1 child, William Zachary. Grad. HS, Butler, Ga. Notary pub., Ga. Staff mem. Fairyland Day Care, Canton, Ga., 1973-74, Small World Child Care, Thomaston, Ga., 1974-77; nurses aide Kenneston Hosp., Marietta, Ga., 1978-80; staff worker Mental Health Ctr., Smyrna, Ga., 1980-81; dir. Kiddie Kollege, Marietta, 1981-85; bus. owner, mgr. Spiffy Clean by Mayfield, Marietta, 1985—95; lead cashier Petsmart, Kennesaw, Ga., 1994—. Choir staff Eastside Bapt. Ch., Marietta, 1988-89; vol. East Valley Elem. Sch., 1989-95, chorus vol., 1994-95; vol. East Cobb Middle Sch., 1995-98; active Nat. Congress Parents and Tchrs., Cobb County Humane Soc., 1991—. Mem. NAFE, Cobb County C. of C., Atlanta High Mus. Art, Dog Lovers Am. Republican. Baptist. Avocations: reading, walking, symphony, art, bicycling. Office: Spiffy Clean By Mayfield 2791 Georgian Ter Marietta GA 30068-3625 Office Phone: 770-424-5226. Personal E-mail: pshortm7@comcast.net.

SHORTRIDGE, JUDY BETH, lawyer; b. Johnson City, Tenn., Feb. 17, 1954; d. George Edd and Anna Louise (Salmon) Copenhaver; m. Michael L. Shortridge, July 27, 1984; children: Sarah Elizabeth, Alexander Blake. BA, Va. Poly. Inst. and State U., 1976; MEd, U. Va., 1982; JD, U. Tenn., 1989. Bar: Va. 1990, U.S. Dist. Ct. (we. dist.) Va. 1990, Ea. Dist. Tenn., 1995. Tchr. Stafford County (Va.) Sch. System, 1976-84, Wise County (Va.) Sch. System, 1984-86; ptnr. Shortridge & Shortridge, P.C., Norton and Abingdon, Va., 1990—. Recipient Am. Jurisprudence award U. Tenn., 1989. Mem. Va. Bar Assn. Home: 340 Winterham Dr Abingdon VA 24211-3800 Office: Shortridge & Shortridge PC 170 Valley St NW Abingdon VA 24210-2836 Home Phone: 276-623-8227; Office Phone: 276-628-5001. E-mail: t10sman@hotmail.com.

SHORTZ, RICHARD ALAN, lawyer; b. Chgo., Mar. 11, 1945; s. Lyle A. and Wilma Warner (Wildes) S.; m. Jennifer A. Harrell; children: Eric, Heidi. BS, Ind. U., 1967; JD, Harvard U., 1970. Bar: Calif. 1971, U.S. Supreme Ct. 1980. Assoc. Gibson, Dunn & Crutcher, LA, 1970-73; sr. v.p., gen. counsel, sec. Tosco Corp., LA, 1973-83; ptnr. Jones, Day, Reavis & Pogue, LA, 1983-95, Rogers & Wells, LA, 1995-97, Morgan Lewis & Bockius, LA, 1997—. Mem. L.A. World Affairs Inst., 1983—, Town Hall L.A., 1983—. 2nd lt. US Army, 1970—71. Mem.: Calif. Bar Assn., L.A. Bar. Assn., ABA, Merion Golf Club (Ardmore, Pa.), Loch Lomond Golf Club (Scotland), L.A. Country Club, Beach Club (Santa Monica, Calif.), Calif. Club. Republican. Episcopalian. Home: 1343 Pavia Pl Pacific Palisades CA 90272-4047 Office: Morgan Lewis & Bockius 300 S Grand Ave Ste 2200 Los Angeles CA 90071-3132 Office Phone: 213-612-2526. Office Fax: 213-612-2501. Business E-Mail: rshortz@morganlewis.com.

SHORTZ, WILL, puzzle editor; b. Crawfordsville, Ind., Aug. 26, 1952; s. Lyle A. and Wilma Warner (Wildes) S. AB, Ind. U., 1974; JD, U. Va., 1977. Editor Penny Press, Stamford, Conn., 1977-78; assoc. editor Games Mag., NYC, 1978-82, sr. editor, 1982-89, editor, 1989-93; crossword editor N.Y. Times, NYC, 1993—. Founder, dir. Am. Crossword Puzzle Tournament, Stamford, Conn., 1978—, World Puzzle Championship, N.Y.C., 1992, Stamford, 2000; puzzlemaster Weekend Edit. Sunday, NPR, Washington, 1987—; U.S. team capt. Internat. Crossword Marathon, 1989-90, World Puzzle Championship, 1993-99; riddle writer Batman Forever, 1995; co-founder, chmn. World Puzzle Fedn., 1999-2004, treas. 2004-; puzzle contb. Reader's Digest, 2002-2007. Author: Brain Games, 1979, The American Quiz Book, 1979, Brain Games 2, 1980, The Bantam Great Masters Winning Crossword Puzzles, vol. 1-3, 1980, World Class Championship Crosswords, 1982, Brain Games 3, 1983, Games Mag. Book of Crossword Puzzles, 1985, American Championship Crosswords, 1990, Games Mag. Giant Book of Games, 1991, Will Shortz's Best Brain Busters, 1991, Games Mag. Best Pencil Puzzles, 1992, Brain Twisters from the First World Puzzle Championships, 1993, NY Times Daily Crossword Puzzles, vol. 40-72, 1995—, The Puzzlemaster Presents, 1996, vol. 2, 2004, Will Shortz's Tournament Crosswords, 1997, NY Times Sunday Crossword Puzzles, vol. 24-32, 1998—, Will Shortz's Favorite Crossword Puzzles, 2002, Will Shortz's Tournament Crosswords, vol. 2, 2005, Sudoku-100 Wordless Crossword Puzzles, vol. 1-3, 2005. Named Wordplay documentary subject, 2006. Mem. Am. Antiquarian Soc., Am. Cryptogram Assn., Authors Guild, Nat. Puzzlers' League (pres. 1977, 81, historian 1992—). Avocations: ping pong/table tennis, book collecting. Office: NY Times 229 W 43rd St New York NY 10036-3959 Office Phone: 212-556-7435.

SHOSKY, JOHN EDWIN, media consultant, speechwriter; b. Colorado Springs, Colo., Nov. 1, 1955; s. Alexander Matthew and Barbara Marie (Middlekamp) Shosky. BA in Polit. Sci., Colo. Coll., 1979; MA in Philosophy, U. Wyo., 1987; PhD in Philosophy, Am. U., 1992. Dep. dir. media and sports commns. White House Conf. for Drug Free Am., Washington, 1987—88; sr. policy analyst White House Office Pub. Affairs, 1988; cons. to sec. HHS, Washington, 1984—91, cons. to Surgeon Gen., 1991—92; cons. to office of nat. drug control policy Exec. Office of the Pres., Washington, 1992—93, cons. to sec. of edn., 2003—05; pres., sr. writer Roncalli Comm., 1991—. Speech writer for govt. ofcls., corp. execs., profl. athletes, congressmen, senators; lectr. in philosophy and internat. studies Am. U., 1987—, asst. prof. philosophy, 1996—97, asst. dir. honors program, 1999—2003; adj. prof. philosophy George Mason U., 1990—94; vis. sr. mem. Linacre Coll., Oxford, England, 1997—; vis. prof. Charles U., Prague, 1998; vis. scholar Ins. of Logic, Acad. Scis., Czech Republic, 1998; vis. fellow Acad. Scis., Czech Republic, 2002—04. Contbr. articles to profl. jours. and publs. Mem.: Mind Assn., Hume Soc., Am. Philos. Assn., Austrian Wittgenstein Soc., U. Wyo. Alumni Assn. Republican. Roman Catholic. Home: 1806 Rollins Dr Alexandria VA 22307-1613

SHOSS, CYNTHIA RENÉE, lawyer; b. Cape Girardeau, Mo., Nov. 29, 1950; d. Milton and Carol Jane (Duncan) S.; m. David Goodwin Watson, Apr. 13, 1986; 1 child, Lucy J. Watson. BA cum laude, Newcomb Coll., 1971; JD, Tulane U., 1974; LLM in Taxation, NYU, 1980. Bar: La. 1974, Mo. 1977, Ill. 1978, N.Y. 1990. Law clk. to assoc. and chief justices La. Supreme Ct., New Orleans, 1974-76; assoc. Stone, Pigman et al, New Orleans, 1976-77, Lewis & Rice, St. Louis, 1977-79, Curtis, Mallet-Prevost, et al, NYC, 1980-82; ptnr. LeBoeuf, Lamb, Greene & MacRae, L.L.P., NYC, 1982—; mng. ptnr. London office LeBoeuf, Lamb, Leiby & MacRae, 1987-89. Assoc. editor Tulane Law Rev., 1972-74; frequent speaker before profl. orgns. and assns. Contbr. articles to profl. jours. Mem. bd. overseers Sch. Risk Mgmt., Ins. and Actuarial Sci., St. John's U. Mem.: Internat. Ins. Soc., The Risk Found. (bd. dirs.), Assn. Life Ins. Counsel (bd. govs.). Office: LeBoeuf Lamb Greene Et Al 125 W 55th St New York NY 10019-5369 Office Phone: 212-424-8129. Business E-Mail: cshoss@llgm.com.

SHOSTAK, BURTON H., lawyer; b. St. Louis, Mar. 20, 1936; AB, Wash. U., 1958, JD, 1960. Bar: Mo. 1960, U.S. Tax Ct. 1973, U.S. Supreme Ct. 1982. Spl. asst. atty. gen., Mo., 1963—68; ptnr. Moline, Shostak & Mehan LLC, St. Louis. Mem. moot ct. Wash. U.; faculty mem. Nat. Criminal Def. Coll., 1988—; counsel com. to investigate dept. revenue Mo. Ho. of Reps., 1982; mem., chmn. Mo. Pub. Defender Commn., 1976—82, 1994—. Recipient Trial Lawyer award, Mo. Bar Found., 1971. Mem.: NACDL (bd. dirs.), Am. Arbitration Assn., Mo. Assn. Trial Lawyers, Assn. Trial Lawyers Am., Lawyers Assn. St. Louis (treas. 1968, mem. exec. com. 1970—71, v.p. 1971—73, pres.-elect 1973—74, pres. 1974—75), Fla. Bar Assn., Mo. Bar Assn. (mem. bd. govs. 1976—86, Pres. award 1984), St. Louis County Bar Assn., Bar Assn. Met. St. Louis, Phi Delta Phi. Office: Moline Shostak & Mehan LLC The Berkley Bldg 8015 Forsyth Blvd Saint Louis MO 63105 Office Phone: 314-725-3200 307. Office Fax: 314-725-3275. E-mail: bshostak@msmattorneys.com.

SHOSTAK, LINDA E., lawyer; b. May 9, 1948; BA, Vassar Coll., 1970; JD, Harvard U., 1973. Bar: NY 1974, Calif. 1975. Lawyer Morrison & Foerster, San Francisco, 1974, ptnr., 1979—. Lectr. CEB, Rutter Grp.; taught (advanced pro. of trial advocacy) Nat. Inst. of Trial Advocacy; spkr. in field. Mem. Phi Beta Kappa. Office: Morrison & Foerster 425 Market St San Francisco CA 94105 Office Phone: 415-268-7202. Office Fax: 415-268-7522. Business E-Mail: lshostak@mofo.com.

SHOSTAK, S. RICHARD, lawyer; b. Omaha, July 16, 1931; s. Max Reubin and Reva Ruth (Gross) S.; m. Carole Ruth Blumenthal; children: Stuart Robert, Dennis Alan, Cynthia Robin. AB, U. Calif., Berkeley, 1951, BA, 1953, JD, 1956. Bar: Calif. 1956, U.S. Dist. Ct. (so. and cen. dists.) 1956, U.S. Ct. Appeals (9th cir.), U.S. Supreme Ct. 1960, U.S. Ct. Appeals (fed. cir.) 1960, D.C. 1980, U.S. Ct. Internat. Trade 1981. Assoc. Geary, Spridgen & Moskowitz, Santa Rosa, Calif., 1956-58; dep. dist. atty. Sonoma County Dist. Atty., Santa Rosa, 1958-59; ptnr. Stein and Shostak, LA, 1960-76; v.p. Stein, Shostak, Shostak & O'Hara, Washington, 1976—2005, San Diego, 1976—2005, ptnr. Washington, 2005—, San Diego, 2005—. Hearing examiner City of L.A. Police Commn., 1964-79; lectr. UCLA Ext., 1975-92. Author: U.S. Customs Laws and Regulations, 1978, 79, 80; contbr. articles to profl. jours. Chmn. World Trade Week, L.A., 1976; sec. Com. for 807, Washington, 1980-88, Com. for Prodn. Sharing, Washington, 1989-92. Mem. ABA, Wilshire Bar Assn., Fgn. Trade Assn. So. Calif. (pres., chmn. bd. 1976-78), L.A. C. of C. Avocation: golf. Home: 4211 Clear Valley Dr Encino CA 91436-3315 Office: Stein Shostak Shostak Pollack and O'Hara 865 S Figueroa St Ste 1388 Los Angeles CA 90071-3329 Home Phone: 818-784-2757; Office Phone: 213-630-8888. Office Fax: 213-630-8890. E-mail: dshostak@steinshostak.com.

SHOTTS, WAYNE J., nuclear scientist, federal agency administrator; b. Des Plaines, Ill., Mar. 20, 1945; s. Norman Russell Shotts and Winnifred Mae (Averill) Shotts Goeppinger; m. Melinda Maureen Antilla, June 24, 1967 (dec. Feb. 1975); children: Kenneth Wayne Shotts, Jeffrey Alan Shotts; m. Jacquelyn Francyle Willis, Aug. 11, 1979. BA in Physics, U. Calif., Santa Barbara, 1967; PhD, Cornell U., 1973. Rsch. physicist E.I. duPont deNemours & Co., Wilmington, Del., 1973-74; physicist U. Calif., Livermore, Calif., 1974—, Lawrence Livermore Nat. Lab., Livermore, 1974-79, group leader, thermonuclear design divsn., 1979-85, divsn leader, nuc. chemistry, 1985-86, divsn. leader, prompt diagnostics, 1986-88, prin. dep. assoc. dir., military applications, 1988-92, prin. dep. assoc. dir. def. and nuc. techs., 1992-95, assoc. dir. nonproliferation arms control/internat. security, 1995—2004, dep. dir. ops., 2004—06; ret., 2006. Sci. advisor Dept. Energy Office of Def. Programs; tech. advisor Nuclear Weapons Council Standing and Safety Com.; mem. Navy Steering Task Group. Recipient Ernest Orlando Lawrence Meml. award U.S. Dept. Energy, Washington, 1990. Mem. Am. Phys. Soc., Am. Assn. Advancement Sci. Office: Lawrence Livermore Nat Lab PO Box 808 Livermore CA 94551-0808

SHOTWELL, MALCOLM GREEN, minister; b. Brookneal, Va., Aug. 14, 1932; s. John Henry and Ada Mildred (Puckett) S.; m. LaVerne Brown, June 19, 1954; children: Donna (dec.), Paula. BA in Sociology, U. Richmond, 1954; MDiv, Colgate Rochester Div. Sch., 1957; D Ministry, Ea. Bapt. Theol. Sem., 1990; DD (hon.), Judson Coll., 1990. Ordained to ministry Am. Bapt. Ch. in U.S.A., 1957. Student asst. Greece Bapt. Ch., Rochester, NY, 1954-57; pastor 1st Bapt. Ch., Cuba, NY, 1957-62, sr. pastor Galesburg, Ill., 1962-71, Olean, NY, 1971-81; area minister Am. Bapt. Chs. of Pa. and Del., 1981-90; regional exec. minister Am. Bapt. Chs. of Great Rivers Region, Ill. and Mo., 1990-96; interim pastor First Bapt. Ch., Jacksonville, Ill., 2002, Galesburg, Ill., 2003, Decatur, Ill., 2005—06. Mem. Midwest Commn. on Ministry Am. Bapt. Chs. U.S.A., 1990—96, mem. task force for So. Bapt. Am. Bapt. Chs. Relationships, 1990—96; cons. for ch. growth and planning. Author: Creative Programs for the Church Year, 1986, Renewing the Baptist Principle of Associations, 1990; contbg. writer Baptists in the Balance, 1997; rschr., writer, performer: (dramatic monologue) Our Neighbors, the Lincolns: A Clergyman Remembers, 1999—. Trustee No. Bapt. Theol. Sem., Lombard, Ill., 1993-96; mem. gen. exec. coun., 1990-96, regional exec. ministers coun., 1990-96; trustee Judson Coll., 1990-2003, trustee emeritus, 2003-, chmn., 1997-00, chmn. presdl. search com., 1997-98; bd. dirs. Ctrl. Bapt. Theol. Sem., Kansas City, Kans., 1990-96, Old State Capitol Found., 2004-; sec. bd. dirs. Shurtleff Fund, Springfield, Ill., 1990-96; tchr., libr. Ctrl. Bapt. Ch., Springfield, 1997-05; mem. Hist. Commn. Am. Bapts. Ill. and Mo., 1998-02; retreat leader in stress mgmt., 1985—; conf., spkr., pulpit supply preacher Bapt. Ch.; mentor ILCS Elem. Sch., Old State Capital Reenactment of Lincoln-Douglas Debates, 1999-01, 03-05; tour guide Old State Capital, Springfield, 2003—, Abraham Lincoln Presdl. Libr. and Mus., 2005-. Recipient George Younge Biennal award The Am. Bapt. Hist. Soc., 2006; Walter Pope Binns fellow William Jewell Coll., 1995. Mem. Ministers Coun. Ill. and Mo., Coun. Ret. Execs., Abraham Lincoln Assn., Am. Bapt. Men of Ill. and Mo. (v.p., coord. disaster relief ministries).

SHOU, SHARON LOUISE WIKOFF, vocational rehabilitation counselor; b. Mpls., Oct. 23, 1946; d. Wallace S. and Phyllis Wikoff; m. James Kouping Shou, Dec. 27, 1969 (dec. June 4, 1989); children: Michelle, Darren. Student, U. Colo., 1971-72, Chinese U. Hong Kong, 1966-67; BA, Macalester Coll., 1968; MA, U. Denver, 1975. Cert. vocat. rehab. counselor, case manager, employment counselor; lic. clin. profl. counselor. Employment counselor Colo. Dept. of Employment, Denver, 1971-74; acad. advisor U. Ky., Lexington, 1978-81; employment advisor DeVry Inst. Tech., Lombard, Ill., 1985-86; trainee asst. specialist County of DuPage, Wheaton, Ill., 1987; sr. rehab. case mgr. CRA Managed Care (Comprehensive Rehab. Assoc.), Boston, 1987-97; rehab. specialist EVR, Batavia, Ill., 1997—2000; sr. vocat. rehab. counselor Unum, 2000—. Vocat. rehab. expert witness. Fellow: Am. Bd. Vocat. Experts; mem. AAUW (internat. rels. com. 1983), Naperville (Ill.) Chinese Assn. (adminstrv. com. 1984), Internat. Assn. Rehab. Profls. in the Pvt. Sector. Office: Unum 655 North Central Ave Ste 900 Glendale CA 91203

SHOULDERS, PATRICK ALAN, lawyer, educator; b. Mar. 26, 1953; m. Lisa Shoulders; children: Samantha Bucur, Andrew. BA in English, Ind. U., Bloomington, 1975; JD magna cum laude, Ind. U., Indpls., 1978. Bar: Ind. 1978, US Dist. Ct. (so. dist.) Ind. 1978, US Ct. Appeals (7th cir.) 1979, US Supreme Ct. 1985, Ky. 1986, US Dist. Ct. (we dist.) Ky. 1987, US Ct. Appeals (6th cir.) 1997. Assoc. Kahn, Dees, Donovan & Kahn, Evansville, Ind., 1978—81, ptnr., 1981—87, Ziemer, Stayman, Weitzel & Shoulders, Evansville, 1987—. Mem. local rules advisory com. US Dist. Ct. (so. dist.) Ind., mem. Civil Justice Reform Act adv. com.; treas., dir. Vanderburgh County Work Release Jobs Program, Inc., 1983—85; mem. Vanderburgh County Pub. Defender Commn., 2000—; pres. Vanderburgh Law Libr. Found., 1983—84. Co-host (public affairs program) Shively & Shoulders WNIN-TV. Judge nat. finals We The People...The Citizen and the Constitution Competition, Washington, 1997—99; past pres. Ind. U. Coll. Arts and Scis. Alumni Bd., Woodburn Guild; gen. chmn. TV auction WNIN Pub. TV, Evansville, 1985; founder Arts Fest River Run, Evansville, 1987; spkr. law-related edn. Evansville-Vanderburgh Sch. Corp.; chmn. Evansville Bill of Rights Bicentennial Celebration, 1991; mem. Evansville Conv. and Visitors Bur., 1993—96; mem. judges panel Entrepreneur of Yr. Awards INC mag., Evansville, 1993; treas. Ind. Equal Justice Fund, 1996—97; trustee Ind. U., 2002—; mem. Bd. Park Commrs. City of Evansville, 1984—87, Ind. State Recount Commn., 1992, Evansville-Vandeburgh County Unification Study Com., 2005; dir. Well House Soc.; mem. alumni bd. Ind. U. Law Sch. Indpls.; mem. med.-ethics com. St. Mary's Med. Ctr., Evansville, 1980—2002, mem. instnl. rev. bd., 1980—2003; pres. bd. dir. Evansville Parks Found., 1982, 1983; bd. dir. Arts Fest River Run, Evansville, 1987—2001; pres. bd. dir. YMCA Southwestern Ind., Inc., Evansville, 1990—94, Evansville Mus. Arts and Scis., 1991—92; bd. dir. Acodia Bus. Benefits Evansville, Inc., 1992—97; dir. Ind. U. Found., 2002—, Ind. U. Ctr. on Philanthropy, 2002. Named a Sagamore of Wabash, Gov. Evan Bayh, 1996; named Boss of Yr., Evansville Legal Sec. Assn., 1988, Vol. of Yr., Evansville YMCA, 1989, Vol. Action Ctr., 1989, Evansville Arts Ctr., 1990; named one of Top 50 Super Lawyers, Indpls. Monthly, 2005, 2006; named to William Henry Harrison HS Hall of Fame, 1996; recipient William L. Brooks Hospitality award, Evansville Conv. and Visitors Ctr., 1996, Roast in Honor of Patrick Shoulders, Albion Fellows Bacon Ctr., 1996, Maynard K. Hine Outstanding Alumni medal, Ind. U. - Purdue U. Indpls., 2005, Herman B. Wells Leadership award, Sigma Nu, 2005, Disting. Citizen award, Ind. Social Studies Tchr.'s Assn., 2001. Fellow: Am. Bar Found., Ind. Bar Found (chmn. fellows Ind. Bar Found. 1996, Pres.'s award 2000, master fellow), Am. Coll. Trial Lawyers; mem.: ABA (mem. trial practice com. litigation sect.), Ind. Trial Advocacy Coll. (co-chair 1996—), 7th Cir. Bar Assn., Am. Bd. Trial Advocates (assoc.), Ky. Bar Assn., Ind. State Bar Assn. (chmn. spring meeting 1991, chmn. litigation sect. 1991—92, mem. BAR-PAC bd. trustees 1991—95, chmn. legal edn. com. 1996—2000, coun. mem. appellate practice sect. 1997—98, mem. bd. govs. 1998—2000, mem. house del., Presidl. citation 2000), Evansville Bar Assn. (pres. 1985—86; James Bethel Gresham Freedom award 1993), Fedn. Ins. and Corporate Counsel, Friends of Kinsey Inst., Ind. U. Alumni Assn. (pres. 2000—01, chmn. 2000—01), Hoosier Hundred, Golden Key, Ky. Col. Office: Ziemer Stayman Weitzel & Shoulders 20 NW 1st St PO Box 916 Evansville IN 47706

SHOUN, ELLEN LLEWELLYN, retired secondary school educator; b. Germantown, Pa., Sept. 8, 1925; d. William Thomas and Ella (Hall) Llewellyn; m. Glenn Harte Shoun, June 25, 1949; children: Mary Deborah, Paul L., Eleanor C., Peter G., Elizabeth A. AB in Chemistry, Oberlin Coll., 1947; MA in Sci. Edn., Western Mich. U., 1972. Cert. libr. (ltd. profl.) Mich., secondary sch. tchr. Mich. Jr. chemist Am. Cyanamid, Stamford, Conn., 1947-49; Charles M. Hall Chem. instr. Oberlin (Ohio) Coll., 1949-51; br. libr. Bronson (Mich.) Pub. Libr., 1966-67; math. and sci. tchr. Bronson H.S., 1967-79; crew leader 1980 U.S. Census, Branch County, Mich., 1980; bus. mgr. Dr. C.F. Cole's Dental Office, Sturgis, Mich., 1982; reference aide Br. Dist. Libr., Coldwater, Mich., 1982-99; ret., 1999. Co-founder Bronson HS Cmty. Recycling Group, 1972—79. Trustee Bronson Pub. Libr., 1968—82, Housing Commn., 1975—, Bronson Cmty. Found., 2003—; instr. CPR Cmty. health Ctr., Coldwater, Mich., 1978—80; cmty. chorus Cmty. Found., 1987—; chair refugee family com. Bronson United Meth. Ch., 1974—82, ch. choir, 1967—, sec. adminstrv. bd., 1987—, chair adminstrv. bd., 1984—86; bd. dirs., treas., mgr. Food Pantry, 5 Ch. Coop., Bronson, 1993—. Named Hon. Grand Marshal, Polish Festival Parade, Bronson, 2002; recipient Cmty. Vol. of Yr. award, Gleaner Life Ins. Soc., 2001. Mem.: Phi Beta Kappa. Democrat. Avocations: photography, knitting, Scrabble.

SHOUP, ANDREW JAMES, JR., retired oil industry executive; b. Monroe, La., Mar. 26, 1935; s. Andrew James Sr. and Ruth (Landis) S.; m. Sue Cowles, Sept. 12, 1959 (dec. May 1998); children: Catherine Shoup Collins, Andrew James III; m. Julia Conger Galloway, May 6, 2000. BS in Petroleum Engring., La. State U., 1957; M in Indsl. Adminstrn., Yale U., 1959. Registered engr., Tex. Prodn. engr. Continental Oil Co., Houston, 1959-65; v.p. DeGolyer and MacNaughton, Dallas, 1965-74; chmn., CEO Sabine Corp., Dallas, 1974-89; pres. Pacific Enterprises Oil Co. U.S.A, Dallas, 1989-90; pres., CEO The Wiser Oil Co., Dallas, 1991-2000; ret., 2000. 2nd lt. U.S. Army, 1959-60. Mem. Soc. Petroleum Engrs. of AIME, Dallas Petroleum Club, Dallas Country Club. Avocations: skiing, golf.

SHOUP, CHARLES SAMUEL, JR., chemicals and materials executive; b. Nashville, Dec. 10, 1935; s. Charles Samuel and Leola Ruth (Turner) S.; m. Frances Carolyn DiCarlo, June 7, 1958 (dec. Apr. 1999); children: Mark Steven, Elizabeth Ann Shoup Kehoe, Margaret Carol Shoup Meyer; m. Sara Jo Denkmann, May 5, 2001. AB, Princeton U., 1957; MS, U. Tenn., 1961, PhD, 1962. Rsch. chemist Oak Ridge (Tenn.) Natl. Lab., 1962-67; mgr. special projects Union Carbide Corp., NYC, 1967-68; mgr. planning and controls Bell and Howell Co., Lincolnwood, Ill., 1968; v.p. Bell and Howell Sch. Inc., Chgo., 1968-69; mgr. tech. planning Cabot Corp., Boston and Billerica, Mass., 1969-70, dir. corp. rsch., Mass., 1970-73; gen. mgr. Aearo Corp., Westwood, Mass and Indpls., 1973-87; v.p., Indpls. Cabot Corp., Boston and Indpls., 1984-87; pres. Alphaflex Ind. Inc., Indpls, 1987-88, bd. dirs., 1988, Cemkote Corp., Indpls., 1988-91. Chmn. bd. dirs. Blasterz Corp., Carmel, Ind., 1992-2001; mem. adv. bd. Technalysis, Inc., Indpls., 1996-99; bd. dirs. Exec. Svc. Corps, Indpls., 1993—2004, mem. exec. com., 1994-2003, vice chmn., sec., 1997-99, chmn. bd. dirs., 2001-03; mem. bd. visitors Coll. Arts and Scis., U. Tenn., Knoxville, 1994-2000, assoc. bd. visitors, 2000—; bd. dirs Nat. Exec. Svc. Corps, Ind., 2001-04. Contbr. articles to profl. jours. Treas. Oak Ridge Arts Ctr., 1965-67; pres. Sherborn Edn. Found., 1974-76; chmn. Met. Div. United Way, 1982; bd. trustees, Ind. Safety Equipment Assn. 1978-81. Fellow Am. Inst. Chemists; mem. AAAS, Am. Chem. Soc., Noise Control Products and Materials Assn. (trustee 1977-87, pres. 1982-84), Sigma Xi. Presbyterian. Home: 13045 Abraham Run Carmel IN 46033-8618

SHOUSE, AUGUST EDWARD, lawyer; b. Houston, Aug. 12, 1949; s. Earl Edward Shouse and Mary Ann (Myers) Carrico; m. Deborah Lee Symonds; children: William Bundy, Edwrd Booth, Tucker Clayton. BS, Stanford U., 1971; JD, U. Tex., 1974. Bar: Tex. 1974. From assoc. to ptnr. Vinson & Elkins, Houston, 1974—. Bd. dirs. Greater Houston area chpt. ARC. Mem. Order of Coif, Phi Beta Kappa, Tau Beta Pi. Episcopalian. Office: Vinson & Elkins 2300 First City Tower 1001 Fannin St Houston TX 77002-6706

SHOWALTER, BETSY S., mathematics educator; b. Rockford, Ill., July 25, 1954; d. Donald James and Grace Lutz Curran; children: Thomas, David. BA in Math., U. Okla., Norman, 1976, MA in Math., 1978; PhD in Math. Edn., Okla. State U., Stillwater, 2005. Cert. secondary math. tchr., k-12 library media Okla. Math. tchr. Midwest City HS, Okla., 1978—80, Drumright HS, Okla., 1986—87, Stillwater HS, 1988—91; adj. math. instr. Okla. State U., 1980—86, 1991—93, Southwestern Okla. State U., Weatherford, 1987—88; instr. math. Langston U., Okla., 1993—. Mem.: Nat. Coun. Tchrs. Math., Phi Kappa Phi, Kappa Delta Pi. Home: 2402 W 8th Ave Stillwater OK 74074 Office: Langston U Math Dept 202A Jones Hall Langston OK 73050

SHOWALTER, BUCK (WILLIAM NATHANIEL SHOWALTER III), former professional baseball team manager; b. DeFuniak Springs, Fla., May 23, 1956; m. Angela Showalter; children: Nathan, Allie. Student, Chipola Jr. Coll., Fla., Miss. State U. Player various minor league teams, 1977-83; minor league coach, 1984; minor league mgr., 1985-89; coach NY Yankees, 1989—92, mgr., 1992-95, Ariz. Diamondbacks, 1998—2000, Tex. Rangers, 2002—06. Named N.Y.-Pa. League Mgr. of Yr., 1985, Eastern League Mgr. of Yr., 1989, Am. League Mgr. of Yr., 1994, Nat. League Mgr. of Yr., 2004 Home: 9736 Hathaway St Dallas TX 75220-2114 *

SHOWALTER, DAVID SCOTT, accounting executive; b. Harrisonburg, Va., May 23, 1953; s. Harold Marvin and Martha (Myers) Showalter; m. Elizabeth Allison, June 1, 1974; children: Braxton, Allison, Mason. AS, Ferrum Coll., 1973; BSBA, U. Richmond, 1975. CPA Ill., 1994, Mo., 1997, Wis., 1995, Ind., 1988, NJ, 2003, NY, 2004; cert. govt. fin. mgr. 1994. Asst. to nat. industry dir. KPMG, NYC, 1981-84, asst. to vice-chmn., 1986-88, ptnr., 1986—, area ptnr. in charge, Indpls., 1993-96; nat. industry dir. state, local govts., Chgo., 1996-98; global mng. ptnr. Assurance & Adv. Svcs. Ctr., Montvale, NJ, 1998—2002, industry sector leader pub. sector, 2002—04, dept. profl. practice, risk mgmt., 2004—. Vis. prof. U. Ill.; vis. scholar Ind. U.; trustee KPMG Found., NYC, co-founder Audit Com. Inst., co-founder Assurance Rsch. Inst.; spkr. in field. Co-editor (newsletters) Govt. Acct. and Auditing Update, Current Issues in Auditing. Pres, Indpls. Youth Hockey Assn., 1990—93; pres. coun. Boy Scouts Am., St. Charles, Ill., 1995—97, chmn. bd. dirs., 1997—98, bd. dirs., 1998—; mem. U.S. C. of C. Homeland Security Task Force; bd. dirs. Greater Indpls. Rep. Fin. Com., 1990—94; elder 1st Presbyn. Ch., Ramsey. Named Ky Col, State of Ky, 1986, Sagamore of Wabash for Serv to State of Ind, 1990, D Scott Showalter Day named in his honor, City of Indianapolis, 1994; named one of Top 100 Most Influential in Acctg., Acctg. Today, 2001; recipient Silver Beaver Award, Boy Scouts Am, 1994, Dist Eagle Scout Award, 1998. Mem.: AICPA (mem. com.), Assn. Sch. Bus. Ofcls., Ill. CPA Soc., NJ CPA Soc., Am. Acctg. Assn (v.p. practice, auditing sect., vice chmn. profl. rels. com., co-editor Current Issues in Auditing jour.), Govt. Fin. Officers Assn. (mem. com.). Presbyterian. Avocations: camping, jogging, backpacking, stamps. Home: 14 Forest Ridge Rd Upper Saddle River NJ 07458 Office: KPMG LLP 757 Third Ave New York NY 10017 Home Phone: 201-934-7913; Office Phone: 212-909-5905. Business E-Mail: dsshowalter@kpmg.com.

SHOWALTER, MARILYN GRACE, trade association administrator, director; AB, Harvard U., 1972, JD, 1975. Bar: Wash. 1975. Dep. pros. atty. King County, Wash., 1975—81, counsel to gov., 1981—83; pvt. practice, 1985—89; counsel house appropriations com. Wash. State House of Reps., 1989—92, dep. chief clk., house counsel, 1992—93, chief clk., 1994—95; advisor to Gov. Gary Locke, 1997—99; chair Utilities and Transp. Com., Portland, Oreg., 1999—2005, exec. dir., 2005—. Office: Pub Power Coun 1500 NE Irving Ste 200 Portland OR 97232 Home Phone: 360-754-7238. Business E-Mail: mshowalter@ppcpdx.org.

SHOWALTER, MARK ROBERT, astronomer; b. Abington, Pa., Dec. 5, 1957; s. James Grove Showalter and Sandra Khuen-Kryk; life ptnr. Frank Yellin, June 10, 1990. BA, Oberlin Coll., Ohio, 1979; PhD, Cornell U., Ithaca, NY, 1984. Prin. investigator SETI Inst., Mountain View, Calif., 2005—. Mgr. Rings Node, NASA's Planetary Data Sys., Mountain View, 1989—2006. Mem.: Am. Astron. Soc., Phi Beta Kappa. Achievements include discovery of outer gossamer ring of Jupiter; Pan, 18th moon of Saturn; Mab, 26th moon of Uranus; Cupid, 27th moon of Uranus; R/2003 U 1 and R/2003 U 2, outer rings of Uranus. Office: SETI Inst 515 N Whisman Rd Mountain View CA 94043 Office Phone: 650-810-0234. Business E-Mail: mshowalter@seti.org.

SHOWALTER, SHIRLEY H., former academic administrator; b. July 30, 1948; BA cum laude in English, Ea. Mennonite U., Harrisonburg, Va., 1970; MA in Am. civilization, U. Tex., Austin, 1974, PhD in Am. civilization, 1981. Tchr. English Harrisonburg HS, Va., 1970—72; tchg. asst. English and Am. Studies depts. U. Tex., Austin, 1973—75, asst. instr. Am. Studies dept., 1976; dir. continuing edn. Goshen Coll., Ind., 1979—82, project dir. Title II tech. and liberal arts devel. grant, 1982—85, project dir. Consortium Advancemet of Pvt. Higher Edn. grant, 1985—86, asst. to prof. English, 1967—, pres., 1997—2004. Coord. Humanities program Harrisonburg (Va.) H.S., 1970—72; co-dir. Study-Svc. Term in Haiti Goshen Coll., 1981—82; rsch. asst. Consortium Advancement of Pvt. Higher Edn., Washington, 1986—87, interim v.p., 1987; chair English dept. Goshen Coll., 1990—93; sr. fellow Lilly Fellows program in Humanities and Arts Valparaiso U., Ind., 1993—94; co-dir. Study-Svc. Term in Ivory Coast Goshen Coll., 1993; lectr. and spkr. in humanities. Contbr. chapters to books, articles to profl. jours. Bd. mem. South Bend Symphony Assn.; mem. blue ribbon adv. group Boys and Girls Club; vice chair and mem. Hist. Com. of Mennonite Ch., 1984—88; co-sponsor Kid's Club No. Va. Mennonite Ch., 1987—88; chair curriculum com. Sojourner's Sunday Sch. class Coll. Mennonite Ch., 1987—88, mem. constn. revision com., 1988—92, tchr. H.S. age class, 1988—91, mem. worship commn., 1994—96; bd. mem. Coun. Christian Coll. and U., 2000—, Ind. Colls. of Ind., 1999—, Lantz Ctr. Christian Vocations, Indpls., 1998—; dir. Coun. Ind. Colls., 1999—; bd. dir. Mennonite Mutual Aid Trust; dir. Elkhart County Cmty. Found. Recipient Tchg. Excellence and Campus Leadership award, Sears Roebuck Found., 1990, Faculty Rsch., Goshen Coll., 1990, Knight Presdl. Leadership award, John S. and James L. Knight Found., 1999, 1999; fellow, George H. Gallup Rsch. Inst., 1999—2000, Coolidge Fellow, Yale U., Assn. Religion in Intellectual Life, 1996; grantee Faculty Rsch., Goshen Coll., 1977, 1982, Summer Stipend, Lilly Endowment, 1991. Mem.: AAUW, Am. Studies Assn., Am. Assn. Higher Edn. (Goshen Coll. rep. Forum on Exemplary Tchg. 1992, bd. dir. 1992—96), No. Ind. Partnership for the Arts, Willa Cather Pioneer Mem., Ind. Hist. Soc., Ellen Glasgow Soc., Blue Sky Assoc. Office: VP Programs Fetzer Inst 9292 West KL Ave Kalamazoo MI 49009-9398

SHOWER, ROBERT WESLEY, corporate financial executive; b. Harvey, Ill., Sept. 5, 1937; s. Glenn Wesley and Chrissie Irene (Ford) S.; m. D. Elaine Crawford, March 25, 2006; children from previous marriage: David Wesley, Lynece Marie. BS, U. Tulsa, 1960; P.MD, Harvard Business Sch., 1972. Sr. auditor Arthur Andersen & Co., Tulsa, 1960-64; with The Williams Cos., Tulsa, 1964-86, asst. v.p., 1968-69, v.p. adminstrn., 1969-71, v.p., treas., 1971, v.p. fin., 1971-73, sr. v.p. fin., 1973-77, exec. v.p. fin. and adminstrn., dir., 1977-86; mng. dir. Shearson, Lehman, Hutton, Dallas, 1986-90; v.p. fin. Ameriserv Food Co., Dallas, 1990-91; sr. v.p. fin., CFO Seagull Energy Co., Houston, 1992-94, exec. v.p., CFO, 1994-96. Mem. Okla. Soc. CPAs, Lambda Chi Alpha, Delta Sigma Pi. Home: 33641 N 79th Way Scottsdale AZ 85262 Fax: 480-575-1286. E-mail: roshower@aol.com.

SHOWERS JOHNSON, VIOLET MARY-ANN IYABO, history professor; b. Lagos, Nigeria; arrived in US, 1985, naturalized, 2002; d. Samuel Dandeson and Edna Taiwo Showers; m. Percy Ayomi Johnson; 1 child, Percy Ayomi Johnson, Jr. BA in History with honors, U. Sierra Leone, Freetown, 1979; MA, U. NB, Fredericton, NB, Canada, 1983; PhD, Boston Coll., Chestnut Hill, Mass., 1992. Lectr. dept. modern history Fourah Bay Coll., U. Sierra Leone, Freetown, 1983—85; history prof. Agnes Scott Coll., Decatur, Ga., 1992—, chair dept. history, 2001—, dir. African studies, 1995—2002. Proposals reviewer NEH Summer Seminars and Insts., 2000; grant screener Am. Coun. Learned Scholars, 2000—01; mem. scholars working group Atlanta Regional Consortium for Higher Edn. Civil Rights Virtual Libr. Project, 2001—03; external reviewer dept. history Spelman Coll., 2003. Author: The Other Black Bostonians: West Indians in Boston, 1900-1950, 2006; mem. editl. bd.: Jour. Am. Ethnic History; contbr. articles to profl. jours. Mem. African Am. initiatives bd. Atlanta History Ctr., 2001—05; applications reviewer, scholarship com. Atlanta Caribbean Assn., 2004; spkr. various events Auburn Ave. Rsch. Libr. on African-American Culture and History, Atlanta. Recipient Durham prize for the best result in the Faculty of Arts, Fourah Bay Coll., U. Sierra Leone, 1979, Vulcan Tchg. Excellence award, Vulcan Materials Co., 2002, Outstanding Woman award, Women Multi-Ethnicity and Nationality, 2004, Joseph R. Gladden Pub. Lecture award for noteworthy scholarship, Bd. Trustees, Agnes Scott Coll., 2005; grantee, NEH, 1998; Jr. Fulbright fellow, Fulbright Found., 1985—92. Mem.: Soc. for Multi-Ethnic Studies: Europe and the Americas, Forum for European Contbns. in African Am. Studies (mem. editl. bd.), Am. Hist. Assn., Assn. for the Study of African Am. Life and History, Immigration and Ethnic History Soc., Collegium African Am. Rsch. (exec. bd. mem.). Office: Agnes Scott College 141 East College Ave Decatur GA 30030 Office Phone: 404-471-6191. Office Fax: 404-471-6369; Home Fax: 404-471-6369. Business E-Mail: vjohnson@agnesscott.edu, vjohnson@agnesscout.edu.

SHPYRKO, OLEG G., physicist; b. Kiev, Ukraine, Apr. 30, 1976; PhD, Harvard U., Cambridge, Mass., 1998—2004. Postdoctoral fellow Harvard U., 2004—05; disting. postdoctoral fellow Argonne Nat. Lab., Ill., 2005—. Contbr. articles to profl. jours. Mem.: Am. Phys. Soc. Office: Argonne Nat Lab 9700 Cass Ave Argonne IL 60559 Home Phone: 630-252-7540.

SHRACK, CHRISTOPHER GEORGE, curator, educator; b. Wichita, Kans., June 17, 1949; s. George William and Phyllis Star Shrack; m. Marsha Carol Gates, Mar. 20, 1986; children: Samuel Cody, Chelsea Christine, Emma Leigh, Gates Kipp. BFA with hons., Wichita State U., Wichita, Kans., 1973; AS, Pratt C.C., Pratt, Kans., 1987; cert. in Tchg., Sterling Coll., Sterling, Kans., 1990. Cert. tchr. Kans. Bd. Edn., 2006, arborist Kans., 1978, housing inspector Kans., 1995, wastewater operator Kans. Dept. Health and Environ., 2004, potable water operator Kans. Dept. Health and Environ., 2004. Graphic design artist Pennypower Shopping News Mag., Wichita, Kans., 1971—74, CGI Assoc. of Local Gov't., Pratt, Kans., 1976—80; instr. art Pratt C.C., 1980—88, Stafford Pub. Schs., Kans., 1991—94; housing insp./crew leader Kans. Weatherization Program, Pratt, 1994—98; instr. art St. John and Hudson Pub. Schs., Kans., 2000—02; curator mus., educator Kans. Dept. Wildlife and Pks., Pratt, 2003—. Presenter in field; spkr. in field. Photo exhibition, Kans. Dept. Wildlife and Pks., 2006; contbr. Active Pratt Teen Ctr., 2003—; leader Stephen Ministry, Pratt, 2006—. Sgt. nat. guard USAF, 1967—72. Named Tchr. of Yr., Stafford County Soil Conservation, 1992, 1994; recipient Outstanding Svc. award, Pratt C.C., 1990. Mem.: Kans. Dept. Wildlife and Parks Employees Group. Meth. Avocations: photography, art. Home: 226 NE 90th St Iuka KS 67066-9541 Office: Kansas Department of Wildlife and Parks 512 SE 25th Ave Pratt KS 67124-8174 Home Phone: 620-546-2594. Business E-Mail: chriss@wp.state.ks.us.

SHRADER, CHARLES REGINALD, historian; b. Nashville, July 3, 1943; s. Reginald Woodrow and Freda Olene (Presley) S.; m. Carole Anne Analore, Aug. 17, 1963; children: Peter Reginald, Sheila Lynne Shrader Bixby. BA cum laude, Vanderbilt U., 1964; MA History, Columbia U., 1970, M Phil, 1974, PhD History, 1976; Grad., U.S. Army Command/Gen. Staff, Coll., 1978, U.S. Army War Coll., 1982, NATO Def. Coll., 1984. Commd. 2d lt. U.S. Army, 1964, advanced through grades to lt. col., ret., 1987; asst. prof. history U.S. Mil. Acad., 1971-74; instr. European Divsn. U. Md., Pirmasens and Landstuhl, Germany, 1974-77; instr. U.S. Army Command and Gen. Staff Coll., 1977-80, U.S. Army War Coll., 1980-84; mem. staff NATO Def. Coll., Rome, 1984-85; independent historian, 1987—; exec. dir. Soc. for Mil. History, Carlisle, Pa., 1992-2000. Pres. Nat. Coalition Ind. Scholars, 2000-2002; adj. instr. Elizabethtown Coll., 1988-89, Penn State U.-Harrisburg, 1988-90; lectr. various Army svc. schs., CIA, U. Kans., U. Victoria/B.C., NATO Def. Coll. Mem. Carlisle Mcpl. Authority, 1993-2003, Carlisle Zoning Hearing Bd, 2005-. Mem. Army and Navy Club, Phi Kappa Psi, Phi Beta Kappa. Roman Catholic. Home and Office: 910 Forbes Rd Carlisle PA 17013-1721 Home Phone: 727-249-5625; Office Phone: 717-249-5625. E-mail: heriger@earthlink.net.

SHRADER, RALPH W., management consultant; BEE, U. Pa.; MSEE minor in Math. and Nuc. Physics, U. Ill., PhD in Elec. Engring. Former pres. worldwide tech. divsn. Booz Allen & Hamilton, Mc Lean, Va., chmn., chmn., CEO, 1999—. Former chmn. bd. Armed Forces Comms. and Electronics Assn., mem. exec. com. bd. dir. Wolf Trap Found. Nat. Park for Performing Arts, Abilities, Inc.; adv. coun. Character Edn. Partnership; chmn. bd. The Neediest Kids, Inc.; corp. chmn. Light the Night Walks, Washington, 2004; bd. dir. Abilities, Inc., ServiceSource, Va. Recipient David Sarnoff award, Armed Forces Comms. and Electronics Assn., Cmty. Leadership award, Northern Va. Cmty. Found., 2001. Office: Booz Allen & Hamilton Inc 8283 Greensboro Dr Mc Lean VA 22102

SHRADER-FRECHETTE, KRISTIN, science educator; m. Maurice Frechette; children: Danielle, Eric. B in Math. summa cum laude, Edgecliff Coll., Xavier U., 1967; PhD in Philosophy, U. Notre Dame, 1972. Asst. prof., philosophy Edgecliff Coll., 1971—73; prof., philosophy, natural sciences U. Louisville, 1973—82; prof., philosophy of sci., environ. studies U. Calif., Santa Barbara, 1982—84; prof., philosophy, natural sciences U. Fla., 1984—87; disting. rsch. prof., philosophy, environ. scis. U. So. Fla., 1987—98; O'Neill Family prof., dept. biol. sci. and dept. philosophy U. Notre Dame. Vis. philosopher Coun. on Philosophical Studies, 1980, 87; US NAS/NRC coun. del. Internat. Union Hist. & Phil. Sci., 1987; chair, internat. geosphere/biosphere program. Internat. Union Hist. & Phil. Sci. & Internat. Conf. Scientific Unions, 1988—91; chair, sci. and ethics com. Internat. Conf. Scientific Unions, 1990—96; mem. adv. bd. Tech., Risk, and Soc.: An Internat. Series in Risk Analysis, 1983—, Earth Ethics Rsch. Group, 1990—, Integration, Environ. Assessment and Environ. Indicators, EPA, 1992—, Planet Ctrl. TV Cable Network (environ. issues), 1993—, Vision for 2010, PBS TV series on the environment, 1993—, Ont. Soc. for Environ. Ethics, 1994—; panelist referee Nat. Endowment for the Humanities, 1979—, NSF, 1980—, EPA, Atmospheric Rsch. and Exposure Assessment, 1992—; mem. Blue Ribbon Panel US Dept. Energy Performance Evaluation of US Nuclear Facilities, 1994—96, US Dept. Energy Performance Evaluation of Sites for Mixed Nuclear Wastes, 1994—97; mem. adv. bd. Inst. Hydrology and Water Quality, 1995—; chair, sci. ethics com. 10th Congress of Logic, Methodology, Philosophy Sci., 1995; chair World Congress Philosophy Sect. on Philosophy and Tech., 1998; chair com. bioethics EPA, mem. sci. adv. bd., 2003—; prin. investigator grants NSF, Nat. Endowment for the Humanities, Coun. Philosophical Studies, U.S. Dept. Energy; dir., Ctr. for Environmental Justice and Children's Health U. Notre Dame; invited lectr. in field. Author: (books) Nuclear Power and Public Policy, 1983, Environmental Ethics, 1991, Four Methodological Assumptions in Cost Benefit Analysis, 1983, Science, Policy, Ethics, and Economic Methodology, 1984, Risk Analysis and Scientific Method, 1985, Nuclear Energy and Ethics, 1991, Risk and Rationality, 1991, Burying Uncertainty: Risk and the Case Against Geological Disposal of Nuclear Waste, 1993, Method in Ecology, 1993, The Ethics of Scientific Research, 1994, Environmental Justice: Creating Equality, Reclaiming Democracy, 2002, Taking Action, Saving Lives: Our Duties to Protect Environmental and Pub. Health, 2007; co-editor: Technology and Human Values, 1996; co-author: Policy for Land: Law and Ethics, 1992; assoc. editor: Bioscience, 1994—2002, editor-in-chief: Oxford U. Press monograph series Environ. Ethics and Sci. Policy, 1988—; mem. editl. bd. Humanities and Tech., 1980—, Environmental Ethics, 1981—, Philosophy and Tech., 1986—, Jour. Agr. and Environ. Ethics, 1986—, Pub. Affairs Quarterly, 1987—, Jour. Law and Pub. Policy, 1987—, Studies in Religion and the Social Order, 1991—, Risk: Issues in Health and Safety, 1991—, Syntheis: An Internat. Jour. in Logic, Epistemology and Philosophy of Sci., 1993—, Eco Spheres, 1993—, Organization and Environ., 1995—, Ethics and the Environment, 1995—, Environmental Values, 1995—, Encyclopedia of Philosophy Sci., 1996—, Poiesis and Praxis, 1999—, Europaische Akademie, 1999—, Bus. Ethics Quarterly, 2002—, Biological Theory, 2004—, Accountability in Rsch., 2004—; Article Referee Behavioral Science, 1975-, Philosophy Sci., 1977-, Sci., Tech., and Human Values, 1980-, Sci., 1982-, Jour. Bus. Ethics, 1983-, Energy Policy Studies, 1984-, Synthese, 1984-, Environment International, 1985-, Risk Analysis, 1985-,Environmental Management, 1985-, Ethics, 1987-, Hypatia, 1988-, Soc. and Natural Resources, 1989-, Biology and Philosophy, 1993, Economics and Philosophy, 1992-, Conservation Biology, 1993-, Bulletin Ecological Soc. Am., 1995-, Environmental Professional, 1995-, Newsletter on Philosophy and Tech., 1995-, Environ. Sci. and Tech., 1996-, Environ. Health Perspectives, 2005-present; Book Referee MIT Press, 1981-, Reidel Press, 1981-, Macmillan Publishers, 1984-, Prentice-Hall, 1984-, Univ. Calif. Press, 1984-, Oxford Univ. Press, 1987-, Kluwer Academic Publishers, 1988-, Cambridge Univ. Press, 1991-, Rowman and Littlefield, 1991-, Univ. Ariz. Press, 1991-, Temple Univ. Press, 1992-, Univ. Press Kans., 1992-, Univ. Georgia Press, 1994-, Yale Univ. Press, 1994-; contbr. several articles to profl jours. including Ethics, Jour. Philosophy, Philosophy of Sci., Synthese, Trends in Ecology Revolution, others Named Kentucky's Outstanding Young Women, 1977; recipient NEH/NSF Interdisciplinary Incentive award, 1982, NSF Scholar's award in Philosophy of Sci., 1982, World Tech. award in Ethics, 2004; Woodrow Wilson Nat. Fellowship, 1967—68, NSF Fellow, 1968—71, Carnegie Found. Fellowship in Philosophy Sci., 1971. Mem.: NAS ((with NRC) bd. dirs. environ. studies and toxicology 1993—96, (with NRC) oversight com. environ. monitoring and assessment program 1993—96, (with NRC) com. risk characterization 1994—96, (with NRC) com. to evaluate zinc-cadmium-sulfide 1995—96, (with NRC) mem. com. on ecosystems svcs. 2002—03), Humanities and Tech. Assn. (bd. mem. 1980—90), Assn. Internat. de Cyberétique (mem. Am. bd. 1976—78), Internat. Soc. Environ. Ethics (mem. nominating com. 1992—, mem. adv. bd. 1995—, pres. 2000—03), Risk Assessment and Policy Assn. (pres. 1995—98, chair, mtg. program com. 1997), Soc. Philosophy and Tech. (v.p./pres.-elect 1983—85, pres. 1985—87, past pres.), Philosophy Sci. Assn. (mem. nominating com. 1981—82, mem. program com. 1986, mem. mtg. program com. 1986, 1996, mem. program com. 1998, mem. mtg. program com. 1998, mem. program com. 2006), Am. Philosophical Assn. (mem. program com. 1981, mem. adv. com. on ethics 1989—92, mam. adv. bd. Newsletter on Feminism and Philosophy 1992—), DAR. Avocations: scuba diving, canoeing, hiking, volunteer work. Office: Dept Philosophy and Dept Biol Scis 100 Malloy Hall Univ Notre Dame Notre Dame IN 46556-5639 Office Phone: 574-631-2647. Office Fax: 574-631-8209. Business E-Mail: kristin.shrader-frechette.1@nd.edu. *

SHRAUNER, BARBARA WAYNE ABRAHAM, electrical engineer, educator; b. Morristown, NJ, June 21, 1934; d. Leonard Gladstone and Ruth Elizabeth (Thrasher) Abraham; m. James Ely Shrauner, 1965; children: Elizabeth Ann, Jay Arthur. BA cum laude, U. Colo., 1956; AM, Harvard U., 1957, PhD, 1962. Postdoc. mrschr. Free U. Brussels, 1962-64, NASA-Ames Rsch. Ctr., Moffett Field, Calif., 1964-65; asst. prof. Washington U., St. Louis, 1966-69, assoc. prof., 1969-77, prof., 1977—2003, sr. prof., 2003—. Sabbatical Los Alamos (N.Mex.) Sci. Lab., 1975-76, Lawrence Berkeley Lab., Berkeley, Calif., 1985-86; cons. Los Alamos Nat. Lab., 1979, 84, NASA, Washington, 1980, Naval Surface Weapons Lab., Silver Spring, Md., 1984. Contbr. articles on transport in semiconductors, hidden symmetries of differential equations, plasma physics to profl. jours. Fellow Am. Phys. Soc. (sr. divsn. plasma physics, exec. com. 1980-82, 96-98); mem. IEEE (sr.; sr. exec. com. of standing tech. com. on plasma sci. and applications 1996-98), AAUP (local sec.-treas. 1980-82), Am. Geophys. Union, Phi Beta Kappa, Sigma Xi, Eta Kappa Nu, Sigma Pi Sigma. Home: 7452 Stratford Ave Saint Louis MO 63130-4044 Office: Washington U Dept Elec and Systems Engring 1 Brookings Dr Saint Louis MO 63130-4899 Home Phone: 314-727-1012; Office Phone: 314-935-6134. Business E-Mail: bas@wustl.edu.

SHREEVE, JEAN'NE MARIE, chemist, educator; b. Deer Lodge, Mont., July 2, 1933; d. Charles William and Maryfrances (Briggeman) Shreeve. BA in Chemistry, U. Mont., 1953, DSc (hon.), 1982; MS in Analytical Chemistry, U. Minn., 1956; PhD in Inorganic Chemistry, U. Wash., 1961. From asst. prof. to assoc. prof. chemistry U. Idaho, Moscow, 1961—67, prof., 1967-73, 2000—, acting chmn. dept. chemistry, 1969-70, 1973, head dept. and prof., 1973-87, v.p. rsch. and grad. studies, prof. chemistry, 1987-99, Jean'ne M. Shreeve chemistry prof., 2004—. Mem. nat. com. Stds. Higher Edn., 1965—67, 1969—73; Lucy W. Pickett lectr. Mt. Holyoke Coll., 1976; George H. Cady lectr. U. Wash., 1993; chmn. com. nat. medal sci. Pres. U.S., 2003—. Mem. editl. bd. Jour. Fluorine Chemistry, 1970—, Jour. Heteroatom Chemistry, 1988—95, Accounts Chem. Rsch., 1973—75, Inorganic Synthesis, 1976—; contbr. articles to sci. jours. Mem. bd. govs. Argonne (Ill.) Nat. Lab., 1992—98. Named Hon. Alumnus, U. Idaho, 1972; named to Idaho Hall of Fame, 2001; recipient Disting. Alumni award, U. Mont., 1970, Outstanding Achievement award, U. Minn., 1975, Sr. U.S. Scientist award, Alexander Von Humboldt Found., 1978, Excellence in Tchg. award, Chem. Mfrs. Assn., 1980; NSF Postdoctoral fellow, U. Cambridge, Eng., 1967—68, U.S. Hon. Ramsay fellow, 1967—68, Alfred P. Sloan fellow, 1970—72. Mem.: AAUW (officer Moscow chpt. 1962—69), AAAS (bd. dirs. 1991—95), Idaho Acad. Sci. (Disting. Scientist 2001), Am. Chem. Soc. (bd. dirs. 1985—93, chmn. fluorine divsn. 1979—81, mem. adv. bd. Petroleum Rsch. Fund 1975—77, mem. women chemists com. 1972—77, Harry and Carol Mosher award Santa Clara Valley sect. 1992, Shirley B. Radding award Santa Clara Valley sect. 2003, Garvan medal 1972, award for creative work in fluorine chemistry 1978), Göttingen (Germany) Acad. Scis. (corr.), Phi Beta Kappa. Avocations: fishing, gardening. Office: U Idaho Dept Chemistry Box 442343 Moscow ID 83844-2343 Office Phone: 208-885-6215. Business E-Mail: jshreeve@uidaho.edu.

SHREM, CHARLES JOSEPH, metals corporation executive; b. Cairo, May 9, 1930; arrived in U.S., 1959; s. Joseph C. and Paula (Cadranel) S.; m. Vivian L. Chalom, Jan. 30, 1955; children: Jeff, Leslie Allen. Degree in bus. and economy, Coll. Français, Cairo, 1951. Export mgr. Stanton Ironworks U.K., Middle East, 1950-57; comml. mgr. Soc. Sovibor, Paris, 1957-59; purchasing dir. Montanore, Inc., NYC, 1959-65; exec. v.p. Commonwealth Metal Corp., Englewood Cliffs, NJ, 1965-85, pres., CEO, 1985-2000, chmn., 2000—02; bus. cons. Pompton Plains, NJ, 2002—. Bd. dirs. Adult Edn., Pequannock, N.J., 1970-80; chmn. bd. govs. Internat. Grad. U., Washington. Mem. U.S. C. of C. (econ. coun., exec. com. U.S. Polish Coun./U.S. C. of C.). Office: 933 Rte 23 Pompton Plains NJ 07444 Office Phone: 973-831-0111. Personal E-mail: charles.shrem@verizon.net.

SHRESTHA, MANOJ LAL, economics professor, policy studies researcher; b. Kathmandu, Nepal, Sept. 5, 1959; arrived in Japan, 1982; s. Mahanta Lal and Nanichhori Shrestha. MA in Econs., Kyoto U., Japan, 1985; PhD, Grad. U. for Advanced Studies, Kyoto, 1997. Rschr. Inst. for Advanced Indsl. Devel., Osaka, Japan, 1988-89; lectr. Ryukoku U., Kyoto, 1989-91; vis. rschr. Internat. Rsch. Ctr. for Japanese Studies, Kyoto,

1991-92; asst. prof. Konan U., Kobe, Japan, 1992-94, assoc. prof., 1994—2000, prof., 2000. Sr. fellow Wharton Sch., U. Pa., 1998—; vis. scholar Ctr. Internat. Studies, MIT, 1998-01; vis. prof. US-Asia Tech. Mgmt. Ctr. Stanford U. Author: Multinationalization of Firms and Technology Transfer (in Japanese), 1996 (Mgmt. Book of Yr. Japan Omni-Mgmt. Assn., Tokyo). Founding dir. Nepal Ednl. Devel. Orgn., Kathmandu, 1991. Mem. Japan Acad. Soc. for Venture and Entrepreneur, Internat. Intellectual Property Assn. Avocations: trekking, music. Office: Konan U Higashinada-ku Okamoto 8-9-1 Kobe 658 Japan Home: Sakaemachi 3-10-12-305 Takarazuka City Japan Address: 43 Park Dr Atherton CA 94027 Home Phone: 650-787-7119; Office Phone: 81 78 431 4341. Business E-Mail: manojlal@stanford.edu.

SHRESTHA, RAM K., economist, researcher; s. Indu Raj and Dil Maya Shrestha; m. Mira Shrestha, Sept. 13, 1970; children: Anima, Anisha. MPA, Tribhuvan U., Kathmandu, Nepal, 1991; MSc, Asian Inst. Tech., Bangkok, Thailand, 1994; PhD, Colo. State U., Fort Collins, 2000. Assoc. econ. affairs officer UN, Bangkok, 1995; program coord. IUCN-World Conservation Union, Bangkok, 1996—97; postdoctoral rsch. fellow U. Fla., Gainesville, 2000—03; economist Ctrs. for Disease Control and Prevention, Atlanta, 2003—. Contbr. chpts. to books, articles to profl. jours. Cmty. coord. Colo. State U., Fort Collins, 1997—2000. Recipient Mahendra Vidhya Bhusan, King of Nepal, 1991; scholar Thai King's scholarship for MSc study, King of Thailand, 1993; Steven M. Teutsch Post-Doctoral fellowship, Ctrs. for Disease Control and Prevention, 2003. Mem.: Am. Econ. Assn. (assoc.), Internat. Health Econs. Assn. (assoc.), Am. Soc. Health Economists (assoc.). Office: Ctrs Disease Control and Prevention 1600 Clifton RdNE MS E-48 Atlanta GA 30333 Home Phone: 678-254-9733; Office Phone: 404-639-6245. Personal E-mail: shrestha1001@hotmail.com.

SHREVE, GENE RUSSELL, law educator; b. San Diego, Aug. 6, 1943; s. Ronald D. and Hazel (Shepherd) S.; m. Marguerite Russell, May 26, 1973. AB with honors, U. Okla., 1965; LLB, Harvard U., 1968, LLM, 1975. Bar: Mass. 1969, Vt. 1981. Appellate atty. and state extradition hearing examiner Office of Mass. Atty Gen., 1968-69; law clk. U.S. Dist. Ct., Dallas, 1969-70; staff and supervising atty. Boston Legal Assistance Project, 1970-73; assoc. prof. Vt. Law Sch., Royalton, 1975-81; vis. assoc. prof. George Washington U., Washington, 1981-83; assoc. prof. law N.Y. Law Sch., NYC, 1983-84, prof., 1984-87; vis. prof. law Ind. U., Bloomington, 1986, prof., 1987-94, Richard S. Melvin Prof. Law, 1994—. Author: A Conflict of Laws Anthology, 1997; co-author: Understanding Civil Procedure, 3d edit., 2002; mem. editl. bd. Am. Jour. Comparative Law, 1994-03, Jour. Legal Edn., 1998-01; contbr. numerous articles to legal jours. Mem. Am. Law Inst., Am. Soc. for Pol. and Legal Phil., Assn. Am. Law Schs. (civil procedure sect. chair 1997, conflict of laws sect. chair 1998). Democrat. Episcopalian. Office: Ind U Sch Law Bloomington IN 47405 Office Phone: 812-855-4230.

SHREVE, SUSAN RICHARDS, writer, educator; b. Toledo, May 2, 1939; d. Robert Kenneth and Helen (Greene) Richards; children— Porter, Elizabeth, Caleb, Kate. BA, U. Pa., 1961; MA, U. Va., 1969. Prof. English lit. George Mason U., Fairfax, Va., 1976—. Vis. prof. Columbia U., NYC, 1982—, Princeton U., 1991-93 Author: (novels) A Fortunate Madness, 1974, A Woman Like That, 1977, Children of Power, 1979, Miracle Play, 1981, Dreaming of Heroes, 1984, Queen of Hearts, 1986, A Country of Strangers, 1989, Daughters of the New World, 1992, The Train Home, 1993, Skin Deep: Women & Race, 1995, The Visiting Physician, 1995; (pseudonym Annie Waters) Glimmer, 1997, Plum & Jaggers, 2000, A Student of Living Things, 2006, A Memoir: Warm Springs: Traces of a Childhood, 2007; (children's books) The Nightmares of Geranium Street, 1977, Family Secrets, 1979, Loveletters, 1979, The Masquerade, 1980, The Bad Dreams of a Good Girl, 1981, The Revolution of Mary Leary, 1982, The Flunking of Joshua T. Bates, 1984, How I Saved the World on Purpose, 1985, Lucy Forever and Miss Rosetree, Shrinks, Inc., 1985, Joshua T. Bates In Charge, 1992, The Gift of the Girl Who Couldn't Hear, 1991, Wait for Me, 1992, Amy Dunn Quits School, 1993, Lucy Forever & the Stolen Baby, 1994, The Formerly Great Alexander Family, 1995, Zoe and Columbo, 1995, Warts, 1996, A Goalie, 1996, Joshua Bates in Trouble Again, 1997, Jonah, The Whale, 1997, Ghost Cats, 1999, The End of Amanda, The Good, 2000, Blister, 2002, Trout & Me, 2003, Under the Watson's Porch, 2004, Kiss Me Tomorrow, 2006; editor: Dream Me Home Safely, 2003; co-editor: How We Want to Live: Narratives on Progress, 1996, (with Porter Shreve) Outside the Law: Narratives on Justice, 1997, How We Want to Live: Narratives on Progress, 1998, Tales Out of School: Narratives on Education, 1999, Blister, 2001, Trout & Me, 2002, Under the Watson's Porch, 2003, Kiss Me Tomorrow, 2006. Recipient Jenny Moore award George Washington U., 1978; John Simon Guggenheim award in fiction, 1980, Nat. Endowment Arts fiction award, 1982 Mem. PEN/Faulkner Found. (pres.), Phi Beta Kappa. Home Phone: 202-363-6528; Office Phone: 703-993-1338. Personal E-mail: srshreve@aol.com.

SHRIBMAN, DAVID MARKS, editor; b. Salem, Mass., Mar. 2, 1954; m. Cindy Skrzycki, Sept. 9, 1978; children: Elizabeth, Natalie. AB summa cum laude, Dartmouth Coll., 1976, AM, 1993; LHD, Salem State Coll., 1995. Mem. city staff and Washington bur. Buffalo Evening News, 1977-80; mem. feature and nat. staff The Washington Star, 1980-81; with Washington bur. N.Y. Times, 1981-84; congl. reporter, nat. polit. corr. The Wall St. Jour., 1984-93; chief Washington bur., asst. mng. editor The Boston Globe, 1993—2003; exec. editor, v.p. Pitts. Post-Gazette, 2003—. Bd. visitors Nelson A. Rockefeller Ctr. for Social Scis. Dartmouth Coll.; panelist Washington Week in Rev. PBS; analyst BBC radio; lectr. in field. Author: I Remember My Teacher, 2002. Trustee Dartmouth Coll. James B. Reynolds scholar Jesus Coll.; recipient Pulitzer Prize for beat reporting, 1995. Mem. Phi Beta Kappa. Office: Pittsburgh Post Gazette 34 Blvd of the Allies Pittsburgh PA 15222 Office Phone: 412-263-1890. *

SHRIER, ADAM LOUIS, investment company executive, consultant; b. Warsaw, Mar. 26, 1938; came to U.S., 1943, naturalized, 1949; s. Henry Leon and Mathilda June (Czamanska) S.; m. Diane Kesler, June 10, 1961; children: Jonathan, Lydia, Catherine, David. BS, Columbia U., 1959; MS (Whitney fellow), MIT, 1960; D. Engr. and Applied Sci. NSF fellow, Yale U., 1965; postdoctoral visitor, U. Cambridge, Eng., 1965—66; JD, Fordham U., 1976. With Esso Rsch. & Engring. Co., Florham Park and Linden, NJ, 1963—65, 1966—72, head. environ. scis. rsch. area, 1969—72; coord. pollution abatement activities, tanker dept. Exxon Internat. Co., NYC, 1972—74; project mgr., energy sys. Exxon Enterprises Inc., NYC, 1974—75, gen. mgr. solar energy projects, 1975—77, pres. solar thermal sys. divsn., 1977—81; corp. planning cons., sec. new bus. investments Exxon Corp., NYC, 1981—82; divsn. mgr. supply and transp. Exxon Internat. Co., NYC, 1983—86, mgr. policy and planning, 1986—88; mng. dir. Splty. Tech. Assocs., Washington, 1988—97; pres. Global Devel. Opportunities, LLC, Washington, 1997—. Adj. lectr. chem. engring. Columbia U., NYC, 1967-69, adj. prof. internat. and pub. affairs, 2005—; adj. prof. internat. bus. Am. U., Washington, 2000—; vis. prof. internat. bus. Xiamen U., China, 2006—; industry adv. bd. Internat. Energy Agy., 1984-88, Energy and Environ. Policy Ctr., Harvard U., 1986-88, Internat. Energy Program, Johns Hopkins U., 1987-88; sr. assoc. Global Bus. Forum, 1988—, Cambridge Energy Rsch. Assocs., 1988-2006, Internat. Exec. Svc. Corps, 2001—, Citizens Devel. Corps, 2006—; course leader CWC Energy, Ltd., 2006—. Contbr. articles to profl. jours. Mem. AIChE, Internat. Assn. Energy Econs., Am. Chem. Soc., U.S. Energy Assn., Mid. East Inst., Acad. Internat. Bus., Cosmos Club, Sigma Xi, Tau Beta Pi, Phi Lambda Upsilon. Achievements include patents in field. Office: 4000 Cathedral Ave NW Washington DC 20016-5249 Personal E-mail: alshrier@verizon.net.

SHRINER, THOMAS L., JR., lawyer; b. Lafayette, Ind., Dec. 15, 1947; s. Thomas L. Sr. and Margaret (Kamstra); m. Donna L. Galchick, June 5, 1971; children: Thomas L. III, John H., Joseph P., James A. AB, Ind. U., 1969, JD, 1972. Bar: Wis. 1972, U.S. Dist. Ct. (ea. dist.) Wis. 1973, U.S. Dist. Ct. (we. dist.) Wis. 1977, U.S. Dist. Ct. Colo. 2005, U.S. Ct. Appeals (7th cir.) 1972, U.S. Ct. Appeals (8th cir.) 1989, U.S. Ct. Appeals (fed. cir.) 1990, U.S. Supreme Ct. 1978. Law clk to Hon. John S. Hastings U.S. Ct. Appeals (7th cir.), Chgo., 1972-73; assoc. Foley & Lardner, Milw., 1973-79, ptnr., 1979—. Adj. prof. Law Sch. Marquette U., Milw., 2005—. Chmn. bd. trustees Cath. Charities of Archdiocese of Milw., 2001—02. Fellow Am. Coll. Trial Lawyers; mem. 7th Cir. Bar Assn. (pres. 1993-94), Phi Beta Kappa. Republican. Roman Catholic. Office: Foley & Lardner LLP 777 E Wisconsin Ave Ste 3800 Milwaukee WI 53202-5306 Home Phone: 414-964-6315; Office Phone: 414-297-5601. Business E-Mail: tshriner@foley.com.

SHRINSKY, JASON LEE, lawyer; b. Pitts., June 15, 1937; s. Abe and Sylvia S.; children: Jeffrey, Steven, Stacy. BA, U. Pitts., 1959; JD, George Washington U., 1962. Sr. ptnr. Shrinsky, Weitzman & Eisen, Washington, DC, 1971-87; ptnr., chair Telecom. Dept. Kaye, Scholer LLP, Washington, DC, 1987—, mem. exec. com., 1998. Panelist Paul Kagan Seminars on Radio and TV Acquisitions, Inst. Soc. Internat. Rsch.; atty.-advisor Complaints and Compliance Div. Broadcast Bur. FCC, Washington, 1961-64; bd. dirs. U.S. Com. Sports for Israel, Phila., FCC Bar Assn. Contbr. articles to Radio and Records mag., Broadcast Cable Fin. Jour. Presdl. del. Mt. Sinai transfer ceremonies, 1978; U.S. basketball chmn. 12th, 13th and 14th Maccabiah games, Israel; bd. dirs. Washington Hebrew Congregation, 1978-85, Spanish Broadcasting Sys., Inc.; mem. adv. bd. Bi-Wak Digital Music, Inc. Mem. Internat. Radio and TV Soc., Nat. Broadcaster's Club (past pres.), U. Pitts. Alumni Assn. (bd. dirs.). Jewish. Office: Kaye Scholer LLP McPherson Building 901 15th St NW, Ste 1100 Washington DC 20005-2327 Office Phone: 202-682-3500. E-mail: jshrinsky@kayescholer.com.

SHRIVER, LIONEL (MARGARET ANN SHRIVER), writer; b. Gastonia, NC, May 18, 1957; married. BA, Barnard Coll., 1978; MFA in Fiction Writing, Columbia Univ., 1982. Author: (novels) The Female of the Species, 1987, Checker & the Derailleurs, 1988, The Bleeding Heart, 1990, Game Control, 1995, A Perfectly Good Family, 1996, Double Fault, 1997, We Need to Talk about Kevin, 2003 (Orange Prize for fiction, Great Britain, 2005); contbr. articles Wall St. Jour., Economist, Phila. Enquirer. Mailing: c/o Author Mail Counterpoint Press 387 Park Ave S New York NY 10016

SHRIVER, MARIA OWINGS, news correspondent; b. Chgo., Nov. 6, 1955; d. Robert Sargent and Eunice Mary (Kennedy) S.; m. Arnold Schwarzenegger, Apr. 26, 1986; children: Katherine, Christina, Patrick & Christopher. BA, Georgetown U. Coll. Am. Studies, Washington, 1977. News producer Sta. KYW-TV, 1977-78; producer Sta. WJZ-TV, 1978-80; nat. reporter PM Mag., 1981-83; news reporter CBS News, Los Angeles, 1983-85; news correspondent, co-anchor CBS Morning News, NYC, 1985-86; co-host Sunday Today, NBC, 1987-90; anchor Main Street, NBC, 1987; co-anchor Yesterday, Today, and Tomorrow, NBC, 1989; anchor NBC Nightly News Weekend Edition, 1989-90, Cutting Edge with Maria Shriver, NBC, 1990, First Person with Maria Shriver, NBC, 1990—2004; First Lady of Calif., 2003—. Co-anchor summer olympics, Seoul, Korea, 1988; substitute anchor NBC News at Sunrise, Today, NBC Nightly News with Tom Brokaw; contbg. anchor Dateline, NBC, 1995-2004. Appeared in Last Action Hero, 1993; correspondent TV series The American Parade, 1984; prodr. (TV Series) Portrait of a Legend, 1981; author What's Heaven, 1999, Ten Things I Wish I'd Known Before I Went Into the Real World, 2000, What's Wrong With Timmy, 2001, What's Happening to Grandpa?, 2003, And One More Thing Before You Go..., 2005 (Publishers Weekly bestseller list). Recipient Christopher award for "Fatal Addictions", 1990, Exceptional Merit Media award Nat. Women's Political Caucus, first-place Commendation award Am. Women in Radio and TV, 1991, Emmy nomination, George Peabody Award, 1998. Democrat. Roman Catholic. Office: First Lady Maria Shriver State Capitol Bldg Sacramento CA 95814-4906

SHRIVER, PHILLIP RAYMOND, academic administrator; b. Cleve., Aug. 16, 1922; s. Raymond Scott and Corinna Ruth (Smith) S.; m. Martha Damaris Nye, Apr. 15, 1944; children: Carolyn (Mrs. William Shaul), Susan (Mrs. Lester LaVine), Melinda (Mrs. David Williams), Darcy, Raymond Scott II. BA, Yale U., New Haven, Conn., 1943; MA, Harvard U., Cambridge, Mass., 1946; PhD, Columbia U., NYC, 1954; LittD, U. Cin., 1966; LLD, Heidelberg Coll., Tiffin, Ohio, 1966, Ea. Mich. U., Ypsilanti, 1972, Ohio State U., 1973; DH, McKendree Coll., Lebanon, Ill., 1973; DPS, Albion Coll., Mich., 1974; LHD, Ctrl. State U., Wilberforce, Ohio, 1976, No. Ky. State U., 1980, Miami U., 1984, U. Akron, Ohio, 1988. Mem. faculty Kent (Ohio) State U., 1947-65, prof. Am. history, 1960-65; dean Coll. Arts and Scis., 1963-65; pres. Miami U., Oxford, Ohio, 1965-81, pres. emeritus, prof. Am. history, 1981-99. Pres. Ohio Coll. Assn., 1974-75; chmn. coun. pres.'s Mid-Am. Conf., 1971-77; chmn. Ohio Bicentennial Commn. for NW Ordinance and U.S. Constn., 1985-89, Ohio Tuition Trust Authority, 1989-92; chmn. coun. pres.'s Nat. Assn. State Univs. and Land Grant Colls., 1975-76, mem. exec. coun., 1976-78. Author: The Years of Youth, 1960, George A. Bowman: The Biography of an Educator, 1963, (with D.J. Breen) Ohio's Military Prisons of the Civil War, 1964, A Tour to New Connecticut in 1811: The Narrative of Henry Leavitt Ellsworth, 1985, Miami University: A Personal History, 1998, (with C.E. Wunderlin Jr.) The Documentary Heritage of Ohio, 2000, (with E.F. Puff) The History of Presbyterianism in Oxford, Ohio, 2000. Bd. dirs. Cin. Ctr. Sci. and Industry, 1965-70; trustee Ohio Coll. Library Center, 1968-74; chmn. bd. Univ. Regional Broadcasting, 1975-76, 78-79. Served to lt. (j.g.) USNR, 1943-46, PTO. Decorated Order of Merit (Grand Duchy of Luxembourg); recipient Disting. Acad. Svc. award AAUP, 1965, Gov.'s award 1969, A.K. Morris award, 1974, Ohioana Career medal, 1987, Converse award, 1990, award of merit Am. Assn. for State and Local History, 1993, Bjornson award Ohio Humanities Coun., 2001, John E. Dolibois History prize, 2003, Statesman award Cin. Soc. Assn. Execs., 2004. Mem. Orgn. Am. Historians, Ohio Acad. History (pres. 1983-84, Disting. Svc. award 1991), Archaeol. Inst. Am., Ohio Hist. Soc. (trustee 1982-91, v.p. 1983-84, pres. 1984-86), Ohio Humanities Coun. (Bjornson award 2001), Am. Studies Assn., Mortar Board, Phi Beta Kappa, Omicron Delta Kappa, Phi Alpha Theta, Alpha Kappa Psi, Kappa Delta Pi, Phi Eta Sigma, Phi Kappa Phi, Kappa Kappa Psi, Alpha Lambda Delta, Beta Gamma Sigma, Sigma Delta Pi, Alpha Phi Omega, Delta Upsilon (Disting. Alumni Achievement award 1985) Clubs: Rotary. Presbyterian. Home: 5115 Bonham Rd Oxford OH 45056-1428 Business E-Mail: shrivepr@muohio.edu.

SHRIVER, TIMOTHY PERRY, sports association executive; b. Aug. 29, 1959; s. Robert Sargent Shriver and Eunice Mary Kennedy; m. Linda Potter Shriver; 5 children. BS, Yale U.; M in Religion and Religious Edn., Cath. U.; DEd, U. Conn.; D (hon.), New Eng. Coll, Albertus Magnus Coll., Loyola U. Balt. Tchr. New Haven Pub. Schs., New Haven; supr. Pub. Schs. Social Devel. Project, New Haven, 1987—96; pres. Spl. Olympics, Inc., Washington, DC, 1996—2003, pres., CEO, chmn., 2003—05, chmn., 2005—. Co-prodr.(film): Amistad, 1997, The Loretta Claiborne Story, 2000. Bd. dirs. Compact for Learning and Citizenship, Frank Porter Child Devel. Ctr. at U. N.C.; co-chair Am.'s Promise Task Force on Youth Svcs., 1997—; chmn. Collaborative for Advancement of Social and Emotional Learning at U. Ill., 1994—; bd. dirs. John F. Kennedy Libr. Found., Boston. Recipient Medal of City of Athens, Order de Manuel Amador Guerrero, Pres. of Panama, Conn. Citizen of Yr.; fellow Yale Child Study Ctrs. Sch. Devel. Program, 1984. Mem.: Am. Assn. on Mental Retardation (bd. mem.). Office: Special Olympics 1133 19th St, NW Washington DC 20036 Office Phone: 202-628-3630. Office Fax: 202-824-0200.

SHRIVER, WILLIAM RUSSELL, secondary school educator; b. Garfield Heights, Ohio, Aug. 15, 1950; s. William Washington and Olive Elizabeth (Doutt) S.; m. Karen Ann Wolfe, June 20, 1987; children: Lauren, Matthew. BA, Coll. of Wooster, 1972; MA, U. Chgo., 1973; postgrad., Cleve. State U., 1973-74. Nat. bd. cert. tchr. soc. studies 2002. Summer staff Philmont Scout Ranch, Cimarron, N.Mex., 1968-76; tchr. Mt. Vernon (Ohio) Sr. H.S., 1974—. Tchr. Kenyon Acad. Partnership Kenyon Coll./Mt. Vernon Sr. H.S., 1983—; vice chair state tchr. edn. cert. adv. commn. Ohio Bd. Edn., Columbus, 1991-99, state tchr. cert. standards revision com., 1992-95; bd. examiners Nat. Coun. Accreditation of Tchr. Edn., Washington, 1993-02; mem. Ohio Gov.'s Commn. on Tchg. Success, 2001-03; mem. Ohio Educators Stds. Bd., 2004-2006, chair, 2004-2006. Bd. of session First Presbyn. Ch., Mt. Vernon, 1980-87, 89-95, 2001—2007. Mem. NEA (assembly del. 1983-99), Ohio Edn. Assn. (exec. com. 1987-93, 96-2002), North Ctrl. Ohio Edn. Assn. (pres. 1984-85, exec. sec. 1993-2004), Mt. Vernon Edn. Assn. (pres. 1976-78), Pi Lambda Theta. Avocations: photography, genealogy. Office: Mt Vernon HS 300 Martinsburg Rd Mount Vernon OH 43050-4246 Business E-Mail: wshriver@mt-vernon.k12.oh.us.

SHROPSHIRE, DONALD GRAY, hospital executive; b. Winston-Salem, NC, Aug. 6, 1927; s. John Lee and Bess L. (Shouse) S.; m. Mary Ruth Bodenheimer, Aug. 19, 1950; children: Melanie Shropshire David, John Devin. BS, U. NC, 1950; postgrad Erickson fellow, U. Chgo., 1958-59; LLD (hon.), U. Ariz., Tucson, 1992, Tucson U., 1994. Personnel asst. Nat. Biscuit Co., Atlanta, 1950-52, asst. personnel mgr. Chgo., 1952-54; adminstr. Eastern State Hosp., Lexington, Ky., 1954-62; assoc. dir. U. Md. Hosp., Balt., 1962-67; adminstr. Tucson Med. Ctr., 1967-82, pres., 1982-92, pres. emeritus, 1992—; pres. Tucson Hosps. Med. Edn. Program, 1970-71, sec., 1971-86; pres. So. Ariz. Hosp. Council, 1968-69; bd. dirs. Ariz. Blue Cross, 1967-76, chmn. provider standards com., 1972-76; chmn. bd. Healthways, Inc., 1985-92. Mem. bd. La Posada at Park Centre, Inc., Green Valley, Ariz., 1996-2000, chmn. bd. emeritus, 2000—. Bd. dirs. Health Planning Coun. Tucson, mem. exec. com., 1969-74; chmn. profl. divsn. United Way, Tucson, 1969-70, vice chmn. campaign, 1988, Ariz. Health Facilities Authority, bd. dirs., 1992-2005; chmn. dietary svcs. com., vice chmn., 1988, Md. Hosp. Coun., 1966-67; bd. dirs. Ky. Hosp. Assn., 1961-62, chmn. coun. profl. practice, 1960-61; past pres. Blue Grass Hosp. Coun.; trustee Assn. Western Hosps., 1974-81, pres., 1979-80; mem. accreditation Coun. for Continuing Med. Edn., 1982-87, chair, 1986; bd. govs. Pima C.C., 1970-76, sec., 1973-74, chmn., 1975-76, bd. dirs. Found., 1978-82, Ariz. Bd. Regents, 1982-90, sec., 1983-86, pres., 1987-88; mem. Tucson Airport Authority, 1987—, bd. dirs., 1990-95, pres., 1995; v.p. Tucson Econ. Devel. Corp., 1977-82; founder, dir., bd. dirs. Vol. Hosps. Am., 1977-88, treas., 1979-82; mem. Ariz. Adv. Health Coun. Dirs., 1976-78; bd. dirs. Tucson Tomorrow, 1983-87, Tucson Downtown Devel. Corp., 1988-95, Rincon Inst., 1992-97, Sonoran Inst., 1992-97, Pima County Med. Res. Corps, 2006—; dir. Mus. No. Ariz., 1988-2002, dir. emeritus, 2002—; nat. bd. advisors Eller Coll. Mgmt. U. Ariz., 1990—, mem. Dean's Bd. Coll. Fine Arts, 1992—, chmn., 1992-96, pres. Ariz. Coun. Econ. Edn., 1993-95; vis. panel Sch. Health Adminstrn. and Policy Ariz. State U., 1990-92; bd. dirs. Cmty. Found. So. Ariz., 1996-2001; mem. adv. bd. Steele Meml. Rsch. Ctr., U. Ariz. Coll. Medicine, 1996-2004; mem. student health adv. com. U. Ariz., 1990-07. Named to Hon. Order Ky. Cols.; named Tucson Man of Yr. 1987, Tucson Father of Yr. 1997, Hon. Alumnus, Coll. Nursing, U. Ariz., 1998; recipient Disting. Svc. award Anti-Defamation League B'nai B'rith, 1989, Sticking-Your-Neck-Out award Pima Coun. on Aging, 1991, Il Magnifico award U. Ariz. Coll. Fine Arts, 1996, Humanitarian award Arthritis Found. S.Am., 2001, Crystal Apple Lifetime Achievement award Tucson Metro Edn. Commn., 2004, Pima Med. Found. award, 2005, Humanitarian Achievement award, Ednl. Enrichment Found., 2005; co-recipient Paloma Family Svcs. Commitment to Children award, 2005; Pima CC Dinner honoree, 1986, 92. Mem. Am. Hosp. Assn. (nominating com. 1983-86, trustee 1975-78, ho. dels. 1972-78, chmn. coun. profl. svc. 1973-74, regional adv. bd. 1969-78, chmn. joint com. with NASW 1963-64, Disting. Svc. award 1989), Ariz. Hosp. Assn. (Salisbury award 1982, bd. dirs. 1967-72, pres. 1970-71), Ariz. C. of C. (bd. dirs. 1988-93), Assn. Am. Med. Colls. (mem. assembly 1974-77), Health Care Execs. Study Soc., Tucson C. of C. (bd. dirs. 1968-69), Nat. League for Nursing, Ariz. Town Hall (bd. dirs. 1982-92, chmn. 1990-92, treas. 1985, Circle of Disting. Svc. award 2002), Pima County Acad. Decathlon Assn. (dir. 1983-85), The Rotary Club of Tucson (pres. 1993-94), U. Ariz. Alumni Assn. Coll. Nursing (hon. alumnus 1998), Pi Alpha Alpha (hon.). Baptist/Presbyterian (ch. moderator, chmn. finance com., deacon, ch. sch. supt., trustee, bd. dirs. ch. found.) Office: Tucson Med Ctr 5301 E Grant Rd Tucson AZ 85712-2805 *It seems important to put something back into life - for all we take from it.*

SHROPSHIRE, KENNETH L., law educator; b. LA, 1955; m. Diane Shropshire; children: Teresa, Samuel. BS in econ., Stanford U., 1977; JD, Columbia U., 1980. Bar: 1982. Assoc. Manatt, Phelps, Rothenberg & Tunney, LA, 1980—82; asst. v.p. (in charge of Olympic Boxing competition and facility during 1984 games) LA Olympic Organizing Com., 1982—85; atty. Gen. Bus., Sports and Entertainment Practice, 1982—86; atty. pvt. practice LA; David W. Hauck prof. legal studies Wharton Sch., U. Pa., 1986—, chmn. legal studies dept., 2000—; acting dir. Afro-Am. Studies Program U. Pa., 1997—98. Mem. US Olympic Com. Budget Com.; chair Mayor's Site Selection Com. New Sports Facilities, Phila. Author: (sports column) Africana.com, Agents of Opportunity: Sports Agents and Corruption in Collegiate Sports (Outstanding Acad. Book award, Choice mag.), The Sports Franchise Game: Cities in Pursuit of Sports Franchises, Events, Stadiums, and Arenas, In Black and White: Race and Sports in America (Outstanding Acad. Book award, Choice mag., 1996, Gustavus Myers Ctr. Study Human Rights in N. Am. Outstanding Book award, 1997), Basketball Jones; co-author: The Sound of Philadelphia. Mem.: Sports Lawyers Assn. (pres. 2004), Phila. Sports Congress, ABA (program chmn. section on sports law), Sports Law Assn. (pres. elect 2003—). Office: Wharton Sch Univ Pa 3730 Walnut St Philadelphia PA 19104-6340 Office Phone: 215-898-3017. Business E-Mail: shropshk@wharton.upenn.edu.

SHROPSHIRE, WALTER, JR., biophysicist, pastor; b. Washington, Sept. 4, 1932; s. Walter and Mary Virginia (Anderson) S.; m. Audrey Marie McConkey, June 28, 1958; children: Janet Marie, Susan Lynn, Edward Allen. BS in Physics, George Washington U., 1954, MS in Botany, 1956, PhD in Plant Physiology, 1958; MDiv summa cum laude, Wesley Theol. Sem., 1990; postdoctoral fellow biophysics, Calif. Inst. Tech., 1957-59. Ordained to ministry United Meth. Ch., 1977. Physicist Smithsonian Instn., Washington, 1954—63; asst. dir. Smithsonian Environ. Rsch. Ctr., Washington, 1963-86; Gast prof. U. Freiburg, Germany, 1968-69; biophysicist, dir. Omega Lab., Cabin John, Md., 1986—. Professorial lectr. botany George Washington U., 1960-85; Gast prof. U. Zurich, Switzerland, 1985-86; part-time adj. prof. Practice Min. and Mission Wesley Theol. Sem., 1990—. Editor: Phytochrome, 1972, Joys of Research, 1981, Photomorphogenesis, Vol 16A, 16B, 1983, Photobiology, 1984-85; Contbr. 50 articles to profl. jours. Pastor, Foundry United Meth. Ch., Washington, 1991-2003. Recipient Smithsonian Outstanding Performance award, 1967, Smithsonian Research award, 1968, Merit award Soc. John Wesley, 1997, Templeton Sci. and Religion Course prize, 1999, 2002; NSF grantee, 1960-66. Fellow Explorers Club, Am. Solar Energy Soc. Office: Omega Lab PO Box 189 Cabin John MD 20818-0189 Home Phone: 301-929-1827; Office Phone: 301-929-3150. E-mail: wshrop@erols.com. *The world* *is an incredible place, rich with unexplored and unexplained interconnections between the biological and physical domains. I am fortunate to have been born when science has begun to unravel some of the mysteries of these interconnections and especially fortunate to have had teachers who shared their enthusiasm for learning. I also have benefited from mystical religious experiences of others and my own that enable me to work at the interface between science and religion. My belief is that the pursuit of both subjective and objective knowledge of ourselves and the universe we live in is necessary to enable humanity to develop to its fullest potential. This is an exciting pursuit I hope to continue to participate in a long time.*

SHRUM, JOHN, equal rights officer; b. Flora, Ill., Apr. 13, 1953; s. William E. and Agnes M. Shrum; children: Jason E., Jarred W. Laborer Labor Union Local 1375, Flora, 1976—2003, bus. agt., 1981—83; dir. asst. employee Fed. Emergency Mgmt. Agy., Chgo., 1993—; equal rights officer Ill. Dept. Transp., Effingham, 2003—. Mem. Clay County Bd., 2004—; precinct committeeman, vice chmn. Dem. Party Clay County, Ill., 1978—; trustee Faith Luth. Ch., 1990—. Named to Wall of Tolerance, So. Poverty Law Ctr., Montgomery, Ala., 2004. Home: 641 W North Ave Flora IL 62839 Personal E-mail: jwshrum@hotmail.com.

SHRUM, ROBERT MATTHEW, political strategist, educator, journalist; b. Connellsville, Pa., 1943; BA, Georgetown U.; JD, Harvard U. Prin. speechwriter to Senator George McGovern, 1972; staff dir., chief counsel US Senate Select Com. on Nutrition and Human Needs; press. sec. to Senator Edward M. Kennedy, 1980—84, speechwriter, 1980; polit. advt. prodr., 1985—2005; sr. advisor Gore-Lieberman campaign, 2000, Kerry-Edwards campaign, 2004; sr. fellow, prof. Robert F. Wagner Grad. Sch. Pub. Svc., NYU, 2005—; polit. analyst MSNBC, 2005—. Tchr. Yale U., Boston Coll. Columnist Slate. Mem.: Am. Assn. of Polit. Cons. (Pollie Award 1986, 1994, 1998). Democrat. Office Phone: 212-998-7556.

SHTERN, VICTOR, computer scientist, educator; b. St Petersburg, Russia, Aug. 5, 1933; arrived in US, 1976, naturalized, 1981; s. Yechiel Shtern and Gitta Foynitsky; m. Ludmila Davidovich, June 1, 1956; 1 child, Katerina Simons. MSEE with highest honors, Leningrad Mining Inst., Russia, 1957; PhD in Control Systems, Nat. Aluminium Inst., Leningrad, Russia, 1967; MBA with high honors, Boston U., 1985. Elec. engr. Paper Industry Design Ctr., Leningrad, Russia, 1958—59; sr. scientist Nat. Aluminum Inst., Leningrad, 1959—75; sys. analyst Eye Rsch. Inst. Retina Found., Boston, 1976—78; mgr. software verification Incoterm Inc., Wellesley, 1978—80; software engr. Atex Systems, Bedford, 1980; assoc. prof. Boston U. Met. Coll., 1980—. Adj. assoc. prof. Leningrad Mining Inst., 1967—75; cons. Prime Computer, Framingham, Mass., 1983, Boston U. Sch. Edn., 1984, Boston U. Coll. Comm., 1985, Keane Inc, Charlestown, 1987—89, Mitre Inc, Bedford, Nat. Tech. U., NYC, 1992—2003, Boston U. Corp. Edn. Ctr., Boston, 1992—2000, Oasys Inc, Lexington, 1992, Sanders Inc, Nasua, NH, 1993—93, Siemens Corp., Danvers, 1998, Quantum Corp., Shrewsberry, 1998—99, Torto Wheaton Rsch., Boston, 2003; panelist Nat. Sci. Found., 2000; book rvr. Author: (book) Core C++: A Software Engineering Approach, 2001, Core C++, in Chinese, 2002, Core C++, in Russian, 2003, Core C++, Inzynieria Programowania, in Polish, 2004, Industrial Experience with the Control System "Aluminum", 1971; co-author: Production of Aluminum, 1971; contbr. articles to profl. jours. Mem. adv. bd. Leningrad Chess Club, 1965—72; mem. resettlement com. absorbtion immigrants from USSR Combined Jewish Philanthropies, Boston, 1978—88. Fellow, Nat. Aluminium Inst., Leningrad, 1959—75, Nat. Aeronautics and Space Adminstrn., Am. Soc. Engring. Edn., 1982, 1983; grantee, Wang Labs., 1984. Independent. Jewish. Achievements include development of electrical and pneumatic instrumentation control systems for pulp and paper mills; training courses on advanced Ada and software testing; training seminars on C, C++, Java, object-oriented design; live satellite broadcasts on Java, C, C++, object-oriented programming; undergraduate and graduate courses on Computer Simulation, Software Testing, Ada, C++, Java, Software Design, Design Patterns; process control systems for production of alumina and aluminium; development of on-line menu-driven programs for Patient Database Management; design of remote communication controller for a programmed airline reservation system; design of newspaper classified ad system; computer-based instruction software for high school introductory physical science course; development of interactive computer troubleshooting simulator with a computer-controlled videodisc player; software for studying subjects' reaction to iconic and textual menus; training courses on advance COBOL and SQL programming. Home: 65 Babcock St Apt 6 Brookline MA 02446 Office: Boston U 808 Commonwealth Ave Rm 250 Boston MA 02215 Home Phone: 617-739-1974; Office Phone: 617-358-0003. Personal E-mail: vshtern@bu.edu.

SHTUTMAN, MICHAEL, biologist; b. Moscow, May 12, 1965; s. Solomon Shtutman and Polina Greenberg; m. Elina Levina, Oct. 31, 2003; children: Julia, Benjamin. PhD, Russian Nat. Cancer Rsch. Ctr., Moscow, 1996. Group leader Quark Biotech., Inc., Nes-Ziona, Israel, 2001—03; rsch. assoc. Ordway Rsch. Inst., Albany, NY, 2003—. Mem.: AACR. Office: Ordway Rsch Inst 150 New Scotland Ave Albany NY 12208 Home Phone: 518-785-6407; Office Phone: 518-641-6484.

SHU, CHI-WANG, mathematics professor, researcher; b. Beijing, Jan. 2, 1957; arrived in U.S., 1982, naturalized, 1993; s. Kuang-Yao and Ding-Zhen (Shi) Shu; m. Din-Sui Loh, May 1, 1984; 1 child, Hai-Shuo. BS, U. Sci. and Tech. of China, 1982; PhD, UCLA, 1986. Rsch. assoc. U. Minn., Mpls., 1986—87; asst. prof. applied math. Brown U., Providence, 1987—91, assoc. prof., 1992—96, prof., 1996—, chmn., 1999—2005. Co-chief editor: Jour. Sci. Computing, 2000—; mng. editor Math. of Computation, 2002—, mem. editl. bd. SIAM Jour. Numerical Analysis, 1993—2001, Jour. Computational Math., 1993—, Comm. in Applied Analysis, 1996—, Acta Mathematicae Applicatae Sinica, —, Jour. Dynamics of Continuous Discrete and Impulsive Sys., Series B., Methods of Analysis, 2000—; contbr. Recipient Pub. Svc. Group Achievement award for pioneer work in computational fluid dynamics, NASA, 1992, First Feng Kang prize of Sci. Computing, Chinese Acad. Sci., 1995, Highly Cited Author in Math., Inst. Scientific Info. Web Sci., 2004—, Computational Sci. and Engring. prize, Soc. for Indsl. and Applied Math./Assn. for Computer Machinery, 2007; grantee, NSF, NASA, Army Rsch. Office. Mem.: Soc. for Indsl. and Applied Math., Am. Math. Soc. Achievements include research in numerical solutions for discontinuous problems. Home: 135 Woodbury St Providence RI 02906-3511 Office: Brown U Div Applied Maths 182 George St Providence RI 02912-9056

SHU, GLEN, lawyer; b. Oakland, Calif., Apr. 4, 1969; BA magna cum laude, U. N.Mex., 1992; JD cum laude, U. Houston Law Ctr., 1996. Bar: Tex. 1996, US Dist. Ct. (so. dist. Tex.) 1999, US Dist. Ct. (we. dist. Tex.) 2000. Briefing atty. to Hon. Leslie Brock Yates Tex. 14th Ct. Appeals, 1996—97; ptnr. Baker Hostetler, Houston, 2000—. Chief articles editor: Houston Law Rev., 1995—96. Named a Rising Star, Tex. Super Lawyers mag., 2006. Mem.: Tex. Bar Assn., Houston Young Lawyers Assn., ABA, Houston Bar Assn. Office: Baker Hostetler 1000 Louisiana St Ste 2000 Houston TX 77002 Office Phone: 713-646-1362. E-mail: gshu@bakerlaw.com. *

SHUART, JAMES MARTIN, retired academic administrator; b. College Point, NY, May 9, 1931; s. John and Barbara (Schmidt) Shuart; m. Marjorie Strunk, Apr. 5, 1953; children: James Raymond, William Arthur. BA, Hofstra U., 1953, MA, 1962; PhD, NYU, 1966; D (hon.), L.I. U., 2000. Group rep. Home Life Ins. Co., 1955—57, N.Y. Life Ins. Co., 1957—59; adminstr. Hofstra U., Hempstead, NY, 1959—70, asst. dir. admissions, asst. dean faculty, asst. pres., exec. dean student svcs., assoc. dean liberal arts scis., trustee, 1973—75, v.p. adminstrv. svcs., 1975—76, pres., 1976—2001, pres. emeritus, 2001—. Mem. higher edn. adv. com. NY State Senate, 1979—95; trustee Commn. on Ind. Colls. and Univs., NY State, 1982—89, 1992—95, chmn., 1988—89; mem. Am. Coun. on Edn.'s Labor/Higher Edn. Coun., 1983—88, Am. Coun. on Edn.'s Commn. on Leadership Devel., 1987—89, Peat Marwick Higher Edn. Pres.'s Adv. Com., 1988—96; bd. dirs. European Am. Bank, 1990—2001, Travelers-Solomon, Smith Barney World Funds, 1995—2000; chair Nassau County Property Tax Relief Commn., 1990—92; co-chair NY State Temporary Commn. for LI Tax Relief, 1990—93; mem. nominating com. NASDQ, 2000—06. Dep. county exec. Nassau County, 1973—75, commr. social svcs., 1971—73; commr. LI Regional Planning Bd., 1978—83, chmn., 1981—83, Nassau Bd. Social Svcs., 1971—73; mem. Nassau County Charter Revision Commn., 1993—96; pres., bd. dirs. Health Welfare Coun., Nassau County, 1971—80; bd. dirs. LI Assn., 1986—90, Winthrop U. Hosp., 1979—86; trustee Molloy Coll., 1973—77, LI Power Authority, 2004—06, Uniondale Pub. Libr., NY, 1966—68, LI Hosp. Planning Coun., 1971—75; mem. adv. bd. Adelphi U. Sch. Social Work, 1973—84. Decorated officer Order of Orange Nassau (Netherlands); recipient Founders Day award NYU, 1967, Alumnus of Yr. award Hofstra U., 1973, George M. Estabrook Disting. svc. award Alumni Assn., 1974, Leadership in Govt. award C.W. Post Coll., L.I. U., 1978, Man of Yr. award Hempstead C. of C., 1978, award L.I. Pers. and Guidance Assn., 1977, Lincoln Day award Syosset-Woodbury Rep. Club, 1981, Disting. Leadership award L.I. Bus., 1982, 96, Joseph Giacalone award 1986, Medal of Honor L.I. Assn., 1988, Achievement award Pub. Rels. Profls. of L.I., 1995, Award L.I. Bus. Devel. Coun., 1994, 98, Educator of Yr. award WLIW Ch 21, 1999, Lifetime Achievement award L.I. Assn., 2001, award L.I. Software and Tech. Network, 2001; others; named to L.I. Hall of Fame, 1985, Lifetime Achievement award Met. Lacrosse Found., 2001. Home: 111 Cherry Valley Ave # M35 Garden City NY 11530-1570

SHUAYTO, MARWAN IBRAHIM, neurologist; s. Ibrahim Khalil and Kamila Ibrahim Shuayto; m. Rima Marwan Ibrahim, July 21, 2001; children: Tia Marwan, Yara Marwan. MD, U. of St. Eustatius, Netherlands-Antilles, 1999—2002; MS in Hyperbaric Medicine, Bachelor of Health Sciences, Saba U. Doctor of Medicine Ala., 2006, Mich., 2005. Neurologist USA Neurology, Mobile, Ala., 2003—. Author: (medical journal publications) Administration of Intravenous Tissue Plasminogen Activator (t-PA) in a Pediatric Patient, (medical journal publication) Chronic Opioid Therapy for Intractable Headache: Great Expectations or Dangerous Liaison?, Borderline Personality Disorder and Migraine: Detection, Epidemiology and Therapeutic Response. Recipient Outstanding Vol. Svc., The Nat. Kidney Found., 2004. Mem.: AMA (assoc.), Am. Assn. of Neuromuscular & Electrodiagnostic Medicine (assoc.), Am. Acad. of Neurology (assoc.). Achievements include research in Co-investigator: A Phase I/II Randomized, Placebo-Controlled Trial to Assess the Safety of IV IgG in Patients with West Nile Virus Encephalitis (NIH — DMID). Avocations: music, travel, sports. Office: USA Neurology 3401 Medical Park Dr Bld 3 Ste 205 Mobile AL 36693 Home Phone: 251-662-7663; Office Phone: 251-660-5506.

SHUB, HARVEY ALLEN, surgeon; b. Bklyn., Oct. 28, 1942; s. Irving and Sara (Levin) S.; m. Susan Jayne Smith, Dec. 26, 1970; children: Carolyn, Todd. Student, NYU, 1960-61, 64-65; BS in Zoology, Physics, U. Miami, 1964; MD, U. Rome, Italy, 1971. Diplomate Am. Bd. Colon and Rectal Surgery. Intern Beth Israel Med. Ctr., NYC, 1971-72, resident in surgery, 1972-76; fellow in colon and rectal surgery Muhlenberg Hosp., Plainfield, NJ, 1976-77; practice medicine specializing in colon and rectal surgery Orlando, Fla., 1977—; chmn. dept. surgery Fla. Hosp., 1988-89, dept. colon and rectal surgery, 1999—2001. Pres. med. staff Fla. Hosp., 1992-93; asst. cons. prof. dept. surgery Duke U., 1995; mem. staff Winter Park Meml. Hosp., South Seminole Cmty. Hosp., Fla. Hosp. and Med. Ctr., Orlando Regional Healthcare Sys.; clin. asst. prof. dept. family medicine U. South Fla., Tampa, 1982—; med. dir. Brevard Profl. Network, 2002-2004. Consulting editor Jour. Fla. Med. Assn.; contbr. articles to profl. jours. Chmn. pub. edn. com. Am. Cancer Soc. Orange County, 1982—86. Capt. M.C., USAR, 1971-77. Recipient Physician's Recognition awards AMA. Fellow ACS, Am. Soc. Colon and Rectal Surgeons, Internat. Coll. Surgeons, Southeastern Surg. Congress, Internat. Soc. Univ. Colon and Rectal Surgeons; mem. AMA, So. Med. Assn., Fla. Med. Assn. (sect. splty. medicine), Orange County Med. Assn., Piedmont Soc. Colon and Rectal Surgeons (pres. elect 1997, pres. 1998-2000), Orange County Ostomy Assn. (med. adviser), Fla. Soc. Colon and Rectal Surgeons (sec.-treas. 1980-82, pres. 1983-84, sec.-treas. 1986-98, pres. 1998-2000, treas. 2005—), Am. Soc. Gastrointestinal Endoscopy, Am. Soc. Laser Medicine and Surgery, Soc. Am. Gastrointestinal Endoscopic Surgeons. Office: 308 Groveland St Orlando FL 32804-4019 Home: 5252 Vista Club Run Sanford FL 32771-7153 Office Phone: 407-894-0481. Personal E-mail: tushmd4@aol.com.

SHUBB, WILLIAM BARNET, judge; b. Oakland, Calif., May 28, 1938; s. Ben and Nellie Bernice (Fruechtenicht) S.; m. Sandra Ann Talarico, July 29, 1962; children: Alisa Marie, Carissa Ann, Victoria Ann. AB, U. Calif., Berkeley, 1960, JD, 1963. Bar: Calif., 1964, U.S. Ct. Internat. Trade 1981, U.S. Customs Ct. 1980, U.S. Ct. Appeals (9th cir.) 1964, U.S. Supreme Ct. 1972. Law clk. U.S. Dist. Ct., Sacramento, 1963-65; asst. U.S. atty., Sacramento, 1965-71; chief asst. U.S. atty. (ea. dist.) Calif., 1971-74; assoc. Diepenbrock, Wulff, Plant & Hannegan, Sacramento, 1974-77, ptnr., 1977-80, 81-90; U.S. atty. Eastern Dist. Calif., 1980-81; judge U.S. Dist. Ct. (ea. dist.) Calif., 1990—, chief judge, 1996-2003; chmn. com. drafting of local criminal rules U.S. Dist. Ct. (ea. dist.) Calif., 1974, mem. speedy trial planning com., 1974-80; lawyer rep. 9th Cir. U.S. Jud. Conf., 1975-78; mem. faculty Fed. Practice Inst., 1978-80; instr. McGeorge Sch. Law, U. Pacific, 1964-66. Mem. ABA, Fed. Bar Assn. (pres. Sacramento chpt. 1977), Calif. Bar Assn., Assn. Def. Counsel, Am. Bd. Trial Advs., Sacramento County Bar Coun., Sacramento Rotary Club.

SHUBERT, JOSEPH FRANCIS, librarian; b. Buffalo, Sept. 17, 1928; s. Joseph Francis and Lena M. (Kohn) Shubert; m. Dorothy Jean Whearty, Feb. 5, 1955 (div. Feb. 1980); children: Julia Ellen, Susan, Alan Joseph. BS, State U. Tchrs. Coll., Geneseo, NY, 1951; MA, U. Denver, 1957. Reference and ext. libr. Nev. State Libr., Carson City, 1951-57, libr. cons., 1957-59, state libr., 1959-61; asst. dir. internat. rels. office ALA, 1962-66; state libr. Ohio, 1966-77; sec., treas. chief officer state Libr. Agys. N.Y. State Edn. Dept., 1973-76, chmn., 1976-78, state libr., asst. commr. librs., 1977-96, state libr. emeritus, 1996—; mem. adv. coun. U.S. Pub. Printer, 1974-77; mem. adv. com. White House Conf. Libr. and Info. Svcs., 1977-79; chmn. steering com. survey state libr. agys. U.S. Nat. Ctr. Edn. Stats., 1992—2003. Trustee Ohio Coll. Libr. Ctr., 1976—78; Disting. Alumnus lectr. U. Denver, 1979; mem. adv. com. Ctr. for Book Libr. of Congress, 1979—82, mem. network adv. coun., 1981—96; mem. adv. coun. Sch. Libr. and Info. Sci., Pratt Inst., 1980—2000; bd. dirs. N.E. Document Conservation Ctr., 1980—82, treas., 1986—89; mem. design task force White House Conf. Libr. and Info. Svcs., 1985; chmn. chief officers State Librs. in N.E., 1987—89; bd. dirs. Capital Dist. Regional Info. Svc. Network State U. Albany, NY, 1994—97. Editor: The Bookmark, 1987—96; contbr. articles to periodicals. Dir. Friends N.Y. State Libr., Inc., 1998—; mem. adv. com. U. Wis. Inst. Edn., Federally Funded Literacy Program, 1992—94; co-chair 50th anniversary com. Coll. Geneseo, 2001. Named Disting. Alumnus, SUNY-Geneseo, 1985; named to Alumni Honor Roll, 1997; recipient Exceptional Achievement award, ALA Assn. Specialized and Coop. Libr. Agy. Assn., 1985, Disting. Pub. Svc. award, SUNY-Albany, Nelson A. Rockefeller Coll. Pub. Affairs and Policy, 1987, Hall of Fame award, Ohio Libr. Assn., 1991, Velma K. Moore award, N.Y. State Assn. Libr. Bds., 1996, Minerva award, SUNY-Geneseo & Friends of Milne Libr., 2006. Mem.: ALA (grass roots adv. 1996), Chief Officers State Libr. Agys. (chmn. 1977—78), N.Y. Libr. Assn. (hon. chair capital campaign 1999—2000, Outstanding Svc. award 1996), Meml. Libr. Assn., North Collins Libr. Assn., Nev. Libr. Assn. (pres.), Assn. Specialized and Coop. Lit. Agys. (pres. 1988—89), Task Force Pub. Libr. Stats. (mem. adv. com. 1990—96, chair steering com. NCES Survey State Libr. Agys. 1993—2003), Nat. Commn. Librs. and Info. Svcs., Nat. Ctr. Ednl. Stats., Nev. Congress Parents and Tchrs., Torch Club Albany. Roman Catholic. Home: 494 Madison Ave Albany NY 12208-3601 also: PO Box 1064 36 Lake Dr South Dennis MA 02660-2838 Home Phone: 518-598-0965. Business E-Mail: jshubert@nycap.rr.com, shubert@nycap.rr.com.

SHUBIK, MARTIN, economics professor; b. NYC, Mar. 24, 1926; s. Joseph Louis and Sara S.; m. Julia Kahn, Aug. 11, 1970; 1 child, Claire Louise. BA, U. Toronto, 1947, MA, 1949; PhD, Princeton U., 1953. Rsch. asst. Princeton U., 1950—53, rsch. assoc., 1953-55; fellow Ctr. for Advanced Study in Behavioral Scis., Palo Alto, Calif., 1955-56; cons. mgmt. consultation svcs. Gen. Electric Co., 1956-60; adj. rsch. prof. Pa. State U., 1957-59; vis. prof. econs. Yale U., New Haven, 1960-61, prof. econs. of orgn., dept. adminstrv. sci., 1963-75, Seymour H. Knox prof. math. instl. econs., 1975—. Bd. dirs. Equity Strategies, 1965-90, Anglo Energy, 1990-91, Third Avenue Funds, 1990-, Perini Corp., 2004-06; mem. staff T.J. Watson Rsch. Labs., IBM Corp., 1961-63; vis. prof. Escuela de Estudios Económicos U. Chile, Santiago, 1965, Inst. Advanced Studies, Vienna, Austria, 1968, 70, U. Melbourne, Australia, 1973; cons. Rand Corp., Santa Monica, Calif., 1963; dir. Cowles Found. for Rsch. In Econs., Yale U., 1973-76; external faculty Santa Fe Inst., 1994—, sci. bd. 1996—; cons. in field. Author or co-author: numerous books, including The War Game, 1979, (with G. Brewer) The Aggressive Conservative Investor, 1979, 2d edit., 2005, (with M.J. Whitman) Market Structure and Behavior, 1980, (with R.E. Levitan) Game Theory in the Social Sciences, vol. 1, 1982, vol. 2, 1984, The Theory of Money and Financial Institutions, vols. 1 and 2, 1999; mem. editorial bd. Conflict Resolution; mem. editl. adv. bd. Internat. Studies Series; assoc. editor Mgmt. Sci, 1965-81; contbr. articles to profl. jours. Served to lt. Royal Can. Navy. Recipient Lanchester prize, 1983, Koopman prize mil. ops. rsch., 1996; named hon. prof. U. Vienna Fellow Econometric Soc., World Acad. Arts and Scis.; mem. Am. Acad. Arts and Scis., Conn. Acad. Arts and Scis. Home: 18 Rockland Park Branford CT 06405 Office: PO Box 208281 30 Hillhouse Ave New Haven CT 06520-8281 Office Phone: 203-432-3694. Business E-Mail: martin.shubik@yale.edu.

SHUBIN, JOANNA, science educator; b. LI City, NY, June 24, 1945; d. Vincent and Theresa Spampanato; m. Jonathan Simon Shubin, Mar. 30, 1980; 1 child, David Jonathan. BA, Queens Coll., 1967, MS, 1972. Cert. Teacher N-6 1973, Social Studies Teacher 1972, Biological Science Teacher 1991, Teacher Nat. Sci. Tchrs. Assn., 1987. Sci. tchr. St. Stanislaus Sch., Bklyn., 1969—71, Most Precious Blood Sch., LI City, 1971—81, Garden Sch., Jackson Heights, NY, 1981—85, Sci. Mus. LI, Manhasset, NY, 1985—86, Garden Sch., 1986—90, Great Neck South Mid. Sch., NY, 1992, Roslyn Mid. Sch., Roslyn, NY, 1992—. Contbr. articles to jours. Sci. tchr. Schneider Children's Hosp., Queens. Recipient Educator of Month, Hofstra U. and News 12, 2001, Excellence in Tchg., Sci. Tchrs. Assn. of NY State, 2002. Mem.: LI Sci. Edn. Leadership Assn. Inc., Astronomical Soc. of the Pacific, Sci. Tchrs. Assn. NY State, Nat. Sci. Tchrs. Assn. Avocations: astronomy, travel, reading. Home: 427 Bellmore Rd East Meadow NY 11554 Office: Roslyn Mid Sch Locust Lane Roslyn NY 11576

SHUCHART, EUGENE JOSEPH, retired accountant; b. New Freedom, Pa., May 22, 1924; s. Albert Alan Shuchart and Victoria Ann Ryer-Shuchart; m. Angelita Rodriguez Shuchart, Nov. 24, 1956; children: Eugene Joseph Jr., Michael Albert, Larry Francis, Lisa Marie, David Alan. BS in Econs., Villanova U., Pa., 1950; MBA, U. Pa., 1951. CPA Dept. Energy State Va., Richmond, Va., 1956—80, ret., 1980. With US Gen. Acctg. Office, 1951—68; assoc. prof. George Washington U., 1968—79; commr. Fed. Power Commn.,/Fed. Energy Regulatory Commn., 1968—80; instr. Edison Coll., 1981—97. With US Army, 1943—46, Pacific. Decorated Purple Heart U.S. Army. Mem.: Nat. Assn. Ret. Fed. Employees (Disting. Career Svc. award 1980), Disabled Am. Vets. (treas. 1996—97). Avocations: organ, piano, swimming, walking. Personal E-mail: eshuchart@comcast.net.

SHUCK, EDWIN HAYWOOD, III, surgeon; b. Chattanooga, 1948; MD, Washington U., St. Louis, 1973. Diplomate Am. Bd. Surgery, Am. Bd. Colon and Rectal Surgery. Intern Tulane U. Hosps., New Orleans, 1973-74, resident, 1974-78; fellow in colon and rectal surgery Carle Clinic, Urbana, Ill., 1978-79; priviliges Meml. Hosp., Chattanooga, Tenn.; pvt. practice Colon & Rectal Surg. Assocs. Asst. prof. clin. surgery U. Tenn. Fellow ACS, Am. Soc. Colon and Rectal Surgery. Office: Colon & Rectal Surg 2341 McCallie Ave #305 Plz Chattanooga TN 37404

SHUCK, ROBERT F., financial executive; s. Robert F. II and Gertrude (Lehr) S.; m. Page Downe, May 30, 1969; children: Robert F. IV, Hollister A. BA in Acctg. with honors, S.E. Mo. Coll., 1959; MBA, Northwestern U., 1961. CPA, Ill.; cert. fin. planner. With Raymond James Fin., Inc., St. Petersburg, Fla., 1969—, vice chmn., 1991—. Bd. dirs. RJ Comm., Inc. Bd. dirs. Southeast Mo. Univ. Found.; trustee All Children's Hosp.; mem. long range devel. com. Fla. Coun. Econ. Edn.; mem. policy bd. Tampa Bay Partnership for Regional Econ. Devel.; mem. devel. found. St. Petersburg Jr. Coll.; stewardship chmn. Our Savior Luth. Ch., St. Petersburg. Mem. Securities Industry Assn. (sales and mktg. com.), Internat. Assn. for Fin. Planning (past bd. dirs.), Nat. Endowment for Fin. Edn. (trustee, mem. exec. com.). Office: Raymond James Fin 880 Carillon Pkwy Saint Petersburg FL 33716-1100 Office Phone: 727-567-5300.

SHUE, ELISABETH, actress; b. Wilmington, Del., Oct. 6, 1963; m. Davis Guggenheim, 1994; children: William, Stella Street, Agnes Charles Student, Wellesley Coll.; BA in Govt., Harvard U., 2000; studied with Sylvie Leigh, Showcase Theater. Appeared in Broadway plays including Some Americans Abroad, Birth and After Birth; Actor (films) The Karate Kid, 1984 (Young Artist award 1984), Link, 1986, Adventures in Babysitting, 1987, Cocktail, 1988, Body Wars, 1989, Back to the Future Part II, 1989, Back to the Future Part III, 1990, Soapdish, 1991, The Marrying Man, 1991, Twenty Bucks, 1993, Heart and Souls, 1993, Radio Inside, 1994, Blind Justice, 1994, The Underneath, 1995, Leaving Las Vegas, 1995 (Oscar nominee for Best Actress), The Trigger Effect, 1996, The Saint, 1996, Palmetto, 1997, Deconstructing Harry, 1997, Cousin Bette, 1997, Molly, 1998, Hollow Man, 2000, Tuck Everlasting, 2002, Leo, 2002, Mysterious Skin, 2004, Hide and Seek, 2005, Dreamer: Inspired by a True Story, 2005; (TV movies) Charles and Diana, Double Switch, 1987, Hale the Hero, 1992, Blind Justice; (TV series) Call to Glory, 1984, Amy & Isabelle, 2001. Office: Creative Arts Agy 9830 Wilshire Blvd Beverly Hills CA 90212-1804

SHUER, LAWRENCE MENDEL, neurosurgery educator; b. Toledo, Apr. 12, 1954; s. Bernard Benjamin and Estelle Rose (Drukker) S.; m. Paula Ann Elliott, Sept. 4, 1976; children: Jenna, Tammy, Nichole. BA with high distinction, U. Mich., 1975, MD cum laude, 1978. Diplomate Am. Bd. Neurol. Surgery, Nat. Bd. Med. Examiners. Fellow in neurology Inst. Neurology, London, 1979; intern in surgery Stanford (Calif.) U. Sch. Medicine, 1978-79, resident in neuropathology, 1980, resident in neurosurgery, 1980-84, clin. asst. prof. surgery and neurosurgery, 1984-90, assoc. prof., 1990—2002, acting chmn. dept. neurosurgery, 1992-95, 96—, assoc. dean, 1996—, chief of staff Stanford Health Sys., 1996—; chief of staff Stanford U. Hosp. and Clinics, 1999—, prof., 2002—. Numerous presentations in field. Contbr. articles and abstracts to med. jours., chpts. to books.

Recipient Kaiser tchr. award Stanford U., 1993; James B. Angell scholar. Mem. AMA, Am. Assn. Neurol. Surgeons, Congress Neurol. Surgeons, Western Neurosurg. Soc., Calif. Assn. Neurol. Surgeons (bd. dirs., treas. 1995—98, 2nd v.p. 1998-99, 1st v.p. 1999-2000, pres.-elect 2000-01, pres. 2002-03), Calif. Med. Assn., Am. Heart Assn. (fellow stroke coun.), Santa Clara County Med. Assn., San Francisco Neurol. Soc., Alpha Omega Alpha. Conservative. Jewish. Avocations: skiing, swimming, travel. Office: Stanford U Med Ctr 300 Pasteur Dr R229 Palo Alto CA 94304-5327 Home Phone: 650-222-5433; Office Phone: 650-723-6093. Business E-Mail: lshuer@stanford.edu.

SHUFELDT, ROBERT CHARLES, bank executive; b. Natick, Mass., May 6, 1950; s. Robert and Barbara Ann (Wasson) S.; m. Margaret Clayton Duval; children: Charles Frederic, Robert Burch. BA in History, Washington and Lee U., Lexington, Va., 1972; MA in Internat. Rels., Johns Hopkins U., Balt., 1976. Mgr. Brown Bros. Harriman & Co., NYC, 1976-84; sr. v.p., mng. dir. SunTrust Corp. fin. divsn. SunTrust Banks, Inc., Atlanta, 1984-90, exec. v.p., head corp. banking Trust Co. Bank subs., 1991, corp. exec. v.p. corp. and investment banking line of bus. Bd. dirs. Young Audiences of Atlanta, 1984, Atlanta Ballet; mem. corp. and found. adv. bd. Washington and Lee U. Republican. Episcopalian. Avocations: flying, golf. Office: SunTrust Banks Inc PO Box 4418 Atlanta GA 30302-4418 Office Phone: 404-588-7711. Office Fax: 404-827-6173. *

SHUFF, RONALD F., lawyer; BA in History, Kenyon Coll., Gambier, Ohio, 1974; JD, Capital U., Columbus, Ohio, 1977; MS, MIT Sloan Sch. Atty. Columbus & So. Electric Co., 1977-81; sec., gen. counsel Accuray Corp., Columbus, 1981—88; gen. counsel, asst. sec. Duriron Co., 1988—89, gen. counsel, sec., 1989—90; v.p., sec., gen. counsel Durco Internat. (formerly Duriron Co.), 1990—97, Flowserve Corp., Irving, Tex., 1997—. Sloan fellow, MIT, 1987-88. Office: Flowserve 5215 N OConnor Blvd Ste 2300 Irving TX 75039

SHUFORD, JACOB L., academic administrator, career military officer; BA, Univ. SC, 1974; MPA, Harvard Univ.; M in nat. security studies & strategy, Naval War Coll.; Olmsted Scholar, Paris Inst. Pol. Sci., France. Commd. ensign USN, advanced through grades to rear adm.; served ops. dept. USS Blakely (FF 1072); ops. & plans officer Comdr. Naval Forces Korea; ops. officer USS Deyo (DD 989), USS Mahan (DDG 42); commdg. officer USS Aries (PHM 5); mem. staff of CNO, Washington; spl. asst., personal aide to Sec. Office of Sec. of the Navy, Washington; commdg. officer USS Rodney M. Davis (FFG 60), USS Gettysburg (CG 64); air warfare comdr. USS Enterprise Battle Group, USS Carl Vinson & USS Enterprise Battle Groups, Operation Desert Fox; dir. Surface Combatant Force Level Study, Washington; chief of staff Roles & Missions organization, Washington; div. chief Force Structure, Resources & Assessment Directorate, Washington; dir. Senate liaison Office of Legis. Affairs, Washington; asst. comdr. Navy Personnel Command; commdg. officer Cruiser Destroyer Group Three, 2003—04; pres. Naval War Coll., Newport, RI, 2004—. Decorated Def. Superior Svc. medal, Legion of Merit (4 awards), Bronze Star, Meritorious Svc. medal (3 awards), Navy Commendation medal (3 awards), Navy Achievement medal. Office: Naval War College Office of President 686 Cushing Rd Newport RI 02841

SHUFTAN, ROBERT L., lawyer; b. Chgo., May 3, 1954; BA summa cum laude with high distinction, U. Ill., 1976; JD, Harvard U., 1979. Bar: Ill. 1979, U.S.D.C. (no. dist.) Ill., 1979, U.S.D.C., (no. dist.,trial bar) Ill., 1983, U.S.D.C., (ea. dist.) Wis., 1988, US Ct. Appeals(7th cir.), 1985, US Ct. Appeals(9th cir), 1991, US Ct. Appeals(5th & 11th cirs), 1993, US Ct. Appeals(3th cir), 1994, US Dist. Ct. (ctrl. dist.) Ill., 2000, US Dist. Ct. (no. dist.) Ind., 2000, Ill. Supreme Ct., 1979, US Supreme Ct., 1989. Lawyer Wildman, Harrold, Allen & Dixon, Chgo.; mng. ptnr. Wildman Harrold, Chgo. Mem. ABA (litig. and natural resources, energy & environ. law sect.), Phi Beta Kappa. Office: Wildman Harrold 225 W Wacker Dr Ste 3000 Chicago IL 60606 Office Phone: 312-301-2000, 312-201-2505. Office Fax: 312-201-2555. Business E-Mail: shuftan@wildmanharrold.com.

SHUGAN, STEVEN MARK, finance educator; b. Chgo., Apr. 21, 1952; s. David Lester and Charlotte Rose Shugan; m. Irene H. Ginter, Dec. 16, 1973; children: Adam Joshua, Elliot Hillel, Ross Isaac, Henry Andrew. BS in Chemistry, So. Ill. U., 1973, MBA, 1974; PhD in Managerial Econs. and Decision Scis., Northwestern U., 1978. Lectr. Grad Sch. Mgmt., Northwestern U., Evanston, Ill., 1975—76; asst. prof. bus. adminstrn. Grad Sch. Mgmt., U. Rochester, NY, 1977—79; asst. prof. mktg. Grad. Sch. Bus., U. Chgo., 1979—82, assoc. prof., 1982—87, prof., 1987—92; Russ Berrie eminent scholar, prof. mktg. U. Fla., Gainesville, 1991—. Chmn., organizer sessions numerous nat. confs., 1979—; cons. various cos., 1976—; chmn. Mktg. Sci. Conf., 1963—96. Editor-in-chief Mktg. Sci., 2002. Fellow Northwestern U., 1978. Mem.: Am. Statis. Assn., Inst. Mgmt. Scis. (pres. coll. mktg.), Assn. Consumer Rsch., Ops. Rsch. Soc. Am., Am. Mktg. Assn. Office: Univ Fla 209 Bryan Hall Gainesville FL 32611-2014 Business E-Mail: sms@ufl.edu.

SHUGART, HOWARD ALAN, physicist, researcher; b. Orange, Calif., Sept. 21, 1931; s. Howard Ancil and Bertha Elizabeth (Henderson) S.; m. Elizabeth L. Hanson, Feb. 6, 1971. BS, Calif. Inst. Tech., 1953; MA, U. Calif., Berkeley, 1955, PhD, 1957. Tchg. asst. physics U. Calif., Berkeley, 1953-56, assoc., 1957, lectr., 1957-58, acting asst. prof., 1958-59, asst. prof., 1959-63, assoc. prof., 1963-67, prof., 1967-93, prof. emeritus, 1993—, vice chmn., 1968—70, 1979—87, 1989—2001, acting chmn., 1979—81, 1983—84, 1987. Cons. Convair divsn. Gen. Dynamics Corp., 1960-61; mem. com. nuc. constants NRC, 1960-63; atomic beam group leader Lawrence Berkeley (Calif.) Nat. Lab., 1965-79, guest rschr., 1999—. Fellow Am. Phys. Soc. (acting sec. Pacific Coast 1961-64, exec. com. divsn. electron and atomic physics 1972-74), Nat. Speleological Soc. (gov. 1954-56); mem. Sigma Xi. Office: U Calif Dept Physics Berkeley CA 94720-7300

SHUGART, JILL, academic administrator; b. Dallas, July 15, 1940; d. Claude Ernest and Allie Merle (Hamilton) S. BA, Baylor U., 1962; MA, Tex. Woman's U., 1972, PhD, 1980. Middle sch. English tchr. Garland (Tex.) Ind. Sch. Dist., 1962-63, high sch. social studies tchr., 1963-76, high sch. asst. prin., 1976-79, dir. communications, 1979-82, asst. supt., 1982-85, supt., 1985—99, ret., 1999—; exec. dir. Region X Edn. Svc. Ctr., 2004—07. Mem. legis. coun. U. Interscholastic League, Tex., 1989-99; chmn. Dist. III music com., Tex., 1989-99; adj. prof. Tex. Women's U., Denton, 1983; chmn. Region X ESC Adv. Coun., rep. to commr.'s supt.'s com., 1993-95; cons. Richardson and Carrollton-Farmers Br. Sch. Dists., 2000-04; coord. Region 10 ESC Supt.'s Acad., 2000-04, mem. commrs. cabinet regional svcs., 2004-07. Gen. chmn. Boy Scouts Am. Scouting Night, Dallas, 1988-89; chmn. City of Garland Comty. Action Com., 1995-99; sec. Tex. Sch. Alliance, 1995-96, chmn., 1998-99; life mem. Tex. and nat. PTA; pres. Garland br. Am. Heart Assn., 1990-91; co-chmn. sustaining dr. Garland YMCA, 1995-96; mem. Adv. Com. to Gov. and State Legisture, 1998; mem. steering com. Garland Econ. Devel. Partnership, 1994-99, Tex. Fast Growth Sch. Coalition; chair Tex. Sch. Alliance, 1998—. Recipient Lamar award for excellence Masons, Award of Distinction, Tex. Ret. Tchrs. Assn.; named Top 100 Educators to Watch, Executive Educator mag., 1985, Finalist as Outstanding Tex. Sch. Supt., 1990, Woman of Distinction, Soroptomist Club, Disting. Alumnus, Garland H.S., 2005; Paul Harris fellow. Mem. Quality Tex. Bd. Examiners, Garland Edn. Found. (bd. dirs. 1999—), Baylor Med. Ctr. Garland (bd. dirs. 2001—). Baptist. Avocations: travel, lake activities. Home: 345 Winding Show Kemp TX 75143 Personal E-mail: jillshugart@aol.com.

SHUGER, DEBORA KULLER, humanities educator; m. Scott Shuger (dec. 2002); 1 child, Dale. PhD, Stanford Univ., 1983. Prof., English UCLA. Co-editor: Religion and Culture in Renaissance England, 1997; author: Sacred Rhetoric, 1988, Habits of Thought in the English Renaissance, 1990, The Renaissance Bible, 1994, Political Theologies in Shakespeare's England, 2001, Censorship and Cultural Sensibility, 2006. Grantee Guggenheim Fellowship, Rockefeller Found. Fellowship. Fellow: Am. Acad. Arts & Scis. Office: Humanities Bldg 297 UCLA PO Box 951417 Los Angeles CA 90095-1417 Office Phone: 310-825-3897. Business E-Mail: shuger@humnet.ucla.edu. *

SHUGHART, WILLIAM FRANKLIN, II, economics professor, consultant; b. Harrisburg, Pa., Dec. 3, 1947; s. William Franklin and Mary Lucille Shughart; m. Hilary Celia Kauffman, Dec. 29, 1986; children: William Franklin III, Frank Jefferson. BA, Tex. A&M U., College Station, 1969, MS, 1970, PhD, 1978. Economist FTC, Washington, 1978—83; asst. prof. econs. Clemson (SC) U., 1984—85; assoc. prof. econs. George Mason U., Fairfax, Va., 1985—88; prof. econs. U. Miss., University, 1988—. Pres. Oxford (Miss.) Economics, Inc., 2004—. Author: Antitrust Policy and Interest-Group Politics, 1990, The Organization of Industry, 1990, Modern Managerial Economics, 1994, The Organization of Industry, 2nd ed., 1997, The Political Economy of the New Deal, 1998; editor: The Causes and Consequences of Antitrust, 1995, Taxing Choice, 1997, The Elgar Companion to Public Choice, 2001, The Economics of Budget Deficits, 2002, Policy Challenges and Political Responses, 2005. Petty officer 3rd class USN, 1971—74. Named F. A. P. Barnard Disting. prof., U. Miss., 1998—; recipient Sir Anthony Fisher Internat. Meml. award, Atlas Econ. Rsch. Found., 1998. Mem.: Pub. Choice Soc., Western Econ. Assn., Am. Econ. Assn., So. Econ. Assn. (trustee 1996—98), Am. Political Sci. Assn. (assoc.). Home: 21 County Rd 3024 Oxford MS 38655 Office: Univ Miss Dept of Economics University MS 38677-1848 Home Phone: 662-236-2620; Office Phone: 662-915-7579. Office Fax: 662-915-6943. Personal E-mail: wfs2@aggienetwork.com. Business E-Mail: shughart@olemiss.edu.

SHUHAN, JANICE-LYNN NAZZIOLA, secondary school educator; b. Passaic, NJ, Sept. 11, 1959; d. Gabriel Anthony and Camille Mary (Monisera) Nazziola. BS in Math., Montclair State U., 1981, MA in Adminstrn. and Supervision, 1999. Cert. tchr. Substitute tchr. Belleville (N.J.) High Sch., 1977-81, long-term substitute tchr., 1981—, secondary math. tchr., 1986—. Sch. choreographer Belleville Mid. and High Schs., 1978—; dir. mus. Belleville H.S., 1991—; performer nat. tour U.S. Coast, 1979-80; performer off-Broadway and dinner theatres, N.Y. and N.J., 1977-86; presenter N.J. Sch. Bds. Curriculum Fair at Conv. Hall, 1989, 90, 91, 92; profl. performer, actress, singer, dancer. Author (poem): Selections of the Heart and Soul, 2000, External Songs, 2000, Between Darkness and Light, 2000; co-author: The Peace to Come, 2001, Secret Hiding Places, 2001, 2001, Math Essentials, Selected Strategies of Teaching Math Essentials, 1992, 93; contbr. articles to profl. jours.; appeared in motion pictures Other People's Money, A Fire in the Dark, Carlito's Way, and nat. comms. Campaign mgr. Belleville B.O.E., 1989; judge Bell/Nutley Columbus Day Parade Bella Signorina, 1988-91; dance class instructor Nutley Italian Am. Club, 1988; bd. dirs. Cranford Dramatic Club Theatre, mem. bd. govs. Recipient Steven's Leadership award Steven's Inst., Hoboken, N.J., 1990, Outstanding Math Nat. Educator award Tandy Corp., 1991, Alumni Citation, Montclair State U., 2003; named Mrs. West Paterson N.J. America, Essex County Tchr. of Yr. 1999-00. Mem. NEA, ASCD, Nat. Coun. Tchrs. Math., Assn. Math. Tchrs. N.J., Belleville Edn. Assn., N.J. Edn. Assn. Republican. Roman Catholic. Avocations: acting, singing, dance, poetry. Office: Belleville High Sch 100 Passaic Ave Belleville NJ 07109-1898 E-mail: janicelyn1@aol.com.

SHUHLER, PHYLLIS MARIE, physician; b. Sellersville, Pa., Sept. 25, 1947; d. Raymond Harold and Catherine Cecilia (Virus) S.; m. John Howard Schwarz, Sept. 17, 1983; 1 child, Luke Alexander. BS in Chemistry, Chestnut Hill Coll., 1971; MD, Mich. State U., 1976; diploma of Tropical Medicine and Hygiene, U. London, 1980. Diplomate Am. Bd. Family Medicine. With Soc. Cath. Med. Missionaries, Phila., 1966-82; ward clk., nursing asst. Holy Family Hosp., Atlanta, 1971-72; resident in family practice Somerset Family Med. Residency Program, Somerville, NJ, 1976-79; physician East Coast Migrant Health Project, Newton Grove, NC, 1980; physician, missionary SCMM, Diocese of Sunyani, Berekum, Ghana, 1980-81; emergency rm. physician Northeast Emergency Med. Assn., Quakertown, Pa., 1981-82; founder, physician Family Health Care Ctr., Inc., Pennsburg, Pa., 1982-90; physician Lifequest Med. Group, Pennsburg, 1990-93; pvt. practice Pennsburg, 1993-99; physician Tri-Valley Primary Care Group, 1999—. Fellow Royal Soc. Tropical Medicine and Hygiene; mem. Am. Acad. Family Practice, Am. Bd. Family Practice, Am. Med. Women Assn. Pa. Acad. Family Practice, Lehigh Valley Women Med. Assn. Roman Catholic. Avocations: guitar, reading, bicycling, hiking. Office: 101 W 7th St Ste 2C Pennsburg PA 18073-1512

SHUKLA, JAGADISH, science educator; m. Anastasia Booras, Oct. 4, 1979; children: Sonia, Pooja Dubey. DS, MIT, Cambridge, 1976. Prof. U. Md., College Park, 1983—93, George Mason U., Fairfax, Va., 1994. Pres. Inst. Global Environment & Soc., Calverton, Md., 1993. Recipient Walker Gold medal, Indian Meteorol. Soc., 2001. Fellow: Third World Acad. Scis. (assoc.). Achievements include research in scientific basis for climate prediction. Office: George Mason U COLA 4041 Powder Mill Rd Ste 302 Beltsville MD 20705 Office Phone: 301-595-7000.

SHULA, DON FRANCIS, retired professional football coach, professional sports team executive; b. Painesville, Ohio, Jan. 4, 1930; s. Dan and Mary (Miller) S.; children: David, Donna, Sharon, Anne, Michael; m. Mary Anne Shula. BS, John Carroll U., Cleve., 1951, H.H.D. (hon.), 1972; MA, Case Western Res. U., 1953; Sc.D. (hon.), Biscayne Coll., 1974, St. Thomas U., 1976, U. Miami, 1992, Fla. Atlantic U., 1999. Profl. football player Cleve. Browns, 1951-52, Balt. Colts, 1953-56, Washington Redskins, 1957; asst. coach U. Va., 1958, U. Ky., 1959, Detroit Lions, 1960-62; head coach Baltimore Colts, 1963-69, Miami (Fla.) Dolphins, 1970-96; vice chmn. Miami Dolphins, 1996—; owner, pres. Shula Enterprises. Author: The Winning Edge, 1972, (with Ken Blanchard) Everyone's A Coach, 1995. Fla. crusade chmn. Nat. Cancer Soc., 1975; co-chmn. Jerry Lewis March Against Dystrophy, 1975; nat. bd. dirs. Boy's Hope; mem. nat. sports com. Multiple Schlerosis Soc., Muscular Dystrophy Assn.; bd. dirs. Heart Assn. Greater Miami; established Don Shula Found., breast cancer rsch., 1991—; sponsor Don Shula Scholarship, 1978—. Coached 6 Superbowl teams, winning teams 1972, 73; recipient Coach of Yr. awards 1964, 66, 70, 71, 72, Coach of decade Profl. Football Hall of Fame, 1980, Pro Football's All-Time Winningest Coach, 1994, Brotherhood award Fla. region NCCJ, 1977, Light of Flames Leadership award Barry Coll., 1977, Concern award Cedars Med. Ctr., 1992, Solheim Lifetime Achievement award, 1992, Jim Thorpe award, 1993,Sportsman of Yr. Sports Illustrated, 1993, Horrigan award Pro Football Writers,1994, Horatio Alger award, 1995, Vince Lombardi Award of Excellence, 1999; named Balt. Colts Silver Anniversary Coach, 1977, elected to Pro Football Hall of Fame, 1997. Roman Catholic. Office: Shula Enterprises Inc 16 Indian Creek Is Miami Beach FL 33154-2904 *Success is never final; defeat is never fatal.*

SHULA, MIKE (MICHAEL JOHN SHULA), professional football coach, former college football coach; b. Balt., June 3, 1965; s. Donald F. and Mary S. Shula. BA in Labor Rels., U. Ala., 1987. Offensive asst. Tampa Bay Buccaneers, 1988—90, quarterbacks coach, 1990—91, offensive coord., 1996—99; coaches asst. Miami Dolphins, 1991—92, quarterbacks coach, 2001—02; asst. coach Chgo. Bears, 1993—95; head coach U. Ala., 2003—06; quarterbacks coach Jacksonville Jaguars, 2007—. Office: Jacksonville Jaguars 1 ALLTEL Stadium Pl Jacksonville FL 32202 *

SHULA, ROBERT JOSEPH, lawyer; b. South Bend, Ind., Dec. 10, 1936; s. Joseph Edward and Bertha Mona (Buckner) S.; m. Gaye Ann Martin, Oct. 8, 1978; children: Deirdre Regina, Robert Joseph II, Elizabeth Martin. BS in Mktg., Ind. U., 1958, JD, 1961. Bar: Ind. 1961. Ptnr. Bingham Summers Welsh & Spilman, Indpls., 1965-82, sr. ptnr., 1982-89; ptnr. Price & Shula, Indpls., 1989-91, Lowe Gray Steele & Darko, Indpls., 1991—2003; of counsel Norris Choplin and Schroeder, Indpls., 2003—05; pvt. practice Indpls., 2005—. Mem. faculty Nat. Inst. Trial Advocacy; guest lectr. Brit. Medicine and Law Soc., 1979, Ind. U. Sch. Law; medico-legal lectr. Ind. U. Schs. Medicine, Dentistry, and Nursing. Bd. dirs. Arts Ind., Indpls., 1995-99; founding pres. Oriental Arts Soc., Indpls., 1975-79, Meridian Women's Clinic, Inc., Indpls.; trustee Indpls. Mus. Art, 1975-78, life trustee, 1984—; bd. dirs. Ind. Repertory Theatre, Indpls., 1982-92, chmn. bd. dirs., pres., 1985-89; pres. Repertory Soc., 1993-96; v.p., bd. dirs. Flanner House of Indpls., Inc., 1977-88, chmn., 1988-99; pres. Internat. Ctr. of Indpls., Inc., 1993-96; commr. Indpls. Met. Devel. Commn., 2005. Maj. JAGC, USAFR, 1961—65. Recipient Gov.'s award of Sagamore of the Wabash, 1998. Master Am. Inns of Ct.; fellow 20th Fighter Wing Assn. (v.p. 2005—); mem. ABA, FBA, Am. Assn. for Justice, Am. Law Inst. (diplomate), Am. Bd. Trial Advs. (pres. 2000), Am. Coll. Legal Medicine, Ind. Bar Assn., Indpls. Bar Assn., Ind. Trial Lawyers Assn., Ind. Trial Lawyers Assn., Am. Assn for Justice. Democrat. Episcopalian. Avocations: flying, art. Home: 7924 Beaumont Green Pl Indianapolis IN 46250-1663 Office: 3891 Eagle Creek Pkwy Ste C Indianapolis IN 46254 Home Phone: 317-845-1857; Office Phone: 317-299-0400. Business E-Mail: shulalaw@sprynet.com.

SHULENBURGER, DAVID EDWIN, educational association administrator, economics educator, former academic administrator; b. Salisbury, NC, Sept. 19, 1945; s. Hubert Ray and Allie (Goodnight) S.; m. Carol Prentice, Aug. 10, 1994; children: Adam Anthony, Neal Gordon, Luke Nathan. BA, Lenoir-Rhyne Coll., 1967; MA, U. Ill., 1968, PhD, 1974. Instr. Clemson U., SC, 1968-71; rsch. asst. U. Ill., Champaign, 1971-72, teaching asst., 1972, 74; staff labor economist U.S. Dept. Labor, Washington, 1973; asst. prof. bus. adminstrn. U. Kans., Lawrence, 1974-77, assoc. prof. bus. adminstrn., 1977-83, prof. bus. adminstrn., 1983—, undergrad. dir., 1982-85, assoc. dean, 1985-88, assoc. vice chancellor, 1989-92, vice chancellor, 1993-96, provost, exec. vice chancellor, 1996—2002, exec. v.p., provost, 2002—06; v.p. academic affairs Nat. Assn. State Univs. and Land-Grant Colls., Washington, 2006—. Cons. Kans. Dept. Human Resources, Topeka, 1975-77, fact-finder, 1979—; panel arbitrator United Mine Workers and P&M Coal Co., Pitts., 1982—; earnings expert for numerous law firms, Kans., Mo., 1979-89. Contbr. articles to profl. jours. Chmn. troop com. Boy Scouts Am., Lawrence, 1984, asst. scoutmaster, 1985—; mem. Kansas City City Coun.; pres. Lawrence Bus./Edn. Partnership, 1995-96. Recipient Alumnus of Yr., Lenoir Rhyne Coll., 2007; Internat. Curriculum grantee US Dept. Edn., 1987. Mem. AAUP (chpt. pres. 1981-82), Indsl. Rels. Rsch. Assn., Am. Econ. Assn., So. Econ. Assn., Swarthout Soc. (bd. dirs. 1989—). Avocations: travel, camping, gardening. Office: NASULGC Ste 400 1307 New York Ave, NW Washington DC 20005-4722 Office Phone: 202-478-6062. Office Fax: 202-478-6061. E-mail: dshulenburger@nasulgc.org.

SHULER, CAROLETTA ALEXIS, criminal justice educator; b. Orangeburg, SC, Mar. 17, 1967; d. Tom and Bernadean Shuler. BA, U. SC, Columbia, 1989, BS, 1994, M of Criminal Justice, 1996; EdD, U. SD, Vermillion, 1998. Asst. mgr. Fast Mart Store, Orangeburg, SC, 1990—92, parking enforcement officer SC State U., Orangeburg, 1992—93; resident adv. divsn. student affairs U. SC, Columbia, 1993—94, asst. hall dir. divsn. of student affairs, 1994, grad. asst. coll. criminal justice, 1995—96, tchg. intern coll. criminal justice, 1996; grad. asst. higher edn. program U. SD, Vermillion, 1997—98; vis. asst. prof. SC State U., Orangeburg, 1998—99, asst. prof., 1999—2007; online faculty criminal justice South U., 2007—. Campus dir. SC Tchg. Fellows Program, Orangeburg, 2000—07. Mem.: Am. Study of Higher Edn., SC Coun. for the Social Studies, Philosopy Edn. Soc., Nat. Coun. for History Edn., Nat. Coun. for the Social Studies, Pi Lambda Theta (faculty liaison 1999), Kappa Delta Pi (faculty counselor 1999), Alpha Kappa Alpha. Democrat. Roman Catholic. Business E-Mail: calexisshuler@msn.com.

SHULER, ELLIE GIVAN, JR., retired military officer, museum administrator; b. Raleigh, NC, Dec. 6, 1936; s. Ellie Givan and Berta (Williams) S.; m. Annette Fontaine Maury, Mar. 22, 1961; children: Ellie Givan III, Franklin Maury, Gray Hays. BSCE, The Citadel, 1959; MS in Mgmt., Rensselaer Poly. Inst., 1967; grad., Squadron Officer Sch., Maxwell AFB, Ala., 1964; postgrad., Naval War Coll.; grad. command and staff course, Nat. War Coll., 1976; grad. cen. flight instr. course, Castle AFB, Calif. Engr. in tng., S.C. Commd. 2d lt. U.S. Air Force, 1959, advanced through grades to lt. gen., 1988, various positions and locations, 1959-68, F-4C pilot, asst. flight comdr. 558th Tactical Fighter Squadron Cam Ranh Bay AFB, Republic of Vietnam, 1968-69, indsl. engr., then asst. dep. chief Engring. Mgmt. Div., Hdqrs. 2d Air Force Barksdale AFB, La., 1969-71; asst. exec. officer to comdr. in chief U.S. Air Force in Europe, Lindsey Air Sta., West Germany, 1972-73, base civil engr., comdr. 86th Civil Engring. Squadron Ramstein Air Base, Fed. Republic Germany, 1973-75; dir. ops. 3902d Air Base Wing, comdr. 3902d Ops. Squadron Offutt AFB, Nebr., 1976; dir. programs Office Dep. Chief of Staff for Engring. and Services SAC, Offutt AFB, Nebr., 1976-77, exec. to comdr. in chief, 1977-79; vice comdr., then comdr. 19th Bombardment Wing Robins AFB, Ga., 1979-80; comdr. 42d Bombardment Wing Loring AFB, Maine, 1980-81; comdr. 4th Air Div. F.E. Warren AFB, Wyo., 1981-84; comdr. 3rd Air Div. SAC, Andersen AFB, Guam, 1984-86; asst. dep. then dep. chief of staff, ops. SAC Hqrs., Offutt AFB, Nebr., 1986-88; comdr. 8th Air Force SAC, Barksdale AFB, 1988-91; retired, 1991; chmn. bd., CEO 8th Air Force Heritage Mus., 1992—98. Trustee, Longs Peak coun. Boy Scouts Am., 1983-84, chair bd. trustees, 1992-2004; trustee Falcon Found., USAF Acad., 8th Air Force Heritage Mus., 1992—. Decorated D.S.M. with oak leaf cluster, Legion of Merit with oak leaf cluster, D.F.C., Air medal with five oak leaf clusters, Air Force Commendation medal with oak leaf cluster; recipient medal of Honor DAR, 2005, Disting. Eagle Scout award Boy Scouts Am., 2006; named Disting. Alumnus, The Citadel, 2007. Mem. Soc. Am. Mil. Engrs. (chpt. pres. 1971), Am. Def. Preparedness Assn. (regional bd. dirs. 1981-84), Order of Dadaelians (hon. flight capt. 1981-85), Council on Am.'s Mil. Past, Mil. Order of World Wars, Kiwanis, Tau Beta Pi. Republican. Episcopalian. Avocations: numismatics, golf, hunting, military, history. Home: 5914 Marthas Glen Rd Columbia SC 29209 Home Phone: 803-776-6462. E-mail: ltgeneshuler@bellsouth.net.

SHULER, (JOSEPH) HEATH, congressman, real estate company executive, retired professional football player; b. Swain Co., NC, Dec. 21, 1971; s. Joe and Margie Shuler; m. Nikol Shuler, 1998; children: Island, Navy. BA in Psychology, U. Tenn., 2001. Quarterback Wash. Redskins, 1994—96, New Orleans Saints, 1997; co-owner, pres. Heath Shuler Real Estate, LLC, Knoxville, Tenn., 1998—2003; mem. US Congress from 11th Tenn. dist., 2007—. Bd. dirs. United Cmty. Bank; mem. Blue Dog Caucus US Congress, 2007—, mem. small bus. com., transp. and infrastructure com., natural resources com., 2007—. Founder Heath Shuler Found.; charter mem. Friends of the Smokies; bd. mem. Knoxville Boys and Girls Club; nat. spokesman Character Counts; mem. scholarship com. N.C. Assn. Advancement of Teaching. Mem.: Blue Dog Coalition, Fell. Christian Athletes. Democrat. Baptist. Office: 356 Biltmore Ave Ste 400 Asheville NC 28801 Office Phone: 828-252-1651. Office Fax: 828-252-8734. *

SHULER, JAMES MANNIE, health physicist; b. Orangeburg, SC, Oct. 23, 1951; s. Ellie Grier Shuler and Gerdene Rickenbaker Shuler. BS in Botany, Clemson U., 1974; MA in Mgmt. and Supervision, Ctrl. Mich. U., 1977; MS in Radiation Sci., Georgetown U., 1988; MPA, U. So. Calif., 1997, DPA, 1999. Regstered radiation protection technologist, environ. profl., environ. mgr.; cert. hazard control mgr., hazardous materials mgr., environ. trainer transp. hazardous materials and waste occupl. health and safety. Health physics technician Allied-General Nuc. Svcs., Barnwell, SC, 1975—79; supr. health physics Chem-Nuc. Sys., Inc., Barnwell, 1979, customer and compliance rep., 1979; radioactive materials enforcement specialist U.S. Dept. Transp., Washington, 1979—81, 1983—88; radwaste/transp. specialist Applied Tech. of Barnwell, Inc., 1981—83; phys. scientist U.S. Dept. Energy, Germantown, Md., 1988—89, health physicist Aiken, SC, 1989—93, from sr. health physicist to phys. scientist Washington, 1993—96, health physicist, 1996—. Assoc. staff instr. U.S. Dept. Transp./Transp. Safety Inst., Oklahoma City, 1981—89; vis. instr. Georgetown U., Washington, 1988—89; assoc. grad. faculty Ctrl. Mich. U., 2001—. Contbr. over 100 articles to profl. jours. and tech. publs. Mem. ASTM (sect. 6 leader radiation protection methods verification 1993-2003), Nat. Environ. Tng. Assn., Assn. of MBA Execs., Am. Nuc. Soc., Health Physics Soc. (environ. radiation sect., govt. sect. 1993—) Home: 12835 Locbury Cir Apt I Germantown MD 20874-3858 Office: US Dept Energy EM-60 CLOV-2047 Washington DC 20585-0001 Office Phone: 301-903-5513. Business E-Mail: James.Shuler@hq.doe.gov.

SHULER, JON EMMETT, securities industry professional; b. Aiken, SC, Sept. 21, 1946; s. Cyril Ovierre and Elizabeth Carolina (Smith) S.; m. Virginia Rose Harris, Aug. 1, 1981; children: Jon Emmett Jr., Kline Martin. BA in Econs., Clemson U., 1968; MBA, U. S.C., 1970. CFP, cert. investment mgmt. cons. Investment Mgmt. Cons. Assn., cert. investment mgmt. analyst Investment Mgmt. Cons. Assn. Broker J.C. Bradford & Co., Spartanburg, S.C., 1972-81, br. mgr., 1981-88, Raymond James & Assocs., Spartanburg, S.C., 1988-94; owner, pres., reg. investment adv. Wealth Mgmt. Assocs., Inc., 1994—. Co-author: Getting to the Heart of the Matter, 1999. Bd. dirs. Habitat for Humanity, Spartanburg, 1990, Spartanburg Music Found., 2007—, Clemson Area Retirement Ctr., 2007—; mem. ARC State Pub. Support Com., Columbia, S.C., 1993; trustee Spartanburg Day Sch., 1997—; v.p. endowments Boy Scouts Am., Palmetto, 1999-2002, mem. exec. bd., 2004-07. Mem. Rotary (pres. North Spartanburg chpt. 1990, chpt. sec., 2006-07, Paul Harris fellow 1989), Soc. Mayflower Descendants. Republican. Presbyterian. Avocations: skiing, antiques, woodworking. Office Phone: 864-591-1099. Personal E-mail: jeshuler@hotmail.com.

SHULER, KURT EGON, chemist, educator; b. Nuremberg, Germany, July 10, 1922; came to U.S., 1937, naturalized, 1944; s. Louis and Donie (Wald) Schulherr; m. Beatrice Gwyn London, Nov. 11, 1944. BS, Ga. Inst. Tech., 1942; PhD, Cath. U. Am., 1949. Fellow Johns Hopkins U., 1949-51; sr. staff mem., asst. group supr., chem. physics group Applied Physics Lab., Johns Hopkins, 1951-55; supervisory phys. chemist Nat. Bur. Standards, 1955-58, cons. to dir., 1958-61, asst. dir., sr. research fellow, 1963-68; rsch. staff, sci. adviser to v.p. rsch. Gen. Motors Corp., 1958; spl. asst. to dir. rsch. Inst. Def. Analyses, 1961-63; vis. prof. chemistry U. Calif., San Diego, 1966-67, prof. chemistry, 1968-91, prof. emeritus, 1991—, chmn. dept., 1968-70, 84-87. Cons. in field; mem. Solvay Conf., 1962, 78; mem. adv. panel, chemistry div. NSF, 1973-75. Author, editor tech. books; assoc. editor: Jour. Math. Physics, 1963-66; bd. editors: Jour. Statis. Physics, 1968-80; mem. adv. bd.: Chem. Engring. News, 1967-70; contbr. articles to profl. jours. Served with U.S. Army, 1944-46. Recipient Distinguished Service award Nat. Bur. Standards, 1959, Gold medal award Dept. Commerce, 1968; Solvay Found. fellow, 1975 Fellow Am. Inst. Chemists, AAAS, Am. Phys. Soc., Washington Acad. Sci.; mem. Am. Chem. Soc., Washington Philos. Soc. Clubs: Rancho Santa Fe Golf. Achievements include the department of chemistry and biochemistry at the University of California San Diego establishing an endowed chair in his name in 2006. Home: PO Box 1504 Rancho Santa Fe CA 92067-1504 Office: Univ Calif San Diego Dept Chemistry La Jolla CA 92093 Business E-Mail: kshuler@ucsd.edu.

SHULER, LAURA, marketing executive; b. Mar. 22, 1961; married; 4 children. BA in Comm., U. Del. Joined Jack Morton Worldwide, 1996, sr. mgmt. position NY offices, sr. mgmt. position ea. ops., sr. mgmt. position, strategic devel. & US brand mktg., pres., chief strategy officer, 2006—. Regular spkr. to bus. and industry audiences. Named a Woman to Watch, Advt. Age, 2007. Mem.: Word of Mouth Mktg. Assn. (WOMMA) (sec.). Office: Jack Morton Worldwide 498 Seventh Ave New York NY 10018 Office Phone: 212-727-0400. Office Fax: 212-401-7016. *

SHULER DONNER, LAUREN, film producer; BS in Film and Broadcasting, Boston U. Assoc. prodr.: (films) Thank God It's Friday, 1978; Mr. Mom, 1983; Ladyhawke, 1985; St. Elmo's Fire, 1985; Pretty in Pink, 1986; Three Fugitives, 1989; Radio Flyer, 1992; Dave, 1993; Free Willy, 1993; prodr.: (TV films) Amateur Night at the Dixie Bar and Grill, 1979; (films) Free Willy 2: The Adventure Home, 1995, You've Got Mail, 1998, Any Given Sunday, 1999, X-Men, 2000, X2: X-Men United, 2003, Timeline, 2003, Constantine, 2005; exec. prodr.: Assassins, 1995; Free Willy 3, 1997; Volcano, 1997; Out Cold, 2001; Just Married, 2003; prodr.: She's The Man, 2006, X-3, 2006, Unaccompanied Minors, 2006. Named one of 100 Most Powerful Women in Entertainment, Hollywood Reporter, 2006. Office: The Donners' Co 9465 Wilshire Blvd Ste 430 Beverly Hills CA 90212 *

SHULEVITZ, URI, writer, illustrator; b. Warsaw, Feb. 27, 1935; came to U.S., 1959, naturalized, 1965; Student, Tel-Aviv Art Inst., 1953-55; Tchrs. Cert., Tchrs. Coll. Israel, 1956; student, Bklyn. Museum Art Sch., 1959-61. Instr. illustrating and writing children's books The New Sch., 1970-86; dir. illustrating and writing children's books Hartwick Coll., 1974-92. Author, illustrator: The Moon In My Room, 1963, One Monday Morning, 1967, Rain Rain Rivers, 1969, Oh What a Noise, 1971, The Magician, 1973, Dawn, 1974, The Treasure, 1978, (Caldecott honor Book 1979), The Strange and Exciting Adventures of Jeremiah Hush, 1986, Toddlecreek Post Office, 1990, The Secret Room, 1993, Snow, 1998 (Caldecott Honor book 1999), What is a Wise Bird like you Doing in a silly tale like this?, 2000, The Travels of Benjamin of Tudela, through three Continents in the Twelfth Century, 2005, So Sleepy Story, 2006; author: Writing with Pictures: How to Write and Illustrate Children's Books, 1985; illustrator: The Mystery of the Woods, 1964, Charley Sang a Song, 1964, A Rose, A Bridge and A Wild Black Horse, 1964, The Second Witch, 1965, The Carpet of Solomon, 1966, Maximilian's World, 1966, The Silk Spinners, 1967, The Fool of the World and the Flying Ship, 1968 (Caldecott medal 1969), Runaway Jonah and Other Tales, 1968, The Twelve Dancing Princesses, 1966, Oh What A Noise!, 1971, Soldier and Tsar in the Forest, 1972, The Fools of Chelm, 1973, The Touchstone, 1976, Hanukah Money, 1978, The Lost Kingdom of Karnica, 1979, The Golem, 1982, Lilith's Cave: Jewish Tales of the Supernatural, 1988, The Diamond Tree, 1991, The Golden Goose, 1995, Hosni The Dreamer, 1997, others. Served with Israeli Army, 1956-59. Guggenheim fellow, 1999. Mem Authors Guild. Office: care Farrar Straus & Giroux Inc 19 Union Sq W New York NY 10003-3304

SHULGASSER-PARKER, BARBARA, critic, writer; b. Manhasset, NY, Apr. 10, 1954; d. Lew and Luba (Golante) S.; m. Norman Parker, Sept. 1999; 1 child: Atticus. Student, Sarah Lawrence Coll., 1973-74; BA magna cum laude, CUNY, 1977; MS, Columbia U., 1978. Feature writer Waterbury (Conn.) Rep., 1978-81; reporter, feature writer Chgo. Sun Times, 1981-84; film critic San Francisco Examiner, 1984-98; freelance book critic N.Y. Times Book Rev., NYC, 1983—; film critic Chgo. Tribune, 1999—2001. Author: Funny Accent, 2001; co-author: (screenplay, with Robert Altman) Ready to Wear, 1994; freelance video columnist N.Y. Times Sunday Arts & Leisure, 1989, features for Vanity Fair, Glamour and Mirabella mags.

SHULKIN, BARRY, health facility administrator; b. Amarillo, Tex., Apr. 2, 1952; s. Stanley and Harriet Shulkin; m. Patricia Ann Mandel, June 17, 1990; children: Zachary David, Jeffrey Daniel. BA, U. Tex., Austin, 1974; MD, U. Tex., Dallas, 1978; MBA, U. Mich., Ann Arbor, 2002. Prof. radiology U. Mich., Ann Arbor, 1999—2004; dir. nuc. medicine St. Jude Children's Rsch. Hosp., Memphis, 2004—. Chair fin. com. Am. Bd. Nuc. Medicine, St. Louis, 2004. Grantee, NIH, 1991—2001. Fellow: ACP. Avocation: running. Office: St Jude Children's Research Hospital 332 North Lauderdale MS 752 Memphis TN 38105 Office Phone: 901-495-3347.

SHULKIN, MARTIN B., lawyer; b. Cambridge, Mass., Apr. 24, 1944; BA, Williams Coll., 1966; JD, Boston Coll., 1969. Bar: Mass. 1969, Fla., US Ct. Appeals 1st Cir., US Dist. Ct. Dist. Mass. Jud. clk. to Hon. G. Joseph Tauro Superior Ct. Mass., 1969-70; assoc. Burns & Levinson LLP, Boston, 1970—71, ptnr., 1980—99, mng. ptnr., 1992—96; founding ptnr. Soble, Soble & Shulkin, Boston, 1972—79; ptnr. Sweeney & Franklin, Boston, 1979—80, Duane Morris LLP, Boston, 1999—, mng. ptnr. Boston office, 1999—. Editor Boston Coll. Law Rev., 1968-69. Mem. ABA, Boston Bar Assn., Order of Coif. Office: Duane Morris LLP Ste 500 470 Atlantic Ave Boston MA 02210 Office Phone: 617-289-9200. Office Fax: 617-289-9201: Business E-Mail: mbshulkin@duanemorris.com.

SHULKINA, TATYANA, botanist, researcher; b. St. Petersburg, Russia, July 16, 1939; arrived in U.S., 1991, naturalized, 1996; d. Vladimir and Elizabeth (Troizky) Borovsky; m. Yuri Shulkin, Mar. 17, 1961; 1 child, Kate Goldenberg. BS with honors, Forest U., St. Petersburg, 1962; MS, Bot. Inst., Acad. Sci., St. Petersburg, 1965, PhD, 1984. Lead rschr. Bot. Inst. Acad. Sci., St. Petersburg, 1962—65, scientist, 1965—84, rschr., 1984—91; asst. prof. Truman Coll., Chgo., 1992—95; asst. curator Mo. Bot. Garden, St. Louis, 1996—99, curator, 2000—. Mem. sci. coun. Bot. Inst. Russia, St. Petersburg, 1985—91, Plant Industry Inst., St. Petersburg, 1986—91; cons. Chgo. Bot. Garden, Glencoe, 1993—. Author (in Russian): Rock Gardens, 1975; author: (in English) Ornamental Plants from Russia, 2004; Healing Herbs in the USA, 2006; contbr. articles to profl. jours. Tchr. Soc. Knowledge, 1966—91. Recipient medal, Internat. Bot. Congress, 1975, 1999. Mem.: Am. Soc. Plant Taxonomists. Office: Mo Bot Garden 4500 Shaw Rsch Ctr Saint Louis MO 63110 Office Phone: 314-577-0853. Business E-Mail: tatyana.shulkina@mobot.org.

SHULL, CLAIRE, documentary film producer, casting director; b. NYC, Oct. 26, 1925; d. Barnet Joseph and Fannie (Florea) Klar; m. Leo Shull, Aug. 8, 1948; children: Lee Shull Pearlstein, David. Student, Am. Acad. Dramatic Arts, NYC, 1943—44, NYU, 1973—74. Editor, assoc. pub. Show Bus. Publs., NYC, 1957-85; owner, founder Claire/Casting, NYC and Miami, Fla., 1972—, Claire/Casting Film Prodns., NYC and Miami, 1978—; cons. dir., prodr., dir. film and TV The Bass Mus., Miami Beach, Fla., 1992—. Miami corr. film, TV, theatre Show Bus. Weekly, 1999—; curator archives Show Bus. Pubs. Performing Arts Theatre Collection, NY Pub. Libr., 2005—. Actress in The Front Page, USO European tour, 1945-46, (on Broadway) Tenting Tonight, 1947; prodr., dir. HBO TV series How To Break into Show Business, 1980-81, Cable-TV series, Join Us at the Bass, 1993-97. Recipient gold award and distinctive merit TV award Advt. Club. Hartford, Conn., 1984, Clio award, 1989. Mem.: Drama Desk, Actors Equity Assn., Ind. Casting Dirs. Assn. NY, South Fla. Internat. Press Club, Miami Internat. Press Club.

SHULL, JOE A., lawyer; b. Houston, Sept. 8, 1945; BBA, U. Tex., 1967, JD, 1969; LLM in Taxation, George Washington U., 1976. Bar: Tex. 1969, D.C. 1973, Va. 1976. Law clerk to trial judges U.S. Ct. Claims; ptnr., Bus. Transactions, Mergers & Acquisitions practices Venable LLP, Washington. Served to capt. US Army, 1970—72. Mem. ABA, D.C. Bar, Va. State Bar. Office: Venable LLP 575 7th St NW Washington DC 20004 Office Phone: 202-344-4821. Office Fax: 202-344-8300. Business E-Mail: jashull@venable.com.

SHULMAN, ABRAHAM, otolaryngology educator, hospital administrator; b. NYC, Feb. 24, 1929; s. Ben and Libby (Sarnoff) S.; m. Arlene P., Sept. 8, 1957; children: Rachel, Melanie. BS, CCNY, 1950; MD, U. Berne, 1955. Bar.; diplomate Am. Bd. Otolaryngology., 1962. Rotating surg. intern Queens County Gen. Hosp., 1955—56; resident in otolaryngology Kings County Hosp., Bklyn., 1957—60; clin. instr. Downstate Med. Ctr. SUNY, 1962—64, assoc. prof. Downstate Med. Ctr., 1975—89; prof. clin. otolaryngology SUNY Health Sci. Ctr., Bklyn., 1989—92, prof. emeritus clin. otolaryngology, 1992—; clin. instr. Albert Einstein Coll. Medicine, 1966—68, asst. clin. prof. otolaryn. surgery, 1968—75. Asst. surgeon Bklyn. Eye & Ear Hosp., 1966-69; otology cons. College Point chief of otolaryngology Lincoln Hosp., 1967-70, Bklyn. VA Med. Ctr., 1977-85, chief otolaryngology, staff attending otolaryngologist, 1985—, acting chief of otolaryngology, 1990-91; lectr., asst. attending otolaryngologist Mt. Sinai Hosp., 1974; chief otolaryngology Lincoln Hosp., 1967-1970; asst. attending otolaryngology Bronx Mcpl. Hosp., 1967-75; chief Otolaryngologist, asst. attending otolaryngologist, Kings County Hosp., 1962-64, dir. otolaryngology, 1975-92, attending otolaryngologist, 1975—, Brookdale Med. Ctr., 1982-86; chief otolaryngology Cath. Med. Ctr., Bklyn. and Queens, 1969-94, attending otololaryngologist St. John's Queens Hosp., 1969-94; chmn. Internat. Tinnitus Forum, 1982—; Martha Entenmann Tinnitus Rsch. Ctr., Inc., dir. otology neurotology 1994—. Editor (co-chief): Internat. Tinnitus Jour., 1994—; editor: (text) Tinnitus Diagnosis and Treatment, 1991—. Cons. Children's Devel. Ctr., 1975; med. cons. Office Vocat. Rehab., 1974; dir. med. svc. Lexington Sch. of the Deaf, 1972-74. Lt. comdr. USNR, 1960-62. Recipient Cert. of Appreciation, Am. Speech and Hearing Assn., 1989—, Hocks award, Am. Tinnitus Assn., 1990, Honor award, Am. Acad. Otolaryngology, 1994, Myrtle Reed award, Hadassah Zionist Orgn. Am., honoree, Neuro Equilibrimetric Soc., 1998. Fellow ACS, AMA, Am. Acad. Ophthalmology and Otolaryngology, Am. Neurotology Soc., Am. Audiology Soc., Am. Soc. Ophthalmologic and Otolaryngology Allergy, Am. Soc. Facial Plastic Surgery, Internat. Coll. Surgeons, Adam Politzer Soc.; mem. Am. Coun. Otolaryngology, Am. Soc. Contemporary Medicine and Surgery, Pan-Am. Assn. Otorhinolaryngology and Bronchoesophagology, N.Y. Acad. Sci., Soc. for Cryosurgery, Queens County Med. Soc., Soc. Univ. Otolaryngologists, Bklyn. Oncology Soc., Assn. for Rsch. in Otolaryngology, Neuroequilibrimetric Soc., Harvey Soc., Centurion Club, Sigma Xi. Office: SUNY Health Sci Ctr Bklyn Div Otolaryngology 450 Clarkson Ave Brooklyn NY 11203-2056 Office Phone: 718-773-8888. Personal E-mail: metrc@inch.com.

SHULMAN, ALLAN T., architect; BArch, Cornell U., Ithaca, NY; MArch in Suburb and Town Planning, U. Miami. Founder, prin. Allan T. Shulman Arch., P.A., Miami, 1996—2007; prin. Shulman & Assocs., Miami, 2007—. Rsch. asst. prof. U. Miami Sch. Architecture. Co-author (with Jean-Francois Lejeune): The Making of Miami Beach: The Architecture of Lawrence Murray Dixon 1933-42, 2000; prin. works include Browns Hotel (AIA Fla. Merit award, 2005), Fairwind Hotel (AIA Fla. Honor award, 2006), 354 Washington (AIA Miami Award of Excellence, 2006), Lindemann Residence (Dade Heritage Trust award, 2007), Anglers Resort and Spa (Dade Heritage Trust award, 2007), Chrysler Bldg./Apple Store (Dade Heritage Trust award, 2007, Miami Design Preservation League award, 2007). Office: Shulman + Assocs 100 NE 38th St Space 2 Miami FL 33137-3654 Office Phone: 305-438-0609. Office Fax: 305-438-0170. E-mail: allan@shulmanarchitect.com. *

SHULMAN, ARTHUR, communications executive; b. NYC, Mar. 4, 1927; s. Jacob and Sarah (Hochman) S.; m. Jan. 30, 1958; children: James, Karen. BA, Syracuse U., 1950. Asst. to pub. TV Guide Mag., Radnor, Pa., 1958-72; pub. Seventeen Mag., NYC, 1972-73; dir. regional ops. TV Guide, 1974-82; dir. comm. B'nai B'rith Internat., Washington, 1983-93. Author: How Sweet It Was, 1966, The Television Years, 1972. Dir. Penn Wynne (Pa.) Civic Assn., 1965-66. S/Sgt. US Army, 1945-46, Japan. Mem. Radio & TV Execs. Soc., Nat. Press Club, Overseas Press Club, Nat. Acad. TV Arts & Scis. Jewish. Address: 4017 Jardin Ln Sarasota FL 34238-4504 Personal E-mail: artshulman@comcast.net.

SHULMAN, GERALD I., physician, scientist, endocrinologist, educator; b. Detroit, Feb. 8, 1953; BS with high honors and distinction, U. Mich., 1974; MD, PhD, Wayne State U., 1979; MA, privatim (hon.), Yale Univ., 1997. Intern Duke U., Durham, NC, 1979-80, residency, 1980-81; fellowship in endocrinology and metabolism Mass. Gen. Hosp., Boston, 1981-84; asst. prof. medicine Harvard U., Boston, 1985-87; assoc. prof. Sch. Medicine Yale U., New Haven, 1989-96; assoc. dir. Yale MD-PhD Program Sch. Medicine Yale U., New Haven, 1993—, prof. internal medicine, cellular and molecular physiology, 1996—. Vis. prof. Vanderbilt U., 1994, Albert Einstein Coll. Medicine, 1999, Washington U. Sch. Medicine, 2001, Cambridge U., 2002, U. Md., 2004; assoc. dir. Yale Diabetes Endocrine Rsch. Ctr., 1996—; investigator Howard Hughes Med. Inst., 1997—; Sipersten lectr. U. Calif., San Francisco, 2006; program dir. Yale/New Haven Hosp. Gen. Clin. Rsch. Ctr.; Pfizer prof. U. Colo.; mem. NIH study sects.; Marble lectr. Joslin Diabetes Ctr., 2007; lectr. in field. Mem. editl. bd. Diabetes, Am. Jour. Physiology; assoc. editor: Diabetic Medicine, Jour. Clin. Investigation, Am. Jour. Medicine, Diabetologia, Internat. Jour. Molecular Medicine, Am. Jour. Physiology, Jour. Biol. Chemistry, Cell Metabolism, 2004—, PLoS Medicine, 2004—; contbr. articles to profl. jours. Recipient Outstanding Investigator award for Clinical Rsch., 1994, Am. Fed. Med. Rsch., 1997, Diabetes Care Rsch. award, Boehriger Mannheim/Juvenile Diabetes Found. Internat., 1997, Young Investigator award in diabetes, Novartis, 1999, Mary June Kugel award, Juvenile Diabetes Rsch. Found. Internat., 1999, E.H. Ahrens Jr. award, Assn. for Patient-Oriented Rsch., 2001, Josiah Brown award in Diabetes, UCLA, 2002, John Shaw Lectureship, Australia-SE Asia- New Zealand, 2006. Fellow: ACP, Am. Coll. Endocrinologists, Internat. Soc. Magnetic Resonance in Medicine; mem.: NAS, European Assn. Study of Diabetes, Am. Physiol. Soc., Inst. Medicine of NAS, Endocrine Soc., Am. Soc. Clin. Investigation, Assn. Am. Physicians, Am. Diabetes Assn. (clin. rsch. grantee 1996, Outstanding Sci. Achievement Lilly Lectr. award 1997, Mentor award 1997, 1999, Disting. Clin. Scientist award 2004), Interurban Clin. Club. Office: Howard Hughes Med Inst Yale U Sch Medicine PO Box 9812 New Haven CT 06536-0812 Address: Dept Cellular & Molecular Physiology Yale U Sch Medicine 333 Cedar St Rm B-147 PO Box 208026 New Haven CT 06520-8026 Fax: 203-737-4059. Business E-Mail: gerald.shulman@yale.edu.

SHULMAN, LAWRENCE EDWARD, biomedical researcher, rheumatologist; b. Boston, July 25, 1919; s. David Herman and Belle (Tishler) S.; m. Pauline K. Flint, July 19, 1946; m. Reni Trudinger, Mar. 20, 1959; children: Kathryn Verena, Barbara Corina. AB, Harvard U., 1941, postgrad., 1941-42; PhD, Yale U., 1945, MD, 1949. Diplomate Nat. Bd. Med. Examiners. Intern Johns Hopkins Hosp., 1949-50, resident and fellow in internal medicine, 1950-53; dir. connective tissue div. Johns Hopkins U., 1955-75, assoc. prof. medicine, 1964—; assoc. dir. div. arthritis, musculoskeletal and skin diseases NIH, Bethesda, Md., 1976-86, dir., 1982-86, dir. Nat. Inst. Arthritis, Musculoskeletal and Skin Diseases, 1986-94, dir. emeritus, 1994—, emissary for clin. rsch., 1995—. Chmn. med. adminstrn. com. Arthritis Found., Atlanta, 1974-75, exec. com., 1972-77; dir. Lupus Found. Am.; med. adv. bd. United. Scleroderma Found., Watsonville, Calif., 1977-88; chmn. sci. group rheumatic diseases WHO, 1989; W.R. Graham meml. lectr., 1973; Cochrane disting. lectr., 1993; vis. prof. Imperial Coll., London, 2002. Discoverer: Eosinophilic Fasciitis, 1974, new med. sign friction rubs in scleroderma, 1961. Recipient Sr. Investigator award Arthritis Found., 1957-62, Disting. Svc. award, 1979, Heberden medal for rsch., London, 1975, Superior Svc. award USPHS, 1985, master Am. Rheumatism Assn., 1986, Spl. Recognition award Nat. Osteoprosis Found., 1991, Spl. award Am. Acad. Orthop. Surgeons, 1992, Presdl. citation for leadership Am. Acad. Dermatology, 1993, Leadership award Lupus Found. Am., 1994, Career Achievement award Am. Coll. Rheumatology, 1994, Outstanding Support Rsch. award Am. Soc. Bone Mineral Rsch., 1994, Gold medal Am. Coll. Rheumatology, 1995, award of Merit, NASA, 1995, Dean's Spl. Recognition award Johns Hopkins Medicine, 2004. Fellow ACP, AAAS; mem. Am. Rheumatism Assn. (pres. 1974-75), Pan-Am. League Against Rheumatism (pres. 1982-86, Morino Gold medal award 2002), Soc. Investigative Dermatology, Am. Soc. Bone Mineral Rsch. Home: Apt 7BC 3900 Watson Pl B NW Washington DC 20016 Office: NIH 9000 Rockville Pike Bethesda MD 20892-0003 Office Phone: 301-496-4574. E-mail: lcshulman@comcast.net.

SHULMAN, LEE S., educational association administrator; b. Chgo., Sept. 28, 1938; BA, MA, U. Chgo., 1959, PhD, 1963; doctorate (hon.), U. Judaism, 1989, Hebrew Union Coll., 1995, Mich. State U., 1996, Drury Coll., 1999, U. Aveiro Portugal, 1999, So. Ill. U., 2001. Prof. ednl. psychology and med. edn. Mich. State U., 1963—82; prof. edn. and psychology Stanford U., Calif., 1982-98, Charles E. Ducommun prof. edn. emeritus, 1998—; pres. Carnegie Found. for the Advancement of Tchg., Stanford, Calif., 1997—. Co-author: Educating Lawyers: Preparation for the Profession of Law, 2007; author: The Wisdom of Practice: Essays on Teaching, Learning, and Learning to Teach, 2004, Teaching as Community Property: Essays on Higher Education, 2004. Recipient Grawemeyer Prize in Edn., 2006; fellow Ctr. Advanced Study in Behavioral Scis.; vis. scholar Guggenheim Fellow. Fellow: AAAS, Am. Acad. Arts and Scis.; mem.: Am. Psychol. Assn. (E.L. Thorndike Award for Disting. Psychol. Contributions to Edn. 1995), Nat. Acad. Edn., Am. Ednl. Rsch. Assn. (past pres.). Office: Carnegie Found for Advancement of Tchg 51 Vista Lane Stanford CA 94305 Office Phone: 650-566-5110. Office Fax: 650-326-0278. *

SHULMAN, MAX REES, lawyer; b. Winston Salem, NC, July 11, 1945; AB, Harvard U., 1967; JD, Columbia U., 1970. Bar: N.Y. 1972, U.S. Dist. Ct. (so. and ea. dists.) N.Y., 1974, U.S. Ct. Appeals (2nd cir.) 1982, U.S. Ct. Internat. Trade, 1982, U.S. Supreme Ct. 1987, U.S. Ct. Appeals (9th cir.) 1987, U.S. Ct. Appeals (fed. cir.) 1988, U.S. Ct. Appeals (5th cir.) 1989. Lawyer Cravath, Swaine & Moore, NYC, ptnr., litig. Office: Cravath Swaine & Moore Worldwide Plz 825 8th Ave Fl 38 New York NY 10019-7475 Office Phone: 212-474-1890. Office Fax: 212-474-3700. Business E-Mail: mshulman@cravath.com.

SHULMAN, MILDRED, artist; b. Perth Amboy, NJ, Aug. 13, 1927; d. Abraham and Estelle Shulman; m. Ben Spina, Feb. 20, 1947 (div. Aug. 1954). Student, Sch. Indsl. Arts, NYC, 1942—45, McDowell Sch. Art, 1946—47, NYU, 1961—62, Art Student's League, 1991—95. Contr. Continental Mdse. Co., Inc., NYC, 1959-65, Famous Fashion Shops, NYC, 1966-69; owner, pres. Luminere Creations, Inc., NYC, 1969-91; self-employed artist NYC, 1991—. Author: Barter "The Silent Giant", 1985, The Talking Mammal, 2006. Mem.: Midtown West Art Assn., Am. Soc. Portrait Artists, Nat. Mus. Women in Arts, Art Students League, New Art Ctr., Salmagundi Club. Achievements include 3 patents flexible screen partitions, electrical lighting design, sculpting method. Avocations: hiking, swimming.

SHULMAN, ROBERT GERSON, biophysics professor; b. NYC, Mar. 3, 1924; s. Joshua S. and Freda (Lipshay) S.; m. Saralee Deutsch, Aug., 1952 (dec. Oct. 1983); children: Joel (dec.), Mark, James; m. Stephanie S.

Spangler, May 11, 1986. AB, Columbia U., 1943, MA, 1947, PhD, 1949. Rsch. assoc. Columbia U. Radiation Lab., NYC, 1949; AEC fellow in chemistry Calif. Inst. Tech., Pasadena, 1949-50; head semicondr. research sect. Hughes Aircraft Co., Culver City, Calif., 1950-53; mem. tech. staff Bell Labs., Murray Hill, NJ, 1953-66, head biophysics rsch. dept., 1966-79; prof. molecular biophysics and biochemistry Yale U., 1979-94, dir. divsn. biol. scis., 1981-87, Sterling prof. molecular biophysics and biochemistry, 1994—2002, Sterling prof. emeritus molecular biophysics and biochemistry, 2002—, sr. rsch. scientist dept. diagnostic radiology, 2002—. Rask Oersted lectr. U. Copenhagen, 1959; vis. prof. Ecole Normale Superieur, Paris, 1962; Appleton lectr. Brown U., 1965; vis. prof. physics U. Tokyo, 1965; Reilly lectr. U. Notre Dame, Ind., 1969; vis. prof. biophysics Princeton U., 1971-72; Regents lectr. UCLA, 1978 Lt. (j.g.) USNR, 1944-46. Guggenheim fellow in lab. molecular biology MRC Cambridge (Eng.) U., 1961-62; recipient Havinga medal Leiden U., 1983, Gold medal Soc. Magnetic Resonance in Medicine, 1984, Mem. Nat. Acad. Scis., Inst. Medicine. Achievements include research in spectroscopic techniques applied to physics, chemistry and biology. Office: Dept Diagnostic Radiology MRRC Yale U PO Box New Haven CT 06520-8043 Home Phone: 203-453-9934; Office Phone: 203-785-6201. Business E-Mail: Robert.Shulman@Yale.edu.

SHULMAN, ROBERT JAY, pediatrician, nutritionist, gastroenterologist, educator; b. Newark; s. Irving Jack and Shirley Shulman; children: David Ian, Hannah Rachel. BA, Emory U., 1972; MD, Chgo. Med. Sch., 1976. Diplomate in pediatrics and pediatric gastroenterology Am. Bd. Pediatrics. Asst. prof. pediat. Baylor Coll. Medicine, Houston, 1982-89, assoc. prof., 1989—96, prof., 1996—; dir. nutritional support team Tex. Children's Hosp., Houston, 1982—; chair pediatric gastroenterology Tex. Children's Hosp. Found., 2003. Chmn. sub-bd. in pediatric gastroenterology Am. Bd. Pediatrics, 2003—06. Author: Young Chef's Nutrition Guide and Cookbook, 1990, Keys to Child Nutrition, 1991; author: (with others) Pediatric Gastroenterology and Nutrition in Clinical Practice, 2001, Principles and Practice of Pediatrics, 2006, Pediatric Nutrition Support, 2007; co-editor: Nutrition in Your Pocket, 2002; mem. editl. bd. Jour. Pediat. Gastroenterology and Nutrition, 1994—96. Fellow: Am. Acad. Pediat.; mem.: Soc. Pediat. Rsch., N.Am. Soc. Pediat. Gastoenterology and Nutrition (exec. coun. 1997—99), Am. Inst. Nutrition, Am. Soc. Patenteral and Enteral Nutrition (chmn. pediatric sect. 1997—99, pres. 1997—99), Am. Gastroent. Assn. Avocation: guitar. Office: Baylor Coll Medicine 1100 Bates Ave Houston TX 77030-2600

SHULMAN, RON E., lawyer; b. Boston, 1955; BA, Amherst Coll., Mass., 1977; JD, Rutgers U., 1981. Bar: N.Y. 1982, Calif. 1995. Ptnr. Fish & Neave, NYC, 1981—95, Wilson Sonsini Goodrich & Rosati, Palo Alto, Calif., 1995—. Named one of Top Ten Jury Trial Lawyers in Country, The Nat. Law Jour., 2002. Office: Wilson Sonsini Goodrich & Rosati PC 650 Page Mill Rd Palo Alto CA 94304-1050 Office Phone: 650-493-9300. Office Fax: 650-493-6811. Business E-Mail: rshulman@wsgr.com.

SHULMAN, STEPHEN NEAL, lawyer; b. New Haven, Apr. 6, 1933; s. Harry and Rea (Karrel) S.; m. Sandra Paula Still, Aug. 14, 1954; children—Harry, Dean, John. BA, Harvard, 1954; LL.B. cum laude, Yale, 1958. Bar: Conn. 1958, D.C. 1960. Indsl. rels. Bendix Aviation Corp., 1954-55; law clk. to Justice Harlan, U.S. Supreme Ct., 1958-59; vis. asst. prof. U. Mich. Law Sch., 1959; assoc. firm Covington & Burling, Washington, 1959-60; asst. U.S. atty. Washington, 1960-61; exec. asst. to sec. labor, 1961-62; dept asst. sec. of def., 1962-65; gen. counsel U.S. Air Force, 1965-66; chmn. Equal Employment Opportunity Commn., 1966-67; mem. Kane, Shulman & Schlei, Washington, 1967-70; mem. firm Cadwalader, Wickersham & Taft, NYC, also Washington, 1971-95, Freedman, Levy, Kroll & Simonds, Washington, 1995-99, O'Connror & Hannan, L.L.P., Washington, 1999—2005; counsel Ivins, Phillips & Barker, Chartered, Washington, 2005—. Vis. asst. prof. law U. Mich., 1959; vis. prof. mgmt. U. Okla., 1965-66. Co-author: The Law of Equal Employment Opportunity, 1990; editor in chief Yale Law Jour., 1957-58. Recipient Medal for Disting. Public Svc., Dept. Defense, 1966, Exemplary Svc. in Public Adminstrn. award, William A. Jump Meml. Found., 1966. Mem. Book and Gavel, Order of Coif, Cum Laude Soc., Phi Alpha Delta. Home: 1332 Skipwith Rd Mc Lean VA 22101-1841 Office: Ivins Phillips & Barker Chartered 1700 Pennsylvania Ave Washington DC 20006-4723 Office Phone: 202-662-3455.

SHULMAN, STEVEN J., health services company executive; Dir. of medical econ. Kaiser Permanente, 1974—82; pres., east ctrl. divsn. CIGNA Healthplans, 1983—86; co-founder Value Health Inc., pres., pharmacy, disease mgmt. group, 1987—96; chmn., pres., CEO Prudential Healthcare Inc., 1997—99; founder Internet HealthCare Group, chmn., CEO, 2000—02; CEO Magellan Health Svcs., Avon, Conn., 2002—, chmn., 2003—. Bd. dir. Lumenos, Digital Ins., RealMed, BenefitPoint Inc., NDCHealth Corp., Internet Health Care Group, HealthMarkets Inc. Office: Magellan Health Svcs 55 Nod Rd Avon CT 06001 Office Phone: 860-507-1900. *

SHULMAN, YECHIEL, engineering educator; b. Tel Aviv, Jan. 28, 1930; came to the U.S., 1950; s. David and Rachel (Chonowski) S.; m. Ruth Danzig, June 29, 1950; children: Elinor D., Ron E., Orna L. BS in Aero. Engring., MIT, 1954, BS in Bus. and Engring. Adminstrn., 1954, MS in Aero. Engring., 1954, DSc Aero. and Astro., 1959; MBA, U. Chgo., 1973. Assoc. prof. mech. engring. Northwestern U., Evanston, Ill., 1959-67; v.p. adv. engring. Anocut, Inc., Elk Grove Vill., Ill., 1967-72; v.p. corp. devel. Alden Press, Elk Grove Vill., Ill., 1973-84; pres. MMT Environ., Inc., Shoreview, Minn., 1984-87; cons. Shulman Assocs., Mpls., 1987-89; prof. mech. engring. dept. U. Minn., Mpls., 1989-2000, H. W. Sweatt chair in technol. leadership and dir. ctr. for devel. technol. leadership, 1989-2000, dir. grad. studies mgmt. of tech. program, 1990-2000, prof. emeritus mech. engring. dept., 2000—. Mem. ASME, Internat. Assn. for Mgmt. of Tech. Business E-Mail: shulman@umn.edu.

SHULMISTER, M(ORRIS) ROSS, lawyer; b. Atlanta, Jan. 6, 1940; s. Morris and Kathryn Sybella (Baker) S.; m. Benita Vee Rosin, Dec. 16, 1974. BEE, U. Fla., 1962, JD, 1973. Bar: Fla. 1973, U.S. Dist. Ct. (so. dist.) Fla. 1974, U.S. Dist. Ct. (mid. dist.) Fla. 1985, U.S. Ct. Appeals (5th and 11th cirs.) 1981. Pvt. practice, Broward County, Fla., 1974—. Spl. master for code enforcement, Pompano Beach, Fla., 1991-92. Mem. Broward County Consumer Protection Bd., 1983-2001, chmn., 1999-2000; chmn. Charter Review Bd., Pompano Beach, Fla., 1994-97; dir. South Pompano Civic Assn., 1989-2000, 2007-, v.p., 1989, pres., 1992-98. Lt. col. USAF, 1964-70, ret., USAFR, 1970-93. Mem. Fla. Bar (mem. constrn. law subcom., civil trial cert. 1984-99), Broward County Bar Assn. (bd. dirs. 2003-06). Office: 590 SE 12th St Pompano Beach FL 33060-9409

SHULRUFF, STUART P., lawyer; b. Chgo., Apr. 28, 1959; BS, U. Ill., 1981; JD cum laude, Loyola U., 1984. CPA Ill., 1981; bar: Ill. 1984. Ptnr. Katten Muchin Zavis Rosenman, Chgo. Mem.: Ill. Bar Assn., Chgo. Bar Assn. Office: Katten Muchin Zavis Rosenman 525 W Monroe St Chicago IL 60661 Office Phone: 312-902-5694, 312-577-8680. E-mail: stuart.shulruff@kmzr.com.

SHULSTAD, ANDREW ROBERT, pediatrician; s. Robert Norman and Carol Ann Shulstad; children: Mary Claire, Christopher, Connor. BSA, U. Ga., Athens, 1992; MD, Med. Coll. Ga., Augusta, 1996. Intern, then resident Med. Coll. Ga., 1996—99; pediatrician Charlotte Pediat. Clinic, NC, 1999—. Camp physician YMCA Camp Thunderbird, Lake Wylie, SC, 2005—; chief pediat. Levine Children's Hosp., Charlotte, 2006—. Chmn. bd. dirs. Reach Out and Read-Charlotte, 2003—05; mem. adv. panel Charlotte Jr. League, 2005—. Recipient Pres. award, Mecklenburg County Med. Soc., Charlotte, 2004. Fellow: Am. Acad. Pediat.; mem.: Carolina Physicians Network (exec. bd. 2007—), NC Pediat. Soc. (exec. bd. 2006—). Avocations: soccer, basketball, water sports, horseback riding, travel. Office: Charlotte Pedia Clinic 4501 Cameron Valley Dr Charlotte NC 28211

SHULTIS, ROBERT LYNN, finance educator, consultant, retired professional society administrator; b. Kingston, NY, June 30, 1924; s. Albert H. and Dorothy Elizabeth (Jenkins) S.; m. Bernice Elizabeth Johnson, Jan. 20, 1946; 1 son, Robert Lee. BS, Columbia Univ. Sch. Bus., 1949, postgrad., 1949-51. Staff acct. Price Waterhouse, NYC, 1949-52; credit mgr., controller Organon, Inc., West Orange, NJ, 1952-68; v.p., treas., chief fin. officer Arwood Corp., Rockleigh, NJ, 1968-72; v.p., controller Technicon, Tarrytown, NY, 1972-80; exec. dir. Inst. of Mgmt. Accts., Montvale, NJ, 1980-86; faculty, exec. dir. Ctr. for Exec. Devel. Coll. William & Mary, Williamsburg, Va., 1987-91. Instr. Rutgers U., 1964-74, Fairleigh Dickinson U., 1967-68; mem. Fin. Acctg. Standards Adv. Coun., 1981-86; lectr., seminar leader, cons. on controllership, activity-based costing, cost mgmt., cost sys. design Boston U., U. Calif., Berkeley, U. Minn., Michigan State U., So. Meth. U., Baldwin Wallace Coll., George Mason U., James Madison U., U. N.C., Colo. State U., others, 1990—. Editor: Management Accountants' Handbook, and supplements, 1991-94; contbr. feature articles to Va. Gazette, 2001—; contbr. articles to profl. jours. Bd. advs. U. Fla. Sch. Accountancy, James Madison U. Sch. Accountancy; fin. and budget com. Kingsmill Cmty. Svcs. Assn.; interpreter Historic Jamestowne Island, 1997—. With USAF, 1943-45 Decorated Presdl. Unit Citation, ETO Ribbon, eight battle stars. Mem. AAUP, Am. Legion, Fin. Execs. Internat. (editl. adv. bd.), Inst. Mgmt. Accts., Assn. for Preservation of Va. Antiquities, Kingsmill Club, Beta Alpha Psi (adv. forum).

SHULTS, ANNA, elementary school educator; BA in Elem. Edn., Anderson Univ., 1996; MA in Elem. Edn., Ind. Wesleyan Univ. Nominee Disney's Am. Tchr. award, 2000; named Fall Creek Elem. Tchr. of Yr., 2006, Hamilton Southeastern Tchr. of Yr., 2006, Ind. Tchr. of Yr., 2007; recipient Hamilton Southeastern Thank An Educator award (five). Office: Fall Creek Elem Sch 12130 Olio Rd Fishers IN 46037 Office Phone: 317-594-4180. Business E-Mail: ashults@hse.k12.in.us. *

SHULTS, ROY L., lawyer; b. Cin., June 10, 1948; BA summa cum laude, UCLA, 1970; JD, Harvard U., 1973. Bar: Calif. 1973. Judge pro tem Small Claims Ct., 1980; mem. Mitchell, Silberberg & Knupp; pvt. practice Santa Monica, Calif. Mem. ABA (mem. antitrust sect. task force 1983), L.A. County Bar Assn. (mem. exec. com. antitrust sect. 1981-88, first vice chair 1986-87), Phi Beta Kappa, Pi Gamma Mu, Pi Kappa Delta. Office: PO Box 7550 Santa Monica CA 90406

SHULTZ, DELRAY FRANKLIN (LUCKY SHULTZ), business coach, consultant; b. South Bend, Ind., Apr. 4, 1948; s. Jack Raymond and Georgina Martha (Johnston) Shultz; m. Catherine Elizabeth Yontz, June 6, 1970; children: Jeremy Frank, Eric Bruce, Jon Karl. BS, USAF Acad., 1970; MS, Air U., 1978. Commd. 2d lt. USAF, 1970, advanced through grades to capt., 1973, navigator Anchorage, 1972—77, adminstrv. contracting officer LA, 1978—81; mgr. purchasing, contracts supr. BP Exploration, Anchorage, 1981—92, internal cons. Bogotá, Colombia, 1992—93; mgr. contracts, internal cons. Alaska Petroleum Contractors, Anchorage, 1994—97; support divsn. mgr., internal cons. Natchiq Inc., Anchorage, 1997—2000; owner Pathways to Leadership, Seattle, 1999—2003, Entrepreneur's Source, Seattle, 2002—03, Lucky Shultz & Assocs., 2003—; pres. IGC Assocs., Inc., 2003; fin. aide Alaska State Senate Senator Fred Dyson, 2004—07, chief of staff, 2007—. Adj. prof. U. Alaska, Anchorage, 1989—96; edn. coord. Bus. Network Internat. (Mill Creek, Wash. chpt.), 2001—03. Bd. dirs., vice chair bd. dirs. Family Connection, Inc., Anchorage, 1981—84; del. Alaska Reps., Anchorage, 1988, 1996; dir., bd. elders Bethany Christian Cmty., Anchorage, 1982—93. Named Outstanding Young Men Am., U.S. Jr. C. of C., 1978; recipient Silver medal, Buckley Sch. Pub. Speaking, 1997. Avocations: commercial pilot, public speaker, personal development teacher/coach, musician. Personal E-mail: akluck@yahoo.com.

SHULTZ, GEORGE PRATT, economics professor, former secretary of state; b. NYC, Dec. 13, 1920; s. Birl E. and Margaret Lennox (Pratt) S.; children: Margaret Ann Shultz Tilsworth, Kathleen Pratt Shultz Jorgensen, Peter Milton, Barbara Lennox Shultz White, Alexander George; m. Charlotte Mailliard, Aug. 15, 1997. BA in Econs., Princeton U., 1942; PhD in Indsl. Econs., MIT, 1949; Hon. degree, Yeshiva U., U. Tel Aviv, Technion-Israel Inst. Tech., Keio U., Tokyo, Brandeis U., U. Notre Dame, Princeton U., Loyola U., U. Pa., U. Rochester, Carnegie-Mellon U., Baruch Coll., Northwestern U., Tblisi State U.; Hon. degree (hon.), Columbia U. Mem. faculty MIT, 1949-57, assoc. prof. indsl. relations, 1955-57; prof. indsl. relations Grad. Sch. Bus., U. Chgo., 1957-68; dean sch. Grad. Sch. Bus. U. Chgo., 1962-68, fellow Ctr. for Advanced Study in Behavioral Scis., 1968-69; sec. US Dept. Labor, 1969-70; dir. Office Mgmt. & Budget Exec. Office of the Pres., 1970-72; sec. US Dept. Treasury, 1972-74; asst. to the Pres. The White House, 1972—74; chmn. Council on Econ. Policy, East-West Trade Policy com.; exec. v.p. Bechtel Corp., San Francisco, 1974-75, pres., 1975-81, vice chmn., 1977-81; also dir.; pres. Bechtel Group, Inc., 1981-82; prof. mgmt. and pub. policy Stanford U., 1974-82, prof. internat. econs., 1989-91, prof. emeritus, 1991—; chmn. Pres. Reagan's Econ. Policy Adv. Bd., 1981-82; sec. US Dept. State, 1982-89; Thomas W. and Susan B. Ford disting. fellow Hoover Instn., Stanford, 1989—. Bd. dirs. Accretive Health, Fremont Group; mem. adv. coun. Bechtel Inc.; chmn. J.P. Morgan Chase Internat. Coun.; chmn. adv. coun. Inst. Internat. Studies, 2002—07; mem. Calif. Gov.'s Econ. Policy Adv. Bd., 1995—98, 2003—; chmn. Govs. Coun. Econ. Advisors, 2004—. Author: Pressures on Wage Decisions, 1950, (with Charles A. Myers) The Dynamics of a Labor Market, 1951, (with John R. Coleman) Labor Problems: Cases and Readings, 1953, (with T.L. Whisler) Management Organization and the Computer, 1960, (with Arnold R. Weber) Strategies for the Displaced Worker, 1966, (with Robert Z. Aliber) Guidelines, Informal Controls and the Marketplace, 1966, (with Albert Rees) Workers and Wages in the Urban Labor Market, 1970, Leaders and Followers in an Age of Ambiguity, 1975, (with Kenneth W. Dam) Economic Policy Beyond the Headlines, 1977, 2d edition, 1998, Turmoil and Triumph: My Years as Secretary of State, 1993; also articles, chpts. in books, reports, and essays. Served to maj. USMCR, 1942—45. Recipient Medal of Freedom, 1989, Seoul Peace prize, 1992, Eisenhower medal for Leadership and Svc., 2001, Reagan Disting. Am. award, 2002, Ralph Bunche award for diplomatic excellence, 2002, Am. Spirit award, Nat. WWII Mus., 2006. Fellow Am. Econ. Assn. (disting.); mem. Indsl. Rels. Rsch. Assn. (pres. 1968), Nat. Acad. Arbitrators. Republican. Office: Stanford U Hoover Instn Stanford CA 94305-6010 Business E-Mail: shultz@hoover.stanford.edu.

SHULTZ, JOHN DAVID, lawyer; b. LA, Oct. 9, 1939; Student, Harvard Coll., Cambridge, Mass., 1960—61; BA, U. Ariz., Tucson, 1964; JD, U. Calif., Berkeley, 1967. Bar: N.Y. 1968, Calif. 1978. Assoc. Cadwalader, Wickersham & Taft, NYC, 1968—77; ptnr. Lawler, Felix & Hall, LA, 1977—83, mem. exec. com., chmn. planning com., co-chmn. recruiting and hiring com.; ptnr. Morgan, Lewis & Bockius, LA, 1983—, chmn. mgmt. com., mem. lateral entry com., chmn. profl. evaluation com., chmn. practice devel. com., chmn. recruiting com. Mem. adv. bd. Internat. and Comparative Law Ctr., Southwestern Legal Found., 1981—; active Practicing Law Inst. Adv. Bd., Corp. and Securities Law, 1992—; Trustee St. Thomas Ch., NYC, 1969—72, Shore Acres Point Corp., Mamaroneck, NY, 1975—77. Mem.: N.Y. State Bar Assn., State Bar Calif., Assn. Bar City of N.Y., ABA. Office: Morgan Lewis & Bockius LLP 300 S Grand Ave Ste 22 Los Angeles CA 90071-3109

SHULTZ, LOIS FRANCES CASHO, nursing supervisor; b. Phila., Apr. 29, 1936; d. Ellwood Francis Casho and Beatrice Mae Gunther Casho; m. Thomas Eugene Shultz, Aug. 15, 1959 (div. June 1983); children: David T., Patricia Shultz Bichefsky, Jeffrey A. Nursing diploma, Temple U. Hosp., 1957; BSN, U. Pa., 1961. RN Pa., 2007, bd. cert. gerontol. nursing, ANCC, 2001. Staff nurse Temple U. Hosp., Phila., 1957, pvt. duty nurse, 1958-59; nursing instr. St. Luke's Hosp. Sch. Nursing, Bethlehem, Pa., 1959-61, Reading (Pa.) Area C.C., 1985-88; asst. DON Reading Nursing Ctr., West Reading, 1988-89; night supr. Berks County Home-BerksHeim, Leesport, Pa., 1989—2004; ret., 2004. Mem. Berks County Bd. Assistance, Reading, 1980—, chmn., 1988-2001, chmn. cmty. rels. com., 2001—; pres., dir. Berks County Med. Soc. Aux.; past bd. dir., chmn., mem. children and youth com. Berks County Mental Health Assn.; organizer, past dir. Reading Is Fun-damental Berks County; past mem., chmn., mem. programs and svcs. sub-com. United Way Home Health Care Study Com.; bd. dir. Berks-Schuylkill unit Arthritis Found., 2005-06, sec., 2006. Mem. Nat. Soc. DAR (1st vice-regent br. Berks County chpt. 1977-80). Republican. Presbyterian. Home: 5 Wendy Rd Reading PA 19601-1031 Personal E-mail: templenurse@1usa.com.

SHULTZ, STEPHEN A., secondary school educator; BS, NYU, NYC, 1972; MA, NYU, 1976; postgrad., Bklyn. Coll., 1992. Social studies tchr. N.Y.C. Schs., 1972—88; asst. prin. social studies Boys and Girls H.S., Bklyn., 1988—2001; dir. social studies, art in edn. Rocky Point Pub. Schs., Rocky Point, NY, 2001—. Author: Teachers Manual - Global History and Geography, Teachers Manual - U.S. History and Government. Named Tchr. of the Yr., Assn. of Tchrs. Social Studies/United Fedn. Tchrs., 1987—88; fellow, Rockefeller Found., 1986, Gilder Lehrman fellow. Mem.: Nat. Coun. for the Social Studies, L.I. Coun. for the Social Studies (exec. bd.). Avocations: race walking, tropical fish, reading.

SHUMACKER, HARRIS B., JR., retired surgeon, educator, author; b. Laurel, Miss., May 20, 1908; s. Harris B. and Corinne (Teller) S.; m. Myrtle E. Landau, Dec. 1, 1933 (dec.); children: Peter D., James N.; m. Grace McConnel, Nov. 9, 1998. BS, U. Tenn., Chattanooga, 1927; A.M., Vanderbilt U., 1928; MD, Johns Hopkins U., 1932; D.Sc. (hon.), Ind. U., 1985. Diplomate Am. Bd. Surgery, Am. Bd. Thoracic Surgery. Asst. in surgery Johns Hopkins U., 1932-35, instr., 1938-41, asst. prof., 1941-46; asst. in surgery Yale U., 1936-37, instr., 1937-38, assoc. prof., 1946-48; prof. surgery Ind. U., 1948-70, chmn. dept., 1948-68, Disting. prof., 1970-78, Disting. prof. emeritus, 1978—. Prof., sr. advisor Uniformed Svcs. U. of Health Scis., Bethesda, Md., 1981-87, Disting. prof. surgery, 1988—; pres. Uniformed Svcs U. Assocs., 1987-88; hon. mem. surg. faculties in Peoples Republic of China, 1979-; dir. sect. cardiovascular-thoracic surgery St. Vincent Hosp., 1973-78, sr. surg. cons., 1978-81. Served from capt. to lt. col. M.C., U.S. Army, 1942-46; cons. surgeon gen., 1949-60 Recipient Roswell Park award, 1968, Medal of Honor, Evansville U., 1970, Disting. Alumus award U. Tenn. at Chattanooga, Curtis medal, 1970, Spl. Alumnus award Johns Hopkins U., 1973, Disting. Svc. award Am. Soc. Abdominal Surgery, letter of commendation Surgeon-Gen. USN, 1987, Disting. Svc. medal Uniformed Svc. U. Health Scis., 1988, René Leriche prize Soc. Internat. de Chir., 1993. Fellow Royal Coll. Surgeons Eng. (hon.); mem. Am. Assn. Surgery of Trauma, Am. Surg. Assn. (1st v.p. 1961, sec. 1964-68), So. Surg. Assn., Ctrl. Surg. Assn., Pan-Pacific Surg. Assn. (trustee 1961-64, v.p., 1964-75, pres. 1975-78), AMA (chmn. sect. gen. surgery), Internat. Surg. Soc., Internat. Soc. Cardiovasc. Surgeons (v.p. 1957-59, pres. N.Am. chpt. 1956-58), Soc. Clin. Surgery (pres. 1961-63), ACS (chmn. forum com. 1955-60, chmn. nat. TV com. 1964-68, Disting. Service award 1968), Soc. U. Surgeons (pres. 1951), Soc. for Vascular Surgery (pres. 1958-59, disting. fellow 2003), Am. Thoracic Surg. Assn., Soc. Thoracic Surgeons (hon.), Internat. Surg. Group (v.p. 1974-75, pres. 1975-76), Polish Surg. Assn. (hon.), Sociedad Cubana de Angiologia (hon.), Societa Italiana di Chirurgia (hon.), Internat. Surg. Group (hon.), Phi Beta Kappa, Sigma Xi, Alpha Omega Alpha.

SHUMAN, ANN, investment company executive; b. 1968; BA in Eng., Trinity Univ., San Antonio, Tex.; JD, Univ. Chgo. Atty., derivatives, investments products group Sidley & Austin, Chgo.; with Chgo. Merc. Exch. Holdings, Inc., Chgo., 2000—, dir., co-head copr. devel., 2005—. Named one of 40 Under Forty, Crain's Bus. Chgo., 2005. *

SHUMAN, CAROLYN RAE (THORBURN), psychologist, columnist, writer, nurse; d. Donald Spencer and Eileen Mary Thorburn; m. Gary H. Shuman, Nov. 22, 1975; m. Dennis Lee Atkin, June 15, 1963 (div. July 20, 1968); 1 child, Dennis Lee Atkin, Jr. PhD, Tex. A&M U., Commerce, 1985—96; MS, East Tex. State U., Commerce, 1985—90; BS, Bapt. Coll. of Charleston, SC, 1977—78; AA, Armstrong State Coll., Savannah, Ga., 1972—76. RN 1975. Owner Ctr. for Cognitive Therapy, Hamilton, Bermuda, 1999—2003; dir. family svc. ctr. USNAS-Bermuda, St David's, 1992—95; psychotherapist/psychologist Ashton Associates, Hamilton, 1994—99; clin. supr. USNAS-Bermuda, St. David's, 1991—94; adj. prof. Webster U., U. of Md., City Colleges of Chgo., USNAS-Bermuda, 1991—97. Cons. King Edward Hosp. VII EAP, Hamilton, 2001—03, Family Learning Ctr., Hamilton, 1994—96. Author: (book) Jenny Is Scared: When Sad Things Happen in the World (Psychology Grad. Faculty Scholarship, Tex. A&M-Commerce, 1987). Mem., spkr. Bermuda Chamber of Commerce, Hamilton, 2000—03; mem. Fairhaven Christian Care/ Nat. Drug Strategy/, Hamilton, 1998—2001. Recipient Journalism Enterprise, Ga. AP, 1972; scholar Honors Scholarship, Armstrong State Coll., 1973-1975, Grad. Faculty Honors, Tex. A&M Psychology Dept., 1987. Mem.: Nat. Writer Assn., Bermuda Psychol. Assn. (assoc.; pub. info. officer 2003—04), APA (life). Achievements include research in cross culture, health, cognitive behavior therapy, hardiness; death studies (Psychology Journal, 1992); presentations, Death & Dying, SWPA, 1993-1997. Avocations: writing, swimming, travel, music. Office: Family and Children First DelPrado Boulevard Cape Coral FL 33904 Office Phone: 441-505-5792. E-mail: drcshuman@datkin.net.

SHUMAN, CHARLES R., medical educator, internist; b. Harrisburg, Pa., Sept. 18, 1918; s. Charles R. and Esther G. Shuman; m. Mary M. Shuman; children: Charles R., Sandra J. DeSante. BA, Gettysburg Coll., Pa., 1940, DS (hon.), 1973; MD, Temple U., Phila., 1943, MS, 1944. Diplomate Am. Bd. Internal Medine. Intern Temple U. Hosp., Phila., 1943—44, resident in internal medicine, 1944—46, 1948—49, instr., 1949—52, asst. prof. medicine, 1952—58, assoc. prof. medicine, 1958—63, prof. medicine, 1966—89, prof. emeritus, 1989—, chief metabolic svcs., 1952—78. Cons. metabolic diseases Phila. Gen. Hosp., 1957—66, VA Hosp., 1957—66, Doylestown Hosp., 1965—80; mem. various editl. bds. Capt. US Army, 1946—48. Recipient Golden Apple awrd, Temple U. Sch. Medicine, 1963. Fellow: ACP, Phila. Coll. Physicians; mem.: AMA, Profl. Diabetes Acad. (bd. dirs.), Endocrine Soc. Phila., J. Aitken Miegs Med. Assn., Am. Geriatric Soc., Am. Diabetes Assn. (coord. Ea. Pa. 1965—74, dir. 5th allied health postgrad. course 1973, co-dir. 21st postgrad. course 1974, chmn. com. on use of therapeutic agts. 1974—75, bd. dirs. 1976—, vice chmn. com. on stats. 1978—80, coord. com. sci. activities 1978—80, ad hoc com. gestational diabetes 1979, Ann. Tchg. award 1978, lifetime achievement award), Am. Fedn. Clin. Rsch., Pa. Med. Soc. (com. on med. econ. 1978—80, nominating com. 1979—80), Phila. County Med. Soc. (dir. postgrad. inst. 1966—67, bd. dirs. 1972—78, pres. 1977), Temple U. Med. Alumni Assn. (trustee, mem. exec. com. 1977—, chmn. awards com.

1992—93, Man of Yr. awrd 1978), Alpha Omega Alpha, Sigma Xi. Republican. Presbyterian. Avocations: travel, music, gardening. Home: 111 Delene Rd Jenkintown PA 19046 Office: Temple U Hosp 3401 N Broad St Philadelphia PA 19140

SHUMAN, EARL STANLEY, songwriter, music publisher; b. Boston, Aug. 2, 1923; s. Benjamin Morris and Mildred Judith (Kaplan) S.; m. Margaret Stein, Nov. 25, 1956; children: Cathy Elizabeth, Daniel James, Steven Lewis. BA, Yale U., 1945. Owner, pres. Earl/Peg Music Cos., NYC, 1957—; pub. BMI, ASCAP, NYC, 1977—. Composer (lyric writer) popular songs including Seven Lonely Days, 1953 (Country and Western award 1970), Hey There Lonely Girl, 1970 (Gold record), Banjo's Back in Town, Caterina, Clinging Vine, Close to Cathy, Hotel Happiness, Left Right Out of Your Heart, Most People Get Married, My Shy Violet, The River, Starry-Eyed, Theme For a Dream, Time, Time, Young New Mexican Puppeteer; lyricist (musicals) Secret Life of Walter Mitty, 1964 (award 1965), (country song) Leaves are the Tears of Autumn, 1968 (Country and Western award 1969), (TV themes) Coronet Blue, ABC TV, 1967, Confidence/NFL-CBS, 1967-76, (Movie Title Songs) The Disorderly Orderly, Dondi, Judith, Situation Hopeless But Not Serious, Robinson Crusoe on Mars, Barrabas, Monica (love theme from The Carpetbaggers), Love Me Longer (love theme from Arrivederci Baby); songs in feature films include Seven Lonely Days featured in Shaq, Persons Unknown, Traveller, Sweet Dreams, Hey There Lonely Girl featured in Nothing to Lose, Must Love Dogs, Love is a Christmas Rose featured in Serving Sarah; pub. Bat Out of Hell album, 1977 (platinum award 1979). Capt. USMCR, 1943-46, 50-51. Mem.: ASCAP. Avocations: music, baseball, travel. Home and Office: 11 E 88th St Apt 3B New York NY 10128-1158 Office Fax: 212-722-3698. Personal E-mail: earlmusic@earthlink.net.

SHUMAN, JOSEPH DUFF, lawyer; b. Pitts., Dec. 27, 1942; s. Joseph and Anna Jane (Phillips) D.; m. Ann Stewart McMillan, Nov. 9, 1969; children: David Stewart, Lauren Forbes. BA, Yale U., 1964; LLB, Harvard U., 1967. Bar: Pa. 1968, U.S. Dist. Ct. (we. dist.) Pa. 1968. Assoc. Thorp, Reed & Armstrong, LLP, Pitts., 1967-73, ptnr., 1974—2004, co-chmn., corp. and bus. law dept., 1990-94, chmn., 1994-97, sr. counsel, 2004—. Republican. Presbyterian. Office: Thorp Reed & Armstrong LLP One Oxford Ctr 301 Grant St 14th Fl Pittsburgh PA 15219-1425 Business E-Mail: jshuman@thorpreed.com.

SHUMAN, R. BAIRD, academic administrator, consultant, language educator, writer; b. Paterson, NJ, June 20, 1929; s. George William and Elizabeth (Evans) Shuman. AB (Trustees scholar), Lehigh U., 1951; M.Ed., Temple U., 1953; PhD (Univ. scholar), U. Pa., 1961; cert. in philology, U. Vienna, Austria, 1954. Tchr. Phila. Pub. Schs., 1953-55; asst. instr. English U. Pa., 1955-57; instr. humanities Drexel U., Phila., 1957-59; asst. prof. English San José (Calif.) State U., 1959-62; asst. prof. English, edn. Duke U., 1962-63, assoc. prof., 1963-66, prof. edn., 1966-77; prof. English, 1977-93, dir. English edn. U. Ill., Urbana-Champaign, 1977-85, dir. freshman rhetoric, 1979-84, coord. Univ. Associates in Rhetoric Program, 1978-84, dir. devel., 1988-93, acting dir. Ctr. for Study of Writing, 1989-90, prof. emeritus, 1993—. Vis. prof. Moore Inst. Art, 1958, Phila. Conservatory Music, 1958—59, Lynchburg Coll., 1965, King Faisal U., Saudi Arabia, 1978, Saudi Arabia, 81, Bread Loaf Sch. English, Middlebury Coll., 1980, E. Tenn. State U., Johnson City, 1980, Olivet Nazarene Coll., 1984, 86, 88, U. Tenn., Knoxville, 1987; com. mem. William Inge Nat. Festival, 1989—95; contbg. cons. Lit. Rsch. Ctr.; cons. in field. Author: Clifford Odets, 1962, Robert E. Sherwood, 1964, William Inge, 1965, Strategies in Teaching Reading: Secondary, 1978, Elements of Early Reading Instruction, 1979, The First R: Strategies in Early Reading Instruction, 1987;: rev. edit., 1989, Classroom Encounters: Problems, Case Studies, Solutions, 1989, Resources for Writers, 1992, American Drama 1918-1960, 1992, Georgia O'Keeffe, 1993; author: (with Robert J. Krajewski) The Beginning Teacher: A Guide to Problem Solving, 1979; author: (with Eric Hobson) Reading and Writing in High School; author: (with Denny T. Wolfe Jr.) Teaching English Through the Arts, 1990; editor: Nine Black Poets, 1968, An Eye for an Eye, 1969, A Galaxy of Black Writing, 1970, Creative Approaches to the Teaching of English: Secondary, 1974, Questions English Teachers Ask, 1977, Educational Drama for Today's Schools, 1978, Education in the 80's-English, 1980, The Clearing House: A Closer Look, 1984, 70th anniversary issue Clearing House, 1995, Great American Writers: 20th Century, 13 vols., 2002, Cyclopedia of Literary Places, 3 vols., 2003, The Clearing House: A Retrospective, 2004, Ednl. Leadership, 1989—96; exec. editor: Clearing House Jour., 1976—2006, cons. editor: Poet Lore, 1977—90, Cygnus, 1978—2001, Jour. Aesthetic Edn., 1978—82, contbg. editor: Reading Horizons, 1975—85. Active Nat. Trust Hist. Preservation. NEH grantee, Trinity Coll., Dublin, Ireland, 1985. Mem.: MLA, Union Profl. Employees (editor newsletter, mem. exec. com. 1988—92, mem. editl. bd. Poeteka 2005—), Am. Fedn. Tchrs., Nat. Soc. Study Edn., Internat. Assn. Univ. Profs. English, Internat. Reading Assn. (coord. symposium cultural literacy Queensland, Australia 1988), Conf. English Edn. (mem. exec. com. 1976—79), Internat. Fedn. Tchrs. English, Nat. Coun. Tchrs. English (evaluator ERIC Clearing House, mem. com. alt. careers English profs.). Democrat. Home: PO Box 27647 Las Vegas NV 89126-1647 Personal E-mail: rbaird@intermind.net. *An education that does not produce people who are vibrantly alive, intoxicated with the wonder of existence, has fallen short. Joy of learning is the fulcrum upon which the human equation is balanced. I have always believed that emotion prevails over intellect and have led my life accordingly with the inevitable result of being extraordinarily happy for most of my days.*

SHUMAN, SAMUEL IRVING, lawyer, educator; b. Fall River, Mass., Aug. 7, 1925; s. Max and Fannie S.; children: Maxim Erric, Michael A.; m. Gordana Potkonjak, Feb. 21, 2007. AB, U. Pa., 1947, MA, 1948, PhD, 1951; JD, U. Mich., 1954; S.JD, Harvard U., 1959. Bar: Mich. 1954, Tex. 1979. Research asst. Legis. Research Center, U. Mich., Ann Arbor, 1953-54, vis. prof. law, 1961; vis. prof. U. Rome, 1963-64; asst. prof. law Wayne State U., Detroit, 1954-55, assoc. prof., 1955-56, prof., 1957-80; prof. dept. psychiatry Wayne State U. Med. Sch. Lectr. Internat. Faculty Comparative Law, Luxembourg, 1964; prof. forensic psychiatry, spl. counsel Lafayette Clinic, Mich. Dept. Mental Health; gen. counsel Mich. Psychiat. Assn., Epilepsy Center Mich. Author: Legal Positivism: Its Scope and Limitations, 1963; (with N.D. West) Introduction to American Law: Cases and Materials, 1971, Psychosurgery and the Medical Control of Violence: Autonomy and Deviance, 1977; mem. editl. bd.: Am. Jour. Jurisprudence, 1969-79. Bd. dirs. Tex. Modern Art Found. Recipient Wayne State U. Bd. Govs. Faculty Recognition award, 1978; Probus Club award Disting. Acad. Achievement in Humanities, 1963; Fulbright fellow Italy, 1961; Rockefeller Found. grantee, 1959, 61; Fulbright travel grantee Germany, 1961; Wayne State U. research grantee, 1960-64; Internat. Research & Exchanges Bd. grantee, 1973 Mem. Am. Law Inst. (life). E-mail: sishuman@sbcglobal.net.

SHUMAN, STANLEY S., investment banker; b. Cambridge, Mass., June 22, 1935; s. Saul A. and Sarah L. (Saxe) S.; m. Ruth H. Lande, 1967 (div. 1979); children: David Lande, Michael Adam; m. Sydney Roberts Gould, 1992. BA, Harvard U., Cambridge, 1956, JD, 1959, MBA, 1961. Bar: Mass. 1959, N.Y. 1991. Mng. dir. Allen & Co., LLC, NYC, 1961—. Bd. dirs. News Corp., 1982—2005, dir. emeritus, 2005—; mem. Pres.'s Fgn. Intelligence Adv. Bd., 1995—2001; bd. dirs. Sesac Inc.; dir. Ripplewood Holdings LLC. Pres. Wiliwyck Sch., 1971—78; alumni charter trustee Phillips Acad., Andover, Mass., 1972—80; v.p. exec. com. Jewish Guild for the Blind, 1973—80; chmn. Nat. Econ. Devel. and Law Ctr., 1978—83, Marc Haas Found., 1995—; mem. Fin. Control Bd., NYC, 1977—97, Coun. on Fgn. Rels., 1995—; bd. trustees The Dalton Sch., 1977—84, hon. trustee, 1984—; trustee Jewish Publ. Soc., 1986—90, NY Law Sch., 1990—96, Carnegie Hall, 1990—, The Markle Found., 1992—, Nat. Pub. Radio Found., 1992—, Mus. TV and Radio, 1996—, Vail Valley Found.; life trustee Channel 13 WNET, 1990—; chmn. adv. bd. Inst. Policy Scis. and Pub. Affairs, Duke U., 1992—96; bd. advisors Harvard Exec. Com. Bd. Overseers Com. U. Resources, 1995—; dir. Lower Manhattan Devl. Corp., 2003—05, Mayors Fund Advance NYC; chmn. adv. com., bd. advisors Palamon Capital Ptnrs. Clubs: Harvard (Boston), Harvard (NYC), Econ. Club NY, Deepdale Golf Club, Atlantic Golf Club, Eagle Springs Golf Club, Quaker Ridge Golf, East Hampton Tennis.

SHUMAN-RILEY, BRENDA, literature and language educator; b. Marietta, Ga. 2 children. BA in English Edn., Ga. So. Univ., Statesboro, specialist degree in Ednl. Adminstrn. and Supervision, PhD in Ednl. Administrn. and Leadership; MA in English Edn., Univ. Ga., Athens. Named Ga. Tchr. of Yr., 2006. Mem.: SPAGE future tchr. org., Profl. Assn. Ga. Educators, Delta Kappa Gamma Soc., Phi Delta Kappa, Kappa Delta Pi. Office: Dublin High Sch 1951 Hillcrest Dr Dublin GA 31021 Office Phone: 478-275-3025. Business E-Mail: bshumanr@doe.k12.ga.us. *

SHUMATE, ALEX, lawyer; b. DeKalb, Miss., June 14, 1950; m. Sharon Louise Holley, Aug. 3, 1974; children: John Alexander, Aaron Michael. BA in Polit. Sci., Ohio Wesleyan U., 1972; JD, U. Akron, 1975. Bar: Ohio 1975, U.S. Dist. Ct. (no. and so. dists.) Ohio 1976, U.S. Supreme Ct. 1980. Asst. atty. gen. State of Ohio, Columbus, 1975-83; atty. Brownfield, Bally & Goodman, Columbus, 1983-85; chief counsel, dep. chief of staff Gov., State of Ohio, Columbus, 1985-88; mng. ptnr.- Columbus, Ohio Office Squire, Sanders & Dempsey L.L.P., Columbus, 1988—. Bd. dirs. Bank One Corp., Chgo, Bank One, N.A., Columbus, Intimate Brands, Inc., Columbus, William Wrigley Jr. Co., Chgo. Bd. trustees Ohio State U., Ohio Wesleyan U., Columbus Mus. of Art; governing com. The Columbus Found.; 1st vice chmn. Columbus Urban League; bd. trustees, exec. com. BalletMet; bd. govs. Pub. Policy Com., United Way of Franklin County; exec. com. 29th Dist. Citizens Caucus, 1992 Commn., Christopher Columbus Quincentennial Jubilee Commn.; founding trustee Participation 2000, Berwick Civic Assn. Recipient Jewish Nat. Fund Tree of Life award 1996, Robert S. Crane Trusteeshp award Leadership Columbus, 1995, Spl. Achievement award NAACP, 1989, Disting. cmty. Svc. award Columbus Urban League, 1987, Cert. of Outstanding Achievement 116th Ohio Gen. Assembly 1985, Polit. Leadership award 29th Dist. Citizens Caucus, 1984, Outstanding Legal Cmty. Svc. award Captial U. Sch. of Law, 1982, Superior Achievement award United Negro Coll. Fund, 1982; named Outstanding Alumni U. Akron Law Sch., 1994, Disting. Alumnus Ohio Wesleyan U., 1992. Fellow Columbus Bar Assn. (governing bd., Cmty. Svc. award 1986), Ohio State Bar Assn. (coun. of dels.); mem. Lambda Boule, John Mercer Langston Bar Assn., Greater Columbus C. of C. (1st vice chair), The Capital Club (bd. govs.). Office: Squire Sanders & Dempsey LLP 41 S High St Ste 1300 Columbus OH 43215-6197 Office Phone: 614-365-2739. Office Fax: 614-365-2499. Business E-Mail: ashumate@ssd.com.

SHUMWAY, ERIC BRANDON, academic administrator; s. James Carroll and Merie Kartchner Shumway; m. Carolyn Merrill, June 1963; 7 children. BA, Brigham Young U., 1964, MA, 1966; PhD in English Lit., U. Va., 1973. Tchr., English Ch. Coll. of Hawaii, 1966—70; academic v.p. Brigham Young U.-Hawaii, 1980—86, 1990—94, prof. English and modern languages, 1966—, pres., 1994—; acting pres. Polynesian Cultural Ctr., 1991. Trainer, Tongan language US Peace Corps, 1967—68. Missionary, Tonga, 1959—62; pres. Tonga Nuku'alofa Mission, 1986—89; Area Authority Seventy Hawaii, Calif.; bishop Hauula 2nd Ward, 1968—70. Office: Brigham Young U-Hawaii 55-220 Kulanui St Laie HI 96762 Business E-Mail: shumwaye@byuh.edu. *

SHUMWAY, HOLLY ANN, art educator; b. Hanover, Pa., Dec. 2, 1966; d. Larry Paul and Bonnie Lee Stover; m. Peter Eldon Shumway, Sept. 8, 1990; children: David Orion, Noah Scott, Elijah Everett. AA, Portland C.C., Oreg., 2006. X-ray technologist St. Francis West Hosp., Ewa Beach, Hawaii, 1990—91; agrl. instr. Mitch Charter Sch., Tigard, Oreg., 2004—05, art tchr., 2004—05, Young Rembrandts, Portland, 2006—. Chair CPO-4B Citizen Participation Orgn., Bull Mountain, Oreg., 2003—04, vice chair, 2005—06. Mem.: Soc. Children Book Writers, Phi Theta Kappa. Democrat. Avocations: writing, painting, drawing, gardening. Home: 14535 SW Woodhue St Portland OR 97224 Office: Ste H Box 242 16200 SW Pacific Hwy Portland OR 97224

SHUPE, DWIGHT A. (IKE), lawyer; b. Bristol, Tenn., July 8, 1946; BS with honors, Ball State U., Muncie, Ind., 1968; MS, MIT, 1970; JD cum laude, So. Meth. U., Dallas, 1981. Bar: Tex. 1982. Atty. to ptnr. Hughes & Luce, LLP, Dallas, 1981—. Mem. Devel. Code Rev. Com. Denton C. of C., Tex.; mem. Greater Dallas Homebuilders Assn., Greater Ft. Worth Homebuilders Assn., Tex. Capt. USAF, 1971—78. Named one of Best Lawyers in Dallas, D Mag., 2001, 2003, 2005. Mem.: Dallas Bar Assn., ABA. Office: Hughes & Luce LLP DR Horton Tower 301 Commerce Ste 3000 Fort Worth TX 76102 Office Phone: 817-347-5280. Office Fax: 817-347-5299. E-mail: ike.shupe@hughesluce.com.

SHUR, MICHAEL, electrical engineer, educator, consultant; b. Kamensk-Uralski, Sverdlovsk, USSR, Nov. 13, 1942; came to US, 1976. s. Saul and Anna (Katz) S.; m. Paulina Gimmelfarb, Sept. 25, 1966; children: Luba, Natasha. MS, Leningrad Elec. Tech. Inst., 1965; PhD, Ioffe Inst., Leningrad, 1967; DSc, Ioffe Inst., St. Petersburg, 1992; Hon. Doctorate, St. Petersburg State Tech. U., 1994. Scientist Ioffe Inst., 1965-75; asst. prof. Wayne State U., Detroit, 1976-77, Oakland U., Rochester, Mich., 1978; prof. U. Minn., Mpls., 1979-92; John Marshall Money prof. U. Va., Charlottesville, Va., 1989-96; Patricia W. and C. Sheldon Roberts prof. Rennselaer Poly. Inst., 1996—; assoc. dir., prof. physics. and info. tech. Ctr. Integrated Electronics and Electronics Mfg., 1997—; dir. Ctr. for Broadband Data Transport Sci. and Tech., 2002—; co-dir. NSF Industry/Univ. Coop. Rsch. Ctr. Connection One, 2004—; co-founder, v.p. Sensor Electronic Tech., Inc., 1999. Editor-in-chief Internat. Jour. High Speed Electronics and Systems, mem. hon. editl. bd. Solid State Electronics, Internat. Semiconductor Device Rsch. Symposium; contbr. over 1000 articles to profl. jours., chapters to books; author: Gunn Effect, 1971, Physics of Semiconductor Devices, 1990, GaAs Devices and Circuits, 1991, Introduction to Electronic Devices, 1996, many others; co-author: Ferroelectrics and Antiferroelectrics, 1971, Gunn Effect, 1975, Semiconductor Device Modeling for VLSI, 1993, Introduction to Device Modeling and Circuit Simulation, 1998, Introduction to Solid State Lighting, 2002; co-editor: Semiconductor Technology: Processing and Novel Fabrication Techniques, 1997, Sensitive Skin, 2000, others; regional editor (USA): physicia status solidi. Recipient Van Der Ziel award, Internat. Semiconductor Device Rsch. Symposium, 1999, Humboldt Sr. Rsch. award, 2002, SOE Rsch. award, Rensselaer Poly. Inst., 2003, Compound SEMI Pioneer award, 2003. Fellow: AAAS, IEEE (v.p. pubs. IEEE Sensor Coun., assoc. editor IEEE Trans. 1990—93, Leon Kirchmaeyr award 2007, MTT Disting. Microwave lectr., EDS Disting. lectr., Donald Fink award 2007), Inst. Engring. and Tech., World Innovation Found., Electrochemical Soc., Am. Phys. Soc.; mem.: ASEE, Humboldt Soc. Am., Materials Rsch. Soc., Sigma Xi, Tau Beta Pi, Eta Kappa Nu. Achievements include more than 30 patents on solid-state devices. Office: Rensselaer Poly Inst CII 9017 110 8th St Troy NY 12180-3590 Office Phone: 518-276-2201. E-mail: shurm@rpi.edu. *When we were penniless refugees, the United States adopted me and my family with compassion and friendship, gave us work and citizenship. Our debt of gratitude to the American people who accepted us as their own we will never be able to repay.* *

SHURE, MYRNA BETH, psychologist, educator; b. Chgo., Sept. 11, 1937; d. Sidney Natkin and Frances (Laufman) Shure. Student, U. Colo., 1955; BS, U. Ill., 1959; MS, Cornell U., Ithaca, NY, 1961, PhD, 1966. Lic. psychologist Pa. Asst. prof. U. RI; head tchr. Nursery Sch., Kingston, 1961-62; asst. prof. Temple U., Phila., 1966-67, assoc. prof., 1967-68; instr. Hahnemann Med. Coll., Phila., 1968-69, sr. instr. psychology, 1969-70, asst. prof., 1970—73, assoc. prof., 1973—80, prof., 1980—2002, Drexel U., Phila., 2002—. Spl. cons. PBS Children's TV Show The Puzzle Place; adv. bd. Parents Mag., 2004—. Author (with George Spivack): Social Adjustment of Young Children, 1974; author: (with George Spivack and Jerome Platt) The Problem Solving Approach to Adjustment, 1976; author: (with George Spivack) Problem Solving Techniques in Childrearing, 1978; author: (child curricula manual) I Can Problem Solve, 1992; author: (trade book) Raising a Thinking Child, 1994; author: (audiotape, workbook, paperback) Raising a Thinking Preteen, 2000 (Parents' Choice award, 2001, Parent's Guide Classic award, 2001); author: Thinking Parent, Thinking Child, 2004; mem. editl. bd. Jour. Applied Devel. Psychology. Recipient Lela Rowland Prevention award, Nat. Mental Health Assn., 1982, Sarah award, Women in Comm. (Phila. chpt., 1998, Psychology in the Media award, Pa. Psychol. Assn., 1999, award, Ctr. for Substance Abuse Prevention, 2001; rsch. grantee, NIMH, 1971—75, 1977—79, 1982—85, 1987, 1988—93, NJ Gov.'s Juvenile Justice and Delinquency Prevention grantee. Fellow: APA (divsn. clin. psychology, child sect. 1994, Disting. Contbn. award divsn. cmty. psychology 1984, Task Force on Prevention award 1987, Task Force on Model Programs award 1994, U. Utah and Juvenile Justice Dept. of Delinquency Prevention award 1996, US Dept. Edn. award 2001); mem.: Phila. Soc. Clin. Psychologists, Soc. Rsch. in Child Devel., Nat. Assn. Edn. Young Children, Nat. Assn. Sch. Psychologists. Office: Drexel U Dept Psychology 245 N 15th St MS 626 Philadelphia PA 19102 Office Phone: 215-762-7205. Business E-Mail: mshure@drexel.edu.

SHURIN, LEONARD JOSEPH, school system administrator; b. Johnstown, Pa., Aug. 18, 1951; s. Leonard Thomas and Betty Elena (Booth) Shurin; m. Sherry Irene Hersh, May 4, 1974; children: Holly Lynne, Amy Lou. BA in English Lit., U. Pitts., 1973, BA in Edn. and Commns., 1986; M in Curriculum and Instrn., The Pa. State U., State College, 2006. Cert. ESL program specialist Pa. Dept. Edn., 2003. Adult and family literacy edn. adminstr. Greater Johnstown Career and Tech. Ctr., Johnstown, Pa., 1986—2002; staff and curriculum developer Appalachia Intermediate Unit 8, Altoona, Pa., 2002—. Pres. Cambria County Literacy Coun., Johnstown, Pa., 1986—90; instr. U. Pitts., 1998—2002; com. mem., ESL proficiency stds. com. Pa. Dept. Edn., Harrisburg, 2003—, com. mem., govs. sch. for ESL strategies, 2003—, com. mem., transl. and interpretation com., 2003—, pde-approved instr. for grad. level courses in ESL. Author: (ednl. rsch. book) Curriculum and the Cultural Body, 2007. Bd. mem. Cambria County Literacy Coun., Johnstown, Pa., 1986—2002. Mem.: TESOL (assoc.). United Methodist. Avocations: hiking, reading. Home: 1013 Granger Dr Johnstown PA 15905 Office: Appalachia Intermediate Unit 8 4500 6th Ave Altoona PA 16602 Home Phone: 814-255-5826; Office Phone: 814-940-0223. Office Fax: 814-949-0984; Home Fax: 814-255-5826. Personal E-mail: sjl@atlanticbb.net. Business E-Mail: ljs@iu08.org.

SHURTLEFF, AKIKO AOYAGI, artist, consultant; b. Tokyo, Jan. 24, 1950; d. Kinjiro and Fumiyo (Sugata) Aoyagi; m. William Roy Shurtleff, Mar. 10, 1977 (div. Jan. 1995); 1 child, Joseph Aoyagi. Grad., Women's Coll. Art, Tokyo, 1971; student, Acad. Art, San Francisco, 1991—92. Fashion designer, illustrator Marimura Co. and Hayakawa Shoji, Inc., Tokyo, 1970-72; co-founder, art dir. Soyfoods Ctr. consulting svcs., Lafayette, Calif., 1976-94; freelance illustrator, graphic designer. Lectr. U.S. Internat. Christian U., Tokyo, 1977, Japanese Tofu Mfrs. Conv., Osaka, 1978; presenter cooking demonstrations; tchr. cooking classes. Co-author, illustrator: The Book of Tempeh, 1979, Tofu and Soymilk Production, 1979, Miso Production, 1979, Tempeh Production, 1980, The Book of Tofu and Miso, 2001, The Book of Tofu, 2005, The Book of Miso, 2005, co-author, illustrator: Chinese edit., 2005 (award Japan External Trade Orgn., 2007), illustrator: Spirulina, 1982, The Book of Shiatsu-The Healing Art of Finger Pressure, 1990, Staying Healthy with Nutrition, 1992, Culinary Treasures of Japan, 1992, Yookoso, An Invitation to Contemporary Japanese, vols. 1 and 2, 1994—95, Blue Collar and Beyond, 1995, Damn Good Ready to Go Resumes, 1995, Homework, 1995, Vegetarian's A to Z Guide to Fruits and Vegetables, 1996, Hubert Keller's Cuisine, 1996, Doctor Generic Will See You Now, 1996, Everyday Pediatrics for Parents, 1996, Angels in My Kitchen-Devine Desserts Recipes, 1997; The Shurtleff and Lawton Families: Genealogy and History, 2005; designer co. logos, greeting cards:. Office: PO Box 443 Lafayette CA 94549-0443

SHURTLEFF, MALCOLM C., plant pathologist, consultant; b. Fall River, Mass., June 24, 1922; s. Malcolm C. and Florence L. (Jewell) S.; m. Margaret E. Johnson, June 14, 1950; m. Freda L. Nothnagel, Aug. 1, 1998; children: Robert Glen, Janet Lee, Mark Steven. BS in Biology, U. R.I., 1943; MS in Plant Pathology, U. Minn., 1950, PhD in Plant Pathology, 1953. Asst. plant pathologist Conn. Agrl. Expt. Sta., New Haven, 1942, R.I. Agrl. Expt. Sta., Kingston, 1943; asst. extension prof. U. R.I., Kingston, 1950-54; assoc. extension prof. Iowa State U., Ames, 1954-61; prof. plant pathology U. Ill., Champaign-Urbana, 1961-92, prof. emeritus, 1992—; cons., writer Urbana, 1992-98. Adj. prof. Tex. A&M U., College Station, 1998—. Author: How To Control Plant Diseases, 1962, 66 (award Am. Garden Guild 1962, 66), How To Control Lawn Diseases and Pests, 1973, How To Control Tree Diseases and Pests, 1975, Controlling Turfgrass Pests, 1987, 97, 2002, A Glossary of Plant Pathological Terms, 1997, The Plant Disease Clinic and Field Diagnosis of Abiotic Diseases, 1997, Diagnosing Plant Diseases Caused by Nematodes, 2000; editor-in-chief Phytopathology News, 1966-69, Plant Disease, 1969-72; contbr. numerous articles to encys., profl. publs. and mags. Lt. (j.g.) USN, 1943-46, PTO. Recipient Disting. Svc. award USDA, Washington, 1986, E.C. Stakman award U. Minn., 2000. Fellow Am. Phytopathological Soc. (councilor at large 1970-71, Excellence in Extension Plant Pathology award 1991); mem. Internat. Soc. Plant Pathology (chmn. extension com. 1975-80), Am. Phytopathological Soc. (mem. various coms.). Avocation: photography. Home: 6730 Heron Ln Pearland TX 77584-6618 Personal E-mail: lmshurt@att.net.

SHURTLEFF, MARK L., state attorney general; BA, Brigham Young U.; JD, U. Utah. Officer, atty. JAG USN, 1985—90; pvt. practice in law Calif., 1990—93; asst. atty. gen. State of Utah, 1993—97; dep. county atty. Salt Lake County, 1997—98; commr. Salt Lake County Commn., 1999—2000, chmn., 2000; atty. gen. State of Utah, 2001—. Leader Boy Scout troops, 1980—; anti-drug lectr., at-risk youth mentor. Republican. Office: Office of Atty Gen State Capitol Rm 236 Salt Lake City UT 84114-0810 Office Phone: 801-538-9600. *

SHURTLIFF, MARVIN KARL, lawyer; b. Idaho Falls, Nov. 6, 1939; s. Noah Leon and Melba Dorothy (Hunting) S.; m. Peggy J. Griffin, Nov. 23, 1963; 1 dau., Jennifer Karyl. BA, Idaho State Coll., 1962; JD, U. Idaho, 1968. Bar: Idaho 1968. Tchr. pub. schs., Jefferson County, Idaho, 1964-65; atty. U.S. Dept. Justice, Washington, 1968-74; commr. Idaho Pub. Utilities Commn., 1974-75, pres., 1975-76; spl. asst., legal counsel Gov. of Idaho, Boise, 1977; U.S. atty. for Dist. of Idaho, Boise, 1977-81; practice law Boise, 1981—. Mem. Idaho Ho. of Reps., 1962-64 Mem. Idaho State Bd. Edn., 1990—95, Idaho Commn. on Redistricting, 2001. Mem. Idaho Bar Assn. Democrat. Home: 62 Horizon Dr Boise ID 83702-4419 Office: PO Box 1652 Boise ID 83701-1652 Office Phone: 208-343-2900.

SHUSHKEWICH, KENNETH WAYNE, structural engineer; b. Winnipeg, Man., Can., Sept. 22, 1952; m. Valdine Cuffe, Sept. 28, 1980. BSCE, U. Man., Winnipeg, 1974; MS in Structural Engring., U. Calif., Berkeley, 1975; PhD in Structural Engring., U. Alta., Edmonton, Can., 1985. Engr. Wardrop and Assocs., Winnipeg, 1974—78, Preconsult Can., Montreal, Que., 1978—80; prof. U. Alta., 1981—85, U. Man., 1985—87; engr. T.Y. Lin Internat., San Francisco, 1988—90, H.J. Degenkolb Assocs., San Francisco, 1990—92, Ben C. Gerwick, Inc., San Francisco, 1993—94, J. Muller Internat., Chgo., 1994—95, T.Y. Lin Internat., San Francisco, 1995—99, KSI Bridge Engrs., San Francisco, 1999—. Prin. works include design of prestressed concrete segmental bridges; design mgr. for long-span west approach bridge of Northumberland Strait Crossing in Can.; contbr. articles to profl. jours. Recipient award for design of Vierendeel truss bridge, Man. Design Inst., 1977. Fellow ASCE; mem. Am. Concrete Inst., Prestressed Concrete Inst., Internat. Assn. Bridge and Structural Engrs. Achievements include invention of strutted box widening method for long-span bridge widening. Office: PO Box 2590 San Francisco CA 94126-2590

SHUSTER, ALVIN, journalist, reporter; b. Washington, Jan. 25, 1930; s. Fred and Dora (Levy) S.; m. Miriam Schwartz, June 22, 1952; children: Fred, Jessica, Beth. AB, George Washington U., 1951. Reporter Washington Bur. N.Y. Times, 1952-61, asst. news editor, 1961-66, reporter London Bur., 1967-70; bur. chief Saigon, Vietnam, 1970-71, London, 1971-75, Rome, 1975-77; dep. editor editorial pages L.A. Times, 1977-83, fgn. editor, 1983-95, sr. consulting editor, 1995—. Pres. Fgn. Corrs. Assn., London, 1973-74; trustee Monterey (Calif.) Inst. Internat. Studies, 1983-99; chmn. Pulitzer Prize Jury Internat. Reporting, 1999. Editor: The Witnesses, 1964, Washington: The New York Times Guide to the Nations' Capital, 1967, International Press Institute Report, 1995-99; assc. editor Global Journalist, 1999-2004; contbg. author: The Kennedy Years, 1964; contbg. editor Columbia Journalism Rev., 1999-2004. Nieman fellow Harvard U., 1966-67. Mem. Reform Club (London). Office: Los Angeles Times 202 W 1st St Los Angeles CA 90012

SHUSTER, BETH, editor; b. Washington; BA in Eng. Lit., Univ. Calif., Santa Cruz. Reporter State News Svc., Wash., Riverside (Calif.) Press-Enterprise; edn. writer LA Daily News, 1987—93; police reporter, edn. writer to state desk LA Times, 1994—2004, edn. editor, 2004—. Office: Edn Editor LA Times 202 W First St Los Angeles CA 90012 Office Phone: 213-237-7847. Office Fax: 213-237-4712. *

SHUSTER, BUD, business executive, former congressman; b. Glassport, Pa., Jan. 23, 1932; s. Prather and Grace (Greinert) S.; m. Patricia Rommell, Aug. 27, 1955; children: Peg, Bill, Debbie, Bobby, Gia. BS, U. Pitts., 1954; MBA, Duquesne U., 1960; PhD in Econs. and Mgmt., Am. U., 1967. Nat. account mgr. Univac divsn. Sperry Rand, 1956, Univac divsn. Remington Rand Co. (now Sperry Rand), 1956-60; dist. mgr. Western Pa. RCA, 1960-62, mgr. ops. Washington, 1962-65, v.p. EPD divsn., 1965-68; pres. computer terminal co., 1968-72; mem. 93rd-106th Congresses from 9th Pa. dist., Washington, 1973-2001, former chmn. U.S. House Transp. Com., former ranking mem. U.S. House Select Com. on Intelligence; pres. Strategic Advisors, Everett, Pa., 2001—; chmn. Safe Extensions, Inc. Vis. prof. St. Francis U., Loretto, Pa., 2001. Author: Believing in America, 1983. Del. Rep. Nat. Conv., 1976, 80, 84, 88, 92, 96; co-chair Energy, Environment & Transp. Platform Subcom.; sr. transp. advisor Bush-Quayle Campaign; also mem. platform com.; chmn. Reagan-Bush Campaign in Western Pa.; sr. advisor to transition team for Dept. Transp., 1980-81; trustee J.F. Kennedy Ctr. for Performing Arts. With Counter-Intelligence US Army, 1954—56. Recipient Watchdog of Treasury award, Guardian of Small Bus. award, Golden Age Hall of Fame award. Mem. Pa. Soc., Chowder and Marching Soc., Capitol Hill Club, Phi Beta Kappa, Omicron Delta Kappa, Sigma Chi (Significant Sig award).

SHUSTER, FREDERICK, retired internist, gastroenterologist; b. Newark, Sept. 12, 1933; s. Ralph and Anne (Weinstein) S.; m. Jane A. Block, June 11, 1958; children: Alan R., Robert G. BS, Rutgers U., 1955; MD, U. Chgo., 1959. Diplomate Am. Bd. Internal Medicine, Am. Bd. Gastroenterology. Intern U. Mich. Hosp., Ann Arbor, 1959-60, resident internal medicine, 1960-62; resident gastroenterology VA Hosp. U. Miami, Fla., 1962-63; pvt. practice N. Miami Beach, Fla., 1963-97; from clin. instr. to assoc. prof. medicine U. Miami, Fla., 1963—; pvt. practice Aventura, Fla., 1997-98; ret., 1998. Chmn. dept. medicine Parkway Regional Med. Ctr., N. Miami Beach, 1967, 70, chief of staff, 1974-75, chief divsn. gastroenterology, 1976-77, chmn. pharmacy and therapeutics com., 1978-98. Chmn. med. advisory com. Crohn's and Colitis Found., S. Fla. chpt., Miami, 1979-81. Major U.S. Army, 1967-69. Recipient Physician's Recognition award in Continung Edn., AMA, Chgo., 1970—. Fellow Am. Coll. Physicians, Am. Coll. Gastroenterology, Alpha Omega Alpha. Jewish. Avocations: bowling, ballroom dancing, stock market research and investing. E-mail: fred991@att.net.

SHUSTER, HELEN M., library director; MA, Edinburgh U.; MLS, Syracuse U. Dir. Gordon Libr. Worcester Poly. Inst., Mass. Chair bd. dirs. New England Libr. Network (NELINET); steering com. mem. Ctrl. Mass. Regional Libr. Sys. Bd. dirs. Seven Hills Found. Office: George C Gordon Libr Worcester Poly Inst 100 Institute Rd Worcester MA 01609-2280 Office Phone: 508-831-5058. E-mail: hshuster@wpi.edu. *

SHUSTER, MARGUERITE, minister, educator; b. Oxnard, Calif., Sept. 10, 1947; d. Carroll Lloyd and Grace Margaret (Hornbeck) S. BA with great distinction, Stanford U., Calif., 1968; MDiv, Fuller Sem., Pasadena, Calif., 1975; PhD, Fuller Grad. Sch. Psychology, Pasadena, 1977. Ordained to ministry Presbyn. Ch. USA, 1980. From asst. to assoc. pastor Arcadia Presbyn. Ch., Calif., 1980-86; pastor Knox Presbyn. Ch., Pasadena, Calif., 1987-92; adj. asst. prof. preaching Fuller Sem., Pasadena, 1988-90; assoc. prof. preaching Fuller Theol. Sem., Pasadena, 1992—2001, prof. preaching, 2001, Harold John Ockenga prof. of preaching and theol., 2007—. Del. gen. Assembly Mission Consultation Planning Team, 1984—85, Inst. Ecumenical and Cultural Rsch., Collegeville, Minn., 1985, Collegeville, 86; com. chair Gen. Assembly, 1988; Staley lectr. Sterling Coll., 2001; Harp lectr. Anderson Sch. Theology, 2004. Author: Power, Pathology, Paradox, 1987, The Fall and Sin: What We Have Become as Sinners, 2004; mem. editl. bd.: Theology, News and Notes, 1986—2005; contbr. articles sermons, and revs. in religious jours. and books; editor (contbr.): Perspectives on Christology, 1991, Who We Are: Our Dignity as Human, 1996. Bd. dirs. Sierra Madre Mountain Conservancy, 2002—. Named one of Outstanding Young Women in Am., 1979, 1983. Mem. Presbytery of San Gabriel (chair, com. on ministry 1991, moderator, permanent jud. commn. 1993-95, moderator Presbytery 1996), Phi Beta Kappa. Home: 675 Mount Wilson Trl Sierra Madre CA 91024-1232 Office: Fuller Theol Sem 135 N Oakland Ave Pasadena CA 91182-0001 Office Phone: 626-584-5248. Business E-Mail: shuster@fuller.edu. *A goal: so to trust in Jesus Christ, especially in times of sorrow and disappointment, that others might find it easier rather than more difficult to believe in a loving, omnipotent God.*

SHUSTER, ROBERT DOUGLAS, archivist; b. Phila., June 26, 1951; s. William L. and Lieselotte Ursula Shuster. BA, Wheaton Coll., Ill., 1973; MA in Am. History, U. Wis., Madison, 1975; MLS, No. Ill. U., Dekalb, 1985. Cert. Acad. of Cert. Archivists, 2002. Dir. of archives Billy Graham Ctr. Archives, Wheaton, 1975—2000, archivist, 2000—. Editor: (collection guide) Researching Modern Evangelicalism: A Guide to the Holdings of the Billy Graham Center, with Information on Other Collections. Named one of Alumni of Yr., Wheaton Coll., 1992; recipient Sister Claude M. Ln. award, Soc. of Am. Archivists, 1987. Mem.: Midwest Archives Conf., Soc. Am. Archivists. Home: PO Box 1184 Wheaton IL 60189-1184 Office: Archives Billy Graham Ctr Wheaton Coll Wheaton IL 60187 Home Phone: 630-690-8641; Office Phone: 630-752-5910. Office Fax: 630-752-5916. Business E-Mail: robert.d.shuster@wheaton.edu.

SHUSTER, ROBERT G., electronics executive, consultant; b. NYC, June 1, 1927; s. Robert Chandler and Therese G. (Giraud); m. Marianne B. Lynski, Apr. 20, 1970 (div. Jan. 1987); m. H. Elizabeth Young, May 20, 1989 (div. Dec. 1995); m. Erika Megas, May 5, 2002. BSEE, CCNY, 1948; MSEE, Columbia U., 1955, postgrad., 1959-64. Test engr. Elec. Testing Labs., NYC, 1948-50; project leader Sperry Gyroscope Co., Great Neck, NY, 1950-59; project mgr. RCA Advanced Communications Lab., NYC, 1959-67; prin. scientist Tracor, Inc., Rockville, Md., 1967-75, v.p. electronics systems div., 1975-87; pres. Tracor Tech. Resources, Inc., Rockville, Md., 1984-90, RGS Assocs., McLean, Va., 1990—; v.p. C-Cubed Corp., Alexandria, Va., 1990-93, pres., 1993-95; sr. cons., 1996—. Mem. IEEE (sr.), N.Y. Acad. Scis. Avocations: photography, hiking.

SHUSTER, WILLIAM (BILL SHUSTER), congressman; b. McKeesport, Pa., Jan. 10, 1961; s. E.G. "Bud" Shuster; m. Rebecca Shuster; children: Ali, Garrett. BA in Polit. Sci. and Hist., Dickinson Coll., Carlisle, Pa., 1983; MBA, American U., Washington. Mgr. retail stores Goodyear Tire and Rubber Corp.; dist. mgr. Bandag Inc.; mem. US Congress from 9th Pa. dist., 2001—. Mem. armed svcs. com. US Congress, mem. transp. and infrastructure com., chmn. econ. devel., pub. bldgs. and emergency mgmt. subcommittee. Mem.: Rural Health Care Coalition, Nat. Fedn. Ind. Bus., NRA, Masons. Republican. Lutheran. Office: 310 Penn St Ste 200 Hollidaysburg PA 16648 Office Phone: 202-225-2431, 814-696-6318. Office Fax: 814-696-6726. *

SHUSTERMAN, NATHAN, underwriter, financial consultant; b. Montreal, Que., Can., Aug. 27, 1927; arrived in US, 1950; s. Aaron and Annie (Nulman) S.; m. Norma Thalblum, Jan. 1950; children: Mark D., Claudia S. Student, Sir George Williams Coll., Montreal, 1944-47; grad., N.Y. Inst. Fin. CLU, chartered fin. cons. Retailing mgr. Jefferson Stores, Miami, Fla., 1950-65; gen. agt. Protective Life Ins. Co., Miami, 1965—. Chmn. emeritus field adv. coun., past pres. Protective Club; pres. Am. Fin. Counseling Corp., Miami; instr. estate and tax planning Am. Coll., Bryn Mawr, Pa., 1972—, U. Miami, Coral Gables, Fla., 1972—; registered rep. Pro Equity Services Inc.; cons. in field. Named Man of Yr., Gen. Agts. and Mgrs. Assn., Miami, 1965-67. Mem. North Dade-South Broward Estate Planning Coun., Million Dollar Round Table (life), Top of Table, Assn. Advanced Life Underwriting, Soc. Fin. Svc. Profls. (past pres. Miami chpt.), Nat. Assn. Ins. and Fin. Advisors (Nat. Sales Achievement award, Nat. Quality award), Fla. Assn. Ins. and Fin. Advisors, Miami Assn. Ins. and Fin. Advisors, Internat. Assn. Fin. Planners, Am. Soc. Pension Actuaries (assoc.), Optimists (pres. North Miami Beach, Fla. chpt. 1971), Masons, Shriners, B'nai B'rith (pres. Miami chpt. 1950). Office: Am Fin Counseling Corp 16121 NE 18th Ave Miami FL 33162-4749 Home: 21050 NE 38th Ave Apt 1701 Miami FL 33180-4078 Office Phone: 305-949-0906.

SHUSTERMAN, NEAL DOUGLAS, writer, scriptwriter; b. NYC, Nov. 12, 1962; s. Milton and Charlotte Ruth (Altman) S.; m. Elaine Gale Jones, Jan. 31, 1987; children: Brendan, Jarrod, Joelle, Erin. BA in Psychology and Drama, U. Calif., Irvine, 1985. Author, screenwriter, 1987—. Author: Guy Talk, 1987, The Shadow Club, 1988 (Children's CHoice award Internat. Reading Assn. 1989), Dissidents, 1989, Speeding Bullet, 1991 (Best Book for Teens award N.Y. Pub. Libr., nominated Calif. Young Reader Medal 1995-96), Kid Heroes, 1991, What Daddy Did, 1991 (Best Book for Young Adults award ALA, Outstanding Work of Fiction award So. Calif. Coun. Lit. for Children and Young People, Children's Choice award and Young Adult Choice award Internat. Reading Assn., Pick of the List award ABA, Best Book for Teens award N.Y. Pub. Libr., Okla. Sequoyah award 1994), The Eyes of Kid Midas, 1992 (ALA Best Book for Reluctant Readers), Darkness Creeping, 1993, Piggyback Ninja, 1994, Scorpion Shards, 1995 (N.Y. Pub. Libr. Best Book for the Teenaged), Darkness Creeping II, 1995, Mindquakes, 1996 (ALA YALSA Quick Pick), Mindstorms, 1996, Mindtwisters, 1997, The Dark Side of Nowhere, 1997 (ALA Best Book, ALA Quick Pick--Top 10 Book), Thief of Souls, 1999, Downsiders, 1999 (ALA Best Book, ALA Quick Pick), MindBenders, 2000, The Shadow Club Rising, 2002, Shattered Sky, 2002, Full Tilt, 2003 (Tex. Lonestar award), The Schwa Was Here, 2004 (Boston Globe Horn Book award, ALA Best Book, ALA Notable), Dread Locks, 2005 (ALA Quick Pick), Red Rider's Hood, 2005 (ALA Quick Pick), Duckling Ugly, 2006, Everlost, 2006, Unwind, 2007; screenwriter: Double Dragon, 1992, Evolver, 1993; dir. Heart on a Chain, 1991 (Golden Eagle award CINE), What About the Sisters, 1993 (Golden Eagle award CINE), Games: How to Host a Teen Mystery, Hot Times at Hollywood High, 1994, Barbecue with the Vampire, 1997, Roswell that Ends Well, 1999, How to Host a Murder: Roman Ruins, 1996, The Good, the Bad and the Guilty, 1997, The Tragical Mystery Tour, 1998, The Maiming of the Shrew, 2000, Saturday Night Cleaver, 2000, An Affair to Dismember, 2003, (TV) Goosebumps: The Werewolf of Fever Swamp, 1996, Goosebumps: Night of the Living Dummy III, 1997, Animorphs (staff writer), 1998, Pixel Perfect, 2004. Mem. PEN, Writers Guild Am. West, Soc. Children's Book Writers and Illustrators. Avocations: swimming, tennis, storytelling. Home: P O Box 80093 Rancho Santa Margarita CA 92688 E-mail: NStoryman@aol.com.

SHUTE, RICHARD EMIL, federal agency administrator, engineer; b. Bklyn., May 1, 1938; s. William Leonard and Doris S.; m. Linda Janan McElhiney, Mar. 7, 1960. BS in Mech. Engring., U. Miami, 1960; MBA, Fla. State U., 1970. Registered profl. engr., Fla. Engr. Pratt and Whitney Aircraft, West Palm Beach, Fla., 1960-62, Gen. Dynamics Corp., San Diego, 1962-64; aerospace engr. NASA/Kennedy Space Ctr., Fla., 1964-71; dir. planning and evaluation Fla. Dept. Health and Human Services, Tallahassee, 1971-76; dir. office program devel. Office Human Devel., HHS, Washington, 1976-87; dir. office of mgmt. and info. systems U.S. Dept. Commerce, Washington, 1987-90; pres. Richard E. Shute and Assocs. Mgmt. Cons., 1990—. Mem. Nat. Assn. Security Dealers (bd. arbitrators).

SHUTLER, MARY ELIZABETH, retired academic administrator; b. Oakland, Calif., Nov. 14, 1929; d. Hal Wilfred and Elizabeth Frances (Gimbel) Hall; m. Richard Shutler Jr., Sept. 8, 1951 (div. 1975); children: Kathryn Allice (dec.), John Hall, Richard Burnett. BA, U. Calif., Berkeley, 1951; MA, U. Ariz., 1958, PhD, 1967. Asst., assoc., full prof. anthropology, chmn. dept. San Diego State U., 1967-75; prof. anthropology, dept. chmn. Wash. State U., Pullman, 1975-80; dean Coll. Arts and Scis., prof. anthropology U. Alaska, Fairbanks, 1980-84; vice chancellor, dean of faculty, prof. anthropology U. Wis. Parkside, Kenosha, 1984-88; provost, v.p. for acad. affairs, prof. anthropology Calif. State U., LA, 1988-94; prof. emeritus, 1994—2007; provost West Coast U., LA, 1994-97; dean Sch. of Arts and Scis. Nat. U., La Jolla, Calif., 1997—2004, dean emeritus, 2004—07; ret., 2007. Mem. core staff Lahav Rsch. Project, Miss. State U., 1975-92. Co-author: Oceanic Prehistory, 1975, Deer Creek Cave, 1964, Archaeological Survey of Southern Nevada, 1963, Stuart Rockshelter, 1962; contbr. articles to jours. in field. Mem. coun. Gamble House; mem. bd. trustees San Diego Archeol. Ctr. 2005-. Fellow Am. Anthropol. Assn.; mem. Soc. for Am. Archaeology, Am. Schs. for Oriental Rsch., Am. Coun. Edn., Am. Assn. for Higher Edn., Am. Assn. State Colls. and Univs., Delta Zeta. Republican. Roman Catholic. Avocations: travel, gardening. Home Phone: 858-673-5200.

SHUTRAN, RICHARD, lawyer; b. New Britain, Conn., Mar. 27, 1952; BA, Trinity Coll., 1974; JD cum laude, NYU, 1978. Bar: N.Y. 1979, US Dist. Ct. (ea. & so. dist. N.Y.). Co-mng. ptnr. & chmn. project fin. group Dewey Ballantine LLP, NYC. Mem.: N.Y. State Bar Assn. Office: Dewey Ballantine LLP 1301 Ave of the Americas New York NY 10019-6092 Office Phone: 212-259-6710. Office Fax: 212-259-6333. Business E-Mail: rshutran@dbllp.com.

SHUTT, ELSIE G., systems analyst, application developer, consultant; m. Philp R. Shutt, Nov. 25, 1953; children: David, Barbara, John. BA, Goucher Coll., Balt., 1948; MA, Harvard U., Cambridge, Mass., 1950. Programmer Raytheon/Datamatic/Honeywell, Waltham and Newton, Mass., 1953—57; pres. Computations Inc., Harvard, Mass., 1957—. Mem.: Assn. Computing Machinery, Am. Math. Soc.

SHUTTLEWORTH, ANNE MARGARET, psychiatrist; b. Detroit, Jan. 17, 1931; d. Cornelius Joseph and Alice Catherine (Rice) S.; m. Joel R. Siegel, Apr. 19, 1959; children: Erika, Peter. AB, Cornell U., 1953, MD, 1956. Intern Lenox Hill Hosp., NYC, 1956-57; resident Payne Whitney Clinic-N.Y. Hosp., 1957-60; practice medicine specializing in psychiatry Maplewood, NJ, 1960—. Cons. Maplewood Sch. System, 1960-62; instr. psychiatry Cornell U. Med. Sch., 1960; mem. Com. to Organize New Sch. Psychology, 1970. Mem. AMA (Physicians Recognition award 1975, 78, 81, 84, 87, 90, 93, 96, 99, 02, 05), Am. Psychiat. Assn., Am. Med. Women's Assn., NY Acad. Scis., Acad. Medicine NJ, Phi Beta Kappa, Phi Kappa Phi. Office: 2066 Millburn Ave Maplewood NJ 07040-3715 Office Phone: 973-763-2929.

SHUTZ, BYRON CHRISTOPHER, real estate company officer; b. Kansas City, Mo., Feb. 16, 1928; s. Byron Theodore and Maxine (Christopher) S.; m. Marilyn Ann Tweedie, Mar. 30, 1957; children: Eleanor S. Gaines, Byron Christopher, Collin Reid, Allison S. Moskow, Lindley Anne Baile. AB in Econs, U. Kans., 1949. Ptnr. Herbert V. Jones & Co., Kansas City, Mo., 1953-72; pres. Herbert V. Jones Mortgage Corp., Kansas City, 1967-72, The Byron Shutz Co., Kansas City, 1973—. Dir. 1st Am. Financial Corp., Rothschild's, Inc., Bus. Men's Assurance Co., Faultless Starch, Bon Ami Co. Chmn. bd. trustees U. Kansas City, 1979-81; trustee Pembroke-Country Day Sch., 1974-77, Midwest Rsch. Inst., 1980-89; chmn., bd. govs. Kansas City Art Inst., 1960-62; chmn. bd. dirs. Ctr. for Bus. Innovation, Inc., 1985-87; bd. dirs. Kansas City Crime Commn. 1st lt. USAF, 1951-53. Mem. Mortgage Bankers Assn. Am. (bd. govs. 1966-74), Am. Inst. Real Estate Appraisers. Clubs: Kansas City Country, University, Mercury (pres. 1978-79); Fla. Yacht (Jacksonville), Ocean Reef (Key Largo, Fla.). Home: 1001 W 58th Ter Kansas City MO 64113-1159 Office: 800 W 47th St Kansas City MO 64112-1251 E-mail: arrowrock3@sbcglobal.net.

SHVARTSMAN, MIKHAIL MEYER, mathematics professor; s. Meyer Gersh Shvartsman and Khava Iosif Kris; children: Marina Chernova, Dina Yushkevich. PhD, U. Md., College Park, 1994. Assoc. prof. U. St. Thomas, Saint Paul, 2006—. Mem.: Am. Meteorol. Soc. (assoc.), Am. Math. Soc. (assoc.). Office: U St Thomas 2115 Summit Ave Mail # OSS 201 Saint Paul MN 55105-1079 Home Phone: 651-699-3952; Office Phone: 651-962-5527. Office Fax: 651-962-5670. E-mail: mmshvartsman@stthomas.edu.

SHVO, MICHAEL, real estate broker; b. Tel Aviv, Dec. 29, 1972; s. Hannah Shvo. With Prudential Douglas Elliman, NYC, 1998—2005, v.p., 2002—05; founder, pres. Shvo Group, 2005—. Mem.: Real Estate Bd. NY. Office: Shvo Group 724 Fifth Ave New York NY 10019 Office Phone: 212-380-2100. E-mail: mshvo@shvo.com. *

SHWAYDER, ELIZABETH YANISH, sculptor; b. St. Louis; d. Sam and Fannie May (Weil) Yaffe; m. Nathan Yanish, July 5, 1944 (dec.); children: Ronald, Marilyn Ginsburg, Mindy; m. M.C. Shwayder, 1988 (dec.). Student, Washington U., 1941, Denver U., 1961; pvt. studies. One-woman shows include Woodstock Gallery, London, 1973, Internat. House, Denver, 1963, Colo. Women's Coll., Denver, 1975, Contemporaries Gallery, Santa Fe, 1963, So. Colo. State Coll. Pueblo, 1967, others; group shows include Salt Lake City Mus., 1964, 71, Denver Art Mus., 1961-75, Oklahoma City Mus., 1969, Joslyn Mus., Omaha, 1964-68, Lucca (Italy) Invitational, 1971, Denver Art Mus., Mus. Natural History, Mizel Mus., Eden Theatrical Workshop, Rose Hosp. Aux., Nat. Mus. Women in the Arts, Colo. Chpt. 8th Air Force Aux., Women's Art Ctr., others; represented in permanent collections Colo. State Bank, Bmh Synagogue, Denver., Colo. Women's Coll., Har Ha Shem Congregation, Boulder, Colo., Faith Bible Chapel, Denver, others. Chmn. visual arts Colo. Centennial-Bicentennial, 1974-75; pres. Denver Coun. Arts and Humanities, 1973-75; co-chmn. visual arts spree Denver Pub. Schs., 1975; trustee Denver Ctr. Performing Arts, 1973-75; chmn. Concerned Citizens for the Arts, 1976; pres. Beth Israel Hosp. Aux., 1985-87; organizer Coat Drive for the Needy, Denver, N.Y.C., 1982-87, Common Cents penny drive for homeless, 1991-93; bd. dirs. Mizel Mus., Srs., Inc.; active Mayor's Com. on Cultural Affairs, Denver Art Mus., Mus. Natural History, Freedom Found. at Valley Forge, Hospice of Metro. Denver; bd. dirs. Rainbow Bridge; bd. dirs. Diabetes Found., Asian Arts Assn. Denver Art Mus., also pres.; historian Childrens Diabetes Found., Univ. Colo. Found. Inc. Humanities scholar Auraria Librs.-U. Colo.; recipient McCormick award Ball State U., Muncie, Ind., 1964, purchase award color Women's Coll., Denver, 1963, Tyler (Tex.) Mus., 1963, 1st prize in sculpture 1st Nat. Space Art Show, 1971, humanitarian award Milehi Denver Sertoma, 1994, The Gleitsman Found., 1994, svc. to mankind awards Freedom Found. at Valley Forge, Mile Hi Sertoma Club, Minoruyasui Found., Gleitsman Found. Mem. Denver Art Mus., Asian Arts Assn. (pres.). Home: Unit 503 2400 Cherry Creek South Dr Denver CO 80209-3259

SHYAMALAN, M. NIGHT (MANOJ NELLIYATTU SHYAMALAN), film director; b. Pondicherry, Tamil-Nadu, India, Aug. 6, 1970; s. Jayalakshmi Shyamalan and Nelliate C; m. Bhavna Vaswani, 1993; 2 children. Grad., NYU, 1992. Actor, dir., prodr., writer: (films) Praying with Anger, 1992, Unbreakable, 2000, Signs, 2002, The Village, 2004, Lady in the Water, 2006; actor, dir., writer: The Sixth Sense, 1999 (Bram Stoker Award for Best Screenplay, 1999, Golden Satellite Award for Best Original Screenplay, 1999, Visionary Award, Palm Springs Internat. Film Festival, 2000, Nebula Award for Best Script, Sci. Fiction and Fantasy Writers Am., 1999, nominated for Best Dir. and Best Original Screenplay, Acad. Awards 2000, Nominated for Best Screenplay, Golden Globes, 2000); dir., writer: Praying Wide Awake, 1998; writer screenplay Stuart Little, 1999; actor (TV appearances) Entourage, 2007 Named one of 50 Most Powerful People in Hollywood, Premiere mag., 2003—05; recipient Samman award, Pravasi Bharatiya Divas, 2005. Office: Creative Artists Agy 9830 Wilshire Blvd Beverly Hills CA 90212

SHYER, JOHN D., lawyer; b. Nashville, May 4, 1956; s. Michael and Hilda (Wertheim) S.; m. Marsha Anne Gisser, May 7, 1989; children: Allison Parcell, Michael Wertheim. AB, Princeton U., 1978; JD, Stanford U., 1981. Bar: NY 1982, US Ct. Appeals (2d cir.) 1983, US Ct. Appeals (3d cir.) 1992. Assoc. Donovan, Leisure, Newton & Irvine, NYC, 1981-85, Latham & Watkins LLP, NYC, 1985-89, ptnr., 1989—. Trustee Princeton Broadcasting Svc., NJ, 1985—. Mem. Assn. Bar City NY, Employment and Labor Lawcast (bd. edit. advisors 1994—), Employment Law Strategist (editl. bd. mem. 2006-). Avocations: travel, hiking, reading. Office: Latham & Watkins LLP 885 3rd Ave Ste 1000 New York NY 10022-4834 Office Phone: 212-906-1200. Business E-Mail: john.shyer@lw.com.

SHYU, HEIDI, defense equipment manufacturing company executive, electrical engineer; b. Taipei, Taiwan, Sept. 28, 1953; came to U.S., 1964; d. Lawrence and Marie (Wu) S. BS in Math., U. New Brunswick, Fredericton, Can., 1976; MS in Math., U. Toronto, Can., 1977; Master's and Engineer's Degree in Elec. Engring., UCLA, 1982. Scientist Hughes Aircraft Co., LA, 1978-89; prin. engr., Joint STARS Self Def. Study Grumman Aerospace, Melbourne, Fla., 1989-90; sr. staff engr. advanced concept dept. Litton Industries, Inc., San Jose, Calif., project mgr., Near Infrared Octane Analyzer commercial develop. project; lab. mgr., electro-magnetic systems Raytheon Co., dir., JSF Antenna Technologies, dir. JSF Integrated Radar/Electronic Warfare Sensors, sr. dir., unmanned combat vehicle prog., dir. Joint Strike Fighter (JSF) prog., Air Combat and Strike Systems, v.p., unmanned and reconnaissance systems, v.p., tech. dir., Space and Airborne Systems, 2004—07, v.p., corp. tech. and rsch., 2007—. Bd. mem. US Air Force Adv. Bd., 2000—, vice chair, 2003—05, chair, 2005—. Mem. San Jose State U. Adv. Coun., 1990—. Hughes fellow Hughes Aircraft Co., 1978-82; named Asian Am. Engr. of Yr., Chinese Inst. of Engineers, 2004. Mem. IEEE, Am. Inst. Aeronautics and Astronautics, Air Force Assn. Avocations: hiking, backpacking, biking, drawing, fgn. travel. Office: Raytheon Co 870 Winter St Waltham MA 02451-1449

SHYU, MEI-LING, information scientist, educator; d. Chun-Jou Shyu and Yu-Hwa Chao; m. Shu-Ching Chen, May 20, 1990; children: Winnie Chen, Tiffany Chen, Jonathan Chen. MS in Restaurant, Hotel, Instl. and Tourism, Purdue U., West Lafayette, Ind., 1997; MS in Computer Sci., Purdue U., 1992, MSEE, 1995, PhD in Electrical and Computer Engring., 1999. Asst. prof. dept. elec. and computer engring. U. Miami, Fla., 2000—05, assoc. prof. dept. elec. and computer engring., 2005—. Grad. student supr. U. Miami, Coral Gables, Fla.; internat. conf. organizer. Contbr. scientific papers. Recipient Metadata Mgmt. award, NOAA, 2004; grantee, NSF, NOAA, FDOI. Mem.: ACM, IEEE (sr. Svc. award 2005). Achievements include design and development of Fishery and Coral Reef databases for NOAA researchers. Office: Univ Miami Dept Elec and Computer Engring Coral Gables FL 33124 Home Phone: 305-278-4787; Office Phone: 305-284-5566. Office Fax: 305-284-4044. Business E-Mail: shyu@miami.edu.

SI, JENNIE, engineering educator; b. Changchun, Jilin, China, Mar. 16, 1963; d. Quanyou Si and Baolin Jiao; m. Jun Shen, July 27, 1988. BS, Tsinghua U., Beijing, 1985, MS, 1988; PhD, U. Notre Dame, 1992. Rsch. asst. U. Notre Dame, South Bend, Ind., 1988-91; asst. prof. Ariz. State U., Tempe, 1991-96, assoc. prof., 1996-2000, prof., 2000—. Cons. Intel Corp., Chandler, Ariz., 1996, Ariz. Pub. Svc., Palo Verde, 1997, Medtronic, Tempe, Ariz., 2002-03; proposal panelist/reviewer NSF/NRC, Washington, 1995—; adviser Assn. Chinese Sci. Engr., Tempe, 1996-99, 2002—; adv. com. Social, Behavioral and Econs. Scis. divsn. NSF, 1998-99, external adv. and sci. review bd.; adv. com. Sci. Learning Ctr., Boston U. Assoc. editor IEEE Transaction on Automatic Control, 1998, 99, IEEE Transaction on Semiconductor Mfg., 1998-2002, Neural Networks, 2001-. Presdl. Faculty fellow The White House/NSF, Washington, 1995-2000; recipient Rsch. Initiation award NSF, Washington, 1993-96, Motorola Excellence award Motorola, Semicon. Prod. Sector, Tempe, 1995. Mem. IEEE (gen. chair internat. joint conf. neural networks 2007), Internat. Neural Networks Soc., Computational Intelligence Soc. (com. mem. 1995—). Avocation: skiing. Office: Ariz State U Dept Elec Engring Tempe AZ 85287 E-mail: si@ash.edu.

SIA, JEFFREY H.K., lawyer; b. Honolulu, June 10, 1956; BA magna cum laude, Brown U., 1978; JD, Villanova U., 1981. Bar: Hawaii 1981. Ptnr. Ayabe Chong Nishimoto Sia & Nakamura LLP, Honolulu. Mem.: Hawaii State Bar Assn. (sec. 2001, treas. 2002, pres.-elect 2006—07). Office: Ayabe Chong Nishimoto Sia & Nakamura LLP Pauahi Tower Ste 2500 1001 Bishop St Honolulu HI 96813 Office Phone: 808-537-6119. Office Fax: 808-526-3491.

SIA, KIMBERLEE JEAN, principal; b. Cedar Rapids, Iowa, Nov. 23, 1975; d. Michael Wayne Unertl and Deborah Jean Frank; m. Andrew Buenaflor Sia, July 24, 2004. BA in German, History, Northwestern U., Evanston, Ill., 1998; MA in Ednl. Leadership, Orgns., U. Calif., Santa Barba, 2006. Cert. mid. child generalist Nat. Bd. Profl. Tchg. Stds. Tchr. Newark Pub. Schs., 1998—2000, Goleta Union Sch. Dist., Calif., 2000—06; prin. Lighthouse Academies, Inc., Gary, Ind., 2006—. Sec. United Tchg. Profession-Goleta, 2001—02, pres., 2002—06. Named Educator of Yr., Goleta Valley C. of C., 2006; Care and Share grant, Santa Barbara County Sch. Dist., 2005. Mem.: Assn. Supervision Curriculum Devel. Office: West Gary Lighthouse Charter Sch 725 Clark Rd Gary IN 46406 Office Phone: 219-977-9583 ext. 208. Business E-Mail: ksia@lighthouse-academies.org.

SIART, WILLIAM ERIC BAXTER, non-profit education organization administrator; b. LA, Dec. 25, 1946; s. William Ernest and Barbara Vesta (McPherson) Baxter; m. Noelle Ellen Reid, Sept. 17, 1966; children—Shayne Allison, Tiffany Ann BS in economics, Santa Clara U., 1968; MBA in fin., U. Calif., Berkeley, 1969. With Bank of Am., 1969-78, v.p. corp. banking Brussels, 1977-78; sr. v.p. charge mktg. Western Bancorp, Los Angeles, 1978-81; pres., COO First Interstate Bank of Nev. N.A., Reno, 1981-82, pres., CEO, 1982-84, chmn. bd., pres., CEO, 1984; formerly chmn., pres., CEO First Interstate Bank Calif., LA, also bd. dirs.; pres. First Interstate Bancorp, LA, 1990-96, CEO, 1994-96; founder, chmn. bd. Excellent Edn. Devel. (ExED), Santa Monica, Calif., 1998—. Bd. trustees J. Paul Getty Trust, 2005—; bd. dirs. Calif. Cmty. Found., 2005—. Mem. Am. Bankers Assn. (mem. govt. relations council), Reno-Sparks C. of C. (dir.). Republican. Roman Catholic. Office: ExED 429 Santa Monica Blvd Santa Monica CA 90401 Office Phone: 310-394-1152. Office Fax: 310-394-7380. E-mail: wsiart@exed.net.

SIAVOSH-HAGHIGHI, ALI, physical chemist, researcher; PhD, U. Mo., Columbia, 2004. Lectr. Persian Gulf U., Boushehr, Iran, 1997—99; post doctoral rsch. assoc. U. Mo., 2004—. Fellow, DOE, 2004—, DOD, 2004—. Mem.: Am. Chem. Soc. (assoc.). Home Phone: 573-874-6731; Office Phone: 573-884-3829.

SIBBALD, JOHN RISTOW, management consultant; b. Lincoln, Nebr., June 20, 1936; s. Garth E.W. and Rachel (Wright) S.; div.; children: Allison, John, Wright. BA, U. Nev., 1958; MA, U. Ill., 1964. Office mgr. Hewitt Assocs., Libertyville, Ill., 1964-66; coll. rels. mgr. Pfizer Inc., NYC, 1966-69; pres., CEO Re-Con Systems, NYC, 1969-70; v.p. Booz, Allen & Hamilton, NYC, 1970-73, Chgo., 1973-75; pres., founder John Sibbald Assocs., Inc., Chgo., 1975. Mem. Nat. Advisory Coun., Nat. Club Assn. Author: The Career Makers, 1990, 92, The New Career Makers, 1995; pub. Club Leaders Forum; contbr. articles to profl. jours. Capt. AUS, 1958-64. Mem. St. Louis Club. Episcopalian. Office: 7733 Forsyth Blvd Saint Louis MO 63105-1817 Home: 3220 Oleander Way Hillsboro Beach FL 33062 Office Phone: 314-727-0227. Business E-Mail: jsibbald@sibbaldassociates.com.

SIBBERNSEN, RICHARD, telecommunications industry executive; b. Omaha; BA, Marquette U., 1971; grad., Creighton U., 1974. Various human resources positions Tenneco, Inc.; head corp. human resources TNT Ltd., Sydney, 1993—97; v.p. human resources Bellsouth Corp., Atlanta, 1997—.

SIBITZ, MICHAEL WILLIAM, school system administrator; b. San Francisco, July 22, 1937; s. Michael Jacob and Erna Anna Elsa (Altendorf) S.; m. Marilyn Joyce Pricco, Nov. 19, 1966; children: Elizabeth, Ryan. BA, San Francisco State U., 1959, MA, 1964; EdD, U San Francisco, 1980; postgrad., Notre Dame Coll. of Calif., Stanford U. Tchr., Pacifica, Calif., 1959—64, Dept. Def., 1964—65, Belmont, Calif., 1965—70; specialist Los Alto, Calif., 1970—71; adminstr. Belmont, Calif., 1971—80; supr. instrn., prin. Los Altos, Calif., 1980—84; asst. supt. Sylvan Union Sch. Dist., Modesto, Calif., 1964—97; supt., interim program dir. St. Mary's Coll., Moraga, Calif., 1998—99. Adj. faculty St. Mary's Coll., Moraga, Calif., 1989—, Edn. Dept. Mills Coll., Oakland, 2006—. Contbr. articles to profl. jours. Bd. dirs. Modesto Symphony, 1993-2002; mem. Stanislaus Arts Commn.; past pres. United Way Stanislaus County, Stanislaus County Industry Edn. Coun. Served with U.S. Army, 1960-66. Mem. NEA (life), ASCD, Assn. Calif. Sch. Adminstrs. (charter-life), Calif. Assn. Supervision and Curriculum Devel. (bd. dirs. 1997, treas. 1999-2001), Phi Delta Kappa. Roman Catholic. Home: 1400 Pinnacle Ct 205 Richmond CA 94801 Personal E-mail: m2sibitz@sbcglobal.net.

SIBLEY, DAVID ALLEN, illustrator, writer, ornithologist; b. 1962; s. Fred Sibley; m. Joan Walsh; 2 children. Illustrator (books) Wind Masters: The Lives of N.Am. Birds of Prey, 1995, author & illustrator Sibley Guide to Birds, Nat. Audubon Soc., 2000, Sibley Guide to Bird Life & Behavior, 2001, Sibley's Birding Basics, 2002, Sibley Field Guide to Birds of Eastern N Am., Birds of Western N.Am., 2003, co-author, illustrator (NY Times Syndicated Column) Sibley on Birds, 2002—. Recipient Roger Tory Peterson award, Am. Birding Assn., 2002. Office: Russell Galen at Scovill Chichak Galen Inc Rm 1020 381 Park Ave S New York NY 10016 also: NY Times Syndication Sales Corp 14th Fl 122 E 42nd St New York NY 10168 Office Phone: 212-679-8686.

SIBLEY, DAVID HURLEY, cardiologist; b. Newport, Ark., June 1, 1952; MD, Tulane Med. Sch., New Orleans, La., 1981. Cert. Internal Medicine, Cardiovascular Disease. Intern, internal medicine U. Ala. Med. Ctr., Birmingham, Ala., 1981—82, resident, cardiology, 1982—84, fellow, 1984—87; clin. cardiologist Baptist Med. Ctr. Princeton, Birmingham, Ala., 1987—. Named one of Golf Digest 2006 Top 250 Golf Doctors in Am. Fellow: Am. Coll. Cardiology; mem.: AMA, Am. Coll. Physicians. Office: 3000 Briarcliff Rd Birmingham AL 35223 Office Phone: 205-879-8065. E-mail: DrDSibleyOffice@cardiologypc.com. *

SIBLEY, JAMES MALCOLM, retired lawyer; b. Atlanta, Aug. 5, 1919; s. John Adams and Nettie Whitaker (Cone) S.; m. Karen Norris, Apr. 6, 1942; children: Karen Mariea, James Malcolm Jr., Jack Norris, Elsa Alexandria Victoria, Quintus Whitaker. AB, Princeton U., 1941; student, Woodrow Wilson Sch. Law, 1942, Harvard Law Sch., 1945—46. Bar: Ga. 1942. Assoc. King & Spalding, Atlanta, 1942-47, ptnr., 1947-91. Bd. dirs. Summit Industries, Inc.; exec. com., mem. pub. affairs com. Coca-Cola Co., 1979-91; chmn. exec. com. John H. Harland Co., 1963-91; chmn. exec. com., mem. compensation com. Trust Co. of Ga., 1975-92; mem. exec. com., mem. compensation com. SunTrust Banks, Inc., 1985-92. Trustee Joseph B. Whitehead Found., Lettie Pate Evans Found., A.G. Rhodes Home, Inc., Robert W. Woodruff Found., Inc. (formerly Trebor Found.); trustee emeritus John H. and Wilhelmina D. Harland Charitable Found., Inc., Berry Coll., The Lovett Sch., Callaway Gardens Found., Emory U. With USAF, 1942—45. Mem. ABA, Ga. Bar Assn., Atlanta Bar Assn., Am. Coll. Probate Counsel, Am. Bar Found., Am. Law Inst., Piedmont Driving Club, Commerce Club. Episcopalian. Home: 3045 Slaton Dr NW Atlanta GA 30305-2006 Office: King & Spalding 1180 Peachtree St Atlanta GA 30309

SIBLEY, WILLIAM ARTHUR, retired academic administrator, physics professor, consultant; b. Ft. Worth, Nov. 22, 1932; s. William Franklin and Sada (Rasor) S.; m. Joyce Elaine Gregory, Dec. 21, 1957; children: William Timothy, Lauren Shawn, Stephen Marshall. BS, U. Okla., Norman, 1956, MS, 1958, PhD, 1960. Tchg., rsch. asst. U. Okla., 1956-60; postdoctoral rsch. in defect solid state Kernforschungsanlage Julich and Tech. U. Aachen, Germany, 1960-61; rsch. solid state divsn. Oak Ridge Nat. Lab., 1961-70; prof., head physics Okla. State U., Stillwater, 1970-76, dir. Sch. Phys. and Earth Scis., 1976-78, asst. v.p. rsch., 1978-88; v.p. acad. affairs U. Ala., Birmingham, 1990-96; program dir. NSF, Washington, 1988-89, acting dir. divsn. materials rsch., 1990, program dir., 1996-99, acting divsn. dir. rsch., evaluation and comm. divsn., 1998-99; pres. Okla. Ctr. for Advancement of Sci. and Tech., 2000—02; CEO, dir. Okla. Sci. and Tech. R & D, 2002—04; ret., 2004. Solid state sci. com. NAS, 1977-83; bd. dirs. Oak Ridge Assoc. Univs., 1982-88, Coun. on Govt. Rels., 1987-93, Okla. Ctr. for Advancement Sci. and Tech., 1987-88; trustee, chmn. materials rsch. counsel Southeastern Univ. Rsch. Assn., 1992-95; cons. in field. Author: University Management 2010, 1998; contbr. articles to profl. jours. Pres. Stillwater Indsl. Found., 1985-86. Served to lt. AUS, 1951-53. Maj. USAR, 1953-60, Korea. Fellow Am. Phys. Soc.; mem. Omicron Delta Kappa, Sigma Xi, Sigma Pi Sigma, Pi Mu Epsilon. Baptist. Home: 2517 Thunderwind Cir Edmond OK 73034-6880 Personal E-mail: sibleybill@aol.com.

SIBLEY, WILLIS ELBRIDGE, anthropology educator, consultant; b. Nashville, Feb. 22, 1930; s. Elbridge and Elizabeth Reynolds (LaBarre) S.; m. Barbara Jean Grant, June 9, 1956 (dec.); m. Marjorie Arielle Hegge, July 6, 2002; children: Sheila Katherine, Anthony Grant, Michael David. BA, Reed Coll., 1951; MA, U. Chgo., 1953, PhD, 1958. Instr. sociology and anthropology Miami (Ohio) U., 1956-58; asst. prof. anthropology U. Utah, 1958-60; from asst. prof. to prof. anthropology Wash. State U., 1960-71; prof. anthropology Cleve. State U., 1971—; chmn. dept., 1971-77, Cleve. (City) faculty fellow, 1987, interim chmn., 1989-90, prof. emeritus, 1990—; sr. program analyst EPA, Washington, 1977-78; Govtl. fellow Am. Coun. on Edn., 1978; Rockefeller Found. vis. prof. anthropology U. Philippines, Quezon City, 1968-69; postdoctoral fellow in society and tech. Carnegie-Mellon U., 1981-82. Fulbright grantee, 1954-55, 64; NIMH grantee, 1959-61; NSF grantee, 1964-71; Nat. Acad. Scis.-NRC travel grantee, 1966; Office Edn., HEW research grantee, 1967 Fellow AAAS, Assn. Profl. Anthropologists (pres. Washington chpt. 1999—), Am. Anthropol. Assn. (treas. 1989-91, com. on pub. policy 2000-2002), Soc. Applied Anthropology (sec. 1977-80, pres. 1981-82, Sol Tax Disting. Svc. award 2006); mem. AAUP (treas. Wash. State U. chpt. 1962-63, v.p. 1963-64, pres. 1965-66, pres. Cleve. State U. chpt. 1979-80, treas. 1980-81, interim pres. 1989-90), ACLU (pres. Pullman chpt. 1963, 66), Ctrl. States Anthropol. Soc. (past mem. exec. bd., treas. 1986-89), Wash. Assn. Profl. Anthropologists, Edgewater Yacht Club (Cleve., commodore 1991), Chesapeake Yacht Club (Shady Side, Md.) (gov. 1999, 2000). Democrat. Unitarian Universalist. Avocation: sailing. Home: 1190 Cedar Ave Shady Side MD 20764 Office: Cleve State U Dept Anthropology Cleveland OH 44115 Home Phone: 301-261-9404; Office Phone: 301-261-9404. Personal E-mail: shadyside1190@comcast.net.

SIBO, ELSA LYNETTE, secondary school educator; d. Lawrence E. and V. Azalee Chapman; m. Richard J. Sibo, Feb. 8, 1964 (dec. Mar. 1, 1986). BA, Blue Mountain Coll., 1962; MEd, U. Nev., 1978. Tchg. cert. Miss., 1962, Tex., 1972, Ga., 1973, Nev., 2002. Tchr. English Greenville H.S., Miss., 1962—64, Schertz-Cibolo Ind. Sch. Dist., Schertz, Tex., 1964—65; tchr. English, speech Randolph Field Ind. Sch. Dist., Universal City, Tex., 1965—72, Clayton County Sch. Dist., Jonesboro, Ga., 1973—74; tchr. English St. Yves H.S., Las Vegas, 1975—76; grad. asst. reading ctr. part time staff U. Nev., 1976—78; tchr. English Clark County Sch. Dist., 1978—2002, CC of So. Nev., Henderson, 2003—. Mem., pres., sec., treas., com. mem. Gamma Chpt., Delta Kappa Gamma, Las Vegas, 1972—2005. Fellow Study Stipend, Delta Kappa Gamma, 1982. Mem.: NEA (life), Delta Kappa Gamma (Rose of Recognition 1983), Kappa Delta Pi (assoc.). Independent. Methodist. Avocations: travel, hiking, ballroom dancing. Personal E-mail: lsibo@earthlink.net.

SIBOLSKI, ELIZABETH HAWLEY, academic administrator; b. Gt. Barrington, Mass., Aug. 18, 1950; d. William Snyder and Frances Harrington (Smith) Gallup; m. John Alfred Sibolski Jr., Aug. 15, 1970. BA, Am. U., Washington, DC, 1973, MPA, 1975, PhD, 1984. Acting dir. acad. adminstrn. Am. U., Washington, 1974, planning analyst, 1974—79, asst. dir. budget and planning, 1980—83, dir. instl. rsch., 1984—85, exec. dir. univ. planning and rsch., 1985—2000; exec. assoc. dir. Middle States Commn. on Higher Edn., Phila., 2000—06, exec. v.p., 2007—. Trustee Mortar Bd. Nat. Found., 1989—95. Recipient Comencement award, Am. U. Women's Club, 1973. Mem. Soc. Coll. and Univ. Planning (bd. dirs. 1995-2000, pres. 1998-99), Mortar Bd. (sect. coord. 1975-82), Pi Alpha Alpha, Phi Kappa Phi (chpt. officer 1986-92), Pi Sigma Alpha, Omicron Delta Kappa. Avocations: breed, raise and show morgan horses. Home: 565 Wayward Dr Annapolis MD 21401-6747 Office: Middle States Commn on Higher Edn 3624 Market St Philadelphia PA 19104-2614 Business E-Mail: esibolski@msche.org.

SIBOLSKI, JOHN ALFRED, JR., educational association executive; b. Nov. 4, 1946; S. John A. and Isabelle Barcaster S.; m. Elizabeth Gallup, Aug. 15, 1970. AA in Data Processing, Andover Inst. Bus., 1966; BS in Tech. of Mgmt., Am. U., 1967; cert. in data processing, 1974, grad. cert. in data processing, 1978. With Automated Systems Corp., Washington, 1969-71, KMS Tech. Ctr., Arlington, Va., 1971-72; ind. cons., 1972-73, 74-76; with Law Enforcement Asst. Adminstrn., Dept. Justice, Washington, 1973-74; D.A. Lewis, Assocs., Clinton, Md., 1974; with Bur. Nat. Affairs, Inc., Washington, 1976-80; mgr. systems. devel. NEA, Washington, 1980-90, Saturn Corp., Cheverly, Md., 1990-91, FBI, Washington, 1991—. Recipient spl. achievement award Dept. Justice, 1974. Mem. Fata Processing Mgmt. Assn., Am. Soc. for Info. Sci. Home: 565 Wayward Dr Annapolis MD 21401-6747 Office: FBI 10th St And Pa Ave Washington DC 20535-0001 E-mail: jsibolski@comcast.net.

SIBONY, GEDI, sculptor; b. NYC, 1973; BA, Brown U., Providence, 1995; student, Skowhegan Sch. Painting and Sculpture, Maine, 1999; MFA, Columbia U., NYC, 2000. Exhibited in group shows at Two Person Show, Gallery 16, San Francisco, 1998, Superimposition, Caren Golden Fine Art, NYC, 2001, Silent Takeover, Staedtische Galerie, Baden, Switzerland, 2002, One Fine Day, Block Gallery, Sydney, Australia, 2003, Breaking Ground, White Columns, NYC, 2003, Playpen: Selections Summer, The Drawing Ctr., NYC, 2004, Slouching Towards Bethlehem, The Project, NYC, 2004, Floorplay, Bklyn. War Meml., 2004, Greener Pastures Contemporary Art, Toronto, Can., 2005, Art Rev. 25, Philips De Pury, NYC, 2005, Make It Now, The Sculpture Ctr., NY, 2005, Walls 'n Things, Nicole Klagsbrun Gallery, NYC, 2005, Poetry in the Backyard, Galerie Art: Concept, Paris, 2006, Whitney Biennial: Day for Night, Whitney Mus. Am. Art, 2006, exhibitions include The Qualities Depend Upon Other Qualities, 2004, Some Places Exist, London, 2005, The Wrong Gallery, NYC, 2005. Grantee, Rema Hort Mann Found., 2004. Mailing: c/o CANADA Gallery 55 Chrystie St New York NY 10002

SIBUL, LEON HENRY, electrical engineer; b. Voru, Estonia, Aug. 30, 1932; arrived in U.S., 1949, permanent resident; s. Aleksander and Helene Sibul; m. Hele Mall Mandel, July 29, 1961; children: Eric Allan, Christina Linda. BEE, George Washington U., 1960; MEE, NYU, 1963; PhD, Pa. State U., 1968. Field engr. Engleman & Co., Inc., Washington, 1958—60; mem. tech. staff Bell Telephone Lab., Holmdel, NY, 1960—64; rsch. asst./assoc. Applied Rsch. Lab. Pa. State U., University Park, 1964—81, prof., sr. scientist Applied Rsch. Lab., 1981—2002, prof. emeritus, 2002—. Cons. NAS, Washington, 1972—74; sr. tech. adv. USN, Washington, 1978—82; vis. prof. Tech. U. Tallinn, Estonia, 2006—. Editor: Adaptive Signal Processing, 1987; mem. editl. bd.: Multidimensional Signal Processing; contbr. articles to profl. jours., chpts. to books. Former faculty advisor Pa. State Sailing Club, University Park, 1974—. Republican. Lutheran. Achievements include development of adaptive array processing techniques for underwater systems, use of wavelet transforms in optimum detectors; first to use application of group theory to signal processing, use info. theoretic concepts for sensor fusion and blind source separation; research in stochastic operator theory. Avocations: sailing, golf, basketball, cross country skiing. Office: Pa State U Applied Rsch Lab PO Box 30 State College PA 16804-0030 Business E-Mail: lhs2@psu.edu.

SICART, PIERRE-ALEXANDRE SERGE HENRY, writer; b. Toulouse, France, Jan. 27, 1975; s. Pierre Alain Thierry Sicart and Micheline Marie Mauricette Ory. DEUG in English, U. Toulouse II, France, 1997; Licentiate Integrated European Studies, U. St. Andrews, Scotland, 1998; PhD in French Lit. with honors, NYU, NYC, 2005; Doctorat es Lettres with highest honors, U. Toulouse II, France, 2005. Computer expert trainee Tocqueville Asset Mgmt., NYC, 1996; web designer, asst. forum mgr. and interpreter Leisure On Line, Saint-Orens, France, 1996—98; tchg. asst. elem. and intermediate French N.Y. U., NYC, 2001—02, tchg. asst. French lang. and lit., 2002—03; freelance voice actor N.Y. Audio Prodns., 2006—. Co-author: Le Web pas cher, 1999; co-editor: Amberzine 12-15, 2005; co-editor and translator: Maîtriser Office 2000 visuel, 1999, Moteurs de recherche pour le WEB, 1999; co-translator Trésors cachés Office 2000, 1999; author: (short stories) État de crise, 1999, Le Crabe et la Fée, 2000, Comment j'ai sauvé la Terre des Martiens, 2000, Sur la digue, 2001 (first text in prose awarded poetry prize Acad. des Jeux Floraux, 2001), 25¢, 2001, Le Temple sous la lune, 2002, L'Adieu aux légendes, 2003, Le Mauvais choix, 2005, Fors l'Honneur, 2005; designer: French phonetic game, 2004; contbr. articles to profl. jours. Capt. N.Y. U. Taekwondo Club, NYC, 2003—04. Named Most Valuable Player Taekwondo, NYU Athletics, 2001—02, Graduation Std. Bearer, Grad. Sch. Arts and Scis. NYU, 2005; recipient Pres.'s Svc. award, NYU, 2003; grantee, Grad. Sch. Arts and Scis. NYU, 2002—03, 2004—05, Tech. and Tchg. Mentoring Program NYU, 2003—04; Socrates-Erasmus scholar, European Union, 1997—98, Merit scholar, French govt., 1998—99, MacCracken fellow, Grad. Sch. Arts and Scis. NYU, 1999—2003, Dean's Dissertation fellow, Grad. Sch. Arts and Scis. NYU., 2003—04. Mem.: MLA, Poetic Genius Soc., Mensa. Home Phone: +33(0)561002277; Office Phone: 917-406-8567. Personal E-mail: sicart@gmail.com. E-mail: french@nyu.edu.

SICHA, CHOIRE, online editor; Editl. dir. Gawker Media, 2004—05; mng. editor Gawker.com, NYC, 2003—04, 2007—; co-founding editor Sploid.com, 2004—05; sr. editor NY Observer, 2005—07. Democrat. Office: Gawker Media 76 Crosby St New York NY 10012 Office Phone: 212-655-9524. E-mail: choire@gawker.com. *

SICHERMAN, MARVIN ALLEN, lawyer; b. Cleve., Dec. 27, 1934; s. Harry and Malvina (Friedman) S.; m. Sue Kovacs, Aug. 18, 1957; children: Heidi Joyce, Steven Eric. BA, Case Western Res. U., 1957, LLB, 1960, JD, 1968. Bar: Ohio 1960, US Dist. Ct. (no. dist.) Ohio 1961, Ct. Appeals (6th cir.) 1969, US Supreme Ct. 1975. Mng. prin. Dettelbach, Sicherman & Baumgart, Cleve., 1971—. Mem. editl. bd.: Case-Western Res. Law Rev, 1958-60; contbr. articles to legal jours. Mem. Beachwood (Ohio) Civic League, 1972-92; mem. Beachwood Bd. Edn., 1978-86, pres., 1981, 85, v.p., 1984; trustee Beachwood Arts Coun., 1977-84. Mem. Ohio Bar Assn. (lectr. truth in lending 1969, lectr. bankruptcy 1972, 81, 84, 99, 2000-06, Meritorious Service awards 1971, 77, 78, 79, 83, 84, 85, 86, 87), Cleve. Bar Assn. (lectr. practice and procedure clinic 1960-80, 82-87, chmn. bankruptcy ct. com. 1971-73; award established in his honor by Bankruptcy & Commercial Law Sect., 2007), Jewish Chautauqua Soc., Tau Epsilon Rho, Zeta Beta Tau. Jewish (trustee Temple brotherhood 1968-76, sec. 1971-73). Jewish. Home: 24500 Albert Ln Cleveland OH 44122-2302 Office: Dettelbach Sicherman & Baumgart 1100 Ohio Savings Plz Cleveland OH 44114 Office Phone: 216-696-6000. Business E-Mail: msicherman@dsb-law.com.

SICHUK, GEORGE, entrepreneur, writer, biochemist, physiologist; b. Butler Twp., Pa., May 10, 1933; s. Stephan Nicholas and Eva (Hawranick)

Sichuk; m. Georgiana Nadya Stroyen, July 27, 1968. BA, Drew U., 1954; DS, Rutgers U., 1962. Rsch. assoc. Sloan-Kettering Inst. Cancer Rsch., NYC, 1961—71; asst. prof. biology Montclair State Coll., Upper Montclair, NJ, 1972—75, William Paterson Coll., Wayne, NJ, 1975; lectr. interdisciplinary studies Bloomfield (N.J.) Coll., 1976; sci. tchr. Eastside H.S., Paterson, NJ, 1988—93; entrepreneur author Lincoln Park, NJ, 1993—. Author: Gabriel's Voice, 1996, Uriel's Light, 1997, One Man's Testament, 1998, Constitutional Imperatives for Rational Government, 2003, Common Sense Plus, 2004, The Pentian Truth: Thomas Paine, the Mozart of Reason, 2004, Miracles of Evolution, Voodoo Religions, 2007; contbr. articles to profl. med. jours. Good will amb. U.S. Govt., Cuba, 1960; coach Police Athletic League, Lincoln Park, 1977—79; CEO NJ Citizens Orgn., 1967—68; exec. and coach Orthodox Citizens' Club, NJ, 1980—90. Achievements include clarification of relationship of the endocrine and immune systems to cancer to direct attention to the nucleic acids (DNA and RNA); clarification of transplantation immunology; proof that "butter yellow" a dibenzanthracene used to give margarine a yellow color is a carcinogen; research in the role of sex hormones in thrombotic disease; dynamic relationship between dietary protein quality and function of adrenal cortex in mammals; harmonic function of the human brain, denial of monotheism; and proof of origin of viruses, identifying vectors of disease; kidney transplantation; proof that DES can cause thromboembolic disease. Avocations: geo-politics, house maintenance engineering, golf, flying, music. Home: 18 Sewanois Ave Lincoln Park NJ 07035-1710

SICILIANO, ROCCO CARMINE, cultural institute executive; b. Salt Lake City, Mar. 4, 1922; s. Joseph Vincent and Mary (Arnone) S.; m. Marion Stiebel, Nov. 8, 1947; children: Loretta, A. Vincent, Fred R., John C., Maria. BA with honors, U. Utah, 1944; LL.B., Georgetown U., 1948; LHD, Hebrew Union Coll., Gettysburg Coll., 2000, U. Utah, 2001. Bar: D.C. bar 1949. Legal asst. to bd. mem. NLRB, Washington, 1948-50; asst. sec.-treas. Procon Inc., Des Plaines, Ill., 1950-53; asst. sec. labor charge employment and manpower Dept. Labor, Washington, 1953-57; spl. asst. to Eisenhower for personnel mgmt., 1957-59; ptnr. Wilkinson, Cragun & Barker, 1959-69; pres. Pacific Maritime Assn., San Francisco, 1965-69; undersec. of commerce Washington, 1969-71; pres., chmn. bd., chief exec. officer Ticor, Los Angeles, 1971-84, chmn., exec. com., 1984-85; of counsel Jones, Day, Reavis & Pogue, 1984-87; chmn. bd., chief exec. officer Am. Health Properties, Inc., 1987-88; chmn. Dwight D. Eisenhower World Affairs Inst., Washington, 1991-2001; apptd. mem. Eisenhower Meml. Commn., 2000, chmn., 2001—. Chmn. Ctr. for Govtl. Studies, 1992—; commr. Calif. Citizens Budget Commn.; mem. Fed. Pay Bd., 1971-73; trustee emeritus J. Paul Getty Trust. Author: Walking on Sand, 2004. Past chmn. Calif. Bus. Roundtable; trustee Com. for Econ. Devel.; co-chmn. Calif. Commn. on Campaign Financing. 1st lt. AUS, 1943-46, MTO, ETO. Decorated Bronze Star for Valor, Combat Infantryman's badge; Order of Merit (Italy); named to Hall of Fame, Inf. Sch., Ft. Benning, Ga. Mem. Nat. Acad. Pub. Adminstrn., Met. Club (Washington), L.A. Philharm. Assn. (life dir.), Calif. Club (L.A.). Home: 612 N Rodeo Dr Beverly Hills CA 90210-3208 Office Phone: 310-276-5912.

SICK, WILLIAM NORMAN, JR., technology company executive; b. Houston, Apr. 20, 1935; s. William Norman and Gladys Phylena (Armstrong) S.; m. Stephanie Anne Williams, Sept. 14, 1963; children: Jill Melanie, David Louis. BA, Rice U., Houston, 1957, BSEE, 1958. With Tex. Instruments Inc., various locations, 1958-87; exec. v.p. Tex. Instruments, Inc., Dallas, 1982-87; pres. semicondr. products group Tex. Instruments Inc., Dallas, 1982-86; bd. dirs. Tex. Instruments, Inc., 1985-87; CEO Am. Nat. Can Co., Chgo., 1988-89; also bd. dirs. Am. Nat. Can. Co., Chgo., 1988-89; mem. exec. com. Pechiney, Paris, 1989; bd. dirs. Pechiney Internat., 1989; vice chmn., bd. dirs. Triangle Industries, NYC, 1988—89; chmn., CEO, Bus. Resources Internat., Winnetka, Ill., 1989—; co-founder, mng. dir. Signature Capital Mgmt., LLC, Northfield, Ill., 1997—2003. Bd. dirs., former chmn. Acoustic Tech., Mesa, Ariz.; co-founder Metasolv, Dallas; bd. dir., co-founder VIRxSYS, Gaithersburg, Md.; former chmn. Aware, Bedford, Mass., Power Trends, Warrenville, Ill.; guest lectr. Sophia U., Tokyo, 1973. Chmn. Fairhill Sch., Dallas, 1980-91; trustee, past chmn. Shedd Aquarium, Chgo., 1990—; trustee Rice U., 1996-2006, Santa Fe Inst., 2000—; bd. dirs. Millennium Park Inc., 2004—; mem. Chgo. Coun. Global Affairs. Mem. Exec. Club Chgo., Glen View Club, Sigma Xi, Tau Beta Pi, Sigma Tau. Episcopalian. Office: Bus Resources Internat 565 Sheridan Rd Winnetka IL 60093-0500

SICKAFUS, KURT EDWARD, materials scientist, researcher; b. Charlottesville, Va., Oct. 14, 1956; s. Edward Nathan and Mary Sue Sickafus; m. Talissa Kay Ralph, Sept. 13, 1983. BA, Ohio Wesleyan U., 1978; MS, PhD, Cornell U., 1985. Postdoctoral rsch. asst. Cavendish Lab. U. Cambridge, England, 1985—87; staff engr./scientist IBM, Tucson, 1987—88; team leader, mem. tech. staff Los Alamos (N.Mex.) Nat. Lab., 1989—. Fellow: The Am. Ceramic Soc.; mem.: Royal Microscopical Soc. (Gt. Britain), Inst. of Physics (Gt. Britain), Minerals, Metals, and Materials Soc., Microscopy Soc. Am., Mineral. Soc. Am., Am. Phys. Soc., Am. Chem. Soc., Am. Nuc. Soc., Materials Rsch. Soc., Böhmische Phys. Soc. Avocations: horseback riding, photography, basketball. Home: HCR 64 Box 28 Santa Cruz NM 87567 Office: Los Alamos Nat Lab PO Box 1663 MS-G755 Los Alamos NM 87545 Office Phone: 505-665-3457. Business E-Mail: kurt@lanl.gov.

SICKING, DEAN L., civil engineer, educator; BSME, Tex. A&M U., 1980, MS in Civil Engring., 1987, PhD in Civil Engring., 1992. Registered Tex.-Mech. Engring., 1985, Ariz.-Civil Engring., 1990, Nebr.-Civil Engring., 1993. Engring. rsch. assoc. Tex. Transportation Inst., 1980—85, asst. rsch. engr., 1985—89, assoc. rsch. engr., 1989—92; lectr., civil engring. dept. Tex. A&M U., 1981—88; asst. prof., civil engring. U. Nebr.-Lincoln, 1992—97, assoc. prof., civil engring., 1997—2001, prof., civil engring., 2001—; dir. Midwest Roadside Safety Facility, 1992—. Invited spkr. in field. Contbr. articles to profl. publications. Named Star of Yr. in recognition of the develop. of steel & foam energy reducing (SAFER) barrier for high speed tracks, Lincoln Jour. Star, 2002, 2005 Nat. Medal Tech. Laureate; recipient C.M. Simmang award-Outstanding Achievement in Thermal Sci., Tex. A&M U., 1980, Fred Burggraf award for paper entitled-Guidelines for Positive Barrier Use in Work Zones, NAS, Transportation Rsch. Bd., 1986, Best Paper award for paper entitled Box-Beam Guardrail End Terminal, Presented by Roadside Safety Features Com. of the Transportation Rsch. Bd., 1994, Best Paper award for paper entitled Slotted Rail Guardrail Terminal, 1995, Best Paper award for paper entitled Development of Flared Energy-Absorbing Terminal for W-beam Guardrails, 1999, Parents Cert. Recognition for Contributions to Students, 1997, FHWA Region 7 Safety award, 1997, Dean's Spl. Recognition for Exemplary Performance, Presented by Dean of Engring. for Outstanding Success of Freshman Engring. Design Project, 1998, Louis Schwitzer award in recognition of develop. of the Steel and Foam Energy Reducing (SAFER) barrier for high speed race tracks, Soc. Automotive Engrs., Ind. Sect. and Borg Warner Inc., 2002, SEMA Motorsports Engring. award, Develop. of the SAFER Barrier, Presented to Midwest Roadside Safety Facility and the Indy Racing League/Indpls. Motor Speedway, 2002, Best Paper award for Develop. of the Midwest Guardrail Sys., Transportation Rsch. Bd. Com. on Roadside Safety Features, 2002, Popular Sci. award for Top 100 Technical Innovations in 2002 (develop. of the steel & foam energy reducing (SAFER) barrier for high speed race tracks, Popular Sci. Mag. Mem.: Pi Tau Sigma, Tau Beta Pi, Phi Kappa Phi. Achievements include Several US Patents in roadside safety features; Recognized for innovative design & development of roadside & racetrack safety technologies that dissipate the energy of high speed crashes, preventing fatalities & countless injuries each year & contributing to the safety & well being of every American who travels the nation's highways. Office: Univ Nebraska-Lincoln Dept Civil Engring Nebraska Hall W527 Lincoln NE 68588-0529 Office Phone: 402-472-9332. Business E-Mail: dsicking1@unl.edu. *

SICKLER, MICHAEL ALLAN, educator, artist; b. Milw., Aug. 11, 1945; s. Harlan E. and Audrey E. (Smith) S.; m. Christine Ann Dall, Sept. 2, 1972; children: Jonas Ian, Beau James. BFA, Layton Sch., 1970; MFA, U. Wis., Milw., 1973. Lectr. U. Wis., Milw., 1973; instr. Syracuse (N.Y.) U., 1973-80, asst. prof., 1981-83, assoc. prof., 1983—. Lectr. various colls. and univs.; recruiter U. Conn., Cin. Art Acad., Pratt Inst., Art Inst. Chgo., Md. Art Inst., others; curator John Mulray Ctr., Syracuse, NY, 2000, Joseph Scala Gallery, New Woodstock, NY, 2006, 07, CNY Watercolor, New Woodstock, 2007; juror various art shows. One-man shows include Bradley Galleries, Milw., 1975, Everson Museum, Syracuse, 1977, Syracuse U. Lubin House Gallery, N.Y.C., 1977, Weber Galleries, North Syracuse, N.Y., 1978, 80, Syracuse Stage Gallery, 1978, Hanover Sq. Gallery, Syracuse, 1980, 83-84, 87, U. Wis./Waukesha Gallery, 1981, Centre for Related Arts City U. London, 1983, Arlene McDaniels Gallery, Simsbury, 1983-84, Chapman Ctr., Cazenovia Coll., 1991; exhibited in group shows at U. Nebr., U. Md., U. Iowa, Edgewood Gallery, Syracuse, NY, 2007, others; curator and exhibitor Milw. Inst. Art and Design, 1989; represented in several permanent collections; assoc. editor Comstock Poetry Rev., 2007; contbr. chpts. to books; contbr. poetry to mags. and revs. Auctioneer five nationally pub. TV stas., 1984-2007; juror local and nat. art exhbns. Recipient Grand prize Kirkland Ann., 1974, 1st prize for painting WCNY Invitational, 1983, 85, Golden Poet award World of Poetry Press, 1984-88, Silver Poet award, 1990. Mem. AAUP (pres. 1991-93), Coll. Art Assn. Lutheran. Home: 91 Ripplebrook Ln Minoa NY 13116-1307 Office Phone: 315-443-4613. Business E-Mail: masickler@syr.edu.

SICOLI, MARY LOUISE CORBIN, psychologist, educator; b. Delaware County, Pa., Nov. 15, 1944; d. C.M. Lewis and Lucille (Weber) Corbin; m. Thomas Sicoli, Aug. 27, 1967; children: Michael, Kathryn Francesca. BS, West Chester U., Pa., 1966, MS, 1974, U. Wis., Madison, 1967; PhD, Bryn Mawr Coll., Pa., 1977. Tchr. music, supr. Unionville-Chadds Ford (Pa.) Sch. Dist., 1967-70; supr. student tchrs. Rosemont (Pa.) Coll., 1976-78; prof. psychology, campus psychologist, coord. psychol. svcs. Cabrini Coll., Radnor, Pa., 1974—. Cons. Children's Svcs. Southea. Pa., 1974-80; supr. doctoral interns in psychology Bryn Mawr Coll., 1979-86; presenter in field. Contbr. articles to profl. jours., scientific papers at profl. Confs. Founding mem. bd. dirs. Maternal Support Sys. Chester County, 1981—; mem. Citizens Action for Better TV, 1981—; founder, chair Psychol. Aspects Popular Culture, Popular Culture Assn. Recipient Legion of Honor award Chapel of the Four Chaplains, 1980, Christian and Mary Lindback award for Disting. Coll. Tchg., 1984; named hon. alumnus Cabrini Coll., 2005. Fellow Pa. Psychol. Assn. (founder campus psychologist network); mem. AAUP, Am. Psychol. Assn., Ea. Psychol. Assn., Jean Piaget Soc., Assn. Moral Devel., Kappa Delta Pi, Psi Chi (founding adv., Ea. Region Chptr. award 2005), Delta Epsilon Sigma. Home: 404 Darlington Dr West Chester PA 19382-2139 Office: Cabrini Coll Dept Psychology Radnor PA 19087 Home Phone: 610-696-8116; Office Phone: 610-902-8310. Business E-Mail: mlsicoli@cabrini.edu. E-mail: mlcorbin@verizon.net.

SIDAMON-ERISTOFF, ANNE PHIPPS, not-for-profit developer; b. NYC, Sept. 12, 1932; d. Howard and Harriet Dyer (Price) Phipps; m. Constantine Sidamon-Eristoff, June 29, 1957; children: Simon, Elizabeth, Andrew. BA, Bryn Mawr Coll., 1954. Chairwoman emerita Am. Mus. Natural History, NYC; dir.-at-large Black Rock Forest Consortium; cons. mem. distbn. com. N.Y. Cmty. Trust. Trustee God Bless Am. Fund, Storm King Art Ctr., Mountainville, NY; hon. trustee World Wildlife Fund; bd. dirs. Greenacre Found., Highland Falls (N.Y.) Libr.; past bd. dirs. Scenic Hudson, St. Bernard's Sch., NYC, Mus. Modern Art, NYC, Mus. Hudson Highlands, Hudson River Found. Address: 120 E End Ave New York NY 10028-7552 Personal E-mail: ananouri@aol.com.

SIDAMON-ERISTOFF, CONSTANTINE, lawyer; b. NYC, June 28, 1930; s. Simon C. and Anne Huntington (Tracy) Sidamon-E.; m. Anne Phipps, June 29, 1957; children: Simon, Elizabeth, Andrew. BSE in Geol. Engring, Princeton U., 1952; LLB, Columbia U., 1957. Clk., then assoc. firm Kelley Drye Newhall Maginnes & Warren, NYC, 1957-64; individual practice law NYC, 1964-65, 74-77; exec. asst. to Congressman John V. Lindsay, 1964-65; city coord. Lindsay Mayoral Campaign, NYC, 1965; asst. to mayor City of NY, 1966, commr. hwys., 1967-68, transp. adminstr., 1968-73; ptnr. Sidamon-Eristoff, Morrison, Warren, & Ecker, NYC, 1978-83; counsel Morrison & de Roos, 1984-88; pvt. practice NYC, 1988-89; regional adminstr. Region II EPA, NYC, 1989-93; of counsel Patterson, Belknap, Webb & Tyler, NYC, 1993-99, Lacher & Lovell-Taylor, NYC, 1999—. Mem. NY State Met. Transp. Authority Bd., 1974—89; commr. NY State Jud. Commn. on Minorities, 1987—91; mem. Gov.'s Coun. on Hudson River Valley Greenway, 1989; trustee United Mut. Savs. Bank, NYC, 1979—82, Phipps Houses, NYC, 1974—, chmn., 1986—2001, chmn. emeritus, 2001—. Trustee Am. the Beautiful Fund, Washington, 1985—97, Allaverdy Found., NYC, 1962—, Carnegie Hall, NYC, 1967—92, Millbrook (NY) Sch., 1971—89, hon. trustee, 1989—; trustee Am. Farm Sch., Thessaloniki, Greece, 1973—79, Orange County (NY) Citizens Found., 1974—81, Coun. Mcpl. Performance, 1981—85, vice chmn., 1986—87; bd. dirs. Mid-Hudson Pattern for Progress, Poughkeepsie, NY, 1975—89, chmn., 1981—85, Am. Friends of Ga., Inc., 1995—, Audubon NY, 1999—; dir. Nat. Audubon Soc., 2005—, Citizens Union Found., 1997—; NY State Rep. committeeman, 1980—89; mem. Orange County (NY) Planning Bd., 1997—; bd. dirs. Tolstoy Found., NYC, 1975—2002, chmn. bd. dirs., 1979—89, 1994—2001; bd. dirs. Caramoor Ctr. Music and Arts, Katonah, NY, 1961—80, Boyce Thompson Inst. for Plant Rsch., Ithaca, NY, 1994—2006. 1st lt. arty. AUS, 1952—54, Korea. Decorated Bronze Star; co-recipient Civic Leadership award (with wife), Citizens Union, 1997, Force for Nature award (with wife), Natural Resources Def. Coun., 1999, Environ. Leadership award (with wife), Nat. Audubon Soc., 2001; recipient Honor award, Kings County chpt. NY State Soc. Profl. Engrs., 1969, Greater NY Coun. Girls Scouts US, 1973, Nat. and NY Parks and Conservation Assn., 1992, Bd. Leadership award, Coun. Mcpl. Performance, 1984, Transp. Man of Yr. award, Greater NY March of Dimes, 1985, award of excellence, Mid-Hudson Pattern for Progress, 1990, Bronze medal, USEPA, 1993. Mem. ABA, NY State Bar Assn., Assn. Bar of City of NY, NY County Lawyers Assn., Kent Moot Ct., AIME, Phi Delta Phi, Delta Psi, Century Assn. (NYC), Knickerbocker Club (NYC), Racquet and Tennis Club (NYC). Republican. Eastern Orthodox. Office: Lacher & Lovell-Taylor 460 Park Ave New York NY 10022 Office Phone: 212-872-1500. Office Fax: 212-872-1630. Business E-Mail: cseristoff@lltlaw.com. E-mail: ananouri@aol.com.

SIDANIUS, JAMES H., psychology professor; b. Dec. 11, 1945; married; 1 child. BA in Psychology, CUNY, 1968; PhD, Univ. Stockholm, 1977. Academic Diagnostician and Counselor Hunter Coll., NYC, 1969—70; asst. instr., psychology Univ. Stockholm, 1974—77, asst. prof., 1977—78, univ. lektor, 1978—80, assoc. prof., 1987; vis. asst. prof., postdoctoral fellow Carnegie Mellon Univ., Pitts., 1983—84; asst. prof., govt. Univ. Tex., 1984, assoc. prof., 1987, UCLA, 1988—2006; prof. psychology, African Am. studies Harvard Univ., 2006—. Author: Social Dominance, 1999, Racialized Politics, 2000, Key Readings in Political Psychology, 2004; assoc. editor Political Psychology, 1998—, editl. bd. Social Justice Research, 2003—. Recipient Hon. Mention, Gordon Allport Intergroup Rels. Prize, 2004—05. Fellow: Am. Acad. Arts & Scis.; mem.: Internat. Soc. Political Psychology (v.p.). Office: Harvard U William James Hall Rm 1544 33 Kirkland St Cambridge MA 02138 Office Phone: 617-495-3804. Business E-Mail: sidanius@wjh.harvard.edu.

SIDDAYAO, CORAZÓN MORALES, economist, educator, consultant; b. Manila, July 26, 1932; came to U.S., 1968; d. Crispulo S. and Catalina T. (Morales) S. Cert. in elem. teaching, Philippine Normal Coll., 1951; BBA, U. East, Manila, 1962; MA in Econs., George Washington U., 1971, MPhil, PhD, 1975. Cert. Inst. de Francais, France, 1989. Tchr. pub. schs., Manila, 1951-53; exec. asst. multinational oil corps., 1953-68; asst. pensions officer IMF, Washington, 1968-71; cons. economist Washington, 1971-75; rsch. assoc. Policy Studies in Sci. and Tech. George Washington U., Washington, 1971-72, teaching fellow dept. econs., 1972-75; natural gas specialist U.S. Fed. Energy Adminstrn., Washington, 1974-75; sr. rsch. economist, assoc. prof. Inst. S.E.A. Studies, Singapore, 1975-78; sr. rsch. fellow energy/economist East-West Ctr., 1978-81, project dir. energy and industrialization, 1981-86; vis. fellow London Sch. Econ., 1984-85; sr. energy economist in charge energy program Econ. Devel. Inst., World Bank, Washington, 1986-94, ret., 1994. Affiliate prof. econs. U. Hawaii, 1979—94; co-dir. UPecon Inst. Resource Studies, 1995—2006; vis. prof. econs. U. Montpellier, France, 1992, France, 1995—96, France, 1997—2006; vis. prof. pub. policy Duke U., 1997; lectr. pub. policy George Mason U., 2000; tchr. coord. English for Hispanic program Parish, 2002; cons., spkr. in field. Author or co-author: Increasing the Supply of Medical Personnel, 1973, The Offshore Petroleum Resources of Southeast Asia: Some Potential Conflicts and Related Economic Factors, 1978, Round Table Discussion on Asian and Multinational Corporations, 1978, The Supply of Petroleum Resources in Southeast Asia: Economic Implications of Evolving Property Rights Arrangements, 1980, Critical Energy Issues in Asia and the Pacific: The Next Twenty Years, 1982, Criteria for Energy Pricing Policy, 1985, Energy Demand and Economic Growth, 1986; editor, co-author: Energy Policy and Planning series, 1990-92, Energy Investments and the Environment, 1993; co-editor: Investissements Energetiques et Environnement, 1993; co-editor: (series) Energy Project Analysis for the CIS Countries (Russian), 1993, Politique d'Efficacité de l'Énergie et Environnement, Expérience pratiques, 1994, Matérial Pedagogique sur la Politique d'Efficacité de l'Énergie et Environnement, 1994; contbr. chpts. to books, articles to profl. jours. Grantee in field; recipient Outstanding Alumni award Arellano Pub. H.S., 1998, Philippine Normal U., 2003 Mem.: Internat. Assn. Energy Economists (charter 1986—2003), Les Amis de l'Abbaye de Chancelade, Perpetual Adoration Soc. of St. Agnes (Arlington) (head scholarship fund), Eucharistic Frat. 3d Order of St. P.J. Eymard, World Bank 1818 Soc. (bd. dirs. 1999—2000), John Carroll Soc., Chorale de St. Louis de France, Omicron Delta Epsilon. Roman Catholic. Office: 1201 S Eads St Ste 1712 Arlington VA 22202-2845 *Power and money were never the stimuli to my endeavors. Spiritual and intellectual challenges are what drive me. In the end, all our achievements mean nothing if we have not learned to appreciate them as gifts and share what we can with others.*

SIDDEEK, M. S.M., marine biologist, educator; arrived in U.S., 2000; s. M. L.M.M. Shareef and I. L.M. Zulaiha; m. Fathima Zeena Siddeek, May 21, 1985; children: Hani, Esra Fathima. PhD, U. of East Anglia, Norwich, Eng., 1981; BSc in Math. with honors, U. of Colombo, Sri Lanka, 1972. Med. lab. tech. Med. Rsch. Inst. Med. lab. technologist Gen. Hosp., Colombo, 1967—74; rsch. officer (biometrics) Nat. Aquatic Resources Agy., Colombo, 1974—85; assoc. rsch. scientist Kuwait Inst. for Sci. Rsch., Kuwait, 1985—90; assoc. prof. fisheries Sultan Qaboos U., Muscat, Oman, 1990—2000; shellfish biometrician Alaska Dept. Fish and Game, Juneau, Alaska, 2000—. Crab plan team mem. NPFMC, 2000—; vis. lectr. fisheries U. of Colombo, 1983—85; keynote spkr. Sultan Qaboos U., 2001, 05; invited spkr., Halifax, Canada, 02; independent rev. on snow crab assessment and mgmt. tech. report DFO, Moncton, Canada, 2007; invited reviewer internat. jour. articles and tech. reports in fisheries. Contbr. articles and tech. reports to profl. publs. Named Outstanding Rschr., Sultan Qaboos U., 1997; recipient Assessment and Mgmt. grant, Kuwait Inst. Sci. Rsch., 1986—89, Shrimp Ecology and Assessment grant, Ministry of Fisheries, Muscat, 1995, Kingfish Stock Assessment and Mgmt. grant, 1998, scholarship for PhD study, Colombo Plan, 1978, Crab Biometrics grant, NOAA, 2000—. Mem.: Sri Lanka Assn. for Advancement of Scis., Am. Fisheries Soc. Office: Alaska Dept Fish and Game PO Box 115526 1255 W 8th St Juneau AK 99811-5526 Home Phone: 907-780-2561; Office Phone: 907-465-6107. Office Fax: 907-465-2604. Business E-Mail: shareef.siddeek@alaska.gov.

SIDDEEQ, BAIYINAH NAWAL RUBYE, secondary school educator; AA, Emory U., 1995, BA in Elem. Edn., 1997. Asst. tchr. Sister Clara Muhammad Sch., Indpls., 1993; co-founder, jr. counselor A Step Up! Summer Enrichment Program, Stone Mountain, Ga., 1995; tutor for academically challenged Cook Elem., Atlanta, 1995; math specialist Medlock Elem., Decatur, Ga., 1996; tchr. Fernbank Elem., Decatur, Ga., 1997; instr. essay, creative writing Md. Homeschoolers, Gaithersburg, Md., 1999—2000; tchr. English Washington Homeschoolers, College Park, Md., 1999—2002; prep instr. English, SAT Muslimah's Alt. to Pub. H.S. (MAPHS), Beltsville, Md., 2001—02; tchr. English Sch. Knowledge, Indpls., 2003; lit./social studies tchr., grades 6-8 Al-Hada Sch., College Park, Md., 2003—. Author: (novels) If I Should Speak, 2001, (children's book) Amir's Cap is Green, 1999, The Show and Tell, 1997, (novels) A Voice, 2003. Recipient Academic Excellence award, Delta Sigma Theta, 1996—97; scholar Phi Theta Kappa scholar, 1993—94. Personal E-mail: baiyinah@hotmail.com.

SIDDIQI, MUNAWAR, anesthesiologist, consultant; b. Karachi, Sindh, Pakistan, June 12, 1959; s. Intikhab Hussain and Nusrat Jehan Siddiqi; m. Samina Munawar Junaid, Apr. 22, 1987; children: Ayesha Anadil, Manahil, Adil. MD, Sindh Med. Coll., Karachi, Pakistan, 1985. Cert. Ednl. Commn. Fgn. Med. Grads., 1995, lic. anesthesiologist Med. Coll. Ohio, 2001. Clin. assoc. Cleve. Clinic Found., Cleve., 2002—04; anesthesiologist So. Ohio Med. Ctr., Portsmouth, 2005—06. Pain specialist Mercy Hosp. Clermont, Batavia, Ohio, 2006—; fellow med. toxicology Hartford Hosp., 1997. Contbr. articles to profl. jours. Mem.: Am. Soc. Anesthesiologists. Achievements include research in silicone breast implants and induction of heat shock proteins. Home: 3004-Old Field Way Lexington KY 40513 Office: Mercy Health Ptnrs 2055 Hospital Dr Ste 200 Batavia OH 45103 Office Phone: 513-735-1701. Office Fax: 513-735-8995.

SIDDIQI, OBAID, retired geneticist; b. Basti, Uttar Pradesh, India, Jan. 7, 1932; s. Mohammad Abdul Qadeer Siddiqi and Umme Kulsum; m. Asiya Siddiqi; children: Imran, Kaleem, Yumna, Diba. PhD, U. Glasgow, Scotland, 1961. Founding dir. Nat. Ctr. for Biol. Sciences; sr. assoc. Nat. Inst. Advanced Studies, Bangalore, Karnataka, India, 1990—95; prof. emeritus Nat. Ctr. for Biol. Sciences, 1996—, sr. Homi Bhahha fellow; chancellor Urdu Univ., India. Mem. editl. bd.: Jour. Biosciences. Pres. Indian Acad. Sciences, Bangalore, 1986—89. Recipient G.M. Modi Sci. Found. award, Modi Sci. Found., 2001, BC Roy award, Indian Coun. Med. Rsch., 2003, Pride of India award, Am. Fedn. Muslims of Indian Origin. Fellow: Royal Soc.; mem.: NAS (assoc.), Nat. Acad. Engring. US (fgn. assoc.). Achievements include discovery of nonsense codonons, the stop signals in the genetic code. Office: Nat Ctr for Biological Sci GKVK Campus PO Box 6501 Karnataka Bangalore 560065 India Home Phone: 080 2364 8507; Office Phone: 080 23636420-432. Office Fax: 080 23636662. E-mail: osiddiqi@ncbs.res.in.

SIDDIQUI, AFZAL A., medical educator; b. Aligarh, U.P., India, 1958; arrived in U.S., 1986, naturalized, 2004; s. Iqbal Siddiqui and Jamal Nizami; m. Shahana Siddiqui; children: Bilal, Sabrina. MS, Aligarh U., India, 1978, MPhil, 1982; PhD, U. Westen Ont., 1986. Post-doctoral rsch. assoc. Morehouse Coll. and Ctrs. Disease Control, Atlanta, 1986—87, U. Ill., Rockford, Ill., 1987—88; rsch. scientist and co-ordinator vaccine program U. We. Ont., London, Ontario, Canada, 1988—95; rsch. fellow

Sch. Pub. Health Harvard U., Boston, 1995—97; asst. prof., health rsch. scientist East Tenn. State U., Johnson City, Tenn., 1997—2000, Veterans Affairs Med. Ctr., Johnson City, 1997—2000; assoc. prof. medicine Health Scis. Ctr. Tex. Tech U., Amarillo, Tex., 2000—. Grant reveiwer in field; paper reveiwer in field. Contbr. chapters to books, articles to profl. jours. Grantee, NIH, 2001—. Mem.: Am. Soc. Microbiology, Infectious Diseases Soc. Am., Am. Soc. Tropical Medicine and Hygiene, Am. Soc. Parasitologists, Sigma Xi. Achievements include research in vaccines and new therapies for parasitic infections. Office: Texas Tech Univ Health Sciences Center 1400 Wallace Blvd Amarillo TX 79106 Office Phone: 806-354-5524. E-mail: afzal.siddiqui@ttuhsc.edu.

SIDDIQUI, RAZIA SULTANA, retired psychotherapisst, educator; d. Gurcharan Singh and Bhupinder Kaur Sangha; m. Mohammed Sadiq Siddiqui, May 2, 1963; children: Niloufer Siddiqi Dennis, Adeeba Sultana Siddiqi, Khalid Mohammed Siddiqi. BA, D.M. Coll., Moga, India, 1956; MA in Psychology, Lucknow U., India, 1958; BT, D.M. Tng. Coll., Moga, 1959; DM and SP, Mysore U., Bangalore, India, 1962; cert. in psychotherapy, Southwestern Med. Sch., Dallas, 1972; PhD in Neuropsychology, Postgrad. Inst. Med. Edn. and Rsch., Chandigarh, India, 1994. Asst. prof. ednl. psychology Saraswati Tng. Coll., Amritsar, India, 1959—60; clin. psychologist Niloufer Pediat. Hosp., Hyderabad, India, 1962—65; asst. prof. med. psychology Nangrahar Med. Sch., Jalalabad, Afghanistan, 1965—80, dir. publs., 1968—80; assoc. prof. psychology Kabul U., Afghanistan, 1980—88, assoc. prof. ednl. psychology Faculty Edn., 1980—88, dir. fgn. rels., 1982—88. Asst. editor Kabul Times, 1967—68. Election officer tech. Registrar of Voters, San Diego, 2006—. Home: 2162 Crystal Clear Dr Spring Valley CA 91978 Home Phone: 619-660-1769. E-mail: goodie65@hotmail.com.

SIDDONS, (SYBIL) ANNE RIVERS, writer; b. Fairburn, Ga., Jan. 9, 1936; m. Heyward Siddons, 1966; 4 stepchildren. BA Auburn U., 1958, student Atlanta Sch. Art, 1958. Mem. advt. dept. bank; sr. editor Atlanta mag., 1960. Author: (novels) John Chancellor Makes Me Cry, 1975, Heartbreak Hotel, 1976, The House Next Door, 1978, Fox's Earth, 1981, Homeplace, 1987, Peachtree Road, 1988, Kings Oak, 1990, Outer Banks, 1991, Colony, 1992, Hill Towns, 1993, Downtown, 1994, Fault Lines, 1995, Up Island, 1997, Low Country, 1998, Nora, Nora, 2000, Islands, 2003, Sweetwater Creek, 2005.

SIDDONS, JOY GARBEE, music educator; b. Lynchburg, Va., July 18, 1952; d. Clyde Lewis and Julia Schmitt Garbee; m. James Siddons, July 2, 1977. BS, Liberty U., 1984; MEd, Lynchburg Coll., 1996; MusEdM, Shenandoah U., 1998. Music educator Bedford County Pub. Schools, Bedford, Va., 1989—2003, Fairfax County Pub. Schools, Springfield, Va., 2003—. Dir. of music United Meth. churches, 1988—. Dir.: children's choirs and musical theater prodns. Mem.: Music Educators Nat. Conf., Phi Delta Kappa. United Methodist. Home: 6020 Woodland Ter Mc Lean VA 22101 Office: Fairhill Elem Sch 3001 Chichester Ln Fairfax VA 22116 Office Phone: 703-208-8100.

SIDEBOTTOM, CHARLES BENTON, engineering executive; s. Oscar H. and Goldia B. Sidebottom; m. Carolyn Sue Padley, May 25, 1969. BSEE, Iowa State U., Ames, 1968; MSEE, U. Mo., Columbia, 1979. Indsl. engr. Kansas City Power & Light Co., 1968—69, sys. planning engr., 1973—74, mgr. tech. svcs., 1974—80; mgr. software systems Medtronic, Inc., Mpls., 1984—85, engring. project mgr., 1985—87, product planner, 1987—89, mgr. engring. dept., 1989—92, mgr. stds., 1992—2000, dir. corp. stds., 2000—. Sec. com. 62a Internat. Electrotech. Commn., Geneva, 1996—. Author: (reference book) International Labeling Requirements for Medical Devcies, Medical Equipment, and Diagnostic Products; contbr. reference book, articles to profl. jours. Co-chmn. planning bd. USE, Inc., Washington, 1983—84; mem. Colonial Williamsburg Capital Soc., Va., 1987; chmn. USE, Inc., Mpls., 1982—84; active Spirit Hope United Meth. Ch., Golden Valley, Minn., 1984—. With USN, 1969—73. Mem.: ASTM (sec. com. 2002—, Robert Fairer award 2005—), IEEE, Internat. Stds. Orgn. (sec. com. ISO/TCISO/SC 5 2007—), Assn. Advancement Med. Instrumentation (co-chiar pacemaker com. 1993—2003, dir. 2000—, industry vice chmn. 2004—06, co-chmn. stds. bd. 2005—, chair elect 2006—, Sds. Developer award), Stds Engring. Soc., Regulatory Affairs Profl. Soc. Office: Medtronic Inc 710 Medtronic Pky Minneapolis MN 55431 Home Phone: 763-559-3755; Office Phone: 763-505-2599.

SIDEBOTTOM, WILLIAM GEORGE, communications executive; b. Greeley, Colo., July 21, 1948; s. William Carroll and Florence Elaine (Krusenstjerna) S.; m. Rosemary Russell, May 16, 1981; children: Faith Ann, William Jeremiah. BS in Mgmt. cum laude, U. West Fla., Pensacola, 1975; MA in Pub. Policy magna cum laude, Regent U., Virginia Beach, 1985. Mgr. Mgmt. Recruiters, Internat., Pensacola, Fla., 1976—79, divsn. mgr. Virginia Beach, Va., 1979—81; dir. comm. Rock Ch., Virginia Beach, 1981—83; dir. devel., v.p. comm. Nat. Freedom Inst., Chesapeake, Va., 1983; pres. William G. Sidebottom & Assocs., 1986—97, InterAct Response Comm., 1997—2004; founder and mng. dir. X'el Commn., 2004—. Author: Who Owns the Children, 1985; sr. editor: The Perspective Papers, 1985, Essential Lectures, 1985. Cons. Am. Ctr. for Law and Justice, 1990-2002, Christian Advocates Serving Evangelism, 1995-2002, Christian Coalition, 1999-2003; v.p. Liberty Coun., 2005—; sr. flight instr. U.S. Navy Aviation Tng. Ctr. Capt. USMC, 1970-76. Mem.: Pi Kappa Delta, Phi Kappa Phi. E-mail: xelcomm@comcast.net.

SIDELSKY, PATRICIA LONEY, science educator; b. Hanover, NH, Jan. 5, 1945; d. Charles Alexander and Mary (Zurbrugg) Loney; m. Richard W. Lippincott, Apr. 17, 1971 (div. Apr. 1980); 1 child, Richard Ryan; m. Michael G. Sidelsky, May 24, 1980; 1 child, Cory Charles. BS in Biology, Bucknell U., 1967; MS in Biology, Rutgers U., 1987; MAT, Mary Grove Coll., 2002. Cert. in comprehensive sci. tchr., N.J. Tchr. sci. Easton (Md.) Mid. Sch., 1972-79; med. technologist Easton Meml. Hosp., 1974-76; tchr. Easton Middle Sch., 1976-79; tchr. advanced placement biology and genetics Cherokee High Sch., Marlton, NJ, 1979—; med. technologist HIP of N.J., Medford, 1979-87, 90-92; lead tchr. Ctr. for Maths., Sci. and Computer Edn. Rutgers U., New Brunswick, NJ, 1988-93; lead tchr. Douglass Summer Sci. Inst., New Brunswick, 1988-92. Mem. Douglas Coll. Bd. for Women in Maths. & Sci., 1988-92. Co-author: Molecular Approaches to the Study of Gene Activity, 1987—. Recipient Outstanding Tchr. award, N.J., Nat. Assn. Biology Tchrs., 1989, Tandy Tchr. Scholar award, 1991; Access Excellence fellow Genentech, 1994; grantee Ptnrs. in Sci. Rsch. Corp., 1994-95; named Tchr. of Yr. Lenape Regional H.S. Dist., 1996. Mem. Biology Tchrs. Assn. N.J. (v.p. 1990, pres. elect 1991-92, pres. 1992—), Nat. Sci. Tchrs. Assn., N.J. Sci. Tchrs. Assn., Nat. Biology Tchrs. Assn., Am. Soc. Clin. Pathologists, Am. Soc. Microbiology. Episcopalian. Home: 8 Rockledge Ct Marlton NJ 08053-9774 Office: Cherokee High Sch Willowbend Rd Marlton NJ 08053

SIDER, RONALD J., theology educator, author; b. Stevensville, Ont., Can., Sept. 17, 1939; m. Arbutus Lichti Sider, Aug. 19, 1961; children: Theodore Ronald, Michael Jay, Sonya Maria. BA with honors, Waterloo Luth. U., Ont., Can., 1962; MA in History, Yale U., New Haven, Conn., 1963, BD, 1967, PhD in History, 1969; D (hon.), Westminster Coll., New Wilmington, Pa., 1998; DHL (hon.), Malone Coll., Canton, Ohio, 2005. Lectr., asst. prof., then assoc. prof. Messiah Coll., New Wilmington, Pa., 1968-78, acting dir., dean, 1971-75; assoc. prof. theology Ea. Bapt. Theol. Sem., Wynnewood, Pa., 1978-84, prof. theology and culture, 1984—2002, Ronald J. Sider prof. theology, holistic ministry and pub. policy, 2002—; dir. Sider Ctr. on Ministry and Pub. Policy Palmer Seminary, Eastern U., 2002—. Coord., chair, convenor workshops in field; coord. Internat. Consultation on Simple Lifestyle, London, 1980; lectr. in field. Author: Christ and Violence, 1979, Karlstadt's Battle with Luther: Documents in a Liberal-Radical Debate, 1978, 82, Evangelism, 1985, Rich Christians in an Age of Hunger: A Biblical Study, 1977, rev. edit., 1984, 90, 97, 2005, German edit., 1979, Dutch edit., 1980, Portuguese edit., 1984, Japanese edit., 1989, Chinese edit., 1998, Korean edit., 1998, Andreas Bodenstein Von Karlstadt, 1974, Genuine Christianity, 1996, (with Richard K. Taylor) Nuclear Holocaust and Christian Hope, 1982, English edit., 1984, (with Oliver O'Donovan) Peace and War: A Debate About Pacifism, 1985, (in Chinese) Evangelical Faith and Social Ethics, 1986, Completely Pro-Life, 1987, (with Michael A. King) Preaching About Life in Threatening World, 1988, (with Kathleen Hayes), JustLife/88: A 1988 Election Study Guide for Justice, Life and Peace, 1988, Testing the Limits of Nonviolence, 1988, One-Sided Christianity? Uniting the Church to Heal a Lost and Broken World, 1993, Cup of Water, Bread of Life: Inspiring Stories About Overcoming Lopsided Christianity, 1994, Korean edit., 1999, Good News and Good Works: A Theology for the Whole Gospel, 1999, Living Like Jesus, 1999, Just Generosity: A New Vision for Overcoming Poverty in America, 1999, 2d edit., 2007, (with Philip N. Olson and Heidi Rolland Unruh) Churches That Make a Difference: Reaching Your Community with Good News and Good Works, 2002, Doing Evangelism Jesus' Way, 2003, The Scandal of the Evangelical Conscience, 2005, (with Heidi Rolland Unruh) Saving Souls, Serving Society: Understanding The Faith Factor in Church Based Social Ministry, 2005, (with Heidi Unruh) Hope for Children in Poverty, 2007; editor: Preaching on Peace, 1982, Lifestyle in the Eighties: An Evangelical Commitment to Simple Life-Style, 1982, Evangelicals and Development: Toward a Theology of Social Change, 1982, Living More Simply, 1980, Cry Justice: The Bible on Hunger and Poverty, 1988, 91, For They Shall Be Fed, 1997, (with Diane Knippers) Toward an Evangelical Public Policy, 2005; co-editor: Transformation mag., 1984-99; editor, contbr.: The Chicago Declaration, 1974; pub. Prism mag., 1993—, Green Cross, 1994-98, Creation Care, 1998-2002; contbr. numerous articles to profl. publs., chpts. to books. Head voter registration drive, New Haven, 1967; pres. Diamond St. Cmty. Ctr., 1986-91; exec. dir. Evangelicals for Social Action, 1987-92, pres., 1992—; exec. dir. Just Life, 1987-91, pres., 1991-94; bd. dirs. Bread for the World, 1978-84, Mennonite Ctrl. Com., 1978-80, Nat. Religious Partnership on the Environ., 1994-, Call to Renewal, 1996— Evangel. Environ. Network, 2005—; co-chair Nat. Workshop on Race and Reconciliation, Atlanta, 1975. Malcolm Chase fellow, 1962-63, R.E. Darling fellow, 1963-64, fellow Yale U., 1967-68, Inst. for Advanced Christian Studies, 1976; co-chair Working Group on Human Needs and Faith-Based and Cmty. Initiatives II, 2002-03. Mem. Nat. Assn. Evangelicals (mem. social action commn. 1975—). Mennonite. Home: 312 W Logan St Philadelphia PA 19144-4120 Office: Palmer Sem 6 E Lancaster Ave Wynnewood PA 19096-3430 Office Phone: 610-645-9354. Business E-Mail: rsider@eastern.edu.

SIDEROW, NEIL, real estate company executive; BA, NYU; MBA, Pace U. Founding ptnr., COO Murray Hill Properties; vice chmn. TCN Worldwide, 2003—, also bd. dirs. Office: Murray Hill Properties LLC 1140 Ave of the Americas New York NY 10036

SIDERYS, HARRY, surgeon, educator; b. NYC, Mar. 2, 1927; s. George and Helen Siderys; m. Cathy Luan Ruby, Apr. 18, 1970; children: George, Robert, William, Christopher. BA, Amhers Coll., 1948; MD, SUNY, 1952. Diplomate Am. Bd Surgery, Am. Bd. Thoracic Surgery, Am. Bd. Vascular Surgery. Asst. prof. surgery Ind. U. Sch. Medicine, Indpls., 1962—; chief surgery St. Francis Hosp., Beech Grove, Ind., 1964—66; chmn. cardiovascular surgery Meth. Hosp., Indpls., 1980—90; chief cardiothoracic surgery Marion County Gen. Hosp., Indpls., 1967—69; sr. surgeon Corvasc, Indpls., 2000—. Founder cardiovascular surgical svcs. Meth. Hosp., Indpls., 1965—, dir. residency thoracic and cardiovascular surgery, 1973—76; examiner grad. program surgery Grad. Edn. Surgery, 1962—80. Contbr. articles various profl. jours. Chmn. Quality Assurance Cardiovascualr Med. and Surgical, 1993—. With USN, 1945—46. Mem.: ACS, AMA, Soc. Clin. Vascular Surgery, Internat. Soc. Heart Transplantation, Am. Soc. Artificial Internal Organ, Midwest Vascular Surgical Soc., Am. Coll. Cardiology, Am. Assn. Thoracic and Cardiovascular Surgery, Soc. Thoracic Surgeons, Internat. Cardiovascular Soc., Marion County Med. Assn., Ind. State Med. Assn., Am. Assn. Thoracic and Cardiovascular Surgery, Midwest Chest Club. Achievements include first coronary bypass in Ind., 1968; first ventricular asst. device in Ind., 1978. Home: 9015 Kirkham Ct Indianapolis IN 46260 Office: Corvasc 1801 N Senate Blvd Indianapolis IN 46202 Personal E-mail: hsiderys@aol.com.

SIDES, JACK DAVIS, JR., lawyer; b. Dallas, Sept. 18, 1939; s. Jack Davis Sr. and Edith Eugenia (Lowrie) S.; m. Nancy Pauline Cantwell, July 22, 1967 (div. Sept. 1976); children: Mary Katharine, Jack Davis III; m. Laura Gail Miller, Aug. 2, 1979; children: Susan Ashley, Stacy Anne. BBA, U. Tex., 1962, JD with honors, 1963. Bar: Tex. 1963. Assoc. Jackson, Walker, et al, Dallas, 1963-67, White, McElroy, White, Sides & Rector, Dallas, 1968-78; sole practice Dallas, 1978—. Editor: U. Tex. Law Review, 1963. Trustee Highland Park Sch. Dist., 1996-2002; With USAFNG, 1963-69. Fellow Dallas Bar Found., Tex. Bar Found. (life); mem. ABA, Tex. Bar Assn. (grievance subcom. 1979-86), Dallas Bar Assn. (ethics com. 1973-77, jud. com. 1988—), Dallas Assn. Def. Counsel (sec. 1973-74). Clubs: Brook Hollow Golf (Dallas). Republican. Methodist. Avocations: reading, tennis, exercise.

SIDES, LARRY EUGENE, advertising executive; b. Albany, Ga., Nov. 14, 1946; s. Robert N. and Florine (Stewart) Sides; m. Kathy Ashworth, Aug. 13, 1950. BA in Radio and TV, U. La., 1970, MS in Communications, 1975. News reporter Sta. KATC-TV, Lafayette, La., 1970-71; account exec. Herbert S. Benjamin Assocs., Lafayette, La., 1971-76; pres. Sides & Assocs., Lafayette, La., 1976—. Vice-chmn. Crimestoppers, Lafayette, 1985; pres. Gateway Found., 1990; active Leadership La., 1989, 1990; mem. Coun. for Better La., 1991—94; bd. dirs. La. Coun. on Child Abuse, 1992—96; active Leadership Lafayette, 1995; mem. exec. com. Cristo en Cuba Coord. Coun.; bd. dirs. Episcopal Sch. Acadiana, Lafayette, 1987; mem. vestry Episcopal Ch. of Ascension, 2002—04, coord. Cuba project, 2001—, jr. warden, 2002; sr. warden Episcopal Diocese of We. La., 2003, chmn. Commn. on Internat. Missions, 2003—; mem. Global Episcopal Mission Network, 2004; bd. dirs. Nat. Cristo En Cuba Coordinating Coun. Named Outstanding Young Men of Am., Lafayette Jaycees, 1976; recipient Disting. Alumni award dept. comms., U. La., 1995. Mem.: Acadiana Advt. Fedn., Pub. Rels. Soc. Am., Am. Soc. Hosp. Pub. Rels., Am. Assn. Advt. Agys. (pres. La. coun. 1989—90), Lafayette C. of C. (pres. 1989, bd. dirs. 2003, Entrepreneur of Yr. 1983), Beaver Club (pres. 1986, Outstanding Club Mem. award 1976), Sigma Nu (alumni pres. Lafayette chpt. 1977). Home: 1015 W Saint Mary Blvd Lafayette LA 70506-3420 Office: 404 Eraste Landry Rd Lafayette LA 70506-2324

SIDHU, JAY S., former bank executive; b. India, Aug. 8, 1951; arrived in U.S. at age 18; BA, Banaras Hindu U.; MBA, Wilkes U., 1973. Vice chmn., COO Penn Savings Bank, 1986—89; treas., CEO Sovereign Bank, 1987—89; pres., CEO Sovereign Bancorp Inc. (formerly Penn Savings Bank), Wyomissing, Pa., 1989—2002, chmn., pres., CEO, 2002—06, non-exec. chmn., 2006. *

SIDHWA, FRANK N., engineering executive; BEE, CUNY, 1980; MBA, Adelphi U., NY, 1984. Cert. project mgmt., U. Calif., 1998. Design engr. Sperry Sys. Mgmt., Great Neck, NY, 1980—83; sys. engr. Harris Corp., Syosset, NY, 1983—85; engring. mgr. Raytheon Corp., Melville, NY, 1985—86; prin. engr. Douglas Aircraft, Long Beach, Calif., 1986—91; sys. engring. mgr. PB/DMJM Metro Rail Projects, LA, 1991—93; sr. mgr. engring. Boeing Co., Long Beach, 1993—. Contbr. scientific papers in field. Recipient Best paper award. Mem.: NSPE, IEEE, Am. Mgmt. Assn. Achievements include research in avionics automated testing. Office: Boeing Co 2401 E Wardlow Rd 52-681 Long Beach CA 90080

SIDICK, ERKIN, optical engineer; arrived in US, 1988; s. Sidick Memet and Patem Ershidin; m. Amangul Eysa, Aug. 16, 1984; children: Dilnare Erkin, Dilshat Erkin. BSEE, Xinjiang U., China, 1983; MS in Physics, Calif. State U., Northridge, 1990; PhD, U. Calif., Davis, 1995. Postdoctoral rschr. Sandia Nat. Labs., Livermore, Calif., 1995—96; sr. optical engr., mgr. CVI Laser Corp., Livermore, 1996—2000, WaveSplitter Tech., Fremont, Calif., 2000—03; sr. mem. tech. staff Jet Propulsion Lab., Pasadena, Calif., 2004—. Contbr. chapters to books, over 60 articles to profl. jours. Recipient Provincial Best Student award, Edn. Commn., Xinjiang Uyghur Autonomous Region, 1981, 1982, Nat. Best Student Leader award, Ministry Edn. People's Republic China, 1982, Anil K. Jain Best Ph.D. Dissertation prize, U. Calif., 1995. Mem.: SPIE. Achievements include patents in field. Office: Jet Propulsion Lab 4800 Oak Grove Dr Pasadena CA 91109 Home Phone: 661-252-1856; Office Phone: 818-393-7585. Office Fax: 818-393-6869. Business E-Mail: erkin.sidick@jpl.nasa.gov.

SIDMAN, RICHARD LEON, neuroscientist, educator; b. Boston, Sept. 19, 1928; s. Manuel and Annabelle (Seltzer) Sidman; m. Ljiljana Lekic, 1974. AB, Harvard U., 1949, MD (Jeffries Wyman scholar), 1953. Intern in medicine Boston City Hosp., 1953—54; asst. resident in neurology Mass. Gen. Hosp., Boston, 1955—56; staff scientist NIH, Bethesda, Md., 1956—58; instr. to prof. neuropathology Harvard U. Med. Sch., Boston, 1959—69, Bullard prof., 1969—99, prof. emeritus, 1999—; chief div. neurogenetics New Eng. Regional Primate Rsch. Ctr. Harvard Med. Sch., Southborough, Mass., 1991—99; prof. neuropathology emeritus dept. neurosurgery Brigham and Womens Hosp., Boston, 1999—; sr. rsch. assoc. dept. neurology Beth Israel Deaconess Med. Ctr., Boston, 2001—. Chief dept. neurosci. Children's Hosp., Boston, 1972—88; 1st Richard Stearns Meml.ml. lectr. Albert Einstein Coll. Medicine, 1958; Bailey Meml. lectr. U. Sask., Canada, 1978; Waisman Meml. lectr. U. Wis. Author (with M. Sidman): Neuroanatomy - A Programmed Text, vol. 1, 1965; author: (with others) Catalog of the Neurological Mutants of the Mouse, 1965; author: (with R.D. Adams) Introduction to Neuropathology, 1968; author: (with others) Atlas of the Mouse Brain and Spinal Cord, 1971; contbr. numerous articles, book chpts., revs. on neuroembryology pathology and genetics to profl. publs. Mem. sci. adv. com. Retinitis Pigmentosa Found.; bd. sci. overseers Jackson Lab., Bar Harbor, Maine. With USPHS, 1956—58. Recipient Soma Weiss student rsch. prizes, Harvard U. Med. Sch., 1951—53, Boylston Soc. Essay prize, 1953; fellow Neuroscis. Rsch. Program fellow, 1971—79; Harvard U. Mosley Travelling fellow, 1954—55. Fellow: Nat. Acad. Sci., Am. Acad. Arts and Scis.; mem.: AAAS, Tissue Culture Assn., Soc. Neurosci., Soc. Devel. Neurosci., Internat. Soc. Devel. Neurobiology, Soc. Devel. Biology, Internat. Brain Rsch. Orgn., Histochem. Soc., Am. Soc. Cell Biology, Am. Assn. Neuropathologists, Am. Assn. Anatomists, Am. Acad. Neurology. Office: Harvard Inst Medicine 855 77 Ave Louis Pasteur Boston MA 02115 Office Phone: 508-341-6552. Business E-Mail: richard_sidman@hms.harvard.edu.

SIDMAN, ROBERT JOHN, lawyer; b. Cleve., Aug. 4, 1943; s. Charles Frances and Louise (Eckert) S.; m. Mary Mato, July 29, 1967; children: Christa Mary, Alicia Mary. BA, Benedictine Coll., 1965; JD, U. Notre Dame, 1968. Bar: Ohio 1968, U.S. Dist. Ct. (so. dist.) Ohio 1970, U.S. Ct. Appeals (6th cir.) 1971, U.S. Supreme Ct. 1971. Law clk. U.S. Dist. Ct. (so. dist.) Ohio, Columbus, 1968-70; assoc. Mayer, Tingley & Hurd, Columbus, 1970-75; judge Bankruptcy Ct. U.S. Dist. Ct. (so. dits.) Ohio, Columbus, 1975-82; ptnr. Vorys, Sater, Seymour & Pease, Columbus, 1982—. Prof. Ohio State U. Law Sch., Columbus, 1984, 85, 86. Mem. Nat. Conf. Bankruptcy Judges (bd. dirs. 1981-82), Assn. Former Bankruptcy Judges (bd. dirs. 1983-89, treas. 1986-87, pres. 1988-89). Office: Vorys Sater Seymour & Pease PO Box 1008 52 E Gay St Columbus OH 43215-3161 E-mail: rjsidman@vssp.com, rsidman843@aol.com.

SIDNAM, ALAN NORTHCOTE, retired advertising executive, venture capitalist; b. Kalamazoo, Mich., July 14, 1916; s. William Northcote and Esther Lulu (Humphrey) S.; m. Shirley S. Meeker, Dec. 31, 1947 (div. Sept. 1975); 1 child, Caroline; m. Gloria Delli-Bovi, Oct. 10, 1975. BA, Kalamazoo Coll., 1937. Apprentice Staake-Schoonmaker, Kalamazoo, 1937-38; acct. exec., copywriter Winternitz & Cairns, NYC, 1938-39, Robert Winternitz, Advt., NYC, 1939-42; acct. exec., exec. v.p. Benton & Bowles, Advt., NYC, 1945-61; vice chmn. Ogilvy & Mather, NYC, 1963-68, cons., 1968-70; venture capitalist NYC, 1970—. Founding investor, dir. Lindblad Travel, N.Y.C., 1961-75; investor, dir. Kelley Oil Corp., Houston, 1970-87. Vestryman St. George's Episcopal Ch., N.Y.C., 1964-65; trustee Kalamazoo Coll., 1971-82, Ch. Heavenly Rest Day Sch., N.Y.C., 1973-79; bd. dirs. Mus. Tower, N.Y.C., 1999—. 1st lt. USAF, 1942-45, PTO. Mem. Univ. Club (coun. 1986-88), Waccabuc Country Club (pres. 1955-56). Republican. Episcopalian. Avocations: tennis, golf.

SIDNEY, CORINNE ENTRATTER, retired journalist, actress; b. LA, Apr. 13, 1937; d. Carl Smith and Alice (Polk) Kegley; m. Jack Entratter (dec. 1971); m. Robert Heffron, 1973 (div. 1980); 1 child, Benjamin Jack; m. George Sidney, Oct. 12, 1991 (dec. 2002). Student, U. Calif., Berkeley; Grad., U. Judaism, LA, 1971; postgrad., UCLA, 1983; fine arts grad., UNLV, 2002—. Feature editor Univ. Man fashion mag., 1972-86; columnist Beverly Hills, 1986-89; writer syndicated entertainment column Real to Real Capital News Svc., 1988-91; chmn. fine arts com. U. (Las Vegas) Nev., 2003, 2004. Stringer USA Today, People weekly, Beverly Hills (Calif.) Post, 1990-91; pub. rels. cons., 1972-86. Film appearances include Murderers' Row, North to Alaska, Speed Limit 65, That Funny Feeling, The Big Mouth, The Journey, (with Peter Sellers) The Party, Road House, (George Sidney's film) The Swinger, Who's Minding the Mint?; TV appearances include Steve Allen, Caine's 100, Cannon, Bob Hope, Hazel, Home Show, Ironside, Monkees, Ozzie and Harriet, Bachelor Father, Tennessee Ernie Ford, General Hospital, FBI, Larry King, Bob Newhart, Shower of Stars, Johnny Carson Players, This is Alice; stage appearances include Born Yesterday, Seven Year Itch, Ninety Day Mistress, Tender Trap, Who Was That Lady I Saw You With?, Getting It; toured with Las Vegas New Frontier Hotel Lounge act, The New Yorkers, also toured 1990-TV cir. with Playboy's playmates of each decade; hostess TV talk show Westcoasting... with Corinne, 1991; co-host Real to Reel. Active civic orgns.; candidate Beverly Hills City Coun., 1980; mem. El Rodeo Sch. PTA, El Rodeo YMCA; established George Sidney award, 5 full 4 yr. student scholarships UNLV. 1st runner-up Miss U.S.A. Contest; named Playboy Ctr. Fold of 50's Decade, 1958; named Pin-up Girl of Atomic Nuclear Submarine Nautilus, 1958, one of 7 Top Playmates Fox-TV Am. Chronicles., 1990. Mem. AFTRA (women's com.), SAG, LWV, Women in Film, Am. Film Inst., C. of C. and Civic Assn. (pres. 1997), Hollywood Women's Press Club (pres. 1997), Bus. and Profl. Women (conv. del., Olympic com., program chmn., founder West Side chpt. 1985), Hadassah (v.p., membership chmn., co-chmn. ann. ball honoring Barbara Sinatra, founder, pres. Haifa chpt.), Israel Tennis Ctrs., UCLA Theatre Arts Alumni Assn, Beverly Hills Cannes' Sister City, Corinne's Beverly Hills Salon (founder). Office Phone: 702-894-5298. Office Fax: 702-894-5291.

SIDRAN, MIRIAM, retired physicist; b. Washington, May 25, 1920; d. Morris Samson and Theresa Rena (Gottlieb) S. BA, Bklyn. Coll., 1942; MA, Columbia U., NYC, 1949; PhD, NYU, 1956. Rsch. assoc. dept. physics NYU, NYC, 1950-55, postdoctoral fellow, 1955-57; asst. prof. Staten Island Community Coll., Richmond, NY, 1957-59; rsch. scientist Grumman Aerospace Corp., Bethpage, NY, 1959-67; prof. N.Y. Inst. Tech., NYC, 1967-72; NSF rsch. fellow Nat. Marine Fisheries Svc., Miami, Fla.,

1971-72; assoc. prof. then prof. physics Baruch Coll., NYC, 1972-89, chmn. dept. natural scis., 1983-89, prof. emerita, 1990—. V.p. Baruch chpt. Profl. Staff Congress, 1983-89. Contbr. numerous articles to profl. and govtl. publs., chpts. to books. N.Y. State Regents scholar, 1937-41; NSF summer fellow, Miami, 1970. Mem. N.Y. Acad. Scis., Am. Assn. Physics Tchrs., Physics Club N.Y., N.Y. Gilbert and Sullivan Soc., Wynmoor Computer Club, Friends of Mozart, Sigma Xi, Sigma Pi Sigma. Avocations: french and hebrew languages, music, bicycling, poetry, opera. Home: 210 W 19th St Apt 5G New York NY 10011-4009

SIDRANSKY, DAVID, molecular biologist; b. El Paso, Tex., June 21, 1960; s. Julia and Amalia Sidransky; m. Lynn R. Clahr, Sept. 26, 1990; children: Elie M., Anina Libi, Yair S. BS in Chemistry, magna cum laude, with highest honors, Brandeis U., 1981; MD, Baylor Coll. Medicine, 1984. Diplomate Am. Bd. Internal Medicine, Am. Bd. Med. Oncology. Intern in internal medicine Baylor Coll. Medicine, Houston, 1984-85, resident in internal medicine, 1985-87, clin. investigator Inst. Molecular Genetics, 1986-87, chief resident in internal medicine, 1987-88; sr. clin. fellow in oncology Johns Hopkins Hosp., Balt., 1988-89, rsch. fellow in oncology, 1989-92, asst. prof. oncology, 1992-94, asst. prof. otolaryngology, head and neck surgery, 1992-94, assoc. prof. oncology, 1994-98, dir. head and neck cancer rsch. divsn., 1994—, prof. otolaryngology, head and neck surgery, 1998—, prof. pathology, 1998—, prof. cellular and molecular medicine, 1998—, prof. urology, 1999—. Mem. external adv. bd. U. Calif., San Diego Cancer Ctr., U. Tex. M.D. Anderson Cancer Ctr., Houston; mem. sci. adv. coun. Israel Cancer Sch. Fund; mem. med. adv. coun. Israel Children's Cancer Found.; mem. devel. diagnostics com. Nat. Cancer Inst., 1996—, mem. cancer prevention and control com., 1996—, bd. sci. counselors, chmn. early detectin rsch. network; bd. dirs. ImClone, 2004-, Alfacell Corp., 2004-; sr. editor Clinical Cancer Research. Contbr. articles to profl. jours. including Sci., Cancer Rsch., Sci., Nature Medicine; chmn., editl. bd. Internat. Jour. Cancer-Predictive Oncology; sr. editor Clin. Cancer Rsch.; assoc. editor Cancer Rsch., Jour. Nat. Cancer Inst., Oral Oncology. Recipient Nat. Rsch. Svc. award, 1989-91, Young Investigators Merit award, 1992, Clinician Scientist award, 1992, award Found. for the Promotion of Cancer Rsch., Japan, 1995, Sarstedt Internat. Rsch. prize German Soc. Clin. Chemistry, 1997, Cheng Suen Man Shook Found. award Hong Kong Cancer Inst., 1998, Walter Hubert award Brit. Assn. Cancer Rsch., 1998, Alton Ochsner award Relating Smoking and Health Am. Coll. Chest Physicians, 1998, Internat. Union Against Cancer Roll of Honour, 1999, Osserman award, Israel Cancer Rsch. Fund, 2001, Richard and Hinda Rosenthal Found. award, Am. Assn. Cancer Rsch., 2004. Mem. AAAS, Am. Soc. for Head and Neck Surgery, Am. Assn. for Cancer Rsch., N.Y. Acad. Scis. Jewish. Avocation: racquetball. Office: Johns Hopkins U Ross Rsch Bldg 720 Rutland Ave Ste 818 Baltimore MD 21205-2109 *

SIDWELL, DAVID H., diversified financial services company executive; b. 1953; BA, Cambridge U., Eng., 1975. Chartered acct. With PricewaterhouseCoopers, 1975—84, J.P. Morgan & Co., 1984—2000; CFO J.P. Morgan Chase & Co., NYC, 2000—04; exec. v.p., CFO Morgan Stanley, 2004—. Office: c/o Morgan Stanley 1585 Broadway New York NY 10036 *

SIEBEL, CARL A., manufacturing executive; b. Bonn, Germany; Grad. in Bus. Studies, Hamburg, Germany. Mng. dir. Perfect Valois Ventil GmbH (subs. of Seaquist Group), Dortmund, Germany, 1969—75; dir. European Ops. Seaquist Group Pittway Corp., 1975—93, v.p., 1982—93; pres., COO AptarGroup, Inc. (formerly Seaquist Group), 1993—96, pres., CEO, 1996—. Bd. trustees Am. Inst. Contemporary German Studies. Office: AptarGroup Inc 475 W Terra Cotta Ave Ste E Crystal Lake IL 60014 Office Phone: 815-477-0424. *

SIEBEL, THOMAS M., software company executive; BA, U. Ill., Urbana-Champaign, MS in Computer Sci., MBA. Various positions including group v.p., gen. mgr. Oracle Corp.; CEO Gain Tech., until 1992, Siebel Systems, San Mateo, Calif., 1993—2004, chmn., 1993—. Author: Virtual Selling, Cyber Rules, Taking Care of eBusiness. Bd. advisors U. Ill., Coll. Engring., Stanford U. Grad. Sch. Bus., Stanford U. Law Sch. Named one of top 25 managers in the world, Business Week mag., 2000, 2001, 400 Richest Americans, Forbes, 2006; recipient David Packard Award, Bus. Executives for Nat. Security, 2002, CEO of the Year, Industry Week mag., 2002.

SIEBEN, JEFFREY SCOTT, lawyer; b. Hastings, Minn., 1975; BA, St. John's U., Collegeville, Minn., 1997; JD, William Mitchell Coll. Law, St. Paul, 2001. Bar: Minn. 2001. Assoc. Sieben, Grose, Von Holtum & Carey, Ltd., Mpls. Named a Rising Star, Minn. Super Lawyers mag., 2006. Mem.: Minn. Trial Lawyers Assn., ABA, Minn. State Bar Assn., Dakota County Bar Assn., Hennepin County Bar Assn. Office: Sieben Grose Von Holtum & Carey Ltd 900 Midwest Plz East Bldg 800 Marquette Ave Minneapolis MN 55402 Office Phone: 612-333-9713. E-mail: jeffrey.sieben@knowyourrights.com. *

SIEBERT, CALVIN D., economist, educator; b. Hillsboro, Kans., Feb. 11, 1934; s. Ira and Margaret (Everett) S.; m. Valerie Dawn Nanninga, Feb. 18, 1960; children— Douglas Erik, Derek Christopher. BA, U. Kans., 1958, MA, 1960; PhD in Econs., U. Calif., Berkeley, 1966. Asst. prof. econs. U. Iowa, 1965-68, assoc. prof., 1968-75, prof., 1975—, chmn. dept., 1969-71, 75-79. Rockefeller Found. vis. asso. prof. U. Philippines, 1971-72 Contbr. articles to profl. jours. With U.S. Army, 1954-56. Ford Found. grantee, 1964-65. Mem. Am. Econ. Assn., Phi Beta Kappa. Home: 341 N 7th Ave Iowa City IA 52245-6003 Office: U Iowa Dept Econs S318 Pbb Iowa City IA 52242 Business E-Mail: calvin_siebert@uiowa.edu.

SIEBERT, DIANE DOLORES, author, poet; b. Chgo., Mar. 18, 1948; m. Robert William Siebert, Sept. 21, 1969. RN. Author: Truck Song, 1984 (Notable Childrens Book award ALA 1984, Sch. Libr. Jour. one of Best Books 1984, Outstanding Childrens Book award NY Times Book Rev. 1984, Reading Rainbow Selection book 1991), Mojave, 1988 (Childrens Editors Choice 1988, Internat. Reading Assn. Tchr. Choice award 1989, others), Heartland, 1989 (award Nat. Coun. for Social Studies/Childrens Book Coun. 1989, on John Burroughs List Nature Book for Young Readers 1989, Ohio Farm Bur. Women award 1991), Train Song, 1990 (Notable Childrens Book award ALA, 1990, Redbook Mag. one of Top Ten Picture Books 1990, one of Best Books award Sch. Libr. Jour. 1990, others), Sierra, 1991 (Outstanding Sci. Trade Book for Children award NSTA 1991, Notable Childrens Trade Book in Field Social Studies award Nat. Coun. Social Studies 1991, Beatty award Calif. Libr. Assn. 1992), Plane Song, 1993 (Outstanding Sci. Trade Book for Children 1994, Reading Rainbow Selection book, Platinum award Oppenheim Toy Portfolio, Tchrs. Choice award Internat. Reading Assn. 1994), Cave, 2000 (Notable children's Book in the english Language Arts, 2001, Nat. Coun. of English Tchr., named to John Burroughs List of Nature Books for Young Readers 2000), Mississippi (named to John Burroughs List 2001), 2001, Motorcycle Song, 2002, Rhyolite, 2003, Tour America, 2006 (Oreg. Book award for children's literature, Eloise Jarvis McGraw award 2006, Lee Bennett Hopkins Honor Book award 2007, Notable Social Studies Trade Books for Young People 2007, Cybils award finalist 2007), Spring, Summer, Autumn, Winter, 2007. Avocations: environmental affairs, running, classical guitar, motorcycle, animals. Home: 9676 SW Jordan Rd Culver OR 97734-9567 Personal E-mail: dsiebert48@msn.com.

SIEBERT, JOHN WESTON, surgeon, plastic surgeon; b. Madison, Wis., Feb. 8, 1955; MD, U. Wis. Med. Sch., 1981. Cert. Surgery, Plastic Surgery. Resident, surgery Mass. Gen. Hosp., 1981—86; resident, plastic surgery NYU Med. Ctr., 1986—88, clin. fellow, microsurgery, 1988—89, assoc. prof., surgery, 1989; attending surgeon Manhatten Ear, Eye and Throat Hosp., NYC, 1989—, Bellevue Hosp. Ctr., NYC, 1989—, NY Ear and Eye Infirmary, NYC, 1989—. Adj. prof., plastic surgery, dept. surgery NYU Med. Ctr. Recipient Golf Digest Top 250 Golf Doctors in Am., 2006. Achievements include pioneering microsurgery on facial deformities, aesthetic surgery. Office: NYU Med Ctr Dept Plastic Surgery 550 First Ave New York NY 10016 *

SIEBERT, KARL JOSEPH, food science educator, consultant; b. Harrisburg, Pa., Oct. 29, 1945; s. Christian Ludwig and Katharine (Springer) S.; m. Sui Ti Atienza, Mar. 14, 1970; children: Trina, Sabrina. BS in Biochemistry, Pa. State U., 1967, MS in Biochemistry, 1968, PhD in Biochemistry, 1970. Chemist Applied Sci. Labs., State College, Pa., 1968-70; rsch. assoc. Stroh Brewery Co., Detroit, 1971, head R & D sect., 1971-73, mgr. R & D lab., 1973-82, dir. rsch., 1982-90; v.p. Strohtech, Detroit, 1986-90; prof. Cornell U., Geneva, NY, 1990—, chmn. dept. food sci. and tech., 1990-95, also assoc. dir. Cornell Inst. Food Sci. Ithaca, NY, 1990-95. Contbr. articles to profl. jours. Bd. visitors Oakland U. Biology Dept., Rochester, Mich., 1985-89; bd. dirs. Cornell Rsch. Found., 1990-96, Geneva Concerts Inc., 1991-98. Capt. USAR, 1967-75. Recipient Presdl. award Master Brewers Assn., 1986, 90; named hon. prof. Moscow State Acad. Food Prodn., 1996. Fellow NSF; mem. Am. Chem. Soc. (divsn. agrl. and food chemistry, computers in chemistry divsn.), Master Brewer Assn. Ams., Am. Soc. Brewing Chemists (chmn. tech. com. 1986-88, mem. editl. bd. 1983-91, 96—, Eric Kneen Meml. award 1998, 99, 2004, award of distinction 1999), Inst. Food Technologists (divsn. fruit and vegetable tech., food chemistry, food microbiology, sensory analysis), Internat. Chemometrics Soc. (N.Am. chpt.), Sigma Xi (pres. Geneva chpt. 2005-06). Avocations: computers, electronics. Home: 9 Parkway St Geneva NY 14456-9765 Home Phone: 315-789-4092; Office Phone: 315-787-2299. E-mail: kjs3@cornell.edu.

SIEBERT, MURIEL (MICKIE), brokerage house executive, retired bank executive; b. Cleve., 1932; d. Irwin J. and Margaret Eunice (Roseman) Siebert. Student, Western Res. U., 1949-52; DCS (hon.), St. John's U., St. Bonaventure U., Molloy Coll., Adelphi U., St. Francis Coll., Mercy Coll., Coll. New Rochelle, St. Lawrence U., Manhattan Coll., Seton Hall Coll., Case Western Res. U., Marymount Manhattan Coll., Hofstra U., U. Rochester, U. NC, Asheville, 2004, U. NC, Greensboro, 2005. Security analyst Bache & Co., 1954-57; analyst Utilities & Industries Mgmt. Corp., 1958, Shields & Co., 1959-60; ptnr. Stearns & Co., 1961, Finkle & Co., 1962-65, Brimberg & Co., NYC, 1965-67; individual mem. (first woman mem.) NY Stock Exch., 1967; chmn., pres. Muriel Siebert & Co., Inc., 1969-77; trustee Manhattan Savs. Bank, 1975-77; supt. banks, dept. banking State of NY, 1977-82; dir. Urban Devel. Corp., NYC, 1977-82, Job Devel. Authority, NYC, 1977-82, State of NY Mortgage Agy., 1977-82; chmn., pres. Muriel Siebert & Co., Inc., NYC, 1983—. Former assoc. in mgmt. Simmons Coll.; former mem. adv. com. Fin. Acctg. Stds. Bd., 1981-84; former mem. adv. bd. Minority and Women-Owned Bus. Enterprise; guest lectr. numerous colls. Author: Changing the Rules - Adventures of a Wall Street Maverick, 2002. Ran for Rep. nomination, U.S. Senate, 1982; former mem. women's adv. com. Econ. Devel. Adminstrn., NYC; former trustee Manhattan Coll.; former v.p., current mem. exec. com. Greater NY Area coun. Boy Scouts Am.; former mem. NY State Econ. Devel. Bd., NY Coun. Economy; bd. overseers NYU Sch. Bus., 1984-88; former bd. dirs. United Way of NYC; former trustee Citizens Budget Commn., LI U.; mem. bus. com. Met. Mus., bus. com. of NY State Bus. Coun.; adv. coun. Women's Campaign Fund.; bd. dirs., past pres. NY Women's Agenda; trustee Guild Hall Mus. EH; current appointee Commn. Jud. Nomination; founding mem. The Mus. Women-The Leadership Coun; founder, bd. dirs. The WISH List; bd. dirs. Breast Cancer Rsch. Found., Animal Rescue Fund of the Hamptons; mem. Bretton Woods Com.; former Tokyo adv. com. Sister City Program NYC Recipient Spirit of Achievement award Albert Einstein Coll. Medicine, 1977, Women's Equity Action League award, 1978, Outstanding Contbns. to Equal Oppty. for Women award Bus. Coun. UN Decade for Women, 1979, Silver Beaver award Boy Scouts Am., 1981, Elizabeth Cutter Morrow award YWCA, 1983, Emily Roebling award Nat. Women's Hall of Fame, 1984, Entrepreneurial Excellence award White House Conf. on Small Bus., 1986, NOW Legal Def. and Edn. Fund award, 1981, Brotherhood award NCCJ. 1989, Women on the Move award Anti-Defamation League, 1990, Bus. Philanthropist of Yr. award So. Calif. Conf. for Women Bus. Owner's, 1990, award Borough of Manhattan, 1991, Benjamin Botwinick prize Columbia Bus. Sch., 1992, Women in Bus. Making History award Women's Bus. Coun. NY C. of C., 1993, Disting. Woman of Yr. award Greater NY Boy Scouts of Am., 1993, Corning Excellence award NYC Bus. Coun., 1993, Woman of Yr. award Fin. Women's Assn. NY, 1994, Medal of Honor award Ellis Island, 1994, Star award N.Y. Women's Agenda, 1994, NY Urban Coalition's Achievement award, 1994, Women of Distinction award Crohn's and Colitis Found., 1994, Entrepreneurial Leadership award Nat. Found. Tchg. Entrepreneurship, 1994, Athena award, 1997, USO Women of Yr. award, 1998, Sara Lee Frontrunner award, 1998, Mattel/Barbie Ambassador of Dreams award, 1999, Town Hall Friend of Arts award, 2000, Pride of NY (PONY) award, 2001, I.O. Salzberger award, 2001, Friars Found. Applause award, 2003, numerous others; honoree Am Bankers Assn., 2003, Enterprising Women's Mag. Lifetime Achiev. award, 2003, Lifetime Achievement award US China Women Bus. Leaders, 2005; inductee Nat. Woman's Hall of Fame, Seneca Falls, NY, 1994, Internat. Women's Forum Hall of Fame, 1994, Ohio Women's Hall Fame, 1994; NY Univ.'s Stern Sch. Bus. 1st Woman Stovall fellow, 1992; established Siebert Entrepreneurial Philanthropic Program, 1990. Mem. Women's Forum (founding mem., pres.), Com. 200, Fin. Women's Assn. (Cmty. Svc. award 1993), Coun. on Fgn. Rels, Nat. Assn. Women Bus. Owners (NAWBO's Veuve Clicquot Bus. Women of Yr. award 1992, Mayor's Lifetime Achievement award for Women Bus. Owners 1993), Econ. Club (exec. com.), Southampton Bath and Tennis Club (founding mem., bd. dirs.), Women's Campaign Fund, Fashion Group Internat., Friars Club, River Club, Doubles Club, Westchester Country Club, Breakers Country Club of Palm Beach. Office: Muriel Siebert & Co Inc 885 3rd Ave Ste 1720 New York NY 10022-4834 Home Phone: 212-758-1904. Personal E-mail: MSiebert@siebertnet.com.

SIEBURTH, RICHARD, literature educator, interpreter; BA, U. Chgo., 1970; PhD, Harvard U., 1976. Prof. French and Comparative Lit. NYU, 1983—. Author: Instigations, 1978; editor: Ezra Pound, A Walking Tour in Southern France, 1992; translator: Walter Benjamin, Moscow Diary, 1986, Friedrich Hölderlin, Hymms & Fragments, 1984, Gerard de Nerval, Selected Writings, 1999. Decorated chevalier Ordre des palmes academiques (France); recipient Book of the Month-Translation prize PEN USA. Fellow Am. Acad. Arts & Scis. *

SIECKERT, KRISTINE ELLEN, school psychologist, consultant; b. Milw., Oct. 25, 1948; d. Jacob George and Leopoldine Christina Schweitzer; m. Dana Jeffery Sieckert, Nov. 11, 1971 (div. June 3, 1992); 1 child, Christopher Jacob. BS, U. Wis., Milw., 1970, MS, 1979; EdS, Pitts. State U., Kansas, 1980. Cert. sch. psychologist NASP, 1986. Sch. psychologist Miami Pub. Schs., Okla., 1980—85, acting dir. spl. edn., 1984—85; sch. psychologist Oconomowoc Area Pub. Schs., Wis., 1986—; coord. English lang. learner svcs. Oconomowoc Area Sch. Dist., 1999—. Crisis response leader Nat. Orgn. Victims Assistance, 1997—; nat. emergency assistance team NASP, 1997—; cons. Wis. Govs. Task Force Sch. Safety, Madison, 1999, Wis. Atty. Gen. Task Force Sch. Safety, Madison, 2000, ARC, Milw., 2001—02. Crisis response leader NASP, 1997—, Nat. Assn. Victims Assistance, Washington, 1997—. Nominee Woman of Distinction award, YWCA, 2001; recipient Educator of Dist. award, Miami Pub. Schs., 1984, Wis. Suicide Prevention Program award, 1992, Wis. Sch. Psychologist of Yr., Wis. Sch. Psychologist Assn., 1999, Nat. Sch. Psychologist of Yr., Nat. Sch. Psychologist Assn., 2000. Mem.: NASP (nat. emergency assistance team charter mem. 1997—, Nat. Sch. Psychologist of Yr. 2000), Nat. Assn. Sch. Psychologists (retirement chair 2007—), Suburban Sch. Psychologist Assn. (pres. 1993—95), Wis. Sch. Psychologist Assn. (pres. 2001—03, crisis chair 2006—, Wis. Sch. Psychologist of Yr. 1999). Roman Catholic. Avocations: walking, swimming, reading, travel. Office: Oconomowoc Area Sch Dist 7077 Brown St Oconomowoc WI 53066 Home Phone: 262-547-5817.

SIEDLE, ROBERT DOUGLAS, management consultant; b. Canton, Ohio, Aug. 08; BA in Econs., Hiram Coll., 1956; profl. cert. edn., Kent State U., Western Res. U., 1963. Tchr., prin. Ohio secondary schs., 1957-65; salesman, area rep. visual products divsn. 3M Co., 1966-68; mgr. market devel. and tng. AV divsn. Bell & Howell, 1968-69; Chgo. br. mgr. info. systems divsn. Am. Std., 1969-72; mgr. edn. systems divsn. Audiotronics Corp., 1972-76; gen. mgr. Niles Entertainment/Wardway Films, 1977-80; pres. The Ultimate Image, Lakeland, Fla., 1985—. Prodr.: (films) New Dimensions in Learning II, 1969, District 65: The Exceptional Child, 1969, Career Exploration: Health, 1976, The Wide World of Work, 1976; author: Multisensory Learning: A Training Guide, 1973, Alphabet Zoo, 1973, City of Boston Young Adult Alternate Career Program, 1974, The Quick Job Hunt Guide, 1991; author, prodr., dir.: (multimedia rd. show) "Rap" With Students, 1975; prodr., editor: (film) Stampin' Ground, 1977; author poetry appearing in books and mags., 1991—; appeared on nat. radio and TV programs in U.S. and Can. Mem. task force Founder Wall Ronald Reagan Ctr., Washington, 2005—. Recipient Internat. Peace prize United Cultural Conv., 2002; named to Nat. Aviation and Space Exploration Wall of Honor Smithsonian Nat. Air and Space Mus. Dulles Ctr., 2000, Roll of Honor Eisenhower Ctr., DC, 2005, Honors Courtyard Ronald Reagan Ctr., Capitol Hill, 2005; VFW Patriot Corps award, 2004; Congl. Order of Merit award, 2005. Mem.: Smithsonian Instn., Profl. Football Rschrs. Assn., Nat. Space Soc., Aerospace Edn. Found., Smithsonian Air and Space Soc., Hat in the Ring Soc. (Bronze Membership award 2005), Am. Air Mus. (Britain) (founding mem.), Exptl. Aircraft Assn. (life), World Nations Congress (life; senator), Navy League U.S. (life), U.S. Naval Inst. (life), Fla. Air Mus. Sun 'n Fun (life), Aircraft Owners and Pilots Assn. Safety Found. (life), Air Force Assn. (life), Aircraft Owners and Pilots Assn. (life), Naval Aviation Mus. Found. (life), Am. Assn. Individual Investors, Smithsonian Inst., Internat. Honour Soc. (charter mem.), Popular Rotorcraft Assn., Inc., Helper Soc. (St. Labre Indian Sch. Edn. Assn.), Century Soc. (St. Labre Indian Sch. Edn. Assn.), Soc. Prevention Cruelty to Animals, Inc., Living Planet Soc. (world wildlife fund, Humanitarian award 2002), Defenders of Wildlife (pres.' coun.), Airship Assn. Ltd., Air Force Meml. Found. (charter sponsor), WW II Meml. Soc. (charter), Lighter-than-Air Soc. (life), Pituitary Network Assn. (life), Steamship Hist. Soc. (life), Great Lakes Hist. Soc. (life). Baptist. Office: The Ultimate Image PO Box 91388 Lakeland FL 33804-1388 E-mail: Office22@webtv.net, metalogenman@aol.com.

SIEDLECKI, NANCY THERESE, lawyer, funeral director; b. Chgo., May 30, 1954; d. LeRoy John and Dorothy Josephine (Wilczynski) Schielka; m. Jonathan Francis Siedlecki, June 18, 1977; children: Samantha Ann, Abigail Marie. Grad. funeral dir., Worsham Coll., 1974; student, Loyola U., Chgo., 1974—76, U. Ill., 1976—77; JD with honors, Chgo.-Kent Coll. Law, 1980. Bar: Ill. 1980. Paralegal in real estate Rosenberg, Savner & Unikel, Chgo., 1974—77; pvt. practice law Burr Ridge, Ill., 1980—; cons. wills, trusts, probate and small bus. corps., Chgo., 1980—. Mem.: ABA, DuPage Bar Assn., DuPage County Bar Assn., Chgo. Bar Assn., Ill. State Bar Assn., NFDA, Ill. Funeral Dirs. Assn., Union League Club of Chgo., Lyric Opera Chgo. Roman Catholic. Office: Village Law Bldg 5300 Main St Downers Grove IL 60515-4846 Office Phone: 630-969-1009. Business E-Mail: nsvillagelaw@aol.com.

SIEDLECKI, PETER ANTHONY, English language and literature educator; b. North Tonawanda, NY, May 19, 1938; s. Anthony Paul and Mary Barbara (Litwin) S.; m. Rose Mary Murphy, June 25, 1960 (div. 1978); children: Christopher, Gregory, Jeffrey, William; m. Lynnette Noreen Mende, Apr. 26, 1980; children: Peter Emmanuel Mende-Siedlecki. BA, Niagara U., 1960, MA, 1966; PhD, SUNY, Buffalo, 1982. Tchr. English Lewiston-Porter Sr. HS, Youngstown, NY, 1960—64, Grand Island Sr. HS, NY, 1964—65; prof. English Rosary Hill Coll., Amherst, NY, 1965—74, Daemen Coll., Amherst, 1974—, dean, divsn. arts and scis., 2001—07, chair divsn. humanities and social scis., 1998—2001; prof. Am. Lit. Jagiellonian U., Cracow, Poland, 1982-84, Friedrich-Schiller U., Jena, 1988-89. Commentator pub. radio, 1995—. Author (poetry) Voyeur; contbr. articles to profl. jours. Bd. dirs., baritone Freudig Singers. Fulbright Sr. lectr., Council for Internat. Exchange of Scholars, 1982-84, 88-89. Mem. MLA, Assn. Am. Colls. and Univs., Coll. English Assn., Fulbright Alumni Assn. Democrat. Avocations: woodworking, racquetball. Home: 249 Winspear Ave Buffalo NY 14215-1035 Office: Daemen College 4380 Main St Buffalo NY 14226-3592 Home Phone: 716-837-2863; Office Phone: 716-839-8304. Business E-Mail: psiedlec@daemen.edu.

SIEDLECKI, SANDRA LEE, nursing educator, researcher; d. Kenneth L. and Kathleen M. Hebebrand; m. Michael David Siedlecki; children: Tracie James, Jonathon Michael. BSN, U. Akron, Ohio, 1987, MSN, 1992; PhD, Case Western Res. U., Cleve., 2005. Faculty MetroHealth Med. Ctr. Sch. Nursing, Cleve., 1985—93, U. Akron, 1993—2005; sr. nurse rschr. Cleve. Clinic, 2005—; adj. asst. prof. nursing Case Western Res. U., Cleve., 2006—. Recipient Tchg. Excellence award, U. Akron, 1998, 1999, Lorain County Cmty. Partnership, 2002; grantee, NINR, NIH, 2000—03; Rsch. grant, Frances Payne Bolton Sch. Nursing Alumni, 2002. Mem.: Midwest Nursing Rsch. Soc., Nat. League for Nursing, Am. Pain Soc., Delta Omega (life), Sigma Theta Tau (life; treas. 2006—, Rsch. grant 2001). Achievements include research in effect of music on power, pain, depression and disability; predictors of self-rated health in patients with chronic non-malignat pain; stress response to non-weight bearing bed rest; nurse/physician relationships: perceptions and impact on the patient care environment; examination of the cummulative effect of music on pain and mood. Avocation: golf. Office: Clev Clinic 9500 Euclid Ave P32 Cleveland OH 44195 Home Phone: 330-225-0836; Office Phone: 216-444-3896. Office Fax: 216-636-0629; Home Fax: 216-636-0629. Business E-Mail: siedles@ccf.org.

SIEDZIKOWSKI, HENRY FRANCIS, lawyer; b. Chester, Pa., Dec. 27, 1953; s. Henry W. and Virginia (Szymanski) Siedzikowski. BA cum laude, Juniata Coll., 1975; JD magna cum laude, Villanova U., 1979. Bar: Pa. 1979, U.S. Dist. Ct. (ea. dist.) Pa. 1979, U.S. Ct. Appeals (3d cir.) 1979, U.S. Ct. Appeals (8th cir.) 1981, U.S. Dist. Ct. (we. dist.) Pa. 1986, U.S. Dist. Ct. (mid. dist.) Pa. 1986. Assoc. Dilworth, Paxson, Kalish & Kauffman, Phila., 1979—86; ptnr. Baskin Flaherty Elliott & Mannino P.C., Phila., 1986—90, Elliott Bray & Riley, Phila., 1990—92, Elliott, Vanaskie & Riley, Blue Bell, Pa., 1992—94, Elliott, Reihner & Siedzikowski PC, 1994—2004, Elliott, Greenleaf & Siedzikowski, P.C., 2004—. Mem. hearing com. disciplinary bd. Supreme Ct. Pa., 1985—91. Mem.: ABA (chmn. Lanham act subcom. bus. torts com. litig. sect. 1986—, rotating editor newsletter antitrust sect. franchise com.), Phila. Bar Assn. (chmn. subcom. disciplinary rules profl. responsibility com. 1984—90), Pa. Bar Assn. Democrat. Roman Catholic. Office: Elliott Greenleaf & Siedzikowski PC 925 Harvest Dr Blue Bell PA 19422-1956 E-mail: hfs@elliottgreenleaf.com.

SIEFERS, ROBERT GEORGE, banker; b. Pitts., Aug. 28, 1945; s. George Francis and Idella Alice (Eiler) S.; m. Janice Lynn Kirkpatrick, Mar. 25, 1970; children: Robert Scott, Jillian Stewart BA, Mt. Union Coll.,

1967; MBA, Kent State U., 1971; JD, Cleveland Marshall Law Sch., 1976. Security analyst Nat. City Bank, Cleve., 1971-76, v.p., investment rsch. dir., 1976-80, v.p. adminstrn. and rsch., 1980-82; sr. v.p. corp. planning Nat. City Corp., Cleve., 1982-85; sr. v.p. corp. banking Nat. City Bank, Cleve., 1985-86; pres., chief exec. officer Ohio Citizens Bank (affiliate Nat. City Corp.), Toledo, 1986-90; vice chmn., CFO Nat. City Corp., Cleve., 1997—. Bd. dirs. HCR Corp. Bd. trustees Mt. Union Coll. Republican. Presbyterian Club: Chagrin Valley Country.

SIEFERT, DAVID MICHAEL, research and development company executive; b. Dayton, Ohio, Apr. 8, 1951; s. Raymond Joseph and Laura Jayne (Blanford) S.; m. Rita Marlene Kuenle, Dec. 12, 1970; children: Christina Marie, Joel David, Jamie Michael, Matthew David, Caroline Marie. BA in Mgmt. Info. Sys., Capital U., Columbus, Ohio, 1988; MA in Bus., Antioch U., Yellow Springs, Ohio, 1994. Cert. sys. profl., quality analyst; cert. assessment profl. Mgr. computer sys. ops. Koehring Bomag, Springfield, Ohio, 1974-77; gen. mgr. bus. ops. Mead Corp., Dayton, 1977-79, mgr. internat. support, 1979-81; sr. cons. computer applied sys. engring., lifecycle methodologies, software engring., edn. systems, software reliability and quality engring. NCR Corp., Dayton, 1981-86, mgr. advanced quality sys., 1986-89, dir. advanced quality sys., 1988-89, dir. strategic processes, 1990-91, program mgr. mergers and acquisitions, 1991, dir. rsch. and tech., 1992—95, dir. R&D corp. global adv. sys., 1996, dir. global learning strategy and arch., 1999—, dir. corp. learning tech., 1996-98. Inventor Continuous Learning Sys., VISIONet Knowledge Ctr., U. Dayton Ctr. for Leaderships Exec. Devel., 1998; developer, reviewer internat. computer stds. Nat. Inst. Stds. and Tech.; founder NCR U., 1998, dir., asst. v.p. 2000—; dir. strategic programs Sinclair C.C.; program dir., prin. investigator NSF Grant; mgr. program dir. Nat. Found. IT grant; founder IT@Sinclair; mem. Nat. Blue Ribbon Panel, chmn. AIAA; mem. natural vis. com., chair Nat. Sci. Foun., Ky., Mass., Tenn., Fla. and W.Va.; cons. in field; profl. paper referee Nat. Computer Conf., 1983, 88, 89; disting. lectr. US Commerce Dept., NIST; spkr. in field. Contbr. articles to profl. jours. Vis. com. chmn. Ky. Nat. Sci. Found. Recipient invention disclosure awards AT&T, 1994, Eureka award for best patent, best patent award AT&T, NCR, 1997-99, Sinclair Visionary award, 2003. Mem. IEEE (sr., profl. paper reviewer IEEE Software Jour. 1988—, sr. mem. stds. com.), Assn. Computing Machinery, Am. Soc. Quality Control, Quality Assurance Inst., Nat. Sci. Found., Futurist Soc. Achievements include patents in field; research in process management, change management innovation, grant management, software reliability, customer satisfaction and continuous improvement of software; knowledge mgmt., decision support systems, learning systems. Personal E-mail: siefert@att.net.

SIEFERT-KAZANJIAN, DONNA, corporate librarian; b. NYC; d. Merrill Emil and Esther (Levins) Siefert; m. George John Kazanjian, June 15, 1974; 1 child, Merrill George. BA, NYU, 1969; MSLS, Columbia U., 1973; MBA, Fordham U., 1977. Asst. librarian Dun & Bradstreet, NYC, 1969-73; rsch. assoc. William E. Hill & Co., NYC, 1973—76; sr. info. analyst Info. for Bus., NYC, 1976-77; librarian Handy Assocs., NYC, 1979-90; mgr. Infoserve Fuchs Cuthrell & Co., Inc., NYC, 1991-94; info. specialist Heidrick & Struggles, Inc., NYC, 1994-2001; learning media specialist St. Mary's Elem. Sch., Manhasset, NY, 2002—03; libr. I Manhasset Pub. Libr., 2003—. Mem.: Rsch. Roundtable, Spl. Librs. Assn., Mensa, Am. Mensa Ltd. Roman Catholic.

SIEG, ALBERT LOUIS, photographic company executive; b. Chgo., Mar. 25, 1930; s. Albert Fredrick and Louise Augusta (Strege) S.; m. Irma Alice Spencer, Sept. 3, 1955; children: Karen, Diane, Susan BS in Chemistry, U. Ill., 1951; PhD in Organic Chemistry, U. Rochester, 1954; P.MD, Harvard Bus. Sch., 1971. Supr. emulsion Eastman Kodak Co., Rochester, NY, 1970-72, corp. mgr. instant, 1972-76, mgr. paper mgmt., 1976-81, v.p., dir., 1981-84; pres. Kodak Japan K.K., Tokyo, 1984-89; pres., rep. dir. Eastman Kodak Japan, Tokyo, 1989-91, also bd. dirs.; pres., rep. dir. Eastman Chems. Japan Ltd., Tokyo, 1989-91; v.p., dir. strategic resources, sec. imaging bd. Eastman Kodak Co., Rochester, 1991-92, ret., 1992; prin., cons. Albert L. Sieg Assocs., Rochester, 1992—. Bd. dirs. Kodak Japan Industries, Ltd., XM Corp.; sr. lectr. U. Rochester, 1960-69; mem. adv. bd. Worldscape, Inc., 2001-. Co-author: 8th Here's How, 1972; co-author (with S. Bennett, Oliver Wight) Tokyo Chronicles, 1994; inventor in field. Bd. dirs., St. John's Home Found., 2000—; chmn. corp. gifts Rochester Philharm. Orch., 1982-84, corp. gifts Internat. Mus. Photography at George Eastman House, 1993, 94; pres. Reformation Luth. Ch., Rochester, 1978-83; bd. dirs. St. John's Home for the Aging, 1994-99, vice chmn. bd. dirs., 1997-99; bd. dirs. St. John's Nursing Home, 1994-99, vice chmn. bd. dirs., 1997-99, chmn., 1999-2001; bd. dirs. St. John's Sr. Svcs., 1997-2001, chair elect, 1997-99, chair, 1999-01, pres., 1997-01; bd. dirs. St. John's Found., 2001—, sec., 2005-06, chmn.-elect, 2006-07. Served with Med. Svc. Corps, U.S. Army, 1955-57. Recipient George Eastman Medal Kodak Camera Clubs, 1980; Kiwanis Club Chgo. fellow, U. Ill., 1947-51; Am. Cyanamide fellow, 1953-54 Fellow Am. Inst. Chemists, Photog. Soc. Am. (v.p. 1969-84, bd. dirs. 1992—, exec. v.p. 1995-99, pres. 1999-2003, Harold Lloyd award 1978, Progress medal 1995); mem. AAAS, N.Am. Nature Photography Assn. (bd. dirs. 2005-06, pres. 2006-07, past pres. 2007—), Am. Chem. Soc., Soc. Photog. Scientists and Engrs., Rochester C. of C., Am. C. of C. in Japan (bd. govs. 1988-91, v.p. 1989-91), Internat. Stereoscopic Union (pres. 1993, 94), Am. Club Tokyo, Fgn. Corrs Club. Republican. Avocations: skiing, photography, gardening. Home and Office: 159 Hillhurst Ln Rochester NY 14617-1938 Personal E-mail: albert4182@aol.com.

SIEG, WILFRIED, philosophy educator; b. Lünen, Fed. Republic of Germany, July 1, 1945; came to U.S., 1971; s. Friedrich and Irma (Jesse) S.; m. Gail C. Francis, Aug. 11, 1979; children: Emily Payne, Clara Francis. MS, Münster U., 1971; MA, Stanford U., 1975, PhD, 1977. From asst. to assoc. prof. Columbia U., NYC, 1977-85; vis. asst. prof. Stanford (Calif.) U., 1981-82; assoc. prof. Carnegie-Mellon U., Pitts., 1985—88, prof. dept. philosophy, 1989—; vis. prof. Ludwig-Maximilians U., Munich, 1987—88. Dir. logic and computation program dept. philosophy Carnegie Mellon U., 1985—94, head dept. philosophy, 1994—2005. Co-author: Iterated Inductive Definitions, 1981; editor: Acting and Reflecting-The Interdisciplinary Turn in Philosophy, 1990, Logic and Computation, 1990, Reflections on the Foundations of Mathematics; contbr. articles to profl. jours. Rsch. grantee, Am. Coun. Learned Socs., 1985, Deutsche Forschungsgemeinschaft, Godesberg, Fed. Republic of Germany, 1987, 1990—2000, Buhl Found., Pitts., 1987—90, NSF, 1994, 1998, 2006—, NEH, 2000—02. Fellow: Am. Acad. Arts and Scis.; mem.: Assn. Symbolic Logic, Am. Math. Soc. Avocations: running, violin. Office: Carnegie Mellon U Dept Philosophy Pittsburgh PA 15213

SIEGAL, ALLAN MARSHALL, journalist, consultant; b. NYC, May 1, 1940; s. Irving and Sylvia Norma (Wrubel) S.; m. Gretchen M-P. Leefmans, May 31, 1977; children: Anna Marianita, Peter Bert Grad., NYU, 1962. With New York Times, 1960—2006, editor Pentagon Papers, 1971, asst. fgn. editor, 1971-76, asst. to exec. editor, 1976-77, news editor, 1977-87, asst. mng. editor, 1987—2006, standards editor, 2003—06, founding editor nat. edit., 1980; tchr. journalism NYU, 1966, Columbia U., 1967-69. Juror Pulitzer Prizes, 1987-89. Co-author: The New York Times Manual of Style and Usage, 1999. Recipient Ethics in Journalism award, Soc. of Profl. Journalists, 2006; Shorenstein fellow in press, politics, and public policy, John F. Kennedy Sch. Govt., Harvard U., 2006. Mem. Century Assn., Am. Soc. Newspaper Editors.

SIEGAL, BURTON LEE, product designer, consultant, inventor; b. Chgo., Sept. 27, 1931; s. Norman A. and Sylvia (Vitz) S.; m. Rita Goran, Apr. 11, 1954; children: Norman, Laurence Scott BS in Mech. Engring., U. Ill., 1953. Torpedo designer U.S. Naval Ordnance, Forest Park, Ill., 1953-54; chief engr. Gen. Aluminum Corp., Chgo., 1954-55; product designer Chgo. Aerial Industries, Melrose Park, Ill., 1955-58; chief designer Emil J. Paidar Co., Chgo., 1958-59; founder, pres. Budd Engring. Corp., Skokie, 1959—. Dir. Dur-A-Case Corp., Chgo.; design cons. to numerous corps. Holder more than 127 patents in more than 40 fields including multimemory for power seats and electrified office panel sys., Piezo ink jet valves; contbr. articles to tech. publs. Mem. math., sci. and English adv. bds. Niles Twp. High Schs., Skokie, Ill., 1975-79; electronic cons. Chgo. Police Dept., 1964. Nominee Presdl. medal Tech., Sen. Paul Simon and Rep. Dan Rostenkowski, 1986; named Winner, Internat. Extrusion Design Competition, 1975, Inventor of Yr., Patent Law Assn. Chgo., 1986, Disting. Alumni, Coll. Engring., U. Ill., 2005. Mem. ASME, Soc. Plastics Engrs., Soc. Mfg. Engrs., Inventors Coun., Soc. Automotive Engrs., Pres.'s Assn. Ill. Office: Skokie IL 60076 *A true professional can perform any time, any place, independent of his mood.*

SIEGAL, JACOB J., management and financial consultant; b. Phila., Apr. 4, 1929; s. Louis and Henrietta (Greenberg) S.; m. Dolores Berg, June 8, 1952; children: Marla, Karen, Leslie. BS, Temple U., 1951, LLB, 1954; postgrad., U. Chgo., 1973. Bar: Pa. 1955, Ill. 1973. With City of Phila., 1954-61, chief counselor, 1959-61, dep. city solicitor, 1958-61; pvt. practice law, partner firm Meltzer & Schiffrin, Phila., 1961-72; v.p., gen. counsel, dir. Bluebird Inc., Phila., 1972-74, exec. v.p., 1974-78, pres., 1978-79, chmn., chief exec. officer, 1979. Chmn. bd. Armen Cadillac-Osmobile, Inc. Mem. Am. Meat Inst. (dir., conv. speaker 1978) Home: 101 Cheswold Ln Haverford PA 19041-1865 Office: PO Box 193 Plymouth Meeting PA 19462-0193

SIEGAL, JOEL DAVIS, lawyer; b. Plainfield, NJ, Feb. 9, 1937; s. Samuel and Florence (Ravitz) Siegal; 2 children. BA in Polit. Sci., U. Pa., 1958; JD, Yale U., 1961; MA in Internat. Rels., U. Stockholm, 1963. Bar: NJ 1962, US Dist. Ct. NJ 1962, US Ct. Appeals (3d cir.) 1963, NY 1965, US Supreme Ct. 1969, US Dist. Ct. (so. and ea. dists.) NY 1975. Law clk. to Hon. Arthur S. Lane US Dist. Ct., Newark, 1961—62; law clk. to Hon. Phillip Forman US Ct. Appeals (3d cir.), 1963-64; assoc. Hellring Lindeman Goldstein & Siegal, Newark, 1967-70, ptnr., 1970—. Commr. Nat. Conf. Commrs. Uniform Laws, 1991—98; mem. US Dist. Ct. Adv. Bd., Newark, 1991—92. Contbr. articles to profl. jours. Fellow: Am. Bar Found.; mem.: ABA, Assn. Fed. Bar NJ (nat. del. NJ 1974, pres. 1990—92, adv. bd. 1993—), Bergen Bar Assn., Essex County Bar Assn., NJ Bar Assn., Harmonie Club NYC. Office: Hellring Lindeman Goldstein Siegal 1 Gateway Ctr Fl 8 Newark NJ 07102-5386 also: 32-40 N Dean St Englewood NJ 07631 Business E-Mail: jdsiegal@hlgslaw.com.

SIEGAL, RITA GORAN, engineering company executive; b. Chgo., July 16, 1934; d. Leonard and Anabelle (Soloway) Goran; m. Burton L. Siegal, Apr. 11, 1954; children: Norman, Laurence Scott. Student, U. Ill., 1951-53; BA, DePaul U., 1956. Cert. elem. tchr. Ill. Tchr. Chgo. Public Schs., 1956-58; founder, chief exec. officer Budd Engring. Corp., Skokie, Ill., 1959—; founder, pres. Easy Living Products Co., Skokie, 1960—; pvt. practice in interior design, Chgo., 1968-73; dist. sales mgr. Super Girls, Skokie, 1976. Guest spkr. nat. radio and TV, 1979—; lectr. Northwestern U., 1983. Contbr. articles to profl. jours. Mem. adv. bd. Skokie HS, 1975—79; advisor Cub Scouts Skokie coun. Boy Scouts Am., 1975; leader Great Books Found., 1972; founder Profit Plus Investment, 1970; bus. mgr. Nutrition Optimal Health Assn., Winnetka, Ill., 1980—82, pres., 1982—84, v.p. med./profl., 1985—93; bd. dirs. Noha, Internat. Named Prominent Alumni, Sullivan HS, 2001; recipient Cub Scout awards, Boy Scouts Am., 1971—72, Nat. Charlotte Danstrom award, Nat. Women of Achievement, 1988, Corp. Achievement award, 1988, Frannie Award, U. Ill., 1998. Mem.: Inventors Coun., Pres. Assn. Ill. (bd. dirs. 1990—94, membership chair 1991—93), North Shore Women Mgmt. (pres. 1987—88), Oriental Art Soc. Chgo. (publicity chair). *Believe in yourself, if others can do it so can you. Prioritize so you are not overwhelmed by your responsibilities.*

SIEGEL, ABRAHAM J., economics professor, academic administrator; b. NYC, Nov. 6, 1922; s. Samuel J. and Dora (Drach) S.; m. Lillian Wakshull, Dec. 22, 1946; children: Emily Jean Siegel Stangle, Paul Howard, Barbara Ann Pugliese. BA summa cum laude, CCNY, 1943; MA, Columbia U., 1949; PhD, U. Calif., Berkeley, 1961. Instr. dept. econs. CCNY, 1947-49; research economist Inst. Indsl. Relations, U. Calif., Berkeley, 1952-54; instr. dept. econs. M.I.T., Cambridge, 1954-56, asst. prof., 1956-59, assoc. prof., 1959-64, prof. dept. econs. Sloan Sch. Mgmt., 1964-93, assoc. dean Sloan Sch. Mgmt., 1967-80, dean, 1980-87, prof. emeritus, sr. lectr., 1993—. Spl. lectr. Trade Union Program, Harvard U., 1961-64; vis. prof. Brandeis U., 1956-60; vis. prin. mem. div. Internat. Inst. Labour Studies, Internat. Labour Office, Geneva, 1964-65; asso. staff dir. Com. Econ. Devel., Study Group on Nat. Labor Policy, 1960-61; trustee, chmn. adminstrv. com. M.I.T. Retirement Plan for Staff Mems., 1970-91. Co-author: Industrial Relations in the Pacific Coast Longshore Industry, 1956, The Public Interest in National Labor Policy, 1961, The Impact of Computers on Collective Bargaining, 1969, Unfinished Business: An Agenda for Labor, Management and the Public, 1978. Bd. dirs. Whitehead Inst. Biomed. Rsch., Analysis Group, Inc., Internat. Data Group; mem. Framingham Sch. Com., South Middlesex Regional Dist. Vocat. Sch. Com., 1968-71. With USAF, 1943-46. Mem. Am. Econ. Assn., Indsl. Relations Research Assn., Nat. Acad. Arbitrators, Am. Arbitration Assn. (mem. various panels), Inst. Mgmt. Scis. Bus. Roundtable (exec. com.), Phi Beta Kappa. Office: MIT Sloan Sch Mgmt 50 Memorial Dr Cambridge MA 02142-1347 Home: 217 Del Pond Dr Canton MA 02021-2754

SIEGEL, ARTHUR HERBERT, finance company executive; b. NYC, Jan. 5, 1938; s. Joseph Kenneth and Gertrude Sylvia (Hecker) Siegel; m. Eleanor Novick, June 5, 1960; children: Joan Aileen, Linda Beth, Mark Eric. AB, Columbia U., 1958, MBA, 1960. With Price Waterhouse, NYC, 1960-97, mgr. LI, 1961-72, ptnr. Boston, 1972-83, nat. dir. acctg. svcs. NYC, 1984-88, vice chmn. bus. adv. and auditing svcs., 1988-95; mem. Fin. Acctg. Stds. Bd. Emerging Issues Task Force, 1985-88, Fin. Acctg. Stds. Adv. Coun., 1985-90; mem. adv. coun. Sch. Acctg., U. So. Calif., 1987-89. Exec. dir. Independence Stds. Bd., 1997—2001; bd. dirs., chmn. audit com. Rotech Healthcare, Inc., 2002—; bd. dirs. Solomon Schechtar Sch., North Jersey, NJ. Bd. dirs. Nat. Multiple Sclerosis Soc., treas., exec. com., chmn. fin. com., 1990—98. Mem.: AICPA (chmn. task force risks and uncertainties 1985—87, chmn. SEC practice exec. com. 1994—97), Mass. Soc. CPAs (pres.-elect 1983), N.Y. Soc. CPAs (Silver Medal award), World Union Progressive Judaism, Assn. Reform Zionists Am. (bd. dirs. 2004—), Beta Gamma Sigma. Home and Office: Apt 3A 179 E 70th St New York NY 10021-5109 Office Phone: 212-327-0794. Personal E-mail: ASiegs@ix.netcom.com.

SIEGEL, BARRY, journalist, writer, literature educator; b. St. Louis, Sept. 7, 1949; m. Marti Devore; 1 child, Alexandra Nicole. BA magna cum laude, Pomona Coll., 1971; MS in Journalism, Columbia U., 1972. Stringer LA bur. Newsweek, 1973; news editor West Coast Women's Wear Daily, 1973—76; writer View sect. LA Times, 1976—78, writer spl. assignment, 1979, corr. Nat., 1980—83, corr./sr. writer, 1983—2003, spl. corr., 2003—; prof. English & comparative lit., dir. Literary Journalism Prog. U. Calif., Irvine, 2003—. Vis. lectr. U. So. Calif., 1988. Author: A Death in White Bear Lake, 1990, Shades of Gray, 1992, The Perfect Witness, 1998, Actual Innocence, 1999, Lines of Defense, 2002; contbr. articles to profl. jours. Recipient USA West Journalism award, PEN Ctr., 1987, USA West Lit. award in Journalism, 2000, Golden Medallion Media award, State Bar Calif., 1984, Silver Gavel award, ABA, 1985, Paul Tobenkin Meml. award, 1997, Pulitzer Prize for Feature Writing, 2002. Office: U Calif Mail Code: 2650 408 Humanities Instructional Bldg Irvine CA 92697 Office Phone: 949-824-3023. Office Fax: 949-824-2916. E-mail: bsiegel@uci.edu, barry@barry-siegel.com.

SIEGEL, BARRY ALAN, radiologist; b. Nashville, Dec. 30, 1944; s. Walter G. Siegel and Lillian B. Ivener; m. Pamela M. Mandel, Aug. 18, 1968 (div. Mar. 1981); children: Peter A., William A.; m. Marilyn J. Siegel, Jan. 29, 1983. AB, Washington U., St. Louis, 1966, MD, 1969. Diplomate Am. Bd. Nuc. Medicine, Am. Bd. Radiology. Intern Barnes Hosp., St. Louis, 1969-70; from resident in radiology to prof. Mallinckrodt Inst. Radiology Washington U., 1970—79, prof. radiology Mallinckrodt Inst. Radiology, 1979—, dir. divsn. nuc. medicine Mallinckrodt Inst. Radiology, 1973—, mem. Siteman Cancer Ctr., 1996—. Dir. Am. Bd. Nuc. Medicine, LA, 1985—90, sec., 1990; chmn. adv. com. on med. uses of isotopes NRC, Washington, 1990—96; chmn. radiopharm. drugs adv. com. FDA, Rockville, Md., 1982—85, radiol. devices panel, 1992—95; mem. U.S. Pharmacopeia Adv. Panel on Radiopharms., 1975—2000, Armed Forces Radiobiol. Rsch. Inst., Bethesda; coun. experts, chair radiopharm. expert com. U.S. Pharmacopoeial Conv., 2000—05; co-chair working group Nat. Oncologic PET Registry, 2005—; cons. in field. Author, editor 33 books; contbr. articles to profl. jours., chpts. in books. Maj. USAF, 1974—76. Recipient Commr.'s Spl. citation U.S. FDA, 1988, Honor citation U.S. Pharmacopeial Conv., 1995, 2000. Fellow: ACP, Am. Coll. Nuc. Physicians, Am. Coll. Radiology (vice chmn. commn. nuc. medicine 1981—93, editor-in-chief profl. self evaluation program 1988—2002, chmn. nuc. medicine com. imaging network 1998—2006, med. dir. PET core lab. imaging network 2006—); mem.: ACS (chmn. diagnostic imaging com. oncology group 1998—, mem. exec. com. 2000—), AMA, Acad. Molecular Imaging (chair inst. Clin. PET coun. 2001—02, bd. dirs. 2004—), Soc. Nuc. Medicine (trustee 1981—85, 1987—91, Georg Charles de Hevesy Nuclear Pioneer award 2003), Radiol. Soc. N.Am., Assn. Univ. Radiologists, Am. Roentgen Ray Soc. Office: Washington U Mallinckrodt Inst Radiology 510 S Kingshighway Blvd Saint Louis MO 63110-1016 Home Phone: 314-367-3650; Office Phone: 314-362-2809. Business E-Mail: siegelb@mir.wustl.edu.

SIEGEL, BERNARD L., lawyer; b. Pitts., Sept. 15, 1938; s. Ralph Robert and Frieda Sara (Stein) S.; m. Marcia Margolis, Sept. 3, 1961 (div. Aug. 1983); children: Jonathan, Sharon; m. Susan Erickson, Aug. 31, 1997 (div. June 2001). BA, Brandeis U., 1960; JD, Harvard U., 1963. Bar: Pa. 1964, US Dist. Ct. (we. dist.) Pa. 1964, US Dist. Ct. (ea. dist.) Pa. 1985, US Ct. Appeals (3d cir.) 1985, US Supreme Ct. 1985. Assoc. Silin, Eckert & Burke, Erie, Pa., 1963-66; ptnr. Silin, Eckert, Burke & Siegel, Erie, 1966-73; 1st asst. dist. atty. Erie County, 1972-76; dep. atty. gen. Pa. Dept. Justice, Phila., 1976-78; dep. dist. atty. Dist. Atty. of Phila., 1978-86; pvt. practice Phila., 1986—. Adj. prof. La Salle U., Phila., 1986—95, 2006; lectr. Fed. Law Enforcement Tng. Ctr., Glynco, Ga., 1986—97, Mercyhurst Coll., Erie, 1974—76, Nat. Coll. Dist. Attys., Houston, 1978—85; adj. prof. Temple U. Law Sch., 1996—, 2006; mem. criminal rules com. Pa. Supreme Ct., Phila., 1976—85; commr. Pa. Crime Commn., Harrisburg, 1976—79. Author: (with others) Pennsylvania Grand Jury Practice, 1983, By No Extraordinary Means, 1986. Mem.: ABA, Phila. Bar Assn. (chmn. criminal justice sect. 1990—91, Justice Thurgood Marshall award 2004), Pa. Bar Assn. (chmn. criminal law sect. 1988—91), Pa. Assn. Criminal Def. Lawyers (bd. dirs. 1988—, treas. 2002—04, v.p. 2004—07, pres. 2007—, Josel Advocacy award 2005), Nat. Assn. Criminal Def. Lawyers. Democrat. Jewish. Avocations: bicycling, reading, hiking. Office: 1515 Market St Ste 1915 Philadelphia PA 19102-1920 Home Phone: 215-632-2515; Office Phone: 215-751-9830. E-mail: bernardlsiegel@comcast.net.

SIEGEL, BETTY LENTZ, university president; b. Cumberland, Ky., Jan. 24, 1931; d. Carl N. and Vera (Hogg) Lentz; m. Joel H. Siegel, June 6; children: David Jonathan, Michael Jeremy. BA, Wake Forest U., 1952; M in Edn., U. NC, 1953; PhD, Fla. State U., 1961; postgrad., Ind. U., 1964-66; doctorate (hon.), Miami U., 1985, Cumberland Coll., 1985, Ea. Ky. U., 1992, Morehead State U., 2002; degree (hon.), Lynchburg Coll., So. Conn. State U. asst. prof. Lenoir Rhyne Coll., Hickory, N.C., 1956-59; assoc. prof., 1961-64; asst. prof. U. Fla., Gainesville, 1967-70, assoc. prof., 1970-72, prof., 1973-76, dean acad. affairs for continuing edn., 1972-76; dean Sch. Edn. and Psychology Western Carolina U., Cullowhee, N.C., 1976-81; pres. Kennesaw State U., Marietta, Ga., 1981—. Bd. dirs. Nat. Services Industries; cons. numerous sch. systems. Author: Problem Situations in Teaching, 1971, Becoming An Invitational Leader, 2002; contbr. articles to profl. jours. Bd. dirs. United Way Atlanta, Ga. Partnership for Excellence in Edn., Ga. Coun. Econ. Edn., Northside Hosp. Found., Atlanta Ballet; Ga. rep. so. growth policy bd. Commn. on Future of South, 1998. Recipient Disting. Tchr. of Yr. award U. Fla., 1969; Mortar Bd. Woman of Yr. award U. Fla., 1973, Mortar Bd. Educator of Yr., Ga. State U., 1983, CASE award, 1986, Alumna of Yr. award Wake Forest U., 1987, "Grad Made Good" award Fla. State U. Alumni Assn, Omicron Delta Kappa, 1991, Spirit of Life award City of Hope, 1992, Woman of Achievement award Cobb Chamber YWCA, 1992, First Lifetime Achievement award YWCA, N.W. Ga., Oak award outstanding Alumni Ky., 1998, Adminstrv. Leadership award Assn. Gerontology in Higher Edn., 2001, Women in Bus. Lifetime Achievement award, 2001, Peabody award UNC-Chapel Hill Sch. Edn., 2003, Justice Robert Benham award outstanding leadership, svc. and commitment equality of all citizens Black's United for Youth of Cobb County, 2004, Howard Washington Thurman Ecumenical award Morehouse Coll.'s Martin Luther King, Jr. Internat. Chapel, 2005, Leita Thompson Lifetime Achievement award; named 50 Most Influential Women in Ga., One of 100 Most Influential People in State of Ga., Ga. Trend Mag., Outstanding Alumni, Fla. State U. Coll. Edn. Alumni Assn., 1992, Cobb Citizen of Yr., 1996, Ga. Woman of Yr. Ga. Commn. Women, 1997, Divas for Life Bus. to Bus. Mag., 2001, 100 Most Disting. Alumni Cumberland Coll.; named to Jr. Achievement Hall of Fame, 1999, 20 Women Making a Mark on Atlanta Atlanta mag., 20 Yrs., 20 Leaders Ga. Trend mag. Mem. Am. Psychol. Assn., Am. Assn. State Colls. and Univs. (bd. dirs., chmn. 1990), Am. Coun. Edn. (bd. dirs., bd. advisors), Am. Inst. Mng. Diversity (bd. dis.), Soc. Internat. Bus. Fellows, Commn. on Women in Higher Edn., Internat. Alliance Invitational Edn. (co-founder, co-dir.), Nat. Ctr. Study of Freshman Yr. Experience, So. Inst. Bus. and Profl. Ethics (mem. gov. bd.), Am. Cancer Soc. (Cobb chpt.), Cobb Exec. Women (founder), Ga. Exec. Women's Network, Internat. Bus. Forum, State Bar Ga., Found. Freedom, Bus./Higher Edn. Forum, mem. exec. com.), Cobb C. of C. (chair 1996), Kiwanis (Atlanta chpt.), Am. Humaries, Inc., Phi Alpha Theta, Pi Kappa Delta, Alpha Psi Omega, Kappa Delta Pi, Pi Lambda Theta, Phi Delta Kappa, Delta Kappa Gamma. Office: Kennesaw State Univ Office of the President 1000 Chastain Rd NW Kennesaw GA 30144-5591

SIEGEL, DAVID B., lawyer; b. 1953; BA summa cum laude, U. Pa., MA, 1975; JD, U. Penn., 1979. Bar: DC 1979. Law clk. to Judge Claerence C. Newcomer U.S. Dist. Ct. Pa. (ea. dist.), 1979—81; with Crowell & Moring LLP, Washington, 1981—, ptnr., mng. ptnr., chmn., 2006—. Contbr. articles to profl. jours. Office: Crowell & Moring LLP 1001 Pennsylvania Ave NW Ste 1100 Washington DC 20004-2595 Office Phone: 202-624-2662. Office Fax: 202-658-5116. E-mail: dsiegel@crowell.com.

SIEGEL, DAVID BURTON, lawyer; b. NYC, Mar. 22, 1949; s. Henry and Ruth (Rosenzweig) S.; m. Barbara Joan Brown, Aug. 6, 1972; children: Jeffrey Spencer, Carolyn Rose, Laura Ellen. AB, Columbia Coll., 1971; JD, NYU, 1974. Assoc. atty. Kelley Drye & Warren, NYC, 1974-77; corp. counsel W.R. Grace & Co., NYC, 1977-87, asst. gen. counsel, 1987-91, assoc. gen. counsel Boca Raton, Fla., 1991-93, v.p., dep. gen. counsel, 1993-98, sr. v.p., gen. counsel and sec., 1998-2001, sr. v.p., gen. counsel, chief restructuring officer, 2001—05. Mem. Econ. Coun. Palm Beach County, Fla., 1993-99; mem. bd. dirs. Edn. Partnership of Palm Beach County, 1994-96, treas., 1995-96. Home and Office: 446 Putnam Forest Rd Stowe VT 05672 Home Phone: 802-253-9264; Office Phone: 802-253-9264. Business E-Mail: david.siegel@grace.com. *

SIEGEL, EDWARD, lawyer; b. Asbury Park, NJ, Jan. 15, 1931; s. Nathan Albert and Fannie Siegel; m. Helen Dorothy Haber, Aug. 29, 1954; children: Sharon, Frances. BA, U. Fla., 1952, JD, 1955. Bar: Fla. 1955. Spl. asst. atty. gen. Office Atty. Gen. Fla., Tallahassee, 1955; ptnr. Adams, Rothstein & Siegel, Jacksonville, Fla., 1957-90. Author: How to Avoid Lawyers, 1969, Defend Yourself! The Moneysworth Legal Advisor, 1972, Just Like a Lawyer, 1993; mem. editorial bd. Fla. Bar Jour., 1979-86. Bd. dirs. Jacksonville Jewish Ctr., 1968-70; bd. dirs., v.p. Jewish Family and Children's Svcs., 1970-75; trustee Jacksonville Libr. Bd., 1978-82. Served as 1st lt. USAF, 1955-57. Mem. ABA, Fla. Bar Assn., Jacksonville Bar Assn. (chmn. fee arbitration com. 1976-77), Blue Key, Order of Coif, Phi Beta Kappa. Democrat. Home: 6855 San Sabastian Ave Jacksonville FL 32217-2731

SIEGEL, EDWARD M., lawyer; b. NYC, Apr. 14, 1934; s. Charles and Rose (Fritzhand) S.; m. Elyse R. Roth, Mar. 9, 1969; children: Eric, Eve-Lynn. BA, Columbia Coll., 1955; MA, Columbia U., 1957, JD, 1960. Bar: NY 1961. Legal asst. to dean Columbia U. Law Sch., NYC, 1960-65; gen. counsel Transp. Displays, Inc., NYC, 1965-75, corp. sec., 1968-75, v.p., 1972-73, sr. v.p., 1973-75; pub. affairs mgr. J.C. Penney Co., NYC, 1975-77; gen. counsel, corp. sec. Electro Audio Dynamics, Inc., Great Neck, N.Y., 1977-85, v.p., 1981-85; v.p. legal affairs East View Co., NYC, 1985-87; ptnr. Bangser Klein Rocca & Blum (formerly Bangser & Weiss), NYC, 1988-92; sr. v.p., gen. coun., corp. sec. Nat. Med. Funding Corp., NYC, 1992-94; atty pvt. practice NYC, 1994—. Mem. N.Y. State Bar Assn., Columbia Law Sch. Alumni Assn. (dir. 1966-70). Home: 1036 Park Ave Apt 6D New York NY 10028-0971

SIEGEL, FREDERIC RICHARD, geology educator; b. Chelsea, Mass., Feb. 8, 1932; s. Louis and Eva (Minsky) S.; m. Felisa Matilde Puszkin, Mar. 3, 1962; children: Gabriela Davina, Galia Dinah. BA, Harvard U., 1954; MS, U. Kans., 1958, PhD, 1961. Prof. titular Universidad Nacional de Tucuman, Argentina, 1961-63; head geochemistry divsn. Kans. Geol. Survey, Lawrence, 1963-65; assoc. prof. geochemistry George Washington U., Washington, 1965-69, prof., 1969-99, prof. emeritus geochemistry, 1999—, dir. geochemistry program, 1965-99, chmn. dept. geology, 1976-86. Tech. cons. UN Devel. program, Havana, Cuba, 1980. Author: Applied Geochemistry, 1974, Geoquimica Aplicada, 1992, Natural and Anthropogenic Hazards in Development Planning, 1996, Environmental Geochemistry of Potentially Toxic Metals, 2001; co-author: Geochimica Ambientale, 2004; editor: Review of Research on Modern Problems in Geochemistry, 1979. With U.S. Army, 1954-56; ETO. Recipient Erasmus Haworth award Dept. Geology, U. Kans., 1958; Fulbright prof., 1970, Best Paper award Energy Minerals divsn. Am. Assn. Petroleum Geologists, 1989. Mem. Assn. Exploration Geochemists (councillor 1988-95), Geochem. Soc., Internat. Assn. Geochemists and Cosmochemists, Soc. Environ. Geochemistry and Health. Jewish. Home and Office: 4353 Yuma St NW Washington DC 20016-2027 Home Phone: 202-362-2545. Business E-Mail: nzkara@gwu.edu.

SIEGEL, GEORGE HENRY, management consultant; b. Bklyn., Oct. 8, 1926; s. Samuel S. and Sara Siegel; m. Lenore D. Greenberg, Oct. 28, 1951; children: Arthur B., Ellen S. BEE, CCNY, 1948; MS Indsl. Engring, NYU, 1951. Registered profl. engr., N.Y. From engr. to gen. mgr. Gen. Electric Corp., Syracuse, Utica and Binghamton, NY, 1951-74; v.p., gen. mgr. flight systems div. Bendix Corp., 1974-77, chief tech. officer, 1977-79, v.p., gen. mgr. diesel engine controls, 1979-82; v.p., group exec. Bendix Automation Co., Cleve., 1983-84; v.p. tech. Allied-Signal Internat., Morristown, NJ, 1984-90; v.p. Volt Tech. Svcs. Co., NYC, 1991-93; pres. Point North Assocs., Inc., Madison, NJ, 1990—. Invited guest lectr. UCLA, 1960-63. Bd. visitors Oakland U., Rochester, Mich., 1977-83. Served with AUS, 1944-46. Mem. IEEE (sr., life, sect. chmn. 1965), Soc. Automotive Engrs. Personal E-mail: siegelgh@att.net.

SIEGEL, HERBERT JAY, communications executive, director; b. Phila., May 7, 1928; s. Jacob and Fritzi (Stern) S.; m. Ann F. Levy, June 29, 1950; children: John C., William D. BA in Journalism, Lehigh U., 1950. Sec., dir. Official Films, Inc., NYC, 1951-54; v.p., dir. Bev-Rich Products, Inc., Phila., 1955-56; chmn. bd. Westley Industries, Inc., Cleve., 1955-58; v.p. Phila. Ice Hockey Club, Inc., 1955-60; chmn. bd. Fort Pitt Industries, Inc., Pitts., 1956-58, Seeburg Corp., 1958-60, Centlivre Brewing Corp., Ft. Wayne, Ind., 1959-61; dir. Baldwin Rubber Co., Pontiac, Mich., Mono-Sol Corp., Gary, Inc., 1959-62; chmn. bd. Baldwin-Montrose Chem. Co., 1960-67; pres., chmn. bd. Gen. Artists Corp., 1960-64, chmn., 1960-62; chmn. bd., pres. Chris-Craft Industries, Inc., 1968—2001; chmn. bd. BHC Comm. Inc., 1977—2001, pres., 1977-96; chmn. bd. dirs. United TV, Inc., 1982—2001, chmn. bd., 1982-96, CEO, 1983-90; bd. dirs. Warner Communications, Inc., 1984-89. Bd. dirs. Piper Aircraft Corp., 1971-77, Paramount Pictures, 1963-64, Harvard-Mahoney Neurosci. Inst., 2000. Bd. dirs. Friends of Israel Defense Forces, 1996—, Research to Prevent Blindness, 2000—, Phoenix House, 1978-81; bd. advisors Vets. Bedside Network, 1980-90; v.p. Friars Nat. Assn. Found., 1980—, Chas. A. Dana Found., Inc., 1996—; trustee Lehigh U., 1989-92, Blair Acad., 1985-92. Named one of Forbes Richest Americans, 2006. Office: News America Inc 767 5th Ave 46th Flr New York NY 10153-0023

SIEGEL, HERRICK JOVE, orthopedic surgeon; s. Michael Elliot and Marsha Rose Siegel; m. Joanna Leigh Fein, Jan. 9, 1999; children: Nicholas Ryan, Dylan Andrew. MD, NY U., 1995. Orthopaedic Surgeon Am. Bd. of Orthopedic Surgery, 2005. Asst. prof. surgery U. of Ala., Ala., 2002—, chief, orthopedic oncology, 2002—06. Orthopaedic Oncology fellow, Mayo Clinic, 2000—02. Mem.: Mid-Am. Orthopedic Soc., Musculoskeletal Tumor Soc., Am. Acad. of Orthopedic Surgeons, Am. Acad. of Orthopedic Surgeons (assoc.). Office: Univ of Ala at Birmingham 1530 3rd Ave South Birmingham AL 35294 Home Phone: 205-967-0607; Office Phone: 205-934-4667. Home Fax: 205-975-5953. Business E-Mail: herrick.siegel@ortho.uab.edu.

SIEGEL, HOWARD JEROME, lawyer; b. Chgo., July 29, 1942; s. Leonard and Idele (Lehrner) S.; m. Diane L. Gerber; children: Sari D., Allison J., James G. BS, U. Ill., 1963; JD, Northwestern U., 1966. Bar: Ill. 1966, U.S. Dist. Ct. (no. dist.) Ill. 1967. Assoc. Ancel, Stonesifer & Glink, Chgo., 1966-70; ptnr. Goldstine & Siegel, Summit, Ill., 1970-75; sole practice Chgo., 1975-77; pres. Wexler, Siegel & Shaw, Ltd., Chgo., 1978-82; ptnr. Keck, Mahin & Cate, Chgo., 1982-95, Neal Gerber & Eisenberg, Chgo., 1995-99; counsel Fagel & Haber, Chgo., 1999—. Bd. dirs. various corps. Mem.: ABA, Chgo. Bar Assn., Ill. Bar Assn., Twin Orchard Country Club (Long Grove, Ill.). Office: FabelHaberLLC 55 E Monroe 40th Fl Chicago IL 60603 Office Phone: 312-580-2248. Business E-Mail: hsiegel@fagelhaber.com.

SIEGEL, JACK MORTON, retired pharmaceutical executive; b. Sioux City, Iowa, June 11, 1922; s. Harry and Rose (Perlman) S.; m. Betty Virginia Collins, Feb. 22, 1946 (dec. Feb. 1986); children: Jennifer L. Mastricola, Marjorie G., Thomas A.; m. Dolores E. Williams Kinert, Dec. 20, 1991. BS in Chemistry, UCLA, 1944; PhD in Chemistry, Washington U., St. Louis, 1950. Chemist The Clinton Labs., Oak Ridge, Tenn., 1944-46; asst. prof. chemistry U. Ark. Sch. Medicine, Little Rock, 1950-55; chemist, v.p. P-L Biochems. Inc., Milw., 1955-82; v.p., gen. mgr. Pharmacia P-L Biochems. Inc., Milw., 1982-87, pres., 1987-89. Contbr. articles to profl. jours. Mem. AAAS, Am. Chem. Soc. Democrat. Jewish.

SIEGEL, JAY STEVEN, chemistry educator; b. Inglewood, Calif., Aug. 16, 1959; s. Erwin and Jeanne (Strzesak) S. BS, Calif. State U., Northridge, 1980; MA, Princeton U., 1982, PhD, 1985. Researcher Princeton (N.J.) U., 1981-83, 84-85, Eidgenossische Technishche Hochschule, Zürich, Switzerland, 1983-84, U. Louis Pasteur, Strasbourg, France, 1985-86; asst. prof. U. Calif., San Diego, 1986—. Observer, mem. com. on stereochemistry Internat. Union of Pure and Applied Chemists, 1985—. Contbr. articles to sci. jours. Calif. State scholar, 1977-70; Swiss U. grantee, 1983-84, NSF-CNRS Sci. Exchange grantee, 1985-86; named Presdl. Young Investigator NSF, 1988—. Mem. Am. Chem. Soc., N.Y. Acad. Scis., Sigma Xi. Office: U Calif San Diego Dept Chemistry B-014 La Jolla CA 92093

SIEGEL, JEFFREY NORTON, lawyer; b. NYC, Nov. 27, 1942; s. George Siegel and Rose (Friedman) Gerber; m. Judith Sharon Chused, June 11, 1966; children: Daniel, Linda. AB, Brown U., 1964; LLB, Harvard U., 1967. Bar: N.Y. 1968. Assoc., ptnr. Golenbock & Barell, NYC, 1967—89; ptnr. Whitman & Ransom, NYC, 1990—93, Shack Siegel Katz & Flaherty, P.C., NYC, 1993—2005, Blank Rome LLP, NYC, 2005—. Mem. bus. com. The Jewish Mus. Mem. ABA, Assn. Bar City N.Y. (com. securities regulation 1987-90, com. profl. responsibility 1979-84), Phi Beta Kappa. Home: 975 Park Ave New York NY 10028-0323 Office: Blank Rome LLP 405 Lexington Ave New York NY 10174-0002 Business E-Mail: jsiegel@blankrome.com.

SIEGEL, JEREMY JAMES, financial analyst, educator; b. Chgo., Nov. 14, 1945; s. Bernard G. and Gertrude (Levite) S.; m. Ellen Ruth Schwartz, Jan. 14, 1980; children: Andrew M., Jeffrey Eric. BA, Columbia U., 1967; PhD, MIT, 1971. Asst. prof. bus. econs. Grad. Sch. Bus. U. Chgo., 1972-76; assoc. prof. fin. Wharton Sch. Bus. U. Pa., Phila., 1976—86, prof. fin. Wharton Sch. Bus., 1986—98, Russell E. Palmer Prof. Fin. Wharton Sch. Bus., 1998—. Macroecons. coord. The Morgan Bank, (Now J.P. Morgan) N.Y.C., 1984-99; acad. dir. Securities Industry Inst., 1987-. Author: Revolution on Wall Street, 1993, Stocks for the Long Run, 1994, 98, 02, Future for Investors, 2005; contbr. numerous articles to profl. jours NSF fellow, 1971-72; recipient Graham and Dodd award Assn. Investment Mgmt., 1992, Nicolas Molodovsky award CFI Inst., 2005; voted best bus. sch. prof. Bus. Week mag., 1994. Office: U Pa Wharton Sch Dept Fin Philadelphia PA 19104

SIEGEL, KENNETH S., lawyer; BA, Cornell U., 1977; JD, NYU, 1980. Assoc. Cravath, Swaine & Moore, NYC, 1980—85, O'Sullivan, Graev & Karabell, LLP, NYC, 1985—87, ptnr., 1987—94, Baker & Botts, LLP, NYC, 1994—97; sr. v.p., gen. counsel Cognizant Corp., Westport, Conn., 1997—98, IMS Health, Westport, Conn., 1998—2000, Gartner Grp., Stamford, Conn., 2000; exec. v.p., gen. counsel Starwood Hotels and Resorts Worldwide Inc., White Plains, NY, 2000—, sec., 2001—, chief adminstrv. officer, gen. counsel, 2006—. Office: Starwood Hotels & Resorts Worldwide Inc 1111 Westchester Ave White Plains NY 10604

SIEGEL, KRISTI ELLEN, language educator; b. Breckenridge, Minn., Jan. 2, 1951; d. Dennis Elton and Cleo Ardell Hjalmer; m. Ronald Siegel, Sept. 30, 1978; children: Aaron, Adam, Ross, Elizabeth. PhD, U. Wis., Milw., 1991. Lectr. Mt. Mary Coll., Milw., 1992-99, asst. prof., 1999—2002, assoc. prof., 2002—, chair dept. English, 2003—, chair divsn. langs., lit. and comm., dir. English grad. program. Author: Word 97 Fundamentals for the Workplace, 1998, Women's Autobiographies, Culture, Feminism, 1999, 2d edit., 2001, Excel 97/Power Point 97 for the Workplace, 1999; editor: Issues in Travel Writing: Empire, Spectacle, and Displacement, 2002, Gender, Genre and Identity in Women's Travel Writing, 2004; contbg. author: Special Needs Adoption Network: A Series on Adoption and Foster Care Issues, 2000. Mem.: MLA, AAUW (bd. dirs.), Internat. Soc. Travel Writing (steering com.), Soc. Tech. Comm., Autobiography Assn., Nat. Coun. Tchrs. English. Avocations: writing, music, tennis. Office: Mt Mary Coll 2900 N Menomonee River Pky Milwaukee WI 53222 Home: W223 N2257 Meadowood Ln Waukesha WI 53186-1182 Office Phone: 414-258-4810 ext. 287. Business E-Mail: siegelkr@mtmary.edu.

SIEGEL, LAURIE, human resources specialist; married; 2 children. B of Gen. Studies, U. Mich.; MBA, Harvard U. Dir. global compensation Avon Products; prin. Strategic Compensation Assocs.; various positions in human resources Honeywell Internat., 1995—2003; sr. v.p. human resources Tyco Internat. Ltd., Princeton, NJ, 2003—. Bd. dirs. Hayes Lemmerz Internat., Inc. Office: Tyco International PO Box 5260 Princeton NJ 08543-5260 Office Phone: 609-720-4200. Office Fax: 603-720-4208.

SIEGEL, LLOYD HARVEY, architect, real estate developer, consultant; b. NYC, Nov. 27, 1928; s. Saul M. and Lillian (Bell) Siegel; m. Margot Kopsidas Phillips, Oct. 25, 1987. BArch, Princeton U., 1949; MArch, MIT, 1953. Registered architect, N.Y., N.J., Conn., Ohio, Ill., Mich., cert. Nat. Coun. Archtl. Registration Bds. Designer Skidmore, Owings & Merrill, then I. M. Pei & Assocs., then Antonin Raymond, NYC, 1955-60; assoc. Kelly & Gruzen, NYC, 1960-66; dep. health svcs. adminstr. City of N.Y., 1966-70; dep. exec. dir. health and hosps. governing commn. Cook County, Chgo., 1970-76; prin. L.H.S. Cons. in Health Planning, Facility Design & Mgmt., Washington, 1976—, Siegel & Schroeder, P.C., Chgo., 1983-87; dir. Office Architecture & Engring. VA, Washington, 1987-94, dir. Facilities Quality Office, 1994-98, dir. Facilities Mgmt. Svc. Delivery Office, 1999-2001; dir. Facilities Strategic Mgmt. Office, 2001—07, dir. constrn. and facilities, 2007—. Prin. Yacht Harbor Devel. Co., South Haven, Mich., 1983—88, Siegel & Schroeder Developers Inc., Chgo., 1983—88; mem. adv. coms. HEW; mem. pub. adv. panels GSA; mem. adv. com. Legislature State of Ill.; mem. fellowship evaluation com. AIA-Am. Hosp. Assn.; mem. tech. adv. com. Northeastern Ill. Planning Commn.; chmn. Com. Architecture for Health, 1984. Author: (book) Hidden Asset? Interstitial Space, A Critical Evaluation, 1987; photography (permanent collections) Met. Mus. Art, N.Y.C., Mus. Modern Art, others; prin. works include N.Y. World's Fair Spanish Pavillion, N.Y.C. (N.Y. chpt. AIA award, 1964), Williams Meml. Residence, Flushing, N.Y. (Queens C. of C. award, 1964), Hebrew Home for Aged, Riverdale, N.Y. (Bronx C. of C. award, 1966). Recipient Presdl. Fed. Design Achievement award, Pres.'s award, Nat. Inst. Bldg. Scis., 2002; Fulbright fellow, Università di Roma, 1954, Politecnico di Milano, 1955. Fellow: AIA; mem.: Urban Land Inst., Univ. Club, Cosmos Club, Arts Club. Avocations: micology, micophagy, oenology. Home: 3133 Connecticut Ave NW Washington DC 20008-5147 Office: VA 810 Vermont Ave NW Washington DC 20420-0001

SIEGEL, LOUIS PENDLETON, retired forest products executive; b. Richmond, Va., Nov. 6, 1942; s. John Boschen Jr. and Francis Beale (Tyler) S.; m. Nancy Dicks Blanton, Apr. 10, 1974 (dec. July 1976); m. Nancy Northon, June 26, 1982; children: Kathryn Tyler. AB in Econs., Dartmouth Coll., 1967. Asst. cashier, security researcher First Nat. Citibank, NYC, 1967-71; v.p. security rsch. Drexel Burnham Lambert, NYC, 1971-79; with Potlatch Corp., San Francisco and Spokane, Wash., 1979—, sr. v.p. fin. and adminstrn. San Francisco, 1989, group v.p. wood products and corp. planning, 1989-92, group v.p. pulp and paperboard and corp. planning, 1992-93, exec. v.p. pulp-based ops. and corp. planning, 1993-94, pres., COO San Francisco and Spokane, Wash., 1994-99, also bd. dirs. Spokane, CEO, 1999—2006, chmn., 1999; ret., 1999. Bd. dirs. San Francisco Fed. Corp., 1985-96. Pres., bd. dirs. Bay Area Sci. Fair, San Francisco, 1989-90; trustee Am. Forest Found., 1999-, chmn. trustees, 2000-; bd. dirs. Nat. Coun. for Air and Stream Improvement, 1999-, chmn. bd., 2003-06; pres. Area One, Boy Scouts Am., 2003-05. With USCG, 1964-65. Mem.: Am. Forest & Paper Assn. (bd. dirs. 1999—). Republican. Episcopalian. Avocations: golf, fishing. Office: Potlatch Corp 601 W Riverside Ave Ste 1100 Spokane WA 99201-0603 Office Phone: 509-835-1565.

SIEGEL, LUCY BOSWELL, public relations executive; b. NYC, July 5, 1950; d. Werner Leiser and Carol (Fleischer) Boswell; m. Henry Winter Siegel, Nov. 11, 1979 (div.); children: David Alan Siegel, Joshua Adam Siegel. BA, Conn. Coll., 1972. Assoc. editor Conn. Western, Litchfield, Conn., 1972-73; assoc. editor, editor United Bus. Publ., NYC, 1974—78; mgr. external communications Equitable Life Assurance Soc., NYC, 1978—86; mgr. internat. affairs Cosmo Pub. Rels. Corp., Tokyo, 1986-87, dir. internat. affairs, 1987-88, pres. NYC, 1988—90, Siegel Assocs. Internat., NYC, 1990—97; sr. v.p. Lobsenz Stevens, NYC, 1997—99; sr. prin., mng. dir. Publicis Dialog, NYC, 1999—2000, exec. v.p., group mng. dir., 2000—04; pres., CEO Bridge Global Strategies LLC, NYC, 2004—. Contbr. articles to jours. and mags. Bd. dirs. NYC chpt. Am. Jewish Com., 1993-2007, sec. 1993-05. Mem. Pub. Rels. Soc. Am. (treas., exec. com. bd., N.Y.C. chpt. 2004-06, exec. bd. internat. sect. 2004, bd. dirs. 2007—), Women Execs. in Pub. Rels. (bd. dirs. 1997-99), Inst. Pub. Rels. (mktg. com. mem., 2004-06). Democrat. Jewish. Home: 41 W 96th St Apt 12B New York NY 10025-6519 Office: 15th Fl 575 Lexington Ave New York NY 10022

SIEGEL, MARC MONROE, television producer, scriptwriter, director; b. NYC, Dec. 8, 1916; s. Isaac and Annie N. (Natelson) S.; m. Anne Dorothy Fishman, Sept. 8, 1940; 1 son, Peter Kieve. BA, Washington Sq. Coll., 1936; MA, N.Y. U. Sch. Edn., 1938. Free-lance mag. writer, especially for: New Yorker mag, 1948-50; writer: Eternal Light radio series, NBC, N.Y.C., 1950-60; writer-dir-producer: Directions, ABC-TV, N.Y.C., 1961-78; exec. producer chief writer: Heritage: Civilization and the Jews, WNET, N.Y.C., 1978-84; author: feature screenplays A Child is Crying, 1961, The Young Adventurers, 1963; ABC News Bicentennial spls. Rendezvous With Freedom, 1973, The Right to Believe, 1975, The Will to Be Free, 1976; ABC News feature The Panama Canal, 1977 (Writers Guild award); (Recipient numerous awards, including: Edinburgh Film Festival award 1948, Venice Film Festival award 1962, Cannes Film Festival award 1964, Eternal Light award Jewish Theol. Sem. Am. 1969). Served with USAAF, 1943-45. Peabody award, 1979, 84; Gabriel award Nat. Assn. Catholic Broadcasters, 1979; Emmy award, 1984, Christopher award, 1984; also several awards Freedoms Found. Mem. Nat. Acad. TV Arts and Scis., Writers Guild Am. East (coun. 1972-73, 78-79, 84-88, awards 1959, 73, 78, 85, Jablow Meml. award 1988, advisor lit. jour. On Writing 1993—), Dirs. Guild Am. Democrat. Home: 75 Central Park W New York NY 10023-6011 Office Phone: 212-787-7326. Personal E-mail: marcsiegel128@verizon.net.

SIEGEL, MARK S., energy executive; b. 1951; BA magna cum laude, Colgate U.; JD, U. Calif., Berkeley. Exec. v.p. Shamrock Holdings, Inc., 1988—92; pres. music divsn. Blockbuster Entertainment Corp., 1992—93; founder, pres. Remy Investors and Consultants, Inc, LA, 1993—; chmn. bd., dir. UTI Energy Corp., 1995—2001, Patterson-UTI Energy Inc., Snyder, Tex., 2001—. Mem. bd. trustees J. Paul Getty Trusy, 2005—. Office: Patterson-UTI Energy Inc 4510 Lamesa Hwy Snyder TX 79549 Office Phone: 325-574-6300. Office Fax: 325-574-6390.

SIEGEL, MARVIN, newspaper editor; b. NYC, June 23, 1935; s. Murray and Belle (Diamond) S.; 1 child, Joshua Murray. BA, U. Mich., 1957. Reporter The Record, Hackensack, NJ, 1957-59; free-lance writer Western Europe, 1960-62; reporter Fairchild Publs., NYC, 1962-63; editor The World Telegram, NYC, 1963-66; copy editor The N.Y. Times, 1966-67, asst. met. editor, 1967-76, founding editor Weekend sect., 1976-82; founding editor World of N.Y., 1982-86; founding editor Edn. Life The N.Y. Times, 1986, dep. editor Week in Rev., 1987, culture news editor, 1988-92, dep. editor Book Rev., 1992-95; asst. to mng. editor, 1995—. Co-author: The World of New York, 1985, The New York Times Great Lives of the 20th Century, 1988; editor: Deadly Sins, 1994, The Last Word: The New York Times Book of Obituaries and Farewells, 1997; Judge Turks and Caicos Internat. Film Festival, 2004, Dubrovnik Internat. Film Festival, 2005. Pfc. U.S. Army. Jewish. Office: NY Times Co 229 W 43d St New York NY 10036-3913 Business E-Mail: marvins@nytimes.com.

SIEGEL, MARY ANN GARVIN, writer; b. Louisville, Apr. 3, 1944; d. Samuel Hughes and Ann Wendell (Smith) Garvin; m. Charles Holladay Siegel, Sept. 2, 1967 (div.); children: Emily Hughes, Charles Holladay, Jr., Margaret Shafer. BA, Conn. Coll., 1966. Photog. rschr. Time Inc., NYC, 1966—67, Nat. Geog. Soc., Washington, 1967—68; content author and editor FundraisingINFO.com, 2000—01. Leadership Atlanta, 1993-94, exec. com., 1995-96. Trustee Conn. Coll., New London, 1985-90; chair Friends of Spelman Coll., Atlanta, 1990-92; active Atlanta/Fulton County adv. bd. United Way Met. Atlanta, 1994-96; Olympic Envoy to Republic of Nauru, Atlanta Com. Olympic Games, 1994-96; formerly active adv. bd. N.C. Outward Bound Sch., Asheville. Recipient Agnes Berkeley Leahy award Conn. Coll. Alumni Assn., 1991. Personal E-mail: seagullwrite@yahoo.com.

SIEGEL, MAX LAURENCE, recording industry executive; b. Dec. 31, 1964; s. William Siegel and Delores Frazier; m. Jennifer Satterfield-Siegel; children: Matthew, Max, Madeline. BA in Psychology and Pre-Profl. Studies, U. Notre Dame, 1986; JD, Notre Dame U., 1992. Assoc. Baker & Daniels LLP, Indpls., 1992—94; pres. SCA Sports & Entertainment Group, LLC, Indpls., 1994—98, Tommy Boy Gospel, 1998—2001; sr. v.p. Tommy Boy Music, 1998—2001; pres. Verify Records (Zomba Gospel), 2001—; sr. v.p. Zomba Label Group, 2001—; v.p. Jive Records Urban A&R, 2001—. Adj. prof. law Ind. U., Seton Hall U. Co-author (with John Ramsey): About My Father's Business: Merging Ministry and Industry, 2006. Named Entrepreneur of the Yr., Ctr. for Leadership Devel., Industry Exec. of the Yr., Gospel Truth Music awards; named one of Indpls. Bus. Jour. 40 under 40, 1997, Crain's NY Bus. 40 under 40, 2004, Network Jour. 40 under 40, 2004; recipient Outstanding Profl. Achievement award, Seton Hall U. Sports & Entertainment Law Soc., 2004, Exec. of the Yr., Gospel Heritage Found., 2004, Black Achievers Alumni award, U. Notre Dame. Mem.: Nat. Bar Assn., Black Entertainment & Sports Lawyer Bar Assn., NY Bar Assn., Ind. Bar Assn., ABA, Nat. Acad. Recording Arts & Sci.(NARAS)- Gospel Music Assn. Office: Max Siegel Inc 112 Russel Ave Edgewater NJ 07020 also: Verity Records 137 W 25th St New York NY 10001 Office Phone: 212-727-0016. E-mail: max@maxsiegel.com.

SIEGEL, MICHAEL ALAN, dental educator; b. Balt., Feb. 6, 1953; s. Harold W. and Ellen Rosenbach Siegel; m. Sharon Crane, July 22, 1979; 1 child, Sarah Emily. BS, U. Md., College Park, 1975; DDS, Balt. Coll. of Dental Surgery, 1979; MS, U. Md., Balt., 1986. Diplomate Am. Bd. of Oral Medicine, 1988. Resident Walter Reed Army Hosp., 1980—82, intern in dentistry and gen. practice, 1982; assoc. prof. oral medicine Balt. Coll. of Dental Sugery, Balt., 1982—2002; assoc. prof. dermatology U. Md. Med. Sch., Balt., 1991—2002; assoc. faculty mem. Grad. Sch., U. Md., Balt., 2002; prof. and chmn. dept. of diagnostic scis. Nova Southeastern U. Coll. of Dental Medicine, Ft. Lauderdale, Fla., 2003—. Cons. Balt. VA Hosp., 1982—2002; mem. editl. bd. Oral Surgery, Oral Medicine, Oral Pathology, Oral Radiology and Endodontics, 1992—. Presenter (400+ continuing dental education courses) Current Concepts in Oral Medicine; author: (100+ articles, chapters and abstracts) Oral Medicine. Capt. U.S. Army Dental Corps, 1979—82, Washington, D.C. Fellowship, Acad. Gen. Dentistry, 1986. Fellow: Acad. Gen. Dentistry, Am. Acad. Oral Medicine (bd. trustees 1990—2003, pres. 2000—02); mem.: ADA (chmn. coun. sci.

affairs 2002—03), Internat. Assn. for Dental Rsch., Omicron Kappa Upsilon (pres. 1999—2000). Achievements include research in over $3,000,000 in research funding. Office: Nova Southeastern Univ 3200 S University Dr Fort Lauderdale FL 33328-2018 Home Phone: 954-473-9998; Office Phone: 954-262-4309. Business E-Mail: masiegel@nova.edu.

SIEGEL, MICHAEL ELLIOT, nuclear medicine physician, educator; b. NYC, May 13, 1942; s. Benjamin and Rose (Gilbert) S.; m. Marsha Rose Snower, Mar. 20, 1966; children: Herrick Jove, Meridith Ann. AB, Cornell U., 1964; MD, Chgo. Med. Sch., 1968. Diplomate Nat. Bd. Med. Examiners. Intern Cedars-Sinai Med. Ctr., LA, 1968-69, resident in radiology, 1969-70; NIH fellow in radiology Temple U. Med. Ctr., Phila., 1970-71; NIH fellow in nuclear medicine Johns Hopkins U. Sch. Medicine, Balt., 1971-73, asst. prof. radiology, 1972-76; assoc. prof. radiology and medicine U. So. Calif., LA, 1976—, prof. radiology, 1989—, dir. divsn. nuclear medicine, 1982-99. Dir. Sch. Nuclear Medicine, Los Angeles County-U. So. Calif. Med. Ctr., 1976-99; dir. divsn. nuclear medicine Kenneth Norris Cancer Hosp. and Rsch. Ctr., L.A., 1983-99; dir. dept. nuclear medicine Orthopaedic Hosp., L.A., 1981-2006, Intercmty. Hosp., Covina, Calif., 1981-2006, U. So. Calif. Univ. Hosp., L.A., 1993—; clin. prof. radiology U. Calif., San Diego, 2000—. Author: Textbook of Nuclear Medicine, 1978, Vascular Surgery, 1983, 88, numerous other textbooks; editor: Nuclear Cardiology, 1981, Vascular Disease: Nuclear Medicine, 1983. Mem. Maple Ctr., Beverly Hills. Served as maj. USAF, 1974-76. Recipient Outstanding Alumnus award Chgo. Med. Sch., 1991. Fellow Am. Coll. Nuclear Medicine (sci. investigator 1974, 76, nominations com. 1980, program com. 1983, trustee 1993, disting. fellow, 1993, bd. reps. 1993—, bd. dirs. 1994—, treas. 1996—, chmn. ann. sci. program 1996—, pres.'s award 1997, v.p. 1997-98, pres. 1999—, CEO 2005—); mem. Soc. Nuclear Medicine (sic. exhbn. com. 1978-79, program com. 1979-80, Silver medal 1975), Calif. Med. Assn. (sci. adv. bd. 1987—), Radiol. Soc. N.Am., Soc. Nuclear Magnetic Resonance Imaging, Friars So. Calif., Alpha Omega Alpha. Achievements include research on development of nuclear medicine techniques to treat recurrent joint effusions, evaluate cardiovascular disease and diagnose and treat cancer; clinical utilization of video digital displays in nuclear medicine development; invention of pneumatic radiologic pressure system. Office: U So Calif Med Ctr Rm 5250 1200 N State St Los Angeles CA 90033-1029 Business E-Mail: mesiegel@usc.edu.

SIEGEL, NATHANIEL HAROLD, sociology educator; b. Bklyn., May 17, 1929; s. Victor and Yetta (Kogel) S.; m. Annabelle Replansky, Mar. 3, 1958; children— Anthony, Jennifer. AB, Bklyn. Coll., 1950; A.M., N.Y.U., 1952, PhD, 1956. Asst. prof. sociology Columbia, 1956-59; sociologist Hillside Hosp., Queens, NY, 1958-63; assoc. dir. behavioral research N.Y.C. Dept. Health, 1963-64; chief social sci. tng. sect. NIMH, 1964-67, cons., 1970-79; prof. sociology Queens Coll., 1967-79, chmn. dept., 1967-70, v.p., dean faculty, 1970-74, provost, 1974-77, acting pres., 1977-78; sr. v.p. acad. affairs SUNY Purchase, 1979-94; prof. sociology SUNY, 1979-2000, prof. emeritus, 2000—. Served with M.C. AUS, 1950-51. Home: 8 Birchfield Rd Larchmont NY 10538-1505

SIEGEL, NED LAWRENCE, real estate developer; b. Newark, Sept. 26, 1951; s. Howard and Esther (Facher) S.; m. Stephanie Moak, Aug. 7, 1976; children: Justin, Joshua, Jillian. BA, U. Conn., 1973; JD, Dickinson Sch. Law, 1976. Law clk. U.S. Dist. Ct., Camden, NJ, 1976-77; assoc. Kimmelman, Wolff & Samson, Roseland, NJ, 1977-78; v.p. Howard Siegel Cos., Manalapan, NJ, 1978-80; pres. The Weingarten-Siegel Group, Manalapan, NJ, 1980-88, Weingarten Siegel Group of Fla., Inc., Boca Raton, Fla., 1985-91, Weingarten, Siegel, Fletcher Group, La Mesa, Calif., 1985-91, The Siegel Schoor Orgn. Fla., INc., Boca Raton, 1991-98, Siegel Group, Studio City, Calif. Pres. SGS Communities Inc., Manalapan, N.J., Boca Raton, 1992— (exec. com. Republican Jewish Coalition, 1995—, steering com.), NLS Cmtys., Inc., 1996—; dir. Marietta Corp., 1996, Blue Lake Ltd., 1997—, Miami One Ctr., L.P., 1998—; chmn. The Siegel Group, 1997—, Siegel-Moskin Realty Group, 1998—; bd. dirs. Palm Beach Internat. Film Festival, mem. of bd. of dir. Marietta Corp., Cenetec LLC, bd of dir. Overseas Pvt Investment Corp, Rep of US 61st Session UNGA Un, Reps of US (7ft) Dept. of State. Bd. govs. Solomon Schechter Sch., West Orange, N.J., 1986-88; mem. bd. adv. Pine Crest Sch. at Boca Raton, 1989-93, mem. bd. dirs. 1992—; bd. trustees Saint Andrew's Sch.; mem. task force City of Boca Raton Affordable Housing, 1995—; founding mem. Treve Brogan Ednl. Inst.; co-chmn. Palm Beach County Gov. George W. Bush Presdl. Exploratory com., Palm Beach County Jeb Bush for Governor Campaign, 1998, Palm Beach County Phil Gray for Pres., 1996. Named Bldr. of the Yr., N.J. Shore Bldrs. Assn., 1986. Mem. Nat. Assn. Homebuilders, Gold Coast Builder's Assn., Fla. Homebuilder's Assn., Internat. Coun. Shopping Ctrs., Found. Fla.'s Future (chmns. adv. bd.), Econ. Coun. Palm Beach County, The Beacon Coun. (Miami chpt.), Republican Eagles, Republican Party of Fla., N.J. Bldrs. Assn., N.J. Shore Bldrs. Assn. (v.p. 1986-88), Urban Land Inst., N.J. Bar Assn., Greater Miami C. of C., Greater Boca Raton C. of C., Phi Beta Kappa. Republican. Jewish. Avocations: tennis, sailing. Office: Overseas Pvt Investment Corp 1100 NY Ave NW Washington DC 20527 Office Phone: 202-336-8400. Office Fax: 202-336-7949.

SIEGEL, NEIL GILBERT, computer engineer, consultant; b. Bklyn, Feb. 19, 1954; s. Bernard Siegel and Judith Love Cohen; m. Robyn Christine Friend, July 8, 1979. BA cum laude, U. So. Calif., 1974, MS, 1976, PhD, 1977. Sr. staff mem. TRW Sys., Inc., Redondo Beach, Calif., 1988—, v.p., gen. mgr. tactical sys.; sector v.p. tech. & v.p. and chief engr. Command, Control and Comm. Northrop Grumman Mission Sys., Redondo Beach, Calif., 2002—. Lectr. UCLA, 1973, cons., 1984—. Contbr. articles to profl. jours, Bd. dirs. Inst. Persian Performing Arts, Calif. State Abalone Cove Landslide Abatement Dist.; mem. various U.S. govt. panels including Def. Advanced Rsch. Project Agy. "command, control, comm., computers and intelligence" (C41) review panel, 1994, Def. Sci. Bd. "summer studies", 1996, 98. Inducted into Order of St. Barbara, U.S. Army. Mem.: NAE. Achievements include 5 U.S. patents. Office: Northrop Grumman Mission Sys 1800 Glenn Curtiss St DH6-2265 Carson CA 90746 Home: 19 Golden Spar Pl Rolling Hills Estates CA 90274-2431 Office Phone: 310-764-3003. E-mail: neil.siegel@ngc.com.

SIEGEL, PAUL, judge; b. Troy, NY, May 7, 1938; s. Benjamin and Mary (Silverman) S.; 1 child, Mark Aron; m. Janique Auvertin, Apr. 30, 1994. BS in Physics magna cum laude, U. Miami, 1958, LLB cum laude, 1962. Bar: Fla. 1963, DC 1964, U.S. Supreme Ct. 1967, U.S. Ct. Appeals (5th cir.) 1967, U.S. Ct. Appeals (11th cir.) 1982; cert. civil trial lawyer Fla. Bar. Mem. gen. counsel's office AEC, Washington, 1962-65; ptnr. Sinclair, Louis, Siegel, Heath, Nussbaum & Zavertnik, P.A., Miami, Fla., 1972-91; judge Dade County (Fla.) Cir. Ct., 1991—. Author: Florida Trial Objections, 2004; editor-in-chief, exec. editor: U. Miami Law Rev. Chmn. bd. dirs. Alliance Francaise of Dade County, 1983-87, pres., 1990-92; pres. Pro-Mozart Soc. Greater Miami, 1984-92. Home: 235 E San Marino Dr Miami FL 33139-1151 Office: Lawson E Thomas Courthouse Ctr 175 NW 1st Ave Ste 2815 Miami FL 33128 Office Phone: 305-349-5726. E-mail: psiegel@jud11.flcourts.org.

SIEGEL, RANDY, publishing executive; BA with honors, Wesleyan U.; MBA, Yale U., 1988. Pub., editor Cleveland Free Times; mktg. mgr. Washington Post; mktg. dir. Newsweek; pres. Venturion, Ltd; cons. Parade, 1999—2001, sr. v.p., 2001—03, assoc. publ., 2003, exec. v.p., pub., 2003—04, pres., pub., 2004—. Siegel's bus. experience includes the launches of Newsweek Interactive, HearSay mag. (a nat. coll. music publ.) and BrassRing.com, a joint venture among The Washington Post, Tribune Co. and Accel Ptnrs.; a major contbr. to Parade's strong positioning in the marketplace; led the sales, mktg. and comm. efforts for The Great Am. Bake Sale, a new program presented jointly by Parade and Share Our Strength, a leading nat. anti-hunger orgn.; he cemented a partnership with ESPN.com to create a program including sales, mktg. opportunities, and the All-Am. HS Sports program; mem. exec. com. The Quills. Office: Parade Publ Inc 711 3rd Ave New York NY 10017-4014 Office Phone: 212-450-0980. Office Fax: 212-450-7091. Business E-Mail: randolph_siegel@parade.com. *

SIEGEL, ROBERT, heat transfer engineer; b. Cleve., July 10, 1927; s. Morris and Mollie (Binder) S.; m. Elaine Jane Jaffe, July 19, 1951; children: Stephen, Lawrence. BS, Case Inst. Tech., 1950, MS, 1951; ScD, MIT, 1953. Heat transfer engr. GE, Schenectady, NY, 1953-54; heat transfer analyst Knolls Atomic Power Lab., Schenectady, 1954-55; rsch. scientist NASA Lewis Rsch. Ctr., Cleve., 1955-99; tech. cons., 1999—. Adj. prof. U. Toledo, 1981, 85, 95, adj. prof. mech. engring. U. Akron (Ohio), 1987, adj. prof. mech. engring. Cleve. State U., 1989, 91; mem. adv. coun. U. Akron, 1989-96. Author: Thermal Radiation Heat Transfer, 1972, 4th edit., 2002; tech. editor ASME, 1973-83, AIAA, 1986-98; author numerous sci. papers. With U.S. Army, 1945-47. Recipient Exceptional Sci. Achievement medal NASA, 1986, Space Act award, 1993, ASME-AIChE Max Jakob Meml. award, 1996. Fellow ASME (Heat Transfer Meml. award 1970, Max Jakob Bd. of award 1999-2002), AIAA (Thermophysics award 1993); mem. Sigma Xi, Tau Beta Pi. Jewish. Avocations: ballroom dancing, piano. Home and Office: 3052 Warrington Rd Shaker Heights OH 44120-2425

SIEGEL, ROBERT (BOB) A., lawyer; AB with great distinction, U. Calif., Berkeley, 1971; JD magna cum laude, U. Mich. Bar: Calif. Ptnr. O'Melveny & Myers LLP, LA, vice-chair LA firm, chair adversarial law dept., mem. office of chair. Tchr., lectr. ALI-ABA, Am. Arbitration Assn., Practisng Law Inst. Sr. editor The Railway Labor Act (BNA). Mem.: ABA (labor and employment law sect., equal opportunity com., railway and airline labor law com. (past co-chmn.)), Order of the Coif, Phi Beta Kappa. Office: O'Melveny & Myers LLP 400 S Hope St Los Angeles CA 90071 Office Phone: 213-430-6005. Office Fax: 213-430-6407. Business E-Mail: rsiegel@omm.com.

SIEGEL, ROBERT CHARLES, broadcast journalist; b. NYC, June 26, 1947; s. Joseph and Edith Ruth (Joffe) S.; m. Jane Claudia Schwartz, June 17, 1973; children: Erica Anne, Leah Harriet. BA, Columbia U., 1968, postgrad. sch. journalism, 1969-70. Newscaster Sta. WGLI, Babylon, N.Y., 1968-69; reporter, news dir. Sta. WRVR-FM, NYC, 1971-76; assoc. producer, editor Nat. Pub. Radio, Washington, 1976-78, sr. editor, 1976-79, dir. news and info., 1983-87, host All Things Considered, 1987—, sr. editor London, 1979-83. Host Ea. Europe: Breaking with the Past, The Learning Channel, Washington, 1990, Earth Scope, Arlington, Va., 1990-91. Editor: The NPR Interviews. Recipient DuPont-Columbia award Columbia U., 1984. Jewish. Avocations: reading, golf, baseball. Home: 1340 19th Rd S Arlington VA 22202-1637 Office: Nat Pub Radio All Things Considered 635 Massachusetts Ave NW Washington DC 20001-3753 E-mail: rsiegel@npr.org.

SIEGEL, ROBERT HAROLD, English literature educator, writer; b. Aug. 18, 1939; married; 3 children. Student, Denison U., 1957-59; BA in English, Wheaton Coll., 1961; MA, Johns Hopkins U., 1962; PhD in English, Harvard U., 1968. Instr. Dartmouth Coll., 1967-68, asst. prof., 1968-75; vis. lectr. Princeton (N.J.) U., 1975-76; poet-in-residence, McManes vis. prof. Wheaton (Ill.) Coll., 1976; asst. prof. U. Wis., Milw., 1976-79, assoc. prof. English, 1979-83, prof., 1983—99, prof. emeritus, 1999—. Poet on faculty Summer Writers' Inst., Wheaton Coll., 1980, Wesleyan U., 1982, 83, New Eng. Young Writers Conf., 2002-2006; vis. prof. J. W. v. Goethe U., Frankfurt, Fed. Republic Germany, 1985; lectr., reader various univs. Author: (fiction) Alpha Centauri, 1980, Whalesong, 1981, The Kingdom of Wundle, 1982, White Whale, 1991, The Ice at the End of the World, 1994; (poetry) The Beasts and the Elders, 1973, In A Pig's Eye, 1980, The Waters Under the Earth, 2005, A Pentecost of Finches: New and Selected Poems, 2006; contbr. poems to Atlantic Monthly, Sewanee Rev., other jours. Recipient Margaret O'Loughlin Foley award Am. mag., 1970, award Cliff Dwellers' Arts Found., 1974, Chgo. Poetry prize Soc. Midland Authors, 1974, Poetry prize Prairie Schooner, 1977, Jacob Glatstein Meml. prize Poetry mag., 1977, award Ingram Merrill Found., 1979, Gold medallion ECPA, 1981, Book of Yr. award Campus Life mag., 1981, 1st Pl. prize for juvenile fiction Coun. for Wis. Writers, 1981, 1st Pl. prize poetry Soc. Midland Authors, 1981, Matson award Friends of Lit., 1982, Golden Archer award Sch. Libr. Sci., U. Wis., Oshkosh, 1986, 1st prize Milton Ctr. Poetry Contest, 1994, EPA 1st place in poetry, 2003; Dartmouth Coll. faculty fellow, 1971; Gilman fellow Johns Hopkins U., 1961-62; tchg. fellow Harvard U., 1965-67, Yaddo Artists' Colony, 1974, 75, Transatlantic Rev. fellow Bread Loaf Writers Conf., 1974, Nat. Endowment for Arts, 1980; grantee U. Wis., 1978, 84, 88-89, 96-97. Office: U Wis English Dept Milwaukee WI 53201 Business E-Mail: grindel@msn.com, siegelrh@uwm.edu.

SIEGEL, ROBERT STEVEN, internist, oncologist, educator; b. Phila., Pa., Feb. 5, 1951; MD, George Washington U. Sch. Medicine, 1977. Cert. Internal Medicine, Hematology, Med. Oncology. Intern, internal medicine Duke U. Med. Ctr., Durham, NC, 1977—78, resident, hematology oncology, 1978—80, fellow, 1980—82; hosp. appointment George Washington U. Med. Ctr., Washington, prof. medicine, dir., divsn. hematology and oncology, mem., Med. Faculty Assocs. Named one of Top Doctors, Washingtonian.com, 2005. Office: George Washington U Med Ctr 2150 Pennsylvania Ave NW Ste 3-428 Washington DC 20037 Office Phone: 202-741-2478, 202-741-2210, Office Fax: 202-741-2487. *

SIEGEL, SAMUEL, metals company executive; b. Elizabeth, NJ, Oct. 30, 1930; s. Morris and Anna (Fader) S.; m. Raenea Kershenbaum, Mar. 29, 1953; children: Daryl Lynn, Annie Roslyn. BBA, CUNY, 1952. CPA, N.Y. Cost accountant Seaporcel Metals, Inc., Long Island City, NY, 1955-56; asst. to controller Deltown Foods, Inc., Yonkers, NY, 1956-57; sr. accountant Touche Ross, NYC, 1957-61; co-founder, vice chmn., chief fin. officer, treas., sec., dir. Nucor Corp., Charlotte, NC, 1961-99; ret., 2000. Mem. AICPA, Am. Soc. Corp. Secs., Fin. Execs. Inst. Office: 3421 Windbluff Dr Charlotte NC 28277-9850 Office Phone: 704-542-8000.

SIEGEL, SARAH ANN, lawyer; b. Providence, Aug. 29, 1956; BA in History cum laude, Brandeis U., 1978; JD, Washington U., St. Louis, 1981. Bar: Mo. 1982, U.S. Dist. Ct. (ea. dist.) Mo. 1983. Assoc. atty., St. Louis, 1982-83; staff atty. Land Clearance for Redevel. Authority, St. Louis, 1983-85, gen. counsel, 1985-88, Econ. Devel. Corp., St. Louis, 1988-90, St. Louis Devel. Corp., 1990-91; spl. counsel for devel. City of St. Louis, 1991-92; assoc. Suelthaus & Walsh, P.C., St. Louis, 1992-95, prin., 1995-99; v.p., gen. counsel Dierbergs Mkts. Inc., St. Louis, 1999—. Pres. Ctrl. Reform Congregation, St. Louis, 1991—93, v.p., 1989—91, bd. dir., 1987—89; bd. dirs. Friends of the Sheldon Concert Hall, 1997—2004, mem. exec. com., 2001—05; bd. dirs. St. Louis Art Fair, 2001—03. Mem.: ABA, Assn. Corp. Counsel (St. Louis chpt., bd. dirs. 2000—, v.p. 2000—05, pres. 2005—06), Women Lawyers Assn. (bd. dirs. 1985—90, v.p. 1989—90), Mo. Bar Assn. (vice chair com. on eminent domain 1990—91, steering com. 1987—89, 1995—96). Avocations: hiking, swimming. Business E-Mail: siegels@dierbergs.com.

SIEGEL, SHELDON C., pediatrician, immunologist, allergist; b. Mpls., Jan. 30, 1922; s. Carl S.; m. Priscilla Rikess, Mar. 3, 1946; children— Linda, Nancy. AA, Va. Jr. Coll., 1940; BA, BS, U. Minn., 1942, MD, 1945. Intern U. Minn. Hosp., 1946, resident in pediatrics, 1947-48; fellow in pediatric allergy Rochester, NY, 1949-50; practice medicine specializing in pediatric allergy and pediatrics St. Paul, 1950-52, San Antonio, 1952-54, Los Angeles, 1954—; clin. instr. pediatrics U. Rochester, 1949-50, U. Minn., 1950-51; asst. prof. pediatrics U. Tex., 1952-54; asst. clin. prof. U. Calif. at Los Angeles Med. Sch., 1955, clin. asso. prof., 1957-62, clin. prof., 1963—, co-chief pediatric allergy clinic, 1957—. Editorial bd.: Jour. Allergy, 1973-75; contbr. articles to med. jours. Fellow Am. Acad. Allergy (pres. 1974), Am. Coll. Allergists, Am. Acad. Pediatrics; mem. AMA, Allergy Found. Am. (pres. 1976), Calif. Med. Assn., LA County Med. Assn., LA Pediatric Soc., Calif. Soc. Allergy, LA Soc. Allergy, Western Pediatric Rsch. Soc., Am. Bd. Med. Specialists, Sigma Xi. Office: 11620 Wilshire Blvd Los Angeles CA 90025-1706 Office Phone: 310-312-5050.

SIEGEL, STANLEY, lawyer, educator; b. NYC, Mar. 2, 1941; s. David Aaron and Rose (Minsky) S. BS summa cum laude, NYU, 1960; JD magna cum laude, Harvard U., 1963. Bar: N.Y. 1963, D.C. 1964, Mich. 1970, Calif. 1976; CPA, Md. Atty. Office Sec. of Air Force, 1963-66; asst. prof. law U. Mich., Ann Arbor, 1966-69, assoc. prof., 1969-71, prof., 1971-74; ptnr. Honigman, Miller, Schwartz & Cohn, Detroit, 1974-76; prof. law UCLA, 1976-86, NYU, 1986—, assoc. dean, 1987-89. Vis. prof. Stanford Law Sch., 1973, Ctrl. European U., Budapest, 1993—2001, U. Konstanz, Germany, 1996, Tel Aviv U., 1998; fellow Max-Planck Inst., Hamburg, 1988; cons. reorgn. U.S. Postal Svc., 1969—71; exec. sec. Mich. Law Revision Commn., 1973; mem. bd. examiners AICPA, 1980—83. Author: (with Schulman and Moscow) Michigan Business Corporations, 1979, (with Conard and Knauss) Enterprise Organization, 4th edit., 1987, (with D. Siegel) Accounting and Financial Disclosure: A Guide to Basic Concepts, 1983, (with others) Swiss Company Law, 1996; mem. editl. bd. Lexis Electronic Author's Press, 1996-98. Served to capt. USAF, 1963-66. Mem. ABA, D.C. Bar Assn., Calif. Bar Assn., Assn. of Bar of City of N.Y., Am. Law Inst., AICPA. Office: NYU Law Sch 40 Washington Sq S New York NY 10012-1099

SIEGEL, STEVEN L., finance company executive, consultant; b. New Rochelle, NY, Feb. 21, 1962; s. Stuart A. Siegel and Stephanie (Kaplita); m. Elizabeth Ellen Starr, Dec. 12, 1987 (div. Jan. 1993). BS in Fin., Calif. Coast U., MBA in Internat. Fin.; DSc magna cum laude in Internat Fin., So. Calif. U., Santa Ana. Fin. analyst Am. Express, Plantation, Fla., 1982-84; investment banker Kidder Peabody & Co., Ft. Lauderdale, Fla., 1985-87, Shearson Lehman Hutton, Boca Raton, Fla., 1987-89; pres. internat. divsn. Cabe Internat. Cons., Inc., Boca Raton, 1989-92; fin. and adminstv. dir. Ensec, Inc., Boca Raton, 1994-95, Art Collectors Internat., Miami, Fla., 1995-96; CFO, COO Enternet Entertainment Group, Inc., Ft. Lauderdale, 1996—97, S.L. Siegel and Assoc. Consulting Group, 1997—2004, Pan Am., 2004—05, Acad. Fire Protection, 2006—. Mng. dir. Fed. Group Ltd., 2001—02, bd. dir., Bought Deal, Inc.; bd. advisors Howa Telco, 1997—2002; pres., CEO Champion Accessories, 2002—03. Mem. Lambda Alpha Epsilon. Avocations: golf, sailing. Address: 2460 Deercreek CC Blvd Suite 209 Deerfield Beach FL 33442 Office Phone: 917-325-0114. Personal E-mail: drsls@earthlink.net.

SIEGEL, STUART ELLIOTT, pediatric oncologist, educator; b. Plainfield, NJ, July 16, 1943; s. Hyman and Charlotte Pearl (Freinberg) S.; m. Linda Wertkin, Jan. 20, 1968 (dec. 2003); 1 child, Joshua; m. Barbara Frankel, May 29, 2005. BA, MD, Boston U., 1967. Diplomate Am. Bd. Pediatrics, Am. Bd. Pediatric Oncology. Intern U. Minn. Hosp., Mpls., 1967-68, resident, 1968-69; clin. assoc. NIH, Bethesda, Md., 1969-72; asst. prof. pediatrics U. So. Calif. Sch. Medicine, LA, 1972-76, assoc. prof., 1976-81, prof., 1981—, vice chmn. dept. pediat., 1994—; head div. hematology-oncology Childrens Hosp. LA, 1976—, dep. physician-in-chief, 1987-90; dir. Childrens Ctr. for Cancer and Blood Diseases, LA, 1996—. Mem. clin. cancer program project com. NIH, Nat. Cancer Inst., HEW, Bethesda, Md., 1978-82; pres. So. Calif. Children's Cancer Services, LA, 1977-95. Bd. dirs. Nat. Leukemia Broadcast Coun., 1987—, Ronald McDonald Children's Charities, 1988-95, Make-A-Wish Found., 1987-95, Children's Hosp. LA Found., 1994-2000, Ronald McDonald House Charities, 1995—, LA Regional Coun. Am. Cancer Soc., 1996—, Nat. Childhood Cancer Found., 1995-2003, 2005—; pres. Ronald McDonald House Charities So. Calif., 1996—; bd. trustees, Children's Hosp., LA, 2000—; treas. Padres Contra El Cancer, 2003-04; mem. steering com. Live Strong Young Adult Alliance, 2005—. Surgeon USPHS, 1969-72. Named to NAt. Caring Hall of Fame, 2001. Fellow Am. Acad. Pediatrics. Office: Childrens Hosp LA Divsn Hematology Oncology MS#54 PO Box 54700 Los Angeles CA 90054-0700 Home Phone: 310-454-0946; Office Phone: 323-669-2205. Business E-Mail: ssiegel@chla.usc.edu.

SIEGEL, VIVIAN, biomedical editor; b. LA, Aug. 24, 1960; d. Edward and Harriet (Greenberg); m. David Alan Zeserson; 1 child, Jacob Edward. AB in Biochemistry and Math., Bowdoin Coll., Brunswick, Maine, 1981; PhD in Genetics, U. Calif., San Francisco, 1987. Postdoctoral fellow U. Calif., San Francisco, 1987-88, 89-93, postgrad. rschr., 1993-94, sr. editor, 2006—; postdoctoral fellow Max Planck Inst. Devel. Biology, Tubingen, Germany, 1988-89; sr. editor Cell, Cambridge, Mass., 1994—98, Molecular Cell, Cambridge, Mass., 1997—98; dep. editor Cell, Molecular Cell, Cambridge, 1998—99, editor-in-chief, 1999—2003, Developmental Cell, Cambridge, 2001—03; exec. dir. Pub. Libr. of Sci., San Francisco, 2003—05; editor PLOS Biology, San Francisco, 2003—05; rsch. prof. Vanderbilt U., Nashville, 2006—. Vis. sci. Whitehead Inst., Cambridge, Mass., 1994—97, Cambridge, 2003; sabbatical rschr. U. Calif., 2005—06. Mem. Am. Soc. Cell Biology, Genetics Soc. Am., Louis Round Wilson Acad. Achievements include functional dissection of signal recognition particle; definition of a translocation-competent state for secretory proteins; demonstration of the existence of a signal recognition particle in ciliates and fungi; demonstration that the bicoid protein of Drosophila is an anterior morphogen; identification of the pipsqueak gene and definition of its role in Drosophila oogenesis and eye development. Personal E-mail: viviansiegel@gmail.com.

SIEGEL, WENDY LOWE, special education educator; m. Rich Siegel, Apr. 4, 2000. PhD, U. New Orleans, 1999. Cert. tchr. La. Asst. prof. Southeastern La. U., Hammond, 2000—. Contbr. articles to profl. jours. Tchr. La. SPCA, New Orleans, 2000—07. Recipient Nat. Jeannie P. Baliles Child Mental Health Rsch. award, 1997; fellow, U. New Orleans, 1995—2000; grantee, 1993—95. Mem.: Coun. Exceptional Children (assoc.), Phi Delta Kappa (assoc.), Delta Kappa Pi (assoc.). Office: Southeastern La U 1300 General Pershing Ste 2004 Hammond LA 70402 Office Phone: 985-549-3421. Business E-Mail: wsiegel@selu.edu.

SIEGERT, BARBARA (BARBARA MARIE SIEGERT), health care administrator; b. Boston, May 22, 1935; d. Salvatore Mario and Mary Kathleen (Wagner) Tartaglia; m. Herbert C. Siegert (dec. Apr. 1974); children: Carolyn Marie, Herbert Christian Jr. Diploma, Newton Wellesley Hosp., Mass., 1956; MEd, Antioch U., 1980. Diplomate Am. Bd. Med. Psychotherapists. Supr. nursing Hogan Regional Ctr., Hathorne, Mass., 1974-78; community mental health nursing advisor Cape Ann area office Dept. Mental Health, Beverly, Mass., 1978-79, dir. case mgmt., 1979-87, dir. case mgmt. north shore area office, 1988-91; dir. case mgmt. Dept. Mental Health-north shore area-Lynn (Mass.) site, Lynn, Mass., 1991-92. Mem. interdisciplinary faculty, profl. cons. com., lecture staff clin. pastoral counseling program Danvers State Hosp./Hogan/Berry Regional Ctrs., Hathorne, Mass., 1982-86; nursing edn. adv. com. North Shore Community Coll., Beverly, 1983-91; tng. staff Balter Inst., Ipswich, Mass., 1987-88. Mem. Internat. Cultural Diploma Honor, 1989—. Recipient Spl. Recognition award Lexington (Mass.) Pub. Schs., 1973, Peter Torci award Lexington Friends of Children in Spl. Edn., 1974. Home: 63 Willow Rd # B Boxford MA 01921-1218

SIEGFRIED, CARY ANN, library director; B, U. Iowa; MLS, La. State U. Positions including support svcs. adminstr., asst. dir. tech. svcs. and asst. dir. libs. City of Arlington, Tex., 1992—2004; interim dir. Arlington, Tex. Pub. Libr., 2004, dir. librs., 2004—. Office: Arlington Tex Pub Libr George W Hawkes Ctrl Libr 101 E Abram St Arlington TX 76010-1183 Office Phone: 817-459-6916. Office Fax: 817-459-6902. E-mail: siegfriedc@pub-lib.ci.arlington.tx.us.

SIEGFRIED, DAVID CHARLES, retired lawyer; b. NYC, Feb. 15, 1942; s. Charles Albert and Marjorie Claire (Young) S.; m. Meri Stephanie (Smith); children: Karin Elisabeth, Christine Elise. BA, Princeton U., 1964; JD, Harvard U., 1967. Bar: N.Y., 1970. Assoc. Milbank, Tweed, Hadley, and McCloy, NYC, 1968-76, ptnr., 1977—98, resident ptnr. Hong Kong and Singapore, 1979-83, 85-88. Spkr. in field. Bd. dirs. Cmty. Agy. Corp. N.J., Inc., pres. alumni assn.; chmn. Princeton U. Alumni Coun.; mem. Millburn Hist. Preservation Commn. 1st lt. USAR, 1967-74. Mem.: Millburn Short Hills Hist. Soc. (bd. dir., past pres.), Assn. Bar City of N.Y., N.Y. State Bar Assn., Cricket Club, Tanglin Club (Singapore), Am. Club (Hong Kong and Singapore), Baltrusrol Golf Club, Short Hills (NJ) Club, Princeton Club. Congregationalist. Avocations: running, tennis, historic reading. Home: 30 Western Dr Short Hills NJ 07078-3230

SIEGLER, KELLY R., lawyer; b. Oct. 1962; m. Sam Siegler. Degree in internat. bus. Asst. dist. atty. Harris County, Houston, 1987—. Named America's Top 50 Women Litigators, Nat. Law Jour., 2002, Named to Winners of Spl. Reports, 2003, 2004; named one of Top 10 Litigators, 2003. Mem.: Tex. Dist. and County Atty. Assn. Office: Harris County District Attorney's Office Ste 600 1201 Franklin St Houston TX 77002-1923 Office Phone: 713-755-5800.

SIEGLER, MARK, internist, educator; b. NYC, June 20, 1941; s. Abraham J. and Florence (Sternlieb) S.; m. Anna Elizabeth Hollinger, June 4, 1967; children: Dillan, Alison, Richard, Jessica. AB with honors, Princeton U., 1963; MD, U. Chgo., 1967. Diplomate Am. Bd. Internal Medicine. Resident, chief resident internal medicine U. Chgo., 1967-71; hon. sr. registrar in medicine Royal Postgrad. Med. Sch., London, 1971-72; asst. prof. medicine U. Chgo., 1972-78, assoc. prof. medicine, 1979-85, acting dir. div. gen. internal medicine, 1983-85, dir. MacLean Ctr. Clin. Med. Ethics, 1984—, prof. medicine, 1985—, Lindy Bergman prof., 1997-2000, Lindy Bergman Disting. Svc. prof., 2000—, dir. fellowship tng. program in clin. med. ethics, 1986—. Vis. asst. prof. medicine U. Wis., Madison, 1977; vis. assoc. prof. medicine U. Va., Charlottesville, 1981-82. Co-author: Clinical Ethics, 1981, 6th edit., 2006, An Annotated Bibliography of Medical Ethics, 1988, Institutional Protocols for Decisions About Life-Sustaining Treatment, 1988; co-editor: Changing Values in Medicine, 1985, Medical Innovations and Bad Outcomes, 1987; editl. bd.: Am. Jour. Medicine, 1979—94, 1997—, Archives Internal Medicine, 1979—90, Bibliography of Bioethics, Jour. Med. Philosophy, 1978—89, Jour. Med. Philosophy, 1978—89, Jour. Clin. Ethics, 1989—; contbr. articles to profl. jours. Mem. adv. bd. Bioethics Inst., Madrid, Notre Dame Ctr. for Ethics and Culture; trustee Princeton U., 2006—. Grantee Andrew W. Mellon Found., Henry J. Kaiser Family Found., Pew Charitable Trusts, Field Found. Ill., Ira De Camp Found., Gaylord & Dorothy Donnelley Found., Irving Harris Found.; Phi Beta Kappa vis. scholar, 1991-92, Chirone prize Italian Nat. Acad. Medicine, 1996; mem. NAS Cloning Panel, 2001-02, others. Fellow ACP (human rights com., ethics com. 1985-90), Hastings Ctr.; mem. ACS (ethics com. 1992—), Assn. Am. Physicians, Chgo. Clin. Ethics Program (pres. 1989-90). Office: Univ Chgo MC 6098 MacLean Ctr Clin Med Ethics 5841 S Maryland Ave Chicago IL 60637-1463 Office Phone: 773-702-1453. E-mail: msiegler@medicine.bad.uchicago.edu.

SIEGRIST, ROBERT L., engineering educator, consultant; b. Waukesha, Wis. m. Sue E. Hintz-Siegrist; 1 child, Jonathan. PhD, U. Wis., Madison, 1986. Registered profl. engr., Wis., 1978. Rsch. specialist U. Wis., Madison, 1975—84; sr. engr. Ayres Assocs., Inc., Madison, 1986—90; vis. sr. scientist Inst. Georesources and Pollution Rsch., Aas, Norway, 1988—89; group leader Oak Ridge Nat. Lab., Tenn., 1990—94; divsn. dir., prof. Colo. Sch. Mines, Golden, 1995—. Contbr. articles to profl. jours. Recipient Outstanding Project of Yr. Award, Dept. of Def., 2005, Tech. Achievement award, Oak Ridge Nat. Lab.; fellow, NATO. Mem.: ASCE, AEESP, NOWRA, NGWA, NEHA, WEF. Achievements include patents for oxidative particle mixture; patents pending for coupling oxidants with surfactacts. Avocations: international travel, rock climbing, mountaineering. Office: Colo Sch Mines Environ Sci and Engring Golden CO 80401-1887 Office Phone: 303-384-2158. Office Fax: 303-273-3413. Business E-Mail: siegrist@mines.edu.

SIEJKA, GEORGE JOHN, artist; b. Vienna, June 24, 1946; came to U.S., 1950; Cert. Fine Arts, Sch. Visual Arts, NYC, 1969; BS in Art Edn. cum laude, NYU, 1974, MA in Fine Arts, 1975. Represented by Nancy Hoffman Gallery, N.Y.C. Group exhbns. include Fitchburg (Mass.) Art Mus., Anchorage (Alaska) Mus. Art, Rockford (Ill.) Coll. Art Gallery, Chgo. Internat. Exposition, Nancy Hoffman Gallery, NY. Recipient Founders Day award NYU, 1974; Hurricane Katrina Relief grant, Pollack-Krasner Found., NY, 2005. Mem. N.Y. Artists Equity Assn. Home: 534 Main St Apt 2 Beacon NY 12508

SIEKERT, ROBERT GEORGE, retired neurologist, retired educator; b. Milw., July 23, 1924; s. Hugo Paul and Elisa (Kraus) S.; m. Mary Jane Evans, Feb. 17, 1951; children: Robert G. Jr., John E., Friedrich A.P. BS, Northwestern U., 1945, MS, 1947, MD, 1948. Diplomate Am. Bd. Psychiatry and Neurology. Instr. anatomy U. Pa., Phila., 1948-49; fellow neurology Mayo Found., Rochester, Minn., 1950-54; cons. Mayo Clinic, Rochester, 1954-91, head neurology sect., 1966-76, bd. govs., 1973-80, prof. neurology med. sch., 1969-91, prof. emeritus neurology, 1991—. Chmn. Internat. Stroke Conf. Am. Heart Assn., 1976-93. Editor Mayo Clinic Procs., 1982-86; cons. editor Jour. Stroke, 1992-2001; contbr. articles to profl. jours.; described transient cerebral ischemic attacks. Trustee Mayo Found., Rochester, 1973-81, chmn. emeritus com., 1997-98. Served to lt. j.g. M.C., USNR, 1950-52. Recipient Disting. Achievement award, Am. Heart Assn., 1984, Merit award, 1989, Robert G. Siekert Young Investigator award Am. Heart Assn., 1986. Fellow Am. Coll. Physicians; mem. Am. Neurol. Assn., Northwestern U. Med. Sch. Alumni Assn. (Service award 1983), Swiss Neurol. Soc. (corr.), Alpha Omega Alpha. Avocation: stamp collecting/philately. Office: Mayo Clinic 200 1st St SW N-10 Rochester MN 55905-0002

SIEKIERSKI, MACIEJ M., curator; b. Poznan, Poland; s. Konrad Siekierski and Helena Buczak-Siekierski; m. Anna Bendisz-Siekierski, Mar. 24, 1979; children: Nicholas, Victoria, Maximilian. BA in History and Russian, San Jose State Coll., 1970; MLS, San Jose State U., 1986; MA in History, U. Calif., Berkeley, 1971, PhD in History, 1984. Curator Hoover Inst., Stanford U., Calif., 1984—. Contbr. articles to profl. jours. Mem.: Polish Inst. Arts and Scis. Am., Am. Assn. Advancement Slavic Studies, Am. Hist. Assn. Home: 1752 Hull Ave Redwood City CA 94061 Office: Hoover Inst Stanford CA Office Phone: 650-725-6955.

SIEKMAN, THOMAS CLEMENT, lawyer; b. Somerville, Mass., Sept. 22, 1941; s. Aloysius C. and Estelle M. (Forte) S.; children: Michael T., James T., Amy K. BS in Engring., Merrimack Coll., 1963; JD, Villanova U., 1966. Bar: Mass. 1966, U.S. Dist. Ct. Mass. 1969. Patent atty. Bethlehem (Pa.) Steel, 1966-68, Mohawk Data Scis., Stoneham, Mass., 1968-72, Chittick, Thompson & Pfund, Boston, 1972-73; from patent atty. to v.p. and gen. counsel Digital Equipment Corp., Maynard, Mass., 1973-98; Sr. v.p., gen. coun., sec. Compaq Computer Corp., 1998—2002; of counsel Skadden, Arps, Slate, Meagher & Flom LLP; chmn. Martha Stewart Living Omnimedia, Inc., 2004—05, lead dir., 2005—. Bd. dirs., chmn. N.E. Legal Found; bd. dirs. Martha Stewart Living Omnimedia, Inc., 2003- Trustee Mass. Taxpayers Found., Merrimack Coll.; mem. New Eng. Legal Found.; mem. Houston cmty. adv. bd. Teach Am.; bd. dirs. Houston African-Am. Mus. Mem. ABA, Am. Corp. Counsel Assn., Assn. Gen. Counsel. Avocations: squash, skiing.

SIEKMANN, DONALD CHARLES, accountant; b. St. Louis, July 2, 1938; s. Elmer Charles and Mabel Louise (Blue) S.; m. Linda Lee Knowles, Sept. 10, 1966; 1 child, Brian Charles. BS, Washington U., St. Louis, 1960. CPA, Ohio, Ga. Regional mng. ptnr. Arthur Andersen & Co., Cin., 1960-98. Trustee Touchstone Group Mut. Funds, Riverfront Group Mut. Funds, Constellation Group Mutual Funds; exec. Duro Bag Mfg. Co. Columnist Cin. Enquirer, 1983-86, Gannett News Services, 1983-86; editor "Tax Clinic" column Tax Advisor mag., 1974-75. Mem. bd. Cin. Zool. Soc., 1985-88; officer, bd. dirs. Cin. Found. for Pub. TV, 1984-88, Cin. Symphony Orch., 1973-85, Cin. Ballet Co., 1973-88, Atlanta Symphony Orch., 1988-91, The Atlanta Opera, 1988-91, Cin. Theatrical Assn., Jewish Hosp., 1993—, Cin. Assn. for Performing Arts, 1992—, Cin. United Way, 1992-99, Cin. Pk. Bd. Found., 1995-98; pres. Greater Cin. Arts and Edn. Ctr., 1996-99; mem. Friends of Sch. for Creative and Performing Arts, 1996-99, Cin. Arts Festival, 1992-96, Ronald McDonald House, 1998—. Mem. AICPA, Ohio Soc. CPAs, Cin. Country Club (trustee 1983-88), Optimists Club (pres. Queen City chpt. 1986). Clubs: Cin. Country (trustee 1983-88). Lutheran. Home: 5495 Waring Dr Cincinnati OH 45243-3933 Office Phone: 859-581-8200. E-mail: dsiekmann@aol.com.

SIELICKI-KORCZAK, BORIS ZDZISLAW, political educator, investigative consultant; b. Wilno, Lithuania, Poland, Feb. 11, 1939; came to U.S., 1980; s. Wiltold and Antonina (Arciszewski) Sielicki-Korczak; m. Barbara Maria Kaniewski, May 29, 1971; children: Robert, Sandra. MSC, Warsaw U., 1964, Kunstindustriskole, Copenhagen, 1971; PhD, Basel U., Switzerland, 1973. Pres. Impolex Ltd., Copenhagen, 1970-79; field operative Europe CIA, 1983-90; pres., educator Anti-Soviet Rsch. Ctr., McLean, Va., 1981-84; export dir. Worldwide Investment Ltd., Arlington, Va., 1985-87; pres. Amexim Internat. Co. Ltd., Arlington, 1986-89, BK & Assocs., Arlington, 1990—, Boris S. de Korczak, Inc., Fairfax Station, Va., 1986—. Pres. R.R. Internat. Ltd., Copenhagen, 1983-89; mng. dir. Securitas Inc., Arlington, 1986-87; multiple appearance on U.S. and fgn. TV shows as expert on terrorism, USSR and Russian intelligence and its ops.; crime scene analyst, 1986—. Author: A Man From Atlantis, 1976; designer anti-drug poster. Dir. Nat. Lyric Opera Co., Washington, 1981-91; chief investigator Nat. Police Def. Found., 1995-98; legis. asst. to Congl. James A. Traficant, U.S. Congress, 2001-2003; sr. analyst 17th Dist. Ohio Congl. Office, Washington. Independent. Avocations: chess, classic music, travel, art, history. Home Phone: 703-503-3350. Business E-Mail: bkorczak@cox.net.

SIEM, PAULINE M., library director; b. Blue Earth, Minn., Nov. 24, 1954; d. Richard Ralph and Neva Theresa (Fischer) Quaday; m. Merlyn Richard Siem, June 30, 1983; 1 child, Steven Richard; m. Patrick Alois Malone, Sept. 20, 1975 (div. May 1981); 1 child, Jason Michael Malone. AA in Liberal Studies, Minn. State U., Mankato, 1991, BSBA (hon.) in Mgmt., 1996; MA in Libr. & Info. Sci., U. Wis., Milw., 2006. Cert. libr. Minn., 2000. Libr. circulation clk. Blue Earth Cmty. Libr., Minn., 1996—97, libr. adminstrv. aid, 1997—99, interim city libr. dir., 2000; interim office mgr. Blue Earth C. of C., 1998; county libr. dir., rotation libr. Faribault County Libr., Blue Earth, 1999—2005; libr. dir. Faribault County Blue Earth, 2005—. Children's program dir. Faribault County Libr., Blue Earth, 2000—, children's program craft instr., Bricelyn, Easton, Minn. Lake, 2003; team leader edn. com. Faribault County Local Redevelopment Agy., Blue Earth, 2001—03, strategic planner edn. com., 2001—03; fund raiser Libr. Friend, Bricelyn, Minn., 2004—05. Philanthropist Am. Liver Found., Mpls., 2001—04; philanthropist Mary V. Garver Scholarship, Chgo., 2004; philanthropist Miriam L. Hornback Scholarship, Chgo., 2004; educator MADD, Irving, Tex., 2003—05; philanthropist Faribault County Food Shelf, Blue Earth, 1983—2004, Blue Earth Cmty. Libr., Blue Earth, 1999, Faribault County Libr. Svc., Blue Earth, 2000—05, Faribault County Children's Toy Drive, Blue Earth, 2002—04, Faribault County Veterans Adminstrn., Blue Earth, 2003, KJLY Radio Sta., Blue Earth, 2003, Libr. Friend, Bricelyn, 2004, 700 Club, Va. Beach, 1998, Samaritan's Purse, Operation Christmas Child, Boone, NC, 2002—04, Living Word Christian Ctr., Brooklyn Park, Minn., 2003—. Pvt. e2 US Army, 1974—75, Texas. Recipient Merit award, Minn. State U., 1992. Mem.: ALA (assoc.), Soc. Am. Archivist (assoc.), Minn. Libr. Assn. (assoc.). Avocation: art. Home: 319 W 1st St Blue Earth MN 56013 Office: Faribault County Libr 120 S Main St Blue Earth MN 56013 Office Phone: 507-526-7182.

SIEMER, DEANNE CLEMENCE, lawyer; d. Edward D. and Dorothy J. (Helsdon) S.; m. Howard P. Willens; 1 child, Jason L. BA, George Washington U., 1962; LLB, Harvard U., 1968. Bar: NY 1968, DC 1969, Md. 1972, Commonwealth of No. Mariana Islands 1976. Economist Office of Mgmt. and Budget, Washington, 1964-67; assoc., then ptnr. Wilmer, Cutler & Pickering, Washington, 1968-77, 80-90; ptnr. Pillsbury, Madison & Sutro, Washington, 1990-95; mng. dir. Wilsie Co., Washington and Saipan, 1995—. Gen. counsel US Dept. Def., Washington, 1977—79; spl. asst. to sec. US Dept. Energy, Washington, 1979—80. Author: Tangible Evidence, 3d edit., 1996, National Security and Self-Determination: United States Policy in Micronesia, 1999, Corel Presentations for Litigators, 2000, PowerPoint for Litigators, 2000, Effective Use of Courtroom Technology: A Judge's Guide to Pretrial and Trial, 2001, An Honorable Accord: The Covenant Between the Northern Mariana Islands and the United States, 2001, Effective Use of Courtroom Technology: A Lawyer's Guide to Pretrial and Trial, 2002, Easy Tech: Cases and Materials on Courtroom Technology, 2002, The Patronus Technique: A Practical Proposal In Asbestos-Driven Bankruptcies, 2002, Power Point 2002 for Litigators, 2002, Basic Power Point Slides, 2003, Argument Slides, 2003, The Evidence Camera, 2004, Oral Histories of the Northern Mariana Islands: Political Life and Developments 1945-1995, 2004, The Digital Projector and Laptop Computer, 2005, PowerPoint 2003: 50 Great Tips for Better, Easier Slides, 2005, From the White House: Documents on the Northern Mariana Islands and Micronesia (1945-1995) Collected from the Presidential Libraries, 2005, The Secret Guam Study: The Documents, 2005, Asbestos Prepackaged Bankruptcies: Apply the Brakes But Retain Flexibility for Debtors, 2005, The Making of a Constitution: Northern Mariana Islands Conventions (1976-1996), 2006, Teaching Legal Strategy, 2007, Teaching E-Discovery, 2007. Mem. Lawyers Com. Civil Rights, Washington, 1973—; mediator US Ct. Appeals, Washington, 1988—; trustee Nat. Inst. Trial Advocacy, 1989—, Am. Law Inst., 1988—; arbitrator Atty. Client Arbitration Bd., 1990-, NASD, 2001-; mem. com. sci. and nat. security NAS, 2002-. Recipient citation Air Force Assn., 1977, Dist. Pub. Svc. medal Sec. of Def., 1979, Commendation Pres. of US 1981; grantee Nat. Endowment Humanities, Commonwealth of No. Mariana Islands Divsn. Hist. Preservation, No. Mariana Islands Coun. Humanities. Mem. DC Bar Assn. (Disting. Svc. award 2006), No. Marianas Bar Assn. Episcopalian. Business E-Mail: wilsieco@aol.com.

SIEMER, PAUL JENNINGS, public relations executive; b. St. Louis, Jan. 24, 1946; s. Robert Vincent and Pauline Mary (Nece) S.; m. Susan MacDonald Arnott, Aug. 26, 1967 Student, U. Notre Dame, 1964-67. Reporter South Bend Tribune, Ind., 1967-69; reporter St. Louis Globe-Democrat, 1969-76; account exec. Fleishman-Hillard Inc., St. Louis, 1976-79, v.p., sr. ptnr., 1979-84, exec. v.p., sr. ptnr., 1984-95; ptnr. Stolberg & Siemer Inc., St. Louis, 1995—. Mem. Pub. Relations Soc. Am. Roman Catholic. Home: 2961 Hatherly Dr Saint Louis MO 63121-4551 Office: Stolberg & Siemer Inc 818 Lafayette Ave Saint Louis MO 63104-3702 Office Phone: 314-436-6577.

SIEMON, JOYCE MARILYN, lawyer, writer; b. Bridgeport, Conn., Dec. 4, 1944; d. George Lewis and Rita (Siegel) Nissenson; m. Robert G. Cash, Oct. 7, 2001; 1 child, Alyssa Karen. BA in English, Carnegie Inst. Tech., 1966; JD with high honors, Fla. State U., Tallahassee, 1980. Bar: Fla. 1981. Tech. writer Computer Sci. Rsch. Ctr. Carnegie Inst. Tech., Pitts., 1966-67; tchr. Leesville Jr. HS, La., 1967-68; mag. editor VanTrump, Zeigler and Shane, Pitts., 1969; news editor Pitts. Press, 1970; staff writer Dade County Pub. Safety Dept., Miami, Fla., 1971-75; reporter North Dade Jour., Miami, 1977; freelance writer, 1977—; instr. legal writing and rsch. Coll. Law Fla. State U., Tallahassee, 1979-80; intern Fla. Supreme Ct., 1980; law clk. Office Gen. Counsel Fla. Dept. Gen. Svcs., Tallahassee, 1980; assoc. Young, Stern & Tannenbaum, P.A., North Miami Beach, Fla., 1981, Greenberg, Traurig, Askew, Hoffman, Lipoff, Quentel & Wolff, Miami, 1981—82, Hornsby & Whisenand, Miami, 1982-85; pvt. practice North Miami Beach, 1985-92, Boca Raton, Fla., 1992—. Editor: Lawrenceville: A Short History, 1969; columnist: Siemon Says North Dade Jour., 1977; contbr. articles to profl. jours. Mem. Dade County Coord. Network, 1983. Mem.: ABA, Dade County Bar Assn., Fla. Bar Assn., Internat. Platform Assn., Am. Jewish Congress (v.p. S.E. region), Am. Judicature Soc., Toastmasters Internat. (area gov. 2004—05), Kiwanis Internat., West Boca Toastmasters Club (pres. 2003—04), Order of the Coif, Phi Alpha Delta. Personal E-mail: gigininini@aol.com.

SIEMON-BURGESON, MARILYN M., education administrator; b. Whittier, Calif., Nov. 15, 1934; d. John Roscoe and Louise Christina (Secoy) Mason; m. Carl J. Siemon, Aug. 18, 1956 (div. Oct. 1984); children: Timothy G., Melanie A. Siemon Imes; Troy M.; m. James K. Burgeson, Jan. 24, 1987. BA, U. Redlands, 1956; MA, Pacific Oaks Coll., 1975; postgrad., Point Loma Coll., 1979—80. Cert. adminstr., elem. and early childhood tchr. Tchr. Sierra Madre Cmty. Nursery Sch., Calif., 1970—77; tchr. parent edn. and music Pasadena Unified Schs., 1977—79, project coord., 1980—82, tchr. curriculum resource dept., 1982—83, adminstr. Washington Children's Ctr., 1983—99; endorsed trainer High Scope Found. Register, 1990—; cons. staff devel. and tng. Pasadena. Trainer Program for Infant/Toddler Care; instr. Citrus Coll., 1996-98; conf. chair Calif. High Scope Educators, 1995-1997. Active Arcadia (Calif.) Bicentennial Commn., 1974-76; mem. policy coun. for cmty. housing svcs. Pasadena Head Start, 1992-95; life mem. Sierra Madre Sch. PTA; mem. Child Care Coalition, Pasadena; Altar Guild, lay Eucharistic minister St. Edmunds, San Marino, Calif., vestry mem., 2003-06. Ednl. Professions Devel. fellow Pacific Oaks Coll., Pasadena, 1969. Mem.: AAUW (pres. Arcadia br. 1973—74, 2007-, co-chair Math.-Sci. Conf. 1983, chair coll./univ. rels. 1988—, v.p. ednl. found. 1996—98, Calif. state divsn. program v.p. 2002—04, leadership devel. com. 2005—07, chmn. L.A. interbr. coun. program 2006—, chmn. 2006—, grantee 1982—83, Woman of Achievement award 2006), Calif. Child Devel. Adminstrs. Assn. (bd. dirs.), Women's Ednl. Leadership (asst. program v.p.), Child Care Info. Svc. (chair parent edn. and family affairs 1986—, bd. dirs.), Nat. Assn. Edn. Young Children (grantee 1970), Pasadena Women's City Club (dir. membership 2000—02, chmn.), Coun. Women's Clubs (pres. 1995—98), Pasadena Coll. Women's Club (pres. 2000—02, pres. Scholarship Found. 2002—04, corr. sec. 2007), Delta Kappa Gamma (pres. Omicron chpt. 1986—88, 1992—94, legis. chmn. Chi state area XIII 2005—). Republican. Episcopalian. Avocation: music. Home: 2266 Kinclair Dr Pasadena CA 91107-1022 Personal E-mail: mburgeson@earthlink.net.

SIEMS, BENNETT A., composer, performing company executive; s. William R. and Mary Louise Siems. BA, Brown U., 1990. Tchr. Princeton (N.J.) Day Sch., 1990—93; prin., owner Bennett Siems Tutoring, Ednl. Svcs., Mpls., 1993—, Willie Aug. Project, Mpls., 1998—. Composer (musician): Surrender to the Wind (named #1 new addition, XM Radio Real Jazz 70, 2006, Hon. Mention award City Pages Top 10 Minn. CDs, 2004), Twin Cities Jazz Society Jazz from J to Z, Shadow Chasers, (theatrical soundtrack) Maggie's Brain, Our Perfectly Wonderful Lives; composer: (co-choreographer, musician) Empire at Twilight (Meet the Composer, Inc. Creative Connections grant, 2005); composer: Dare to Dream (Am. Composers Forum, Harriet Tubman Ctr. Composer fellowship, 2001), Timescape, Off-Leash Area Movement Theater Co., 2006, 2007, Walker Art Ctr. Momentum Series, 2007; musician: Grand Marais Jazz Festival, Mainstage All-Star Guitar Summit; author: (scholarly essay) Brer Robert: The Bluesman and the African American Trickster Tale Tradition, in Southern Folklore. Nominee Six Minn. Music awards, Minn. Music Acad., 2000-2005; recipient Tchr. Recognition award for Outstanding Letter of Recommendation, Duke U., 1997, Outstanding Vol. Achieve. award, Sierra Club North Star Chpt., 2004, All-Time Top Fifty Daily Downloads award, All About Jazz web site, 2005; grantee, Meet the Composer, Inc., NYC, 2001, 2002, 2006, 2007, Am. Composers Forum, 2002. Mem.: ASCAP (ASCAPlus award 2000-2005, 2006), Am. Composers Forum (grantee 2006), Nature Conservancy, Phi Beta Kappa. Avocations: hiking, wilderness advocacy, canoeing, volleyball. Home Phone: 612-827-0966; Office Phone: 612-825-9952. Business E-Mail: willieaugust@hotmail.com.

SIEPI, CESARE, opera singer; b. Milan, Feb. 10, 1923; Operatic debut in Rigoletto, Schio, 1941, Il Nabucco, LaScala Opera, Milan, 1946, Don Carlo, Met. Opera, N.Y.C., 1950; soloist debut in, Carnegie Hall, N.Y.C., 1951; sang in Mozart and Verdi requiems, Edinburgh Festival, Albert Hall, London; leading bass at, Salzburg Festival, LaScala, Milan; appeared in: play Bravo Giovanni, 1962; appeared: play Vienna Staatsoper; made many opera recordings for, London Records. (Winner Nat. Singing Competition, Florence 1941, recipient Italy's Orfeo award 1956). Home: 12095 Brookfield Club Dr Roswell GA 30075-1261

SIEPMANN, JAMES PATRICK, research and development company executive, retired physician; b. Rochester, Minn., Jan. 16, 1960; s. Richard James and Mary Margaret Siepmann; m. Victoria Lynn Ewert, Sept. 4, 1982; children: Jeffrey Michael (dec.), Justine Nicole, Jennifer Ashley, Jessica Raquel, Joelle Kristina, Jarett James. BA, U. St. Thomas, St. Paul, 1982; MD, Mayo Med. Sch., Rochester, Minn., 1986. Diplomate Am. Bd. Family Practice. Resident in family practice Mayo Grad. Sch. Medicine, Rochester, 1986—89; pvt. practice Oshkosh, Wis., 1989—2000; founder, chmn. LightTime, Winnebago, Wis., 2000—. Med. dir. United Health Wis., Appleton, 1993-95; chmn. dept. family practice Mercy Med. Ctr., Oshkosh, 1992-94; team physician Lourdes H.S., Oshkosh, 1993-99. Editor Jour. Theoretics, 1999-2004. Founding pres. sch. bd. Oshkosh Area Cath. Sch. Sys. (now consol.), 1991-93 Mem. IEEE, AMA, Math. Assn. Am., Optical Soc. Am., Internat. Soc. Optical Engring., Wis. Med. Soc. (del. 1994-98, bd. dirs. polit. action com. 1994—99, Wis. Physician-Citizen of Yr. award 1993). Roman Catholic. Achievements include patents for humidifier and in the optoelectronic field. Avocations: inventing, theoretics, writing, computer science, collecting fine wines. Home: 2941 Prairie Wood Dr Oshkosh WI 54904-8478 Office: 3555 Moser St Oshkosh WI 54904 E-mail: siepmann@lighttime.com.

SIERACKI, ERIC P., diversified financial services company executive; BS in Econs., U. Pa. Mgr. Grant Thornton; sr. v.p. Countrywide Asset Mgmt. Corp., 1988—89; exec. v.p. corp. fin. Countrywide Fin. Corp., Calabasas, Calif., 1989—94, mng. dir., 1994—2002, sr. mng. dir. corp. fin., treas., & corp. develop., investor rels., 2002—05, exec. mng. dir., CFO, 2005—. Recipient Best Fin. Exec., Am. Bus. Awards, 2007. Office: Countrywide Fin Corp 4500 Park Granada Calabasas CA 91302-1613 *

SIERLES, FREDERICK STEPHEN, psychiatrist, educator; b. Bklyn., Nov. 9, 1942; s. Samuel and Elizabeth (Meiselman) S.; m. Laurene Harriet Cohn, Oct. 25, 1970 (div. Aug. 1990); children: Hannah Beth Alterson, Joshua Caleb. AB, Columbia U., 1963; MD, Rosalind Franklin U., 1967. Diplomate Am. Bd. Psychiatry and Neurology. Intern Cook County Hosp., Chgo., 1967-68; resident in psychiatry Mt. Sinai Hosp., NYC, 1968-69, assoc. attending psychiatrist Chgo., 1973-74; resident in psychiatry Rosalind Franklin U., North Chgo., Ill., 1969-71, chief resident, 1970-71, asst. prof., 1974-78, assoc. prof., 1978-88, dir. med. student edn., 1974—94, instr. psychiatry, 1973—; staff psychiatrist U.S. Reynolds Army Hosp., Ft. Sill, Okla., 1971-73. Cons. psychiatry Cook County Hosp., 1974-79, St. Mary of Nazareth Hosp., 1979-84, Gt. Lakes Naval Hosp., 1987-90, Jackson Park Hosp., 1987-89, Mt. Sinai Hosp., 1988—, Elgin Mental Health Ctr., 1997—; chief mental health clinic, North Chicago VA Hosp., 1982-85, chief psychiatry svc., 1983-85. Author: (wth others) General Hospital Psychiatry, 1985, Behavioral Science for the Boreds, 1987, rev. 2d edit., 1989, rev. 3d edit., 1993, USMLE Behavioral Science Made Ridiculously Simple, 1998; editor: Clinical Behavioral Science, 1982, Behavioral Science for Medical Students, 1993; mem. editl. bd. Acad. Psychiatry, 2000—; contbr. articles to profl. jours. Coach Glenview (Ill.) Youth Baseball, 1987-89, mgr. 1990 (age 10-12 Glenview World Series winner 1990), Glenview Tennis Club, 1986-90 (3.5 Men's Doubles League winner 1989-90). Maj. M.C., U.S. Army, 1971-73. N.Y.State Regents scholar, 1959-63; NIMH grantee, 1974-83, Chgo. Med. Sch. grantee, 1974-83; recipient Seymour Vestermark award NIMH/Am. Psychiat. Assn., 2003. Fellow Am. Psychiat. Assn. (disting. life fellow, 2006-, coun. edn. and career devel. 1993-95); mem. Ill. Psychiat. Soc. (fellowship com. 1985-99), Columbia Coll. Alumni Secondary Schs. Com., Assn. Dirs. Med. Student Edn. in Psychiatry (exec. coun. 1985-99, chmn. program com. 1987-88, treas. 1989-91, pres-elect 1991-93, pres. 1993-95, immediate past pres. 1995-99), Alliance for Clin. Edn., Am. Assn. Dirs. Psychiat. Residency Tng. (exec. coun. 2000-03, chair workforce coalition 2000-03), Sigma Xi, Alpha Omega Alpha, Phi Epsilon Pi. Office: Rosalind Franklin Univ Chgo Med Sch 3333 Green Bay Rd North Chicago IL 60064-3037 Business E-Mail: frederick.sierles@rosalindfranklin.edu.

SIEROCKI, JOHN STANLEY, oncologist; b. New Haven, 1947; MD, Hahnemann U., 1973. Diplomate Am. Bd. Internal Medicine, Am. Bd. Med. Oncology. Intern Hahnemann U., Phila., 1973—74, resident in medicine, 1974—76; fellow in med. oncology Meml. Sloan-Kettering Cancer Ctr., NYC, 1976—78; attending physician in medicine, hematology and med. oncology Med. Ctr. at Princeton, NJ, 1983—. Assoc. clin. prof. medicine U. Medicine and Dentistry N.J.-R.W. Johnson, 1985—. Named one of Top Drs. in N.Y. Metro Area, Castle Connolly, Top Drs. 2003, N.J. Monthly Mag. Office: Princeton Med Group 419 N Harrison St Princeton NJ 08540-3521 Home Phone: 609-575-4809; Office Phone: 609-924-9300. E-mail: jsierocki@princetonhcs.org.

SIERRA MEJIA, MAURICIO ANDRES, communications engineer; b. Armenia, Quindio, Colombia, Apr. 24, 1977; s. Guillermo Sierra Penagos and Stella Mejia Maya; m. Monica Andrea Rincon Barragan. BS in Biomed. Engring., U. Antonio Narino, Bogota, Colombia, 2001; BS Electronic Engring., U. El Bosque, Bogota, 1999; MS in Telecomm. Sys., U. Okla., Tulsa, 2005. Network engr. Teledifusion, SA, Bogota, 2000—03; adj. faculty prof. U. Los Libertadores, Bogota, 2002—03; rsch. asst. U. Okla., 2004—05; sr. network engr. Sci. Games Internat., Alpharetta, Ga., 2006—. Contbr. articles to profl. jours. Independent. Roman Catholic. Achievements include research in CWDM, EPON, next generation SONET/SDH. Avocations: travel, swimming, movies. Home: 1435 Deerfield Point Alpharetta GA 30004 Personal E-mail: andres.sierra@ou.edu.

SIES, TIMOTHY RAY, music educator; s. Terry R. and Marian D. Sies. MusB Edn., Wright State U., 2001; postgrad., Ohio State U. Cert. K-12 music tchr. Ohio. Student tchr. Huber Heights (Ohio) City Schs.; lead music educator Marburn Acad., Columbus, 2002—04; music dir. Bishop Ready HS, Columbus, 2004; dir. vocal studies North Coll. Hill City Schs., Cin., 2004—. Asst. tchr. Gospel Music Workshop of Am., New Orleans; musical instrument digital interface lab instr. Wright State U., Dayton, Ohio, 1999—2001; pvt. practice music theory tutor, voice tutor, trumpet tchr.; head coach jr. high wrestling North Coll. Hill City Schools, 2004—05, varsity wrestling head coach. Recipient Outstanding Service in Music award, Aley Meth. Ch., Music Edn. award, Wright State U., 1999; Juanita C. Burns scholar. Mem.: SW Ohio Wrestling Coaches Assn., Ohio Wrestling Coaches Assn., North Coll. Hill Edn. Assn., Ohio Edn. Assn., Ohio Music Edn. Assn., Music Educators Nat. Conf., Golden Key Internat. Honor Soc. (life), Kappa Delta Pi. Office: North Coll Hill City Schs 1620 W Galbraith Rd Cincinnati OH 45239 Home Phone: 513-337-5701; Office Phone: 513-931-8181.

SIESS, ALFRED ALBERT, JR., engineering executive, management consultant; b. Bklyn., Aug. 16, 1935; s. Alfred Albert and Matilda Helen (Suttmeier) S.; m. Gale Murray Scholes, Dec. 17, 1966; children: Matthew Alan, Daniel Adam. BCE, Ga. Inst. Tech., 1956; postgrad. in bus., Boston Coll., 1968; MBA, Lehigh U., 1972. With fabricated steel constrn. divsn. Bethlehem Steel Corp., Pa., 1958-76, project mgr. Pa., 1969-76, engr. projects and mining divsn. Pa., 1976-86; sr. cons. T.J. Trauner Assocs., Phila., 1986-87; assoc. S.T. Hudson Internat., Phila., 1987-90; dir. mktg. SWIN Resource Sys., Inc., Bloomsburg, Pa., 1989-90; mem. adj. faculty Drexel U., 1976-96. Weekly columnist Economic and Environmental Issues, East Pa. edit. The Free Press, 1981-86; co-patentee suspension bridge erection equipment. Founder S.A.V.E. Inc., Coopersburg, Pa., 1969, pres., 1970, 75, 81, bd. dirs. 1970—. Served with C.E., USN, 1956-58. Recipient Environ. Action award, S.A.V.E., Inc., 1975. Mem. ASCE (chmn. environ. tech. com. Lehigh Valley sect. 1971-83, life), Lions, Chi Epsilon. Republican. Mem. United Church of Christ. Home: 6460 Blue Church Rd Coopersburg PA 18036-9371 Office: C E Resource Group PO Box 39 Coopersburg PA 18036-0039 Office Phone: 610-965-3263. Business E-Mail: newmill05@earthlink.net.

SIEVING, PAUL A., federal agency administrator, ophthalmologist, educator; BS in Physics and History with honors, Valparaiso U., Ind., 1970, DS (hon.), 2003; MS in Physics, Yale U., New Haven, Conn., 1973; postgrad., Yale Law Sch., New Haven, Conn., 1974; MD, U. Ill. Med. Sch., 1978; PhD in Bioengring., U. Ill. Grad. Sch., 1980. Diplomate Nat. Bd. Med. Examiners, 1978, Am. Bd. Ophthalmology, 1983. Med. resident in ophthalmology U. Ill. Eye and Ear Infirmary, 1978—82; post-doctoral fellow in retinal physiology U. Calif., San Francisco, 1982—84; clin. fellow in retinal degenerations Harvard, Berman-Gund Lab, Mass. Eye and Ear Infirmary, 1984—85; asst. prof. ophthalmology U. Mich., Ann Arbor, 1985—89, assoc. prof., 1989—94, prof., 1994—2001, Paul R. Lichter prof. of ophthalmic genetics, 1990—2001; dir. Nat. Eye Inst., NIH, Bethesda, Md., 2001—. Chair Retinal Diseases NEI, Vision Rsch.: A Nat. Plan, 1999—2003. Named one of Best Drs. in Am., 1996, 1998, 2001, 2005; recipient Olga Keith Weiss scholar, 1989, Disting. Alumnus, Valparaiso U., 1991, Sr. Sci. Investigator award, 1998, Alcon Rsch. award, Alcon Rsch. Inst., 2000; James scholar, U. Ill. Med. Sch., 1978. Mem.: Nat. Acad. Scis. Inst. Medicine, Academia Ophthalmol. Internat., RP Found. Fighting Blindness (Sci. Adv. Bd. 1989—2001, vice-chair rsch. 1995—2001), Internat. Soc. Clinical Electrophysiology of Vision (tres. 1986—94), Am. Ophthal. Soc., Sigma Xi. Achievements include specializing in the treatment of human genetic retinal and macular degenerations and research to prevent blindness. Office: Nat Eye Inst NIH Bldg 31 6A03 31 Center Dr Bethesda MD 20892-2510

SIEVWRIGHT, JULIA ANN, elementary school educator; d. Ronald Irvin and Ann Julia Budd; m. Curtis James Sievwright, Mar. 31, 1982; children: Dane Wyatt, Drew Tanner. BS in Elem. Edn., U. Minn., 1992; MEd, St. Mary's U. Minn., 1999. Cert. tchr. Nat. Bd. Profl. Tchg. Standards, 2001. Tchr. elem. sch. Dist. 196, Eagan, Minn., 1992—. Founder, prin. PaW Print Pub., Eagan, 2002—. Fundraiser Shrine Children's Hosp., Minn., 1993—95. Mem.: ASCD. Office: Pinewood Community School 4300 Dodd Road Eagan MN 55123 Home Phone: 651-423-4656.

SIFF, MARLENE IDA, artist, designer; b. NYC; d. Irving Louis and Dorothy Gertrude (Lahn) Marmer; m. Elliott Justin Siff, July 11, 1959; children: Bradford Evan, Brian Douglas. BA, Hunter Coll., 1957. Cert. tchr. elem. edn., NY, NJ. Tchr. Stewart Manor (NY) Sch. Sys., 1957-59, Teaneck (NJ) Sch. Sys., 1959-60; freelance interior designer Westport, Conn., 1966-70; designer Varo Inertial Products, Trumbull, Conn., 1970; designer signature collections J.P. Stevens & Co. Inc., NY, 1974-78, J.C. Penney Co., NY, 1978, C.R. Gibson Co., Norwalk, Conn., 1980. Corp. sec., treas., bd. dirs. Belmar Corp., Westport, 1972—; chmn. bd. Marlene Designs Inc., Westport, 1973-77; owner Marlene Siff Design Studio, Westport, 1978—; aesthetic cons. Alcide Corp., Norwalk, 1980-88; art adv. coun. Herbert F. Johnson Mus. Art Cornell U., Ithaca, NY. One-person shows include David Segal Gallery, NYC, 1987, Conn. Pub. TV Gallery, Hartford, 1987, Paul Mellon Art Ctr., Choate Rosemary Hall, Wallingford, Conn., 1989, Conn. Nat. Bank Hdqs., Norwalk, 1990, Michael Stone Collection, Washington, 1992, Bergdorf Goodman Men, NYC, 1993, Joel Kessler Fine Art, Miami Beach, Fla., 1994, Park Pl., Stamford, Conn., 1995, Westport Arts Ctr., 1995, Mitchells, Westport, 1998, NIH, Bethesda, Md., 1999, Durst Lobby Gallery, NYC, 1999, Rosenthal Gallery at Rich Forum, Stamford, Conn., 2005, Walter Wickiser Gallery, NYC, 2007, exhibitions include Cheesebrough Pond's Gallery, Westport Arts Ctr., Conn., 1984-87, 1991, 1995, Conn State Cap. Bldg., 1990, Aldrich Mus., Ridgefield, Conn., 1991-92, Galleri Seven, Danbury, Conn., 1991, Funding Ctr., Alexandria, Va., 1992-93, Michael Stone Collection, Washington, DC, 1992-93, Am. Soc. Interior Designers Nat. Hqds., Washington, DC, 1992-93, Joel Kessler Fine Arts, Miami Beach, 1993-94, Wave Gallery, New Caanan, Conn., 1993-94, Galerie Début, Nagoya, Japan, 1993-94, Internat. Cancer Alliance, Nat. Inst. Health, Bethesda, Md., 1993, Boston Corp. Art, 1994, Art Miami Internat. Exposition, 1994, Share Gallery, Funibashi, Japan, 1995, Reece Gallery, NYC, 1995, Whitney Gallery, Westport, Conn., 1996, B'nai B'rith Klutznick Nat. Jewish Mus. Washington, DC, 1998, Studio Tour, Westport Arts Ctr., 2000, Kenneth Raymond Gallery, Boca Raton, Fla., 2001-06, River Rd. Gallery, Wilton, Conn., 2002-05, Hall-Brooke Behavioral Health Services Art Show, Westport, Conn., 2004, Bendheim Gallery, Greenwich, Conn., 2007; represented in permanent collections B'nai B'rith Klutznick Nat. Jewish Mus., Washington, 1997. Decorator Easter Seal Home Svc. Charity Ball, 1976; bd. dirs. United Jewish Appeal, Westport, 1982-86; com. mem. Levitt Pavillion of the Performing Arts, Westport, 1982-89. Recipient award for creating the most beautiful working environment in an indsl. facility in lower Conn., Lower Conn. Mfrs. Assn., 1970. Mem.: LVW, Am. Israel Pub. Affairs Com., Anti Defamation League, Nat. Coun. Jewish Women, Kappa Pi. Jewish. Avocations: tennis, swimming, race walking, gardening. Home: 15 Broadview Rd Westport CT 06880-2303 Home Phone: 203-227-4270. Office Fax: 203-227-4273. Business E-Mail: marlene@marlenesiff.com.

SIFFERT, JOHN SAND, lawyer, educator, writer; b. NYC, Mar. 26, 1947; s. Robert Spencer and Miriam (Sand) S.; m. Goldie Alfasi-Siffert, June 1, 1975; children: David Alfasi, Matthew Alfasi. BA, Amherst Coll., 1969; JD, Columbia U., 1972. Bar: N.Y. 1973, U.S. Dist. Ct. (so. dist.) N.Y. 1974, (ea. dist.) N.Y. 1974, U.S. Ct. Appeals (2d cir.) 1974, U.S. Supreme Ct. 1979. Law clk. to Hon. Murray I. Gurfein U.S. Dist. Ct. (so. dist.) N.Y., 1972-74; asst. U.S. atty. (so. dist.) N.Y., 1974-79; ptnr. Fulop & Hardee and predecessor firm Barovick, Konecky et al, NYC, 1979-83, Lankler & Siffert, NYC, 1983-84, Lankler Siffert & Wohl LLP, NYC, 1984—. Adj. prof. NYU, 1979—; adv. coun. procurement policy bd. City of NY, 1991-95; adv. bd. NY Civil Rights Coalition, 1995-; spl. master First Dept. Appellate Divsn., 1999—; mem. divsn. first dept. Indigent Def. Orgn. Oversight Com., 2003-2004; mem. appellate divsn. Dept. Disciplinary Com. 1st Jud. Dept., 2005—. Co-author: Business Crime, 1981, Modern Federal Jury Instructions-Criminal, Modern Federal Jury Instructions-Civil. Mem. adv. bd. N.Y. Civil Rights Coalition, 1995—; bd. dirs. N.Y. Lawyers for Pub. Interest, 1998—, sec., 2003—06, chair, 2006—. Fellow: Am. Coll. Trial Lawyers (chmn. com. on admission to fellowship 2001—04, chmn. N.Y. downstate com. 2004—06, bd. regents 2006—); mem.: ABA, N.Y. Coun. Def. Lawyers (bd. mem. 2004—), Fed. Bar Coun. (pres. Inns of Ct. 2001—02), Assn. Bar City N.Y. (chmn. fed. legis. com. 2003—06, exec. bd. 2006—), N.Y. State Bar Assn. Democrat. Jewish. Office: Lankler Siffert & Wohl LLP 500 5th Ave Fl 33 New York NY 10110-3398 Business E-Mail: jsiffert@lswlaw.com.

SIFFERT, ROBERT SPENCER, orthopedic surgeon; b. NYC, June 16, 1918; s. Oscar and Sadye (Rusoff) Siffert; m. Miriam Sand, June 29, 1941; children: Joan, John. AB in Biology with honors, NYU, 1939, MD, 1943. Diplomate Am. Bd. Orthrop. Surgery, Nat. Bd. Med. Examiners. Intern Kings County Hosp., Bklyn., 1943; resident in orthop. surgery Mt. Sinai Hosp., NYC, 1946-49, fellow in pathology, 1949-52, mem. staff, 1949—, attending orthop. surgeon, 1986—, dir. orthop. surgery, orthop. surgeon in chief, 1960-86, Lasker/Siffert Disting. Svc. prof., 1986—, chmn. emeritus, 1990—; pvt. practice NYC, 1949—. Sr. orthop. cons. N.Y.C. Dept. Health, 1952—60; attending orthop. surgeon Blythedale Children's Hosp., Valhalla, 1960—86, cons., 1986—90; dir. dept. orthops. City Hosp., Elmhurst, 1965—86; prof., chmn. dept. orthrops. Mt. Sinai Sch. Medicine, 1966—86, Dr. Robert K. Lippman prof., 1983—86, acting chmn., 1993—94, emeritus prof. and chair, 1986—. Author (with J. F. Katz): Management of Hip Disorders in Children, 1983; author: See How They Grow, 1985; contbr. articles to profl. jours. Bd. dirs., mem. profl. adv. com. Easter Seal Soc. Crippled Children and Adults, 1st v.p., 1977—79; mem. adv. bd. CARE-MEDICO, 1972—83, bd. dirs., chmn., 1981—83; bd. dirs. CARE, 1983—90; mem. adv. bd. Orthopaedics Overseas, 1981—93. Capt. USAAF, 1944—46, CBI. Decorated 4 Battle Stars; recipient Am. award in medicine, N.Y. Pub. Health Assn., 1956, N.Y. Philanthropic League, 1959, Richman award for humanism in medicine, Mt. Sinai Sch. Medicine, 1989, Lifetime Achievement award, NY Arthritis Found., 2004. Fellow: APHA, ACS; mem.: N.Y. State Med. Soc. (chmn. orthrop. sect. 1967—68), N.Y. Acad. Medicine (fellow orthop. sect. 1952, sec. 1962—63, chmn. 1963—64), Orthop. Rsch. Soc., Internat. Skeletal Soc., Internat. Soc. Orthop. Surgery and Traumatology, Assn. Bone and Joint Surgeons, Am. Acad. Orthop. Surgery (chmn. com. care handicapped child), Am. Orthop. Assn., Century Assn. (N.Y.C.), Phi Beta Kappa, Alpha Omega Alpha. Personal E-mail: rssiffert@aol.com.

SIFTON, CHARLES PROCTOR, federal judge; b. NYC, Mar. 18, 1935; s. Paul F. and Claire G. S.; m. Susan Scott Rowland, May 20, 1986; children: Samuel, Tobias, John. AB, Harvard U., 1957; LL.B., Columbia U., 1961. Bar: N.Y. 1961. Assoc. Cadwalader, Wickersham & Taft, 1961-62, 64-66; staff atty. U.S. Senate Fgn. Rels. Com., 1962-63; asst. U.S. atty. NYC, 1966-69; ptnr. LeBoeuf, Lamb, Leiby and MacRae, NYC, 1969-77; judge U.S. Dist. Ct. (ea. dist.) N.Y., Bklyn., 1977—, chief judge, 1995-2000, sr. judge, 2000—. Mem.: Bar Assn. City of NY. Office: US Dist Ct US Courthouse 225 Cadman Plz E Rm 244 Brooklyn NY 11201-1818

SIFTON, DAVID WHITTIER, retired magazine editor; b. NYC, Sept. 12, 1940; s. David William and Dorothy (Whittier) S. BA, Trinity Coll., Hartford, Conn., 1962; MA, Stanford U., 1967. Editor Inside Edn., N.Y. State Edn. Dept., 1968-70; adminstrv. editor Med. Econs., Oradell, NJ, 1970-72; editor Drug Topics, Oradell, 1972-75; editor in chief Current Prescribing, Oradell, 1975-78, RN mag., Oradell, 1978-83; dir. spl. editorial projects Med. Econs. Co., 1983-90; editor PDR Publs., Montvale, 1990—2003; ret., 2003. Founder Physicians' Desk Reference on CD-ROM, PDR's Drug Interactions and Side Effects Index, PDR's Indications Index, Pocket PDR (handheld electronic database), The PDR Family Guide to Prescription Drugs, The PDR Family Guide to Women's Health, The PDR Family Guide to Nutrition and Health, The PDR Family Guide to Lifelong Health, The PDR Family Guide Encyclopedia of Medical Care, The PDR Family Guide to Over-the-Counter Drugs, The PDR Family Guide to Natural Medicines and Healing Therapies, The PDR Family Guide to Common Ailments, The PDR Family Guide to Nutritional Supplements, The PDR Guide to Biological and Chemical Warfare Response, The PDR Drug Guide for Mental Health Professionals. Served to 1st lt. USAF, 1963-66. Decorated Air Force Commendation medal; grantee Ford Found., 1967 Mem. Am. Bus. Press (chmn. editorial com. 1975-76) Republican. Episcopalian. Personal E-mail: david.sifton@verizon.net.

SIFTON, SAM, editor; AB, Harvard U., 1988. Asst. editor Am. Heritage, 1988—90; media critic NY Press, restaurant critic, mng. editor; founding editor Talk Mag.; dep. dining editor NY Times, NYC, 2001, dep. culture editor, 2004—05, culture editor, 2005—. Tchr. NYC Pub. Schs., 1990—94. Office: Culture Editor NY Times 229 W 43rd St New York NY 10036 Office Phone: 212-556-7411. Office Fax: 212-556-1516.

SIGAL, ELLIOTT, pharmaceutical executive; BS in Indsl. Engring., MS in Indsl. Engring., Purdue U., 1973, PhD, 1977; MD, U. Chgo., 1981. V.p., co-founder Pritsker Assocs., 1973—75; clin. fellow, rsch. fellow pulmonary medicine U. Calif., San Francisco, 1984—88, instr. medicine, 1988—89, asst. prof. medicine, 1989—92, asst. dir. Cystic Fibrosis R & D prog., 1990—92; exec. dir. Ctr. Inflammation Rsch. Syntex, 1992—95; v.p. inflammation and immunology rsch. Roche Bioscience, 1995—96; pres., CEO Mercator Genetics, 1996—97; v.p. dept. applied genomics Bristol-Myers Squibb, 1997—99, sr. v.p. early discovery and applied tech., 1999—2001, mem. exec. com., 2001—, sr. v.p. drug discovery and exploratory devel., 2001—02, sr. v.p. global clin. and pharm. devel., co-chair brand devel. oper. com., 2002—04, exec. v.p., chief sci. officer, pres. R & D, 2004—. Asst. adj. prof. medicine U. Calif., San Francisco, 1992—94, assoc. adj. prof., 1994. Office: Bristol Myers Squibb 345 Park Ave New York NY 10154-0037 *

SIGAL, JILL LEA, nuclear energy industry executive, former federal agency administrator; b. 1961; m. Bob Muth; 1 child. BA, Vermont U.; JD, George Washington U. Pres. Jill Sigal Assocs.; adv. Office Gen. Counsel US Dept. Energy, dep. asst. sec. for environ. & sci., 2003—04, prin. dep. asst. sec., 2004—05, acting asst. sec. for cong. & intergovernmental affairs, 2005, asst. sec., 2005—07; sr. v.p. govt. rels. EnergySolutions, Salt Lake City, 2007—. Office: EnergySolutions 423 W 300 S Ste 200 Salt Lake City UT 84101 *

SIGAL, LEONARD H., physician; b. NYC, Aug. 26, 1951; s. Morris Lloyd and Theresa (Green) S.; m. Judith Halden, June 6, 1976 (div. May 31, 1981); m. Barbara K. Snyder, June 15, 1986; children: Merissa, Caroline SB, MIT, 1972; MD, Stanford U., 1976. Intern, resident Mt. Sinai Hosp., NYC, 1976-79; chief internal medicine Westchester Community Health Plan, White Plains, NY, 1979-81; fellow rheumatology Yale U. Sch. Medicine, New Haven, 1981-84, fellow immunology, 1982-84; chief rheumatology Syracuse (N.Y.) VA Med. Ctr., 1984-88; asst. prof. medicine and immunology SUNY Health Sci. Ctr., Syracuse, 1984-88; asst. prof. medicine UMDNJ - R.W. Johnson Med. Sch., New Brunswick, NJ, 1988—, asst. prof. molecular genetics and microbiology, 1988—91, prof., chief divsn. rheumatology, dept. medicine, 1991—2003; dir. Immunology Pharm. Rsch. Inst. Bristol-Myers Squibb, Princeton, NJ, 2003—. Speaker in field. Author (editor): Immunology to Inflammation: Basic Mechanisms and Clinical Consequences, 1990. Recipient Research Grant Arthritis Found., 1988, Research Grant Am. Heart Assn., 1989. Fellow ACP, Am. Coll. Rheumatology; mem. Am. Assn. Immunologists, Clin. Immunology Soc., Soc. Exptl. Biology and Medicine, MIT Club. Democrat. Jewish. Avocations: reading, tennis, sailing, photography, kayaking. Home: 26 Hastings Rd Belle Mead NJ 08502 Office: J3100 Pharm Rsch Inst Bristol Myers Squibb Rte 206 and Provinceline Rd PO Box 4000 Princeton NJ 08543-4000 Office Phone: 609-252-6050. Business E-Mail: leonard.sigal@bms.com.

SIGAL-IBSEN, ROSE, artist; b. Bucharest, Romania, Aug. 22; arrived in U.S., 1957; d. Joseph and Tilly (Eckstein) Cohen; m. Albert D. Sigal, Dec. 25, 1941 (dec. May 1970); 1 child, Daniel M.; m. Joseph Ibsen, Oct. 1973 Diploma, Fashion Inst. Technology, NYC, 1978; Parson, Sch. of Design, NYC, 1985—86; student, Koho Sch. of Sumi-E, NYC, 1979—90, Zhejiang Acad. Fine Arts, China, 1990. Curator Metro N.Y. Chpt. of Sumi-E Soc., 1990—, v.p., 1990—. One-woman shows include China-Gallery Weizhi Schubert, Hanover, Germany, 1991, Manhattan Savs. Bank, N.Y.C., 1993—94, Chem. Bank, 1993—95, N.Y. Pub. Libr., 1996, Bankers Fed., N.Y.C., 1996, Rep. Bank for Savs., 1996, Romanian Cultural Found., Bucharest, 1998, World Fine Art Gallery, N.Y.C., 1998, Romanian Embassy, Washington, 2000, Berkeley Coll. Gallery, 2006, others, numerous group shows including most recently, exhibited in group shows at Broome St. Gallery, NYC, 2001—02, 2005—06, Sumi-e Soc. Am. Inc. at Courthouse Galleries of Portsmouth Va., 2001 (Hallie Hazen Meml. award, 2001), Pen and Brush Ann. Mixed Media, 2002, Korean Cultural Ctr., L.A., 2002, Japanese Artists Assn. N.Y., 2002, Mobile Mus. Art, 2004, NY Hall of Sci., 2005, Hammond Mus., 2005, Keith and Janet Kelly U. Art Gallery, Calif. State Poly. U., Pomona, 2005, Courage Card design, 1998. Recipient Manhattan Arts award Cover Art Competition, N.Y.C., 1992, 94, 95, 97, King Point award, Fla., 1991, Tenth Japanese Internat. Calligraphy Exhbn. award, N.Y.C., 1996, Manhattan Arts Internat. Showcase award, Emily N. Hatch Meml. award Pen and Brush, Inc., Spring Watercolor Exhbn., 1998, Hallie Hazen Meml. award Sumi-e Soc. Am., Inc., 2001. Mem. Nat. Mus. of Women in the Arts, Artist Equity of N.Y., Am. Soc. Contemporary Artists, Art of Ink in Am., The Oriental Brushwork Soc. of Am., Sumi-e Soc. (hon.). Avocations: sculptor in clay, dance. Home: One Irving Pl Apt 2-22B New York NY 10003-9741 Office Phone: 212-979-2459.

SIGALL, HAROLD FRED, psychology professor; b. NYC, June 29, 1943; s. Walter and Regine (Goldenberg) S.; m. Brenda Ann Alpert, Aug. 8, 1965; children: Elana, Jennifer, Emily. BS, CUNY, 1964; PhD, U. Tex., 1968. Asst. prof. psychology U. Rochester, NY, 1968-72; assoc. prof. U. Md., College Park, 1972-78, prof., 1978—, dir. grad. program in social psychology, dir. grad. studies dept. psychology, 2000—, chair dept. psychology, 2006—; cons. editor Jour. Applied Social Psychology, 1992—. Cons. social rsch. and decision making to numerous orgns., lectr. Smithsonian Inst., Washington, 1984, 85; vis. prof. U. Bologna, 1997, 2002. Editor Personality and Social Psychology Bull., 1977-81. Bd. dirs. Columbia (Md.) Jewish Congregation, 1985-87, Howard County (Md.) Jewish Cmty. Sch., Columbia, 1986-87; mem. Human Rights Commn., Howard County, 1994-99. NDEA fellow, 1967-68, Danforth Found. fellow, 1970-71. Fellow APA, Am. Psychol. Soc.; mem. Soc. Exptl. Social Psychology. Home: 5060 Castle Moor Dr Columbia MD 21044-1871 Office: U of Md Dept Psychology College Park MD 20742-0001 Office Phone: 301-405-0424. Business E-Mail: hsigall@psyc.umd.edu.

SIGANGA, WALTER, physics professor; Asst. prof. U. Toledo, 1992—97, assoc. prof., 1997—2006; prof. So. Ill. U. Edwardsville, Ill., 2006—.

SIGEL, ANTHONY B., art conservator; Conservator objects Straus Ctr. Conservation, Harvard Art Mus., Cambridge, Mass. NEA Rome Prize Fellowship for Historic Preservation and Conservation, 2004—05. Office: Straus Ctr Conservation Harvard Art Museums 32 Quincy St Cambridge MA 02138

SIGEL, JOHN D., lawyer; b. 1953; BA, Middlebury Coll., 1975; JD, Cornell Univ., 1980. Bar: Mass. 1980. Ptnr., chmn. Bankruptcy & Comml. dept. Wilmer Cutler Pickering Hale & Dorr, Boston. Editor (mng.): Cornell Law Rev.; contbr. articles to profl. jours. Fellow: Am. Coll. of Bankruptcy; mem.: Mass. Bar Assn., Boston Bar Assn. Office: Wilmer Cutler Pickering Hale & Dorr 60 State St Boston MA 02109 Office Phone: 617-526-6728. Office Fax: 617-526-5000. Business E-Mail: john.sigel@wilmerhale.com.

SIGEL, MARSHALL ELLIOT, financial consultant; b. Hartford, Conn., Nov. 25, 1941; s. Paul and Bessie (Somer) Sigel; m. Sybil R. Miller, Nov. 23, 1995. BS in Econs., U. Pa., 1963; JD, U. Miami, 1982, LLM in Taxation, 1983. Exec. v.p. Advo-Sys. divsn. KMS Industries, Inc., Hartford, 1963—69, pres., 1969—72, Ad-Type Corp., Hartford, 1963—69, Ad-Lists, Inc., Hartford, 1963—69; fin. cons. Hartford, 1972—83, Boca Raton, Fla., 1987—; pvt. practice law, 1983—87. Bd. dir. Wharton Sch. Club S. Fla. Mem.: World Pres. Orgn., Fraternal Order Police Assocs., Boca Grove Club, 100 Club So. Palm Beach County. Home and Office: PO Box 273408 Boca Raton FL 33427-3408

SIGERSON, MARJORIE LORRAINE, librarian; b. Pitts., June 11, 1923; d. Roy Allen and Myrtle Mae (Bering) Parke; m. David Kinley Sigerson, Apr. 9, 1943 (div. Dec. 1985); children: Diane Parke, David Kinley. Student, Carnegie Inst. Tech., 1941—42, U. Pitts., 1942—43. Libr. Mus. Arts and Scis., Daytona Beach, Fla., 1963—, trustee, 1978—81, pres. Guild, 1978—79. Mem. com. Halifax Art Festival, 1963—99; mem. coun. Garden Clubs of Halifax Dist., 1965—67; charter mem. Ormond Beach (Fla.) Meml. Hosp. Aux., 1967—76; pres. Street Sch. PTA, New City, NY, 1958—59; leader Girl Scouts U.S.A., 1956—58. Recipient award for disting. svc., Mus. Arts and Scis., 1977, 1979, 1996, 2003, award, Fla. Assn. Mus., 2006. Mem.: Guild Mus. of Arts and Sci. (pres. 1978—79), Friendship Force of Daytona Beach, Cherry Laurel Garden Club (pres. 1966—67), Harvard Dames Club (sec. 1946—47). Presbyterian. Home: 210 Royal Dunes Blvd Ormond Beach FL 32176-4769 Office: Mus Arts & Scis 1040 Museum Blvd Daytona Beach FL 32114-4510

SIGETY, CHARLES BIRGE, investment company executive; b. NYC, Sept. 30, 1952; s. Charles Edward and Katharine Kinne (Snell) S.; m. Elizabeth Ross Pennington, Nov. 27, 1976; children: Austin Douglas, Katharine Colyer, Alexander Birge. BA in English Lit., Bates Coll., 1975. Lic. nursing home adminstr. Adminstr. in tng. Florence Nightingale Nursing Home, NYC, 1972, asst. dir. facility ops., 1975, dir. facility ops., 1975-78, assoc. adminstr., 1978-81, exec. dir., 1981-82; pres., CEO Profl. Med. Products, Inc., Greenwood, SC, 1982-96; pres. Upper Savannah Internat. Trade Assn., Greenwood, 1993; CEO Bison Investments, Inc., Tampa, Fla., 1996—, Aerial Machine & Tool Corp., Vesta, Va., 1998—2006, Polyten Plastics, LLC, Washington, 1998-2000, Coeur Acquisition, LLC, Washington, NC, 1999, Polyten, LLC, Washington, NC, 2000—03; mem. bd. advisors MD Internat., 2003—. Mem. adv. bd. Liberty Mut. Ins. Cos. S.C., 1986—96, NationsBank (Bank of Am.), Greenwood, SC, 1984—96; vice chmn. Upper Savannah Bus. Group on Health Care, 1981—87, S.C. Bus. Roundtable for the Initiative for Work Force Excellence, Columbia, 1988—92; dir. exec. com. Osteo Am., Inc., 1993—96; bd. advisors Capital South Ptnrs., 2004—06; pres. Petersburg Landing Devel., Inc., 2005—, Boonsborough, LLC, 2006—; mem. bd. adv. MD Internat., 1992—2000, 2003—. Bd. visitors Med. U. S.C., 1988; treas. YPO HealthCare Focus Forum, 1997; bd. dirs. Stewards Found., 2003-; active SIBF 1999-2006, DOCA 2004-. Mem. Health Industry Mfrs. Assn. (ofcl. rep. 1982-96, 99-2002), Upper Savannah Internat. Trade Assn. (pres. 1993), Young Pres.'s Orgn., Chief Execs. Orgn., World Pres.' Orgn., Def. Orientation Conf. Assn. Avocations: hunting, sailing. Office: Bison Investments Inc 3225 S Macdill Ave # 236 Tampa FL 33629-8171 Office Phone: 813-832-6359.

SIGETY, CHARLES EDWARD, lawyer, financial planner; b. NYC, Oct. 10, 1922; s. Charles and Anna (Toth) S.; m. Katharine K. Snell, July 17, 1948; children: Charles, Katharine, Robert, Cornelius, Elizabeth. BS, Columbia U., 1944; MBA, Harvard U., 1947; LLB, Yale U., 1951; LHD (hon.), Cazenovia Coll., 1994. Bar: NY 1952, DC 1958. With Bankers Trust Co., 1939-42; instr. adminstrv. engring. Pratt Inst., 1948; instr. econs. Yale U., 1948-50; vis. lectr. acctg. Sch. Gen. Studies Columbia U., NYC, 1948-50, 52; rapporteur com. fed. taxation for U.S. coun. Internat. C. of C., 1952-53; asst. to com. fed. taxation Am. Inst. Accts., 1950-53; with Compton Advt. Agy., NYC, 1954; vis. lectr. law Yale U., 1952; pvt. practice law NYC, 1952—67; pres., dir. Video Vittles, Inc., NYC, 1953—67; dep. commr. FHA, 1955-57; of counsel Javits and Javits, 1959-60; 1st asst. atty. gen. NY, 1958-59; dir., mem. exec. com. Gotham Bank, NYC, 1961—63; dir. NY State Housing Fin. Agy., 1962—63; chmn. Met. Ski Slopes, Inc., NYC, 1962—65; pres., exec. adminstr. Florence Nightingale Health Ctr., NYC, 1965—85; dir. Schaerer AG, Wabern, Switzerland, 1982-88; chmn. Kenbar Group, NYC, 1997—, Internat. Bioimmune Sys., Inc., Great Neck, NY, 1999—. Professorial lectr. Sch. Architecture, Pratt Inst., NYC, 1962-66; mem. Sigety Assocs., cons. in housing mortgage financing and urban renewal, 1957-67; ho. cons. Govt. of Peru, 1956; mem. missions to Hungary, Poland, Fed. Republic Germany, Malta, Czechoslovakia, Russia, Israel, Overseas Pvt. Investment Corp., 1990-92; owner, operator Peppermill Farms, Pipersville, Pa., 1956—. Bd. dirs., sec., v.p., treas. Nat. Coun. Health Ctrs., 1969-85; bd. dirs. Am.-Hungarian Found., 1974-76, Pritikin Rsch. Found., 1991—, Stratford Arms Condo Assn., 1992-93, 2002-, Global Leadership Inst., 1993—, Hepatitus B Found., Doylestown, 2005-; founding mem., bd. dirs., Natl. Assn. for Continence, 1982, trustee Cazenovia Coll., NY, 1981-2002, Delaware Valley Coll. Sci. and Agr., Doylestown, Pa., 1998-2005; trustee, v.p. Woodmere Art Mus. Phila., 2000-05, Navy Supply Corps Found., Athens, Ga., 2000—; del. White House Conf. on Aging, 1971, White House Conf. on Mgmt. Tng. and Market Econs. Edn. in Ctrl. and Ea. Europe, 1991; bd. visitors Lander Coll., U. SC, Greenwood, 1982-84; mem. fin. com. World Games, Santa Clara, 1981, London, 1985, Karlsruhe, 1989, The Hague, 1993, Confrerie des Chevaliers du Tastevin, Confrerie de la Chaine des Rotisseurs, Wine and Food Soc., Wednesday 10; chmn. Alumni Assn. Townsend Haris HS, NYC, 2005-. Lt. (j.g.) Supply Corps, USNR, 1942-46. Recipient President's medal Cazenovia Coll., 1990, George Washington laureate Am. Hungarian Found., 1996; named Prin. for Day, Townsend Harris HS NYC Bd. Edn., 1997-2001, 2006, Disting. Alumnus US Navy Supply Corps Sch., Athens, Ga., 1998; Baker scholar Harvard U., 1947. Mem. DOCA (Defense Orientation Conf. Assn.). Presbyterian. Personal E-mail: sigety@msn.com.

SIGETY, CORNELIUS EDWARD, real estate developer, director; b. NYC, June 6, 1958; s. Charles Edward and Katharine (Snell) Sigety; m. Virginia White, Oct. 28, 1995; children: Charles Edgar, Bradford Earle, Cornelia Ring. BA, U. Rochester, NY, 1980; MBA, Harvard U., Boston, 1985. Asst. adminstr. Florence Nightingale Health Ctr., NYC, 1980-83; v.p. Profl. Med. Products, Greenwood, SC, 1985-88; mng. dir. Kenbar Mgmt., NYC, 1988—. Bd. dirs. Heritage Conservancy. Mem. sch. bd. Buckingham Friends Sch., Lahaska, Pa. Mem. Union Club, Doylestown Country Club, Bay Head Yacht Club, Mantoloking Yacht Club. Presbyterian. Avocations: sailing, golf, skiing. Office: Kenbar Mgmt 1500 Lexington Ave New York NY 10029 Personal E-mail: cesigety@hotmail.com.

SIGETY, ELIZABETH DONNEM, lawyer; b. NYC, Apr. 8, 1964; d. Roland William and Sarah (Lund) Donnem; m. Robert Griswold Sigety; children: Sarah Katharine, William Hall, Elizabeth Brandon, George Lund. BA cum laude, Yale U., New Haven, 1986; JD, U. Chgo., 1989. Bar: Conn. 1989, NY 1990, Pa. 1997. Atty., assoc. Debevoise and Plimpton, NYC, 1989—97; atty. Antheil, Maslow and MacMinn, Doylestown, Pa., 1997—2004; ptnr. Fox Rothschild LLP, Warrington, Pa., 2004—. Asst. mng. dir., co-founder Del. Crossing Investor Group, Warrington, 2005—; co-chair franchising and distbn. group Fox Rothschild LLP, 2005—. Bd. mem. East Side Ho. Settlement, Bronx, NY, 1991—, exec. v.p., 2000—04; bd. mem., v.p. Child, Home and Cmty., Doylestown, Pa., 1999—2004; bd. mem. Village Improvement Assn., Doylestown, 2000—, Doylestown Hosp., 2004—06; chair ann. fund Buckingham Friends Sch., Pa., 2004—06; bd. mem. Doylestown Hosp. Found., Pa., 2006—. Mem.: Bucks County Bar Assn., Internat. Franchise Assn., NYC Bar Assn., Pa. Bar Assn., Am. Bar Assn., Montgomery County Bar Assn. (assoc.). Avocations: tennis, sailing, cooking, skiing. Office: Fox Rothschild LLP 2700 Kelly Rd Ste300 Warrington PA 18976 Home Phone: 215-795-2555; Office Phone: 215-918-3554. Business E-Mail: esigety@foxrothschild.com.

SIGGINS, JACK ARTHUR, university librarian; b. Arp, Tex., July 11, 1938; s. Wilbur McCulla and Dayle Marie (Hensley) S.; m. Maureen Ellen Sullivan, Sept. 1, 1984 BA, Princeton U., 1960; postgrad. law, U. Va., 1961-62; MA, Am. U., 1967, U. Chgo., 1969. Research analyst Library of Congress, Washington, 1965-66; Librarian Far Eastern Library, U. Chgo., 1968-70; head East Asia Coll. U. Md., College Park, 1970-75, asst. dir. libraries, 1975-77, assoc. dir. libraries, 1977-82; dep. univ. librarian Yale U., New Haven, 1982-92; pvt. practice orgnl. cons. New Haven, 1993-94; univ. libr. George Washington U., Washington, 1995—. Cons. Boston Coll. 1994, U. Mo., 1994, Harvard U., 1994, Nat. Libr. of Australia, 1993, Ctrl. Mich. U., 1993, Tulane U., 1993; advisor Md. Dept. Edn., Balt., 1978-82; mem. adv. com. Sch. Libr. Sci. So. Conn. State U., New Haven, 1981-88; vis. com. Princeton U. Libr., 1987-96. Contbr. articles to profl. jours. Served with US Army, 1961—64, Japan. Far Eastern Studies fellow Ford Found., 1966; Title II fellow U. Chgo., 1967-70; fellow Davenport Coll., Yale U., 1983-92. Mem. ALA (univ. libr. standards com. 1985-88), Beta Phi Mu. Clubs: Princeton (N.Y.C.). Office: George Washington U Melvin Gelman Libr 2130 H St NW Washington DC 20052-0001 Office Phone: 202-994-6455. E-mail: siggins@gwu.edu.

SIGH, ROBERT VIRGIL, public health physician; b. Houston, Aug. 9, 1964; s. Odea D. and Rosie L. Sigh; m. Miriam Lynette Sigh, July 21, 1991; 1 child, Caleb Robert. BA, Oakwood Coll., Huntsville, Ala., 1985; MPH, Loma Linda U., Calif., 1992, MD, 1996. Residency in family practice Fla. Hosp., Orlando, 1996—99; residency in preventative medicine, pub. health Loma Linda Univ., Calif., 1999—2000; med. dir. Adventist Whole Health Network, Reading, Pa., 2001—03, Margaret J. Weston Cmty. Health Ctr., Clearwater, SC, 2003—06; clin. dir., ready responder HRSA/NHSC, Rockville, Md., 2003—; with USPHS, 2003—. Recipient Crisis Response award, Health Rescue Svc. Adminstrn., Rockville, 2006. Mem.: Commd. Officers Assn., Rres. Officer Assn., Delta Sigma Phi. Avocations: saxophone, woodworking, hiking, camping. Home: 2066 Canada Falls Ct Lithonia GA 30058 Office Phone: 404-298-8998.

SIGLAIN, HELEN See DE LUCA, ANDREA

SIGLER, MARY ANN, investment company executive, accountant; BA, Calif. State Univ., Fullerton; M bus. taxation, Univ. So. Calif. CPA. Assoc. Ernst & Young LLP, 1980—87, ptnr. to sr. ptnr., 1987—2004; CFO Platinum Equity, Beverly Hills, Calif., 2004—. Office: Platinum Equity 360 N Crescent Dr Beverly Hills CA 90210 *

SIGLER, PAULETTE TERRY, music educator; d. Wallace Roland Terry, Jr. and Apphia Adele Terry; m. Thomas Burke Sigler, Feb. 28, 1976; children: James Adam, Catherine Adele. MusB in Edn., U. So. Miss., 1976; postgrad., Meredith Coll., 1989—92. Cert. tchr. Ga., 1998. Choir dir. Waynesboro (Miss.) So. Meth. Ch., 1980—88; tchr. Wayne Acad., Waynesboro, 1987—88; music tchr. band, chorus, voice Raleigh (N.C.) Christian Acad., 1989—92; dir. youth music Northside Bapt. Ch., Charlotte, NC, 1993—95; voice tchr. Johnson Ferry Bapt. Music Conservatory, Marietta, Ga., 1996—99; choral dir. Hightower Trail Mid. Sch., Marietta, 1998—2005; choral specialist Mt. Bethel Christian Acad., Marietta, 2005—. Singer and soloist Charlotte Choral Soc., 1994—95; chorus mem. Opera Carolina, Charlotte, 1995—96; founder Cantare Youth Choirs of St., 2005—; ind. cons. Choral Clinician; adj. voice tchr. Dir.: (choral performance-featured choir) Allegro Mixed Chorus Georgia Music Educator's Annual State Conf., Hightower Trail Mid. Sch. (Cert. of Appreciation, 2005), Allegro Treble Chorus Georgia Music Educator's Annual Conf. (Cert. of Appreciation, 2004); singer: (vocal performance) Concerto Performance with the Raleigh Symphony (Winner of Competition-Symphony Performance, 1992). Music provider for elder citizens Sunrise Assisted Living, Marietta, 2000—04; active Mt. Bethel United Meth. Ch., Marietta, 2003—05. Mem.: DAR, Profl. Assn. Ga. Educators, Am. Choral Dirs. Assn., Ga. Music Educator's Assn. (choral chair dist. 12 2002—05, music festival adjudicator and clinician 2004—). Republican. Avocations: swimming, acting, reading, skiing. Office: Mt Bethel Christian Acad 4385 Lower Roswell Rd Marietta GA 30068 Home Phone: 770-579-1606; Office Phone: 770-971-2880 ext. 234. Personal E-mail: paulettesigler@yahoo.com.

SIGLER, THERESA JANE, school system administrator; b. Marion, Ohio, Mar. 24, 1951; d. William Howard and Joanna Elizabeth Byrd; m. Timothy Joseph Sigler, July 11, 1981; 1 child, Andrew Joseph. BA summa cum laude, Walsh U., North Canton, Ohio, 1972; MA, U. Mo., Kansas City, 1979. Cert. elem. edn. K-8 Walsh U., 1972, reading edn. K-12 U. Mo., 1979, gifted edn. K-12 Ashland U., 1985, gen. supervision K-12 Ashland U., 1985, elem. prin. Ashland U., 1987, asst. supt. cert. Ashland U., 1988, supt. Ashland U., 1990. Tchr. grade 1 Sandy Valley Local Sch. Dist., Canton, Ohio, 1972—73; tchr. multiage 3/4 Ctr. City Sch., Dayton, Ohio, 1973—74; tchr. grade 6 St. Pius X, Reynoldsburg, Ohio, 1974—76; reading specialist Canton Local Sch. Dist., 1980—84; reading/lang. arts supr. Stark County Bd. Edn., Canton, 1984—86; dir. curriculum and staff devel. Barberton (Ohio) City Sch. Dist., 1986—2000, Woodridge Local Sch. Dist., Peninsula, Ohio, 2000—. Cons. Am. Book Co., NYC, 1976—80; adj. prof. Ashland U., Mussillon, Ohio, 1984—; presenter in field. Designed/developed (how to teaching audio visual vhs tape) Implementing and Integrating a New Language Arts Program at Grades K-8. Com. mem. United Way, Barberton, Ohio; mem. Barberton Head Start, 1996—2000, Decker Family Devel. Ctr., Barberton, 1996—2000; sec. Magical Theatre Co., Barberton, 1996—2000. Recipient Title I Program of the Yr. - Barberton City Schools, Ohio Dept. Edn. - Fed. Programs, 1994, Star Partnership award - Decker Family Devel. Ctr., Summit Edn. Initiative Found., 2000; grantee, Ohio Dept. Edn., 1986—2004, Barberton Found., 1996—2000; scholar, Kiwanis, 1970—72. Mem.: ASCD (assoc.), Internat. Reading Assn. (assoc.), Nat. Staff Devel. Coun. (assoc.), Ednl. Rsch. Svc. (assoc.), Delta Kappa Gamma (assoc.), Phi Delta Kappa (assoc.). Avocations: golf, reading, theater, bicycling, music. Home: 6516 Shenandoah Ave NW Canton OH 44718 Office: Woodridge Local Schools 4411 Quick Rd Peninsula OH 44264

SIGMAN, DANIEL M., geochemist, educator; BS in Geology with distinction, Stanford U., Calif., 1991; PhD in Oceanography, MIT/Woods Hole Oceanog. Inst., 1997. Harry Hess postdoctoral fellow dept. geosciences Princeton U., NJ, 1998—99, asst. prof. geosciences, 2000—06, prof., 2006—. Dusenbury preceptor Princeton U., 2004—06. Contbr. articles to sci. jours.; assoc. editor: Paleoceanography, 2004—. Recipient James B. Macelwane, Am. Geophys. Union, 2004, Friedrich Wilhelm Bessel award, Alexander von Humboldt Found., 2004, CAREER award, NSF, 2005. Office: Dept Geosciences Princeton U Guyot Hall Princeton NJ 08544 Office Phone: 609-258-2194. E-mail: sigman@princeton.edu. *

SIGMAN, STANLEY T., telecommunications industry executive; b. Lubbock, Tex. m. Gerry Lynn Sigman; 2 children. BBA, W. Tex. State U., 1970. Stockman Southwestern Bell Telephone, Hereford, Tex., 1965; exec. v.p. Southwestern Bell Mobile Sys., 1986—91, mng. dir., cellular and paging, SBC Comm., Teléfonos de México Mexico City, 1991—93, v.p., gen. mgr. Okla., 1993—94, exec. v.p., 1994—95, pres., CEO, 1995—99, group pres., SBC opers., 1999; sr. exec. v.p., svcs. Southwestern Bell Telephone Co., CEO, pres.; group pres., COO SBC Communications Inc., 2001—02; pres., CEO Cingular Wireless LLC, Atlanta, 2002—. Office: Cingular Wireless Glenridge Highlands Two 5565 Glenridge Connector Atlanta GA 30342

SIGMON, J. LEWIS, JR., medical educator; b. Newton, NC, July 8, 1940; MD, U. N.C., 1966. Intern David Grant USAF Hosp., 1966-67; resident Charlotte (N.C.) Meml. Hosp., 1969-71; chmn. dept. family medicine Carolinas Med. Ctr., Charlotte, 1984-95, clin. coord. Charlotte Ofcl Reg. Primary Care Edn., 1995—2001, sr. ind. cons. in grad. med. edn., family and ins. medicine, 2001—, dir. family medicine residency program Monroe, 1997—2001; prof. family medicine U. NC, 1993—2004, prof. emeritus, 2004—. Acad. coun. Nat. Inst. for Program Dir. Devel., Kansas City, Mo., 1999—2003; pres. Am. Bd. Family Medicine Found., 2000—07; residency rev. com. for family medicine ACGME, 1997—2003, specialist site visitor for residency rev. com., 2004—; step 3 test com. USMLE/NBME, 2005—. Recipient Disting. Svc. award, U. NC Sch. Medicine, 2005. Mem. AMA, N.C. Acad. Family Physicians, Am. Acad. Ins. Medicine. Personal E-mail: sigmonjr@aol.com.

SIGMON, JOYCE ELIZABETH, professional society administrator; b. Stanley, NC, Oct. 4, 1935; d. Rome Alfred and Pearl Elizabeth (Beal) S. BS, U. N.C., 1971; MA, Loyola U., 1980. Cert. assn. exec. Dental asst. Dr. Paul A. Stroup, Jr., Charlotte, N.C., 1953-63; instr. Wayne Tech. Inst., Goldsboro, N.C., 1963-65, Ctrl. Piedmont CC, Charlotte, 1965—69; dir. Dental Assisting Edn. ADA, Chgo., 1971-85, asst. sec. Coun. Prosthetics Svcs., 1985-87, mgr. Office Quality Assurance, 1987—90, exec. dir. Aux., 1990-92; dir. adminstrv. activities Am. Acad. of Implant Dentistry, Chgo., 1993—; exec. sec. Am. Bd. of Oral Implantology/Implant Dentistry, 1993-99. Deacon 4th Presbyn. Ch., 1973-75, elder 1975-77, 88-91, 2002-05, trustee, 1991-94; moderator Presbyn. Women in 4th Ch., 1987-91, Stephen min., 1997-99 Mem. Am. Soc. Assn. Execs., Chgo. Soc. Assn. Execs. (chair CAE com. 1991-92), Am. Dental Assts. Assn., N.C. Dental Assn. (pres. 1968-69), Charlotte Dental Assts. Soc. Presbyterian. Home: 260 E Chestnut St Chicago IL 60611-2401 Office: Am Acad Implant Dentistry 211 E Chicago Ave Chicago IL 60611-2637 Home Phone: 312-642-8242. Personal E-mail: jesigmon@aol.com.

SIGMOND, CAROL ANN, lawyer; d. Irwin and Mary Florence (Vollmer) S. BA, Grinnell Coll., 1972; JD, Cath. U., 1975. Bar: Va. 1975, D.C. 1980, Md. 1988, N.Y. 1990, U.S. Dist. Ct. (ea. dist.) Va. 1975, U.S. Dist. Ct. (so. and ea. dist.) N.Y. 1991, U.S. Ct. Appeals (4th cir.) 1976, U.S. Ct. Appeals (fed. cir.) 1987, U.S. Ct. Appeals (2d cir.) 2000, Fed. Claims Ct. 2002, Ct. Internat. Trade 2006. Asst. gen. counsel Washington Met. Area Transit Authority, 1978-85; acting assoc. gen. counsel for appeals and gen. law, 1985-86; assoc. Patterson, Belknap, Webb & Tyler, Washington, 1986-89, Berman, Paley, Goldstein & Kannry, NYC, 1991—93; prin. Law Offices of Carol A. Sigmond, NYC, 1993—97; of counsel Pollack & Greene, LLP, NYC, 1998—2000; pvt. practice NYC, 2000—03; ptnr. Kehl, Katzive, & Sigmond, NYC, 2004—05, Dunnington, Bartholomew & Miller, LLP, NYC, 2005—. Mem. ABA, DC Bar Assn., NY State Bar Assn. (House of dels. 2007—), Assn. Bar City NY, NY County Lawyers Assn. (chair constrn. law com. 2007-), Women's Nat. Dem. Club. Democrat. Avocations: piano, bridge. Office: Dunnington Bartholow & Miller LLP 477 Madison Ave 12th Fl New York NY 10022 Office Phone: 212-682-8811. Business E-Mail: csigmond@dunnington.com.

SIGMOND, RICHARD BRIAN, lawyer; b. Phila., Dec. 7, 1944; s. Joseph and Jean (Nissman) S.; children: Michael, Catherine, Alina; m. Susan Helen Peteraf, Dec. 24, 1984. BS, Phila. Coll. Textiles & Sci., 1966; JD, Temple U., 1969. Bar: Pa. 1969, U.S. Supreme Ct. 1973, U.S. Dist. Ct. (ea. dist.) Pa. 1975, U.S. Ct. Appeals (3d cir.) 1975, N.Y. 1982, D.C. 1995. Atty. Pub. Defender Assn., Phila., 1969-70; ptnr. Meranze, Katz, Spear & Wilderman, Phila., 1970-84; sr. ptnr. Spear, Wilderman, Sigmond, Borish & Endy, Phila., 1985-89, Jennings Sigmond, Phila., 1989—; gen. counsel Internat. Brotherhood Painters and Allied Trades, 1997-2000. Chmn., bd. dirs. Gatehouse Phila., 1972-83; lectr. Pvt. Industry Coun., Phila., 1985—, labor studies div., Pa. State U., 1978-82, 85-86; gen. counsel Stabilization Agreement, Sheet Metal Industry Trust Fund, 1994—, Internat. Painters and Allied Trades Industry Pension Fund, 1997—. Mem. ABA (labor law com., litigation com.), AFL-CIO (lawyers coordinating com.), Pa. Bar Assn. (labor law com.), Phila. Bar Assn. (labor com.), Phi Alpha Delta. Avocations: sailing, writing. Office: Penn Mutual Towers 510 Walnut St Fl 16 Philadelphia PA 19106-3601 Office Phone: 215-351-0609. Business E-Mail: r.sigmond@jslex.com.

SIGMUND, DIANE WEISS, judge; b. NYC, Mar. 1, 1943; BS, Pa. State U., 1963; JD magna cum laude, Temple U., 1977. Bar: Pa. 1977. Atty. Blank, Rome, Cominsky & McCauley, Phila.; judge U.S. Bankruptcy Ct. (Pa. ea. dist.), 3rd circuit, Phila., 1993—, chief judge, 2004—. Mem. steering com. Ea. Dist. Pa. Bankruptcy Conf., 1995—, 3d Cir. Task Force Equal Treatment in Cts., Gender Commn., 1995-97; chmn. endowment edn. Nat. Conf. Bankruptcy Judges, 1996—, bd. govs., 1998-2002; mem. com. on automation and tech. Jud. Conf. U.S., 1997-2004. Fellow Am. Coll. Bankruptcy. Office: Robert NC Nix Courthouse 900 Market St Rm 203 Philadelphia PA 19107-4237

SIGMUND, GREG S., investment company executive; M, St. Louis Univ. Securities analyst, REITs, utilities & household products A.G. Edwards, St. Louis, 1983—2002, asst. dir. securities rsch., 2002—04, sr. v.p., dir. rsch., 2004—. Named Best on the Street in REIT industry, Wall Street Jour., 2001. Office: AG Edwards 1 N Jefferson Saint Louis MO 63103 *

SIGNORILE, VINCENT A., lawyer; b. Jersey City, Mar. 22, 1959; s. Ralph R. and Rita (DeRosa) S. BS, St. Peter's Coll., Jersey City, 1981; JD, Seton Hall U., 1985. Bar: N.J. 1985, Pa. 1985. Aide Jersey City Mcpl. Coun., 1980-81, Office of Mayor, City of Jersey City, 1981; law clk. Corp. Counsel Jersey City, 1981-85; law sec. Superior Ct. N.J. for Hudson County, Jersey City, 1985-86; assoc. atty. Jersey City, 1986-89; ptnr. Signorile & Saminski, Jersey City, 1989-97; atty. Jersey City Zoning Bd. Adjustment, 1994-97, Bayonne City Ethics Bd., 1995-97; judge Jersey City Mcpl. Ct., 1996—, chief judge, 1999—2003. Elected mem. Hudson County Dem. Com., 1977-81, Jersey City Environ. Com., 1989-93, Jersey City Planning Bd. Com., 1991-93, Jersey City Ins. Fund Com., 1989-93; co-chmn. Hudson County Columbus Parade, 1984-85; elected to Mcpl. Coun. Jersey City, 1989-93. Mem. Hudson County Bar Assn., Univ. Club Hudson County (pres. 2003-04). Roman Catholic. Home: 1691 John F Kennedy Blvd Jersey City NJ 07305-1841 Office: Jersey City Municipal Ct 365 Summit Ave Jersey City NJ 07306

SIGNOROVITCH, DENNIS J., communications executive, educator; b. Norristown, Pa., July 23, 1945; s. James and Regina S.; m. Susan M. McLaughlin, 1968 (dec. 2002); children: James Edward, Sarah Elizabeth.

BS in Fgn. Svc., Georgetown U., 1967; MA, Old Dominion U., 1972. Instr. U. Toledo, 1972-77; writer/editor Doehler Jarvis div. NL Industries, Toledo, 1977-78; mgr. pub. rels. Eltra Corp., NYC, 1979, mgr. planning, 1980; various assignments AlliedSignal Corp., Morristown, N.J., 1980-92; v.p. pub. affairs AlliedSignal Inc., Torrance, Calif., 1992-98; v.p. mktg. and comm. AlliedSignal Aerospace, Torrance, 1998-99; v.p. comms. Honeywell Aerospace, 1999—2003; sr. counselor Hawthorn Group. Adj. prof. Mt. St. Mary's Coll., L.A.; program dir. Vantage Point Spkrs. Svc.; mem. Exec. Comm. Forum. With U.S. Army, 1967-70. Decorated Bronze Star with oak leaf cluster. Mem. The Conf. Bd. (corp. comm. coun. 1991), San Francisco Acad. (trustee), Aerospace Industries Assn. (chmn. comms. coun. 2001-02). Office: Hawthorne Group 1199 N Fairfax St Ste 1000 Alexandria VA 22314 *

SIGULER, GEORGE WILLIAM, diversified financial services company executive; b. Cleve., Apr. 26, 1947; s. John Frederick and Helen Alice (Popp) S.; m. Pamela Ann Mallon, Oct. 31, 1981; children: George William Jr., Emily Ann, Charles Arthur, Mary Elizabeth, Andrew Cooper. AB, Amherst Coll., 1970; MBA, Harvard U., 1972. Ptnr. Harvard Mgmt. Co., Boston, 1974-83; chief of staff HHS, Washington, 1983-84; exec. v.p. Monarch Capital Corp., Springfield, Mass., 1984-87, vice chmn. bd., 1987-91; pres. Associated Capital Investor, San Francisco, 1990-91; mng. dir. Mitchell Hutchins Instl. Investors, Inc., NYC, 1991-95; founder Siguler Guff & Co., 1995—. Assoc. treas. Harvard U., 1973-88; bd. dirs. Venture Lending and Leasing, Inc., Russia Ptnrs., L.P.; dir. Emerging Mkt. Pvt. Equity Assn., Rand Corp., Siguler Guff Distressed Oportunities Fund, Siguler Guff B.R.I.C. Opportunities Fund; mem. Bus. Forum, 1999—; mem. adv. bd. Rand Corp. Ctr. Asia Pacific Policy, 2004. Mem. vis. com. Harvard U. Med. Sch., Boston, 1986—; mem. nat. adv. com. on community health resources HHS, Washington, 1985-90; trustee Perkins Sch. Blind, Watertown, Mass., 1976-83, New Eng. Aquarium, 1989-91, Bement Sch., 1999-. Recipient Disting. Svc. award HHS, 1984. Republican. Presbyterian. Office: Siguler Guff & Co 825 Third Ave 29th Fl New York NY 10022

SIHLER, WILLIAM WOODING, finance educator; b. Seattle, Nov. 17, 1937; s. William and Helen Alice (Wooding) S.; m. Mary Elizabeth Unwin, Aug. 21, 1963; children: Edward Wooding, Jennifer Sihler Zysman. AB summa cum laude in Govt., Harvard U., 1959, MBA with high distinction, 1962, DBA, 1965. Instr., asst. prof. Harvard U. Bus. Sch., 1964-67; assoc. prof. Darden Grad. Bus. Sch., U. Va., Charlottesville, 1967-72, prof., 1972-76, A.J. Morris prof., 1976-84, Ronald E. Trzcinski prof., 1984—, assoc. dean acad. affairs, 1972-77; exec. dir. Bankers Assn. Fgn. Trade/Ctr. for Internat. Banking Studies, 1977-91; dir. Tayloe Murphy Ctr. U. Va. Bd. dirs. Curtiss-Wright Corp.; pres. Southeastern Cons. Group, Ltd. Coauthor: Financial Management: Text and Cases, 2d edit., 1991, The Troubled Money Business, 1992, Financial Service Organizations: Cases in Strategic Management, 1993, Cases in Applied Corporate Finance, 1994, Building Value with Capital-Structure Strategies, 1998, Financial Turnarounds--Preserving Value, 2001, Smart Financial Management: The Essential Reference for the Successful Small Business, 2004; editor: Classics in Commercial Bank Lending, vol. 1, 1981, vol. 2, 1985; contbr. articles to profl. jours. Vis. com. Sch. Mgmt., Case Western Res. U., 1976-86, bd. overseers, 1980-86. Recipient DeL. K. Jay prize Harvard U., Disting. Prof. award U. Va. Alumni Assn., 1982; C.J. Bonaparte scholar Harvard U.; Sheldon fellow 1955-60. Mem. Fin. Mgmt. Assn., Am. Econ. Assn., Am. Fin. Assn., Eastern Fin. Assn., Univ. Club (N.Y.C.), Harvard Club (N.Y.C.), Greencroft Club (Charlottesville), Phi Beta Kappa, Beta Gamma Sigma. Home: 3215 Heathcote Ln Keswick VA 22947-9160 Office: PO Box 6550 Charlottesville VA 22906-6550 Office Phone: 434-924-7489.

SIIROLA, JEFFREY JOHN, chemical engineer; b. Patuxent River, Md., July 17, 1945; s. Arthur Raymond and Nancy Ellen (Harris) S.; m. Sharon Ann Atwood, Apr. 24, 1971; children: John Daniel, Jennifer Ann. BS in Chem. Engring., U. Utah, 1967; PhD, U. Wis., 1970. Rsch. engr. Eastman Chem. Co., Kingsport, Tenn., 1972-74, sr. rsch. engr., 1974-80, rsch. assoc., 1980-88, sr. rsch. assoc., 1988-95, tech. fellow, 1995—. Trustee CACHE Corp., Austin, Tex., 1983—. Co-author: Process Synthesis, 1973. Appalachian tr. maintenance Eastman Hiking Club, Kingsport, 1973—. With US Army, 1970—72. Fellow AIChE (A.E. Marshall award 1967, Computing Practice award 1991, bd. dirs. 1999-2001, pres. 2005); mem. Nat. Acad. Engring., Accreditation Bd. for Engring. and Tech. (bd. dirs. 2006-), Am. Chem. Soc., Am. Soc. for Engring. Edn., Assn. for Advancement of Artificial Intelligence. Achievements include development of the AIDES chem. process flowsheet invention procedure. Home: 2517 Wildwood Dr Kingsport TN 37660-4748 Office: Eastman Chem Co 200 S Wilcox Dr PO Box 1972 Kingsport TN 37662-5150 Office Phone: 423-229-3069. Business E-Mail: siirola@eastman.com.

SIKANDER, SHAHZIA, artist; b. Lahore, Pakistan, 1969; BFA, Nat. Coll. Arts, Lahore, Pakistan, 1992; MFA, RISD, Providence, 1995. Artist-in-residence Otis Coll. Art and Design, LA, 2005. Work represented in numerous newspapers and mags., represented in solo and group exhibitions at MoMA, NY, Hirshhorn Mus. and Sculpture Garden, Nat. Gallery Canada, Musée d'Art moderne de la Ville de Paris, one-woman shows include Barbara Davis Gallery, Houston, 1996, Hosfelt Gallery, San Francisco, 1997, Deitch Project, N.Y.C., 1997, Renaissance Soc. U. Chgo., 1998, Kemper Mus. Contemporary Art and Design, Kansas City, Mo., 1998—88, Hirshhorn Mus., Washington, 1999, exhibited in group shows at Rhotas Gallery, Islamabad, Pakistan, 1992, Pacific Asia Mus., Pasadena, Calif., 1994—95, Bradford (Eng.) City Mus., 1996, Glassell Sch. Art Mus. Fine Arts, 1996, 1997, Laing Gallery, Newcastle, Eng., 1997, Whitney Mus. Am. Art, 1997, Queens Mus. Art, Flushing Meadows, N.Y., 1997, Yerba Buena Gardens Ctr. Arts, San Francisco, Forum for Contemporary Art, St. Louis, 1998, Bard Coll., Annandale-on-Hudson, N.Y., 1998, Ludwig (Austria) Mus., 1998, Aldrich Mus. Contemporary Art, Conn., 1998, also exhbns. in Portugal, Johannesburg, South Africa, Mexico City, Drawing to Drawing, Hosfelt Gallery, 2003, Vancouver Art Gallery, 2003, Venice Biennale, 2005, Queens Mus. Art, 2006. Recipient Haji Sharif award for miniature painting, Shakik Ali award and Kipling award, Nat. Coll. Art, Lahore, 1993; grad. fellow, RISD, 1993—95, core program fellow, Glassel Sch. Art Mus. Fine Arts, Houston, 1995—97, grantee, Louis Comfort Tiffany Found., 1997, Joan Mitchell grantee, 1998—99, MacArthur Fellow, John D. and Catherine T. MacArthur Found., 2006. Address: care Deitch Projects 76 Grand St New York NY 10013-2220

SIKER, EPHRAIM S., anesthesiologist; b. Port Chester, NY, Mar. 24, 1926; s. Samuel S. and Adele (Weiser) S.; m. Eileen Mary Bohnel, Aug. 5, 1951; children— Kathleen Ellen, Jeffrey Stephen, David Alan, Paul William, Richard Francis. Student, Duke U., 1943-45; MD, N.Y.U., 1949. Diplomate: Am. Bd. Anesthesiology (dir. 1971—, sec.-treas. 1974-82, pres. 1982-83) Nat. Bd. Med. Examiners. Intern Grasslands Hosp., Valhalla, N.Y., 1949-50, resident in anesthesia, 1950; resident dept. anesthesiology Mercy Hosp., Pitts., 1952-53, assoc. dir. dept., 1955-62, chmn., 1962-92; practice medicine, specializing in anesthesiology Pitts., 1954—; pres. Pitts. Anesthesia Assocs., Ltd., 1967-89; dir. anesthesia services Central Med. Ctr., Pitts., 1973-89. Courtesy staff St. Clair Meml. Hosp., Pitts., 1954—89; clin. prof. dept. anesthesiology U. Pitts. Sch. Medicine, 1968—; mem. exec. com. Am. Bd. Med. Spltys., 1978—81; Exch. cons. Welsh Nat. Sch. Medicine, Cardiff, 1955—56; mem. Pa. Gov.'s Commn. on Profl. Liability Ins., 1968—70; mem. adv. panel U.S. Pharmacopeia, 1970—76; mem. Am. Acupuncture Anesthesia Study Group NAS to Peoples Republic China, 1974; mem. adv. com. on splty. and geog. distbn. of physicians Inst. Medicine NAS, 1974—76; trustee Ednl. Coun. for Fgn. Med. Grads., 1980—82, Mercy Hosp. Found., 1983—95; bd. dirs., sec. Anesthesia Patient Safety Found., 1985—89, mem. exec. com., 1985—92, exec. dir., 1992—97. Author: (with F.F. Foldes) Narcotics and Narcotic Antagonists, 1964; sect. on narcotic: (with F.F. Foldes) numerous other publs. in med. lit. Ency. Brittanica. Served to lt. M.C. USNR, 1950-52. USPHS postdoctoral research fellow, 1954; hon. fellow faculty anaesthetists Royal Coll. Surgeons, Eng., 1974; hon. fellow faculty anesthetists Coll. Medicine South Africa, 1983; recipient Hippocratic award Mercy Hosp., 1982 Fellow Royal Coll. Surgeons Ireland, Faculty Anaesthetists (hon. 1988); mem. Am. Soc. Anesthesiologists (pres. 1973—, bd. dirs. Disting. Svc. award 1984), AMA (alt. del. 1962), Pa. Med. Soc., Allegheny County Med. Soc., Pa. Soc. Anesthesiologists (pres. 1965, Disting. Svc. award 1986), Royal Soc. Medicine (Eng.), Pitts. Acad. Medicine, Am. Coll. Anesthesiologists (bd. govs. 1969-71), World Fedn. Anesthesiologists (chmn. exec. com. 1980-84, v.p. 1984-88), Assn. Anesthesia Program Dirs. (pres. 1987-89), Japanese Soc. Anesthesiologists (hon.). Achievements include developing Siker Laryngoscope, 1956. Home: 185 Crestvue ManorDr Pittsburgh PA 15228-1814 E-mail: r.siker@msn.com. *If you have to tell someone who you are, then you probably aren't. People are measured by more than their deeds, and such estimations are frequently made on the basis of their inter-personal relationships. While achievement and effort usually bear a linear relationship to each other, the impact that the achiever has on society depends upon the impact he makes on individuals.*

SIKES, MARY TAGGART, librarian; b. Oceanside, Calif., Aug. 29, 1964; d. Billy Ray and Joycln Ruth Taggart; m. Clay Daniel Sikes, Dec. 17, 1995; children: Victoria Celeste, Zachary Daniel. AA, Weatherford Coll., Tex., 1984; BA, U. N. Tex., 1987, MLS, 1993. Receiving clk. Walden Books, Denton, Tex., 1986, asst. store mgr. Denton, Irving, Tex., 1986-90, store mgr. Sherman, Tex., 1990-93; reference libr. Ft. Worth Pub. Libr., 1993-95, reference asst. mgr., 1995-98, interlibrary loan supr., 1998—2007, periodicals/government docs. supr., 2007—. Big Bros. Big Sisters, Tarrant County; Junior Girl Scouts troop leader. Mem.: ALA, Tex. Libr. Assn. (alt. counselor interlibr. loan roundtable 1999—2000, counselor interlibr. loan roundtable 2001—03, mem. Woll meml. grant com. 2002—07, sec.-treas. 2003—04, vice chair interlibrary loan roundtable 2005—06, chair interlibr. loan roundtable 2006—07, chair PLD scholarship com. 2007), Phi Theta Kappa, Beta Sigma Phi. Republican. Home: 637 Catalpa Rd Fort Worth TX 76131 Office: Fort Worth Pub Libr 500 W 3d St Fort Worth TX 76102 Office Phone: 817-871-7733.

SIKES, MICHELLE M., health sciences scholar; d. Bonnie S. BS in Math. Econ., Wake Forest Univ., NC, 2007; MSc. student in Global Health Sci., Oxford Univ., 2007—. Named a NCAA All-American; Rhodes Scholar. Achievements include conducting health policy rsch. and designing alternative econ. models for the US organ donation system. Avocation: running. *

SIKLOS, RICHARD, reporter; Media editor BusinessWeek; editor-in-chief Inside mag.; corp. media reporter NY Times, 2005—07; media reporter Fortune, 2007—. Author: Shades of Black, 1995, Shades of Black: Conrad Black - His Rise and Fall, 2004. Office: Fortune 16th Fl 1271 6th Ave New York NY 10020 Office Phone: 212-556-1474. Office Fax: 212-556-1448.

SIKORA, CLIFFORD S., lawyer; b. Harrisburg, Pa., 1962; BS, Cornell Univ., 1984; MPA, Univ. Del, 1986; JD, Univ. Dayton, 1989. Bar: Pa. 1989, DC 1999. Adv. atty., office of gen. counsel, dept. elec. rates and corp. regulation Fed. Energy Regulatory Commn., 1989—91, supervising atty., office of gen. counsel, dept. elec. rates and corp. regulation, 1991—93, legal adv. to Commr. Donald F. Santa, Jr., 1993—95; counsel, com. on energy and natural resources US Senate, 1995—96; of counsel Troutman Sanders LLP, Washington, 1996—99, ptnr., energy group, 1999—, energy practice group leader, 2001—. Named to BTI Client Service All-Star Team for Law Firms, 2005. Office: Troutman Sanders LLP Ste 1000 401 Ninth St NW Washington DC 20004-2134 Office Phone: 202-274-2966. Office Fax: 202-654-5627. Business E-Mail: clifford.sikora@troutmansanders.com.

SIKOROVSKY, EUGENE FRANK, retired lawyer; b. Jackson, Mich., Nov. 27, 1927; s. Frank Joseph and Betty Dorothy (Malik) S.; m. Patricia O'Byrne, July 11, 1953; children: Paul, Charles, Catherine, Elizabeth, Emily. BSEE, U. Mich., 1948; LLB, Harvard U., 1951. Bar: N.Y. 1952, Va. 1970, Ill. 1978. Assoc. predecessor firms Cahill, Gordon & Reindel, 1954-63, ptnr., 1964-68; v.p., gen. counsel, dir. Reynolds Metals Co., Richmond, Va., 1969-76; gen. counsel Gould Inc., Rolling Meadows, Ill., 1977-79, v.p., 1977-81; dep. gen. counsel Bell & Howell Co., Skokie, Ill., 1981-83, v.p., 1983-88, gen. counsel, 1983-92, sec., 1984-92, sr. v.p., dir., 1988-92. Lt. USNR, 1951—54. Mem. Ill. State Bar Assn., Tau Beta Pi, Eta Kappa Nu, Phi Eta Sigma, Phi Delta Theta. Episcopalian. Home: 720 Grandview Ln Lake Forest IL 60045-3953 Personal E-mail: genesikor@earthlink.net.

SIKORSKI, GERRY, congressman; b. Breckenridge, Minn., Apr. 26, 1948; s. Elroy and Helen S.; m. Susan Jane Erkel, Aug. 24, 1974; 1 dau., Anne. BA with highest honors, U. Minn., 1970; JD with high honors, U. Minn. Law Sch., 1973. Bar: Minn. 1973, DC 1997. Mem. Minn. Senate, 1976-82, majority whip, 1980-82; mem. 98th-102nd Congresses from 6th Minn. dist., 1983—93; freshman whip 98th-99th Congresses; ptnr. Holland & Knight LLP, Washington, gov. sect. leader, former chmn. dirs. com., former chair, pub. law dept. Mem. Energy and Commerce Com., Post Office and Civil Service Com., Select Com. on Children Youth and Families; served with Chmn. John D. Dingell, Subcommittee on Oversight and Investigations; vice chair to Henry Waxman, Health and Environment Subcommittee; sponsor Clean Air Act. Author: Community Right to Know Law, Acid Rain Control Act. Mem.: ABA, DC Bar, Phi Beta Kappa. Office: Holland & Knight LLP 2099 Pennsylvania Ave NW Ste 100 Washington DC 20006 Office Phone: 202-828-5007. Business E-Mail: gsikorsk@hklaw.com.

SIKORSKI, JAMES ALAN, research chemist; b. Stevens Point, Wis., Nov. 9, 1948; s. John Paul and Florence Lucille (Wierzba) S.; m. Jeanne Delaney, Apr. 15, 1968 (div. 1975); 1 child, Christine René; m. Georgina Weber, Nov. 19, 1977. BS, Northeast La. State Coll., 1970; MS, Purdue U., 1976, PhD, 1981. With Monsanto Agrl. Co., St. Louis, 1976-91, sci. fellow, 1987-91, Monsanto Corp. Rsch., St. Louis, 1991-93; sci. fellow med. chem. G.D. Searle R&D, St. Louis, 1994-2000; sci. fellow med. chemistry Pharmacia Discovery Rsch., St. Louis, 2000—. Instr. organic chemistry St. Louis C.C., 1977-78; adj. prof. biochemistry Ctrl. Meth. Coll., 1995-97; invited spkr. tech. presentations and seminars. Contbr. chpts. to books, rev. articles, symposia-in-print and articles to profl. jours.; patentee and co-patentee in field. Mem. AAAS, Am. Chem. Soc. (St. Louis ACS award St. Louis Mo. sect. 1994, Kenneth A. Spencer award Kansas City Mo. sect. 1999, Internat. Soc. Heterocyclic Chemistry. Avocations: hiking, canoeing, skiing, photography, snorkeling. E-mail: james.a.sikorski@pharmacia.com.

SILAK, CATHY R., lawyer, former state supreme court justice; b. Astoria, NY, May 25, 1950; d. Michael John and Rose Marie (Janor) S.; m. Nicholas G. Miller, Aug. 9, 1980; 3 children. BA, NYU, 1971; M in City Planning, Harvard U., 1973; JD, U. Calif., 1976. Bar: Calif. 1977, U.S. Dist. Ct. (no. dist.) Calif. 1977, D.C. 1979, U.S. Ct. Appeals (D.C. cir.) 1979, U.S. Dist. Ct. (so. dist.) N.Y. 1980, Idaho 1983, U.S. Dist. Ct. Idaho 1983, U.S. Ct. Appeals (2nd cir.) 1983, U.S. Ct. Appeals (9th cir.) 1985. Law clk. to Hon. William W. Schwarzer U.S. Dist. Ct. (no dist.), Calif., 1976-77; pvt. practice San Francisco, 1977-79, Washington, 1979-80; asst. U.S. atty. So. Dist. of N.Y., 1980-83; spl. asst. U.S. atty. Dist. of Idaho, 1983-84; pvt. practice Boise, Idaho, 1984-90; judge Idaho Ct. Appeals, 1990-93; justice Idaho Supreme Ct., Boise, 1993—2000; ptnr. Hawley, Troxell, Ennis, and Hawley, 2001—. Assoc. gen. counsel Morrison Knudsen Corp., 1989-90; mem. fairness com. Idaho Supreme Ct. and Gov.'s Task Force on Alternative Dispute Resolution; instr. and lectr. in field. Assoc. note and comment editor Calif. Law Rev., 1975-76. Land use planner Mass. Dept. Natural Resources, 1973; founder Idaho Coalition for Adult Literacy; bd. dirs. Literacy Lab., Inc.; mem. adv. bd. Boise State U. Legal Asst. Program. Recipient Jouce Stein award Boise YWCA, 1992, Women Helping Women award Soroptimist, Boise, 1993. Fellow Idaho Law Found (ann., lectr.); mem. ABA (nat. conf. state trial judges jud. adminstrn. divsn.), Nat. Assn. Women Judges, Idaho State Bar (corp./securities sect., instr.), Am. Law Inst., Fellows of the Am. Bar Found, Am. Judicature Soc. (bd. dirs.). Office: Hawley Troxell Ennis & Hawley PO Box 1617 Boise ID 83702-1617

SILANO, LAWRENCE, music educator; b. Orange, NJ, Sept. 19, 1944; s. Lawrence and Mildred Silano; m. Karen Ann Vaughn, Aug. 25, 1978; children: Christian, Jason, Jessica. BA, West Liberty State Coll., 1966; MusM, W.Va. U., 1968. Cert. tchr. NJ, 1968. Music tchr. Wayne Bd. Edn., NJ, 1968—. Named an Outstanding Educator, Coll. NJ, 2001. Mem.: NRA. Roman Catholic. Avocations: pistol shooting, high power rifle, golf, tennis. E-mail: lsilano44@aol.com.

SILANTIEN, JOHN JOSEPH, music educator; b. Pawtucket, RI, Nov. 20, 1947; s. John and Lucy Helen Silantien; children: John Andrew, Ryan Danek. BA in Music Edn., Hartt Coll. Music, West Hartford, Conn., 1964—68; MusM, Cath. U., DC, 1968—71; MusD, U. Ill., Urbana, 1975—80. Soloist The U. S. Army Band, Washington, DC, 1968—71; choral, gen. music tchr. Andrew Jackson Jr. H.S., Suitland, Md., 1971—72; dir. choral activities Northwood H.S., Silver Spring, Md., 1972—75; asst. prof. Eastman Sch. Music, Rochester, NY, 1977—80; editor The Choral Jour., Lawton, Okla., 1992—98; music dir. San Antonio Symphony Mastersingers, 1983—; dir. choral activities U. Tex., San Antonio, 1980—; dir. choral music U. Presbyn. Ch., San Antonio. Lectr. in field. Contbr. articles to profl. jours. Specialist five US Army, 1968—71, Ft. Myer, Arlington, Va. Recipient, Fulbright-Hays Award, 1978—79; grantee, Rockefeller Found., 1973; scholar, Presser Found., 1964—65. Mem.: Tex. Choral Directors Assn., Tex. Music Educators Assn., Coll. Music Soc., Internat. Fedn. for Choral Music, Chorus Am., Am. Choral Directors Assn., Pi Kappa Lambda, Phi Mu Alpha Sinfonia. Office: Dept Music Univ Texas San Antonio TX 78249 Home Phone: 210-695-9579; Office Phone: 210-458-5328. Office Fax: 210-458-4381. Business E-Mail: john.silantien@utsa.edu.

SILAS, CECIL JESSE, retired petroleum company executive; b. Miami, Fla., Apr. 15, 1932; s. David Edward and Hilda Videll (Carver) S.; m. Theodosea Hejda, Nov. 27, 1965; children: Karla, Peter, Michael, James. BSChemE, Ga. Inst. Tech., Atlanta, 1953. With Phillips Petroleum Co., Bartlesville, Okla., 1953-94, pres. Europe-Africa, Brussels and London, 1968-74, mng. dir. natural resource group Europe/Africa London, 1974-76, v.p. gas and gas liquids div. natural resources group Bartlesville, 1976-78, sr. v.p. natural resources group, 1978-80, exec. v.p. exploration and prodn., minerals, gas and gas liquids, 1980-82, pres., chief operating officer, 1982-85, chmn., CEO, 1985-94. Bd. dirs. Boys/Girls Clubs Am., Atlanta, parton councillor Atlantic Coun. of the U.S.; bd. dirs. Okla. Found. for Excellence, Ga. Tech. Found.; trustee Frank Phillips Found. Served to 1st lt. Chem. Corps, AUS, 1954-56. Decorated comdr. Order St. Olaf (Norway); inducted into Ga. Inst. Tech. Athletic Hall of Fame, 1959, recipient Former Scholar-Athlete Total Person award, 1988; inducted into Okla. Bus. Hall of Fame, 1989; named CEO of Yr., Internat. TV Assn., 1987. Mem. Am. Petroleum Inst., U.S. C. of C. (past chmn. bd. dirs.), 25 Yr. Club, Phi Delta Theta. Avocations: fishing, golf, hunting. Office: PO Box 2127 Bartlesville OK 74005-2127

SILBER, JOHN ROBERT, retired academic administrator, law and philosophy educator; b. San Antonio, Aug. 15, 1926; s. Paul G. and Jewell (Joslin) S.; m. Kathryn Underwood, July 12, 1947 (dec.); children: David Joslin (dec.), Mary Rachel, Judith Karen, Kathryn Alexandra, Martha Claire, Laura Ruth, Caroline Jocasta. Postgrad., Northwestern U., 1944; BA summa cum laude, Trinity U., 1947; postgrad., Yale Div. Sch., 1948, U. Tex. Sch. Law, 1949; MA, Yale, 1952, PhD, 1956; L.H.D., Kalamazoo Coll., 1970; many others. Instr. dept. philosophy Yale U., 1952—55; asst. prof. U. Tex., Austin, 1955—59, assoc. prof., 1959—62, prof. philosophy, 1962—70, chmn. dept. philosophy, 1962—67, Univ. prof. arts and letters, 1967—70, chmn. (Comparative Studies Program), 1967, dean Coll. Arts and Scis., 1967—70; Univ. prof., prof. philosophy and law Boston U., 1971—, pres., 1971-96, prof. internat. rels., 1996—2003, chancellor, 1996—2003, pres. emeritus, 2003—. Vis. prof. Bonn U., 1960; fellow Kings Coll. U. London, 1963-64; bd. dirs. Mut. Am. Inst. Funds, Inc. Author: The Ethical Significance of Kant's Religion, 1960, Straight Shooting: What's Wrong With America and How to Fix It, 1989, Ist Amerika zu retten?, 1992; editor: Kant's Religion Within the Limits of Reason Alone, 1960, Works in Continental Philosophy, 1967—; assoc. editor: Kant-Studien, 1968-; contbr. to profl. jours. Chmn. Tex. Soc. to Abolish Capital Punishment, 1960-69; mem. Nat. Commn. United Meth. Higher Edn., 1974-77; exec. bd. Nat. Humanities Inst., 1975-78; trustee Coll. St. Scholastica, 1973-85, U. Denver, 1985-89, WGBH Ednl. Found., 1971-96, Adelphi U., 1989-97; bd. visitors Air U., 1974-80; bd. dirs. Greater Boston coun. Boy Scouts Am., 1981-93, v.p. fin., 1981-93, Silver Beaver award, 1989, Disting. Eagle, 1997; mem. Nat. Humanities Faculty, 1968-73, Nat. Captioning Inst., 1985-94; bd. advisors Matchette Found., 1969-70; mem. Nat. Bipartisan Commn. on Ctrl. Am., 1983-84, U.S. Strategic Inst., 1983-2001; Presdl. Adv. Bd. Radio Broadcasting to Cuba, 1985-92, v.p. 1984-98, vice chmn., 1998-2001; bd. dir. US Strategic Inst., 1983-2001, v.p., 1984-98, vice chmn., 1998-2001; adv. bd. Schurman Libr. of Am. Hist., Ruprecht-Karl U., Heidelberg, 1986—; mem. def. policy bd. U.S. Dept. Def., 1987-90; mem. internat. coun.advisors Inst. for Humanities at Salado, 1988—; bd. dirs. New Eng. Holocaust Meml. Com., 1989-95, Brit. Inst. of U.S., 1989—, Bette Davis Found., 1997—, Boston Police Found., 1997—; Dem. gubernatorial candidate of Mass., 1990; bd. dirs. U.S. Strategic Inst., 1983-2001, vice chmn., 1998-2001; bd. dirs., vice chmn. Americans for Med. Progress, 1992—, chmn., 1994-95, mem. exec. com. 1995—; chmn. Mass. Bd. Edn., 1996-99; bd. advisors Nat. Assn. Scholars. Recipient E. Harris Harbison award for disting. tchg. Danforth Found., 1966, Wilbur Lucius Cross medal Yale Grad. Sch., 1971, Outstanding Civilian Svc. medal U.S. Army, 1985, Disting. Pub. Svc. award Anti-Defamation League of B'nai B'rith, 1989, Horatio Alger award, 1992, Am.-Swiss Friendship award, 1991, Israel Peace medal, 1985, Ehrenmedaille U. Heidelberg, 1986, White House Small Bus. award for entrepreneurial excellence, 1986, Cross of Paideia, Greek Orthodox Archdiocese of North and South Am., 1988, Pro Bene Meritis award U. Tex., Austin, 1997; Fulbright rsch. fellow Germany, 1959-60; Guggenheim fellow Eng., 1963-64; decorated with Knight Comdr.'s Cross with Star of Order of Merit Fed. Republic of Germany, 1983; commandeur Nat. Order of Arts and Letters (France), 1985. Fellow Royal Soc. Arts; mem. Am. Philos. Assn., Am. Soc. Polit. and Legal Philosophy, Royal Inst. Philosophy, Am. Assn. Higher Edn., Nat. Assn. Ind. Colls. and Univs. (dir. 1976-81), Phi Beta Kappa. Office: Boston Univ 73 Bay State Rd Boston MA 02215-1708 Office Phone: 617-353-2208.

SILBER, MICHAEL H., neurologist; s. Wolf and Leila Silber; m. Sandra Feldman; children: Bradley, Taryn, Ryan. M.B.Ch.B., BS, U. Cape Town, South Africa. Neurologist, lectr. U. Cape Town, 1987—91; cons. neurologist Mayo Clinic, Rochester, Minn., 1991—; assoc. prof. neurology Mayo Clinic Coll. Medicine, Rochester, 1999—2005, prof. neurology, 2005—; assoc. dean acad. and faculty affairs Mayo Sch. Health Scis., Rochester,

2007—. Author: (textbook) Sleep Medicine in Clinical Practice; dep. editor: Jour. SLEEP, 2006—; contbr. articles to profl. jours. Recipient Helmut S. Schmidt award Meritorous Svc., Am. Bd. Sleep Medicine, 2000, Outstanding Physician Scientist award, Mayo Sch. Health Scis., 2002. Fellow: Am. Acad. Sleep Medicine (pres. 2006—07), Am. Acad. Neurology; mem.: Am. Bd. Sleep Medicine (pres. 2000—03), Am. Neurol. Assn. Office: Mayo Clinic Coll Medicine 200 1st St SW Rochester MN 55905 Office Phone: 507-266-7456.

SILBER, NORMAN JULES, lawyer; b. Tampa, Fla., Apr. 18, 1945; s. Abe and Mildred (Hirsch) Silber; m. Linda Geraldine Hirsch, June 10, 1979; 1 child, Michael Hirsch. BA, Tulane U., 1967, JD, 1969; postgrad. in bus. adminstrn., NYU, 1970—72. Bar: Fla. 1970, U.S. Dist. Ct. (so. dist.) Fla. 1975, U.S. Tax Ct. 1975, U.S. Ct. Appeals (5th cir.) 1975, U.S. Ct. Appeals (11th cir.) 1981. With legal dept. Fiduciary Trust Co. N.Y., NYC, 1969—72, asst. trust officer, 1971—72; exec. v.p. I.R.E. Fin. Corp., Miami, Fla., 1972—76; mng. atty. Norman J. Silber, P.A., Miami, 1973—85; ptnr. McDermott, Will & Emery, 1985—2001, Ruden, McClosky, Smith, Schuster & Russell, P.A., 2001—. Mem.: Fla. Bar (chmn. 11th jud. cir. grievance com. 1982—84). Republican. Jewish. Office: Ruden McClosky Smith Schuster & Russell PA 701 Brickell Ave Fl 19 Miami FL 33131 Office Phone: 305-789-2790. Business E-Mail: norman.silber@ruden.com.

SILBERBERG, DONALD H., neurologist; b. Washington, Mar. 2, 1934; s. William Aaron and Leslie Frances (Stone) S.; m. Marilyn Alice Damsky, June 7, 1959; children: Mark, Alan. MD, U. Mich., 1958; MA (hon.), U. Pa., 1971. Intern Mt. Sinai Hosp., NYC, 1958-59; clin. assoc. in neurology NIH, Bethesda, Md., 1959-61; Fulbright scholar Nat. Hosp., London, 1961-62; NINDB spl. fellow in neuro-ophthalmology Washington U., St. Louis, 1962-63; assoc. neurology U. Pa., 1963-65, asst. prof., 1965-67, assoc. prof., 1967-71, prof., 1971-73, acting chmn. dept., 1973-74, prof., vice chmn. neurology, 1974-82, chmn., 1982-94, sr. assoc. dean, dir. internat. programs, 1994—2004. Active staff U. Pa. Med. Ctr., Phila.; cons. Children's Hosp., Phila.; pres., CEO Betasteron Found., Inc., 1994—. Contbr. articles to profl. jours., abstracts, chpts. in books. Recipient grants in study of multiple sclerosis. Mem.: Global Network for Rsch. on Mental and Neurol. Health (founding v.p.), World Fedn. Neurology, Phila. Neurol. Soc. (pres. 1978—79), Assn. Univ. Profs. Neurology (pres.-elect 1993), Nat. Multiple Sclerosis Soc. (trustee 1997—99, 2001—03), Coll. Physicians Phila., Am. Soc. Neurochemistry, Am. Neurol. Assn., Am. Acad. Neurology, Alpha Omega Alpha. Office: U Pa Med Ctr Dept Neurology 3400 Spruce St Philadelphia PA 19104-4206

SILBERBERG, RICHARD HOWARD, lawyer; b. NYC, Feb. 20, 1951; BA, U. Wis., 1972; JD, NYU, 1975. Bar: NY 1976, US Dist. Ct. (so. and ea. dists.) NY, 1976, US Ct. Appeals (2d cir.) 1981, US Ct. Internat. Trade 1983, U.S. Ct. Appeals (fed. cir.) 1988, US Ct. Appeals (3d cir.) 1991, US Supreme Ct. 1994, US Ct. Appeals (11th cir.) 1996, US Ct. Appeals (1st cir.) 1997. Assoc. Delson & Gordon, NYC, 1975-83, ptnr., 1983—87; ptnr., trial group Dorsey & Whitney, NYC, 1988—, mng. ptnr., 1994—97, co-chair global trial group, 2004—06, chmn. global advocacy group, 2007—. Mem. panel arbitrators U.S. Dist. Ct. for Ea. Dist. N.Y., 1987-; mem. panel mediators US Dist. Ct. So. Dist. NY, 1992—; trustee Lawyers Com. Civil Rights Under Law, 1992-; dir. Fund Modern Cts., 1999-, High 5 Tickets to the Arts, 1999—, NYU Law Alumni Assn., 2002-06. Mng. editor NYU Jour. Internat. Law and Politics, 1974-75. Mem.: Am. Arbitration Assn. (mem. panel neutrals 1992—). Office: Dorsey & Whitney LLP 250 Park Ave New York NY 10177-0001 Office Phone: 212-415-9231. Office Fax: 212-953-7201. Business E-Mail: silberberg.richard@dorsey.com.

SILBERFARB, PETER MICHAEL, psychiatrist, educator; b. Jersey City, Oct. 28, 1938; m. Anne Wagner, 1962; children: Benjamin, Leah S. BS, Bucknell U., 1960; postgrad., NYU, 1960-61; MD, Hahnemann Coll., 1965; MA (hon.), Dartmouth Coll., 1986. Diplomate Nat. Bd. Med. Examiners, Am. Bd. Psychiatry and Neurology (pres. 1998). Intern Hahnemann Med. Coll. Hosp., Phila., 1965-66; resident in internal medicine Dartmouth Affiliated Hosps., Hanover, NH, 1966-68, resident in internal medicine and psychiatry, 1968-69, psychiatry resident, 1971-72, chief resident in psychiatry, 1972-73; instr. in psychiatry Med. Sch., Dartmouth Coll., Hanover, 1972-73, asst. prof. of psychiatry, 1973-77, dir. tng. and edn., 1976-86, assoc. prof. clin. psychiatry, assoc. prof. clin. medicine, 1977-80, dir. grad. edn. and residency tng., 1978-86, assoc. prof. psychiatry, assoc. prof. medicine, 1980-82, dir. tng. and edn., 1984—2002, prof. psychiatry, prof. medicine, 1986—2002, chmn. dept. psychiatry, 1986—2002, Raymond Sobel prof. psychiatry, 1993, prof. emeritus. Cons. psychiatrist Mary Hitchcock Meml. Hosp., Hanover, 1973—; dir. psychiat. in-patient svc. Dartmouth-Hitchcock Med. Ctr., 1973-75, dir. cancer psychiatry program Norris Cotton Cancer Ctr., 1975-2002, acting dir. psychiatry consultation svc., 1977-79, assoc. dir. cancer control Norris Ctr., 1981-86; sec. psychiatry com. Cancer and Leukemia Group B, 1976-79, vice chmn., 1979-2000; mem. grant rev. com. for cancer control Nat. Cancer Inst., 1979, 80, mem. spl. grant rev. com., 1981, 82, 85, cons. to bd. sci. counselors, 1982, mem. cancer control grant rev. com., 1986-90; vice chmn. adv. com. for psychosocial and behavioral rsch. Am. Cancer Soc., 1982-88, chmn., 1988-89; cons. collaborative ctr. for cancer pain relief WHO, Milan, 1985; mem. accreditation coun. for grad. med. edn. Appeals Bd. for Psychiatry, Chgo., 1983, specialist site visitor, 1985-90, mem. residency rev. com. for psychiatry, 1991-96; dir. Am. Bd. Family Practice, 1996-2000; mem. exec. com. Am. Bd. Med. Specialties, 1996-99. Author chpts. to books; mem. editl. bd. Jour. Psychosocial Oncology, 1983-91, Internat. Jour. Psychiatry in Medicine, 1986-90, Contemporary Psychiatry, 1987-91, Psychooncology, 1991-96; referee numerous manuscripts; contbr. articles to profl. jours. Surgeon USPHS, 1969-71. Fellow Am. Psychiat. Assn. (cons. to task force on treatment if psychiat. disorders 1989), Am. Coll. Psychiatrists; mem. AMA, Am. Soc. Psychiat. Oncology/AIDS, Am. Soc. Clin. Oncology, Am. Assn. Dirs. Psychiat. Residency Tng. (mem. curriculum com. 1979-88, mem. task force on med. students and residents, chmn. com. regional dirs. 1984-88, mem. exec. com. 1984-88), Am. Psychosomatic Soc., N.H. Psychiat. Soc. (chmn. membership com. 1974-76, chmn. continuing edn. com. 1977-79), N.H. Med. Soc., Assn. Rsch. in Nervous and Mental Disease, Assn. Acad. Psychiatry, Benjamin Rush Soc. Home: Bragg Hill Norwich VT 05055 Office: Dartmouth Coll Med Sch Dept Psychiatry Lebanon NH 03756-0001

SILBERG, JAY ELIOT, lawyer; b. NYC, Apr. 5, 1941; s. Arnold and Lillian (Liberman) S.; m. Ruth Vogel, June 22, 1975; children: Eric, Karen, Joanne. BA cum laude, Amherst Coll., 1963; LLB, Harvard U., 1966. Bar: N.J. 1966, US Dist. Ct. NJ 1966, US Ct. Appeals (DC cir.) 1970, US Ct. Appeals (7th cir.) 1982, US Supreme Ct. 1983, US Ct. Appeals (6th cir.) 1986, US Ct. Appeals (9th cir.), 1990, US Ct. Appeals (fed. cir.), 1997, US Ct. Appeals (11th cir.), 2000, US Ct. Appeals (2d cir), 2003, US Ct. Appeals (3d cir.) 2007. Atty. Office Gen. Counsel AEC, Washington, 1966-69; assoc. Shaw, Pittman, Potts & Trowbridge, Washington, 1969-72, ptnr., 1973—2005, Pillsbury, Winthrop, Show and Pittman, 2005—. Republican. Jewish. Home: 6109 Neilwood Dr North Bethesda MD 20852-3706 Office: Pillsbury Winthrop Shaw and Pittman LLP 2300 N St NW Washington DC 20037-1128

SILBERGELD, ARTHUR F., lawyer; b. St. Louis, June 1, 1942; s. David and Sabina (Silbergeld) S.; m. Carol Ann Schwartz, May 1, 1970; children: Diana Lauren, Julia Kay. BA, U. Mich., 1968; M in City Planning, U. Pa., 1971; JD, Temple U., 1975. Bar: N.Y. 1976, Calif. 1978, D.C. 1983, U.S. Ct. Appeals (2nd cir.), U.S. Ct. Appeals (9th cir.), U.S. Ct. Appeals (D.C. cir.), U.S. Supreme Ct. 1999. Assoc. Vladeck, Elias, Vladeck & Lewis, NYC, 1975-77; field atty. NLRB, LA, 1977-78; ptnr., head employment law practice group McKenna, Conner & Cuneo, LA, 1978-89; ptnr. Graham & James, LA, 1990-96; labor ptnr. Sonnenschein Nath & Rosenthal, LA, 1996-99; ptnr. Proskauer Rose LLP, LA, 1999—. Instr. extension divsn. UCLA, 1981-89. Author: Doing Business in California: An Employment Law Handbook, 2nd edit., 1997, Advising California Employers, 1990-95 supplements; contbr. articles to profl. jours. Founding mem. L.A. Mus. Contemporary Art; bd. dirs. Bay Cities unit Am. Cancer Soc., Calif., 1981-85, Jewish Family Svc., L.A., 1981-85, So. Calif. Employers Roundtable, Leadership coun., So. Poverty Law Ctr., Leadership Task Force, Drs. Without Borders; pres. Mo. Valley Fedn. of Temple Youth, 1959-60, Exec. Com., Calif. Com. South Human Rights Watch, 2005-; treas. L.A. Child Devel. Ctr., 2001-. Mem. ABA (labor and employment law sect.), L.A. County Bar Assn. (mem. exec. com. 1984-, chmn. labor and employment law sect. 1999-2000, trustee 2000-01), Mus. Modern Art (N.Y.C.), Coll. of Labor and Employment Lawyers. Office: Proskauer Rose LLP 2049 Century Park E Fl 32 Los Angeles CA 90067-3101 Office Phone: 310-557-2900.

SILBERGELD, ELLEN KOVNER, epidemiologist, toxicologist, researcher; b. Washington, July 29, 1945; d. Joseph and Mary (Gion) Kovner; m. Alan Mark Silbergeld, 1969; children: Sophia, Nicholas. AB, Vassar Coll., 1967; PhD, Johns Hopkins U., 1972. Kennedy fellow Johns Hopkins Med. Sch., Balt., 1974—75; scientist NIH, Bethesda, Md., 1975—81; chief toxics scientist Environ. Def. Fund, Washington, 1982—90; prof. epidemiology, toxicology and pharmacology U.Md., Balt., 1990—2001, affil. prof. environ. law, 1990—2001, dir. program in human health and environ., 1996—2000, prof. dept. pathology, 1995—2000, adj. prof. dept. pharmacology and exptl. therapeutics, 1995—2000; prof. environ. health scis. epidemiology, and health policy and mgmt. Bloomberg School Public Health, Johns Hopkins U., Balt., 2001—. Mem. sci. adv. bd. EPA, 1983—89, 1993—99, Dept. Energy, 1994—95; mem. bd. on environ. sci. and toxicology NAS-NRC, 1983—89; mem. Com. Geosci. Environ. and Resources, 1994—98; mem. bd. biotech. and agr., 1999—2004; mem. bd. sci. councellors Nat. Inst. Environ. Health Scis., 1987—93; cons. Oil and Chem. Atomic Workers, 1970, NSF, 1974—75, OECD, 1987—90. Mem. editl. bd.: Neurobehavioral Toxicology, 1979—87, Am. Jour. Medicine, 1980—, Neurotoxicology, 1981—86, Environ. Rsch., 1983—, editor-in-chief:, 1994—. Mem. Homewood Friends Meeting. Recipient Wolman award, Md. Pub. Health Assn., 1991, Barsky award, APHA, 1992, Md. Gov. Excellence citation, 1990, 1993; Fulbright fellow, London, 1967, Woodrow Wilson and Danforth fellow, 1967, NAS Exch. fellow, Yugoslavia, 1976, MacArthur Found. fellow, 1993—98, Baldwin scholar, Coll. Notre Dame. Mem.: APHA, AAAS, Soc. for Neurosci., Soc. Toxicology, Soc. for Occupl. and Environ. Health (sec.-treas. 1983—85, pres. 1987—89), Collegium Ramazzini (councillor), Delta Omega, Phi Beta Kappa. Office: Bloomberg Sch Pub Health 615 N Wolfe St Baltimore MD 21205

SILBERMAN, ALAN HARVEY, lawyer; b. Chgo., Oct. 22, 1940; s. Milton J. and Mollie E. (Hymanson) S.; m. Margaret Judith Auslander, Nov. 17, 1968; children: Elena, Mark. BA with distinction, Northwestern U., 1961; LLB, Yale U., 1964. Bar: Ill. 1964, U.S. Dist. Ct. (no. dist.) Ill. 1966, U.S. Ct. Appeals (7th cir.) 1970, (5th and 9th cir.) 1977, (D.C. cir.) 1979, (4th cir.) 1980, (11th cir.) 1981, (3rd cir.) 1982, (8th and 10th cirs.) 1993, U.S. Supreme Ct. 1978. Law clk. U.S. Dist. Ct., Chgo., 1964-66; assoc. Sonneschein Nath & Rosenthal, Chgo., 1964-71, ptnr., 1972—. Mem. antitrust adv. bd. Bur. Nat. Affairs, Washington, 1985—; mem. Ill. Atty. Gen. Franchise Adv. Bd., 1996—; bd. dirs., mem. exec. com. Mercaz, USA. Contbr. articles to profl. jours. Bd. dirs., v.p., sec. Camp Ramah in Wis., Inc., Chgo., 1966-86, pres., 1986-94; bd. govs. Northwestern U. Libr., 2004-; bd. dirs. Nat. Ramah Commn., Inc. of Jewish Theol. Sem. Am., N.Y.C., 1970—, v.p., 1986-94, pres., 1994-99, sr. v.p., 1999-2003; mem. U.S. del. 33d World Zionist Congress, Jerusalem, 1997, 34th World Zionist Congress, Jerusalem, 2002, 35th World Zionist Congress, Jerusalem, 2006; bd. dirs., mem. exec. com. Masorti Olami/World Coun. of Conservative Synagogues, 2002—, v.p. 2005, pres., 2005—; bd. govs. Jewish Agy. Israel, 2006-; mem. presidium World Zionist Orgn. Gen. Cou., 2006-. Mem. ABA (chmn. antitrust sect. FTC com. 1981-83, chmn. nat. insts. 1983-85, mem. coun. antitrust sect. 1985-88, fin. officer 1988-90, sect. del. ho. of dels. 1990-92, chmn.-elect 1992-93, chmn. 1993-94), Ill. Bar Assn. (chmn. antitrust sect. 1975-76), Northwestern U. 1851 Soc. (chair 1994-97), Lex Mundi Assn. Ind. Law Firms (bd. dirs. 2005—, vice chmn. com. antitrust competition and trade 1999-2003, internat. chair elect 2003-05, chair 2005—). Home: 430 Oakdale Ave Glencoe IL 60022-2113 Office: Sonnenschein Nath Ste 7800 233 S Wacker Dr Chicago IL 60606-6491 Office Phone: 312-876-8103. Business E-Mail: ASilberman@sonnenschein.com.

SILBERMAN, ENRIQUE, physicist, director; b. Buenos Aires, Dec. 9, 1921; came to U.S., 1966; m. 1949; 2 children. PhD in Engring., U. Buenos Aires, 1945. Investigator physics Argentina Atomic Energy Commn., Buenos Aires, 1953-58; head dept. Arg AEC, 1958-63; prof. U. Buenos Aires, 1963-66; prof. physics Fisk U., Nashville, 1966—; dir. photonic materials and devices NASA Ctr., 1992—. Guest prof. U. Notre Dame, 1963; cons. Arg Nat. Coun. Sci. Rsch., 1964; vis. prof. Vanderbilt U., 1967—. Mem. AAAS, Am. Assn. Physics Tchrs., Am. Phys. Soc., Arg Physics Assn. Office: Fisk U Dept Physics Nashville TN 37208-3051 Home Phone: 615-385-3584; Office Phone: 615-329-8620. Business E-Mail: esilber@fisk.edu.

SILBERMAN, H. LEE, public relations executive, consultant; b. Newark, Apr. 26, 1919; s. Louis and Anna (Horel) S.; m. Ruth Irene Rapp, June 5, 1948; children: Richard Lyle, Gregory Alan, Todd Walter. BA, U. Wis., 1940. Radio continuity writer Radio Sta. WTAQ, Green Bay, Wis., 1940-41; reporter Bayonne Times, NJ, 1941-42; sales exec. War Assets Adminstrn., Chgo., 1946-47; copy editor Acme Newspictures, Chgo., 1947; reporter, editl. writer Wichita Eagle, Kans., 1948-55; reporter Wall St. Jour., NYC, 1955-57, banking editor, 1957-68; 1st v.p., dir. corp. rels. Shearson-Hamill & Co., NYC, 1968-74; N.Y. corr. Economist of London, 1966-72; from contbg. editor to editor in chief Finance mag., 1970-76; from v.p., dir. to exec. v.p. Fin. Svcs. Group, Carl Boyir & Assos., Inc., NYC, 1976-86, exec. v.p., 1981-86; sr. counselor Hill & Knowlton, Inc., NYC, 1986-93, sr. v.p., 1993-96, sr. mng. dir., 1996; pres. LSA Media Cons., 1997—. Cons. in field. Contbr. articles to profl. jours. Capt. C.E. AUS, 1942-46. Recipient Loeb Mag. award U. Conn., 1965; Loeb Achievement award for disting. writing on fin. Gerald M. Loeb Found., 1968 Mem.: Soc. Profl. Journalists, Soc. Silurians, NY. Fin. Writers Assn., Deadline Club NY, Zeta Beta Tau. Republican.

SILBERMAN, JOHN ALAN, lawyer; b. Balt., Sept. 20, 1951; s. Ronnie A. and Dovera (Gogel) S. BA, Northwestern U., 1973; JD, Harvard U., 1976. Bar: N.Y. 1977, U.S. Dist. Ct. (so. and ea. dists.) N.Y. 1977. Assoc. Paul, Weiss, Rifkind, Wharton & Garrison, NYC, 1976-84, ptnr., 1985-96; pvt. practice NYC, 1996—. Bd. dirs., Pres.'s adv. coun. on the Arts John F. Kennedy Ctr., Washington, 1998—. Found. for Contemporary Performance Arts, N.Y.C., 1998—. Mem.: NY Bar Assn., NY City Bar Assn., Phi Beta Kappa. Office: 145 E 57th St New York NY 10022-2141 Office Phone: 212-319-3737. Office Fax: 212-319-8188. *

SILBERMAN, LARRY (LAURENCE HIRSCH), federal judge; b. York, Pa., Oct. 12, 1935; s. William and Anna (Hirsch) S.; m. Rosalie G. Gaull, Apr. 28, 1957 (dec. Feb. 23, 2007); children: Robert Stephen, Katherine DeBoer Balaban, Anne Gaull Otis. BA, Dartmouth Coll., 1957; LLB, Harvard U., 1961. Bar: Hawaii 1962, DC 1973. Assoc. Moore, Torkildson & Rice and Quinn & Moore, Honolulu, 1961-64; ptnr. Moore, Silberman & Schulze, Honolulu, 1964-67; atty. appellate divsn. gen. counsel's office NLRB, Washington, 1967-69; solicitor US Dept. Labor, Washington, 1969-70, under sec., 1970-73; ptnr. Steptoe & Johnson LLP, Washington, 1973-74; dep. atty. gen. US Dept. Justice, Washington, 1974-75; US amb. to Yugoslavia US Dept. State, Belgrade, 1975-77; mng. ptnr. Morrison & Foerster LLP, Washington, 1978-79, 83-85; exec. v.p. Crocker Nat. Bank, San Francisco, 1979-83; judge US Ct. Appeals (DC cir.), Washington, 1985—2000, sr. judge, 2000—. Lectr. labor law and legis. U. Hawaii, 1962—63; adj. prof. adminstrv. law Georgetown U., Washington, 1987—94, 1997, 1999—2001, NYU, 1995, 96, Harvard U., 1998; adj. prof. labor law Georgetown U., Washington, 2001, disting. visitor from the Judiciary tchr. adminstrv. law and labor law, 2002—; Pres.' spl. envoy on ILO affairs, 1976; gen. adv. com. on Arms Control and Disarmament, 1981—85; mem. Def. Policy Bd., 1981—85; vice-chmn. State Dept.'s Commn. on Security and Econ. Assistance, 1983—84. Bd. dirs. Com. on Present Danger, 1978-85, Inst. for Ednl. Affairs, 1981-85; mem US Fgn. Intelligence Surveillance Act. Ct. of Rev., 1996-2003; co-chmn. Commn. on Intelligence Capabilities of the US Regarding Weapons of Mass Destruction, 2004; vice chmn. adv. coun. on gen. govt. Rep. Nat. Com., 1977-80. With AUS, 1957-58. Am. Enterprise Inst. sr. fellow, 1977-78, vis. fellow 1978-85. Mem. Coun. on Fgn. Rels. *

SILBERMAN, ROBERT A. S., lawyer; b. Lebanon, Pa., Mar. 4, 1945; s. Henry T. and Genevieve (Mensh) S.; m. Nancy D. Netzer, Nov. 10, 1974. BA magna cum laude, Yale U., 1967; JD, Harvard U., 1970. Bar: Mass. 1970, Pa. 1984. Assoc. Csaplar & Bok, Boston, 1970—78, ptnr., 1978—90, Gaston & Snow, Boston, 1990—91, Edwards & Angell, Boston, 1991—2000, Israel & Silberman PC, Wellesley, Mass., 2000—. Mem. editl. bd. Managed Care Law Strategist, Am. Lawyer Media newsletter, 1999-2001. Citizens rev. com. United Way Mass. Bay, Boston, 1981-89; bd. dirs. All Newton (Mass.) Music Sch., 1994-96, v.p., 1995-96; bd. overseers Boston Baroque, 1998-2000, bd. dirs., chmn. bd. overseers, 2000-02, chmn. bd. dirs., 2003—. Mem. ABA (vice chmn. health law com. sect. bus. law 1992-95, chmn., 1995-99), Internat. Bar Assn., Boston Bar Assn., Phi Beta Kappa. Office: Israel & Silberman PC 15 Walnut St Ste 100 Wellesley MA 02481 Office Phone: 781-235-1500. Business E-Mail: rsilberman@israelsilberman.com.

SILBERSACK, JOHN WALTER, literary agent; b. NYC, Dec. 8, 1954; s. Walter Roy and Joan Small Silbersack; m. Elionora van Tyen Wilking, June 29, 1985; children: Nichols Clay, Johanna van Tyen, Catryn Center. AB, Brown U., 1977. Pub. dir. Roc Books Penguin Pub. Group, NYC, 1986—92; editor in chief Warner Aspect, Warner Books, NYC, 1992—93; sr. vice pres./pub. dir. Harper Entertainment/Harper Children's Entertainment, Harper Collins Publishers, NYC, 1993—99; exec. v.p. Trident Media Group, 2001—; sr. v.p. Epicom Media, NY, 2001—. Author: No Frills Science Fiction, 1983, Rogers Rangers, 1983; editor: The Berkley Showcase: New Writings in Science Fiction and Fantasy, 1980—83, The Magic of Christmas, 1992; contbr. introductions, revs. and literary criticism. Mem.: Trap Door Spiders, Sci. Fiction Writers Am., Thurs. Evening Club, Manhasset Bay Yacht Club (trustee 2006—), Century Assn. Home: 5 Harbor Road Sands Point NY 11050 Office: Trident Media Group 41 Madison Avenue New York NY 11050 Home Phone: 516-883-8456; Office Phone: 212-333-1513. Office Fax: 212-262-4849. Personal E-mail: quidnetma@aol.com. E-mail: jsilbersack@tridentmediagroup.com.

SILBERSACK, MARK LOUIS, lawyer; b. Cin., Dec. 27, 1946; s. Joseph Leo and Rhoda Marie (Hinkler) S.; m. Ruth Ann Schwallie, Sept. 7, 1985. AB, Boston Coll., 1968; JD, U. Chgo., 1971. Bar: Ohio 1971, U.S. Dist. Ct. (so. dist.) Ohio 1973, U.S. Ct. Appeals (6th cir.) 1974, U.S. Supreme Ct. 1975. Atty. Dinsmore & Shohl LLP, Cin., 1971—. Lectr. Ohio CLE Inst., Columbus, 1981-91. Co-author: Managed Care: The PPO Experience, 1990, Information Sharing Among Health Care Providers, 1994. Bd. dirs. United Way, Cmty. Chest, 1985-89, 2001—, chmn. pub. policy com., 1998—; vice-chmn. Ohio United Way, Columbus, 1989-94, chmn. bd. dir., 1994-96; pres. Hyde Park Neighborhood Coun., Cin., 1989-91, Hyde Park Ctr. for Older Adults, 1989-91; active Cin. Bd. Health, 1991-97, chmn., 1995-97; bd. dirs. Cath. Social Svc. of S.W. Ohio, 1998-2003, Children, Inc., 2003-; mem. Cincinnatus Assn., 2000—. Mem. ABA, FBA, Ohio State Bar Assn. (chmn. antitrust sect. 2005-07), Cin. Bar Assn., Cin. Assn., Cincinnatus Assn., Hyde Park Golf and Country Club. Republican. Roman Catholic. Avocations: reading, travel, theater. Home: 3465 Forestoak Ct Cincinnati OH 45208-1842 Office: Dinsmore & Shohl LLP 1900 Chemed Ctr 255 E 5th St Cincinnati OH 45202-4700 Home Phone: 513-321-1806; Office Phone: 513-977-8243. Business E-Mail: mark.silbersack@dinslaw.com.

SILBERSCHATZ, ABRAHAM (AVI SILBERSCHATZ), computer scientist, educator, researcher; arrived in US, 1968, naturalized; s. Joseph and Vera (Rosenblum) S.; children: Lemor, Sivan, Aaron. MS, SUNY, Stonybrook, 1973, PhD, 1976. From asst. prof. to assoc. prof. U. Tex., Austin, 1976-84, prof., 1984-96; v.p. Info. Sci. Rsch. Ctr. Bell Labs., Murray Hill, NJ, 1993—2003; Sidney J. Weinberg Prof., Dept. Computer Sci. Yale Univ., 2003—, also chmn., Dept. Computer Sci. Author: Database System Concepts, 1996, 2004 Operating System Concepts, 1998, 2005. Sgt. Israel mil., 1965-68. Recipient Pres. award, Bell Labs., 1998, 1999, 2004. Fellow IEEE (Taylor L. Booth Edn. award 2002), Assn. for Computing Machinery (Carl V. Karlstrom Educator of Yr. award 1999, SIGMOD Contbn. award 1997). Jewish. Achievements include 48 patents. Office: Yale Univ Dept Computer Sci PO Box 208285 New Haven CT 06520-8285 Office Fax: 203-436-4918.

SILBERSTEIN, ALAN MARK, financial services executive; b. Munich, Dec. 22, 1947; came to U.S., 1949; s. Leon and Rose S.; m. Carol Krongold, Aug. 30, 1970; children: Eric, Adam, Meredith. BS in Engring., Columbia U., 1969; MBA, Harvard U., 1972. Design engr. Ford Motor Co., Dearborn, Mich., 1969-70; budget analyst N.Y.C. Bur. of Budget, 1972-74; various positions Chem. Bank, NYC, 1974-88, exec. v.p., head Consumer Banking Group, 1990-92; exec. v.p. and dir. of retail banking Midlantic Corp., Edison, N.J., 1992-95; CEO claims divsn. Travelers Property Casualty Corp., Hartford, Conn., 1995-96, exec. v.p., 1997-98; pres. Allston Assocs., 1998—; pres., CEO Western Union Fin. Svcs., Inc., 2000—01. Bd. dirs. global Payments Inc., Capital Access Network, Debt Resolve, Inc. Trustee Tenafly Bd. Edn., N.J., 1983-86, Yeshiva U. Sy Syms Sch. Bus., 1989—; mem. consumer adv. coun. Fed. Res. Bd., 1989-91; bd. dirs. N.Y. State Tree Consortium Inc., 1990-92; mem. exec. No. N.J. Boy Scouts Am., 1992-2003; adv. coun. Columbia U. Sch. Engring., 1998-2004. Mem. Am. Bankers Assn. (chmn. retail banking exec. com. 1992—), Harvard Bus. Sch. Club N.Y. (sec. 1981-85, bd. dirs. 1982-83, 85-88), Coun. Fgn. Rels., Bus. Execs. for Nat. Security.

SILBERSTEIN, EDWARD BERNARD, nuclear medicine educator, oncologist, researcher; b. Cin., Sept. 3, 1936; s. Bernard Gumpert and Harriet Louise (Kahn) S.; m. Jacqueline Rose Mervis, Oct. 2, 1988; children: Scott, Lisa. BS magna cum laude, Yale U., 1958; MD, Harvard U., 1962; postgrad. in art history, U. Cin. Bd. cert. in Internal Medicine, Hematology, Nuclear Medicine, Med. Oncology Am. Bd. Internal Medicine. Intern Cin. Gen. Hosp., 1962—63, resident in internal medicine, 1963—64; resident Univ. Hosps. Cleve., 1966—67; NIH fellow in hematology New Eng. Med. Ctr., Boston, 1967—68; asst. prof. radiol. medicine U. Cin. Med. Ctr., 1968—72, assoc. prof. radiol. medicine, 1972—76, prof. radiol. medicine, 1976—. Eugene L. and Sue R. Saenger prof. radiol. scis., 1998—2000, prof. emeritus of radiology and medicine, 2000—. Assoc. dir. E.L. Saenger Radioisotope Lab., 1980—; chmn. Environ. Safety Health Com. Dept. Energy Fernald Facility, 1986-91; mem. U.S. Pharmacopeia Com. of Revision, 1990—; mem. Nat. Coun. on Radiation Protection and

Measurement, 1997—; cons. Nuc. Regulatory Commn., 1988—; dir. divsn. nuc. medicine Jewish Hosp., 1976-95; cancer pain panel Agy. for Health Care Planning and Rsch., 1992-93; mem. Am. Nuclear Soc. Com. on Isotope Assurance, 2003-05; vis. prof. various lecturerships; reviewer in field. Author: Differential Diagnosis in Nuclear Medicine, 1984, Bone Scintigraphy, 1984, Diagnostic Patterns in Nuclear Medicine, 1998; contbr. articles to profl. jours., chpts. to books. Active Race Rels. Commn. Greater Cin., 1995—2000; trustee Cin. Opera Assn., 1993—, v.p., 2003—; active Jewish Cmty. Rels. Coun., 1992—; trustee Isaac M. Wise Temple, 1992—2000, treas., 1997—2000; bd. dirs. Talbert House, 1969—, Air Pollution Control League, Cin., 1980—95. Capt. US Army Med. Corps, 1964—66. Recipient Pearl S. Gantz award for Cmty. Svc., United Way of Cin., 2002, VIP Volunteerism award, Hamilton County Mental Health Bd., 2005; fellow, Am. Col. Nuc. Physicians. Mem.: Am. Bd. Nuclear Medicine (chmn. 1999), Soc. Nuc. Medicine (sec. 1989—92, 1989—92, bd. dirs. 1989—99, pres. S.E. chpt. 1990—91, chair sci. program 1992—94, spkr. Ho. of Dels. 2002—04, Speaker's award 2004, Marshall Brucer award 2002), Literary Club, Sigma Xi, Phi Beta Kappa. Jewish. Avocations: tennis, history of art, archaeology, travel. Office: U Cin Med Ctr Mont Reid Pavilion G026 234 Goodman St Cincinnati OH 45219-2364 Office Phone: 513-584-9032. Business E-Mail: silbereb@healthall.com.

SILBERT, EARL J., lawyer; b. Boston, Mar. 8, 1936; s. Coleman and Lillian (Rosenberg) S.; m. Patricia Allott, Oct. 18, 1969; children: Sarah, Leslie. BA magna cum laude, Harvard U., 1957, LLB cum laude, 1960. Bar: Mass. 1970, D.C. 1963, U.S. Supreme Ct. 1975, U.S. Ct. Appeals (Fed. cir.) 1985. Lawyer tax divsn. US Dept. Justice, Washington, 1960-64, asst. U.S. atty. for D.C., 1964-69, atty. advisor office criminal justice Office of Dep. Atty. Gen., 1969-70, exec. asst. to U.S. atty. for D.C., 1972-73, U.S. atty. for D.C., 1974-79; prin. Schwalb, Donnenfeld, Bray & Silbert, Washington, 1979—98; ptnr. DLA Piper Rudnick Gray Cary, 1998—. Commr. Law Rev. Commn. of D.C., 1975-79; mem. com. on grievances U.S. Dist. Ct. D.C., 1980-87, chairperson, 1989—; master of bench Charles Fahy Am. Inn of Ct., 1984-87, Edward Bennett Williams Inn of Ct., 1989—; chairperson hearing com. Bd. on Profl. Responsibility, 1983-86; mem. adv. com. for rev. of admissions process D.C. Ct. Appeals, 1988; mem. adv. com. on rules criminal procedure Superior Ct. of D.C., 1985—; practicioners adv. bd., US Sentencing Commn.; DC Adv. Commn. on Sentencing. Contbr. articles to profl. jours. Pres. Nat. Assn. Former U.S. Attys., 1985-86, Asst. U.S. Attys. Assn. for D.C., 1985-86; former chmn, Hearing Com., Bd. of Profl. Responsibility, District of Columbia; former chmn, Grievance Com., US District Ct., District of Columbia; master bench, Edward Bennett Williams Inn Ct. Named one of 75 Best Lawyers in Washington, Washingtonian survey mag., 2002. Fellow Am. Coll. Trial Lawyers (chairperson D.C. 1989, 90, regent 1993—; pres, 2000-2001); mem. ABA (chairperson Ethics in Govt. Act white collar crime com. 1989—, standing com. on assn. standards for criminal justice 1976-79, com. on law and nat. security, taxation and criminal justice), Nat. Assn. Criminal Def. Lawyers, Phi Beta Kappa. Jewish. Office: DLA Piper Rudnick Gray Cary 1200 19th St NW Washington DC 20036-2412 E-mail: earl.silbert@dlapiper.com.

SILBEY, JOEL HENRY, history professor; b. Bklyn., Aug. 16, 1933; s. Sidney and Estelle (Mintzer) S.; m. Rosemary Johnson, Aug. 13, 1959; children: Victoria, David. BA, Bklyn. Coll., 1955; MA, U. Iowa, 1956, PhD, 1963. Asst. prof. San Francisco State Coll., 1960-64, U. Md., College Park, 1965-66; asst. prof. Am. History Cornell U., Ithaca, NY, 1966-67, assoc. prof., 1967-68, prof., 1968-86, Pres. White prof. history, 1986—2002, prof. emeritus, 2002—; Harold V. Harmsworthy prof. Am. history U. Oxford, 2004—05. Vis. asst. prof. history U. Pitts., 1964-65. Author: The Shrine of Party, 1967, The Transformation of American Politics, 1968, A Respectable Minority: The Democratic Party in the Civil War Era, 1977, The Partisan Imperative: The Dynamics of American Politics before the Civil War, 1985, The American Political Nation, 1838-1893, 1991, The American Party Battle, 1828-1876, 1999, Martin Van Buren and the Emergence of American Popular Politics, 2002, Storm Over Texas: The Annexation Controversy and the Road to Civil War, 2005; editor: (with others) Voters, Parties and Elections, 1972, American Political Behavior, 1974, The History of American Electoral Behavior, 1978; editor-in-chief: Encyclopedia of the American legislative System, 1993; editorial cons. numerous publs.; contbr. numerous articles to profl. jours Am. Philos. Soc. fellow, 1969-70; NSF fellow, 1970-74; NEH fellow, 1980-81; vis. fellow Ctr. for Advanced Study in the Behavioral Scis., 1985-86; vis. scholar Russell Sage Found., 1988-89; John Simon Guggenheim Meml. fellow, 1989-90. Mem. Am. Hist. Assn. (program com. 1977), Orgn. Am. Historians (chmn. program com. 1983), So. Hist. Assn., Social Sci. History Assn. (co-chmn. membership com., mem. exec. com). Home: 105 Judd Falls Rd Ithaca NY 14850-2715 Office: Cornell U 140 Mcgraw Hall Ithaca NY 14853-4601 Office Phone: 607-255-4966. Business E-Mail: jhs@cornell.edu.

SILBEY, ROBERT JAMES, chemistry professor, researcher, consultant; b. NYC, Oct. 19, 1940; s. Sidney Richard and Estelle (Mintzer) S.; m. Susan Sorkin, June 24, 1962; children: Jessica, Anna. BS, CUNY Bklyn. Coll., 1961; PhD, U. Chgo., 1965; PhD (hon.), Bklyn. Coll., 2004. From asst. prof. to assoc. prof. MIT, Cambridge, 1966-76, prof., 1976—, chmn. dept. chemistry, 1990-95, dir. ctr. for materials sci. and engring., 1998-2000, dean sci., 2000—07. Vis. prof. U. Utrecht, The Netherlands, 1972-73, 97, U. Grenoble, France, 1983; cons. Exxon Rsch., Clinton, N.J., 1984-98. Author: Physical Chemistry, 1991, 4th edit., 2004; editor: Conjugated Polymers, 1991; contbr. articles to profl. jours. Recipient Alexander von Humboldt Found. Sr. Scientist award, 1989, Max Planck award, 1992; Alfred P. Sloan fellow, 1968, John S. Guggenheim fellow, 1972; Dreyfus Found. Tchr.-Scholar grantee, 1969. Fellow AAAS, Am. Acad. Arts and Sci., Am. Phys. Soc.; mem. NAS. Avocations: sailing, swimming. Office: MIT Dept Chemistry 77 Mass Ave Cambridge MA 02139-4307 Office Phone: 617-253-1470. Business E-Mail: silbey@mit.edu.

SILBEY, VICTORIA E., lawyer; Atty. Morgan, Lewis & Bockius LLP, Phila., 1991—97; joined SunGard Data Sys. Inc., Wayne, Pa., 1997, v.p. legal, asst. gen. counsel, 2004—05, v.p. legal, gen. counsel, 2005—. Office: SunGard Data Sys Inc 680 E Swedesford Rd Wayne PA 19087 Office Phone: 484-582-5542. E-mail: victoria.silbey@sungard.com. *

SILBIGER, MARTIN L., radiologist, educator, dean; b. Ravenna, Ohio, Mar. 17, 1938; s. Alfred James and Evelyn Norma (Cheswick) Silbiger; m. Ruth Hope Steele, June 4, 1957; children: Martin, Eve, Jonathan, Holly, Wendy. BA, U. Pa., 1958; MD, Western Reserve U., 1962; MBA, U. South Fla., 1989. Diplomate Am. Bd. Radiology, Am. Bd. Nuc. Medicine. Intern Univ. Hosps. Cleve., 1962—63; resident Johns Hopkins Hosp., 1963—66; with NIH, 1966—68; radiologist Tampa (Fla.) Gen. Hosp., 1968—; prof. U. South Fla., Tampa, 1982—; chief of staff Tampa Gen. Hosp., 1978—80; chmn. dept. radiology U. South Fla. Coll. Medicine, 1982—95; dean coll. medicine U. South Fla., 1995—2000, v.p. health scis., 1995—2000. Founder Hillsborough County Med. Assn. Found., Tampa, 1992; treas. Cmty. Found. Tampa, 1993—95; bd. dirs. Moffitt Cancer Ctr., Tampa, 1985—2000, Moffitt Cancer Ctr. Found., 1994—2000. Avocations: reading, rollerblading, golf, tennis. Home: 1827 Bayshore Blvd Tampa FL 33606-3210 Office: 3301 Alumni Dr Tampa FL 33612-9413 also: 1209 Bruce B Downs Blvd PO Box 66 Tampa FL 33601-0066

SILCOCK, RAYMOND P., food products executive; MBA, Univ. Pa. Fin. mgmt. positions Campbell Soup Co., 1979—97; CFO Delimex, San Diego, 1997—98; exec. v.p., CFO Cott Corp., Toronto, Canada, 1998—2005, Swift & Co., Greeley, Colo., 2006—. Fellow: Chartered Inst. Mgmt. Accountants UK. Office: Swift & Co 1770 Promontory Circle Greeley CO 80634

SILCOX, FRANCES ELEANOR, museum and exhibits planning consultant; b. Orange, California, Sept. 26, 1956; d. William Henry and M. Eleanor (Saulpaugh) S.; m. David William Smith, June 21, 1986; children: Lena Celeste and Reid Whitney. BA in English, U. San Francisco, 1979; MA in Mus., George Washington U., 1984. Intern divsn. performing arts Smithsonian Instn., Washington, 1978; adminstrv. asst. exhibits dept. Calif. Acad. Sci., San Francisco, 1979—81; gallery coord. The George Washington U., Washington, 1981—83; intern art dept. aide Smithsonian Instn., Washington, 1983—84; asst. dir. Torpedo Factory Arts Ctr., Alexandria, Va., 1983—84; accreditation coord. Am. Assn. Mus., Washington, 1984—86; interpretive planner Design and Prodn. Inc., Lorton, Va., 1986—88; mus. planner West Office Exhbn. Design, San Francisco, 1988—91; ind. mus. and exhibits planner; owner Dallas, 1991—99; prin., owner Exhibi Tree, Moraga, Calif., 2000—. Bd. mem. St. Gerard Circle, St. Rita Cath. Cmty., Dallas, 1995-98; contbr. numerous natural and cultural resources orginazations. Scholar Nat. Endowment for the Arts, Am. Law Inst., ABA, Washington, 1982. Mem. Am. Assn. for State and Local History, Am. Assn. Mus., Internat. Coun. Mus., Nat. Assn. for Mus. Exhbn., Western Mus. Assn., Cultural Connections, Calif. Assn. Mus., World Monuments Fund. Democrat. Avocations: travel, corresponding, photography, reading, walking. Home and Office: 463 Fernwood Dr Moraga CA 94556-2119

SILCOX, GORDON BRUCE, executive coach; b. Takoma Park, Md., May 11, 1938; s. Walter Bruce and Ruth May (Davis) S.; m. Judith Andrea Smith, Mar. 7, 1970 (div. Apr. 1998); children: Andrea Davis, Jessica Lyn. AB, Princeton U., 1960; MBA, U. Pa., 1965. Trust investment officer Am. Security Bank, Washington, 1967—69; v.p., trust investment officer, head trust investment divsn. First Am. Bank, N.A., 1969—77; v.p., prin. Paul Stafford Assocs., Ltd., Washington, 1977-83; v.p., mgr. MSL Internat. Ltd., Washington, 1983-86; v.p. Manchester, Inc., Washington, 1987-91, sr. v.p., 1991—2003; prin. Words on Purpose LLC, Fairfax, Va., 2003—. Pres. Wash. Human Resource Forum, 1993-95. Treas. Princeton U. Class of 1960, v.p., 1980-85. Lt. (j.g.) USN, 1962-63. Mem. Univ. Club, Princeton Club (treas. Washington 1972-74, N.Y.C.). Methodist. Home and Office: 3159 Colchester Brook Ln Fairfax VA 22031-2609 Home Phone: 703-280-1041; Office Phone: 703-280-1041. E-mail: gsilcox@wordsonpurpose.com.

SILER, EUGENE EDWARD, JR., federal judge; b. Williamsburg, Ky., Oct. 19, 1936; s. Eugene Edward and Lowell (Jones) Siler; m. Christy Dyanne Minnich, Oct. 18, 1969; children: Eugene Edward, Adam Troy. BA cum laude, Vanderbilt U., 1958; LLB, U. Va., 1963; LLM, Georgetown U., 1964, U. Va., 1995. Bar: Ky. 1963, Va. 1963, DC 1963. Pvt. practice, Williamsburg, 1964—65; county atty. Whitley County, Ky., 1965—70; US atty. (ea. dist.) Ky. US Dept. Justice, Lexington, 1970—75; judge (ea. & we. dist.) Ky. US Dist. Ct., 1975—91, chief judge (ea. dist.) Ky., 1984—91; judge US Ct. Appeals (6th Cir.), 1991—2001, sr. judge, 2001—. Trustee Cumberland Coll., Williamsburg, 1965—73, 1980—88; campaign co-chmn. Congressman Tim L. Carter, 1966, 5th Congl. Dist., US Senator J.S. Cooper, 1966; 1st v.p. Ky. Bapt. Convention, 1986—87, 2002—03, pres., 2003—04; bd. dirs. Bapt. Healthcare System Inc., 1990—2004, 2006—. With USN, 1958—60, with USNR, 1960—83. Recipient Freedom's Found. medal, 1968; E. Barrett Prettyman fellow, 1963—64. Mem.: Va. State Bar, DC Bar Assn., Ky. Bar Assn. (Judge of Yr. 1992), Fed. Bar Assn. Republican. Baptist. Home: PO Box 129 Williamsburg KY 40769-0129 Office: US Ct Appeals 310 S Main Street Room 333 London KY 40741 *

SILHAVY, THOMAS JOSEPH, molecular biology educator; b. Wauseon, Ohio, Jan. 13, 1948; s. W.J. and Helen (Batdorf) S.; Daileen K. Stutzman, June 27, 1969; children— Marc Thomas, Ned Thomas BS in Pharmacy, summa cum laude, Ferris State Coll., 1971; A.M. in Biochemistry, Harvard U., 1974, PhD in Biochemistry, 1975; DSc (hon.), Ferris State Coll., 1982. Instr. Harvard U. Med Sch., Boston, 1978-79; head genetics sect. Nat. Cancer Inst., Frederick, Md., 1979-81, dir. genetics, 1981-84; instr. Advanced Bacterial Genetics, Cold Spring Harbor, NY, 1981-85; prof. molecular biology Princeton U., 1984—. Co-author: Experiments with Gene Fusions, 1984, The Power of Bacterial Genetics: A Literature-based Course, 1992; contbr. over 100 articles to profl. jours. Editor, Proceedings of NAS, 2005-. Recipient Advanced Tech. Achievement award Litton, 1982, Wellcom vis. professorship in microbiol. scis., 1990, Pres.'s award for disting. teaching, 1993; Jane Coffin Childs fellow, 1975-77, Med. Rsch. Found. fellow, 1978-79. Fellow Am. Soc. Microbiology, Am. Acad. Microbiology, AAAS, Am. Acad. Arts and Sciences; mem. Am. Soc. Biol. Chemists, Am. Soc. Cell Biology, NAS. Achievements include patents in field. Home: 22 Van Doren Way Belle Mead NJ 08502-5508 Office: Princeton U Dept Molecular Biology Princeton NJ 08544-0001 Office Phone: 609-258-5899. E-mail: tsilhavy@princeton.edu.

SILIANOFF, DAVID, secondary school educator, educator, mathematics educator; BS in Math., Westminster Coll., New Wilmington, Pa., 1986; MEd in Adult Edn., Pa. State U., U. Pk., Pa., 1994; MS in Ednl. Tech. Mgmt., Carnegie-Mellon U., Pitts., Pa., 2006; cert. in Tchg. Math., Westminster Coll., 2000; cert. in Prin., Saint Francis Coll., 2000. Tchr. math. Norwin Sch. Dist., North Huntingdon, Pa., 1995—. Recipient Outstanding Master's Paper award, Pa. State U., 1994, Norwin Outstanding Educator award, Norwin Sch. Dist., 1998, Tchr. of Yr. award, Wal-Mart and Sam's Club, 2002. Mem.: Nat. Coun. Tchrs. Math., Math. Assn. Am.

SILJAK, DRAGOSLAV D., engineering educator, researcher; b. Belgrade, Serbia, Sept. 10, 1933; came to U.S. 1964, naturalized; s. Dobrilo T. and Ljubica Z. (Zivanovic) S.; m. Dragana T. Todorovic, Sept. 28, 1967; children— Ana, Matija. BSEE, U. Belgrade, 1958, MSEE, 1961, ScD, 1963. Docent prof. U. Belgrade, 1963-64; assoc. prof. U. Santa Clara, Calif., 1964-70, prof. engring., 1970-84, B. and M. Swig Univ. chair, 1984—. Author: Nonlinear Systems, 1969, Large Scale Systems, 1978, Decentralized Control of Complex Systems, 1991; mem. editl. bd. Jour. Difference Equations, Nonlinear World, Comm. in Applied Analysis, Internat. Jour. Computer Rsch., Nonlinear Analysis: Theory, Methods and Applications, Dynamics of Cont., Disc. and Impulsive Systems, Math. Problems in Engring., Stability and Control: Theory and Applications. Disting. prof. Fulbright Found., 1984. Life fellow IEEE; mem. Serbian Acad. Scis. and Arts (hon.) Mem. Christian Orthodox Ch. E-mail: dsiljak@scu.edu.

SILK, FREDERICK C.Z., financial consultant; b. Pretoria, Transvaal, South Africa, July 29, 1934; arrived in Canada, 1964; s. Frederick Charles and Edythe D'Olier S.; m. Margaret Colbourne, May 12, 1962; children: Michael, Alison, Jennifer. BS, Rhodes U., Grahamstown, Republic South Africa, 1954; cert. in acctg. theory, U. Witwatersrand, Johannesburg, Republic South Africa, 1957. Acct., cons. Deloitte, Plender, Haskins & Sells, Johannesburg, London and NYC, 1954-64; mgmt. cons. P.S. Ross & Ptnrs., Montreal, Que., Canada, 1964-68; v.p. fin. and adminstrn. J&P Coats Ltd., Montreal, Que., Canada, 1968-74; treas. Standard Brands, Ltd., Montreal, Que., Canada, 1974-75; asst. treas. Standard Brands, Inc., NYC, 1975-78; treas. Harlequin Enterprises, Ltd., Toronto, Ont., Canada, 1978-82; v.p., treas. Nabisco Brands, Ltd., Toronto, 1982-95; pvt. treas. cons. Toronto, 1995—. Fellow Inst. Chartered Accts. (Eng., Wales), Inst. Chartered Accts. (South Africa), Fin. Execs. Internat. Avocations: music, choral music, Gilbert and Sullivan operettas. Office: 80 Front St E Ste 602 Toronto ON Canada M5E 1T4 Personal E-mail: fczsilk@hotmail.com.

SILK, MARK REUEL, religious studies educator, writer; b. Cambridge, Mass., May 12, 1950; s. Leonard and Bernice Silk; m. Tema Kaiser, June 25, 1978; children: Abraham, Ezra, Isaac. AB, Harvard U., Cambridge, Mass., 1972, PhD, 1982. Lectr. Harvard U., 1982—85; editor Boston Rev., Boston, 1985—86; staff writer, editl. writer, columnist Atlanta Jour. Constn., 1987—96; dir. Leonard E. Greenberg Ctr. Study Religion in Pub. Life Trinity Coll., Hartford, Conn., 1996—, assoc. prof. religion in pub. life, 1996—2007, dir. pub. values program, 2005—, prof. religion in pub. life, 2007—. Adv. bd. Inst. Advanced Study of Religion Yale U., New Haven, 1999—2002; adv. bd. Gralla Fellows Program for Religion Journalists Brandeis U., Waltham, Mass., 1999—; adv. bd. nat. program First Freedom Ctr., Richmond, Va., 2003—. Author: Spiritual Politics: Religion and America Since World War II, 1988, Unsecular Media: Making News of Religion in America, 1995; editor: Religion by Region, Religion in the News; contbg. editor: The Rev. Faith and Internat. Affairs, 2006—, mem. editl. bd.: Jour. Media and Religion, 2001—; contbr. articles to profl. jours. Mem. cmty. relations coun. Hartford Jewish Fed., Conn. Recipient Best article of Yr. award, editl. bd. Am. Quarterly, 1984; fellow, Harvard U., 1975—76. Mem.: Am. Acad. Religion, Phi Beta Kappa. Democrat. Jewish. Home: 63 Highland St West Hartford CT 06119 Office: Trinity Coll 300 Summit St Hartford CT 06106 Home Phone: 860-232-9586; Office Phone: 860-297-2352. Office Fax: 860-297-5125. Business E-Mail: mark.silk@trincoll.edu.

SILK, THOMAS, lawyer; b. Beaver, Pa., Dec. 12, 1937; s. Thomas and Alice Genevieve (Beck) S.; m. Arlene Schlaifer, 1959 (div.); 1 child, Nicole Amory; m. Susan Clark, 1979 (div.); m. Suzanne Vinson, 1996. AB, U. Calif., Berkeley, 1959, LLB, 1963. Bar: Calif. 1964, U.S. Dist. Ct. (no. dist.) Calif. 1964, U.S. Ct. Appeals (D.C., 2-10th cirs.) 1966-68, U.S. Tax Ct. 1966, U.S. Supreme Ct. 1967. Appellate atty. tax divsn. U.S. Dept. Justice, Washington, 1964-66, spl. asst. to asst. atty. gen. tax divsn., 1966-68; assoc. Brobeck, Phleger & Harrison, San Francisco, 1968-71; founder, chmn. Silk, Adler & Colvin, San Francisco, 1972—. Lectr., author, advisor in field; advisor project on the principles of law of nonprofit orgns. Am. Law Inst., 2004—. Editor, co-author: Philanthropy and Law in Asia, 1999; author: Corporate Philanthropy and Law: A Guide to Tax Charities and An Introduction to Compliance with Anti-Terrorist Laws, 2003, Good Governance Practices for 501(c) (3) Organizations: Should the IRS Become Further Involved, 2007—. Trustee CompassPoint; trustee, sec. Hertz Found. Office: Silk Adler & Colvin Ste 1220 235 Montgomery St San Francisco CA 94104-2902 Office Phone: 415-421-7555. Business E-Mail: tom@silklaw.com.

SILKENAT, JAMES ROBERT, lawyer; b. Salina, Kans., Aug. 2, 1947; s. Ernest E. and Mildred R. (Iman) S.; children: David Andrew, Katherine Anne. BA, Drury Coll., 1969; JD, U. Chgo., 1972; LLM, NYU, 1978. Bar: N.Y. 1973, D.C. 1980. Assoc. Cravath, Swaine & Moore, NYC, 1972-80; counsel Internat. Fin. Corp., Washington, 1980-86; ptnr. Morgan, Lewis & Bockius, NYC, 1986-89, Morrison & Foerster, NYC, 1989-92, Pillsbury, Winthrop, NYC, 1992—2002, Arent Fox, NYC, 2002—. Chmn. Council N.Y. Law Assocs., 1978-79, Lawyers Com. Internat. Human Rights, 1978-80. Editor ABA Guide to Fng. Law Firms, Moscow Conf. on Law Bilateral Econ. Rels., ABA Guide to Internat. Bus. Negotiations, The Imperial Presidency and the Consequences of 9/11, The Law of International Insolvencies and Debt Restructurings; contbr. articles to profl. jours. Capt. U.S. Army, 1972-73. Fellow NEH, 1977, U.S. Dept. State, 1981. Fellow Am. Bar Found. (chmn. 2004-05); mem. ABA (chmn. internat. law and practice sect. 1989-90, chmn. sect. officer's conf. 1990-92, mem. ho. of dels. 1989—, bd. govs. 1994-97). Office: Arent Fox 1675 Broadway New York NY 10019 Home Phone: 212-245-5815; Office Phone: 212-492-3318. E-mail: silkenat.james@arentfox.com.

SILL, ROBERT MICHAEL, curator; b. Racine, Wis., Jan. 28, 1957; s. Robert Leroy and Eleanor Mildred Sill; m. Jean Ellen Tweet, Jan. 16, 1982; children: Andrew William, Peder Adrian, Robert Eliot. BFA, No. Ill. U., Dekalb, 1980; MA, U. Minn., Mpls., 1987. Exhibit designer Ill. State Mus., Springfield, 1987—89, curator I, 1989—96, curator II, 1996—2001, curator III, 2001—, asst. dir. art, 2005—. Adj. prof. studio & art history U. Ill., Springfield, 1996—2001; art advisor Old Capitol Art Fair Bd., Springfield, 2002—04; juror numerous exhibitions & competitions Mid-west Arts Orgns. Mem.: Am. Assn. Mus. Avocations: painting, drawing.

SILLARS, MALCOLM O., communications educator; b. Union City, NJ, Feb. 12, 1928; s. Malcolm Osgood and Dorothy Edna (Browning) S.; m. Charlotte Jane Grimm, June 1, 1948; children: Paul Louis, Bruce Malcolm, Alan Leslie. BA, U. Redlands, 1948, MA, 1949; PhD, U. Iowa, 1955. Asst. prof. comm. Iowa State U., Ames, 1949-53; asst. prof. Calif. State U., LA, 1954-56, prof., 1956—71, dean, 1970-71; pres. Calif. State U. Northridge, 1969-70; prof. U. Mass., Amherst, 1971-74; prof. communication U. Utah, Salt Lake City, 1974-97, dean humanities, 1974-81, ret., 1998. Author: Speech: Content and Communications, 6th edit., 1991, Argumentation and Critical Decision Making, 6th edit., 2005, Communication Criticism, 2d edit., 2001; contbr. articles to profl. jours. Recipient Silver Beaver award Boy Scouts Am. Mem. ACLU, Nat. Comm. Assn. (pres.), We. States Comm. Assn. (pres.). Democrat. Home: 3508 Eastoaks Dr Salt Lake City UT 84124-3811 E-mail: m.sillars@utah.edu.

SILLER, STEPHEN I., lawyer; b. May 8, 1949; m. Helen Seewald, June 6, 1971. BA, Bklyn. Coll., 1970, JD cum laude, 1973; LLM, NYU, 1978. Bar: N.Y. 1974, U.S. Dist. Ct. (so. and ea. dists.) N.Y. 1974, U.S. Ct. Appeals (2d cir.) 1974. Assoc. Fried, Frank, Harris, Shriver & Jacobson, NYC, 1973-78, Feit & Ahrens, NYC, 1978-80, ptnr., 1981-87; founder, sr. ptnr. Siller Wilk LLP, NYC, 1987—. Mem. ABA (partnership law com., negotiated acquisitions com.), Internat. Bar Assn., Assn. Bar City of N.Y. (transp. com. 1978, U.S. in global economy com. 1996-97). Office: Siller Wilk LLP 675 3rd Ave Fl 9 New York NY 10017-5704 Office Phone: 212-421-2233. Business E-Mail: ssiller@sillerwilk.com.

SILLERMAN, ROBERT F. X., communications executive, banker; b. NYC, Apr. 12, 1948; s. Michael McKinley and Estelle (Levande) Sillerman; m. Jane Waxenberg, July 13, 1969 (div. Dec. 1970); m. Laura Baudo, Feb. 25, 1974. BS magna cum laude, Brandeis U., 1969. CEO, chmn. bd. Youth Markets Cons., Inc., Boston, 1966-74, Nat. Discount Mktg., Great Neck, NY, 1974-78, Sillerman-Morrow Broadcasting Group, Middletown, NY, 1978-85; co-chmn. bd. Legacy Broadcasting, LA, 1985-89; CEO, chmn. bd. Sillerman-Magee Comm. Mgmt. Corp. (now Sillerman Comm. Mgmt. Corp.), NYC, 1985, TV Programs of Am., Hollywood, Calif., 1985; founder, CEO, chmn. SFX Broadcasting, Inc.(acquired by Hicks, Muse, Tate & Furst), 1992—95, exec. chmn., 1995—98; founder, exec. chmn., mem. of the office of the chmn., dir. SFX Entertainment, Inc. (acquired by Clear Channel Communications), 1997—2000; chmn. FXM, Inc., 2000—05; founder, mng. mem. FXM Asset Mgmt. LLC, 2003—; mng. mem. MJX Asset Mgmt., 2003—; CEO, pres., chmn. bd. CKX, Inc., Las Vegas, Nev., 2005—. Co-chmn. Legacy Broadcasting, Inc., 1986—; chmn. Met. Broadcasting, Inc., 1988-89. Recipient Bearer of the Torch award Anti-Defamation League, N.Y.C., 1982. Mem. Nat. Assn. Broadcasters, Nat. Radio Broadcasters Assn. Office: CKX Inc 6730 S Las Vegas Blvd Las Vegas NV 89119 Address: Southampton Coll LI Univ 239 Montauk Hwy Southampton NY 11968-4196 Office Phone: 702-798-7777, 631-283-4000. Office Fax: 702-798-6847, 631-283-4081.

SILLERUD, ARLEN ROGER, retired secondary school educator; b. Nov. 28, 1934; BS, Moorhead State U., Minn., 1958; postgrad., Bemidji State U., Minn., 1969-70, U. Minn., 1988-90. Tchr. Ada School Dist., Ada, Minn., 1958-90. Chmn. Norman County Reps., Ada, Minn., 1996—, county, dist., and state del., 1994-2000,, 2002—, state ctrl. del., 1997-2001, alt., 2000—; elder Zion Luth. Ch., Ada, 1994-2005, Gideon spkr., 1971—. Achievements include rsch. in heart fibrillation, that the heart can be restarted by electric shock; creator five solutions to clean up oil spills; inventor wind deflector for trucks. Home: 807 3rd Ave E Ada MN 56510-1120

SILLMAN, AMY, painter, art educator; b. Oct. 1955; Student, Beloit Coll., NYU; BFA, Sch. Visual Arts, Manhattan; MFA, Bard Coll. Milton Avery prof. arts, faculty Milton Avery Grad. Sch. Arts, Bard Coll., 1996—. One-man shows include Brent Sikkema Gallery, 2000, exhibitions include Casey Kaplan Gallery, Manhattan, N.Y., 1996, 1998, White Columns, 1996, Postmasters Gallery, N.Y.C., 1997, Sixth@Prince Fine Art, 1999, Exit Art, 2000, Whitney Biennial, Whitney Mus. Am. Art, NY, 2004. Recipient Tiffany Found. award, 1999—2000; Guggenheim fellow, 2001—02. Home Phone: 845-757-3636. Personal E-mail: amyfelix@aol.com.

SILLMAN, ARNOLD JOEL, physiologist, educator; b. NYC, Oct. 10, 1940; s. Philip and Anne L. (Pearlman) S.; m. Jean Fletcher Van Keuren, Sept. 26, 1969; children: Andrea Jose Callaway, Diana Van Keuren Taylor. AB, UCLA, 1963, MA, 1965, PhD, 1968. Asst. prof. UCLA, 1969-73, U. Calif., Davis, 1975-78, assoc. prof., 1978-85, prof., 1985—; asst. prof. U. Pitts., 1973-75, interim dir. aquaculture and fisheries program, 1994—95, vice chair sect. neurobiology, physiology and behavior, 1998—, acting chair, 2001. Contbr. articles to profl. jours. USPHS trainee, UCLA, 1966-67; fellow NSF, 1967-68, Fight for Sight, Inc., 1968-69. Recipient Acad. Senate Disting. Tchg. award, 1996. Jewish. Avocations: backpacking, gardening, woodworking. Home: 1140 Los Robles St Davis CA 95618-4927 Office: U Calif Sect Neurobiology Physiology & Behavior Coll Biol Scis Davis CA 95616 Office Phone: 530-752-3207. Business E-Mail: ajsillman@ucdavis.edu.

SILMAN, ROBERTA KARPEL, writer, critic; b. Bklyn., Dec. 29, 1934; d. Herman and Phoebe Karpel; m. Robert Silman, June 14, 1956; children: Miriam, Joshua, Ruth. BA, Cornell U., 1956; MFA, Sarah Lawrence Coll., 1975. Sec. Saturday Rev. Mag., NYC, 1957, sci. writer, 1958—60; freelance fiction writer Ardsley, NY, 1961—. Author: Somebody Else's Child, 1976 (award Child Study Assn.), Blood Relations, 1977 (Hon. Mention Pen Hemingway prize, Hon. Mention Janet Kafka prize), (novels) Boundaries, 1979 (Hon. Mention Janet Kafka prize), The Dream Dredger, 1986, Beginning The World Again, 1990, short stories; contbr. articles to newspapers. Mem. adv. coun. Coll. Arts & Scis. Cornell U. Fellow, Guggenheim Found., 1979—80, Nat. Endowment for Arts, 1982—83. Mem.: PEN, Poets and Writers, Authors Guild, Phi Beta Kappa. Democrat. Jewish. Avocations: piano, classical music, hiking, travel. Home: 18 Larchmont St Ardsley NY 10502 Office Phone: 914-693-2816. Personal E-mail: rsilman@verizon.net.

SILSBY, PAULA D., prosecutor; b. Ellsworth, Maine, 1951; JD, U. Maine, 1976; BA, Mt. Holyoke Coll. Bar: Maine 1976. US atty. dist. Maine US Dept. Justice, Portland, 2001—. Fellow: Maine Bar Found. Office: US Attys Office 100 Middle St Ste 6 Portland ME 04101-4182 *

SILVA, CLARENCE, bishop; b. Honolulu, Aug. 6, 1949; Student, St. Joseph Sem., Mountain View, Calif., St. Patrick Sem., Menlo Pk. Ordained priest Diocese of Oakland, Calif., 1975; parochial vicar St. Bernard Parish, Oakland, St. Bede Parish, Hayward, Calif.; pastor St. Peter Martyr Parish, Pittsburgh, Pa., St. Anthony Parish, Oakland, Calif., St. John the Baptist Parish, El Cerrito, Calif., St. Andrew-St. Joseph Parish, Oakland, Calif., St. Leonard-St. Paul Parish, Fremont, Calif.; vicar gen. & moderator of curia Diocese of Oakland, 2004—05; Bishop of Honolulu, 2005—. Roman Catholic. Office: Diocese of Honolulu 1184 Bishop St Honolulu HI 96813-2858 Office Phone: 801-533-1791.

SILVA, CLARICE F. (CLARICE F. CHAVIRA-SILVA), lawyer; b. LA, Sept. 14, 1973; BA cum laude, Calif. State Univ., Northridge, 1998; JD, Loyola Univ., 2001. Bar: Calif. 2001. Assoc., real estate practice Shumaker Steckbauer Weinhart LLP, LA. Named a Rising Star, So. Calif. Super Lawyers, 2006. Mem.: ABA, State Bar Calif., Women Lawyers Assn. LA, LA County Bar Assn. Office: Shumaker Steckbauer Weinhart 36th Fl 333 S Hope St Los Angeles CA 90071 Office Phone: 213-229-2868. Office Fax: 213-229-2870. Business E-Mail: csilva@sswesq.com.

SILVA, DANIEL JOSEPH, writer; b. Kalamazoo, Dec. 19, 1960; s. Richard and Carol Ann (Koerber) S.; m. Jamie Sue Gangel, Oct. 8, 1988; children: Lily Elizabeth, Nicholas Jacob (twins). BA, Calif. State U., Fresno, 1983. Fgn. news editor UPI, Washington, 1985-86; Mideast corr. Cairo, Egypt, 1986-87; exec. prodr. CNN, Washington, 1988—. Author: The Unlikely Spy, 1997 (NY Times bestseller list), Mark of the Assassin, 1998, Marching Season, 1999, Kill Artist, 2000, English Assassin, 2002, Confessor, 2003, Death in Vienna, 2004, Prince of Fire, 2005 (NY Times bestseller list), The Messenger, 2006, The Secret Servant, 2007. Office: c/o Marilyn Duckworth Putnam 375 Hudson St New York NY 10014 *

SILVA, EUGENE JOSEPH, lawyer; b. Gloucester, Mass., May 23, 1942; s. Edward Joseph and Rose (Lebre) Silva; m. Nancy Blue-Pearson, Jan. 8, 1972; children: Eugene Joseph II, Michael Joseph. BS with honors, Maine Maritime Acad., Castine, 1964; JD, U. Notre Dame, Ind., 1972. Bar: Calif. 1972, US Dist. Ct. (so. and cen. dists.) Calif. 1972, Tex. 1977, US Dist. Ct. (so. and ea. dists.) Tex. 1978, US Ct. Appeals (5th, 9th, 2d and 11th cirs.) 1978, US Supreme Ct. 1981; lic. Master Mariner. Assoc. Luce, Forward, Hamilton & Scripps, San Diego, 1972-77, Vinson & Elkins, Houston, 1977-79, ptnr., 1980—2003. Mem. adv. bd. Admiralty Law Inst. Tulane U., 1999—. Bd. dirs. Cabrillo Festival Inc., San Diego, 1974—77, San Jose Clinic, Inc., 1990—97, pres., 1993—95; bd. dirs. Portuguese Heritage Scholarship Found., 1995—, St. Joseph Hosp. Found., 1995—2000. Decorated Knight Grand Cross Equestrian Order Holy Sepulchre Jerusalem; named one of Best Lawyers in Am., 1991—; recipient Outstanding Alumni award, Maine Maritime Acad., 1990. Mem. Calif. Bar Assn., Tex. Bar Assn., Grays Inn U. Notre Dame Sch. Law (pres. 1970-72), Maritime Law Assn. US (proctor in admiralty 1974-2005), Portuguese Union Calif. (bd. dirs. 1973-74), Portuguese Am. League San Diego (pres. 1974-75), Portuguese Am. Leadership Coun. US, Notre Dame Club (pres. San Diego chpt. 1976-77). Roman Catholic. Home: 8 Smithdale Estates Dr Houston TX 77024-6600 Personal E-mail: ejsilva@swbell.net.

SILVA, JOSEPH, JR., dean, medical educator; BA in biol. scis., Rutgers U., 1962; MD, Northwestern U., 1966. Diplomate Am. Bd. Internal Medicine, 1972. Intern Johns Hopkins Hosp., Balt., 1962—66, asst. resident in medicine, 1967—68, sr. resident in medicine, 1968—69; fellow in infectious diseases U. Mich. Med. Ctr., Ann Arbor, 1969—70; asst. prof. internal medicine divsn. infectious diseases U. Mich., prof., 1980—82; prof. and chair. of internal med. U. Calif. Davis, 1982—97; dean U. Calif. Davis Sch. Medicine, 1997—2005, sr. adv. to chancellor health sciences, 2005—, dean emeritus; CEO U. Calif. Davis Health Sys.1, 1997—. Served 2 yrs. in USAF. Fellow: Royal Soc. Medicine, London, Infectious Diseases Soc. Am., ACP (regent); mem.: Sociedad Medica de Santiago, Chile (assoc. mem.), Internat. Immunocompromised Host Soc., Sacramento/Sierra Med. Soc., Western Assn. Physicians, Western Assn. Clin. Investigation, Soc. Intestinal Microecology and Disease, Soc. Hosp. Epidemiologists of Am., Sacramento/El Dorado Med. Soc. (affiliate), Reticuloendothelial Soc., Mich. Soc. Med. Rsch., Mich. Soc. Infection Control, Ctrl. Soc. Clin. Rsch., Calif. Acad. Medicine, Am. Soc. Tropical Medicine and Hygiene, Am. Soc. Internal Medicine, Am. Fedn. Clin. Rsch., Calif. Med. Assn., AMA, AAAS, Alpha Omega Alpha. Office: U Calif Sch Medicine 2315 Stockton Blvd Rm 1501 Sacramento CA 95817 Office Phone: 530-752-0321. E-mail: josilva@ucdavis.edu.

SILVA, MARY BARNES, retired elementary school educator; d. Walter Howard and Rosalinda M. Barnes. BS Edn., Kent State U., 1964; M Edn., U. Hawaii, 1976. Provisional Ohio, profl. Hawaii. Tchr. St. Louis Sch., Louisville, Ohio, 1960—62, Elyria Pub. Schs., Ohio, 1962—68, Kailua Elem., Hawaii, 1968—78, tchr. academically gifted and talented, 1978—88; tech. coord. Royal Sch., Honolulu, 1988—2001; ret., 2001. Adviser student coun., newspaper, yearbook Kailua Elem., 1979—88, chair grade level, 1975—78, Royal Sch., Honolulu, 1993—2001, chair sch. cmty.-based mgmt., 1994—99, sch. facilitator, 1995—99, tech. trainer, 1996—2001. Pres., vp., sec., treas. Assn. of Apt. Owners, Honolulu, 1979—2004. Named Tchr. of Yr., Honolulu Dist., 1997. Mem.: NEA (life), Hawaii State Ret. Tchrs. Assn., Hawaii Edn. Assn. (life), Contemporary Mus., Bishop Mus., Acad. Arts. Avocations: travel, the arts. Home: 410 Magellan Ave 808 Honolulu HI 96813 Home Phone: 808-533-4325. Personal E-mail: malia.aloha@hawaiiantel.net.

SILVA, SUSAN See NIKIRK, SUSAN

SILVA, TONY, education educator, editor; b. Bethlehem, Pa., Oct. 3, 1953; s. Anthony and Regina (DeSantis) Silva; m. Margie Berns. AA in Liberal Arts, Northampton County Area C.C., 1975; BA in Spanish, Kutztown State U., 1977; MA, U. of Ill., 1981; PhD in English, Purdue U., 1990. Prof. Auburn U., Ala., 1990—91, Purdue U., West Lafayette, Ind., 1991—. Consulting; jour. editing; profl. conf. planning. Mem.: Conf. on Coll. Composition and Comm., Tchrs. of English to Spkrs. of Other Languages, Nat. Coun. Tchrs. of English. Achievements include research in Second Language Writing. Home: 2315 Sycamore Lane West Lafayette IN 47906 Office: Purdue University English Dept 500 Oval Dr West Lafayette IN 47907-2038 Home Phone: 765-497-1452; Office Phone: 765-494-3769. Office Fax: 765-494-3780. Personal E-mail: tony@purdue.edu.

SILVER, ADAM, sports association executive; b. 1962; BA in Polit. Sci., Duke U., 1984; JD, U. Chgo., 1988. Legis. aide to Rep. Les AuCoin US Congress, Washington; law clk. to Hon. Kimba Wood US Dist. Ct. (so. dist.) NY, NYC; litig. assoc. Cravath, Swaine & Moore LLP, NYC; spl. asst. to commr. NBA, 1992—93, chief of staff, 1993—95; sr. v.p., COO NBA Entertainment, Secaucus, NJ, 1995—97, pres., 1997—2006, COO, 2000—06; COO, dep. commr. NBA, 2006—. Prodr.: Michael Jordan to the Max, 2000. Mem. Spl. Presdl. Coun. on Campus Life and Culture at Duke U.; mem. vis. com. U. Chgo. Law Sch.; bd. mem. PENCIL, Hands on Network Corp. Svc. Coun., Partnership for a Drug-Free Am., Duke U. Libr., NYC Sports Devel. Corp., 2003—. Named one of The Most Influential People in Sports Bus. Jour., Sports Bus. Jour., The Most Powerful People in Sports, The Sporting News, 2005. Jewish. Office: NBA Olympic Tower 645 5th Ave Fl 10 New York NY 10022-5986 *

SILVER, ALAN IRVING, lawyer; b. St. Paul, Sept. 17, 1949; s. Sherman J. Silver and Muriel (Bernstein) Brawerman; m. Janice Lynn Gleekel, July 8, 1973; children: Stephen, Amy. BA cum laude, U. Minn., 1971, JD cum laude, 1975. Bar: Minn. 1975, U.S. Dist. Ct. Minn. 1975, U.S. Dist. Ct. (ea. dist.) Wis. 1975, U.S. Ct. Appeals 8th and 10th cirs.) 1975. Assoc. Doherty, Rumble & Butler, P.A., St. Paul, 1975-80, ptnr. Mpls., 1980-99, Bassford, Remele (formerly called Bassford, Lockhart, Truesdell & Briggs, P.A.), Mpls., 1999—. Mem. 2d Jud. Dist. Ethics Com., St. Paul, 1985-88, 4th Jud. Dist. Ethics Com., Mpls., 1990-97. Author: Building a New Foundation: Torts, Contracts and the Economic Class Doctrine, 2000, other numerous continuing edn. seminar material. Vol. atty. Legal Assistance Ramsey County, St. Paul, 1975-82; mem. St. Louis Park (Minn.) Sch. Bd., 1993-99, chair, 1995-97; mem. St. Louis Park Human Rights Commn., 1987-91; chmn. site mgmt. coun. Susan Lindgren Sch., St. Louis Park, 1986-93; bd. dirs. Jewish Cmty. Rels. Coun., Anti-Defamation League Minn. and Dakotas, 1987-93, 97—, treas., 1992-93, v.p., 2003-06, pres., 2006-. Mem. ABA, Minn. Bar Assn. (exec. bd. antitrust sect. 1984, litigation chair probate and trust sect.), Hennepin County Bar Assn. Avocations: running, guitar, reading. Home: 4320 W 25th St Minneapolis MN 55416-3841 Office: Bassford Remele Ste 3800 33 S 6th St Minneapolis MN 55402-1501 Office Phone: 612-376-1634. Business E-Mail: alans@bassford.com.

SILVER, ARNOLD HERBERT, retired physicist; s. Louis and Fannie Silver; m. Irene Mary Silver, 1952; children: Pamela Ann Townsend, Nancie Gail, Mark Edward, Lynn Alison Abelson, Susan Deborah Lane. BS in Physics, Rensselaer Poly. Inst., Troy, NY, 1948—52, MS in Physics, 1952—54, PhD in Physics, 1954—57. Dir. electronics rsch. lab. Aerospace Corp., El Segundo, Calif., 1969—81; mgr. superconductor electronics TRW, Inc., Redondo Beach, Calif., 1981—98, tech. fellow, 1991—98; cons. Northrop Grumman, Redondo Beach, 1998—2005, Jet Proplusion Lab., Pasadena, Calif., 2005—; scientist sci. lab. Ford Motor Co., Dearborn, Mich. Sec. US Com. Superconductor Electronics, Rancho Palos Verdes, 2005—. Bd. dirs. Com. Superconductivity in Am. Competitiveness, DC. Recipient Chairman's award for innovation, TRW, Inc., 1992. Fellow: Am. Phys. Soc.; mem.: NAE, IEEE (life Continuing & Significant Contributions award in fields of applied superconductivity 2000). Achievements include development of superconducting quantum interference device; patents for superconducting analog to digital converters; applications of superconducting devices. Home: 6670 Eddinghill Dr Rancho Palos Verdes CA 90275 Home Phone: 310-541-2650. Personal E-mail: arnold.silver@ieee.org.

SILVER, AUDREY WILMA, nurse, educator, writer; b. Nashville, Nov. 29, 1945; d. David and Roslyn Silver; m. Lawrence Claster Falk (div. June 1973); children: Wendy Falk MacGregor, Laurie Falk Fields, PJ MacGregor, Jason Fields; m. Stuart Alan Berney, May 20, 1988; stepchildren: Elizabeth Berney Weiskopf, Joshua Forrest Berney. AS in Nursing, Tenn. State U., Nashville, 1992, BS in Psychology cum laude, 1997. RN Tenn., Fla., cert. case mgr.; lic. real estate broker Tenn., Fla. Consumer health writer, editor Healthy Earth Comms., Nashville, Columbia/Hosp. Corp. Am., Nashville; nurse educator, case mgr., disease mgr. Health Integrated, Tampa, Healthways, Nashville, 1999—. Contbr. articles to profl. publs., ency. Vol. Great Harvest Food Bank; precinct county chmn. Kerry for Pres., Pinellas County, Fla.; health edn. coord. Hadassah, 2006. Recipient Top Internet Content award, US News and World Report, 1996, Top Health Content award, AOL and Dow Jones, 1997, award, USA Today; grantee Virtual Body feature award, CNN, 1997. Mem.: LWV, Sierra Club, Fla. Assn. Realtors, Nat. Assn. Realtors, Case Mgmt. Soc. Am., Mensa, Planned Parenthood, Habitat for Humanity, So. Poverty Law Ctr. Jewish. Avocations: bicycling, photography, reading, exercise.

SILVER, BARNARD JOSEPH STEWART, mechanical and chemical engineer, consultant, inventor; b. Salt Lake City, Mar. 9, 1933; s. Harold Farnes and Madelyn Cannon (Stewart) S.; m. Cherry Bushman, Aug. 12, 1963; children: Madelyn Stewart Palmer, Cannon Farnes. BSME, MIT, 1957; MS in Engring. Mechanics, Stanford U., 1958; grad. Advanced Mgmt. Program, Harvard Grad. Sch. Bus., 1977. Registered profl. engr. Colo. Engr. aircraft nuclear propulsion divsn. GE Co., Evandale, Ohio, 1957; engr. Silver Engring. Works, Denver, 1959-66, mgr. sales and tech. svcs., 1966-71, pres., 1998-99, chmn. bd., 1999—; chief engr. Union Sugar divsn. Consol. Foods Co., Santa Maria, Calif., 1971-74; directeur du complex SODESUCRE Abidjan, Cote d'Ivoire, 1974-76; supt. engring. and maintenance U and I Inc., Moses Lake, Wash., 1976-79; pres. Silver Enterprise Denver, Moses Lake, 1971—, Silver Energy Systems Corp., Moses Lake, 1980-98, chmn. bd., 1998—; pres., gen. mgr. Silver Chief Corp., 1983—; pres. Silver Corp., 1984—; chmn. bd. Silver Pubs., Inc., 1986-87, 90—; exec. v.p. Cascadian Inulin L.L.C., Sedro-Wooley, Wash., 1996—99; mgr. Silver Inulin LLC, Moses Lake, 1996-98; dir. processing rsch. Inuloa, Wyo., 1999—2001; bd. mgrs. Inula, Wyo., Lovell; v.p. Barnard J. Stewart Cousins Land Co., 1987—88, 1992—2003; chmn. Mid. East Peace Inst., 1998—; founder, pres. Life Energy Food, LLC, Holladay, 2001—. Dir. Isle Piquant Sugar Found., 1993-94; steering com. World Botanical Inst., 1993-99; instr. engring. Big Bend C.C., 1980-81. Patentee in field, including patent for novel inulin fractions extracting soluable substances from subdivided solids, 1995. Explorer adv. Boy Scouts Am., 1965-66, 89-90, pack com. chmn., 1968-74, 94-96, troop com. chmn., 1968-74, vice chmn. Columbia Basin Dist., 1986-87; pres. Silver Found., 1961-87, v.p., 1987-97, sec.-treas. 1997—; ednl. conselor MIT, 1971-89; pres. Chief Moses Jr. HS Parent Tchr. Student Assn., 1978-79; missionary Ch. of Jesus Christ of Latter-day Saints, Can., 1953-55, Hawaii, P.R., Ctrl. and South Am., Asia, 1959-68, West Africa, 1988, Cote d'Ivoire, 1988-89, Zaire, 1989, Holladay North Stake, 1991, 95-97, Cheyenne Stake, 1998-99, Salt Lake Inner-City Project Mission, 2000-03; Sunday Sch. 2d counselor Wasatch br. Utah Correctional Facility; dist. pres. No. B.C., No. Alberta, Yukon and N.W. Ters., 1955; stake high counselor, Santa Maria, Calif., 1971-72, Moses Lake Wash., 1977-79; presiding elder Cote d'Ivoire, 1974-76, 88; 2d counsleor Moses Lake Stake Presidency, 1980-88; bd. dirs. Columbia Basin Allied Arts, 1986-88; mem. Health Sci. Coun. U. Utah, 1991—; Sunday sch. gen. bd. Ch. of Jesus Christ of Latter-Day Saints, 1991-93, com. for mems. with Disabilities, 1992-93, CHOICE adv. bd., 1993-95; emergency preparedness dir. Holladay North Stake, 1993-95. With Ordnance Corps., US Army, 1958-59, USAR, 1960-63. Decorated Chevalier Ordre National (Repbulic of Cote d'Ivoire). Mem. ASME (life), Assn. Energy Engrs., AAAS, Am. Soc. Sugar Beet Technolgists, Internat. Soc. Sugar Cane Technologists, Am. Soc. Sugar Cane Technologists, Environ. Engrs. & Mgrs. Inst., Sugar Industry Technicians, Nat. Fedn. Ind. Bus., Utah State Hist. Soc. (life), Mormon Hist. Assn., G. Polysopnical Chowder and Marching Soc., Western Hist. Assn., Sons of Utah Pioneers (life), Univ. Archeol. Soc. (life), Kiwanis, Cannon-Hickley Study Group, Sigma Xi (life, sec., treas., Utah chpt. 1994-99), Pi Tau Sigma, Sigma Chi, Alpha Phi Omega. Republican. Mem. Lds Ch. Office: 4390 S 2300 E Holladay UT 84125-3651 Office Phone: 801-272-5433. Business E-Mail: barnardsilver@lifeenergyfood.com.

SILVER, BARRY MORRIS, lawyer; b. Mt. Vernon, NY, Nov. 18, 1956; s. Samuel Manuel and Elaine Martha (Shapiro) Silver. BA, Fla. Atlantic U., 1979; JD, Nova U., 1983. Bar: Fla. 1983. Atty. pvt. practice, Boca Raton, 1986—. Tchr. bilingual edn. Palm Beach County Schs., Delray Beach, Fla., 1981—83; faculty Palm Beach Jr. Coll., Boca Raton, 1990—; atty. NOW, South Palm Beach County. Vol. Haitian Refugee Ctr., Miami, 1982; mem. Fla. Ho. Reps., 1997—98; asst. rabbi Congregation L'Dor Va-Dor, Boynton Beach, Fla. Mem.: Palm Beach County Bar Assn., Fla. Bar Assn., Sierra Club. Democrat. Jewish. Avocations: languages, tennis, frisbee, chess. Office: 1200 S Rogers Cir Ste 8 Boca Raton FL 33487- Home: 18624 Cape Sable Dr Boca Raton FL 33498-6374 Office Phone: 561-483-6900. Personal E-mail: barryboca@aol.com.

SILVER, CHARLES MORTON, communications company executive; b. New Haven, Sept. 22, 1929; s. Sam and Rose (Fischman) S.; m. Rose Charek, Mar. 27, 1960; children: Ronni Ellen, Suzanne Paula, Steven Mitchell. BS, U Conn., 1954. With Arthur Andersen & Co., NYC, 1954-61, ITT, NYC, 1961-88, ret. as v.p. and assoc. treas., 1988. Served with U.S. Army, 1947-48, 50-51. Mem. Roxbury Swim and Tennis Club. Home: 51 Akbar Rd Stamford CT 06902-1401 E-mail: rosecs50@aol.com.

SILVER, DAVID, lawyer; b. NYC, Jan. 27, 1931; s. Sol and Fannie (Stein) S.; m. Meryl Young, Sept. 14, 1952 (dec.); children: Daniel, Matthew, Joshua; m. Ann Schwartz, June 4, 1993. BA, CCNY, 1953; LL.B. cum laude, Harvard U., 1958. Bar: N.Y. 1958, D.C. 1979. Pvt. practice law, NYC, 1960-61; spl. counsel SEC, Washington, 1961-65; gen. counsel Investors Planning Corp., NYC, 1965-66; asst. counsel Investment Co. Inst., Washington, 1966-69, gen. counsel, 1969-77, pres., 1977-91, ICI Mut. Ins. Co., Washington, 1987-2001. Cons. securities regulation Govt. of India, 1964; mutual fund regulation Govt. of China, 1999; lectr. Law Sch. Boston U., 1995—98; mem. individual investor adv. com. N.Y. Stock Exch., 1994—99; dir. PGAM, Milan, 2001—. Served with U.S. Army, 1953-55. Mem. Fed. Bar Assn. (exec. coun. securities com., past chmn. investment co. com.). Home and Office: 9410 Brooke Dr Bethesda MD 20817-2110 Business E-Mail: anndave@verizon.net.

SILVER, DEE EDWARD, physician, neurologist; b. Keystone, Iowa, Dec. 8, 1939; s. Grant Mason and Cora Ann (Larson) S.; m. Penelope Neena Diumenti (div. May 1988); 1 child, Helen Diumenti Silver; m. Marilyn Janet Lyddy, Mar. 8, 1998. BA, Iowa State Tchrs. Coll., Cedar Falls, 1961; MD, U. Iowa, Iowa City, 1967. Diplomate Am. Bd. Neurology. Head dept. electroencephalography and neurophysiology Balboa Naval Hosp., San Diego, 1971—73; physician, ptnr., head dept. neurology Coastal Neurol. Med. Group, La Jolla, Calif., 1973—. Med. dir. San Diego Parkinsons Disease Info. Ctr., 1986—; bd. dirs. Ellen Browning Scripps Soc., San Diego, 1986-94, 1996-2005; mem. exec. cabinet Scripps Inst. Medicine and Sci., San Diego, 1994-2004; head neurology dept. Balboa Naval Hosp., 1972-73 Author and editor publs. in field Lt. comdr. USN, 1971-73 Mem. AMA, Calif. Med. Assn. (del. 1981-84), Am. Acad. Neurology, Movement Disorder Soc., Rotary Internat. (Paul Harris fellow 1986), Purple Key Soc Republican. Avocations: tennis, fly fishing, hunting, golf, trumpet. Home: PO Box 224 Rancho Santa Fe CA 92067-0224 Office: 9850 Genesee Ave Ste 740 La Jolla CA 92037-1218 Office Phone: 858-453-3842.

SILVER, ELAINE TERRY, lawyer; b. Balt., May 11, 1953; Student, Hebrew U., 1972-73; BA with honors, Bucknell U., 1974; JD, NYU, 1977. Bar: Conn. 1977, U.S. Dist. Ct. Conn. 1977, U.S. Ct. Appeals (2d cir.) 1980. Assoc. Glazer, Seelig & Glazer, Stamford, Conn., 1977-81, 82-83; vis. prof. law Beijing U., 1981-82; ptnr. Fleisher, Trow & Silver, Stamford, 1983-87, Silver, Golub & Sandak (now Silver Golub & Jeitell LLP), Stamford, 1987—2000; founder Law Office of Elaine T. Silver, Lake Mary, Fla., 2005—. Counsel Domestic Violence Service, Stamford, 1983-85; founder Silver Divorce Ctr., 2004-; adj. family law instr., Barry U. Sch. Law, 2007 Pres., bd. dirs. Rape and Sexual Abuse Crisis Ctr., Inc., Stamford, 1985-87. Mem. ABA (family law sect.), Conn. Bar Assn. (exec. com. family law sect.), Stamford Bar Assn., The Regional Bar (co-chair family law sect.), Midday Club, Newfield Club. Office: Silver Dovorce Ctr Park Pl at Heathrow 1515 Internat Pkwy Ste 1019 Lake Mary FL 32746 E-mail: ESilver@SilverDivorce.com. *

SILVER, GEORGE, metal trading and processing company executive; b. Warren, Ohio, Dec. 17, 1918; s. Jacob and Sophie (Bradlyn) S.; m. Irene Miller, Aug. 5, 1945. Student, U. Ala., 1938; BA, Ohio U., 1940; postgrad. law sch., Ohio State U., 1940—41; grad., Adj. Gen. Sch., 1944. Pres. Riverside Indsl. Materials, Bettendorf, Iowa, 1947-70, Metalpel subs. Continental Telephone Co., Bettendorf, Iowa, 1970-71, Riverside Industries Inc., Bettendorf, Iowa, 1971—. Pres. Scott Resources Inc., Davenport, Iowa; v.p. Durbin Midwest, Davenport, 1987—90; mktg. dir. NAMCO Internat., Miami; cons. Waste Mgmt.-Non Ferrous Mktg., 1990—, Snyer Steel Casting, Iowa, Riverside Products, Ill., 1992—93, Tamron Internat. Ltd., Shanghai, 2002; founder Iowa Steel Mills (named changed to North Star Steel), Cargill and Wilton; mktg. dir. NAMCO Environ. Svcs. Corp.,

Miami, Fla., 1995—; bd. dirs. NAMCO Trading Co., Miami; cons. metal trading Cricket Club, Miami. Contbr. articles to profl. jours. Mem. Nat. UN Day Com., 1975-83. Capt. AC, USAF, 1941-46, 50-51, Korea. Named to Hon. Order Ky. Cols., 1991. Mem. Nat. Assn. Recycling Industries (co-chmn. nat. planning com., bd. dirs.), N.Y. Acad. Scis., Copper Club, Paper Stock Inst. Am. (exec. com.), Bur. Internat. de la Recuperation (chmn. adv. com.), Inter Global Trading Group (chmn. bd. dirs.), Mining Club N.Y.C., Outing Club, Hatchet Men's Chowder and Protective Assn., Copper Club, Jockey Club Miami, Williams Island Club, Rock Island Arsenal Officer's Club, Chemist Club (N.Y.C.), Crow Valley Country Club, Elks, Phi Sigma Delta.

SILVER, HARRY R., lawyer; b. Phila., Aug. 8, 1946; s. Jerome Benjamin Silver and Josephine Sandler (Steinberg) Furr; m. Jessica Dunsay, Nov. 23, 1972; children: Gregory, Alexander. BA, Temple U., 1968; JD, Columbia U., 1971. Bar: N.Y. 1972, D.C. 1973, U.S. Dist. Ct. D.C., U.S. Ct. Claims, U.S. Ct. Appeals (1st, 4th, 5th, 7th, 8th, 9th, 10th, fed. and D.C. cirs.), U.S. Supreme Ct. Law clk. to Hon. Harold R. Medina, U.S. Ct. Appeals (2d cir.), NYC, 1971-72; assoc. Arent, Fox, Kintner, Plotkin & Kahn, Washington, 1972-74; atty. U.S. Dept. Justice, Washington, 1974-77, U.S. Dept. Energy, Washington, 1977-78; assoc. Akin, Gump, Strauss, Hauer & Feld, Washington, 1978-81, ptnr., 1981-88, Oppenheimer, Wolff & Donelly, Washington, 1988-91, Davis Wright Tremaine, Washington, 1991-94, Ober, Kaler, Grimes & Shriver, Washington, 1994—2004, Patton Boggs, Washington, 2004—. Mem.: ABA, Fed. Bar Assn. Avocations: running, music, travel. Home: 6829 Wilson Ln Bethesda MD 20817-4948 Office: Patton Boggs 2550 M St NW Washington DC 20037 Home Phone: 301-229-2295; Office Phone: 202-457-6453. E-mail: hsilver@pattonboggs.com.

SILVER, HERBERT, physician; b. Bklyn., Feb. 18, 1932; s. Ben and Sylvia (Weinstock) S.; m. Judith Elaine Miller, Aug. 28, 1966; children: Rand Kenneth, David Jeffrey. BA, Adelphi U., 1953; MD, SUNY, Buffalo, 1957. Diplomate Am. Bd. Pathology. Intern Maimonides Med. Ctr., 1957-58; resident Nassau Univ. Med. Ctr., 1958-60, Hosp. of U. of Pa., 1960-62; assoc. pathologist, dir. blood bank/hematology Barnes-Jewish Hosp., St. Louis, 1964-70; dir. transfusion medicine Hartford (Conn.) Hosp., 1970—2001; assoc. prof. U. Conn. Med. Ctr., Farmington, 1970-90, U. Conn. Sch. of Allied Health, Storrs, 1977—2002. Cons. St. Francis Med. Ctr., Hartford, Conn., 1978-2002, Conn. Children's Med. Ctr., 1980-2002; med. dir. Hartford Med. Lab, 1985-99; adv. coun. Capital Cmty. Coll. Found., Hartford, Conn., 2002—. Author, editor: Probability of Inclusion in Paternity Testing, 1982, Problem Solving in Immunohematology, 1987; guest editor Transfusion Jour., 1992-96; contbr. articles to profl. jours. Bd. dirs. Emanuel Synagogue, West Hartford, Conn. Capt. U.S. Army Med. Corps, 1962-64. Mem.: AMA, Coll. Am. Pathologists, Am. Soc. Clin. Pathology, Am. Assn. Blood Banks (bd. dirs. 1987—92, Disting. Svc. award 1993, John Elliott Meml. award 2000). Democrat. Jewish. Avocations: bicycling, clarinet. Home: 32 Beacon Hill Dr West Hartford CT 06117-1003

SILVER, JEFFREY, film producer; Films produced include Rappin', 1985, Shag: The Movie, 1989, Don't Tell Mom the Babysitter's Dead, 1991, Crossing the Bridge, 1992, Mr. Baseball, 1992, The Opposite Sex...And How to Live with Them, 1993, Indian Summer, 1993, The Santa Clause, 1994, Born to Be Wild, 1995, Addicted to Love, 1997, How to Be a Player, 1997, Three to Tango, 1999, Ready to Rumble, 2000, Gossip, 2000, Training Day, 2001, The Santa Clause 2, 2002, National Security, 2003, If Only, 2004, Mindhunters, 2004, Assault on Precinct 13, 2005, The Thing About My Folks, 2005, The Santa Clause 3: The Escape Clause, 2006, The Return, 2006, 300, 2006, Breach, 2007. Office: Outlaw Prodns 12103 Maxwellton Rd Studio City CA 91604-3623 *

SILVER, JOAN MICKLIN, film director, screenwriter; b. Omaha, May 24, 1935; d. Maurice David and Doris (Shoshone) Micklin; m. Raphael D. Silver, June 28, 1956; children: Dina, Marisa, Claudia. BA, Sarah Lawrence Coll., 1956. Writer, dir. (movies) Hester Street, 1975 (Writers Guild best screenplay nomination), Chilly Scenes of Winter, 1981, (TV film PBS) Bernice Bobs Her Hair starring Shelly Du Vall, 1975; dir. (TV films HBO) Finnegan, Begin Again with Robert Preston and Mary Tyler Moore, Parole Board, A Private Matter with Sissy Spacek and Aidan Quinn, (TV film Showtime) In The Presence of Mine Enemies, 1997, (films) Between the Lines, 1976, Crossing Delancey with Amy Irving, 1988, Loverboy, 1989; dir. stage plays and musicals including Album, Maybe I'm Doing It Wrong, Off-Broaday prodn. A...My Name is Alice; prodr. On The Yard, (radio) Great Jewish Stories from Eastern Europe and Beyond, 1995; dir. (feature film) A Fish in the Bathtub, 1998, (TV film Lifetime) Invisible Child, 1999, (TV film Showtime) Charms for the Easy Life, 2001, TV film LifeTime) Hunger Point, 2003. Office: Silverfilm Prodns Inc 510 Park Ave New York NY 10022-1105 Office Phone: 646-282-0312.

SILVER, JOEL, film producer; b. South Orange, NJ, July 14, 1952; m. Karyn Fields, July 10, 1999. Attended, Lafayette Coll. Owner Silver Pictures; co-owner (with Robert Zemenckis) Dark Castle Entertainment. Film producer: The Warriors, 1979, Xanadu, 1980, 48 Hours, 1982, Jekyll & Hyde...Together Again, 1982, Streets of Fire, 1984, Brewster's Millions, 1985, Weird Science, 1985, Commando, 1985, Jumpin' Jack Flash, 1986, Lethal Weapon, 1987, Predator, 1987, Action Jackson, 1988, Die Hard, 1988, Lethal Weapon 2, 1989, Roadhouse, 1989, The Adventures of Ford Fairlane, 1990, Die Hard 2, 1990, Predator 2, 1990, Hudson Hawk, 1991, Ricochet, 1991, The Last Boy Scout, 1991, Lethal Weapon 3, 1992, Demolition Man, 1993, Richie Rich, 1994, Demon Knight, 1995, Assassins, 1995, Fair Game, 1995, Executive Decision, 1996, Bordello of Blood, 1996, Father's Day, 1997, Conspiracy Theory, 1997, Lethal Weapon 4, 1998, Made Men, 1999, The Matrix, 1999, The House on Haunted Hill, 1999, Romeo Must Die, 2000, Dungeons and Dragons, 2000, Exit Wounds, 2001, Proximity, 2001, Swordfish, 2001, Thir13en Ghosts, 2001, Ghost Ship, 2001, Cradle 2 the Grave, 2003, The Matrix Reloaded, 2003, The Matrix Revolutions, 2003, Gothika, 2003, House of Wax, 2005, Kiss Kiss Bang Bang, 2005, V for Vendetta, 2005, The Reaping, 2007; TV prodr.: W.E.I.R.D. World, 1995, Action, 1999, The Strip, 1999, Freedom, 2000, Jane Doe, 2001, Newton, 2003, Next Action Star, 2004, Bet Your Life, 2004, Veronica Mars, 2004, The Studio, 2005. Office: Silver Pictures care Warner Bros Pictures 4000 Warner Blvd Bldg 90 Burbank CA 91522-0001 *

SILVER, MALCOLM DAVID, pathologist, educator; b. Adelaide, South Australia, Apr. 29, 1933; s. Eric Bertram and Stella Louisa (Riley) S.; m. Meredith May Galloway, Jan. 19, 1957; children: Stuart Faulkner, Claire Eleanor, Caryl Louise. MD, U. Adelaide; PhD, McGill U. Diplomate: Am. Bd. Pathology. Resident med. officer Royal Adelaide Hosp., 1957-58; resident in pathology Royal Victoria Hosp.-Pathol. Inst., McGill U., Montreal, Que., Canada, 1958-63; research fellow dept. exptl. pathology John Curtin Sch. Med. Research, Australian Nat. U., Canberra, 1963-65; asst. prof. pathology U. Toronto, 1965-68, assoc. prof., 1968-74, prof., 1974—79, chmn. dept. pathology, 1985-95, prof. dept. lab. medicine and pathobiology, 1996—98; staff pathologist Toronto Gen. Hosp., 1965-72, sr. staff pathologist, 1972-79; prof., chmn. dept. pathology U. Western Ont., London, Ont., Canada, 1979-85; chief pathology Univ. Hosp., London, 1979-85; pathologist in chief Toronto Gen. Hosp., 1985-89, The Toronto Hosp. (Toronto Gen. and Toronto Western Divs.), 1989-91, sr. staff pathologist, 1991-98. Prof. emeritus U. Toronto, 1998—. Contbr. articles to profl. jours. Fellow Royal Coll. Pathologists Australasia, Royal Coll. Physicians and Surgeons Can.; mem. Can. Assn. Pathologists, Ont. Assn. Pathologists, Internat. Acad. Pathology, Can. Cardiovasc. Soc., Soc. for Cardiovasc. Pathology. E-mail: md.silver@utoronto.ca.

SILVER, MICHAEL, education educator; b. Landsberg, Germany, Jan. 30, 1948; came to U.S., 1949; s. Norman and Esther Silver; m. Beverley Ann Moss, May 16, 1971; children: Sabina, Joseph. AB, Washington U., 1970, MEd, 1973, PhD, 1982. Cert. supt. Mo., Wash. Tchr. Normandy Sch. Dist., St. Louis, 1970-72, Parkway Sch. Dist., St. Louis, 1972-75, asst. prin., 1976-79, adminstrv. asst., 1979-83, asst. to supt., 1983-84, asst. supt., 1984-86; supt. Tukwila Sch. Dist., Seattle, 1986—2003; asst. prof. ednl. adminstrn. Seattle U. Bd. dirs. Cities in Schs., Seattle; mem. adv. bd. Sta. KCTS, Seattle, 1990-2003; vis. exec. Seattle U. Sch. Edn., 1995. Author: Values Education, 1976, Facing Issues of Life and Death, 1976. Pres. SeaTac Task Force, Seattle, 1989; bd. dirs. Anti-Defamation League, Seattle, 1987—; mem. City of Tukwila (Wash.) 2000 Com., 1988-90. Recipient A Plus award Wash. Coun. Econ. Edn., 1992, Excellence in Ednl. Leadership award Univ. Coun. for Ednl. Adminstrn., 1998, Art Tribute award, Wash. Art Edn. Assn., 2001; named Exec. Educator, 100 Exec. Educator Mag., 1985, 1996 Assoc. for Inst. for Ednl. Inquiry Leadership Program; named to Homework Ctrl.; 100 Most Influential People in U.S. Pub. Edn.; I/D/E/A fellow Charles F. Kettering Found., 1978, 88, Title VI fellow Washington U., 1971-73, Svc. Learning Faculty fellow Seattle U., 2005-06; New Prin. grantee Wash. Mutual, 2005; named Supt. of Yr. Wash. Libr. Media Assn., 2000. Mem. ASCD, Am. Assn. Sch. Adminstrs., Wash. Assn. Sch. Adminstrs. (met. chpt., pres. 1989-90), King County Supts. (chmn. adv. com. 1989-90, 95-96), Southcenter Rotary Club (Paul Harris fellow 1994), Southwest King County C. of C., Phi Delta Kappa. Home: 14127 SE 50th St Bellevue WA 98006-3409 Office: Seattle U Sch Edn PO Box 222000 901 12th Ave Seattle WA 98122 Office Phone: 206-296-5798. Personal E-mail: silver@eskimo.com. Business E-Mail: silverm@seattleu.edu.

SILVER, MICHAEL JOEL, lawyer; b. Balt., Feb. 8, 1955; s. Edgar P. and Ann W.S.; m. Abbe Rebecca Levitt, May 14, 1983; children: Rachel, Lucy. AB, Harvard U., 1977; JD, U. Chgo., 1980. Bar: Md. 1980. Assoc. Piper & Marbury, Balt., 1980-87, ptnr. Balt. & NYC, 1987-92; now ptnr. Hogan & Hartson LLP, Balt. Office: Hogan & Hartson LLP 111 S Calvert St Fl 16 Baltimore MD 21202-6174 Office Phone: 410-659-2741. Business E-Mail: mjsilver@hhlaw.com.

SILVER, MORRIS, economist, educator; b. NYC, July 9, 1931; s. Julius and Lilly Silver; m. Sondra P. Hartman, Jan. 26, 1958; children: Gerald David, Ronald Alan. BA, CCNY, 1958; PhD (Earhart Found. fellow, Ford Found. fellow), Columbia U., 1964. Mem. faculty City Coll. CUNY, 1964—, assoc. prof. econs., 1968—, prof., 1972—, chmn. dept., 1969-95. Rsch. assoc. Nat. Bur. Econ. RSch., 1967—71; cons. crime deterrence and offender career Nat. Ctr. Health Svcs. Rsch., 1970—, Hudson Inst., 1974. Author (with r. D. Auster): The State as a Firm, 1979; author: Affluence, Altruism, and Atrophy: The Decline of Welfare States, 1980, Prophets and Markets: The Political Economy of Ancient Israel, 1983, Enterprise and the Scope of the Firm, 1984, Economic Structures of the Ancient Near East, 1985, Foundations of Economic Justice, 1989, Taking Ancient Mythology Economically, 1992, Economic Structures of Antiquity, 1995. With US Army, 1953—55. Mem.: Am. Econ. Assn. Jewish. Office: Dept Econs City Coll 133 D St New York NY 10031 E-mail: msilver12@nyc.rr.com.

SILVER, PAUL G., geophysicist; b. LA, Nov. 30, 1948; s. Theodore L. and Rose (Cohen) S.; m. Nathalie Valetie, June 21, 1980; children: Karen, Celine. BA in Psychology magna cum laude, UCLA, 1970; BA in Geology, U. Calif., Berkeley, 1976; PhD in Geophysics, U. Calif., San Diego, 1982. Sr. staff scientist Carnegie Inst. DTM, Washington, 1982—; rsch. assoc. prof. dept. earth and planetary scis. Johns Hopkins U., Balt., 1986—. Participant various sci. expdns.; rep. to Am. Geol. Inst., Seismol. Soc. Am., 1997—; mem. com. of charis Inc. Rsch. Instns. for Seismology, 1996—. Assoc. editor Jour. Geophys. Rsch., 1987-90; contbr. articles to profl. jours. Recipient Carl Eckart award Scripps Inst. Oceanography, 1982; UNESCO lectr., 1988. Fellow Geol. Soc. Am., Am. Geophys. Union, Am. Acad. Arts & Scis.; mem. AAAS, Seismol. Soc. Am., Phi Beta Kappa. Office: Carnegie Inst DTM 5241 Broad Branch Rd NW Washington DC 20015-1305 E-mail: silver@dtm.ciw.edu. *

SILVER, R. PHILIP, packaging products executive; b. 1942; Grad., U. Mo., 1967. With Amour & Co., Atlanta, 1967—68, Boise Cascade Corp., Idaho, 1968—75; exec. v.p. Fla. Gas Co., Orlando, Fla., 1975—80; pres. Continental Can, Norwalk, Conn., 1980—86; pres., treas. Silgan Holdings Inc., Stamford, Conn., 1987—93, chmn., co-CEO, 1994—2004, co-chmn., co-CEO, 2004—06, co-chmn., 2006—. Office: Silgan Holdings Inc 4 Landmark Sq Stamford CT 06901 *

SILVER, RALPH DAVID, financial planner; b. Chgo., Apr. 19, 1924; s. Morris J. and Amelia (Abrams) S.; m. Lois Reich, Feb. 4, 1951; children: Jay, Cappy. BS, U. Chgo., 1943; postgrad., Northwestern U., 1946-48; JD, DePaul U., 1952. Bar: Ill. bar 1952. Staff accountant David Himmelblau & Co. (C.P.A.'s), 1946-48; internal revenue agt. U.S. Dept. Treasury, 1948-51; practice in Chgo., 1952-55; atty. Lawrence J. West, 1952-55; exec. v.p.-fin., bd. dirs. Barton Inc., Chgo., 1955-92. Arbitrator N.Y. Stock Exch., Cir. Ct. of Cook County, Ill. Bd. dirs., pres. Ralph and Lois Silver Found. Lt. (j.g.) USNR, 1943-46. Mem. ABA, Chgo. Bar Assn., AICPA. Clubs: Green Acres Country. Home: 1124 Old Elm Ln Glencoe IL 60022-1235

SILVER, RICHARD TOBIAS, oncologist, educator; b. Jan. 18, 1929; m. Barbara Silver; 1 son, Adam Bennett. BA, Cornell U., 1950, MD, 1953. Diplomate Nat. Bd. Med. Examiners, Am. Bd. Internal Medicine, Am. Bd. Clin. Oncology. Intern N.Y. Hosp.-Cornell Med. Ctr., NYC, 1953-54, asst. resident in medicine, 1956-57, resident in hematology, 1957-58; clin. assoc. gen. medicine br. Nat. Cancer Inst., NIH, Bethesda, Md., 1954-56; asst. in medicine Cornell U. Med. Coll., NYC, 1956-58, instr. medicine, 1958-62, clin. asst. prof., 1962-67, clin. assoc. prof., 1967-73, clin. prof., 1973—2002; asst. attending physician NY Hosp., 1964-67, assoc. attending physician, 1967-73, attending physician, 1973—, dir. clin. oncology and chemotherapy rsch., divsn. Hematology & Med. Oncology, 2000; prof. medicine, med. dir. Leukemia and Myeloproliferative Ctr., Weill Med. Coll. of Cornell U., 2002—. Asst. vis. physician 2d Cornell Med. div. Bellevue Hosp., NYC, 1963-66; vis. Fulbright prof. U. Bahia Sch. Medicine, Brazil, 1958-59; vis. prof. Hershey Hosp.-Pa. State Hosp., 1976, Mayo Clinic, 1977, Upstate Med. Ctr., Binghamton, NY, 1977, Med. Coll. Va., 1979, Med. Sch. Colubia U., 1982, NJ Coll. Medicine, New Brunswick, 1983, Meml. Med. Ctr. U. Ga., 1984, 86; invited lectr. and presenter in field; chair 1st, 2d, 3d and 4th Internat. Congresses Myelproliferative and Myelodysplastic, 2001, 03, 05, 07; vis. faculty curriculum devel. Annenberg Ctr. Rancho Mirage, Calif., 1994—; mem. rev. bd. NIH, Nat. Cancer Inst.; cons. Cancer Chemotherapy Investigative Rev. Bd., 1980, clin. trials com., 1979-81; mem. Cornell U. Coun., 1987—; spl. site visitor medicine A Roswell Park Meml. Inst., NIH-Nat. Cancer Inst., 1976, mem. combined modality com. divsn. cancer treatment, 1977-79, clin. trials com., 1979-81, cons. cancer chemotherapy rev. bd., 1980, ad hoc site visitor, MD Anderson Hosp., Houston, 2003, prin. investigator Internat. Myeloprolifentive Rsch. Consortium, 2006-, chmn. membership com., 2006-, vice-chmn. Internat. Working Group for Myelofibrosis Rsch. and Treatment, 2006-; vis. Fulbright lectr. Sch. Medicine U. Bahia, Brazil, 1958-59; lectr., presenter in field. Author: Morphology of the Blood and Marrow in Clinical Practice, 1970; co-author: (with R.D. Lauper, C.I. Jarowski) A Synopsis of Cancer Chemotherapy, 1977, 2ndedit., 1986, monographs; editor: Clinical Topics in Cancer: Diagnosis and Treatment, 1982; cons. editor Am. Jour. Medicine, 1974-84, mem. editl. adv. bd., 1984; editor, contbr.: Topics in Cancer, 1982; mem. editl. adv. bd. Cancer Investigation, 1983-94; ad-hoc rev. New Eng. Jour. Medicine, Annals of Internal Medicine, Mayo Clinic Procs., Blood, Cancer, Am. Jour. Hematology, Med. Rsch. Coun., Eng., others; contbr. chpts. to books and articles to profl. jours. Trustee Frances and Edwin Cummings Meml. Fund, 1985-92, Rectory Sch., Pompret, Conn., 2004-; med. dir. Rsch. for Blood Health, Inc., 1968-85, Arnold K. Krakower Hematology Found., 1966-75, Cancer Rsch. and Treatment Fund, 1985—. Recipient Pasmantier award, Timothy Gee award for outstanding tchr., clinician, inventor and humanist, 2001; N.Y. State scholar for profl. study of medicine. Fellow ACP; mem. Cornell U. Med. Coll. Alumni Assn. (pres. 1973-76, sr. advisor 1976—), Am. Soc. Clin. Oncology (mem. com. clin. practice 1976, com. on pub. affairs 1981-83, chmn. program com. 1977), Internat. Soc. Hematology (chmn. bone marrow biopsy wokshop XV congress 1974, internat. adv. com. XX Congress 1984, lectr.), Am. Soc. Hematology (chmn., guidelines com., mem. devel. com. 2003-06), Leukemia Soc. Am. (med. dir., v.p. NYC chpt. 1968-78), Chronic Myeloid Leukemia (mem. devel. com., 2003-06), Sass Found Hematologic Rsch. (bd. advs.), NY Soc. Study of Blood, NY County Med. Soc., NY State Med. Soc. Oncologists and Hematologists (pres. 1991-2001, mem. exec. com. 1991—, chmn. nominating com.), Harvey Soc., Am. Fedn. Clin. Rsch., Am. Assn. Cancer Rsch., Explorers Club (bd. dirs., chmn. sci. adv. com. 1987), Sigma Xi. Office: NY Presby Hosp Weill Cornell Med Ctr 525 E 68th St Box 581 New York NY 10021 Home Phone: 212-746-2541; Office Phone: 212-746-2098. Business E-Mail: rtsilve@med.cornell.edu. E-mail: rtsilvermd@gmail.com.

SILVER, RICHARD V., lawyer, diversified financial services company executive; b. 1955; BA, JD, St. John's Univ. Bar: NY 1982. Assoc. Cahill Gordon & Reindel, NYC; v.p., sr. securities atty. Merrill Lynch; atty. AXA Equitable, 1986—88, v.p., 1988—91; pres., COO Equico Securities, 1991—95; sr. v.p., chief compliance officer AXA Equitable, 1995—96; sr. v.p., dep. gen. counsel AXA Financial, 1996—2001, exec. v.p., gen. counsel, 2001—. AXA rep., variable ins. products & ind. dealer com. NASD. Editor: St. John's Law Rev. Office: AXA Financial Inc 1290 Ave of the Americas New York NY 10104 Office Phone: 212-314-3916. Office Fax: 212-554-2320.

SILVER, RICK, marketing professional; Grad. cum laude, U. SC, 1974. Pvt. practice, 1976—. Office: 1411 Gervais St Columbia SC 29201 Home Phone: 803-254-8158; Office Phone: 803-254-8158. E-mail: rick.silver@cnsg.com.

SILVER, ROSLYN OLSON, federal judge; b. Phoenix, Feb. 28, 1946; BA, U. Calif. Santa Barbara, 1968; JD cum laude, Ariz. State U., 1971. Bar: Ariz. 1971, U.S. Ct. Appeals (9th cir.) 1980, U.S. Supreme Ct. 1984. Law clk. Hon. Lorna E. Lockwood Ariz. Supreme Ct., Phoenix, 1971-72; advisor, litigator Navajo Nation Native Am. Rights Fund, Phoenix, 1974-76; legal labor counsel Dial Corp., Phoenix, 1976-78; ptnr. Logan and Aguirre, Phoenix, 1978-79; legal counsel EEOC, Phoenix, 1979-80; asst. U.S. Atty. Dist. Ariz., Phoenix, 1980-84; asst. atty. gen. Ariz. Atty. Gen.'s Office, Phoenix, 1984-86; acting 1st asst., chief criminal divsn. dist. Ariz. U.S. Atty. Office, Phoenix, 1986-94; judge Dist. Ariz. U.S. Dist. Ct., Phoenix, 1994—. Chair local rules com. Ariz. Dist. Ct.; mem. regional sect. panel Harry S Truman Scholarship Found. Contbg. editor: Rutter Group Practice Guide; contbr. articles to profl. jours. Mem. bd. visitors U. Ariz. Law Sch.; mem. adv. panel Lodestar Mediation Clinic, Ariz. State U. Law Sch. Named one of 100 Significant Women and Minorities in Ariz.'s Legal History, 2000. Mem. ABA, Fed. Bar Assn., Nat. Assn. Women Judges, Ariz. Bar Assn. (Pub. Lawyer of Yr. 1990), Ariz. Women Lawyers Assn. (outstanding legal practitioner award 1999), Ariz. State U. Alumni Assn. (outstanding alumnus award 1996). Office: US Dist Ct 401 W Washington SPC 59 Phoenix AZ 85003 Office Phone: 602-322-7520.

SILVER, SHELDON, state legislator, lawyer; b. NYC, Feb. 13, 1944; s. Nathan and Frieda (Bearman) S.; m. Rosa Mandelkern, June 25, 1967; children: Edward, Janine, Michelle, Esther. BA, Yeshiva U., 1965; JD, Bklyn. Coll., 1968. Bar: N.Y. 1969, U.S. Dist. Ct. (so. and ea. dists.) N.Y. 1970. Assoc. Schechter & Schwartz, NYC, 1968-71; law sec. to Judge Francis Pecora NYC, 1971-76; ptnr. Agri, Bilder & Silver, NYC, 1976-81; pvt. practice NYC, 1981—. Mem. N.Y. State Assembly, 1977—, chmn. ways and means com., 1992, speaker, 1994. Vice pres. Bialystoker Synagogue, Young Israel Synagogue. Named Man of Yr., Harry S. Truman Dem. Club, 1977, United Jewish Appeals, 1983, also others. Democrat. Office: 250 Broadway Ste 2301 New York NY 10007

SILVER, WARREN M., state supreme court justice; m. Evelyn Silver. Grad., Tufts U., 1970; JD, Am. U. Wash. Coll. of Law, 1973. Atty., priv. practice, Bangor, 1977—2005; justice Maine Supreme Ct., 2005—. Bd. dir. Bangor Museum and Ctr. History. Mem.: Maine Trial Lawyers Assn. (bd. govs. 1987—97, pres. 2001—05, liaison supreme judicial court civil rules com. 2005—). Office: Maine Supreme Ct Penobscot Cty Courthouse 97 Hammond St Bangor ME 04401 Office Phone: 207-561-2325.

SILVERBERG, JAY LLOYD, lawyer; b. NY, Oct. 1, 1961; s. Sheldon and Elissa (Nenner) S.; children: Jennifer, Rebecca, Sabrina. BA, Brandeis U., 1983; JD, Boston U., 1986. Bar: N.Y. 1987, N.J. 1987, U.S. Dist. Ct. (so. dist.) N.Y. 1990, U.S. Dist. Ct. (ea. dist.) N.Y. 1991. Assoc. McCarter & English, Newark, 1986-87, Proskauer Rose, NYC, 1987-91; mem. Silverberg, Stonehill & Goldsmith, P.C., NYC, 1991—. Lectr. Nat. Assn. Credit Mgmt., Columbia U. Sch. Bus., 1996. Editor: Annual Review of Banking Law, 1986. Paul J. Liacos scholar Boston U. Sch. Law, 1985, G. Joseph Tauro scholar, 1984. Mem. N.Y. Inst. Credit, Manhattan Credit Club (pres. 1998), Turnaround Mgmt. Assn. Office: Silverberg Stonehill & Goldsmith PC 111 W 40th St New York NY 10018-0968 Office Phone: 212-730-1900. Business E-Mail: jlsilverberg@ssghlaw.com.

SILVERBERG, MARK VICTOR, lawyer, educator; b. Akron, Ohio, Sept. 26, 1957; s. Alvin Harold and Marilyn (Bierman) S.; m. Marsha Phyllis Mermelstein, Aug. 11, 1979; childern: Samantha Michele, Marissa Jill. BS, Rider Coll., 1979; JD, Pace U., 1983. Bar: N.J. 1983, N.Y. 1984, U.S. Dist. Ct. (so. dist.) N.Y., U.S. Dist. Ct. N.J. Atty. Met. Life Ins. Co., NYC, 1983—84; corp. counsel H & N Chem. Co., Totowa, NJ, 1984—85; pvt. practice East Brunswick, NJ, 1985—90; gen. coun. East Coast Title Ins., 1990—91; CEO Nalmar Captial Mortgage Corp., 1991—. Prof. law Middlesex County Coll., Edison, N.J., 1985—, Mercer County Coll., Trenton, N.J., 1985—, Upsala Coll., East Orange, N.J., 1991—. Mem. ABA (real estate, probate and property law sect., corp. law sect.), N.Y. State Bar Assn., N.J. Bar Assn. (real estate, probate and property law sect., corp. law sect.), Middlesex County Bar Assn., Rotary. Republican. Jewish. Avocations: basketball, golf, hockey, woodworking, gardening.

SILVERBERG, MICHAEL JOEL, lawyer; b. Rochester, NY, Aug. 12, 1932; s. Goodman and Minnie (Krovetz) S.; m. Charlotte Goldman, June 19, 1955; children: Mark (dec. 1999), Daniel. BA, U. Rochester, 1954; JD, Columbia U., 1957. Bar: N.Y. 1958, U.S. Dist. Ct. (so. dist.) N.Y. 1965, U.S. Dist. Ct. (ea. dist.) N.Y. 1990, U.S. Ct. Appeals (2d cir.) 1975, U.S. Supreme Ct. 1967. Instr. Columbia U. Law Sch., NYC, 1957—58; assoc. Phillips Nizer LLP (formerly Phillips, Nizer, Benjamin, Krim & Ballon), NYC, 1960—67, ptnr., 1967—2006, counsel, 2006—. Vol. civil rights lawyer Miss. Lawyers Com. for Civil Rights Under Law, 1965; cons. sci. program com. Am. Psychiat. Assn., 2000—01. Bd. editors Columbia Law Rev., 1955—57. Bd. dirs. Nat. Alliance on Mental Illness of NY State, 1998-2004, 2005-, pres., 1999-2004, 2005-06, 1st v.p. 2006—; pres. Nat. Alliance on Mental Illness NYC, 1997-2003, pres. emeritus, 2006; mem. adv. bd. NYC Vis. Nurse Svc.; mem. nat. adv. coun. Columbia Teen Screen Program; mem. bd. editors Columbia Law Rev., 1955-57. Fulbright scholar U. Strasbourg, France, 1958-59; named one of NY Super Lawyers Gen. Litig., 2006. Mem. ABA, N.Y. State Bar Assn., Assn. Bar City N.Y. Home:

205 W End Ave New York NY 10023-4804 Office: Phillips Nizer LLP 666 Fifth Ave New York NY 10103 Home Phone: 212-787-2771; Office Phone: 212-841-0533. Personal E-mail: msilverberg@phillipsnizer.com.

SILVERBERG, ROBERT, writer; b. NYC, 1935; s. Michael and Helen (Baim) S.; m. Barbara Brown, 1956; m. Karen Haber, 1987. BA, Columbia U., 1956. Author: (novels) Thorns, 1967, The Masks of Time, 1968, Hawksbill Station, 1968, Nightwings, 1969, To Live Again, 1969, Tower of Glass, 1970, The World Inside, 1971, Son of Man, 1971, A Time of Changes, 1971, Dying Inside, 1972, The Book of Skulls, 1972, Born with the Dead, 1974, Shadrach in the Furnace, 1976, Lord Valentine's Castle, 1980, Majipoor Chronicles, 1982, Lord of Darkness, 1983, Valentine Pontifex, 1983, Gilgamesh the King, 1984, Tom O'Bedlam, 1985, Star of Gypsies, 1986, At Winter's End, 1988, To the Land of the Living, 1989, The New Springtime, 1990, (with Isaac Asimov) Nightfall, 1990, The Face of the Waters, 1991, (with Isaac Asimov) The Ugly Little Boy, 1992, Kingdoms of the Wall, 1993, (with Isaac Asimov) The Positronic Man, 1993, Hot Sky at Midnight, 1994, Mountains of Majipoor, 1995, Starborne, 1996, Sorcerers of Majipoor, 1997, The Alien Years, 1998, Lord Prestimion, 1999, The King of Dreams, 2001, The Longest Way Home, 2002, Roma Eterna, 2003, Phases of the Moon, 2004, In the Beginning: Tales from the Pulp Era, 2006; (non-fiction) Lost Cities and Vanished Civilizations, 1962, The Great Wall of China, 1965, The Old Ones: Indians of the American Southwest, 1965, Scientists and Scoundrels: A Book of Hoaxes, 1965, The Auk, the Dodo and the Oryx, 1966, The Morning of Mankind: Prehistoric Man in Europe, 1967, Mound Builders of Ancient America: The Archaeology of a Myth, 1968, If I Forget Thee, O Jerusalem: American Jews and the State of Israel, 1970, The Pueblo Revolt, 1970, The Realm of Prester John, 1971. Recipient Hugo award World Sci. Fiction Conv., 1956, 69, 87, 90; Nebula award Sci. Fiction Writers Am., 1970, 72, 75, 86, Grand Master Nebula award, 2004. Mem. Sci. Fiction Writers Am. (pres. 1967-68) Address: PO Box 13160 Oakland CA 94661-0160 E-mail: ragberg@attglobal.net.

SILVERBERG, STEVEN MARK, lawyer; b. Bklyn., June 7, 1947; m. Arlene Leopold, July 4, 1971; 2 children. BA, Bklyn. Coll., 1969; JD, NYU, 1972. Bar: N.Y. 1973, U.S. Dist. Ct. (so. and ea. dists.) N.Y. 1974, U.S. Supreme Ct. 1976, U.S. Ct. Appeals (2nd cir.) 1978. Asst. dist. atty. Kings County Dist. Atty., Bklyn., 1972-75; dep. town. atty. Town of Greenburgh, N.Y., 1975-79; ptnr. Stowell, Kelly & Silverberg, White Plains, N.Y., 1979-83, Hoffman, Silverberg & Wachtell, Elmsford, N.Y., 1983-86, Hoffman, Silverberg, Wachtell & Koster, White Plains, N.Y., 1986-89; pvt. practice White Plains, 1989-92; ptnr. Kirkpatrick & Silverberg LLP, White Plains, 1993—2000, Wilson, Elser, Moskowitz, Edelman & Dicker LLP, White Plains, 2001—. Adj. assoc. prof. N.Y. Law Sch., 1990—93. Co-author: Wetlands and Coastal Zone Regulations and Compliance, 1993; contbr. to profl. publs. Counsel Greenburgh Housing Authority, 1979-84, Town of Mamaroneck, N.Y., 1984-96, Village of Mamaroneck, 1999-2003, planning and zoning bd. Town of Haverstraw, 2001—; bd. dirs. Temple Beth Torah, Upper Nyack, N.Y., 1977-89, 2000-03, pres. 1984-86; bd. dirs. N.J. West Hudson Valley Region Union of Am. Hebrew Congregations, 1986-88, Westchester Mcpl. Planning Fedn. Mem. ABA, N.Y. State Bar Assn., Westchester County Bar Assn. (chair environtl. law com. 1997—). Office: Wilson Elser Moskowitz Edelman & Dicker LLP 3 Gannett Dr White Plains NY 10604 E-mail: silverbergs@wemed.com.

SILVERMAN, ALAN HENRY, lawyer; b. NYC, Feb. 18, 1954; s. Melvin H. and Florence (Green) S.; m. Gretchen E. Freeman, May 25, 1986; children: Willa C.F., Gordon H.F. BA summa cum laude, Hamilton Coll., 1976; MBA, JD, U. Pa., 1980. Bar: N.Y. 1981, U.S. Dist. Ct. (so. and ea. dists.) N.Y. 1981, U.S. Ct. Internat. Trade 1981, D.C. 1986, U.S. Supreme Ct. 1990. Assoc. Hughes, Hubbard & Reed, NYC, 1980-84; asst. counsel Newsweek, Inc., NYC, 1984-86; v.p., gen. counsel, sec., dir. adminstrn. Cable One, Inc., Phoenix, 1986—. Contbr. articles to profl. jours. Mem. prevention adv. com. Gov. Pa. Justice Commn., 1975-79; bd. dirs. Lawyers' Alliance for N.Y., 1982-85, N.Y. Lawyers Pub. Interest, 1983-85, Nat. Assn. JD-MBA Profls., 1983-85, Bus. Vols. for Arts, Inc., Phoenix, 1989-93, Ariz. Vol. Lawyers for the Arts, Inc., 1994-97, First Amendment Coalition Ariz., Inc., 1991—, Phoenix Falcons Fencing Club, Inc., 2003-05; mem. Maricopa County Citizens Jud. Adv. Coun., 1990-93; mem. citizens' bond com. City of Phoenix, 2000. Mem. ABA, Assn. of Bar of City of N.Y., D.C. Bar Assn., Phi Beta Kappa. Home: 5833 N 30th St Phoenix AZ 85016-2401 Office: Cable One Inc 1314 N 3d St Phoenix AZ 85004 Office Phone: 602-364-6190. E-mail: alan.silverman@cableone.net.

SILVERMAN, ALLISON, scriptwriter, television producer, actress; Actor, prodr., writer (TV series) The Colbert Report, 2005—, writer Late Night with Conan O'Brien, 1993—94, The Daily Show, 1996—2001 (Emmy award for outstanding writing for variety, music or comedy prog., 2001), Late Night with Conan O'Brien: 10th Anniversary Special, 2003, The Daily Show with Jon Stewart: Indecision 2006 Election Night, 2006, (video game) You Don't Know Jack!, 1999, You Don't Know Jack!: Mock 2, 2000. Office: Viacom 1515 Broadway New York NY 10036 *

SILVERMAN, AMY JOCELYN, psychiatrist; b. Royal Oak, Mich., Apr. 6, 1972; d. Fredrick and Evelyn Simon; m. Stephen Silverman, Sept. 15, 2001; 1 child, Alexandra Joy. BA in Psychology, Brandeis U., Waltham, Mass., 1994; MD, Mt. Sinai, NYC, 1998. Resident Harvard Longwood Psychiatry Residency Tng. Program, Boston, 1998—2001; fellow Ny Presbyn. Hosp.-Payne Whitney, Manhattan, 2001—03; psychiatrist NY Presbyn. Hosp., Weill Cornell Med. Ctr., White Plains, NY, 2003—. Recipient Physician of Yr., NY Presbyn. Hosp.-Westchester Divsn., 2005. Mem.: Am. Acad. Child and Adolescent Psychiatry, Am. Psychiat. Assn. Office: New York Presbyterian Hospital 21 Bloomingdale Rd White Plains NY 10605 Home Phone: 914-686-1595; Office Phone: 914-997-5991. Personal E-mail: ams9012@med.cornell.edu.

SILVERMAN, ARNOLD BARRY, lawyer; b. Sept. 1, 1937; s. Frank and Lillian Lena (Linder) S.; m. Susan L. Levin, Aug. 7, 1960; children: Michael Eric, Lee Oren. B of Enging. Sci., Johns Hopkins U., 1959; JD cum laude, U. Pitts., 1962. Bar: US Dist. Ct. (we. dist.) Pa. 1963, Pa. 1964, U.S. Patent and Trademark Office 1965, US Supreme Ct. 1967, Can. Patent Office 1968, US Ct. Claims 1975, US Ct. Appeals (3d cir.) 1982, US Ct. Appeals (fed. cir.) 1985, US Ct. Appeals (4th cir.) 2000. Patent atty. Alcoa, New Kensington, Pa., 1962-67, 68-72, sr. patent atty., 1972-76; ptnr. Price and Silverman, Pitts., 1967-68; v.p., gen. patent counsel Joy Mfg. Co., Pitts., 1976-80; ptnr. Murray Silverman & Keck, Pitts., 1980-81, Buell, Blenko, Ziesenheim & Beck, Pitts., 1984; ptnr. intellectual property dept. Eckert, Seamans, Cherin & Mellott, Pitts., 1984—, chmn., 1992—2005, chmn. info. tech. practice group, 1992-97; spl. asst. atty. gen. State of W.Va., 1985—; spl. counsel patents U. Pitts., 1975—. Nat. panel of arbiters Am. Arbitration Assn., 1987—; spkr. in field. Contbr. 90 articles to profl. jours. Mem. Churchill CSC, Pa., 1967-90, chmn., 1975-90; mem. Pitts. law com. Anti-Defamation League, 1981—, regional adv. bd., 1982—, ch-chmn. Pitts. region ann. dinner, 1983, mem. chmn. by-laws com., 1983; bd. govs. Slippery Rock U. Found., 1985-91; Pitts. steering com. MIT Enterprise Forum, 1986-87. With US Army, 1963-64. Recipient Am. Spirit Honor medal, Ft. Knox, 1963; named Pa. Super Lawyer Pa. Law and Politics Mag., 2004, 05, 06, 07. Fellow: Mensa (nat. assoc. counsel patents and trademarks copyrights 1980—82, inventors' spl. interest group 1980—86, chmn. trademark and logo com. 2006—); mem.: ASME, ABA, U. Pitts. Gen. Alumni Assn., Assn. Corp. Patent Counsel (emeritus mem.), Intertel (treas. Pitts. Forum 1983—), Stratford Cmty. Assn. (v.p. 1966—67, gov. 1966—70, pres. 1967—68), Golden Panthers, U. Pitts. Law Alumni Assn. (bd. dirs. 1992—2002, treas. 1997—98, v.p. 1998—99, pres.-elect 1999—2000, pres. 2001—02), Johns Hopkins Soc. Engring. Alumni, Johns Hopkins U. Alumni Assn. (chmn. publicity com. 1963—66, exec. com. 1966—87, v.p. 1969—70, pres. 1971—72, nat. alumni coun. 1989—92, 2003—), Brit. Inst. Chartered Patent Agts. (fgn. mem.), Licensing Execs. Soc. (co-chmn. Pitts. chpt. 1994—96), Am. Chem. Soc. (chemistry and the law sect.), Nat. Assn. Coll. and Univ. Attys., Pa. Bar Assn. (sports/entertainment arts law com. 1999—), DC Bar Assn., US Trademark Assn. (chmn. task force on advt. agys. 1981, membership com. 1987—89), Am. Intellectual Property Law Assn. (membership com. 1985—88, pub. rels. com. 1994—), Pitts. Intellectual Property Law Assn. (chmn. pub. rels. com. 1968—69, chmn. patent laws com. 1970—72, chmn. legis. action com. 1972—75, chmn. nominating com. 1973, bd. mgrs., newsletter editor 1974—88, sec.-treas. 1976—84, v.p. 1984—85, pres. 1985—86, pub. rels. com. 1994—95, program com. 1995—96, co-chmn. 2001—03), U. Pitts. Gen. Alumni Assn. (life; bd. dir. 2001—06, exec. com. 2002—06, sec. 2003—06, strategic planning com. 2003—06, awards com. 2006—, leadership coun. 2006—), Robert Bruce Assn. Law Fellows (life), Allegheny County Bar Assn. (chmn. pub. rels. com. 1978—80, vice-chmn. intellectual property sect. 1981—83, chmn. 1984—85), Duquesne Club, Order of Coif, Psi Chi, Tau Epsilon Rho. Republican. Jewish. Home: 2019 High Pointe Ct Murrysville PA 15668-8515 Office: 600 Grant St 44th Fl Pittsburgh PA 15219-2703 Office Phone: 412-566-2077. Business E-Mail: abs@escm.com. *Welcome challenge and perform all tasks with enthusiasm, in a moral manner and to the very best of your ability.*

SILVERMAN, ARTHUR CHARLES, lawyer; b. Lewiston, Maine, June 13, 1938; s. Louis A. and Frances Edith (Brownstone) S.; BS in Elec. Engring., BS in Indsl. Mgmt., MIT, 1961; JD, Columbia U., 1964; m. Donna Linda Zolov, June 18, 1961; children: Leonard Stephen, Daniel Edward. Bar: N.Y. 1965, U.S. Supreme Ct. 1971. Engr., engring. asst. Gen. Electric Co., Pittsfield, Mass. and Phila., 1958-62; assoc. Baer & Marks, N.Y.C., 1965-68; assoc. Golenbock and Barell, N.Y.C., 1968-72, ptnr., 1972-89; ptnr. Reid & Priest LLP, N.Y.C., 1989-98, dep. chair, 1996-98; ptnr. Thelen Reid & Priest LLP, N.Y.C., 1998-2006, Thelen Reid Brown Raysman & Steiner LLP, N.Y.C., 2006—. Treas., trustee Ramaz Sch., 1977-84, vice chmn., 1984-85, 86-88, chmn., 1988-92, hon. chmn., 1992—; bd. govs. MIT Hillel Found., 1979-84; mem. Bd. Jewish Edn. of City of N.Y., 1981-84; mem. exec. com. Nat. Jewish Ctr. for Learning and Leadership, 1984-90. Mem. IEEE, ABA, NSPE, N.Y. State Bar Assn., Fed. Bar Council, Assn. Bar City N.Y., N.Y. Soc. Architects, Internat. Bar Assn., Inter-Pacific Bar Assn., Constrn. Mgmt. Inst., Constrn. Specifications Inst. Home: 200 E 74th St New York NY 10021-3618 Office: Thelen Reid Brown Raysman & Steiner LLP 900 Third Ave New York NY 10022 Office Phone: 212-895-2138.

SILVERMAN, BARRY G., federal judge; b. NYC, Oct. 11, 1951; 1 child, Bagel Ann. BA summa cum laude, Ariz. State U., 1973, JD, 1976. Bar: Ariz. 1976, US Dist. Ct. Ariz. 1976, US Ct. Appeals (9th cir.) 1976, US Supreme Ct. 1980. Asst. city prosecutor, Phoenix, 1976—77; dep. atty. Maricopa County, 1977—79; ct. commr., 1979—84; judge Superior Ct. Ariz. Maricopa County, 1984—95; apptd. magistrate judge US Dist. Ct. Ariz., 1995—98; judge US Ct. Appeals (9th cir.), 1998—. Instr. constnl. law Coll. Law, Ariz. State U., 1983, adj. prof. advanced criminal procedure, 89; lectr. cmty. property BAR/BRI Ariz., Idaho and Nev. Bar Rev. Courses, 1989—94. Recipient Exel award, Soc. Nat. Assn. Publs., 1992. Mem.: ABA, Maricopa County Bar Assn. (Henry Stevens award 1991), State Bar Ariz. Avocations: magic, beagles, baseball, wine tasting. Office: US Ct of Appeals 401 W Washington St SPC 78 Phoenix AZ 85003 *

SILVERMAN, BEN, broadcast executive, television producer; b. Pittsfield, Mass., Aug. 15, 1970. BA History magna cum laude, Tufts U. V.p. New World/Marvel Entertainment; head of internat. packaging divsn. & NY cons. br. William Morris Agy.; founder, exec. prodr. Reveille Prodns., 2002—07; co-chmn. NBC Entertainment & NBC Universal TV Studio (name changed to Universal Media Studios), 2007—. Writer (TV series) The Restaurant, 2003—04, co-creator & exec. prodr. Nashville Star, 2003—, The Biggest Loser, 2004—; exec. prodr.: (TV series) Coupling, 2003, $25 Million Dollar Hoax, 2004, Blow Out, 2004—, The Club, 2004—05, 30 Days, 2005, The Office, 2006—, Ugly Betty, 2006—07, Are You Smarter Than a 5th Grader?, 2007—; (TV miniseries) The Tudors, 2007; prodr.: (TV films) 9/11, 2002. Active in Seeds of Peace. Named one of 40 Under 40, Advt. Age, 2007. Office: Universal Media Studios 100 Universal City Plaza Universal City CA 91608 *

SILVERMAN, BRUCE GARY, advertising executive, consultant; b. NYC, Feb. 16, 1945; s. Edward E. and Lillian (Brill) S.; children: Jennifer, Matthew; m. Nancy Cole, 1996; children: Christen Cole, Larry Cole. BA, Adelphi U., 1965; JD, Albany Law Sch., 1967. Sr. v.p., exec. creative dir. Ogilvy & Mather Inc., NYC, 1967-80; exec. v.p., exec. creative dir. Bozell & Jacobs Inc., Dallas, 1981-83, Batten, Barton, Durstine & Osborn Inc., LA, 1984-85; exec. v.p., creative dir. Asher/Gould Advt. Inc., LA, 1986-89, pres., chief creative officer, 1989-95, pres., COO, 1996-97; pres. Western Internat. Advocacy Group, LA, 1997-98; exec. v.p., mng. dir. Initiative Media, LA, 1998—; pres., CEO Initiative Ptnrs., USA, 1999—2002; pres. WONGDOODY Advt., LA, 2003—05; chmn., CEO Pocket Billboards, Inc., Studio City, Calif., 2005—. V.p., bd. dirs. L.A. Children's Mus., 1984-88; chmn. Resource Devel. com. Starbright Pavillion Found., 1993. Mem. Acad. TV Arts and Scis., Am. Assn. Advt. Agys. (bd. dirs., vice chmn. western region 2002). Home: 3168 Dona Mema Pl Studio City CA 91604-4264 Office: Pocket Billboards Inc 12750 Ventura Blvd Ste 202 Studio City CA 91604 Personal E-mail: bgsla@adelphia.net.

SILVERMAN, BURTON PHILIP, artist; b. Bklyn., June 11, 1928; s. Morris Daniel and Anne (Firstenberg) S.; m. Claire Guss, June 12, 1969; children: Robert Arthur, Karen Lila. BA, Columbia Coll., 1949. Freelance illustrator Life, Fortune, Esquire, Time, Newsweek, Sports Illus., New York, The New Yorkers mags., 1959—; instr. Sch. Visual Arts, NYC, 1964-67. Co-author: Abel, 1968, A Portfolio of Drawings, 1968; author: Painting People, 1977, Breaking the Rules of Watercolor, 1983, Sight and Insight: The Art of Burton Silverman, 1999; contbr. articles and drawings to profl. jours.; one-man exhbns. include Davis Gallery, N.Y.C., 1956, 58, 62, Kenmore Galleries, Phila., 1963, 67, 70, FAR Gallery, N.Y.C., 1965, 70, 75, 77, Genesis Gallery, N.Y.C., 1979, Sindin Galleries, N.Y.C., 1983, Capricorn Galleries, Bethesda, Md., 1979, 91, Gallery 52, South Orange, N.J., 1967, 70, 77, Harbor Gallery, L.I., 1971, 74, U. Utah, 1967, Doll and Richards, Boston, 1980, Grand Ctrl. Galleries, N.Y.C., 1988, Cudahy's Gallery, N.Y.C., 1990, Joseph Keiffer, Inc., N.Y.C., 1993, Gerold Wunderlich & Co., N.Y.C., 1996, 97, Merrill Gallery, Denver, 1996, 98, Butler Inst. of Am. Art, 1999, Brigham Young Mus., Provo, 1999, Gallery Henoch, N.Y.C., 2001, 04; group exhbns. include Butler Inst. Am. Art, Youngstown, Ohio, 1954-71, 74, 76, 79, 88, 90, 93, 2002, NAD, N.Y.C., 1958-96, 98, 2001, 03, Am. Watercolor Soc., N.Y.C., 1978-82, 84-87, 89-91, 95-96, 97, 99, 2002, Pa. Acad. Fine Art, 1949, New Britain (Conn.) Mus. Am. Art, 1964, Wadsworth Atheneum, Hartford, Conn., 1961, Am. Acad. Arts and Letters, 1967, 74, 76, 79, N.Y. Hist. Soc., 1976, Pa. State Mus. Art, Portsmouth (Va.) Mus. Art, 1976, 79-80, 82 (Purchase prize, 1979, 82), Mexico City Mus. Art, 1990, Nat. Portrait Gallery, Washington, 1993, Hofstra Mus., N.Y.C., 1993, South Bend (Ind.) Mus. Art, 1994, Old Forge (N.Y.) Mus. and Gallery, 1994, Qgunquit Mus., 1997, Del. Art Mus., Wilmington, 2004. With AUS, 1951-53. Named to Hall of Fame, Soc. of Illustrators, N.Y., 1990, Pastel Soc. Am., 1992; named Artist of Am., 1991, 94, 2000; recipient Gold medal Nat. Portrait Soc., 2004. Mem. NAD (numerous awards and prizes including Joseph Isidor Gold medal 1992, Ranger Purchase prize 1962, 84, Benjamin Altman figure prize 1969, academician, 1972-), Am. Watercolor Soc. (numerous awards and prizes including Gold medal 1979, Silver medal 1984, 95, annuals), Pastel Soc. Am. (hon.). E-mail: bpsart@aol.com. *In art I am wary of things too facile, or appealing. My painting is rooted in a realist tradition that is equally concerned with objective facts and subjective realities. It is a visual language that allows me to explore the tensions and ambiguities engendered by this dual aspect of human experience. Art is my life and my life is in my art.*

SILVERMAN, DAVID, film director, television producer, television director, animator; b. NYC, Mar. 15, 1957; Attended, U. Md., 1975—77, UCLA. Dir.: (TV series) The Simpsons, 1989—2006 (named Outstanding Animated Prog., Emmy Awards, 1990, 1995, 1997, 2006); prodr.:, 1991—; visual designer (TV series) The Critic, 1994—95; dir.: (films) The Strange Case of Mr. Donnybrook's Boredom, 1981, The Road to El Dorado, 2000, Monsters, Inc., 2001 (Best Fgn. Language film, Hochi Film Awards, 2002), The Simpsons Movie, 2007. Recipient Outstanding Individual Achievement in Field of Animation, Annie Awards, 1992. Office: The Simpsons c/o Twentieth Television PO Box 900 Beverly Hills CA 90213 *

SILVERMAN, DAVID A., lawyer, finance company executive; b. 1958; BS, Drexel U.; JD, U. Calif. Sch. of Law, LA. Bar: NJ 1984, PA 1984. Assoc. Duane, Morris & Heckscher, 1987—91; gen. counsel Meridian Mortgage Corp., 1991—97; sr. v.p., gen. counsel, sec. Sovereign Bancorp, Phila., 1997—. Office: Sovereign Bancorp Inc 1500 Market St Philadelphia PA 19146 E-mail: dsilverm@sovereignbank.com.

SILVERMAN, DAVID IRVING, cardiologist; b. New Bedford, Mass., Aug. 24, 1954; s. Seymour and Roslyn S.; m. Adrienne Bentman, May 26, 1985; children: Gabriel, Alexandra. BA, Yale Coll., 1976; MS, U. Chgo., 1977; MD, U. Ill., 1982. Diplomate Am. Bd. Internal Medicine in medicine and cardiovascular disease. Resident Boston City Hosp., 1982-85; fellow West Roxbury (Mass.) VA/Harvard Med., 1985-87; rsch. fellow Beth Israel Hosp., Boston, 1987-90; asst. prof. U. Conn. Health Ctr., Farmington, 1990-99, assoc. prof., 1999—. Dir. Lipid Disorders Clinic, U. Conn., Farmington, 1991—. Fellow Am. Coll. Cardiology; mem. ACP, Am. Heart Assn., Conn. State Med. Soc. Office: U Conn Health Ctr Cardiology Dv Farmington CT 06030-0001

SILVERMAN, ERIC F., lawyer; b. Phila., Sept. 21, 1954; s. Robert L. and Marilyn L. S.; m. Joann B. Silverman, Oct. 7, 1979; children: Amy, Laura, Charlie. BA, Middlebury Coll., 1976; JD, Georgetown U., 1982. Bar: N.Y. 1982. Energy/environ. planner Henningson, Durham, Richardson, Washington, 1976-79; mgmt. cons. Booz Allen & Hamilton, Washington, 1980; ptnr. & chmn. global project fin. group Milbank Tweed Hadley & McCloy, NYC, 1982—. Author: Resource Recovery - A Plan for Small Communities and Institutions, 1976; editor, Project Finance newsletter. Mem. Fed. Energy Bar Assn., ABA (energy/environ. natural resources div.), N.Y. State Bar Assn., Bar Assn. City of N.Y. Office: Milbank Tweed Hadley McCloy 1 Chase Manhattan Plz Fl 54 New York NY 10005-1401 Office Fax: 212-530-5219. Business E-Mail: esilverman@milbank.com.

SILVERMAN, GARY R., lawyer; b. 1961; BA, Brandeis U., 1983; JD, Northwestern U., 1986; MBA, U. Chgo., 1990, MLA, 2006. Bar: Ill. 1986, Colo. 1987, DC 1988, NY 1994. Ptnr. Corp. & Fin. Dept. Kaye Scholer LLP, Chgo., NYC. Mem.: ABA. Office: Kaye Scholer LLP Ste 4100 3 First Nat Plaza Chicago IL 60602 also: 425 Park Avenue New York NY 10022 Office Phone: 312-583-2330. Business E-Mail: gsilverman@kayescholer.com.

SILVERMAN, GILBERT B., retired real estate developer, art collector; b. May 1925; 3 children. B, U. Calif., Berkeley. Chmn. CEO Silverman Companies, Bingham Farms, Mich.; owner Amurcon. Named one of Top 200 Collectors, ARTnews Mag., 2004, 2005, 2006. Mem.: Bldg. Industry Assn. (pres. 1996). Avocation: collector of Fluxus-related materials & conceptual art. Office: Silverman Companies Ste 220 32100 Telegraph Rd Bingham Farms MI 48025

SILVERMAN, HENRY RICHARD, real estate company executive; b. NYC, Aug. 2, 1940; s. Herbert Robert and Roslyn (Moskowitz) S.; m. Susan H. Herson, June 13, 1965 (div. Jan. 1977); children: Robin Lynn, Deborah Leigh; m. Nancy Ann Kraner, Jan. 22, 1978; 1 child, Catherine Anne Grad. cum laude, Hackley Sch., Tarrytown, NY, 1957; BA with honors, Williams Coll., 1961; LLB, U. Pa., 1964; postgraduate student in Corp. Fin. and Taxation, NYU, 1965. Bar: NY 1965, US Tax Ct. 1965, US Ct. Appeals (2nd cir.) 1965. Atty., 1965—66; with White, Weld & Co., beginning 1966; gen. ptnr. Oppenheimer & Co., until 1970; pres., CEO ITI Corp., 1970—72; founder, pres. Trans-York Securities Corp., 1972; exec. v.p., chmn. exec. com. Ladenburg, Thalmann & Co., 1973; pres., CEO Vavasseur Am. Ltd., subs. UK mcht. bank, 1974—75; gen. ptnr. Brisbane Ptnrs., 1976-77; prin. various investment groups, 1977—, Silverman Energy Co., NYC, 1977, NBC Channel 20, Springfield, Ill., 1977—83, ABC Channel 9, Syracuse, NY, 1977—81; prin., dir. Delta Queen Steamboat Co., New Orleans, 1977—86; prin. outdoor advt., music pub., motion picture prodn., radio broadcasting & hardware mfg. cos.; pres., CEO Reliance Capital Corp., subs. Reliance Group Holdings, Inc., NYC, 1982—90; sr. v.p. bus. devel. Reliance Group Holdings, Inc., NYC, 1982—90; chmn., CEO Days Inns Am., Inc., Atlanta, 1984—89; pres., CEO Telemundo Group, Inc., NYC, 1986—90; gen. ptnr. Blackstone Group, NYC, 1990—91; chmn., CEO, pres. HFS Inc., NYC, 1990—97; chmn., pres., CEO Cendant Corp., NYC, 1996—2004, chmn., CEO, 2004—06, Realogy Corp., Parsippany, NJ, 2004—. Bd. dirs. NYU Hosp., NYC, 1987. Served to lt. USNR, 1965-73. Recipient Am. Heritage Award, Anti-Defamation League, 1998. Mem.: Harmonie (NYC). Republican. Jewish. Avocation: tennis. Office: Realogy Corp 1 Campus Dr Parsippany NJ 07054 *

SILVERMAN, HUGH J., philosophy educator; b. Boston, Aug. 17, 1945; s. Leslie and Eleanore (Riffin) S.; m. L. Theresa Watkins, June 22, 1968 (div. Apr. 1983); children: Claire Christine, H. Christopher; m. Gertrude Postl, Sept. 1, 1987. BA, Lehigh U., 1966, MA, 1967; postgrad., U. Paris, 1968, 71-72; PhD, Stanford U., 1973. Lectr. Stanford U., Calif., 1973-74; asst. prof. SUNY, Stony Brook, 1974-79, assoc. prof., 1979-83, prof. philosophy and comparative lit., 1983—, affiliated faculty mem. dept. European langs., lits. and cultures, 2004, dept. art, 2005—. Vis. sr. lectr. U. Warwick, Coventry, Eng., 1980, U. Nice, France, 1980, 81; vis. prof. Duquesne U., Pitts., 1978, 2000, NYU, 1978-80, 85-86, U. Leeds, Eng., 1988, U. Torino, Italy, 1989, U. Vienna, Austria, 1993, 94, 97, 2000, U. Nice, France, 1994, U. Helsinki, Finland, 1997, 99, U. Sydney, Australia, 1998, U. Milan, U. Rome II, 2001, U. Trondheim, Norway, 2002, Ul Klagenfurt, Austrlia, 2003, 05; co-dir. Internat. Philos. Seminar, Alto Adige, Italy, 1991—; Fulbright Disting. chair humanities U. Vienna, 2000-01. Author: Inscriptions: Between Phenomenology and Structuralism, 1987, Textualities: Between Hermeneutics and Deconstruction, 1994 (German translation 1997), Inscriptions: After Phenomenology and Structuralism, 1997; editor: Piaget, Philosophy and the Human Sciences, 1980, 97 (Spanish translation 1989), Philosophy and Non-Philosophy since Merleau-Ponty, 1988, 97, Derrida and Deconstruction, 1989, (Korean translation 1999), Postmodernism - Philosophy and the Arts, 1990 (Korean translation 1990), Gadamer and Hermeneutics, 1991, Writing the Politics of Difference, 1991, Questioning Foundations: Truth/Subjectivity/Culture, 1993, Cultural Semiosis: Training the Signifier, 1997, Philosophy and Desire, 2000, Lyotard: Philosophy, Politics and the Sublime, 2002; co-editor: Jean-Paul Sartre: Contemporary Approaches to His Philosophy, 1980, Continental Philosophy in America, 1983, Hermeneutics and Deconstruction, 1985, Descriptions, 1985, Critical and Dialectical Phenomenology, 1987, Horizons of Continental Philosophy, 1987, Postmodernism and

Continental Philosophy, 1988, The Textual Sublime: Deconstruction and its Differences, 1990, Merleau-Ponty: Texts and Dialogues: On Philosophy, Politics and Culture, 1992, 96, Textualität der Philosophie-Philosophie und Literatur, 1994, Derrida und Die Politiken der Freundschaft, 2003, co-editor; series editor: Routledge Continental Philosophy series, 1986—; co-editor: Humanities Press Humanity Books Contemporary Studies in Philosophy and the Human Sciences series, 1989—, assoc. editor, 1979-89; editor: Humanities Press Humanity Books Series in Philosophy and Literary Theory, 1989—, SUNY Press Contemporary Studies in Philosophy and Literature, 1988-96, Northwestern U. Press Series in Philosophy, Literature, and Culture, 1996-2001; Bull. for Rsch. in Humanities, 1983-84, Continuum Books Textures: Philosophy/Literature/Culture Series, 2001—; mem. editorial bd. Rsch. in Phenomenology, 1981—, Rev. of Existential Psychology and Psychiatry, 1979—, Symploké, 2000-, Chiasmi: Intz Merleau-Ponty Studies, 2001-; translator: Consciousness and the Acquisition of Language, 1973; contbr. numerous articles to profl. jours., and chpts. in books. Fulbright-French Govt. and Alliance Francaise fellow, Paris, 1971-72; faculty rsch. fellow SUNY-Stony Brook, 1977, 78, 81; rsch. fellow Am. Coun. Learned Socs., 1981-82; Experienced Faculty Travel fellowship SUNY, 1985, 88, 93, 99; Fulbright travel grant, Netherlands and Germany, 2001; recipient MLA travel grant (Brazil), 1993, N.Y. Coun. for Humanities grant, 1976-77, SUNY Chancellor's award for excellence in teaching, 1977, medal U. Helsinki, 1997. Mem. Soc. Phenomenology and Existential Philosophy (exec. co-dir. 1980-86), Internat. Assn. Philosophy and Lit. (exec. com. 1976—, exec. sec. 1979-87, exec. dir. 1987—), Brit. Soc. Phenomenology (exec. com. 1980-95), Merleau-Ponty Circle (chmn. publs. com. 1978-2001), Heidegger Conf., Am. Soc. Aesthetics, Am. Philos. Assn. (program adv. com. 1986-89, 2003-, lectures publs. and rsch. com. 1991-94). Office: Stony Brook U Dept Philosophy Stony Brook NY 11794-3750 Business E-Mail: hugh.silverman@stonybrook.edu.

SILVERMAN, IRA NORTON, news producer; b. Bklyn., May 17, 1935; s. Joseph and Mildred (Axelrod) S.; m. Elizabeth Parsons Aspray, June 16, 1979; children by previous marriage: Gary, Bruce; stepchildren: Elizabeth, Aime, Alison. AB, Columbia U., 1957. Newspaper, mag. and book editor, 1957—67; prodr., writer NBC News, 1967—79; sr. prodr. spl. projects NBC Nightly News, Washington, 1977—95; contbr. The New Yorker, NYC, 1995—, editl. cons., 1995—96; cons. NBC News, 1998, PBS, 1999, 2002. Co-author: The Pleasant Avenue Connection, 1976. Recipient Nat. Headliner award, 1977, 78, 81, 87, Alfred I. DuPont-Columbia U. award, 1983-84, 85-86, Emmy award for news and documentary, 1985, 87, award Overseas Press Club Am., 1987, 90, George Polk award L.I. U., 1988, Excellence in TV award Channels mag., 1990, George Foster Peabody award U. Ga., 1991, Citation for Excellence Overseas Press Club, 1992.

SILVERMAN, JOSEPH, chemistry professor; b. NYC, Nov. 5, 1922; s. Jakob and Mary (Chechick) S.; m. Joan Aline Jacks, Jan. 14, 1951; children: Joshua Henry, David Avrom. BA, Bklyn. Coll., 1944; A.M., Columbia U., 1948, PhD, 1951. Head research dept. Walter Kidde (nuclear labs.), Garden City, N.Y., 1952-54; v.p., tech. dir. RAI Research Corp., L.I. City, N.Y., 1954-59; assoc. prof. chemistry State U. N.Y., Stony Brook, 1959-60; prof. dept. materials and nuclear engring. U. Md., College Park, 1960-92, dir. Inst. for Phys. Sci. and Tech., 1976—83, prof. emeritus, 1992—. Cons. Danish AEC, Indsl. Research Inst., Japan, Boris Kidric Inst., Yugoslavia, Bechtel Co., GPU Nuclear Corp., GE, IAEA, Vienna; disting. vis. prof. Tokyo U., 1974; gen. chmn. 2d Internat. Meeting on Radiation Processing, Miami, Fla., 1978, 3d Tokyo, 1980, hon. chmn. 6th, Ottawa, 1987; trustee Washington Inst. Values in Pub. Policy, 1981-87. Editor Internat. Jour. Applied Radiation and Isotopes, 1973-78, Trans. 1st Internat. Meetings on Radiation Processing, 1977, 3d edit., 1981; mem. editorial adv. bd. Radiation Physics and Chemistry, 1978-95. Served with AUS, 1944-46. Recipient Founders award 6th Internat. Meeting on Radiation Processing, 1987, Centennial medal U. Md. Coll. Engring., 1994; grad. rsch. fellow Brookhaven Nat. Lab., 1949-51; Guggenheim fellow, 1966-67. Fellow Nordic Soc. Radiation Chemistry and Tech., Am. Phys. Soc., Am. Nuclear Soc. (Radiation Industry award 1975); mem. Am. Chem. Soc., Sigma Xi. Home: 8101 Connecticut Ave Apt S407 Chevy Chase MD 20815-2839 Office: U Md Dept Materials Sci and Enging College Park MD 20742-2115 E-mail: jagman@umd.edu.

SILVERMAN, JOSEPH HILLEL, mathematics professor; b. NYC, Mar. 27, 1955; s. Harry and Shirley (Seiner) S.; m. Susan Leslie Greenhaus, June 13, 1976; children: Deborah, Daniel, Jonathan. ScB, Brown U., 1977; MA, Harvard U., 1979, PhD, 1982. Moore instr. MIT, Cambridge, 1982-86; assoc. prof. Boston U., 1986-88; assoc. prof. math. Brown U., Providence, 1988-91, prof., 1991—, chmn., 2001—04. Founder and v.p. rsch., NTRU Cryptosystems, Inc., 1997—. Author: Arithmetic of Elliptic Curves, 1986; editor: Arithmetic Geometry, 1987, Rational Points on Elliptic Curves, 1992, Advanced Topics in Arithmetic of Elliptic Curves, 1995, Diophantine Geometry (with M. Hindry), 2000, Arithmetic of Dynamical Systems, 2007. Fellow NSF, 1983-86, Sloan fellow Sloan Found., 1987, Guggenheim Found. fellow, 1998. Mem. Am. Math. Soc. (Steele prize 1998). Avocation: bridge. Office: Brown U Dept Math PO Box 1917 Providence RI 02912-1917

SILVERMAN, KENNETH EUGENE, language educator, writer; b. NYC, Feb. 5, 1936; s. Gustave and Bessie (Goldberg) S.; children: Willa Zahava, Ethan Leigh. BA, Columbia U., 1956, MA, 1958, PhD, 1964. Instr. English U. Wyo., Laramie, 1958-59; preceptor in English Columbia U., NYC, 1962-64; prof. English, co-dir. The Biography Seminar NYU, NYC, 1964-2001. Adv. coun. Inst. Early Am. History and Culture, 1984-87. Author: Timothy Dwight, 1969, A Cultural History of the American Revolution, 1976, The Life and Times of Cotton Mather, 1984, Edgar A. Poe: Mournful and Never-ending Remembrance, 1991, Houdini!!! The Career of Ehrich Weiss, 1996, Lightning Man: The Accursed Life of Samuel F.B. Morse, 2003; editor: anthology Colonial American Poetry, 1968; compiler: Selected Letters of Cotton Mather, 1976; mem. editl. bd. Early Am Lit., 1969-72, 77-80, William and Mary Quar., 1984-87, Am. Lit. 1987-90. Recipient Bancroft prize in Am. history, 1985, Pulitzer Prize for biography, 1985, Edgar Allan Poe award Mystery Writers Am., 1992; grantee Bicentennial award NEH, 1972-74, Am. Philos. Soc., 1986, Am. Coun. Learned Socs., 1986; Guggenheim fellow, 1989-90. Mem. Am. Acad. Arts and Scis., Soc. Am. Historians, Am. Antiquarian Soc., Authors Guild, Soc. Am. Magicians. Jewish. Personal E-mail: ks2@nyu.edu.

SILVERMAN, LAURENCE A., lawyer; b. NYC, Sept. 9, 1953; s. Jacob and Julia (Melnick) S. BA summa cum laude (hon.), Columbia U., 1974; JD, Yale U., 1977. Bar: NY 1978, US Dist. Ct. (so. dist.) NY 1978, US Ct. Appeals (2d cir.) 1979, US Ct. Appeals (10th cir.) 1980, US Dist. Ct. (ea. dist.) NY 1982. Law clk. to justice Hon. Thomas P. Griesa US Dist. Ct. (so. dist.), NYC, 1977-78; assoc. David Polk, NYC, 1978-79; spl. counsel N.Y.C. Dept. Ports and Terminals, 1979-80; assoc. Cahill, Gordon & Reindel, NYC, 1980-86, ptnr., 1986, Covington & Burling LLP, NYC. Pro bono bd. mem. Tibet House. Named Best Lawyers in Am. Mem. ABA, NY County Lawyers Assn., Downtown Athletic Club. Democrat. Jewish. Avocations: running, tennis, hiking. Office: Covington & Burling LLP 1330 Avenue of Americas New York NY 10019 Office Phone: 212-841-1092. Business E-Mail: lsilverman@cov.com.

SILVERMAN, LESLIE E., commissioner; b. Needham, Mass. Grad., U. Vt.; JD, Am. U.; M with distinction, Georgetown U. Bar: D.C., Mass. Law clk. U.S. Atty.'s Office; assoc. Keller & Heckman, 1990—97; labor counsel Senate Health, Edn., Labor and Pensions Com., 1997—2002; commr. US Equal Employment Opportunity Commn., Washington, 2002—. Office: US Equal Employment Opportunity Commn 1801 L St NW Washington DC 20507

SILVERMAN, MARTIN MORRIS BERNARD, secondary school educator; b. Boston, May 27, 1936; s. Joseph Lazarus and Sonya Lillian (Feldman) S.; m. Joseph Harvey. BS in Chemistry, U. Mass., 1960, MEd, 1962; EdM, Columbia U., 1974, EdD, 1985. Math. and sci. tchr. Northampton (Mass.) Pub. Schs., 1960-62, U.S. Dept. of Def., Korea and Bermuda, 1963-66; tchr. math, sci. N.Y.C. Bd. Edn., 1966-91. Rsch. scholar biophysics NYU, 1986—; biochemistry rsch. asst. Harvard U. Med. Sch., Boston, 1960; supr., dir. sci. fairs and competitions; cons. in field. Writer, musician, composer and performer; photographer Explorers Jour., U. Mo. Archives Collection, Jour. Violin Soc. Am. Curator musical instrument collection, instrument restorer Abrons Arts Ctr., Henry Street Settlement, 2000—03; mem. Violin Craftsmanship Inst., U. N.H., 1995, 1996, String Inst. Restoration Workshop, Oberlin Coll., 1995, 1996. Internat. Ctr. Photography scholar, N.Y.C., 1975. Mem. Violin Soc. Am., Jour. Violin Soc. Am., Nat. Assn. Watch Clock Collectors Assn., Musical Box Soc. Internat., Mensa, Explorers Club. Home: 25 Montgomery St New York NY 10002-6557

SILVERMAN, MOSES, lawyer; b. Bklyn., Mar. 3, 1948; s. Bernard and Anne Silverman; m. Betty B. Robbins, Jan. 19, 1980; children: Benjamin, Rachel. AB, Colby Coll., 1969; JD, NYU, 1973. Bar: NY 1974, Washington 1982, US Dist. Ct. (so. and ea. dists.) N.Y. 1974, US Dist. Ct. D.C. 2001, US Ct. Appeals (2d cir.) 1974, US Ct. Appeals (D.C. cir.) 1977, US Ct. Appeals (fed. cir.) 1985, US Ct. Appeals (11th cir.) 2001, US Ct. Appeals (9th cir.) 2002, US Ct. Appeals (6th cir.) 2006, US Supreme Ct. 1977, US Ct. Appeals (6th cir.) 2006. Assoc. Paul, Weiss, Rifkind, Wharton & Garrison, NYC, 1973-81, ptnr., 1981—. Vol. U.S. Peace Corps., Istanbul, Turkey, 1969-70; bd. dirs. Legal Aid Soc., 1998-05; overseer Colby Coll., 2002-. Mem. ABA, N.Y. State Bar Assn., Assn. Bar City N.Y. Home: 7 Gracie Sq New York NY 10028-8001 Office: Paul Weiss Rifkind Wharton & Garrison 1285 Ave of Americas New York NY 10019-6064 Office Phone: 212-373-3355. Business E-Mail: msilverman@paulweiss.com.

SILVERMAN, NORMAN ALAN, cardiac surgeon; b. Boston, Dec. 19, 1946; BA, Dartmouth Coll., 1968; MD, Boston U., 1971. Prof. surgery U. Ill., Chgo., 1980-89; divsn. head Henry Ford Hosp., Detroit, 1989—; prof. surgery Case-Western Res. U., Cleve., 1992—. Contbr. 200 scientific articles to profl. jours. Lt. comdr. USPHS, 1973-75. Fellow Am. Coll. Surgeons, Am. coll. Cardiology, Am. Coll. Chest Physicians. Avocation: sailing. Office: Henry Ford Hosp 2799 W Grand Blvd Detroit MI 48202-2689 Home Phone: 313-881-0302; Office Phone: 313-916-2695. Business E-Mail: nsilver1@hfhs.org.

SILVERMAN, NORMAN HENRY, cardiologist, educator; b. Johannesburg, Sept. 29, 1942; came to U.S., 1972; s. Simon Cecil and Jean (Krawitz) S.; m. Heather Silverman. DSc in Medicine, U. Witwatersrand, Johannesburg, 1985, postgrad. Diplomate Am. Bd. Pediatrics. Asst. prof. pediatrics Stanford U. Med. Ctr., Palo Alto, Calif., 1974—75, prof. pediat. cardiology, 2002—; asst. prof. pediatrics U. Calif., San Francisco, 1975—79, assoc. prof. radiology, 1979—85, prof. pediat. in residence, 1985—2002, prof. radiology in residence, 1985—2002. Co-author: Two Dimensional Echocardiography, 1982, Congenital Heart Disease, 1990; author: Pediatric Echocardiography, 1993; co-editor: Fetal Cardiology, 2003. Lt. South African Def. Force, 1968-69. Grantee March Dimes, 1977-79, Am. Heart Assn., 1978-80, 90-92; Roma and Marvin Auerback scholar pediat. cardiology Lucile Packard Children's Hosp. and Stanford U. Med. Ctr. Fellow Am. Coll. Cardiology, Coll. Physicians South Africa, Soc. Pediatric Rsch., Am. Pediatric Soc., Am. Heart Assn., Am. Soc. Echocardiography. Achievements include research in echocardiography of congenital heart disease in infants and children; fetal echocardiography and treatment. Office: Stanford U Med Ctr 750 Welch Rd #305 Palo Alto CA 94304 Office Phone: 650-723-7913. E-mail: norm.silverman@stanford.edu.

SILVERMAN, OZZIE, consulting strategist; b. Montreal, Que., Can., Jan. 30, 1939; s. Louis and Fanny (Black) S.; m. Sheela Marsha Zangwill, Aug. 22, 1962; children: Caroline, Marjorie. BSME, McGill U., 1963, diploma in mgmt., 1968, MBA, 1969. Cert. Que. Order of Engrs. Supr. quality control engring. Pratt and Whitney, Montreal, 1964-68; sr. mktg. rschr. United Aircraft, Montreal, 1969-70; asst. chief internat. Dept. Industry, Trade and Commerce, Ottawa, Ont., Canada, 1972-77; dir. industry projects Ministry of State for Sci. and Tech., Ottawa, 1978-85; dir. strategic techs. policy Industry, Sci. and Tech. Can., Ottawa, 1986-91; dir. gen. sci. strategy and innovation policy Industry Can., Ottawa, 1992-98; cons. ptnr. SECOR Cons., Inc., Ottawa, 1998—. Chmn. com. for sci. and tech. policy Orgn. for Econ. Coop. and Devel., Paris, 1995-98. Avocation: Inuit and Japanese graphic art. Home and Office: 112 Pigeon Terr Ottawa ON Canada K1V 9H7 Office Phone: 613-737-5596. E-mail: osilverman@secor.ca.

SILVERMAN, RICHARD BRUCE, chemist, educator, biochemist; b. Phila., May 12, 1946; s. Philip and S. Ruth (Simon) Silverman; m. Barbara Jean Kesner, Jan. 9, 1983; children: Matthew, Margaret, Philip. BS, Pa. State U., 1968; MA, Harvard U., Cambridge, Mass., 1972, PhD, 1974. From asst. prof. to prof. Northwestern U., Evanston, Ill., 1976—86, prof., 1986—, mem. Inst. Neurosci., 1990—. Mem. adv. panel NIH, Bethesda, Md., 1981, 83, 85, 87-91, 2001; expert analyst CHEMTRACTS; scientific adv. bd. Influx, Inc., 1998-2003, Protez Pharml., 2004—, Synchem, 2003—. NIGMS adv. coun., 2002, 2005; mem. Faculty of 1900; cons. in field. Mem. editl. bd.: Jour. Enzyme Inhibition, 1988—2002, Archives Biochem. & Biophys., 1993—, Jour. Medicinal Chemistry, 1995—2000, Enzyme Inhibition and Medicinal Chemistry, 2002—, Letters in Drug Design & Discovery, 2003—, Bioorganic & Medicinal Chemistry, 2003—, Bioorganic & Medicinal Chemistry Letters, 2003—, Current Enzyme Inhibition, 2004—. Mem. adv. bd. Ill. Math. & Scis. Acad., 1988. With U.S. Army, 1969-71. Recipient Career Devel. award USPHS, 1982-87, E. LeRoy Hall award for tchg. excellence, 1999, Northwestern Alumni Tchg. award, 2000; postdoctoral fellow Brandeis U., Waltham, Mass., 1974-76, DuPont Young Faculty fellow, 1976, Alfred P. Sloan Found. fellow, 1981-85; grantee various govt. and pvt. insts., 1976—. Arthur C. Cope. Sr. scholar ACS, 2003. Fellow: AAAS; mem.: Am. Chem. Soc. (nat. elected nominating com. divns. biol. chemistry 1993—96, long-range planning com. divsn. med. chem. 1999—2002), Am. Soc. Biochem. Molecular Biology, Am. Inst. Chemists. Avocations: golf, tennis. Office: Northwestern U Dept Chemistry 2145 Sheridan Rd Evanston IL 60208-3113 Office Phone: 847-491-5653. Business E-Mail: Agman@chem.northwestern.edu.

SILVERMAN, ROSS O., lawyer; b. Toledo, Aug. 3, 1960; BA, Ohio State U., 1982; JD cum laude, U. Toledo, 1985. Bar: Ga. 1986, DC 1989, Ill. 1995, NY 2003, US Dist. Ct., So. and Ea. Dist. NY, No Dist. Ill., US Ct. Appeals, 7th Cir. Trial atty. Criminal Sect. Tax Div., US Dept. Justice, 1988—90; asst. US atty. No. Dist. Ill., 1990—94; ptnr. Katten Muchin Zavis Rosenman, Chgo. Mem.: DC Bar, State Bar Ga., Ill. State Bar Assn., Chgo. Bar Assn. Office: Katten Muchin Zavis Rosenman 525 W Monroe St Chicago IL 60661 Office Phone: 312-902-5240. Office Fax: 312-577-8989. E-mail: ross.silverman@kmzr.com.

SILVERMAN, SAM MENDEL, physicist, lawyer; b. NYC, Nov. 16, 1925; s. Moshe Aaron and Gitel (Korenbaum) S.; m. Jacqueline Greenberg, Sept. 12, 1948 (div. Apr. 1965); children: Ann, William, Nancy; m. Phyllis Rolfe, June 26, 1966; children: Gila, Aaron. BChE, CCNY, 1945; PhD, Ohio State U., 1952; JD, Suffolk U., Boston, 1982. Bar: Mass. 1982, US Dist. Ct. Mass. 1982, US Ct. Appeals (1st cir.) 1982, NY 1983, US Supreme Ct. 1986, NH, 2007. Assoc. Ohio State U., Columbus, 1952-55; asst. prof. chem. physics U. Toledo, 1955-57; rsch. physicist Air Force Cambridge Rsch. Labs., Bedford, Mass., 1957-80, chief polar atmospheric processes br. and dir. geopole obs., 1963-74, cons., 1980—. Vis. rsch. assoc. Queens U., Belfast, 1963-64; vis. prof. Osmania U., Hyderabad, India, 1965-66; mem. adv. bd. Inst. Space and Atmospheric Studies, U. Sask., Can., 1965-69; sr. rsch. physicist Boston Coll., 1981-97; co-chmn. interdivisional commn. history Internat. Assn. Geomagnetism and Aeronomy, 1987-91; lectr. palliative care courses, Poland, 1993, 94, 2000. Contbr. articles to profl. jours. Mem. Town Meeting Lexington, Mass., 1973-79, 84—; elected mem. Lexington Dem. Town Com., 1996—; legal counsel Internat. Work Group on Death, Dying and Bereavement. With USAAF, 1945-46. Recipient Thurgood Marshall award, com. pub. counsel svcs. Mass. Pub. Defender's Agy., 2002. Fellow Am. Phys. Soc., Explorers Club; mem. Am. Geophys. Union (editor History of Geophysics newsletter 1983-91), Internat. Work Group on Death, Dying and Bereavement. Home: 18 Ingleside Rd Lexington MA 02420-2522 Office Phone: 781-861-0368. E-mail: smpr@rcn.com.

SILVERMAN, SARAH, comedian, actress; b. Bedford, NH, Dec. 1, 1970; Actor: (TV series) Saturday Night Live, 1993—94, Mr. Show with Bob and David, 1995—97, Greg the Bunny, 2002, The Sarah Silverman Program, 2007—, (voice only) Crank Yankers, 2002,: (TV miniseries) Pilot Season, 2004; (TV films) Mr. Show and the Incredible, Fantastical News Report, 1998, Smog, 1999, Late Last Night, 1999, Rocky Times, 2000, (voice only) Saddle Rush, 2002,: (films) Overnight Delivery, 1998, Bulworth, 1998, There's Something About Mary, 1998, The Bachelor, 1999, The Way of the Gun, 2000, Black Days, 2001, Say It Isn't So, 2001, Heartbreakers, 2001, Evolution, 2001, Run Ronnie Run, 2002, The School of Rock, 2003, Nobody's Perfect, 2004, (voice only) Hair High, 2004, Rent, 2005, I Want Someone to Eat Cheese With, 2005, School for Scoundrels, 2006; actor, co-prodr.: Who's the Caboose?, 1997; writer, actor Sarah Silverman: Jesus is Magic, 2005; actor: (TV appearances) Star Trek: Voyager, 1996, The Larry Sanders Show, 1996, Seinfeld, 1997, Brotherly Love, 1997, JAG, 1997, The Naked Truth, 1997, Futurama, 2000, V.I.P., 2002, Frasier, 2003, Monk, 2004, Entourage, 2004, (voice only) Aqua Teen Hunger Force, 2004, Drawn Together, 2004, American Dad, 2005. Recipient Nightlife award for comic female stand-up, 2007. Office: Creative Artists Agy Inc 9830 Wilshire Blvd Beverly Hills CA 90212 *

SILVERMAN, STANLEY WAYNE, chemical company executive; m. Ellen J. Seligsohn, June 7, 1970. BSChemE, Drexel U., 1969, MBA, 1974; AMP, Harvard U., 1989. Process engr. Atlantic Richfield Co., Phila., 1969-71, PQ Corp., Phila., 1971-74, mgr. oper. planning Valley Forge, Pa., 1974-76, product mgr., 1976-80, mktg. mgr., 1980-82, nat. sales mgr., 1982-84, pres. Nat. Silicates Ltd. subs. Toronto, Ont., Can., 1984-87, pres. ind. chem. group Valley Forge, 1987-90, exec. v.p., COO, 1990-99, pres., CEO, bd. dirs., 2000—05; dir. C&D Techs., 2003—. Chmn. adv. coun. Drexel U. Coll. Engring, 1991-93, alumni bd. govs., 1998, bd. trustees, 2000—; bd. dirs. Phila. Acad., Inc., 1999—2004. Named among 100 most accomplished grads. Drexel U., 1992; recipient Alumni Achievement award Drexel U., 1995. Mem. Soap and Detergent Assn. (bd. dirs. 2004—, chmn bd. 2004—), Am. Chemistry Coun. (bd. dirs. 2001—). Business E-Mail: stan.silverman@comcast.net.

SILVERMAN, VICTOR, history professor, writer, filmmaker; BA, MA, U. Calif., Berkeley, PhD, 1990. Assoc. prof. history Pomona Coll., Claremont, Calif., 1993—. Dir.(prodr., writer): (films) Screaming Queens: the Riot at Compton's Cafeteria (Regional Emmy award, 2006); author: (book) Imagining Internationalism. Office: Dept History Pomona Coll 551 N College Ave Claremont CA 91711 Office Phone: 909-607-3395. Business E-Mail: vsilverman@pomona.edu.

SILVERMAN, WILLIAM A., lawyer; b. Phila., Mar. 1, 1945; BA, Univ. Pa., 1966; JD, Univ. Chgo., 1969. Bar: Ill. 1969, DC 1974, lic.: US Ct. Internat. Trade 1980, US Ct. Appeals, Fed. Cir. 1982. Asst. prof. Univ. Ill. Ctr. for Urban Studies, Coll. Edn., Chgo., 1969—71; ptnr., regulated industries, govtl. rels. Hunton & Williams LLP, Washington. Office: Hunton & Williams LLP 1900 K St NW Washington DC 20006-1109 Office Phone: 202-419-2013. Office Fax: 202-778-2201. Business E-Mail: wsilverman@hunton.com.

SILVERS, GERALD THOMAS, retired publishing executive; b. Cin., Aug. 26, 1937; s. Steve Allen and Tina Mae (Roberts) S.; m. Ann Gregory Woodward, July 25, 1964. BA, U. Ky., Lexington, 1960. Asst. rsch. svcs. mgr. Cin. Enquirer, 1963-72, rsch. svcs. dir., 1972-74, rsch. dir., 1974-90, v.p. mktg. svcs., 1990-94, v.p. market devel., 1994—2003; ret., 2003. Active U. Ky. Devel. Coun., Lexington, 1986—; trustee Neediest Kids of All, 1991—; region 5 exec. com. Ohio Sch. to Work, 1997-2000; corps. com. St. Elizabeth Med. Ctr. Found., 1998—; bd. overseers Taft Mus. Art, 1999—, treas., bd. govs., 2002—, vice chmn., 2007. 1st lt. U.S. Army, 1960-62. Recipient Thomas H. Copeland award of merit, 1991. Mem. U. Ky. Alumni Assn. Cin. Chpt. (pres. 1985), Newspaper Rsch. Coun. (pres. 1985-86), Internat. Newspaper Market Assn., Am. Mktg. Assn., Am. Art Soc. Cin. (pres. 1999-2001). Presbyterian. Home: 229 Watch Hill Rd Fort Mitchell KY 41011-1822

SILVERS, ROBERT B., editor; b. NY, Dec. 31, 1929; s. James J. and Rose (Roden) S. AB, U. Chgo., 1947; cert., Ecole de Sci. Politiques, Paris, 1956; LittD (hon.), Harvard U., 2007. Paris editor Paris Rev., 1954-59; asst. editor Harpers Mag., NYC, 1959-63; co-editor N.Y. Rev. of Books, NYC, 1963—. Editor: Writing in America, 1962, Hidden Histories of Science, 1995, Doing It: Five Performing Arts, 2001; co-editor: The Legacy of Isaiah Berlin, 2001, Striking Terror: America's New War, 2002, The Company They Kept: Writers on Unforgettable Friendships, 2006. Trustee NY Pub. Libr., 1997—, Ditchley Found., 1996—, Am. Acad. in Rome, 1998-, Paris Rev. Found., 2002-. With SHAPE US Army, 1952. Decorated Legion d'Honneur, l'Ordre Nat. du Merite France; recipient Literarian award outstanding svc. to Am. lit. cmty., Am. Book Found., 2006. Mem. Am. Acad. Arts and Scis., Coun. Fgn. Rels., Century Assn., Knickerbocker Club. Office: NY Rev of Books 1755 Broadway New York NY 10019-3743 Office Phone: 212-757-8070.

SILVERS, SALLY, choreographer, performing company executive; b. Greeneville, Tenn., June 19, 1952; d. Herbert Ralston and Sara Elizabeth (Buchanan) S.; life ptnr. Bruce Erroll Andrews. BA in Dance and Polit. Sci., Antioch Coll., 1975. Artistic dir. Sally Silvers & Dancers, NYC, 1980—. Mem. faculty Leicester Poly., 1986, 87, 89, summer choreography project Bennington Coll., 1988-92, Chisenhale Dance Space, London, 1989, 91, Am. Dance Festival, Durham, N.C., 1990, 92; guest tchr. European Dance Devel. Ctr., Arnhem, The Netherlands, 1992—. Choreographer (performances) Politics of the Body Microscope of Conduct, 1980, Social Movement, 1981, Connective Tissue, 1981, Less Time You Know Praxis, 1981, Don't No Do And This, 1981, Lack of Entrepreneurial Thrift, 1982, Celluoid Sally and Mr. E, 1982, Mutate, 1982, Being Red Enough, 1982, Disgusting, 1982, Bedtime at the Reformatory, 1982, Eat the Rich, 1982, They Can't Get It in the Shopping Cart, 1982, Blazing Forceps, 1982, And Find Out Why, 1983, Choose Your Weapons, 1984, Extend the Wish for Entire, 1985, No Best Better Way, 1985, Every All Which is Not Us, 1986, Swaps Ego Say So, 1986, Be Careful Now, You

Know Sugar Melts in Water, 1987, Fact Confected, 1987, Both, Both, 1987, Tizzy boost, 1988, Moebius, 1988, Whatever Ever, 1989, Get Tough, Sports and Divertissement, 1989, Flap, 1989, Swan's Crayon, 1989, Fanfare Tripwire, 1990, Harry Meets Sally, 1990, Along the Skid Mark of Recorded History, 1990, Matinee Double-You, 1991, Grand Guignol, 1991, Dash Dash Slang Plural Plus, 1992, The Bubble Cut, 1992, Vigilant Corsage, 1992, Oops Fact, 1992, Small Room, 1993, Exwhyzee, 1993, Elegy, 1993, Now That It Is Now, 1994, Give Em Enough Rope, Swoon Noir, 1994, Radio Rouge, 1995, Braceletizing, 1995, Hush Comet, 1995, Bite the Pillow, 1995, Pandora's Cake Stain, 1996, Secrets Of, 1997, HUSHHUSH, Sugar Raised, 1998 Capture, Teddy Growl, 1999, Storming Heaven, 2000, Swaphot Trouble, 2001, Strike Me Lightning, 2002, Spaced Out, 2003, Dreams Do Come True, 2004, Dang Me, 2004, Versus, The Professionals, 2005, 25th Anniversary Season: RUPT, Puppy Skills, Oven Rack, 2005; video and performance filmmaker: (films) Little Lieutenant, 1993 (Silver); N.Y. Dance on Camera Festival, Mechanics of the Brain, 1997; dancer (with) Yvonne Lainer, 2006—07; co-author: (book) Resurgant New Writings By Women, 1992; contbr. articles to profl. jours. Grantee Nat. Endowment Arts, 1987, 89, 90, 91, 98, Jerome Found., 1993, 1996, Meet the Composer N.Y. Found. for the Arts, 1995; Guggenheim Found. fellow, 1988; Found. Contemporary Performance Arts, 2001. Mem. Segue Found. (bd. dirs. Segue Performance Space 1992-2002). Avocations: reading, writing, art events, costume design. Home: 303 E 8th St Apt 4F New York NY 10009-5212

SILVERS, WILLYS KENT, geneticist; b. NYC, Jan. 12, 1929; s. Lewis Julian and Miriam Elizabeth (Rosenzweig) Silvers; m. Abigail M. Adams, Sept. 29, 1956 (dec. June 18, 2005); children: Deborah Elizabeth, Willys Kent. BA, Johns Hopkins U., 1950; PhD, U. Chgo., 1954. Assoc. staff scientist Jackson Lab., Bar Harbor, Maine, 1956-57; assoc. mem. Wistar Inst., Phila., 1957-65; mem. faculty U. Pa. Med. Sch., 1965—, prof. genetics, 1967-98, prof. emeritus, 1998—. Mem. allergy and immunology study sect. NIH, 1962—66, adv. bd. primate rsch. ctrs., 1968—71; mem. com. cancer immunobiology Nat. Cancer Inst., 1974—78; bd. sci. overseers Jackson Lab., Bar Harbor, 1980—89. Author: The Immunobiology of Transplantation, 1971, The Coat Colors of Mice: A Model for Mammalian Gene Action and Interaction, 1979; mem. editl. bd. Transplantation, 1963—71, Jour. Exptl. Zoology, 1965—70, 1981—86, Jour. Immunology, 1973—77, Jour. Reticuloendothelial Soc., 1974—77; contbr. articles to profl. jours. Mem.: Am. Genetic Assn. (coun. 1980—83, pres. 1983). Home: 210 Millcreek Rd Ardmore PA 19003-1506 Personal E-mail: wsilvers@aol.com.

SILVERSTEIN, BARBARA ANN, conductor, artistic director; b. Phila., July 24, 1947; d. Charles and Selma (Brenner) S.; m. Bernard J. Taylor II, Aug. 19, 1978. Student, Bennington Coll., 1965-67; BMus, Phila. Coll. Performing Arts, 1970; MA, U. Del., 1997. Assoc. music dir. Suburban Opera Co., Chester, Pa., 1967-75; asst. condr. Toledo Opera Assn., 1975-76; asst. condr., coach Curtis Inst. Music, Phila., 1973-77; asst. condr. Phila. Lyric Opera, 1971-74, Des Moines Opera Festival, Indianola, Iowa, 1974-78; music dir., condr. Savoy Co., Phila., 1977-80, Miss. Opera, Jackson, 1979-82; artistic dir., condr. Pa. Opera Theater, Phila., 1976-93; guest condr. Opera Del., Wilmington, 1981, 83, Anchorage Opera, 1982, Utah Festival Opera Co., 1993-96, Lyric Opera Kansas City, 1995, Opera Roanoke, Va., 1995, 98, Hollins U., 1999; prof. English U. Del., Ursinus, 1996—2004; mng. editor Epotec Inc., 1999-2000, dir. comm., 2000—01; freelance writer, translator, 1980—. Recipient alumni award U. of Arts. Mem. Am. Fedn. Musicians, Music Fund Soc., Pa. Coun. on the Arts (adv. panel 1987-90, OPERA Am. (bd. dirs. 1987-93, exec. com. 1988-93). Jewish. Avocations: scuba diving, reading.

SILVERSTEIN, LARRY A., real estate developer; m. Klara Silverstein; children: Roger, Lisa, Sharon. BA, NYU, 1952; JD, Brooklyn Law Sch. Bar: N.Y. Pres. Silverstein Properties, Inc., NYC; owner 529 Fifth Ave., 570 Seventh Ave., One River Place, Two River Place, 120 Wall St., 120 Broadway, Seven World Trade Ctr.; 99 year leaseholder World Trade Ctr., 2001—. Gov., past chmn. Real Estate Bd. N.Y.; founder, chmn. emeritus NYU Real Estate Inst.; chmn. Realty Found. Trustee NYU, vice chmn. bd. trustees; trustee South St. Seaport Mus., Mus. Jewish Heritage; bd. chmn. United Jewish Appeal, Fedn. Jewish Philanthropies, NY. Avocations: classical music, yachting. Office: Silverstein Properties Inc 120 Broadway Suite 230 New York NY 10271

SILVERSTEIN, LEONARD A., lawyer; b. Mobile, Ala., Apr. 18, 1958; s. Burton Howard and Fannye Mitchell Silverstein; m. Ellen Sue Frauenthal, May 25, 1986; children: Andrew, Laura, Anna. BA magna cum laude, Vanderbilt U., Nashville, 1980; JD, Vanderbilt U., 1983. Bar: Ga. 1983. Assoc./ptnr. Powell Goldstein Frazer & Murphy LLP, Atlanta, 1983—94; ptnr. McKenna Long & Aldridge LLP, Atlanta, 1994—. Mem. Ga. Biomed. Partnership, Atlanta, 2002—; mem., biosciences exec. com. Met. Atlanta C. of C., 2002—. Contbr. articles to profl. jours.; assoc. mng. editor, Vanderbilt Law Rev., 1982—83. Pres. Vanderbilt U. Alumni Club, Atlanta, 1991; co-pres. Bach n' Rollers, Divsn. of The Atlanta Symphony Assocs., 1992—93; bd. mem. and exec. com. mem. Zoo Atlanta, 1996—2001, bd. mem., 2003, Am.-Israel C. of C., S.E. Region, Atlanta, 1995—; bd. mem. and exec. com. mem. Am. Jewish Com., Atlanta, 1999—; bd. of trustees The Atlanta Symphony Assocs., 1992—93. Recipient IPO Rainmaker, IPO Counsel - The Corp. Fin. Inst., 1996. Mem.: Vanderbilt U. Alumni Assn. (bd. dirs. 1992—96), Ga. Bar Assn. (vice chair/chair elect of securities subcom. 2001—02), Atlanta Bar Assn. Achievements include patents pending for Reloadable Rights Plan for Preferred and Common Stock Rights Plans. Avocations: triathlons, golf. Office: McKenna Long & Aldridge LLP 303 Peachtree St Ste 5300 Atlanta GA 30308 Office Phone: 404-527-4390. Business E-Mail: lsilverstein@mckennalong.com.

SILVERSTEIN, MARTIN J., lawyer, former ambassador; b. NYC; married; 6 children. BA in Polit. Sci., Rutgers U., 1976; JD, Temple U., 1979. Bar: Pa., N.J., U.S. Ct. Internat. Trade, U.S. Ct. Customs and Patent Appeals. Founder Martin J. Silverstein and Assocs.; U.S. amb. to Uruguay US Dept. State, Montevideo, 2001—05; sr. counsel Greenberg Traurig LLP, Washington, 2005—. Mem. Fed. Jud. Nominating Commn., Pa. Active M.D. Anderson Cancer Ctr., Lower Merion Hist. Soc., U.S. Negro Coll. Fund, Phila. C. of C.; bd. mem. Vietnam Vets. Com. for Better Legislation. Recipient Citizens Commendation for Bravery, Phila. Police Dept. Mem.: Internat. Rep. Inst., Am. Fgn. Svc. Assn., Ctr. for Security Policy, Fgn. Policy Rsch. Inst., Am. Enterprise Inst., Heritage Found., World Affairs Coun. Office: Greenberg Traurig LLP 800 Connecticut Ave NW Ste 500 Washington DC 20006

SILVERSTEIN, PAUL N., lawyer; b. NYC, 1955; BFA, CUNY, 1977; JD, Bklyn. Law Sch., 1981. Bar: NY 1982. Ptnr., Bankruptcy Andrews Kurth LLP, NYC, mem. mgmt. com. Mem.: ABA, NY State Bar. Office: Andrews Kurth LLP 450 Lexington Ave New York NY 10017 Office Phone: 212-850-2819. Office Fax: 212-813-8158. Business E-Mail: paulsilverstein@andrewskurth.com.

SILVERSTEIN, ROBERT P., lawyer; BA magna cum laude, UCLA, 1990; JD, Univ. Calif., Hastings, 1996. Bar: Calif. Judicial extern Assoc. Justice Marvin Baxter Calif. Supreme Ct., 1995; assoc. Demetriou, Del Guerico, Springer & Moyer LLP, LA, 1996—99; assoc. to ptnr., bus. & real estate litigation Hill, Farrer & Burrill LLP, LA, 1999—2005; founder, principal, real estate & bus. litigation Silverstein Law Firm, LA, 2005—. Editor (articles): Hastings Internat. & Comparative Law Rev. (Am. Jurisprudence award in legal writing & rsch.). Named a Rising Star, So. Calif. Super Lawyers, 2006. Mem.: Calif. State Bar, LA County Bar Assn., Phi Beta Kappa. Office: Silverstein Law Firm 3d Fl 215 N Marengo Ave Pasadena CA 91101-1504 Office Phone: 626-449-4200. Office Fax: 626-449-4205. Business E-Mail: robert@robertsilversteinlaw.com.

SILVERSTEIN, SAMUEL CHARLES, cellular biology and physiology professor, researcher; b. NYC, Feb. 11, 1937; s. Paul Robert and Jeanette (Kamen) S.; m. Jo Ann Kleinman, Apr. 2, 1967; children: David Paul, Jennifer Kate. AB, Dartmouth Coll., 1958; MD, Albert Einstein Coll. Medicine, 1963. Intern in medicine U. Colo. Med. Center, 1963-64; postdoctoral fellow dept. cell biology Rockefeller U., 1964-67; resident in medicine Mass. Gen. Hosp., 1967—68; asst. prof. cellular physiology and immunology Rockefeller U., 1968-71, assoc. prof., physician, 1972—; John Dalton prof. physiology, prof. medicine Columbia U. Coll. Physicians and Surgeons, NYC, 1983—, chmn. dept., 1983—2003. Founder, dir. Columbia U. Summer Rsch. Program for Secondary Sch. Sci. Tchrs., 1990—; prin. investigator, program dir. Pre and Post-doctoral Tng. Immunology, 1997—2005. Editor: Transport of Macromolecules in Cellular Systems, 1979; chmn. editl. bd. Jour. Cell Biology, 1979-82, editor, 1978-89. Bd. dirs. Arnold P. Gold Found., 1998—, Cancer Rsch. Fund, Damon Runyon Found., 1990—; bd. dirs. Rsch. Am., 1993-2005, mem. exec. com., 1996-2006. Recipient John Oliver LaGorce medal, Nat. Geog. Soc., 1967, Marie Bonazinga Rsch. award, Soc. Leukocyte Biology, 1984, Disting. Alumnus award, Albert Einstein Coll. Medicine, 1987, N.Y.C. Mayor's award Publ. Understanding of Sci. and Tech., 2003, Westy award Contbns. Sci. Edn. N.Y.C. Schs., 2004, Fountain Valley Sch. Trustees 75th Anniversary award, Colorado Springs, 2005, Mt. Silverstein, Sentinel Range, Antarctica named in his honor by, US Geol. Survey, 2006; fellow Helen Hay Whitney, 1964—67, John Simon Guggenheim, 2005, Pres. Lasker/Funding First, 2001—04. Fellow: AAAS (chair sect. medicine 1998), N.Y. Acad. Sci. (edn. com.), Am. Soc. Microbiology; mem.: Am. Acad. Arts and Scis., Inst. Medicine Nat. Acad. Scis., Fedn. Am. Socs. for Exptl. Biology (bd. dirs. 1991—96, v.p. 1993—94, pres. 1994—95, chmn. pub. affairs adv. com. 1995—96), Practitioners Soc. N.Y., Assn. Am. Physicians, Am. Physiol. Soc., Am. Soc. Biol. Chemists, Infectious Diseases Soc. Am., Am. Assn. Immunologists, Am. Soc. Clin. Investigation, Am. Soc. Cell Biology (Bruce Alberts award for Excellence in Sci. Edn. 2005), Century Assn., Explorers Club, Am. Alpine Club (dir. 1963—64, 1969—74). Achievements include research and numerous publications in field of virology, cell biology, immunology, seconary science education, science policy, and mountaineering. Office: Columbia U Coll Physicians & Surgeons 630 W 168th St New York NY 10032-3795 Home Phone: 212-595-3903; Office Phone: 212-305-3546. Business E-Mail: scs3@columbia.edu.

SILVERSTEIN, SUZANNE, art therapist; b. LA, Jan. 14, 1948; d. Lita (Factor) Kilpatrick; m. Andrew Chiaramonte, July 4, 1988; 1 child, Jaysen Pascal. BFA, Calif. Inst. of the Arts, LA, 1971; MA, Immaculate Heart Coll., LA, 1975. Art therapy coord., supr. family and child program Thalians Mental Health Ctr., LA, 1977—; art therapy coord., supr. famil and child program dept. psychiatry Cedars-Sinai Med. Ctr., LA, 1977—; pres., co-founder Psychol. Trauma Ctr., LA, 1981—. Faculty clin. art therapy dept. Immaculate Heart Coll., 1975-81, Loyola Marymount U., 1981-82, leader, group dynamics class, 1975-82; adminstr. Psychol. Trauma Ctr., 1981—, pres. 1981—. Author: (with others) Expanding Mental Health Interventions in Schools, 1988. Fellowship Thalians Mental Health Ctr./Cedars Sinai Med. Ctr., L.A., 1975-76. Mem. Am. Art Therapy Assn., So. Calif. Art Therapy Assn. Office: Psychol Trauma Ctr 8730 Alden Dr Rm C212 Los Angeles CA 90048-3811 Office Phone: 310-423-3541. Business E-Mail: suzanne.silverstein@cshs.org.

SILVERSTONE, HARRIS J., chemistry professor; b. NYC, Sept. 18, 1939; s. Sidney M. and Estelle Silverstone; m. Ruth C. Federman, 1960; children: Robert, Aron, Nancy, Murray. AB, Harvard U., 1960; PhD, Calif. Inst. Tech., 1964. Asst. prof. Johns Hopkins U., Balt., 1965-68, assoc. prof., 1968-71, prof., 1971—. Contbr. articles to profl. jours. NSF Postdoctoral fellow Yale U., 1964. Mem. Am. Phys. Soc., Am. Chem. Soc., Internat. Soc. Theoretical Chem. Physics. Office: Johns Hopkins U 3400 N Charles St Baltimore MD 21218-2685

SILVERTHORN, ROBERT STERNER, JR., lawyer; b. Oklahoma City, Dec. 22, 1948; s. Robert Sterner and Marilyn I. Silverthorn; m. Mary Russell Cofer, June 26, 1982; children: Robert Sterner III, Christine Elizabeth. BA, Dickinson Coll., 1969; JD, U. Louisville, 1974; postgrad., Nat. Def. U., 1988, U.S. Army War Coll., 1993. Bar: Ky. 1975, U.S. Dist. Ct. (we. dist.) Ky. 1975, U.S. Tax Ct. 1975, U.S. Dist. Ct. (ea. dist.) Ky. 1980, U.S. Dist. Ct. (so. dist.) Tex. 1981, U.S. Dist. Ct. (no. dist.) Ohio 1983, U.S. Dist. Ct. (so. dist.) Ind. 1993, U.S. Supreme Ct. 1983, U.S. Ct. Appeals (6th cir.) 1995. Pvt. practice, Louisville, 1975; assoc. Pallo White & O'Conner, Louisville, 1975-76, Hargadon Lenihan & Harbolt, Louisville, 1976-82; ptnr. White Diamond & Silverthorn, Louisville, 1982-83; of counsel Nutt & Mayer, Louisville, 1983-91; mng. ptnr. Morris, Silverthorn & Dutton, Louisville, 1991-92, Silverhorn Law Offices, 1993—; commd. 2d lt. U.S. Army, 1970, advanced through grades to maj. gen., 2000, comdr. gen. 84th Divsn., 1998, comdr. gen. 95th divsn., 2000-04; bd. dirs. Maroco Leasing, Inc., Louisville, Akima Intra-Data, Charlotte, NC, Meth. Retirement Homes Ky. Inc., Louisville; repeat guest radio talk show Ask the Lawyers Sta. WHAS; mil. commentator WAVE-TV (NBC). Pres. Windhurst Acres Homeowners Assn., St. Matthews, Ky., 1981-85; chmn., pres. Hurstbourne Village Office Condo, Louisville, 2005—; bd. dirs. Am. Cherokee dist. Boy Scouts Am., dePaul Sch., Louisville, 1997-99. Decorated Disting. Svc. medal, Meritorious Svc. medal with 6 oak leaf clusters, Bronze Star with 1 oak leaf cluster, Air medal, Army Commendation medal with 3 oak leaf clusters, Army Achievement medal; recipient Constl. Book award U. Louisville, 1975. Mem. ABA (past vice chair real property sect.), Ky. Bar Assn. (chmn. civil litigation sect. 2001-02), Louisville Bar Assn., Ky. Acad. Trial Attys., Res. Officers Assn., Assn. of Century (pres. 1993-95), Assn. U.S. Army (chmn. Louisville Armed Forces com. 1986-88), Sr. Army Res. Comdrs. Assn. (pres. 2001-04), Louisville Area C. of C. (mil. affairs com.), Hurstbourne Country Club, Jefferson Club, Rotary Club of Jeffersontown, Ky. (pres. 1995-96, dist. 6710 asst. gov. 1997-2000), Masons, Delta Theta Phi (dean), Sigma Chi. Methodist. Office: Silverthorn Law Offices Ste 200 2305 Hustbourne Village Dr Louisville KY 40299-1861 Office Phone: 502-495-2300. Personal E-mail: RSilvertho@aol.com. Business E-Mail: silverthornlaw@bellsouth.net.

SILVESTON, PETER LEWIS, engineering educator, consultant; b. NYC, Mar. 10, 1931; s. Barnett Silveston and Hannah Hendelman; m. Helen Storin Brown (dec.); children: Rachel, Rebecca, Matthew. ScB, MIT, Cambridge, 1951, ScM, 1953; DEng, Tech. U. Munich, 1956. Cert. profl. engr., NJ, 1959, Va., 1967, Ont., Can., 1970. Devel. engr. Esso Rsch. & Engring., Linden, NJ, 1957—59; rsch. engr. Am. Std., Union, NJ, 1960—63; asst. prof. U. BC, Vancouver, Canada, 1963—65, prof., 1972—97; from assoc. prof. to prof. U. Waterloo, Ont., Canada, 1965—97, disting. prof. emeritus, 1997—. V.p. rsch. Claritek, Toronto, 1987—92, pres. Rsch. & Engring., Waterloo, 1992—2006; prin. B & P Silveston Engring., Johns Island, SC, 1972—; gen. mgr. Gargoyles & Windlocks, Johns Island, SC, 1996—. Editor, author: Pollution Reader, 1969, Multiphase Chemical Reactors, 1986, Composition Modulation, 1998, Cyclic Separating Reactors, 2006; contbr. articles to profl. jours. Fellow, Deutsche Akad. Austavahdienst, 1952—56, Japan Soc. Promotion Sci., 1986; Erskine fellow, U. Canterbury, 1992. Fellow: AIChE, Can. Soc. Chem. Engrs.; mem.: Am. Chem. Soc. Achievements include patents in field. Office: B and P Silveston Engrs 51 Crested Flycatcher Johns Island SC 29455

SILVESTRI, ALAN ANTHONY, film composer; b. NYC, Mar. 26, 1950; s. Louis and Elizabeth (Clarke) S.; m. Sandra Dee Shue; children: Alexandra, Joseph, James. PhD in Music (hon.), Berklee Coll. Music, Boston, 1995. Film scores include The Doberman Gang, 1972, The Amazing Dobermans, Las Vegas Lady, 1976, Romancing the Stone, 1984, Par ou t'es rentre? On t'as vu sortir, 1984, Fandango, 1984, Cat's Eye, 1984, Back to the Future, 1985 (Grammy award nominations best instrumental composition and best album of original score for a motion picture, 1985), Summer Rental, 1985, Clan of the Cave Bear, 1986, The Delta Force, 1986, American Anthem, 1986, Flight of the Navigator, 1986, No Mercy, 1986, Critical Condition, 1987, Outrageous Fortune, 1987, Predator, 1987, Overboard, 1987, Who Framed Roger Rabbit?, 1988 (Grammy award nominations best instrumental composition and best album of original score for a motion picture, 1988), My Stepmother Is an Alien, 1988, Mac and Me, 1988, She's Out of Control, 1989, Downtown, 1989, The Abyss, 1989, Back to the Future II, 1989, Back to the Future III, 1990, Young Guns II, 1990, Predator II, 1990, Soapdish, 1991, Dutch, 1991, Ricohet, 1991, Shattered, 1991, Father of the Bride, 1991, Ferngully: The Last Rainforest, 1992, Death Becomes Her, 1992, Stop! Or My Mom Will Shoot, 1992, The Bodyguard, 1992, Cop and a Half, 1993, Sidekicks, 1993, Super Mario Bros., 1993, Judgment Night, 1993, Grumpy Old Men, 1993, Clean Slate, 1994, Blown Away, 1994, Forrest Gump, 1994 (Academy award nomination best original score, Grammy award nomination best instrumental performance for "Feather Theme from Forrest Gump," Golden Globe award nomination best original score), Richie Rich, 1994, The Quick and the Dead, 1994, The Perez Family, 1995, Judge Dredd, 1995, Father of the Bride II, 1995, Sgt. Bilko, 1995, Grumpier Old Men, 1995, Eraser, 1996, Long Kiss Goodnight, 1996, Fools Rush In, 1996, Volcano, 1997, Contact, 1997, Mousehunt, 1997, Odd Couple II, 1998, Parent Trap, 1998, Holyman, 1998, Practical Magic, 1998, Siegfried & Roy, The Magic Box, 1999, Stuart Little, 1999, Reindeer Games, 2000, What Lies Beneath, 2000, What Women Want, 2000, Castaway, 2000 (Grammy award winner for best instrumental composition for "Theme from Castaway"), The Mexican, 2001, What Women Want, 2000,The Mummy Returns, 2001, Serendipity, 2001, Showtime, 2002, Lilo & Stitch, 2002, Stuart Little 2, 2002, Maid in Manhattan, 2002, Identity, 2003, Lara Croft Tomb Raider: The Cradle of Life, 2003, Two Soldiers, 2003, Van Helsing, 2004, The Polar Express, 2004, The Wild, 2006, Night at the Museum, 2006 (ASCAP award); TV themes include CHiPs, 1978-83, Manimal, 1983. Recipient ACE award Nat. Acad. Cable Programming for Tales from the Crypt - All Through the House, 1990, Saturn award Acad. Arts and Sci. for fantasy and horror film, 1987, Grammy award for Best Song Written for Motion Picture for The Polar Express, 2006; Grammy nominations for Back to the Future, 1985, Who Framed Rger Rabbit?, 1988, Forrest Gump, 1994, Castaway, 2001, Henry Mancini award, ASCAP, 2002; nominated for Golden Globe, Forrest Gump, 1994.

SILVESTRI, GINA, lawyer; b. NJ, Feb. 18, 1972; BA magna cum laude, Seton Hall U., NJ, 1994; JD, Thomas M. Cooley Law Sch., Mich., 1995. Bar: NY 1999, NJ 2001, U.s. Dist. Ct. of NJ (Dist. Ct. NJ) 2001. Atty. Gina Silvestri, Esq., Jackson, NJ, 2003—04; assoc. atty. Law Office Of Terence G. Van Dzura, Edison, NJ, 2001—03, William J. Leininger, PC, SI, 2000—01, Law Office Of Mahipal Singh, PC, Jackson Heights, NY, 1999—2000. Fla. notary pub., Fla., 2004—. Mem.: NJ Bar Assn., NY Bar Assn., Alpha Phi (life). Home Phone: 386-761-5228. Personal E-mail: gsilvst@prodigy.net.

SILVESTRI, VITO NICHOLAS, communications educator; b. Vandergrift, Pa., Nov. 23, 1932; s. Vito Antonio Silvestri and Elvira DiVincenzo; 1 child, Marc. Student, Wayne U., Detroit, 1952; BS in Edn., Indiana State Tchrs. Coll., Pa., 1958; MS in Speech, Emerson Coll., Boston, 1959; PhD in Rhetoric and Pub. Address, Ind. U., Bloomington, 1966. Prof. English NY State Coll., Potsdam, 1959—64; prof. comm. studies Emerson Coll., Boston, 1964—96; founder, pres. The Bach Ensemble, Naples, Fla., 2002—. Vis. prof. U. ND, Grand Forks, 1969, Boston U., 1979, Stonehill Coll., Easton, Mass., 2001; cons. Nat. Fire Protection Assn., Quincy, Mass., 1980—86; adj. prof. comm. Fla. Gulf Coast U., Ft. Myers, 2002—05; mediator small claims Quincy Dist. Ct., Mass., 1988—92; cons. St. Lawrence Mental Health Agy., Potsdam, NY, 1960—64. Author: (textbook) Interpersonal Communication, 3d edit., 1991, JFK: Profile in Communication, 2000; contbr. articles to profl. jours. Cpl. US Army, 1952—54. Recipient Pro Arts Pub. Svc. in Arts award, City of Boston, 1992; Theodore Sorenson fellow, Kennedy Libr. Found., 1998—99. Democrat. Avocations: singing, cooking, reading, dance, travel. Home and Office: 3667 Arctic Cir Naples FL 34112

SILVESTRO, CLEMENT MARIO, museum director, historian; b. New Haven, Sept. 7, 1924; s. Joseph and Rose (Griego) S.; m. Betty C. Mack, June 26, 1950; 1 dau., Elizabeth J. Silvestro Casner. BS, Central Conn. State Coll., 1949; MS, U. Wis., 1951; PhD, 1959. Asst. to dir. Wis. Hist. Soc., 1956-57; dir. Am. Assn. State and Local History, 1957-64; editor History News, 1957-64; assoc. dir. Chgo. Hist. Soc., 1964-65, dir., 1965-74, sec., 1970-74; dir. Mus. of Our Nat. Heritage, Lexington, Mass., 1974-92. Mem. exec. com. Am. Assn. Museums, 1965-71, v.p., 1966-71; vis. lectr. Northeastern U., 1983-85 Co-author: A Decade of Collecting: Maps, 1985 Mem. Chgo. Archtl. and Landmark Com., 1968-74; mem. Ill. Historic Sites Adv. Council, 1970-74, U.S. ICOM, Nat. Com., 1970-74; chmn. Pres.'s Adv. Council on Historic Preservation, 1974-77; mem. adv. bd. Eleutherian Mills-Hagley Found., 1973-76; U.S. rep. to UNESCO Internat. Adv. Com. to Safeguard City of Venice, 1975; trustee U.S. Capitol Hist. Soc.; trustee, pres. Fruitlands Mus., 1982-85. Served with USAAF, 1943-45. Decorated Air medal with oak leaf clusters. Mem. Am. Assn. Mus., Orgn. Am Historians (chmn. hist. sites com. 1973-78), Chgo. Hist. Soc., Colonial Soc. Mass., Bostonian Soc., Mass. Hist. Soc. (resident), Union Club Boston, Masons. Home: 200 West Shore Rd Hancock ME 04640 Personal E-mail: silvestro@adelphia.net.

SILVESTRY, FRANK E., cardiologist; BS in Biochemistry, SUNY, Binghamton, 1986; MD, U. Pa., Phila., 1990. Resident U. Pa. Sch. Medicine, Phila, 1990—94, fellow in cardiology, 1994—97, assoc. prof. medicine, 1997—. Office: Univ Pa Health Sys 250 King Prussia Rd Radnor PA 19087 Office Phone: 610-902-2273. Office Fax: 610-902-2311.

SILVEY, ANITA LYNNE, editor; b. Bridgeport, Conn., Sept. 3, 1947; d. John Oscar and Juanita Lucille (McKitrick) Silvey. BS in Edn., Ind. U., 1969; MA in Comm. Arts, U. Wis., 1970. Editorial asst. children's book dept. Little Brown and Co., Boston, 1970-71; asst. editor Horn Book Mag., Boston, 1971-75; mng. editor, founder New Boston Rev., 1975-76; mktg. mgr. children's books, libr. svcs. mgr. trade divsn. Houghton Mifflin, Boston, 1976-84; editor-in-chief Horn Book Mag., Boston, 1985-95; v.p., pub. Children's Books Houghton Mifflin Co., Boston, 1995—2001. Editor: Children's Books and Their Creators, 1995, Help Wanted: Stories About Young People and Work, 1997, Essential Guide to Children's Books and their Creators, 2002, 100 Best Books for Children, 2004, 500 Great Books for Teens, 2006. Named one of 70 Women Who Have Made a Difference, Women's Nat. Book Assn., 1987. Mem.: ALA (chmn. children's librs., Laura Ingalls Wilder award 1987—89), Assn. Am. Pubs. (mem. libr. com.), Internat. Reading Assn. (mem. IRA Book award com. 1985—87), New Eng. Round Table (chmn. 1978—79). Personal E-mail: anitasilvey@aol.com.

SILVIA, DAVID ALAN, insurance broker; b. Taunton, Mass., Mar. 5, 1953; s. Edward J. and Loretta (Sousa) S.; m. Janet E. McMahon, Apr. 16, 1988 (div. Jan. 1996); 1 child, David. BA, Roger Williams U., 1975. Sales rep. New England Brass, Taunton, Mass., 1976-81; ins. agt. Prudential Ins., Raynham, Mass., 1981-82; owner, ptnr. CS Assocs., North Attleboro,

Mass., 1982-86; asst. ice hockey coach New England Hockey Inst., 2002—. Independent. Office: 495 Somerset Ave North Dighton MA 02764-1809 Office Phone: 508-880-0650. Business E-Mail: dsilviabroker@aol.com.

SIM, CRAIG STEPHEN, retired investment banker; b. Bklyn., Apr. 23, 1942; s. William Henry Craig and Lenore (Overton) S.; m. Susan Hart; children: Brandon Craig William, Stephanie Brooke. BA, Gettysburg Coll., 1965. Account exec. Francis I. duPont & Co., NYC, 1969-72; v.p. E.F. Hutton & Co., NYC, 1972-75; sr. v.p. Donaldson, Lufkin & Jenrette, NYC, 1975-83; exec. v.p. Shearson Am. Express, NYC, 1983-84; mng. dir. Donaldson, Lufkin & Jenrette, NYC, 1984-2001, Credit Suisse First Boston, 2001—. Trustee Gettysburg Coll., 1995-2001, Vt. Hist. Soc. Served to capt. USMC, 1965-69. Mem. Bond Club N.Y. (gov. 1979-80, 84-85, 90-93), Lawrence Beach Club (gov.), St. Andrew's Soc. (N.Y.C.), Burns Soc. City of N.Y. (trustee), L.I. Wyandanch Club, Seawanhaka Corinthian Yacht Club, Army and Navy Club (Washington), Union Club. Address: PO Box 57 Charlotte VT 05445

SIM, FRANKLIN H., orthopedic surgery educator; children: Leslie, Sheridan. MD, Dalhousie U. Med. Sch., 1964. Cert. orthopedic surgeon MN, 1972. Prof. orthop. surgery Mayo Clinic, Rochester, Minn., 1983—. Chair, divsn. orthop. oncology Mayo Clinic, 2000—. Physician US Nat. Hockey Team. 2d. lt. Black Watch Rgt., 1961, Germany. Recipient Outstanding Svc award, Canadian Orthop. Assn., 2000, Disting. award, Mayo Clinic, 2003. Fellow: Royal Australian Coll. Surgeons (hon.); mem.: SICOT, AMA, Orthop. Practice Soc., Orthop. Rsch. Soc., Musculoskeletal Tumor Soc., Minn. Orthop. Soc., Mid-Am. Orthop. Assn., Internat. Soc. Limb Salvage, Internat. Soc. Intraoperative Radiation Therapy, Internat. Skeletal Soc., Internat. Orthop. Assn., Canadian Orthop. Found. (bd. dirs.), Am. Orthop. Assn., Am. Orthop. Soc. Sports Medicine, Am. Coll. Sports Medicine, Am. Acad. Orthop. Surgeons, 20th Century Orthop. Soc., Ruth Jackson Orthop. Soc. (hon.), Sigma Xi (sci. rsch. soc.). Office: Mayo Clinic 200 First St SW Rochester MN 55905

SIM, JAI-HOON, electronics researcher; b. Seoul, Korea, Oct. 20, 1967; s. Kisub Sim and Joonghee Choi; m. Heaseung Oh, April 12, 1999; 1 child, Janie. BSEE, Nat. Taiwan U., Taipei, 1990, PhD in Elec. Engring., 1993. Assoc. rschr. Samsung Electronics Co., Ltd., Kyungki-Do, Korea, 1993-94, tech. mgr., 1995-98; adv. rschr. IBM, Hopewell Junction, NY, 1999—. Contbr. articles to profl. jours. Mem. IEEE. Roman Catholic. Avocations: skiing, swimming, ancient chinese literature. E-mail: jaihoons@us.ibm.com.

SIMA, ANDERS ADOLPH FREDRIK, pathologist; b. Jönköping, Sweden, Dec. 3, 1943; came to the U.S., 1990; s. Karl Jonas Simon Sima and Svea Gunhild (Nilsson) S.; children: Patricia, Alexander, Vanessa. BS, U. Vienna, Austria, 1967; MD, U. Göteborg, Sweden, 1973, PhD, 1974. Asst. prof. pathology U. Goteborg, Sweden, 1973-83, U. Toronto, Ont., 1978-81, assoc. prof. pathology Ont., 1981-82, U. Manitoba, Winnipeg, 1982-85, prof. pathology, 1985-90, dir. Diabetes Rsch. Ctr., 1988-90; prof. pathology U. Mich., Ann Arbor, 1990-96, prof. internal medicine, 1991-96; dir. neuropathology core MADRC Mich. Alzheimer Disease Rsch. Ctr., Ann Arbor, 1992—; prof. pathology, neurology and neurosurgery Wayne State U., Detroit, 1996—, dir. Morris Hood Jr. Comprehensive Diabetes Ctr., 1998—. Hon. prof. neuroscis. Med. Univ., Shanghai, China, 1988; cons. Pfizer, Inc., N.Y.C., 1987—, FDA, Washington, 1988—, Miles Pharm. Inc., West Haven, Conn. 1990—; mem. internat. adv. bd. Hoffman La Roche, Basel, Switzerland, 1992—, Takeda Pharm., Chicago, 2002-, Aventis, Bridgewater, NJ, 2003-, Novo Nordisk, Copenhagen, 2004-. Assoc. editor: Jour. PNS, Internat. Jour. Diab., Diabetes/Metabolism Rsch. and Revs., Jour. of Clinical Neurology; editor-in-chief: Frontiers in Animal Diabetes Research, Internat. Jour. Exptl. Diabetic Rsch., Internat. Jour. Diabetes Rsch.; mem. editl. bd. for 8 nat. and internat. jours.; contbr. numerous articles to profl. jours. Recipient Chinese Acad.'s award for Sci. Achievement, 1981, Acad. Achievement award Toku Med. Soc., Sendai, Japan, 1985, Gold medal Consiglio Nat. delle Ricerche, Rome, 1987, Internat. Order of Merit, 1999, Order of Internat. Ambs., 1999, Paulescu award, 2002; Diabetes Rsch. grantee NIH, Bethesda, Md., 1991, 92, Dementia Related grantee NIH, Bethesda, Md., 1994, Ednl. Tng. grantee Pfizer, Inc., N.Y.C., 1994. Fellow Royal Coll. Physicians and Surgeons Can., Internat. Study Group on Diabetes in Animals, Am. Assn. Pathologists, Juvenile Diabetes Found. (hon. chmn. 1984, Appreciation award 1984, Spl. Achievement award 1989, 97). Achievements include major contributions to the pathogenesis of diabetic neuropathy; original description of diffuse Lewy Body disease; description of genetically linked senile dementias. Office: Wayne State U Dept Pathology 540 E Canfield St Detroit MI 48201-1928 Home Phone: 313-640-8918; Office Phone: 313-577-1150. E-mail: asima@med.wayne.edu.

SIMAAN, MARWAN, electrical engineering educator; b. July 23, 1946; m. Rita Simaan. MSEE, U. Pitts., 1970; PhDEE, U. Ill., 1972. Registered profl. engr., Pa. Rsch. engr. Shell Devel. Co., Houston, 1974-76; assoc. prof. elec. engring. U. Pitts., 1976-85, prof., 1985-89, Bell of Pa./Bell Atlantic prof., 1989—, chmn. dept. elec. engring., 1991—. Cons. Gulf Rsch. and Tech., Pitts., 1979-85, ALCOA, Pitts., 1986-89. Editor: Vertical Seismic Profiles, 1984, Two-dimensional Transforms, 1985, Artificial Intelligence in Petroleum Exploration, 1989, Expert Systems in Exploration, 1991, (series) Advances in Geophysical Signal Processing; co-editor jour. Multidimensional Sys. and Signal Processing; mem. editl. bd. profl. jours., including IEEE Procs., IEEE Transactions on Cirs. and Sys., IEEE Transactions on Geosci. and Remote Sensing, Jour. Optimization Theory and Applications, Integrated Computer-aided Engring. Jour., Jour. Cirs., Sys. and Computers; contbr. over 300 articles on signal processing and control to profl. publs. Grantee NSF, NIH, ONR, Def. Advance Rsch. Project Adminstrs., Ben Franklin, Westinghouse, Gulf, ALCOA; recipient Outstanding ECE Alumnus U. Ill. Fellow: AAAS (sec. engring. sect. M 2003—), IEEE (Best Paper award 1985, 1999), Am. Soc. Engring. Edn.; mem.: NAE, Am. Assn. Artificial Intelligence, Soc. Exploration Geophysics, Sigma Xi (Best Paper award Alcoa chpt. 1988), Eta Kappa Nu. Achievements include patent in application of signal processing technology in aluminum manufacturing. Office: Univ Pitts Dept Elec Engring Pittsburgh PA 15261-0001 E-mail: simaan@engr.pitt.edu.

SIMANDLE, JEROME B., federal judge; b. Binghamton, NY, 1949; s. Paul R. Sr. and Mary F. Simandle; married; children: Roy C., Liza Jane. BSE magna cum laude, Princeton U., 1971; JD, U. Pa., 1976; diploma in Social Scis., U. Stockholm, 1974-75. Bar: Pa. 1977, N.J. 1978. Law clk. to Hon. John F. Gerry U.S. Dist. Ct., NJ, 1976-78; asst. U.S. atty. Dist. N.J., 1978-83; U.S. magistrate judge U.S. Dist. Ct., NJ, 1983-92, judge NJ, 1992—. Mem. lawyers adv. com. U.S. Dist. Ct., NJ, 1984—95; mem. ct. adminstrn. case mgmt. com. Jud. Conf. U.S., 1991—97; mem. joint adv. coun. of Adminstrv. Office of U.S. Cts., 2002—; mem. CPR Inst. for Dispute Resolution Commn. on Ethics and Stds. in Alternative Dispute Resolution, 1996—2002; chair Third Cir. Com. on Rules of Practice and Procedure, 2003—; mem. Third Cir. Model Civil Jury Instrns. Com., 2004—. Internat. grad. fellow Rotary Found., 1974-75. Master: Camden Inn of Ct. (program chmn. 1990—93, vice chmn. 1996—2004); fellow: Am. Bar Found.; mem.: Camden County Bar Assn., Am. Judicature Soc., Fed. Judges Assn. (bd. dirs. 1997—, treas. 2003—, co-editor In Camera 2004—). Office: Mitchell H Cohen US Courthouse Rm 6010 1 John F Gerry Pl Camden NJ 08101-0888

SIMANSKI, CLAIRE DVORAK, art educator; d. George James and Gertrude Louise Dvorak; m. Robert Simanski, June 20, 1970 (div. Sept. 2000); children: Joseph Brian, John Francis. BFA, Md. Inst. Coll. Arts, Balt., 1968. Cert. art tchr. K-12 Va. Dept. Edn. Tchr. Ann Arundle County Bd. Edn., Annapolis, 1969—71; day care provider Andover, 1973—77; fine arts instr. Bolling AF Base, Md., Md. Nat. Capital Parks, 1981—84; sales Loudon Jewelers, Loudon, 1989—90; vol. coord. Telecom. Exch. for Deaf, Great Falls, Va., 1990; tchr. Fairfax County Schs., Herndon, Va., 1992—. Mem. character counts com. Herndon Mid. Sch., 1999—2001; prodr., writer, bd. dirs. Herndon Cable TV, 1999—2006, sec., 2001, 03, 05; dept. chair Fine & Performing Arts, Herndon, 2000—06; mem. P.A.R. com. Johns Hopkins U., Balt., 2003—06. Active Art in Pub. Places, Herndon, Reston, 1998—2007; com. mem. Cmty. Arts Ctr., Herndon, 2001—02. Recipient Partnership in Edn. award, Optomists of Herndon, 1998, Fairfax County Police Dept. award, 2001, Outsanding Vol. award, Mayor, Herndon, Va., 2003, 2005, 2007, Hon. Commn., Congl. Youth Leadership Coun., Outstanding Vol. award, Herndon Cable TV, 2003. Mem.: Va. Edn. Assn., Fairfax Educators Assn. Avocations: antiques, writing. Office: Herndon Mid Sch Herndon VA 20170

SIMAO, PAUL, news agency executive; Writer Reuters Am., Inc., Canada, bur. chief Atlanta, 2000—. Office: Reuters America 3340 Peachtree Rd NE Ste 200 Atlanta GA 30326-1028 Business E-Mail: paul.simao@reuters.com.

SIMBERLOFF, DANIEL, biologist, educator; b. Easton, Pa., Apr. 7, 1942; s. Isaac and Ruth (Koplowitz) S. A.B., Harvard U., 1964; Ph.D., 1969. Asst. prof. biology Fla. State U., Tallahassee, 1968-73, assoc. prof., 1973-78, prof., 1978—1997, Robert O. Lawton Disting. prof., 1986; Nancy Gore Hunger prof. environ. studies, dept. ecology and evolutionary biology, U. Tenn., 1997-; vis. prof. U. Mich., 1974, U. Minn., 1980, Hebrew U., Jerusalem, 1984, bd. dirs. Nat. Sci. Bd.; mem. species survival commn. Internat. Union Conservation Nature and Natural Resources; contbr. articles to sci. jours; editor Jour. Biogeography, 1974—, Biodiversity and Conservation; mem. editl. bd. Jour. Biogeography, Northeast Gulf Sci., Environ. and Ecological Statistics, Raffles Bulletin of Zoology, Ecologie, Oecologia, BioScience, Biological Invasions. Co-editor: Ecological Communities: Conceptual Issues and the Evidence, 1984, (with D. Schmitz and T. Brown) Strangers in Paradise: Impact and Management of Nonindigenous Species in Florida, 1997. Recipient Developing Scholar award Fla. State U., 1977, Rector's medal U. Helsinki, Finland, 1983, Disting. Statistical Ecologist award, Internat. Assn. Ecology, 1994. Mem. Am Acad. Arts and Scis., British Ecol. Soc., Soc. Conservation Biology, Nature Conservancy, Ecol. Soc. Am. (Mercer award 1971), Am. Soc. Naturalists, Soc. for Study Evolution, Brit. Ecol. Soc., Soc. for Systematic Zoology. Jewish. Home: 2145 Indian Hills Dr Knoxville TN 37919-8914 Office: Ecology and Evolutionary Biology Univ Tenn 480 Dabney Hall Knoxville TN 37996-1610 Office Phone: 865-974-0849. Office Fax: 865-974-3067. E-mail: dsimberloff@utk.edu.

SIMECKA, BETTY JEAN, marketing executive; b. Topeka, Apr. 15, 1935; d. William Bryan and Regina Marie (Rezac) S.; m. Alex Pappas, Jan. 15, 1956 (div. Apr. 1983); 1 child, Alex William. Student, Butler County C.C., 1983—85. Freelance writer and photographer, L.A., also St. Marys, Kans., 1969-77; co-owner Creative Enterprises, El Dorado, Kans., 1977-83; coord. excursions into history Butler County C.C., El Dorado, 1983-84; dir. Hutchinson Conv. & Visitors Bur., Kans., 1984-85; dir. mktg. divsn. Exec. Mgmt., Inc., Wichita, 1985-87; exec. dir. Topeka Conv. and Visitors Bur., 1987-91, pres., CEO, 1991-96; pres. Internat. Connections, Inc., 1996-97, Simecka and Assoc., 1996-99, Pinnacle Prodns., L.L.C., 1997-99; pres., CEO Cultural Exhbns. and Events, L.L.C., 1999—2003; organizer Czars: 400 Years of Imperial Grandeur exhbn., 2002—04; v.p. mktg. Sunflower Exhbns., LLC, 2003—04; mktg. cons., 2003—06; employment cons. Joblink, Cottonwood, Inc., Lawrence, Kans., 2006—. Dir. promotion El Dorado Thunderboat Races, 1977-78. Contbr. articles to jours. and mags.; columnist St. Marys Star, 1973-79. Pres. El Dorado Art Assn., 1984; chair Santa Fe Trail Bike Assn., Kans., 1988-90; co-dir. St. Marys Summer Track Festival, 1973-81; chair spl. events Mulvane Art Mus., 1990, sec., 1991-92; membership chair, 1993-94, bd. dirs., 1995-96; bd. dirs. Topeka Civic Theater, 1991-96, co-chair spl. events, 1992; Kans. chair Russian Festival Com., 1992-93; vice-chair Kans. Film Commn., 1993-94, chair, 1994; bd. dirs. Kans. Expoctr. Adv. Bd., 1990-96, Brain Injury Assn. Greater Kansas City, Concerned Citizens Topeka, 1998-2000; pres. Kans. Internat. Mus., 1994-96. Recipient Kans. Gov.'s Outstanding Tourism award Kans. Broadcaster's Assn., 1993, Disting. Svc award City of Topeka, 1995, Hist. Ward Meade Disting. award Topeka Parks and Recreation Dept., 1995; named Kansan of Yr., Topeka Capitol-Jour., 1995, Sales and Mktg. Exec. of Yr., 1995, Internat. Soroptomists, Topeka chpt., Woman of Distinction, 1996. Mem. Nat. Tour Assn., Sales and Mktg. execs. (bd. dirs. 1991-92), Internat. Assn. Conv. and Visitors Burs. (co-chair rural tourism com. 1994), Am. Soc. Assn. Execs., Travel Industry Assn. Kans. (membership chair 1988-89, sec. 1990, pres. 1991-92, Outstanding Merit award 1994), St. Marys C. of C. (pres. 1975), I-70 Assn. (v.p. 1989, pres. 1990), Optimists (social sec. Topeka chpt. 1988-89). Independent. Methodist. Holder Nat. AAU record for 100-yard dash, 1974.

SIMENDINGER, THEODORE JOHN, writer, publishing executive; b. Phila., Oct. 6, 1954; s. Theodore John and Margaret Smith Simendinger; m. Bonita Ann Kolish; 1 child, Grace. BS, Jacksonville U., 1976. Founder, chmn. Pro Leisure Tour, Inc., Greenwood Village, Colo., 2000—. Career devel. cons. Airplane Reader Pub., Greenwood Village, 2000—. Author: Critters, Fish & Other Troublemakers, 2001, Rich Without Money, 2002, 12 Miles to Paradise, 2003, Searching for Tendulkar, 2004, Jurassic Trout, 2004, The Rise And Fall of Piggy Church, 2006, Tuki Banjo, Superstar, 2007, Maximum Horsepower: How to Strengthen Your Sales Force, 2007. Founder, chmn. No Bats Baseball Club, Global Ambassadors for the Good of the Game. Greenwood Village, Colo., 1991—. Named Alumnae of the Yr., Jacksonville U., 2003. Avocations: reading, writing, comedy, fishing. Office Phone: 877-611-6222.

SIMEONE, WENDY FRANCES, secondary school educator, department chairman; b. Middleboro, Mass., Sept. 2, 1951; d. Carl Thurston and Pauline Mary (Springer) Matheson; m. Robert Paul Simeone; children: Paul, Adam, Matthew. BA in English and Edn., Southeastern Mass. U., 1973; MA in English, U. Mass., Boston, 1998. Tchr. English Plymouth (Mass.)-Carver Schs., 1975—87; tchr. English, chair Carver (Mass.) HS, 1987—. Cons. Edn. Testing Svc., Princeton, NJ, 1992—, Nat. Coun. Tchrs. English, Urbana, Ill., 1997—, Mass. Dept. Edn., 1999—; presenter in field. Leader Boy Scouts Am., Mass., 1989—92; coach Kingston (Mass.) Youth Soccer, 1989—93; teacher, counselor Harvest of Hope World Hunger, Ashland, Va., 1997; youth min. COAP Ministry, Harlan, Ky., 1996—. Finalist Tchr. of the Yr., Mass. Dept. Edn., 2000; named S. Boston's Best Tchr., 1993, Tchr. Who Inspires, Simmons Coll., 1993, Tufts U., 1995, 1997, Inspriational Tchr., Nat. Found. Advancement Arts, 1994; fellow, Nat. Bd. Profl. Tchg. Stds., 1999—, NEH, 2004; Tchg. fellow, Mass. Tchr. Leadership Acad., 2002—. Mem.: Nat. Coun. Tchrs. English (chair commn. lit., chair world lit. commn. 1997—). Democrat. United Ch. Of Christ. Avocations: reading, yoga, hiking, writing, skiing. Home: PO Box 37 91 Winnetuxet Rd Plympton MA 02367 Office: Carver HS 60 S Meadow Rd Carver MA 02330

SIMEONOV, SIMEON, computer scientist; BS in Computer Sci., Economics and Math., Macalester Coll.; MS in Computer Sci., Boston U. V.p. Emerging Technologies; chief arch. Macromedia Corp.; prin. Polaris Ventures, 2002—. Author: Building Web Services with Java, 2001. Named one of Top 100 Young Innovators, MIT Tech. Review, 2004. Office: Polaris Ventures 1000 Winter St Waltham MA 02451

SIMERAL, WILLIAM GOODRICH, retired chemical company executive; b. Portland, Oreg., May 22, 1926; s. Claire Cornelius and Geneva G. Simeral; m. Elizabeth Louise Ross, June 25, 1949; children: Linda Simeral McGregor, Karen Simeral Schousen, William Goodrich Jr., John David; m. Marion Poore Anderson, Nov. 3, 2001. BS in Physics, Franklin and Marshall Coll., Lancaster, Pa., 1948; PhD in Physics, U. Mich., 1953. With E.I. duPont de Nemours and Co., Inc., 1953-87, v.p., gen. mgr. plastics dept. Wilmington, Del., 1974-76, v.p., gen. mgr. plastic products and resins dept., 1976-77, sr. v.p., dir., mem. exec. com., 1977-81, exec. v.p., dir., mem. exec. com., 1981-87; vice chmn. bd., chief operating officer Conoco Inc., 1984-85. Trustee Franklin and Marshall Coll., 1977—, chmn. bd., 1991-94; trustee, bd. dirs. Wilmington Med. Ctr., 1978-93, chmn. bd., 1982-86; bd. dirs. YMCA Wilmington and New Castle County, 1978-81. Mem. Chem. Mfrs. Assn. (vice chmn. bd. 1980-81, chmn. exec. com. 1981-82, chmn. bd. 1982-83), Am. Phys. Soc., Phi Beta Kappa, Sigma Xi, Wilmington Country Club.

SIMES, MICHAEL LOUIS, lawyer; b. Hartsdale, NY, Oct. 8, 1969; s. Irwin M. and Ann L. Simes; m. Deborah Tamara Schaefer, Jan. 21, 2007. BA, SUNY, Albany, 1988—91; JD, U. Ariz., Tuscon, 1991—94; MBA, Ariz. State U., Tempe, 2001—03. Bar: Ariz. 1994, Colo. 1996. Atty. Michael Simes, LLC, Tempe, 2000—. Contbr. articles to profl. jours. Sec. Ariz. Coalition for Tomorrow, Phoenix, 1995—99. Recipient Pres. award, Ariz. Coalition for Tomorrow, 1998. Achievements include being a recognized expert in website and electronic services by the state bar of Arizona. Office: Michael Simes LLC 903 S Rural Rd #101-323 Tempe AZ 85281 Business E-Mail: info@michaelsimes.com.

SIMES, STEPHEN MARK, pharmaceutical executive; b. NYC, Nov. 23, 1951; s. Herbert H. and Mimi (Maurer) S.; m. Anita H. Herzog, Aug. 23, 1975. BS in Chemistry, Bklyn. Coll., 1973; MBA in Mktg., NYU, 1980. Sales rep. G.D. Searle and Co., NYC, 1974-78, supr. sales tng. Chgo., 1978-79, dist. sales mgr. NYC, 1979-81, product mgr. Chgo., 1981-82, sr. product mgr., 1982-83, dir. pub. affairs and communications, 1983-84; v.p. Gynex Inc., Chgo., 1984-88; dir. Gynex Pharms. Inc., Deerfield, 1985-93; pres., dir. Gynex Labs., Chgo., 1985-88; pres., CEO Contracap Inc., 1988-89, Gynex Pharms., Inc., Chgo., 1989-93, chmn., 1992-93; sr. v.p., dir. Bio-Technology Gen. Corp., 1993-94; pres., CEO, dir. Unimed Pharms., Inc., 1994-97; bd. dirs., CEO, pres. Simes Pharm. Cons., 1997-98. Vice chmn., CEO, pres., BioSante Pharms., Inc., Lincolnshire, Ill., 1998—. Mem.: Internat. Soc. For Study of Women's Sexual Health, Drug Info. Assn., iBio, Biotech. Industry Orgn., N.Am. Menopause Soc., Endocrine Soc., Licensing Exec. Soc., Chgo. Coun. Fgn. Rels. Office: 111 Barclay Blvd Lincolnshire IL 60069

SIMIC, CHARLES, language educator, poet; b. Beograd, Yugoslavia, May 9, 1938; arrived in U.S., 1954, naturalized, 1971; s. George and Helen (Matijevich) Simic; m. Helen Dubin, Oct. 1964; children: Anna, Philip. BA, NYU, 1967. Editl. asst. Aperture, Quar. of Photography, NYC, 1966—69; prof. English Calif. State U., Hayward, Calif., 1970—73, U. N.H., Durham, NH, 1973—. Author: What the Grass Says, 1967, Somewhere Among us a Stone is Taking Notes, 1969, Dismantling the Silence, 1971, White, 1972, Return to a Place Lit by a Glass of Milk, 1974, Biography and a Lament, 1976, Charon's Cosmology, 1977, Classic Ballroom Dances, 1980, Austerities, 1982, Weather Forecast for Utopia and Vicinity, 1983, Selected Poems, 1985, rev. edit., 1990, Unending Blues, 1986, The World Doesn't End, 1989 (Pulitzer Prize for poetry, 1990), The Book of Gods and Devils, 1990, Hotel Insomnia, 1992, A Wedding in Hell, 1994, Frightening Toys, 1995, Walking the Black Cat, 1996, Looking for Trouble, 1997, Selected Early Poems, 1999, Jackstraws, 1999, rev. edit., 2000, Night Picnic, 2001, Voice at 3 A.M., 2003, My Noiseless Entourage, 2005, (essays) The Uncertain Certainty, 1985, (novels) Wonderful Words, Silent Truth, 1990, Dimestore Alchemy, 1992, The Unemployed Fortune Teller, 1994, Orphan Factory, 1998, A Fly in the Soup, 2000, Metaphysician in the Dark, 2003, Memory Piano, 2005; translator (with C.W. Truesdale): Fire Gardens, 1970; translator: The Little Box, 1970; translator: (with Mark Strand) Another Republic, 1976; translator: Four Modern Yugoslav Poets, 1970, Homage to the Lame Wolf, 1979; translator: (with P. Kastmiler) Atlantis, 1987; translator: Roll Call of Mirrors, 1987, Some Other Wine and Light, 1989, Bandit Wind, 1991, The Horse Has Six Legs, 1992, Night Mail, 1992, Devil's Lunch, 1999, A Wake for the Living, 2002; contbr. Selected Poems of Tomaz Salamun, 1987, RollCall of Mirrors, 1987, poems to mags. and anthologies. With US Army, 1961—63. Named US Poet Laureate, Libr. Congress, 2007—; recipient PEN Internat. award for transl., 1970, 1980, Edgar Allan Poe award, Am. Acad. Poets, 1975, award, Nat. Inst. Arts and Letters, 1976, AAAL award, 1976, Harriet Monroe poetry award, U. Chgo., 1980, CiCastignola award, Poetry Soc. Am., 1980; fellow Guggenheim fellow, 1972—73, Nat. Endowment for the Arts, 1974—75, 1979—80, Fulbright Travelling fellow, 1982, Ingram Merrill fellow, 1983—84, Mac Arthur fellow, 1984—89. Mem.: Acad. Arts and Letters. Home: PO Box 192 Strafford NH 03884-0192 Office: U NH Dept English Durham NH 03824 *

SIMINI, JOSEPH PETER, accountant, financial consultant, writer, former educator; b. Buffalo, Feb. 15, 1921; s. Paul and Ida (Moro) S.; m. Marcelline McDermott, Oct. 4, 1968. BS, St. Bonaventure U., 1940, BBA, 1949; MBA, U. Calif.-Berkeley, 1957; DBA, Western Colo. U., 1981. CPA, Calif. Insp. naval material Bur. Ordnance, Buffalo and Rochester, N.Y., 1941-44; mgr. Paul Simini Bakery, Buffalo, 1946-48; internal auditor DiGiorgio (Fruit) Corp., San Francisco, 1950-51; tax acct. Price Waterhouse & Co., San Francisco, 1953; sr. acct. Richard L. Hanlin C.P.A., San Francisco, 1953-54; prof. acctg. U. San Francisco, 1954-79, emeritus prof., 1983—. Mem. rev. bd. Calif. Bd. Accountancy, 1964-68; host The Bus. Doctor Stas. WALE and KCCF, 1998. Author: Accounting Made Simple, 1967, rev. edit., 1987, Cost Accounting Concepts for Nonfinancial Executives, 1976, Become Wealthy! Using Tax Savings and Real Estate Investments, 1982, Balance Sheet Basics for the Nonfinancial Managers, 1989, Petals of the Rose, 1990, How to Become Financially Independent, 1996, 10 Steps to Financial Independence Guaranteed, 2000, Entwined Lives, 2003; tech. editor Accounting Essentials, 1972; patentee Dial-A-Trig and Verbum Est card game. Mem. coun. com. Boy Scouts Am., Buffalo, San Francisco, 1942-65, Souters Key, San Francisco coun.; bd. dir. Nat. Italian Am. Found., Washington, 1979-85. Lt. j.g. USNR, 1944-46. Recipient Bacon-McLaughlin medal St. Bonaventure U., 1940, Laurel Key, 1940; Outstanding Tchr. award Coll. Bus. Adminstrn., U. San Francisco, 1973, Disting. Tchr. award U. San Francisco, 1975, Joseph Per Simini award, 1977, Crown Zellerbach Found. fellow, 1968-69, Gold Medal Associazione Piemontese nel Mondo, Turin, Italy, 1984; decorated Knight Order of Merit, Republic of Italy, 1982. Mem. AICPA's, MENSA, Calif. Soc. CPAs (past chmn. ednl. stds., student rels. com. San Francisco chpt.), Inst. of Mgmt. Accts. (past pres. San Francisco chpt.), Am. Acctg. Assn., Am. Mgmt. Assn. (lectr. 1968-78), Serra (past pres. Golden Gate chpt.), Il Cenacolo (past pres.), Toastmasters (past pres. Magic Word, treas. Dist. 4, 1996-97), K.C., Rotary (past pres. Daly City), Delta Sigma Pi (past pres. San Francisco alumni club), Beta Gamma Sigma. Roman Catholic. Office: PO Box 31420 San Francisco CA 94131-0420 Home: 5235 Diamond Heights Blvd #209 San Francisco CA 94131 *Personal philosophy: You can succeed! but you must program yourself for success and know what you want.*

SIMIS, THEODORE LUCKEY, investment banker, information technology executive; b. NYC, June 17, 1924; s. Theodore William Ernest and Helen (Luckey) S.; m. Laura Cushman Ingraham, Sept. 8, 1946; children—Nancy Simis Ricca, Theodore Steven, Karen Simis Woods, June Simis Sobocinski BS, NYU, 1950, MBA, 1952. With Bell System, 1941-79; various positions to officer level with N.Y. Telephone Co., N.J. Telephone

Co., and AT&T; v.p. Warner Amex Cable Co., 1980-81; sr. v.p. E.F. Hutton, Sarasota, Fla., 1982-87; vice chmn., bd. dirs. XMX Corp., Burlington, Mass., 1986-2000, 2005—, OPIX Corp., Burlington, 2000—04; pres. Pvt. Transatlantic Telecommunication System Inc., McLean, Va.; 1987-89; chmn. Value Added Network System, Inc., Sarasota, Fla., 1990-91. Dir. Liebenzell Mission, Schooleys Mountain, N.J.; vis. Nieman fellow Harvard U., 1977. Life mem. Republican Nat. Com., 1981—. 1st lt. U.S. Army, 1942-53, ETO Mem. N.Y. Acad. Scis., U.S. C. of C., NYU Club. Lutheran. Home: 6025 Manasota Key Rd Englewood FL 34223-9245 Office Phone: 941-474-8690. Fax: 941-475-1128. Personal E-mail: tlslns@verizon.net.

SIMITIS, SPIROS, legal educator; b. Athens, Greece, Oct. 19, 1934; s. George and Fanny (Christopoulo) S.; m. Ilse Grubrich, Aug. 3, 1963. JD, U. Marburg, Fed. Republic Germany, 1956. Assoc. prof. U. Frankfurt, Fed. Republic Germany, 1963, prof., 1969, U. Giessen, Fed. Republic Germany, 1964-69; vis. prof. London Sch. Econs., U. Calif. - Berkeley, 1976, U. Pa., 1980, U. Strasbourg, France, 1987-88, Paris, 1990—2001, Yale U., New Haven, 1981—. Sec. gen. Internat. Civil Status Commn., 1966—80; chmn. Data Protection Experts Com. of the Coun. of Europe, Strasbourg, 1982—86; with Hesse Data protect commr., 1975—91; mem. rsch. coun. European Univ. Inst.; chmn. social rights com. European Commn., 1998; chmn. German Nat. Ethic Coun., 2000—05. Contbr. numerous articles to legal publs. Mem.: Athens Acad. Scis., German Coun. Pvt. Internat. Law, German Lawyers Assn. (bd. dirs. 1970—82). Office: Johann Wolfgang Goethe U Senckenberganlage 31 Postfach 111932 60054 Frankfurt Germany Office Phone: 0049-69-79822733. E-mail: simitis@jur.uni-frankfurt.de.

SIMJEE, AISHA, ophthalmologist, educator; b. Surat, India, Jan. 23, 1944; came to U.S., 1970; d. Yusuf Esmail Simjee and Amina Ahmed Badat; m. Sabbir A. Dadabhai, Apr. 28, 1978; children: Alia Dadabhai, Sufia Dadabhai. Intermediate Sci. degree, Rangoon U., Burma, 1963; MB, BS, Inst. Medicine, Rangoon, 1968. Diplomate Am. Bd. Ophthalmology. Intern Rangoon Gen. Hosp., 1968-69, South Balt. Gen. Hosp., 1970-71; rschr. in ophthalmology Johns Hopkins Hosp., Balt., 1971-72; resident in ophthalmology Eye Dept. Howard U. Hosp., D.C. Gen. Hosp., Armed Forces Inst. Pathology, Washington, 1972-75; fellow in cornea external diseases Wills Eye Hosp., Phila., 1975-76; fellow in ophthalmic pathology and med. retina Scheie Eye Inst., Phila., 1976-77; asst. prof. ophthalmology Howard U., Washington, 1977-78; clin. assoc. prof. ophthalmology U. Calif., Irvine, 1978—; pvt. practice Orange, Calif. Mem. med. adv. bd. Orange County Eye & Tissue Bank, 1990—; attending physician St. Joseph Hosp., Orange, 1978—, U. Calif. Irvine Med. Ctr., 1978—. Contbr. articles to profl. jours. Vol. ophthalmologist La Amistad de Jose Clinic, Sponsor Care Program of St. Joseph Hosp., 1988—, Testing 1-2-3 Screening Clinic St. Joseph Hosp., ann. eye screening for local sch. children, Project Orbis, S.E.E. Internat., Santa Barbara, Am. Eye Care Project, Hope World Wide, 2002—, Internat. Asst. Mission, 2002—. Named Woman of Achievement, Rancho Santiago Coll., Santa Ana, 1990; recipient certs. of recognition Calif. state senator John Seymour, Calif. congressman Christopher Cox, Calif., lt. gov. Leo McCarthy; recipient Pride in the Profession award AMA Found., 2005, Woman of Vision award We Give Thanks or Orange County, 2006. Fellow ACS, Am. Acad. Ophthalmology (Nat. Eye Care Project 1986—); mem. AMA (Pride in Profession award 2005), Calif. Med. Assn., Orange County Med. Assn. (bd. dirs. 1995-02), Orange County Soc. Ophthalmology (exec. com. 1992-02). Office: 1310 W Stewart Dr Ste 501 Orange CA 92868-3856 Home Phone: 714-771-2033; Office Phone: 714-771-2020. Personal E-mail: drsimjee@sbcglobal.net.

SIMKIN, STEVEN, lawyer; b. NYC, Aug. 6, 1947; BS cum laude, U. Pa., 1969, MCP, JD cum laude, 1973. Bar: N.Y. 1974, U.S. Dist. Ct. (so. dist.) N.Y., U.S. Ct. Appeals (2nd cir.). Ptnr. Paul, Weiss, Rifkind, Wharton & Garrison, NYC, 1982—, chair, Real Estate Dept. Assoc. editor U. Pa. Law Rev., 1972-73. Mem. N.Y. State Bar Assn. (exec. com. real property law sect. 1988-90), Order of Coif, Pi Gamma Nu, Beta Gamma Sigma. Office: Paul Weiss Rifkind Wharton & Garrison 1285 Avenue Of The Americas Fl 22 New York NY 10019-6064 Office Phone: 212-373-3073. Office Fax: 212-373-2058. Business E-Mail: ssimkin@paulweiss.com.

SIMKO, JAN, English, foreign language and literature educator; b. Zlaté Moravce, Slovakia, Oct. 30, 1920; arrived in U.S., 1967; s. Simon Simko and Terezia Simkova; m. Libusa Safarikova, Dec. 20, 1950 (div. 1970, dec. 2004); children: Jan, Vladimir (dec.). Diploma in English, U. Bratislava, 1942, Diploma in German, 1943, PhD in English, 1944; MPhil in English, U. London, 1967. Tchr. English and German various bus. schs., 1942-45; asst. depts. English and German U. Bratislava, 1945-46; instr. English Econom U., 1946-47; faculty U. Bratislava, 1950-68, from asst. prof. to prof. English, 1957-68; prof. English Rio Grande Coll., Ohio, 1968-75. Instr. Shakespeare Georgetown U., 1982-84; vis. prof. English, scholar-in-residence W. Va. U., Parkersburg, 1989-90; instr. Slovak Fgn. Svc. Inst., Washington, 1974, 96, fed. govt., 1989, 91-93, IMF & World Bank, 1994-95; examiner critical langs. program Kent (Ohio) State U., 1974-91; feature writer Voice of Am., 1983-94; translator U.S. Dept. State, 1997—2005; bd. linguistics Slovak Acad. of Scis., 1957-67. *Mr. Simko is the author of many works on linguistics such as Word-Order in the Winchester Manuscript as well as articles on the origin of Standard English, the criteria of linguistic relationships, and relations of vocabulary and grammar. His writings on lexicography include the English-Slovak Dictionary and his writings on literature include Malory's Creed, Shakespeare in Slovakia, and King Lear and Timon of Athens. He has written an autobiography entitled Education of a Slovak Anglicist: My Contacts with Foreign Anglicists. His other works include Slovak Musicians Abroad, Slovak Singers at New York's Met, Global Thoughts for Our Times, Martina Hingis — No One in Tennis, and Thoughts on Soccer.* Author: 3 English textbooks, 2 bilingual dictionaries, 1 linguistic monograph; editor: Lectures in the Circle of Modern Philology, 2 vols., 1965-66; chief consulting editor: textbooks of Slovak and Czech, 1993-96; contbg. writer: The Review, 1995-2002; Am./Can.-Slovak press; contbr. articles to profl. jours. With Czechoslovak infantry, 1946. Grantee Brit. Coun., 1947-49, Folger Shakespeare Libr./U.S. Dept. State, 1967-68; Internat. Rsch. and Exch. Bd., 1982, others; recipient awards W.Va. U., 1990, Bratislava U., 1995, medal Pres. of Slovakia, 2002. Mem. MLA (life), Slovak Studies Assn., Soc. for Scis. and Arts, Met. Opera Guild, Shakespeare Theater Guild, Nat. Symphony Orch. Assn., English-Speaking Union. Roman Catholic. Avocations: classical music, opera, theater, fine arts, swimming. Home: Apt 511 725 24th St NW Washington DC 20037 Office Phone: 202-429-8899. Personal E-mail: jansimko@hotmail.com.

SIMMONDS, ROBERT MAURER, education educator; b. Beaver Falls, Pa., Apr. 16, 1947; s. Harold Maurer and Mary Simmonds; m. Deborah Lynne Carawan, June 25, 1977; children; Stephen Maurer, Kent Hayes. BS, Youngstown State U., 1973, MS, 1975; advanced cert. edn., Coll. William and Mary, 1983, EdD, 1985; grad. sr. exec. fellows program JFK Sch. Govt., Harvard, 2004. Assoc. prof. St. Leo Coll., Ft. Eustis, Va., 1985—88; assoc. prof. ops. rsch. US Army Transp. Sch., Ft. Eustis, 1988—2001; dept. chmn. sys. engring. dept. US Army Logistics Mgmt. Coll., Ft. Lee, 2001—06; sr. ops. rschr., analyst US Army Human Resources Command, Washington, 2006; sr. fellow US Army, 2006—. Contbr. articles to profl. jours. With USN, 1965—68. Avocations: walking, golf. Office Phone: 703-325-4479. Personal E-mail: orsased1@comcast.net. Business E-Mail: robert_simmonds@us.army.mil.

SIMMONS, ADELE SMITH, foundation executive, former educator; b. Lake Forest, Ill., June 21, 1941; d. Hermon Dunlap and Ellen T. (Thorne) Smith; m. John L. Simmons; children: Ian, Erica, Kevin BA in Social Studies with honors, Radcliffe Coll., 1963; PhD, Oxford U., Eng., 1969; LHD (hon.), Lake Forest Coll., 1976, Amherst Coll., 1977, Franklin Pierce Coll., 1978, U. Mass., 1978, Alverno Coll., 1982, Marlboro Coll., 1987, Smith Coll., 1988, Mt. Holyoke Coll., 1989, Am. U., 1992, Tufts U., 1994. Asst. prof. Tufts U., Boston, 1969-72; dean Jackson Coll., Medford, Mass., 1970-72; asst. prof. history, dean student affairs Princeton U., NJ, 1972-77; pres. Hampshire Coll., Amherst, Mass., 1977-89, John D. and Catherine T. MacArthur Found., Chgo., 1989—99; vice chair, sr. exec. Chgo. Metropolis 2020, 1999—; sr. assoc. Ctr. for Internat. Studies U. Chgo., 1999—2005. Bd. dirs. Marsh & McLennan Cos., N.Y.C., Shorebank Corp., Chgo., Union Concerned Scientists, Synergos Inst., Environ. Def., bd. mem., Am. Prospect; bd. dirs. Field Mus., Chgo., Mexican Fine Arts Ctr. Mus., Chgo. Coun. on Fgn. Rels., Winning Worlplaces; emeritus mem. bd. dirs. Rocky Mountain Inst.; former corr. in Mauritius and Tunisia for N.Y. Times, The Economist; high level adv. bd. UN, 1993—; mem. adv. com. World Bank Inst.; mem. bd. overseers Harvard U., 1972-78; chair Fair Labor Assn.; sr. advisor World Econ. Forum. Co-author: (with Freeman, Dunkle, Blau) Exploitation from 9 to 5: Twentieth Century Fund Task Force Report on Working Women, 1975; author: Modern Mauritius, 1982; contbr. articles on edn. and pub. policy in The N.Y. Times, Christian Sci. Monitor, The Bulletin of Atomic Scientist, Harper's, The Atlantic Monthly and others. Commr. Pres.'s Commn. on World Hunger, Washington, 1978-80, Pres.'s Commn. on Environ. Quality, 1991-92; mem. Commn. Global Governance; trustee Carnegie Found. for Advancement Teaching, 1978-86; chair Mayor Richard Daley's Youth Devel. Task Force, 1993-95. Named one of Chgos. 100 Most Influential Women, Crain's Chgo. Bus., 2004. Fellow Am. Acad. Arts and Scis.; mem. Phi Beta Kappa. Office: Chgo Metropolis 2020 30 W Monroe St Chicago IL 60603 Home Phone: 773-404-5566; Office Phone: 312-332-8161. Business E-Mail: adele.simmons@cm2020.org.

SIMMONS, ANNE L., federal official; b. Spencer, Iowa, Jan. 4, 1964; d. Donald Lewis and Lois Amber (Blass) S. B in Spl. Studies, Cornell Coll., 1986. Intern for Congressman Berkley Bedell, Washington, 1986; field staff Iowans for Clayton Hodgson, Sioux City, Iowa, 1986; exec. sec. Atomic Indsl. Forum, Bethesda, Md., 1986-87; staff asst. House Armed Svcs. Com., Washington, 1987; legis. asst. to Congressman Tim Johnson Washington, 1988-93; staff dir. gen. farms commodities subcom. House Agriculture Com., Washington, 1993, staff dir. environ., credit and rural devel. subcom., 1994, minority resource conservation rsch. and forestry subcom., 1995-96. Profl. Staff Ho. Com. on Agrl., 1997—. Music scholar Cornell Coll., 1982-86. Mem. Delta Phi Alpha. Democrat. Office: House Agriculture Com 1301 Longworth House Ofc Bldg Washington DC 20515-0001 E-mail: anne.simmons@mail.house.gov.

SIMMONS, ANTHONY, virology educator, physician, researcher; b. Leicestershire, U.K., Mar. 12, 1954; s. Alfred William and Sarah Sylvia Simmons; m. Mary-Jane Potter, June 8, 2002; children: Katie Anne, Matthew James. MD, PhD, Cambridge, UK, 1976—86. FRCPath Royal Coll. Pathologists, 1986. Sr. med. specialist Inst. Med. and Vet. Sci., Adelaide, Australia, 1986—2001; prof. pediat. pathology: microbiology and immunology U. Tex., Galveston, 2001—. Mem. editl. bd. Jour. Virology, Herpes Jour.; contbr. articles to profl. jours. Mem.: Australian Herpes Mgmt. forum (founding mem.), Am. Social Health Assn. (sci. adv. com.), Am. Soc. Virology, Am. Assn. Immunologists. Achievements include patents for compositions and methods for herpes simplex prophylaxis and treatment. Avocations: sailing, rock climbing, snowboarding. Home: 1001 Postoffice St Galveston TX 77550 Office: U Tex Med Br 301 University Blvd Galveston TX 77555-0372 Office Phone: 409-772-0423. Business E-Mail: ansimmon@utmb.edu.

SIMMONS, BILL, sportswriter; b. Boston, Mass., 1969; m. Kari Simmons, Apr. 1, 1999. BA, Holy Cross Univ., Springfield, Mass., 1991. Free-lance website journalist, 1992—98; writer Jimmy Kimmel Live, 2003—04; Page 2 columnist ESPN.com, 1999—; columnist ESPN The Mag., 2003—. Appeared in (films) Doing Time on The Longest Yard, 2005, The Mean Machine, 2005; author: (sports book) Now I Can Die in Peace, 2005. Office: c/o ESPN 935 Middle St Bristol CT 06010

SIMMONS, CHARLES B., JR., lawyer; b. Wilmington, NC, Mar. 19, 1961; BA summa cum laude, Yale Univ., 1984; JD, Univ. Va., 1987. Bar: NC 1987. Ptnr., capital mkts group, ptnr.-in-charge, Charlotte Alston & Bird LLP, Charlotte, NC. Bd. dir. Junior Achievement Carolinas; adv. com. Queens Univ. Law Sch. Mem.: ABA, NC Bar Assn., Phi Beta Kappa. Office: Alston & Bird LLP Ste 4000 Bank of Am Plz 101 S Tryon St Charlotte NC 28280-4000 Office Phone: 704-444-1035. Office Fax: 704-444-1111. Business E-Mail: csimmons@alston.com.

SIMMONS, CHARLES BEDFORD, JR., judge; b. Greenville, SC, Dec. 4, 1956; s. Charles Bedford and Mary Margaret (Mason) S.; children: Charles B. III, Elizabeth S., Mason W. AA magna cum laude, Spartanburg Meth. Coll., 1977; BS magna cum laude, E. Tenn. State U., 1979; JD, U. S.C., 1982. Bar: S.C. 1982, U.S. Dist. Ct. S.C. 1983, U.S. Ct. Appeals (4th cir.) 1986. Law clk. to presiding justice S.C. Cir. Ct., Greenville, 1982-83; with Carter Law Firm, Greenville, 1983-86; ptnr. Wilkins, Nelson, Kittredge & Simmons, Greenville, 1986-89; civil ct. judge Greenville, 1989—; presiding judge 13th Circuit Drug Ct. Mem. bench-bar com. S.C. Supreme Ct., 1992-97; presiding judge 13th cir. Drug Ct; bd. mem. Nat. Assn. Drug Ct. Profls Mem. adv. com. paralegal program Greenville Tech. Coll., 1989-97, chmn., 1990-91; mem. Friends of 200 Adv. Bd., 1991-99. Named Big Brother of Yr., Big Bros.-Big Sisters, 1988; recipient Svc. to Manking award Rotary Club, 1989, Outstanding Young Disting. Svc. award Greenville Jaycees, 1990-91. Mem. ATLA, S.C. Bar Assn. (young lawyer liason 1985-89, named Outstanding Young Lawyer of Yr. 1989), Nat. Assn. Drug Ct. Profls. (bd. dirs.), Greenville Bar Assn., S.C. Trial Lawyers Assn., Greenville Young Lawyers (pres. 1988—1990), Gamma Beta Phi, Pi Gamma Mu, Phi Delta Phi. Clubs: Greenville City, Textile (v.p. 1985-87), Revelers (Greenville). Presbyterian. Office: Ste 313 County Courthouse Greenville SC 29601 Office Phone: 864-467-8556. Business E-Mail: csimmons@greenvillecounty.org.

SIMMONS, CLINTON CRAIG, human resources executive; b. Cleve., Nov. 25, 1947; s. Benjamin F. and Catharin (Thornton) R.; m. Cheryl LeRoy, June 16, 1973; 1 child, Eric. BBA, Miami U., Oxford, Ohio, 1969; grad. quality mgmt. course, Winter Park, Fla., 1986. Cert. quality edn. system instr. Specialist employee, cmty. rels. Euclid Lamp Plant, GE, Cleve., 1970-75; employee, indsl. rels. rep. Bailey Controls Co., Wickliffe, Ohio, 1975-78; mgr., coll. recruiting Gen. Tire and Rubber, Akron, Ohio, 1978-81, profl. staffing coord., 1981-82; regional human resource mgr. Gilbane Bldg. Co., Cleve., 1982-86, human resource mgr. Western regions, 1987-88; asst. v.p., dir. human resources St. Alexis Hosp. Med. Ctr. CA Div. Sisters of St. Francis, 1988-90; corp. pers. mgr. MK-Ferguson Co., 1990-94, mgr. human resources, 1993-94; mgr. human resources engring., constrn. and environ. group Washington Group Internat., Cleve., 1994-2001, sr. mgr. human resources, 2001—; human resources cons. Key Source HCI, LLC, 2003—, Highbridge Assoc., 2003—07; chmn. human resource consultors Health, Human Svcs. Secretariat Cath. Diocese Cleve., 2005—; pres. Diversity Leaders, LLC, Cleve., 2005—; diversity practice lead, sr. recruiting cons. Qualigence, Inc., Cleve., 2007—. Author: (with w.J. McBurney Jr.) College Recruitment: Effective Programs and Practices, 1982. Past chmn. orgn. and extension com. Newton D. Baker Dist., Greater Cleve. coun. Boy Scouts Am., 1970-71; mem. Human Resource Com. for Greater Cleve. United Way, NAACP, Urban League of Cleve.; mem. pension and benefit coms. Greater Cleve. Hosp. Assn., 1988-90; Bd. Edn. commr. Villa Angela Acad. (pres., 1986-87, U.S. Edn. Dept. award 1987); founder, advisor Explorer Post, Gilbane Bldg. Co., Cleve., 1984-88; Cleve., 1988—; v.p. adv. bd. Cath. Social Svcs. Cuyahoga County, chmn. coun. advisors, 1992-93; mem. urban regional bd. Cath. Edn. Cleve., 1986; trustee Marotta Montessori Sch. of Cleve., 1993—, pres.-elect, 1993, pres., 1993-2000; founding trustee Harambee Svcs. Orgn. Cleve., 1987—; trustee Cath. Charities Svcs. Corp. N.E. Ohio, 1992—, Laurel Lake Retirement Cmty., 2006—; vice chmn. bd. trustees Benedictine H.S., 2006—; mem. edn. commn. Villa Angela St. Joseph High Sch., 1990—, pres., 1993—; chmn. coun. advisors Cath. Social Svcs. Cuyahoga County, 1992—; bd dirs CSA Health Sys., 2005-. Recipient commendation Nat. Alliance of Bus., Akron, 1979, Cmty. Svc. award WJW-Northwest Orient Airlines, 1975. Mem. Cleve. EEO Assn., Soc. Human Resources Mgmt., Soc. Am. Mil. Engrs., U.S. Naval Inst., Mid-West Coll. Placement Assn. (chmn. rubber industry com. 1979-81), Ctr. for Human Svcs. (v.p., trustee, vice chmn. bd. trustees), Internat. Human Resources Assn., Indsl. Rels. Rsch. Assn., Human Resources Systems Assn., Alpha Phi Alpha. Democrat. Roman Catholic. Home: 24400 Emery Rd Cleveland OH 44128-5614

SIMMONS, DEBRA ADAMS, editor; m. Jonathan Simmons; children: Jacob, Jonathan. BA, Syracuse U., NY; diploma in Advanced Exec. Program, Northwestern U. Reporter Syracuse (NY) Herald-Jour., The Hartford (Conn.) Courant; metro editor The Virginian Post; asst. metro editor and reporter Detroit (Mich.) Free Press; dep. mng. editor The Virginian-Pilot, Norfolk, Va., 2000—03; mng. editor Akron (Ohio) Beacon Jour., 2003, editor & v.p., 2003—06. *

SIMMONS, DEIDRE WARNER, retired performing company executive, arts consultant; b. Easton, Pa., May 11, 1955; d. Francis Joseph and Irene Carol (Burd) Mooney; m. Robert D. Jacobson, June 27, 1981 (div. Mar. 1989); m. William Richard Simmons, Aug. 18, 1990; children: Caitlin Dawn, Abigail Patricia, Samantha Irene. BA in Music, Montclair State Coll., 1978. Music tchr. Warren Hills Regional Sch., Washington, NJ, 1978-80; devel. dir. N.J. Shakespeare Festival, Madison, 1981-83; dir. contbns. Parent Found., Lancaster, Pa., 1983-86; exec. dir. Fulton Opera House, Lancaster, 1986—95, capital campaign counsel, 1995—2000, dir. theatre advancement, 2000—03; arts cons., 2003—. Bd. dirs. WITF, vice chmn., 2005—; chmn. Lancaster Arts, 2005; bd. dirs. Lancaster Country Day Sch. Vice chmn. bd. dirs. Ind. Eye, Lancaster, 1986—89; bd. dirs. Pa. Dutch Conv. and Visitors Bur., Lancaster Campaign; chair Destination Downtown. Recipient Exemplar award, Lancaster C. of C. and Industry, 2003. Mem.: League Hist. Theatres, Theatre Comm. Group. Avocations: piano, singing. E-mail: dwsimmons@comcast.net.

SIMMONS, DONNA MARIE, neuroscientist, histotechnologist, neuroendocrine anatomist, researcher; b. Hartford, Conn., Oct. 13, 1943; d. John Henry and Ellen Louise (Meehl) Strayer; m. Corvin Gale Simmons, Sept. 17, 1964. Student, U. Wash., We. Wash. State U.; PhD, U. So. Calif., 2005. Histologic technician, instr. Tacoma Gen. Hosp. Sch. Med. Tech., Tacoma, 1963; lab. technician Med. Sch. U. Wash., 1964; histologic technician Northgate Med. Lab., Seattle, 1964—67; rsch. technologist in neuroanatomy Regional Primate Rsch. Ctr. U. Wash., 1967—82; rsch. asst. Devel. Neurobiology Lab. Salk Inst., La Jolla, Calif., 1982—85, sr. technician. lab. mgr. Neural Sys. Lab. Howard Hughes Med. Inst., 1985—90; vis. faculty neurosciences dept. Baylor U. Med. Sch., 1990; rsch. assoc. dept. biol. scis.-neurobiology U. So. Calif., LA, 1990—, Neurosci. Rsch. Inst., 2002—. Cons., lectr. in field; judge Greater San Diego Sci. and Engring. Fair, 1987-89, Calif. Sci. Fair, 1992—; leader sci. del. to People's Rep. of China, 1986; chair China Scientist Exch. Fund, 1986-87; mem. Swiss Histology Meeting Exch., 1990. Author tech. articles, revs. in field; mem. editl. bd. Jour. Histotech., 1982-2002. Recipient Diamond Cover award Jour. Histotech., 1990; various svcs. awards; best non-clin. pub. in field, 1985; Hudson Hoagland USA-Australia Exch. Med. Rsch. fellow Prince Henry's Rsch. Inst. Monash U., 1996. Mem. AAAS, APA, Am. Soc. Clin. Pathologists (affiliate), Am. Physiol. Soc., Wash. State Histology Soc. (past pres., histology liason Am. Soc. Med. Tech.), Nat. Soc. Histotech. (charter, regional dir. 1980-82, jud. chair 1983-86), Calif. Soc. Histotech. (San Diego dir. protem 1985-86), Assn. Women in Sci. (San Diego charter, bd. dirs. 1985-90), Soc. for Neurosci., Women in Neurosci., NY Acad. Sci., J.B. Johnston Club, Cajal Club, Sierra Club, NOW, Am. Alpine Club, Sigma Xi. Office: U So Calif Mc 2520 Los Angeles CA 90089-0001

SIMMONS, EILEEN, librarian; m. Roger Berger. BA in Studio Art, DePauw U., 1972; MLS, Ind. U., 1984. Asst. head Art, Music & Video Sect. Wichita Pub. Libr., Kans.; asst. dir. Everett Pub. Libr., Wash., 1998—2007, dir. Wash., 2007—. Named one of the Movers & Shakers, Libr. Jour., 2007. Avocations: gardening, knitting, reading, cooking, yoga. Office: Everett Public Library 2702 Hoyt Ave Everett WA 98201 E-mail: esimmons@ci.everett.wa.us.

SIMMONS, GENE (CHAIM WITZ, GENE KLEIN), musician; b. Haifa, Israel, Aug. 25, 1949; came to U.S., 1958, naturalized, 1963; s. Flora Witz; children Nicholas, Sophie (with Shannon Tweed). BE, SUNY, 1970; BA in Edn., Richmond Coll., CUNY, 1972. Tchr., Spanish Harlem, NY; asst. to editor Glamour and Vogue; asst. to dir. Puerto Rican InterAgeny Coun.; member in bands called Bullfrog Beer, Coffee, Long Island Sounds, Cathedral, and Wicked Lester; co-founder Kiss, 1973—; founder $immons Records; ptnr. Simmons Abramson Mktg., 2006—; chmn. NGTV (No Good TV), 2006—. Albums (with Kiss): Kiss, 1974, Hotter Than Hell, 1974, Dressed to Kill, 1975, Alive, 1975, Destroyer, 1976, Rock & Roll Over, 1976, Love Gun, 1977, Alive II, 1977, Double Platinum, 1978, Dynasty, 1979, Unmasked, 1980, Music From the Elder, 1981, Killers, 1982, Creatures of the Night, 1982, Lick It Up, 1983, Animalize, 1984, Asylum, 1985, Crazy Nights, 1987, Hot In The Shade, 1989, Smashes, Thrashes and Hits, 1989, Revenge, 1992, Alive III, 1993, Kiss My Ass, 1995, MTV: Kiss Unplugged, 1996, Carnival of Souls, 1997, You Wanted the Best You Got the Best!, 1997, Greatest Kiss, 1997, Psycho Circus, 1998, Kiss: The Box Set, 2001, The Very Best of Kiss, 2002, Kiss Symphony Alive VI, 20th Century Masters: Millenium Collection Vol. 1 and 2, Kiss Gold, Kiss Rock the Nation; (solo albums) Gene Simmons, 1978, ***Hole, 2004; actor (films) Runaway, 1984, Never Too Young To Die, 1986, Trick or Treat, 1986, Wanted: Dead or Alive, 1987, The Decline of Western Civilization Part II: The Metal Years, 1988, The Return of Bruno, 1988, Red Surf, 1990, Detroit Rock City, 1999, Wish You Were Dead, 2000, The New Guy, 2002; (TV series) My Dad the Rock Star, 2003 Gene Simmons' Rock School, 2005, Gene Simmons Family Jewels, 2005-; (TV appearances) The Paul Lynde Halloween Special, 1976, KISS Meets the Phantom of the Park, 1978, Miami Vice, 1985, Hitchhiker, 1986, Millennium, 1996, Talk to Me, 2000, (voice only) Family Guy, 2001, 2002, 2005, King of the Hill, 2003 Who Wants to Be a Millionaire, 2001, At Any Cost, 2002, (voice only) King of the Hill, 2003, Gene Simmons TV Special '24/7', 2004, Third Watch, 2004; creater (TV) Baby 101, Mr. Romance, The Apprentice 3, 2005; guest judge American Idol: The Search for a Superstar, 2005; composer (films) Reform School Girls, 1986, Less Than Zero, 1987, (TV) Kiss: The Last Kiss, 2000, Kiss: Beyond the Makeup, 2001, (video game) Underground, 2003; prodr. (TV series) Detroit Rock City, 1999, Smash, 2001; writer (video) KISS: eXposed, 1987; author: Kiss and Makeup, 2001, Sex Money Kiss (both NY Times Best Selling Books), 2005; founder Simmons Publishing; published(magazine) Gene Simmons Tongue, 2001-(Sterling/Macfadden), Gene Simmons Game mag.; released (audio visual, CD) Speaking in Tongues; launched fashion label, Gene Simmons-Dragonfly, 2002; perfomer, writer (song) I Am Indy, 2006; TV commericals, shows and advertising associated with KISS include Cannon Camera (Japan), NASCAR, Nat. Hot Rod Assn. (NHRA), Pepsi Cola, Coca Cola, Holiday Inn, VISA cards, KISS/Platinum online comics, KISS Girls; sponsor Worldwide Mktg. and Branding of Indy Racing League, 2006-. Winner 27 Gold Record Albums, 9 Platinum Record Albums, 7 Multi-Platimun Record Albums. Mem. Am. Fedn. Musicians, AFTRA, ASCAP.

Discovered Van Halen in 1977 and produced 15 song demo album; inventor of Axe bass guitar in 1980; speaks several languages English, Hungarian, Hebrew, German, learning Japanese and Mandarin Chinese; Kiss has been America's Number One Gold Record award winning group of all time according to RIAA; in honor of Gene Simmons US Postage Stamp; self-titled debut from the group BAG to mark first release from Gene Simmons' Simmons Records in over a decade in 2005. Office: $immons Records PO Box 15097 Beverly Hills CA 90210 *Listen to everyone around you, but do only what you believe.*

SIMMONS, GEORGE FINLAY, retired mathematics professor; b. Austin, Tex., Mar. 3, 1925; s. George Finlay and Armede Victoria (Hatcher) S.; m. Hope Bridgeford, Sept. 11, 1954; 1 child, Nancy Bingham. BS, Caltech, 1946; MS, U. Chgo., 1948; PhD, Yale U., 1957. Instr. U. Chgo., 1947-50, U. Maine, Orono, 1950-52, Yale U., New Haven, 1952-56; asst. prof. U. R.I., Kingston, 1956-58, Williams College, Williamstown, Mass., 1958-62; assoc. prof. math. Colo. Coll., Colorado Springs, 1962-65, prof., 1965-90, prof. emeritus, 1990—. Author: Introduction Topology and Modern Analysis, 1962, Differential Equations, 1972, 3d edit., 2006, Precalculus Mathematics in a Nutshell, 1981, Calculus with Analytic Geometry, 1985, 2nd edit., 1995, Calculus Gems: Brief Lives and Memorable Mathematics, 1992, repub., 2007. Mem. Math. Assn. Am. Avocations: travel, cooking, fishing, billiards. Home: 1401 Wood Ave Colorado Springs CO 80907-7348 Office: Colorado College Dept Math Colorado Springs CO 80903

SIMMONS, HAROLD C., investment company executive, sugar company executive; b. 1931; m. Annette Simmons; 6 children. BA, MA with Phi Beta Kappa key, U. Tex., 1952. Investigator U.S. Civil Service, Dallas, 1952-55; book examiner Fed. Deposit Ins. Corp., Dallas, 1955-56; loan officer Republican Nat. Bank, Dallas, 1956-61; with Amalgamated Sugar Corp., Dallas, 1961—, chmn., chief exec. officer, also bd. dirs. Ogden, Utah; pres., chief exec. officer, dir. Contran Corp., Dallas; chmn., dir. NL Industries Inc., Houston, 1961—; chmn. Nat. City Lines, Dallas; chmn. bd. dir. Valhi, Inc., Dallas. Founder Harold C. Simmons Comprehensive Cancer Ctr., 1988; founder, chmn. Simmons Found., 1988. Named one of Forbes' Richest Americans, 1999—, World's Richest People, Forbes mag., 2001—. Office: Valhi Inc Three Lincoln Centre 5430 Lbj Fwy Ste 1700 Dallas TX 75240-2620 also: NL Industries Inc 300 N Sam Houston Pky E Houston TX 77060-3301 Office: The Amalgamated Sugar Company 3184 Elder St Boise ID 83705-4709 *

SIMMONS, HARRIS H., bank executive; b. Salt Lake City, June 25, 1954; s. Roy William and Elizabeth (Ellison) S. BA in Econs., U. Utah, 1977; MBA, Harvard U., 1980. Comml. loan officer Allied Bancshares, Houston, 1980-81; asst. v.p. Zions Bancorp, Salt Lake City, 1981, fin. v.p., 1981-82; sr. v.p. fin. Zions Utah Bancorp, Salt Lake City, 1982-83, exec. v.p., sec., treas., 1984-86, pres., 1986—90; pres., CEO Zions 1st Nat. Bank, Salt Lake City, 1990—98, chmn., 1990—; pres., CEO Zions Bancorporation, Salt Lake City, 1990—, chmn., 2002—. Bd. dirs. Questar, Inc., Salt Lake City, Entrada Industries, Inc., Salt Lake City, Keystone Comm., Salt Lake City, Simmons Family, Inc., Salt Lake City, Zions 1st Nat. Bank, Salt Lake City, Nat. Bank Ariz., Tucson, Nev. State Bank, Las Vegas. Bd. dirs. United Way, Salt Lake City, 1983-89; bd. dirs. Utah Symphony, 1986—, vice chmn., 1990-95, chmn., 1995—; trustee Salt Lake City C.C., 1993—; v.p. fin. Great Salt Lake coun. Boy Scouts Am., 1991-95; co-chair Greater Salt Lake Shelter-the-Homeless Com., 1986-89, v.p., 1989—. Pres., dir., past vice-chmn. ABA; mem. Utah Bankers Assn. (bd.dirs. 1987-92, chmn. 1990-91), Salt Lake Area C. of C. (bd. dirs. 1991-94), Phi Beta Kappa. Mem. Lds Ch. Office: Zions Bancorporation 1 S Main St Salt Lake City UT 84111 *

SIMMONS, JANET BRYANT, writer, publishing executive; b. Oakland, Calif., Apr. 22, 1925; d. Howard Pelton and Janet Horn (McNab) Bryant; m. William Ellis Simmons, May 17, 1944 (div. 1979); children: William Howard, Janet Margaret Simmons McAlpine. BA, San Jose State U., Calif., 1965; MA, U. San Francisco, 1979. Social worker Santa Clara County Social Svcs., San Jose, Calif., 1965-91; editor, pub. Enlightenment Press, Santa Clara, 1994—. Author: The Mystical Child, 1996. Mem. AAUW, Am. Booksellers Assn., Pubs. Mktg. Assn., Bay Area Ind. Pubs. Assn., Audubon Soc., Jacques Cousteau Soc. Avocations: playing piano, swimming, tai chi, travel, gardening. Office: Enlightenment Press PO Box 3314 Santa Clara CA 95055-3314 Office Fax: 408-248-3222. Personal E-mail: simmonsj@aol.com.

SIMMONS, JEAN BYERS, academic administrator, director; b. Ft. Worth, July 29, 1956; d. James Clifford and Don Jean Carter; m. Jim Allen Simmons, Sept. 20, 1973; children: Jeffrey Brent, Joshua Allen. B of Arts History magna cum laude, Columbia Coll., Mo., 2002; M of History, Tarleton State U., 2004. DataTel Columbia Coll., 2000. Office mgr. Columbia Coll., 2002—03, acad. advisor, 2003—05; dir. Embry Riddle Aeronautical U., 2005—. Trainer Columbia Coll., Columbia, Mo., 2000—05. Fund raising Little League, White Settlement, Tex., 1984—90; mem. PTA, 1980—93; treas. Brewer Bear Athletic Booster Club, 1990—93. Mem.: Phi Alpha Theta (life), Alpha Sigma Lambda (life). Democrat-Npl. Baptist. Avocations: travel, reading, swimming, researching. Home: 508 Meadow Park Dr White Settlement TX 76108 Office: Embry-Riddle Aeronautical Univ NAS JRB Bldg 1525 Fort Worth TX 76127 Home Phone: 817-246-2116; Office Phone: 817-737-8180. Personal E-mail: js114729@sbcglobal.net. Business E-Mail: jean.simmons@erau.edu.

SIMMONS, JOHN DEREK, retired financial consultant; b. Essex, Eng., July 17, 1931; arrived in U.S., 1952; s. Simon Leonard and Eve (Smart) Simmons; m. Rosalind Wellish, Mar. 5, 1961; children: Peter Lawrence, Sharon Leslie. BS, Columbia U., 1956; MBA, Rutgers U., 1959; postgrad., NYU, 1959-62. Chief cost acct. Airborne Accessories, Hillside, NJ, 1952-57; sr. cost analyst Curtiss-Wright Corp., Wood Ridge, NJ, 1957; sr. fin. analyst internat. group Ford Motor Co., Jersey City, 1958-60; rsch. assoc. Nat. Assn. Accts. (now Inst. Mgmt. Accts.), NYC, 1960-64; asst. to v.p. fin. Air Reduction Co., Inc., 1965—67; mgr. corp. planning Anaconda Wire & Cable Co., NYC, 1968; assoc. cons. Rogers, Slade & Hill, Inc., NYC, 1969-71; v.p., security analyst, economist Moore & Schley, Cameron & Co. (name now Fourteen Rsch. Corp.), 1972-81; v.p., security analyst Merrill Lynch Capital Markets, NYC, 1981-88; security analyst Arnhold and S. Bleichroeder, Inc., 1988—89; v.p., security analyst, corp. fin. specialist Smith Barney, Harris Upham & Co., Inc. (now Salomon Smith Barney, Inc.), 1989—90; sr. cons. Carl Byoir & Assocs., 1991—94; assoc. mng. dir. Commonwealth Assocs., 1994—95; mng. dir. State St. Capital Markets Corp., 1996; v.p. GKN Securities Corp., 1996—97; dir. instnl. sales Gabelli & Co., Rye, 1997; assoc. Manning, Selvage & Lee, NYC, 1998—2001; ret., 2001. Lectr. fin. bus. Rutgers U., NJ, 1957—64; lectr. Marymount Manhattan Coll., NYC, 2002—. Contbr. articles to profl. jours. Docent Asia Soc. and Mus., NYC, 2002—05. 1st lt. Brit. Army, 1950—52. Grantee personal coat of Arms, by Queen Elizabeth II: manorial Lord of Ash, Suffolk, Eng. Mem.: Knight Templar Sovereign Mil. Order Temple of Jerusalem. Avocations: photography, travel, fishing. Home: 360 E 72d St New York NY 10021-4753 Personal E-mail: johnlordash@aol.com.

SIMMONS, JOSEPH (RUN SIMMONS, REVEREND RUN), musician; b. Hollis, Queens, NY, Nov. 24, 1964; s. Daniel and Mary Simmons; m. Justine Jones Simmons, June 25, 1994; children: Daniel, Russell II; children: Angela, Vanessa, Joseph Jr. Founding mem. Run-D.M.C., 1983—2002. Co-owner & pres. Phat Farm Footwear; co-owner & CEO Run Athletics. Musician: (albums) Run-D.M.C., 1984, King of Rock, 1985, Raising Hell, 1986, Tougher Than Leather, 1988, Back from Hell, 1990, Down With the King, 1993, Crown Royal, 1999, (solo albums) Distortion; actor: (films) Krush Groove, 1986, Tougher Than Leather, 1988, Who's the Man?, 1993, Red Dragon, 2002; co-exec. prodr., actor (TV series) Run's House, 2005—. Ordained min. Zoe Ministries, NYC. Office: Phat Farm Corp Office 512 Fashion Ave New York NY 10018 also: Zoe Ministries 310 Riverside Dr New York NY 10025

SIMMONS, KIMORA LEE, apparel designer, television personality, model; b. St. Louis, May 3, 1975; d. Vernon Whitlock and Joanne Perkins; m. Russell Simmons, 1998; 2 children. Former model Chanel; founder, CEO, dir. Baby Phat Clothing. Appearances include (films) Unzipped, 1995, Catwalk, 1996, Brown Sugar, 2002, The Big Tease, 1999, Beauty Shop, 2005, Rebound, 2005, (TV series) America's Next Top Model, 2003, Life & Style, 2004—, Fashion Week Diaries, 2005; exec. prodr.: (Broadway plays) Def Poetry Jam, 2003 (Tony award). Established Kimora Lee Simmons Scholarship Fund, Kimora Lee Simmons Foundation. Named Vibe Vixen, Vibe mag., 2005, Outstanding Stylemaker, Asian Excellence Awards, 2006. Office: Sony Pictures Entertainment 10202 W Washington Blvd Culver City CA 90232 *

SIMMONS, LEE GUYTON, JR., zoological park director; b. Tucson, Feb. 20, 1938; s. Lee Guyton and Dorothy Esther (Taylor) S.; m. Marie Annette Geim, Sept. 6, 1959; children: Lee Guyton, Heather, Heidi. Student, Cen. State Coll.; DVM, Okla. State U. Resident veterinarian Columbus Zoo, Powell, Ohio, 1963-66, Henry Doorly Zoo, Omaha, 1966-70, dir., 1970—. Research cons. VA Hosp.; assoc. instr. U. Nebr. Med. Ctr., Omaha; assoc. clin. prof. Creighton U. Sch. Dentistry. Contbr. articles to profl. jours. Bd. dirs. Nebr. State Mus., Lincoln. Served with USAR. Recipient Nat. Idealism award City of Hope, 1979; named Man of Yr., Lions Club, 1978. Fellow AVMA, Am. Assn. Zool. Veterinarians (pres.), Am. Assn. Zool. Parks, Nebr. Vet. Med. Assn. (Veterinarian of Yr. 1979). Lodges: Rotary. Office: Henry Doorly Zoo Office of the Director 3701 S 10th St Omaha NE 68107-2200

SIMMONS, LYNDA MERRILL MILLS, retired principal; b. Salt Lake City, Aug. 31, 1940; d. Alanson Soper and Madeline Helene (Merrill) Mills; m. Mark Carl Simmons, Nov. 17, 1962; children: Lisa Lynn Simmons Morley, William Mark, Jennifer Louise, Robert Thomas. BS, U. Utah, Salt Lake City, 1961, MS, 1983. Cert. sch. adminstr., Utah. Tchr. Wasatch Jr. H.S./Granite Dist., Salt Lake City, 1961-64, Altamont (Utah) H.S./Duchesne Dist., 1964-66; tchr. spl. edn. Park City (Utah) H.S., 1971-73; resource tchr. Eisenhower Jr. H.S., Salt Lake City, 1979-88; tchr. specialist Granite Sch. Dist., Salt Lake City, 1985-90; asst. prin. Bennion Jr. H.S., Salt Lake City, 1990-93; prin. Hartvigsen Sch., Salt Lake City, 1993—2002; ret., 2002. Adj. prof. spl. edn. U. Utah, Salt Lake City, 1987—, Utah Prin. Acad., 1994-95, co-chair Utah Spl. Educators for Computer Tech., Salt Lake City, 1988-90; adv. com. on handicapped Utah State Office Edn., 1990-93; cons., presenter in field. Author: Setting Up Effective Secondary Resource Program, 1985; contbr. articles to profl. jours. Dist. chmn. Heart Fund, Cancer Dr., Summit Park, Utah, 1970-82; pack leader Park City Area coun. Boy Scouts Am., 1976-80; bd. dirs. Jr. League Salt Lake City, 1977-80, cmty. bd., 1997—; cookie chmn. Park City area Girl Scouts U.S., 1981; dist. chmn. March of Dimes, 1982—. Recipient Amb. award Salt Lake Conv. and Vis. Bur., 1993; named Bus. Woman of Yr., South Salt Lake C. of C., 2001. Mem. Nat. Assn. Secondary Sch. Prins., Park City Young Women's Mut. (pres. 1989-93, family history cons. 1993-95), Women's Athanaeum (v.p. 1990-93, pres. 1994-2001), Gen. Fedn. Women's Clubs (pres. Salt Lake dist. 1998-02, cmty.-improvement chairperson Utah 1996-98, chairperson Woman of Yr. 1998—, state treas. 2006-) Coun. for Exceptional Children (pres. Salt Lake chpt. 1989-90, pres. Utah Fedn. 1991-93, Spl. Educator of Yr. 1995), Granite Assn. Sch. Adminstrs. (sec.-treas. 1992-94); Mission for Ch. of Jesus Christ of Latter Day Saints, Blacksburg, Va., 2003-04. Mem. Lds Ch. Avocations: reading, cooking, writing, sports, handiwork.

SIMMONS, LYNDA TEEL, nurse, healthcare executive; d. A. Stokes. A in Nursing, Columbus Coll., 1969, BA in Psychology, 1973; BSN, Troy State U., 1984, MSN magna cum laude, 1986. RN State Med. Agy., Clin. Nurse Specialist. Head nurse emergency room Columbus Med. Ctr., Ga., 1972—75; hosp. supr. Drs. Hosp. Hosp. Corp. Am., 1975—80; dir. surgical nursing divsn. Columbus Med. Ctr., 1980—82; critical care instr. BSN Program Auburn U., Auburn, Ala., 1985; RN State Med. Agy., Columbus, Ga., 1988—93; CEO Simmons Healthcare Enterprises, 1996—. Lectr. seminars, 2004. Mem.: Am. Assn. Critical Care Nurses, Emergency Nurse Assn., Soc. Critical Care Medicine, Am. Assn. Legal Nurse Cons., Sigma Theta Tau. Avocations: horseback riding, fencing, tennis, swimming. Office: Simmons Healthcare Enterprises 1303 Pagoda Dr Columbus GA 31907

SIMMONS, MARK ISAAC, voice educator, director; b. Bloomington, Ind., May 31, 1971; s. Bruce F. Simmons and Robin Simmons Pape; m. Amy Parks, May 24, 2003. MusB, Ithaca Coll., NY, 1993; MusM, Eastman Sch. Music, Rochester, NY, 1994; D in Musical Arts, Ariz. State U., Tempe, 2002. Dir. music St. Mary's Sch., Medford, Oreg., 1994—97; asst. prof. music Ithaca Coll., 1999—2000; dir. choral activities Briar Cliff U., Sioux City, Iowa, 2001—03; music educator U. Evansville, Ind., 2003—04; dir. choral activities U. Tenn., Martin, 2004—. Office Phone: 731-881-7412.

SIMMONS, MARVIN GENE, retired geophysics educator; b. Dallas, May 15, 1929; s. Burt H. and Mable (Marshall) S.; m. Dorothy Richter; children by previous marriage: Debra Lynn, Sandra Kay, Pamela Jean. BS, Tex. Agrl. and Mech. Coll., 1949; MS, So. Methodist U., 1958; PhD, Harvard U., 1962. Registered profl. geologist, N.H., Ky. Petroleum engr. Humble Oil Co., 1949-51; propr. gravel business, 1953-58; asst. prof. So. Meth. U., 1962-65; prof. geophysics MIT, 1965-89, prof. emeritus, 1989—; ret., 1989; prin. Hager-Richter Geoscience Inc., 1989—. Cons. NASA, 1965-72; chief scientist NASA (Manned Spacecraft Center), Houston, 1969-71; cons. on siting of nuclear facilities; sec. Internat. Heat Flow Com., 1967-71; chmn. com. drilling for sci. purposes Nat. Acad. Scis., 1965; Mem. geophysics panel NSF. Served with USAF, 1951-53. NSF postdoctoral fellow, 1961-62 Fellow Geol. Soc. Am., Am. Geophys. Union; mem. ASTM (com. C-18 on dimension stone 1986—), Boston Geol. Soc. (pres. 1967-68), Soc. Exploration Geophysicists, Sigma Xi, Tau Beta Pi. Achievements include research on physical properties of materials, lunar exploration, marine geophysics, temperature of earth, regional geophysics, engineering geology and geophysics. Home: 140 Range Rd Windham NH 03087 Office: 8 Industrial Way Unit D10 Salem NH 03079-2837

SIMMONS, MICHAEL, entrepreneur, publishing executive; b. 1982; m. Sheena Lindahl. Grad., NYU Stern Sch. Bus., 2005. Co-founder Princeton WebSolutions; CEO, co-founder Extreme Entrepreneurship Edn. Corp., NYC. Co-author: The Student Success Manifesto, 2003, All or Nothing, Now or Never. Named one of Best Entrepreneurs Under 25, BusinessWeek mag., 2006; recipient Entrepreneur of Yr. award, Nat. Found. Tchg. Entrepreneurship, 2002, Fleet, Nat. Coalition Empowering Youth Entrepreneurship. Achievements include launching a nationwide speaking tour called the Extreme Entrepreneur Tour in 2005. Office: Extreme Entrepreneurship Edn Corp 120 Wall St 29th Fl New York NY 10005 Office Phone: 800-930-8021. E-mail: michael@extremee.org.

SIMMONS, PETER, law and urban planning educator; b. NYC, July 19, 1931; s. Michael L. and Mary A. S.; m. Ruth J. Tanfield, Jan. 28, 1951; children: Sam, Lizzard. AB, U. Calif., Berkeley, 1953, LLB, 1956; postgrad., U. Wis., 1956—58. Prof. SUNY, Buffalo, 1963-67; mem. faculty Ohio State U., 1967-75, U. Ill., 1972, Case Western Res. U., 1974-75; prof. law and urban planning Rutgers U. Sch. Law, Newark, 1975—, dean, 1975-93; univ. prof. Rutgers U., Newark, 1993—. Contbr. articles to profl. jours. Mem. Ohio Housing Commn., 1972-74; commr. Ohio Reclamation Rev. Bd., 1974-75; chmn. N.J. Criminal Disposition Commn., 1983-84; mem. N.J. Law Revision Commn., 1987—. Alvord fellow, 1956—58. Mem. Am. Planning Assn., Urban Land Inst., Am. Law Inst., AAUP (nat. coun. 1973-75). Office: Rutgers U Law Sch 123 Washington St Newark NJ 07102-3192 Office Phone: 973-353-1589. E-mail: psimmons@andromeda.rutgers.edu.

SIMMONS, PETER LAWRENCE, lawyer; b. NYC, May 1, 1965; s. John Derek and Rosalind (Wellish) S.; m. Corinne Ryan, Apr 7, 2001; children: Mark R., Matthew S. AB magna cum laude, Columbia U., 1985, JD, 1987. Bar: NY 1987, US Dist. Ct. (so. and ea. dists.) NY 1988, US Ct. Internat. Trade 1991, US Spreme Ct. 1991, US Ct. Appeals (2d cir.) 1992, US Ct. Appeals (1st cir.) 1993, US Ct. Appeals (6th cir.) 2001, US Ct. Appeals (9th cir.) 2006. Law clk. to Hon. Lawrence W. Pierce U.S. Ct. Appeals (2d cir.), NYC, 1987-88; assoc. Fried, Frank, Harris, Shriver & Jacobson LLP, NYC, 1988-94, ptnr., 1994—. Treas., sr. editor Columbia Law Rev., 1985-87. Harlan Fiske Stone scholar, 1985-87. Mem.: ABA, Assn. Bar City NY (profl. responsibility com. 1998—2001, civil rights com. 1989—92), NY Bar Assn., Fed. Bar Coun., Phi Beta Kappa. Home: 91 West Rd Short Hills NJ 07078 Office: Fried Frank Harris Shriver & Jacobson LLP 1 New York Plz Fl 22 New York NY 10004-1980 Office Phone: 212-859-8455. Business E-Mail: peter.simmons@friedfrank.com.

SIMMONS, RICHARD DE LACEY, mass media executive; b. Cambridge, Mass., Dec. 30, 1934; s. Ernest J. and Winifred (McNamara) S.; m. Mary DeWitt Bleecker, May 20, 1961; children: Christopher DeWitt, Robin Bleecker Turner. Grad., 1951; AB, Harvard Coll., 1955; LLB, Columbia U., 1958. Bar: N.Y. 1959. V.p., gen. counsel Dun & Bradstreet Corp., NYC, 1969-73, exec. v.p., 1976-79, vice chmn., 1979-81; pres. Moody's Investors Svc., NYC, 1973-75, Dun & Bradstreet, Inc., NYC, 1975; pres., chief oper. officer Washington Post Co., Washington, 1981-91; pres. Internat. Herald Tribune, Paris, 1989-96. Bd. dirs. Washington Post Co. Office: 105 N Washington St Ste 202 Alexandria VA 22314-3022

SIMMONS, RICHARD J., lawyer; b. Brockton, Mass., Nov. 26, 1951; BA summa cum laude, U. Mass., 1973; JD, U. Calif., Berkeley, 1976. Bar: Calif. 1976. Ptnr. Sheppard, Mullin, Richter & Hampton LLP, LA, 1995—. Lectr. State of Calif., 1977-88; instr. UCLA, 1980-87; appointed to bd. Calif. Minimum Wage Bds. 1982, 84, 87; adv. bd. U. Calif. Boalt Hall Law Sch. Indsl. Relations Law Journal, 1985—. Reviews editor, editor in chief: Indsl. Relations Law Jour. 1975-76; Author: Wrongful Discharge and Employment Practices Manual, 1989, 2001, Employee Handbook and Personnel Policies Manual, 1983, 87, 92, 2004, Wage and Hour Manual for California Employers, 1982, 86, 88, 89, 91, 2001, 04, 05, Employment Discrimination and EEO Practice Manual for California Employers, 1982, 85, 91, 2000, 05, Employer's Guide to the American with Disabilities Act, 1990, 91, 92, The Employer's Guide to the California Family Rights Act of 1991, 92, 2000, Employer Obligations Under the Federal Plant Closing Law, 1989, 90, The New Federal Polygraph Law, 1989, The New Federal Immigration Law: The Immigration Reform and Control Act of 1986, 1987, COBRA: The Federal Health Insurance Rules for the 1990's, 1987,90, 2001; contbr. articles to profl mags. and jours. Commonwealth scholar. Mem. ABA (labor, employment law, tax sect.), L.A. County Bar Assn. (tax, labor sect.), The State Bar Calif., Calif. Soc. Health Care Attys., Am. Soc. Health Care Attys., Phi Kappa Phi. Office: Sheppard Mullin Richter & Hampton 333 S Hope St Ste 4700 Los Angeles CA 90071-1448 Office Phone: 213-617-5518. Business E-Mail: rsimmons@smrh.com.

SIMMONS, RICHARD L., surgeon; b. Boston, Feb. 23, 1934; s. Nathanial J. and Anne Dorothy (Levenson) S.; widowed (Feb. 1993); children: Nicole, Janine. AB in Biochem. Scis. magna cum laude, Harvard U., 1955; MD summa cum laude, Boston U., 1959. Diplomate Am. Bd. Surgery. Intern, resident in surgery Columbia Presbyn. Med. Ctr., NYC, 1959-66; clin. and rsch. fellow Mass. Gen. Hosp., Boston, 1965; rsch. fellow in surgery Harvard Med. Sch., Boston, 1965; instr. surgery Columbia U. Coll. P&S, NYC, 1965-68; from asst. prof. to assoc. prof. surgery U. Minn., Mpls., 1968-72, prof. surgery and microbiology, 1972-87; George V. Foster prof. surgery U. Pitts., 1987—98; chmn. dept. surgery U. Pitts. Med. Ctr., 1987-98; chmn. emeritus, 1998—; assoc. dean for clin. affairs Sch. Medicine U. Pitts., 1989-92, prof. molecular genetics and biochemistry, 1992—; med. dir. U. Pitts. Med. Ctr., 1996—. Chief of surgery Presbyn.-Univ. Hosp., Pitts., 1987—98. Author/co-author 15 books; contbr. more than 1200 articles to profl. jours. Recipient Disting. Svc. Prof. Surgery, 1994, other awards and grants. Mem. AMA, AAAS, ACS (pres. Southwestern Pa. chpt. 1992), NAS Inst. Medicine, Am. Soc. for Microbiology, Am. Soc. Transplant Surgeons (pres. 1980-81), Am. Assn. Immunologists, Am. Assn. Pathologists, Am. Surg. Assn. (chmn. program com. 1990), Assn. for Acad. Surgery, Ctrl. Surg. Assn., Cell Transplant Soc., Halsted Soc., Infectious Diseases Soc. Am., Midwest Surg. Soc. (hon.), Reticuloendothelial Soc., Soc. for Leukocyte Biology, Soc. for Microbiology, Soc. Clin. Oncologists, Surg. Infection Soc. (pres. 1988), Soc. Surg. Chmn., Soc. Univ. Surgeons (exec. coun. 1973-81, pres. 1977-78), Allegheny County Med. Soc., Transplantation Soc. (councillor 1974-80, Peter Medawar prize 2004—), others. Office: Univ Pittsburgh Med Ctr 200 Lothrop St Pittsburgh PA 15213-2582 Home Phone: 412-767-4642; Office Phone: 412-647-0680. Business E-Mail: simmonsrl@upmc.edu.

SIMMONS, RICHMOND HOGLE, retired obstetrician, gynecologist; b. Novi, Mich., Mar. 31, 1925; s. George Richmond Simmons and Eva Norine Hogle; m. Audrey Irene Hunt, June 21, 1952; children: Audrey Anne, Richmond Hunt, Clark David, Lauren Lucile, Scott Daniel. BA, U. Mich., Ann Arbor, 1951, MD, 1954. Intern, resident ob-gyn. Mt. Carmel Mercy Hosp., Detroit, 1954—58; assoc. Jacksonville Ob-gyn. Assocs., Ill., 1958—85. Med. staff pres. Pssavant Meml. Hosp., Jacksonville, 1964, chmn., ob-gyn. dept.; pres. Morgan-Scott Counties Med. Soc., Jacksonville, 1973. Author: (books) Joshua Simmons III and His Descendants, 1996, rev. edit., 2007. Co.-chmn. United Fund. Dr., Jacksonville, 1968—69; v.p. Elm City Rehab. Ctr., Jacksonville, 1970; treas. St. Malthias Episcopal Ch., Clermont, Fla., 1989—2001, sr. warden, 2002—05; bd. mem. South Lake Cmty. Hosp., Clermont, 1988—95; charter bd. mem. South Lake County Cmty. Found., 1995—2000; bd. dirs. YMCA, Jacksonville, 1972—75; charter mem. Elm City Rehab. Bd., Jacksonville. Recipient Gem of Hills award, South Lake, Fla. C. of C., 2005. Mem.: AMA (life), Am. Coll. Ob-gyn. (life), Ill. State Med. Soc. (life; mem. maternal welfare com. 1980—85), Rotary Club (pres. 1961). Republican. Episcopalian. Avocations: genealogy, history, stamp collecting/philately, numismatics.

SIMMONS, ROBERT RANDOLPH, principal; b. Phila., Aug. 27, 1935; s. Aaron J. Simmons and Lou (Randolph) Higgs; m. Patricia Ann Grace, June 26, 1975; children: Darris, William, Cynthia L., Tricia M., Robby R. BA in History, Mich. State U., 1958; MA in Community Sch. Leadership, Ea. Mich. U., 1967, Specialist of Arts, 1976; EdD, U. Mich., 1978; doctoral postgrad., Marygrove Coll., Detroit, 2004. Cert. tchr., elem. sch. adminstr., Mich., cert. primary and elem. sch. tchr., elem. prin. Flint Cmty. schs., N.Y. Tchr. Flint (Mich.) Community Schs., 1962-68, asst. prin., 1968-70, prin., 1970—, elem. liaison prin., 1992—. Adj. prof. edn. Ea. Mich. U., Ypsilanti, 1988-97; NEA Mastery In Learning sch. renewal site-based cons., 1987-92, cons. parent edn. Flint Community Schs., 1970—, cons. sch. improvement, Mich., 1989—; presenter Mich. Dept. Edn., MSU, 1987—; co-sponsor Mentor's for At-Risk Males Program, Stewart Sch., 1989-2005; sch. reform peer reviewer State of Mich., 2002; peer mentor and reviewer Nat. Youth Leadership Coun., 2000-. Contbr. to book: Parents and Schools:

From Visitors to Partners, 1993; contbr. articles to profl. jours.; contbg. author in-dist. teaching materials Flint Cmty. Schs; contbr. Nat. Soc. Experiential Edn., 1997-, Family Literacy Ctr., 2000. Deacon bd. New Jerusalem Full Gospel Bapt. Ch., security ministry Flint Jr. C. of C., 1965-1968; adv. bd. Cmty. Alliance Resource Environment, Flint, 1989—; bd. dirs., co-sponsor Stewart/Brennan Youth Clubs, Inc., 1987—; active Coalition for Positive Youth Devel., 1990—, Urban League Flint; Leonard Floyd scholarship com. New Jerusalem Full Gospel Bapt. Ch., pres. Inspirational Voice Choir, 1983-85, 90—; Nat. Youth Leadership Coun. Svc. Learning Peer Mentor Nat. 2003—. Recipient Drum Maj. award Mayor Woodrow Stanley, City of Flint, 1992, 96, Staff Devel. Policy Bd. award Mich. State Bd. Edn., 1987, Chpt. 1 Excellence in Edn. scholarship award, 1986, Flint Tchr.'s Golf Champaionship award, 1974, 78-79, 81, 83-84, Golf award Greater Flint Olympian-CANUSA Assn., 1981, 84, Outstanding Achievement in Edn. cert. Ctrl. Flint Optimist, 1993, Gov. and Mich. Cmty. Svc. Commn. award, 1993, Vol. Action award, Flint Cmty. Schs. Neighborhoods Pride award, 1994, Pres. Bill Clinton, 1994, African Am. Men of Achievement award, 1996, Nat. Burtley Golf Champion award, 1998, Exec. Declaration Reading award, State of Mich., 2000, Pupil Pers. Golf trophy Flint Cmty. Sch., 2002, Mich. Adaptive Golf McClaren Hosp. award, 2006, Internat. 40 Yr. Mem. award, Phi Delta Kappa, 2007. Mem. NAESP (Presenter award 1988), ASCD, NAACP, Nat. Community Edn. Assn. (Presenter award 1973), Mich. Elem. and Mid. Sch. Prin. Assn. (Presenter awards 1987-91), Flint Assn. Elem. Sch. Prins., Congress Flint Sch. Adminstrs. (pres. 1991—), Mich. Community Edn. Assn. (Presenter award 1973), Phi Delta Kappa (treas. Flint chpt. 1985-87, 25 Yr. Svc. award 1992), Alpha Phi Alpha. Democrat. Baptist. Avocations: golf, jazz, reading, music, sports. Home: PO Box 804 2262 NOLEN DRIVE Flint MI 48501-0804 Personal E-mail: rsimm1002@aol.com.

SIMMONS, ROBERT RUHL, former congressman; b. NYC, Feb. 11, 1943; s. Charles Herbert Jr. and Roxane Page (Ruhl) S.; m. Edith Heidi Paffard, June 22, 1974; children: Jane Adams, Robert Waldo Ruhl. BA, Haverford Coll., 1965; MPA, Harvard U., 1979; LLD (hon.), U. New Haven, 2003; DHL (hon.), U. Bridgeport, 2005. Ops. officer CIA, Washington, 1969-79; legis. asst. to Senator John H. Chafee US Senate, Washington, 1979-81, staff dir. intelligence com., 1981-85; vis. lectr. Yale U., New Haven, 1986—95; tchg. asst. U. Conn., Storrs, 1988—91; mem. Conn. Gen. Assembly, Hartford, 1991—2001, US Congress from 2d Conn. Dist., Washington, 2001—07. Contbr. articles to profl. jours. Mem. Republican Nat. Com. Col. USAR, 1970-2003. Decorated Bronze Star with 1 oak leaf cluster, Meritorious Svc. medal, Army Commendation medal with 1 oak leaf cluster, Vietnam Svc. medal with four campaign stars, Nat. Def. medal, Army Res. Achievement medal, Vietnam Civilian Svc. medal; named to Infantry Officer Candidate Sch. Hall of Fame, 2003; assoc. fellow Berkeley Coll., Yale U., 1986-2007. Republican. Episcopalian. Avocations: chinese art, forestry. Office: PO Box 268 Stonington CT 06378-0268 Office Phone: 860-270-8012. Business E-Mail: rob.simmons@ct.gov.

SIMMONS, RUSSEL, Internet company executive, entrepreneur; b. 1978; BS in computer sci., U. Ill., 1998. Co-founder & lead software architect Confinity, 1999, PayPal, 1999—2002; co-founder & chief tech. officer Yelp Inc., San Francisco, 2004—. Office: Yelp Inc 650 Mission St #2 San Francisco CA 94105 E-mail: info@yelp.com.

SIMMONS, RUSSELL, recording industry executive; b. Queens, NY, Oct. 4, 1957; s. Daniel and Evelyn Simmons; m. Kimora Lee, Dec. 20, 1998 (separated 2006); children: Ming, Aoki Lee. Attended, CCNY. Co-founder, owner Def Jam Records, NYC, 1983—; chmn., CEO, pres. Rush Communications, 1990—; owner Rush Artist Mgmt., PHAT Fashion. Rush Prodr. Mgmt.; partner Rush Model Mgmt. Represents Public Enemy, LL Cool J, others. Co-prodr.: (films) Krush Groove, 1985, The Funeral, 1996; prodr.: Tougher Than Leather, 1988, The Nutty Professor, 1996, How to Be a Player, 1997; exec. prodr.: The Addiction, 1995, Gridlock'd, 1997, Waist Deep, 2006; prodr.: (TV special) Def Comedy Jam Primetime, 1994; (TV series) Def Poetry Jam, 2002; co-author (with Nelson George): Life and Def: Sex, Drugs, Money & God, 2001; co-author: (with Chris Morrow) Do You!: 12 Laws to Access the Power in You to Achieve Happiness and Success, 2007. Founder Rush Philanthropic Arts Found. 10 gold albums, 6 platinum albums, 2 multiplatinum albums; named one of 100 Most Influential Black Americans, Ebony mag., 2006. Achievements include bringing hip-hop culture into the American mainstream. *

SIMMONS, RUTH J., academic administrator; b. Grapeland, Tex., July 3, 1945; d. Isaac and Fannie Stubblefield; m. Norbert Simmons, 1968 (div. 1989); children: Khari, Maya. Student, Universidad Internacional, Saltillo, Mex., 1965, Wellesley Coll., 1965—66; BA, Dillard U., 1967; postgrad., Universite de Lyon, 1967—68, George Washington U., 1968—69; AM, Harvard U., 1970, PhD in Romance Langs., 1973; LLD (hon.), Amherst Coll., 1995; LHD (hon.), Howard U., 1996, Dillard U., 1996; LLD (hon.), Princeton U., 1996, Lake Forest Coll., 1997; LHD (hon.), U. Mass., 1997; LLD (hon.), Dartmouth Coll., 1997, Mt. Holyoke Coll., 2001, U. Pa., 2001, Harvard U., 2002, George Washington U., 2002, Columbia U., 2002, Washington U., 2002, U. So. Calif., 2003, Boston U., Rensselaer Polytechnic Inst., N.Y. U., Northeastern; D of Women's Studies (hon.), Ewha Woman's U., Rep. of Korea, 2002; LittD (hon.), U. Toronto, 2004; LHD, Jewish Theol. Sem., 2004, Taugaloo Coll., 2004. Interpreter lang. svcs. divsn. U.S. Dept. State, Washington, 1968—69; instr. French George Washington U., 1968—69; admissions officer Radcliffe Coll., 1970—72; asst. prof. French U. New Orleans, 1973—75, asst. dean coll. liberal arts, asst. prof. French, 1975—76; adminstrv. coord. NEH liberal studies project Calif. State U., Northridge, 1977—78, acting dir. internat. programs, vis. assoc. prof. Pan-African studies, 1978—79; asst. dean grad. sch. U. So. Calif., 1979—82, assoc. dean grad. sch., 1982—83; dir. studies Butler Coll. Princeton U., NJ, 1983—85, acting. dir. Afro-Am. studies, 1985—87, asst. dean faculty, 1986—87, assoc. dean faculty, 1986—90, vice provost, 1992—95; provost Spelman Coll., 1990—91; pres. Smith Coll., Northampton, Mass., 1995—2001; pres Brown U., Providence, 2001—, prof. comparative lit. and African studies. Peer reviewer higher edn. divsn. NEH, 1980—83, bd. cons., 1981; mem. grad. adv. bd. Calif. Student Aid Commn., 1981—83; chair com. to visit dept. African-Am. studies Harvard U., 1991; mem. strategic planning task force N.J. Dept. Higher Edn., 1992—93; mem. nat. adv. commn. EQUITY 2000 Coll. Bd., 1992—95; mem. adv. bd. ctrl. N.J. NAACP Legal Def. Fund, 1992—95; mem. Mid. States Assn. Accreditation Team, Johns Hopkins U., 1993; chmn. accreditation team Bryn Mawr Coll., 1999; chair rev. panel for model instns. planning grants NSF, 1993; mem. Conf. Bd., 1995; bd. dirs. MetLife, JSTOR, Pfizer Inc., 1997—, COFHE, Com. Econ. Devel., Goldman Sachs, 1999—, Tex. Instruments, 1999—; mem. adv. coun. dept. Romance Langs. and Lit. Princeton U., 1996; trustee Carnegie Corp., 1999—; presenter, spkr. and panelist in field. Mem. editl. bd.: World Edn. series Am. Assn. Collegiate Registrars and Admissions Officers, 1984—86; contbr. articles to profl. jours. Named mem. Women's Progress Commemoration Commn. by Pres. Bill Clinton, 1999; mem. adv. coun. Bill and Melinda Gates Millennium Scholars Found.; chmn. Congl. Black Caucus Found. Washington, 2004; mem. adv. bd. N.J. Master Faculty Program Woodrow Wilson Nat. Fellowship Found., 1987—90, trustee, 1991—96, Inst. Advances Study, 1995—98, The Clarke Sch. for Deaf, 1995—; chmn. bd. trustees Acad. Music, 1995—98; mem. adv. com. Healthy Steps for Young Children Program, 1996—98; mem. bd. advisors 1st Internat. Conf. on AIDS, Ethiopia, 1998. Named Women of Yr., CBS, 1996, Glamour Mag., 1996, Disting. Fulbright Alumna, Inst. Internat. Edn., 1997, Woman of World, NASA, 1998, Am. Best Coll. Pres., Time mag., 2001, Woman Yr., Ms. mag., 2002; named one of Newsweek Person to Watch, 2002; recipient Disting. Svc. award, Assn. Black Princeton Alumni, 1989, Dillard U., 1992, Pres.'s Recognition award, Bloomfield Coll., 1993, TWIN award, Princeton Area YWCA, 1993, Women's orgn. Tribute award, Princeton U., 1994, Leadership award, Third World Ctr. Princeton U., 1995, Tex. Excellence award, Leap Program, 1995, Benjamin E. Mays award, A Better Chance, 1995, Centennial medal, Harvard U. Grad. Sch. Arts & Scis., 1997, Achievement award, Nat. Urban League, 1998, Tchr. Coll. Medal for Disting. Svc., Columbia U., 1999, Pres. award, United Negro Coll. Fund, 2001, "Drum Major for Justice" Edn. award, So. Christian Leadership Conf./W.O.M.E.N., 2002, Fulbright Lifetime Achievement Medal, 2002, R.I. History Makers award, 2002, Amelia Earhart award, 2002, ROBIE Humanitarian award, The Jackie Robinson Found., 2004, The Eleanor Roosevelt Val-Kill medal, 2004, fellowship, DAAD, Presdl. Medal of Honor, Dillard U., 2006; fellow, Danforth Found., 1967—73, Sr. Fulbright fellow, 1981; scholar, KYOK, 1963, Worthing Found., 1963—67, Fulbright scholar, U. de Lyon, 1967—68. Fellow: Am. Acad. Arts & Scis.; mem.: AAAS, Coun. Foreign Rels., Am. Philos. Soc. Office: Office of Pres Brown U One Prospect Street, Campus Box 1860 Providence RI 02912 Office Phone: 401-863-2234. Office Fax: 401-863-7737. E-mail: president@brown.edu. *

SIMMONS, SARAH R., lawyer; b. Ducktown, Tenn., Jan. 23, 1948; BA magna cum laude, U. Ariz., 1970, postgrad.; JD magna cum laude, U. Denver, 1973. Bar: Colo. 1974, Ariz. 1975. Mem. Molloy, Jones & Donahue, Tucson, Brown & Bain, P.A., Lewis & Roca LLP, 2002—05; judge Ariz. Superior Ct. Pima County, 2006—. Mem. Davis Monthan 50, 1991—, pres., 1998-2000; trustee Tohono Club Park, 1995-2004, sec., 1997-99, v.p. 1999-2001, pres., 2001-03; trustee Tucson Airport Authority, 1996-2006, bd. dir., 2005-06; mem. Law Coll. Assn. Bd., 1996—, sec. 1998-99, pres. 2000-01; 4th R bd. Tucson Unified Sch., 1996-2003; bd. dir. United Way Tucson, 1995-2000, Family Advocacy Resource and Wellness Ctrs., Resources Women, 1995-2000; bd. dir. Ariz. Town Hall, 1998-2003; mem. adv. bd. Ariz. Drug Free Workplace, 1991-2002, So. Ariz. Sports Devel. Corp., U. Ariz. Social and Behavioral Scis., 1994-96; sec. So. Ariz. Minutemen, 1996-98; mem. bd. visitors Coll. Law, chair, 2002-06; v.p. Met. Tucson Conv. and Visitors Bur., 2003-05, pres. 2005-07. Recipient Outstanding Alumni award U. Ariz. Coll. of Law, 1993, Tucson Woman of Yr. C. of C., 1994, Women on the Move award YWCA, 1995, Alice Truman Leadership award, 2003; named one of 100 Women and Minorities in the Law, 2000, Women Who Lead, U. Ariz. Women's Studies Adv. Coun., 2003. Fellow ABA, Ariz. Bar Assn.; mem. Nat. Assn. Bond Lawyers, State Bar Ariz. (bd. govs. 1987-95, sec.-treas. 1989-90, 2d v.p. 1990-91, 1st v.p. 1991-92, pres.-elect 1992-93, pres. 1993-94, employment law sect., profl. conduct com., fee arbitration com., co- mem. of yr. 2004), Ariz. Women Lawyers Assn. (charter), Colo. Bar Assn., Pima County Bar Assn. (bd. dirs. 1985-94), Am. Judicature Soc., So. Ariz. Legal Aid (bd. dir. 1990-93), Lawyers Against Hunger, Order St. Ives, Phi Beta Kappa, Phi Kappa Phi, Phi Alpha Theta, Kappa Beta Pi. Office: Ariz Supreme Ct in Pima County 110 W Congress Tucson AZ 85701 Office Phone: 520-740-8441. E-mail: ssimmons@sc.pima.gov.

SIMMONS, SHERWIN PALMER, lawyer; b. Bowling Green, Ky., Jan. 19, 1931; AB, Columbia U., 1952, LLB, 1954, JD, 1969. Bar: Tenn. 1954, Fla. 1957. Assoc. Fowler, White, Collins, Gillen, Humkey & Trenam, Tampa, Fla., 1956-60, ptnr., 1960-70, Trenam, Simmons, Kemker, Scharf & Barkin, Tampa, 1970-77; stockholder, pres. Trenam, Simmons, Kemker, Scharf, Barkin, Frye & O'Neill, PA, Tampa, 1977-94; ptnr., chair tax group Steel Hector & Davis, LLP, Miami, Fla., 1994—2005; shareholder, vice chair tax group, chair tax practice Buchanan Ingersoll PC, Miami, 2005—. Atty. adv. U.S. Tax Ct., Washington, 1954—56, mem. nominating commn., 1978—81; mem. adv. group Commr. of IRS, 1978—79, 1989—90, U.S. Dept. Justice, 1979—80; adj. prof. U. Miami, 1995—. Contbr. articles to profl. jours. Trustee Hillsborough County Soc. Crippled Children & Adults, 1956—85, pres., 1960—61; mem. adv. bd. Salvation Army, 1959—62, 1964—66, sec., 1960—61; treas., chmn. Hillsborough County Pub. Edn. Study Commn., 1965—66; chmn., bd. dirs. Fla. Orch., 1987—89; founding trustee, pres. Am. Tax Policy Inst., 1996—99; trustee Tampa Bay Performing Arts Ctr., Inc., 1984—93, mem. program adv. com., 1985—89, mem. investment com., 1986—91. Fellow: Am. Coll. Tax Counsel (regent 1987—93, vice chmn. 1989—91, chmn. 1991—93), Am. Bar Found. (mem. devel. com. 1992—94), Am. Coll. Trust and Estate Counsel (bd. regents 1982—88); mem.: ABA (vice chmn. adminstrn. taxation sect. 1972—75, chmn. 1975—76, ho. of dels. 1985—90, bd. govs. 1990—93, chmn. bd. govs. fin. com. 1992—93, chmn. commn. multidisciplinary practice 1998—2000), Am. Law Inst. (mem. coun. 1985—, mem. exec. com. 1994—97, 1999—, mem. com. 1997—, chmn. 1999—), Internat. Fiscal Assn., Internat. Acad. Estate and Trust Law, So. Fed. Tax Inst. (trustee, pres. 1974, chmn. 1975, trustee emeritus 1999—), Am. Judicatrue Soc., Fla. Bar Assn. (chmn. taxation sect. 1964—65), Am. Law Network ABA-Am. Law Inst. (mem. com. continuing profl. edn. 1973—), Am. Bar Retirement Assn. (bd. dirs. 1984—90, v.p. 1987—88, pres. 1988—89). Office: Buchanan Ingersoll PC 34th Fl Bank Am Tower 100 SE 2d St Miami FL 33131 Home Phone: 305-971-4800; Office Phone: 305-347-4060. Business E-Mail: spstax@bipc.com.

SIMMONS, STEPHEN JUDSON, lawyer; b. Columbus, Ohio, Feb. 19, 1946; s. Samuel A. and Jane A. (McGrath) S.; m. Claire Maxine Schriber, Aug. 15, 1970; children: Darren, Judson. BA, Ohio State U., 1968; JD, U. Cin., 1972. Bar: Ohio 1973, Tex. 1982. Sr. law clk. U.S. Dist. Ct. (ea. dist.) Tenn., Knoxville, 1972-74; asst. atty. gen. Office of Atty. of Ohio, Columbus, 1974-75; assoc. McGrath & Shirey, Columbus, 1975; corp. counsel Wendys, Inc., Columbus, 1975-79; sr. v.p., gen. counsel Precision Tune, Inc., Beaumont, Tex., 1979-87, also dir.; sr. v.p. adminstrn., dir. Kwik-Kopy Corp., Cypress, Tex., 1988-90; v.p. Deli Mgmt., Inc., 1990-94; pvt. practice Houston, 1994—. Bd. editors U. Cin. Law Rev., 1971-72. Mem. Tex. Bar Assn. Roman Catholic. Home: 13603 Balmore Cir Houston TX 77069-2703 Office: 3845 Fm 1960 Rd W Ste 250 Houston TX 77068-3548 Office Fax: 281-586-0088. Personal E-mail: sjsimmons@aol.com.

SIMMONS, SUE, newscaster; b. NY, May 27, 1943; d. John Simmons. Corr. WTNH-TV, New Haven, 1973-74, WBAL-TV, Balt., 1974, anchor, host Balt. at One, 1975—76; corr./anchor. WRC-TV, Washington, 1976—80; co-anchor News Channel 4/Live at Five/News Channel 4 at 11 p.m WNBC News, NYC, 1980—; host Images: A Year in Review, WNBC, 2002—. Recipient four Emmy awards, award for Outstanding Performance by a News Commentator, Barnabus McHenry, Vice-Chmn. Pres.'s Task Force on Arts and Humanities, 1981; named to the NY State Broadcasters Assn. Hall of Fame, 2005 Office: WNBC-TV 30 Rockefeller Plz New York NY 10112-0002

SIMMONS, SYLVIA JEANNE QUARLES (MRS. HERBERT G. SIMMONS JR.), academic administrator, educator; b. Boston, May 8, 1935; d. Lorenzo Christopher and Margaret Mary (Thomas) Quarles; m. Herbert G. Simmons, Jr., Oct. 26, 1957; children: Stephen, Alison, Lisa. BA, Manhattanville Coll., 1957; MEd, Boston Coll., 1962, PhD, 1990; DHL (hon.), St. Joseph's Coll., 1994; EdD (hon.), Merrimack Coll., 1999. Montessori tchr. Charles River Park Nursery Sch., Boston, 1970-76; registrar Boston Coll. Sch. Mgmt., Chestnut Hill, 1966-70; dir. fin. aid Radcliffe Coll., Cambridge, Mass., 1970-75, assoc. dean admissions and fin. aid, 1972-75, assoc. dean admissions, fin. aid and women's edn., 1975; assoc. dean admissions and fin. aid Harvard and Radcliffe, from 1975; assoc. v.p. for acad. affairs ctrl. adminstrn. U. Mass., Boston, 1976-79, spl. asst. to chancellor, 1979; v.p. field svcs. Am. Student Assistance, 1982-84, sr. v.p., 1984-93, exec. v.p., 1983-95, pres., 1996; mem. faculty Harvard U., 1970-77, pres. faculty, 1995-96; lectr. Boston U., 1991—. Cons. Mass. Bd. Higher Edn., 1973—77. Co-editor: Student Loans Riches and Realities, 1987. Past bd. dirs. Rivers Country Day Sch., Weston, Mass., Simons's Rock Coll., Great Barrington, Mass., Wayland (Mass.) Fair Housing, Cambridge Mental Health Assn., Family Svcs. Greater Boston, Concerts in Black and White, Mass., Higher Edn. Assistance Corp.; chmn. bd. dirs. North Shore Cmty. Coll., 1986-88, mem. bd. dirs., 1985—; trustee and alumnae bd. dirs. Manhattanville Coll., 1986—; mem. adv. com. Upward Bound, Chestnut Hill Boston Coll., 1972-74, Women in Politics John McCormick Inst., 1994-2000; Camp Chimney Corners, Becket, Mass., 1971-77; bd. dirs. Am. Cancer Soc. Mass., 1987-89, Boston Coll., 1990-98, Merrimack Coll., 1992-2000, Mass. Found. for Humanities, 1990-92, Mass. Bay United Way, 1990-94, Grimes King Found., 1992—, St. Elizabeta's Hosp., 1991-2005, Anna Stearns Found., 1996—, Regis Coll., 1997-2004, Edn. Resources Inst., 1998—, Supreme Ct. Jud. Hist. Soc., 2001—, Newton Country Day Sch., 2002-2005, Shirley Eustis House, 2002—; trustee Mt. Ida Coll., 1990—, Exec. Svc. Corp., 1997—, Supreme Ct. Judicial Hist. Soc., 2001—, Newton County Day Sch., 2002—; overseer Mus. Fine Arts, Boston, Mass., 2002-2005; chair Coll. Club Scholarship com., 1997. Recipient Educator of Yr. award Boston and Vicinity Club, 1989, Bicentennial medal Boston Coll., 1976, Achievement award Greater Boston YMCA, 1977, Human Rights award Mass. Tchrs. Assn., 1988, Pres'. award Mass. Ednl. Opportunity Assn., 1988, Archbishop Timothy Healy award, 1997, Outstanding Alumna award Girl's Latin Sch., 1998; named One of Ten Outstanding Yung Leaders, Boston Jr. C. of C., 1971, Sojourner's Daus.: 25 African women who have made a difference, 1991. Mem. Eastern Assns. Fin. Aid Officers (2st v.p. 1973), Coll. Scholarship Svc. Coun., Links (pres. local chpt. 1967-69), Nat. Inst. Fin. Aid Adminstrs. (dir. 1975-77), Jack and Jill Am. (pres. Newton chpt. 1972-74), Manhattanville Club (pres. Boston 1966-68), Delta Sigma Theta, Delta Kappa Gamma (pres. 1988-90). Home: 19 Clifford St Roxbury MA 02119-2120 Office: 330 Stuart St Boston MA 02116-5237 Personal E-mail: ssimm38414@aol.com.

SIMMONS, TERRY L., lawyer; b. Santa Anna, Tex. BBA cum laude, Baylor U., Waco, Tex., 1977; JD, Baylor Law Sch., 1978; LLM, So. Meth. U. Dedman Sch. Law, Dallas, 1984. Bar: Tex. 1978, Colo. 1998, NY 2006. Ptnr. Thompson & Knight, LLP, Dallas. Contbr. articles to profl. jours.; pub., co-editor: Charitable Gift Planning News. Bd. trustees Baptist Child & Family Svcs., Tex. Christian U. Brite Divinity Sch., Adv. Coun. of Dallas Found., Dallas Women's Found. Planned Giving Adv. Com.; founding pres. North Tex. Chpt. Nat. Com. Planned Giving, 1988—97, nat. bd. dirs. Indpls., 1990—92; pres., bd. mem. Charitable Accord, 1994—; bd. dirs. Am. Coun. Gift Annuities. Named a Tex. Super Lawyer, Tex. Monthly, 2004—06; named Planned Giving Profl. of Yr., Planned Giving Today, 1994, Exec. of Yr., The NonProfit Times, 1997; named one of Top 100 Attys. in Am., Worth mag., 2005—06; recipient David M. Donaldson Disting. Svc. award, Planned Giving Grp. New Eng., 1996, Disting. Svc. award, Nat. Com. Planned Giving, 1996. Mem.: ABA. Office: Thompson & Knight LLP Ste 3300 1700 Pacific Ave Dallas TX 75201 Office Phone: 214-969-1419. Office Fax: 214-880-3373. Business E-Mail: Terry.Simmons@tklaw.com.

SIMMONS, TIMOTHY F., military officer; b. 1985; s. Kent and Barb S. BS in Econ., US Military Acad., West Point, 2007; MPhil. student in Devel. Studies, Oxford Univ., 2007—. Intern President's Coun. Econ. Advisors. Rhodes Scholar. Avocation: lacrosse. *

SIMMONS, WILLIAM, retired aerospace engineer, research and development company executive; b. Chgo., Apr. 24, 1932; s. Walter Garfield and Edna Dean (Winch) S.; m. Barbara Millet Haury, Oct. 4, 1954; children: Sheryl Lee, Cynthia Jane, Shelly Jean. BA in Physics, Carleton Coll., 1953; MS in Physics, U. Ill., 1955, PhD in Physics, 1960. Mem. tech. staff Space Tech. Labs., Redondo Beach, Calif., 1960-62; sr. rsch. scientist Gen. Tech., Torrance, Calif., 1962, TRW, Redondo Beach, 1962-71, dir. rsch., 1984-89, chief engr. spl. projects assigned to Lawrence Livermore (Calif.) Labs., 1989-92; engring. mgr. Lawrence Livermore Labs., 1972-84, rsch. reviewer, 1985-89; prof. engring. UCLA, 1968-72. Tech. panel mem. U. Calif., Berkeley, 1985; tech. reviewer Dept. Energy, Washington, 1986—, mem. rev. com., 1987—; cons. in field, 1992-2006. Editor, reviewer 2 books, 1982, 83; contbr. numerous articles to profl. jours. Named Disting. Engring. Prof. of Yr. UCLA, 1972, one of Top 100 Innovators in U.S.A, Sci. Digest, 1986; George F. Baker Found. scholar Carleton Coll., 1949-53. Mem. IEEE (sr., life, gen. chmn. symposia 1988, 89, Simon Ramo Major medal 1987), Laser Engring. and Optical Soc., Am. Phys. Soc., Soc. of Photographic and Instrumentation Engrs., U.S. Chess Club, Phi Beta Kappa, Sigma Xi. Republican. Achievements include 11 patents for electro-optics devices. Avocations: chess, ping pong/table tennis, bridge. Office: Sys Solutions 1621 W 25th St Ste 231 San Pedro CA 90732-4300 Office Phone: 310-541-4140. Business E-Mail: wwsimmons@cox.net.

SIMMONS-WELBURN, JANICE, dean, library director; BA, Bishop Coll.; MA in Am. History, Atlanta U., MLS, 1978. Libr. Bishop Coll., Dallas, Indpls.-Marian County Pub. Libr., NYU, Ga. Inst. Tech.; interim head Med. Scis. Libr. Ind. U.; head Psychology Libr. Princeton U.; head info. and instrnl. svcs. U. Iowa Librs., 1990—95, dir. human resources and ctrl. processing, 1995—2000, dir. ctrl. pub. librs., 2000—03; assoc. dean U. Ariz. Librs., 2003—06; dean univ. libr. Marquette U., Milw., 2006—. Spkr. in field. Contbr. articles to profl. jours. Office: Marquette U Raynor Meml Librs 1355 W Wisconsin Ave Milwaukee WI 53233 Office Phone: 414-288-7214. Business E-Mail: janice.simmons-welburn@marquette.edu. *

SIMMS, LOIS AVERETTA, retired secondary school educator; b. Charleston, SC, May 27, 1919; d. Jasper Simeon and Anna Inez (Ferguson) Simms. BA, Johnson C. Smith U., 1941; MA, Howard U., 1954. Cert. English and social studies educator SC. Directive tchr. Avery Normal Inst., Charleston, 1941-42; tchr. English and French Laing H.S., Mt. Pleasant, SC, 1942-44; tchr. English and math. Henry P. Archer Sch., Charleston, 1944-45; tchr. social studies and English Burke H.S., Charleston, 1945-52; tchr. English Avery H.S., Charleston, 1952-54, Burke H.S., Charleston, 1954-73; tchr. English and history Charleston H.S., 1973-76; ret., 1976. Co-advisor Dramatic Club Burke HS, Charleston, 1945—46, trainer sect. chorus, 1945—47, chief advisor Bulldog Yearbook, 1960—61; advisor Crochet Club Avery HS, 1952—54, Charleston HS, 1973—76. Author: Growing Up Presbyterian: Life in Presbyterian Colleges and Churches, 1991, Profiels of African American Females in Low Country of South Carolina, 1992, A Chalk and Chalkboard Career in Carolina, 1995, A History of Zion, Olivet, and Zion-Olivet Churches 1850-1885, 1989; editor: The Scroll newsletter, 1984—94. Sec. exec. bd. YWCA Greater Charleston, 1950; active YWCA, SC Hist. Soc., SC ETV Endowment; chmn. Super Grandchild Contest fundraiser Barber-Scotia Coll., 2007. Recipient plaque, Zion-Olivet Presbyn. Ch., 1987, C.L. Campbell award, Presbyn. Ch., 1988, plaque, Staff of the Scroll, 1990, Educator's award, Moja Arts Festival, 2003; Honoree, Women's Resource Project, Inc., 2007, Centenniel Celebration of YWCA of Greater Charleston, 2007. Mem.: NAACP (Silver life, Trailblazer award 2002), Presbyn. Women's Assn. (chair com. quar. birthday celebration and grad. ceremony 1999—2003), Barber-Scotia Coll. Alumni, Johnson C. Smith U. Alumni Assn., Assn. Study African-Am. Life and History, SC Soc., Avery Inst. Afro-Am. History and Culture (editor The Bull. 1990—2000, cert.), Charleston County Ret. Educators Assn. Unit 2, Pres.'s Club (plaque 1991). Avocations: reading, music, Scrabble, gardening, creative writing. Home: 28 Jasper St Charleston SC 29403-6006

SIMMS, MARIA ESTER, health facility administrator; b. Bahia Blanca, Argentina; arrived in U.S., 1963; d. Jose and Esther (Guays) Barberio Esandi; m. Michael Simms, July 15, 1973 (dec. Aug. 1993); children: Michelle Bonnie Lee Carla, Michael London Valentine, Matthew Brandon.

MD, Facultad del Centenario, Rosario, Argentina, 1962; cert. physician asst. with honors, U. So. Calif., 1977. Diplomate. Pres. Midtown Svcs. Inc., LA, 1973—; dir. internat. affairs, speaker Gov. of Papua, New Guinea, 1996—; dir., CFO, pres. World Film Inst., 1996—; commr. Inmate Welfare Commn. Los Angeles County Sheriff's Dept., 1977—. Dir. internat. affairs, spkr. on humanitarian, cultural and econ. matters Govt. of Papua New Guinea; adv., internat. spkr. women, children and animal rights; bd. dirs. Kohtakt, Raduga. Chmn. bd. dirs. Am. Film Inst., Washington; chmn. bd. trustees World Film Inst., dir. internat. affairs; spkr.-humanitarian Econ. and Cultural Consulate of Papua New Guinea, LA; bd. dirs. Glendale Symphony Orch.; mem. Tumate Welfare Commn.; commr. Los Angeles County Sheriff Dept. Fellow: Am. Acad. Physician's Assts.; mem.: Physicians Social Responsibility, Bus. Law Enforcement (N.E. divsn.), So. Calif. Alliance Survival, Inst. Noetic Scis., Noetic Scis. Soc., Mercy Crusade Inc., Internat. Found. Survival Rsch., Supreme Emblem Club U.S., Shriners, Flying Samaritans, Order Eastern Star. Avocations: coin collecting/numismatics, designing, writing, painting, flying. Home Phone: 323-255-0734; Office Phone: 323-255-0734. Personal E-mail: msimms1234@aol.com.

SIMMS, MARSHA E., lawyer; b. St. Louis, Sept. 15, 1952; AB, Barnard Coll., 1974; JD, Stanford U., 1977. Bar: NY 1978. Ptnr., corp. dept. Weil, Gotshal & Manges LLP, NYC. Bd. trustees Lawyers' Com. Civil Rights Under Law, Ednl. Broadcasting Corp. (Channel 13). Mem. editl. bd.: Bus. Lawyer. Former trustee Stanford Alumni Assn.; former mem. campaign steering com. Stanford Law Sch. Named one of Am. Top Black Atty., Black Enterprise, 2003. Mem.: ABA, Am. Law Inst., Met. Black Bar Assn., NY State Bar Assn., Am. Arbitration Assn. (past bd. dirs.). Office: Weil Gotshal & Manges LLP 767 Fifth Ave New York NY 10153 Home Phone: 212-686-8218; Office Phone: 212-310-8116. Office Fax: 212-310-3007. Business E-Mail: marsha.simms@weil.com.

SIMMS, PHIL, sports commentator, retired professional football player; b. Lebanon, Ky., Nov. 3, 1956; m. Diana Simms; children: Christopher, Matthew, Deirdre. Grad., Morehead State U., 1979. Quarterback N.Y. Giants, 1979-94; studio analyst ESPN, Prime Time Monday, 1994—95; game analyst NBC, 1995—98; lead analyst CBS Sports, 1998—. Co-author (with Rick Meier): Phil Simms on Passing: Fundamentals of Throwing the Football, 1996; (with Vic Carucci) Sunday Morning Quarterback: Going Deep on the Strategies, Myths, and Mayhem of Football, 2004. Named to Pro Bowl Team, 1985, 1993; Named All-Pro, 1986; recipient Pro Bowl Player of Game award, 1986, MVP award Super Bowl XXI, 1987. Mem. NFL Championship Teams, 1986, 1990. Office: CBS 51 W 52nd St New York NY 10019 *

SIMNJANOVSKI, RISTE, counseling administrator; b. Escondido, Calif., Dec. 24, 1979; s. Djoko and Zorka Simnjanovski. BA, U. Redlands, Calif., 2002, MA, 2004. Cert. tchr. Calif., 2003. Resident dir. U. Redlands, Calif., 2002—04, asst. dir. cmty. svc., 2002, asst. dir. student leadership, 2003, admissions counselor, 2005—. Named to All-SCIAC Men's Soccer, 1999—2001; recipient Player of Yr., san Diego Soccer Club, 1998, Male Athlete of yr., 1998, Resident Advisor of Yr., U. Redlands, 2001, MA Student of Yr., 2002; cummings Endowed scholarship, 1998—2002. Mem.: CCPA, National Assn. Student Pers. Admstrs., Am. Coll. Pers. Assn., Phi Alpha Theta. Avocations: soccer, computers, drums, linguistics, research. Office: U Redlands 1200 E Colton Redlands CA 92373

SIMOKAITIS, FRANK JOSEPH, military officer, lawyer; b. St. Louis, Dec. 12, 1922; s. Frank and Constance (Ladish) S.; m. Mary Jane Feeny; children: Peggy, Mary, Frank (dec.). Student, Washington U., St. Louis, 1945-47; LL.B., St. Louis U., 1950, JD, 1970. Bar: U.S. Supreme Ct. U.S 1950, Mo. 1950, also other fed. cts. 1950. Commd. 2d lt. USAAF, 1943; advanced through grades to maj. gen. USAF, 1973; plans and ops. officer Hdqrs. Pacific Air Force, 1960-63; staff officer Hdqrs. USAF, Washington, 1963-69, exec. asst. to sec. air force, 1969-73; comdt. Air Force Inst. Tech., 1973-78; dir. Dept. Def. affairs Hdqrs. NASA, Washington, 1978-83, cons., 1983—. Bd. dirs. Dayton chpt. ARC, Greater Miami chpt., arbitrator Better Bus. Bur. Decorated D.S.M. with oak leaf cluster, Legion of Merit, Air medal with 4 oak leaf clusters, Air Force Commendation medal. Mem. Miami Air Force Assn. (bd. dirs.), Navy League (v.p. U.S. Miami coun.), Univ. Club of Washington D.C., Patrick AFB Officers Club. Home: 1594 Frontier Dr Melbourne FL 32940

SIMON, ALBERT, retired physicist, engineer, educator; b. NYC, Dec. 27, 1924; s. Emanuel D. and Sarah (Leitner) S.; m. Harriet E. Rubinstein, Aug. 17, 1947 (dec. June 1970); children: Richard, Janet, David; m. Rita Shiffman, June 11, 1972. BS, CCNY, 1947; PhD, U. Rochester, 1950. Registered profl. engr., N.Y. State. Physicist Oak Ridge Nat. Lab., 1950-54, assoc. dir. neutron physics divsn., 1954-61; head plasma physics divsn. Gen. Atomic Co., San Diego, 1961-66; prof. dept. mech. engring. U. Rochester, NY, 1966—2005, prof. physics, 1968—2005; prof. emeritus, 2005; chmn. dept. mech. engring. U. Rochester, 1977-84. Mem. Inst. for Advanced Study, Princeton, 1974-75; sr. vis. fellow U.K. Sci. Rsch. Coun., Oxford U., 1975 Author: An Introduction to Thermonuclear Research, 1959; contbr. to: Ency. Americana, 1964, 74; editor Advances in Plasma Physics, 1967—. With USN, 1944—46. Recipient Univ. Mentor award, 1988-89; John Simon Guggenheim fellow, 1964-65. Fellow Am. Phys. Soc. (chmn. plasma physics divsn. 1963-64); mem. ASME, ASEE (chmn. nuc. engring. divsn. 1985-86). Home: 7340 Amberly Ln #309 Delray Beach FL 33446 Office Phone: 585-275-4431. Business E-Mail: simo@me.rochester.edu.

SIMON, ARTHUR JOSEPH, lawyer; b. Berwyn, Ill., June 4, 1954; s. Frank and Bessie (Bauer) S.; m. Donna Casey, July 30, 1977; children: James Casey, John Arthur, Jane Mayer. BS, Vanderbilt U., 1975; JD, Northwestern U., 1979. Bar: U.S. Dist. Ct. (no. dist.) Ill. 1979. Assoc., then ptnr. Gardner, Carton & Douglas, Chgo.; ptnr. Sonnenschein, Nath & Rosenthal, Chgo.; gen. counsel William Blair & Co., Chgo. Mem. ABA, Union League (Chgo.). Avocations: sports, woodworking. Office: William Blair & Co LLC 222 W Adams St Chicago IL 60606 Office Phone: 312-236-1600.

SIMON, BARRY S., lawyer; b. New Haven, Nov. 13, 1949; BA magna cum laude, Harvard U., 1971, JD magna cum laude, 1974. Bar: D.C. 1976. Law clk. to Hon. J. Skelly Wright U.S. Ct. Appeals (D.C. Cir.), 1974-75; law clk. to Justice William J. Brennan, Jr. U.S. Supreme Ct., 1975-76; mem. Williams & Connolly, Wash., ptnr. Vis. lectr. in law U. Mich. Law Sch. 1979; adj. prof. criminal procedure Georgetown U. Law Ctr., 1981-84. Mem. D.C. Bar Assn., Phi Beta Kappa. Pres. Harvard Law Review, 1973-74. Office: Williams & Connolly 725 12th St NW Washington DC 20005-5901 Office Phone: 202-434-5005. Office Fax: 202-434-5029. Business E-Mail: bsimon@wc.com.

SIMON, BERNECE KERN, retired social worker; b. Denver, Nov. 27, 1914; d. Maurice Meyer and Jennie (Bloch) Kern; m. Marvin L. Simon, Feb. 26, 1939 (dec.); 1 child, Anne Elizabeth. BA, U. Chgo., 1936, MA, 1942. Social worker Jewish Children's Bur. Chgo., 1938-40, U. Chgo. Hosps. and Clinics, 1940-44; mem. faculty U. Chgo., 1944-81, instr., 1944-48, asst. prof., 1948-60, prof. social casework, 1960—81, prof. emeritus, 1981—, Samuel Deutsch prof. Sch. Social Service Adminstrn., 1960—. Mem. bd. editors 17th Edit. Ency. Social Work, 1975—77, Social Svc. Rev., 1975—99, Social Work, 1978—82; book rev. editor: Social Work, 1982—87, cons. editor: Jour. Social Work Edn., 1991—94; contbr. articles to profl. jours., chapters to books. Mem.: NASW, Nat. Acads. Practice Social Work, Acad. Cert. Social Workers, Coun. Social Work Edn. (mem. nat. bd. dirs., sec. 1972—74).

SIMON, BRUCE HARVEY, lawyer; b. NYC, Dec. 27, 1934; s. Morris and Pearl (Mandelstein) S.; m. Arlene Bartfield, June 16, 1957; children: Douglas, Charles, Rachel. BA, Bklyn. Coll., 1956; LLB, Harvard U., 1959. Bar: N.Y. 1961, U.S. Ct. Appeals (2d, 3d, 4th and 5th cirs.) U.S. Dist. Ct. (so., ea. and no. dists.) N.Y. Assoc. Cohen & Weiss, NYC, 1960-66; ptnr. Cohen, Weiss & Simon, NYC, 1966—. Mem. NYC Bd. Collective Bargaining, 1999-2006; bd. dirs. AFL-CIO Lawyers Coordinating Com., 1982—; disting. practitioner in residence Cornell Law Sch., 1995. Contbr. articles to legal publs. Served with U.S. Army, 1959-60. Mem. ABA, Fed. Bar Coun. Democrat. Jewish. Office: Cohen Weiss & Simon 330 W 42nd St Fl 25 New York NY 10036-6976 E-mail: bsimon@cwsny.com.

SIMON, DAVID, real estate company officer; BS, Ind. U.; MBA, Columbia U. Assoc. First Boston Corp., NYC; CFO, COO Melvin Simon & Assocs., Inc.; v.p. Wasserstein Perella & Co., NYC, til 1990; pres., CEO Simon Property Group, 1990-96, CEO, 1996—. 2d. vice-chmn. Nat. Assn. Real Estate Investment Trusts, Inc.; trustee Internat. Coun. Shopping Ctrs.; dir. 1st Health Corp. Mem. urban Land Inst. Office: Simon Property Group Inc 115 W Washington St Ste 1465 Indianapolis IN 46204-3464 *

SIMON, DAVID FREDERICK, lawyer; b. El Paso, Tex., Apr. 14, 1953; s. Maurice and Susan (Bendekovits) S.; m. Deborah Hart, Mar. 1, 1980; children: Alison Mallory, Joshua Alan, Rebecca Elizabeth, Nathaniel Cody. BS magna cum laude, U. Buffalo, 1974; JD cum laude, U. Pa., 1977. Bar: Pa. 1977, N.J. 1978. Law clk. to presiding judge Phila. Ct. Common Pleas, 1977-79; assoc. Wolf, Block, Schorr & Solis-Cohen, Phila., 1979-85, ptnr., 1985-90; sr. v.p. U.S. Healthcare Inc., Blue Bell, Pa., 1990-96; chief legal officer Aetna U.S. Healthcare, Inc., Blue Bell, 1996—2000; chief counsel Pa. Ins. Dept., Harrisburg, 2001—03; sr. v.p. Jefferson Health Sys., Inc., Radnor, Pa., 2003—05; gen. counsel Mt. Lauren Risk Retention Group, Inc., 2003—. Adv. coun. Pa. Dept. Conservation and Natural Resources, 1996-97, Pa. MCare Commn., 2006; bd. mgrs. U. Pa. Law Sch. Alumni, 1997-2003; dean's adv. coun. SUNY Buffalo Sch. Mgmt., 1999—, chmn., 2003-2005. Mem. Phila. Bar Assn. (exec. com. young lawyers sect. 1983-85, chmn. computer law com. 1984-85), Pa. Bar Assn. (chmn. in-house counsel com. 1993-94), Pa. Bar Inst. (bd. dirs. 1992-96). Avocations: photography, electronics. Home: PO Box 551 Gwynedd Valley PA 19437-0551 Office: Jefferson Health Sys Inc 259 N Radnor-Chester Rd Radnor PA 19087-5288 Home Phone: 215-646-6528; Office Phone: 610-225-6298.

SIMON, DAVID JUDAH, reporter; b. Washington, Sept. 2, 1960; s. Bernard and Dorothy (Ligeti) S.; m. Kayle Tucker, 1991; 1 child, Ethan Simon. BS in Gen. Studies, U. Md., 1983. Editor in chief Besthesda-Chevy Chase (Md.) High Sch. Tattler, 1977-78; editor U. Md., Diamondback, College Park, 1978-81; editor in chief U. Md. Diamondback, College Park, 1981-82; corr. Balt. Morning Sun, 1982-83, city reporter, 1983-95. Author: Homicide: A Year on the Killing Streets, 1991; co-author (with Ed Burns): The Corner: A Year in the Life of an Inner-City Neighborhood, 1997; writer, prodr.: (TV series) Homicide: Life on the Street, 1993—99; exec. prodr.: (TV miniseries) The Corner, 2000 (Emmy for Outstanding Writing for a Miniseries or a Movie, 2000); exec. prodr., writer, creator: (TV series) The Wire, 2002— (Peabody award, 2003). Recipient 5 nat. and 13 regional newspaper writing awards. Jewish. *

SIMON, DAVID L., art historian; s. Abe M. and Thelma D. Simon; m. Sonia Chalif Simon, June 11, 1971; 1 child, David L. Jr. BA, Boston U., 1969, MA, 1971; PhD, U. London, 1977. Instr. Boston U., 1973—74; from asst. to assoc. prof. SUNY, Cortland, 1974—81; prof. Colby Coll., Waterville, Maine, 1981—. Author: La Condesa Dona Sancha, 1995; editor: (jour.) Gesta, 1998; co-author: Janson's History of Art, 2006. Recipient award, Am. Coun. Learned Societies, 1978, Basset Tchg. award, Colby Coll., 2005;, Met. Mus. Art fellow, 1980—81. Mem.: Internat. Ctr. Medieval Art, Coll. Art Assn. Office: Colby Coll 5640 Mayflower Hill Waterville ME 04901 Business E-Mail: dlsimon@colby.edu.

SIMON, DIANE ROSE, music educator, writer, poet; b. Appleton, Wis., Oct. 19, 1945; d. Raymond George and Violet Beatrice (Behnke) Rippl; m. Ronald Philip Simon, Sept. 18, 1938; children: David Clarence, Mary Anne. Student, Stevens Point State Tchrs. Coll., 1966; BMus, Ariz. State U., Tempe, 1969, post grad., 1971—94; student, Paris Am. Acad., 1970, Union Coll., Schenectady, NY, 1970, Westminster Choir Coll., Princeton, NJ, 1979, Grand Canyon Coll., 1992, Inst. Children's Lit., 1998—2003, Poetry Laureate Program, Owings Mills, Md., 2002—04. Dir. band, chorus, gen. music Wellton Elem. Sch. Dist., Ariz., 1969—70; saxophone instr. Ariz. We. Coll., Yuma, 1969—70; woodwind specialist Yuma Sch. Dist., 1970—72; dir. band Balsz Sch. Dist., Phoenix, 1972—76, Paradise Valley Sch. Dist., Phoenix, 1976—77; dir. band, chorus, gen. music Mesa Pub. Schs., Ariz., 1978—94; ret., 1994; pvt. music lessons, 1965—. Mem. Yuma Symphony, 1969—72; dir. saxophone ensembles Yuma Sch. Dist. #1, 1970—72; saxophone clinician, adjudicator Ariz. Music Educators Assn., 1972—76, 2002. Author: Expressions of the Heart, 1997, Family Treasures, 1998, With a Giggle and a Tear, 1998, Butterflies in the Meadow, 1999, The Rat and The Hat, 1999, Into the Millennium, 2000, Nature's Lavender Lap of Love, 2006; pub.: Beneath the Mesquite, 1999, Sunrise Over the Desert, 1999; poet (poetry) pub. numerous anthologies (Editors Choice Award cert., 1996, 1997, 1998, 1999, 2000, 2001, 2002, 2003); contbr. articles to profl. publs. Recipient The Muse of Fire trophy, medallion, The Famous Poets Soc., 2000, The Shakespeare Trophy of Excellence award, 2004. Mem.: Internat. Libr. Poetry, Internat. Soc. Poets (Disting. Membership 1996, Internat. Poet of Merit award Medallion and Commemorative Plaque 1996, 1998, Poet of Merit award medallion 2002, Silver award bowl trophy 2002, Poet of Merit award medallion 2004, Outstanding Achievement in Poetry Silver award cup 2004, Outstanding Achievement in Poetry Crystal award trophy 2006). Republican. Roman Catholic. Home: 732 W Curry St Chandler AZ 85225

SIMON, DOLORES DALY, copy editor; b. San Francisco, Nov. 18, 1928; d. Francis Edward and Jeannette (Cooke) Daly; m. Sidney Blair Simon, Aug. 24, 1952 (div. Nov. 1955); children: John Roderick, Douglas Brian. BA in Journalism, Pa. State U., 1950. County editor Centre Daily Times, State College, Pa., 1950-51; soc. editor Bradford (Pa.) Era, 1951-52; copy editor Harper & Bros., Pubs., NYC, 1955-60; copy chief Harper & Row, Pubs., NYC, 1960-88; freelance editor, copy editor Warwick, NY, 1988—. Co-author: Recipes into Type, 1993 (Best Food Reference 1994). Mem. James Beard Found., Phi Mu. Democrat. Avocation: book collecting. Office: Editl Svcs 63 Blooms Corners Rd Warwick NY 10990-2403 Office Phone: 845-986-4442.

SIMON, DONALD JOHN, financial planner, small business owner; b. Chgo., July 16, 1947; s. Nicholas J. and Alice R. (Vaughn) S.; 1 child, Joshua K. BSBA, Oglethorpe U., 1969. CFP, CLU, ChFC. Sales rep. D. W. Shaw, Inc., Berlin, NJ, 1969-74; owner Simon Fin. Co., Vero Beach, Fla., 1975—. Mem. Nat. Assn. Ins. and Fin. Advisors. Avocations: music, bicycling, boating.

SIMON, ECKEHARD (PETER), foreign language educator; b. Schneidemühl, Germany, Jan. 5, 1939; came to U.S., 1955, naturalized, 1960; s. Herbert and Doris (Keiler) S.; m. Eileen Higginbottom, Dec. 19, 1959; children: Anders, Conrad (dec.), Matthew, Frederick. AB, Columbia U., 1960; A.M., Harvard U., 1961, PhD, 1964. Instr., German Harvard U., Cambridge, Mass., 1964-65, asst. prof., 1965-69, assoc. prof., 1969-71, prof., 1971—, Victor S. Thomas prof. Germanic langs. and lit., 1996—2007, Victor S. Thomas rsch. prof. German, 2007—, head tutor and lang. coordinator, 1965-76, chmn. dept. German, 1976—82, 1996—99, chmn. com. on medieval studies, 1992—95, 2001—02. Author: Neidhart von Reuental: Geschichte der Forschung und Bibliographie, 1968, Neidhart von Reuental, 1975, The Türkenkalender (1454) Attributed to Gutenberg and the Strasbourg Lunation Tracts, 1988, Die Anfänge des weltlichen deutschen Schaupiels, 1370-1530, 2003; editor: The Theatre of Medieval Europe, New Research in Early Drama, 1991; mem. editl. bd.: Dictionary of the Middle Ages, 1982-89; contbr. articles to profl. jours. Woodrow Wilson fellow, 1960-61, NEH Younger Scholar fellow, 1968-69, Rsch fellow, 1977-78, Guggenheim fellow, 1968-69, Fulbright fellow U. Cologne, 1983, Sr. Exchange fellow Dumbarton Oaks, Washington, 2001. Mem. MLA, Am. Assn. Tchrs. German, Medieval Acad. Am. (asst. editor Speculum 1981-94, book review editor 1994-2000). Home: 11 Hayes Ave Lexington MA 02420-3521 Office: Harvard U Barker Ctr 345 Cambridge MA 02138-3879 Home Phone: 781-862-5326; Office Phone: 617-496-9359. Business E-Mail: simon2@fas.harvard.edu.

SIMON, ERIC JACOB, neuroscientist, educator; b. Wiesbaden, Germany, June 2, 1924; came to U.S., 1938, naturalized, 1945; s. Joseph and Paula (Meyer) S.; m. Irene M. Ronis, Aug. 9, 1947; children: Martin A., Faye Ruth, Lawrence D. BS, Case Inst. Tech., Cleve., 1944; MS, U. Chgo., 1947, PhD, 1951; doctorate (hon.), U. René Descartes Sorbonne, Paris, 1982. Postdoctoral trainee in biochemistry Columbia U. Coll. Physicians and Surgeons, 1951-53; lectr. in chemistry CCNY, 1952-59; research assoc. Cornell U. Med. Coll., 1953-59; asst. prof. medicine NYU Med. Center, 1959-64, assoc. prof. exptl. medicine, 1964-72, prof. exptl. medicine, 1972-80, prof. psychiatry and pharmacology, 1980—. Harry Williams Meml. lectr. Dept. Pharmacology Emory U., Atlanta, 1986; mem. initial rev. com. Nat. Inst. Drug Abuse, 1976-80, chmn. 1979-80, mem. Nat. Adv. Coun. on Drug Abuse, 1989-92; Sterling-Winthrop lectr. Albany Med. Coll., 1977; vis. prof. Coll. de France, Paris, 1990; vis. lectr. Shanghai and Beijing, 1985. Trustee Teaneck (N.J.) Bd. Edn., 1975-79. Served with U.S. Army, 1944-46. Recipient Rsch. Pace Setter award Nat. Inst. Drug Abuse, 1977, Louis and Bert Freedman Found. award N.Y. Acad. Scis., 1980, Nathan B. Eddy Meml. award Coll. on Problems of Drug Dependence, Lexington, Ky., 1983, Alumni Profl. Achievement award U. Chgo., 1986, Founder's Lectr. award Internat. NArcotics Rsch. Conf., 1999; Health Rsch. Coun. NYC career scientist, 1959-75. Fellow AAAS, N.Y. Acad. Scis. (trustee 1986-89); mem. Am. Soc. Biol. Chemists, Am. Soc. Neurochemistry, Am. Soc. Pharmacology, Internat. Soc. Neurochemistry, Am. Chem. Soc., Sigma Xi. Lodges: B'nai B'rith. Research, publs. on opiate receptors, endorphins, biochemistry of analgesic action, vitamin E metabolism, acyl-coenzyme A synthesis. Office: 550 1st Ave New York NY 10016-6402 Office Phone: 212-263-5637. Business E-Mail: eric.simon@nyu.edu.

SIMON, EVELYN, lawyer; b. NYC, May 13, 1943; d. Joseph and Adele (Holzschlag) Berkman; m. Fredrick Simon, Aug. 18, 1963; children: Amy Jocelyn, Marcie Ann. AB in Physics, Barnard Coll., 1963; MS in Physics, U. Pitts., 1964; JD, Wayne State U., 1978; LLB, Monash U., Melbourne, Australia, 1980. Bar: Mich. 1980, Victoria (Australia) 1981. Supr. engring. Chrysler Corp., Detroit, 1964-72; edn. and profl. mgr. Engring. Soc. Detroit, 1972-78; solicitor Arthur Robinson & Co., Melbourne, 1980-81; sr. atty. Ford Motor Co., Detroit, 1981-89; assoc. gen. counsel Sheller-Globe Corp., Detroit, 1989-90; v.p. planning, gen. counsel United Techs. Automotive Inc., Dearborn, Mich., 1991-94, v.p. bus. devel. and legal affairs, 1995-96, v.p. Asian bus. devel., 1997-98; pvt. practice, 1999—. Cons. internat. bus. devel., 1998—. Mem.: Mich. Bar Assn. Office: 1787 Alexander Dr Bloomfield Hills MI 48302-1204 Home Phone: 248-855-5664; Office Phone: 248-539-0969. E-mail: evelynsimon@prodigy.net.

SIMON, GARY LEONARD, internist, educator; b. Bklyn., Dec. 18, 1946; s. Bernard and Dorothy (Ligeti) Simon; m. Vicki Thiessen, Aug. 29, 1970; children: Jason, Jessica. BS, U. Md., 1968, MD, 1975; PhD, U. Wis., 1972. Diplomate Am. Bd. Internal Medicine, Am. Bd. Infectious Diseases. Resident in internal medicine U. Md. Hosp., Balt., 1975—78; fellow infectious diseases Tufts-New Eng. Med. Ctr., Boston, 1978—80; asst. prof. dept. medicine George Washington U., Washington, 1980-84, assoc. prof., 1984-89, assoc. chmn. medicine, 1984-97, prof., 1989—, dir. divsn. infectious diseases, 1993—, vice chmn. medicine, 1997—, Walter G. Ross Prof. Medicine, 2006. Cons. on AIDS Assn. Am. Med. Coll., Washington, 1990—. Contbr. articles to profl. jours. Named Walter G. Ross Prof. in Clinical Rsch., George Washington U., 2006; named one of Best Doctors in Am., 2004—; recipient Outstanding Attending Physician award, George Washington U., 1981, Disting. Rschr. award, 2002, Oscar and Shoshana Trachtenburg award, 2005. Fellow: ACP (Laureate award 2000), Infectious Disease Soc.; mem.: Internat. AIDS Soc., Assn. Subspecialty Profs., Am. Soc. Microbiology, Alpha Omega Alpha. Office: George Washington U 2150 Pennsylvania Ave NW Washington DC 20037-3201 Home Phone: 301-983-2873; Office Phone: 202-741-2234. Business E-Mail: gsimon@mfa.gwu.edu.

SIMON, GEORGE T., lawyer; BA, Trinity Coll., 1969; JD, Harvard U. Law Sch., 1972. Bar: N.Y. 1973, Ill. 1982. Staff atty. SEC, Washington, 1976—81; ptnr. Foley & Lardner LLP, Chgo., 1991—, mem. mgmt. com. Mem.: SEC Hist. Soc. (chmn., market regulation com.), Trinity Coll. (bd. fellows 1998—2002), Securities Industry Assn., ABA, Northwestern U. Law Sch. Garrett Inst. (exec. com.). Office: Foley & Lardner LLP 321 N Clark St Ste 2800 Chicago IL 60610-4764 Office Phone: 312-832-4554. Business E-Mail: gsimon@foley.com.

SIMON, GREGORY, lawyer; b. Blytheville, Ark., Nov. 18, 1951; s. Michael F. and Marcella (Kallile) S.; m. Jennifer Lee Marberg, Dec. 21, 1978 (div. Mar. 1982); m. Margo Lynn Reid, Sept. 5, 1988; children: Michael Reid Simon, Kallile Speice Simon. Student, U. Wien, Vienna, 1971-72; BA, U. Ark., 1973; JD, U. Wash., 1983. Bar: Wash. 1983. Press sec. Barry Commoner for Pres., Flushing, NY, 1980; law clk. Riddell, Williams et al, Seattle, 1982; atty. Roberts & Shefelman, Seattle, 1983-85; counsel, staff dir. Investigation and Oversight subcom. House Com. on Sci., Washington, 1985-91; legis. dir. Senator Al Gore, Washington, 1991-93; chief domestic policy advisor Vice Pres. Al Gore, Washington, 1993—2001; chair Infotech Strategies, 2002—03; pres. Fastercures/Ctr. Accelerating Med. Solutions, Washington, 2003—. Named Outstanding Oralist, N.W. Round, Jessup Internat. Law Competition, 1983; European Cmty. Visitors Program fellow, Brussels, Strasbourg, London, Rome, Madrid, 1989; Sharon Nelson Leadership award, Shidler Ctr. Law, Commerce, Tech., U. Wash. Law Sch., 2004. Office: FasterCures Ctr Accelerating Med Solutions 509 Seventh St NW Washington DC 20004 Office Phone: 202-654-7090. Office Fax: 202-654-7079.

SIMON, HANS-JOERG WALTER, lawyer; s. Walter and Gertrud Simon; m. Isabell Maria Decker. M in German and Fgn. Law, U. Mainz, U. Tor Vergata II, Rome, 1998. Bar: Bavaria 2000, Munich 2004. Lawyer Noerr Stiefenhofer Lutz, Munich, 2000—06, SJ Berwin LLP, Berlin, 2006—. Author: Finance; contbr. articles to profl. jours. With Arty. German Army, 1991—92. Avocations: sailing, history of cars. Office: SJ Berwin LLP Kurfuerstendamm 63 Berlin D-10707 Germany Home Phone: +493088717156; Office Phone: +493088717156. Office Fax: +493088717166. Business E-Mail: hans-joerg.simon@sjberwin.com.

SIMON, HAROLD, radiologist; b. Trenton, NJ, May 13, 1930; s. John and Rae B. Simon; m. Jane L. Ludwig, Feb. 25, 1956; children: Steven Gregg, John Gregory. MD, Duke U., Durham, NC, 1955. Diplomate Am.

Bd. Radiology, Am. Bd. Nuc. Medicine. Intern U.S. Naval Hosp., Chelsea, Mass., 1955-56; resident in radiology Mass. Gen. Hosp., Boston, 1958-61, Oak Ridge Inst. Nuc. Medicine, 1959; instr. radiology Med. Sch., Tufts U., Boston, 1961-63, clin. asst. prof., 1965, assoc. clin. prof., 1971-77, clin. prof., 1977-98; pvt. practice Newton Lower Falls, Mass., 1963-95; mem. staff Newton Wellesley Hosp., Mass., assoc. chief radiology, 1977—, radiologist-in-chief, 1987-95; cons. VA Med. Sys., 1997—. Dir. Sch. Nuc. Med. Tech.; bd. dirs., mem. CRC com., mem. audit com. Grove Bank, chmn. audit com., 1995—96; bd. dirs., treas. Newell Physicians, Inc., 1986—93; mem. staff Intracoastal Med. Sys., West Palm Beach, Fla., 1997—2001; bd. overseers Newell Health Corp.; cons. VA Hosp., Boston, 1999—, Charitas Norwood Hosp., Mass., 1998—2002, Beth Israel Deaconess Hosp., 2007. Contbr. articles to profl. jours. With USNR, 1955—58, med. officer USN, 1956—58. Fellow: Am. Coll. Radiology; mem.: Mass. Radiology Soc., Mass. Med. Soc. (mem. ins. com. 1992—95), New Eng. Roentgen Ray Soc., Am. Roentgen Ray Soc., Radiol. Soc. N.Am., Banyon Country Club, Belmont Country Club, Pinebrook Country Club (pres. 1982—85), Phi Beta Kappa, Phi Eta Sigma. Home: 252 Atlantic Ave Palm Beach FL 33480-3709

SIMON, HERBERT, real estate developer, professional sports team owner; b. Bklyn., Oct. 23, 1934; s. Max and Mae Simon; m. Bui Simon; children: Jennifer, Stephen, Sarah, Rachel, Asher, Sean. Grad., CCNY. With Albert Frankel Co., Indpls., 1959; co-founder Melvin Simon and Assocs., Inc., Indpls., 1959—; co-owner NBA Ind. Pacers, Indpls., 1983—; went pub. and became Simon Property Group, 1993; CEO Simon Property Group, Inc., 1993—95; merged with DeBartolo Realty Corp. and became Simon DeBartolo Group, 1996; name changed back to Simon Property Group, 1998; co-chmn. bd. Simon Property Group, Inc., 1995—. Named one of Forbes' Richest Ams., 2006. Office: Ind Pacers 125 S Pennsylvania St Indianapolis IN 46204 also: Simon Property Group Inc 225 W Washington St Indianapolis IN 46204 *

SIMON, HERBERT BERNHEIMER, sculptor; s. Jacob Bernheimer and Emma Mellon Simon. BA, MA, NYU, 1964. Instr. Sch. Design NC State Coll., Raleigh, 1966—68; prof. Wilkes U., Wilkes-Barre, Pa., 1969—92. With USN, 1946—47, with USN, 1950—51. Avocations: reading, travel, visiting museums. Home: 25 E Center St Shavertown PA 18708

SIMON, HORST D., computer scientist; b. Aug. 8, 1953; married; 2 children. Diploma in Math., Technische U. Berlin, 1978; PhD, U. Calif., 1982. Asst. prof. SUNY, Stony Brook, NY, 1982—83; with Boeing Computer Svcs., 1983—89, coord. engring. and tech. applications divsn., 1983—86, mgr. computational math. group, 1986—87; mgr. rsch. dept. computer sci. corp. NASA Ames Rsch. Ctr., Moffett Field, Calif., 1989—94; rsch. market devel. mgr. advanced sys. divsn Silicon Graphics, 1994—96; dir. Nat. Energy Rsch. Sci. Computing Divsn., Computational Rsch. Divsn. Lawrence Berkeley Nat. Libr., 1996—. Spkr. in field; mem. indsl. adv. bd. dept. computer sci. U. Calif., Davis; mem. internat. adv. panel Inst. HPC, Singapore. Editor: (books) Scientific Applications of the Connection Machine, 1989, Parallel Computational Fluid Dynamics, 1992, Parallel Processing for Scientific Computing, 1995, Solving Irregularly Structured Problems in Parallel, 1998; contbr. articles to profl. jours., chapters to books; mng. editor: Internat. Jour. High Speed Computing, 1989—97, mem. editl. bd.: SIAM Jour. Sci. and Statistical Computing, 1989—95, Jour. Sci. Programming, NHSE Review, Advances in Engineering Software (formerly Computing Systems Engineering), others. Recipient (with NAS Parallel Benchmarks Team) H. Julian Allen award, 1995, (with group from Cray and Boeing) Gordon Bell Prize, 1988. Office: NERSC Divn Dir Berkeley Lab MS 50B4230 One Cyclotron Rd Berkeley CA 94720-8150

SIMON, H(UEY) PAUL, lawyer; b. Lafayette, La., Oct. 19, 1923; s. Jules and Ida (Rogére) S.; m. Carolyn Perkins, Aug. 6, 1949 (dec. Dec. 1999); 1 child, John Clark. BS, U. Southwestern La., 1943; JD, Tulane U., 1947. CPA La., 1947; bar: La. 1947. Pvt. practice, New Orleans, 1947—; asst. prof. advanced acctg. and taxation U. Southwestern La., 1944-45; staff acct. Haskins & Sells (now Deloitte & Touche), New Orleans, 1945-53, prin., 1953-57; ptnr. Deutsch, Kerrigan & Stiles, 1957-79; sr. founding ptnr. Simon, Peragine, Smith & Redfearn, 1979—. Mem. New Orleans Bd. Trade. Author: Community Property and Liability for Funeral Expenses of Deceased Spouse, 1946, Income Tax Deductibility of Attorney's Fees in Action in Boundary, 1946, Fair Labor Standards Act and Employee's Waiver of Liquidated Damages, 1946, Louisiana Income Tax Law, 1956, Changes Effected by the Louisiana Trust Code, 1965, Gifts to Minors and the Parent's Obligation of Support, 1968; co-author: Deductions—Business or Hobby, 1975, Role of Attorney in IRS Tax Return Examination, 1978; assoc. editor: The Louisiana CPA, 1956-60; mem. bd. editors Tulane Law Rev., 1945-46, adv. bd. editors, 1992—; estates, gifts and trusts editor The Tax Times, 1986-87. Bd. dirs., mem. fin. com. World Trade Ctr., 1985-86; mem. New Orleans Met. Crime Commn., Coun. for a Better La., New Orleans Met. Area Com., Bur. Govtl. Rsch., Pub. Affairs Rsch. Coun.; co-chmn. NYU Tax Conf., New Orleans, 1976; mem. dean's coun. Tulane U. Law Sch. Named one of Best Lawyers in Am., 1985—. Fellow Am. Coll. Tax Counsel; mem. ABA (com. ct. procedure tax sect. 1958—), AICPA, La. Bar Assn. (com. on legis. and adminstrv. practice 1966-70, bd. cert. tax atty.), New Orleans Bar Assn., Internat. Bar Assn. (com. on securities issues and trading 1970-88), Am. Judicature Soc., Soc. La. CPAs, New Orleans Assn. Notaries, Tulane U. Alumni Assn., New Orleans C. of C. (coun. 1952-66), Tulane Tax Inst. (program com. 1960-96, emeritus 1997--), Internat. House (bd. dirs. 1976-79, 82-85), Internat. Platform Assn., City Energy Club, Press Club, New Orleans Country Club, Phi Delta Phi (past pres. New Orleans chpt.), Sigma Pi Alpha. Roman Catholic. Achievements include becoming the 11th attorney-CPA in Louisiana history. Office: 30th Fl Energy Ctr New Orleans LA 70163 Mailing: PO Box 2759 Covington LA 70434 Home: 323 Kirkwood Dr Covington LA 70433 Office Phone: 504-258-9177. Personal E-mail: hpsimon@aol.com. Business E-Mail: hpsimon@spsr-law.com. *Developing and maintaining consistency and constancy in feeling and showing genuine respect towards others, nourish and stimulate an individual to day by day become a better person. Whether alone or in the presence of others, one who abides by the guidance and rules he would advocate to others invariably finds the greatest reward of all--true respect for one's self.*

SIMON, J. STEPHEN, oil industry executive; BS in Civil Engring., Duke U.; MBA, Northwestern U., Evanston, Ill. With Exxon U.S.A., 1967, mgr. refinery Baton Rouge; supply and transp. mgr. Esso Europe, Esso U.S.A.; exec. asst. to the pres. Exxon Corp.; gen. mgr. Esso Caribbean and Ctrl. Am.; pres. Esso Italiana; exec. v.p. Exxon Co. Internat., 1997—99; pres. ExxonMobil Refining and Supply Co., 1999—2004; v.p. ExxonMobil Corp., 1999—2004, sr. v.p., 2004—. Bd. dir. ExxonMobil Corp., 2006—, Am. Petroleum Inst.; past bd. dir. NAM. Mem. governance com. Nat. Action Council for Minorities in Engring.; bd. dir. U.S.-China Bus. Council; mem. bd. vis., mem. Pres. Council Duke Univ. Sch. Engring.; mem. Kellogg adv. bd. Northwestern Univ. Office: ExxonMobil Corp 5959 Las Colinas Blvd Irving TX 75039 *

SIMON, JACOB MATTHEW, lawyer; b. Pitts., Pa., June 22, 1979; s. J. Matthew and Janet DiPasquale Simon. BA, Allegheny Coll., Meadville, Pa., 2001; M in Pub. and Internat. Affairs, U. Pitts., 2005, JD, 2005. Bar: Pa. 2006. Office asst. Western Pa. Sch. for Blind Children, Pitts., 1995—2004; rschr. Goldberg, Persky and White, PC, Pitts., 2004; project asst. Eckert, Seamans, Cherin and Mellot LLC (Choice Counsel, Inc.), Pitts., 2005; law clk. to assoc. Morton B. DeBroff and Assoc., PC, Pitts., 2005—06; assoc. Lieber and Hammer, PC, Pitts., 2006—. Legal extern Edn. Law Ctr. Pa., Pitts., 2002; project intern Pitts. Coun. for Internat. Visitors, 2003; mem. U. Pitts. Niagara Internat. Moot Ct. Team, 2005. Mem. Am. Civil Liberties Union, Pitts., 2001—. Young Dem. Allegheny County, Pitts., 2004—, World Affairs Coun. Pitts., 2004—. Mem.: ABA, Pa. Bar Assn., Allegheny County Bar Assn. Home: 114 Yorkshire Dr Pittsburgh PA 15208 Office: Lieber and Hammer PC 5528 Walnut St 2d Flr Pittsburgh PA 15232 Office Phone: 412-687-2231. Business E-Mail: jacob.simon@worldnet.att.net.

SIMON, JACQUELINE ALBERT, political scientist, writer; d. Louis and Rose (Axelroad) Albert; m. Pierre Simon; children: Lisette, Orville. BA cum laude, NYU, MA, 1972, PhD, 1977. Adj. assoc. prof. Southampton Coll., 1977-79; mng. editor Point of Contact, NYC, 1975-76; assoc. editor, US bur. chief Politique Internationale, Paris, 1979—. Sr. fellow Inst. French Studies, NYU, 1980—, adj. assoc. prof., 1982-85, assoc. prof. govt., 1982-83; frequent appearances French TV and radio. Author: A Century of Artists' Letters: Delacroix to Leger, 2004; contbg. editor: Harper's mag., 1984—92; contbr. numerous articles to French mag., revs., books on internat. affairs. Bd. dirs. Fresh Air Fund, 1984—, Overseas Press Club Found. Mem. Overseas Press Club of Am. (bd. dirs., treas. 2000-04, sec. 2006-), Phi Beta Kappa. Home: 988 5th Ave New York NY 10021-0143 Personal E-mail: jasimon@verizon.net.

SIMON, JAMES LOWELL, lawyer; b. Nov. 8, 1944; s. K. Lowell and Elizabeth Ann (Unholz) S.; m. RuthAnn Beck, July 4, 1997; children: Heather Lyn Small, Brandon James; stepchildren: Gary G. Mower, Richard M. Nazareth II, Juliet A. Nazareth. Student, U. Ill., 1962-63, JD with honors, 1975; BSEE magna cum laude, Bradley U., 1967. Bar: Fla. 1975, Utah 1999, Calif. 2002, U.S. Dist. Ct. (mid. dist.) Fla. 1976, U.S. Dist. Ct. Utah 1999, U.S. Dist. Ct. (no. dist.) Calif. 2002, U.S. Ct. Appeals (11th cir.) 1981, U.S. Patent Office 1983. Engr. Pan Am. World Airways, Cape Kennedy, Fla., 1967-68; assoc. Akerman, Senterfitt & Eidson, Orlando, Fla., 1975-80; ptnr. Bogin, Munns, Munns & Simon, Orlando, 1980-87, Holland & Knight, LLP, 1987-99; corp. counsel Agilent Technologies Inc., Palo Alto, Calif., 2000—. With Seminole County Sch. Adv. Coun., Fla., 1981-88, chmn., 1982-83; with Forest City Local Sch. Adv. Com., Altamonte Springs, Fla., 1981-84, Code Enforcement Bd., Altamonte Springs, 1983-84, Cen. Bus. Dist. Study com., Altamonte Springs, 1983-85, Rep. Coun. of '76, Seminole County, 1982-87; mem. Seminole County Libr. Adv. Bd., 1989-92, sec., 1990, pres., 1991, Seminole County Citizens for Quality Edn., 1990-92; mem. Seminole County Sch. Dist. Strategic Planning Com., 1991-99, Leadership Orlando Alumni, 1992-99; bd. dirs. Found. for Seminole County Pub. Schs., Inc., 1992-95, chmn., 1993-94; bd. dirs. Greater Seminole C. of C., 1993; active Lake Brantley HS Band Boosters, 1995-2000, Lake Brantley HS PTSA, 1995-2000, Chorus Boosters, 1997, Leadership Club-Heart of Fla. United Way, 1997; sponsor concerts Orlando Philharm. Orch. for Boys and Girls Clubs. Cen. Fla., 1996-97; regional dir. region 5 Holocaust Remembrance Project, 1997-99. Capt. USAF, 1968-72. Mem. ABA, Am. Corp. Counsel Assn., Am. Intellectual Property Law Assn., Intellectual Property Owners Assn. (chmn. copyright law com. 2003-05), U. Ill. Alumni Club, Phi Kappa Phi, Tau Beta Pi, Sigma Tau, Eta Kappa Nu Republican. Home: 1675 Tupolo Dr San Jose CA 95124-4754 Office: M/S 1A-PB 5301 Stevens Creek Blvd Santa Clara CA 95051 Office Phone: 408-553-2772. Personal E-mail: JimandRuthann@comcast.net. Business E-Mail: jim_simon@agilent.com.

SIMON, JANICE CROWDER, language educator, consultant; b. Mobile, Ala., Oct. 24, 1961; d. Hal and Sarah Snow Crowder; m. David Alan Simon, Mar. 13, 1982; children: Catherine Ann, David Alan Jr. BS, U. South Ala., Mobile, 1986; Cert. COMP Trainer, Peabody Coll., Vanderbilt U., Nashville, Tenn. Cert. adult reading grades 1-6 Ala. Bd. Edn., 1986. Secondary English tchr. Baldwin County Sch. Bd., Bay Minette, Ala., 2000—, secondary reading coach, 2002. Comp trainer Baldwin County Sch. Bd., 1997; sch. improvement com. Bay Minette Mid. Sch., 2002—, chmn. so. assn. of schools com., 2006. Bd. mem. South Ala. Inservice and Rsch. Ctr., Mobile, 2000. Grantee, Heritage Jr. Women's Club, 2004, Ala. Legislators, 2006. Mem.: Alpha Delta Kappa (assoc.). Home: 603 Lakeview Dr Bay Minette AL 36507 Office: 1311th W 13th St Bay Minette AL 36507 Home Phone: 251-605-6431; Office Phone: 251-580-2961. Business E-Mail: jsimon@bcbe.org.

SIMON, JIMMY LOUIS, pediatrician, educator; b. San Francisco, Dec. 27, 1930; s. Sylvain L. and Hilda H. (Netter) S.; m. Marilyn S. Wachter, June 21, 1953; children: Kent, Nancy. AB, U. Calif.-Berkeley, 1952; MD, U. Calif.-Berkeley, San Francisco, 1955. Diplomate Am. Bd. Pediats. Intern U. Calif., San Francisco, 1955-56; resident Grace-New Haven Hosp., 1956-57; sr. asst. resident Boston Children's Hosp., 1957-58; instr., asst. prof. pediats. U. Okla., Oklahoma City, 1960-64; asso. prof. U. Tex. Med. Br., Galveston, 1966-72, prof. pediatrics, 1972-74; prof., chmn. pediats. Bowman Gray Sch. Medicine, Wake Forest U., Winston-Salem, NC, 1974-96; prof., chmn. emeritus Wake Forest U. Sch. Medicine, Winston-Salem, NC, 1996—. With USAF, 1958-60. Mem. Am. Pediat. Soc., Am. Acad. Pediats., Am. Bd. Pediats., Ambulatory Pediat. Assn., Alpha Omega Alpha. Office: Wake Forest U Sch Medicine Dept Pediatrics Medical Center Blvd Winston Salem NC 27157-0001

SIMON, JOEL, music producer, advertising executive; b. 1968; B. in Bus. Mgmt. & Mktg., Cornell U., 1989. With JSM Music Inc., NYC, 1994—97, pres. & CEO, 1997—; co-founder Artemis JSM LLC, 2004—. Music prodr. for commercials including Pinata, for Juicy Fruit, 2003 (AdAge Best Spots of 2003), Car Carrier, for Chevrolet, 2006 (Assn. Ind. Comml. Prodrs. award for Best Musical Arrangement in a TV ad, 2006), Bold Moves, for Ford, 2006, Be Anyone, for Las Vegas Conv. & Visitors Authority, 2006 (AdWeek's Best Spots of Yr.), prodr. (song & music video) Unleashed, 2005. Named one of 40 Under 40, Crain's NY Bus., 2007. Achievements include winning NY State Battle of the Bands, 1984. Office: JSM Music Inc 5th Fl 59 W 19th St New York NY 10011 Office Phone: 212-627-2200. Office Fax: 212-645-0484. *

SIMON, JOHN A., investment company executive; Bachelor's degree, Princeton U.; M in Pub. Policy, Harvard U. Various positions including dep. dir. rsch. and devel. Exec. Office Adminstrn. Commonwealth of Mass.; dir. bus. fin. and strategic planning Harvard Pilgrim Health Care; dep. asst. adminstr. U.S. Agy. Internat. Devel., 2002—03; spl. asst. to Pres., sr. dir. for relief, stabilization and devel. Nat. Security Coun. The White House, dir. devel. issues, 2003—05; exec. v.p. Overseas Pvt. Investment Corp. (OPIC), 2006—. Office: Overseas Pvt Investment Corp 1100 New York Ave NW Washington DC 20527

SIMON, JOHN BERN, lawyer; b. Cleve., Aug. 8, 1942; s. Seymour Frank and Roslyn (Schultz) S.; children: Lindsey Helaine, Douglas Banning. BS, U. Wis., 1964; JD, DePaul U., 1967. Bar: Ill. 1967. Asst. U.S. atty. U.S. Justice Dept., Chgo., 1967-70, dep. chief civil div., 1970-71, chief civil div., 1971-74; spl. counsel to dir. Ill. Dept. Pub. Aid, Chgo., 1974-75; legal cons. to Commn. on Rev. of Nat. Policy Toward Gambling, Chgo., 1975-76; ptnr. firm Friedman & Koven, 1975-85, mem. exec. com., 1983-85; ptnr. firm Jenner & Block, 1986—. Spl. cons. to adminstr. DEA Dept. Justice, 1976-77; counsel to Gov.'s Revenue Study Commn. on Legalized Gambling, 1977-78; spl. counsel Ill. Racing Bd., 1979-80; lectr. tng. seminars and confs.; instr. U.S. Atty. Gen.'s Advocacy Inst., Washington, 1974; lectr. Nat. Conf. Organized Crime, Washington, 1975, Dade County Inst. Organized Crime, Ft. Lauderdale, Fla., 1976; faculty Cornell Inst. Organized Crime, Ithaca, N.Y., 1976, judge Miner Moot Ct. competition Northwestern U., 1971-73; mem. law coun. DePaul U., 1974-83, mem. alumni assn., 1984-85, chmn., 1975-79; adj. prof. DePaul U. Coll. Law, 1977, 81; faculty Practising Law Inst., Chgo., 1984. Contbr. articles to profl. jours. Bd. dirs. Lawyer's Trust Fund of Ill., 1998-2004, treas., 2000-01, v.p., 2002-03, pres., 2003-04, Cmty. Film Workshop of Chgo., 1977-90, Friends of Glencoe Parks, 1977-78, sec., 1978-79; mem. nominating com. Glencoe Sch. Bd., 1978-81, chmn. rules com., 1980-81; pres. Glencoe Hist. Soc., 1979-82; mem. Glencoe Zoning Bd. Appeals, Zoning Commn., Sign Bd. Appeals, 1981-86, chmn., 1984-86; mem. Ill. Inaugural Com., 1979, 83, 87, 95; bd. dirs., mem. exec. com. Chgo. World's Fair 1992 Authority, 1983-85; mem. Chancery divsn. task force Spl. Commn. on Adminstrn. of Justice in Cook County, 1985-87; trustee De Paul U., 1990, chair phys. plant and property com., 1992-94, vice chair, 1995-2004, chair, 2004—; commr. Ill. Racing Bd., 1990—2006; gen. trustee Lincoln Acad. Ill., 1993—, regent, 1999—, chancellor, 2001—; mem. Ill. Supreme Ct. Planning and Oversight Com. for Jud. Performance Evaluation Program, 1997-98, 2000-05, Ill. Supreme Ct. Rules Com., 2004—. Recipient Bancroft-Whitney Am. Jurisprudence award, 1965, 66, Judge Learned Hand Human Rels. award Am. Jewish Com., 1994, award for outstanding svc. to legal profession DePaul U. Coll. Law, 1996, Am. ORT Jurisprudence award, 1999. Mem. ABA (com. on liaison with the judiciary 1983-95), Fed. Bar Assn., Chgo. Bar Assn. (fed. civil procedure com. 1979-85, chmn. 1985-86, bd. mgrs. 1987-89, chmn. house com. 1989-90, treas. 1990-91, 2d v.p. 1991-92, 1st v.p. 1992-93, pres. 1993-94), Ill. State Bar Assn., Women's Bar Assn., Ill. Police Assn., Ill. Sheriffs Assn., U.S. Treasury Agts. Assn., Chgo. Bar Assn., DePaul U. Alumni Assn. (pres. 1985-87, chmn. spl. gifts com. campaign, chmn. Simon Commn. 1989-91, nat. chair for ann. giving 1991-94), Std. Club. Office: Jenner & Block One IBM Plz 42nd Fl Chicago IL 60611

SIMON, JOHN DOUGLAS, academic administrator; b. Cin., Feb. 11, 1957; s. Thomas Henry and Sally Sussler Simon; m. Diane Marie Szaflarski, Dec. 7, 1991; 1 child, Katherine Anne (dec.). BA, Williams Coll., 1979; MA, Harvard U., 1981, PhD, 1983. Postdoctoral rschr. UCLA, 1983-85; prof. chemistry U. Calif., San Diego, 1985—97; George B. Geller prof., dept. chemistry Duke Univ., 1997—, chmn. dept. chem., 1999—2004, vice provost academic affairs, 2005—. Mem. molecular and cellular biophysics study sect. NIH, Bethesda, Md., 1994-99. Author: Braving the Elements, 1985; contbr. articles to profl. jours. Recipient Fresenius award Nat. Chemistry Fraternity, 1993; Alfred P. Sloan fellow Sloan Found., 1988-90; Camille and Henry Dreyfus Tchr. scholar Dreyfus Found., 1990-95. Fellow AAAS, Am. Physical Soc.

SIMON, JOHN R., utilities executive; B, Colo. Coll., Colo. Springs; law degree, Georgetown U., Washington. Ptnr. Hallenbeck, Lascell, LLP, Rochester, NY; exec. v.p. global human capital TeleTech Holdings, Inc., Denver; sr. v.p. human resources PG&E Corp., San Francisco, sr. v.p. human resources Pacific Gas & Electric Co. subs. Office: PG&E Corp One Market Spear Tower Ste 2400 San Francisco CA 94105-1126 Office Phone: 415-267-7070. Office Fax: 415-267-7268. *

SIMON, KEITH R., safety engineer, petroleum engineer, radio personality; b. Lafayette, La., July 2, 1955; s. Jean Raymond and Ranelle T. (Touchet) S.; m. Martha Simon, Oct. 16, 1976 (div. Oct. 1979); 1 child, Jamie. BSN, BS, postgrad., U. La., 1980, student, 1981. Cert. nurse, nursing instr.; crane operator, first aid, offshore orientation lead abatement 1991, API thread inspector 1985, safety profl. 1991. Ops. mgr. Boco of Lafayette, 1980-82, exec. v.p., 1982-84, sr. project supr. La., 1980—82, exec. v.p., 1982—84; safety dir., corp. security Petro-Drive, Inc., 1989—91; divsnl. mgr. Petro-Drive/Boco of Lafayette, Inc., La., 1984—86, v.p., 1991—; offshore internat. sector mgr. Sigma Coatings USA, 1998—; ofshore internat. project mgr. Sigmakalon, Houston, 2000—03; v.p. ops. Chavez Svc. Cos., 2004—. Pres. and owner Silver Bullet Prodns. Inc., 1983—, Silver Bullet Limousine, 1983—. Mem. ARC, 1986—. Named Coors Lite Nat. Disc Jockey, 1984, named in Men Achievement, 1991, 2000 Notable Am. Men, 1992, Personalities Am., 1993; recipient Silver Shield of Valor award, 1992, Lifetime Achievement award, 1993. Mem.: ARC, Assn. Gen. Contractors, Am. Bldg. Contractors, Ind. Am. Drilling Contractors, Nat. Safety Coun., Acadiana Safety Assn., Nat. Assn. of Corrosion Engrs., Steel Structure Painting Coun., Lafayette Soc. Tng. and Devel., Am. Soc. Safety Engrs. Achievements include engineered, developed new techs., methodologies for offshore oil drilling. Avocations: skiing, softball, football, disc jockey. Office: 1401 Destrehan Ave Harvey LA 70058-2436 Home: 104 Pomerol Pl Lafayette LA 70503-6527 E-mail: ksimon007@bellsouth.net.

SIMON, KENNETH MARK, lawyer; b. Pitts., Apr. 25, 1952; s. Harvey and Jean (Busis) S.; m. Janet Hahn, June 24, 1979; children: Eliza, Jessica, Zachary. BA magna cum laude, U. Pitts., 1974; JD, Georgetown U., 1977. Bar: DC 1977. Assoc. Dickstein, Shapiro & Morin, Washington, 1977-85; ptnr. Dickstein, Shapiro Morin & Oshinsky LLP, Washington, 1985—, co-head Corp. & Fin. Practice Group, 1999—2004; practice leader Energy Transactions Dickstein Shapiro LLP, Washington, 2004—. Mem.: Electric Generation Assn. (gen. counsel 1992—95), DC Bar Assn. Democrat. Office: Dickstein Shapiro LLP 1825 Eye St Washington DC 20006 Office Phone: 202-420-2227. Office Fax: 202-887-0689. Business E-Mail: simonk@dsmo.com.

SIMON, KINDRA LEE, language educator, translator; b. Cheraw, SC, Jan. 09; d. Lee N. and Dianne Crawford Simon. BA in English & Psychology, Clemson U., SC, 1993—97. Cert. English tchr. SC Dept. Edn., 2005, ESOL SC Dept. Edn., 2005. Sales rep., trainer ALLTEL Comm., Charlotte, NC, 2000—02; ESOL tchr. Chesterfield County Sch. Dist., SC, 2002—. Translator Chesterfield County Sch. Dist., 2002—. Singer ch. choir, Pageland, SC, 2004. Grantee, Office English Lang. Acquisition, 2003—05. Mem.: Golden Key Honor Soc. (life). Avocations: photography, singing, travel, reading, writing. Home: 695 Virgil Griffin Rd Pageland SC 29728 Home Phone: 843-672-3459. Office Fax: 843-623-5513. Personal E-mail: kindrasimon@yahoo.com.

SIMON, LOTHAR, publishing executive; b. Wuppertal, Germany, Sept. 17, 1938; arrived in U.S., 1961, naturalized, 1973; s. Fritz and Erna (Backhaus) S.; m. Jeannine Rechtman, Oct. 30, 1964; 1 child, Charles. Mgr. book dept. Franz Bader Book Shop and Globe Book Shop, Washington, 1961-66; sales mgr. Humanities Press Inc., NYC, 1966-73; pres. Longman Inc., NYC, 1973-81; pub. cons., 1981-82; pres., CEO Sheridan House, Inc., Dobbs Ferry, NY, 1982—. Mem. Assn. Am. Pubs., Town Club (Scarsdale, N.Y.). Democrat. Office: Sheridan House Inc 145 Palisade St Dobbs Ferry NY 10522-1617 Office Phone: 914-693-2410. Business E-Mail: lothars@sheridanhouse.com.

SIMON, LOU ANNA KIMSEY, academic administrator; BA in Math., Ind. State U., 1969, MS in Student Personnel and Counseling, 1970; PhD in Higher Edn., Mich. State U., 1974. Faculty mem. Mich. State U., asst. dir. Office Instl. Rsch., 1974—78, asst. provost gen. academic adminstrn., 1981—87, assoc. provost, 1987—92, v.p. acad. affairs, 1993—2004, interim pres., 2003, pres., 2005—. Office: Mich State U 450 Administration Bldg East Lansing MI 48824-1046 Office Phone: 517-355-6560. Business E-Mail: presmail@msu.edu.

SIMON, MARTIN STANLEY, economist, consultant; b. St. Louis, Sept. 6, 1926; s. Elmer Ellis and Bee Marion (Werner) S.; m. Rita Edith Scheinhorn, June 18, 1950; children: Deborah, Richard. BBA, CCNY, 1949; MA, NYU, 1953. Econ. statistician Indsl. Commodity Corp., NYC, 1949-52; agrl. econ. statistician Dept. Agr., Washington, 1952-58; commodity analyst Connell Rice & Sugar Co., Inc., Westfield, NJ, 1958-62, asst. to pres., 1962-67, v.p., 1967-74; sr. v.p. Connell Rice & Sugar Co., Inc. (now The Connell Co.), Berkeley Heights, NJ, 1974-99; pres. Eureka

Group, LLC, Westfield, NJ, 1999—, The Rice Econs. Group, LLC, Westfield, NJ, 1999—; cons. AID, Jamaica, 1963; mem. Rice Insp. Industry Adv. Com., Washington, 1971-72; adv. U.S. Del. to UN FAO Intergovtl. Meetings on Rice, 1981; export dir., bd. dirs. Assn. Administrn. Rice Quotas, Inc., 1997-99. Served with U.S. Army, 1944-46, ETO. Recipient Class of 1920 award for merit in econ. stats. CCNY, 1949 Mem. Am. Econ. Assn., Rice Millers Assn. (chmn. legis. options working group 1984-86, govt. programs com. 1986-87, chmn. PL480 subcom. 1988-90), Nat. Economists Club. Office: The Rice Econs Group LLC PO Box 2446 Westfield NJ 07091-2446 E-mail: rice.economics@prodigy.net.

SIMON, MELVIN, real estate developer, professional sports team owner; b. Oct. 21, 1926; s. Max and Mae Simon; m. Bren Burns, Sept. 14, 1972; children: Deborah, Cynthia, Tamme, David, Max. BS in Acctg., CCNY, 1949, MBA in Real Estate, 1983; PhD (hon.), Butler U., 1986, Ind. U., 1991. Leasing agt. Albert Frankel Co., Indpls., 1955-60; co-founder Melvin Simon & Assocs., Indpls., 1959—, pres., 1960-73, co-chmn. bd., 1973; co-owner NBA Ind. Pacers, Indpls., 1983—; went pub. becoming Simon Property Group, 1993; chmn. bd. Simon Property Group, Inc., Indpls., 1993—95, co-chmn. bd. dirs., 1995—; merged with DeBartolo Realty Corp. to become Simon DeBartolo Group, 1996; reverted to Simon Property Group, 1998. Adv. bd. Wharton's Real Estate, Phila., 1986—. Prodr.: (films) Porky's. Adv. bd. dean's coun. Ind. U., Bloomington; bd. dirs. United Cerebral Palsy, Indpls., Muscular Dystrophy Assn., Indpls., Jewish Welfare Found., Indpls.; trustee Urban Land Inst., Internat. Coun. Shopping Ctrs. Served in US Army. Recipient Horatio Alger award Boy's Club Indpls., 1986; named Man of Yr., Jewish Welfare Found., 1980; named one of Forbes' Richest Ams., 1999—, World's Richest People, 2005—. Democrat. Jewish. Office: Simon Property Group Inc 225 W Washington St Indianapolis IN 46204 also: Indiana Pacers 125 S Pennsylvania St Indianapolis IN 46204 *

SIMON, MELVIN I., molecular biologist, educator; b. NYC, Feb. 8, 1937; s. Hyman and Sarah (Liebman) S.; m. Linda, Jan. 7, 1959; children— Joshua, David, Rachel BS, CCNY, 1959; PhD, Brandeis U., 1963. Postdoctoral fellow Princeton U., N.J., 1963-65; prof. biology U. Calif.-San Diego, La Jolla, 1965-82, Calif. Inst. Tech., Pasadena, 1982—, chmn., 1995-2000, prof., 2000—. Pres., dir. Agouron Inst., La Jolla, 1980— Contbr. articles to profl. jours. Mem. Nat. Acad. Scis. (Selman A. Waksman microbiology award 1991), Am. Soc. Microbiology

SIMON, NANCY LYNN, performing arts educator, director; b. Chgo., June 20, 1942; d. Otis Benjamin Simon and Virginia Ruth Gilliland. BA, Whitman Coll., Walla Walla, Wash., 1959—63; MA, Tufts U., Somerville, Mass., 1963—65; PhD, U. Wash., Seattle, 1965—75. Paul Garrett prof. dramatic arts Whitman Coll., 1967—, dir. Harper Joy Teater, 1967—. Freelance theatre/opera dir. Tacoma Opera, 1983—, Seattle Opera Cmty. Outreach, 1983—, Bellevue Civic Theatre, 1983—, Walla Walla Opera, 1983—, Juneau Lyric Opera, Alaska, 1983—, Shepherd Sch. Music Rice U., Houston, 1983—. Recipient George Ball Advising Excellence award, Whitman Coll., 1997, Thomas D. Howells award for disting. tchg. in humanities and arts, 2005, Paul Garrett Endowed Professorship award, 2006, Faculty award, Whitman Alumni Assn., 2007. Mem.: Artists Trust, Theatre Comm. Group, US Inst. Theater Tech., Actors' Equity Assn. Office: Whitman Coll 345 Boyer Ave Walla Walla WA 99362

SIMON, NEIL, playwright, screenwriter, television writer; b. Bronx, NY, July 4, 1927; s. Irving and Mamie Simon; m. Joan Baim, Sept. 30, 1953 (dec. 1973); children: Ellen, Nancy; m. Marsha Mason, 1973 (div. 1981); m. Diane Lander, 1987 (div. 1988); 1 child, Bryn; m. Diane Lander, 1990 (div. 1998); m. Elaine Joyce, 1999. Student, NYU, 1946; LLD (hon.), Hofstra U., 1981, Williams Coll., 1984. Sports editor Rev-Meter, Lowry Field, Colo., 1945—46; owner Eugene O'Neill Theatre, NYC. Author: materials for Tamiment (Pa.) revues, 1952—53, (Broadway plays) (with Danny Simon) Catch a Star, 1955, New Faces of 1956, 1956, (book for Broadway musical) Little Me, 1962 (Tony award nom. best book of a musical, 1963), Promises, Promises, 1970 (Tony award nom. best musical, 1969), They're Playing Our Song, 1980 (Tony award nom. best book of a musical, 1979), (Broadway plays) Come Blow Your Horn, 1961, Barefoot in the Park, 1964 (Tony award nom. best play, 1963), The Odd Couple, 1966 (Tony award best author, 1965, Writers Guild of Am. award best comedy, 1968), Sweet Charity, 1966 (Evening Standard Drama award, 1968, Tony award nom. best musical, 1966), The Star-Spangled Girl, 1967, Plaza Suite, 1969 (Tony award nom. best play, 1969), Last of the Red Hot Lovers, 1970 (Tony award nom. best play, 1970), The Gingerbread Lady, 1971, The Prisoner of Second Avenue, 1972 (Tony award nom. best play, 1972), The Sunshine Boys, 1973 (Tony award nom. best play, 1973), The Good Doctor, 1974 (Tony award nom. best score, 1974), God's Favorite, 1975, California Suite, 1977, Chapter Two, 1978 (Tony award nom. best play, 1978), I Ought to be in Pictures, 1981, Fools, 1982, Brighton Beach Memoirs, 1983 (NY Drama Critics Circle award best play, 1983), Biloxi Blues, 1986 (Tony award best play, 1986), The Odd Couple (female version), 1986, Broadway Bound, 1987 (Tony award nom. best play, 1987, Pulitzer prize nom. in drama, 1987), Rumors, 1990, Lost in Yonkers, 1991 (Tony award best play, 1991, Pulitzer prize in drama, 1991, Outer Critics Circle award outstanding play, 1991, Drama Desk award outstanding new play, 1991), Jake's Women, 1993, Laughter on the 23rd Floor, 1995, London Suite, 1995, Proposals, 1997, The Dinner Party, 2000, 45 Seconds From Broadway, 2001, (screenplay adaptations of plays) Come Blow Your Horn, 1963, Barefoot in the Park, 1967, The Odd Couple, 1968 (Acad. award nom. best adapted screenplay, 1969, Writers Guild of Am. award best comedy, 1969), Sweet Charity, 1969, Plaza Suite, 1971, The Star-Spangled Girl, 1971, Last of the Red Hot Lovers, 1972, The Prisoner of Second Avenue, 1975, The Sunshine Boys, 1975 (Writers Guild of Am. award best comedy adaptation, 1975, Acad. award nom. bext adapted screenplay, 1976, BAFTA award nom. best adapted screenplay, 1977, Golden Globe nom. best adapted screenplay, 1976), California Suite, 1978 (Acad. award nom. best adapted screenplay, 1979), Chapter Two, 1979, Brighton Beach Memoirs, 1986, Biloxi Blues, 1988, Broadway Bound, 1992, Lost in Yonkers, 1993; author & prodr. (screenplay adaptations of plays) Only When I Laugh (adapted from play The Gingerbread Lady), 1981, I Ought to be in Pictures, 1982; author: (screenplays) After the Fox, 1966, The Out-of-Towners, 1970 (Writers Guild of Am. award best comedy screenplay, 1970), The Heartbreak Kid, 1973 (Golden Globe nom. best screenplay, 1973), Murder by Death, 1976, The Goodbye Girl, 1977 (Golden Globe award best screenplay, 1977, Acad. award nom. best screenplay, 1978, BAFTA award nom. best screenplay, 1979), The Cheap Detective, 1978, Seems Like Old Times, 1980, The Lonely Guy (adaptation), 1984, The Sluggers Wife, 1984, The Marrying Man, 1991; author & prodr. (screenplays) Max Dugan Returns, 1983, The Odd Couple II, 1997; author: (TV series) Cavalcade of Stars, 1949—52, The Tallulah Bankhead Show, 1951, Stanley, 1956, The Sid Caesar Show, 1956—57 (Emmy award, 1956, 1957), The Phil Silvers Arrow Show, 1958—59 (Emmy award, 1958), The Garry Moore Show, 1959—60, The Odd Couple (based on play), 1970—75, also NBC spl. The Trouble with People, 1972, (TV films) Kibbe Hates Fitch, 1964, (teleplay) The Good Doctor, 1978, Sonny Boys, 1982, (teleplay) Jake's Women, 1996, London Suite, 1996, (autobiography) Rewrites: A Memoir, 1996. Cpl. USAF, 1945—46. Recipient Sam S. Shubert award, Shubert Found., 1968, Special Tony award for overall contribution to theater, 1975, Am. Comedy award for lifetime achievement, 1989, Drama League Unique Contribution to Theater award, 1991, Kennedy Ctr. Honors Lifetime Achievement award, 1995, Mark Twain prize, Kennedy Ctr., 2006. Mem.: Writers Guild Am. (Laurel award 1979), Dramatists Guild. *

SIMON, NORMA PLAVNICK, psychologist; d. Mark and Mary Plavnick; m. Robert G. Simon, Dec. 18, 1949; children: Mark Allan, Susan. BA, NYU, 1952, cert. in psychoanalysis, 1977; MA, Columbia U., 1953, EdD, 1968. Diplomate Am. Bd. Profl. Psychology, Am. Bd. Counseling Psychology, Am. Bd. Psychoanalysis. Psychologist Queens Coll. Counseling Ctr., Flushing, NY, 1968-70, asst. dir., 1970-76, dir., 1976; gen. practice psychology NYC, 1970—. Faculty, supr. New Hope Guild, Bklyn., 1976—, dir. child and adolescent tng. prog., 1988-98; adj. prof. clin. psychology Columbia U., N.Y.C., 1986-2002; supr. NYU Postdoctoral Prog. in Psychoanalysis, 1988—; mem. com. on profl. practice and ethics Nat. Register Health Svc. Providers, 1998-2003. Author: (with Robert G. Simon): Choosing a College Major: Social Science, 1981; co-author 3 book chpts. on licensure and ethics in psychology; mem. editl. bd. The Counseling Psychologist jour., 1986-89, Profl. Practice and Rsch. in Psychology, 1994-99, Jour. Infant, Child and Adolescent Psych Therapy, 1999—. Vice chair N.Y. State Bd. for Psychology State Edn. Dept., Albany, 1978-82, chair, 1982-88; bd. dirs. Pelham (N.Y.) Guidance Coun., 1980-83; pres.-elect Assn. State and Provincial Psychology Bds., 1990, pres., 1991. Recipient Morton Berger award, Assn. State and Provincial Psychology Bds., 1998, Outstanding Psychologist award, Acad. Counseling Psychology, 2003. Fellow: APA (mem. bd. profl. affairs 1987—89, chair bd. profl. affairs 1988—89, policy and planning bd. 1991—93, mem. ethics com. 1995—97, vice chair ethics com. 1996—97, chair ethics com. 1997, workgroup on telehealth 1998—2000, mem. accreditation com. 2004—, non-govtl. orgnl. UN team assoc. mem. 2006—, John Black award 1994, Disting. Psychologist of Yr., Divsn. Ind. Practice 2004, Karl Heiser award 1993), Am. Bd. Counseling Psychology (bd. dirs. 1992—2000, pres.-elect 1999, pres. 2001—03), Nat. Acads. of Practice (elected disting. practitioner), Am. Bd. Profl. Psychology (trustee 1998—2001, pres.-elect 2001—, pres. 2004—05).

SIMON, PETER E., publishing executive; b. Bklyn., July 29, 1953; BA in English, CCNY, 1971; MA in Libr. Sci., Columbia U., 1980. Database mgr. R.R. Bowker, NYC, 1982-84; v.p. R.R. Bowker/Reed Reference Pubs., 1984-93; sr. v.p. Reed Reference Pub., New Providence, N.J., 1993-95, exec. v.p., 1995-97; v.p. bus. devel. Nat. Info. Svcs./Lexis-Nexis, Horsham, Pa., 1997-98; v.p. new product planning and devel. The Gale Group, Farmington Hills, Mich., 1998—, v.p. product mgmt., 1999, v.p. bus. devel., 1999-2000; dir. content lic. The Deal, LLC, NYC, 2000-2001; v.p. strategic devel. Digital Owl, Orlando, Fla., 2001—02; dir. new bus. devel. Nstein Techs. Corp., 2002—03; v.p. product mgmt. NewsBank, Inc., Naples, Fla., 2003—. Mem. Info. Industry Assn. (chmn. content divsn., bd. dirs.), Phi Beta Kappa.

SIMON, RAYMOND JOSEPH, federal agency and former school system administrator; b. Conway, Ark. m. Phyllis Simon; 1 child, Sandy. BS math./acctg., U. Ctrl. Ark., MS math.; MSE, sch. adminstrn., U. Ark. Math tchr. North Little Rock H.S.; with sch. food svcs. and computer svcs.; asst. supt. for fin. Conway Sch. Dist., Ark., supt. Ark., 1991—97; dir. Ark. Dept. Edn., Little Rock, 1997—2003; asst. sec., elem. and secondary edn. US Dept. Edn., Washington, 2004—05, acting dep. sec., 2005, dep. sec., 2005—. Adj. prof. U. Ctrl. Ark. Grad. Sch., U. Ark. Little Rock, Ark. State U., Beebe. Mem. Conway Planning Commn.; exec. bd. Quapaw Area Coun., Boy Scouts Am.; bd. dirs. Conway Civic Orch. Office: US Dept Edn 400 Maryland Ave SW Rm 7E308 Washington DC 20202 Office Phone: 202-401-0113. *

SIMON, ROBERT G., lawyer; b. NYC, Feb. 21, 1927; s. Monroe and Claire S. S.; m. Norma Plavnick, Dec. 18, 1949; children: Mark A., Susan. BA, Cornell U., 1947; LLB, JD, Georgetown U., 1950; LLM, NYU, 1961. Bar: D.C. 1950, N.Y. 1951, U.S. Supreme Ct. 1955. Assoc. firms in, NYC, 1950-52; legal sec. to judge U.S. Dist. Ct. So. Dist. N.Y., 1953-58; assoc. Jaffe & Wachtell, NYC, 1958-61; legal adv. TV series The Verdict Is Yours, 1958-60; successively dir. bus. affairs, v.p., sr. v.p., mgr. bus. affairs dept. McCann-Erickson, Inc., NYC, 1961-80; sr. broadcast atty. The Interpublic Group of Cos., NYC, 1980-95. Adj. faculty Manhattan Community Coll., 1967, Baruch Coll., 1968, CCNY, 1968, New Sch. Social Research, 1972-73; speaker in field. Author: (with Norma Simon) Choosing a College Major: The Social Sciences, 1981; contbr. articles to profl. jours. Dem.-Liberal candidate for county clk. Westchester County, N.Y., 1952; chmn. Narcotics Guidance Coun., Pelham, N.Y., 1973; mem. Nat. Media Coun. on Disability, 1986-90; bd. dirs., gen. counsel Nat. Challenge Com. on Disability, 1986-88; mem. adv. bd. The Caption Ctr. WGBH Found., 1987—; mem. state bd. for podiatry N.Y. State Dept. Edn., 2000—. With USAAF, 1944-46. Mem.: NATAS (chpt. gov. 1972—85, treas. 1976—81, 1st v.p. 1981—83, nat. trustee 1981—85, pres. 1983—85, chpt. gov. 1996—97, nat. trustee 1996—98), Am. Assn. Advt. Agy.s (com. on broadcast adminstrn. policy 1985—93), N.Y. County Lawyers Assn. (com. on comms. and entertainment law 1990—, not-for-profit orgns., alternate dispute resolution com. 1998—), Hemlock Soc. N.Y. (bd. dirs. 2000—02).

SIMON, RONALD CHARLES, curator, educator; b. Phila., Feb. 23, 1951; s. Samuel Charles and Emily (Luzenberg) Simon. BA, Dickinson Coll., 1973; postgrad., Brit. Film and TV Inst., Stirling, Scotland, 1973, Columbia U., 1973-75. Researcher NBC, NYC, 1976—77; mgr. media prodn. 1st Boston Corp., NYC, 1979; curator TV, Mus. TV and Radio, NYC, 1979—. Adj. prof. Hunter Coll., CUNY, 1987—, Columbia U., NYC, 1991—; cons., lectr. to mus. and colls. including Smithsonian Instn., Whitney Mus. Am. Art, NYU, Cooper Hewitt Mus., 1985—. Exhbns. curated include The Television of Dennis Potter, 1992, Witness to History, Jack Benny: The Radio and Television Work, 1991, contbg. author Encyclopedia of TV, 1997, Encyclopedia of Radio, 2002, creative cons., host CD-ROM Total TV, 1997; author: Worlds Without End: The Art and History of Soap Opera, 1997; advisor, contbg. author St. James Ency. Popular Culture, 1999, Violence in America: An Encyclopedia, 1999; author: The Television of Dennis Potter, 1992. Mem. George Foster Peabody Awards Bd., 2003—; bd. dirs. United Action for Animals, 2004—. Decorated chevalier of Art and Sci. Ministry of French Culture; Metzger Conway Fellow, Dickinson Coll., 2002, Cogan Alumni fellow, 2006. Mem.: NATAS (panelist and juror for numerous awards 1985—, mem. editl. bd. TV Quar. 1987—), TV Ltd. (bd. dirs. 2000—). Home: 141 E 17th St New York NY 10003-3402 Office: Television & Radio 25 W 52nd St New York NY 10019-6104 Home Phone: 212-475-6801; Office Phone: 212-621-6680. Personal E-mail: ronsimonnyc@yahoo.com. Business E-Mail: rsimon@mtr.org.

SIMON, RONALD ISAAC, financial executive; b. Cairo, Nov. 4, 1938; came to U.S., 1942; s. David and Helene (Zilkha) S.; m. Anne Faith Hartman, June 19, 1960; children: Cheryl, Eric, Daniel. BA, Harvard U., 1960; MA, Columbia U., 1962, PhD, 1968. V.p. Harpers Internat., NYC, 1959-62; fin. analyst Amerace Corp., NYC, 1965-66; v.p. Am. Foresight Inc., Phila., 1966-67; asst. to pres. Avco Corp., Greenwich, Conn., 1967-70; exec. v.p. Avco Community Developers Inc., La Jolla, Calif., 1970-73; pres. Ronald I. Simon Inc., La Jolla, 1973—99; pres., CEO Delta Data Systems Corp., Phila., 1980-81; exec. v.p. Towner Petroleum Corp., Houston, 1983-85; mng. dir., chief fin. officer The Henley Group Inc., La Jolla, 1986-90; pvt. practice fin. cons. La Jolla, 1990—2000. Vice-chmn. bd. dirs. Softnet Corp., San Francisco, 1998—2002, acting chmn. and CEO, 2001; CFO WingCast LLC, San Diego, 2001—02; bd. dirs. Collateral Therapeutics, Inc., San Diego, 1999—2002; exec. v.p., CFO/bd. dirs. Western Water Co., San Diego, 1997—2000; bd. dirs. Am. Independence Corp., NY, 2002—, WFS Fin., Inc., Irvine, Calif., 2003—06, BDI Investments, San Diego, 2003—05, Cardium Therapeutics, 2006—. Bd. dirs. San Diego Opera Co., 1988-90, Univ. Art Gallery U. Calif., San Diego, 1991-95; bd. dirs., treas. Lyric Opera, San Diego, 2003-2005. Ford Found. fellow, 1963-65.

SIMON, SHELDON WEISS, political science professor; b. St. Paul, Jan. 31, 1937; s. Blair S. and Jennie M. (Dim) S.; m. Charlann Lilwin Scheid, Apr. 27, 1962; 1 child, Alex Russell BA summa cum laude, U. Minn., 1958, PhD, 1964; MPA, Princeton U., 1960; postgrad., U. Geneva, 1962—63. Asst. prof., then prof. U. Ky., 1966-75; prof. polit. sci. Ariz. State U., 1975—, chmn. dept., 1975-79, dir. Ctr. Asian Studies, 1980-88. Vis. prof. George Washington U., 1965, U. B.C., Can., 1972-73, 79-80, Carleton U., 1976, Monterey Inst. Internat. Studies, 1991, 96, Am. Grad. Sch. Internat. Mgmt., 1991-92; cons. USIA Rsch. Analysis Corp., Am. Enterprise Inst. Pub. Policy Rsch., Hoover Instn., Orkand Corp.; cons., dir. S.E. Asian Projects, Nat. Bur. Asian Rsch., 1998—; Smithsonian Instn. lectr. internat. politics Crystal and Radisson Cruise Lines, 2000—. Author: Asian Neutralism and U.S. Policy, 1975, The ASEAN States and Regional Security, 1982, The Future of Asian-Pacific Security Collaboration, 1988; editor: The Military and Security in the Third World, 1978, East Asian Security in the Post-Cold War Era, 1993, Southeast Asian Security in the New Millenium, 1996, The Many Faces of Asian Security, 2001, Disrupting Violence: Religion and Conflict in South and Southeast Asia, 2006, others; contbr. articles to profl. jours., chpts. to books. Mem. Com. Fgn. Relations, Phoenix, 1976—; bd. dirs. Phoenix Little Theater, 1976-79 Grantee Am. Enterprise Inst., 1974, Earhart Found., 1979, 81, 92, 84, 88, U.S. Inst. Peace, 1994-96, 2000-01, Nat. Bur. Asian Rsch., 1998, W. Alton Jones Found., 2000, U.S. Pacific Command, 2002-03; Hoover Instn. fellow, 1980, 85; named Outstanding Alumni Notable Achievement, U. Minn., 2007. Mem. Am. Polit. Sci. Assn., Assn. Asian Studies, Internat. Studies Assn. (profl. ethics com. 1987-91, v.p. 1991-93), Asia Soc. (contemporary affairs com. 1987-92), U.S. Coun. for Asia-Pacific Security (exec. bd. 1998-2003), Phi Beta Kappa. Democrat. Jewish. Avocations: acting, singing, tennis. Home: 5630 S Rocky Point Rd Tempe AZ 85283-2134 Office: Ariz State U Polit Sci Dept Tempe AZ 85287-3902 Office Phone: 480-965-1317. Business E-Mail: shells@asu.edu.

SIMON, TREVOR, management consultant, educator, human resources specialist; s. Thelma Corrica and Patrick Simon; m. Julia Ruffins; 2 children. BS in Profl. Aeronautics, Embry-Riddle Aero. U., 1996; MBA in Human Resources Mgmt., Wayland Bapt. U., 2001; PhD, Capella U., Mpls., 2001—04. With USAF, 1986, dir. tng., 2003—; USAF tng. course developer 362nd Tng. Wing, Wichita Falls, Tex., 1990—98; dir., tng. Field Tng. Detachment, Clovis, N.Mex., 1998—; tchr. U. Phoenix, ITT Tech. Inst. Owner TS Consulting, Clovis, N.Mex., 1995—. Co-chair C. of C. Amb., Clovis, N.Mex., 2004. Decorated Global War on Terrorism Svc. medal, Korean Defense Svc. medal, NATO medal, Kuwait Liberation medal Kingdom of Saudi Arabia, Govt. Kuwait. Mem.: Nat. Bus. Edn. Assn., Toastmasters, Soc. Human Resource Mgmt., Acad. Mgmt. Achievements include development of a training program to eliminate backlogs in current training system. Avocations: reading, flying, travel. Home Phone: 505-762-1450; Office Phone: 505-784-4085. Personal E-mail: trevorsimon@email.uophx.edu.

SIMON, WILLIAM, retail executive; 2 children. B. in Economics, U. Conn., MBA. Various mktg. and devel. positions Cadbury-Schweppes, Pepsico, RJR-Nabisco; v.p. consumer mktg. Diageo PLC, 1998, pres. Southeast region; sec. Fl. Dept. Mgmt. Services, 2003—05; senior v.p. global bus. devel. Brinker Internat., Dallas, 2005—06; exec. v.p. specialty divsn. Wal-Mart Stores Inc., Bentonville, Ark., 2006—07, COO, 2007—. Served USN, served USNR. Office: Wal-Mart Stores Inc 702 SW Eighth St Bentonville AR 72716 *

SIMON, WILLIAM LEONARD, scriptwriter, television producer, writer, film producer; b. Washington, Dec. 3, 1930; s. Isaac B. and Marjorie (Felsteiner) Simon; m. Arynne Lucy Abeles, Sept. 18, 1966; 1 child, Victoria Marie 1 stepchild, Sheldon M. Bermont. BEE, Cornell U., 1954; MA in Ednl. Psychology, Golden State U., 1982, PhD in Comm., 1983. Writer features and TV movies, documentary and indsl. films, TV programs, 1958—; lectr. George Washington U., Washington, 1968-70. Juror Coun. Nontheatrical Events Film Festival, 1975—90, Cindy Festival Blue Ribbon Panel, 1985—; jury chmn., bd. dirs. CINE Film Festival, 1988—. Author: more than 600 produced works for motion pictures and TV; author: (screenplays) Fair Woman Without Discretion, Majorca, Swindle, A Touch of Love, In the Shadows of Her Life; author: (teleplays and documentaries) From Information to Wisdom, Flight of Freedom II, Missing You; writer, prodr. The Star of India: Setting Sail; co-author: Profit from Experience-The Story of Transformation Management, 1995, Lasting Change, 1997; author: Beyond the Numbers, 1996; co-author: On the Firing Line, My 500 Days at Apple Computer, 1998, High Velocity Leadership--The Mars Pathfinder Approach to Faster, Better, Cheaper, 1999, Driving Digital--What Microsoft is Learning from its Customers about Thriving in the Digital Revolution, 2000, The Afterlife Experiments--Breakthrough Scientific Evidence of Life After Death, 2002, The Art of Deception, 2002, In Search of Business Value, 2004, The Art of Intrusion: The Real Stories Behind the Exploits of Hackers, Intruders and Decievers, 2005, iCon: Steve Jobs - The Greatest Second Act in the History of Business, 2005, The Truth About Medium-Extraordinary Experiments with the Real Allison Du Bois of NBC's Medium, 2005, The G.O.D. Experiments, 2006, Gorgeous Disaster--The Tragic Story of Debra LaFave, 2006, The Healing Energy Experiments -- Science Reveals Our Natural Power to Heal, 2007, A Cat by the Tail, 2007, Think India--The Rise of the Next Superpower and What it Means for Every American, 2007. Pres. Foggy Bottom Citizens Assn., 1963—65, mem. exec. bd., 1965—69; v.p. Shakespeare Summer Festival, 1966—67, trustee, 1965—70. Mem. interview com. Cornell U., 1987—88. Lt. USN, 1954—58. Named 30 Best Bus. Books of 1997, Exec. Book Summaries; recipient 12 Golden Eagle awards, Cine Film Festival, Gold medal, N.Y. Internat. Festival, Freedoms Found., Gold Cindy, IFPA, awards, Berlin, Belgrade and Venice Film Festivals, others. Mem.: NATAS (gov. DC chpt. 1970—73, gov. San Diego chpt. 1998—2002), Writers Guild Am., Silver Cir., Rotary (bd. dirs., program chmn.), Tau Beta Pi, Eta Kappa Nu (chpt. pres. 1953—54). Republican. Avocations: crew member square-rigged brig Pilgrim, San Diego Museum ship Star of India, tennis. E-mail: bill@simon1.com.

SIMONCINI, MATTHEW J., manufacturing executive; BA in Acctg., Wayne State U., Detroit, 1985. With United Technologies Automotive; v.p. fin. Europe Lear Corp., 2001—04, v.p. operational fin., 2004—06, v.p. global fin., chief acctg. officer, 2006, sr. v.p. operational fin., 2006—. Office: Lear Corp 21557 Telegraph Rd PO Box 5008 Southfield MI 48086 Office Phone: 248-447-1500. Office Fax: 248-447-1722. *

SIMONDS, CHARLES FREDERICK, artist; b. NYC, Nov. 14, 1945; s. Robert and Anita I. (Bell) S. BA, U. Calif., Berkeley, 1967; MFA, Rutgers U., 1969. One man shows include Ctr. Nat. d'Art Contemporain, Paris, 1975, Mus. Modern Art, N.Y.C., 1976, Westfälischer Kunstverein, Munster, 1978, Mus. Ludwig, Cologne, 1979, Mus. Contemporary Art, Chgo., 1981, Phoenix (Ariz.) Mus. Art, 1982, Brooks Meml. Art Gallery, Memphis, 1982, Solomon R. Guggenheim Mus., N.Y., 1983, Leo Castelli Gallery, N.Y., 1984, Architekturmuseum, Bâle, 1985, Corcoran Gallery Art, Washington, 1988, Fundació "la Caixa," Barcelona, 1994, Galerie nat. Jeu Paume, Paris, 1994, retrospective IVAM, Valencia, Spain, 2003; exhibited in group shows Whitney Mus. Am. Art, N.Y., 1975, 77, Mus. d'Art moderne Ville de Paris, 1975, Stedelijk Mus., Amsterdam, 1978, Mus. Modern Art, N.Y., 1979, Hayward Gallery, London, 1980, Tate Gallery, London, 1983, Solomon R. Guggenheim Mus., N.Y., 1985, 87, 89; works included in publs. including Artforum, 1980, Art/Cahier, 1977, Sprache im Technischen Zeitalter, 1978, Art in America, 1983, Images and Issues, 1982, ARTnews, 1978, Beaux Arts, 1986. Fellow Am. Acad. Rome. Home: 26 E 22nd St New York NY 10010-6107 E-mail: simondse@aol.com.

SIMONDS, JOHN EDWARD, retired newspaper editor; b. Boston, July 4, 1935; s. Alvin E. and Ruth Angeline (Rankin) S.; m. Rose B. Muller, Nov. 16, 1968; children— Maximillian P., Malia G.; children by previous marriage— Rachel F. Cobb, John B. BA, Bowdoin Coll., 1957. Reporter Daily Tribune, Seymour, Ind., 1957-58, UPI, Columbus, Ohio, 1958-60; reporter, asst. city editor Providence Jour. Bull., 1960-65, Washington Evening Star, 1965-66; corr. Gannett News Svc., Washington, 1966-75; mng. editor Honolulu Star Bull., 1975-80, exec. editor, 1980-87, sr. editor, editl. page editor, 1987-93; exec. Hawaii Newspaper Agy., Honolulu, 1993-99; reader rep. The Honolulu Advertiser, Honolulu, 1999—2002; ret., 2002. Served with U.S. Army, 1958. Mem. Am. Soc. Newspaper Editors, AP Mng. Editors, Soc. Profl. Journalists, Nat. Conf. Editl. Writers, Orgn. News Ombudsmen, Hawaii Lit. Arts Coun. Home: 5316 Nehu Pl Honolulu HI 96821-1941 Office: The Honolulu Advertiser 605 Kapiolani Blvd Honolulu HI 96813-5195 Home Phone: 808-373-3609; Office Phone: 808-383-7984. Personal E-mail: simondsj001@hawaii.rr.com.

SIMONDS, MARSHALL, retired lawyer; b. Boston, Sept. 17, 1930; s. Sidney Lawrence and Evelyn (Peterson) S.; m. Katharine Blewett, May 9, 1969; children: Robert Bradley, Joshua Lawrence. BA, Princeton U., 1952; LLB, Harvard U., 1955. Bar: Mass. 1955. Since practiced in Boston; ptnr. Goodwin, Procter & Hoar, Boston, 1965-2000; counsel Mass. Crime Commn., 1963-65; spl. asst. atty. gen. Commonwealth of Mass., 1964-66. Dir. Dynatech Corp., 1960-85, Data Packaging Corp., 1972-79; trustee Middlesex Instn. Savs., 1974-79 Moderator of Carlisle, Mass., 1967-2000; trustee Trustees for Reservations, 1972-78; bd. dirs. South Boston Neighborhood House, 1972-78. Served with USMCR, 1955. Fellow Am. Coll. Trial Lawyers, Am. Bar Found., Mass. Bar Found.; mem. ABA, Mass. Bar Assn., Boston Bar Assn. (coun. 1980-82), New Eng. Legal Found. (dir.), Am. Kennel Club (del.), Labrador Retriever Club (bd. dirs.), Orthopedic Found. for Animals (bd. dirs.), Harvard Club (Boston). Address: Bliss Hill Rd Morrisville VT 05661 E-mail: coppertoot@aol.com.

SIMONE, JOSEPH R., lawyer; b. NYC, Jan. 7, 1949; m. Virginia E. Simone, May 29, 1971; children: Jacquelyn, Robert. BA cum laude, Queens Coll., 1971; LLM in Taxation, NYU, 1977; JD cum laude, Fordham U., 1974. Bar: N.Y. 1975, U.S. Dist. Ct. (so. dist.) N.Y. 1975, U.S. Ct. Appeals (2d cir.) 1975. Ptnr. Patterson, Belknap, Webb & Tyler, NYC, 1982-88, Schulte, Roth & Zabel, NYC, 1988—2002; spl. prof. law Hofstra U. Sch. Law, 1998—2006; of counsel Pitney Hardin LLP, NYC, 2003—, ptnr., 2004—06, Day Pitney LLP, NYC, 2007—. Author: (textbooks) Pension Answer Book, 5th edit., 1990, Essential Facts: Pension and Profit-sharing Plans, 1999; editl. advisor Jour. of Pension Planning. Mem. Am. Arbitration Assn. (panel on multiemployer pension plans), Am. Coll. Employee Benefits (counsel 2003—), Phi Beta Kappa. Office: Day Pitney LLP 7 Times Sq New York NY 10036 Office Phone: 212-297-5859. Business E-Mail: jsimone@daypitney.com.

SIMONE, RENATA, television producer; MPhil, Harvard U. Prodr. & reporter WGBH Nat. Prodns., Boston; exec. prodr. documentaries Sundance Inst. Prodr.: (TV series) The AIDS Quarterly, 1987—, The Health Quarterly, 1991—, Growing Up in the Age of AIDS, 1992; (documentaries) AIDS Research: The Story So Far, 1994, Frontline: A Whale of a Business, 1997, Frontline: The Age of AIDS, 2006. Co-recipient George F. Peabody award, 2002; recipient Robert F. Kennedy Journalism award, 1990, 2007, Sci. Journalism award, AAAS, 2003, Alfred I. duPont-Columbia U. award, 2007. Office: WGBH PO Box 200 Boston MA 02134 *

SIMONEAU, CYNTHIA LAMBERT, editor, educator; b. Central Falls, RI, May 18, 1958; d. Roland and L. Jean Simoneau; m. Paul E. Lambert, Oct. 24, 1981; children: Thomas S. Lambert, Marc S. Lambert. BA, U. R.I., 1980. Asst. news editor Newtown (Conn.) Bee, 1980-82; reporter Bridgeport (Conn.) Post & Telegram, 1982-83, bur. chief, 1983-91; editor Woman Wise Conn. Post, Bridgeport, 1991-97, asst. mng. editor, 1997—2004, cons. newspaper editor, 2004—. Adj. prof. So. Conn. State U., New Haven, 19932007, asst. prof., 2007—, Fairfield (Conn.) 2003—, Sacred Heart U., Fairfield, Conn., 2004-2007, Quinnipiac U., Hamden, Conn., 2005-2007. Eucharistic min., mem. parish adv. coun., former religious edn. tchr., St. Thomas Aquinas Ch., Fairfield, Conn. Mem. Soc. Profl. Journalists (bd. dirs. Conn. chpt. 1983-2003, treas. Conn. chpt. 1985-95, 2003—, pres. Conn. chpt. 1995-97, Journalism Excellence awards for news stories and columns, 3 Pres.'s awards Conn. chpt., Women of Dist. award Girl Scout Coun.). Avocation: reading. Office: Conn Post 410 State St Bridgeport CT 06604 E-mail: csimonea@aol.com.

SIMONEAU, DANIEL ROBERT, application developer, accountant, educator, artist; b. Lewiston, Maine, Aug. 3, 1962; s. Robert Eugene and Rolande Muriel (Plante) S. BFA, U. So. Maine, 1984. Reconciling specialist Fleet/Norstar Bank of Maine, Lewiston, 1981—84, acct., 1984—88, Sterling Engineered Products, Auburn, Maine, 1988—89; fin. analyst Pioneer Plastics Corp., Auburn, Maine, 1989—91; acct. Aeroquip Corp., New Haven, Ind., 1992, coord. adminstrv. sys. Maumee, Ohio, 1992—93, acct., 1993—94, Trinova Corp., Maumee, 1994—96, chmn. employee activities com. ann. outing Toledo, 1995; fin. edn. specialist PeopleSoft, Inc., Westchester, Ill., 1996—98, instr. master tech., 2000—02; sr. cons. Revere Group, Deerfield, Ill., 1998—2000, functional specialist, 2000; PeopleSoft developer Robert W. Baird, Milw., 2002—. Asst. v.p. Robert W. Baird, Milw., 2003—06, v.p., 2007—, leader application devel. team, 2005—; treas. Cream City Found., 2003—05. Contbr. article to mag. Chmn. award winners show Spectrum Friends of Fine Art, Toledo, 1995. Recipient Recognition award Spectrum Friends of Fine Art, 1994, Com. award Spectrum Gallery, 1994, 3d pl. award Toledo Fedn. Art Socs., 1992, 3d Judge's award Lewiston Art Festival Com., 1988, 90, 91, Purchase award Portland Art Festival Com., 1981, 91. Mem. Northwestern Ohio Watercolor Soc., Coll. Art Assn., Friends of Arts Chgo., Transparent Watercolor Soc. Am. (life, membership chair 2003-05), Midwest Water Color Soc. (life), Wis. Watercolor Soc., Wis. Painters and Sculptors. Office: Robert W Baird 777 E Wisconsin Ave Milwaukee WI 53201-0672 Home: 9507 74th St Kenosha WI 53142-8194

SIMONIAN, SIMON JOHN, surgeon, scientist, educator, health science association administrator; b. Antioch, French Ter., Apr. 20, 1932; arrived in U.S., 1965, naturalized, 1976; s. John Simon and Marie (Tomboulian) Simonian; m. Arpi Ani Yeghiayan, July 11, 1965; children: Leonard Armen, Charles Haig, Andrew Hovig. MD, U. London, 1957; BA in Animal Physiology, St. Edmund Hall, U. Oxford, Eng., 1964; MSc in Nutrition, Immunology and Genetics, Harvard U., 1967, ScD in Nutrition, Immunology and Genetics, 1969; MA in Animal Physiology, U. Oxford, 1969; DSc (hon.), Nat. Acad. Scis., Armenia, 1998. Diplomate Am. Bd. Surgery, 1977. Rschr., team mem. smallpox vaccine lyophilization immunology unit Lister Inst. Preventive Medicine, Elstree, Essex, England, 1951—52; intern in medicine Univ. Coll. Hosp., London, 1957; intern in surgery Edinburgh Royal Infirmary, Scotland, 1957—58, resident in surgery, 1961—62; clin. clk. Nat. Hosp. & Inst. of Neurology, 1958; resident Edinburgh Western Gen. Hosp., 1958-59, City Hosp., Edinburgh, Birmingham Accident and Burns Hosp., U. Birmingham, Eng., 1959-60; demonstrator dept. anatomy Edinburgh U., 1960-61; rsch. fellow in pathology Lab. Chem. Pathology Harvard U., Harvard Med. Sch., Boston, 1965-68; trainee NIH US Army Devel. Command Immunology Rsch. Harvard Med. Sch., 1967; instr. immunology Harvard Med. Sch., Boston, 1966-70, instr. in surgery and immunology, 1968—69, surg. dir. course on transplantation, biology and medicine, 1968-70, assoc. in surgery and immunology, 1969—70; vis. prof., invited spkr. Harvard Med. Sch., Mass. Gen. Hosp., Brigham and Womens Hosp., New Eng. Deaconess Hosp., 1982; dir. transplantation immunology unit, lab. asst. in surgery Brigham and Womens Hosp., Boston, 1968-70; resident in surgery Boston City Hosp., 1970-74; attending surgeon in transplantation and gen. surgery services U. Chgo. Med. Ctr., 1974-77; asst. prof. surgery, mem. com. immunology U. Chgo., 1974-77; dir., surgeon-in-chief divsn. renal transplantation Hahnemann U. Sch. Medicine and Hosp., 1978-87, prof. surgery, 1978-88, chmn. Transplantation Com., 1983-88, chmn. quality assurance of surgery com., 1986-88; dept. surgery coord. with joint commn. for accreditation of hosps. Hahnemann U. Sch. Medicine, 1986—88; chief and chmn. dept. surgery twelve divsns. St. John Hosp. and Med. Ctr., Detroit, 1988-89, chmn. credentials com. of surgery and oper. rm. com., 1988-89, assoc. v.p. for med. affairs, 1989-90; pres., CEO Vein Inst. Met. Washington, Inc., 1990—2006; assoc. attending staff Fairfax Hosp., Falls Church, Va., 1990-92, active attending faculty, 1992—; guest lectr., 1994, 99; clin. assoc. prof. surgery Georgetown U. Sch. Medicine, Washington, 1992-95, guest lectr., 1994—, clin. prof. surgery, 1995—. Vis. prof., invited spkr. Vanderbilt U., 1968, Cedars-Sinai Med. Ctr., UCLA, 1977, Addenbroke's Hosp., Cambridge U., 1977, Karolinska Inst., Stockholm, 1977, Huddinge Hosp., U. Stockholm, 1977, Med. Coll. Pa. and Hosp., 1980, 81, 85, Grad. Hosp., U. Pa., 1981, 85, U. Athens, 1981, U. Coll. Hosp., U. London, 1981, Western Gen. Hosp. Edinburg U., 1981, VA Hosp., Tufts U., 1982, John Radcliffe Hosp., U. Oxford, 1982, Nat. Acad. Scis., Yerevan, Armenia, 1995, St. Edmund Hall, U. Oxford, 1997, Christ Ch. Hosp., Chgo., 1974—77, South Chgo. Hosp., 1974—77, Del. Med. Ctr., Wilmington, 1977, Wilkes Barre (Pa.) Gen. Hosp., 1979, Robert Packer Hosp., Guthrie Clinic, Sayre, Pa., 1980, Abington Meml. Hosp., Phila., 1982, Crozer Chester Med. Ctr., Pa., 1982, St. Agnes Hosp. Med. Ctr., Phila., 1982, Sacred Heart Hosp., 1982, Riverview Hosp., Red Bank, NJ, 1983, Easton (Pa.) Hosp., Allentown, 1983, Newcombe Med. Ctr., Vineland, NJ, 1983, Cath. Med. Ctr., Manchester, NH, 1984, Burlington County Med. Ctr., Mount Holly, NJ, 1984; cons. Michael Reese Hosp., Chgo., 1976—77; cons. gen. surgery City of Phila., 1986—88; cons. vascular surgery Coll. Podiatry, Phila., 1986—88; cons. venous vascular surgery Podiatry Residence Program, No. Va. Med. Coll., Richmond, 1994—; cons. surgery John F. Kennedy Meml. Hosp., Stratford, NJ, 1982—86, St. Agnes Hosp. Med. Ctr., Phila., 1982—86; cons. Am.-Armenian Cultural Assn., 2001; surgeon in chief, med. team support U.S. Pres. Ronald W. Reagan, 1988, George H. W. Bush, 1989, U.S. Presdl. visits to Detroit; vis. surgeon Inst. Vein Disease, Mich., 1989—90; vis. scientist Argonne Nat. Lab., Ill., 1969, vis. scientist, collaborator, 1974—77; founding mem. sci. bd. ctr. regenerative biology and medicine Ind. U., 2001—; invited spkr., panelist 8th Internat. Congress of Nephrology, Athens, 1981, 1st Internat. Soc. for Edn. and Rsch. in Vascular Disease, San Diego, 1992, 4th Internat. Dialogue Transition to Global Soc., U. Md., College Park, 1995; invited spkr. 3d Armenian Med. World Congress, Montreal, 1986, 4th Armenian Med. World Congress, LA, 1989; invited spkr., chairperson of session 5th Armenian Med. World Congress, Paris, 1992; invited spkr. 6th Armenian Med. World Congress, Boston, 1995, 7th Armenian Med. World Congress, Lyon, France, 1998, Internat. Forum Plebology, Frankfurt, 2000, 01, 03, 04, 8th Armenian Med. World Congress, Toronto, 2001, Internat. Soc. Lymphology, 2001; eminent scholar external assessor dept. surgery U. Zambia, Lusaka, 1994; mem. faculty, moderator internat. consensus panel The Investigation Chronic Venous Insufficiency, Paris, 1997; mem. internat. consensus panel Thromboembolism, Rhodes, Greece, 1999, Thrombophilia, Limasol, Cyprus, 2003, The Prevention, Investigation and Treatment of Venous Thromboembolism and Thrombophilia, Windsor, England, 2005; sci. advisor, invited spkr., panelist 8th Pan-Am. Congress Phlebology and Lymphology, Campo Grande, Brazil, 1998; lectr, invited spkr., panelist 9th Pan-Am. Congress Phlebology and Lymphology, Cordoba, Argentina, 2000; hon. mem. Internat. Forum Phlebology and Minisurgery of Varicose Veins, Frankfurt, Germany, 2000; Guthrie lectr. Robert Packer Hosp., 1980; Venus lectr., Rhodes, Greece, 99, Internat. Union Angiolo European Chpt. Congress, 2003; Diomed. lectr., 03; Kwang Dong lectr. Phlebological Soc. Korea Ann. Congress, Seoul, 2003; BSN Jobst lectr. Internat. Union Phlebology USA Congress, San Diego, 2003; keynote spkr. 18th Internat. Union Angiolo World Congress, Tokyo; Jonathan E. Rhoads ann. orator Phila. Acad. Surgery, 1984. Co-author: (books) Manual of Vascular Access Procedures, 1987, Prevention of Venous Thromboembolism, 2002, Diagnosis and Treatment of Lymphedema, 2006, Prevention and Treatment of Venous Thromboembolism, 2006; cons. to editl. bd. Dateline: Issues in Transplantation, 1985—87, mem. editl. bd. Phila. Medicine, 1988, Transplantation Procs., 1987—96, Jour. Transplantation Abstracts, 1969—70, Internat. Angiology, 1998—, assoc. editor Am. Coll. Phlebology Vein Line, 2000—06, reviewer Jour. Oncology and Dermatologic Surgery, 1993, Jour. Dermatologic Surgery, 1997, Jour. Vascular Surgery, 2000—, The Surgeon Journal Royal College of Surgeons Edinburgh and Ireland, Venous Digest, 2002; editor (translator in English): Short Saphenous Vein issue, Jour. de Phlebologie, 1999; contbr. articles to profl. jours. and books; appeared in med. movie Giving. Co-founder Armenian Youth Soc., London, Eng., 1953, pres. 1953-54; Armenian Studies Program U. Chgo., 1975; bd. govs. Friends Sch., London, 1964-65; Mass. del., co-founder Armenian Assembly of Am., Washington, 1970-74; fellow-trustee, co-founder Entry into Manhood of Armenian Youth at Age 13, 1981; co-founder Armenian Am. Health Assn. of Greater Washington, 1992, mem. pharms. com. 1992—, chmn. nominating com., 1993; sec., bd. dirs. Woodrock Inc., Potomac, Md., 1993-94; mem. Am. Friends of St. Edmund Hall, U. Oxford, 1992—, U.S. Campaign for St. Edmund Hall, 1995—, mem. bd. advisors, 1999-03, mem. campaign steering bd., 2000—; mem. St. Mary's Armenian Apostolic Ch., Washington, guest preacher, 1994, 95, 96; guest spkr. Armenian Ch. Youth Orgn. Am., Washington, 1998; bd. dirs. Am. Friends State U. Armenia, Yerevan, 1994-, mammography unit and wellness ctr. State Med. U., Yerevan, Armenia, 1997-98, Arlington (Va.) Symphony Orch., 1992-96, sci. com. Armenia-U.S.A., 1996—; mem. regional com. U.S. Campaign for Univ. Oxford, 1993; active amphitheatre endowment fund Boston City Hosp., 1994; fundraiser Eurasia Found., 1996; sci. advisor, chmn. session, invited spkr. Internat. Union Plebology, World Congress, 11th, Monreal, Can., 1992, 12th, London, Eng., 1995, 13th, Sydney, Australia, 1998, 14th, Rome, 2001; sci. advisor, chmn. session, invited spkr. Internat. Union Angiology World, Congress 17th, London, Eng., 1995, 18th, Tokyo, 1998, 19th, NYC, 2001, 20th, Rome, 2004, 15th, Brazil, 2005; bd. advisors Georgetown U. Ctr. for Advancement, 2007—, Am. U. of Armenia Devel. Coun., 2007—; bd. visitors Brigham and Women's Hosp., Boston Harvard U. Med. Sch., 2007—, Cornell U. Weill Med. Coll., 2007-, NY Presbyn. Hosp., 2007—, U. Mich. Med. Ctr., Ann Arbor, 2007—, Tufts U., Boston, 2007. H.J. Turtle scholar, 1943-46, R. Wright scholar, 1943-46, A. Koundakjian scholar, 1943-48, K. Clay scholar, 1946-48, Nairn scholar London U., 1949-52, Middlesex scholar London U., 1952-57; recipient N.K. Harris award, 1946, Leadership award, 1949, Suckling prize obstetric rsch. U. London, 1956, Brit. Med. Rsch. Coun. award Lab. Physiology Oxford U., 1962-64, NIH award transplantation and immunology rsch. Harvard Med. Sch. and Peter Bent Brigham Hosp., 1970, R. Alt prize surg. rsch. Boston City Hosp. and Beverly Hosp., 1973, Thompson award immunological rsch. U. Chgo., 1974-77, Johnson award immunological rsch. U. Chgo., 1975-77, Upjohn award, 1982, Presdl. Rep. Ronald Reagan Medal of Merit, 1982, U.S. Pres. Ronald W. Reagan Seal and Medal, 1988, Richard Kabakjian award eradication of small pox Armenian Student Assn. Am., 1986, Disting. Alumni award Med. Soc. St. Edmund Hall, U. Oxford, 1997, Kaken award Tokyo, 1998, STD award Cordoba, Argentina, 2000, Contbns. to Health Rsch. award; named Outstanding New Citizen of Citizenship Coun. Met. Chgo. and Dept. Justice, Washington, 1976; Businessman of Yr. Leadership award Nat. Rep. Congl. Com., 2003, Physician of Yr. Leadership award, 2003, Stanley N. Gershoff PhD prize Friedman sch. nutrition, sci. and policy Tufts U., Boston, 2006; co-endowed The John and Marie J. Simonian award, St. Nerces Sem., 1981, John R. Pfeifer, MD Rsch. award, Providence Hosp., Southfield, Mich., 1992, Joseph E. Murray, MD prof. plastic surgery Harvard Brigham Women and Children's Hosps., Boston, 1999, John R. Pfeifer MD prof. vascular surgery U. Mich., Ann Arbor, 2006, David B. Skinner MD prof. thoracic surgery Weill Cornell Med. Coll. NY Presbyn. Hosp., 2006; endowed Marie J. Simonian Prize, Georgetown U. Hosp. Med. Ctr., 1991 (prize com. 1991—), The Thomas J. Gill III MD prize dept. pathology Brigham Women's Hosp., Boston, 2003, Simon J. and Arpi A. Simonian Prize for scholastic excellence for doctoral candidates, dept. nutrition sch. pub. health Harvard U., 2006; Philanthropy Recognition award Hahnemann U., 1980—; named to Wall Inova's Claude Moore Health Edn. Ctr., Fairfax, Va., 2006, Guide to Am.'s Top Surgeons, Consumer's Rsch. Coun., 2006—; grantee U.S. Govt., industry cos., founds. Fellow: ACS (Phila., Mich. and Washington chpts.), Am. Coll. Phlebology (invited spkr. La Quinta 2001, invited spkr. Ft. Lauderdale 2005), Phila. Acad. Surgery (Jonathan E. Rhoads ann. orator 1984—, Samuel D. Gross prize com. 1988), Royal Coll. Surgeons Edinburgh; mem.: APHA, AAAS, AAUP (hon.), AMA, Leadership Coun., Harvard Sch. Pub. Health (founding mem. 2003—), Phlebological Surgery Sect., Am. Coll. Phlebology (founding chair, bd. dirs. 2002—03, past chair 2003—), Ambulatory Phlebectomy Sect., Am. Coll. Phlebology (chmn. program com. and sec. treas. 1999—2001, sect. chair elect 2000—01, chair, bd. dirs. 2001—02), European Acad. Scis. and Arts (fgn.), Northern Va. Med. Soc., North Am. Soc. Phlebology, Chgo. Soc. Gastroenterology, Transplantation Soc. (membership com. 1980—82), Pa. Med. Soc., Phila. County Med. Soc. (rep. ctr. city br. 1981—83, pres. 1984, bd. dirs. 1985—87, chairperson long range planning com. 1986—98), Greater Del. Valley Soc. Transplant Surgeons (councilor 1978—80, pres. elect 1980—82, pres. 1982—85, councilor 1985—88), Phila. Acad. Scis. (invited spkr. 1982, co-chmn. membership com. 1982—88), Chgo. Soc. Gastroenterology, Assn. of Ill. Transplant Surgeons, Am. Venous Forum (co-chair session, ofcl. disscussant 10th ann. meeting 1999, invited spkr. Ft. Myers 2001, chair Internat. Rels. Com. 2001—02, invited spkr. La Jolla 2002), Am. Soc. Transplant Surgeons (co-founding mem. 1974, chair immunosuppression studies com. 1974—77, membership com. 1980—82), NY Acad. Scis., Internat. Forum Phelbology (hon.), Samuel Hahnemann Surg. Soc., Am. Coll. Phlebology (curriculum devel. projects com. 1992—2006, co-chmn. symposiums and session 1992—, faculty 1993—2006, panelist 10th ann. congress 1996, membership com. 1998—2006, chmn. sci. program com. 13th ann. congress 1999, program chair 14th ann. congress 2000, invited spkr. Atlanta 2000, invited spkr. Ft. Lauderdale 2002), Internat. Cardiovasc. Soc. (chair session 22d world congress 1995, N.Am. chpt.), European Soc. Organ Transplant, Am. Soc. Artificial Internal Organs, Am. Technion Soc., Wayne County Med. Soc., Greater Washington Telecomm. Assn. (pres.' club 1994), Korean Soc. Phlebology (hon.), Am. Soc. Lymphology (nat. adv. bd., chair sci. com. 1999—, pres.-elect 2000—01, invited spkr. La Quinta 2001, pres. 2001—03, invited spkr. Kansas City 2002, re-elected pres. 2003—06), Am. Fedn. Clin. Rsch., Transplantation Soc. Mich., Assn. Acad. Surgery, Armenian Med. and Dental Assn. Greater Phila. (co-founder 1983, pres. 1983—85, Outreach award 1986), Assn. for Study of Med. Edn., Physicians for Social Responsibility, Cancer Rsch. Assn. Boston, Am. Venous Found. (bd. dirs. 2002—06), Brit. Med. Assn., Am. Armenian Med. Assn. (co-founder 1972, 25th anniversary co-founder award 1997), Nat. Assn. Armenian Studies and Rsch. (rep. Midatlantic region 1994—2003, bd. dirs. 2004—06), Royal Coll. Physicians of London Licentiates, Med. Soc. Va., Fairfax County Med. Soc., Mich. State Med. Soc., Chgo. Assn. Immunologists, Detroit Surgical Assn., Detroit Acad. Surgery, Am. Coll. Physician Execs., Am. Assn. Vascular Surgery (invited spkr. 2000), Royal Coll. Surgeons of Eng., Nat. Acad. Scis. Armenia (fgn.), Organ Procurement Agy. Mich. (adv. bd. 1988—89), Soc. Brigham Surg. Alumni, Armenian Gen. Benevolent Union (invited spkr. 1982, pres.' club 1990—), End Stage Renal Disease Network 24 (med. rev. bd. 1980—82, 1986—87), Oxford and Cambridge Soc., Immunology Club Boston, Med. Club (Phila.), Harvard Club, Oxford Soc., Sigma Xi. Mem. Soc. Of Friends. Achievements include bilateral lung reimplantation resulting in normal function without vagus nerves; reversal of renal allograft rejection using IgG concentrate of antilymphocyte serum (ALS) and of antihymocyte globulin (ATG); prevention and treatment of massive gastroduodenal hemorrhage from hemorrhagic gastritis using pioneering antacids to neutralize gastric acid pH7; co-discovered essential amino acids phenylalanine and tryptophan that are essential for antibody formation; participated in the lyophilization of the smallpox vaccine which was used by the WHO in 1966; to vaccinate everybody resulting in eradication of smallpox in 1977 which was the first and only major disease eradicated in the history of medicine and public health; co-discoverer of immunogenetic control of antibody formation that will lead to design future drugs to treat patients as genetically unique to the prevention of hypertension and arthritis; research advantages and disadvantages and prevention of splenectomy in renal transplant recipients; stage-enmasse cardiopulmonary reimplantation that resulted in normal function without vagus nerves; zinc deficiency depresses the action of zinc dependent enzymes, priming the recipient with donor antigen improves kidney transplant survival; discovery of stable bonding protein carriers and cytotoxic agents for treatment of organ transplant rejection and cancer; combined surgery and sclerotherapy corrects abnormal structure, function and aesthetics of leg varicose veins; pioneering conversion of arteriovenous shunt to arteriovenous fistula for immediate long term hemodialysis; first to use needle phlebectomy in USA; first to use beaver microblade phlebectomy; first to use bupivacaine wound infiltration in venous surgery wounds to minimize post operative pain; abolition of concurrent deep and perforator vein incompetence by surgical correction of superficial vein incompetence; evolving concepts in management of accute superficial and deep thromboembolism, phlebolymphedema; first to develop the largest phlebology organization participating with insurance in the United States; first to use the name Vein Institute.

SIMONIN, HOWARD A., biologist; b. Ypsilanti, Mich., Mar. 13, 1949; s. Joe W. and Myrtle D. Simonin; m. Martha M. Cavanaugh, Feb. 19, 1983; children: Paul W., Mark A. BS, SUNY, Syracuse, 1971; MS, Mich. State U., East Lansing, 1973. Aquatic biologist NY State Dept. Environ. Conservation, Rome, 1974—79, 1983—; fish pond specialist U. S. Peace Corps, Roseau, Dominica, 1979—81; biologist aid Nat. Park Svc., Ind., 1982—83. Contbr. articles to profl. jours. Scoutmaster, asst. scoutmaster Boy Scout Troop 55, Holland Patent, NY, 1995—; bldg. chmn. First United Meth. Ch., Rome, 2005—. Mem.: Am. Chem. Soc., NY Chpt. Am. Fisheries Soc. (environ. concerns chmn. 1994—2000), Am. Fisheries Soc. (cert. fisheries profl. 1984). Achievements include research in effects of pesticides, acid rain, and mercury on aquatic life. Avocations: camping, fishing, canoeing. Office: New York State Dept Environmental Cons 8314 Fish Hatchery Rd Rome NY 13440 Office Phone: 315-337-0910. Office Fax: 315-337-0988. Business E-Mail: hasimoni@gw.dec.state.ny.us.

SIMONS, ALBERT, III, lawyer; b. Charleston, SC, Nov. 22, 1950; s. Albert Jr. and Caroline Pinckney (Mitchell) S.; m. Theodora Bonnell Wilbur, Jan. 28, 1970; children: Albert IV, Charles A., Theodora B. BA, U. Va., 1972, JD, 1976. Bar: S.C. 1977, N.Y. 1978. Ptnr. Orrick, Herrington & Sutcliffe, NYC, 1984—. Mem. S.C. Bar Assn., N.Y. State Bar Assn. Office: Orrick Herrington & Sutcliffe 666 5th Ave Rm 203 New York NY 10103-1798 Business E-Mail: asimons@orrick.com.

SIMONS, ANNEKE PRINS, artist, educator; b. Amsterdam, The Netherlands, Feb. 15, 1930; arrived in U.S., 1940; d. Raphael Hugo and Charlotte Prins. BA, Vassar Coll., Poughkeepsie, NY, 1952; MAT, Harvard-Radcliffe, Cambridge, Mass., 1953; PhD, Pa. State U., Univ. Park, Pa., 1968; MA in Social Sci., Jersey City State Coll., Jersey City, NJ, 1975. Tchr., originator adult art edn. South End House, Boston, 1953—54; part-time asst. tchr. Boston Mus. Children's Rm., Boston, 1954—56; with Met. Mus. Art, NYC, 1957—61; tchr., art dir. Twin Pines, Oakland, Calif., 1961—62; grad. rsch. asst. tchr. art edn. Pa. State. U., Univ. Park, Pa., 1962—64; prof. N.J. City U., 1967—2000; prof. emeritus. Senator-at-large Jersey City State Coll., mem. personnel com. art dept., dir. art program gifted H.S. students. One-woman shows include The Courtney Gallery, Jersey City State Coll., 1979, The Gallery, Jersey City, NJ, 1981, Stevens Inst. Tech., Hoboken, NJ, 1984, Jersey City Mus., 1996, exhibited in group shows at Gallery Stendhal, NYC, 1991, Jersey City State Coll., 1992, juried show, C.A.S.E. Mus., Jersey City, NJ, 1982, exhibitions include Lemmerman Gallery, NJ City U., 1999, City Spirit Cultural Arts Festival, Jersey City, NJ, 1981 (Best in Show, 1981), Visceglia Art Ctr. Caldwell Coll., Caldwell, NJ, 1994, The Rotunda Gallery, City Hall, Jersey City, NJ, 1995, Viridian Gallery, NYC, 1997, numerous others; contbr. articles to profl. jours. Co-founder Genesis Project, Jersey City, 1986—2004. Recipient Martin Luther King, Jr. Cmty. Svc. award, Jersey City U., 1999; grantee Chinese Art Hist. Coll. Tchrs. summer seminar, Nat. Endowment Humanities, 1975; grad. sch. fellowship, Pa. State U., 1964—65. Mem.: Harvard Club NY, NJ.

SIMONS, BARBARA, retired elementary school educator; b. NYC, May 25, 1947; d. Abraham William and Gertrude (Monash) Cohn; m. Bernard Louis Simons, Dec. 23, 1972. BA, Bklyn. Coll., 1969; MS, Syracuse U., 1970. Lic. tchr., N.Y. Tchr. Pub. Sch. 209K, Bklyn., 1970-71, Pub. Sch. 177K, Bklyn., 1971-75, Pub. Sch. 95K, Bklyn., 1975-92, Pub. Sch. 215K, Bklyn., 1993—2002; ret., 2002. Mem. Am. Fedn. Tchrs., United Fedn. Tchrs. (del. 1976-90), N.Y. United Tchrs., N.Y. Edn. Guild. Avocations: tennis, travel, bowling, golf. Home: 2428 E 27th St Brooklyn NY 11235-2004

SIMONS, BARBARA M., lawyer; b. NYC, Feb. 7, 1929; d. Samuel A. and Minnie (Mankes) Malitz; m. Morton L. Simons, Sept. 2, 1951; 1 child, Claudia. BA, U. Mich., 1950, JD, 1952. Bar: N.Y. 1953, U.S. Supreme Ct. 1963, U.S. Ct. Appeals (D.C. cir.) 1971, (5th cir.) 1992, (1st cir.) 1994. Ptnr. Simons & Simons, Washington, 1962—. Pres. Forest Hills Citizens Assn., Washington, 1998-2002; past pres. D.C. chpt. U. Mich. Alumnae, Washington. Alumnae scholar U. Mich., 1946-50. Mem. Washington Coun. Lawyers, Nat. Partnership Women & Families, Sierra Club, Nat. Symphony Orch. Assn., Phi Beta Kappa, Phi Kappa Phi, Alpha Lambda Delta. Office: Simons & Simons 5025 Linnean Ave NW Washington DC 20008-2042

SIMONS, BARRY THOMAS, lawyer; b. Lynn, Mass., Dec. 14, 1946; s. Emanuel Isador and Betty (Darish) S.; m. Laurie Jean Louder, May 5, 1985; children: Britton Eugene, Brett Jacob. BS in Govt., Am. Univ., 1968; JD, NYU, 1971. Bar: Calif. 1971, U.S. Dist. Ct. (ctrl. dist.) Calif. 1972, U.S. Ct. Appeals (9th cir.) 1972, U.S. Supreme Ct. 1978, U.S. Dist. Ct. (so. and no. dists.) Calif. 1979. Pvt. practice, Laguna Beach, Calif., 1971—. Co-author: California Drunk Driving Law, 2005; editor (law rev.) N.Y. Law Forum, 1971. Apptd. mem. gen. plan revision com. and local coastal task force City of Laguna Beach, 1980. Mem. Orange County Bar Assn. (bd. dirs. 1981), Newport/Harbor Bar Assn. (bd. dirs. 1979), South Orange County Bar Assn. (pres. 1986, bd. dirs. 1980-95), Calif. Attys. for Criminal Justice (chair misdemeanor com. 1995), Nat. Assn. Criminal Def. Attys. (vice chair D.U.I. com.), Nat. Coll. D.U.I. Def. (founding mem., dean), Assn. Calif. D.U.I. Defenders (bd. dirs.), Deuce Defenders Assn. (specialist mem.). Office: 260 Saint Anns Dr Laguna Beach CA 92651-2737 Office Phone: 949-497-1729. Fax: 949-497-3971. E-mail: simonslaw@aol.com, info@simonslaw.com.

SIMONS, DOLPH COLLINS, JR., publishing executive, editor; b. Lawrence, Kans., Mar. 11, 1930; s. Dolph Collins and Marie (Nelson) S.; m. Pamela Counseller, Feb. 7, 1952; children: Pamela, Linda, Dolph Collins, Dan. AB, U. Kans., 1951; LLD (hon.), Colby Coll., 1972. Reporter Lawrence Jour.-World, 1953, asso. pub., 1957, pub., 1962—2004, editor, 1978—, pres., 1969—2004; reporter The Times, London, 1956, Johannesburg (South Africa) Star, 1958; chmn. World Co. Mem. Pulitzer Awards Jury, 1977, 78, 80, 81. Trustee, past pres. William Allen White Found.; trustee Midwest Rsch. Inst.; former trustee Menninger Found., Nat. Parks Conservation Assn.; former mem. governing bd. Children's Mercy Hosp., Kansas City, Mo.; former trustee, former chmn. U. Kans. Endowment Assn.; past bd. dirs. Greater Kansas City Cmty. Found., Commerce Bancshares, Kansas City, Mo.; former trustee The Freedom Forum, Kans. Nature Conservancy; mem. Kans. Biosci. Authority Bd. Served to capt. USMRC, 1951—53. Recipient Elijah Parish Lovejoy award, 1972; Fred Ellsworth award for significant service to U. Kans., 1976; Disting. Service citation, 1980 Mem. Newspaper Advt. Bur. (past dir.), Am. Soc. Newspaper Editors, Inland Daily Press Assn. (past dir.), Kans. Press Assn. (past pres., dir.), AP (past dir.), Am. Newspaper Pubs. Assn. (past dir., past nat. sec.), Lawrence C. of C. (past pres., dir.), U. Kans. Alumni Assn. (past pres., dir.), Lawrence Country Club, Kansas City Country Club, Kansas City River Club, Masons, Rotary, Sigma Delta Chi, Phi Delta Theta. Republican. Episcopalian. Home: 2425 Vermont St Lawrence KS 66046-4761 Office: 609 New Hampshire St Lawrence KS 66044-2243 Personal E-mail: dsimonsjr@ljworld.com.

SIMONS, ELIZABETH R(EIMAN), biochemist, educator; b. Vienna, Sept. 1, 1929; came to U.S., 1941, naturalized, 1948; d. William and Erna Engle (Weisselberg) Reiman; m. Harold Lee Simons, Aug. 12, 1951; children: Leslie Ann Mulert, Robert David. BChemE, Cooper Union, NYC, 1950; MS, Yale U., 1951, PhD, 1954. Rsch. chemist Tech. Ops., Arlington, Mass., 1953-54; instr. chemistry Wellesley (Mass.) Coll., 1954-57; rsch. asst. Children's Hosp. Med. Ctr. and Cancer Rsch. Found., Boston, 1957-59, rsch. assoc. pathology, 1959-62; rsch. assoc. Harvard Med. Sch., 1962-66, lectr. biol. chemistry, 1966-72; tutor biochem. scis. Harvard Coll., 1971-94; assoc. prof. biochemistry Boston (Mass.) U., 1972-78, prof., 1978—, asst. dir. Office Med. Edn., 2000—. Contbr. articles to profl. jours. Grantee in field. Mem.: AAAS, Soc. for Neurosci., Biophys. Soc., Am. Soc. Hematology, Am. Soc. Cell Biology, Am. Soc. Biol. Chemists, Am. Chem. Soc. Office: Boston U Sch Medicine 80 E Concord St Roxbury MA 02118-2307 Home Phone: 617-527-6560; Office Phone: 617-638-4332. Business E-Mail: esimons@bu.edu.

SIMONS, ELWYN LAVERNE, physical anthropologist, primatologist, paleontologist, educator; b. Lawrence, Kans., July 14, 1930; s. Verne Franklin and Verna Irene (Cuddeback) S.; m. Friderun Annursel Ankel, Dec. 2, 1972; children: Cornelia Verna Mathilde, Verne Franklin Herbert; 1 child by previous marriage: David Brenton. BS in Biology, Rice U., 1953; MA, Princeton U., 1955, PhD in Paleobiology, 1956; D.Phil., Oxford U., Eng., 1959; MA (hon.), Yale U., 1967; DSc, Oxford U., 1995. Demonstrator, exhibitor Oxford U., 1956-58; lectr. geology Princeton (N.J.) U., 1958-59; asst. prof. zoology U. Pa., Phila., 1959-61; vis. assoc. prof. geology, curator vertebrate paleontology Yale U., New Haven, 1960-61, head divsn. vert. paleontology, 1961-77, prof. paleontology, 1967; prof. geology, curator charge div. vertebrate paleontology Peabody Mus., 1965-77; prof. biol. anthropology, anatomy Duke U., Durham, NC, 1977-82, 1982, prof. zoology, dir. Duke Primate Center, 1977-91, sci. dir., 1991—2001, head, div. fossil primates, 2001—. Dir. Paleontol. Expdns., Egypt, 1961—68, Egypt, 1977—99, India, 1968—69, India, 1996, India, 98, India, 1999—2000; rsch. expdns. for fossil mammals, Wyo., 1960—96, Wyo., 1998—99, Iran, 1970, Spain, 71, Madagascar, 1983—2004; Barbour-Schramm Meml. lectr. U. Nebr., 1974; David French lectr. Claremont Coll., 1974; traveling lectr. French Bur. Fgn. Affairs, 1976; bd. dirs. Ctr. Tropical Conservation, NC. Author: Primate Evolution: An Introduction To Man's Place In Nature, 1972; co-editor: Macmillan Series in Physical Anthropology; A Simons Family History in England and America, 1975, Candebec in France and England, 2005; contbr. numerous articles to profl. publs. Decorated chevalier Ordre Nat., Madagascar; named hon. citizen, Fayum Province of Egypt, 1981; recipient Annadale Meml. medal, Asiatic Soc. Bengal, 1973, Sr. U.S. Scientist award, Alexander von Humboldt Found., 1975. Mem. AAAS, Am. Philos. Soc., Nat. Acad. Scis., Soc. Vertebrate Paleontology, Inst. Human Paleontology, Am. Assn. Zool. Parks and Aquariums (primate specialist group, advisor prosimian taxon group), Assn. Phys. Anthropology (Charles R. Darwin award 2000), Madagascar Fauna Group (bd. dirs.), Internat. Assn. Human Biologists, Sigma Xi. Democrat. Achievements include research in on early mammals, prosimians and primate and human evolution, with special interest in living prosimians, higher primate and human origin and evolution; discovery of 1st tarsiers and 1st marsupials in Africa; naming of earliest known ape Aegyptopithecus in Oligocene of Africa; discovery of Gigantopithecus in India, 1968; naming of earliest anthropoids Oligopithecus, 1962, Qatrania, 1983, Serapia and Arsinoea, 1992; discovery of and naming of new species of Propithecus: Golden Crowned Sifaka in Madagascar, 1989; conservation of lemurs and rain forest of Madagascar. Office: Duke Primate Ctr Divsn Fossil Primates 1013 Broad St Durham NC 27705 Office Phone: 919-416-8420 x 27. Office Fax: 919-416-8584. Business E-Mail: esimons@duke.edu.

SIMONS, GALE GENE, nuclear and electrical engineer, educator; b. Kingman, Kans., Sept. 25, 1939; s. Robert Earl and Laura V. (Swartz) S.; m. Barbara Irene Rinkel, July 2, 1966; 1 child, Curtis Dean. BS, Kans. State U., 1962, MS, 1964, PhD, 1968. Engr. Argonne Nat. Lab., Idaho Falls, Idaho, 1968-77, mgr. fast source reactor, head exptl. support group, 1972-77; prof. nuc. engring. Kans. State U., Manhattan, 1977—2001, assoc. dean for rsch., dir. rsch. coun. Coll. Engring., 1988-97, emeritus prof., 2001—, bd. dirs. Rsch. Found., 1988-97, Presdl. lectr., 1983-96, career counselor, 1984-96. Bd. dirs. Kans. Tech. Enterprise Corp., Topeka; com. mem. Kans. Gov.'s Energy Policy Com., Topeka, 1992-97; presenter, cons. in field Contbr. over 100 articles to sci. jours.; patentee radiation dosimeter. Expert witness State of Kans., Topeka, 1986. Fellow AEC, 1964-67; recipient numerous rsch. grants Mem. AAAS, IEEE, Am. Nuclear Soc., Health Physics Soc., Am. Soc. for Engring. Edn., Masons, Rotary, Phi Kappa Phi, Tau Beta Pi, Pi Mu Epsilon. Home: 2395 Grandview Ter Manhattan KS 66502-3729

SIMONS, HELEN, school psychologist, psychotherapist, educator; b. Chgo., Feb. 13, 1930; d. Leo and Sarah (Shrayer) Pomper; m. Broudy Simons, May 20, 1956 (div. May 1972); children: Larry, Sheri. BA in Biol., Lake Forest Coll., 1951; MA in Clin. Psychology, Roosevelt U., 1972; D of Psychology, Ill. Sch. Profl. Psychology, 1980. Intern Cook County Hosp., Chgo., 1979-80; pvt. practice psychotherapist Chgo., 1980—; sch. psychologist Chgo. Bd. Edn., 1974-79, 80—. Faculty Internat. Soc. for Prevention of Child Abuse and Neglect; lectr., presenter at workshops. Contbr. articles to profl. jours. Mem.: APA, Internat. Sch. Psychologists Assn., Internat. Assn. Applied Psychology, Internat. Soc. for Prevention of Child Abuse and Neglect, Chgo. Sch. Psychol. Assn., Ill. Sch. Psychologists Assn., Nat. Sch. Psychologists Assn. Avocations: music, dance, reading. Home: 6145 N Sheridan Rd Apt 29D Chicago IL 60660-6855 Office: Gladstone Sch 1231 S Damen Ave Chicago IL 60608 Personal E-mail: hpompers@aol.com.

SIMONS, JAMES HARRIS, technology company executive; b. Apr. 25, 1938; married; 5 children. BS, MIT, 1958; PhD in Math., U. Calif., Berkeley. Tchr. math. MIT and Harvard U., 1961—64; chmn. math. dept. SUNY, Stony Brook, 1968; pres., founder Renaissance Techs. Corp., East Setauket, NY, 1982—. Chmn. Stony Brook Found., 1989—; chmn. bd. dirs. Franklin Electronic Pubs., Segue Software; bd. dirs. Brookhaven Sci. Assocs.; founder Renaissance Institutional Equity Fund, 2005. Co-author (with Shiing-Shen Chern): Characteristic Forms and Geometric Invariants, 1974. Supporter of autism rsch.; founder Math for America, 2004; sec. Simons Found., treas.; trustee Rockefeller U., MIT, Inst. for Advanced Study. Named one of Forbes' Richest Americans, 2005—, World's Richest People, Forbes mag., 2005—; recipient Oswald Veblen prize in Geometry, Am. Mathematical Society, 1976, Financial Engr. of Yr., Internat. Assn. Fin. Engineers, 2006. Office: Renaissance Techs Corp 600 Route 25A East Setauket NY 11733-2841 also: 800 3rd Ave Fl 33 New York NY 10022-7604 *

SIMONS, JOHN NELSON, surgeon, consultant; b. Lawrence, Kans., Sept. 19, 1932; s. Dolph Collins and Marie Nelson Simons; m. Ann Marie Leyendecker, July 2, 2005; children: John Jr., Andrea, James, Suzanne, Melissa. BA, U. Kans., 1954; MD, U. Pa., 1958; M in Surgery, U. Minn., 1963. Cert. Am. Bd. Surgery, 1965, Am. Bd. Plastic Surgery, 1967. Cons. plastic surgery Mayo Clinic, Rochester, Minn., 1965—66, asst. prof. plastic surgery, 1965—72, assoc. prof. plastic surgery, 1972—73, head sect. plastic surgery. Founder, CEO Health Campus Internat. Consultants in Health Care Delivery, East Gulf Lake, Minn., 1995—. Republican. Home: 10999 Pine Beach Rd East Gull Lake MN 56401

SIMONS, LAWRENCE BROOK, lawyer; b. NYC, Oct. 19, 1924; s. Harry A. and Marion B. (Brook) Simons; m. Annalou Kadin, Aug. 24, 1947; children: Barbara Flexner, Kenneth. Student, Duke U., 1941-43, 46-47; JD, Columbia U., 1949. Bar: N.Y. 1949, U.S. Dist. Ct. (so. dist.) N.Y. 1949, DC 1984, U.S. Supreme Ct. 1987. Assoc. Spring & Eastman, NYC, 1949-53; v.p., gen. mgr. Caribe Knitting Mills, San Juan, 1953-58; pres. LBS Constrn. Co. Inc., SI, NY, 1958-77; asst. sec. housing FHA commn. HUD, Washington, 1977-81; ptnr. Powell, Goldstein, Frazier & Murphy, Washington, 1981—. Mem. task force quality life Dept. of Def., 1995. Mem. Nat. Housing Task Force, 1988, Nat. Housing Trust, 1990—; chmn. bd. dirs. NY State Urban Devel. Corp., 1975—77, Pa. Ave. Devel. Corp., 1981—87; trustee Bayley Seton Hosp., SI, 1981—90, NHP Found., Inc., 1991—2003, Affordable Housing Found., 1990—92, Ctr. Democracy, 1990—96; pres. Ctr. Housing Policy, 1992—96, bd. dirs., 1996—; commr. Beaufort (S.C.) Housing Authority, 1997—, Affordable Housing Commn., Hilton Head, SC, 1997—99. With US Army, 1943—46, ETO. Named Man of the Yr., Nat. Housing Conf., 1985. Mem.: ABA, Nat. Assn. Home Builders (named to Housing Hall of Fame 2002), Sea Pines Country Club, Lambda Alpha. Democrat. Jewish. Avocation: golf. Home: 40 Plantation Dr Hilton Head Island SC 29928-4402 Office: Powell Goldstein Frazier Murphy 1001 Pennsylvania Ave NW Washington DC 20004-2505 Home Phone: 843-671-4990. Personal E-mail: simonshil1@roadrunner.com.

SIMONS, LEWIS MARTIN, journalist; b. Paterson, NJ, Jan. 9, 1939; s. Abram and Goldie (Fleisher) S.; m. Carol Lenore Seiderman, Feb. 7, 1965; children: Justine, Rebecca, Adam P.D. BA, NYU, 1962; MS, Columbia U., 1964. Corr. AP, Kuala Lumpur, Singapore, Saigon, Denver, 1965-70, Washington Post, Bangkok, New Delhi, Washington, 1971-82; bur. chief Knight-Ridder Newspapers, Tokyo and Beijing, 1982-95; fgn. policy corr. Time mag., 1996-97; freelance writer, 1997—. Author: Worth Dying For, 1987; contbg. author: Crimes of War, 1999, The World of Islam, 2001, Breach of Faith, 2002; contbr. to Nat. Geog. mag., Smithsonian mag., Atlantic Monthly, N.Y. Times, Washington Post. With USMC, 1962-64. Recipient Grand prize and Investigative Reporting award Am. Newspaper Guild, 1981, Citation for Excellence, Overseas Press Club Am., 1983, Jessie Meriton White award Friends World Coll., 1986, Investigative Reporters and Editors award U. Mo., 1986, Award of Excellence, World Affairs Coun., 1984, 86, 89, 92, Pulitzer Prize, 1986, George Polk award, 1985, Malcolm S. Forbes award Overseas Press Club Am., 1986, 92, Gerald Loeb award UCLA, 1993, Alumni award Columbia U. Grad. Sch. Journalism, 2004; Edward R. Murrow fellow Coun. of Fgn. Rels., 1970-71. Mem. Fgn. Corrs. Club Japan (bd. dirs. 1991-92, pres., 1993-94), Washington Inst. Fgn. Affairs. E-mail: clsimons@ix.netcom.com.

SIMONS, LYNN OSBORN, educational consultant; b. Havre, Mont., June 1, 1934; d. Robert Blair and Dorothy (Briggs) Osborn; m. John Powell Simons, Jan. 19, 1957; children: Clayton Osborn, William Blair. BA, U. Colo., 1956. Tchr. Midvale (Utah) Jr. H.S., 1956-57, Sweetwater county Sch. Dist. 1, Rock Springs, Wyo., 1957-58, U. Wyo., 1959-61, Natrona County Sch. Dist. 1, Casper, Wyo., 1963-64; credit mgr. Gallery 323, Casper, 1972-77; Wyo. state supt. pub. instrn. Cheyenne, 1979-91; sec.'s regional rep. region VIII U.S. Dept. Edn., Denver, 1993—2001; mem. Denver Fed. Exec. Bd., 1995-2001; mem. exec. bd. combined Fed. campaign, 1994—2001; ednl. cons., 2001—03; state planning coord. Capitol Bldg., Cheyenne, Wyo., 2003. Mem. State Bds. Charities and Reform, Land Commrs., Farm Loan, 1979-91; mem. State Commns. Capitol Bldg., Liquor, 1979-91; Ex-officio mem. bd. trustees U. Wyo., 1979-91; ex-officio mem. Wyo. Community Coll. Commn., 1979-91; mem. steering com. Edn. Commn. of the States, 1988-90; mem. State Bd. Edn., 1971-77, chmn., 1976-77; advisor Nat. Trust for Hist. Preservation, 1980-86; bd. visitors coll. arts and scis. U. Wyo., 1998—. Bd. dirs. Cheyenne Bot. Gardens Found., 2004—. Mem. LWV (pres. 1970-71). Democrat. Episcopalian.

SIMONS, RICHARD DUNCAN, lawyer, retired judge; b. Niagara Falls, NY, Mar. 23, 1927; s. William Taylor and Sybil Irene (Swick) S.; m. Muriel (Penny) E. Genung, June 9, 1951 (dec. 1992); m. Esther (Esi) Turkington Tremblay, May 21, 1994; children: Ross T., Scott R., Kathryn E., Linda A. AB, Colgate U., 1949; LLB, U. Mich., 1952; LLD (hon.), Albany Law Sch., 1983. Bar: N.Y. 1952. Pvt. practice, Rome, NY, 1952-63; asst. corp. counsel City of Rome, 1955-58, corp. counsel, 1960-63; justice 5th jud. dist. N.Y. Supreme Ct., 1964-83, assoc. justice appellate divsn. 3d dept., 1971-72, assoc. justice appellate divsn. 4th dept., 1973-82; assoc. judge N.Y. Ct. Appeals, 1983—97, acting chief judge, 1992-93; counsel McMahon & Grow, Rome, NY, 1997—; dir. N.Y. State Capital Defender Office, 1997-2000; chief judge Oneida Indian Nation, 1997—. Jurist in residence Syracuse U. Law Sch., 1998; mem. Law Sch. Admission Svcs., Bar Passage Study Com.; mem. chief judges commn. Future of NY Govts.; mem. 4 Cts. on the Judiciary. Editorial staff: N.Y. Pattern Jury Instructions, 1979-83. Chmn. Republican City Com., 1958-62; vice chmn. Oneida County Rep. Com., 1958-62; bd. mgrs. Rome Hosp. and Murphy Meml. Hosp., 1953; trustee Rome Arts and Cmty. Ctr., 2003-2004, mem. chief judge's commn. fiduciary appointments, chief judge's com. promote trust and confidence in legal sys., chair jud. election qualification commn. 5th Jud. Dist., N.Y. Fair Elections Project, Inc., Campaign for Effective Justice; trustee First Presbyn. Ch. Rome. Served with USN, World War II. NEH fellow U. Va. Law Sch., 1979. Fellow Am. Bar Found., N.Y. State Bar Found. (chmn. 1997-98); mem. ABA, N.Y. State Bar Assn. (chair task force on ct. reorgn. 1999-2003, chair spl. com. ct. structure and jud. selection 2004-05, Disting. Svc. award 2000), Oneida County Bar Assn., Rome Bar Assn., Am. Law Inst., Inst. Jud. Adminstrn. Home: 6520 Pillmore Cir Rome NY 13440-7337 Office: McMahon & Grow 301 N Washington St Rome NY 13440-5152

SIMONS, STEPHEN, mathematics professor, researcher; b. London, Aug. 11, 1938; came to U.S., 1965; s. Jack Isidore Simons and Ethel Esther (Littman) Harris; m. Jacqueline Mania Berchadsky, Aug. 13, 1963; 1 son, Mark. BA, Cambridge U., Eng., 1959, PhD, 1962. Instr. U. B.C., Vancouver, Can., 1962-63; asst. prof. U. BC., Vancouver, Can., 1964-65, U. Calif., Santa Barbara, 1965-67, assoc. prof., 1967-73, prof., 1973—2002, prof. emeritus, 2002—, chmn. dept., 1975-77, 88-89. Trustee Math. Scis. Rsch. Inst., Berkeley, Calif., 1988-94. Peterhouse rsch. fellow, Cambridge U., 1963-64. Mem. Am. Math. Soc. Office: Univ Calif Dept Math Santa Barbara CA 93106

SIMONSON, DAVID C., retired newspaper association executive; b. NYC, May 9, 1927; s. Simon and Rebecca (Coolman) S.; m. Lois E. Sneider, Nov. 1, 1952; children: Peter, Eric, John Frederick. BA, Hamilton Coll., 1948; postgrad., U. Vt., 1949, Art Student League of N.Y., 1949. Copywriter Forwell & Mart Advt., NYC, 1949-50; reporter, editor Croton-Cortlandt News, Croton, N.Y., 1950-52; gen. mgr. Colony Publs., NYC, 1952-54; editor, mgr. County Press Newspapers, Croton, 1955-59; promotion dir. Amcrete Corp., Peekskill, N.Y., 1959-60; various positions in mgmt. Patent Trader, Mt. Kisco, N.Y., 1960-72, pub., 1972-77; pres./pub. Pioneer Press Newspapers, Wilmette, Ill., 1977-86; exec. v.p., chief exec. officer Nat. Newspaper Assn., Washington, 1987-92; retired, 1992. Bd. dirs. Christian Herald Assn., NYC; lectr. Medill Sch. Journalism, Meridian House, U.S.A., numerous state press assns.; media cons.; seminar leader Ea. Europe for World Pres Freedom Com.; cons. to Slovenian publs. for U.S. Info. Agy., 1993—94; cons. to Slovakian publs. for USIA, 1995; cons. to African publs. for UNESCO, 95; cons. to Bulgarian Publs. for USIA, 96, 97; cons. to U.S. State dept. World Freedom Com., 2002—; cons. to Bulgarian Publs. for USIA Croatian Publs. for USIA, 1999; seminar leader Voice of Am. for Bulgarian Publs., 1997, Bosnian pubs., 2000, Albanian publs., 2000; U.S. rep. Media Conf., Prague, 2001; DVTV U.S. rep. with Chinese journalists, 01; participant Freedom Forum Roundtables; media panel cons. U.S. Dept. of State, 2003. Author: What a Free Press Means to Me, 2004, Global Issues, 2005. Chmn. planning bd. Town of Croton-on-Hudson, N.Y., 1962-67, trustee, 1967, mayor, 1969. With USNR, 1945-46. Recipient Lesher award Suburban Newspapers of Am., 1998. Mem. Suburban Newspapers Am. (pres. 1984-85, bd. dirs. 1980-84), Ill. Press Assn (bd. dirs. 1980-84, 1st v.p. 1986), N.Y. Press Assn. (bd. dirs. 1966-76, 1st v.p. 1976), Nat. Newspaper Assn. (bd. dirs. 1985-86), Cook County Pubs. Assn. (pres. 1983-84). Avocations: painting, cartooning. Home: 1805 28th St S Arlington VA 22202-1536 Personal E-mail: simonsona6@aol.com. E-mail: simonsondc@aol.com.

SIMONSON, ERIC A., insurance company executive; AB, Princeton Univ.; MBA, Columbia Univ. Investment mgmt. positions Prudential Ins. Co.; pres., CEO Prudential Asset Mgmt. Group, Prudential Pvt. Asset Mgmt. Group; sr. v.p. chief investment officer John Hancock Mutual Life Ins. Co., 1996—2002; sr. v.p., chief investment officer Allstate Ins. Co., Northbrook, Ill., 2002—. Lectr. Darden Sch., Univ. Va.; masters degree prog. adv. Boston Univ. Grad. Sch. Bus.; corp. adv. Samsung Life Ins. Co. Served USN, 1967—73. Office: Allstate Corp 2775 Sanders Rd Northbrook IL 60062 *

SIMONSON, JAMES S., lawyer; b. Madison, Wis. BA, U. Wis., 1956; LLB, Harvard U., 1959. Bar: Minn. 1959. Ptnr., comml. litigation, chmn. trial dept. Gray Plant Mooty, Mpls. Fellow: Am. Coll. Trial Lawyers; mem.: Fed. Bar Assn., Eighth Cir. Ct. Appeals Bar Assn., Minn. State Bar Assn. Office: Gray Plant Mooty 500 IDS Ctr 80 S 8th St Minneapolis MN 55402 Office Phone: 612-632-3300. Office Fax: 612-632-4300. Business E-Mail: james.simonson@gpmlaw.com.

SIMONSON, LEE STUART, broadcast executive; b. Balt., July 3, 1948; s. Theodore and Sara (Silver) S.; m. Nancy Paula Levin, Mar. 25, 1973; children: Laura Todd, Michael Theodore. BA, U. Md., 1970. Acct. exec. WGMS-AM-FM (subs. RKO Gen.), Washington, 1971-73, retail sales mgr., 1973-76; sales mgr. WFYR-FM (subs. RKO Gen.), Chgo., 1976-80; v.p., gen. mgr. WRKS-FM (subs. RKO Gen.), NYC, 1980-84, WOR-AM (subs. RKO Gen.), NYC, 1984-88; vice chmn., COO, owner radio stas. Broadcasting Ptnrs., Inc., NYC, 1988-95; chmn., CEO Broadcasting Ptnrs. Holdings, LP, NYC, 1997-2000; pres. Simonson Assocs., 2000—. Bd. dirs. TheaterMania.com, MIVA, Inc. Bd. dirs. NY state chpt. March of Dimes, 1982—; bd. mgrs. Border Media Ptnrs., 2007—. With US Army, 1970—76. Jewish. Office Phone: 201-767-9551. Personal E-mail: SIMONSONLS@aol.com.

SIMONSON, STEWART GERARD, retired federal agency administrator; b. May 11, 1963; BA, U. Wis., 1986, JD, 1994. Bar: Wis., DC. Legal counsel to gov. of Wis., 1995—99; corp. sec., counsel AMTRAK, 1999—2001; dep. gen. counsel U.S. Dept. Health & Human Svcs., 2001—03, spl. counsel to sec., 2003—04, asst. sec. pub. health emergency preparedness, 2004—; ret., 2006. Office: US Dept Health & Human Svcs 200 Independence Ave SW Washington DC 20201 Office Phone: 202-619-0257.

SIMONSON, SUSAN KAY, hospital clinical care coordinator; b. La Porte, Ind., Dec. 5, 1946; d. George Randolph and Myrtle Lucille (Opfel) Menkes; m. Richard Bruce Simonson, Aug. 25, 1973. BA with honors, Ind. U., 1969; MA, Washington U., St. Louis, 1972. Perinatal social worker Yakima Valley Meml. Hosp., Yakima, Wash., 1979-81, dir. patient support program, 1981—, dir. social svc., 1982-98; instr. Spanish, ethnic studies, sociology Yakima Valley Coll., Yakima, Wash., 1981—. Pres. Yakima Child Abuse Council, 1983-85; developer nat. patient support program, 1981. Contbr. articles to profl. jours. Mem. adv. council Robert Wood Johnson Found. Rural Infant Health Care Project, Yakima, 1980, Pregnancy Loss and Compassionate Friends Support Groups, Yakima, 1982—, Teen Outreach Program, Yakima, 1984—. Recipient NSF award, 1967, discharge planning program of yr. regional award Nat. Glasrock Home Health Care Discharge Planning Program, 1987; research grantee Ind. U., 1968, Fulbright grantee U.S. Dept. State, 1969-70; Nat. Def. Edn. Act fellowship, 1970-73. Mem. NASW, Soc. Hosp. Social Work Dirs. Am. Hosp. Assn. (regional award 1989), Phi Beta Kappa. Office: Yakima Valley Meml Hosp 2811 Tieton Dr Yakima WA 98902-3799 Office Phone: 509-575-8151.

SIMONT, MARC, artist; b. Paris, Nov. 23, 1915; arrived in US, 1927, naturalized, 1936; s. Josep and Dolors (Basté) Simont; m. Sara Dalton, Apr. 7, 1945; 1 child, Marc Dalton. Attended, Academie Julian, Academie Ranson, André Lhote Sch., all Paris, 1932-35, NAD, NYC, 1936. Jefferson Wing mural Libr. Congress, 1940, 80 books, —; author, illustrator: 9 children's books, 1939—, Opera Soufflé, 1950, Poly Oats, 1951, The Lovely Summer, 1952, Mimi, 1955, The Plumber Out of the Sea, 1955, The Contest at Paca, 1959, How Come Elephants?, 1965, Afternoon in Spain, 1965, A Child's Eye View of the World, 1972, The Goose That Almost Got Cooked, 1997, author, illustrator (with Red Smith): Hot to Get to First Base, 1952, translator, illustrator: The Lieutenant Colonel and The Gypsy, 1971, The Stray Dog, 2001 (Caldecott honor, NEBA award, 2005), translator: Ibrahim, 1989. Recipient Caldecott honor, 1950, Caldecott award, 1957, citation merit, Soc. Illustrators, 1965, Il-lustrad'Or, Profl. Assn. Illustrators Catalonia, 1997, Horn Book award, Boston Globe, 2001; Tiffany Found. fellow, 1937. Mem.: Authors Guild, Am. Vets. Com. Home: 336 Town St West Cornwall CT 06796-1304

SIMONTON, DEAN KEITH, psychology professor; b. Glendale, Calif., Jan. 27, 1948; s. Dean Clair Simonton and Laverne (Merkobrad) Williams; m. Susan Youel, June 21, 1971 (div. 1982); m. Melody Boyer, Dec. 29, 1984 (div. 2004); m. Karen Horobin, Mar. 20, 2005. BA in Psychology magna cum laude, Occidental Coll., 1970; MA in Social Psychology, Harvard U., 1973, PhD with distinction, 1975. Asst. prof. psychology U. Ark., Fayetteville, 1974-76; from asst. prof. to prof. U. Calif., Davis, 1976—2004, disting. prof., 2004—. Cons. Wissenschaftzentrun, Berlin, 1979, Ctr. for Creative Leadership, Greensboro, N.C., 1983, NATO, Brussels, Belgium, 1980-81, Dept. Def., Washington, 1983, Creative Problem Solving Inst., 1984, Arvin Perlmutter, Inc., 1992, Milken Family Found., 1994, Templeton Found., 2002. Author: Genius, Creativity and Leadership, 1984, Why Presidents Succeed, 1987, Scientific Genius, 1988, Psychology, Science, and History, 1990, Greatness, 1994, Genius and Creativity, 1997, Origins of Genius, 1999, Great Psychologists and Their Times, 2002, Creativity in Science, 2004; editor Jour. Creative Behavior, 1993-99; contbr. numerous articles to profl. jours. Recipient Excellence award Mensa Adn. and Rsch. Found., 1986, Francis Galton award Internat. Assn. Empirical Aesthetics, 1996, Theatrical Innovation prize, Soc. Personality and Soc. Psychology, 2004. Fellow AAAS, Am. Psychol. Soc., Am. Assn. Applied and Preventive Psychology, Am. Psychol. Assn. (mem.-at-large 1979-82, pres. psychology and the arts divsn. 1985-86, Rudolf Arnheim award Outstanding Contbn. to Psychology and the Arts, 1996, George A. Miller award 1997, William James Book award, 2000, Robert S. Daniel Four Yr. Coll./Univ. Tchg. award, 2006); mem. Phi Beta Kappa, Sigma Xi. Home: 1331 Arena Dr Davis CA 95616-0274 Office: U Calif Dept Psychology Davis CA 95616 Office Phone: 530-752-1677. Business E-Mail: dksimonton@ucdavis.edu.

SIMONYI, CHARLES, software engineer; b. Budapest, Hungary, Sept. 10, 1948; BS in Engring. Math., U. Calif., Berkeley, 1972; PhD in Computer Sci., Stanford U., 1976; PhD (hon.), U. Pecs, Hungary, 2001. Developer Xerox Palo Alto Rsch. Ctr. (PARC), Calif., 1972-80; dir. application develop., chief architect, and disting. engr. Microsoft Rsch. Corp., Redmond, Wash., 1981—2002; co-founder, pres., CEO Intentional Software Corp., Bellevue, Wash., 2002—. Trustee Inst. for Advanced Study, Princeton, NJ, 1997—, pres. of the corp., 2003—. Named one of 400 Richest Americans, Forbes mag., 2006; recipient Whaton Infosys Bus. Transformaton award, 2004. Mem. NAE, Hungarian Acad. Sci. (corres. mem.) Achievements include development of new approaches in programming technology; program representation where new abstraction mechanisms can be introduced without invalidating legacy code; created the first WYSIWYG (what you see is what you get) text editor called Bravo; endowed a chair for the Public Understanding of Science at Oxford University and a chair for Theoretical Physics at the Institute for Advanced Study, Princeton, NJ, among many other educational and charitable contributions through the Charles Simonyi Fund for Arts and Sciences; fulfilled a lifelong dream and became the fifth space tourist for $25 million to take a trip to the International Space Station with Russian cosmonauts on the Russian Soyuz TMA-10 in April, 2007. The trip lasted a total of 13 days. Returned to Earth on April 21, 2007. Office: Intentional Software Corp 500 108th Ave NE #1050 Bellevue WA 98004 Office Phone: 425-467-6600. Office Fax: 425-467-6601. E-mail: charles@intentsoft.com. *

SIMOWITZ, LEE H., lawyer; b. Augusta, Ga., Sept. 7, 1946; BA cum laude, Harvard U., 1968; JD, Yale U., 1972, Bar: DC 1973, US Ct. Appeals (10th cir.) 1979, US Ct. Appeals (3rd cir.) 1983, US Ct. Appeals (4th cir.) 1985, US Ct. Appeals (2nd cir.) 1998, US Ct. Appeals (DC cir.) 1980, US Supreme Ct., 1984. Law clk. to Hon. Harold H. Greene, chief judge Superior Ct., Washington, 1972-73; asst. to dir. bur. consumer protection FTC, Washington, 1975-76, atty.-adviser Calvin J. Collier, chmn., 1976-77; ptnr. Baker & Hostetler, Wash., 1977—. Mem. ABA (antiturst law sect., pub. utility law sect.), DC Bar. Office: Baker & Hostetler 1050 Connecticut Ave NW Wash Square Ste 1100 Washington DC 20036-5304 Office Phone: 202-861-1608. Office Fax: 202-861-1783. Business E-Mail: lsimowitz@bakerlaw.com.

SIMPKINS, NEIL P., investment and automotive company executive; Grad. with honors, Oxford U.; MBA, Harvard Bus. Sch. Consultant Bain & Co., London; principal Bain Capital, 1993—99; sr. mng. dir., private equity group Blackstone Group L.P., 1999—; chmn. TRW Automotive, Livonia, Mich., 2003—. Bd. dirs. Vanguard Health Systems Inc. Office: Blackstone Group 345 Park Ave New York NY 10154 also: TRW Automotive 12001 Tech Ctr Dr Livonia MI 48150 *

SIMPLOT, JACK (JOHN RICHARD SIMPLOT), diversified food products company executive; b. Dubuque, Iowa, Jan. 4, 1909; m. Esther Becker; children: Richard, Don, Scott, Gay Simplot Otter. Potato sorter during Great Depression; founder, chmn. J.R. Simplot Co., Boise, Idaho, 1923—73, chmn. emeritus, 1973—. Bd. dir. Micron Tech., First Security Corp., Continental Life and Accident Co., Morrison-Knudsen, Inc.; former chmn. bd. trustees Coll. Idaho. Named one of Forbes' Richest Americans, 1999—, World's Richest People, Forbes mag., 2000—; named to Manitoba Agrl. Hall of Fame. Achievements include patents for commercial frozen french fries in 1950's; having January 4, 2004 named J.R. "Jack" Simplot Day by gov. Idaho. Avocations: skiing, horseback riding, hunting, fishing. Office: J R Simplot Co PO Box 27 1 Capitol Ctr Boise ID 83707 *

SIMPLOT, SCOTT R., diversified food products company executive; b. Boise, Idaho, Oct. 11, 1946; s. John Richard and Ruby Simplot; m. Maggie Simplot. BA, U. Idaho, 1968; MBA, U. Pa., 1973; D Adminstrv. Sci (hon.), U. Idaho, 2004. Chmn. The J.R. Simplot Co., Boise, 1994—. Named one of Forbes' Richest Americans, 2006. Office: The J R Simplot Co PO Box 27 Boise ID 83707-0027 *

SIMPSON, ALAN KOOI, retired senator, lawyer; b. Cody, Wyo., Sept. 2, 1931; s. Milward Lee and Lorna (Kooi) S.; m. Ann Schroll, June 21, 1954; children: William Lloyd, Colin Mackenzie, Susan Lorna Simpson Gallagher. BS, U. Wyo., 1954, JD, 1958; LLD (hon.), Calif. Western Sch. of Law, San Diego, 1983, Colo. Coll., Colo. Springs, 1986, Notre Dame U., South Bend, Ind., 1987, Am. U., DC, 1989, Rocky Mountain Coll., Billings, Mont., 1996, U. Wyo., Laramie, 1999. Bar: Wyo. 1958, U.S. Supreme Ct. 1964. Asst. atty. gen. State of Wyo., 1959; city atty. City of Cody, 1959-69; ptnr. Simpson, Kepler, and Simpson, Cody, Wyo., 1959-78; mem. Wyo. Ho. of Reps., 1964-77, majority whip, 1973-75, majority floor leader, 1975-77, speaker pro tem, 1977; US Senator from Wyo., 1979—97; asst. majority leader, 1985—87; asst. mimority leader, 1987—95; chmn. vets. affairs com., 1980—84; chmn. fin. subcom. on Social Security and Family Policy; chmn. subcom. on Immigration and Refugee Policy; mem. Spec. Com. on Aging; dir. Inst. Politics Kennedy Sch. Govt. Harvard U., 1999—2000; ptnr. & shareholder Burg Simpson Eldredge Hersh Jardine and Simpson Kepler & Edwards PC, Cody, Wyo. Guest lectr. London exchange program Regent's Coll., London, 1987; vis. lectr. Lombard chair Shorenstein Ctr. for Press, Politics and Pub. Policy, Kennedy Sch. Govt., Harvard U., 1997-2000; mem. Presdl. Debate Commn.; former commr., Am. Battle Monuments Commn., co-chair Continuity in Govt. Commn., 2002-; mem. Iraq Study Group, 2006; mem. external adv. bd. BP Am.; bd. visitors Kennedy Sch. Govt.; co-chmn. Ams. Campaign Reform, adv. com. The Common Good. Author: Right in the Old Gazoo: A Lifetime of Scrapping with the Press, 1997. Chmn. bd. trustees Buffalo Bill Hist. Ctr., Cody; trustee emeritus, Grand Teton Music Festival; former regent Smithsonian Inst., Washington; past adv. bd. Folger Shakespeare Libr., Washington, past bd. mem. Kennedy Ctr. for Performing Arts, Washington. Recipient Nat. Assn. Land Grant Colls. Centennial Alumni award U. Wyo., 1987, Disting. Alumnus award, 1985, Lifetime Svc. award Vietnam Vets. Am., 1993, Thomas Jefferson award in Law U. Va., 1998. Mem. Wyo. Bar Assn., Park County Bar Assn., U. Wyo Alumni Assn. (pres. 1962, 63, Disting. Alumnus award 1985), VFW (life), Am. Legion, Amvets. (Silver Helmet award). Lodges: Eagles, Elks, Masons (33 deg., Order of Grand Cross), Shriners, Rotary. Republican. Office: Burg Simpson Eldredge Hersh & Jardine 1135 14th St PO Box 490 Cody WY 82414

SIMPSON, ALLAN BOYD, real estate company executive; b. Lakeland, Fla., Nov. 24, 1948; s. Alfred Forsythe and Ruth Jeanette (Coker) S.; m. Melody Elaine Mann; 1 child, Lauren Leigh. B in Indsl. Ingring., Ga. Inst. Tech., 1970; MBA, U. Pa., 1972. Cert. rev. appraiser; lic. realtor, Ga. Dir. mortgage banking Ackerman & Co., Atlanta, 1972-73; v.p. B.F. Saul & Co., Atlanta, 1973-79; pres. L.J. Hooker, Atlanta, 1979-88; also bd. dirs. Hooker/Barnes, Atlanta. Bd. dirs. Hooker Holdings (USA), Inc., Century Ins. Co., Hooker Internat. Devels. Ltd., Hooker Internat. Fin. BV, Charter Credit Corp. Ltd., Simpson Spring, Inc., Strategic Land, Inc., Dunwoody Retail, Inc., 750 Park Ave.; chmn., CEO The Simpson Orgn. Inc. Coker Capital Corp., 1989—. Bd. dirs. YES Atlanta, 1991—, Atlanta Coll. Art, Theatrical Outfit; bd. dirs., treas. Midtown Bus. Assn., 1979-88. Mem. Am. Inst. Indsl. Engrs., MBA Execs. Assn., Bldg. Owners and Mgrs. Assn., Nat. Assn. Realtors, U.S. C. of C., Atlanta C. of C., Internat. Coun. of Shopping Ctrs., Urban Land Inst., Nat. Assn. of Office and Indsl. Pks., Ctrl. Atlanta Progress, Amelia Island Club, Mystic Krewe of Ga. (capt.), Loch Lomond Golf Club, Pinehurst Country Club. Democrat. Methodist. Home: 750 Park Ave NE Atlanta GA 30326-3266 Office: 1401 Peachtree St Ste 400 Atlanta GA 30309-3607 Office Phone: 404-253-6350. E-mail: boyd@simpsonorg.com.

SIMPSON, ANDREA LYNN, communications executive; b. Altadena, Calif., Feb. 10, 1948; d. Kenneth and Barbara Simpson; 1 child, Christopher Ryan Myrdal. BA, U. So. Calif., 1969, MS, 1983; postgrad., U. Colo., Boulder Sch. Bank Mktg., 1977. Mktg. officer United Calif. Bank, LA, 1969-73; asst. v.p. mktg. 1st Hawaiian Bank, Honolulu, 1973-78; v.p. corp. comms. Pacific Resources Inc., Honolulu, 1978-89, BHP Hawaii, Inc., 1989-98; v.p. corp. rels. Tesoro Petroleum Corp., San Antonio, 1998-2000; v.p. corp. comms. Edison Internat., Rosemead, Calif., 2000—01; pres. Simpson Comm., 2001—. Bd. dirs. Arts Coun., Hawaii, 1977-81, Hawaii Heart Assn., 1978-83, Coun. Pacific Girls Scouts USA, 1982-85, Child and Family Svcs., 1984-86, Honolulu Symphony Soc., 1985-91, Sta. KHPR Hawaii Pub. Radio, 1988-92, Kapiolani Found., 1990-95, Hanahauoli Sch., 1991-98, Hawaii Strategic Devel. Corp., 1991-98, Children's Discovery Ctr., 1994-98, Pacific Asian Affairs Coun., 1994-96, Hawaii MADD, 1992-96, Girl Scout Coun. Mt. Wilson Dist., 2005—; adv. dir. Hawaii Kids at Work, 1991-98; bd. dirs., 2d v.p. Girl Scout Coun. Hawaii, 1994-96, adv. bd., 1996-98; trustee Hawaii Loa Coll., 1984-86, Kapiolani Women's and Children's Hosp., 1988-97, Hawaii Sch. for Girls at LaPietra, 1989-91, Kapiolani Med. Ctr. at Pali Momi, 1994-98; bd. dirs. Aloha coun. Boy Scouts Am., 1998, Alamo coun., 1998-2000; found. bd. dirs. Hawaii Pub. TV, 1998, bd. dirs., San Pedro Playhouse, 1999-2000; bd. dirs. Red Cross of San Antonio, 1999-2000; commr. Hawaii State Commn. on Status of Women, 1985-87, State Sesquecentennial of Pub. Schs. Commn., 1990-91. Named Advt. Woman of Yr., Honolulu Advt. Fedn., 1982, Pub. Rels. Profl. of Yr., Honolulu Pub. Rels. Soc., 1993, Communicator of Yr., Utilities Communicators Internat., 1983. Mem. Internat. Pub. Rels. Assn. (Golden World award 1997), Am. Mktg. Assn., Pub. Rels. Soc. Am. (bd. dirs. Honolulu chpt. 1984-86, Silver Anvil award 1984, Pub. Rels. Profl. Yr. 1991), U. So. Calif. Alumni Assn. (bd. dirs. Hawaii 1981-83), Outrigger Canoe Club, Rotary (pub. rels. chmn. 1988-97, Honolulu chpt., bd. dirs. 1998), Alpha Phi (past pres., dir. Hawaii), Hawaii Jaycees (Outstanding Young Person of Hawaii 1978).

SIMPSON, A.W. BRIAN, law educator; b. 1931; Degree (hon.), Dalhousie Law Sch., Can., 2003, U. Kent at Canterbury, Eng., 2003. Fellow Oxford U., Eng., 1955-72; prof. U. Kent, Canterbury, Eng., 1972-84, U. Chgo., 1984-87, U. Mich. Law Sch., Ann Arbor, 1987—, Charles F. and Edith J. Clyne Prof. of Law. Lectr. Centre for Human Rights, London Sch. Econs., 2003. Author: Human Rights and the End of Empire: Britain and the Genesis of the European Convention, History of the Common Law of Contract, Biographical Dictionary of the Common Law, Cannibalism and the Common Law, A History of the Land, Law, Legal Theory and Legal History, In the Highest Degree Odious: Detention Without Trial in Wartime Britain, Leading Cases in the Common Law; contbr. articles to law jours. Named Hon. Queen's Coun., 2001. Fellow: Am. Acad. Arts and Scis., Lincoln Coll., Oxford (hon.); mem.: British Acad. Office: U Mich Law Sch 409 Hutchins Hall 625 S State St Ann Arbor MI 48109-1215 Office Phone: 734-763-0413. Business E-Mail: bsimpson@umich.edu.

SIMPSON, BENNETT, art critic, art museum curator; BA, Univ. Virginia, 1994. Former editor ArtByte Mag., NYC, Purple Mag., NYC; Whitney Lauder curatorial fell. Inst. Contemporary Art, 2001—02, assoc. curator Phila., 2002—03, Boston, 2004—. Exhibitions include Apex Art, NYC, 1999, Elysian Fields, Centre Pompidou, Paris, 2000, Shoot the Singer: Music on Video, ICA, Phila., 2002, Make Your Own Life: Artists in and out of Cologne, 2004; contbr. articles to numerous profl. jours. Office: ICA Boston 955 Boylston St Boston MA 02115

SIMPSON, BERYL BRINTNALL, botany educator; b. Dallas, Apr. 28, 1942; d. Edward Everett and Barbara Frances (Brintnall) S.; children: Jonathan, Meghan. AB, Radcliffe Coll., 1964; MA, PhD, Harvard U., 1968. Rsch. fellow Arnold Arboretum/Gray Herbarium, Cambridge, Mass., 1969-71; curator Smithsonian Instn., Washington, 1971-78; prof. U. Tex., Austin, 1978—. Chmn. U.S. Com. to IUBS, 1985-88; co-pres. Internat. Congress Systematic and Evolutionary Biology, 1980-85. Author: Economic Botany, 1994, 3d edit., 2001; editor: Mesquite, 1977; contbr. over 160 articles and notes to profl. jours. Recipient Greenman award Mo. Bot. Garden, 1970. Fellow AAAS, Am. Acad. Arts and Sci., Soc. for Study Evolution (coun. 1975-80, pres. 1985-86), Bot. Soc. Am. (pres. 1990-91, Merit award 1992), Bot. Soc. Washington (v.p. 1975), Am. Soc. Plant Taxonomists (pres. 1994, Cooley award, Asa Gray award), Am. Inst. Biol. Scis. (bd. dirs. 1993-95), U.S.-Mex. Found. for Sci. (bd. govs.), Soc. Econ. Botany (pres. 1999). Office: 1 University Station A6700 Univ Tex Sect Integrative Biology Austin TX 78712 Business E-Mail: beryl@mail.utexas.edu.

SIMPSON, BOB R., energy executive; BS Acctg. with honors, Baylor U., MBA. Tax mgr. Southland Royalty Co., 1976—79, v.p. Fin. & Corp. Devel., 1979—86; co-founder, CEO XTO Energy Inc., Fort Worth, Tex., 1986—96, dir., 1990—, chmn., CEO, 1996—. Mem. Nat. Petroleum Council. Office: XTO Energy Inc 810 Houston St Fort Worth TX 76102-6298 *

SIMPSON, CAM, reporter; State Dept. corr. Chgo. Tribune, Washington. Recipient George Polk award for Internat. Reporting, 2006, Madeline Dane Ross award, Overseas Press Club, 2006. Office: Chicago Tribune Washington Bur Ste 700 1025 F St NW Washington DC 20004 Office Phone: 202-824-8237. Office Fax: 202-824-8302. E-mail: csimpson@tribune.com.

SIMPSON, CAROL MANN, librarian, educator, editor; b. Aberdeen, Md., Nov. 28, 1949; d. Joey Mathew and Grace Winifred (Fielman) Pirrung; m. Robert Smith Mann, Jan. 4, 1969 (div. May 1986); children: Stephen, David (dec.), Sarah; m. Douglas Michael Simpson, Jan. 18, 1992; stepchildren, Brian, Kevin. BS in Edn., Southwestern U., 1971; MA, U. Tex., 1975, MLS, 1977; EdD, East Tex. State U., 1987. Cert. art and French tchr., libr., learning resources specialist, supr., Tex. Tchr. Round Rock (Tex.) Ind. Sch. Dist., 1970-74; libr. Mesquite (Tex.) Ind. Sch. Dist., 1977-90, coord. libr. and media svcs., 1990-92, facilitator libr. tech., 1992—98; assoc. prof. U. North Tex. Sch. Libr. and Info. Scis., Denton, 1998—. Adj. prof. Tex. Women's U., 1992-93; fellow Tex. Ctr. for Digital Knowledge, 2000—; cons. Orex Petroleum, Dallas, 1988, Mesquite Pub. Libr., 1989-90, HBW Assocs., Dallas, 1988-89; reviewer Booklist, 1984-95, Sch. Libr. Jour., 1984-95, Video Rating Guide for Libs., 1989-92. Author: Copyright for School Libraries, 1994, Internet for Library Media Specialists, 1995, Copyright for Schools, 1997, 2005, Copyright Catechism, 2005, Internet for Schools, 1997, 2003, Ethics for School Librarianship, 2003; editor: Technology Connection, 1995—99, The Book Report, 1999—2003, Library Talk, 1999—2003, Library Media Connection, 2003—; contbr. articles to profl. jours. Mem. ALA, Assn. for Ednl. Comms. and Tech., Tex. Libr. Assn., Am. Assn. Sch. Libs., Tex. Assn. Sch. Libs. Methodist. Avocations: genealogy, computers, gardening. Home: 1086 Holly Ln Lewisville TX 75067-5710 Office: U North Tex Sch Libr and Info Scis PO Box 311068 Denton TX 76203

SIMPSON, CARTER B., lawyer; b. Pitts., July 19, 1950; s. John W. Simpson; m. Paulette Peters, May 1, 1982; children: Christina B., Carter B. Jr. BSE in Elec. Engring., Princeton U., 1972; JD, U. Mich., 1976. Assoc. Cadwalader, Wickersham & Taft, NYC, 1976—86, counsel, 1986—88; counsel, antitrust and litig. Mobil Corp., Fairfax, Va., 1988—91, sr. counsel, antitrust, 1991—96, sr. counsel, antitrust and trade regulation, 1996—99; downstream antitrust counsel Exxon Mobil Corp., Fairfax, 2000—06; sr. counsel antitrust and trade regulation Downstream Cos., 2006—. Adv. bd. mem.: Antitrust Counselor, Bus. Laws Inc., 1995—. Dir. Overlook Condo Assn., Wintergreen, Va., 2005—06. Mem.: ABA Anitrust Sect. (vice chair Clayton Act com. 1995—99, vice chmn. teleseminars com. 2007—). Home: 10007 Thompson Ridge Ct Great Falls VA 22066 Office: Exxon Mobil Corp 3225 Gallows Rd Fairfax VA 22037 Home Phone: 703-759-4118; Office Phone: 703-846-2829. E-mail: carter.b.simpson@exxonmobil.com.

SIMPSON, CHARLES R., III, judge; married; 3 children. BA, U. Louisville, 1967, JD, 1970. Bar: Ky. 1970, U.S. Dist. Ct. (we. dist.) Ky. 1971, U.S. Cir. Ct. (6th cir.) 1985. With Rubin, Trautwein & Hays, Louisville, 1971-75, Levin, Yussman & Simpson, Louisville, 1975-77; judge U.S. Dist. Ct. (we. dist.) Ky., Louisville, 1986—, chief judge, 1994—2001; pvt. practice Louisville, 1977-86. Part-time staff counsel Jefferson County Judge/Exec., 1978-84; adminstr. Jefferson County Alcoholic Beverage Control, 1983-84. Roman Catholic. Office: We Dist Ct Ky 247 US Courthouse 601 W Broadway Louisville KY 40202-2238 E-mail: judgesimpson@kywd.uscourts.gov.

SIMPSON, DANIEL H., ambassador; b. Wheeling, W.Va., July 9, 1939; married; 4 children. BA, Yale U., 1961; cert. in African studies, Northwestern U., 1973. Joined Fgn. Svc., U.S. Dept. State, Washington, 1966—, staff asst. Bur. Security and Consular Affairs, 1966-67, speech writer for asst. sec. state for African affairs, 1968, desk officer for Rhodesia, Botswana, Lesotho, and Swaziland, 1973-74; tng. officer USIA, Washington, 1967-68; polit., econ. and consular officer Am. Embassy, Bujumbura, Burundi, 1968-70, polit. officer Pretoria, Republic South Africa, 1970-72, dep. chief mission Beirut, until 1989; amb. to Cen. African Republic, Bangui, 1989-92; dep. comdr. Army War Coll., Carlisle, Pa., 1993-94; ambassador to Somalia Mogadishu, 1994-95; ambassador to Congo Kinshasa, 1995-98; v.p. Nat. Def. U., Washington, 1998-2000; regional dir. OSCE, Bosnia-Herzegovina, 2000—01; assoc. editor Pitts. Post-Gazette and Toledo Blade, 2001—. Address: Pitts Post-Gazette 34 Blvd of the Allies Pittsburgh PA 15222 Home: 112 Washington Pl #20A Pittsburgh PA 15219 Office Phone: 412-263-1976. E-mail: dsimpson@post-gazette.com.

SIMPSON, DAVID WILLIAM, artist, educator; b. Pasadena, Calif., Jan. 20, 1928; s. Frederick and Mary Adeline (White) S.; m. Dolores D. Debus, July 30, 1954; 1 stepchild, Gregory C. Vose; 1 child, Lisa C. B.F.A., Calif. Sch. Fine Arts, 1956; MA, San Francisco State Coll., 1958. Instr. art Am. River Jr. Coll., Sacramento, 1958-60, Contra Costa Jr. Coll., San Pablo, Calif., 1960-65; prof. art U. Calif., Berkeley, 1967-91, prof. emeritus, 1991—. One-man shows include Robert Elkon Gallery, NYC, 1961, 63-64, San Francisco Mus. Art, 1967, Henri Gallery, Washington, 1968, Oakland Mus., 1978, Modernism, San Francisco, 1980-81, 84, 86, 2001, Sheldon Meml. Art Gallery, Lincoln, Nebr., 1990, Mincher/Wilcox Gallery, San Francisco, 1991-93, Angles Gallery, Santa Monica, Calif., 1991-92, 94, 99, Bemis Found., Omaha, 1991, Anthony Ralph Gallery, NYC, 1992, John Berggruen Gallery, San Francisco, 1994, Charlotte Jackson Fine Art, Santa Fe, 1995, 2005, Laguna Art Mus., Laguna Beach, Calif., 1995 Haines Gallery, San Francisco, 1997, 99, 2004, 07, Studio La Citta, Verona, Italy, 1998, 2002, Renate Schröder Gallery, Cologne, Germany, 2000-02, Artothek, Cologne, 2002, James Kelly Contemporary, Santa Fe, 2003, Studio G-7, Bologna, Italy, Sonja Roesch Gallery, Houston, 2005, 07; exhibited in group shows at Mus. Modern Art, NYC, 1963, Carnegie Internat., Pitts., 1961-62, 66-67, LA Mus. Art, 1964, U. Ill., 1969, Expo '70, Osaka, Japan, 1970, Josly Art Mus., Omaha, 1970, John Berggruen Gallery, San

Francisco, 1979, 93, Angles Gallery, Santa Monica, 1988, 90, John Good Gallery, NY, 1992, Cheryl Haines Gallery, San Francisco, 1996, Mus. di Arte Moderna e Contemporanea, Trento, Italy, 1996, Studio La Citta, Verona, Italy, 1996-2005, Llonja, Palma De Majorca, Spain, 1997, Mus. Cantonale d'Arte, Lugano, Switzerland, 1997, Haines Gallery, San Francisco, 1997, Palazzo Ducale, Gubbio, Italy, 1999, Palazzo Ducale, Panza Della Gran Guardia, Verona, 2002, Albright-Knox Gallery, Buffalo, NY, 2005, Fondazione Marenostrum Porto Venere, Italy, Kunstverein Lingen Kuntshauz, Germany, 2005, Lausberg Gallery, Toronto, Can., 2007, Dusseldorf, Germany, 2007, others; represented in permanent collections including Phila. Mus. Art, Nat. Collection Fine Arts, Wash., Seattle Art Mus., La Jolla (Calif.) Mus. Art, Mus. Modern Art, NYC, San Francisco Mus. Art, Oakland (Calif.) Mus., Panza Collection, Italy, Laguna Art Mus., Laguna Beach, Calif., U. Art Mus., Berkeley, Calif., Mus. Cantonale d'Arte Lugano, Switzerland, Mus. Di Arte Moderna e Contemporanea Di Trento e Roverato, Sassuolo, Panza Collection, Italy, Albright Knox Gallery, Buffalo, San Jose Mus., Calif. Home: 565 Vistamont Ave Berkeley CA 94708-1244 Office: U Calif Dept Art Berkeley CA 94720

SIMPSON, DEBORAH, medical educator; BA, U. Calif., Santa Barbara, 1974; MA, Ohio State U., Columbus, 1976; PhD, U. Minn., Mpls., 2003. Assoc. dean ednl. support and evaluation, dir. office ednl. svcs., prof. family and cmty. medicine Med. Coll. Wis., Milw., 1984—. Recipient Disting. Svc. award, Med. Coll. Wis., 2001, Excellence in Edn. award, Soc. Tchrs. Family Medicine, 2001; McCann Faculty scholar, Joy McCann Found., 2005. Mem.: Soc. Dirs. Rsch. Med. Edn., Assn. of Am. Med. Coll. (chair 1999—2001, ctrl. group ednl. affairs, chair 2003—04, Med. Edn. Laureate 1999, Merrill Flair award 2007). Avocations: hiking, recreational sports. Office: Med Coll Wis 8701 Watertown Plank Rd Milwaukee WI 53226 Office Phone: 414-456-4332. Office Fax: 414-456-6506.

SIMPSON, DENNIS DWAYNE, psychologist, educator; b. Lubbock, Tex., Nov. 9, 1943; s. Homer Arnold and Georgie Lee (Barrett) S.; m. Sherry Ann Johnson, Aug. 20, 1965; children: Jason Renn, Jeffrey Todd, Jennifer Lynn. BA, U. Tex., 1966; PhD, Tex. Christian U., 1970. Asst. prof. psychology Tex. Christian U., Ft. Worth, 1970-74, assoc. prof., 1974-79, prof., 1979-82, dir., prof., 1989—, S.B. Sells prof. psychology, 1992—; dir., prof. Tex. A&M U., College Station, 1982-89. Mem. sci. adv. bd. NICA Rsch. Ctrs., Washington, 1992—; mem. adv. bd. Nat. Drug Treatment Evaluation Studies, Washington, 1992—; cons. WHO, fgn. govts. regarding drug rsch. Mem. editl. bd. Am. Jour. Drug and Alcohol Abuse, Substance Abuse Treatment, Substance Use and Misuse; contbr. over 250 articles to profl. jours.; author: 9 books. Recipient Disting. Rsch. Achievement award Tex. Commn. on Alcohol and Drug Abuse, 1987; recipient numerous grants. Mem.: APA, Southwestern Psychol. Assn., Acad. for Health Svcs. Rsch. and Health Policy, The Coll. on Problems of Drug Dependence. Achievements include research emphasis on the process of treatment service delivery in relation to client attributes and how they related to retention rates, relapse and posttreatment outcomes; research in drug use in the workplace; organizational behavior and its role in transferring evidence-based innovations into practice in community-based treatment agencies as well as criminal justice settings; other areas. Office: Tex Christian U Inst Behavioral Rsch PO Box 298740 Fort Worth TX 76129-0001 Business E-Mail: ibr@tcu.edu.

SIMPSON, DICK WELDON, political science educator; b. Houston, Nov. 8, 1940; s. Warren Weldon and Ola Ela (Felts) S.; m. Sarajane Avidon, Mar. 22, 1987 (dec. March 29, 2006); children: Kate Donley, August Donley. BA, U. Tex., 1963; MA, Ind. U., 1964, PhD, 1968; MDiv, McCormick Theol. Sem., 1984. Ordained to ministry United Ch. of Christ, 1985. Rsch. asst. Ind. U., Bloomington, 1965; fgn. area fellow Ford Found., Africa, 1966-67; instr. U. Ill., Chgo., 1967-68, asst. prof., 1968-71, assoc. prof. polit. sci., 1972-96, prof., 1996—, head dept., 2006—. Exec. dir. Inst. on Ch., Chgo., 1984-86, Clergy and Laity Concerned, Chgo., 1987-89. Author: Winning Elections, 1972, 74, 81, 96, Strategies for Change, 1976, Politics of Compassion, 1989; editor: Chicago's Future, 1976, 80, 83, 88, 93, Rogues, Rebels, and Rubber Stamps, 2001, Inside Urban Politics, 2004; prodr., polit. advisor 8 documentary films including By the People, 1970, Teaching Politics, 2006. Alderman Chgo. City Coun., 1971-79; campaign mgr. McCarthy for Pres., Ill., 1967-68; transition team Mayors Washington and Byrne, 1979, 83, State's Atty. O'Malley and County Clk. Orr, 1990, 91, Ill. Atty. Gen. Lisa Madigan, 2003, Cook County Bd. Pres. Todd Stroger, 2006-07; congl. candidate, 1992, 94. Humanities Inst. fellow U. Ill., Chgo., 1985-86, Great Cities fellow, 1997-98, 2005-06; rsch grantee Joyce, Amoco, Woods, McArthur, Carnegie, Wieboldt Founds., 1972-2003; recipient award Clarence Darrow Cmty. Ctr., Clergy and Laity Concerned, IVI-IPO. Mem. Am. Polit. Sci. Assn. (Excellence in Tchg. award, 2002), Midwest Polit. Sci. Assn., Ill. Polit. Sci. Assn. (past pres.), City Club Chgo. (v.p., award). Office: Dept Polit Sci U Ill M/C 276 1007 W Harrison St Chicago IL 60607-7137 Home Phone: 773-728-1110; Office Phone: 312-413-3780. Business E-Mail: simpson@uic.edu.

SIMPSON, DOROTHY AUDREY, retired speech educator; b. Las Vegas, N.Mex., Feb. 29, 1944; d. Clyde Joseph and Audrey Shirley (Clements) Simpson; m. Gary Alan Beimer, May 13, 1972 (div. Apr. 1986); children: Laura Lea Beimer Mitchell, Rose; m. Ian B. Croxton, Dec. 27, 1992 (div. Oct. 1993); m. Doyle W. Hauschulz, Feb. 23, 2001 (div. June 2003). BA, N.Mex. Highlands U., 1965; MS, U. Utah, 1968; EdD, U. N.Mex., 1989. Cert. secondary edn., N.Mex. Tchr. West Las Vegas (N.Mex.) H.S., 1966-67, Santa Rosa (N.Mex.) H.S., 1968-71, Questa (N.Mex.) Consol. Schs., 1972-73; prof. speech comm., assoc. dean coll. arts and scis. N.Mex. Highlands U., Las Vegas, 1975—2003, prof. emeritus, 2003—. Ednl. cons. Rancho Valmora, 2003—. Author: Hovels, Haciendas, and House Calls: The Life of Carl H. Gellenthien, M.D., 1986, Speaking for Life: A Speech Communication Guide for Adults, 1990, Wreck of the Destiny Train, 1993; From Pajarito to Lungchow, 2003. Active 1st Bapt. Ch., Las Vegas, 1959—. Recipient Educator of Yr. award Pub. Svc. Co. of N.Mex., Albuquerque, 1990. Mem. P.E.O. Republican. Avocation: writing. Home: PO Box 778 Las Vegas NM 87701-0778

SIMPSON, ELBERT C., utilities executive; BS in Elec. Engring. and Nuc. Engring., U. Fla., Gainesville. Various managerial positions including dir. nuc. ops. engring. and projects, dir. nuc. ops. site support and dir. nuc. ops. engring. and licensing Fla. Power Corp.; v.p. nuc. engring. Ariz. Pub. Svc. Co., 1990—93, v.p. nuc. support, 1993; sr. v.p. nuc. engring. PSEG Nuc., sr. v.p., chief adminstrv. officer; sr. v.p. info. tech., chief info. officer PSEG Svcs. Corp., pres., COO, 2006—. Office: PSEG Svcs Corp PO Box 570 Newark NJ 07101 Office Phone: 973-430-7000. *

SIMPSON, EUGENE THAMON, music educator, singer; b. North Wilkesboro, NC, Apr. 10, 1932; s. Eugene Tyra and Roxie Johnson Simpson; m. Ingres La Verne Hill, June 9, 1973 (div.); children: Eugene Tyra II, Adrienne Adele. MusB, Howard U., 1951, Yale U., 1953, MusM, 1954; EdD, Columbia U., 1968. Tchr. music Chelsea High Sch., NYC, 1956; asst. choral dir. Second Army Chorus, Ft. Meade, Md., 1956—58; tchr. music N.Y.C. High Schs., 1959—68; chmn. voice and choral Va. State U., Petersburg, 1968—70; chmn. music dept. Bowie State U., Md., 1970—75; prof. music Rowan U., Glassboro, NJ, 1980—2000, chmn. dept. music, 1980—2000. Author: Analysis and Performance of Schwanengesang of Schubert, 1968, Black Genius: The Life, Spirit and Music of Hall Johnson, 2005; composer: Hold On, 1973, Steal Away, Sinnuh Please Don't Let Dis Harvest Pass, Nobody Knows De Trouble I've Seen, True Religion, Too Late Sinnuh, Sistuh Mary Had-a-But One Child, Let Us Break Bread Together; singer: (albums) Danse Calinda, Swing Low Sweet Chariot, Born to Sing the Blues, Life, I Love You Because, 18 Yellow Roses, St. Martin De Porres Mass, The Cascading Voices with Brass, I Hear America Singing, Just A Closer Walk, Melodies of the World, The Wonderful World of Folk, Belefonte at the Greek Theater, Special for Young Lovers, Great Movie Themes, James Brown Showtime, An Evening with Belafonte/Mouskouri, Belafonte, Ballads, Blues and Boasters, King of the Gospel Singers, Porgy and Bess, Mother Nature, Father Time, On the Country Side, Tell Me Why, It's Magic, The Dinah Washington Years, Simon Estes, Singin' Through the Storm, (TV series) The Night They Saved Christmas, The Ed Sullivan Show, Those Ragtime Years, Camera Three. Founding chair Nat. Com. Ethnic Com., 1979—86; mem. adv. bd. Nat. Choral Coun., 1980—85; choral panelist NEA, 1987—88. With US Army, 1956—59. Fellow, Ford Found.; scholar, Howard U., Washington, 1947—51, Yale U., 1951—54; Tanglewood fellow. Mem.: SAG, Am. Coun. Edn., Am. Soc. Composers, Authors and Pubs., Am. Guild Musical Artists, Am. Fedn. Tchrs., Nat. Assn. Tchrs. Singing (gov. 1978—82, mem. com. 1982—87), N.J. Choral Dirs. Assn. (pres. 1977—79), Am. Choral Dirs. Assn. (life; chair ethic music com. 1977—79), Alpha Phi Alpha, Phi Mu Alpha, Pi Kappa Lambda, Kappa Delta Pi, Phi Delta Kappa, Pi Lambda Kappa. Home: 10 Aspen Rd Sicklerville NJ 08081 E-mail: thamspx1@verizon.net.

SIMPSON, FREDERICK JAMES, retired science administrator; b. Regina, Sask., Can., June 8, 1922; s. Ralph James and Lillian Mary (Anderson) S.; m. Margaret Christine Simpson, May 28, 1947 (dec. Apr. 2003); children: Christine Louise, Steven James, Leslie Coleen, Ralph Edwin, David Glen. B.Sc., U. Alta., Can., 1944, M.Sc. in Agr., 1946; PhD in Bacteriology, U. Wis., 1952. With Nat. Research Council Can., 1946-84; asst. dir. Atlantic Research Lab., Halifax, N.S., 1970-73, dir., 1973-84; sci. cons., 1985-90. Vis. scientist U. Ill., Urbana, 1955-56, vis. prof., 1964; mem. exec. council Atlantic Provinces Interuniv. Com. on Scis., 1976-79, chmn., 1981-84; pres. Fed. Inst. Mgmt., Halifax, 1981-82 Contbr. numerous articles to profl. jours. Treas. Lunburg Condominium Corp. No. 1, 1998—. Decorated Queen's Silver Anniversary medal. Fellow Royal Soc. of Arts (London); mem. Can. Soc. Microbiologists (hon., sec.-treas. 1969-70, v.p. 1971-72, pres. 1972-73), Nova Scotian Inst. Sci. (v.p. 1975-76, pres. 1977-78), Internat. Phycological Soc., Aquaculture Assn. Can., Sigma Xi. Mem. United Ch. of Canada.

SIMPSON, H. RICHARD (DICK SIMPSON), retail buyer; b. Oct. 10, 1928; s. Bert M. and Violet K. (Mathias) S.; m. Marion Welty, 1950; children: Carla Sue, Barry Nelson, Richard Drew, Catherine Irene; m. Joan Rose Marshall, March 22, 1970; m. Charlotte S. Fox, Dec. 12, 1999. Student, U. Akron, 1949-50; BS, U. Md., 1955. Mgr. Tex. GMC, Detroit, 1959-62. Pres. Friendly Pontiac, Friendly Toyota, Derrick Chrysler, Simpson Oil Corp., Corp. S., Dick Tiger Homes, Austin, 1962-85, Simpson Hill Country Realty and Builders, 1989-2003, 05. Served to lt. col. USAF, 1953-75; Korea. Decorated D.F.C., Air Medal. Mem. Soc. Automotive Engrs., Res. Officers Assn., Horseshoe Bay Yacht Club, Horseshoe Bay Country Club, Rotary Internat., Masons. Methodist. Office: PO Box 8186 Horseshoe Bay TX 78657-8186 Personal E-mail: dicksimpson_hsb@yahoo.com.

SIMPSON, HUGH L., news correspondent, newswriter; b. Kingston, Jamaica, Jan. 17, 1942; s. Melville Herbert (Stepfather) and Aldina Poulton (Willis) Simpson; m. Stephanie Anna Harcken, Jan. 7, 1988; children: Star, Susan, Andrew(dec.). AA, Maui Cmty. Coll. Radio stringer WWRL, NYC, 1964; radio news reporter WMCA, NYC, 1964—68; press sec. for black media Robert F. Kennedy Presdl. Campaign, 1968; news writer WABC-TV, NYC, 1968; on-camera news reporter WCBS-TV, NYC, 1968—72; freelance Minn., SD and ND, 1973—. Recipient John B. Russwurm award, Nat. Urban League. Mem.: AFTRA, Profl. Assn. Photographers, Phi Theta Kappa. Personal E-mail: blake19060@aol.com.

SIMPSON, JACK BENJAMIN, medical technologist, business executive; b. Tompkinsville, Ky., Oct. 30, 1937; s. Benjamin Harrison and Verda Mae (Woods) S.; m. Winona Clara Walden, Mar. 21, 1957; children: Janet Lazann, Richard Benjamin, Randall Walden, Angela Elizabeth. Student, Western Ky. U., 1954-57; grad., Norton Infirmary Sch. Med. Tech., 1958. Asst. chief med. technologist Jackson County Hosp., Seymour, Ind., 1958-61; chief med. technologist, bus. mgr. Mershon Med. Labs., Indpls., 1962-66; founder, dir., officer Am. Monitor Corp., Indpls., 1966-77; founder, pres., dir. Global Data, Inc., Ft. Lauderdale, Fla., 1986—. Mng. ptnr. Astroland Enterprises, Indpls., 1968—, 106th St. Assocs., Indpls., 1969-72, Keystones Ltd., Indpls., 1970-82, Delray Rd. Assoc. Ltd., Indpls., 1970-71, Allisonville Assocs. Ltd., Indpls., 1970-82, Grandview Assocs. Ltd., 1977—, Rucker Assocs. Ltd., Indpls., 1974—; mng. ptnr. Raintree Assocs. Ltd., Indpls., 1978—, Westgate Assocs. Ltd., Indpls., 1978—; pres., dir. Topps Constrn. Co., Inc., Bradenton, Fla., 1973-91, Acrovest Corp., Asheville, N.C., 1980—; dir. Indpls. Broadcasting, Inc.; founder, bd. dirs. Bank of Bradenton, 1986-92; founder, CFO Biomass Processing Tech., Inc., West Palm Beach, Fla., 1996—; also bd. dirs. Mem. Am. Soc. Med. Technologists (cert.), Indpls. Soc. Med. Technologists, Fla. Soc. Med. Technologists, Am. Soc. Clin. Pathologists, Am. Assn. Clin. Chemistry, Royal Soc. Health (London), Internat. Platform Assn., Am. Mus. Natural History, Columbia of Indpls. Club, Harbor Beach Surf Club, Fishing of Am. Club, Marina Bay Club (Ft. Lauderdale), Elks. Republican. E-mail: jack_simpson@msn.com.

SIMPSON, JAMES S., federal agency administrator; BS magna cum laude, St. John's U. Commr. NY State Met. Transp. Authority, 1995—2005; fed. transit adminstr. US Dept. Transp., 2006—. Mem. NY State Job Devel. Authority Bd., NYC Work Force Investment Bd.; observer NY State Fin. Control Bd.; hon. dep. police commr. NYC Police Dept.; chmn. St. Lawrence Seaway Adv. Bd. Dir. NYC Partnership and C. of C.; chmn. Staten Island C. of C.; vice chmn. Snug Harbor Cultural Ctr.; bd. dirs. Staten Island U., St. Vincent's Hosp. Finalist Nat. Entrepreneur of Yr. award, Ernst & Young/NASDAQ; recipient Medal of Achievement, St. John's U., Employer of Yr. award, Am. Moving and Storage Assn. Mem.: NYC Police Dept. Honor Legion (hon.), Nat. Bus. Honor Soc., Nat. Honor Soc. of Economics. Office: Fed Transit Adminstrn 400 7th St SW Washington DC 20590

SIMPSON, JESSICA ANN, singer, actress; b. Abilene, Tex., July 10, 1980; d. Joe and Tina Simpson; m. Nick Lachey, Oct. 26, 2002 (div. June 30, 2006). Launched edible fragrance, cosmetic and body care line, Dessert Beauty, 2004; co-creator and launched, edible fragrance, cosmetic, and body care line, Taste, 04; nat. spokesperson for Operation Smile; designer swimwear line, 2007. Singer: (albums) Sweet Kisses, 1999, Irresistible, 2001, In This Skin, 2004, Rejoyce: The Christmas Album, 2004, A Public Affair, 2006, (songs) These Boots are Made for Walkin', 2005 (People's Choice award for Favorite Song from a Movie (The Dukes of Hazzard), 2006); actor: (films) The Dukes of Hazzard, 2005, Employee of the Month, 2006; (TV series) Newlyweds: Nick and Jessica, 2003—05, (TV) Nick & Jessica's Variety Hour, 2004, Nick & Jessica's Family Christmas, 2004, Nick & Jessica's Tour of Duty, 2005; co-author: I Do: Achieving Your Dream Wedding, 2003; co-host with husband: Saturday Night Live, 2004; co-host with Dane Cook Teen Choice Awards, 2006, guest appearances (TV series) MadTV, 2000, 2001, That '70s Show, 2002, 2003, Punk'd, 2003, Twilight Zone, 2003, Top of the Pops, 2004, Ashlee Simpson Show, 2004, The Apprentice, 2004. Recipient Movies-Choice Breakout (Female), Teen Choice Awards, 2006. Office: c/o Creative Artists Agy 9830 Wilshire Blvd Beverly Hills CA 90212-1825 also: Epic Records 550 Madison Ave New York NY 10022-3211 *

SIMPSON, JOANNE MALKUS, meteorologist; b. Boston, Mar. 23, 1923; d. Russell and Virginia (Vaughan) Gerould; m. Robert H. Simpson, Jan. 6, 1965; children by previous marriage: David Starr Malkus, Steven Willem Malkus, Karen Elizabeth Malkus. BS, U. Chgo., 1943, MS, 1945, PhD, 1949; DSc (hon.), SUNY, Albany, 1991. Instr. physics and meteorology Ill. Inst. Tech., 1946-49, asst. prof., 1949-51; meteorologist Woods Hole Oceanographic Instn., 1951-61; prof. meteorology UCLA, 1961-65; dir. exptl. meteorology lab. NOAA, Dept. Commerce, Washington, 1965-74; prof. environ. scis. U. Va., Charlottesville, 1974—79, W.W. Corcoran prof. environ. scis., 1974—79; head Severe Storms br. Goddard Lab. Atmospheres, NASA, Greenbelt, Md., 1979—88; chief scientist for meteorology, earth scis. dir. Goddard Space Flight Ctr., NASA, 1988—2004, chief scientist emeritus for meteorology, 2004—; project scientist tropical rainfall measuring mission, 1986—98. Mem. Bd. on Atmospheric Scis. and Climate, NRC/NAS, 1990-93, 97-2000, Bd. on Geophys. and Environ. Data, 1993-96, com. on climate, ecosystems, infectious diseases and human health, 1998-2000; mem. sr. adv. bd. NOAA, 1998-2003. Author: (with Herbert Riehl) Cloud Structure and Distributions Over the Tropical Pacific Ocean; assoc. editor: Revs. Geophysics and Space Physics, 1964-72, 75-77; contbr. articles to profl. jours. Mem. Fla. Gov.'s Environ. Coordinating Coun., 1971-74. Recipient Disting. Authorship award NOAA, 1969, Silver medal Dept. Commerce, 1967, Gold medal, 1972, Vincent J. Schaefer award Weather Modification Assn., 1979, Cmty. Headliner award Women in Comm., 1973, Profl. Achievement award U. Chgo. Alumni Assn., 1975, 92, Lifetime Achievement award Women in Sci. Engring., 1990, Exceptional Sci. Achievement award NASA, 1982, William Nordberg award NASA, 1994, NASA Medal Outstanding Leadership, 1998, I.M.O. prize World Meteorol. Orgn., 2002, U.S. Gov. Presdl. Rank award, 2003, 04; named Woman of Yr., L.A. Times, 1963; Guggenheim fellow, 1954-55, Goddard Sr. fellow, 1988-2004. Fellow Am. Geophys. Union, Am. Meterol. Soc. (mem. coun. 1975-77, 79-81, mem. exec. com. 1977, 79-81, commr. sci. and tech. activities 1982-88, pres.-elect 1988, pres. 1989, publs. commr. 1992-98, hon. mem. 1995, Meisinger award 1962, Rossby Rsch. medal 1983, Charles Franklin Brooks award 1992, Charles E. Anderson award 2001), World Meterol. Orgn. (IMO prize 2002), Explorers Club, Nat. Acad. Engring., Am. Acad. Arts & Sciences; mem. Royal Meteorol. Soc. (hon.), Cosmos Club, Phi Beta Kappa, Sigma Xi. Office: NASA Goddard Space Flight Ctr Earth Scis Greenbelt MD 20771-0001 Personal E-mail: nasajoanne@earthlink.net. Business E-Mail: simpson@agnes.gsfc.nasa.gov, joanne.simpson_1@nasa.gov.

SIMPSON, JOE LEIGH, obstetrics and gynecology educator; b. Birmingham, Ala., Apr. 4, 1943; s. Robert S. and Winnie (Leigh) S.; m. Sandra A. Carson, May 6, 1978; children: Scott, Reid MD, Duke U., Durham, NC, 1968. Diplomate Am. Bd. Ob-Gyn, Am. Bd. Med. Genetics. Fellow in ob-gyn Cornell Med. Coll., NYC, 1968-73; clin. assoc. NY Blood Ctr., NYC, 1969-73; asst. clin. prof. ob-gyn U. Tex., San Antonio, 1973-75; assoc. prof., head ob-gyn Northwestern U. Med. Sch., Chgo., 1975-79, prof. ob-gyn, 1979-86; Faculty prof. chmn. dept. ob-gyn U. Tenn., Memphis, 1986-94; prof., chmn. dept. ob-gyn Baylor Coll. Medicine, Houston, 1994—2006, prof. dept. molecular and human genetics, 1994—2006. Mem. genetics grant rev. and adv. bd. HHS, 1979-82; mem. clin. rsch. panel March of Dimes, 1986-94, chmn. adv. panel reproductive hazards, 1988-92, mem. sci. adv. bd., 1994—; mem. accreditation coun. grad. med. edn. Residency Rev. Com. Med. Genetics, 1993-98; mem. adv. com. Nat. Inst. Child Health and Devel., 1994-97; mem. bd. sci. counselors Intramural Rsch. Nat. Inst. Child Health and Devel., 2005—. Author: Disorders of Sexual Development, 1976; author: (with others) Genetics in Obstetrics and Gynecology, 1982, 3d edit., 2003, Obstetrics: Normal and Problem Pregnancies, 1986, 5th edit., 2007; co-editor: Genetic Diseases in Pregnancy, 1981, Material Serum Screening for Fetal Genetic Disorders, 1992, Essentials of Prenatal Diagnosis, 1993; contbr. articles to profl. jours. and chpts. to books. Maj. US Army, 1973-75. Recipient numerous awards Nat. Insts. Child Health and Devel., March of Dimes, Wyeth-Ayerest pub. recognition award Assn. Profs. Ob-Gyn, 1992. Fellow ACOG (chmn. genetics subcom. 1981-84), Am. Coll. Med. Genetics (treas. 1996-02, pres., 2007-), Royal Coll. Obstetricians and Gynecologists (hon.); mem. NAS, Inst. Medicine, Am. Gynecol. and Obstet. Soc. (mem. coun. 1997-99), Am. Soc. Reproductive Medicine (bd. dirs. 1984-87, pres. 1993-94), Soc. Gynecologic Investigation (pres. 1998-99, Pres.'s Achievement award 1986, Pres. Disting. Scientist award 2002), Soc. Advancement Contraception (pres. 1995-98), Am. Soc. Human Genetics (mem. program com. 1988-91), Internat. Soc. Prenatal Diagnosis (pres. 1994-98), Internat. Fedn. Fertility Socs. (treas. 2007-), Preimplantation Genetic Diagnosis Internat. Soc. (pres. 2006-). Office: Fla Internat Univ Coll Medicine 11200 SW 8th St HCSII 693 Miami FL 33199 Office Phone: 305-348-0570. Business E-Mail: simpsonj@fiu.edu.

SIMPSON, JOHN BARCLAY, academic administrator; b. Oakland, Calif., June 8, 1947; s. Barclay and Joan (Devine) S.; children: Matthew, Melissa. BA, U. Calif., Santa Barbar, 1969; MA, Northwestern U., 1972, PhD, 1973. Research assoc. U. Pa., Phila., 1973-75; from asst. prof. to prof. psychology U. Wash., Seattle, 1975—98, dir. physiology-psychology program, 1984-88, head of the physiological psychology area, 1986—90, assoc. dean for computing, rsch. and facilities, 1991—94, dean of College of Arts and Sciences, 1994—98; exec. vice chancellor, provost U. Calif., Santa Cruz, 1998—2003; president U. at Buffalo, SUNY, 2004—. Vis. researcher U. Calif., San Francisco, 1976-80; vis. prof. Howard Florey Inst. U. Melbourne, Australia, 1983. Contbr. articles to profl. jours. Grantee NIH. Mem. AAAS, Soc. for Neurosci., Soc. Study Ingestive Behavior. Avocations: skiing, sailing, bicycling. Office: U at Buffalo 501 Capen Hall Buffalo NY 14260-1600 Office Phone: 716-645-2901. Office Fax: 716-645-3728. Business E-Mail: simpson@buffalo.edu. E-mail: UBOfficeOfThePresident@vpsa.buffalo.edu. *

SIMPSON, JOHN M., lawyer; AB, Harvard U., 1972; JD, Columbia U., 1978. Bar: D.C. 1979, N.C. 1988. Mem. Fulbright & Jaworski L.L.P., Washington. With USMC, 1972—75. Office: Fulbright & Jaworski LLP Market Square 801 Pennsylvania Ave NW Washington DC 20004-2615 Office Phone: 202-662-0200. E-mail: jsimpson@fulbright.com.

SIMPSON, JOHN NOEL, health facility administrator; b. Durham, NC, Feb. 27, 1936; m. Virginia Marshall, June 27, 1959; children: John Noel, William M. Asst. adminstr. Riverside Health Sys., Newport News, Va., 1962-65, assoc. adminstr., 1965-70, Richmond (Va.) Meml. Hosp., 1970-74, sr. v.p., adminstr., 1974-77, exec. v.p., 1977-80, pres., 1980-85, Health Corp. Va., 1985-96; chmn. bd. Bon Secours-Richmond Health System, 1996-97, regional v.p., CEO, 1997-2000, divisional cons., 2000—. Preceptor Sch. Health Adminstrn. Duke U. and Med. Coll. Va., Washington U., St. Louis; bd. dirs. Sun Health, Inc./Sun Alliance, 1979-92, vice-chmn., 1984, chmn., 1985-87; vice-chmn. Med./Bus. Coalition, 1981-83; participant Leadership Met. Richmond; bd. dirs. Ctrl. Va. Health Sys. Agy., 1980-84, Richmond chpt. ARC, 1980-83; mem. Va. Bd. Med. Assistance, 1980-84; mem. joint subcom. studying Va. med. malpractice laws divsn. legal svcs. Gen Assembly of Comm. of Va., 1984; chmn. Va. Health Network, 1989-91; chmn. Hanover Bus. Coun., 1994-95; mem. Gov. Regional Econ. Devel. Adv. Coun., 1994-95. Served with Med. Svc. Corps U.S. Army, 1959-62. Fellow Am. Coll. Healthcare Execs. (Coun. of Regents 1976-82, Edgar C. Hayhow award 1976, bd. govs. 1990-94, regents award sr. exec. level 1995). Fellow Am. Coll. Healthcare Execs. (coun. of regents 1976-82, Edgar C. Hayhow award 1976, bd. govs. 1990-94, regents award sr. exec. level 1995); mem. Am. Hosp. Assn. (chmn. RPBIII 1994-97, del. 1989-93, mem. bd. trustees 1994-97, Va. Hosp. Assn. (dir. 1974-97), del. 1989-93, mem. bd. trustees 1994-97, Va. Hosp. Assn. (dir. 1974-97, chmn.-elect, chmn. 1984-85, Disting. Svc. award 1998), Va. Ins. Reciprocal (chmn.

1977-79), Met. Richmond C. of C. (bd. dirs), Richmond Acad. Medicine (Disting. Svc. award 2000). Republican. Presbyterian. Home Phone: 804-740-0283; Office Phone: 804-379-2930. Personal E-mail: JSIMP22736@aol.com.

SIMPSON, JOHN W., lawyer; b. Wichita, Kans., 1960; BA with highest distinction, U. Kans., 1982, JD, 1985. Bar: Mo. 1985, US Dist. Ct., We. Dist. of Mo., US Ct. of Appeals, Tenth Cir. 1986, US Tax Ct. 1989, US Dist. Ct., Dist. of Kans. Ptnr., chmn Tax Practice Group Shook, Hardy & Bacon LLP, Kansas City, Mo. Mem. bd. dirs. Higher M-Pact. Mem.: Kansas City Met. Bar Assn., Phi Kappa Phi, Phi Beta Kappa. Office: Shook, Hardy & Bacon LLP 2555 Grand Blvd Kansas City MO 64108 Office Phone: 816-559-2453. Office Fax: 816-421-5547. E-mail: jsimpson@shb.com.

SIMPSON, LISA ANN, physician, educator; b. Lagos, Nigeria, Feb. 9, 1958; (parents Am. citizens); d. Howard Russell and Mary Alice (Turner) Simpson; m. Richard L. Wittenberg; children: Ethan Simpson Wittenberg, Sydney Simpson Wittenberg. MB, B of Surgery, Trinity Coll., Dublin, Ireland, 1981; MPH, U. Hawaii, 1986. Diplomate Am. Bd. Pediat. Resident in pediat. U. Hawaii, Honolulu, 1982-85; resident in preventive medicine U. NC, Chapel Hill, 1987-88; dir. Maternal and Child Health Bur. State Dept. Health, Honolulu, 1988-90, acting dir. family health svcs. divsn., 1990; policy advisor Office of Asst. Sec. for Health HHS, Washington, 1993-94, sr. advisor Agy. for Health Care Policy and Rsch. Rockville, Md., 1994-95, acting dep. adminstr. Agy. for Health Care Policy and Rsch., 1995-96, dep. adminstr. Agy. for Health Care Policy and Rsch., 1996-99, dep. dir. Agy. Healthcare Rsch. and Quality, 1999—2002; prof., All Children's Hosp. Guild endowed chair child health policy dept. pediat. U. South Fla., St. Petersburg, 2003—07; dir., prof. Child Policy Rsch. Ctr., Cin. Children's Hosp. Med. Ctr., 2007—. Mid-career fellow Inst. Health Policy Studies, San Francisco, 1991-93; adj. faculty dept. health policy and mgmt. Johns Hopkins U., Balt., 1995—; vis. prof. U. Wash., 2000, U. Mich., 2000; nat. dir. child health policy, Nat. Initiative Children's Healthcare Quality, 2004-. Mem. editl. bd. Future Children, Maternal and Child Health Jour., 1996-2005; contbr. articles to profl. jours. Recipient Preventive Medicine traineeship Pub. Health Svc., 1986, Sec. Disting. Svcs. award Dept. HHS, 2000, Dir. Disting. Svc. award AHRQ, 2001, Meritorious Rank SES Presdl. award, 2002. Fellow: Am. Acad. Pediat. (Excellence in Pub. Svc. award 2002); mem.: APHA (governing coun. 1994—96), Nat. Acad. for Social Ins., Ambulatory Pediat. Assn. (chair pub. policy and advocacy com. 2005—), Acad. Health (bd. dirs. 2006—). Avocations: hiking, cuisine, gardening. Office: Child Policy Rsch Ctr Cin Children's Hosp Med Ctr 3333 Burnet Ave MLC 7014 Cincinnati OH 45229-3039 Office Phone: 513-636-2781. Office Fax: 513-636-0117. Business E-Mail: lisa.simpson@cchmc.org.

SIMPSON, LOUIS A., insurance company executive; b. Chgo., Dec. 23, 1936; s. Irving and Lillian (Rubin) S.; m. Margaret Rowley, Dec. 16, 1959; children: Irving, Kenneth, Edward Student, Northwestern U., 1954-55; BA, Ohio Wesleyan U., 1958; AM, Princeton U., 1960. Instr. econs. Princeton U., 1961-62; assoc., ptnr. Stein Roe & Farnham, Chgo., 1962-69; v.p. Shareholders Mgmt., Los Angeles, 1969-70; sr. v.p., exec. v.p., pres. Western Asset Mgmt., Los Angeles, 1970-79; vice chmn. bd. Geico Corp., Washington, 1979-93, pres., chief exec. officer capital ops., 1993—. Bd. dirs. AT & T, Pacific Am. Income Shares, Western Asset Funds, Inc., HNC Software, ResMed, Inc. Trustee Cate Sch., U. Calif. San Diego Found., Urban Inst.; vice chair Woodrow Wilson Nat. Fellowship Found. Woodrow Wilson fellow, 1958 Mem. San Diego Soc. Fin. Analysts, Scripps Inst. Oceanography Coun., Calif. Club, Arts Club Chgo., Chevy Chase Club, Met. Club. Episcopalian. Office: Geico Corp 1 Geico Plz Washington DC 20076-0005

SIMPSON, LOUIS ASTON MARANTZ, language educator, writer; b. Jamaica, W.I., Mar. 27, 1923; s. Aston and Rosalind (Marantz) S.; m. Jeanne Claire Rogers, 1949 (div. 1954); 1 child, Louis Matthew; m. Dorothy Mildred Roochvarg, 1955 (div. 1979); children: Anne Borovoi, Anthony Rolf; m. Miriam Butensky Bachner, 1985 (div. 1998). Higher schs. certificate, Munro Coll., Jamaica, 1939; BS, Columbia U., 1948, A.M., 1950, PhD, 1959; D.H.L., Eastern Mich. U., 1977; DLitt, Hampden Sydney Coll., 1990. Editor Bobbs-Merrill Pub. Co., NYC, 1950-55; instr. Columbia U., 1955-59; prof. English U. Calif., Berkeley, 1959-67, SUNY, Stony Brook, 1967-91, Disting. prof., 1991—. Author: (poems) The Arrivistes, 1949, Good News of Death, 1955, A Dream of Governors, 1959, At the End of the Open Road, 1963 (Pulitzer prize for poetry 1964), Selected Poems, 1965, Adventures of the Letter I, 1971, Searching for the Ox, 1976, Caviare at the Funeral, 1980, The Best Hour of the Night, 1983, People Live Here: Selected Poems 1949-83, 1983, Collected Poems, 1988, In the Room We Share, 1990, Jamaica Poems, 1993, There You Are, 1995, The Owner of the House, New Collected Poems, 1940-2000, (transl.) Nombres et poussière, 1996, Modern Poets of France, 1997, Kaviar pä begravningen, 1998, François Villon: The Legacy and The Testament, (prose) Riverside Drive, 1962, James Hogg: A Critical Study, 1962, North of Jamaica, 1972, Three on the Tower: The Lives and Works of Ezra Pound, T.S. Eliot and William Carlos Williams, 1975, A Revolution in Taste: Studies of Dylan Thomas, Allen Ginsberg, Sylvia Plath and Robert Lowell, 1978, A Company of Poets, 1981, The Character of the Poet, 1986, Selected Prose, 1989, Ships Going into the Blue, 1994, The King My Father's Wreck, 1995; editor: The New Poets of England and America, 1957, An Introduction to Poetry, 1967. Served with AUS, 1943-45. Decorated Purple Heart, Bronze Star with oak leaf cluster; Hudson Rev. fellow, 1957, Guggenheim fellow, 1962, 70; Am. Coun. Learned Socs. grantee, 1963; recipient Prix de Rome, 1957, Millay award, 1960, Distinguished Alumnus award Columbia U., 1960, medal for excellence Columbia U., 1965; American Acad. of Arts and Letters award in literature, 1976; Centenary medal Inst. of Jamaica, 1980, Jewish Book Coun. award for poetry, 1981, Elmer Holmes Bobst award, 1987, Harold Morton Landon award for translation, 1997. Fellow Am. Acad. in Rome. Home: 7 Stony Rd Stony Brook NY 11790 Office Phone: 631-689-0498. Personal E-mail: louissimpson1@yahoo.com.

SIMPSON, LYLE LEE, lawyer; b. Des Moines, Oct. 15, 1937; s. R. Clair and Martha B. (Accola) S. BA, Drake U., 1960, JD, 1963. Bar: Iowa 1963, U.S. Dist. Ct. (so. and no. dists.) Iowa 1963, U.S. Ct. Appeals (8th cir.) 1963, U.S. Tax Ct. 1963, U.S. Supreme Ct. 1970, U.S. Ct. Mil. Appeals 1972. Pvt. practice, Des Moines, 1963—; mem. Beving and Swanson, Des Moines, 1964-68; sr. ptnr. Peddicord, Simpson & Sutphin, Des Moines, 1968-83; pres. Dreher, Simpson & Jensen, PC, 1984—. Gen. counsel campaign com. Gov. Iowa, 1978-98. Contbr. articles to profl. jours. Chmn. bd. trustees Broadlawns Med. Ctr., 1974-80; mem. Iowa Inaugural Com., 1983, 87, 89, 91, 95; bd. dirs. YMCA Boys Camp, 1967-86, Home, Inc., 1981-85, Project H.E.L.P.E.R., 1983-87, Batten Found.; pres., bd. dirs. Polk County Health Svcs., 1972-88; chmn. Iowa Health Facilities Coun., 1988-93; pres. First Unitarian Ch., 1958-70, Iowa Humanities Bd., 1988-94, Humanist Found., 1980—, East High Alumni Found., 1992-2000; treas. Iowa Humanities Found., 1994-99; chmn. Iowa Health Found., 1993—; mem. investment com., fin. com. Iowa Health Sys., 2000—; bd. Iowa Health System, Des Moines, 2005—. Recipient Oren E. Scott award, Class of 1915 award in liberal arts Drake U., 1960. Mem. ABA, Iowa Bar Assn., Polk County Bar Assn., Am. Arbitration Assn., Am. Humanist Assn. (pres. 1979-84), Prairie Club (pres. 1992), Morning Club (pres. 1965), Le Chevaliers de vin Club (pres. 1976-85), YMCA Heritage Club (pres.), Masons, Scottish Rite, Shriner 33 degree, Rotary. Republican. Congregationalist. Address: 222 Equitable Bldg 604 Locust St Des Moines IA 50309-3723 Office Phone: 515-288-5000. Business E-Mail: lsimpson@dreherlaw.com.

SIMPSON, MARY MICHAEL, priest, psychotherapist; b. Evansville, Ind., 1925; d. Link Wilson and Mary Garrett (Price) S. BA, BS, Tex. Women's U., 1946; grad., N.Y. Tng. Sch. Deaconesses, 1949, Westchester Inst. Tng. in Psychoanalysis and Psychotherapy, 1976; S.T.M., Gen. Theol. Seminary, 1982. ordained priest Episcopal Ch., 1977. Missionary Holy Cross Mission, Bolahun, Liberia, 1950-52; mem. Order of St. Helena, 1952—; acad. head Margaret Hall Sch., Versailles, Ky., 1958-61; sister in charge Convent of St. Helena, Bolahan, 1962-67, dir. novices, 1968-74; pastoral counselor on staff St. John the Divine, NYC, 1974-87, canon residentiary, canon counselor, 1977-87, hon. canon, 1988—. Pvt. practice psychoanalyst, 1974—; dir. Cathedral Counseling Svc., 1975-87; cons. psychotherapist Union Theol. Seminary, 1980-83; bd. dirs. Westchester Inst. Tng. in Psychoanalysis and Psychotherapy, 1982-84; priest-in-charge St. John's Ch., Wilmot, New Rochelle, N.Y., 1987-88; trustee Coun. Internat. and Pub. Affairs, 1983-87;interim pastor St. Michael's Ch., Manhattan, 1992-94; cons. Diocese of N.Y., 1990—. Author: The Ordination of Women in the American Episcopal Church: The Present Situation, 1981; contbg. author: Yes to Women Priests, 1978. Mem. Nat. Assn. Advancement of Psychoanalysis, N.Y. State Assn. Practicing Psychotherapists, N.Y. Soc. Clin. Psychologists. Home and Office: 151 E 31st St Apt 8H New York NY 10016-9502 Office Phone: 212-951-4316. Personal E-mail: mmsimpson@rcn.com.

SIMPSON, MICHAEL, retired metals service center executive; b. Albany, NY, Dec. 10, 1938; s. John McLaren Simpson and Constance (Hasler) Ames; m. Barbara Ann Bodtke, Jan. 5, 1963; children: Leslie Ann, Elizabeth S. Wessel. BA, U. Mich., 1965, MBA, 1966. Product mgr. Armour & Co., Chgo., 1966-68; with A.M. Castle & Co., Franklin Park, Ill., 1968—, pres. Hy-Alloy Steels Co. divsn., 1974-79, v.p. Midwestern region, 1977-79, chmn. bd., 1979—2004, also bd. dirs.; chmn. emeritus, 2004—. Trustee Rush U. Med. Ctr., Chgo., 1978—, mem. exec. com., 1980—, vice chmn., 1991—; trustee Oldfields Sch., Glencoe, Md., 1982-87, 95-2003, chmn. bd., 1998-2000; bd. dirs. Lake Forest (Ill.) Hosp. Found. and Lake Forest Hosp., 1998—; chmn. bd. overseers Rush U., Chgo., 1996-. Office: AM Castle & Co 3400 N Wolf Rd Franklin Park IL 60131-1319 Office Phone: 847-349-2500. Business E-Mail: msimpson@amcastle.com.

SIMPSON, MICHAEL K., congressman; b. Burley, Idaho, Sept. 8, 1950; m. Kathy Johnson, 1971. Student, Utah State U.; DDS, Washington U., St. Louis, 1978. Dentist, Blackfoot, Idaho, 1978—; councilmember Blackfoot City Coun., 1980—84; mem. Idaho Ho. Reps., 1985—99, asst. majority leader, 1989, speaker, 1991—99; mem. US Congress from 2nd Idaho dist., Washington, 1999—. Mem. Ho. Appropriations com., Agr., Resources, Transp. & Infrastructure com., Vet. Affairs com. Served as spkr. majority caucus chmn. and asst. majority leader in Idaho Ho. Reps. Mem. Idaho's Rep. Party Hall of Fame. Recipient Friend of Edn. award, 1994, Citizen of the Yr. award Idaho Family Forum, 1996, Boyd A. Martin award Assn. Idaho Cities. Mem. Idaho State Dental Assn. (Pres.'s award 1998), Am. Legis. Exch. Coun. (state chmn., nat. bd. dirs., Jefferson award 1994). Republican. Avocations: golf, chess, painting. Office: US Ho Reps 1339 Longworth Ho Office Bldg Washington DC 20515-1202 Office Phone: 202-225-5531. Office Fax: 202-225-8216. *

SIMPSON, MICHAEL MARCIAL, science specialist, consultant; b. Honolulu, Sept. 24, 1954; s. Marcial Tolentino and Beatrice (Martin) S. AB in Biol. Scis., U. Calif., Berkeley, 1976; MS in Biol. Scis., U. San Francisco, 1977; MS in Energy and Resources, U. Calif., Berkeley, 1979; PhD in Environ. Scis. and Engring., UCLA, 1986. Assoc. researcher NASA, Moffett Field, Calif., 1973; radio program host, producer Sta. KUSF-FM, San Francisco, 1976-78; rsch. asst. Lawrence Berkeley Lab., Berkeley, Calif., 1977-79; rsch. assoc. UCLA/U.S. Dept. Energy, 1979-81; congl. fellow, environ. health U.S. Congress, Washington, 1981-82; specialist in environ. techs., life scis., and terrorism U.S. Congl. Rsch. Svc., Washington, 1982—2006, sci. policy advisor on Homeland Security issues, 2006—; cons. CSC Inc. Adv. bd. Banbury Ctr., Cold Spring Harbor, N.Y., 1985—; adj. faculty The Washington Ctr., 1992—. Contbr. articles to profl. jours. Fellow AAAS (Named Congl. Sci. fellow 1981-82); mem. Washington Acad. Sci., Library of Congress Profl. Assn., UCLA in Washington (exec. steering com. 1986-92). Avocations: photography, bicycle touring, short story writing, travel. Home Phone: 703-239-8050; Office Phone: 703-461-2011. Business E-Mail: msimpson8@csc.com, DrMichaelMSimpson22015@yahoo.com.

SIMPSON, MIKE, talent agent; b. Tampa, Fla. BS in Communications, U. Tex., Austin; MA, U. Tex., 1978. Agent trainee program William Morris Agy., 1979, head motion picture packaging dept., 1986, co-head West Coast motion picture dept., 1989—, exec. v.p., mem. bd. dirs. Beverly Hills, Calif. Named one of The 100 Most Powerful People in Hollywood, Premiere Mag., 1998; recipient Warren Skaaren Lifetime Achievement award, Tex. Film Commn., 2001. Office: William Morris Agy 151 S El Camino Dr Beverly Hills CA 90212-2775

SIMPSON, MURRAY, electrical engineer, consultant; b. NYC, July 27, 1921; s. George and Sonia (Vernov) Simpson; m. Ethel Gladstein, June 29, 1947; children: Anne Simpson, David, Mindy, Jonathan. BEE, CCNY, 1942; MEE, Polytech. Inst. of NY, 1952. Engr. ITT, NYC, 1942-44; sr. engr. Raytheon Co., Waltham, Mass., 1946-48; sect. mgr. Fairchild Guided Missles div., Farmingdale, NY, 1948-50; v.p. Maxson Elec. Co., NYC, 1950-62; pres. SEDCO Sys. Inc. subs. Raytheon Co., Melville, NY, 1963-86; cons. M. Simpson Assocs., Ft. Lauderdale, Fla., 1986—. Former chmn. bd. dirs. Radyne Corp. Contbr. articles to profl. jours. Former bd. dirs. United Way, LI. Served to lt. (j.g.) USNR, 1944—46, PTO. Fellow: IEEE (chmn. L.I. sect. 1963—64). Avocations: boating, skiing, golf, tennis. *Don't be afraid to take risk in the hope of great reward and satisfaction. The worst that could happen is that you may fail. A much greater loss is that you never tried and perhaps missed the great opportunity of your life.*

SIMPSON, MURRAY L., lawyer; b. Chgo., 1937; BA, U. Ill., 1959; JD, DePaul U., 1961. Staff atty. Securities and Exchange Commn., 1961—64; atty. priv. practice, 1964—91; CEO, mng. dir. Franklin Templeton Investments-Asia, Hong Kong, 1994—2000; exec. v.p., gen. counsel Franklin Resources, Inc., San Mateo, Calif., 2000—06, exec. v.p., 2006—. Mem. unit trust com. Securities and Futures Commn., 1998—2000; chmn. Hong Kong Investment Funds Assn., 2000; mem. financial services advisory com. Hong Kong Trade Devel. Council; former bd mem. Franklin Resources, Inc. Office: Franklin Resources Inc One Franklin Pkwy San Mateo CA 94403 Business E-Mail: mlsimpson@frk.com.

SIMPSON, ROBERT G., waste management executive; BS in Acctg., Ind. U.; JD, U. Ill. Dir. fed. taxes Kraft Gen. Foods divsn. Phillip Morris; v.p. tax, gen mgr. Tenneco Bus. Svcs., 1997—98; v.p. taxation Waste Mgmt. Inc., Houston, 1998—2002, v.p., chief acctg. officer, 2002—03, sr. v.p., chief acctg. officer, 2003—04, sr. v.p., CFO, 2004—. Office: Waste Mgmt Inc 1001 Fannin St Ste 4000 Houston TX 77002 Office Phone: 713-512-6200. *

SIMPSON, ROBERT GLENN, lawyer; b. Seattle, June 27, 1932; s. Harold Vernon and Anna Rondeau (McCabe) S.; m. Josephine Anne Heald, June 7, 1959; children: Jenifer Jane, Thomas Glenn, Mary Elizabeth. BS, U. Oreg., 1954; LLB, Willamette U., 1959. Bar: Oreg. 1959. Assoc. William B. Adams Law Office, Portland, Oreg., 1959-67; ptnr. Adams McLaughlin & Simpson, Portland, 1967-70, Schwabe Williamson & Wyatt, P.C., Portland, 1970—. Trustee, sec. Legacy Good Samaritan Hosp. and Med. Ctr., Portland, 1983-89, mem. cmty. bd., 1989-98; trustee, chancellor Episcopal Diocese of Oreg., Portland, 1988—. Mem. Oreg. State Bar (exec. com. health law sect. 1987-90), Am. Health Lawyers Assn. (program com. 1987-88), Oreg. Health Lawyers Assn.(pres. 1977-78, legis. com. 1989), Multnomah Athletic Club, Univ. Club. Home: 13345 SW Iron Mountain Blvd Portland OR 97219-9306 Office: Schwabe Williamson & Wyatt, PC 1211 SW 5th Ave Ste 1800 Portland OR 97204-3795

SIMPSON, ROBERT HOMER, meteorologist, consultant; b. Corpus Christi, Tex., Nov. 19, 1912; s. Clyde Robert and Annie Laurie (Rainey) S.; m. Mazie Houston, Dec. 22, 1935 (div. Dec. 1949); m. Joanne Gerould Malkus, Jan. 6, 1965; children: Peggy A., Lynn S.; stepchildren: David Malkus, Steven Malkus, Karen Malkus. BS, Southwestern U., Tex., 1932, DSc (hon.), 1963; MS, Emory U., 1935; PhD, U. Chgo., 1962. Cert. cons. meteorologist. Observer U.s. Weather Bur., Brownsville, Tex., 1940-42, forecaster New Orleans and Miami, Fla., 1942-45, exec. asst. to dep. chief Washington, 1946-48; established Pacific Region of U.S. Weather Bur., Honolulu, 1948-52; rsch. scientist U.S. Weather Bur., Washington, 1952-56, founding dir. Nat. Hurricane Rsch. Project West Palm Beach, Fla., 1956-61, dep. dir. rsch. severe storms Washington, 1961-64; assoc. dir. ops. Nat. Weather Svc., NOAA, Washington, 1964-67, dir. Nat. Hurricane Ctr. Miami, 1967-74; founding dir. Simpson Weather Assoc., Inc., Charlottesville, Va., 1974—; rsch. prof. environ. sci. U. Va., Charlottesville, 1974-80. Established Mauna Loa Summit Obs., Hawaii, 1951. Author: (with Herbert Riehl) The Hurricane and Its Impact, 1981; chief editor: Hurricane: Coping with Disaster, 2002; contbr. articles to profl. jours. Recipient Gold medal Dept. Commerce, 1962, Profl. Achievement award U. Chgo. D.C. Alumni Group, 1998. Fellow Am. Meteorol. Soc. (hon. mem., Cleveland Abbe award 1991), Explorers Club NY; mem. steering com. Wash. Group. Achievements include (with Herbert Saffir) development and implementation of the Saffir-Simpson scale for hurricane damage potential; pioneering research flight in hurricane, Caribbean Sea, W. Pacific Ocean, first over-the-top flight in hurricane, Atlantic Ocean, 1947; many research penetrations of hurricane eyes. Personal E-mail: r.h.simpson@verizon.net.

SIMPSON, ROBERT LEE, academic administrator, department chairman, biologist, educator; b. San Francisco, Apr. 3, 1942; s. Robert Lee and Valerie Brinley (Serrick) S.; m. Penelope Sue Flint, June 12, 1970; children: Robert Lee III, Elizabeth Jean. BA in Zoology, Fresno State Coll., 1965, MA in Biology, 1967; PhD in Limnology, Cornell U., 1971. Instr. Cornell U., Ithaca, N.Y., 1970; from asst. prof. to prof. biology Rider Coll., Lawrenceville, N.J., 1970-85, chairperson biology dept., 1972-80; acting dean sch. health professions and nursing William Paterson Coll., Wayne, N.J., 1986-87, prof. biology, 1985-91, dean sch. sci. and maths., 1985-91; provost, vice chancellor acad. affairs U. Mich., Dearborn, 1991—2006, prof. biology, 1991—. Adj. grad. prof. Rutgers U., Camden, N.J., 1976-91; vis. scientist Smithsonian Environ. Rsch. Ctr., Edgewater, N.J., 1977; mem. grad. degree adv. com. N.J. Dept. Higher Edn., Trenton, 1989-91; interim provost, v.p. academic affairs Kettering U., Flint, Mich, 2006-07. Editor: (with D. Whigham, R. Good) Freshwater Wetlands: Ecological Processes & Management Potential, 1978, (with M. Leck, V.T. Parker) Ecology of Soil Seed Banks, 1989; contbr. articles to profl. jours. Mem. N.J. Wetlands Mitigation Coun., Trenton, 1988-91; trustee Chilton Meml. Hosp., Pompton Plains, N.J., 1989-91; bd. dirs. Granville Acad., Detroit, 1991-93; chair acad. affairs affairs subcom. Pres. Coun. of State Univs. of Mich., 1997-2007. Rsch. grantee Office Water Rsch. & Tech., 1975, 79, U.S. EPA, 1976, 78, NSF, 1975, 80, U.S. Geol. Survey, 1983, Challenge to Excellence grantee N.J. Dept. Higher Edn., 1987. Mem. N.J. Acad. Sci. (pres. 1983-85, Outstanding Svc. award 1989), Ecol. Soc. Am., Brit. Ecol. Soc., Soc. Wetland Scientists, Am. Soc. Limnology and Oceanography, Sigma Xi. Home: 2470 Harness Dr West Bloomfield MI 48324-3733 Office Phone: 313-593-5678. Business E-Mail: rlsumd@umich.edu.

SIMPSON, ROBERT LOUIS, music educator; b. Orange, NJ, Apr. 17, 1948; s. Robert Gage and Frances Dean Simpson; m. Marianna Parnas, May 29, 1994; children: Laura Helen, Robert Kirkpatrick. AB, Brown U., 1970; M Sacred Music, Union Theol. Sem., Sch. Sacred Music, 1972. Cert. Assoc. Am. Guild of Organists, NY, 1989, Choirmaster Am. Guild of Organists, NY, 1989. Organist-choirmaster Cathedral Ch. St. Luke, Orlando, Fla., 1974—79, Cathedral St. Philip, Atlanta, 1979—93, Christ Ch. Cathedral, Houston, 1993—; founder and artistic dir. Houston Chamber Choir, 1995—; lectr. ch. music Shepherd Sch. Music, Rice U., Houston, 2003—. Musician (conductor): (choral performances) The Blue Estuaries. Recipient S. Lewis Elmer Award, Am. Guild of Organists, 1988. Mem.: Chorus Am. (bd. mem. 2000—06), Assn. Anglican Musicians, Am. Choral Dirs. Assn. Office: Houston Chamber Choir PO Box 53388 Houston TX 77052-3388 Home Phone: 713-906-9017. Office Fax: 713-222-2412. E-mail: robertsimpson@houstonchamberchoir.org.

SIMPSON, SANDRA KAY, operations research specialist; b. Rutland, Vt., Feb. 26, 1949; d. Freeman Edward and Ruth Gail (Smith) Campbell. BA, U. Vt., Burlington, 1971; MPA, Troy State U., Europe, 1988, MSc in Internat. Rels., 1991. Isntr., trainer US Govt., Ft. McClellan, Ala., 1975-79, asst. logistics officer Kitzingen, Germany, 1979-82, property acctg. officer Ft. Hood, Tex., 1982-86, Wiesbaden, Germany, 1986-93, maintenance mgmt. coord., 1994—, dep. dir. internal logistics, 1999—2002, theater level logistics mgr., 2002—03, 2005—06, def. logistics agy., 2003—05, 2007—, theater level logistics mgr., 2005—07; exec. mgmt. asst. Sport and Sound, Mainz Kastel, Germany, 1993-94. Cons. U.S. Govt., Heidelberg, Germany, 1994—. With US Army, 1973—93. Mem. Women in Mil. Svc. to Am. Found. (charter mem.), USAREUR Retiree Coun., Wiesbaden/Mainz Retiree Coun. (sec. 1994—), Oxford Club. Avocations: photography, marathons. Home: Cmr 467 Box 1505 APO AE 09096-1505 Office Phone: 49-6314-604584. Business E-Mail: sandy.simpson@us.army.mil.

SIMPSON, STEVEN DREXELL, lawyer; b. Sturgis, Mich., Sept. 20, 1953; s. Rex and Lorraine Simpson; m. Peggy Deibert, Apr. 28, 1979; children: Andrew Drexell, Christine Elizabeth, Marianne Tyner. BA, Hillsdale Coll., Mich., 1975; JD, Wake Forest U., 1978; LLM in Taxation, Georgetown U., 1981. Bar: Fla. 1978, D.C. 1980, N.C. 1984. Assoc. Bradford, Williams et al, Miami, Fla., 1978-80, Webster & Chamberlain, Washington, 1980-82, Fisher, Wayland et al, Washington, 1982-84, Maupin, Taylor & Ellis, P.A., Raleigh, NC, 1984-98; pvt. practice, 1998—2006; counsel Wyrick Robbin Yates & Ponton, LLP, 2007—. Author: Tax-Exempt Organizations: Organizational and Operational Requirements, 2000, Tax-Exempt Organizations: Reporting, Disclosure and Other Procedural Aspects, 2000, Taxable Expenditures, 2000, Tax Compliance for Tax-Exempt Organizations, 2007, Multistate Guides to Regulation and Taxation of Nonprofits, 2007; contbr. articles to profl. jours. Mem. ABA (exempt orgns. com.). Republican. Methodist. Avocations: golf, running. Home: 409 Hillandale Dr Raleigh NC 27609-7036 Office: PO Drawer 17803 4101 Lake Boone Trail Ste 300 Raleigh NC 27619 Office Phone: 919-781-4000. Business E-Mail: ssimpson@wyrick.com.

SIMPSON, VINSON RALEIGH, manufacturing executive, director; b. Chgo., Aug. 9, 1928; s. Vinson Raleigh and Elsie (Passeger) S.; m. Elizabeth Caroline Matte, Sept. 9, 1950; children: Kathleen Simpson Zier, Nancy Simpson Ignacio, James Morgan. SB in Chem. Engring, MIT, 1950; MBA, Ind. U., 1955. With Trane Co., LaCrosse, Wis., 1950-75, mgr. mktg. services, 1957-64, mgr. dealer devel., 1964-66; mng. dir. Trane Ltd., Edinburgh, Scotland, 1966-67; v.p. internat. Trane Co., LaCrosse, Wis., 1967-68, exec. v.p., 1968-70; exec. v.p., gen. mgr. comml. air conditioning div., 1970-73; pres., dir., 1973-75, Simpson and Co., La Crosse, 1975-76; pres., chief operating officer, dir. Marathon Electric Mfg. Corp., Wausau, Wis., 1976-80; chmn., pres., chief exec. officer Marion Body Works, Inc., Wis., 1980-93, chmn., 1993—. Bd. dirs. Clintonville Area Found. Past trustee, treas. Fox Valley Tech. Coll.; bd. dirs., past pres. Fox Valley Tech. Coll. Found.; past pres., bd. dir. Wausau Area Jr. Achievement; mem. Marion Minutemen; past 20 yr. trustee, chair endowment com., trustee emeritus Northland Coll.; past dir. Wis. Mfrs. and Commerce; mem. investments com. Comty. Found. for Fox Valley Region, Inc. Decorated Korean War Commendation ribbon. Mem. Am. Legion, Kappa Kappa Sigma, Alpha Tau Omega, Beta Gamma Sigma (dirs. table). Lodges: Masons, Shriners, Rotary (past. pres. Marion club, Paul Harris fellow). Congregationalist. Avocations: running, snorkeling, cross country skiing, playing the trombone. Home: 171 Fairway Dr Clintonville WI 54929-1071

SIMPSON, WILLIAM, information technology manager, consultant; b. Escondido, Calif., 1953; m. Deborah Simpson. BA in Social Sci., San Diego State U., 1976; MA in Ednl. Tech., U.S. Internat. U., San Diego, 1993. Profl. adminstr. credential Calif. Commn. Tchr. Credentialing, 2003, preliminary adminstrv. svcs. credential Calif. Commn. Tchr. Credentialing, 1993, secondary tchr. credential Calif. Commn. Tchr. Credentialing, 1977. Tchr. Escondido Union Sch. Dist., Calif., 1979—92, coord. tech. and media svcs., 1992—99; dir. staff devel. svcs. San Diego County Office Edn., 1999—. Edn. adv. bd. mem. Apple Computer, Inc., San Diego, 1997—99; co-founder and dir. Innovative Video in Edn., 2001—; dir. Innovative Video in Edn. Adv. Bd.; project dir. techsets San Diego County Office Edn., 2004—; mem. product adv. bd. Learning Frameworks, Inc. Developer: Innovative Video in Education Program (iVIE). Bd. dir. Classroom of the Future Found., San Diego, 1999—2001; mem. program com. San Diego Natural History Mus., 2002—04; edn. com. co-chair Pacific Southwest chpt. NATAS, 2004—. Named Apple Disting. Educator, Apple Computer, Inc., 2003; grantee, Calif. Tech. Assistance Project Region 9 Calif. Dept. Edn., 2003—05, 2005—. Mem.: ISTE, ASCD, Calif. Computer Using Educators (membership chair 1996—97, Tech. Learning Leadership award 2004), Internat. Soc. Tech. in Edn. (Outstanding Leadership 2004). Office: San Diego County Office Edn 6401 Linda Vista Rd San Diego CA 92111 Office Phone: 858-292-3608.

SIMPSON, WILLIAM ARTHUR, insurance company executive; b. Oakland, Calif., Feb. 2, 1939; s. Arthur Earl and Pauline (Mikalasic) S.; m. Nancy Dougery Simpson, Mar. 31, 1962; children: Sharon Elizabeth, Shelley Pauline BS, U. Calif.-Berkeley, 1961; postgrad. Exec. Mgmt. Program, Columbia U. CLU. V.p. mktg. Countrywide Life, LA, 1973-76; v.p. agy. Occidental Life of Calif., LA, 1976-79; pres., CEO Vol. State Life, Chattanooga, 1979-83; exec. v.p. Transam. Occidental Life Ins. Co., LA, 1983-86, pres., 1986-88, pres., CEO, COO, 1988-90, also bd. dirs.; dir. USLIFE Corp., NYC, 1990—; pres., CEO All Am. Life Ins. Co., Pasadena, Calif., 1990-94, USLIFE Life Ins. div. USLIFE Corp., 1994, USLIFE Corp., 1995-97. Chmn. Franklin Life Ins. Co. Pres. Chattanooga coun. Boy Scouts Am., 1982, bd. dirs., LA, 1983, v.p., 1983-85, vice-chmn LA area, 1989, chmn., 1989; pres. bd. councillors LA County Am. Cancer Soc.; trustee Verdugo Hills Hosp. Found., Ill. Symphony Orch.; bd. dirs. Abraham Lincoln coun. Boy Scouts Am., Meml. Medical Ctr., Springfield, Ill. 1st lt. US Army, 1961—64. Mem. Am. Soc. CLUs, Life Ins. Mktg. and Rsch. Assn. (bd. dirs. 1986-89), Ctl. Ill. Ins. Co. (bd. dirs.), Rotary. Republican. Presbyterian. Avocations: golf, skiing. Office: Franklin Life Ins Co 1 Franklin Sq Springfield IL 62713-0002 E-mail: neswas@aol.com.

SIMPSON, WILLIAM KELLY, curator, Egyptologist, educator; b. NYC, Jan. 3, 1928; s. Kenneth Farrand and Helen L.K. (Porter) S.; m. Marilyn E. Milton, June 19, 1953; children: Laura Knickerbacker Simpson Thorn, Abby Rockefeller Simpson Mydland. BA, Yale U., 1947, MA, 1948, PhD, 1954; DHL (hon.), Am. U. in Cairo, 2001. Asst. in Egyptian art Met. Mus. Art, 1948-54; rsch. fellow Center Middle East Studies, Harvard U., 1957-58; faculty Yale U., New Haven, 1958—65, prof. Egyptology, 1965—2004, chmn. dept. Near Eastern langs., 1966-69; curator Egyptian and ancient Near Eastern art Mus. Fine Arts, Boston, 1970-86; ltd. partner Kin and Co., 1967-69; ltd. ptnr. Venrock, 1970—. Dir. editor of papers Penn-Yale Archaeol. Expdn. to Egypt, 1960—; mem. adv. council fgn. currency program Smithsonian Instn., 1966-69 Author: Papyrus Reisner I-Records of a Building Project, 1963, Hekanefer and the Dynastic Material from Toshka, 1963, Papyrus Reisner II-Accounts of the Dockyard Workshop, 1965, Papyrus Reisner III: Records of a Building Project in the Early Twelfth Dynasty, 1969, The Terrace of the Great God at Abydos, 1974, The Mastabas of Qar and Idu, 1976, The Offering Chapel of Sekhem-ankh-ptah, 1976, The Offering Chapel of Kayemnofnet in the Museum of Fine Arts Boston, 1992, Papyrus Reisner IV: Personnel Reports, 1986, The Inscribed Material from the Pennsylvania-Yale Excavations at Abydos, 1995, (with others) The Ancient Near East, A History, 2d edit., 1998, The Literature of Ancient Egypt, 1972, The Mastaba of Queen Mersyankh III, 1994. Trustee Am. Sch. Classical Studies, Athens, Am. U. in Cairo, Katonah Mus. Art; mem. internat. council Mus. Modern Art, N.Y.C.; pres. Wrexham Found., 1965-67. Fulbright fellow Egypt, 1955-57; Guggenheim fellow, 1965 Mem. Am. Oriental Soc., Am. Philos. Soc., Archaeol. Inst. Am., Internat. Assn. Egyptologists, Egypt Exploration Soc., Soc. française d'egyptologie, German Archaeol. Inst., Foundation egyptologique Reine Elisabeth. Clubs: Century (N.Y.C.), Met. Opera (N.Y.C.), University (N.Y.C.), Union (N.Y.C.), River (N.Y.C.); Bedford (N.Y.); Golf and Tennis. Home: 129 Katonah Woods Rd Katonah NY 10536-3846 Personal E-mail: william.simpson@yale.edu.

SIMPSON, WILLIAM M., history professor; b. Oct. 25, 1948; BA, Millsaps Coll., Jackson, Miss., 1970; MA, Miss. State U., Starkville, 1972, PhD, 1974. Instr. Miss. State U., 1974—75; instr. dept. history Hinds CC, Raymond, Miss., 2006—; asst. prof., full time prof. La. Coll., Pintville, 1975—2006. Mellon fellow in so. history, Mellon Found. Rice U., 1984, Hist. Archeol. Study fellow, Friends of Poplar Forest, Lynchburg, Va., 2005. Mem.: Miss. Hist. Assn., La. Hist. Assn., So. Hist. Assn. Office: Hinds CC Dept History PO Box 1100 Raymond MS 39154-1100 Office Phone: 601-857-3636.

SIMPSON, WILLIAM M., JR., family medicine educator; b. Louisville, Aug. 20, 1947; s. William Maynard and Mary Glynn (Chambers) S.; m. Margaret Elaine Bath, Dec. 20, 1969; children: Jonathan Marc, Kimberly Anne. BS, Clemson U., 1968; MD, Med. U. S.C., 1972. Diplomate Am. Bd. Family Medince; cert. of added qualification in geriatrics, 1988. Resident in family medicine Med. U. S.C., Charleston, 1972—74, chief resident and instr., 1974—75, asst. prof. family medicine, 1977—84, assoc. prof., 1984—91, prof. family medicine, 1991—, acting chmn. family medicine, 1989—90. With U.S. Army, 1975-77. Grantee HHS, 1986—. Fellow Am. Acad. Family Physicians; mem. Am. Geriatric Soc., Soc. of Tchrs. of Family Medicine. Avocations: tennis, exercise, stamps, coins, guitar. Home: 49 Montagu St Charleston SC 29401-1738 Office: Med U SC PO Box 250192 Charleston SC 29425-0192 Home Phone: 843-577-6822; Office Phone: 843-792-3607. Business E-Mail: simpsowm@musc.edu.

SIMS, ASHLEY JANE, accountant; b. Lake Ozark, Mo., Feb. 11, 1978; d. James Rance and Linda Lee Stith; m. Albert Earl Sims III, July 27, 2002. BBA, Ga. Southwestern State U., Americus, 2002. Staff acct. Draffin & Tucker, Albany, Ga., 2003—04; sr. acct. Templeton & Co., West Palm Beach, Fla., 2004—05; fiscal & grant mgr. Legal Aid Soc. Palm Beach County, West Palm Beach, 2005—. Mem.: Am. Mensa. Republican. Baptist. Office: Legal Aid Soc Palm Beach County 423 Fern St Ste 200 West Palm Beach FL 33401

SIMS, DALE, state official; b. Charlotte, NC; m. Debbie Davis; 1 child. BS, We. Carolina Univ., 1978; grad. work, Murray (Ky.) State Univ. Program auditor Comptroller of Treas., 1980—82; staff asst. Dept. Treas., 1982—87, exec. asst., treas, 1987—2003; state treas. State of Tenn., 2003—. Mem.: Nat. Assn. State Auditors, Comptrollers and Treas. (exec. com.), Nat. Assn. State Treas. (So. Regional v.p. 2006). Meth. Office: State Treas State Capitol Nashville TN 37243 Office Phone: 615-532-9910. *

SIMS, DAVID LLOYD, lawyer; b. Pine Bluff, Ark., Dec. 31, 1960; s. Lloyd H. Sims Jr. and Betty S. (Wilson) Sims; m. Joan M. Bennett, Aug. 17, 1985; 1 child, Wilson D. BA cum laude, Ouachita Bapt. U., 1983; JD with honors, U. Ark. Sch. Law, 1986. Bar: Ark. 1986, US Dist. Ct., Ea. Dist. Ark. 1987, US Claims Ct. 1989, US Ct. Appeals 8th Circuit 1989, U.S. Supreme Ct. 2005. Assoc. Bridges, Young, Matthews, Holmes & Drake, Pine Bluff, Ark., 1986—91; mem. Bridges, Young, Matthews & Drake PLC, 1991—. Chmn. Am. Cancer Soc. Relay for Life, Pine Bluff, Ark., 1999—2000; adv. bd. Student Cmty. Svc. Project, 1991—94; dir. United Way of SE Ark., 1992—98, Youth Ptnrs. of Pine Bluff/Jefferson County, 2002—07; asst. scoutmaster Boy Scouts of Am., 2002—. Mem.: ABA, Ark. Bar Assn. (ho. of delegates 1997—2004), Jefferson County Bar Assn., Greater Pine Bluff C. of C., Rotary Club of West Pine Bluff (pres. 1995—96, Paul Harris Fellow 1998). Methodist. Avocations: tennis, hiking, reading, music. Office: Bridges Young Matthews & Drake PLC 315 East 8th Ave Pine Bluff AR 71601 Home Phone: 870-535-8323; Office Phone: 870-534-5532. Business E-Mail: davidsims@bridgesplc.com.

SIMS, DOUGLAS D., bank executive; b. 1946; Grad., U. Ill., Urbana, 1968. With St. Louis Bank for Cooperatives, St. Louis, 1969-74; v.p. Ctrl. Bank for Coops., 1974-78; pres. St. Louis Bank for Coops., 1978-84; exec. v.p. Farm Credit Banks of St. Louis, 1984-86, pres., 1986-88, Nat. Bank for Cooperatives, Englewood, Colo., 1988-93; CEO CoBank, Englewood, 1994—. Office: CoBank 5500 S Quebec St Greenwood Village CO 80111-1914

SIMS, EDWARD HOWELL, editor, writer; b. Orangeburg, SC, May 29, 1923; s. Hugo Sheridan and Jesse Lucile (Howell) S.; m. Frances Dell Hartt, Jan. 5, 1946; m. Martha Lurene Bass, July 18, 1960; children: Edward H., Robert; m. Bente Thorlund Christensen, Oct. 4, 1969; children: Edward Christian, Frederik. AB, Wofford Coll., 1943; postgrad., Emory U., 1946-47. Mng. editor Orangeburg Times and Democrat, 1946, editor, 1952—; Washington corr., founder Washington bur. for number S.C. dailies, 1947. Dir. Sims Pub. Co., Orangeburg. Columnist: Looking South From Washington, 1948—; Washington Bur. chief: Editor's Copy syndicate, 1950-52; editor-pub., 1952—; radio news analyst: The News of The Week In Washington, 1951—; Author: American Aces, 1958, Greatest Fighter Missions, 1962, The Fighter Pilots, 1967, Fighter Tactics 1914-70, 1972, Aces Over the Oceans, 1987; contbr. articles to publs. White House corr. covering Pres.''s confs., 1948—; mem. Senate and House press galleries, 1947—; Am. consul Munich, Germany, 1963-65; cons. Exec. Office of White House, 1966-67; consul gen. Zurich, 1992; apptd. mem. Commn. to Preserve Am. Heritage Abroad, 1987. Served to 1st lt. USAF, World War II. Recipient Young Man of the Year award S.C. Jr. C. of C., 1959 Mem. White House Corrs. Assn., Am. Legion, V.F.W. Clubs: Rotary, Nat. Press; Metropolitan (Washington); R.A.F. (London). Methodist. Home: 3803 Pin Oaks St Sarasota FL 34232-1241 also: PO Box 400 Fairview NC 28730-0400 Office: PO Box 532 Orangeburg SC 29116-0532

SIMS, ELIZABETH LANEAL, retired healthcare association executive; b. Manila, Ark., May 22, 1948; d. Aaron Neal and Mary Elizabeth (Butler) Shedd; m. Jared Preston Sims, Aug. 31, 1968; children: Jared Neal, David Paul, Christopher Wayne. BA in English, James Madison U., Harrisonburg, Va., 1974. Tchr. English Buffalo Gap HS, Augusta County, Va., 1977—79, Wilson Meml. HS, 1981—88, tchr., sponsor, high sch. yr. book The Hornet's Nest, 1981—88; vol. coord., case mgr. Family Children's Svc., Richmond, 1989—93, program adminstr. sr. svcs., 1993—98; exec. dir. Hanover Mental Health Assn., Inc., Ashland, 1998—2005; exec. dir. Va. affiliate Nat. Alliance on Mental Illness, 2005—06; ret., 2007. Pres. bd. dirs. Hanover Mental Health Assn., 1996-98; bd. dirs. Va. Coalition for Aging Mem. adminstrv. bd. Ctr. United Meth. Ch., 1981—83; mem. staff/parish com. Duncan Meml. United Meth. Ch., 2002—, sec. to adminstrv. bd., 2003—, mem. lay leadership com., 2006—; bd. dirs. United Way, Richmond, 1995—97, campaign cabinet, 1998—2000; v.p. bd. dirs. Urban League Greater Richmond, 1999—2004; bd. dirs. Urban League Found., 2002—04, Friends of Hanover, 2003—05. Recipient Cert. of Appreciation for Profl. Excellence in Edn., Aug. Co., 1987, Cert. of Appreciation, Urban League, 1998, United Way Svcs., 1997, 1998, 1999, 2000. Mem. Internat. Assn. Psychosocial Rehab. Svcs., Mental Health Assn. Va. (bd. dirs. 1998—), Beta Sigma Phi (Laureate Rho chpt. pres. 2003—) United Methodist. Avocation: Boy Scout counseling. Personal E-mail: simseliz@gmail.com.

SIMS, EZRA, composer; b. Birmingham, Ala., Jan. 16, 1928; s. Ezra G. and Kathryn W. (Wallace) S. BA, Birmingham So. Coll., 1947; postgrad., Birmingham Conservatory Music, 1945-48; MusB in Composition, Yale U. Sch. Music, 1952; MA in Composition, Mills Coll., 1956. Librarian Harvard Music Library, Cambridge, Mass., 1958-62, 65-74; music dir. New Eng. Dinosaur Dance Theatre, Boston, 1968-78; instr. theory New Eng. Conservatory Music, Boston, 1976-78; instr. microtonal theory Mozarteum, Salzburg, 1992-93; freelance composer Cambridge, 1974—. Dir. Dinosaur Annex Music Ensemble, Cambridge, pres. 1977-2003; guest composer 23d Ann. Contemporary Music Festival, Ill. Wesleyan U., 1977; lectr. various colls. including Warwick U., Cleve. Inst. Music, Internat. Christian U., Westport Friends of Music, Schlumberger-Doll Rsch., Webster U., Mozarteum, Northwestern U., Hochschule für Musik, Hamburg. Composer over 100 works, predominantly microtonal music for various mediums including Chamber Cantata on Chinese Poems, 1954, Mass, 1955, Two Folk Songs, 1958, String Quartet, 1959, Sieben-Spencer Lieder, 1960, Sonate Concertanti, 1961, Third Quartet, 1962, Buchlein for Lyon, 1962, Cantata III, 1963, Octet for Strings, 1964, In Memoriam Alice Hawthorne, 1967, Antimatter: Three Dances for Toby, 1968, A Frank Overture: Four Dented Interludes and Coda, 1969, Pastorale, 1970, Clement Wenceslaus Lothaire Nepomucene, Prince Mettermich (1773-1859), In Memoriam, 1970, Real Toads, 1970, Interlope, 1971, Tango Variations, 1971, Museum Piece, 1972, Where the Wild Things Are, 1973, String Quartet #2 (1962), 1974, After Lyle or Untitled, 1975, When the Angels Blow Their Trumpets, 1976, Celebration of Dead Ladies, 1976, Elegie-nach Rilke, 1976, Collage XIII, 1977, Aeneas on the Saxophone, 1977, Come Away, 1978, Midorigaoka, 1978, 5 Songs, 1979, -And, As I Was Saying..., 1979, Two for One, 1980, Sextet, 1981, All Done From Memory, 1980, Phenomena, 1981, Solo After Sextet, 1981, Quartet, 1982, Pictures for an Institution, 1983, Tune and Variations, 1983, Brief Elegies, 1983, String Quartet #4, 1984, The Conversions, 1985, Wedding Winds, 1986, Quintet, 1987, Chase, 1987, Solo in four movements, 1987, AEDM in memoriam, 1988, Flight, 1989, Night Piece: IN Girum Imus nocte et Consuminur Igni, 1989, Concert Piece, 1990, Duo, 1992, Invocation, 1992, Stanzas, 1995, If I Told Him, 1996, Duo, 1996, 97, Encores: Three Parlor Songs, 2000, String Quartet #5, 2000, Musing and Recollection, 2003, -furthermore..., 2004, Concert Piece, 2005, im Mirabell, 2006; contbr. articles to profl. jours. Served as pvt. U.S. Army, 1952-54. Recipient Composers Forum award, 1959, Koussevitzky Found. commn., 1983, Am. Acad. Arts and Letters award, 1985; grantee Cambridge Arts Coun., 1975, 76, Martha Baird Rockefeller Found., 1977; fellow Guggenheim Found., 1962, McDowell Colony, 1966, Nat. Endowment for Arts, 1976, 78, Mass. Artists Found., 1979, Djerassi Found., 1990, Fulbright Sr. Scholar, 1992, Wurlitzer Found., 1998, Camargo Found., 2000. Mem. Broadcast Music, Inc. Home and Office: 229 Hurley St Cambridge MA 02141-2133 Address: Rosalie Calabrese Mgmt Box 20580 Park West St New York NY 10025-1521 Office Phone: 617-864-8781. Personal E-mail: ezrsims@aol.com.

SIMS, GARY WAYNE, music educator; b. Pevely, Mo., Mar. 31, 1949; s. George Alvin and Eva Clara Sims. AA in Music, Jefferson Coll., Hillsboro, Mo., 1969; BS in Music, William Jewell Coll., Liberty, Mo., 1971; MusM, Southwestern Bapt. Theol. Sem., Ft. Worth, 1974. Prof. music Brewton-Parker Coll., Mt. Vernon, Ga., 1974—79; instr. voice Webster U., St. Louis, 1980—; instr. music So. Ill. U., Edwardsville, 2005—. Composer art songs, sacred songs, children's cantata, handbell arrangements, folk song arrangements; singer: Bach Soc. St. Louis, St. Louis Symphony, Ft. Worth Oratorio Orch., Ga. Chamber Orch., St. Louis Chamber Chorus and Orch., Savannah Symphony, Jerusalem Symphony, others. Named Tchr. of Yr., Brewton-Parker Coll., 1974; named one of Outstanding Young Men of Am. Mem.: Nat. Assn. Tchrs. of Singing, Phi Mu Alpha. Avocations: classic cars, interior decorating. Home: 1535 Grant Rdd Saint Louis MO 63119 Office: Webstre Univ Dept Music Saint Louis MO 63119

SIMS, HENRY P., JR., management educator; Prof. mgmt. U. Md., College Park. Author: The Thinking Organization: Dynamics of Organizational Social Cognition, 1986, SuperLeadership: Leading Others to Lead Themselves, 1989, The New Leadership Paradigm: Social Learning and Cognition in Organizations, 1992, Business Without Bosses: How Self-Managing Teams Are Building High-Performance Companies, 1993, Company of Heroes: Unleashing the Power of Self Leadership, 1996, Team Work and Group Dynamics, 1999, The New Superleadership: Leading Others to Lead Themselves, 2001. Office: U Md Van Munching Hall College Park MD 20742-0001 Business E-Mail: hsims@rhsmith.umd.edu.

SIMS, JOE, lawyer; b. Phoenix, Sept. 29, 1944; s. Joe and Pauline Jane (Saunders) S.; m. Robin Ann Reed, Jan. 30, 1965; 1 child, Shannon Dane. BS in Fin., Ariz. State U., 1967, JD, 1970. Bar: Ariz. 1970, U.S. Supreme Ct. 1975, D.C 1978. Trial atty. antitrust div. Dept. Justice, Washington, 1970-73; spl. asst. to asst. atty. gen., 1973-75; dep. asst. atty. gen. for policy planning and legislation, 1975-77, dep. asst. atty. gen. for regulatory matters and fgn. commerce, 1977-78; mem. firm Jones, Day, Washington, 1978-79, ptnr., 1979—. Resident fellow Am. Enterprise Inst. for Pub. Policy Rsch., Washington, 1978-79, vis. fellow, 1979-81; prin. Coun. for Excellence in Govt. Contbr. articles to profl. jours. Co-recipient US Antitrust award, Chambers Awards for Excellence Ceremony, 2006; named one of 15 Dealmakers of the Yr., Am. Lawyer mag., 2000, World's Top 10 Antitrust Lawyers, Global Counsel mag., 2001. Mem. ABA (chmn. antitrust law sect. one com. 1987-90, bus. law sect. antitrust law com. 1988-91, antitrust law civil practice and procedure com. 1990-91), Am. Law Inst., D.C. Bar Assn., Firestone Country Club (Akron, Ohio), Mirabel Club (Scottsdale, Ariz.), Talking Rock Club (Prescott, Ariz.). Republican. Office: Jones Day 51 Louisiana Ave NW Washington DC 20001-2113 Office Phone: 202-879-3863. Office Fax: 202-626-1747. Business E-Mail: jsims@jonesday.com.

SIMS, JOHN R., lawyer; b. 1950; B, U. Mo., 1972, JD, 1975. Various legal positions to v.p., dep. gen. counsel Federated Dept. Stores, Inc., Cin., 1980—2002; exec. v.p., gen. counsel Albertson's-Inc., Boise, Idaho, 2002—. Mem.: Law Review, Phi Beta Kappa. *

SIMS, KENT OTWAY, economist; b. Chickasha, Okla., Nov. 2, 1940; s. Jesse Otway and Mable Vela (Bear) S.; m. Jeanette McCollum, June 9, 1961; children: Marketa, Adam. BA, U. Colo., 1963, PhD, 1966. registered investment advisor. Economist Urban Renewal Authority, Denver, 1965-66, U.S. Dept. State mission to Pakistan, 1966-69, Fed. Res. Bank of San Francisco, 1969-71, asst. v.p., 1971-72, v.p., dir. research, 1972-74, sr. v.p., 1974-82, exec. v.p., chief fin. officer, 1982-85; fin. advisor, investment mgr., mgmt. cons. Theodore R. Seton, 1985-86; ptnr. C&K Partnership, 1987-89. Pres. Her Equal Share, Inc., 1986-89, San Francisco Econ. Devel. Corp., 1988-91; dir. econ. planning and devel. Mayor's Office, San Francisco, 1992-93, San Francisco Redevel. Agy., 1993-96; dir. spl. projects City Mgr.'s Office, Oakland, Calif., 1997; dep. dir. Com. Econ. Devel., Oakland, 1997-98; cons. Bay Area Life Scis. Alliance, 1999, San Francisco Planning and Urban Rsch. Assn., 2000, Golden Gate Restaurant Assn., 2001-05, San Francisco Small Property Owners, 2003, San Francisco Small Bus. Alliance, 2003, Burnham & Brown, Attys., 2003-05. Bd. govs. Econ. Lit. Coun. Calif., Long Beach, 1983-88; trustee Strybing Arboretum Soc. Golden Gate Park, San Francisco, 1983-96; bd. dirs. Jewish Community Mus., San Francisco, 1986-93, Design Coun. San Francisco Bay Area, 1989-90, Career Resources Devel. Ctr., 1991-92; adv. bd. St. Lukes Hosp., San Francisco, 1988-96. Mem. Am. Econs. Assn., Nat. Audubon Soc. Am. Clubs: Sierra. Home Phone: 419-383-5049. Personal E-mail: kentsims@pacbell.net.

SIMS, LOWERY STOKES, museum curator and administrator, writer, educator; b. Washington, Feb. 13, 1949; d. John Jacob and Bernice Marion (Banks) S. BA in Art History, Queens Coll., 1970, MPhil, 1989; PhD in Art History, CUNY, 1995; MA in Art History, Johns Hopkins U., 1972; LHD (hon.), Md. Coll. Art, Balt., 1988; ArtsD (hon.), Moore Coll. Art, Phila., 1990; ArtsD, Brown U., Providence, 2003. Mus. edn. assoc. Met. Mus. Art, NYC, 1972-75, asst. curator, 1975-79, assoc. curator, 1979-95, curator, 1995—99; exec. dir. Studio Mus. in Harlem, NYC, 1999—2005, pres., 2005—06, adj. curator, 2006—. Prin. author: (catalogue) Stuart Davis, American Painting, 1991; co-author: (book) Wifredo Lam and the International Avant Guide, 1923, 1982, (catalogue) Wifredo Lam and His Contemporaries, 1992, (catalogue) Challenge of the Modern: African American Arts, 1925-1945, 2002-03, Persistence of Geometry, Cleve. Mus. Art, 2006. Bd. dirs. Caribbean Cultural Ctr., N.Y.C., 1975-80, 90—99, Tiffany Found., N.Y.C., 2005—, Met. Mus. Art, 2005—, Art 21, 2006—. Recipient award of distinction Am. Women's Econ. Devel., 1993. Mem. Internat. Assn. Art Critics, Coll. Art Assn. (bd. dirs. 1993-97, Mather award for art criticism 1991). Democrat. Avocations: needlepoint, collecting black memorabilia. Personal E-mail: lsimssmh@aol.com. Business E-Mail: lsims@studiomuseum.org.

SIMS, MARCIE LYNNE, language educator, writer; b. Monrovia, Calif., Feb. 22, 1963; d. Charles Eugene and Delores May (Wonert) S.; m. Douglas Todd Cole; children: Marcus Anthony Cole, Thomas Halvor Cole. BA in English, Calif. State Poly., 1986; MA in English, San Diego State U., 1990. Page U.S. Senate, Washington, 1979; instr. Calif. Conservation Corps, San Diego, 1990; instr. in English Shoreline C.C., Seattle, 1990-94, Seattle Ctrl. C.C., 1990-94, Green River C.C., Auburn, Wash., 1994—. Founder Wild Mind Women Writers Workshop, Seattle, 1992—. Author: The Write Stuff, 2007; contbg. author Moms on Line, 1996-; editor Espial Lit. Jour. Vol. cons. Camp Fire, Wash., 1994-96. Mem. Am. Fedn. Tchrs., The Keats-Shelley Orgn., Wash. Fed. Tchrs. (exec. bd. mem. 1993-94), Phi Kappa Phi, Sigma Tau Delta. Democrat. Avocations: cooking, tennis. Office: Green River CC 12401 SE 320th St Auburn WA 98092-3622

SIMS, MARCY (MARTHA J. SIMS), library director; b. Portsmouth, NH, Oct. 26, 1946; m. Hunter Sims; children: Hunter III, Clara. BA in English, Mary Baldwin Coll.; MLS, U. NC, 1969; MPA, Old Dominion U. Positions up to dir. Va. Beach Pub. Libr. Vice chair United Way Va. Beach campaign, 1994, chair, 1995; bd. dirs. Va. Literacy Found. Recipient Award for Excellence in Humanities, Va. Found. Humanities, 2005. Mem.: Va. Libr. Assn. (sec. 1977—78). Avocations: tennis, skiing, reading. Office: Va Beach Pub Libr Adminstrn Municipal Ctr Bldg 19 2416 Courthouse Dr Virginia Beach VA 23456 Office Phone: 757-385-8244. E-mail: msims@vbgov.com.

SIMS, PAMELA JAN (CERUSSI), writer, minister; b. Little Rock, Sept. 10, 1933; 2 children. Attended, Mt. St. Mary's Acad., St. Scholastica's Coll., Sydney, Delgado Coll., Nola, Tulane U., 1951; DD (hon.). Lic. rev.

in Christian ministry specialized svcs. Fla., 2006. Past pres. Ikebana Internat., Le Gals, Inc., 1979—89; pres. Titanic Bead Co.; journalist, notary pub. Fla., 1986—. Tchr. legal secretarial classes, Nola; support writer Pres. George W. Bush, 1999—2007. Author: Pensacola Today mag., Climate mag., introduction to Bonsai & Basic Ikebara; featured on local TV Guide mag. cover Anskebara Design; prin. works include Bonsai and Ikebana design articles; contbr. articles in mags. and newspapers. Vol. Pensacola Art Mus.; team leader Bush/Cheney Inc., 2002—07; mem. Rep. Nat. Com., Rep. Nat. Woman's Club, Pensacola Christian Women's Club, United Intercessors Inc. Recipient Cert. of Recognition, Rep. Nat. Party, 2002, 2006, Congl. Award of Merit, 2004, 8 Blue ribbons and 3 Tri-Color ribbons, Fla. Fedn. Garden Clubs, 2004, Cert. of Appreciation, Rep. Nat. Com., 2005. Mem.: Pensacola Camellia Club. Achievements include patents pending for AIDS cure. Office Phone: 850-607-1786. Office Fax: 850-457-1022.

SIMS, PATTERSON, curator; b. Phila., Nov. 17, 1947; m. Katy Homans, 1987; 2 children. Student, Trinity Coll., Hartford, Conn.; BA, New Sch. Social Rsch., 1972. Asst. dir. O.K. Harris Works Art, NYC, 1969-76; assoc. curator permanent collection Whitney Mus. Am. Art, NYC, 1976-87; part-time instr. Sch. Continuing Edn. NYU, 1975-77, 84-86; assoc. dir. art and exhbns., curator modern art Seattle Art Mus., 1987—96; dep. dir. edn. and rsch. support Mus. Modern Art, NYC, 1996—2001; dir. Montclair Art Mus., NJ, 2001—. Mem. adv. bds., panels the Fabric Workshop, Phila., Studio in a Sch. Assn., N.Y.C, Robert Lehman Coll. Art Gallery, N.Y.C., Santa Fe Chamber Mus. Festival., N.Mex., Seattle, Laumier Sculpture Pk., St. Louis, NEA Mus. Implementation Panel, Washington; lectr. in field. Exhbns. include 30 Years Am. Art, 1977, Am. Art 1920-45, Am. Art 1950—, 1977-78, Tradition and Modernism in Am. Art, 1900-25, Gibbes Art Gallery, Charleston, S.C., 1978, Jan Matulka Retrospective Exhbn., 1979-80, Concentration, 1980-81, Biennial Exhbn., Decade of Transition: 1940-50, 1981, (with Ann D'Harnoncourt) John Cage: Scores and Prints, 1882, (with Emily Rauh Pulitzer) Ellsworth Kelly: Sculpture, 1982-83, (with 3 other curators) Biennial Exhbn.: Minimalism to Expressionism: Painting and Sculpture since 1965, 1983, Viola Frey, 1984, Clare Zeisler, 1984-85, Biennial Exhbn., 1985, Figure as Subject: The Last Decade, 1986, John Storrs Retrospective Exhbn., 1986-87. Figure as Subject: The Revival of Figuration since 1975, 1988, Twentieth Century Am. Art Highlights of the Permanet Collection of the Whitney Mus. Am. Art, 1988, Documents Northwest Series: C.T. Chew, Seattle Art Mus., 1988, Made in N.Y.: The N.Y. Sch.: 1945-65: Jasper Johns: A Selected View: New Work N.Y., Seattle Art Mus., 1989, Documents Northwest Series: Crossed Cultures, Figures of Translucence, Seattle Art. Mus., 1989, Mark Tansey: Art and Source, Seattle Art Mus., 1990; author brochures, catalogs. Home: 11 W 53rd St New York NY 10019-5401 Office: Montclair Art Mus 3 South Mountain Ave Montclair NJ 07042

SIMS, REBECCA LITTLETON, lawyer; b. Macon, Ga., May 24, 1957; d. William Harvey and Carlan Patricia (Hammond) Littleton; m. Charles Neil Sims, Jr., Dec. 29, 1984; children: Charles Neil III, William Vickers, Caroline Greer. Student, Tex. A&M U., 1977; JD, Baylor U., 1981; BA in Polit. Sci. with honors, U. South, 1979; MPA, Valdosta State U., 2002. Bar: Ga. 1983, U.S. Dist. Ct. (so. dist.) Ga. 1984, U.S. Dist. Ct. (no. dist.) Ga. 1985, U.S. Dist. Ct. (mid. dist.) Ga. 1992, U.S. Supreme Ct. 2001. Law clk., Waco, Tex., 1981, Waycross Jud. Cir., Waycross and Douglas, Ga., 1982-83; asst. dist. atty. Waycross cir. Dist. Atty.'s Office, Douglas, 1983-84; spl. asst. to atty. gen. Dept. Family and Children's Svcs., Coffee County, 1988-90; pvt. practice Douglas, 1985-92; state ct. solicitor Coffee County, Ga., 1989-96; in-house counsel Sims Funeral Home, 1997-99; asst. prof. polit. sci. South Ga. Coll., Douglas, 2000—. Mem. altar guild St. Andrew's Episcopal Ch., Douglas, 1983-90, 2000—, vestryman, clk. of vestry, 1986-88, 2002—04; bd. dirs. Shelter for Abused Women, Waycross, 1986-87; trustee U. South, Diocese of Ga., Savannah, 1988-91; mem. First Meth. Ch., Douglas, Ga., 1991-99, United Meth. Women Cir. # 8, 1991-98; dir. Vacation Bible Sch., 1997, 98; legis. aide Charles Neil Sims, Jr., Ga. Ho. Reps., 1997—; mem. Ga. Regents Adv. Com. on Polit. Sci. Mem. State Bar Ga., Rsch. Club. Avocations: gardening, reading, cooking, antiques. Office: PO Box 2352 Douglas GA 31534-2352 E-mail: rsims@sga.edu.

SIMS, RICHARD LEE, retired hospital administrator; b. Columbus, Ohio, Jan. 6, 1929; s. Dorwin Delos and Christine Anna (Hanstein) Sims; m. Marilyn Lou Atkinson, June 2, 1951 (dec. July 2005); children: John Christopher, Steven Paul; m. Norma W. Shilliday, Nov. 17, 2006. BS, Ohio State U., Columbus, 1951. Pres. Doctors Hosp. Found., Columbus, 1977-95; preceptor faculty Ohio State U. Coll. Health Care Adminstrn.; past chmn. Hosp. Coun. Franklin County; ret., 1995. Past chmn. Hosp. Shared Svc. Inc. Past chmn. 1st Cmty. Village Bd.; past chmn. governing bd. 1st Cmty. Ch.; pres. Scioto Valley Health Systems Agy., 1999-2002; pres. Employment for Srs., 1999-2000, Probus, 2003; past chair Columbus area chpt. ARC, emeritus bd. dirs.; mem. 1st Cmty. Found., Drs. Hosp. Devel. Found. Recipient Disting. Svc. award Columbus Jr. C. of C., 1960-63. Fellow Am. Coll. Healthcare Execs. (life), Am. Coll. Osteo. Healthcare Execs. (life); mem. Am. Osteo. Healthcare Assn. (chmn. 1988), Ohio Soc. of Assn. Execs. (past pres.), Ohio Hosp. Assn. (past chmn. bd.), Ohio Osteo. Hosp. Assn. (past pres.), Am. Legion (past post comdr.), Rotary (pres. 1978-79), Columbus Club, Sigma Chi (named Significant Sig 2003). Home: 4848 Slate Run Ct Columbus OH 43220

SIMS, ROBERT JOHN, financial planner; b. Phila., Mar. 18, 1926; s. Stanley Joseph and Marie (Kendrick) S.; m. Gloria MacCarter, Nov. 27, 1965 (dec. June 21, 2005); children: Lisa Byrne, Dana Hospodar, Ernest, William, Peter, Moira. Student, Temple U., 1947-51; MSFS, CLU, ChFC, Am. Coll., Bryn Mawr, Pa., 1957; CFP, Coll. Fin. Planning, Denver. With Provident Mut. Life Ins., Phila., 1947-56, Aetna Life Ins., Phila., 1956-58, Mut. of N.Y., Phila., 1958-68; chmn. Fin-Plan Investments, Inc., Wayne, Pa., 1960—; pres. Fin-Plan Cons., Inc., Wayne, 1960—, Fin-Plan, Inc., Wayne, 1960—; chmn. Sims Fin. Svcs. LLC. Mem. fin. com. Archdiocese of Phila., investment com., trustee Lay Employees Pension Plan. Past trustee Notre Dame Acad. Bd., Radnor, Pa., United Fund; past pres. Phila. Jaycees, past nat. dir. U.S. Jaycees; bd. dirs. Gwynedd Mercy Coll., Phila.; active Big Bros.; mem. adv. bd. St. Charles Borremmeo Sem.; past pres., active Cath. Philopatrian Lit. Inst. With U.S. mil., 1944-46. Mem. Internat. Assn. Fin. Planners (founding pres. Delaware Valley chpt.), Inst. CFPs, Am. Soc. CLU, Phila. Estate Planning Coun., Phila. Assn. Life Underwriters, Golden Key Soc., Union League Phila., Phila. Country Club, Ocean Reef Club, Sky 700 Club. Republican. Roman Catholic. Avocation: golf. Home: 219 Orchard Way Saint Davids PA 19087-4805 Office: Sims Fin Svcs LLC 531 E Lancaster Ave Wayne PA 19087-5112

SIMS, ROGER W., lawyer; b. Cleve., Aug. 3, 1950; BA with high honors, U. Fla., 1972, JD, 1974. Bar: Fla. 1975. Mem. Holland & Knight, Orlando, Fla. Mem. Moot Ct. U. Fla.; contbr. to profl mag. and jour. Mem. ABA (mem. standing com. on environ. law 2000-2003), Fla. Bar Assn. (chmn. environ., land use law sect. 1988-89), Fla. Assn. Water Quality Control (pres. 2006-07), Phi Beta Kappa, Phi Kappa Phi, Omicron Delta Kappa, Phi Alpha Delta, Fla. Blue Key. Office: Holland & Knight PO Box 1526 200 S Orange Ave Ste 2600 Orlando FL 32801-3453 Office Phone: 407-425-8500. Business E-Mail: roger.sims@hklaw.com.

SIMS, WILLIAM D., JR., lawyer; b. Kosciusko, Miss., Nov. 19, 1947; BA, U. Miss., 1969; JD, Harvard U., 1972. Bar: Tex. 1972, US Supreme Ct., US Ct. Appeals (5th cir.), US Dist. Ct. (no., ea. we. so. districts) Tex., Tex. Supreme Ct. Ptnr. Vinson & Elkins LLP, Dallas, co-chair Dallas Litig. sect. Named one of The Best Lawyers in Dallas, D mag., 2002—03. Fellow: The Ctr. for Am. & Internat. Law, Internat. Acad. Trial Lawyers. Office: Vinson & Elkins LLP Trammell Crow Ctr 2001 Ross Ave Ste 3700 Dallas TX 75201 E-mail: bsims@velaw.com.

SIMS, WILSON, lawyer; b. Nashville, Dec. 24, 1924; s. Cecil and Grace (Wilson) S.; m. Linda Bell, Aug. 12, 1948; children: Linda Rickman; Suzanne, Wilson. BA, U. N.C., 1946; JD, Vanderbilt U., 1948. Bar: Tenn. 1948. Since practiced in, Nashville; ptnr. Bass, Berry & Sims; gen. counsel, dir. Baird Ward Printing Co., Southeastern Capital Corp., Martha White Foods, Synercon Corp., Forrest Life Ins. Co., Charter Co., The Bailey Co., Kenworth of Tenn., Inc. Chmn. Tenn. Commn. for Human Devel., Tenn. Commn. on Continuing Legal Edn.; mem. Tenn. Gen. Assembly, 1959-60; bd. dirs. Nashville YMCA, United Cerebal Palsy, Kidney Found., Matthew 25, McKendree Village; trustee Meharry Med. Coll., Webb Sch., Bell Buckle, Tenn.; adv. bd. Jr. League; mem. bd. visitors U. N.C. 1st lt. USMCR, 1942-45, 50-52. Fellow Am. Bar Found. (life), Nashville Bar Found.; mem. ABA, Tenn. Bar Assn. (past spkr. ho. of dels., past pres.), Nashville Bar Assn. (past pres., dir., Pub. Svc. award), Tenn. Bar Found. (past chmn.), Am. Judicature Soc., Am. Acad. Polit. Sci., Vanderbilt U. Law Alumni Assn. (past pres., Disting. Svc. award), Nashville C. of C. (2 terms bd. govs.), Belle Meade Country Club (bd. dirs.), High Hampton Colony Club (bd. dirs., pres.). Methodist. Home: 22 Foxhall Close Nashville TN 37215-1862 Office: Bass Berry & Sims Ste 2700 315 Deaderick St Nashville TN 37238-3001 Business E-Mail: wsims@bassberry.com.

SIMS-CURRY, KRISTY, women's college basketball coach; b. Olla, La., 1967; m. Kelly Curry, 2 dau. BS in Health and Phys. Edn., N.E. La. U., 1988; MS in Kinesiology, Stephen F. Austin U., Nacogdoches, Tex., 1992. Coach Weston H.S., Mansfield H.S., La.; women's asst. basketball coach Tulane U., 1991-93, Stephen F. Austin U., 1993-94, Tex. A&M U., 1994-96; asst. coach La. Tech. U., 1996-99; head coach Purdue U., West Lafayette, 1999—. Office: care Women's Basketball 1790 Mackey Arena Rm 44 West Lafayette IN 47907-1790 *

SIMSON, BEVLYN, artist; b. Columbus, Ohio, Sept. 9, 1917; d. Amon and Fannie Florence (Gilbert) Thall; m. Theodore Richard Simson, Mar. 25, 1938; children: Sherran Blair, Douglas A. BFA, Ohio State U., 1969, MFA, 1972. Author: Prints and Poetry, 1969. One woman shows include J.B. Speed Art Mus., Louisville, 1970, Huntington Gallery, Columbus, Ohio, 1970, 73, United Christian Ctr., Columbus, 1970, Bodley Gallery, NY, 1971, 74, Gilman Galleries, Chgo., 1971, Gallery 200, Columbus, 1972, Hopkins Hall Gallery, Ohio State U., Columbus, 1972, Meth. Theol Sch., Deleware, Ohio, 1973, Columbus Public Lib., 1973, Garfinkels, Washington, 1973, City Hall, Mayor's Office, Columbus, 1974, 82, Capital U., Bexley, Ohio, 1977, Hillel Found., Ohio State U., 1978, Columbus Tech. Inst., 1979, Springfield Art Mus., Ohio, 1980, Peace Luth. Ch., Gahanna, Ohio, 1981, Franklin U. Gallery, Columbus, 1981, Columbus Mus. Art Collectors Gallery, 1983, Ohio State U., 2006; exhibited in juried and invitational shows at Columbus Mus. Art-Ohio Art League, 1968, 70, 71, 73, 74, 75, 77, 78, 79, 80, 86, Ohio Statehouse and State Office Tower, Columbus, 1968-78, Battelle Meml. Inst., Columbus, 1969-73, 75, 78, 81-82, Schumacher Gallery, Capital U., Columbus, 1969-85, 87, 88, Salles d'Exposition, Paris, 1969, Am. Cultural Ctr., Kyoto, Japan, J.B. Speed Art Mus. Collector's Gallery, Louisville, 1970-85, Studio San Guiseppe, Mt. St. Joseph Coll., Cin., 1971, Silver Anniversary Coll. Arts, 2nd Biennial Alumni Exhbn., Hopkins Hall Gallery, 1972, 2nd Internat. Art Exhbn., Paramaribo, Serinam, 1974, Mansfield Art Ctr., Ohio, 1971, Collector's Showroom, Chgo., 1971-82, Gov.'s MansionState of Ohio, 1972, 74, We. Ill. U., 1972, Albatross Gallery, Rome, 1972, Palazzo Dell Exprizioni, Rome, 1972, Place-Allrich Gallery, San Francisco, 1973-75, Chautauqua Assn., NY, 1973, Butler Inst. Am. Art, Youngtown, Ohio, 1973, 76, Huntington Gallery, Columbus, 1973, 74, Gallery 200, Columbus, 1972-76, Columbus C. of C., 1974, 75, Zanesville Art Ctr., Ohio, 1976, Columbus Inst. Contemporary Art, 1978, Nationwide Plaza Gallery, Columbus, 1980, Franklin U., Columbus, 1980, Ohio State U., 1993, Ohio Art League, 1987, Jeffrey Mansion, Bexley, Ohio, 1996, 10th Ann. Women Artists Expo Seal of Ohio Girl Scout Coun., Inc. Columbus, 1996, Financial Group Gallery, Worthington, Ohio, 1997, Ohio Art League, 1997, 4th Hall Gallery, Ohio State U., 1997, Concourse Gallery, Upper Arlington, Ohio, 1998, 13th Ann. Women Artists Expo Art in The Nation Wide Atrium, Columbus, Ohio, 1999, Bexley Art League, Ohio, Jeffrey Mansion, 2000, State Office Towers Exhbn. Gallery, 2003; Art League Mem. Curated Exhbn., Structure/Consequences, 1997, Fourth Biennial Alumni Exhbn-.:ReSiDivist, Hopkins Hall Gallery, Ohio State U., 1997, Concourse Gallery, Arlington Ohio, 1998, Bexley Art League, Precision Concepts, Dublin, Ohio, 1999, Art in the Atrium, Columbus, Ohio, 1999, Art on Main Street, Schumacher Gallery, 2002, others; represented in permanent collections Columbus Mus. Arts, J.B. Speed Art Mus., Louisville, Capital U., Bexley, Fordham U., NYC, Kyoto City U. Fine Arts, Springfield Art Mus., Ohio, Tyler Mus. Art, Tex., Wichita Mus. Art, Kans., Zanesville Art Ctr., Ohio State U., Columbus, Meth. Theol. Sch., Delaware, Ohio, Yerke Mortgage Co., Columbus, Marcorp, NY, Kresge Co., Detroit, IBM, Columbus, Chase Manhattan Bank, NYC, Chase Bank Ohio, Am. Bancorp., Columbus, Ohio Nat. Bank Plaza, Columbus, Pan Western Life Ins. Co., Columbus, First Investment Co., Columbus, Children's Hosp., Phila., Franklin County Crippled Children's Ctr., Columbus, Zenith East, NYC, First Cmty. Bank, Columbus, First City Bank, Columbus, Ohio, Ronald McDonald House, Columbus, Columbia Gas of Ohio, Columbus, Midland Title Security Co., Columbus, Huntington Nat. Bank Ctr., Columbus, Lehman Bros., NYC, Columbus Sch. for Girls, Grand Prix Assocs., Inc., Columbus, Grant Hosp. Med Ctr., Columbus, Libr. and Rsch. Ctr. Nat. Mus. Women in Arts, Washington, DC, Ohio State U. Libr. Rare Books Room Collection, Laredo Pub. Libr., Tex.; represented in private collections. Mem. Nat. League Am. Pen Women, Nat. Artists Equity Assn., Bexley Art League, Columbus Mus. Art, Ohio Art League (bd. dirs. 1965-96, treas., sec., pres. 1977), Ohio State U. Alumni Assn., Pres.'s Club (Ohio State U.), Phi Sigma Sigma. Studio: Bevlyn Simson Studio 4300 E Broad St 1st Cmty Bank Bldg Columbus OH 43213-1243 Office Phone: 614-239-4610. Personal E-mail: sherblair@aol.com.

SIMSON, CLAUDINE, computer company executive; married; 2 children. BEE, INSA, Toulouse, France, PhD in Semiconductor Physics, 1978; three hon. degrees. Device physicist Bell-Northern Rsch., France; R&D and sr. exec. positions, including gen. mgr. global microelectronics & microwave components bus. Nortel Networks, v.p., global tech rsch. & intellectual property, 1997; v.p., chief tech. officer, semiconductor products sector (now Freescale Semiconductor) Motorola, Inc., 2003—07; exec. v.p., chief tech. officer LSI Logic Corp., Milpitas, Calif., 2007—. Established the Nat. Chair for Women in Engring., 1988; involved with Adv. Coun. for Sci. & Tech. to the Prime Minister Can., NRC; Can. rep. US President's Adv. Com. on Internat. Cooperation Policy; hon. chair US Nat. Task Force on Intellectual Property and Knowledge Mgmt.; chmn. bd. directors Micronet R&D, Inc.; spkr. in field. Named to Hall of Fame of Women in Tech. Internat., 1999; recipient Chevalier de l'Ordre Nat. du Merite, Pres. France, 1998; Disting. Fellow, Field Inst., 2004. Fellow: Royal Soc. Can. Achievements include being the youngest PhD in France. Office: LSI Logic Corp 1621 Barber Ln Milpitas CA 95035 *

SIMSON, GARY JOSEPH, dean, law educator; b. Newark, Mar. 18, 1950; s. Marvin and Mildred (Silberg) S.; m. Rosalind Slivka, Aug. 15, 1971; children: Nathaniel, Jennie Anne. BA summa cum laude, Yale Coll., 1971; JD, Yale U., 1974. Bar: Conn. 1974, N.Y. 1980. Law clk. to judge U.S. Ct. Appeals 2d Cir., 1974-75; asst. prof. law U. Tex., 1975—77, prof. law, 1977—80, Cornell U., Ithaca, NY, 1980—2006, assoc. dean faculty devel., 1997—2000, assoc. dean acad. affairs Ithaca, NY, 2000—04; dean, Hostetler-Baker & Hostetler prof. law Case Western Reserve U., 2006—. Vis. prof. law Cornell U., Ithaca, 1979-80, U. Calif., Berkeley, 1986; chmn. adv. bd. law casebook series Carolina Acad. Press. Author: Issues and Perspectives in Conflict of Laws, 1985, 4th edit., 2005; contbr. articles to profl. jours. Mem. ABA, ACLU, Am. Law Inst., Phi Beta Kappa. Office: Case Western Reserve U Sch Law 11075 E Blvd Cleveland OH 44106 Office Phone: 216-368-3283. Business E-Mail: gary.simson@case.edu.

SIMSON, JO ANNE, retired anatomy and cell biology educator; b. Chgo., Nov. 19, 1936; d. Kenneth Brown and Helen Marjorie (Pascoe) Valentine; m. Arnold Simson, June 1961 (div.); 1 child, Maria; m. Michael Smith, Nov. 10, 1971 (div.); children: Elisabeth Smith, Briana Smith. BA, Kalamazoo Coll., 1959; MS, U. Mich., 1961; PhD, SUNY, Syracuse, 1969. Fellow Temple U. Health Sci. Ctr., Phila., 1968-70; asst. prof. Med. U. S.C., Charleston, 1970-76, assoc. prof., 1976-83, prof. anatomy and cell biology, 1983-96, prof. emerita, 1996—. With overseas program UMUC, 1999—2004; featured in Smithsonian exhibit Sci. in Am. Life, 1994—. Contbr. articles to profl. jours.; author short stories and poems. Active adult edn. Unitarian Ch., Charleston, 1973-75, social action, 1990-92. Grantee NSF, 1959-60, NIH, 1966-67, 72-87, 91-95. Mem. Am. Assn. Anatomists, Am. Soc. Cell Biology, Histochem. Soc. (sec. 1979-82, exec. com. 1985-89), Fogarty Internat. Fellowship Bioctr. (Basel, Switzerland, 1987-88), Amnesty Internat. (newsletter editor Group 168 1982-86), Phi Beta Kappa. Business E-Mail: joanne.simson@comcast.net. *In the end, it is only what a person has created and given to the rest of the world that endures.*

SINAGRA, JACK G., former state senator; b. Queens, NY, Mar. 18, 1950; m. Eileen Cook, 1978; children: Jacklyn, Alexandra, Patrick. BA, Emporia Coll., 1972. Mayor Town of East Brunswick, NJ, 1989—91; mem. NJ State Senate from Dist. 18, Trenton, 1992—2002; chmn. bd. The Port Authority of NY & NJ, 2001—07. V.p. Turtle & Hughes, Linden, N.J. Mem. Assn. for a Better Middlesex County.

SINAI, ALLEN LEO, economist, educator; b. Detroit, Apr. 4, 1939; s. Joseph and Betty Paula (Feinberg) Sinai; m. Lee Davis Etsten, June 23, 1963; children: Lauren Beth, Todd Michael. AB, U. Mich., 1961; MA, Northwestern U., 1966, PhD, 1969. From asst. prof. to prof. econs. U. Ill., Chgo., 1966-75; sr. v.p., chmn. fin. info. group, chief fin. economist Data Resources, Lexington, Mass., 1971-83; chief economist, mng. dir. Lehman Bros. and Shearson Lehman Bros. Inc., NYC, 1983—88; chief economist, exec. v.p. The Boston Co. Inc., 1988-93; pres., CEO Boston Co. Econ. Advisors Inc., Boston, NYC, 1988-93; mng. dir., chief global economist, dir. global econs. Lehman Bros., NYC, 1993-96; pres., chief global economist, strategist Decision Econs., Inc., Boston, NYC, London, 1996—; chief global economist, vice-chmn. WEFA Group, 1997-2000; global chief economist, exec. v.p. Global Insight, Inc., Lexington, Mass., 2001—03. Cons. Laural Cons., Lexington, Mass.; vis. assoc. prof. econs. and fin. MIT, Cambridge, 1975—77, vis. faculty Sloan Sch., 1989—91; adj. prof. econs. Boston U., 1977—78, 1981—83, NYU, NYC, 1984—88; adj. prof. econs. and fin. Lemberg Sch., Brandeis U., 1988—95; bd. economists Time Mag., 1991—2003; bd. dirs. Boston Pvt. Fin. Holdings, Inc., NACB; spkr. nationally and internationally. Contbr. articles to profl. jours., chapters to books. Mem. reducing fed. budget deficit task force Roosevelt Ctr., Washington, 1984; econ. policy adviser Rep. and Dem. Adminstrns., Washington, 1975—; bd. govs. Com. Developing Am. Capitalism, 1984—96, chmn., 1990—95. Named Top Forecaster, Bus. Week, 1997, USA Today, 2003, 2005, Wall St. Jour., 2006, Market Watch, 2004—; named one of Ten Smartest Men in Boston, Boston Mag., 1993; recipient Alumnus Merit award, Northwestern U., 1985, Otto Eckstein prize, 1988. Mem.: Am. Econ. Assn., Econometric Soc., Western Econ. Assn. (bd. dirs. 1995—97), Ea. Econs. Assn. (v.p. 1988—89, pres. 1990—91), N.Am. Econ. Fin. Assn. (pres. 2004—05, v.p. 2003—04). Jewish. Avocations: tennis, skiing, golf, bicycling. Home Phone: 781-861-0950, 617-686-7954; Office Phone: 617-994-0503. Office Fax: 212-884-9451. Business E-Mail: asinai@pdeeco.com.

SINAI, YAKOV G., theoretical mathematician, educator; b. Moscow, Sept. 21, 1935; BS, Moscow State U., 1957, PhD in Math., 1960, Doctor Degree, 1963; D Honoris Causa, Warsaw U., 1993, Budapest U. Sci. and Tech., 2002, Hebrew U., Jerusalem, 2005. Sci. rschr. lab. probabilistic and statis. methods Moscow State U., 1960-71; sr. rschr. Landau Inst. Theoretical Physics Acad. Scis., Moscow, USSR, 1971—; prof. math. Moscow State U., 1971-93; prof. math. dept. Princeton (N.J.) U., 1993—. Loeb lectr. Harvard U., 1978; plenary speaker Internat. Congresses Math. Physics, Berlin, 1981, Marseille, 1986, Internat. Congress Math., Kyoto, 1990; disting. lectr., Israel, 1989; S. Lefshetz lectr., Mex., 1990. Recipient Boltzman Gold medal, 1986, Heineman prize, 1989, Markov prize, 1990, Paul Adrian Maurice Dirac medal Internat. Centre for Theoretical Physics, 1992, Wolf prize in math. Wolf Found., Israel, 1997, Moser Prize, 2001, Nemmers Prize in Mathematics, 2002. Mem. Am. Acad. Arts and Sci. (fgn. hon.), Russian Acad. Scis., Hungarian Acad. Scis. (fgn.), London Math. Soc. (hon.), Nat. Acad. Scis. of USA (fgn. assoc.), Brazilian Acad. Scis. (fgn.). Office: Princeton University Dept of Mathematics 708 Fine Hall Washington Rd Princeton NJ 08544-0001 Home Phone: 609-924-6094; Office Phone: 609-258-4199.

SINAK, DAVID LOUIS, lawyer; b. Detroit, Oct. 3, 1953; s. Joseph and Edwina Mae (Collarini) S.; m. Elisabeth Crook; children: Jeffrey David, Margaret Louise, Slade Henry, Calder Crook. BA, U. Notre Dame, 1975; student, London Sch. Econs., 1975-76; JD, Boston Coll., 1979. Bar: Tex. 1979, U.S. Ct. Claims 1981, U.S. Tax Ct. 1981, U.S. Dist. Ct. (no. dist.) Tex. 1984, U.S. Ct. Appeals (fed. cir.) 1982, U.S. Ct. Appeals (5th cir.) 1984. Assoc. Hughes and Luce, Dallas, 1979-84, ptnr., 1984—2002, Gibson, Dunn & Crutcher LLP, Dallas, 2002—. Speaker on taxes to tax insts., law insts. and assns. and legal founds., 1981—. Mem. ABA, Tex. Bar Assn., Dallas Bar Assn. Office: Gibson Dunn & Crutcher LLP 2100 McKinney Ave Ste 1100 Dallas TX 75201 Office Phone: 214-698-3107. Office Fax: 214-571-2914. Business E-Mail: dsinak@gibsondunn.com.

SINAKIN, HERBERT MORRIS, dermatologist; b. Jersey City, Jan. 26, 1931; s. Richard and Florence Sinakin; m. Inga Silberberg Sinakin; 1 child, William Elias. BS, Rutgers U., New Brunswick, NJ, 1952; MD, SUNY, Bklyn., 1956. Dermatologist pvt. practice, Jersey City, 1960—75, Vineland, NJ, 1975—97; ret., 1997. Mem.: AMA, Am. Acad. Dermatology, NJ State Med. Soc. Avocations: bicycling, exercise, bowling. Home: 1083 E Landis Ave Vineland NJ 08360

SINANAN, MIKA NARAD, surgeon, educator; b. Helsinki, Finland, July 13, 1954; PhD, U. BC, 1991; MD, John Hopkins U. Sch. Medicine, 1980. Cert. Gen. Surgery. Fellow U. BC, Vancouver, Canada, 1983—86; acting asst. prof. U. Wash., Seattle, 1988—90, resident, gen. surgery, 1980—83, asst. prof., 1990—96, assoc. prof., 1996—2003, prof., 2003—; co-dir., Ctr. for Videoendoscopic Surgery U. Wash. Med. Ctr., Seattle. Office: U Wash Dept Surgery Box 356410 Seattle WA 98195-6410 Office Phone: 206-543-5511. Office Fax: 206-543-8136. Business E-Mail: mssurg@u.washington.edu. *

SINAY, JOSEPH, retail executive; b. Chgo., Dec. 5, 1920; s. Hyman and Ella S.; m. Ruth Milman, Mar. 7, 1961; 1 dau., Elise Sinay Spilker. Student, Herzl Jr. Coll., 1939. Gen. mgr. Fanchon & Marco Theatres, LA, 1943-54; v.p., founder Interstate United, Chgo., 1953-56; ptnr. Josam Investment Co., LA, 1956-97, Sinay Co. L.L.C., LA, 1997—; pres., CEO R B Industries Inc., LA, 1956-89, also chmn. bd. dirs., cons.; chmn. bd. dirs. Gorian Sinay Land Co., Inc., LA, 1997—. Bd. dirs. Am. Acad. Dramatic Arts; pres. Variety Clubs Internat., 1985-87; gen. chmn. United Jewish

Welfare L.A., 1976; pres. We. region Am. Friends Hebrew U., 1980; Calif. fin. chmn. Muskie for Pres., 1972; trustee Idyllwild Arts Found., 1968-73; bd. dirs. Constl. Rights Found., 1973-78. Mem. Nat. Home Furnishing Assn. Jewish. Office: Sinay Co LLC 1801 Century Park E Los Angeles CA 90067-2302 Home Phone: 310-553-2340. Business E-Mail: joe@sinaycompany.com.

SINCLAIR, ALASTAIR JAMES, geology educator; b. Hamilton, Ont., Can., Aug. 1, 1935; s. Burton Leslie and Grace (Isherwood) S.; m. Elizabeth Mary Sylvia Hill, June 13, 1964; children: Alison Trevena, Fiona Tamsin. BS, U. Toronto, Can., 1957, MS, 1958; PhD, U. B.C., Can., 1964. Asst. prof. U. Wash., Seattle, 1962-64, U. B.C., Vancouver, 1964-68, assoc. prof., 1968-74, prof., 1974-98, prof. emeritus, 1999—, head dept. geol. scis., 1985-90, dir. Geol. Engring., 1979-80, 81-82, 92-98. Pres. Sinclair Cons. Ltd., Vancouver, 1980—. Internat. Croesus Venture Corp. (now Zikco Mining Corp.), 2004—07, Deal Capital, 2006—. Author: Applied Mineral Inventory Estimation, 2002, Applied Ore Microscopy and Minerolography, 2003, Quality Control of Assay Data, 2004, Empirical Methods of Resource/Reserve Estimation, 2006; contbr. articles to profl. jours. Killam Sr. fellow, 1990—91. Fellow Geol. Assn. Can. (treas. mineral deposits divsn. 1978-89, Disting. Svc. award 2001), Soc. Econ. Geologists; mem. Assn. Profl. Engrs. B.C., Assn. Exploration Geochemists (councillor 1992-96), Can. Inst. Mining, Metallurgy and Petroleum (life, disting. lectr. 1999-2000, Robert Elver award 1991), Geol. Soc. Brazil (hon. mem. sci.-tech. commn. geochemistry 1982), Brazilian Geochem. Soc. (hon.). Avocations: classical music, skiing, golf. Home: 2972 W 44th Ave Vancouver BC Canada V6N 3K4 Office: U BC Dept Earth and Ocean Scis Vancouver BC Canada V6T 1Z4 Home Phone: 604-261-8477; Office Phone: 604-822-3086. E-mail: asinclai@eos.ubc.ca, ajsincon@shaw.ca.

SINCLAIR, CAMERON, architect; b. London, 1973; BArch, U. Westminster, London; student, Bartlett Sch. Architecture, London. Arch. Lauster and Radu Archs.; project arch. Gensler; co-founder, exec. dir. Architecture for Humanity, 1999—. Adj. prof. Mont. State U. Sch. Architecture; Cass Gilbert vis. prof. U. Minn. Coll. Architecture and Landscape Architecture, 2006; mem. adv. bd. Detroit Collaborative Design Ctr., Kids With Cameras, NYC. Internat. lectr.; co-editor: Design Like You Give a Damn, 2006. Co-recipient WIRED Rave award-Architecture, 2006; recipient Nice Modernist award, Dwell Mag., 2003, Design for Humanity award, Am. Soc. Interior Designers, 2004, TED prize, 2006. Achievements include providing design services to communities in need; selection as one of the Aspen Seven, Fortune Mag., 2004; selection as one of the Fast 50, Fast Co. Mag., 2004. Office: Architecture for Humanity 900 Bridgeway Ste 2 Sausalito CA 94965-2100 *

SINCLAIR, CAROLE, publishing executive, editor; b. Haddonfield, NJ, May 13, 1942; d. Earl Walter and Ruth (Sinclair) Dunham; 1 child, Wendy. Student, U. Florence, Italy, 1963; BA in Polit. Sci., Bucknell U, 1964. Advt. copywriter BBD&O Advertising, NYC, 1966-67; sales promotion mgr. Macmillan Pub. Co., NYC, 1967-71; mktg. mgr. Doubleday & Co., Inc., NYC, 1972-74, promotion dir., 1974-76, advt. mgr., sales and promotion, chmn. mktg. com., 1976-80; v.p. mktg., editorial dir. Davis Pubs., NYC, 1980-83; founder, pub., editorial dir., sr. v.p. Sylvia Porter's Personal Fin. Mag., NYC, 1983-90; pres. The Sylvia Porter Orgn., Inc., NYC, 1980—; founder, pres. Sinclair Media Inc., NYC, 1990—. Mktg. dir. Denver Pub. Inst., summers 1975-78; lectr. Columbia U. Bus. Sch. and Sch. of Journalism, 1976; host nationally syndicated TV show, Sylvia Porter's Money Tips, syndicated daily radio show, Sylvia Porter's Personal Fin. Report, audio cassette series on fin. topics. Author: Keys for Women Starting and Owning a Business, 1991, Keys to Women's Basic Professional Needs, 1991, When Women Retire, 1992; contbg. editor Pushcart Prize, 1977; contbr. The Business of Publishing, 1980. Renaissance Art Program fellow, Florence, Italy, 1963; White House intern, 1962. Mem. Women's Forum, Intercorp. Communications Group, Mag. Pubs.' Assn., Advt. Women in N.Y., Spence Sch. Parent's League. Clubs: Pubs. Lunch. Presbyterian. Avocation: boating.

SINCLAIR, DAISY, communications executive; b. Perth Amboy, NJ, Mar. 22, 1941; d. James Patrick and Margaret Mary (McAniff) Nieland; m. James Pratt Sinclair, May 25, 1978; children: Duncan, Gibbons. BA, Caldwell Coll., 1962. Jr. copywriter Young & Rubican, NYC, 1962-64; various positions in casting dept. Ogilvy & Mather, NYC, 1964-90, sr. v.p., dir. casting, 1990—. Mem.: Drama League N.Y. (3d v.p. 1982—), Am. Assn. Advt. (talent agt. com. 1972—), N.Y. Yacht Club, Union Club, Tuxedo Club, Chapaquoit Yacht Club, Edgartown Yacht Club, Knickerbocker Greys (pres.). Republican. Episcopalian. Avocations: opera, theater, sailing, skiing. Home: 4 E 95th St New York NY 10128-0705

SINCLAIR, FRANCES TERESA, music educator, musician; d. Joe Neal Sinclair, Jr. and Ruth Spears Smith; m. John Jay Galland, July 31, 1999; 1 stepchild, Hill Autumn Galland. MusB with distinction, U. N.C., Chapel Hill, 1986; MusM, Fla. State U., Talahassee, 1989; DMA, U. N.C., Greensboro, 1997. Choral dir. Pinecrest HS, Southern Pines, NC, 1989—93; asst. prof. and asst. dir. choral activities Clemson U., SC, 1998—2000; instr. music applied and class piano Sandhill's CC, Pinehurst, NC, 2000—03; asst. prof., interim dir choral activities U. NC, Charlotte, 2003—04, dir. choral music, coord. vocal studies Asheville, 2005; asst. prof., dir. choral activities Coastal Carolina U., Conway, SC, 2005—. Guest condr.; clinician; adjudicator local to regional festivals, competitions and clinics. Contbr. articles to profl. jours. Mem. Moore County Choral Soc., Pinehurst, NC, 1989—91, Moore County Music Soc., 1989—93, So. Pines Bus. and Profl. Women, 2000—02; dir. music Cmty. Presbyn. Ch., Pinehurst, 1991—; mem. bd. dir. Moore County chpt. N.C. Symphony, So. Pines, 1989—93. Finalist Tchr. of Yr., Pinecrest H.S., 1991, Prof. of Yr., Coastal Carolina U., 2006; recipient Outstanding Young Musician of Yr., Moore County Music Soc., 1991. Mem.: Am. Choral Dir. Assn. (exec. bd. N.C. and S.C. chpt. 1998—), Coll. Music Soc., Music Educators Nat. Conf. (sec. jr. high exec. bd. 1991—93). Home: 5 Wampanoag Ln Pinehurst NC 28374 Office: Coastal Carolina U Conway SC 29528

SINCLAIR, GLENN BRUCE, mechanical engineering educator, researcher; b. Auckland, New Zealand, Mar. 7, 1946; came to U.S., 1969; s. Alan John and Piri (Vincent) S.; m. Della Jane Sutton, Dec. 23, 1972; children: Heidi Lee, Heather Ann, Hillary Colleen, Christopher Alan B.Sc., U. Auckland, 1967, B.E., 1969; PhD, Calif. Inst. Tech., 1972. J. Willard Gibbs instr. mech. engring. Yale U., New Haven, 1972-74; lectr. U. Auckland, 1974-77; asst. prof. Carnegie-Mellon U., Pitts., 1977-80, assoc. prof., 1980-82, prof., 1982-2000, head, 1986-92; vis. prof. Cambridge U., England, 1981; Junneau prof. La. State U., Baton Rouge, 2000—, chmn. dept. mech. engring., 2000—. Research scientist Dept. Sci. and Indsl. Research, Wellington, New Zealand, 1968-69; summer prof. Pratt & Whitney, Hartford, Conn., 1978, Aircraft Corp., West Palm Beach, Fla., 1979; cons. in field. Contbr. articles to profl. jours. Fulbright scholar, 1969-72. Mem. Am. Acad. Mechanics Office: La State U Dept Mech Engring Baton Rouge LA 70803 Office Phone: 225-578-5899. Business E-Mail: sinclair@me.lsu.edu.

SINCLAIR, JAMES BURTON, retired plant pathology educator, consultant; b. Chgo., Dec. 21, 1927; s. James Lawrence Sinclair and Helen Marie (Thompson) Owens. BSc, Lawrence U., 1951; PhD, U. Wis., 1955. Grad. rsch. asst. U. Wis., Madison, 1951-55, grad. rsch. assoc., 1955-56; from asst. prof. to assoc. prof. La. State U., Baton Rouge, 1956-65, prof., 1965-68, adminstrv. asst. to chancellor, 1966-68; prof. U. Ill., Urbana, 1968-96, dir. nat. soybean rsch. lab., 1992-96; ret. Co-author: Basic Plant Pathology Methods, 1985, 1995, Principles of Seed Pathology, 1987, 1997, Anatomy and Physiology of Diseased Plants, 1991; contbr. articles to profl. jours. Pres. bd. dirs. W.R. and C.V. Spurlock Mus., Urbana, 1998-00; sec., editor Greater Cmty. AIDS Project, 1996-00; sec. Econ. Devel. Commn., Savoy, 2004-; fin. planning com. Carle Hospice, 2001-02; mem. (docent), dir bd. Spurloch Mus. World Culture, 1998-, mem. pub. com., 2005—; mem., chmn. catalogue collection com. Coun. Krannert Art Mus. and Kincaid Pavilion, 1998-, docent; active Village Savoy Econ. Devel. Com., 2004-. Sgt. US Army, 1946-47. Recipient Soybean Rsch. Recognition award, Am. Soybean Assn., 1983, Prodn. Rsch. award, 1989, Paul A. Funk award, 1984, Disting. Svc. award, USDA, 1988, Phytopathol. Soc. (north ctrl. divsn.), 1991, Rsch. award, Land of Lincoln Soybean Assn., 1992, Lucia R. Briggs Disting. Achievement award, Lawrence U., 2001. Fellow Am. Phytopathol. Soc., Nat. Acad. Scis. (India); mem. Ill. Crop Improvement Assn. (hon.), Am. Soc. Agronomy (hon.), Rotary (chmn. internat. com. Savoy chpt. 1990-91, v.p. 1991-93, pres. 1993-94, chmn. club svc. conf. 2003-04). Home: 408 Arbours Dr Savoy IL 61874-9752 Personal E-mail: jsinclai@uiuc.edu.

SINCLAIR, LINDA DRUMWRIGHT, educational consultant; b. Norfolk, Va., Aug. 4, 1942; d. Raymond Edward and Evelyn Elizabeth (Edwards) Drumwright; m. Charles Armstrong Sinclair, Oct. 5, 1962; children: William, Dianne, Sandy. BS, U. S.C., 1974, MA, 1976, postgrad. Cert. tchr. in biology, chemistry, physics. Sci. tchr. Keenan H.S., Columbia, S.C., 1976-77; chemistry/physics tchr. Lexington (S.C.) H.S., 1977-93; talented/gifted tchr. U. S.C., Columbia, 1988; tchr. rsch. program Oak Ridge (Tenn.) Nat. Lab., 1989; rschr. Savannah River Ecology Lab., Aiken, S.C., 1991-92; state sci. edn. cons. S.C. Dept. Edn., Columbia, 1993—. Cons. Prentice Hall Pub., Princeton, N.J., 1992-93. Author: Operation Radon, 1993. Adv. bd. S.C. Forestry Commn., Columbia, 1993—, S.C. Environ. Coalition, Columbia, 1993—, S.C. Sci. Coun., Columbia, 1989—; mem., com. chair Lexington Woman's Club, 1986—; v.p. Lexington Garden Club, 1983—. Named S.C. Sci. Tchr. of the Yr., S.C. Acad. Sci., 1986, Sigma Xi, 1986, S.C. Chemistry Tchr. of the Yr., S.C. Chem. Soc., 1992; recipient Presdl. Award for Excellence in Sci. Teaching, NSF, 1993. Mem. S.C. Sci. Coun. (v.p., pres.), S.C. Chemistry Tchrs. Assn. (bd. dirs. 1987—), S.C. Acad. Sci. (bd. dirs. 1982—), S.C. Jr. Acad. Sci. (bd. dirs. 1980—), S.C. Environ. Edn. Assn. (bd. dirs. 1990—), Nat. Sci. Tchrs. Assn. (bd. dirs. 1992-94). Lutheran. Avocations: horseback riding, gardening, swimming, water sports. Home: 107 Hermitage Rd Lexington SC 29072-2221 Office: SC Dept Edn 801-B Rutledge Bldg 1429 Senate St Columbia SC 29201-3730 Home Phone: 803-359-4449; Office Phone: 803-734-0887. Business E-Mail: lsinclai@ed.sc.gov.

SINCLAIR, ROBERT EWALD, retired physician; b. Columbus, Jan. 19, 1924; s. George Albert and Bertha Florence (Ewald) S.; m. Mary Almira Underwood, Mar. 31, 1945; children: Marcia Ann, Bonnie Sue. BA, Ohio State U., Columbus, 1948, MD, 1952. Lic. physician, Ohio, Colo., Ala., Kans. Intern Mt. Carmel Hosp., Columbus, 1952—53; resident neurology and psychiatry Columbus State Hosp., 1964—66, chief psychiat. resident adolescent unit, 1965—66; pvt. practice medicine Columbus, 1953—57, Granville, Ohio, 1957—64; dir. student health svc., prof. health edn., team physician Denison U., 1957—64; dir. student health svc., team physician U. Cin., 1966—70; dir. Lafene Student Health Ctr. and U. Hosp.; team physician Kans. State U., Manhattan, 1970—80; dir. Russell Student Health Ctr. and Hosp.; prof. medicine U. Ala., University, 1980—88, ret., 1988. Physician Westinghouse Electric Corp., Columbus, 1953-57; asst. zone chief Civilian Def., Columbus, 1954-57; mem. Licking County Bd. Health, Ohio, 1958-59. Bd. dirs. social health com. Cin. and Hamilton County, Ohio, 1967-70, drug abuse and edn. com., 1968-70. With USNR, 1943-46. Mem. AMA, Ohio Med. Soc., Kans. Med. Soc., Ala. Med. Soc., Columbus Acad. Medicine, Licking County Med. Soc., Riley County Med. Soc. (Kans.), Tuscaloosa County Med. Soc., Nat. Athletic Trainers Assn., Ohio Coll. Health Assn. (editor Newsletter 1968-70, pres. 1970-71), Central Coll. Health Assn. (pres. 1972-73), So. Coll. Health Assn. (pres. 1986), St. Andrews Soc., So. Medicine Assn., Delta Tau Delta (faculty advisor), Nu Sigma Nu, Nu Sigma Nu Ohio State Alumni Assn. (pres. 1953-54), Kiwanis, Rotary. Home: 1 Rollingwood Tuscaloosa AL 35406-2261 Personal E-mail: unsink2@comcast.net.

SINCLAIR, ROLF MALCOLM, retired physicist; b. NYC, Aug. 15, 1929; s. Nathan and Elizabeth S.; m. Margaret Lee Andrews, June 13, 1959 (div. 1978); children: Elizabeth Ann, Andrew Caisley; m. Allyn J. Miner, July 29, 1991 (div. 1998); m. Sarah Richards, Mar. 18, 2004. BS, Calif. Inst. Tech., 1949; MA (Reade scholar), Rice U., 1951, PhD (Inst. fellow), 1954. Physicist Westinghouse Rsch. Labs., 1953—56; vis. scientist U. Hamburg, Germany, 1956—57, U. Paris, 1957—58, U.K. Atomic Energy Authority, Culham Lab., England, 1965—66; rsch. physicist Princeton U., 1958—69; program dir. NSF, Washington, 1969—98; ret., 1998. Mem. Solstice Project, 1978-91; NSF rep. U.S. Solar Eclipse Expdn. to Can., 1979, to India, 1980, Amundsen-Scott South Pole Sta., 1995, 96; Disting. vis. prof. N.Mex. State U., 1985; vis. prof. No. Ariz. U., 1986; vis. scientist Los Alamos Nat. Lab., 1988-89, guest scientist, 1989—; cons. to industry, 1960-69, 98—; sr. advisor Centro de Estudios Cientificos, Valdivia, Chile, 1999—. Fellow Am. Phys. Soc. (panel pub. affairs 1976-77, nominating com. 1988-90), AAAS (sec. physics sect. 1972-2000, chair 2005—2006, ret. chair 2006-2007, coun. 1972-73, nominating com. 1982-83); mem. Soc. Am. Archaeology, Sigma Xi. Achievements include research and publs. on physics, archaeoastronomy, tech. and instrumentation. Home: 7508 Tarrytown Rd Chevy Chase MD 20815-6027 E-mail: rolf@santafe.edu.

SINCLAIR, STEPHEN LAWRENCE RABEHL, psychologist, educator; b. Balt., Aug. 4, 1958; s. Lawrence Albert and Jean Rabehl Sinclair. PhD, LaSalle U., Mandeville, La., 1993—96. Cert. sch. psychologist Wis. Dept. Pub. Instrn., 1984, pvt. practice sch. psychologist Wis. Dept. Regulation & Licensing, 1987. Sch. psychologist Inst. Motivational Devel., Wauwatosa, Wis., 1986—2000, Milw. Pub. Schs., 1998—. Instr. U. Phoenix, 2003—. Bd. mem. Phantom Lake YMCA Camp, Mukwanago, Wis., 1997. Mem.: NASP, Wis. Sch. Psychologist's Assn. R-Liberal. Presbyn. Achievements include research in analysis of children's reading indices. Avocations: travel, boating, snowboarding. Home: 309 N 95 St #104 Milwaukee WI 53226 Office: Milw Pub Schs 3815 W Kilbourn Ave Milwaukee WI 53208 Home Phone: 414-443-0441. Personal E-mail: psychman22@aol.com. Business E-Mail: sinclasl@email.milwaukee.k12.wi.us.

SINCLAIR, WILLIAM DONALD, state legislator, retired church official; b. LA, Dec. 27, 1924; s. Arthur Livingston and Lillian May (Holt) S.; m. Barbara Jean Hughes, Aug. 9, 1952; children: Paul Scott, Victoria Sharon. BA cum laude, St. Martin's Coll., Olympia, Wash., 1975; postgrad., Emory U., 1978-79. Commd. 2d lt. USAAF, 1944; advanced through grades to col. USAF, 1970; served as pilot and navigator Italy, Korea, Vietnam, Japan; ret., 1975; bus. adminstr. 1st United Mth. Ch., Colorado Springs, Colo., 1976-85, Village Seven Presbyn. Ch., 1985-87, Sunrise United Meth. Ch., 1987-89; vice chmn. coun. fin. and adminstrn. Rocky Mountain Conf., United Meth. Ch. U.S.A., 1979-83; mem. Colo. Ho. of Reps., Denver, 1996—, majority whip, 2001—. Pres. Pioneers Mus. Found., 1985—; Rep. candidate for Colo. State Chmn., 1992—93; chmn. bd. dir. Pikes Peak Performing Arts Ctr., 1985—92; bd. dir. Chins Up, Colorado Springs, Colo., 1983—86, Prostate Cancer Edn. Coun., 2000—. Decorated Legion of Merit with oak leaf cluster, DFC, Air medal with six oak leaf clusters, Dept. Def. Meritorious Svc. medal, Vietnam Cross of Gallantry with palms; named Legislator of Yr., Colo. Assn. Commerce and Industry, 1998—99, Colo. Sheriff's Assn., 2001; recipient Frying Pan award, Colo. Restaurant Assn., 1999, 2003, Guardian Small Bus. award, Nat. Fedn. Ind. Bus., 1999—2001, 2003, 2004, Disting. Legislator award, United Vets. Com. of Colo., 2002, Common Sense in the Courtroom award, Colo. Civil Justice League, 2003, 2004, Legis. Yr. award, Colorado Springs C. of C., 2004. Fellow Ch. Bus. Adminstrn. Nat. Assn. (nat. dir., regional v.p., v.p. 1983-85, pres. 1985-87, Ch. Bus. Adminstr. of Yr. award 1983, inducted into Hall of Fame 1995), Colo. Assn. Ch. Bus. Adminstrs. (past pres.), United Meth. Assn. Ch. Bus. Adminstrs. (nat. sec. 1978-81), Christian Ministries Mgmt. Assn. (dir. 1983-85), USAF Acad. Athletic Assn., Colorado Springs Country Club, Garden of Gods Club, Winter Night Club, Rotary (pres. Colorado Springs 1985-86), Order of Daedalians, Tower Club (Dallas). Home: 3007 Chelton Dr Colorado Springs CO 80909-1008

SINCLITICO, DENNIS J., lawyer; b. St. Louis, Jan. 9, 1947; BA, U. San Diego, 1968; JD cum laude, U. Wis., 1971. Bar: Wis. 1971, Calif. 1972, U.S. Dist. Ct. (cen. and so. dists.) Calif. 1972. Prof. Calif. Coll. Law, 1972; ptnr. Sinclitico & Burns PLC, Long Beach, Calif. Arbitrator spl. arbitration plan Los Angeles County Superior Ct., 1975—. Mem. Am. Bd. Trial Advocates (nat. exec. com. 1978—, pres. L.A. chpt., editor newsletter), Long Beach Bar Assn., State Bar Wis., State Bar Calif., Assn. So. Calif. Def. Counsel (program chmn. 1980-81, bd. dirs. 1980—), Cal-Abota (chair 1994), Ball-Hunt Ins of Ct. (barrister), Phi Alpha Delta. Office: Sinclitico & Burns PLC 330 Golden Shore # 410 Long Beach CA 90802 Office Phone: 562-628-1919. Business E-Mail: dsinclitico@sin-burns.com.

SINCOFF, MICHAEL Z., human resources and marketing executive, educator; b. Washington, June 28, 1943; s. Murray P. and Anna F. (Jaffe) S. m. Kathleen M. Dunham, Oct. 9, 1983. BA, U. Md., 1964, MA, 1966; PhD, Purdue U., 1969. Instr. U. Tenn., Knoxville, 1968; asst. prof. Ohio U., Athens, 1969-74, dir. Ctr. for Comm. Studies, 1969-76, assoc. prof., 1974-76; vis. prof. U. Minn., St. Paul, 1974; dir. personnel devel. Celanese Corp., NYC, 1976-79; dir. employee comm. The Mead Corp., Dayton, Ohio, 1979-81, dir. edn. and tng., 1981-83; assoc. dean Sch. of Bus. Adminstrn., Georgetown U., Washington, 1983-84; v.p. human resources ADVO-Sys., Hartford, Conn., 1984—87; v.p. human resources, corp. officer DIMAC Direct Inc., St. Louis, 1987-88; sr. v.p. human resources and adminstrn., sr. corp. officer DIMAC Mktg. Corp. (parent of DIMAC Direct Inc.), St. Louis, 1988-97, also sec., asst. treas., exec. com., 1988-97; sr. v.p. human resources, exec. corp. officer Brooks Fiber Properties, Inc., St. Louis, 1997-98; pres., CEO Michaelson Group Ptnrs., Dayton, Ohio, 1969—. Vis. prof. Wright State U., Dayton, Ohio, 1999-2001, assoc. prof., 2001-07, prof., 2007-; assoc. grad. faculty mem. Ctrl. Mich. U., Mt. Pleasant, 1999—. Author, editor human resources sect. Am. Mgmt. Assn. Mgmt. Handbook, 3d edit.; author approximately 50 books and articles; mem. edtl. adv. bd. Jour. Applied Comm. Rsch., 1991-97. Life mem. Internat. Comm. Assn. (bus. mgr.-exec. sec. 1969-73, fin. com. 1982-85); mem. Am. Mgmt. Assn. (human resources coun. 1990-2000), Printing Industries of Am. (employer resources group 1989-97).

SINDEN, HARRY, professional sports team executive; b. Collins Bay, Ont., Can., Sept. 14, 1932; m. Eleanor Sinden; children: Nancy, Carol, Donna, Julie. Defenseman Oshawa Generals, 1951—53, Whitby Dunlops, 1956—59, Hull-Ottawa Canadiens, 1959—60, Kingston Frontenacs, 1960—63, Minneapolis Bruins, 1963—65, Oklahoma City Blazers, 1965—66; head coach Minneapolis Bruins, 1963—64, Boston Bruins, 1966—70, 1979, 1984, gen. mgr., 1972—2000, pres., alt. gov., 1989—2006, sr. advisor to owner, 2006—; chmn. TD Banknorth Garden, Boston, 2002—. Coach Team Can., Summit Series, 1972; mem. bd. dirs. Hockey Hall of Fame. Named to Hockey Hall of Fame, 1983, Internat. Ice Hockey Fedn. Hall of Fame, 1997; recipient Lester Patrick Award, 1999. Achievements include being the coach of Stanley Cup Champion Boston Bruins, 1970. Office: Boston Profl Hockey Assn, Inc TD Banknorth Garden 100 Legends Way Boston MA 02114

SINDON, GEOFFREY STUART, lawyer; b. Dec. 3, 1952; s. Arlen Earle and Rita Nathalie (Dillon) S.; children: Jennifer Lorraine, Darryl Aaron. BS cum laude, U. Utah, 1973; JD, Pepperdine U., 1976. Bar: Calif. 1976, U.S. Dist. Ct. (cen. dist.) Calif. 1977, U.S. Dist. Ct. (no. dist.) Calif. 1980, U.S. Dist. Ct. Appeals (9th cir.) 1980. Mem. Litt and Wells, LA, 1977—78, Cohen and Steinhart, LA, 1978—82, Trope and Trope, LA, 1982—83, Sindon and Vogt, LA, 1983—88; pvt. practice, 1988—. Mediator L.A. Superior Ct., 1996—2000. Mem.: State Bar Calif., L.A. County Bar Assn., San Fernando Valley Bar Assn. Home: 1239 Willowgreen Ct Westlake Village CA 91361-1422

SINEATH, TIMOTHY WAYNE, librarian, educator, dean; b. Jacksonville, Fla., May 21, 1940; s. Holcombe Asbury and Christine Marcel (Cook) S.; m. Patricia Ann Greenwood, June 8, 1962; children: Philip Greenwood, Paul Byron. BA, Fla. State U., 1962, MS, 1963; PhD (Higher Edn. Act fellow), U. Ill., 1970. Reference librarian U. Ga., 1963-64, catalog librarian, 1964-66; acad. coordinator continuing edn. in library sci. U. Ill., 1966-68; asst. prof. library sci. Simmons Coll., 1970-74, coordinator doctoral program, 1974-77; prof., dean Coll. Libr. Sci. and Info. Sci. U. Ky., Lexington, 1977-87, prof., 1987-97, dir. sch. Libr. and Info. Sci., 1997—. Cons. to libraries, schs., chs., industry; mem. Lexington (Ky.) Public Library Bd., 1978— Author profl. reports; contbr. articles on library and info. sci., gen. info. mgmt., organizational and small group behavior to profl. jours. Mem. ALA, Am. Soc. Info. Sci. and Tech., Assn. for Libr. and Info. Sci. Edn. (pres. 1993). Episcopalian. Office: U Ky M King Bldg Lexington KY 40506-0039 E-mail: tsineath@uky.edu.

SINEGAL, JAMES D., wholesale distribution executive; b. 1936; BA, San Diego State U., 1959. With Fed-Mart Corp., 1954-77, exec. v.p.; v.p. Builders Enporium, 1977-78; exec. v.p. Price Co., 1978-79; with Sinegal/Chamberlin & Assocs., 1979-83; COO Costco Wholesale Corp., Issaguah, Wash., 1983—93, pres., 1993—, CEO, 1988—, bd. dir. Named one of 100 Most Influential People, Time mag., 2006. Address: Costco Wholesale PO Box 34331 999 Lake Dr Ste 200 Issaquah WA 98027-8982 *

SINEL, NORMAN MARK, lawyer; b. New Haven, Dec. 8, 1941; s. Nathan and Mona S.; m. Ellen Winnick, June 16, 1963; children: Joshua, Natasha. BA, Yale U., 1963; LL.B., Stanford U., 1966. Bar: Calif. 1967, D.C. 1968. Law clk. to Judge Weigel, Dist. Ct. No. Dist., Calif., 1966-67; assoc. firm Wilmer, Cutler & Pickering, Washington, 1967-71; gen. counsel Public Broadcasting Service, Washington, 1971-73, v.p., gen. counsel, 1973-76, sr. v.p. for corp. mgmt., gen. counsel, 1976-79; ptnr., Telecom. Practice Group Arnold & Porter, Washington, 1979—. Mem. Calif. Bar Assn., D.C. Bar Assn. Office: Arnold & Porter 555 12th St NW Washington DC 20004-1206 Office Phone: 202-942-5222. Office Fax: 202-942-5999. Business E-Mail: norman.sinel@aporter.com.

SINENSKY, JEFFREY, lawyer; b. 1948; BA cum laude, Bklyn. Coll. City U. NY; JD with honors, St. John's U. Bar: NY, admitted to practice: US Ct. Appeals (2nd Cir.), US Supreme Ct. Dep. chief Indictment Bur. Bronx County Dist. Atty. Office, sr. mem. Appeals Bur.; legal affairs and civil rights dir. Anti-Defamation League; gen. counsel & dir. Domestic Policy Dept. American Jewish Com., 1998—. Office: American Jewish Com PO Box 705 New York NY 10150

SINES, RANDY DWAIN, retail executive; b. Spokane, Jan. 16, 1948; s. Myron Jones and Paula Inez (Walls) S.; m. Irene Cheng, Mar. 18, 1981. Student, Wash. State U., 1966—67, U. Wash., 1968—69. Lic. water well contractor, Wash., Mont. With Boeing Co., 1967, Winchell's Donut House, Inc., Seattle, 1968—71; owner, mgr. bakeries Wash. and Mont., 1972—78; owner, mgr. Sonsine Inc., Great Falls, Mont., 1976—79; pres. Gardian Port Corp., Oxnard, Calif., 1980—82; pres., chmn. SNS Motor Imports, Inc.,

Oxnard, 1982—86; chmn. Karakal Corp. of Ams., Ventura, Calif., 1986—89; CEO, chmn. Steel Stix, U.S.A., 1990—; chmn. MITT U.S.A. Corp., 1991—; mng. ptnr. Sharps Internat., 1999—. CEO Casinovations Inc., 1995-96; founder, CEO Inven Corp., Spokane, 1996-97; chmn. Digideal Corp., Las Vegas, 1998-2005; chmn. eCardless Bancorp., Spokane, 2000-; CEO VeriCard, Inc., Spokane, 2000-. Holder more than 50 utility patents. Recipient alumni grant Wash. State U., 1967. Home: 4056 S Madelia St Spokane WA 99203-4227 E-mail: rsines@ecardless.com.

SINFELT, JOHN HENRY, chemist; b. Munson, Pa., Feb. 18, 1931; s. Henry Gustave and June Lillian (McDonald) Sinfelt; m. Muriel Jean Vadersen, July 14, 1956; 1 child, Klaus Herbert. BS, Pa. State U., 1951; PhD, U. Ill., 1954, DSc (hon.), 1981. Research engr. Exxon Research Engring. Co., Linden, NJ, 1954—57, sr. research engr., 1957—62, research assoc., 1962—68, sr. research assoc., 1968—72, sci. advisor, 1972—79, sr. sci. advisor, 1979—96, sr. sci. advisor emeritus, 1996—. Vis. prof. chem. engring. U. Minn., 1969; Lacey lectr. Calif. Inst. Tech., 1973; Reilly lectr. U. Notre Dame, 1974; Frontiers in Chemistry lectr. Case Western Res. U., Cleve., 1978; Matthew Van Winkle lectr. U. Tex., 1979, disting. vis. lectr. in chemistry, 81; Francois Gault lectr. catalysis Coun. Europe Rsch. Group Catalysis, 1980; Mobay lectr. in chemistry U. Pitts., 1980; Robert Welch Found. lectr. Confs. on Chem. Rsch., 1981; Camille and Henry Dreyfus lectr. UCLA, 1982; Edward Clark Lee Meml. lectr. U. Chgo., 1983; Dow disting. lectr. in chemistry Mich. State U., 1984; Arthur D. Little lectr. Northeastern U., 1985; Vollmer W. Fries lectr. Rensselaer Poly. Inst., 1986; disting. lectr. Ctr. Chem. Physics U. Fla., 1988; David M. Mason lectr. Stanford U., 1995, cons. prof. dept. chem. engring., 1996—. Contbr. articles to profl. jours. Named to N.J. Inventors Hall of Fame, 1991; recipient Dickson prize, Carnegie-Mellon U., 1977, Internat. prize for new materials, Am. Phys. Soc., 1978, Nat. medal of sci., 1979, Perkin medal in chemistry, Soc. Chem. Industry, 1984, Disting. Alumnus award, Pa. State U., 1985. Fellow: AIChE (Alpha Chi Sigma award 1971, Profl. Progress award 1975), Am. Inst. Chemists (Chem. Pioneer award 1981, Gold medal 1984), Am. Acad. Arts and Scis.; mem.: NAE, NAS (award for indsl. application of sci. 1996), Am. Philos. Soc., Catalysis Soc. (Emmett award 1973), Am. Chem. Soc. (Carothers lectr. Del. sect. 1982, Petroleum Chemistry award 1976, Murphree award 1986). Methodist. Achievements include development of bimetallic clusters as catalysts; invention of polymetallic cluster catalysts used commercially in petroleum reforming. Home: PO Box 364 Oldwick NJ 08858

SING, ROBERT FONG, physician; b. Camden, NJ, May 29, 1953; s. William Fong and Elizabeth (Maxwell) S.; m. Lauren McNamee, May 11, 1991. BS in Biology, Ursinus Coll., 1975; DO, Coll. Osteo. Medicine and Surgery, 1978. Intern Met. Hosp., Phila., 1978-79, resident in family practice, 1979-80; dir. emergency dept. Springfield (Pa.) Hosp., 1984—2000; dir. sports medicine Sports Sci. Ctr., 1987—; med. dir. Emergency Ambulance Svcs., Inc., 1994-95, Universal Ambulance Svcs., 2005—; owner J. Enright Jewelers, Inc., Swarthmore, Pa., 1995-97; owner, pres. Springfield Sports Emergency Med. Corp., 1999—. Owner, pres. Finish Line Sports, Inc., Phila., 1988-94; sch. and team physician Springfield Sch. Dist., 1989—, Rose Tree-Media (Pa.) Sch. Dist., 1987—; chief med. officer Kent Profl. Bicyling Tour of China, 1995, U.S. Olympic Cycling Trials, 1996. Author: Dynamics of the Javelin Throw, 1984. Med. dir. Springfield Ambulance Corp., 1988—. Named to Ursinus Coll. Athletic Hall of Fame, 1985. Fellow Am. Coll. Sports Medicine, Am. Osteo. Acad. Sports Medicine; mem. Am. Coll. Osteo. Emergency Physicians, Am. Coll. Emergency Physicians. Avocations: track and field, classical music, bicycling. Home: 1274 Gradyville Rd Glen Mills PA 19342-9614 Office: Sports Sci Ctr 166 Saxer Ave Springfield PA 19064-2335 Office Phone: 610-328-7262. Personal E-mail: sing3035@aol.com.

SING, WILLIAM BENDER, lawyer; b. Houston, Oct. 16, 1947; s. William Bender, Sr. and Alice Irene Sing; m. Doris Anne Sing, Sept. 1, 1967; children: Erin Elaine, Emily Elizabeth. BS cum laude, U. Houston, 1968, JD magna cum laude, 1971; MLA, U. St. Thomas, 1995. Bar: Tex. 1971. Assoc. Fulbright & Jaworski, LLP, Houston, 1973-80, ptnr., 1980—. Past pres., bd. dirs. St. Andrew's Presbyn. Sch., Houston; past pres. Houston CC Place civic Assn.; elder, trustee St. Andrew's Presbyn. Ch., Houston. 1st lt. US Army, 1971—77. Mem.: ABA, Houston Bar Assn., Tex. Bar Assn., U. Houston Alumni Orgn. (life), Order of Barons Law Honor Soc., Omicron Delta Epsilon, Phi Kappa Phi, Phi Delta Phi (life). Avocations: history, literature. Office: Fulbright and Jaworski LLP 1301 Mckinney St Houston TX 77010-3095 Office Phone: 713-651-3709.

SINGER, ALAN DANIEL, artist; b. NYC, June 19, 1950; s. Arthur B. and Edith (Goulfine) S.; m. Anna K. Sears, Sept. 1, 1979; 1 child, Nathaniel. BFA, Cooper Union, 1972; MFA, Cornell U., 1975; student, Yale U., 1971; postgrad., Pratt Inst., 1976-77. Artist, painter, freelance writer, educator, designer, illustrator and curator, 1974—; prof. dept. fine art Rochester Inst. Tech., 1987—; adult edn. instr. N.Y. Bot. Garden, 1985-88; instr. Asa Wright Nature Ctr., Trinidad, W.I., 1978-80. Designer program Franklin Mint Graphics for TDK/Impressions Illustration and Design Exhibits, Bklyn. Bot. Garden, 1987, designs and mechanicals for L.I. U. Brochures/N.C. Zool. Assn., 1986, others; designer, illustrator stamps U.S. Postal Svc., 1980-81; illustrator for Levaquin (Johnson & Johnson), 2006; vis. lectr. and artist Syracuse U., 2006. One-man shows include Hobart William and Smith Coll., Geneva, NY, 2001, The Mill Art Ctr., Honeoye Falls, NY, 2001, Century Club, Rochester, 1999, Upstairs Gallery: Gallery Arabesque, Ithaca, NY, 1998, Germanow-Coffey Gallery, 1997, Angel Fire Gallery, Rochester, NY, 1993, 55 Mercer St. Gallery, NYC, 1985, 92, Haenah-Kent Gallery, NYC, 1991, Bali Miller Gallery, NYC, 1988, Smithsonian Mus. of Natural History, Washington, 1987, Dyer Art Gallery, R.I.T., Rochester, NY, 2004, Art and Cultural Coun., 2005, Red House Gallery, Syracuse, 2007, others; group shows include Everson Mus., Syracuse, NY, 1999, 06, Norman Rockwell Mus., Stockbridge, Mass., 2000, Sonnenberg Gardens, Canandaigua, NY, 2000, Kew Gardens, Eng., 1997, Buffalo Mus. Sci., 1997, Monroe C.C., 1997, Meml. Art Gallery, Rochester, 1991, 93, Angel Fire Gallery, 1992, Rochester Inst. Tech., 1988, Nat. Acad. Design, NYC, 1986, Cmty. Gallery, Bklyn. Mus., 1985, Coffey Germanow Gallery, 1995, Mill Art Ctr., Honeyoye Falls, NY, 2003, Nat. Postal Svc. Mus., 2003, Bausch & Lomb Hdqrs., Rochester, NY, Mercer Gallery Monroe CC, Rochester, others; author: Wildlife Art, 1999, Botanica 2000, 2000—, Traveling the Erie Canal by Watercolor, 2001; author essays in mus. catalogs, newspapers and jours. Recipient cert. Merit Soc. Illustrators, 1985, Best of Yr. award Postal Commemorative Soc., 1983, Purchase award Nassau C.C., 1976, Pres.'s award Nat. Arts Club, N.Y.C., 1975; Rochester Inst. Tech. grantee, 1991, Faculty Devel. grantee, 1997. Mem. Rochester Print Club (pres.). Avocations: gardening, guitar, hiking. Office: Rochester Inst Tech One Lomb Memorial Dr Rochester NY 14623 E-mail: alan@singerarts.com.

SINGER, ALLEN MORRIS, lawyer; b. Mpls., Dec. 30, 1923; s. William and Ida (Simenstein) S. JD, U. Chgo., 1948; LLM, Harvard U., Cambridge, Mass., 1958. Bar: Ill. 1948, Calif. 1949. Pvt. practice, 1950-55, 59—; v.p., sec., gen. counsel ABM Industries, San Francisco, 1969-85. Assoc. prof. law U. Oreg., 1955-59; lectr. law Stanford (Calif.) U., 1960-62; of counsel Cooper, White & Cooper, San Francisco, 1970-97. Contbr. articles to profl. jours. Mem. U. Chgo. Nat. Alumni Cabinet, 1978-80. 2nd lt., USAAF, 1943-45. Mem. ABA, San Francisco Bar Assn., Calif. Bar Assn. Office: 1070 Green St Ste 703 San Francisco CA 94133-5414 Home Phone: 415-447-5495; Office Phone: 415-673-9149.

SINGER, BARBARA HELEN, photographer, radiographer; b. NYC, Jan. 29, 1927; d. Robert and Rose (Kaplowitz) S.; m. Nat Herz, Jan. 15, 1956 (dec. Nov. 1964); m. Melvin C. Zalkan, Sept. 7, 1983 (dec. Nov. 1993). BA in Biology, NYU, 1947; studied with Eli Siegel, 1944-76. Registered in diagnostic radiography AART, 1964, in mammography AART, 1991, cert. Women's Bus. Enterprise, 2001. Radiographer, 1951—2007; instr. Meth. Hosp. Sch. Radiologic Tech., Bklyn., 1968-72; asst. to Benedict J. Fernandez NYC, 1985-91; asst. to Lucien Clergue New Sch., Parsons, NYC, 1989; photographer NYC, 1983—. Lectr. NY Film Acad., NYC, 2000; panel mem. Phoenix Gallery, NYC, 1999, St. Francis Coll., NYC, 2001. Represented by Bridgeman Art Library Internat. Ltd., Getty Images, workbookstock.com, Getty Images; exhibited in numerous group shows including most recently John Stevenson Gallery, NYC, 1999, 2003, Pietra di Luna Gallery, Fla., 1999, 2000, Park Ave. Armory, NYC, 1999, AIPAD, NYC, 1999, George A. Spiva Ctr. for Arts, Mo., 2000, Hist. Yellow Springs, Chester, Pa., 2000, Nat. League Am. Pen Women Art Exhbn., NYC, 2000, AIR Gallery, NYC, 2000, Pietra di Luna Gall., Hollywood FL., 2000, St. Francis Coll., NYC, 2001, Modernage, NYC, 2001, Ashforth-Warburg Downtown, NYC, 2002, Gallery in Stamford, Conn., 2003, WBENC Conf. and Bus. Fair, NYC, 2003, Photo-Plus Expo, NYC, 2003, 04, APA, NYC, 2003, John Stevenson Gallery, 2003, MFA Exhbn. Space, 2005-06, Great Hall at Cooper Union, Nye, 2007; CD-ROM Urbane Photography, 1996; photography published in Murray Hill News, 1983, Profl. Women Photographers Newsletter, 1985, 95, Light and Shade, 1985, Best of Photography Annual 1990, Women of Vision, 1990, Tear Sheet, 1995, Wildlife Conservation Soc. Annual Report, Photonica 21, 1996, In Shape, 1996, Summer of Betrayal, Farrar Straus Giroux, 1997, Wildlife Conservation Mag., 1997, Worldcare Annual Report, 1997, Svenska Missions, 1997, Photonica 25, 1997, Fotophile, 1997, Photonica 34, 1998, Photonica 38, 44, 1999, 49, 2000, Shots, vol. 63, 1999, Photo Dist. News Online, 2003, How Success Happens, 2003, The Picture Professional, 2003, Women's Winners Circle, 2004, Breaking Through, 2004, Roseanne Backstedt, 2005, Partnering For Profit, 2005, www.modernwomentoday-.com, 2004, www.thejewishpost.com, 2004, www.montlyherald.net, 2004, Fancy Living mag., 2005; lit. published in PWP Newsletter, 2001, Tear Sheet, vol. 3, 1995, Today's Great Poems, 1994, Evangelism in America, 1988, Radiologic Tech., 1969, 71; editor, pub. The Impossible Landscapes of Nat Herz and Kurt Seligmann, 1999; appeared in website video, 2003, Manhattan Neighborhood Network TV, 2004; contbr. articles to profl. jours. Photographers' Forum Finalist, 1990; recipient Photography award Beaux Arts Soc., 1994, fiscal sponsorship NY Found. for Arts, 2000, 2d pl. winner for poetry E.F.S. 1999 Ann. Writing Competition, 2000. Cert. by Women Pres. Ednl. Orgn., 2002, Editor's Choice award Poetry.com and Internat. Lib. Poetry, 2007; named to Jewish Post list of American's Brightest, Most Talented and Hottest Women of Yr., 2004, Outstanding Jewish Woman of Yr., 2004, others; subject of articles US and the World Face to Face, 2006, ARRT Ann. Report, NY Monthly Herald, 2006. Mem.: Am. Soc. Radiologic Technologists, Advt. Photographers Am., Acad. Am. Poets, Poetry Soc. Am., Am. Soc. Media Photographers, Am. Soc. Picture Profls. Avocation: ballroom dancing. Office: 319 East 24 St #3A New York NY 10010 Home Phone: 212-686-4890; Office Phone: 212-689-0395. Fax: 212-684-1051. Personal E-mail: barbara@barbarasinger.com.

SINGER, BRYAN, film producer, director, writer, actor; b. NYC, Sept. 17, 1965; s. Norbert and Grace Singer. Grad., USC School of Cinema, LA, 1989. Founder Bad Hat Harry Prodn. Co. Dir. (films) Lion's Den, 1988; exec. prodr., dir., writer: (films) Public Access, 1993 (Grand Jury Prize, Sundance Film Festival, 1993); exec. prodr. (films) Burn, 1998, exec. prodr., dir., writer X2, 2003, prodr., dir., writer Superman Returns, 2006, prodr., dir. The Usual Suspects, 1995 (Best Dir. award, Soc. Tex Film Critics, 1995, Best Dir. award, Seattle Film Festival, 1995), Apt Pupil, 1998, prodr., dir., writer Superman Returns, 2006 (WIRED Rave Award in Film, 2006), dir., writer X-Men, 2000 (Saturn Best Dir. award, 2001); actor: (films) Star Trek: Nemesis, 2002, X2, 2003; appearances (films) Cannes Man, 1996, The Book That Wrote Itself, 1999, Round Up: Deposing 'The Usual Suspects', 2002, Keyser Soze: Lie or Legend, 2002, The Uncanny Suspects, 2003, The Visual Effects of X-Men, 2003, X-Factor: The Look of X-Men, 2003, X-Men Production Scrapbook, 2003, My Life with Count Dracula, 2003, The Second Uncanny Issue of X-Men! Making 'X2', 2003, Requiem for Mutants: The Score of 'X2', 2003, Introducing the Incredible Nightcrawler!, 2003, The Secret Origin of X-Men, 2003, Access Nation, 2004, The Shark is Still Working, 2006, (TV specials) Hitchcock: Shadow of a Genius, 1999, The 100 Greatest Movie Stars, 2003, 2nd Annual Spaceys, 2004, (TV series) HBO First Look, 2003, House, M.D., 2005, Sunday Morning Shootout, 2005, exec. prodr., writer The Triangle, 2005, exec. prodr., dir. House, M.D., 2005, exec. prodr. (TV films) The Science of Superman, 2006. Named one of 50 Most Powerful People in Hollywood, Premiere mag., 2006. Office: Bad Hat Harry Productions Inc 150 S Rodeo Dr 3rd Fl Beverly Hills CA 90212

SINGER, BURTON HERBERT, statistics educator; b. Chgo., June 12, 1938; married; 3 children. BS, Case Inst. Tech., 1959, MS, 1961; PhD in Stats., Stanford U., 1967. From asst. to assoc. prof. stats. Columbia U., NYC, 1967-77, prof. math. stats., 1977-85, chmn. dept. math. stats., 1985-89; chmn. biostats. Yale U., New Haven, 1989—91, chmn. and assoc. dean pub. health dept. epidemiology and pub. health, 1989—91, chmn. epidemiology and pub. health, 1991-93, Ira Vaughan Hiscock prof. epidemiology and pub. health, 1991-94, prof. econs. and stats. dept. epidemiology and pub. health, 1991-94; prof. demography and pub. affairs Princeton U., NJ, 1994—, Charles & Marie Robertson prof. pub. & internat. affairs. Research assoc. statistician Princeton U., 1972—73; scientific adv. bd. Santa Fe Inst.; adv. bd. Fogarty Internat. Ctr., NIH; editorial bd. Frontiers of Primary Medicine, Series in Statistics. Commn. Behavioral & Social Sciences & Ed. Nat. Rsch. Coun.; coord. Malaria Task Force, UN Millennium Project. Mem. AAAS, Nat. Acad. Scis., Am. Statis. Assn., Psychometric Soc., Inst. Medicine. Office: Princeton Univ Office Population Rsch 21 Prospect Ave Princeton NJ 08544-2007 Office Phone: 609-258-5938. Office Fax: 609-258-1039. E-mail: singer@princeton.edu.

SINGER, CAROL ANN, librarian, researcher; b. Tarentum, Pa., Mar. 13, 1953; d. Richard Meade and Eleanor (Weir) S. BA, Bowling Green State U., 1975; MLS, Ind. U., 1979. Instr. info. svc. Wayne (Nebr.) State Coll., 1979-84; govt. documents libr. U. Nebr., Omaha, 1984-85, Kenyon Coll., Gambier, Ohio, 1985-91; sr. ref. libr. U.S. Dept. Energy, Washington, 1991-92; ref. libr. USDA, Washington, 1992-97; asst. libr. U.S. Dept. Justice, Washington, 1997-98; ref. libr. Bowling Green (Ohio) State U., 1998—. Instr. Kent State U., Bowling Green, Ohio, 1999; rschr. in field. Contbr. articles to profl. jours. Mem. ALA, Acad. Libr. Assn. Ohio, Ohio Govt. Documents Roundtable. Office: Bowling Green State U Jerome Libr Rm 152 Bowling Green OH 43403 Office Phone: 419-372-9412. Business E-Mail: singerc@bgsu.edu.

SINGER, CECILE DORIS, bank executive, former state legislator; BA, Queens Coll.; DHL (hon.), Pace U., 1997. Past rep. Spl. Svcs. for Children, NYC; past exec. dir. N.Y. State Assembly Social Svcs. and Judiciary Coms., Joint Legis. Com. on Corps., Authorities and Commns.; past pub. rep. Yonkers (N.Y.) Emergency Control Bd.; past coord. Westchester County Assembly Dels.; past chief of staff for dep. minority leader; mem. N.Y. State Assembly, Albany, 1988—94, leadership sec. Rep. Conf., mem. assembly children & families com., mem. various other coms.; bd. dirs. Hudson Valley Bank; prin. Cecile D. Singer Cons. Past rep. Temp. Commn. to Revise Social Svcs. Law; mem. Presdl. Commn. on Privacy Conf., NY State Senate Transp. Conf.; task force on substance abuse Am. Legis. Exch. Coun., task force on econ. devel., crime victims' rights, hosp. crisis, women's issues, com. on mass transit; sec. Rep. Conf. Nat. Adv. Panel Child Care Action Campaign; chmn. Westchester County Commn. on Pub. Financing of Campaigns; chmn. Lower Hudson Valley Adv. Com. NY State Divsn. for Women; past dir. commn. on poverty and pregnancy, dir. Yonkers IDA, NY; treas. Riverside Corp.; chair, NY State Hudson Valley Coun.; pres. Women's Enterprise Devel. Ctr.; mem. Westchester County Women's advisory bd.; bd. dirs. Hudson Valley Holding Corp., Hudson Valley Bank, NY; prin. Cecile D. Singer Cons. Chair adv. com. Westchester C.C. Found., Westchester 2000 Rsch., Womens Adv. Bd. Westchester County; task force on certiorari Westchester County Sch. Bds. Assn.; sch. and cmty. chmn. Yonkers PTA; bd. dirs. Yonkers chpt. United Jewish Appeal; v.p. Westchester Sr. Housing; chair Women's Networking, Women in Bus. and the Professions award; v.p. Westchester Srs. Housing; trustee, treas. St. John Hosp. Recipient Jenkins Meml. award, Nat. PTA award, Bus. and Profl. award Yonkers C. of C., Yonkers Fedn. Tchrs. Friend Edn. award, Lillian Vernon award West Chester Assn. Women Bus. Owners, 2002, Star award Mental Health Assoc., Yonkers Woman Valor award, Trustee award St. Johns Hosp., 2005; inducted into Women's Hall of Fame, 1996, Sr. Citizens Hall of Fame, 1996, Westchester County Cert. Svc. Mem. Rotary. Office: 21 Scarsdale Rd Yonkers NY 10707-3204 Home: 1 Scarsdale Rd Tuckahoe NY 10707-3215 E-mail: ceds@optonline.net.

SINGER, CLIFFORD, mathematics educator, artist; b. Great Neck, NY, May 19, 1955; BFA, Alfred U., NYC, 1977; MFA, CCNY, NYC, 1990. Tchr. math. Clark County Sch. Dist., Las Vegas, Nev., 2004—. Exhibit curator Geometric Abstraction Nat. Endowment Arts and N.Y. State Coun. Arts Bklyn. Law Sch., 1980, Art & Math. 200 Cooper Union and Albert Nerken Sch. Engring. SUNY, Albany, 2000; commissioned artist Lincoln Ctr. List Art Posters, NYC, 1991, Mostly Mozart Festival, Tokyo, 1991; contr. art and papers to conf. proceedings; lectr. in field. One-man shows include Art Investors Internat., West Palm Beach, Fla., 1986, Vasarely Ctr., N.Y.C., 1988, Thesis Exhibn, Eisner Gallery, CCNY, 1990, Art Rsch. Ctr., Kansas City, Mo., 1992, Fine Arts Forum, Compuserve, 1994, Eich Space, N.Y.C., 1996, Non-Euclid Wide World Web Gallery, Rice U., Tex., 1997, Emden Rm. St. Edmund Hall, U. Oxford, Eng., 2000, Truly Virtual Wab Art Mus., Lastplace.com, 2000, exhibitions include Soho Ctr. Visual Artists Aldrich Mus. Contemporary Art, N.Y.C., 1980, Aldrich Mus. Contemporary Art, Ridgefield Conn., 1981, 1986, Pace Editions, N.Y.C., 1981, Branchville Soho Gallery, Ridgefield, Conn., 1982, Original Print Collectors Group, N.Y.C. and Paris, 1982, 80 Wash. Sq. East Galleries, N.Y.C., 1983, Thirteen Collection Exhibn. Sotheby Parke Bernet, Inc., 1983, 1984, Hammer Publishing, 1984, The Gallery Albany Inst. History and Art, 1986, Vasarely Ctr., 1987, Art Rsch. Ctr., Kansas City, Mo., 1988, 1995, Ann Jacob Gallery, Atlanta, 1989, Gemini Gallery, West Palm Beach, Fla., 1989, N.Y. Area MFA Ehibn. Coll. Art Assn., Hunter Coll., N.Y.C., 1990, Lincoln Ctr./ Tokyo Bunkamura, N.Y.C. and Tokyo, 1991, 30th Anniversary Lincoln Ctr. Poster and Print Program, N.Y.C., 1993, Bruce McGraw Graphics, N.Y.C., 1994, Am. Online Keyword: Art, 1994, Fine Arts Forum, Compuserve, 1994, Cercle et Carre, Vallejo, Calif., 1996, 1998, Abstract-Art Repository Portfolio Gallery, abstract-art.com, 1997, Boca Raton Mus. Art. Dir.'s Choice, Fla., 1997, Presidents Gallery Darbeth Fine Arts Ctr., Winfield, Kans., 1998, 2001, Bechtel Ctr. U. Caluf., Berkeley, 1998, Mondiale Echo's Mondriinhuis, Amersfoort, Netherlands, 2000—01, Joint Meeting Am. Math. Soc. and Math. Assn. Am., New Orleans, 2001, Ann. Meeting Assn. Women in Math., 2001, Ann. Meeting Nat. Assn. Mathematicians, 2001, Art & Math. 2001 Koussevitsky Art Gallery, Pittsfield, Mass., 2001, Internat. Soc. Interdisciplinary Study of Symmetry Red Ctr. U. NSW, Paddington and Sydney, Australia, 2001, Ringling Sch. Art and Design, Sarasota, Fla., 2002, Monique Goldstrom Gallery, N.Y.C., 2002, AULA Gallery Pedagogical U. FReiburg, Germany, 2002, Holzmann Art Gallery Towson U., Md., 2002, Fire Patrol No. 5 Art, N.Y.C., 2003, U. Granada Art Gallery, Spain, 2003, Cork Gallery Lincoln Ctr., N.Y.C., 2003, Broome St. Gallery, 2004, Joint Math. Meeting Exhibit of Math. Art, Atlanta, 2005, prin. works include Lemma III, Mobil Oil Corp. Hdqs., N.Y.C., 1983, Didecameter Suite, 1985, prin. works include cover art Stagebill Lincoln Ctr. July-Aug., 1992, MUDFISH 9, 1996, FOCUS, 2000, Represented in permanent collections Aldrich Mus. Contemporary Art, Conn., Armand Hammer Collection, N.Y.C., Art Rsch. Ctr., Kansas City, Mo., AT&T, Atlanta, Bank Julius Baer, N.Y.C. and Zurich, Boca Raton Mus. Art, Chemical Bank, N.Y., Citibank, N.A., The Continental Group, Inc., Conn., Gen. Electric Co., Fairfield, Conn., Giant Foods, Mo., IBM Corp., N.Y., Lincoln Ctr. List Art Posters, N.Y.C., McGraw Hill, Mobil Oil Corp., Washington, Mondriaanhuis Archive 90 Reference Collection, Netherlands, Namura Computer Sys., N.Y.C., Needham Harper Worldwide, Inc., Oppenheimer & Co., Inc., Reader's Digest, Pleasantville, N.Y., Revlon, N.Y.C., Southwestern Coll., Winfield, Kansas, Texaco, Inc., N.Y.C., N.Y. Trust Co., Xerox Pub. Group; contbr. chapters to books, scientific papers, articles to profl. jours. Recipient hon. mention, Summit Art Ctr., 1985; grantee, Change, Inc., 1989, IMPACT II, Tchrs. Network, 2001. Home: 4477 El Campana Way Las Vegas NV 89121 Personal E-mail: CliffordhS@aol.com.

SINGER, CRAIG, entrepreneur, inventor, executive, investor, consultant; b. NYC, Aug. 13, 1947; s. Albert and Dorothy (Blackman) Singer; m. Ellen Rappaport, Aug. 31, 1969 (div. Oct. 26, 2006); children: Chad Adam, Cara Danielle. BS, Cornell U., 1969; JD, Columbia U., 1972. Bar: N.Y. 1973. Exec. Continental Wingage Co., Inc., NYC, 1972-74, Integrated Resources, Inc., NYC, 1974-87; pres. Westminster Fin. Group, Inc., Bedford Corners, NY, 1989—2006; mng. dir. Richman Mortgage Assets Mgr. LLC, 2007—. Chmn. bd. dirs. Integrated Resources Funding Corp., AIM Capital Mgmt. Corp., 1983—87; bus. exec., 2007—; entrepreneur; inventor; cons., broker, investor, Bedford Corners, NY, 1988—2006. Former mem. editl. adv. bd. Bur. Nat. Affairs Housing and Devel.; former dir. Assn. Govt. Assisted Housing, Inc., 1976—84; former mem. exec. com. Coalition Low and Moderate Income Housing. Home and Office: 148 Meeting House Rd Bedford Corners NY 10549-4241

SINGER, DANIEL MORRIS, lawyer; b. Bklyn., Oct. 10, 1930; s. Samuel W. and Fannie G. (Sabloff) S.; m. Maxine Frank, June 15, 1952; children: Amy E., Ellen R., David B., Stephanie F. BA with honors, Swarthmore Coll., 1951; LLB, Yale U., 1954. Bar: N.Y. 1956, U.S. Dist. Ct. D.C. 1957, U.S. Ct. Appeals (D.C. cir.) 1957, U.S. Supreme Ct. 1959. Motions clk. U.S. Ct. Appeals for D.C. Circuit, Washington, 1956-57, law clk. to Judge George T. Washington, 1957-58; assoc. Fried, Frank, Harris, Shriver & Jacobson, Washington, 1958-64, ptnr., 1965-87, counsel, 1987—. Arbitrator complex comml. case and constrn. nat. panels; mediator US Dist. Ct., Washington; vol. atty. Lawyers Com. for Civil Rights Under Law, 1965, 66; mem. exec. com. Washington Lawyers Com. for Civil Rights Under Law, 1973—; spl. asst. corp. counsel, D.C., 1995-2000. Bd. mgrs. Swarthmore Coll., 1987—91; dir., sec.-treas. Coun. for a Livable World, 1962—64; dir. Am. Soc. for Protection of Nature in Israel, 1986—; mem. governing coun., mem. exec. com. Am. Jewish Congress, 1986—96, v.p., 1988—92; bd. dirs., sec.-treas. Nat. Com. Tithing in Investment, 1964—65; bd. dirs. D.C. Developing Families Ctr., 1999—, D.C. Appleseed Ctr., 1996—, chmn. bd., 2000—04. With Signal Corps US Army, 1954—56. Mem.: ABA, D.C. Bar. Home: 5410 39th St NW Washington DC 20015-2902 Office: Fried Frank Harris Shriver & Jacobson 1001 Pennsylvania Ave NW Washington DC 20004-2596 E-mail: daniel.singer@ffhsj.com.

SINGER, DAVID MICHAEL, marketing and public relations executive; b. Bklyn., Feb. 11, 1957; s. Seymour Allen and Ellen Sybil (Pavnick) S.; m. Pamela Rae Silton, July 20, 1986; children, Max!, Bobby. BA in History, NYU, 1978; MA in Comms., Syracuse U., 1979; MA in Media, New Sch. Social Rsch., 1983; JD, Yeshiva U., 1981. Cons. pub. rels. Burson-Marsteller, NYC, 1979-81, The Haas Group, NYC, 1981-84, Braff & Co., NYC, 1987-89; pub., editor-in-chief Lodestone Pub., NYC, 1984-87; chief oper. officer Pentagon Ltd., NYC, 1989-91; v.p. pub. rels. Braff & Co., NYC, 1991-92; v.p. G.S. Schwartz & Co., NYC, 1993-97; v.p. mktg. comm. Imedia, Morristown, NJ, 1998-99; pres. S&S Mktg. Comms. Inc. Lectr. evening div. NYU, 1982-96; dir. media rels. Braff & Co. Contbr.

articles and poems to profl. and consumer jours. and mags. Pres. Jewish Cultural Found., N.Y.C., 1976. Named to Outstanding Young Man of Am., Jaycees, 1977; recipient Cert. Recognition Am. Film Inst., 1982, ANDY Design award Advt. Club N.Y., 1983, Proclamation Bklyn. Borough Pres., 1987. Mem. Alpha Epsilon Pi (Bro. of Yr. 1976). Avocations: baseball, politics, ping pong/table tennis, films, theater.

SINGER, DINAH S., federal agency administrator, immunologist, researcher; Grad., MIT, 1969; MPhil, PhD, Columbia U. Post-doctoral fellow Lab. Biochemistry Nat. Cancer Inst., sr. investigator Immunology Branch; sr. scientific officer Howard Hughes Med. Inst., 1998—99; dir. Divsn. Cancer Biology Nat. Cancer Inst., 1999—, also chief Molecular Regulation Sect. of Exptl. Immunology Branch. Mem.: Am. Assn. Immunologists. Office: Nat Cancer Inst Divsn Cancer Biology Executive Plaza North Ste 5000 Bethesda MD 20892-7390 Office Phone: 301-496-8636. E-mail: ds13j@nih.gov.

SINGER, DONNA LEA, writer, editor, educator; b. Wilmington, Del., Oct. 6, 1944; d. Marshall Richard and Sara Emma (Eppihimer) S. BA in English cum laude, Gettysburg Coll., 1966; postgrad., Montclair State Coll., 1972-73, U. Birmingham, Eng., 1977; M of Letters, Drew U., 1985. Asst. to dir. student activities Fairleigh Dickinson U., Madison, crw., 1966-68; tchr., drama coach Morris Hills High Sch., Rockaway, N.J., 1968-84; free-lance editor Basic Books, Inc., NYC, 1983-86; adj. instr. Fairleigh Dickinson U., Madison, 1986-87; free-lance writer, editor Visual Edn. Corp., Princeton, N.J., 1988—, Fact's on File, Bantam, Random House, Fodor's Travel Books, NYC, 1990—, John Wiley & Sons, NYC, 1990—; tchr. Sylvan Learning and Tech. Ctr., Sarasota, Fla., 1999—. Co-founder, co-dir. Traveling Hist. Troupe, Rockaway, 1976-78; tour leader Am. Leadership Study Groups, 1976, 78, 82; theatre studies participant Royal Shakespeare Co., Stratford, Eng., 1978-79, 81; docent, lectr. acting co. Hist. Spanish Point, Osprey, Fla., 1989-2001; grant facilitator NEA, Sarasota, Fla. Author: numerous poems; contbr. chapters to books, articles to profl. jours. Big sister Big Bros./Big Sisters, Sarasota, Fla., 1990-98; NEA grant facilitator Asolo Theater, Sarosota, Fla. Mem. Internat. Women's Writing Guild, West Coast Writers, Met. Mus. Art, Royal Shakespeare Company Assocs., Emerald Coast Writers, Travel Writers Internat. Network. Avocations: dance, theater, travel, antiques. E-mail: shakesds@aol.com.

SINGER, ERIC T., investment banker; b. NYC, 1952; s. Roger M. and Meredith Singer; m. Aet Paaro, Aug. 10, 1974; children: Brett A., Jamison P. BA, SUNY, Stony Brook, 1974; JD, Cornell U., 1977. Assoc. Barrett, Smith et al, NYC, 1977-80; v.p. Smith Barney, NYC, 1980-84; sr. v.p. PaineWebber, NYC, 1984-88; exec. v.p. Metromedia Hotels, NYC, 1988-90; exec. v.p., dir. corp. fin. Gerard Klauer Mattison, NYC, 1990-99; mng. dir., pres. H.C. Wainwright & Co., Inc., NYC, 1999—2003; mng. dir. Pali Capital, Inc., NYC, 2003—; mng. ptnr. Singer Congl. Fund Singer Funds, 2004—. Mem. Cornell Law Rev. Mem. U.S. Maccabiah Squash Team, 1997, 2001, 2005. Mem. Heights Casino Club, Yale Club, Phi Beta Kappa. Home: 72 Hicks St Brooklyn NY 11201-1709 Home Phone: 718-522-6893; Office Phone: 212-259-2039.

SINGER, FREDERICK RAPHAEL, medical researcher; b. St. Louis, June 27, 1939; s. Meyer and Lee (Minkle) S.; m. Sandra Joy Barnes, Aug. 16, 1964; children: Stefanie, Jeffrey. Student, UCLA, 1956—59; BS, U. Calif., Berkeley, 1960; MD, U. Calif., San Francisco, 1963. Diplomate Am. Bd. Internal Medicine, Am. Bd. Endocrinology and Metabolism. Intern UCLA Affiliated Hosp., 1963-64; resident VA Hosp., LA, 1964-65, 68-69; instr. in medicine Harvard U., Boston, 1971-72; asst. prof. medicine UCLA, 1972-73, U. So. Calif., LA, 1973-74, assoc. prof., 1974-78, prof., 1978-89, prof. orthop. surgery, 1980-89; dir. Bone Ctr. Cedars-Sinai Med. Ctr., LA, 1989-92, clin. prof. medicine, 1993—. Dir. Osteoporosis/Metabolic Bone Disease program St. Johns Hosp. and Health Ctr., Santa Monica, Calif., 1992—; dir. Skeletal Biology Lab, John Wayne Cancer Inst., Santa Monica, 1992—; mem. endocrine and metabolic drug adv. com. FDA, USPHS, Bethesda, Md., 1983-87. Author: Paget's Disease of Bone, 1977; contbr. numerous articles, revs. to profl. jours. Vice chmn. cmty. adv. com. Univ. H.S., L.A., 1984. Capt. USAF, 1965-67. Calif. State scholar, 1956-60; clin. investigator VA, 1971-73. Mem. Endocrine Soc., Am. Soc. Clin. Investigation, Am. Soc. Bone and Mineral Rsch. (chmn. pub. affairs 1981-86, coun. 1987, pres.-elect 1989, pres. 1990), Paget's Disease Found. (chmn. bd. dirs. 1990—2006), Fibrosis Dysplasia Found. (bd. dirs. 2006—). Office: John Wayne Cancer Inst 2200 Santa Monica Blvd Santa Monica CA 90404-2302 Personal E-mail: singerf@yahoo.com.

SINGER, GARY JAMES, lawyer; b. LA, Oct. 8, 1952; s. Stanley Merle and Ernestine Alice (Brandstatter) S.; m. Melanie Carol Rabin, Mar. 19, 1978; children: Brian, Kimberly, Andrew. BA magna cum laude, U. Calif., Irvine, 1974; JD cum laude, Loyola U., 1977. Bar: Calif. 1977, U.S. Dist. Ct. (fed. dist.) 1978. Assoc. O'Melveny & Myers LLP, LA, 1977-84, Newport Beach, Calif., ptnr., head Irvine, Calif., 1985—, ptnr., head bus. practice group Newport Beach, Calif. Bd. dirs. Irvine Barclay Theatre, 1990-98, chmn. 1993-96; chair bd. dir. Com. on Product Liability and Tort Reform, 1999-; lectr. Continuing Legal Edn., Merger and Acquisition Practice (1997, 1999), Calif. Continuing Edn. of the Bar, Calif. State Bar Assn., Euromoney Conf. Editor-in-chief Loyola of LA Law Review, 1976—77. Bd. dir. Calif. C. of C., Orange County Bus. Com. Arts, 1999—, U. Calif. Irvine Found., 1998—, Human Options, 1982—86, Big Canyon Country Club, 1990—93; past pres. U. Calif. Irvine Chancellor's Club. Named Disting. Alumni Recipient; recipient Lauds and Laurels, 1998. Mem.: ABA, Orange County Bar Assn. (past chmn., corp. and bus. law sect.), St. Thomas More Law Honor Soc., Phi Beta Kappa, Alpha Sigma Nu. Avocations: golf, skiing, reading. Office: O'Melveny & Myers LLP 610 Newport Center Dr 17th Fl Newport Beach CA 92660

SINGER, GEORGE ALAN, oil and gas company executive, arts association administrator; b. Tulsa, Mar. 6, 1948; s. Alexander Simon and Marjorie (Teller) S.; m. Judith Marie Sanditen, June 20, 1970 (div. May 1975); m. Hilary Kitz, Dec. 18, 1975 (div. 1993); children: Samuel Jacob, Nicholas John William, Jeremy Daniel. BA, Yale U., 1970; JD, Harvard U., 1973. Ptnr. Denner & Singer, Cambridge, Mass., 1974-78; v.p. Pedestal Oil Co., Inc., Tulsa, 1978-80; gen. ptnr. Singer Bros., Tulsa, 1980—. Bd. dir. Tulsa Metro Chamber. Chmn. State Arts Coun. Okla., Task Force 2000, Okla., 1989—; mem. Gov.'s Constn. Revision Commn., 1988. Recipient Friend of Edn. award Okla. Edn. Assn., 1991, Share the Excellence award Support Ctr., Tulsa, 1990. Democrat. Jewish. Avocations: running, biking, fishing, reading. Office: Singer Bros PO Box 755 Tulsa OK 74101-0755 Business E-Mail: ChamberBoard@tulsachamber.com.

SINGER, HOWARD JACK, biology professor, researcher; b. Newark, Sept. 4, 1940; s. Nat I. and Rose (Alboum) S.; m. Helena Liisa Niskanen, May 29, 1986; children: Jamie Alexander Niskanen-Singer. BA, Oberlin Coll., 1962; MS, U. Minn., 1966; PhD, Tufts U., 1970. Prof. biology N.J. City U. (formerly Jersey City State Coll.), Jersey City, 1970—. Cons. Proforma Base Corp., Jersey City, 1985-87, Instructivision, Inc., Livingston, N.J., 1988-89; researcher SUNY Downstate Med. Ctr., Bklyn., 1987-89. Contbr. articles to profl. jours. Pres. Van Vorst Pk. Assn., Jersey City, 1977-78; treas. Environ. Voters Alliance, N.J., 1984-90; dir. Hudson County (N.J.) Toxic Task Force, 1980-86; active Scientists Com. for Pub. Info., N.Y.C., 1976-80. Am. Chem. Soc. scholar, 1958-62; fellow NIH, 1966-70, NSF, 1961. Mem.: Am. Fedn. Tchrs. (membership chmn. 1989—), Theobald Smith Soc. (pres. 1996—97, alt. nat. councilor 1997—99, nat. councilor 2000—01, alt. nat. councilor 2002—03, nat. councilor 2003—05, chmn. program com., co-pres. 2006—07), Am. Soc. for Microbiology. Avocations: skiing, art nouveau, scuba, tennis. Home: 297 York St Jersey City NJ 07302-4016 Office: NJ City U 2039 John F Kennedy Blvd Jersey City NJ 07305-1527 Office Phone: 201-200-3310. Business E-Mail: hsinger@njcu.edu.

SINGER, ISADORE MANUEL, mathematician, educator; b. Detroit, May 3, 1924; married; 5 children. BS, U. Mich., 1944; MS, U. Chgo., 1948, PhD in Math., 1950; ScD (hon.), Tulane U., 1981; LLD (hon.), U. Mich., 1989, U. Ill., Chgo. Moore instr. math. MIT, Cambridge, 1950—52, prof. math., 1956—70, Norbert Wiener prof., 1970—79, John D. MacArthur prof. math. (1st holder), 1983—, Inst. prof., 1987—; asst. prof. UCLA, 1952—54; vis. prof. math U. Calif., Berkeley, 1977—79, prof., 1979—83, Miller prof. math., 1982—83, prof. math., 1977—83. Vis. asst. prof. math. Columbia U., NYC, 1954—55; mem. Inst. Advanced Study, 1955—56; past steering com. Ctr. for Non-Linear Scis., Los Alamos Nat. Labs.; adv. bd. Inst. Theoretical Physics, U. Calif., Santa Barbara; bd. dirs. Santa Fe Inst.; mem. various organizing coms.; editor procs. for confs. in field. Former editor profl. jours. Recipient Nat. medal of Sci., 1983, Steele prize Lifetime Achievement, 2000, Abel prize, Norwegian Academy of Sci. and Letters, 2004; fellow Alfred P. Sloan, 1959—62, Guggenheim, 1968—69, 1975—76. Mem.: NAS (past councillor, former mem. com. math. and phys. scis., other coms.), Internat. Congress Mathematicians (program com.; 1986, Wigner prize 1989), Am. Phys. Soc., Am. Math. Soc. (v.p. 1970—72, past exec. com., Bocher Meml. prize 1969, Pub. Svc. award 1993), Am. Acad. Arts and Scis., Am. Philos. Soc. Office: MIT Dept of Math Bldg 2 Rm 387 77 Massachusetts Ave Cambridge MA 02139-4307

SINGER, JEFFREY ALAN, surgeon; b. Bklyn., Feb. 2, 1952; s. Harold and Hilda (Ginsburg) S.; m. Margaret Sue Gordon, May 23, 1976; children: Deborah Suzanne, Pamela Michele. BA cum laude, Bklyn. Coll., 1973; MD, N.Y. Med. Coll., 1976. Diplomate Am. Bd. Surgery. Intern Maricopa County Gen. Hosp., Phoenix, 1976-77, resident, 1977-81, mem. teaching faculty, 1981-96; trauma cons. John C. Lincoln Hosp., Phoenix, 1981-83; pvt. practice Phoenix, 1981-87; group pvt. practice Valley Surg. Clinics, Ltd., Phoenix, 1987—, S.W. Surg. Clinics, P.C., Phoenix, 1996-97. Sec.-treas. med. staff Humana Desert Valley Hosp., Phoenix, 1987-89, chief surgery, 1985-87, 91-93, exec. com., 1993-95; adj. asst. prof. divsn. clin. edn. Ariz. Coll. Osteo. Med., Midwestern U., 1998—; mem. adj. clin. faculty Kirksville (Mo.) Coll. Osteo. Medicine. Assoc. editor Ariz. Medicine, 1994-2000, contbg. writer, 2001—. Rep. precinct committeeman, Phoenix, 1986-2000; exec. com. bd. dirs. Goldwater Inst. for Pub. Policy Rsch., 2002—; bd. dirs. Ariz. Fedn. Taxpayers, 2007—. Named Top Doc, Phoenix Mag., 1999. Fellow: ACS, Am. Soc. Abdominal Surgeons, Southwestern Surg. Congress, Internat. Coll. Surgeons; mem.: Maricopa County Med. Soc. (v.p. 1998, bd. dirs. 1998—2002), Ariz. Med. Assn. (bd. dirs. polit. com. 1985—, legis com. 1986—, chmn. bd. dirs. polit. com. 1991—93, Walk the Talk award 2001), Ariz. Sch. Choice Trust (bd. dirs. 1998—2004, adv. bd. 2004—), Alpha Omega Alpha. Avocations: philosophy, politics, history, travel, underwater sports, writing. Office: Valley Surg Clinics Ltd 16601 N 40th St Ste 216 Phoenix AZ 85032-3353 Office Phone: 602-996-4747. Personal E-mail: dr4liberty@aol.com. Business E-Mail: jsinger@valleysurgicalclinics.com.

SINGER, JOEL, real estate company executive; m. Karen Singer; 2 children. BA, UCLA; ed., Albert-Ludwigs U., Germany. Chief economist Calif. Assn. Realtors, LA, head, pub. affairs dept., head, rsch. dept., exec. v.p., 1989—; pres. Real Estate Bus. Services Inc., bd. dirs. Exec. com. Civil Justice Assn. Calif. Named one of Real Estate's 25 Most Influential Thought Leaders, Realtor Mag., 2006; recipient William R. Magel Award of Excellence, Nat. Assn. Realtors, 2004. Mailing: California Assn Realtors 525 S Virgil Los Angeles CA 90020 Office Phone: 213-739-8200. Office Fax: 213-480-7724. *

SINGER, JON DOUGLAS, foundation administrator, writer; b. NYC; s. Jerome Leonard and Dorothy Gottlieb Singer. BA, NYU, 1974, MA, 1978. Shelver libr. books Yale U. Med. Sch., New Haven, Conn., 1987-88, Wilbur Smith Assocs., New Haven, 1996; receptionist Fellowship Club, 2000—. Author: Lost Lands and Cities, 1987, Lost Lands and Cities Beneath the Sea, 1997, Ireland's Mysterious Lands and Sunken Cities, 2001. Campaign asst. Dem. Party, NYC, 1980; active Rep. Nat. Com., 2003-06, Dem. Nat. Com., 2007—, US Naval Inst., 2003. Mem.: Artship Art Coop., Fellowship Club (membership v.p. 2006). Jewish. Avocations: archaeology, astronomy, quantum physics. Home: 305 Audubon Ct New Haven CT 06510

SINGER, JOY DANIELS, journalist, consultant; b. NYC, Feb. 22, 1928; d. Maurice Blumberg and Anna S. (Kleegman) Daniels; m. Jack Singer, July 30, 1955; children: Meriamne B., Daniel C., Richard K. BA, Cornell U., 1948; postgrad., The Sorbonne, Paris, 1949. Advt. copywriter Franklin Spier, George Knoerr & Assocs., Parents Mag., Diener & Dorskind, March Advt., NYC, 1950-68; CEO J.D. Singer, NYC, 1968—. Scriptwriter Can. TV show, Magistrate's Court, 1968-69; syndicated columnist with Marlies Wolf, Women at Work, Feature Assocs., San Rafael, Calif., 1979—. Author: My Mother, The Doctor, 1970. Dem. County committeewoman, 1960-61. Mem. Direct Mktg. Creative Guild (v.p., corp. sec.), Friends Com., Gen. Soc. Libr. (chmn.), NATAS. Home and Office: 1725 York Ave Apt 19F New York NY 10128-7811 Office Phone: 212-348-0881. E-mail: imrejoysing@aol.com.

SINGER, LINDA J., attorney general; b. 1966; m. Joseph D. Singer; children: Erin, Lucas. Grad., Harvard Coll., 1988; JD magna cum laude, Harvard Law Sch., 1991. Bar: NY 1992, DC 2007. Staff atty. criminal def. divsn. Legal Aid Soc., NYC; exec. dir. Appleseed, 1993—2006; acting atty. gen. DC, 2007—. Bd. mem., chair Jessie Smith Noyes Found., NYC; mem. adv. bd. Family Econ. Self Sufficient prog. Wider Opportunities for Women. Office: Office of Atty Gen John A Wilson Bldg Ste 409 1350 Pennsylvania Ave NW Washington DC 20009 Office Phone: 202-724-1305. E-mail: oag@dc.gov. *

SINGER, MARKUS MORTON, retired trade association administrator; b. NYC, Dec. 20, 1917; s. Isadore and Nettie (Stromer) S.; m. Phyllis Berger, June 26, 1945; children: Fredric L., Robert B. B.C.S., NYU, 1939; postgrad., George Washington U., 1951-55. With Nat. Food Brokers Assn., Washington, 1946—, v.p., 1961-65, exec. v.p., 1965-71, pres., 1972-83, pres. emeritus, 1983—, acting pres., chief exec. officer, 1987-88. Lifetime hon. trustee Nat. Food Brokers Assn. Edn. and Tng. Found. Served with AUS, 1942-45. Recipient Pres.'s award as Man of Yr. Can. Food Brokers Assn., 1976 Mem. European Food Brokers Assn. (hon. life), Frozen Food Industry Disting. Order of Zerocrats. Jewish.

SINGER, MARTIN DORI, lawyer; b. Bklyn., Apr. 25, 1952; BA, CCNY, 1974; JD, Bklyn. Law Sch., 1977. Bar: Calif. 1977, US Dist. Ct., DC 1978, US Ct. Appeals (9th Cir) 1990. Ptnr. Lavely & Singer Profl. Corp., 1982—. Calif. labor commr. Author: (Law Handbook) Regulation of Talent Agent, 1983. Named to The Top 100 Attorneys in California, Daily Jour., 2005, 2006. Mem.: Beverly Hills, Century City and LA County Bar Associations. Office: Lavely & Singer 2049 Century Pk E Ste 2400 Los Angeles CA 90067 Office Phone: 310-556-3501. Office Fax: 310-556-3615. E-mail: msinger@lavelysinger.com. *

SINGER, MAXINE FRANK, retired biochemist, science association director; b. NYC, Feb. 15, 1931; d. Hyman S. and Henrietta (Perlowitz) Frank; m. Daniel Morris Singer, June 15, 1952; children: Amy Elizabeth, Ellen Ruth, David Byrd, Stephanie Frank. AB, Swarthmore Coll., 1952, DSc (hon.), 1978; PhD, Yale U., 1957, DSc (hon.), 1994, Wesleyan U., 1977, U. Md.-Baltimore County, 1985, Cedar Crest Coll., 1986, CUNY, 1988, Brandeis U., 1988, Radcliffe Coll., 2000, Williams Coll., 1990, Franklin and Marshall Coll., 1991, George Washington U., 1991, NYU, 1992, Lehigh U., 1992, Dartmouth Coll., 1993, Harvard U., 1994, Yale U., 1994, U. Nebr., 2004; PhD honoris causa (hon.), Weizmann Inst. Sci., 1995. USPHS postdoctoral fellow NIH, Bethesda, Md., 1956—58, rsch. chemist biochemistry, 1958—74; head sect. on nucleic acid enzymology Nat. Cancer Inst., 1974—79; chief Lab. of Biochemistry, Nat. Cancer Inst., 1979—87, rsch. chemist, 1987—88; pres. Carnegie Inst. Washington, 1988—2002, pres. emeritus, 2002—. Regents vis. lectr. U. Calif., Berkeley, 1981; bd. dirs. Perlegen Sci., Inc. Mem. editl. bd.: Jour. Biol. Chemistry, 1968—74, Sci. mag, 1972—82, chmn. editl. bd.: Procs. of NAS, 1985—88; co-author (with Paul Berg): 3 books on molecular biology and a sci. biog.; contbr. articles to scholarly jours. Chmn. Smithsonian Coun., 1992—93; trustee Wesleyan U., Middletown, Conn., 1972—75, Yale Corp., New Haven, 1975—90, Carnegie Inst. Wash., 2002—; bd. govs. Weizmann Inst. Sci., Rehovot, Israel, 1978—; bd. dirs. Whitehead Inst., 1985—94, chmn. bd., 2003—04. Named to Washington D.C. Hall of Fame, 2000; recipient award for achievement in biol. scis., Washington Acad. Scis., 1969, award for rsch. in biol. scis., Yale Sci. and Engring. Assn., 1974, Superior Svc. Honor award, HEW, 1975, Dirs. award, NIH, 1977, DSM, HHS, 1983, Presdl. Disting. Exec. Rank award, 1987, U.S. Disting. Exec. Rank award, 1987, Mory's Cup, Bd. Govs. Mory's Assn., 1991, Wilbur Lucius Cross Medal for Honor, Yale Grad. Sch. Assn., 1991, Nat. Medal Sci., NSF, 1992, Pub. Svc. award, NIH Alumni Assn., 1995, Vannevar Bush award, Nat. Sci. Bd., 1999, Pub. Welfare award, NAS, 2007. Fellow: Am. Acad. Arts and Scis.; mem.: AAAS (Sci. Freedom and Responsibility award 1982, Philip Hauge Abelson prize 2004), NAS (coun. 1982—85, com. sci., engring. and pub. policy 1989—91, chmn. 1999—2005, Pub. Welfare medal 2007), Am. Soc. Cell Biology, Pontifical Acad. of Scis., Inst. Medicine of NAS, Am. Philos. Soc., Am. Chem. Soc., Am. Soc. Microbiologists, Am. Soc. Biol. Chemists. Home: 5410 39th St NW Washington DC 20015-2902 Office: Carnegie Inst Washington 1530 P St NW Washington DC 20005-1933

SINGER, MICHAEL HOWARD, lawyer; b. NYC, Nov. 22, 1941; s. Jack and Etta (Appelbaum) S.; m. Saundra Jean Kupperman, June 1, 1962; children: Allison Jill, Pamela Faith. BS in Econs., U. Pa., 1962; JD, NYU, 1965, LLM in Taxation, 1968. Bar: N.Y. 1965, U.S. Ct. Claims 1968, U.S. Supreme Ct. 1969, U.S. Ct. Appeals (6th cir.) 1970, D.C. 1972, U.S. Tax Ct. 1972, Nev. 1973, U.S. Ct. Appeals (9th cir.) 1973. Law asst. Appellate Term Supreme Ct., NYC, 1965-68; trial lawyer Ct. Claims Tax Div., Washington, 1968-72; tax lawyer Beckley, DeLanoy & Jemison, Las Vegas, 1972-74; ptnr. Oshins, Singer, Segal & Morris, Las Vegas, 1974-87, Singer, Brown, and Barringer, LLC, Las Vegas, 1996-99; pvt. practice Las Vegas, 1987—. Settlement judge Nev. Supreme Ct., 1997—, judge pro tempore short trials, 2007—; short trial judge Nev. Dist. Ct., 2007—. Pres. Las Vegas chpt. NCCJ, 1980—82. Mem. ABA, Nev. Bar Assn., Clark County Bar Assn., Las Vegas Country Club (bd. dirs. 1999-04, v.p. 2001-02, chmn. membership com. 2002-05). Democrat. Jewish. Avocations: golf, tennis. Office: 4475 S Pecos Rd Las Vegas NV 89121 Home: 3684 Rick Stratton Dr Las Vegas NV 89120 Office Phone: 702-454-2111. Business E-Mail: msinger@mhsingerlaw.com. *Personal philosophy: A reasonable settlement is more economically beneficial for the client than protracted litigation of a great lawsuit.*

SINGER, MYER R(ICHARD), lawyer; b. Everett, Mass., Oct. 24, 1938; s. Nathan and Celia (Rudin) Singer; m. Elaine Doris Ginesky, June 17, 1962; children: Andrew L., Stephen D., Jocelyn G. BSBA, Boston U., 1960, LLB, 1963. Bar: Mass. 1963, U.S. Ct. Appeals (1st cir.) 1963. Atty. Boston Legal Aid Soc., 1963—64; pvt. practice Dennis Port, Mass., 1965—2001; ptnr. Singer & Singer, LLC, 2001—. Trustee, corporator, mem. bd. investment Cape Cod Five Cents Savs. Bank, Harwich Port, Mass.; trustee Cape Cod Mus. of Natural History, 2001—; faculty Mass. Continuing Legal Edn., Inc., 1985, 1990—98; program chmn. Real Estate Devel. Cape Cod-Mass. Bar Inst., 1999; corporator Heritage Mus. and Gardens, 2003—; spkr. in field. Co-author: (book) Creation and Care of Condominiums, 1985, Everything You Need to Know about the Cape Cod Commission Act, 1990. Pres. Dennis Yarmouth Band Parents, 1986—87; mem. adv. bd. Cape Mus. Fine Arts, Dennis, 1988—96; mem. exec. com. Cape Cod Five Cents Savs. Bank Charitable Found. Trust, 2006—; former trustee Cape Cod Synagogue; mem., clk. Yarmouth (Mass.) Zoning Bd. Appeals, 1980—86; former bd. dirs. Cape Cod and Island chpt. of Mass. Heart Assn.; former pres. Legal Svcs. of Cape Cod and Island, Inc. Mem.: ABA, Barnstable County Bar Assn. (mem. exec. com. 1999—2003), Mass. Bar Assn. (chmn. bar assn. program real estate devel. Cape Cod 1999). Avocations: boating, photography. Home: 238 Greenland Circle East Dennis MA 02641-1302 Office: PO Box 67 26 Upper County Rd Dennis Port MA 02639-0067 Office Phone: 508-398-2221. Business E-Mail: mrsinger@singer-law.com.

SINGER, PAUL MEYER, lawyer; b. Pitts., May 20, 1943; s. Sidney Morris and Doris (Lyttle) S.; m. Laurie Stern, 1989. BS in Bus., U. Minn., 1965; JD, U. Pitts., 1968; LLM, Harvard U., 1970. Law clk. to presiding justice Pa. Supreme Ct., Pitts., 1970-71; atty. Am. Express Credit Corp., NYC, 1971-73; ptnr. Reed Smith LLP, Pitts., 1973—. Mem. Am. Coll. Bankruptcy (v.p.), Harvard-Yale-Princeton Club, Duquesne Club. Office: Reed Smith LLP 435 6th Ave Pittsburgh PA 15219-1886 E-mail: psinger@reedsmith.com.

SINGER, PAUL RICHARD, ophthalmologist; b. NYC, Feb. 1, 1947; m. Katherine W. Singer, June 13, 1970; children: Amy E., Evan P. BA with honors, U. Rochester, NYC, 1969, MD, 1973. Diplomate Am. Bd. Ophthalmology. Internal medicine intern U. N.C., Chapel Hill, 1973-74, resident in neurology, 1974-75; resident in ophthalmology Washington U. Sch. Medicine, St. Louis, 1975-78, Fight for Sight postdoctoral rsch. fellow dept ophthalmology, 1978-79; pres. Hartford (Conn.) Eye Physicians, 1980—; sr. staff dept. ophthalmology Hartford Hosp., 1980—. Chmn. bd. dirs. Prevent Blindness Conn., Middletown, 1990-92, Combined Health Appeal, Hartford, 1993-95. Recipient Cmty. Svc. award Hartford County Med. Assn., 1993, Robert Polk award for outstanding vol. svc. Prevent Blindness Conn., 1993. Office: Hartford Eye Physicians 55 Nye Rd Ste 103 Glastonbury CT 06033-4394

SINGER, PAULA NOYES, lawyer, computer company executive; b. Portsmouth, NH, Aug. 2, 1944; d. Paul Snowman and Grace Marion (Smith) Noyes; m. Wayne Allen Goodrich, Sept. 6, 1964 (div. 1973); 1 child, Beth Ann; m. Gary Philip Singer, June 1, 1976; 1 child, Samantha Anne. BA, U. Maine, Orono, 1966; JD, U. Maine, Portland, 1978. Bar: Maine 1978, Mass. 1978, U.S. Dist. Ct. Maine 1978, U.S. Dist. Ct. Mass. 1979, U.S. Tax Ct. 1985, U.S. Ct. Appeals (1st cir.) 1996, U.S. Supreme Ct. 1986. Programmer New Eng. Mut. Life Ins. Co., Boston, 1966-67; programmer to sr. systems analyst Union Mut. Life Ins. Co., Portland, 1968-77; tax specialist Peat, Marwick, Mitchell & Co., Portland, 1977-79; internat. personnel specialist Arthur D. Little, Cambridge, Mass., 1979-85; lawyer Vacovec, Miller & Rothenberg, Brookline, Mass., 1985-88; ptnr. Vacovec, Rothenberg, Mayotte & Singer, Newton, Mass., 1988-90, Vacovec, Mayotte & Singer LLP, Newton, Mass., 1990—; co-founder, chmn. Windstar Techs., Inc., 1994—; co-founder, pres. Windstar Publ., Inc., 2000—. Author: 8 books on tax and immigration; contbr. articles pub. to profl.jour. Bd. dirs. U. Maine Law Sch. Alumni, 1989-95. Mem. ABA, Mass. Bar Assn., Boston Bar Assn., Am. Immigration Lawyers Assn., Women in World Trade (bd. dirs. 1987-89), ADL Alumni Assn. (bd. dirs. 1987-95, clerk 1987—), Internat. Fiscal Assn., Phi Beta Kappa, Phi Kappa

Phi. Democrat. Jewish. Avocation: reading. Office: Windstar Tech Inc 1400 Providence Hwy Bldg 3 Ste 3250 Norwood MA 02062-0800 also: Vacovec Mayotte & Singer LLP 255 Washington St Ste 340 Newton MA 02458-1634

SINGER, PETER ALBERT DAVID, philosophy educator, writer; b. Melbourne, Victoria, Australia, July 6, 1946; s. Ernest and Cora Renata (Oppenheim) S.; m. Renata Diamond, Dec. 16, 1968; children: Ruth, Marion, Esther. BA with honors, U. Melbourne, 1967, MA, 1969; BPhil, U. Oxford, Eng., 1971. Radcliffe lectr. Univ. Coll., U. Oxford, 1971-73; vis. asst. prof. dept. philosophy NYU, 1973-74; sr. lectr., dept. philosophy La Trobe Univ., 1975—76; prof. dept. philosophy Monash U., Clayton, Australia, 1977-99, prof. dept. philosophy, on secondment to the Ctr. for Human Bioethics (part-time), 1983—87, 1997—99, prof. dept. philosophy, on secondment to the Ctr. for Human Bioethics (full time), 1987—97, chair, dept. philosophy, 1977—78, 1980—81, acting dean, faculty of arts, 1982, dir. Ctr. for Human Bioethics, (part time) Clayton, Australia, 1983—87, dir. Ctr. for Human Bioethics, (full time), 1987—91, dep. dir., Ctr. for Human Bioethics, 1992—97, co-dir., Inst. for Ethics and Pub Policy, 1992—95; Ira W. DeCamp prof. bioethics, U Princeton U., 1999—2004, Ira W. DeCamp prof. bioethics, 2005—; laureate prof., Ctr. for Applied Philoosphy (part time) Univ. Melene, 2005—. Sr. scholar, Fulbright prog., 1978; guest scholar Inst. for Soc., Ethics, and the Life Sciences, Hastings-on-Hudson, NY, 1979; Cecil Green vis. prof. U. BC, Vancouver, Can., 1981; vis. disting humanist U. Colo., Boulder, 1984; disting vis. prof. U. Calif., Irvine, 1987; Sissela Bok lectr. program for ethics in the professions J.F. Kennedy Sch. Govt. Harvard U., 1987; Italian Nat. Rsch. Coun. Vis. Scholar, U. Rome La Sapienza, 1991, Erskine Fellow, U. Canterbury, Christchurch, 1997, Ferrator Mora Chair Comtemporary Thought, U. Girono, 2003; scientific advisor, Aufklarung und Kritik, 1994-; co-founder, pres., The Great Ape Project, 1993-2005, chair bd. dirs., 2005-; invited lectr. in field. Author: Democracy and Disobedience, 1973, Animal Liberation: A New Ethics for our Treatment of Animals, 1975, 2nd edit., 1990, Animal Rights and Human Obligations: An Anthology, 1976, 2nd edit., 1989, Practical Ethics, 1979, 2d edit., 1993, Marx, 1980, The Expanding Circle: Ethics and Sociobiology, 1981, Hegal, 1982, reissued as Hegel: A Very Short Introduction, 2001, (with J. Mason) Animal Factories, 1980, 2nd edit., 1990, (with D. Wells) The Reproduction Revolution: New Ways of Making Babies, 1984, (with H. Kuhse) Should the Baby Live? The Problem of Handicapped Infants, 1985, (with L. Gruen) Animal Liberation, A Graphic Guide, 1987, (with Barbara Dover & Ingrid Newkirk) Save the Animals, 1991, How Are We to Live? Ethics in an Age of Self-Interest, 1993, (with Helga Kuhse) Individuals, Humans & Persons: Questions of Life and Death, 1994, Rethinking Life and Death: The Collapse of Our Traditional Ethics, 1994, (with Bob Brown) The Greens, 1996, (with John McKie, Jeff Richardson and Helga Kuhse) The Allocation of Health Care Resources: An Ethical Evaluation of the "QALY" Approach, 1998, Ethics in Action: Henry Spira and the Animal Rights Movement, 1998, A Darwinian Left, 1999, Writings on an Ethical Life, 2000, Unsanctifying Human Life: Essays on Ethics, 2001, One World: Ethics and Globalization, 2002, Pushing Time Away: My Grandfather and the Tragedy of Jewish Vienna, 2003, The President of Good & Evil: The Ethics of George W. Bush 2004, Comment Vivre Avec Les Animaux, 2004, (with Tom Gregg) How Ethical is Australia? An Examination of Australia's Record as a Global Citizen, 2004, (with Jim Mason) The Way We Eat: Why Our Food Choices Matter, 2006; editor: In Defense of Animals, 1985, Applied Ethics, 1986, (with W. Walters) Test-Tube Babies: A Guide to Moral Questions, Present Techniques, and Future Possibilities, 1982, (with H. Kuhse, Stephen Buckle, Karen Dawson & Pascal Kasimba) Embryo Experimentation, 1990, (with Paola Cavalieri) The Great Ape Project" Equality Beyond Humanity, 1993, Ethics, 1994, (with Helga Kuhse) A Companion to Bioethics, 1998, Bioethics: An Anthology, 1999, 2nd edit. 2006, (with Renata Singer) A Moral of the Story: An Anthology of Ethics Through Literature, 2005; co-editor Bioethics, 1985-99, mem. editl. bd., 1999-; gen. editor, Studies in Bioethics, 1984-92; mem. editl. bd. Australasian Jour. Philosophy, 1978-99, Ethics, 1979-82, Internat. Jour. for the Study of Animal Problems, 1978-82, Philosophy and Geography, 2000-, Reason in Practice, 2001-; adv. bd. Jour. of Medicine and Philosophy, 1984-85, editorial bd. 1985-; mem. adv. bd. Centre for Philosophy & Pub. Affairs, Univ. St. Andrews, Scotland, 1984-; adv. editor (Australia) Jour. of Applied Philosophy, 1985-85, editl. bd. 1985-; appeared on various televison programs; contbr. articles to profl. journals. Patron Farm and Food Soc. U.K., 1978-2001, Animal Liberation, Australia, 1978-; mem. animal welfare adv. com. Dept. Agr., Victoria, 1981-92; chmn. Australian Fedn. Animal Socs., 1980-83; v.p. Australian and New Zealand Fedn. Animal Socs., 1984-94, pres., 1994-99; mem. Commonwealth Sci. and Indsl. Orgn. Adv. Com. on Ethics Animal Rsch., 1984-91; v.p. Royal Soc. for the Prevention of Cruelty to Animals, 2001, Oxfam Am. Leadership Coun., 2003-, World Coun. Religious Leaders Global Ethics Initiative, 2003-; mem. adv. bd. Ctr. for Philosophy and Pub. Affairs, U. St. Andrews, Scotland, 1984-. Fellow Woodrow Wilson Internat. Ctr. for Scholars, Smithsonian Instn., 1979; recipient World Tech. Network Ethics award, 2003, Emperor Has No Clothes award, Freedom from religion Found. named one of 100 Most Influential People of 2005, Time mag. Fellow Acad. Humanities in Australia, Acad. Social Scis. in Australia, Internat. Assn. Bioethics (found. pres. 1992-95, bd. dir. 1992-1999); mem. Am. Philos. Assn., Eastern Divsn, adv. com. to the program com., 2000-. Avocations: surfing, hiking. Office: Univ Ctr for Human Values Princeton Univ 5 Ivy Ln Princeton NJ 08544-1013 Office Phone: 609-258-2202. Office Fax: 609-258-1285. Business E-Mail: psinger@princeton.edu. *

SINGER, RICHARD M., lawyer; b. Mt. Vernon, NY, 1946; BA, Univ. Pa., 1968, JD, 1971. Bar: NY 1972, DC 1972. Mng. ptnr, ptnr.-in-charge, mem., comm. law practice group Drinker Biddle & Reath LLP, Washington. Mem.: ABA, Fed. Comm. Bar Assn. Office: Drinker Biddle & Reath LLP Ste 1100 1500 K St NW Washington DC 20005-1209 Office Phone: 202-342-8814. Office Fax: 202-842-8465. Business E-Mail: richard.singer@dbr.com.

SINGER, ROBERT, plastic surgeon; b. Buffalo, Oct. 22, 1942; s. Murray and Fay Singer; m. Judith Harris. Student, SUNY, Buffalo, 1960-63; MD, SUNY, 1967. Lic. physician, Calif.; diplomate Am. Bd. Plastic and Reconstructive Surgery. Resident in gen. surgery Stanford Med. Ctr., Palo Alto, Calif., 1967-69, Santa Barbara Cottage and Gen. Hosp., 1972-74; resident in plastic surgery Vanderbilt U., 1974-76; pvt. practice specializing in emergency and trauma San Diego, 1971-72; pvt. practice plastic, reconstructive and aesthetic surgery La Jolla, Calif., 1976—. Prior asst. clin. prof. plastic surgery U. Calif., San Diego; sr. staff, chief plastic surgery Scripps Meml. Hosp., La Jolla, 1980-86, vice chmn. dept. surgery, 1989-91. Contbr. articles to profl. jours. Active San Diego Opera, San Diego Mus. of Man, La Jolla Playhouse, Voices for Children, San Diego Zoo, Mus. Photog. Arts, KPBS, others. Fellow ACS; mem. AMA, Calif. Med. Assn., San Diego County Med. Soc., San Diego Internat. Soc. Plastic Surgeons (pres. 1988-89), Calif. Soc. Plastic Surgeons (pres. 1995-96), Am. Soc. Aesthetic Plastic Surgeons (pres. 1994-95), Internat. Soc. Clin. Plastic Surgeons, Am. Soc. Plastic and Reconstructive Surgeons (trustee 1996—, chmn. bd. trustees 1998-99), J.B. Lynch Soc., Royal Soc. Medicine, Am. Assn. for Accreditation of Ambulatory Surgery Facilities (pres. 1991-2000), San Diego Plastic Surgery Soc. (pres. 1989-90), Aesthetic Surgery Edn. and Rsch. Found. (pres., 2000—) Avocations: tennis, travel, pre-columbian art. Office: 9834 Genesee Ave Ste 100 La Jolla CA 92037-1214

SINGER, ROSS, library and information scientist; BA in Theater, U. Tenn., 2000. Web and applications coord. Emory U. Gen. Libr.; formerly with internet.com (now Jupiter Media); application developer Ga. Tech. Library and Info. Ctr. Contbr. articles to numerous profl. tech. jours. Named one of the Movers and Shakers, Libr. Jour., 2007. Mem.: Metro Atlanta Libr. Tech. Assn. (founder). Achievements include creating The Umlaut Open URL Link Resolver, A9 Opensearch interface for SRU, WebTribute (a Web-based alternative to Macromedia's Contribute 2). Office: Ga Tech Libr 704 Cherry St Atlanta GA 30332-0900

SINGER, STEVEN D., lawyer; b. 1954; BA summa cum laude, Tufts U., 1976; JD magna cum laude, Harvard U., 1979. Bar: Mass. 1979. Ptnr., vice chmn. Corp. dept., co-chmn. Life Sci. dept. Wilmer Cutler Pickering Hale & Dorr, Boston. Mem. bd. overseers Beth Israel Deaconess Med. Ctr.; bd. dir. Beelzebubs Found.; past pres. Temple Beth Shalom, Needham, Mass. Named a Mass. Super Lawyer, Boston Mag., 2004. Mem.: ABA, Mass. Biotechnology Council, Biotechnology Ind. Org. Jewish. Office: Wilmer Cutler Pickering Hale & Dorr 60 State St Boston MA 02109 Office Phone: 617-526-6410. Office Fax: 617-526-5000. Business E-Mail: steven.singer@wilmerhale.com.

SINGER, SUE, academic administrator; Grad. Bus. Mgmt. & Personnel Mgmt. prog, Humber Coll., Toronto. Founder, pres. Pacific Inst. Culinary Arts, Vancouver, 1995—. Mem. exec. bd. go2 Tourism. Mem.: Granville Island Merchants Assn., Internat. Assn. Culinary Professionals, Can. Fedn. Ind. Bus., BC Career Colleges Assn. (dir.), BC Restaurant Assn. Office: Pacific Inst Culinary Arts 1505 W 2nd Ave Vancouver BC V6H 3Y4 Canada Office Phone: 604-734-4488. Office Fax: 604-734-4408. Business E-Mail: info@picachef.com. *

SINGER, WILLIAM HARRY, retired artificial intelligence application developer, retired research scientist; b. Lancaster, Pa., Jan. 25, 1947; s. Wilbur Weitzel and Mildred (Myers) S.; m. Nanette Platt Willis, July 28, 1989. BS, U. Pitts., 1973; MS, Drexel U., 1982; PhD, U. Basel, 1991. Rsch. asst. dept. molecular biology Ea. Pa. Psychiatric Inst., Phila., 1976-81; rsch. fellow dept. biophys. chemistry Biozentrum, Basel, Switzerland, 1981-83; ltd. ptnr. Tech. Systems Software, 1983-86; gen. ptnr. Singer and Singer Assocs., 1993—2004; ret., 2007. Vis. scientist, rsch. fellow, dept. biophysical chem. Biozentrum, Basel, Switzerland, 1981—83; co-founder, prin. ptnr. Singer Cons. Inc., Palmyra, Pa., 1983—2000; adj. lectr. Wilson Coll., Chambersburg, Pa., 1994—96; founder Blue Dragon Ceramic Studio, 2003; adj. lectr. Ctrl. Pa. Bus. Coll., Summerdale, 2005; lectr. in field; cons. in field. Contbr. articles to profl. jours.; co-author: Diabetic's Daily Diary, 1987; world wide web site designer; prodr. abstract nonfunctional ceramic art, 2000—, mentor to several ceramic artists at Blue Dragon Studio. Served with USAF, 1966—69, Vietnam. Swiss Nat. Sci. Found. rsch. fellow, 1981-83. Mem. NRA, Okinawa Isshinryu Karate Assn. (life), Wasserfahrverein Horburg of Basel (Switzerland) (life mem.), Am. Potters Council, Am. Ceramics Soc. Democrat. Roman Catholic. Achievements include research in drug and chemically induced membrane fusion, determination of rates of protein lateral diffusion in membrane monolayers and bilayers; discoveries of new quantum effects in fields of fluorescence quenching, recovery, and determination of extinction coefficients in new radicals; design and construction of several diagnostic devices including devices to measure membrane fusion directly, and protein lateral diffusion rate constants in monolayered and bilayered membranes; design and coding of several Industrial Process Control software systems; design and production of various educational CD-ROM titles; design and production of various educational and business level worldwide web sites; statistical analysis and control of serum glucose levels in Type II diabetics; and design and production of ceramic works of art. Home and Studio: 1533 Cambridge Ct Palmyra PA 17078-9375 Home Phone: 717-838-6706; Office Phone: 717-838-6906. Personal E-mail: whsinger@comcast.net.

SINGER-CHANG, GAIL LESLIE, medical and social sciences educator, consultant; d. Frank Max (Stepfather) and Rona Jane Singer; m. Anthony Chang. BA in Journalism, San Diego State U., 1988; MS in Counseling, Calif. State U., Fullerton, 1992; MA in Clin. Psychology, Calif. Sch. Profl. Psychology, 1994, D of Psychology in Clin. Psychology, 1996. Pupil pers. svcs. credential Calif. Asst. prof. family medicine Western U. of Health Scis., Coll. Osteopathic Medicine of the Pacific, Pomona, Calif., 1999—2005, asst. prof. social and behavioral scis., asst. dean student affairs, 2003—05, program dir., doctor-patient communication program, 1999—2005; med. edn. consultant, 2005—. Orgnl. cons., Irvine, Calif., 1998—99; post-doctoral psychology intern El Toro Marine Base Family Services Ctr., El Toro, Calif., 1997—99; psychology intern Kaiser Permanente, Tustin, Calif., 1995—96, Orange Coast Coll. Student Health Ctr., Costa Mesa, Calif., 1994—95; counseling intern Teen-Age Pregnancy and Parenting Program, Fullerton, Calif., 1991—91; adj. prof. Concordia U., Irvine, Calif., 1998—99, Calif. State U., Fullerton, 1999; presenter in field. Presenter (profl. presentation) Enabling Disability Education: The Value of Using Disabled Persons as Standardized Patients, 10th Internat. Ottawa Conf. Med. Edn., 2002 (Greatest Profl. Promise, 1992), Creative Use of Assessment and Feedback: Increasing Deep Learning and Professionalism, Western Assn. Schs. and Colls., 2002, Psychosocial Aspects of the Physician-Patient Intervention, Soc. Psychol. Anthropology, 2003. Recipient Dedicated Svc. award, Calif. State U., 1998, Recognition cert., El Toro Marine Base Family Svcs. Ctr., 2001—03. Mem.: Assn. Profl. Cons., Am. Anthropol. Assn., Assn. for the Behavioral Scis. and Med. Edn., Soc. of Tchrs. of Family Medicine. Office Phone: 909-469-5563. Personal E-mail: doctorgail@msn.com. Business E-Mail: gsingerchang@westernu.edu.

SINGER-GRANICK, CAROL J., pediatric endocrinologist, educator; b. NYC, Jan. 6, 1952; d. Alan and Gloria Francine (Kaplan) Singer; m. Mark Stephen Granick, Feb. 17, 1974; children: Michelle, Jaclyn. BS with distinction, Cornell U., 1974; MD, Boston U., 1978. Diplomate Nat. Bd. Med. Examiners, Am. Bd. Pediatrics, Am. Bd. Pediatric Endocrinology. Clin. instr. pediats. U. Pitts., 1985-87; attending physician Pediat. Med. Assn., Abington/Norristown, Pa., 1987-90; asst. prof. pediats. Hahnemann U., Phila., 1990-94, Temple U., Phila., 1994-97, Allegheny U.- St. Christopher's Hosp. for Children, Phila., 1997-98; pediat. endocrinologist MCP/Hahnemann Sch. Medicine, Drexel U., St. Christophers Hosp. for Children, Phila., 1998-2000; assoc. prof. pediat. Temple U. Children's Med. Ctr., 2000—. Dir. pediat. residency Hahnemann U., 1990-94; lectr. in field. Contbr. articles to profl. jours. Fellow Am. Acad. Pediats.; mem. Am. Diabetes Assn., Endocrine Soc., Phila. Pediat. Soc., Lawson Wilkens Pediat. Endo Soc. Avocations: tennis, reading, bicycling.

SINGH, DEVINDER, chemical engineer; b. Nilokheri, Haryana, India, Aug. 28, 1977; s. Joga and Balwinder (Kaur) Singh; m. Gurjeet Kaur, July 30, 2006. BChemE, Panjab U., Chandigarh, India, 2000; MSChemE, U. ND, Grand Forks, 2005; postgrad., Kans. State U., Manhattan, 2005—. Grad. rsch. asst., grad. tchg. asst. dept. chem. engring. U. ND, Grand Forks, 2002—04; grad. rsch. asst. dept. chem engring. Kans. State U., Manhattan, 2005—. Presenter in field. Contbr. articles to profl. jours. Honstead scholar, Dept. of Chem. Engring., 2006. Mem.: AIChE, North Am. Membrane Soc. Achievements include research in partial hydrogenation of vegetable oil with less trans fatty acids using membrane reactor technology; development of solid oxide fuel cells. Office: Kansas State Univ Dept Chem Engring 105 Durland Hall Manhattan KS 66506 Home Phone: 785-317-5301; Office Phone: 785-532-4324. Business E-Mail: dsingh@ksu.edu.

SINGH, HARBACHAN, solicitor, barrister; b. Klang, Malaysia, Mar. 11, 1939; arrived in U.S., 1969; s. Kishen Singh and Dhan Kaur; m. Susil Kaur, Jan. 12, 1963; children: Sukhwant, Ramesh, Praveen. Barrister-at-law, Honorable Soc. Lincoln's Inn, London, 1967; MA, St. John's U., 1981. Police interpreter Royal Malaysian Police, Malaysia, 1957-63; advocate, solicitor Allen & Gledhill Law Firm, Kuala Lumpur, Malaysia, 1967-69; chief of travel UN, NYC, 1969-79, chief of transp., 1979-90, chmn. hdqrs. com. on contracts, 1995—99, chmn. hdqrs. property survey bd., 1987—99; mng. dir. Triangle Mortgage Svcs., Inc., 2000—01. UN team leader Return of Property from Iraq to Kuwait, UN Security Coun. Resolution, 1994-95; sr. exec. officer UN Mission East Timor, 1999; chmn. UN Appointments and Promotion Com., 1987-89; elected mem. UN Panel of Counsel Joint Appeals bd., 1987-92; mem. U.S. Presdl. Gateway Improvement Task Force; mem. Staff Union, 1969-99. Mem. Queens Borough County Cmty. Bd. 8, 2000—; ofcl. del. Queens Borough Gen. Assembly, 2003—; com. mem. Annual Meml. Day March and Celebrations Com., 2003—, Queens Health Congress, 2003—; mem. adv. bd. Flushing Meadows Corona Park Conservancy Com., 2003—, Holocaust Resource and Archieves Ctr., Queensboro Cmty. Coll., 2004—; com. mem. Queensboro Borough Pres. Com.; mem. Queensboro residents com. African-Am. Annual Heritage celebrations, 2005—; mrm. steering com. Friends Cunningham Pk., 2005—; pres., CEO Sikh Am. Friendship Found., 2002—. Recipient numerous achievement awards and accolades, US Congressmen, NY State Senators, NY State Assemblymen, NYC Councilmen, Comptroller of NY. Mem.: Hollis Park Gardens Assn. (bd. dirs. 2002—), True Potential Toastmasters Internat. Inc. (pres.), Saul Wopin Regular Dem. Club (pres. 2007—). Home: 193-12 Foothill Ave Hollis NY 11423-1259 Personal E-mail: hsingh19@nyc.rr.com.

SINGH, HARJIT, medical educator, artist; b. Shimla, Himachal Pradesh, India, Sept. 26, 1936; s. Achal Singh and Sunder Kaur; m. Cecilia Sepulveda, July 17, 1993; children: Namrita, Arshdeep. MB, BS, Govt. Med. Coll., Patiala, India, 1958; MD, Punjabi U., Patiala, 1964. Lic. Punjab Med. Coun., Ludhiana, India, 1958, cert. Ednl. Coun. for Fgn. Med. Grads., 1962, lic. pediat. specialist Dept. Health, Dubai, UAE, 1990. Sr. lectr. in pediat. Govt. Med. Coll., Patiala, Punjab, India, 1965—66, Med. Coll., Rohtak, Haryana, India, 1966—70, asst. prof. pediat., 1970—75, reader in pediat., 1975—76, assoc. prof. pediat., 1976—77, 1978—82, prof. pediat., 1977—78, 1982—84, Arab Med. U., Benghazi, Libya, 1984—88; cmty. pediatrician Am. Hosp., Dubai, United Arab Emirates, 1997—2000; CME program dir. Hackettstown Regional Med. Ctr., NJ, 2002—. Examiner in pediat. Arab Med. U., Benghazi, 1985—88; vis. prof. Sch. Tropical Medicine, Liverpool, 1986—95. Exhibitions include Dubai Internat. Art Ctr., 1991—99, Yolo County Art Coun., 2001, Sussex County Art & Heritage Coun., 2002, Warren County Art Coun., 2002, Triveni Art Gllery, New Delhi, 1970, Represented in permanent collections, India, Can., UK, UAE, US. Grantee, Indian Coun. Med. Rsch., New Delhi, 1975—88; fellowship in pediat. hematology, WHO, 1974-75. Mem.: Alliance of CME (corr.), Indian Assn. Advancement Med. Edn. (life), Perinatology Forum (life). Office: Hackettstown Regional Med Ctr 651 Willow Grove St Hackettstown NJ 07840 Home Phone: 908-850-3367. Office Fax: 908-950-6815. E-mail: hsingh@hrmend.org.

SINGH, JAY, director, researcher; b. Mumbai, Maharashtra, India, Mar. 8, 1971; s. Surinder Singh; m. Neetu Bali. PhD, Mich. State U., East Lansing, 2002. Rsch. assoc. Mich. State U., 2002—03; dir. packaging program Calif. Poly. State U., San Luis Obispo, 2003—. Prin. Cal Pack Solutions, San Luis Obispo, 2005—. Mem.: ASTM (licentiate), PolyGAIT-RFID R & D Lab., Cal Poly (founding mem. 2004), Nat. Assn. for Indsl. Tech. (licentiate), Internat. Safe Transit Assn. (licentiate), Internat. Assn. Packaging Rsch. Inst. (licentiate). Achievements include research in comparison of radio frequency identification tag performance for fresh produce containers. Office: Calif Polytechnic State U 1 Grand Ave San Luis Obispo CA 93407 Home Phone: 805-756-2129; Office Phone: 805-756-2129. Office Fax: 805-756-6111; Home Fax: 805-756-6111. Business E-Mail: jasingh@calpoly.edu.

SINGH, JYOTI SHANKAR, international organization executive; b. Pathalgaon, India, Apr. 15, 1935; arrived in U.S., 1972; s. Brijnath Kumar and Tirthmani (Singh) S.; m. Maria Luz Molares, 1962; children: Anil, Rajeev, Ajit. BA, Banaras U., India, 1952, MA, 1954, LLB, 1955; MA, NYU, 1979; D (honoris causa), Internat. Inst. Integration, Bolivia, 1980. Assoc. sec. coordinating secretariat, Leiden, The Netherlands, 1960-61; sec. gen. coordinating secretariat, 1961-64; programme cons. Internat. Youth Centre, New Delhi, 1965-66; sec. gen. World Assembly of Youth, Brussels, 1966-72; liaison officer Fund for Population Activities UN, NYC, 1972-73, asst. exec. sec. World Population Yr., 1973-74, dep. chief info. and pub. affairs, 1975-80, dir. info. and external rels., 1980—90; dir. tech. and evaluation div. UN Population Fund, NYC, 1990-95, dep. exec. dir., 1995-96; spl. adviser to exec. dir. UNFPA, NYC, 1996-99; exec. coord. 23rd spl. session UN Gen. Assembly, 2000; exec. coord. World Conf. Against Racism, Geneva, 2000—01; pres. Population 2005, 1999—2005. Hon. prof. Ctrl. Am. U., Managua, Nicaragua, 1975; exec. coord. UN Internat. Conf. on Population, 1982-84, permanent observer to UN, Ptnrs. in Population and Devel., NY, 2003—; exec. coord. Internat. Conf. on Population and Devel., 1992-94; chmn. The Earth Times, 1996-98. Author: Creating a New Consensus on Population, 1998; editor-in-chief Populi, 1980-90. Mem. Ams. for UNFPA (bd. dirs.). Home: 10 Waterside Plz Apt 26D New York NY 10010-2606 Office Phone: 212-286-1082. Personal E-mail: jyotissingh@hotmail.com.

SINGH, K. PAUL, telecommunications industry executive; MSEE, SUNY; MBA, Harvard U. Vice-pres. global prod. mktg. M.C.I., 1991—94; found., chmn., CEO Overseas Telecommunications Inc.; found. Cygnus Satellite Corp.; found., chmn., CEO Primus Telecommunications Group, 1994, also pres. Office: Primus Telecommunications Group Ste 900 7901 Jones Branch Rd Mc Lean VA 22102

SINGH, LOREN CHAN, writer, educator; b. Palo Alto, Calif., Sept. 10, 1943; s. Shau Wing and Anna Mae Chan; m. Frances Anastasia Chow, Apr. 19, 1975 (div. Jan. 1988); children: Karen Monique Chan, Pierre Benedict Chan, Marc Henri Chan; m. Sandra Marie Miner, Mar. 14, 2000. AB, Stanford U., Calif., 1965, AM, 1966; MS, Golden Gate U., San Francisco, 1988; PhD, UCLA, 1971. Tchg. asst. UCLA, 1968—69, tchg. assoc., 1969—70; lectr. in history Calif. State U., Northridge, 1970—71, San Jose State U., Calif., 1971—72, asst. prof. history, 1972—76, assoc. prof. history, 1976—80; lectr. history Calif. State U., East Bay, 1980—81; prodn. test technician Nicolet Paratronics Corp., Fremont, Calif., 1982; computer svc. technician Bell-No. Rsch., Mountain View, Calif., 1982—83, rsch. analyst, 1984—85, tech. writer, 1985—87; sr. tech. writer StrataCom, Inc., Campbell, Calif., 1987—88; tech. writer Sun Microsystems, Palo Alto, 1988—90, sr. tech. writer, 1990—2000; tech. editor Brocade Comms. Sys., Inc., San Jose, 2000—02; instr. adult edn. Santa Clara Unified Sch. Dist., Calif., 2002—03; bus driver Serendipity Land Yachts, Ltd., Santa Clara, 2002—05; adminstrv. asst. Microcontroller Pros Corp., Morgan Hill, Calif., 2005—. Author: Sagebrush Statesman, 1973, Collected Technical Support Notes, 1988, SPARCstation 1 Installation Guide, 1989, Desktop Storage Pack Installation Guide, 1989—90, SPARCstation 2 Installation Guide, 1990, SPARCstation 10 Installation Guide, 1992, SPARCstation 10 Networking and Communication Guide, 1993, SPARCstation 10SX VSIMMs Installation, 1993, SPARCstation 20 HyperSPARC Module Upgrade, 1995, SPARCstation 20 SuperSPARC-II Module Upgrade, 1995, Sun Ultra 1 Reference Material, 1995—96, Sun Ultra 2 Reference Manual, 1996, Sun Ultra 30 Installation Guide, 1997, SPARCstorage FlexiPack Removable Storage Tray Installation Guide, 1997, Sun StorEdge Long Wave Gigabit Interface Converter Service Manual, 1999, Sun StorEdge PCI Dual Fibre Channel Host Adapter Installation, 2000; editor: Chinese-American History Reader, 1976; contbr. articles to profl. jours. Radio sta. trustee ARC, Menlo Park, Calif., 1975—80. Recipient Presdl. Sports award, Pres.'s Coun. Phys. Fitness and Sports, 1973. Mem.: Am. Radio Relay League, South Valley YMCA. Democrat. Sikh. Avocations: swimming, amateur radio, stamp collecting/philately. Home: 195 Blossom Hill Rd # 123 San Jose CA 95123-2348 Office: Microcontroller Pros Corp 17408 Blue Jay Dr Morgan Hill CA 95037-6402 Personal E-mail: ad6yu@ecoisp.com.

SINGH, MEENAKSHI, pathologist, educator; MB, BChir, MD, Christian Med. Coll., India. Cert. in anatomic and clin. pathology Am. Bd. Pathology, 1997. Asst. prof. pathology U. Colo. Health Scis. Ctr., Denver and Aurora, 1999—2003, assoc. prof. pathology, 2003—, assoc. dir. surg. pathology. Author: Digital Atlas of Breast Pathology and Digital Atlas of Gynecologic Pathology. Recipient Tchg. awards, Med. Students of the U. Colo. Sch. Medicine, 1994—2005, William S. Hammond, MD. Excellence in Tchg. award, Dept. Pathology, U. Colo. Health Scis. Ctr. Fellow: Coll. Am. Pathologists (state commr. for co and wy 2006); mem.: Colo. Soc. Clin. Pathologists (pres. 2005—06, Leadership, Dedication and Svc. awards 1999—2006). Achievements include research in biomarkers of breast cancer and gynecological cancers.

SINGH, NARENDRA, cardiologist, researcher, medical educator; b. Saraiya, Uttar Pradesh, India, June 10, 1963; Can., US; s. Rudra Prasad and Manorma Singh; m. Mitra Kumari Kandhal, June 26, 1993; children: Shailin Raj, Ishaan Vivek. BS in Biochemistry, Dalhousie U., Halifax, Can., 1983, MD, 1987. Diplomate Am. Bd. Internal Medicine, Am. Bd. Cardiovascular Disease, Am. Bd. Nuclear Cardiology, NASPE Testamur. Rotating intern St. Michael's Hosp., U. Toronto, 1987—88, resident in internal medicine, 1988—91, rsch. fellow in cardiology, 1993—94; cardiologist Centenary Cardiology Assocs., Toronto, Ont., Canada, 1994—2002; dir. Scarborough Cardiology Rsch., Toronto, 1996—2002; cardiologist Northside Cardiology P.C., Atlanta, 2002—, dir. rsch., 2003—; cardiology sect. chair Northside Hosp., Atlanta, 2003—06. Lectr. U. Toronto, 1994—2002; med. dir. Pacemaker/ICD Programme, 1995—2002, Cardiac Cath Lab., 1999—2001; co-founder Greater Toronto Area Cmty. Cardiologists, 1995—2001; clin. asst. prof. Emory U. Sch. Medicine, Atlanta, 2002—; mem. regional lipid adv. bd. Merck, Canada; mem. nat. adv. bd. Pfizer, Canada; spkr. in field. Contbr. articles to profl. jours. Bd. dirs. Hosp. Found., Toronto, 1998—2002. Recipient award plaque in recognition for contbns., Greater Torotno Area Cmty. Cardiologists; scholar, Dalhousie U., 1981, 1983, 1985; Rsch. fellow, U. Toronto, 1993. Fellow: Am. Coll. Cardiology, Royal Coll. Physicians and Surgeons Can. (cert. in cardiology/internal medicine), Am. Heart Assn. (bd. dirs. Atlanta 2005—); mem.: Internat. Soc. Hypertension Blacks, Am. Soc. Nuc. Cardiology, Hearth Rhythm Soc., Med. Assn. Atlanta, Med. Assn. Ga., Can. Med. Assn., Med. Staff Soc. (bd. govs., mem. med. adv. com. 1995—97, pres. Centenary site, mem. strategic planning com. 1996), Can. Cardiovasc. Soc. (nat. sec. 2000—02, sec., mem. exec. com., chairperson membership com. 2000—02, coun. mem. 1999—2002). Avocations: travel, golf, theater. Office: Northside Cardiology PC 5670 Peachtree-Dunwoody Rd Ste 880 Atlanta GA 30342 Office Phone: 404-256-2575. Office Fax: 404-256-2535. Business E-Mail: nsingh@nscatl.com.

SINGH, OM V., biotechnologist, researcher; b. Chandosi, Uttar Pradesh, India, Jan. 8, 1972; s. Uday V Singh and Indu B Devi; m. Rashmi Singh; 1 child, Manav V. BS in Biol. Science, Meerut U., 1992; MS in Zoology, CCS U., 1994; PhD, Indian Inst. Tech., India, 2000. Rsch. scholar Indian Inst. Tech., Roorkee, Uttaranchal, India, 1995—2000; rsch. assoc. Inst. Microbial Tech., Chandigarh, Punjab, India, 2000—02; postdoctoral rsch. assoc. U. Mo., Rolla, 2002—03; postdoctoral rsch. fellow U. Louisville, 2003, Johns Hopkins Sch. Medicine, Balt., 2003—. Mem. editl. bd.: World Jour. Microbiol. Biotech., Optics: A Jour. of Integrative Biology, Jour. Jnd. Microbiol. Biotech., Proteome Sci. Post-doctoral Rsch. Assoc. fellowship, Monsanto Inc. St. Louis, 2002, Post-doctoral Rsch. fellowship, Nat. Inst. Aging, NIH, 2003, Eudowood Divsn. Pediatric Respiratory Scis., Johns Hopkins U. Sch. Medicine, 2003. Mem.: Soc. Applied Microbiology (assoc.), Water Environment Fedn. (assoc.), Internat. Soc. for Computational Biology (assoc.), Internat. Proteome Soc. (assoc.), Am. Soc. Cell Biology (assoc.), Assn. Environ. Engring. and Sci. Profs. (assoc.), Am. Soc. Microbiology (assoc.), Indian Sci. Congress Assn. (life), Assn. Microbiologist of India (life). Achievements include discovery of novel fermentation techniques and microorganism; novel therapeutic targets for cystic fibrosis using 2D gel electrophoresis and mass spectrometry; pharmacoproteomics for cystic fibrosis. Avocations: billiards, chess, horseback riding, reading. Office: Johns Hopkins Sch Medicine 600 N Wolfe St Pk 316 Baltimore MD 21287 Home Phone: 410-467-3887; Office Phone: 410-614-1804. Personal E-mail: ovs11@yahoo.com.

SINGH, RAJENDRA, mechanical engineering educator, director; b. Dhampur, India, Feb. 13, 1950; came to U.S., 1973; s. Raghubir and Ishwar (Kali) S.; m. Veena Ghungesh, June 24, 1979; children: Rohit, Arun. BS with honors, Birla Inst., 1971; MS, Indian Inst. Tech., 1973; PhD, Purdue U., 1975. Grad. instr. Purdue U., West Layfayette, Ind., 1973-75; sr. engr. Carrier Corp., Syracuse, NY, 1975-79; asst. prof. Ohio State U., Columbus, 1979-83, assoc. prof., 1983-87, prof., 1987—, Donald D. Glower chair in engring., 2001—, dir. Smart Vehicle Concepts Ctr., 2006—, sr. fellow Ctr. Automotive Rsch., 2006—. Adj. lectr. Syracuse (N.Y.) U., 1977-79; bd. dirs. Inst. of Noise Control Engring., 1994-96, 99—, v.p. tech. activities, 2000-02, pres., 2003; gen. chmn. Nat. Noise Conf., Columbus, 1985; leader U.S. delegation to India-U.S.A. Symposium on Vibration and Noise Engring., 1996; vis. prof. U. Calif., Berkeley, 1987-88; pres. Inter-Noise 2002 Congress; chmn. India-USA Symposium on Vibration and Noise, 2001; cons., lectr. in field. Author: Emerging Trends in Vibration and Noise Engineering, 1996; contbr. more than 350 articles to profl. jours.; guest editor jours. Recipient Gold medal U. Roorkee, 1973, R. H. Kohr Rsch. award Purdue U., 1975, Excellence in Tchg. award Inst. Noise Control Engring., 1989, Rsch. award Ohio State U., 1983, 87, 91, 96, 01, 06, Educator of Yr. award GM Tech. Edn. Program, 1998. Fellow ASME, Acoustical Soc. Am., Soc. Auto Engring.; mem. Inst. Noise Control Engring.(cert.), Am. Soc. Engring. Edn. (George Westinghouse award 1993). Achievements include patent for rolling door; development of new analytical and experimental techniques in machine dynamics, acoustics, vibration and fluid control. Home: 4772 Belfield Ct Dublin OH 43017-2592 Office: Ohio State U Mech Engring Dept 201 W 19th Ave Columbus OH 43210 Home Phone: 614-761-8855; Office Phone: 614-292-9044.

SINGH, RESHMI L., medical educator; b. Mumbai, Maharashtra, India, Aug. 22, 1977; d. Lalchand and Meera Singh; m. Rajivkumar Dhingra, July 18, 2001. BPharm, Bombay U., Mumbai, India, 1999; MS, U. Toledo, Ohio, 2001; PhD, U. Minn., Mpls., 0205. Tchg. asst. U. Toledo, 1999—2001, U. Minn., 2001—05, rsch. asst., 2002—04, Pfizer Inc., Mpls., 2004; asst. prof. MA Coll. Pharmacy & Health Scis., 2005—. Contbr. chapter to book, articles to profl. jours. Vol. Internat. Pharm. Congress Assn., Mumbai, 1998; co- chair admissions com. Mass. Coll. Pharmacy, Boston, 2006—; primary organizer Biennial Pharmacy Adminstrn. Midwest Conf., Toledo, 2000—01. Recipient Leadership in Pharmacy award, Albert Wertheimer, Faculty Development Seed Grant award. Mem.: Internat. Soc. Pharmacoeconomics and Outcomes Rsch., Acad. Pharm. Rsch. and Sci., Am. Soc. Health Sys. Pharmacists, Am. Assn. Colls. Pharmacy, Am. Pharmacists' Assn. (reviewer 2001—06). Hindu. Avocations: travel, reading. Office: Mass Coll Pharmacy & Health Sci 179 Longwood Ave Boston MA 02115 Personal E-mail: reshmi_l_singh@hotmail.com. Business E-Mail: reshmi.singh@mcphs.edu.

SINGH, SANGITA, information technology and marketing executive; With HCL Technologies, Wipro Technologies, Mountain View, Calif., 1992—, jr. exec., mktg. mgr. e-bus. portfolio, 1999, chief mktg. officer, 2001—, v.p. strategic mktg. Office: Wipro Technologies 2nd Fl 1300 Crittenden Lane Mountain View CA 94043 Office Phone: 650-316-3555. Office Fax: 650-316-3468.

SINGH, VIJAY, professional golfer; b. Lautoka, Fiji, Feb. 22, 1963; m. Andrea Seth Singh; 1 child, Qass Seth. Profl. golfer, 1993—. Player The President's Cup, 1994, 96, 98, 2000, 03, 05, World Cup, 2002. Named Hon. Chairperson, National Golf Day, 1999; named to World Golf Hall of Fame, PGA Tour, 2006; recipient Samman award, Pravasi Bharatiya Divas, 2005. Achievements include 31 Career PGA Tour victories; winner PGA Championship, 1998, 2004, Masters Tournament, 2002; 22 international victories; set single season record for earnings, 2004; Ranked No. 1 in the world, 2004; holds record for most wins on PGA Tour after turning 40 (18). Avocations: snooker, cricket, rugby, soccer. Office: PGA Tour 112 TPC Blvd Ponte Vedra FL 32802 *

SINGHAL, AVINASH CHANDRA, engineering administrator, educator; b. Aligarh, India, Nov. 4, 1939; s. Shiam Sunder and Pushpa Lata (Jindal) S.; m. Uma Rani Sharma, Sept. 5, 1967; children: Ritu Chanchal, Anita, Neil Raj. BSc, Agra U., India, 1957; BSc in Engring., St. Andrews U., Dundee, Scotland, 1959, degree (hon.) in engring., 1960; MS, MIT, 1961, CE, 1962, ScD, 1964; certificate in bus. mgmt., UCLA, 1971; postgrad., 2005. Registered profl. engr., N.Y., Que., Ariz. Rsch. engr. Kaman Aircraft, Burlington, Mass., 1964-65; prof. Laval U., Quebec, Can., 1965-69; asst. program mgr. TRW, Redondo Beach, Calif., 1969-71; mgr. GE, Phila., 1971-72; mgr. tech. svcs. Engrs. India Ltd., New Delhi, 1972-74; project engr. Weidlinger Assocs., NYC, 1974-77; prof. Ariz. State U., Tempe, 1977—; dir. Cen. Bldg. Rsch. Inst., 1992-93. Dir. Earthquake Rsch. Lab., Ariz. State U., Tempe, 1978—89, grad. coord. structural engring., 1991—92, senator acad. senate, 1995—98, chmn. governance grievance, 1995—96, faculty ombudsman, 1996—97, coord. Computer Aided Design and Modeling, 1997—98, com. acad. freedom and tenure, 1998—99, com. promotion and tenure; cons. McDonnel Aircraft Corp., St. Louis, 1977—78, Sperry Corp., 1979—80, McDonnell Douglas Helicopter Co., 1990—91, Ariz. Nuc. Power Plant, 1991—92; U.S. del. U.S./China Workshop on Arch Dams, Beijing, 1987; Can. del. Shell Structures, USSR, Ukraine, 1964; session chmn. Internat. Conf. on Soil Dynamics and Earthquake Engring., Karlsruhe, Germany, 1991; rsch. prof. Nat. Ctrl. U. Taiwan, 1990; vis. prof. U. Melbourne, Australia, 1983—84, U. Auckland, New Zealand, 1983—84; nodal dir. wood substitute rsch. program, India, 1992—93; instr. Indian Inst. Tech., Madras, 1997—98, Indian Inst. Sci., Bangalore, 1997—98. Mem. editl. bd. Soil Dynamics and Earthquake Engring., 1991—, Advances in Earthquake Engring., 1995—; reviewer Jour. Psychol. Reports, Perceptual and Motor Skills; contbr. Nuclear Waste Storage, 1986, (proc. publ.) Earthquake Behavior of Buried Pipelines, 1989, Wood Substitute: A National Priority, 1992, System Flexibility and Reflected Pressures, 1993, Simulation of Blast Pressures on Flexible Panels, 1994, Dynamic Analysis of Dams with Nonlinear Slip Joints, 1998, Performance of Retrofit Arch Dams, 1998, Ariz. Emergency Ctr. Retrofit, 1998, others; editor: Seismic Performance of Pipelines & Storage Tanks, 1985, Recent Advances in Lifeline Earthquake Engineering, 1987, Seismic Ground Motions Response, Repair and Instrumentation of Pipes and Bridges, 1992; contbr. articles to Jour. Performance of Constructed Facilities, ASCE, Jour. Computers and Structures, Jour. ASME, Jour. Aerospace Engring. ASCE; reviewer, bd. editors Jour. Earthquake Engring. and Structural Dynamics, Structural Engring. Papers Jour. ASCE. Bd. dirs., pres. Las Estadas Homeowner's Assn., Tempe, 1996-97; chmn. bd. dirs. India Assn. Greater Phoenix, 1985-86; pres. India Assn. Greater Boston, 1964-65; v.p., treas. Dobson Ranch Homeowners Assn., Mesa, Ariz., 1988-91; founding mem. Asian Am. Assn. Ariz., Phoenix, 1987-89; founding mem., pres. Asian Am. Faculty Assn., Ariz. State U., Tempe, 1986-88; cons. UN Devel. Program New Delhi, 1991-92. McLintock fellow MIT, 1960, Carnegie fellow MIT, 1960-63, fellow Royal Astron. Soc., London, 1961-64, rsch. fellow Kobe U., Japan, 1990; Denninson scholar Instn. Civil Engrs., London, 1959; Henry Adams Rsch. medal Structural Engrs., London, 1972; grantee Can. Def. Rsch. Bd., 1966-69, NSF, 1978-82, Engring. Found., 1978-79, U.S. Army Corps Engrs., 1984-86, U.S. Dept. Interior, 1986-88, Office Naval Rsch., 1994. Ariz. Dept. Emergency Mgmt., 1997-98; recipient 1st prize bridge bldg. Instn. Strucural Engrs., Merit award Inst. Engrs., India. Fellow ASCE, Ctrl. Bldg. Rsch. Inst. (chmn. mgmt. coun., chmn. APEX com.), Sigma Xi, Tau Beta Pi, Chi Epsilon. Achievements include research in computer modeling, blast effects on structures, in lifeline engineering, earthquake strengthening of deteriorated dams, steel and concrete buildings, bridges, materials, and non-linear finite element dynamics. Home: 2258 W Monterey Ave Mesa AZ 85202-7330 Office: Ariz State U Dept Civil Engring 2258 W Monterey Cir Mesa AZ 85202-7330 Business E-Mail: singhal@asu.edu. *Service to mankind and love for the family and friends is the key to success and happiness.*

SINGHAL, SUBHASH C., engineer; BE, Indian Inst. Sci., 1965; BS, Agra U., 1963; PhD in Materials Sci. and Engring., U. Pa., 1969; MBA, U. Pitts., 1977. Mgr. fuel cell technology Siemens Westinghouse Power Corp.; Battelle fellow, dir. fuel cells rsch. Pacific N.W. Nat. Lab., US Dept. Energy, Richland, Wash., 2000—. Contbr. articles to profl. jours. Fellow: AAAS, ASM Internat., Electrochem. Soc., Am. Ceramic Soc.; mem.: NAE, Mineral, Metals and Materials Soc. Office: Pacific NW Nat Lab PO Box 999 Richland WA 99352 Home Phone: 509-628-2365; Office Phone: 509-375-6738. E-mail: singhal@pnl.gov.

SINGHVI, SURENDRA SINGH, financial consultant; b. Jodhpur, Rajasthan, India, Jan. 16, 1942; came to U.S., 1962, naturalized 1986; s. Rang Raj and Ugam Kanwar (Surana) S.; m. Sushila Bhandari, July 7, 1965; children: Seema, Sandeep. B in Commerce, Rajasthan U., 1961; MBA, Atlanta U., 1963; PhD, Columbia U., NYC, 1967. CPA; cert. mgmt. acct. Asst. prof. fin. Miami U., Oxford, Ohio, 1967-69, assoc. prof. fin., 1969-70; adj. prof. fin., 1970-95; fin. mgr. ARMCO Inc., Middletown, Ohio, 1970-79, asst. treas., 1979-83, gen. fin. mgr., 1983-86; v.p. and treas. Edison Bros. Stores, Inc., St. Louis, 1986-90; pres. Singhvi & Assocs., Inc., Dayton, Ohio, 1990—. Bd. dirs. Columbia Indsl. Sales Corp., Hauer Music Co., Oasis Property Inc., Om Hospitality, Inc.; part owner Hilton Garcia Inn, Hampton Inn, Cin. Author: Planning for Capital Investment, 1980; co-editor: Frontiers of Financial Management, 4th edit., 1984, Global Finance 2000-A Handbook of Strategy and Organization (The Conference Board), 1996; contbr. over 90 articles to profl. jours. Bd. trustees South Ctrl. Ohio Minority Bus. Coun., 2000—. Recipient Singhu prize in recognition of profs. for excellence in classroom, Columbia U., 1970, Chancellor's Gold medal Rajasthan U., Ahimsa (Non-Violence) award Fedn. Jaina Assns. in N.Am., 1999. Mem. Inst. Mgmt. Accts. (Bayer Silver medal 1978), Fin. Execs. Inst., Fin. Mgmt. Assn., Dayton Minority Supplier Devel. Coun. (dir. 1997—, chmn. 2000), Rotary (dir. internat. program Middletown chpt. 1973-86, Dayton chpt. 1995—, treas., dir. 2001—02), India Club (pres. Dayton chpt. 1980). Avocations: swimming, kanasta, travel, writing. Home and Office: Singhvi and Assocs Inc 439 Ridge Line Ct Dayton OH 45458-9546 Office Phone: 937-885-7414. Personal E-mail: s.singhvi@yahoo.com.

SINGLETARY, ALVIN D., lawyer; b. Sept. 27, 1942; s. Alvin E. and Alice (Pastoret) Singletary; m. Judy Louise Singletary, Dec. 3, 1983; children: Kimberly Dawn, Shane David, Kelly Diane. BA, La. State U., 1964; JD, Loyola U., New Orleans, 1969. Bar: La. 1969, U.S. Dist. Ct. (ea. dist.) La. 1972, U.S. Ct. Appeals (5th cir.) 1972, U.S. Ct. Appeals (11 cir.) 1981, U.S. Ct. Internat. Trade 1981, U.S. Ct. Customs and Patent Appeals 1982, U.S. Supreme Ct. 1978. Instr. Delgado Coll., New Orleans, 1976—77; sole practice Slidell, La., 1970—. Spl. asst. dist. atty 22d Judicial Dist. Ct., Parish of St. Tammany, La.; sec., treas. St. Tammany Pub. Trust Fin. Authority, 1978—2002. Chmn. sustaining membership enrollment Cypress dist. Boy Scouts Am., 1989—; treas. Slidell Centennial commn.; councilman-at-large City of Slidell, 1978—2002, interim mayor, 1985; mem. Dem. State Ctrl. Com., 1978—82; mem. Rep. State Ctrl. Com. Dist. 76, La., 1996—2000; del. La.Constl. Conv., 1972—73; chmn. Together We Build Program First Baptist Ch. of Slidell, La.; bd. dir. St. Tammany Coun. on Aging. Mem.: Lions, Delta Theta Phi. Baptist. Office: PO Box 1158 Slidell LA 70459-1158

SINGLETARY, DEJUAN THERESA, child and adolescent psychiatrist; b. Berkeley, Calif., Apr. 7, 1965; d. Wilbert Paul and Frances Mahala Thomas; m. Craig Singletary, Jan. 31, 2003. AA in Gen. Edn., Chalot Coll., Hayward, Calif., 1986; BS in Physiology, U. Calif., Davis, 1989; MD, U. So. Calif., LA, 1995. Diplomate Am. Bd. Psychiatry and Neurology. Intern LAC/USC Med. Ctr., LA, 1995—96; resident U. Calif.-Davis Dept. Psychiatry, 1996—98; fellow U. Ariz. Health Sci. Ctr., Tucson, 1998—2000; child and adolescent psychiatrist Carmel Psychiat. Assocs., Charlotte, NC, 2001—03, N.E. Psychiat. and Psychol. Inst., Concord/Harrisburg, NC, 2003—05, Elon Homes for Children, 2005, The Keys of the Carolinas, Charlotte, 2005, DeJuan T. Singletary LLC/St. Charles Med. Ctr., Bend, Oreg., 2005—. Cons. Best Care Treatment Svcs., Madras, Oreg., 2006—, Luth. Family Svcs., 2006—. Mem.: AMA (polit. action com. 2000—), Am. Acad. Child and Adolescent Psychiatrists, Am. Psychiat. Assn. (Psychiatry Resident of the Yr. 1999), Golden Key (life). Avocations: gourmet cooking, antiques, travel. Office: 2100 NE Wyatt Ct Ste 202 Bend OR 97701

SINGLETON, DONALD EDWARD, journalist; b. Morristown, NJ, Nov. 8, 1936; s. Edward Leslie and Charlotte (Angerbauer) S.; m. Maureen Ann McNiff, Aug. 8, 1959 (div. 1977); children: Nancy Ann, Mark Aram, Jill Susan. Student, Fairleigh Dickinson U., 1955-58. Reporter Dover (N.J.) Advance, 1959-61, Morristown Daily Record, 1961-63, Newark Eve. News, 1963-64; feature reporter-writer N.Y. Daily News, 1964—. Organizer Com. to Save Church Sq. Park, Hoboken, N.J.; vice chmn. Hoboken Environment Com.; mem. due process com. ACLU., Mem. bd. edn., City of Hoboken, 1974-77. Recipient Pub. Service award N.Y. Council Civic Affairs, 1967; President's Distinguished Service award N.Y.C. Council, 1969; Newspaper award merit Women's Press Club N.Y.C., 1970, 79; citation VFW, 1970; Heywood Broun Meml. award Am. Newspaper Guild, 1970; Silver medal for pub. service journalism N.Y. chpt. Pub. Relations Soc. Am., 1970; certificate merit Am. Bar Assn., 1971; Page One award Newspaper Guild N.Y., 1970; Feature award Newspaper Reporters Assn. N.Y., 1972; Consistent Excellence award Uniformed Firefighters Assn., 1991. Mem. Am. Newspaper Guild. Clubs: Press (N.Y.C.). Home: 366 Ogden Ave Jersey City NJ 07307-1115 Office: 220 E 42nd St New York NY 10017-5806 E-mail: donaldnj@sprynet.com. *In reporting, I try very hard to avoid gathering facts in such a way as to fulfill a preconception. I also attempt to force myself to review constantly my opinions about my subjects, and to keep my mind as open as possible. In writing, I try to ask myself the following questions regularly: "Is this what I really believe? Or am I simply writing this way because I believe that this is what some other person or group would like me to write?" Unless I can answer the first question in the affirmative, and the second in the negative, I am not satisfied with a particular story.*

SINGLETON, HARRY MICHAEL, lawyer; b. Meadville, Pa., Apr. 10, 1949; s. Getdins T. and Rose Ann Singleton; children: Harry M. Jr., Leah Rose. BA, Johns Hopkins U., 1971; JD, Yale U., 1974. Bar: D.C. 1975, Pa. 1976, Calif. 1999, Md. 1999, U.S. Dist. Ct. D.C. 1975, U.S. Dist. Ct. Md. 2001, U.S. Ct. Appeals (D.C. cir.) 1975, U.S. Ct. Mil. Appeals 1975; lic. realtor Va., 2004, D.C., 2004. Assoc. Houston & Gardner, Washington, 1974-75, Covington & Burling, Washington, 1976-77; atty. FTC, Washington, 1975-76; dep. minority counsel Com. on D.C./U.S. Ho. of Reps., Washington, 1977-79, minority chief counsel, staff dir., 1979-81; dep. asst. sec. U.S. Dept. Commerce, Washington, 1981-82; asst. sec. U.S. Dept. Edn., Washington, 1982-86; pres. Harry M. Singleton & Assocs., Washington, 1986-91; pvt. practice law Washington, 1991—; pres. Singleton Entertainment, LLC, Washington, 1999-2000; pres., gen. counsel Single Source Tech. Solutions, LLC, Washington, 2001—03; realtor D.C., Va., 2004—, Va. Assn. Realtors, 2004—, Nat. Assn. Realtors, 2004—. Legis. cons. Am. Enterprise Inst., Washington, 1975. Pres. bd. trustees Barney Neighborhood House, Washington, 1978-80; corp. bd. dirs. Children's Hosp. Nat. Med. Ctr., Washington, 1984-88; mem. crime com. Boys and Girls Clubs of Greater Washington, 1994-97; mem. D.C. Rep. State Com., 1991—2004, Rep. Nat. Com., 1992-2000, R.N.C. exec. coun., 1993-95, resolutions com., 1997-2000; mem. Rep. Nat. Hispanic Assembly Washington, 1991-92. Mem. Rep. Nat. Lawyers Assn. (bd. dirs. D.C. chpt. 1990-91), Coun. of 100 Black Reps. (bd. dirs. 1991-92), D.C. Black Rep. Coun. (chmn. 1992-93), Rep. Nat. African-Am. Coun. (nat. chmn. 1993-2001), D.C. Rep. Nat. African-Am. Coun. (chmn. 1993-2001). Republican. Presbyterian. Office: 1250 Connecticut Ave NW Ste 200 Washington DC 20036

SINGLETON, JOAN VIETOR, publishing executive, writer, film producer; b. LA, Nov. 8, 1951; d. Carl William and Elizabeth Anne (Caulfield) Vietor; m. W. Alexander Sheafe, Apr. 23, 1977 (div. 1981); m. Ralph Stuart Singleton, Dec. 21, 1984. Premiere degre, Universite de Paris, 1971; BA, Hollins Coll., 1972. Asst. to pres. Calif. Fed. Savs., Los Angeles, 1972-73, dir. promotion, publicity, 1973-74; publicist Dave Mirisch Enterprises, Beverly Hills, Calif., 1974-75; owner, pres. Joan Vietor Enterprises, Los Angeles, 1975-79; bus. affairs staff Warner Bros., Inc., Burbank, Calif., 1979-80; pres. Lone Eagle Pub. Co., Los Angeles, 1981—. Assoc. prodr. Stephen King's Graveyard Shift, 1990; prodr., writer Because of Winn-Dixie, 2005. Bd. dirs. The Curtis Sch., 1993—, Crestwood Hills Sch., 1993-95. Mem. Pubs. Mktg. Assn. (bd. dirs. 1984-87). Democrat. Presbyterian. Avocations: skiing, needlepoint, tennis, scuba diving, reading. Office: Lone Eagle Pub Co 2337 Roscomare Rd Los Angeles CA 90077-1851

SINGLETON, JOHN, director, screenwriter; b. LA, Jan. 6, 1968; s. Danny Singleton and Sheila Ward.; m. Akosua Busia, Oct. 12, 1995 (div. June 15, 1997); children: Hadar, Cleopatra. BA, U. So. Calif., 1990. Writer, dir.: (films) Boyz N the Hood, 1991 (Acad. award nominee Best Dir. and Best Screenplay 1992), Shaft, 2000; writer, dir., prodr. Poetic Justice, 1993, Higher Learning, 1995, Shaft, 2000, Baby Boy, 2001; dir.: Rosewood, 1997, 2 Fast 2 Furious, 2003, Four Brothers, 2005 (NAACP Image award for Outstanding Direction in a Feature Film, 2006); exec. prodr.: Woo, 1998, Time Out, 2004; prodr.: Hustle & Flow, 2005, Black Snake Moan, 2006. Named to Hollywood Walk of Fame, 2003; recipient New Generation award, LA Film Critics Assn., 1991, Best New Director, NY Film Critics Cir., 1991, MTV Movie award for Best New Filmmaker, 1992. Achievements include being the first African-American and youngest person to be nominated for an Academy Award for Best Director. *

SINGLETON, JONETTA WILLIAMS, poet, retired special education educator; b. Bunkie, La., June 9, 1920; d. Josephus and Carrie Smith Williams; m. Jonetta W. Singleton; children: Carrie Elizabeth, Lafayette Jr. AA, Balt. Jr. Coll., 1971; BS in Biology and English, Coppins State Coll., 1973, Master's in Spl. Edn., 1974, Master's in Counseling, 1975. Tchr. Balt. Pub. Sch., Baltimore City, Md., 1974—94; ret., 1994. Poet: Poems from the Heart, 2004. Active ARC. Mem.: AAUW, ACLU. Democrat. Methodist.

SINGLETON, MARVIN AYERS, state legislator, otolaryngologist; b. Baytown, Tex., Oct. 7, 1939; s. Henry Marvin and Mary Ruth Singleton. BA, U. of the South, 1962; MD, U. Tenn., 1966. Diplomate Am. Bd. Otolaryngology. Intern City of Memphis Hosps., 1966-67; resident in surgery Highland Alameda City Hosp., Oakland, Calif., 1967-68; resident in otolaryngology U. Tenn. Hosp., Memphis, 1968-71; fellow in otolaryngic pathology Armed Forces Inst. Pathology, Washington, 1971; fellow in otologic surgery U. Colo. at Gallup (N.Mex.) Indian Med. Ctr., 1972; practice medicine specializing in otolaryngology/allergies Joplin, Mo., 1972—. Founder, operator Home and Farm Investments, Joplin, 1975—, staff mem. Freeman Hosp., St. John's Hosp., Joplin; cons. in otolaryngology Mo. Crippled Children's Service; pres. Ozark Mfg. Co., Inc., Joplin; mem. St. Joaquin Commn. on Aging, 2005—; dir. St. Mary's Interfaith Svcs., Stockton, 2007—; med. dir. Health Choice NW Mo. Mem. Internat. Arabian Racing Bd., 1983-88; mem. Mo. State Senate, 1990-2003; del. Rep. Nat. Conv., 1988, 92. Served with USNG, 1966-72. Fellow Am. Coll. Surgeons, Am. Acad. Otolaryngologic Allergy (past pres.), Am. Assn. Acad. Asthma, Allergy and Immunology; mem. AMA (Mo. del.), Mo. State Med. Assn., So. Med. Assn., Mo. State Allergy Assn., Ear Nose & Throat Soc. Mo. (past pres.), Calif. Med. Assn. (trustee 2005—), San Joaquin Med. Soc. (pres. 2006-07), Masons (32d degree), Sigam Alpha Epsilon, Phi Theta Kappa, Phi Chi. Republican. Episcopalian. Home: 1637 W Swain Rd Stockton CA 95207-4172 Office: 7373 W Lake Stockton CA 95210 Home Phone: 209-951-7273; Office Phone: 209-476-5623. Personal E-mail: senatorsingleton@hotmail.com.

SINGLETON, ROBERT CULTON, academic administrator, theology studies educator; b. Amarillo, Tex., Oct. 17, 1950; s. William Madison and Doris (Culton) S.; m. Stephanie Diane Lawrence, May 17, 1975; children: Kristin Michelle, Robert Culton Jr. BSEE, U. Tex., 1973; ThM in Bible Exposition, Dallas Theol. Sem., 1977; PhD in Higher Edn., U. Tex., 1993. Ordained to ministry Cmty. Bible Chapel, 1981. Campus staff Campus Crusade for Christ, Dallas, 1974-77; dean Nairobi (Kenya) Internat. Sch. Theology, 1978-83; grad. studies staff Campus Crusade for Christ, Austin, Tex., 1984-92; dean faculty East Asia Sch. Theology, Singapore, 1993-96; faculty The Orlando (Fla.) Inst., 1997—. Bd. dirs. Nairobi Internat. Sch. Theology, 1981-83. Contbr. articles to profl. jours. Mem. Kappa Delta Pi, Phi Kappa Phi. So. Bapt. Avocations: personal computers, tennis. Personal E-mail: drbobsing@netscape.net.

SINGLETON, TANYA, nursing educator; b. Tuscaloosa, Ala., July 23, 1958; d. Crimpton and Inez Virginia (Powe) Singleton; children: David, Edward, Brittany Summerhill; m. Michael B. Brown, Nov. 2003. BS in Nursing, U. Ala., 1982; MPH in Maternal-Child Health, George Washington U., 1997. Cert. high risk perinatal nurse, childbirth educator; cert. lactation cons. Commd. 2d lt. U.S. Army, 1986, advanced through grades to capt., 1988; staff nurse labor and delivery Druid City Hosp., Tuscaloosa, 1982—83, Huntsville (Ala.) Hosp., 1983—86; perinatal counselor Cen. North Ala. Health Svcs. Inc., Huntsville, 1984—86; staff nurse Tripler Army Med. Ctr., Honolulu, 1986—90; asst. head nurse newborn nursery, staff nurse labor and delivery, childbirth counselor and inpatient lactation cons. DeWitt Army Hosp., Ft. Belvoir, Va., 1990—92; maternal infant health educator Providence Hosp., Washington, 1992—95; instr. Montgomery Coll. Sch. of Nursing, 1994; founder Sacred Conceptions Childbirth and Parenting Svcs., 1996—; exec. dir. Women's Wellness Ctr., Fredericksburg, Va., 1999—2000; tobacco cessation coord. MediCorp Health Sys., Fredericksburg, 2001—03; perinatal bereavement coord. Prince William Health Sys., 2002—04, nurse recruiter, 2004—, 2004—. Mem. low risk neonatal test com. Nat. Certification Corp., 1994—95; rsch. assoc. NIH-DC Initiative to Decrease Infant Mortality in D.C. Pride in Parenting Study, 1995—; pres. Rappahannock Teen Abstinence Program; organizer Rappahannock Healthy Families Initiative Planning Bd., Ptnrs. in Prevention VA Planning Dist. XVI. Chair health com. Stafford County br. NAACP. Maj. USAR, 1995—2000, instr. 91C program 80th Tng. Divsn. USAR, res. comp. cmdr. 91W transition program USAR, 2001—04, Ft. Lee. Mem. ANA, Assn. Women's Health, Obstetric and Neonatal Nurses, Internat. Childbirth Edn. Assn., Sigma Theta Tau. Home: 6917 Smith Station Rd Spotsylvania VA 22553-1808 Home Phone: 540-898-0560; Office Phone: 703-369-8007. Personal E-mail: singmo40@aol.com. Business E-Mail: tsinglet@pwhs.org.

SINGLETON, WILLIAM DEAN, publishing executive; b. Graham, Tex., Aug. 1, 1951; s. William Hyde and Florence E. (Myrick) S.; m. Adrienne Casale, Dec. 31, 1983; children: William Dean II, Paige, Adam Nicholas. Student, Tyler Jr. Coll., Tex., El Centro Coll., Dallas; BS, U. Tex., Arlington. Vice chmn. and CEO MediaNews Group Inc., Denver, 1983—. Chmn. and pub. Denver Post; chmn. bd. Denver Newspaper Agency; pub. Salt Lake City Tribune; bd. dir. Associated Press, chmn. bd. dir., 2006—; former chmn. Newspaper Assn. Am. Mem. Salvation Army, Am. Heart Assn. of Ft. Bend County. Mem. Newspaper Assn. Am. (bd. govs.), So. Newspapers Assn., New Eng. Newspaper Assn., NJ Press Assn., Tex. Daily Newspaper Assn., Greater Houston Partnership Assn. Baptist. Office: Denver Post 101 W Colfax Ave Denver CO 80202 *

SINGLEY, JOHN EDWARD, JR., retired environmental scientist, consultant; b. Wildwood, NJ, July 31, 1924; s. John Edward Singley and Dorothy Mae (Pfrommer) S.; children: Gladys, Ann, Margaret, Patricia; m. June Walden Calohan, Apr. 28, 2001; stepchildren: Daniel, Christopher Calohan. BS, Ga. Inst. Tech, 1950; MS, Ga. Inst. Tech., 1952; PhD, U. Fla., 1966. Chemist Redstone Arsenal, Huntsville, Ala., 1950-51; dir. tech. svs. Tenn. Corp., College Park, Ga., 1951-64; lectr. chemistry Ga. State U., Atlanta, 1954-64, assoc. prof., 1964-67; prof. environ. engring. sci. U. Fla., Gainesville, 1967-90, prof. emeritus, 1990—; dir. TREEO Ctr., Gainesville, 1978-86; v.p. James M. Montgomery, Cons. Engrs., Inc., Gainesville, 1984-93, Montgomery Watson Cons. Engrs. Inc., Gainesville, 1993-96; sr. v.p. Environ. Scis. Engring. Inc., Gainesville, 1977-84; prin. Water and Air Rsch., Gainesville, 1970-77; v.p. Metcalf & Eddy, Gainesville, 1996-99; ret., 1999. Cons. Carollo Engrs., Sarasota, Fla., Jones, Edmunds Assocs., Gainesville. Patentee in field of polymers. Mem. Fulton County Rep. Exec. Com., 1962-64; mem. founding bd. Water for People, 1990-92. With USN, 1943-45. Recipient Donald R. Boyd award Met. Water Agys., 1992. Fellow Am. Inst. Chemists, Inst. Water and Environ. Mgmt.; mem. Am. Water Works Assn. (hon., life, bd. dirs. 1984-87, exec. com. 1986-87, 89-93, v.p. 1989-90, pres.-elect 1990-91, pres. 1991-92, Fuller award 1974, rsch. award 1983, Abel Wolman Excellence award 1995, Disting. Pub. Svc. award 1995, Water Industry Hall of Fame 2000), Fla. Water and Pollution Control Operators Assn. (Flanigan award 1979), Nat. Lime Assn. (Recognition award), Internat. Water Supply Assn., Nat. Assn. Corrosion Engrs., Internat. Ozone Assn. (bd. dirs. 1985-93). Clubs: Gainesville, Civitan (pres. 1972, lt. gov. Fla. dist. 1973-76). Presbyterian. Home: 1719 NW 23rd Ave # PHE Gainesville FL 32605-3027 Office: 1719 NW 23rd Ave PHE Gainesville FL 32605-3027 Office Phone: 352-372-2590. E-mail: h2odoceds@aol.com.

SINGSTOCK, DAVID JOHN, military officer; b. Oshkosh, Wis., July 19, 1940; s. Arnold William and Viola Rufine (Gerdener) S.; children: Susan, Brian, Elissa, Timothy. BS distinction, Maine Maritime Acad., 1964; student, U.S. Mcht. Marine Acad., 1959—62; BSBA distinction, George Washington U., 1973, MS, 1975. Lic. profl. marine engr. Commd. ensign USN, 1964, advanced through grades to comdr., 1984, various sea assignments including combat duty in Vietnam, 1964—69, engr. officer USS Harold J. Ellison Norfolk, Va., 1969—71, ADP fin. mgr. Cinclantflt, 1971—73, planning and quality assurance officer supr. shipbuilding Portsmouth, Va., 1973—76, prodn./repair officer supr. shipbuilding Bath, Maine, 1976—79, ship maintenance mgr. chief naval ops. Washington, 1980—83, dir. fleet modernization program space/naval warfare systems command, 1983—86, program mgr. USS Stark restoration naval sea systems command, 1986—88, tech. dir. dep. asst. sec. Navy for internat. programs, 1988—93; mgr. ships program ROH, Inc., Arlington, Va., 1993—95; mgr. ship self def. Vitro, Corp., Arlington, 1996—97; R&D mgr. theater ballistic missile def. Tracor Sys. Techs., Inc., Arlington, 1998—99; mgr. theater ballistic missile def. Marconi Sys. Techs., Inc., Arlington, 1999—2001; dep. dir. Applied Ordnance Tech. Internat., Arlington, 1999—2001; sr. tech. dir. Aegis Ballistic Missile Def. Gen. Dynamics Info. Tech., Arlington, 2001—. Sr. tech. advisor Royal Saudi Naval Forces Ops. Desert Shield and Desert Storm, 1990-91; sr. naval tech. mem. to Sec. of Def. chartered delegation of sr. U.S. ofcls., Saudi Arabia, 1991; retired U.S. Navy, 1993 Asst. scoutmaster Boy Scouts Am., Dumfries, Va., 1985-90; coach Youth Soccer, Maine, Va., 1976-84; active local property owners civic orgns., Va., Maine, 1970—; instr. ARC, Seattle, 1967-68 Decorated Navy Commendation medal, Navy Achievement medal, Vietnamese Cross of Gallantry, Meritorious Svc. medal, Joint Svc. Commendation medal, Bronze Star, Purple Heart; recipient Cert. Appreciation and Gratitude Comdr. Saudi Arabian Armed Forces, Missile Def. award Nat. Def. Indsl. Assn., 2005. Mem. Am. Soc. Naval Engrs. (dep. com. chmn., spkr. 1988), Nat. Contract Mgmt. Assn. (cert. contracts mgr.), Ret. Officers Assn., Nat. Eagle Scout Assn., Mason (32 degree), Scottish Rite, Shriner Presbyterian. Avocations: sailing, jogging, camping, golf, music. Home: 1125 Portner Rd Alexandria VA 22314-1314 Office: Gen Dynamics IT Divsn 2231 Crystal Dr Ste 600 Arlington VA 22202-3723 Office Phone: 703-892-7966. Business E-Mail: david.singstock.ctr@mda.mil.

SINHA, AKHOURI A., cell and development biologist, researcher; b. Churamanpur, Bihar, India, Dec. 17, 1933; arrived in U.S., 1961; s. Akhouri Chandra B. and Bittan Devi Sinha; m. Dorothy Kay Pamer, Sept. 29, 1979. BSc, Allahabad U., India, 1954; MSc, Patna U., India, 1956; PhD, U. Mo., 1965. Lectr. Ranchi (India) U., 1956—61; asst. prof. U. Wis., Eau Claire, 1965—67; sr. scientist U. Minn., Mpls., 1967—69; rsch. scientist VA Med. Ctr., Mpls., 1969—. Prof. U. Minn., 1981—. Contbr. articles to profl. jours. Hindu. Avocations: cross country skiing, photography, travel, reading. Office: Rsch Svcs One Veterans Dr Minneapolis MN 55417 Office Phone: 612-467-2846. Business E-Mail: sinha001@tc.umn.edu.

SINHA, NEETI, biophysicist, researcher; married; 1 child. PhD, U. Oxford, England, 1998. Postdoctoral rschr. NIH, Frederick, Md., 1998—2003; assoc. rsch. scientist Johns Hopkins U., Balt., 2003—. Asst. dir. Ctrl. Drug Rsch. Inst., Lucknow, India, 2004. Author: (book) Absolute: Multidimensional Biengness, 2006; mem. editl. bd.: Protein and Peptide Letters, Current Protein and Peptide Science, Open Biochemistry Journal, International Reviewers Panel Medical Science Monitor; contbr. articles to profl. jours. Office: Johns Hopkins U Mudd Hall 3400 N Charles St Baltimore MD 21218 Home Phone: 410-366-1877; Office Phone: 410-516-5379.

SINHA, PAWAN, research scientist, educator, entrepreneur; B Tech, Indian Inst. Tech., New Delhi, 1988, MS, 1992; PhD in Computer Sci., MIT, 1995. Co-founder Imagen, Inc.; rsch. fellow Max Planck Inst.; asst. prof., psychology U. Wis., Madison; assoc. prof., vision and computational neuroscience, dept. brain and cognitive sciences MIT, 1999—. Vis. scientist Mass. Gen. Hosp.; affiliated faculty mem. Athinoula A. Martinos Ctr. for Biomedical Imaging. Contbr. articles to profl. jours. Co-recipient Troland Rsch. award, NAS, 2007; recipient AT&T Rsch. award, NEC Rsch. award, John Merck Scholars Program award in Biology Develop. Disabilities in Children, Wade award for Creative Rsch. Contributions towards understanding of how the brain interprets and encodes visual information to perform complex tasks such as face recognition; launched Project Prakash, combines social, humanitarian, and scientific relevance. It focuses on the large population of blind children in India. This project will improve the lives of several children by helping them with treatment and rehabilitation, and answering some of the basic questions of neuroscience regarding brain plasticity and cognitive development; creator of the world's smallest book in the Guinness Book of World Records. Office: Dept Brain and Cognitve Sciences Bldg 46-4077 Sinha Lab Mass Inst Tech 77 Massachusetts Ave Cambridge MA 02139-4307 Office Phone: 617-253-1434. Office Fax: 617-253-2964. Business E-Mail: psinha@mit.edu. *

SINHA, RAKESH KUMAR, computer scientist, researcher; s. RamKrishna and Sanyukta Sinha. PhD in Computer Sci., U. Wash., Seattle, 1995. Asst. prof. Sch. Computer Sci., Miami, Fla., 1995—98; mem. tech. staff Bell Labs., Murray Hill, NJ, 1998—2000; prin. engr. Ciena Core Switching Divsn., Cupertino, Calif., 2000—01; tech. cons. AT&T Labs Rsch., Middletown, NJ, 2001—. Contbr. articles to profl. jours. Mem.: IEEE, Assn. Computing Machinery. Achievements include patents in field. Home Phone: 732-420-9045; Office Phone: 732-420-9045. Personal E-mail: rakesh_sinha100@yahoo.com. Business E-Mail: sinha@research.att.com.

SINHA, SUNIL K., aerospace engineer, consultant; b. Patna, Bihar, India, Aug. 19, 1949; arrived in US, 1973; s. Awadh Bihari and Sumitra Kumari Sinha; m. Suman Sinha, Apr. 23, 1978 (dec. July 2006); children: Neena P., Anjuli M. BS, Patna U., India, 1968; MS, So. Ill. U., 1974; PhD, U. Ill., Urbana-Champaign, 1977—77; MTech., Indian Inst. of Tech., Bombay, 1973. Sr. rsch. asst. Indian Inst. of Tech., Bombay, 1969—73; grad. tchg. asst. U. of Ill., Urbana-Champaign, 1974—77; stress and vibration analyst Foster Wheeler Energy Corp., Livingston, NJ, 1977—79; sr. tech. analyst Westinghouse Electric Corp., Boston, 1979—83; sr. engr. GE Appliances, Louisville, 1983—89; sr. staff engr. GE Aircraft Engines, Evendale, Ohio, 1989—2001; prin. engr. GE Aviation, Evendale, 2002—. Mem. LS-Dyna Aerospace Working Group, Livermore, 2000—. Contbr. articles to profl. jours. Mem. Elfun Soc., Cin., 1989—2006. Mem.: ASME. Non-Partisan. Achievements include research in Pioneering transient dynamics work in the area of rotordynamics such as blade-out and tip-rub, contained and uncontained failure of rotating components; Missile Impact on a Commercial Jet engine; Dynamic Stability of Airfoils; High-speed impact dynamics. Home: 11025 Woodlands Way Cincinnati OH 45241 Office: Imapct Dynamics 1 Neumann Way Cincinnati OH 45215 Business E-Mail: sunil.sinha@ae.ge.com.

SINHA, SUNIL KUMAR, physicist; b. Calcutta, India, Sept. 13, 1939; came to U.S., 1965; s. Sushil Kumar and Romola Sinha; m. Lonny Linde Olsen, Jan. 27, 1962; children: Arjun, Ranjan. BA in Natural Scis., Cambridge U., Britain, 1960, PhD in Physics, 1964. Vis. scientist Bhabha Atomic Rsch. Ctr., Trombay, India, 1965; asst. prof. physics dept. Iowa State U., Ames, 1966-69, assoc. prof., 1969-71, prof. physics, 1972-75; sr. physicist Argonne (Ill.) Nat. Lab., 1975-82; sr. rsch. assoc. Corp. Rsch., Exxon Rsch., Annandale, NJ, 1982-95; sr. scientist and assoc. dir., exptl. facilities div. Argonne (Ill.) Nat. Lab., 1995-2001; prof. physics U. Calif., San Diego, 2001—. Chmn. Div. Condensed Matter Physics Fellowship Com. of Am. Phys. Soc., 1990-91, Conf. X-Ray Physics, 1999; mem. adv. com. US Dept. Energy, 1997-02; co-chair Basic Energy Scis. Advisry Com. subcom. Dept. Energy facilities, 2003. Editor: Ordering in Two Dimensions, 1980, Spin Waves and Magnetic Excitations, 1990; contbr. articles to profl. jours. Recipient Dept. Energy Rsch. Achievement award, 1981, Ernest Orlando Lawrence Meml. award, 1996, Arthur H. Compton award Advanced Photon Source, 2000; Guggenheim fellow, 1982; MRS medal, 2004. Fellow AAAS, Am. Phys. Soc.; mem. Materials Rsch. Soc., Am. Crystallographic Assn. Achievements include research in antiferromagnetism in High Tc materials by neutron diffraction; theory of diffuse X-ray scattering from surfaces.

SINICK, MARSHALL S., lawyer; b. Hartford, Conn., 1942; BA, Boston U., 1964; JD with honors, Ind. U., 1968. Bar: Conn. 1968, DC 1972. Trial atty., Bur. Oper. Rights Civil Aeronautics Bd., 1968—71; ptnr. Squire, Sanders & Dempsey LLP, Washington, chmn., Transp. Practice Group. Editl. bd. Ind. U. Law Jour., 1967—68. Mem.: Conn. Bar, DC Bar, Order of Coif. Office: Squire Sanders & Dempsey LLP 1201 Pennsylvania Ave NW PO Box 407 Washington DC 20044-0407 Office Phone: 202-626-6651. Office Fax: 202-626-6780. Business E-Mail: msinick@ssd.com.

SINISCALCHI, MARCIANO, economist; b. Milan, July 18, 1967; s. Lucio and Tranquilla Marialuisa (Covini) Siniscalchi. PhD in Bus., Stanford Grad. Sch. Bus., Calif., 1998. Asst. prof. dept. econs. Princeton U., 1998—2002, Northwestern U., Evanston, Ill., 2002—. Assoc. editor: Theoretical Econs., Jour. Econ. Theory, 2005—; author: articles in profl. jours. Grantee, NSF, 1999-2002, 2005—. Office: Northwestern Univ Econs Dept 2001 Sheridan Rd Evanston IL 60208-2600 Office Phone: 847-491-5398.

SINISCALCO, GARY RICHARD, lawyer; b. NYC, Aug. 14, 1943; BA in Econs., Le Moyne Coll., 1965; JD, Georgetown U., 1969. Bar: Calif. Regional counsel, sr. trial atty. EEOC, San Francisco, 1969-78; ptnr. Orrick, Herrington & Sutcliffe, San Francisco, 1978—, past co-chair employment law dept. Mem. adv. bd. Nat. Employment Law Inst.; lectr. in field. Co-author: Manager's Guide to Lawful Terminations, 1991; author: (with others) Employment Discrimination Law, 1979, 3rd edit., 1996; contbr. articles to profl. jours. Mem. ABA (mem. com. on internat. labor rels. and equal employment opportunity, mgmt. co-chair equal employment opportunity com. 1996-98, co-chair internat. labor law com. 2006—), State Bar Calif., Bar Commonwealth Va., Am. Employment Law Coun. (founder). Office: Orrick Herrington 405 Howard St San Francisco CA 94105 Office Phone: 415-773-5833. E-mail: grsiniscalo@orrick.com.

SINISE, GARY, actor; b. Blue Island, IL, Mar. 17, 1955; s. Robert L. Sinise; m. Moira Harris, 1981; children: Sophie, McCanna, Ella. Ph.D (hon.), Amherst Coll., 2003. Co-founder, artistic dir. Steppenwolf Theatre, 1974-, Chgo. Appeared in (plays) The Indian Wants The Bronx, 1977, Getting Out, 1980 (Joseph Jefferson award), Of Mice And Men, 1980, Loose Ends, 1982, True West, 1983 (also dir., Obie award best dir. 1982-83), Balm in Gilead, 1984, Streamers, 1985, The Caretaker, 1986, Grapes of Wrath, 1990 (Tony award and Drama Desk), Buried Child, 1996 (Tony award nominee, Joseph Jefferson award, 1996), One Flew Over the Cuckoos Nest, 2001; film appearances include A Midnight Clear, 1991, Jack The Bear, 1991, Forrest Gump, 1994 (Acad. award nomination for Best Supporing Actor, 1994, Disabled Am. Veterans Nat. Commanders award, 1994), The Quick and the Dead, 1995, Apollo 13, 1995, Ransom 1996, Albino Alligator, 1996, Snake Eyes, 1998, That Championship Season, 1999, Being John Malkovich, 1999, Reindeer Games, 1999, Mission to Mars, 1999, Bruno, 1999, All the Rage, 1999, The Green Mile, 1999, A Gentleman's Game, 2001, Made-Up, 2002, Mission: Space, 2003, The Human Stain, 2003, The Big Bounce, 2003, This Old Cub, 2004, The Forgotten, 2004, (voice) Open Season, 2006; (TV films) True West, 1984, Family Secrets, 1984, The Final Days, 1989, The Grapes of Wrath, 1991, The Witness, 1992, My Name is Bill W., 1989, The Stand, 1994, Truman, 1995 (Cable Ace award 1996, Golden Globe, 1996, Screen Actors Guild Award, 1996), Wallace, 1997 (Emmy award, 1998, Screen Actors Guild award, 1998, Cable ACE Award), That Championship Season, 1999, Path to War, 2002, Fallen Angel, 2003; (TV series) CSI: NY, 2004-; (TV appearances) Knots Landing, 1980, Crime Story, 1986, 1987, Hunter, 1990, Frasier, 1995, CSI: Miami, 2004, 2005; actor, dir. prodr., (films) Of Mice and Men, 1991; actor, prodr. Impostor, 2002; dir., Miles from Home, 1988; dir. (plays) Frank's Wild Years, Action, The Miss Firecracker Contest, Waiting for the Parade, Tracers, Orphans, Landscape of the Body, 1984 Office: care Creative Artists Agy 9830 Wilshire Blvd Beverly Hills CA 90212-1804 also: Licker & Ozurovich 2029 Century Park E Ste 1060 Los Angeles CA 90067-2919 *

SINK, ADELAIDE ALEXANDER, state official; b. Mt. Airy, NC, June 5, 1948; d. Kester Andrew and Adelaide (Bunker) S.; m. William Howard McBride, Jr., July 10, 1986; children: William Albert (Bert), Cheryle Alexander (Lexie). BS, Wake Forest U., 1970. Tchr. Meth. Girls High Sch., Freetown, Sierra Leone, 1970-71, Am. Sch. of Liberia, Monrovia, 1971-72; v.p. NCNB, Charlotte, N.C., 1974-81, sr. v.p. NYC, 1981-84, Miami, Fla., 1984-89; exec. v.p. Nations Bank, Tampa, Fla., 1989-93; pres., Fla. Banking Divsn. Nations Bank (now Bank of America), Fla., 1993—2000; CFO, dept. financial services State of Fla., 2007. Appointed to Commn. on Govt. Accountability to the People; vice chair Fla. TaxWatch. Campaign chair United Way of Hillsborough County, Tampa, 1993; trustee Wake Forest U., 1992—; chair Hillsborough Edn. Found., 1994-96, bd. dir.; chair Take Stock in Children; svc. with Fla. Chpt. Nature Conservancy, Jr. Achievement of West Ctrl. Fla., Beth El Farm Workers Ministry, Redlands Christian Migrant Assn. Recipient Disting. Alumnus award Wake Forest U., 1993. Mem. Leadership Fla., Fla. Coun. 100, So. Growth Policies Bd., Fla. Taxwatch, Bus./Higher Edn. Partnership. Democrat. Presbyterian. Avocations: fishing, politics, reading. Home: PO Box 219 Thonotosassa FL 33592-0219 Office: Fla Dept Financial Services 200 E Gaines St Tallahassee FL 32399-0300 Office Phone: 850-413-3100.

SINK, KAYCEE M., geriatrician, medical educator; d. Paul Sink and Pauline Sorensen. MD, U. Calif., San Francisco, Calif., 1998, MA in Advanced Studies, 2005. Diplomate Am. Bd. Internal Medicine, 2001, added qualifications in geriatric medicine Am. Bd. Internal Medicine, 2002. Resident internal medicine U. Calif., San Francisco, 1998—2001, clin. fellow in geriat., 2001—02, postdoctoral fellow in clin. rsch., 2002—04; asst. prof. medicine Sch. Medicine Wake Forest U., Winston-Salem, NC, 2004—. Med. dir. Kulynych Memory Assessment Clinic, Winston-Salem, NC, 2005—. Recipient Kathryn Grupe Excellence in Alzheimer's Rsch. award, Alzheimer's Assn. No. Calif. and Nev., 2004; scholar, Claude Pepper Independence Ctr., Wake Forest U., 2005—. Mem.: AMA, Am. Geriat. Soc. (Presdl. Poster award 2004, Best Paper award 2003), Phi Beta Kappa. Avocations: tennis, scuba diving. Office: Wake Forest University One Medical Center Blvd Winston Salem NC 27157 Office Phone: 336-713-8560. Business E-Mail: kmsink@wfubmc.edu.

SINK, ROBERT C., lawyer; b. Racine, Wis., 1938; AB, Duke U., 1959, LLB, 1965. Bar: N.C. 1965. Ptnr. Robinson, Bradshaw & Hinson, P.A., Charlotte, N.C., 1965—. Assoc. editor Duke Law Jour., 1964-65. Trustee Pub. Libr. Charlotte and Mecklenburg County, 1985-90, chmn., 1989-90; bd. dirs. Mus. New South, 1991-97, chmn., 1996-97. Lt. USN, 1959-62, USNR. Mem. ABA (ho. dels. 2001—), N.C. State Bar (councilor 1988-96, pres. 1998-99), Mecklenburg County Bar (pres. 1986-87), Order of Coif, Phi Beta Kappa. Office: Robinson Bradshaw & Hinson PA 101 N Tryon St Ste 1900 Charlotte NC 28246-0103

SINKFORD, JEANNE CRAIG, dental association administrator, retired dentist, dean, educator; b. Washington, Jan. 30, 1933; d. Richard E. and Geneva (Jefferson) Craig; m. Stanley M. Sinkford, Dec. 8, 1951; children: Dianne Sylvia, Janet Lynn, Stanley M. III. BS, Howard U., 1953, MS, 1962, DDS, 1958, PhD, 1963; DSc (hon.), Georgetown U., 1978, U. Med. and Dentistry of N.J., 1992, Detroit Mercy U., 1996. Instr. prosthodontics Sch. Dentistry Howard U., Washington, 1958—60, faculty dentistry, 1964—, rsch. coord., co-chmn. dept. restorative dentistry, assoc. dean, 1968—75, dean, 1975—91, prof. Prosthodontics Grad. Sch., 1977—91, dean emeritus, prof., 1991—; spl. asst. Am. Assn. Dental Schs., 1991—93, dir. office women and minority affairs, 1993—97, assoc. exec. dir., 1998—. Instr. rsch. and crown and bridge Northwestern U. Sch. Dentistry, 1963—64; cons. prosthodontics and rsch. VA Hosp., Washington, 1965—;

resident Children's Hosp. Nat. Med. Ctr., 1974—75; cons. St. Elizabeth's Hosp.; mem. attending staff Freedman's Hosp., Washington, 1964—; adv. bd. DC Gen. Hosp., 1975—; mem. nat. adv. dental rsch. coun. Nat. Bd. Dental Examiners; mem. ad hoc adv. panel Tuskegee Syphilis Study for HEW; sponsor DC Pub. Health Apprentice Program; mem. adv. coun. to dir. NIH; adv. com. NIH/NIDR/NIA Aging Rsch. Coun.; mem. dental devices classification panel FDA; mem. select panel for promotion child health, 1979—80; mem. spl. med. adv. group VA; bd. overseers U. Pa. Dental Sch., Boston U. Dental Sch.; bd. advisors U. Pitts. Dental Sch.; mem. bd. visitors Temple U. Sch. Dentistry, Howard U Coll. Dentistry, Ind. U. Sch. Dentistry, W.Va. U. Health Ctr.; mem. anat. rev. bd. DC NRC Governing Bd.; cons. FDA; mem. Nat. Adv. Dental Rsch. Coun., 1993—96; active NRC Governing Bd. Mem. Mayor's Block Grant Adv. Com., 1982; mem. parents' coun. Sidwell Friends, 1983; adv. bd. United Negro Coll. Fund, Robert Wood Johnson Health Policy Fellowships; mem. women's health task force NIH; bd. dirs. Girl Scouts U.S.A., 1993—95; bd. visitors Temple U. Sch. Dentistry, W.Va. U. health Scis. Ctr., Howard U. Coll. Dentistry. Fellow Louise C. Ball fellow grad. tng., 1960—63. Fellow: Internat. Coll. Dentists (Merit award), Am. Coll. Dentists (mem. editl. bd. 1988—2006, sec.-treas. Wash. met. sect.); mem.: ADA (chmn. appeal bd. coun. on dental edn. 1975—82), Children's Dental Health Found. (mem. adv. bd.), Fedn. Dentistry Internat., Links Inc., Dean's Coun. (chair), Smithsonian Assocs., NY Acad. Scis., Am. Soc. Dentistry for Children, Inst. Medicine of NAS (coun.), Nat. Dental Assn., Fed. Prosthodontic Orgn., Am. Prosthodontic Soc., Am. Pedodontic Soc., Leadership in Acad. Medicine (adv. bd.), Health Professions Partnership Initiative (adv. bd.), Assn. Am. Women Dentists, Wash. Coun. Adminstrv. Women, So. Conf. Dental Deans (chmn.), Inst. Grad. Dentists (trustee), Am. Inst. Oral Biology, Dist. Dental Soc., Internat. Assn. Dental Rsch., Am. Soc. for Geriatric Dentistry (bd. dirs.), North Portal Civic League, Golden Key, Beta Kappa Chi, Psi Chi, Omicron Kappa Upsilon, Phi Beta Kappa, Sigma Xi (pres.). Achievements include first female dental dean at Howard U., and in the U.S.A.

SINMA, BINOD K., urologist, consultant; arrived in US, 1979; m. Renu Sinma, June 14, 1978; 1 child, Tara. MBBS, Prince Wales, Patra, 1976. Urology resident U. Minn., Mpls., 1981—85. Office: Urology Care 4 Program St Ste A-9 Edison NJ 08820

SINN, JERRY L., army officer; m. Cheryl Parant; children: Jacob, Andrew. Grad., U. Mo., Rolla, Command and Gen. Staff Coll. Math. instr. U.S. Mil. Acad., West Point; enlisted U.S. Army, 1968, commd. 2d lt., 1969, advanced through grades to comdr.; dir. for ops. and and support, asst. to Sec. of Army for Fin. Mgmt. and Compt., 1995-97; divsn. engr. U.S. Army C.E., Bklyn., 1997-98, comdg. gen. North Atlantic divsn., 1998-99; dep. asst. sec. U.S. Army Budget Office, Washington, 1999—2003; mil. dep. for budget ASA (FM&C), 2003—. Decorated Legion of Merit with 3 oakleaf clusters, Bronze Star medal with V device, Purple Heart with oakleaf cluster, others. Office: ASA/DAS 109 Army Pentagon Rm 3a662 Washington DC 20310-0109

SINN, RYAN, musician; b. Fremont, Calif., Apr. 23, 1979; Bassist The Distillers, 2003—05, Angels & Airwaves, 2005—. Musician: (albums) (with The Distillers) Coral Fang, 2003, (with Angels & Airwaves) We Don't Need to Whisper, 2006. Co-recipient Woodie of Yr. award, mtvU Woodie Awards, 2006. *

SINNARD, ELAINE JANICE, painter, sculptor; b. Fort Collins, Colo., Feb. 14, 1926; d. Elven Orestes and Catherine (Bennet) S. Student, Art Students League, 1948, NYU, 1953, Sculpture Ctr., NYC, 1954, Academie Grande Chaumiere, Paris, 1956. Painter, sculptor. Works exhibited Riverside Mus., NYC, 1955, City Ctr., NYC, 1954-56, Nat. Arts Club, NYC, 1959-90, Lord & Taylor, NYC, 1963-78, Bergdorf Goodman, NYC, 1980-90, Zantman Art Galleries, Carmel-by-the-Sea, Calif., 1970-73, Chevy Chase Gallery, Washington, 1981-88; one woman shows and group exhbns. include: Bergdorf Goodman Nena's Choice Gallery, Sinnard Art Studios; tchr. open workshop for artists, (murals) Trinity Assembly of GOD, Middletown, NY. Mem. Nat. Arts Club NYC. Home and Studio: PO Box 304 New Hampton NY 10958-0304 Office Phone: 845-374-8128. Personal E-mail: sinnard@warwick.net.

SINNER, STEVE, sculptor; b. Omaha, Nebr., 1942; BS in Industl. Edn., Iowa St. Univ., 1965. Presenter in field. Exhibitions include Minn. Mus. Am. Art, St. Paul, Minn., 2001, Univ. Calif. Davis, 2001, Defining Craft: Collecting for the new Millenium, Davenport Mus. Art, 2002, Put a Lid on It: Containing Human Experience, Am. Assn. Woodturners, 2003, Turned Wood-Small Treasures, del Mano Galleries, LA, 2003—07, Selected Works, 2006, Functional Art Exposition, NYC, 2003—07, Cheongiu Internat. Craft Bienalle, Republic of Korea, 2003 (Spl. citation, 03, Hon. mention, 05), Beneath the Bark: 25 Years of Woodturning, BYU, 2004, Against the Grain: Contemporary Turned Wood Urns, Dubuque Mus. Art, 2006, Our Turn Now: Artists Speak out in Wood, 2006, Pritchard Gallery, U. Idaho, 2006, Ohio Craft Mus., 06, Dubuque Mus. Art, 2006, exhibitions include numerous others. Office: c/o del Mano Gallery 11981 San Vicente Blvd Los Angeles CA 90049

SINNING, MARK ALAN, thoracic and vascular surgeon; b. Holton, Kans., Apr. 24, 1953; s. Henry Harold and Valere Madelene (Davey) S.; m. Kathy Diann Pugh, Sept. 25, 1982 (div.); m. Srinuan Williamson, Sept. 3, 2003; children: Sarah, Emily, Mark, Rachel, Walter, Madalyn, Robert Campbell. BA, U. Kans., 1975; MD, U. Kans., Kansas City, 1978. Diplomate Am. Bd. Surgery, Am. Bd. Thoracic Surgery. Gen. surgery resident St. Luke's Hosp., Kansas City, Mo., 1978-83, thoracic surgery resident, 1983-85; pvt. practice Coastal Surg. Specialists, PA, New Bern, NC, 1986—. Attending staff Danbury (Conn.) Hosp., 1985-86, Craven Regional Med. Ctr., New Bern, 1986—; asst. clin. prof. East Carolina U., Greenville, 1992—. Fellow ACS, Am. Coll. Chest Physicians; mem. Soc. Thoracic Surgeons, So. Assn. Thoracic Surgery, N.C. Med. Soc., Phi Beta Kappa, Alpha Omega Alpha. Avocations: golf, skiing, music. Office: 2203 Neuse Blvd New Bern NC 28560

SINNOTT, JOHN PATRICK, lawyer, educator; b. Bklyn., Aug. 17, 1931; s. John Patrick and Elizabeth Muriel (Zinkand) Sinnott; m. Rose Marie Yuppa, May 30, 1959; children: James Alexander, Jessica Michelle. BS, US Naval Acad., 1953; MS, USAF Inst. Tech., 1956; JD, No. Ky. U., Highland Heights, 1960. Bar: Ohio 1961, NY 1963, NJ 1970, Ga 2000, US Patent Office 1963, US Supreme Ct 1977. Assoc. Brumbaugh, Graves, Donohue & Raymond, NYC, 1961-63; patent atty. Bell Tel. Labs., Murray Hill, NJ, 1963-64, Schlumberger Ltd., NYC, 1964-71; asst. chief patent counsel Babcock & Wilcox, NYC, 1971-79; chief patent and trademark counsel Am. Std. Inc., NYC, 1979-92; of counsel Morgan & Finnegan, NYC, 1992-99, Langdale & Vallotton, Valdosta, Ga., 2000—. Adj lectr NJ Inst Technology, Newark, 1974—89; adj prof Seton Hall Univ Sch Law, Newark, 1989—98. Author: Counterfeit Goods Suppression, 1998, World Patent Law and Practice, 1999; co-author: To Paris! August, 1914 and Now-Belgian and Northern French Battlefields, 2006, Document Authentication, 2007; contbr. articles to profl. jours. Mem. local Selective Serv Bd., Plainfield, NJ, 1971; bd dirs New Providence Community Swimming Pool, NJ, 1970. Capt. USAF, 1953—61, col. AUS ret., 1977—91. Decorated Legion of Merit, others. Mem.: Ga. State Bar Assn., Squadron A Assn., Valdosta Country Club, Cosmos Club. Republican. Roman Catholic. Home: 2517 Rolling Rd Valdosta GA 31602-1244 Office: Langdale & Vallotton 1007 N Patterson St PO Box 1547 Valdosta GA 31603 Office Phone: 229-244-5400. Fax: 229-244-9646.

SINNOTT, WILLIAM F., lawyer; b. 1958; BA, Holy Cross Coll., Springfield, Mass.; JD, Suffolk Univ. Law Sch. Former dist. atty. Office US Atty., former asst. US atty.; corporation counsel Legal Dept., Boston, 2006—. Colonel US Army, reserve mem. USAR, 2005, Iraq. Office: Boston City Law Dept Rm 615 One City Hall Plz Boston MA 02201 Office Phone: 617-635-4034. Fax: 617-635-3199. E-mail: law@cityofboston.gov.

SINOFF, HARRY, religious studies educator, director; b. Denver, Apr. 16, 1951; s. Abraham Sinoff and Beatrice Cohen; m. Linda Joy Stacy, Apr. 2, 1989; children: Abraham, Eliana, Annabelle, Amalya. BA, Columbia U., NYC, 1976; JD, Boston U., 1979. Ordained Rabbi Pvt.: Rabbi Pinchas Hirschprung, 1987; cert. Mandel Tchr. Mandel Inst., 2004. Atty. Solo Practice, Boston, 1979—87; tchr. Ida Crown Jewish Acad., Chgo., 1987—89; orthodox rabbinic advisor Harvard Hillel, Cambridge, 1989—96; tchr. Maimonides Sch., Brookline, Mass., 1989—95, Hebrew Coll., Newton, Mass., 1995—2005; talmud dept. head Gann Acad., Waltham, Mass., 1996—2004, dean faculty, 1998—2004; dir. judaic studies Herzl/RMHA, Denver, 2005—. Jerusalem Fellow, Mandel Inst., 1995—96. Jewish. Achievements include design of new method for teaching talmud. Office: Herzl/RMHA 2450 S Wabash St Denver CO 80231 Home Phone: 303-394-2254; Office Phone: 303-369-0663. Business E-Mail: hsinoff@dcje.org.

SINOR, DENIS, history professor, linguist; b. Kolozsvar, Hungary, Apr. 17, 1916; s. Miklos and Marguerite (Weitzenfeld) S.; m. Eugenia Trinajstic (dec.); children: Christophe (dec.), Sophie. BA, U. Budapest, 1938; MA, Cambridge U., Eng., 1948; doctorate (hon.), U. Szeged, Hungary, 1971. Attache Centre National de la Recherche Scientifique, Paris, 1939-48; univ. lectr. Altaic studies Cambridge U., 1948-62; prof. Uralic and Altaic studies and history Ind. U., Bloomington, 1962-81, disting. prof. Uralic and Altaic studies and history, 1975-86, disting. prof. emeritus Uralic and Altaic studies and history, 1986—, chmn. dept. Uralic and Altaic studies, 1963-1981, dir. Lang. and Area Ctr., 1963-88, dir. Asian studies program, 1965-67, dir. Asian Studies Rsch. Inst., 1967-79, dir. Rsch. Inst. for Inner Asian Studies (renamed Denis Sinor Inst. for Inner Asian Studies), 1979-1981, 85-86. Sec. gen. Permanent Internat. Altaistic Conf., 1961—; rsch. project dir. U.S. Office Edn., 1969-70; sec. Internat. Union Orientalists, 1954-64; vis. prof. Inst. Nat. des Langues et Civilisations Orientales, Paris, spring 1974; scholar-in-residence Rockefeller Found. Study Ctr., Bellagio, 1975; vice chmn. UNESCO Commn. for History Civilization Cen. Asia, 1981-2005, consultative com. UNESCO Silk Rd. Project, 1990-97; summer seminar dir. NEH, 1988, 2005; hon. prof. Inst. Oriental Studies, Russian Acad. Scis. Author: Orientalism and History, 1954, History of Hungary, 1959, Introduction à lètude de l'Eurasie Centrale, 1963, Aspects of Altaic Civilization, 1963, Inner Asia, 1968, Inner Asia and Its Contacts with Medieval Europe, 1977, Tanulmányok, 1982, Essays in Comparative Altaic Linguistics, 1990, Studies in Medieval Inner Asia, 1997; editor, contbr.: Modern Hungary, 1977, Studies in Finno-Ugric Linguistics, 1977, Uralic Languages, 1988, Essays on Uzbek History, Culture and Languages, 1993, Cambridge History of Early Inner Asia, Handbook of Uralic Studies, Jour. Asian History, Ind. U. Uralic and Altaic Series; mem. editl. bd. Britannica-Hungarica. Served with Forces Françaises de l'Intérieur, 1943-44; with French Army, 1944-45. With Free French Army, 1944—45. Rsch. grantee Am. Coun. Learned Soc., 1962, Am. Philos. Soc., 1963, NEH grant, 1981, 87-88; Guggenheim fellow, 1968-69, 1981-82; recipient Jubilee prize U. Budapest, 1938, Barczi Geza Meml. medal, 1981, Gold medal Permanent Internat. Altaistic Conf., 1982, 1996, Arminius Vambery Meml. medal, 1983, Thomas Hart Benton Mural medal Hungarian Order of Star, 1986, UNESCO Avicenna medal, 1998, medal for outstanding svcs. U. Szeged, 2002, UNESCO 60th Anniversary medal, 2005, Middle Cross Hungarian Order of Merit, 2006, John W. Ryan award, Ind. U., 2006; named Denis Sinor Inst. for Inner Asian Studies in his honor, 2006. Fellow Körösi Csoma Soc. (hon.); mem. Royal Asiatic Soc. (hon. sec. 1954-64, Denis Sinor medal for Inner Asian Studies named in his honor 1992), Am. Oriental Soc. (pres. Midwest br. 1968-70, nat. pres. 1975-76, medal of honor 1999), Assn. Asian Studies, Am. Hist. Soc., Soc. Asiatique (hon.), Tibet Soc. (pres. 1969-74), Mongolia Soc. (pres. 1987-94), Correspondant de l'Académie des inscriptions et belles lettres (Paris), Hungarian Acad. Scis. (hon.), Acad. Europaea (fgn.), Deutsche Morgenlandische Gesellschaft, Suomalais-Ugrilaisen Seura (hon.), Soc. Uralo-Altaica (v.p. 1964-94, hon.), Internat. Union Oriental and Asian Studies (v.p. 1993—), Cosmos Club Washington, Explorers Club NYC, United Oxford and Cambridge Club London. Achievements include reached the North Pole on a Russian icebreaker, 2004. Home: 5581 E Lampkins Ridge Rd Bloomington IN 47401-8674 Office: Indiana U Dept Ctrl Eurasian Studies Goodbody Hall Bloomington IN 47405 E-mail: sinord@indiana.edu.

SINOR, HOWARD EARL, JR., lawyer; b. New Orleans, Sept. 6, 1949; s. Howard E. and Beverly M. (Bourgeois) S.; m. Katy K. Sinor; children: Sally, Vera Sue, Sarah, Sadie. BA with honors, U. New Orleans, 1971; JD cum laude, Harvard U., 1975. Bar: La. 1975, U.S. Supreme Ct. 1983, U.S. Ct. Appeals (3rd, 5th and 11th cir.), U.S. Dist. Ct. (ea., middle, we.) Dist. La. Ptnr. Jones, Walker, Waechter, Poitevent, Carrere & Denegre, 1975-98, Gordon Arata, New Orleans, 1999—. Contbg. author: La. Appellate Practice Handbook, 1990, 97; editor: CLE Manual of Recent Developments, 1985; contbr. articles to profl. jours. Recipient Pres.'s award, La. State Bar Assn., 1987. Fellow La. Bar Found.; mem. ABA, FBA, La. State Bar Assn. (chmn. antitrust sect. 1987-89). Avocations: golf, hiking.

SINSHEIMER, ROBERT LOUIS, retired academic administrator, educator; b. Washington, Feb. 5, 1920; s. Allen S. and Rose (Davidson) S.; m. Flora Joan Hirsch, Aug. 8, 1943 (div. 1972); children: Lois June (Mrs. Wickstrom), Kathy Jean (Mrs. Vandagriff), Roger Allen; m. Kathleen Mae Reynolds, Sept. 10, 1972 (div. 1980); m. Karen Current, Aug. 1, 1981. S.B., MIT, 1941, MS, 1942, PhD, 1948. Staff mem. radiation lab. MIT, Cambridge, 1942-46; assoc. prof. biophysics, physics dept. Iowa State Coll., Ames, 1949-55, prof., 1955-57; prof. biophysics Calif. Inst. Tech., Pasadena, 1957-77, chmn. div. biology, 1968-77; chancellor U. Calif., Santa Cruz, 1977-87, chancellor emeritus, 1987—, prof. Santa Barbara, 1988-90, prof. emeritus, 1990—. Editor: Jour. Molecular Biology, 1959-67, Ann. Rev. Biochemistry, 1966-72. Named Calif. Scientist of Year, 1968; recipient N.W. Beijerinck-Virologie medal Netherlands Acad. Sci., 1969 Fellow Am. Acad. Arts and Scis.; mem. Am. Soc. Biol. Chemists, Biophys. soc. (pres. 1970), AAAS, Nat. Acad. Scis. (mem. council 1970-73, chmn. bd. editors Proc. 1972-80), Inst. Medicine. Achievements include discovery of single-stranded DNA, circular DNA; research in first in vitro replication of infective DNA. Avocations: photography, travel. Office: U Calif MCD Biology Santa Barbara CA 93106 Home Phone: 805-683-2247; Office Phone: 805-893-8038. Business E-Mail: sinsheim@lifesci.ucsb.edu.

SINSHEIMER, WARREN JACK, lawyer; b. NYC, May 22, 1927; s. Jerome William and Elizabeth (Berch) S.; m. Florence Dubin, Mar. 30, 1950; children: Linda Ruth, Ralph David, Alan Jay, Michael Neal. Student, Ind. U., 1943-47; JD cum laude, NY Law Sch., 1950; LLM, NYU, 1957; MPhil, Columbia U., 1977; HLD (hon.), Drew U., 2002. Bar: NY bar 1950. Ptnr. Sinsheimer, Sinsheimer & Dubin, NYC, 1950-78, Satterlee & Stephens, NYC, 1978-86, Patterson, Belknap, Webb & Tyler, NYC, 1986-91; counsel Patterson Belknap Webb & Tyler, NYC, 1991-96; pres., bd. dirs. Neighborhood Bagel Corp., 1994—. Pres. Plessey Inc., NYC, 1956-70, chmn., CEO, 1970-89; dir. oversees ops. devel. Plessey Co., Ltd., Illford, Essex, Eng., 1969-70, dep. chief exec., dir., 1976-89; dir. Plessey, Inc.; trustee NYU Sch. Law, 1996—; pres., bd. dirs. Partnership for Children's Rights, 1998—. Chmn. Com. of 68, 1964-67; Mem. Westchester County Rep. Com., 1956-73; chmn. Nat. Scranton Pres. Com., 1964; mem. NY State Assembly, 1965-66; Bd. visitors Wassaic State Sch., 1962-64; trustee Sch. Law, NYU, 1996—, bd. dirs. Shalom Hartman Inst., Jerusalem, 1991—, treas., 1996—; trustee Citi Bar Fund, 1998-2004. Served with USNR, 1944-45; with USAF, 1950-52. Mem. ABA, Assn. Bar City NY, Torch and Scroll, Century Club (Purchase, NY, gov., treas. 1997—), Century Assn. NYC, Univ. Club, Zeta Beta Tau. Jewish. Home: 22 Murray Hill Rd Scarsdale NY 10583-2828 Office: 271 Madison Ave New York NY 10016-1001 Office Phone: 212-683-7999. Business E-Mail: Sinsheimer@kidslaw.org.

SINTZ, EDWARD FRANCIS, librarian; b. New Trenton, Ind., Feb. 6, 1924; s. John and Edith E. (Rudicil) S.; m. Donna Norris, Apr. 12, 1952; children: Ann Kristin, Lesley Elizabeth, Julie Melinda. BA, U. Kans., 1950; MA in L.S, U. Denver, 1954; MS in Pub. Adminstrn, U. Mo., 1965. With Kansas City (Mo.) Pub. Library, 1954-66, asst. dir., 1964-66; asso. librarian St. Louis Pub. Library, 1966-68; dir. pub. libraries Miami-Dade Pub. Libr., 1968—89, ret. Instr. Washington U., St. Louis, 1966-67; library surveys for Mo. State Library, 1967-68; library bldg. cons., 1965—. Editor: Mo. Library Assn. Quar., 1956—58. Served with USAAF, 1942-45. Mem. ALA, Fla. Library Assn. (pres. 1975-76), Southeastern Library Assn. Clubs: Kiwanian. Home: 7105 Lakeside Dr Charlotte NC 28215 Personal E-mail: edanddonna9@bellsouth.com.

SIO, JIMMY ONG, embryologist; b. Manila, Philippines, Mar. 9, 1954; arrived in U.S., 1973; s. Vicente and SiokBee (Ong) Sio. Biology major, U. Philippines, 1971—73; BS in Biology, Calif. State Coll. Bakersfield, 1976; PhD of Cell Biology, U. Tex. Health Sci. Ctr., Dallas, 1985; MD, Emory U., 1985. Diplomate Nat. Bd. Med. Examiners, Am. Bd. Hosp. Physicians, Am. Coll. Ethical Physicians. Resident in anat. pathology Emory U., Atlanta, 1985—86; resident in internal medicine Kem Med. Ctr., Bakersfield, Calif., 1990—93; physician Kaiser So. Calif. Permanente Med. Group, Bakersfield, 1993—, asst. area med. dir., 2006—. Pvt. Philippine Armed Forces, 1971—73. Recipient Businessman of Yr., NRCC, 2003, Man of Yr., IBC and ABI, 2004. Fellow: Am. Biog. Inst.; mem.: Internat. Biog. Assn., NY Acad. Scis., Order of Internat. Fellowship, InterNet Assocs. Avocation: reading. Home: 8604 Dinard Pl Bakersfield CA 93311 Office: Kaiser So Calif Permanente Med Group 8800 Ming Ave Bakersfield CA 93311 Office Phone: 661-664-3706. Personal E-mail: doctorsio@aol.com.

SION, MAURICE, mathematics professor; b. Skopje, Yugoslavia, Oct. 17, 1928; came to Can., 1960; s. Max and Sarah (Alalouf) S.; m. Emilie Grace Chisholm, Sept. 15, 1957; children: Crispin, Sarah, Dirk. BA, NYU, 1947, MA, 1948; PhD, U. Calif., Berkeley, 1951. Mathematician Nat. Bur. Stds., Washington, 1951-52; instr. U. Calif., 1952-53; asst. prof. U. Calif., 1957-60; mem. Inst. for Advanced Study, Princeton, NJ, 1955-57, 62; asst. prof. U. B.C., Vancouver, Canada, 1960, assoc. prof., 1961, prof., 1964-89, prof. emeritus, 1989—, head math. dept., 1984-86, dir. Quadra Inst. Math., 1970-89. Author: Introduction to Methods of Real Analysis, 1969, Theory Semi Group Valued Measures, 1973; contbr. articles to profl. jours. With U.S. Army, 1953-55. Mem. Am. Math. Soc., Can. Math. Soc. (v.p. 1972-74). Office: U BC Dept Math Vancouver BC Canada V6T 1Z2

SIPE, LAWRENCE ROBERT, education educator; b. York, Pa., Dec. 1, 1949; BA in English Lit., U. Chgo., 1967; BS in Elem. Edn., Bloomsburg State Coll., Pa., 1973; MEd in Reading and Spl. Edn., Temple U., Phila., 1980; PhD, Ohio State U., Columbus, 1996. Tchr. grades 1-8 Ocean View Sch., Petites, Newfoundland, Canada, 1971—73; tchr. grades k-2 Stuart Country Day Sch., Princeton, NJ, 1976—80; asst. prof. Grad. Sch. Edn. U. Pa., Phila., 1996—2002, assoc. prof. Grad. Sch. Edn., 2002—. Editor: Children's Lit. in Edn. jour., 2006—. Recipient Student Outstanding Rsch. award, Nat. Reading Conf., 1997, Outstanding Dissertation award, Coll. Reading Assn., 1997, Promising Rschr. award, Nat. Coun. Tchrs. English, 1998, Outstanding Dissertation award, Internat. Reading Assn., 1998, Early Career Achievement award, Nat. Reading Conf., 2001, Outstanding Tchg. award, Grad. Sch. Edn., U. Pa., 2005; Rsch. and Grad. Coun. fellow, Ohio State U., 1993—96, Martha King scholar, 1993—96. Office: Grad Sch Education Univ of Pa 3700 Walnut St Philadelphia PA 19104 Home Phone: 215-417-8229; Office Phone: 215-898-1920.

SIPES, KAREN KAY, communications executive; b. Higginsville, Mo., Jan. 8, 1947; d. Walter John and Katherine Marie (McLelland) Heins; m. Joel Rodney Sipes, Sept. 24, 1971; 1 child, Lesley Katherine. BS in Edn., Ctrl. Mo. State U., 1970. Reporter/news editor Newton Kansan, 1973—76; sports writer Capital-Jour., Topeka, 1976—83, spl. sects. editor, 1983—85, editl. page editor, 1985—92, mng. editor/features, 1992—2002, asst. editl. page editor, 2002—03; dir. commn. Kans. Dept. Aging, Topeka, 2003—. Co-chair Mayor's Commn. on Literacy, Topeka, 1995-96; mem. Act Against Violence Com., Topeka, 1995-96, Mayor's Task Force on Race Rels., 1998; planning com. Leadership Greater Topeka, 1997; Great Am. Cleanup, 1999-2001, ERC/Resource and Referral, 2001-07; com. mem. Martin Luther King Living the Dream Bus. Ptnrs., 2001-2004; Centennial planning com. Family Svc. and Guidance Ctr., 2003-04; mem. Project Topeka Com., 2004—, Arthritis Walk Com., 2004-05, Faith in Action-No Place Like Home Coalition, 2003—; bd. dirs. Western Swing Music Soc. Kans., 2003—. Mem. Ctrl. Mo. State U. Alumni Assn. (bd. dirs. 1996-2002, v.p. 1999, pres. 2000). Avocations: music, gardening, art. Office: Kans Dept Aging New England Bldg 503 S Kans Ave Topeka KS 66603-3404 Home Phone: 785-862-4119; Office Phone: 785-368-7196. Personal E-mail: critterkaren@aol.com. Business E-Mail: karen.sipes@aging.state.ks.us.

SIPHO, ELLA P., artist; b. Kansas City, Mo., Aug. 12, 1964; d. John H. I. Sipho Sr. and Paulette Sipho; m. Anthony M. Ferguson, July 11, 1997. AA, U. Mo., Columbia, 1989. Represented by ArtReps, Woodland Hills, Calif., 2003—05, Art A LA Internat. Co., Longwood, Fla., 2003—04. One-woman shows include Commerce Bank, Kansas City, Mo., 2003, The View, Grandview, Mo., 2004, exhibitions include Whitney Mus. Am. Art, NY, 2003 (prize), Manhattan Arts Internat., NYC, 2003 (award of merit), City of Overland Park, Kans. Convention Ctr., 2003, Lessedra World Print Annual, Sofia, Bulgaria, 2004, Period Gallery, Omaha, 2004, Kansas City Artist Coalition, 2004, Open Studios, Grandview, 2004, Internat. VideoArt Festival, Ferrara, Italy, 2005, Mus. TV and Radio Art Film Screening, Beverly Hills, Calif., 2005, Bohemian Gallery, Kansas City, 2005, MGM Grand, Las Vegas, Nev., 2005, Florean Mus., Romania, 2005, 2006, Snap to the Grid, LA, 2006, ARC Gallery, 2006, Mus. Florean, 2006, Marlene Tseng Yu Studio, NYC, 2006—, 30+ KCAC Invitational Group Exhibition, 2007, numerous others, Represented in permanent collections Florean Mus., Spring Corp., Overland Park, Kans., Grandview Parks and Recreation, Urban Lofts, TV exhbn., Amsterdam Whitney Gallery, 2003, NBC's BRAVO Network, 2007. Recipient Frontice Piece Cover award, Book Art Press, 2004, award, ARTV, Las Vegas, 2005, Prize of Excellence award, Art Addiction Medial Mus., 2007. Mem.: Chgo. Artist Coalition, Kansas City Artist Coalition. Home: 8309 E 110th St Kansas City MO 64134

SIPIERA, PAUL P., JR., foundation administrator, retired geology and astronomy professor; b. Chgo., Nov. 30, 1948; s. Paul P. and Frances A.; m. Diane M. Vidmar, May 22, 1993; children: Paula Frances, Caroline Antarctica. BA in History, Northeastern Ill. U., 1971, MS in Earth Sci., 1975; PhD in Natural Sci., U. Innsbruck, Austria, 2004. Prof. geology and astronomy Harper Coll., Palatine, Ill., 1976—2006, prof. emeritus, 2006—. Rsch assoc. Field Mus. Natural History, Chgo., 1976—92; exec. bd. Ill. State Acad. Sci., Springfield, 1978—83; rsch. sci. Antarctic search for meteorites NSF, Washington, 1983—84; pres. and CEO Planetary Studies Found., Algonquin, Ill., 1989—. Author: Gerald Ford, 1989, Amundsen & Scott: Race to the South Pole, 1990, Ernest Shackleton: A Life of Antarctic Exploration, 2002; contbr. chapters to books, to profl. publ. Adv. bd. mem.

X-Prize Found., St. Louis, 1996—. Recipient Nininger Meteorite Rsch. award, Ariz. State U., 1975—76, Antarctic Svc medal, U.S.A, 1984, Disting. Faculty award, Harper Coll., 1996. Fellow: Ill. State Acad. Sci.; mem.: New Zealand Antarctic Soc., Geol. Soc. New Zealand, Meteoritical Soc. Achievements include asteroid 31931 named in his honor. Avocations: photography, farming. Home and Office: 10 Winterwood Ln Galena IL 61036 Home Phone: 815-858-3362; Office Phone: 847-854-0468. Business E-Mail: psipiera@planets.org.

SIPIORA, LEONARD PAUL, retired museum director, art appraiser; b. Lawrence, Mass., Sept. 1, 1934; s. Walter and Agnes S.; m. Sandra Joyce Coon, 1962; children— Alexandra, Erika. AB cum laude, U. Mich., 1955, MA, 1956. Dir. museums, City of El Paso, Tex., 1967-90; ret. Co-founder, pres. El Paso Arts Coun., 1969-71; sec.-treas. El Paso Coun. Internat. Visitors, 1968-71; trustee El Paso Mus. Art; bd. dirs. Tex. Com. Humanities, Assn. Southwestern Humanities Coun.; adv. bd. S.W. Arts Found.; expert Antiques Roadshow-U.S.A. Bd. dirs. Cmty. Concert Assn. El Paso, El Paso Symphony Orch., El Paso Hist. Soc. Mem. Assn. Mus. Dirs., Mountain Plains Mus. Assn. (pres. 1978-79), Tex. Assn. Museums (pres. 1977-79), Appraisers Assn. Am., Knights of Malta (decorated Grand Cross), Prior of Tex., Kappa Pi. Republican. Lutheran. Home: 1012 Blanchard Ave El Paso TX 79902-2727

SIPKINS, PETER W., lawyer; b. Mpls., 1944; BA, U. Minn., 1966, JD, 1969. Bar: Minn. 1969, Wis. 1982. Spl. asst. atty. gen. State Minn., 1971-73, solicitor gen., 1974-76; mem. Dorsey & Whitney, Mpls., ptnr., trial practice group; co-chmn., products & tech. liability litig. group. Adj. prof. law, legal writing, appellate advocacy William Mitchell Coll. Law, 1974-77. Mem. Phi Delta Phi. Office: Dorsey & Whitney Ste 1500 50 S 6th St Minneapolis MN 55402-1498 Office Phone: 612-343-7903. Office Fax: 612-340-2807. Business E-Mail: sipkins.peter@dorsey.com.

SIPPEL, WILLIAM LEROY, lawyer; b. Fond du Lac, Wis., Aug. 14, 1948; m. Barbara Jean Brost, Aug. 23, 1970; children: Katharine Jean, David William. BA, JD, U. Wis. Bar: Wis. 1974, U.S. Dist. Ct. (we. dist.) Wis. 1974, Minn. 1981, U.S. Dist. Ct. Minn. 1981, U.S. Ct. Appeals (10th cir.) 1984, U.S. Ct. Appeals (8th cir.) 1985. Research assoc. dept. agrl. econs. U. Wis., Madison, 1974-75; counsel monopolies and comml. law subcom. Ho. Judiciary Com., Washington, 1975-80; spl. asst. to asst. gen. antitrust div. U.S. Dept. of Justice, Washington, 1980-81; from assoc. to ptnr. Doherty, Rumble & Butler, Mpls. and St. Paul, Minn., 1981-99; ptnr. Oppenheimer, Wolff & Donnelly, LLP, Mpls., 1999—. Bd. dirs. Music in the Park, Inc.; adj. faculty antitrust William Mitchell Coll. Law, 2000-01; adj. faculty grad. program U. Minn. Carlson Sch. Mgmt., 2007—. Co-author: The Antitrust Health Care Handbook, 1988; contbg. author: ABA Energy Antitrust Handbook, 2002. Mem. program com. Minn. World Trade Assn., Mpls., St. Paul, 1985-86, bd. dirs., 1986, Minn.; former dir. Music in the Park, Mpls.; former dir. Person to Person Inc.; chmn. antitrust mktg. orders com. Nat. Coun. Farmer Coops., 2001—. With USAR, 1971-77. Mem. ABA (vice chmn. ins. industry com. 1990-91, contbr. ABA Joint Ventures in Health Care), Minn. Bar Assn. (co-chmn. antitrust sect. 1986-88, internat. law sect. coun. 1986-89, treas. 1989-90, sec. 1990-91, vice chmn. 1995-96, chmn. 1996-97), Minn. Med. Alley Assn. (co-chmn. internat. bus. com. 1990-95, Hennepin County Office Internat. Trade (bd. dirs. 1988-93), Phi Beta Kappa. Roman Catholic. Avocations: reading, photography, computers. Home: 2151 Commonwealth Ave Saint Paul MN 55108-1730 Office: Oppenheimer Wolff Donnelly LLP Plaza VII 45 S Seventh St Ste 3400 Minneapolis MN 55402-1609 Home Phone: 651-645-3630; Office Phone: 612-607-7251. Business E-Mail: bsippel@oppenheimer.com.

SIPPEL-WETMORE, FRANCES MARIE, microbiologist, retired business owner; b. Phila., Apr. 17, 1930; d. Jacob Harry Jr. and Catharine Seachrist (Hershey) Pickle; m. Roy Joseph Sippel, Feb. 8, 1958 (div. June 1979); m. Orville Chase Wetmore, June 14, 1997. BA Biology and Chemistry with honors, Hood Coll., 1952; postgrad., Women's Med. Coll., Pa., 1952—54; MS Microbiology, U. Pitts., 1956. Rsch. asst. to Dr. Jonas Salk U. Pitts., 1955; rsch. asst. to Dr. T.S. Danowski Children's Hosp., Pitts., 1956; bacteriologist Shadyside Hosp., Pitts., 1956—57; rsch. asst. to Dr. Leonard Hayflick Wistar Inst., Phila., 1958—59; asst. editor Biol. Abstracts, Phila., 1959—60; lit. chemist E.I. du Pont de Nemours & Co., Wilmington, Del., 1960—66; sec.-treas. Can-Am Sales Corp., West Chester, Pa., 1972—73; sales rep. Quick Courier Svc., Phila., 1977—82; owner Color Profile, West Chester, 1982—97. Bd. dirs. Chester County Emergency Med. Svcs., Pa., 1980-97; co-chair Holiday House Tour, 1989-93, chair House Acquisitions, 1995; vol. YWCA. Mem. AAUW (Outstanding Woman from West Chester br. 1991), LWV (chmn. Chester County coun. 1993-95), Am. Soc. Microbiologists, Phila. Hood Coll. Club (past pres.), Chester County Hist. Soc. (antiques show com.), Wilmington Country Club, Sigma Xi Republican. Unitarian Universalist. Avocations: art, music, downhill skiing, travel. Home: 1007 Oriente Ave Wilmington DE 19807-2260

SIPPRELL, GEORGE SIDNEY, aerospace engineer, consultant; b. Buffalo, Jan. 10, 1949; s. George Gilbert and Eleanor M. Sipprell; m. Kathleen Ann Meyer, July 22, 1972; children: Jeffrey David, Benjamin Daniel. BS in Aero. Engring., Rensselaer Poly. Inst., 1970, MEng in Aero. Engring., 1972. Joined Sikorsky Aircraft Corp., Stratford, Conn., 1972, propulsion sys. analyst, 1972—74, helicopter icing lead rsch. engr., 1974—76, UH-60A Black Hawk project engr., 1972—76, engring. mgr. USCG SRR/S76, 1976—79, sr. sys. analyst, LHX, 1979, program mgr., engring. mgr. UH60A Black Hawk ESSS, 1979—83, engring. mgr. LHX Program, 1983—90, engr. mgr. LHX simulation and SHADOW program, 1988—91, dep. program mgr. RAH-66 Comanche Helicopter Program, 1990—2002, chief engr. U.S. Army/DARPA Unmanned Combat Armed Rotorcraft program, 2002—03, dir. engring., sys. requirements and analysis and advanced concepts, 2003—04; ret., 2004. Ind. aerospace sys. engring. cons., 2004—. Recipient AHS Grover Bell award, 1990, U.S. Army Chief Staff award, 1993, Bd. Dirs. Trophy award, United Techs. Corp., 2001. Mem.: Am. Helicopter Soc. (mem. qua. century group), Sikorsky Ski Club (pres. 1980—82, Outstanding Member award 1982). Avocations: sailing, model railroading, skiing, toy collecting, British cars and Corvettes. Home and Office: 4 Featherbed Ln Branford CT 06405-6113 Home Phone: 203-481-4866; Office Phone: 203-747-9618. Personal E-mail: gsipprell@excite.com.

SIPPY, DAVID DEAN, dentist; b. Waukesha, Wis., June 22, 1953; s. Lawrence Vern and Myrtle (Lawton) S.; m. Sharon Eleanor Komar, Jan. 8, 1977; children: Sharon Kay, Derek Bradley. MB, U. Wis., Milw., 1972; M in Dental Surgery, Marquette U., 1987. Dentist, New Glarus, Wis., 1988—. Owner Zenter Haus Bed and Breakfast Inn; part-time faculty Sch. Dental Hygiene Madison Area Tech. Coll. Bd. dirs. C. of C., 1989-91. Mem. ADA, Internat. Assn. for Orthodontics, Nat. Trust for Hist. Preservation, Oreg. Geneal. Soc., Am. Orthodontics Soc. (bd. dirs.). Mem. Seventh-Day Aventists. Avocations: genealogy, history, historical architecture, astrophysics. Home: N8588 Zentner Rd New Glarus WI 53574 Office: New Glarus Dental Clinic 119 6th Ave New Glarus WI 53574 also: Family Dental Care 405 1/2 Iowa St Dodgeville WI 53533 Office Phone: 608-930-2121. Personal E-mail: tremeau@tds.net.

SIQUELAND, EINAR, psychologist, educator; b. Glasgow, Mont., Nov. 15, 1932; s. Harald and Anna Lydia (Kristensen) S.; m. Marian McGrail, Dec. 1960 (div. May 1970); children: Lynne Ruth, Beth Ann; m. Jillian E.A. Godfree, June 29, 1973. BA, Pacific Luth. U., 1954; MS, U. Wash., 1962, PhD, 1963. Rsch. assoc. pharmacology U. Wash., Seattle, 1958-59; clin. intern psychology VA Mental Hygiene Clinic, Seattle, 1960-61; asst. prof. dept. psychology Brown U., Providence, 1965-69, assoc. prof., 1969-88, prof., 1988-99; rsch. scientist dept. Pediatrics Women's and Infants' Hosp., Providence, 1975-93; prof. emeritus Brown U., 1999—. Contbr. articles to profl. jours., chpts. to books. With U.S. Army, 1956-58, Korea. Predoctoral fellow USPHS, 1961-63, postdoctoral fellow, 1963-65. Fellow Am. Psychol. Soc.; mem. AAUP, APA, Soc. Rsch. in Child Devel., Sigma Xi. Office: Brown U Dept Psychology PO Box 1853 Providence RI 02912-1853 Personal E-mail: siquel-e@cox.net.

SIRACUSA, PAUL J., automotive executive; b. NYC, Mar. 26, 1945; m. Anna Siracusa. Fin. mgmt. positions Hertz Corp., 1969—94; staff v.p., controller Hertz Worldwide Rent A Car, 1994—95; v.p. fin., CFO Hertz Internat. Ltd., England, 1996—97; exec. v.p., CFO Hertz Corp., 1997—2005, Hertz Global Holdings Inc., Park Ridge, NJ, 2005—. Bd. dir. Hertz Corp., 2004—05. Office: Hertz Global Holdings 225 Brae Blvd Park Ridge NJ 07656 *

SIRAGUSA, CHARLES J., judge; b. Rochester, NY, 1947; BA, Lemoyne Coll., 1969; JD, Albany Law Sch., 1976. Asst. dist. atty. Monroe County Dist. Atty.'s Office, NY, 1977—92; state supreme ct. justice (dist. 7) NY State Supreme Ct., 1993—97; judge US Dist. Ct. (we. dist.) NY, 1997—. Office: 1360 US Courthouse 100 State St Rochester NY 14614-1350 Office Phone: 585-613-4050.

SIRCAR, SHIVAJI, chemical engineer, researcher; b. Calcutta, India, Oct. 21, 1944; s. Sachindra N. and Binapani (Bose) S.; m. Shukla Sinha, Mar. 12, 1971; 1 child, Sanjoy. BSChemE, Jadavpur U., Calcutta, 1964; MSChemE, U. Pa., 1968, PhDChemE, 1970. Sr. rsch. fellow Ctrl. Fuel Rsch., India, 1964-65; postdoctoral fellow U. Pa., Phila., 1970-73; sr. rsch. engr. Air Products & Chems., Inc., Allentown, Pa., 1973-76, prin. rsch. engr., 1976-78, rsch. assoc., 1978-82, sr. rsch. assoc., 1982-86, prin. rsch. assoc., 1986-96, chief scientist, 1996—2001; prof. practice Lehigh U., Bethlehem, Pa., 2002—. Mem. adv. bd. Adsorption Sci. Tech., 1996-99. Mem. adv. bd. Adsorption, I&EC Rsch., 1996-99; contbr. more than 160 articles to profl. jours. NSF fellow. Mem. NAE, AIChE (chmn. adsorption com. 1992-93, Profl. Progress award 1988, Excellence in Indsl. Gases Tech. award 2001), Am. Chem. Soc., Internat. Adsorption Soc. (dir. 1995-97). Achievements include 55 U.S. patents and 65 internat. patents; inventor of five adsorptive separation processes which have been commercialized by Air products. Office: Chemical Engring Dept Iacocca Hall Lehigh U 111 Research Drive Bethlehem PA 18015-4469 Personal E-mail: sircar@aol.com.

SIRES, ALBIO, congressman, former state legislator; b. Bejucal, Cuba, Jan. 26, 1951; arrived in USA, 1962; m. Adrienne Sires; 1 stepchild, Tara Kole. BA in Spanish & Mktg., St. Peter's Coll., 1974; MA in Spanish, Middlebury Coll., 1985. Dir Hispanic Outreach Dept. Cmty. Affairs, State of NJ, 1987—88; owner A.M. Title Agy., Inc.; mayor Town West NY, NJ, 1995—2006; mem. NJ Gen. Assembly from Dist. 33, 2000—06, spkr., 2002—06; acting gov. State of NJ, 2002, 2005; mem. US Congress from 13th NJ dist., 2006—, mem. fin. svcs. com., fgn. affairs com. Named Mayor of the Yr., NJ Conf. Mayors, 2004; recipient Community That Works award, State of NJ, William J. Brennan Citation for Justice, NJ Bar Assn., Legal Services NJ, 2005. Mem.: Legis. Svcs. Commn. Democrat. Roman Catholic. Office: 1024 Longworth House Office Bldg Washington DC 20515 also: 5500 Palisade Ave Ste A West New York NJ 07093 Office Phone: 201-558-0800. Office Fax: 201-617-2809. *

SIRGADO, JO ANNE E., lawyer; b. Meadville, Pa., May 16, 1960; BA magna cum laude, Villa Maria Coll., 1982; JD, Pace Univ., 1990. Bar: NY 1991. Ptnr., project devel., fin., leasing Hunton & Williams LLP, NYC, and co-chmn. recruitment com. Office: Hunton & Williams LLP 43rd Fl 200 Park Ave New York NY 10166-0136 Office Phone: 212-309-1093. Office Fax: 212-309-1100. Business E-Mail: jsirgado@hunton.com.

SIRICA, ALPHONSE EUGENE, pathology educator; b. Waterbury, Conn., Jan. 16, 1944; s. Alphonse Eugene and Elena Virginia (Mascolo) S.; m. Annette Marie Murray, June 9, 1984; children: Gabrielle Theresa, Nicholas Steven. MS, Fordham U., 1968; PhD in Biomed. Sci., U. Conn., 1977. Asst. prof. U. Wis., Madison, 1979-84; assoc. prof. Med. Coll. Va., Va. Commonwealth U., Richmond, 1984-90, prof. of pathology, 1990—, divsn. chair exptl. pathology, 1992-99, divsn. chair cellular and molecular pathogenesis, 1999—. Vis. prof. Pa. State U. Coll. Medicine, 2000; regular mem. sci. adv. com. on carcinogenesis and nutrition Am. Cancer Soc., Atlanta, 1989—92; metabolic pathology study sect. NIH, Bethesda, 1991—95, ad hoc mem. study sect., 1997—2006. Editor, author: The Pathobiology of Neoplasia, 1989, The Role of Cell Types in Hepatocarcinogenesis, 1992, Cellular and Molecular Pathogenesis, 1996; co-editor, author: Biliary and Pancreatic Ductal Epithelia: Pathobiology and Pathophysiology, 1997; mem. editl. bd. Pathobiology, 1990-99, Hepatology, 1991-94; rev. bd. In Vitro Cellular and Devel. Biology-Animal, 1987—, Exptl. and Molecular Pathology, 1999—, World Jour. Gastroenterology, 2006-; contbr. articles to profl. jours. including Am. Jour. Pathology, Cancer Rsch., Hepatology, and other. Recipient Rsch. Recognition award, Va. Commonwealth U. Sch. Medicine, 2002, 2007. Mem.: AAAS, Soc. Toxicology, Han. Popper Hepatopathology Soc., Soc. Exptl. Biology and Medicine, NY Acad. Scis., Am. Gastroenterological Assn., Am. Assn. Study Liver Diseases, Am. Soc. Investigative Pathology (chair program com. 1994—96), Assn. Clin. Scientists, Soc. for In Vitro Biology, Am. Assn. Cancer Rsch. (chmn. Va. state legis. com. 1992—95), Am. Soc. Cell Biology. Achievements include development of collagen gel-nylon mesh system for culturing hepatocytes; first establishment and characterization of hyperplastic bile ductular epithelial cells in culture; research in hepato and biliary carcinogenesis, pathobiology of hepatocyte and biliary epithelial cells and molecular pathogenesis and experimental therapeutics of biliary cancer. Office: Med Coll Va Va Commonwealth U PO Box 980297 Richmond VA 23298-0297 Home Phone: 804-346-9210; Office Phone: 804-828-9549. Business E-Mail: asirica@mcvh-vcu.edu.

SIRIGNANO, MONICA ANN, performing company executive, playwright; b. Princeton, NJ, May 18, 1971; d. William Alfonso and Molly Wilhelmina Sirignano. BA in English, Stetson U., 1993; postgrad., CUNY. Mng. editor Encore Mag., Miami, Fla., 1993—95; asst. mng. editor PC Mag., NYC, 1995—2000; performer, playwright NYC, 1995—; artistic dir., pres. Screaming Venus Prodns., NYC, 1999—, also bd. dirs. Adjudicator Fringe NYC, 2000, 01; mem. adv. bd. Blue Allied Theatre Co., NYC, 2002—. Contbr. articles to jours.; author: On Zither & Autobiography, 2004, short story publs. Mem. membership com., mem. creative black tie invitation com. Am. Cancer Soc., Miami, 1993—94; mem. Habitat for Humanity, Ft. Lauderdale, Fla., 1994. Recipient award, Off-Off Broadway Rev., 2001; grantee, Harburg Found., 2000. Mem.: Theatre Comm. Group, Dramatists Guild. Avocations: photography, painting, graphic design. Office: Screaming Venus Prodns 29-22 Hoyt Ave S # 21 Astoria NY 11102 Personal E-mail: nicasiri@gmail.com.

SIRIGNANO, WILLIAM ALFONSO, aerospace and mechanical engineer, educator; b. Bronx, NY, Apr. 14, 1938; s. Anthony P. and Lucy (Caruso) S.; m. Lynn Haisfield, Nov. 26, 1977; children: Monica Ann, Jacqueline Hope, Justin Anthony. B.Aero.Engring., Rensselaer Poly. Inst., 1959; PhD, Princeton U., 1964. Mem. research staff Guggenheim Labs., aerospace, mech. scis. dept. Princeton U., 1964-67, asst. prof. aerospace and mech. scis., 1967-69, assoc. prof., 1969-73, prof., 1973-79, dept. dir. grad. studies, 1974-78; George Tallman Ladd prof., head dept. mech. engring. Carnegie-Mellon U., 1979-85; dean Sch. Engring., U. Calif.-Irvine, 1985-94, prof., 1994—. Cons. industry and govt., 1966—; lectr., cons. NATO adv. group on aero. rsch. and devel., 1967, 75, 80; chmn. nat. and internat. tech. congs.; chmn. acad. adv. coun. Indsl. Rsch. Inst., 1985-88; mem. space sci. applications adv. com. NASA, 1985-90, chmn. combustion sci. microgravity disciplinary working group, 1987-90; chmn. com. on microgravity rsch. space studies bd. NRC, 1991-94, Henry Samueli endowed chair in engring., 2004-. Spl. issues editor: Combustion Sci. and Tech., 1969-70, 2000-06; assoc. tech. editor Jour. Heat Transfer, 1986-92; contbr. articles to profl. jours. Recipient Disting. Alumni Rsch. award U. Calif. Irvine, 1992, Recognition award Am. Electronics Assn., 1994, Excellence award Orange County Engring. Coun., 1994; United Aircraft rsch. fellow, 1973-74. Fellow: AAAS, ASME (Freeman scholar 1992), AIAA (Pendray Aerospace Lit. award 1991, Propellants and Combustion award 1992, Energy Systems award 2004, Sustained Svc. award 2006), Am. Phys. Soc.; mem.: NAE, Soc. Indsl. and Applied Math., Combustion Inst. (treas. internat. orgn., chmn. ea. sect., Alfred C. Egerton Gold medal 1996), Inst. Dynamics Explosives and Reactive Sys. (v.p. 1991—95, pres. 1995—99, Oppenheim award 1993). Office: U Calif Irvine Sch Engring S3202 Engring Gtwy Irvine CA 92697-3975 Business E-Mail: sirignan@uci.edu.

SIRILLA, GEORGE M., lawyer; b. Perryopolis, Pa., May 1, 1929; s. Michael and Helen Sirilla; m. Floranne Zalewski Sirilla, Nov. 23, 1968; children: Michael George, Joseph David. BSME, Rensselaer Poly. Inst., Troy, NY, 1952; LLB, Georgetown Law Sch., Washington, JD, 1956. Bar: Va. 1956, DC 1956. Assoc. Cushman, Darby & Cushman, Washington, 1955—59, ptnr., 1960, 1968—96, Pillsbury, Madison & Sutro, 1996—, Pillsbury Winthrop, McLean, Va., 2001—05, Pillsbury Winthrop Shaw Pittman, 2005—. Adj. prof. George Washington Law Sch., Washington, 1982—83; mem. mng. bd. Cushman, Darby & Cushman, 1988—89, Pillsbury, Madison & Sutro, 1999—2000. Contbr. articles to law revs. Sgt. US Army, 1946—47, Korea. Named Master, Giles S. Rich Inn of Ct., 1992—2001. Mem.: Am. Coll. Trial Lawyers. Office: Pillsbury Winthrop Shaw 1650 Tysons Blvd Mc Lean VA 22102 Office Phone: 703-770-7784.

SIRKEN, MONROE GILBERT, statistician; b. NYC, Jan. 11, 1921; s. Irving and Henrietta (Oram) S.; m. Blanche Skalak Hurwitz (div. 1960); children: Robert, Philip. BA, UCLA, 1946, MA, 1947; PhD, U. Wash., 1950. Lectr. Med. Sch. U. Wash., Seattle, 1949; fellow Stats. Lab. U. Calif., Berkeley, 1950; statistician Census Bur., Suitland, Md., 1951-54, Pub. Health Svc., Washington, 1954-60, Nat. Ctr. Health Stats., Hyattsville, Md., 1961—. Cons. NIH, 1980-85, Nat. Inst. Drug Addiction, 1976-80, NSF, 1986—, Health Care Fin. Adminstrn., 1989-90. Contbr. articles to Jour. Am. Statis. Assn., Biometrics, Demography, Jour. APHA, Pub. Health Reports, also others. Home: 3309 Claridge Ct Silver Spring MD 20902-2201 Home Phone: 301-946-6757; Office Phone: 301-458-4505. Personal E-mail: mgsirken@aol.com. Business E-Mail: mgs2@cdc.gov.

SIRKIN, JOEL H., lawyer; b. Pitts., Jan. 7, 1946; s. Sidney and Marion (Wolkin) S.; m. Karen Sargent, Aug. 7, 1977; children: Alex S., Jacob O. BA magna cum laude, Johns Hopkins U., 1967; JD cum laude, Harvard U., 1972. Bar: Mass. 1972. Prin. Cambridge (Mass.) Pilot Sch., 1970-71; staff atty. Cambridge-Somerville Legal Services, 1972-74; sr. ptnr., chmn. Real Estate dept. Hale & Dorr, Boston, 1974—2004; ptnr., chmn. Real Estate dept., mem. exec. com. Wilmer Cutler Pickering Hale & Dorr, Boston, 2004—. Author: Public School Law. Dir. Mass. Children's Lobby, Boston, 1980-84; mem. fin. com. Town of Wayland, Mass., 1993-96. Named a Mass. Super Lawyer, Boston Mag., 2004. Mem. Phi Beta Kappa. Avocations: gardening, tennis, golf. Home: 10 Wildwood Rd Wayland MA 01778-2122 Office: Wilmer Cutler Pickering Hale & Dorr 60 State St Boston MA 02109-1816 Office Phone: 617-526-6279. Office Fax: 617-526-5000. Business E-Mail: joel.sirkin@wilmerhale.com.

SIRKIN, MICHAEL S., lawyer; b. Newark, Feb. 21, 1947; BS in industl. engring., Rutgers U., 1969; JD, Columbia U., 1972. Bar: N.Y. 1973. Mem. Proskauer Rose LLP, NYC, 1989—. Office: Proskauer Rose LLP 1585 Broadway Fl 27 New York NY 10036-8299 Home Phone: 212-734-1947; Office Phone: 212-969-3840. E-mail: msirkin@proskauer.com.

SIRMANS, BARBARA C., library director; Dir. Birmingham Pub. Libr., Ala., 2002—. Mem. exec. coun. Ala. Libr. Assn., 1999, conv. chair, 2004; bd. dirs. Workshops, Inc., 2004. Office: Birmingham Pub Libr 2100 Park Pl Birmingham AL 35203 Office Phone: 205-226-3614. Office Fax: 205-226-3731. Business E-Mail: barbara@bham.lib.al.us.

SIRNA, GAIL CAROLYN, artist, educator, writer; b. Detroit, Apr. 7, 1943; d. John Arthur and Viola Rose McKeown; m. Robert G. Sirna, May 28, 1966; children: Michele Lee Grace, Cheryl Lynn, Anthony McKeown. AB, St. Louis U., 1965; MA, U. Mich., 1969. Tchr., counselor Hazel Park (Mich.) Pub. Schs., 1972—82; shopowner The Fancyworks, Sterling Heights, Mich., 1982—85. Author: (bi-monthly column) Needlepoint Now, 2001—, In Praise of the Needlewoman: Embroiderers, Knitters, Lacemakers, & Weavers in Art, 2007. Mem.: Am. Needlepoint Guild (nominating com. 2000—03, Best of Show 1999), Nat. Embroidery Tchrs. Assn. (pres. 1985—88, sec. 2002—07), Embroiderers' Guild Am. (region dir. 1990—92, chmn. cert. grad. tchr. program 2001—04, cert. grad. tchr.), Nat. Acad. Needlearts (dir. 1990—2000, treas. 2000—, cert. tchr. needlearts, cert. judge, Lifetime Achievement award 2004), Mensa, Phi Kappa Phi. Roman Catholic. E-mail: gigigail@speakeasy.net.

SIROIS, CHARLES, communications executive; b. Chicoutimi, Que., Can., May 22, 1954; children: François-Charles, Marie-Hèlène. Doctorate (hon.), U. Québec, Montréal, Ottawa U., Can., Concordia U., Montreal, Laval U., Que.; B Fin., Sherbrooke U., Qué.; M Fin., Laval U., Qué. Founder Telesystem Ltd., Montreal, 1984—, Nat. Pagette Ltd., Montreal, 1986-88; chmn., CEO BCE Mobile Comms. Inc., Montreal, 1988-90, Teleglobe Inc., Montreal, 1992-2000; founder, chmn., CEO Telesystem Ltd., Montreal, 1990—; chmn. Microcell Telecomms. Inc., Montreal, 1993—, Telesys. Internat. Wireless, 1997—; global bd. dirs. Enablis. Bd dirs Can Imperial Bank Commerce; mem Global Info Infrastructure Comn, Can Info Hwy. Co-author: (book) The Medium and the Muse, 1995, Organic Management-Creating a Culture of Innovation, 2000. Mem.: Knight Order nat du Que, Order Can (hon.). Office: Telesystem Ltd 38th Fl 1250 René Lévesque Blvd W Montreal PQ Canada H3B 4W8 E-mail: csirois@telesystem.ca.

SIROONI, ANAHID ALICE, composer, musician; Postgrad. diploma, Juilliard Sch., NYC. Concert pianist; piano tchr. Composer: Prelude in E Minor, 1976, Rondo Eb, 1976, Poéme, 1976. Home: 188 Ryder Rd Manhasset NY 11030

SIROTA, WILBERT H., lawyer; b. Balt., 1937; BA, Johns Hopkins Univ., 1958; JD, Univ. Md., 1961; LLM, Georgetown Univ., 1964. Bar: Md. 1961. Law clk. Md. Ct. Appeals, 1961—62; atty., office of chief counsel IRS, 1963; ptnr. DLA Piper, Balt. Lectr. Georgetown Univ. Sch. Law, Univ. Md. Sch. Law, Loyola Coll. Bd. dir. & treas. World Trade Ctr. Inst., Balt.; counsel Econ. Alliance Greater Balt.; mem. bd. vis. Univ. Md. Balt. County; mem. bd. U. Md. Med. Sys. Office: Duane Morris LLP 111 S Calvert St Ste 2000 Baltimore MD 21202

SIROTY, WILLIAM CHARLES, physician; b. NYC, June 9, 1951; s. Daniel Hirsch and Eileen (Gusman) S. BS, SUNY, Stony Brook, 1973; MD, Georgetown U., Washington, DC, 1977. Diplomate Am. Bd. Internal Medicine, Am. Bd. Allergy-Immunology. Intern in internal medicine Beth Israel Med. Ctr., NYC, 1977-78, resident in internal medicine, 1977-78; fellow allergy and immunology NY Hosp.-Cornell U. Med. Ctr., 1980-82;

pvt. practice NYC, 1982-94; staff physician Nashua (NH) Med. Group, 1994—. Editor: NH News Links, 2000—. Co-founder, first co-chair Gay People in Medicine Caucus Am. Med. Student Assn., 1976—77; active NH State Dem. Com., 1998—2006, Hillsborough County Dem. Com., NH, 1998—2006, vice-chmn., 2004—06; del. Dem. Nat. Conv., 2000, 2004; chair Dems. Amherst, 2002—06; bd. dirs. Democracy for NH, 2006—, Elizabeth Streb Ringside, Inc., NH Civil Liberties Union. Mem. Am. Acad. Allergy, Asthma and Immunology, NH Med. Soc. Office: Nashua Med Group 173 Daniel Webster Hwy Nashua NH 03060-5224

SIRRI, ERIK R., federal agency administrator, economist; BS in Astonomy, Calif. Inst. of Technology, 1979; MBA, U. of Calif.: Irvine, 1984; PhD in Finance, UCLA, 1990. Rsch. scientist Nichols Rsch. Corp., Newport Beach, Calif., 1979—83; asst. prof. Harvard Bus. Sch., Boston, 1989—95, Babson Coll., Babson Park, Mass., 1995—96, assoc. prof., 1999—2004, prof., Walter H. Capenter chair, 2004—; chief economist US SEC, 1996—99, dir. divsn. market regulation, 2006—. Econ. advisory bd. Nasdaq Stock Market, 2000—02, Nat. Assn. Securities Dealers, 2001—05; gov. Boston Stock Exch., 2003—; bd. mem. Boston Options Exch., 2004—; advisory bd. Proxy Governance Inc., 2004—; visiting scholar Harvard Law Sch., 2005—06. Recipient Morgan Stanley Microstructure award, 2005; Olin Fellow, Cornell Law Sch., 2000. Mem.: Am. Fin. Assn., Quantitative Work Alliance for Applied Fin., Edn., and Wisdom (QWAFAFEW), Soc. Fin. Studies. Office: SEC 100 F St NE Washington DC 20549

SIRVÉN, JOSÉ E., lawyer; b. Camaguey, Cuba, Aug. 28, 1956; AA with honors, Miami-Dade CC, 1976; BBA in Acctg. with honors, Fla. Internat. U., 1978; JD cum laude, U. Miami, 1981. Ptnr. Holland & Knight LLP, Miami, Fla., mem. dir. com. Articles and comment editor U. Miami Law Review, 1980—81. Mem.: Cuban Am. Bar Assn., Fla. Bar, Dade County Bar Assn. Office: Holland & Knight LLP 701 Brickell Ave Ste 3000 Miami FL 33131 Office Phone: 305-789-7784. Business E-Mail: jsirven@hklaw.com.

SISCHY, INGRID BARBARA, editor, art critic; b. Johannesburg, Republic of South Africa, Mar. 2, 1952; came to U.S., 1967; d. Benjamin and Claire S. BS, Sarah Lawrence Coll., 1973; PhD (hon.), Moore Coll. Art, 1987. Assoc. editor Print Collector's Newsletter, NYC, 1974-77; dir. Printed Matter, NYC, 1977-78; curatorial intern Mus. Modern Art, NYC, 1978-79; editor ArtForum Mag., NYC, 1979-88; editor-in-chief Interview, NYC, 1989—. Office: Interview Magazine 575 Broadway Fl 5 New York NY 10012-3230

SISIOPIKU, VIRGINIA P., civil engineer; b. Thessaloniki, Greece, July 16, 1965; d. Poulios and Paraskevi (Rammou) S.; m. Yiannis Argyropoulos, Sept. 12, 1993; 2 children. BSCE, Aristotelian U. Thessaloniki, 1988; MS in Civil Engring., U. Ill., Chgo., 1991, PhD in Civil Engring., 1994. Registered profl. engr., Greece. Rsch. and tchg. asst. U. Ill., Chgo., 1989-93; rsch. fellow Fed. Hwy Adminstrn., McLean, Va., 1992-93; transp. cons. P/R Michaels Assocs., Ltd., Chgo., 1994-95; assoc. rsch. scientist U. Ill./IVHS Lab., Chgo., 1994-95; adj. asst. prof. Ill. Inst. Tech., Chgo., 1994-95; asst. prof. Mich. State U., East Lansing, Mich., 1995—2002; assoc. prof. U. Ala., Birmingham, 2002—. Com. mem. Mich. Dept. Transp., Lansing, 1995—, ITS Soc. Mich., Detroit, 1996—. Faculty advisor UABITE Student Chpt., 2002—. Recipient Grant Shaw Meml. award Ill. Assn. Hwy. Engrs., Palatine, Ill., 1992, Faculty Fellowship award Fed. Hwy. Adminstrn., Washington, 1995, 98, 2003, Pres.'s Tchg. Excellence award U. Alabama, Birmingham, 2007; Helen Overly scholarship Women Transp. Seminar, Seattle, 1991, scholar NSF ADVANCE, 2005, 06, 07. Mem. Transp. Rsch. Bd., Inst. Transp. Engrs. (pres. 1993-94, Outstanding Student Paper Nat. award 1991), Intelligent Transp. Soc. Mich., Safety Mgmt. Systems. Avocations: travel, baking, stamp collecting/philately. Office: U Ala Birmingham 1075 13th St S Birmingham AL 35294

SISK, CHERYL, neuroscientist, educator; b. Waco, Tex., July 4, 1954; BA in Psych., Baylor U., Waco, Tex., 1974; MS in Psych., Fla. State U., Tallahassee, 1976, PhD in Psychobiology/Neuroscience, 1980. Postdoctoral rschr. dept. neurobiology and physiology Northwestern U., 1980—82; rsch. assoc. dept. zoology U. Tex. Inst. Reproductive Biology, Austin, 1983—85; asst. prof. dept. psych. and neuroscience prog. Mich. State U., 1985—89, assoc. prof., 1989, prof., 1995—, adj. assoc. prof., prof. dept. physiology, 1990—. Dir. Interdepartmental Grad. Neuroscience Prog. Mich. State U., 1998—. Contbr. articles to profl. jours., chapters to books; mem. adv. bd.: Jour. Biol. Rhythms, 1995—97, mem. editl. bd.: Endocrinology, 1999—2002, Jour. Exptl. Biology and Medicine, 2004—. Mem.: Soc. Study Reproduction, Soc. Neuroscience, Soc. Behavioral Neuroendocrinology (treas. 2004—), Endocrine Soc., AAAS, Am. Neuroendocrine Soc. Office: Dept Psych Neuroscience Prog Mich State U East Lansing MI 48824 Office Phone: 517-355-5253. Office Fax: 517-432-2744. E-mail: sisk@msu.edu.

SISK, DANIEL ARTHUR, lawyer; b. Albuquerque, July 12, 1927; s. Arthur Henry and Myrl (Hope) S.; m. Katharine Banning, Nov. 27, 1954; children: John, Sarah, Thomas. BA, Stanford U., 1950, JD, 1954. Bar: N.Mex. 1955, Calif. 1954. Ptnr. firm Modrall, Sperling, Roehl, Harris & Sisk, Albuquerque, 1954-70, 71—; justice N.Mex. Supreme Ct., Santa Fe, 1970. Chmn. bd. Sunwest Fin. Svcs., Inc., Albuquerque, 1975-90. Pres. Legal Aid Soc., Albuquerque, 1960-61; trustee Sandia Sch., 1968-72, Albuquerque Acad., 1971-73, A.T. & S.F. Meml. Hosps., Topeka, 1966-82; bd. dirs. N.Mex. Sch. Banking Found., 1981-85. Served with USNR, 1945-46, PTO; to capt. USMCR, 1951-52, Korea. Mem. N.Mex. Bar Assn., Albuquerque Bar Assn. (dir. 1962-63), ABA, State Bar Calif. Presbyn. (elder). Office: 500 4th St NW Albuquerque NM 87102-5324

SISK, EILEEN VICTORIA, writer, journalist; b. Henderson, Nev., Nov. 8, 1952; d. Hugh Albert and Susan Apathy (Kuyrkendall) S.; m. Richard James Adams, Dec. 28, 1974 (div. Mar. 1979); m. Stephan Rudolph Tetreault, Aug. 29, 1981 (div. Oct. 1993); children: Jeffrey Hugh Tetreault, Douglas Gerard Tetreault; m. Samuel Ragan Mellar, Apr. 14, 1995 (div. June 2001). BA in Comm., Calif. State U., Fullerton, 1979. Feature writing intern L.A. Times, 1977-78; pub. info. asst. Orange County Transit Dist., Garden Grove, Calif., 1978; copy editor Las Vegas Rev. Jour., 1978-79, Sunday editor, 1979-81; copy editor U.S. C. of C., Washington, 1981-83, The Washington Post, 1982-86, design editor, 1987-92; copy editor II The Tennessean, Nashville, 2000—. Freelance journalist various media outlets including XM Satellite Radio, Continuum Ency., Popular Music of the World, Am. Cowboy, Nev., others. Author: Honky-Tonks: Guide to Country Dancin' and Romancin', 1995. Vol. NOW, Washington, 1981, Gloucester County Pub. Schs., 1992-99. Recipient 4 Merit awards Calif. Photographers Pro Show, 1978. Mem.: Investigative Reporters and Editors, Soc. Newspaper Design (4 awards of excellence 1990, 1992), Soc. Profl. Journalists (profl. devel. com. 1986—92). Avocations: running, reading, racquetball, cooking, dance. E-mail: eileensisk@earthlink.net.

SISK, FRED DEAN, retired cartographer; b. Johnson City, Tenn., May 26, 1940; s. Aubrey Mackenzie and Violet Mae (McCartt) S.; m. Martha Lynn Robinson, Aug. 25, 1963. BS, East Tenn. State U., 1962; MS, George Mason U., 1984. Cartographer Def. Mapping Agy., Brookmont, Md., 1965—79, sr. cartographer, sr. instr., master instr. Ft. Belvior, Va., 1979—81, course mgr., 1981—88, dep. divsn. chief, 1983—88, new employees tng. coord. Bethesda, Md., 1988—89; tng. coord. Def. Mapping Agy. Reston Ctr., Va., 1989—90, security analyst, 1990—95; ret., 1995. Mem. scholarship com. George Mason U. Alumni Assn., Fairfax, 1990; mem. Rep. Nat. Com., Rep. Presdl. Task Force, Washington, 1990—, adv. com. House of Dels., 54th Dist., 1995-2002; officer of election City of Fredericksburg, 1995—, mem. pub. transit adv. bd., 1996—, chmn. memls. adv. commn., 2000-03; notary public, 1996—, security officer, 1996—; pres. Fox Run Homeowners Assn., 1996—. 1st lt. battery commdr. U.S. Army, 1962-64. Mem.: NRA, Internat. Freelance Photographers Orgn. (master photographer 2004—, Lifetime Achievement award in Photography, Master Photographer Regnant), Civil War Round Table. Baptist. Home: 18 Devonshire Dr Fredericksburg VA 22401-2100

SISK, GREGORY CHARLES, lawyer, educator; b. Des Moines, May 29, 1960; s. James Anderson and Roberta Jean (Thornburg) S.; m. Melinda Fay Gilchrist, June 14, 1981; 1 child, Caitlin Anne. Student, Western Mont. Coll., 1978; BA in Polit. Sci., Mont. State U., 1981; JD, U. Wash., 1984. Bar: Wash. 1985, Iowa 1992, US Ct. Appeals (3d cir. and 9th cir.) 1986, US Ct. Appeals (2d, 5th, 11th and DC cir.) 1987, US Ct. Appeals (4th, 8th and fed. cir.) 1988, US Ct. Appeals (1st cir.) 1989, US Supreme Ct. 1988. Legis. asst. US Senate, Washington, 1984-85; jud. clk. US Ct. Appeals (9th cir.), Seattle, 1985-86; appellate staff atty. civil div. US Dept. Justice, Washington, 1986-89; assoc. Karr, Tuttle & Campbell, Seattle, 1989-91; asst. prof. Drake U., Des Moines, 1991-94, assoc. prof., 1994-97, prof., 1997—2003, Richard M. and Anita Calkins disting. prof., 1999—2003; prof. U. St. Thomas, Mpls., 2003—. Mem. ABA, Am. Law Inst., Fed. Bar Assn., Christian Legal Soc., Order of Coif, Nat. Order of Barristers, Law and Soc. Assn., Am. Polit. Sci. Assn. Republican. Roman Catholic. Office: Univ St Thomas Sch Law 1000 La Salle Ave Minneapolis MN 55403-2005 Office Phone: 651-962-4923. Business E-Mail: gcsisk@stthomas.edu.

SISK, JANE ELIZABETH, economist, educator; b. West Reading, Pa., Sept. 23, 1942; 2 children. BA with honors, Brown U., 1963; MA, George Washington U., 1965; PhD, McGill U., Montreal, Que., Can., 1976. Cons. Nat. Planning Assn., Washington, 1976; scholar VA, Washington, 1978-81; rsch. dir. Office Tech. Assessment, U.S. Congress, Washington, 1976-78, sr. analyst, 1981-84, sr. assoc., 1984-91. Vis. prof. Columbia U. Sch. Pub. Health, N.Y.C., 1990-91, prof., 1992—99; prof. Mt. Sinai Sch. Medicine, N.Y.C., 1999—, dir. divsn. health care stats. Nat. Ctr. for Health Stats., Ctrs. for Disease Control, Hyattsville, Md., 2004—. Co-author: Toward Rational Technology in Medicine, 1981; mem. editl. bd. Internat. Jour. Tech. Assessment in Health Care, 1987—, vol. editor, 1990, 98; asst. editor Am. Jour. Pub. Health, 1990-91; mem. editl. bd. Health Svcs. Rsch., 1994—; contbr. articles to profl. jours. Pres. Internat Soc. Tech. Assessment in Health Care, 1991-93, bd. dirs., 1987-95; mem. N.Y. State Task Force on Clin. Guidelines & Med. Tech. Assessment, 1994-96; mem. study sect. on health care quality and effectiveness rsch. U.S. Agy. for Health Care Policy and Rsch., 1997-2001. Elisah Benjamin Andrews scholar Brown U., 1961, 63; Bronfman fellow McGill U., 1971. Fellow Assn. for Health Svcs. Rsch.; mem. Inst. of Medicine, NAS (mem. cancer policy bd. 1997-2000, inst. medicine, 2001—), Phi Beta Kappa. Office Phone: 301-458-4157.

SISKA, JOHN EDWARD, foundation administrator, publishing executive; b. Gary, Ind., Oct. 15, 1940; s. Andrew and Ann Mary Siska. AA in Mktg., Ivy Tech., Gary, Ind., 1978; student, Edison 5th Coll., Trenton, NJ, 1959—67. Printer/proofreader Post TriBune, Gary, Ind., 1958—67, Chgo. Tribune, Chgo., 1967—73, Chgo. Sun Times, Chgo., 1967—73, Hammond Times, Ind., 1967—73; owner/mgr. Compass Newspaper, Hammond, Ind., 1973—76; sales WNWI Radio, Valparaiso, 1976—77; adv. mgr. CEN Flo Publs., Chgo., 1978—89; owner, CEO, rep., broker John Edward Siska Mfg., 1989—95. Dir. Portage Twp. Food Pantry, Ind., 2003, Gabriel's Shelter, Ind., 2004, North Shore Health Ctrs., Ind., 2004; CEO John Edward Siska Found., Valparaiso, 2004—. Mem.: Porter County Triad, United Nations Assn. of Am., Chgo. Coun. on Foreign Rels., Acad. Polit. Sci., Portage C. of C. Democrat. Presbyn. Avocations: skiing, birdwatching. Office Phone: 219-764-2158.

SISKA, ROBERT JOHN, software engineer; b. Evergreen Park, Ill., May 28, 1949; s. Emil Thomas and Marie Clara Siska; m. Jane Suzan Dwyer, May 25, 1979; children: Johanna, Charlotte. BA, U. Mass., 1974. Advt. coord. Goldblatt Bros., Chgo., 1976-79; tech. writer Calif Fed., LA, 1980-82; software engr. Informatics Gen. Corp., Canoga Park, Calif., 1982-84, Team Quest Corp., Clear Lake, Iowa, 2005; software programmer Great We. Bank, Northridge, Calif., 1984-86; sr. software engr. Litton Computer Svcs., Woodland Hills, Calif., 1986-90; sr. software devel. Legent Corp., Woodland Hills, 1990-94; sr. systems programmer Nat. Computer Sys., Iowa City, 1994-97; sr. software devel. Storage Tek, Louisville, 1997—2003; sys. programmer State of Colo., Lakewood, 2003—05; software engr. TeamQuest Internat., Clear Lake, Iowa, 2005—. Cons. advisor Johnson County, Iowa City, 1996—97; creator, coord. Craven Maven Record Co., pres., 1995—. Cons. advisor Johnson County Computer Com., Iowa City, 1996—97. Mem.: Network and Sys. Profls. Assn., Johnson County Blues Soc., Colo. Blues Soc. Avocations: record company, marathon running, literature, music. Office: TeamQuest Corp One Team Quest Way Clear Lake IA 50428 Home: 412 Main Ave Clear Lake IA 50428 Home Phone: 303-579-1972; Office Phone: 641-357-2700. Personal E-mail: bobsiska@aol.com. Business E-Mail: bob.siska@teamquest.com.

SISKE, REGINA, artist; b. Varen Muritz, Germany, Oct. 11, 1944; d. Peter Paul and Olga Vanda Markunas; m. Roger Charles Siske, May 31, 1969 (dec.); children: Kelly, Jennifer, Kimberly. BSN, U. Ill., 1966; postgrad. in MSN program, U. Mich., 1968—69; ind. fine art studies, North Shore Art League, Winnetka, Ill., 1970s, Alain Gavin, Art Inst. Chgo., 1980s, Tom James, Wilmette, Ill., 2000—; Asian brush painting and calligraphy studies Lampo Leong, U. Mo., 1998—; Asian brush painting and Chinese calligraphy studies Madeleine Jossem and Qi-Gu Jiang, Art Inst., Chgo., 1999—2002; Asian brush painting and Chinese calligraphy studies Moon Yan Huen, City Coll., San Francisco, 1999—2002; Asian brush painting and Chinese calligraphy studies, Charles Liu, Westmont, Ill., 1999—, numerous workshops, NYC and Chgo. RN Ill., 1966. Staff med.-surg. nurse Presbyn.-St. Luke's Hosp., Chgo., 1966—67, Mass. Gen. Hosp., Boston, 1967—68; nursing staff devel. VA Rsch. Hosp., Chgo., 1969—70, Evanston/Northwestern Hosp., Evanston, Ill., 1971, St. Francis Hosp., Evanston, Ill., 1971—73; nursing cons. Evanston Hosp., 1971; rsch. and quality control studies VA Hosp., Chgo., 1969—70; cmty. outreach and edn. Evanston and St. Francis Hosps., 1971—73. Chair Asian art exhibit and workshop Suburban Fine Arts Ctr., 2004. Exhibitions include Mobile Mus. Art, Ala., 1998, Bayard Cutting Arboretum, LI, NY, 1999, Suburban Fine Arts Ctr., Highland Park, Ill., 1999—2007 (award, 2001), Alliance Gallery, Indpls. Mus. Art, 2000—01, Strathmore Hall of Arts, Bethesda, Md., 2000 (award, 2000), 2003 (award, 2003), Courthouse Gallery, Norfolk, Va., 2001, Nat. Juried Virtual Exhbn., Internet, 2002, 2004, Chinese Fine Arts Soc., Westmont, Ill., 2001, Chgo. Bot. Gardens, Art League Alliance, 2004, J. Harrison Smith Fine Art Gallery, Clearwater, Fla., 2005, Bloomington Art Ctr., Minn., 2006, Represented in permanent collections. Vol. Kellogg Cancer Rsch. Ctr., Evanston Hosp., 1988—89; bd. dir. St. Elizabeth Nursery Sch., Glencoe, Ill., 1981—82, Josselyn Ctr. for Mental Health, Northfield, Ill., 1989—93, devel. chmn., 1992—93. Named hon. lifetime trustee, Josselyn Ctr. Mental Health, 1993—, Honoree, Josselyn Ctr. Ann. Benefit, 2006. Mem.: Nat. Sumi-e Soc. Am., Midwest Sumi-e Soc. (program dir. 2000—07). Avocations: piano, jewelry design, skiing, swimming, tennis. Home and Studio: 248 Hawthorn Ave Glencoe IL 60022 Fax: 847-835-2836. E-mail: sisker@aol.com.

SISKIN, EDWARD JOSEPH, engineering and construction company executive; b. Bklyn., Apr. 30, 1941; s. Haskell and Sylvia (Steckler) S.; m. Patricia Ann Moore, June 26, 1965 (div. Apr. 1990); children: Candice P. Howard, Cristin Jo Blackman; m. Jean Elizabeth Bowen, Dec. 17, 1994. BSEE, U. Pa., 1963; cert., Bettis Reactor Engring. Sch., West Mifflin, Pa., 1965; postgrad., George Washington U., 1963—67. Registered profl. engr., Pa., Mass., N.Y., N.J., Ill., Mich., Fla., W.Va., Ind., S.C., Tex., La., Nebr., Calif., Ala. Engr. U.S. Atomic Energy Commn., Washington, 1963-67, field office mgr. Pitts., 1967-70, Groton, Conn., 1970-77; project mgr. Stone & Webster Engring. Corp., Boston, 1977-78, asst. engring. mgr., 1978-79, engring. mgr. NYC, 1979-83, v.p., mgr., 1984-86, sr. v.p., mgr. Cherry Hill, NJ, 1987-88, exec. v.p., 1988-90, also bd. dirs. Boston; gen. mgr. Superconducting Supercollider Lab., Dallas, 1990-94; pres. Enerjoin Svcs., Inc., 1994—, 2005—; dir. office fissile materials disposition US Nat. Nuc. Security Adminstrn., 2000—05. Mem. adv. com. Inst. of Nuc. Power Ops., Atlanta, 1987-90, adv. bd. Ctr. for Chem. Plant Safety, N.Y.C., 1988-90. Bd. dirs. PenJerDel Coun., Phila., 1987-90. Lt. USN, 1963-69. Office: PO Box 445 Voorhees NJ 08043 Personal E-mail: jeananded@comcast.net.

SISKIND, ARTHUR MICHAEL, lawyer; b. NY, Oct. 11, 1938; s. William and Sylvia (Schuman) S.; m. Mary Ann Silverman, Nov. 10, 1962; children: Laura, Julie, Kenneth. BA in Liberal Arts, Cornell U., 1960, LLB with distinction, 1962. Ptnr. Squadron, Ellenoff, Plesent & Lehrer, NYC, 1970-91; group gen. counsel News Corp., NYC, 1991—2004, exec. v.p., 1991—96, sr. exec. v.p., 1996—2004, sr. advisor to chmn., 2005—, bd. dirs.; sr. exec. v.p., gen. counsel Fox Entertainment Group. Inc., 1998—2004. Adj. prof. Georgetown Law Ctr., Washington, 2005—07, Cornell Law Sch., Ithaca, 2007—; bd. dirs. Brit. Sky Broadcasting Group, PLC, NDS, PLC; adv. coun. sch. journalism CUNY, 2005. Active Cornell Law Sch. Adv. Coun., 1996—; nat. chmn. Cornell Law Sch. Alumni Fund, 1998-01, Citizens Budget Commn. NYC. Capt. U.S. Army, 1963-65. Mem. ABA, City Bar Assn., Cornell Club, Stockbridge Golf Club. Office: News Corp 1211 Avenue Of The Americas New York NY 10036-8795 Office Phone: 212-852-7007. Business E-Mail: asiskind@newscorp.com.

SISKIND, DONALD HENRY, lawyer; b. Providence, Dec. 25, 1937; s. Samuel and Sadie (Wasserman) S.; m. Beth Mohel, July 15, 1962; children: Steven M., Edward M. BS, U. Pa., 1959; LLB, Columbia U., 1962. Bar: Mass. 1962, N.Y. 1963. Assoc. Marshall Bratter Greene Allison & Tucker, NYC, 1962-69, ptnr., 1969-82, Katten Muchin Rosenman, 1982—99, of counsel, 1999—. Mem. adv. bd. Chgo. Title Ins. Co.; chmn. various seminars Practicing Law Inst., 1974—; vis. lectr. Columbia U. Sch. Law, 1993-95; mem. adv. bd. Wharton Real Estate Ctr. Contbr. articles to profl. jours. Pres. Greenville Community Coun., 1974-76; pres. bd. edn. Union Free Sch. Dist., Scarsdale, N.Y., 1978-81 Mem.: ABA, Am. Coll. Real Estate Lawyers (past pres.), Anglo Am. Real Property Inst. (past chmn.), N.Y. State Bar Assn., Assn. of Bar of City of N.Y., Phi Alpha Psi. Home: 876 Park Ave New York NY 10021-1832 Office: Katten Muchin Rosenman 575 Madison Ave Fl 15 New York NY 10022-2585 Home Phone: 212-772-9061; Office Phone: 212-940-8610. Business E-Mail: donald.siskind@kattenlaw.com.

SISLEY, EMILY LUCRETIA, psychologist, writer; b. North Charleroi, Pa., May 7, 1930; d. Frederick William and Harriet Watkins (Litman) S. PhD in Clin. Psychology, L.I. U., 1972. Diplomate Am. Bd. Med. Psychotherapists. Mng. editor Med. Jours., Harper & Row, NYC, 1960-67; freelance med. writer-editor NYC, 1967-95; supervising psychologist, dept. psychiatry Roosevelt Hosp., NYC, 1972-77; clin. instr. Columbia Univ. Coll. Physicians and Surgeons, NYC, 1975-77; chief psychologist Gramercy Park Inst., NYC, 1978-84; staff therapist MedcoBehavioral Care Sys., NYC, 1984-95; ret., 1995. Cons. Internat. Jour. Group Tensions, N.Y.C., 1968-72. Illustrator: You and Your Brain, 1963, Thomas Alva Edison award, 1963; co-author: The Vitamin C Connection, 1983; contbr. articles to profl. and lit. jours. Fellow Am. Bd. Med. Psychotherapists; mem. APA, N.Y. Acad. Scis. Democrat. Episcopalian. Avocations: music, golf, skiing, sailing.

SISLEY, NINA MAE, physician, public health service officer; b. Jacksonville, Fla., Aug. 19, 1924; d. Leonard Percy and Verna (Martin) S.; m. George W. Fischer, May 16, 1962 (dec. 1990). BA, Tex. State Coll. for Women, 1944; MD, U. Tex., Galveston, 1950; MPH, U. Mich., 1963. Intern City of Detroit Receiving Hosp., 1950-51; resident in gen. practice St. Mary's Infirmary, Galveston, Tex., 1951-52; sch. physician Galveston Ind. Sch. Dist., 1953-56; dir. med. svcs. San Antonio Health Dept., 1960-63, acting dir., 1963-64; resident in pub. health Tex. Dept. Pub. Health, San Antonio, 1963-65; dir. cmty. health svcs. Corpus Christi-Nueces County Dept. Health, Tex., 1964-67; dir. Tb control region 5 Tex. Dept. Health, Corpus Christi, 1967-73; chief chronic illness control City of Houston Health Dept., 1973-78; dir. pub. health region 11 Tex. Dept. Health, Rosenberg, 1978-87; dir. Corpus Christi-Nueces County Dept. Pub. Health, 1987—2002. Lectr. Incarnate Word Coll., San Antonio, 1963-64; adj. prof. U. Tex. Sch. Pub. Health, Houston, 1980—2002; adj. prof. Tex. A&M U., Corpus Christi, 1997—2002; pvt. practice Galveston, Stockdale, Hereford and Borger, Tex., 1952-59; mem. adv. bd. Cmty. Adv. Coun.; clin. instr. U. Tex. Health Sci. Ctr., San Antonio, 1997-2002 Mem. Nueces County Child Fatality REv. Com.; mem. adv. com. Nueces County Hosp. Dist.; mem. adv. bd. Alzheimers Assn.; mem. health adv. bd. Corpus Christi Ind. Sch. Dist.; bd. dirs. Coastal Bend chpt. ARC, Corpus Christi, 1990—94, 2003—07, pres., 1990—91; bd. dirs. United Way-Coastal Bend, Coastal Bend Coalition on AIDS, 1988—94, Charlie's Place Alcohol and Drug Rehab. Ctr. Fellow Am. Coll. Preventive Medicine; mem. Tex. Med. Assn., Nueces County Med. Soc. (pres. 1997-98), Tex. Assn. Pub. Health Physicians, Tex. Pub. Health Assn. (pres. 1991-92), Local Emergency Planning Assn., Long Term Health Assn., Asthma Coalition. Episcopalian. Avocations: fishing, crossword puzzles, raising african violets. Home: 62 Rock Creek Dr Corpus Christi TX 78412-4214 E-mail: nsisley@sbcglobal.org.

SISNEY, NED, education educator; b. Kansas City, Mo., Feb. 9, 1947; s. Dwight E. and Jeann A. Sisney; m. Mary A. Petersen, Sept. 9, 1988; 1 child, Kaitlyn J. Master's, Concordia U., Mequon, Wis., 2003. Cert. tchr. Wis., 2006. Prof. Concordia U., 1988—. Actor(and dir.): ednl. and profl. theatre. Mem.: Pi Kappa Delta (life), Actor's Equity Assn. (life), Phi Delta Kappa (life), Alpha Psi Omega (life; chpt. pres. 1968—69). Home: 7808 W Rolling Field Dr Mequon WI 53097 Home Phone: 262-512-1590.

SISNEY, PHILIP LYNN, retired pilot; b. Tulsa, Okla., Nov. 20, 1939; s. Edgar Lynn and Mary Elizabeth Sisney; m. Debora Ann Noble, June 4, 1988; children: Christopher Leland, Steven Douglas. BS, U. of Okla., Norman, 1960. Lic. airline transport pilot FAA. Airline capt. Continental Airlines, Houston, 1966—2001; ret. Naval aviator USN. Local rep. USGA, El Paso, Tex. Lt. comdr. USNR. Avocation: golf. Home: 6171 Los Felinos Cir El Paso TX 79912 Home Phone: 915-581-3421.

SISNEY, SHERLEEN SUE, secondary education educator; b. Stillwater, Okla., Oct. 19, 1946; m. Lee Sisney, June 11, 1969; 1 child, Shara Lee. B.S. in Secondary Edn., Okla. State U., 1968; M.Ed., U. Louisville, 1975. Tchr. Merrill Jr. High Sch., Denver, 1968-69, Monterey High Sch., Calif., 1969-71, Ballard High Sch., Louisville, 1971—92; exec. dir., Ky. Gov.'s Scholars Program, dir., Career Acad., Louisville; mem. pub.'s adv. council Quantum Communications, Inc.; dir. New Foundations in Edn., 1984—; mem. adv. council tchr. and edn. div. Met. Life Found.; mem. Gov.'s Council on Edn. Reform, Joint Council Econ. Edn.; mem. task force social studies Ky. Dept. Edn. Mem. Okla. State U. Centennial Adv. Commn., Jr. League Louisville. Named Nat. Tchr. of Yr., 1984. Recipient Chris Mattingly award for Outstanding Leadership in Ky., Univ. Louisville, 1999. Mem. Ky. Edn. Assn. (Outstanding Tchr. 1979-80), Phi Delta Kappa, others. Home: 8002 Montero Ct Prospect KY 40059-9424 Office: Gov Scholars Program Ste 210 1024 Capital Ctr Dr Frankfort KY 40601 *

SISSEL, GEORGE ALLEN, manufacturing executive, lawyer, engineer; b. Chgo., July 30, 1936; s. William Worth and Hannah Ruth (Harlan) S.; m. Mary Ruth Runsvold, Oct. 5, 1968; children: Jenifer Ruth, Gregory Allen. BSEE, U. Colo., 1958; JD cum laude, U. Minn., 1966. Bar: Colo. 1966, Ind. 1973, U.S. Supreme Ct. 1981. Assoc. Sherman & Howard, Denver, 1966-70; with Ball Corp., Broomfield, Colo., 1970—2002, CEO, 1995-2001, chmn. bd., 1996—2002, also bd. dirs. Bd. dirs. Ciber, Inc. Assoc. editor: U. Minn. Law Rev., 1965-66. Served with USN, 1954-65. Mem. Colo. Assn. Commerce & Industry, Order of Coif, MIT Soc. Sr. Execs. (bd. govs. 1987-95), Sigma Chi, Sigma Tau, Eta Kappa Nu. Lodges: Rotary. Methodist.

SISSMAN, LIRON, artist, painter; d. Arie and Atara Sissman. BSc magna cum laude, The Hebrew U., Jerusalem, 1987; attended, Avni Fine Art Inst., Tel Aviv, 1988, NY Acad. Art, 1999; MBA, NYU, 1991. One-man shows include Taro Pharms., Hawthorne, NY, 2002 (Purchase award, 2002), Sound Fed. Savs., Cos., Cob, Conn., 2004, Patriot Bank, Old Greenwich, Ct., 2004, Waltuch Gallery, Tenafly, NJ, 2004, Block Gallery, Montclair, NJ, 2005, Shimon and Sara Birnbaum Gallery, Bridgewater, NJ, 2005, The Synaptic Art Gallery, Paramus, NJ, 2005, ADP Hdqrs., 2005, Watchung Arts Ctr., NJ, 2005, Johnson & Johnson World Hdqrs. Gallery, New Brunswick, NJ, 2006, The Pk. Ave Club, Florham Pk., NJ, 2006, Walter Skulski Art Gallery, Clark, NJ, 2007, The Donald B. Palmer Museum, Springfield, NJ, 2007, The Atrium Gallery, YJCC, Washington Township, NJ, 2007, two person show, Synagogue for the Arts, NYC, 2006, 2007, three person show, Best Little Art Gallery, Mahwah, NJ, 2005, Perkins Gallery, Stoughton, Mass., 2005, Euro Art Gallery, Montclair, NJ, 2006, Pomona Cultural Center, Pomona, NY, 2007, commd. oil painting, Bar Scene, 2002, Donna, 2003, Donna II, 2004, Hanna, 2004, Sea Scape, 2004, Leaving the Nest, 2004, Steve Finley, 2005, Coupling, 2006, Aviv, 2007, Alpine Golf, 2007, exhibitions include Cmty. Arts Assn., Ridgewood Art Inst., 2002, Salmagundi Club, NYC, 2002, 2003, Westminster Gallery, 2003, St. John on the Mountain, Bernardville, NJ, 2004, Audobon Artists, 2004, Gallery 214, Montclair, NJ, 2005, Am. Artists Profl. League, Salmagundi Club, NYC, 2005, Hudson Valley Art Assn., Newington-Cropsey Mus., Hastings-on-Hudson, NY, 2005, The Art Center of Northern NJ, New Milford, NJ, 2007, exhibited in group shows at Madison Gallery, NYC, 2000, Limner Gallery, NYC, 2000, The Artist Gallery, Ridgewood, 2001, Midday Gallery, Englewood, NJ, 2004, Montclair State U. Art Galleries, Montclair, NJ, 2004, Port of Call Gallery, Warwick, NY, 2004, Geneva Gallery, Morristown, NJ, 2004, Galleria Nuova, Warwick, NY, 2005, C. Magor Gallery, Ridgewood, NJ, 2005, Geary Gallery, Darien, Conn., 2007 (ongoing representation), Peter McPhee Fine Arts, Stone Harbor, NJ, 2007 (ongoing representation), Also represented by JSO Art Assoc., Westport, CT. Represented in permanent collections PeproTech, Inc., NJ, Taro Pharms., NY, Sq. Bus. Products, Inc., NJ, Potomac Homes, NJ, Lounge Zen, NJ, AtlantiCare Med. Ctr., NJ, pvt. collections, Can., US, UK, and Israel; contbr. articles to varoius publs. featuring artist work; featured guest: PKRG-TV. Named Best in Show, Mid Rockland Arts Festival, Nanuet Hebrew Ctr., 2004; recipient Cert. of Achievement, 2004, 1st Pl. Oil award, Bergenfield Arts Festival Collection, 2005, Best of Art, Edgewater Arts Festival, 2006, hon. mention, Renewal Interpreted, Art Ctr. Northern NJ, 2007, 1st prize, Oil and Acrylic Painting, Trees, Waltuch Gallery, 2007. Mem.: Landscape Artists Internat., Studio Montclair (assoc.), Audubon Artists (assoc.), Allied Artists Am. (assoc.), Am. Artists Profl. League (assoc.). Office Phone: 201-952-1666. Business E-Mail: liron@liron.com.

SISSOM, LEIGHTON ESTEN, engineering educator, dean, consultant; b. Manchester, Tenn., Aug. 26, 1934; s. Willie Esten and Bertha Sarah (Davis) S.; m. Evelyn Janelle Lee, June 13, 1953; children: Terry Lee, Denny Leighton. BS, Middle Tenn. State Coll., 1956; BS in Mech. Engring., Tenn. Technol. U., 1962; MS in Mech. Engring., Ga. Inst. Tech., 1964, PhD, 1965. Diplomate Nat. Acad. Forensic Engrs.; registered profl. engr., Tenn. Draftsman Westinghouse Electric Corp., Tullahoma, 1953-57; mech. designer ARO, Inc., Tullahoma, 1957-58; instr. mech. engring. Tenn. Technol. U., Cookeville, 1958-62, chmn. dept. mech. engring., 1965-79, dean engring., 1979-88, dean of engring. emeritus, 1988—; prin. cons. Sissom & Assocs., Cookeville, Tenn., 1962—. Bd. dirs. Accreditation Bd. Engring. and Tech., N.Y.C., 1978-86, treas., 1982-86. Author: (with Donald R. Pitts) Elements of Transport Phenomena, 1972, Heat Transfer, 1977, 1,000 Solved Problems in Heat Transfer, 1991; contbr. An Attorney's Guide to Engineering, 1986; contbr. articles to various publs. Fellow ASME (sr. v.p. 1982-86, gov. 1986-88, Golden medallion), Am. Soc. Engring. Edn. (bd. dirs. 1984-87, pres. 1991-92), Accreditation Bd. Engring. and Tech.; mem. NSPE, Soc. Automotive Engrs., Nat. Engring. Deans Coun. (chmn. 1984-87), Order of the Engr. (chmn. bd. govs. 1994-96), Tau Beta Pi (v.p. 1986-89, councillor 1986-89). Home and Office: 1151 Shipley Church Rd Cookeville TN 38501-7730 Office Phone: 931-526-9123. Business E-Mail: sissom@frontiernet.net.

SISSON, BERNICE BELAIR, advocate; b. St. Paul, Oct. 25, 1922; d. Kenneth Theodore Belair and Bernadette Josephine Cormier; m. John McCormick Sisson, May 8, 1948 (dec. Feb. 12, 2005); children: Hilde, Lydwine, John, Catherine, Angela, Paul, Kenneth, David, Marie, Joseph. BA, Minn. Met. State U., St. Paul, 1986. LPN. Maternity nurse Miller Hosp./United Hosp., St. Paul, 1966—80; dir. Region XI Battered Women's Consortium, St. Paul, 1980—84; coord., legal adv. older battered women's program St. Paul Intervention Project, 1989—; co-founder, first chair Minn. Network on Abuse in Later Life, St. Paul, 2002, also bd. dirs. Co-founder, early pres. Women's Advocate Shelter, St. Paul, 1974—84; facilitator Home Free Shelter Support Groups, Plymouth, Golden Valley, Minn., 1984—87. Co-author: Old Women: Breaking the Silence, 1987. Tutor reading East Side Literacy, St. Paul, 2001—03. Named Marvelous Minn. Woman, Minn. Gov., Minn. Women's Consortium, 1993, Woman of Vision and Courage award, Minn. Met. State U., 2001; recipient Sunshine Peace award, Nat. Coalition Against Domestic Violence, 1998, Disting. Svc. award, Office of Justice, Dept. Pub. Safety, 2005. Mem.: Minn. Women's Consortium, Minn. Coalition Against Domestic Violence. Avocations: reading, music, Sudoku, card and board games, theater. Home: 932 Westminster St Saint Paul MN 55130-4038 Office: St Paul Intervention Project 1509 Marshall Ave Saint Paul MN 55104 Office Phone: 651-645-2824. Personal E-mail: bernicesisson@comcast.net.

SISSON, ELISABETH JOANNE, elementary school educator; d. George Hale and Dinah Lynn Sisson. BA, Coll. Notre Dame, Balt.; MS, CCNY, NYC; postgrad., Bank St. Coll., NYC. Reading recovery tchr. Bronx Sch. Dist., NY, grades K-12 tchr. Fellow: Met Life Action Rsch.; mem.: Internat. Reading Assn., Nat. Coun. Tchrs. Math., Reading Recovery Coun. N.Am. Office: PS 64X 1425 Walton Ave Bronx NY 10452

SISSON, LAURENCE P., artist; b. Boston, Apr. 27, 1928; s. Arthur Foster and Gertrude Davis Sisson; m. Judy Haslee Zimmermann, May 17, 1990; m. Beatrice Bachelder Sisson (div.); children: Mark D., Kerry, David B., Derek Phoenix. Student, Yale U., 1948—49; grad., Worcester Mus. Sch., Mass., 1949; DFA, Maine Coll. Art (formerly Portland Sch. Art), 1992. Artist-in-residence Publick House, Sturbridge, Mass., 1950; guest lectr. Cin. Mus., 1954; instr., dir. Portland Sch. Art, Maine, 1954—58; corporator Worcester Art Mus., Mass., 1972. Artist (cover) Fortune Mag., 1951, artist, actor (film) Maine Harvestors of the Sea, 1969; author: (book) Along Time River, 1975; Represented in permanent collections include Boston U., Berkshire Mus., Bowdin Coll., Clark U., Columbia Mus. Fine Art, Boston Mus. Fine Arts, DeCordova Mus., Darthmouth Coll., and others. With US Army, 1946—47. Recipient 4th Am. prize, Hallmark Internat. Show, 1949, 1st prize, Boston Arts Festival, 1956, 1964, Boston Watercolor Soc., 1957. Avocations: golf, croquet. Home: 1408 Camino Amparo NW Albuquerque NM 87107 E-mail: LPSisson@comcast.net.

SISSON, RAY L., retired dean, author; b. Pueblo, Colo., Apr. 24, 1934; s. William Franklin and Lillie Mae (Hall) S.; m. Dixie Lee McConnell, Oct. 5, 1952; children: Mark Lynn, Bryan Keith, Tammy Sue Ann. AA, Pueblo Coll., 1958; BSEE, U. Colo., 1960; MSEE, Colo. State U., 1966; EdD, U. No. Colo., 1973. Electronic technician TV Svcs. Co., Pueblo, 1958, Sid's Appliance Ctr., Tucson; from instr. engring. to asst. prof. So. Colo. State Coll., Pueblo, 1960-63, assoc. prof., 1963-76, engring., electronics dept. head, 1968-70; dean Sch. Applied Sci. and Engring. Tech. U. So. Colo., Pueblo, 1973-84, prof., 1976—, interim dean Coll. Engring. and Sci., 1984-85, dean Coll. Applied Sci. and Engring. Tech., 1985-96, dean, prof. emeritus, 1996—; curator Pueblo Weisbrod Aircraft Mus. Cons. Escuela Superior Politecnica del Litoral, Ecuador, 1979-82, SUNY, Alfred, Farmingdale, 1982, Moorhead U., 1985, N.Mex. Highlands U., 1985, 90, Kans. State U., Salina, 1994, Ministry Edn., Republic of Yemen, 1996, Min. Edn., State of Kuwait, 1998. Author: Pueblo Army Air Base 1942-46 A Chronological History, 2001. Bd. dirs. Colo. Transp. Inst., 1993-96; exec. dir. So. Colo. Bus. and Tech. Ctr., 1994-96. With USN, 1952-56. Recipient James H. McGraw award Am. Soc. Engring. Edn., 1990; NSF grantee, 1964, 65, 67, 68, 80-83. Mem. IEEE, ABET (tech. accreditation commn. 1990-96, chmn. definition com. 1991, vice chmn. tech. accreditation commn., 1993-96), Am. Soc. Engring. Edn. (active, spectrum com. 1989-90, chmn. definition com. 1991, fellow 1993), Engring. Tech. Leadership Inst. (founding mem., bd. dirs. 1983-88, chmn. 1984-85), Profl. Engrs. Colo. (So. chpt., assoc. mem., chair young engrs. 1969, scholarship, edn. com. 1969, chair state scholarship com. 1968), Pueblo Pachyderm Club (pres. 1986, 89, 98), Pueblo Hist. Aircraft Soc. (historian 1999—, curator 2003—), Retirees Assn. (pres. 1998, 99), Phi Delta Kappa, Eta Kappa Nu, Tau Alpha Pi. Home: 403 Starlite Dr Pueblo CO 81005-2685 Office Phone: 719-948-9219. Personal E-mail: sisson@email.com. Business E-Mail: Ray.Sisson@colostate-pueblo.edu.

SISTO, FERNANDO, mechanical engineering educator; b. La Coruña, Spain, Aug. 2, 1924; s. Fernando Cartelle and Clara (Reiss) S.; m. Grace Jeanette Wexler, June 27, 1946; children: Jane Caroll, Ellen Gail, Todd Frederic. Student, NYU, 1940-43; BS, U.S. Naval Acad., 1946; ScD, MIT, 1952; M Engring. (hon.), Stevens Inst. Tech., 1962. Registered profl. engr., N.J. Commd. ensign USN, 1946, service in the Pacific, ret., 1949; propulsion div. chief Curtiss-Wright Research, Clifton, N.J., 1952-58; prof. mech. engring. Stevens Inst. Tech., Hoboken, N.J., 1959-96, chmn. dept., 1966-79, George Meade Bond prof., 1978-96, prof. emeritus, 1996—, dean of the grad. sch., 1993-94. Bd. dirs., trustee Am. Capital Mut. Funds, Houston, 1960—, chmn. bd., 1992-95; co-chmn. merged bd. Van Kampen Am. Capital, 1995-97, dir. emeritus, 2001—; bd. dir. Dynalysis of Princeton; cons. UN Devel. Program at Nat. Aero. Lab., Bangalore, India, 1978. Co-author: (textbook) A Modern Course in Aeroelasticity, 1978, 5th edit., 2004. Lt. USNR, 1943—49. R.C. DuPont fellow MIT, 1951-52. Fellow ASME; mem. Adirondack Mountain Club. Avocations: skiing, tennis, woodworking, sculling. Office: Stevens Inst Tech Dept Mech Engring Hoboken NJ 07030-5991 Personal E-mail: gsandfs@aol.com. E-mail: sisto_fred@yahoo.cm.

SISTO, JEREMY MERTON, actor; b. Grass Valley, Calif., Oct. 6, 1974; s. Dick Sisto and Reedy Gibbs; m. Marisa Ryan, Aug. 30, 1993 (div. June 2002). Attended, UCLA. Founder Dima Entertainment, 2003—. Actor: (films) Grand Canyon, 1991, The Crew, 1994, Hideaway, 1995, Clueless, 1995, White Squall, 1996, Three Women of Pain, 1997, Bongwater, 1997, Suicide Kings, 1997, Some Girl, 1998, Without Limits, 1998, Trash, 1999, The Auteur Theory, 1999, This Space Between Us, 2000, Dead Dog, 2000, Dragon Kin, 2001, Don's Plum, 2001, Angel Eyes, 2001, Robbing 'Hef, 2002, Manfast, 2002, Now You Know, 2002, Something More, 2003, Wrong Turn, 2003, The Movie Hero, 2003 (Spl. Jury award, Cinequest San Jose Film Festival, 2003, D.I.F.F. Jury award, Dahlonega Internat. Film Festival, 2003), In Enemy Hands, 2004, Method, 2004, Dean & Breakfast, 2004, The Nickel Children, 2005, A Lot Like Love, 2005, In Memory of My Father, 2005, Broken, 2006, Population 436, 2006, The Thirst, 2006, Unknown, 2006, Waitress, 2007; (TV films) Moonlight and Valentino, 1995, The Day Lincoln Was Shot, 1998, The 60's, 1999, Jesus, 1999, Julius Caesar, 2002; (TV series) Six Feet Under, 2001—05, Kidnapped, 2006—07, Law & Order, 2007—. Avocation: guitar. *

SISULU, SHEILA VIOLET MAKATE, international organization official, diplomat; m. Lungi Sisulu. BA, U. Lesotho; BE, Witwatersrand U. Various sr. positions South African Com. for Higher Edn., 1978-88; edn. coord. African Bursary Fund South African Com. Chs., 1988-91; dir. Joint Enrichment Project, 1991-94; spl. advisor Min. Edn., 1994-97; consul-gen. South African Consulate-Gen., NY, 1997-99; amb. extraordinary and plenipotentiary to the U.S. South African Govt., 1999—2002; deputy exec. dir. U.N. World Food Programme, 2003—. Organizer, coord. several confs., workshops and seminars on youth and edn.; presenter in field. Mem. ANC Nat. Edn. Com., U.S.A./South Africa Leadership Tng. Program, Cmty. Bank Found.; coun. mem. U. Witwatersrand; trustee Equal Opportunity Found., Women's Devel. Found., Women's Devel. Bank, South African Broadcasting Cooperation. Office: via CG Viola 68 Parco Dei Medici 00148 Rome Italy Fax: 202-265-1607. E-mail: wfpinfo@wfp.org. *

SITARZ, ANNELIESE LOTTE, pediatrician, educator, physician; b. Medellin, Colombia, Aug. 31, 1928; arrived in US, 1935; d. Hans and Elisabeth (Noll) Sitarz. BA cum laude, Bryn Mawr Coll., Pa., 1950; MD, Columbia U., 1954. Diplomate Nat. Bd. Med. Examiners, Am. Bd. Pediatrics, Am. Bd. Pediatric Hematology and Oncology. Intern Children's Med. Ctr., Boston, 1954—55; resident in pediat. Babies Hosp.-Columbia-Presbyn. Med. Ctr., NYC, 1955—57; mem. faculty Columbia U., NYC, 1957—74, assoc. prof. clin. pediat., 1974—83, prof., 1983—2000, prof. emerita, spl. lectr. in pediat., 2000—; attending in pediat. Babies and Children's Hosp., NYC, 1983—2007. Cons. pediatrics, hematology and oncology Harlem Hosp., NYC, 1967—72, Overlook Hosp., Summit, NJ, 1975—2001. Contbr. articles to profl. jours. Pres. Mt. Prospect Assn., Summit, 1987—. Fellow: Am. Acad. Pediat.; mem.: Internat. Soc. Hematology, Am. Soc. Hematology, Am. Soc. Clin. Oncology, Am. Assn. Cancer Rsch., Harvey Soc. Republican. Episcopalian. Avocations: gardening, sewing, hiking, stamp collecting/philately, photography. Office: Childrens Hosp of NY Presbyn Irving Pavilion 161 Ft Washington Ave New York NY 10032-3710 Office Phone: 212-305-5808. Business E-Mail: als4@columbia.edu.

SITES, JAMES PHILIP, lawyer; b. Detroit, Sept. 17, 1948; s. James Neil and Inger Marie (Krogh) Sites; m. Barbara Teresa Mazurek, Apr. 9, 1978; children: Philip Erling, Teresa Elizabeth. Student, U. Oslo, Norway, 1968-69; BA, Haverford Coll., 1970; JD, Georgetown U., 1973, ML in Taxation, 1979. Bar: Md. 1973, DC 1974, U.S. Supreme Ct. 1978, Mont. 1984, U.S. Dist. Ct. Mont. 1984, U.S. Tax Ct. 1984, U.S. Ct. Appeals (9th cir.) 1988. Law clk. to Hon. James C. Morton, Jr. Ct. Spl. Appeals Md., Annapolis, 1974-75; law clk. to Hon. Orman W. Ketcham Superior Ct. DC, Washington, 1975-76; gen. atty. U.S. Immigration & Naturalization Svc., Washington, 1976-77; trial atty. tax divsn. U.S. Dept. Justice, Washington, 1977-84; ptnr. Crowley, Haughey, Hanson, Toole & Dietrich, Billings, Mont., 1984—; consul for Govt. of Norway State of Mont., Billings, 1987—. Instr. Norwegian Eastern Mont. Coll., 1987—88, Sons of Norway, 1989—; instr. polit. sci. Mont. State U., Billings, 1997—; v.p. Scandinavian Studies Found., 1989—; bd. dirs. Billings Com. Fgn. Rels., Festival Cultures; mem. Mont. Coun Internat. Visitors, Norsemen's Fedn. Chmn. local exec. bd. Mont. State U., Billings, 1993—. Decorated knight 1st class Royal Norwegian Order Merit; scholar, U. Oslo, 1969. Mem.: Am. Imigration Lawyers Assn., DC Bar Assn., Mont. State Bar (co-chmn. com. income and property taxes 1987—91, chair tax and probate sect. 1991—92), Md. Bar Assn., Billings C. of C. (bd. dirs. 1998—, chair), Norwegian-Am. C. of C., Kenwood Golf and Country Club, Hilands Golf Club. Avocations: hiking, Nordic skiing. Office: Crowley Haughey Hanson Toole & Dietrich Consulate for Norway 490 N 31st St Billings MT 59101-1256 Office Phone: 406-252-3441. Business E-Mail: jsites@crowleylaw.com.

SITES, KEVIN, news correspondent, journalist, web blogger; Masters Degree, Medill Sch. Journalism, Northwestern U. Corr. covering wars and disasters for nat. networks (Iraq, Afghanistan, Columbia and Kosovo, Indonesia 2004 Tsumami, Katrina Hurricane, New Orleans), 2000—; freelance solo journalist NBC News in Asia, 2004, NBC and MSNBC News (Northern and Eastern Alliance forces prior to fall and after fall of Taliban); corr. CNN; war news corr., online news svc., Kevin Sites in the Hot Zone Yahoo! News, 2005—. Covered US Anti-Drug effort in Columbia, 2000—01; broadcast lectr. in journalism dept. Calif. Polytechnic State, San Luis Obispo, 2000—01. Prodr.: NBC News (Edward R. Murrow award for coverage of the war in Kosovo, nominated for nat. Emmy award for contributions to a series on landmines); worked in local, cable, and network news, including (ABC) This Week with David Brinkley & (NBC) Nightly News with Tom Brokaw, published numerous articles in newspapers and magazines, author of monthly media column NY Times alternative weekly. Named Disting. Lectr. 2000-2001 Academic Yr., Calif. Faculty Assn., Best News Site (Hot Zone) in Online Film & Video Cat., Webby awards, 2007; named one of Top 25 Web Celebs, Forbes mag., 2007; recipient Payne award for Ethics, RAVE award (Blogs), WIRED mag., 2005, Daniel Pearl award for Courage and Integrity in Journalism, LA Press Club, 2006. Travels to major hotspots of the world and reports on various armed conflicts occurring to date; while covering initial invasion of Iraq in 2003 for CNN, was captured and briefly held by Saddam Hussein's militia. Business E-Mail: kevin@kevinsites.net. *

SITES, RICHARD LOREN, lawyer, educator; b. Feb. 16, 1948; s. Loren Richard and Frances Mary (Tellaro) Sites; m. Karen Ann Heazlit, Oct. 6, 1979; children: Brian, David. BA, Coll. Wooster, 1970; JD, U. Denver, 1973, MS, 1975. Bar: Colo. 1973, Ohio 1975, U.S. Dist. Ct. 1973, U.S. Supreme Ct. 1977; cert. health care fin. mgmt. Ohio State U., 1984. Sole practice, Columbus, Ohio, 1973—; atty. HHS, Columbus, 1975—85, Ohio Hosp. Assn., Columbus, 1985—. Academic adv. Ctrl. Mich. U., 1992—2005, adj. faculty, 1992—; faculty Franklin U., Ohio, 1999—2001, Wittenberg U., Ohio, 2002—; exec. dir. OHA Purchasing Solutions, 2004—; trustee eHealth Ohio, Inc., 2002—; mem. newborn genetic screening adv. coun. and others Ohio Dept. Health; co-founder Ohio Bleeding Disorders Coun., 2004—. Co-editor: OHA Hosp. Law Handbook, 2005—; contbr. articles to profl. jours. Co-founder FAMOHIO, Inc., 1992, pres., 1996—98, v.p. legal, 1992—95; leader Boy Scouts Am., 1992—2002; alumni admissions rep. Coll. Wooster, Ohio, 1979—85, fund raiser, 1984; v.p. Sycamore Hills Residents Assn., Columbus, 1983, pres., 1984; chair hemophilia adv. coun. Ohio Dept. Health, 1995—2000. Recipient Spl. Contbn. award, Ohio Soc. for Hosp. Engring., 1988, 1993, Ira Gaffin Meml. award, Famohio, Inc., 1999, Rosie Hass Adv. award, N.W. Ohio Hemophilia Found., 2002. Mem.: Am. Health Lawyers Assn. Office: Ohio Hosp Assn 155 E Broad St Fl 15 Columbus OH 43215-3609 Home Phone: 614-457-0027; Office Phone: 614-221-7614.

SITKEI, GYÖRGY, engineer, educator; b. Orosháza, Hungary, Feb. 13, 1931; s. Lajos Sitkei and Erzsébet Szabó; m. Emilia Bereczky, Aug. 18, 1959 (dec. 1993); 1 child, Zsuzsanna. MS, Tech. U., Budapest, Hungary, 1954, PhD, 1960; D Engring. Sci., Hungarian Acad. Scis., Budapest, 1964; D (hon.), U. Gödöllo, 1999, U. Sopron, 2000. Doctorant U. Agr., Moscow, 1954-57; rschr. Tech. U., Budapest, 1957-75; head dept. Agrl. Machinery Trust, Budaörs, Hungary, 1975-80; prof., head U. Sopron, Hungary, 1980-97, prof. emeritus, 1997—. Mem. State Sci. Accreditation Com., Budapest, 1993—. Author: Mixture Formation and Combustion in Diesel Engines, 1964, Heat Transfer and Thermal Loading in IC Engines, 1974, Soil Mechanics Problems of Agricultural Machines, 1976, Mechanics of Agricultural Materials, 1986 (Acad. award 1988). Recipient Szent-Györgyi Albert award Ministry of Edn., 1993, Pattantyus Á. Géza award Sci. Soc. Mech. Engring. Budapest, 1994. Mem. N.Y. Acad. Scis., Hungarian Acad. Scis. (mem. com. for agrl. mechanization 1975—, com. for thermal engines 1978—), Internat. Soc. for Terrain Vehicle Sys. Avocation: ornamental trees and shrubs. Home: Széher ut 19 H-1021 Budapest Hungary Office: U Sopron Ady E u 5 H-9401 Sopron Hungary E-mail: dwoodma@fmk.nyme.hu.

SITNYAKOVSKY, ROMAN EMMANUIL, scientist, writer, inventor, translator; b. Kiev, Ukraine, Jan. 5, 1934; arrived in U.S., 1988; s. Emmanuil I. and Yevgeniya N. (Glazova) S.; m. Bella Baram, Oct. 4, 1968 (div. Mar. 1992); 1 child, Art. MS in Mech. and Heat Engring., Polytech. Inst., Kiev, Ukraine, 1956; PhD in Heat Theory/Engring., USSR Acad. Scis., Minsk, Belarus, 1967. Project engr. Ural Turbomotor, Sverdlovsk, USSR, 1956-58; mech. engr. Engring Factory, Kiev, Ukraine, 1958-61; project engr. Design Inst., Kiev, Ukraine, 1961-63; sr. engr. Heat and Mass Transfer Inst., Minsk, Belarus, 1963-68; prin. engr. Thermophysics Inst., Kiev, Ukraine, 1968-87; project engr. Hirt Combustion Engring., Montebello, Calif., 1989-90. Cons. Socio-Econ. Sys., LA, 1988-93; translator, Kiev, 1979-87, LA, 1988—, journalist Panorama, LA, 1989-98. Author: I Disagree with Guberman, 1995, Chernobyl is our Fate, 2006, Mollify, not harass hearts, 2007, What is Love?, 2007, Democrats, Communists, Nationalists, Fascists, 2007, Fundamentals, 2007, To the Point, 2007; contbr. articles to profl. jours., newspapers and mags. Achievements include over 100 inventions; patentee in field; discoveries of discreteness property of internal heat-mass transfer processes in three-phase media; wave nature of moisture transfer into wet bodies; resonances at heat-mass transfer in three-phase media.

SITOMER, ALAN LAWRENCE, literature and language educator; m. Tracy Sitomer; 1 child, Sienna. Lang. arts tchr. Lynwood (Calif.) H.S.; and instr., grad. sch. edn. Loyola Marymount Univ. Co-author (with Michael Cirelli): Hip-Hop Poetry and the Classics, 2004; author: The Hoopster, 2005, Hip-Hop High School, 2006, Homeboyz, 2007. Named Tchr. of Yr., Calif. Literacy, 2003, Calif. Tchr. of Yr., 2007; recipient Classroom Excellence award, So. Calif. Tchrs. of English, 2006. Office: Lynwood High Sch 4050 E Imperial Hwy Lynwood CA 90262 Address: Milk Mug Pub– Ste #253 9190 W Olympic Blvd Beverly Hills CA 90212 E-mail: alanlawrencesitomer@yahoo.com. *

SITOMER, RICHARD, air transportation executive; m. Lori Levy; children: Jordan Mark, Taylor Nicole. Grad., Emory U., 1987. Chief exec. TRS Trading Co., NYC; founder, CEO Millenium Securities, NYC; co-founder, CEO Blue Star Jets, LLC, NYC, 2001—. Mem.: Beta Kappa Alumni Assn. Office: Blue Star Jets 28th Fl 805 3rd Ave New York NY 10022 Office Phone: 212-446-9037. Office Fax: 212-446-9061. *

SITOMER, SHEILA MARIE, television producer and director; b. Hartford, Conn., Aug. 25, 1951; d. George W. and Mary E. (Chaponis) Bowe; m. Daniel J. Sitomer, Aug. 25, 1985. BA, Smith Coll., 1973. Field producer, dir. Good Morning Am., ABC-TV, NYC, 1981-86; field producer Evening Magazine, WWOR-TV, KDKA-TV, Pitts. and Secaucus, NJ, 1978-79, 88; supervising producer The Reporters, Fox Broadcasting, NYC, 1988; producer Inside Edition, King World Prodns., NYC, 1988-95; co-exec. prodr. Inside Edition and Am. Jour., 1995-98; exec. prodr. Extra,

1998-2000; exec. prodr. program devel. ABC News, NYC, 2000—. Recipient Peabody award, Columbia Dupont award, AWRT Gracie award, 3 Emmys, New England chpt. TV Acad. Arts & Scis., 1975-78, 2 Emmys, N.Y. chpt. TV Acad. Arts & Scis., 1979, 89, recipient first prize Internat. Film & TV Festival N.Y., 1988, No. N.J. Press Club award, 1988, George Polk award, Sigma Delta Chi award, IRE award Nat. Headliners, Columbus Film Festival. Mem. Dirs. Guild Am., Actors Equity Assn. Office: ABC News 47 W 66th St New York NY 10023 E-mail: sheila.sitomer@abc.com.

SITRICK, MICHAEL STEVEN, communications executive; b. Davenport, Iowa, June 8, 1947; s. J. Herman and Marcia B. (Bofman) S.; m. Nancy Elaine Eiseman, July 1, 1969; children: Julie, Sheri, Alison. BS in Bus. Adminstrn. and Journalism, U. Md., 1969. Coordinator press services Western Electric, Chgo., 1969-70; asst. dir. program services City of Chgo., 1970-72; asst. v.p. Selz, Seabolt & Assocs., Chgo., 1972-74; dir. communications and pub. affairs Nat. Can Corp., Chgo., 1974-81; dir. communications Wickes Cos., Inc., San Diego, 1981-82, v.p. communications Santa Monica, Calif., 1982-84, sr. v.p. communications, 1984-89; chmn., CEO Sitrick & Co., L.A. and NYC, 1989—. Bd. dirs. Turnaround Mgmt. Assn., Jewish Television Network; mem. adv. bd. The 1939 Club. Author: Spin--How to Turn the Power of the Press to Your Advantage, 1998. Office: Sitrick and Co 1840 Century Pk E Ste 800 Los Angeles CA 90067 *

SITTIG, JAMES CHRISTOPHER, art dealer, painter, sculptor, landscape artist, poet; b. East Stroudsburg, Pa., Mar. 9, 1954; s. Edgar Hans and Charlotte Frances Sittig. Pres., ex. dir. Worthington Ave. Gallery, Shawnee-on Del., Pa., 1992—2001; owner James C. Sittig Fine Arts Am. Paintings, Waverly, 1989—. Juror many art exhbns., pvt. art dealer, collector, rschr. and restorer early 19th to early 20th century Am. paintings. Prin. biographer Strauser on Strauser Video Biography, 1994, Sterling Strauser Sterling Strauser: A Modernist Revisited, 1999; author: Salvage Style for the Garden, Found Object Sculptures, 2003. Appraiser paintings Monroe County Hist. Soc., Stroudsburg, 1999—2003, Western Pocono Libr., Bradheaderville, Pa., 1999—2006, WYOU TV, Scranton, Pa., 2001. Recipient Albert Handell Stewart Klonis award, Art Student League, NY, 1977. Mem.: Nat. Trust Hist. Preservation, Pocono Arts Coun., Am. Mus. Britain, Mus. Am. Folk Art, Allentown Art Mus., Smithsonian Instn., Phila. Mus. Art, Reading Pub. Mus. Avocations: tennis, skiing, hiking, bicycling.

SITTLER, RYAN LEE, librarian; b. Reading, Pa., Mar. 17, 1979; s. Barry Lee and Deborah Colleen Sittler. BS in Secondary Edn., Kutztown U. Pa., 2002; MS in Librs., Clarion U. Pa., 2005. Reference, instrn. libr. Shippensburg U., Pa., 2004—05, Raritan Valley CC, North Branch, NJ, 2006—; adj. reference instrn. libr. Reading Area CC, 2006—. Named Berks County Poet Laureate, Berks County Bd. Commissioners, 2002—; recipient Cert. Appreciation, Oley Valley Sch. Dist., 2003; H.W. Wilson scholar, 2005. Mem.: ALA (assoc.), Am. Mensa, Ltd. (assoc.), Sigma Tau Delta (life), Kappa Delta Pi (life), Beta Phi Mu (life). Home: 108 Arrowhead Ct Apt E3 Phillipsburg NJ 08865 Office: Raritan Valley CC Route 28 and Lamington Rd North Branch NJ 08876 Home Phone: 610-780-2661; Office Phone: 908-526-1200 8412. Personal E-mail: rlsittler@aol.com. Business E-Mail: rsittler@raritanval.edu.

SIU, WANG-NGAI, solicitor; b. Hong Kong, Feb. 14, 1938; s. Man-Wan and Wai-Ying (Cheung) S.; m. Yuen-Ling April Lee. Grad., St. Francis Xavier's Coll., 1959, Coll. Law, London, 1967. Solicitor T.S. Tong & Co., Hong Kong, 1971-73, Chan & Ho, Hong Kong, 1973-77; solicitor, ptnr. Gallant Y.T. Ho & Co., Hong Kong, 1977—97; ret., 1998. Chmn. Fedn. Hong Kong-Macau Photographic Assns., Hong Kong; co. photographer Hong Kong Ballet, 1994—. Author: Chinese Opera: Images and Stories, 1997, Hong Kong Ballet, 2003. Royal Photographic Soc. Gt. Britain fellow, Bath, 1985, 89. Mem. Law Soc. Hong Kong, Soc. Notaries, Photographic Soc. Am. Avocations: photography, classical music, Go.

SIUTA, ABBY MAE, primary school educator; b. Racine, Wis., Feb. 3, 1980; d. Jeffrey Charles and Mary Margaret Siuta. BS in Edn., U. of Wis., Stevens Point, 2002. Cert. gifted edn. State of Ga. Tchr. Savannah Chatham COunty Pub. Schs., Savannah, Ga., 2002—. Coord. holiday program Savannah Chatham Pub. Sch., 2006—; liaison edn. support fundrasing Windsor Forest Elem. Sch., Savannah, 2005—. Unitarian Univaersalist. Office: Windsor Forest Elem Sch 414 Briarcliff Cir Savannah GA 31419 Home Phone: 912-844-2682; Office Phone: 912-961-3353.

SIVAK-CALLCOTT, JENNIFER A., ophthalmologist; MD, Ohio State U., Columbus, 1996. Diplomate Am. Bd. Ophthalmology, 2002. Asst. prof. W.Va. U., Morgantown, 2001—. Office Phone: 304-598-6944.

SIVANANTHAN, SIVALINGAM, science educator; PhD. Dir., microphysics lab. U. Ill., 1994—. Pres. EPIR Technologies Inc., Boolingbrook, Ill., 2003. Author over 160 publications. Mem.: Adv. Bd. for Ill. Coll. of Tech., Nat. Adv. Bd. for Micro fabrication Applications Lab., Editl. Bd. of Jour. of Infrared and Millimeter Waves, Proceeding US workshop on the physics and chemistry of II-VI materials, SPIE (assoc.). Achievements include first to use mercury cadmium telluride (MCT) semiconductor materials in some devices. Office: Dept Physics- UIC 845 W Taylor Str (M/C 273) Room 2236 Chicago IL 60607

SIVANESAN, SIVARUBAN, mechanical engineer; s. Sinniah and Meenalogani Sivanesan; m. Nishiya Das, Feb. 1, 1998; children: Maathanggi Maijuu Sivaruban, Eashwar Arya Sivaruban. BSc in Mech. Engring., Ryerson U., Toronto Can., 1994; MBA, U. Nebr., Kearney, 2002. Auditor corp. quality systems C.R. Bard, Murray Hill, NJ, 2002—05; sr. supplier quality engr. Ethicon Inc., Somerville, NJ, 2005—. Contbr. articles to profl. jours. Site coord. SAI Orgn., Easton, Pa., 2005—07. Mem.: Am. Soc. Quality (assoc. cert. quality auditor), Profl. Engs. Ont. (assoc. cert.). Avocation: yoga. Office: Ethicon Inc a Johnson and Johnso Co Rt 22W Somerville NJ 08876 Home Phone: 610-252-4560; Office Phone: 908-218-3371. Personal E-mail: rsivanesan@hotmail.com.

SIVCO, DEBORAH LEE, materials scientist, researcher; b. Somerville, NJ, Dec. 21, 1957; d. Lawrence M. Skurkay and Elizabeth J. McCulla; m. Gregory Charles Sivco, July 11, 1981; children: Scott Gregory, Michelle Elizabeth, Carolyn Suzanne, David Charles. BA in chem. edn., Rutgers U., 1980; MS in material sci., Stevens Inst., 1988. III-V processing tech. Laser Diode Labs, New Brunswick, NJ, 1980-81; materials scientist Alcatel-Lucent, Murray Hill, NJ, 1981—. Contbr. articles to profl. jours. Recipient Newcomb Cleveland prize AAAS, 1993-94, Electronics Letters premium Instn. Elec. Engrs. U.K., 1995, Group Achievement award NASA, 2000. Achievements include 30 patents in field. Office: Alcatel-Lucent 600 Mountain Ave New Providence NJ 07974-2008 Office Phone: 908-582-2041. Business E-Mail: dls@alcatel-lucent.com.

SIVE, REBECCA ANNE, public relations executive; b. Jan. 29, 1950; d. David and Mary (Robinson) S.; m. Clark Steven Tomashefsky. BA, Carleton Coll., 1972; MA in Am. History, U. Ill., Chgo., 1975. Asst. to chmn. of pres.' task force on vocations Carleton Coll., Northfield, Minn., 1972; rsch. asst. Jane Addams Hull House, Chgo., 1974; instr. Loop Coll., Chgo., 1975, Columbia Coll., Chgo., 1975-76; dir. Ill. Women's History Project, 1975-76; founder, exec. dir. Midwest Women's Ctr., Chgo., 1977-81; exec. dir. Playboy Found., 1981-84; v.p. pub. affairs/pub. rels. Playboy Video Corp., 1985—85; v.p. pub. affairs Playboy Enterprises, Inc., Chgo., 1985-86; pres. The Sive Group, Inc., Chgo., 1986—. Instr. Roosevelt U., Chgo., 1977-78; dir. spl. projects Inst. on Pluralism and Group Identity, Am. Jewish Com.; trainer Midwest Acad. Contbr. articles to profl. jours. Commr. Chgo. Park Dist., 1986-88; del.-at-large Nat. Women's conf., 1977; mem. Ill. Human Rights Commn., 1980-87, Ill. coordinating com., Internat Womens Yr.; coord. Ill. Bicentennial Photog. Exhbn., 1977; mem. Ill. Employment and Tng. Coun.; bd dirs. Nat. Abortion Rights Action League and NARAL Found., Ill. div. ACLU, Midwest Women's Ctr. Recipient award for outstanding cmty. leadership YWCA Met. Chgo., 1979, award for outstanding cmty. leadership Chgo. Jaycees, 1988. Office: The Sive Group Inc 1235 N Astor St Chicago IL 60610-5213 Office Phone: 312-397-9857. Business E-Mail: rsive@sivegroup.com.

SIVELL, JOHN NORMAN, language educator; b. Toronto, Ont., Can., June 14, 1946; s. Arthur Leslie and Josephine Ruth Sivell; m. Chirawibha Pongruang; children: Vincent, Florent, Wasintara, Chonsawat. BA in English with honors, U. Toronto, 1969; diploma in English, Cambridge U., Eng., 1970; PhD in English, U. East Anglia, Norwich, Eng., 1974; MEd, U. Wales, Cardiff, 1983. Asst. prof., head English dept. Jundi Shapur U., Ahwaz, Iran, 1974-78; asst. prof. U. Riyadh, Abha, Saudi Arabia, 1978-79; maî de confs. Faculty of Letters, Rabat, Morocco, 1980-82; vis. lectr. Inst. Am. Univs., Aix-en-Provence, France, 1982-83; instr. English as a 2d lang. Brock U., St. Catharines, Ont., Canada, 1983-86, asst. prof. applied linguistics, 1986—88, chair dept. applied linguistics, 1988—89, 1990—92, 2001—04, assoc. prof. applied lang. studies, 1988-91, prof. applied linguistics, 1991—, interim dean faculty of humanities, 1994-95, dean faculty of humanities, 1995—2000, founding dir. ctr. intercultural studies, 1996—2000, 2001—. Co-editor: Cooperative Learning and Social Change, 1990, Of Special Interest, 1990, Reading Into the Future, 1991; editor: Freinet Pedagogy, 1994; translator: The Wisdom of Matthew, 1990, Education Through Work, 1993; co-author French Elementary Education and the Ecole Moderne, 2000; editor TESL Canada Jour., 2006-; series editor Full Blast Prodns., 1991—; mem. editorial bd. Lang. Teaching Strategies, 1991-94; author ESL pedagogical texts; contbr. articles to profl. publs. Mem. adv. bd. alphabase project Alpha Ont., Toronto, 1992-96. Can. Coun. fellow, 1970-73. Mem. Internat. Assn. Tchrs. of English for Speakers of Other Langs., Ont. Tchrs. ESL (bd. dirs. 1991—, conf. chmn. 1989, 90), Internat. Reading Assn., Comparative and Internat. Edn. Soc., Am. Ednl. Rsch. Assn., Can. Assn. ESL Tchrs. Avocations: gardening, angling, writing. Office: Brock Univ Saint Catharines ON Canada L2S 3A1 Business E-Mail: jsivell@brocku.ca.

SIVERD, ROBERT JOSEPH, lawyer; b. July 27, 1948; s. Clifford David and Elizabeth Ann (Klink) S.; m. Bonita Marie Shulock, Jan. 8, 1972; children: Robert J. Jr., Veronica Leigh. AB in French, Georgetown U., 1970, JD, 1973; postgrad., The Sorbonne, Paris, 1969. Bar: N.Y. 1974, U.S. Dist. Ct. (so. and ea. dists.) N.Y. 1974, U.S. Ct. Appeals (2d cir.) 1974, U.S. Supreme Ct. 1980, U.S. Dist. Ct. (ea. dist.) Pa. 1984, U.S. Ct. Appeals (3d cir.) 1984, U.S. Ct. Appeals (6th cir.) 1985, Ohio 1991, Ky. 1992. Assoc. Donovan Leisure Newton & Irvine, NYC, 1973-83; staff v.p., litigation counsel Am. Fin. Group, Inc., Greenwich, Conn., 1983-85, v.p. litigation counsel, 1986-87, v.p. assoc. gen. counsel Cin., 1987-92; sr. v.p., gen. counsel and sec. Gen. Cable Corp., 1992-94, exec. v.p., gen. counsel and sec., 1994—. Mem. Ky. Bar Assn. Republican. Office: Gen Cable Corp 4 Tesseneer Dr Newport KY 41076-9167 Business E-Mail: rsiverd@generalcable.com.

SIVILL, JASON RYAN, music educator; b. Kankakee, Ill., Sept. 22, 1975; s. Joel Franklin and Julie Ray Sivill. BA, We. Ill. U., 1999; MusM, Bowling Green State U., Ohio, 2004. Grad. tchg. asst. Coll. of Musical Arts Bowling Green (Ohio) State U., 2002—04; dir. bands Talawanda H.S., Oxford, Ohio, 2004—. Designer marching band drill Bowling Green (Ohio) State U. Falcon Marching Band, 2003—. Mem.: Music Educators Nat. Conf. Republican. Methodist. Home Phone: 513-839-1206. Personal E-mail: sivijys@aol.com.

SIVINSKI, TINA M., human resources specialist; Grad. magna cum laude, Springfield Coll. Various positions including v.p. Data Gen. Corp., 1980—99; corp. v.p. mktg. and innovation Sci. Applications Internat. Corp., 2000; v.p. strategic mktg., sales and bus. devel. GrandBasin, 2000—01; pres. energy glow industry solutions group Elec. Data Systems, Plano, Tex., 2001—02, sr. v.p., 2002—03, exec. v.p. human resources, 2003—. Bd. dirs. Tranxition. Office: Elec Data Systems 5400 Legacy Dr Plano TX 75024-3199 Office Phone: 972-604-6000. Office Fax: 972-605-2643.

SIVORI, JOHN P., health and medical products executive; BBA, Calif. State U., Chico. CPA. Audit mgr. KPMG Peat Marwick; various fin. positions Sutter Health, Sacramento; various sr. mgmt. positions Found. Health Corp., 1994—98; sr. v.p., CFO Health Net Pharm. Svcs. (formerly Integrated Pharm. Svcs.), 1998—2001, pres., 2001; sr. v.p. Health Net, Inc. Office: Health Net Inc 21650 Oxnard St Woodland Hills CA 91367 Office Phone: 818-676-6000. *

SIZEMORE, DEBORAH LIGHTFOOT, writer, editor; b. Lamesa, Tex., Mar. 18, 1956; d. Glenn Billy and Francis Earlene (Cable) Lightfoot; m. O.E. Gene Sizemore, June 19, 1981. BS in Agrl. Journalism summa cum laude, Tex. A&M U., 1977. Writer Tex. Agrl. Extension, College Station, 1976—77; copy editor Abilene (Tex.) Reporter-News, 1978; customer svc. rep. Motheral Printing Co., Ft. Worth, 1978—79; prodn. coord. Graphic Arts, Inc., Ft. Worth, 1980—81; writer, editor Crowley, Tex., 1981—; freelance writer, editor Boy Scouts Am., Irving, Tex., 1981—; mng. editor Seven Rivers Pub., Crowley, 2003—. Author: The LH7 Ranch, 1991, 2000, Trail Fever, 1992, 2003, co-author: (with Simon W. Freese) A Century in the Works, 1994; contbg. writer New Handbook of Texas, 1996; contbg. writer: Folklore: In All We Do, 2006; contbg. editor Dairymen's Digest, Arlington, Tex., 1981-89, 95-97, Longhorn Scene, Ft. Worth, 1982-84, Lone Star Horse Report, Ft. Worth, 1985-86; acting assoc. editor Boy's Life mag., Boy Scouts Am., 1995; writer, photographer Harvest Times, Dallas, 1983-84, Simbrah World, Ft. Worth, 1985-87; contbr. photographs to mags.; contbr. articles to mags. Women's issues chmn., v.p. membership, pub. info. officer, newsletter editor, yearbook editor AAUW of Tarrant County, 1981-86, 90-92, vice chmn. devel. com. Friends of Ft. Worth Pub. Lib., 1991-93, bd. mem., 1994-97, v.p. 1995-97. Finalist sci. fiction/fantasy novel, SW Writers Contest, 2002; recipient Sr. Merit award in agrl. journalism, Tex. A&M U., 1978, cert. of merit, Livestock Publs. Coun., 1984, 1986, 2d pl. Nonfiction Book award, Tex.-Wide Writers' Competition, 1988, 1989, Publ. awards, San Antonio Conservation Soc., 1993, History and Heritage award, Tex. sect. ASCE, 1997, Grand prize, Laura Bower Van Nuys writing contest, 2002, Sci. Fiction/Fantasy Category award, Lu Spurlock Black Gold Writing Contest, 2004, Paul Gillette Meml. Writing Contest, 2005, Frontiers in Writing, 2005, 2006. Mem.: Tex. Libr. Assn., Tchrs. and Writers Collaborative, Tex. Coalition Authors, Tex. Folklore Soc., Sci. Fiction and Fantasy Workshop, Soc. Children's Book Writers and Illustrators (publicity dir. North Ctrl. Tex. chpt. 1991—92, program dir. 1994—95, newsletter designer 2002—03, newsletter editor 2006), Authors Guild. Office: PO Box 682 Crowley TX 76036-0682 Office Phone: 817-297-1533. Personal E-mail: djls@djlightfoot.com.

SIZEMORE, GRADY, III, professional baseball player; b. Seattle, Aug. 2, 1982; s. Grady and Donna Sizemore. Student, U. Wash., Seattle. Draft pick Montreal Expos, 2000; outfielder Cleve. Indians, 2004—. Named to Am. League All-Star Team, 2006—07. Achievements include leading the Am. League in runs scored (134), 2006, doubles (53), 2006, extra-base hits (92), 2006. Office: Cleve Indians Jacobs Field 2401 Ontario St Cleveland OH 44115-4003 *

SIZEMORE, MICHAEL MAYNARD, architectural firm executive; b. Detroit, July 20, 1943; s. Arthur Logan and Evelyn (Willer) S.; m. Christine Wick, June 1, 1968; children: Christine Corsaut, James Gawne. BArch, Ga. Inst. Tech., 1966; MArch in Urban Design, Carnegie-Mellon U., 1968. Registered arch. Owner Sizemore & Assocs., Atlanta, 1974-76; v.p. CRS, Sizemore/CRS, Houston and Atlanta, 1976-78; sr. prin. Sizemore Floyd (now Sizemore Group), Atlanta, 1973—. Mem. bd. advisors dist. coun. Urban Land Inst.; trustee The Ga. Conservancy. Author: Energy Planning in Buildings, 1979; prin. works include redesign of hqrs. AIA, Washington, Emory U. Clinic, Hale Ctr. Theatre, Salt Lake City, Atlanta C. of C., master plan of Centennial Olympics, Atlanta, 1996, master plan, feasibility Centennial Olympic Park, hqrs. Atlanta Com. Olympic Games, Smyrna Town Ctr. Design and Devel. (Nat. award Urban Land Inst. 1997). Fellow AIA; mem. Atlanta C. of C. (bd. advisors). Office: 1700 Commerce Dr NW Atlanta GA 30318-3123 Home Phone: 404-355-0839; Office Phone: 404-605-0690.

SIZEMORE, NICKY LEE, computer scientist; b. NYC, Feb. 13, 1946; s. Ralph Lee and Edith Ann (Wangler) S.; m. Frauke Julika Hoffmann, Oct. 31, 1974; 1 child, Jennifer Lee Sizemore; 1 stepchild, Mark Anthony Miracle. BS in Computer Sci., SUNY, 1989. Sgt. first class U.S. Army, 1964-68, 70-86; computer operator UNIVAC, Washington, 1968-69, programmer, 1969-70; programmer/analyst Ultra Systems, Inc., Sierra Vista, Ariz., 1986-87; computer scientist Comarco, Inc., Sierra Vista, 1987-92, ARC, Profl. Svcs. Group, Sierra Vista, 1992-93, Computer Scis. Corp., Ft. Huachuca, Ariz., 1994; sr. cons. Inference Corp., 1995; subject matter expert Northrop Corp., Sierra Vista, Ariz., 1995—; sr. info. sys. engr. Harris Corp., Sierra Vista, Ariz., 1996—2001; systems analyst EWA Svcs., Inc., Ft. Huachaca, 2002—. Speaker numerous confs., seminars, symposia; tech. columnist Sierra vista Herald. Mem.: IEEE, Internat. Coun. Sys. Engring., IEEE Computer Soc., Assn. Computing Machinery, Am. Assn. Artificial Intelligence (validation and test of knowledge-based sys. 1988, co-dir. workshop on verification). Avocations: chess, jogging, tai chi. Home: 880 E Charles Dr Sierra Vista AZ 85635-1611 Office Phone: 520-538-2527. Personal E-mail: sizemorn@fhu.disa.mil.

SIZEMORE, WILLIAM HOWARD, JR., journalist; b. South Boston, Va., Dec. 18, 1948; s. W. Howard and Genevieve T. (Walton) S.; m. Mary K. Lamont, Jan. 29, 1972; children: Justin, Jennifer, Julie. BA in Philosophy, Coll. William and Mary, 1971. Editor The Clarksville (Va.) Times, 1972-75; reporter The Roanoke (Va.) Times, 1975-76, The Times-Herald, Newport News, Va., 1976-81; editor, pub. The York Town Crier, Yorktown, Va., 1981-88; copy editor The Ledger-Star, Norfolk, Va., 1982-89, news editor, 1989-95; writer, editor The Virginian-Pilot, Norfolk, Va., 1995—. Recipient various Journalism awards Va. Press Assn., 1972-2007. Avocations: tennis, music, bicycling, camping. Home: 4704 Yarrow Ct Williamsburg VA 23188-2427 Office: Virginian-Pilot 150 W Brambleton Ave Norfolk VA 23510-2075 Office Phone: 757-446-2276. Business E-Mail: bill.sizemore@pilotonline.com.

SIZER, PHILLIP SPELMAN, gas industry executive, retired oil industry executive; b. Whittier, Calif., Apr. 11, 1926; s. Frank Milton and Helen Louise (Saylor) S.; m. Evelyn Sue Jones, Aug. 16, 1952; children: Phillip Spelman Jr., Ves Warner. BSME, So. Meth. U., 1948. Registered profl. engr., Tex. With Otis Engring. Corp., Dallas, 1948-91, project engr., 1958-62, chief devel. engr., 1962-70, v.p. R & D, 1970-73, v.p. engring. and rsch., 1973-76, sr. v.p., tech. dir., 1977-91, bd. dirs., 1975-91; pres. Sizer Engring. Inc., 1992—; prin. Crawford-Sizer Devel. Co., 1996—. Cons. in field; mem. exec. com. Offshore Tech. Conf., 1976-79. Patentee in field Mem. vis. com. dept. mech. engring. U. Tex., 1977-83. Named to Hall of Achievement Coll. Engring., U. Tex., Arlington, 1983 Fellow ASME (chmn. 1972, exec. com. petroleum divsn. 1974-75, SPPE-1 chmn. main com. 1981-88, Engr. of Yr. award North Tex. sect. 1971, centennial medal 1980, OILDROP award petroleum divsn. 1982, Dedicated Svc. award 1985, Silver Patent award 1990, region x Clifford H. Shumaker award 1993); mem. Soc. Petroleum Engrs., S.W. Rsch. Inst. (trustee 1981—), Assn. Wellhead Eq. Mfrs. (pres. 1976), Petroleum Engrs. Club of Dallas, Rotary Internat., Kappa Sigma, Tau Beta Pi, Kappa Mu Epsilon. Home: 14127 Tanglewood Dr Dallas TX 75234-3851 Office Phone: 972-247-6087. Personal E-mail: sizer26@tx.rr.com.

SIZER, THEODORE R., education educator; b. New Haven, June 23, 1932; m. Nancy Faust; 4 children. BA in English Lit., Yale U., 1953; MAT in Social Studies, Harvard U., 1957, Phd in Edn. and Am. History, 1961; PedD (hon.), Lawrence U., 1969; LittD (hon.), Union Coll., 1972; LLD (hon.), Conn. Coll., 1984; LHD (hon.), Williams Coll., 1984; MA ad eundem, Brown U., 1985; LHD (hon.), U Mass., Lowell, 1985, Dartmouth Coll., 1985, Lafayette Coll., 1991, Webster U., 1992, Ind. U., 1993, Mt. Holyoke Coll., 1993, U. Maine, 1993, Iona Coll., 1995, L.I. U., 1996, Bridgewater State Coll., 1996. English and math. tchr. Roxbury Latin Sch., Boston, 1955-56; history and geography tchr. Melbourne (Australia) Grammar Sch., 1958; asst. prof. edn., dir. MA in tchrs. program Harvard U., Cambridge, Mass., 1961-64, dean grad. sch. edn., 1964-72; headmaster, instr. in history Phillips Acad., Andover, Mass., 1972-81; chmn. A Study of High Schs., 1981-84; prof. edn. Brown U., Providence, 1984-96, chmn. edn. dept., 1984-89, Walter H. Annenberg prof. edn., 1993-94, dir. Annenberg Inst. Sch. Reform, 1994-96, univ. prof. emeritus, 1997—. Chmn. Coalition of Essential Schs., 1984—97, chmn. emeritus, 1997—; vis. prof. U. Bristol, England, 1971, Brown U., Providence, 1983; vis. prof. edn. Brandeis U., 2001—. Author: Secondary Schools at the Turn of the Century, 1964, The Age of the Academies, 1964, Religion and Public Education, 1967; author: (with Nancy F. Sizer) Moral Education: Five Lectures, 1970; author: Places for Learning, Places for Joy: Speculations on American School Reform, 1972, Horace's Compromise: The Dilemma of the American High School, 1984, rev. edit., 2004, Horace's School: Redesigning the American High School, 1992, Horace's Hope: What Works for the American High School, 1996; author: (with Nancy Faust Sizer) The Students Are Watching: Schools and the Moral Contract, 1999; author: (with Deborah Meier & Nancy F. Sizer) Keeping School: Letters to Families from Principals of Two Small Schools, 2004; author: The Red Pencil: Convictions from Experience in Education, 2004. Capt. U.S. Army, 1953-55. Named Guggenheim fellow, 1971; recipient citations Am. Fedn. Tchrs., Nat. Assn. Secondary Sch. Prins., Phillips Exeter Acad., Boston C. of C., Andover C. of C., Lehigh U. Edn. Alumni, 1991, Nat. Assn. Coll. Admissions Counsellors, 1991, Anthony Wayne award Wayne State U., 1981, Gold medal for excellence in undergrad. teaching CASE, 1988, Tchrs. Coll. medal Tchrs. Coll., Columbia U., 1991, Harold W. McGraw prize in edn., 1991, James Bryant Conant award Edn. Commn. States, 1992, Disting. Svc. award Coun. Chief State Sch. Officers, 1992, Coun. Am. Private Edn., 1993, Nat. award of Distinction U. Pa., 1993, Alumni award Harvard Grad. Sch. Edn., 1994. Fellow Am. Acad. Arts and Scis., Am. Philos. Soc.; mem. Nat. Acad. Edn. Office: FW Parker Charter Essential Sch Tchrs Ctr 49 Antietam St Ayer MA 01432

SJOBLOM, THOMAS V., lawyer; BA summa cum laude, U. Minn., 1974; JD, William Mitchell Coll. Law, 1978; LLM, Georgetown U., 1982. Bar: Minn. 1978, DC 1978, Pa. 2000, NY 2003. Branch chief Div. Market Regulation, Securities and Exchange Commn. (SEC), 1980—82, spl. counsel, 1982—87, asst. chief litig. counsel, 1987—99; spl. asst. US atty. Ctrl. Dist., Calif., 1990—92, We. Dist., NY, 1991—92, Ea. Dist., Pa., 1996—98; litig. ptnr., chair securities practice grp. Dilworth Paxson LLP, Phila., 1999—2002; ptnr. Chadbourne & Parker LLP, NYC, 2002—06, Proskauer Rose, Washington, 2006—. Named to NY Super Lawyers, 2006. Mem.: ABA (mem. litig. sect. & bus. law sect.), Swedish-Am. Chamber Commerce, Assn. Trial Lawyers of Am., Washington DC Bar Assn., NY Bar Assn., Fed. Bar Counsel NY, Am. Conf. Inst. (co-chair "The Corporate

Counsel's Guide to Internal Investigations" 2003), Phi Beta Kappa. Office: 30 Rockefeller Plaza New York NY 10112 also: Proskauer Rose LLP 1001 Pennsylvania Ave NW Ste 400 S Washington DC 20004 Office Phone: 202-416-5805. *

SJOERDSMA, ALBERT, research and development company executive; b. Lansing, Ill., Aug. 31, 1924; s. Sam and Agnes S.; m. Fern E. MacAllister, Dec. 2, 1950; children— Leslie, Ann, Albert, Britt. Ph.B., U. Chgo., 1944, BS, 1945, PhD, 1948, MD, 1949. Research asst. U. Chgo., 1947-49, NIH postdoctoral research fellow, 1950; intern U. Mich. Hosp., Ann Arbor, 1949-50; resident physician Michael Reese Hosp., Chgo., 1951; resident in internal medicine USPHS Hosp., Balt., 1951-53; sr. investigator, chief exptl. therapeutics br. Nat. Heart and Lung Inst., Bethesda, Md., 1953-71; v.p. Merrell Internat. Co., Strasbourg, France, 1971-78; v.p. pharm. research and devel. Richardson-Merrell Inc., 1978-81; v.p. pharm. research Merrell Dow Pharms., Cin., 1981-83; pres. Merrell Dow Research Inst., Cin., 1983-89, pres. emeritus, 1989-94; med. scis. cons., 1994—. Vis. spl. fellow Gen. Hosp., Malmo, Sweden, 1959-60; spl. lectr. George Washington U., 1959-71; Anton Julius Carlson lectr. U. Chgo., 1984; hon. chmn. 2d World Conf. on Clin. Pharmacology and Therapeutics, Washington, 1983; clin. prof. medicine U. Cin. Med. Ctr., 1986-91. Mem. AAAS (Theobold Smith award med. scis. 1958), Am. Soc. Pharm. and Exptl. Therapeutics (Harry Gold award in clin. pharmacology 1977, Exptl. Therapeutics award 1990), Am. Soc. Clin. Pharmacology and Therapeutics (Oscar B. Hunter Meml. award in therapeutics 1981, 50 Yr. Membership cert. 2007), Internat. Soc. Hypertension, Coun. High Blood Pressure Rsch., Am. Heart Assn., Am. Fedn. Clin. Rsch., Am. Soc. Clin. Investigation, Am. Soc. Exptl. Biology and Medicine, Assn. Am. Physicians, Am. Coll. Neuropsychopharmacology. Home and Office: 263 N Dogwood Trail Kitty Hawk NC 27949-3138

SJOSTRAND, FRITIOF STIG, biologist, educator; b. Stockholm, Nov. 5, 1912; s. Nils Johan and Dagmar (Hansen) S.; m. Marta Bruhn-Fahraeus, Mar. 24, 1941 (dec. June 1954); 1 child, Rutger; m. Ebba Gyllenkrok, Mar. 28, 1955; 1 child, Johan; m. Birgitta Petterson, Jan. 23, 1969; 1 child, Peter. MD, Karolinska Institutet, Stockholm, 1941, PhD, 1945; PhD (hon.), U. Siena, 1974, North-East Hill U., Shillon, India, 1989. Asst. prof. anatomy Karolinska Institutet, 1945-48, assoc. prof., 1949-59, prof. histology, 1960-61; research assoc. MIT, 1947-48; vis. prof. UCLA, 1959, prof. zoology, 1960-82, prof. emeritus molecular biology, 1982—. Author: Über die Eigenfluoreszenz Tierischer Gewebe Mit Besonderer Berücksichtigung der Säugetierniere, 1944, Electron Microscopy of Cells and Tissues, Vol. I, 1967, Deducing Function from Structure, Vols. I and II, 1990; also numerous articles. Decorated North Star Orden Sweden; recipient Jubilee award Swedish Med. Soc., 1959, Anders Retzius gold medal, 1967; Paul Ehrlich-Ludwig Darmstaedter prize, 1971 Fellow Royal Micros. Soc. (hon., London), Am. Acad. Arts and Scis.; mem. Electron Microscopy Soc. Am. (hon., Disting. Scientist award 1992), Japan Electron Microscopy Soc. (hon.), Scandinavian Electron Microscopy Soc. (hon.). Achievements include development technique for high resolution electron microscopy of cells, fluorescence microspectrography; inventor ultramicrotome. E-mail: fsjostra@ucla.edu.

SKAFF, JOSEPH JOHN, state agency administrator, retired military officer; b. Charleston, W.Va., June 13, 1930; s. Michael Joseph and Zahia S.; m. Maree A. Fleming, Aug. 4, 1957; children: Joseph M., Lynn M. Johnson, Gregory M., Nancy E. Kochman. BS, U.S. Mil. Acad., 1955; MS, George Wash. U., 1968. Commd. 2d. lt. U.S. Army, 1955, commd. 1/27 FA bn. Vietnam, 1968-69; mem. staff and faculty U.S. Mil. Acad., 1972-76; advance through grades to maj. gen.; dep. dir. internat. negotiations U.S. Army Joint Chiefs of Staff, Washington, 1979-81; also dep. commr. U.S. Del. Standing Consultative Commn., Geneva, 1979-81; dep. dir. ops. readiness and moblzn. hdqrs. U.S. Army, Washington, 1981-83, dep. commdg. gen., chief staff Japan, 1982—84; dep. comdg. gen. 1st U.S. Army, Fort Devens, Mass., 1985-89; cabinet sec. mil. affairs and pub. safety W.Va., 1989-97. Decorated DSM U.S. Army, Def. Superior Svc. medal, Legion of Merit, Bronze Star, Air medal, others; recipient Disting. W. Va. award. Mem. Assn. Grads. US Mil. Acad., Assn. US Army, Adj. Gens. Assn. US, N.G. Assn. U.S., Fellowship Christian Athletes (regional bd.), Union Mission Ministries (mem. bd.). Eastern Orthodox. Avocations: golf, travel.

SKAGGS, BEBE REBECCA PATTEN, college dean, clergywoman; b. Berkeley, Calif., Jan. 30, 1950; d. Carl Thomas and Bebe (Harrison) P. BS in Bible, Patten Coll., 1969; BA in Philosophy, Holy Names Coll., 1970; MA in Bibl. Studies New Testament, Wheaton Coll., 1972; PhD in Bibl. Studies New Testament, Drew U., 1976; MA in Philosophy, Dominican Sch. Philosophy & Theology, 1990; postgrad., U. Calif., Berkeley, 1991-92. Ordained to ministry Christian Evang. Ch., 1963. Co-pastor Christian Cathedral, Christian Evang. Chs. Am., Inc., 1964—; assoc. prof. Patten Coll., Oakland, Calif., 1975-82, dean, 1977—, prof. N.T., 1982—. Presenter in field. Author: Before the Times, 1980, The World of the Early Church, 1990; contbg. author: Internat. Standard Bibl. Ency., rev. edit., 1983, Women's Study Bible, Pneuma Faculty Dialogue. Active Wheaton Coll. Symphony, 1971-72, Drew U. Ensemble, 1971-75, Young Artists Symphony, N.J., 1972-75, Somerset Hill Symphony, N.J., 1973-74, Peninsula Symphony, 1977, 80-81, Madison Chamber Trio, N.J., 1973-75. Named one of Outstanding Young Women of Am., 1976, 77, 80-81, 82; St. Olaf's Coll. fellow, 1990. Mem. AAUP, Am. Acad. Religion, Soc. Bibl. Lit., Internat. Biographical Assn., Christian Evang. Chs. of Am., Inc. (bd. dirs. 1964—), Inst. for Bibl. Rsch., Soc. for Pentecostal Studies (pres. 1998-99), Phi Delta Kappa.

SKAGGS, DAVID L., orthopedist, educator; BA in Neurosci. and Psychology, Amherst Coll., Mass., 1985; MD, Columbia U. Coll. of Physicians and Surgeons, NYC, 1989; Masters of Med. Mgmt., Marshal Sch. Bus., U. So. Calif., 2005—06. Diplomate Am. Bd. of Orthop. Surgery, 1998. Intern Columbia-Presbyterian Med. Ctr., NY, 1989—90, resident, 1990—94; Frank E. Stinchfield orthop. rsch. fellowship Columbia U., NY, 1991—92; pediatric orthop. fellowship U. So. Calif., Children's Hosp., LA, 1994—95; asst. prof., divsn. orthop. surgery U. Ala. Sch. Medicine, 1995—96; asst. prof. orthop. surgery U. of So. Calif.-Keck Sch. of Medicine, 1996—2002, assoc. prof. of orthop. surgery, 2002—; assoc. dir. Children's Orthop. Ctr., Children's Hosp. LA, endowed chair, pediatric spinal disorders. Cons. Stryker Spine, Allendale, NJ; instr. Am. Acad. of Orthop. Surgeons, Rosemont, Ill.; cons. Medtronics Sofamor Danek, Memphis; instr., rschr. Stryker Spine, Westchester, Pa. Author: (textbook) Staying Out of Trouble in Pediatric Orthopaedics; contbr. articles to profl. jours.; featured on Miracle Workers (ABC), 2006. Recipient Young Investigator Award, Pediatric Orthopaedic Soc. of N.Am., 2000, Sandoz award, Columbia U. of Coll. of Physicians and Surgeons, 1989; fellow Am., Brit., Can. Traveling Fellow, Am. Orthop. Assn., 2003, Traveling fellow, Pediatric Orthop. Soc. of N.Am., 2002. Mem.: Am. Acad. of Pediat., Sect. of Orthopedics (exec. com.), Am. Acad. of Orthop. Surgeons, Pediatric Orthop.Soc. of N.Am. (bd. of directors, Young Investigators Award, Traveling Fellos 2000, 2002), Scoliosis Rsch. Soc. (program com.), LA Tennis Club, Salt Air Club. Achievements include design of Pediatric spinal instrumentation. Avocations: meditation, tennis, weightlifting, boogie boarding, yoga. Office: Childrens Hospital Los Angeles 4650 Sunset Blvd #69 Los Angeles CA 90027 Office Phone: 323-669-4658. Office Fax: 323-666-4409.

SKAGGS, MERRILL MAGUIRE, humanities educator; b. Florala, Ala., Oct. 1, 1937; d. John Henry and Clyde Louise (Merrill) M.; m. Calvin Lee Skaggs, Aug. 19, 1960 (div. Feb. 1994); children: Sylvia Merrill, John Adam. BA, Stetson U., DeLand, Fla., 1958, LLD, 1988; MA, Duke U., 1960, PhD, 1965. Tutor Duke U., 1961-62; lectr. Bklyn. Coll., 1965; assoc. editor The MacMillan Co., NYC, 1966-67; adj. asst. prof. English Drew U., Madison, NJ, 1975-76, adj. assoc. prof., 1976-79, assoc. prof., 1979-85, prof., 1985-86, dean-elect, 1985-86, dean Grad. Sch., 1986-92, Baldwin prof. of humanities, 1992—. Author: The Folk of Southern Fiction, 1972 (Edd Winfield Parks award), After the World Broke in Two: The Later Novels of Willa Cather, 1990, Axes: Willa Cather and William Faulkner, 2007; co-author: The Mother Person, 1975; editor: Willa Cather's New York: New Essays on Cather in the City, 2000 (with Joseph R. Urgo) Violence, the Arts and Cather, 2007. Bd. dirs. Willa Cather Found., Red Cloud, Nebr., 1991—, NJ Com. for the Humanities, New Brunswick, 1990-95; clk. Summit Monthly Meeting, 2003-05. Recipient Book of Yr. award, Am. Jour. Nursing., Presdl. award, Drew U., 2006, Lifetime Scholarly Achievement award, 2006. Mem. Soc. Values in Higher Edn. (bd. dir. 1988-94), Soc. Study of So. Lit. (bd. dir. 1982, 83-85, 87-89). Democrat. Mem. Soc. Of Friends. Home: 9 Woodcliff Dr Madison NJ 07940-2006 Office Phone: 973-408-3491. Business E-Mail: mskaggs@drew.edu.

SKAGGS, ROBERT C., JR., utilities executive, lawyer; BA, Davidson Coll.; JD, W. Va. Univ.; MBA, Tulane Univ. With Columbia Energy Group, 1981—2000, law dept., 1981—96, pres., Columbia Gas Ohio & Ky., 1996—2000; pres. Bay State Gas, No. Utilities, other Columbia cos. NiSource Inc., 2000—03, exec. v.p., 2003—04, pres., 2004—, CEO, 2005—. Bd. dir. Southeastern Gas Assn.; mem. Midwest Energy Assn.; mem. leadership council Am. Gas Assn. Mem.: ABA, Energy Bar Assn., W. Va. Bar Assn. Office: NiSource Inc 801 E 86th Ave Merrillville IN 46410 *

SKAGGS, SANFORD MERLE, lawyer; b. Berkeley, Calif., Oct. 24, 1939; s. Sherman G. and Barbara Jewell (Stinson) Skaggs; m. Sharon Ann Barnes, Sept. 3, 1976; children: Stephen, Paula Ferry, Barbara Gallagher, Darren Peterson. BA, U. Calif., Berkeley, 1961; JD, U. Calif., 1964. Bar: Calif. 1965. Atty. Pacific Gas and Electric Co., San Francisco, 1964-73; gen. counsel Pacific Gas Transmission Co., San Francisco, 1973-75; ptnr. Van Voorhis & Skaggs, Walnut Creek, Calif., 1975-85, McCutchen, Doyle, Brown & Enersen, San Francisco and Walnut Creek, 1985—2002, Bingham McCutchen LLP, 2002—, mng. ptnr. Walnut Creek, Calif.; dir. John Muir Mt. Diablo Health Sys., 1997—2005. Mem. Calif. Law Revision Commn., 1990—2001, chmn., 1993. Councilman City of Walnut Creek, 1972-78, mayor 1974-75, 76-77; bd. dirs. East Bay Mcpl. Utility Dist., 1978-90, pres., 1982-90; dir. Episcopal Homes Found., 2005-. Mem.: Contra Costa County Bar Assn., Calif. State Bar Assn., Phi Delta Phi, Alpha Delta Phi, Lambda Alpha. Episcopalian. Office: Bingham McCutchen LLP 1333 N California Blvd Ste 210 Walnut Creek CA 94596-4585 Office Phone: 925-975-5310. Office Fax: 925-975-5390. Business E-Mail: s.skaggs@bingham.com.

SKAGGS, WAYNE GERARD, retired diversified financial services company executive; b. Bonneterre, Mo., Dec. 12, 1929; s. Jasper Pinkney and Lattie May (Duren) S.; m. Hana Kaneko, June 1, 1952; children: Robert Kenneth, Melody Jane, Joy Elizabeth. Student, Mo. Inst. Acctg. and Law, 1947-48, U. Mo., Columbia, 1954-55. With Advantage Capital Corp. (formerly Am. Capital Corp.), Houston, 1955-96, ret., 1996; pres., COO Mktg. Group of Cos., Houston, 1976-80, corp. v.p., cons., 1972-90. Served with USAF, 1950-54, Korea. Mem. Nat. Assn. Securities Dealers (nat. vice-chmn. 1977, dist. chmn. 1972), Nat. Bus. Conduct (gov., chmn. 1976), Investment Co. Inst., Am. Legion (life), VFW (life), Optimists (life, pres. 1966). Home: PO Box 726 Wimberley TX 78676-0726 Personal E-mail: hanawayn@anvilcom.com.

SKAINE, JAMES C., retired communications educator; b. Monongahela, Pa., Jan. 3, 1936; s. James Skaine, Jr. and Ruth Stamper Skaine; m. Rosemarie Keller, June 4, 1957; children: James Keller, Forrest Todd. BA, Sioux Falls Coll., SD, 1957; MA, U. SD, Vermillion, 1958; Doctoral study, Cornell U., Ithaca, NY, 1958—60, U. Iowa, Iowa City, 1968—78. Lic. to preach Ctrl. Pk. Bapt. Ch., Buffalo, NY, 1954. Grad. asst. U. SD, 1957—58, Cornell U., 1958—60; tchr. George Jr. Republic, Freeville, NY, 1960; prof., comm. Ithaca Coll., Ithaca, NY, 1960—63; asst. prof., comm. Mid. Tenn. State Coll., Murfreesboro, 1963—65, U. No. Iowa, Cedar Falls, 1965—99. Faculty advisor, UNI chpt., Iowa pub. interest rsch. group U. No. Iowa, Cedar Falls, 1976—78, presenter, ofcl. guest, exch. program with China at universities: Beijing Normal, Hebei tchrs., Shaanxi, & Guangxi tchrs., 1991, founders days presdl. com., 1988—90, coll. of humanities & fine arts senator, 1982—83, sec., United Faculty, 1978—79, academic freedom & profl. rights chair, United Faculty, 1980—86, treas., United Faculty, 1986—89, pres., United Faculty, 1989—94; exec. sec. NY State Debate Assn., Ithaca, 1962—63; mem. Speech Comm. Assn., Des Moines, 1965—72, Iowa Comm. Assn., Des Moines, 1972—85; cons., pub. speaking and voice improvement, Cedar Falls - Waterloo, Iowa. Co-author: (book) A Man of the Twentieth Century: Recollections of Warren V. Keller, A Nebraskan; contbr. chapters to books, articles to profl. pubs. Pres. Friends of the Accused, Waterloo, Iowa, 1974—76; parliamentarian Iowa LWV, Des Moines, 1979—81; host in our home Zhu Qizhen, the amb. extraordinary & plenipotentiary of the People's Republic of China to the USA and his wife, Wang Yude Iowa US Senator Charles Grassley's Iowa Internat. Trade Symposium III, Cedar Falls, Iowa, 1990; candidate US Congress, Iowa, Dem. Primary Election, Third District, Iowa, 1972—74; min. Presbyn. Ch., Rockvale, Tenn., 1964—65, Bapt. Ch., Enfield, NY, 1960—62, Bapt. Churches, Turkey Valley and Viborg, SD, 1957—58. Mem.: NEA, Iowa State Edn. Assn., Pi Kappa Delta (life). Democrat. Baptist. Avocations: travel, gardening. Home: 2215 Clay St Cedar Falls IA 50613 Office: Author's Castle Publisher 2215 Clay St Cedar Falls IA 50613 Home Phone: 319-266-8163; Office Phone: 319-266-8163. Office Fax: 319-266-1406; Home Fax: 319-266-1406. Business E-Mail: jskaine@cfu.net.

SKAINE, ROSEMARIE KELLER, writer, consultant, publisher; d. Warren V Keller and Marie W Kuehner Keller; m. James Cole Skaine, June 4, 1957; children: James Keller, Forrest Todd. BA, U. SD, Vermillion, 1958; MA, U. No. Iowa, Cedar Falls, 1977. Cert. secondary edn. tchr. NY, 1959, SD, 1958. English tchr. Ovid Ctrl. Sch., NY, 1958—60; adminstrv. and legislative asst. Pres. Kennedy's Consumer Adv. Coun. Chairperson, Ithaca, NY, 1963; adj. instr., sociology Wartburg Coll., Waverly, Iowa, 1979—80; adj. instr., composition Hawkeye C.C., Waterloo, Iowa, 1998—98. Cons., institutes on sexual harassment Adult Edn. Bd. YWCA, Waterloo, Iowa, 1992; cons., sexual harassment KCET Pub. TV, Los Angeles, Calif., 1991—94; ct. testimony, sexual harassment Dist. Ct., Waterloo, Iowa, 1989—99; US del. XII Internat. Congress on Family Law, Havana, Cuba, 2002; speaking tour, women of Afghanistan under the Taliban SD Ctr. for the Book's three day program, Maintaining Democracy in an Unstable World, Aberdeen, Brookings, Mitchell and Sioux Falls, SD, 2002; presenter, Am. family, Guilin, Shijiazhuang, Xian, China U. No. Iowa, Cedar Falls, 1993; featured author 4th anniversary hostage-taking Radio Free Europe, Moscow Dubrovka House of Culture, 2006. Co-author (with Warren V. Keller and James C. Skaine): (book) A Man of the Twentieth Century: Recollections of Warren V. Keller, A Nebraskan, 1999; author: Women at War: Gender Issues of Americans in Combat, 1999, Power and Gender: Issues in Sexual Dominance and Harassment, 1996 (Gustavus Myers Ctr. award for the study of human rights in N.Am. for the outstanding work on intolerance in N.Am., 1997), Sexual Harassment: Questions and Answers, 2d revised edit., 1990, (nonfiction book) Female Genital Mutilation: Legal, Cultural and Medical Issues, 2005, (short stories) Lessons in Love and Life, (book) The Cuban Family: Custom and Change in an Era of Hardship, 2004, Questions and Answers about Sexual Harassment, 1980, Paternity and American Law, 2003, The Women of Afghanistan Under the Taliban, 2002, Women College Basketball Coaches, 2001, Female Suicide Bombers, 2006; contbr. articles to profl. jours. Panel mem., women in Afghanistan Cable TV Here and There, Cedar Falls, Iowa, 2001; voters svc. chair, pres. LWV of Waterloo-Cedar Falls, Cedar Falls, Iowa, 1964—69; nat. steering com., hon. mem. Gore 2000 Presdl. Campaign, 2000, Clinton-Gore Presdl. Campaign, 1996; campaign mgr. James Skaine for U.S. Congress, Cedar Falls, Iowa, 1972—74. Recipient award, Women's Studies Undergraduate and Grad. Programs, U. of No. Iowa, Cedar Falls, 1998, So. Poverty Law Ctr., Montgomery, Ala., 2003—. Mem.: Alpha Kappa Delta, Pi Kappa Delta (life). Office: Author's Castle Publishing PO Box 1044 Cedar Falls IA 50613 Office Phone: 319-266-8163. Office Fax: 319-266-1406; Home Fax: 319-266-1406. Personal E-mail: rskaine@cfu.net.

SKAINS, THOMAS E., gas industry executive; BBA, Sam Houston State Univ.; JD, Univ. Houston. Sr. atty. Trans-Continental Gas Pipeline Corp., 1981—86, v.p., 1986—89, sr. v.p. transp. & customer svc., 1989—95; sr. v.p. mktg. & supply svc. Piedmont Natural Gas, Charlotte, NC, 1995—2002, pres., COO, 2002—03, chmn., pres., CEO, 2003—. Bd. dir., mem. exec. com. Am. Gas Assn.; chmn. So. Gas Assn.; regional bd. adv. Wachovia Bank. Bd. dir., mem. exec. com. Charlotte C. of C.; bd. mem. United Way Ctrl. Carolinas; chmn. bd. trustees Providence Day Sch. Mem.: State Bar Tex. Office: Piedmont Natural Gas 4720 Piedmont Row Dr Charlotte NC 28210 Mailing: Piedmont Natural Gas PO Box 33068 Charlotte NC 28233 *

SKAISTIS, RACHEL G., lawyer; b. Phila., June 7, 1970; BA, Yale Coll., 1992; JD cum laude, Cornell U., 1997. Bar: NY 1998, US Dist. Ct., So and Ea. Dists. NY 2000. Reporter Fort Worth Star-Telegram, Tex.; assoc. Cravath, Swaine & Moore LLP, NYC, 1997—99, 2000—05, ptnr., litig., 2005—; law clk., Hon. Shira Ann Scheindlin US Dist. Ct., So. Dist. NY, 1999. Mng. editor Cornell Law Rev. Mem.: NY State Bar Assn. Office: Cravath Swaine & Moore LLP Worldwide Plz 825 Eighth Ave New York NY 10019-7475 Office Phone: 212-474-1934. Office Fax: 212-474-3700. Business E-Mail: rskaistis@cravath.com.

SKALA, GARY DENNIS, management consultant; b. Bay Shore, NY, Oct. 15, 1946; s. Harry A. and Emily Skala. BS in Mgmt. Engring., Rensselaer Polytech. Inst., 1969; MA in Psychology, Hofstra U., 1972; postgrad., Chgo. Theol. Sem., 1996—. Engr. L.I. Lighting Co., Hicksville, NY, 1969-71, labor rels. coord., 1971-73; mgmt. cons. Gilbert/Commonwealth, NYC, 1973-74; sr. mgmt. cons. Booz, Allen & Hamilton, San Francisco, 1974-78; mgr. utility cons. A.T. Kearney, Chgo., 1978-81; mng. cons. Cresap, div. Towers Perrin, Chgo., 1981-85; pres. Gary D. Skala & Assocs. Mgmt. Cons., Chgo., 1985—. Lectr. utility bus. issues Edison Electric Inst., Utility Exec. Mgmt. Com., Internat. Maintenance Conf., Assn. Rural Electric Coops., Inst. Indsl. Engrs.; subcontracting cons. Arthur D. Little, Inc., Liberty Cons. Group, Ernst & Young, Cresap, A. T. Kearney, Towers Perrin, Michael Paris Assocs. Ltd., Planmetrics. Contbr. articles to profl. jours. Trustee Samaritan Inst. for Religious Studies, 1995—97, chair instnl. advancement com., 1995; bd. dirs. Bailiwick Repertory Theater, 1999—2005, pres., 2001—02, chair mktg./pub. rels. com.; bd. dirs. Good Shepherd Parish Met. Cmty. Ch. of Chgo., 1995—99, vice moderator, 1996—97; mem. bd. Ordained Ministry of Gt. Lakes Dist. of Universal Fellowship Met. Cmty. Chs., 1996—99; vol. The Night Ministry of Chgo. Mem.: Am. Inst. Indsl. Engrs. (chmn. Midwest chpt. utility divsn. 1980—81), Inst. Indsl. Engrs. (sr.; mem. utility divsn. 1978—, charter). Home Phone: 773-935-1362; Office Phone: 773-935-1362.

SKALAGARD, HANS MARTIN, artist; b. Skuko, Faroe Islands, Feb. 7, 1924; came to U.S., 1942, naturalized, 1955. s. Ole Johannes and Hanna Elisa (Fredriksen) S.; m. Mignon Diana Haack Haegland, Mar. 31, 1955; 1 child, Karen Solveig Sikes. Pupil, Anton Otto Fisher, 1947. Joined U.S. Mcht. Marine, 1942, advanced through grades to chief mate, 1945; ret., 1965; owner, operator Skalagard Sq. Rigger Art Gallery, Carmel, Calif., 1966—; libr. Mayo Hays O'Donnel Libr., Monterey, Calif., 1971-73; painter U.S. Naval Heritage series, 1973—. Lectr., bd. dirs. Allen Knight Maritime Mus., 1973—, mem. adv. and acquisitions coms., 1973-77; spkr. in field. One-man shows include Palace Legion of Honor, San Francisco, 1960, J.F. Howland, 1963-65, Fairmont Hotel, San Francisco, 1963, Galerie de Tours, 1969, 72-73, Pebble Beach (Calif.) Gallery, 1963, Laguna Beach (Calif.) Gallery, 1969, Arden Gallery, Atlanta, 1970, Gilbert Gallery, San Francisco, Maritime Mus. of Monterey, 1993, 97, Rigger Art Gallery, Carmel, Stanton Ctr., Monterey, 1993, Monterey Maritime Mus., 1993, 1997, St. Francis Yacht Club, San Francisco, 1995, Ventura County Maritime Mus., Oxnard, Calif., 1998, Monterey Maritime Mus., 2006, Santa Barbara Maritime Mus., 2007, Petaluma Carnegie Mus., 2007; exhibited in group shows at Am. Artists, Eugene, Oreg., Robert Louis Stevenson Exhibit, Carmel Valley Gallery, Biarritz and Paris, David Findley Galleries, N.Y.C. and Faroe Island, Maritime Mus., Calif., 1993, 94, 95, Pacific Coast Lumber Schooners, 1994,, San Francisco Art Expo, 2000, Herrschoff Marine Mus., Bristol, R.I., 2002, Cavalier Galleries, Inc., Nantucket, Mass., 2003, Cavalier Galleries, Inc., Greenwich, Conn., 2003, numerous others; represented in permanent collections Naval Post Grad. Sch. and Libr., Allen Knight Maritime Mus., Salvation Army Bldg., Monterey, Robert Louis Stevenson Sch., Pebble Beach, Anenberg Art Galleries, Chestlibrook Ltd., Skalagard Art Gallery, Carmel; work represented in numerous books including Modern Masters of Marine Art, 1993; featured artist KTEH-TV On-Air Art Auction, 1998; profiled in profl. jours.; subject of cover and article Palette Talk, 1980, Compass mag., 1980; artist (series of paintings) American Revolutionary War at Sea, 2003. Chairperson Mayor's Choice Exhibit, Carmel, 1993-95; co-founder Carmel Gallery Alliance, 2000-. Recipient Silver medal Tommaso Campanella Internat. Acad. Arts, Letters and Scis., Rome, 1970, Gold medal, 1972, Gold medal and hon. life membership Acad. Italia dell Arti e del Honoro, 1980, Gold medal for artistic merit Acad. d'Italia, Statue of Victory award Acad. d'Italia, 2003. Mem. Navy League (bd. dirs. Monterey), Internat. Platform Assn., Sons of Norway (cultural dir. 1974-75, 76-77), Am. Mcht. Marine Vets. Assn. (Goden Gate chpt.), Combat Mcht. Marine WWII Assn. (coun.), Mariners (San Francisco Bay area chpt.). Home: 602 Stony Point Rd Petaluma CA 94952-1048 Home Phone: 707-769-9340; Office Phone: 707-769-9340. Home Fax: 707-776-4889. E-mail: skalagard@aol.com.

SKALKA, ANNA MARIE, molecular biologist; b. NYC, July 2, 1938; AB, Adelphi U., 1959; PhD in Microbiology, NYU, 1964. Am. Cancer Soc. fellow molecular biology genetics rsch. unit Carnegie Inst., 1964-66, fellow, 1966-69; asst. mem. dept. cell biology lab. molecular and biochemical genetics Roche Inst. Molecular Biology, 1969-71, assoc. mem., 1971-76, mem., 1976-80, head, 1980-87; now dir. Inst. Cancer Rsch., Phila., 1987—; sr. v.p. basic sci. Fox Chase Cancer Ctr., Phila., 1987—. Adj. prof. microbiology, Sch. Medicine, U. Pa., 1973—, Rockefeller U., 1975. Mem. AAAS, Am. Soc. Microbiology, Am. Soc. Biol. Chem., Assn. Women Sci., Sigma Xi. Achievements include research in the structure and function of DNA, host and viral functions in the synthesis of viral DNA and RNA, phage DNA as a vehicle for the amplification and study of eukaryotic genes, molecular biology of avian retroviruses. Office: Inst for Cancer Rsch Fox Chase Cancer Ctr 7701 Burholme Ave Philadelphia PA 19111-2412

SKALKA, MICHAEL B., insurance company executive, lawyer; b. 1951; BA, Long Island U. C.W. Post Coll.; JD, Kent Coll. of Law, Chicago, 1977. Bar: Ill. 1977. Pres. Stewart Title Insurance Co., NY, 1988—93, chmn. NY, 1993; exec. v.p., gen. counsel Stewart Title Guaranty Co., 1993—2005, exec. v.p. internat., 2005—; chmn., CEO Stewart Internat., 2005—. Mem.:

ABA, NY State Land Title Assn. (past pres.), Am. Land Title Assn. (mem. underwriting counsel Com., mem. indian lands com.). Office: Stewart Internat 1990 Post Oak Blvd Ste 100 Houston TX 77056

SKALL, GREGG P., lawyer; b. El Paso, Tex., Mar. 28, 1944; s. Ben Milton and Lottie (Berger) S.; m. Monte Kaye Leake; 1 child, Brandon Cornell. BS, Ohio State U., 1966; JD, U. Cin., 1969. Bar: Ohio 1969, D.C. 1971, D.C. Dist. Ct. 1971, U.S. Dist. Ct. (no. dist.) Ohio 1972, D.C. Ct. Appeals 1971, U.S. Supreme Ct. 1978. Atty. gen. State of Ohio, Cleve., summer 1967; intern U.S. Dept. Justice, div. Civil Rights, Washington, summer 1968; tax law specialist IRS, Washington, 1969; gen. atty. FCC, Washington, 1970-72; ptnr. Garber, Simon, Haiman, Gutfeld, Werthiemer & Friedman, Cleve., 1972-75; acting gen. counsel Office Telecommunications Policy Exec. Office of the Pres. of the U.S., Washington, 1975-78; chief counsel Nat. Telecommunications and Info. Adminstrn., Washington, 1978-80; ptnr. Blum, Nash & Railsback, Washington, 1980-84, Baker & Hostetler, Washington, 1984-91, Pepper & Corazzini LLP, Washington, 1991—; with Womble Carlyle Sandridge & Rice PLLC, Washington, 2005—. Professorial lectr. telecomms. law George Washington U. Grad. Sch., Washington, 1978-83; adv. bd. Pike & Fischer Radio Regulation, 1991—; comms. counsel to Minn., Calif. and Nev. Broadcasters Assns., 1990—. Co-author: The Broadcaster's Survival Guide: A Handbook of FCC Rules and Regulations for Radio and TV Stations, 1988; contbr. articles to profl. jours. Named to, Broadcasting Hall Fame, 2003; recipient Corp. Leadership award, Mo. Broadcasters Assn., 2003, Friend Mo. Broadcasters award, 2004. Mem. Fed. Bar Assn. (chmn. regulated industries com. 1979-81), ABA, Fed. Communications Bar Assn., Minn. Broadcasters Assn., Calif. Broadcasters Assn. Lodges: Masons. Office: Womble Carlyle Sandridge & Rice PLLC 1401 I St NW Ste 700 Washington DC 20005-2225 Office Phone: 202-857-4441. Business E-Mail: gskall@wcsr.com.

SKAMBIS, CHRISTOPHER CHARLES, JR., lawyer; b. Painesville, Ohio, Jan. 21, 1953; s. Christopher Charles and Anne (Haritos) S.; m. Susan Elaine Adrianson, Dec. 18, 1976 (div. Mar. 1997); m. Kathleen Louise Maloney, Feb. 1999; children: Adrianne Elaine, Christopher Roy. Student, U. Pa., 1970-72; BA, U. Conn., 1972-74; JD, Ohio State U. Coll. Law, Columbus, 1975-78. Bar: Fla. 1978, US Dist. Ct. (mid. dist.), 1979, US Dist. Ct. (no. and so. dists.) 1997, US Ct. Appeals (5th and 11th cir.) 1981, US Supreme Ct. 1989. Assoc. VandenBerg, Gay & Burke, Orlando, Fla., 1978-81, ptnr., 1982, VandenBerg, Gay, Burke, Wilson & Arkin, Orlando, Fla., 1982-85, Foley & Lardner, Orlando, Fla., 1985—95, Moran & Shams PA, Orlando, Fla., 1996-99, The Skambis Law Firm, Orlando, 2000—. Mem. Orange County Bar Assn., Orlando, Fla., 1978, Fla. Bar 9D Grievance Commn., Orlando, Fla., 1989; arbitrator Fla. Bar 9th Cir. Fee Arbitration Commn., Orlando, 1987; co-chair Federal and State Trial Practice Co., Orlando, 1992-93. Mem. Am. Judicature Soc., ABA. Avocation: amateur ham radio operator. Office: The Skambis Law Firm 715 Vassar St Orlando FL 32804-4920 Office Phone: 407-649-0090. Office Fax: 407-649-0191. Business E-Mail: cskambis@cfl.rr.com.

SKANCKE, NANCY J., lawyer; b. Mar. 24, 1950; d. Frank and LaVerne Hubbard; m. Steven Lynn Skancke, Nov. 29, 1975; children: Matthew David, Carolyn Elizabeth. BS in Math. (hon.), Purdue U., West Lafayette, Ind., 1972; JD (hon.), George Washington U., DC, 1975. Bar: Va. 1975, D.C. 1975, U.S. Ct. Appeals (5th, D.C. 11th cirs.), U.S. Supreme Ct. Ptnr. Ross, Marsh & Foster, Washington, 1980—92, Baller Hammett, Washington, 1992-93, Grammer, Kissel, Robbins & Skancke, Washington, 1993-96, Grammer, Kissel, Robbins, Skancke & Edwards, Washington, 1996—2000, GKRSE, 2000—. Bd. dirs. Found. of Energy Law Jour., 1986—89, 1998—2001. Contbr. articles to profl. jours. Master, Prettyman-Leventhal Am. Inns of Ct., 1988—2001, pres., 1992—93. Named Disting. Sci. Alumnus, Purdue U., 2006. Fellow: Am. Bar Found.; mem.: ABA (sect. natural resources energy law, sect. adminstrv./regulatory law), Internat. Mcpl. Lawyers' Assn. (chmn. mcpl. contracts and franchises tech. sects. 2005—07, program planning com., Pres. award 2003), Nat. Hydropower Assn. (bd. dirs. 2002—05, treas. 2003—05), Energy Bar Assn. (bd. dirs. 1985—88). Home: 833 Nethercliffe Hall Rd Great Falls VA 22066-2717 Office: Law Offices of GKRSE Ste 330 1500 K St NW Washington DC 20005 Home Phone: 703-759-4927; Office Phone: 202-408-5400. Business E-Mail: njskancke@gkrse-law.com.

SKANDERA TROMBLEY, LAURA ELISE, academic administrator, literature educator; b. LA, Nov. 1, 1960; d. John and Mary Ruth (Chaney) S.; m. Nelson Edmund Trombley, July 13, 1991. BA, Pepperdine U., 1981, MA summa cum laude, 1993; PhD in English Lit., U. So. Calif., 1989. Asst. prof. Dept. English SUNY, Potsdam, 1990—92, assoc. prof., 1993—97, spl. asst. to pres., 1994—97, dir. Tchg., Tenure and Promotion Assistance Program, 1994—97, asst. provost, 1995—97; v.p. academic affairs, dean faculty Coe Coll., Cedar Rapids, Iowa, 1997—2002; pres. Pitzer Coll., Claremont, Calif., 2002—. Asst. lectr. writing program U. So. Calif., 1983—85, 1987; vis. prof. Am. studies U. Eichstaett, Bavaria, Germany, 1985—86, Bavaria, 1987—88; vis. asst. prof. Dept. English Pepperdine U., 1988—90. Author: Epistemology: Turning Points in the History of Poetic Knowledge, 1986, Mark Twain's Literary Marriage, 1992, Mark Twain in the Company of Women, 1994; editor: Critical Essays on Maxine Hong Kingston, 1998; co-editor: Constructing Mark Twain: New Directions in Scholarship, 2001; contbr. articles to profl. jours. Named Quarry Farm fellow Ctr. for Mark Twain Studies, 1988, Finklestein fellow U. Soc. Calif., 1988. Mem.: Internat. Assn. Univ. Prof. English, Internat. Assn. Univ. Pres., Am. Assn. Univ. Women, Mark Twain Circle of Am. Office: Office of Pres Pitzer Coll 1050 N Mills Ave Claremont CA 91711 Office Phone: 909-621-8198. E-mail: president@pitzer.edu. *

SKARE, ROBERT MARTIN, lawyer, director; b. Jan. 13, 1930; s. Martin Samuel and Verna Adelle (Forseth) S.; m. Marilyn Hutchinson, Aug. 28, 1954; children: Randolph, Robertson, Rodger, Richard. Student, St. Olaf Coll., Northfield, Minn., 1947-48; BS, U. Minn., 1951, JD, 1954. Bar: Minn. 1956. Clk. Minn. Supreme Ct., 1953-54; assoc. Best and Flanagan, Mpls., 1956-60, ptnr., 1960-90, sr. ptnr., 1970-90, of counsel, 1990—. Corp. mcpl. counsel City of Golden Valley, Minn., 1963—88; founder, dir., gen. counsel, v.p. Luth. Brotherhood-Thrivent Mut. Funds, Mpls., 1969—93; bd. dirs. Vesper Soc. Group, San Francisco, Son of Heaven, Seattle, Aspen Inst. Cmty. Forum; bd. dirs., vice chair of bd. Nat. Coun. Search Inst. Youth Initiative; bd. dirs. Venture Catalysts of Calif.; nat. pres. Luth. Human Rels. Assn. Am., 1977—79; founder, dir. Episc. Found. of Aspen, Vinland Nat. Ctr. Disabled; founder Westwood Luth. Found.; adv. bd. P.F. Drucker Grad. Sch. Venture Fin. Inst. Claremont (Calif.) U., 2003—; co-founder Venture Catalysts Mexico, 2006—, SME Mexico Growth Fund, 2006—, Social Enterprise Expansion Fund USA, chmn. sponsor bd.; exec. com. Vesper Svc. Network, Inc. Trustee Nat. Bd. Am. Luth. Ch., 1980—88; bd. mgmt. U. Minn. YMCA. Officer Counter-Intelligence Corps US Army, 1954—56. Recipient Pres. award Luth. Human Rels. Assn. Am., 1979, Citizenship award Am. Legion, 25 Yr. Pub. Svc. award City of Golden Valley, 1988, Minn., Presdl. award Search Inst., 1997, Disting. Svc. award Luth. Brotherhood, 1992; named Disting. Mil. Student Res. Officers Tng. Corps., U. Minn., 1954. Fellow Vesterheim Norwegian-Am. Soc.; mem. ABA, Minn. State Bar Assn., U. Minn. Alumni Club (charter), Mpls. Club, Torske Klubben, Sigma Alpha Epsilon (Alumni Svc. award 1978), Vesper Soc. San Francisco (officer, exec. com. 2004-07). Office: 4000 US Bank 225 South 6th St Ste 4000 Minneapolis MN 55402-4690 also: 780 Mt Laurel Aspen CO 81611 Home (Winter): Box 1390 Fallbrook CA 92088 Home (Summer): 1931 Westhaven Lodge Resort Tower MN 55790 Office Phone: 612-339-7121, 970-920-3162. Personal E-mail: marskare@aol.com.

SKARIE, DAVID P., food products executive; BBS, Minn. State Univ. Mgmt. positions through v.p. field sales Ralcorp Holdings Inc., St. Louis, 1986—93, v.p., dir. sales human foods, 1993—94, corp v.p., dir. customer devel. group, 1994—2000, corp. v.p., 2000—03, pres. Ralston Foods, 2000—, pres. Carriage House Co., 2002—, co-CEO, pres., 2003—. Chmn. Private Label Mfr. Assn. Office: Ralcorp Holdings Inc 800 Market St Saint Louis MO 63101 *

SKEEN, DAVID RAY, systems engineer, consultant, engineering executive, educator; b. Bucklin, Kans., July 12, 1942; s. Claude E. and Velma A. (Birney) S.; m. Carol J. Stimpert, Aug. 23, 1964; children: Jeffrey Kent, Timothy Sean, Kimberly Dawn. BA in Math., Emporia State U., Kans., 1964; MS, Am. U., DC, 1972; grad., Fed. Exec. Inst., 1983, Naval War Coll., 1984; DSc in Engring. Mgmt., George Washington U., DC, 1998. Cert. office automation profl. Computer sys. analyst to comdr.-in-chief U.S. Naval Forces-Europe, London, 1967-70; computer sys. analyst Naval Command Sys. Support Activity, Washington, 1970-73; dir. data processing Office Naval Rsch., U.S. Navy Dept., Arlington, Va., 1973-78; dir. mgmt. info. sys. Naval Civilian Pers. Command, Washington, 1978-80; dep. dir. manpower, pers. tng. automated sys. Dept. Naval Mil. Pers. Command, Washington, 1980-85; dir. manpower, pers. tng. info. resource mgmt. Chief Naval Ops., Washington, 1985-91; assoc. dir. Office of IRM, USDA, Washington, 1992-96; dir. modernization of adminstrn. processes program, 1996-98; dep. dir. office of ops. USDA, Washington, 1998; sr. engring. mgr., cons. Lockheed Martin, Washington, 1998—2004; sys. engr., cons. GCI, 2004—. Lectr. Inst. Sci. and Pub. Affairs, 1973-76; cons. Electronic Data Processing Career Devel. Programs, 1975—; detailed to Pres.'s Reorgn. Project for Automated Data Processing, 1978, spl. Navy IRM studies, SECNAV, 1991, USDA/Office of Mgmt. and Budget IRM, 1993, spl. USDA Field Structure Studies, 1997; adj. prof. Sch. Engring. and Applied Sci. George Washington U., 1985—, Dept. Pub. Adminstrn. George Mason U., 2005—; mem. Pres.'s Fed. Automated Data Processing Users Group, Washington, 1978-80 Contbr. articles to profl. jours. Capt. USNR, 1960-91. Recipient Outstanding Performance award Interagy. Com. Data Processing, 1976, Adminstrv. Staff Performance award, 1998, Sec.'s cert. Appreciation, 1998. Mem. IEEE, Internat. Coun. on Sys. Engring., Sr. Exec. Assn., Assn. Fed. IRM, Naval Res. Assn., Pres. Fed. Automated Data Processing Users Group. Home: 544 Hidden Cove Ln Lynch Station VA 24571-2410 Personal E-mail: docskeen@earthlink.net.

SKEES, WILLIAM LEONARD, JR., lawyer; b. Indpls., Jan. 26, 1947; s. William Leonard and Marian Catherine (Fagan) S.; m. Cindy Lee Keeton; children: Kristina Suzanne Carlsen, Elizabeth Ann Garrison, Catherine Fagan, William Leonard III (dec.), Samuel Jackson. BA, Ball State U., 1969; JD magna cum laude, Ind. U., 1971. Bar: Ind. 1971, Ky. 1981. Law clk. U.S. Dist. Ct. (no. dist.), Fort Wayne, Ind., 1971-72; mem. Frost Brown Todd, LLC, Louisville, 1981—. Contbr. articles to jours. in field. Mem. bd. visitors Ind. U. Sch. Law, 1975-91; bd. dirs., past pres. Louisville Housing Partnership, 1978—; bd. dirs. Stage One, Louisville Children's Theatre, pres., 1990-91; bd. dirs. Ky. chpt. Nat. SIDS Found.; grad. Leadership Ky., 1996. Mem. ABA, Ky. Bar Assn., Ind. Bar Assn., Louisville Bar Assn., Nat. Assn. Bond Lawyers. Office: Frost Brown Todd LLC 400 W Market St Fl 32D Louisville KY 40202-3346 Office Phone: 502-568-0301. Business E-Mail: bskees@FBTLaw.com.

SKELTON, IKE (ISAAC NEWTON SKELTON IV), congressman; b. Lexington, Mo., Dec. 20, 1931; s. Isaac Newton and Carolyn (Boone) S.; m. Susan B. Anding, July 22, 1961 (dec. Aug. 23, 2005); children: Ike, Jim, Page. AA, Wentworth Mil. Acad., 1951; student, U. Edinburgh, Scotland, 1953; AB in Hist., U. Mo., Columbia, 1953, LLB, 1956. Bar: Mo. 1956. Atty. pvt. practice, Lexington, Mo.; pros. atty. Lafayette County, Mo., 1957-60; spl. asst. atty. gen. Mo., 1961-63; mem. Mo. State Senate from 28th dist., 1971—76, US Congress from 4th Mo. dist., 1977—, chmn. armed svcs. com. Vice chmn. bd. trustees Harry S. Truman Scholarship Found. Named Minuteman of Yr., Res. Officers Assn. of US, 1995; recipient W. Stuart Symington award, Air Force Assn., 1994, Henry M. Jackson Disting. Svc. award, Jewish Inst. Nat. Security Affairs, 1999, Hon. commandant award, Indsl. Coll. Armed Forces, 2005, Mil. Order of Iron Mike award, Marine Corps League. Mem. Phi Beta Kappa, Sigma Chi, Masons, Shriners, Elks, Boy Scouts Am., Mo. Bar Assn. Democrat. Mem. Christian Ch. Office: US House Reps 2206 Rayburn House Office Bldg Washington DC 20515-2504 Office Phone: 202-225-2876. *

SKELTON, ROBERT W., lawyer, food products executive; b. 1947; AB, Bates Coll., 1970; JD, U. Md. Bar: 1974. V.p., gen. counsel, sec. McCormick & Co., Inc., 1997—2002, sr. v.p., gen. counsel, corp. sec., 2002—. Mem.: ABA, Soc. of Corp. Secretaries & Governance Professionals (mem. Corp. Practices Comm., adv. com. Mid-Atlantic Chapter). Office: McCormick & Co Inc 18 Loveton Circle Sparks MD 21152

SKELTON, WILLIAM DOUGLAS, physician; MD, Emory U., 1963. Sr. v.p. rsch. and health affairs Mercer U., Macon, Ga., 1985—2004; dist health dir. Coastal Health Dist., Savannah, Ga., 2004—. Office: Coastal Health Dist 24 Oglethorpe Professional Blvd Savannah GA 31416 Home Phone: 912-598-0762; Office Phone: 912-356-2233, 912-644-5210. Business E-Mail: wdskelton@dhr.state.ga.com.

SKENDER, JOSEPH, construction executive; s. Joseph Skender, Sr.; m. Cheryl Skender. BSBA, DePaul U., Chgo. Founding shareholder, prin. Skender Constrn. Co., Palos Hills, Ill., 1980—, pres. Regional adv. dir. Great Lakes Bank. Former pres. bd. dirs. SOS Children's Villages Ill. Achievements include leading Skender Construction Company when it was named one of the 50 fastest growing companies in the Chicago area by Crain's Chicago Business, 2007. Office: Skender Constrn Co 10101 Roberts Rd Palos Hills IL 60465 Office Phone: 708-430-8488. Office Fax: 708-430-8472. *

SKERRITT, TOM, actor; b. Detroit, Aug. 25, 1933; 4 children. Student, Wayne State U., UCLA. Films: War Hunt, 1962, One Man's Way, 1964, Those Calloways, 1964, M*A*S*H, 1970, WIld Rovers, 1972, Fuzz, 1972, Big Bad Mama, 1974, Thieves Like Us, 1974, The Devil's Rain, 1975, The Turning Point, 1977 (Nat. Bd. Rev. Best Supporting Actor), Up In Smoke, 1978, Alien, 1979, Ice Castles, 1979, Silence of the North, 1981, A Dangerous Summer, 1981, Savage Harvest, 1981, Fighting Back, 1982, The Dead Zone, 1983, Top Gun, 1986, Space Camp, 1987, The Big Town, 1987, Wisdom, 1987, Opposing Force, 1987, Maid to Order, 1987, Poltergeist III, 1988, Steel Magnolias, 1989, Big Man On Campus, 1990, The Rookie, 1991, Blue Movie Blue, 1991, Poison Ivy, 1991, A River Runs Through It, 1992, Contact, 1997, The Other Sister, Texas Rangers, 2000, Tears of the Sun, 2003, Swing, 2003,; TV shows: Ryan's Four, 1983, Contact, 1997, On The Edge, 1987, Cheers, 1987-88, Picket Fences, 1992-96 (Emmy award Outstanding Lead Actor in a Drama Series, 1993), Brothers & Sisters, 2006; guest star Will and Grace, 2003, West Wing, 2003, Law & Order: Special Victims Unit, 2004, Huff, 2006; TV films: The Bird Man, The Last Day, Maneaters Are Loose!, Calendar Girl Murders, Miles to Go, True Believer, Parent Trap II, A Touch of Scandal, Poker Alice, Nightmare At Bitter Creek, Moving Target, The Heist, Red King White Knight, The China Lake Murders, Child of the Night, In Sickness and In Health, Getting Up and Going Home, Divided By Hate, 1997, What the Deaf Man Heard, The Heart of the Unicorn Killer, 1999, Aftershock, 1999, American Daughter, 2000, High Noon, 2000, Jacqueline Bouvier Kennedy Onassis: Alife, 2000, Path to War, 2002, Jaqueline Bouvier Kennedy Onassis: A Life, Vinegar Hill, 2004, Desperation, 2006. Office: Guttman Assocs 118 S Beverly Dr Beverly Hills CA 90212-3003

SKIDD, THOMAS PATRICK, JR., lawyer; s. Thomas Patrick and Anna Skidd; m. Judith Chase Roberts, Sept. 10, 1960; children: Suanne C., Sherry E., Thomas Patrick III, Jody E. BA in Econs. cum laude, Georgetown U., 1958; LLB, Yale U., 1961. Bar: Conn. 1961, U.S. Supreme Ct. 1963. Ptnr., prin. Cummings & Lockwood LLC, Stamford, Conn., 1961—. Mem.: Fairfield County Bar Assn., Conn. Bar Assn. (real estate sect. and land use sect.). Office: Cummings & Lockwood LLC 6 Landmark Sq 9th Fl Stamford CT 06904-0120 Office Phone: 203-327-1700. Business E-Mail: tskidd@cl-law.com.

SKIDMORE, HOWARD FRANKLYN, public relations counsel; b. Bklyn., Sept. 24, 1917; s. William F. and Mae (White) S.; m. Zaza Irina O'Hara, Dec. 4, 1943; children: Joel Michael, Susan Irina. Student, Coll. City N.Y., 1938-39. Editorial staff N.Y. Herald Tribune, 1937-42, 45-47; asst. to dir. pub. relations C. & O. Ry., NYC, 1948, exec. asst. to v.p. passenger traffic, pub. relations, advt. Cleve., 1949-53, dir. pub. relations, 1954-59, spl. asst. to chmn. bd., 1954-77, dir. pub. relations and passenger traffic, 1959-63; v.p. C. & O. Ry., also B. & O. Ry., 1963-77, Western Md. Ry., 1973-77, Chessie System, Inc., 1974-77; pres. Howard Skidmore Co., Inc., Cleve., 1977-83. Trustee Cleve. Music Sch. Settlement, 1958—. Served with USNR, 1942-45. Mem. Soc. Silurians, R.R. Pub. Rels. Assn. (pres. 1958), Pub. Rels. Soc. Am., Soc. Profl. Journalists, Nat. Press Club (Washington), Carmel Valley Racquet Club, Canterbury Golf Club (Cleve.). Home: 26360 Monte Verde St Carmel CA 93923-9233 Personal E-mail: howzaco@aol.com.

SKIDMORE, JAMES ALBERT, JR., management, computer technology and engineering services company executive; b. Newark, June 30, 1932; s. James A. and Frances W. (Barker) S.; m. Peggy Ann Young, July 10, 1954; children: Jacqueline Sue, James Albert III. BA, Muhlenberg Coll., 1954; postgrad., Duke U., 1984. Customer sales rep. N.J. Bell Tel. Co., Newark, 1957-65, then dist. sales mgr., divsn. mktg. mgr.; asst. to pres. for pub. affairs Pepsi Co., Inc., NYC, 1967—69; asst. to Pres. of U.S., 1968-69; v.p. Handy Assoc., NYC, 1969—71, pres., 1972; pres., CEO Sci. Mgmt. Corp., Basking Ridge, NJ, 1972—; chmn. bd. dirs. Newark Brush Co., 1974-79. Bd. dirs. United Jersey Banks, United Jersey Bank, Franklin State Bank; mem. exec. com. UJB Fin.-Summit Bank, 1985-93, Blue Cross & Blue Shield N.J., Inc., Enterprise Holding Co., Inc.; exec. com., trustee Blue Cross of N.J., 1983—; dir. Coca Cola, N.Y., 1980-85, Mariner Comm., 1983-85, Horizon Blue Cross Blue Shield N.J., Pa., N.Y., Del., 1998—; mem., chmn. mktg. com. Seton Hall Commn., 1987; trustee Rutgers U. Grad. Sch. Mgmt., 1989—; trustee Pub. Affairs Rsch. Inst. N.J., 1988-99; lectr. U. Amsterdam, 1967, U. Toronto, U. Helsinki, 1967, Tokyo U. Guest columnist Rotary Internat. mag., 1966-68, Kiwanis mag., 1966-68, Japan Times on Cmty. Responsibility and Leadership, 1965-67. Mem. Nat. Commn. on Crime and Delinquency, 1965-66; mem. Nat. Commn. on Youth Employment, 1966-67; state chmn. N.J. Nat. Found. March of Dimes, 1966-73; mem. exec. bd. Watchung Area coun. Boy Scouts Am., 1972-77, dir. N.E. region, 1983-90; mem. Citizen's Adv. Bd. on Youth Opportunity, 1969-75; state chmn. United Citizens for Nixon-Agnew, N.J., 1968; nat. bd. govs. Alpha Tau Omega Found., 1967-73; treas. Jr. Chamber Internat., 1967-68; bd. dirs. Muhlenberg Coll., Allentown, Pa., 1980-92, 2001—, chair governance com., N.E. region Boy Scouts Am., 1983—; trustee Brick Twp. Hosp., Inc., Brick Town, N.J., 1976-80; bd. dirs. Am. Christmas Trains and Trucks, chmn., 1966-67; pres. Project Concern, San Diego, 1966-78; trustee The Scholarship Fund for Inner-City Children, 1997—, Ctr. for Analysis of Pub. Issues, 1999—. Served to capt. USMCR, 1954-57. Decorated Order of St. John (Eng.); recipient Internat. Understanding award, Brussels, 1966, Disting. Svc. award, St. Paul, 1966, Freedom Found. George Washington Medal of Honor award, 1965, Outstanding Achievement in Life award Muhlenberg Coll. Alumni, 1966, Amb. award U.S. Jaycees, 1977, Trinidad and Tobago award Prime Minister of Ireland, 1970, Human Rels. award Soc. Advancement of Mgmt., 1982, Statesman award N.J. Jaycees, 1983, Disting. Citizens award Boy Scouts Am., 1983, Pvt. Sector Initiative award Pres. Reagan, 1985; named among Am.'s Ten Outstanding Young Men, Look Mag. and U.S. Jaycees, 1968; inducted into U.S. Jaycees Hall of Leadership, 1983. Mem. NJ State C. of C. (bd. dirs. 1984-2003), Jr. C. of C., Muhlenberg Coll. Alumni Assn., Alpha Tau Omega, Sky Club (NYC), Baltusrol Golf Club, Longboat Key Club, The Players Club (chair fin. com., trustee), Union League Club NY. Office: Sci Mgmt Co LLC 745 US Hwy 202/206 Bridgewater NJ 08807-1760 Office Phone: 908-722-0300.

SKIDMORE, MICHELLE MARIE, elementary school educator, principal; b. Newport Beach, Calif., Oct. 11, 1969; d. Rene and Jan Sommer; m. James Jonathan Skidmore, June 28, 2002. BA in Psychology, U. Calif., Davis, 1991; MS in Edn., Calif. State U., Fullerton, 2002. Tchr. 4th & 5th grade, tchg. asst. prin. Capistrano Unified Sch. Dist., San Juan Capistrano, Calif., 1996—; faculty reading dept. Calif. State U., Coll. Edn., Fullerton, 2003—. Coord. Ladera Ranch Sch. Improvement Coun., Calif., 2003—; beginning tchr. support & assistance support provider Calif. Commn. for Tchr. Credentialing, 2003—; asst. dir. CSUF Coll. Kids Reading Clinic, Mission Viejo, 2002—02. Keynote spkr. conf. Contitutional Rights Found., Irvine, Calif., 2006—06; vol. Ladera Ranch Ednl. Found., Ladera Ranch, 2003—06; dir. Change Change Program, 2004—06. Recipient Tchr. Yr., Capistrano Unified Sch. Dist., 2005, Orange County Dept. Edn., 2006, award, Hines Found., 2006; grantee, Capistrano Unified Sch. Dist., 2005, Ladera Ranch Edn. Found., 2006; Japan Fulbright Meml. scholar, 2005. Mem.: Calif. Assn. Gifted, Computer Using Educators, Internat. Reading Assn., Calif. Tchrs. Assn., Golden Key, Phi Beta Kappa, Pi Beta Phi. Home: 112 Sellas Road South Ladera Ranch CA 92694 Office: Ladera Ranch School 29551 Sienna Parkway Ladera Ranch CA 92694 Home Phone: 949-218-4797; Office Phone: 949-234-5915. Home Fax: 949-218-4795. Personal E-mail: mmskidmore@capousd.org.

SKIENA, STEVEN SOL, computer scientist, educator; b. NYC, Jan. 30, 1961; s. Morris and Ria Skiena; m. Renee Michelle Skiena, Aug. 17, 1997; children: Bonnie, Abby. BS in Computer Sci., U. Va., Charlottesville, 1983; PhD in Computer Sci., U. Ill., Champaign-Urbana, 1988. Prof. computer sci. Stony Brook U., NY, 1988—. Author: (book) The Algorithm Design Manual, Calculated Bets: Computers Gambling, and Mathematical Modeling to Win, Programming Challenges, Computational Discrete Mathematics. Fulbright scholar, Univ. Haifa, Israel, 2001—02. Achievements include patents in field.

SKIGEN, PATRICIA SUE, lawyer; d. David P. and Gertrude H. (Hirschhaut) Skigen; m. Irwin J. Sugarman, May 1973 (div. Nov. 1994); 1 child, Alexander David Sugarman; m. Gary W. Guttman, May 2001. BA with distinction, Cornell U., 1964; LLB, Yale U., 1968. Bar: NY 1968, US Dist. Ct. (so. dist.) NY 1969. Law clk. Anderson, Mori & Rabinowitz, Tokyo, 1966-67; assoc. Rosenman Colin Kaye Petschek Freund & Emil, NYC, 1968-70, Willkie Farr & Gallagher, NYC, 1970-75, ptnr., 1977-95, J.P. Morgan Chase & Co., NYC, 1995—2002, mng. dir., assoc. gen. counsel, 2002—04; gen. coun. fin. svcs. Am. Internat. Group, Inc., 2005—, Dep. supt., gen. counsel NY State Banking Dept., NYC, 1975-77, first dep. supt. banks, 1977; adj. prof. Benjamin Cardozo Law Sch. Yeshiva U., 1979. Contbr. articles to profl. jours. Cornell U. Dean's scholar, 1960-64, Regent's scholar, 1960-64, Yale Law Sch. scholar, 1964-68. Mem.: ABA (corp. banking and bus. law sect.), Assn. of Bar of City of N.Y. (chmn. com. banking 1991—94, long range planning com. 1994—96, audit com. 1994—2001), Phi Kappa Phi, Phi Beta Kappa. Office Phone: 212-770-8805. Business E-Mail: patricia.skigen@aig.com.

SKILES, JAMES JEAN, electrical and computer engineer, educator; b. St. Louis, Oct. 16, 1928; s. Coy Emerson and Vernetta Beatrice Skiles; m. Deloris Audrey McKenney, Sept. 4, 1948; children: Steven, Randall,

Jeffrey. BSEE, Washington U., St. Louis, 1948; MS, Mo. Sch. Mines and Metallurgy (now U. Mo.-Rolla), 1951; PhD, U. Wis., Madison, 1954. Engr. Union Electric Co., St. Louis, 1948-49; instr. U. Mo., Rolla, 1949-51; instr. elec. engring. U. Wis., Madison, 1951—54, prof., 1954-89, prof. emeritus, 1989—, chmn. dept. elec. engring., 1967-72, dir. univ. industry rsch. program, 1972-75, dir. Energy Rsch. Ctr., 1975-95. Cons. in field. Contbr. articles to profl. jours. Mem. Monona Grove Dist. Schs. Bd., Wis., 1961—69; mem. adv. com. Wis. Energy Office, Madison, 1979—80, Wis. Pub. Svc. Commn., 1980—81. Recipient Kiekhofer Tchg. award, 1955, Wis. Electric Utilities Professorship in Energy Engring., U. Wis., 1975—89, Benjamin Smith Reynolds Tchg. award, 1980, Acad. Elec. Engring. award, U. Mo. - Rolla, 1982. Mem.: IEEE (sr.), Am. Soc. Engring. Edn. Home: 8099 Coray Ln Verona WI 53593-9073 Office: Univ of Wisconsin Dept Elec & Computer Engring 1415 Engineering Dr Madison WI 53706-1607 Business E-Mail: skiles@engr.wisc.edu.

SKILES, SCOTT ALLEN, professional basketball coach; b. LaPorte, Ind., Mar. 5, 1964; m. Kim Skiles; children: Scott Jr., Sean, Shelby. Grad., Mich. State U. Profl. basketball player Milw. Bucks, 1986—87, Ind. Pacers, 1987—89, Orlando Magic, 1989—94, Washington Bullets, 1994—95, Phila. 76ers, 1995—96; head coach PAOK, Greece; asst. coach Phoenix Suns, 1997-99, head coach, 1999—2002, Chgo. Bulls, 2003—. Named Most Improved Player, NBA, 1991. Achievements include holding the NBA record for most assists in a game at 30. Office: Chgo Bulls United Ctr 1901 W Madison St Chicago IL 60612-2459 *

SKILLERN, MICHAEL PHILLIP, museum administrator; b. Long Beach, Calif., Aug. 30, 1940; s. Robert Earl and Ruby Page Skillern; m. Tracey Lynn Tate, Jan. 10, 2002; children: James, Deborah, Angela, Shauna, Dana, Stephen, Allen. ASEE, Portland CC, Oreg., 1994. Elec. engr. Wyo. Hwy. Dept., Cheyenne, 1979—84; design engr., prodn. supr. Internat. Game Tech., Reno, 1984—87; contract elec. engr. Christiansen Motoryacht Corp., 1988—94, West State Inc., Portland, Oreg., 1988—94; v.p. S.W. Wash. Vets. Meml. Mus., Vancouver, 1994—. Dir. H. J. Kaiser Ships Victory Hist. Preservation Project; N.W. coord. APA Hist. Preservation Project, Vancouver, 1999—2004, Save the USS Gage Hist. Preservation Project, Vancouver, 1999—2004. Vol. Walk for Life March of Dimes, Vancouver, 1999—2001, vol. Jail and Bail Project, 1999—2001; bd. dirs. Adonais Haven and Christian Bookstore. Chief petty officer USN, 1957—78. Named Instr. of the Yr., USN, 1969. Mem.: NRA (life), VFW (life; bd. dirs., officer 1999—2002), Fleet Res. Assn., Destroyer Escort Sailors Assn. (life), Naval Inst. (life), N.Am. Hunting Club (life), Masons. Republican. Avocations: fishing, model building, painting. Home: PO Box 1336 Goldendale WA 98620 Office: SW Wash Vets Meml Mus PO Box 1336 Goldendale WA 98620

SKILLING, RAYMOND INWOOD, lawyer; b. Enniskillen, Eng., July 14, 1939; s. Dane and Elizabeth (Burleigh) Skilling; m. Alice Mae Welsh, Aug. 14, 1982; 1 child from previous marriage, Keith A. LLB, Queen's U., Belfast, UK, 1961; JD, U. Chgo., 1962. Solicitor: English Supreme Ct. 1966, bar: Ill. 1974. Assoc. Clifford-Turner (name now Clifford Chance), London, 1963-69, ptnr., 1969-76; exec. v.p., chief counsel Aon Corp. (and predecessor cos.), Chgo., 1976—2003, sr. advisor, 2004—. Recipient McKane medal, Queen's U., Belfast, 1961; Commonwealth fellow, U. Chgo., 1961—62, Bigelow Tchg. fellow, U. Chgo. Law Sch., 1962—63, Fulbright scholar, U.S. Ednl. Commn., London, 1961—63. Mem.: Bucks Club London, Racquet Club Chgo. Office: Aon Corp 200 E Randolph Chicago IL 60601

SKILLINGSTAD, CONSTANCE YVONNE, social services administrator, educator; b. Portland, Oreg., Nov. 18, 1944; d. Irving Elmer and Beulah Ruby (Aleckson) Erickson; m. David W. Skillingstad, Jan. 12, 1968 (div. Mar. 1981); children: Michael, Brian. BA in Sociology, U. Minn., Mpls., 1966; MBA, U. St. Thomas, St. Paul, 1982. Cert. lay spkr. United Meth. Ch.; lic. social worker; cert. vol. adminstr., lic. real estate agt. Social worker Rock County Welfare Dept., Luverne, Minn., 1966-68, Hennepin County Social Svc., Mpls., 1968-70, vol. coord., 1970-78, St. Joseph's Home for Children, Mpls., 1978-89, mgr. cmty. resources, 1989-94; exec. dir. Mpls. Crisis Nursery, 1994-97; mem. cmty. faculty Met. State U., St. Paul and Mpls., 1980-97; faculty U. St. Thomas Ctr. Non Profit Mgmt., 1990—2001; asst. adminstr. St. Joseph's Home Children, Mpls., 1997-98; asst. dir. Cath. Charities Archdiocese of St. Paul and Mpls., 1998-2000; dir. mem. svc. Minn. Coun. Founds., 2001—02; pres. Golden Girl Homes, Inc., 2001—; exec. dir. Prevent Child Abuse Minn., St. Paul, 2002—. Trainer, mem. adv. commn. Mpls. Vol. Ctr., 1978—90, cons., 1980—, chmn. Contbr. articles to profl. jours. Mem. adv. bd. MADD, Minn., 1986—88, Congregations Concerned for Children, 2002—, Stop It Now!, Minn., 2003—, Grandkids and Me; bd. dirs. Survivors Network Minn., 2005—, Authentic Voices Internat., Ctr. Giref, Loss and Transition, U. Minn. Children Youth and Family Consortium; vice chmn., chmn. adminstrv. coun., lay leader Hobart United Meth. Ch.; lay rep. ann. conf. Spencer Brook United Meth. Ch., 1989—92; chmn. social concerns commn. Park Ave. United Meth. Ch., 1992—; bd. dirs. Sexual Abuse Prevention Network, 2006—. Named Woman of Distinction, Mpls. St. Paul Mag./Sta. KARE-TV, 1995; named one of Outstanding Young Women in Am., 1974. Mem.: Minn. Social Svcs. Assn. (pres. 1981, 1998—99, bd. dirs. 1996—2001, mem. legis. com., Disting. Svc. award 1987), Assn. Vol. Adminstrn. (v.p. regional affairs 1985—87, mem. assessment panel 1986—94, coord. nat. tng. team, cert. process vol. adminstr. 1986—92, profl. devel. chair 1990—92), Minn. Assn. Vol. Dirs. (pres. 1975, sec., ethics chmn. 1987—). Dfl. Avocations: bridge, volleyball, travel, reading, accordion. Office: Prevent Child Abuse Minn Ste 202 S 1821 University Ave Saint Paul MN 55104 Home: 28544 Lakewood Dr NW Isanti MN 55040 Business E-Mail: cskillingstad@pcamn.org.

SKILLMAN, BECKY SUE, lieutenant governor, former state legislator; b. Bedford, Ind., Sept. 26, 1950; d. Jack Delmar and Catherine Louise (Flinn) Foddrill; m. Stephen E. Skillman, 1969; 1 child, Aaron. Dep. recorder Lawrence County, 1971-76, county recorder, 1977-84; clk. Lawrence County Cir. Ct., 1985—92; mem. Ind. State Senate from 44th dist., 1992—2005; lt. gov. State of Ind., Indpls., 2005—. Co-dir. Lawrence County Young Reps., 1973-78; co-chmn. State Young Reps. Conv., 1975, 77; vice chmn. Lawrence County Rep. Ctrl. Com. Named The Outstanding Elected Official of 2000, Ind. Assn. Area Agencies, "Legislator of the Year", Ind. Library Found., 2002; recipient "Champion of Small Bus." award, Small Bus. Coun, 1995, Disting. Pub. Policy award, Ind. Rural Health Policy award, 2003. Republican. Office: Office Lt Governor State Capitol Rm 333 Indianapolis IN 46204 Office Phone: 317-232-4545. Office Fax: 317-232-4788. *

SKILLMAN, WILLIAM ALFRED, consulting engineering executive; b. Lakehurst, NJ, Jan. 22, 1928; s. Wilbur Newton and Greta Alfreda (Ekman) S.; m. Anne Marie Cavender, Sept. 19, 1948; children: Thomas R., Gregory A., Karen L. BS in Engring. Physics, Lehigh U., 1952; MS in Physics, U. Rochester, 1954. Assoc. engr. Westinghouse Electric Corp., Balt., 1954-56, engr., 1956-58, sr. engr., 1958-61, supervisory engr., 1961-64, adv. engr., 1964-73, sr. adv. engr., 1973-85, cons. engr., 1986-93, cons. electronic systems group, 1993—. Author: Radar Calculations Using the TI-59 Programmable Calculator, 1983; author: (with others) Radar Handbook, 2d edit., 1990; patentee in field Served with USN, 1946-48. Fellow IEEE (life, Dennis J. Picard medal for radar technologies and applications 2003); mem. Aerospace and Electronic Sys. Soc. (Pioneer award 1995), Phi Beta Kappa. Republican. Methodist. Avocations: photography, travel, genealogy, programming. Home and Office: 605 Forest View Rd Linthicum Heights MD 21090-2819 E-mail: wskillman@aol.com.

SKILLRUD, HAROLD CLAYTON, minister, retired bishop; b. St. Cloud, Minn., June 29, 1928; s. Harold and Amanda Skillrud; m. Lois Dickhart, June 8, 1951; children: David, Janet, John. BA magna cum laude, Gustavus Adolphus Coll., 1950; MDiv magna cum laude, Augustana Theol. Sem., Rock Island, Ill., 1954; STM, Luth. Sch. Theology, Chgo., 1969; DD (hon.), Augustana Coll., 1978, Newberry Coll., 1988. Ordained to ministry Evang. Luth. Ch. in Am., 1954. Supply pastor Saron Luth. Ch., Big Lake, Minn., 1950-51; mem. staff 1st Luth. Ch., Rock Island, Ill., 1951-52; intern, organizer new mission Faith Luth. Ch., Syosset, NY, 1952-53; sr. pastor St. John's Luth. Ch., Bloomington, Ill., 1954-79, Luth. Ch. of the Redeemer, Atlanta, 1979-87; bishop Southeastern Synod Evang. Luth. Ch. in Am., Atlanta, 1987-95, regional rep. bd. pensions, 1995—2007. Del. to various convs. Luth. Ch. in Am., Luth. World Fedn. in Helsinki, 1963, mem. bd. publ., 1976-84, pastor-evangelist Evang. Outreach Emphasis program, 1977-79, mem. exec. bd. Ill. synod, 1977-79, pres. bd. publ., 1980-84, leader stewardship cluster Southeastern synod, 1983, mem. exec. bd. Southeastern synod, 1984-87; mem. exec. coun., Luth. Ch. in Am., 1984-87; mem. task force on new ch. design Commn. on New Luth. Ch., task force on ch. pub. house, 1985; del. constituting conv. Evang. Luth. Ch. in Am., 1987, del. assemblies Evang. Luth. Ch. in Am., 1989, 91, 93, 95; mem. commn. on clergy confidentiality Luth. Coun. in USA, 1987; co-chair USA Luth.- Roman Cath. Dialogue, 1990-97; mem. Task Force on Theol. Edn. Author: LSTC: Decade of Decision, 1969; co-editor Scripture and Tradition, Lutherans and Catholics in Dialogue, 1995; mem. edtl. bd. Partners mag., 1978-80; contbr. articles and sermons to religious jours. Former bd. dirs. Augustana Theol. Sem.; bd. dirs. Augustana Coll., 1969-77, chmn. bd., 1976-77; bd. dirs. Kessler Reformation Collection, Newberry Coll., Luth. World Relief, Augsburg Fortress; chmn. bd. dirs. Luth. Sch. Theology, Chgo., 1962-69; mem. Leadership Atlanta, 1980-81, United Way, Atlanta, 1980-81; mem. Bishop's Commn. on Econ. Justice, 1985-86; pres. bd. dirs. Atlanta Samaritan House, 1986-87. Recipient Alumni award Luth. Sch. Theology, Chgo., 1976, award Leadership Atlanta, 1981, The Rev. John Bachman award, Luth. Theol. Sem., Columbia, S.C., 1996. Mem. Luth. Sch. Theology Alumni Assn. (pres. 1975-77), Conf. of Bishops, Kiwanis (pres. Midtown chpt. 1984-85). Lutheran. Avocations: travel, photography. Home: 104 Hawthorne Lake Dr Bloomington IL 61704 Personal E-mail: hcskillrud@aol.com.

SKILTON, JOHN SINGLETON, lawyer; b. Washington, Apr. 13, 1944; s. Robert Henry and Margaret (Neisser) S.; m. Carmen Fisher, Jan. 28, 1967; children: Laura Anne, Susan Elizabeth, Robert John. BA, U. Wis., 1966, JD, 1969. Bar: Wis. Supreme Ct. 1969, U.S. Dist. Ct. (ea. and we. dists.) Wis. 1969, U.S. Ct. Appeals (7th cir.) 1969, U.S. Supreme Ct. 1989, U.S. Ct. Appeals (Fed. cir.) 1991. Law clk. 7th Cir. Ct. Appeals, Milw., 1969-70; assoc. Foley & Lardner, Milw., 1970-77, ptnr. Madison, Wis., 1977-2000; shareholder Heller, Ehrman, White & McAuliffe, Washington, 2000—. Bd. visitors U. Wis. Law Sch., Madison, 1982-90, chmn., 1988-89; chair Wis. Fed. Nominating Commn., 1994; mem. Gov.'s Task Force on Bus. Ct., 1994-95, Govs. Internat. Trade Coun., 2004-; pres. Wis. Law Found., 2000-02 Recipient Lifetime Achievement award, Equal Justice Fund, 2003. Fellow Am. Bar Found., Am. Coll. Trial Lawyers, Internat. Acad. Trial Lawyers; mem. ABA (chmn. standing com. on delivery of legal svcs. 1996-2000, chmn. consortium legal svcs. and pub. 2000-02), Am. Law Inst., Am. Acad. Appellate Lawyers, 7th Cir. Bar Assn. (pres. 1985-86, chmn. 7th cir. adv. com. on rules 1994-2000), State Bar Wis. (pres. 1995-96, Pres.'s award of excellence 1989, Sinykin award for publ svc. 1996), Western Dist. Wis. Bar Assn. (pres. 1992-93), Western Dist. Adv. Group (chmn. 1991), Wis. Law Found. (pres. 2000-02), James E. Doyle Am. Inn of Ct. (coun. 1992-94), Am. Inns of Ct. Found. (trustee 1995-98), U. Wis. Law Alumni Assn. (bd. dirs. 1991-97, pres. 1993-95), Lawyers Com. Civil Rights (co-chair, 2003-2005). Home: 917 Woodward Dr Madison WI 53704 Office: 1 E Main St Madison WI 53703-5118 Office Phone: 608-663-7474.

SKINNER, BRIAN JOHN, geologist, educator; b. Wallaroo, South Australia, Dec. 15, 1928; came to U.S., 1958, naturalized, 1963; s. Joshua Henry and Joyce Barbara Lloyd (Prince) S.; m. Helen Catherine Wild, Oct. 9, 1954; children: Adrienne Wild, Stephanie Wild, Thalassa Wild. B.Sc., U. Adelaide, Australia, 1950; A.M., Harvard U., 1952, PhD, 1955; D Engring. (hon.), Colo. Sch. Mines, 1998; DSc (hon.), U. Toronto, 1998. Lectr. U. Adelaide, 1955-58; research geologist U.S. Geol. Survey, 1958-62, chief br. exptl. geochemistry and mineralogy, 1962-66; prof. geology and geophysics, chmn. dept. Yale U., New Haven, 1966-73, Eugene Higgins prof., 1972—. Hugh Exton McKinstry Meml. lectr. Harvard U., 1978; Alex L. du Toit lectr. Combined Socs. South Africa, 1979; Cecil H. and Ida Green lectr. U. B.C., 1983; Thayer Lindsley Meml. lectr. Soc. Econ. Geologists, 1983; Soc. Econ. Geologists Overseas lectr., 1985; Hoffman lectr. Harvard U., 1986, Joubin-James lectr. U. Toronto, 1987; mem. exec. com. divsn. earth scis. NRC, 1966-69; chmn. com. mineral resources and the environ. Nat. Acad. Scis.-NRC, 1973-75; mem. Lunar Sample Analysis Planning Team, 1968-70, Lunar Sci. Rev. Bd., 1971-72, U.S. Nat. Com. for Geochemistry, 1966-67, U.S. Nat. Com. for Geology, 1973-77, 85-93, chmn., 1987-93, chmn. bd. earth scis. NRC, 1987-88, earth scis. and resources, 1989-90; mem. bd. Internat. Geol. Correlation Program, UNESCO-IUGS, 1985-89, 90-96, chmn., 1986-89; cons. Office Sci. and Tech. Policy, 1977-80, NSF, 1977-82; dir. Econ. Geology Pub. Co.; chmn. governing bd. Am. Jour. Sci., 1972-2004; pres. Econ. Geology Pub. Co., 1996-2000. Author: Earth Resources, 1969, 77, 86, Man and the Ocean, 1973, Physical Geology, 1974, 77, 87, Rocks and Rock Minerals, 1979, The New Iron Age Ahead, 1987, Resources and World Development, 1987, The Dynamic Earth, 1989, 92, 95, 2000, 03, The Blue Planet, 1995, 99, 2000, Environmental Geology, 1996, Geology Today, 1999, Oxford Companion to the Earth, 2000, Visualizing Geology, 2007; editor: Econ. Geology, 1969-96, Oxford Univ. Press Monographs in Geological Sciences, 1979-2005, Internat. Geology Rev., 1995-2007; mem. editl. bd. Am. Scientist, 1974-90, chmn., 1987-90. Trustee Hopkins Grammar Sch., 1978-83. Recipient Disting. Contbns. award, Assn. Earth Sci. Editors, 1979, medal, Geol. Assn. Can., 1998, Futer's medal, Inst. of Mining and Metallurgy, London, 2002; fellow, Guggenheim fellow, 1970. Fellow Geol. Soc. Am. (councillor 1976-78, chmn. spl. publs. com. 1980-81, chmn. com. on coms. 1983, pres. 1985); mem. Geochem. Soc. (pres. 1972-73), Conn. Acad. Sci. and Engring. (div. chmn. 1978-80, coun. 1982-87), Soc. Econ. Geologists (pres. 1995, Silver medal 1981, Marsden medal 2003, Penrose medal 2005). Home: PO Box 894 Woodbury CT 06798-0894 Personal E-mail: brian.skinner@yale.edu.

SKINNER, DANIEL THOMAS, language educator; b. Boston, May 1, 1916; s. Thomas Henson and Esther Hannetta (Jennings) Skinner; m. Vyna May Wingood, Oct. 15, 1944 (dec. Jan. 1995); children: David Edward, John Arnold. AB magna cum laude, Harvard U., 1938, PhD in Romance Lang., 1953; MA in Romance Lang., Boston Coll., 1939. Substitute instr. in French Va. State Coll., Ettrick, 1939—40; instr. in French and Spanish Dillard U., New Orleans, 1940—42; from asst. prof. to prof. French and Latin Morgan State Coll., Balt., 1946—81. Vis. prof. Tex. So. U., Houston, 1953—54, Houston, 1956, Towson State Coll., Balt., 1969; part-time prof. Sojourner-Douglass Coll., Balt., 1981—85, Coppin State Coll., Balt., 1985—90; mem. adv. bd. Directory of Am. Scholars, NYC, 1970—80. Author: U.S. Teacher-Training Program: for France, 1959, Victor Hugo and L. Frechette, 1972, Ustaz Aswad (Black Professor), 1996, Ustaz Aswad No. II (Black Professor), 2005. Pres. PTA, Balt., 1957. Named Rosenwald fellow, Rosenwald Found., Chgo., 1947—48, Fulbright prof. in France, Fulbright Found., Washington, 1956—57; recipient Nat. award, Urban League, Boston, 1949, congratulatory dinner in his honor, French Embassy, Washington, 2003. Mem.: Frisby Hist. Soc. (fin. sec. 2001—02), Henson Family Soc., Phi Beta Kappa. Democrat. Roman Catholic. Avocations: movies, pinochle, sports, foreign travel.

SKINNER, HALCYON E., lawyer; b. Yonkers, NY, 1946; BA, Wesleyan U., 1968; JD, Duke U., 1973. Bar: Fla. 1973. Ptnr. Mahoney, Adams & Criser (merged with McGuireWoods in 1998), Jacksonville, Fla., McGuire Woods LLP, Jacksonville, Fla., 1998—, mng. ptnr. Jacksonville office, 2000—. Served US Army. Mem.: ABA (bus. law sect.), Jacksonville Bar Assn., Fla. Bar (bus. law sect.). Office: McGuireWoods LLP Bank of Am Tower Ste 3300 50 N Laura St Jacksonville FL 32202-3661 Office Phone: 904-798-2626. Office Fax: 904-360-6324. Business E-Mail: hskinner@mcguirewoods.com.

SKINNER, JAMES A. (JAMES A. SKINNER), food products executive; b. Davenport, IA; m. Kathleen Skinner; 1 child. Grad, Roosevelt U. Restaurant mgr. trainee to numerous positions within the US Co. McDonald's Corp., 1971—, US zone v.p., 1987—92; sr. v.p., relationship ptnr., 1992—95; exec. v.p., internat. relationship ptnr. McDonald's Ctrl. Europe, Middle East, Africa, India, 1995—97; pres. McDonald's Europe, 1997—2001; pres., COO McDonald's Europe/Asia/Pacific and Middle East, 2001—02, McDonald's Restaurant Group, 2002—03; vice chmn. McDonald's Corp., 2003—04, vice-chmn., CEO, 2004—. Adv. dir. bd. dirs. (twice) McDonald's Corp.; bd. dirs. Walgreen Co., 2005—. Bd. mem. Ronald McDonald House Charities. Office: McDonald's Corp McDonald's Plz 2111 McDonalds Dr Oak Brook IL 60523 *

SKINNER, JAMES LAURISTON, chemist, educator; b. Ithaca, NY, Aug. 17, 1953; s. G. William and Carol (Bagger) S.; m. Wendy Moore, May 31, 1986; children: Colin Andrew, Duncan Geoffrey. AB, U. Calif., Santa Cruz, 1975; PhD, Harvard U., 1979. Rsch. assoc. Stanford U., Calif., 1980-81; from asst. prof. to prof. chemistry Columbia U., NYC, 1981-90; Joseph O. Hirschfelder prof. chemistry, dir. Theol. Chemistry Inst. U. Wis., Madison, 1990—. Vis. scientist Inst. Theol. Physics U. Calif., Santa Barbara, 1987; vis. prof. physics U. Jos. Fourier, Grenoble, France, 1987, U. Bordeaux, France, 1995. Contbr. articles to profl. jours. Recipient Fresenius award Phi Lambda Upsilon, 1989, Camille and Henry Dreyfus Tchr.-Scholar award, 1984, NSF Presdl. Young Investigator award, 1984, Humboldt Sr. Scientist award, 1993; NSF grad fellow, 1975, NSF postdoctoral fellow, 1980, Alfred P. Sloan Found. fellow, 1984, Guggenheim fellow, 1993. Fellow: AAAS, Am. Acad. Arts & Sciences, Am. Phys. Soc. Achievements include fundamental research in condensed phase theoretical chemistry. Office: U Wis Dept Chemistry Theoretical Chem Inst 1101 University Ave Madison WI 53706-1322

SKINNER, JAUNETH, art educator, graphic artist; b. Waco, Tex., Mar. 19, 1958; d. Owen George and Patricia Ann Skinner; 1 child, Miriam Reneé Kessler. AS in Comml. Art Tech., Ind. U., Ft. Wayne, 1990, BFA, 1991; MFA, Bowling Green State U., 1993. Cert. Italian lang. and culture tchr. Università per Stranieri, Perugia, Italy, 2004. Curator Lillie M. Kleven print collection dept. visual arts Bemidji State U., Minn., 1994—2007, asst. prof. visual arts, 1994—99, assoc. prof. visual arts, 1999—2004, prof. visual arts, 2004—, chair visual arts dept., 2005—06. Bemidjicreative dir. Endion Studio, Bemidji, 1986—; assoc. editor, sr. designer Mid Am. Print Coun. Jour., Chgo., 1994—97; creative dir., master printer The Quiet Crow Press, Bemidji, 2000—; vis. prof., interim chair visual comm. and design Ind. U. Purdue U.- Ft. Wayne, 2007—08. Exhibited in group shows at Lessedra World Art Print Annual, Sofia, Bulgaria., 4th Annual Mini Print International Exhibition 2000, 1st Biennial International Miniature Print Exhibition, The World's Women On-Line!, Acm Siggraph, The Solarplate Revolution, Women's Work, Traditional and Contemporary: 100 Years of Etchings and Woodblock Prints, APA Memorial Print Project, Minnesota Journal Project 2000, The Foot in the Door Show, Border to Border, Ada: Women and Information Technology, Contemporary Prints - National Invitational, Hare of the Dog Press: Printed Works, Ohio Women's Caucus for Art Exhibition, Chicago Printmakers Collaborative: Paradise Lost, Holograms and Computer Prints, From Greenware to Software, The Little Prints Exhibit, The 21st National Print Exhibition, 23rd National Small Works Exhibition, Vital Signs:Drawing as Inquiry, Counterpoint 2000; 32nd Annual National Printmaking, Drawing, and Photography Exhibition, Outside Impressions: A Showcase of Contemporary Printmaking, Annual National Small Works Competition, Innovations in Printmaking, Paperworks '99, Community Visual Art Association, Jackson Hole, Wyoming, 12th Annual Parkside National Small Print Exhibition, Hand-Pulled Prints IV, National Works on Paper, Printwork '95, Americanism: Breaking the Mold, Positive/Negative IV, Regional '93, 16th Annual Proscenium 1992, Concepts and Dimensions, Issues of Color and Gender, Reverent/Irreverent, Women's Caucus for Art Third Annual Juried Exhibit, Digital Images 1990, 54th Annual Tri Kappa Regional Artists Exhibition, Indiana: Works on Paper, Women's Self Image, one-woman shows include Impressions: The Graphic Art of Jauneth Skinner, Away: Sabbatical Exhibition, Landscape and Memory, Imprimere: Imprinted on Memory, The Extraordinary in the Prosaic (Works on Paper), All Labels Female, Naked Singularity, print portfolio, Catch Phrase, Women's Self Image, Woman, Sheep, Water, print with Gendron Jensen, Umingmaq, broadside print portfolio, Italia, Lake Songs, Horizon Club Print, Out of the Woods, print published with John Hitchcock, Isolation, with Gendron Jensen, Mandan, print portfolio, Memorial, Women's Work, Past-Tense, A Half Mile From Home, nat. juried exhbn/, The Payne Gallery Print Exhibition, Hunterdon Art Center 32nd National Print Exhibition, North Arlington Library Print Exhibition. Recipient Best of Drawing, Beck Ctr., 1992, First and Second Pl., Preble County Art Assn., 1991, Merit Award, Drawing, Wassenburg Art Ctr., 1991, Third Pl. and Merit Award, Studio Mag. Computer Art Competition, 1989, Merit Award, Third Ann. Liquitex Art Awards Program, 1989, Artist in Residence, Scuola Internazionale di Grafica, Venice, Italy, 2005, Vis. Artist, Kelliher Pub. Sch., Mpls., 2003, Sch. of Art, U. of SD, Vermilion, SD, 2002, 2001, ND State Coll., Wahpeton, ND, 2002, Artist in Residence, Santa Reparata Stamperia d'Arte Grafica, Florence, Italy, 2001, 2000, Am. U., Corciano, Italy, 2001, Voyageurs Nat. Pk., Internat. Falls, MN, 1999, Vis. Artist, Valley City State U., Valley City, ND, 1997, Ctrl. Lakes Coll., Brainerd, MN, 1997, Disting. Artist Award, McKnight Found. and Region 2 Arts Coun., 1996, Manhattan Arts Internat. Merit Award, 1995, Someone Spl. Vol., United Way, 1995, Charles F. Wassenburg Award, Drawing, Wassenburg Art Ctr., 1993, Best of Show Purchase Award, East Tenn. State U., 1993; grantee McKnight Found. Grant with Dust & Fire: Women's Stories, Region 2 Arts Coun., 1999, Individual Artist Grant with poet CarolAnn Russell, McKnight Found. and Region 2 Arts Coun., 1999, McKnight Found. Grant with Loonfeather Press, 1997, Q-7 Ventures Grant, Minn. State Colleges and Universities, 1996, 1995; scholar Paralyzed Veterans of Am., Paralyzed Veterans of Am., 1989, Fine Arts Scholarship, Dept. of Fine Art, Ind. U., 1986, 1987, 1988, 1989, 1990, 1991, Grad. Tchg. Assoc., Sch. of Art, Bowling Green State U., 1992, Fellowship in Graphic Arts, 1992, 1993, Ely Lilly Scholarship, Ely Lilly Found., 1991. Mem.: Coll. Art Assn., No. Printmakers Alliance, Am. Print Alliance, MidAmerica Print Coun., So. Graphics Print Coun. Achievements include Art work in Cradle Oak Press Collection, Bradley University, Peoria, Illinois; Scuola Internazionale di Grafica collection, Venice, Italy; Rossi Library Archives collection, American Academy in Rome; St. Cloud State University collection, Minnesota; University Print Library collection, Università di Palermo, Italy; University of Montana collection, Bozman; Lillie M. Kleven Print Collection, Bemidji State University, Minnesota; University Print Society Collection, Iowa State University, Ames; University of Nebraska, Omaha; Fogg Art Museum collection, Harvard, Cambridge, Massachusetts; Harwood Museum of Art collection, University of New Mexico, Santa Fe; Jerome Library Archives collection, School of Art Print Collection, Bowling Green State

University, Ohio; Kennaraháskóli Íslands University Print Collection, Stakkahlíð, Reykjavík, Iceland; Arizona State University Print Collection, Tempe; King Jigme Singhe Wangchuk of Bhutan Palace Art Collection; Anoka Ramsey Foundation collection, Anoka Ramsey Community College, Minnesota; Bob Leian Library, Oxford University, UK, Beijing University, China. Avocations: travel, reading, gardening. Office: Ind U Purdue U Ft Wayne Visual Arts Bldg Room 213 2101 E Coliseum Blvd Fort Wayne IN 46805-1499 Office Phone: 260-481-6053. Business E-Mail: skinnerj@ipfw.edu.

SKINNER, JOAN, dancer, choreographer, educator; b. St. Paul, Jan. 29, 1924; BA, Bennington Coll., Vt., 1946; MA, U. Ill., Urbana, 1963. Mem. Martha Graham Dance Co., NYC, 1947—50, Merce Cunningham Dance Co., NYC, 1950—53; featured dancer John Butler, The Am. Dance Theater, 1953—55; artist in residence U. Minn., Mpls., Walker Art Ctr., Mpls., 1964—66; faculty U. Wash., Seattle, 1967—89, prof. emeritus, 1989—; artistic dir. Skinner Releasing Dance Co., Seattle, 1977—85. Guest artist Mpls. Civic Orch., 1959—61, NH Music Festival, 1961, Guthrie Theatre, Mpls., 1964—66; chair dance dept. faculty U. Wash., Seattle, 1982—87; dir. summer tchg. cert. program Skinner Releasing Technique, Seattle, 1990—; artist in residence New Dance Festival, Caracas, Venezuela, Sch. New Dance Devel., Amsterdam. Lead dancer Mary Hunter's Musical Americana, 1953, soloist Am. Dance Festival, NYC, 1950—53, U. Ill. Contemporary Arts Festival, Urbana, 1950—53, choreographer Water Piece, Quartet, Etudes 1 and 2, Juxtapositions, music by Ernst Krenek, Dawn Travelers, music by James Knapp, Dialogues in Dance, Dialogues in Dance II, Songs of Transformation, Pulsare, Interludes, music by Denney Goodhew, Floating Sounds - Fleet Feet, with Charles Stokes, Bill Ritchie Who's When Where, music by James Knapp, Echoes. Achievements include research in kinesthetic training; development of Skinner Releasing System. Mailing: 827 NE 130th St Seattle WA 98125-3951

SKINNER, JONATHAN SNOWDEN, economics educator; b. Boston, Aug. 29, 1955; s. Walter Jay and Sylvia (H.) S.; m. Martha Amy McLafferty, Oct. 17, 1987; children: Owen, Lucy. BA, U. Rochester, 1977; MA, UCLA, 1978, PhD, 1983. Asst. prof. to prof. U. Va., Charlottesville, 1981—95, prof., 1995—; vis. assoc. prof. Harvard U., Cambridge, Mass., 1992—93; prof. Dartmouth Coll., 1999—.

SKINNER, KNUTE RUMSEY, poet; b. St. Louis, Apr. 25, 1929; s. George Rumsey and Lidi (Skjoldvig) S.; m. Jeanne Pratt; 1953; divorced 1954; 1 child, Frank; m. Linda Kuhn, 1961 (div. 1977); children: Dunstan, Morgan; m. Edna Kiel, 1978. Student, Culver-Stockton Coll., 1947-49; BA, U. No. Colo., 1951; MA, Middlebury Coll., 1954; PhD, U. Iowa, 1958. Instr. English U. Iowa, Iowa City, 1955-56, 57-58, 60-61; asst. prof. English Okla. Coll. for Women, 1961-62; lectr. creative writing Western Wash. U., Bellingham, 1962-71, asso. prof. English, 1971-73, prof. English, 1973-97; pres. Signpost Press Inc., nonprofit corp., 1983-95. Author: Stranger with a Watch, 1965, A Close Sky Over Killaspuglonane, 1968, 75, In Dinosaur Country, 1969, The Sorcerers: A Laotian Tale, 1972, Hearing of the Hard Times, 1981, The Flame Room, 1983, Selected Poems, 1985, Learning to Spell "Zucchini," 1988, The Bears and Other Poems, 1991, What Trudy Knows and Other Poems, 1994, The Cold Irish Earth: New and Selected Poems of Ireland, 1965-1995, 1996, An Afternoon Quiet and Other Poems, 1998, Greatest Hits, 1964-2000, 2001, Stretches, 2002, The Other Shoe, 2005; editor: Bellingham Rev., 1977-83, 93-95; contbr. poetry, short stories to anthologies, textbooks, periodicals. Nat. Endowment for the Arts fellow, 1975 Mem. Am. Conf. Irish Studies, Wash. Poets Assn. E-mail: knuteskinner@eircom.net.

SKINNER, MARY JACOBS, lawyer; b. 1957; m. Sam Skinner, Aug. 17, 1989; stepchildren: Thomas, Steven, Jane. BA cum laude, Harvard U., 1978; JD, Northwestern U., 1981. Bar: Ill. 1981, D.C. 1990, U.S. Supreme Ct. 1990. With Sidley Austin Brown & Wood, Chgo., 1981—, ptnr., 1989—; counsel to spkr. Ill. Ho. of Reps., Springfield, Ill., 1983—85. Intern White House, 1979, Former trustee RAdcliffe Coll.; participant leadership coun. Greater Chgo. Fellowship Program, 1984. Named One of Forty under 40 Most Outstanding Leaders in Chco., Crain's Chgo. Bus. Mem. Harvard Alumni Assn. (bd. dirs.), Radcliffe Coll. Alumni Assn. (past pres.). Office: Sidley Austin Brown and Wood Bank One Plz 10 S Dearborn St Chicago IL 60603

SKINNER, MICHAEL DAVID, lawyer, lobbyist, consultant; b. Shreveport, LA, Jan. 5, 1950; s. Roger Gilman and Jerry Ann (Sneed) S.; m. Janet Louise Horaist, Jan. 7, 1978. JD, La. State U., 1976. Bar: La. 1977, U.S. Dist. Ct. (we. dist.) La. 1978, U.S. Ct. Appeals (5th and 11th cirs.) 1978, U.S. Dist. Ct. (mid. dist.) La. 1982, U.S. Supreme Ct. 1982, U.S. Dist. Ct. (so. dist.) Tex. 1983. Pvt. practice, Lafayette, La., 1976-84; asst. dist. atty. Lafayette Parish, 1983—84; ptnr. Guilliot, Skinner & Everett, 1984-86; asst. parish atty. Lafayette Parish, 1988—93; ptnr. Goode, Skinner & Hawkland, 1986-93; U.S. atty. West Dist. La., 1993-2000; atty. Onebane Law Firm, Lafayette, La., 2001—. Chmn. La. Democratic Party, 2003—05. Mem. La. State Bar Assn. (mem. ho. of dels.). Democrat. Office: 1200 Camellia Blvd Ste 300 Lafayette LA 70508 Office Phone: 337-237-2660.

SKINNER, PAMELA J., adult education educator; b. St. Paul, Jan. 20, 1967; d. Neal Herbert and Claudia Jac Skinner; m. Adam Forbes Carpenter, Aug. 14, 2002; children: Spencer John Tichenor, Benjamin Lee Carpenter. BS in Genetics and Cell Biology, U. Minn., St. Paul, 1995; postgrad., St. Olaf Coll., Northfield, Minn., 1985—86; PhD in Pathobiology, U. Minn., Mpls., 1998. Jr. scientist microbiology U. Minn., St. Paul, 1993—95, grad. asst. lab. medicine and pathology, 1995—98, post-doctoral assoc. Lab. Medicine and Pathology, 1998—99, post-doctoral fellow microbiology, 1999—2001, rsch. assoc. microbiology, 2002, asst. prof. vet. and biomed. scis., 2002—. Ad hoc reviewer: Jour. Gen. Virology, 1200, Jour. Neurochemistry, 2006; contbr. chapters to books, articles to profl. jours. Watershed dist. mgr. Ramsey Wash. Metro Watershed Dist., Little Canada, Minn., 1994—2007. Mem.: AAAS, Soc. for Neurosci., Am. Soc. for Microbiologists, Am. Assn. Immunologists, Sigma Xi. Office: Univ Minnesota 1971 Commonwealth Ave 205 VSB Saint Paul MN 55108 Office Phone: 612-624-2644. Office Fax: 612-625-5203. Business E-Mail: skinn002@umn.edu.

SKINNER, PATRICIA MORAG, state legislator; b. Glasgow, Scotland, Dec. 3, 1932; d. John Stuart and Frances Charlotte (Swann) Robertson; m. Robert A. Skinner, Dec. 28, 1957; children: Robin Ann, Pamela. BA, NYU, 1953. Mdse. trainee Lord & Taylor, NYC; adminstrv. asst. Atlantic Products, NYC; newspaper corr. Salem Observer, NH, 1964-84; mem. N.H. Ho. of Reps., 1972-94, chmn. labor, human resources, and rehab. com., 1975-86, mem. House edn. com., 1987, chmn., 1989-94, exec. com. Nat. Conf. State Legislatures, 1987-90; chmn. N.H. Adv. Coun. Unemployment Compensation, 1984-94. Mem. State Libr. Adv. Coun., 2001—. Bd. dirs. Castle Jr. Coll., 1975, chmn. bd., 1988-96; v.p. bd. Swift Water coun. Girl Scouts U.S., v.p., 1987-92; N.H. Voc-Tech. Coll., Nashua, 1978-83; trustee Nesmith Libr., Windham, N.H., 1982—, chmn. bd. trustees, 1994-99; pres. N.H. Fedn. Rep. Women's Clubs, parliamentarian, legis. chmn., 1984-86, 94-96. Mem. Windham Woman's Club (pres. 1981-83), Order Ea. Star. Christian Scientist.

SKINNER, PETER GRAEME, retired lawyer; b. London, Ont., Can., July 27, 1944; naturalized, U.S., 1952; s. George Woodley and Marjorie Grace S. AB, Princeton U., 1966; JD, MBA, Columbia U., 1970. Bar: NY 1971. Assoc. Patterson, Belknap, Webb & Tyler, NYC, 1970-77, ptnr., 1977-85; gen. counsel, sec. Dow Jones & Co., NYC, 1985—2004, v.p., 1985—89, sr. v.p., 1989—98, exec. v.p., 1998—2004; ret., 2004. Mem.: ABA, Assn. Bar City N.Y., N.Y. State Bar Assn. Office: Dow Jones & Co Inc 200 Liberty St Fl 12 New York NY 10281-1003 Office Phone: 212-416-3030. E-mail: peter.skinner@dowjones.com.

SKINNER, RICHARD L., federal agency administrator; BS, Fairmount State U.; MPA, George Washington U. Asst. inspector gen. audits Fed. Emergency Mgmt. Agency Dept. Homeland Security, Washington, 1991—96, dep. inspector gen., 1996, acting inspector gen., 2002—03; dep. inspector gen. US Dept. Homeland Security, Washington, 2003—05, acting inspector gen., 2004—05, inspector gen., 2005—. Office: Dept Homeland Security Naval Security Station Nebraska and Massachusetts Avenues NW Washington DC 20528 Office Phone: 202-254-4100. Office Fax: 202-254-4285. E-mail: rick.skinner@dhs.gov.

SKINNER, ROBERT C., JR., retail executive; BA in Political Sci., Middlebury Coll., 1976; grad., Harvard Bus. Sch. Advanced Mgmt. Program, 1992. Pres. Oxford Shirt Group, 1987—99; v.p. Oxford Industries, 1999—2000; pres. Kellwood Menswear, 2000—02; from v.p. to pres., COO Kellwood Co., St. Louis, 2002—03, pres., COO, 2003—05, pres., CEO, 2005—06, chmn., pres., CEO, 2006—. Bd. govs. Young Mens Assn. Office: Kellwood Co 420 Fifth Ave 28t Fl New York NY 10018 Business E-Mail: Bob_Skinner@kellwood.com.

SKINNER, ROBERT EARLE, librarian, writer; b. Alexandria, Va., June 25, 1948; s. Earl Woodrow and Pearle Labar (Capper) S.; m. Linda Sue Long, June 12, 1970 (div. 1976); children: Christopher William, Kelly Sue; m. Patricia Ann Friedmann, Mar. 17, 1979 (div. 1996); children: Esme F., Werner H.; m. Bettye Jean Harrison, June 20, 2001. BA in History, Old Dominion U., 1970; MLS, Ind. U., 1977; postgrad. student, U. New Orleans, 1991-93. Search analyst Strughold Aeromed. Libr., Brooks AFB, Tex., 1977-79; from reference libr. to head med. edn. libr. La. State U. Med. Ctr., New Orleans, 1979-85; spl. cons. Robert L. Siegel & Assocs., New Orleans, 1985-87; univ. libr. Xavier U., New Orleans, 1987—; mng. editor Xavier Rev. Press, 1989—. Vis. lectr. in Am. studies U.S. Air Force Acad., 2002; spkr. Symposium on African-Am. Detective Fiction, Bucknell U., 2005. Author: The Hard-Boiled Explicator, 1985, The New Hard-Boiled Dicks, 1987, rev. edit., 1995, Two Guns From Harlem, 1989, (with Michel J. Fabre) Chester Himes: An Annotated Primary and Secondary Bibliography, 1992, Fiction in Ellipsis, 1992, (with Thomas Bonner, Jr.) Above Ground, 1993, Immortelles, 1995; (with Michel J. Fabre) Plan B, 1993, Conversations with Chester Himes, 1995, Fiction in Hard Boiled, 1994, Fiction in Crime Yellow, 1994, Skin Deep, Blood Red, 1997, Cat-Eyed Trouble, 1998, Daddy's Gone-A-Hunting, 1999, Blood to Drink, 2000, Pale Shadow, 2001, The Righteous Cut, 2002; guest editor La. Lit., 1998, contbg. guest editor Plots With Guns, 2002-03, contr., 2005; contbr. articles to profl. jours. With USCG, 1970-74. Grantee Mellon Found., 1987-95, La. Divsn. of the Arts, 1993, 95, NEH, 1991—. Mem. ALA. Avocations: hiking, reading, book collecting, antique radios. Home: 6824 General Haig St New Orleans LA 70124-4029 Office: Xavier U 1 Drexel Dr New Orleans LA 71245-1098 Business E-Mail: rskinner@xula.edu.

SKINNER, ROBERT EARLE, JR., civil engineer, engineering executive; b. Washington, Aug. 10, 1946; s. Robert Earle and Dorothy Inez (Ballance) S.; m. Dianne Lynette Sands; children: Martha, Jeffrey. BSCE, U. Va., 1969; MS in Civil Engring., MIT, 1971. Registered profl. engr., Va. Sr. assoc. PRC Voorhees, McLean, Va., 1971-79, v.p., 1979-83; sr. staff officer Transp. Rsch. Bd., Washington, 1983-86, dir. studies and info. svc., 1986-94, exec. dir., 1994—. Exec. com. Hwy. Innovative Tech. Evaluation Ctr., Washington, 1994—; adv. com. Ctr. for Transp. and the Environment, Raleigh, N.C., 1995—; bd. dirs. Innovation Pavement Rsch. Found., Washington, 1999-2002; mem. adv. bd. Ctr. for Urban Transp. Rsch., U. South Fla., 2003—; mem. vis. com. engirng. sys. divsn. MIT, 2004—. Contbr. articles to profl. jours.; mem. editorial bd. Jour. Trans. and Stats., 1996. Mem. adv. coun. U. Va., 1995—; mem. vis. com. Engring. Sys. Ctr., MIT, 2003—. With U.S. Army N.G., 1970-76. Mem.: ASCE. Methodist. Avocations: woodworking, tennis. Office: Transportation Research Bd of the Nat Acads 500 5th St NW Washington DC 20001-

SKINNER, SUE DOSSETT, retired vocational director; b. Geneva, Ky., Dec. 4, 1928; d. Ural Morrison and Nellie Susan (Long) Dossett; m. William Thomas Skinner III, Sept. 7, 1952 (dec.); children: William Thomas IV, John Little Clay. BS, U. Ky., Lexington, 1951; EdM, NC State U., Raleigh, 1972. Asst. home demonstration agt. NC Ext. Svc., Warren County, 1952—60; food svcs. dir. Warren County Schs., 1968—72, tchr. home econ., 1972—88, dir. vocat. edn., 1988—92; ret., 1992. Past chair and vice chair Region III Home Econ. Leadership Coun.; v.p. NC Assn. Educators, Warren County, NC, sec., past pres. home econ. tchrs. sect.; Warren County del. NC Vocat. Assn.; past state sec. NC Home Econ. Assn., past state scholarship chair; mem. state scholarship com. NC Sch. Food Svc. Assn.; past advisor Region III Future Homemakers Am. Contbr. articles to periodicals. Participant Internat. Farm Youth Exch., Finland; local club leader 4-H; past dist. pres. Fedn. Woman's Clubs; past pres., com. chair Warrenton Woman's Club; v.p. Valley Investors; past pres. Littleton Womans Club; elder, choir dir. Presbyn. Ch. Finalist runner-up, Mrs. NC Contest; named county and state winner, 4-H Alumni Recognition Program; recipient state poetry prizes (4), Fedn. Woman's Clubs. Mem.: DAR (state chaplain 1997—2000, pres. 2004—06, chpt. regent 1976—78, 1983—85, 1988—93, 2007—), Gavel Soc., Am. Assn. Career and Tech. Edn., Order of the Merovingian Dynasty, Sons and Daus. Pilgrims, Order Ancient Planters (nat. pres. 2004—05, nat. sec. 2005—07), Jamestowne Soc. (hon. gov. 1st NC chpt. 2005—), Dau. Colonial Wars (state chaplain 2005—06, state pres. 2007—), Dames Ct. Honor (state sec. 2006, state chaplain 2006—), Charlemagne Soc., Colonial Dames Am., Little Garden Club, Delta Kappa Gamma (past pres.). Presbyterian. Avocations: knitting, antiques. Home: PO Drawer 520 Littleton NC 27850-0520

SKINNER, THOMAS, broadcast executive; b. Poughkeepsie, NY, Aug. 17, 1934; s. Clarence F. and Frances D. S.; m. Elizabeth Burroughs, June 22, 1957; children: Kristin Jon, Karin Anne, Erik Lloyd. BS, SUNY, Fredonia, 1956; MA, U. Mich., Ann Arbor, 1957, PhD, 1962. Instr. speech U. Mich., 1960; assoc. prof., exec. producer dept. broadcasting San Diego State U., 1961-66; asst. mgr. Sta. WITF-TV, Hershey, Pa., 1966-70; v.p. Sta. WQED-TV, Pitts., 1970-72; exec. v.p., COO QED Communications Inc. (WQED-TV, WQED-FM, Pittsburgh mag., WQEX-TV), 1972-93; founder, pres., exec. prodr. Windrush Assocs., 1993—; v.p. Programming Resolution Prodns., Burlington, Vt., 1996—; mng. dir. Inland Seas Edn. Assn., 2000—; exec. prodr. Free to Choose Media, 2004—. Exec. prodr.: spls. and series including (for PBS) Nat. Geog. spls. Planet Earth, The Infinite Voyage, Conserving America, (for TBS) Pirate Tales, (for A&E) Floating Palaces, California and the Dream Seekers, The Story of Money, (for Discovery) Battleship, The Secret World of Air Freight, (for PBS) The Power of Choice: The Life and Ideas of Milton Friedman, (for HDNET) The Ultimate Resource. Recipient award as exec. prodr. DuPont Columbia, 1979, Oscar award as dir. Acad. Motion Picture Arts and Scis., 1967, Emmy award as exec. prodr. Nat. Acad. TV Arts and Scis., 1979, 83-84, 86-87, Peabody award as exec. prodr., 1980, 86. Office Phone: 231-883-1659. Personal E-mail: ski361@aol.com.

SKINNER, THOMAS V., federal agency administrator; BA, Lawrence U.; JD, Northwestern U., 1987. Ptnr. Winston & Strawn, Chgo., 1991—99; dir. Ill. EPA, 1999—2001; regional adminstr. Region 5 U.S. EPA, Chgo., 2001—04, acting asst. adminstr. enforcement & compliance assurance Washington, 2004—. Office: EPA Ariel Rios Fed Bldg 1200 Pennsylvania Ave NW Rm 3204 Washington DC 20460

SKINNER, WILLIAM PHILIP, JR., manufacturing executive; b. Youngstown, Ohio, June 24, 1957; s. William Philip Skinner and Lois Jean Brauninger. Student, Youngstown State U., Ohio, 1982, Palm Beach C.C., Lake Worth, Fla., 1990; cert. in clay modeling, Ctr. Creative Studies, Detroit, 1993. Owner Youngstown Reconditioning, 1982—85; with Nat. Water Svc., Rivera Beach, Fla., 1990—92; treas., head ops. Skinner Interiors, Blkln., 1992—93; contract employee Modern Engring., Detroit, 1993—2001; owner, pres. Complete Coating Inc., Youngstown, 2001—. Founding mem. Lowellville Hist. Soc., 2005. Mem.: Internat. High IQ Soc., Youngstown Club, Phi Theta Kappa. Avocations: reading, travel. Home: 7100 Lockwood Blvd #405 Boardman OH 44512

SKINSTAD, ANNE HELENE, psychologist, researcher; b. Bergen, Hordaland, Norway, July 8, 1949; d. Alfhild (Hektoen) and Leif Sigurd Skinstad; 1 child, Siri Ødegaard. D in Psychology, U.of Bergen, Norway, 1977; PhD, U.of Bergen, 2001. Diplomate in Clin. Psychology Coll. Problems of Drug Dependence, 1985. Staff psychologist Hjellestad Clinic and Dr. Martens Clinic, Bergen, Norway, Hordaland, Norway, 1977—79; leading psychologist Blå-Kors Social Ctr., Bergen, Norway, 1979—83; facullty mem. U. Iowa, Iowa City, 1990—2001, asst. prof. Coll. Pub. Health, 2001—. Rsch. fellow The U. of Bergen, Norway, 1983—87; leading psychologist treatment ctr. substance abusing women Hjellestad Clinic, Bergen, Norway, 1987—90; program dir. Prairielands Addiction Tech. Transfer Ctr., Iowa City, 1995—2005. Contbr. articles to profl. jours. Recipient numerous grants, Norway, U.S. Mem.: APA, Am. Public Health Assn., Rsch. Soc. Alcoholism, European Roschach Assn. (founding mem. 1989), Nat. ATTC (chmn. liaison com., mem. curriculum com.), Norwegian Psychol. Assn. Avocations: owning Australian sheppards, piano. Office: U Iowa Coll Pub Health E239GH Iowa City IA 52242 Business E-Mail: anne-skinstad@uiowa.edu.

SKIPPER, JAMES HULETT, JR., music educator; b. Griffin, Ga., Oct. 27, 1937; s. James Hulett and Kathleen Grace Skipper; m. Velma B. Brannon, Aug. 28, 1960; children: Jacob, Zena. BFA, U. Ga., 1959, M Music Edn., 1963, specialist in edn., 1975; PhD, Pacific Western U., 1995. Band dir. Rockdale County Bd. Edn., Conyers, Ga., 1960—68, 1973—90, Henry County Bd. Edn., McDonough, Ga., 1968—69, DeKalb County Bd. Edn., Decatur, Ga., 1969—73, Rockdale County Bd. Edn., 1973—90; pvt. piano and brass instr. Conyers, 1991—. Performer Norwegian and QE2 cruise ships. Mem.: Music Educators Nat. Conf., Music Tchrs. Nat. Assn. (past pres. Ga. chpt.), Ga. Music Educators Assn. (past vice chmn.). Republican. Baptist. Avocations: trumpet, piano, crossword puzzles. Home: 2131 Christian Cir Conyers GA 30013 E-mail: vebskipp@bellsouth.net.

SKIPPER, JOHN, publishing executive; BA in Eng. Lit., UNC; MA in Eng. Lit., Columbia Univ., NYC. Formerly with Straight Arrow Publ., editor, Rolling Stone Mag., publ. US Mag.; v.p. Disney Mag. Publ. Co.; sr. v.p. Disney Publ. Group; sr. v.p., gen. editor ESPN The Mag.; sr. v.p., gen. mgr. ESPN.com; sr. v.p. programming, exec. v.p. content ESPN, 2005—. Office: ESPN ESPN Plz 935 Middle St Bristol CT 06010 *

SKIRNICK, ROBERT ANDREW, lawyer; b. Chgo., Apr. 23, 1938; s. Andrew and Stella (Sanders) S.; children: Rebecca, David; m. Maria Ann Castellano, Oct. 4, 1974; 1 child, Gabriella. BA, Roosevelt U., 1961; JD, U. Chgo., 1966. Bar: U.S. Dist. Ct. (no. dist.) Ill. 1966, U.S. Ct. Appeals (7th cir.) 1968, U.S. Supreme Ct. 1970, U.S. Ct. Appeals (5th and 9th cirs.) 1982, N.Y. 1989, U.S. Ct. Appeals (11th cir.) 1992, U.S. Dist. Ct. (so. dist.) Tex. 1992, U.S. Dist. Ct. Ariz. 1993, U.S. Ct. Appeals (4th, 6th and 8th cirs.) 2002. Atty. office gen. counsel honors program HEW, Washington, 1966-68; ptnr. Fortes, Eiger, Epstein & Skirnick, Chgo., 1975-77, Much, Shelist, Freed, Chgo., 1977-79, Wolf, Popper, Ross, Wolf & Jones, NYC, 1979-87, Kaplan, Kilsheimer & Foley, NYC, 1988-89, Wechsler, Skirnick, Harwood, Halebian & Feffer, NYC, 1989-95, Lovell & Skirnick, LLP, NYC, 1995-97, Meredith Cohen Greenfogel & Skirnick, P.C., NYC, 1997—. Cons. Nat. Legal Aid and Def. Assn., Chgo., 1968—69; instr. NYU, 1979—80; spl. asst. atty. gen. Ill. Atty. Gen. Office, Chgo., 1972—73; spl. antitrust counsel State of Conn., 1976—77; mem. adv. bd. Small Bus. Legal Def. Commn., San Francisco, 1982—; lectr. Practicing Law Inst., NYC, 1986—87; spl. master So. Dist. N.Y., 1988—91; ct. apptd. co-lead counsel NASDAQ market makers antitrust litigation, 1994—; ct. apptd. local counsel for instnl. plaintiff AOL TW Securities Litigation, 2002—; adv. bd. Am. Antitrust Inst., Washington, 2004—; sponsor Skirnick Fellowships for Pub. Interest Law Harvard Law Sch. Author: (with others) Federal Subject Matter Jurisdiction of U.S. District Courts, Federal Civil Practice, 1974, Antitrust Class Actions-Twenty Years Under Rule 23, 1986, The State Court Class Action-A Potpourri of Difference in the ABA Forum, Summer 1985; contbg. author: Multiparty Bargaining in Class Actions, Attorneys' Practice Guide to Negotiations, 2d edit., 1996, Survery of Securities Class Actions and Derivative Suits, 2001, ABA Section of Litigation, 2003; bd. editors Ill. Bar Antitrust Newsletter, 1969-73; topic and articles editor Jour. Forum Com. on Franchising, 1981-86. Atty. Office Gen. Counsel Honors Program, U.S. Dept. HEW, 1966-68; chmn. Ill. Legis. Com. Antitrust Section Ill. Bar., 1970-71; Topic and Articles Editor, Jour. Forum Com. on Franchising, 1981-86; ct. apptd. local counsel for instl. plaintiff in AOLTW securities litigation, 2002-. Mem.: ATLA, ABA (co-chair securities law subcom. litigation sect. 1987, mem. com. on regulation of futures and derivative instruments, mem. forum com. on franchising, mem. com. on class actions and derivative suits, mem. internat. antitrust and fgn. competition laws com.), Am. Antitrust Inst. (mem. adv. bd. 2004—), Assn. of the Bar of the City of N.Y. (antitrust and trade regulation com. 2004—), Assn. Bar N.Y. (mem. antitrust and trade regulation com. 2004—), Nat. Assn. Pub. Interest Law (bd. dirs. 1997—, nomination and election com. 1998—99, mem. fin. and investment com. 1998—, chair nominations and elections com. 1999—2000, chair fin. and investment com. 2000—03), Nat. Assn. for Pub. Interest Law Fellowships (bd. dirs. 1991—97, v.p. 1994—97, bd. dirs. 1997—2003, nomination and election coms. 1998—99, mem. budget com. 1998—2003, treas. 2000—03, mem. exec. com., mem. selection com., mem. investment and fin. com.), Ill. Bar Assn. (chmn. antitust sect. Ill. legis. com. 1970—71), N.Y. State Trial Lawyers Assn., N.Y. State Bar Assn. (mem. class action com.), Fed. Bar Coun. (mem. com. on second cir. cts. 1983—86, dir. Maria and Robert A. Skirnicle Fund for New Works at Carnegie Hall 2004—), Navy League of U.S. (mem. jour. com. 1995—97, N.Y. coun.), Plandome Country Club, Carlton Club. Office: Meredith Cohen Greenfogel & Skirnick One Liberty Plaza 35th Fl New York NY 10006-1404 Office Phone: 212-240-0020.

SKIRPAN, RICHARD MICHAEL, conductor, music educator; b. Phila., Sept. 17, 1980; s. Richard John and Deborah Ann (Gliick) Skirpan; m. Diane Marie Clark, Aug. 19, 2006. MB, Duquesne U., 2002, MusM, 2004. Dir. choral music Calvert Hall Coll. H.S., Balt., 2004—; choirmaster Ch. of the Nativity, Timonium, Md., 2007—. Grad. asst. for choral activities Duquesne U., Pitts., 2002—04; asst. condr. Bach Choir of Pitts., 2003—04. Composer: (one-act opera) Masque of the Red Death. Recipient Excellence in Choral Conducting, Beaver Valley (Pa.) Choral Soc., 2002. Mem.: Nat. Assn. for Music Edn., MENC, Am. Choral Dirs. Assn., Golden Key, Pi Kappa Lambda. Roman Catholic. Office: Calvert Hall Coll HS 8102 LaSalle Rd Baltimore MD 21286-8022

SKIVER, STEPHEN ALLEN, lawyer, physician; b. Toledo, Feb. 14, 1949; s. Arnold Leroy and Elizabeth Jane (Boyer) S.; m. Catherine Ann Reynolds, June 26, 1971; children: Tonia, Justin, Ryan, Laura, Elyssa. BS, Ohio U., 1971; MD, Med. Coll. Ohio, 1974; JD, U. Toledo, 1988. Bar: Ohio 1989, U.S. Dist. Ct. (no. dist.) Ohio 1991; Cert. Am. Bd. Internal Medicine. Physician, Maumee, Ohio, 1977-89; clin. asst. prof. medicine

Med. Coll. Ohio, Toledo, 1983-89; physician Toledo, 1989—; assoc. Jacobson, Maynard, Tuschman, Toledo, 1990-97; ptnr. Buckley, King & Bluso, Toledo, 1997—adr. Home: 30025 E River Rd Perrysburg OH 43551-3430 Office: Buckley King & Bluso 420 Madison Ave Ste 1100 Toledo OH 43604-1209

SKJERVOLD, GERALDINE REID See REID, GERALDINE

SKLANSKY, JACK, electrical and computer engineering educator, researcher; b. NYC, Nov. 15, 1928; s. Abraham and Clara S.; m. Gloria Joy Weiss, Dec. 24, 1957; children: David Alan, Mark Steven, Jeffrey Paul. BEE, CCNY, 1950; MSEE, Purdue U., 1952; D in Engring. Sci., Columbia U., 1955. Research engr. RCA Labs., Princeton, NJ, 1955-65; mgr. Nat. Cash Register Co., Dayton, Ohio, 1965-66; prof. elec. and computer engring. U. Calif., Irvine, 1966—94; pres. Scanicon Corp., Irvine, 1980-89; prof. radiology Charles R. Drew U. of Medicine and Sci., LA, 1995—2004. Author: (with others) Pattern Classifiers and Trainable Machines, 1981; editor: Pattern Recognition, 1973, (with others) Biomedical Images and Computers, 1982; editor-in-chief: Machine Vision and Applications, 1987. Recipient best paper award Jour. Pattern Recognition, 1977, 2000; rsch. grantee NIH, 1971-84, Army Rsch. Office, 1984-91, NSF, 1992-96, Office of Naval Rsch., 1995-97, Naval Air Warfare Ctr., 1997-98, Calif. Breast Cancer Rsch. Program, 1997-99, US Army Med. Rsch. and Materiel Command, 1999-2004, Calif. Telehealth and Telemedicine Ctr., 2000-02. Fellow IEEE, Internat. Assn. for Pattern Recognition; mem. ACM. Office: U Calif Dept Elec Engring & Computer Sci MSTB 211 Irvine CA 92697 E-mail: sklansky@uci.edu.

SKLAR, ALAN CURTIS, lawyer; b. NYC, Aug. 19, 1959; s. Jerry and Martha (Kolin) S.; m. Linda Susan Catalan, Dec. 26, 1982; twins: Daniel Jay and Jennifer Rachel. BA summa cum laude, U. Pa., 1980, JD, 1982. Bar: Calif., Nev. Assoc. Wolf Block Schorr & Solis-Cohen, Phila., 1980, 81, Rifkind & Sterling, Beverly Hills, Calif., 1982-84, Mitchell Silberberg & Knupp, LA, 1984-86; mng. dir. Coastal Investment Group, Beverly Hills, 1986-89; ptnr. Warren Clark & Sklar, LA, 1989—, Gordon & Silver, Las Vegas, Nev., 1991-95, Sklar Warren Conway & Williams LLP, Las Vegas, Nev., 1995—. Bd. dirs. Consolidated Mgmt., Inc., N.Y.C., L.A., Las Vegas. Author: Tactics and Techniques in Mergers and Acquisitions, 1985, Recent Developments in Mergers and Acquisitions, 1985, California Corporate Securities Laws, 1985, Corporate Law Overview, 1985, Secured Real Estate Transactions, 1993. Bd. trustees Las Vegas Bowl Organizing Com., 1995, 96, So. Nev. Housing Corp., 1995-98; mem. U. Pa. Alumni Secondary Sch. Com., 1998—; counsel Chabad of So. Nev., Las Vegas, 1991-2000. Named Top Corp. Atty., Nev. Bus. Jour. Mem. ABA, State Bar Nev., State Bar Calif., TPC Summerlin Country Club, World Zionist Orgn., Phi Beta Kappa, Phi Alpha Theta. Democrat. Jewish. Office: 8363 W Sunset RD #300 Las Vegas NV 89113-2092 Business E-Mail: asklar@sklar-law.com.

SKLAR, ERIC B., neurologist; m. Andrea L. Schaffer; children: Alexander Michael, Jordan Zachary. MD, Temple U., Phila., 1994—98. Lic. dr. VA. Neurologist, clinical neurophysiologist Alexandria Fairfax Neurology, Va., 2003—.

SKLAR, KATHRYN KISH, historian, educator; b. Columbus, Ohio, Dec. 26, 1939; d. William Edward and Elizabeth Sue (Rhodes) Kish; m. Robert A. Sklar, 1958 (div. 1978); children: Leonard Scott, Susan Rebecca Sklar Friedman; m. Thomas L. Dublin, Apr. 30, 1988. BA magna cum laude, Radcliffe Coll., 1965; PhD, U. Mich., 1969. Asst. prof., lectr. U. Mich., Ann Arbor, 1969-74; assoc. prof. history UCLA, 1974-81, chmn. com. to administer program in women's studies Coll. Letters and Sci., 1974-81, prof., 1981-88; Disting. prof. history SUNY, Binghamton, 1988—, co-dir. Ctr. Hist. Study of Women and Gender, 1998—; Harmsworth prof. U.S. history U. Oxford, 2005—. Pulitzer juror in history, 1976; fellow Newberry Libr. Family and Community History Seminar, 1973; active Calif. Coun. for Humanities, 1981-85, N.Y. Coun. for Humanities, 1992—; Harmsworth prof. Am. history Oxford U., 2005—. Author: Catharine Beecher: A Study in American Domesticity, 1973 (Berkshire pri e 1974); editor: Catharine Beecher: A Treatise on Domestic Economy, 1977, Harriet Beecher Stowe: Uncle Tom's Cabin, or Life Among the Lowly: The Minister's Wooing, Oldtown Folks, 1981, Notes of Sixty Years: The Autobiography of Florence Kelley, 1849-1926, 1984, (with Thomas Dublin) Women and Power in American History: A Reader (2 vols.), 1991, (with Linda Kerber and Alice Kessler-Harris) U.S. History as Women's History: New Feminist Essays, 1995, Women's Rights Emerges within the Antislavery Movement: A Short History with Documents, 1830-1870, 2000; co-editor: The Social Survey Movement in Historical Perspective, 1992, Florence Kelley and the Nation's Work: The Rise of Women's Political Culture, 1830-1900, 1995 (Berkshire prize 1996). Social Justice Feminists in the United States and Germany: A Dialogue in Documents, 1885-1933, 1998, Women's Rights Emerges within the Anti-Slavery Movement: A Short History with Documents 1830-1870, 2000, (with James Brewer Stewart) Women's Rights and Transatlantic Anti-Slavery in the Era of Emancipation, 2007; mem. edit. bd. Jour. Women's History, 1987—, Women's History Rev., 1990—, Jour. Am. History, 1978-81; contbr. chpts. to books; co-dir. Women and Social Movements in the U.S. 1600-2000: An Online Jour. and Datebase, 1997—. Fellow Woodrow Wilson Found., 1965-67, Danforth Found., 1967-69, Radcliffe Inst., 1973-74, Nat. Humanities Inst., 1975-76, Rockefeller Found. Humanities, 1981-82, Woodrow Wilson Internat. Ctr. for Scholars, 1982, 1992-93, Guggenheim Found., 1984, Ctr. Advanced Study Behavioral and Social Scis., Stanford U., 1987-88, AAUW, 1990-91; Daniels fellow Am. Antiquarian Soc., 1976, NEH fellow Newberry Library, 1982-83; Ford Found. faculty rsch. grantee, 1973-74; grantee NEH, 1976-78, UCLA Coun. for Internat. and Comparative Studies, 1983. Mem. Am. Hist. Assn. (chmn. com. on women historians 1980-83, v.p. Pacific Coast br. 1986-87, pres. 1987-88), Orgn. Am. Historians (exec. bd. 1983-86, Merle Curti award com. 1978-79, lectr. 1982—), Am. Studies Assn. (coun. mem.-at-large 1978-80), Berkshire Conf. Women Historians, Am. Antiquarian Soc., Phi Beta Kappa. Avocation: photography. Office: SUNY Dept History Binghamton NY 13902 Office Phone: 607-777-6202.

SKLAR, MARTY (MARTIN A. SKLAR), entertainment company executive; b. New Brunswick, NJ; m. Leah Sklar. Grad., UCLA. Asst. news editor Media Agy. Clients Publs.; with Walt Disney Co., Burbank, Calif., 1956—; v.p. concepts/planning Walt Disney Imagineering, Walt Disney Co., Burbank, Calif., 1974—79, v.p. creative devel., 1979—87, pres., 1987—96, vice chmn., prin. creative exec., 1996—2006, internat. amb., 2006—. One of founders Ryman Program for Young Artists. Contbr. articles to Showman of the World films. Mem. bd. edn. Anaheim City Sch. Dist., 1969, 1973; pres. Orange County, Calif. Sch. Bds. Assn.; commr. Anaheim City; founding chmn. Michael L. Roston Creative Writing Awards. Recipient Cmty. Svc. award for Anaheim, Cypress Coll., 1977, Lifetime Achievement award, Themed Entertainment Assn., 1995; inducted into, Hall of Fame, Internat. Assn. Amusement Pks. and Attractions, 2002. Office: Walt Disney Co 500 S Buena Vista St Burbank CA 91521-9722

SKLAR, RICHARD LAWRENCE, political science professor; b. NYC, Mar. 22, 1930; s. Kalman and Sophie (Laub) S.; m. Eva Molineux, July 14, 1962; children: Judith Anne, Katherine Elizabeth. AB, U. Utah, 1952; MA, Princeton U., 1957, PhD, 1961. Mem. faculty Brandeis U., U. Ibadan, Nigeria, U. Zambia, SUNY-Stony Brook, UCLA; now prof. emeritus polit. sci. UCLA. Mem. fgn. area fellowship program Africa Nat. Com., 1970-73; Simon vis. prof. U. Manchester, Eng., 1975, Fulbright vis. prof. U. Zimbabwe, 1984; Lester Martin fellow Harry S. Truman Rsch. Inst., Hebrew U. Jerusalem, 1979; fellow Africa Inst. of South Africa, 1994—. Author: Nigerian Political Parties: Power in an Emergent African Nation, 1963, Corporate Power in an African State, 1975, African Politics in Postimperial Times, 2002; co-author: Postimperialism: International Capitalism and Development, 1987, African Politics and Problems in Development, 1991; co-editor: Postimperialism and World Politics, 1999; contbr. articles to profl. jours. Served with U.S. Army, 1952-54. Rockefeller Found. grantee, 1967 Mem. Am. Polit. Sci. Assn., African Studies Assn. (dir. 1976-78, 80-83, v.p. 1980-81, pres. 1981-82), AAUP (pres. Calif. Conf. 1980-81) Home: 1951 Holmby Ave Los Angeles CA 90025-5905 E-mail: sklar@polisci.ucla.edu.

SKLAR, WILFORD NATHANIEL, lawyer, real estate broker; b. Salt Lake City, Dec. 13, 1916; s. Benjamin B. Sklar and Blanche Blau; m. Sarah Cohen, Jan. 16, 1945 (dec. Dec. 2000); children: Beth-Lynn (dec.), Teri Helene. BBA, U. Pitts., 1942; JD, Southwestern Sch. Law, 1960. Bar: Calif. 1960, U.S. Dist. Ct. Calif. 1962, U.S. Supreme Ct. 1965. Pvt. practice, Riverside, Calif., 1960-98; ret., 1998. Co-comdr. mil. affairs com. March AFB, Calif.; active Riverside Family Svcs., 1965-85, Am. Legion. Sgt. USAF, PTO, 1942-46. Mem. B'nai B'rith (Akiba Dist. award 1970, 74), Riverside Jewish War Vets. Democrat. Jewish. Avocations: golf, coin collecting/numismatics, real estate investments. Home: 5904 Copperfield Ave Riverside CA 92506-4510 Office Phone: 951-684-1248.

SKLAREW, ROBERT JAY, biomedical research educator, consultant; b. NYC, Nov. 25, 1941; s. Arthur and Jeanette (Laven) S.; m. Toby Willner, July 15, 1970; children: David Michael, Gary Richard. BA in Zoology, Cornell U., 1963; MS, NYU, 1965, PhD in Biology, 1970. Assoc. rsch. scientist NYU Sch. Medicine, NYC, 1965-70, rsch. scientist, 1971-73, sr. rsch. scientist, 1973-79; rsch. asst. prof. pathology Goldwater Meml. Hosp. Sch. Medicine, NYC, 1979-87, rsch. assoc. prof. pathology, 1987-88; dir. cytokinetics and imaging lab. NYU rsch. svc. Goldwater Meml. Hosp., NYC, 1980-88; prof. cell biology, anatomy and medicine N.Y. Med. Coll., Valhalla, 1988-98. Rsch. assoc. dept. pathology Lenox Hill Hosp., N.Y.C., 1981-88; pres., CEO R.J. Sklarew Imaging Assoc., Inc., Larchmont, N.Y., 1990—2003; chmn. consensus panel for diagnostic cancer imaging Nat. Cancer Inst., 1994. Author: Microscopic Imaging of Steroid Receptors, 1990; sr. author: Cytometry, Jour. Histochem. Cytochem., Cancer, Exptl. Cell Rsch. Group leader Boy Scouts Am., Larchmont, 1978—80; bd. dir. Pinelake Park Coop, 1998—2001, 2006—. Grantee Am. Cancer Soc., Nat. Cancer Inst./NIH Conc. for Tobacco Rsch., R.J. Reynolds Industries Found., NYU; recipient Shannon award Nat. Cancer Inst., 1991. Mem. AAAS, Cell Kinetics Soc. (sec. 1983-85, 85-87, v.p. 1987-88, pres. 1988-89, chmn. nominations 1991, 93), N.Y. Acad. Sci., Soc. for Analytic Cytology, Soc. for Cell Biology, Tissue Culture Assn., Union Concerned Scientists, Kappa Delta Rho. Democrat. Achievements include development of methodology, algorithms and Receptogram analytic software for application of microscopic imaging in medical research and in pathodiagnosis of cancer, imaging methods for simultaneous densitometry and autoradiographic analysis; research in diagnostic imaging of steroid receptors, oncogenes and DNA ploidy in cancer, proliferative patterns and cell cycle kinetics of human solid tumors. Home: 8 Vine Rd Larchmont NY 10538-1247 Office: RJ Sklarew Imaging Assoc Inc 8 Vine Rd Larchmont NY 10538-1247 Personal E-mail: rjsklarew@aol.com.

SKLAROW, MARK HOWARD, educational association administrator; b. Phila., Oct. 11, 1956; s. Eugene Jay and Lois Francine (Shapiro) S.; m. Mindy Ellen Halbkram, June 22, 1980; children: Michelle Gail, Jaimie Lynn. BA, Temple U., 1978, MA, 1980, postgrad., 1981-83. Social sci. tchr. Penn Ctr. Acad., Phila., 1980-83, dean students, 1983-87; polit. analyst Sta. WWBZ (ABC affiliate), Vineland, NJ, 1984-87; exec. dir. Phila. Assn. Student Couns., 1985-87; dir. Pa. Student Leadership Workshops, Bloomsburg, Pa., 1985-87; curriculum dir. Presdl. Classroom, Washington, 1987-89, exec. dir., 1989-90; contbg. editor Classroom Role Call, 1990-93; exec. dir. Creative Response, 1990-94, Ind. Ednl. Cons. Assn., Fairfax, Va., 1995—. Commr. Phila. Youth Svcs. Commn., 1986-87; cons. Am. Heart Assn., Harrisburg, Pa., 1984-87; ednl. cons., Alexandria, Va., 1988—; mem. accreditation com. Middle States Assn. Colls. & Schs., 1981-82. Author: Outlook: A Guide to Current American Government, 1989; contbr. articles to profl. jours. Committeeman Dem. City Com., Phila., 1976-82; del. candidate, Pa., 1976; security dir. Dem. Nat. "Mini Conf.", Phila., 1978; exec. com. Somerton Civic Assn., Phila., 1972-76. Recipient Resolution for Community Svc., City Coun. Phila., 1986, Community Svc. award State Senate Pa., 1974; Temple U. fellow, 1979-80. Mem. Nat. Coun. for the Social Studies, Coun. for the Advancement of Citizenship (bd. dirs.), Nat. Assn. Student Activity Advisors, Nat. Assn. Leadership Workshop Dirs. Democrat. Jewish. Office: Ind Edl Cons Assn 3251 Old Lee Highway, Ste 510 Fairfax VA 22030-1504 Office Phone: 703-591-4850. Office Fax: 703-591-4860. E-mail: MSklarow@IECAonline.com. *

SKLARSKY, CHARLES B., lawyer; b. Chgo., June 13, 1946; s. Morris and Sadie (Brenner) S.; m. Elizabeth Ann Hardzinski, Dec. 28, 1973; children: Jacob Daniel, Katherine Gabrielle, Jessica Leah. AB, Harvard U., 1968; JD, U. Wis., 1973. Bar: Wis. 1973, Ill. 1973, U.S. Dist. Ct. (no. dist.) Ill. 1973, U.S. Ct. Appeals (7th cir.) 1978, U.S. Ct. Appeals (2nd cir.) 1986. Asst. states atty. Cook County, Chgo., 1973-78; asst. U.S. atty. (no. dist.) Ill. US Dept. Justice, Chgo., 1978-86; ptnr. Jenner & Block LLP, Chgo., 1986—. Mem. ABA, Am. Coll. Trial Lawyers, Chgo. Bar Assn. Office: Jenner & Block One IBM Plz Chicago IL 60611-3586 Office Phone: 312-923-2904. E-mail: csklarsky@jenner.com.

SKLARSKY, FRANK S., imaging company executive; b. Buffalo; married; 2 children. B in Acctg., Rochester Inst. Tech., 1978; MBA, Harvard Bus. Sch., 1983. CPA. Sr. acct. Ernst and Young, Rochester, NY, 1978—81; analyst DaimlerChrysler Corp., Auburn Hills, Mich., 1983, v.p. corp. fin. activities, v.p. product fin., asst. contr. prod. quality, cost mgmt. and procurement, 2001—04, v.p. corp. fin. control, 2004; v.p. fin. consumer divsn. Dell Computer Corp., Austin, Tex., 2000—01; exec. v.p., CFO ConAgra Foods, Omaha, 2004—06; exec. v.p. Eastman Kodak Co., Rochester, NY, 2006—, CFO, 2006—. Avocations: piano, swimming. Office: Eastman Kodak Co 343 State St Rochester NY 14650 Office Phone: 585-724-4000. *

SKLENAR, HERBERT ANTHONY, industrial products manufacturing company executive; b. Omaha, June 7, 1931; s. Michael Joseph and Alice Madeline (Spicka) S.; m. Eleanor Lydia Vincenz, Sept. 15, 1956; children: Susan A., Patricia I BSBA summa cum laude, U. Omaha, 1952; MBA, Harvard U., 1954; LLD (hon.), Birmingham-So. Coll., 1996. CPA W.Va. V.p., comptr. Parkersburg-Aetna Corp., W.Va., 1956—63; v.p., dir. Marmac Corp, Parkersburg, 1963-66; mgr. fin. control Boise-Cascade Corp., Idaho, 1966-67; exec. v.p. fin. and adminstrn., sec. Cudahy Co., Phoenix, 1967-72; chmn. emeritus Vulcan Materials Co., Birmingham, Ala., 1972-97, chmn. bd. dirs. emeritus, 1997—. Author (with others): The Automatic Factory: A Critical Examination, 1955. Trustee Leadership Birmingham, Birmingham-So. Coll Recipient Alumni Achievement award U. Nebr.-Omaha, 1977, cert. merit W.Va. Soc. CPAs, Elizah Watts Sells award AICPA, 1965, Brotherhood award NCCJ, 1993; inductee Ala. Acad. Honor, 1997 Mem.: Rotary Club Birmingham (pres.), Birmingham Country Club, Shoal Creek Club, Phi Eta Sigma, Phi Kappa Phi, Omicron Delta Kappa, Delta Sigma Pi. Republican. Presbyterian. Home: 2809 Shook Hill Cir Birmingham AL 35223-2618 Office: Vulcan Materials Co 1200 Urban Center Dr Birmingham AL 35242-2545 Office Phone: 205-298-3225.

SKLOVSKY, ROBERT JOEL, naturopathic physician, pharmacist, educator; b. NY; BS summa cum laude, Bklyn. Coll., 1975; MA in Sci. Edn., Columbia U., 1976; PharmD, U. Pacific, 1977; D in Naturopathic Medicine, Nat. Coll. Naturopathic Medicine, 1983. Intern Tripler Army Med. Ctr., Honolulu, 1977; pvt. practice Milwaukie, Oreg., 1983—. Recipient Bristol Labs. award Bklyn. Coll. Pharmacy, 1975, Coll. Gold medal, 1975, NYC Sci. Tchg. award Chemist's Club NY, 1976. Mem.: NY Acad. Sci. Avocations: classical and jazz music, art, gardening, painting. Office: 6910 SE Lake Rd Milwaukie OR 97267-2101 Office Phone: 503-654-3938.

SKLUTE, ADAM, performing company executive, dancer; b. Waterville, Maine; Scholarship student, The Joffrey Ballet Sch., NYC. Dancer Ballet Am. Concert Dancers, 1985-86, Joffrey II Dancers, NYC, 1986-88, The Joffrey Ballet, NYC, 1988, schedule coord., asst. ballet master, 1995—98, ballet master, artistic coord., 1998—2004, asst. artistic dir., 2004—05, assoc. artistic dir., 2005—07; artistic dir. Ballet West, Salt Lake City, 2007—. Office: Ballet West 50 W 200 South Salt Lake City UT 84101 Office Phone: 801-323-6908. Office Fax: 801-359-3504. *

SKLYAR, ADELINA M., lawyer; d. Joseph and Klafira Sklar. BA, NYU, NYC, 1993, JD, 1998. Bar: US Dist. Ct. (ea. dist.) NY 2001. Assoc. Ferro & Kuba, P.C., NYC, 1998—2001, Ferro, Kuba, Bloom, Mangano, Gacovino & Lake, P.C., NYC, 2001—05; ptnr. Ferro, Kuba, Mangano, Sklyar, Gacovino & Lake, P.C., NYC, 2005—. Mem.: ACLU, ATLA, NY State Bar Assn., NY County Lawyers' Assn. (assoc.). Office: Ferro Kuba Mangano Sklyar Ste 1100 360 West 31st St New York NY 10001 Office Phone: 212-244-7676. Office Fax: 212-244-9393. Business E-Mail: asklyar@ferrokuba.com.

SKOBLAR, BARRY, neuroscientist; b. Akron, Ohio, June 3, 1976; s. Richard and Jean Skoblar. PhD in Psychology, Fla. Inst. Tech., Melbourne, 2001—05. Neuropsychology internship Ctrl. Ark. Veterans Healthcare Sys., Little Rock, 2004—05; neuropsychology fellow U. Fla., Gainesville, 2005—. Contbr. articles to profl. jours. Constrn. vol. Habitat Humanity, Akron, 1991—95, Little Rock, 2004; mem. cmty. mental health svc. Gainesville, 2005. Recipient Outstanding Rsch. award, Fla. Inst. Tech., 2004. Mem.: APA, Nat. Acad. Neuropsychology, Internat. Neuropsychological Soc. Achievements include research in Parkinson's disease. Home: 333 NW 48th Blvd Gainesville FL 32607 Home Phone: 321-271-8017. Personal E-mail: bskoblar@hotmail.com. Business E-Mail: bskoblar@phhp.ufl.edu.

SKOCHELAK, SUSAN E., dean; BS, Mich. Tech. U., 1975, MS in Biol. Sci., 1977; MD, U. Mich., 1981; MPH, U. N.C., 1986. Diplomate Am. Bd. Family Medicine. Intern, resident family medicine U. N.C.-N.C. Meml. Hosp., Chapel Hill, 1977-81; assoc. dean Academic Affairs U. Wis., Madison, 1993—. Cons. in field; assoc. prof. U. Wis. Author: (with others) Preceptor Education Project, Handbook for Clerkship Directors. Mem. Wis. Rural Health Dev. Council, Consortium Primary Care in Wis.; co-dir. Wis. Area Health Edn. Sys. Recipient National award Patient Care mag., 1997. Mem. AMA, Soc. Tchrs. Family Medicine, Assn. Am. Med. Colls., Am. Med. Women's ssn., ACPHE. Office: Univ Wisconsin Med School 1300 University Ave Madison WI 53706-1510

SKOCPOL, THEDA RUTH, sociology and political science educator, former dean; b. Detroit, May 4, 1947; d. Allan Earnest and Jennie Mae (Becker) Barron; m. William John Skocpol, June 10, 1967; 1 child, Michael Allan. BA in Sociology, Mich. State U., 1969; MA in Sociology, Harvard U., 1972, PhD in Sociology with distinction, 1975; DSc (hon.), Mich. State U., 1997. Asst. prof. sociology Harvard U., Cambridge, Mass., 1975—78, assoc. prof. sociology, 1978—81, prof. sociology, 1986—94, prof. govt. sociology, 1995—97, Victor S. Thomas Prof. govt. and sociology, 1995—, dir., Ctr. for Am. Polit. Studies, 2000—06, dean Grad. Sch. Arts and Scis., 2005—07, sr. advisor social scis. Radcliffe Inst. Advanced Study, 2006—; assoc. prof. sociology and polit. sci. U. Chgo., 1981—84, prof. sociology and polit. sci., 1984—86, dir. Ctr. for Study of Indsl. Socs., 1982—85. Mem. Sch. for Social Sci., Inst. for Advanced Study, Princeton, 1980—81; vis. disting. prof. Amsterdam Sch. for Social Science Rsch., Netherlands, 1997. Author: States and Social Revolutions: A Comparative Analysis of France, Russia and China, 1979, edits. in Italian, 1981, Korean, 1980, French, 1985, Spanish, 1985, Portuguese, 1985 (Wright Mills award Soc. Study of Social Problems, 1979, Am. Sociol. Assn. award, 1980), Protecting Soldiers and Mothers: The Political Origins of Social Policy in the U.S., 1992 (Woodrow Wilson Found. award, 1993, J. David Greenstone award, 1993, Best Book award Am. Sociol. Assn., 1993, Allan Sharlin Meml. award Soc. Sci. History Assn., 1993, Ralph Waldo Emerson award Phi Beta Kappa, 1993), Boomerang: Clinton's Health Security Effort and the Turn Against Govt. in the U.S., 1996, Diminished Democracy: From Membership to Mgmt. in American Civil Life, 2003; author: Social Revolutions in the Modern World, 1994, Japanese edit., Iwanami, 1997, Social Policy in the U.S.: Future Possibilities in Hist. Perspective, 1995; author: (with Kenneth Finegold) State and Party in America's New Deal, 1995; author: Boomerang: Health Reform and the Turn Against Govt., paperback edit., 1997, The Missing Middle: Working Families and the Future of Am. Social Policy, 2000; editor: Vision and Method in Hist. Sociology, 1984, Japanese edit. by Bokutakusha, 1995, Democracy, Revolution, and History, 1998, Turkish edit. by Tarih Vakfi Yayinlari, 1999; co-editor, with Peter Evans and Dietrich Rueschemeyer: Bringing the State Back In, 1985;; co-editor: (with Margaret Weir and Ann Shola Orloff) The Politics of Social Policy in the U.S.; co-editor: (with John L. Campbell) Am. Soc. and Politics: Institutional, Hist., and Theoretical Perspectives, 1994; co-editor: (with Dietrich Rueschemeyer) States, Social Knowledge, and the Origins of Modern Social Policies, 1996; co-editor: (with Stanley B. Greenberg) The New Majority: Toward a Popular Progressive Politics, 1997; co-editor: (with Morris P. Fiorina) Civic Engagement in Am. Democracy, 1999; contbr. articles to profl. jours. Recipient Johan Skytte Prize in Polit. Sci., 2007; fellow Danforth Found., 1969—74, Woodrow Wilson Found., NSF, 1969—72, John Simon Guggenheim Found., 1990; grantee Russell Sage Found., 1983—84, 1990—92, Ford Found., 1986—87; sr. vis. scholar, Russell Sage Found., 1984—85, Nat. Merit scholar, 1965—69. Fellow: Nat. Acad. of Arts and Sci.; mem.: Nat. Acad. Social Ins., Social Sci. History Assn. (pres. 1996), Am. Sociol. Assn., Am. Polit. Sci. Assn. (pres. politics and history sect. 1991—92, coun. mem. 1994—96, chair Hubert Humphrey award com. 1995, pres. 2002—03), Sociol. Sci. Rsch. Assn. (founder, co-chair 1985—94), Phi Beta Kappa. Democrat. Home: 66 Huron Ave Cambridge MA 02138-6708 Office: Radcliffe Inst Advanced Study 10 Garden St Cambridge MA 02138 Office Phone: 617-496-0966. Business E-Mail: skocpol@fas.harvard.edu. *

SKODON, EMIL MARK, ambassador; b. Chgo., Nov. 25, 1953; s. Emil John and Anne F. (Soltes) S.; m. Dorothea Shaffer, Mar. 6, 1982; children: Catherine Marie, Christine Louise. BA, U. Chgo., 1975, MBA, 1976. Consular officer Am. Embassy, Bridgetown, Barbados, 1977-79, econ. officer East Berlin, Germany, 1979-81; econ. officer Office So. African Affairs, US Dept. State, Washington, 1982-84; econ. officer Am. Embassy, Vienna, 1984-88, Kuwait City, Kuwait, 1989-91; consul gen. Am. Consulate Gen., Perth, Australia, 1991-94; dep. chief mission Am. Embassy, Singapore, 1995-98, dir. office Australia, New Zealand, Pacific Island Affairs Washington, 1998-2000, polit. advisor to USAF chief of staff, 2000—02, deputy chief of Mission Rome, 2002—05, amb. to Brunei Bandar Seri Begawan, 2005—. Decorated Outstanding Civilian Svc. medal U.S. Army, Exceptional Civilian Svc. medal USAF Mem.: Chaine des Rotisseurs, Nat. Trust Historic Preservation. Avocations: visiting historic sites, good food, spending time with family. Office: Am Embassy Bandar Seri Begawan 4020 Bandar Seri Begawan Pl Dulles VA 20189

SKOGEN, HAVEN SHERMAN, investment company executive; b. Rochester, Minn., May 8, 1927; s. Joseph Harold and Elpha (Hemphill) S.;

m. Beverly R. Baker, Feb. 19, 1949; 1 child, Scott H. BS, Iowa State U., 1950; MS, Rutgers U., 1954, PhD, 1955; MBA, U. Chgo., 1970. Registered profl. engr., Wis. Devel. engr. E.I. duPont, Wilmington, Del., 1955—57; prof. Elmhurst (Ill.) Coll., 1957—58; chief engr. Stackpole, St. Marys, Pa., 1958—62; plant mgr. Magnatronics, Elizabethtown, Ky., 1962—65; mgr. Allen-Bradley, Milw., 1965—70; v.p. Dill-Clithrow, Chgo., 1970—74; oil co. exec. Occidental Oil Co., Grand Junction, Colo., 1974—92; ptnr. H&B Investment Co., 1992—. Author: Synthetic Fuel Combustion, 1984; inventor radioactive retort doping, locus retorting zone. Naval Rsch. fellow, 1951-55. Fellow Am. Inst. Chemists; mem. Internat. Platform Assn., Masons, Elks, Sigma Xi, Phi Beta Kappa, Phi Lambda Upsilon. Republican. Avocations: fly fishing, travel, reading, teaching. Home: 3152 Primrose Ct Grand Junction CO 81506-4147

SKOGLUND, MARILYN, state supreme court justice; b. Chgo., Aug. 28, 1946; BA, So. Ill. U., 1971; clerkship, 1977-81. Bar: Vt. 1981, U.S. Dist. Ct. Vt. 1981, U.S. Ct. Appeals (2d cir.) 1983. Asst. atty. gen. Civil Law Divsn., 1981—89, chief, 1988—93, Pub. Protection Divsn., 1993-94; judge Vt. Dist. Ct., 1994-97; assoc. justice Vt. Supreme Ct., 1997—. Office: Vt Supreme Ct 109 State St Montpelier VT 05609-0001 *

SKOL, MICHAEL, counter-money laundering consultant; b. Chgo., Oct. 15, 1942; s. Ted and Rebecca (Williams) S.; m. Claudia Serwer, Sept. 29, 1973. BA, Yale U., 1964. U.S. fgn. svc. officer Dept. State, 1965-96; polit. officer U.S. Embassy, Buenos Aires, 1966-67, Saigon, Viet Nam, 1968-70; desk officer Dept. State, Washington, 1970-72; comml. attache U.S. Embassy, Santo Domingo, Dominican Republic, 1972-75; econ. comml. officer U.S. Consulate Gen., Naples, Italy, 1975-76; comml. attache U.S. Embassy, Rome, 1976-78, polit. counselor San Jose, Costa Rica, 1978-82; dep. dir. policy planning Inter-Am. Affairs Bur. Dept. State, Washington, 1982-85; dep. chief of mission U.S. Embassy, Bogota, Colombia, 1985-87; dir. Andean affairs Dept. State, Washington, 1987-88; dep. asst. sec. state for S.Am. U.S. Dept. of State, Washington, 1988-90; amb. U.S. Embassy, Caracas, Venezuela, 1990-93; prin. dep. asst. sec. for Latin Am./Caribbean Dept. State, Washington, 1993-96; sr. v.p. Diplomatic Resolutions, Inc., Washington, 1996-97; pres. Skol & Assoc. Inc., NY, Washington, Bogota, 1998—; chmn. US Colombian Bus. Partnership, 1996-99; mng. dir. L.Am. Decision Strategies, NYC, 1998—2005. Pres. Skol, Ospina & Serna, NYC, Washington and Bogota, 2001—03; prin. Skol & Serna, Washington, Bogota, 2003—. Mem.: Coun. on Fgn. Rels., Yale Club of N.Y. Office: 1710 Rhode Island Ave NW Ste 300 Washington DC 20036 Office Phone: 202-331-9464. Personal E-mail: mikeskol@aol.com.

SKOLDBERG, PHYLLIS LINNEA, musician, educator; d. August Theodore Skoldberg and Esther Amanda Carlson. MusB with honors, New Eng. Conservatory, 1955, MusM, 1957; M in Music Edn. with high distinction, Ind. U., 1964, Mus D in Performance, 1967. Violinist Houston Symphony Orch., 1957—59, Cin. Symphony Orch., 1959—62; assoc. instr. Ind. U., Bloomington, 1962—64; prof. music SUNY, Oswego, 1964—77; asst. dean fine arts Ariz. State U., Tempe, 1977—84, prof. music, 1977—2001, prof. emeritus, 2001—. Vis. artist Paris Conservatoire, 1973; vis. prof., cons. Australian String Tchrs. Assn., Brisbane and Sydney, 1984, Shanghai Conservatory Music, 1984; artist-in-residence U. Hong Kong, 1984; adj. prof., coord. string dept. Mesa (Ariz.) CC, 2001—. Author: The Strings: A Comparative View, Vol. I, 1981, Vol. 2, 1982; performer: (solos) Reston (Va.) Music Festival, 1972, 1973, Charles Ives Music Festival, 1975, 1976, Western Music Festival, 1980, (1st violin) Concert Quartet, 2003; soloist Philharmonic. Named winner performance competition, Seattle Philharm. Orch., 1952; recipient Boston Civic Music award, 1954. Mem.: The Phoenix Inst. of Music (founding dir. 2005), Red Rock Music Festival (bd. dirs. 2002—), Music Tchrs. Nat. Assn., Am. String Tchrs. Assn. (adv. bds. 1970—84, Ariz. pres. 1984—86). Home: 12002 S Tuzigoot Ct Phoenix AZ 85044-3467 Office: Mesa CC 1833 W Southern Ave Mesa AZ 85202 Office Phone: 480-461-7575. Office Fax: 480-461-7422. Business E-Mail: phyllis.skoldberg@asu.edu.

SKOLDS, JOHN L. (JACK SKOLDS), utilities executive; m. Marilyn Skolds; 3 children. Grad. with distinction, US Naval Acad.; MBA, U. SC. With Impell Corp. and Nuc. Regulatory Commn., 1977—83; gen. mgr. sta. ops. Virgil C. Summer Nuc. Plant SC Electric and Gas, 1986, various positions including plant mgr., site v.p. and sr. v.p. nuc. ops., sr. v.p. generation, 1995—96, pres., COO, 1996—2000; sr. v.p. Unicom and ComEd, 2000; COO Nuc. Generation Group ComEd, 2000; pres., chief nuc. officer Exelon Nuc. Exelon Corp., exec. v.p., pres. Exelon Energy Delivery, 2004—, pres. Exelon Generation, 2005—. Bd. dirs. Zolo Techs., Inst. Nuc. Power Ops. Bd. dirs. Lyric Opera Chgo., Northwestern Meml. Healthcare. Office: Exelon Corp 10 S Dearborn St 37th Fl PO Box 805398 Chicago IL 60680-5398 Office Phone: 800-483-3220. *

SKOLER, LOUIS, architect, educator; b. Apr. 5, 1920; s. Harry and Etta (Mitkoff) S.; m. Celia Rebecca Stern, 1952; children: Elisa Anne, Harry Jay. BArch, Cornell U., 1951. Maj. designer Sargent, Webster, Crenshaw & Folley, Syracuse, NY, 1951-59; design critic Cornell U., Ithaca, NY, 1956-57; pvt. practice arch. Syracuse, 1956-69; faculty Sch. Arch. Syracuse U., 1959-92, prof. emeritus, 1990—, Head of arch. masters program, 1980-82, head undergrad. program, 1989-90, arch. programs abroad, London, 1977, Scandinavia, 1985, Japan, 1988; ptnr. Arch. Partnership, Syracuse, 1969-71; pres. Skoler & Lee Archs., P.C., Syracuse, 1971-89; lectr. Nanjing Inst. Tech., China, summer 1986. Named Best in Residential Design, Design-in-Steel, 1968-69. Mem.: AIA. Home: 213 Scottholm Ter Syracuse NY 13224-1737 *A guiding principle over many years of teaching and practice, is the interrelationship of theory and work-of idea and circumstance, of imagination and the forces generated by day to day life.*

SKOLL, JEFFREY S., philanthropist, former internet company executive; b. Montreal, Jan. 16, 1965; BSEE, U. Toronto, 1987; MBA, Stanford U., 1995; LLD (hon.), U. Toronto, 2003. Founder Skoll Engring., 1987, Micros on the Move Ltd., 1990; mgr. distbn. channels online news info. Knight-Ridder Info.; co-founder, pres., v.p. strategic analysis and planning eBay Inc., San Jose, Calif., 1995—99; founder, CEO Participant Productions, LA, 2004—. Exec. prodr.: (films) Good Night, and Good Luck, North Country, Syriana, American Gun, An Inconvenient Truth, The World According to Sesame Street, Fast Food Nation. Bd. dirs. e-Bay Found., 1998—; founder, chmn. Skoll Found., 1999—; bd. dirs. Cmty. Found. Silicon Valley; mem. advisory bd. Stanford Grad. Sch. Bus. Named a WIRED Renegade, WIRED Rave Awards, 2006; named one of the most innovative philanthropists of the past decade, BusinessWeek, 2002, 2003, 50 Most Generous Philanthropists, Fortune Mag., 2005, World's Richest People, Forbes, 1999—, 100 Most Influential People, Time Mag., 2006; recipient Leafy award, 1999, Visionary award, Software Development Forum, 2001, Outstanding Philanthropist award, Silicon Valley chapter Assn. Fundraising Professionals, 2002, Internat. Assn. Fundraising Professionals, 2003, Nat. Leadership Award, Commonwealth Club Silicon Valley, 2004. Office: Skoll Foundation 250 University Ave Ste 200 Palo Alto CA 94301 Office Phone: 650-331-1031. Office Fax: 650-331-1033. *

SKOLNICK, LAWRENCE, neonatal physician, medical association administrator; b. NYC, July 29, 1947; s. Harry and Sylvia Skolnick; m. Tamar Tumarkin, Apr. 7, 1970; children: Daniel, Michael, Rachel. BS, CUNY, 1968; MD, NYU, 1972; MPH, U. N.C., 1980. Dir. newborn medicine Hosp. of Albert Einstein Coll. Medicine, Bronx, NY, 1977-80; dir. neonatology Morristown (N.J.) Meml. Hosp., 1980—, Overlook Hosp., Summit, NJ, 1999—, Atlantic Health Sys., 1999—; assoc. prof. med. pediat. UNDNJ-N.J.Sch. Medicine, 2001—. E-mail: larry.skolnick@ahsys.org.

SKOLNICK, MARILYN, civic worker; b. NYC, Jan. 17, 1925; d. Max and Annie Ruth (Stern) Kassel; n. Herbert Skolnick, Aug. 2, 1948; 1 child, Tamara. BA, Bklyn. Coll., 1946; MA, U. Okla., 1948; postgrad., State U. Iowa, 1948-52. Host, prodr. cable TV program Focus on Issues, 1983—; chair citizen participation com. Transp. Rsch. Bd., Nat. Acad. Sci., 1987-94; sec. local transp. fin. com., 1987—. Bd. dirs. Port Authority of Allegheny County, 1982-95; pres. Allegheny County Transp. Coun., 1997-99, v.p., 1999-2000; mem. Pa. Small Bus. Compliance Adv. Com., 1992-2007, Penndot Mobility Plan for Pa., 2004-06. Chair Monroeville Planning Commn., 1983-85; bd. dirs. Pa. Planning Assn., 1983-85, Group Against Smog and Pllution; mem. Pa. Transp. Adv. Com., 1983-86; mem. air pollution ctrl. adv. com. Allegheny County Health Dept., 1985—, pollution prevention com. chair, 2004—; mem. Allegheny County Local Emergency Planning Com., 1987—, Allegheny County Comprehensive Plancomm. Pub. Participation Team. Mem. LWV (former bd. dirs.), N.Y. Acad. Scis., Pa. Acad. Scis., Sierra Club (bd. dirs. Pa. chpt. 1986—, chair Allegheny Group 1988-91), Sigma Xi. Home: 109 South Ridge Dr Monroeville PA 15146-4739

SKOLNICK, S. HAROLD, lawyer; b. Woonsocket, RI, June 17, 1915; s. David and Elsie (Silberman) S.; m. Shirley Marshall. AB cum laude, Amherst Coll., Mass., 1936; JD, Boston U., 1940. Bar: RI 1940, US Supreme Ct. 1946, DC 1947, Fla. 1952, US Dist. Ct. (so. dist.) Fla. 1953, US Ct. Appeals (5th cir.) 1960, US Ct. Appeals (11th cir.) 1981. Atty. Dept. of War, Washington, 1940-42; asst. gen. counsel, asst. chief legal dept. Office Chief Ordnance, Dept. of Army, Washington, 1947-50; assoc. Francis I. McCanna, Providence, 1951-52; ptnr. French & Skolnick, Miami, Fla., 1953-60; sole practice Miami, Fla., 1961—. Served to lt. col. US Army, 1942—47. Mem. ABA, Am. Judicature Soc., Nat. Def. Indsl. Assn. (life), RI Bar Assn., DC Bar Assn., Dade County Bar Assn., Estate Planning Coun. Greater Miami, Masons, Shriners. Home and Office: 6521 SW 122d St Miami FL 33156-5550

SKOLNIK, BARNET DAVID, retired lawyer; b. NYC, Feb. 8, 1941; s. Jack and Edythe (Savitz) S.; m. Patricia L. Krohn; children: Sarah, Deborah, Daniel, Joseph, Benjamin, Rebecca, Zachary. AB in Am. Govt. cum laude, Harvard U., 1962, LLB, 1965. Bar: D.C. 1966, Md. 1984, Maine 1991. Atty. criminal div. U.S. Dept. Justice, Washington, 1966-68; asst. U.S. atty. for Dist. Md., Balt., 1968-78; chief public corruption unit U.S. Atty.'s Office, Balt., 1973-78; pvt. practice law Balt. and Washington, 1978—91, Portland, Maine, 1991—94; ret. Tchr., lectr. on trial practice, white collar criminality, pub. corruption. Recipient Spl. Achievement award Dept. Justice, 1972, 74, Spl. Commendation for Outstanding Svc., Dept. Justice, 1978, Younger Fed. Lawyer award Fed. Bar Assn., 1974, Atty. Gen.'s Disting. Service award, 1974, Legal award Assn. Fed. Investigators, 1977 E-mail: bskolnik@gwi.net.

SKOLNIK, MERRILL I., electrical engineer; b. Balt., Nov. 6, 1927; s. Samuel and Mary (Baker) S.; m. Judith Magid, June 4, 1950; children: Nachama, Martin Allen, Julia Anne, Ellen Charlotte. BEng, Johns Hopkins U., 1947, MSEng, 1949, DEng, 1951. Research scientist Johns Hopkins U., Balt., 1947-54, vis. prof., 1973-74; engring. specialist Sylvania Electric, Boston, 1954; staff mem. MIT Lincoln Lab., Lexington, Mass., 1954-59; research mgr. Electronic Communications, Timonium, Md., 1959-64, Inst. Def. Analyses, Arlington, Va., 1964-65; supr. radar divsn. Naval Research Lab., Washington, 1965-96, radar sys. cons., 1996—. Mem. bd. visitors Duke U. Engring. Sch., Durham, N.C., 1976-93; disting. vis. sci. Jet Propulsion Lab., 1990-92; mem. Md. Gov.'s Exec. Adv. Com., 1993-95. Author: Introduction to Radar Systems, 1962, 3d edit., 2001, Radar Handbook, 1970, 3d edit., 2008; editor: Radar Applications, 1988. Recipient Heinrich Hertz premium Instn. Electronic and Radio Engrs., London, 1964, Disting. Alumnus award Johns Hopkins U., 1979, Disting. Civilian Svc. award USN, 1982, Meritorious Exec. award Sr. Exec. Svc., 1986, Johns Hopkins Engring. and Applied Sci. Excellence in Tchg. award, 1998; named to Soc. of Scholars, Johns Hopkins U., 1975. Fellow IEEE (editor Proceedings 1986-89, Harry Diamond award 1983, Centennial medal 1984, Dennis J. Picard medal for radar technologies and applications 2000); mem. Nat. Acad. Engring. Home: 8123 McDonogh Rd Baltimore MD 21208-1005 Office: Naval Rsch Lab Washington DC 20375-5320 E-mail: merrill.skolnik@nrl.navy.mil.

SKOLNIK, RICHARD ALAN, plastic surgeon; b. NYC, Jan. 7, 1951; BA in Biology summa cum laude, C.W. Post Coll., 1972; MD, Cornell U., 1976. Cert. Am. Bd. Plastic and Reconstructive Surgery. Resident gen. surgery Mt. Sinai Med. Ctr., NYC, 1976-79, resident plastic surgery, 1979-82; clin. instr. Mt. Sinai Sch. Medicine, NYC, 1982-84, asst. clin. prof., 1985—2005, assoc. clin. prof., 2005—; assoc. attending Mt. Sinai Med. Ctr., NYC, 1982—, Beth Israel Med. Ctr., NYC, 1984—; courtesy staff Beth Israel North (Doctor's Hosp.), NYC, 1987—. Fellow cleft lip and palate Children's Hosp., Lima, Peru, 1982; vis. prof. Reconstructive Surgery Found., Maceo, Brazil, 1990, Pune, India, 1994, Beijing, China, 1998. Fellow ACS; mem. Am. Soc. of Plastic and Reconstructive Surgeons, N.Y. Regional Soc. Plastic and Reconstructive Surgeons, AMA, Barsky Soc., N.Y. State Med. Soc. Avocations: ceramics, cooking, golf, tennis. Office: 21 E 87th St New York NY 10128-0506 Office Phone: 212-722-1977. E-mail: shanepunum@aol.com.

SKOLNIK, SANDRA J., educational association administrator; b. NYC, Jan. 23, 1938; m. Leonard Skolnik; children: Rachel Cogan, Adam. Student, Balt. Jr. Coll., U. Md. Exec. dir. Md. Com. for Children Inc., 1994—. Mem. Nat. Child Care Policy Rsch. Consortium; founding pres. Md. Assn. Nonprofit Orgns.; mem. Friends of the Family Inc., Leadership Network on Children and Welfare Reform, U. Md. Hosp. for Children; mem. fund adv. bd. Md. After-Sch. Opportunity; mem. adv. bd., com. mem. Md. State Dept. Edn., Jr. League Balt.; mem. Judith P. Hoyer Blue Ribbon Commn. on Funding of Early Child Care and Edn.; mem. adv. bd., com. mem. Md. State Dept. Human Resources. Named one of Md.'s Top 100 Women, Daily Record, 1998, Balt. Power Couples, Balt. Mag., 2000; recipient Leadership Distinction award, United Way Cen. Md., Woman of Excellence award, Nat. Assn. Women Bus. Owners, Pres.'s award, Healthy Mothers, Healthy Babies, honoree, NA'AMAT USA, Celebration of Women. Mem.: Nat. Assn. Resource and Referral Agys. (treas., bd. dirs., leadership coun.). Office: 608 Water St Baltimore MD 21202

SKOLNIKOFF, EUGENE B., political science professor; b. Phila., Aug. 29, 1928; s. Benjamin H. and Betty (Turoff) S.; m. Winifred S. Weinstein, Sept. 15, 1957; children: Matthew, Jessica. BS, MS, MIT, 1950, PhD, 1965; BA, Oxford U., Eng., 1952, MA, 1955. Registered profl. engr. Rsch. asst. in elec. engring. Uppsala U., Sweden, 1950; prof. polit. sci emeritus M.I.T., 1965—, chmn. polit. sci. dept., 1970-74; dir. Center for Internat. Studies, 1972-87. Vis. rsch. prof. Carnegie Endowment Internat. Peace, Geneva, 1969-70; vis. fellow Balliol Coll., U. Oxford, 1989; vis. scholar Yale U., 1997; sys. analyst Inst. Def. Analyses, Washington, 1957-58; mem. White House staff Office Spl. Asst. to Pres. Sci. and Tech., Washington, 1958-63; adj. prof. Fletcher Sch. Law and Diplomacy, Tufts U., Medford, Mass., 1965-72; sr. cons. White House Office Sci. and Tech. Policy, 1977-81, vice chmn. adv. com. on sci., tech. and devel.; mem. policy rev. com. on nat. low-level nuclear waste mgmt., 1980-86; cons. Dept. State, Office of Tech. Assessment, AID, OECD, MacArthur Found., Resources Future, Am. Soc. Internat. Law, Ford Found., Inst. Def. Analyses; chmn., pres. Sci. and Public Policy Studies Group, 1967-73; mem. Internat. Council Sci. Policy Studies; Montague Burton vis. prof. U. Edinburgh, 1977, mem. NRC coms.; chmn. bd. UN U. Inst. New Tech. (INTECH), Maastricht, Holland, 1998-2005; Michael Dukakis vis. prof. pub. policy Am. Coll. Thessaloniki, Greece, 2000. Author: Science, Technology and American Foreign Policy, 1967, International Imperatives of Technology, 1972, The Elusive Transformation: Science, Technology, and the Evolution of International Politics, 1993; co-editor: World Eco-Crisis, 1972, Visions of Apocalypse, End or Rebirth?, 1985, The Implementation and Effectiveness of International Environmental Commitments, 1998; contbr. articles to publs.; chmn. editorial bd. Pub. Sci., 1971-75; mem. editorial bd. Tech. Rev., 1976-78, Social Studies of Sci., 1970-75, Internat. Orgn., 1974-80, Internat. Rels. of Asia Pacific, 2000-; mem. MIT Press Editl. Bd., 2005—; patentee hybrid circuits. Trustee German Marshall Fund, 1979-87, chmn., 1980-86; trustee UN Rsch. Inst. for Social Devel., 1979-85; bd. dirs. Saco Def., 1984-86; mem. Overseas Devel. Coun.; mem. U.S. del. UN Commn. for Social Devel., 1979; mem. State Dept. Adv. Com. on Sci. and Tech., 1987-90. Served with U.S. Army Security Agy., 1955-57. Decorated Comdr.'s Cross Fed. Republic Germany, Order of Rising Sun, Golden Rays, Neck Ribbon, Japan; Rhodes scholar, 1950—52, Rockefeller Found. fellow, 1963—65. Fellow Am. Acad. Arts and Scis. (councillor 1973-77), AAAS (sec. sect. K 1967-69, mem. com. on sci. and pub. policy 1973-74, com. on sci., engring. and pub. policy 1984-89); mem. UN Assn., Fedn. Am. Scientists, (coun. 1981-85), Coun. Fgn. Rels., Am. Assn. Rhodes Scholars, Soc. for Social Studies of Sci., Sigma Xi, Tau Beta Pi, Eta Kappa Nu. Home: 3 Chandler St Lexington MA 02420-3601 Office: MIT E53-373 77 Massachusetts Ave Cambridge MA 02139-4307 Office Phone: 617-253-3140. Business E-Mail: ebskol@mit.edu.

SKOMAL, EDWARD NELSON, aerospace company executive, electromagnetic environments consultant; b. Kansas City, Mo., Apr. 15, 1926; s. Edward Albert and Ruth (Bangs) S.; m. Elizabeth Birkbeck, Mar. 4, 1951 (dec. June 1987); children: Susan Beth, Catherine Anne, Margaret Elaine; m. Joan Kerner, Apr. 9, 1988. BA, Rice U., Houston, 1947, MA, 1949. Engr., Socony Rsch. Labs., Dallas, 1949-51; asst. sect. head Nat. Bur. Standards, Washington, 1951-56; project engr. Sylvania Microwave Rsch. Lab., Palo Alto, Calif., 1956-59; mgr. solid state sys. and components applications engring., chief applications engr. Motorola Solid State Systems Div., Phoenix, 1959-63; dir. comms. engring. dept. Aerospace Corp., El Segundo, Calif., 1963-86, ret., 1986; mem. Presdl. Joint Tech. Adv. Com. on Electromagnetic Compatibility, Washington, 1965-70, 71-75. Author: Man Made Radio Noise, 1978, Automatic Vehicle Locating Systems, 1980; Measuring the Radio Frequency Environment, 1985; contbr. articles to profl. jours. Patentee in field of radio systems, solid state devices, radar cross sect. reduction of ballistic rentry vehicles and solid state microwave components. Elder Riverside Presbytery. With USN, 1944-6. Fellow IEEE (asst. editor Trans. Electromatic Compatibility 1978-86, chmn. tech. adv. com. 1982-86, chmn. tech. com. electromagnetic environments 1976-82, standards com. 1980-86, fellow nominating com. 1980-83, nat. com. standards coordinating com. on definitions 1986—, Richard A. Stoddart award 1980, cert. of Achievement 1971, Paper of Yr. award 1970); mem. IEEE Electromagnetic Soc. (life), Am. Phys. Soc., Internat. Union Radio Scientists, Friends A.H. Smiley Pub. Libr., Am. Leghion, Sigma Xi. Republican. Presbyterian. Achievements include research on the theory of man-made radio noise, development of solid state microwave components, the application of stochastic processes to man-made radio noise analysis. Home: 1802 Morning Dove Ln Redlands CA 92373

SKONEY, SOPHIE ESSA, educational administrator; b. Detroit, Jan. 29, 1929; d. George Essa and Helena (Dihmes) Cokalay; m. Daniel J. Skoney, Dec. 28, 1957; children: Joseph Anthony, James Francis, Carol Anne. PhB, U. Detroit, 1951; MEd, Wayne State U., 1960, EdD, 1975; postgrad., Ednl. Inst. Harvard Grad. Sch., 1986—. Tchr. elem. sch. Detroit Bd. Edn., 1952-69, remedial reading specialist, 1969-70, curriculum coord., 1970-71, region 6 article 3 title I coord., 1971-83, area achievement specialist, 1984-88; adminstrv. asst. Office Grant Procurement and Compliance, 1988-2000. Mem. dean's adv. coun. Coll. Edn. Wayne State U., 1995—; cons. in field. Editor newsletter Alliance to the Mich. Dental Assn., 1993-2000. Recipient Disting. Alumni award Wayne State U., 1993. Mem. ASCD, Wayne State U. Edn. Alumni Assn. (pres. bd. govs. 1979-80, newsletter editor 1975-77, 80—), Macomb Dental Aux. (pres. 1969-70), Mich. Dental Aux. (pres. 1980-81), Alliance Mich. Dental Assn. (pres. 1998-2000), Am. Assn. Sch. Adminstrs., Wayne State U. Alumni Assn. (dir., v.p. 1985-86), Internat. Reading Assn., Mich. Reading Assn., Mich. Assn. State and Fed. Program Specialists, Profl. Women's Network (newsletter editor 1981-83, pres. 1985-87, Anthony Wayne award for leadership 1981), Retirees Orgn. Sch. Adminstrs. and Suprs. (pres. 2003—), Anthony Wayne Soc., Delta Kappa Gamma, Beta Sigma Phi, Phi Delta Kappa (v.p. 1988-90, pres. 1990-91, Educator of Yr. 1985, 91, 96, 2000). Roman Catholic. Home: 20813 Lakeland St Saint Clair Shores MI 48081-2104 Home Phone: 586-776-3809. Personal E-mail: skoneys@aol.com.

SKOOG, DONALD PAUL, retired pathologist, educator; b. Sioux City, Iowa, Sept. 29, 1931; m. Mary Ann Bunn, 1955; children: Robert Eugene, David Alan (dec.), Kristin Marie. BA magna cum laude, Midland Lutheran Coll., Fremont, Nebr., 1953; MD cum laude, U. Nebr., 1958; DSci (hon.), Midland Luth. Coll., 1993. Diplomate Am. Bd. Pathology. Intern, then resident in pathology Bishop Clarkson Meml. Hosp., Omaha, 1958-62; resident in pathology Parkland Meml. Hosp., Dallas, 1962-63; fellow in pathology U. Tex. Southwestern Med. Sch., Dallas, 1962-63; practice medicine specializing in pathology Omaha, 1963-92. Pathologist Bishop Carlson Meml. Hosp., 1963-88, chmn. dept. pathology, 1978-80, chmn. med. edn. com., 1978-83, sec.-treas. med. staff, 1982-87, dir. dept., 1986-87; prof. pathology and microbiology U. Nebr. Coll. Med., 1977-93, mem. dean's faculty adv. coun., 1977-79, mem. grad. and continuing edn. com., 1980-85, mem. coun. affilitated instns., 1981-83, mem. admissions com., 1986-91, sr. cons. pathology and microbiology, 1993—; assoc. med. dir. ARC Blood Svcs., Midwest Region, Omaha, 1988, med. dir./dir. 1989-91, dir./prin. officer, 1991-92; mem. computer sys. selection com., 1991, ARC Blood Svcs., Washington, 1981-, mem. med. affairs com., 1991-92; mem. exec. com. Nebr. Med. Edn. Fund, 1981-, bd. dirs., 1981-, chmn. loan com., 1983-91, sec.-treas., 1984-91; mem. comm. com. Pvt. Practice Assocs., Omaha, 1998-03, mem. credentials and quality improvement com., 1998-03; chmn. com. Clarkson Legends, Nebr. Med. Ctr., 2005; vol. cons. dept. devel. Nebr. Med. Ctr., 2005-. Mem. editl. bd. Lab. Medicine, 1979—03; editor, lead author: Swedes, Danes, and Norwegians: Oral Histories from Nebraska, 2000; contbr. articles to med. jours. Councilman Luther Meml. Luth. Ch., Omaha, 1966-72, 87-91, vice chmn., 1969-72; trustee Midland Luth. Coll., 1968-87, chmn., 1973-75; mem. Swedish Cultural Com., Omaha, 1975—. Recipient Alumni Achievement award Midland Luth. Coll., 1972, Disting. Svc. award Sch. of Allied Health Program, U. Nebr. Med. Ctr., 1990, Disting. Alumnus award U. Nebr. Coll. Medicine Alumni Assn., 1998. Fellow Am. Soc. Clin. Pathologists (hematology profl. self-assessment com. 1972, 75,78, adv. coun. 1972-78, chmn. coun. hematology 1978-81, editor Hematology Check Sample 1983-88, Disting. Svc. award Commn. on Continuing Edn. 1985, mem. bd. censors 1987-89, mem. nat. meeting activities com. 1989-92, chmn. 1990-92, Israel Davidsohn disting. svc. award 1993), Coll. Am. Pathologists (hematology resource com. 1981-86, vice chmn. 1982-85); mem. AMA, Nebr. Assn. Pathologists, Nebr. Med. Assn., Met. Omaha Med. Soc. (coun. on grievances and profl. ethics 1983-91), Midland Luth. Coll. Alumni Assn. (pres. 1969-70), Alpha Omega Alpha (pres. U. Nebr. chpt. 1976-77, counsellor 1984-90). Republican. Lutheran. Home: 706 S 96th St Omaha NE 68114 Personal E-mail: dpsmd@cox.net.

SKOOG, DOUGLAS ARVID, retired chemistry educator, writer; b. Willmar, Minn., 1918; s. Arvid C. and Hilma E. (Erickson) S.; m. Judith Bone, 1942; children: James Arvid, Jon Douglas. BS, Oreg. State U., 1940; PhD, U. Ill., 1943. Research chemist Standard Oil Co. of Calif., Richmond,

Calif., 1943-47; asst. prof. chemistry Stanford (Calif.) U., 1947-53, assoc. prof., 1953-62, prof., assoc. exec. head dept. chemistry, 1963-76, prof. emeritus, 1976—; writer Stanford, 1976—. Author: Fundamentals of Analytical Chemistry, 8th rev. edit., 2003, Principles of Instrumental Analysis, 1998, 5th rev. edit., 1992, Analytical Chemistry, 7th rev. edit., 2000; contbr. articles to profl. jours. Fellow AAAS; mem. Am. Chem. Soc. (pres. Santa Clara Valley sect. 1962, Fisher award in analytical chemistry 1999), Sigma Xi, Phi Kappa Phi, Alpha Chi Sigma. Clubs: Bohemian (San Francisco). Avocations: flying, skiing. Home: 401 Webster St Apt 302 Palo Alto CA 94301-1249 Personal E-mail: skoog@stanford.edu.

SKOOG, GERALD DUANE, science educator; b. Sioux City, Iowa, Feb. 27, 1936; s. Paul and Mary Ann Skoog; m. Elizabeth Ann Lee, Dec. 28, 1962; children: Jeffrey, John, Sarah. BS, U. Nebr., 1958. Tchr. various schs., Nebr., Ill., 1958-69; instr. U. Nebr., Lincoln, summer 1969; asst. prof. curriculum and instrn. Tex. Tech U., Lubbock, 1969-72, assoc. prof., coordinator program, 1972-74, assoc. prof., chmn. secondary edn., 1976-80, prof., chmn. secondary edn., 1980-90, prof., chmn. curriculum and instrn., 1990-97, Helen DeVitt Jones prof., 1997-2001, pres. faculty senate, 1986-87, dean Coll. Edn., 2002—03, Paul Whitfield Horn prof., 2000—04, prof. emeritus, 2005; dir. Ctr. Integration Sci. and Edn. Rsch., 2004—. Vis. prof. We. Ill. U., summer 1972; lectr. in field; participant, facilitator numerous workshops; cons. Contbr. numerous articles to profl. jours., also reviewer articles and papers; co-author secondary sch. science textbooks. Bd. dirs. Gloria Dei Luth. Ch., Lubbock, 1971-74, 92-93; bd. dirs. Luth. Coun. Cmty. Action, 1970-71, Good Neighbor Ministry, 1982-84; leader Boy Scouts Am., 1978-79; foster parent Luth. Social Svcs. Tex.; bd. dirs. Triangle Coalition for Sci. and Tech., 1986-95. Recipient Pres.'s Faculty Achievement award Tex. Tech. U., 1986, Disting. Leadership award, 1996, Award of Excellence, U. Nebr., Lincoln Tchrs. Coll. Alumni Assn., 2003; named Notable Alumnus, U. Nebr., Lincoln, Tchrs. Coll., 1998; named to Tex. Sci. Hall of Fame, 2000. Fellow AAAS; mem. ASCD, NSTA (life, bd. dirs. 1977-79, pres. 1985-86, various coms., Disting. Svc. to Sci. Edn. award 1994, Robert H. Carleton award 2004), Nat. Assn. Rsch. Sci. Tchg, Assn. Edn. Tchrs. Sci., Sci. Tchrs. Assn. Tex. (hon., past pres., Skoog Cup award), Nat. Assn. Biology Tchrs., Soc. Study Edn., Phi Delta Kappa. Lutheran. Office: Tex Tech U Coll Edn Lubbock TX 79409 Home: 4709 116th St Lubbock TX 79424 Office Phone: 806-742-1997 x 259. E-mail: gerald.skoog@ttu.edu.

SKOOG, WILLIAM ARTHUR, retired oncologist; b. Culver City, Calif., Apr. 10, 1925; s. John Lundeen and Allis Rose (Gatz) Skoog; m. Ann Douglas, Sept. 17, 1949; children: Karen, William Arthur, James Douglas, Allison. AA, UCLA, 1944; BA with great distinction, Stanford U., 1946, MD, 1949. Intern in medicine Stanford Hosp., San Francisco, 1948-49, asst. resident in medicine, 1949-50, N.Y. Hosp., NYC, 1950-51; sr. resident in medicine Wadsworth VA Hosp., LA, 1951, attending specialist in internal medicine, 1962-68; pvt. practice internal medicine Los Altos, Calif., 1959-61; pvt. practice hematology and oncology, Santa Monica, Calif., 1971-72; pvt. practice med. oncology, San Bernardino, Calif., 1972-94; ret. Assoc. staff Palo Alto-Stanford Med. Ctr., 1959-61, U. Calif. Med. Ctr., San francisco, 1959-61; assoc. attending physician UCLA Hosp. and Clinics, 1961-78; vis. physician in internal medicine Harbor Gen. Hosp., Torrance, Calif., 1962-65, attending physician, 1965-71; cons. in chemistry Clin. Lab., UCLA Hosp., 1963-68; affiliate cons. staff St. John's Hosp., Santa Monica, 1967-71, courtesy staff, 1971-72; courtesy attending med. staff Santa Monica Hosp., 1967-72; staff physician St. Bernardine (Calif.) Hosp., 1972-94, hon. staff, 1994—; staff physician San Bernardino Cmty. Hosp., 1972-90, courtesy staff, 1990-94; chief sect. oncology San Bernardino County Hosp., 1972-76; cons. staff Redlands(Calf.) Cmty. Hosp., 1972-83, courtesy staff, 1983-94, hon. staff, 1994—; asst. in medicine Cornell U. Med. Coll., N.Y.C., 1950-51; jr. rsch. physician UCLA Atomic Energy Project, 1954-55; instr. medicine, asst. rsch. physician dept. medicine UCLA Med. Ctr., 1955-56, asst. prof. medicine, asst. rsch. physician, 1956-59; clin. assoc. in hematology VA Ctr., L.A., 1956-59; co-dir. metabolic rsch. unit UCLA Ctr. for Health Scis., 1955-59, 61-65; co-dir. Health Scis. Clin. Rsch. Ctr., 1965-68, dir., 1968-72; clin. instr. medicine Stanford U., 1959-61; asst. clin. prof. medicine, assoc. rsch. physician U. Calif. Med. Ctr., San Francisco, 1959-61; lectr. medicine UCLA Sch. Medicine, 1961-62, assoc. prof., 1962-72, assoc. clin. prof., 1973—. Contbr. articles to med. jours. Active duty USNR, 1943—46, lt. M.C. USNR, 1951—53. Fellow: ACP, Am Soc. Internal Medicine; mem.: AMA, San Bernardino County Med. Soc., Am. Soc Clin. Oncology, L.A. Acad. Medicine, Am. Fedn. Clin. Rsch., Western Soc. Clin. Rsch., So. Calif. Acad. Clin. Oncology, Calif. Med. Assn., Redlands Country Club, Alpha Omega Alpha, Sigma Xi, Phi Beta Kappa, Alpha Kappa Kappa. Episcopalian (vestryman 1965-70). Home: 1119 Kimberly Pl Redlands CA 92373-6786 Home Fax: 909-798-5016. Personal E-mail: wasredarrow@aol.com.

SKOPIL, OTTO RICHARD, JR., federal judge; b. Portland, Oreg., June 3, 1919; s. Otto Richard and Freda Martha (Boetticher) Skopil; m. Janet Rae Lundy, July 27, 1956; children: Otto Richard III, Casey Robert, Shannon Ida, Molly Jo. BA in Econs., Willamette U., 1941, LLB, 1946, LLD (hon.), 1983. Bar: Oreg. 1946, US Dist. Ct. Oreg., US Ct. Appeals (9th cir.), US Supreme Ct. 1946. Assoc. Skopil & Skopil, 1946—51; ptnr. Williams, Skopil, Miller & Beck (and predecessors), Salem, Oreg., 1951—72; judge US Dist. Ct., Portland, 1972—79, chief judge, 1976—79; judge US Ct. Appeals (9th cir.), Portland, 1979—85, sr. judge, 1986—. Chmn. com. adminstrn. of fed. magistrate sys. US Jud. Conf., 1980—86; co-founder Oreg. chpt. Am. Leadership Forum; chmn. 9th cir. Jud. Coun. Magistrates Adv. Com., 1988—91; chmn. US Jud. Conf. Long Range Planning Com., 1990—95. Hi-Y adviser Salem YMCA, 1951—52; appeal agt. SSS Marion County (Oreg.) Draft Bd., 1953—66; master of ceremonies 1st Gov.'s Prayer Breakfast for State Oreg., 1959; citizens adv. com. City of Salem, 1970—71; Gov.'s Com. on Staffing Mental Instns., 1969—70; pres., bd. dirs. Marion County Tb and Health Assn., 1958—61; bd. dirs. Willamette U., 1969—71; elder Mt. Park Ch., 1979—81; bd. dirs. Willamette Valley Camp Fire Girls, 1946—56, Internat. Christian Leadership, 1959, Fed. Jud. Ctr., 1979. Lt. USNR, 1942—46. Recipient Oreg. Legal Citizen of Yr. award, 1986, Disting. Alumni award, Willamette U. Sch. Law, 1988. Mem.: ABA, Internat. Soc. Barristers, Assn. Ins. Attys. U.S. and Can. (Oreg. rep. 1970), Def. Rsch. Inst., Oreg. Assn. Def. Counsel (bd. dirs.), Am. Judicature Soc., Marion County Bar Assn., Oreg. Bar Assn. (bd. dirs.), Prayer Breakfast Movement (fellowship coun.), Illahe Hills Country Club (pres., bd. dirs. 1964—67), Exchange Club (pres. 1947), Salem Club. Office: Sr Circuit Judge 827 US Courthouse 1000 SW 3rd Ave Portland OR 97204-2930 *

SKORA, SUSAN SUNDMAN, lawyer; b. Chgo., Jan. 5, 1947; d. Gordon Manley and Julia Walker (Firebaugh) Sundman; m. Alan Patrick Skora, May 1, 1977. AB, U. Ill., Chgo., 1970; JD, Ill. Inst. Tech., Chgo., 1980. Bar: Ill. 1980, Mich. 1983, US Dist. Ct. (we. dist.) Mich. 1983. Dir. Chgo. programs U. Ill. Found., 1973—79; asst. dir. bus. affairs U. Ill., Chgo., 1980—81, exec. asst. to exec. v.p., 1981—83; 2d v.p. Nat. Bank Detroit, Grand Rapids, 1983—88; v.p., dept. head bus. devel. NBD Grand Rapids Bank, 1985—88; v.p., trust divsn. head, mem. exec. com. First Bank, Davenport, Iowa, 1988—91; v.p., trust Firstar Bank, Davenport, 1992—97; asst. prof. dept. bus. adminstrn. Black Hawk Coll., 1992; v.p. pvt. client svcs. Wells Fargo Bank, Davenport, 1998—2004; pres., CEO Cmty. Found. of Gt. River Bend, Davenport, 2004—. Author: Cuneen Linguist, 1975 Mem. Scott County Osteo. Physicians and Surgeons Aux., 1988-99, treas., 1989, 91-99, v.p., 1990; v.p. West Mich. U. Ill. Alumni Club, 1983-86; mem. Quad City Osteo. Found., 1988—, bequest and fin. com., 1988-95, 97-2004, bd. dirs., 1992-95; lead gift com. Davenport Mus. Art, 1988; endowment com. St. Ambrose U., 1988, Quad City Arts, 1992-94; devel. and fin. com. CASI, 1998-2004, bd. govs., 1992-98, chair trustees com., 1994-98; bd. dirs. Cmty. Found. of Great River Bend, 1998-2003, chair major gifts com., 1998, 2d v.p. 1998-2000, 1st vice chair, 2001, chair, 2002-03; bd. dirs. Quad City Planned Giving Coun., pres., 2000, treas., 2007—; capital campaign com. Luth. Social Svcs., 1994; mem. Quad City Estate Planning Coun., 1988—; planned giving com. Am. Cancer Soc., 2000-03. Mem. U. Ill. Alumni Assn. (various offices to sec. 1989-91, exec. com. bd. dirs. 1985-91, nominating com. 1991), Quad City Employee Benefits Group (treas. 1993-95, 96-99), Davenport C. of C. (com. 1996-97), Davenport Country Club (fin. com. 1996-2000), Pi Alpha Tau. Avocations: gardening, reading, golf, auctions. Home: 1139 Brookview Dr De Witt IA 52742-9290 Office: Cmty Found Gt River Bend 852 Middle Rd Bettendorf IA 52722 Home Phone: 563-659-2199; Office Phone: 563-326-2840. Personal E-mail: SusanSkora@mail.com. Business E-Mail: susanskora@cfgrb.org.

SKORA, WAYNE PHILIP, retired air force officer; b. Chgo., Jan. 16, 1944; s. Felix Anthony Skora and Lillie (Goshko) St. Thomas; m. Dorothy Mae Barrett, June 13, 1966; children: Tanya Christine, Christopher Michael. BS in Engring. Sci., USAF Acad., 1966; MS in Human Resource Mgmt., U. Utah, 1976. Commd. 2d lt. USAF, 1966, advanced through grades to col., 1988, F-4 pilot various locations, 1967-69, 71-79; flight safety officer Hdqrs. Tactical Air Command, Langley AFB, Va., 1979-82; chief safety, A-10 pilot 23d Tactical Fighter Wing, England AFB, La., 1982-84; chief Office Mil. Cooperation, Am. Embassy, Manama, Bahrain, 1984-87; asst. chief logistics 507th Tactical Air Control Wing, Shaw AFB, SC, 1987-88; dep. comdr. for ops. So. Air Div., Howard AFB, Panama, 1988-90; dep. for safety Air Force Devel. Test Ctr., Eglin AFB, Fla., 1990-92; pres. Skora Enterprises, Inc., Colorado Springs, Colo., 1994—. Decorated Legion of Merit, DFC with oak leaf cluster, Air medal with 21 oak leaf clusters, Def. Meritorious Svc. medal, AF Meritorious Svc. medal with oak leaf cluster, AF Commendation medal with oak leaf cluster. Mem. Order of Daedalians (sec. 1988-90), Sertoma. Roman Catholic. Home: 24 Luxury Ln Colorado Springs CO 80921-3300 Office Phone: 719-488-8314. E-mail: wayne@skorateam.com.

SKORTON, DAVID JAN, academic administrator; b. Milw., Nov. 22, 1949; s. Samuel and Pauline (Millstein) Skorton; 1 child, Joshua Samuel. BA, Northwestern U., 1970; MD, Northwestern U., Chgo., 1974. Diplomate Nat. Bd. Med. Examiners, Am. Bd. Internal Medicine, Am. Bd. Cardiovascular Disease. Resident UCLA, 1974—77, fellow in cardiology, 1977—80, chief resident in medicine, 1978—79, adj. asst. prof., 1978—80; instr. medicine U. Iowa, Iowa City, 1980—81, asst. prof., 1981—82, asst. prof. elec. and computer engring., 1982—84, assoc. prof. medicine and elec. and computer engring., 1984—88, prof. medicine, elec. and computer engring. and biomed. engring., 1988—; acting dir., then dir. div. gen. internal medicine U. Iowa Coll. Medicine, Iowa City, 1985—89, assoc. chmn. for clinical programs, 1989—92, v.p. for rsch. and external rels., 1992—2002; pres. U. Iowa, 2003—06, Cornell U., Ithaca, NY, 2006—. Dir. echocardiology lab. VA Med. Ctr., Iowa City, 1980—89; mem. internat. and coop. projects study sect. NIH, 1988—92, chmn., 1990—92; lectr. in field numerous sci. sessions, nat. and internat. meetings; manuscript reviewer maj. jours. in field. Editor: (book) Cardiac Imaging and Image Processing, 1986, Cardiac Imaging, 1990, Cardiac Imaging, 2d edit., 1996; contbr. articles and abstracts to profl. jours., chapters to books. Named Intern-of-Yr., UCLA, 1975; recipient Rsch. Assoc. Career Devel. award, VA, 1981—84, Rsch. Career Devel. award, Nat. Heart Lung & Blood Inst., 1984—89; scholar Regents', UCLA, 1967—68. Fellow: ACP, Am. Physiol. Soc., Am. Heart Assn., Am. Coll. Cardiology; mem.: AAAS, Internat. Soc. Adult Congenital Cardiac Disease, Assn. Univ. Cardiologists. Jewish. Office: Cornell U Office of Pres 300 Day Hall Ithaca NY 14853 Office Phone: 607-255-5201. Office Fax: 607-255-9924. E-mail: president@cornell.edu. *

SKOSNIK, PATRICK DAVID, neuroscientist, researcher; b. Pitts., Pa., Aug. 21, 1973; s. Ronald J. and Linda L. Skosnik. BA in Psychology, W.Va. U., Morgantown, 1996; PhD, Northwestern U., Evanston, Ill., 2000. Postdoctoral fellow Northwestern U., Evanston, Ill., 2000—02, Ind. U., Bloomington, 2003—05, rsch. scientist, 2005—. Prodr.: (music single) The Chicago Allstars EP, Moments, Redemption/Cydonia, Forests of Azure / Invisible Landscape, Sola Fide, Faith in the Elders/Prophecy, Zion, The Unthinkable; contbr. articles to profl. jours. Grantee, Nat. Alliance Rsch. Schizophrenia and Affective Disorders, 2005—07, Nat. Inst. Drug Abuse, 2005—07. Mem.: Internat. Cannabinoid Rsch. Soc., Soc. Neuroscience. Independent. Buddhist. Avocations: painting, poetry. Office: Indiana Univ 1101 E 10th St Bloomington IN 47405 Home Phone: 812-320-2521. Personal E-mail: morphius777@hotmail.com.

SKOTHEIM, ROBERT ALLEN, retired academic administrator, educator; b. Seattle, Jan. 31, 1933; s. Sivert O. and Marjorie F. (Allen) S.; m. Nadine Vail, June 14, 1953; children: Marjorie, Kris, Julia. BA, U. Wash., 1955, MA, 1958, PhD, 1962; LLD (hon.), Hobart and William Smith Colls., Geneva, NY, 1975; LittD (hon.), Whitman Coll., 1988; LHD (hon.), Coll. Idaho, 1988, Occidental Coll., 1989, Ill. Wesleyan U., 1990; DFA (hon.), Willamette U., 1989; DFA (hon.), Whittier Coll., 2000, Gustavus Adolphus Coll., 2000. Prof. history U. Wash., 1962-63; prof. history Wayne State U., Detroit, 1963-66; prof. UCLA, 1966-67, U. Colo., Boulder, 1967-72; provost, dean faculty Hobart and William Smith Colls., 1972-75; pres. Whitman Coll., Walla Walla, Wash., 1975-88, Huntington Libr., Art Collections & Bot. Gardens, San Marino, Calif., 1988-2001, ret., 2001. Author: American Intellectual Histories and Historians, 1966, Totalitarianism and American Social Thought, 1971; Editor: The Historian and the Climate of Opinion, 1969; co-editor: American Social Thought: Sources and Interpretations, 2 vols, 1972. Guggenheim fellow, 1967-68 Mem. Phi Beta Kappa (hon.) Home: 10866 Bill Point Dr Bainbridge Island WA 98110

SKOTZKO, CHRISTINE, psychiatrist, department chairman; b. Lawton, Okla. MD, U. Rochester, NY, 1988. Lic. Psychiatrist ABPN, 1994. Vice chair clin. affairs dept. psychiatry UMDNJ-RWJMS, New Brunswick, 2004—. Fellow: Acad. Psychosomatic Medicine (coun. mem. 2005—).

SKOV, ARLIE MASON, petroleum engineer, consultant; b. Perry, Okla., Sept. 21, 1928; s. Arnold and Mary (Mason) S.; m. Luella Luticia Sloan, July 31, 1951; children: Gregory Morgan, Jeffrey Markham, Tamara Kay. BS in Petroleum Engring., U. Okla., 1956; postgrad., U. Va., 1966. Engr., Sohio Petroleum Co., Pauls Valley, Oklahoma City, Okla., 1958-66, mgr. spl. projects Oklahoma City, 1966—76; mgr. prodn. planning BP Alaska Inc., San Francisco, 1977-80; project advisor Sohio Gas Pipeline Co., San Francisco, 1980-81; mgr. new tech. devel. Sohio Petroleum Co., San Francisco, 1981-83; dir. prodn. tech. Sohio Petroleum Co. and Standard Oil Prodn., Dallas, 1983-88; sr. cons. BP Exploration, Inc., Houston, 1989-92; owner Arlie M. Skov, Inc. Petroleum Consulting, Houston, 1993—2001. Chair Santa Barbara City Water Commn., 2003—04. Recipient Disting. Svc. award Okla. Petroleum Coun. 1973. Mem. AIME (bd. dirs. 1977-79, trustee 1990-92, 95-97, 2007-) Soc. Petroleum Engrs. (hon.; bd. dirs. 1972-74, exec. com. 1990-92, pres. 1991, pres. Found. 2003-04, Disting. Mem.), Santa Barbara Club, Cosmopolitan Club of Santa Barbara. Avocations: reading, travel. Home Phone: 805-963-2904. Personal E-mail: askov@earthlink.com.

SKOWRONEK, STEPHEN LEE, political scientist, educator; b. Somerville, NJ, Mar. 8, 1951; s. Sidney Daniel and Esther (Gordon) S.; m. Susan Jacobs, Dec. 5, 1982; children: Michael, Samuel. AB, Oberlin Coll., 1973; MA, Cornell U., 1976, PhD, 1979. From asst. to assoc. prof. UCLA, 1978-85; Pelatiah Perit prof. of Pol. & Social Sci. Yale U., New Haven, 1986—. Author: Building A New American State: The Expansion of National Administrative Capacities 1888-1920, 1982, The Politics Presidents Make: Leadership From John Adams to George Bush, 1993, rev. ed. The Politics Presidents Make: Leadership from John Adams to Bill Clinton, 1997; mng. editor Studies in Am. Polit. Devel., 1986—. Woodrow Wilson Internat. Ctr. for Scholars fellow, Washington, 1985-86. Fellow Am. Acad. Arts & Sci.; mem. Am. Political Sci. Assn., Am. Hist. Assn., Social Sci. History Assn., Phi Beta Kappa, Phi Kappa Phi. Office: Yale Univ Dept Polit Sci PO Box 208301 New Haven CT 06520-8301 Business E-Mail: stephen.skowronek@yale.edu.

SKOWRONSKI, NANCY, library director; m. Dennis Skowronski. Acting dir. Detroit Pub. Libr., 2001—02, interim dir., 2002, dir., CEO. Bd. dirs. ProLiteracy Detroit, 2006—. Mem.: ALA, Univ. Cultural Ctr. Assn. (bd. mem.), Mich. Libr. Assn. Office: Detroit Pub Libr 5201 Woodward Ave Detroit MI 48202 Office Phone: 313-833-3997. Office Fax: 313-833-2327. E-mail: nskowro@detroit.lib.mi.us. *

SKOWRONSKI, VINCENT PAUL, musician, recording industry executive; b. Kenosha, Wis., Jan. 22, 1944; MusB, Northwestern U., 1966, MusM, 1968. V.p. Eberley-Skowronski, Inc., Evanston, Ill., 1973-92; internat. dir. mktg. and pub. rels. Vincent Skowronski: Producer of Classical Recordings, Evanston, 1993—. Internat. broker rare instruments Strings & Things, Evanston, 1973-92; owner Vincent Skowronski: Fine Violins, Evanston, 1993—; internat. dir. mktg. and pub. rels. EB-SKO Prodns., Evanston, 1978-92; dir. media comm. E-S Mgmt., Evanston, 1985-92; instr. violin Northwestern U., 1969-71; asst. prof. violin U. Wyo., 1971-72; pvt. violin tchr., chamber music coach, lectr., master classes. Solo violinist debut Chgo. Youth Orch., 1959; soloist Chgo. Civic Orch., 1968, guest solo artist Am. Artist Gala, Nat. Puerto Rican TV, 1960, guest solo artist Peninsula Music Festival, Fish Creek, Wis., 1965, 66; guest solo artist Young Am. Musicians Sta. WKAR-TV Mich. State U., 1966, N.Am. premiere R. Nanes' Rhapsody Pathetique for violin and orch., Chgo. Cultural Ctr., 1994, Beijing, 1994, DePaul U. Ctr., Chgo., 1994, Skowronski in Recital: 20 Years Remembered, Northwestern U., Evanston, Ill., 1994, IV Internat. Tchaikovsky Competition Commemorative Recital-Moscow Remembered: 1970-95, Evanston, Ill., 1995, J.L. Kellogg Sch. Mgmt. Recital Northwestern U., Ill., 1996; featured soloist Artist Showcase, Sta. WGN-TV Chgo., 1966-71, Honors Concert-Northwestern U., 1966, guest solo artist A.M. Am., Sta. ABC-TV, 1977—, Continental Bank Concerts Sta. WFMT-FM Chgo., 1983, 85-86, 88, 90, United Airlines Presents, Live! Sta. WFMT-FM Chgo., Schumann, 1986, Szymanowski, 1987, Bloch, 1988, Saint-Saens, 1989, Grieg, 1991, Excursions in Music: The Artistry of Vincent P. Skowronski, Sta. KQED-FM San Francisco, 1979, Skowronski: Musical Giant, Interlake Profiles, Sta. WFMT-FM Chgo., 1980, Skowronski at 50: A Birthday Celebration Sta. WNIB-FM, Chgo., 1994, Chgo. Musicians Sta. WNIB-FM, 1996-97, Skowronski at 55: A Birthday Celebration Sta. WNIB-FM, Chgo., 1999; guest solo artist, prodr., annotator for LPs Separate But Equal, 1976, All Brahms, 1977; solo artist, exec. prodr., annotator for LPs Gentleman Gypsy, 1978, Strauss and Szymanowski, 1979, Franck and Szymanowski, 1982; exec. prodr., prodr. CDs Skowronski Alone, 1996, Skowronski Plays, Strauss and Szymanowski, 1998, Skowronski Plays, Live in Concert, 2000, Skowronski Plays! Franck, Szymanowski, Bacewicz and Saint-Saens, 2002, Skowronski Plays! Gentleman Gypsy, 2003, Skowronski Plays Beethoven, Live in Concert, 2003 (Top Ten Best Classical CD award, Chgo. Daily Herald, 2003), Skowronski Plays, Avec et Sans, Live in Concert, 2004 (Top Ten Best Classical CD award Chgo. Daily Herald), Skowronski Plays! Avec et Sans, Vol. II, Honegger, Milhaud, Engel, Bloch & Szymanowski, Live in Concert, 2006 (Top Ten Best Classical CD award Chgo. Daily Herald), Skowronski Plays! Schumann and Strauss, Live in Concert, 2007; prodr., annotator for LPs Opera Lady I, 1978, Eberley Sings Strauss, 1980, American Girl, 1983, Opera Lady II, 1984; guest performances numerous TV stas. Bd. dirs. Chgo. Youth Orch., 1973-77, v.p., 1974-77; artistic cons. Classical and Protege Symphony Orchs., Chgo., 1994—; spl. cons. Beck Inst. for Arts, Schaumburg, Ill., 1998-2000; adjudicator ice skating shows and competitions Wilmette (Ill.) Park Dist., 1985-89; guest panelist classical performance-career forum Sch. of Music, Northwestern U., Evanston, 1992, 94; guest cons. career symposium Edwin G. Foreman High Sch., Chgo., 1989; mem. mayor's founding com. Evanston Arts Coun., 1974-75; pres. Vincent Skowronski Music Found., Evanston, 1997—. Recipient Excellence in Performance award Northwestern U., 1958, 59, 60, Nat. H.S. Inst., 1958-60, Roy Harris award Inter-Am. U., San German, P.R., 1960, award Am. Fedn. Musicians, 1961, award Soc. Am. Musicians, 1961, McCormick Found. award Chgo. Tribune, 1965, Wade Fetzer award for excellence in performance Northwestern U., 1966, award Crescendo Musical Club, 1967; selected as one of 7 violinists to represent U.S. in IV Internat. Tchaikovsky Competition, Moscow, 1970; Grammy award entry list Best Chamber Music Performance, 2001, 04—; guest dignitary Papal Audience, The Vatican, 1995. Mem. Internat. Platform Assn. (voting mem.), Nat. Acad. Arts and Scis., Sigma Nu Home Phone: 847-491-9155; Office Phone: 847-491-9155. Personal E-mail: skowronskirecordings@ameritech.net.

SKRAINKA, ALAN FREDERICK, securities analyst; b. St. Louis, May 8, 1961; s. Frederick Ralph and Yvonne M. (Oelawder) S.; m. Julie Lynn Wussler, Jan. 24, 1987. BBA in Acctg. and Fin., U. Mo., 1983; MBA, Washington U., 1990. Chartered fin. analyst. Utility analyst Edward D. Jones & Co., St. Louis, 1983—, ltd. ptnr. Maryland Heights, Mo., 1986-88, gen. ptnr., 1988—, chief market strategist, Investment Policy Adv. Com., 1996—. Mem. Fin. Analysts Fedn. Office: Edward D Jones & Co PO Box 190489 Saint Louis MO 63119-6489

SKRAMSTAD, HAROLD KENNETH, JR., museum consultant; b. Washington, June 3, 1941; s. Harold K. and Sarah (Shroat) S.; m. Susan Chappelear, Dec. 28, 1963; children: Robert, Elizabeth. AB, George Washington U., 1963, PhD, 1971. Asst. dir. Am. studies program Smithsonian Instn., Washington, 1969-71, spl. asst. to dir. Nat. Mus. Am. History, 1971, chief spl. projects Nat. Mus. Am. History, chief exhibit programs Nat. Mus. Am. History, 1971-74; dir. Chgo. Hist. Soc., 1974-80; pres. Henry Ford Mus. and Greenfield Village, Dearborn, Mich., 1981—96; mus. cons., 1996—. Mem. Nat. Coun. on Humanities, 1994-2000; mem. mus. mgmt. adv. com. J. Paul Getty Trust, L.A., 1984-90; mem. presdl. commn., action plan, Nat. Mus. African Am. Hsitory and Culture, 2003. Chmn. bd. Met. Detroit Conv. and Visitors Bur., 1993, chmn., mem. exec. com., 1985—; trustee Coll. Art and Design, Detroit, 1981—; mem. Mich. Travel Commn., 1989—. Recipient Charles Frankel prize Nat. Endowment for the Humanities, 1992; named to Centennial Honor Roll Am. Assn. Museums, 2006. Mem. Am. Assn. Mus. (v.p. 1984-88, accreditation commn. 1982, ethics commn. 1992-93), Smithsonian Instn. Nat. Air and Space Mus. (pub. programming adv. com. 1990—), Smithsonian Coun.

SKRETNY, WILLIAM MARION, federal judge; b. Buffalo, Mar. 8, 1945; s. William S. and Rita E. Skretny; m. Carol Ann Skretny; 3 children. AB, Canisius Coll., 1966; JD, Howard U., 1969; LLM, Northwestern U., 1972. Bar: Ill. 1969, U.S. Dist. Ct. (no. dist) Ill. 1969, N.Y. 1972, U.S. Ct. Appeals (7th cir.) 1972, U.S. Dist. Ct. (we. dist.) N.Y. 1973, U.S. Ct. Appeals (2d cir.) 1976, U.S. Supreme Ct. 1980. Asst. U.S. atty. Office of U.S. Atty. No. Dist. Ill., Chgo., 1971-73, Office of U.S. Atty. We. Dist. N.Y., Buffalo, 1973-81, 1st asst., 1975-81; gen. ptnr. Duke, Holzman, Yaeger & Radlin, Buffalo, 1981-83; 1st dep. dist. atty. Office Dist. Atty Erie County, Buffalo, 1983-88; with Gross, Shuman, Brizdle and Gillfillan, PC, Buffalo, 1988, Cox, Barrell, Buffalo, 1989-90; judge U.S. Dist. Ct. (we. dist.) N.Y., Buffalo, 1990—. Mem. jud. conf. com. on security and facilities, 1994; chair subcom. on planning and space mgmt.; com. liaison for long range planning; spl. counsel U.S. Atty. Gen.'s Advocacy Inst., 1979; staff atty., Office of Spl. Prosecutor U.S. Dept. Justice, 1980. Mem.

ABA, Fed. Judges Assn., Bar Assn. of Erie County, Di Gamma, Phi Alpha Delta, Alpha Sigma Nu. Republican. Roman Catholic. Office: US District Court 68 Court St Rm 507 Buffalo NY 14202-3405 Office Phone: 716-332-7820.

SKRIP, CATHY LEE, psychologist; b. Berwyn, Ill., July 19, 1948; d. Raymond Joseph and Gladys Catherine (Mazanec) Jirsa; m. Paul Joseph Skrip, Aug. 29, 1970; children: Carrie Anne, Christie Ellen, Jonathan Paul. AB in English, Miami U., Ohio, 1969; MS in Counseling, Calif. State U., LA, 1971. Cert. counselor, Calif.; lic. psychologist Minn. 1990. Counselor, instr. Rio Hondo Coll., Whittier, Calif., 1971-73; instr. N. Shore C.C., Beverly, Mass., 1974-75, counselor, dir. of placement, 1973-75; instr. Western Wis. Tech. Inst., La Crosse, Wis., 1975; asst. dir. Cmty. Care Orgn. of La Crosse County, Inc., Wis., 1976-79; planning analyst Dept. Health and Social Svcs., Madison, Wis., 1979-80; vol. co-facilitator battered women's support group Alexandra House, Circle Pines, Minn., 1985-88; pvt. practice Hugo, Minn., 1992—98, Crystal, Minn., 1993—98, New Hope, Minn., 1998—2003, Forest Lake, Minn., 1998—. Charter trustee 621 Found., Shoreview, Minn., 1988-91, co-chair, 1990-91, chair, 1991-92, mem. 20th anniversary com.; sec. Rio Hondo Coll. Faculty Assn., Whittier Calif., 1972-73. Author: (with Kristin Kunzman) Women With Secrets: Dealing With Domestic Abuse and Childhood Sexual Abuse in Treatment, 1991. Treas. LWV, La Crosse, 1978-81; mem. Ramsey County Cmty. Initiative to End Family Violence, 1990—, Family Violence Tng. Task Force, St. Paul, 1991, Mounds View Violence Prevention Coun., 1993—97, Anoka County Domestic Violence Coun., 1994—97, Forest Lake C. of C., 2003-; chair sch. adv. com. Chippewa Elem. Ctr., St. Paul, 1986-87; bd. dirs. YWCA, La Crosse, 1980-81; adv. com. Social Work Dept. U. Wis., La Crosse, 1981-82; bd. dirs. Ret. Sr. Vol. Program, La Crosse, 1980-82; founder, exec. dir. Abuse Resource Ctr., St. Paul, 1988-92; exec. dir. Abuse Resource Ctr. Hugo, 1992-93. Recipient Bertha Provine Oxford Coll. scholarship, Miami U., Oxford, Ohio, 1968, Alumni Assn. Departmental Honors award Calif. State U., LA, 1971. Mem. Minn. Women in Psychology (social action chair 1992-94, Greater Minn. co-chair 1993-94, steering com. 1992—, vice-chair 1994-95, chair 1995-97, Founding Mother's award 2007), Minn. Psychol. Assn., Minn. Soc. Clin. Hypnosis, Alpha Omicron Pi. Roman Catholic. Avocations: sewing, bicycling, crafts, running, canoeing. Office: 20 North Lake St Ste 308 Forest Lake MN 55025 Office Phone: 651-468-8918.

SKROBELA, KATHERINE CREELMAN, music producer, data processing executive; b. NYC, Jan. 18, 1941; d. George Douglas and Marjorie Ethel (Broer) Creelman; m. Paul John Skrobela, May 23, 1970 (dec. Feb. 1999). AB, Vassar Coll., 1962; MLS, Columbia U., 1964. Music cataloger Bklyn. Coll., 1964-71; music libr. Middlebury (Vt.) Coll., 1971-80; programmer ADT Co., NYC, 1981-83; sr. cons. Marathon Software & Svcs. Inc., 1983-90; sr. programmer analyst Chase Manhattan Bank, 1990-2000; dir. tech. info., agt. support Brown Harris Stevens, 2003—. Pres. Miranda Music, Inc., 1995—. Editor Music Cataloging bull., 1970-75; prodr. Blame It On My Youth: Berri Blair Sings Ballads, 1999, Karen Oberlin: My Standards, 2000, Christopher Gines: The Way It Goes, 2001, Karen Oberlin: Secret Love: the Music of Doris Day, 2002, John Wallowitch & Bertram Ross: Wallowitch & Ross, 2002; author:(dance) I care not for these ladies; composer Magnificat. Treas., bd. dirs. Middlebury Farmers Market, 1979; dir. St. Stephen's Motet Choir, Middlebury, 1975-78; membership chair Bklyn. Bot. Garden Aux.; treas. Vassar Class of 1962, 2002-05. Mem. ALA, Music Libr. Assn. (chmn. com. on cataloging, rep. to ALA catalog code revision com.), Music OCLC Users Group, UFO-Cobol/XE Internat. Users Group (v.p. 1989-91), Country Dance and Song Soc. Am., Manhattan Assn. Cabarets and Clubs. Home: 234 Lincoln Rd Brooklyn NY 11225-3432 Office: Brown Harris Stevens 129 Montague St Brooklyn NY 11201 Office Phone: 718-858-5736. Personal E-mail: ceo@mirandamusic.com. Business E-Mail: kskrobela@bhsusa.com.

SKROCKI, EDMUND STANLEY, II, health fair promoter, executive; b. Schenectady, NY, Sept. 6, 1953; s. Edmund Stanley I and Lorraine (Nocian) S.; m. Diane Carolyn Sittig, Sept. 6, 1976 (div. 1992); children: Carolyn, Michelle, Edmund III, Johnathan Edmund; m. Deborrah Anne Allen, June 4, 1998 (div. Mar. 2000). AA, LaValley Coll., 1981; BA, Sonoma State U., 1982, MA, 1987; postgrad., Am. Inst. Hypnotherapy, 1988. Pres. Skrocki's Philos. Svc., Lakeview Terrace, Calif., 1971—81, Redding, Calif., 1982—; pres., CEO Skrocki's Superior Svc., Lakeview Terrace, 1971—76, Redding, 1976—; pres., CEO, promoter, prodr. Realife Expositions, 1991—; prodr. Realife Expo Stars Over Hollywood, 1997. Founder Realife Found., 2003. Prodr. Superstars of Excellence, 2000—. Bd. govs., deacon Ch. of Universal Knowledge, 1991—; founder, exec. dir. Real Life Found., 2003; active Rep. Party, 1966-86, Young Ams. for Freedom, 1968-82, Nixon for Pres., 1968, 72, Regan for Gov., 1970, Murphy for Senate, 1970, Arklin for Assembly, 1970-72, Christian Anti Communist Crusade, 1970-72, Ford for Pres., 1976, Regan for Pres., 1980, 84. Named one of Outstanding Young Men Am., 1980. Mem. Shasta Submarine Soc. (pres. 1984—). Avocations: chess, basketball, reading, health, exercise. Office Phone: 530-241-1540. Personal E-mail: edskrockrii@hotmail.com.

SKROMME, LAWRENCE H., consulting agricultural engineer; b. Roland, Iowa, Aug. 26, 1913; s. Austin G. and Ingeborg B. (Holmedal) S.; m. Margaret Elizabeth Gleason, June 24, 1939; children: Cherlyn Sue Granrose, Inga Jean Hill, Karen Ann Sequino. BS with honors, Iowa State U., Ames, 1937. Registered profl. engr., Pa. Design and test engr. Goodyear Tire and Rubber Co., Akron, Ohio, 1937-41; project engr., asst. chief engr. Harry Ferguson Inc., Detroit, 1941-51; chief engr. Sperry New Holland div. Sperry Corp., New Holland, Pa., 1951-61, v.p. engring., 1961-78; cons. agrl. engr. Lancaster, Pa., 1978—. Mem. adv. bd. U.S. Congresss Com. on Sci. and Tech., 1989—93; cons. AID, World Bank, others, 1978—85, Saudi Arabia, 1985—86. Patentee; contbr. articles to profl. jours. Dir., pres. Farm and Home Found., Lancaster County, 1968—90, Lancaster County Agrl. Land Preservation Bd., 1978—2002, sec.-treas., 1989—99, dir. emeritus, 2002—; rsch. adv. com. U.S. Dept. Agr., Washington, 1964—68; gov.'s com. agr. and land preservation Gov. of Pa., 1969; bd. dirs. awards com. Engrs. Joint Coun., NYC, 1967—75. Fellow: Am. Soc. Agrl. Engrs. (v.p. 1952—55, pres. 1959—60, Gold medal 1974); mem.: NAE (peer and membership com. 1978—82), Am. Soc. Engring. Edn., Internat. Assn. Agrl. Engrs. (v.p. 1974—79, pres. farm machine divsn.), Nat. Soc. Profl. Engrs., Tau Beta Pi, Alpha Zeta, Phi Kappa Phi. Republican. Methodist. Avocations: collecting old tools and antiques, farm machinery history. Office Phone: 717-392-6127. E-mail: lhsae@aol.com.

SKROWACZEWSKI, STANISLAW, conductor, composer; b. Lwow, Poland, Oct. 3, 1923; came to U.S., 1960; s. Pawel and Zofia (Karszniewicz) S.; m. Krystyna Jarosz, Sept. 6, 1956; children: Anna, Paul, Nicholas. Diploma faculty philosophy, U. Lwow, 1945; diploma faculties composition and conducting, Acad. Music Lwow, 1945, Conservatory at Krakow, Poland, 1946; L.H.D., Hamline U., 1963, Macalester Coll., 1972; L.H.D. hon. doctorate, U. Minn.; Doctorate (hon.), U. Wroclaw, Poland, 2003. Guest condr. in, Europe, S.A., U.S., 1947—; Composer, 1931—; pianist, 1928—; violinist, 1934—; condr., 1939—; permanent condr., music dir. Wroclaw (Poland) Philharmonic, 1946-47, Katowice (Poland) Nat. Philharmonic, 1949-54, Krakow Philharmonic, 1955-56, Warsaw Nat. Philharmonic Orch., 1957-59, Minnesota Orch., 1960-79; prin. condr., mus. adviser Halle Orch., Manchester, Eng., 1984-91; musical advisor St. Paul Chamber Orchestra, 1986—87, Milw. Symphony, 1995—97; prin. condr. Yominri Nippon Symphony Orch., Tokyo, 2007—; prin. conductor Nippon Symphony Orch., Tokyo, 2007—. First symphony and overture for orch. written at age 8, played by Lwow Philharm. Orch., 1931; adv. music Milw. Symphony, 1994-97. Composer: 4 symphonies Prelude and Fugue for Orchestra (conducted first performance Paris), 1948, Overture, 1947 (2d prize Szymanowski Concours, Warsaw 1947); Cantiques des Cantiques, 1951, String Quartet, 1953 (2d Prize Internat. Concours Composers, Belgium 1953), Suite Symphonique, 1954 (first prize, gold medal Composers Competition Moscow 1957), Music at Night, 1954, Ricercari Notturni, 1978 (3d prize Kennedy Center Friedheim Competition, Washington), Concerti for Clarinet and Orch., 1980, Violin Concerto, 1985, Concerto for Orch., 1985, Fanfare for Orch., 1987, Sextett for Oboe, Violin, Viola, Orchestra, 1980, String Trio for Violin, Viola, 1990, Triple Concerto for Violin, Clarinet, Piano, Orchestra, 1992, Fantasie per Tre (Flute, Oboe, Cello), 1993, Chamber Concerto, 1993, Passacaglia Immaginaria for Orch., 1995, Musica a Quattro for Clarinet, Violin, Viola, Cello, 1998, Concerto for Orch., 1998, Symphony, 2003; also music for theatre, motion pictures, songs and piano sonatas, English horn concerto; rec. by Mercury, Columbia, RCA, Albany, Victor, Vox, EMI, Angel. Decorated comdrs. cross Polonia Restituta, Highest Polish award Gold medal, Gloria Artist, 2007; recipient nat. prize for artistic activity Poland, 1953, 1st prize Santa Cecilia Internat. Concours for Condrs., Rome, 1956, Cannes Festival award for best rec. of 19th century symphonic music, 2002, Disting. Artist award McKnight Found., 2004. Mem. Union Polish Composers, Internat. Soc. Modern Music, Nat. Assn. Am. Composers-Condrs., Am. Music Center. Office: PO Box 700 Wayzata MN 55391

SKRUPKY, ELAINE CHARLOTTE, art educator; b. Amery, Wis., Nov. 11, 1927; d. Herbert Roy Peterson and Nina Louise Olson; m. Hartferd Gay Elaine Charlotte Peterson, June 24, 1950 (dec. Aug. 2, 1982); children: Lynn, Jenene, Van(dec.), Renée, Shawndel(dec.). BSc in Art and English, River Falls U., 1949. Art supr. Rice Lake (Wis.) Schs., 1949—50; art tchr. U. Wis. Ctr., Rice Lake, 1968—69, VIII Pk., Jensen Beach, Fla., 1993—. Author: Poetry Guild Anthology, 1996 (Editors Choice award, 1996), The Best Poems of the 90's, 1997 (named Internat. Poet of Merit, Internat. Soc. Poetry, 1997), Of Moonlight and Wishes, 1997, A Celebration of Poets, 1998, sound of Poetry, 1998. Chmn. and organizer Aquafest Art Show, Rice Lake, 1960—75; chmn. state fine arts Wis. Fedn. Women's Clubs, 1972—74, state drama chmn., 1974—76, dist. art chmn., 1976; pres. Daubers Guild, Rice Lake, 1976—77; chmn. Am. Cancer Dr., Rice Lake, 1979—80, Heart Drive, Rice Lake, 1980; organizer The Red Barn Theatre, Rice Lake. Named Outstanding Woman in Arts, Wis. Federated Woman's Club, 2000; named to Internat. Hall of Fame, Internat. Soc. Poetry, 2000; recipient State Art award, Rural Artists Wis., 1979, 4th runner-up, Ms. Nat. Sr Queen Contest, 1998, State Achievement award, Wis. Federated Woman's Club, 2000, 2001. Mem.: Art League, Alpha Psi Omega, Art Gallery Coop, Poetry Club. Avocations: painting, writing, piano, singing, acting. Home (Winter): 10701 S Ocean Dr Jensen Beach FL 34957 E-mail: peterson@mailstation.com.

SKRUTSKIE, MICHAEL F., science educator; PhD, Cornell U., 1987. Prof. U. Mass., Amherst, 1987—2001; prof. astronomy U. Va., Charlottesville, Va., 2001—. Contbr. articles to profl. jours. Co-recipient James Craig Watson medal, NAS, 2007. Achievements include being the private investigator on the development of a near-infrared cameras & spectrographs; one of scientists on the execution of the Two Micron All Sky Survey (2MASS). Office: Dept Astronomy U Va 262 Astronomy Bldg PO Box 400325 Charlottesville VA 22904-4325 Office Phone: 434-924-4328. Office Fax: 434-924-3104. Business E-Mail: skrutskie@virginia.edu. *

SKULINA, THOMAS RAYMOND, lawyer; b. Cleve., Sept. 14, 1933; s. John J. and Mary B. (Vesely) S. AB, John Carroll U., 1955; JD, Case Western Res. U., 1959, LLM, 1962. Bar: Ohio 1959, U.S. Supreme Ct. 1964, ICC 1965. Ptnr. Skulina & Stringer, Cleve., 1967-72, Riemer Oberdank & Skulina, Cleve., 1978-81, Skulina, Fillo, Walters & Negrelli, 1981-86, Skulina & McKeon, Cleve., 1986-90, Skulina & Hill, Cleve., 1990-97; atty. Penn Ctrl. Transp. Co., Cleve., 1960-65, asst. gen. atty., 1965-78, trial counsel, 1965-76; with Consol. Rail Corp., 1976-78; pvt. practice Cleve., 1997—. Tchr. comml. law Practicing Law Inst., N.Y.C., 1970; practicing labor arbitrator Fed. Mediation and Conciliation Svc., 1990—; arbitrator Mcpl. Securities Rulemaking Bd., 1994-98, N.Y. Stock Exch., 1995—, NASD, 1996—; mediator NASD, 1997—, AAA Comml., 1997—; mediator vol. panel EEOC, 1997-99, contract panel, 1999-2000; arbitrator Better Bus. Bur., 2000—. Contbr. articles to legal jours. Income tax and fed. fund coord. City of Warrensville Heights, Ohio, 1970—77; spl. counsel City of North Olmstead, Ohio, 1971—75; spl. counsel to Ohio Atty. Gen., 1983—93, Cleve. Charter Rev. Commn., 1988, referee, 1986—; fact-finder State Employees Rels. Bd., Ohio, 1986—; hearing officer Human Resource Commn., Summit County, Ohio, 2000—03. With US Army, 1959. Mem. ABA (R.R. and motor carrier com. 1988-96, jr. chmn. 1989-96, alt. dispute resolution com. 1998—), FBA, Assn. Conflict Resolution, Cleve. Bar Assn. (grievance com. 1987-93, chmn. 1997-98, trustee 1993-96, ADR com. 1997—), Ohio Bar Assn. (bd. govs. litigation sect. 1986-98, negligence law com. 1989-96, ethics and profl. responsibility com. 1990-91, alt. dispute resolution com. 1996—), Am. Arbitration Assn. (practicing labor arbitrator 1987—), Nat. Acad. Arbitrators, Nat. Assn. R.R. Trial Counsel (emeritus), Internat. Assn. Law and Sci., Pub. Sector Labor Rels. Assn., Internat. Indsl. Rels. Rsch. Assn., Soc. Fed. Labor and Employee Rels. Profls. Democrat. Roman Catholic. Home: 3162 W 165th St Cleveland OH 44111-1016 Office: 24803 Detroit Rd Westlake OH 44145 Home Phone: 216-221-4910; Office Phone: 440-899-1911. E-mail: tskulina@sbcglobal.net.

SKUNDRIC, DUSANKA S., medical educator, researcher; b. Beograd, Serbia-Montenegro; d. Strahinja N. and Jelka D. (Dimic) Skundric. MD, PhD, U. Beograd. Assoc. prof. pathophysiology Sch. Medicine U. Beograd, Serbia and Montenegro; Fogarty internat. fellow Albert Einstein Sch. Medicine, NYC; Javits rsch. fellow Wayne State U., Detroit, asst. prof. neurology, asst. prof. immunology and microbiology. Recipient Jr. Faculty Travel award, Am. Assn. Immunologists, 2003, Travel award, Fedn. Clin. Immunol. Socs., 2005; grantee Career Devel. award, Am. Diabetes Orgn., 1999—2003, Nat. Multiple Sclerosis Soc., 2000—01, 2003—04, 2005—; Rsch. fellow, Brit. Coun. Mem.: NY Acad. Scis., Am. Diabetes Assn., Am. Assn. Immunologists. Achievements include design of novel experimental models and identification of novel molecular and immune mechanisms, which foster studies of regulation and therapy of autoimmune diseases of nervous system. Office: Wayne State Univ School of Medicine 421E Canfield Detroit MI 48201 Office Phone: 313-993-4002. Office Fax: 313-577-7552. Business E-Mail: skundric@cmb.biosci.wayne.edu.

SKUTNIK, BOLESH J., optics scientist, lay worker, lawyer; b. Passaic, NJ, Aug. 19, 1941; s. Boleslaw Stanley and Helen Marie (Dzierzynska) S.; m. Phyllis Victoria Wojciechowski, Sept. 2, 1967 (div. July 1991); m. Anita Marie Bacon, Aug. 2, 1997; children: Pam, Janeen, Todd, Darren. BS, Seton Hall U., 1962; MS, Yale U., 1964, PhD, 1967; JD, U. Conn., 1995. Bar: N.Y. 1996, Conn. 1996, U.S. Patent and Trademark Office 1992. Chief scientist Ensign Bickford Coating Co., Simsbury, Conn., 1979-91; prin. B.J. Assocs., New Britain, Conn., 1991-97, West Hartford, Conn., 1997—; patent atty., rsch. scientist Fiberoptic Fabrications, Inc., East Longmeadow, Mass., 1995-97; dir. rsch., dir. patents and licensing Sci. Fiberoptic Fabrications, Inc., East Longmeadow, Mass., 1997—2002; corp. counsel, dir. rsch. CeramOptec Industries, Inc., East Longmeadow, Mass., 2003—. Lector, mem. parish coun. St. Catherine of Siena, West Simsbury, Conn., 1980-85, St. Maurice, New Britain, Conn., 1985-2000, St. Thomas Apostle, West Hartford, 2000-06; chmn., del. synod Archdiocese of Hartford, Conn., 1990-96; chmn. parish Holy Family Retreat League, New Britain, 1989-2000; pres. Enbic Employees Credit Union, Simsbury, 1988-91; asst. prof. chemistry Fairfield U., Conn., 1973-79. Contbr. articles to profl. jours. Interviewer Yale Alumni Schs. Com., L.I. and Hartford, Conn., 1969—; rep. New Britain Club, 1997-2000; mem. New Britain Mus. Am. Art, Hillstead Mus., Wadsworth Mus., Smithsonian, Ctr. Polish Culture, DC, Bushnell Soc. Mem. ABA (subcom. chair 1993, 94, 96), Conn. Bar Assn., N.Y. State Bar Assn., Conn. Intellectual Property Lawyers Assn., Am. Intellectual Property Lawyers Assn., Soc. Photo-optical Engrs. (conf. co-chair, 1987-90, 2006), Optical Soc. Am., Am. Ceramic Soc., (coord. symposium 1991), Materials Rsch. Soc. (chair symposium 1987-89), Am. Chem. Soc. (alt. coun. 1988-90. sect. chair 1994, vice chair 1993, bd. dirs. 1985-2002), Porsche Club Am. (various positions Conn. Valley region), Yale Club New Britain (dir. 1994-2000), Yale Club Hartford, Yale Alumni Assn. Roman Catholic. Achievements include patents in field. Home: 51 Banbury Ln West Hartford CT 06107-1102 Office: CeramOptec Industries Inc 515 Shaker Rd East Longmeadow MA 01028-3126 Office Phone: 413-525-8222. Personal E-mail: boleshsj@aol.com. Business E-Mail: bolesh.skutnik@ceramoptec.com. *The human spirit is stronger than anything that can happen to it.*

SKVORECKY, JOSEF VACLAV, literature educator, writer; b. Nachod, Czechoslovakia, Sept. 27, 1924; arrived Can., 1969; s. Josef Karel and Anna (Kurazova) S.; m. Zdenka Josefa Salivarova, Mar. 30, 1958 PhD, Charles U., Czechoslovakia, 1951; PhD (hon.), SUNY, 1986, Masaryk U., 1991, U. Calgary, 1992, U. Toronto, 1992. Vis. lectr. U. Toronto, Ont., Canada, 1969-70, writer-in-residence, 1970-71, assoc. prof., 1971-75, prof. English, 1975-90; prof. emeritus, 1990—. Lectr. on lit. topics Voice of Am., 1973—; adv. to Pres. Vaclav Havel, 1990. Editor: Sixty Eight Publ. Corp., 1972—; author: The Cowards, 1958, The End of the Nylon Age, 1967, Republic of Whores, 1969, The Miracle Game, 1972, The End of Lieutenant Boruvka, 1980, The Engineer of Human Souls, 1984, Miss Silver's Past, 1985, Dvorak in Love, 1986, The Bride of Texas, 1992, Headed for the Blues, 1996, The Two Murders in My Double Life, 1996; co-author (with Zdena Salivarova): Brief Encounter, With Murder, 1999, Brief Encounter After Many Years with Murder, 2000, Brief Encounter at the End of an Era, With Murder, 2001, Brief Encounter in the White Lady, With Murder, 2003; co-author: Pulchra, 2003, Ordinary Lives, 2004, An Inexplicable Story, 2002, Brief Encounter in Prague with Murder, 2004; author: (short stories) The Menorah, 1964, The Life of High Society, 1965, The Mournful Demeanor of Lieutenant Boruvka, 1966, A Babylonian Story, 1967, The Bitter World, 1969, Sins for Father Knox, 1973, Oh, My Papa!, 1972, The Edenvale Stories, 1996, When Eve Was Naked, 2001, (plays) The New Men and Women CBC Radio, 1977, God in Your House, 1980 (1st prize Multicultural Theatre Festival Hamilton, 1980), (films) The Tank Battalion, 1991, The Swell Season, 1994, Eine Kleine Jazzmusik, 1996, Poe and the Death of a Beautiful Girl, 1997, The Legend of Emoke, 1998, The Detective Agency, 2000, The Ostrozrak Detective Agency, 2002, (essays) Reading Detective Stories, 1965; author They-Which is We, 1968, All the Bright Young Men and Women, 1972, Working Overtime, 1979, Talkin' Moscow Blues, 1989. Decorated Order of White Lion; apptd. mem. Order of Can., 1992; recipient Neustadt Internat. prize for lit., U. Okla., 1980, Gov. Gen. Can.'s award, 1985, lit. prize Echoing Green Found., 1990, Czech Republic's State Prize for Lit., 1999, Pangea prize 2001, Jaroslev Seifert prize, 2004. Fellow Royal Soc. Can.; mem. Can. Writers' Union, Authors' League Am., Crime Writers Can., Mystery Writers Am., The Internat. PEN Club, Can. br. Czechosolovak Nat. Assn. Can., Order of Can. Conservative. Roman Catholic. Avocation: swing music. Home: 487 Sackville St Toronto ON Canada M4X 1T6 Office Phone: 416-964-8372. Personal E-mail: j.skvorecky@utoronto.ca.

SKWARA, ERICH WOLFGANG, writer, poet, critic, literature educator; b. Salzburg, Austria, Nov. 4, 1948; came to U.S., 1975, naturalized, 1981. s. Alois Gaigg and Hermine Maria Skwara; m. Victoria Anne Dufresne, July 10, 1974 (div. Mar. 1978); m. Gloria Elaine Winniski, June 8, 1978; children: Gabriella Maria, Alexandra Felicitas. BA, U. Paris VII, 1970; MA, Salzburg U., 1972; PhD, SUNY, Albany, 1985. Instr. U. Md., Balt., 1975-77; freelance author Balt. and Paris, 1977-82; vis. lectr. Georgetown U., Washington, D.C., 1982-84; freelance author Salzburg, 1984-86; prof. humanities, comparative lit. and German San Diego State U., 1986—. Dep. editor-in-chief for cultural affairs Die Welt, Berlin, 1993; cultural and lit. corr. for a number of German and Austrian newspapers and media, 1979—; worldwide readings and lecture tours. Author: (novels) Black Sails, 1979, 99, The Cool Million, 1990, Tristan Island, 1992, Die Heimlichen Könige, 1995, Plague in Siena, 1994, 95, Ice on the Bridge, 1997, Versuch einer Heimkehr, 1998, Nach dem Norden, 1998, The Angel of Death, 1998, Anruf aus Rom, 1999, Pest in Siena, 2001, Zerbrechlichkeit, 2002, Träumeerzählen, 2002; translated (from English and French to German) works by T. Williams, Thomas Wolfe, J.J. Rousseau, Gustave Flaubert; own works translated into English, French, Japanese, Arabic, Latvian. Named Hon. citizen, City of Trois-Rivières, Que., Can., 2004; recipient Hermann-Lenz-Preis, Germany, 2002; awarded title of prof., Republic of Austria, 2003. Mem. Internat. PEN Club (Austria, France ctrs). Roman Catholic. Avocations: fine wines, travel, walking. Office: San Diego State U Dept Classics Humanities San Diego CA 92182 also: Suhrkamp Verlag Linden Str 29-35 D60325 Frankfurt am Main Germany E-mail: poetskwara@aol.com.

SKWARCZYŃSKI, HENRYK ADAM (HENRYK SKWAR), writer; b. Felicjanow, Poland, Aug. 13, 1952; arrived in US, 1980; s. Zdzislaw and Stanislawa Ewa (Laszczyk) S.; m. Eglé Juodvalkis, Sept. 2, 1989 MA, U. Warsaw, 1977; postgrad., Polish Acad. Sci., 1978-80, Sorbonne U. Freelance writer Radio Free Europe, NYC, 1980—81, Voice of Am., Washington, 1981-82; instr. Defense Lang. Inst., Monterey, Calif., 1982-84; staff writer Libertas, Paris, 1984-86; free-lance writer Radio Free Europe, Munich, 1987-95; writer Chgo., 1995—. Author: Man in a Cleft, 1979, The Anguish of Becoming American, 1989, Sweeney Among the Nightingales, 2000, The Straw Sea, 2002, With a Rose and the Moon in My Crest, 2004; editor-in-chief: Ephemeron, 1974—75; contbr. short stories to mags. Activist Solidarity Movement, 1980—89. Rotary Club grantee, 1982, Hoover Inst. grantee, 1985. Avocation: travel in Africa.

SKWARYK, ROBERT FRANCIS, judge; b. Erie, Pa., Nov. 4, 1948; s. Frank and Gloria (Hinkle) S. BS, Pa. State U., 1973; JD, U. Kans., 1977. Bar: Pa. 1977, US Dist. Ct. (we. dist.) Pa. 1977. Legal intern legal svcs. Clallum and Jefferson Counties, Port Angeles, Wash., 1977; assoc. Galbo, McNelis, Restifo & Held, Erie, 1977-80; instr. bus. law Behrend Coll. Pa. State U., Erie, 1978-80; appeals referee Commonwealth of Pa., Harrisburg and Pottsville, 1981, Pitts. and Erie, 1985-88, adminstrv. law judge Allentown, 1988-96, Pitts., 1996—. Contbg. author ct. opinions Pa. Liquor Control Bd., 1988—. Mem. Behrend Coll. Soccer Alumni Assn., Erie, 1974-90. Sgt. USMC, 1967-70, lt. (j.g.) USN, 1981-85, lt. USNR, 1986-92, Saudi Arabia, lt. comdr. USNR, 1992-98, comdr., 1998—. Fellow Theatre-Sciptworks, Pa. Coun. Arts, 2002. Mem. ABA, Pa. State Bar Assn., Erie County Bar Assn., Pa. Conf. Adminstrv. Law Judges, First Marine Air Wing Assn., Pa. State U. Alumni Assn. Avocations: soccer, flying, orienteering. Home: 833 Greentree Rd Apt 2-6 Pittsburgh PA 15220-3418 Office: Commonwealth Pa Office Adminstrv Law Judge 875 Greentree Rd Pittsburgh PA 15220-3508 Office Phone: 412-920-2008.

SKYLER, JAY S., medical educator, consultant; b. Phila., Feb. 14, 1947; m. Mercedes Armas Bach, Aug. 9, 2003; children: Jennifer Anne, Alexandra Regina Bach, Marcus Richard Bach. BS, Pa. State U., 1967; MD, Jefferson Med. Coll., 1969. Diplomate in internal medicine, also endocrinology, diabetes and metabolism Am. Bd. Internal Medicine. Intern, resident in internal medicine, fellow in endocrinology and metabolism Duke U., Durham, NC, 1969—73, assoc. then asst. prof., 1972—76; assoc. prof. then prof., medicine, pediatrics and psychology, divsn. endocrinology, diabetes, and metabolism, dept. medicine U. Miami, Fla., 1976—. Pres. Am. Diabetes Assn., Alexandria, Va., 1991—92; v.p. Internat. Diabetes Fedn., Brussels, 1994—2000; bd. dirs. Amylin Pharms., San Diego,

DexCom, Inc, San Diego. Founding editor-in-chief (med. jour.) Diabetes Care, 1978—82, scientific editor Internat. Diabetes Monitor, 1989—, assoc. editor Diabetes Technology & Therapeutics, 2006—. With USPHS, 1973—75. Master: ACP (mem. bd. regents 1996—99, chmn., coun. of subspecialty societies); mem.: Internat. Diabetes Fedn. (past v.p.), So. Soc. for Clin. Investigation, Internat. Diabetes Immunotherapy Group, Am. Diabetes Assn. (past pres.). Independent. Achievements include research in multiple developments for treatment of diabetes. Office: Univ of Miami Diabetes Research Institut Ste 3054 1450 NW 10th Ave Miami FL 33136 Home Phone: 305-361-8035; Office Phone: 305-243-6146. Office Fax: 305-243-4484. Business E-Mail: jskyler@miami.edu.

SLAATTE, HOWARD ALEXANDER, minister, philosophy educator; b. Evanston, Ill., Oct. 18, 1919; s. Iver T. and Esther (Larsen) S.; m. Mildred Gegenheimer, June 20, 1951; children: Elaine Slaatte, Mark, Paul. AA, Kendall Coll., 1940; BA cum laude, U. ND, 1942; B.D. cum laude, Drew U., 1945, PhD, 1956; Drew fellow, Mansfield Coll., Oxford U., Eng., 1949-50. Ordained to ministry Meth. Ch. as elder, 1943. Pastor Detroit Conf. United Meth. Ch., 1950-65; assoc. prof. systematic theology Temple U., 1956-60; vis. prof., prof. philosophy and religion McMurry Coll. (now named McMurry U.), 1960-65; prof. dept. philosophy Marshall U., Huntington, W.Va., 1965-89, prof. emeritus, 1989—, chmn. dept., 1966-81, mem. grad. council, 1970-73, mem. research bd., 1974-76, mem. acad. standards and policy com., 1975-77, research grantee, 1976, 77; mem. bd. Campus Christian Center, 1973-75; prof. ethics St. Leo (Fla.) Coll., 1993. Lectr. Traverse City (Mich.) State Hosp., 1966-71, Am. Ontoanalytical Assn. internat. conf., Acapulco, Mex., 1970, World Congress Logotherapy, San Diego, 1980, other orgns. Author: Time and Its End, 1962, Fire in the Brand, 1963, The Pertinence of the Paradox, 1968, The Paradox of Existentialist Theology, 1971, Modern Science and the Human Condition, 1974, The Arminian Arm of Theology, 1977, The Dogma of Immaculate Perception, 1979, Discovering Your Real Self, 1980, The Seven Ecumenical Councils, 1980, The Creativity of Consciousness, 1983, Contemporary Philosophies of Religion, 1986, Time, Existence and Destiny, 1988, Critical Survey of Ethics, 1988; co-author: The Philosophy of Martin Heidegger, 1983, Religious Issues in Contemporary Philosophy, 1988, Our Cultural Cancer and Its Cure, 1995, A Re-Appraisal of Kierkegaard, 1995, Plato's Dialogues and Ethics, 1999, A Purview of Wesley's Theology, 2000; contbr. Analecta Frankliana, 1981; gen. editor: (series) Contemporary Existentialism; contbr. to theol. and philos. jours. Mem. W.Va. Conf. United Meth. Ch., 1966-87, ret., 1987; bd. dirs. Inst. for Advanced Philos. Research, 1979-90; chmn. bd. dirs. Salvation Army of Huntington, W. Va.; courtesy prof. U. South Fla., 1993-99. Recipient Outstanding Educators of Am. award, 1975, Profl. Excellence award Faculty Merit Found., State of W.Va., 1986, U. N.D. Found. award, 2000; named to Honorable Order of Ky. Colonels, W.Va. Ambassador of Good Will; named Internat. Man of Yr., 1993; NSF fellow, 1965, Benedum Found. rsch. grantee, 1970, NSF rsch.-grantee, 1965, 71. Mem. W.Va. Philos. Assn. (pres., 1966-67, 83-84), Am. Philos. Assn., AAUP, Am. Acad. Religion. Home: 10820 Penny Rd Apt 119 Cary NC 27518 *Most knowledge is relative, a balanced existential position with empirical implications, except for the divine Absolute encountered by faith in existence. The revealed principles opened up thereby, especially the ultimacy of sacrifical love (Agape), give basis and motivation for vital morality and a healthy culture. True freedom springs from commitment to these principles.*

SLABACH, STEPHEN HALL, lawyer; b. Nov. 15, 1934; s. Carl Edward and Alvine A. Slabach; m. Elizabeth Havard Cartwright, Feb. 15, 1958; children: Elizabeth Slabach Schmit, Stephen Edward, William Cartwright. BSME, Northwestern U., 1957; postgrad., George Washington U. Sch. Law, 1957—59; LLB, Stanford U., 1961. Bar: Calif., US Dist. Ct. Calif. 1962, US Ct. Appeals (9th cir.) 73, US Supreme Ct. 76. Law clk. to judge Calif. First Dist. Ct. Appeal, San Francisco, 1961—62; assoc. Cooley, Corwley, Gather, Godward, Castro & Huddleson, San Francisco, 1962—65, Cushing, Cullinan, Hancock & Rothert, San Francisco, 1965—73, ptnr., 1973—75; sole practice Burlingame, Calif., 1975—88, San Mateo, Calif., 1988—. Legal aid vol. San Mateo County; trustee San Mateo County Law Libr. Com., 1993—2002, v.p., 1998—2002; pres. Pacific Locomotive Assn., 1988—90, gen. counsel, 1980—. Mem.: ABA, State Bar Calif. Republican. Episcopalian. Office: PO Box 369 Burlingame CA 94011 Office Phone: 650-347-7776. Business E-Mail: stephen@slrbachlaw.com.

SLABE, JAMES F., publishing executive; b. Johnstown, Pa., Nov. 29, 1940; s. Frank and Antoinette Marie (Draksler) S.; m. Elaine Werner, July 14, 1973. BA, Washington and Jefferson Coll., 1962; postgrad., U. Md., 1962—64. Divsn. contr. Pfizer, Inc., NYC, 1967—72; treas., contr. Pharmacaps, Inc., Elizabeth, NJ, 1972—73; dir. profit planning McGraw-Hill, Inc., NYC, 1973—78; v.p. fin. Parade Publs., Inc., NYC, 1978—79; pres. Exec. Enterprises, Inc., NYC, 1979—95, Sabor & Co., Inc., Mountainside, NJ, 1995—. Bd. dirs. Nat. Assn. Visually Handicapped, Washington and Jefferson Coll., pres. Youth and Family Counseling Svc.; mem. investment com. Westfield YMCA. Capt. U.S. Army, 1964-66. Mem. Fin. Execs. Inst., Assn. Am. Planners, Assn. Am. Contrs., Phi Beta Kappa. Roman Catholic. Office: Sabor & Co 50 E 83d St New York NY 10028 Business E-Mail: jfslabe@quantumforce.net.

SLACIK, CLAUDIA, bank executive; b. 1957; AB, Smith Coll.; MBA, NYU; grad., French Culinary Inst., NYC. V.p., Strategic Planning World Color Press, 1992; group head, Asset Based Fin. Grp., Global Fixed Income Grp. Citigroup, NYC, sr. credit officer, global head of trade, Global Trans. Services, 2004—. Mem., Bd. Dirs. Jonathan Woodner Co., Wickes Co.; founding dir. North Fork Women's Health Fund, LI; co-chair, Bd. Dirs. Callen-Lorde Cmty. Health Ctr., NYC. Named one of 25 Women to Watch, US Banker, 2006. Avocation: golf. Office: Citigroup Inc 399 Park Ave New York NY 10043 *

SLACK, DONALD CARL, agricultural engineer, educator; b. Cody, Wyo., June 25, 1942; s. Clarence Ralbon and Clara May (Beightol) S.; m. Marion Arline Kimball, Dec. 19, 1964; children: Jonel Marie, Jennifer Michelle. BS in Agrl. Engring., U. Wyo., 1965; MS in Agrl. Engring., U. Ky., 1968, PhD in Agrl. Engring., 1975. Registered profl. engr., Ky., Ariz. Asst. civil engr. City of LA, 1965; research specialist U. Ky., Lexington, 1966—70, agrl. engring. advisor Tha Phra, Thailand, 1970—73, rsch. asst. Lexington, 1973—75; from asst. prof. to assoc. prof. agrl. engring. U. Minn., St. Paul, 1975—84; prof. U. Ariz., Tucson, 1984—, head dept. agrl. and biosystems engring., 1991—, prof. watershed mgmt., Cecil H. Miller endowed chair, 2006—. Mem. Mid. East and Mediterranean Desert Devel. Program, 1997—; vis. prof. dept. atmospheric sci. Fed. U. Paraiba, Campina Grande, Brazil, 1997; vis. prof. dept. irrigation Chapingo Autonomous U., Mexico, 2000; tech. adv. Ariz. Dept. Water Resources, Phoenix, 1985—, Tucson active mgmt. area, 1996—; cons. Winrock Internat., Morrilton, Ark., 1984, Water Mgmt. Synthesis II, Logan, Utah, 1985, Desert Agrl. Tech. Sys., Tucson, 1985—, Portek Hermosillo, Mexico, 1989—, World Bank, Washington, 1992—, Malawi Environ. Monitoring Project, 1996, Mex. Inst. for Water Tech., 1997, Nat. Agrl. Rsch. Inst., La Serema, Chile, 1997; cons. F.J. Hansen Inst. for World Peace San Diego State U., 1997—; cons. Internat. Ctr. for Agrl. Rsch. in Dry Areas, 2005; dep. program support mgr. Rsch. Irrigation Support Project for Asia and the Near East, Arlington, Va., 1987—94; mem. adv. team Cearan Found. for Meteorology and Hydrology, Fortaleza, Brazil, 1995—; mem. internat. adv. panel Matrou Resources Mgmt. Project, World Bank, Egypt, 1996—2000; bd. dirs. Sonoita Vineyards, Ltd., Watershed Mgmt. Group, Inc. Contbr. articles to profl. jours. Named Adminstr. of Yr., Coll. Agrl. & Life Scis., 2004—05. Fellow ASCE (Outstanding Jour. Paper award 1988), Am. Soc. Agrl. Engrs. (Ariz. sect. Engr. of Yr. 1993); mem. US Com. on Irrigation and Drainage (life), Am. Soc. Engring. Edn. (program evaluator accreditation bd. for enring. and tech., 2001—), SAR, Brotherhood of Knights of the Vine (master knight), Rocky Mountain Elk Found. (life), Wyo. Wildlife Fedn. (life); Sigma Xi, Tau Beta Pi, Alpha Epsilon, Gamma Sigma Delta. Democrat. Lutheran. Achievements include patents pending in field; development of infrared based irrigation scheduling device. Avocations: hunting, camping, hiking, model railroading. Home: 9230 E Visco Pl Tucson AZ 85710-3167 Office: U Ariz Agrl Biosystems Engring Tucson AZ 85721-0038 Home Phone: 520-722-2162; Office Phone: 520-621-7230. Business E-Mail: slackd@email.arizona.edu. *Personal philosophy: Don't take yourself too seriously and don't take anyone else too seriously either.*

SLACK, EDWARD DORSEY, III, financial systems professional, consultant; b. Fairmont, W.Va., June 2, 1942; s. Edward Dorsey Jr. and Margaret Elaine (Higgs) S.; m. Donna Jean Carter, Oct. 19, 1944; children: Ted, Robyn. BS in Indsl. Engring., W.Va. U., Morgantown, 1965, postgrad., 1965—66. Registered profl. engr., W.Va. Assoc. sys. and procedures analyst Westinghouse Atomic Power divsn., Pitts., 1966—69; sys. and procedures analyst Westinghouse Nuc. Energy Sys., Pitts., 1969—72, sr. sys. analyst, 1972—75, mgr. payroll and fin. sys., 1975—77; mgr. std. ledger conversion Westinghouse Energy Sys., Pitts., 1977, mgr. fin. sys. and control, 1978—90, mgr. fin. sys. and std. ledger, 1990—91, mgr. payroll, cost and fin. sys. control, 1991—94; data processing analyst & decision support coord. Braddock Med. Ctr., Pa., 1995—96; sys. analyst, decision support coord. U. Pitts. Med. Ctr., Braddock, 1996—. Developer computer programs; designer and installer computer modules, report writer. Mem. NSPE, W.Va. Soc. Profl. Engrs. Avocations: walking, spectator sports, sports and other memorabilia, ballroom dancing. Home: 179 Autumn Dr Trafford PA 15085-1448 Office: U Pitts Med Ctr Braddock 400 Holland Ave Braddock PA 15104-1599

SLACK, JEFFERY E, lawyer; b. Salt Lake City, June 3, 1973; s. Eugene B. and Janie Slack; m. Renae Caverhill Slack, Apr. 17, 2005; children: Rylee M., Hutson J., Asher G. B, U. Utah, Salt Lake City, 1998, JD, 2001. Dep. iron county atty. Iron County Attys. Office, Cedar City, Utah, 2003—06; owner Law Offices Jeffery E. Slack, Cedar City, 2006—. Office: Law Offices of Jeffery E Slack 141 N Main Ste 215 Cedar City UT 84720 Home Phone: 435-867-5608; Office Phone: 435-586-2384. Office Fax: 866-606-4278; Home Fax: 866-606-4278. Business E-Mail: jeff@slacklawfirm.com.

SLACK, MOLLY JOHANNA, theater educator; b. Baytown, Tex., Dec. 1, 1951; d. Thomas Edward and Bonnie Burkman Slack. AA, Lon Morris Coll., Jacksonville, Tex., 1972; BA, Trinity U., San Antonio, 1975; M in Liberal Arts, Houston Bapt. U., 1994. Asst. program dir. Houston Bapt. U., 1994—96; tchr. theatre arts Lamar Consol. Sch. Dist., Rosenberg, 1996—. Supts. secondary adv. com. Lamar Consol. Ind. Sch. Dist., Rosenberg, Tex., 1999—2001; site-based mgmt. com. Wessendorff Mid. Sch., 1997—2001, chair dept. fine arts, 2003—, campus coord. U. Interscholastic League, 1996—, bd. mem. PTO, dist. coord. U. Interscholastic League, 2005—. Dir.(designer): Beauty & the Beast, The Pirates of Penzance, Cinderella, H.M.S. Pinafore, Reynard the Fox (Superior One Act Play Festival, 1999), The Adventures of Tom Sawyer, Peter Pan, You're A Good Man, Charlie Brown; set designer Annie, Once Upon a Mattress, Bye, Bye Birdie, Rodger's and Hammerstein's Cinderella, Guys and Dolls. Coord. fine arts related activities Wessendorff Parent/Tchr. Orgn., 2003—06. Recipient Tchr. Yr., Wessendorff Faculty and Staff, 2001; grantee, Lamar Ednl. Found., 2001—02. Mem.: Tex. Ednl. Theatre Assn., Tex. Assn. Gifted and Talented. Avocations: travel, reading, painting, orchids. Home: 14207 Whitecross Drive Houston TX 77083 Office: Wessendorff Middle Sch 5201 Mustang Rosenberg TX 77471 Home Phone: 281-530-3378; Office Phone: 832-223-3300. E-mail: mslack@lcisd.org.

SLACK, RYAN, entrepreneur; b. 1972; BCE, U. Calif. Davis; MBA, Stanford Bus. Sch. COO Champion Trailers, Calif.; sr. mgr. KPMG Germany, Berlin; CEO PropertyShark.com, Bklyn., 2004—. Named one of 200 Most Influential New Yorkers, NY Mag., 40 Under 40, Crain's NY Bus., 2007. Office: Property Rsch Ptnrs LLC Ste 307 181 N 11th St Brooklyn NY 11211 Office Phone: 718-715-1758. Office Fax: 646-349-1132. *

SLACK, WARNER VINCENT, medical educator, researcher; b. East Orange, NJ, June 10, 1933; s. Charles Morse Slack and Evelyn Francis Slack; m. Carolyn Paxton Slack, June 23, 1956; children: Alison Townsend, Charles Warner, Jennifer Cora. AB, Princeton U., NJ, 1955; MD, Columbia U., NYC, 1959; MS (hon.), Harvard U., Cambridge, Mass. Lic. physician Mass., 1970. Intern then resident in neurology U. Wis., Madison, 1959—61; mem. divsn. clin. computing dept. medicine Beth Israel Deaconess Med. Ctr., Boston, 1970—; prof. of medicine Harvard Med. Sch., 1999—. Co-pres. Ctr. Clin. Computing Beth Israel Med. Ctr., Boston; editor-in-chief MDComputing, 1989—99. Author: Cybermedicine, 2001; contbr. articles to profl. jours. Mem. Med. Com. for Human Rights, Chgo., 1964—70; bd. dirs. Com. of Responsibility, Boston, 1968—73, Princeton Project 55, Princeton, NJ, 1993—99; physician doing primary care medicine in Honduras Cape Cares, Cape Cod, Mass. Capt. Med. Corp USAF, 1962—64. Recipient Outstanding Contributions to Soc. award, Princeton U. Class of 1955, 1995, Morris F. Collen award for Excellence, Am. Coll. of Med. Informatics, 2001. Fellow: Am. Coll. of Medial Informatics (life; one of 50 founding fellows 1986). Achievements include ealy contributor to study of uses of computers in medicine; one of first to offer the idea of patient power that patients who want to should be helped and encouraged to particpate as co-equals with their doctors in medical decisions; research in patient-computer dialogue-the use of a computer to interview patients about their medical histories and to help patients help themselves with medical problems; use and misuse of the SAT and other tests of mental ability; psychology of interviewing. Home: 75 Homer St Newton Centre MA 02459 Office: Beth Israel Deaconess Med Ctr 330 Brookline Ave Boston MA 02215 Office Phone: 617-667-1511. Office Fax: 617-667-1518. Business E-Mail: wslack@bidmc.harvard.edu.

SLADE, BERNARD, playwright; b. St. Catharines, Ont., Can., May 2, 1930; s. Frederick and Bessie (Walbourne) Newbound; m. Jill Florence Hancock, July 25, 1953; children: Laurel, Christopher. Actor: Garden Ctr. Theatre, Vineland, Ont., Crest Theatre, Toronto, CBC-TV, Citadel Theatre, Edmonton, Alta.; screenwriter of over 20 hour TV plays for CBC, CBS, ABC, NBC, 1957—; writer/creator (TV series) Love on a Rooftop, The Partridge Family, The Flying Nun, The Girl with Something Extra, Bridget Loves Bernie; story editor, writer 15 episodes of TV series Bewitched; writer/creator (plays) A Very Close Family, 1962, Same Time Next Year (Drama Desk award 1975, Tony award nomination 1975), Tribute, 1978, Romantic Comedy, 1979, Special Occasions, 1981, Fatal Attraction, 1984, Return Engagements, 1986, Sweet William, 1987, An Act of the Imagination, 1987, I Remember You, 1991, You Say Tomatoes, 1993, Everytime I See You, 1994, Same Time, Another Year, Fling!, 2000, Les Grande Occasions, Paris, 2007; feature films: Same Time, Next Year, 1977, Tribute, 1978, Romantic Comedy, 1979, Shared Laughter-a memoir, 2000, Moving Day, 2005, (film biography) Comedic Genius of Bernard Slade, 2003. Recipient Acad. award nomination Motion Picture Arts and Scis., 1978. Mem. Dramatists Guild Am., Writers Guild Am. (award nomination), Acad. Motion Picture Arts and Scis. (Acad. award nomination 1978), Soc. Authors and Artists (France). Avocation: tennis. Address: Apt 1201 1100 Alta Loma RD West Hollywood CA 90069-2439 Office Phone: 310-360-6532. Personal E-mail: bernslade@aol.com. *I am a prisoner of a childhood dream: to write for the theatre. The fulfillment of that dream has lived up to all my expectations. I believe the theatre should be a celebration of the human condition and that the artist's job is to remind us of all that is good about ourselves. I feel privileged to be given a platform for my particular vision of life, and, whether my plays succeed or fail, I am always grateful for the use of the hall.*

SLADE, BERNARD NEWTON, electronics executive; b. Sioux City, Iowa, Dec. 21, 1923; s. William Charles and Katherine Gertrude Slotsky; m. Margot Friedlein, Aug. 18, 1946; children: Steven P., Eric J. BSEE, U. Wis., 1948; MS, Stevens Inst. Tech., Hoboken, NJ, 1954. Devel. engr. tube divsn. RCA, Harrison, NJ, 1948-55; devel. engr. RCA Labs., Princeton, NJ, 1955-56; mgr. tech. program IBM, Poughkeepsie, NY, 1956-60, mgr. product ops. Hopewell Junction, NY, 1960-64; mgr. mfg. tech. IBM World Trade Corp., Armonk, NY, 1964-65; corp. dir. of mfg. tech. IBM Corp., Armonk, 1965-84; sr. cons. Arthur D. Little, Inc., Cambridge, Mass., 1984-86, Gemini Cons., Morristown, NJ, 1986-93; founder, v.p., bd. dirs. Yieldup Internat. Corp., 1993-97; bd. dirs. V3 Semiconductors, 1996—2003, Anon, Inc. Co-author: Winning the Productivity Race, 1985; author: Compressing the Product Develop. Cycle, 1992; contbr. articles to profl. jours.; patentee in field; contbg. author: Transistors, 1956, Handbook of Semiconductor Electronics, 1962. 2nd lt. AUS, 1943-46. Mem.: IEEE (sr.), Sigma Xi. Home: 12 Merry Hill Rd Poughkeepsie NY 12603-3214

SLADE, JOHN DANTON, lobbyist; b. Balt., Apr. 5, 1939; s. Eldon and Marie (Smith) S.; m. Dale Iris Walden, Mar. 14, 1964 (dec. Dec. 1965); 1 child, Kenyatta Conrad; m. Deborah Faye Douglas, Dec. 11, 1987. BA in Sociology, Morgan State U., 1964; MA in Sociology, CUNY, 1966. Mgmt. trainee IBM, NYC, 1966-69; producer, dir. WBAL-TV, Balt., 1969-71, WGBH-TV, Boston, 1971-73, KPIX-TV, San Francisco, 1973-75; announcer KEST Radio, San Francisco, 1975-76; gen. mgr. Channel 8 Access TV, San Francisco, 1975-79; owner Swansbriar Plantation, Cumberland, Va., 1979-85; asst. prof. military sci., dept. chmn. Howard U., Bowie State U., Georgetown U., Washington, 1985-88; acting chief Nat. Guard Bur., Washington, 1988-92; exec. dir. Assn. Reserve Minority Svc. Members, Inc., Washington, 1992—; founder Iota Phi Theta, Inc. Talk show host WOL Radio, Washington; bd. dirs. Meridian Distributors, St. Thomas, V.I.; guest lectr. Stanford (Calif.) U., Northeastern U., Boston, Morgan State Coll., Balt., Merritt Coll., Oakland, Calif., U. Mass., Amherst; mem. spl. com. San Francisco Chronicle; mem. Balt. Community Rels. Commn.; mem. N.G. Drug Reduction Bd., 1990-91. Author: Last Testament of an American, 1993, Flight of an Angel, 1993, The Founding and Ascendancy of Iota Phi Theta, 1994; Man-Made (Guide to Single Mothers Raising Black Boys Alone), 1994, Iota Phi Theta (Ascending to the Next Millenium), 1999; film producer Breaking the Chains of Bondage, 1972. Mem. exec. council, AARP, DC, 2002; Lt. col. U.S. Army, 1985-92. Recipient Roy Wilkens Renown Svc. award, 1991, Award of Honor, NAACP, Balt., Community Svc. award Les Hommes Civic and Social Club, Hampton, Va., 1991. Mem. Iota Phi Theta (founding mem., bus. mgr. 1963-64, chmn. 2003-). Republican. Personal E-mail: iotabooks@comcast.com.

SLADE, LYNN, lawyer; b. Santa Fe, Jan. 29, 1948; m. Susan Zimmerman, 1 child, Benjamin, 1 child from a previous marriage, Jessica. BA in Econs., U. N.Mex., 1973, JD, 1976. Bar: N.Mex. 1976, U.S. Dist. Ct. N.Mex. 1976, U.S. Ct. Appeals (10th cir.) 1978, U.S. Ct. Appeals (D.C. cir.) 1984, U.S. Supreme Ct. 1984. Ptnr. Modrall, Sperling, Roehl, Harris & Sisk, PA, Albuquerque, 1976—. Adj. prof. U. N.Mex. Sch. Law, Albuquerque, 1990. Editor N.Mex. Law Rev., 1975-76; contbr. articles to profl. jours. Bd. dirs. N.Mex. First, 1999—, chair, 2005—06; trustee-at-large Rocky Mountain Min. L. Found., 1995—97, 2005—; mem. bd. adv. Utton Ctr. for Teens Boundary Resources, 2005—. Mem. ABA (sect. environ., energy and resources, membership officer 1998-00, chair com. on Native Am. natural resources 1991-94, 2002-, coun. mem. 1995-98, mem. sects. litig., dispute resolution, pub. utilities and comm., and transp. law), N.Mex. State Bar (chair, bd. dirs. sect. natural resources 1983-87, bd. dirs. Indian law sect. 2002-04). Home: 143 Olguin Rd Corrales NM 87048-6930 Office: Modrall Sperling Roehl Harris & Sisk PA 500 4th St NW Ste 1000 Albuquerque NM 87102-2186 Office Phone: 505-848-1828. E-mail: lynn.slade@modrall.com.

SLADE, ROY, artist, college president, museum director; b. Cardiff, U.K., July 14, 1933; came to U.S., 1967, naturalized, 1975; s. David Trevor and Millicent (Stone) S. N.D.D., Cardiff Coll. Art, 1954; A.T.D., U. Wales, 1954; D of Arts, Art Inst. So. Calif., 1994. Tchr. art and crafts Heolgam High Sch., Wales, 1956-60; lectr. art Clarendon Coll., Nottingham, Eng., 1960-64; sr. lectr. fine art Leeds Coll. Art, Eng., 1964-67; prof. painting Corcoran Sch. Art, Washington, 1967-68, assoc. dean, 1969-70, dean, 1970-77; dir. Corcoran Gallery of Art, Washington, 1972-77; pres., dir. Cranbrook Acad. Art, Bloomfield Hills, Mich., 1977-94, now dir. emeritus. Sr. lectr. Leeds Coll. Art, England, 1968—69; vis. Boston Mus. Fine Arts, 1970; dir. emeritus Cranbrook Art Mus., 2000—. Exhibited one-man shows Howard Roberts Gallery, Cardiff, Wales, 1958, New Art Ctr., London, 1960, U. Birmingham, 1964, 69, Herbert Art Gallery and Mus., Coventry, 1964, Va. State Art League, 1967, Mus. of Arts and Crafts, Columbus, Ga., 1968, Jefferson Place Gallery, Washington, 1968, 70, 72, 73, Park Sq. Gallery, Leeds, 1969, St. Mary's Coll., Md., 1971, Guelph U., Ont., Can., 1971, Hood Coll., 1974, Pyramid Gallery, Washington, 1976, Robert Kidd Gallery, 1981, 92, Herman Miller, Inc., Mich., 1985; group shows in U.K., Washington, Can.; represented in permanent collections Arts Council Gt. Brit., Contemporary Art Soc., Nuffield Found., Ministry of Works, Eng., Brit. Embassy, Washington, Brit. Overseas Airways Corp., U. Birmingham, Wakefield City Art Gallery, Clarendon Coll., Cadbury Bros., Ltd., Eng., Lord Ogmore, Local Edn. Authorities. Mem. D.C. Commn. on Arts.; bd. dirs. Artists for Environment Found., Nat. Assn. Schs. Art; chmn. Nat. Council Art Adminstrs., 1981. Served with Brit. Army, 1954-56. Decorated knight 1st class Order of White Rose (Finland), Royal Order of Polar Star (Sweden); recipient award Welsh Soc., Phila., 1974, Gov.'s Arts Orgn. award, 1988; Fulbright scholar, 1967-68. Mem. Nat. Soc. Lit. and Arts, AIA (hon. Detroit chpt.), Assn. Art Mus. Dirs. (hon.). Home; 31 Island Way Apt 801 Clearwater FL 33767-2206 Personal E-mail: royslade@verizon.net.

SLADE, SCOTT, radio personality; Traffic reporter WSB-AM 750, Atlanta, morning show host, 1992—. Host (radio shows) Atlanta's Morning News, 1992—. Recipient Marconi Radio Award for Large Market Personality of Yr., Nat. Assn. Broadcasters, 2004, Marconi Radio Award for Major Market Personality of Yr., 2006. Office: Atlanta's Morning News WSB-AM/FM 1601 W Peachtree St NE Atlanta GA 30309-2663 Office Phone: 404-897-6287. Office Fax: 404-876-5126. E-mail: scott.slade@wsbradio.com.

SLADE, TOM, manufacturing executive, political organization worker; b. Albany, Ga., Mar. 13, 1936; s. T.H. and Flora Bell (Jackson) S.; divorced; children: Thomas, Jack, Jeff, Shad. Owner Slade Gas Co., Jacksonville, Fla., 1958-71; pres. Gen. Environ., Jacksonville, 1971-75, Slade & Co., Jacksonville, 1975-80; pres., owner Dozier & Jay Paint Co., Green Cove Springs, 1980—; pres. Tidewater Cons., 1998—. Mem. Fla. Ho. of Reps., Tallahassee, 1962-64, Fla. Senate, 1966-70; vice chmn. Fla. Tax and Budget Reform Commn., 1990—; mem. Fla. High Speed Rail Commn., 1991; active in numerous polit. and civic orgns. Recipient numerous pub. svc. awards. Republican. Avocations: tennis, boating. Office: Dozier & Gay Paint Co 3529 Enterprise Way Green Cove Springs FL 32043-9334 Home: 825 Shipwatch Dr E Jacksonville FL 32225-5416

SLADEK, JOHN R., JR., academic administrator, neurobiology and anatomy educator; b. Chgo., Feb. 6, 1943; s. John R. and Marie (De Benedictis) S.; m. Celia Davis; children: Jonathan Andrew, Stefan Zachary, Jessica Anne. BA, Carthage Coll., 1965; MS, Northwestern U., 1968; PhD,

U. Health Scis./Chgo. Med. Sch., 1971. Teaching asst. Chgo. Med. Sch., 1968-70, asst. prof. anatomy, 1971-73, U. Rochester Sch. Medicine, NY, 1973-77, assoc. prof. NY, 1977-82, assoc. prof. brain rsch. NY, 1979-82, prof. NY, 1982-83, prof. neurobiology and anatomy NY, 1982-91, Kilian and Caroline Schmitt prof. NY, 1987-91, chmn. dept. NY, 1982-91, dir. neurosci. grad. program NY, 1987-91; prof., chmn. dept. Neuroscience., dir. Neuroscience. Inst. U. Health Scis./Chgo. Med. Sch., 1991—2001, dir. med. neurosci. course, 1993—2001; vice chancellor rsch. U. Colo. at Denver and Health Scis. Ctr., 2001—06; pres., CEO Calif. Luth. U., Thousand Oaks, 2006—. Vernon Roosa lectr. Trinity Coll., Hartford, Conn., 1989; 1st Irving S. Cooper vis. prof. Mayo Clinic, Rochester, Minn., 1989. Editor: Monoamine Transmitter Histochemistry, 1982, Neural Transplants: Development and Function, 1984, Transplantation into the Mammalian CNS, 1988; editor-in-chief Exptl. Neurology, 1988—; editor Brain Rsch. Bull., 1980-88, Cell and Tissue Rsch., 1992—; mem. editorial adv. bd. Neurobiology of Aging, 1980—; contbr. over 150 articles to profl. jours. Pres. Residents of Bergen (N.Y.) Believe in the Environment and Democracy, 1989-91; mem. spl. com. bd. trustees Carthage Coll., mem. natural scis. adv. com., 1992—, mem. adv. com. career placement and continuing edn. programs, 1993—. Recipient Disting. Alumnus award Carthage Coll., 1983, U. Health Scis./Chgo. Med. Sch., 1990. Mem. Soc. for Neurosci. (nominating com. 1990, fin. com. 1990—), Am. Assn. Anatomists (exec. com. 1972—), Am. Assn. Anatomy Chmn., N.Y. Acad. Scis., Histochem. Soc., Alzheimers Assn. (med. sci. adv. bd.), Coun. Biology Editors. Office: Calif Luth U 60 West Olsen Rd Thousand Oaks CA 91360

SLADEK, LYLE VIRGIL, mathematician, educator; b. Pukwana, SD, Oct. 13, 1923; s. Charles Frank and Emma Margaret (Swanson) S.; m. Patricia Knotts, Sept. 12, 1948; children: Susan, Ann, Laura, Karen. BS, SD State U., Brookings, 1948; MA, U. SD, Vermillion, 1949, Stanford U., Calif., 1963; PhD, UCLA, 1970. Tchr. high sch., Mitchell, S.D., 1950-56; asst. prof. math. Black Hills State Coll., S.D., 1957-62; prof. math. Calif. Luth. Univ., Thousand Oaks, 1963-94, prof. emeritus, 1994—. Lectr. history WWII. Author, contbr. Lucky Stars and Gold Bars, 2005 (Benjamin Franklin award 2005); contbr. short stories, poems to mags. and newspapers. Pres. congregation Our Savior's Lutheran Ch., Spearfish, S.D., 1961. Served as officer US Army, 1943-46, PTO, ETO. Shell Merit fellow, 1956; NSF fellow, 1956-57, 62-63; recipient Meritorious Achievement award edn. S.D. Mines and Tech., 1957; Fulbright-Hays lectr. Bahamas, 1980-81 Mem. Math. Assn. Am., Blue Key, Pi Kappa Delta, Phi Delta Kappa Home: 3243 Pioneer St Thousand Oaks CA 91360-2730 Personal E-mail: patlyle@hotmail.com. *I learned from my parents during the dust bowl years that adversity often can be overcome through patience and determination, and that problems provide challenges that add spice to life. I have sought to return full measure to society for all the opportunities and joys of life that have come my way.*

SLADEK, RONALD JOHN, physics professor; b. Chgo., Sept. 19, 1926; s. James Joseph and Rose (Vachulka) S.; m. Jeanne T. McFadden, Sept. 19, 1953; children: Linda, James, Frances, Stephen, Rosemarie, Edward. PhB, U. Chgo., 1947, SB, 1949, SM, 1950, PhD, 1954. Rsch. physicist Westinghouse Rsch. Labs., Pitts., 1953-60, fellow scientist, 1960-61; assoc. prof. physics Purdue U., West Lafayette, Ind., 1961-66, prof., 1966-91, prof. physics emeritus, 1992—, acting head dept. physics, 1969-71, assoc. dean sci., 1974-87. Vis. scientist Sci. Center, N.Am. Rockwell Corp., Thousand Oaks, Calif., summer 1967; sabbatical scientist Xerox Rsch. Ctr., Palo Alto, Calif., 1976-77 Contbr. articles to profl. jours. With USNR, 1945-46. AEC fellow U. Chgo., 1952-53. Fellow Am. Phys. Soc. Home: 963 Ridgeview Dr Reno NV 89511-8506

SLADKUS, HARVEY IRA, lawyer; b. Mar. 5, 1929; s. Samuel Harold and Charlotte Dorothy Sladkus; m. Harriet Marcia Barske, Nov. 26, 1967 (div.); children: Steven David, Jeffrey Brandon; m. Roberta Frances Pope, Oct. 24, 1986. AB, Syracuse U., 1950; JD, NYU, 1961. Bar: NY 1962, U.S. Supreme Ct. 1967, Conn. 1981. Assoc. Morris Ploscowe, NYC, 1961-66; pvt. practice NYC, 1968—95, 1997—; ptnr. Dweck & Sladkus and Feiden, Dweck & Sladkus, NYC, 1968-95, Dweck & Sladkus, LLP, NYC, 1996; pres. Harvey I. Sladkus, P.C., 1997—. Small claims arbitrator Civil Ct. City of NY, 1977—; adj. prof. law Benjamin N. Cardozo Sch. Law, 1994—95; lectr. family and matrimonial law. Co-author: (book) Practice Under New York's Matrimonial Law, 1971—79; editor-in-chief: Family Law Practice, 1982, contbg. columnist: It's the Law, Suffolk Times, 1999—2002, Bottom Line, 2000—; contbr. articles to profl. jours. 1st lt. US Army, 1952—53, Korea. Decorated Bronze Star, War Svc. medal Korean Govt.; named Arbitrator of Yr., NY Civil Small Claims Ct., 2002, Civil Ct. NY County, 2002; recipient George Washington Honor medal, Freedoms Found., Valley Forge, 1953. Mem.: Suffolk County Bar Assn., Am. Arbitration Assn. (nat. panel arbitrators), Internat. Acad. Matrimonial Lawyers, Am. Acad. Matrimonial Lawyers, Assn. Bar City of NY, NY State Bar Assn. Jewish. Office: 425 Park Ave New York NY 10022-3506 Office Phone: 212-754-9400. E-mail: hisatty@nyc.rr.com. *Notable cases include: Burns vs. Burns, first to constitute a tenant in occupancy to subscribe to shares of an apt. corp. going coop.; Brown vs. Brown, case of first impression reclause in agreement of ex-wife living with another man.*

SLAFF, ALLAN PAUL, military officer, academic administrator, educator, entrepreneur; b. Mt. Vernon, NY, Feb. 2, 1923; s. Frank Alfred and Augusta Raye (Scher) S.; m. Mary Lee Schaeffer; children: Randolph Elliott, Valerie Anne. BS, U.S. Naval Acad., 1944; postgrad., U.S. Naval Post Grad Sch., 1949-50, U.S. Naval War Coll., Newport, RI, 1959-60, Harvard U., 1967. Commd. ensign USN, 1944, advanced through grades to capt., 1965, WWII Battleship Mass. Fast Carrier TF, 1944-46, personal aide to CNO Adm. Arleigh Burke, 1950-51, spl. security officer commd. in Korean War Navy, comdr. USS Lester, Davis, Luce, Albany, 1957-70, sr. naval advisor to Vietnam Navy, 1967-68, ret., 1970; dean, mem. faculty Bus. Sch. Harvard U., Boston, 1970-80; chmn. Luzerne Co. News Co., Wilkes Barre, Pa., 1980-86, LABSPHERE, Inc., N. Sutton, N.H., 1983-94. Cons. Harvard Bus. Sch., 1980-84. Author (autobiography): A Sailor's Story, 2004; contbr. articles to profl. jours. and mags. Decorated Legion of Merit, Bronze Star, Nat. Order of Vietnam, numerous other decorations U.S. Navy, 1941-70; recipient Disting. Grad. award Wyoming Sem., Kingston, Pa., 1990. Mem. Port Royal Club (sec. bd. dirs.), Naples Yacht Club (treas., bd. dirs.), Royal Poinciana Golf Club, Port Royal Property Owners Assn. (bd. dirs.). Republican. Episcopalian. Avocations: golf, travel, photograrphy, gardening. Home: 4151 Gulf Shore Blvd N 601 Naples FL 34103-2292 Personal E-mail: allanslaff@aol.com.

SLAFKA, KRISTI LYNNE, journalist; b. McKeesport, Pa., Aug. 18, 1978; d. Kenneth Edward and Debra Lynne Slafka. BA, Washington and Lee U., 2000; web prodr. cert., Georgetown U., 2002. Assoc. editor Hotline, Washington, 2000—04; assoc. prodr./booker Fox News Channel, Washington, 2004—05; stringer People mag., Washington, 2002; prodr. Washington Jour. C-SPAN, Washington, 2005—. Mem.: Radio and TV News Dirs. Assn., Soc. Profl. Journalists, Washington and Lee U. Alumni Assn., Kappa Delta. Office: C-SPAN 400 N Capitol St NW Ste 650 Washington DC 20001

SLAGER, DONALD W., waste management executive; Various mgmt. positions Gen. Waste Svcs., 1985—90, gen. mgr., 1990—92; dist. mgr. Chgo. metro dist. Allied Waste Industries, Scottsdale, Ariz., 1992—96, regional v.p. west region, 1996—97, asst. v.p. ops., 1997—98, v.p. ops., 1998—2001, sr. v.p. ops., 2001—03, exec. v.p., COO, 2003—04, pres., COO, 2005—. Office: Allied Waste Industries Ste 100 15880 N Greenway-Hayden Loop Scottsdale AZ 85260 *

SLAGLE, TOM, medical products executive; BBA, U. Toledo. With ortho diagnostics divsn. Johnson & Johnson; with Baxter Healthcare; mem. staff to exec. v.p. East Coast Distbn. Cardinal Health, Inc., Dublin, Ohio, 1996—99, exec. v.p. franchise devel. Medicine Shoppe Internat., pres., CEO Medicine Shoppe Internat., grp. pres. Med. Supply Chain bus. Office: Cardinal Health Inc 7000 Cardinal Pl Dublin OH 43017

SLAIHEM, AMEER ABDULLAH, career officer; b. Madina Munuwara, Saudi Arabia, July 7, 1959; s. Abdullah Ahmed Slaihem; Noaf, Nada, Scarlett, Gazzi. Diploma in Acctg., Valencia C.C., Orlando, Fla., 1981; B in Acctg., U. N. Fla., Jacksonville, 1984, cert. of Merit in Cost, 1984. Cert. computer mgmt. Commd. lt. Royal Saudi Airforce, 1984, advanced through grades to lt. col., 1998, base level contract officer, 1984-85, central level contract officer, 1985-88, contract officer, 1988-90, capt., 1989-94, O&M squadron asst. comdr., 1990-93, O&M squadron comdr., 1993-98; ret., 1998. Pres. Soccer Club, U. N. Fla., 1983-84, social dir. Alpha Sigma Pi, 1983-84, pre. govt. students, 1984, pres. Internat. Student Assn., 1984. Decorated Desert Storm Shield, 1992. Avocations: flying scuba diving, marina sport, volleyball, athletics, soccer playing. Mailing: 5815 SE Federal Hwy Stuart FL 34997-7883 Office Phone: 5612198803.

SLAMAN, THEODORE A., mathematics professor; BS in physics, Pa. State U., 1976; PhD in math., Harvard U., 1981. Prof. U. Chgo., 1983—96, U. Calif. Berkeley, 1996—, chair math. dept., 2003—06. Office: Dept Math 719 Evans Hall U Calif Berkeley CA 94720

SLANSKY, JERRY WILLIAM, investment company executive; b. Chgo., Mar. 8, 1947; s. Elmer Edward and Florence Anna (Kosobud) S.; m. Marlene Jean Cannella, Jan. 29, 1950; children: Brett Matthew, Blake Adam. BA, Elmhurst Coll., 1969; MA, No. Ill. U., 1971. Mktg. rep. Bantam Book Co., Chgo., 1972-73, Charles Levy Circulating Co., Chgo., 1973-76; account exec. Merrill Lynch, Chgo., 1976-77, Oppenheimer & Co., Inc., Chgo., 1977—, asst. v.p., 1978, v.p., 1979, sr. v.p., 1981, mng. dir., 1986, ptnr., 1986—. Bd. dirs. Lake Geneva (Wis.) Beach Assn., 1987-02, Glen Ellyn Youth Ctr., Glenbard West H.S., pres., 1998-99; bd. dirs. Buttonwood Cove, Longboat Key, Fla., 2006-; mem. bus. affairs com. Presbytery of Chgo., 1999-04. Mem. Nat. Assn. Securities Dealers (arbitrator 1988—), N.Y. Stock Exch., Chgo. Bd. Options, Am. Arbitration. Assn, Omaha C. of C. Presbyterian. Avocations: swimming, water-skiing, golf, skiing, kayaking. Office: Oppenheimer & Co Ste 4000 500 W Madison St Chicago IL 60661 Office Phone: 312-360-5553. Personal E-mail: jerry.slansky@opco.com.

SLARK, MARTIN P., electronics executive; BSE, Reading Univ., England, 1977; MBA, Ea. London Univ. Mgmt. positions Molex Inc., Lisle, Ill., 1976—99, exec. v.p., 1999—2001, pres., COO, 2001—05, vice-chmn., CEO, 2005—. Bd. dir. Hub Group Inc. Office: Molex Inc 2222 Wellington Ct Lisle IL 60532 *

SLASH, (SAUL HUDSON), guitarist; b. Stoke-on-Trent, Eng., July 23, 1965; s. Anthony and Ola Hudson; m. Renée Suran, Oct. 10, 1992 (div. 1997); m. Perla Ferrar Oct. 15, 2001-; children: London Emilo, Cash Anthony. Guitarist Guns n' Roses, 1985—96; founder, guitarist Slash's Snakepit, 1994—2001; guitarist Velvet Revolver, 2002—. Albums: (with Guns N' Roses) Live Like a Suicide, 1986, Appetite for Destruction, 1987 (Am. Music awards Favorite Hard Rock Album, 1990, VH1: 100 Greatest Albums, 2001, #1, Spin mag.'s Greatest Metal Albums, 2002, one of 500 Greatest Albums of All Time, Rolling Stone, 2003), GN'R Lies, 1988, Use Your Illusion I, 1991, Use Your Illusion II, 1991, The Spaghetti Incident?, 1993, (with Slash's Snakepit) It's Five O'Clock Somewhere, 1995, Ain't Life Grand, 2000, (with Velvet Revolver) Contraband, 2004, Libertad, 2007; songs: (with Guns N' Roses) Welcome to the Jungle, 1987 (one of 500 Songs That Shaped Rock & Roll, Rock & Roll Hall of Fame, 1997, one of 100 Greatest Videos Ever Made, MTV, 1999), Sweet Child O' Mine, 1987 (Am. Music awards Favorite Rock Single, 1989, MTV Video Music awards Best Heavy Metal video, 1989), November Rain, 1991 (MTV Video Music awards Best Cinematography, 1992); contbr.: (films) The Dead Pool, 1988, Cocktail, 1988, Lean on Me, 1989, Black or White, 1991, Interview with the Vampire, 1994, Jackie Brown, 1997, Rated X, 2000, Hulk, 2003, Ray, 2004 (video games) Grand Theft Auto: San Andreas, 2004; worked as guitarist with Iggy Pop, Bob Dylan, Michael Jackson, Lenny Kravitz. Named Best New Artist, MTV Video Music awards, 1988, Favorite Hard Rock Artist, Am. Music awards, 1990, 1992, World's Best Selling Hard Rock Artist of Yr., World Music awards, 1993; named one of 100 Greatest Artists of Hard Rock, VH1, 2001, Sexiest Artists, 2002; recipient Video Vanguard award, MTV Video Music awards, 1992.

SLATE, FLOYD OWEN, retired engineering educator; b. Carroll County, Ind., July 26, 1920; s. Ora George and Gladys Marie (Miller) Slate; m. Margaret Mary Magley, Oct. 14, 1939; children: Sally Lee Slate McEnteer, Sandra Kay Slate Miller, Rex Owen. BS, Purdue U., 1941, MS, 1942, PhD, 1944. Chemist Manhattan Project, Columbia U., NYC and Decatur, Ill., 1944-46; asst. prof. civil engring. Purdue U., Lafayette, Ind., 1946-49; v.p., dir. Geotechnics & Resources Inc., White Plains, NY, 1959—63; prof. engring. materials Cornell U., Ithaca, NY, 1949—87, prof. emeritus, 1987. Internat. lectr.; cons. concrete, low-cost housing. Author; contbr. articles to profl. jours. Recipient Excellence in Engring. Tchg. award, Cornell U., 1976; sr. fellow, East-West Ctr., 1976, rsch. grantee, NSF, 1960—86. Fellow: Am. Inst. Chemists, Am. Concrete Inst. (hon. Wason Rsch. medal 1957, 1965, 1974, 1986, Anderson award 1983); mem.: ASTM, ASCE, Am. Chem. Soc. Achievements include research in internal structure of concrete vs. properties; chemistry applied to engineering problems and low-cost housing for developing countries. Home: 255 The Esplanade N Apt 306 Venice FL 34285-1518 *Think positively and be optimistic. Be considerate of others, try to help others, and enjoy life.*

SLATE, JOE HUTSON, psychologist, educator; b. Hartselle, Ala., Sept. 21, 1930; s. Murphy Edmund and Marie (Hutson) S.; m. Rachel Holladay, July 1, 1950; children: Marc Allan, John David, James Daryl. BS, Athens Coll., 1960; MA, U. Ala., 1965, PhD, 1970. Mem. faculty Athens (Ala.) State Coll., 1965-92, prof. psychology, 1974-92, chmn. behavioral scis., 1974-92; pvt. practice psychology Athens, 1970-92, Hartselle, 1992—; v.p. Slate Security Systems, Hartselle, Ala., 1984—. Author: Psychic Phenomena, 1988, Self-Empowerment, 1991, Psychic Empowerment, 1995, Psychic Empowerment for Health and Fitness, 1996, Astral Projection, 1998, Aura Energy for Health Healing, and Balance, 1999, Rejevenation: Strategies for Living Younger, Longer and Better, 2001, Psychic Vampires, 2002, Beyond Reincarnation, 2005. Named hon. prof. U. Montevallo, 1973, prof. emeritus Athens State U., 1992. Mem. APA, Am. Soc. Clin. Hypnosis, Inst. Parapsychol. Rsch. (founder), Coun. for Nat. Register Health Svc. Providers in Psychology, NEA, Ala. Edn. Assn., Delta Tau Delta, Phi Delta Kappa, Kappa Delta Pi. Home: 1807 Highway 31 NW Hartselle AL 35640-4442 Office: 310 E Main St Hartselle AL 35640 Personal E-mail: joehslate@aol.com.

SLATE, JOHN BUTLER, biomedical engineer; b. Schenectady, NY, Sept. 27, 1953; s. Herbert Butler and Violet (Perugi) S. BSEE, U. Wis., 1975, MEE, 1977, PhDEE, 1980. Spl. fellow of cardiovascular surgery U. Ala., Birmingham, 1980-81, dept. biomed. research engr., 1981-82; microbiology fellow, 1981-82; sr. research engr. IMED Corp., San Diego, 1982-83, sr. research scientist, 1983-86; sci. dir. Pacesetter Infusion Ltd. (dba MiniMed Technologies), Sylmar, Calif., 1986-87; v.p. tech. MiniMed Technologies, Sylmar, Calif., 1987-91; v.p. R & D Siemens Infusion Systems, Sylmar, Calif., 1991-93; v.p. tech. devel. Via Med., San Diego, 1993-94; pres. Slate Engring., San Diego, 1997—2003, Avant Drug Delivery Sys., Inc., San Diego, 1997—2002; v.p. ops. Avant Med. Corp., San Diego, 2002—, pres., 2002—. Mem. IEEE (IEE Ayrton award), Sigma Xi. Office: Avant Med Corp 10225 Barnes Canyon Rd Ste A113 San Diego CA 92121 Home Phone: 858-273-3674; Office Phone: 858-202-1560 Ext. 1. E-mail: jslate@avantmedical.com.

SLATER, ALLEN J., music educator; s. Kermit and Ruth Slater; m. Rebecca Slater, Sept. 3, 1977; children: Benjamin, Megan. MusB in Edn., U. Mont., Missoula, Mont., 1978; MusM in Edn., VanderCook Coll., Chgo., Ill., 1989. Dir. choir First Immanuel Luth. Ch., Missoula, Mont., 1978—79; tchr. music Harlem (Mont.) Schs., 1979—80, Shelby (Mont.) Pub. Schs., 1980—88; dir. bands Flathead H.S., Kalispell, Mont., 1988—, chmn. Dept. Music, 1991—. Dir. choir United Meth. Ch., Shelby, 1980—83; pres. dist. music festival, Shelby, Mont., 1980—88, Kalispell, Mont., 1989—2007. Bd. dirs. Glacier Symphony Orch., Kalispell, Mont., 1996—2001. Named Arts Educator of Yr., Kalispell Arts Assn., 1999; recipient Gold Star Excellence award, Sta. KCFW-TV, Staples, 2001; fellow, Flubright Meml. Fund, Japanese Govt., 2001. Mem.: NEA, Mont. Music Educators Assn. (state mgr. 2006—, chmn. membership 2006—), Nat. Bandmasters Assn. (state pres. 1988—2006), Mont. Bandmaster Assn. (pres. 1988—93), Am. Sch. Band Dirs. Assn., Mortor Bd. (v.p. 1977—78), Phi Beta Mu (treas. 1990—98). Meth. Avocations: music, woodworking. Home: 468 2nd Ave WN Kalispell MT 59901 Office: Flathead High School 644 4th Ave W Kalispell MT 59901 Office Phone: 406-751-3554. Office Fax: 406-751-3505. Business E-Mail: slatera@sd5.k12.mt.us.

SLATER, C. STEWART, chemical engineering educator; b. Feb. 24, 1957; s. Clarence S. and Elizabeth Slater. BS, Rutgers U., Piscataway, NJ, 1979, MS, 1981, MPh, 1982, PhD, 1983. Process devel. engr. Procter & Gamble Co., Cin., 1979-81; teaching asst., project mgr. Rutgers U., 1981-83; prof. chem. engring. Manhattan Coll., Riverdale, NY, 1983-95; prof. chem. engring. dept. Rowan U., Glassboro, NJ, 1995—. Cons. to major U.S. corps. Contbr. over 100 articles to profl. publs., several chpts. to books. Recipient Ralph R. Teetor award Soc. Automotive Engrs., 1986. Fellow Am. Soc. for Engring. Edn. (divsn. chmn. 2003, program chmn. 1990, New Engring. Educator Excellence award 1987, Dow Outstanding Faculty award 1989, John Fluke award 1992, George Westinghouse award 1996, Chester Carlson award 1999, Joseph J. Martin award 1998, 99), Mem. Am. Chem. Soc., Am. Inst. Chem. Engrs., N. Am. membrance Soc., Sigma Xi, Tau Beta Pi, Omega Chi Epsilon. Achievements include research in membrane technology. Office: Rowan Univ Dept Chem Engring 201 Mullica Hill Rd Glassboro NJ 08028-1702 Business E-Mail: slater@rowan.edu.

SLATER, CHRISTIAN, actor; b. NYC, Aug. 18, 1969; s. Michael Hawkins and Mary Jo Slater; m. Ryan Haddon, Feb. 12, 2000; children: Jaden Zach Haddon-Slater, Eliana Sophia Haddon-Slater. Actor: (films) Legend of Billie Jean, 1985, Name of the Rose, 1986, Twisted, 1986, Tucker, 1988, Gleaming the Cube, 1989, Heathers, 1989, Beyond the Stars, 1989, The Wizard, 1989, Tales from the Darkside: The Movie, 1990, Young Guns II, 1990, Pump Up the Volume, 1990, Robin Hood: Prince of Thieves, 1991, Mobsters, 1991, Star Trek VI: The Undiscovered Country, 1991, Kuffs, 1992; (films, voice) FernGully: The Last Rainforest, 1992; (films) Where the Day Takes You, 1992, Untamed Heart, 1993, True Romance, 1993, Jimmy Hollywood, 1994, Interview with the Vampire: Vampire Chronicles, 1994, Murder in the First, 1995, Bed of Roses, 1995, Broken Arrow, 1996, Austin Powers: Internat. Man of Mystery, 1997, The Tears of Julian Po, 1997, (& co-prodr.) Hard Rain, 1998, Basil, 1998, (& exec. prodr.) Very Bad Things, 1998, Love Stinks, 1999, White Lies, 1999, The Contender, 2000, 3000 Miles to Graceland, 2001, Who Is Cletis Tout, 2001, Windtalkers, 2002, Run for the Money (aka Hard Cash), 2002, Masked & Anonymous, 2003, Mindhunters, 2004, The Good Shepherd, 2004, Pursued, 2004, Churchill: Hollywood Years, 2004, (& exec. prodr.) The Deal, 2004, Alone in the Dark, 2005, A License to Steal, 2005, Bobby, 2006; dir.: Mus. of Love, 1996; actor: (TV films) Sherlock Holmes: The Strange Case of Alice Faulkner, 1981, The Hunted Mansion Mystery, 1983, Living Proof: The Hank Williams Jr. Story, 1983, Secrets, 1986, Desperate for Love, 1989, Merry Christmas, George Bailey, 1997; (TV series) One Life to Live, 1977, Ryan's Hope, 1985, LA Law, 1988, Saturday Night Live, 1991, 1993, 1994; (TV series, voice) Prehistoric Planet, 2002; (TV series) The West Wing, 2002, (voice) Adventures of Jimmy Neutron: Boy Genius, 2003, Alias, 2003; (plays) Music Man, 1980, Between Daylight & Boonville, 1980, Copperfield, 1981, Macbeth, 1982, Merlin, 1983, Landscape of the Body, 1984, Dry Land, 1986, One Flew Over the Cuckoo's Nest, 2004—05, The Glass Menagerie, 2005. Named one of 100 Sexiest Stars in Film History, Empire Mag., 1995. Office: Creative Artists Agy 9830 Wilshire Blvd Beverly Hills CA 90212 *

SLATER, EVE E., former federal agency administrator; b. May 16, 1945; 2 children. Grad., Vassar Coll. Cert. internal medicine and cardiology. Intern and resident Mass. Gen. Hosp., chief resident medicine, 1976; chief hypertension unit, asst. prof. medicine Harvard Med. Sch., 1977—82; sr. dir. biochem. endocrinology Merck Rsch. Labs., 1983—88, sr. v.p. clinical & regulatory devel., 1994—2001, sr. v.p. external policy, v.p. corp. pub. affairs, 2001—02; acting asst. sec. for health US Dept. Health & Human Services, Washington, 2001—02, asst. sec. for health, 2002—03; Lloyd H. Smith vis. prof. med. U. Calif., San Francisco, 2003. Adj. assoc. clinical prof. med. Columbia U., 1983—2002; chmn. Internat. Conf. on Harmonization Com. on the Structure and Content of Clin. Studies Reports; chmn. regulations adv. bd. Ctr. for Medicine Rsch.; mem. Keystone Nat. Policy Dialogue on HIV; founder Forum for HIV Rsch.; bd. dirs. Vertex Pharmaceuticals Inc., Cambridge, Mass., 2004—, AnorMED, 2005—, Theravance, Inc., 2005—, Phase Forward Inc., 2005—. Recipient Virginia Kneeland Frantz '22 Disting. Women in Med. award, Columbia U. Coll. Physicians & Surgeons, 2003, Caring Heart award, NJ Assn. for Biomedical Rsch., 2004. Mem.: Phi Beta Kappa. Avocation: flute.

SLATER, JAMES MUNRO, radiation oncologist; b. Salt Lake City, Jan. 7, 1929; s. Donald Munro and Leone Forestine (Fehr) S.; m. JoAnn Strout, Dec. 28, 1948; children: James, Julie, Jan, Jerry, Jon. BS in Physics, U. Utah, Utah State U., 1954; MD, Loma Linda U., 1963; PhD (hon.), Andrews U., Berrien Springs, Mich., 1996. Diplomate Am. Bd. Radiology. Intern Latter Day Saints Hosp., Salt Lake City, 1963-64, resident in radiology, 1964-65; resident in radiotherapy Loma Linda U. Med. Ctr., White Meml. Med. Center, LA, fellow in radiotherapy, 1967-68, U. Tex.-M.D. Anderson Hosp. and Tumor Inst., Houston, 1968-69; dir. radiation oncology sect. Loma Linda U. Med. Ctr., Calif., 1970—79, dir. radiation sect. Calif., 1975—79, chmn. dept. radiation scis. Calif., 1978—90, chmn. dept. radiation medicine Calif., 1990—2001, dir. Cancer Inst., 1993—97, treas. Calif., 1995-96, exec. v.p. Calif., 1994—95; founder, dir. Loma Linda U./NASA Radiation Biology Lab., Calif., 1997—; vice chair radiation medicine Loma Linda U. Med. Ctr., 2003—. Co-dir. cmty. radiology oncology program L.A. County-U. So. Calif. Comprehensive Cancer Ctr., 1978-83; mem. cancer adv. coun. State of Calif., 1980-85; clin. prof. U. So. Calif., 1982—; founding mem. Proton Therapy Coop. Group, 1985—, chmn. 1987-91; cons. charged particle therapy program Lawrence Berkeley Lab., 1986-94; cons. R&D monoclonal antibodies Hybritech Inc., 1985-94, bd. dirs., 1985-94; cons. Berkeley lab., 1986-94; mem. panel cons. Internat. Atomic Energy Agy. UN, 1994-98; cons. Sci. Applications Internat. Corp., 1979, 89-91. Bd. dirs. Am. Cancer Soc., San Bernardino/Riverside, 1976-84, exec. com., 1976—; pres. Inland Empire chpt., 1981-83. NIH fellow, 1968-69; recipient exhbn. awards Radiol. Soc. N.Am., 1973, exhbn. awards European Assn. Radiology, 1975, exhbn. awards Am. Soc. Therapeutic Radiologists, 1978. Alumnus of Yr. award, 1993-94. Fellow Am. Coll. Radiology; mem. AAAS, AMA, ACS (liaison mem. to commn. on cancer 1976-84), Am.

Radium Soc., Am. Soc. Clin. Oncology, Am. Soc. Therapeutics Radiologists, Assn. Univ. Radiologists, Soc. for Clinical Trials, N.Y. Acad. Scis., Calif. Med. Assn., Calif. Radiol. Soc., Gilbert H. Fletcher Soc. (pres. 1981-82), Loma Linda U. Med. Sch. Alumni Assn., Radiol. Soc. N.Am., Bernardino County Med Soc., Soc. Chairmen Of Acad. Radiation Oncology Programs, Alpha Omega Alpha. Achievements include development of proton accelerator system for treating patients with cancer and some benign diseases in a hospital environment; development of computer assisted radiation treatment planning system utilizing patient's digitized anatomic images with overlying radiation distribution images. Office: Loma Linda Univ Med Ctr 25590 Prospect Ave Apt 27c Loma Linda CA 92354-3150 Business E-Mail: jmslater@dominion.llumc.edu.

SLATER, JEFFREY KEITH, banker; s. Kenneth and Bette Mae Slater; m. Catherine Jean Slater (div.); 1 child, Brittany Danielle. BA, U. Washington, Seattle, 1971; MBA, Western Washington U., Bellingham, 1984. Notary Washington. V.p. US Bank N.A., Everett, Wash., 1986—2003; asst. v.p., loan offier Prime Pacific Bank, Kenmore, Wash., 2003—05; lan officer Bank Washington, Lynnwood, 2005—06; v.p., loan officer Frontier Bank, Lynnwood, 2006—. With US Army, 1971—73, Germany. Mem.: Kiwanis Club Lynnwood, Wash. (pres., treas. 1978—, Outstanding Achievement award 1990). Avocation: collector of 20th century advertising. Personal E-mail: jkalenslater@yahoo.com.

SLATER, JIM, sportswriter, journalist; b. Williamsburg, Va., May 31, 1961; s. James and Iva Slater. BA in Journalism and Sociology, Ind. U., Bloomington, 1982. Sports journalist UPI, Indpls., 1983—91, Watertown Daily Times, NY, 1991—93; sports editor Agence France-Presse, Washington, 1993—. Recipient Second pl. nat. sports news writing/circulation 50, 000 and under, AP, 1992, 1993, Hon. Mention sports features and in-depth investigative sports reporting/circulation 50, 000 or less, 1992, 1993. Office: Agence France Presse 1500 K St NW Ste 600 Washington DC 20005-1200

SLATER, KELLY (ROBERT KELLY SLATER), professional surfer; b. Cocoa Beach, Fla., Feb. 11, 1972; s. Steve Slater and Judy; 1 child. With Quicksilver, 1990—. Actor: Baywatch, 1992—93; musician: The Surfers, 1998. Named one of 50 Most Beautiful People, People mag., 1991; named to Surfing Hall of Fame. Achievements include winning 8 world titles, 1992, 94-98, 2005-06; winner, 36 career events, 33 World Championship Tour events; became first to score two perfect rides according to the Association of Surfing Professionals two-wave scoring system, Billabong Tahiti Pro, May, 2005. Mailing: c/o Quicksilver Inc 15202 Graham St Huntington Beach CA 92649 *

SLATER, RALPH EVAN, lawyer; b. Bklyn., July 14, 1948; s. Ralph Groff and Silvia Helen (Montanelli) S.; m. Cynthia Elaine Mahn, Aug. 29, 1970; children: Robert Evan, Andrew Montgomery, Steven Edward. AB, Princeton U., 1970; JD, U. Pa., 1973. Bar: Conn. 1973, U.S. Dist. Ct. Conn. 1984, U.S. Tax Ct. 1984, U.S. Supreme Ct. 1987. Assoc. Gregory & Adams, Wilton, Conn., 1973-79, ptnr., 1980-93; prin. Gregory & Adams P.C., 1994—, pres., 1996—. Chmn. bd. The Wilton Bank, 1986—; atty. Planning and Zoning Commn., Zoning Bd. Appeals, Ridgefield, Conn., 1979—81. Chmn. bd. edn. 1st Congl. Ch., Ridgefield, Conn., 1982—84, chmn. bd. trustees, 1985—87. Mem. Conn. Bar Assn. (exec. com. estates and probate sect. 1984-86, 93-99), Western Conn. Estate and Tax Planning Coun. Inc. (dir. 1992-96), Wilton C. of C. (dir., 2004—). Republican. Mem. Ch. of Christ. Home: 30 Strawberry Ridge Rd Ridgefield CT 06877-6019 Office: Gregory & Adams 190 Old Ridgefield Rd Wilton CT 06897-4023 Office Phone: 203-762-9000. E-mail: rslater@gregoryandadams.com.

SLATER, RODNEY E., lawyer, emergency management executive, former secretary of transportation; b. Tutwyler, Miss., Feb. 23, 1955; m. Cassandra Wilkins; 1 child. BS, Ea. Mich. U., 1977; JD, U. Ark., 1980. Asst. atty. gen. State of Ark., 1980-82; spl. asst. for community and minority affairs Gov. of Ark., 1983-85, exec. asst. for econ. and community programs, 1985-87; dir. intergovernmental rels. Ark. State U., 1987-93; adminstr. fed. hwy. adminstrn. U.S. Dept. Transp., Washington, 1993-97, sec., 1997-2001; ptnr. Patton Boggs LLP, Washington, 2001—; and vice chair & sr. advisor James Lee Witt Associates, LLC, Washington, 2004—. Mem. Ark. State Hwy. and Transp. Commn., 1987-93, chair, 1992-93; dep. campaign mgr., sr. traveling advisor Clinton for Pres. Campaign, 1992; dep. to chair Clinton/Gore Transition Team, 1992-93; bd. dirs. Africare, 2001—, Joint Ctr Polit. and Econ. Studies, 2001— Ark. liaison Martin Luther King, Jr. Fed. Holiday Commn., 1983-87; mem. Ark. Sesquicentennial Commn., 1986. Mem. Ark. Bar Assn. (sec.-treas. 1989-93), W. Harold Flowers Law Soc. (pres. 1985-92). Democrat. Office: Patton Boggs 2550 M St NW Washington DC 20037

SLATER, THOMAS GLASCOCK, JR., lawyer; b. Washington, Mar. 15, 1944; s. Thomas G. and Hylton R. Slater; m. Scott Newell Brent, Aug. 31, 1996; children: Thomas Glascock, Tacie Holden Norris, Andrew Fletcher. BA, Va. Mil. Inst., 1966; LLB, U. Va., 1969. Bar: Va. 1969, US Dist. Ct. (ea. dist.) Va. 1970, US Ct. Appeals (4th cir.) 1975, DC 1980, US Ct. Appeals (5th cir.), US Ct. Appeals DC 1980, US Supreme Ct. 1981. Assoc. Hunton & Williams LLP, Richmond, Va., 1969-76, ptnr., 1976—. Group head litig., intellectual property competition and labor group Hunton & Williams LLP; bd. dirs. Tredegar Industries. Pres. VMI Found., 1995—97, VMI Bd. Visitors, 2003—; bd. trustees Va. Hist. Soc.; mem. vestry St. Mary's Episcopal Ch.; bd. dirs. Central Va. Legal Aid Soc. Fellow: Va. Law Found., Am. Coll. Trial Lawyers, Am. Bar Found.; mem.: Richmond Bar Assn. (pres. 1989—90), DC Bar Assn., Va. State Bar Coun. (exec. com.), 4th Cir. Jud. Conf., Va. Mil. Inst. Alumni Assn. (past pres.). Office: Hunton & Williams LLP Riverfront Plz East Tower 951 E Byrd St Richmond VA 23219-4074 Office Phone: 804-788-8475. Business E-Mail: tslater@hunton.com.

SLATER, VALERIE A., lawyer; b. Passaic, NJ, Oct. 13, 1952; BA magna cum laude, Allegheny Coll., 1974; JD, Cath. U. Am., 1977. Bar: DC 1977, US Ct. Appeals (DC cir.) 1978, US Dist. Ct. (DC dist.) 1982, US Ct. Internat. Trade 1984, US Ct. Appeals (fed. cir.) 1984. Ptnr. Akin Gump Strauss Hauer & Feld LLP, Washington, 1990—2003, ptnr., chair internat. trade practice group, 2003—. Mem.: Phi Beta Kappa. Office: Akin Gump Strauss Hauer & Feld LLP 1333 New Hampshire Ave NW Washington DC 20036-1564 Office Phone: 202-887-4112. Office Fax: 202-887-4288. Business E-Mail: vslater@akingump.com.

SLATKIN, LEONARD EDWARD, musician, conductor, director; b. LA, Sept. 1, 1944; s. Felix and Eleanor (Aller) Slatkin; m. Linda Hohenfeld, Mar. 29, 1986; 1 child, Daniel. Began violin study, 1947; piano study with, Victor Aller and Selma Cramer, 1955; composition study with, Castelnuovo-Tedesco, 1958; viola study with, Sol Schoenbach, 1959; conducting study with, Felix Slatkin, Amerigo Marino and Ingolf Dahl; student, Ind. U., 1962, L.A. City Coll., 1963, Juilliard Sch.; student (Irving Berlin fellow in musical direction), beginning 1964; student of, Jean Morel and Walter Susskind; doctorate (hon.), Juliard Sch. Music dir. Nat. Symphony Orch., Washington, 1996—; chief condr. BBC Symphony Orch., 2000—04. Condr. St. Louis Symphony Orch., 1968—96, musical dir., 1979—96, condr. laureate, 1996—; founder, music dir., condr. St. Louis Symphony Youth Orch., 1969—, mus. advisor, 1979—80; prin. guest condr. LA Philharmonic, Hollywood Bowl, 2005—, Royal Philharmonic Orch., 2005—; with Columbia Artists Mgmt. Inc., Askonas Holt, Ltd., Konzertdirektion/Schmidt; founder, dir. Nat. Conducting Inst.; music advisor Nashville Symphony Orch., 2006—. Conducting debut as asst. condr. Youth Symphony of N.Y., Carnegie Hall, 1966, asst. condr. Juilliard Opera Theater and Dance Dept., 1967, St. Louis Symphony Orch., 1968—71, assoc. condr., 1971—74, guest condr. Concertgebouw, Royal Danish Orch., Tivoli, English Chamber Orch., BBC Manchester, London Philharm., London Symphony Orch., Royal Philmarm. Orch., 1974, Nat. Orch. Paris, Scottish Nat. Orch., NHK Tokyo, 1986, Vienna State Opera, Lyric Opera Chgo., Stuttgart Opera, Stockholm, Oslo, Israel, Goteborg, Berlin, debut Chgo. Symphony Orch., 1974, NY Philharm., 1974, Phila. Orch., 1974, USSR Orchs., 1976—77, Met. Opera, 1991, prin. guest condr. Minn. Orch., 1974—, summer artistic dir., 1979—89, music dir. New Orleans Philharm. Symphony Orch., 1977—78, artistic dir. Great Woods, 1990, artistic adminstr. Blossom, 1991; composer: The Raven, Dialogue for Two Cellos and Orchestra, Ext. 1, 2, 3, 4; rec. artist RCA, Angel EMI, Vox, Telarc, Philips, Warner Bros.; condr.: Arthur R. Metz Found., Ind. U. Recipient 5 Grammy awards, Declaration of Honor in Silver, Austrian Govt., 1986. Mem.: NARAS (bd. govs. Chgo. chpt.). Office: John F Kennedy Ctr 2700 F St NW Washington DC 20566 also: Askonas Holt Ltd Lonsdale Chambers 27 Chancery Ln London WC2A 1PF England Office Phone: 20 7400-1700. Office Fax: 20 7400-1799. *

SLATNER, THOMAS ALLEN, bookseller; b. Marple, Cheshire, Eng., May 1, 1940; arrived in U.S., 1947; s. Hugo and Edith (Elsner) S.; m. Eve Naomi Silberberg, Aug. 11, 1961; children: Nicole, Claude, Genevieve. BA, CCNY, 1961. Mgr. Richard Abel & Co., London, 1968-73; dir. Thomas Slatner & Co., London and N.J., 1978—. Home: 2 Wellfield Ave London N10 2EA England Office: 151 Pritchard Dr Palm Coast FL 32164 E-mail: tslatnerco@blueyonder.co.uk.

SLATOPOLSKY, EDUARDO, nephrologist, educator; b. Buenos Aires, Dec. 12, 1934; married, 1959; 3 children. BS, Nat. Coll. Nicolas Avellaneda, 1952; MD, U. Buenos Aires, 1959. Postdoctoral rschr. renal USPHS, renal divsn., Dept. Internal Medicine Washington U. Sch. Medicine, 1963—65, instr. med. nephrology, 1965—67, asst. prof. to assoc. prof. medicine dept. nephrology, 1967—75, dir. Chromalloy Am. Kidney Ctr. St. Louis, 1967—97, co-dir. renal divsn. Chromalloy Am. Kidney Ctr., 1972—97, prof. medicine, nephrology dept. Chromalloy Am. Kidney Ctr., 1975—, Joseph Friedman Prof. renal disease medicine Chromalloy Am. Kidney Ctr., 1991—. Adv. mem. regional med. prog., renal prog. sch. medicine Washington U., 1970-75; chmn. transplantation com. Barne Hosp., 1975—; fellow com. Kidney Found. Ea. Mo. and Metro.-East, 1978; mem. adv. com. artificial kidney-chronic uremia prog. NIH, 1978-90, rep. Latin-Am. nephrology, 1983-88; mem. study sect. Gen. Med., NIH, 1984-88. Recipient Frederick C. Bartter award, 1991. Mem. AAAS, Am. Fedn. Clin. Rsch., Internat. Soc. Nephrology (Amgen Internat. prize for Therpeutic Advancement in Nephrology), Am. Soc. Nephrology, Endocrine Soc., Sigma Xi. Achievements include research in pathogenesis and treatment of secondary hyparathyroidism and bone disease in renal failure; studies conducted at both levels: clinical, on patients maintained on chronic dialysis and on animals with experimentally induced renal feilure; detailed studies of the effects of calcitriol on PTH MRNA and the extra-renal production of calcitriol by macrophages; vitro studies in primary culture of bovine parathyroid cells used to understand the mechanisms that control the secretion of PTH. Office: Washington U Chromalloy Am Kidney Ctr PO Box 8126 Saint Louis MO 63156-8126 Office Phone: 314-362-7208. Office Fax: 314-362-7875. E-mail: eslatopo@wustl.edu. *

SLATTERY, CHARLES WILBUR, biochemistry educator; b. La Junta, Colo., Nov. 18, 1937; s. Robert Ernest Slattery and Virgie Belle (Chamberlain) Tobin; m. Arline Sylvia Reile, June 15, 1958; children: Scott Charles, Coleen Kay. BA, Union Coll., 1959; MS, U. Nebr., 1961; PhD, 1965. Instr. chemistry Union Coll., Lincoln, Nebr., 1961-63; asst. prof., assoc. prof. chemistry Atlantic Union Coll., South Lancaster, Mass., 1963-68; rsch. assoc. biophysics MIT, Cambridge, Mass., 1967-70; asst. prof., then prof. biochemistry Loma Linda U., Calif., 1970-80; prof. biochemistry-pediatrics, 1980—2003; prof. emeritus biochemistry-microbiology, 2003—; chmn. dept., 1983-99. Vis. prof. U. So. Calif., L.A., 1978-79. Contbr. articles to profl. jours. NIH grantee, 1979-82, 86-89, AHA (Calif.), 1981-83, 83-84. Mem. AAAS, Am. Chem. Soc. (biochemistry divsn.), Am. Dairy Sci. Assn., N.Y. Acad. Scis., The Protein Soc., Am. Soc. Biochemistry and Molecular Biology, Sigma Xi. Republican. Adventist. Office: Loma Linda U Sch Medicine Dept Biochemistry Loma Linda CA 92350-0001

SLAUGH, LYNN H., retired chemist; With Shell Devel. Co., Houston, 1956—98; ret., 1998. Contbr. articles to profl. jours. Recipient Indsl. Chemistry award Am. Chem. Soc., 1995. Achievements include 162 patents; development of two indsl. processes.

SLAUGHTER, ALEXANDER HOKE, lawyer; b. Charlottesville, Va., Nov. 24, 1937; s. Edward Ratliff and Mary (Hoke) S.; m. Virginia Borah, 1964 (div.); 1 child, David A.; m. Mary Peeples, 1971. BA, Yale U., 1960; LLB, U. Va., 1963. Ptnr. McGuire, Woods, Richmond, Va., 1969—. Episcopalian. Home: 3016 Rugby Rd Richmond VA 23221-3936 Office: McGuire Woods One James Ctr 901 E Cary St Richmond VA 23219-4030 Home Phone: 804-353-1405; Office Phone: 804-775-4346. E-mail: aslaughter@mcguirewoods.com.

SLAUGHTER, ANNE-MARIE, dean; m. Andrew Moravcsik; children: Edward, Alexander. Grad. magna cum laude, Princeton U., 1980; JD cum laude, Harvard U., 1985; MPhil, Oxford U., 1982, DPhil, 1992. Tchr. law U. Chgo.; rschr. Harvard U., J. Sinclair Armstrong prof. internat., fgn., and comparative law, dir. internat. legal studies program; Bert G. Kerstetter univ. prof. politics and internat. affairs Princeton U., dean Woodrow Wilson sch. pub. and internat. affairs, 2002—. Bd. dirs. Coun. Fgn. Rels., New Am. Found., Can. Inst. Internat. Governace Innovation; spkr. in field. Author: (book) A New World Order, The Idea That is America; contbr. articles to profl. jours. Covener, acad. co-chair Princeton Project on Nat. Security. Recipient Francis Deak Prize, Am. Jour. Internat. Law, 1990, 1994. Fellow: Am. Acad. Arts and Scis.; mem.: Am. Soc. Internat. Law (pres. 2002—04). Office: Princeton Univ 424 Robertson Hall Princeton NJ 08544-1013 E-mail: slaughtr@princeton.edu.

SLAUGHTER, DJUANIQUE NATÉ, healthcare analyst, project manager, consultant; BS in Criminal Justice, Grambling State U., La., 1993; MPA, Calif. State U., Dominiguez Hills, 1998. Med. clinic asst. Green Clinic, Ruston, La., 1993—97; pub. health intern Dept. Health and Human Svcs., Long Beach, Calif., 1997—98; project mgmt. specialist Scan Health Plan, Long Beach, 1998; adminstrv. asst. Salick Healthcare, LA, 1998—99, healthcare analyst, cons., project mgr., 1999; managed care report analyst Health Care Ptnrs., Torrance, Calif., 1999—2000; project mgr. Ops. Health Care Ptnrs., Torrance, 2000—03; mgr. claims adminstrn. Kaiser Permanent, Pasadena, Calif., 2003—04, cons. quality and risk mgmt., 2004—. HIV/AIDS peer counselor Campus Awareness Prevention, Grambling, La., 1993; sr. cons. Health Plan Regulatory Svcs., 2007—. Mem. Reach 2010, Reach 2010 Project, 2001—. Am. scholar, Grambling State U. Personal E-mail: dedeaka@aol.com.

SLAUGHTER, EDWARD RATLIFF, JR., lawyer; b. Raleigh, NC, Sept. 15, 1931; s. Edward Ratliff and Mary McBee (Hoke) S.; m. Anne Limbosch, July 25, 1957; children: Anne-Marie, Hoke, Bryan. AB, Princeton U., 1953; postgrad. (Rotary Found. fellow), U. Brussels, 1955-56; LLB, U. Va., 1959. Bar: Va. 1959, D.C. 1981. Assoc. firm McGuire, Woods & Battle (now McGuire Woods) and predecessors, Charlottesville, Va., 1959-64; ptnr. McGuire, Woods & Battle and predecessors, 1964-79, head dept. litig., 1964-79, spl. asst. for litig. to atty. gen. U.S., 1979-81; ptnr. firm Whitman & Ransom, Washington, 1981-84; prin. Slaughter & Redinger, P.C., Charlottesville, 1984-95, Slaughter, Izakowitz, Clarke & Nunley, P.C., 1995-96, Woods, Rogers & Hazlegrove, P.L.C., 1996—2002, of counsel, 2002—03, Michie, Hamlett, Lowry, Rasmussen, & Tweel, PLLC, 2003—. Vis. lectr. trial advocacy U. Va., 1970-77, Va. procedure, 1986-91; disting. lectr. U. Tunis, 1996; mem. standing com. on commrs. of accounts Jud. Coun. of Va., 1993—, chmn., 1995-2001. Chmn. Albemarle County (Va.) Dem. Com., 1969-73; pres. Charlottesville-Albemarle United Way, 1972; commr. accounts Albemarle County, 1986—; trustee Lime Kiln Arts, Inc., 1992-98. Served with USNR, 1953-55. Recipient William J. Brennan award U. Va. Trial Advocacy Inst., 1996. Fellow Am. Bar Found., Am. Coll. Trial Lawyers; mem. D.C. Bar, Charlottesville-Albemarle Bar Assn. (pres. 1976-77), Va. Bar Assn. (pres. 1978), Va. State Bar (bd. govs. internat. practice sect. 1992-2000, bd. govs. sr. lawyers conf. 2004—), Thomas Jefferson Inn Ct. (pres. 1995-96), Farmington Country Club. Home: 200 Tuckahoe Farm Ln Charlottesville VA 22901-5531 Office: Michie Hamlett Lowry Rasmussen & Tweel PLLC 500 Court Sq Ste 300 PO Box 298 Charlottesville VA 22902-0298 Home Phone: 434-975-3079; Office Phone: 434-295-8310. Business E-Mail: eslaughter@mhlrt.com.

SLAUGHTER, FREEMAN CLUFF, retired dentist; b. Estes, Miss., Dec. 30, 1926; s. William Cluff and Vay (Fox) S.; m. Genevieve Anne Parks, July 30, 1948; children: Mary Anne, Thomas Freeman, James Hugh. Student, Wake Forest U., 1944, Emory U., 1946-47; DDS, Emory U. Sch. of Dentistry, 1951. Lic. real estate broker. Practice gen. dentistry, Kannapolis, N.C., 1951-89; ret. Mem. N.C. State Bd. Dental Examiners, 1966-75, pres., 1968-69, sec.-treas., 1971-74; chief dental staff Cabarrus Meml. Hosp. (now Carolinas Med. Ctr. NE), Concord, N.C., 1965-66, 75; mem. N.C. Adv. Com. for Edn. Dental Aux. Pers.-N.C. State Bd. Edn., 1967-70; advisor dental asst. program Rowan Cabarrus C.C., 1974-76; Duke Med. Ctr. Davison Century Club. Trustee N.C. Symphony Soc., 1962-68, pres. Kannapolis chpt., 1961; mem. Cabarrus County Bd. Health, 1977-83, chmn., 1981-83, acting health dir., 1981; vice chmn. Kannapolis Charter Commn., 1983-84; mem. City Coun. Kannapolis, 1984-85; Mayor protem, Kannapolis, 1984-85; past active Boy Scouts Am., Eagle scout with silver palm. QM2C asst. navigator on USS Xenia AKA 51, co-navigator on USS Gen. George O. Squier AP 130 with USN, 1944-46, WW II, ETO, MTO. Recipient Kannapolis Citizen of Yr. award, 1982. Fellow Am. Coll. Dentists (life); mem. ADA (life), Am. Legion, Kannapolis Jr. C. of C. (v.p. 1952), Toastmasters Internat. (pres. Kannapolis chpt. 1963-64), Am. Assn. Dental Examiners (Dentist Citizen of Yr. 1975, v.p. 1977-79, Recognition plaque, 1980), So. Conf. Dental Deans and Examiners (v.p. 1969), N.C. Dental Soc. (resolution of commendation 1975), N.C. Dental Soc. Anesthesiology (pres. 1964), Southeastern Acad. Prosthodontics, So. Acad. Oral Surgery, Am. Soc. Dentistry for Children (pres. N.C. unit 1957), Internat. Assn. Dental Rsch., Cabarrus County Dental Soc. (pres. 1953-54, 63-64, 69), N.C. Assn. Professions (dir. 1976-80), Kannapolis Music Club (pres. 1962-63), Emory U. Corpus Cordis Aureum (Emory U. disting. alumnus award 2006), Masons, Shriners, Rotary (dir. 1977-80), Omicron Kappa Upsilon, Alpha Epsilon Upsilon.

SLAUGHTER, JAMES H., lawyer; b. Concord, NC, July 29, 1964; s. Freeman C. and Genevieve A. (Parks) S.; m. Tamara A. Vincent, Oct. 1, 1988; children: Freeman J., McKinley J., Wyatt T. BA with highest honors, U. N.C., 1986, JD, 1989. Bar: N.C., 1989, U.S. Dist. Ct. (mid. and we. dists.) N.C., 1989, U.S. Ct. Appeals (fed. cir.) 1992, Supreme Ct. US; cert. profl. parliamentarian; profl. reg. parliamentarian. Assoc. Henson, Henson, Bayliss & Sue, Greensboro, NC, 1989—91, Floyd & Jacobs, LLP, Greensboro, NC, 1991—96; ptnr. Floyd & Jacobs, Greensboro, NC, 1996—2001, Forman Rossabi Black, Pa., 2001—, pres. Pa., 2003—. Mem. of faculty Williamsburg Practicum of the Am. Inst. of Parliamentarians, 1994-2002. Tech. editor: The Complete Idiot's Guide to Robert's Rules, 2004; contbg. author: Labor Union Law and Regulation, 2005; legal guest columnist News & Record, Greensboro, 1991-95. Pres. Young Dems. of N.C., 1992-93; chmn. State Dem. Coun. of Rev., N.C., 1994-96, 2001—; chmn. Triad chpt. Nat. Conf. Com. Justice, 2004-06; mem. Gov.'s Crime Commn., N.C., 1982-85; mem. N.C. Progress Bd., 1996-98; bd. dirs. Greensboro chpt. ARC, 1996-99, sec., 1997-98; bd. dirs. Greensboro chpt. NCCJ, 1996-99; trustee Greensboro Hist. Mus., 1996-99, pres.-elect, 2006—; elder First Presbyn. Ch., 2000-03, clk. of session, 2001-02. U.S. Truman Scholar, 1984. Master Am. Inns Court; mem. Rotary (Greensboro Crescent club 1993—, Paul Harris fellow), Greensboro Bar Assn. (treas. 1991-92), Nat. Assn. Parliamentarians Ethics (chmn., 2005-), Am. Inst. Parliamentarians (chmn., 2005-), Coll. Cmty. Assn. Lawyers, Ethics Phi Beta Kappa. Presbyterian. Home: 2206 Granville Rd Greensboro NC 27408-5012 Office: Forman Rossabi Black PA PO Box 41027 Greensboro NC 27404

SLAUGHTER, JERRY, medical association administrator; Exec. dir. Kans. Med. Soc. Recipient Med. Exec. Lifetime Achievement award, AMA, 2006. Office: Kans Med Soc 623 SW 10th St Topeka KS 66612 Office Phone: 785-235-2383. Office Fax: 785-235-5114. Business E-Mail: jslaughter@KMSonline.org. *

SLAUGHTER, KENNETH S., lawyer; b. Washington, July 5, 1951; AB, Brown Univ., 1973; JD, Georgetown Univ., 1976. Bar: DC 1976. Atty. advisor U.S. Dept. Treasury, Washington, 1976—79; asst. gen counsel Nat. Cooperative Bank, 1979—83, corp. v.p., gen. counsel, 1983—87; ptnr., State & Local Govt. practice Venable LLP, Washington & Baltimore. Bd. mem. SEED Public Charter Sch., Heads Up, Boys & Girls Clubs of Greater Washington, Venture Philanthropy Ptnrs. Mem.: Nat. Bar Assn., Internat. Assn. Gaming Attorneys, DC Bar Assn. Office: Venable LLP 575 7th St NW Washington DC 20004 also: Venable LLP 1800 Mercantile Bank & Trust Bldg 2 Hopkins Plz Baltimore MD 21201 Office Phone: 202-344-8385, 410-244-7715. Office Fax: 202-344-8300. Business E-Mail: ksslaughter@venable.com.

SLAUGHTER, LOUISE MCINTOSH, congresswoman; b. Lynch, Ky., Aug. 14, 1929; d. Oscar Lewis and Grace (Byers) McIntosh; m. Robert Slaughter, 1956; children: Megan Rae, Amy Louise, Emily Robin. BS in Microbiol., U. Ky., Lexington, 1951, MPH, 1953; D (hon.), U. Ky., 2006. Bacteriologist Ky. Dept. Health, Louisville, 1951-52, U. Ky., 1952-53; market rschr. Procter & Gamble, Cin., 1953-56; mem. Monroe County Legislature, NY, 1976—79; regional coord. Staff of Sec. State Mario Cuomo, NY, 1976—78, Staff of Lt. Gov. Mario Cuomo, NY, 1979—82; mem. NY State Assembly, 1982—86, US Congress from 28th NY dist., 1987—, chairwoman rules com., co-chair Congl. Arts Caucus, co-chair Congl. Bipartisan Pro-Choice Caucus, mem. Dem. steering and policy com., mem. Commn. Security and Cooperation in Europe. Del. Dem. Nat. Conv., 1972, 76, 80, 88, 92, 96; mem. Nat. Ctr. for Policy Alternatives Adv. Bd., League of Women Voters, Nat. Women's Polit. Caucus. Named Lay Educator of Yr., Phi Delta Kappa Internat., Rochester chpt., 1999; recipient Disting. Pub. Health Legislator award, Pub. Health Assn., 1997, Award for Outstanding Arts Leadership in the US Ho. Reps., US Conf. Mayors and Ams. for the Arts, 1998, Humane Legislator of Yr., Am. Humane Assn., 2003, Woman of Vision award, Women in Film and Vision, 2004, Sidney R. Yates Nat. Arts Advocacy award, Nat. Assembly State Arts Agencies. Democrat. Episcopalian. Office: US House Reps 2469 Rayburn House Office Bldg Washington DC 20515-3228 Office Phone: 202-225-3615, 585-232-4850. Office Fax: 202-225-7822, 585-232-1954. *

SLAUGHTER, MATTHEW J., economics professor, former federal official; b. 1969; BA in Econ., Notre Dame, 1990; PhD in Econ., MIT, 1994. Asst. prof. econ. Dartmouth Coll., Hanover, NH, 1994—2001, assoc. prof. econ., 2001—02, assoc. prof. bus. adminstrn. Tuck Sch. Bus., 2002—; mem. Coun. Econ. Advisers Exec. Office of the Pres., Washington, 2005—07. Faculty rsch. fellow Nat. Bur. Econ. Rsch., 1995—2002; vis.

fellow Inst. for Internat. Economics, 1997—; mem. Coun. Fgn. Rels., 2000—05, sr. fellow for bus. & globalization, 2007; vis. scholar Fed. Reserve Bank, 1998, 2002, IMF, 1996, 97; panel mem. NAS, 2004—; bd. acad. advisors Internat. Tax Policy Forum, 2005—; bd. economists Time mag., 2004; cons. The World Bank, 1995—97, 2000, 02, Emergency Com. for Am. Trade, 1996—2003, Nat. Fgn. Trade Coun., 2003, Com. for Fair Internat. Taxation, 2004, Org. for Internat. Investment, 2004. Recipient Bronze award, AMEX Bank Review Essay Competition, 1994, John M. Manley Huntington Teacher award, Dartmoth Coll., 2001; fellow, NSF, 1990—93; grantee MIT Industrial Performance Ctr. Doctoral Fellowship, Sloan Found., 1993—94, Nat. Fellowship, Nat. Bur. Econ., 2000—01, Elizabeth R. & Roland A. Jeffe Fellowship, Dartmouth Coll., 2001—02. Office: Tuck Sch Bus Dartmouth Coll 100 Tuck Hall Hanover NH 03755 E-mail: matthew.j.slaughter@dartmouth.edu. *

SLAUGHTER, MICHAEL WAYNE, education educator; b. Waco, Tex., Nov. 1, 1952; s. Theodore Todd Slaughter and Ethel Mae Massingale; 1 child, Fredrick Wayne Hampton. BS in Edn., Paul Quinn Coll., Waco; M in Edn., Prairie View A&M U., Tex., 1993; PhD in Theology, Christian Bible Coll., Rock Mount, 1993. Cert. Tex. State Bd. Examiners Profl. Counselors Tex., 1994. Counselor McLennan C.C., Waco, Tex., 1993—98; ednl. aide Meadowbrook Elem., Waco, 1999—. Tax preparer, notary Slaughter's Tax and Notary Svcs., Waco, 2003—. Mem. Hillcrest Hosp., Valley Mills, Tex., 1996—98. E-5 U.S. Army, 1972—80, Fort Hood, Texas. Decorated Good Conduct medal U.S. Army. Mem.: Am. Legion (life), Disable Veterans (life), Benevolent Protective Order Elks of The World (life; e.l. k. 2005—06), Order Ea. Star (life; worthy patron 1994), United Most Scottish Rite Grand Lodge Tex. (life; worshipful master 1994). R-Consevative. Baptist. Avocations: billards, reading, travel, shopping, writing. Home: 316 Wilson Rd Waco TX 76705 Office: Slaughter's Tax and Notary Svcs 316 Wilson Rd Waco TX 76705-4860 Home Phone: 254-412-2725; Office Phone: 254-716-3550. Office Fax: 254-412-2725; Home Fax: 254-412-2725. Business E-Mail: mwslaug3@netscape.com.

SLAUGHTER, RICHARD ARTHUR, political scientist, economist, educator; b. Twin Falls, Idaho, Nov. 20, 1943; s. Walter Arthur and Mary Viola Slaughter; m. Susan Kay Clark, Aug. 11, 1966; children: Scott, Ryan. BA in Polit. Sci., U. Idaho, 1966; MA in Internat. Rels., U. Denver, 1968, PhD in Internat. Politics, 1974. Asst. prof. polit. sci. West Ga. Coll., Carrollton, 1972-76; economist divsn. fin. mgmt. State of Idaho, Boise, 1976-80, chief economist, 1980-84; pres. Richard Slaughter Assocs., Boise, 1984—; dir. Martin Inst. for Peace Studies U. Idaho, 1996—2000; internat. economist Cen. Asia, 1998—2001; cons. economist Climate Impacts Group, U. Wash., 2000—. Vol. exec. dir. Boise Com. on Fgn. Rels., 1989-; mem. adv. bd. Martin Inst., U. Idaho, 1990-96, 2005—; co-founder Am. Coms. on Fgn. Rels., treas. 1995-2001, v.p., 2005—. Editor Idaho Econ. Forecast jour., 1977-84; author articles on Third World econ. devel. and nation-bldg., global climate change policy. Bd. dirs. Capitol Youth Soccer Assn., Boise, 1980-89, soccer commr., 1983-86. Mem. Coun. Fgn. Rels. Home and Office: 907 Harrison Blvd Boise ID 83702-4052 Home Phone: 208-345-9633; Office Phone: 208-850-1223. Business E-Mail: richard@rsaboise.com.

SLAVENS, THOMAS PAUL, library science educator; b. Cincinnati, Iowa, Nov. 12, 1928; s. William Blaine and Rhoda (Bowen) S.; m. Cora Hart, July 9, 1950; 1 son, Mark Thomas. BA, Phillips U., 1951; MDiv, Union Theol. Sem., 1954; MA, U. Minn., 1962; PhD, U. Mich., 1965. Ordained to ministry Christian Ch., 1953. Pastor First Christian Ch., Sac City, Iowa, 1953-56, Sioux Falls, SD, 1956-60; librarian Divinity Sch., Drake U., Des Moines, 1960-64; teaching fellow Sch. Info., U. Mich., Ann Arbor, 1964-65; instr. U. Mich., Ann Arbor, 1965-66, asst. prof., 1966-69, assoc. prof., 1969-77, prof., 1977—2003, prof. emeritus, 2003—. Vis. prof. U. Minn., 1967, U. Coll. of Wales, 1978, 80, 93; vis. scholar U. Oxford, Eng., 1980; cons. Nutrition Planning Abstracts-UN, N.Y.C., 1977-79. Author-editor: Library Problems in the Humanities, 1981, (with John F. Wilson) Research Guide to Religious Studies, 1982, (with W. Eugene Kleinbaur) Research Guide to the History of Western Art, 1982, (with Terrence Tice) Research Guide to Philosophy, 1983, Theological Libraries at Oxford, 1984, (with James Pruett) Research Guide to Musicology, 1985, The Literary Adviser, 1985, A Great Library through Gifts, 1986, The Retrieval of Information, 1989, Number One in the U.S.A.: Records and Wins in Sports, Entertainment, Business, and Science, 1988, Doors to God, 1990, Sources of Information for Historical Research, 1994, Introduction to Systematic Theology, 1992, Reference Interviews Questions and Materials, 3d edit., 1994, Using the Financial and Business Literature, 2004. Served with U.S. Army, 1946-48. Recipient Warner Rice Faculty award U. Mich., 1975; H.W. Wilson fellow, 1960; Lilly Endowment fellow Am. Theol. Libr. Assn., 1963. Mem. Assn. Libr. and Info. Sci. Edn. (pres. 1972), Beta Phi Mu.

SLAVICK, ANN LILLIAN, retired art educator; b. Chgo., Sept. 29, 1933; d. Irving and Goldie (Bernstein) Friedman; m. Lester Irwin Slavick, Nov. 21, 1954 (div. Mar. 1987); children: Jack, Rachel. BFA, Sch. of Art Inst. of Chgo., 1973, MA in Art History, Theory, Criticism, 1991. Dir. art gallery South Shore Commn., Chgo., 1963-67; tchr. painting, drawing, crafts Halfway House, Chgo., 1972-73; tchr. studio art Conant H.S., Hoffman Estates, Ill., 1973-74; tchr. art history and studio arts New Trier H.S., Winnetka and Northfield, Ill., 1974-80; tchr. 20th century art history New Trier Adult Edn. Program, Winnetka, 1980-81; tchr. art adult edn. program H.S. Dist. 113, Highland Park, Ill., 1980-81; rschr., writer Art History Notes McDougall-Littel Pub., Evanston, Ill., 1984-85; tchr. art and art history Highland Park and Deerfield (Ill.) H.S., 1980-2000; tchr. art history Coll. of Lake County, Grayslake, Ill., 1986-88; ret., 2000. Faculty chair for visual arts Focus on the Arts, Highland Park H.S., 1981-85, faculty coord. Focus on the Arts, 1987-2005; panelist Ill. Arts Coun. Arts Tour, 1999, Evanston Arts Coun., 2000-02, Ill. Arts Coun. Multidisciplinary Grant Awards, 2001-03; reader advanced placement art history exams, 2003, 04, 06. One woman show Bernal Gallery, 1979, U. Ill., Chgo., 1983, Ann Brierly Gallery, Winnetka, 1984; exhibited paintings, drawings, prints and constrns. throughout Chgo. area; work represented by Art Rental and Sales Gallery, Art Inst. Chgo., 1960-87, Bernal Gallery, 1978-82; group shows at Bernal Gallery; work in pvt. collections in Ill., N.Y., Calif., Ariz., Ohio. Recipient Outstanding Svc. in Art Edn. award Ea. Ill. U., 1992, Mayors award for contbn. to the arts, Highland Park, 1995. Mem.: Ill. Art Edn. Assn., Nat. Art Edn. Assn. Avocations: cooking, reading, theater. Home: 5057 N Sheridan Rd Chicago IL 60640-3127 Office: Highland Park High Sch 433 Vine Ave Highland Park IL 60035-2099 E-mail: annlslavick@aol.com.

SLAVICKAS, RIMAS ANTHONY, electrical engineer, educator, researcher; s. Silvestras Kasimeras and Sofija (Koncavicius) Slavickas; m. Wilma Johanna Van Sinderen, Sept. 13, 1969; 1 child, Paul Anthony. Diploma Elec.Engring., Gordon Inst. Tech., Geelong, Victoria, Australia, 1962; BSc in Math. & Physics magna cum laude, Laurentian U., Sudbury, Ont., Can., 1969; BSc in Elec. Engring. with honours, Queens U., Kingston, Ont., Can., 1971; MSc in Applied Sci., U. Toronto, Can., 1974; PhD, McMaster U., Can., 1998. Profl. Engr., Ont., 1972. Pres., CEO Welland Hydro-Electric Sys. Corp., Ont., Canada, 1974—2003; prof. industry U. Fla., Gainesville, 2004—. Adv. bd. mem. Savo Tech Inc., Toronto, 2003—; cons. W&E Internat. Corp., Markham, Ont., Canada. Assoc. editor: Internat. Jour. Power and Energy Sys., 1998—; contbr. articles to profl. jours. Recipient Best Paper award, Internat. Conf., 2000. Mem.: IEEE (life A number of awards for tech. excellence at confs.), Assn. Profl. Engrs. Australia, Profl. Engrs. Ont. (licentiate; chmn. Niagara chpt. 1985—86). Achievements include arranging a meeting of Chinese delegation from Shanghai Municipal Electric Power Company, with Ontario's Minister of Energy to foster business opportunities between Canada and China. Home: 76 Bridlewood Drive Ontario Welland Canada L3C 6K8 Office: University Florida 320 Benton Hall Gainesville FL 32611-6200 Home Phone: (905) 735-5600; Office Phone: 352-392-3291. Personal E-mail: lpa@collaborative-research.com. E-mail: ras@ece.ufl.edu.

SLAVIK, DONALD HARLAN, lawyer; b. Milw., June 17, 1956; s. Donald Jean and Sally Ann (Croy) S.; m. Cynthia Sue Barfknecht, Jan 5, 1980. BS in Nuclear Engring., U. Wis., 1978, JD, 1981. Bar: Wis. 1981, U.S. Dist. Ct. (ea. and we. dists.) Wis. 1981, Tex. 2002, Colo. 2002, Wash. 2004. Mem. Habush, Habush & Rottier, Milw., 1981—. Lectr. engring. extension U. Wis., Madison, 1985—95. Author: (with others) Anatomy of a Roof Crush Case, 1985, Seat Belt Handbook, 1987, Crashworthiness, 1989, 98; contbr. articles to profl. jours. Mem. Assn. Trial Lawyers Am. (co-chair exch. com. 1986-87, 91-93, chmn. computer law office tech. 1993-97, 2000—), Wis. Bar Assn., Attys. Info. Exch. Group (bd. dirs., exec. com. 1987—, lectr. 1987—, pres. 2001-2003), Assn. for Advancement of Automotive Medicine (sci. program com. 1996-2001). Office: Habush Habush & Rottier Ste 2300 777 E Wisconsin Ave Milwaukee WI 53202-5381 Office Phone: 414-271-0900.

SLAVIN, ARLENE, artist; b. NYC, Oct. 26, 1942; d. Louis and Sally (Bryck) Eisenberg; m. Neal Slavin, May 24, 1964 (div. 1979); m. Eric Bregman, Sept. 21, 1980; 1 child, Ethan. BFA, Cooper Union for the Advancement of Sci. and Art, 1964; MFA, Pratt Inst., 1967. One-woman shows include Fischbach Gallery, N.Y., 1973, 1974, 2003, Brooke Alexander Gallery, 1976, Alexander Milliken Gallery, N.Y.C., 1979, 1980, 1981, 1983, U. Colo., 1981, Pratt Inst., N.Y.C., 1981, Am. Embassy, Belgrad, Yugoslavia, 1984, Heckscher Mus., Huntington, N.Y., 1987, Katherine Rich Perlow Gallery, 1988, Chauncey Gallery, Princeton, N.J., 1990, The Gallery Benjamin N. Cardoza Sch. Law, 1991, Norton Ctr. for Arts, Danville, Ky., 1992, Kavesh Gallery, Ketchum, Idaho, 1993, exhibited in group shows at Bass Mus. Art, Fla., Whitney Museum of Art, 1973, The Contempory Arts Center, Cin., 1974, Indpls. Mus. Art, 1974, Madison (Wis.) Art Ctr., Santa Barbara (Calif.) Mus., Winnipeg (Can.) Art Gallery, Gensler Assocs., San Francisco, 1986, Eliane Benson Gallery, Bridgehampton, N.Y., 1987, 1989, 1991, 1993, 2004, City of N.Y. Parks and Recreation Central Park, N.Y.C., 1989, Benton Gallery, Southampton, N.Y., 1991, Parish Mus., Southampton, 1991, Michele Miller Fine Art, 1993, Dillon Gallery, N.Y.C., 1998, Hebrew Union Coll., 2000—01, Fischbach Gallery, 2003, Am. Inst. Archs., 2003, Represented in permanent collections Met. Mus. of Art, N.Y.C., Fogg Art Mus., Cambridge, Mass., Hudson River Mus., Yonkers, N.Y., Heckscher Mus., Huntington, N.Y., Cin. Art Mus., Readers' Digest, Pleasantville, N.Y., pub. commns., N.C. Zoo, 1999, N.Y.C. Parks and Recreation, 1999, NJ Transit, Hoboken Terminal and Middletown Station, NJ, 1999—2002, Forest City Ratner, Ct. St Devel., 2000, Assunpink (NJ) Wildlife Ctr., 2004; subject: bibliography Arlene Slavin: Mediating Public Space, 2001; pub. commns., Town of Chapel Hill, N.C., 2002, PS 89, NYC, 2003, Island Beach State Pk., N.J., 2006, one-woman shows include Fischbach Gallery, N.Y., 2003; artist mem. design team Hillsborough Area Regional Transit, Tampa, Fla., 2003—05. Grantee, Nat. Endowment for Arts, 1977—78, Threshold Found., 1991. Home: 119 E 18th St New York NY 10003-2107 Office Phone: 212-777-3042. E-mail: slavin@arleneslavin.com.

SLAVIN, PETER L., hospital administrator; AB, Harvard U., 1979, MD, 1984, MBA, 1990. Sr. v.p., chief med. officer Mass. Gen. Hosp., Boston, 1994—97; pres. Barnes-Jewish Hosp., St. Louis, 1997-99; med. dir. Mass. Gen. Physicians Orgn., Boston, chair., CEO, 1999—2003; pres. Mass. Gen. Hosp., Boston, 2003—. Office: Mass Gen Hosp 55 Fruit St Boston MA 02114-2622 Office Phone: 617-724-9300.

SLAVIN, RAYMOND GRANAM, allergist, immunologist; b. Cleve., June 29, 1930; s. Philip and Dinah (Baskind) S.; m. Alberta Cohrt, June 10, 1953; children: Philip, Stuart, David, Linda. AB, U. Mich., 1952; MD, St. Louis U., 1956; MS, Northwestern U., 1963. Diplomate Am. Bd. Internal Medicine, Am. Bd. Allergy and Immunology (treas.). Intern U. Mich. Hosp., Ann Arbor, 1956-57; resident St. Louis U. Hosp., 1959-61; fellow in allergy and immunology Northwestern U. Med. Sch., 1961-64; asst. prof. internal medicine and microbiology St. Louis U., 1965-70, assoc. prof., 1970-73, prof., 1973—, dir. divsn. allergy and immunology, 1965—. Mem. NIH study sect., 1985-89; cons. U.S. Army M.C. Contbr. numerous articles to med. publs.; editl. bd.: Jour. Allergy and Clin. Immunology, 1975-81. Chmn. bd. Asthma and Allergy Found. Am., 1985-88. With M.C., U.S. Army, 1957-59. Grantee NIH, 1967-70, 84—, Nat. Inst. Occupl. Safety and Health, 1974-80. Master: ACP; fellow: Am. Acad. Allergy and Immunology (exec. bd., historian, pres. 1983—84, Disting. Svc. award 1995, Disting. Clinician award 2005); mem.: AAAS, Ctrl. Soc. Clin. Rsch., Am. Assn. Immunologists. Democrat. Jewish. Home: 631 E Polo Dr Saint Louis MO 63105-2629 Office: 1402 S Grand Blvd Saint Louis MO 63104-1004 Office Phone: 314-977-8829. Business E-Mail: slavinrg@slu.edu.

SLAVIT, DAVID HAL, otolaryngologist; b. NYC, Sept. 5, 1960; s. Leonard S. and Barbara H. (Levine) S.; m. Robin E. Feldman, July 31, 1983; children: Danielle, Evan, Roni. BS, Cornell U., 1982; MD, Mt. Sinai U., 1986. Cert. in otolaryngology. Intern Mayo Clinic, Rochester, Minn., 1986-87, resident in otolaryngology, 1987-91; with Lenox Hill Hosp., NYC. Asst. prof. Health Sci. Ctr.-SUNY Downstate; cons. Juilliard Sch. Music, N.Y.C., 1994-99; dir. Ames Vocal Dynamics Lab., N.Y.C., 1998-2001. Author, editor: (book) Essentials of Otolaryngology, 1993; author: (books) Voice Disorders, 1995, Rhinologic Diagnosis and Treatment, 1996, Systemic Disease of the Nasal Airway, 1993; contbr. articles to profl. jours. Fellow ACS; mem. AMA, Am. Acad. Otolaryngology-Head and Neck Surgery, Am. Acad. Facial Plastic and Reconstructive Surgery, Am. Rhinologic Soc. Office Phone: 212-517-9177.

SLAVITT, DAVID WALTON, retired lawyer; b. Chgo., Mar. 15, 1931; s. Isaac and Fay (Goldstein) S.; m. Roberta Chelnek, July 26, 1953; children: Steven, Denise, Howard. BS, UCLA, 1952, JD, 1955. Bar: Calif. 1956; C.P.A., Calif. Since practiced in Los Angeles; pres. Slavitt & Borofsky (P.C.), 1969-87. Moderator continuing edn. programs. Author articles in field. Served with USNR, 1955. Mem. Am. Assn. Atty.-C.P.A.s (pres. 1964), ABA, State Bar Calif., Calif. Assn. Atty.-C.P.A.s (pres. 1963), Beverly Hills Bar Assn. (vice chmn. continuing edn. of bar 1970, asst. chmn. law practice mgmt. com. 1973).

SLAVKIN, HAROLD CHARLES, dean, biologist; b. Chgo., Mar. 20, 1938; m. Lois S. Slavkin; children: Mark D., Todd P. BA in English lit., U. So. Calif., 1961, DDS, 1965; Doctorate (hon.), Georgetown U., 1990, U. Paris, 1996, U. Md., 1997. Mem. faculty U. So. Calif. Sch. Dentistry, LA, 1968—, mem. faculty gerontology inst., 1969, chmn. dept. biochemistry and nutrition, 1969—75, prof., 1974—, chmn. grad. program in craniofacial molecular biology, 1975-85, founding dir. Ctr. for Craniofacial Molecular Biology, 1989-95, George & Mary Lou Boone prof. craniofacial molecular biology, 1989-95, dean, 2000—, G. Donald and Marian James Montgomery Dean's Chair in Dentistry, 2000—; dir. Nat. Inst. Dental and Craniofacial Rsch., NIH, Bethesda, Md., 1995—2000. Vis. prof. Israel Inst. Tech., Haifa, 1987-88; cons. U.S. News and World Report, 1985-95, L.A. Edn. Partnership, 1983-95, Torstar Books, Inc., 1985-95. Contbr. articles to profl. jours. Mem. sci. adv. bd. Calif. Mus. Sci. and Tech., 1985-95. Rsch. scholar U. Coll. London, 1980. Mem. AAAS, Am. Assn. Anatomists, Am. Inst. Biol. Scis., Am. Soc. for Cell Biology, Am. Assn. for Dental Rsch. (pres. 1993-94), N.Y. Acad. Scis., Inst. Medicine of NAS, Internat. Coll. Dentistry, Am. Coll. Dentistry, Los Angeles County Art Mus. Assocs. Office: 925 W 34th St Los Angeles CA 90089 Office Phone: 213-740-2811. Office Fax: 213-740-1509. E-mail: slavkin@usc.edu.

SLAWKOWSKI, DAVID JOHN, lawyer; b. Chgo., Sept. 18, 1950; s. Edward John and Loretta (Guminski) S.; m. Penny Ann Al-Greene, June 16, 1972; children: Amanda, Holly. AB magna cum laude, U. Notre Dame, 1972; JD, Harvard U., 1975. Bar: Ill. 1975, US Dist. Ct. (no. dist.) Ill. Assoc. Lord, Bissell & Brook, Chgo., 1975-83, ptnr., 1984—, Anderson, Rasor & Ptnrs., Chgo. Author: (with others) Medical Malpractice Defense, 1983, Hospital Quality Assurance, 1984, Do the Courts Understand the Realities of Hospital Practices?, Adolescent Medicine and Law, 1993. Mem. ABA, Am. Acad. Hosp. Attys., Union League. Avocations: tennis, photography. Office: Anderson Rasor & Ptnrs 55 E Monroe St Ste 3650 Chicago IL 60603 Office Phone: 312-673-7802. Office Fax: 312-673-7781. Business E-Mail: david.slawkowski@arandpartners.com.

SLAWTER, JOHN DAVID, JR., oil industry executive; b. Winston-Salem, May 11, 1917; s. John David and Carrie Wess (Linville) S.; children: Suzanne Marie, Sheila Margaret; m. Joan Margaret Pirek, July 7, 1966. Student, U. N.C., 1935—37, U.N.C., 1938—40. V.p. B&B Gas and Petroleum, Corpus Christi, Tex., 1950-59; exec. v.p. Cal-O-Tex Oil, Columbus, Ohio, 1959-65; pres. Atlantic Internat. Oil, Charleston, W.Va., 1966-73; CEO Interstate Hotels, Inc., 1975, Pacific Internat. Prodn. Holding Co. for Activated Carbon Corp. Am., Dallas, 1989, Mid-Continent Oil, 1974—, OFG Corp., 1995—, EMTEC, 1997—, HTS, 1999—. Chmn. adv. bd. Cal-O-Tex, 1966—, Atlantic Internat. Oil, 1974—, Pacific Internat., 1974—, Black Diamond Coal Co., 1978—, Southwest Interstate Support Sys., 1985—, Activated Carbon Corp., 1989—; vice chair AIOC Trust, Slawter Trust (lifetime). Author: (patents and copyrights) purification and desalination sys., 1991, pumping unit tech., 1995, oil field gen., 1996, oil field mobile remote control unit, 1998, heat transfer sys., 1999. Mem. Rep. Nat. Nom. Com., Washington, 1994-2000. Maj. Engrs. 1941-45, WWII, PTO. Decorated Purple Heart, Silver Star, Bronze Star with oak leaf cluster, Presdl. Citation, 4 Battle Stars. Mem. internat. petroleum clubs, Geneva Exec. Club (v.p. 1970-78), Chi Phi. Avocations: aviation, golf. Office: Pacific Internat Prodn/Subs Ste 8108 4350 Trinity Mills Rd Dallas TX 75287-7037 also: PO Box 795273 Dallas TX 75379-5273 Home Phone: 972-380-0744; Office Phone: 972-380-5560. Personal E-mail: joslawter2@earthlink.net.

SLAYDEN, JAMES BRAGDON, retired retail executive; b. Seattle, Sept. 28, 1924; s. Philip Lee and Ruth Alwin (Bragdon) Slayden; m. Barbara Marie McBride, May 7, 1955; children: Tracy Anne, James Bragdon. BA, U. Wash., 1948; MBA, U. So. Calif., 1949. Buyer Frederick & Nelson, Seattle, 1949-59, div. mdse. mgr., 1959-65; gen. mgr. Bullocks Westwood, Los Angeles, 1965-69; exec. v.p., gen. mdse. mgr. May D&F Co. dept. store, Denver, 1969—72; exec. v.p. Robinson dept. store, LA, 1972—73; pres. J.W. Robinson dept. store, 1974—78; exec. v.p. ops. Marshall Field & Co., Chgo., 1978—80; gen. mgr. Bullocks Del Amo, 1980—85; lectr. mktg. U. So. Calif., 1985—93. Active United Crusade United Way, LA, 1973—78, Chgo. Heart Assn., Chgo., 1978—79; chmn. Pvt. Industry Coun., 1982—95; cons. Internat. Exec. Svc. Corps., 1987—; mem. traffic com. Rancho Palos Verdes, 1994—97; mem. planning commn., 1997—2000; mem. view restoration com., 2000—04. With US Army, 1943—45. Mem.: Phi Kappa Psi. Republican. Christian Scientist. Home: 37 Mela Ln Palos Verdes Peninsula CA 90275-5086

SLAYMAN, CAROLYN WALCH, geneticist, educator; b. Portland, Maine, Mar. 11, 1937; d. John Weston and Ruth Dyer (Sanborn) Walch; m. Clifford L. Slayman; children: Andrew, Rachel BA with highest honors, Swarthmore Coll., Pa., 1958; PhD, Rockefeller U., NYC, 1963; DSc (hon.), Bowdoin Coll., Brunswick, Maine, 1985. Instr., then asst. prof. Case Western Res. U., Cleve., 1967; from asst. prof. to prof. genetics Yale U. Sch. Medicine, New Haven, 1967—, Sterling prof. genetics, 1991—, chmn. dept. genetics, 1984-95, dep. dean acad. and sci. affairs, 1995—. Chmn. genetic basis of disease rev. commn. NIH, 1981—85, nat. adv. gen. med. scis. coun., 1989—93; bd. dirs. J. Weston Walch Pub., Portland, Maine, Applera Corp.; mem. sci. rev. bd. Howard Hughes Med. Inst., 1992—97. Mem. editl. bd. Jour. Biol. Chemistry, 1989-94; contbr. articles to sci. jours. Trustee Foote Sch., New Haven, 1983—89, Hopkins Sch., New Haven, 1988—93; bd. overseers Dartmouth Med. Sch., 1997—2003, Woods Hole Oceanographic Instn., Mass., 1997—2007, Bowdoin Coll., 1976—88, trustee, 1988—2001. Recipient Deborah Morton award Westbrook Coll., 1986. Mem. Am. Soc. Biol. Chemists, Genetics Soc. Am., Soc. Gen. Physiologists, Am. Soc. Microbiology, Inst. Medicine, Phi Beta Kappa Office Phone: 203-737-1770.

SLAYTON, GUS, foundation administrator; b. Pocahontas, Ark., Jan. 20, 1937; s. Alvin M. and Eula Inis (Milam) S.; m. Ruth Virginia Furr, May 27, 1961 (dec. Nov. 1989). BA, U. Md., College Park, 1973. Enslited U.S. Army, 1957, commd. 2nd lt., 1963, advanced through grades to lt. col., 1978; various operational and research and devel. assignments, including The Pentagon, 1974-78; ret., 1980; exec. dir. Assn. of Old Crows, Alexandria, Va., 1980-92, AOC Ednl. Found., 1992—. Decorated Legion of Merit (2), Bronze Star (2) Republican. Avocation: real estate investment. Home: 152 Mill Cove Ln Ponte Vedra Beach FL 32082-4135 E-mail: slaytonag@earthlink.net.

SLAYTON, JOHN HOWARD, lawyer, corporate financial executive; b. Sparta, Wis., July 6, 1955; s. Rex Gordon and Elizabeth (Ward) S.; m. Judith Hughes. BA in Polit. Sci. cum laude, Marquette U., 1977; JD cum laude, George Washington U., 1980, MBA in Fin., 1982; LLM in Taxation, Georgetown U., 1986. Bar: D.C. 1981, U.S. Ct. Appeals (D.C. cir.) 1981, U.S. Dist. Ct. D.C. 1981, Va. 1993. Assoc. Metzger, Shadyac & Schwarz, Washington, 1980—83, Pillsbury, Madison & Sutro, Washington, 1983—87; gen. counsel Leland & Assocs., Inc., Washington, 1987—95; cons. Gordon Getty Family trust, Washington, 1995—96; pres., CEO The Trust Co. of the South, Burlington, NC, 1996—. Instr. real estate syndication Arlington County Continuing Edn., Realty Bd., 1982; adj. prof. fin. Love Sch. Bus., Elon U., 2006—; expert witness fed. cts. investment and fiduciary issues. Contbr. articles to profl. jours. Mem.: N.C. Bar Assn. (chmn. legis. com. of estate planning com., chmn. uniform trust code subcom. of estate planning legis. com., mem. joint com. between N.C. Bankers Assn. and N.C. Bar Assn., coun. mem.), D.C. Bar Assn., Va. Bar Assn., ABA (chmn. trusts and investments subcom. of banking com., com. fed. regulation of securities). Roman Catholic. Office: The Trust Co of the South 3041 S Church St Burlington NC 27215-5154 Office Phone: 336-538-1000. Business E-Mail: jslayton@tcts.com.

SLEAD, ROGER W, lawyer; b. Marshall, Mo., Jan. 11, 1962; s. Roger V. Slead and Carolyn Susie Saxton; m. Brenda L. Weber, Oct. 17, 1987; children: Tanner S., Griffen N., Logan D. BA in Polit. Sci. and History, U. Mo., Columbia, 1984; JD, Northwestern U., Chgo., 1987. Bar: Supreme Ct., Mo. 1987, Supreme Ct., Kans. 1988, US Dist. Ct. (we. dist.), Mo. 1987, US Dist. Ct., Kans. 1988, Supreme Ct., Nebr. 1996, US Dist. Ct., Nebr. 1998. Atty. Blackwell Sanders Peper Martin, LLC, Kansas City, Mo., 1987—2000; atty., ptnr. Horn Aylward and Bandy, LLC, Kansas City, 2000—. Mem. Def. Rsch. Inst., Chgo., 1987—, Mo. Orgn. Def. Lawyers, Jefferson City, Mo., 1996—. Contbr. Accelerated Cure Project, Boston, 2004—; pres. Hampton Pl. Homes Assn., Overland Park, Kans., 2001—05, Prairie Village Homes Assn., Kans., 1991—94; mem. Friends of Zoo, Kansas City. Mem.: ARC, Kans. Bar Assn., Mo. Bar Assn., Kans. City Met.

Bar Assn. Democrat-Npl. Office: Horn Aylward and Bandy LLC 2600 Grand Blvd Ste 500 Kansas City MO 64108 Home Phone: 913-681-0268; Office Phone: 816-421-0700. Office Fax: 816-421-0899. Business E-Mail: rslead@hab-law.com.

SLECHTA, JIRI, theoretical physicist; b. Havlickuv Brod, Bohemia, Czechoslovakia, Apr. 26, 1939; came to Eng., 1969; s. Josef and Marie (Posikova) S.; m. Miriam Vydrarova, July 17, 1971; children: Vera, Martin. Dr rer. nat., Charles U., Prague, Czechoslovakia, 1962. Sr. lectr. dept. theoretical physics Charles U., Prague, 1964-69; rsch. fellow dept. physics U. Warwick, Conventry, Eng., 1969-71; sr. rsch. assoc. Sch. Math. and Physics U. East Anglia, Norwich, Eng., 1971-74; rsch. fellow dept. physics U. Leeds, England, 1976-77. Chair 3 Symposiums 13th Internat. Congress on Cybernetics, Namur, Belgium, 1992; co-chmn. symposium 17th World Congress SVU, Prague, 1994, chair symposium 14th Internat. Congress on Cybernetics, Namur, 1995, Knowledge Transfer 96, London; rschr. and presenter in field. Author 67 papers and 42 contbns. at nonpub. confs.; editor Informatica; patentee in field 2d lt. Czechoslovakia mil., 1962-64. Benevolent Fund Inst. of Physics ann. grantee, London, 1979—; recipient Gold Coins Am. Biog. Inst., 1994, 95, 96. Assoc. fellow Inst. Math. and Applications; mem. Am. Phys. Soc., Internat. Acad. Scis. San Marino, Inst. Physics, European Phys. Soc., Brit. Cybernetic Soc., Internat. Assn. Cybernetics, Internat. Cybernetics Acad., NY Acad. Scis., Czechoslovak Math. Phys. Union, Czech Soc. Arts and Sci. Mem. Conservative party. Achievements include theory of disordered materials and self-organizing systems (brain, economy, society) and cybernetics; mathematical theory of Darwinism. Home and Office: 5 Beckhill Chase Leeds LS7 2RQ England Home Phone: 44113-2165654; Office Phone: 44 113 216 5654. E-mail: jirislechta@hotmail.com, jiri_slechta@yahoo.co.uk.

SLEDD, ROBERT C., food products executive; Dir. Taylor & Sledd Industries, 1974—87, pres. & CEO, 1984—87; dir. Performance Food Group, 1987—, pres., 1987-95, CEO, 1987—2001, 2004—06, chmn., 1995—. Bd. dir. SCP Pool Corp., Internat. Foodservice Distributor Assn. Vice chmn. Homeward, 2000—; bd. dir. Better Housing Coalition, 2000—, Va. Found. for Performing Arts; trustee Va. Found. of Independent Colleges; chmn. bus. adv. bd. Hilliard House. Office: Performance Food Group 12500 West Creek Pkwy Richmond VA 23238 *

SLEDJESKI, EVE MARY, psychologist, researcher; b. Manassas, Va., Sept. 14, 1978; d. William Francis and Barbara Ann Sledjeski; m. Tom James Dinzeo, June 25, 2004; 1 child, Lucius James Dinzeo. BS, Mary Wash. Coll., Fredericksburg, Va., 2000; MA, Kent State U., Ohio, 2003, PhD, 2005. Rsch. scientist Wesleyan U., Middletown, Conn., 2005—; instr. Kent State U., 2002—04. Contbr. articles to profl. jours. Mem.: Internat. Soc. Traumatic Stress Studies, Phi Beta Kappa.

SLEED, JOEL, columnist; b. NYC, Jan. 29, 1929; m. MaryLou Kalwara, Nov. 15, 1983; children: Jodie, Jill, Jeffrey, Kristin Kalwara, Karen Hepler. Former travel editor The Star-Ledger, Newark, Newhouse News Svc., Washington; columnist travel sect. Sunday Rep., Springfield, Mass.; travel editor Palm Beach Soc. mag. Office: Newhouse Newspapers 711 Third Ave New York NY 10017 E-mail: joelsleed@msn.com.

SLEEMAN, BILL, library and information scientist; BA, Oakland U., 1984; MLS, U. Mich., 1986; MA in Legal and Ethical Studies, U. Balt., 1997. Reference libr. Enoch Pratt Free Libr.; sr. law libr. US Dept. Interior Law Libr.; bibliographic control and govt. documents libr. Thurgood Marshall Law Libr., U. Md., 1994—2004, asst. dir. tech. services, 2004—. Named one of the Movers and Shakers, Libr. Jour., 2007. Mem.: Palinet, Md. Libr. Assn., ALA (Govt. Documents Roundtable). Office: Marshall Law Library 500 W Baltimore St Baltimore MD 21201 Office Phone: 410-706-0783. E-mail: bsleeman@law.umaryland.edu.

SLEEPER, NANCY JOANN, mental health services professional; d. John Harold and Helen Amelia Sagdahl; m. John Edward Tracy (div.); children: Christopher Tracy, Heidi Thorley, Jeffrey Tracy, Scott Tracy; m. Richard Edwin Sleeper, Jan. 26. BS in Psychology, Wash. State U., Pullman, 1977; MA in Clin. Psychology, John F. Kennedy U., Orinda, Calif., 1985. LCSW Wis.; lic. profl. counselor Ill., mental health counselor Nat. Bd. Addiction Examiners, nat. cert. counselor. Mental health profl. KTSAP Mental Health Svcs., Bremerton, 1988—90; exceptional family mem. program coord. Army Comty. Svc., Schofield Barracks, Hawaii, 1991—93; new parent support team counselor Navy Family Svc. Ctr., Great Lakes, Ill., 1993—95; therapist Luth. Social Svcs., Bremerton, 1995—96; MICA specialist, older adults therapist KTSAP Mental Health Svcs., Bremerton, 1996—2000; substance abuse counselor Dept. Army, 104th ASG, Germany, 2000—03, Dept. Army, Ft. Huachuca, Ariz., 2003—. Mem. Comty. Emergency Response Team, Sierra Vista, Ariz., 2004—. Mem.: ACA, Am. Psychotherapy Assn. (diplomate). Mem. Lds Ch. Office: Army Substance Abuse Program Bldg 22414 Fort Huachuca AZ 85613 Business E-Mail: nancy.sleeper@us.army.mil.

SLEIGH, SYLVIA, artist, educator; b. Llandudno, North Wales; came to U.S., 1961; d. John Harold and Katherine Amy (Miller) S.; m. Lawrence Alloway, June 28, 1954. Student, Sch. Art, Brighton, Sussex, Eng., 1932-36; diploma, U. London Extra-Mural Dept., 1947. Vis. asst. prof. SUNY-Stony Brook, 1978; instr. New Sch. Social Research, NYC, 1974-77, 78-80; Edith Kreeger Wolf disting. prof. Northwestern U., Evanston, Ill., 1977; vis. artist Baldwin Seminar Oberlin Coll., Ohio, 1982, New Sch. Social Rsch., NYC. One person shows include Bennington (Vt.) Coll., 1963, Soho 20 Art Gallery, N.Y.C., 1974, 76, 80, 82, A.I.R. Gallery, N.Y.C., 1974, 76, 78, Ohio State U., Columbus, 1976, Matrix, Wadsworth Atheneum, Hartford, Conn., 1976, Marianne Deson Gallery, Chgo., 1990, G.W. Einstein, Inc., N.Y.C., 1980, 83, 85, U. Mo., Saint Louis, 1981, Zaks Gallery, Chgo., 1985, 95, Milw. Art Mus., Butler Inst., Youngstown, Ohio, 1990, Stiebel Modern, N.Y.C., 1992, 94, Gallery 609, Denver, Canton (Ohio) Art Inst., Soho 20 Gallery, 1999, Deven Golden Fine Arts, N.Y., 1999, The Art of Sylvia Sleigh and Lawrence Alloway Phila. Art Alliance, Phila., 2001; exhibited in group shows Newhouse Gallery, S.I., N.Y., Stamford (Conn.) Mus., 1985, Albany (N.Y.) Inst. Art, Cin. Art Mus., New Orleans Mus. Art, Denver Art Mus., Pa. Acad. Fine Arts, 1989, Carlsten Art Gallery, Stevens Point, Wis., 1993, Stiebel Modern, N.Y.C., 1994, Soho 20, N.Y.C., 1993, 96, Katzen Brown Gallery, N.Y.C., 1989, Zaks Gallery, Chgo., 1986, Steinbaum Krauss Gallery, 1997, Deven Golden Fine Arts, Ltd., N.Y.C., 1997, Rutgers U., New Brunswick, N.J., 1984, 86, RioArriba Gallery, Abiquiu, N.Mex., 1996, Milw. Art Mus., 1996, Steinbaum Krauss Gallery, 1997, N.Y. Mus. exhbn. traveling until 2001, David and Alfred Smart Mus., Chgo., Broome St. Gallery, N.Y.C., Deven Golden Fine Arts, N.Y.C., A.I.R. Gallery, N.Y.C., Apex Art Co., N.Y.C., 1998, McKee Gallery, N.Y.C., 1998, Royal Coll. Art, London, 1998, Heckscher Mus. Art, Huntington, N.Y., 1999, Printworks Gallery, 2000, SoHo 20, N.Y.C., 2004, Snug Harbor Cultural Ctr., N.Y.C., 2005, Mason Gross at Rutgers U., N.J., 2005, Mus. Contemp. Art, L.A., 2006. Panelist Creative Artists Pub. Service Program, N.Y.C., 1976. Nat. Endowment for Arts grantee, 1982, Pollock-Krasner Found. grantee, 1985. Home: 330 W 20th St New York NY 10011-3302 Personal E-mail: ssallway@verizon.net.

SLEIK, THOMAS SCOTT, lawyer; b. La Crosse, Wis., Feb. 24, 1947; s. John Thomas and Marion Gladys (Johnson) S.; m. Judith Mattson, Aug. 24, 1968; children: Jennifer, Julia, Joanna. BS, Marquette U., 1969, JD, 1971. Bar: Wis. 1971, U.S. Dist. Ct. (we. dist.) Wis. 1971. Assoc. Hale Skemp Hanson Skemp & Sleik, La Crosse, 1971-74, ptnr., 1975—. Bd. mem. Wis. Lawyer Mut. Ins. Co., 1999—. State pres. Boy Scouts Am., 1981—83, bd. dirs. Gateway Area Con., 1973—99, pres., 1980—81; trustee La Crosse Pub. Libr., 1981—, chair, bd. trustees, 2006—; bd. dirs. Children's Mus. of La Crosse, 1997—2002, Greater La Crosse Area United Way, 1985—92, campaign chmn., 1986, pres., 1987; mem. Sch. Dist. La Crosse Bd. Edn., 1973—77, v.p., 1977; festmaster Oktoberfest (LaCross Festivals Inc.), 2001, trustee, 2001—; bd. mem. Franciscan Skemp Healthcare, 2003—. Fellow Am. Acad. Matrimonial Lawyers (pres. Wis. chpt. 1999-2000); mem. ABA, State Bar Wis. (bd. govs. 1987-94, pres. 1992-93). Roman Catholic. Home: 4082 Glenhaven Dr La Crosse WI 54601-7503 Office: Hale Skemp Hanson Skemp & Sleik 505 King St Ste 300 La Crosse WI 54602-1927 Business E-Mail: tss@haleskemp.com.

SLEMMER, CARL WEBER, JR., retired lawyer; b. Camden, NJ, Mar. 28, 1923; s. Carl and Annetta (Donner) S.; m. Renée Jeannette Kinsey, Oct. 11, 1952; children: Michael, John, Sandra. BS, Muhlenberg Coll., 1948; JD, Temple U., 1963. Bar: N.J. 1972, Pa. 1972, U.S. Dist. Ct. N.J. 1972, Fla. 1974. Various pers. positions RCA, Camden, 1950-55; mgr. labor rels. Allied Chem. Corp., Morristown, N.J., 1955-67; dir. employee rels. Exide Corp., Phila., 1967-82; pvt. practice Cherry Hill, N.J., 1982-83; dir. labor rels. Columbia U., NYC, 1983-89; mgr. tax office H & R Block, Marlton, N.J., 1991-93; ret., 1993. Mem. labor coun. U. Pa., Phila., 1967-82. Lt. (j.g.) USN, 1943-46, PTO. Republican. Presbyterian. Avocations: tennis, reading, travel, legal research. Home: 888 Heritage Rd Moorestown NJ 08057-1330 Personal E-mail: carlslemmer@verizon.net.

SLEMMONS, ROBERT SHELDON, architect; b. Mitchell, Nebr., Mar. 12, 1922; s. Matthew Garvin and K. Fern (Borland) S.; m. Dorothy Virginia Herrick, Dec. 16, 1945; children: David (dec.), Claire, Jennifer, Robert, Timothy. AB, U. Nebr., 1947, BArch, 1948. Draftsman Davis & Wilson, Archs., Lincoln, Nebr., 1947-48; chief designer, project arch. Office of Kans. State Arch., Topeka, 1948-54; assoc. John A. Brown, Arch., Topeka, 1954-56; ptnr. Brown & Slemmons, Arch., Topeka, 1956-69; v.p. Brown-Slemmons-Krueger, Archs., Topeka, 1969-73; owner Robert S. Slemmons, A.I.A. & Assocs., Archs., Topeka, 1973—. Cons. Kans. State Office Bldg. Commn., 1956-57; lectr. in design U. Kans., 1961; bd. dirs. Kaw Valley State Bank & Trust Co., Topeka, 1978-92. Prin. archtl. works include Kans. State Office Bldg., 1954, Topeka Presbyn. Manor, 1960-74, Meadowlark Hills Ret. Cmty., 1979, Shawnee County Adult Detention Facility, 1985. Bd. dirs. Topeka Civic Symphony Soc., 1950-60, Midstates Ret. Cmtys., Inc., 1986-92, Topeka Festival Singers; cons. Ministries for Aging, Inc., Topeka, 1984-97; mem. Topeka Bd. Bldg. and Fire Appeals, Kans., 1977-97, Com. for Employer Support of the Guard and Res. With USNR, 1942-48. Mem. AIA (Topeka pres. 1955-56, Kans. dir. 1957-58, com. on housing, com. for hist. resources), Internat. Conf. Bldg. Ofcls., Topeka Art Guild (pres. 1950), Am. Corrections Assn., Kans. Coun. Chs. (dir. 1961-62), Shawnee County Hist. Soc., Greater Topeka C. of C. (sr. coun., pres.), Downtown Topeka Inc. (v.p. 1992-99), Topeka, Shawnee County Libr. (dir. friends of the libr.), St. Andrews Soc. (pres.), SAR (pres. state soc., pres. chpt.), Soc. of Antiquaries of Scotland (fellow), U. Nebr. Alumni Assn. (life), Band Alumni Assn., Kiwanis (pres. 1966-67), Topeka Knife and Fork Club. Presbyterian (elder, deacon, chmn. trustees). Office: Slemmons Assocs Archs 534 S Kansas Ave Ste 140 Topeka KS 66603-3473 Personal E-mail: rdslem@hotmail.com.

SLEMON, GORDON RICHARD, electrical engineering educator; b. Bowmanville, Ont., Can., Aug. 15, 1924; s. Milton Everitt and Selena (Johns) S.; m. Margaret Jean Matheson, July 9, 1949; children: Sally, Stephen, Mark, Jane. BASc., U. Toronto, 1946, MASc., 1948; D.I.C., Imperial Coll. Sci., London U., Eng., 1951, PhD, 1952; D of Engring. (hon.), Meml. U. Nfld., 1994. Asst. prof. elec. engring. N.S. Tech. Coll., Can., 1953-55; assoc. prof. U. Toronto, Ont., Can., 1955-63, prof. Ont., 1964-90, chmn. dept. elec. engring. Ont., 1966-76, dean of faculty of applied sci. and engring. Ont., 1979-86, prof. emeritus Ont., 1990—. Colombo plan adviser, India, 1963-64; pres. Elec. Engring. Consociates, 1976-79; bd. dirs. Inverpower Controls Ltd., Innovations Found. Author: (with J.M. Ham) Scientific Basis of Electrical Engineering, Magnetoelectric Devices, (with A. Straughen) Electric Machinery; (with S.B. Dewan, A. Straughen) Power Semiconductor Drives, Electric Machines and Drives; contbr. articles to profl. jours. Chmn. Innovations Found., 1980-93, vice chmn., 1993—97; chmn. Microelectronics Devel. Ctr., 1983-88. Decorated officer Order of Can.; recipient excellence in tchg. award Western Electric, 1965, Can. Centennial medal, 1967, Ross medal, 1978, 83, Gold medal Jugoslav Union of Nikola Tesla Socs., Engring. Alumni medal, Educator of Yr. award Can. Engrs., 1992, Hall of Distinction award U. Toronto, 1992, Achievement award IEEE Magnetics Soc., 1997, Arbor award U. Toronto, 1997. Fellow Can. Acad. Engring. (pres. 1998-99), Engring. Inst. Can., Instn. Elec. Engrs. (hon. fellow 1995), IEEE (Centennial medal 1984, Nikola Tesla award, Millennium medal 2000, Prof. Engrs. Engring. Excellence award 2005); mem. Am. Soc. Engring. Edn., others. Achievements include patents in field. Home: 40 Chatfield Dr Don Mills ON Canada M3B 1K5 Office: U Toronto Fac Applied Sci and Engring Toronto ON M5S 3G4 Canada Business E-Mail: g.slemon@utoronto.ca.

SLEMP, DENNETT CLINTON, priest, counselor; b. Washington, Mar. 7, 1932; s. Patton Wise and Dorothy Dixon (Dennett) Slemp; m. Mary Virginia Clarke, June 22, 1957; children: Catherine Branam, Rebecca Villeda. AB, Johns Hopkins U., Balt., 1957; MDiv, Va. Theol. Sem., Alexandria, 1961; STM, Episcopal Theol. Sem. S.W., Austin, Tex., 1968. Ordained deacon Episcopal Ch., 1961, ordained priest Episcopal Ch., 1962; cert. profl. counselor Va. Vicar Episcopal Chs. Botetourt County, Va., 1962—66; priest-in-charge Our Saviour Epsicopal Ch. Chesterfield County, Va., 1968—73; pastoral counselor VA. Inst. Pastoral Care, Richmond, Va., 1970—. Chair pers. com., bd. dirs. Chaplain Svc. Chs. Va., 1970—. With USN, 1951—53. Mem.: Am. Assn. Pastoral Counselors (diplomate), Phi Beta Kappa. Avocations: hiking, writing. Office: Va Inst Pastoral Care 2000 Bremo Rd Ste 105 Richmond VA 23226

SLEZAK, SHERI, plastic surgeon; b. Fort Riley, Kans., Dec. 30, 1953; MD, Harvard U., 1980. Cert. Gen. Surgery, Plastic and Reconstructive Surgery. Resident, gen. surgery Columbia-Presbyterian Med. Ctr., NYC, 1980—85; fellow, plastic surgery John Hopkins Hosp., Balt., 1986—89; assoc. prof., plastic surgery U. Md. Sch. Medicine; dir., breast reconstruction U. Md. Med. Ctr. Office: U Md Med Ctr 22 S Greene St Baltimore MD 21201 *

SLEZKINE, YURI, history professor; b. Moscow, Feb. 7, 1956; came to U.S., 1983; s. Lev Y. and Karma M. (Goldstein) S.; m. Lisa C. Little, Nov. 21, 1984; 1 child, Peter A. BA, MA, Moscow State U., 1978; PhD, U. Tex., 1989. Transl., Port Beira, Mozambique, 1978-79; editor Progress Pub., Moscow, 1980-82; instr. Linguacoop Lang. Inst., Lisbon, Portugal, 1982-83; instr. Slavic Studies U. Tex., 1983-86; asst. prof. history Wake Forest U., Winston-Salem, NC; prof. of history, dir. Inst. Slavic, East European & Eurasian studies Univ. Calif., Berkeley. Author: The Jewish Century, 2004, Arctic Mirrors: Russia and the Small Peoples of the North, 1994; co-author: Speak Russian, 1990; asst. editor Slavic Rev., 1985-87; co-editor: In the Shadow of Revolution: Life Stories of Russian Women from 1917 to the Second World War, 2000, Between Heaven and Hell: The Myth of Siberia in Russian Culture, 1993. Pew grantee Wake Forest U., 1990; Postdoctoral fellow Social Sci. Rsch. Coun., 1990—, Fgn. Lang. and Area Studies fellow U. Tex., 1988-89, Univ. fellow U. Tex., 1987-88. Mem. Am. Hist. Assn., Am. Assn. Advancement Slavic Studies. Office: UC Berkeley History Dept 2220 Dwindle Hall Berkeley CA 94720 also: UC Berkeley ISEES 260 Stephens Hall 2304 Berkeley CA 94720-2304 Office Phone: 510-642-3230, 510-642-2224. Office Fax: 510-643-5045. E-mail: isees@berkeley.edu, slezkine@berkeley.edu. *

SLICKER, FREDERICK KENT, lawyer; b. Tulsa, Aug. 21, 1943; s. James Floyd and Lucille Geneva (Nordling) S.; children: Laura, Kipp. BA, U. Kans., Lawrence, 1965, JD with highest distinction, 1968; LLM, Harvard U., Cambridge, Mass., 1973. Bar: Kans. 1968, U.S. Ct. Mil. Appeals 1968, U.S. Supreme Ct. 1972, Tex. 1973, Okla. 1980. Prin. founder Slicker Law Firm, P.C., 2000—. Author: A Practical Guide to Church Bond Financing, 1985, Angels All Around, 1999, Seeking God's Heart, 2004, A Treasury of Truth and Wisdom, 2007. Capt. US Army, 1965—72. Mem. ABA, Okla. Bar Assn., Order of Coif. Democrat. Methodist. Avocation: Christian men's ministries. Office: 4444 E 66th Ste #201 Tulsa OK 74136-4206 Home Phone: 918-749-8786; Office Phone: 918-496-9020. Business E-Mail: fslicker@swbell.net.

SLIFKA, ERIC, oil industry executive; s. Alfred A. Slifka. With Global Cos. LLC, 1987—, various sr. positions in acctg., supply, distbn. and mktg. to predecessor cos., COO, dir., 1998—2004, pres., CEO, dir., 2004, Global Ptnrs., 2005—. Office: Global Ptnrs PO Box 9161 Waltham MA 02454-9161 Office Phone: 781-894-8800. *

SLIFKIN, DANIEL, lawyer; b. London, Eng., June 14, 1965; BA first class honors, Oxford Univ., Eng., 1987, BCL first class honors, 1988; JD magna cum laude, Harvard Univ., 1991. Bar: NY 1991. Assoc. Cravath Swaine & Moore LLP, NYC, 1991—98, ptnr., litig., 1998—. Articles editor Harvard Law Rev. Mem.: ABA, NY State Bar Assn. Office: Cravath Swaine & Moore LLP Worldwide Plz 825 Eighth Ave New York NY 10019-7475 Office Phone: 212-474-1438. Office Fax: 212-474-3700. Business E-Mail: dslifkin@cravath.com.

SLIGER, BERNARD FRANCIS, academic administrator, economist, educator; b. Chassell, Mich., Sept. 30, 1924; s. Paul and Hazel (MacLauchlin) S.; m. Greta Taube, Sept. 1, 1945; children: Nan, Paul, Greta Lee, Sten. BA in Econs. with high hons., Mich. State U., 1949, MA, 1950, PhD, 1955; postgrad., U. Minn., 1961-62. Mem. faculty La. State U., 1953-61, prof. econs., 1961, head dept., 1961-65, vice chancellor, dean academic affairs, 1965-68; sec. adminstrn. State of La., 1968—69; sec.-treas. La. Office Bldg. Corp., 1969-72; organizer, exec. dir. La. Coordinating Council Higher Edn., 1969-72; prof. econs. Fla. State U., Tallahassee, 1973—2003, prof. econ. emeritus, 2003—, exec. v.p. Tallahassee, 1972-76, chief acad. officer, 1973-76, pres., 1977-91, interim pres., 1993, dir. univ.'s London Study Ctr., 1975, pres. emeritus, 1992—2003; ret., 2003. Mem. staff sci. and tech. com. Fla. Ho. of Reps., 1979; mem. V.P. Mondale's Select Com. on Sci. and Tech., 1980; mem. bd. dirs. Fed. Res Bank of Atlanta, 1983-88; cons. econ. theory and pub. fin. to pvt. and pub. commns., orgns.; mem., chief cons. Gov. La.'s tax study com., 1968; formerly La. commr. adminstrn. and chief budget officer; mem. NCAA pres.'s commn., 1987-91. Author: (text) Public Finance, 1964, rev. edit., 1970, (with others) Municipal Finance Administration, 1976, rev.; contbr. to profl. publs. Vol. economist Tallahassee C. of C., 1977, Fla. C. of C., 1978; mem. Acad. Task Force for Review of the Ins. and Tort Systems, 1986-88; trustee The Nature Conservancy, 1986—; trustee Am. Coll. Testing Corp., 1981-87, chmn. 1985-87; ex-officio mem. Fla. Coun. 100. With C.E., U.S. Army, 1943-46. Named Dir. Practical Politics La. Ho. of Reps., 1969; Bernard F. Sliger Eminent scholar Chair in Econ. Edn. created in his name by Fla. State U., 1987, Bernard F. Sliger Bldg. dedicated at univ.-related rsch. park, Bernard F. Sliger Tower in Univ. Ctr. Bldg. dedicated, 1999. Mem. Kiwanis, Phi Beta Kappa, Omicron Delta Kappa, Phi Kappa Phi, Omicron Delta Epsilon, Alpha Kappa Psi, Beta Gamma Sigma, Phi Eta Sigma. Presbyterian. Home: 3341 E Lakeshore Dr Tallahassee FL 32312-1440 Office: Gus A Stavros Ctr Adv Free Enterprise & Economic Edu 250 S Woodward Ave Tallahassee FL 32306-4220 Office Fax: 850-644-9866. Business E-Mail: sliger@mailer.fsu.edu.

SLIGER, HERBERT JACQUEMIN, JR., lawyer; b. Urbana, Ill., Nov. 21, 1948; s. Herbert Jacquemin and Marina (Mantia) Sliger; m. Sandra Ann Ratti, May 3, 1996; children: Lauren Christine, Matthew Ryan, Nicholas Adam, Claire Nicole, Adam Gregory. BS in Fin., U. Ill., 1970; JD, U. Ariz., 1974. CPA Okla.; bar: Ariz. 1974, Ill. 1975, US Supreme Ct. 1983, Okla. 1984, US Ct. Appeals (7th cir.) 1980, US Tax Ct. 1980. Lawyer Charles W. Phillips Law Offices, Harrisburg, Ill., 1974—75; trust counsel Magna Trust Co., F/K/A Millikin Nat. Bank, Decatur, Ill., 1976—80, First of America Trust Co., Springfield, Ill., 1980—83; trust counsel personal fin. svcs. group First Interstate Bank Okla. NA, Oklahoma City, 1983—86; mgr. employee benefits trust dept. First Interstate Bank of Okla., NA, Oklahoma City, 1986—89; v.p., pension counsel Star Bank, NA, Cin., Cin., 1989—90; asst. gen. counsel Bank One Ariz. Corp., Phoenix, 1990—95; asst. gen. counsel, nat. practice group head Banc One Corp., Columbus, Ohio, 1995—98, state gen. counsel Phoenix, 1996—97; sec. of bd. and cashier Bank One, Ariz. NA, 1996—97; sec. of bd. and statutory agt. Banc One Ariz. Corp., 1996—97; sec. bd. Bank One Trust Co. N.A., Columbus, 1996—2006; asst. gen. counsel, trust counsel practice group head law dept. Bank One Corp., 1999—2003, sr. counsel, 2003—04, J.P. Morgan Chase & Co., Phoenix, 2004—05, v.p., asst. gen. counsel, 2005—. Co-chmn. Nat. Conf. Lawyers and Corp. Fiduciaries, 1992—94, 2006—; instr. Chaminade U., Hawaii, Hawaii Tax Inst., 1999. Contbr. articles to profl. jours. Mem.: ABA (sect. real property, probate and trust law 1974—, banking law com. 1991—99, sect. taxation, employee benefits com. 1991—2001, fiduciary environ. problems com. 1993—99, sect. bus. law), Am. Corp. Counsel Assn., Am. Bankers Assn. (chmn. trust counsel com. 1992—94, trust and investment divsn. exec. com. 1992—94, mem., head fiduciary dept. Nat./Grad. Trust Sch. Bd. Faculty Advisors 1994—95, spokesman environ. risk task force 1994—95, faculty mem. under ERISA Nat. Employee Benefit Trust Sch. 1994—96, mini-adv. bd. chmn. trusts and estates 1995—99, trust counsel com. 2006—), Okla. Bar Assn., State Bar Ariz. (chmn. ethics com. 2002—05, exec. com. probate and trust sect.). Roman Catholic. Office Phone: 480-333-4472. Business E-Mail: herb.j.sliger@jpmchase.com.

SLIM, MICHEL S., surgeon, educator, health facility administrator; b. Nov. 18, 1929; s. Saliba and Julia Slim; m. Norma Gebara, Sept. 4, 1958; children: Julie, Lina, Nayla. MD, Am. U., Beirut, Lebanon, 1954. Diplomate Am. Bd. Surgery, Am. Bd. Pediatric Surgery, Am. Bd. Thoracic Surgery. Prof. surgery Am. U., Beirut, 1963-86, N.Y. Med. Coll., 1986—2006, prof. emeritus NY, 2006—; attending Westchester Med. Ctr., Valhalla, 1986—, chief pediatric trauma, 1991—2006, chief pediatric surgery, 1994—2002. Editl. cons. Pediatric Surg. Internat., 1985-2004; reviewer Ann. Thoracic Surgery, Jordan Med. Jour. Jour. Jordan Royal Med. Svcs.; contbr. articles to profl. jours Evarts Graham Traveling fellow Am. Assn. Thoracic Surgery, 1970-71. Fellow ACS, Am. Acad. Pediat., Am. Coll. Chest Physicians, Soc. Critical Care Medicine; mem. Am. Pediatric Surgery Assn., Brit. Assn. Pediatric Surgery, Internat. Soc. Surgery, Eastern Assn. for Surgery of Trauma. Office Phone: 914-493-7620. Personal E-mail: normichslim@gmail.com. E-mail: mslimpedsurg@hotmail.com.

SLINGER, MICHAEL JEFFERY, law librarian, director; b. Pitts., Apr. 12, 1956; s. Maurice and Mary Helen (Kengerski) S.; m. Cheryl Blaney, Apr. 19, 1980; children: Rebecca, Sarah. BA, U. Pitts., 1978; M Librianship, U. S.C., 1979; JD, Duquesne U., 1984. Reference libr. Duquesne U. Sch. Law, Pitts., 1983-84; rsch. libr. U. Notre Dame Sch. Law, Ind., 1984-85, head rsch. svcs., 1985-86, assoc. dir. pub. svcs., 1986-90; law libr. dir., assoc. prof. law Suffolk U. Sch. Law, Boston, 1990-93, law libr. dir., prof. law, 1994-95; law libr. dir., prof. law, assoc. dean Cleve. State U., 1995—. Contbr. articles to profl. jours., chpt. to book. Mem.: ALA, ABA, Ohio Regional Assn. Law Librs. (v.p. 1987—88, pres. 1988—89, Pres. award 1989), New Eng. Law Libr. Consortium (treas. 1992—95), Am. Assn. Law Schs. (exec. bd. sect. on law librs. 1993—94), Am. Assn. Law

Librs. (chair acad. law libr. spl. interest sect. 2005—). Avocations: reading, sports. Office: Cleve-Marshall Coll Law Law Libr 1801 Euclid Ave Cleveland OH 44115-2223 Office Phone: 216-687-3547. Business E-Mail: michael.slinger@law.csuohio.edu.

SLIPSAGER, HENRIK C., building services company executive; CFO ISS Internat. Svc. Sys., Inc., 1984-85, exec. v.p., COO, 1985-88, pres., CEO, 1988-94; exec. v.p. janitorial svcs. ABM Industries Inc., San Francisco, 1994-99, sr. v.p., 1997-99, pres. Am. Bldg. Maintenance Co., 1999-2000, CEO, pres., 2000—. Office: ABM Industries 160 Pacific Ave San Francisco CA 94111 *

SLIVE, SEYMOUR, museum director, art educator; b. Chgo., Sept. 15, 1920; s. Daniel and Sonia (Rapoport) S.; m. Zoya Gregorevna Sandomirsky, June 29, 1946; children: Katherine, Alexander, Sarah. AB, U. Chgo., 1943, PhD, 1952; MA (hon.), Harvard U., 1958, Oxford U., Eng., 1972. Instr. fine arts Oberlin (Ohio) Coll., 1950-51; chmn. art dept. Pomona (Calif.) Coll., 1952-54; mem. faculty Harvard U., Cambridge, Mass., 1954—, prof. fine arts, 1961—, Gleason prof. fine arts, 1973-91, Gleason prof. fine arts emeritus, 1991—, chmn. dept. fine arts, 1968-71, dir. Fogg Art Mus., 1975-82; Elizabeth and John Moors Cabot dir. emeritus Harvard art museums, 1982. Exchange prof. Leningrad (USSR) U., 1961; Ryerson lectr. Yale U., 1962; Slade prof. Oxford (Eng.) U., 1972-73 Author: Rembrandt and His Critics, 1630-1730, 1953, The Rembrandt Bible, 1959, Catalogue of the Paintings of Frans Hals, 1962, Drawings of Rembrandt, 1965, (with Jakob Rosenberg and E.H. ter Kuile) Dutch Art and Architecture 1600-1800, 2nd edit., 1978, Rembrandt's Drawings, 1965, Frans Hals, 3 vols., 1970-74, Jacob van Ruisdael, 1981, Frans Hals, 1989, Dutch Painting: 1600-1800, 1995, 2d edit., 1998, Jacob van Ruisdael: A Complete Catalogue of His Paintings, Drawings and Etchings, 2001, Jacob Van Ruisdael: Master of Landscape, 2005. Trustee Solomon R. Guggenheim Found., 1978—, Norton Simon Mus., 1989-91; bd. dirs. Burlington mag. Found., 1987—. Lt. (j.g.) USNR, 1943-46, PTO. Decorated officer Order Orange Nassau Netherlands, 1962; Fulbright fellow Netherlands, 1951-52; Guggenheim fellow, 1956-57, 78-79; Fulbright research scholar Utrecht (Netherlands) U., 1959-60 Fellow Am. Acad. Arts and Scis.; mem. Karel van Mander Soc. (hon.), Coll. Art Assn. (dir. 1958-62, 65-69), Renaissance Soc., Dutch Soc. Scis. (fgn. mem.), Brit. Acad. (corr. fellow). Office: Harvard U Sackler Art Museum Cambridge MA 02138 Office Phone: 617-495-9151.

SLIVKA, MICHAEL ANDREW, lawyer; b. Ambridge, Pa., Jan. 14, 1955; s. Andrew and Veronica (Yanko) S. AB in Psychology, Cornell U., 1977; JD, U. Miami, 1980. Bar: Fla. 1980, U.S. Dist. Ct. (so. dist.) Fla. 1981, U.S. Ct. Appeals (5th cir.) 1981, U.S. Ct. Appeals (11th cir.) 1981, Colo. 1997, U.S. Dist. Ct. Colo. 1999, U.S. Tax Ct. 2001; cert. arbitrator Coun. Better Bus. Burs. Va. Pvt. practice, Ft. Lauderdale, Fla., 1990-99; pvt. practice Colorado Springs, 1999—. Precinct capt., exec. com. Broward County Rep. Party, 1991-92; v.p. West Broward Rep. Club, 1991-92; sec. North Dade/South Broward Estate Planning Coun., 1991-92; founding bd. mem. Peak Venture Group, 2000-02. Albert C. Murphy scholar Cornell U., 1973. Mem. Fla. Bar Assn., Assn. for Objective Law, Weston Area Jaycees (past sec.), Colo. Sport Compact Racing (bd. dirs.). Republican. Avocations: objectivist philosophy, weightlifting, motorcycling, gardening. Home and Office: 225 Thames Dr Colorado Springs CO 80906-5952 Home Phone: 719-576-6990; Office Phone: 719-576-6990. Personal E-mail: michaelslivka@earthlink.net.

SLIWA, CURTIS, radio personality, volunteer; b. Bklyn., Mar. 26, 1954; s. Chester and Francesca Sliwa; m. Lisa Evers, Dec. 24, 1981 (div. 1993); m. Mary Sliwa; 1 child, Anthony Chester. Founder, head Guardian Angels, 1979—; talk show host WNYW, 1993—96, Monday Night Flights, 1996, WABC, 1990—92, talk show host, Curtis and Kuby in the Morning, 2002—, MSNBC, 2002—03. Spkr. in field. Actor: (films) The Siege, 1998; contbr. articles to numerous profl. jours. Named Top Talk Show Host Yr., Radio and Records Mag., 2004. Mem.: Guardian Angels. Achievements include host of number one rated morning talk-show in NYC. Office: The Guardian Angels Ste 401 717 Fifth Ave New York NY 10022 Office Fax: 212-545-7666.

SLJIVIC-SIMSIC, BILJANA B., Slavic and Baltic languages educator; b. Belgrade, Yugoslavia, Jan. 20, 1933; arrived in US, 1962; d. Branko M. and Radoyka (Pesic) S.; m. Branislav S. Simsic, Jan. 21, 1953 (div. 1963); 1 child, Violet Ljubica. Diploma, U. Belgrade, 1955; MA, Harvard U., 1963, PhD, 1966. Asst. U. Belgrade, 1957-62; lectr. U. Clermont-Ferrand, France, 1959-61; vis. lectr. UCLA, 1964—65, vis. asst. prof., 1965-66; asst. prof. U. Ky., Lexington, 1966-67, U. Pa., Phila., 1967-73; vis. lectr. Princeton (N.J.) U., 1967-69; assoc. prof. U. Ill., Chgo., 1973-86, head of dept., 1981—96, prof. dept. Slavic and Baltic langs. and lit., 1986—. Exch. prof. U. London and Cambridge (Eng.) U., 1989—90, U. Amsterdam, 2000, 02; cons., panelist U.S. Dept. Edn., Fulbright Fellowship, Washington; sr. writer Ohio State U., summers, 1983, 84, 85, 86, 88. Co-author: Serbo-Croatian-English Dictionary, 1972 (grant), Judeo-Spanish Ballads from Bosnia, 1972 (grant); author: Serbo-Croatian, Just For You, 1985 (grant 1983-84); major author 8 vols. of Serbo-Croatian Textbooks for Individualized Studies, 1983-88. Grantee, U. Pa., Phila., 1972; scholar, Radcliffe Coll., 1962—63, Harvard U., 1963—64. Mem.: Am. Assn. for Advancement of Slavic Studies, N.Am. Soc. Serbian Studies (sec.-treas. 1978—84, pres. 1984—86, mem. exec. bd. 1986—88), Assn. Serbian Writers Belgrade, Chgo. Hort. Soc., Harvard and Radcliffe Clubs Chgo. Serbian Orthodox. Avocations: photography, travel, gardening. Office: U Ill Chgo Dept Slavic & Baltic Langs & Lit 601 S Morgan St Chicago IL 60607-1716 Office Phone: 312-996-4412. Personal E-mail: simsic711@comcast.net. Business E-Mail: bibi@uic.edu.

SLOAN, ALLAN HERBERT, journalist; b. Bklyn., Nov. 27, 1944; s. Samuel and Doris (Shanblott) Sloan; m. Nancy Nolan, June 29, 1969; children: Sharon R., Susan M., Dena A. BA, Bklyn. Coll., 1966; MS, Columbia U., 1967. Reporter, sports writer Charlotte Observer, NC, 1968-72; reporter Detroit Free Press, 1972-79; assoc. editor, staff writer Forbes Mag., NYC, 1979-81, sr. editor, 1984-88; staff writer Money Mag., NYC, 1982-84; columnist NY Newsday, NYC, 1989-95; Wall St. editor Newsweek Mag., NYC, 1995—2007; sr. editor-at-large Fortune Mag., NYC, 2007—. Contbr., Marketplace Pub. Radio Internat.; frequent commentator, Nightly Bus. Report PBS TV. Author: Three Plus One Equals Billions: The Bendix-Martin Marietta War, 1982. Named Alumnus of Yr., Columbia Grad. Sch. Journalism, 1999; recipient Hancock award for fin. journalism, Hancock Found., 1992, Loeb award for fin. journalism, Loeb Found., UCLA Anderson Sch. Mgmt., 1974, 1984, 1991, 1993, 1998, Lifetime Achievement award, 2001, Disting. Achievement award, Am. Bus. Editors and Writers, 2001. Office: Newsweek 251 W 57th St New York NY 10019-1802

SLOAN, ANNE ELIZABETH, food scientist, writer; d. Thomas and Anne Sloan; m. James Murtland, June 14, 2003. BS, Rutgers U., 1973; PhD, U. Minn., 1976. Mgr. nutrition comm. Gen. Mills, Mpls., 1976—78; dir. Good Housekeeping Inst., NYC, 1978—85; editor-in-chief McCall's Mag., NYC, 1985—92; pres. Sloan Trends and Solution, Stuart, Fla., 1993—2003, Sloan Trends, Escondido, Calif., 2004—. Author: Food For Thoughts, 1977, Contemporary Nutrition Controversies, 1979; contbr. articles to numerous profl. jours. and mag. Recipient Pub. Rels. award, John W. Hill Found.; George Cook scholar, Rutgers U., 1973. Office: Sloan Trends PO Box 461149 Escondido CA 92046

SLOAN, CAROLYN, music educator, composer, lyricist; d. Myron and Susanne Sloan; m. Stuart Zagnit; 1 child, Sam Zagnit. BA, N.Y. U., NYC, 1982. Cert. Orff instr. N.J., 2004. K-12 music chair Berkeley Carroll Sch., Bklyn., 2005—. Author: (book) Finding Your Voice-A Practical and Spiritual Approach to Singing and Living, Hyperion, 1999; composer (lyricist): (theatrical) I Have Found Home, 1986, My Name is Still Alice, 1992—, Pets, 1992—93, That's Life, 1993—94. Recipient Founder's Day Acad. Excellence award, N.Y. U., 1981, 1982. Mem.: ASCAP (assoc.). Achievements include development of new voice technique for singers and actors; two volumes of children's songs currently being used around the country. Avocations: cooking, travel, swimming, bicycling. Home Phone: 718-643-9578. Personal E-mail: sloantone@aol.com.

SLOAN, CLIFFORD M., lawyer, publishing executive; b. 1957; m. Mary Lou Hartman; children: Sarah, Annie, Nick. BA, Harvard U., 1979; JD, Harvard Law Sch., 1984. Bar: Ill. 1986. Law clk. to Hon. J. Skelly Wright U.S. Ct. of Appeals (DC Cir.), 1984—85; law clk. to Justice Paul Stevens US Supreme Ct., 1985—86; assoc. counsel Office of Ind. Counsel Investigating the Iran-Contra affair, 1987—88; assoc. Onek, Klein & Farr, Washington, 1988—89; asst. to solicitor gen. US Dept. Justice, 1989—91; assoc. then ptnr. Mayer, Brown & Platt, 1991—93; assoc. counsel to Pres. The White House, Washington, 1993—95; prtnr., co-chair Internet Practice Group Wiley, Rein & Fielding LLP, Washington, 1995—2000; v.p. bus. devel., gen. counsel Washingtonpost.Newsweek Interactive, 2000—; pub. Slate mag., 2005—. Adjunct prof. cyberspace and internet law Georgetown U. Law Sch., George Wash. U. Law Sch., Am. U. Wash. Law Ctr.; mem. adv. bd. Corp. Pro Bono. Mem.: ABA. Office: Washingtonpost Newsweek Interactive PO Box 17370 Arlington VA 22216 *

SLOAN, DAVID B., lawyer; b. Martin, Ky., Sept. 20, 1950; BA, Berea Coll., 1972; JD, No. Ky. Univ., 1976. Bar: Ky. 1976, US Dist. Ct. (Ea. Dist. Ky.) 1977, US Ct. Appeals (6th Cir.) 1979. Atty. Stephens, Combs, and Page, Pikeville, Ky., 1976; assoc. O'Hara, Ruberg, Taylor, Sloan & Sergent, Covington, Ky., 1978—82, ptnr., 1982—. Mem.: Am. Bar Assn., Ky. Bar Assn. (pres.-elect 2004, pres.), No. Ky. Bar Assn. (bd. dir.). Office: O'Hara Ruberg Taylor Sloan & Sergent Ste 201 25 Crewstview Hills Mall Rd Covington KY 41017-0411 Office Phone: 859-331-2000. Office Fax: 859-578-3365. Business E-Mail: dsloan@ortlaw.com. *

SLOAN, DONNIE ROBERT, JR., lawyer; b. Nashville, July 24, 1946; s. Donnie R. Sr. and Mary Catharine (Willis) S. BS in Indsl. Engring., Ga. Inst. Tech, 1968; JD cum laude, U. Ga., 1971; LLM, Harvard U., 1975. Bar: Ga. 1971, U.S. Dist. Ct. (no. dist.) Ga. 1971, U.S. Ct. Appeals (11th cir.). Atty. Southwire Co., Carrollton, Ga., 1971-74; assoc., ptnr. Hyatt & Rhoads, P.C., Atlanta, 1975-89; pvt. practice, 1989-96; ptnr. Davidson, Fuller & Sloan, LLP, 1996—. Instr. legal rsch. U. Ga., Athens, 1970-71; instr. music law Ga. State U., Atlanta, 1976. Mem. editl. bd. Ga. Law Rev., 1969-71. Treas. Ga. Wheelchair Athletic Assn., Atlanta, 1981-84; pres., treas. Dixie Wheelchair Athletic Assn., Atlanta, 1984-87. Recipient Appreciation award Ga. Wheelchair Sports and Recreation Assn., 1979; named one of Outstanding Young Men of Am., 1981; named to Dixie Wheelchair Athletic Assn. Hall of Fame, 1990. Mem. Am. Judicature Soc., Phi Kappa Phi, Alpha Phi Mu, Ga. Tech. Club, Harvard Club. Presbyterian. Avocations: skiing, jogging, swimming. Home: 820 Saddlehill Rd Roswell GA 30075 Office: 11330 Lakefield Dr Bldg 1 Ste 250 Duluth GA 30097-1578 Office Phone: 770-662-4700. Business E-Mail: drsloan@dfslaw.com.

SLOAN, EARLE DENDY, JR., chemical engineering educator; b. Seneca, SC, Apr. 23, 1944; s. Earle Dendy and Sarah (Bellotte) S.; m. Marjorie Nilson, Sept. 7, 1968; children: Earle Dendy III, John Mark. BSChemE, Clemson U., 1965, MSChemE, 1972, PhD in Chem. Engring., 1974. Engr. Du Pont, Chattanooga, 1965-66, Seaford, Del., 1966-67, cons. Parkersburg, W.Va., 1967-68, sr. engr. Camden, S.C., 1968-70; postdoctoral fellow Rice U., 1975; prof. chem. engring. Colo. Sch. Mines, Golden, 1976—, dir. Ctr. for Rsch. on Hydrates and Other Solids, 1990—, Gaylord and Phyllis Weaver dist. prof. chem. engring., 1992—. Inaugural pres. faculty senate Colo. Sch. Mines, 1989-90, disting. lectr., 1997-98, appointed senator, 1998; Tokyo Electric Power Co. chair Keio U., Japan, 1996; Erskine fellow U. Canterbury, Christchurch, N.Z., 2002; chmn. Codata Corps Hydrate Database Task Force Group, 2005-, Fed. Methane Hydrate Adv. Com., USA Hydrate Database Com. Author: Clathrate Hydrates of Natural Gases, 1990, 2d edit., 1998, Hydrate Engineering, 2000; chmn. pub. bd. Chem. Engring. Edn., 1990-2006. Scoutmaster local Cub Scouts, 1978-81; elder Presbyn. Ch., Golden, Colo., 1977-79, 92-94; elder Ctrl. Presbyn. Ch., Denver, 1999—. Recipient Donald L. Katz award for rsch., Gas Processors Assn. Fellow AIChE (chmn. area Ia thermodynamics and transport 1990-93); mem. Am. Soc. for Engring. Edn. (chmn. ednl. rsch. methods divsn. 1983-85, chmn. chem. engring. divsn. 1984), Am. Chem. Soc., Soc. Petroleum Engrs. (Disting. Lectr. 1996-97). Avocations: bicycling, cello, philosophy. Office: Colo Sch of Mines Ctr for Hydrate Rsch Golden CO 80401 Personal E-mail: edendysloan@comcast.net. Business E-Mail: esloan@mines.edu.

SLOAN, F(RANK) BLAINE, retired law educator; b. Geneva, Nebr., Jan. 3, 1920; s. Charles Porter and Lillian Josephine (Stiefer) S.; m. Patricia Sand, Sept. 2, 1944; children: DeAnne Sloan Riddle, Michael Blaine, Charles Porter. AB with high distinction, U. Nebr., 1942, LLB cum laude, 1946; LLM in Internat. Law, Columbia U., 1947. Bar: Nebr. 1946, N.Y. 1947. Asst. to spl. counsel Intergovtl. Com. for Refugees, 1947; mem. Office Legal Affairs UN Secretariat, NYC, 1948—78; gen. counsel Relief and Works Agy. Palestine Refugees, Beirut, 1958—60; dir. gen. legal divsn., dep. to legal counsel UN Legal Office, NYC, 1966—78, rep. of Sec. Gen. to UN Commn. Internat. Trade Law, 1969—78, rep. to Legal Sub-com. on Outer Space, 1966—78; rep. UN Del. Vietnam Conf., Paris, 1973, UN Conf. on Carriage of Goods by Sea, Hamburg, 1978; prof. internat. law orgn. and water law Pace U., 1978—87, prof. emeritus, 1987—. Law lectr. Blaine Sloan Internat., 1988—. Author: United Nations General Assembly Resolutions in Our Changing World, 1991, United Nations Memories, 2005, (with Kathryn Sloan Ashby) A History of the Sloan, Porter, Fournell and Stiefer Families, 2005; contbr. articles to legal jours. Cons. UN Office of Legal Affairs, 1983-84, UN Water Resources Br., 1983; supervisory com., Pace Peace Ctr.; legal advisor Korean Missions, 1951, 53, UNTSO, Jerusalem, 1952, UNEF I, Gaza, 1957-58; prin. sec.UN Commn. to investigate Sec.-Gen. Hammarskjold's crash, 1961-62. Navigator AC, U.S. Army, 1943-46 Decorated Air medal. Mem. Am. Soc. Internat. Law, Am. Acad. Polit. and Social Sci., Am. Arbitration Assn., Order of Coif, Phi Beta Kappa, Phi Alpha Delta (hon.). Republican. Roman Catholic. Home: HCR-68 Box 72 Foxwind-Forbes Park Fort Garland CO 81133 Office: 78 N Broadway White Plains NY 10603-3710 also: 375 Soubry Pl Forbes Park Fort Garland CO 81133

SLOAN, HARRY EVANS, film company executive; BA, UCLA, 1971; JD, Loyola Law Sch., 1976. Founder, entertainment lawyer Sloan, Kuppin and Ament, LA, 1976—83; co-chmn. New World Entertainment Ltd., Los Angeles, 1983—89; chmn. SBS Broadcasting S.A., Luxembourg, 1990—2002, CEO, 1993—2001, exec. chmn., 2002—05; chmn., CEO Metro-Goldwyn-Mayer Inc., 2005—. Dir. ZeniMax Media Inc. Office: Metro Goldwyn Mayer Inc 10250 Constellation Blvd Los Angeles CA 90067

SLOAN, HERBERT ELIAS, physician, surgeon; b. Clarksburg, W.Va., Oct. 10, 1914; s. Herbert Elias and Luella (Dye) S.; m. Doris Edwards, May 3, 1943; children: Herbert, Ann, Elizabeth, John, Robert. AB, Washington and Lee U., 1936; MD, Johns Hopkins U., 1940. Diplomate Am. Bd. Surgery, Am. Bd. Thoracic Surgery (bd. dirs. 1966-86, v.p. 1971-73, sec.-treas. 1973-86). Resident in surgery Johns Hopkins Hosp., 1941-44; instr. dept. surgery Johns Hopkins U., 1943-44; resident in thoracic surgery U. Mich. Hosp., Ann Arbor, 1947-49, instr. thoracic surgery, 1949-50; asst. prof. U. Mich., Ann Arbor, 1950-53, assoc. prof., 1953-62, prof. surgery, 1962-87, head sect. thoracic surgery, 1970-85; chief clin. affairs U. Mich. Hosps., Ann Arbor, 1982-86, med. dir. operating room, 1986-87, prof. emeritus surgery, 1987—; med. dir. managed health care U. Mich., Ann Arbor, 1989-96, Herbert Sloan Collegiate Professorship in cardiac surgery, 2003. Mem. staff VA Hosp., Ann Arbor, 1953—, cons., 1968—. Author: The American Board of Thoracic Surgery: A Fifty Year Perspective, 1998, (with Marvin M. Kirsh) Blunt Chest Trauma, General Principles of Management, 1977; editor Annals of Thoracic Surgery, 1969-85; contbr. (with Marvin M. Kirsh) chpts. to books, articles to profl. jours. Served to maj. M.C. U.S. Army, 1944-47. Recipient Bruce Douglas award in thoracic diseases, 1974, Med. Alumni Svc. award Johns Hopkins Sch. Medicine, 1973, Disting. Svc. award Johns Hopkins U. Sch. Medicine, 1983, Disting. Svc. award Mich. Med. Ctr. Alumni Soc., 1988, Herbert Sloan Collegiate Prof. Cardiac Surgery award, 2003; named to Hall of Honor, U. Mich. Med. Sch., 2006. Mem. ACS, Am. Surg. Assn., Am. Heart Assn., Am. Assn. Thoracic Surgery (pres. 1979-80), Soc. Thoracic Surgeons (pres. 1974-75, Disting. Svc. award 1981), Central Surg. Assn., Soc. Univ. Surgeons, So. Thoracic Surgery Assn. (hon.), Thoracic Soc. Gt. Britain (hon.), John Alexander Soc., Western Thoracic Surg. Assn. (hon.), Cardiovascular Surgeons Club, Detroit Heart Club, Am. Trudeau Soc., Mich. Heart Assn., Mich. Trudeau Soc., Am. Acad. Pediatrics, Soc. Vascular Surgery, Frederick A. Coller Surg. Soc., U. Mich. Med. Alumni Soc. (Disting. Svc. award 1988), U. Mich. James Angell Soc., Rsch. Club, Phi Beta Kappa, Alpha Omega Alpha, Omicron Delta Kappa, Sigma Xi. Clubs: Ann Arbor Figure Skating (pres. 1965-66). Home: 471 Barton North Dr Ann Arbor MI 48105-1017 Office: 1500 E Medical Center Dr Ann Arbor MI 48109 Business E-Mail: hsloan@umich.edu.

SLOAN, HUGH WALTER, JR., automotive executive; b. Princeton, NJ, Nov. 1, 1940; s. Hugh Walter and Elizabeth (Johnson) Sloan; m. Deborah Louise Murray, Feb. 20, 1971; children: Melissa, Peter, Jennifer, William. AB in History with honors, Princeton U., 1963. Staff asst. to Pres. U.S. White House, Washington, 1969-71; treas. Pres. Nixon's Re-election Campaign, Washington, 1971; spl. asst. to pres. Budd Co., Troy, Mich., 1973-74, exec. asst. internat., 1974-77, mgr. corp. mktg., 1977-79; pres., gen. mgr. Budd Can. Inc., Kitchener, Ont., Canada, 1979-85; pres. automotive Woodbridge Group, Troy, 1985-98, dep. chmn., 1998—. Bd. dirs. Woodbridge Foam Corp., Mfrs. Life Ins. Co., Wescast Industries. Trustee Spartan Motors, Inc., Beaumont Hosp.; gov. Cranbrook Schs. Lt. USNR, 1963—65. Recipient Outstanding Bus. Leader award, Wilfrid Laurier U., 1987. Mem.: Bloomfield Hills (Mich.) Country Club. Republican. Office: Woodbridge Group 1515 Equity Dr Troy MI 48084-7146 Office Phone: 248-280-6571. Business E-Mail: hugh_sloan@woodbridgegroup.com.

SLOAN, JEANETTE PASIN, artist; b. Chgo., Mar. 18, 1946; d. Antonio and Anna (Baggio) Pasin; children: Eugene Blakely, Anna Jeanette. BFA, Marymount Coll., Tarrytown, NY, 1967; MFA, U. Chgo., 1969. One-woman shows include G.W. Einstein Gallery, NYC, 1977—85, Landfall Press Gallery, Chgo., NYC, 1978, 1987, Roger Ramsay Gallery, Chgo., 1987, 1989, 1992, Tatischeff Gallery, Santa Monica, Calif., 1989, Steven Scott Gallery, Balt., 1989, Butters Gallery, Portland, Oreg., 1989, 1991, 1994, 1996, 1999, Tatistcheff & Co. Inc., 1995, 1997, 1999, Ouartet Editions, NYC, 1995, Elliot Smith Gallery, St. Louis, 1994, Peltz Gallery, Milw., 1994—95, 1999, 2006, Gerhard Wurzer Gallery, Houston, 1997, 2001, Cline Fine Arts Gallery, Santa Fe, 1998, 2001, J. Cacciola Gallery, NYC, 2004—05, Amarillo Mus. Art, Tex., 2006, William Havu Gallery, Denver, 2007, Landfall Press Gallery, Santa Fe, 2007, Klaudia Marr Gallery, 2007, Represented in permanent collections Art Mus. Chgo., Cleve. Mus. Art, Ill. State Mus., Indpls. Mus. Art, Canton Art Inst., Ohio, Ball State Bus., Mpls. Inst. Art, Fogg Mus. Harvard U., Yale U. Art Gallery, Snite Mus. U. Notre Dame, Met. Mus. Art, NYC, Herbert F. Johnson Mus. Cornell U., Ithaca, NY, Valpariaso Mus. Art, Ind., Nat. Gallery Art, Washington, exhibited in group shows; subject of book by Gerritt Henry Jeanette Pasin Sloan, 2000, subject of book by by James Yood The Prints of Jeanette Pasin Sloan, 2003. Studio: 301 Loma Arisco Santa Fe NM 87501 Home Phone: 505-989-9660; Office Phone: 505-699-9234. Personal E-mail: jeanettepasin@aol.com.

SLOAN, JERRY (GERALD EUGENE SLOAN), professional basketball coach; b. McLeansboro, Ill., Mar. 28, 1942; m. Bobbye (dec. 2004); 3 children: Kathy, Brian, Holly. Student, Evansville Coll., Ind., 1965. Player Balt. Bullets, 1965—66, Chgo. Bulls, 1966—76, scout, 1976—77, asst. coach, 1977—79, head coach, 1979—82; scout Utah Jazz, Salt Lake City, 1983—84, asst. coach, 1984—88, head coach, 1988—. Named NBA Coach of Yr., The Sporting News, 2004; named to NBA All-Star Team, 1967, 1969, NBA All-Def. First Team, 1969, 1972, 1974, 1975. Office: Utah Jazz EnergySolutions Arena 301 W South Temple Salt Lake City UT 84101 *

SLOAN, KATHERINE (KAY SLOAN), college president; DArts in English, Carnegie Mellon U. Pres. Greenfield C.C., 1988—94, North Hennepin C.C., Mpls., 1994—96, Mass. Coll. Art, Boston, 1998—. Office: Office of President Mass College of Art 621 Huntington Ave Boston MA 02115 Office Phone: 617-879-7100. *

SLOAN, MACEO KENNEDY, lawyer, investment company executive; b. Phila., Oct. 18, 1949; s. Maceo Archibald and Charlotte (Kennedy) S.; m. Melva Iona Wilder, July 3, 1971; children: Maceo S., Malia K. BA, Morehouse Coll., 1971; MBA with honors, Ga. State U., 1973; JD with honors, N.C. Cen. U., 1979. CFA. Investment analyst N.C. Mut. Life Ins. Co., Durham, 1973-77, asst. to treas., 1977-78, asst. v.p., 1978-83, treas., 1983-85, v.p., treas., 1985-86; pres. NCM Devel. Group subs. N.C. Mut. Life Ins. Co., Durham, 1985-86; of counsel Moore & Van Allen, Durham, 1985-86; pres., CEO NCM Capital Mgmt. Group, Inc., Durham, 1986-91, chmn., pres., CEO, 1991—, Sloan Fin. Group, Inc., Durham, N.C., 1991—. Adj. vis. prof. N.C. Ctrl. U., Durham, 1978-86, workshop rev. leader Study Seminar for Fin. Analysts, Windsor, Ont., Can., 1980—; bd. dirs. Mechanics & Farmers Bank, Durham, 1979—, chmn. trust com., 1979-93; networking leader Black Enterprise mag., 1987—; bd. trustees Coll. Retirement Equities Fund, 1991—, ERISA Adv. Coun. U.S. Dept. Labor, 1991-93; bd. dirs. News and Observer Pub. Co. Bd. dirs. United Way, Durham, 1980-87, Urban Ministries, Durham, 1983-88, Internat. Found. Edn. and Self Help, 1993—, N.C. Air Cargo Airport Authority, 1993—; bd. visitors N.C. Ctrl. U. Sch. Law, Durham, 1979-86, U. N.C., Chapel Hill, 1990—. Recipient Outstanding Svc. award Better Bus. Bur., 1980, Freedom Guard award Durham Jaycees, 1982, Outstanding Leadership award United Way Durham, 1984, Resolution in Appreciation Durham City Coun., 1983. Fellow Life Mgmt. Inst.; mem. ABA, Fin. Analysts Fedn., N.C. Soc. Fin. Analysts (v.p. 1977-78), N.C. State Bar Assn., Durham C. of C., Nat. Investment Mgrs. Assn. (founder, chmn.), Nat. Assn. Securities Profls., Treyburn Country Club (Durham), Univ. Club (Durham), The George Town (Washington). Democrat. Baptist. Avocations: reading, jogging, weight training, golf, tennis. Home: 24000 S Lowell Rd Bahama NC 27503-9693 Office: Sloan Fin Group Inc 103 W Main St Fl 4 Durham NC 27701-3638 also: NCM Mgmt/Sloan Financial 2634 Durham-Chapel Hill Blvd Ste 206 Durham NC 27707-1958

SLOAN, MARK HAMILTON, art gallery director, educator, author; b. Durham, NC, Nov. 16, 1957; s. William Lee and Ruth (Hamilton) S.; m. Elise Labe, 1982 (div. 1986); 1 child, Mara Daile; m. Michelle Van Parys, Mar. 10, 1990; 1 child, Andre. BA, U. Richmond, 1980; MFA, Va. Commonwealth U., 1984. Exec. dir. The Light Factory, Charlotte, N.C.,

1985-86; assoc. dir. San Francisco Camerawork, 1986-89; ind. curator META Mus., Brasher Falls, N.Y., 1989-92; dir. Roland Gibson Gallery, Potsdam, N.Y., 1992-94, Halsey Inst. Contemporary Art, Charleston, SC, 1994—. Adj. prof. SUNY, Potsdam, 1992-94; assoc. prof. Coll. Charleston, 1994—; mem. adv. bd. Office of Cultural Affairs City of Charleston, 1994—; mem. collections com. Gibbes Mus. Art, Charleston, 1997-2005. Author: Hoaxes, Humbugs and Spectacles, 1990, Wild, Weird and Wonderful, 2002; co-author: Dear Mr. Ripley, 1993, Self-Made Worlds, 1997, The Rarest of the Rare, 2004, Force of Nature: Site Intallation by Ten Japanese Artists, 2007. Grantee S.C. Arts Commn., 1996-2000. Mem. Soc. Photographic Edn., Coll. Art Assn. Office: Halsey Inst Contemporary Art Coll of Charleston 66 George St Charleston SC 29424 Office Phone: 843-953-7891. E-mail: sloanm@cofc.edu.

SLOAN, MARY JEAN, retired media specialist; b. Lakeland, Fla., Nov. 29, 1927; d. Marion Wilder and Elba (Jinks) Sloan. BS, Peabody Coll., Nashville, 1949; MLS, Atlanta U., 1978, SLS, 1980. Cert. libr. media specialist. Music dir. Pinecrest Sch., Tampa, Fla., 1949-50, Polk County Schs., Bartow, Fla., 1950-54; pvt. music tchr. Lakeland, 1954-58; tchr. Clayton County Schs., Jonesboro, Ga., 1958-59; media specialist Eastualley Sch., Marietta, Ga., 1959-89; ret., 1989. Coord. conf. Ga. Libr. Media Dept., Jekyll Island, 1982-83, sec., Atlanta, 1982-83, com. chmn. ethnic conf., Atlanta, 1978, pres., 1984-85, state pres., 1985-86; program chmn. Ga. Media Orgns. Conf, Jekyll Island, 1988. Contbr. to bibliographies. Recipient Walter Bell award Ga. Assn. Instrnl. Tech., 1988, Disting. Svc. award, 1991. Mem. ALA (del. 1984, 85, 90), NEA, Southeastern Libr. Assn., Am. Assn. Sch. Librs., Soc. for Sch. Librs., Internat., Ga. Assn. Educators (polit. action com. 1983), Beta Phi Mu, Phi Delta Kappa. Republican. Methodist. Home: 797 Yorkshire Rd NE Atlanta GA 30306-3264

SLOAN, MELANIE TOGMAN, lawyer, former prosecutor; b. Washington, Dec. 16, 1965; d. Leonard Seymour and Barbara (Kaufman) T. BA in English, U. Chgo., 1987, JD, 1991. Bar: Calif. 1991, D.C. 1992. Student atty. Mandel Legal Aid Clinic, Chgo., 1988-91; assoc. Sonnenschein, Nath & Rosenthal, LA, 1991-92, Howrey & Simon, Washington, 1992-93; nominations counsel com. on judiciary U.S. Senate, Washington, 1993-94; counsel U.S. Ho. Subcom. on Crime and Criminal Justice, Washington, 1994-95; minority counsel Ho. Jud. Com., Washington, 1995—98; asst. US atty. DC dist. US Dept. Justice, 1998—2003; exec. dir. Citizens for Responsibility & Ethics in Washington, Washington, 2003—. Office: Citizens for Responsibility & Ethics in Washington 1400 Eye St NW Ste 450 Washington DC 20005 Office Phone: 202-408-5565.

SLOAN, MICHAEL ALLAN, neurologist; b. Detroit, July 26, 1954; s. Eugene and Mildred Jody Sloan (Stepmother); children: Jessica Barry, Brittany Erin. MD, Wayne State U., 1980; MS, Rush U., 2003. Diplomate internal medicine Am. Bd. Internal Medicine, 1984, neurology Am. Bd. Psychiatry and Neurology, 1988, vascular neurology Am. Bd. Psychiatry and Neurology, 2005. Assoc. prof. neurology U. Md. Med. Ctr., Balt., 1988—97; neurologist Harbin Clinic, Rome, Ga., 1998—2000; assoc. prof. neurology U. Rush, Chgo., 2000—05; dir. stroke ctr. Carolinas Med. Ctr., Charlotte, NC, 2005—07; adj. prof. neurology U. NC, Chapel Hill, 2005—07; prof. neurology U. Southern Fla, Tampa, 2007. AMA del. Am. Soc. Neuroimaging, 2001. Fellow: Am. Coll. Cardiology, Am. Acad. Neurology; mem.: Am. Coll. Physicians. Avocations: politics, music, performing arts, travel, sports. Office Phone: 813-259-8577. Business E-Mail: msloan@health.isf.edu.

SLOAN, MICHAEL DANA, information systems specialist, management consultant; b. Santa Monica, Calif., Sept. 30, 1960; s. Avery and Beverly Rae (Krantz) S.; m. Barbara Rogers; 1 child, Ashley Harrison. BS in Bus. Adminstrn., Calif. State U., Northridge, 1983; MBA, Pepperdine U., 1987. Programmer/analyst TICOR, Inc., LA, 1979-80; data processing analyst Deluxe Check Printers, Inc., Chatsworth, Calif., 1980-83; fin. systems analyst Wismer & Assocs., Inc., Canoga Park, Calif., 1983-84; sr. systems analyst Coast Savs. & Loan, Granada Hills, Calif., 1984-86; microcomputer systems specialist Litton Industries, Woodland Hills, Calif., 1986-87; systems mgr., info. resources mgr. TRW, Inc.- Space and Def., Redondo Beach, Calif., 1987-93; project mgr. Health Net, Woodland Hills, 1993-95; mgr. fin. and sales systems Merisel Ams. Inc., El Segundo, Calif., 1995-97; sr. mgr. web tech. & devel. Ingram Micro Inc., Santa Ana, Calif., 2000—01; with Ptnrs. Cons. Svcs., Inc., Laguna Beach, Calif., 2001—02, Consulting Solutions, Inc., Calabasas, Calif., 2002—05; sr. mgr. IT ops. DirecTV, 2006—. Cons. Data Most, Inc., Chatsworth, 1982—83, Home Savs. & Loan, North Hollywood, Calif., 1987, Micro Tech., LA, 1987, TRW, Inc.-Space and Def., Redondo Beach, Calif., 1993—2000, Pacificare Health Sys., Inc., 1997, Nissan N.Am. (formerly Nissan Motor Corp., USA), 1998—99, Prosum Info. Techs., Inc., 2000—01, Am. Honda Motors, Inc., 1999—2000, Toyota Fin. Svcs., 2001—02, Warner Bros. Studios, 2002—05, Oakwood Worldwide, 2005—06; mgmt. cons. Strategic Cons. Solutions, Ltd., Redondo Beach, Calif., 2005—. Mem. IEEE Computer Soc., Salle Gascon Fencing Club, U.S. Fencing Assn., Delta Sigma Pi. Republican. Avocations: fencing, comedy improvisation, tennis, volleyball, travel. Office: Strategic Consulting Solutions Ltd Ste 1 2607 Vanderbilt Ln Redondo Beach CA 90278 Office Phone: 310-964-5883.

SLOAN, O. TEMPLE, JR., automotive equipment executive; b. Sanford, NC, Feb. 21, 1939; s. Orris Temple and Thelma (Hamilton) S.; m. Carol Carson; children: C. Carson Henline, O. Temple Sloan III, Mark H. Sloan. BA in Bus. Adminstrn., Duke U., 1961; LLD (hon.), Northwood U., Midland, Mich., 2007. Founder, chmn., CEO Gen. Parts Internat. Inc., Raleigh, NC, 1961—. Chmn. bd. dir. Highwoods Properties Inc., Raleigh; bd. dir. CARQUEST Corp., Raleigh, Bank Am., Charlotte, Lowe's Cos., Inc., Golden Corral, Global Transpark Found. Trustee Boys and Girls Homes N.C., Lake Waccamaw, 1973; campaign chmn. Wake County United Way, 2001; mem. Centennial Authority, 1995—2005, trustee, former chmn. fin. com.; elder Presbyn. Ch.; exec. bd. Occoneechee coun. Boy Scouts Am., capital campaign chmn. Occoneechee coun., 2004—05, past v.p.Occoneechee coun., past treas. Occoneechee coun.; bd. visitors Peace Coll., Raleigh, 1985—87, trustee, 1987—97, vice chmn. bd. trustees. Recipient Silver Beaver award Boy Scouts Am., Disting. Eagle Scout award Boy Scouts Am., Disting. Svc. citation Automotive Hall of Fame, 1997; named Northwood U. Outstanding Bus. Leader, 1999. Mem. Automotive Warehouse Distbrs. Assn. Inc. (dir. 1969—, chmn. 1976-77, Scholarship award 1977, Automotive Man of Yr. award 1989), The Fifty Group (past pres.), Carolina Country Club (Raleigh). Avocations: fishing, hunting, ranching. Home: 3026 Randolph Dr Raleigh NC 27609-6942 Office: Gen Parts Internat Inc PO Box 26006 Raleigh NC 27611 Business E-Mail: licanipe@gpi.com.

SLOAN, ROBERT BRYAN, JR., academic administrator; b. Coleman, Tex., 1949; m. Sue Collier; children: Charissa, Bryan, Eraina, Michael, Alathea, Sophia, Paul. BA cum laude, Baylor U., 1970; MDiv magna cum laude, Princeton Theol. Sem., 1973; doktor der theologie insigni cum laude, U. Basel, 1978. Faculty Hardin-Simmons U., Abilene, Southwestern Bapt. Theol. Sem., Fort Worth, 1980—83; faculty, religion Baylor U., Waco, Tex., 1983, George W. Truett chair in Evangelism, 1990—95, dean Truett Sem., 1993—95, pres., CEO, 1995—2005, chancellor, 2005—. Mem. Cooper Found. Bd., Compass Bank Adv. Bd.; pastor, interim pastor over 20 chs., Tex., Okla., N.J., Germany; mem., treas. Big 12 Exec. Com.; bd. dirs. Salado Inst. for the Humanities. Inducted Little League Hall of Excellence. Mem. Studiorum Novi Testamenti Societas, Soc. of Bib. Lit., Inst. for Bib. Rsch. Office: Baylor U Office of Chancellor PO Box 97132 Waco TX 76798-7132 Office Phone: 254-710-2012. Office Fax: 254-710-3126. *

SLOAN, ROBERT D., energy executive, lawyer; b. Ill., Oct. 27, 1947; m. Dauphine de Montlaur Sloan; children: Alexandra, Caroline, Edward. BA, U. Mich.; JD, Harvard U. Gen. counsel to Minority U.S. Senate Permanent Subcommittee on Investigations; asst. legal adviser, worked on nuclear non-proliferation and politico-military matters U.S. State Dept.'s Office of Legal Adviser; gen. counsel Multinational Force and Observers, Rome, 1981—84; v.p., dir. Sovereign Credit Mgmt. Divsn. 1st Nat. Bank Chgo., 1985—92; ptnr. Pepper, Hamilton and Sheetz Law Firm, Washington, Sloan, Lehner & Ruiz; mng. ptnr. Brussels office McKenna and Cuneo LLP, 1993—98; v.p., gen. counsel GE Indsl. Sys., Plainville, Conn., 1998—2003; sr. v.p., gen. counsel, sec. Entergy Corp., New Orleans, 2003—. Adj. prof. law Georgetown Law Ctr., Washington. Bd. dir. Ctr. for Internat. Bus. Edn., U. Mich., New Orleans Ballet Theatre. Office: Entergy Corp PO Box 61000 New Orleans LA 70160 *

SLOAN, SHELDON HAROLD, lawyer; b. Mpls., Dec. 25, 1935; s. Leonard Norman Sloan and Mary (Wasserman); m. Loraine Bayer, Nov. 28, 1964; children: Stephen Howard, Jennifer Blair; m. Shelby Jean Sloan. BSBA, UCLA, 1958; JD, U. So. Calif., 1961. Bar: Calif. 1962, US Dist. Ct. (so. and cen. dists.) Calif. 1962, US Claims Ct. 1962, US Supreme Ct. 1962. Atty. US Dept. Justice, Washington, 1962-63; assoc. Brown & Brown, LA, 1963-73, ptnr., 1976-79; judge LA Mcpl. Ct., 1973-76; sole practice, 1980—; of counsel Lewis, Brisbois Bisgaard & Smith LLP. Bd. dirs. ACA JOE, San Francisco, Pioneer Magnetics Inc., Santa Monica, Calif. Trustee, treas. Westlake Sch. for Girls, Los Angeles, 1980; pres., chmn. Coro Found., LA, 1980-81, Frater Friends Music Ctr., LA, 1981-85; chmn. Senator Pete Wilson's Jud. Selection Com., 1982-84, 85—; pres. Guardians Jewish Homes for the Aged, LA, 1986. Mem.: State Bar Calif. (pres. 2006—07), LA County Bar Assn. (chmn. Jud. Appointments Com. 1984, pres. 1996—97). Republican. Avocations: tennis, golf, skiing. Office: Lewis, Brisbois Bisgaard & Smith LLP Ste 1200 221 N Figueroa St Los Angeles CA 90012-2601 also: 11111 Santa Monica Blvd Ste 230 Los Angeles CA 90025-3347 Office Phone: 310-268-0622. E-mail: Sloan@lbbslaw.com. *

SLOAN, STEVEN RICHARD, medical educator, director; b. Chgo., Dec. 19, 1960; s. Bernard Richard and Ethel Mae Sloan. MD, PhD, NYU. Cert. transfusion medicine Am. Bd. Pathology, 2006. Asst. prof. Harvard Med. Sch., Boston, 2000—; blood bank med. dir. Children's Hosp. Boston, 2000—. Office: Children's Hospital Boston 300 Longwood Ave - Bader 406 Boston MA 02115 Office Phone: 617-355-6268. Business E-Mail: steven.sloan@childrens.harvard.edu.

SLOANE, BEVERLY LEBOV, writer, instructor, consultant; b. NYC, May 26, 1936; d. Benjamin S. and Anne (Weinberg) LeBov; m. Robert Malcolm Sloane, Sept. 27, 1959 (dec. May 16, 2002); 1 child, Alison Lori Sloane Gaylin. AB, Vassar Coll., 1958; MA, Claremont Grad. U., 1975, postgrad., 1975—76; cert. in exec. mgmt., UCLA Grad. Sch. Mgmt., 1982, grad. exec. mgmt. program, 1982, cert. in advanced exec. mgmt., 1995, grad. advanced exec. mgmt. program, 1995; grad. profl. pub. course, Stanford U., 1982, grad. exec. refresher course in profl. pub., 1994; grad. intensive bioethics course Kennedy Inst. Ethics, Georgetown U., 1987, advanced bioethics course, 1988; grad. Summer Bioethics Inst., Loyola Marymount U., 1990; grad. Ann. Summer Inst. on Tchg. of Writing, Columbia U. Tchrs. Coll., 1990; grad. Ann. Summer Inst. on Advanced Tchg. of Writing, Columbia Tchrs. Coll., 1993; grad. Ann. Inst. Pub. Health and Human Rights, Harvard U. Sch. Pub. Health, 1994; grad. women's campaign sch., Yale U., 1998; grad. numerous courses, Inst. Writing and Thinking, Bard Coll., 2005—07; grad. memoir writing, Omega Inst., Rhinebeck, NY, 2006; Ethics Fellow, Loma Linda U. Med. Ctr., 1989. Circulation libr. Harvard Med. Libr., Boston, 1958-59; social worker Conn. State Welfare, New Haven, 1960-61; tchr. English Hebrew Day Sch., New Haven, 1961-64; instr. creative writing and English lit. Monmouth Coll., West Long Branch, NJ, 1967-69; writer, cons., 1970—. V.p. coun. grad. students, Claremont Grad. U., 1971-72, adj. dir. Writing Ctr. Speaker Series, 1993-2000, spkr., 1996-98, Claremont Grad. U.; mem. Strategic Planning Task Force Com. Campaign Pre-eminence. 1986-87, Alumni Coun., bd. dirs. Alumni Assn., 1993-96; mem. Vol. Devel. Com., 1994-96, Alumni Awards Com., 1993-96; bd. visitors Claremont Grad. U. Ctrs. for Arts and Humanities, 2001—; adv. coun. tech. and profl. writing Dept. English, Calif. State U., Long Beach, 1980-82; adv. bd. Calif. Health Rev., 1982-83; mem. Foothill Health Dist. Adv. Coun. LA County Dept. Health Svcs., 1987-93, pres., 1989-91; vis. scholar Hastings Ctr., 1996; adj. instr. English composition Marist Coll., Poughkeepsie, NY, 2005-06; instr. memoir writing Lifetime Learning Inst. Bard Coll., Annandale-on-Hudson, NY, 2006-; spkr. in field. Author: From Vassar to Kitchen, 1967, A Guide to Health Facilities: Personnel and Management, 1971, 2nd edit., 1977, 3d edit., 1992, Introduction to Healthcare Delivery Organization: Functions and Management, 4th edit., 1999. Co-chmn. Vassar Christmas Showcase Vassar Club, New Haven, 1965—66; pub. rels. bd. Monmouth County Mental Health Assn., 1968—69; co-chmn. Vassar Club So. Calif. Annual Book Fair Vassar Coll., 1970—71; chmn. creative writing group Calif. Inst. Tech. Woman's Club, 1975—79; mem. task force edn. and cultural activities City of Duarte, 1987—88; class rep. Vassar Coll. Alumnae Assn., 1989; chmn. creative writing group Yale U. Newcomers, 1965—66; dir. creative writing group Yale U. Women's Orgn., 1966—67; mem. Exec. Program Network UCLA Grad. Sch. Mgmt., 1987—2000; trustee Ctr. Improvement Child Caring, 1981—83; mem. League Crippled Children, 1982—, treas. for gen. meetings, 1990—91, chmn. hostesses com., 1988—89, pub. rels. com., 1990—91; del. Task Force on Minorities in Newspaper Bus., 1987—89; rep. cmty. County Health Network Tobacco Control Program, 1991; mem. NY Citizens Com. Health Care Decisions, bd. dirs., 2005—; mem. Vassar Coll. Class Gift Com., 1998; chmn. 1st ann. Rabbi Camillus Angel Interfaith Svc. Temple Beth David, 1978, v.p., 1983—86; cmty. rels. com. Jewish Fedn. Coun. Greater LA, 1985—87; bd. dirs. League Crippled Children, 1988—91; ethics com., human subjects protection com. Jewish Home for Aging, Reseda, Calif., 1994—97; various positions and coms. Claremont Grad. U., 1986—; bd. visitors Claremont Grad. U. Ctr. Arts and Humanities, 2001—; bd. dirs. LA Commn. Assaults Against Women, 1983—84; class corr. Vassar Coll. Quar. Alumnae Mag., 1993—98; class of 1958 coms. Vassar Coll., class v.p., 1998—2000, class co-pres., 2000—01, class pres., 2001—03, program chmn. 40th reunion, 1998, program com. 50th reunion 2008, 2007—. Recipient cert. of appreciation City of Duarte, 1988, County of LA, 1988, Ann. Key Mem. award LA Dept. Health Svcs., 1990, cert. of appreciation Alumni Coun. Claremont Grad Sch., 1996; Coro Found. fellow, 1979, Ethics fellow Loma Linda U. Med. Ctr., 1989; named Calif. Communicator of Achievement, Woman of Yr. Calif. Press Women, 1992. Fellow: Am. Med. Writers Assn. (Pacific SW del. to nat. bd. 1980—87, dir. 1980—93, chmn. nat. book awards trade category 1982—83, chmn. Nat. Networking Luncheon 1983—84, nat. chmn. freelance sect. 1984—85, workshop leader, Nat. Ann. Conf. 1984—92, gen. chmn. Asilomar Western Regional Conf. 1985, workshop leader, Asilomar Western Regional Conf. 1985, nat. exec. bd. dirs. 1985—86, nat. adminr. sects. 1985—86, pres.-elect Pacific Southwest chpt. 1985—87, chmn. gen. session nat. conf. 1986—87, chmn. Walter C. Alvarez Mem. Found award 1986—87, program co-chmn. 1987, program chmn. nat. conf. 1987, moderator gen. session. nat. conf. 1987, pres. Pacific S.W. chap. 1987—89, workshop leader, Asilomar Western Nat. Conf. 1988, spkr. Pacific S.W. chpt. 1988—89, program co-chmn. 1989, workshop leader, Asilomar Western Nat. Conf. 1989, Pacific Southwest deleg. to nat. bd. 1989—91, immediate past pres. 1989—91, workshop leader, Nat. Ann. Conf. 1990—92, bd. dirs. 1991—93, workshop leader, Nat. Ann. Conf. 1995, chmn. conv. coms., workshop leader, Nat. Ann. Conf. 1995, Appreciation award for outstanding leadership 1989, named to Workshop Leaders Honor Roll 1991); mem.: AAUP, APHA, AAUW (creative writing chmn. 1969—70, books and plays chmn. Arcadia Br. 1973—74, 1st v.p. program dir. 1975—76, legis. chmn. Arcadia Br. 1976—77, networking chmn. 1981—82, spkr. 1987, chmn. task force promoting individual liberties 1987—88, pres.-elect 1998—99, educ. equity chmn. 1998—99, chmn. deleg. to national conv. 1999, chmn. Technical Trek Sci. Camp Scholarship for Girls 1999, Career Day 1999, pres. Arcadia br. 1999—2000, writer in res Calif. State Am. Assn. Univ. Women 1999—2000, diversity chmn. Arcadia br. 2000—01, LA Interbr. Coun. Arcadia br. repr. 2000—02, Calif. State diversity com. 2000—02, program vice-chmn. LA County Interbr. Coun. 2000—02, Woman of Achievement Arcadia br. 1986, cert. of appreciation 1987), Calif. State AAUW (program co-v.p. 2002), Town Hall Calif. (vice chmn. cmty. affairs sect. 1982—87, faculty-instr. Exec. Breakfast Inst. 1985—86, Exec. Breakfast Inst. spkr. 1986), Pasadena Athletic, Claremont Cols. Faculty House, Women's City (Pasadena), Nat. Writer's Union, Authors Guild, Assn. Writing Programs, NY Acad. Medicine (met. NY Ethics Network), Soc. Health and Human Values, Kennedy Inst. Ethics, Nat. Fedn. Press Women (chmn. state women of achievement comt. 1986—87, nat. co-chmn. task force recruitment minorities 1987—89, del. 1987—89, bd. dirs. 1987—93, bd. dir. spkrs. bur. 1989—93, Plenary past pres. state 1989—, workshop leader, spkr. annual nat. conf. 1990, editor spkrs. bur. directory 1991—92, editor spkrs. bur. addendum dir. 1992, cert. of appreciation 1991, 1st runner up, Nat. Communicator of Achievement 1992, cert. of appreciation 1993), Hastings Cent. (vis. scholar 1996), Ind. Writers So. Calif. (bd. dirs. corp. 1988—89, bd. dirs. 1989—93, dir. at large 1989—90, dir. specialized groups 1989—90, dir. speech writing group 1991—92), NY Acad. Scis., Calif. Press Women (v.p. programs L.A. chpt. 1982—85, pres. 1985—87, state pres. 1987—89, immediate past state pres. 1989—91, chmn. state speakers bur. 1989—95, deleg. nat. bd. 1989—95, dir. family literacy day Calif. 1990, moderator, ann. spring conv. 1990, chmn. nominating comt. 1990—91, Calif. literacy dir. 1990—92, dir. state literacy com. 1990—92, moderator, ann. spring conv. 1992, Cert. of Appreciation 1991, Calif. Communicator of Achievement 1992), Am. Soc. Law, Medicine, Ethics, AAUW Calif. State Comns. Comt. (writer in residence 1999—2000), Coro Nat. Alumni Assn. (bd. dirs. 1999—, continuing edn. com. 2003—), Am. Assn. Higher Edn., Women in Comm. Inc. (NE area rep. 1980—81, bd. dirs. 1980—82, v.p. cmty. affairs 1981—82, chmn. awards banquet 1982, chmn. LA chpt. Agnes Underwood Freedom Info. Awards banquet 1982, nominating com. 1982—83, seminar leader, spkr., ann. nat. profl. conf. 1985, program adv. com. LA chpt. 1987, com. Women of the Press awards luncheon 1988, bd. dirs. 1989—90, v.p. activities 1989—90, Recognition award 1983), Duarte Rotary Club. Home and Office: 22 East Knoll Rhinebeck NY 12572 Office Phone: 845-876-0738.

SLOANE, CARL STUART, corporate executive, educator, management consultant; b. NYC, Feb. 9, 1937; s. George and Dorothy (Cohen) S.; m. Toby Tattlebaum, Dec. 27, 1958; children: Lisa Beth, Amy Rachel, Todd Cowan. BA, Harvard U., 1958, MBA, 1960. Asst. to pres. Revlon, Inc., NYC, 1960-62; mgmt. cons. Harbridge House, Inc., Boston, 1962-69; pres., CEO, chmn. Temple, Barker & Sloane, Inc., Lexington, Mass., 1970—91; prof. bus. adminstrn. Harvard Grad. Sch. Bus. Adminstrn., Cambridge, Mass., 1991—2001; co-chair Alex Ptnrs. and Questor Funds, 2005—06. Policyholders' examining com. N.W. Mut. Life Ins. Co.; bus. adv. com. Transp. Ctr., Northwestern U., 1984-91; adv. com. Ctr. for Sci. and Internat. Affairs, Kennedy Sch. Govt., Harvard U., 1984-94; dir. Harvard med. faculty physicians at BIDMC, 2007-; bd. dirs. Rayonier, Inc., Brinks Co., Cardiovasc. Assoc., Inc. Bd. dirs. Harvard-Radcliffe Hillel, Cambridge, Mass., 1987-98, chmn., 1994-98; bd. dirs., trustee Beth Israel Deaconess Med. Ctr., Boston, 1993—, vice-chmn., 1996-2002, chmn. 2002-05; nat. fund chmn. Harvard Bus. Sch., 1987-89, vis. com. Mem. Assn. Mgmt. Cons. Firms (chmn. 1984-86), Harvard U. Bus. Sch. Alumni Assn. (v.p. 1989, pres. 1989-91), Boston Yacht Club (Marblehead), Kernwood County Club (Salem), Harvard Club NYC. Office: Harvard Bus Sch Soldiers Fld Boston MA 02163-1317 Home: 402 Paradise Rd Apt 2G Swampscott MA 01907 Office Phone: 617-495-6984. Business E-Mail: csloane@hbs.edu.

SLOANE, HOWARD G., lawyer; b. San Francisco, Dec. 7, 1950; BA, Wesleyan U., Ohio, 1972; JD, Suffolk U., 1976. Bar: NY 1977, DC 1981. Law clk. US Dist. Ct. (Ea. Dist.) NY, 1976—77; co-adminstr. ptnr. Cahill Gordon & Reindel LLP, ptnr., Litig. Practice Group. Chmn. bd. Heckscher Found. for Children, 1995—; trustee Horace Mann Sch., 1998—, Sisulu Victory Acad. Charter Sch., 2000—03, Leadership for a Diverse Am., 2004—; bd. dir. Mcpl. Art Soc., 1990—. Office: Cahill Gordon & Reindel LLP 80 Pine St New York NY 10005-1702 Office Phone: 212-701-3321. Office Fax: 212-378-2369. Business E-Mail: psloane@cahill.com.

SLOANE, J.P., television producer, theologian, entertainer, writer; b. Hollywood, Calif., Sept. 6, 1942; s. Jimmy Jackson and Anita (Coleman) Barrios. Cert. in TV prodn., Purdue U., 1981; grad., Oral Roberts U., 1985; diploma, Inst. Jewish-Christian Studies, Dallas, 1992; grad., Moody Bible Inst., Chgo., 1998; student, IBEX Campus, Abu Ghosh, Israel, 2001; BA summa cum laude, Master's Coll., 2003, MA, 2004; PhD, Trinity Theol. Sem., 2006—. Biblical scholar and lectr.; appeared on major Christian networks. Guest Art Linkletter's House Party (age 5), CBS Radio Network; played Billy Kettle in Ma and Pa Kettle movie series; appeared on Memory Lane TV show, Hollywood; recorded High on a Mountain, 1960, Linda Darling, 1960; lead singer The Brothers Grim, 1965-68; featured act with Charlie Rich; mem. J.P. Sloane & Co. group, 1973-78; albums include Solid Gold; co-author (with dau. Shannon Sloane) You Can Be a Virgin Again (Execellence in Media Angel award, 2007), The Christian Counselor's Guide for Restoring Virginity, 2007; radio host, What in the World!; tv and radio prodr. Recipient Excellence in Media Angel awards for Outstanding TV Prodr., Outstanding Male Vocalist and Outstanding Music Video, Medal of Merit, Pres. Ronald Reagan; named Hon. Sheriff, L.A. County, Hon. Ky. Col., Hon. Lt. Gov. State of Ind., Hon. Citizen, Tulsa, Met. Nashville, 22d Internat. Angel award best multiple character voices, 1999, others; nominee Cleo award, 1980; key to cities Nashville and New Orleans, others. Mem.: Nat. Scholars Honor Soc. (life). Office: Angeles Crest Productions Ste 407 2219 E Thousand Oaks Blvd Thousand Oaks CA 91362-2930 Business E-Mail: jp@jpsloane.com.

SLOANE, NEIL JAMES ALEXANDER, mathematician, researcher; b. Beaumaris, Wales, Oct. 10, 1939; came to U.S., 1961; s. Charles Ronald and Jessie (Robinson) S.; m. Susanna Stevens Cuyler, Mar. 8, 1980. BA with honors, U. Melbourne, Australia, 1959, BEE, 1960; MS, Cornell U., 1964, PhD, 1967. Asst. prof. Cornell U., Ithaca, NY, 1967-69; mem. tech. staff AT&T Bell Labs., Murray Hill, NJ, 1969-96; prin. mem. tech. staff AT&T Rsch. Labs, 1996—, fellow, 1998. Author: Handbook of Integer Sequences, 1973; co-author: (with F.J. MacWilliams) Theory of Error-Correcting Codes, 1977, (with J.H. Conway) Sphere-Packings, Lattices and Groups, 1988, 32d edit., 1998, (with A.D. Wyner) Claude Elwood Shannon:Collected Papers, 1993, (with S. Plouffe) Encyclopedia of Integer Sequences, 1995, (with A.S. Hedayat and J. Stufken) Orthogonal Arrays, 1999, (with P. Nick) Rock Climbing New Jersey, 2000, (with G. Nebe and E.M. Rains) Self-Dual Codes and Invariant Theory, 2006. Fellow IEEE (editor in chief Trans. Info. Theory jour. 1978-80, Hamming medal 2005); mem. NAE, Math. Assn. Am. (Chauvenet prize 1979, Earle Raymond Hedrick lectr. 1984), Am. Math. Soc., Am. Stat. Assn. Avocation: rock climbing. Office Phone: 973-360-8415. E-mail: njas@research.att.com.

SLOAT, BARBARA FURIN, cell biologist, educator; b. Youngstown, Ohio, Jan. 20, 1942; d. Walter and Mary Helen (Maceyko) Furin; m. John Barry Sloat, Nov. 2, 1968; children: John Andrew, Eric Furin. BS, Denison U., Granville, Ohio, 1963; MS, U. Mich., Ann ARbor, 1966, PhD, 1968. Lic. and cert. emergency med. technician, paramedic. Lab. asst. U. Ghent, Belgium, 1964; tchg. fellow, lectr. U. Mich., Ann Arbor, 1964-66, 68-70, asst. rsch. biologist Mental Health Rsch. Inst., 1972-74, vis. asst. prof., lectr. Ann Arbor and Dearborn, 1974-76, dir. women in sci. Ann Arbor, 1980-84, assoc. dir. honors, 1986-87, rsch. scientist, 1976—, lectr. Residential Coll., 1984—, assoc. Inst. Humanities, 1991—. Author: Laboratory Guide for Zoology, 1979, Summer Internships in the Sciences for High School Women (CASE Silver medal, 1985, Excellence in Edn. award, U. Mich., 1993). Bd. dirs. HIV/AIDS Resource Ctr., Ypsilanti, Mich., 1994—2000, Jewel Heart Health Ctr. and Cmty. Hospice, Ann Arbor, 2003—, Jewel Heart Tibetan Cultural Ctr., Ann Arbor, Mich., 2005—, Jewel Heart Tibetan Buddhist Ctr., 2005—. Recipient Sarah Goddard Power award U. Mich., 1984, Grace Lyon Alumnae award Denison U., 1988; grantee NSF, U.S. Dept. Edn., Warner Lambert Found., others. Mem. AAAS, Am. Soc. Cell Biology, N.Y. Acad. Scis., Nat. Assn. Women Deans, Adminstrs. and Counselors, Assn. for Women in Sci. (councilor 1988-90, pres. elect 1990, mentor of yr. award Detroit area chpt. 1994), Phi Beta Kappa, Sigma Xi. Avocations: hiking, yoga, tibetology. Home: 240 Indian River Pl Ann Arbor MI 48104-1825 Office: U Mich Residential Coll 216 Tyler East Quad Ann Arbor MI 48109-1245 Business E-Mail: bsloat@umich.edu.

SLOAT, RICHARD JOEL, artist; b. Easton, Pa., Sept. 18, 1945; s. Samuel Michael and Florence Elizabeth (Cohen) S.; m. Su-Li Hung, Aug. 18, 1972; 1 child, Benjamin Hung-Hur. BA, U. Pa., 1969; postgrad., Art Students League, NYC, 1971-72. One-man shows include Moon St., Westport, Conn., 1974, Spring Gallery, Taipei, 1979, Martin Summers, N.Y.C., 1987, Wood and Stone Gallery, Taipei, 1990, F.D.R. Gallery, N.Y.C., 1993, The Old Print Shop, N.Y.C., 1995, The Ottendorfer Libr., N.Y.C., 1996, Sonnenshein, Nath & Rosenthal, N.Y.C., 1998, Paul McCarron, N.Y.C., 2001, Howard Salon, Taiwan, 2001, Old Print Shop, 2004, Safe-T-Gallery, N.Y.C., 2005; two-person show Falkenstern Fine Art, N.Y.C., 1990, Port Washington Pub. Libr., 1998, Michael Ingbar Gallery, N.Y.C., 2005; exhibited in group shows at NAD, 1974, 86, 88, 94, 1999, 2000, 03, 04, 05, 07, Taipei Mus., 1976, Terry/Chassman, N.Y.C., 1990, Blum Helman Warehouse, N.Y.C., 1989, Fine Arts Assn., Hanoi, 1991, Curtiba Print Mus., Brazil, 1992, Michael Ingbar Gallery, N.Y.C., 1993, 94, 96, 97, 98, 2000, 01, 05, 06, Duxbury (Mass.) Mus., 1994, 97, 2004, Paul McCarron Gallery, N.Y.C., 1994, 2004, Child's Gallery, Boston, 1994, Br. Consulate, N.Y.C., 1995, Mus. Fine Art, Springfield, Mass., 1995, Kanagawa Prefectural Gallery, Japan, 1995, 97, Roopankar Mus. Fine Arts, India, 1995, Kala Inst., Calif., 1996, Frederick Baker, Chgo., 1996, Fed. Hall, N.Y.C., 1996, N.Y. Transit Mus., N.Y.C., 1997, 2003, Mass. Coll. Art, Boston, 1997, Boston U., 2001, 03, 07, Newark Pub. Libr., 1997, 2000, Daniel Peretz Gallery, N.Y.C., 1997, The Old Print Shop, 1998, 2001, 03, 04, 05, 07, Krasdale Gallery, N.Y.C., 1998, Housatonic Mus. Art, Conn., 1998, Macau Mus. Art, 2000, Albrecht-Kemper Mus. Art, Mo., 2000, Springfield Art Mus., 2001, 05, Mus. Modern Art, N.Y.C., 2002, Mus. City N.Y., 1982, 2002, N.Y. Hist. Soc., N.Y.C., 2002, 04, Susan Teller Gallery, 2004, UBS Paine Weber Art Gallery, 2002, NobleMaritime Collection, 2006, Hollar Soc., Prague, 2006, Graphic Studio Gallery, Dublin, 2006; group shows inlcude AFP Gallery, N.Y.C., 2006, Noble Maritime Collection, S.I., N.Y., 2006, ICPNY, Boston U., 2007; represented in permanent collections Mus. City of N.Y., N.Y. Pub. Libr., Taipei Mus., Printmaking Workshop, N.Y.C., Fogg Mus., Cambridge, Mass., Nat. Mus. Fine Art, Hanoi, Boston Pub. Libr., Davison Art Ctr., Middletown, Conn., Israel Mus., Jerusalem, Brit. Mus., London, Libr. of Congress, Washington, Portland (Oreg.) Art Mus.; author: Journey of Faces, 1985, Mythic City and Friends. Recipient 1st Presbyn. Ch. award Washington Square Art Show, N.Y.C., 1976, Leo Meissner prize NAD, 1986, 94, Annual prize Audubon Artists, 1974, 96, 97, 98, 99, 2001, 02, Cash award Springfield Mus., 2005. Mem. Alliance Figurative Artists (program dir. 1982-85), Print Consortium, Printmaking Workshop, Boston Printmakers, Soc. Am. Graphic Artists (coun. 1995—2007, v.p. 1999-2002, pres. 2003-06), Fedn. Modern Painters and Sculptors, Nat. Acad. Design (coun. 2006—, rec. sec. 2006—). Jewish. Avocations: bird watching, travel. Home: 170 2nd Ave 7B New York NY 10003-5754 Studio: 27 Essex St Apt 5A New York NY 10002-4662

SLOBOZHANIN, LEV ARKADIEVICH, fluid mechanics engineer, researcher; b. Nylga, Russia, Sept. 1, 1941; arrived in US, 1995; s. Arkadii Alexandrovich and Iraida Stepanovna (Vlasova) S.; divorced; children: Andrei L., Darya L. Degree in mech. engring. with honors, Kharkov Aviation Inst., Ukraine, 1963; PhD in Physics and Math., Inst. for Low Temperature Physics and Engring., Kharkov, 1968; cert. sr. rsch. scientist, Acad. Scis. of Ukraine, 1975; DSc in Physics and Math., Lavrentyev Inst. Hydrodynamics, Novosibirsk, Russia, 1989. Engr. B. Verkin Inst. Low Temperature Physics and Engring. Nat. Acad. Scis. of Ukraine, Kharkov, 1963-66, sr. engr., 1966-69, jr. scientist, 1969-71, sr. scientist, 1971-89, leading scientist, 1989-98. Sr. tchr. Kharkov Aviation Inst., 1969—71, prof., 1989—90; vis. prof. Madrid Poly. U., 1993—94; vis. scholar U. Ala., Huntsville, 1995—2002; vis. rschr. Case Western Res. U., Cleve., 1999—2002, prin. rschr., 2002—. Co-author: Fluid Mechanics of Weightlessness, 1976, Low-Gravity Fluid Mechanics, 1987, Solution Methods for Fluid Mechanics Problems Under Weightlessness Conditions, 1992; contbr. articles to profl. jours. Chmn. trade union com. B. Verkin Inst. for Low Temperature Physics and Engring., 1986-89. Mem.: Am. Phys. Soc. Office: Case Western Res U 305 Olin Bldg 10900 Euclid Ave Cleveland OH 44106-7222 Office Phone: 216-368-2984. Business E-Mail: lion@mae.cwru.edu.

SLOCOMBE, WALTER BECKER, lawyer, former federal official; b. Albuquerque, Sept. 23, 1941; m. Ellen Seidman; children: Sarah Cody, Merrin Hayes, Benjamin William. BA, Princeton U., 1963; Rhodes scholar, Balliol Coll., Oxford U., 1963-65; LL.B., Harvard U., 1968. Bar: D.C. 1970. Law clk. to Justice Abe Fortas, US Supreme Ct., Washington, 1968-69; mem. staff Nat. Security Coun., 1969-70; rsch. assoc. Internat. Inst. Strategic Studies, London, 1970-71; assoc. Caplin & Drysdale, Washington, 1971—74, mem., 1974-76, 81-93, 2001—03, 2003—; prin. dep. asst. sec. for internat. security affairs US Dept Def., Washington, 1977—79, dep. under-sec. for policy planning, 1979-81, prin. dep. under-sec. for policy, 1993-94, under-sec. for policy, 1994—2001; sr. advisor for nat. def. Coalition Provisional Authority, Baghdad, Iraq, 2003. Dir. US Dept. Def. Task Force on Strategic Arms Limitation Talks II (SALT II), 1977—81; mem. Commn. on the Intelligence Capabilities of the US Regarding Weapons of Mass Destruction, 2004. Rhodes scholar, 1963-65; recipient Disting. Pub. Svc. medal, 1981, 85, 97, 2001, 04, Joseph Kruzel award for Disting. Svc. in the Pursuit of Peace, 2000. Mem. ACLU, Coun. Fgn. Rels., Internat. Inst. Strategic Studies. Democrat. Office: Caplin & Drysdale 1 Thomas Cir Washington DC 20005 Office Phone: 202-862-5060. Business E-Mail: wbs@capdale.com.

SLOCUM, DONALD WARREN, chemist, researcher; m. Laurel Hopper, 1990 (dec. May 1997); children from previous marriage: Warren, Matthew. BS in Chemistry, BA in English, U. Rochester; PhD in Chemistry, NYU, 1963. Postdoctoral rsch. assoc. Duke U., Durham, NC, 1963—64; asst. prof. chemistry Carnegie Inst. Tech., Pitts., 1964—65; from asst. to assoc. prof. chemistry So. Ill. U., Carbondale, 1965—72, prof., 1972—81, adj. prof., 1981—84; program dir. chem. dynamics sect., chemistry divsn. NSF, Washington, 1984—85; program leader divsn. ednl. programs, sr. scientist chem. tech. divsn. Argonne Nat. Lab., Ill., 1985—90; head dept. chemistry We. Ky. U., Bowling Green, 1990—95, prof. chemistry, 1995—2005, rsch. prof. chemistry emeritus, 2005—. Sr. scientist Gulf R&D Co., Pitts., 1980-82; vis. prof. U. Ill., 1970, U. Bristol, Eng., 1973, U. Cin., 1976; vis. fellow U. Bristol, 1972; vis. lectr. Carnegie-Mellon U., 1983-84, U. Pitts., 1983-84; organizer symposia on organometallic chemistry and catalysis; bd. dir. Ctrl. States Univs., Inc., 1986-88, Arts at Argonne, 1988-90; mem. nat. organizing com. XV Internat. Conf. on Organometallic Chemistry Wayne State U., Detroit, 1990; mem. internat. adv. bd. XV Internat. Conf. on Organometallic Chemistry, Warsaw, 1992; mem. NSF/EPSCoR subcom., Ky., 1993-94; mem. coun. on undergrad. rsch. Instnl. Liaison Rep. to We. Ky. U., 1995-2005; cons. in field. Co-editor: Advances in Chemistry Series of Am. Chem. Soc., Vol. 230, 1992, Methane and Alkane Activation (Plenum), 1995; mem. editl. bd. Synthesis and Reactivity in Inorganic, Metal-Organic and Nano-Metal Chemistry, 1971—, Natural Product Rsch., 2006—; regional editor Letters in Organic Chemistry, 2004-05, mem. editl. bd., 2005—; contbr. over 80 articles to profl. jours., chpts. to books Recipient Rsch./Creativity award Ogden Coll. of Sci., Tech. and Health, We. Ky. U., 1996, Sci. award honoring Brian Andreen, Cottrell Coll. Sci., 1999. Mem. Am. Chem. Soc. (sec. gen. elect catalysis and surface sci. secretariat 1992, sec. gen. 1993, organic divsn. rep. to catalysis and surface sci. secretariat, 1993-98, co-chmn. symposium, San Diego, 1994), Chem. Soc. Gt. Britain, Catalysis Soc., Bowling Green Chamber Singers, Sigma Xi. Avocations: music, literature, sports. Office: Western Ky U Dept Chemistry Bowling Green KY 42101 Office Phone: 270-745-5239. Business E-Mail: donald.slocum@wku.edu.

SLOCUM, ROBERT BIGNEY, retired librarian; b. Brockton, Mass., Apr. 6, 1922; s. George Weeden and Florence Alice (Heustis) S.; m. Christine Stanfield, Aug. 23, 1953; children: Robert Stanfield, Kathryn Slocum Goodwin. BA, Boston U., 1946; MA, Columbia U., 1947; BSLS, Simmons Coll., 1949. Libr. intern Libr. of Congress, Washington, 1949-50; asst. to dir. librs. Simmons Coll., Boston, 1950-51; libr. cataloger, instr. U. Ill. Libr., Urbana, 1951-54; assoc. catalog libr. Cornell U. Libr., Ithaca, N.Y., 1954-88. Author: Sample Catalog Cards, 1962, Biographical Dictionaries and Related Works, 1967-78, 2d edit., 1986, Sample Cataloging Forms, 1968, rev. edit., 1980; editor Manual of Cataloging Procedures, 1959, rev. edit., 1969, New England in Fiction, 1994; contbr. articles to profl. jours. Active Am. for Dem. Action, Pub. Citizen, Am. Farmland Trust, steering bd. Cornell U. Retirees Vols. in Svc.; co-chmn. Dryden Bicentennial Com. With U.S. Army, 1942-45, ETO. Mem.: AARP, ALA, AAUP, Cornell U. Libr. Assoc., Newark Valley Hist. Soc., N.Y. State Hist. Assn., Libr. Congress Assoc., Dryden Hist. Soc., Am. Hist. Assn. (founder Nat. History Ctr.), Peace Action, Common Cause, Wilson Ctr. Assoc., Drake Group, Cornell Assn. Profs. Emeriti, Smithsonian Assoc. Presbyterian. Avocations: hiking, movies, literature. Home: 92 W Main St Dryden NY 13053-9706 Personal E-mail: rbs8@cornell.edu.

SLOCUM, ROSEMARIE, physician services consultant, recruiter; b. Port Arthur, Tex., Dec. 19, 1948; d. Edly and Ella (McNeely) Raccard; m. James Rubenstein; 1 child from previous marriage, Blair Ashton Slocum. BS in Secondary Edn., La. State U., Baton Rouge, 1971; MA in Bus. Comm., Jones Internat. U., Englewood, Colo., 1999. Cert. tchr. La. Edn. specialist La. Dept. Occupl. Stds., Baton Rouge, 1971—74; account exec. UARCO, Inc., 1974—77; owner, broker Rosemarie Slocum Real Estate, 1977—85; physician recruiter MSI, New Orleans, 1985—86; assoc. dir. physician recruitment Physician Svcs. Cons., Fairfax, Va., 1986-88; spl. cons. Caswell/Winters Physician Search Cons., Milw., 1988—89; v.p. U.S. Med. Search, Inc. subs. of Caswell/Winters, 1988—89; dir. physician recruitment/mktg. East Range Clinics, Ltd., Virginia, Minn., 1989—91; pres. RSI Physician Svcs. Cons., Virginia, 1991—96, Mpls., 1996—. Office: RSI Physician Svcs Cons 3622 W 44th St Minneapolis MN 55410-1366 Office Phone: 612-703-0410. Personal E-mail: rsrsi@earthlink.net.

SLOMAN, MARVIN SHERK, lawyer; b. Fort Worth, Apr. 17, 1925; s. Richard Jack and Lucy Janette (Sherk) S.; m. Margaret Jane Dinwiddie, Apr. 11, 1953; children: Lucy Carter, Richard Dinwiddie. AB, U. Tex., Austin, 1948, LLB with honors, 1950. Bar: Tex. 1950, N.Y. 1951. Assoc. Sullivan & Cromwell, NYC, 1950-56, Carrington, Coleman, Sloman & Blumenthal LLP and predecessors, Dallas, 1956-60, ptnr., 1960-97; sr. counsel, 1998—. Office: Carrington Coleman Sloman & Blumenthal LLP 901 Main St Ste 5500 Dallas TX 75202-3767

SLOMANSKI-WARD, PATRICIA ANN, minister; b. Wilmington, NC, Mar. 6, 1951; d. Robert Homer and Annie Grace Parker; m. Henry Slomanski (dec.); children: Randall Edward Slomanski, Patricia Grace Slomanski. BA in Music, U. NC, Wilmington, 1992; MA in Christian Edn., Presbyn. Sch. Christian Edn., Richmond, Va., 1995; MDiv, Union Theol. Sem., Richmond, 1998; postgrad., Columbia Theol. Sem., Decatur, Ga., 2006—. Ordained min. Presbyn. Ch., 2002. Tchr. New Hanover HS, Wilmington, NC, 1993—94; dir. adult ministries St. Giles' Presbyn. Ch., Richmond, 1998—2000; supply pastor Louisa Presbyn. Ch., Va., 2000, Westminster Presbyn. Ch., Richmond, 2001, Milford Presbyn. Ch., Va., 2002, Genito Presbyn. Ch., Powhatan, Va., 2005—06; mem. small ch., new ch. devel. com. Salem Presbytery, 2007; pastor Ashland Presbyn. Ch., Va., 2002—04; min. Hill and Pine Ridge Presbyn. Chs., 2006—. Chaplain Hermitage United Meth. Retirement Home, 2005; supply ch. organist, pianist; mem. nurturing congregations com. Presbytery of James, 2002, 05. Sunday sch. tchr. Gayton Kirk, Richmond, 1996; organist, choirmaster Grace United Meth. Ch., Wilmington, 1973—74; Sunday sch. tchr. Westminster Presbyn. Ch., Richmond, 1993, Three Chopt Presbyn. Ch., Richmond, 1997; pianist, organist Winter Pk. Bapt. Ch., Wilmington, NC, 1993. A.J. Fletcher Music scholar, U. NC, 1990—92. Mem.: Union/PSCE Alumni Assn., Presbyn. Older Adult Ministry Network, Am. Assn. Christian Counselors. Home: 210 Old Westfield Rd PO Box 580 Pilot Mountain NC 27041 Office: Hills Presbyn Ch Hills Presbyterian Church Rd Pilot Mountain NC 27041

SLOMANSON, LLOYD HOWARD, architect, musician, photographer; b. NYC, July 31, 1928; s. Albert Jerome and Dorothea (Jacobson) S.; m. Joan Barbara Kanel; children: Peter, Eric. BArch, Syracuse U., 1949. Registered architect, 18 states including N.Y. and N.J.; NCARB; registered profl. planner, N.J. Archtl. draftsman Rich & Conn Architects, Bklyn., 1949-50; project architect Fordyce & Hamby/Raymond Loewy, NYC, 1951-53; project architect, assoc. ptnr. Serge P. Petroff, Architect, NYC, 1953-58; project dir. Robert W. Hegardt, Architect, NYC, 1959-60; project architect, ptnr. Fordyce & Hamby Assocs., NYC, 1960-67; ptnr. Fordyce, Hamby & Kennerly, NYC, 1967-69, Hamby, Kennerly & Slomanson, NYC, 1969-72, Kennerly, Slomanson & Smith, NYC, 1972-81; mng. ptnr. Slomanson, Smith & Barresi, NYC, 1981-99; pvt. practice, 1999—. Arbitrator Am. Arbitration Assn. and NASD Dispute Resolution, N.Y.C. Author articles. Served with U.S. Army, 1950-51. Recipient 1st prize for design S.I. C. of C., 1967, 84. Mem. AIA, N.Y. Soc. Architects (Store of Yr. award 1985, Design award 1993), N.Y. State Assn. Architects, Bldg. Ofcls. Conf. Am., Univ. Club, The Players. Avocations: music, photography. Office: 137 W 78th St New York NY 10024-6702 Home Phone: 212-724-8451; Office Phone: 917-441-0067. Personal E-mail: woodpics@aol.com.

SLONAKER, NORMAN DALE, lawyer; b. Havre, Mont., Sept. 16, 1940; s. Frederick and Agnes (Monson) S.; m. Helen Bogumil, Aug. 29, 1964. BS, U. Wash., Seattle, 1962; LLM, Harvard U., 1965. Bar: NY 1966. Assoc. Sidley Austin LLP, NYC, 1965—72, ptnr., 1973—. Office Phone: 212-839-5356. Business E-Mail: nslonaker@sidley.com.

SLONE, SANDI, artist; b. Boston, Oct. 1, 1939; d. Louis and Ida (Spind) Sudikoff; children: Erric Solomon, Jon Solomon. Student, Boston Mus. Fine Arts Sch., 1970-73; BA magna cum laude, Wellesley Coll., 1974. Sr. grad. painting faculty Boston Mus. Fine Arts Sch./Tufts U., 1975—; instr. grad. program Sch. Visual Art, NYC, 1989-90; lectr. painting Harvard U., Cambridge, Mass., 1982; artist-in-residence City Hall, Barcelona, 1987, 1989; NY Artists resident Santa Fe Art Inst., 2002. Vis. artist Triangle Artists Workshop, NY, 1982, 87, 90; co-founder, dir. Art/Omi Internat. Artists Found., NYC, 1992—; bd. dirs. The Fields Sculpture Pk. and ART OMI, 1991-. One-woman shows include ICA, Boston, 1977, Harcus Krakow Gallery, Boston, 1978, 79, 80, 82, 84, 86, Acquavella Contemporary Art, N.Y., 1977, 79, 80, 82, 84, Stephen Rosenberg Gallery, N.Y., 1988, Levinson Kane Gallery, Boston, 1989, Smith Jariwala Gallery, London, 1990, Jersey City Mus., 1996, The Artists Mus., Lodz, Poland, 1997, Cristinerose Gallery, N.Y.C., 1999, Savage Gallery, Portland, Oreg., 2001, Art Resources Transfer, NYC, 2002, The Santa Fe Art Inst., N.Mex., 2002, The Tower Gallery, Hong Kong, 2004; exhibited in group shows at Mus. Fine Arts, Boston, 1977, Corcoran Gallery of Art 35th Biennial, Washington, 1977, Edmonton Art Mus., 1977, 85, Hayden Gallery MIT, Cambridge, Mass., 1978, New Generation Andre Emmerich Gallery, N.Y., 1980-81, Am. Ctr., Paris, 1980-81, Amerika Haus, Berlin, 1980-81, Carpenter Ctr., Harvard U., Ctr. de la Cultura Contemporania, Barcelona, 1987, Federated Union of Black Artists, Johannesburg, South Africa, 1989, Jan Weiss Gallery, N.Y., 1990, Olympia Internat. Art Fairs, London, 1991, Gallery Korea, N.Y., 1992, Klarfeld Perry Gallery, N.Y., 1994, Out of the Blue Gallery, Edinburgh, Scotland, 1994, Gallery One, Toronto, 1996, Fine Arts Ctr., U. R.I., Kingston, 1996, Crieger Dane Gallery, Boston, 1996, Visual Arts Gallery, N.Y., 1997, TransHudson Gallery, N.Y., 1997, Butler Inst. of Am. Art, Youngstown, Ohio, 1998, 45th Biennial Corcoran Mus. Art, Washington, 1998, Lombard-Freid Fine Arts, N.Y., 1999, 00, Cyclorama, Boston, 2000, Cristinerose Gallery, N.Y., 2001, Queens U., Toronto, 2001, Art Resources Transfer, 2002, U. Cambridge, Eng., 2003, Art in Gen., NYC, 2004, Savage Gallery, Portland, Oreg., 2004, The Transformer Rm. Queens U. Belfast, Ireland, 2006, Dashanzi Int. Art Festival, Beijing, 2006, Queen's U. Art Festival, Belfast, Ireland, 2006, others; represented in permanent collections Mus. Modern Art, N.Y.C., Mus. Contemporary Art, Barcelona, Mus. Fine Arts, Boston, Hirshhorn Mus., Washington, Corcoran Gallery & Mus. Art, Washington. Mus. Fine Arts Boston fellow, 1977, 81; Ford Found. grantee, 1979. Studio: 13 Worth St New York NY 10013-2922 E-mail: sslone@rcn.com.

SLOOP, JOSEPH C., chemistry professor; m. Lisa Sloop; 1 child, Joseph D. BS, Davidson Coll., 1983; PhD, NCSU, Raleigh, 2000—03. Chem. officer 7th SFG(A), Ft. Bragg, NC, 1983—87; asst. prof. USMA, W.Point, NY, 1990—93; comdr./staff officer 10th Inf. Rgt., Ft. Leonard Wood, Mo., 1993—96; chem. surety officer USACAP, Johnston Atoll, 1996—97; chem. officer 101st ABN Divsn., Ft. Campbell, Ky., 1998—2000; assoc. prof. USMA, W. Point, NY, 2003—. Contbr. articles to profl. jours. Ltc US Army, 1983—, Chem. Corps. Mem.: Am. Chem. Soc. (assoc.), Gamma Sigma Epsilon (assoc.; faculty sponsor), Phi Lambda Upsilon (life), Phi Kappa Phi (life).

SLOSBERG, MIKE, advertising executive; b. Phila., Aug. 29, 1934; s. Sam. M. and Florence (Frank) S.; m. Joan Shidler, Aug. 29, 1957 (div. 1984); children: Sydney Ellen (dec.), Robert Morton; m. Janet Cohn, June 10, 1987. BSBA, U. Denver, 1960. With Young & Rubicam, Inc., NYC, 1960-78; pres. Wunderman, Rocotta & Kline, NYC, 1978-83; exec. v.p., exec. creative dir. Marsteller, Inc., NYC, 1983-84, Bozell Jacobs, Kenyon & Eckhardt, NYC, 1984-86, pres. direct mktg. div., 1986-87; exec. creative dir. Bronner Slosberg Humphrey, Boston, 1987-96; vice chmn., chief creative officer Digitas (formerly Bronner Slosberg Humphrey), Boston, 1996-2000; co-founder Digitas, Inc.; ret., 2003. Author: The August Strangers, 1978, The Hitler Error, 2006. Bd. dirs. Keen Co. Theater, The Atlantic Theater Co. Avocation: writing novels. Personal E-mail: mslosberg@digitas.com.

SLOSBURG-ACKERMAN, JILL ROSE, artist, educator; b. Omaha, Aug. 28, 1948; d. Harold Walter and Marion (Gill) Slosburg; m. James Sloss Ackerman, Aug. 8, 1987; 1 child, Jesse August Ackerman. Diploma, Boston Mus. Sch., 1971; BFA, Tufts U., 1971, MFA, 1983. Prof. art Mass. Coll. Art, Boston, 1973—; vis. artist Cranbrook Acad. Art, Bloomfield, Mich., 1993. One-woman shows include Harcus-Krakow-Rosen-Sonnabend Gallery, Boston, 1978, 1980, Helen Shlien Gallery, 1980, 1982, Cohen Arts Ctr., Tufts U., Medford, Mass., 1982, Van Buren/Brazellon/Cutting Gallery, Cambridge, Mass., 1985, Genovese Gallery, Boston, 1995, Manwaring Gallery Cumings Art Ctr., Conn. Coll., New London, 1995, Rose Art Mus., Brandeis U., Waltham, Mass., 1996, Atrium Gallery, U. Mass., Dartmouth, 1999, Judy Ann Goldman Fine Art, Boston, 1999, 2004, exhibited in group shows at Naga Gallery, 1980, DeCordova Mus., Lincoln, Mass., 1980, Jewett Art Ctr., Wellesley, Mass., 1982, Helen Shlien Gallery, Boston, 1982, Cherry Stone Gallery, Wellfleet, Mass., 1984, Quadrum Gallery, Chestnut Hill, Mass., 1985, Fed. Res. Gallery, Boston, 1986, Danforth Mus., 1986, Conseil de la Sculpture, Montreal, 1986, North Hall Gallery, Boston, 1987, Artists Found. Gallery, 1990, Mus. Decorative Arts, Prague, 1991, Nancy Margolis Gallery, N.Y.C., 1991, Bellevue (Wash.) Art Mus., 1992, Artwear, N.Y., 1992, Genovese Gallery, Albany, N.Y., 1992, Judy Ann Goldman Fine Art, Boston, 1997, 2002, 2007, Mills Gallery, 1997—98, 2004, Boston Mus. Fine Arts, 1999, DeCordova Mus., Lincoln, 2000, Nat. Art Mus. China, Beijing, 2001, Forest Hills Cemetery, Boston, 2002, 2004, Coll. Holy Cross, Worcester, Mass., 2003, Concord Art Assn., Mass., 2003, Fuller Craft Mus., 2005, AASpace Gallery, Maynard, Mass., 2007, N.Am. Costa Rica Cultural Ctr., San Jose, 2007, Trustman Gallery, Simmons Coll., Boston, 2007, Paul Kotula Projects, Ferndale, Mich., 2007, Represented in permanent collections J. L. Brandeis & Sons, Omaha, Mass. Coll. Art, Boston, Boston Pub. Libr., City of Cambridge, Forest Hills Cemetery, Jamaica Plain, Mass.; contbr. articles to profl. jours. Founder, mem. Boston Women's Action Coalition; bd. dirs. Cambridge (Mass.) Multi-Cultural Ctr., Gallery at Green St., 1993—2006. Recipient Patricia Jellinek Hallowell prize for Jewelry, 1984, Disting. Svc. award, Mass. Coll. Art, 1980, 4th prize sterling silver design competition, Nat. Guild Sterling Silversmiths, 1970, Traveling Scholar's award, Sch. Boston Mus. Fine Arts, 1998; fellow, Haystack Mountain Sch. Crafts, 1972, 1976, Nat. Endowment Arts, 1974, 1986, The Artists Found., 1984, Mary Ingraham Bunting Inst., 1985—86; grantee, Artist's Resource Trust, 2001, New Eng. Art Critics Assn., 2004, 2006; Profl. Devel. grantee, Mass. Coll. Art, 1987, Polaroid Corp. Photography grantee, 1988, New Eng. Found. Arts fellow, 1998, Mass. Cultural Coun. Artist's grantee, 1999, 2006. Jewish. Home: 12 Coolidge Hill Rd Cambridge MA 02138-5510 Studio: One Fitchburg St Apt C415 Somerville MA 02143-2128 Office Phone: 617-625-4056. Personal E-mail: jsackerman4@comcast.net.

SLOTKIN, RICHARD SIDNEY, literature educator; b. Bklyn., Nov. 8, 1942; s. Herman and Roselyn B. (Seplowitz) S.; m. Iris F. Shupack, June 23, 1963; 1 child, Joel Elliot. BA, Bklyn. Coll., 1963; PhD, Brown U., 1967; MA (hon.), Wesleyan U., Middletown, Conn., 1976. Mem. faculty Wesleyan U., 1966—, prof. English, 1976—, Olin prof., 1982—, chmn. dept. Am. studies, 1976—. Author: Regeneration Through Violence: The Mythology of the American Frontier, 1600-1860, 1973 (Albert Beveridge award Am. Hist. Assn.), (with J.K. Folsom) So Dreadfull a Judgement: Puritan Responses to King Philip's War, 1675-1677, 1978, The Crater: A Novel of the Civil War, 1980, The Fatal Environment: The Myth of the Frontier in the Age of Industrialization, 1800-1890, The Return of Henry Starr, 1988, Gunfighter Nation: The Myth of the Frontier in Twentieth Century America, 1992 (National Book award nominee, 1993), Abe: A Novel of the Young Lincoln, 2000 (Michael Shaara Civil War Fiction award, 2000), Lost Battalions: The Great War and the Crisis of American Nationality, 2005; and articles. Fellow Center Humanities; fellow Wesleyan U., 1969-70, 74-75, 80—; fellow NEH, 1973-74, Rockefeller Found., 1976-77; recipient Don D. Walker prize AQ; lit. award Little Big Horn Assocs., 1986 Fellow Soc. Am. Historians; mem. AAUP, PEN, Am. Film Inst., Am. Studies Assn. (Mary Turpie prize for tchg. and program-bldg. 1995), Am. Hist. Assn., Orgn. Am. Historians, Authors Guild. Jewish. Office: Wesleyan U Ctr For The Americas Middletown CT 06459-0001

SLOTKIN, TODD, diversified financial services company executive; b. Detroit, Mar. 19, 1953; s. Hugo and Babette Slotkin; m. Judy Scavone, Jan. 30, 1988; children: Matthew, William, Thomas, Peter. BS, Cornell U., 1974, MBA, 1975. With Citicorp, 1975-92, sr. credit officer, 1984-92, head divsn. corp. fin., 1988-90, sr. mng. dir., 1990-92; with MacAndrews & Forbes Holdings, Inc., NYC, 1992—2006, sr. v.p., 1992-98, exec. v.p., 1998—2006, CFO, 1999—2006. Bd. dirs. CBIZ, Inc., Allied Barton. Dir. Food Allergy Initiative, 1999—. Home: 888 Park Ave Apt 12 B New York NY 10021 Office: MacAndrews & Forbes Holding 35 E 62nd St New York NY 10021-8032

SLOTNICK, BARRY IVAN, lawyer; b. NYC, June 18, 1939; s. Meyer and Rose Ann (Hurwitz) S.; m. Donna Miriam Auerbach, July 12, 1968; children: Stuart Philip, Melissa Lynne, Deborah Anne-Shoshana, Melanie Judith-Chani. BA, CCNY, 1959; JD, NYU, 1961. Bar: N.Y. 1961, U.S. Ct. Appeals (2d cir.), U.S. Dist. Ct. (ea. dist., so. dist.) N.Y., U.S. Supreme Ct., 1966. Pvt. practice, NYC, 1966-68; sr. ptnr. Slotnick & Baker, NYC, 1986-94, Slotnick, Shapiro, & Crocker LLP, NYC, 1994—2005; ptnr. Buchanan Ingersoll PC, NYC, 2005—. Adj. prof. in trial practice Cardozo Law Sch., N.Y.C.; judge moot ct. competition NYU and Bklyn. Law Sch. Contbr. articles to profl. jours. Recipient Anti-defamation and Anti-discrimination award Italian Am. Civil Rights League, 1970, Honor plaque Jewish Def. League, 1973, Champion of Youth award B'nai B'rith, 1973, Masada award Jewish Identity Ctr., 1978, AMMY award for best criminal lawyer Am. Lawyer, 1981, Humanitarian award Crime Victims' Polit. Platform, 1982, Award on Behalf of Crime Victims N.Y. Supreme Ct. Officers Assn., 1983, Israel Leadership Peace award Greater Westchester Div., 1984; named Man of Yr. Young Israel Scarsdale, 1982. Mem. N.Y. State Bar Assn. (criminal justice sect.-Outstanding Practitioner award 1987, fed. judiciary com.), Fed. Bar Assn., Inter-Am. Bar Assn., Assn. of Bar of City of N.Y., N.Y. County Lawyer's Assn., Bronx County Bar Assn., P.R. Bar Assn. (assoc. selective svc. examiner 1968-70, spl. dep. atty. gen. 1972). Clubs: Atrium, Downtown Athletic (N.Y.). Republican. Avocation: boating. Office: Buchanan Ingersoll PC Floor 35 One Chase Manhattan Plaza New York NY 10005-1417 *

SLOTSVE, GEORGE AARON, economist, educator, consultant; b. Estevan, Saskatchewan, Can., Sept. 5, 1959; s. Stanley and Mary Elizabeth Slotsve. BA honors, Queen's U., Kingston, 1981; MA in Econ., U. We. Ont., 1982; MS in Econ., U. Wis., 1985, PhD in Econ., 1989. Prof. Vanderbilt U., Nashville, 1988—96, No. Ill. U., DeKlab, 1996—. Vis. prof. Queen's U., Kingston, Ont., Canada, 1992, U. Philippines, Quezon City, 1999. Author: (book) Are We Becoming Two Societies?: Income Polarization and the Myth of the Declining Middle Class in Canada. Office: Northern Ill Univ Dept Econ Zulauf Hall Dekalb IL 60115 Business E-Mail: gslotsve@niu.edu.

SLOTTA, OLIVEANN DAVIS, mathematics educator, consultant; m. James G. Slotta; children: Lizann, James D., Jon, Karen Larson. BA, Hiram Coll., Ohio, 1963; MA, U. Colo., Denver, 1992, PhD, 1999. Lic. profl. tchr. Colo., 1991, cert. tchr. Ohio, 1963, Ohio, 1991. Tchr. secondary math Painesville City Schs., Ohio, 1965—69; facilitator Montreal Cath. Sch. Commn., Montreal, Quebec, 1976—79, Inst. Cultural Affairs, Denver, 1979—83; exec. dir. Cornerstone Ctr., Denver, 1983—85; tchr. math. Denver Pub. Schs., 1986—94, 1998—, math. program specialist, 1994—98. Mem. selection com. Am. Tchr. awards, 1993—2005; charter mem. Internat. Assn. Facilitators, 1988—2000; facilitator town meeting program US and Canada, 1975—80. Named Outstanding Math Tchr., Colo. Coun. Tchrs. Math, 1992; named one of Mirabella's 1000, 1994; recipient Am. Tchr. award, Disney Co., 1991, Alumni award, U. Colo. Denver, 1993, Mayor's award, City of Denver, 2005; fellow, U. Colo. Denver, 1997. Mem.: NEA, Nat. Coun. Tchrs. Math., Colo. Edn. Assn. Avocations: knitting, skiing. Home: 1685 Steele St Denver CO 80206-1780

SLOUJITEL, JACOB BEN, mathematics professor, researcher; b. Moscow, Nov. 1, 1945; arrived in U.S., 1994; s. Ben Leo Sloujitel and Bertha Gilel Sloujitel-Shamis; m. Mira Noah Rudaya, Aug. 31, 1968; children: Kate, Lev. BS, Inst. Elecs. and Mining Mechanics, 1966; MS, Moscow Mining U., 1968; PhD, State Rsch. Inst., 1976. Cons. Acad. Natural Sci., Moscow, 1993—95; prof., chairperson math. Globe Inst. Tech., NYC, 1997—. Adj. prof. physics CUNY, NYC, 1995—98; vis. prof. math. Ramapo Coll., Mahwah, NJ, 1997—, Fairleigh Dickinson U., Madison, 2002—; pres. J and M Smartel Cons. Ctr., Fair Lawn, 1999—. Author: Underground Melting of Sulphur, 1981. Mgr. Soccer Club, Fair Lawn, 1994—. Fellow, State Rsch. Inst., Moscow, 1968—94. Mem.: Math. Assn. Am. Avocations: soccer, ping pong/table tennis, chess. Home: 38 Beverly Ct Fair Lawn NJ 07410 Office: Globe Inst Tech 291 Broadway New York NY 10007 Office Phone: 212-624-1806. Business E-Mail: jsloujit@globe.edu.

SLOVACHEK, DONN RICHARD, obstetrician, gynecologist; s. Charles Edward and Jane Caroline Slovachek; m. Sharon Kay Lantern, Apr. 19, 1985. BA in Psychology, U. Wis., Milw., 1975; MD, U. Wis., Madison, 1979. Diplomate Am. Bd. Ob-Gyn., 1985. Resident ob-gyn. Wright State U., Dayton, Ohio, 1983; chief dept. ob-gyn. Mt. Home AFB Hosp., Idaho, 1983—87; ob-gyn. Medcenter One, Dickinson, ND, 1987—2002, Welborn Clinic, Evansville, Ind., 2002—. Maj. USAF, 1975—85. Fellow: ACS, ACOG. Avocations: motorcycling, scuba diving. Home: 1877 Lares Edge Dr Newburgh IN 47630

SLOVER, WILLIAM LEWIS, lawyer; b. Aug. 15, 1937; AB, Yale U., New Haven, 1959; JD, Columbia U., NY, 1962. Bar: DC. Assoc. Pope, Ballard & Loos, Washington, 1962—65, Hogan & Hartson, Washington, 1966; ptnr. Slover & Loftus, Washington, 1967—. Recipient award, Law Profls., Disting. Svc. award, Assn. Transp., Washington, 1996.

SLOVITER, DOLORES KORMAN, federal judge; b. Phila., Sept. 5, 1932; d. David and Tillie Korman; m. Henry A. Sloviter, Apr. 3, 1969 (dec. May 2003); 1 child, Vikki Amanda. AB in Econs. with distinction, Temple U., 1953, LHD (hon.), 1986; LLB magna cum laude, U. Pa., 1956; LLD (hon.), Dickinson Sch. Law, 1984, U. Richmond, 1992, Widener U., 1994. Bar: Pa. 1957. From assoc. to ptnr. Dilworth, Paxson, Kalish, Kohn & Levy, Phila., 1956—69; mem. Harold E. Kohn PA, Phila., 1969—72; assoc. prof. Temple U. Law Sch., Phila., 1972—74, prof., 1974—79; judge US Ct. Appeals (3rd cir.), Phila., 1979—, chief judge, 1991—98. Bd. overseers U. Pa. Law Sch., 1993—99; bd. trustees Nat. Constitution Ctr., 1998—; mem. Jud. Conf. of US, 1991—98. Chair Pa. Rhodes Scholarship Selection Com., 2003—04; mem. Dist. IV Selection Com., Rhodes Scholarship Competitions, 2005—, chair, 2006—; mem. Pa. Women's Forum, 1996—, Pa. Gov.'s Conf. on Aging, 1976—79, Com. of 70, 1976—79; US com. Bicentennial Constn., 1987—90; com. on Rules of Practice and Procedure, 1990—93; com. on judicial conduct and disability, 2004—; trustee Jewish Publ. Soc. Am., 1983—89; mem. Am. Soc. Internat. Law Jud. Adv. Bd., 2007—. Recipient Juliette Low medal, Girl Scouts Greater Phila., Inc., 1990, Honor award, Girls High Alumnae Assn., 1991, Jud. award, Pa. Bar Assn., 1994, James Wilson award, U. Pa., 1996, Cert. of Honor award, Temple U., 1996; Disting. Fulbright scholar, Chile, 1990. Mem.: ABA, Phila. Bar Assn. (gov. 1976—78, Sandra Day O'Connor award 1997), Am. Judicature Soc. (bd. dirs. 1990—95), Nat. Assn. Women Judges, Am. Law Inst., Fed. Judges Assn., Fed. Bar Assn., Order of Coif (pres. U. Pa. chpt. 1975—77), Phi Beta Kappa. Office: US Ct Appeals 18614 US Courthouse 601 Market St Philadelphia PA 19106-1713 *

SLOYAN, GERARD STEPHEN, theology studies educator, priest; b. NYC, Dec. 13, 1919; s. Jerome James and Marie (Kelley) S. AB, Seton Hall U., 1940; S.T.L., Cath. U. Am., 1944, PhD, 1948; DLitt, Seton Hall U., 1984; HHD, St. Ambrose U., 1995. Ordained priest Roman Cath. Ch., 1944. Asst. pastor in, Trenton, Maple Shade, N.J., 1947-50; mem. faculty Cath. U. Am., Washington, 1950-67, chmn. dept. religion, 1957-67; prof. N.T. studies Temple U., Phila., 1967-90, chmn. dept. religion, 1970-74, 84-86. Disting. lectr. Georgetown U., 1997—; vis. prof. Cath. U. Am., Washington, 1992—, Iowa State U., 1995. English editor: N.T., The New American Bible, 1970; author: Jesus on Trial: A Study of the Gospels, 2d edit., 2006, Historical Atlas of the Religions of the World, 1974, Is Christ the End of the Law?, 1978, Jesus in Focus, 1983, 2d edit., 1993, The Jesus Tradition, 1986, John: "Interpretation" Commentary, 1988, Jesus, Redeemer and Divine Word, 1989, What Are They Saying About John?, 1991, rev. edit., 2006, Walking in the Truth: 1, 2, and 3 John, 1995, The Crucifixion of Jesus, History, Myth, Faith, 1995, Open Catholicism, The Tradition at Its Best, 1997, Holy Week and Easter, 1999, What Men Owe to Women, Men's Voices from World Religions, 2001, Preaching from the Lectionary: An Exegetical Commentary, 2005, Why Jesus Died, 2004. Recipient Pro Ecclesia et Pontifice medal, 1970, Johannes Quasten medal Cath U. Am., 1985, Michael Mathis award Notre Dame Ctr. Pastoral Liturgy, 1994. Mem. AAUP, Cath. Bibl. Assn., Soc. Bibl. Lit., Cath. Theol. Soc. Am. (John Courtney Murray award 1981, pres. 1993-94), Coll. Theology Soc. (pres. 1964-66), Liturg. Conf. (pres. 1962-64, v.p. 1970-71, 75-88, chmn. bd. dirs. 1980-88), N.Am. Acad. Liturgy (Berakah award 1986). Democrat. Personal E-mail: gerard.sloyan@att.net.

SLOYAN, PATRICK JOSEPH, journalist; b. Stamford, Conn., Jan. 11, 1937; s. James Joseph and Annamae (O'Brien) Sloyan; m. Phyllis Hampton, Nov. 19, 1960; children: Nora, Amy, Patrick, John. BS, U. Md., 1963. Reporter Albany (N.Y.) Times-Union, 1957—58, Balt. News Post, 1958—60, UPI, Washington, 1960—69, Hearst News Svc., Washington, 1969—74, Newsday, Washington, 1974—81, bur. chief London, 1981—86, Washington, 1986—88, sr. corr., 1988—2001; assoc. editor Digital Journalist.org, 2002—. Dir. Fund for Investigative Journalism, Washington, 1987—. With US Army, 1955—57. Recipient Best Writing award, Am. Soc. Newspaper Editors, 1982, War Reporting award, George Polk Awards, 1992, Pulitzer Prize for internat. reporting, 1992, Raymond Clapper award, 1996; Alicia Patterson Found. fellow, 2000. Mem.: Gridiron Club. Roman Catholic. Avocations: gardening, swimming, tennis. Home: 17115 Simpson Cir Paeonian Springs VA 20129-1735 Personal E-mail: pjs338@yahoo.com.

SLUBERSKI, THOMAS RICHARD, international educator, journalist, theologian; b. Jersey City, Dec. 7, 1939; s. Walter and Anna Louise (Gall) S. BA with honors, Concordia U., St. Louis, 1962; MDiv with high honors, Concordia Sem., St. Louis, 1966; postgrad., U. Vienna, Austria, 1966, U. Erlangen-Nuremberg, Fed. Republic Germany, 1966-68; MA in English Lit., Washington U., 1970; ThD with honors, U. Heidelberg, Fed. Republic Germany, 1973, NYU, 1978. Ordained to ministry Luth. Ch.-Mo. Synod, 1969. Vicar Zion Luth. Ch., Wausau, Wis., 1964-65; asst. to dean chapel., lectr. dept. theology Valparaiso (Ind.) U., 1969-70; prof. English, religion, humanities Concordia Univ. Sys., Bronxville, N.Y., 1972—, Duda Endowed chair in religion, 2000—07; pastor St. Matthew's Luth. Ch., Hastings-on-Hudson, N.Y., 1977-87; exec. dir. Am. Luth. Publicity Bur., 1987-89; guest prof. Luth. U. of Brazil, Canoas, Brazil, 2004—. Rsch. asst., editor Luth. World Fedn., Geneva, 1968—69; coord. 9th and 10th Inter-Luth. forums, 1988—90; bd. dirs. Luth. Soc. Worship, Music and Arts, 1971—73; lectr. U. St. Petersburg, U. Omsk, Merchant Marine Acad., Vladivostok, Russia, U. Khabarovsk, U. Vladivostok, Alexander von Herzen U., Russia; staff Russian-Am. Press Ctr.; warden U.S. Consulate at St. Petersburg; coord. vols. St. Petersburg Goodwill Games, 1994; tchr. sports mktg. Sports Couns. of Singapore, Hong Kong and Kuala Lumpur, Malaysia, 1995; prof. Russian Luth. Sem., 1992—94, Deacon's Tng. Sch., 1992—94; instr., bd. mem. Ben Weider Coll. Bodybldg., St. Petersburg, 1993—94; advisor Internat. Shaping Fedn., 1992—94; mem. exec. bd. 15th Ann. Workshop on Jewish Christian Rels., Stamford, Conn.; bd. dirs. Peterschule, St. Petersburg, 1993—94. Asst. editor Seminarian jour., 1965-66; lit. survey editor, rsch. asst. Luth. World Fedn., Geneva, Switzerland, 1968-69; judge (TV) Emmy's, 1995—; contbr. articles to profl. jours. Juror Am. Film Festival, NYC, 1976-87; mem. nat. faculty of US Sports Acad., Daphne, Ala., 1995—; judge Nat. Physique Com., 1983-87, Russian Fedn., Body Builders, 1992-94, Brazilian Fitness and Body Bldg. Confederation, 2004-. Austrian State scholar, 1966, Bavarian State scholar, 1966-67; World Coun. Chs. fellow, 1967, Nat. Merit scholar, 1958, Luth. World Fedn. scholar, 1967, Deutscher Akademischer Austauschdienst fellow, 1970-72, Ctr. for Creative Persons fellow, 1975, 76; Aid Assn. for Luths. Faculty Study grantee, 1972. Fellow Christian Writers Inst.; mem. Am. Soc. Rio De Janeiro (bd. govs. 2006—), Nat. Acad. TV Arts and Scis., Polish Inst. Arts and Scis., Am. Film Inst., Soc. Arts, Religion and Culture, Salmagundi Club. Home: 529 Bastogne Dr Akron OH 44303-1606 Office: Rua Santo Amaro 29 Gloria Rio deJaneiro Brazil Personal E-mail: sluberski@aol.com.

SLUSAR, LINDA, library and information scientist; MLS, No. Ill. Univ., 1985. Asst. prof. to prof., coord. libr. & info. tech. prog. Coll. of DuPage, Glen Ellyn, Ill., co-founder Soaring to Excellence teleconference prog. Author: (Book & DVD) Creating Your Professional Portfolio; co-author: (Book & VHS prog.) Ranganathan's Five Laws of Library Science. Named one of the Movers & Shakers, Libr. Jour., 2007; recipient Outstanding Supporter of Support Staff award, Libr. Mosaics, 2000. Office: College of DuPage 425 Fawell Blvd Glen Ellyn IL 60137 Office Phone: 630-942-2597. Office Fax: 630-858-8757. Business E-Mail: slusar@cdnet.cod.edu.

SLUSHER, RICHART ELLIOTT, physicist, researcher; b. Higginsville, Mo., May 20, 1938; BS, U. Mo., Rolla, 1960; PhD in Physics, U. Calif., Berkeley, 1965. Mem. tech. staff to dir. quantum info. rsch. Lucent Technologies/Bell Labs., Murray Hill, NJ, 1965—. Co-editor (with Benjamin J. Eggleton): Nonlinear Photonic Crystals, 2002. Recipient Einstein prize for laser sci., 1989. Fellow Am. Phys. Soc. (Arthur L. Schawlow prize 1995), Optical Soc. Am. (Max Born award 2006). Office: Lucent Technologies Bell Labs 600 Mountain Ave New Providence NJ 07974-2008 *

SLUSS, DOROTHY LOUISE, education educator, researcher; b. Hurley, Va., Aug. 02; d. Monroe Irvin and Mildred A. Dotson Justus; m. James Roger Sluss, Sr.; 1 child, James Roger II. BS, U. of Va., 1978; MS (magna cum laude), Va. Tech., 1983, PhD, 1995. Commonwealth of Va. Postgrad. Profl. Cert. Va. State Dept. of Edn., 1983. Elem. tchr. Coeburn Primary and Mid. Schs., Va., 1978—92; adj. prof. Va. Tech., Blacksburg, 1993—94; vis. prof. Emory & Henry Coll., Va., 1994—95; from asst. prof. to assoc. prof. East Tenn. State U., Johnson City, 1995—2001, program coord., 2000—01; assoc. prof., program coord. Clemson (SC) U., 2001—. V.p. Va. Assn. for the Edn. of Young Children, 1994—95; dir. project TIES East Tenn. State U., Johnson City, SC, 1996—2001; panel chair, grants reviewer U.S. Dept. of Edn., Washington, 2000; pres. The Assn. for the Study of Play, 2000—01; adv. bd. Playing for Keeps, Wilmette, Ill., 2003—. Editor (guest editor): National Newsletter; editor: The Association for the Study of Play; contbr. chapters to books; author: Supporting Play: Birth to Age Eight, Effects of Peer Interaction on Play. Clk. of the session, elder Castlewood Presbyn. Ch., Va., 1985—99. Recipient Darden Soc. award, U. of Va. at Wise, 1978, W.D. Richmond award in Edn., 1978; grantee Towards Inclusion in Edn. Project (TIES), U.S. Office of Edn., 1996—2002. Mem.: Nat. Assn. for the Edn. of Young Children, Soc. for Rsch. in Child Devel. (assoc.), Kappa Omicron Nu (treas. 1993—94), Phi Delta Kappa (assoc.; sec. 2002—03), Phi Kappa Phi (assoc.). Office: Clemson U 406 Tillman Hall Clemson SC 29634 Office Phone: 864-656-5099. Personal E-mail: dsluss@charter.net. Business E-Mail: djsluss@clemson.edu.

SLUSSER, EUGENE ALVIN, electronics executive, consultant; b. Denver, Mar. 13, 1922; s. Jesse Alvin and Grace (Carter) S.; m. Anne L. Longley, Oct. 2, 1943; children: Robert, Jon, Carolyn BS Physics, U. Denver, 1947. Registered profl. engr., N.H. Mem. staff Radiation Lab. MIT, Cambridge, 1942—45; project engr. Heiland Rsch. Co., Denver, 1945—47; cons. Gen. Tel. Sys., NYC, 1947—51; project engr. Airborne Inst. Lab., Mineola, NY, 1951—53; v.p. N.E. Electronics Corp., Concord, NH, 1953—58; pres. Aerotronic Assocs., Inc., Contoocook, NH, 1958—84, N.H. Automatic Equipment Corp., Concord, 1962—90, N.H. Realty Corp., Concord, 1990—96; pres., cons. E.A. Slusser & Assocs., Concord, 1996—. Patentee electronics field Chmn. Hopkinton (N.H.) Water Bd., 1962-69, Hopkinton Planning Bd., 1971-77, Hopkinton Precinct Bd. Adjustment, 1977 Mem. Aircraft Owners and Pilots Assn. (cert. pilot), Captiva Island (Fla.) Yacht Club (past commodore), Wharf Rat Club, Anglers Club, Pacific Club (Nantucket, Mass.), Masons (32d degree) Personal E-mail: easlusser@comcast.net.

SLUSSER, ROBERT WYMAN, aerospace transportation executive; b. Mineola, NY, May 10, 1938; s. John Leonard and Margaret McKenzie (Wyman) S.; m. Linda Killeas, Aug. 3, 1968. BS, MIT, 1960; MBA, U. Pa., 1962; ERC, Ft. Belvior Def. Sys. Mgmt. Sch., 1977; AMP, Claremont, 1982. Assoc. adminstr.'s staff NASA Hdqrs., Washington, 1962-65; with Northrop Corp., Hawthorne, Calif., 1965-96; adminstr. Space Labs., 1965-68; mgr. bus. and fin. Warnecke Electron Tubes Co. divsn., Chgo., 1968-71; mgr. bus. adminstrn. YF-17 Program Aircraft Divsn., 1971-75, mgr. adminstrn. F-18/Cobra programs, also mgr. F-18 design to cost program, 1975-79, mgr. engring. adminstrn., 1980-82, acting v.p. engring., 1982, v.p. info. resources, 1983-91, mgr. long range planning, 1991-93, program mgr.-bus. F/A-18E/F program, 1994-96, cons., 1996—. Bd. dirs., CFO So. Calif. Hist. Aviation Found., 1987-90, chmn. bd., pres., 1990-97; treas. Flight Path Learning Ctr. So. Calif., 1996-2001; contracting officer, PDES, 1988-91; dirs. adv. bd. SC Rsch. Authority, 1991-95. Grumman Aircraft Engring. scholar, 1956—60. Fellow AIAA (assoc., membership chmn. L.A. sect. 1996-98); mem. So. Calif. Soc. Info. Mgmt. (mem. exec. com. 1987-91), Northrop Mgmt. Club (bd. dirs. 1992-93, Man of Yr. 1991-92). Avocation: private pilot. Home and Office: 7270 Berry Hill Dr Palos Verdes Peninsula CA 90275-4402

SLUSSER, WILLIAM PETER, investment banker; b. June 20, 1929; s. Eugene and Thelma (Donovan) S.; m. Joanne Eleanor Briggs, June 20, 1953; children: Kathleen E., Martin E., Wendelin M., Caroline E., Sarah A. BA cum laude, Stanford U., 1951; MBA, Harvard U., 1953. Mgr. spl. situations dept. Dean Witter & Co., NYC, 1955-60; ptnr., sr. v.p., mgr. corp. fin. dept. Shields & Co., NYC, 1960—75; sr. v.p. Paine Webber, Inc., NYC, 1975-80; mng. dir., head merger and acquisitions dept., mem. mgmt. com. Blyth Eastman Paine Webber, Inc., NYC, 1980—88; pres. Slusser Assocs., Inc., NYC, 1988—. Bd. dirs. Ampex Corp., Sparton Corp., Magellan Group Ltd., Unigene Labs., Inc. Contbr. articles to profl. jours. Founding stockholder Assoc. Mortgage Cos., Cap Gemini Sogetti; bd. fin. advisors Columbia U. Bus. Sch.; mem. Calif. Senate Commn. on Local Govt. Investments; mem. senate commn. corp. governance, Calif., 1985-95. 1st lt. USAF, 1953—55. Mem. Soc. Calif. Pioneers, Knickerbocker Club, Stanford Assoc., Harvard (N.Y.C.) Club, Lawrence Beach Club, Stanford of N.Y. Club, Alpha Delta Phi (exec. coun. 1956-62, treas. 1961). Home: 901 Lexington Ave New York NY 10021-5924 also: Slusser Ranch Windsor CA 95492 Office: Slusser Assoc Inc 1 Citicorp Ctr Ste 5100 153 E 53d St New York NY 10022-4611

SLUTSKY, KENNETH JOEL, lawyer; b. NYC, Sept. 18, 1953; s. Clement and June (Gross) S.; m. Nancy Ellen Goldfarb, Jan. 15, 1978; children: Rachel, Jason, Jenna. BA summa cum laude, Columbia U., 1975; JD magna cum laude, Harvard U., 1978. Bar: NJ 1978, US Dist. Ct. NJ 1978, US Tax Ct. 1980. Assoc. Lowenstein, Sandler, Brochin, Kohl, Fisher & Boylan, Roseland, N.J., 1978-83; mem. Lowenstein, Sandler, Kohl, Fisher & Boylan, P.A., Roseland, NJ, 1984, Lowenstein Sandler PC, Roseland, NJ. Mem. met. N.J. chpt. Am. Jewish Com., Millburn, Jewish Family Svc. Metrowest N.J., Florham Park. Named NJ Super Lawyer, 2005, Best Lawyers Am. Mem. ABA, NJ State Bar Assn. Office: Lowenstein Sandler PC 65 Livingston Ave Ste 9 Roseland NJ 07068-1725 Office Phone: 973-597-2510. Office Fax: 973-597-2511. E-mail: kslutsky@lowenstein.com.

SLUTSKY, LEONARD ALAN, finance executive, consultant; b. NYC, July 25, 1945; s. Hyman and Ruth (Neuman) S.; m. Sharlene Alexis Farber, Oct. 20, 1968; children: Jacquelyn Anne, Jason Ian, Adam Jeffrey. Student, U. Ariz., 1963-66. Chmn., pres., chief exec. officer Republic Pension Svc. Inc., Melville, N.Y., 1981-83; pres., chief exec. officer Am. Money Svc. Corp., Huntington, N.Y., 1977-97; chmn. bd. Peoples Nat. Bank of Rockland, N.Y., 1983-85, Millbrook Equity Corp., NYC, 1985-86; chmn., chief exec. officer Republic Advisors, Inc., Lake Success, N.Y., 1981-95; chmn. Am. Money Co., Inc., Huntington, 1982-90; pres. Windsor Funding Corp., West Hills, N.Y., 1987-90. Bd. dirs. Triad Temporary Agy., Inc., Triad Employee Leasing LLC. Sgt. N.Y. N.G., 1966-71. Recipient Disting. Service award Rockland County, 1984, Com. Service award Dist. Atty. Rockland, 1984, Distinguished Service award 6th Congl. Dist., Washington, 1984, Yeshiva U., N.Y.C., 1984. Mem. Am. Soc. C.L.U., KP. Republican. Jewish. Avocations: swimming, fishing, camping, golf. Home: 20 Equestrian Ct Huntington NY 11743-6636 Office: 790 Management Co 790 New York Ave Huntington NY 11743-4499 Office Phone: 631-424-2400. E-mail: americanmoneyco@aol.com.

SLUTSKY, LORIE A(NN), foundation executive; b. NYC, Jan. 5, 1953; d. Edward and Adele (Moskowitz) S. BA, Colgate U., 1975; MA in Urban Policy Analysis, New Sch. Social Rsch., NYC, 1977. Program officer NY Cmty. Trust, NYC, 1977-83, v.p., 1983-87, exec. v.p., 1987-89, pres., CEO, 1990—. Former mem. and chmn. bd. Coun. on Founds., Inc., Washington, 1986-95. Trustee emerita, former chmn. budget com. Colgate U., Hamilton, N.Y., 1989-98; former mem. bd. dirs. Found. Ctr., Inc., N.Y.C., L.A. Wallace Fund for Met. Mus. Art, N.Y.C., D. Wallace Fund for Meml. Sloan Kettering, United Way of N.Y.C.; bd. dirs. BoardSource, Alliance Bernstein, AXA Fin.; trustee New Sch. U. Office: NY Community Trust 22d Fl 909 3d Ave New York NY 10022

SLUTZ, PAMELA JO HOWELL, ambassador; b. Chgo., 1949; d. Robert and Rose Slutz; m. Ronald Deutch; 2 children. B in Politics, Hollins U., 1970; M in Asian Studies and Polit. Sci., U. Hawaii, 1972. Office of Korean Affairs Bur. East Asian and Pacific Affairs US Dept. of State (FSO), 1981—82, Office of China and Mongolia Affairs Bur. East Asian and Pacific Affairs, 1995—97, Office of East Asian and Pacific Regional Security and Policy Planning Bur. East Asian and Pacific Affairs, 1997—99, amb., fgn. svc. officer Shanghai, 1991—94, Am. Inst. Taiwan, 2001—03; US amb. to Mongolia Dept. State, 2003—06. Mem. U.S. Del. to Nuc. and Space Talks with Russia, Geneva, 1987—89. Fellow, East West Ctr., 1970—72.

SLY, RIDGE MICHAEL, pediatrician, allergist, immunologist, educator; b. Seattle, Nov. 3, 1933; s. Ridge Joseph and Eva Jean (Ruddell) S.; m. Ann Turner Jennings, June 12, 1957; children: Teresa Ann Perper, Cynthia Marie Schattenfield. AB, Kenyon Coll., Gambier, Ohio, 1956; MD, Washington U., St. Louis, 1960. Diplomate Am. Bd. Pediat., Am. Sub-Bd.

Pediat. Allergy, Am. Bd. Allergy and Immunology. Intern, resident in pediat. St. Louis Children's Hosp, 1960—62; chief resident in pediat. U. Ky. Med. Ctr., Lexington, 1962—63; fellow in allergy and immunology UCLA Med. Ctr., 1965—67; from asst. prof. to prof. pediat. La. State U. Med. Ctr., New Orleans, 1967—78; head sect. allergy and immunology Children's Nat. Med. Ctr., Washington, 1978—; prof. pediat. George Washington U., Washington, 1978—. Author: Textbook of Pediatric Allergy, 1985; mem. editl. bd. Annals of Allergy, Asthma, & Immunology, 1982-98, 99-2002, Jour. Asthma, 1982-93, Clin. Revs. in Allergy, 1982-2001, Pediat. Asthma, Allergy, & Immunology, 1987—; assoc. editor Annals of Allergy, Asthma, & Immunology, 1989-90, editor, 1990-98; contbr. articles to profl. jours. Served to capt. USAF, 1963-65 Recipient La. plaque Am. Lung Assn. of La., 1978 Fellow Am. Acad. Allergy, Asthma & Immunology (chmn. com. on drugs 1981-87), Am. Acad. Pediats. (sect. on allergy com. 1972-75), Am. Coll. Allergy, Asthma, and Immunology (Disting. Fellow award 1993, Bela Schick award 1997, chmn. ethics com. 1997-99); mem. Am. Thoracic Soc., Assn. for Care of Asthma (pres. 1980-81, dir. postgrad. courses 1980—, Peshkin Meml. award 1983), Ctr. for Bioethics and Human Dignity, Phi Beta Kappa. Republican. Baptist. Avocations: music, piano, organ. Office: Children's Nat Med Ctr 111 Michigan Ave NW Washington DC 20010-2970

SLY, WILLIAM S., biochemist, educator; b. East St. Louis, Ill., Oct. 19, 1932; MD, St. Louis U., 1957. Intern, asst. resident ward medicine Barnes Hosp., St. Louis, 1957-59; clin. assoc. nat. heart inst. NIH, Bethesda, Md., 1959-63, rsch. biochemist, 1959-63; dir. divsn. med. genetics, dept. medicine and pediatrics, sch. medicine Washington U., St. Louis, 1964-84, from asst. prof. to prof. medicine, 1964-78, from asst. prof. to prof. pediatrics, 1967-78, prof. pediatrics, medicine and genetics, 1978-84; prof. biochemistry and pediat. St. Louis U., 1984—, chmn. Edward A. Doisy dept. biochemistry-molecular biology, 1984—. Vis. physician Nat. Heart Inst., 1961-63, pediatric genetics clinic U. Wis., Madison, 1963-64; Am. Cancer Soc. fellow lab. enzymol Nat. Ctr. Sci. Rsch., Gif-sur-Yvette, France, 1963, dept. biochemistry and genetics U. Wis., 1963-64; attending physician St. Louis County Hosp., Mo., 1964-84; asst. physician Barnes Hosp., St. Louis, 1964-84, St. Louis Children's Hosp., 1967-84; genetics cons. Homer G. Philips Hosp., St. Louis, 1969-81; mem. genetics study sect. divsn. rsch. grants NIH, 1971-75; mem. active staff Cardinal Glennon Children's Hosp., St. Louis, 1984—; mem. med. adv. bd. Howard Hughes Med. Inst., 1989-92. Recipient Merit award NIH, 1988; elected to Nat. Acad. Sci., 1989; named Passano Found. laureate, 1991. Mem. NAS, AMA, AAAS, Am. Soc. Human Genetics (mem. steering com. human cell biology program 1971-73, com. genetic counseling 1972-76); Am. Soc. Clin. Investigation, Am. Chem. Soc., Genetics Soc. Am., Am. Soc. Microbiology, Soc. Pediatric Rsch., Sigma Xi. Achievements include research on lysosomal enzyme replacement in storage diseases, inherited carbonic anhydrase deficiencies, and hereditary hemochromatosis. Office: St Louis U Med Sch Dept Biochemistry 1402 S Grand Blvd Saint Louis MO 63104-1004 Business E-Mail: slyws@slu.edu.

SMAGALSKI, CAROLYN M., publishing executive, webmaster, director; b. Phila., Aug. 28, 1952; d. Raymond L and Mary K Hanisco; children: Michael M, Tyler A. BA Cum Laude, Temple U., Philadelphia, 1971—75. Lic. private pilot SEL with IFR rating and Complex Aircraft Rating US Dept. of Transp./Fed. Aviation Adminstrn., 1996. Account mgr. Brown Printing Co., East Greenville, Pa., 1996—; exec. dir., author, webmaster, internetwork marketer CQ Web Wide LLC, Harleysville, Pa., 2002—. Beer and brewing advisor Gluten Free Beer Festival U.K., 2006—. Author (editor): (website mag.) Beer and Brewing, 2004—; creator Beer Fox, 2004, guest appearance Beer Fox/Beer Chef, Beer Radio. Beer and brewing advisor Gluten Free Beer Festival, England, 2006—. Mem.: Better Internet Bur., Internat. Assn. Home Bus. Entrepreneurs, Aircraft Owners & Pilot's Assn. Avocations: information technology, aviation, psychology of brain & socio-emotional challenges, gourmet cooking, public relations & travel. Home: 805 Continental Drive Harleysville PA 19438 Office: CQ Web Wide LLC 805 Continental Drive Harleysville PA 19438 Office Phone: 215-541-2723. Personal E-mail: carolsmagalski@comcast.net. E-mail: cs1@cqwebwide.com.

SMAGNER, JOHN PATRICK, applied behavior analyst, educator; b. Jamestown, NY, July 27, 1974; s. Linda Smagner. B, Edinboro U., Pa., 1996; MA, U. Chgo., 1998; M, PhD, U. Kans., Lawrence, 2003. Applied behavior analyst, Chgo., 2003—. Adj. prof. U. Chgo., 2004—, Chgo. Sch. for Profl. Psychology, 2004—. Author: Research on Social Work Practice, Behavioral Interventions. Mem.: Assn. for Behavior Analysis. Home: 4677 N Virginia Ave Chicago IL 60625 Office: U Chgo 969 E 60th St Chicago IL 60637 Home Phone: 312-520-4657. Personal E-mail: johnsmag@uchicago.edu.

SMAGORINSKY, PETER, education educator; b. Princeton, NJ, Oct. 24, 1952; s. Joseph and Margaret (Knoepfel) Smagorinsky; m. Anne O'Gorman, July 10, 1982 (dec. Aug. 1982); m. Jane E. Farrell, Oct. 12, 1985; children: Alysha, David. BA, Kenyon Coll., 1974; MA in Tchg., U. Chgo., 1977, PhD, 1989. English tchr. Westmont (Ill.) H.S., 1977-78, Barrington (Ill.) H.S., 1978-85, Oak Park (Ill.) and River Forest H.S., 1985-90; asst. prof. U. Okla., Norman, 1990-95, assoc. prof., 1995-98, U. Ga., Athens, 1998-2001, prof., 2001—. Author: Standards in Practice, 1996; co-author: How English Teachers Get Taught, 1995, The Language of Interpretation, 1995; co-editor: Rsch. Tchg. English, 1996—2003, Reading Rsch. Quar. Rev. Ednl. Rsch., Am. Jour. Edn., Written Comm., Reading and Writing Quar. Recipient Steve Cahir award for Rsch. in Writing, Am. Ednl. Rsch. Assn., 1991, Raymond B. Cattell award for Disting. Programmatic Rsch., 1999. Mem.: Nat. Coun. Tchrs. English (chair standing com. rsch. 1995—96, co-chair assembly rsch. 1996, trustee rsch. found. 1997—2003, chair 2000—03, pres. nat. conf. rsch. lang. and literacy 2001, English Jour. Writing award 1989, Edwin M. Hopkins award 2000, Janet Emig award 2003). Home: 121 Inverness Rd Athens GA 30606 Office: U Ga 125 Aderhold Hall Athens GA 30602 Business E-Mail: smago@uga.edu.

SMAIL, KAREN MARY, physical education educator, consultant; children: Jacob, Abey, Kristen. PhD, U. Ga., Athens, 2003. Lic. teacher Alta., Ont., NY (Provisional). Phys. edn. tchr. Calgary Cath. Sch. Bd., Alberta, Canada, 1998—2000; tchr. U. Ga., Kinesiology Dept., Athens, Ga., 2000—03; asst. prof. Coll. Charleston, SC, 2003—. Office: College of Charleston 66 George St Charleston SC 49424 Business E-Mail: smailk@cofc.edu.

SMAIL, LESLIE ANNE, librarian; b. Pitts., July 25, 1958; d. Laurence Mitchell and Nancy (Fried) S.; m. Eric D. Hunley, July 10, 1998. BA, Christopher Newport Coll., 1980; MSLS, Cath. U., 1982. Libr. intern Tng. and Doctrine Command, Ft. Monroe, Va., 1982-84; libr. Ft. Story (Va.) Libr., 1985-2000; libr. dir. Bryant & Stratton Coll. Libr., Virginia Beach, Va., 2000; libr. Gwinnett County Pub. Libr., Lawrenceville, Ga., 2000—01; contractor retrospective conversion project Tortolita Vet. Svcs., PC, Tucson, 2002—03; reference libr. Davis-Monthan AFB Libr., 2003—04; libr. dir. Bateman Libr., Langley AFB, Va., 2004—. Recipient Exceptional Performance award U.S. Army, Ft. Eustis, Va., 1985-99, Comdr.'s award for civilian svc., 1995, 2000; named Outstanding Program Mgr. TRADOC, Ft. Monroe, 1988-89, Contractor of Yr., First Svcs., 2005. Mem.: Sigma Tau Delta. Avocations: arts and crafts, antiques, gardening, genealogy. Office: Bateman Libr 42 Ash Ave Langley Afb VA 23665 Office Phone: 757-764-2906. Business E-Mail: leslie.smail@langley.af.mail.

SMALDONE, EDWARD MICHAEL, composer; b. Wantagh, NY, Nov. 19, 1956; m. Karen Ajamian, Aug. 5, 1979; children: Laura, Gregory, Julia. BA in Music, Queens Coll., 1978, MA in Music, 1980; PhD in Music, CUNY, 1986. Lectr. SUNY, Purchase, 1986-90; adj. asst. prof. Hofstra U., Hempstead, NY, 1988-90; vis. asst. prof. New Sch. for Social Rsch., NYC, 1988; adminstrv. dir. Speculum Musicae, NYC, 1988-89; artistic dir. Sounds for the Left Bank, Rego Park, NY, 1985-92; asst. prof. Copland Sch. of Music, CUNY, Flushing, 1990-99, assoc. prof., 1994—2005, prof., 2005—; dir. Copland Sch. Music CUNY, Flushing, 2002—. Composer in residence N.Y.C. Pub. Schs., 1994, 95; Carlisle Project Choreographer and Composer Collaboration Commn., 1994; assoc. composer Atlantic Ctr. Arts, 1999, vis. fac. Univ. Coll. Chichester, Eng., 1999, 01. Composer: Two String Quartets, 1980, 86, Dialogue for orch., 1987, Double Duo (flute, clarinet, violin, cello), 1987, Transformational Etudes (solo piano), 1990, Rhapsody for piano and orch., 1992, Suite for violin and piano, 1993, Three Scenes from "The Heartland" for solo piano, 1994, Saxophone Quartet, 1995, Rituals: Sacred and Profane for flute, cello and piano, 1996, American Spiritual Fantasy for string orch., 1997, Psalm of the Phoenix for Shakuhachi and cello, 1998, Suite for violin and 12 instruments, 2000, Letters from Home, mezzo soprano, flute, clarinet, and piano, 2000, String Quartet No. 3, 2001, Life Imagined, Life Engaged for piccolo and chamber orch., 2001, Trio Concertante for violin, horn and piano with string orch., 2004; dance compositions: The Chair, The Table and Tatyana's Letter (choreography by Yin Mei), 1999; albums include Scenes from the Heartland, Transformational Etudes, String Quartet No. 2. Recipient Standard award ASCAP, 1986—, Creative Incentive award CUNY Rsch. Found., 1992, 95, 97; residency fellow Yaddo Corp., 1986, 87, Composer's fellow Charles Ives Ctr. for Am. Music, 1990, residency fellow MacDowell Colony, 1994, Goddard Lieberson fellow Am. Acad. Arts and Letters, 1993; prize winner Percussive Arts Soc., 1994. Home: 228 Manhasset Ave Manhasset NY 11030-2220 Office: Copland Sch of Music Queens College Flushing NY 11030 Business E-Mail: edward.smaldone@qc.cuny.edu.

SMALE, STEPHEN, mathematics professor; b. Flint, Mich., July 15, 1930; BS, U. Mich., 1952, MS, 1953, PhD, 1957; PhD (hon.), U. Warwick, 1974, Queens U., Kingston, Ontario, 1987; DSc (hon.), U. Mich., 1996; Doctor Honoris Causa, Universite Pierre et Marie Curie Paris, 1997; DSc (hon.), City U. Hong Kong, 1997; PhD (hon.), Rostov State U., 1999. Assoc. prof. math. U. Calif., Berkeley, 1960—61, prof. math., 1964—94, prof. emeritus math. and economics, 1994—; prof. math. Columbia U., 1961—64; disting. univ. prof. City U. Hong Kong, 1995—2001; prof. Toyota Technological Inst. at Chgo., 2002—. Instr. U. Chgo., 1956—68; mem. Inst. for Advanced Study Princeton, 1958—60, 1966; vis. prof. Coll. of France, Paris, 1962, Yale U., 1974, Inst. de Matematica Pura e Aplicado Rio de Janeiro, 1976, 94, 98, Columbia U., 1987; rsch. prof. Miller Inst. for Basic Rsch. in Sci., Berkeley, 1967—68, Berkeley, 1978—80; vis. mem. Inst. des Hautes Etudes Scientiques, 1969—70, 1972—73, vis. prof., 1976; vis. mem. U. Paris, Orsay, 1972—73; vis. scientist IBM Corp., Yorktown Heights, 1987; fellow Japan Soc. for the Promotion Sci., 1994; hon. prof. U. Yunnan, Kunming, 1997; spkr. in field. Contbr. articles to profl. jours. Co-recipient 2006/2007 Wolf Found. prize in Math., Israel; recipient U. Mich. Sesquicentennial Award, 1967, Chauvenet prize, Math Assn. Am., 1988, Von Neumann award, Soc. Industry and Applied Math., 1989, Jurgen Moser prize, Soc. Industry and Applied Math., Dynamics Group, 2005, Nat. medal of Sci., NSF, 1996; fellow Alfred P. Sloan rsch. fellow, 1960—62. Mem.: NAS, Brazilian Acad. Scis. (foreign mem.), Econometric Soc., Am. Math. Soc. (Veblen prize for geometry 1965), Internat. Union of Math. (Fields medal 1966), Am. Acad. Arts and Scis., Moscow Math. Soc. (hon.), London Math. Soc. (hon.), Trinity Math. Soc. (hon.), Instituto de Matematica Pura e Aplicada (IMPA) (hon.), Brazilian Nat. Order of Scientific Merit (Class of Grand Cross). Office: Toyota Technological Inst Chgo 5801 S Ellis Ave Chicago IL 60637 Address: Toyota Technological Inst University Press Bldg 1427 E 60th St Second Fl Chicago IL 60637 *

SMALL, CLARENCE MERILTON, JR., lawyer; b. Birmingham, Ala., July 24, 1934; s. Clarence Merilton and Elva (Roberts) S.; m. Jean Russell, Nov. 18, 1935; children: William Stephen, Elizabeth Ann, Laura Carol. BS, Auburn U., 1956; LLB, U. Ala., 1961. Founding ptnr. Christian & Small, Birmingham, 1961—. Served to 1st lt., arty. AUS, to capt. JAGC. Fellow Am. Bar Found., Internat. Acad. Trial Lawyers, Am. Coll. Trial Lawyers, Ala. Law Found.; mem. ABA (ho. of dels. 1984-86), Ala. Bar Assn. (pres. 1992-93), Birmingham Bar Assn. (pres. 1979), Ala. Def. Lawyers Assn., Internat. Assn. Def. Counsel. Office: 1800 Financial Ctr Birmingham AL 35203-4611 Home Phone: 205-871-5994; Office Phone: 205-795-6588. Business E-Mail: cmsmall@csattorneys.com.

SMALL, DANIEL I., lawyer; b. Boston, Jan. 2, 1954; s. Martin I. and Joanne (Goldfine) S. BA cum laude, Harvard U., 1975, JD, 1979. Bar: Mass. 1979, Fla, US Ct. Appeals (1st, 5th, 11th and DC cirs.). Trial atty. U.S. Dept. Justice, Washington, 1979-82; asst. U.S. atty. State of Mass., Boston, 1983—88; spl. counsel Dem. Nat. Com., 1988; with Portue, Widett Slater & Goldma, 1989—93; gen. counsel InPhynet Med. Mgmt., 1993—95; ptnr. Bottes, Brasilian & Sundl, 1995—2003, Duane Morris, 2004—. Lectr. Harvard U. Law Sch.; commentator TV, radio and newspaper. Author: Preparing Witnesses, 2d edit., 2004; contbr. articles to profl. journs. Recipient Dir.'s award Tex. Dept. Pub. Safety, 1983. Mem.: ABA, Am. Health Lawyers Assn., Fed. Bar Assn., Mass. Bar Assn., Fla. Bar Assn. Avocations: sailing, football referee. Office: Duane Morris LLP 200 S Biscayne Blvd Ste 3400 Miami FL 33131 Office Phone: 305-960-2207. Office Fax: 305-960-2201. Business E-Mail: dsmall@duanemorris.com.

SMALL, DONALD MACFARLAND, biophysics professor, gastroenterologist, department chairman, researcher; b. Newton, Mass., Sept. 15, 1931; s. Grace (MacFarland) S.; m. Elisabeth Chan, July 8, 1957 (div. 1979); children: Geoffrey, Philip; m. Kathryn Ross, July 26, 1986 (div. 1999); 1 child, Samuel. BA, Occidental Coll., 1954; MA (hon.), Oxford U., Eng., 1964; MD, UCLA, 1960. Intern, asst. resident in medicine Mass. Meml. Hosps., Boston, 1960-62; sr. resident Boston City Hosp., 1962-63, vis. physician med. svcs., 1965—90; asst. prof. medicine Boston U. Sch. Medicine, 1968-69, assoc. prof. medicine and biochemistry, 1969-73, prof., 1973—, prof. biophysics, chmn. dept., 1989-2000, dir. Biophysics Inst., 1972—, prof. chmn. dept. physiology and biophysics, 2000—. Spl. tng. in phys. chemistry of lipids Inst. Pasteur, Paris, 1963-65; mem. adv. bd. Gladstone Found Labs., San Francisco, 1980—; George Lyman Duff Meml. lectr. Coun. Arteriosclerosis, Am. Heart Assn., 1986; cons. Nat. Inst. Arthritis and Metabolic Diseases, NIH, 1968-72, mem. task force Nat. Heart, Lung and Blood Inst., 1990; also others. Author, editor: Physical Chemistry of Lipids, 1986; mem. editl. bd. Gastroenterology, 1967-74, Arteriosclerosis, Thrombosis and Vascular Biology, 1980-2002, Jour. Biol. Chemistry, Current Opinions in Structural Biology, 1990—, Structure, 1992-98; sub-editor: Jour. Lipid Rsch., 1974-78, editor, 1979-83; editor: (with R. Havel) Advances in Lipid Rsch., 1989-99; mem. internat. bd. editors Jour. Nutritional Biochemistry, 1989—; contbr. articles and revs. to profl. jours.; author: (with A. Adams) The Healthy Meateaters Cookbook, 1991. Recipient Eppinger prize IV Internat. Congress on Liver Disease, 1976, Disting. Achievment award Modern Medicine, 1978, Disting. Alumni award UCLA Sch. Medicine Alumni Assn., 1988; Marshall scholar Magdalen Coll., Oxford, 1956-58, Aesculapian scholar UCLA, 1958-60, Markle scholar, 1966-70; others. Mem. AAAS, Am. Heart Assn. (fellow coun. arteriosclerosis, chmn. program com. 1988-90, chmn. coun. 1992-94), Am. Assn. Physicians, Am. Soc. Biol. Chemists, Biophys. Soc., Am. Soc. Clin. Investigation, Am. Gastroent. Assn. (Ann. Disting. Achievement award 1972, Beaumont prize 2000), Am. Oil Chemists Soc. (Alton E. Bailey award 1998), Am. Fedn. Clin. Rsch., Am. Chem. Soc., Mass. Med. Soc., Suffolk Dist. Med. Soc., Phi Beta Kappa, Alpha Omega Alpha, Sigma Xi. Achievements include patents for on method for making meat products having a reduced saturated fat and cholesterol content. Office: Boston U Sch Medicine Dept Physiology and Biophysics 715 Albany St W302 Boston MA 02118-2526 Office Phone: 617-638-4001. E-mail: dmsmall@bu.edu.

SMALL, ELISABETH CHAN, psychiatrist, educator; b. Beijing, July 11, 1934; came to U.S., 1937; d. Stanley Hong and Lily Luella (Lum) Chan; m. Donald M. Small, July 8, 1957 (div. 1980); children Geoffrey Brooks, Philip Willard Stanley; m. H. Sidney Robinson, Jan. 12, 1991 (div. 2001). Student, Immaculate Heart Coll., LA, 1951-52; BA in Polit. Sci., UCLA, 1955, MD, 1960. Intern Newton-Wellesley Hosp., Mass., 1960-61; asst. dir. for venereal diseases Mass. Dept. Pub. Health, 1961-63; resident in psychiatry Boston State Hosp., Mattapan, Mass., 1965-66, Tufts New Eng. Med. Ctr. Hosps., 1966-69, psychiat. cons. dept. gynecology, 1973-75; asst. clin. prof. psychiatry Sch. Medicine Tufts U., 1973-75, assoc. clin. prof., 1975-82, asst. clin. prof. ob-gyn, 1977-80, assoc. clin. prof. ob-gyn, 1980-82; from assoc. prof. to prof. psychiatry U. Nev. Sch. Med., Reno, 1982-95; practice psychiatry specializing in psychological effects of bodily changes on women, 1969—; emeritus prof. psychiatry and behavioral scis. U. Nev. Sch. Medicine, Reno, 1995—, from assoc. prof. to clin. assoc. prof. ob-gyn, 1982-88; mem. staff Tufts New Eng. Med. Ctr. Hosps., 1977-82, St. Margaret's Hosps., Boston, 1977-82, Washoe Med. Ctr., Reno, 1983—2006, St. Mary's Regional Med. Ctr., Reno, Truckee Meadows Hosp., Reno, St. Mary's Hosp., Reno; chief psychiatry svc. Reno VA Med. Ctr., 1989-94. Lectr., cons. in field; mem. psychiatry adv. panel Hosp. Satellite Network; mem. office external peer rev. NIMH, HEW; psychiat. cons. to Boston Redevelopment Authority on Relocation of Chinese Families of South Cove Area, 1968-70; mem. New Eng. Med. Ctr. Hosps. Cancer Ctr. Com., 1979-80, Pain Control Com., 1981-82; reproductive sys. curriculum com. Tufts Univ. Sch. Medicine, 1975-82. Mem. editorial bd. Psychiat. Update Am. (Psychiat. Assn. ann. rev.), 1983-85; reviewer Psychosomatics and Hosp. Community Psychiatry, New Eng. Jour. of Medicine, Am. Jour. of Psychiatry Psychosomatic Medicine; contbr. articles to profl. jours. Immaculate Heart Coll. scholar, 1951-52, Mira Hershey scholar UCLA, 1955; fellow Radcliffe Inst., 1967-70. Fellow Am. Coll. Psychiatrists (sci. program com. 1989-98); mem. AMA, Am. Psychiat. Assn. (life, rep. to sect. com. AAAS, chmn. ad hoc com. Asian-Am. Psychiatrists 1975; task force 1975-77, task force cost effectiveness in consultation 1984—, caucus chmn. 1981-82, sci. program com. 1982-88, courses subcom. chmn. sci. program com. 1986-88), Nev. Psychiat. Assn., Assn. for Acad. Psychiatry (fellowship com. 1982), Washoe County Med. Assn., Nev. Med. Soc. Avocations: skiing, cooking. Home and Office: 825 Caughlin Crossing Reno NV 89519-0647

SMALL, GEORGE LEROY, geographer, educator; b. Malden, Mass., Mar. 27, 1924; s. George Arthur and Alice Mildred (Weston) S.; m. Geraldine H. Koepke, July 4, 1970; 1 dau., Elizabeth Mary. BA, Brown U., 1950; M.I.A., Columbia U., 1952, PhD, 1968. French tchr. pvt. schs., Ariz., 1955-62; instr. geography Hunter Coll., 1964-68; asso. prof. geography Coll. S.I., CUNY, 1968—. Cons. in field. Author: The Blue Whale, 1971. Served with U.S. Army, 1942-46. Recipient Nat. Book award, 1972; Rotary Found. fellow, 1952-53 Mem. Assn. Am. Geographers. Office: CUNY Coll Staten Is New York NY 10314

SMALL, GUS H., lawyer; b. Macon, Ga., Mar. 17, 1943; AB, Emory U., Atlanta, 1965; JD, Mercer U., Macon, Ga., 1969. Bar: Ga. 1970. Dir., pres. Southeastern Bankruptcy Law Inst., Atlanta, 1976—2007; ptnr. Cohen Pollock Merlin & Small, Atlanta, 2000—. 1st lt. US Army, 1969—71. Mem.: State Bar Ga. (chmn. bankruptcy sect.), Atlanta Bar Assn. (chmn. sect. bankruptcy). Office: Cohen Pollock Merlin & Small PC 3350 Riverwood Pky Ste 1600 Atlanta GA 30339 Home Phone: 770-857-4806; Office Phone: 770-857-4806. Office Fax: 770-857-4807. Business E-Mail: gsmall@cpmas.com.

SMALL, HAMISH, chemist; b. Newtown Crommelin, No. Ireland, Oct. 5, 1929; s. Johnston and Jean (Wilson) S.; m. Beryl Maureen Burley, Mar. 27, 1954; children: Deborah Jane, Claire Leslie. BS, Queens U., Belfast, Northern Ireland, 1949, MS, 1953. Chemist U.S. Atomic Energy Authority, Harwell, England, 1949-55; rsch. scientist Dow Chem. Co., Midland, Mich., 1955-83; chemist Rsch. and Invention, 1983—. Author: Ion Chromatography, 1990; contbr. articles to profl. jours. Recipient Albert F. Sperry award Instrument Soc. Am., 1978, A.O. Beckman award, 1983, Herbert H. Dow Gold Medal Dow Chem. Co., 1983, Stephen Dal Nogare award, 1984, Am. Chem. Soc. award in Chromatography, 1991. Mem. Am. Chem. Soc. Achievements include 46 patents in field. Avocations: painting, sketching. Home: 4176 Oxford Dr Leland MI 49654-9716 E-mail: montalto1929@msn.com.

SMALL, JEFFREY, lawyer; b. NYC, Oct. 11, 1941; s. I Maxwell and Norma Small; children: Lara, David. AB, Cornell U., 1963; LLB, NYU, 1966. Bar: NY 1967. Assoc. in law U. Calif., 1968; assoc. Davis, Polk & Wardwell, NYC, 1968-76, ptnr., 1976—, co-head global capital markets group. Assoc. adj. prof. NYU Sch. Law, 1979—86. Fulbright scholar, Madrid, 1967. Mem.: ABA, Assn. of Bar of City of NY, NY State Bar Assn. Office: Davis Polk & Wardwell 450 Lexington Ave New York NY 10017 Office Phone: 212-450-4500. Office Fax: 212-450-3500. E-mail: jeffrey.small@dpw.com.

SMALL, JONATHAN ANDREW, lawyer, consultant; b. NYC, Dec. 26, 1942; s. Milton and Teresa Markell (Joseph) S.; m. Cornelia Mendenhall, June 8, 1969; children: Anne, Katherine. BA, Brown U., 1964; student, U. Paris, 1962-63; LLB, Harvard U., 1967; MA, Fletcher Sch. of Law and Diplomacy, 1968; LLM, NYU, 1974. Bar: NY 1967. VISTA vol., Washington and Cambridge, Mass., 1968; law clk. to judge US Ct. Appeals (2d cir.), 1968-69; assoc. Debevoise & Plimpton, NYC, 1969-75, ptnr., 1976-99; pres. Nonprofit Coord. Com. NY, 2000—05; spl. cons. Govt. Rels., 2005—. Cons. Spl. Task Force of NY State Taxation, 1976; bd. overseers Fletcher Sch. Law and Diplomacy Tufts U., 2003—. Trustee Brearley Sch., 1985-95; bd. dirs. Nonprofit Coordinating Com. of NY, 1985-2005, Muscular Dystrophy Assn., 1986-88, Human Svcs. Coun. NYC, Inc., 2000-05, Investor Responsibility Rsch. Ctr., Inc., 2000-2006, Lawyers Alliance for NY, 2000-2007, Americans for the UN Population Fund, 2000—07. Mem. ABA, Am. Law Inst., NY State Bar Assn. (chmn. tax sect. com. exempt orgns. 1980-82, co-chmn., 1995), Assn. Bar City NY, Nonprofit Forum, Phi Beta Kappa. Home: 60 E End Ave New York NY 10028-7907 Office: Debevoise & Plimpton 919 Third Ave New York NY 10022 Office Phone: 212-909-6461.

SMALL, LAWRENCE M., former museum executive; b. NYC, Sept. 14, 1941; m. Sandra Small; 2 children. BA in Spanish Lit. with highest honors, Brown U., 1963; LLD (hon.), Morehouse Coll.; LHD (hon.), Brown U.; D Pub. Svc. (hon.), Am. U., 2002; D Arts & Sciences (hon.), Dickinson Coll., 2004; LHD (hon.), Coll. St. Rose, Albany. Mgmt. trainee Citibank, Chile, 1964, sr. exec. in charge comml. banking, info. tech., human resources and worldwide corp. banking, vice chmn., chmn. exec. com., 1964-91; pres., COO Fannie Mae, Washington, 1991-2000; sec. Smithsonian Instn., Washington, 2000—07. Creator Nat. Air and Space Mus. Smithsonian Instn., creator Nat. Mus. Am. Indians; bd. dirs. Chubb Corp., Marriott Internat., Paramount Comm. Inc. Bd. trustees Spanish Repertory Theatre, John F. Kennedy Ctr. Performing Arts, Washington, Nat. Gallery Art, Washington, Woodrow Wilson Internat. Ctr. for Scholars; trustee emeritus Brown U., 1984—90, Morehouse Coll., Atlanta, 1973—99, Collegiate Sch., Mt. Sinai-NYU Med. Ctr. and Health Sys., Joffrey Ballet, Am. Women's Econ. Devel. Corp., Internat. Exec. Svc. Corps, Inst. de Estudios

Superiores de la Empresa, Barcelona, Greater NY Councils of Boy Scouts of Am.; mem. Com. for Preservation of the White House, Washington. Avocations: collecting and restoring masks and tribal art, flamenco guitar playing. *

SMALL, MELVIN, historian, educator; b. NYC, Mar. 14, 1939; s. Herman Z. and Ann (Ashkinazy) S.; m. Sarajane Miller, Oct. 23, 1958; children: Michael, Mark. BA, Dartmouth Coll., 1960; MA, U. Mich., 1961, PhD, 1965. Asst. prof. history Wayne State U., Detroit, 1965-68, assoc. prof., 1968-76, prof., 1976—, chmn. dept. history, 1979-86, disting. prof., 2004—. Vis. prof. U. Mich., Ann Arbor, 1968, Marygrove Coll., Detroit, 1971, Aarhus (Denmark) U., 1972—74, 1983, Windsor (Ont., Can.) U., 1977—78; Fulbright sr. specialist CIES, 2007—. Author: Was War Necessary, 1980, Johnson, Nixon and the Doves, 1988, Covering Dissent, 1994, Democracy and Diplomacy, 1996, The Presidency of Richard Nixon, 1999, Antiwarriors, 2002, At The Water's Edge, 2005; co-author: Wages of War, 1972, Resort to Arms, 1982; editor: Public Opinion and Historians, 1970; co-editor: International War, 1986, Appeasing Fascism, 1991, Give Peace a Chance, 1992, The Good Fight Continues, 2006; mem. editl. bd. Internat. Interactions, 1987-91, Peace and Change, 1989—; restaurant critic Detroit Metro Times, 1982-95, 2006—; reviewer Detroit Free Press, 1988-95. Hon. bd. Swords into Plowshares Mus., 1992—; bd. dirs. Abraham Lincoln Brigade Archives, 1998—, Ctr. on Peace and Liberty, 2003-, David S. Wyman Inst. for Holocaust Studies, 2003-. Recipient Disting. Faculty award Mich. Assn. Governing Bds., 1993; Am. Coun. Learned Socs. fellow, 1969; Stanford Ctr. for Advanced Study fellow, 1969-70, Rsch. fellow NATO, 1996; grantee Am. Coun. Learned Socs., 1983, Johnson Libr., 1982, 88, Can. Govt., 1987; named to Hewlett-Woodmere Alumni Hall of Fame, 2005. Mem. Coun. on Peace Rsch. in History (nat. coun. 1986-90, pres. 1990-92), Am. Hist. Assn., Atlantic Coun. (acad. assoc.), Orgn. Am. Historians, Soc. Historians of Am. Fgn. Rels. (Warren Kuehl prize 1989). Home: 1815 Northwood Blvd Royal Oak MI 48073-3919 Office: Wayne State U Dept History 3119 Fab Detroit MI 48202 Office Phone: 313-577-6138. Business E-Mail: M.Small@Wayne.edu.

SMALL, MELVIN D., physician, educator; b. Somerville, Mass., May 22, 1925; s. Sidney J. and Ida (Gelbsman) Small; m. Judith Nogee, Dec. 23, 1962; children: Michael Dorian, Michele. AB, U. Wis., 1953; MD, Duke U., Durham, NC, 1959; studied under Dr. Gregory Pincus, Worcester Found. Exptl. Biol. and Medicine, 1950-53; studied under Prof. Brian Abel-Smith, London Sch. Econs, 1986-90, MPhil, 1988. Lic. physician Fla., Md., DC, Va. Intern Georgetown U. Med. Ctr., Washington, 1959-60, resident, 1960-61, chief gastrointestinal rsch., 1961-64, instr. medicine, 1961-66, asst. prof., 1966-67, asst. clin. prof., 1967—81, 1993; chief gastroenterology sect. Georgetown divsn. DC Gen. Hosp., Washington, 1964-68; cons. pain mgmt. and addiction treatment Advanced Med. Ctrs., Wilton Manors, Fla., 2006—. Chief animal experimentation cancer rsch. under Dr. Sidney Farber Children's Med. Ctr., Boston, 1948—50; rsch. asst. Boston U. Sch. Medicine, 1956—57; lectr. hygiene and preventive medicine Peace Corps groups, Ethiopia, Turkey, Brazil, and Columbia Georgetown U., 1961—62; active staff Fairfax Hosp., Va., 1961—73, Arlington Hosp., Va., 1961—85, Cir. Terr. Hosp., Alexandria, 1965—85, Commonwealth Drs. Hosp., Fairfax, 1969—74, Mt. Vernon Hosp., Alexandria, 1976—85; attending physician DC Gen. Hosp., 1961—68, Georgetown U. Hosp., 1961—81, 1993—, Mt. Sinai Hosp., Miami Beach, Fla., 1992—; cons. Children's Hosp., Washington, 1962—66; physician mem. presdl. appeals bd. (under Pres. John F. Kennedy) VA, 1962—63; chmn. dept. medicine Alexandria Hosp., 1974—75, hon. staff mem., 1985—89, 1992—; founder, chmn. No. Va. Consortium Continuing Med. Edn., 1974—86, chmn. emeritus No. Va. Consotium Continuing Med. Edn., 1986; witness subcom. small bus. US Senate, 1967; founder, chmn. Nat. Coun. State Coms. Continuing Med. Edn., 1977—79; lectr in field. Author: publs. in field. Nominated candidate Palm Beach Town Coun., Fla., 1995—96; mem. presdl. appeals bd. under Pres. John F. Kennedy VA Adminstrn., 1961; trustee Jefferson Meml. Hosp., 1965—74, mem. founding group, 1965, chmn. pharmacy com., 1965—76, co-chmn. tissue com., 1965—74. Fellow, Mallory Inst. Pathology, 1953—59, Gastroenterology Rsch., Evans Meml. Hosp., 1951—53. Mem.: ACP, AMA, Am. Acad. Addiction Psychiatry, Palm Beach County Med. Soc., Alexandria Med. Soc. (v.p. 1979—80), Med. Soc. Va. (chmn. commn. continuing med. edn. 1978—81), DC Med. Soc., Am. Soc. Gastrointestinal Endoscopy, Am. Physiol. Soc., Am. Inst. Nutrition, Am. Gastroent. Assn., Am. Coll. Gastroenterology. Office Phone: 800-551-9876. Personal E-mail: drmelv@comcast.net.

SMALL, NATALIE SETTIMELLI, retired pediatric mental health counselor; b. Quincy, Mass., June 2, 1933; d. Joseph Peter and Edmea Natalie (Bagnaschi) Settimelli; m. Parker Adams Small, Jr., Aug. 26, 1956; children: Parker Adams III, Peter McMichael, Carla Edmea. BA, Tufts U., 1955; MA, EdS, U. Fla., 1976, PhD, 1987. Cert. child life specialist. Pediatric counselor U. Fla. Coll. Medicine, Gainesville, 1976-80, Shands Hosp.-U. Fla., Gainesville, 1980-87, supr. child life dept. patient and family resources, 1987—2003; pres. Small Group Cons.com, 2003—06. Adminstrv. liaison for self-dir. work teams, mem. faculty Ctr. for Coop. Learning for Health and Sci. Edn., Gainesville, 1988-2003, assoc. dir., 1996, supr. pastoral svcs., 1998-2003; cons. and lectr. in field. Author: Parents Know Best, 1991; co-author team packs series for teaching at risk adolescent health edn. Building Strong Families, 1998. Bd. dirs. Ronald McDonald House, Gainesville, 1980-2007, mem. exec. com., 1991-05; bd. dirs. Gainesville Assn. Creative Arts, 1994—; mem. health profl. adv. com. March of Dimes, Gainesville, 1986-96, HIV prevention planning partnership, 1995-96; mem. Teen Pregnancy Prevention Action Com., 1998-00, exec. com. Children's Hosp., 1998-03. Recipient Thayer Acad. Humanitarian award, 2006, Caring and Sharing award Ronald McDonald House, 1995, Appreciation award March of Dimes, 1996; Boston Stewart Club scholar, Florence, Italy, 1955; grantee Jessie Ball Du Pont Fund, 1978, Children's Miracle Network, 1990, 92-95, 97, 2000, 01-03. Mem. ACA, Nat. League Am. Pen Women. Roman Catholic. Avocations: travel, reading, swimming. Home: 3454 NW 12th Ave Gainesville FL 32605-4811 E-mail: smallgroup2@aol.com.

SMALL, PARKER ADAMS, JR., pediatrician, educator; b. Cin., July 5, 1932; s. Parker Adams and Grace (McMichael) S.; m. Natalie Settimelli, Aug. 26, 1956; children: Parker Adams, Peter McMichael, Carla Edmea. Student, Tufts U., 1950-53; MD, U. Cin., 1957; BS extraordinem, 1986. Med. intern Pa. Hosp., Phila., 1957-58; rsch. assoc. Nat. Heart Inst. NIH, Washington, 1958-60; rsch. fellow St. Mary's Hosp., London, 1960-61; sr. surgeon NIMH, Washington, 1961-66; prof. immunology and med. microbiology U. Fla., 1966-95, chmn. dept., 1966-75, prof. pediat., 1979—2003, prof. emeritus, 2003—, prof. pathology, 1995—2003, prof. emeritus, 2003—, adj. clin. prof. large animal sci., 1999—2003; pres. PigVax Inc., 2000—01. Dir. Ctr. for Coop. Learning for Health Sci. Edn., U. Fla., 1988-2003; vis. prof. U. Lausanne, Switzerland, 1972, U. Lagos, Nigeria, 1982, Al Hada Hosp., Saudi Arabia, 1983; vis. scholar Assn. Am. Med. Colls., Washington, 1973; assoc. life scis. panel Nat. Acad. Scis., 1981-88, co-chmn., 1982-83; bd. dirs. Biol. Sci. Curriculum Study, 1984-90, exec. bd., 1987-90; mem. edn. adv. com. Nat. Fund Med. Edn., 1984-87; mem. study com. Nat. Bd. Med. Examiners, 1983-85, mem. nat. vaccine adv. com., 1987-91, chmn. subcom. on new vaccines, 1987-91; v.p. smallgroupconsultants.com, 2003-; mem. Truro Shellfish Advisory Com.; cons. in field. Creator patient oriented problem solving system/POPS, for tchg. immunology and coop. learning to med. students and Team Packs for tchg. K-12 & coll. students health edn. and coop. learning; co-dir. Fla. Ptnrs. in Prevention of Substance Abuse, 1997-2003; editor: The Secretory Immunologic System, 1971; mem. editl. bd. Infection and Immunity, 1974-76, Jour. Med. Edn., 1978-80; cons. editor Microbios, Cytobios; patentee in field; contbr. more than 150 articles to profl. jours. Sec., treas. Oakmont, Md., 1964-65, mayor, 1965-66; chmn. Citizens for Pub. Schs. Gainesville, Fla., 1969-70; mem. Teen Pregnancy Prevention Action Com., 1998-2000, Truro Shellfish Adv. Com., 2004-. With USPHS, 1958-60, 61-66. Named Tchr. of Yr. U. Fla. Coll. Medicine, 1978-79, Disting. Lectr. AMA, 1986; recipient Presdl. medallion U. Fla., 1987, Nat. Basic Sci. Disting. Tchg. award Alpha Omega Alpha, 1993, Jacob Ehrenzeller award, 1995, Pres.'s Faculty Humanitarian award U. Fla., 1996, Pep award U. Fla., 1998, Lifetime Achievement award U. Fla. Coll. Medicine, 2003; NIH spl. fellow, 1960-61, rsch. grantee, 1966-91, U. Fla. Tchr./Scholar and commencement spkr., 1987; invited lectr. Assn. Am. Med. Colls., 1992. Mem. AAAS, Am. Assn. Immunologists (edn. com. 1983-86), Physicians for Social Responsibility, Fla. Med. Assn., Phi Beta Kappa, Sigma Xi, Alpha Omega Alpha, Theta Delta Chi. Office: U Fla Coll Med PO Box 100275 Gainesville FL 32610-0275 Personal E-mail: smallgroup2@aol.com. Business E-Mail: small@pathology.ufl.edu.

SMALL, RICHARD DONALD, travel company executive; b. West Orange, NJ, May 24, 1929; s. Joseph George and Elizabeth (McGarry) S.; m. Arlene P. Small; children: Colleen P., Richard Donald, Joseph W., Mark G., Brian P. AB cum laude, U. Notre Dame, 1951. With Union-Camp Corp., NYC, 1952-62, Chgo., 1952—62; chmn. Alumni Holidays, Inc., 1962—, Alumni Holidays Internat. Corp., 1962—2003; pres. All Horizons, Inc., 1982—2000; travel industry cons., 2003—. Chmn. AHI, Inc., 1982-89; bd. dirs. French Cruise Lines, Des Plaines, Ill., Russian Cruise Lines, Alumni Campus Abroad, 1994—. Recipient Munich Ptnr. award, 1989. Mem.: Carlton Club (Chgo.), Univ. Club Chgo. Home: Water Tower Pl 180 E Pearson St # 3306 Chicago IL 60611-6730 also: Wailea Golf Estates 3954 Waakaula Pl Wailea HI 96753-5415 Personal E-mail: royals@hawaii.rr.com.

SMALL, SARAH MAE, volunteer; b. Salisbury, NC, Nov. 16, 1923; d. Clint and Lillie Mae (Wilbourn) Evans; m. Jesse Small Sr., May 4, 1941; children: Jesse Jr., Jean Carol Small Bell. Cert., Cortez Bus. Sch., 1948. File clk. gen. acctg. office Fed. Govt., Washington, 1941—47; sec., stenographer CIA, Washington, 1948—52, adminstrv. asst. McLean, Va., 1952—65, ret., 1965. Pres. Energetic Crusaders, Inc., 1993; bd. dirs. ARC, Washington, 1986-87, Children's Edn. Found., Inc., 1989—. Recipient Outstanding and Dedicated Vol. Svc. award Kiwanis Club of Capital Centre, 1985, Plaque in Recognition of Dedicated and Outstanding Vol. Svc. to the Corps and Washington D.C., Cmty. Jr. Citizen's Corps., 1989, Appreciation award for Outstanding and Dedicated Vol. Svc. to Corps, Jr. Citizens Corps., Inc., 1990, Appreciation award Jr. Citizens Corp., Inc., 1990, Cmty. Svc. award for leadership and youth advocacy Bus. and Profl. Women's League, Inc., 1991, Vol. award achievement excellence svc. youths of Jr. Citizens Corps., Inc., 1992, others. Mem. Jr. Citizens Corps (life, pres. 1985—, Dedicated Cmty. Svc. award 1983, Bus. and Cmty. Svc. award 1986), Bus. and Profl. Women's League (treas. 1982-86), Women in Arts (chartered, pres. 1984—), Nat. Coun. Negro Women, World Affairs Coun. Washington, Agrl. Coun. Am. Democrat. Baptist. Avocations: travel, photography, walking, swimming.

SMALL, WILLIAM EDWIN, JR., association and recreation executive; b. Jackson, Mich., Jan. 18, 1937; s. William Edwin and Lena Louisa (Hunt) S.; m. Ruth Ann Toombs, Mar. 28, 1959; children: Suzanne Marie, William Edwin III, Bryan Anthony. AS, Jackson C.C., 1959; BS in Geology, Mich. State U., 1961, MA in Journalism, 1964. Reporter Sci. Svc., Washington, 1961-62; writer sci. U. Chgo., 1963-64; sci. info. officer Pa. State U., State College, 1964-66; corr. McGraw-Hill, Washington, 1966-69; staff com. pub. works U.S. Senate, 1969—71; founding editor Biomed. News, 1969-71; dir. pub. info. Nat. Bur. Standards, Washington, 1972-76; editor Am. Pharmacy Jour., 1979-82; dir. media and info. svcs. AMA, Washington, 1982-86; exec. dir. Nat. Found. Infectious Diseases, Washington, 1986-91, Assn. Biotech. Cos., 1991-93; CEO, Bioconfs. Internat., Bethesda, Md., 1993-95, WESmall & Assocs., Assn. Execs., Louisa, Va., 1976—. Owner recreation resort Small Country Campground, Louisa, 1976—; exec. dir. Va. Biotech. Assn., 1996-2000, Va. Campground Assn., 2001-03; developer Weswood Estates properties, Louisa, 2004-. Author: Third Pollution, 1971. With Security Agy., AUS, 1955-59. Recipient Superior Accomplishment award U.S. Dept. Commerce, 1974. Fellow AAAS; life mem. Nat. Assn. Sci. Writers. Office: PO Box 343 Louisa VA 23093-0343

SMALLEY, DONNA WESSON, lawyer, educator; b. Ft. Sill, Okla., Oct. 8, 1955; d. Robert Eugene and Frances Marie (Yates) Wesson; m. Jack Smalley Jr., July 31, 1978 (div. Jan. 1987); 1 child, Jack Smalley III. BA in Journalism, U. Ala., 1975, JD, 1978; cert. instr. Nat. Inst. Trial Advocacy, U. Calif. Berkeley, San Francisco, 1994. Bar: Ala. 1978. State lobbyist U. Ala., Tuscaloosa, 1974-75; personal injury claims adjuster State Farm Mutual Auto Ins., Birmingham, 1978-82; assoc. Williams & Pradat, Tuscaloosa, 1982-83; legal clk., adminstrv. asst. Tuscaloosa County Dist. Ct., 1983-84; assoc. atty., ptnr. Gibson & Smalley, P.C., Tuscaloosa, 1984-88; pvt. practice Tuscaloosa, 1988-95; ptnr., gen. practitioner Smalley & Carr, L.L.C., Tuscaloosa, 1996—2005; sr. assoc. Ivey & Ragsdale, Jasper, Ala., 2005—. Adj. English instr. U. Ala., Tuscaloosa, 1988-91, adj. trial advocacy instr., 1991—; bd. mem. Ala. Lawyers for Children, Montgomery, 1993-96, Ala. Children's Trust Fund Bd., Montgomery, 1994—; cir. judge pro-tem Ala. Adminstrv. Office of Cts., Tuscaloosa, 1995; chair citizen's edn. Ala. State Bar Assn., Montgomery, 1995-96; spkr. in field. Paintings exhibited Jr. League, 1990 (3d place), Lawyers for Children Charitable Auction, 1996. Chair mediation com. Tuscaloosa County Bar, 1989-91; task force mem. Lt. Gov.'s Task Force-Juvenile Crime, Montgomery, 1993-96; exec. com. Ala. State Dem. Party, Birmingham, 1994—; parent-bd. liason Tuscaloosa Acad., 1994-95. Named Outstanding Young Businesswoman, Jaycees, Tuscaloosa, 1984, Outstanding Young Careerist, Bus. and Profl. Women, Tuscaloosa, 1985; recipient Outstanding Achievement-CLE award Ala. State Bar, Montgomery, 1994, 95, Pro Bono award Ala. State Bar, 1997. Fellow Am. Acad. Matrimonial Lawyers; mem. Ala. Trial Lawyers (exec. bd. 1994—). Methodist. Avocations: reading, walking, computers. Office: Smalley & Carr LLC Attys 601 Greensboro Ave Tuscaloosa AL 35401-1730 also: Ivey & Ragsdale Attys 315 W 19th St Jasper AL 35501 Home Phone: 205-799-6078; Office Phone: 205-221-4644.

SMALLEY, ROBERT MANNING, diplomat; b. Los Angeles, Nov. 14, 1925; s. William Denny and Helen (McConnell) S.; m. Lois Louisa Williamson, Nov. 28, 1948 (div.) m. Rosemary Sumner, Jan. 4, 1957; children: Leslie Estelle, David Christian. Student, UCLA, 1946-48. Radio news editor Mut. Radio Broadcasting System, Los Angeles, 1950-55; mgr. Agrl. Info. Inc., Sacramento, 1957-59; with Whitaker & Baxter, San Francisco, 1956-57, 59-61; sec. Mayor, San Francisco, 1961-63; asst. dir. pub. relations Republican Nat. Com., 1964; press sec. Republican vice presdl. candidate William E. Miller, 1964; dir. pub. relations Republican Nat. Com., 1965; v.p. Whitaker & Baxter, San Francisco, 1966-68; asst. press sec. Republican vice presdl. candidate Spiro Agnew, 1968; spl. asst. Sec. Commerce, Washington, 1969-72; adminstrv. asst. U.S. Senator Robert P. Griffin, Washington, 1972-73; dir. corp. affairs Potomac Electric Power Co., Washington, 1973-75; U.S. rep. devel. assistance com. O.E.C.D., Paris, 1975-77; spl. asst. U.S. Senator Robert P. Griffin, Washington, 1977-78; asst. to campaign mgr. Reagan for Pres. Com., Washington, 1979; sr. advisor mgmt. communications IBM, 1979-82; dep. asst. sec. of state pub. affairs Dept. of State, Washington, 1982-87, U.S. amb. to Kingdom of Lesotho, 1987-89; lectr. in U.S. politics and pub. policy. Author: (book) The Admiralities at War 1944-45, 2002. Campaign mgr. Senator Robert P. Griffin, MIch., 1966, 72. Served with USN, 1944-46, PTO. Republican. Episcopalian. Home: 3131 Connecticut Ave NW Apt 2302 Washington DC 20008

SMALLING, WILLIAM E., pediatrician, neonatologist; b. NYC, Oct. 12, 1967; MD, U. Miami Sch. Medicine, 1993. Cert. Pediatrics, Neonatal-Perinatal Medicine. Intern, pediatrics Jackson Meml. Hosp., Miami, Fla., 1993—94, resident, neonatology, 1994—96; fellow Jackson Meml. Hosp.U. Miami, Miami, Fla., 1996; private practice Coral Gables, Fla. Office: Critical Care Newborn Svcs 5955 Ponce de Leon Blvd Miami FL 33146 Office Phone: 305-661-1515. Office Fax: 305-662-3823. *

SMALLWOOD, CAROL, writer; b. Cheboygan, Mich., May 3, 1939; d. Lloyd Gouine and Lucille Drozdowska; m. T.M. Smallwood, 1963 (div. 1976); children: Michael, Ann. BS, Ea. Mich. U., Ypsilanti, 1961, M in History, 1963; MLS, We. Mich. U., Kalamazoo, 1976. Tchr. Mich. Pub. Sch., 1961—64; grad. asst. Western Mich. U., Kalamazoo, 1975-76; Title I libr. cons. Northland, Grand Traverse Library Systems, Mich., 1976-77; head media dir. Pellston Pub. Schs., Mich., 1977—97; writer, libr. cons. classes Mt. Pleasant, 1998—. Asst. dir. Northland Libr. System, Alpena, Mich., 1977; developer, operator ednl. materials clearinghouse, 1981-83; adult edn. tchr. Cheboygan Area Schs., 1985-86. Author: Free Michigan Materials for Educators, 1980, 2nd edit., 1986, Free Materials Resource Disk, 1983, Exceptional Free Library Resource Materials, 1984, Free Resource Builder, 1985, 2d edit., 1992, A Guide to Selected Federal Agency Programs and Publications for Librarians and Teachers, 1986, Health Resource Builder, 1988, An Educational Guide to the National Park System, 1989, Current Issues Builder, 1989, Library Puzzles and Word Games, for Grades 7-12, 1990, Reference Puzzles and Word Games for Grades 7-12, 1991, Michigan Authors, 1993, Helpful Hints for the School Library, 1993, Recycling Tips for Teachers and Librarians, 1995, An Insider's Guide to Libraries, 1997, Free or Low-Cost Health Information, 1998; (with S. McElmeel) WWW Almanac, 1999; (with B. Hudson, A. Riedling, J. Rotole) Internet Sources on Each U.S. State, 2005, Educators as Writers: Publishing for Personal and Professional Development, 2006; author 100 poems in English Jour., Poesia, others; contbr; columnist Detroit News; others. Charter bd. mem., publicity chmn. Cheboygan Area Arts Coun.; founder, pres. Cheboygan County Humane Soc.; co-founder Humane Animal Treatment Soc. Recipient 1st prize for fiction, Byline Mag., 2004. Mem.: Doris Day Animal Found. Mailing: PO Box 1485 Mount Pleasant MI 48804 E-mail: smallwood@tm.net.

SMALLWOOD, DAVID ANDREW, language educator, education educator; b. Cape Girardeau, Mo., Apr. 21, 1964; s. Darlene Ruth Smallwood; 1 child, John Joseph. BA in Spanish & Linguistics, U. Mo., Columbia, 1983—89; MA in Spanish, St. Louis U., 1998—99; PhD in Spanish & Latin Am. Lit., Tex. Tech U., Lubbock, 1999—2005. Cert. K-12 Spanish tchr. Mo., 1994. Spanish tchr. Chaminade Coll. Prep. Sch., St. Louis, 1994—95, Sikeston Pub. Schs., Sikeston, Mo., 1995—98; Spanish grad. tchg. assistantship St. Louis U., 1998—99; part-time grad. instr. Tex. Tech U., Lubbock, 1999—2001; Spanish & mid. and secondary edn. instr. SE Mo. State U., Cape Girardeau, 2005—06, asst. prof. Spanish & mid. and secondary edn., 2006—. Pres. MSTA fgn. lang. divsn. SE Mo. State U., 1997—98, advisor Spanish & fgn. lang. edn., 2005—, chairperson, curriculum designer for global studies maj., 2005—, curriculum and assessment com. mem., 2005—, mem. univ. disability awareness com., 2005—, advisor Spanish lang. program, 2005—, advisor mid. & secondary edn.; co-coord. cefiro fgn. lang. conf. Tex. Tech U., 2000—01. Translator: (poetry) Translation of Pablo Neruda's El tigre. Presenter Wal Mart, Cape Girardeau, Mo., 2006. Recipient Faculty Mem. of Month award, Delta Delta Delta Chpt., SE Mo. State U., 2006; grantee Part-time Grad. Instr. scholarship, Tex. Tech U., 1999—2002; scholar Grad. Tchg. assistantship, St. Louis U., 1998—99. Mem.: MLA, Am. Assn. Applied Linguistics, Tchrs. English Speakers Other Langs., Nat. Assn. Bilingual Edn., Am. Assn. Tchrs. Spanish & Portuguese, Am. Coun. Tchg. Fgn. Langs., Rotary Internat., Sigma Delta Pi Nat. Spanish Honor Soc., Alpha Sigma Phi Nat. Frat. (treas., v.p., pledge edn. 1984—87). R-Consevative. Home: 324 S Spring Cape Girardeau MO 63703 Office: SE Mo State Univ 1 University Plz Cape Girardeau MO 63701 Home Phone: 573-335-1240. Business E-Mail: dsmallwood@semo.edu.

SMALLWOOD, GLENN WALTER, JR., utility marketing management executive; b. Jeffersonville, Ind., Oct. 12, 1956; s. Glenn Walter and Darlene Ruth (Zeller) S. BSBA, SE Mo. State U., 1978, BS in Engring. Tech., 2006; MA in Bus., Webster U., 1992, MBA, 1993. Cert. econ. developer Inst. Econ. Devel., counselor, energy mgr. Customer svc. advisor Union Electric Co., Mexico, Mo., 1979—95, Cape Girardeau, Mo., 1995—97; cmty. devel. exec. Ameren Svcs., Cape Girardeau, 1997—98, bus. devel. exec., 1998—. Instr. Mexico Vo-Tech Sch., 1981; panelist on home design Mo. Extension Svc., 1984; co. advisor Mo. Bus. Week. Coord. local United Way, 1984; mem., chair Gt. Rivers coun. Boy Scouts Am., chair Shawnee dist. Eagle Scout advancement com., 1999-2001, chair Shawnee Dist. com., 2002--; panelist Mo. Freedmon Forum, 1990; charter mem. class Mo. Leadership; chmn. Leadership Mexico Program; coordinating advisor Jr. Achievement, Mexico H.S.; committeeman, chmn. Republican Party of Audrain County; bd. dirs. Mo. Rep. Grassroots Caucus, S.E. Mo. Univ. Found., 1998— chmn. Cape Girardeau Planning and Zoning Commn., 2004—; adv. coun. Cape Girardeau County Jr. Achievement, 2005-06. Named among Ten Outstanding Young Missourians, Mo. Jaycees, 1993; recipient Disting. Svc. award, Mexico, Mo. Jaycees, 1993. Mem. Am. Mktg. Assn. (profl.), Nat. Eagle Scout Assn. (bd. dirs. St. Louis coun.), Cooper Dome Soc., Boy Scouts Am. Alumni Family, Mexico Area C. of C. (bd. dirs. 1993-95), Cape Girardeau C. of C. (chair govtl. affairs com.), S.E. Mo. U. Alumni Assn., Inst. Cert. Profl. Mgrs. (cert. mgr.), Assn. Energy Engrs. (cert. energy mgr.), Adminstrv. Mgmt. Soc., Optimists (Youth Appreciation award 1974), Kiwanis (cert. appreciation 1984), Mexico Noon (bd. dirs. 1990, treas. 1990-91, v.p. 1991-92, pres. 1993-94), Audrain County Pachyderm Club (bd. dirs., 2d v.p. 1990-92, pres. 1993), S.E. Mo. Univ. Found. (bd. dirs.), S.E. Mo. Pachyderm Club (founder, pres. 1997-98), Mo. Fedn. Pachyderm Clubs (bd. dirs.), Honorable Order Ky. Cols. (commd. Ky. col. 1995), Sons of Confederate Vets., Disting. Hoosier Com. (State of Ind. 1999), Rotary (treas. 2004-05, pres. elect 2005-06), 1889er Soc. Republican. Avocations: music, sports, baseball, basketball, tennis. Office: Ameren Svcs 2222 Kent Dr Cape Girardeau MO 63701 Business E-Mail: gsmallwood@ameren.com.

SMALLWOOD, ROBERT ALBIAN, JR., retired secondary education educator; b. Phila., Oct. 3, 1946; s. Robert Albian and Mildred May (Miller) S.; m. Geraldine Ann Boozan, May 27, 1972; children: Amy Lynn, Daniel James. BS in Commerce, Bus. Adminstrn., Rider Coll., Lawrenceville, NJ, 1969, MA in Sch. Adminstrn. and Supervision, 1976; EdS in Ednl. Adminstrn. and Supervision, Rutgers U., New Brunswick, NJ, 1983. Cert. social studies tchr., secondary sch. prin., supr. curriculum and instrn., Pa.; cert. social studies and gen. bus. tchr., prin., supr., sch. bus. adminstr., asst. supt. bus., sch. adminstr. (supt.) NJ. Tchr. social studies Trenton Bd. Edn., 1973-76, tchr. bus. edn., 1975-76, sch. disciplinaerian, 1976-84, 94-97; acting asst. prin. Jr. High Sch. 2, 1980-83, tchr. U.S. history, 1983-87, chmn. social studies dept., 1984-85; acting asst. prin. Carroll Robbins Elem. Sch., Jr. High Schs. #1 and #5, 1987-88; tchr. gifted and talented social studies Dunn Jr. High Sch., 1989-93, social studies tchr., 1997-99, whole sch. reform site facilitator, 1999—2005; ret., 2005. Mem. Dist.'s Affirmative Action Adv. Council; mem. Nat. Tchr. Corps Project, Trenton Area; fin. advisor M.S. Prin., 1998-2005. Asst. ops. officer Trenton CD Unit, 1974-76, asst. disaster analysis officer, 1976, disaster analysis officer, 1976-79; trustee N.J. Coun. for Alcohol/Drug Edn., 1983-99, mem.

exec. com., 1985-95, 96-99, chmn. nominating com., 1985, 86, treas., 1987-95, acting exec. dir., 1994-95, v.p., 1996-98, pres. 1998-99. With U.S. Army, 1969-72. With US Army, 1969—72. Decorated Bronze Star, Army Commendation medal with oak leaf cluster, Joint Svc. Commendation medal, Good Conduct medal, Nat. Defense Svc. medal, Vietnam Svc. medal, Vietnam Campaign medal with 2 campaign stars. Mem. NEA Ret., Vietnam Vets. Am. (life), Va. Geneal. Soc. (life), Md. Geneal. Soc., Md. Hist. Soc., Geneal. Soc. Pa. (life), Nat. Geneal. Soc., Assn. Profl. Genealogists, Franklin County Hist. Soc., Adams County Hist. Soc., Pa., Assn., Colonial Williamsburg Found., Va. Republican. Baptist. Avocations: genealogy, history. Home: 2 Leese Ave Trenton NJ 08609-1828 Home Phone: 609-587-2364. Personal E-mail: RASteach@aol.com.

SMALLY, DONALD JAY, consulting engineering executive; b. Cleve., 1922; s. Daniel James and Alice (Rohrheimer) S.; m. Ruth Janet Glasser, July 8, 1944; children: Alan Jon, Leonard Arthur. BME, U. Cin., 1949. Prodn. engr. N. Ransohoff, Inc., Cin., 1949-50; chief engr. Mosby Engring. Assocs., Sarasota, Fla., 1952-55; prin. Smally, Wellford & Nalven, Inc., Sarasota, 1956-91. Mem. tech. adv. com. Manatee Community Coll., Sarasota, 1965-90; mem. adv. com. Vocat.-Tech. High Sch., Sarasota, 1968-80 V.p. Sarasota YMCA, 1968-71, Sarasota Opera Assn., 1975-88, pres., 1988-89; chmn. Sarasota Vol. Talent Pool, 1973-76; sec.-treas. Civitan Found., 1965-79; bd. dirs. Suncoast Heart Assn., 1976; mem. Fla. Coordinating Coun. for Vocat. and Adult Edn., 1984-95, chmn., 1987-88; chmn. Sarasota Hist. Preservation Bd., 1988-91; pres. Sarasota County Rd. Improvement Task Force, 1990-93; mem. Sarasota County Pub. Sch. Found., 1990-95, chmn., 1990-91; v.p. Hist. Soc. Sarasota, 1990-91, Children's Haven and Adult Cmty. Svcs., 1983-99, pres., 1991-94; pres. John Ringling Ctr. Found., 1991-98; mem. Plymouth Harbor Bd., 1994-99; bd. dirs. Sarasota Alliance for Hist. Preservation, 2004—. Recipient Good Citizenship award SAR, 1975, Disting. Alumni award U. Cin. Engring. Coll., 1985, Outstanding Svc. award Myakica Chpt. Fla. Engring. Soc., 1993; named Citizen of Yr. Sarasota Civitan Club, 1975, Engr. of Yr. Sarasota-Manatee Engrs. Soc., 1976. Fellow Am. Coun. Engring. Cos. (treas. 1980-82), Fla. Engring. Soc. (pres. Sarasota-Manatee chpt. 1956-58); mem. Sarasota County C. of C. (past dir., v.p. 1983), Cons. Engrs. Council Fla. (pres. 1968), Fla. Soc. Profl. Land Surveyors (chpt. pres. 1973), Am. Water Works Resources Assn. (pres. Fla. Soc. 1981), Sarasota-Manatee Engring. Soc. Personal E-mail: donsmally@earthlink.net.

SMARAGDIS, PARIS, audiologist, researcher; s. Ioannis Gryparis and Kalliope Smaragdis. MusB, Berklee Coll. Music, Boston, 1995; MS, MIT, Cambridge, Mass., 1997, PhD, 2001. Postdoctoral assoc. MIT, 2001—02; rsch. scientist Mitsubishi Electric Rsch. Labs., Cambridge, 2002—. Named one of Top Young tech. Innovators, MIT tech. rev.; named to Top GreekScientist Shortlist, Status; fellow, Interval Rsch.; Riverland fellow, Starlab. Mem.: IEEE. Achievements include research in enabling machines to understand sound; patents for audio synchronization techniques; patents pending for in audio technology; invention of multiple tools for interactive performance of electronic music; audio based surveillance systems for improvement of automotive traffic and personal security; development of highlight detection techniques for commercial products such as PVRs and TV enabled cell phones; research in mathematical foundations of human hearing processes; sound separation; development of secure speech recognition systems that preserve the privacy of communicating parties. Home Phone: +1 617 731-9523; Office Phone: +1 617 621-7561.

SMARDON, RICHARD CLAY, landscape architect, environmental studies professor; b. Burlington, Vt., May 13, 1948; s. Philip Albert and Louise Gertrude (Peters) Smardon; m. Anne Marie Graveline, Aug. 19, 1973; children: Regina Elizabeth, Andrea May. BS cum laude, U. Mass., 1970, MLA, 1973; PhD in Environ. Planning, U. Calif., Berkeley, 1982. Environ. planner, landscape architect Wallace, Floyd, Ellenzweig, Inc., Cambridge, Mass., 1972-73; assoc. planner Exec. Office Environ. Affairs, State of Mass., Boston, 1973-75; environ. impact assessment specialist USDA extension svc. Oreg. State U., Corvallis, 1975-76; landscape architect USDA Pacific S.W. Forest and Range Expt. Sta., Berkeley, 1977; rsch. landscape architect U. Calif., Berkeley, 1977-79; prof. landscape architecture, sr. rsch. assoc. SUNY Coll. Environ. Sci. and Forestry, Syracuse, 1979-86, prof. environ. studies, 1987—, dir. Inst. for Environ. Policy and Planning, 1987-95, chair faculty of environ. studies, 1996—. Co-dir. Gt. Lakes Rsch. Consortium, Syracuse, 1986—2007; guest lectr. numerous univs.; adj. asst. prof. U. Mass., Amherst; dir. R. G. Pack Environment Inst., 1996—; Sea Grant trainee Inst. Urban and Regional Devel., Berkeley, 1976; condr., presenter numerous seminars and workshops; cons. numerous orgns.; mem. com. environ. design and landscape Transp. Rsch. Bd.-NAS, 1985—95; mem. tech. adv. bd. Wetlands Rsch., Inc., Chgo., 1985; mem. adv. bd. Wetlands Fund, NY, 1985; v.p. Integrated Site, Syracuse, 1990—2002. Co-editor: Our National Landscape, 1979, (spl. issue) Coastal Zone Mgmt. Jour., 1982, The Future of Wetlands, 1983, Foundations for Visual Project Analysis, 1986, The Legal Landscape, 1993, Protecting Floodplain Resources, 1995, Adirondacks and Beyond, 1998, Environmental Knowledge, 2001, (spl. issue) Landscape and Urban Planning, 2005; mem. editl. bd. Northeastern Environ. Sci. Jour., 1981—85, Landscape and Urban Planning, 1991—, Environ. Sci. and Policy, 1999—, The Sci. World, 2001—, Internat. Jour. Environ. Scis., 2005; contbr. articles to profl. jours. Pres. Save the County, Inc., Fayetteville, NY, 1986—88, 2002—04; apptd. to Gt. Lakes Adv. Commn., NY, chmn. NY, 1993—98, Gt. Lakes Legal Found., 1999—, NY State Wetlands Forum Bd., 2000—07; bd. dirs. Sackets Harbor Area Hist. Preservation Found., Watertown, NY, 1984—90. Recipient Beatrice Farrand award, U. Calif., 1979, Am. Soc. Landscape Archs. award, 1972, Pub. Svc. award in edn., 1990, Progressive Architecture mag. award, 1992, Pres.'s Pub. Svc. award, 1994. Mem.: NAEP, AAAS, Coastal Soc., Internat. Assn. Impact Assessment, Land Resource Assn. (charter), NY Acad. Sci., Sigma Lambda Alpha, Alpha Zeta (life). Avocations: folk guitar, hiking, skiing, travel. Office: SUNY Faculty Environ Studies Syracuse NY 13210 Office Phone: 315-470-6576. Business E-Mail: rsmardon@esf.edu.

SMARSH, JAMES DAVID, retired military officer; b. Great Bend, Kans., Feb. 21, 1938; s. Jerome Arthur Smarsh and Bernetta Marie Blubaugh; m. Nancy Carol Topham Chadwick (div.); 1 child, Nancy Kim. BS in Chem. Engring., U. Kans., Lawrence, 1961; MS in Nuc. Engring., Kans. State U., Manhattan, 1971; cert. occupl. health, San Diego State U., 95. Commd. 2d lt. US Army, 1961, advanced through grades to col.; chem. staff officer 82d Airborne Divsn., 3d Infantry Divsn., Wurzburg, Germany, 1961—66; ret. US Army, 1994; chem. staff officer US Army Infantry Ctr., Columbus, Ga., 1966—67; gen. staff officer Hdqrs. III Marine Amphibious Force, Danang, 1968—69; nuc. facility mgr. Armed Forces Radiobiology Rsch., Bethesda, Md., 1971—74; nuc. and chem. surety program mgr. USA Test and Evaluation Command, Aberdeen, Md., 1974—77; sci. and tech. info. program mgr. Def. Logistics Agy., Alexandria, Va., 1977—81; intelligence analyst USA Intelligence Command, Arlington, Va., 1981—82; radiation safety officer Naval Hosp., Long Beach, Calif., 1982—87. Instr. Palomar Coll., San Marcos, Calif., 1988, U. Alaska, Palmer, 1996—97; nuc. med. sci. officer Office Surgeon Gen., Washington, 1977—87; cons. in field; vis. scholar U. Sydney, 1972—87, 2003—04. Democrat. Roman Catholic. Home: 7224 Pintail Dr Carlsbad CA 92011

SMART, ALLEN RICH, II, retired lawyer; b. Chgo., July 3, 1934; s. Jackson W. Smart and Dorothy (Byrnes) Bowles. Student, Deerfield Acad., 1949-52; AB magna cum laude, Princeton U., 1956; LLB, Harvard U., 1961. Bar: Ill. 1961. Assoc. Bell Boyd & Lloyd, Chgo., 1961-69, ptnr., 1970-91, of counsel, 1992—2001. Bd. dirs. Rec. for Blind, Inc., Chgo., 1984-95, vice-chmn., 1987-90; co-chmn. zoning com. Old Town Triangle Assn., Chgo., 1987-94; bd. dirs. Lawrence Hall Sch. for Boys, 1965-70, Old Masters Soc., Art Inst., 1987—; governing mem. Orchestral Assn. Lt. USNR, 1956-58. Mem.: ABA, Chgo. Opera Theater (dir. 2002—), Renaissance Soc. Chgo. (bd. dirs. 1988—), Inst. for Psychoanalysis (dir. 2001—), Friends of the Pks. Chgo. (bd. dirs. 1986—), Infant Welfare Soc. Chgo. (bd. dirs. 1971—95, pres. 1982—86), Racquet Club Chgo., Arts, Lawyers Econ. Clubs of Chgo., Univ. Club (bd. dirs. 1986—89). Home: 1732 N North Park Ave Chicago IL 60614-5710 Office: Bell Boyd & Lloyd 3200 Three First Nat Pl Chicago IL 60602

SMART, FRANK WILSON, physician; b. New Orleans, Apr. 12, 1956; s. Foch Mahlon and Laura Gladys Smart; m. Jaclyn Cutrone, Nov. 16, 1996; children: Daniel, Katherine, Michael. BS in Zoology, So. La. U., 1978; MD, La. State U., New Orleans, 1985. Diplomate Am. Bd. Internal Medicine, Am. Bd. Cardiovascular Disease. Intern Ochsner Found. Hosp., New Orleans, 1985-86, resident, 1986-88; fellow Baylor Coll. Medicine, Houston, 1988-90, fellow in transplant rsch., 1990-91; co-sect. head heart failure and cardiac transplantation Ochsner Med. Instn., New Orleans, 1991-97, dir. med. transplant svcs., multi-organ transplant ctr., 1994-97; dir. transplant Ochsner Clinic, New Orleans, 1991-97; prof. medicine, co-dir. to dir. cardiac transplant program Tulane U. Med. Ctr., New Orleans, 1997; med. dir., adv. heart failure, cardiac transplantation, Tex. Heart Inst. St. Luke's Episcopal Hosp., Houston; dir. cardiology Morristown (NJ) Meml. Hosp., 2006—, chmn., cardiology, vice chmn., cardiovascular medicine, 2006—. V.p., co-founder Rsch. Congestive Heart Failure, New Orleans, 1998—; rep. region 3 United Network Organ Sharing, Richmond, Va., 1999—; mem. adv. bd. Action Heart Failure, Parsippany, N.Y. Mem. editl. bd. Cardiology Today, 1996, Congestive Heart Failure, Jour. Heart & Lung Transplantation; author: The Transplantation & Replacement of Thoracic Organs, 1997, Primer on Transplantation, 1998; reviewer Am. Jour. Cardiology. Recipient Richard Van Reet award Baylor Coll. Medicine, Houston, 1991. Fellow ACP, Am. Coll. Cardiology (Syntex award 1990); mem. AMA, Internat. Soc. Heart or Lung Transplantation, Am. Soc. Transplantation, So. Med. Assn., Alpha Omega Alpha. Office: Morristown Meml Hosp 100 Madison Ave Morristown NJ 07962 Office Phone: 973-290-7316. *

SMART, GEORGE M., energy executive, former packaging company executive; BS, Defiance Coll.; MBA, Wharton Sch., U. Penn. With Central States Can Co. (div. of Van Dorn Co.), 1970—78, pres., CEO, 1978—93; chmn., pres. Phoenix Packaging Corp., 1993—2001; pres. Sonoco- Phoenix, Inc., 2001—03; bd. dirs. FirstEnergy Corp., Akron, Ohio, 1997—, chmn., 2004—. Bd. dirs. Ohio Edison Co., 1988—, Ball Corp., 2005—. Office: FirstEnergy Corp 76 S Main St Akron OH 44308 *

SMART, JAMES ANTHONY, music educator; b. Marietta, Ga., July 21, 1959; s. James Bryant Smart and Patricia Morgan Williams; m. Robin Arlene McDaniel, May 26, 1990; children: Laurel Morgan, Andrew Forrest. MusB, Jacksonville State U., 1982; MusM, Ga. State U., 1985; student in Music Edn., Boston U., 2006—. Adj. prof. U. West Ga., Carrollton, 1995—2001; dir. of bands Cobb County Schs., Mableton, Ga., 2000—; tchg. asst. Auburn U., 1994—96. Orch. dir. First Bapt. Ch., Lithia Springs, Ga., 1995—2005. Home Phone: 770-420-9496; Office Phone: 770-819-2496. Personal E-mail: james.smart@cobbk12.org.

SMART, JILL BELLAVIA, financial consultant; b. Chgo., Oct. 16, 1959; d. Salvatore and patricia (Foran) B.; m. Stephen D. Smart; two children. BS, U. Ill., 1981; MBA, U. Chgo., 1991. Assoc. ptnr. Accenture Ltd., Chgo., 1981—89, mng. ptnr. human resource delivery/Chgo. office, lead ptnr., 1989—. Bd. trustee Accenture Found. Vol. Treehouse Animal Found., Chgo., 1986-90, Chgo. Area Runners Assn., 1986—; bd. dirs. Goodman Theater, Chgo.; dir. United Way Met. Chgo.; mem. pres. adv. com. U. Ill. Named one of Chgos. 100 Most Influential Women, Crain's Chgo. Bus., 2004. Republican. Roman Catholic. Avocations: jogging, aerobics, travel, reading, skiing. Office Phone: 312-693-0161.

SMART, JUDITH ANN, mathematics professor; d. Paul Frederick and Keneta Mae Decker; m. Philip Amos Smart, Aug. 22, 1970; children: Renée Annette, Eric Philip. BS in Edn. and Math., Otterbein Coll., Westerville, Ohio, 1970; MA in Edn., Heidelberg Coll., Tiffin, Ohio, 1999. Math. tchr. Lakota H.S., Rising Sun, Ohio, 1970, Upper Arlington Schs., Ohio, 1970—71, Newport News Schs., Va., 1971—73; subsitute math tchr. Clyde-Green Springs Schs., Ohio, 1973—80; math. instr. Terra C.C., Fremont, Ohio, 1983—. Mem. adv. bd. for apprentices Terra C.C., Fremont, 2005—. Choir mem. Trinity United Meth. Ch., Fremont, 1965—, Sunday sch. tchr., 1973—, fin. sec., 1976—. Recipient Adj. Faculty Excellence award, Terra C.C., 1991, Nat. Inst. Staff and Devel. ORgnl. Devel. Excellence award, 2001, U. Tex., Austin, 2001, Cir. Excellence award, Terra C.C., 2006. Mem.: Beta Sigma Phi (v.p., Order of the Rose). Republican. Avocations: crocheting, flower arranging, gardening, playing piano for quartet. Home: 1455 CR 31 Fremont OH 43420 Office: Terra CC 2830 Napolean Rd Fremont OH 43420

SMART, MARY-LEIGH CALL (MRS. J. SCOTT SMART), civic worker; b. Springfield, Ill., Feb. 27, 1917; d. S(amuel) Leigh and Mary (Bradish) Call; m. J. Scott Smart, Sept. 11, 1951 (dec. 1960). Diploma, Monticello Coll., 1934; student, Oxford U., 1935; BA, Wellesley Coll., 1937; MA, Columbia U., 1939, postgrad., 1940—41, NYU, 1940—41; painting student, with Bernard Karfiol, 1937—38. Dir. mgmt. Cen. Ill. Grain Farms, Logan County, 1939—; owner Lowtrek Kennel, Ogunquit, Maine, 1957-73, Cove Studio Art Gallery, Ogunquit, 1961-68; art collector, patron, publicist, 1954—. Cons. in field. Editor: Hamilton Easter Field Art Found. Collection Catalog, 1966; originator, dir. show, compiler of catalog Art: Ogunquit, 1967; Peggy Bacon-A Celebration, Barn Gallery, Ogunquit, 1979. Program dir., sec. bd. Barn Gallery Assoc., Inc., 1958-69, pres., 1969-70, 82-87, asst. treas., 1987-92, hon. dir., 1970-78, adv. trustee, 1992-94, v.p., 1994-2003; curator Hamilton Easter Field Art Found. Collection, 1978-79, curator exhbn., 1979-86, chair exhbn. com., 1987-94; acquisition com. DeCordova Mus., Lincoln, Mass., 1966-78; chancellor's coun. U. Tex., 1972—; pres. coun. U. NH, 1978—; bd. dir. Ogunquit C. of C., 1966, treas., 1966-67, hon. life mem., 1968—; bd. overseers Strawbery Banke, Inc., Portsmouth, NH, 1972-75, 3d vice chmn., 1973, 2d vice-chmn., 1974; bd. advisors U. Art Galleries, U. NH, 1973-89; pres., 1981-89; bd. dir. Old York Hist. and Improvement Soc., York, Maine, 1979-81, v.p., 1981-82; adv. com. Bowdoin Coll. Mus. Art Invitational exhibit, 1975, '76 Maine Artists Invitational Exhbn., Maine State Mus., Maine Coast Artists, Rockport, 1975-78, All Maine Biennial '79, Bowdoin Coll. Mus. Art juried exhbn.; mem. jury for scholarship awards Maine com. Skowhegan Sch. Painting & Sculpture, 1982-84; nat. com. Wellesley Coll. Friends of Art, 1983—; adv. trustee Portland Mus. Art, 1983-85, fellow, 1985—; mus. panel Maine State Commn. on Arts and Humanities, 1983-86; adv. com. Maine Biennial, Colby Coll. Mus. Art, 1983; coun. advisors Farnsworth Art Mus., Rockland, Maine, 1986-98; collections com. Payson Gallery, Westbrook Coll., Portland, 1987-91; dir. Greater Piscataqua Cmty. Found., NH Charitable Fund, 1991-97; com. to establish artist's advancement grant, 2001; mem. corp. Ogunquit Mus. Am. Art, 1988-90, 95-2000; active Maine Women's Forum, 1993—; mem. art com. York Pub. Libr., 2002—; pres. Class of 1937, Wellesley Coll., 2001-07. Lt. (j.g.) WAVES, 1942-45. Recipient Deborah Morton award Westbrook Coll., 1988, Friend of the Arts award Maine Art Dealers Assn., 1993. Mem. Springfield Art Assn., Jr. League Springfield Ill., Western Maine Wellesley Club. Episcopalian. Address: 30 Surf Point Rd York ME 03909-5053

SMART, THOMAS A., lawyer; AB summa cum laude, Dartmouth Coll., 1971; JD, U. Pa., 1974. Bar: NY 1976, So. and Ea. Dist. NY, US Ct. Appeals, 2nd, 3rd, 9th and 10th Cir., US Supreme Ct. Ptnr. litig., co-chair trademark, copyright & false advt. litig. group Kaye Scholer LLP, NYC. Mem.: Phi Beta Kappa. Office: Kaye Scholer LLP 425 Park Ave New York NY 10022 Office Phone: 212-836-8761. E-mail: tsmart@kayescholer.com.

SMARTSCHAN, GLENN FRED, educational consultant; b. Allentown, Pa., Dec. 11, 1946; s. Fred Gotfred and Joyce Isabel (Hensinger) S.; m. Linda Susan Bastinelli, Mar. 18, 1972; children: Erin Joy, Lauren Nicole. BS in Edn., Kutztown U., 1968; MS in Edn., Temple U., 1972; EdD in Ednl. Adminstrn., Lehigh U., 1979. Cert. tchr. history and comprehensive social studies, secondary prin., supt., Pa. Tchr. 8th grade social studies South Mountain Jr. H.S., 1968-76; adminstrv. asst. to prin. to prin. Raub Jr. H.S., 1976-80, dist. dir. curriculum, 1980-84, asst. to supt. for curriculum and cmty. svcs., 1984-86; supt. schs. Brandywine Hts. Area Sch. Dist., Topton, Pa., 1986-90, Mt. Lebanon Sch. Dist., Pitts., 1990—2003. Adj. prof. Cedar Crest Coll., 1986-88, Duquesne U., 1997, 2005, 06, U. Pitts., 2001; CEO Ednl. Dynamics Cons.; spkr. and cons. Multiple Client Feedback (MCF), Stakeholder Surveys Pay for Performance Plans, Match of Written, Taught and Tested Curriculum, Criterion Referenced Testing, Strategic Planning; ednl. planner Burt Hill, 2003—; cons. Tri-State area study coun. U. Pitts for planning and accountability, 2003— Bd. dirs. Alternative House, Inc., Bethlehem, Pa., 1976-81, chmn. program com., 1977-78, v.p., 1979, pres., 1980; adv. com. Lehigh County (Pa.) Hist. Mus., 1980-86; bd. dirs. Girls Club Allentown, 1983-86, v.p., 1985. Named Pa. Superintendent of Yr., 1999. Mem. ASCD, Pa. Assn. Supervision and Curriculum Devel. (exec. com., registrar ea. regional meeting, v.p. Ea. region, pres. 1988), Am. Assn. Sch. Adminstrs. (Pa. State Supt. of Yr. 1999), Pa. Assn. Sch. Adminstrs. (pres. 1996), Pa. Sch. Bds. Assn., Juvenile Diabetes Assn. (bd. dirs.), Alumni Coun. Lehigh U. (pres. 1986), Phi Delta Kappa, Fleetwood Club, Rotary (charter mem. Allentown club, exec. com. 1985). Roman Catholic. Home: One Spalding Cir Pittsburgh PA 15228 Office Phone: 412-344-8663. Business E-Mail: edcsmartschan@adelphia.net.

SMATHERS, JAMES BURTON, medical physicist, educator; b. Prairie du Chien, Wis., Aug. 26, 1935; s. James Levi and Irma Marie (Stindt) S.; m. Sylvia Lee Rath, Apr. 20, 1957; children: Kristine Kay, Kathryn Ann, James Scott, Ernest Kent. B.Nuclear Enging., N.C. State Coll., 1957, MS, 1959; PhD, U. Md., 1967. Diplomate Am. Bd. Radiology, Am. Bd. Health Physics, Am. Bd. Medical Physics; cert. in radiation oncology physics; registered profl. engr., D.C., Tex., Calif. Research engr. Atomics Internat., Canoga Park, Calif., 1959, Walter Reed Army Inst. Research, Washington, 1961-67; prof. nuclear engring. Tex. A. and M. U., College Station, 1967-80, prof., head bioengring., 1976-80; prof., head med. physics, dept. radiation oncology UCLA, 1980-2001, prof. emeritus, 2001—. Cons. U.S. Army, Dept. Energy, also pvt.; industry. Served with U.S. Army, 1959-61. Recipient Excellence in Teaching award Gen. Dynamics, 1971; Excellence in Research award Tex. A. and M. U. Former Students Assn., 1976 Mem. Health Physics Soc., Am. Assn. Physcists in Medicine, Am. Coll. Med. Physics, Am. Soc. Therapeutic Radiation Oncology, Am. Coll. Radiology. Home: 18229 Minnehaha St Northridge CA 91326-3427 E-mail: smathers@ucla.edu.

SMAY, CONNIE R., educational media specialist, educator; b. Benton Harbor, Mich., May 27, 1953; d. Victor Wier and Lois Reynolds; m. James Robert Smay, Aug. 11, 1979; children: Robert James, Thomas Victor, Rebekah Josephine. Student, Western Mich. U., Kalamazoo, 1975-76; BS in Edn., Ctrl. Mich. U., Mt. Pleasant, 1975; MS in Edn. with honors, No. Ill. U., DeKalb, 1979. Tchr.'s aide Coloma (Mich.) Migrant Program, 1971, 73-76, tchr., 1977; factory prodn. line worker Voice of Music, Benton Harbor, 1972; student tchr. Wyoming (Mich.) Sch. Dist., 1975; libr., media specialist Cmty. Sch. Dist. 300, Dundee, Ill., 1975-79, Cmty. Sch. Dist. 115, Oquawka, Ill., 1980; children's libr. Warren County Pub. Libr., Monmouth, Ill., 1980-81; ednl. media specialist Parsippany Troy Hills (N.J.) Bd. Edn., 1990—. Computer liaison Parsippany Troy Hills Bd. Edn., 1993-98, insvc. trainer for dist., 1995—, integrator of technology and NJ Core Content Stds. into content curriculum areas, 1990—; Internet trainer, 1997—, dist. tech. com., 2002-, coord. NetDay, 1997-98. Grantee EBSCO Pub., Ipswich, Mass., 1996-97; recipient dist. mini-grant Sci. Is for Everyone, 1996, Hit the Nail on the Head, 1997, Integrating Core Curriculum Stds. in Sci. and Math. Mem. DAR, ALA, Am. Assn. Sch. Libr., NJ Reading Assn., NJ Statewide Systemic Initiative, NJ Edn. Assn., Parsippany Tech. Com. (sci. standing com., learning resources and media svcs. com.), Ednl. Media Specialists Assn., Ednl. Media Assn. NJ, Morris County Media Specialist Assn., Disting. Flying Cross Soc. (assoc.). Methodist. Home: 152 Orben Dr Landing NJ 07850-1828 Office: Parsippany Troy Hills Sch Dist Brooklawn Mid Sch Parsippany NJ 07054 Office Phone: 973-428-7551 x 3003. Business E-Mail: csmay@pthsd.k12.nj.us.

SMEAD, WILLIAM LEWIS, surgeon, educator; b. Hartsdale, NY, Mar. 3, 1946; s. George Lewis and Margaret Boyd Smead; m. Anne Crimmins, 1968; 1 child, Jennifer Anne. BA, Amherst Coll., Mass., 1968; MD, Vanderbilt U., Nashville, 1972. Diplomate Am. Bd. Vascurlar Surgery, Am. Bd. Gen. Surgery, Am. Bd. Surgery. Resident surgeon Mass. Gen. Hosp., Boston, 1972—78; from asst. to assoc. prof. Ohio State U., Columbus, 1978—2006, Luther M. Keith prof., 1996—; chief staff Ohio State U. Med. Ctr. Contbr. chapters to books, articles to profl. jours. Named Prof. of the Yr., Ohio State U. Med. Sch., 1980. Fellow: ACS; mem.: Columbus Surg. Soc. (pres.), Midwestern Vascular Surgery, Eastern Surg. Soc., Ctrl. Surg. Soc. Avocations: skiing, golf, fly fishing. Home: 2530 Sherwin Rd Columbus OH 43221 Office: Ohio State U 1654 Opham Dr Means 325 Columbus OH 43210 Office Phone: 614-293-8536. Business E-Mail: william.smead@osumc.edu.

SMEAL, KEMP LESLIE, psychotherapist, musician; s. Ronald Leslie and Patricia Ann Smeal. MusB, Westminister Choir Coll., Princeton, NJ, 1981; MA in Clin. Psychology, Azusa Pacific U., Calif., 1994. Lic. marital and family therapist Bd. Behavioral Scis., Calif., 2000. Min. music Cmty. Presbyn. Ch., Danville, Calif., 1982—92; organist/pianist Glendale Presbyn. Ch., Calif., 1992—99, Glendale City Seventh-day Adventist Ch., 1997—, La Canada Presbyn. Ch., Calif., 1999—; assoc. prof. of accompanying Vanguard U., Costa Mesa, Calif., 2001—03; pvt. practice psychotherapy Newport Beach, Calif., 2000—. Organist Welsh Choir So. Calif., North Hollywood, 2001—02; organist for the glory of easter Crystal Cathedral, Garden Grove, 2002—03, interim assoc. organist, 2003; recitalist Cathedral of Our Lady of the Angels, LA, 2003—07. Musician: (CD) Beside Still Waters, Hearts Afire, (featured pianist on time-life video) A Walk With Jesus: A Holy Land Journey With Hymns and Scripture. William and Mary Renneckar scholar, Westminster Choir Coll., 1978—79. Mem.: Calif. Assn. Marriage and Family Therapists (assoc.), Am. Guild Organists Orange County Chpt. (assoc.), Am. Guild Organists LA Chpt. (assoc.). Office: 1151 Dove St Ste 205 Newport Beach CA 92660 Home Phone: 714-848-2287; Office Phone: 714-647-7577. Personal E-mail: ksmeal@aol.com. Business E-Mail: kempsmeal@aol.com.

SMEALL, CHRISTOPHER, lawyer; b. Aug. 17, 1951; BA, U. Mich., 1973; MA, U. Calif., Berkeley, 1975, CPhil, 1976; JD, Yale U., 1979. Law clerk US Ct. Appeals, Second Cir., 1979—80; assoc. Debevoise & Plimpton LLP, NYC, 1980—88, corp. ptnr., 1988—. Mem.: ABA, Coun. Foreign Rels., Assn. of Bar of City of NY, Internat. Bar Assn. Office: Debevoise & Plimpton LLP 919 Third Ave New York NY 10022 Office Phone: 212-909-6457. E-mail: csmeall@debevoise.com.

SMEALLIE, KEVIN WAYNE, engineering company executive, consultant; b. Willoughby, Ohio, Sept. 24, 1965; s. Wayne Henry and Nancy Jane Smeallie; 1 child, Devin Wayne. AS, ETI, 1984; BS in mech. engring. magna cum laude, U. Wexford, 1994. Designer Barce Equipment, Painesville, Ohio, 1984—90; project mgr., sr. designer SMS Engring., Painesville, 1990—93, project engr., mgr., sr. designer; project mgr., sr. designer Leveltek Internat., Grand River/Painesville, 1998—2000, gen. mgr., 2000—04; ret., 2004. Mem.: AISE. Achievements include invention of cart for a golf bag and method for usage. Avocation: golf. Personal E-mail: kwaynes@netzero.net.

SMEDINGHOFF, THOMAS J., lawyer; b. Chgo., July 15, 1951; s. John A. and Dorothy M. Smedinghoff; m. Mary Beth Smedinghoff. BA in Math., cum laude, Knox Coll., 1973; JD cum laude, U. Mich., 1978. Bar: Ill. 1978, U.S. Dist. Ct. (no. dist.) Ill. 1978. Assoc. McBride, Baker & Coles and predecessor McBride & Baker, Chgo., 1978—84, ptnr., 1985—99, Baker & McKenzie, Chgo., 1999—2006, Wildman, Harrold, Allen & Dixon LLP, Chgo., 2006—. Adj. prof. info. tech. & privacy law John Marshall Law Sch., Chgo., 1985-; adj. prof. bus. law Brennan Grad. Sch. Bus. Dominican U., Chgo., 2004—; chair Ill. Commn. on Electronic Commerce and Crime, 1996—; mem. US Del. to UN Commn. on Internat. Trade Law; mem. legal working group, UN Ctr. For Trade Facilitation and Elec. Bus., 2004-. Author: The Legal Guide to Developing, Protecting & Marketing Software, 1986, Multimedia Law Handbook, 1995, Online Law, 1996. Fellow: Am. Bar Found.; mem.: ABA (chair electronic commerce divsn. 1995—2003, chair sect. Sci. and Tech. Law 1999—2000, chair Internat. Policy Coord. Com. 2003—). Office: Wildman Harrold Allen & Dixon LLP 225 W Wacker Dr Ste 3000 Chicago IL 60606 Home Phone: 708-366-2329; Office Phone: 312-201-2021. Business E-Mail: smedinghoff@wildman.com.

SMEDLEY, LAWRENCE THOMAS, retired organization executive; b. Lorain, Ohio, Sept. 2, 1929; s. Robert E. and Gerda Sofia (Johnson) S.; m. Carmen Nancy Suarez, June 29, 1962; children: Lorraine, Robert, Lawrence, Richard. BA, Bowling Green State U., 1952; MA, U. Mich., 1957; PhD, Am. U., 1972. Analyst Social Security dept. AFL-CIO, Washington, 1962-65, asst. dir. dept., 1965-73, assoc. dir. dept. occupation safety-health-social security, 1973-88; exec. dir. Nat. Coun. Sr. Citizens, Inc., Washington, 1988-96. Former mem. numerous presdl. task forces and coms. on older Ams. and disabled; planning and adv. coms. White House Conf. on Aging, 1971, 81; former adv. coun. on employee welfare and pension plans Dept. Labor, former spl. task force examining policies relating to asset reversions from over-funded pension plans; bd. dirs. Nat. Coun. Sr. Citizens. Co-chmn. Leadership Coun. Aging Orgns., Washington, 1988-95; exec. bd. Com. for Nat. Health Ins., WAshington, 1989—; mem. policy conv. White House Conf. on Aging, 1995; chair Montgomery County Com. Aging. With M.I., U.S. Army, 1952-55, Korea. Recipient Svc. award Commn. on Accreditation of Facilities of Rehab., 1975, Dedicated Svc. award White House Conf. on Handicapped, 1977, award of honor Industry-Labor Coun., 1981, Outstanding Svc. award Pres.'s Com. on Employment of Handicapped, 1987. Democrat. Lutheran. Home: 3154 Grace Field Rd Apt 217 Silver Spring MD 20904 Home Phone: 301-890-4115. Personal E-mail: ltsmed@comcast.net.

SMEDS, EDWARD WILLIAM, retired food company executive; b. Chgo., Feb. 15, 1936; s. Sigvard A. and Ida S.; m. Alice J. Lawler, Jan. 26, 1957; children: Ellen R., Brad W. BS, Carthage Coll., 1957; MS, U. Ill., 1959; grad. advanced mgmt. program, Harvard U., 1977. With Borg Warner Corp., 1958-61, Kraft Foods div. Kraft Inc., 1961-75, v.p., dir. personnel, ops. group, 1976-78, v.p. human resources, 1978-79, sr. v.p. human resources, 1979-80, sr. v.p. fin. and adminstrn., 1980-84; pres. Kraft Asia Pacific, 1984-88; chmn. Kraft Foods Ltd., Australia, 1984-88; pres. Kraft Ltd. Can., 1988-89; sr. v.p. ops. and logistics Kraft Gen. Foods, Glenview, Ill., 1990-94; pres. customer svc. and ops. Kraft, Northfield, Ill., 1993-94, ret., 1994. Chmn. bd. Thrivent Mut. Funds. Chmn. bd. trustees Carthage Coll. Mem. Econ. Club of Chgo., Sunset Ridge Country Club, Club at Pelican Bay, Olde Fla. Home: 10 Regentwood Rd Northfield IL 60093-2728 also: 7575 Pelican Bay Blvd Naples FL 34108-8218 E-mail: esmeds@comcast.net.

SMEETON, THOMAS ROONEY, government affairs consultant; b. Evanston, Ill., Sept. 26, 1934; s. Cecil Brooks, Jr. and Florence Mary (Rooney).; m. Susan Diane Tollefson, Feb. 23, 1963; children: Sean, Timothy, Shannon, Brendan, Colin. BS in History, Marquette U., 1958; postgrad., U. Notre Dame, 1958-59; grad., Armed Forces Staff Coll., 1972. Intelligence officer U.S. CIA, Langley, Va., 1962-73; vp., gen. mgr. Nowicki Fla. Devel. Corp., Ft. Lauderdale, 1973-75; cons. spl. projects com. on fgn. affairs U.S. House Reps., Washington, 1975-86, minority counsel permanent select com. on intelligence, 1986-92, minority staff dir. Iran/Contra com., 1987-88, exec. dir. Rep. policy com., 1993-94; adminstr., chief investigator House Judiciary Com., Washington, 1995-96; govtl. affairs cons., 1996—. Contbg. author: (with Hyde) For Every Idle Silence, 1985. Bd. dirs. Sylvan Beach Found. With U.S. Army, 1959-62. Recipient Agy. Seal medallion CIA, 1993. Mem. Assn. Former Intelligence Officers, Ctrl. Intelligence Retirees Assn., Am. Legion, Amelia Island Club, Capitol Hill Club, The Notre Dame Club of North Fla. Republican. Roman Catholic. Avocation: golf. Home and Office: PO Box 8029 Fernandina Beach FL 32035-8029

SMEGAL, THOMAS FRANK, JR., lawyer; b. Eveleth, Minn., June 15, 1935; s. Thomas Frank and Genevieve (Andreachi) S.; m. Susan Jane Stanton, May 28, 1966; children: Thomas Frank, Elizabeth Jane. BS in Chem. Engring., Mich. Technol. U., 1957; JD, George Washington U., 1961. Bar: Va. 1961, D.C. 1961, Calif. 1964, U.S. Supreme Ct. 1976. Patent examiner U.S. Patent Office, Washington, 1957-61; staff patent atty. Shell Devel. Co., San Francisco, 1962-65; patent atty. Townsend and Townsend, San Francisco, 1965-91, mng. ptnr., 1974-89; sr. ptnr. Graham and James, San Francisco, 1992-97; ptnr. Knobbe, Martens, Olson & Bear, San Francisco, 1997—2005, Law Offices Thomas F. Smegal, Jr., 2006—. Mem. U.S. del. to Paris Conv. for Protection of Indsl. Property; mem. adv. com. Ct. of Appeals for Fed. Cir., 1992-96. Contbr. articles to profl. jours. Pres. bd. dirs. Legal Aid Soc. San Francisco, 1982-84, Youth Law Ctr., 1973-84; bd. dirs. Nat. Ctr. for Youth Law, 1978-84, San Francisco Lawyers Com. for Urban Affairs, 1972—, Legal Svcs. for Children, 1980-88; bd. dirs., presdl. nominee Legal Svcs. Corp., 1984-90, 1993-2003. Capt. Chem. Corps, U.S. Army, 1961-62. Recipient St. Thomas More award, 1982. Mem. ABA (chmn. PTC sect. 1990-91, ho. of dels. 1988-2000,2006, mem. standing com. Legal Aid and Indigent Defendants 1991-94, 2004—07, chair sect. officer conf. 1992-94, bd. govs. 1994-97, standing com. on Pro Bono and Pub. Svc. 1997-2001, standing com. on Gavel awards 2001-04), Intellectual Property Law Assn. (chmn. nat. coun. 1989), Nat. Inventors Hall of Fame (pres. 1988), Calif. Bar Assn. (v.p. bd. dirs. 1986-87), Am. Patent Law Assn. (pres. 1986), Internat. Assn. Intellectual Property Lawyers (pres. 1995-2001), Bar Assn. San Francisco (pres. 1979), Patent Law Assn. San Francisco (pres. 1974), Olympic Club, Golden Gate Breakfast Club, Claremont Country Club (Oakland). Republican. Roman Catholic. Office: One Sansome Ste 3500 San Francisco CA 94104 Home: 107 King Ave Piedmont CA 94610 Home Phone: 510-547-5309; Office Phone: 415-217-8383. Business E-Mail: tomsmegal@smegallaw.com.

SMELSER, NEIL JOSEPH, sociologist; b. Kahoka, Mo., July 22, 1930; s. Joseph Nelson and Susie Marie (Hess) S.; m. Helen Thelma Margolis, June 10, 1954 (div. 1965); children: Eric Jonathan, Tina Rachel; m. Sharin Fateley, Dec. 20, 1967; children: Joseph Neil, Sarah Joanne. BA, Harvard U., 1952, PhD, 1958; BA, Oxford U., Eng., 1954, MA, 1959; grad., San Francisco Psychoanalytic Inst., 1971. Mem. faculty U. Calif., Berkeley, 1958-94, prof. sociology, 1962—, asst. chancellor ednl. devel., 1966-68; assoc. dir. Inst. of Internat. Studies, Berkeley, 1969-73, 80-89; prof. sociology U. Calif., Berkeley, 1972-94; prof. emeritus, 1994—; dir. edn. abroad program for U. Calif., Berkeley, 1977-79, spl. advisor Office of Pres., 1993-94, dir. Ctr. for Advanced Study in Behavioral Scis., 1994-2001. Bd. dirs. Social Sci. Rsch. Coun., chmn., 1971-73, com. econ. growth, 1961-65; trustee Ctr. for Advanced Study in Behavioral Scis., 1980-93, 94-, chmn., 1984-86; trustee Russell Sage Found., 1990-2000; subcom. humanism Am. Bd. Internal Medicine, 1981-85, 89-90, adv. com., 1992-99, chmn. adv. com., 1995-99; chmn. sociology panel Behavioral and Social Scis. survey NAS and Social Sci. Rsch. Coun., 1967-69; com. on basic rsch. in behavioral and social scis. NRC, 1980-89, chmn., 1984-86, co-chmn., 1986-89; chmn. com. of selection Guggenheim Found., 1996-; chmn. Commn. for Behavioral and Social Scis. and Edn. (NAS/NRC), 1996-2003, German-Am. Acad. Coun., 1999-2000. Author: (with T. Parsons) Economy and Society, 1956, Social Change in the Industrial Revolution, 1959, Theory of Collective Behavior, 1962, The Sociology of Economic Life, 1963, 2d edit., 1975, Essays in Sociological Explanation, 1968, Sociological Theory: A Contemporary View, 1971, Comparative Methods in the Social Sciences, 1976, (with Robin Content) The Changing Academic Market, 1980, Sociology, 1981, 2d edit., 1984, 3d edit., 1987, 4th edit., 1991, 5th edit., 1995, Social Paralysis and Social Change, 1991, Effective Committee Service, 1993, Sociology, 1994, Problematics of Sociology, 1997, The Social Edges of Psychoanalysis, 1999; editor: (with W.T. Smelser) Personality and Social Systems, 1963, 2d edit., 1971, (with S.M. Lipset) Social Structure and Mobility in Economic Development, 1966, Sociology, 1967, 2d edit., 1973, (with James Davis) Sociology: A Survey Report, 1969, Karl Marx on Society and Social Change, 1973, (with Gabriel Almond) Public Higher Education in California, 1974, (with Erik Erikson) Themes of Work and Love in Adulthood, 1980, (with Jeffrey Alexander et al) The Micro-Macro Link, 1987, Handbook of Sociology, 1988, (with Hans Haferkamp) Social Change and Modernity, 1992; (with Richard Munch) Theory of Culture, 1992; (with Richard Swedberg) The Handbook of Economic Sociology, 1994; (with Jeffrey Alexander) Diversity and Its Discontents, 1999; (with William Julius Wilson and Faith Mitchell) American Becoming: Racial Trends and their Consequences, 2001, (with Paul B. Baltes) International Encyclopedia of the Social and Behavioral Sciences, 2001; editor Am. Sociol. Rev., 1962-65; adv. editor Am. Jour. Sociology, 1960-62. Rhodes scholar, 1952-54; Jr. fellow Soc. Fellows, Harvard U., 1955-58, fellow Russell Sage Found., 1989-90. Mem. Am. Sociol. Assn. (coun. 1962-65, 67-70, exec. com. 1963-65, pres. elect 1995-96, pres. 1996-97), Pacific Sociol. Assn., Internat. Sociol. Assn. (exec. com. 1986-94, v.p. 1990-94), Am. Acad. Arts and Scis. (hon.), Fedn. State Med. Bds. (bd. dirs. 2006-), (Am. Philos. Soc. (hon.), Nat. Acad. of Scis. (hon.). Business E-Mail: nsmelser@berkeley.edu.

SMELSER, THELMA ANN, writer, tax specialist; b. Piedmont, Ala., June 7, 1941; d. Rufus Milton and Florence Inez Steward; m. William Guy Smelser, Jr., June 11; children: Joseph Milton, William Preston. BA in English, Huntingdon Coll., 1964; postgrad., U. Ga., 1973—77. Lic. SEC. Tchr. Montgomery (Ala.) Bd. Edn., 1964—66, DeKalb County Bd. Edn., Decatur, Ga., 1966—85; owner Everlasting Images Wholesale, Snellville, Ga., 1985—98; tax profl. H&R Block, Loganville, Ga., 1998—; owner TAS Publs., 2004—. SEC fin. advisor H&R Block, Loganville, Ga., 2003—. Author: Strawberries & Honeysuckle, 1985; columnist: Loganville Post, 2004—. Tax advisor The Loganville Post, 2004; team mom Little League Baseball Team, Gwinnett County, Ga., 1986; mem. charity com. First Bapt. Ch., Loganville, 1997. Recipient Yearbook award, Walker H.S., 1977, Scrapbook award, Snellville Middle Sch., 1988. Republican. Baptist. Avocations: wildlife, boating, rug hooking, painting, reading. Home: 4201 Cannon Rd Loganville GA 30052 Office: H&R Block 4325 Atlanta Hwy Loganville GA 30052 Office Phone: 404-444-7279. E-mail: asmelser@bellsouth.net.

SMERDON, ERNEST THOMAS, engineering educator; b. Ritchey, Mo., Jan. 19, 1930; s. John Erle and Ada (Davidson) Smerdon; m. Joanne Duck, June 9, 1951; children: Thomas, Katherine, Gary. BS in Engring., U. Mo., 1951, MS in Engring., 1956, PhD in Engring., 1959, DSc (hon.), 2003. Registered profl. engr., Ariz. Chmn. dept. agrl. engring. U. Fla., Gainesville, 1968-74, asst. dean for rsch., 1974-76; vice chancellor for acad. affairs U. Tex. System, Austin, 1976-82; dir. Ctr. for Rsch. in Water Resources U. Tex., 1982-88; dean Coll. Engring. and Mines U. Ariz., Tucson, 1988-92, vice provost, dean Engring, 1992-97; sr. edn. assoc. NSF, Arlington, Va., 1997-00; prof. civil engring. and hydrology U. Ariz., Tucson, 2000—01, dean emeritus, 2001—. Mem. bd. sci. and tech. internat. devel. NRC, 1990—94, mem. com. planning and remediation irrigation-induced water quality problems, 1990—96, chair com. Yucca Mountian peer rev., 1995, mem. com. study rsch.-doctorate programs U.S., 1991—95, mem. com. Missouri River Ecosystem Sci., 1999—2001; chair com. Water Resources Mgmt. Instream Flow and Salmon Survival in Columbia River, 2002—04, Sci. Bases Colorado River Water Mgmt., 2005—, others. Editor: Managing Water Related Conflicts: The Engineer's Role, 1989. Mem. Ariz. Gov.'s Sci. and Tech. Coun., Tucson, 1989—96; bd. dirs. Greater Tucson Econ. Coun., 1990—95. Recipient Disting. Svc. in Engring. award, U. Mo., 1982, Lifetime Achievement award, Environ. and Water Resources Inst., 2002. Fellow: NAE (acad. adv. bd. 1989—95, tech. policy options com. 1990—91, chair com. career-long edn. engrs. 1997—2000, acad. adv. bd. 1998—99, peer com. 2002—05, chmn. sect. 12 2003—04, com. capacity U.S. Engr. Rsch. Enterprise 2004, peer com. 1986—90, 2002—, steering com. engr. 2020, policy com. Engr. 2020), ASCE (hon. Outstanding Svc. award irrigation and drainage divsn. 1988, Royce Tipton award 1989, Robert C. Park Outstanding Civil Engr. award 2005); mem.: Ariz. Soc. Profl. Engrs. (Engr. of Yr. award 1990), Univ. Coun. Water Resources, Am. Geophys. Union, Am. Soc. Engring. Edn. (chmn., bd. dirs. engring. dean's coun. 1995—97, pres. 1998—99), Am. Water Resources Assn. (Icko Iben award 1989), Am. Soc. Agrl. Engrs., Pi Mu Epsilon, Tau Beta Pi, Phi Kappa Phi, Sigma Xi. Avocations: hiking, golf, scuba diving, painting. Office: U Ariz AME Bldg Rm N521 Tucson AZ 85721-0001

SMERGE, RAYMOND G., finance company executive; b. Portales, N.Mex. m. Patricia Smerge; children: Paul, Jessica, Mark. BS, No. Ill. U., 1967; JD, De Paul U. Law, 1971. Closing officer Centex Corp., 1968—72, v.p., gen. counsel, 1972—85, v.p., 1985—93, chief legal officer, 1985—, sec., chief legal officer, 1993—2005, exec. v.p., 1997—2005; ret., 2005. Mem.: Dallas Bar Assn., ABA. Home: 315 Tonkawa Trail Corsicana TX 75109-0699 Office Phone: 214-981-6530. E-mail: rsmerge@centex.com.

SMETANA, MARK, food products executive; CFO Eby-Brown Co., Naperville, Ill. Office: 280 Shuman Blvd Ste 280 Naperville IL 60563-2578

SMETANKA, MARY JANE, reporter; Grad., U. Minn.-Twin Cities. Reporter, Minn., ND, Conn.; higher edn. reporter Mpls. Star Tribune, Mpls. Mem.: Edn. Writers Assn. (pres.). Achievements include being a Minn. Master Gardener. Office: Mpls Star Tribune 425 Portland Ave Minneapolis MN 55488-1511

SMETANKA, SALLY S., small business owner; b. Athens, NY, Aug. 26, 1944; AS, Valencia C.C., Orlando, Fla., 1981; BA, Rollins Coll., Winter Park, Fla., 1991. With labor rels. Walt Disney World, Orlando, Fla., 1978—81, asst. to pres., 1983—2005; owner Carriage Ho. Antiques, Orlando, Fla., 2005—. Home and Office: 1253 Nottingham St Orlando FL 32803 Office Phone: 321-217-1687.

SMETHERAM, HERBERT EDWIN, management consultant; b. Seattle, Sept. 9, 1934; s. Francis Edwin and Grace Elizabeth (Warner) S.; m. Beverly Joan Heckert, Sept. 7, 1963; children: Alice, Helen, Charles. BA, U. Wash., 1956; diploma, Naval Intelligence Sch., 1962; MA, U. Md., 1971; diploma in Swedish, U.S. Fgn. Svc. Inst., 1978; MBA, Rollins Coll., 1991. Ensign USN, 1956, advanced through grades to capt., 1976; comdr. USS Lind (DD-703), 1971-73; attache to Sweden USN, Stockholm, 1978-81; comdr. Naval Adminstrn. Command, Orlando, Fla., 1981-84; ret. USN, 1984; strategic planner electronics, info. and missiles group Martin Marietta Corp., Orlando, 1985-93; exec. dir. re-use com. Naval Tng. Ctr., Orlando, 1993-97, mil. base closure cons., 1991-98. Mgmt. cons., ZHA, Inc., 1998—. Mem. ARC Ctrl. Fla.; mem. Ctrl. Fla. coun. USO, Orlando, 1981—93, pres., 1991—93; mem. steering com. U.S. Congressman McCollum for Re-election, 1992—96; mem. U.S. Senator Hawkins Naval Acad. Nominating Com., Orlando, 1982—86, Fla. Gov.'s Def. Reinvestment Task Force, 1992—93; treas. St. Mathews Episcopal Parish, Orlando, 2000—03; bd. dirs. Episcopal Diocese Ctrl. Fla., 2002—05, exec. com. commn. on ministry. Decorated Royal Order of North Star (Sweden). Mem. SAR, Electronics Industry Assn. (requirements com. 1985-93), Nat. Assn. Installation Developers (southeast regional dir. 1996-97, treas. 1996-2000, bd. dirs. 1996-2000), Fla. Def. Alliance, Ret. Officers Assn., Fla. Econ. Devel. Coun., Navy League, Univ. Club of Winter Park, Fla. (bd. dirs. 2003-06), U.S. Tennis Assn., Fla. Tennis Assn., Army Navy Country Club, Orlando Tennis Ctr., Royal Lawn Tennis Club Stockholm, Winter Park (Fla.) Tennis Ctr., Delta Kappa Epsilon. Republican. Episcopalian. Avocation: tennis. Home: 3985 Lake Mira Dr Orlando FL 32817-1643 E-mail: hesmetheram@msn.com.

SMETHURST, E(DWARD) WILLIAM, JR., investment banker; b. Newark, Apr. 15, 1930; s. Edward William and Helen Lea (Wiener) S.; m. Ludlow Bixby, June 30, 953; children: James, Andrew, Katherine. AB, Amherst Coll., 1952; MBA, Harvard U., 1958. Credit analyst Chase Manhattan Bank, NYC, 1958-60; mgr. securities Irwin Mgmt. Co., Columbus, Ind., 1961-64; ptnr. Wertheim & Co., NYC, 1965-79; sr. v.p. Cyrus J. Lawrence Inc., NYC, 1980-87; mng. dir. Wertheim Schroder & Co. Inc., NYC, 1988-95; pres., chief investment officer Schroder Wertheim Investment Svcs., NYC, 1990-96; chmn., trustee Wertheim Series Trust, NYC; retired, 1996; mng. dir. Byram Capital Mgmt., Greenwich, Conn., 2002—. Trustee Mount Holyoke Coll., South Hadley, Mass., 1982—98. Lt. USN, 1952—55. Episcopalian. Home: 861 Bingham Rd Ridgewood NJ 07450-2111 Office: Byram Captial Mgmt 41 West Putnam Ave Greenwich NY 06830 Office Phone: 203-869-5570 225. Personal E-mail: wsmeth@optonline.net.

SMIALOWSKI, JOSEPH A., finance company executive; b. 1949; BA in Philosophy, Merrimack Coll., Andover, MA; MS in Computer Systems Mgmt., Rochester Inst. Tech., NY. Mgr. Xerox Corp., 1974—83, Dennison Mfg., 1983—84; ptnr. Price Waterhouse, 1984—93; v.p., chief info. officer Sears, Roebuck & Co., 1993—95, sr. v.p., chief info. officer, 1995—98; exec. v.p. BankBoston, 1998—99; vice chmn., tech. and ops. FleetBoston Fin. Corp., Boston, 1999—2002, exec. v.p., 2002—04; exec. v.p. ops. and tech. Fed. Home Loan Mortgage Corp., 2004—. Mem. Rochester Inst. Tech. Presdl. Roundtable, Banking Info. Tech. Secretariat, Pvt. Sector Coun. Active mem. United Way of Mass. Bay. Named a Premier 100 IT Leader, Computerworld Mag., 2000; named one of Top 25 People To Watch, 1998. Office: Fed Home Loan Mortgage Corp 8200 Jones Branch Dr Mc Lean VA 22102-3110 Office Phone: 703-903-2000. *

SMIDDY, JOSEPH CHARLES, retired academic administrator; b. Jellico, Tenn., June 20, 1920; s. Joseph F. and Sara Nan (Tye) Smiddy; m. Reba Graham, Sept. 6, 1985; children: Joseph F., Elizabeth Lee. BA, Lincoln Meml. U., 1948, LHD (hon.), 1970; MA, Peabody Coll., 1952; LLD, U. Richmond, 1975; LHD (hon.), Coll. William and Mary, 1986; DAm (hon.), Cumberland Coll., 1993. Tchr. Jonesville HS, 1948—51, prin., 1951—52; sec.-treas. Powell Valley Oil Co., Big Stone Gap, Va., 1952—53; prof. biology Clinch Valley Coll., U. Va., Wise, 1956—57, dean, 1957—68, dir., 1968—85, chancellor, 1968—85, chancellor emeritus, 1985—. Mem. Charter Day Award Emory and Henry Coll., 1980; mem. Commonwealth Day Award James Madison U., 1985. Musician, singer. Trustee Lincoln Meml. U. With US Army, 1942—45, PTO. Recipient Laurel Leaves award, Appalachian Consortium, 1995, Kanto Ednl. award, Wise County, 1995. Mem.: Bapt. Gen. Assn. Va. (pres. 1974—), Kiwanis, Shriners, Masons. Home: Ridgefield Acres Wise VA 24293 Office: PO Box 3160 Wise VA 24293-3160

SMIDT, SEYMOUR, economics professor; b. Chgo., Nov. 2, 1928; s. Joseph and Harriet (Morrison) S.; m. Rita Barbara Liss, Jan. 28, 1951; children— Tamar Rachelle, Stanley Adam. AB, U. Chgo., 1948; MA, 1952, PhD, 1954. Asst. prof. econs. and fin. Cornell U. Johnson Grad. Sch. Mgmt., Ithaca, NY, 1956-59, assoc. prof., 1959-65, prof., 1965-78, Nicholas H. Noyes prof., 1978—2005, prof. emeritus, 2005—. Assoc. dir. Instl. Investor Study, SEC, 1969-70; dean faculty of adminstrv. scis. Koç U., Istanbul, Turkey, 1993-95. Author: (with Harold Bierman, Jr.) The Capital Budgeting Decision, 1960, 66, 71, 75, 80, 84, 88, 92, 2007, Advanced Capital Budgeting, 2007, (with others) Management Decision-Making Under Uncertainty, 1969; contbr. articles to profl. jours. Mayor Village of Lansing, N.Y., 1975-81. Served with U.S. Army, 1954-56. Mem. Am. Econ. Assn., Am. Fin. Assn., Fin. Mgmt. Assn. Office: Cornell U Johnson Grad Sch Mgmt Ithaca NY 14853-4201

SMIDTS, CAROL, mechanical engineer, educator; d. Freddy and Julienne Smidts. PhD, U. Libre, Brussels, 1991. Faculty rsch. assoc. Ecole Poly. U. Libre, Brussels, 1991—92; faculty rsch. assoc. dept. materials and nuc. engring. U. Md., College Park, 1992—94, asst. prof. dept. materials and nuc. engring., 1994—2000, assoc. prof. dept. materials and nuc. engring., 2000—03, assoc. prof. dept. mech. engring., 2003—; assoc. dir. rsch. Nat. Ctr. Sci. Rsch., Toulouse, France, 2000. Assoc. chair reliability engring. program U. Md., College Park, 2000—01; CEO TestSolvers, Bethesda, Md., 2005—; vis. scientist Inst. for Systems Engring. & Informatics, Italy, 1992, JRC, Italy, 1992, European Communities Commn., Italy, 1992. Organizing com. Jeunesses Scientifiques Belgique, Brussels, 1987—91. Recipient award, Belgian Nuc. Soc., 1986, Flight Safety award, NASA, 1998, Rotary Nat. award, 1998, Achievement award, 1998, Software Assurance Symposium award, 2003; fellow, Inst. pour l=Encouragement de la Rsch. Sci. dans l'Industrie Agr., Belgium, 1986—88, Fonds Nat. de la Rsch. Sci., Belgium, 1989; grantee, TEDCO, 2005. Mem.: AIAA, ANS (Best Paper award 1991), IEEE (sr.). Achievements include patents for QRAS 1.0 software; method and apparatus for a common-cause failure module for probabilistic risk assessment tools; patents pending for domain specific test design automation, domain specific test design automation. Office: 3125 Glenn Martin Hall College Park MD 20742 Office Phone: 301-405-7314. Business E-Mail: csmidts@umd.edu.

SMILEY, JANE GRAVES, author, educator; b. LA, Sept. 26, 1949; d. James La Verne and Frances Nuelle (Graves) S.; m. John Whiston, Sept. 4, 1970 (div.); m. William Silag, May 1, 1978 (div.); children: Phoebe Silag, Lucy Silag; m. Stephen Mark Mortensen, July 25, 1987; 1 child, Axel James Mortensen. BA, Vassar Coll., 1971; MFA, U. Iowa, 1976, MA, PhD, U. Iowa, 1978. Asst. prof. Iowa State U., Ames, 1981-84, assoc. prof., 1984-89, prof., 1989-90, Disting. prof., 1992-96. Vis. asst. prof. U. Iowa, Iowa City, 1981, 87. Author: (fiction) Barn Blind, 1980, At Paradise Gate, 1981 (Friends of American Writers prize 1981), Duplicate Keys, 1984, The Age of Grief, 1987 (Nat. Book Critics Circle award nomination 1987), The Greenlanders, 1988, Ordinary Love and Goodwill, 1989, A Thousand Acres, 1991 (Pulitzer Prize for fiction 1992, Nat. Book Critics Circle award 1992, Midland Authors award 1992, Amb. award 1992, Heartland prize 1992), Moo: A Novel, 1995; Ten Days in the Hills (2007); (non-fiction) Catskill Crafts: Artisans of the Catskill Mountains, 1987, The All-True Travels and Adventures of Lidie Newton, 1998, Horse Heaven, 2001, Good Faith, 2003, Thirteen Ways of Looking at the Novel, 2005. Grantee Fulbright U.S. Govt., Iceland, 1976-77, NEA, 1978, 87; recipient O. Henry award, 1982, 85, 88. Mem. Author's Guild, Screenwriters Guild. Avocations: cooking, swimming, playing piano, quilting. Office: c/o Molly Friedrich Dept English 708 3rd Ave Fl 23 New York NY 10017-4201 *

SMILEY, MARILYNN JEAN, musicologist; b. Columbia City, Ind., June 5, 1932; d. Orla Raymond and Mary Jane (Bailey) S. BS (State scholar), Ball State U., 1954; MusM, Northwestern U., 1958; cert., Ecoles d'Art Americaines, Fontainebleau, France, 1959; PhD (Grad. scholar, Delta Kampa Gamma scholar), U. Ill., 1970. Public sch. music tchr., Logansport, Ind., 1954-61; faculty music dept. SUNY-Oswego, 1961—, Disting. Teaching prof., 1974—, chmn. dept., 1976-81. Presenter papers at confs. Contbr. articles to profl. jours. Bd. dirs. Oswego Opera Theatre, 1978—, Oswego Orch. Soc., 1978—, Penfield Libr. Assocs., 1985—. Recipient Chancellor's award for Excellence in Tchg., 1973; SUNY Rsch. Found. fellow, summers, 1971, 1972, 1974, NEH grantee, 1990—91. Mem.: AAUW (grantee 1984, pres. Oswego br. 1984—86, br. coun. rep. dist. III, N.Y. State divsn. 1986—88, br. coun. coord. N.Y. State divsn. 1988—90, N.Y. divsn. area intererst rep. cultural interests 1990—92, N.Y. divsn. diversity dir. 1993—96, Oswego br. diversity chair 1995—, N.Y. state unofcl. historian 2000—04, N.Y. state historian 2004—, co-pres. Oswego br. 2007—), NOW, Oswego County Hist. Soc., Early Music Am., Am. Recorder Soc., Soc. Am. Music (membership chair 1998—2003, mem. membership com. 2003—), Renaissance Soc. Am., Coll. Music Soc., Music Libr. Assn., Medieval Acad. Am., Am. Musicol. Soc. (chmn. N.Y. chpt. 1975—77, chpt. rep. to AMS coun. 1993—96, bd. dirs. N.Y. State-St. Lawrence chpt. 1993—96, mem. status of women com. 1997—2000), Oswego Recorder Consort, Ontario Singers, Heritage Found. of Oswego, Phi Kappa Phi, Kappa Delta Pi, Sigma Tau Delta, Sigma Alpha Iota, Pi Kappa Lambda, Delta Phi Alpha, Phi Delta Kappa, Delta Kappa Gamma (music chair State of Ind. 1961, music chair State of N.Y. 1968). Methodist. Office: SUNY Dept Music Oswego NY 13126 Office Phone: 315-312-3054. Business E-Mail: smiley@oswego.edu.

SMILEY, RICHARD WAYNE, researcher; b. Paso Robles, Calif., Aug. 17, 1943; s. Cecil Wallace and Elenore Louise (Hamm) S.; m. Marilyn Lois Wenning, June 24, 1967; 1 child, Shawn Elizabeth. BSc in Soil Sci., Calif. State Poly. U., San Luis Obispo, 1965; MSc in Soils, Wash. State U., 1969, PhD in Plant Pathology, 1972. Asst. soil scientist Agrl. Rsch. Svc., USDA, Pullman, Wash., 1966-69; rsch. asst. dept. plant pathology Wash. State U., Pullman, 1969-72; soil microbiologist Commonwealth Sci. and Indsl. Rsch. Orgn., Adelaide, Australia, 1972-73; rsch. assoc. dept. plant pathology Cornell U., Ithaca, NY, 1973-74, asst. prof., 1975-80, assoc. prof., 1980-85; supt. Columbia Basin Agr. Rsch. Ctr., 1985-2000; prof. Oreg. State U., 1985—. Vis. scientist Plant Rsch. Inst., Victoria Dept. Agr., Melbourne, Australia, 1982-83. Author: Compendium of Turfgrass Diseases, 1983, 3d edit., 2005; contbr. more than 200 articles to profl. jours. Postdoctoral fellow NATO, 1972. Fellow Am. Phytopath. Soc. (sr. editor APS Press 1984-87, editor-in-chief 1987-91); mem. Coun. Agrl. Sci. and Tech., Rotary (pres. Pendleton chpt. 1991-92, Paul Harris fellow 1993). Achievements include discovery of the etiology of a serious disease of turfgrasses, which led to a redefinition of studies and disease processes in turfgrasses. Office: Oreg State U Columbia Basin Agr Rsch Ctr PO Box 370 Pendleton OR 97801-0370 Home Phone: 541-276-0909. Business E-Mail: richard.smiley@oregonstate.edu.

SMILEY, ROBERT WILLIAM, JR., investment banker; b. Lansing, Mich., Nov. 17, 1943; s. Robert William Sr. and Rebecca Lee (Flint) S. AB in Econs., Stanford U., 1970; postgrad., San Fernando Valley Coll. Law, 1973—75; MBA in Corp. Fin., City U. L.A., 1979; LLB, LaSalle U., 1982. Bar: Calif. 1984. Sr. v.p. mktg. Actuarial Systems Inc., San Jose, Calif., 1972-73; founder, chmn. Benefit Systems Inc., L.A. and S.E. Nev., 1973-84, Brentwood Sq. Savs. and Loan, LA, 1982-84; chmn., CEO The Benefit Capital Cos. Inc., L.A. and S.E. Nev., 1984—. Lectr. U. Calif. Ext., L.A. and Berkeley, 1977—; instr. Am. Coll. Life Underwriters. Editor, contbg. author: Employee Stock Ownership Plans: ESOP Planning, Implementation, Law and Taxation, 1989, 3d edit. 2006; contbg. author: The Handbook of Employee Benefits, 1984, 7th edit., 2005; contbr. articles to profl. jours. Mem. nat. adv. coun., trustee Reason Found., L.A., 1983-91; bd. dirs. Nat. Ctr. for Employee Ownership, Oakland, Calif.; former trustee The Employee Ownership Found., Washington, 2000-04. With USN, 1961-64, Vietnam. Recipient Spl. Achievement award Pres.' Commn. on Pension Policy, 1984. Fellow Life Mgmt. Inst.; mem. Employee Stock Ownership Plan Assn. (founder, pres., bd. dirs., lifetime dir.), Assn. for Corp. Growth, Western and SW Pension Confs., Nat. Assn. Bus. Economists, ABA, Calif. Bar Assn. Office: The Benefit Capital Cos Inc PO Box 542 Logandale NV 89021-0542 Office Phone: 702-398-3222.

SMILEY, TAVIS, radio talk show host, writer; b. Bilox, Miss., Sept. 13, 1964; s. Emory G. and Joyce M. Smiley. Grad., Ind. U., 1986, D (hon.). Asst. to Mayor Tomilea Allison, LA, 1984—85; coun. aide, 1987; spl. asst. to exec. dir., 1978—88; adminstrv. aide to Mayor Tom Bradley, 1988—90; commentator The Smiley Report, 1990—2001; contbr. CNN, 2001—, HuffingtonPost.com; spl. correspondent ABC-TV, 2001—; commentator Tom Joyner Morning Show; pres., CEO Smiley Group, Inc. Host (TV series) BET Tonight with Tavis Smiley, 1998—2001, supervisory prodr. Tavis Smiley, 2004— (Outstanding TV News, Talk or Information (Series or Spl.), NAACP Image award, 2006), TV appearances include For Your Love, 1999, The Parkers, 2000, Any Day Now, 2001, American Dreams, 2004; author: Hard Left: Straight Talk about the Wrongs of the Right, 1996, Doing What's Right: How to Fight for What You Believe and Make a Difference, 2000, How to Make Black America Better: Leading African Americans Speak Out, 2002, Keeping the Faith: Stories of Love, Courage, Healing and Hope from Black America, 2002; co-author (with David Ritz): What I Know for Sure: My Story of Growing up in America, 2006; editor: The Covenant with Black America, 2006; host TavisTalks.com. Founder Tavis Smiley Found.; bd. dirs. Challengers Boys and Girls Club, Black Coll. Tour, LA; mem. adv. bd. Martin Luther King Jr. Ctr. Non-Violent Social Change, 1992—93, Inner City Found. Excellence in Edn., 1989—91, After Class Scouting, Scouting USA, 1991; chmn. ops. com. Young Black Profls., LA, 1988—90; mem. steering com. United Way Greater L.A., 1989—90. Named one of 50 Most Promising Young Leaders, Time Mag., 100 Most Influential Black Americans, Ebony mag., 2006; named to Hall of Fame, Vanity Fair, 1996; recipient Outstanding Bus. Profl. award, Dollars & Sense Mag., 1992, Image award, NAACP, 2000, Mickey Leland Humanitarian award, Nat. Assn. Minorities in Communications, NAACP Image award for News, Talk or Information, Series or Spl. for Katrina-One Year Later, 2007. Office: 3870 Crenshaw Blvd Ste 391 Los Angeles CA 90008 *

SMILLIE, DOUGLAS JAMES, lawyer; b. Glen Ridge, NJ, Aug. 16, 1956; s. James and Nancy (Albright) Smillie; m. Nancy Marie McKenna, Jan. 27, 1990; children: Sara Grace, Jeffrey Douglas, Heather Patricia. BA in Polit. Sci. cum laude, Muhlenberg Coll., 1978; JD, Villanova U., 1982. Bar: Pa. 1982, U.S. Dist. Ct. (ea. dist.) Pa. 1982, U.S. Ct. Appeals (3d cir.) 1983, N.J. 1984, U.S. Dist. Ct. N.J. 1984, U.S. Dist. Ct. (mid. dist.) Pa. 1995. Assoc. Clark, Ladner, Fortenbaugh & Young, Phila., 1982-90, ptnr., 1991-96; chair exec. com., dir., shareholder, v.p. Fitzpatrick Lentz & Bubba, P.C., Ctr. Valley, Pa., 1996—. Lectr. bus. bankruptcy Lehigh-Carbon CC, 1999; chmn. litig. sect. Fitzpatrick Lentz & Bubba, P.C., 1996—, chmn. exec. com., 2007; spkr. in field. Author: When Worlds Collide: The Impact of the Bankruptcy Stay on Environmental Clean-Up Litigation, 1989; editor (newsletter) Environ. Impact, 1985—96, Villanova Law Rev.; contbr. articles to profl. jours. Named one of Pa. Superlawyers, Phila. Mag., 2004, 2005, 2006; recipient Rev. Joseph Ullman award. Mem.: ABA (litig. sect.), Ea. Dist. Bankruptcy Conf., Lehigh County Bar Assn. (fed. cts. com.), Phila. Bar Assn., N.J. Bar Assn. (bankruptcy sect.), Assn. Comml. Fin. Attys., Comml. Law League Am. (bankruptcy and insolvency sect., creditors rights sect.), Turnaround Mgmt. Assn., Am. Bankruptcy Inst., Nat. Bus. Inst. Avocation: Second City Troop Rugby Football Club Alumni. Office: Fitzpatrick Lentz and Bubba PO Box 219 Stabler Corp Ctr 4001 Schoolhouse Ln Center Valley PA 18034-0219 Office Phone: 610-797-9000. Office Fax: 610-797-6663. Business E-Mail: dsmillie@flblaw.com.

SMIRNOVA, ALEVTINA LEONIDOVIA, physical chemistry educator, researcher; b. St. Petersburg, Russia, June 22, 1955; arrived in US, 2000; d. Leonid Shugalov and Vera Shugalova; children: Mikhail Smirnov, Kate. MS, St. Petersburg State U., 1976, PhD, 1989. Jr. scientist Russian Acad. Scis., St. Petersburg, 1976—78; jr./sr. scientist St. Petersburg State U., 1978—90; Ford intern U. Mich., Dearborn, 2000; prof. St. Petersburg State U., 1990—99; asst. rsch. prof. U. Conn., Storrs, 2000—. Vis. prof. Autonoma U. Barcelona, 1997; invited prof. Inst. Chemistry and Biosciences, Muenster, Germany, 1998—99; cons. in field. Co-editor: Fuel Cell Technologies: State and Perspective, 2005; contbr. articles to profl. jours. Named Vis. Women and Minority Lectr., State of Mich. King-Chavez Initiative, 2006; grantee, George Soros Found., 1997, Sci. Coun. St. Petersburg U., 1999. Mem.: ASME, Materials Rsch. Soc., Electrochemical Soc. Achievements include 4 patents in field. Avocations: violin, reading. Office: Univ Conn Weaver Rd U-5233 Storrs Mansfield CT 06269 Business E-Mail: alevtina@engr.uconn.edu.

SMISEK, JEFFERY A., air transportation executive; b. Washington, Aug. 17, 1954; married; 2 children. AB, Princeton U., 1976; JD, Harvard U., 1982. Bar: Mass., 1982, Tex. 1983. Ptnr., exec. v.p. Vinson & Elkins, LLP, Houston, 1983-95; sr. v.p., gen. counsel Continental Airlines, Inc., Houston, 1995—96, exec. v.p., gen. counsel and sec., 1996—2001, exec. v.p., corp., 2001—03, exec. v.p., 2003—04, pres., 2004—. Bd. dirs. Varco Internat., Inc., Orbitz, Inc. Office: Continental Airlines PO Box 4607 Houston TX 77210 *

SMISKO, NICHOLAS RICHARD, bishop, educator; b. Perth Amboy, NJ, Feb. 23, 1936; s. Andrew and Anna (Totin) S. BTh, Christ the Saviour Sem., 1959; BA, U. Youngstown, 1961; Lic. in Theology, Halki (Greece) Sch. Theology, 1965. Ordained priest Carpatho-Russian Orthodox Greek Cath. Ch., 1959; elevated to rank of met. bishop, 1997. Pastorate Sts. Peter and Paul Ch., Windber, Pa., 1959-62; prefect of discipline Christ the Saviour Sem., Johnstown, Pa., 1963-65; pastor Sts. Peter and Paul Ch., Homer City, Pa., 1965-71, St. Michael's Ch., Clymer, Pa., 1971-72; pastorate St. Nicholas Ch., NYC, 1972-77; abbot Monastery of the Annunciation, Tuxedo Park, NY, 1978-83; bishop of Amissos Carpatho-Russian Orthodox Diocese, 1983—. Mem. del. Ecumenical Patriarchate World Coun. Chs. 6th Gen. Assembly, Vancouver, B.C., Can.; mem. standing conf. Canonical Orthodox Bishops in Ams.; active Orthodox-Cath. Consultation of Hierarchs. Mem. Halki Alumni Assn. Am., Christ the Saviour Sem. Alumni Assn., Am. Soc. Constantinople. Carpatho-Russian Orthodox. Home and Office: 312 Garfield St Johnstown PA 15906-2122

SMIT, NEIL, telecommunications industry executive; BS, Duke U.; M in internat. bus., Tufts U. Mgmt. positions Pillsbury Co.; regional v.p. Nabisco; with Am. Online, Inc., 2000—05, COO Mapquest.com, COO AOL Local, sr. v.p. product and programming team, exec. v.p. mem. services, 2002—03, exec. v.p. mem. devel., 2003—04, pres. access bus., 2004—05; pres., CEO Charter Comm., Inc., St. Louis, 2005—, also dir., 2005—. Served to lt. comdr. Navy SEALS USN. Office: Charter Comm Inc Ste 1000 12405 Powerscourt Dr Saint Louis MO 63131-3660 *

SMITH, A. ROBERT, editor, author; b. York, Pa., Feb. 13, 1925; s. Arthur R. and Inez (Dunnick) S.; m. Yvonne Franklin, 1945 (div. 1965); 1 child, Dana C.; m. Elizabeth McDowell Morgan, 1967 (div. 1988); children: Philip S. Morgan IV, Edward A. M. Morgan, Elizabeth A. Morgan; m. Jane Dreifus, 1993 (dec. 1999). BS, Juniata Coll., 1950; postgrad., George Washington U., 1950. Reporter Huntingdon (Pa.) Daily News, 1947, Evening Star, Washington, 1950; Washington corr. Eugene (Oreg.) Register-Guard, 1951-78, Portland Oregonian, 1952-72, King Broadcasting, 1976-78; assoc. editor Virginian-Pilot, Norfolk, 1978-83; editor Venture Inward, Assn. Rsch. and Enlightenment mag., Virginia Beach, Va., 1984—2003. Author: The Tiger in the Senate, 1962, Hugh Lynn Cayce: About My Father's Business, 1988, The Lost Memoirs of Edgar Cayce, 1997, Misdiagnosed: Was My Wife a Casualty of America's Medical Cold War?, 2001, No Soul Left Behind, 2005; co-author: (with Eric Sevareid and Fred J. Maroon) Washington: Magnificent Capital, 1965; (with James V. Giles) An American Rape, 1975 With USNR, 1943-46, PTO. E-mail: abob@cox.net.

SMITH, ADA LAVERNE, state legislator; b. Amherst County, Va. d. Thomas and Lillian Smith. Grad., CUNY. Dep. clk. N.Y.C.; state senator N.Y. Legislature, Albany, 1988—, mem. various coms., ranking corp. commn. and authorities, 1994, minority whip, 1994—2003, chair Senate Dem. Conf., 2003—05, asst. Dem. leader, policy and adminstrn., 2005—. Mem. Senate Minority Puerto Rican and Hispanic Task Force. Trustee, life dir. Coll. Fund Baruch Coll. Recipient Outstanding Alumni award Baruch Coll. Mem. NY Assn. State Black and Puerto Rican Legislators, Baruch Coll. Alumni Assn. (pres., Disting. Svc. award, Outstanding Achievement award), Nat. Black Caucus of State Legislators (bd. dirs., vice chair telecomms. com.), Women in Govt. (state bd. dirs.). Office: NY State Senate Rm 808 Legis Office Bldg Albany NY 12247 also: Queens Dist Office 11643 Sutphin Blvd Jamaica NY 11434-1526 Office Phone: 518-455-3531. E-mail: smith@senate.state.ny.us.

SMITH, ADAM See GOODMAN, GEORGE

SMITH, ADAM, congressman; b. Washington, June 15, 1965; s. Ben Smith; m. Sara Bickle-Eldridge, Aug. 1993; 2 children. BA, Fordham U., 1987; JD, U. Wash., 1990. Driver United Parcel Svc., 1985-87; mem. Wash. State Senate, 1990-96; atty. Cromwell, Mendoza and Belur, 1991—92; asst. pros. atty. Seattle, 1993—95; pro tem judge, 1996; mem. US Congress from 9th Wash. dist., 1997—, mem. armed svcs. com., mem. internat. rels. com. Mem. Kent Drinking Driver Task Force, Highline Citizens for Schs., Kent Meridian HS Site-Based Coun.; bd. mem. Judson Pk. Retirement Home. Mem.: Kiwanis Internat. Democrat. Office: US Ho Reps 227 Cannon Ho Office Bldg Washington DC 20515 Office Phone: 202-225-8901. *

SMITH, ADRIAN DEVAUN, architect; b. Chgo., Ill., Aug. 19, 1944; s. Alfred D. and Hazel (Davis) S.; m. Nancy L. Smith, Aug. 17, 1968; children: Katherine, Jason. Student, Tex. A&M U., 1962-66; BArch, U. Ill., Chgo., 1969. Registered architect, Ill., Mass., Fla. Design ptnr. Skidmore, Owings, & Merrill, Chgo., 1980—2003, cons. ptnr., 2003—06; CEO Adrian Smith & Gordon Gill Arch., 2006—. Vis. faculty Sch. Architecture, U. Ill., Chgo., 1984; chmn. U. Ill. Sch. Archtl. Alumni Assn., AIA Jury on Inst. Honors; adv. jury AIA gold metal and architecture firm award, 2000; chmn. nat. AIA awards jury for architecture and 25 yr. award, 2004; chmn. Skidmore Owings Merrill Found., 1989-95; pres. Chgo. Ctrl. Area, 1997-99; bd. dirs. Greater State Street Coun. trustee; bd. govs. Sch. Art Inst. Chgo., 1999—; repr., RIBA British Archtl. Libr. Trust, British Schs. and Univ. Found.; dir., U. Ill. Alumni Found., 88-89; cons. and lectr. in field. Designer numerous projects including 919 North Michigan Ave, Chgo., 1982, Chgo. Ctrl. Area Plan, 1984, 1992 Chgo. World's Fair, 1980-85, Olympia Ctr., Chgo., 1986, Trump Tower Chgo., GM Hdqrs., Renn Ctr., Detroit, 222 N. LaSalle, Chgo., 1986, Art Inst. Chgo. 2nd Fl. Galleries, 1987, Arthur Anderson Tng. Ctr., St. Charles, Ill., 1987, Rowes Wharf, Boston, 1988, Chgo. Transit Authority Red Line, AT&T Corp. Ctr., Chgo., 1989, NBC Tower at Cityfront Ctr., Chgo., 1989, 75 State St., Boston, 1989, Continental Bank First Fl. Renovation, Chgo., 1990, Dearborn Tower, Chgo., 1991, USG Hdqs., Chgo., 1991, Washington Univ. Psychology Bldg., Lab., & Animal Facility, St. Louis, 1996, Chgo. Transit Authority, Green Line Rehabilitation, Chgo., 1995, Heller Internat. Tower, Chgo., State St. Renovation, 1997 (AIA honor award urban design, 1998), Metro. Ctr. II, Mpls., Minn., 1997, Washington Univ. Arts & Scis. Bldg., St. Louis, Mo., 2000, Campus Crusade for Christ Internat., Orlando, Fla., 2000, Millennium Park, Chgo., 2002, 7 South Dearborn Tower, Chgo., 2002, Manulife Fin., Boston, 2003, GM Hdqrs. at Resaissance Ctr., Detroit, 2003, Lakeshore East, Chgo., Trump Internat. Hotel & Tower, Chgo., Monterey Cultural Ctr., Mex., 1978, Hyatt Regency Surabaya, Indonesia, 1979, Banco de Occidente, Guatemala City, 1980, Bally of Switzerland, 1982, Hdqs. Canary Wharf Fin. Ctr., London, Eng., 1988, United Gulf Bank, Manama, Bahrain, 1986, 10 Ludgate, 10 Fleet Place, Ludgate Office Bldg., London, 1992, 100 Ludgate Hill, Ludgate Office Bldg., London, 1992, Aramco Hdqrs., Dhahran, Saudi Arabia, 1993, Aramco Hdqrs. Office Bldg., 1993, Xiamen Posts & Telecommunications Bldg., China, 1994, Frankfurter Allee, 1991, Phase I implementation, Berlin, Germany, 1995, Tower Palace III, Seoul, Korea, 1996, Kowloon MTR Tower, Hong Kong, Pidemco GSCP MSCP Towers, Singapore, 1997, McGraw Hill European Headquarters, Canary Wharf (FC-2), London, 1990, Canary Wharf, London, 1991, Canary Wharf (DS4), CSFB European Headquarters, Canary Wharf (DSI), Morgan Stanley Headquarters for Europe (HQI), Canary Wharf, Burj Dubai Tower (World's Tallest Bldg.), United Arab Emirates, Jin Mao Tower (World's Tallest Mixed-Use Project), Shanghai, China (Nat. AIA award for interior architecture 2000), 1998, BankBoston Hdqrs., Sao Paulo, Brazil, 2000, 201 Broadgate, London, Eng., 2008, Nanjing Guozi Greenland Fin. Ctr., Nanjing, China, Chemsunny Office Bldg., Beijing, Russia Tower, Moscow, Tower Palace for Samsung Group,Seoul, Korea, 2003, Shanghai Grand Office Tower, 2008, Shanghai, Pearl River Zero Energy Tower, Guanghou, China; author: Monograph of Adrian P. Smith, 2002, The Architecture of Adrian Smith 1980-2006: Toward a Sustainable Future, 2007; contbr. articles to profl. jours.; subject numerous pubs. in architecture. Mem. com. Task Force for New City Plan, Chgo., Light Up Chgo., Ctrl. Area Com. Task Force Chgo.; chmn. Senator Richard A. Newhouse Bldg. Competition Jury, 1982, Progressive Architecture Design Jury, 1985; bd. dirs. State St. Coun.; lifetime gov., Urban Land Inst. Found.; trustee, Chgo. Architecture Found., 93-99, Bldg. Experiences Trust, 91-95. Recipient silver award, Ill. Ctr. Masonry Coun., 1981, Gold award, 1982, Urban Design and Planning First award, 32nd Annual Progressive Architecture Mag., 1986, Energy award program, Am. Refrigerating & Air Conditioning Engrs., NBC 1988, AT&T 1988, Build Am. award, Assoc. General Contractors of Am. and Motorola, 1989, Excellence on the Waterfront Honor award, 1990, Civic Trust award, Ludgate Office Complex, 1994, Alumni Achievement award, U. Ill., 1995, First Prize, European Commercial Property Development Awards, 1995, Excellence in Engring., ASHRAE, 1995, spl. achievement award, Internat. Downtown Assn., 1997, Best Structure award, Structural Engineers Assn. Ill. 1998, Architect Creation award, World Architect Conf., 2001, Merit award, Illuminating Engring. Soc. N. Am., 2001, award of excellence, ULI, 2004, Pres. award, Korea Inst. Architects, 2005, Am. Architecture award, Chgo. Athenaeum; named Best of Competition, Inst. Bus. Designers, Interior Design Mag., Bally Switzerland, Chgo., 1982. Fellow AIA (mem. Young Architects Award Design July, 1987, Mich. Jury 1988, chmn. nat. jury arch. and 25 yr. award 2004, Banco de Occidente, 1980, 81, Interior Architecture Award, Citation of Merit, 1984, Interior Architecture award, 1989, Disting. Bldg. award 1981, 87, 90, 91, 92, 94, 97, 98, 2003, 04, 06, Nat. Honor award, 1988, 94, 98), Royal Inst. Brit. Architects, Archtl. Registration Coun., U.K., Nat. Coun. Archtl. Registration Bds., Architecture Soc. of Art Inst. Chgo., Chgo. Arch. Found., Chgo. Archtl. Club, Urban Found. (bd. trustees) University Club, Arts Club; Am. Acad. Rome (Midwest dir., 85-86); mem. Economic Club Chgo. Office: Adrian Smith & Gordon Gill Architecture 111 W Monroe St #2300 Chicago IL 60603 Office Phone: 312-920-1888. Office Fax: 312-920-1775.

SMITH, ADRIAN M., congressman, real estate agent; b. Scottsbluff, Nebr., Dec. 19, 1970; BS in Mktg. Edn., U. Nebr., 1993, postgrad., Portland State U. Legis. page Nebr. Legislature, 1992; mem. Nebr. Legislature from 48th dist., Lincoln, 1998—; staff internat., mktg. specialist Nebrs. Gov.'s Office, 1992; rsch. asst. U. Nebr. Found., 1992-93; educator, staff devel. project mgr. Ednl. Svc. Unit 13, 1994-97; real estate agt., mktg. specialist Buyers Realty, 1997—; mem. US Congress from 3rd Nebr. dist., 2007—, asst. whip, 2007—. Mem. Scotts Bluff County Bd. Realtors. Mem. Gering City Coun., 1994-98, We. Nebr. Regional Airport Ops. Bd., Scotts Bluff County Visitors Adv. Com., 1995-96, N. Platte Valley Hist. Soc., Riverside Zool. Soc., Wyo-Braska Mus. Natural History, Calvary Meml. Evang. Free Ch., Farm and Ranch Mus. Assn.; chmn. land use task force Vision 2020; bd. dirs. Twin Cities Devel. Mem. Scottsbluff Kiwanis Club (bd. dirs. Camp Kiwanis). Republican. Office: US House Reps 503 Cannon House Office Bldg Washington DC 20515 Office Phone: 202-225-6435. Office Fax: 202-225-0207. *

SMITH, AGNES MONROE, history professor; b. Hiram, Ohio, Aug. 8, 1920; d. Bernie Alfred and Joyce (Messenger) Monroe; m. Stanley Blair Smith; children: David, Doris, Darl, Diane. BA, Hiram Coll., 1940; MA, W.Va. U., 1945; PhD, Western Res. U., 1966. Social sci. tchr. Freedom (Ohio) High Sch., 1940-44; instr. of history W.Va. U., Morgantown, 1945; instr. of social sci. Hiram Coll., 1946; inst. history and social sci. Youngstown (Ohio) State U., 1964-66, asst. prof. to prof. of history, 1966-84, prof. history emeritus, 1984—; vis. prof. history Hiram Coll., 1988-90. Co-editor: Bourgeois, Sans Culottes and other Frenchmen, 1981; contbr. articles to profl. jours. Mem. Ohio Acad. History, Delta Kappa Gamma, Phi Alpha Theta, Pi Gamma Mu. Mem. Christian Ch. (Disciples Of Christ). Home: 16759 Main Market Rd West Farmington OH 44491-9608

SMITH, A.J., professional sports team executive; b. Feb. 28, 1949; m. Susan Smith; children: Andrea, Kyle. Grad. in Health and Phys. Edn., Ky. Wesleyan Coll., Owensboro, 1971. Tchr. health and phys. edn. Providence Jr. HS Sys., 1971—85; asst. coach Cranston West HS, RI, 1971—76, U. RI, 1978; wide receiver Ea. Football League Attleboro Kings, Mass., 1972—74; head coach Ea. Football League RI Kings, 1976; vol. part-time scout NFL NY Giants, 1977; part-time scout NFL New Eng. Patriots, 1978—80, NFL Houston Oilers, 1981; scouting position US Football League Chgo. Blitz., 1982—83, US Football League Pitts. Maulers, 1984; dir. pro pers. NFL San Diego Chargers, 1985—86, asst. gen. mgr., dir. pro pers., 2001—03, exec. v.p., gen. mgr., 2003—; area scout NFL Buffalo Bills, 1987—89, asst. dir. coll. scouting, 1989—93, dir. pro pers., 1993—2000. Named NFL Exec. of Yr., Pro Football Weekly, 2004, Profl. Football Writers of Am., 2004, FoxSports.com, 2004, CBSSportsline.com, 2004; named to Am. Football Assn. Minor/Semi-Pro Football Hall of Fame, 1990. Office: San Diego Chargers PO Box 609609 San Diego CA 92160-9609 *

SMITH, ALAN JAY, computer science educator, consultant; b. NYC, Apr. 10, 1949; s. Harry and Elsie Smith. SB, MIT, 1971; MS, Stanford U., Calif., 1973, PhD in Computer Sci., 1974. From asst. prof. to full prof. U. Calif., Berkeley, 1974—; assoc. editor ACM Trans. on Computers Systems, 1982-93. Vice-chmn. elec. engring. and computer sci. dept. U. Calif., Berkeley, 1982-84; nat. lectr. ACM, 1985-86; mem. editl. bd. Jour. Microprocessors and Microsystems, 1988—2005, Microprocessor Report, 2005-; subject area editor Jour. Parallel and Distbn. Computing, 1989—; mem. IFIP working group 7.3.; program chmn. Sigmetrics 89, Performance 1989, Hot Chips Symposium, 1990, 94, 97. 2005. Recipient AA Michaelson award, Comp. Measurement Group, 2003, Harry Goode award, IEEE computer Soc., 2006. Fellow: AAAS, IEEE (disting. visitor 1986—87), Assn. for Computing Machinery (chmn. spl. interest group on ops. sys. 1983—87, nat. lectr. 1985—86, bd. dirs. spl. interest group on performance evaluation 1989—89, chmn. spl. interest group on computer architecture 1991—93, bd. dirs. spl. interest group on computer architecture 1993—2003); mem.: Computer Measurement Group. Office: U Calif Dept Computer Sci Berkeley CA 94720-1776

SMITH, ALAN MICHAEL, music educator, musician; b. Austin, Tex., Oct. 2, 1945; s. Jackson Buford Smith and Katherine Elizabeth Webb; m. Diana Lou Barker, Dec. 28, 1968; 1 child, Hillary Kay. MusB, U. Tex., 1967, MusM, 1969, D of Musical Arts, 1977. Instr. cello Shenandoah U., Winchester, Va., 1970—72; asst. prof. cello U. NC, Chapel Hill, 1974—80; prof. cello Bowling Green (Ohio) State U., 1980—. Vis. assoc. prof. cello Oberlin (Ohio) Conservatory of Music, 1990; vis. prof. cello U. Ariz., Tucson, 1992—93; music dir., coord. Bowling Green Symphony Orch., 1994—2004; assoc. dean Coll. Musical Arts Bowling Green State U., 2001—; mem. adv. bd. STRINGS Mag., San Rafael, Calif., 2003—; performing tours of U.S., Mex., Taiwan, China, Netherlands, Belgium, Korea, Romania and Greece; performed at Ionian Music Acad. and Festival, Corfu, Greece, 2005—06. Performer (CD) The Guarneri Duo, 2004. Tech. sgt. USAF, 1969—72. Recipient Young Artist award, Midland-Odessa (Tex.) Symphony, 1965, Eric Sorantin award, San Angelo (Tex.) Symphony, 1968, Young Artist award, Denver Symphony Orch., 1970. Mem.: Am. Fedn. Musicians, Chamber Music Am., Coll. Music Soc.

SMITH, ALAN WADE, music educator; b. Elizabeth City, NC, Oct. 8, 1964; s. Gilbert Richard and Marilyn Kay Smith. AA in Music Edn., St. Petersburg Jr. Coll., Fla., 1986; BS, U. South Fla., 1990. Cert. Secondary Social Studies Edn. S.C., 2005, Fla., 2004. Social studies tchr. Seminole (Fla.) Mid. Sch., 1993—2004; global studies tchr. Dorman HS Freshman Campus, Roebuck, SC, 2004—06; assoc. marching band dir. Dorman HS, Roebuck, SC, 2004—06. Visual designer (marching band competitive field shows) Marching Band Competitive Field Show (Bands of Am. Regional Champions/Nat. Finalists). Recipient Tchr. of the Yr., Seminole Mid. Sch., 1997. Mem.: Music Educator's Nat. Conf., Nat. Coun. for Social Studies (assoc.). Home: PO Box 665 Roebuck SC 29376 Office: Dorman HS Freshman Campus 1225 Cavalier Way Roebuck SC 29376 Home Phone: 864-266-7873. Personal E-mail: alan88888@aol.com. Business E-Mail: smithaw@spart6.org.

SMITH, ALBERT CROMWELL, JR., investment company executive, writer; b. Norfolk, Va., Dec. 6, 1925; s. Albert Cromwell and Georgie (Foreman) Smith; m. Laura Thaxton, Oct. 25, 1952; children: Albert, Elizabeth, Laura. BSCE, Va. Mil. Inst., 1949; MS in Govtl. Adminstrn., George Washington U., 1965; MBA, Pepperdine U., 1975; PhD in Bus. Adminstrn., LaSalle U., 1994. Enlisted USMC, 1944, advanced through grades to col., 1970, comdr. inf. platoons, cos., landing force; assigned to staffs, U.K. Joint Force, U.S. Sec. Navy, Brit. Staff Coll., Marine Staff Coll., U.K. Staff Coll. and Latimer Staff Coll.; advisor, analyst amphibious sys. USMC; ret., 1974; pres. A. Cromwell-Smith, Ltd., Charlottesville, Va., 1973; head broker, cons. A. Cromwell Smith, Investments, La Jolla and Coronado, Calif., 1975—. Author: The Individual Investor in Tomorrow's Stock Market, 1977, The Little Guy's Stock Market Survival Guide, 1979, rev. edit., 2000, Wake Up Detroit: The EVs are Coming, 1982, The Little Guy's Tax Survival Guide, 1984, Little Guy's Real Estate Success Guide, 1990, Little Guy's Stock Market Success Guide, 1992, Little Guy's Stock Market Future Effectiveness, 1994, The Little Guy's Sailboat Success, 1996, The Little Guy's Business Success, 1997, Business Success, 1997, Stock Market Success, 1998, Semper Fidelis in Peace and War, 1999, revised edit., 2003, Sailboat Success, 1999, Tax Survival Guide, 1999, The EVs are Coming, 1999, Real Estate Success, 2000, The EVs and Hybrids Are Here, 2005; contbr. articles to profl. jours. Bd. dirs. La Jolla Reps., 1975—76; vestryman St. Martin's Episcopal Ch., 1971—73. Decorated Legion of Merit with oak leaf cluster with V device, Bronze Star with V device with oak leaf cluster, Air medal with two oak leav clusters, Purple Heart, Vietnamese Galantry Cross with gold star. Mem.: VFW, SAR, ASCE, So. Calif. Options Soc., Stockbrokers Soc., Coronado Bd. Realtors, San Diego Bd. Realtors, Calif. Assn. Realtors, Nat. Assn. Realtors, Mil. Order Purple Heart. Address: 1810 Ave del Mundo # 106 Coronado CA 92118 Office Phone: 619-435-1928.

SMITH, ALEX, professional football player; b. Seattle, Wash., May 7, 1984; s. Doug, Pam. Bachelor's degree in Econ., Utah Univ., 2003. Quarterback San Francisco 49ers. Named Nat. Player Yr., The Sporting News, 2004. Achievements include first over-all selection in NFL draft, 2005. Office: San Francisco 49ers Marie P DeBartolo Sports Ctr 4949 Centennial Blvd Santa Clara CA 95054

SMITH, ALEXANDER W., retail executive; Chmn. Winners Merchant Internat. LP; pres. UK ops. T.J. Maxx, 1995—2001; exec. v.p. and group exec. internat. The TJX Companies Inc., 2001—04, sr. exec. v.p. and group exec. internat., 2004—07; pres., CEO Pier 1 Imports, Inc., 2007—. Office: Pier 1 Imports Inc 100 Pier 1 Pl Fort Worth TX 76102 Office Phone: 817-252-8000. Office Fax: 817-252-8174. *

SMITH, ALEXANDER WYLY, JR., lawyer; b. Atlanta, June 9, 1923; s. Alexander Wyly and Laura (Payne) S.; m. Betty Rawson Haverty, Aug. 31, 1946; children: Elizabeth Smith Crew, Clarence Haverty, Laura Smith Brown, James Haverty, Edward Kendrick, Anthony Marion, William Rawson. Grad., Marist Sch., 1941; student, Holy Cross Coll., 1941-42; BBA, U. Ga., 1947, LL.B. cum laude, 1949. Bar: Ga. 1948. Practiced in Atlanta, 1948-98; ret. ptnr. Smith, Gambrell & Russell and predecessor, 1994—. Bd. dirs. Our Lady of Perpetual Help Free Cancer Home; bd. dirs., planning and devel. coun. Cath. Archdiocese Atlanta, Marist Sch., Atlanta, John and Mary Franklin Found. Served with USAAF, 1943-46. Mem. Ga. Bar Assn., Atlanta Bar Assn., Phi Delta Phi, Chi Phi, Piedmont Driving Club Atlanta, Peachtree Golf Club Atlanta (pres. 1989-91). Home: 2771 Peachtree Rd #5 Atlanta GA 30305-3523 Office: 3100 Promenade II Atlanta GA 30309-3574 Office Phone: 404-815-3507.

SMITH, ALISON LEIGH, lawyer; b. Brownsville, Tex., Sept. 24, 1952; d. Arthur Lee and June (Allen) Smith; m. Dean A. Burkhardt, Apr. 24, 1981. B in Journalism summa cum laude, U. Tex., 1974, JD cum laude, 1977. Bar: Tex. 1977, US Dist. Ct. (so. dist.) Tex. 1978, US Ct. Appeals (5th cir.) 1981, US Dist. Ct. (no. dist.) Tex. 1987, US Ct. Appeals (DC cir.) 1989. Assoc. Vinson & Elkins LLP, Houston, 1977-84, ptnr., 1984—89, 1991—2004; dep. asst. atty. gen. antitrust divsn. U.S. Dept. Justice, Washington, 1989-91; ptnr. Dewey Ballantine LLP, Houston, 2004—05, Haynes and Boone, LLP, Houston, 2005—. Adj. prof. law U. Tex., Austin, 1992-93. Alternate del. Rep. Nat. Conv., New Orleans, 1988; mem. ethics com. City of Houston, 1988-89; chair Mayor's Animal Protection Task Force, 2005. Mem. ABA (antitrust law sect., chair transp. industry com., 1992-95, co-chmn. pvt. antitrust litig. com. 2001-04, long range planning task force, 2002, vice chmn. Sherman Act sect. one com. 2004-05, econ. evidence task force 2005-06, editl. bd. State Antitrust Practice and Statutes, 2006-, litig. sect. chair, 1999-2000, animal law sect. chair-elect, 2007-), Am. Law Inst., Tex. Bar Found., Houston Bar Assn. Home: 2125 Bolsover St Houston TX 77005-1617 Office: Haynes and Boone LLP 1221 McKinney Ste 2100 Houston TX 77010 Home Phone: 713-520-1979; Office Phone: 713-547-2673. Business E-Mail: alison.smith@haynesboone.com.

SMITH, ALLIE MAITLAND, engineering educator; b. Lumberton, NC, June 9, 1934; s. Allie McCoy and Emma Hattie (Wright) S.; m. Sarah Louise Whitlock, June 16, 1957; children: Sara Leianne, Hollis Duval, Meredith Lorren. BME with honors, N.C. State U., Raleigh, 1956, MS, 1961, PhD, 1966. Assoc. engr. Martin Co., Balt., 1956-57; devel. engr. Western Electric Co., 1957-60; mem. tech. staff Bell Tel. Labs., Burlington, NC, 1960-62; instr., then asst. prof. extension N.C. State U., 1958-62; rsch. project engr. Rsch. Triangle Inst., Durham, NC, 1962-66; rsch. supr. Sverdrup/ARO, Inc., Arnold Air Force Sta., Tenn., 1966-79; adj. prof. U. Tenn., Tullahoma, 1967-79; prof. mech. engring. U. Miss., University, 1979—, dean Sch. Engring., 1979—2000. Bd. dirs., scholarship bd. Miss. Mineral Resources Inst.; exec. chmn. 14th conf. Southeastern Conf. on Theoretical and Applied Mechanics, exec. com. 13th-16th confs., ops. com. and policy com., 1990-99, session chair, 1994; organizing com., internat. sci. adv. bd., plenary session presiding officer Internat. Conf. on Hydrosci. and Engring., 1993, 95; organizing com., plenary session chair Conf. on Mgmt. of Landscapes Disturbed by Channel Incision, 1997; keynote lecture and plenary sessions chair, 3rd Internat. Conf. on Hydrosci. and Engring., Berlin, 1998 Author: Fundamentals of Silicon Integrated Device Technology, Vol. I: Oxidation, Diffusion and Epitaxy, 1967, also articles, revs.; editor: Radiative Transfer and Thermal Control, 1976, Thermophysics of Spacecraft and Outer Planet Entry Probes, 1977, Fundamentals and Applications of Radiation Heat Transfer, 1987, Developments in Theoretical and Applied Mechanics, Vol. XIV, 1988, Radiation Heat Transfer: Fundamentals and Applications, 1990, Fundamentals of Radiation Heat Transfer, 1991, Radiative Heat Transfer: Theory and Applications, 1993, Solution Methods for Radiative Heat Transfer in Participating Media, 1996, Radiative Heat Transfer, 1997. Fellow AIAA (chmn. thermophysics tech. com. 1975-77, ASME (aerospace heat transfer com. 1975—; chmn. radiative heat transfer I and II sessions, Pitts. 2000, chmn. radiation heat transfer II session, St. Louis, 2002), chmn. terrestrial energy sys. tech. com. 1979-81, chmn. confs. 1975, 79, assoc. editor jour. 1975-77, 1986—, nat. publ. com. 1979-83, Nat. Thermophysics award 1978, Hermann Oberth award 1984-85, Space Shuttle Flag Challenger plaque 1984, supernumerary dir. Ala.-Miss. sect. 1994—2000); mem. AAUP, NSPE (pres. N.E. Miss. chpt. 1990-91), Am. Soc. Engring. Edn. (host Nat. Engring. Deans' Inst. 1991), NY Acad. Scis., Sigma Xi, Phi Kappa Phi, Tau Beta Pi, Pi Tau Sigma, Upsilon Pi Epsilon, Sigma Pi (scholar 1955), Order of the Engr., Rotary Achievements include discovery of anomalous refraction maxima phenomenon. Home: PO Box 1857 University MS 38677-1857 Office: U Miss 205 Carrier Hall University MS 38677 Office Phone: 662-915-5842. Business E-Mail: enas@olemiss.edu.

SMITH, ALVY RAY, computer graphics designer; b. Mineral Wells, Tex., Sept. 8, 1943; m. Zu Smith; children: Sam, Jesse. BSEE with high honors, N.Mex State U., 1965, LLD (hon.), 1999; MS, Stanford U., 1966, PhD, 1970. Jr. engr. N.Mex State U., 1962—65; assoc. prof. Elec. Engring. and Computer Sci. Dept. NYU, 1969—73; sr. scientist Computer Graphics Lab. NY Inst. Tech., 1975—79; cons. Jet Propulsion Lab. Calif. Inst. Tech., 1979; dir. computer graphics rsch. Lucasfilm Ltd., 1980—86; co-founder, exec. v.p., bd. mem. Pixar, 1986—91; founder, pres., bd. mem. Altamira Software Corp., 1991—94; graphics fellow Microsoft Corp., 1994—2000; founder, pres. Ars Longa. Vis. assoc. prof. U. Calif., Berkeley, 1974; vis. scientist Xerox Palo Alto Rsch. Ctr., 1974; Forsythe lectr. Stanford U., 1997. Contbr. articles to profl. jours.; spkr. in field. Mem.: NAE, Descendants of Founders of NJ, NY Genealogical and Biog. Soc., Soc. of Colonial Wars in State of NY, New England Historic Genealogical Soc. (bd. trustees), Old Derby Hist. Soc. (hon.), Nat. Huguenot Soc. (life), Genealogical Soc. of NJ (life). E-mail: alvy@alvyray.com.

SMITH, AMOS BRITTAIN, III, chemist, educator; b. Lewisburg, Pa., Aug. 26, 1944; s. Amos Brittain and Mildred (Cornelius) S.; m. Janet L. Duyckinck; children: Amos Matthew MacMillan, Kathryn Schuyler. BS, MS, Bucknell U., 1966; PhD, Rockefeller U., 1972; MA (hon.), U. Pa., 1978. Rsch. assoc. Rockefeller U., NYC, 1972-73; asst. prof. U. Pa., Phila., 1973-78, assoc. prof., 1978-81, prof., 1981—, chmn. dept. chemistry, 1988—96, Rhodes-Thompson prof. chemistry, 1990—, mem. Lab. Rsch. Structure Matter, 1976—2000. Vis. dir. Kitasato Inst., Tokyo, 1990—; ad hoc mem. medicinal chemistry A and bioorganic and natural products chemistry rev. panel, NIH, 1980-83, mem. medicinal chemistry study sect., 1983-87, chmn. study sect. workshop on medicinal chemistry, 1986, mem. study sect. for AIDS and related rsch., 1989; vis. prof. Columbia U., N.Y.C., 1980, Cambridge (Eng.) U., 1982; Arthur D. Little lectr. Northeastern U., 1986, H. Martin Friedman lectr. Rutgers U., 1988, Merck-Frosst lectr., Ottawa, Can., 1988, U. Sherbrooke, Québec, Can., 1993; Phillips lectr. Haverford Coll, 1992; Soc. Francaise de Chimie lectr., Paris, 1988, lectr. at French-speaking univs., Switzerland, 1989; bd. dirs. Organic Reactions, Inc. Mem. editl. bd. Jour. Organic Chemistry, 1982-86, 94-97, Jour. Am. Chem. Soc., 1988-93, Organic Reactions, 1987—, Organic Syntheses, 1990—, Jour. Chem. Soc., Perkin I., 1992—, Synlett, 1995-97, Fullerene Sci. and Tech., 1993—; guest editor Tetrahedur Symposium in Print, Fullerene Chemistry, 1995; regional editor Fullerene Sci. and Tech., 1997—; bd. cons. editors Tetrahedron Publs., Jour. of Antibiotics, 1999—; editor-in-chief Organic Letters, 1999—; editl. adv. bd. Synlett, 1995-98; contbr. numerous articles to profl. jours., chpts. in books, revs., others. Recipient Camille and Henry Dreyfus Tchr.-Scholar award, 1978-83, Career Devel. award NIH, 1980-85, Arthur C. Scholar award, 1991, Alexander von Humboldt Rsch. award for sr. U.S. scientists, 1992, Ernest Guenther award in the chemistry of essential oils, 1993, Alumni award for outstanding profl. achievement Bucknell U., 1993, Centenary medal Royal Soc. Chem., London, 2002, Yamada prize Tokyo, Japan, 2003, Order of Rising Sun Gold Rays with Neck Ribbon, Govt. Japan, 2004; J.S. Guggenheim Found. fellow, 1985-86, Japan Soc. for Promotion Sci. fellow, 1986-87. Mem. Am. Chem. Soc. (chmn. nominating com. organic chemistry divsn. 1985, exec. com. 1987-90, chmn. fellowship com. 1988-89, symposium exec. officer Nat. Organic Symposium 1993, chair-elect, chair, past chair Divsn. Organic Chemistry, 1995, 96, 97, canvassing com. 1989—, Phila. sect award 1986), Internat. Soc. Chem. Ecology (counselor), Gordon Rsch. Conf. (vice chmn. organic reaction and processes 1979, chmn. 1980), Franklin Inst. (com. on scis. and arts 1985—), Phila. Organic Chemists Club (chmn. 1978, award 1991), Pharm. Soc. of Japan (hon. mem. 1999); fellow AAAS, 2002, Am. Acad. Arts and Sciences, 2006. Avocations: hunting, fishing. Office: Univ Penn Dept Chemistry 231 S 34th St 440 N Philadelphia PA 19104-3803 Office Phone: 215-898-4860. E-mail: smithab@sas.upenn.edu.

SMITH, AMY B., mechanical engineer, educator; BSc, MIT, 1984, MSE, 1995. Vol. Peace Corps, Botswana, 1986—90; inventor, instr. MIT Edgerton Ctr., Cambridge, Mass., 2000—. Co-founder MIT IDEAS competition (Innovation, Devel., Enterprise, Action, Svc.); and co-founder Internat. Devel. Initiative. Named a MacArthur Fellow, 2004; recipient Lemelson-MIT Student prize, 2000.

SMITH, ANDREW DONALD, plastic surgeon; s. Donald Raymond and Susan Blair Smith; m. Erin Patricia Wayne, Aug. 10, 1997; children: Hunter James, Claire Emma, Jillian Erin. BS, U. Mich., 1991; MD, George Washington U., 1995. Diplomate Am. Bd. Plastic Surgery, Am. Bd. Surgery. Resident gen. surgery George Washington U., Washington, 1995—98; postdoctoral rsch. fellow plastic and reconstructive surgery U. Calif., LA, 1998—99, resident, 2001—03; resident gen. surgery Med. Ctr. The U. Calif., Irvine, Calif., 1999—2001; pvt. practice Irvine, Calif., 2003—; staff Salleback Meml. Med. Ctr., 2003—, Orange Coast Meml. Med. Ctr., 2003—, Irvine (Calif.) Regional Med. Ctr., 2003—, Mission Hosp., 2003—05, Laguna Hills (Calif.) Surgery Ctr., 2003—, Saddleback Valley Outpatient Surgery Ctr., 2003—. Fellow pathology George Washington U., Washington, 1991; surgeon Hosp. Regional Univ., Lille, France, 1992; asst. rschr. surg. oncology NIH, Bethesda, Md., 1995. Contbr. chapters to books, articles to profl. jours. Mem.: AMA, ACS, Orange County Soc. Plastic Surgeons, Calif. Soc. Plastic Surgery, Am. Soc. Plastic Surgeons, Alpha Omega Alpha. Office: 16300 Sand Canyon Ave 911 Irvine CA 92618 also: 720 Magnolia Ave #B-1 Corona CA 92879 Office Phone: 951-734-2500. *

SMITH, ANDREW JAMES THOMAS, music educator; b. Isleworth, England, Sept. 9, 1968; arrived in U.S., 1996; s. James Smith and Ann Madelaine Veronica (Collette) Gane; m. Andrea Elizabeth Mills, May 25, 2003; m. Margaret Mary Kane. Diploma, Royal Acad. Music, 1991, cert. in Advanced Solo Studies, 1992; D in Musical Arts, Hartt Sch., 2003. Concertmaster European Chamber Opera, London, 1992—95; asst. prof. Valparaiso (Ind.) U., 2000—05; dir. Suzuki Music Sch., Westport, Conn., 2005—. Concertmaster Orquestra da Fafe, Portugal, 1992; assoc. concertmaster D'Oyly Carte Opera Orchestra, Birmingham, England, 1992—94; dir. Stamford (Eng.) Internat. Music Festival, 2004—; guest artist Andrews U., Mich., 2002, Shanghai (China) Conservatory, 2003, Am. String Tchrs. Assn., Valparaiso, 2002, 05, Dame Myra Hess Concerts, Chgo., Fetzer Soc. Concerts, 2004; artist in residence La Porte Symphony; asst. Emerson String Quartet; guest concertmaster Ill. Philharmonic, Kalamazoo Symphony; asst. concertmaster London Pops Orch. Musician: (albums) Glazunov Violin Concerto, 2001, My True Gift's To Come, 2004, Castillon Piano Trio. Dir. The Copland Century Festival, Hartford, Conn., 2000; artistic dir. Bach At The Brauer Mus., Valparaiso, 2002—05; artistic dir. Da Capo Concert Series Southport, Conn., 2005—. Recipient Farjeon prize, Royal Acad. Music, 1992, Celt award, Valparaiso (Ind.) U., 2002, Alumni award, 2002. Mem.: Suzuki Assn. The Americas, Cobbett Assn. Chamber Music, Am. String Tchrs. Assn. Office: Suzuki Music School Westport 212 Post Road West Westport CT 06880 Office Phone: 203-227-9474. Personal E-mail: violin@att.net.

SMITH, ANNA DEAVERE, actress, playwright, educator; b. Balt., Sept. 18, 1950; d. Deavere Young and Anna (Young) S. BA, Beaver Coll., Pa., 1971, doctorate (hon.), 1973; MFA, Am. Conservatory Theatre, 1977; doctorate (hon.), U. NC, 1995; degree (hon.), Wheelock Coll., 1995, Colgate U., 1997, Sch. Visual Arts, 1997, Wesleyan U., 1997, Northwestern U., 1997, Coll. Holy Cross, 1997. Ann O'Day Maples prof. arts and drama Stanford U. Artist-in-residence Ford Found., 1997. Playwright, performer one-woman shows On the Road: A Search for American Character, 1983, Aye, Aye, Aye, I'm Integrated, 1984, Piano, 1991 (Drama-Logue award), Fires in the Mirror, 1989 (Obie award 1992, Drama Desk award 1992, N.Y. Drama Critics spl. citation 1993-94), Twilight: Los Angeles 1992 (Obie award, 2 Tony award nominations, Drama Critics Cir. spl. citation, Outer Critics Cir. award, Drama Desk award, Audelco award, Beverly Hills, Hollywood NAACP theatre awards), House Arrest, 1997; writer libretto for Judith Jamison, performer Hymn, 1993; appeared in (films) Dave, 1993, Philadelphia, 1993, The American President, 1995, Twilight: Los Angeles, 2000. Founding dir. The Inst. on Arts and Civic Dialogue Harvard U., 1998; trustee, Mus. Modern Art, N.Y.C. Named One of Women of Yr., Glamour mag., 1993; fellow Bunting Inst., Radcliffe Coll.; genius fellow The MacArthur Found., 1996. also: Stanford U Dept Drama Memorial Hall Stanford CA 94305

SMITH, ANNE DAY, writer; b. Bath, Maine, Oct. 14, 1937; d. Harry L. Day; m. Gerald H. Smith, Dec. 21, 1957; children: David, Frederick, Stephen. AA, Lasell Coll., Auburndale, Mass., 1957. Contbg. editor Nutshell News Mag., 1979-96; freelance writer various newspapers and mags., 1979—. Author: Interior Design in Miniature, 1986, Masters in Miniature, 1987, The Andrews Collection, 1988, The Period Rooms of Ruth McChesney, 1997; contbg. editor Dollhouse Miniatures mag., 1996—; contbr. articles to publs. Mem. Nat. Assn. Miniature Enthusiasts, Acad. Honor (chmn. 1996-2000), Internat. Guild Miniature Artisans. Avocations: reading, research, travel, antique collecting.

SMITH, ANNE MARIE SCHOEFER, application developer; d. Walter Hellmann Schoefer and Helen MacNeil Fox; children: Jonathan Michael, Jessica Lauren, Matthew Andrew. BA, LaSalle U., Phila., 1980. Cert. artificial intelligence DARPA, Wash. D.C., 1986; programming and macro, Sas Inst., Cary NC, 1995, software engring., GE, Valley Forge, PA, 1984. Software engr. cons. Rainbow Comm. and Software, Palm Beach, Fla., 1986—. Book, Poetry for Lovers and Romanticists: Art in Poetry and Photography. Tour guide MacAuthor Pk., Palm Beach Gardens, Fla., 2003—04. Recipient Alumni Honor Soc. Kappa Mu Epsilon, LaSalle Coll., 1979—80. Mem.: PhilaSUG (assoc.; bd. mem., sec. 1995—2000). R-Conservative. Achievements include development of webpages with poems, art and music. Avocations: travel, swimming, writing, sports. Home Phone: 561-797-0344; Office Phone: 561-797-0344. Personal E-mail: rainbowangel@myway.com. Business E-Mail: rainbow_softwr@geocities.com.

SMITH, ANNICK, writer; b. Paris, May 11, 1936; came to U.S., 1937; d. Stephen and Helene Deutch; m. David James Smith (dec. 1974); children: Eric, Stephen, Alex, Andrew. Student, Cornell Univ., 1954-55, U. Chgo., 1955-57; BA, U. Wash., 1961. Editor U. Wash. Press, Seattle, 1961-64, Montana Bus. Quarterly, U. Montana, Missoula, 1971-72; founding bd. mem. Sundance Film Inst., Sundance, Utah, 1981-85; founding mem. Ind. Film Project, NYC, 1981-84; acting dir. Montana Com. for the Humanities, Missoula, 1983-84; devel. dir. Hellgate Writers, Inc., Missoula, 1986-96; creative dir. Yellow Bay Writers Workshop, U. Montana Continuing Edn. Dept, Missoula, 1987-98. Freelance filmmaker, producer, arts administrator, writer, Mont., 1974—; past H.S. tchr., cmty. organizer, environ. worker. Exec. prodr. Heartland, 1981; co-prodr. A River Runs Through It, 1992; co-editor: (with William Kittredge) The Last Best Place; author: Homestead, 1994, Big BlueStem A Journey into the Tall Grass, 1996, In This We Are Native, 2001; contbr. to anthologies including Best Am. Short Stories, 1992. Recipient Western Heritage award Cowboy Hall of Fame, 1981; Mont. Humanites award Mont. Com. for Humanities, 1988, Okla. Book award, 1997, Bancroft Prize Denver Pub. Libr., 1998. Mem. Trout Unlimited, Blackfoot Challenge. Democrat. Office: 898 Bear Creek Rd Bonner MT 59823

SMITH, ARLAN ROBERT, plastic and reconstructive surgeon; b. Surabaja, Indonesia, Aug. 3, 1948; arrived in Holland, 1954; m. Paulina Jacoba de Jong, May 25, 1990; children: Darryl Nathaniël, Beau Aurora Fabiana, Chloé Aphrodite Zoë. Student, St. Ignatius Coll., Amsterdam, The Netherlands, 1961-66; PhD, U. Amsterdam, The Netherlands, 1972, MD, 1974. Cert. plastic and reconstructive surgeon. Gen. surgery tng. dept gen. surgery U. Maastricht, The Netherlands, 1975-79; clin. and rsch. fellow Mass. Gen. Hosp., Harvard Med. Sch., Boston, 1977-79; specialist in plastic and reconstructive surgery dept. plastic surgery U. Hosp. Dijkzigt Rotterdam, The Netherlands, 1979-82, chef de clinique in microsurgery and hand surgery dept. plastic and reconstructive surgery, 1979-86; head dept. plastic and reconstructive surgery Holy Hosp. Vlaardingen, The Netherlands, 1985-96; vis. prof. plastic and reconstructive surgery U. Kristen Idonesia Jakarta, Indonesia, 1989-91; dir. and owner Clinic Holystaete Vlaardingen, Netherlands, 1991—. Contbr. articles to profl. jours. Mem. Dutch Soc. for Hand Surgery, Dutch Soc. Esthetic Surgery, Dutch Soc. Plastic and Reconstructive Surgery, Internat. Microsurg. Soc., Found. Moshe Yemin clinic Holystaete (chmn. bd.), the Netherlands. Avocations: gardening, pre-Columbian art, modern art, Egyptian and African art. Office: Clinic Holystaete Churchillsingel 480 3137XB Vlaardingen Netherlands Business E-Mail: info@kliniekholystaete.nl. E-mail: abr.smith@planet.nl.

SMITH, ART, chef; b. Jasper, Fla. Attended, Fla. State U., Walt Disney Magic Kingdom Coll. Prog. Tchr. Williams-Sonoma, Chgo.; internship Greenbrier Resort; exec. chef Fla. Gov. Mansion; chef Am. European Express Train; spl. event chef Martha Stewart Living Mag.; personal chef to Oprah Winfrey, 1997—. Spkr. Celebration of Reading, Barbara Bush Found. for Family Literacy; mem., bd. dirs. Kid's Cafe, Mpls.; chef's coun. Chefs for Humanity, 2005—. Author: Back to the Table: The Reunion of Food and Family, 2001 (James Beard Found. award, 2002, Gourmand World Cookbook award, 2001), Kitchen Life (Gourmand World Cookbook award, 2004); contbg. editor: O Mag. Co-founder Common Threads, 2002—. Office: Common Threads c/o Linda Novick 345 N Canal Ste 1601 Chicago IL 60606 Office Phone: 312-876-1289. Office Fax: 312-876-1038.

SMITH, ARTHUR B., JR., lawyer; b. Abilene, Tex., Sept. 11, 1944; s. Arthur B. and Florence B. (Baker) S.; m. Marya Argetsinger, 1968 (div. 1996); children: Arthur C., Sarah R.; m. Tracey L. Truesdale, 1999; children: Thomas A. BS, Cornell U., 1966; JD, U. Chgo., 1969. Bar: Ill. 1969, N.Y. 1976. Assoc. Vedder, Price, Kaufman & Kammholz, Chgo., 1969-74; asst. prof. labor law N.Y. State Sch. Indls. and Labor Rels., Cornell U., 1975-77; ptnr. Vedder, Price, Kaufman & Kammholz, Chgo., 1977-86; founding mem. Murphy, Smith & Polk, Chgo., 1986-98; shareholder Ogletree, Deakins, Chgo., 1999—. Guest. lectr. Northwestern U. Grad. Sch. Mgmt., 1979, Sch. Law, spring 1980; chmn. hearing bd. Ill. Atty. Registration and Disciplinary Commn. Author: Employment Discrimination Law Cases and Materials, 6th edit., 2006, Construction Labor Relations, 1984, supplement, 1993; co-editor-in-chief: 1976 Annual Supplement to Morris, The Developing Labor Law, 1977; chpt. editor: The Developing Labor Law, 5th edit., 2006; contbr. articles to profl. jours. Recipient award for highest degree of dedication and excellence in tchg. N.Y. State Sch. Indsl. and Labor Rels., Cornell U., 1977; listed in The Best Lawyers in Am., 2003—. Fellow Coll. Labor and Employment Lawyers; mem. ABA (co-chmn. com. on devel. law under Nat. Labor Rels. Act, Sect. Labor Rels. Law 1976-77), N.Y. State Bar Assn., Phi Eta Sigma, Phi Kappa Phi, Chgo. Athletic Assn., Mid-Day Club. Presbyterian. Office: Ogletree Deakins et al 2 First National Plz Fl 25 Chicago IL 60603 Office Phone: 312-558-1230. Business E-Mail: Arthur.Smith@odnss.com.

SMITH, ARTHUR EDWARD, JR., lawyer; b. Oct. 8, 1949; s. Arthur and Audre Smith; m. Janis O'Hara; children: Gregory, Jeffrey. BA in Biology, Columbia U., 1971, MA in Environ. Sci., 1972, MS in Environ. Sci., 1973; JD with distinction, U. Puget Sound, 1976. Bar: Wash. 1976. Assoc. regional counsel Region V, EPA, Chgo., 1976-91; spl. asst. US Atty. (no. dist.) Ill., 1989; environ. officer, counsel NIPSCO Industries (now NiSource), Merrillville, Ind., 1991—2000; sr. v.p., environ. counsel NiSource Inc., Merrillville, Ind., 2000—. Recipient bronze medal EPA, 1985, 91, Silver medal Am. Gas Assn., 2007; environ. fellow Columbia U. 1972; scholar U. Puget Sound. Home: 300 S Ashland Ave La Grange IL 60525-6308 Office: 801 E 86th Ave Merrillville IN 46410

SMITH, ARTHUR JOHN STEWART, physicist, researcher; b. Victoria, BC, Can., June 28, 1938; s. James Stewart and Lillian May (Geernaert) S.; m. Norma Ruth Askeland, May 20, 1966; children: Peter James, Ian Alexander. BA, U. B.C., 1959, MSc., 1961; PhD, Princeton U., 1966. Postdoctoral fellow Deutsches Electronen-Synchrotron, Hamburg, Germany, 1966—67; mem. faculty dept. physics Princeton U., 1967—, prof., 1978—, Class of 1909 prof., 1992—, assoc. chmn. dept., 1979—83, chmn. dept. physics, 1990—98, chair Rsch. Bd., 2005—, dean rsch., 2006—. Vis. scientist Brookhaven Nat. Lab., 1967—, chair sci. and tech. steering com. Brookhaven Sci. Assocs., 1997—2005, bd. dirs., 2005—; vis. scientist Fermilab, 1974—, Stanford Linear Accelerator Ctr., 1996—, vis. prof., 2000—02, spokesperson BaBar experiment, 2000—02. Assoc. editor Phys. Rev. Letters, 1986-89; contbr. articles to profl. jours. Fellow Am. Phys. Soc. (chmn. divsn. of particles and fields 1991). Achievements include research on experimental high-energy particle physics; kaon decays, physics of the B particles and quark structure of hadrons. Home: 4 Ober Rd Princeton NJ 08540-4918 Office: PO Box 708 Princeton NJ 08544-0001

SMITH, ARTHUR KITTREDGE, JR., academic administrator, political scientist, educator; b. Derry, NH, Aug. 15, 1937; s. Arthur Kittredge and Rena Belle (Roberts) S.; m. June Mary Dahar, Nov. 28, 1959; children: Arthur, Valerie, Meredith. BS, U.S. Naval Acad., 1959; MA, U. N.H., 1966; PhD, Cornell U., 1970. Vis. prof. El Colegio de Mexico, Mexico City, 1968-69; asst. prof. polit. sci. SUNY-Binghamton, 1970-74, assoc. prof., 1974-84, prof., 1984-88, provost for grad. studies and research, 1976-83, v.p. for adminstrn., 1982-88; prof. govt. and internat. studies U. S.C., Columbia, 1988-91, exec. v.p. for acad. affairs, provost, 1988-90, 91, interim pres., 1990-91; pres., prof. polit. sci. U. Utah, Salt Lake City, 1991-97; chancellor U. Houston Sys., 1997—2003; pres. U. Houston, 1997—2003, prof., 2003—. Author: (with Claude E. Welch, Jr.) Military Role and Rule: Perspectives on Civil-Military Relations, 1975; contbr. articles to profl. jours. Officer USN, 1959—65. Lehman fellow, 1966-69, NDEA fellow, 1969-70 Mem. Am. Polit. Sci. Assn., L.Am. Studies Assn., Inter-Univ. Sem. on Armed Forces and Soc., Am. Coun. on Edn., World Affairs Coun. (pres. Binghamton chpt. 1976-76), Bus.-Higher Edn. Forum, Phi Beta Kappa, Pi Sigma Alpha, Omicron Delta Kappa, Phi Delta Kappa, Beta Gamma Sigma, Phi Kappa Phi. Office: Univ Houston 4500 University Dr Rm 2000K Houston TX 77204-6056 Office Phone: 832-443-3008.

SMITH, ARTHUR LEE, lawyer; b. Davenport, Iowa, Dec. 19, 1941; s. Harry Arthur Smith and Ethel (Hoffman) Duerre; m. Georgia Mills, June 12, 1965 (dec. Jan. 1984); m. Jean Bowler, Aug. 4, 1984; children: Juliana, Christopher, Andrew, Wendy. BA, Augustana Coll., Rock Island, Ill., 1964; MA, Am. U., 1968; JD, Washington U., St. Louis, 1971. Bar: Mo 1971, DC 1983. Telegraph editor Davenport Morning Democrat, 1962-64; ptnr. Peper Martin Jensen Maichel & Hetlage, 1971-95, Husch & Eppenberger, St. Louis, 1995—. Arbitrator Nat Asn Security Dealers, 1980—, Am Arbitration Assn, 1980—2004; dir. St. Louis Bar Found., 2005—, v.p., 2005—. Columnist: St Louis Lawyer, syndicated columnist: Technolawyer.com and other publications. Dir. P. Buckley Moss Found. for Children's Edn., 2001—03; mem. Sedona Conf. Working Group on Electronic Document Prodn.; mem. electronic discovery and ethics com. DRI, Inc., 2007—. Lt USN, 1964—68. Named Mo.-Kans. Superlawyer, 2006; named one of Best Lawyers in Am., 2005, 2006, 2007, Best Lawyers in Info.-Tech. in Am., 2006. Mem.: ABA (co-chair electronic discovery subcom.), Bar Assn. Met. St. Louis (chmn law mgt comt 1993—96, chair technology comt 1996—99, Pres.'s award Exceptional Service 1995, 1997), P. Buckley Moss Soc. (dir 1994—2006, v.p. 1998—2000, exec vpres 2001—02, pres. 2002—06), Mo. Bar Assn. (vice-chair ins programs comt 1981—83, vice-chair antitrust comt 1981—83, chair admin law comt 1995—97), D.C. Bar Assn. (chmn law practice mgt 1990—91), Order of Coif. Office: Husch & Eppenberger Ste 600 190 Carondelet Plz Saint Louis MO 63105-3441 Home Phone: 636-532-0354; Office Phone: 314-480-1500. Business E-Mail: arthur.smith@husch.com.

SMITH, B. SCOTT, automotive executive; Grad., Rollins Coll., 1991. Gen. mgr. Town & Country Ford, Charlotte, NC, 1992—97; pres., COO Sonic Automotive Inc., Charlotte, NC, 1997—2002, vice chmn., chief strategic officer, 2002—07, pres., chief strategy officer, 2007—. Office: Sonic Automotive Inc 5401 Independence Blvd Charlotte NC 28212 *

SMITH, BAKER ARMSTRONG, management executive, lawyer; b. Oct. 3, 1947; s. William Armstrong and Priscilla (Baker) S.; m. Deborah Elizabeth Ellis, Nov. 13, 1982; children: Ellis Armstrong, Elizabeth Anne, Everett Baker, Emery Manning. BS, U.S. Naval Acad., 1969; MBA, Northeastern U., 1975; JD cum laude, Suffolk U., 1977; LLM in Labor, Georgetown U., 1981. Bar: Ga. 1977, D.C. 1978, U.S. Supreme Ct. 1980; cert. turnaround profl., 1994; fellow Family Firm Inst. Commd. ensign USN, 1969, advanced through grades to lt., 1974; exec. dir., founder Ctr. on Nat. Labor Policy, Inc., North Springfield, Va., 1977-81; asst. to sec., dir. labor rels. U.S. Dept. HUD, Washington, 1981-83; exec. v.p. U.S. Bus. and Indsl. Coun., Nashville, 1983-84; pres. Am. Quality Builders, Inc., Nashville, 1984-86; v.p. Hopeman Bros., Inc., Waynesboro, Va., 1986-88, Morris, Anderson, Atlanta, 1988—. Sec., founder U.S. Constnl. Rights Legal Def. Fund, Inc., Atlanta, 1983—; trustee Leadership Inst., Springfield, Va., 1978—; v.p., 1998—; v.p. Turnaround Mgmt. Assn., Chgo., 1998-99; pres. Assn. Cert. Turnaround Profls., Boston, 1997-98; mem. Coun. for Nat. Policy, Washington, 1981—, Civil Rights Reviewing Authority U.S. Dept. Edn., Washington, 1984-88; transition team leader Office of the Pres.-Elect of the U.S., NLRB, Occupl. Safety and Health Rev. Commn., Fed. Mediation and Conciliation Svc., Nat. Mediation Bd., Fed. Labor Rels. Authority, Washington, 1980-81; instr. law, faculty sec. No. Va. Law Sch., Alexandria, Va., 1980-83; instr. law D.C. Law Sch., Washington, 1978-80. Contbg. author: Mandate for Leadership, 1981; contbr. articles to profl. jours. Bd. dirs. Atlanta Opera, 2006—. Recipient Outstanding Contbn. to the Turnaround Profession award, 1999. Fellow Family Firm Inst.; mem. ABA (Nat. Law Day chmn. 1976-77, Silver Key award 1977), St. George's House, Windsor Castle (assoc.), Phila. Soc., U.S. Supreme Ct. Hist. Soc., Federalist Soc., Beta Gamma Sigma, Phi Delta Phi (pres. 1989-91), Capitol Hill Club (Washington), Piedmont Club (Winston-Salem). Republican. Presbyterian. Home: 3360 E Terrell Branch Ct Marietta GA 30067-5164 Home Phone: 770-980-0921. Business E-Mail: bsmith@morris-anderson.com.

SMITH, BARBARA, bank executive; b. Bryan County, Ga. m. Gary Smith. Teller The Heritage Bank, Hinesville, Ga., 1972, sr. v.p. Vol. fundraiser United Way, Am. Cancer Soc., Am. Heart Assn., Am. Diabetes Assn. Named one of 25 Most Powerful Women in Banking, US Banker, 2006. Mem.: Independent Cmty. Bankers Am. Avocation: quilting. Mailing: The Heritage Bank PO Box 1009 Hinesville GA 31310 Office Fax: 912-408-6102, 912-369-9397. E-mail: bsmith@the-heritage-bank.com. *

SMITH, BARBARA BARNARD, music educator; b. Ventura, Calif., June 10, 1920; d. Fred W. and Grace (Hobson) S. BA, Pomona Coll., Claremont, Calif., 1942, DMus (hon.), 2001; MusM, U. Rochester, NY, 1943, performer's cert., 1945. Mem. faculty piano and theory Eastman Sch. Music, U. Rochester, 1943-49; mem. faculty U. Hawaii, Honolulu, 1949—, assoc. prof. music, 1953-62, prof., 1962-82, prof. emeritus, 1982—; sr. fellow East-West Center, 1973. Lectr., recitals in Hawaiian and Asian music, US, Europe and Asia, 1956—; field rschr. Asia, 1956, 60, 66, 71, 80, Micronesia, 1963, 70, 87-88, 90-91, Solomon Islands, 1976. Contbr. articles to profl. jours. Mem. Soc. Ethnomusicology, Internat. Coun. for Traditional Music, Am. Mus. Instrument Soc., Coll. Music Soc., Soc. for Asian Music, Music Educators Nat. Conf., Pacific Sci. Assn., Phi Beta Kappa, Mu Phi Epsilon.

SMITH, BARBARA JANE, computer scientist, educator; d. Kenneth O. and Jane Louise Campbell; m. Douglas Brian Smith, Dec. 29, 1984; children: Michael Douglas, James Kenneth. MS in Math., Purdue U., 1981. Assoc. prof. Purdue U., Ft. Wayne, Ind., 1979—84; pres. Software Profls., Inc, Ft. Wayne, 1980—84; sr. sys. analyst Burroughs Corp., Camarillo, Calif., 1984—86, W. L. Gore, Flagstaff, Ariz., 1986—89; instr. Cochise Coll., Sierra Vista, Ariz., 1989—, U. Ariz., South, Sierra Vista, 1996—. Author: Programming Logic and Design. Mem. White Cross, Ft. Wayne, 2005—. Office: Cochise Coll 901 N Colombo Sierra Vista AZ 85635 Home Phone: 520-439-4183; Office Phone: 520-515-5441. Personal E-mail: barbaraj@email.arizona.edu.

SMITH, BARBARA JEAN, lawyer; b. Washington, Jan. 9, 1947; d. Harry Wallace and Jean (Fraser) S.; m. Philip R. Chall, July 13, 1991; children: Brian C.S. Brown, Craig F.S. Brown, Amy E. Spiers, Carrie A. Chall. BA, Old Dominion Coll., 1968; MBA, Pepperdine U., 1974; JD, Case Western Res. U., 1977. Bar: Ohio 1977. Assoc. Squire, Sanders & Dempsey, Cleve., 1977—88, ptnr., 1988—93; shareholder McDonald, Hopkins, Burke & Haber Co., L.P.A., Cleve., 1993—2003; ptnr. Shottenstein, Zox & Dunn Co., LPA, Cleve., 2003—05; founding mem. Smith & Hultin LLC, Chagrin Falls, Ohio, 2005—. Bd. editors Health Law Jour. of Ohio, 1989-95; contbr. articles to health jours. and periodicals. Trustee Urban Community Sch., Cleve., 1984-86, Alzheimer's Assn. Greater Cleve., 2000-2005. Mem. Ohio Women's Bar Assn. (pres. 1994-95), Cleve. Bar Assn. (pres. 1998-99, trustee 1992-95, chair health law sect. 1991-92), Am. Health Lawyers Assn., Ohio State Bar Assn. (health law com. 1991—), Soc. Ohio Hosp. Attys., Sci. Edn. Coun. Ohio. Democrat. Mem. United Ch. of Christ. Avocations: reading, hiking. Home: 416 Fairway Vw Chagrin Falls OH 44023-6718 Office: Smith & Hultin LLC 100 N Main St Ste 350 Chagrin Falls OH 44022 Office Phone: 440-247-2620. Business E-Mail: smith@smithhultin.com.

SMITH, BARBARA JEANNE, retired librarian; b. Jersey Shore, Pa., Apr. 14, 1939; d. Moyer Emmerson and Mary Kathryn (Ebner) S. BS in Edn. (Biology), Pa. State U., 1961, DEd in Higher Edn., 1981; MS in Edn. (English), SUNY, Oswego, NY, 1967; MLS, U. Pitts., 1970. Reference libr. Pa. State U. Librs., University Park, 1970-75, commonwealth campus coord., 1975-82, asst. dean librs., head commonwealth campus librs. divsn., 1982-89; dir. Smithsonian Instn. Librs., Washington, 1989-98. Gen. sci. tchr., Binghamton (N.Y.) City Schs., 1961-62; English tchr., North Syracuse (N.Y.) Ctrl. Schs., 1970-75; mem. Smithsonian Instn. Rsch. Info. Svc. (chair 1993-95), Planning Adv. Group, 1989-93; chair Internet Implementation Com., Smithsonian Instn. Librs. User Adv. Com., 1989-97; founding dir. Chesapeake Info. and Rsch. Libr. Alliance, 1996-98. Contbr. articles to profl. jours.; speaker in field. UCLA Grad. Sch. of Libr. and Info. Sci. Sr. fellow, 1982. Mem. AAUW, ALA (mem. coun. 1987-91), Centre County (Pa.) Hist. Soc. (life), U. Pitts. Alumni Assn. (bd. dirs. 1991-94), Beta Phi Mu. E-mail: bsmith5598@pennswoods.net.

SMITH, BARBARA RODERICK, health and social services administrator, nursing consultant; b. Peoria, Ill., Mar. 5, 1948; d. Fremont August and Jessie May (Burdess) Roderick; children: Yvette, Roderick, Jennifer. Student, Peoria Sch. Practical Nursing, Ill., 1967-68; A, Ill. Cen. Coll. Registered Nursing, 1971; BS, Coll. St. Francis, Joliet, 1981; postgrad., U. Ill., 1985-90, U. Iowa, Iowa City, Bradley U., Peoria, Ill., 1991-93; MS in Nursing, Columbia State U., 1995, PhD in Social Work, 1997. Cert. sch. nurse, LPN; Ordained to ministry Meth. Ch.; cert. social worker. Med. coord. Covenant Children's Home, Princeton, Ill.; cons. Donna Home Care, Bartonville, Ill.; nursing cons. Rose Shelter, Peoria; adminstr. health svc. Cath. Social Svc., Peoria; dir. Alzheimer unit Americana Health Care Manor Corp.; mem. faculty Ill. Cen. Coll., East Peoria, 1992—; asst. nurse mgr. Tuba City Indian Hosp., Navajo Hopi Reservation, Twin City, Ariz. Guest spkr. St. Francis Coll. Nursing; adminstr. detox, nursing programs White Oaks Detox Ctr.; exec. dir. Rural Peoria County Coun. on Aging; asst. to chief nurse State of Ill. Health Svc. Mgmt. Health Policy Divsn.; minority adv. coun. Ill. Dept. Pub. Health; cons. in field. Mem. subcom. on nursing Forward Peoria; adv. coun. Native Am. Child Welfare. Mem. Ill. Nursing Assn. (bd. dirs.), Ill. Assn. Maternal Child Health (bd. dirs.), Am. Indian Coun. of Ill.; Sigma Theta Tau. Personal E-mail: bsmith1980@aol.com.

SMITH, BARNARD ELLIOT, management educator; b. Mpls., May 6, 1926; s. Sheldon Strong and Jessie (Gould) S.; m. Betty Lou Strohschein, Aug. 28, 1949; children: Carolyn Louise, Eileen Elizabeth. BS in Mech. Engring. with distinction, U. Minn., 1949, MS, 1950; PhD, Stanford U., Calif., 1961; MA (hon.), Dartmouth Coll., Hanover, NH, 1971. Asst. prof. mech. engring. U. ND, 1950-51; mfg. specialist A.O. Smith Co., Milw., 1951-54; asst. prof. indsl. engring. Oreg. State Coll., 1954-58, Stanford U., 1958-61; asso. prof. mgmt. Sloan Sch. Mgmt., MIT, 1961-68; prof. mgmt. Indian Inst. Mgmt., Calcutta, 1965-68; prof. engring. Thayer Sch. Engring. Dartmouth Coll., 1968-71; dean Stuart Sch. Mgmt. and Finance, Ill. Inst. Tech., 1971-75, prof. mgmt., 1975-80; David M. French disting. prof. mgmt. U. Mich., Flint, 1980-89, emeritus, 1989; pres. Vineyards of the Acad., 1989, The Acad. of Wine of Oreg. Inc., 1993—. Cons. in field. Served with USNR, 1944-46. Mem. Phi Tau Sigma, Beta Gamma Sigma. Home: 18200 Highway 238 Grants Pass OR 97527-8631 Office Phone: 541-846-6817.

SMITH, BARRY HAMILTON, foundation administrator, physician; b. Orange, NJ, Oct. 6, 1943; s. Kenneth Wright and Harriet (Barr) S.; m. Carley Eldredge, Dec. 13, 1969; children: Christopher, Sara. BA, Harvard U., 1965; PhD, MIT, 1968; MD, Cornell U., 1972. Intern, resident N.Y. Hosp., NYC, 1971—75; resident Mass. Gen. Hosp., Boston, 1975—78; program dir. Neuroscis. Rsch. Program MIT, Boston, 1975—78; dep. dir. Surg. Neurology Br. NIH, Bethesda, Md., 1978—83; dir. sci. & med. Dreyfus Med. Found., NYC, 1983—88; dir. Dreyfus Health Found., NYC, 1988—. Sr. v.p. Rogosin Inst., 1998—; prof. surgery Cornell U., Peking U. Med. Coll.; bd. dirs. pub. health sys. rsch. panel US Dept. Health and Human Svcs. Editor Ency. Neurosci., 1995-2005; contbr. articles to profl. jours. Bd. dirs. Desmond Tutu Peace Found., Kornfeld Found., N.Y.C. Rescue Mission, Global Health Action Comdr. USPHS, 1978—83. Recipient Commendation Medal award, USPHS, 1982, EEO award, 1983. Mem. AMA, AAAS, Soc. Neurosci., Am. Pain Soc. (audit com. 1983-85), Nat. Coun. Internat. Health (governing bd. 1990-95, chair 1993-95), Global Health Coun. Soc. Critical Care Medicine, Phi Beta Kappa, Sigma Xi, Alpha Omega Alpha Avocations: sailing, writing. Home: 1192 Park Ave Apt 10B New York NY 10128-1314 Office: Dreyfus Health Found 205 E 64th St Rm 404 New York NY 10021-6635 Office Phone: 212-750-5075. Business E-Mail: bsmith@dhfglobal.org.

SMITH, BERNALD STEPHEN, retired pilot; b. Long Beach, Calif., Dec. 24, 1926; s. Donald Albert and Bernice Merrill (Stephens) Smith; m. Marilyn Mae Spence, July 22, 1949; children: Lorraine Ann Smith Foute, Evelyn Donice Smith DeRoos, Mark Stephen, Diane April(dec.). Student, U. Calif., Berkeley, 1944-45, 50-51. Cert. airline transport pilot, flight engr. FAA. Capt. Transocean Airline, Oakland, Calif., Transocean Air Lines, Tokyo, 1951-53, Hartford, Conn., 1954-55; 1st officer United Air Lines, Seattle, 1955, San Francisco, 1956-68, tng. capt. Denver, San Francisco, 1961—68, capt., 1968-86, 2d officer, 1986-93; ret., 1993. Founder, v.p. Avia Am., Palo Alto, Calif., 1970—72, Avia Internat., Palo Alto, 1972—74; founder, trustee AirSailing, Inc., 1970—, Soaring Safety Found., 1985—; cons. Caproni Vizzola, Milan, 1972—84; instr. aviation Ohlone Coll., Fremont, 1976; prin., cons. Internat. Aviation Cons. and Investments, Fremont, Calif., 1985—; founder Pacific Soaring Coun. Author, editor: American Soaring Handbook, 1975, 1980, pub.: Technical Soaring, 2004—; contbr. articles to profl. jours. Trustee Nat. Soaring Mus., 1975—2001, pres., 1975—78; active RTCA; SSA del., 1992—; FAI del., 1996—. Comdr. USNR. Named Barnaby Lectr., Nat. Soaring Mus., 2003; recipient Gold medal, 2002. Fellow: Internat. GPS Svc. Geodynamics; mem.: AIAA (pub. bd. 1977—94), Civil GPS Svc. Interface Com., Inst. Navigation, Commn. de Vol A Voile (US del. 1981—97, v.p. 1988—96), Fedn. Aeronatique Internat. (environ. commn. v.p., U.S. del. 1995—, mem. airspace mgmt. group 1998—, del. environ. com. 2002—, Paul Tissandler diploma 1992, Lilienthal medal 1993, Bronze medal 2003, Companion du Hon. 2007), Seaplane Pilots Assn., Orgn. Scientifique et Technique Internat. du Vol a Voile (hon.; bd. dirs., U.S. del. 1981—97, pub. Tech. Soaring 2004—, bd. dirs.), Airline Pilots Assn., Exptl. Aircraft Assn., Nat. Aero. Assn., Soaring Soc. Am. (bd. dirs. 1963—97, pres. 1969—70, chmn. pub. bd. 1971—84, chmn. ins. com. 1975—93, hon. vice-chmn. bd. dirs. 2000—, Exceptional Svc. award 1970, 1975, Warren Eaton Meml. trophy 1977, Exceptional Svc. award 1982, named to Hall of Fame 1984, Exceptional Svc. award 1988, 1991, Exceptional Achievement award 1996, Warren Eaton Meml. trophy 1997, Schweizer Lifetime Svc. award 2003), Aircraft Owners and Pilots Assn., U. Calif. Alumni Assn. (life). Democrat. Methodist. Office: Internat Aviation Cons Investments PO Box 3075 Fremont CA 94539-0307

SMITH, BETTY, writer, not-for-profit developer; b. Bonham, Tex., Sept. 16; d. Sim and Gertrude (Dearing) S. Student, Stephens Coll.; BJ, U. Tex. Women's editor Daily Texan; pres. Hope Assocs. Corp., NYC; pres., owner Betty Smith Assocs., NYC. Author: A Matter of Heart, 1969, Journey to Valhalla: The Life of Lauritz Melchior, 2007. Bd. dirs. Melchior Heldentenor Found., N.Y.C., 1968—, pres., 1987-97; pres., CEO Gerda Lissner Found., 1994-2006; bd. dirs. Herman Lissner Found., 1990—, CEO, 2004—. Mem. Author's Guild. Office: care Lissner Found 135 E 55th St 8th Fl New York NY 10022-4049 Office Phone: 212-826-6100. E-mail: bsmithassocs@aol.com.

SMITH, BETTY DENNY, county official, administrator, fashion executive; b. Centralia, Ill., Nov. 12, 1932; d. Otto and Ferne Elizabeth (Beier) Hasenfuss; m. Peter S. Smith, Dec. 5, 1964; children: Carla Kip, Bruce Kimball. Student. U. Ill., 1950-52; student, L.A. City Coll., 1953-57, UCLA, 1965, U. San Francisco, 1982-84. Freelance fashion coordinator, L.A., NYC, 1953-58; tchr. fashion Rita LeRoy Internat. Studios, 1959-60; mgr. Mo Nadler Fashion, LA, 1961-64; showroom dir. Jean of Calif. Fashions, LA, 1965—. Freelance polit. book reviewer for community newspapers, 1961-62; staff writer Valley Citizen News, 1963. Bd. dirs. Pet Assistance Found., 1969-76; founder, pres., dir. Vol. Services to Animals L.A., 1972-76; mem. County Com. To Discuss Animals in Rsch., 1973-74; mem. blue ribbon com. on animal control L.A. County, 1973-74; dir. L.A. County Animal Care and Control, 1976-82; mem. Calif. Animal Health Technician Exam. Com., 1975-82, chmn., 1979; bd. dirs. L.A. Soc. for Prevention Cruelty to Animals, 1984-94, Calif. Coun. Companion Animal Advocates, 1993-97; dir. West Coast Regional Office, Am. Humane Assn., 1988-97; mem. adv. com. Moorepark Coll., 1988-97; CFO Coalition for Pet Population Control, 1987-92; trustee Gladys W. Sargent Found., 1997—, Coalition to End Pet Overpopulation, 1998—; cons. Jungle Book II, Disney Studios, 1997; mem. adv. com. Wishbone Prodn., 1995-97; mem. govt. rels. and pub. affairs com. Motion Picture & TV Industry Assn., 1992-97; mem. Coalition to Protect Calif. Wildlife, 1996-97, Spl. Commn. Spay/Neuter City L.A., 1998-99; adv. com. La. Dept. of Animal Reg. 2000; mem. adv. com. Calif. Dept. Fish & Game Animal Care, 2003; pres., bd. dirs. Fauna Found., 2004-; mem. Calif. Rep. Cen. Com., 1964-72, mem. exec. com., 1971-73; mem. L.A. County Rep. Cen. Com., 1964-70, mem. exec. com., 1966-70; chmn. 29th Congl. Cen. Com., 1969-70; sec. 28th Senatorial Cen. Com., 1967-68; mem. speakers bur. George Murphy for U.S. Senate, 1970; campaign mgr. Los Angeles County for Spencer Williams for Atty. Gen., 1966; mem. L.A. County Art Mus., L.A. Libr. Assn. Mem. Internat. Platform Assn., Mannequins Assn. (bd. dirs. 1967-68), Lawyer's Wives San Gabriel Valley (bd. dirs. 1971-74, pres. 1972-73), L.A. Athletic Club, Town Hall. Home: 1766 Bluffhill Dr Monterey Park CA 91754-4533 Office Phone: 323-262-1815.

SMITH, BETTY W., librarian; b. Lincoln, Nebr., June 29, 1919; d. Clem and Edith Margaret (Stanley) Wilder; m. Dulaney Dale Smith, Mar. 20, 1946; children: Douglas D., Diane E., Richard W. BA, Wayne U., 1940; BS, U. Minn., 1941; MA, Mich. State U., 1955. Cert. libr. Br. libr. Pub. Libr., Park Ridge, Ill., 1941-42, reference libr. Dearborn, Mich., 1942-44; U.S.C.G. SPAR, libr. asst. U.S.C.G. Acad., New London, Conn., 1945-46; reference libr. Libr. Hawaii, Honolulu, 1946-47; libr. Hawaiian Econ. Found., Honolulu, 1947-49; reference libr. Lansing Pub. Libr., Mich., 1967-86, substitute libr., 1986-98. Mem. Citizens for Actions in Mental Health, 1980—86; steering com. Long-Range Planning Mich. Dept.

Mental Health, 1986—90; bd. dirs. Tri-Co. Cmty. Mental Health, Lansing, 1992—98; founding and exec. com. mem. Alliance for Mentally Ill, Mich., 1985—2003, now v.p.; adv. coun. Mich. Forensic Ctr., 1988—, Lafayette Clinic, Detroit, 1986—92. Mem. LWV, Mental Health Assn., Mich. Assn. Emotionally Disturbed Children (bd. dirs. 1963-68), Mich. Mental Health (adv. coun. 1986-90), Phi Alpha Theta. Home: 1782 Eifert Rd Holt MI 48842-1976

SMITH, BOB, lawyer, educator, state senator; b. Scranton, Pa., Mar. 25, 1947; s. Philip and Ruth (Delmar) S.; m. Ellen Theresa Foster; children: Karen Elizabeth, Lisa. BA in History, U. Scranton, 1969, MS in Chemistry, 1970; MS in Environ. Sci., Rutgers U., 1973; JD, Seton Hall U., 1981. Bar: N.J. 1981. Sci. tchr. Lourdesmont H.S., Clark Summit, Pa., 1968-70; environ. health sci. curriculum coord. Middlesex County Coll., Edison, NJ, 1972-73, adminstrv. asst. to dean sci., 1974-77, instr., 1970-74, asst. prof., 1974-76, assoc. prof., 1976-79, prof. chemistry and environ. sci., 1979-86; law clk. N.J. Dept. Environ. Protection, Trenton, 1980; prin., pvt. practice law Bob Smith and Assocs., Piscataway, NJ, 1981—. Prosecutor East Brunswick, 1997—2005, South Brunswick, 1998—. Mayor of Piscataway Twp., 1981-86; N.J. assemblyman N.J. 17th Legis. Dist., 1986-2001, mem. appropriations com. and environ. quality com., assembly select com. on ocean pollution, 1988, assembly energy and hazardous waste com. policy and rules, 1994; mem. N.J. State Senate, 2002—, chmn. environ. com., 2004-, mem. jud. com. and environment com.; parliamentarian Assembly Dem. Caucus, 1988-90, chmn. task force on environment, 1987; chmn. Piscataway Dem. Orgn., 1981-90; counsel N.J. State Dem. Platform Com., 1987, 89; chmn. Middlesex County Dem. Orgn., 1991-92; Assembly Dem. Dept. Minority Leader, 1993-95; councilman-at-large Piscataway Twp., 1977-80, pres. coun., 1979, v.p., 1978; mem. Middlesex County Transp. Coordinating Com., 1980-86; chmn. Piscataway Planning Bd, 1981-86, sec., 1975, chmn., 1976; bd. dirs. N.J. Conf. Mayors, 1984-86; mem. tech. adv. com. air pollution Middlesex County Planning Bd., 1973-74; mem. Greenbrook Basin com. Area 208 Mgmt. Planning Program, 1975-76; mem. commr.'s adv. com. N.J. Dept. Environ. Protection, 1972-86. Recipient Disting. Citizen award Piscataway Jewish Congregation B'nai Shalom, 1982; named Legis. of Yr. Eden Inst., N.J. State VFW, 1998, Environ. Legislator of Yr., N.J. Environ. Fedn., 1990, Environ. Legislator of Yr., N.J. Environ. Lobby, 2005; Presdl. scholar U. Scranton, 1965-69. Mem. Middlesex County Bar Assn., NJ State Bar Assn Roman Catholic. Office: 216 Stelton Rd B-1 Piscataway NJ 08854-3284 also: 216 Stelton Rd E-5 Piscataway NJ 08854-2600

SMITH, BRAD, journalist; Picture editor Sports Illustrated, Sports Illustrated Women; sports photo editor New York Times. Spkr. in field. Co-editor: (books) Sports of the Times, 2003. Office: NY Times Sports Desk 229 W 43rd St New York NY 10036 Office Phone: 212-556-7371. Office Fax: 212-556-5848.

SMITH, BRAD M., political science scholar; BA summa cum laude in govt., Harvard Coll., 2005; MPhil. student in Comparative Social Policy, Oxford Univ., 2007—. Campaign asst. Senator Bob Corker, 2005—06. Former chmn. Mass. Alliance of Coll. Republicans. Rhodes Scholar. Mem.: Phi Beta Kappa. *

SMITH, BRADFORD LEE, information technology executive, lawyer; b. Milw., Jan. 17, 1959; m. Kathy Surace-Smith; 2 children. AB. summa cum laude, Princeton U., 1981; JD, Columbia U., 1985; student, U. Geneva Grad. Inst. Internat. Studies, Geneva, Switzerland, 1984. Former ptnr. Covington & Burling, Washington; mgr., European Law & Corp. Affairs group, Microsoft, Paris, 1993—96, dep. gen. counsel for worldwide sales Redmond, Wash., 1996—2001, sr. v.p., gen. counsel for law and corp. affairs, 2001—. Lectr. Hague Acad. Internat. Law. Contbr. articles. Office: Microsoft One Microsoft Way Redmond WA 98052-6399 *

SMITH, BRADFORD T., lawyer; b. Phila., 1953; BA, Rutgers U., 1975, JD, 1978. Asst. gen. counsel Hoffmann-La Roche, 1988—95, asst. sec., 1989—95, asst. v.p., 1992—93; chief compliance officer Lab. Corp. of Am., Burlington, NC, 1996—2001, 2004—, exec. v.p., gen. counsel, sec., 1995—2001, exec. v.p., chief legal officer, sec., 2001—, vice chmn. bd. dirs., 2007—. Bd. mem. Alamance Regional Med. Ctr., Alamance County Chamber of Commerce, Alamance Arts Council, Alamance Cares AIDS Support Group, Paramount Community Theater. Office: Lab Corp of Am 358 S Main St Burlington NC 27215

SMITH, BRADLEY E., anesthesiologist; b. Cedar Vale, Kans., Jan. 4, 1933; MD, U. Okla., Norman, 1957. Diplomate Am. Bd. Anesthesiologists. Resident U.S. Naval Hosp., NYC, 1957-60; fellow Columbia Presbyn. Hosp., NYC, 1960—61; faculty Yale U., 1962-63, U. Miami, 1963-69; chmn., prof. dept. anesthesiology Vanderbilt U., Nashville, 1969-93, prof., 1993—, prof. emeritus, 2004—, prof. clin. anesthesiology, 2005—. Mem.: AMA, ACOG (assoc.), Am. Soc. Anesthesiologists. Office: Vandy Med Ctr Rm 209 Oxford House Nashville TN 37232-4125 Office Phone: 615-936-0718.

SMITH, BRADLEY YOULE, lawyer; b. NYC, Feb. 11, 1948; s. Bradley and Christine (Brown) S.; m. Anne Barre, Dec. 31, 1986; children: Evelyn McLaren, Andrew Robert, Lauren Barre, Timothy James, Lynden Eleanor, Christina McLaren. BA in History cum laude, Yale U., 1970; JD, NYU, 1974. Bar: N.Y. 1975, U.S. Dist. Ct. (so. dist.) N.Y. 1975, U.S. Ct. Appeals (2d cir.) 1975. With Davis Polk & Wardwell, NYC, 1974—, ptnr., 1980—. Trustee Royal Coll. Surgeons Found., Inc. Mem. ABA (chmn. subcom. secured transactions 1983-87, moderator and panelist com. banking law and uniform comml. code), Am. Law Inst., N.Y. State Bar Assn. (mem. banking law com.). Office: Davis Polk & Wardwell 450 Lexington Ave New York NY 10017-3982 Office Phone: 212-450-4000. Business E-Mail: bradley.smith@dpw.com.

SMITH, BRIAN D., lawyer; AB, Brown U., 1972; JD, U. Va. Law Sch., 1977; PhD, Cambridge U., 1986. Bar: Calif., NY, Am. Bar Assn. Atty., real estate, shareholder Heller, Ehrman, White, & McAuliffe LLP, San Francisco, 1991—. Mem.: Lambda Alpha Internat. Office: Heller Ehrman 333 Bush St San Francisco CA 94104 Office Phone: 415-772-6534. Fax: 415-772-6268. E-mail: bsmith@hewm.com.

SMITH, BRIAN J., lawyer; b. 1951; BA in Polit. Sci., Bradley U., 1973; JD, U. Mich., 1976. Bar: Mich. 1976. Mem. legal dept., specialty prods. div., Hospital Prods. Div., Specialty Prods. Div. Hospira, Inc., Chgo., 1979—84, div. counsel Abbott Diagnostics Division and the Pharmaceutical Products Division, 1984—91, intl. legal dept., 1991—95, v.p., domestic legal ops., 1995—2001, now sr. v.p., gen. counsel, sec. Sec. Clara Abbot Found. Office: Hospira Inc 275 North Field Dr Lake Forest IL 60045

SMITH, BRIAN RICHARD, hematologist, oncologist, pathologist; b. Glen Cove, NY, May 7, 1952; s. Frank C. and Gloria R. S.; m. Keiren Donovan, Apr. 17, 1993. AB in Chemistry summa cum laude, Princeton U., 1972; MD, Harvard U., 1976; MA (hon.), Yale U., 1997. Diplomate Am. Bd. Internal Medicine, Hematology and Med. Oncology, Am. Bd. Pathology Hematopathology. Resident/fellow Harvard U., Brigham and Women's Hosp., 1976-80; instr. medicine Harvard Med. Sch., 1981—84; assoc. physician Brigham & Women's Hosp., Children's Hosp., Dana-Farber Cancer Ins, Boston, 1981-88; asst. prof. medicine Harvard Med. Sch., 1985-88; assoc. prof. medicine, lab. medicine & pediatrics sch. med. Yale U., New Haven, 1988-96, prof. medicine, lab medicine & pediatrics, 1996—, dir. immunohematology; vice chmn. dept. lab. medicine Yale Med. Sch.-Yale New Haven Hosp., 1997—2005, chmn. dept. lab. medicine, 2006—; DeCamp lectr. biomed. ethics Princeton U., NJ, 1992. Contbr. over 150 articles to med. publs. Trustee Richard D. Frisbee III Found.; chair study sect. Am. Heart Assn. Recipient George A. Howe prize Princeton U., 1976; Am. Cancer Soc. fellow, 1981-84, Leukemia Soc. fellow, 1982-88; Leukemia Soc. Am. scholar, 1989, Stohlman scholar, 1993, Nat. Blood Found. scholar, 1996. Fellow ACP, Coll. Am. Pathologists; mem. NIH (recombinant DNA adv. com. 1992-97), Acad. Clin. Lab. Physicians and Scientists (pres. 2006-), Phi Beta Kappa, Sigma Xi, Alpha Omega Alpha. Roman Catholic. Office: Yale U Sch Med PO Box 208035 333 Cedar St New Haven CT 06520-8035

SMITH, BRIAN WILLIAM, lawyer, former government official; b. NYC, Feb. 3, 1947; s. William Francis and Dorothy Edwina (Vogel) S.; m. Donna Jean Holverson, Apr. 24, 1976; children: Mark Holverson, Lauren Elizabeth. BA, St. John's U., NYC, 1968, JD, 1971; MS, Columbia U., 1981. Bar: N.Y. 1972, D.C. 1975, U.S. Dist. Ct. (ea. and so. dists.) N.Y. 1975, U.S. Supreme Ct. 1976, U.S. Dist. Ct. D.C. 1986. Atty. Am. Express Co., NYC, 1970-73, CIT Fin. Corp., NYC, 1973-74; assoc. counsel, mng. atty. Interbank Card Assn. (named changed to Master Card Internat., Inc.), NYC, 1974-75, sr. v.p., corp. sec., gen. counsel, 1975-82; chief counsel Compt. of Currency, Washington, 1982-84; ptnr. Stroock & Stroock & Lavan, Washington, 1984-92, mng. ptnr., 1986-92; ptnr. Mayer, Brown, Rowe & Maw, LLP, Washington and NYC, 1992—2004, Latham & Watkins LLP, Washington, 2004—. Lectr. fin. industry. Capt. USAR, 1970—78. Mem. ABA, N.Y. State Bar Assn., D.C. Bar Assn., Assn. Bar City N.Y., Fed. Bar Assn., N.Y. Athletic Club, Met. Club (N.Y.), Met. Club (Washington). Home: 35 W Lenox St Chevy Chase MD 20815-4208 Office: Latham & Watkins LLP 555 11th St NW Washington DC 20004-1304 Office Phone: 202-637-2288.

SMITH, BRUCE ALFRED, oil industry executive; b. Coffeyville, Kans., Oct. 12, 1943; s. George Alfred and Isabel (Andrews) S.; m. Cynthia Denton Doughat, Aug. 7, 1969 (div. Jan. 1987); children: Denton Todd, Bruce Chandler, John Paul, Joseph Willimas, Charles Pinson Smith; m. Gail Hutchison, Nov. 10, 1990. BA, Westminster Coll., 1965; MBA, U. Kans., 1967; postgraduate student, U. Chgo., 1971. With Ford Motor Co., Dearborn, Mich., 1967-69; banking officer met. divsn. Continental Ill. Nat. Bank and Trust Co. Chgo., Chgo., 1971-73, 2nd v.p. multinational divsn., 1973-75, v.p. mining divsn., 1975-77, v.p., sect. mgr. Chgo. and London, 1977-80, v.p., mgr. internat. energy divsn. Chgo., 1980-82, v.p., mgr. SW group, comml. banking Houston, 1983-86; corp. v.p., treas. Valero Energy Corp. and Valero Natural Gas Ptnrs., San Antonio, 1986-92; v.p. Tesoro Petroleum Corp., San Antonio, 1992-93, CFO, 1992-95, exec. v.p., 1993-95, exec. v.p. Tesoro Exploration and Prodn. Co., 1993-95, exec. v.p., COO, dir., 1995, pres., CEO, 1995-96, chmn., CEO, pres., 1996—. Bd. dirs. Noble Energy, Inc., Nat. Petrochemical & Refiners Assn. Bd. dirs. San Antonio Sports Found. Served in US Army, 1969—71. Mem. Fin. Execs. Inst. (past pres. San Antonio chpt.). Office: Tesoro Petroleum Corp 300 Concord Plz San Antonio TX 78216-6999 *

SMITH, BRUCE ARTHUR, lawyer; b. Terre Haute, Ind., Jan. 4, 1952; s. Wayne Coakley and Stella Inez S.; m. Lora L. Smith, May 16, 1992; children: Ashley Nicole, Haley Marie, Nathan Wayne, Evan McKean. BS, Ind. State U., 1973; JD cum laude, Ind. U., 1976. Bar: Ind. 1976, Ill. 1984, Ky. 2002, U.S. Dist. Ct. (so. dist.) Ind. 1976, U.S. Tax Ct. 1977, U.S. Supreme Ct. 1983; cert. in bus. bankruptcy law and consumer bankruptcy law Am. Bd. Cert. Ptnr. Sturm, Smith & Parmenter, Vincennes, Ind., 1976—. Instr. paralegal edn. Vincennes U., 1977-81, mem. adv. bd. dept. small bus. edn., 1984-86; dep. pros. atty. Knox County Prosecutor's Office, Vincennes, 1976-82; instr. Ind. Continuing Legal Edn. Forum, 1995, 97, 99, 2001. Mem. Ind. Bar Assn. (chair bankruptcy law sect., 1994-95), Ill. Bar Assn., Knox County Bar Assn. (pres. 1982-83), Kiwanis (pres. 1981-82), Elks (exalted ruler 1983-84), Phi Delta Phi. Home: 564 N Deer Creek Dr Vincennes IN 47591-9600 Office: Sturm Smith & Parmenter 302 Main St PO Box 393 Vincennes IN 47591-0393

SMITH, BRUCE CAMERON, physician; b. Seattle, May 7, 1957; s. Roderick Kay and Rhoda Ann Smith; m. Denise Doherty Smith. MD, U. Wash., Seattle, 1984. Physician Overlake Sr. Health Ctr., Bellevue, Wash., 1999—. Asst. scoutmaster Boy Scouts Am., Issaquah, Wash., 2005—06; bd. mem. Luth. Outdoor Ministries, Issaquah, 2003—06. Fellow: ACP (v.p. 1997—2006); mem.: Am. Med. Dirs. Assn. (pub. policy com. 2003—04, cert. long-term care med. dir. 2001, cert. med. dir.), Am. Geriatric Soc., Am. Acad. Hospice and Palliative Care (cert. hospice med. dir.). Office: Overlake Senior Health Center Ste A101 1750 112th Ave NE Bellevue WA 98004 Home Phone: 425-392-9339; Office Phone: 425-688-5569. Personal E-mail: bsmd@hotmail.com.

SMITH, BRUCE VAUGHN, electrical engineer; b. Kingsville, Tex., July 28, 1953; s. Robert Vaughn and June Estelle (Link) S.; m. Astrid Marie Ryerson, July 17, 1976; 1 child, Leslie Michelle. BSEE, Iowa State U., 1975, MSEE, 1980, PhD, 1991. Prof. engr., Iowa. Sr. prin. sys. engr. Rockwell-Collins Avionics, Cedar Rapids, Iowa, 1975—. Owner Cottonwood Sys. Design, Co., 2001—; adj. prof. Iowa State U., Ames, 1991—, grad. faculty, 1999—; program evaluator, engr. commr., exec. com. Accreditation Bd. Engring. & Tech., Balt., 1995—, mem. exec. com.; state problem capt. Odyssey of the Mind, 1996-2000. Bd. dirs. North Linn Sch. Dist., Troy Mills, Iowa, 1993-95. Mem. IEEE (com. on engring. accreditation activities), Internat. Coun. Sys. Engring. (sec.-treas. Heartland chpt. 2000-), Sigma Xi. Avocations: target shooting, auto racing. Office: Rockwell Collins Inc 400 Collins Rd NE Cedar Rapids IA 52498-0001

SMITH, BURTON JORDAN, computer designer; b. Durham, NC, Mar. 21, 1941; s. Sherman Everett and Rebecca Frances (Jordan) S.; m. Dorothy Nan Duncan, Dec. 28, 1966; children: Katherine Page, Julia Jordan. BSEE, U. N.Mex., Albuquerque, 1967; SM, MIT, Cambridge, 1968, Elec. Engring. Diploma, 1969, ScD, 1972. Asst. prof. U. Colo., Denver, 1972-78, assoc. prof., 1978-79; v.p. R&D Denelcor, Inc., Denver, 1979-85; fellow Supercomputing Rsch. Ctr., Lanham, Md., 1985-88; co-founder, chief scientist Tera Computer Co. (purchased Cray Rsch. from Silicon Graphics, Inc. in 2000, renamed Cray, Inc.), Seattle, 1988—2005; chmn. Cray, Inc., Seattle, 1988—99, also bd. dir., 1988—2005; tech. fellow Microsoft Corp., Redmond, Wash., 2005—. Adv. com. on computer rsch. NSF, Washington, 1984-87; fellow, Supercomputing Rsch. Ctr. (now Ctr. for Computing Sciences), divsn. Inst. for Def. Analysis, 1985-88; sci. coun. Universities Space Rsch. Assn., Washington, 1987-91; blue ribbon panel on high performance computing NSF, Washington, 1993, presdl. faculty fellows final selection panel, Washington, 1992-93; principal architect of the MTA (Multithreaded Architecture) system and head, Cascade project, Cray, Inc. Editor: (book) Multithreaded Computer Architecture, 1994. Precinct committeeman Dem. Party, Denver, 1980-84. With USN, 1960-64. Recipient Eckert-Marchly award, 1990, awarded jointly by IEEE Computer Soc. and Assn. for Computer Machinery, Seymour Cray award IEEE Computer Soc., 2003. Fellow IEEE, Assn. for Computing Machinery; mem. NAE, Eta Kappa Nu, Sigma Xi. Democrat. Avocation: choral singing. Office: Microsoft Corp 1 Microsoft Way Redmond WA 98052-6399

SMITH, C. D., civil engineering educator; BSc in Civil Engring., U. Alta, Can., 1948; MSc in Hydraulic Engring., U. Sask., 1963. Cons. hydraulic engr., prof. civil engring. U. Sask., Saskatoon, Can., to 1991, prof. emeritus civil engring., cons. hydraulic engr., 1991—. Author: two books; contbr. to over 70 profl. jours. Recipient C. Dagenais award Can. Soc. Civil Engring., 1986, T.C. Keefer medal, 1962, 91, Engring. Achievement Silver medal Profl. Engrs. of Sask., 1991,Engr. of Yr., Saskatoon Engring. Soc., 1993, Julian Smith medal Engring. Inst. Can., 2000. Fellow ASCE; mem. Can. Soc. Civil Engring. (past pres.). Home: 120 7th St E Saskatoon SK Canada S7H 0W8 Office Phone: 306-242-8421.

SMITH, C. GRANT, film producer, scriptwriter; b. St. Louis, Mar. 1, 1967; s. Lynwood M. and Peggy M. Smith; m. Hannah King, June 17, 1971; children: Caroline K., Samuel Owen, William Francis, Conrad Lucas. Cert., Am. Film Inst., LA, 1998; MA, Webster U., 2007. Cert. Acctg., Sanford Brown Bus. Coll., 1988. Co-owner BlackSmith Pictures, Inc., 1994; mcht. developer Maritz, Inc., Fenton, Mo., 1995—97; flight attendant coord. TWA, St. Louis, 1999—2001; prodn. engr. Quick Study Radiology. Co-writer, prodr.: screenplays Hunting Ground; co-author Jersey Shore (finalist L.A. Screenwriting Expo., 2003), Hawkins, The Wild Willows, 2006, Mythos, Ley of the Land, 2006. Democrat. Achievements include development of screenwriting application through MS Access. Home: 1075 Wilson Ave Saint Louis MO 63130 Home Phone: 314-725-7472; Office Phone: 314-713-6872. Personal E-mail: cgsgrant@yahoo.com.

SMITH, C. LEMOYNE, retired publishing executive; b. Atkins, Ark., Sept. 15, 1934; s. Cecil Garland and Salena Bell (Wilson) S.; m. Selma Jean Tucker, May 23, 1964; 1 child, Jennifer Lee BS, Ark. Tech. U., 1956; M.Ed., U. Ark., 1958. Tchr. pub. schs., Little Rock, 1956-58; instr. bus. adminstrn. Ark. Tech. U., Russellville, 1958-60; sales rep. South-Western Pub. Co., Cin., 1960-67, editorial staff, 1967-82, pres., chief exec. officer, 1982-90, chmn., 1990-91, ret., 1991. Bd. dirs. Cin. Council on World Affairs, 1983-95. Mem.: Nat. Bus. Edn. Assn., Delta Pi Epsilon. Republican. Presbyterian. Avocations: bridge, travel, golf. Office: South-Western Pub Co 5191 Natorp Blvd Mason OH 45040-7980

SMITH, CARL BERNARD, education educator; b. Feb. 29, 1932; s. Carl R. and Elizabeth Ann (Lefeld) S.; m. Virginia Lee Cope, Aug. 30, 1958; children: Madonna, Anthony, Regina, Marla. BA, U. Dayton, 1954; MA, Miami U., Oxford, Ohio, 1961; PhD, Case Western Res. U., 1967. Tchr. Cathedral Latin H.S., Cleve., 1954-57; customer corr. E.F. MacDonald Co., Dayton, 1958-59; tchr. Kettering (Ohio) H.S., 1959-61; editor Reardon Baer Pub. Co., Cleve., 1961-62; tchr., rschr. Case Western Res. U., Cleve., 1962-65, Cleve. Pub. Schs., 1966-67; asst. prof. edn. Ind. U., Bloomington, 1967-69, assoc. prof., 1970-72, prof., 1973—99, prof. emeritus, 1999—. Dir. ERIC Ctr., 1988-2004, Family Literacy Ctr., 1990—; pres. Grayson Bernard Pub. Co., 1988—, Am. Family Learning Corp., 1996—. Author: Reading Instruction through Diagnostic Teaching (Pi Lambda Theta Best Book in Edn. award 1972), Getting People to Read, 1978; sr. author: Series r, 1983, New View, 1993, Teaching Reading and Writing Together, 1984, Connect! Getting Your Kids to Talk to You, 1994, Word History A Resource Book, 1995, Self-Directed Learner Curriculum, 1998, (videotape) Make a Difference, 1996, Improving Your Child's Writing Skills, 1999, Gotcha Grandpa, 2000, Talk to Your Children About Books, 2001, Teaching Children to Learn, 2002, Reading to Learn, 2003, Parents Guide to Character Development, 2003, The Spriritual Family, 2005, Teaching Parents How To Listen and Learn, 2007. Pres. Bd. Edn., St. Charles Sch., Bloomington, 1976-80. Recipient Sch. Bell award NEA, 1967, Literacy award Ind. State Reading Assn., 1997. Mem. ASCD, Internat. Reading Assn., Nat. Coun. Tchrs. of English, Am. Ednl. Rsch. Assn., Phi Delta Kappa. Republican. Roman Catholic. Home: 4915 E Cedarcrest Dr Bloomington IN 47401 Office: Reading and English Clearinghouse Smith Rsch Ctr Bloomington IN 47405 Home Phone: 812-336-1800; Office Phone: 812-345-0985. Business E-Mail: smith2@indiana.edu.

SMITH, CARNICE, music educator, director; b. Jackson, Mississippi, Miss., June 8, 1954; d. James Edward and Mary Lee Smith. B in Music Edn., Jackson State U., 1976, M in Music Edn., 1979; Orff cert., Miss. State U., 1993. Nat. bd. cert. tchr. Music tchr. Morrison Elem. Sch. Jackson Pub. Sch., Miss., 1987—95; choral dir. Blackburn Mid. Sch. Jackson Pub. Schools, Miss., 1995—. Dir., sponsor Miss. Songfest Jackson Pub. Schools, 1998—2005. Music scholar, Jackson State U., 1972—76. Mem.: Delta Sigma Theta (life). Democrat. Baptist. Home: 3627 Fontaine Ave Jackson MS 39213 Office: Blackburn Mid Sch 1311 W Pearl St Jackson MS 39203 Home Phone: 601-366-7682. Personal E-mail: csharp54@yahoo.com.

SMITH, CAROL L., human services administrator, consultant; MA, Purdue U., West Lafayette, Ind., 1978; PhD, U. Ill., Champagne-Urbana, 1984; Cert. in mng. ind. and orgnl. change, U. Va., Charlottesville, 1993. Cert. bus. ethics specialist Ethics Inst., 1988. Pres. First Priority, Inc., Atlanta, 1998—. Cons. Team UK Sable Group, Weston, Conn., 2002—. Author (proposal for creation of acad.): (math. and sci. acad.) Making A Difference (Achievement award Lockheed Martin, 1997). Creator Dabbling Decorators, Kennesaw, Ga., 2004—07. Nat. Mental Health fellowship, NIMH, 1979-81. Mem.: Nat. Coalition Black Women (chair edn. 1994—98), YMCA (assoc.; mentor 1990—91, Nat. Black Achiever 1990), Toastmasters Internat., Phi Beta Kappa. Achievements include development of anti-bullying initiative. Avocations: travel, mentoring. Office: First Priority Inc PO Box 384 Kennesaw GA 30144

SMITH, CAROLE DIANNE, retired lawyer, editor, writer, product developer; b. Seattle, June 12, 1945; d. Glaude Francis and Elaine Claire (Finkenstein) S.; m. Stephen Bruce Presser, June 18, 1968 (div. June 1987); children: David Carter, Elisabeth Catherine. AB cum laude, Harvard U., Radcliffe Coll., 1968; JD, Georgetown U., 1974. Bar: Pa. 1974. Law clk. Hon. Judith Jamison, Phila., 1974—75; assoc. Gratz, Tate, Spiegel, Ervin & Ruthrouff, Phila., 1975—76; freelance editor, writer Evanston, Ill., 1983—87; editor Ill. Inst. Tech., Chgo., 1987—88; mng. editor LawLetters, Inc., Chgo., 1988—89; editor ABA, Chgo., 1989—95; product devel. dir. Gt. Lakes divsn. Lawyers Coop. Pub., Deerfield, Ill., 1995—96; product devel. mgr. Midwest Market Ctr. West Group, Deerfield, Ill., 1996—97; mgr acquisitions, bus. and fin. group CCH, Inc., Riverwoods, Ill., 1997—2002; ret. Author Jour. of Legal Medicine, 1975, Selling and the Law: Advertising and Promotion, 1987; (under pseudonym Sarah Toast) 79 children's books and stories, 1994-2002; editor The Brief, 1990-95, Criminal Justice, 1989-90, 92-95 (Gen. Excellence award Soc. Nat. Assn. Pubs. 1990, Feature Article award-bronze Soc. Nat. Assn. Pubs. 1994), Franchise Law Jour., 1995; mem. editl. bd. The Brief, 1995-2000, editor-in-chief, 1998-2000. Dir. Radcliffe Club of Chgo., 1990-93; mem. parents coun. Latin Sch. Chgo., 1995-96; trustee Winnetka-Northfield Libr. Dist., 2003—, pres. trustees, 2005-; mem. Winnetka Plan Commn. 2003-05, Winnetka Forestry Commn., 2004-05 Mem. ABA (editor-in-chief The Brief 1998-2000, mem. publs. editl. bd. tort trial and ins. practice sect. 2003-05, chair 2005—).

SMITH, CARRIE VERONICA, psychology professor; m. James Walter Parrett, Nov. 1, 2003. PhD, U. Houston, Tex., 2004. Vis. asst. prof. U. Del., Newark, 2004—. Office: Univ Delaware 108 Wolf Hall Newark DE 19716 Home Phone: 302-478-5104; Office Phone: 302-831-1511. Business E-Mail: cvsmith@psych.udel.edu.

SMITH, CATHERINE H., bank executive; b. 1953; 2 children. BA, Hampshire Coll.; M in pub. and pvt. mgmt., Yale Sch. Orgn. and Mgmt. Sr. positions in investment and healthcare bus., 1983—98; CFO Aetna Fin. Services; pres., healthcare, edn., govt. distbn. ING US Worksite Fin. Services, broker dealer ops., customer svc., USFS retail and worksite bus. groups; pres., US Retail Fin. Services ING Grp. Bd. mem. Outward Bound USA, Conn. Fund for Environment; adv. Conn. Trust for Pub. Land. Named one of 25 Women to Watch, US Banker, 2006. Avocations: hiking, skiing. *

SMITH, CATHERINE JEAN, artist, educator; b. Washington, Oct. 19, 1950; d. Albert Eugene and Catherine Virginia Smith. MFA, Sch. of the Art Inst. of Chgo., 1990. Prof. of art Mott C.C., Flint, Mich., 1991—. Bd. dirs. Buckham Fine Arts Gallery, Flint, Mich., 1992—. Author: Women in Pants: Manly Maidens, Cowgirls and Other Renegades, 2003 (Amelia Bloomer List, ALA, 2004); curator and author (art exhbn. and book) Witness and Warriors: The 1936-1937 Flint Sitdown Strike, 1999; one-woman shows include Flint Inst. Art, 1977. Recipient Jurors award, Mich. Outdoor Sculpture 5, Southfield, 1995; scholarship, Sch. of the Art Inst. of Chgo., 1989, Creative Artist grant, Arts Found. of Mich., 1993-4, Animating Democracy Initiative grant, C.S. Mott Found., 2001. Mem.: Coll. Art Assn. (assoc.). Democrat. Home: 824 S Leroy St Fenton MI 48430 Office: Mott CC 1401 E Court St Flint MI 48503 Home Phone: 810-714-2441; Office Phone: 810-762-0443. E-mail: womeninpants1@sbcglobal.net.

SMITH, CATHERINE MARIE, science educator; b. Bridgeport, Conn., Dec. 28, 1958; d. Arthur Vincent Giles, Sr. and Lila Catherine (Auger) Giles; m. Roger K. Smith, July 16, 1982. BS, U. Bridgeport, 1980; MBA, Sacred Heart U., 1994. Cert. Med. Technologist Am. Soc. Clin. Pathologists, 1981. Medical technician Bridgeport Hosp., Conn., 1980—88; med. technologist St. Joseph Med. Ctr., Stamford, Conn., 1988—94; lab. mgr. Stamford Medical Group, Stamford, 1994—99; chemistry and biology tchr. Wilbur Cross HS, New Haven, 1999—2003, New Canaan HS, Conn., 2003—. Donor Am. Red Cross, Conn., 1984—; tchr. participant Jr. Sci. & Humanities Symposium, U. Conn., 2000—03; youth min. Our Lady of Assumption, Fairfield, Conn., 1989—2004; emmaus team mem. Holy Family, Fairfield, Conn., 2000—, St. Aloysius, New Canaan, Conn., 2004—. Mem.: NSTA, So. Poverty Law, Am. Soc. Clin. Pathologists, Conn. Nat. Sci. Tchrs. Assn., Pi Lambda Theta, Delta Mu Delta. Roman Catholic. Avocations: car racing, dog training. Personal E-mail: cmbgs@aol.com.

SMITH, CATHERINE R., construction executive; B in Bus. Econs., U. Calif., Santa Barbara; MBA, U. So. Calif. Various fin. positions including v.p., CFO intelligence and info. systems bus. Raytheon Co., 1986—2003; exec. v.p., CFO Bell Systems Textron, Inc., 2003—05; exec. v.p., CFO Kennametal, Inc., 2005—06, Centex Corp., 2006—. Office: Centex Corp PO Box 199000 Dallas TX 75219-9000 Office Phone: 214-981-5000. *

SMITH, CHAD GAYLORD, musician, recording artist; b. St. Paul, Oct. 25, 1962; m. Maria St. John, 1996 (div. 1997); 1 child; m. Nancy Mack Smith, May 2004; 1 child. Drummer The Red Hot Chili Peppers, 1988—. Musician: (albums) The Red Hot Chili Peppers, 1984, Freaky Styley, 1985, The Uplift Mofo Party Plan, 1987, Mother's Milk, 1989, Blood Sugar Sex Magik, 1991, One Hot Minute, 1995, Californication, 1999, By the Way, 2002, Live in Hyde Park, 2004, Stadium Arcadium, 2006 (Best Album, MTV Europe Music Awards, 2006, Best Rock Album, Best Ltd. Edit. Package, Grammy awards, 2007), (songs) Dani California, 2006 (MTV Video Music award for best Art Direction, 2006, Best Rock Vocal Performance, Best Rock Song, Grammy awards, 2007). Co-recipient Favorite Band, Duo or Group, Am. Music Awards, 2006, Favorite Alternative Artists, 2006. Office: care Q Prime 131 S 11th St Nashville TN 37206 Office Phone: 615-258-1050. Office Fax: 615-258-1040. E-mail: info@qprime.com. *

SMITH, CHADWICK FITZHUGH, orthopaedic surgeon, educator; s. Roy Ledson Smith and Minnie Jewel Chadwick; m. Corinna Carr Smith, June 6, 1958; children: Laura Sweeney, Chuck, Stephanie, Michael, E.K. BA, So. Meth. U., Dallas, 1954; MD, U. Tex., Galveston, 1959; PhD, U. Madrid, 1999; PhD (hon.), U. Mexico City, 2001. Cert. Am. Bd. Orthopaedic Surgery, Internat. Bd. Orthopaedic Surgery. Intern Harbor Gen. Hosp., LA, 1958—59; resident orthopaedic surgery Orthopaedic Hosp., LA, 1962—65; fellow upper extremity surgery and acad. orthopaedic medicine Orthopaedic Hosp., U. So. Calif., LA, 1965—67; clin. prof. orthopaedic surgery U. So. Calif. Sch. Medicine, LA; med. dir. Internat. Children's Program Orthopaedic Hosp., LA. Chmn. Internat. Soc. Orthopaedic Surgery and Traumatology Found., 1991—; examiner Am. Bd. Orthopaedic Surgery; med. staff Orthopaedic Hosp., LA, U. So. Calif. U. Hosp., LA, LAC/U. So. Calif. Med. Ctr., LA, Hosp. Good Samaritan, LA, St. Vincent's Med. Ctr., LA; chmn. bd. trustees Pitzer Coll.; vice chmn. bd. fellows Claremont Colls.; mem. bd. councilors U. So. Calif. Sch. Medicine; chmn. bd. dirs. Laser Medics, Inc.; bd. dirs. Directed Energy, Inc.; trustee Chadwick Sch., 1980—91, chmn. bd. trustees, 1985—90; chmn. LA Doctors for United Way; med. adv. bd. Universal Pain Tech., 1997; lectr. in field. Mem. exec. com.: Jour. Internat. Orthopaedics; contbr. articles to profl. jours. Capt. US Army, 1959—62, PTO. Recipient Outstanding Intern award, Outstanding Non-Alumnus Physician award, U. So. Calif., 1987. Fellow: ACS, Internat. Coll. Surgeons; mem.: AMA, Western Orthopaedic Assocs., Orthopaedic Sports Medicine, Soc. Internat. Rsch. Orthopaedic and Traumatology (v.p.), Internat. Soc. Orthopaedic Surgery and Traumatology (pres. US sect.), Salerni Collegium, Royal Soc. Medicine, Pediat. Orthopaedic Soc. N.Am., Pan Pacific Surg. Assn., Osteon, Orthopaedic Laser Soc. N.Am. (pres., founding pres.), Orthopaedic Rsch. and Edn. Found. (chmn. LA), Nat. Am. Arthroscopy Assn., Nat. Osteonecrosis Found., Inc., LA County Med. Assn., Internat. Orthopaedic Assn., Internat. Musculoskeletal Laser Soc., Internat. Arthroscopy Assn., German Orthopaedic Assn. (hon.), Mexican Orthopaedic Assn. (hon.), Calif. Med. Assn. (bd. dirs.), Calif. Orthopaedic Assn., Biomed. Engring. Soc., Arthroscopy Assn. N.Am., Am. Soc. Laser Therapy (founder), Am. Orthopaedic Foot and Ankle Soc., Am. Acad. Neurol. Orthopaedic Surgeons, Am. Orthopaedic Assn., Am. Bd. Laser Surgery (diplomate), Am. Acad. Pediat., Am. Acad. Orthopaedic Surgeons (gen. chmn. 1991, gen. chmn. Anaheim meeting 1991), Fraternity of Friends of the Music Ctr., Jack Kramer Tennis Club, Calif. Club. Achievements include co-developer R.A.M. total knee prosthesis; co-developer Smith elbow prosthesis; development of CFS patellofemoral prosthesis; multiple laser tools for use in orthopaedic surgery; research in effects of motor vehicle accidents on shoulders, spines and knees; the relationship between orthpaedic problems and repetitive trauma. Avocations: scuba diving, tennis, skiing, windsurfing, chess. Office: 1127 Wilshire Blvd Ste 912 Los Angeles CA 90017

SMITH, CHARLES ANTHONY, foundation administrator, director; b. Santa Fe, Sept. 16, 1939; s. Frances (Mier) Vigil; m. Paula Ann Thomas, June 26, 1965; 1 child, Charlene Danielle. Student various adminstrv. & law courses. Circulation mgr. Daily Alaska Empire, 1960-63; agt. Mut. of N.Y. Life Ins. Co., Juneau, Alaska, 1964-65; mng. ptnr. Future Investors in Alaska and Cinema Alaska, Juneau, 1961-62; SE Alaska rep. K & L Distbrs., 1966-68; mgr. SE Alaska Alaska Airlines Newspapers, 1969; dep. Alaska Retirement Sys., Juneau, 1970-71; apptd. dir. hwy. safety, gov.'s hwy. safety rep. Juneau, 1971-83; pres. Valley Svc. Ctr., I Nc., 1984-94; chmn. S.E. Alaska Employee Support of the Guard and Reserve, 1992—; pres. 3-S Corp., 1995—. Apptd. chmn. S.E. Alaska for ESGR, 1995; apptd. Alaska state dir. Selective Svc., 1996—. Author various hwy. safety manuals and plans. Alaska pres. Muscular Dystrophy Assn. Am.; pres. SE Alaska Emergency Med. Svcs. Coun., 1965-72; state dir. Selective Svc., 1996. Served to maj. Army N.G., 1964-88. Named Alaska Safety Man of Yr., 1977. Mem. Am. Assn. Motor Vehicle Adminstrs., Alaska Peace Officers Assn., Nat. Assn. Gov.'s Hwy. Safety Reps., N.G. Assn., Internat. Platform Assn., Elks (Juneau). Roman Catholic. Home: PO Box 32856 Juneau AK 99803-2856

SMITH, CHARLES COURTLAND, JR., lawyer, state legislator; b. Edgewood, Md., Feb. 27, 1946; s. Charles Courtland and Nell Jeanette (Martin) S.; m. Patricia Arlene Cassens, Aug. 31, 1974; children: Brian Courtland, Joel McQuarrie. BA, U. Ga., 1968, JD, 1973. Ptnr. Nichols, Lavigao, Smith & Rice, Conyers, Ga., 1973-74, Smith & Floyd, St. Marys, Ga., 1976—2006; trial asst. dist. atty. Fulton County Dist. Atty., Atlanta, 1974-76; rep. Ga. Gen. Assembly, Atlanta, 1993—2003, adminstrn. fl. leader, 1999—2003; of counsel Gilbert, Harrell, Sumerford & Martin, PC, 2002—. City atty. City of St. Marys, 1979-81. Chmn. bd. dirs. St. Marys United Meth. Ch., 1983. Fellow Kiwanis Internat.; mem. USN League (life), Am. Numis. Assn., Am. Radio Relay League (life), Camden-Kings Bay Navy League (charter), Camden-Kings Bay C. of C. (charter), St. Marys Kiwanis Club (pres. 1979). Democrat. Avocations: flying, scuba diving, skiing, amateur radio, woodturning. Office: Gilbert Harrell Sumerford & Martin PO Drawer 768 1815 Osborne Rd Saint Marys GA 31558

SMITH, CHARLES HADDON, geologist, consultant, retired federal agency administrator; b. Dartmouth, NS, Can., Sept. 3, 1926; s. Albion Benson and Dora Pauline (McGill) S.; m. Mary Gertrude Saint, Sept. 5, 1949; children: Charles Douglas, Richard David, Alan Michael, Timothy McGill. B.Sc. and Diploma in Engring, Dalhousie U., Can., 1946, M.Sc. in Geology, 1948; MS, Yale U., 1951, PhD in Econ. Geology, 1952. Instr. Dalhousie U., Halifax, N.S., 1946-48; geologist Cerro de Pasco Copper Corp., Morococha, Peru, 1949, Geol. Survey of Can., Ottawa, Ont., 1952-64, chief petrological scis. div., 1964-67, chief crustal geology div., 1967-68; sci. adviser Sci. Council Can., Ottawa, 1968-70; dir. planning Dept. Energy Mines and Resources, Ottawa, 1970-71, asst. dep. minister sci. and tech., 1971-75, sr. asst. dep. minister, 1975-81; pres. Charles H. Smith Cons., 1982-94. Mem. adv. coun. dept. geology and geophysics Princeton U., 1967-76; sci. advisor Can. Commn. for UNESCO, 1983-89; exec. dir. Can. Nat. Com./World Energy Conf., 1983-90; bd. govs. Can. Inst. Radiation Safety, 1983-86; hon. mem. Energy Coun. Can., 1991—; coord. 150th anniversary Geol. Survey Can., 1990-93. Mem. editl. bd. Am. Jour. Sci., 1967-72, Mineralium Deposita, 1968-83, Jour. Petrology, 1966-70, Econ. Geology, 1966-70; contbr. articles to profl. jours. Fellow Royal Soc. Can. (fgn. sec. 1986-90), Canadian Acad. Engring., Mineral. Soc. Am., Soc. Econ. Geologists (v.p. N.Am. 1968-70); mem. Can. Inst. Mining and Metallurgy (life mem., v.p. 1982-84), Assn. Profl. Engrs. Ont., Geol. Assn. Can., Can. Geosci. Coun. (pres. 1984), Rotary.

SMITH, CHARLES HYDE, librarian, historian, geographer; b. Winsted, Conn., Sept. 30, 1950; s. George Nelson and Hazel Munson Smith; m. Alesia Maltz, 1978 (div. 1984). BA in Geology, Wesleyan U., Middletown, Conn., 1972; MA in Geography, Ind. U., Bloomington, 1980; PhD in Geography, U. Ill., Champaign-Urbana, 1984; MLS, U. Pitts., 1995. Sci. libr., asst. prof. libr. pub. svcs. Western Ky. U., Bowling Green, 1995—2000, sci. libr., assoc. prof. libr. pub. svcs., 2000—04, sci. libr., prof. libr. pub. svcs., 2004—. Author: (monographic analysis) Alfred Russel Wallace: The Evolution of an Evolutionist, 2003—; editor: (anthology and bibliography) Alfred Russel Wallace: An Anthology of His Shorter Writings, 1991, (anthology) Alfred Russel Wallace: Writings on Evolution 1843-1912, 2004; compiler (bibliography) Biodiversity Studies: A Bibliographic Review, 2000 (The Oberly award, 2001), compiler/maintainer (informational website) Nineteenth Century Exploration of Australia, 2002—, Early Classics in Biogeography, Distribution, and Diversity Studies: 1951-1975, 2003—, Some Biogeographers, Evolutionists and Ecologists: Chrono-Biographical Sketches, 2005—, Malvina Reynolds: Song Lyrics and Poems, 2006—, The 111 Greatest Acts of the Anglo-American Folk Music Tradition, 2006—, The Alfred Russel Wallace Page, 2000— (Sci. Am. Best Five History of Sci. Websites, 2003), HERPFAUN, 1998, The Classical Music Navigator, 2000—, MAMMFAUN, 2001, Early Classics in Biogeography, Distribution, and Diversity Studies: To 1950, 2002—; author/maintainer: website The Once and Future Wallace, 2006—; contbr. articles to profl. jours. Mem.: Internat. Biogeography Soc., History of Sci. Soc., Soc. for the History of Natural History, Ky. Libr. Assn. Home Phone: 270-842-8927; Office Phone: 270-745-6079. Business E-Mail: charles.smith@wku.edu.

SMITH, CHARLES ISAAC, geology educator; b. Hearne, Tex., Feb. 9, 1931; s. Walter Lee and Nellie Lucille (Clearwater) S.; m. Anita Lou Howell, Aug. 22, 1961; children: Lanita Maylene, James Emmett, Timothy Stephen, Sheila Nell. BS, Baylor U., 1952; MA, La. State U., 1955; PhD, U. Mich., 1966. Geologist Shell Devel. Co., Houston, 1955-60, 62-65; prof. geology U. Mich., Ann Arbor, 1965-77, chmn. dept., 1970-77; prof. geology U. Tex., Arlington, 1977-93, prof. emeritus, 1994—, chmn. dept., 1977-89, cons. geologist, 1993—. Contbr. articles to profl. jours. Home: 3814 Tridens Trl San Angelo TX 76904-7223 Office: Univ Tex Dept Geology Arlington TX 76019-0001

SMITH, CHARLES JOE, SR., music educator; b. Tuskegee, Ala., Aug. 24, 1951; s. Jim Smith and Mattie (Burrell) Wilson; m. Susie Marie Jones, May 9, 1970; children: Charles J., Jr., Yashica C. Profl. diploma, Am. Sch. Photography, Chgo., 1972; B in Music Edn., Jackson State U., Miss., 1973; M in Music Edn., Vandercook Coll. Music, 1982; PhD, Kennedy-Western U., Augoura Hills, Calif., 1988. Cert. music educator, Ga. Dir. bands D.C. Wolfe High Sch., Shorter, Ala., 1973-77, T.W. Josey Comprehensive High Sch., Augusta, Ga., 1977—; adminstrv. asst. Richmond County Band Programs, 1977. Guest condr. Amos Alonzo Stagg Bowl, 1979-81; coord. Cen. Savannah River Area Jazz Fest, 1980-85; adjudicator Alcorn State U. Jazz Fest, 1982-85; asst. dir. John Phillip Sousa Nat. High Sch. Hon. Band, 1985; cons. Ga. Dept. Edn. Tchr. Cert. Test Revision; chmn. Richmond County Bd. Edn. Spring Fling; other activities. Recipient award Augusta Black History Com., badge of merit John Phillip Sousa Found., 1985, Bridge Builders award Upsilon Gamma Gamma chpt. Omega Psi Phi, 2006, Pres.'s award Ga. State Conf. NAACP, 2007; named with D.C. Wolfe High Sch. Band as Ala.'s Bicentennial Band State of Ala., 1976, Hon. Lt. Col. Aide-de-Camp, 1976, one of Outstanding Young Men of Am., 1977, 83, 85, 87, 88, 90, Tchr. of Yr. Augusta, Ga.-Richmond County, 1988-89, Educator of Yr. Augusta Jaycees, 1989, State Citizen of Yr. Omega Psi Phi, 1989, Local Citizen of Yr., 7th Dist. Citizen of Yr., Citizen of Yr. local Psi Omega chpt. Omega Psi Phi, 2006. Mem. NAACP, Nat. Assn. Jazz Educators (chmn. jazz 10th dist. Ga. 1985—, cert. 1986—), Nat. Band Assn., Music Educators Nat. Conf., Richmond County Band Dirs. Assn. (chmn. budget, all-county coms. 1985—), Inst. Cert. Photographers, Inc. (life), Profl. Photographers Am., Ga. Music Educators Assn., 100 Black Men Am., Inc., 100 Black Men Augusta, Omega Psi Phi (chmn. talent hunt, scholarship coms. 1985— Local Citizen of Yr. 1989, State Citizen of Yr. 1989, 7th Dist. Citizen of Yr. Ala., Ga., Fla., Miss., 1989). Clubs: Band Boosters (Augusta) (chmn. budget com. 1977—). Democrat. Baptist. Avocations: music, basketball, tennis, football, golf. Home: 2910 Inwood Dr Hephzibah GA 30815-4158

SMITH, CHARLES LEE, writer; b. Colo., June 23, 1925; s. Alferd and Hattie Smith; m. Anne Smith; children: Gregory, Jay. Student, Napa Jr. Coll., 1946, student, 1949—50, San Francisco State Coll., 1950—52, U. Wash., 1952—53, U. Calif., Berkeley, 1956. Surveyor Pacific Gas & Electric, 1945—46, 1947—48; with Calif. Divsn. Hwy., 1951, 1953—87. Lectr. in field. Contbr. articles to newspapers and mags.; author: numerous pamphlets on social issues. Mem. svc. com. Am. Friends, 1949. With US Army, 1943—45. Recipient Outstanding Svc. award, Napa Coll., 1950, Meritorious Svc. award, Am. Vet. Com., 1963. Home: 37 San Mateo Rd Berkeley CA 94707

SMITH, CHARLES WILLIAM, social sciences educator; b. Providence; s. Joseph and Clara (Loitman) S.; m. Rita Cope, Sept. 3, 1963; children: Abigail Cope Suguy, Jonathan Cope. AB, Wesleyan U., 1960; MA, Brandeis U., 1966, PhD in Sociology, 1966. Instr. sociology Simmons Coll., Boston, 1964-65; from lectr. to assoc. prof. Queens Coll., Flushing, NY, 1965-71, from assoc. to prof. sociology, 1979—; grad. faculty Grad. Ctr. CUNY, 1986—. Vis. scholar Nuffield Coll., Oxford, Eng., 1979-80, Wesleyan U., Middletown, Conn., 1987-88; chair dept. sociology Queens Coll., Flushing, 1988-91, 97-00, acting dean of faculty social sci., 1991-92, dean faculty social sci., 1992-97; cons. auctions, 1986—. Author: Critique of Sociological Reasoning: An Essay in Philosophic Sociology, 1979, Auctions: The Social Construction of Values, 1989, Success and Survival on Wall Street: Understanding the Mind of the Market, 1999, Market Values Im American Higher Education, 2000; editor Jour. for Theory of Social Behavior, 1983—. Bd. dirs., pres. Cmty. Action Program of White Plains, N.Y., 1974-79; bd. trustees, v.p. Temple Israel Ctr. of White Plains, 1975-94; class agt., alumni activities Wesleyan U., Middletown, Conn., 1960—. Recipient FIPSE award, Dept. Edn., 1993—96, Ford Found. Diversity grant, 1990—93, 1996—98. Office: Queens Coll CUNY 65-30 Kissena Blvd Flushing NY 11367-1575 Office Phone: 718-997-2840. Business E-Mail: charles.smith@qc.cuny.edu.

SMITH, CHARLES Z., retired state supreme court justice; b. Lakeland, Fla., Feb. 23, 1927; s. John R. and Eva (Love) S.; m. Eleanor Jane Martinez, Aug. 20, 1955; children: Carlos M., Michael O., Stephen P., Felica L. BS, Temple U., 1952; JD, U. Wash., 1955. Bar: Wash. 1955. Law clk. Wash. Supreme Ct., Olympia, 1955-56; dep. pros. atty., asst. chief criminal div. King County, Seattle, 1956-60; ptnr. Bianchi, Smith & Tobin, Seattle, 1960-61; spl. asst. to atty. gen. criminal div. U.S. Dept. Justice, Washington, 1961-64; judge criminal dept. Seattle Mcpl. Ct., 1965-66; judge Superior Ct. King County, 1966-73; former assoc. dean, prof. law U. Wash., 1973—83; justice Wash. Supreme Ct., Olympia, until 2002. Mem. adv. bd. NAACP, Seattle Urban League, Wash. State Literacy Coun., Boys Club, Wash. Citizens for Migrant Affairs, Medina Children's Svc., Children's Home Soc. Wash., Seattle Better Bus. Bur., Seattle Foundation, Seattle Symphony Orch., Seattle Opera Assn., Community Svc. Ctr. for Deaf and Hard of Hearing, Seattle U., Seattle Sexual Assault Ctr., Seattle Psychoanalytic Inst., The Little Sch., Linfield Coll., Japanese Am. Citizens League, Kawabe Meml. Hous, Puget Counseling Ctr, Am. Cancer Soc., Hutchinson Cancer Rsch. Ctr., Robert Chinn Found.; pres. Am. Bapt. Chs. U.S.A., 1976-77, U.S. Commn. on Internat. Religious Freedom, 1999-2000. lt. col. ret. USMCR Mem. ABA, Am. Judicature Soc., Washington Bar Assn., Seattle-King County Bar Assn., Order of Coif., Phi Alpha Delta, Alpha Phi Alpha. Mailing: PO Box 146 Olympia WA 98507-0146 Home Phone: 360-273-0964; Office Phone: 360-273-0964. Business E-Mail: czsmith@usa.net.

SMITH, CHARLOTTE REED, retired music educator; b. Eubank, Ky., Sept. 15, 1921; d. Joseph Lumpkin and Cornelia Elizabeth (Spenser) Reed; m. Walter Lindsay Smith, Aug. 24, 1949; children: Walter Lindsay IV, Elizabeth Reed. BA in Music, Tift Coll., 1941; MA in Mus. Theory, Eastman Sch. of Music, 1946; postgrad. Juilliard Sch., 1949. Asst. prof. theory Okla. Bapt. U., 1944-45, Washburn U., 1946-48; prof. music Furman U., Greenville, S.C., 1948-92; chmn. dept. music, 1987-92. Editor: Seven Penitential Psalms with Two Laudate Psalms, 1983; author: Manual of Sixteenth-Century Contrapuntal Style, 1989. Mem. Internat. Musicological Soc., Am. Musicological Soc., Soc. for Music Theory, AAUP (sec.-treas. Furman chpt. 1984-85), Nat. Fedn. Music Clubs, Pi Kappa Lambda. Republican. Baptist.

SMITH, CHRISTOPHER (KIT SMITH), lawyer; b. Evanston, Ill., Nov. 12, 1947; AB, Wabash Coll., 1969; JD, U. Kans., 1972. Bar: Kans. 1972, DC 1973, US Supreme Ct. 1976. Ptnr. Arent Fox Kintner Plotkin & Kahn, Washington, mng. ptnr., 1997—2002; ptnr. Sonnenschein Nath & Rosenthal LLP, Washington, 2003—. Office: Sonnenschein Nath & Rosenthal LLP Ste 600, E Tower 1301 K St NW Washington DC 20015 Office Phone: 202-408-9231. Office Fax: 202-408-6399. Business E-Mail: kitsmith@sonnenschein.com.

SMITH, CHRISTOPHER ALLEN, information technology executive, financial executive; b. Rockford, Ill., Nov. 16, 1961; s. Robert Lee and Martha Ann (Moody) S.; m. Mary G. Meany, Apr. 13, 1991. BA, postgrad., Ind. U., 1983, Golden Gate U., San Francisco, 1986—87; MA, U. Phoenix, Ariz., 2003. Rates analyst North American Van Lines, Ft. Wayne, Ind., 1984-85; mgr., investor rels. BRAE Corp., San Francisco, 1985-87; fin. analyst CIS Corp., San Francisco, 1987-89; dir., corp. devel. Affiliated Computer Systems, Inc., San Francisco, 1989-96; v.p. Sci. Applications Internat. Corp., San Francisco, 1996—. Alumni Dept. of Def. Joint Civilian Orientation Conf. Contbr. articles to profl. jours. Vol. Rep. Party, Foster City, Calif., 1988; apptd. dir. Pvt. Industry Coun. Contra Costa County; apptd. bd. mem. St. Perpetua Sch., 2005-06. With USMCR, 1982-83. Mem. Equipment Leasing Assn. Am. (Jour. award 1991), Ind. U. Alumni Assn. Republican. Roman Catholic. Avocations: writing, photography, gardening. Office: Sci Applications Internat Corp 1000 Broadway Ste 675 Oakland CA 94607 Office Phone: 510-466-7174. Business E-Mail: christopher.a.smith-2@saic.com.

SMITH, CHRISTOPHER HENRY, congressman; b. Rahway, NJ, Mar. 4, 1953; s. Bernard Henry and Katherine Joan (Hall) Smith; m. Marie Hahn, July 2, 1977; children: Melissa, Christopher, Michael, Elyse. Student, Worcester Coll., Eng., 1973-74; BA in Bus. Adminstrn., Trenton State Coll., NJ, 1975. Exec. dir. NJ Right to Life Com., Inc., 1976-78; dir. instl. sales Leisure Unlimited Inc., Woodbridge, NJ, 1978-80; legis. agt. NJ Gen. Assembly, 1979; mem. US Congress from 4th NJ dist., 1981—, mem. fgn. affairs com., ranking mem. security and cooperation in Europe commn., co-chair Pro-Life Caucus. US rep. to UN internat. conf. on immunizing world's children. Active in human rights movements Romania, China, former Soviet Union, Vietnam Named Legislator of Yr. VFW, Internat. Assn. Chiropractors, JWV of Am., 1996, Leader of the Yr., NJ State Postal Workers Union, 2002, William Wilberforce award, 2002; recipient Leader for Peace award Peace Corps, George (Buck) Gillispie Congl. award, Meritorious Svc. Blinded Am. Vets. Found., 2003. Mem.: Nat. Fedn. Ind. Bus. Republican. Roman Cath. Office: US House Reps 2373 Rayburn House Office Bldg Washington DC 20515-3004 Office Phone: 202-225-3765. Office Fax: 202-225-7768. *

SMITH, CHRISTOPHER T., environmental health officer; BS Environ. Health Sci., Ea. Ky. U., Richmond, 2001; MPH, Fla. Internat. U., Miami, 2004. Registered Environ. Health Specialist Ky, 2006. Regulatory ops. officer US FDA, Rockville, Md., 2004—. Lt. US Pub. Health Svc., 2001. Scholar Environ. Health, Ky Assn. Milk, Food, and Environ. Sanitarians, 2000. Mem.: Nat. Environ. Health Assn. Office Phone: 240-276-0115.

SMITH, CLARE, art appraiser; Grad, Oxford Univ., Courtauld Inst. Art, London. Specialist, Victorian picture dept. Christie's, NYC, 1999, now specialist, sporting art, also US rep. for British & Irish art. Project coord., sale, Forbes collection, Victorian art Christie's, 2003. Office: Christie's 20 Rockefeller Plz New York NY 10020 Office Phone: 212-636-2084. Office Fax: 212-636-4925. Business E-Mail: claresmith@christies.com.

SMITH, CLYDE CURRY, historian, educator; b. Hamilton, Ohio, Dec. 16, 1929; s. Charles Clyde and Mabel Ethel Ola (Curry) S.; m. Ellen Marie Gormsen, June 13, 1953; children: Harald Clyde, Karen Margaret Boettge. BA in Physics cum laude and MS, Miami U., Oxford, Ohio, 1951; BDiv, U. Chgo., 1954, MA, 1961, PhD, 1968; DLitt honoris causa, Fairfax U., 1999. Ordained to ministry Christian Ch. (Disciples of Christ), 1954. Exec. asst. to dean Disciples Div. House, Chgo., 1956-57; lectr. in O.T., Univ. Coll. U. Chgo., 1957; asst. prof. St. John's Coll. U. Manitoba, Winnipeg, Can., 1958-63; instr. Brandeis U., Waltham, Mass., 1963-65; prof. ancient history and religions U. Wis., River Falls, 1965-90, prof. emeritus, 1990—. Vis. prof. religious studies Culver-Stockton Coll., Canton, Mo., 1990, U. Newcastle-upon-Tyne, Eng., 1992-94; vis. lectr. div., Edge Hill Coll. of Edn., Ormskirk, Eng., 1970-71; postdoctoral fellow Johns Hopkins U.,

Balt., 1977; NEH fellow-in-residence U. Calif., Santa Barbara, 1978-79; vis. rsch. fellow, lectr. religious studies U. Aberdeen, Scotland, 1980, 85-86; sr. acad. visitor Wolfson Coll., Cambridge U., 2001—; scholar-in-residence Mesopotamian Studies Ctr., New Haven, 2004—. Contbr. articles to profl. jours. Mem. Pierce County Hist. Assn., River Falls, 1965—, Wis. Dems., 1965—, Dem. Nat. Com., 1983—; charter mem. Sci. Mus. of Minn., St. Paul, 1973—; charter assoc. Libr. of Congress, 1994—; founding mem. River Falls Cmty. Arts Base, 1996—, Kinnickinnic River Land Trust, 1996—; bd. dirs. River Falls Libr. Found., 1997—. Recipient Gov.'s Spl. award State of Wis., 1990, several grants. Mem. Assn. Ancient Historians, Can. Soc. Ch. History (founder, treas. 1960-63), N.Am. Patristics Soc., Can. Soc. for Mesopotamian Studies, Soc. Old Testament Study (Gt. Britain), Soc. for Promotion Roman Studies of London, Hellenic Soc. London, Brit. Sch. Archaeology in Iraq, Brit. Inst. Archaeology in Ankara, Internat. Soc. Anglo-Saxonists, Oriental Inst. U. Chgo., Phi Beta Kappa. Democrat. Avocations: outerspace, battleships, dinosaurs. Home: 2642 Golf View Dr River Falls WI 54022-7502 Office Phone: 715-425-6383. *We can begin thought with the assumption that there is a world which knows neither origin nor end but which includes us; we can conclude with the affirmations that there was a "when" whatever is was not, and that whatever is will with time cease to be. Our concern then can be to enhance value and empower others, especially those who follow.*

SMITH, CLYDE RAY, dean; b. Bassett, Va, Apr. 21, 1935; s. William Henry and Ava I. (Roberson) S.; m. Phyllis Jane Watkins, Mar. 25, 1959; children: Anthony William, Cheryl Ann, Theresa Jane. BA, Bridgewater Coll., 1956; MBA, U. Va., 1958; D in Bus. Adminstrn. (hon.), Bridgewater Coll., 2004. Instr. U. Va. - Darden, Charlottesville, Va., 1961-64, asst. prof., 1964-67, assoc. prof., 1967-72, prof., 1972—, assoc. dean MBA program, 1972-94, assoc. dean exec. edn., 1994-97, interim dean, 1997-98; exec. dir. Darden Sch. Found., 1998—2003; prof. emeritus U. Va. - Darden, Charlottesville, Va., 2003—. Adminstrv. dir. Inst. Chartered Fin. Analysts, Charlottesville, 1962-69; bd. trustees Bridgewater Coll. Co-author: (books) Executive's Guide to Mgmt. Accounting and Control Sys., 1998, Fin. Accounting for Mgmt., 1981. Capt. (res.) US Army, 1958-68. Named Disting. Alumnus Bridgewater Coll., Va., 1991. Mem. AICPA, Am. Real Estate Soc., Colonade Club, Farmington Country Club, Raven Soc., Beta Gamma Sigma, Omicron Delta Kappa. Home: 39 Canterbury Rd Charlottesville VA 22903-4700 Office: Univ Va - Darden Sch PO Box 6550 Charlottesville VA 22906-6550 Office Phone: 434-924-4799. E-mail: crs6n@virginia.edu.

SMITH, CONNIE, hospital administrator; b. Moline, Ill., Feb. 7, 1947; d. Phillip and Betty (McSparin) Warrick. Diploma, Moline Pub. Sch. Nursing, 1969; BSN, U. Iowa, 1975; MSN, Rush U., 1981. Cert. nurse operating rm. Staff nurse operating rm. Moline (Ill.) Pub. Hosp., 1969-70; head nurse operating rm./recovery Resurrection Hosp., Chgo., 1970-72; staff nurse operating rm. Mennonite Hosp., Bloomington, Ill., 1973-74; instr. Franciscan Hosp. Sch. Nursing, Rock Island, Ill., 1975-77; staff nurse intensive care unit Moline Luth. Hosp., 1977-79; MICU staff nurse, unit leader operating rm., univ. faculty mem. Rush Presbyn-St. Luke's Med. Ctr., Chgo., 1979-85; dir. operating rm. Albert Einstein Med. Ctr., Phila., 1985-88; dir. operating rm. svcs. St. Joseph Hosp., Houston, 1988-90; regional dir. surg. svcs. Sharp HealthCare, San Diego, 1990-93; surg. svcs. cons. Coast Assocs., 1993-99; dir. Fountain Valley (Calif.) Surgery Ctr., 1999—2003, interim mgr., cons. surg. svc., 2004—. Presenter in field.

SMITH, CORINNE ROTH, psychologist; b. Reading, Pa., May 22, 1945; d. Zoltan and Elizabeth (Foldes) Roth; m. Lynn Helden Smith, June 9, 1968; children: Juliette Sarah, Rachael Eliza. BA in Psychology cum laude, Syracuse U., 1967, PhD, 1973; MA, Temple U., Phila., 1969. Lic. psychologist, NY. Psychologist experimental presch. program Syracuse City Schs., 1970-71; psychologist reading clinic Syracuse U., 1969-70, coordinator lab. sch. and clinic, 1971-72, asst. prof., 1971—84, founder, dir. psychoednl. teaching lab., 1971—, founder, dir. comprehensive assessment ctr., 1981-83, psychologist Devel. Evaluation Ctr., 1984—96, assoc. dean edn., 1992—2000, prof., 1997—, dean, 2000—02, chair inclusive elem. and spl. edn. program, 2005—, chair inclusive spl. edn. 1-6 MS program, 2005—, chair tchg. and leadership programs, 2006—. Mem. Coun. for Exceptional Children; reviewer Aspen, Ablex, Mc Graw Hill, Little Brown & Co., NY, Allyn & Bacon, Pergammon, 1985—; apptd. mem. Gov. NY Coun. for Youth, Albany, 1984-91; chair hon. degrees com., Meredith selection com., sexual harassment com., human svcs. and health professions formation com., Syracuse U., 1993-2007; spkr. in field. Author: Learning Disabilities: The Interaction of Learner, Task and Setting, 1983, 2d edit., 1991, 3rd edit, 1994, 4th edit., 1998, 5th edit., 2004, (retitled) Learning Disabilities: The Interaction of Students and Their Environments, The People's Guide to Drug Education, 1992, Learning Disabilities A to Z: The Complete Parent Guide to Learning Disabiltities from Preschool to Adulthood, 1997, reprinted in Portuguese, Latvian, Korean; contbr. articles to profl. jours. and chpts. to books. Bd. dirs. Ctrl. NY United Way, 1987-93, leadership giving chair, 2003-06; pres. Jewish Comm. Ctr., Syracuse, 1978-81; bd. dirs., chair career womens network Syracuse Jewish Fedn., 1985-87, womens campaign chair, 1987-89, gen. campaign chair, 1990-92. Recipient Disting. Svc. award Jewish Comm. Ctr., 1976, Comm. Leadership award Syracuse Jewish Fedn., 1986, 89, Jewish Family Svc. Humanitarian award, 1991, Roth Humanitarian award, 1992, Citizen of Yr. award, 2000; named Woman of Yr. Post Std., 1990; grantee NY State Office Mental Retardation and Devel. Disabilities, 1985-93; Leadership award Coun. Jewish Women, 1999. Mem. Am. Psych. Assn., Nat. Assn. Sch. Psychologists, NY State Learning Disabilities Assn., Learning Disability Assn. Am., Winnick Hillel (pres. nat. bd. 2003-06, treas. 2007). Avocations: tennis, gardening. Office: Syracuse U 136 Huntington Hl Syracuse NY 13244-0001 Office Phone: 315-443-1468.

SMITH, CRAIG BENNETT, lawyer; b. Wilmington, Del., Oct. 16, 1943; s. Wilfred Winter and Louetta Beatrice (Bennett) S.; m. Charlotte Anne Boucheron, May 27, 1967; 1 child, Stuart Evan. BA in English, Carleton Coll., 1966; MA in Creative Writing, Syracuse U., 1969, JD summa cum laude, 1975. Bar: U.S. Dist. Ct. Del. 1975. Assoc. Morris, Nichols, Arsht & Tunnell, Wilmington, 1975-83; ptnr. Biggs & Battaglia, Wilmington, 1983-84, Lassen, Smith, Katzenstein & Furlow, Wilmington, 1984-91, Smith, Katzenstein & Furlow, L.L.P., Wilmington, 1992—. Mem. adv. bd. Bur. Nat. Affairs Corp. Practices Series, Washington, 1988—. Co-author: State Limited Partnership Laws, 1987, Guide to the Takeover Law of Delaware, 1988, Limited Partnerships: Legal Aspects of Organization, Operation and Dissolution, 1992 (book chpts.) New York and Delaware Business Entities, 2001; mem. editorial bd. State Ltd. Partnership Laws-Prentice Hall Law & Bus., 1987—; sr. notes and comments editor Syracuse Law Rev., 1974-75; contbr. articles to profl. jours. Mem. Del. Gov's High Tech. Task Force, Wilmington, 1986, com. bus. & indsl. devel. cos. Del. Econ. Devel. Office, Wilmington, 1988. Named to Justinian Soc., 1974. Fellow ABA (litigation sect. 1985—, bus. law sect. 1975—); mem. Del. State Bar Assn. (corp. law sect. com. 1987-90, 93—, com. Del. Revised Uniform Ltd. Partnership Act 1984—, chancery ct. fiduciary rules adv. com. 1986-89), Order of Coif. Republican. Avocations: classical guitar playing, sculpturing. Home: 318 Spalding Rd Wilmington DE 19803-2422 Office: Smith Katzenstein & Furlow LLP The Corporate Plaza 800 Delaware Ave Wilmington DE 19801-1322

SMITH, CRAIG R., health products executive; m. Cynthia Smith; 2 children. BA, Univ. So. Calif. With Owens & Minor, Glen Allen, Va., 1989—, divsn. v.p., group v.p., sr. v.p. distbn. and info. sys., 1989—95, exec. v.p., COO, 1995—99, pres., COO, 1999—2005, pres., CEO, 2005—. Bd. mem. Inst. for Diversity in Health Mgmt., Health Ind. Dist. Assn.; mem. bd. vis. St. Gertrude High Sch., Richmond; mem. bus. council Va. Mus. Fine Arts; bd. dir. Greater Richmond YMCA. Office: Owens & Minor Inc 9120 Lockwood Blvd Mechanicsville VA 23116 *

SMITH, CRAIG R., lawyer; BS in Civil Engring., Manhattan Coll., 1992; MS in Environmental Engring., U. Ill., 1994; JD, NYU, 1997. Bar: Mass. 1997. Principal Fish & Richardson, Boston. Mem. bd. dirs. Greater Boston Legal Svcs. Named a Super Lawyer-Rising Star, Boston Mag., 2005; named Up and Coming Lawyer, Mass. Lawyers Weekly, 2006; recipient Norman S. Ostrow Moot Ct. award, 1996. Mem.: ABA. Office: Fish & Richardson 225 Franklin St Boston MA 02110-2804 Office Phone: 617-542-5070. Office Fax: 617-542-8906.

SMITH, CRAIG RICHEY, thoracic surgeon; b. Cleve., Nov. 17, 1948; AB, Williams Coll., 1970; MD, Case Western Res. U., 1977. Diplomate Am. Bd. Thoracic Surgery, Am. Bd. Surgery. Intern U. Rochester Hosp., NY, 1977-78, resident, gen. surgery NY, 1978-82; fellow in cardiothoracic surgery Columbia-Presbyn. Med. Ctr., NYC, 1982-84, chief, divsn. cardiothoracic surgery, 1996—; prof. surgery Columbia U. Coll. Physicians & Surgeons, 1997—2001, Calvin F. Barber prof. surgery, 2001—. Assoc. prof. surgery Columbia U. Hosp., N.Y.C. Mem. AMA, ACS, Am. Assn. Thoracic Surgery, Am. Heart Assn., Am. Surgical Assn., Internat. Soc. for Heart Transplantation, Am. Coll. Cardiology, NY Soc. for Thoracic Surgery, Assn. for Academic Surgery. Office: 177 Fort Washington Ave New York NY 10032-3713 *

SMITH, CULLEN, lawyer; b. Waco, Tex., May 31, 1925; s. Curtis Cullen and Elizabeth (Brient) S.; m. Laura Risher Dossett, Mar. 6, 1948 (dec.); children: Sallie Smith Wright, Alethea Risher Smith Gilbert, Elizabeth Brient Smith. Student, Emory U., 1943-44, Duke U., 1944; BBA, Baylor U., 1948, JD, 1950. Bar: Tex. 1950. Ptnr. firm Smith, McIlheran & Smith, Weslaco, Tex., 1950-53, Naman, Howell, Smith & Lee LLP, Waco, 1953—. Lectr. law Baylor U. Sch. Law, 1964-72 Contbr. articles to legal publs. Mem. standing com. Episcopal Diocese of Tex., 1960-63, 74-75; trustee Episcopal Theol. Sem. of S.W., 1962-67; mem. Waco City Coun., 1983-86; chmn. bd. Vanguard Sch., 1975; bd. dirs. G.H. Pape Found., 1993-94; bd. dirs., vice chmn. Tex. Ctr. for Legal Ethics and Professionalism, 1994-99; mem. adv. coun. Baylor U. Coll. Arts and Scis., 1998-2003. 1st lt. USMCR, 1943—46, inactive, 1946—58. Named one of 5 Outstanding Young Texans Tex. Jr. C. of C., 1957, Baylor Lawyer of Yr., 1980; recipient Disting. Alumnus award Waco Ind. Sch. Dist. Edn. Found., 2002; named Outstanding Mentor of Tex., Tex. Young Lawyers Assn., 2007. Fellow Am. Bar Found., Tex. Bar Found. (chmn. bd. 1973-74, 50 Yr. Lawyer award 2000), fellow Coll. of Law Practice Mgmt.; mem. ABA (chmn. standing com. econs. law practice 1965-69, chmn. spl. com. on law book pub. practices 1970-72, chmn. gen. practice sect. 1973-74, mem. house of dels. 1974-81), Am. Law Firm Assn. (chmn. 1989-90), Waco-McLennan County Bar Assn. (pres. 1956-57), Mont. Bar Assn. (hon.), State Bar Tex. (pres. jr. bar 1957-58, chmn. profl. econs. com. 1959-61, chmn. spl. com. on revision Tex. Canons Ethics 1969-71, dir. 1971-74, pres. 1978-79), Philos. Soc. Tex., Baylor U. Law Alumni Assn. (pres. 1962-63), Order of Coif, Delta Sigma Phi, Phi Delta Phi, Am. Inns Ct. (master), Ridgewood Country Club (pres. 1965), Hedonia Club (pres. 1957), Rotary. Avocation: photography. Home: Oak Grove Farm 447 Meandering Way China Spring TX 76633-2905 Office: Naman Howell Smith & Lee LLP Tex Ctr PO Box 1470 Waco TX 76703-1470 Office Phone: 254-755-4100.

SMITH, CURT, think tank executive, journalist; b. Richmond, Ind., May 11, 1957; s. John Robert and Rena Carolyn Smith; m. Debra Diane Sutter, Aug. 21, 1980; children: Stephen, Julie, Andrew, Kimberly. BA, Ind. U., 1978. Press sec. Rep. Dan Coats, Washington, 1983-88, campaign mgr. Fort Wayne, Ind., 1988; comms. dir. U.S. Senator Dan Coats, Washington, 1989-91, state dir., comms. dir., 1991-95; chief of staff U.S. Rep. John Hostettler, Washington, 1995-98; v.p. external affairs Hudson Inst., Indpls., 1998-99, v.p., COO, 1999—2001; pres. Ind. Family Inst., 2001—06. Acting city editor Fort Wayne Jour. Gazette, 1983, staff writer, 1980-83; staff writer Palladium-Item, Richmond, Ind., 1979-80. Stringer for N.Y. Times, 1982-83. Vice chmn., bd. elders, Traders Point Christian Ch., Indpls., 1999, past chmn., elder, 1996—; led UN sanction Election Observer Team, 1999. Named Outstanding Environtl. reporter Izack Walton League of Am., 1983; recipient Voice of Dem. Ind. winner VFW, 1975. Republican. Office: Indiana Family Inst 55 Monument Cir Ste 322 Indianapolis IN 46204 Office Phone: 317-423-9178. E-mail: curt@hoosterfamily.org.

SMITH, D. BROOKS, federal judge; b. 1951; BA, Franklin and Marshall Coll., 1973; JD, Dickinson Sch. Law, 1976. Pvt. practice Jubelirer, Carothers, Krier, Halpern & Smith, Altoona, Pa., 1976-84, mng. ptnr., 1981—83; judge Ct. Common Pleas of Blair County, Pa., 1984-88, US Dist. Ct. (we. dist.) Pa., 1988—2002, chief judge, 2001—02; judge US Ct. Appeals (3d cir.), 2002—. Asst. dist. atty. Blair County, part-time, 1977-79, spl. prosecutor, 1981-83, dist. atty. part-time, 1983-84; instr. Pa. State U., Altoona campus, 1977—, St. Francis Coll., 1986—; adv. com. on criminal rules U.S. Jud. Conf., 1993-99. Trustee St. Francis Coll., 1992—2004, Phila. U., 2005—. Mem. Am. Law Inst., Pa. Bar Assn., Am. Judicature Soc., Pa. Soc., Amen Corner, Blair County Game, Fish and Forestry Assn., Fed. Judges Assn. (bd. dirs. 1993-97, 2002—), Inns of Ct., Allegheny County Bar Assn., Pi Gamma Mu. Office: Allegheny Profl Ctr 1798 Old Rte 220 N Ste 203 Duncansville PA 16635 *

SMITH, D. JASON, music educator, composer; b. Hinesville, Ga., Sept. 1, 1970; s. Carolyn Ruth Smith; m. Sarah Elizabeth Ginn, Apr. 8, 1998; 1 child, Elaina Isabel. BFA in Music Composition, Marshall U., Huntington, W.Va., 1998; MusM in Music Composition, Ball State U., Muncie, Ind., 2000, postgrad., 2000—. Music collection coord. Ball State U., U. Libraries, Muncie, 2004—. Chair staff assembly U. Libraries, Muncie, 2005—; presenter in field. Mem.: ACLU, Soc. for Music Theory, Coll. Music Soc., Am. Mensa. Democrat. Home Phone: 765-288-6974.

SMITH, D. NEIL, lawyer; b. Beaumont, Tex., June 12, 1971; BS in Constrn. Engring., Tex. A&M U., 1993; JD, Baylor Sch. Law, 1996. Bar: Tex. 1996, US Dist. Ct. (ea. dist. Tex.), US Ct. Appeals (5th cir.), US Ct. Fed. Claims. Ptnr. Nix, Patterson & Roach, L.L.P., Daingerfield, Tex. Adj. prof. Baylor Sch. Law. Named a Rising Star, Tex. Super Lawyers mag., 2006. Mem.: Tex. Mex. Bar Assn., Lawyer-Pilot Bar Assn., Assn. Trial Lawyers of Am., East Tex. Trial Lawyers Assn., Tex. Trial Lawyers Assn., N.E. Tex. Bar Assn., Morris County Bar Assn. Office: Nix Patterson & Roach LLP 205 Linda Dr Daingerfield TX 75638 Office Phone: 903-645-7333. E-mail: dnsmith@nixlawfirm.com. *

SMITH, D(AISY) MULLETT, publisher; b. Washington, Aug. 17, 1948; d. Gordon Hunt and Suzanne Myrick (Mullett) Smith. BA, Am. U., 1970; cert. computer programming, U. So. Calif., Arlington, Va., 1986; cert. in records mgmt., Assn. Records Mgrs. Am., Prairie Village, Kans., 1987. Christian Sci. practitioner The First Ch. of Christ, Scientist, Boston, 1970-86; clk. Fifth Ch. of Christ, Scientist, Washington, 1971-74; Christian Sci. campus counsellor The Am. U., Washington, 1976-81; editor, computer specialist, desktop pub. Mullett-Smith Press, Washington, 1984-89, owner, pub., 1989—, music copyist, pub. on computer, 1990—, web weaver, 1996—, pub., typesetting, 2004—. Cons., spkr. in field. Author, editor: AB Mullett, His Relevance in American Architecture, 1990 (Printers award 1990); editor: AB Mullett, Architect Engineer 1862-90, 1985; contbr. articles to profl. jours. Participant White House Conf. on Children, 1970; active Save Pioneer Post Office, Portland, Oreg., 1996—; fundraising com. U.S. Treasury Bill Restoration Fund, 1998-2000; libr. Christian Sci. Reading Rm., 1999-2002; renovator TH-7, 2003, Hist. Townhouse Wheat Row, 2003-06; commrs. Jefferson County, W.Va., 2003; interviewer PBS radio, saving Jefferson County Jail. Recipient Key to the City, Mayor Lincoln, Nebr., 1989. Mem. Nat. Soc. Arts and Letters (editor/pub. directory 1971-2006, treas. 1988-90, web weaver 1996—, web host 2006—), Nat. Trust for Hist. Preservation, Assn. Records Mgrs. and Adminstrs., Assn. for Info. and Image Mgmt. Internat., U.S. Treasury Hist. Assn., U.S. Capitol Hist. Soc. Achievements include helping to make Charlestown, West Virginia's County Jail a historial landmark; started webhosting service partnership with H. James Enterprises and Bluebird-artworks.com. Avocations: art, design, guitar, windsurfing, computers. Home Phone: 202-554-2718; Office Phone: 202-479-4333. Business E-Mail: mspress@mullett-smithpress.com.

SMITH, DAN, chef; b. NYC; life ptnr. Steve McDonagh; 1 adopted child, Nate. Actor; model; chef Francine Maroukian; co-founder The Hearty Boys catering co., Bethel, Maine, Chgo., The Cafe at Hearty Boys, Lakeview, Ill., 2003—, HB restaurant, The Cafe at Hearty Boys, Lakeview, Ill., 2005—. Co-host Party Line with the Hearty Boys; co-author: Solving the Run of the Mill; featured in Chgo. Mag., guest appearances on ABC, NBC, CBS, FOX, CLTV. Achievements include co-winning The Next Food Network Star with ptnr. Steve McDonagh, 2005. Office Phone: 773-244-9866. Office Fax: 773-244-8088.

SMITH, DAN F., chemicals executive; With Atlantic Richfield Co, Los Angeles, Calif., 1967—88; exec. v.p., CFO Lyondell Chem. Co., Houston, dir., 1988—, COO, 1993—96, pres., 1994—, CEO, 1996—. Bd. dir. Cooper Industries. Office: Lyondell Chemical Co 1221 McKinney St Ste 700 Houston TX 77010 *

SMITH, DANIEL, oncologist, gynecologist; b. Cushing, Okla., Feb. 12, 1946; MD, Harvard Med. Sch., 1972. Diplomate Am. Bd. Surgery, Am. Bd. Obstetrics and Gynecology with subspecialty in gynecologic oncology. Intern Mass. Gen. Hosp., Boston, 1972—73, resident, 1973—75, 1978, L.A. County/U. So. Calif. Med. Ctr., LA, 1975—78; fellow Meml. Sloan-Kettering Cancer Ctr., 1979—81; oncologist, ob-gyn. Columbia Presbyn. Med. Ctr., NYC, 1981—2003; assoc. prof. ob-gyn. Columbia Coll. Physicians and Surgeons. Office: 20 Prospect Ave Ste 703 Hackensack NJ 07601 Office Phone: 201-996-5373. Business E-Mail: dsmith@humed.com.

SMITH, DANIEL BRIGGS, JR., lawyer; s. Daniel Briggs and Imojean Murphy Smith; m. Dorothy Eleanor Fancher, July 6, 1968; children: Daniel Briggs III, Carter Pearce, Stephen Fancher. BS in Pharmacy, U. Miss., Oxford, 1962, JD, 1966. Bar: Miss. 1966, US Dist. Ct. (no. and so. dist.) Miss. 1971, US Ct. Appeals (5th cir.) 2002, cert.: Nat. Bd. Trial Advocacy Miss. 1995; registered pharmacist Miss., 1962. Atty. Cliff Finch & Assoc., Batesville, Miss., 1968—74; ptnr. Smith, Phillips, Mitchell, Scott & Nowak, LLP, Batesville, 1974—. Contbr. articles to profl. jours. Elder Batesville Presbyn. Ch.; pres. Rotary, Batesville. Staff sgt. USNG, 1968—72. Named Law Alumni of Yr., U. Miss., 2003; recipient Pres. award, U. Miss. Law Alumni Assn., 2000, Pres.-Lamar Order award, 2002. Fellow: Miss. Bar Found. Presbyterian. Avocations: travel, hunting, art. Office: Smith Phillips Mitchell Scott & Nowak 695 Shamrock Dr Batesville MS 38606 Office Phone: 662-563-4613. Office Fax: 662-563-1546. Business E-Mail: briggs@smithphillips.com.

SMITH, DANIEL C., dean, finance educator; BBA, U. Toledo, 1980, MBA, 1982; PhD in bus. adminstrn., U. Pitts., 1988. Asst. prof. U. Wis. Sch. Bus., Madison; asst. to assoc. prof. U. Pitts. Joesph M. Katz Grad. Sch. Bus.; joined faculty Kelley Sch. Bus., Ind. U., 1996, MBA program chair, 1998—2001, chair mktg. dept., 2002—03, Clare W. Barker chair mktg., 2002—, assoc. dean academics, 2003—04, interim dean, 2004—05, dean, 2005—. Mem. editl. rev. bd. Jour. Mktg., Jour. Acad. Mktg. Sci., Jour. Competitive Intelligence, Jour. Personal Selling and Sales Mgmt., Jour. Market Focused Mgmt. Avocations: fly fishing, food and wine. Office: Indiana Univ Kelley Sch Business 1575 E 10 St Ste 2010 Bloomington IN 47405 Office Phone: 812-855-8489. Business E-Mail: dansmith@indiana.edu. *

SMITH, DANIEL CLIFFORD, lawyer; b. Cin., Aug. 9, 1936; s. Clifford John and Vivian Aileen (Stone) S.; m. Carroll Cunningham; children: Edward, Andrew, Scott. BS, Ariz. State U., 1960; postgrad., George Washington U., 1961—62; JD, Am. U., 1965. Bar: D.C. 1965, U.S. Ct. Appeals (D.C. cir.) 1966, U.S. Ct. Appeals (Fed. cir.), U.S. Dist. Ct. D.C. 1966, Va. 1967, U.S. Supreme Ct. 1969, U.S. Ct. Appeals (4th, 5th, 6th, 7th, 9th and 11th cirs.), U.S. Ct. Claims, U.S. Ct. Customs and Patent Appeals, U.S. Tax Ct. Assoc. Alpern & Feissner, Washington, 1963-66; atty. FTC, Washington, 1966-70; ptnr. Arent, Fox, Kintner, Plotkin & Kahn, Washington, 1970-93, Canfield & Smith, Washington, 1993—. Pres., dir. Country Pl. Citizens Assn., Inc., 1974-77; bd. dirs. Sea Watch Condominium, Ocean City, Md., 1978—, treas., 1982-86, pres. 1986—; active Supreme Ct. Hist. Soc., The Federalist Soc., Smithsonian Inst. Assocs., Ariz. State Soc. Served with USMC. Mem. D.C. Bar Assn. (bd. dirs. 1974-76, chmn. consumer protection com. 1972-74, chmn. D.C. affairs sect. 1975-76), Va. State Bar Assn., Fed. Bar Assn., Assn. Trial Lawyers Am., Nat. Field Selling Assn. (gen. counsel), Ariz. State U. Alumni Assn., Rotary Club (pres. 1987-88, 96-97), Optimist (pres. 1972-73), Internat. Town and Country Club (dir. 1969-73), Masons, Delta Theta Phi. Office: Canfield & Smith Ste 800 910 17th St NW Washington DC 20006-2606

SMITH, DAVID, music educator; b. Newton, Kans., June 17, 1962; s. Bobby Smith, Twyla and Roy Rumfelt (Stepfather); m. Audry Johnson, June 2, 2001. AA with honors, Cowley County CC, 1984; BSc, S.W. Bapt. U., 1986; MSc, Pittsburg State U., 1990; M in Ch. Music, Midwestern Bapt. Theol. Sem., 1997. Cert. in Microsoft Word 2003, 2006, in Microsoft Power Point 2003, 2006; Voice Music Tchr. Music Tchrs. Nat. Assn., 2004. Admissions counselor, adj. instr. music Cowley County CC, Arkansas City, Kans., 1990—91; instr. vocal music Highland CC, Kans., 1992—94, Ctrl. CC, Columbus, Nebr., 2000—01; min. music edn. First Bapt. Ch., Kearney, Mo., 1994—95; coll. coord. Blue River CC, Blue Springs, Mo., 1995—2000; grad. tchg. asst. U. Kans., Lawrence, 1997—2000; instr. music Neosho County CC, Chanute, Kans., 2001—. Mem. First Bapt. Ch., Independence, Kans., 2005—. Named an Outstanding Music Grad., S.W. Bapt. U., 1986; recipient Excellence award, Nat. Inst. Staff and Orgnl. Devel., 2006. Mem.: Coll. Music Soc., Music Tchrs. Nat. Assn., Am. Choral Dirs. Assn., Music Educators Nat. Conf. R-Conservative. Avocations: reading, golf, travel. Office: Neosho County Community Coll 800 W 14th Chanute KS 66720 Home Phone: 620-331-2784. Business E-Mail: dksmith@neosho.edu.

SMITH, DAVID A., medical services executive; BS, U. No. Fla. CPA. Public acctg., 1983—87; regional mgr., gen. mgr., sales mgr. and opers. mgr. PSS/World Medical Inc., Jacksonville, Fla., 1987—93, v.p., 1992—96, chmn. bd. dirs., 1993—, exec. v.p., 1996—2000, pres., 2000—, CFO, 1992—2002, CEO, 2002—, chmn., 2007—. Mem. exec. bd. Health Industry Distributors Assn. Office: PSS World Med Inc 4345 Southpoint Blvd Jacksonville FL 32216 *

SMITH, DAVID BURNELL, lawyer, state legislator; b. Charleston, W.Va., Apr. 8, 1941; s. Ernest Dayton and Nellie Dale (Tyler) S.; m. Rita J. Hughes, Sept. 25, 1967. BA, U. Charleston, 1967; JD, U. Balt., 1972; MJS, U. Nev., 1995. Bar: Colo. 1972, Md. 1972, U.S. Supreme Ct. 1980, Ariz. 1983, U.S. Dist. Ct. Md. 1972, U.S. Dist. Ct. Colo. 1972, U.S. Ct. Appeals (4th Cir.) 1972, U.S. Ct. Appeals (9th cir. 1972, U.S. Ct. Appeals

(10th cir.) 1983. Sales rep. Gulf Oil, Washington, 1967-72; pvt. practice Littleton, Colo., 1972-83, Glendale, Ariz., 1983-86, Phoenix, 1986-88, Scottsdale, Ariz., 1988—; mem. Ariz. Ho. of Reps., 2005—, vice-chmn. judiciary com., 2005—. Pro-tempore judge Wickenburg Mcpl. Ct., 1986—; presiding judge Peoria (Ariz.) Mcpl. Ct., 1987-94, Cave Creek Mcpl. Ct., 1995-98. Appeared as actor in movie Dead Girls Don't Tango, 1990. V.p. South Jefferson County Reps., Lakewood, Colo., 1979, pres., 1990; candidate Dist. 6 for Congress; 2nd vice-chmn. Dist. 7 Rep. Party, pres. Ariz. Rep. Assembly Dist. 28, bd. dirs. Scottsdale (Ariz.) Constitution Commemorative Com., 1995-2003, pres., 2002-; elected Ariz. Ho. of Reps., Dist. 7, 2005—. With USCG, 1959-66. Mem. ATLA, ABA (vice-chmn. family law 1983), Nat. Assn. Criminal Lawyers, Am. Judicature Soc., Nat. Assn. Criminal Def. Attys., Ariz. Magistrates Assn., Colo. Bar Assn., Ariz. Bar Assn., Scottsdale (Ariz.) Bar Assn. (sec. 2001-2002, v.p. 2002-2003, pres., 2003-2004), Md. Bar Assn., Colo. Trial Lawyers Assn., Maricopa County Bar Assn., Scottsdale Bar Assn. (bd. dirs., sec. 1996—, pres.), Masons, Shriners, Elks. Home: PO Box 5145 36418 N Wildflower Rd Carefree AZ 85377-5145 Office: 4310 N 75th St Scottsdale AZ 85251-3578 Office Phone: 480-990-7500. Personal E-mail: dbsdbsatty@yahoo.com.

SMITH, DAVID CLARK, research scientist; b. Owensboro, Ky., Feb. 8, 1937; s. Robert Emmitt and Mary Margaret (Flaherty) S.; m. Kathleen Sue Kohne, June 27, 1964; children: Christine, Jennifer, Paula. BSME, U. Dayton, 1959; MS, Northwestern U., 1961, PhD, postgrad., Northwestern U., 1964. Rsch. scientist United Techs. Rsch. Ctr., East Hartford, Conn., 1965-67, sr. rsch. scientist, 1967-68, prin. scientist, 1968-80, mgr. exptl. optics, 1980-82, mgr. optical physics, 1982-91; cons. DCS Assoc., Inc., 1992-99, Conn. Tech. Assocs., 1992—, DCS Lasers/Optics LLC, 1997—. Author: (with G. Bekefi) Principles of Laser Plasmas, 1976; contbr. articles to profl. jours. Chmn. Youth and Family Resource Ctr. Commn., 1979-84; bd. dirs. Glastonbury A Better Chance, Conn., 1970-78; mem. Glastonbury Energy Com., 1979-83; tutor YMCA Read to Succeed Literacy; vol. Habitat for Humanity. Recipient Outstanding Svc. award, 1985, Glastonbury, Conn., United Techs. Outstanding Svc. award, 1987; named Man of Yr., Friends of Glastonbury Youth, 1984. Fellow: Am. Soc. Laser Medicine and Surgery; mem.: SPIE, IEEE, AIAA, AAAS, Am. Phys. Soc., Sigma Xi. Democrat. Roman Catholic. Achievements include patentee in field. Home: 514 Main St Old Saybrook CT 06475 Office: DCS Lasers & Optics LLC 514 Main St Old Saybrook CT 06475 Office Phone: 860-510-0554. E-mail: kohne@aol.com.

SMITH, DAVID COVENTRY, lawyer; BA cum laude, Wake Forest Univ., 1981, JD cum laude, 1984. Bar: NC 1984, Maine 1986, US Dist. Ct. (ea., we., middle dist. NC), US Ct. Appeals (4th cir.). Ptnr., bus. litigation Kilpatrick Stockton LLP, Winston-Salem, NC. Co-author (& co-editor): North Carolina Trial and Appeal, 1998; contbr. articles to profl. jours. Bd. dirs. Legal Aid Soc., Children's Law Ctr. Named NC Lawyer of the Year, Legal Aid Soc. N.W. NC, 2001—04, Best Lawyers in Am. Bus. Litig., 2004—06; named to NC Legal Elite, 2006. Mem.: NC Bar Assn. (Commendation pub. svc. 2005), NC Acad. Trial Lawyers, Forsyth County Bar Assn., Am. Inns of Ct. Barrister. Office: Kilpatrick Stockton LLP 1001 W 4th St Winston Salem NC 27101-2400 Office Phone: 336-607-7392. Office Fax: 336-734-2611. Business E-Mail: dcsmith@kilpatrickstockton.com.

SMITH, DAVID EDWARD, small business owner, aerospace engineer, aerospace scientist; b. Battle Creek, Mich., Sept. 16, 1939; s. Hebdin Leslie and Dureatha Rosella (Stephens) S.; m. Margaret Eugenia Clark, June 13, 1964; 1 child, Wendy Leigh. Student, Kellogg C.C., 1957—58; BSME, Mich State U., 1962; MS in Real Estate Investing (hon.), Meta U., Salt Lake City, 1992. Engr., scientist Douglas Aircraft Co., Santa Monica, Calif., 1962-63, McDonnell Douglas Astronautics Co., Cape Kennedy, Fla., 1963-78; broker salesman Cape Kennedy Realty, Inc., Cape Canaveral, Fla., 1978-87; pres., founder Cash Flow Seminars, Merritt Island, Fla., 1979—, Cash Flow Systems, Inc., Merritt Island, Fla., 1983—; prof. fin. Meta U., Salt Lake City, 1992-94. Lectr. fin. convs. and orgns. including Fed. GSA, Pub. Bldg. Svc., Am. League of Savs., Fin. Instns. Mktg. Assn., Acad. Real Estate, Am. Congress Real Estate; prof. fin. Meta U., Salt Lake City, 1992-94; distbr. Hewlett Packard Corp., 1985-88; dir. comml. investment divsn. CKBOR, Merritt Island, 1978-79; adv. bd., lectr. Fin. Freedom Report, Nat. Inst. Fin. Planning, both Salt Lake City, 1985-92; instr. Fla. Real Estate Commn., La. Real Estate Commn., Fla. Bd. Accountancy, Am. Inst. Real Estate Appraisers. Author: Turbo-Diesel, The Time Value of Money, Creative Financing Techniques; contbr. articles to profl. jours. and mags. Mem.: Internat. Platform Assn., Fla. Real Estate Exchangors, Iron Butt Assn., Gold Wing Rd. Riders Assn. Republican. Avocations: flying, transcontinental bicycling, motorcycle touring. Office: Cash Flow Seminars PO Box 540634 Merritt Island FL 32954-0634

SMITH, DAVID ELVIN, physician; b. Bakersfield, Calif., Feb. 7, 1939; s. Elvin W. and Dorothy (McGinnis) S.; m. Millicent Buxton; children: Julia, Suzanne, Christopher Buxton-Smith, Sabree Hill-Smith. BS, U. Calif., Berkeley; MS in Pharmacology, U. Calif., San Francisco, 1964, MD, 1967. Intern San Francisco Gen. Hosp., 1965; fellow pharmacology and toxicology U. Calif., San Francisco, 1965-67; clin. prof. U. Calif., San Francisco Med. Ctr., 1967—, dir. psychopharmacology study group, dir. Inst. of Health, 1966-70, assoc. clin. prof., rsch. physician Med. Sch.; clin. prof. U. Calif., San Francisco; practice specializing in toxicology/addiction medicine San Francisco, 1965—. Physician Presbyn. Alcoholic Clinic, 1965—67, Contra Cost Alcoholic Clinic, 1965—67; dir. alcohol and drug abuse screening unit San Francisco Gen. Hosp., 1967—68; co-dir. Calif. drug abuse info. project U. Calif. Med. Ctr., 1967—72; founder, pres., med. dir. Haight-Ashbury Free Med. Clinic, San Francisco, 1967—2006; rsch. dir. Merritt Peralta Chem. Dependency Hosp., Oakland, Calif., 1984—2003; med. dir. Drug Abuse Scis., 1999—2003, Calif. Alcohol and Drug Programs, U. Calif. San Francisco Substance Abuse Policy Ctr., 1999; exec. med. dir. Prometa Ctr., Santa Monica and San Francisco, Calif.; assoc. med. dir., med. rev. officer Betty Ford Ctr. Profl. Recovery Program; chmn. Nat. Drug Abuse Conf., 1996—2006, Calif. Gov.'s Comm. on Narcotics and Drug Abuse, 1977—; nat. health adviser to former U.S. Pres. Jimmy Carter; mem. Pres. Clinton's Health Care Task Force on Addiction and Nat. Health Reform, 1993; with Office Drug Abuse Policy, White House Task Force Physicians for Drug Abuse Prevention; dir. Benzodiazepine Rsch. and Tng. Project, Substance Abuse and Sexual Concerns Project, PCP Rsch. and Tng. Project; med. editor AlcoholMD.com, OpiateMD.org, Alcohol MD (CD-ROM); vis. assoc. prof. U. Nev. Med. Sch., 1975—; clin. prof. U. Calif. San Francisco Med. Ctr.; v.p. corp. med affairs Hythiam; cons. in field; chief Addiction Medicine Svcs. Bayside Marin, San Rafael, 2006—; med. dir. Centerpoint, 1996—. Author: Love Needs Care, 1970, The New Social Drug: Cultural, Medical and Legal Perspectives on Marijuana, 1971, The Free Clnic: Community Approaches to Health Care and Drug Abuse, 1971, Treating the Cocaine Abuser, 1985, The Benzodiazepines: Current Standard Medical Practice, 1986, Physicians' Guide to Drug Abuse, 1987; co-author: It's So Good, Don't Even Try it Once: Heroin in Perspective, 1972, Uppers and Downers, 1973, Drugs in the Classroom, 1973, Barbiturate Use and Abuse, 1977, A Multicultural View of Drug Abuse, 1978, Amphetamine Use, Misuse and Abuse, 1979, PCP: Problems and Prevention, 1981, Sexological Aspects of Substance Use and Abuse, Treatment of the Cocaine Abuser, 1985, The Haight Ashbury Free Medical Clinic: Still Free After All These Years, Drug Free: Alternatives to Drug Abuse, 1987, Treatment of Opiate Dependence, Designer Drugs, 1988, Treatment of Cocaine Dependence, 1988, Treatment of Opiate Dependence, 1988, The New Drugs, 1989, Crack and Ice in the Era of Smokeable Drugs, 1992, Clinical Guide to Substance Abuse, 2001, others; also drug edn. films; founder, editor Jour. Psychedelic Drugs (now Jour. Psychoactive Drugs), 1967—; co-author: Clinical Guide to Substance Abuse; contbr. over 300 articles to profl. jours. Mem. Physicians for Prevention White House Office Drug Abuse Policy, 1995; pres. Youth Projects, Inc.; founder, chmn. bd., pres. Nat. Free Clin. Coun., 1968-72; med. dir. Calif. Alcohol and Drug Programs, 1998, U. Calif. Drug Policy Ctr., San Francisco, 1998—, Drug Abuse Scis., 1998—. Named one of Best Drs. in US, 1995, 1996, 1997, 2002; recipient Rsch. award, Borden Found., 1964, AMA Rsch. award, 1977, Cmty. Svc. award U. Calif., San Francisco, 1974, Calif. State Drug Abuse Treatment award, 1984, Vernelle Fox Drug Abuse Treatment award, 1985, UCLA Sidney Cohen Addiction Medicine award, 1989, U. Calif. San Francisco medal of honor, 1995, Lifetime Achievement award for sr. workers, Gov. of Calif., 2003. Mem. AMA (alt. del.), Calif. Med. Assn. (alt. del.), Am. Soc. on Addiction Medicine (bd. dirs., pres. 1995), San Francisco Med. Soc., APHA, Calif. Soc. on Addiction Medicine (pres., bd. dirs.), Am. Soc. Addiction Medicine, Cosmos Club, 2006-, Sigma Xi, Phi Beta Kappa. Methodist. Home: 289 Frederick St San Francisco CA 94117-4051 Office: David E Smit MD and Assocs 856 Stanyan San Francisco CA 94117 Office Phone: 415-518-8380. Personal E-mail: dsmith4619@aol.com.

SMITH, DAVID ENGLISH, pathologist, educator; b. San Francisco, June 9, 1920; s. David English and Myrtle (Goodin) S.; m. Margaret Elizabeth Bronson, June 9, 1948; children: Ann English Smith Elbert, David Bronson, Mary Margaret. AB, Central Coll. Mo., 1941; MD cum laude, Washington U., St. Louis, 1944. Intern, resident pathology Barnes Hosp., St. Louis, 1944-46; instr. pathology Washington U. Med. Sch., 1948-51, asst. prof., 1951-54, asst. head dept., 1953-54, assoc. prof., 1954-55; prof. pathology U. Va. Sch. Medicine, 1955-73, chmn. dept., 1958-73; dir. div. U. Va. Sch. Medicine (Cancer Studies), 1972-73; prof. pathology Northwestern U. Sch. Medicine, 1974-75, U. Pa. Sch. Medicine, 1976-80, Tulane U. Sch. Medicine, 1980-85, assoc. dean, 1980-85; prof. pathology U. Tex. Med. Br., 1986—. Assoc. dir. Am. Bd. Med. Spltys., 1974-75; v.p., sec., dir. undergrad. evaluation Nat. Bd. Med. Examiners, 1975-80; trustee Am. Bd. Pathology, 1966-73, v.p., 1973; mem. Nat. Bd. Med. Examiners, chmn. pathology test com., 1966-72; chmn. test com. Ednl. Commn. for Fgn. Med. Grads., 1979-91; eligibility & due process com. Nat. Commn. Cert. Physician Assts., 1990-2001. Editor: Survey of Pathology in Medicine and Surgery, 1966-70; contbr. articles to profl. publs. Pres. Va. div. Am. Cancer Soc., 1967-69. Served from 1st lt. to capt. M.C. AUS, 1946-48. Named Disting. Alumnus, Wash. U. Med. Sch., 2004; recipient Preclin. Tchr. award, U. Tex. Med. Br., 1999; Paul Brindley Disting. scholar, 1997. Mem. Va. Soc. Pathology (pres. 1960), Am. Assn. Pathologists, Internat. Acad. Pathology (council 1956-59, pres. 1964-65), Am. Soc. Clin. Pathologists (co-dir. self assessment program 1970-75, Path Educator award 2000), AMA, Am. Assn. Neuropathologists, AAAS, Sigma Xi, Alpha Omega Alpha, Phi Beta Pi, Alpha Epsilon Delta. Home: 59 Colony Park Cir Galveston TX 77551-1737 E-mail: descolpkga@aol.com.

SMITH, DAVID EUGENE, business administration educator; b. Boise, Idaho, Dec. 14, 1941; s. Roy Arthur and Anna Margaret (Fries) S.; m. Patricia Stroy, Aug. 4, 1973; 1 child, Zachary Adam. BS in Applied Stats., San Francisco State Coll., 1964, MS in Mgmt. Sci., 1966; MBA, PhD in Bus. Adminstrn., U. Santa Clara, 1969. Asst. to dir. mgmt ctr. Grad. Sch. Bus., U. Santa Clara, Calif., 1966-69, lectr. mktg. Calif., 1968; asst. prof. bus. adminstrn. dept. mktg./decision Scis. San Jose State U., Calif., 1969—71, assoc. prof. bus. adminstrn. dept. mktg./decision Scis., 1971—76, prof. bus. adminstrn. dept. mktg./decision Scis., 1976—, chmn. dept. mktg./decision Scis., 1986—89. Author: Quantitative Business Analysis, 1977, Internat. Edit., 1979, 1982; contbr. articles to profl. jours. Mem.: DSI, INFORMS, Beta Gamma Sigma, Phi Kappa Phi. Republican. Avocations: tennis, fishing, skiing. Home: 22448 Tim Tam Ct Los Gatos CA 95033-8521 Office: San Jose State U Mktg/Decision Scis One Washington Sq San Jose CA 95192

SMITH, DAVID HORTON, retired social sciences educator; b. LA, May 2, 1939; s. Paul Roosevelt Smith and Helen Ethel (Frechem) Mitchell; divorced; children: Gregory David, Laura Ghislaine. AB magna cum laude, U. So. Calif., 1960; MA, Harvard U., 1962, PhD, 1965. Asst. prof. U. So. Calif., LA, 1966-68; assoc. prof. Boston Coll., Chestnut Hill, Mass., 1968-76, prof., 1976—2004. Rsch. fellow, lectr. Harvard U., 1965-66; cons. Nat. Ctr. for Voluntary Action, Brit. Nat. Vol. Ctr., Ctr. for Voluntary Soc., Filer Commn. on Pvt. Philanthropy and Pub. Needs, Union of Internat. Assns., others. Author: Latin American Student Activism, 1973, Grassroots Associations, 2000; co-author: Becoming Modern, 1974 (award 1975), Voluntary Sector Policy Research Needs, 1974, Participation in Social and Political Activities, 1980, Why People Recreate, 1987, A Dictionary of Nonprofit Terms and Concepts, 2006; editor: Voluntary Action Research, 1972, 73, 74, Voluntary Transnational Cultural Exch. Orgns. of the US, 1974, Volunteerism, Voluntary Assns. and Devel., 1981, Internat. Perspectives on Voluntary Action Rsch., 1983; contbr. numerous articles to profl. jours., chpts. to books; founding editor-in-chief Jour. Voluntary Action Rsch. (now Nonprofit and Voluntary Sector Quar.), 1971-76. Founding bd. dirs. Nat. Com. for Responsive Philanthropy, 1976-78, Alliance for Volunteerism; dir. rsch. Ctr. for Voluntary Soc., Washington, 1970-74. NSF grad. fellow, 1960-63; Woodrow Wilson Hon. fellow, 1960. Mem. Assn. Rsch. on Non-Profit Orgns. and Voluntary Action (founder, pres. 1971-73, Lifetime Achievement award 1993), Authors Guild, Sarasota Fiction Writers, Harvard Club of Sarasota, Phi Beta Kappa, Phi Kappa Phi. Mem. Unity Ch. Avocations: reading, photography, fiction writing, jazz, foreign travel. E-mail: dhortonsmith@hotmail.com.

SMITH, DAVID HUNT, systems analyst, educator; b. Columbus, Ohio, Nov. 3, 1950; s. Philip George and Wilanna Smedley Smith; m. Darla Rae Groth, May 5, 1990; children: James Kenneth Wray, Sarah Shannon. AAS in Electronic Comm., Ind. Vocat. Tech. Coll., Bloomington, 1984; AAS in Indsl. Design & Drafting, Ind. Vocational Tech. Coll., Bloomington, 1985; BS, Excelsior Coll., Albany, NY, 1982—84; MBA, Ind. U., Bloomington, 1985—87. Cert. computing profl. Inst. Cert. Computing Professionals, 1993, client server profl. Learning Tree Internat., 2000. Knowledge engr. Cummins Engine Co., Columbus, Ind., 1987—92, systems arch., 1992—94; bus. systems cons. dhuntsmith.com, Bloomington, 1994—. Sr. instr. Learning Tree Internat., Reston, Va., 1996—. Scouting leader Boy Scouts Am., Bloomington, 1990—. Recipient Clan Macneil Order Merit award, The Clan Macneil Assn. Am., 1997. Mem.: ARC (disaster svcs. vol. 2005—), NRA (life; benefactor 2000—), Nat. Assn. United Meth. Scouters (life; dist. rep. 2005—06), Clan MacLaren Soc. N.Am. (life; woodbadge mem. 2005—), Clan MacNeil Assn. Am. (life; commr.-at-large 1996—). Independent. Meth. Avocations: scuba diving, photography, bicycling, camping, backpacking. Office: Dhuntsmith.com PO Box 5152 Bloomington IN 47407-5152 Home Phone: 812-334-1009. Business E-Mail: dhs@dhuntsmith.com.

SMITH, DAVID JAMES, lawyer; b. 1955; BS, Western Ill. U.; JD, John Marshall Law Sch. Asst. sec. Archer Daniels Midland, Decatur, Ill., 1988-97, asst. gen. counsel, 1995-97, v.p., sec., gen. counsel, 1997—2001, sr. v.p., sec., gen. counsel, 2002—03, exec. v.p., sec. and gen. counsel, 2003—. Office: Archer Daniels Midland Co 4666 E Faries Pkwy Decatur IL 62526-5666 Office Phone: 217-424-5200. *

SMITH, DAVID JOHN, physicist, researcher; b. Melbourne, Australia, Oct. 10, 1948; arrived in U.S., 1984; s. Arthur and Agnes Frances Smith; m. Gwenneth Paula Bland, Sept. 18, 1971 (div. 1992); children: Heather F., Marion J. BSc with honors, U. Melbourne, Australia, 1970, PhD, 1978, DSc, 1988. Post-doctoral rsch. asst. Cavendish Lab. U. Cambridge, England, 1976-78, sr. rsch. assoc., 1979-84; assoc. prof. Ariz. State U., Tempe, 1984-87, prof., 1987—, regents prof., 2000—, dir. Ctr. Solid State Sci., 2001—04. Dir. high resolution electron microscope Cambridge U., 1979—84; dir. Ctr. High Resolution Electron Microscopy NSF, Tempe, 1991—96, Ariz. State U., Tempe, 1991—2006; presenter in field. Contbr. chapters to books, articles to profl. jours. Recipient Faculty Achievement award, Burlington Resources Found., 1990. Fellow: Am. Phys. Soc., Inst. Physics (U.K.) (Charles Vernon Boys prize 1985); mem.: Microscopy Soc. Am., Material Rsch. Soc. Office: Ariz State U Dept Physics Tempe AZ 85287-1504 Office Phone: 480-965-4540. Business E-Mail: david.smith@asu.edu.

SMITH, DAVID JOHN, JR., plastic surgeon; b. Indpls., Feb. 20, 1947; s. David John and Carolyn (Culp) S.; m. Nancy Loonsten, June 7, 1975; children: Matthew, Peter, Hadley. BA, Wesleyan U., 1969; MD, Ind. U., 1973. Diplomate Am. Bd. Plastic Surgery. Resident Emory U.-Grady Hosp., Atlanta, 1973-78; resident Ind. U. Med. Ctr., Indpls., 1978-80; Christine Kleinert fellow in hand surgery, 1979; asst. prof. surgery Ind. U. Sch. Medicine, 1980-84; assoc. prof. of surgery Wayne State U. Sch. Medicine, 1984-87; assoc. prof. plastic surgery, surgery sect. head U. Mich. Med. Ctr., Ann Arbor, 1987-92, prof. surgery sect. head, 1992—2001; prof. surgery Coll. Medicine U. South Fla., 2004—, Juan Bolivar chair in surg. oncology, dir. divsn. plastic and reconstructive surgery, 2004—. Mem. Residency Rev. Com. for Plastic Surgery, 1992-2000, vice chmn., 1994, chmn. 1996-99; vis. prof. Ctr. Cutaneous Rsch. Queen Mary U., London, Eng., 2004—, Anglia Polytech. U., Cambrige, Eng., 2004—. Mem. editl. bd. Jour. of Surg. Rsch., 1989-95, Annals of Plastic Surgery, 1992-2002, assoc. editor, 1994-2002, Yearbook of Hand Surgery, 1989—; guest reviewer Surgery, 1988—, Plastic and Reconstructive Surgery, 1988—; contbr. articles to profl. jours. Recipient numerous grants. Fellow ACS (com. mem.), Am. Assn. Plastic Surgeons, Am. Surg. Assn., Am. Bd. Plastic Surgeons (vice chmn. 1997-98, chair-elect 1998-99, chmn. oral exam 1995-97, chmn. 1999-2000), Ctrl. Surg. Assn., Am. Soc. for Surgery of the Hand, Am. Soc. Plastic Surgeons, Plastic Surgery Ednl. Found. (bd. dirs. 1988-99, treas. 1994, v.p., pres.-elec., pres., chair nominating com. 1997-98), Plastic Surgery Rsch. Coun., Am. Burn Assn. (chmn. com. on organization and delivery of burn care 1995-98), Am. Burn Life Support Nat. Faculty, Am. Assn. for Hand Surgeons (pres. 1994), Assn. Acad. Chmn. Plastic Surgery (pres.-elect 1997, pres. 1998-99, chmn. nominating com. 1999-2000). Home: 3107 Prospect Rd Tampa FL 33629 Office: Divsn Plastic Surgery 4 Columbia Dr Ste 650 Tampa FL 33606 Home Phone: 813-250-9160. Business E-Mail: dsmith3@health.usf.edu.

SMITH, DAVID JULIAN, educational consultant; b. Boston, Apr. 24, 1944; s. Julian John and Anita Regina (Goldman) S.; m. Suzanne Marilla Shaw, June 18, 1966. AB, Harvard U., 1966; MAT, Reed Coll., 1967. Cert. elem. tchr., Mass., Hawaii, Oreg. 10th grade tchr. Punahou Sch., Honolulu, 1967-69; 7th, 9th grades tchr. U. Hawaii Lab. Sch., Honolulu, 1969-70; 7th grade head tchr. Shady Hill Sch., Cambridge, Mass., 1970-92; pvt. practice ednl. cons. Cambridge, Mass., 1992—. Author: Mapping the World By Heart, 1992, CEESA Web-Site Manual, 1998, If the World Were a Village, 2002, Emergency Procedures Manual for Overseas Schools, 2004; contbr. articles to profl. jours. Bd. dirs. Cambridge Mental Health Assn., 1991-96, Cambridge Ctr. for Adult Edn., 1988-98; active Cambridge Civic Assn. Recipient Breaking the Mold award US Dept. Edn., 1992. Mem. Nat. Coun. Social Studies, Nat. Coun. Geog. Edn., Assn. Am. Geographers (chair cartographic splty. group 1997). Office: Mapping the World by Heart 4 Blanchard Rd Cambridge MA 02138-1009 Personal E-mail: djsmapping@gmail.com.

SMITH, DAVID KINGMAN, retired oil company executive, consultant; b. Malone, NY, June 5, 1928; s. Ernest DeAlton and Louisa Kingman (Bolster) S.; m. Lois Louise Wing, June 13, 1959; children: Mara Louise, David Andrew. BS in Engring., Princeton U., 1952. Registered profl. engr., Tex. Civil engr., supt. Raymont Internat. Inc., NYC, 1952-55, asst. v.p., 1970-71, v.p., 1971-74, group v.p. Houston, 1974-80; mgr. Raymond-Brown and Root, Maracaibo, Venezuela, 1955-70; sr. engring. assoc. Exxon Prodn. Rsch. Co., Houston, 1980-81, supr., 1982-95; cons. project mgmt., 1995—. Pres. Yorkshire Civic Assn., Houston, 1979-80, trustee, 1985-97. With U.S. Army, 1946-48, PTO. Mem. ASCE, NSPE, Soc. Petroleum Engrs. (continuing edn. com. Gulf Coast chmn. 1989-93, treas. 1987-88, nat. continuing edn. com. 1991-93, dir. Gulf Coast sect. 1994-95), Tex. Soc. Profl. Engrs., Men's Garden Club Houston, Am. Legion, Princeton Alumni Assn. (dir. Houston sect.), Cen Ners In Square Dance Club (pres. 1996-97), Exxon Mobil Meml. Area Retirees Club (pres. 2005-06, treas. 2007). Republican. Methodist. Avocations: photography, gardening, tennis, golf, square dancing. Home: 611 W Forest Dr Houston TX 77079-6915 Personal E-mail: smithdktx@aol.com.

SMITH, DAVID LEE, retired editor; b. Shelby, Ohio, Apr. 4, 1939; s. Ferris Francis and Rita Ann (Metzger) Smith; m. Betty Stewart Walker, Sept. 10, 1960; children: Stacie Lynn, Stefanie Linn, David Lee II(dec.). Student, Pontifical Coll. Josephinum, Worthington, Ohio, 1953-56, Ohio State U., Mansfield, 1961. Sports writer Mansfield News-Jour., 1960-61; sports editor Ashland Times-Gazette, Ohio, 1961-63, Miami News, Fla., 1963-67, Ft. Lauderdale News, Fla., 1967-70, Boston Globe, 1970-78, Washington Star, 1978-81; dep. mng. editor, exec. sports editor Dallas Morning News, 1981—2005, sports dir. AH Belo pub. and new media divsns., 1998—2003, v.p., 2003—05; ret., 2005. Condr. seminars. Mem. adv. bd. Dallas Stars Found., Dallas Alliance for the Mentally Ill, SMU Athletics, Jesuit Sch. Found.; bd. govs. Bethesda Home Boys, Savannah, Ga.; bd. dirs. Field Scovell Scholarship Found., Doak Walker Nat. Running Back Award, GTE-SMU Athletic Forum. With USMC, 1957—60. Mem.: Golf Writers Assn., Football Writers Assn., Baseball Writers Assn. (Red Smith award for major contbns. to sports journalism 1990), AP Sports Editors Assn. (1st pres. 1974—75), SMU Athletic Forum (bd. dirs.), Salesmanship Club Dallas, Bent Tree Country Club. Roman Catholic. Home: 16 Mad Turkey Crossing Savannah GA 31411 Personal E-mail: studie.dave@comcast.net.

SMITH, DAVID MARTYN, retired forestry educator; b. Bryan, Tex., Mar. 10, 1921; s. John Blackmer and Doris (Clark) S.; m. Catherine Van Aken, June 16, 1951; children: Ellen, Nancy. BS, U. R.I., 1941; postgrad., NYU, 1942; MF, Yale U., 1946, PhD, 1950; DSc (hon.), Bates Coll., 1986, U. R.I., 1993. From instr. to prof. Sch. Forestry and Environ. Studies, Yale U., 1946-90, asst. dean, 1953-58; Morris K. Jesup prof. silviculture Yale U., 1967-90, ret., 1990, Morris K. Jesup prof. emeritus, 1990—. Vis. prof. U. Munich, 1981. Author: Practice of Silviculture, 1954, 4th edit., 1997. Capt. Weather Svc., USAAF, 1942-45. Fellow Soc. Am. Foresters (Disting. Svc. New Eng. sect. award 1969, 93); mem. Am. Forests (Disting. Svc. award 1990), Nat. Acad. Forest Scis. Mex. (corr.), Ecol. Soc. Am., Conn. Forest and Park Assn. (dir.), Sigma Xi, Phi Kappa Phi. Mem. United Ch. of Christ. Home: 200 Leeder Hill Dr Apt 425 Hamden CT 06517-2728 Personal E-mail: david.m.smith@wcres.org.

SMITH, DAVID MICHAEL, financial planner; b. Fresno, Calif., Dec. 29, 1944; s. Ralph S. and Verla Fern Smith; m. Barbara J. Bryson, June 27, 1964; children: Brandon, Eric. AA, Fresno City Coll., 1964; AB, Calif. State U., Fresno, 1966. Tchr. English Fresno Unified Sch. Dist., 1967-79; registered rep. TMI Equities, Inc., Fresno, 1979-82, regional mgr. Camarillo, Calif., 1982-85; fin. planner Associated Planners Securities Corp., Camarillo, 1985-89, David M. Smith & Assocs., Camarillo, 1989—2002, Lifetime Planning, Inc., 2003—. Coun. mem. City of Camarillo, 1988—96, mayor, 1991, 1996; pres. Fresno Dem. Coalition, 1979. Mem.: Fin. Planners Assn. Ventura County (pres. 2004), Fin. Planning Assn., Camarillo Noontime Optimists Club. Office: Lifetime Planning Inc 1200 Paseo Camarillo Ste 190 Camarillo CA 93010-6085 Home Phone: 805-987-5919; Office Phone: 805-987-8938. Personal E-mail: dms.planners@verizon.net.

SMITH, DAVID STUART, anesthesiology educator, physician; b. Detroit, May 29, 1946; s. Philip and Eleanor (Bishop) S.; m. Suzanne Wanda Zeleznik, Aug. 17, 1969; children: Katherine Michele, Lisa Anne. BA, Oakland U.; MD, PhD, Med. Coll. Wis., 1975. Intern dept. medicine Med. Coll. Wis., Milw., 1975-76; resident dept. anesthesia U. Pa., Phila., 1976-78, fellow dept. anesthesia, 1978-80; dir. divsn. neuroanesthesia Hosp. U. Pa., Phila., 1982-2001, attending anesthesiologist, 1980—; asst. prof. U. Pa., Phila., 1980-89, assoc. prof., 1989—. Co-editor: Anesthesia and Neurosurgery, 3d edit., 1994, 4th edit., 2001; mem. editl. bd. Jour. Neurosurg. Anesthesia, N.Y.C., 1987-97; author and co-author of numerous sci. papers, revs., and book chpts. Sr. fellow, Nat. Rsch. Svc. award, Phila., 1985-87. Fellow Coll. Physicians Phila.; mem. Am. Soc. Anesthesiologists, Soc. Neurosurg. Anesthesia and Critical Care (sec., treas. 1987-89, v.p. 1989-90, pres. elect 1990-91, pres. 1991-92), Assn. U. Anesthesiologists, Internat. Soc. Cerebral Blood Flow and Metabolism. Jewish. Office: Hosp U Pa Dept Anesthesia 3400 Spruce St Philadelphia PA 19104-4206

SMITH, DAVID THORNTON, lawyer, educator; b. Pawtucket, RI, Dec. 11, 1935; s. Herbert Jeffers and Harriet Amelia (Thornton) S.; m. Sandra June Gustavson, Dec. 20, 1958; children: David T., Douglas A., Daniel H. BA, Yale U., 1957; JD cum laude, Boston U., 1960. Bar: Mass. 1961, U.S. Supreme Ct. 1964. Instr. law Ind. U., Bloomington, 1960-62; asst. prof. law Duquesne U., Pitts., 1962-63, Case Western Res. U., Cleve., 1963-65, assoc. prof., 1965-68; assoc. prof. law U. Fla., Gainesville, 1968-69, prof., 1969—2003, prof. emeritus, 2003—. Lectr. Fla. Bankers Assn., Fla. Trust Sch., 1973—; vis. prof. law U. Ga., 2004, Wake Forest U., 2006. Author: (with M. Sussman and J. Cates) The Family and Inheritance, 1970, Florida Probate Code Manual, 1975. Mem. Am. Bar Assn., Mass. Bar Assn., Am. Law Inst., Am. Judicature Soc., AAUP (past pres. U. Fla. chpt.), Fla. Blue Key, Selden Soc., Omicron Delta Kappa, Phi Alpha Delta. Lutheran. Office: Univ Fla Coll Law Gainesville FL 32611

SMITH, DAVID WAYNE, psychologist, educator; b. Ind., Apr. 16, 1927; s. Lowell Wayne and Ruth Elizabeth (Westphal) S.; m. Marcene B. Leever, Oct. 20, 1948; children: David Wayne, Laurreen Lea. BS, Purdue U., 1949; MS, Ind. U., 1953, PhD, 1955. Diplomate Am. Bd. Psychol. Specialities. Prof. rehab., dir. Rehab. Ctr.; assoc. dean, later asst. v.p. acad. affairs Ariz. Health Scis. Ctr., U. Ariz., Tucson, 1955-80; rsch. prof. rehab., adj. prof. medicine, cons. in rsch. S.W. Arthritis Ctr., Coll. Medicine, 1980-87; prof. rehab. and rheumatology, dept. medicine U. Ariz., 1987—, also dir. disability assessment program; assoc. dir. Ariz. Arthritis Ctr., 2007—. Pres. allied health professions sect. Nat. Arthritis Found.; bd. dirs. Nat. Arthritis Found. (S.W. chpt.); nat. vice chmn. bd. dirs.; mem. NIH Nat. Arthritis Adv. Bd., 1977-84; also chmn. subcom. community programs and rehab.; mem. staff Ariz. Legislature Health Welfare, 1972-73; Mem. Gov.'s Council Dept. Econ. Security, 1978-85; pres., bd. dirs. Tucson Assn. for Blind, 1974-86; chmn. Gov.'s Council on Blind and Visually Impaired, 1987—; active Gov.'s Coun. on Arthritis and Musculoskeletal Disease, 1987—, Gov.'s State wide Coun. on Rehab., 1998—, Am. Bd. Forensic Examiners, 1997—. Author: Worksamples; contbr. chpts. to books and articles to profl. jours. Mem. Gov.'s State Rehab. Coun., 1998—, commr. Commn. on Civil Rights, Az., 2002. Recipient Gov.'s awards for leadership in rehab., 1966, 69, 72, 73; awards for sci. and vol. services Nat. Arthritis Found., 1973, 75; 1st nat. Addie Thomas award Nat. Arthritis Found., 1983, Benson award, 1989, Govt. Affairs award, 1989; Arthritis Found. fellow, 1983. Fellow Am. Coll. Forensics; mem. Am. Psychol. Assn. (div. 17 counseling psychology), Assn. Schs. Allied Health Professions, Nat. Rehab. Assn., Ariz. Psychol. Assn. Home: 5765 N Camino Real Tucson AZ 85718-4213 Office: U Ariz Arizona Health Scis Ctr Tucson AZ 85724-0001 Personal E-mail: davesfolly@earthlink.net.

SMITH, DEAN, communications advisor, arbitrator; b. NYC, Aug. 10, 1925; s. Franklin Grant and Anna Lucille (Kranebell) S.; m. Andree Marie Praileur, Aug. 9, 1947; children: David F., Christopher P. Student, NYU, 1945-46, Columbia U., 1946-47, N.Y. Sch. Printing, 1946-47. Editor ShowBill Mag., NYC, 1945-47; news editor Boulder City (Nev.) Daily News, 1947-49; owner, pub., editor Tucson Sun-News, NYC, 1949-51; dir. radio and TV news Sta. WBEN/WBEN-TV, Buffalo, 1951-53; dir. pub. svc. and promotion Indpls. Times, Buffalo, 1953-56; v.p., gen. mgr Kendall Assocs., Inc., NYC, 1956-60; dir. Office Publs. and Info., Commerce Dept., Washington, 1961-70, dir. publs. div., 1970; asst. dir. Nat. Tech. Info. Svc., Springfield, Va., 1971-81, dir. office of market devel., 1982-83; assoc. dir. NTIS, Springfield, Va., 1984-85, self-employed communications advisor, 1986—. Chmn. for fed. mail list policy Vice Pres.'s Com. on Right of Privacy; chmn. presdl. domestic policy rev. work group on fed. acquisition of fgn. tech., 1979; bd. dirs. Commerce Fed. Credit Union. Served with AUS, 1943-45 Decorated Silver Star with oak leaf cluster, Bronze Star, Purple Heart with oak leaf cluster; recipient award Ariz. Newspaper Assn., 1950, Ind. Photo Journalism award, 1954 Mem. Am. Arbitration Assn. (panelist), Washington Book Pubs., Soc. Mayflower Descs., Sons of Revolution (treas.), Flagon and Trencher, Soc. for the Descs.of the Colonial Clergy, Soc. Descs. of Founders of Hartford, Oldest Inhabitants of DC., St. Nicholas Soc. of N.Y.C. Democrat. Home and Office: 2325 49th St NW Washington DC 20007-1002 Personal E-mail: dc49@comcast.net.

SMITH, DEAN EDWARDS, retired men's college basketball coach; b. Emporia, Kans., Feb. 28, 1931; s. Alfred Dillon and Vesta Marie (Edwards) S.; m. Linnea Weblemoe, May 21, 1976; children: Sharon, Sandy, Scott, Kristen, Kelly. BS in Math. and Phys. Edn., U. Kans., 1953. Asst. basketball coach USAF Acad., 1955-58; asst. basketball coach U. N.C., 1958-61, head basketball coach, 1961-97, now cons. basketball and athletic dept. Mem. U.S. and Canadian Basketball Rules Com., 1967-73; U.S. basketball coach Olympics, Montreal, Que., Can., 1976; lectr. basketball clinics, Germany, Italy. With USAF, 1954-58. Named Coach of Yr., Atlantic Coast Conf., 1967, 68, 71, 76, 77, 79, Nat. Basketball Coach of Yr., 1977, Nat. Coach of Yr., US Basketball Writers, 1979, one of Top 5 Coaches of the 20th Century, ABC-TV and ESPN; named to Naismith Basketball Hall of Fame, 1982, Nat. Collegiate Basketball Hall of Fame, 2006. Mem. Nat. Assn. Basketball Coaches (Nat. Basketball Coach of Yr. 1976, dir. 1972—, pres. 1981-82), Fellowship Christian Athletes (dir. 1965-70) Baptist. Office: U NC Basketball Office PO Box 2126 Chapel Hill NC 27515-2126

SMITH, DEIRDRE O'MEARA, lawyer; b. NYC, June 2, 1946; d. Thomas Francis and Mary Veronica (Meehan) O'Meara; children: Thomas Brady Ahr, Andrew Travers Ahr; m. Gerald Monroe Smith, Aug. 15, 1992. BA cum laude, Trinity Coll., 1968; MEd, Va. Commonwealth U., 1976; JD, U. Mo., 1982. Bar: Mo. 1982, U.S. Dist. Ct. (we. dist.) Mo. 1982. Tchr. Prince George's County Schs., Md., 1968-70, St. Michael's Sch., Richmond, Va., 1976-78; staff lawyer Mo. Supreme Ct., Jefferson City, 1982-83; gen. counsel State of Mo. Detention Facilities Commn., Jefferson City, 1983, State of Mo. Jud. Fin. Commn., Jefferson City, 1983-85; clk. of the ct. Mo. Ct. Appeals Eastern Dist., St. Louis, 1985-98. Bd. dirs. Downtown St. Louis, 1994-95; bd. dirs. Beaufort Boys and Girls Club, 2004-06, v.p., 2005, pres., 2005-06; bd. dirs. Low Country Boys and Girls Club, 2006—, sec., 2006-07, pres., 2007—. Recipient Acad. Excellence award in environ. law U. Mo. Sch. Law, 1981; disting. fellow St. Louis Bar Found. Fellow Am. Bar Found., Mo. Bar Found.; mem. ABA (jud. divsn. lawyers conf., exec. com. 1997-2000), Nat. Conf. Bar Pres., Nat. Conf. Bar Founds., Mo. Bar Assn. (Mo. Client Security Security Trust Fund bd. dirs. 1991-95, chmn. 1995-96), St. Louis County Bar Assn., Lawyers Assn. St. Louis (Outstanding Svc. award 1998), Met. St. Louis Bar Assn. (exec. com. 1988-96, pres. 1994-95), Beaufort, S.C. Art Assn. (bd. dirs. 1999-2002, v.p., 2004-05), Dataw Island Owners Assn. (sec. 2001-02, v.p. 2002-03, pres. 2003-04), St. Louis Bar Found. (bd. dirs. 1989-96, pres. 1995-96), St. Louis Women Lawyers Assn. (bd. dirs. 1989-94, pres. 1992-93), Am. Judicature Soc. (bd. dirs. 1990-92, bd. exec. com. 1993-2003, v.p. 1995-97, sec. 1997-99, treas. 1999-2001, pres. 2001-03, chmn. nat. nominating com., 2003-05), Nat. Conf. Appellate Ct. Clks. (exec. com. 1990-92), Phi Delta Phi, Media Club -St. Louis (sec. bd. dirs. 2006-07, pres.), Dataw Island Club (bd. sec. 2006-07, pres. 2007—). Roman Catholic.

SMITH, DEMAURICE F., lawyer; b. Anacostia, Washington, 1964; BA, Cedarville Coll., 1985; JD with honors, U. Va., 1989. Bar: DC, Md. Asst. U.S. atty. DC dist. US Dept. Justice, 1991—98; counsel to dep. atty. gen. DC, 1999—2001; with US Secret Svc. Multi-Agy. Command Ctr., 2001; ptnr. Latham & Watkins LLP, Washington, 2001—06, Patton Boggs LLP, Washington, 2006—. Commentator MSNBC, CNN, NBC, Court-TV, Fox TV; tchr. U. Va., George Washington U., Am. U.; bd. governors DC Bar Assn.; bd. dirs. Good Samaritan Found.; faculty mem. Nat. Trial Advocacy Coll., Nat. Inst. Trial Advocacy. Named one of Young Guns Washingtonian's Top 40 Lawyers Under 40; recipient U.S. Atty. Gen. Dir. award, 2000, John Evans Trial Advocacy award, U.S. Atty.'s Assn., Leadership Team award, U.S. atty.'s office, commendation, U.S. Secret Svc., DEA, U.S. Marshal's Svc., Met. Police Dept., others. Office: Patton Boggs LLP 2550 M St NW Washington DC 20037 Office Phone: 202-457-5636. Office Fax: 202-457-6315. E-mail: dfsmith@pattonboggs.com. *

SMITH, DENA MICHELE, physical education educator; d. Edward I. Smith and Beverly M. Metz. BS, U. Wis., La Crosse, 1992. Tchr. phys. edn. and health Shell Lake Schs., Wis., 1993—2000, Sch. Dist. Jefferson, Jefferson, Wis., 2000—. Head coach girls basketball Shell Lake Schs., 1993—2000, head coach girls softball, 1994—2000; head coach girls basketball Sch. Dist. Jefferson, 2000—. Mem.: Wis. Basketball Coaches Assn. Office: Sch Dist Jefferson 700 W Milwaukee St Jefferson WI 53549 Office Phone: 920-675-1185.

SMITH, DENNIS (EDWARD SMITH), publishing executive, writer; b. NYC, Sept. 9, 1940; s. John and Mary (Hogan) S.; m. Patricia Ann Kearney, Aug. 24, 1963 (div. May 1988); children: Brendan, Dennis, Sean, Deirdre and Aislinn (twins); m. Katina Arts Meyer, Dec. 25, 1997. BA, NYU, 1970, MA, 1972. Adj. asst. prof. Coll. New Rochelle, 1973-74; fireman City of N.Y., 1963-80; founder, pub., editor in chief Firehouse Mag., NYC, 1976-89; chmn. First Responders Fin., LLC, 2005—. Author: Report from Engine Co. 82, 1972, Final Fire, 1975, Firehouse, 1977, Dennis Smith's History of American Firefighting, 1978, Glitter and Ash, 1980, The Aran Islands—A Personal Journey, 1980, Steely Blue, 1985, Firefighters, Their Lives in Their Own Words, 1988, The Little Fire Engine That Saved the City, 1990, A Song for Mary, 1999, Report From Ground Zero, 2002, Brassy the Fire Engine, 2005, San Francisco Is Burning, 2005. Chmn. First Responders Fin., LLC; mem. bd. advisors Boys and Girls Clubs Am., N.Y.C., The New York Fire Safety Found.; bd. dirs. Kips Bay Boys and Girls Club, N.Y.C., N.Y. Police & Fire Widows' & Children's Benefit Fund; bd. dirs., chmn. emeritus N.Y. Acad. Art; bd. dirs., pres. First Responders Found. With USAF, 1957-60. Recipient Christopher award for non-fiction, 1973. Mem. Century Assn. Club. Roman Catholic. Home and Office: 545 Fifth Ave New York NY 10017 Personal E-mail: dennissmith@mindspring.com, dennis@dennissmith.com.

SMITH, DEREK ARMAND, information technology executive; b. Hamilton, Ont., Can., Sept. 2, 1953; came to U.S., 1981; s. Alastair A.G. and Jessie Mead (Maben) S.; m. Rebecca Oldfield, Oct. 10, 1981; 1 child, Alastair Maben Oldfield. BCom., U. Toronto, 1976. Chartered acct.; CPA, Mass. Staff acct. Office of Auditor Gen., Ottawa, 1976-78; chartered acct. Peat Marwick Thorne, Ottawa, 1978-79; v.p. fin. adminstrn. Can. Dry Bottling Ltd., Kingston, Ont., 1979-81; supervising sr. Peat Marwick, Boston, 1981-82; mgr. corp. reporting Warren, Gorham & Lamont, Inc., Boston, 1981-82, asst. contr. NYC, 1982-84, sr. v.p., CFO, 1988-90, Penguin Books USA Inc., NYC, 1990-96; exec. v.p., 1995-96; exec. v.p., CFO Addison Wesley Longman Inc., Reading, Mass., 1996-98; v.p., chief adminstrv. officer Orgnl. Dynamics., Inc., Burlington, Mass., 1998-2000; CFO First Knowledge Ptnrs. Inc., Boston, 2000—02; CFO, v.p. adminstrn. Castel, Inc., Beverly, 2002—. Pres. Trinity Coll. Sch. Fund, Beverly, Mass., 1992; bd. govs. Trinity Coll. Sch., Port Hope, Ont., 1992-2003, trustee, 2003—. Trustee John Hart Hunter Ednl. Found., N.Y.C., 1992. Mem. AICPA (bd. examiners 1998-2003), Assn. Chartered Accts. U.S. Ltd. (treas. 1990-93, dir. 1989-94, hon. dir. 1994—), Kappa Alpha Soc. (exec. com., v.p. 1991-93, pres. 1993-95). Episcopalian. Avocations: skiing, sailing, tennis, paddle tennis, golf. Office: Castel Inc 100 Cummings Ctr Ste 152F Beverly MA 01915 Office Phone: 978-232-7612. Personal E-mail: derekasmith@comcast.net.

SMITH, DIANA BARKER, music educator; b. Houston, Sept. 1, 1941; d. Irving Willis Barker and Mary Martine Kelly; m. Alan Michael Smith, Dec. 28, 1968; 1 child, Hillary Kay. Student, Aspen Sch. Music, Colo., 1961; MusB, U. Houston, 1963; MusM, U. Tex., 1966. Instr. piano SW Tex. State U., San Marcos, 1968—69, Colo. Coll., Colorado Springs, 1969—71; adj. prof. piano Duke U., Durham, NC, 1974—79, Bowling Green State U., Ohio, 1998—. Mem. JDC-Guarneri Duo, US, 1980—; musician: Houston Symphony, Kennedy Ctr., Phillips Collection, Nat. Gallery of Art, Sala Chopin, Sala Carlos Chavez, Chautauqua Inst., 1999, 2001, Ionian Music Acad. and Festival, 2005, 2006. Recipient 1st pl. award Young Artist Competition, Houston Symphony, 1955, Phi Beta award, Nat. Young Artist Competition, 1960, Franklin Academic award, U. Houston, 1961, Young Artist Competition award, KRBE FM, Tex., 1962. Mem.: Phi Kappa Phi.

SMITH, DIANA MARIE, business educator; b. Des Moines, Oct. 25, 1940; d. Nathan Henry and Helen (Hall) Kitchen; m. Robert Nelson Smith, Jan. 26, 1971 (dec. 12-7-2004); 1 child, Stephen BA, Drake U., Des Moines, Iowa, 1968, MA, 1971. Cert. tchr., Iowa. Stenographer Polk County Welfare Dept., Des Moines, 1960—67; typist Polk County Auditor, Des Moines, 1968, Ctrl. Life Assurance Co., Des Moines, 1976—79; computer oper. IRS, Des Moines, 1988; lead specialist II Norwest Bank, Des Moines, 1978—2002; sec. Shive-Hattery Engrs., Des Moines, 1976—90; instr. adult edn. Des Moines Ind. Dist., 1969—2001; tchr. bus., computers Des Moines Pub. Schs., 1968—2000; instr. computers St. Paul Ch. and Saks Inc., Des Moines, 2000—06. Ind. computer cons.; instr.-authorized tng. assoc. program for WordPerfect, 1994; Mary Kay beauty cons., 1993— Chair meml. com. Burns United Meth. Ch., Des Moines, 1988—, Sunday sch. tchr., 1961-83, 92-98, 2006—, sec. adminstrv. bd., 1983-2004 Democrat. Avocations: reading, computers. Office: Chim Cherie Fireplaces 534 35th St Des Moines IA 50312 Personal E-mail: dsmith1034@aol.com.

SMITH, DONALD ARCHIE, religious business executive, consultant; b. Dayton, Ohio, Feb. 23, 1934; s. Archie Ford and Catherine Rosella (Rabold) S.; m. Joan Sandra Speedie, May 18, 1955; children: Douglas Alan, Keith Cameron, Deirdre Lynn, Neal Ramsey. BA in Sci. and Math., Harvard U., 1956; cert., Indsl. Coll. of Armed Forces, 1971. Mgmt. Acct., 1977, Enrolled Agt., 1996. Nuclear rsch. and project engr. N.Am. Aviation Co., 1956-62; fin. software specialist Nat. Cash Register, 1962-63; mgr. sys. engring. N.Am. Aviation, 1963-67; mgr. bus. planning, mktg. svcs. and pub. rels. N.Am. Rockwell, Columbus, Ohio, 1967-72, mgr. internat. sales and mktg., 1968-73; mgr. strategic planning Rockwell Internat. Corp., Columbus, 1973-76, program mgr. Condor weapons sys., 1976-77, dir. guided bomb programs, 1977-78, dir. bus. devel. and legis. liaison, 1978-80; v.p. fin. applied tech. group Arvin Industries, Columbus, Ind., 1980-84; v.p. fin. Calspan Corp., Columbus, Ind., 1980-82, v.p. fin. and adminstrn., 1982-84, CFO, treas., dir., 1983-84; bus. dir. Franklin United Meth. Home, 1984-86; dir. fin. and adminstrn. North Ind. Conf. of the United Meth. Ch., 1986-92; sr. assoc. gen. sec. health benefits/gen. bd. of pensions United Meth. Ch., 1992-96; staff devel. cons. logal ednl. software, 1996-2000; pres. Kid Solve, Inc., 1999—. Ops. rsch. cons., 1962-64; instr. math. Sinclair Coll., Dayton, Ohio, 1961-63; mem. U.S.-U.K. Bipartite Com. on Nuclear Weapons, 1958-61; industry chmn. Mil. Specifications and Stds. Rev. Com,. 1972-79; mgmt. cons., 1984—. Author: Financial Recordkeeping Handbook for Local Churches. Past pres., treas., trustee Players Theatre of Columbus, 1975—80; v.p. Ohio Assn. U.S. Army, 1979—80; dist. commr. Boy Scouts Am., 1970—73, cubmaster, 1965—70; squadron comdr. CAP, 1976; treas., dir. Franklin United Meth. Home, 1982—84; auditor First United Meth. Ch., 1981—84; ch. adminstr. Greenwood United Meth. Ch., 1997—2002; dir., treas. South Ind. United Meth. Found., 2002—; treas., trustee Columbus Arts Guild, 1980—83; mem. audit and rev. com. Gen. Coun. on Fin. and Adminstrn., 1988—92; chmn. Commn. on Racism in Columbus Pub. Schs., 1972; trustee Indpls. East Dist. United Meth. Ch., 2002—. Recipient Nat. award Jr. Achievement, Inc., 1954; Letters of Commendation govt. agys., Am. Def. Preparedness Assn., Boy Scouts Am., 1958-78; Leadership award Nat. Mgmt. Assn., 1979. Mem.: NAEA, NAA, NRA, SAR, AIA (nat. chmn. soc. and aerospace tech. com. 1980—83, nat. pub. policy com.), AARP (state chmn. Ill. 1993—95, mem. nat. tech. com. 1996—98, state adminstr. Ind. 1996—2003), Royal Inst. Nav., Nat. Mgmt. Assn. (v.p., trustee), Nat. Tng. Com. (chmn. 1998—2003, Gt. Lakes regional coord. 2003—05), Army and Navy Club, Harvard Club (Ind.), Palatines to Am., Shriners, Masons. Home and Office: 7 E Hill Valley Dr Indianapolis IN 46227-2624 Office Phone: 319-889-0771.

SMITH, DONALD CAMERON, retired preventive medicine physician; b. Peterborough, Ont., Can., Feb. 2, 1922; arrived in U.S., 1952, naturalized, 1960; m. Jean Morningstar, Sept. 11, 1946. MD, Queen's U., 1945; MSc in Medicine, U. Toronto, Ont., 1948, DPH, 1949. Diplomate Am. Bd. Preventive Medicine, Am. Bd. Pediatrics. Intern Victoria Hosp., London, Ont., Canada, 1945-46; fellow in physiology U. Toronto, 1947—49; med. officer health Kent County (Ont.) Health Unit, 1950—52; Commonwealth Fund fellow in pediat. U. Mich. Hosp., 1952-55; prof. maternal and child health Sch. Pub. Health U. Mich., prof. pediat. Med. Sch., chmn. dept. health and human devel., 1961-79; prof. psychiatry and behavioral scis. Northwestern U. Med. Sch., Chgo., 1979-85; ret., 1985. Chmn. Medicaid Adv. Coun., 1969—72; vis. prof. maternal and child health Harvard U., 1969—72; prin. advisor health and med. affairs to gov., Mich., 1972—78; dir. Mich. Dept. Mental Health, 1974—78; chmn. State Pub. Health Adv. Coun., 1982—90; chmn. health care policy bd. Mich. Dept. Corrections, 1986—91; med. dir. Sisters Mercy Health Corp., 1981—91. Surgeon lt. Royal Can. Navy, 1946—47. Address: # 408 807 Asa Gray Dr Ann Arbor MI 48105 Business E-Mail: leelo@umich.edu.

SMITH, DONALD E., broadcast engineer; b. Salt Lake City, Sept. 10, 1930; s. Thurman A. and Louise (Cardall) S.; m. Helen B. Lacy, 1978. BA, Columbia U., 1955; BS, U. Utah, 1970; postgrad., U. So. Calif., U. Utah, Harvard U.; PhD (hon.), Columbia U., 1985. Engr. Iowa State U. (WOI-TV), 1955-56; asst. chief engr. KLRJ-TV, Las Vegas, 1956-60; studio field engr. ABC, Hollywood, Calif., 1960; chief engr. Teletape, Inc., Salt Lake City, 1961; engring. supr. KUER, U. Utah, Salt Lake City, 1962-74, gen. mgr., 1975-85. Freelance cinematographer, 1950—; cons. mgmt., 1965—. Mem. Soc. Motion Pictures and TV Engrs., Lambda Chi Alpha. Home: 2233 S 500 E Unit 115 Salt Lake City UT 84106-1485 Personal E-mail: donald.smith2@comcast.net.

SMITH, DONALD RAY, magazine dealer; b. Louisville, Dec. 12, 1934; s. Henry Bland and Margaret Frances (Corbett) S. Student pvt. schs., Louisville. Clerk Huber & Huber Motor Express, Louisville, 1951-52, Retail Credit Co., Louisville, 1952-53, Louisville & Nashville R.R., Louisville, 1953-65; owner, appraiser, cons. Don Smith's Nat. Geog. Mags., Louisville, 1969—. Author: Nat. Geog. Mag. for Collectors, 1975, 2d edit., 1978, 3d rev. edit., 1985, 4th rev. edit., 1988, 5th rev. edit., 1992, 6th rev. edit., 1996, Gone With the Wagons, 1980; composer song My Dreams Desire Another Way, 1968, poem Calico Waltz, 1986, Beyond Repast, 1986, The Essence of Darkness, 1986, The Dominant Submissive, 1987, Agony's Prelude, 1987, The Unmoving Distance, 1988, Exercise, 1997, Doris Jean, 1998, Crantling's Release, 1998, Mr. Gally, 1999, Every Time I Hear My Favorite Song, 1999; price guide booklet for collectors of Nat. Geog. Mag., 2000, Nat. Geog. Collector's Newsletter, 2000, Torell's First Love, 2001, Put Your Dreams in a Cup, 2001, I Heard Your Melody of Words, 2002, The Sealed Doorway, 2003, The Picture of Helga Harwell, 2004, Hopeless Surrender, 2004, The Valley of the Morons, 2005, The Lady on the Wall, 2005, Symbols are Written on the Walls, 2005, The Third Profile, 2005, A Gift from the Heavens, 2006, My Melody of Words, 2007; contr. pamphlets and articles on collecting mags. Independent. Roman Catholic. Avocations: finger style guitar, drawing, painting. Home and Office: 3930 Rankin St Louisville KY 40214-1748 Office Phone: 502-366-7504.

SMITH, DONALD RAYMOND, librarian; b. Highland, Ill., Sept. 25, 1946; s. Raymond Stanley and Gladys Loraine (Martin) S.; m. Elaine Marie Neudecker, Apr. 12, 1969; 1 child, Benjamin Christopher. BA, So. Ill. U., Edwardsville, 1968, MA, 1972, MS, 1978; MLS, U. Mo., Columbia, 1976. Acad. adv. So. Ill. U., Edwardsville, 1970-73, libr. instr., 1973-78, edn. libr., 1978-82; assoc. dir. pub. svc. and collection devel. U. Tulsa, 1982-88, assoc. dir. gen. svcs., 1988-93; dir. libr. N.E. La. U., Monroe, La., 1993-96; dean info. svcs. U. La., Monroe, 1996—2003, dean libr., 2003—. Cons. Hayner Pub. Libr., Alton, Ill., 1977-82, Tulsa City County Libr., 1984; cons. facilitator Tulsa Area Libr. Coop., 1987-88, 90; collection evaulator Okla. Jr. Coll., Tulsa, 1984; planning cons. Delgado C.C., New Orleans, 2006; libr. cons. Temple B'nai Israel, Monroe, La., 2007-. Author: Newspaper Indexing Handbook, 1981; editor and compiler newspaper index, 1976-77. Cataloger Our Lady Queen of Peace Sch., Belleville, Ill., 1979-82; campaign worker Dem. Party, Belleville, 1972; chair bd. dirs. Tulsa Area Libr. Coop., 1991-93; mem. La. Libr. Network Commn., 2004—; cons. libr. Temple B'nai Israel, 2007—. With US Army, 1969-70. Recipient Millicent C. Palmer award Friends of Lovejoy Library, So. Ill. U., 1974, H.W. Wilson scholar, 1974, Higher Edn. Coordinating Act grantee Ill. State Library, 1980-81, Workshop award U. Okla. Sch. Library Sci., 1984. Mem.: ALA, La. Libr. Network (commn. 2004—07), Tech. Consortium Tchr. Edn., Trailblazer Libr. Dirs. Bd. and Commn., La. Acad. Libr. Info. Network Consortium (at-large exec. bd. dirs. 1994—96, chmn. rsch. and devel. com. 2001—03), La. Assn. Coll. and Rsch. Librs. (automation and tech. com. 2000—, v.p., pres.-elect 2003—05), La. Libr. Assn. (sec. scholarship trust 1994—2004, co-chair ann. conf. 2003—04, network commn. 2004—), Okla. Libr. Assn. (chmn. contg. edn. com. 1985—86, chmn. adminstrn. roundtable 1989—90, chair automation roundtable 1991—92), Assn. Coll. and Rsch. Librs., Phi Delta Kappa, Phi Kappa Phi. Roman Catholic. Avocations: travel, history, reading. Office: U La Univ Libr 700 University Ave Monroe LA 71209-0720 Office Phone: 318-342-1051. Business E-Mail: dosmith@ulm.edu.

SMITH, DONNIE KAY, state agency administrator, retired military officer; b. Franklin, Ky., Dec. 4, 1947; s. Norris Justin and Ruby Evelyn Smith; m. Rhonda Joan Cowan; children: Haley Ann, Jennifer Leigh, Justin Patrick, Heather Marie. BA, Western Ky. U., Bowling Green, 1970. Deliveryman Nashville Surg. Supply, 1965—66; radio announcer WPHC Radio, Waverly, Tenn., 1966—67; music dir., announcer WBGN Radio, Bowling Green, 1967—70; 2d lt. US Army, Augusta, Ga., 1970—71; music dir., announcer WBGN Radio, 1971—72; music dir., radio announcer WSM Radio and TV, Inc., Nashville, 1972—75; capt., adminstrv. asst. HQ, Office of the Adj. Gen., Dept. of Mil., Tenn., Nashville, 1975—79; tchr. Trevecca Nazarene Coll., Nashville, 1978—79; capt., state recruiting and retention mgr. HQ, Tenn. Army NG, Nashville, 1979—80; maj., tng. officer 130th Rear Area Ops. Ctr., Smyrna, Tenn., 1980—85; lt.

col., plans, ops. and mil. support officer HQ, Tenn. Army NG, 1985—88, lt. col., tng. adminstr., 1988—90; lt. col., pers. mgmt. officer HQ, Tenn. Army and Air NG, Nashville, 1990—91; col., dep. chief of staff for pers. HQ, Tenn. Army NG, 1991—2000; col., dep. chief of staff for human resources Joint Forces HQ, Tenn. Army and Air NG, Nashville, 2000—03; exec. adminstrn. officer Tenn. Emergency Mgmt. Agy., Nashville, 2004—. Assoc. editor Volstate Guardsman Newspaper, Nashville, 1974—75. Decorated Legion of Merit US Army, Meritorious Svc. medal (3), Army Commendation medal (4), Army Achievement medal, Commendation medal USAF, Fla. Meritorious Svc. medal Fla. N.G., Iowa Meritorious Svc. medal Iowa N.G., Pa. DSM Pa. N.G., Tex. Lone Star Medal Tex. N.G., Wis. NG Commendation medal Wis. N.G., Commendation Ribbon (3) Tenn. N.G., Individual Achievement Ribbon (5), Tenn. DSM (2), Ala. DSM Ala. N.G., Ky. DSM Ky. N.G., Miss. Magnolia medal Miss. N.G.; recipient Eagle Trophy, Nat. Mil. Pers. Adv. Com., NG Bur., Washington, 1997—2000, plaque, Bulgarian Army Gen. Staff, 2000, Minuteman Trophy, N.G. Assn. Tenn., 2000. Democrat. Presbyterian. Home: 116 Deer Rd Smyrna TN 37167-9743 Office: Tenn Emergency Mgmt Agy 3041 Sidco Dr Nashville TN 37204-1502 Home Phone: 615-459-7408; Office Phone: 615-741-1453. Office Fax: 615-741-0006. Personal E-mail: donnieksmith@yahoo.com. Business E-Mail: dsmith@tnema.org.

SMITH, DOROTHY OTTINGER, apparel designer, volunteer; b. Indpls., 1922; d. Albert Ellsworth and Leona Aurelia (Waller) Ottinger; m. James Emory Smith, June 25, 1943 (div. 1984); children: Michael Ottinger, Sarah Anne, Theodore Arnold, Lisa Marie. Student, Herron Art Sch. of Purdue U. and Ind. U., 1941-42. Comml. artist William H. Block Co., Indpls., 1942-43, H.P. Wasson Co., 1943-44; dir. Riverside (Calif.) Art Ctr., 1963-64; jewelry designer Riverside, 1970—; numerous design commns. Adviser Riverside chpt. Freedom's Found. of Valley Forge; co-chmn. fund raising com. Riverside Art Ctr. and Mus., 1966-67, bd. dirs. Art Alliance, 1980-81; mem. Riverside City Hall sculpture selection panel Nat. Endowment for the Arts, 1974-75; chmn. fundraising benefit Riverside Art Ctr. and Mus., 1973-74, trustee, 1980-84, chmn. permanent collection, 1981-84, co-chmn. fund drive, 1982-84, trustee, 1998—; chmn. Riverside Mcpl. Arts Commn., 1974-76, Silver Anniversary Gala, 1992; juror Riverside Civic Ctr. Purchase Prize Art Show, 1975; mem. pub. bldgs. and grounds subcom., gen. plan citizens com. City of Riverside, 1965-66; mem. Mayor's Commn. on Civic Beauty, Mayor's Commn. on Sister City Sendai, 1965-66; bd. dirs., chmn. spl. events Children's League of Riverside Community Hosp., 1952-53; bd. dirs. Crippled Children's Soc. of Riverside, spl. events. chmn., 1952-53; bd. dirs. Nat. Charity League, pres. Riverside chpt., 1965-66; mem. exec. com. bd. trustees Riverside Arts Found., 1977-91, fund drive chmn., 1978-79, project rev. chmn., 1978-79, advisor Eveing for the Arts, 1998, juror Gemco Charitable and Scholarship Found., 1977-85; mem. bd. women deacons Calvary Presbyn. Ch., 1978-80, elder, 1989-92; mem. incorporating bd. Inland Empire United Fund for the Arts, 1980-81; bd dirs. Hospice Orgn. Riverside County, 1982-84; trustee Riverside Art Mus., 1998—; mem. Calif. Coun. Humanities, 1982-86. Recipient cert. Riverside City Coun., 1977, plaque Mayor of Riverside, 1977, Spl. Recognition Riverside Cultural Arts Coun., 1981, Disting. Svc. plaque Riverside Art Ctr. and Mus., Jr. League Silver Raincross Community Svc. award, 1989, Cert Appreciation Outstanding Svc. to the Arts Community Riverside Arts Found., 1990, Top Dog award Riverside Art Mus., 1999. Mem. Riverside Art Assn. (pres. 1961-63, 1st. v.p. 1964-65, 67-68, trustee 1959-70, 80-84, 87-92), Art Alliance of Riverside Art Ctr. and Museum (founder 1964, pres. 1969-70). Address: 3979 Chapman Pl Riverside CA 92506-1150

SMITH, (J.) DORRANCE, federal agency administrator; BA, Claremont Men's Coll. Asst. to the Pres. for media affairs The White House; exec. prodr. Nightline ABC News, exec. prodr. This Week with David Brinkley; sr. media advisor & cons. Fed. Emergency Mgmt. Agy. (FEMA); sr. media advisor Coalition Provisional Authority, Iraq; media cons. Joint Com. on Inaugural Ceremonies US Ho. Reps.; asst. sec. for pub. affairs US Dept. Def., Washington, 2006—. Office: US Dept Defense 1400 Defense Pentagon Rm 2E556 Washington DC 20310-1400 Office Phone: 703-697-9312. Office Fax: 703-695-4299.

SMITH, DWIGHT CHICHESTER, III, lawyer; b. Ft. Meade, Md., June 24, 1955; s. Dwight Chichester Jr. and Rachel (Stryker) S.; m. Mindy L. Kotler, Aug. 18, 1985; children: Dwight C. IV, Cornelia R. BA, Yale U., 1977, JD, 1981. Bar: DC 1982, NY 1982. Para-legal House Ethics Com., Washington, 1977-78; law clk. to Hon. Hugh Bownes U.S. Ct. Appeals (1st cir.), Concord, NH, 1981-82; assoc. Kaye, Scholer, Fierman, Hays & Handler, Washington, 1982-84, Covington & Burling, Washington, 1984-90; dep. chief counsel for legal policy Office of Thrift Supervision, Dept. of Treasury, Washington, 1990-94, dep. chief counsel for bus. transactions, 1995-99; counsel Alston & Bird, LLP, Washington, 1999—2001, ptnr., fin. svcs., products group, 2002—. Article and book rev. editor Yale Law jour., 1980-81; contbr. articles to profl. jours. Mem. Potomac Boat Club, City Tavern Club. Presbyterian. Avocation: rowing. Home: 1606 32nd St NW Washington DC 20007-2930 Office: Alston & Bird LLP North Bldg 11th Fl 601 Pennsylvania Ave NW Washington DC 20004-2601 Office Phone: 202-756-3325. E-mail: dcsmith@alston.com.

SMITH, DWIGHT MORRELL, chemistry professor, academic administrator; b. Hudson, NY, Oct. 10, 1931; s. Elliott Monroe and Edith Helen (Hall) S.; m. Alice Beverly Bond, Aug. 27, 1955 (dec. 1990); children—Karen Elizabeth, Susan Allison, Jonathan Aaron; m. Elfi Nelson, Dec. 28, 1991. BA, Ctrl. Coll., Pella, Iowa, 1953; PhD, Pa. State U., 1957; ScD (hon.), Ctrl. Coll., 1986; LittD (hon.), U. Denver, 1990. Postdoctoral fellow, instr. Calif. Inst. Tech., 1957—59; sr. chemist Texaco Rsch. Ctr., Beacon, NY, 1959—61; asst. prof. chemistry Wesleyan U., Middletown, Conn., 1961—66; assoc. prof. Hope Coll., Holland, Mich., 1966—69, prof., 1969—72; prof. chemistry U. Denver, 1972—, chmn. dept., 1972—83, 1999—2001, vice chancellor for acad. affairs, 1983—84, chancellor, 1984—89; pres., bd. trustees Hawaii Loa Coll., Kaneohe, 1990—92. Mem. Registry for Interim Coll. and Univ. Pres.; mem. adv. bd. Solar Energy Rsch. Inst., 1989—91; mem. vis. com. Zettlemoyer Ctr. for Surface Studies Lehigh U., 1990—96; dept. chemistry and geochemistry Colo. Sch. Mines; mem. sci. adv. bd. Denver Rsch. Inst.; sr. advisor Rocky Mountain Ctr. Homeland Def. Editor Revs. on Petroleum Chemistry, 1975-78; editl. adv. bd. Recent Rsch. Devels. in Applied Spectroscopy, 1998—; contbr. articles to profl. jours. Chmn. Chs. United for Social Action, Holland, 1968-69; mem. adv. com. Holland Sch. Bd., 1969-70; bd. commrs. Colo. Adv. Tech. Inst., 1984-88, Univ. Senate, United Meth. Ch., Nashville, 1987-88, 91-93; mem. adv. bd. United Way, Inst. Internat. Edn., Japan Am. Soc. Colo., Denver Winter Games Olympics Com.; mem. ch. bds. or consistories Ref. Ch. Am., N.Y., Conn., Mich., United Meth. Ch., Colo. DuPont fellow, 1956-57, NSF fellow Scripps Inst., 1971-72; recipient grants Rsch. Corp., Petroleum Rsch. Fund, NSF, Solar Energy Rsch. Inst., Camille & Henry Dreyfus Found., Inc. Mem. AAAS, Am. Assn. Aerosol Rsch., Am. Chem. Soc. (chmn. Colo. 1976, sec. we. Mich. 1970-71, joint coun. and bd. com. on sci. 1997-98, award Colo. sect. 1986), Soc. Applied Spectroscopy, Mile High Club, Sigma Xi. Achievements include patents for selective hydrogenation and fuel, lubricant additives. Home: 1931 W Sanibel Ct Littleton CO 80120-8133 Office: U Denver Dept Chem & Biochem Denver CO 80208-0001 Office Phone: 303-871-2938. Personal E-mail: elfidwight@comcast.net. Business E-Mail: dwismith@du.edu.

SMITH, E. ASHLEY, lawyer, insurance company executive; LLM, U. Houston. V.p., gen. counsel Southwestern Group Fin.; pres., CEO Inst. for Rehab. and Rsch. (TIRR); vice chancellor govtl. rels. and policy U. Tex. Sys.; exec. v.p., gen. counsel, chief legal officer Stewart Info. Svcs. Corp., 2006—. Mem. Tex. Ho. of Reps., Harris County. Office: Stewart Info Svcs Corp 1980 Post Oak Blvd Houston TX 77056 Office Phone: 713-625-8100. *

SMITH, E. BERRY, television and radio consultant; b. Daytona Beach, Fla., Feb. 21, 1926; s. Samuel Rogers and Rosemary (Berry) S.; m. Mary Terese Hoffman, Apr. 3, 1948 (dec.); children: Kevin B., Martin J. BS, Butler U., 1949. Account exec. Sta. WIRE Radio, Indpls., 1949-54; dir. advt. and pub. relations Franklin Fin. Co., Hartford City, Ind., 1954-56; account exec. CBS Radio Network, Detroit, 1956-57; v.p. Sta. WFIE-TV, Evansville, 1957-61, Sta. WFRV-TV, Green Bay, Wis., 1961-62; exec. v.p. Sta. WLKY-TV, Louisville, 1962-64; pres. Sta. WTVW-TV, Evansville, 1964-80, Sta. WSBT, South Bend, Ind., 1981-89; sr. v.p. Schurz Comm. Inc., South Bend, 1989-2001, cons., 2001—. Dir. adv. bd. CBS-TV Affiliates Assn., 1984-87, sec., treas., 1988-90, chmn., 1990-91. Dir. Goodwill Industries, South Bend, 1984-85, Jr. Achievement Michiana, South Bend, 1984-91. 1st lt. U.S. Army, 1944-46, PTO. Recipient Silver medal Am. Advt. Fedn., Evansville, Ind., 1973; named to Ind. Broadcasters Assn. Hall of Fame, 1989; appointed Sagamore of the Wabash, 1993. Mem. South Bend C. of C. (bd. dirs. 1988-92), Ind. Soc. Chgo., Nat. Press Club, Mensa, Notre Dame U. Club, Elks. Roman Catholic. Office: 5182 Finch Dr South Bend IN 46614-5491 Office Phone: 574-291-9664.

SMITH, E. FOLLIN, retired energy executive; b. Miss. m. John Gerdy; children: E. Wallace Gerdy, James F. Gerdy. BA, Davidson Coll.; MBA, U. Va. With treas.'s office GM, NYC, 1985; treas. GM Canada Ltd., 1994-97; v.p. fin. GMAC; asst. treas. GM, 1994-97; CFO Delphi Cahssis, Dayton, Ohio, 1997-98; v.p., treas. Armstrong World Industries, Inc., Lancaster, Pa., 1998-2000, sr. v.p., CFO, 2000—01, Constellation Energy, Balt., 2001—03, exec. v.p., CFO, CAO, 2003—07. Bd. dir. Ryder Sys. Inc., Discover Fin. Services, 2007—. Trustee, chair audit com. Darden Sch., Univ. Va.; mem. bd. vis. Davidson Coll.; bd. dir. Balt. Mus. Art. Mailing: Discover Fin Services Bd Directors 2500 Lake Cook Rd Riverwoods IL 60015 *

SMITH, EARL CHARLES, nephrologist, educator; b. Pitts., Mar. 1, 1936; s. Mose and Irene Smith. BS, Tufts U., 1957; MD, U. Pitts., 1961. Diplomate in internal medicine and nephrology Am. Bd. Internal Medicine. Intern Montefiore Hosp., Pitts., 1961-62; resident, fellow Cleve. Clinic, 1964-68; physician Cook County Hosp., Chgo., 1968-71; chief nephrology divsn. Mt. Sinai Hosp., Chgo., 1971—, pres. med. staff, 1985-87, vice chair medicine, 1987—, interim chair medicine, 1994—95, 2005—06; chief nephrology divsn. Chgo. Med. Sch., 1994—, prof. medicine, 1995—. Cons. Internat. Jour. Artificial Organs, Milan, 1986—; med. adv. bd. Kidney Found. Ill., Chgo., 1980—. Co-author: Medical Exam Book-Nephrology, 1976, Self Assessment in Internal Medicine, 1980; assoc. editor Kidney jour., 1991—; contbr. articles to profl. jours. Chair hypertension com. Chgo. Heart Assn., 1973-75. Capt. USAF, 1962-64. Recipient Meritorious Svc. award, Chgo. Heart Assn., 1975. Fellow Am. Coll. Physicians, Am. Soc. Nephrology; mem. Am. Soc. Artificial Internal Organs, Am. Soc. Hypertension Specialist in Clin. Hypertension, Internat. Soc. Nephrology, Phi Beta Kappa, Alpha Omega Alpha, Sigma Xi. Office: Mount Sinai Hosp 15th and California Ave Chicago IL 60608 Business E-Mail: smie@sinai.org.

SMITH, EDWARD KENDRICK, lawyer; b. Atlanta, Dec. 9, 1956; s. Alexander Wyly and Elizabeth (Haverty) Smith; m. Caryl Greenberg Smith, Oct. 16, 1983; children: Gina Leigh, Jacob Ryan. BA, U. NC, Chapel Hill, 1974—78; JD, U. Ga., Athens, 1978—81. Bar: Ga. 1981, US Ct. Appeals (4th and 11th cirs.), US Dist. Ct. (no., mid. & so. dist)., US Supreme Ct. Ptnr. Smith Gambrell & Russell, LLP, Atlanta, 1981—2005, Jones Day, Atlanta, 2005—. Instr. Lorman Bus. Inst, 1989—, Inst. Continuing Legal Edn., Nat. Bus. Inst., Inc., Tax Exec. Inst., Faculty for Advanced Tax Sch., Leadership Atlanta, 1997. Chmn. Rsch. Atlanta, 1993—97; program chair Leadership Ga., Atlanta, 1997—98; chmn. Servants Relief for Incurable Cancer, Atlanta, 2000—07; mem. exec. com. Atlanta Downtown Partnership, 1990—92; pres. The Bridge, Atlanta, 1991—99; trustee SW Hosp. & Med. Ctr., Atlanta, 1991—2002; bd. dirs. Ctrl. Atlanta Progress, Atlanta, 1994—2007, Zoo Atlanta, Atlanta, 2004—07; mem. bd. visitors U. Ga. Law Sch., Athens, 2004—07; co-chmn. Fernbank Soc., 2005—06; pres. Tate Mt. Assocs., 2005—06; trustee John & Mary Franklin Found., 2002—07. Recipient Ga. Legal Elite, Ga. Trend Mag., 2003, 2004, 2005, 2006, Ga. Super Lawyer, Atlanta Mag., 2003, 2004, 2005, 2006, 2007, Ga. Legal Leader, James Mag., 2005, 2006, Top Ga. Lawyer, 2007. Mem.: ABA, Inst. Profls. Taxation, Ctrl. Atlanta Progress, Piedmont Driving Club. Avocations: squash, hiking, piano, bicycling. Office: Jones Day 1420 Peachtree St Ste 800 Atlanta GA 30309 Office Fax: 404-581-8330. Business E-Mail: eksmith@jonesday.com.

SMITH, EDWARD PAUL, JR., lawyer; b. Westbury, NY, Jan. 13, 1939; s. Edward Paul Sr. and Margaret (Eisenhauer) S.; m. Mary Elizabeth Neagle, Mar. 29, 1980; children: Nora, Edward, Brian, Thomas, Brendan. BA, Coll. of the Holy Cross, 1960; LLB, Columbia U., 1963. Bar: NY 1964, Fla. 1966. Assoc. Chadbourne & Parke LLP, NYC, 1964-75, prin., 1975—, ptnr. corp. dept., employment dept. Corp. sec. Am. Bur. Metal Statis., NYC, 1978—. Contbr. articles to profl. jour. Capt. USAF, 1964-67. Mem. NY State Bar Assn., Fla. Bar Assn. Roman Catholic. Office: Chadbourne & Parke LLP 30 Rockefeller Plz Fl 31 New York NY 10112-0129 Home Phone: 914-787-8350; Office Phone: 212-408-5100. Office Fax: 212-541-5369. Business E-Mail: esmith@chadbourne.com.

SMITH, EDWIN DUDLEY, lawyer; b. NYC, Oct. 4, 1936; s. Edwin Dudley Jr. and Mary Jane (Bannigan) S.; m. Joan Joyce Mortenson, June 29, 1963; children: Edwin Dudley V, Patrick Townshend. BA, U. Kans., 1960, JD, 1963. Bars: Kans. 1963, Mo. 1992, U.S. Dist. Ct. Kans. 1963, U.S. Ct. Appeals (10th cir.) 1967, U.S. Supreme Ct. 1972, U.S. Dist. Ct. (we. dist.) Mo., 1998. Assoc. Fisher Patterson Sayler & Summers, Topeka, 1963-66; ptnr. Fisher Patterson Sayler & Smith, L.L.P., Topeka, Overland Park, 1966—2007, of counsel, 2007—. Contbg. author: Pharmacy Law Annual, 1991. Past mem. adv. bd. Florence Crittenton Svcs., Topeka; past chmn. legis. com. U.S. Swimming; past chmn. Missouri Valley Swimming. Fellow Kans. Bar Found.; mem. ABA, Kans. Bar Assn. (bd. govs. 1986-92, Outstanding Svc. award 1978), Topeka Bar Assn., Johnson County Bar Assn., Kansas City Met. Bar Assn., Internat. Assn. Def. Counsel, Am. Judicature Soc. (bd. dirs. 1984-89), Am. Bd. Trial Adv. (past pres. Kans. chpt.), Kans. Assn. Def. Counsel, Def. Rsch. Inst., Am. Soc. Pharmacy Law, Assn. Atty. Mediators. Home: 4344 W 124th Ter Leawood KS 66209-2277 Office: Fisher Patterson Sayler & Smith LLP 51 Corporate Woods Ste 300 9393 W 110th St Shawnee Mission KS 66210 also: Fisher Patterson Sayler & Smith LLP 3550 SW 5th St Topeka KS 66606-1998 Office Phone: 913-339-6757. E-mail: dsmith@fisherpatterson.com.

SMITH, EDWIN ERIC, lawyer; b. Louisville, Sept. 29, 1946; s. Lester Henry and Nancy Joy (Heyman) S.; m. Katharine Case Thomson, Aug. 16, 1969; children: Benjamin Clark, George Louis, Andrew Laurence. BA, Yale U., 1968; JD, Harvard Law Sch., 1974. Bar: Mass. 1974, NY, 2005, US Dist. Ct. Mass. 1974. Assoc. Bingham McCutchen LLP, Boston, 1974—81, ptnr., 1981—, co-chmn. fin. instn. practice group. Lectr. in field; Mass. commr. on uniform state laws; articles 5 and 9 drafting com. Uniform Comml. Code, chmn. payments article divsn. drafting com., editl. bd., 2005—; U.S. del. to receivables assignment working group UN Commn. on Internat. Trade Law Trustee Uniform Law Found. Lt. USNR, 1969-71. Recipient Achievement Medal USN, 1971. Mem. ABA (chmn. uniform comml. code com. bus. law sect. 1995-99, permanent editl. bd. uniform comml. code 1999-), Am. Law Inst. (Uniform Comml. Code article 9 study com.), Am. Coll. Comml. Fin. Lawyers (pres. 2002-03), Assn. Comml. Fin. Attys., Nat. Bankruptcy Conf., Am. Coll. Bankruptcy. Office: Bingham McCutchen LLP 150 Federal St Boston MA 02110-1713 Office Phone: 617-951-8615. Office Fax: 617-951-8736. Business E-Mail: edwin.smith@bingham.com.

SMITH, ELAINE DIANA, foreign service officer; b. Glencoe, Ill., Sept. 15, 1924; d. John Raymond and Elsie (Gelbard) S. BA, Grinnell Coll., 1946; MA, Johns Hopkins U., 1947; PhD, Am. U., 1959. Commd. fgn. svc. officer U.S. Dept. State, 1947; assigned to Brussels, 1947-50, Tehran, Iran, 1951-53, Wellington, New Zealand, 1954-56, Dept. State, Washington, 1956-60, Ankara, Turkey, 1960-69, Istanbul, Turkey, 1969-72, Dept. Commerce Exch., 1972-73; dep. examiner Fgn. Svc. Bd. Examiners, 1974-75; Turkish desk officer Dept. State, Washington, 1975-78. Consul gen., Izmir, Turkey, 1978—. Author: Origins of the Kemalist Movement, 1919-1923, 1959. Recipient Alumni award Grinnell Coll., 1957. Mem. U.S. Fgn. Svc. Assn., Phi Beta Kappa. Home: The Plaza 800 25th St NW Apt 306 Washington DC 20037-2207

SMITH, ELDEN LEROY, recreational vehicle company executive; b. Berwyn, Ill., June 1, 1940; s. Frederick M. and Margaret I. (Larson) S.; m. Barbara G. Whaley, Apr. 4, 1963; children: Jill Marie, David Elden. BA in Bus. Adminstrn., Whittier Coll., Calif., 1962. Market analyst autonetics div. N.Am. Aviation, Anaheim, Calif., 1963-66; sales mgr. Pendleton Tool Industries, LA, 1966-68; plant gen. mgr. Fleetwood Enterprises, Inc., Hancock, Md., 1969-71, v.p. recreational vehicle group, Riverside, Calif., 1972-88, sr. v.p., 1988-97, pres., dir., CEO 2005-. Trustee Whittier Coll., 1991-99. Served with USNR, 1962-63. Mem. Recreation Vehicle Industry Assn. (chmn. 1980-82, dir. 1975-97). Office: Fleetwood Enterprises 3125 Myers St Riverside CA 92503 *

SMITH, ELDON, cardiologist, physiologist, educator; MD, Dalhousie U., Halifax, NS, Can., 1967. From asst. prof. to assoc. prof. medicine and physiology Dalhousie U., 1973—80; prof. medicine and physiology and biophysics U. Calgary, Canada, 1980—2004, prof. emeritus, 2004—, chief divsn. cardiology, 1980—86, chair dept. medicine, 1985—90, assoc. dean clin. affairs, 1990—92, dean faculty of medicine, 1992—97. Corp. dir. Can. Natural Resources, Ltd., 1997—, Vasogen, Inc., 1998—, Sernova Corp., 2000—, Overlord Fin., Inc., 2005—. Editor-in-chief: Can. Jour. Cardiology, 1997—. Bd. dirs., pres. Peter Lougheed Med. Rsch. Found., 1999—, Premier's adv. coun. health, 2000—02, health professions adv. bd., 2002—; trustee Alta. Heritage Found. for Med. Rsch., Canada, 2000—07. Recipient officer Order of Can. Fellow: Can. Acad. Health Scis., Am. Heart Assn., Internat. Acad. Cardiovasc. Scis., Am. Coll. Cardiology, Royal Coll. Physicians and Surgeons Can. Office: U Calgary Faculty Medicine 3330 Hosp Dr Calgary AB Canada T2N 4N1 Home Phone: 403-286-6800; Office Phone: 403-220-5500. Business E-Mail: esmith@ucalgary.ca.

SMITH, ELDRED GEE, church leader; b. Lehi, Utah, Jan. 9, 1907; s. Hyrum Gibbs and Martha E. (Gee) S.; m. Jeanne A. Ness, Aug. 17, 1932 (dec. June 1977); children: Miriam Smith Skeen, Eldred Gary, Audrey Gay Smith Vance, Gordon Raynor, Sylvia Dawn Smith Isom; m. Hortense H. Child, May 18, 1978; stepchildren: Carol Jane Child Burdette (dec.), Thomas Robert Child. Employed with sales div. Bennett Glass & Paint Co., Salt Lake City, 6 years; mech. design engr. Remington Arms Co., 2 years; design engr., prodn. equipment design Tenn. Eastman Corp., Oak Ridge, Tenn., 3 years; now presiding patriarch Ch. Jesus Christ of Latter-day Saints. Mem. Lds Ch. Home: 2942 Devonshire Cir Salt Lake City UT 84108-2526 Office: 47 E South Temple Salt Lake City UT 84150-9701

SMITH, ELEANOR JANE, retired university chancellor, consultant; b. Circleville, Ohio, Jan. 10, 1933; d. John Allen and Eleanor Jane (Dade) Lewis; m. James L. Banner, Aug. 10, 1957 (div. 1972); 1 child, Teresa M. Banner Watters; m. Paul M. Smith Jr. (dec. Apr. 30, 2004). BS, Capital U., 1955; PhD, The Union Inst., Cin., 1972. Tchr. Columbus (Ohio) Pub. Schs., 1956-64, Worthington (Ohio) Pub. Schs., 1964-72; from faculty to administrator U. Cin., 1972-88; dean Smith Coll., Northampton, Mass., 1988-90; v.p. acad. affairs, provost William Paterson Coll., Wayne, NJ, 1990-94; chancellor U. Wis.-Parkside, Kenosha, 1994-97, ret., 1997; ind. cons. in higher edn. Dir. Afrikan Am. Inst., Cin., 1977-84; adv. bd. Edwina Bookwalter Gantz Undergrad. Studies Ctr., Cin.; mem. Gov.'s Tobacco Tax adv. coun.; lectr. in field. Performances include (concert) Black Heritage: History, Music and Dance, 1972—. Spl. Arts Night Com., Northampton, 1988-89; bd. dirs. Planned Parenthood No. and Ctrl. Ariz., Am. Lung Assn. Ariz./N.Mex. Named career woman of achievement YWCA, Cin., 1983. Mem. AAUW, Nat. Assn. Women in Higher Edn., Am. Assn. for Higher Edn., Leadership Am. (bd. dirs., treas. 1993-95), Nat. Assn. Black Women Historians (co-founder, co-dir. 1979-82), Am. Coun. on Edn. (mem. com. on internat. edn. 1994-97, bd. dirs. 1995-97), Am. Assn. State Colls. and Univs. (mem. com. on policies and purposes 1994-97). Avocations: music, pen and ink drawing, travel, reading. Home: 1208 Verona Way Keller TX 76248

SMITH, ELISE FIBER, international non-profit development agency administrator; b. Detroit, June 14, 1932; d. Guy and Mildred Geneva (Johnson) Fiber; m. James Frederick Smith, Aug. 11, 1956 (div. 1983); children: Gregory Douglas, Guy Charles; life ptnr. Jac Smit, 1990. BA, U. Mich., 1954; postgrad., U. Strasbourg, France, 1954-55; MA, Case Western Res. U., 1956. Tchr. US Binat. Ctr., Caracas, Venezuela, 1964-66; instr. English Am. U., 1966-68; prof. lang. faculty Catholic U., Lima, Peru, 1968-70; coord. English lang. culture program, lang. faculty El Rosario U., Bogota, Colombia, 1971-73; lang. specialist, mem. faculty Am. U., English Lang. Inst., 1975-78; exec. dir. OEF Internat. (name formerly Overseas Edn. Fund), Washington, 1978-89, bd. dirs.; dir. Global Women's Leadership Program Winrock Internat., 1989-98, sr. policy advisor on gender, 1998—2005, ex officio bd. mem., 2005—. Co-founder, founding chair Women's EDGE, 1997—; v.p. Pvt. Agys. Collaborating Together, NYC, 1983-89; trustee Internat. Devel. Conf., Washington, 1983-2001, exec. com., 1985-90; hon. com. for Global Crossroads Nat. Assembly, Global Perspectives in Edn., Inc., NYC, 1984, Washington, 1984-92, gen. assembly, 1992; nat. com. Focus on Hunger '84, LA; ofcl. observer UN Conf. on Status Women, 1980, UN 3rd World Conf. on Women, 1985, del. NGO Forum, UN 4th World Conf. on Women, del. NGO Forum, 1995; mental health adv. com. Dept. State, 1974-76; U.S. del. planning seminar integration women in devel. OAS, 1978; participant Women, Law and Devel. Forum; exec. com., chair commn. advancement women interaction Am. Coun. for Vol. Internat. Action,1994-97, co-founder, 1985-88, chmn. bd., 1985-88; adv. bd. Global Links Devel. Edn., Washington, 1985-86; adv. coun. Global Fund for Women, 1988-93; US del. Vital Voices Conf. Women and Democracy, Iceland, 1999, Women in Democracy Conf., Lithuania, 2000, Baltic Women in Democracy Conf., Estonia, 2003. Co-editor: Toward Internationalism: Readings in Cross-cultural Communication, 1979, 2d edit. 1986; author: (book chpt.) Developing Power: How Women Transformed International Development, 2004. Mem. USAID Adv. Com. on Vol. Fgn. Aid, 1994—; mem. women and conservation adv. com. World Wildlife Fund, 1998—2002; mem. State Dept. Adv. Com. US Internat. Econ. Policy, 2000—; bd. dirs. Internat. Ctr. Rsch. on Women, 1992—2001, Sudan-Am. Found. Rotary Internat. ambassadorial scholar Strasbourg, France, 1954-55; grantee Dept. State, 1975. Mem. Assn. Women in Devel., UNIFEM, Coalition Women in Internat. Devel. (co-founder 1979, chair 1993-96),pvt. Agys. in Internat. Devel. (co-chmn.

1980-82, pres. 1982-85), Nat. Assn. Fgn. Student Affairs (grantee 1975), U. Mich. Alumni Assn., Women's Fgn. Policy Group, Rotary Internat. (mem. global com. Women in Future Soc. 1996). Unitarian Universalist. Business E-Mail: esmith@winrock.org.

SMITH, ELIZABETH ANGELE TAFT, curator; Degree in Art History, Columbia U. Curator Mus. Contemporary Art, LA, 1983—99, James W. Alsdorf Chief Curator Chgo., 1999—. Adj. prof. pub. art studies program U. So. Calif., 1992—98; bd. advisors Independent Curators Internat., NYC; bd. overseers, Sch. Architecture, Ill. Inst. Tech., Chgo. Curator (exhibitions) Blueprints for Modern Living: History and Legacy of the Case Study Houses, Mus. Contemporary Art, LA, 1989, Urban Revisions: Current Projects for the Public Realm, 1994, Cindy Sherman: Retrospective, 1997, At the End of the Century: One Hundred Years of Architecture, 1998, The Architecture of R.M. Schindler, 2001 (Named Best Architecture or Design Exhibition of Yr., Internat. Assn. Art Critics/USA, 2001), Matta in America: Painting and Drawings of the 1940s, Mus. Contemporary Art, Chgo., 2001, Donald Moffett: What Barbara Jordan Wore, 2002, Lee Bontecou: A Retrospective, 2003 (Named Best Monographic Mus. Show Nationally, Internat. Assn. Art Critics/USA, 2004); author: (books) Techno Architecture, 2000, Case Study Houses: The Complete CSH Program 1945-66, 2002; co-editor: Lee Bontecou: A Retrospective of Sculpture and Drawing, 1958-2000, 2003. Named Woman of Yr., Chgo. Soc. Artists, 2004. Office: Mus Contemporary Art 220 E Chgo Ave Chicago IL 60611

SMITH, ELIZABETH LEIGH, literature and language professor; b. Lufkin, Tex., May 1, 1969; d. Allen Martin and Joan Ruth Richman; m. Charles Michael Smith, Feb. 29, 1992. BA, Rice U., Houston, 1991; MA, U. Houston, 1994, PhD, 1999. Tchg. asst. U. Houston, 1992—98, adj. instr., 1998—2000, Houston CC, 1996—2000, instr., 2000—01; vis. prof. Stephen F. Austin State U., Nacogdoches, Tex., 2001—02; prof. English East Stroudsburg U., Pa., 2002—. Recipient Sensitivity to Students with Disabilities award, Office of Disabilities, 2006, 1st pl. Pa. State Powerlifting, US Assn. Powerlifting, 2005, 1st pl. Tex. State Powerlifting, US Powerlifting Fedn., 1995, 1996, 1998, 1999; scholar for supervision of peer tutors, Prudential, 1998—99; travel grantee, Faculty Devel. and Rsch., 2004, 2006, 2007. Mem.: NJ Coll. English Assn., English Assn. Pa. State Colls. and Univs., Internat. Arthurian Soc., Hagiography Soc., Phi Kappa Phi (life). Democrat. Jewish. Home: 110 Orchard Ln Tobyhanna PA 18466 Office: E Stroudsburg U 200 Prospect St East Stroudsburg PA 18301 Home Phone: 570-894-2398; Office Phone: 570-422-3385. Business E-Mail: lsmith@po-box.esu.edu.

SMITH, ELIZABETH MACKEY, retired financial consultant; b. Phila., Mar. 23, 1941; d. William Norman and Celeste (Parvin) Mackey; m. George Van Riper Smith, Aug. 15, 1964; children: Douglas George, Todd Mackey. BA, Gettysburg Coll., 1963; MAT in French, Ga. State U., 1978. ChFC. Tchr. fgn. lang. Haverford (Pa.) H.S., 1963-65; registered rep. Am. Express Fin. Advisors, Inc., Macon and Savannah, Ga., 1979-2000, br. mgr. Tybee Island, Ga., 2000—05, ret., 2005. Reader Atlanta Serv for the Blind, 1968; hostess Atlanta Coun Int Visitors, 1972—74; foreign exchange student coord Loisirs Culturels a l'Etranger, 1990; staff protocol vol sailing venue Olympic Games, Savannah, 1996. Mem.: Delta Gamma, Delta Phi Alpha, Phi Sigma Iota. Avocations: tennis, swimming. Home: 104 Landings Way North Savannah GA 31411-1512 Personal E-mail: islandwoman64@earthlink.net.

SMITH, ELMER, telecommunications industry executive; Grad., Tulane U. Various positions Berry Co. (now Bellsouth Corp.), pres., CEO, pres. advt., pub. Atlanta, 2001—. Mem.: Assn. Directory Mktg. (bd. dirs.), Yellow Pages Integrated Media Assn. (chmn. 2003—04).

SMITH, ELWIN EARL, mining and oil company executive; b. Ellicottville, NY, Sept. 30, 1922; s. Henry B. and Beatrice M. (Spellman) S.; m. Mary Ellen Kirchmaier, Nov. 4, 1944; children: Peter E., Michael E., Timothy E. Student, U. Ala., 1940, NYU, 1954, Harvard Bus. Sch., 1962. Sales engr. Cities Service Oil Co., NYC, 1949-55; gen. sales mgr. Climax Molybdenum Co., NYC, 1955-64; exec. v.p., dir. Lithium Corp. Am., Gastonia, N.C., 1964-69, pres., CEO, 1969-77; v.p. Gulf Resources & Chem. Co., Houston, 1970-77; pres., dir. Asia Lithium Corp., Osaka, Japan, 1970-77; pres. Amax Iron Ore, Greenwich, Conn., 1977-80, corp. v.p., group exec. for indsl. minerals and resources group, 1978-80; exec. v.p. Amax Inc., Greenwich, 1981-82, sr. exec. v.p., 1982-85; prin. Elwin Smith Internat. Sales Engrs., Darien, Conn., 1986—. Bd. dirs. Am. Metal & Coal Co., Greenwich, Conn., Freeport Copper & Gold, Ethanol Corp., Sydney, Australia, First Dynasty Mines, Denver, IMR Industries, Ltd., London; chmn. Seven Seas Cinema, Stamford, Conn., 1985-95. 1st lt. U.S. Army Paratroopers, 1943-48. Decorated Combat Inf. badge, Bronze Star, sr. parachute badge. Mem. AIME, Am. Petroleum Inst., Am. Chem. Soc., Am. Australian Assn., Japan Soc., Asia Soc., Mining and Petroleum Club of Sydney, Copper Club N.Y., Weeburn Country Club, Masons. Republican. Home and Office: 7 Tokeneke Trl Darien CT 06820-6126 Home Phone: 203-655-9408; Office Phone: 203-655-9129. E-mail: thesquare@aol.com.

SMITH, EMIL L., biochemist, educator; b. NYC, July 5, 1911; s. Abraham and Esther (Lubart) S.; m. Esther Press, Mar. 29, 1934; children: Joseph Donald, Jeffrey Bernard BS, Columbia U., 1931, PhD, 1936. Instr. biophysics Columbia U., NYC, 1936-38; John Simon Guggenheim fellow Cambridge U., Eng., 1938-39, Yale U., New Haven, 1939-40; fellow Rockefeller Inst., NYC, 1940-42; biophysicist, biochemist E. R. Squibb & Sons, New Brunswick, N.J., 1942-46; assoc. prof. to prof. biochemistry U. Utah, Salt Lake City, 1946-63; prof. biol. chemistry Sch. Medicine UCLA, 1963-79, prof. emeritus, 1979—. Cons. NIH, Am. Cancer Soc., Office Naval Research Author: (with others) Principles of Biochemistry, 7th edit., 1983; also numerous articles Recipient Stein-Moore award Protein Soc., 1987. Mem. NAS, Am. Acad. Arts and Scis., Am. Philos. Soc., Am. Soc. Biochemistry and Molecular Biology, Am. Chem. Soc., Acad. Scis. Russia (fgn.). Office: UCLA Sch Medicine Los Angeles CA 90095-1737

SMITH, EMMITT (EMMITT JAMES SMITH III), sportscaster, retired professional football player; b. Pensacola, Fla., May 15, 1969; s. Emmit Jr. and Mary Smith; m. Patricia Southall, Apr. 22, 2000; 4 children. BA in Pub. Recreation, U. Fla., 1996. Running back Dallas Cowboys, 1990—2003, Ariz. Cardinals, 2003—04; football analyst ESPN, 2007—. Named NFL Offensive Rookie of Yr., 1990, NFL All-Pro, Sporting News, 1992, 1993, NFL Player of Yr., 1993; named to NFC Pro-Bowl Team, 1990—95, 1998—99, Coll. Football Hall of Fame, 2006; recipient NFL MVP award, 1993, Super Bowl XXVIII MVP, 1993. Achievements include recognized as NFL's all-time leading rusher, 2002; leading NFL in rushing, 1991-93, 95; leading NFL running backs in scoring, 1992, 95; leading NFL in rushing touchdowns, 1992, 1994-95; being a member of Super Bowl Champion Dallas Cowboys, 1992, 1993, 1995; winner, Dancing With the Stars, 2006. Office: ESPN Plz 935 Middle St Bristol CT 06010 *

SMITH, EPHRAIM PHILIP, academic administrator; b. Fall River, Mass., Sept. 19, 1942; s. Jacob Max and Bertha (Horvitz) S.; m. Linda Sue Katz, Sept. 3, 1967; children: Benjamin, Rachel, Leah. BS, Providence Coll., 1964; MS, U. Mass., 1965; PhD, U. Ill., 1968. Chmn. dept. acctg. U. R.I., Kingston, 1972-73; dean Sch. Bus. Shippensburg State Coll., Pa., 1973-75; dean Coll. Bus. Adminstrn. Cleve. State U., 1975-90; dean Sch. Bus. Adminstrn. and Econ. Calif. State U., Fullerton, 1990-98, v.p. acad. affairs, 1998—. Co-author: Principles of Supervision: First and Second Level Management, 1984, Federal Taxation-Advanced Topics, 1995, Federal Taxation-Basic Principles, 2007, Federal Taxation Comprehensive Topics, 2007; contbr. articles to profl. jours. Mem. Am. Acctg. Assn., Am. Taxation Assn., Am. Inst. Decision Scis., Fin. Execs. Inst., Beta Gamma Sigma, Beta Alpha Psi. Office: Calif State Univ - Fullerton VPAA Office MH-133 800 N State College Blvd Fullerton CA 92831-3599 Business E-Mail: esmith@fullerton.edu.

SMITH, ERIC LEDELL, historian; b. Detroit, Oct. 9, 1949; s. Warren Cornelius and Hernrietta Volena Smith. BA in Humanities, Mich. State U., 1971, MA in Philosophy, 1973, student, 1973—78; MLS, U. Mich., 1980; MA in Performance Studies, NYU, 1985. Sales clk. Dawn Treader Bookshop, Ann Arbor, Mich., 1980—90; asst. Libr. U. Mich., Ann Arbor, 1980—90; curator jr. edn. Detroit (Mich.) Hist. Mus., 1990—92; curator African Am. Mus., Phila., 1992—93; historian Pa. State Archives, Harrisburg, Pa., 1993—2001, State Mus. Pa., Harrisburg, 2001—. Archivist R.E. Olds Mus., Lansing, Mich., 1985; curator jr. edn. Dossin Great Lakes Mus., Detroit, 1989; curator exhbns. Author: Bert Williams: A Biography of the Pioneer Black Comedian, 1992 (nominee Pulitzer prize in biography, 1992), Blacks in Opera: A Biographical Dictionary of People and Companies, 1873-1993, 1995, African Americans in Pennsylvania: Shifting Historical Perspectives, 1997, Commemorating African American History in Pennsylvania: The First Twenty-five Years of the Conference on Black History in Pennsylvania, 2002, African American Theater Buildings, 2003 (Ray and Pat Browne Book award, 2003), The State Museum of Pennsylvania: A Centennial History, 2005; co-author: The African Americans in Pennsylvania, 1997, African Americans of Harrisburg, 2005; mem. editl. bd.: Pa. History, 1999—2001, Pa. Mag. History and Biography, 2004—; author: (plays) African Americans at the Capital Making Jazz History, 1999, When Lincoln Came to Harrisburg, 2000, The Liberation of Jim Phillips, 2001; contbr. articles to profl. jours. and mags. Bd. dirs. U.S. Colored Troops Inst., Harrisburg, Pa., 2002—03, African Am. Mus., Harrisburg, 1994—97; dir. exec. bd. Fedn. State Cultural Ednl. Profls., 2005—. Finalist Excellence Hist. Recorded Sound Rsch. award, Assn. Recorded Sound Collections, 1993; recipient Contbn. award, Pa. Dept. Edn., 1999, Individual Achievement award, Pa. Fedn. Mus. and Hist. Socs., 2003. Mem.: Hist. Harrisburg Assn., Dauphin County Hist. Soc. (bd. dirs. 1994—97), African Am. Mus. Phila., Assn. Study African Am. History, Pa. Hist. Assn. (Philip S. Klein award 1999), Org. Am. Historians. Democrat. Roman Cath. Home: 101 S 2nd St 1202 Harrisburg PA 17101 Office: The State Mus of Pa 300 North St Harrisburg PA 17120

SMITH, ERNEST KETCHAM, electrical engineer; b. Peking, China, May 31, 1922; (parents Am. citizens); s. Ernest Ketcham and Grace (Goodrich) S.; m. Mary Louise Standish, June 23, 1950; children: Priscilla Varland, Nancy Smith Johnson, Cynthia Jackson. BA in Physics, Swarthmore Coll., 1944; MSEE, Cornell U., 1951, PhD, 1956. With Mut. Broadcasting Sys., 1946-49, chief plans and allocations engr., 1949; with radio propagation lab. Nat. Bur. Stds., Boulder, Colo., 1951-65, chief ionosphere rsch. sect., 1957-60, divsn. chief, 1960-65; dir. aeronomy lab. Environ. Sci. Svcs. Adminstrn., Boulder, 1965-67; dir. Inst. Telecom. Scis., 1968, dir. univ. rels., 1968-70; assoc. dir. Inst. Telecom. Scis. Office of Telecom., Boulder, 1970-72, cons., 1972-76; tech. staff Jet Propulsion Lab. Calif. Inst. Tech., Pasadena, 1976-87; adj. prof. dept. elec. and computer engrng. U. Colo., Boulder, 1987—. Vis. fellow Coop. Inst. Rsch. on Environ. Scis., 1968; assoc. Harvard Coll. Obs., 1965-75; adj. prof. U. Colo., 1969-76; internat. vice-chmn. study group 6, Internat. Radio Consultative Com., 1958-70, chmn. U.S. study group, 1970-76; mem.-at-large U.S. nat. com. Internat. Sci. Radio Union, 1985-88; convenor Boulder Gatekeepers to the Future, 1990—. Author: Worldwide Occurrence of Sporadic E, 1957; (with S. Matsushita) Ionospheric Sporadic E, 1962. Contbr. numerous articles to profl. jours. Editor: Electromagnetic Probing of the Upper Atmosphere, 1969; assoc. editor for propagation IEEE Antennas and Propagation Mag., 1989—. Mem. 1st Congl. Ch., moderator, 1995-97. Recipient Diplôme d'Honneur, Internat. Radio Consultative Com., Internat. Telecom. Union, 1978; named to Gallery of Disting. Scientists, Engrs. and Adminstrs., Nat. Bur. Stds., Nat. Inst. Stds. and Tech., Gaithersburg, Md., 2003. Fellow IEEE (fellow com. 1993, 94, 95), AAAS; mem. Am. Geophys. Union, Electromagnetics Acad., Athenaeum (Pasadena), UN Assn. of US (convenor Boulder chpt., treas. 1994-2005), Sigma Xi (pres. U. Colo. chpt. 1994-95, v.p. 95-98). Home: 350 Ponca Pl Apt 179 Boulder CO 80303-3802 Office: U Colo Dept Elec & Computer Engring Campus Box 425 Boulder CO 80309-0425 Personal E-mail: n6hqksmithek@yahoo.com. *A weakness of many large organizations is that it is difficult for senior administrators to step down after peaking in their 40s. I'm grateful for a crisis at age 50 which resulted in my taking early retirement at age 54 and then accepting a more modest job until age 65.*

SMITH, ESTHER THOMAS, communications executive; b. Jesup, Ga., Mar. 13, 1939; d. Joseph H. and Leslie Thomas; m. James D. Smith, June 2, 1962; children: Leslie, Amy, James Thomas. BA, Agnes Scott Coll., 1962. Staff writer Sunday women's editor Atlanta Jour.-Constn., 1961-62; mng. editor Bull. of U. Miami Sch. Medicine, 1965-66; corr. Atlanta Jour.-Constn. and Fla. Times-Union, 1964, 67-68; founding editor Bus. Rev. of Washington, 1978-81; founding editor, gen. mgr. Washington Bus. Jour., 1982; pres., bd. dirs. TechNews, Inc., 1986-96, CEO, 1995-96; founder, editor-at-large Washington Tech., 1986-97, Tech. Transfer Bus. Mag., 1992-95; co-chair editl. bd. TechCapital Mag., 1997-99; prin. Poretz Group Investor Rels., McLean, Va., 1998—2000; ptnr. Qorvis Comm. LLC (successor to Poretz Group), McLean, 2000—. Bd. dirs. Provant Inc., Women Connect.com, telezoo inc., World Affairs Coun. Washington, Atlantic Coun., Netpreneur Program Morino Inst., 1996—2002; mem. internat. adv. bd. Kilby Awards Found.; mem. MIT Enterprise Forum of Washington/Balt., 1981—82, Internat. Women's Forum, 1981—, No. Va. Bus. Round Table, exec. com., 1993—98; mem. adv. bd. Va. Math Coalition, 1991—94; commr. NACD Blue Ribbon Commn., 2001; trustee Ctr. for Excellence in Edn., 1993—96; bd. dirs., trustee Capital Region Technology Investors Conf.; bd. advisors George Washington U., Va., 1996—99; trustee George Mason U. Found., 2004—. Named to, Washington Bus. Hall of Fame, 2002; recipient Lifetime Achievement award, Women in Tech., 2000. Mem.: Md. High Tech. Coun., No. Va. Tech. Coun. (sr. adv. bd. 1998—2000, exec. com., bd. dirs., Earle C. Williams Leadership award 1999), Assn. Tech. Bus. Couns. (chmn. bd. advisors 1989—94), Econ. Club Washington. Office: Qorvis Comm LLC 8484 Westpark Dr 8th Fl Mc Lean VA 22102 Home Phone: 703-893-2195; Office Phone: 703-744-7800. Business E-Mail: esmith@qorvis.com.

SMITH, EUGENE WILSON, retired academic administrator, education educator; b. Forrest City, Ark., June 10, 1930; s. Milton Saumel and Frank Leslie (Wilson) S.; m. Rebecca Ann Slaughter, May 27, 1956; children: Lucinda Anne, Bradley Eugene. BA, Ark. State U., 1952; M.Ed., U. Miss., 1955, Ed.D., 1958. Mem. faculty Ark. State U., State University, 1958-92, prof. edn., 1971-92, v.p. adminstrn., 1968-71, dean Grad. Sch., 1971-84, interim pres., 1980, sr. v.p., 1980-84, pres., 1984-92, 94-95, pres. emeritus, 1992—, interim pres., 1994-95. Pres. Jonesboro Indsl. Devel. Corp., 1983-94; mem. exec. com. Conf. So. Grad. Schs., 1973-74, Ark. State Coun. on Econ. Edn., 1987-90; pres. Am. South Athletic Conf., 1987-89; dir. Mercantile Bank of Jonesboro, Union Planters Bank of Northeast Ark., Regions Bank of N.E. Ark. Alderman, City of Jonesboro, 1982-84, dir., pres. The Kays Found. Served to 1st lt. AUS, 1952-54, Korea. W.K. Kellogg Found. rsch. fellow, 1954-58 Mem. Ark. Adv. Coun. Elem. and Secondary Edn., Jonesboro C. of C. (dir. 1967-69, 80-85, v.p. 1981-82, pres. 1982-83), Phi Kappa Phi, Phi Delta Kappa, Kappa Delta Pi. Clubs: Rotary (pres. 1974-75). Home: 407 Lynne Ct Jonesboro AR 72401-8807

SMITH, FERN M., judge; b. San Francisco; children: Susan, Julie. AA, Foothill Coll., 1970; BA, Stanford U., 1972, JD, 1975. Bar: Calif. 1975. Assoc. Bronson, Bronson & McKlinnon, San Francisco, 1975-81, ptnr., 1981—86; judge San Francisco County Superior Ct., 1986-88, U.S. Dist. Ct. (no. dist.) Calif., 1988—. Dir. Fed. Jud. Ctr., Wash., 1999-2003; mem. adv. com. on Jud. Conf. U.S., Rules of Evidence, 1993-96, chair, 1996-99; mem. exec. com. Ninth Cir. Jud. Conf., 1994-96, Ninth Cir. State-Fed. Jud. Coun., 1990-93, Calif. Jud. Coun. 1987-88, mem. adv. Task Force on Gender Bias, 1988-90, hiring, mgmt. and pers. coms., active recruiting various law schs.; faculty Inst. Study and Devel. Legal Sys., 1992, Egypt & Bolivia, 1994, Mexico and Tunisia, 1995, Israel, Jordan, Greece and Egypt, 1996, India, 1998, Jordan and Italy, 1998, Italy, Israel and France, 2000, India, Israel and Russia, 2001, Morocco, Thailand and China, 2002, Turkey, Bahrain, the Netherlands and Russia, 2003, Jordan and Brazil, 2004, ISDLS Rule of Law Conf., Berkeley, Calif.; bd. vis. Law Sch. Stanford U., 1990-92, 99—; chair U.S. Jud. Conf. Com. on Internat. Jud. Rels., 2003—. Contbr. articles to legal publ. Mem. ABA, Queen's Br. Nat. Assn. Women Judges, Calif. Women Lawyers Assn., Bar Assn. San Francisco, Fed. Judges Assn., 9th Cir. Dist. Judges Assn., Am. Judicature Soc., Calif. State Fed. Jud. Coun., Phi Beta Kappa.

SMITH, FLOYD LESLIE, insurance company executive; b. Silver Creek, NY, Nov. 12, 1931; s. Harry Lee and Fanny Diem (Arnold) S.; m. Jane Kathryn Elters, Feb. 18, 1956; children: Keith Arnold, Bruce Erik. AB, Oberlin Coll., (Ohio), 1953; MBA, NYU, 1962. Investment analyst Mut. of N.Y., NYC, 1953-64, dir. investments, 1964-66; asst. v.p. securities investment Mut. of. N.Y., NYC, 1966-69; 2d v.p. securities investment Mut. of N.Y., NYC, 1969-74, v.p. securities investment, 1974-78, sr. v.p., 1978-81, chief investment officer, 1981-83, exec. v.p., chief investment officer, 1983-89, vice chmn., chief investment officer, 1989-91; trustee The Mut. Life Ins. Co. of N.Y., 1988-91; dir. MONY Series Fund, 1983—2005, Empire Fidelity Investments Life Ins. Co., 1994—. Trustee MONY Real Estate Investors, N.Y.C., 1981-90; bd. dirs., chmn. exec. com. Ins. Systems Am., Atlanta, 1974-82. Trustee Friends Sem., N.Y.C., 1975-84, Village of Saltaire, 1984-87; dir. St. Maarten Condo. Assn., Naples, Fla., 1993—; mem. Saltaire (N.Y.) Zoning Bd. Appeals, 1982-84; mem. fin. com. N.Y. Quarterly Meeting Soc. of Friends, 2004-07. With Signal Corps, U.S. Army, 1954-56. Mem. Ft. Worth Boat Club, Edgewater Club.

SMITH, FRANK EARL, retired trade association administrator; b. Fremont Center, NY, Feb. 4, 1931; s. Earl A. and Hazel (Knack) S.; m. Caroline R. Gillin, Aug. 14, 1954; children: Stephen F., David S., Daniel E. BS, Syracuse U., 1952. With Mellor Advt. Agy., Elmira, NY, 1954-55; asst. mgr. Elmira Assn. of Commerce, 1955-56; retail dept. mgr. C. of C., Binghamton, NY; mgr. Better Bus. Bur., Broome County, NY, 1956-60; exec. v.p. C. of C., Chemung County, Elmira, 1960-65, Schenectady County (N.Y.) C. of C., 1965-69, Greater Cin. C. of C., 1969-78; pres. Greater Detroit C. of C., 1978-95; ret., 1995. Bd. dirs., sec. Presbyn. Devel. Corp. of Detroit, Inc., 1995-2006. 1st lt. USAF, 1952-54. Named Young Man of Yr. Jr. C. of C. Elmira, 1964. Mem. C. of C. Execs. Mich., Am. C. of C. Execs. (past chmn.), N.Y. State C. of C. Execs. (past pres.), Ohio C. of C. Execs. (past pres.), C. of C. of U.S. (past bd. dirs. Ctr. Internatl Pvt. Enterprise, past chmn. nat. bd. regents, Inst. for Orgn. Mgmt.). Presbyterian. Home: 1626 Shallow Shores Dr Gaylord MI 49735

SMITH, FRANK G., III, lawyer; b. Greenville, Miss., June 6, 1952; BA cum laude, Davidson Coll., 1974; JD, Stanford Univ., 1977. Bar: Ga. 1977. Ptnr., head, intellectual property litig. group Alston & Bird LLP, Atlanta. Contbr. articles to profl. journals. Mem.: Order of Coif, Phi Beta Kappa. Office: Alston & Bird LLP One Atlantic Ctr 1201 W Peachtree NW Atlanta GA 30309-3424 Office Phone: 404-881-7240. Office Fax: 404-253-8184. Business E-Mail: fsmith@alston.com.

SMITH, FRANK M., lawyer; b. Mineola, NY, Mar. 27, 1966; s. Nita R. Smith-Delman and Frank Delman (Stepfather); m. Ruth E. Winick, Apr. 1, 1995; children: Martina J., Bryan C. JD, Hofstra U., Hempstead, NY, 1993. Bar: NY 1994, Fla. 1996. Atty. Atkinson Diner, et al, Ft. Lauderdale, Fla., 2001—. Office: Atkinson Diner Stone Mankuta & Ploucha 100 SE 3rd Ave Ste 1400 Fort Lauderdale FL 33394 Office Phone: 954-925-5501. Office Fax: 954-920-2711. Business E-Mail: fs@atkinson-diner.com.

SMITH, FREDERICK COE, retired manufacturing executive; b. Ridgewood, NJ, June 3, 1916; s. Frederick Coe and Mary (Steffee) S.; m. Ruth Pfeiffer, Oct. 5, 1940; children: Frederick Coe, Geoffrey, Roger, William, Bart. BS, Cornell U., 1938; MBA, Harvard U., 1940. With Armstrong Cork Co., Lancaster, Pa., 1940-41; with Huffy Corp., Dayton, Ohio, 1946-86, pres., chief exec. officer, 1961-72, chmn., chief exec. officer, 1972-76, chmn., 1976-78, chmn. exec. com., 1979-86. Past chmn. Sinclair C.C. Found.; past chmn. nat. bd. dirs. Planned Parenthoo Fedn.; past dir. Internat. Parenthood Fedn.; past chmn. Dayton Found.; trustee emeritus Alan Gutmacher Inst., Ohio United Way; past chmn. employment and tng. com. Gov.'s Human Investment Coun. Lt. col. USAAF, 1941-46. Decorated Legion of Merit. Home Phone: 937-434-1654. Office Fax: 937-223-1441. Personal E-mail: dotti8@aol.com.

SMITH, FREDERICK ORVILLE, II, agricultural products executive, retired military officer; b. Cambridge, Mass., July 17, 1934; s. Harry Francis and Dorothy Spaulding (Zeller) S.; m. Mabel Roxy Moore, June 6, 1965; children: Sarah Zeller, Jennifer Joy, Erika Hildred. BA, Bowdoin Coll., 1956; MA in Polit. Sci., U. Vt., 2000. Deck officer, 1st lt. USS The Sullivans USN, 1957-59; officer US Naval Sta., Adak, Alaska, 1959-60; clk. & exec. Fred O. Smith Mfg. Co., New Vineyard, Maine, 1960-71, pres., treas., 1971—; res. officer Naval Res. Tng. Ctr., Augusta, Maine, 1960-69, Bangor, Maine, 1970-79 (ret.). Co-owner Sugarwood Gallery, Inc., Farmington, Maine, 2000—, corp. sec., 2007—. Editor: New Vineyard, Maine 1802-2002, Its Settlement, Its People, Its History, A New Vineyard Historical Society Document, 2002. Notary pub., 1978—; chair, mem. nat. com. Young Reps., Maine, 1960—68, pres. New Eng. coun., 1962—64; chmn. Franklin County (Maine) Rep. Com., 1976—80, v.p. state conv., 1994; mem. Maine Rep. State Com., 1980—86, 1992—94, 1998—2002, 2006—; mem. state com. ASCO, 1998—2002; town chmn. Rep. Com., New Vineyard, 1972—86, Farmington, Maine, 1992—; ecumenical rep. Old South Congl. Ch., 2007—. Paul Harris fellow Farmington Rotary Club, 1996. Mem.: Porter Lake Assn. (bd. dirs. 2005—), Franklin County Arts and Crafts (v.p. 2002—05, pres. 2006—), Up Country Artists (bd. dirs. 1996—2003, v.p. 1997, pres. 1998—2000, bd. dirs. 2000—03, v.p., bd. dirs. 2005—06), Shriners, Am. Legion, Masons, Kora Temple Shrine. Avocations: photography, cabinet making & design, skiing, hiking, writing. Home: 127 Anson St Farmington ME 04938-5734 Office: The Fred O Smith Mfg Co PO Box 248 New Vineyard ME 04956-0248 Office Phone: 207-778-4177. Fax: 207-779-0716. E-mail: fosmith@somtel.com.

SMITH, FREDERICK WALLACE, delivery service executive; b. Marks, Miss., Aug. 11, 1944; s. Frederick Smith; m. Diane Avis., div. BS in Econs., Yale U., 1966. Cert. comml. pilot. Owner Ark Aviation, 1969-71; founder FedEx Express Corp., Memphis, 1971—, pres., 1971—75, CEO, 1977—98, chmn. bd., 1975—; chmn. bd., pres., CEO FedEx Corp., 1998—. Served with USMC, 1966-70, co-chmn. WWII Meml. Campaign. Named one of 400 Richest Ams., Forbes mag., 2006; recipient Eagle of Aviation award, Embry-Riddle Aero. award, 2001, Champion of Workplace Learning and Performance award, Amer. Soc. Tng. and Devel., 2002. Office: FedEx Corp 942 S Shady Grove Rd Memphis TN 38120-4117 *

SMITH, FREDRICA EMRICH, rheumatologist, internist; b. Princeton, NJ, Apr. 28, 1945; d. Raymond Jay and Carolyn Sarah (Schleicher) Emrich; m. Paul David Smith, June 10, 1967. AB, Bryn Mawr Coll., Pa., 1967; MD, Duke U., Durham, NC, 1971. Intern, resident U. N.Mex. Affiliated Hosps., 1971-73; fellow U. Va. Hosp., Charlottesville, 1974-75;

pvt. practice, Los Alamos, N.Mex., 1975—. Chmn. credentials com. Los Alamos Med. Ctr., 1983—, chief staff, 1990, 2003; bd. dirs. N.Mex. Physicians Mut. Liability Ins. Co., Albuquerque, 1988-97; regional adv. bd. Am. Physicians Assurance, 1997-. Contbr. articles to med. jours. Mem. bass sect. Los Alamos Symphony, 1975—; active Los Alamos County Parks and Recreation Bd., 1984-88, 92-96, 2007-, Los Alamos County Med. Indigent Health Care Task Force, 1989—2003; ops. subcom. Aquatic Ctr., Los Alamos County, 1988—. Fellow ACP, Am. Coll. Rheumatology; mem. N.Mex. Soc. Internal Medicine (pres. 1993-96), Friends of Bandelier. Democrat. Avocations: swimming, music, reading, hiking. Office: Los Alamos Med Ctr 3917 West Rd Los Alamos NM 87544-2275 Office Phone: 505-662-9400.

SMITH, GARY RICHARD, technology educator; b. Little Rock, Ark., Jan. 21, 1929; s. C. Ray and Maureen (Martin) S.; m. Mary Clare Beacom, June 16, 1956; children: Raymond, Timothy, Daniel, Laura, Carolyn. BA, Cornell Coll., 1952; MEd, Nat. Coll. Edn., Evanston, Ill., 1954; PhD, Northwestern U., 1960. Asst. editor Chem. Processing Mag., Chgo., 1952-53; tchr. various elem. schs. Evanston, Ill., 1954-58; instr. Northwestern U., Evanston, 1958-60; asst. prof. Wayne State U., Detroit, 1960-63, assoc. prof., 1964-69, prof., 1970—. Edn. rsch. cons. Mich. Senate Edn. Com., Lansing, 1973-74, Mich. Com. to Redistrict Detroit Pub. Schs., 1981. Contbr. articles to profl. jours. With U.S. Army, 1948-49. Mem. Internat. Soc. for Technology in Edn. Home: 3514 Arrowvale St Orchard Lake MI 48324-1506 Office: Wayne State U Rm 227 Edn Bldg Detroit MI 48202

SMITH, GENE, athletic director; m. Sheila Smith; children: Matt, Lindsay, Nicole, Summer. BA, U. Notre Dame, 1977. Asst. football coach U. Notre Dame, 1977—81; mktg. rep. IBM; athletic dir. Ea. Mich. U., 1983—93, Iowa State U., 1993—2000, Ariz. State U., 2000—05, Ohio State U., 2005—. Named one of 50 Most Powerful Blacks in Sports, Black Enterprise mag., 2005. Mem.: NCAA (mem. Football Rules Com. and Com. on Infractions). Office: Ohio State U 224 St John Arena 410 Woody Hayes Dr Columbus OH 43210 Office Phone: 614-292-7572. Office Fax: 614-292-0506. *

SMITH, GEOFFREY ARTHUR, museum staff member, surgeon; b. Loma Linda, Calif., July 23, 1946; s. Gerald Arthur and Maxine McGowan Smith; children: Ashley, Courtland. BA, UCLA, 1964; MD, U. Calif., Davis, 1972. Diplomate Am. Bd. Otolaryngology, Am. Bd. Plastic Surgery. Clin. prof. surgery U. Calif., San Diego, 1977—79; mus. exhibit antiquities cons., owner Antiqueties in Design, Del Mar, Calif., 1994—; med. dir. Latino Health, Calif., 1999—. Vis. prof. UCLA, 1977—93; mem. nat. faculty Am. Acad. Ootlarungology; owner La Jolla Limousines, Calif., 1984—94; presenter in field. Contbr. articles to profl. publs. Fellow: ACS. Avocation: archaeology. Home: 14730 Caminito Barbuda Del Mar CA 92014 Office Phone: 858-759-7838.

SMITH, GEORGE, marketing professional; Assoc. Sci. in Liberal Arts, Monroe Community Coll., Rochester, NY. Field sales rep. Elec. Components, Avnet, Inc., 1978—80, gen. mgr. Rochester, NY, 1980—84, Boston, 1984—88; N.E. regional v.p. Avnet, Inc., 1989—91; ea. area mgr. Avnet Computer Mktg. Group, 1991; sr. v.p. sales North Am. Avnet Computer Mktg. Group, 1992—94; exec. v.p. Avnet Computer, 1994; exec. v.p. Hall-Mark Computer Products Avnet, Inc., 1995, pres. Hall-Mark Computer Products, 1996; regional pres. Avnet Computer Mktg. Europe, 1997; pres. Avnet Electronics Mktg. EMEA, Phoenix, 1998—2003; pres. computer mktg. Europe Avnet Computer Mktg.-Avnet Applied Computing, 2001—03; pres. Avnet Computer Mktg.-Avnet Applied Computing, Asia, 2003—; v.p. Avnet, Inc., 1996—. Office: Avnet Inc 2211 S 47th St Phoenix AZ 85034

SMITH, GEORGE BUNDY, lawyer, retired state appeals court judge; b. New Orleans, Apr. 7, 1937; s. Sidney R. & Beatrice (Bundy) Smith; m. Alene L. Smith, 1964; children: George, Jr., Beth Beatrice. Cert. Polit. Studies, Institut d'Etudes Politiques, Paris, 1958; BA, Yale U., 1959, JD, 1962; MA in Polit. Sci., NYU, 1967, PhD, 1974; LLM of Jud. Process, U. Va., 2001; LLD (hon.), Fordham U. Sch. Law, 2004, Albany Law Sch., 2006. Staff atty. NAACP, 1962-64; law sec. to Hon. Jawn Sandifer, 1964-67; law sec. to Hon. Edward Dudley, 1967-71; law sect. to Hon. Harold Stevens, 1972-74; adminstr. model cities City of NY, 1974-75; interim judge Civil Ct. NYC, 1975-76, judge, 1976-79, NY State Supreme Ct., 1980-86, assoc. justice appellate divsn., 1st dept., 1987-92; assoc. justice NY State Ct. Appeals, NYC, 1992—2006; ptnr. Chadbourne & Parke LLP, NYC, 2006—. Apptd. mem. NY State Ethics Commn. Unified Ct. System, 1989-90; adj. prof. law Fordham U., 1981—. Co-author: (with Alene L. Smith) You Decide: Applying the Bill of Rights to Real Cases; contbr. articles to profl. jours. Trustee Grace Congl. Ch., Harlem, NY, Horace Mann-Barnard Sch., Bronx, NY, 1977-99; bd. dirs. Harlem-Dowling Westside Ctr. for Children and Family Svcs., NYC; former alumni trustee Phillips Acad., Andover, Mass. Mem. Met. Black Bar Assn. (founding, former pres. Harlem Lawyers Assn., bd. dirs., chmn. 1984-88), Assn. of Bar of City of NY (v.p. 1988-89), Judicial Friends. Office: Chadbourne & Parke LLP 30 Rockefeller Plz New York NY 10112 E-mail: gsmith@chadbourne.com. *

SMITH, GEORGE CURTIS, judge; b. Columbus, Ohio, Aug. 8, 1935; s. George B. and Dorothy R. Smith; m. Barbara Jean Wood, July 10, 1963; children: Curtis, Geoffrey, Elizabeth Ann. BA, Ohio State U., 1957, JD, 1959. Bar: Ohio 1959, U.S. Dist. Ct. (so. dist.) Ohio 1987. Asst. city atty. City of Columbus, 1959-62; exec. asst. to Mayor of Columbus, 1962-63; asst. atty. gen. State of Ohio, 1964; chief counsel to pros. atty. Franklin County, Ohio, 1965-70; pros. atty., 1971-80; judge Franklin County Mcpl. Ct., Columbus, 1980-85, Franklin County Common Pleas Ct., 1985-87; sr. judge U.S. Dist. Ct., 2002—. Mem. 2003 Ohio Bicentennial Com.; mem. Historical Marker com., 2003; mem. Ohio Supreme Ct. Coun. on Victims Rights; judge in residence Law Sch. U. Cin.; chair Fed. Ct. Case Settlement Seminar; faculty Ohio Jud. Coll., Litig. Practice Inst.; chmn., Fed. Bench-Bar Conf.; lectr. ABA Anti-Trust Sec.; alumni spkr. law graduation Moritz Coll. Law, Ohio State U.; pres. Young Rep. Club; chmn. Perry Group, 2005; exec. com. Franklin County Rep. Party, 1971-80 Elder Presbyn. Ch. Recipient Superior Jud. Svc. award Supreme Ct. Ohio, Outstanding Pub. Svc. award Fr. Co. Rep. Orgn., 2001, Judge W.K. Thomas award Ohio State U. Law Alumni, 2005, Disting. Jurist, 2006, Ohio Pros. of Yr. award Ohio Pros. Attys. Assn., 1976, Hon. Leadership award, 1977. Mem. Columbus Bar Assn., Columbus Bar Found., Columbus Athletic Club (pres. 1980, dir.), Lawyers Club of Columbus (pres. 1975), Masons (pres. 33d assn.), Shriners, Gyro Club (pres. 2003), Putin Bay Yacht Club (commodore 2007). Office: 85 Marconi Blvd Columbus OH 43215-2823 Office Phone: 614-719-3220.

SMITH, GEORGE DRURY, publishing executive; b. Dayton, Ohio, Mar. 10, 1927; s. Martin Jefferson and Viola (Haas) Smith; m. Anne Liard Jennings, Apr. 1967 (div. 1977); life ptnr. Leston Chandler Buell, 1996. AB cum laude, Marietta Coll., 1953; Diplome de Phonetique, U. Grenoble, 1950; student, U. Madrid, 1950-51, Heidelberg U., 1951-52, U. Minn., 1953-55, U. Calif.-Berkeley, 1965, UCLA, 1968. CFO Argonaut newspaper, 1972—. Editor: Beyond Baroque, 1968—80, NewLetters, 1969—75, NewBooks, 1976—78. Founder Beyond Baroque Found., Venice, Calif., 1968, chmn., 1968—80, chmn. emeritus, 1980—; active Mcpl. Arts Adv. Bd., LA, 1980—82; chmn. Save Westminster Auditorium Com., Venice, 1977—80. With US Army, 1945—47. Grantee, Nat. Endowment Arts, 1973—80, Calif. Arts coun., 1977—80, Mcpl. Arts Commn., 1977—80, Coordinating Coun. Lit. Mags., 1974—80. Home Fax: 323-443-3808. Personal E-mail: georgedrurysmith@yahoo.com. *I believe that if we have faith we can live without fear; that the universe is benevolent if we can love unconditionally; that we can live righteously and prosper if we are honest and seek divine guidance; and that our mission is to enjoy life and strive for beauty.*

SMITH, GEORGE FLOYD, medical educator; b. St. Paul, Dec. 13, 1947; s. George Floyd and Dorothy Charlene (Tator) Smith; m. Christine Ruth Meyer, June 7, 1972; children: Randall, Ryan, Kathryn. BA, Macalester Coll., St. Paul, 1969; MS, MD, U. Minn., Mpls., 1972. Physician Eastside Med. Ctr., St. Paul, 1975—2000; tchr. medicine U. Minn., Mpls., 2000—. Contbr. articles to profl. jours. Presbyterian. Office: 1414 Maryland Ave E Saint Paul MN 55106

SMITH, GEORGE PATRICK, II, lawyer, educator; b. Wabash, Ind., Sept. 1, 1939; s. George Patrick and Marie Louise (Barrett) S. BS, Ind. U., 1961, JD, 1964; certificate, Hague Acad. Internat. Law, 1965; LLM, Columbia U., 1975; LLD, Ind. U., 1998. Bar: Ind. 1964, U.S. Supreme Ct. 1968. Kannert teaching fellow Ind. U. Sch. Law, 1964-65; instr. law U. Mich. Sch. Law, 1965-66; practiced in Ind. and Washington, 1965—; legal adviser Fgn. Claims Settlement Commn., Dept. State, Washington, 1966; asst. prof., asst. dean State U. N.Y. at Buffalo Law Sch., 1967-69; vis. asst. prof. law George Washington U., Nat. Law Center, summer 1968; assoc. prof. law U. Ark., 1969-71; spl. counsel EPA, Washington, 1971-74; adj. prof. law Cath. U. Law Sch., Washington, 1973-74, prof., 1977—. Spl. counselor environl. affairs Gov. Ark., 1969—71; mem. Ark. Waterway Commn., 1970—71; mem. com. hwy. rsch. NRC, NAS, 1971—81; adj. prof. law Georgetown U., 1971—75; assoc. prof. law U. Pitts., 1975—78; vis. prof. U. New South Wales, Australia, 2001, U. Sydney, Australia, 2003, others; disting. vis. prof. Macquarie U., Sydney, 2005; cons., lectr. in field. Author: Restricting the Concept of Free Seas, 1980, Legal, Ethical and Social Issues of the Brave New World, 1980, Genetics, Ethics and the Law, 1981, Medical-Legal Aspects of Cryonics, 1983, The New Biology, 1989, Final Choices: Autonomy in Health Care Decisions, 1989, Bioethics and the Law, 1993, Legal and Healthcare Ethics for the Elderly, 1996, Family Values and the New Society: Dilemmas of the 21st Century, 1998; Human Rights and BioMedicine, 2000, The Christian Religion and Biotechnology, 2005 (nominated Pulitzer prize, 2005); contbr. articles to profl. jours. U. Ark. del. Pacem In Maribus Conf., Malta, 1970. Recipient Disting. Alumni award Ind. U. Bd. Trustees, 1985, citation for Path-Breaking Work; vis. fellow Law Sch. Fordham U., 1999, fellow Emmanuel Coll. Cambridge (England) U., 1999, vis. fellow Program Law and Pub. Health Johns Hopkins U., Washington, 2001—2002; vis. fellow Australioan Inst. Ethics and Professions U. Queensland, Brisbane, Australia, 2003, vis. fellow Inst. Health Law Loyola U., Chgo., 2004, vis. fellow Ctr. Interdisciplinary Study Religion Emory U., Atlanta, 2005, vis. fellow U. Ctr. Law, Ethics and Health, U. Mich., Ann Arbor, 2007; vis. scholar Ctr. Clin. Bioethics Georgetown U., Washington, 1998—1999, vis. scholar Ctr. Theology and Natural Scis. U. Calif., Berkeley, 1999, vis. scholar Ctr. Study Sci. and Religion Columbia U., 2002, vis. scholar Reily Ctr. Sci., Tech. and Values Notre Dame U., 2002, vis. scholar Law Sch. Cardiff (Wales) U., 2002, vis. scholar Ctr. Ethics in Culture, 2003, vis. scholar Inst. Spirituality and Health George Washington U., 2006, vis. scholar Ctr. for the Study of Religion and Politics U. St. Andrews, Scotland, 2006, vis. fellow Rothermere Am. Inst. Oxford U., England, 2006, vis. scholar The Hastings Ctr., NY, 2006, vis. scholar Inst. Ethics, AMA, 2006; establishment of George P. Smith II Disting. Professorship of Law, Ind. U., Bloomington, 1986; inducted Ind. U. Acad. Law Alumni Fellows, 2007. Mem. ABA (rep. UN Conf. on Human Environ., Stockholm 1972, rep. Law of Sea Conf., UN, N.Y.C. 1976, Switzerland 1979, cons. UNESCO Declaration on the Production of the Protection of the Human Genome, Paris 1995-97), Am. Law Inst., Soc. Ind. Pioneers, Am. Friends of Cambridge U., Order of St. John Hospitaller, Alpha Kappa Psi, Phi Alpha Delta, Sigma Alpha Epsilon, Order of Omega. Clubs: Cosmos (Washington). Republican. Office Phone: 202-319-5140. Business E-Mail: smithg@law.edu. *Think big, work hard and, above all, have a dream: these are the simple guideposts for a fulfilling life.*

SMITH, GEORGE THORNEWELL, retired state supreme court justice; b. Camilla, Ga., Oct. 15, 1916; s. George C. and Rosa (Gray) S.; m. Eloise Taylor, Sept. 1, 1943 (dec.). Grad., Abraham Baldwin Agrl. Coll., 1940; LLB, U. Ga., 1948. Bar: Ga. 1947. Assoc. Cain & Smith, Cairo, Ga., 1947-71; city atty. Cairo, 1949-58; atty. Grady County, 1950-59; solicitor Cairo City Ct., 1951-59; mem. Ga. Ho. of Reps., 1959-67, speaker of the house, 1963-67; lt. gov. State of Ga., 1967-71; city atty. East Point, Ga., 1973-76; judge Ga. Ct. Appeals, 1976-81; justice Ga. Supreme Ct., Atlanta, 1981-91, presiding justice, 1990-91; of counsel Browning & Smith LLC, Marietta, Ga., 1992—. Past mem. exec. com. Nat. Conf. Appellate Judges; vice chmn. Nat. Conf. Lt. Govs. Trustee Nat. Arthritis Found. Lt. comdr. USN, 1940-45. Only person in the state's history to serve in an elective capacity in all 3 brs. of govt. Mem. State Bar Ga., Cobb County Bar Assn., Lawyers Club Atlanta, Am. Legion, VFW, Moose, Kiwanis. Avocations: hunting, golf. Office: Browning & Smith 31 Atlanta St Ste 201 Marietta GA 30060 Home Phone: 770-516-7074; Office Phone: 770-424-1500.

SMITH, GEORGE VINAL, librarian; b. Chgo., May 14, 1943; s. Earl Wesley and Frances (Kenney) S.; m. Chrystal Jean Stillings, Jan. 29, 1966; children: Rebecca Tyson, Morgen Elizabeth. BA, Whitman Coll., 1965; MA, Wash. State U., 1967; PhD, No. Ill. U., 1974; MS, U. Ill., 1975. Reference libr. Illinet/U. Ill., Urbana, 1975-76; info. svcs. cons. Lincoln Trail Libr. System, Champaign, Ill., 1977-79; circulation and network svcs. supr. Oreg. State Libr., Salem, 1979-81, adminstr. of libr. devel., 1983-85; dir. Canby (Oreg.) Pub. Libr., 1981-82, Woodburn (Oreg.) Pub. Libr., 1982-83; dep. dir. Alaska State Div. of Librs., Archives and Mus., Juneau, Alaska, 1985—2002, acting dir., 2002—05; assoc. dep. dir. state programs Inst. of Mus. and Libr. Svcs., Washington, 2005—. Vol. Peace Corps, Thailand, 1967-69; vis. asst. prof. Grad. Sch. Libr. Sci., U. Ill., 1977-78; instr. Chemekata C.C., Salem, 1980-83, Marylhurst Coll., Lake Oswego, Oreg., 1982; course mentor Grad. Sch. Libr. Sci., U. Ariz., Juneau, Alaska, 1992-94; mem. State of Alaska Personnel Reinvention Com., 1996; Library Fellow to Bulgaria, US State Dept., 2000. Author: The Dutch in 17th-Century Thailand, 1977; co-editor and author: Contributions to Asian Studies, 15, 1980. Pres., bd. dirs., coach Juneau Soccer Club, 1992-94; dir., adminstrv. staff Arctic Winter Games/Team Alaska, Fairbanks, 1992-2005; coach, referee, referee trainer, Juneau Parks and Recreation Dept., 1986-2005; vol., patron Alaska Folk Festival, 1986—. NDEA fellow No. Ill. U., 1972-73; recipient Gov.'s Mgmt. Recognition award, Gov. Oreg., 1985. Mem. ALA (Libr. fellow to Nat. Libr. Cambodia 1994-95), Pacific N.W. Libr. Assn. (pres., v.p. 1987-89), Alaska Libr. Assn., Oreg. Libr. Assn. (pres., v.p. 1984-85). Avocations: fishing, hiking, backpacking, soccer coaching and refereeing. Office: Inst of Mus and Libr Svcs 1800 M St NW Washington DC 20036 Office Phone: 202-653-4650. E-mail: vinal2@verizon.net.

SMITH, GEORGE WOLFRAM, physicist, researcher; b. Des Plaines, Ill., Sept. 19, 1932; s. Murray Sawyer and Alice Lucile (Wolfram) S.; m. Mary Lee Sackett, Sept. 7, 1956; children: Dean, Grant. BA, Knox Coll., 1954; MA, Rice U., 1956, PhD, 1958. Welch Found. fellow Rice U., 1958-59; sr. rsch. physicist GM, Warren, Mich., 1959-76, dept. rsch. scientist, 1976-81, sr. staff rsch. scientist, 1981-87, prin. rsch. scientist, 1987-99; retired, 1999. Lectr. physics and astronomy Cranbrook Inst. Sci., Bloomfield Hills, Mich., 1963-87, mem. sci. adv. com., 1989—; instr. Lawrence Inst. Tech., 1963-65; vice chmn. Gordon Rsch. Conf. on Orientational Disorder in Crystals, 1976, chmn., 1978; co-chmn. Internat. Symposium on Particulate Carbon, 1980; mem. rev. com. Liquid Crystal Inst., Kent (Ohio) State U., 1984-85; mem. adv. com. Conf. on Electrorheological Fluids, 1991, 93; mem. adv. bd. NSF Sci. and Tech. Ctr. for Advanced Liquid Crystalline Optical Materials, 1996-00; physics co-chair Internat. Sci. and Engring. Fair, 2000; invited spkr. Ill. Assn. Physics Tchrs., 2003. Co-editor: Particulate Carbon: Formation During Combustion, 1981; editl. cons. Ency. Applied Physics, 1988-00; contbr. Handbook of Chemistry and Physics; contbr. 100 articles to sci. and tech. jours.; patentee on temperature measuring device, liquid crystal device tech., dielectric heating, graphite fiber growth, polymer-dispersed liquid crystals. Mem. Mich. Regtl. Civil War Roundtable, 1965—, pres., 1971-72. Recipient Knox Coll. Achievement award 1977, John M. Campbell Research award, 1980, Charles L. McCuen Achievement award, Gen. Motors, 1985. Fellow Am. Phys. Soc. (com. on applications of physics 1988-91, chmn. 1991, chmn. com. on tutorials 1991, mem. Pake Prize Com. 1993-94); mem. Soc. Info. Display (program com. 1990-93), Detroit Zool. Inst. (docent 2001-03, sr. docent 2003—), Am. Contract Bridge League, Phi Beta Kappa, Sigma Xi (chpt. pres. 1980-81), Phi Delta Theta, Alpha Delta. Home: 1882 Melbourne St Birmingham MI 48009-1163

SMITH, GERARD PETER, neuroscientist; b. Phila., Mar. 24, 1935; s. Stanley Alward and Agnes Marie (McLarney) S.; m. Barbara McInnis, May 12, 1962; children: Christopher, Mark, Hilary, Maura. BS, St. Joseph's U., Phila., 1956; MD, U. Pa., 1960; ScD (hon.), U. Camerino, Italy, 2002. Intern, resident N.Y. Hosp., 1960-62; with dept. neuroendocrinology Walter Reed Army Inst. Rsch., 1962—64; asst. prof. physiology U. Pa. Sch. Medicine, Phila., 1964-68; from asst. to assoc. prof. Cornell U., NYC, 1968—, prof. psychiatry (behavioral neurosci.), 1973—. Vis. prof. MIT, 1973—74, Rockefeller U., 1979—80, adj. prof., 1982—86; cons. NIH; Curt Richter lectr. Johns Hopkins U., 1976; Leon lectr. U. Pa., 1990, Stellar lectr., 93; Rushton lectr. Fla. State U., 1992; Merck, Sharpe, and Dohm prof. neurosci. U. Flinder, Australia, 1992; Loucks lectr. U. Wash., 1995; dir. Eating Disorders Inst. N.Y. Hosp.-Cornell Med. Ctr., 1984—88. Recipient Rsch. Scientist, USPHS, 1982; grantee, NIH. Mem. AAAS, Am. Physiol. Soc., Soc. for Study Ingestive Behavior (pres., Disting. Career award 2004), Internat. Behavioral Neurosci. Soc. (pres., Myers Lifetime Achievement award 2001), Alpha Omega Alpha, Alpha Sigma Nu. Office: NY Presbyn Hosp Westchester Divsn 21 Bloomingdale Rd White Plains NY 10605-1504 Office Phone: 914-682-9100 x 2666. Business E-Mail: gpsmith@med.cornell.edu.

SMITH, G(ODFREY) T(AYLOR), college president; b. Newton, Miss., Nov. 12, 1935; s. Taylor and Edna (Blanton) S.; m. Joni Eaton, Sept. 1, 1956; children: Paul Brian, Sherry Lynn. BA, Coll. of Wooster, 1956; MPA with distinction, Cornell U., 1960; LLD (hon.), Bethany Coll., 1979. Assoc. dir. devel. Cornell U., Ithaca, NY, 1960-62; dir. devel. Coll. Wooster, Ohio, 1962-66, v.p., 1966-77; pres. Chapman U., Orange, Calif., 1977-88, pres. emeritus, 1988—; exec. dir. Talaris Rsch. Inst., Seattle, 2001—03; pres. Bethany Coll., Bethany, W.Va., 2004—. Lectr. in field. Contbr. numerous articles to profl. publs. Bd. dirs. Wayne County (Ohio) Indsl. Devel. Corp., 1966-72, World Affairs Coun. Orange Coun., Calif., 1978-89, Orange County chpt. NCCJ, 1979-86, Orange County coun. Boy Scouts Am., 1980-85, Coun. Ind. Colls., 1985-87; bd. dirs. div. higher edn. Christian Ch. (Disciples of Christ), 1980-86, chmn., 1984-86; bd. dirs., mem. exec. com. Ind. Colls. So. Calif., 1979-88, pres., 1981-82; mem. exec. com. Assn. Ind. Calif. Colls. and Univs., 1980-88, treas., 1982-87. Recipient William A. Galpin prize The Coll. Wooster, 1956, Steuben Apple award for tchg. excellence Coun. for Advancement and Support Edn., 1984, Disting. Alumnus award Coll. of Wooster, 1991, Faith and Reason award Christian Ch. (Disciples of Christ), 1993, Laureate award for Lifetime Achievement Inst. for Charitable Giving, 1997; Smith Hall dedicated at Chapman U., 1988; Alfred P. Sloan fellow Cornell U., 1960. Presbyn. Home: PO Drawer S Bethany WV 26032 Office: Bethany Coll 110 Old Main Bethany WV 26032 Office Phone: 304-829-7111. Business E-Mail: buck@bethanywv.edu. *If we treat people as they are, they will stay as they are. But if we treat them for what they might be and might become, they will become those better selves.*

SMITH, GOFF, industrial equipment manufacturing executive; b. Jackson, Tenn., Oct. 7, 1916; s. Fred Thomas and Mabel (Goff) S.; m. Nancy Dall, Nov. 28, 1942 (dec. 1972); children: Goff Thomas, Susan Knight; m. Harriet Schneider Oliver, June 23, 1973 (dec. 1998). BSE, U. Mich., 1938, MBA, 1939; MS, MIT, 1953. Trainee Bucyrus Erie, South Milwaukee, Wis., 1939-40; mem. sales staff Amsted Industries, Chgo. and NYC, 1946-55, subsidiary pres. Chgo., 1955-60, v.p., 1960-69, pres., dir., 1969-74, pres., CEO, dir., 1974-80, chmn., 1980-82. Pres. Village of Winnetka, Ill., 1967—69; pres., bd. dirs. United Way Chgo., 1976—85; bd. dirs. Rehab. Inst., Chgo., 1979—99, Chgo. Theol. Sem., 1979—99, Presbyn. Home, Evanston, Ill., 1979—2005. Maj. US Army. Sloan Fellow MIT, 1952-53. Republican. Avocations: hunting, fishing, golf. Office Phone: 847-446-5756.

SMITH, GORDON A., bank executive; Mgmt. positions through sr. v.p. Am. Express Co., 1978—2000, exec. v.p. svc. del., 2000—01; pres. consumer card services Am. Express Travel Related Services, 2001—05, pres., global comml. card group, 2005—07; CEO cardmember services JP Morgan Chase, NYC, 2007—. Bd. dir. Choice Hotels Internat. Office: JP Morgan Chase 270 Park Ave New York NY 10017-2070 *

SMITH, GORDON EUGENE, pilot; b. Corpus Christi, Tex., Nov. 22, 1953; s. Orvis Alvin and Helen Lucille (Lockhart) A.; m. Crisanta Lacson Oqueriza, Jan. 5, 1979; children: Pia Marie, Helena Irita. AAS in Electronics, Riverside City Coll., 1985; BSEE, Calif. Polytech., 1987. Electronics technician Lear Siegler, Inc., Ontario, Calif., 1981-86, Rockwell Internat., Palmdale, Calif., 1986-87; pilot Orion Air Inc., Raleigh, NC, 1987-90; pilot, dir. maintenance, asst. dir. ops. Nat. Air, Riverside, Calif., 1990-93; pilot MGM Grand Air, 1993—96, Sun Pacific Internat., Tucson, 1996-99, Sunworld Internat., Cin., 1999—2002, Aramco, Houston, 2002—04, Custom Air Transport, Ft. Lauderdale, 2004—06, So. Air, Inc., Norwalk, Conn., 2006—. With USAF, 1972-79, with USAFR 1979-2005. Mem. Aircraft Owners and Pilots Assn., Team One (v.p. 1980—). Republican. Dunkard Brethren. Avocations: flying, golf, bowling, baseball, computers. Office: Southern Air Inc 117 Glover Ave Norwalk CT 06850 Personal E-mail: zsparkman@hotmail.com.

SMITH, GORDON H., civil and forensic engineer, consultant; b. NYC, Mar. 17, 1936; s. Henry and Theodora (Augenstern) S.; m. Norma Kaplan, Feb. 28, 1960; children: Randy Smith Aberg, Robin Smith. B in Engring., Yale U., 1957. Registered profl. engr., Mich., NY, Fla. V.p., chief engr. Albro Metal Products Corp., NYC, 1957-69, pres., 1969-75, Gordon H. Smith Corp., NYC, 1975—, Gordon H. Smith PE, PC, NYC, 1998—. Guest lectr. Yale U. Sch. Arch., MIT, Am. Inst. Archs., Constrn. Specification Inst., Nat. Glass Assn., Glass Assn. N.Am.; protective glazing coun. N.Y. Inst. Tech. Contbr. articles to Archtl. Record, Progressive Arch., ASTM, Chgo. High Rise Com. Mem. NSPE, ASTM, ASCE, AIA (Inst. Honors 1994, 2003), Nat. Assn. Archtl. Metal Mfrs. (v.p., pres., bd. dirs.), Archtl. Aluminum Mfrs. Assn. (v.p., bd. dirs.), Nat. Assn. Miscellaneous, Ornamental and Archtl. Metal Mfrs. (bd. dirs.), Constrn. Specifications Inst. Office: Gordon H Smith Corp 200 Madison Ave New York NY 10016-3903 Home Phone: 212-879-9004. Business E-Mail: ghsmith@gordonhsmithcorp.com.

SMITH, GORDON HAROLD, senator; b. Pendleton, Oreg., May 25, 1952; s. Milan Dale and Jessica (Udall) S.; m. Sharon Lankford; children: Brittany, Garrett (dec.), Morgan. BA in History, Brigham Young U., 1976; LLB, Southwestern U., 1979. Law clk. to Justice H. Vernon Payne N.Mex. Supreme Ct.; pvt. practice Ariz.; pres., CEO Smith Frozen Foods, 1981—97; mem. Oreg. State Senate, 1992-95, pres., 1995-96; US Senator from Oreg., 1997—. Mem. com. Indian affairs US Senate, com. fin., com. energy and natural resources, com. commerce, sci. and transp., commn.

security and cooperation in Europe; mem. Presdl. Adv. Commn. Holocaust Assets in US. Author: Remembering Garrett: One Family's Battle with a Child's Depression, 2006. Recipient Torch of Liberty award, Nat. Conf. Soviet Jewry, 2001, Cmty. Health Defender award, Nat. Assn. Cmty. Health Centers, 2003, Homeownership Hero award, Homeownership Alliance, 2004. Republican. Lds Ch. Office: US Senate 404 Russell Senate Off Bldg Washington DC 20510-0001 also: Jager Bldg Ste 3 116 South Main St Pendleton OR 97801 Office Phone: 202-224-3753, 541-278-1129. Office Fax: 202-228-3997, 541-278-4109. *

SMITH, GORDON PAUL, management consultant; b. Salem, Mass., Dec. 25, 1916; s. Gordon and May (Vaughan) S.; m. Daphne Miller, Nov. 23, 1943 (div. 1968); m. Ramona Chamberlain, Sept. 27, 1969; children: Randall B., Roderick F. BS in Mgmt., U. Mass., 1947; MS in Govt. Mgmt, U. Denver, 1948; postgrad. in polit. sci, NYU, 1948-50; DHL (hon.), Monterey Inst. Internat. Studies, 1994. With Econ. Rsch. Tax Found., Inc., NYC, 1948—51, Booz, Allen & Hamilton, 1951-70, partner San Francisco, 1959-62, v.p., 1962-67, mng. ptnr. Western U.S., 1968-70; ptnr. Harrod, Williams and Smith, San Francisco, 1962—69; dir. fin. State of Calif., Calif., 1967—68; pres. Gordon Paul Smith & Co., Mgmt. Cons., 1968—; pres., CEO Golconda Corp., 1972—74, chmn. bd., 1974-85. Pres. Cermetek Corp., 1978-80; adviser task force def. procurement and contracting Hoover Commn., 1954-55; spl. asst. to pres. Republic Aviation Corp., 1954-55; cons., Hawaii, 1960-61, Alaska, 1963; cons. Wash. Hwy. Adminstrn., 1964, Am. Baseball League and Calif. Angels, 1960-62, others; bd. dirs. Monterey Coll. Law; chmn. Ft. Ord Econ. Devel. Adv. Group, 1991; chmn. Coalition on Rsch. and Edn., 1993—97; spkr. in field. Contbr. articles to profl. jours. Mem. Calif. Select Com. on Master Plan for Edn., 1971—73; mem. alumni coun. U. Mass., 1950—54, bd. dirs. alumni ass., 1964—70; chmn. West Coast Cancer Found., 1976—87, Coalition Rsch. and Edn., 1993—, Jim Tunney Youth Found., 1994—; trustee, chmn. Monterey Inst. Internat. Studies, 1978—92, trustee emeritus, 1995—; trustee Northfield Mt. Hermon Sch., 1983—93, Robert Louis Stevenson Sch., 1993—; mem. devel. coun. Cmty. Hosp. of Monterey Peninsula, 1983—84; sr. advisor Pres. Calif. State U., Monterey, Calif., 1998—; mem. 15 bds. and commns. State of Calif., 1967—72; bd. dirs. Alumni Assn. Mt. Hermon Prep. Sch., 1963; bd. dirs. Stanford Med. Ctr., 1960—62, pres., chmn., 1962—66; bd. dirs. Friends of the Performing Arts, 1985—, Monterey County Symphony Orch., 1991—96, Monterey Bay Futures Project, 1992—, Ctr. for Nonproliferation of Weapons of Mass Destruction, 1998—, Calif. Inst. for Local Self Govt., 2000—. Recipient spl. commendation Hoover Commn., 1955, Alumni of Yr. award U. Mass., 1963, Trustee of Yr. award Monterey-Peninsula, 1991, Monterey-Peninsula Outstanding Citizen of Yr. award, 1992, Laura Bride Powers Heritage award, 1991, U.S. Congl. award, 1992, Calif. Senate and Assembly Outstanding Citizen award, 1992, Wisdom award of honor Wisdom Soc., 1992; permanent Gordon Paul Smith Disting. Chair for Internat. Studies established at Monterey Inst. Internat. Studies; named Gordon Paul Smith Scholarship Fund in his honor Northfield Mt. Hermon Sch.and Robert Louis Stevenson Sch.; named to Honorable Order of Ky. Cols. Mem. Monterey History and Art Assn. (bd. dirs. 1987-92, pres. 1985-87, chmn. 1987-92, hon. lifetime dir. 1992—), The Stanton Heritage Ctr. (chmn. 1987-92, chmn. emeritus 1992—), Salvation Army (bd. dirs., chmn. hon. cabinet), Monterey Peninsula Mus. Art, Carmel Valley (Calif.) Country Club, Monterey Peninsula Country Club, Old Capitol Club, Edgartown Yacht Club. Home: 253 Del Mesa Carmel CA 93923 Personal E-mail: gp1225@aol.com. *If the quest for personal success is only for an accumulation of prestige, power or wealth, then personal failure will be assured. Genuine personal success can surely be found, however, through a significant and lasting contribution toward helping the progress of others and raising the human worth. This is the true mark of leadership.*

SMITH, GRANT WILLIAM, language educator, volunteer; b. Bellingham, Wash., July 26, 1937; s. George Whitfield and Hazel (Speirs) S.; m. Lelia Dickinson, June 9, 1961; children: Kathryn, Gavin. BA, Reed Coll., 1964; MA, U. Nev., 1966; PhD, U. Del., 1975. Asst. prof. Eastern Wash. U., Cheney, 1968-76, assoc. prof., 1976-79, prof., 1979—. Faculty pres. Eastern Wash. U., Cheney, 1976-77, chair English dept., 1978-84, acting vice provost, 1987-88, coord. humanities, 1979—, dir. cultural outreach, 1995-97; host Pub. TV, Here's Shakespeare, 1980, 81; mem. Wash. Bd. Geog. Names, 1987—; guest editor: NAMES, 1989, ONOMA; dissertation rsch. advisor Mukogawa Women's U., Japan, 2007—. Editor Procs. of Am. Name Soc., 1997, 98, 99; contbr. articles to profl. jours. and conf. procs. Chair devel. Spokane Symphony, 2000—01; program chair Coun. Geo. Names Authorities, 1999; moderator Cheney United Ch. of Christ, 1982—84. With US Army, 1957—60. Grantee U.S. Geol. Survey, State Humanities Commn., NEH; Fulbright faculty assoc., 2005-06. Mem. MLA, AAUP, Placename Survey U.S. (chair 1990—), Connoisseur Concerts Assn. (pres. 1992-95), Am. Dialect Soc. (regional sec. 1982-98), Rocky Mountain MLA (program chair 1987, 95), Internat. Coun. Onomastic Scientists (exec. bd. dirs. 1999—, v.p. 2002—, editl. bd. ONOMA 2000—), Internat. Soc. Dialectology and Geolinguistics, Am. Name Soc. (v.p. 1996-98, pres. 1999-2001). Avocations: jogging, reading, singing. Home: 905 Gary St Cheney WA 99004-1341 Address: Eastern Wash Univ 250 Patterson Hall Dept of English Cheney WA 99004-2430 Office Phone: 509-359-6023. E-mail: gsmith@ewu.edu.

SMITH, GREGORY ALLGIRE, academic administrator; b. Washington, Mar. 31, 1951; s. Donald Eugene and Mary Elizabeth Smith; m. Susan Elizabeth Watts, Oct. 31, 1980; 1 child, David Joseph Smith-Watts. BA, Johns Hopkins U., 1972; MA, Williams Coll., 1974. Adminstrv. asst. Washington Project for Arts, 1975; intern Walker Art Ctr., Mpls., 1975—76; asst. devel. officer Sci. Mus. Minn., St. Paul, 1977; asst. dir. Akron Art Inst., Ohio, 1977—80; asst. to dir. Toledo Mus. Art, 1980—82, asst. dir. adminstrn., 1982—86; exec. v.p. Internat. Exhbns. Found., Washington, 1986—87; dir. Telfair Mus. Art, Savannah, Ga., 1987—94, Art Acad. Cin., 1994—98, pres., 1998—. Trustee Greater Cin. Consortium of Colls. and Univs., vice chmn., 2001—03, chmn., 2003—05; trustee Assn. Ind. Colls. of Art and Design; grad. Leadership Savanah, 1990—92, Leadership Cin., 2003—04. Mem.: Coll. Art Assn., Ohio Found. on the Arts (v.p. 1981—83, trustee 1981—84), Assn. Art Mus. Adminstrs. (founder 1984—85), Am. Assn. Mus., Rotary (dir. Cin. club 2000—01, sec.-treas. 2001—02, pres. 2002—03), Univ. Club. Avocation: collecting arts and crafts movement objects, landscape design, gardening. Home: 8380 Springvalley Dr Cincinnati OH 45236-1356 Office: Art Academy Of Cincinnati 1212 Jackson St Cincinnati OH 45202-7106 Office Phone: 513-562-8743. E-mail: gasmith@artacademy.edu.

SMITH, GREGORY C., lawyer; b. Salt Lake City, 1963; BA with distinction, Stanford U., 1985; JD Harlan Fiske Stone Scholar, Columbia Law School, 1988. Bar: Calif. 1988. Ptnr. Skadden, Arps, Slate, Meagher & Flom LLP. Contbg. author, gen. editor Start-up and Emerging Companies, 2004. Dir. Friends of Music, Stanford U. Named one of The World's Leading Lawyers Bus., Chambers Global, 2002—04, 2004—05, Am.'s Leading Bus. Lawyers, Chambers USA, 2004—05. Mem.: Phi Beta Kappa. Office: Skadden 525 University Avenue Suite 1100 Palo Alto CA 94301 Office Phone: 650-470-4590.

SMITH, GRIFFIN, JR., executive editor; b. Fayetteville, Ark., June 29, 1941; s. Griffin and Mildred Smith; m. Mary Elizabeth Routh, Sept. 1, 1979. BA in History, Rice U., 1963; MA in Polit. Sci., Columbia U., 1965; postgrad. in philosophy, Oxford U., 1966; JD, U. Tex., 1969. Bar: Tex. 1969, US Dist. Ct. (ea., we., no. and so. dists.) Tex. 1969, Ark. 1981, US Dist. Ct. (ea. and we. dists.) Ark. 1981. Spl. asst. to Senator Fulbright US Senate, Washington, 1968-69; atty. estate and gift tax div. IRS, Houston, 1970; rsch. dir. Tex. gubernatorial campaign Paul Eggers, 1970; chief counsel constl. amendments com. Tex. Senate, 1971, chief counsel drug law reform com., 1971-73; editor natural areas survey Lyndon B. Johnson Sch. Pub. Affairs U. Tex., Austin, 1973-77; sr. editor Tex. Monthly mag., 1973—77; speech writer Pres. of US, 1977-78; ptnr. Smith & Nixon (formerly Smith, Smith, Nixon & Duke), Little Rock, 1984-92; exec. editor Ark. Democrat-Gazette, Little Rock, 1992—. Author: (book) A Consumer Viewpoint on Taxation, 1971, Marijuana in Texas, 1972, The Best of Texas Monthly, 1978, Texas Monthly's Political Reader, 1978, 1980, Journey into China, 1982, Forgotten Texas: A Wilderness Portfolio, 1983, The Great State of Texas, 1985. Recipient Disting. Alumni award, Rice U., 1999; fellow Woodrow Wilson, 1964. Mem.: Tex. Inst. Letters (award for best work of journalism in Tex. 1974, 1976), State Bar Tex., Ark. Episcopalian-Reformed. Office: Ark Democrat-Gazette 121 E Capitol Ave Little Rock AR 72201-3819 also: Ark Democrat-Gazette PO Box 2221 Little Rock AR 72203 Office Phone: 501-399-3610.

SMITH, GROVER C(LEVELAND), language educator; b. Atlanta, Sept. 6, 1923; s. Grover C. and Lillian Julia (McDaniel) S.; m. Phyllis Jean Snyder, June 19, 1948 (div. 1965); children: Alice Elizabeth, Charles Grover; m. Dulcie Barbara Soper, Dec. 29, 1965; children: Stephen Kenneth, Julia Margaret. BA with honors, Columbia U., 1944, MA, 1945, PhD, 1950. Instr. English Rutgers U., 1946-48, Yale U., 1948-52, Duke U., 1952-55, asst. prof., 1955-61, assoc. prof., 1961-66, prof., 1966-93, prof. emeritus, 1993—. Mem. summer faculty CUNY, 1946, 47, 48, Columbia U., 1963, 64, NYU, 1963, Wake Forest U., 1966, vis. lectr., 1963, 64; instr. coll. entrance exam bd. Summer Inst. Commn. on English, 1962. Author: The Poems of T.S. Eliot 1909-1928: A Study in Symbols and Sources, 1950, T.S. Eliot's Poetry and Plays: A Study in Sources and Meaning, 1956 (Poetry Chapbook award) rev. edit., 1974, Archibald MacLeish, 1971, Ford Madox Ford, 1972, The Waste Land, 1983, T.S. Eliot and the Use of Memory, 1996; editor: Josiah Royce's Seminar, 1913-1914: As Recorded in the Notebooks of Harry T. Costello, 1963, Letters of Aldous Huxley, 1969. Mem. Christian Gauss Award com., 1973-75; mem. com. of sponsors Sir Julian Huxley Tribute, NY Soc. for Ethical Culture, 1975. With U.S. Army, 1943. Alexander M. Proudfit fellow Columbia U., 1945-46; Guggenheim fellow, 1958; Am. Philos. Soc. grantee, 1965; Am. Learned Socs. grantee, 1965; NEH grantee, 1979, fellow, 1980. Mem. T.S. Eliot Soc. (hon., Eliot Meml. Lectr. 1986, bd. dirs. 1986-94, 96-99, v.p. 1986-88, editor News and Notes, 1987-88, 90-91, pres. 1989-91, supr. elections 1992-94, sec. 1996-99), Am. Lit. Assn. (rep. to coun.of Am. Author Socs. 1990-91), Nat. Assn. Scholars. Home: 2 Silver Maple Ct Durham NC 27705-5642

SMITH, H. MORGAN, environmental scientist, educator; b. Orlando, Fla., Dec. 31, 1926; s. Claude Earle Smith and Pearl Adelaide Morgan; m. Marjori Blank (div. 1962); m. Charles V. Smith. BS in Anthropology, Fla. State U., 1953; postgrad., U. Ala., Troy State U.; PhD (hon.), U. Peru, Iquitos, 2002. Prof. environ. sci. State of Ala., U. USAF; rsch. scientist, tchr., adminstr. fed. svc.; ret., 1981. Lectr. univs., schs., profl. and civic groups; conductor security, survival tng. people, India, Australia, Europe, and US, 2001—; tchr. rainforest ecology workshops ethnobotany, Peruvian Amazon, Panama; vol. prof. environ. sci. Selwyn Sch., Denton, Tex. Author (editor) numerous pubs.; scriptwriter (5 major ednl. videos cross-cultural comm. and emergency survival). Decorated WWII Asia Pacific Combat medal. Home Phone: 940-891-1133; Office Phone: 940-891-1133. Business E-Mail: vieje7@charter.net.

SMITH, HAMILTON OTHANEL, molecular biologist, educator; b. NYC, Aug. 23, 1931; s. Bunnie Othanel and Tommie Harkey S.; m. Elizabeth Anne Bolton, May 25, 1957; children: Joel, Barry, Dirk, Bryan, Kirsten. Student, U. Ill., 1948-50; AB in Math, U. Calif., Berkeley, 1952; MD, Johns Hopkins U., 1956. Intern Barnes Hosp., St. Louis, 1956-57; resident in medicine Henry Ford Hosp., Detroit, 1959-62; USPHS fellow dept. human genetics U. Mich., Ann Arbor, 1962-64, rsch. assoc., 1964-67; asst. prof. molecular biology and genetics Sch. Medicine Johns Hopkins U., Balt., 1967-69, assoc. prof., 1969-73, prof., 1973—, emeritus prof. molecular biology and genetics; scientist Celera Genomics. Asso. Inst. für Molekularbologie der U. Zurich, Switzerland, 1975-76; assoc. Rsch. Inst. Molecular Pathology, Vienna, 1990-91; trustee The Inst. for Genomic Rsch. Contbr. articles to profl. jours. Served to lt. M.C. USNR, 1957-59. Recipient Nobel prize in physiology or medicine, 1978; Guggenheim fellow, 1975-76. Mem. Am. Soc. Microbiology, AAAS, Am. Soc. Biol. Chemists, Nat. Acad. Sci.

SMITH, HARMON LEE, JR., clergyman, theology studies educator; b. Ellisville, Miss., Aug. 23, 1930; s. Harmon Lee Sr. and Mary (O'Donnell) S.; children: Pamela Lee, Amy Joanna, Harmon Lee III. AB, Millsaps Coll., 1952; BD, Duke U., 1955, PhD, 1962. Ordain to priest Episcopal Ch., 1972. Asst. dean Duke U. Divinity Sch., Durham, NC, 1959-65, asst. prof. Christian ethics, 1962-68, assoc. prof. moral theology, 1968-73, prof. moral theology, 1973-99, prof. community and family medicine, 1974-99, ret., 1999, prof. emeritus moral theology and cmty. family medicine. Cons. med. ethics; vis. prof. U. N.C., 1964, 70, 72, U. Edinburgh, Scotland, 1969, U. Windsor, Ont., 1974 Author books on Christian theology, ethics and med. ethics; sr. editor Social Science and Medicine, 1973-89; contbr. articles on Christian ethics to various publs. Lilly Found. fellow, 1960; Gurney Harris Kearns Found. fellow, 1961; Nat. Humanities Ctr. fellow, 1982-83 Mem. Am. Assn. Theol. Schs., Am. Soc. Christian Ethics, Am. Acad. Religion, Soc. for Religion in Higher Edn., Soc. Health and Human Values. Home: 3510 Randolph Rd Durham NC 27705-5347 E-mail: orare@aol.com.

SMITH, HAROLD B., manufacturing executive; b. Chgo., Apr. 7, 1933; s. Harold Byron and Pauline (Hart) S. Grad., Choate Sch., 1951; BS, Princeton U., 1955; MBA, Northwestern U., 1957. With Ill. Tool Works Inc., Chgo., 1954—, exec. v.p., 1968-72, pres., 1972-81, vice chmn., 1981, chmn. exec. com., 1982—, also bd. dirs. Bd. dirs. W.W. Grainger, Inc., No. Trust Corp Mem. Rep. Nat. Com., 1976-99; chmn. Ill. Rep. Com., 1993-99; del. Rep. Nat. Conv., 1964, 76, 88, 92, 96, 2000, 04; bd. dirs. Adler Planetarium, Boys and Girls Clubs Am., Northwestern U., Rush U. Med. Ctr., Newberry Libr. Mem.: Chicago, Commercial, Commonwealth, Economic, Northwestern, Princeton (Chgo.). Office: Ill Tool Works Inc 3600 W Lake Ave Glenview IL 60026-1215

SMITH, HAROLD CHARLES, pension fund administrator; b. NYC, Jan. 11, 1934; s. Harold Elmore and Hedwig Agnes (Gronke) S. BA cum laude with honors, Ursinus Coll., 1955; MBA, NYU, 1958; M in Div., Union Theol. Sem., NYC, 1958; DD (hon.), 1993; DD (hon.), Ursinus Coll., 1997; DHum (hon.), Springfield Coll., 1998. CFA; ordained minister United Ch. Christ, 1959. V.p. YMCA Retirement Fund, Inc., NYC, 1958-69, portfolio mgr., 1960—, assoc. sec., 1969-77, v.p., 1977-80, exec. v.p., 1980-82, pres. elect, 1982-83, pres., 1983-2000; assoc. prof. bus. and fin. L.I. U., 1969-71. Trustee Bank Mart, Bridgeport, Conn., 1983-91; bd. dirs. Y Mut. Ins. Co., treas. 1988—. Author: Getting It All Together in Retirement, 1977. Trustee YWCA Greater Bridgeport, 1975—79, Pension Funds United Ch. of Christ, 1968—, Springfield Coll., Mass., 1983—, United Ch. Found., 1968—, vice chmn., 1995—98, chmn., 1998—99; chmn. bd. trustees NY State YMCA; pastor 1st E&R Ch., Bridgeport, Conn., 1958—88, Unity Hill United Ch. of Christ, 1988—2000, 1st Congl. Ch., Union, NJ, 2001—02, River Edge, NJ, 2002—03; treas. United H. Homes of N.J. Inc., 2001—; exec. coun. UCC, 2000—; bd. dirs. United Ch. Residencies, 1962—65, YMCA Greater N.Y., 2002—04, 1983—97, Bridgeport Area Found., 1989—2000, Ursinus Coll., Pa., 1994—, Coun. of Chs. Greater Bridgeport, 1995—96, Silver Bay Christian Conf. Ctr., 1997—2003. Mem. Am. Econs. Assn., N.Y. Soc. Security Analysts, Fin. Analysts Fedn., Masons, Order Ea. Star. Office Phone: 212-566-4452. Personal E-mail: hcsmith2@email.msn.com.

SMITH, H(AROLD) LAWRENCE, lawyer; b. Evergreen Pk., Ill., June 27, 1932; s. Harold Lawrence and Lorna Catherine (White) Smith; m. Madonna Jeanne Koehl, June 9, 1956 (div. 1968); children: Lawrence Kirby, Sandra Michele, Madonna Clare Galloway; m. Nancy Leigh Baum, May 2, 1970 (dec. 1983); m. Louise Fredericka Jeffrey, Nov. 2, 1984 (div. 1994); m. Marianne Lorraine Laug, Apr. 19, 1997. BS, US Naval Acad., 1956; JD, John Marshall Law Sch., 1965. Bar: Ill. 1965, Mich. 1986, U.S. Dist. Ct. (no. dist.) Ill. 1965, U.S. Ct. Appeals (7th cir.) 1967, U.S. Ct. of Customs and Patent Appeals, 1976, U.S. Ct. Appeals (fed. cir.) 1982, U.S. Patent and Trademark Office 1968. Asst. prof. naval sci. U. Notre Dame, 1960-61; tech. asst. Langner, Parry, Card & Langner, Chgo., 1961-65, assoc., 1965-69; patent atty. Borg-Warner Corp., Chgo., 1970-74; sr. patent atty. Continental Can Co., Inc., Chgo. and Oak Brook, Ill., 1974-82, asst. gen. counsel Stamford and Norwalk, Conn., 1982-86; ptnr. Varnum, Riddering, Schmidt & Howlett, Grand Rapids, Mich., 1986-96, counsel, 1996-97; ptnr. Rader, Fishman, Grauer & McGarry, Grand Rapids, 1997—2001; of counsel McGarry Bair LLP, Grand Rapids, 2001—03; cons., 2003—. Adj. prof. patent law Cooley Law Sch., 1991—. Served to lt. USN, 1956-61. Fellow Mich. State Bar Found.; mem. Intellectual Property Law Assn. Chgo., Chartered Inst. Patent Agts. (London 1971-2003), World Affairs Coun. Western Mich. (bd. dirs. 1996-2002, treas. 1998-2000. Office: 39533 Woodward Ave Ste 140 Bloomfield Hills MI 48304 Business E-Mail: hls@mcgarrybair.com.

SMITH, HARRISON HARVEY, journalism consultant; b. Wilkes-Barre, Pa., Oct. 24, 1915; s. Ernest Gray and Marjorie (Harvey) S.; m. Joanne Christopher, June 7, 1940 (div.); children: Barbara DeWitt, Marjorie Harvey, Susan C. (dec. 1999); m. Margaret Simons, July 18, 1947 (dec. May 1978); children: Rosanne Jameson, Elizabeth Simons; m. Dorothy Wright Welborn, June 22, 1989. Diploma in lit., Wyoming (Pa.) Sem., 1936; postgrad., Northwestern U., 1937-38. Asst. to pub. Wilkes-Barre Times-Leader, 1938-39, v.p., asst. sec., 1939-46, pres., 1946-79; editor Wilkes-Barre Record, 1962-72; newspaper cons. Key Biscayne, Fla., 1979—. Dir. emeritus 1st Ea. Bank Wilkes-Barre; pres. Pa. AP, 1953. Chmn. Wyoming Valley ARC, 1954-55; v.p. bd. dirs. Wilkes-Barre Gen. Hosp., 1954-76. With U.S. Army, 1945-46, Korea. Mem. Am. Soc. Newspaper Editors, Nat. Conf. Editl. Writers, Soc. Profl. Journalists, Pa. Newspaper Pubs. Assn. (mem. exec. com. 1954-62), Wyoming Valley Hist. Soc. (pres. 1971-74), Newcomen Soc., Am. Legion, VFW, Poor Richard Club (Phila.), Mirador Club (Geneva), Westmoreland Club, Sankaty Head Golf and Beach Club (Nantucket Island, Mass.), Country Club Coral Gables, Key Biscayne Yacht Club, Masons (33 degree). Republican. Presbyterian. Home (Summer): 10 Lyons Ln PO Box 180 Siasconset MA 02564-0180 Office Phone: 508-257-6177.

SMITH, HARVEY ALVIN, mathematics professor, consultant; b. Easton, Pa., Jan. 30, 1932; s. William Augustus and Ruth Carolyn (Krauth) S.; m. Ruth Wismer Kolb, Aug. 27, 1955; children: Deirdre Lynn, Kirsten Nadine, Brinton Averil. BS, Lehigh U., 1952; MS, U. Pa., 1955, AM, 1958, PhD, 1964. Asst. prof. math Drexel U., 1960-65; mem. tech. staff Inst. Def. Analyses, Arlington, Va., 1965-66; assoc. prof. math Oakland U., 1966-68; ops. rsch. scientist Exec. Office of Pres., Washington, 1968-70; prof. math. Oakland U., 1970-77; prof. Ariz. State U., Tempe, 1977—2003, prof. emeritus, 2003—. Cons. U.S. Army Security Agy., 1967—68, Inst. Def. Analyses, 1967—69, Exec. Office Pres., 1967—73, U.S. Arms Control and Disarmament Agy., 1973—79, Los Alamos Nat. Lab., 1980—93. Author: Mathematical Foundations of Systems Analysis, 1969. NSF fellow, 1964-65; recipient Meritorious Service award Exec. Office of Pres., 1970 Mem. Soc. Indsl. and Applied Math., Am. Math. Soc., AAAS, Sigma Xi Home: 18 E Concorda Dr Tempe AZ 85282-3517 Office: Ariz State U Dept Math Tempe AZ 85287-1804 Home Phone: 480-968-6813; Office Phone: 480-968-6813. Business E-Mail: hsmith@math.asu.edu.

SMITH, HEATHER LYNN, psychotherapist, recreational therapist; b. Modesto, Calif., May 31, 1956; d. Gary Fremont and Marilyn Rae (Brown) S. BS, Calif. State U., Fresno, 1979; MA, U. San Francisco, 1989. Lic. marriage, family and child counselor, Calif. Recreational therapist Casa Colina Rehab. Hops., Pomona, Calif., 1979-82; evaluator developmentally delayed, coord. family edn. Cath. Charities, Modesto, 1982-87; bereavement counselor Hospice, Modesto, 1983-87; high risk youth counselor Ctr. Human Svcs., Modesto, 1987—; pvt. practice, family therapist Modesto, 1988—. Program dir. chemically dependent treatment program Stanislaus County Juvenile Hall, 1990—; program adminstr. First Step, 1999—. Named Outstanding Young Woman of Stanislaus County, 1986, Citizen of Yr., Civitan, 1986, Outstanding Individual award Stanislaus County, 1992. Mem. Calif. Assn. Marriage and Family Therapists, Kappa Kappa Gamma. Republican. Roman Catholic. Avocations: skiing, running, backpacking, tennis. Office: PO Box 577456 Modesto CA 95357-7456 Office Phone: 209-521-7254. Business E-Mail: serenitymft@comcast.net.

SMITH, HEDRICK LAURENCE, journalist, television producer; b. Kilmacolm, Scotland, July 9, 1933; s. Sterling L. and Phebe (Hedrick) S.; m. Ann Bickford, June 29, 1957 (div. Dec. 1985); children: Laurel Ann, Jennifer Laurence, Sterling Scott, Lesley Roberts; m. Susan Zox, Mar. 7, 1987. BA, Williams Coll., 1955, LittD (hon.), 1975; postgrad. (Fulbright scholar), Balliol Coll., Oxford, Eng., 1955-56; LittD (hon.), Wittenburg U., 1985, N.H. Coll., 1991; LHD (hon.), Columbia Coll., 1992; LittD (hon.), Amherst Coll., 1992; LHD (hon.), U. S.C., 1992; LittD (hon.), Furman U., 1996. With U.P.I., Memphis, Nashville, Atlanta, 1959-62; with N.Y. Times, 1962-88, Washington and S.E., 1962-63, Vietnam, 1963-64; Middle East corr. N.Y. Times, Cairo, U.A.R., 1964-66, diplomatic news corr. Washington, 1962-64, 66-71, Moscow Bur. chief, 1971-74, dep. nat. editor, 1975-76, Washington Bur. chief, 1976-79, chief Washington corr., 1980-85; Washington correspondent N.Y. Times mag., 1987-88. Vis. journalist Am. Enterprise Inst., 1985-87; fellow Fgn. Policy Inst., Johns Hopkins U. Sch Advanced Internat. Studies, 1989-97; panelist Washington Week in Rev., PBS, 1969-95. Author: The Russians, 1975 (Overseas Press Club award, 1976), The Power Game: How Washington Works, 1988, The New Russians, 1990 (Overseas Press Club citation, 1991), Rethinking America, 1995; co-author: The Pentagon Papers, 1972, Reagan the Man, the President, 1981, Beyond Reagan: The Politics of Upheaval, 1986, Seven Days That Shook the World, 1991, (TV documentaries) Star Wars, 1985, Moscow Jews, 1986, Space Bridge, Chernobyl: Three Mile Island, 1987, 4-part Power Game series, PBS, 1989, Countdown to White House: The Bush Transition, 1989, 4-part series Inside Gorbachev's USSR, 1990 (George Polk award, Gold Baton award Columbia-DuPont), Guns, Tanks and Gorbachev (Frontline), 1991, Soviets, 1991 (George Peabody award), After Gorbachev's USSR (Frontline), 1992, 4-part series PBS, Challenge to America, 1994 (Cine Golden Eagle award, Rias award), Across the River, PBS, 1995 (Hillman award), The People and the Power Game, 1996 (Silver award Houston Film Festival), Surviving the Bottom Line, 1998 (Cine Golden Eagle award), Seeking Solutions, 1999 (nat. award for pub. svc. Sigma Delta Chi, spl. gold medal Houston Film Festival), Duke Ellington's Washington, 2000 (N.Y. Film Festival Bronze prize), Critical Condition, 2000 (Emmy nomination), Dr. Solomon's Dilemma (Frontline), 2000 (Chris award), Juggling Work and Family, 2001, Rediscovering Dave Brubeck, 2001, Inside the Terror Network (Frontline), 2002 (co-winner Columbia-Dupont Gold Baton), Bigger Than Enron (Frontline), 2002 (Cine Gold Eagle), The Wall Street Fix (Frontline), 2003 (Emmy award, Cine Gold Eagle, Chris award), Tax Me If You Can (Frontline), 2004 (Emmy nomination), Is Walmart Good for America?, 2004 (Writer's Guild award nomination), Making Schools Work With Hedrick Smith, 2005, Can

You Afford to Retire, 2006 (Emmy), Spying on the Home Front, 2007. Trustee Williams Coll., 1982-97, Nat. Ctr. for Humanities, 2005—; mem. Aspen Inst. Domestic Strategy Group, 1997-2002; bd. dirs. New American Schs., 1996-2004; mem. steering com. Concerned Journalists, 2001—. With USAF, 1956-59. Recipient Pulitzer prize for pub. svc. Pentagon Papers Series, 1972, for internat. reporting from Soviet Union and Ea. Europe, 1974, William Allen White award U. Kans., 1996; Nieman fellow Harvard U., 1969-70. Mem. Gridiron Club, Phi Beta Kappa. Office: Hedrick Smith Prodns Inc 6935 S Wisconsin Ave Chevy Chase MD 20815 Office Phone: 301-654-9848. E-mail: hsmithprod@aol.com.

SMITH, HENRY CHARLES, III, symphony orchestra conductor; b. Phila., Jan. 31, 1931; s. Henry Charles Jr. and Gertrude Ruth (Downs) S.; m. Mary Jane Dressner, Sept. 3, 1955; children: Katherine Anne, Pamela Jane, Henry Charles IV. BA, U. Pa., 1952; artist diploma, Curtis Inst. Music, Phila., 1955. Solo trombonist Phila. Orch., 1955-67; condr. Rochester (Minn.) Symphony Orch., 1967-68; assoc. prof. music Ind. U., Bloomington, 1968-71; resident condr., ednl. dir. Minn. Orch., Mpls., 1971-88; prof. music U. Tex., Austin, 1988-89, Frank C. Erwin Centennial Prof. of Opera, 1988-89; music dir. S.D. Symphony, Sioux Falls, 1989-2001; prof. Ariz. State U., Tempe, 1989-93, prof. emeritus, 1993—. Vis. prof. U. Tex., Austin, 1987-88; founding mem. Phila. Brass Ensemble, 1956—; music dir. World Youth Symphony Orch., Interlochen, Mich., 1981-96; artistic advisor, prin. guest conductor Cedar Rapids Symphony, Iowa, 2004-. Composer 5 books of solos for trombone including Solos for the Trombone Player, 1963, Hear Us As We Pray, 1963, First Solos for the Trombone Player, 1972, Easy Duets for Winds, 1972; editor 14 books 20th century symphonies lit. Served to 1st lt. AUS, 1952-54. Recipient 3 Grammy nominations, 1967, 76, 1 Grammy award for best chamber music rec. with Phila. Brass Ensemble, 1969. Mem. Internat. Trombone Assn. (dir.), Am. Symphony Orch. League, Music Educators Nat. Conf., Am. Guild Organists, Am. Fedn. Musicians, Tubist Universal Brotherhood Assn., Acacia Fraternity. Republican. Congregationalist. Home: 8032 Pennsylvania Rd S Bloomington MN 55438-1135

SMITH, HERBERT G., II, lawyer; b. Newport News, Va., Mar. 15, 1958; BA cum laude, Washington & Lee Univ., 1980, JD, 1983. Bar: Va. 1984, DC 1996. Ptnr., Comml. Litigation, Product Liability & Toxic Torts practices Venable LLP, Washington. Contbr. articles to profl. jours. Mem.: Va. State Bar Assn., DC Bar Assn. Office: Venable LLP 575 7th St NW Washington DC 20004 Office Phone: 202-344-4858. Office Fax: 202-344-8300. Business E-Mail: hgsmith@venable.com.

SMITH, HILARY CRANWELL BOWEN, investment banker; b. Balt., Nov. 1, 1937; s. Henry Bowen and Clayton (Cranwell) S.; m. Janet Simmons, June 9, 1962; children: Kent C.B., Kendall S., Hillary E. BA, Colgate U., 1960; MBA, U. Va., 1967. V.p. Merc. Safe Deposit & Trust, 1967—69, Goldman, Sachs & Co., NYC, 1969-74, E. F. Hutton & Co., NYC, 1974-77; sr. v.p. Blyth Eastman Dillon, NYC, 1977—79; mng. dir. Salomon Bros., NYC, 1979—2004, UBS, NYC, 1990—2004; sr. advisor Greenhill & Co., NYC, 2004—. Trustee Wheaton Coll., 1997-2003, Chesapeake Maritime Mus., 1998-2004, Greenwich Acad., 1988-94, Mystic Seaport, 2005, Nat. Maritime Hist. Soc., 2006—; treas. Riverside Theater, 2007; bd. dirs. Forest 2 Market, 2002—. Lt. USN, 1960-63. Office: Greenhill and Company 300 Park Ave New York NY 10022 Office Phone: 212-389-1557.

SMITH, HOWARD RUSSELL, manufacturing executive, director; b. Clark County, Ohio, Aug. 15, 1914; s. Lewis Hoskins and Eula (Elder) S.; m. Jeanne Rogers, June 27, 1942; children: Stewart Russell, Douglas Howard, Jeanne Ellen Smith James. AB, Pomona Coll., 1936. Security analyst Kidder, Peabody & Co., NYC, 1936-37; economist ILO, Geneva, 1937-40; asst. to pres. Blue Diamond Corp., Los Angeles, 1940—; v.p., gen. mgr., dir. Avery Dennison Corp., Pasadena, Calif., 1946-56, pres., 1956-75, chmn. bd., 1975-84, chmn. exec. com., 1984-95; dir. emeritus, 1995—; chmn. bd. Kinsmith Fin. Corp., San Marino, Calif., 1979—. Bd. dirs., past pres., chmn. Los Angeles Philharm. Assn.; chmn. emeritus, bd. trustees Pomona Coll., Claremont, Calif.; past chmn. bd. Children's Hosp. Los Angeles, Community TV of So. Calif. (Sta. KCET), Los Angeles. Lt. USNR, 1943-46. Home: 1458 Hillcrest Ave Pasadena CA 91106-4503 Office: Avery Dennison Corp 150 N Orange Grove Blvd Pasadena CA 91103-3534 Office Phone: 626-304-2153.

SMITH, HOWARD THOMPSON, manufacturing executive; b. Camden, Ark., Apr. 30, 1937; s. Howard Thompson and Pauline Virginia (Rogers) S.; m. Ann Monroe; children: Paul R., Elizabeth M. BS, Tulane U., 1960; postgrad. studies, La. State U., 1961-63; EPBA, Columbia U., 1978. Dir. planning Ethyl Corp., Baton Rouge, La., 1970-76; exec. v.p., gen. mgr. William Bonnell Co. subs. Ethyl Corp., Newman, Ga., 1976-81; pres. Steelcraft, Cin., 1981-84; v.p., group exec. Am. Standard, Cin., 1984-89, sr. v.p. NYC, 1989-94, also bd. dirs., 1989—; pres., CEO The Trane Co., NYC, 1989-94; mng. ptnr. Septa Assocs., 1994—; gen. ptnr. Rutledge Capital, 2000—. Pres. Thompson Smith Found., 1993—; chmn. bd. dirs. Trinity Mother Francis Health Sys., 1996—, Adobe, 2000—, Framed Picture Enterprises, 1999-,; bd. dirs. CROM Corp. Bd. dirs. Salvation Army, 1988—, Tex. Rsch. League, Austin, 1989, U. Tex., Tyler, 1990—, Mother Francis Hosp. Found., 1991—; chmn. bd. dirs. East Tex. Communities Found., 1993—; elder, trustee 1st Presbyn. Ch.; trustee U. Tex., Tyler, East Tex. Pres. Found., Union Theol. Sem., 1994— Mem. Tex. Assn. Taxpayers (dir.), Smith County C. of C. (bd. dirs. 1988-91), Tyler Petroleum Club, Hollytree Country Club, Willowbrook Country Club, Sawgrass Country Club. Republican. Presbyterian. Avocations: golf, tennis. Office: The Trane Co PO Box 9010 Tyler TX 75711-9010 also: 819 Spinnakers Reach Dr Ponte Vedra Beach FL 32082-3408

SMITH, HOWARD WELLINGTON, education educator, retired dean; b. Granby, Mo., Jan. 19, 1929; s. Howard W. and Margaret L. (Sanderson) S.; m. Margaret E. Bell, Mar. 1, 1953; 1 child, Christopher Alan. BS, S.W. Mo. State U., 1954; MEd, U. Mo., 1955, EdD, 1959. Tchr. Newton County (Mo.) Pub. Schs., 1948-51; instr. U. Mo., Columbia, 1955-59; asst. prof. So. Meth. U., Dallas, 1959-61; from asst. to full prof. U. North Tex., Denton, 1961-97, dean emeritus. Assoc. dean Coll. Edn. U. North Tex., 1972-76, assoc. v.p. acad. affairs, 1976-79, v.p. acad. affairs, 1979-82, interim dean, 1994-97; interim chancellor U. North Tex. Coll. Osteo. Medicine, Denton and Ft. Worth, 1981; sr. cons. Am. Assn. State Colls. and Univs., Washington, 1982; cons. Srinakharinwirot U., Thailand, 1986, Tex. Internat. Edn. Consortium, Austin, 1992, sr. author Operation Manual Al Akhawayn U., 1993; vis. prof. Shanxi Ednl. Coll. Taiyuan, China, 1993. Contbr. articles to ednl. jours. Prin. investigator Micro Tchg. Lab., 1967—69; chair Ret. Instrs., Pers. and Spouses U. North Tex., 2001; accreditation cons. Art Inst. Dallas, 2001—; chair Denton County Hist. Soc., 1999—2004; exec. coun. U. North Tex. Friends of Libr., 2005—; trustee Art Inst. Dallas, 2005—; adv. bd. Coll. Edn. U. North Tex., 1997—2005, adv. bd. Bill J. Priest Ctr. for C.C. Edn., 1999—2002, Coll. of Edn. devel. bd., 1999—2002, devel. bd. Coll. Edn., 2006—; pres. bd. dirs. Tex. Lakes Trail, 2002—04; bd. dirs. HOPE, Inc., 2007—. With USAF, 1951—53. Democrat. Presbyterian. Avocations: travel, reading. Office: U North Tex Coll Edn PO Box 311337 Denton TX 76203-1337

SMITH, IAN CORMACK PALMER, biophysicist; b. Winnipeg, Man., Can., Sept. 23, 1939; s. Cormack and Grace Mary Smith; m. Eva Gunilla Landvik, Mar. 27, 1965; children: Brittmarie, Cormack, Duncan, Roderick. BS, U. Man., 1961, MS, 1962; PhD, Cambridge U., Eng., 1965; PhD (hon.), U. Stockholm, 1986; DSc (hon.), U. Winnipeg, 1990, Brandon U., 2001, Cracow Polish Acad. Sci., 2006; diploma in tech. (hon.), Red River Coll., 1996. Fellow Stanford U., 1965-66; mem. rsch. staff Bell Tel. Labs., Murray Hill, NJ, 1966-67; rsch. officer divsn. biol. scis. NRC, Ottawa, Canada, 1967-87, dir. gen., 1987-91, Inst. Biodiagnostics, Winnipeg, Canada, 1992—. Adj. prof. chemistry and biochemistry Carleton U., 1973—90, U. Ottawa, 1976—92; adj. prof. biophysics U. Ill., Chgo., 1974—80; adj. prof. chemistry, radiology, physics and anatomy U. Man., 1992—; allied scientist Ottawa Civic Hosp., 1985—98, Ottawa Gen. Hosp., 1989—98, Ont. Cancer Found., 1989—91, St. Boniface Hosp., 1992—, Health Scis. Ctr., 1993—, Econ. Tech. Innovation Coun., Man., 1994—98, exec. com., Man., 1996—98, Man. Health Rsch. Coun., 1996—98, chmn., 1998—2002, 2007; mem. adv. bd. Loeb Inst., Ottawa, 1999—2001, Keystone Ventures, 1999—2002, Western LIfe Scis. Fund, 2002—, Novadaq, 2004—, St. Boniface Hosp. Rsch. Enterprise, 2006—, Cancer Care Man.; bd. dirs. ENSIS Growth Fund, DIASPEC Holdings, IMRIS Inc., Magnetic Resonance Vets., Photonics Rsch. Ont., Spectex Pty., Biomed. Commercialization Can., Ontario Centres of Excellence, Genome Prairie, Cancer Care Man. Contbr. chapters to books, articles to profl. jours. Mem. adv. bd. Smart Winnipeg, 2000—03; mem. Premier's Econ. Adv. Bd., Man., 2001—, exec. com. Man., 2004—; bd. govs. U. Man., 2000—06. Decorated Order of the Star of Romania; recipient Barringer award, Can. Spectroscopy Soc., 1979, Herzberg award, 1986, Organon Teknika award, Can. Soc. Clin. Chemists, 1987, Sr. Scientist award, Sigma Xi, 1995, Queen's Jubilee medal, 2003, Star of Romania, 2004, Paul Harris award, Rotary Club, 2006. Fellow: Soc. Magnetic Resonance Medicine (mem. exec. com. 1989—94), Royal Soc. Can. (Flavelle medal 1996), Chem. Inst. Can. (Merck award 1978, Labatt award 1984); mem.: Internat. Union Pure and Applied Biophysics (mem. coun. 1993—, v.p. 1996—99, 2002—05, pres. 2005—), Biophys. Soc. Can. (pres. 1992—94), Can. Biochem. Soc., Biophysical Soc., Internat. Coun. Sci. Unions (mem. gen. com. 1989—94), U. Man. Alumni Assn. (bd. dirs. 1994—2000, v.p. 1997—98, pres. 1998—99). Office: Inst Biodiagnostics Winnipeg MB Canada R3B 1Y6 Home Phone: 204-897-0650; Office Phone: 204-983-7526. Business E-Mail: ian.smith@nrc-cnrc.gc.ca.

SMITH, IAN K., writer, columnist, physician; AB, Harvard U., 1991; MA, Columbia U., 1992; attended, Dartmouth Coll.; MD, U. Chgo. Med. Sch., 1997. Med. corr. NBC Nightly News, Today Show, The View, Men's Health Mag., Celebrity Fit Club, VH1. Host Meet the Faith, Black Entertainment TV, HealthWatch; author: Dr. Ian Smith's Guide to Medical Websites, 2001, The Blackbird Papers, 2004 (Black Caucus ALA fiction Hon. Book award, 2005), The Take-Control Diet, 2005, The Fat Smash Diet, 2006, The Extreme Fat Smash Diet, 2007. Bd. mem. NYC Mission Soc., Cancer Rsch. Found. Am., Am. Coun. on Exercise, North Shore-Long Island Jewish Rsch. Inst., Henry H. Kessler Found., Bldg. with Books. Office: PO Box 765 FDR Station New York NY 10150 Business E-Mail: ian@doctoriansmith.com. *

SMITH, IRENE HELEN-NORDINE, music educator; d. John J. and Dorothy J. Horzepa; m. Thomas Carlyle Smith, Dec. 19, 1982; children: Julie Ann Nordine, Ryan Carlyle. AA in Music Edn. K-12, Broward C.C., Fort Lauderdale, Fla., 1973; BA in Music Edn. K-12, Fla. Atlantic U., 1975; BA in Elem. Edn., Kennesaw State U., 1991. Cert. tchr. Ga. Profl. Stds. Commn., 2003. Elem. music tchr. Tedder Elem. Broward County Sch. Sys., Pompano, Fla., 1976—77, elem. music tchr. Harbordale Elem. Fort Lauderdale, 1979—83, elem. music tchr. Meadowbrook Elem., 1979—83, elem. music tchr. Banyan Elem., 1979—83; pvt. piano and voice tchr. Roswell, Ga., 1983—; tchr. Mabry Mid. Sch. Cobb County Bd. Edn., Marietta, Ga., 1993—. Organist, choir dir. Coral Springs (Fla.) United Meth. Ch., 1976—83; organist / choir dir. Birmingham United Meth. Ch., Alpharetta, Ga., 1994—99; accompanist Ga. Music Educators Assn. Dist. 12 Mid. Sch. Honor Chorus, Marietta, 1999—. Composer: (Rocky Mount Elem. spirit song) Rocky Mountain Warriors, (Shallowford Falls Elem. spirit song) The Foxy Foxes, (Tritt Elem. Sch. spirit song) I Am A Tritt Tiger, (music high school alma mater) Alan Pope High School Alma Mater. Dir., accompanist Roswell United Meth. Ch., 1983—90. Scholar, Broward C.C., 1971—73, Fla. Atlantic U., 1973—75. Mem.: Music Educators Nat. Conf., Ga. Music Educators Assn., Phi Theta Kappa. Republican. Methodist. Avocations: travel, piano, art, reading, football. Office: Mabry Middle School 2700 Jims Rd Marietta GA 30066 Personal E-mail: irenesmith@bellsouth.net.

SMITH, IRVING, gerontologist; b. Washington, June 4, 1948; s. Alfonso Marcellus and Nannie (Hunter) S.; children: Bryan, Rashard, Irving, Nevada, Ryan. M in Human Svcs., Lincoln U., 1995, grad. cert. advanced gerontology, 1995; PhD in Health and Human Behavior, Walden U., 2002. Lic. profl. counselor D.C. Dir. Sr. Ctr. Md.-Nat. Capital Park and Planning Commn., Prince George's County, Md., 1969—71, 1989—; prof. psychology Grad. Sch. Internat., nat. forum spkr. on leisure and aging issues; founder Prince George's County Centenarian Celebration; prin. investigator Prince George's County, Md. Centenarian Rsch. Study; bd. dirs., regional dir. Leisure and Aging. Mem. Nat. Recreation and Park Assn. (state rep. leisure and aging, bd. dirs. leisure and aging sect., dir. Mid-Atlantic region), Pi Gamma Mu. Democrat. Baptist. Home: 4311 23d Pky #505 Temple Hills MD 20748 Personal E-mail: ismith@starpower.net.

SMITH, ISABEL FRANCIS, financial planner; b. Detroit, May 21, 1935; d. Edward Hugh and Isabel (Winegar) Francis; m. Lawrence Smith, June 7, 1958; children: Mark, Hugh, Claire. Student, Newton Coll., 1953—54; BA, U. Mich., 1957, MA, 1958, postgrad., 1975—76. Registered investment adviser. Tchr. Edison Sch., Hazel Park, Mich., 1958—61, Warren Valley Sch., Dearborn Heights, Mich., 1958—61; counselor Riverside HS, Dearborn Heights, 1961—62; pres. Isabel Francis Smith Ltd., Farmington Hills, Mich., 1980—2004, Integrated Fin. Strategies Ltd., Farmington Hills, 1980—. Registered rep., dist. mgr. Investors Diversified Svcs., Oak Park, Mich., 1978—80; instr. Oakland CC, 1979—; cons. to women's orgns.; dir. pres. Oakland County Fin. and Estate Planning Coun., 1988—94; writer, profl. radio and TV personality. Lectr., trustee Bloomfield Twp. Libr., 1978—99, Interlochen Ctr. Arts, 1989—; founder Interlochen Friends, Vol. Network for Women. Recipient Heart of Gold award, United Found., 1976, Outstanding New Rep. award, Investors Diversified Svcs., 1979, Bravo award, Interlochu Alumni Assn., 2005. Mem.: AAUW, Inst. Cert. Fin. Planners (nat. dir. 1980—86, dean retreat 1987, 1989, past regional dir., leadership devel. com., cert. fin. planner), Internat. Assn. Fin. Planners (past pres. S.E. Mich. chpt.), Nat. Assn. Women Bus. Owners, U. Mich. Alumni Assn., Interlochen Alumni Founder Assn. (past pres., award), Village Club, Mut. Svcs. Corp. (pres. club 1992—2002, Outstanding Rep. award 1981—90), Women's Econ. Club, Phi Beta Kappa (nat. chmn., past pres., exec. com. Pres. award Detroit assn.). Home: 7110 Paterese Dr Bloomfield Hills MI 48301-3764 Office: 31884 Northwestern Hwy Farmington Hills MI 48334-1628 Business E-Mail: isabel@ifs-ltd.com.

SMITH, J. GORDON, automotive executive; BBA in Acctg., U. Mass.; grad., GE Fin. Mgmt. Program. Fin. mgmt. positions GE, 1977—90, CFO corp. fin. services, comml. equip. fin., capital markets units, 1990—2003; sr. v.p., chief fin. officer Asbury Automotive Group, NYC, 2003—. Office: Asbury Automotive Group 37th Fl 622 Third Ave New York NY 10017 *

SMITH, J. KELLUM, JR., foundation administrator, lawyer; b. NYC, June 18, 1927; s. James Kellum and Elizabeth Dexter (Walker) S.; m. Sarah Tod Lohmann, July 22, 1950 (div. 1993); children: Alison Andrews, Timothy Kellum, Jennifer Harlow, Christopher Lohmann; m. Angela Marina Brown, Feb. 3, 1995. Grad., Phillips Exeter Acad., 1945; AB magna cum laude, Amherst Coll., 1950; LL.B., Harvard, 1953. Bar: N.Y. 1955. Assoc. Lord, Day & Lord, NYC, 1953-59; asst. sec. John Simon Guggenheim Meml. Found., 1960-62; mem. staff Rockefeller Found., 1962-74, asst. sec., 1963-64, sec., 1964—74; v.p., sec. Andrew W. Mellon Found., NYC, 1974—89, sr. fellow, 1989-92; sr. advisor, 1992-98; pres. Hill and Hollow Music, Inc., 1995—; pvt. practice cons. and writer. Trustee Nat. Sculpture Soc., 1955-71, Nat. Ins. Archtl. Edn., 1961-69, St. Bernard's Sch., N.Y.C., 1968-78, Found. for Child Devel., 1968-74; trustee Brearley Sch., N.Y.C., 1964-80, pres., 1973-78; trustee Am. Acad. in Rome, 1964-95, treas., 1965-66, 2d v.p., 1968-72, 84-88, sec., 1973-84, 89-95. With USAAF, 1945-46. Mem. Phi Beta Kappa. Clubs: Century Association (N.Y.C.). Home: 550 Number 37 Rd Saranac NY 12981-2956

SMITH, JACK CARL, import/export company executive; b. Cleve., Sept. 11, 1928; s. John Carl and Florence Agnes (O'Rourke) S.; m. Nannette June Boyd, Dec. 1, 1962; 1 dau., Colleen Wentworth. Student, Baldwin Wallace Coll., 1948-51, postgrad., 1958; BA, Ohio U., 1954. Rep. Flying Tiger Line, Inc., Los Angeles, 1958-61; prin. Pub. Rep. bus., Cleve., 1961-64; pub. Penton Pub., Cleve., 1964-90; spl. advisor Am. Fgn. Policy Coun., Washington, 1990—. Dir. Central Cleve. Corp., Nat. Distbn. Terminals; graduated Air Tng. Command Intelligence Officer Sch., served from 1958-62 AFR. Trustee Presdl. task force, Rep. Senatorial Inner Circle, Coun. of Logistics Mgmt., U.S. Bus. and Indsl. Coun. With USAF, 1954-58. Mem. Am. Mgmt. Assn., Material Handling Inst., Am. Trucking Assn., Nat. Council Phys. Distbn. Mgmt., Family Motor Coach Assn., Recreation Vehicle Industry Assn., Am. Bus. Press, Mag. Pubs. Assn., Sci. Research Soc., Internat. Platform Assn., Sigma Xi, Sigma Chi Clubs: Wings (N.Y.C.). Home: 457 Devonshire Ct Bay Village OH 44140-3009 Office: Am Fgn Policy Coun 1521 16th St NW Washington DC 20036-1463 *Do your best and God will forgive you the rest.*

SMITH, JACK DAVID, lawyer; b. Honolulu, Jan. 4, 1946; s. Jack David and Gloria June (Slater) S.; m. Alexa Drubay, June 12, 2006; children: Amy Elizabeth, Amanda Marie. BA in Polit. Sci., George Washington U., 1968, JD, 1971. Bar: Va. 1971, U.S. Ct. Mil. Appeals 1971, U.S. Ct. Appeals (1st and D.C. cirs.) 1975, U.S. Ct. Appeals (2d and 7th cirs.) 1976, U.S. Supreme Ct. 1976, D.C. 1986. Atty. litig. div. FCC, Washington, 1974-81, dept. chief common carrier bur., 1981-83, chief common carrier bur., 1983-84, gen. counsel, 1984-86; dep. gen. counsel Fed. Home Loan Bank Bd., Washington, 1986-89, Fed. Deposit Ins. Corp., Washington, 1989—2006; dir. Internat. Ctr. Asset Recovery, Basel, Switzerland, 2006—. Served to capt. USMC, 1971-74. Mem. Va. Bar Assn., D.C. Bar Assn. Avocations: tennis, running, skiing. Home Phone: 4161-271-0801; Office Phone: 4161-290-2957. Business E-Mail: jack.smith@baselgovernance.org.

SMITH, JACK LEE, bank executive; b. Yale, Okla., Feb. 2, 1948; s. George W. and Alta E. (Tilley) S.; m. Rose Mary Cantrell, Feb. 3, 1968 (div. Feb. 1980); children: Anissa Kay, Melany Elaine; m. Janice A. Houston, Aug. 2, 1981(div. Feb. 2000). BS, Okla. State U., 1972. Asst. v.p. Production Credit Assn., 1972-76; v.p., office mgr. Mountain Plains Prodn. Credit Assn., Ft. Collins, 1976-81; dist. mgr. Ralston Purina, St. Louis, 1981-83; 2d v.p. Omaha Nat. Bank, 1983-85; v.p., office mgr. FirsTier Bank, N.A., Omaha, Ft. Collins, 1985-93, mgr. western area agrl. lending Omaha, 1993-96; sr. v.p. agribus. fin. group Farm Credit Svcs., Greeley, Colo., 1996—. Bd. dirs. Colo. Cattle Feeders Assn.; chmn. Allied Industry Coun. for Agr. Mem. Am. Bankers Assn., Colo. Bankers Assn., Nat. Cattlemen's Assn., Kans. Livestock Assn., Colo. Cattlemen's Assn., Elks. Republican. Avocations: photography, hiking, fishing, camping. Home: 2613 Jewelstone Ct Fort Collins CO 80525-6118 Office: AgriBusiness Finance Group Farm Credit Svcs 4505 29th St Greeley CO 80634-8763

SMITH, JACKSON BARKLEY, JR., retired judge; b. Houston; s. John Barkley and Buelah Floyce (Oldham) Smith; m. Jessie Myrtle Scheidemantel, Jan. 29, 1928; children: John Barkley Jr., Stephen Louis, Stephanie Alison, Robert Kevin. BS, JD, U. Houston, 1950. Pvt. practice, 1950—62; city. atty. Hedwig Village, Tex., 1958—60; exec. asst. to county judge, 1960—62; probate judge Harris County, 1963—69, family ct. dist. judge, 1969—72, dist. judge civil jurisdiction, 1972—80; justice 1st Ct. Appeals, 1980—88; ret., 1988. Vis. judge, 1989—. Deacon, elder Presbyn. Ch.; lay leader, past chmn. bd. dirs., trustee Meth. Ch. Maj. USAAF, 1942—46. Fellow, Houston Bar Found. Mem.: Fed. Bar Assn., State Bar Tex., Masons, Alpha Phi Omega. Avocation: golf.

SMITH, JACLYN, actress; b. Houston, Oct. 26, 1947; d. Jack and Margaret Ellen S.; m. Dennis Cole (div. 1981); m. Tony Richmond, Aug. 4, 1981; 1 dau., Spencer Margaret. Student, Trinity U., San Antonio. Worked as model. Motion picture appearances include The Adventurers, 1970, Bootleggers, Deja Vu; TV film appearances include Bogen County, 1977, The Users, 1978, Rage of Angels, 1980, Nightkill, 1980, Jacqueline Bouvier Kennedy, 1981, Sentimental Journey, 1984, George Washington (miniseries), 1984, Florence Nightingale, 1985, The Night They Saved Christmas, 1986, Wind Mills of the Gods (miniseries), 1988, The Bourne Identity, 1988, Settle the Score, 1989, Danielle Steele's Kaleidoscope, 1990, Lies Before Kisses, 1991, The Rape of Dr. Willis, 1991, In The Arms Of A Killer, 1992, Love Can Be Murder, 1992, Family Album, 1994, Cries Unheard: The Donna Yaklich Story, 1994, My Very Best Friend, 1996, Married to a Stranger, 1997, Before He Wakes, 1998, Three Secrets, 1999, Freefall, 1999; one of prin. roles TV series Charlie's Angels, 1976-80, (ABC Saturday Night Movie) Christine Cromwell, 1989-90; other TV appearances include Get Christy Love, McCloud, The Rookies, Love Boat, Switch, Navigating the Heart, 2000, The District, 2000; appeared in numerous TV commls. Mem. AFTRA. Office: ICM 8942 Wilshire Blvd Beverly Hills CA 90211-1934

SMITH, JAMES A., lawyer; b. Akron, Ohio, June 11, 1930; s. Barton H. and Myrna S. (Young) S.; m. Melda I. Perry, Jan. 17, 1959; children: Hugh, Sarah Louise. AB, Western Res. U., 1952; postgrad., Columbia U., 1954-56, LLB, 1961; postgrad., Yale U., 1956-58. Bar: Ohio 1961, U.S. Dist. Ct. (no. dist.) Ohio 1963, U.S. Ct. Appeals (6th cir.) 1973, U.S. Supreme Ct. 1974, U.S. Ct. Appeals (11th cir.) 1983, U.S. Ct. Appeals (D.C. cir.) 1984. Assoc. Squire, Sanders and Dempsey, Cleve., 1961-70, ptnr., 1970-91, counsel, 1991-96; adj. prof. Case Western Res. U. Sch. Law, 1997-98, ret., 1994. Mem. spl. adv. com. Nat. Conf. Commrs. on Uniform State Laws, 1972-74. Trustee Chagrin Falls Park Cmty. Ctr., 1968-78, Greater Cleve. Neighborhood Ctrs. Assn., 1973-78, Legal Aid Soc. Cleve., 1977-80, Cleve. Inst. Music, 1994—; mem. Charter Rev. Commn., Chagrin Falls, 1966. Lt. (j.g.) USNR, 1952-54. Fellow Am. Coll. Trial Lawyers; mem. ABA, Ohio Bar Assn., Cleve. Bar Assn. (trustee 1988-92), U.S. Ct. Appeals for 6th Cir. Jud. Conf. (life), Ohio Ct. Appeals for 8th Jud. Dist. Conf. (life), Ct. of Nisi Prius (clk. 1975-76, judge 1994-95), Appalachee Vill. Assn. (pres. 2004-05), Phi Beta Kappa, Omicron Delta Kappa, Delta Sigma Rho. Democrat. Personal E-mail: jasasmith1@aol.com.

SMITH, JAMES ALBERT, lawyer; b. Jackson, Mich., May 12, 1942; s. J. William and Mary Barbara (Browning) S.; m. Lucia S. Santini, Aug. 14, 1965; children: Matthew Browning, Aaron Michael, Rachel Elizabeth. BA, U. Mich., 1964, JD, 1967. Bar: Mich. 1968, U.S. Dist. Ct. (ea. dist.) Mich., U.S. Ct. Appeals (6th and D.C. cirs.), U.S. Supreme Ct. Assoc. Bodman, Longley & Dahling, Detroit, 1967-75, ptnr., 1975—. Mem. panel Atty. Discipline Bd., Wayne County, Mich., 1987—; arbitrator Am. Arbitration Assn., 1975—; mem. Banking Commrs. com. on Contested Case Adminstrn., 1978. Mem. pro bono referral group Call For Action, Detroit, 1982—. Mem. ABA, State Bar Mich., Detroit Bar Assn. Roman Catholic. Avocations: sailing, travel. Office: Bodman LLP 1901 Antoine St 6th Fl Detroit MI 48226

SMITH, JAMES COPENHAVER, bank executive; s. Harold Webster Smith; m. Cathy Smith, 1987; 2 children. BA, Dartmouth Coll., 1971. Adminstrv. banking officer First Federal (renamed Webster Bank in 1995),

1975; pres. Webster Bank, 1982—87, CEO, 1987—, Webster Financial Corp., 1987—, chmn., 1995—. Mem. Fed. Advisory Coun.; bd. dirs. MacDermid Inc. Bd. dirs., exec. com. St. Mary's Hosp., Waterbury, Conn.; chmn. bd. dirs. Palace Theater, Waterbury, Conn. Mem.: Conn. Bankers Assn. (exec. com.). Avocations: running, bicycling, golf, hiking. Office: Webster Fin Corp Webster Plaza WFD730 Waterbury CT 06702

SMITH, JAMES FINLEY, economist, educator; b. Dallas, Nov. 4, 1938; s. Emerson Russell and Achsah Elizabeth (Foster) S.; children: Carter Emerson, Jade, Curtis Noel, Marshall Edward; m. Linda M. Topp, Aug. 5, 2001. BA, So. Meth. U., 1961, MA, 1964, PhD, 1971. Math. analyst Sears, Roebuck & Co., Oak Brook, Ill., 1965-68, adminstrv. asst. to v.p. and treas. Chgo., 1968-69, dir. econometric rsch., 1969-75; sr. economist Bd. Govs. FRS, Washington, 1975-77; dir. credit rsch. Sears, Roebuck & Co., Chgo., 1977-80; chief economist Union Carbide Corp., Danbury, Conn., 1980-85; dir. regional svcs. and U.S. cons. Wharton Econometric Forecasting Assocs., Phila., 1986; dir., chief economist Bur. Bus. Rsch. U. Tex., Austin, 1987-88; prof. fin. U. NC, Chapel Hill, 1988—, sr. fellow Kenan Inst. Pvt. Enterprise, 2002—; chief economist Nat. Assn. Realtors, Washington, 1999—2000; dir. Ctr. for Bus. Forecasting, U. N.C., 2002—; chief economist Soc. Indsl. and Office Realtors, Washington, 2002—06, Parsec Fin., Asheville, NC, 2006—; prof. of practice Inst. for Economy and the Future, Western Carolina U., Cullowhee, NC, 2006—. Econ. adv. bd. U.S. Dept. Commerce, 1977-80, 83-93; cons. Pres.'s Coun. of Econ. Advisers, Washington, 1978-83; dir. Nat. Bur. Econ. Rsch., Cambridge, Mass., 1992-95; bd. advisors Thurston Arthritis Rsch. Ctr., Chapel Hill, N.C., 1994-99; dir. Am. Fin. Svcs. Assn. Edn. Found., 1997—. Author: (quarterly) UNC Business Forecast, 1988-2005, Jim Smith's Econ. Outlook, 2005—; (with others) Economic Growth and Investment in Higher Education, 1987, The New Texas Economy, 1988; (with Elsie Echeverri-Carroll) The Economic Impact of Travel on Texas Counties: 1986, 1988; contbr. articles to profl. jours. Served to lt. U.S. Army, 1961-62. Fellow NDEA, 1962—65. Fellow Nat. Assn. Bus. Econ. (v.p. 1988-89, pres. 1989-90, dir. 1980-84, 85-92); Nat. Economists Club (bd. govs. 1984-87), Am. Econ. Assn., Economists Group Switzerland, Fin. Mgmt. Assn., Bus. Economists UK, Nat. Bus. Econ. Issues Coun. (pres. 1981-83). Methodist. Office: Parsec Fin 6 Wall St Asheville NC 28802 Business E-Mail: j_smith@unc.edu.

SMITH, JAMES LAWRENCE, research physicist; b. Detroit, Sept. 3, 1943; s. William Leo and Marjorie Marie (Underwood) S.; m. Carol Ann Adam, Mar. 27, 1965; children: David Adam, William Leo. BS, Wayne State U., 1965; PhD, Brown U., 1974. Mem. staff Los Alamos Nat. Lab., N.Mex., 1973—82, fellow, 1982—86, 1987—, dir. Ctr. Materials Sci., 1986—87; chief scientist Superconductivity Tech. Ctr., 1988—99. Sci. editor: Los Alamos Rsch. Quar., 2002-03; N.Am. editor: Philos. mag., 1990-95, 03-06; editor: Philos. mag. B, 1995-02, Philos. Mag., 2003-06; contbr. articles to profl. jours. Recipient E.O. Lawrence award, 1986, Disting. Alumni award Wayne State U., 1993. Fellow Am. Phys. Soc. (internat. prize for new materials 1990); mem. AAAS, Materials Rsch. Soc., Minerals Metals Materials Soc., Am. Crystallographic Assn., Brown Alumni Assn. (bd. govs. 1998-2000), Phi Beta Kappa. Achievements include patents for design of magnetic field and high-strength conductors. Office: Los Alamos Nat Lab Mail Stop G770 Los Alamos NM 87545-0001 Office Phone: 505-667-4476. Business E-Mail: jlsmith@lanl.gov.

SMITH, JAMES LESLIE, minister, educator, counselor; 2 children. B of Gen. Studies, Ohio U., Lancaster, 1974; MDiv, Asbury Theol. Seminary, Wilmore, Ky., 1977; MA in Pastoral Psychology and Counseling, Ashland Theol. Seminary, Ohio, 1981; D of Ministry and Pastoral Counseling, Louisville Seminary, 2000. Lic. profl. clin. counselor Ohio, 1999, ordained elder United Meth. Ch., 1977; lic. ind. chem. dependency counselor Ohio, 1992. Alcoholism counselor Alcoholism Recover Cmty., Lexington, Ky., 1976—78; pastor Emmanuel United Meth. Ch., Lucasville, Ohio, 1978—80, Oakland Park United Meth. Ch., Columbus, Ohio, 1981—87; pastoral counseor Pastural Counseling Svcs., Columbus, 1984—97; supr. counselor, profl. counselor Well Spring Counseling, Columbus, 1997—; assoc. prof. substance abuse counseling Ohio Chirstian U., Circleville, 1994—. Presenter in field. Writer (curriculum) Aim Adult Degree Curriculum, 2003—. Fellow: Am. Assn. Pastoral Counselors. Avocations: reading, walking, weightlifting. Office: Ohio Christian Univ PO Box 460 1476 Lancaster Pke Circleville OH 43113

SMITH, JAMES O., history professor, writer; b. Dreux Air Force Base, France, Mar. 13, 1959; s. Lyle Eugene and Barbara Jean Smith; m. Jennifer Sue Duzan; children: George H., Jessie E. Roberts. PhD, U. Mo., Columbia, 1996. Interim instr. history Kemper Mil. Sch., Boonville, Mo., 1998—99; adj. instr. history Moberly Area CC, Moberly, Mo., 1999—2001, Columbia Coll., Mo., 2001; interim instr. history SW Bapt. U., Bolivar, Mo., 1999—2001, assoc. prof. history, 2001—. Substitute Sun. sch. tchr. Mt. Olive Bapt. Ch., Bolivar, Mo., 2001—. Mem.: Conf. Faith and History (assoc.). Home: 1125 S Birum Bolivar MO 65613 Office: SW Bapt Univ 1600 University Ave Bolivar MO 65613 Home Phone: 417-777-9196; Office Phone: 417-328-1720. Business E-Mail: jsmith@sbuniv.edu.

SMITH, JAMES ORMAL, engineering educator; b. South Bend, Ind., Oct. 7, 1949; s. George Ormal and Sylvia R. Smith; children: Laurie Ann Larime, Jamie Susanne. Student, Buchanan Trade Sch., Mich., 1969—73. Mgr. chem. engring. support svcs. U. Notre Dame, Ind., 1999—. Blood donor South Bend Med. Found. Ctrl. Blood Bank, Ind., 1982—2007; youth vol. Camp Evergreen Hospice and Palliative Care, South Bend, 1995—2007, patient care vol., 2003—07; team capt. Relay for Life Am. Cancer Soc., Notre Dame, 2002—07. Named Outstanding Ski Patrol Dir., Royal Valley Ski Patrol, 1982. Mem.: ASME, Soc. Mfg. Engrs. (sr.). Achievements include development of automation of electronics assembly lines; design of Nano CNC Milling Machine; adjustable volume adjustable flow acid re-action vessals; vacuum hood variable speed sample spinner; blood filtration/seperation research equipment. Home: 50911 Rothbury Dr Granger IN 46530 Office: University Notre Dame B-01 Fitzpatrick Hall Notre Dame IN 46556 Home Phone: 574-271-0445; Office Phone: 574-631-6606. Office Fax: 574-631-8366. Business E-Mail: jsmith1@nd.edu.

SMITH, JAMES PATRICK, economist; b. Aug. 3, 1943; s. James P. and Winefred (Harrison) S.; m. Sandra Berry, Oct. 25, 1983; children: Gillian Clare, Lauren Theresa. BS, Fordham U., 1965; PhD, U. Chgo., 1972. Rsch. assoc. Nat. Bur. Econ. Rsch., NYC, 1972-74; sr. economist Rand Corp., Santa Monica, Calif., 1974—, dir. of rsch. labor and population, 1977-93. Bd. dirs. Occupl. Safety and Health Standards State Calif. Editor: Female Labor Supply, 1980, The New Americans, 1997, The Immigration Debate, 1998, Wealth, Work, and Health, 1999; bd. editors: Am. Econ. Rev., 1980-83; contbr. articles to profl. jours. Recipient Merit award NIH, 1995—. Mem. NIA (monitoring com., health and retirement survey, chair NAS panel on immigration, prin. investigator New Immigrant Survey), Am. Econ. Assn., Phi Beta Kappa. Office: RAND PO Box 2138 Santa Monica CA 90407-2138 Business E-Mail: smith@rand.org.

SMITH, JAMES W., JR., state supreme court justice; b. Louisville, Miss., Oct. 28, 1943; BS, U. So. Miss., 1965; JD, Jackson Sch. Law, 1972; MEd with honors, Miss. Coll., 1973. Bar: Miss. 1972, U.S. Dist. Ct. (no. and so. dists.) Miss. 1973, U.S. Ct. Appeals (5th cir.) 1974. Pvt. practice, Pearl, Miss., 1972-78, Brandon, Miss., 1979-80; pros. atty. City of Pearl, 1973-80; prosecutor Rankin County, Miss., 1976; dist. atty. 20th Jud. Dist., Miss., 1977-82; judge Rankin County, 1982-92; justice Miss. Supreme Ct., 1993—, chief justice, 2004—. With U.S. Army, 1966-69. Named Wildlife Conservationist of Yr. Rankin County, 1988, Lawyer Yr. Miss. Coll. Sch. Law, 2006, Ams. 500 Leading Judges, 2006; recipient Alumnus of Yr. award Hinds C.C., 1996, Disting. Pub. Servant award U. So. Mo., 2006, Amicus award Miss. Coll.; Juris Sodalitas fellow 2006; named to Hall Fame, U. So. Miss., 2006. Fellow Miss. Bar Found. (bd. dirs. 1998); mem. Miss. State Bar Assn., Rankin County Bar Assn. Office: Carroll Gartin Justice Bldg PO Box 117 Jackson MS 39205-0117 Office Phone: 601-359-2093.

SMITH, JAMES WALKER, lawyer; b. SI, NY, May 11, 1957; s. James Patrick and Ann Catherine (Sullivan) S.; m. Erin Patricia Murphy, Aug. 15, 1982; children: Patrick James, Daniel Timothy, Meghan Kathleen, James John. BA magna cum laude, Fordham U., 1979, JD, 1982; LLM, NYU, 1988. BAr: N.Y. 1983, N.J. 1984, Pa. 1993, U.S. Supreme Ct. 1994. Assoc. Mendes & Mount, NYC, 1982, Costello Shea & Gaffney, NYC, 1982-86; ptnr. Anderson Kill Olick & Oshinsky P.C., NYC, 1986-96, Smith Abbot, LLP, NYC, 1996—. Arbitrator N.Y.C. (N.Y.) Civil Ct., 1987-89; faculty chairperson hosp. law Fordham Law Sch., N.Y.C., 1989-93; mediator U.S. Dist. Ct. (so. dist.) N.Y., N.Y.C., 1992-96. Author: Hospital Liability, 1985—; editor-in-chief: New York Practice Guide, 1993-97; contbg. editor: Medical Malpractice Law and Strategy, 1993—; bd. editors Fordham Urban Law Jour., 1981-82. Mem. N.Y. County Lawyer's Assn. (com. on tort law 1993-95), Assn. of the Bar of the City of N.Y. (com. on tort law 1990-92, com. on state cts. 1994—). Roman Catholic. Avocations: golf, coaching youth basketball. Home: 15 Flagg Ct Staten Island NY 10304-1157 Office: Smith Abbot LLP 100 Maiden Ln New York NY 10038-4818

SMITH, JAMES WARREN, pathologist, educator, microbiologist, parasitologist; b. Logan, Utah, July 5, 1934; s. Kenneth Warren and Nina Lou (Sykes) S.; m. Nancy Chesterman, July 19, 1958; children: Warren, Scott. BS, U. Iowa, 1956, MD, 1959. Diplomate Am. Bd. Pathology. Intern Colo. Gen. Hosp., Denver, 1959—60; resident U. Iowa Hosps., Iowa City, 1960—65; asst. prof. pathology U. Vt., Burlington, 1967—70; prof. pathology Ind. U., Indpls., 1970—98, chmn. dept. pathology and lab. medicine, 1992—98, Nordshow prof. of lab. medicine, 1997—98, prof. emeritus, 1998—. Contbr. articles to profl. jours. Served to lt. comdr. USN, 1965-67. Recipient Outstanding Contbn. to Clin. Microbiology award South Ctrl. Assn. Clin. Microbiology, 1977. Fellow Coll. Am. Pathologists (chmn. microbiology resource com. 1981-85); mem. AMA, Infectious Disease Soc. Am., Am. Soc. Investigative Pathology, Royal Soc. Tropical Medicine and Hygiene, Am. Soc. Clin. Pathology, Am. Soc. Microbiology, Am. Soc. Tropical Medicine and Hygiene, U.S.-Can. Acad. Pathology, Assn. Pathology Chairs, Binford Dammin Soc. Infectious Disease Pathologists, Soc. Protozoologists. Home: 4375 Cold Spring Rd Indianapolis IN 46228-3327 Office: Ind U Med Ctr 635 Barnhill Dr Rm A128 Indianapolis IN 46202-5126

SMITH, JANE SCHNEBERGER, retired city administrator; b. Chgo., Aug. 9, 1928; d. Frank R. and Marion (Durante) Schneberger; m. Z. Erol Smith Jr., Oct. 28, 1950 (div. 1974); children: Suzan MacKenzie Smith, Tracy Smith Cawley, Cameron Farley, Z. Erol III, Kimberly Van Den Elzen, Scott. BA in Chemistry, U. Colo., 1950; MA in Comm., Mich. State U., East Lansing, 1978, PhD in Ednl. Adminstrn., 1987. Chemist Kellogg Switchboard, Chgo., 1950-51; v.p. South Cook County Girl Scouts, Harvey, Ill., 1967-69, staff advisor, 1970-72; tchr. Crab Orchard Sch., Palos Heights, Ill., 1969-70; program and tng. dir. Mich. Capitol. Coun. Girl Scouts, Lansing, Mich., 1972-75; dir. svc. learning ctr. Mich. State U., East Lansing, 1975-81; city clk. City of Ashland, Wis., 1981-89, interim city adminstr., 1989-90; ret., 1990; acting city clk. City of Ashland, 2003, 2006. Cons. vol. adminstrn., Mich., Wis., 1975—. Co-editor: Looking Backward Moving Forward, 1987, Roots and Wings, 2002; contbr. articles to profl. jours. v.p. Mich. Capitol Girl Scout Coun., Lansing, 1976-78; bd. dirs. Lansing RSVP, 1976-81, Ashland Mus., 1985-87, Ptnrs. in Recovery, 1985-87; v.p. Friends of the Libr., 1992-97, pres., 1997-99; sec. New Horizons, 1985-90, New Day Shelter, 1990-99, v.p., 1993-95, pres., 1995-97, sec., 1997-99; pres. LWV of Ashland Bayfield County, 1992-93, 96-98; sec. No. Wis. History Ctr., 1992-94; commr. Ashland Water and Wastewater Utility, 1993-96; mem. Ashland Beautification Com., 1993—, Big Top Chautauqua, 1996-2003, vice chair Alliance for Sustainability, 1994-99; v.p. GFWC/Ashland Monday Club, 1994-98, pres., 1998-2000, 1st v.p. 10th Dist. GFWC-W1, 2000-02; mem. Ashland County Human Svcs. Bd., 1998—, vice chair, 2003-04, Restore the Depot Com., 2001—; co-chair comprehensive plan update com., 2002—05. co-chair comprehensive plan implementation com., 2006—; mem. tree bd. City of Ashland, 2002—, planning commn., 2004—. Recipient cert. appreciation Mich. Capitol Girl Scout Coun., 1975, Thanks Badge, 1972, Tribute to Excellence award LWV of Wis., 1999. Mem. Internat. Assn. Mcpl. Clks., Wis. Mcpl. Clks. Assn. (bd. dir. 1984-86), Am. Bus. Women's Assn. (scholarship chmn. 1985), Zonta (pres. 1979-81), Ashland Hist. Soc. (bd. dirs.). Roman Catholic. Avocations: stained glass, gardening, stamp collecting/philately, genealogy. Home: 700 MacArthur Ave Ashland WI 54806-2903 Personal E-mail: smith023@centurytel.net.

SMITH, JANET HUGIE, lawyer; b. Logan, Utah, Aug. 1, 1945; BA magna cum laude, Utah State U., 1967; MA cum laude, Stanford U., 1969; JD, U. Utah, 1976. Bar: Utah 1976, US Supreme Ct. 1992, U.S. Ct. Appeals (10th cir.) 1977, (9th cir.) 2003, US Dist. Ct. Colo. 2004. Shareholder, exec. com. Ray, Quinney & Nebeker, Salt Lake City, 1983—. Mem. ABA (labor and employment law sect.), Utah State Bar (labor and employment law sect.), CUE (labor lawyers adv. coun.), Am. Law Coun., Am. Coll. Trial Lawyers, Aldon J. Anderson Am. Inns of Ct. Office: Ray Quinney & Nebeker 36 S State St Ste 1400 Salt Lake City UT 84111-1431 Business E-Mail: jhsmith@rqn.com.

SMITH, JANET SUE, systems process specialist; b. Chgo., Jan. 15, 1945; d. Curtis Edwin and Margaret Louise (Yost) Smith. BA, Ind. U., 1967. Sales mgr. Marshall Field & Co., Chgo., 1968-70, programmer, 1970-72; sr. programmer, analyst Trailer Train Co., Chgo., 1972-75; mgr. data base and systems devel. Railinc-Assn. Am. R.R., Washington, 1975-85, asst. v.p., corp. sec., 1985-93, asst. v.p. strategic systems, 1994-98; exec. dir. Interline Svc., 1998-99, asst. v.p. bus. svc., 1999—2001; owner JSSmith Consulting LLC, Chapel Hill, NC, 2002—05, Bloomington, Ind., 2005—. Nat. student v.p. YWCA, 1966-67; bd. dir., v.p. planning and fin. Guide Internat.; advisor Jr. Achievement; mem. alumni bd. dir. Coll. Arts and Scis. Ind. U., co-chair colloquium for women, mem. internat. studies adv. coun. Mem.: Woodburn Guild, Ind. U. Alumni Assn. (life). Home and Office: JSSmith Cons LLC 3141 E Wyndam Ct Bloomington IN 47401-4495

SMITH, JARED RUSSELL WILLIAM, research executive, research scientist, consultant, poet; b. Cleve., Mar. 24, 1950; s. Russell Floyd William Smith and Mary Wiltrude Lee; m. Deborah Jane Parriott; children: Russell Jared Webster, Heather Frances. BA cum laude, NYU, 1973, MA, 1976. V.p. The Energy Bur., Inc., NYC, 1976—86; assoc. dir. Inst. Gas Tech., Des Plaines, Ill., 1986—99; spl. appointee Argonee Nat. Lab., Ill., 1999—2000; cons., 2001—. Adj. faculty NYU, N.Y.C., 1974-76; mem. adv. bd. La. State U., Baton Rouge, 1999—; adviser to Pres.'s Commn. on Critical Infrastructure Protection, Washington, 1997—; bd. dirs., adviser N.Y. Quar. Literary Found., N.Y.C., 1986. Author: (poetry books) Song of the Blood, 1983, Dark Wing, 1986, Keeping the Outlaw Alive, 1988, Walking the Perimeters of the Plate Glass Window Factory, 2000, Lake Michigan adapted to stage by David Lightner, 2003, Lake Michigan and Other Poems, 2005, Where Images Become Imbued with Time, 2007, (CD) Seven Minutes Before the Bombs Drop, 2006; editor: (books) Integrating Microelectronics into Gas Distribution, 1987, Gas, Oil and Coal Biotechnology, 1990 Election dist. leader Dem. Party, White Plains, N.Y., 1972; chmn. nominating com. Sch. Dist. 181, Hinsdale, Ill., 1993; adv. bd. mem. N.Y. Quar., 2005; bd. dirs. DuPage Symphony Orch., 2006. Mem. Acad. Am. Poets, Chgo. Poets Club, Poets and Patrons (pres.), Ill. State Poetry Soc. Democrat. Avocations: literature, fishing, hiking, painting, music. Home: 2630 Longview Dr Lisle IL 60532 E-mail: smithjrw@comcast.net.

SMITH, JASON A. B., lawyer; b. Washington, Aug. 21, 1971; BA, Columbia Univ., 1993; JD, NYU, 1996. Bar: NY 1998. Ptnr., structured fin. and derivatives practice Weil Gotshal & Manges, NYC. Mem.: ABA, NY State Bar Assn. Office: Weil Gotshal & Manges 767 Fifth Ave New York NY 10153 Home Phone: 212-586-4726; Office Phone: 212-310-8914. Office Fax: 212-310-8007. Business E-Mail: jason.smith@weil.com.

SMITH, JEAN KENNEDY, former ambassador; b. Brookline, Mass., Feb. 20, 1928; d. Joseph P. and Rose Kennedy; m. Stephen E. Smith (dec. 1990); 4 children. BA, Manhattanville Coll.; Degree (hon.), NYU, Fordham U., Nat. U. Ireland, Dublin City U. Founder, dir., chair Very Spl. Arts, 1974—; amb. to Ireland Dublin, 1993-98. Author: (with George Plimpton) Chronicles of Courage, 1993; contbr. articles on the disabled to profl. jours. Trustee John F. Kennedy Ctr. Performing Arts, 1964—. Recipient Sec.'s award Dept. Vets. Affairs, Vol. of Yr. award People-to-People Com. Handicapped, Margaret Mead Humanitarian award Coun. Cerebral Palsy Auxs., Jefferson award Am. Inst. Pub. Svc., Spirit of Achievement award Yeshiva U., Humanitarian award Capital Children's Mus., Irish Am. of Yr. award Irish Am. Mag., 1995, Rotary One Internat. award Rotary Club Chgo., 1997, Terence Cardinal Cooke Humanitarian award, 1997.

SMITH, JEAN WEBB (MRS. WILLIAM FRENCH SMITH), civic worker; b. LA; d. James Ellwood and Violet (Hughes) Webb; m. George William Vaughan, Mar. 14, 1942 (dec. Sept. 1963); children: George William Vaughan, Merry Vaughan; m. William French Smith, Nov. 6, 1964. BA summa cum laude, Stanford U., Calif., 1940. Mem. Nat. Vol. Svc. Adv. Coun., 1973—76, vice chmn., 1974—76; dir. Beneficial Std. Corp., 1976—85; bd. dirs. Cmty. TV So. Calif., 1979—93. Bd. dirs. United Way, Inc., 1973—80, Nat. Symphony Orch., 1980—85; nat. bd. dirs. Boys' Club Am., 1977—80; mem. Pres.'s Commn. White House Fellowships, 1980—90, Nat. Coun. Humanities, 1987—90, Calif. Arts Commn., 1971—74, vice chmn., 1973—74; bd. dirs. The Founders, Music Ctr., LA, 1971—74; bd. dirs. costume coun. Los Angeles County Mus. Art, 1971—73; bd. dirs. LA chpt. NCCJ, 1977—80, LA World Affairs Coun., 1990, LA chpt. ARC, 1994—95; mem. adv. bd. Salvation Army, 1979—; bd. overseers Hoover Instn. War, Revolution and Peace, 1989—94; bd. govs. Calif. Cmty. Found., 1990—; bd. dirs. Hosp. Good Samaritan, 1973—80, mem. exec. com., 1975—80; bd. fellows Claremont U. Ctr. and Grad. Sch., 1987—; bd. regents Children's Hops. LA, 1993—. Named Woman of the Yr. for Cmty. Svc., LA Times, 1958; recipient Citizens of the Yr. award, Boys Clubs Greater LA, 1982, Life Achievement award, LA Coun. Boy Scouts Am., 1985. Mem.: Kappa Kappa Gamma, Assn. Jr. Leagues Am. (dir. region XII 1956—58, pres. 1958—60), Jr. League LA (pres. 1954—55, Spirit of Volunteerism award 1996), Phi Beta Kappa. Home: 11718 Wetherby Ln Los Angeles CA 90077-1348

SMITH, JEFFERY W., architect; m. Nancy Smith. Grad., La. State U., Baton Rouge. With Obst Assocs., pres., 1985; founder, prin. Smith Architectural Group, Inc., Palm Beach, Fla., 1989—. Prin. works include La Follia, 1993, Villa Venezia, La Reverie, Serenity (Elizabeth L. and John H. Schuler award, Preservation Found. Palm Beach, 2007). Chmn. Palm Beach Archtl. Commn., Landmark Preservation Commn. Mem.: AIA. Office: Smith Archtl Group Inc 206 Phipps Plz Palm Beach FL 33480 Office Phone: 561-832-0202. Office Fax: 561-832-3443. *

SMITH, JEFFREY A., lawyer; b. Trenton, Tenn., Sept. 27, 1963; s. Nathan L. and Mary Jane (Ledsinger) S. BS in Acctg., U. Tenn. at Martin, 1985; JD, MBA, Memphis State U., 1991. Cost acct. Goodyear Tire & Rubber, Union City, Tenn., 1986-88; atty. Bill Barron, Atty., Trenton, Tenn., 1991-93, Kizer, Bonds, Crocker & Hughes, Milan, Tenn., 1993-95, Jeffrey A. Smith, Trenton, Tenn., 1995—. City atty. City of Dyer, Tenn., 1993-95, City of Kenton, Tenn., 1996—; bd. dirs. United Way of West Tenn., Jackson, 1997—. Elected mem.-alderman Bd. of Mayor & Aldermen, Rutherford, Tenn., 1993—; elected mem.-commr. Gibson County Bd. County Commrs., 1994—. Office: Jeffrey A Smith Atty PO Box 462 Trenton TN 38382-0462 Home: 16 Mcwherter Ln Rutherford TN 38369-9605

SMITH, JEFFREY ANDREWS, musician, educator, sound recording engineer; b. Tulsa, Aug. 25, 1955; s. Charles Lee Smith and Dorothy Gernon Babcock; m. Robin Karen Hock, 1986. MusB with distinction, U. Kans., Lawrence, 1977; MusB in Edn. with honors, U. Tulsa, 1978, MA in Music Edn., 1979; MusM, Cleve. Inst. Music, 1983. Cert. tchr. State of Okla., 1983. Prin. violist Signature Symphony Orch., Tulsa, 1978—, Bartlesville Symphony Orch., Bartlesville, Okla., 1985—, Internat. String Orch., Graz, Austria, 1996; instrumental music dir. Allison Jr. HS, Wichita, Kans., 1979—83, Bell Mid. Sch., Tulsa, 1983—88, Edison Prep. Sch., Tulsa, 1988—; pres., CEO SongSmith Records, Tulsa, 1986—; violist Signature String Quartet, Tulsa, 2000—; adj. faculty Okla. Wesleyan U., Bartlesville, Okla., 2002—. Prodr.: (CD) All Strings Attached, 2002, Christmas at the Capital, 2001, Tulsa Bagpipe Band, 2003. Recipient Excellence award, Tulsa Pub. Schs., 1998; scholar U. So. Calif. String Congress, Am. Fedn. Musicians, 1973. Mem.: NEA, Tulsa Classroom Tchrs. Assn., Okla. Music Educators Assn. (all state chmn. 1992), Am. Fedn. Musicians, Local 94, Am. String Tchrs. Assn., Okla. Chpt. (pres. 1996—98, Tchr. of Yr. 2003). Avocations: model aircraft, racecars, motorcycling. Home: 4205 N Lions Ave Broken Arrow OK 74012 Home Phone: 918-355-8693. Personal E-mail: songsmithrecords@cox.net.

SMITH, JEFFREY AUSTEN, lawyer; b. Queens, NY, Sept. 6, 1952; AB cum laude, Harvard U., 1974; JD, U. Pa., 1981. Bar: Pa. 1982, NY 1992, US Ct. of Appeals (3d cir.) 1982. Assoc. Cravath Swaine & Moore LLP, NYC, 1992—98, ptnr., 1998—, mng. ptnr. adminstrn., 2000—05. Contbr. articles to profl. jours. Mem. adv. bd. Urban Assembly. Mem.: ABA (chmn. com. environ. disclosure), Urban Assembly (adv. bd.). Office: Cravath Swaine & Moore LLP Worldwide Plz 825 Eighth Ave New York NY 10019-7475 Office Phone: 212-474-1514. Office Fax: 212-474-3700. Business E-Mail: jsmith@cravath.com.

SMITH, JEFFREY CHIPPS, art educator; MA, Columbia U., 1975, MPhil, 1977, PhD, 1979. Kay Fortson chair in European art U. Tex., Austin, 1979—. Author: Nuremberg, A Renaissance City, 1500-1618, 1983, German Sculpture of the Later Renaissance, c. 1520-1580: Art in an Age of Uncertainty, 1994, Sensuous Worship: Jesuits and the Art of Early Catholic Reformation in Germany, 2002, The Northern Renaissance, 2004, The Art of the Goldsmith in Late Fifteenth Century Germany: The Virgin and Her Bishop, 2006; editor: New Perspectives on the Art of Renaissance Nuremberg: Five Essays, 1985; editor: (introduction to) E. Panofsky, The Life and Art of Albrecht Durer, 1943—2005; reviewer in field, —; contbr. articles to profl. jours. Alexander von Humboldt-Stiftung fellow, Bonn, Germany, ACLS grantee, NEH grantee, Getty Found. grantee, Guggenheim Found. grantee, Kimbell Art Found. grantee, Zentralinstitut Kunstgeschicht fellow. Mem.: Sixteenth Century Soc. and Conf. (bd. dir. 2004—), Renaissance Soc. Am. (bd. dirs. 2000—, editor Renaissance Quarterly 2003—06), Coll. Art Assn. (bd. dir. 1996—2000). Office: U Tex Dept Art and Art History Austin TX 78712 Home Phone: 512-451-0097; Office Phone: 512-232-2609. Business E-Mail: chipps@mail.utexas.edu.

SMITH, JEFFREY G., lawyer; b. Mineola, NY, Feb. 21, 1948; s. Robert R. and Helen E. (Graham) S.; m. Lynn J. Fielden, June 16, 1974; children: Allyson M., Graham H., Brendan C. AA, Dutchess C.C., Poughkeepsie, NY, 1972; AB, Vassar Coll., 1974; M in Pub. Adminstrn., Princeton U., NJ, 1977; JD, Yale U., New Haven, Conn., 1978. Bar: N.Y. 1979, Calif. 1988, U.S. Dist. Ct. (so. and ea. dists.) N.Y. 1979, U.S. Dist. Ct. (so. dist.) Calif. 1989, U.S. Dist. Ct. (ctrl. dist.) Calif. 1990, U.S. Dist. Ct. Colo. 1998, U.S. Dist. Ct. Nev. 2000, U.S. Ct. Appeals (6th, 8th and 9th cirs.) 1985, U.S. Ct. Appeals (2d cir.) 1987, U.S. Ct. Appeals (3d cir.) 1992, U.S. Ct. Appeals (4th cir.) 1998, U.S. Ct. Appeals (5th cir.) 2000, U.S. Tax Ct. 1979, U.S. Supreme Ct. 1983. Assoc. Fried, Frank, Harris, Shriver & Jacobson, NYC, 1978-81, Wolf Haldenstein Adler Freeman & Herz, LLP, NYC, 1981-86, ptnr., 1987—. Bd. dirs. Osborne Assn., NYC, chair, 2004—; bd. dirs. Dutchess C.C. Found., Poughkeepsie. Mem. ABA, N.Y. State Bar Assn., Calif. State Bar Assn., Assn. Bar of City of N.Y. Avocations: scuba diving, sailing. Office: Wolf Haldenstein et al 270 Madison Ave New York NY 10016-0601 Home Phone: 914-941-0886; Office Phone: 212-545-4600. E-mail: smith@whafh.com.

SMITH, JEFFREY GREENWOOD, retired military officer; b. Ft. Sam Houston, Tex., Oct. 14, 1921; s. Henry Joseph Moody and Gladys Adrienne (Haile) S.; m. Dorothy Jane Holland, June 2, 1948; children: Meredith B. Exnicios, Jennifer H. Smith, Jeffrey Greenwood, Tracy E. McDonald, Melissa A. Deutsch, Ashley A. Pollock. BS in Civil Engring, Va. Mil. Inst., 1943; MS in Mech. Engring, Johns Hopkins U., 1949; MA in Internat. Affairs, George Washington U., 1964. Commd. 2d lt. U.S. Army, 1944, advanced through grades to lt. gen., 1975; service in CBI, Korea, Germany and Vietnam; comdr. 2d Inf. Div., Korea, 1971-73; dep. chief staff ops. Hdqrs. Army Forces Command, Ft. McPherson, Ga., 1973-74, chief staff, 1974-75; comdr. 1st U.S. Army, Ft. Meade, Md., 1975-79; ret., 1979; dir. govt. rels. Ethyl Corp., Washington, 1980—, v.p. govt. rels., 1992—, ret., 1994. Decorated D.S.M., Silver Star, Legion of Merit with 3 oak leaf clusters, D.F.C., Bronze Star with V device and 2 oak leaf clusters, Air medal with 12 oak leaf clusters, Army Commendation medal with oak leaf cluster, Purple Heart with oak leaf cluster, Combat Inf. badge (2); breast Order Yun Hui Republic China; Order Security Merit Korea; Gallantry Cross with silver and gold stars (Vietnam) Army Distinguished Service Order Mem. Assn. U.S. Army (dir. army hist. found.), Mil. Order Carabao, U.S. Cavalry Assn., Kappa Alpha, Tau Beta Pi. Clubs: Army and Navy. Home: 3000 Sevor Ln Alexandria VA 22309-2221 E-mail: genjeffrey@aol.com.

SMITH, JEFFREY HARTMAN, lawyer; b. Salina, Kans., Oct. 24, 1944; s. Robert B. and Alice Mae (Williams) S.; m. Claudia Jean Chyle, June 18, 1966; children: Amy Elisabeth, Katherine Ann. BS, U.S. Mil Acad., 1966; JD, U. Mich., 1971. Bar: Mich. 1971, D.C. 1989. Asst. legal advisor Office of Legal Advisor Dept. of State, Washington, 1975-84; minority counsel Senate Armed Svcs. Com., Washington, 1984—86, gen. counsel, 1986-88; ptnr. Arnold & Porter, Washington, 1988—95; gen. counsel CIA, 1995—96; ptnr., Govt. Contracts Practice Group & Public Policy/Legislative Practice Group Arnold & Porter, Washington, 1996—. Mem. bd. dirs. The Henry L. Stimson Ctr., Washington, 1990-; mem. Commn. to Review Roles & Missions of Armed Svcs. & chmn., Joint Security Commn., US Dept. Def.; chief, Clinton Transition team, US Dept. Def., 1992-1993. Mem. Bd. Vis., US Mil. Acad., 1993-; bd. vis., Univ. Mich. Law Sch.; gen. counsel The Goldwater Found., Washington, 1988—; trustee Aerospace Corp., El Segundo, Calif., 1990—. Atty. JAG Corps US Army, 1971—75. Mem. Am. Soc. Internat. Law, Coun. Fgn. Rels. Office: Arnold & Porter 555 12th St NW Washington DC 20004-1206 Office Phone: 202-942-5115. Office Fax: 202-942-5999. Business E-Mail: jeffrey.smith@aporter.com.

SMITH, JEFFREY MICHAEL, lawyer; b. Mpls., July 9, 1947; s. Philip and Gertrude E. (Miller) S.; 1 son, Brandon Michael. Student, U. Malaya, Kuala Lumpur, 1967—68; BA summa cum laude, U. Minn., Mpls., 1970, JD magna cum laude, 1973. Bar: Ga. 1973. Assoc. Powell, Goldstein, Frazier & Murphy, 1973-76; ptnr. Rogers & Hardin, 1976-79, Bondurant, Stephenson & Smith, 1979-85, Arnall, Golden & Gregory, 1985-92, Katz, Smith & Cohen, 1992-98; prin. shareholder Greenberg Traurig LLP, 1998—. Vis. lectr. Duke U., 1976-77, 79-80, 89-93; adj. prof. Emory U., 1976-79, 81-82; lectr. Vanderbilt U., 1977-82. Editor, reviewer Accountant's Legal Liability, 1981; co-author: Preventing Legal Malpractice, 1999, Legal Malpractice, 2007, Legal Opinions in Business Transactions, 2007. Bd. visitors Law Sch. U. Minn., 1976-82. Mem. ABA (vice-chmn. com. profl. liability 1980-82, mem. standing com. lawyer's profl. liability 1981-85, chmn. 1985-87, standing com. lawyer competency 1993-95), State Bar Ga. (chmn. profl. liability and ins. com. 1978-89, trustee Inst. Cont. Legal Edn. in Ga. 1979-80), Order of the Coif, Phi Beta Kappa. Home: 145 15th St NE Unit 811 Atlanta GA 30309-3559 Office Phone: 678-553-2333. Business E-Mail: smithj@gtlaw.com.

SMITH, JENNIE, artist; b. San Francisco, 1981; Student, Burren Coll Art, Ireland, 2002; BFA in Drawing, Mpls. Coll. Art & Design, 2004. Prin. works include Migration, 2003, Animal Its Habitat, 2004, Animals Slumber, 2004, Kite Wars, 2004, We'll Never Tell You Where We Have Gone, 2004, exhibited in group shows at Made at MCAD, Mpls., 2005, Sr. Exhbn., Mpls. Coll. Art & Design, 2005, Drawing Show, Soo Vac Gallery, Mpls., 2005, Grp. Drawing Show, The Gen. Store, Milw., 2005, Four Color Drawing Show, Van Harrison Gallery, Chgo., 2005, Whitney Biennial: Day for Night, Whitney Mus. Am. Art, 2006, exhibitions include Bull. Bd. Project 008, Calif. Coll. Arts Wattis Inst. Contemporary Arts, San Francisco, 2006, Rena Bransten Gallery, San Francisco, 2006. Mailing: c/o Rena Bransten Gallery 77 Geary St San Francisco CA 94108

SMITH, JEROME (DR. JEROME SMITH), not-for-profit developer, film producer, writer; b. Birmingham, Ala., Sept. 10, 1956; s. Herny Horace and Susie Govan Smith. BS in Edn., Daniel Payne Coll., Birmingham, Ala., 1979. Cert. tchr. Ala., Ohio. Tchr. Birmingham Bd. of Edn., Ala., 1979—84, Cleve. Bd. of Edn., 1984—95; CEO Poise Entertainment Edn., Cleve., 1999—. Ednl. prodr. Urban League, Cleve., 2001—03, United Black Fund, Cleve., 2000—03, Rock and Roll Hall of Fame, Cleve., 1999—, dir. cmty. svc., 2003—; songwriter Hilltop Records, Hollywood, Calif., 2004—; TV host You Can Do It Program. Author: Greatest You Can Do It Program, 2004; host, prodr. Poise Entertainment Edn. Co.'s "You Can Do It Program" Hall of Fame and Mus. Named to Nat. Dean's List; recipient Best Song honors, Hilltop Records, Best Songwriter honors, Americord, Cmty. Svc. award, Help Educate for Svc.; grantee, Urban League, 2002, United Black Fund, 2003, Ward 7 City of Cleve., 2004. Baptist. Avocations: songwriting, horseback riding. Office: Poise Entertainment Edn Co 15115 Elm Ave Cleveland OH 44112 Office Phone: 216-561-0277. Personal E-mail: poiseed@aol.com. E-mail: jeromesmith@sbcglobal.net.

SMITH, JERRY EDWIN, federal judge; b. Del Rio, Tex., Nov. 7, 1946; s. Lemuel Edwin and Ruth Irene (Henderson) Smith; m. Mary Jane Blackburn, June 4, 1977; children: Clark, Ruth Ann, J.J. BA, Yale U., 1969, JD, 1972. Bar: Tex. 1972. Law clk. to judge US Dist. Ct. (no. dist.) Tex., Lubbock, 1972—73; assoc. then ptnr. Fulbright & Jaworski, Houston, 1973—84; dir. Harris County housing auth., Tex., 1978—80; special asst. office of atty. gen., Tex., 1981—82; Chmn. Houston Civ. Svc. Comm., 1982—84; city atty. City of Houston, 1984—87; cir. judge US Ct. Appeals (5th cir.), Houston, 1988—. Chmn. Harris County Rep. Party, Houston, 1977—78; committeeman State Rep. Exec. Com., Tex., 1976—88. Mem.: Houston Bar Assn., State Bar Tex. Methodist. Office: US Ct Appeals Bob Casey US Courthouse 515 Rusk St Rm 12621 Houston TX 77002-2698 *

SMITH, JESSE GRAHAM, JR., dermatologist, educator; b. Winston-Salem, NC, Nov. 22, 1928; s. Jesse Graham and Pauline Field (Griffith) S.; m. Dorothy Jean Butler, Dec. 28, 1950; children: Jesse Graham, Cynthia Lynn, Grant Butler. BSM, Duke U., 1962, MD, 1951. Diplomate: Am. Bd. Dermatology (dir. 1974-83, pres. 1980-81). Intern VA Hosp., Chamblee, Ga., 1951—52; resident in dermatology Duke U., 1954—56, assoc. prof. dermatology, 1960—62, prof., 1962—67; resident U. Miami, 1956—57, asst. prof., 1956—60; prof. dermatology Med. Coll. Ga., 1967—91, chmn. dept. dermatology, 1967—91, acting chmn. dept. pathology, 1973—75, acting v.p. devel., 1984—85; chief staff Talmadge Meml. Hosp., Augusta, Ga., 1970—72; chief divsn. of dermatology U. South Ala., Mobile, 1991—98, prof. dermatology, 1991—99, prof. emeritus, 1999—. Mem. adv. coun. Nat. Inst. Arthritis, 1975-79 Mem. editl. bd. Archives of Dermatology, 1963-72, Jour. Investigative Dermatology, 1966-67, Jour. AMA, 1974-80; mem. editl. bd. So. Med. Jour., 1976-2000, assoc. editor, 1991-92, editor, 1992-2000; editor Jour. Am. Acad. Dermatology, 1978-88; contbr. chpts. to books, articles to profl. jours. Served with USPHS, 1952-54. Recipient Disting. Alumnus award Duke U. 1981 Fellow ACP, Royal Soc. Medicine; mem. Am. Acad. Dermatology (hon., dir. 1971-74, 78-88, pres.-elect 1988-89, pres. 1989-90, master 2003), Can. Dermatol. Assn. (hon.), Am. Dermatol. Assn. (hon. sec. 1976-81, pres. 1981-82), Soc. Investigative Dermatology (dir. 1964-69, pres. 1979-80), S.E. Dermatol. Assn. (sec. 1970-71, pres. 1975-76), Ga. Soc. Dermatology (pres. 1979-80), So. Med. Assn. (chmn. sect. dermatology 1973-74, Disting. Svc. award 2005), Assn. Profs. Dermatology (dir. 1976-77, 80-82, pres. 1984-86), Med. Rsch. Found. Ga. (bd. dir. 1967-91, pres. 1974-75), Alpha Omega Alpha Home: 4272 Bit and Spur # 4 Mobile AL 36608 Office: Diagnostic and Med Clinic 1700 Spring Hill Ave Mobile AL 36604-1407 Office Phone: 251-435-1200. E-mail: skeesmith@mindspring.com.

SMITH, JESSIE P. DOWLING, retired social services administrator; b. Sturgills, NC, June 15, 1918; d. Rohe V. and Stella Pennington (Eller) Smith; m. F. P. Smith, July 22, 1983. AB, Berea Coll., 1939; MSW, Columbia U., 1945. Social work assignments WPA, Ky., 1939—43; social worker ARC, New Orleans, 1943—45, Bklyn., 1943—45, Huntington, W.Va., 1946—56, Washington, 1946—56; instr. Sch. Social Work W.Va. U., Morgantown, 1953—54; cons. W.Va. Dept. Mental Health, Charleston, 1954—55; program supr. USPHS Clin. Ctr., Bethesda, Md., 1956—62; cons., social work NIMH, Chgo., 1962—66, NYC, 1962—66; assoc. regional health dir. Mental Health Programs, NYC, 1966—81; ret., 1981; v.p. adv. bd. Mental Retardation Substance Abuse Programs Davidson County Mental Health, NC, 1987—89, pres., 1988—89. Mem.: NASW (exec. bd. 1968—70, pres. Washington Met. Area chpt., pioneer steering com. 1999—), Columbia U. Alumni Fedn. Bd., Columbia U. Sch. Social Work Alumni Assn. (pres. 1979—81), Columbia U. Sch. Social Work (adv. coun.), Social Casework (editl. adv. bd. 1968—70), NC Coun. of Cmty. Mental Health Programs (adv. bd. 1987—92). Home: Apt 703 1330 Massachusetts Ave NW Washington DC 20005-4154

SMITH, JIMMIE DEE, lawyer; BBA, No. Ariz. U.; JD, Ariz. State U., 1970. Solo law practice, Yuma, Ariz., 1971—. Mem.: State Ariz. Bar Assn. (sec.-treas., 2nd v.p., 1st v.p., pres.-elect 2005—06, pres. 2006—07), Yuma County Bar Assn. (former pres.). Office: Atty at Law 221 S 2nd Ave Yuma AZ 85364-2265 Office Phone: 928-783-7809. Office Fax: 928-783-7800. E-mail: jimmiedeesmith@azbar.org.

SMITH, JO ANNE, writer, retired communications educator; b. Mpls., Mar. 18, 1930; d. Robert Bradburn and Virginia Mae S. BA, U. Minn., 1951, MA, 1957. Wire and sports editor Rhinelander (Wis.) Daily News, 1951-52; staff corr., night mgr. UPI, Mpls., 1952-56; interim instr. U. N.C., Chapel Hill, 1957-58; instr. U. Fla., Gainesville, 1959-65, asst. prof. journalism, communications, 1965-68, assoc. prof., 1968-76, prof., 1976-88, disting. lectr., 1977, prof. emeritus. Author: JM409 Casebook and Study Guide, 1976, Mass Communications Law Casebook, 1979, 3d edit., 1985. Active, Friends of Libr., Alachua County Humane Soc. Recipient outstanding Prof. award Fla. Blue Key, 1976; Danforth assoc., 1976-85. Mem. Women in Communications, Assn. Edn. in Journalism, Phi Beta Kappa, Kappa Tau Alpha. Democrat. Unitarian Universalist. Home: 208 NW 21st Ter Gainesville FL 32603-1732

SMITH, JOAN LOWELL, syndicated columnist, feature writer; b. Orange, NJ, June 20, 1933; d. William Jr. and Katherine Margaret (Macpherson) Lowell; m. John A. Nave, Dec. 14, 1957 (div. May 1961); children: Deborah Lowell Kelly, Nancy Nave Ferguson; m. Warren W. Smith, July 19, 1969. Student, Lasell Coll., 1951—52, Drake Bus. Sch., NYC, 1952—53. Exec. sec. Amb. Ernest A. Gross, NYC, 1954-57; adminstrv. asst., v.p. J.B. Williams Co. (Geritol), Clark, NJ, 1966-74; pub. rels. dir. NJ State Opera, Newark, 1974-78; weekly talk show host-radio Stas. WJDM-AM, WFME-AM, FM, Elizabeth and West Orange, NJ, 1974-82; weekly talk show host Sta. WCTV, Wometco, 1975-79; exec. dir. C. of C., Westfield, NJ, 1976-79; legis. aide Assemblyman C. Hardwick, NJ, 1980-82; exec. dir. Alzheimer's Disease Fund, Westfield, 1986-87; pub. rels. dir. Children's Specialized Hosp., Mountainside, NJ, 1993-94; pres., owner Media Mgmt., Westfield, 1974-95; feature writer, weekly columnist on animals The Star-Ledger, Newark, 1996—. Named one of 40 Women of Achievement, NJ State Assembly, 2001; recipient 46 awards, NJ Press Woman, 1991—, Humane Edn. award, Jersey Animal Coalition, 2001, Hero to Animals award, Animal Welfare Fedn. NJ, 2003, Dedication to Animals award, Humane Soc. U.S. N.E. Region, 2003, Hartz Mountain Top Cat Writer, Cat Writers Assn., 2005. Mem.: DAR (regent 1987—89), Westfield Day Care Ctr. (bd. dirs.), Nat. Fedn. Press Women (2d pl. award 1997, 1st pl. columnist award 1998), Assn. Children with Learning Disabilities (chmn. bd. dirs. 1980—82), Cat Writers Assn. Am. (2d pl. columnist 1999, top CAT writer 2005), Dog Writers Assn. Am. (top features writer 1999, top columnist award 2001, top features writer 2003), Daus. of Cin., Geneal. Soc. of West Fields (bd. dirs. 1984—88). Republican. Presbyterian. Avocations: bible studies, swimming, bridge, genealogy. Office: PO Box 302 Garwood NJ 07027-0302 E-mail: jsmith@startledger.com.

SMITH, JOANN CARROLL, library and information scientist; m. Michael Smith; children: Jenifer Jeané Wilkinson, Jonna Jarie Hawkins. BS, U. Ala., Tuscaloosa, 1972; MA, U. of Ala., Tuscaloosa, 1974; EdS, U. Ala., 1979; M in Libr. Svc., U. of Ala., Tuscaloosa, 1984, EdS level in Libr. Svc., 1993. Cert. Tchr. Tenn., 1997, Ala., 1972. Libr. media specialist Sullivan East HS, Bluff City, Tenn., 1997—2001, Sullivan South HS, Kingsport, Tenn., 2001—. Mem. bd. examiners Nat. Coun. Accreditation Tchr. Edn., bd. dirs. Treas. PACE Polit., North Johnson City Bapt., Johnson City, Tenn., 2004—06; dist. 1 dir. Tenn. Edn. Assn., Nashville, 2002—05. Recipient Oustanding Svc. to Ala. Librs., Libr. and Media Profls., 1996—97. Mem.: NEA, Tenn. Edn. Assn. (chair nea concerns com. 2002—04, bd. dirs. 2002—05, chair human rels. com. 2004—05), Sullivan County Edn. Assn. (pres. 1999—2001, treas. 2001—06, pres. 2006—), Tenn. Assn. Sch. Librs. (chair constn. and bylaws 2006—), Delta Kappa Gamma. Baptist. Avocations: reading, singing, travel. Home: 141 Bentley Parc Johnson City TN 37615 Office: Sullivan South HS Libr 1236 Moreland Dr Kingsport TN 37664 Home Phone: 423-283-9037; Office Phone: 423-354-1312. Home Fax: 423-283-9037. Personal E-mail: joannsmi@yahoo.com.

SMITH, JOANNE, marketing executive; Mgr. aviation mktg. & cargo sales DHL, v.p. mktg. planning; v.p. mktg. customers Song Airlines, 2003—05, pres., 2005—06; v.p. mktg. Delta Air Lines Inc., 2006—07, sr. v.p. flight services & global product devel., 2007—. Named a Woman to Watch, Advt. Age, 2007. Office: Delta Air Lines Inc PO Box 20706 Atlanta GA 30320-6001 Office Phone: 404-715-2600.

SMITH, JOANNE C., physiatrist; b. 1962; BS, Oakland U.; MD, Michigan State U.; MBA, U. Of Chgo. Grad. Sch. Of Bus. Cert. Physical Medicine and Rehabilitation. Chief residency Northwestern U. Med. Sch.; attending physician Rehabilitation Inst. of Chgo., 1992—94, med. dir. Day Rehabilitation Centers program, 1994—95, sr. v.p., COO Corp. Partnerships, 1995—97, sr. v.p. Corp. Strategy and Bus. Devel., 1997—2002, pres. nat. divsn., 2005—06, pres. CEO, 2006—. Asst. prof. Physical Medicine and Rehabilitation at Northwestern U. Feinberg Sch. of Medicine; founder Women's Health Rehabilitation program, Rehabilitation Inst. of Chgo.; vice-chmn. Hillenbrand Industries Inc., mem. bd. dirs., AptarGroup Inc. Named a Woman to Watch, Crain's Chgo. Bus., 2007; named one of Chicago's 'Top Doctors', Chgo. Mag., 2004, 2005, 2006. Mem.: The Chgo. Network. Office: Rehabilitation Inst of Chgo 345 E Superior St Chicago IL 60611 Office Phone: 312-238-6044. *

SMITH, JOE DORSEY, JR., retired newspaper executive; b. Selma, La., Apr. 6, 1922; s. Joe Dorsey and Louise (Lindsay) S.; 1 child, Lawrence Dorsey. BA, La. Coll. Pineville, 1939-43. Gen. mgr. Alexandria Daily Town Talk, La., 1958—, pub., 1965—; pres. McCormick & Co., Inc., 1968—, chmn., 1990-96. Served with USAF, 1942-45. Mem. Alexandria Golf and Country Club, Boston Club, New Orleans Club. Democrat. Episcopalian. Home: 2804 Georges Ln Alexandria LA 71301-4723 Office: Ste 1003 Hibernia Bldg 934 3rd St Alexandria LA 71301-8383 Home Phone: 318-443-1227; Office Phone: 318-448-3598. Personal E-mail: smith7462@aol.com.

SMITH, JOHN B., publishing executive; b. LaGrange, Ga. s. John Watson and Pressarene Whitfield Smith; m. Frances M. Evans; children: Pamela, Lori, John Jr. BS, Morehouse Coll.; MA, Atlanta U. Pub., CEO Atlanta Inquirer. Bd. dirs. Atlanta Fair & Exposition, Grade Homes Boys' Club, Boy Scouts of Am. Named one of Most Influential Black Americans, Ebony mag., 2006. Mem.: Nat. Newspaper Publishers Assn. (mem. bd. dirs., pres., Publisher of Yr. Award). Office: Nat Newspaper Pub Assn 3200 13th St, NW Washington DC 20010

SMITH, JOHN BREWSTER, library administrator; b. Bryan, Tex., June 26, 1937; s. Elmer Gillam and Sara Roland (Lull) S.; m. Ida Hawa, Dec. 28, 1963; children: Susan Helen, Rona Esther. BA, Tex. A & M U., 1960; MS, Columbia U., 1963, cert. advanced librarianship, 1984, DLS, 1991. Asst. law librarian Columbia U., NYC, 1963-66; asst. library dir. for pub. services Tex. A & M U., College Station, 1966-69, dir. libraries, 1969-74; dir. libraries, dean library scis. SUNY, Stony Brook, 1974-96, dir. library and info. sci. tchg. program, 1996-97; chief libr. Bronx Cmty. Coll., CUNY, 1997-2000, cons. on libr. mgmt., 2000—. Named Librarian of Year Tex. Library Assn., 1972 Mem. ALA. Home and Office: 115 Stetson Trail Georgetown TX 78628 Office Phone: 512-863-2835. Personal E-mail: jscounterpoint@yahoo.com.

SMITH, JOHN EDWIN, philosophy educator; b. Bklyn., May 27, 1921; s. Joseph Robert and Florence Grace (Dunn) S.; m. Marilyn Blanche Schulhof, Aug. 25, 1951; children: Robin Dunn, Diana Edwards. AB, Columbia U., 1942, PhD, 1948; BD, Union Theol. Sem., NYC, 1945; MA, Yale U., 1959; LL.D., U. Notre Dame, 1964. Instr. religion and philosophy Vassar Coll., 1945-46; instr., then asst. prof. Barnard Coll., 1946-52; mem. faculty Yale U., 1952—, prof. philosophy, 1959—, chmn. dept., 1961—, Clark prof. philosophy, 1972-91, Clark prof. philosophy emeritus, 1991—. Vis. prof. Union Theol. Sem., 1959, U. Mich., 1958; guest prof. U. Heidelberg, Germany, 1955-56; Fagothey chair of philosophy U. Santa Clara, 1984, vis. prof. Boston Coll., 1992; Dudleian lectr. Harvard, 1960; lectr. Am. Week, U. Munich, Germany, 1961; Suarez lectr. Fordham U., 1963; pub. lectr. King's College, Univ. London, 1965; Aquinas lectr. Marquette U., 1967; Warfield lectr. Princeton Theol. Sem., 1970; Fulbright lectr. Kyoto U., Japan, 1971; Sprunt lectr. Union Theol. Sem., Va., 1973; Mead-Swing lectr. Oberlin Coll., 1975; H. Richard Niebuhr lectr. Elmhurst Coll., Ill., 1977; Merrick lectr. Ohio Wesleyan U., 1977; Roy Wood Sellars lectr. Bucknell U., 1978; O'Hara lectr. U. Notre Dame, 1984; Winston Churchill lectr. Bristol (Eng.) U., 1985; Hooker disting. vis. prof. Mc Master U., 1985; mem. adv. com. Nat. Humanities Inst., New Haven, 1974, dir., 1977-80; Winston Churchill lectr. Bristol U., Eng., 1985. Author: Royce's Social Infinite, 1950, Value Convictions and Higher Education, 1958, Reason and God, 1961, The Spirit of American Philosophy, 1963, 2d edit., 1983, The Philosophy of Religion, 1965, Religion and Empiricism, 1967, Experience and God, 1968, revised edit., 1995, Themes in American Philosophy, 1970, Contemporary American Philosophy, 1970, The Analogy of Experience, 1973, Purpose and Thought: The Meaning of Pragmatism, 1978, America's Philosophical Vision, 1992, Jonathan Edwards, Puritan, Preacher, Philosopher, 1992, Quasi-Religions: Humanism, Marxism, Nationalism, 1994, Reason, Experience, and God, 1997; translator: (R. Kroner): Kant's Weltanschauung, 1956; editor: (Jonathan Edwards): Religious Affections, Vol. 2, 1959, An Edwards Reader, 1995; gen. editor, Yale edit.: Works of Jonathan Edwards, 1965-91, gen. editor emeritus, 1992—; Editorial bd.: Monist, 1962—, Jour. Religious Studies, Philosophy East and West, Jour. Chinese Philosophy, The Personalist Forum, Jour. Faith and Philosophy, Jour. Speculative Philosophy. Named Hon. Alumnus, Harvard Div. Sch., 1960; recipient Herbert W. Schneider award Soc. for Advancement of Am. Philosophy, 1990, Founder's medal Metaphys. Soc. Am., 1996; Am. Coun. Learned Socs. fellow, 1964-65. Mem. Culinary Inst. Am. (dir. New Haven affiliate), Am. Philos. Assn. (v.p. 1980, pres. 1981), Am. Theol. Soc. (pres. 1967-68), Metaphys. Soc. Am. (pres. 1970-71, founder's medal, 1996), Hegel Soc. Am. (pres. 1971), Charles S. Peirce Soc. (pres. 1992). Home: 300 Ridgewood Ave Hamden CT 06517-1428 Office: PO Box 201562 New Haven CT 06520-1562 E-mail: john.smith@yale.edu.

SMITH, JOHN FRANCIS, materials science educator; b. Kansas City, Kans., May 9, 1923; s. Peter Francis and Johanna Teresa (Spandle) S.; m. Evelyn Ann Ross, Sept. 1, 1947 (dec. July 1994); children— Mark Francis, Letitia Ann Smith Harder; m. Eileen R. Ross, Apr. 12, 1997. BA with distinction, U. Mo., Kansas City, 1948; PhD, Iowa State U., Ames, 1953. Grad. asst. Iowa State U., Ames, 1948-53, faculty and rsch. scientist, 1953—88, dept. chmn., div. chief Ames Lab., 1966-70, prof. emeritus, 1988. Cons. Tex. Instruments, Inc., Dallas and Attleboro, Mass., 1958-63, Argonne Nat. Lab., Ill., 1964-70, Iowa Hwy. Commn., Ames, Los Alamos Nat. Lab., N.Mex., 1984-88, bur. standards Nat. Inst. Standards and Tech., Gaithersburg, Md., 1988-91, Sandia Nat. Lab., Albuquerque, N.M., 1991-92, ASM Internat., Cleve., 1992—. Patentee ultrasonic determination of texture in metal sheet and plate, lead-free solder; author: Phase Diagrams of Binary Vanadium Alloys; Hellcats Over the Philippine Deep; co-author: Thorium: Preparation and Properties, 1975; editor: Calculation of Phase Diagrams and Thermochemistry of Alloy Phases, 1978, Jour. Phase Equilibrium and Diffusion, 1988-; contbr. articles to profl. publs. Mem. former comdr. Ames-Boone Squadron CAP, 1970-75. With USN, 1942-46, PTO, comdr. USNR, 1946-64. Decorated Air medal with cluster; recipient Disting. Svc. award CAP, Maxwell AFB, Ala., 1979, faculty citation Iowa State U. Alumni Assn., Ames, 1977. Fellow Am. Inst. Chemists, ASM (chmn. Des Moines chpt. 1966); mem. AIME, Materials Rsch. Soc., Polish Acad. Arts and Scis. (fgn.), Am. Legion, Silent Knights, Inc. (trustee 1980-96), Exptl. Aircraft Assn., Alpha Sigma Mu (trustee 1984-86). Roman Catholic. Avocation: flying. Home: 2919 S Riverside Ames IA 50010-8605 Office: Iowa State U Ames Lab 136F Wilhelm Hall Ames IA 50010

SMITH, JOHN FRANCIS, JR., (JACK SMITH), retired automotive executive; b. Worcester, Mass., Apr. 6, 1938; s. John Francis and Eleanor C. (Sullivan) S.; children: Brian, Kevin; m. Lydia G. Sigrist, Aug. 27, 1988; 1 stepchild, Nicola. BBA, U. Mass., 1960; MBA, Boston U., 1965. Fisher Body divsn. mgr. GM, Framingham, Mass., 1961-73, asst. treas. NYC, 1973-80, comptr. Detroit, 1980-81, dir. worldwide product planning,

1981-84, pres., gen. mgr. Oshawa, Ont., Canada, 1984-85, exec. v.p. internat. ops. Detroit, 1988-90, vice chmn. internat. ops., 1990, bd. dirs., mem. fin. com., 1990-98, COO, 1992, CEO, 1992—2000, pres., 1992—98, chmn. bd., 1996—2003; exec. v.p. GM Europe, Glattbrugg, Switzerland, 1986-87, pres., 1987-88. Mem. US Japan Bus. Coun.; bus. coun. Meml. Sloan-Kettering Cancer Ctr.; bd. dirs. Procter & Gamble Co., Swiss Re, Delta Air Lines Inc., 2000-, non-exec. chmn., 2004-; chmn. adv. bd. Alix Ptnrs. LLC/Questor Ptnrs. Funds. Mem. chancellor's exec. com. U. Mass., dir.; trustee United Way SE Mich., New Am. Revolution, Boston U.; bd. dirs. The Nature Conservancy. Mem. Am. Soc. Corp. Execs., Am. Auto Mfrs. Assn. (bd. dirs.), Econ. Club Detroit (bd. dirs.), The Bus. Coun., Beta Gamma Sigma (pres.), Dirs. Table. Roman Catholic. Office: Delta Air Lines Inc PO Box 20706 Atlanta GA 30320-6001 Office Phone: 404-715-2600. *

SMITH, JOHN FRANCIS, III, lawyer; b. White Plains, N.Y., Sept. 24, 1941; s. John Francis and Mary Dake (Mairs) S.; m. Susan Brown; children: John, Stephen, Peter. AB, Princeton U., 1963; LLB, Yale U., 1970. Bar: Pa. 1970, U.S. Supreme Ct. 1985. Assoc. Dilworth, Paxson, Kalish & Kauffman, Phila., 1970-75, ptnr., 1975-86, sr. ptnr., 1986-91; sr. litigation ptnr. Reed Smith LLP, Phila., 1991—, mem. exec. com., 1993-04; chancellor Reed Smith U., 2004—. Mem. exec. com. Employment Discrimination Referral Project, 1971-74; pres. Society Hill Civic Assn., 1975-76, Phila. Chamber Ensemble, 1977-80; bd. govs. Pa. Economy League (ea. divsn.), 1983—, sec. 1995-97; vice chair Health Care Task Force, 1993-96; bd. dirs. World Affairs Council Phila., 1983-87, chmn. program com., 1986-87; Burn Found., 1987-95, Internat. House Phila., chmn. bd. trustees, 2005-; moderator Main Line Unitarian Ch., 1986-89, 00—; founder and pres. Found. for Individual Responsibility and Social Trust (FIRST), 1995—. Served to lt. (j.g.) USNR, 1963-67; Vietnam. Fellow Am. Bar Found.; mem. ABA, Phila. Bar Assn., Unitarian Universalist Assn. (pres.'s coun.), Yale Law Sch. Alumni Assn. (exec. com. 1982-88, sec. 1987-88), Princeton Club (Phila.). Office: Reed Smith LLP 2500 One Liberty Pl Philadelphia PA 19103 Home Phone: 610-527-3320; Office Phone: 215-241-7920. E-mail: jsmith@reedsmith.com.

SMITH, JOHN KERWIN, lawyer; b. Oct. 18, 1926; 1 child, Cynthia. BA, Stanford U.; LLB, Hastings Coll. Law. Ptnr. Haley, Purchio, Sakai & Smith, Hayward, Calif.; pres. Calhoun Heights LLC, Garin Vista LLC. Pres. bd. dirs. Rowell Ranch Rodeo, Hastings Coll. Lawpres. Gen. ptnr. Oak Hills Apts., City Ctr. Commercial, Creekwood I and II Apts.; Road Parks commn. 1957; city coun. 1959-66, mayor 1966-70; chmn. Alameda County Mayors conf. 1968, revenue taxation com. League Calif. Cities, 1968; former vice chmn. Oakland-Alameda County Coliseum; vol. Hastings 1066 Found. (pres., vol. svc. award 1990), chmn. Martin Kauffman 100 Club; bd. dirs. Hastings Coll. of Law, 1999—, pres. bd. dirs., 2004—. Named Alumnus of Yr., Hastings Coll. Law, 1989. Mem. ABA, Calif. Bar Assn., Alameda County Bar Assn., Am. Judicature Soc., Rotary, 100 Club (chmn. bd. dirs.) Office: Haley Purchio Sakai & Smith 22320 Foothill Blvd Ste 620 Hayward CA 94541-2700 Office Phone: 510-538-6400. Personal E-mail: hpssem@aol.com.

SMITH, JOHN LEROY, mathematician, educator; b. Cooper, Tex., July 15, 1944; s. John Jr. and Annie (West) Smith; m. Barbara Ann Frazier, Dec. 27, 1965 (div. Apr. 1972); m. Mary Anne Anthony, June 17, 1978; children: Alexander Anthony, Anastasia Marie, Jeannette Joy. BS in Math., U. Wash., 1966; MA in Math., San Diego State U., 1971; BS in Info. & Computer Sci., U. Calif., Irvine, 1986. Computer operator U. Wash., Seattle, 1964-66; tchr. math., sci., English Highline (Wash.) Sch. Dist., 1966-70; tchr. math. & computer scis. Kwajalein (Marshall Islands) Jr./Sr. HS, 1973-75; instr. scuba diving Santa Ana (Calif.) Coll., 1978-91; prof. math., computer sci. Rancho Santiago CC Dist., Santa Ana, 1975—; math dept. chair Santiago Canyon Coll., Orange, Calif., 1998—2002. Spkr. Internat. Conv. Underwater Edn., 1978, 86, 87; treas. faculty assn. Rancho Santiago CC, 1988—, FARSCCD PAC, 1990—, v.p., 2001—, mem. OR.Co leg task force, 2001—02; mem. adv. bd. govs. Faculty Assn. Calif. CC, Sacramento, 1991—99, 2006—; pres. Santiago Canyon Coll. Acad. Senate, 1999—2004; treas. C.C.C. Ind. Unions, 2004—. Editor: Dive Boat Calendar, 1987—91, (newsletter) FARSIGHT, 1989—. Asst. scoutmaster Boy Scouts Am., Irvine, 1994—2002; choir mem. St. Paul's Greek Orthodox Ch., Irvine, 1993—, mem. parish coun., 1987—89, 1998—2000, choir pres., 1999—2005; mission church builder Tanzania, 2007. Recipient Tchr. of the Yr. award, Santa Ana C. of C., 1997, NISOD Excellence award, U. Tex., 1998; NSF fellow, 1970. Mem.: NEA, Am. Math. Assn. Two Yr. Colls., Math. Assn. Am., Calif. Math Coun. Cmty. Colls., Nat. Coun. Tchrs. Math. Avocations: scuba diving, camping, hiking, boating. Home: 1 Caraway Irvine CA 92604-3217 Office: Santiago Canyon Coll 8045 E Chapman Ave Orange CA 92869 Home Phone: 949-559-8189; Office Phone: 714-628-4922. Business E-Mail: smith_john@sccollege.edu.

SMITH, JOHN W(ESLEY), JR., data processing executive, consultant; b. Bklyn., Jan. 6, 1946; s. John Wesley and Eunice (Davis) S.; m. Carolyn Ferrebbee, Aug. 19, 1971 (div. 1980); children: John Wesley III, Janine Carol. Student, NYU, 1989—. Supr. computer ops. Shearson Lehman Stone, Inc., NYC, 1967—70; sr. ops. analyst Fin. Data Svcs., Inc., NYC, 1970—77; coord. tng. program Chem. Bank, NYC, 1977—78; sr. hardware analyst ADP, Clifton, NJ, 1978—79; adminstr. data base Depository Trust Co., NYC, 1979—81; mgr. data ctr. ops. Leviton Mfg. Co., Littleneck, NY, 1981—83; dir. corp. info. svcs. Reed Robert's Assocs., Inc., Uniondale, 1983—86; dir. prodn. planning and control Human Resource Adminstrn., NYC, 1986—87; mgmt. cons. Asbach/Sci., Inc., NYC, 1987—. Mem. Data Processing Mgmt. Assn., Am. Soc. Notaries, Am. Mgmt. Assn., Am. Arbitration Assn. (comml. panel 1983—), Inst. Certification Computer Profls. (cert systems profl.). Avocation: real estate. Office Phone: 757-265-4457.

SMITH, JONATHAN DAVID, medical educator; b. Cleve., Jan. 10, 1955; BS, U. Calif., Santa Cruz, 1978; PhD, Harvard U., 1984. Postdoctoral Lab. Biochem. Genetics and Metabolism The Rockefeller U., NYC, 1984-89, asst. prof., 1989-96, assoc. prof., 1996—. Contbr. articles to profl. jours. Recipient Nat. Rsch. Svc. award NIH, 1985-87, Program Project award, 1995—. Mem. AAAS, Am. Heart Assn. (Investigatorship award N.Y.C. affiliate 1989-92, Grant-in-Aid 1989-92, 92-95, Established Investigator 1994—). Achievements include identification of genes that regulate atherosclerosis; development of animal models useful for testing therapies to proevent atherosclerosis; characterization of novel functions of apolopoprotein E which are relevant to Alzheimer's disease, cardiovascular disease and longevity. Home: 22687 Westchester Rd Shaker Heights OH 44122-2976

SMITH, JOSEPH A., JR., state agency administrator; b. Charleston, W.Va., Nov. 9, 1949; m. Elizabeth Marion; children: Joseph A. III, Matthew M. BA in History, Davidson Coll., 1971; JD, U. Va., 1975. Bar: NY 1975, NC 1989. Assoc. atty. pub. fin. Brown, Wood, Ivey, Mitchell & Petty (now Sidley, Austin, Brown & Wood), NYC, 1975—79; corp. counsel PepsiCo, Inc., Purchase, NY, 1979—84; asst. gen. counsel Emery Air Freight Corp., Wilton, Conn., 1984—88; ptnr. Poyner & Spruill, Raleigh, NC, 1988—91; gen. counsel, sec. Centura Banks, Inc., Rocky Mount, NC, 1991—2000; counsel Thacher, Proffitt & Wood, Washington, 2000—02; commr. of banks NC Banking Comm., 2002—. Contbr. articles to profl. publs. Mem. steering com. UNC Law Sch. Ctr. Banking & Fin. Office: Commr Banks 4309 Mail Svc Ctr Raleigh NC 27699-4309 Office Phone: 919-733-3016. Office Fax: 919-733-6918. E-mail: jsmith@nccob.org.

SMITH, JOSEPH LORENZO, II, otolaryngologist; s. Joseph Lorenzo and Judy Peterson Smith; m. Sarah Loos Smith; children: Benjamin Joseph, Ava Elizabeth. AB, Cornell U., Ithaca, NY, 1993; MD, Jefferson Med. Coll., Phila., 2001. Physician ENTACC, Exton, Pa., 2006—. Mem.: Am. Acad. Otolaryngic Allergy, Am. Acad. of Otolaryngology Head and Neck Surgery. Office: Entacc 80 W Welsh Pool Rd Ste 103 Exton PA 19341 Home Phone: 484-924-8901; Office Phone: 610-363-2532.

SMITH, JUANITA BÉRARD, lawyer, artist; b. St. Martinsville, La., Oct. 23, 1947; d. Zachary Joseph and Lucille Bourque Bérard; m. Mark Christian Smith III, Mar. 16 (dec. 2003); children: Mark IV, Brett, Robyn, Tara. BA in History, Loyola U., La., 1979, JD, 1982. Bar: La. 1982. Pvt. practice, New Orleans, 1982—; pres. Marie Antoinette Hotel, New Orleans, 2003, owner, 2004; pres. 730 Bienville Inc., New Orleans, 2003—, TSL Properties Inc., New Orleans, 2003—, Century Hotels Inc., New Orleans, 2003—; owner, pres. St. Louis Hotel, New Orleans, 2003—, St. Ann Hotel, New Orleans, 2003—, Louis XVI Restaurant, New Orleans, 2003—, La Louisiane Restaurant, New Orleans, 2003—, Woodstone Subdivsn., Mandeville, 2003—, McCrory's, New Orleans, 2003—, Mark Smith Enterprises, New Orleans, 2004. Exhibited in group shows at Alexander and Victor Gallery Fine Art, New Orleans, Alexander and Victor Gallery, Coral Gables, Fla., Palma Gallery, New Orleans, one-woman shows include La Louisiana Gallery, Louis XVI, 2004—07. Named one of Women of Yr., New Orleans City Bus., 2004. Mem.: La. State Bar Assn., New Orleans Bar Assn. Avocations: skiing, theology. Home: 730 Rue Bienville St New Orleans LA 70130 Office: 730 Bienville Partners Ltd 1000 Iberville St New Orleans LA 70130 Studio: 106 Mariners Island Mandeville LA 70448 Mailing: PO Box 57929 New Orleans LA 70157 Personal E-mail: smith_jb@bellsouth.net.

SMITH, JULES LOUIS, lawyer; b. NYC, Oct. 7, 1947; s. Henry Newman and Leonora (Fuerth) S.; m. Alexandra Remington Northrop, Feb. 15, 1986. BS, Syracuse U., 1969, JD, 1971. Bar: N.Y. 1972, U.S. Dist. Ct. (no. dist.) N.Y. 1972, U.S. Dist. Ct. (we. dist.) N.Y. 1973, U.S. Ct. Appeals (2d cir.) 1975, U.S. Supreme Ct. 1982. Assoc. Blitman and King LLP, Syracuse, N.Y., 1971-77, ptnr., 1977-88, resident ptnr., 1988—. Lectr. to legal and profl. assns., confs., colls., 1980—, including AFL-CIO Union Lawyers Conf., 1991, ABA Labor and Employment Law, 1992, 25th Pacific Coast Labor Law Conf., 1992, ABA Satellite Seminar, 1992, N.Y. State Bar Assn. Labor and Employment Law Sect. Ann. Meeting, 1993; lectr. Inst. Indsl. Labor Rels.; mem. N.Y. State Bar Assn. Task Force on Adminstrv. Hearings, Albany, 1986—; bd. advisors LeMoyne Inst. Labor Rels., LeMoyne Coll., Syracuse Inst. Labor Rels.; mem. exec. bd. Greater Mem. editl. bd. Syracuse Law Rev., 1970-71; contbr. articles to legal publs. Sec. Onondaga Neighborhood Legal Svcs., 1978, pres., 1979, v.p. bd. dirs., 1983-87; chair Prevention Ptnrs., 1994-97, pres. 1994-96; co-chair legal divsn. fund raising activities Syracuse Symphony Orch., 1985-86; bd. dirs. fundraising activities Am. Heart Assn., 1985-86; bd. dirs. Greater Rochester Fights Back, 1990-92, vice chair, 1992-93, chair, 1994; pres. Prevention Ptnrs., 1994-96, bd. dirs., 1999—; bd. dirs. United Way Greater Rochester, Cmty. Legal Intake Project, 1998—; v.p. Rochester Com. on Fgn. Rels., 1990-94. Fellow N.Y. Bar Found.; mem. ABA (union chmn. EEO com. labor and employment law sect. 1985-88, co-chairperson labor and employment law sect., mem. ad hoc com. to comment on EEO com. Ams. with Disabilities Act regulations, Coll. of Labor and Employment Lawyers award 1996), FBA, N.Y. State Bar Assn. (chmn. membership and fin. com. 1980-83, mem. spl. com. on specialization 1983-85, chmn. labor and employment law sect. 1984-85, mem. ho. dels. 1989-92), Onondaga County Bar Assn., Monroe County Bar Assn., N.Y. State Trial Lawyers Assn., Am. Trial Lawyers Assn., Fed. Bar Coun., Indsl. Rels. Rsch. Assn., Assn. Ctrl. N.Y. (co-founder, v.p. 1981), Justinian Honor Soc., Order of Coif. Democrat. Jewish. Avocations: skiing, running, cooking, reading. Home Phone: 585-381-7428; Office Phone: 585-232-5600. Business E-Mail: jlsmith@bklawyers.com.

SMITH, JULIA LADD, oncologist, physician; b. Rochester, NY, July 26, 1951; d. John Herbert and Isabel (Walcott) Ladd; m. Stephen Slade Smith; 1 child. BA, Smith Coll., 1973; MD, N.Y. Med. Coll., 1976. Diplomate Am. Bd. Internal Medicine, Am. Bd. Med. Oncology, Am. Bd. Hospice and Palliative Medicine. Intern in medicine N.Y. Med. Coll., NYC, 1976-77; resident in medicine Rochester Gen. Hosp., 1977-79; internist Genesee Valley Group Health, Rochester, 1979-80; oncology fellow U. Rochester, 1980-82, asst. prof. oncology in medicine sch. medicine and dentistry, 1986—2003; oncologist Med. Ctr. Clinic, Ltd., Pitts., 1982-83; oncologist, internist Rutgers Community Health Plan, New Brunswick, N.J., 1983-86; med. dir. Genesse Region Home Care Assn./Hospice, Rochester, 1988—; med. oncologist Genesee Hosp., Rochester, 1996—2001, chief hematology/oncology, 1996—2001; med. oncologist Rochester Gen. Hosp., 2001—. Bd. dirs. Am. Cancer Soc., Monroe County, 1988-92. Nat. Cancer Inst. rsch. grantee, 1993—95. Fellow Acad. Hospice Physicians; mem. ACP, Am. Soc. Clin. Oncology. Unitarian-Universalist. Avocations: sailing, reading, movies, bridge. Office: Lipson Blood and Cancer Ctr 1425 Portland Ave Rochester NY 14621 Office Phone: 585-922-4020.

SMITH, JULIAN CLEVELAND, JR., chemical engineering professor; b. Westmount, Que., Can., Mar. 10, 1919; s. Julian Cleveland and Bertha (Alexander) S.; m. Joan Elsen, June 1, 1946; children: Robert Elsen, Diane Louise Smith Brook, Brian Richard. B.Chemistry, Cornell U., 1941, Chem. Engr., 1942. Chem. engr. E. I. duPont de Nemours and Co., Inc., 1942-46; mem. faculty Cornell U., 1946—, prof. chem. engring., 1953-86, prof. emeritus, 1986—, dir. continuing engring. edn., 1965-71; assoc. dir. Cornell U. (Sch. Chem. Engring.), 1973-75, dir., 1975-83. Vis. lectr. U. Edinburgh, 1971-72; cons. to govt. and industry, 1947-2001; UNESCO cons. Universidad de Oriente, Venezuela, 1975 Author: (with W. L. McCabe and P. Harriott) Unit Operations of Chemical Engineering, 1956, 7th edit., 2005, also articles; sect. editor: Perry's Chemical Engineers' Handbook, 1963. Fellow Am. Inst. Chem. Engrs.; mem. Am. Chem. Soc., Paleontologic Rsch. Instn., Ithaca Country Club, Savage Club, Sigma Xi, Tau Beta Pi, Phi Kappa Phi, Alpha Delta Phi. Home: 427 Savage Farm Dr Ithaca NY 14850-6507 Business E-Mail: jcs29@cornell.edu.

SMITH, JULIE ANN, pharmaceutical executive; BS, Cornell Univ. Mktg. div. Bristol-Myers Squibb; comml. team Novazyme Pharmaceutical Corp.; v.p. product strategy and devel. Genzyme Corp., v.p. global mktg.; v.p., mktg. Jazz Pharmaceuticals, 2006—. Clinical rschr. neuroendocrinology Mass. Gen. Hosp. Named one of 40 Under 40, Boston Bus. Jour., 2005. Office: Jazz Pahrmaceuticals 3180 Porter Dr Palo Alto CA 94304

SMITH, JULIOUS PERRY, JR., lawyer; b. Richmond, Va., Jan. 10, 1943; s. Julious Perry and Mary Inez (Whitlow) S.; m. Sherrill Marie Poehler, July 28, 1967; children: Julious P. III, S. Hayes, Sarah Graham. BS, Hampden-Sydney Coll., Va., 1965; LLB, U. Va., 1968. Bar: Va. 1968, U.S. Dist. Ct. (ea. dist.) Va. 1969. Assoc. Williams Mullen, Richmond, 1968-73, shareholder, 1973—, pres., 1983—99, chmn., CEO, 1999—. Bd. dirs. Quarles Petroleum, Inc., Mut. Assurance Soc. of Va., LandAm. Fin. Group, Inc., Hilb Rogal and Hobbs Co.; spkr. Joel A. Rose Conf. on Law Firm Mgmt., 1995, 98, 2000, 04. Chmn. profl. divsn. United Way, 1990—92, campaign chmn., 1994—95, de Tocqueville Chair, 2000; Va. state chair U.S. Olympic Com., 1996—2000; trustee Hampden-Sydney Coll., 1996—2005, vice chmn., 2004—06; bd. dirs. Theater Va., pres., 2001—02; chair Multiple Sclerosis Dinner, 2002, CCA-Fin.-Am. Cancer Soc. Golf Championship, 2004; mem. sch. bd. St. Bridget's Cath. Ch., Richmond, 1981—88, chmn. capital fund raising campaign, 1991. Recipient Micheli award Richmond Touchdown Club, 1981, Patrick Henry award Hampden-Sydney Coll., 2003; named to Salvation Army Boys and Girls Club Hall of Fame, 1997 Fellow: Va. Law Found., Am. Coll. Trust and Estate Coun.; mem.: ABA, Chambers Internat. Lawyers, Va. Super 50 Lawyers, Best Lawyers in Am., Va. Legal Elite, Richmond Mgmt. Round Table, Soc. Internat. Bus. Fellows (Va. chair 1996—97), Richmond Bar Assn. (chmn. young lawyers sect. 1973—74, bd. dirs. 1985—87, 1989—92, pres. 1995—96, Hill-Tucker Pub. Svc. award 2005), Va. Bar Assn., Kinloch Golf Club, Farmington Country Club, Forum Club, Country Club Va., Commonwealth Club (bd. govs. 1997—2000, v.p. 2005—07, pres. 2007—). Roman Catholic. Avocations: reading, sports, travel. Office Phone: 804-783-6408. Business E-Mail: jsmith@williamsmullen.com.

SMITH, JUSTIN STUART, mathematics educator; b. Dixon, Ill., Apr. 15, 1976; s. James Michael and Karen Ann Smith; m. Megan Kay Wolford, Aug. 5, 2000; 1 child, Austin. Bachelors Degree, Iowa State U., Ames, 1999; Masters Degree, Aurora U., Ill., 2004. Math. tchr. Lake Park H.S., Roselle, Ill., 1999—2000, Grant Cmty. H.S., Fox Lake, Ill., 2000—. Named Educator of Yr., Grant Cmty. H.S., 2004, Most Influential Tchr., Western Ill. U., 2005. Mem.: Nat. Coun. Tchrs. Math. Avocations: golf, coaching sports, boating. Home: 25727 W Woodland Dr Round Lake IL 60073 Office: Grant Cmty HS 285 E Grand Ave Fox Lake IL 60020

SMITH, K. CLAY, machinery transport company executive; b. New Orleans, Aug. 29, 1937; s. Kenneth Eugene and Yvonne Smith; children: Elizabeth, K. Clay, Andrew. BBA, U. Notre Dame, 1960; JD, Georgetown U., 1964; DBA (hon.), Marian Coll., Indpls., 1988. Bar: Ind. 1964. Spl. agt. FBI, Los Angeles, 1964-68; assoc. Kightlinger, Gray, Indpls., 1968-71; pres., chief exec. officer Underwood Machinery Transport, Indpls., 1971—. Bd. dirs. Specialized Carriers; former vice chmn. Ind. Horse Racing Commn. Chmn. lic. rev. bd., City of Indpls., 1974; mem. reciprocity com., State of Ind., 1988. Mem. Ind. Bar Assn., Indpls. Bar Assn., Indpls. Athletic Club (bd. dirs. 1986-92, pres. 1992), Highland Country Club, Meridian Hills Country Club, Columbia Club. Republican. Roman Catholic. Avocations: reading, music, golf, tennis. Home: PO Box 977 Indianapolis IN 46206-0977 Office: Underwood Cos 940 W Troy Ave Indianapolis IN 46225-2244

SMITH, KAREN A., lawyer; b. Newark, May 26, 1962; BA, Lafayette Coll., 1984; JD, Cornell U., 1987. Bar: NJ 1987, NY 1988, DC 1989. Ptnr., co-head Bus. & Internat. Sect. Vinson & Elkins LLP, NYC. Mem.: ABA. Office: Vinson & Elkins LLP 666 Fifth Ave, 26 Fl New York NY 10103-0040

SMITH, KAREN ANN, visual artist; b. Trenton, NJ, May 25, 1964; d. James Roy and Clara Patricia (Walton) S. A in Comml. Art, Art Inst. Phila., 1984; BFA in Graphic Design and Art Therapy, U. Arts, Phila., 1989; grad. in graphic design, Basel Sch. for Design, 1991; MA in Expressive Therapies, Lesley Coll., 1993. Graphic designer Mercer County C.C., Trenton, 1984-86; mural painter, supr. Anti-Graffiti Network, Phila., 1988; tchr. drawing and set design Chestnut Hill (Mass.) Sch., 1995, 96; freelance graphic designer Swiss Fed. Rys., Bern, 1993-95; tchr. drawing Wentworth Inst. Tech., Boston, 1996, 97; tchr. design Northeastern U., Boston, 1997. Fireworks crew Pyrotech. Inc., Boston, 1997; apprentice Johnson Atelier Tech. Inst. of Sculpture, Trenton, 1997-99; artist Airtex Interiors, Fallsington, 2000-03; artist, instr. intergenerational program Pennswood Village and Newtown Friends Sch., 2003-; visual artist. Author numerous poems; one-woman shows include Contempo Galerie, Bern, Switzerland, 1994, Boston Archtl. Ctr. Atelier, 1997, George Sch., Newtown, Pa., 1997, exhibited in group shows at Howard Yezerski Gallery, Boston, 1994, Kingston Gallery, 1995, Phillips' Mill, New Hope, Pa., 1997, Woodmere Art Mus., Chestnut Hill, Pa., 1998, Princeton (NJ) Day Sch., 1999, Trenton City Mus., 1999, Vorpal Gallery, N.Y.C., 2000—02, Artsbridge, Prallsville Mills, N.J., 2000, Riverbank Arts, Stockton, N.J., 2000—, Nat. Bottle Mus., Ballston Spa, N.Y., 2001, Artsbridge Photography Exhbn., Lambertville, NJ, 2003, Artists at the Farm, Langhorne, Pa., 2003—, Rosenberg-Wila, Switzerland, 1994, 2005—07. Scholar Women in Graphic Arts, 1987-89; grantee Mystic Studios Trust, 1994-97, Artists at the Farm, Langhorne, Pa., 2003—. Mem. Coll. Art Assn., Soc. Artists in Healthcare, Origami USA, Artsbridge. E-mail: sunbellsmith@msn.com.

SMITH, KAREN E., mathematician, educator; b. Red Bank, New Jersey, May 9, 1965; married; children: Sanelma, Tapio, Helena. BA in Math., Princeton U., 1987; PhD, U. Mich., 1993. Tchr. math. N.J. Pub. Schs., 1987—88; NSF postdoctoral fellow Purdue U., West Lafayette, Ind., 1993—94; Moore instr., asst. prof. MIT, Cambridge, 1994—97; prof. math. U. Mich., Ann Arbor, 1997—. Vis. prof. U. Jyvaskyla, Finland, 2001. Author: An Invitation to Algebraic Geometry, 2000; assoc. editor Jour. Am. Math. Soc., mem. edit. bd. Am. Math. Monthly. Recipient Ruth Lyttle Satter prize, 2001; fellow, Fulbright Found.; grantee, NSF, Alfred P. Sloan Found. Mem.: Nat. Rsch. Coun. (bd. dirs. Math. Scis.). Office: Dept Math Rm 2832 East Hall Univ Michigan 530 Church St Ann Arbor MI 48109 Office Phone: 734-763-5048. Fax: 734-763-0937. E-mail: kesmith@umich.edu.

SMITH, KAREN JODY, education educator; d. Glen A. Davis and Grace H. Nelson; m. G. Michael Smith; 1 child, Nathan. BS, Ill. State U., Normal, 1973; M, Maryville U., St. Louis, 1987; PhD, St. Louis U., 2003. Ednl. coord. St. Francis Med. Ctr., Peoria, Ill., 1973—74; asst. dir. Meml. Med. Ctr., Springfield, Ill., 1974—76, dir. med. recs., 1976—81; instr. med. recs. adminstrn. Ill. State U., Normal, 1981—82; dir. med. recs. St. Louis U. Hosp., 1982—84; asst. prof. dept. health info. mgmt. St. Louis U., 1988—96, assoc. prof., chair dept. health informatics and info. mgmt., 1992—. Author: (book) Delmar's Handbook for Health Information Careers; contbr. articles to profl. jours. Mem.: Mo. Health Info. Mgmt. Assn. (pres. 2002—03), Am. Med. Informatics Assn., Health Info. and Info. Sys. Soc., Am. Health Info. Mgmt. Assn. Office: St Louis U 3437 Caroline Saint Louis MO 63104 Office Phone: 314-977-8710.

SMITH, KATHY L., elementary school educator, cosmetics executive, consultant; b. Gillespie, Ill., Mar. 8, 1959; d. William G. and Phyllis L. Russell; m. Thomas A. Smith, Aug. 30, 1980; children: Ashley M., Blake T. BA, So. Ill. U., Edwardsville, 1981, MA, 1988. Cert. Nat. Bd. Cert. Tchr. Fla., 2002. Tchr. 1st, 4, th and 6th Bunker Hill Sch. Dist., Bunker Hill, Ill., 1984—89; tchr. kindergarten, 1st, and 2nd Marion County Sch. Dist., Weirsdale, Fla., 1989—96; tchr. 1st grade Lake County Sch. Dist., Eustis, Fla., 1996—99, intensive reading tchr. Leesburg, Fla., 1999—; beauty cons. Mary Kay, Fruitland Park, Fla., 2003—. Facilitator U. Ctrl. Fla., Orlando, Fla., 2004—. Author: (novels) Powerful Classroom Stories from Accomplished Teachers. Family fun Women of the Moose, Leesburg, Fla., 2005—; vol. Morrison United Meth. Ch., Leesburg, Fla., 1989—2001. Mem.: Cert. Accomplished Tchrs. (assoc.), So. Ill. U. Alumni Assn. (life), Women of the Moose (assoc.). Avocations: reading, travel, swimming. Home: 4209 Idlewild Dr Fruitland Park FL 34731 Office: Carver Mid Sch 1200 N Beecher St Leesburg FL 34748 Home Phone: 352-787-6316; Office Phone: 352-787-7868. Personal E-mail: kathysmarykay4u@aol.com.

SMITH, KEITH E., hotel and gaming company executive; b. 1960; Corp. controller Boyd Gaming Corp., 1990, sr. v.p., controller, exec. v.p., ops., 1998—2001, COO, 2001—, pres., 2005—. Dir., bd. of dirs. Boyd Gaming Corp; vice-chmn., bd. of dirs. NV Resort Assn., Las Vegas Convention and Visitors Authority. Office: Boyd Gaming Corp 3883 Howard Hughes Pkwy Ninth Fl Las Vegas NV 89118 Office Phone: 702-792-7200. Office Fax: 702-792-7263. *

SMITH, KELLY M., pharmacist, educator, researcher; b. Statesboro, Ga. d. Kenneth P. and Janice A. Smith. BS, PharmD, U. Ga., Athens, 1993. Registered pharmacist Ga., 1993, Ky., 1995. Clin. asst. prof. U. Ky. Coll. Pharmacy, Lexington, 1996—2001, clin. assoc. prof., 2001, assoc. prof., 2002—, dir. residency program advancement, 2007—; dir. PGY1 pharmacy residency U. Ky. HealthCare, Lexington, 1998—, dir. drug info. ctr., 2001—05, clin. specialist medication use policy, 2005—. Presenter in field. Contbr. articles to profl. jours. Fellow: Am. Soc. Health Sys. Pharmacists (chair commn. on credentialing); mem.: Univ. HealthSystem Consortium Pharmacy Coun. (vice chair rsch. and edn. com.), Am. Assn. Colls. of Pharmacy, Am. Coll. Clin. Pharmacy (chair drug info. PRN, tchg. and learning steering com), Zeta Tau Alpha.

SMITH, KENNETH ALAN, chemical engineer, educator; b. Winthrop, Mass., Nov. 28, 1936; s. James Edward and Alice Gertrude (Walters) S.; m. Ambia Marie Olsson, Oct. 14, 1961; children: Kirsten Heather, Edward Eric, Andrew Ian Beaumont, Thurston Garrett. BS, MIT, 1958, MS, 1959, DSc, 1962; postgrad., Cambridge U., Eng., 1964-65. Asst. prof. chem. engrng. MIT, 1961-67, assoc. prof., 1967-71, prof., 1971—, Edwin R. Gilliland prof. chem. engrng., 1989—, acting head dept., 1976-77, assoc. provost, 1980-81, assoc. provost, v.p. rsch., 1981-91, dir. Whitaker Coll. Health Sci. and Tech., 1989-91. Cons. chem. and oil cos. NSF fellow, 1964-65, Overseas fellow, Churchill Coll., (Eng.), 1993, 01. Mem. Am. Inst. Chem. Engrs., Nat. Acad. Engring., Am. Chem. Soc., AAAS, Sigma Xi, Phi Lambda Upsilon, Tau Beta Pi. Episcopalian. Home: 32 School St Manchester MA 01944-1336 Office: MIT Bldg 66-540 Cambridge MA 02139 Home Phone: 978-526-1743; Office Phone: 617-253-1973. E-mail: kas@mit.edu.

SMITH, KENNETH JUDSON, JR., chemistry professor; b. Raleigh, NC, Sept. 4, 1930; s. Kenneth Judson and Irene (Strickland) S.; m. Dorothy Margaret Ratcliffe, Mar. 6, 1953; children: Patricia Lynne Smith Pittman, Pamela Jean. AB, East Carolina U., 1957; MA, Duke U., 1959, PhD, 1961. Research chemist Chemstrand Research Center, Durham, N.C., 1961-65, sr. research chemist, 1965-68; asst. prof. polymer research SUNY Coll. Environ. Sci. and Forestry, Syracuse, 1968-70, assoc. prof., 1970-73, prof., 1973-95, emeritus prof., 1995—, asst. dir. Polymer Research Center, 1971-79, acting dir., 1979-83, dir. Organic Materials Sci. Program, 1971-75, chmn. dept. chemistry, 1972-84. Vis. prof. Instituto di Chimica Industriale, U. Genoa, Italy, 1979; cons. U.S. Army Materials and Mechanics Rsch. Ctr., Watertown, Mass., 1973-75, cert. of appreciation 1973, NRC, Washington, 1980-87; mem. adv. coun. Syracuse Met. Transp. Coun., 1975-84; mem. adv. bd. confs. in polymer sci. and tech. SUNY, New Paltz, 1977-85; mem. rsch. found. joint com. on procedures SUNY, Albany, 1974-81; cons. Hong Kong Rsch. Coun., 1995—. Contbr. articles to profl. jours. Served with USMC, 1951-54. Recipient cert. Appreciation U.S. Army Materials and Mechanics Rsch. Ctr., 1973. Mem. AAAS, Am. Chem. Soc. (dir. Syracuse sect. 1977-79, chmn. 1978, councilor 1979-82), Am. Phys. Soc. (com. on internat. freedom of scientists, small coms.), Am. Inst. Chemists, Soc. Plastics Engrs., Math. Assn. Am., N.Y. Acad. Scis., Sigma Xi, Phi Lambda Upsilon, Kappa Delta Pi. Achievements include research on statistical mechanics, mechanical properties and theoretical studies of polymers; rubber elasticity and thermoelasticity; crystallization of networks; structure-property relationships; ultimate properties of fibers; thermodynamic theory of polymer fiber properties; thermodyanic theory of fiber strength. Office: Coll Environ Sci and Forestry Suny Syracuse NY 13210

SMITH, KENNETH RODGER, finance educator; b. Vancouver, BC, Can., May 12, 1942; arrived in US, 1962; s. John Douglas and Marion (Cannon) S.; m. Esther J. Davenport, July 26, 1977; children from previous marriage: Morgen Jennifer, Jason Andrew BA, U. Wash., 1964; PhD, Northwestern U., 1968. Vis. rsch. fellow Universite Catholique de Louvain, Belgium, 1968-69; asst. prof. economics Health Economics Rsch. Ctr., U. Wis., Madison, 1969-71, assoc. prof., 1971-75; prof., program dir. Grad. Sch. Mgmt., Northwestern U., Evanston, Ill., 1975-79; Eller Disting. Svc. prof. Eller Coll. Mgmt., U. Ariz., Tucson, 1980—, dean, 1980—95, interim dean, 2004—05; vice provost U. Ariz., Tucson, 1992—95. Vis. assoc. prof. U. Calif.-San Diego, 1971-72; bd. dirs. The FINOVA Group, Apache Nitrogen Products, Ventana Corp. Co-author: Hospital Cost Containment Programs: A Policy Analysis, 1978 Bd. dirs. Jr. Achievement of Tucson, 1980-88, St. Joseph Hosp., Tucson, 1980-83; vice chmn. Ariz. Commn. on Long Term Care, 1983-84; mem. nat. adv. com. Robert Wood Johnson Found. Program for Prepaid Health Care, 1983-88. Mem. Assn. to Advance Collegiate Schools of Bus. (bd. dirs., 1990-96, pres., 1994-95). Office: U Ariz Eller Coll Mgmt Dept Economics PO Box 210108 Tucson AZ 85721-0108 Office Phone: 602-621-2633. Office Fax: 520-621-8450. Business E-Mail: ksmith@eller.arizona.edu.

SMITH, KENNETH T., retail executive; BS acctg., Wake Forest Univ. CPA. Acctg. positions Ernst & Young LLP; mgmt. positions Beall's Dept. Stores; mgmt. positions through sr. v.p. fin. Family Dollar Stores, Charlotte, NC, 1990—2007, sr. v.p., CFO, 2007—. Mailing: Family Dollar Stores PO Box 1017 Charlotte NC 28201-1017 *

SMITH, KENT ASHTON, information scientist, consultant; b. Boston, Sept. 3, 1938; s. Kent Wooliscroft and Dorothy Patten Smith; m. Mary Margaret Gaffney; children: Holly L. Smith, Kent W. BA, Hobart Coll., 1960; MBA, Cornell U., 1962; postgrad., Am. U., 1978-79. Mgmt. analyst Office of Sec., HEW, Washington, 1962-65; adminstrv. officer divsn. rsch. facilities and resources NIH, Bethesda, Md., 1965-67, asst. exec. officer divsn. rsch. facilities and resources, 1967-68, exec. officer divsn. rsch. resources, 1968-71, asst. dir. adminstrn. Nat. Libr. Medicine, 1971-78, dep. dir., 1978—2004, PHS spl. expert-info. scientist, 2000—02; cons. Nat. Ctr. for Biotechnology Info., 2004—, Office Sci. and tech. Info. Dept. Energy, 2005—. Mem. exec. bd. and bur. Internat. Coun. Sci. and Tech. Info., Paris, 1983—2001; v.p. U.S. Nat. Com. of UNESCO-PGI, Washington, 1983—85; mem. exec. adv. bd. Fed. Libr. and Info. Ctr. Com., Washington, 1984—89; exec. com. CENDI-Info. Consortia, Washington, 1985—; treas. Internat. Coun. Sci. and Tech. Info., Paris, 1986—89; pres. Nat. Fed. Abstracting and Info. Sci., Phila., 1988—89, v.p., 1987—88; chmn. Info. Policy Com., 1988—89, CENDI-Info. Consortia, Washington, 2001—04; mem. US Nat. Commn. for CODATA, 1990—2001, Science.gov Alliance, 2002—04, NISO Blue Ribbon Panel, 2004; pres. Internat. Coun. Sci. and Tech. Info., Paris, 1990—94; mem. panel US Dept. Energy info. infrastructure NAS, 2000, 07; reviewer study digital strategy for Libr. Congress NRC, 2000; mem. panel on Nat. Tech. Info. Svc. Nat. Commn. Libr. and Info. Sci., 2000; long-range planning panel mem. Nat. Libr. Medicine, 2005—07; bd. mem. Nat. Tech. Info. Svc. Adv. Bd., 2006—; mem. Dept. Energy panel on accelerating knowledge diffusion NAS, 2007. Contbr. articles to profl. jours., chpt. to book: Management of Federally Sponsored Libraries, 1995. Mem. Citizens Com. for Pub. Libr. Montgomery County, Bethesda, 1981-82; fin. dir. Christ Ch., Rockville, Md., 1990-91. Recipient Asst. Sec. for Health Exceptional Achievement award USPHS, 1978, Sr. Exec. Svc. award, 1996, 97, 98, 99, HEW Superior Svc. medal 1974, Nat. Fedn. Abstracting Info. Sci., 1998, Miles Conrad hon. lectureship, Hammer award V.P. US, 1999. Fellow Nat. Fedn. Abstracting and Info. Svcs.; mem. ASPA (vice chmn. 1971-72), AAAS, Int. Assn. Sci. Tech. and Med. Pubs., Am. Mgmt. Assn., Am. Soc. Info. Svc., Med. Libr. Assn. (hon.; Pres. award 1997, ICSTI Disting. Svc. award 2001, Joseph Leiter Hon. Lecturship, 2007), Assn. Rsch. Librs. (Alfred Zipf fellow com. chair 2001-04), Cosmos Club. Episcopalian. Avocations: golf, baseball, genealogy, theater, bird-watching, antiques. Home and Office: 17517 Hidden Garden Ln Ashton MD 20861 Office Phone: 301-496-5359.

SMITH, K(ERMIT) WAYNE, computer company executive; b. Newton, NC, Sept. 15, 1938; s. Harold Robert and Hazel K. (Smith) S.; m. Audrey M. Kennedy, Dec. 19, 1958; 1 son, Stuart W. BA, Wake Forest U., 1960; MA, Princeton U., 1962, PhD, 1964; postgrad., U. So. Calif., 1965; LLD (hon.), Ohio U., 1992; LHD (hon.), Ohio State U., 1998. Instr. Princeton U., 1963; asst. prof. econs. and polit. sci. U.S. Mil. Acad., 1963-66; spl. asst. to asst. sec. def. for sys. analysis Washington, 1966-69; program mgr. def. studies RAND Corp., Santa Monica, Calif., 1969-70; dir. program analysis NSC, Washington, 1970-72; group v.p. planning Dart Industries, LA, 1972-73, group pres. resort devel. group, 1973-76; exec. v.p. Washington Group, Inc., 1976-77; mng. ptnr. Coopers & Lybrand, Washington, 1977-80, group mng. ptnr., 1980-83; chmn., CEO World Book, Inc., 1983-86; prof. Wake Forest U., 1986—88, 2001—; CEO OCLC Online Computer Libr. Ctr., Inc., Dublin, Ohio, 1989-98, pres. emeritus, 1998—. Sr. cons. Dept. Def., Dept. State, NSC, NASA, Dept. Energy, OMB, GAO; bd. dirs. Nat. City Bank, K. Wayne Smith and Assocs.; con. prof. (hon.) Tsinghua U., Beijing, 1996; chmn. Rainbow Care For Kids Found., 1999-2000. Author: How Much is Enough? Shaping the Defense Program, 1961-69, 1971, reprinted as RAND classic, 2005; editor: OCLC 1967-97: Thirty Years of Furthering Access to the World's Information, 1998; contbr. articles to profl. jours. Mem. vis. com. Brookings Instn., Washington, 1971-79; mem. bd. visitors Wake Forest U., 1974-78, 82-90, chmn. bd. visitors, 1976-78, trustee, 1991-95, 96-00, 01-05, 06-, vice chmn., 2006-07, chmn., 2007—; mem. bd. visitors Def. Sys. Mgmt. Coll., 1982-85, Lenoir Rhyne Coll., 1988-94, Mershon Ctr. Ohio State U., 1990-92, Columbus Assn. for Performing Arts, 1991-95, U. Pitts. Sch. Libr. and Info. Sci., 1992-95; mem. bd. visitors Bowman Gray Bapt. Hosp. Med. Ctr., 1992-95, chmn. bd. visitors, 1993-95; bd. dirs. Wake Forest U. Bapt. Med. Ctr., 2007—. Danforth fellow, Woodrow Wilson fellow Princeton U., 1962-64. Mem. ALA (hon., life), Coun. Fgn. Rels., Internat. Inst. Strategic Studies, Inst. Internat. Edn., Coun. Higher Edn., Am. Assn. Higher Edn., Chgo. Club, Lakes Golf and Country Club, Capital Club, Phi Beta Kappa, Omicron Delta Kappa, Kappa Sigma. Methodist. Home: 2606 Sigmon Dairy Rd Newton NC 28658-7609 Office: Online Computer Libr Ctr Inc 6565 Frantz Rd Dublin OH 43017-5308

SMITH, KERRY CLARK, lawyer; b. Phoenix, July 12, 1935; s. Clark and Fay (Jackson) S.; m. Michael Waterman, 1958; children: Kevin, Ian. AB, Stanford U., 1957, JD, 1962. Bar: Calif. 1963, U.S. Supreme Ct. 1980. Assoc. Chickering & Gregory, San Francisco, 1962-70, ptnr., 1970-81, Pettit & Martin, San Francisco, 1981-95, Hovis, Smith, San Francisco, 1995-99; pvt. practice San Francisco, 1999—. Mem. editl. bd. Stanford Law Rev., 1961-62. Lt. USN, 1957-60. Mem. ABA (bus. law sect.), Calif. Bar Assn., San Francisco Bar Assn., Orinda County Club, Palms Golf Club, La Quinta Citrus Golf Club, San Francisco World Trade Club. Office: Smith Law Offices 601 California St Ste 1600 San Francisco CA 94108-2821 E-mail: kerrysmith50965@msn.com.

SMITH, KEVIN, film director, writer, actor; b. Red Bank, NJ, Aug. 2, 1970; m. Jennifer Schwalbach, Apr. 25, 1999; 1 child, Harley Quinn. LHD (hon.), Illinois Wesleyan University. Owner Jay and Silent Bob's Secret Stash Comic Book Store, Red Bank, NJ, View Askew Productions, 1996—. Dir., writer, actor (films): Clerks, 1994, Mall Rats, 1996, Chasing Amy, 1997, Dogma, 1999; dir., writer, actor: Jay and Silent Bob Strike Back, 2001; exec. prodr.: Good Will Hunting, 1997, Vulgar, 2000, Reel Paradise, 2005, Small Town Gay Bar, 2006; dir., producer, writer (films): Jersey Girl, 2004, Clerks II, 2006; screenwriter: (TV film) Roadside Attractions, 2002; dir., screenwriter: (TV film) The Flying Car, 2002; writer, actor, exec. prodr. (TV series) Clerks, 2000; appeared in films: Scream 3, 1999, Daredevil, 2003, Bottom's Up, 2006, Southland Tales, 2006, Catch and Release, 2006, (voice) Doogal, 2006, TMNT, 2007; Author: Silent Bob Speaks: The Collected Writings of Kevin Smith, 2005 *

SMITH, KIKI, artist; b. Nuremberg, Germany, Jan. 18, 1954; d. Tony Smith. One-woman shows include The Kitchen, N.Y.C., 1982, Fawbush Gallery, 1988, 1992, 1993, Galerie René Blouin, Montreal, 1989, 1991—92, 1994, Dallas Mus. Art, 1989, Ezra and Cecile Zilkha Gallery Ctr. for the Arts Wesleyan U., Middletown, Conn., 1989, Tyler Gallery Tyler Sch. Art Temple U., Phila., 1990, Ctr. d'Arte Contemporaine, Geneva, 1990, Inst. Art and Urban Resources The Clocktower, Long Island, N.Y., 1990, Inst. Contemporary Art, Amsterdam, 1990, Mus. Modern Art, N.Y.C., 1990—91, Shoshana Wayne Gallery, Santa Monica, Calif., 1991, 1992, 1992—93, MAK Galerie, Vienna, 1991, U. Art Mus., Berkeley, Calif., 1991, Art Awareness, Inc., Lexington, N.Y., 1991, Corcoran Gallery Art, Washington, 1991, Greg Kucera Gallery, Seattle, 1991, Rose Art Mus. Brandeis U., Waltham, Mass., 1992, Österreichisches Mus. angewandte Kunst, Vienna, 1992, Moderna Mus., Stockholm, 1992, Bonner Kunstverein, Bonn, 1992, Galerie M*& R Fricke, Düsseldorf, Germany, 1992—93, Williams Coll. Mus. Art, Williamstown, Mass., 1992—93, Ohio State U., Columbus, 1992—93, Anthony d'Offay Gallery, London, 1993, 1995, Phoenix Art Mus., 1993, U. Art Mus., Santa Barbara, Calif., 1994, La. Mus. Modern Art, Humlebaek, Denmark, 1994, The Israel Mus., Jerusalem, 1994, Barbara Gross Galerie, Munich, 1994, Laura Carpenter Fine Art, Santa Fe, 1994, Pace Wildenstein, N.Y., 1994, Royal LePage Gallery, Toronto, 1994—95, Barbara Krakow Gallery, Boston, 1994—96, Whitechapel Art Gallery, London, 1995, San Francisco Mus. Modern Art, 2005, Contemporary Art Mus., Houston, 2006, numerous others, exhibited in group shows at Brooke Alexander Gallery, N.Y., 1980, 1991, White Columns, N.Y., 1981, 1983, 1990, Artists Space, 1981, 1990, Barbara Gladstone Gallery, 1982, Hallwalls, Buffalo, N.Y., 1983, Susan Caldwell Gallery, N.Y., 1984, 1987, Galerie Engstrom, Stockholm, 1984, Art City, N.Y., 1985, Moderna Mus., Stockholm, 1985, Cin. Art Mus., 1985, Bklyn. Mus., 1986, 1989, Curt Marcus Gallery, N.Y., 1986, Fawbush Gallery, 1987, 1989, 1990, Mus. Modern Art, N.Y.C., 1988, 1992, IBM Gallery, N.Y., 1988, Arch Gallery, Amsterdam, 1988, Tom Cugliani Gallery, 1989, Simon Watson Gallery, N.Y., 0190, Mus. Fine Arts, Boston, 1990, Hunter Coll. Art Gallery, 1991, Milw. Art Mus., 1992, Paula Cooper Gallery, 1993, Serpentine Gallery, London, 1994, PaceWildenstein, N.Y., 1995, 1997, 1998, Ace Gallery, Mex., 1997, Yale U. Art Gallery, New Haven, Conn., 1998, John Berggruen Gallery, San Francisco, 2005, numerous others. Named one of 100 Most Influential People, Time Mag., 2006. Mem.: AAAL. Office: c/o Pace Wildenstein 32 E 57th St New York NY 10022-2513

SMITH, KIMMIE CHRISTINE, small business owner; b. Redding, Calif., Apr. 28, 1971; d. Steven Burton Tyler and Kim Kassina Hern; m. Kenneth Thomas Smith, Nov. 12, 1988; 1 foster child, Savannah children: Stephanie, Shannon, Steven, Shelby, Danika. AAS, U. Alaska, Sitka, 2003, AA, 2004, BLA, 2005; postgrad. in Psychology, Walden U. Owner, adminstr. Krissy's Playland Childcare Ctr., Wrangell, Alaska, 1995—. Facilitator Wrangell Spl. Needs Team, 2003—; mem. elem. advisory com., 2007—; early childhood cmty. liaison Assn. for Edn. of Young Children-S.E. Alaska. V.p. Emblem Club #87, 2006—. Named Family Childcare Provider of Year, AEYC-SEA, 2005. Avocations: hunting, scrapbooks, fishing. Home: PO Box 615 Wrangell AK 99929 Office: Krissy's Playland PO Box 615 Wrangell AK 99929 Office Phone: 907-874-4307. Business E-Mail: krissysplayland@aptalaska.net. E-mail: shelby@aptalaska.net.

SMITH, KINGSTON EARL, lawyer; b. Newport News, Va., Apr. 11, 1946; s. John Howard and Jane Elizabeth (Fawcett) S.; m. Juliana Parker, June 10, 1978; children: Andrew Earl, Christina Louise. BA, Duke U., 1968; JD, U. Richmond, 1977. Bar: Va. 1977, U.S. Ct. Appeals (4th cir.) 1977, U.S. Dist. Ct. (ea. dist.) Va. 1977, U.S. Dist. Ct. (we. dist.) Va. 1979, U.S. Supreme Ct. 1981, Air Force Mil. Rev. 1992. Tchr. high sch., coach Poquoson (Va.) Pub. Schs., 1973-74; assoc. May, Miller & Parsons, Richmond, 1977-80; gen. atty. Office Gen. Counsel, Vets. Adminstrn., Washington, 1980-84; gen. counsel & dep. staff dir., Subcommittee on Oversight & Investigations Com. Vet. Affairs, U.S. Ho. Rep., Washington, 1985—2001, dep. chief counsel, 2001—04, chief counsel Washington, 2004—. Mem., st. advisor for vets. and nat. security task force Bush-Quayle campaign, 1987, sr. advisor for vets. and nat. security press conf., 1991, mem. vets. adv. bd.; vol. Dole-Kemp campaign, 1995. Capt. USAF, 1968-72, Vietnam, Lt. col. USAFR (ret.). Decorated DFC, Air medal with bronze oak leaf cluster. Republican. Presbyterian. Office: Committee on Veterans' Affairs Room 335 Cannon House Office Building Washington DC 20515-6335

SMITH, L. DENNIS, former academic administrator; b. Muncie, Ind., Jan. 18, 1938; s. Thurman Lewis and Dorothy Ann (Dennis) S.; m. Suzanne F. Metcalfe; children: Lauren Kay, Raymond Bradley. AB, Ind. U., 1959, PhD, 1964; DSc (hon.), Purdue U., 2000. Asst. embryologist Argonne (Ill.) Nat. Lab., 1964-67, assoc. biologist, 1967-69; assoc. prof. Purdue U., West Lafayette, Ind., 1969-73, prof. biology, 1973-87, assoc. head dept. biol. scis., 1979-80, head dept., 1980-87; prof. dept. devel. and cell. U. Calif., Irvine, 1987-94, dean Sch. Biol. Scis., 1987-90, exec. vice chancellor, 1990-94; pres. U. of Nebr., 1994—2004, pres. emeritus, prof. biol. scis., 2004—. Instr. embryology Woods Hole (Mass.) Marine Biology Lab., 1972-74, mem. Space Studies Bd., Washington, 1986-91; chmn. Space Biology and Medicine, space sci. bd., 1986-91; cell biology study sect. NIH, Bethesda, Md., 1971-75; chmn., 1977-79, bd. sci. counselors Nat. Inst. Child Health and Human Devel., 1990-95, chmn. 1992-95; space biology peer rev. bd. AIBS, 1980-85. Mem. Bus. Higher Edn. Forum, 1995—, chair, 2000—02; bd. dirs. Nebr. Arts Coun., Nebr., Nebr. Indsl. Competitiveness Alliance. Fellow Guggenheim, 1987; Sci. Freedom and Responsibility award, AAAS, 2002. Mem. AAAS, Am. Soc. Biochemistry and Molecular Biology, Internat. Soc. for Devel. Biology, Soc. for Devel. Biology, Am. Soc. Cell Biology, Am. Soc. for Microbiology. Office: Alex West Ste 135 312 No 14th St Lincoln NE 68588-0430 Office Phone: 402-472-7154.

SMITH, LAMAR SEELIGSON, congressman; b. San Antonio, Nov. 19, 1947; s. Campbell and Eloise Keith (Seeligson) Smith; m. Elizabeth Schaefer, Mar. 20, 1992; children: Nell Seelligson, Tobin Wells. BA, Yale U., New Haven, 1969; JD, So. Meth. U. Sch. Law, Dallas, 1975. Mgmt. intern SBA, Washington, 1969-70; bus. writer Christian Sci. Monitor, Boston, 1970-72; assoc. Maebius & Duncan, Inc., San Antonio, 1975-76; chmn. Rep. Party of Bexar County, San Antonio, 1978—82; mem. Tex. State Ho. Reps. from Dist. 57-F, San Antonio, 1981-82; commr. Bexar County Precinct 3, Tex., 1982—85; mem. US Congress from 21st Tex. dist., 1987—, mem. judiciary com., chmn. courts, the internet and intellectual property subcommittee, mem. sci. com., mem. homeland security com., mem. standards of ofcl. conduct com. Ptnr. Lamar Seeligson Ranch, Premont, Tex., 1975—. Named Legislator of Yr., Info. Tech. Industry Coun., 2005; named one of 50 Most Influential People in the World of Intellectual Property, Mng. IP Mag., 2006, 100 Most Influential People in Washington, DC, Nat. Jour.; recipient Congl. Leadership award, Semiconductor Industry Assn. Republican. Christian Scientist. Office: US Ho Reps 2184 Rayburn Ho Office Bldg Washington DC 20515-4321 Office Phone: 202-225-4236. *

SMITH, LANCE L., career military officer; BA in Bus. Mgmt., Va. Poly. Inst., 1969; MA in Bus. Mgmt, Ctrl. Mich. U., 1978; grad., Air command Staff Coll., 1982, Army War Coll., 1990, J. L. Kellog Grad. Sch. Mgmt., 1994. Commd. 2d. lt. USAF, 1970, advanced through grades to gen., 2005; pilot tng. Columbus AFB, Miss., 1970-71; A-1 combat crew tng. Hurlburt Field, Fla., 1971-71; A-1 pilot 1st Spl. Ops. Squadron, Nakhom Phanom Royal Thai AFB, Thailand, 1971-72; instr. pilot tng. Randolph AFB, Tex., 1972-73; instr. pilot, chief 96th Flying Tng. Squadron, Williams AFB, Ariz., 1973-77; staff ofice Air Staff Tng. Program, Washington, 1977-79; A-7 Corsair Conversion Tng., A-7D aircraft comdr., flight comdr. and asst. ops. officer 76th Tactical Fighter Squadron Eng. Airforce Base, La., 1979-81; air staff officer The Pentagon, Washington, 1982-86; chief safety, asst. dep. comdr. for ops. 354th Tactical Fighter Wing, Myrtle Beach AFB, S.C., 1986-89; comdt. NATO Sch., Obermammergau, Germany, 1992-93; vice comdr, then comdr. 27th Fighter Wing, Cannon AFB, N.Mex., 1992-93; asst. dir. ops. Hdqs. Air Combat Command, Langley AFB, Va., 1993-95; comdr. 4th Wing, Seymour Johnson AFB, N.C., 1995-97; vice comdr. 7th Air Force, U.S. Air Forces Korea, chief staff, Osan Air Base, South Korea, 1997-98; comdt. Air War Coll., 1998-99; vice comdr. Air Univ., Maxwell AFB, Ala., 1998-99; comdr. Airforce Doctrine Ctr., Maxwell AFB, Ala., 1999—2001; dep. comdr. UN Command, Osan AFB, Republic of Korea, 2001—03; dep. comdr. US Forces Korea, comdr. Air Component Command Republic of Korea/US Combines Forces Command, 2001—03; comdr. 7th Air Force, Pacific Air Forces, Osan AFB, 2001—03; dep. comdr. US Ctrl. Command, MacDill AFB, Fla., 2003—05; comdr. US Joint Forces Command, Norfolk, Va., 2005—; supreme allied comdr. for transformation NATO, 2005—. Decorated Silver Star with two oak leaf clusters, Def. Superior Svc. medal, Dinsting. Svc. medal, Legion of Merit with oak leaf cluster, D.F.C. with two oak leaf clusters, Purple Heart, Meritorious Svc. medal with three oak leaf clusters, Air medal with one silver and four bronze oak leaf clusters, Aerial Achievement medal with oak leaf cluster, Air Force Commendation medal, Army Commendation medal, Humanitarian Svc. medal, Armed Forces Expeditionary medal, Rep. Vietnam Gallantry Cross with Palm, Honor Cross of the Bundeswehr medal (Republic of Germany), Order Nat. Sec. Merit Cheonsu medal, Order Nat. Security Merit Gukseon medal (Rep. Korea). Office: US Joint Forces Command 1562 Mitscher Ave Ste 200 Norfolk VA 23551 *

SMITH, LANTY L(LOYD), lawyer, corporate financial executive; b. Sherrodsville, Ohio, Dec. 11, 1942; s. Lloyd H. and Ellen Ruth (Newell) S.; m. Margaret Hays Chandler, June 11, 1966; children: Abigail Lamoreaux Presson, Margaret Ellen Smith-Rhee, Amanda Prescott Lacoff. BS in Math. with honors, Wittenberg U., Springfield, Ohio, 1964; LLB with honors, Duke U., 1967. Bar: Ohio 1967. Assoc. Jones, Day, Cockley & Reavis, Cleve., 1967-73; ptnr. Jones, Day, Reavis & Pogue, Cleve., 1974-77; exec. v.p., sr. gen. counsel Burlington Industries, Inc., Greensboro, NC, 1977-86, pres., 1986-88; chmn. Precision Fabrics Group Inc., Greensboro, 1988—, The Greenwood Group, Inc., Raleigh, NC, 1992—, Soles Brower Smith & Co., 1998—. Bd. dir., chmn. exec. com., lead ind. dir. Wachovia Corp.; bd. dir. Nat. Humanities Ctr.; pres., CEO MediWave Star Tech. Inc., 1999—. Mem. bd. visitors Duke U. Sch. Law; trustee The Duke Endowment; vice chmn. exec. com. Duke U. Mgmt. Co. Mem.: NC Inst. Medicine. Home: 1401 Westridge Rd Greensboro NC 27410-2912 Office: Soles Brower Smith & Co Wachovia Tower Ste 925 Greensboro NC 27401-2167 Business E-Mail: lsmith@solesbrower.com.

SMITH, LARRY STEVEN, financial analyst, accountant, farmer; b. Jasper, Tenn., Sept. 30, 1950; s. Samuel Lester and Stella Mae (Barnes) Smith. BA in Econs., U. Ala., Tuscaloosa, 1972, MBA, 1975. Laborer Lester Smith Farms, Scottsboro, Ala., 1975-76; acct. Ala. Hwy. Dept., Montgomery, 1976-77, Ala. State Agy. Social Security, Montgomery, 1977-78; acct., analyst Ala. Pub. Svc. Commn., Montgomery, 1978-79, utilities analyst II, 1980-81, supr., 1981-89, chmn. computer oversight com., 1988-91, supr. telecom. divsn., 1989—; sales assoc. Jack Hendrix Real Estate, Montgomery, 1979-80. Interim dir. telecom. divsn. Ala. Pub. Svc. Commn., Montgomery, 1993, mem. telecom. task force, 1996—99. Mem. Montgomery Jaycees, 1978—81, bd. dirs., 1979, 1980, Ala. Jr. Miss, Montgomery, 1979—81; mem. Ala. Reps., 1983—. Nat. Grad. Coun. Fellowship grantee, 1973. Mem.: Sierra Club, Nat. Wildlife Fedn., Amnesty Internat., Environ. Def. Fund, Wilderness Soc., N.Am. Limousin Found. Baptist. Avocations: photography, skiing, hunting, hiking, fly fishing, backpacking. Home: 1600 Cobblestone Ct Montgomery AL 36117-1702 Office: Alabama Public Service Commission PO Box 304260 Montgomery AL 36130-4260

SMITH, LAUREN ASHLEY, lawyer, clergyman, physicist, journalist; b. Clinton, Iowa, Nov. 30, 1924; s. William Thomas Roy and Ethel (Cook) S.; m. Barbara Ann Mills, Aug. 22, 1947; children: Christopher A., Laura Nan

Smith Pringle, William Thomas Roy II. BS, U. Minn., 1946, JD, 1949; postgrad., U. Chgo., 1943-49; MDiv, McCormick Theol. Sem., 1950; postgrad., U. Iowa, 1992. Bar: Colo. 1957, Iowa 1959, Ill. 1963, Minn. 1983, U.S. Supreme Ct. 1967; ordained to ministry Presbyn. Ch., 1950. Pastor Presbyn. Ch., Fredonia, Kans., 1950-52, Lamar, Colo., 1952-57, Congl. Ch., Clinton, 1975-80; editor The Comml., Pine Bluff, Ark., 1957-58; ptnr. Schoenauer Smith & Fullerton ASP, Clinton, 1995—. CEO LASCO Pub. Group, Clinton, 1995—; CEO, founder Interlink for the Internet Generation; internat. conferee Stanley Found., Warrenton, Va., 1963—72; legal observer, USSR, 1978; co-sponsor All India Renewable Energy Conf., Bangalore, 1981; law sch. conferee U. Minn., China, 1983; lectr. law, religion, physics, nat. policy U. Wis., 2001, Spl. lectr. contemporary physics and religion, 01. Author: (jurisprudence treatise) Forma Dat Esse Rel, 1975; co-author: India On to New Horizons, 1989; columnist Crow Call, 1968—; co-editor Press and News of India, 1978-82; pub. Crow Call; pseudonym Christopher Crow, 1981—; writer BBC World Svc., London; editor Asian Econ. Cmty. Jour.; contbr. articles to religious publs. Assoc. Westar Inst. (The Jesus Seminar), Santa Rose, Calif.; active Quad City Estate Planning Coun.; minister-at-large Presbyn. Ch. U.S.A., Iowa, 1987—; bd. dirs. Iowa divsn. UN Assn. U.S.A., Iowa City, 1970—85; fellow Molecular Nanotechnology Foresight Inst., Palo Alto, Calif., Franciscans UN Non Govt. Orgn.; founder, CEO Interlink relating quantum mechanics and religion, Clinton, Iowa, 1998—; founding dir. Project 67/74, Clinton, 2002—. Recipient World Wide Essay Contest award, Radio China Internat., 2003—04. Mem. ABA, Iowa Bar Assn., Ill. Bar Assn., St. Andrews Soc., Clinton County Bar Assn. (pres. 1968, Best in Iowa citation), Clinton Ministerial Assn., Samaritan Health Systems Chaplain Corps. (pres.), European Soc. for Study of Sci. and Religion, Quad City Estate Planning Coun., Quaker Internat. Yokefellow, Nat. Network for New Spiritual Formation Presbyn. Ch. USA, Franciscans Internat., Parish Without Walls (founding dir.), City Club of Quad Cities (bd. dirs.), Cath. Order St. Francis (assoc., founder project 67/74), New Rd. Map for Am. (founder). Office: 230 4th Ave S Clinton IA 52732-4311

SMITH, LAURENCE ROGER, journal editor; b. NYC, Sept. 30, 1939; s. John and Edith (Haabestad) S.; m. Betty Ann Larsen, Oct. 9, 1965; children: Erik Lars, Alesa Ann. AAS, Staten Island Community Coll., 1962; BS, SUNY, Oswego, 1965; MBA, St. John's U., 1975. Cert. in bus. and exec. coaching NLP & Coaching Inst. Calif., Inst. HeartMath, Heart Math. Inner Quality Mgmt., bus. tchr. NY, indsl. arts tchr. NY. Dir. cmty. devel. S.I. (N.Y.) C. of C., 1965-77; exec. v.p., CEO, Yonkers (N.Y.) C. of C., 1977-78; chief exec. officer Greater Lawrence (Mass.) C. of C., 1978-91; pres. The LeaderShip, North Andover, Mass., 1991-94; editor in chief, dir. knowledge mgmt. Jour. Innovative Mgmt. (Goal/QPC), Salem, NH, 1994—; chief knowledge officer Goal/QPC and Ctr. Quality Mgmt., 2007—. Dir., clk. Lawrence Downtown Parking Assocs., 1979-91; dir., asst. treas. Greater Lawrence Revolving Loan Fund, 1979-91; mem. U.S. C. of C. Com. on Edn. and Tng., 1990-91; dir. Mgmt. Innovations Group, GOAL/QPC, 1997—. Author: Godfidence, 1991. Chmn. Lower Merrimack Valley Pvt. Industry Coun., Lawrence, 1981; treas. Lawrence YMCA, 1985; vice-chmn. literacy com. Mass. Regional Employment Bd., 1989-90; bd. dirs. Greater Lawrence Red Cross; apptd. to Mass. Dept. Edn. Sch.-Bus. Partnership Com., 1990-91; chmn. bd. dirs. St. Paul's Ch., North Andrew, 2007—. With USCG, 1958-60. Recipient Pvt. Sector award Presdl. Commn., 1985, Flood Relief award ARC, 1987; named to U. Notre Dame Acad. Orgn. Mgmt., 1989, CUNY Hall of Fame. 1990. Mem. Am. C. of C. Execs., New Eng. Assn. C. of C. Execs. (pres., 1986), Mass. Assn. C. of C. Execs. (pres. 1984). Democrat. Episcopalian. Avocations: writing, golf. Home: The LeaderShip 233 Osgood St North Andover MA 01845-4025 Office: Jour Innovative Mgmt Goal/QPC 12B Manor Pkwy Salem NH 03079 Office Phone: 603-890-8800. E-mail: lsmith@goalqpc.com.

SMITH, LAVENSKI R. (VENCE), federal judge; m. Trendle Smith; 2 children. BA, U. Ark., 1981, JD, 1987. Law clerk Hall, Wright & Morris, 1985—87; staff lawyer Ozark Legal Svcs., 1987-91; pvt. practice Springdale, 1991-94; asst. prof. John Brown U., 1994-96; regulatory liaison Ark. Gov. Off., 1996—97; interim assoc. justice Ark. State Supreme Ct., 1999—2000; commr. Ark. Pub. Serv. Commn., 2001; judge US Ct. Appeals (8th cir.), 2002—. Bd. dirs. N.W. Ark. Christian Justice Ctr.; trainer Ptnrs. for Family Tng., 1993-96; chmn. Ark. Pub. Svc. Commn., 1996-98. Republican. Office: Fed Bldg Rm 316 35 E Mountain St Fayetteville AR 72702 *

SMITH, LEE ELTON, surgery educator, retired military officer; b. Ventura, Calif., July 19, 1937; s. Raymond Elroy and Edith Irene (Jordan) S.; m. Carole Sue Smith; children: Justine Diane, Alexander Loren. BS, U. Calif., Berkeley, 1959; MD, U. Calif., San Francisco, 1962. Diplomate Am. Bd. Surgery, Am. Bd. Colon and Rectal Surgery (pres. 1992-93). Commd. ens. USN, 1960, advanced through grades to capt., 1977; intern U. Utah, Salt Lake City, 1962-63; resident USN, San Diego, 1966-70, staff surgeon Bremerton, Wash., 1970-72; resident colorectal surgery U. Minn., Mpls., 1972-73; dir. colorectal surgery Nat. Naval Med. Ctr. USN, Bethesda, Md., 1973-82, ret., 1983, Seattle, 1982; clin. prof. surgery Uniformed Svcs. U., Bethesda, 1976—; prof. surgery George Washington U., Washington, 1983-96, Georgetown U., Washington, 2001—; dir. sect. of colon and rectal surgery Washington Hosp. Ctr., 1996—. Pres. Am. Bd. Colon and Rectal Surgery, 1993-94. Editor: Practical Guide to Anorectal Physiology, 1990, 2d edit., 1995; assoc. editor Diseases of the Colon and Rectum, 1984-96, Perspectives in Colon and Rectal Surgery, 1989-2000. Mem. ACS (pres. Met. Washington chpt. 1993-94), Soc. Am. Gastrointestinal Endoscopic Surgeons (pres. 1989-90), Am. Cancer Soc. (v.p. D.C. chpt. 1985-93), Am. Soc. Colon & Rectal Surgeons (pres. 1998-99). Home: 7512 16th St NW Washington DC 20012 Office: Washington Hosp Ctr 106 Irving St NW Washington DC 20010-2975 Office Phone: 202-877-8484. E-mail: lee.e.smith@medstar.net.

SMITH, LEILA HENTZEN, artist; b. Milw., May 20, 1932; d. Erwin Albert and Marian Leila (Austin) Hentzen; m. Richard Howard Smith, Sept. 12, 1959; 1 child, Jennie. BFA, Miami U., 1955; cert., Famous Artists Schs., 1959. Quilting tchr. Milw. Pub. Schs., 1975-79. One-woman shows include Boerner Bot. Gardens, Whitnall Park, Wis., 1995, 2 person show, Firefly Gallery, Wauwatosa, Wis., 2003, exhibited in group shows at Milw. Art Ctr., 1961, West Bend Gallery Fine Arts, 1963, 1993, 1996, 1999, 2002, 2005, Wustum Mus. Art, Racine, Wis., 1966, Mount Mary Coll., Milw., 1969—2001, Mapledale Sch. Gallery, Bayside, Wis., 1977, 1981, Artist's World Gallery, Cedarburg, Wis., 1975, Ozaukee Art Ctr, 1982—86, John Michael Kohler Arts Ctr., Sheboygan, Wis., 1984, 1987, 1989—2002, 2005, Cedarburg Cultural Ctr., 1988—2001, Ozaukee Art Ctr, Cedarburg, Wis., 1993, Rahr-West Art Mus., Manitowoc, Wis., 1994, Gallery 110 North, Plymouth, Wis., 1996, Rahr-West Art Mus., Manitowoc, Wis., 1997, Cardinal Stritch U., 1998—2003, Represented in permanent collections Milw. County Art Commn. Women's aux. vol. Salvation Army, Milw.; mem. dean's adv. coun. U. Wis. Milw. Sch. Arts. Recipient Honorable Mention for painting Bayshore Merchants Assn, 1969, Delta Gamma Art Fair, 1981, Best of Show for painting John Michael Kohler Arts Ctr., 1988. Mem. AAUW, Cedarburg Artists Guild, Wis. Watercolor Soc., Seven Arts Soc. Milw. (pres. 1967-68, painters group chmn. 1962-63), DAR (Milw. chpt. Holiday Folk Fair chmn. 1965-76, libr. historian 1974-77, corr. sec. 1977-80, dir. 1983-86, rec. sec. 1992-95, regent 1995-98, Outstanding Jr. Mem. 1966), Wis. Soc. Daus. of Founders and Patriots of Am. (pres. 1964-66, 2d v.p. 1966-68, 70-73, corr. sec. 1976-79), Wis. Ct. Assts., Nat. Soc. Women Descendants Ancient and Hon. Arty. Co. Boston, Wis. Soc. Mayflower Descendants (sec. 1999-02), Delta Zeta. Congregationalist. Avocations: needlecrafts, swimming, quilting.

SMITH, LEONORE RAE, artist; b. Chgo. d. Leon and Rose (Hershfield) Goodman; m. Paul Carl Smith, Apr. 17, 1943; children: Jill Henderson, Laurie Christman. Student, Chgo. Art Inst., 1935-40, U. Chgo., 1939—. Performer in many Broadway shows, with Met. Opera Quartet, Carnegie Hall, nat. concerts; portrait, landscape painter; signature artist Oil Painters of Am., Chgo., 1992-2006, Am. Acad. of Women Artists, 1997-98; ofcl. artist U.S. Coast Guard, Washington, 1989-2000; cert. artist Am. Portrait Soc., Huntington Harbor, Calif., 1985; nat. adv. bd. The Portrait Club, N.Y.C., 1983. Pres. Pacific Palisades Rep. Women, Calif. Named one of Master Artists of the World, Internat. Artist Mag., 1996; recipient Best of Show awards, Salamagundi U.S. Coast Guard, 1989, Pacific Palisades Art Assn., 1987, 1st prize in oils, Greater L.A. Art Competition, Santa Monica, Calif., 1995, prize, The Artist's Mag., 1995, Internat. Soc. Artists, 1977, 1st pl. award, Dream Studio competition, 1996, 1st pl. in portrait, O.P.A. Nat. Show, 2001, award, Northlight Art Mag., 2002, Internat. Artist Mag., 2002, several awards, Calif. Art Club, shown at Nat. Mus. Naval Aviation, Carnegie Mus., Frederick Weisman Mus., Malibu, Calif. Mem. Am. Acad. Women Artists (signature), Salmagundi Club, Pacific Palisades Art Assn. (past pres.), Oil Painters Am. (signature, 1st Pl. 2001), Am. Portrait Soc. (cert.). Achievements include completing over 90 oil paintings of fallen military in Iraq and Afghanistan. Avocations: singing, acting, poetry. Office Phone: 310-454-4096. Personal E-mail: leonorpaul@aol.com.

SMITH, LEROY HARRINGTON, JR., mechanical engineer, consultant; b. Balt., Nov. 3, 1928; s. Leroy Harrington and Edna (Marsh) S.; m. Barbara Ann Williams, July 7, 1951; children: Glenn Harrington, Bruce Lyttleton, Cynthia Ann. BS in Engring., Johns Hopkins U., 1949, MS, 1951, Dr. Engring., 1954. Compressor aerodynamacist Gen. Electric Co., Cin., 1954-61, mgr. turbomachinery devel., 1961-68, mgr. compressor & fan design tech., 1968-75, mgr. turbomachinery aerodynamics tech., 1975-92, cons. technologist Turbomachinery Aerodynamics, 1992-94, cons., 1994—. Contbr. articles to ASME Trans. Recipient Perry T. Egbert Jr. awards, 1969, 83, Charles P. Steinmetz award, 1987 Gen. Electric Co. Fellow ASME (Gas Turbine award 1981, 87, R. Tom Sawyer award 1987, Aircraft Engine Tech. award 1993); mem. NAE, Internat. Soc. Air Breathing Engines (award 2001), Ohio River Launch Club. Achievements include patents in field. Office: GE Aviation 30 Merchant St Princeton Hill P20 Cincinnati OH 45246 Office Phone: 513-552-5702. E-mail: leroy.smith@ae.ge.com.

SMITH, LESLIE EDGAR, vocational school administrator; b. Pitts., Dec. 28, 1950; s. Joel David and Margaret Elizabeth Smith; m. Pamela S. Ghost, June 17, 1994; children: Bethani E. Thomas, Kylene D. Clickner, Andrew J. Clickner. BA, Calif. U. Pa., 1972, MEd, 2006. Vocat. instr. Steel Ctr. AVTS, Jefferson Hills, Pa., 1989—99, vocat. adminstr., 1999—. Baptist. Home: 400 Bunola River Rd Bunola PA 15020 Office: Steel Center AVTS 565 Lewis Run Rd Jefferson Hills PA 15025 Home Phone: 412-384-3841; Office Phone: 412-469-3200 129. Personal E-mail: lps50@msn.com. Business E-Mail: leslie.smith@aiu3.net.

SMITH, LEWIS J., medical educator, researcher; b. NYC, Oct. 17, 1948; m. Ellen J. Jarrow; children: Laura M.Lang, Deborah S. Wood. BA, CCNY, 1969; MD, U. Rochester, 1973. Diplomate in internal medicine and pulmonary medicine Am. Bd. Internal Medicine. Intern, resident Strong Meml. Hosp., Rochester, NY, 1973—76; pulmonary fellow Boston U., 1976—79; prof. medicine Northwestern U. Feinberg Sch. Medicine, Chgo., 1991—. Office: Northwestern Univ 750 N Lake Shore Dr Ste 707 Chicago IL 60611 Office Phone: 312-503-0501. Business E-Mail: ljsmith@northwestern.edu.

SMITH, LEWIS MOTTER, JR., retired advertising and direct marketing executive; b. Kansas City, Mo., Nov. 4, 1932; s. Lewis Motter and Virginia (Smith) S.; m. Alice Allen, June 28, 1975; children: Katherine Allen, Patience Allen. Student, Kenyon Coll., 1951-53, Columbia U., 1956-58. Copywriter mail order divsn. Grolier Soc., Inc., NYC, 1957-59; free lance copywriter Santa Fe, 1960-61; v.p. creative svcs. Grolier Enterprises Inc., NYC, 1962-67; v.p., creative planning dir. Wunderman, Ricotta & Kline, Inc., NYC, 1968-72; exec. v.p., creative dir., 1972-79; exec. v.p. Young & Rubicam Direct Mktg. Group, 1980; sr. v.p., dir. mktg. Book-of-the-Month Club, Inc., 1980-84, dir., 1981-84; exec. v.p., creative dir. SSC&B: Vos Direct Inc., NYC, 1985-87; pres., dir. creative services Lintas: Direct Inc. (formerly SSC&B: Vos Direct Inc.), NYC, 1987-89; pres. Lew Smith & Assocs., Inc., Hyde Park, NY, 1989—2001. Bd. dirs. Young Concert Artists, Inc., N.Y.C., 1966-67, Harlem Sch. Arts, 1967-68. Served with U.S. Army, 1953-56. Mem. Delta Phi. Episcopalian. Home: 215 East Dr Hurley NY 12443 E-mail: lmsjr@earthlink.net.

SMITH, LINDA A., retired congresswoman; m. Vern Smith; children: Sheri, Robi. Office mgr.; former mem. Wash. State Ho. of Reps.; mem. Wash. State Senate; congresswoman, Wash. 3rd Dist. U.S. House Reps., Washington, 1995-98; mem. resources com., small bus. com.; founder, dir. Shared Hope Internat., Vancouver, Wash., 1998—. Republican. Home: 10009 NW Ridgecrest Ave Vancouver WA 98685-5159 Office: Shared Hope Internat PO Box 65337 Vancouver WA 98665

SMITH, LINDA B., psychology professor; BS, Univ. Wis., Madison, 1973; PhD, Univ. Pa., 1977. Asst. prof., psychology Univ. Ind., 1977—81, assoc. prof., 1981—85, prof., 1985—97, chancellor's prof., 1997—. Recipient Rsch. Career Devel. award, NIH, 1984—89, Award for Early Career Contribution, APA, 1985, James McKeen Cattell Sabbatical award, 1985. Fellow: Am. Acad. Arts & Scis.; mem.: Soc. Experimental Psychologists, Cognitive Sci. Soc. (governing bd.). Office: Psychological & Brain Sci Indiana Univ 1101 E Tenth St Bloomington IN 47405 Office Phone: 812-855-6052. Business E-Mail: Smith4@indiana.edu. *

SMITH, LISA J., lawyer; d. Thomas F. and Carol M. (Severson) Smith. BS, Towson State U.; MA, Auburn U.; JD, U. Md. Jud. clk. Hon. Carol E. Smith Cir. Ct. Balt. City, 1999—2000; assoc. atty. Saul E. Kerpelman & Assocs., P.A., Balt., 2000—06, Schochor, Federico & Staton, P.A., Balt., 2006—. Recipient Adv. for Justice award, Md. Trial Lawyers Assn., 2006. Mem.: Md. Trial Lawyers Assn. Office: Schochor Federico & Staton PA 1211 Saint Paul St Baltimore MD 21202 Office Phone: 410-234-1000.

SMITH, LIZ (MARY ELIZABETH SMITH), columnist, newscaster; b. Ft. Worth, Feb. 2, 1923; d. Sloan and Sarah Elizabeth (McCall) S. BA in Journalism, U. Tex., Austen, 1948. Editor Dell Publns., NYC, 1950-53; assoc. producer CBS Radio, 1953-55, NBC-TV, 1955-59; assoc. Cholly Knickerbocker newspaper column, NYC, 1959-64; film critic Cosmpolitan mag., 1966; columnist Chgo. Tribune-N.Y. Daily News Syndicate (now Tribune Media Services), 1976-91; TV commentator WNBC-TV, NYC, 1978-91; commentator Fox-TV, NYC, 1991—; columnist Newsday, L.A. Times Syndicate, 1991—2005, Family Circle mag., 1993—; freelance mag. writer; commentator Gossip Show E! Entertainment, 1993—; columnist N.Y. Post, NYC, 1995—. Author: The Mother Book, 1978, Natural Blonde, 2000, Munich at Your Door, 2003, Dishing, 2005. Recipient Emmy award for reporting, 1995. Office: Ny Post 1211 Ave of Am New York NY 10036-8790 *A career in Journalism? Any career at all? I say learn to type. Read a lot. Keep on keeping on. Work is its own reward and success is loving your work. And remember, never give up. After the Middle Ages comes the Renaissance.* *

SMITH, LLOYD, musician; b. Cleve., Dec. 1, 1941; s. Thomas George Russell and Anita May (Speer) S.; m. Rheta R. Naylor, Mar. 30, 1967 (div. Nov. 1994); 1 child, Peter Eldon; m. Nancy R. Bean, June 6, 1995. MusB, Curtis Inst. Music, 1965. Tchr. Settlement Music Sch., 1970-72, 92—. Cellist Pitts. Symphony, 1965-67, Phila. Orch., 1967—, asst. prin. cello, 1988-2002, acting assoc. prin. cello, 2002-2003, ret., 2003; soloist Indpls. Symphony, 1958, 68, Garden State Philharm., 1964, Lansdowne Symphony, 1965, West Jersey Chamber Orch., 1991, Haverford-Bryn Mawr Symphony, 1992, The Phila. Orch., 1994, Ocean City Symphony, 2001, The Brn Athym Orch., 2003, The Everett Symphony, 2004; mem. Huntingdon Trio, 1974-93, Wister quartet, 1988—; composer Sonata for cello and piano, Op. 1, 1997, Quintet, Op. 2 for Saratoga Chamber Music Festival, 1998, duet for cello Four Hands, 1999, "You're Invited" for string quartet and violin, 1999, Suite for accordion and strings, Op. 4, 2000, String Quartet Op. 3, 2000, Full Circle for cello Op. 5, 2003, Ceremonial, Op. 6 for 8 cellos, 2004, Trio for cellos, Op. 7, 2004, Cherry Blossoms for Double Quartet, Op. 8, 2006, Zephyr for Double Quartet, Op. 9, 2007, Memorial Op. 10, Cherish the Life, Op. 11, 2007. Alumni rep. Curtis Inst. Music Bd. Trustees, chmn. Parents' Com., 1989-90; bd. dirs. Phila. Youth Orch., 1987-91, Cmty. Out Reach Partnership, 1988-90, Musical Fund Soc. Phila., 2005—. Recipient C. Hartman Kuhn award for outstanding achievement, Phila. Orch., 2002. Mem. Am. Soc. Ancient Instruments (asst. artistic dir. 1975-77, music dir. 1977-80), Curtis Inst. Music Nat. Alumni Assn. (treas., bd. dirs. 1989-90), 1807 & Friends (bd. dirs. 1994—). Home and Office: 5639 E Wister St Philadelphia PA 19144-1522 E-mail: frnd1807@verizon.net.

SMITH, LLOYD HOLLINGSWORTH, physician; b. Easley, SC, Mar. 27, 1924; s. Lloyd H. and Phyllis (Page) S.; m. Margaret Constance Avery, Feb. 27, 1954; children— Virginia Constance, Christopher Avery, Rebecca Anne, Charlotte Page, Elizabeth Hollingsworth, Jeffrey Hollingsworth. AB, Washington and Lee U., 1944, D.Sc., 1969; MD, Harvard, 1948. Intern, then resident Mass. Gen. Hosp., Boston, 1948-50, chief resident physician, 1955-56; mem. Harvard Soc. Fellows, 1952-54; asst. prof. Harvard Soc. Fellows (Med. Sch.), 1956-63; vis. investigator Karolinska Inst., Stockholm, 1954-55, Oxford (Eng.) U., 1963-64; prof. medicine, chmn. dept. U. Calif. Med. Sch., San Francisco, 1964-85, assoc dean, 1985-2000. Mem. Pres.'s Sci. Adv. Com., 1970-73 Bd. overseers Harvard, 1974-80. Served to capt., M.C. AUS, 1950-52. Mem. Am. Acad. Arts and Scis., Am. Soc. Clin. Investigation (pres. 1969-70), Western Soc. Clin. Rsch. (pres. 1969-70), Assn. Am. Physicians (pres. 1974-75), Am. Fedn. Clin. Rsch. Achievements include special research genetic and metabolic diseases. Home: 309 Evergreen Dr Kentfield CA 94904-2709 Office: U Calif San Francisco Med Ctr San Francisco CA 94143-0001 E-mail: lloydhsmith@aol.com.

SMITH, LOIS ARLENE, actress, writer; b. Topeka, Kans., Nov. 3, 1930; d. William Oren and Carrie D. (Gottshalk) Humbert; m. Wesley Dale Smith, Nov. 5, 1948 (div. 1973); 1 child, Moon Elizabeth. Student, U. Wash., Seattle, 1948-50; studied with Lee Strasberg, Actor's Studio, NYC, 1955—. Guest dir. Juilliard Sch., 1987; Clarence Ross fellow Am. Theater Wing at Eugene O'Neill Theater Ctr., 1983; mem. adv. panel program fund Pub. Broadcasting Service, 1981-82; hon. founder Harold Clurman Theatre Artists Fund, Ctr. for Arts, SUNY-Purchase, 1981 Author: play All There Is, 1982; debut in Time Out for Ginger, 1952; actress Broadway and off-Broadway prodns., 1952—; stage appearances include Theater of the Living Arts, Mark Taper Forum, Long Wharf Theater, Balt. Centerstage and Steppenwolf Theater Co.; appears on network and pub. TV programs; stage appearances include, The Young and the Beautiful, 1955, The Glass Menagerie, 1956, Blues for Mr. Charlie, 1964, Orpheus Descending, 1957, Miss Julie, 1966, Uncle Vanya, 1965, 69, The Iceman Cometh, 1973, Harry Outside, 1975, Hillbilly Women, 1979, 81, the Vienna Notes, 1985, The Stick Wife, April Snow, 1987, The Grapes of Wrath, 1988-89, 90, Measure for Measure, Beside Herself, 1989, Escape from Happiness, 1993, Buried Child, 1995-96, Defying Gravity, 1997, Impossible Marriage, 1998, Mrs. Warren's Profession, 1999, Give Me Your Answer, Do, 1999, Mother Courage, 2001, The Trip to Bountiful, 2005 (Lucille Lortel award, outstanding actress 2006, Outer Critics' Cir. award outstanding actress in a play 2006, OBIE award Village Voice 2006, Drama Desk award outstanding actress in a play, 2006, Kingsley-Evans award, 2006), Surface to Air, 2007; films include East of Eden, 1955, Five Easy Pieces, 1970, Next Stop Greenwich Village, 1975, Resurrection, 1980, Four Friends, 1981, Green Card, 1990, Fried Green Tomatoes, 1991, Falling Down, 1993, How to Make an American Quilt, 1995, Dead Man Walking, 1995, Larger than Life, 1996, Twister, 1996, Tumbleweeds, 1998, Minority Report, 2002, The Laramie Project, 2002, Iron-Jawed Angels, 2004, Best Thief in the World, 2004, P.S., 2004, Sweet Land, 2005, Hollywoodland, 2006, Kill Shot, 2006. Named Best Supporting Actress for Five Easy Pieces, Nat. Soc. Film Critics, 1971; named to named to Filmdom's Famous Fives for East of Eden, Failm Daily mag., 1955; recipient Tony nominations, for Grapes of Wrath, 1990, Buried Child, 1996, Steppenwolf Ensemble Nat. Medal of Arts, 1998. Mem. SAG, AFTRA, Actors Equity Assn., Dramatists Guild, Actors Studio, Ensemble Studio Theater, Steppenwolf Theatre Co. Ensemble, Acad. Motion Picture Arts and Scis. *

SMITH, LOREN ALLAN, federal judge; b. Chgo., Dec. 22, 1944; m. Catherine Yore; children: Loren Jr., Adam (dec.). BA in Polit. Sci., Northwestern U., Evanston, Ill., 1966, JD, 1969; LLD (hon.), John Marshall Law Sch., 1995, Capital U. Law Sch., 1996, Campbell U., Buies Creek, NC, 1997. Bar: Ill. 1970, US Ct. Mil. Appeals 1973, US Ct. Appeals (DC cir.) 1974, US Supreme Ct. 1974, US Ct. Claims, 1985, US Ct. Appeals (fed. cir.) 1986, US Ct. Fed. Claims. Host nightly radio talk show What's Best for Am.?, 1972; cons. Sidney & Austin, Chgo., 1972-73; gen. atty. FCC, 1973; asst. to spl. counsel to the pres. The White House, Washington, 1973-74; spl. asst. US atty US Dept. Justice, Washington, 1974-75; chief counsel Reagan for Pres. campaigns, 1976, 80; prof. Del. Law Sch., 1976-84; dep. dir. Office Exec. Br. Mgmt. Presdl. Transition, 1980-81; chmn. Adminstrv. Conf. US, 1981-85; judge US Ct. Fed. Claims, Washington, 1985—2000, chief judge, 1986-2000, sr. judge, 2000—. Disting. lectr. Columbus Sch. Law, Cath. U. Am., 1996—; Disting. adj. prof. law George Mason U. Sch. Law, 1998—; past mem. Pres.'s Cabinet Coun. Legal Policy, Pres.' Cabinet Coun. on Mgmt. and Adminstrn.; chmn. Coun. Ind. Regulatory Agys.; served as disting. jurist in residence U. Denver; Allen chair U. Richmond Sch. Law, 1995, internat. elections observer Chile and Serbia; internat. speaker in field; internat. appearances on TV and radio. Co-author: Black America and Organized Labor: A Fair Deal?, 1979; contbr. articles to profl. jours. Adv. bd. mem. WETA Pub. Radio Cmty. Adv. Bd. Recipient Presdl. medal Cath. U. Am. Law Sch., 1993, Romanian medal of justice Romanian Ministry Justice, 1995, Ronald Reagan Pub. Svc. award Nat. Property Rights Conf., 1997. Mem. Bar Assn. DC (hon. mem., jud. honoree award 1997), Univ. Club (Washington, named club mem. of yr. 1991, chmn. entertainment com., centennial com.). Republican. Jewish. Office: US Ct of Fed Claims 717 Madison Pl NW Washington DC 20005

SMITH, LOUIS JOHN, historian; b. Harvey, Ill., Mar. 6, 1940; s. Louis and Agnes Smith; m. Sharon Ann Moeller, June 13, 1965; children: David Louis, Deborah Ann Tully. BA in History, Carthage Coll., Kenosha, Wis., 1963; MA in History, Ill. State U., Normal, 1967; PhD in History, Mich. State U., East Lansing, 1977. Asst. prof. Ill. State U., Normal, 1969—70; sr. editor, chief European and gen. divsn. historian's office US Dept. State, Washington, 1971—2005; dir. oral history program Hist. Office, Office of Sec. of Def., Washington, 2006—. Author: Yorktown: Cornerstone of Independence, 1981; editor: The Foreign Relations of the United States, 20 vols., 1974—2005; contbg. editor: American Foreign Relations: Current Documents, 10 vols., 1980—90. Sec. Chapel Sq. West Civic Assn., Annandale, Va., 1985—2005; pres. bd. dirs. Queen of Peace Ch., Arlington, Va., 1975—80. Named to Hall of Fame, Coll. Arts and Scis., Ill. State U., 2005; recipient Superior Honor and Franklin awards, US Dept. State, 1980—2004, Sec. of State's Lifetime Achievement award, 2005. Mem.: Soc. Historians of Am. Fgn. Rels., Orgn. Am. Historians, Am. Hist. Assn.

Avocations: opera, gardening, golf, youth athletics. Home: 8327 Epinard Ct Annandale VA 22003 Office: Hist Office Office of Sec of Defense 1777 Kent St Arlington VA 22209 Office Phone: 703-688-7575.

SMITH, LOVIE, professional football coach; b. Gladewater, Tex., May 8, 1958; m. MaryAnne Smith; children: Mikal, Matthew, Miles. BA, U. Tulsa, 1979. Head coach Big Sandy HS Football Team, 1980, Cascia Hall Prep, Tulsa, 1981, U. Tulsa, 1983—86, U. Wis., 1987, Ariz. State U., 1988—91, U. Ky, 1992, U. Tenn., 1993—94, Ohio State U., 1995, Chgo. Bears, 2004—; linebacker coach Tampa Bay Buccaneers, 1996—2001; defensive coord. St. Louis Rams, 2001—03. Named two-time All-American, three-time All-Mo. Conf., Coach of Yr., AP, 2005. Achievements include becoming one of two first African-Am. Coaches in Super Bowl, 2007. Office: Chgo Bears 1000 Football Dr Lake Forest IL 60045 *

SMITH, LUELLA MARGARET, special education educator; b. Greensburg, Pa., Nov. 8, 1947; d. William Elmer Peace and LaRue (Matson); m. Edwin Stewart Smith, Oct. 17, 1970; children: Laura LaRue Zendarski, William Daniel. BS, Indiana U. of Pa., 1990; MEd, Gannon U., Erie, Pa., 2000. Cert. prin. Spl. edn. tchr. Blairsville-Saltsburg Sch. Dist., Blairsville, Pa., 1990—. Mem.: ASCD (assoc.), Coun. for Exceptional Children (assoc.). Democrat-Npl. Lutheran. Avocations: golf, scrapbooks. Home: 4416 Rte 819 Avonmore PA 15618 Home Phone: 724-727-7070. Personal E-mail: edwlue@kiski.net.

SMITH, MABEL HARGIS, retired secondary school educator, musician; b. Ruby, La., Sept. 29, 1917; d. Ildephonso Albinos Hargis and Stella Gertrude Baker; m. Thomas Leonard Smith, Jr., Dec. 29, 1950; 1 child, Susan Claire Smith McLaughlin. BA, La. Coll., 1938; MusM, Northwestern U., 1952. Tchr. Tioga H.S., La., 1938—75; pianist-organist children's choir Tioga First Bapt. Ch., Tioga, 1941—2002. Named Sr. Adult of Yr., First Bapt. Ch., 1989, Disting. Alumna, La. Coll., 1977; named one of Women of Century, Daily Town Talk, Alexandria, La., 1999; recipient Cmty. Svc. award, Matinee Music Club, 1953—54, Recognition for musical contbns., Curtis T. Hines Masonic Lodge, 1997. Mem.: La. Music Educators (Hall of Fame 1999), Music Educator's Nat. Conf., Delta Omicron Internat., Delta Kappa Gamma. Baptist. Avocations: sewing, cooking, reading, gardening. Home: 415 McMahon St Deridder LA 70634

SMITH, DAME MAGGIE (MARGARET NATALIE SMITH CROSS), actress; b. Ilford, Eng., Dec. 28, 1934; d. Nathaniel and Margaret Hutton (Little) S.; m. Robert Stephens, 1967 (div. 1974), 2 children; m. Beverley Cross, 1974 (dec. 1998). Grad., Oxford High Sch. Girls; D.Litt. (hon.), St. Andrews, 1971; DLitt (hon.), Oxford U., 1994. Asst. stage mgr., actor Oxford Playhouse, 1951—53. Stage and film actress, 1952—, stage appearances include New Faces, debut N.Y.C, 1956, Share My Lettuce, 1957, The Stepmother, 1958, Rhinoceros, 1960, Strip the Willow, 1960, The Rehearsal, 1961, The Private Ear and the Public Eye, 1962 (Evening Standard award for best actress, 1962), Mary, Mary, 1963 (Variety Club award named actress of yr., 1963), Othello, 1964, Twelfth Night, 1952, Hay Fever, 1964, 1977, Master Builder, 1964, Much Ado About Nothing, 1965, 1980, Miss Julie, 1965, Black Comedy, 1965, Hedda Gabbler, 1970 (Evening Standard award, 1970), Three Sisters, 1970, 1976, Private Lives, 1972, 1974 (Variety Club award, 1972), 1978, Cleopatra, 1976, Way of the World, 1976, 1984—85 (Evening Standard award for best actress, 1984), A Midsummer Night's Dream, 1977, Richard III, 1977, As You Like It, 1977, Macbeth, 1978, Night and Day, 1979—80, Virginia, 1980 (Evening Standard award for best actress, 1982), Interpreters, 1985—86, Lettice and Lovage, 1987—88 (Tony Award for best actress, 1990), 1990, The Importance of Being Earnest, 1993, Three Tall Women, 1994—95 (Evening Standard award for best actress, 1994, Variety Club award for best actress, 1994), Talking Heads, 2004, Bed Among the Lentils, 1996, A Delicate Balance, 1997—98, Lady in the Van, 1999—2000, Breath of Life, 2002—03, and several others, The Lady from Dubuque, 2007, appearances at Old Vic, 1959—60, charter mem. Royal Nat. Theatre, London, 1963—; actor: (films) Child in the House, 1956, Nowhere to Go, 1958, Go to Blazes, 1962, The VIPs, 1963, The Pumpkin Eater, 1964, Young Cassidy, 1965, Othello, 1965, The Honey Pot, 1967, Oh What a Lovely War, 1968, Hot Millions, 1968, The Prime of Miss Jean Brodie, 1969 (Brit. Acad. of Film & TV Arts for best actress, 1969, Film Critic's Guild for best actress, 1969, Acad. award for best actress, 1970, Variety Club for film actress of yr., 1988), Travels with My Aunt, 1973, Love and Pain and the Whole Damn Thing, 1973, Murder by Death, 1976, Death on the Nile, 1978, California Suite, 1978 (Golden Globe for best supporting actress, 1979, Acad. award for best supporting actress, 1979), Quartet, 1981 (Evening Standard award for best actress, 1981), Clash of the Titans, 1981, Evil under the Sun, 1981, Better Late Than Never, 1982, The Missionary, 1983, A Private Function, 1984 (Brit. Acad. of Film & TV Arts for best actress, 1984), A Room with a View, 1986 (Brit. Acad. of Film & TV Arts for best supporting actress, 1986, Golden Globe for best supporting actress, 1986), The Lonely Passion of Judith Hearn, 1988 (Brit. Acad. of Film & TV Arts for best actress, 1989), Paris by Night, 1988, Hook, 1991, Sister Act, 1992, The Secret Garden, 1993, Sister Act 2: Back in the Habit, 1993, Richard III, 1995, The First Wives Club, 1996, Washington Square, 1997, Tea with Mussolini, 1999 (Brit. Acad. of Film & TV Arts for best supporting actress, 2000), The Last September, 2000, Harry Potter and the Sorcerer's Stone, 2001 (Golden Satelite (Internat. Press Assn.) for best supporting actress, 2002), Gosford Park, 2001 (NY Critics Online for best supporting actress, 2002, SAG award for best ensemble in a motion picture, 2002), Divine Secrets of Ya-Ya Sisterhood, 2002, Harry Potter and the Chamber of Secrets, 2002, Harry Potter and the Prisoner of Azkaban, 2004, Ladies in Lavender, 2004, Harry Potter and the Goblet of Fire, 2005, Keeping Mum, 2005; (TV films) Night of the Plague, 1957, Boy Meets Girl, 1957, The Widower, 1958, The Curious Savage, 1958, Sunday Out of Season, 1958, A Phoenix Too Frequent, 1959, For Services Rendered, 1959, Guardian Angel, 1960, The Savages, 1961, Hay Fever, 1965, Penelope, 1965, Much Ado About Nothing, 1967, Home and Beauty, 1967, On Approval, 1968, Man and Superman, 1968, The Merchant of Venice, 1972, The Millionairess, 1972, Mrs. Silly, 1983, Lily in Love, 1983, Bed Among the Lentils, 1988 (Brit. Acad. of Film & TV Arts for best actress, 1987, Baniff (Can.) for best actress, 1987), Memento Mori, 1992, Suddenly Last Summer, 1993, Curtain Call, 1998, David Copperfield, 1999, All the King's Men, 1999, My House in Umbria, 2003 (Emmy award for best actress miniseries or movie, 2003);, performer albums and tapes. Recipient Best Film Actress award Soc. Film and TV Arts U.K., 1968, Best Actress LA Critics, 1970, Taomina Gold award, 1985, Hanbury Shakespeare prize, FVS Found. 1991, Lifetime Achievement award, Brit. Acad. of Film & TV Arts, 1992, William Shakespeare award for Classical Theatre, Wahington, DC's Shakespeare Theatre, 1999; decorated Commdr. British Empire, 1970, Dame of the British Empire, 1990; named to Theater Hall of Fame, 1994. Fellow: British Film Inst., British Acad. Film & Television Arts. Office: 41 Warbeck Rd London W12 8NS England

SMITH, M(AHLON) BREWSTER, retired psychologist, educator; b. Syracuse, NY, June 26, 1919; s. Mahlon Ellwood and Blanche Alice (Hinman) S.; m. Jean Dresden Schwartz, June 1942 (div. 1945); m. Deborah Anderson, June, 1947; children: Joshua H., T. Daniel, Rebecca M., J. Torquil. Student, Reed Coll., Portland, Oreg., 1935-38; AB, Stanford U., 1939, AM, 1940; PhD, Harvard U., 1947. Jr. analyst Office Coordinator of Info., U.S. Govt., 1941; Rantoul scholar Harvard U., 1940-41, Social Sci. Research Council fellow, 1946-47, asst. prof. social psychology, dept. social rels., 1947-49; prof. psychology, chmn. dept. Vassar Coll., 1949-52; staff Social Sci. Rsch. Coun., 1952-56; prof. psychology NYU, 1956-59, U. Calif. at Berkeley, 1959-68, dir. Inst. Human Devel., 1965-68; prof., chmn. dept. psychology U. Chgo., 1968-70; prof. psychology U. Calif. at Santa Cruz, 1970-88, prof. emeritus, 1988—, vice chancellor social scis., 1970-75, ret., 1988. Fellow Ctr. Advanced Studies Behavioral Scis., 1964-65; v.p. Joint Commn. Mental Illness and Health, 1955-61. Author: Social Psychology and Human Values, 1969, Humanizing Social Psychology, 1974, Values, Self and Society, 1991, For a Significant Social Psychology, 2003; co-author: The American Soldier, vol. 2, 1949, Opinions and Personality, 1956; editor: Jour. Social Issues, 1951-55, Jour. Abnormal Soc. Psychology, 1956-61; contbr. articles to profl. jours. Rsch. officer Info. and Edn. divsn. War Dept., 1943-46; rsch. assoc. spl. com. on soldier attitudes Social Sci. Rsch. Coun. 1946. Maj. AUS, 1942-46 Decorated Bronze Star medal; NIMH fellow, 1964-65, NEH fellow, 1975-76; Belding scholar Found. for Child Devel., 1982-83; Gold medal award Am. Psychol. Found., 1992 Fellow AAAS, APA (pres. 1978, Disting. Contbn. to Pub. Interest award 1988, Henry A. Murray award 1993); mem. Soc. Psychol. Study Social Issues (pres. 1959, Kurt Lewin Meml. award 1986, Presdl. citation 2004), Western Psychol. Assn. (pres. 1986, Lifetime Contbn. award 1996), Psychologists for Social Responsibility (pres. 1987-90), Internat. Soc. Polit. Psychology (Harold Lasswell award 1993), Internat. Assn. Applied Psychology (pres. divsn. polit. psychology 1994-98), Soc. Peace, Conflict and Violence (Lifetime Contbn. to Peace Psychology award 1999), Cosmos Club (Washington), Phi Beta Kappa, Sigma Xi. Democrat. Home: 316 Escalona Dr Santa Cruz CA 95060 Business E-Mail: brsmith@ucsc.edu.

SMITH, MALCOLM BARRY ESTES, philosopher, educator, lawyer; b. Houston, Oct. 24, 1939; s. Fairleigh Estes and Norna Barry (McNab) S.; m. Patricia Sweetser; children: Malcolm, Eric. BA, Va. Mil. Inst., 1961; PhD, Cornell U., 1969; JD, U. Calif., Berkeley, 1984. BarL Mass. 1985, U.S. Supreme Ct. 1992. Instr. philosophy Smith Coll., Northampton, Mass., 1967-69, asst. prof. philosophy, 1969-74, assoc. prof., 1974-79, prof., 1979—2002, prof. emeritus, 2002—. Served to capt. USAR, 1964-66. Mem. Mass. Bar Assn., Am. Philos. Assn. Home: 9 Park St Northampton MA 01062-1236 Office: Smith Coll Dept Philosophy PO Box 839 Northampton MA 01061-0839 Office Phone: 413-586-0679. Business E-Mail: mbsmith@smith.edu.

SMITH, MALCOLM BERNARD, investment company executive; b. Lynn, Mass., May 27, 1923; s. Philip and Ida (Zenis) S.; m. Betty Booth, June 20, 1948; children: Eric, Daniel. BA summa cum laude, Dartmouth Coll., 1944; MA in Econs., Harvard U., 1948; degree (hon.), New Sch. Social Rsch., 1995. Sec. Gen. Am. Investors Co., NYC, 1956-57, treas., 1957-59, v.p., 1958-61, pres., 1961-89, vice chmn., 1989-97; sr. cons., 1997—. Chmn. fin. com. N.Y. Found., 1973—82, treas., 1979—82, trustee, 1973—89; chmn. N.Y. Found., 1982—85; chmn. New Sch. for Social Rsch., NYC, 1985—95, trustee, 1982—, treas., 1982—84, chmn. ednl. policy com., 1984—85, chmn. exec. com., 1985—95; mem. investment com. Phi Beta Kappa Found., 1987—96; bd. dirs. Learning Smith, Inc., 1992—93, Cybersmith, Inc., 1994—97; mem. investment com. Fedn. Jewish Philantrophies, NY, 1975—96; bd. dirs. Human Rights Watch, 1993—2001, emeritus, 2001—; trustee John Simon Guggenheim Meml. Found., 1982—95, chmn. fin. com., 1985—95; mng. trustee Permanent Fund of MLA, 1987—. With US Army, 1943—46. Mem. AAAS (chmn. investment and fin. com. 1975—), Investment Co. Inst. (bd. govs. 1987-95), Assn. Publicly Traded Investment Funds (bd. dirs. 1970-87, chmn. 1971-79, Coun. on Fgn. Rels., N.Y. Soc. Security Analysts, Harvard Club (bd. mgrs. 1984-86), Century Assn. N.Y.c. (treas., bd. mgrs. 1999-2003), Phi Beta Kappa Fellows (adv. com. 1984-93, bd. dirs. 1993—), Phi Beta Kappa. Home: PO Box 358 Pound Ridge NY 10576-0358 Office: 1150 Park Ave New York NY 10128-1244

SMITH, MALCOLM SOMMERVILLE, bass; b. Rockville Centre, NY, June 22, 1933; s. Carlton Newell and Margaret (Sommerville) S.; m. Margaret Yauger, Oct. 4, 1975. B.Music Edn., Oberlin Coll., 1957, B.Mus., 1960; MA in Ednl. Adminstrn, Columbia Tchrs. Coll., 1958; student, Ind. U. Sch. Music, 1960-62. Dir. choral music Ramapo Regional H.S., Wyckoff, NJ, 1958—60. Mem. artist faculty U. So. Maine, 2003—07. Bass: Lyric Opera, bass soloist: Russian tour, Robert Shaw Choral, 1962; leading bass N.Y.C. Opera, 1965—70, Deutsche Oper Am Rhein, Dusseldorf, Germany, 1971—, Vienna State Opea, 1973—74, 86 Met. Opera, Japan tour, 1975, Met. Opera, N.Y.C., 1975—77, Paris Opera, 1978, Barcelona Opera, 1978, Sao Paulo, Brazil, 1978, Mexico City, 1979, 80, Berlin Opera, 1979, 80, Montreal Symphony, 1979, 80, 81, 82, Hamburg Opera, 1981, Koln Opera, 1980, Stuttgart Opera, 1980, Frankfurt Opera, 1980, Rome Opera, 1980, Trieste (Italy) Opera, 1981, Berlin Staatsoper, 1982, 85, Lyric Opera Phila., 1982, L.A. Philharm. at Hollywood Bowl, 1984, Mannheim Opera, Germany, 1986, Turin Opera, Italy, 1986, 88, Bordeaux, France, 1987, Dresden Opera, Germany, 1987, Staats Opera Berlin Japan tour, 1987, Polish TV, 1989, Oslo Opera, 1987, Paris Radio, 1988-89, Orange Festival, France, 1988, Penderecki Festival, Krakow, Poland, 1988, maj. soloist Schleswig Holstein Festival, Germany, 1989, Krakow Philharmonic, Poland, 1988, Maggio Musicale, Florence, Italy, 1988, Boston Symphony, Minn., Cin., Houston, Utah, Seattle, Chgo., Phila., Balt. Symphony, 1993, Mex. Nat. Symphony, 1993, nat. symphonies, also Cin. Summer Opera, Central City (Colo.), Summer Opera, Festival of Two Worlds, Spoleto, Italy, Saratoga Festival, 1985, debut La Scala, Milan, Italy, 1982, Salzburg Festival, 1986, Athens Festival, 1987, Bordeaux (France) Opera, 1987, Ft. Worth Opera, 1988, Orange Festival, France, 1988, Staatsoper Munich, 1990, Bastille Opera, Paris, 1991, Heidelberg Summer Festival, 1991, 92, Brussels Opera, 1992, 93, 94, 97, Opera Nice, France, 1992, Opera Montpelier, France, 1992, Cin. Opera, 1994, 2000, Dusseldorf Opera, 1994, Japan tour, 1994, Bregenz (Austria) Festival, 1996, Honolulu Opera, 1996, 98, Balt. Opera, 1996, Prague Autumn Festival, 1997, Cin. Opera, 1998, 2000, Grand Rapids Opera, 2000, Dusseldorf Opera, 2001, 2002, Portland Opera, 2001, Portland Symphony, 2002, recorded War and Peace, 1986, Penderecki Requiem, 1990, Aspen Music Festival, 1997; musician: Portland Symphony Orch., 2002—05, Schwerin Opera Festival, 2003, Opera Orch. NY, 2005, Springfield Festival, 2006, Spoleto Festival, 2006, Port Opera, 2006, Helena Mont. Symphony, 2007. Served with AUS, 1954-56. Recipient Kämmersanger title Dusseldorf (Germany) Opera, 1996. Congregationalist. Office: care Thea Dispeker Artists Rep 59 E 54th St New York NY 10022-4211 *Hard work and a sense of humor.*

SMITH, MARGARET TAYLOR, volunteer; b. Roanoke Rapids, NC, May 31, 1925; d. George Napoleon and Sarah Luella (Waller) T.; m. Sidney William Smith Jr., Aug. 15, 1947; children: Sarah Smith, Sidney William Smith III, Susan Smith, Amy Smith. BA in Sociology, Duke U., 1947. Chair emeritus bd. trustees Kresge Found., Troy, Mich., 1985—; chmn. Nat. Coun. for Women's Studies Duke U., NC, 1986—, chmn. Trinity Bd. Visitors NC, 1988-98; chair emeritus. Chmn. bd. visitors Wayne State U. Med. Sch., 1993; bd. dirs., mem. exec. com. Detroit Med. Ctr.; mem. bd. govs. Detroit Med. Ctr. Recipient the Merrill-Palmer award Wayne State U., Detroit, 1987, Zimmerman award Gtr. Detroit Health Coun., Athena award C. of C., 1998, Women of Achievement award Mich. Women's Fedn., 1999, disting. svc. award Wayne State U., 1999; named disting. alumna award Duke U. Mem. The Village Club, Internat. Women's Forum, Pi Beta Phi, Phi Beta Kappa. Methodist. E-mail: sidmyth@aol.com.

SMITH, MARIE EDMONDS, real estate agent, property manager; b. Quapaw, Okla., Oct. 5, 1927; d. Thomas Joseph and Maud Ethel Edmonds; m. Robert Lee Smith, Aug. 14, 1966 (dec. 1983). Grad. vocat. nurse, Hoag Hosp., Costa Mesa, Calif., 1953; BA, Vanguard U., 1955; MS, U. Alaska, 1963. Lic. vocat. nurse, Calif.; cert. sci. tchr., Alaska. Nurse Calif. Dept. Nurses, Costa Mesa, 1952-60; tchr. Alaska Dept. Edn., Aniak and Anchorage, 1955-60; tchr. sci. Garden Grove (Calif.) Sch. Dist., 1960-87; property mgr. Huntington Beach, Calif., 1970—; agent Sterling Realtors, Huntington Beach, 1988—. Author: Ocean Biology, 1969. Bd. dirs., tchr. Newport Mesa Christian Ctr., Costa Mesa, 1983-2001; com. chmn. Garden Grove Unified Sch. Dist. PTA, 1977. NSF grantee, 1960-62. Mem. AAUW, Vangaurd U. Alumnae Assn. Republican. Avocations: skin diving, travel. Home: 83ll Reilly Dr Huntington Beach CA 92646 Office: L8l53 Brookhurst St Fountain Valley CA 92708

SMITH, MARIE F., lobbyist, small business owner, writer; b. East St. Louis, Ill., Mar. 12, 1939; d. David and Christina Ford; m. Richard Stanley Smith, Dec. 13, 1986; stepchildren: Jeffrey, Reginald, Laurie Debrotz. BA, Fisk U., 1961. Dir. manpower mgmt. and orgn. planning Social Security Adminstrn.; realtor assoc., 1987—; small bus. owner, 1987—; freelance writer, 1987—; commr. Status of Women; chair Nat. Legis. Coun. AARP, Washington, spokesperson Women's Initiative Program, mem. audit and fin. com., 2000—02, mem. exec. dir. search com., 2000—02, treas. found. bd. dirs., 2000—02, pres. elect, 2002—04, pres., 2004—06. Active Interfaith Vol. Caregivers; sec. bd. dirs. Maui Adult Day Care Ctr.; pres. bd. dirs. Maui Vol. Ctr. Named one of Am.'s 100 most influential African Am. leaders, Ebony mag., Most Influential Black Americans, 2006; recipient Woman of Excellence award, Commn. on the Status of Women, Circle of Women award, County Commn. on the Status of Women. Mem.: Zonta Internat., Nat. Assn. Ret. Fed. Employees (pres.), African Am. Heritage Found. Maui (pres.). Avocations: writing, travel, golf.

SMITH, MARILYN NOELTNER, retired science educator; b. LA, Feb. 14, 1933; d. Clarence Frederick and Gertrude Bertha (Smith) Noeltner; m. Edward Christopher Smith, Sept. 11, 1971 (dec. Oct. 1999). BA, Marymount Coll., 1957; MA, U. Notre Dame, 1966; MS, Boston Coll., 1969. Cert. tchr.; cert. community coll. tchr., Calif.; cert. adminstr., Calif. Tchr., chmn. sci. dept. Marymount High Sch., Santa Barbara, Calif., 1954-57, LA, 1957-58, 69-79, tchr., chmn. sci. and math. depts. Palos Verdes, Calif., 1959-69; tchr., chmn. math. dept. Corvallis High Sch., Studio City, Calif., 1958-59; instr. tchr. tng. Marymount-Loyola U., LA, 1965-71, instr. freshman interdisciplinary program, 1970-71; tchr. math. Santa Monica (Calif.) HS, 1971-72; instr. math., chemistry, physics Santa Monica Coll., 1971—79; tchr. sci. Beverly Vista Sch., Beverly Hills, Calif., 1972—2002; ret., 2002. Cons. Calif. State Sci. Framework Revision Com., LA, 1975; chmn. NASA Youth Sci. Congress, Pasadena, Calif., 1968-69, Hawaii, 1969-70; participant NASA Educators Conf. Jupiter Mission, Ames Research, San Francisco, 1973, NASA Educators Conf. Viking-Mars Ames Project, San Francisco, 1976-77, NASA Landsat Conf., Edward's AFB, Calif., 1978, NASA Uranus Mission, Pasadena, Calif., 1986, NASA Uranus-Voyager Mission, Pasadena, 1989, NASA Neptune-Voyager Mission, Pasadena, 1989; test scoring com. Calif. Learning Assessment System, U. Santa Barbara, 1993, writing com. Trainers Manual, 1993. Author books and computer progs. including NASA Voyager-Uranus Sci. Symposium for Educators, 1989, NASA Voyager 2 Neptune Encounter Conf., 1989, others; contbr. articles to profl. jours. Sponsor Social Svc. Club, Palos Verdes, 1959-69, moderator, sponsor ARC Youth Svc. Chmn., Beverly Hills, 1974-77, judge L.A. County Sci. Fair, 1969—, blue ribbon com. NATAS, 1971—; bd. dirs. Children First, Beverly Hills, 1990-91; vol. sch. initiative, Beverly Hills, 1989-90; steering com. on tech. Beverly Vista Sch., 1994-95; del. Congress of Am. Women Scientists to Cuba, People to People Amb. Program, 2001; active U. Notre Dame Badin Guild, 1989—. Recipient Commendation in Teaching cert. Am. Soc. Microbiology, 1962, Salute to Edn. award So. Calif. Industry Edn. Council, 1962, Outstanding Teaching citation Cons. Engrs. Assn. Calif., 1967, Cert. Honor, Silver Plaque Westinghouse Sci. Talent Search, 1963-68, Tchr. award Ford-Future Scientists of Am., 1968, Biomed. award Com. Advance Sci. Tng., 1971, Outstanding Tchr. award LA County Sci. Fair Com., 1975-76, Contbns. to Youth Service citation ARC, 1976-77, Outstanding Tchr. award Kiwanis, Beverly Hills, 1987, NAST Pres'. award, 1990, Woman of Yr. award, 1990, cert. appreciation Profl. Leadership and Support for Advancing Sci. Edn. Calif. Dept. Edn., 1992-93, Outstanding Tchr. Gifted Students award Johns Hopkins U., 1999-2000. Mem. We. Assn. Schs. and Colls. (vis. com. 1968, writing com. 1969—), Assn. Advancement Biomed. Edn. (pres. 1970-71), 1st Internat. Sci. Tchrs. Conf. (presider, evaluator 1977), Nat. Sci. Tchrs. Assn. (presider, evaluator 1976, chmn. contributed papers com. 1977-78, presenter 1990), Beverly Hills Edn. Assn.(pres. faculty coun. 1980-81, 85-86, sch. rep. 1990—, Ann. WHO award 1995, 96), Chemist's Club, Calif. Statewide Math. Adv. Com., So. Calif. Industry Edn. Council, Calif. Assn. Chemistry Tchrs. (program chmn. 1960), Calif. Sci. Tchrs. Assn., Am. Chem. Soc., AAAS, South Bay Math. League (sec. 1967-68, pres. 1968-69, 72, 1969-70), Calif. Math. Council, Nat. Assn. Biology Tchrs., U. Notre Dame Sorin Soc. Republican. Roman Catholic. Avocations: stone age architecture, Gaelic, Irish fisheries population samplings and contributions to data bank. Office: Beverly Vista Sch 200 S Elm Dr Beverly Hills CA 90212-4011

SMITH, MARILYNN, retired professional golfer; b. Topeka, Apr. 13, 1929; d. Lynn Smith. Grad. in Phys. Edn. and Journalism, U. Kans., 1951. Profl. golfer, 1949; founder LPGA, 1950, pres., 1957—60. Named to Kans. Golf Hall of Fame, 1991, Tex. Golf Hall of Fame, 1994, Kans. U. Sports Hall of Fame, 1999, Tchg. and Club Profl. Hall of Fame, LPGA, 2000, Kans. Sports Hall of Fame, 2000, Wichita Sports Hall of Fame, 2005, World Golf Hall of Fame, 2006; recipient Patty Berg award, LPGA, 1979, LPGA Founders Cup, Golf Digest, 1983, Commr.'s award, LPGA, 2000. Achievements include winning 21 LPGA events; five career holes-in-one; first female TV commentator for a men's golf tournament, US Open, 1973. Avocations: photography, politics. Office: c/o LPGA 100 Internat Golf Dr Daytona Beach FL 32124-1092 *

SMITH, MARION PAFFORD, retired avionics company executive; b. Waycross, Ga., Dec. 12, 1925; s. Rossa Elbert and Lillian Solee (Pafford) S.; m. Esther Pat Davis, Nov. 23, 1952; children: Bryan P., Danton D., Patricia Anne. Student, Okla. State U., 1944, Yale U., 1945; BS in EE, La. State U., 1949; postgrad., U. So. Fla., 1966-70. Engr. Bell Telephone Co., Baton Rouge, 1949-51; mgr. engring. Vitro Labs., Silver Spring, Md., 1952-57; design engring. mgr. dept. design and constrn. flight hand contrs. Space Shuttle and Space Sta. Honeywell Avionics Div., Clearwater, Fla., 1957-98. Vice chmn., bd. dirs. First Union, Largo, Fla., 1985-93; cons. U.S. Army Mgmt. Engring. Tng. Agy., 1975-79; U.S. Del. Internat. Elec. Tech. Commn., 1965-85, chmn. chief U.S. tech. adviser com. on reliability and maintainability, 1975-85, v.p., exec. com. U.S. nat. com., 1975-84; U.S. del. NATO Quality Conf., 1973; mem. White House Summit Conf. on Inflation, 1975; del. White House Conf. on Handicapped, 1977; mem. nat. adv. coun. on devel. disabilities HEW, 1974-78, Fla. Devel. Disabilities Coun., 1974-78; pres. Fla. Advocacy Ctr. for Persons with Disabilities, Inc., 1997-2000; commr. State of Fla. Occupl. Access Commn., 2000-2002; mem. devel. coun. Morton Plant Hosp., Clearwater, 1971-74. 1st lt. Signal Corps, AUS, 1944-45, 51-52. Served to 1st lt. Signal Corps AUS, 1944-45, 51-52. Recipient McDonald award Fla. Rehab. Assn., 1968; Bilgore award Citizen of Year Clearwater, Fla., 1969; Outstanding Svc. award Am. Soc. Quality Control, 1968-69; United Comml. Travelers award Most Outstanding Svc. Retarded Fla., 1970; named Engr. of Year Fla. W. Coast, 1970; Svc. to Mankind award Sertoma Clubs, 1977 Fellow IEEE (dir., Nat. Reliability award 1979); mem. Assn. Retarded Citizens USA (pres. 1973-75, nat. govt. affairs chmn. 1975-83), Am. Assn. Mental Deficiency, Nat. Symposium Reliability Quality Control (gen. chmn.), Sigma Chi. Presbyterian elder. Club: Kiwanis (Marion P. Smith award established in his honor). Home: 1884 Oakdale Ln N Clearwater FL 33764-6441 Personal E-mail: m.paffordmps2@aol.com. *True turning points in life are sometimes difficult to recognize, but for those who have become parents of a handicapped child, particularly a mentally retarded child, then that turning point is easy to recognize. After the difficult period of adjustment, one becomes aware of a realization that all persons have human dignity and worth and can make a contribution to humanity and to society.*

SMITH, MARK ANTHONY, neuroscientist, educator; b. Leicester, Eng., Aug. 15, 1965; came to U.S., 1992; s. John and Rita Joyce (Haywood) S. BSc with honors, Durham U., Eng., 1986; PhD, Nottingham U., Eng., 1990. Postdoctoral biochemist Sandoz Forschungsinstitut, Vienna, 1990-91, Karl Landsteiner rsch. fellow, 1991-92; rsch. assoc. Case Western Res. U., Cleve., 1992-94, instr. pathology, 1994-95, asst. prof., 1995—99, assoc. prof., 1999—2002, prof., 2002—. Cons. StressGen Biotechs. Corp., Victoria, BC, 1999, Panacea Pharms, Potomac, 2000—05, Prion Devel. Labs, Vernon Hills, 2001—04, Voyager Pharmacies, Raleigh, NC, 2001—07, Newpharm, England, 2006—. Author: (peer-reviewed publication) Science, Nature, Journal of Biological Chemistry, Journal of Neurochemistry, 2001 (Jordi Folch-Pi Award, American Society of Neurochemistry, 2000); editor-in-chief: Jour. Alzheimer's Disease, mem. editl. bd.: Jour. Neurochemistry; contbr. articles to profl. jours. Dalland fellow Am. Philos. Soc., 1995; recipient Ruth Salta Investigator award, 1995, Young Scientist Lectr. award Internat. Soc. Neurochem., Nathan Shock New Investigator award Gerontol. Soc. Am. Mem. AAAS, Am. Assn. Neuropathology, Microscopic Soc. Northeast Ohio (pres. elect 1997—), N.Y. Acad. Scis., Internat. Soc. Neurochemistry. Avocations: golf, soccer, music, current affairs. Office: Case Western Res U Dept Pathology 2103 Cornell Rd Cleveland OH 44106 Home: 7416 Chagrin Rd Chagrin Falls OH 44023-4435 Business E-Mail: mark.smith@case.edu.

SMITH, MARK ARTHUR, information scientist, educator; s. Marvin (Mark) Ira and Cora S. Smith. AAS in Music, Nassau CC, 1977; MusB in Music Edn., SUNY, Fredonia, 1980; MS in Edn., Elmira Coll., Fredonia, 1987; MLS, U. Buffalo, 1992. Cert. music edn. tchr. N.Y., 1980, sch. libr. media specialist N.Y. Dept. Edn., 1992. Vocal music tchr. Canisteo Ctrl. Sch., NY, 1981—91; info. sys. libr. NY State Coll. Ceramics, Alfred U., 1994—; mem. adv. com. info. techs. South Ctrl. Rsch. Coun., 2002—. Provost adv. com., liaison SUNY Librs., Albany, 1998—; pres. State Univ. of N.Y. Librs. Assn., 1999—2000. Musician (choral condr.): Hornell Cmty. Choir; contbr. articles to profl. jours. Actor, dir. Hornell Rotary Club, NY, 1992; dir. Orpheus Chorale Hornell; bd. dirs. Hornell Area Arts Coun., NY, 2004—06. Recipient Chancellors Award for Excellence in Librarianship, SUNY, 2004. Mem.: ALA, South Ctrl. Rsch. Libr. Coun. (chair adv. com. on info. techs. 2005), Libr. and Info. Tech. Assn., Assn. of Coll. and Rsch. Librs., Am. Choral Dirs. Assn., SUNY Librs. Assn., Phi Beta Mu, Phi Kappa Phi. Avocations: music performance, theatrical perfomance, choral directing. Office: NYS Coll of Ceramics Alfred Univ 2 Pine St Alfred NY 14802 Home Phone: 607-871-2942; Office Phone: 607-871-2942. Personal E-mail: mark@opus57.com. Business E-Mail: msmith@alfred.edu.

SMITH, MARK EUGENE, nuclear engineering service company executive; b. Wareham, Mass., Apr. 1, 1951; s. Mark Alvin and Evelyn Marie (Somers) S.; m. Brigid Ann Murray, Oct. 17, 1979; children: Hugh Talmidge, Patrick Morgan. AS, New England Inst. Tech., 1981. Owner Marks Motor Co., Wareham, 1965-69; chief designer HF Scientific Instrument, Ft. Myers, Fla., 1981-83; chief designer HVE Keltron Corp., Waltham, Mass., 1984-85; CEO Home Svcs., Ft. Myers, 1985-90, Gen. Capitol, Mocksville, N.C., 1990—. Cons. Underwood & Assocs., Cape Coral, Fla., 1981-89, Shaban Mfg. Co., Ft. Myers, 1982-83; chief designer Keltron Corp., Waltham, 1984-85; sr. designer Proctor & Schwartz, Lexington, NC, 1990-99; lead discipline designer Mixed Oxide Fabrication Facility (MOX-MFFF), Shaw, Ariva Mox Svcs., Aiken, SC, 2003—. Co-author: The Art of Custom Painting, 1978. With USMC, 1969-72. Named Advanced Designer, Metalflake Design Group, Springfield, Mass., 1977. Mem. Soc. Mech. Engrs., Soc. Automotive Engrs., Am. Inst. Design and Drafting (nat. drafting award 1981), Am. Nuc. Soc. Republican. Avocations: antiquarian, numismatics. Home: PO Box 906 Jackson SC 29831-0906 Home Phone: 803-643-6290; Office Phone: 803-643-5290, 803-819-8600. Personal E-mail: markussmithium@email.com. Business E-Mail: mesmith1@duke-energy.com, mesmith@moxproject.com.

SMITH, MARK LEE, architect; b. LA, Nov. 16, 1957; s. Selma (Moidel) Smith. BA in History of Architecture, UCLA, 1978, MA in Architecture, 1980, MA in History, 2006. Registered architect Calif., Nev., Oreg., Wash., Tenn., Colo., N.Y., Ohio. Designer, drafter John B. Ferguson and Assocs., LA, 1976-83, architect, 1983; pvt. practice architecture LA, 1984—. Mem. L.A. County Archtl. Evaluation Bd., 1990-2004; spkr. Western Pool and Spa Show, 1997—2001. Author: A Bridge Across the Continents, 2003; essay columnist AIA/SFV monthly, 1997—; founding editor ARCHimpressions.org mag., 2003-2005, When Stones Could Speak, 2005; contbr. articles to profl. jours Bd. govs. UCLA John Wooden Ctr., 1978-80; judge Bank Am. Achievement Awards, 1998—2000, chair, 1999-2000. Regents scholar, U. Calif., Berkeley, UCLA, 1975-78; UCLA Grad. Sch. Architecture Rsch. fellow, 1979-80. Mem. AIA (treas. San Fernando Valley chpt. 1986, bd. dirs. 1986—, v.p. 1987, pres. 1988, Design award 1988, 89, 90, 91, 99, chmn. Design awards 1994, bd. dirs. Calif. coun. 1989-94, v.p. 1991-94, chmn. continuing edn. 1991-93, chmn. 1992 conf.), Phi Beta Kappa. Office: 18340 Ventura Blvd Ste 225 Tarzana CA 91356-4278

SMITH, MARK P., foundation administrator; b. Charleston, W. Va., July 27, 1949; s. Bernard Henry and Josephine S. (Polan) Smith; m. Jane Stephens, May 6, 1978; children: Stephen Noble, Allison Baxter. BA, Princeton U., 1971; JD, Yale U., 1978. Asst. to exec. dir. ABA, Chgo., 1976—79; v.p. Ctr. Am. and Internat. Law, Richardson, Tex., 1989—; dir. Inst. for Transnational Arbitration, 1993—98, Mcpl. Legal Studies Ctr., 1998—; sec. W. Va. Legal Svc. Plan, Inc., Charleston, 1987—88. Pres. bd. dirs. Kanawha County Coalition for Homeless, 1986—87; pres. Vol. Ctr. Collin County, 2001—03; mem. bd. Vol. Ctr. North Tex., 2001—; chair Dallas Com. for Internat. Visitors, 2003—. Mem.: Nat. Assn. Bar Execs. (chmn. continuing ed. com. 1981—82, mem. exec. com. 1984—86), Saigling Elem. Sch. PTA (pres. 1991—92). Office: Ctr Am and Internat Law PO Box 799030 Richardson TX 75379-9030

SMITH, MARK W., management consultant; BA in Acctg., Hillsdale Coll., Mich. CPA AICPA. Mgr. Arthur Andersen; various fin. positions Ryder Sys., Inc., Miami; from v.p. fin. to CFO Spherion Corp., Ft. Lauderdale, Fla., 1997—2003, CFO, 2003—. Mem.: Mich. Assn. CPAs and Fin. Execs. Internat. Office: Spherion corp 2050 Spectrum Blvd Fort Lauderdale FL 33309

SMITH, MARSCHALL IMBODEN, lawyer; b. San Antonio, Oct. 3, 1944; s. Lowell B. and Jacqueline I. Smith; m. Elizabeth Braswell (div. 1973); m. Ann McNamara, June 3, 1976; children: Catherine, Elizabeth, Margaret, Austin, Lillian. AB cum laude in Hist., Princeton U., NJ, 1966; JD, U. Va., 1973; MBA, U. Chgo., 1987. Bar: NY 1974, US Ct. Appeals (2nd cir.) 1974, US Dist. Ct. (so. dist. NY) 1974, Ill. 1980. Assoc. Debevoise & Plimpton, NYC, 1973-75, Paul, Weiss, Rifkind, Wharton & Garrison, NYC, 1975-81; atty. Baxter Travenol Labs., Deerfield, Ill., 1980-82, Baxter Internat. Inc., Deerfield, Ill., 1982-83, 1983-85, asst. gen. counsel, 1985-87, assoc. gen. counsel, 1987—92; v.p., gen. counsel Am. Med. Holdings Inc., 1992—93; sr. v.p., gen. counsel, sec. IMC Global Inc. (formerly IMC Fertilizer Group Inc.), Northbrook, Ill., 1993—99; exec. v.p., gen. counsel Digitas Inc., Boston, 1999—2001; v.p., gen. counsel, corp. sec. Brunswick Corp., Lake Forest, Ill., 2001—07; sr. v.p. legal affairs, gen. counsel 3M Co., St. Paul, 2007—. Adj. faculty Lake Forest Grad. Sch. Mgmt., 1985—88. Maj. USMC, 1966—73, Vietnam. Mem.: Assn. Corp. Counsel, Christian Legal Soc., Chgo. Bar Assn. Office: 3M Co 3M Corp HQ 3m Ctr Saint Paul MN 55144-1000 Office Phone: 847-735-4430. *

SMITH, MARSHA H., state agency administrator, lawyer; b. Boise, Idaho, Mar. 24, 1950; d. Eugene F. and Joyce (Ross) Hatch; 2 children. BS in Biology/Edn., Idaho State U., 1973; MLS, Brigham Young U., 1975; JD, U. Wash., 1980. Bar: Idaho, U.S. Dist. Ct. Idaho, U.S. Ct. Appeals (9th cir.), U.S. Ct. Appeals (D.C. cir.). Dep. atty. gen. Bus./Consumer Protection Divsn., Boise, 1980-81, Idaho Pub. Utilities Commn., Boise, 1981-89, dir. policy and external rels., 1989-91, commr., 1991—, pres., 1991-95. Mem. Harvard Electricity Policy Group, Nat. Coun. on Electricity Policy; com. for regional electric power coop. Western Interstate Energy Bd., 1999-2005; dir. Western Electricity Coordinating Coun., 2002—; mem. adv. coun. Electric Power Rsch. Inst. Legis. dist. chair Ada County Democrats, Idaho, 1986-89. Mem. Nat. Assn. Regulatory Utility Commrs. (bd. dirs. 1999—, chair electricity com. 2000-03, 2nd v.p. 2005). Office: Idaho Pub Utilities Commn PO Box 83720 Boise ID 83720-0074 Office Phone: 208-334-3912.

SMITH, MARSHALL SAVIDGE, foundation executive; b. East Orange, NJ, Sept. 16, 1937; s. Marshall Parsons and Ann Eileen (Zulauf) S.; m. Carol Goodspeed, June 25, 1960 (div. Aug. 1962); m. Louise Nixon Claiborn, Aug. 1964; children: Adam, Jennifer, Matthew, Megan. AB, Harvard U., 1960, EdM, 1963, EdD, 1970. Systems analyst and computer programmer Raytheon Corp., Andover, Mass., 1959-62; instr., assoc. prof. Harvard U., Cambridge, Mass., 1966-76; asst., assoc. dir. Nat. Inst. Edn., Washington, 1973-76; asst. commr. edn. HEW, Washington, 1976-79, chief of staff to U.S. Dept. Edn. sec., 1980; prof. U. Wis., Madison, 1980-86, Stanford (Calif.) U., 1986—2003, dean Sch. Edn., 1986—94; under-sec. edn. U.S. Dept. Edn., 1993-2000, acting dep. sec. edn., 1996-2000; program dir. Hewlett Found., 2001—. Task force, chmn. Clinton Presdl. Transition Team, 1992-93; chmn. PEW Forum on Ednl. Reform; chmn. bd. internat. com. studies in edn. NAS, 1992-93. Author: The General Inquirer, 1967, Inequality, 1972; contbr. articles to profl. jours., chpts. to books. Pres. Madison West Hockey Assn., 1982-84. Mem. Am. Ednl. Rsch. Assn. (chmn. orgn. instl. affiliates 1985-86), Nat. Acad. Edn. Democrat. Avocations: environmental issues, philanthropy. Home: 1256 Forest Ave Palo Alto CA 94301 Office: Wm & Flora Hewlett Found Menlo Park CA Business E-Mail: msmith@hewlett.org.

SMITH, MARTHA A., academic administrator; b. Bradford, Pa., Aug. 31, 1948; BA, Slippery Rock State U., Pa., 1970; MEd, U. Hawaii, 1972; PhD, U. No. Colo., 1974. Dir. Hawaii Open program U. Hawaii, 1975—77; v.p. student affairs Coll. of St. Teresa, 1977—81; dean of students Dundalk CC, 1982—87, acting pres., 1987, pres., 1988—94, Anne Arundel CC, Arnold, Md., 1994—. Bd. dir. Inst. CC Devel. at Cornell U.; mem. Gov.'s Workforce Investment Bd., Md. Ednl. Coun., Nat. Edn. Commn. of the States; charter mem. Nat. Cmty. Coll. Adv. Bd. Campaign chair Anne Arundel County United Way, 1999; mem. adv bd. Chesapeake Innovation Ctr.; mem ACE Commn. on Adult Learning and Ednl. Credentials; bd. dirs. League for Innovation in the C.C., Leadership Anne Arundel, Greater Balt. Com. Named Bus. Leader of Yr., Anne Arundel Trade Coun., 1996—97, Power Elite, Daily Record, 2003; named one of Md.'s Top 100 Women, 1998, 2000, 2002; recipient First Women award, YWCA of Annapolis and Anne Arundel County, 1995, Tribute to Women in Industry award, YWCA, 1995, Cmty Trustee award, Leadership Anne Arundel, 2001, Inside the Field Nat. Leadership award, Nat. Coun. Continuing Edn., 2001, Fannie Lou Hamer award, Dr. Martin Luther King awards com., 2002, Kathleen Kennedy Townsend award of excellence, Women in Govt. Studies, 2001, Employer of the Yr., BWI Bus. Partnership, 2004. Mem.: Md.Assn. of CC (exec. com.). Office: Anne Arundel CC 101 College Pkwy Arnold MD 21012-2222 Office Phone: 410-777-1177. E-mail: masmith@aacc.edu.

SMITH, MARTHA LEE, lawyer; b. Austin, Tex., 1968; BA in English, cum laude, Washington & Lee U., 1990; JD, U. Tex., 1993. Bar: Tex. 1993. Ptnr., Banking/Fin. Andrews Kurth LLP, Houston, chmn. recruiting com., mem. policy com. Mem.: Houston Bar Assn., ABA, State Bar Tex. Office: Andrews Kurth LLP 600 Travis St Ste 4200 Houston TX 77002-3090 Office Phone: 713-220-4372. Office Fax: 713-238-7202. Business E-Mail: martysmith@andrewskurth.com.

SMITH, MARTIN BERNHARD, retired journalist; b. San Francisco, Apr. 20, 1930; s. John Edgar and Anna Sophie (Thorsen) S.; m. Joan Lovat Muller, Apr. 25, 1953; children: Catherine Joan, Karen Anne. AB, U. Calif., Berkeley, 1952, M Journalism, 1968. Reporter, city editor Modesto (Calif.) Bee, 1957-64; reporter, mng. editor Sacramento Bee, 1964-75; polit. editor, columnist McClatchy Newspapers, Sacramento, 1975-92; ret., 1992. Episcopalian. Personal E-mail: Joan_and_Marty@msn.com.

SMITH, MARTIN CRUZ, author; b. Reading, Pa., Nov. 3, 1942; s. John and Louisa (Lopez) S.; m. Emily Stanton Arnold, June 15, 1968; children: Ellen, Luisa, Samuel. BA, U. Pa., 1964. Author: Gorky Park, 1981, Stallion Gate, 1986, Polar Star, 1989, Red Square, 1992, Rose, 1996, Havana Bay, 1999, December 6, 2002, Wolves Eat Dogs, 2004.

SMITH, MARTIN HENRY, retired pediatrician; b. Gainesville, Ga., Nov. 3, 1921; s. Charles E. and Mamie Mae (Emmett) S.; m. Mary Gillis, Feb. 25, 1950; children: Susan, Margaret, Mary MD, Emory U., 1945. Diplomate Am. Bd. Pediatrics. Intern City Hosp. System, Winston-Salem, NC, 1945-46; fellow in infectious diseases Grady Meml. Hosp., Atlanta, 1948-49; resident Henrietta Egleston Hosp., Atlanta, 1949-50, Children's Hosp., Washington, 1950-51; practice medicine, specializing in pediatrics Gainesville, Ga.; ret., 1988; clin. asst. prof. Emory U. Hosp., Atlanta; chief of staff Hall County Hosp., Gainesville, 1965-66. Mem. Nat. Vaccine Adv. Commn., 1990—, chmn., 1991. Contbr. articles to profl. jours. Chmn. Nat. Vaccine Adv. Com., 1991—. Capt. M.C., U.S. Army, 1946-48 Fellow Am. Acad. Pediatrics (chpt. chmn. 1966-69, dist. chmn. 1977-83, pres.-elect 1984-85, pres. 1985-86); mem. Hall County Med. Soc. (pres. 1960), Ga. Pediatric Soc. (pres. 1965-66), Med. Assn. Ga., AMA, Alpha Omega Alpha Clubs: Chattahoochee Country (Gainesville); Piedmont Driving (Atlanta). Episcopalian. Personal E-mail: drmsmith@earthlink.net.

SMITH, MARTIN JAY, advertising and marketing executive; b. NYC, Feb. 1, 1942; s. Nathan and Helen (Schwartz) S.; m. Ellen Susan Chadakoff, Dec. 20, 1964; children: Hilary, Nancy. BA, U. Pitts., 1963. With sta. clearance dept. ABC Radio Network, NYC, 1965-66; asst. account exec. Norman Craig & Kummel, NYC, 1966-67, account exec., 1967-68, Gotham, Inc., NYC, 1968-72, account supr., 1972-74, v.p., 1974-78, sr. v.p., 1978-80, exec. v.p., 1980-84, vice chmn., 1995—2005; chief strategy officer Agency Sacks, NYC, 2005—. Sgt. USAR, 1963-69. Mem. Am. Advt. Assn. Am. (mem. mgmt. com. 1987). Avocations: flying, tennis, golf. Home: 920 Park Ave New York NY 10028-0208 Office: Agency Sacks 345 7th Ave New York NY 10001 Home Phone: 212-861-0543; Office Phone: 212-225-9327. Business E-Mail: msmith@agencysacks.com.

SMITH, MARTIN JAY, physician, biomedical research scientist; b. Bklyn., May 21, 1934; s. I. Richard and Marilyn (Bernard) S.; m. Joyce Ellen Gleason, June 26, 1960 (div. Nov. 1968); children: Danielle, Robert, Alexander; m. Ruby Helen Rhodes, Apr. 7, 1972. BA, Hofstra Coll., 1955; MD, Columbia U., 1959. Diplomate Am. Bd. Internal Medicine, Am. Bd. Internal Medicine in Hematology, Am. Bd. Pathology in Clin. Pathology, Am. Bd. Pathology in Immunopathology. Intern Meth. Hosp., NYC, 1959-60, resident in medicine, 1960-61, Montefiore Hosp., NYC, 1963-64; rsch. fellow in medicine Harvard Coll., Cambridge, Mass., 1964-66; clin. and rsch. fellow in medicine Mass. Gen. Hosp., Boston, 1964-66; physician Gundersen Clinic and Luth. Hosp., La Crosse, Wis., 1966-99, chmn. dept. internal medicine, 1971-73; dir. spl. hematology lab. Gundersen Clinic, La Crosse, 1967-99, chmn. dept. lab. medicine, 1973-96; dir. lab. medicine Luth. Hosp., La Crosse, 1973-96. Dir. rsch. Gundersen Med. Found., 1975-88; med. dir. Med. Lab. Tech. Program Western Wis. Tech. Inst., 1978-99. Contbr. articles to New Eng. Jour Medicine, Jour. Lab. Clin. Medicine, Blood, Ann. Internal Medicine, Biochim, Biophys. Acta, Jour. Infectious Diseases, Thrombosis and Haemostasis, Clin. Chemistry. Capt. USNR, ret. Fellow ACP, Coll. Am. Pathologists (inspector labs. 1983-99); mem. Am. Assn. for Cancer Rsch., Am. Soc. Hematology, Internat. Soc. Hematology, Assn. Med. Lab. Immunologists, Phi Beta Kappa. Home: 1428 Main St La Crosse WI 54601-4225

SMITH, MARY ELLEN, educational program facilitator; b. Provo, Utah, Aug. 2, 1954; d. Lloyd Coltrin McEwan and Barbara Jean Saxey; m. Samuel Adam Smith, Oct. 4, 1988; children: Brandy Lee Wilbur, Jeremy Mark Penrod. BS in Elem. Edn., So. Utah U., 1987; MA in Elem. Edn. Diverse Learners, U. Phoenix, Provo, Utah, 1998. Spl. edn./resource tchr. Jordan Sch. Dist., Eastmont Mid. Sch., Sandy, Utah, 1987—90; 6th grade tchr. Jordan Sch. Dist., Sprucewood Elem., Sandy, 1990—95, kindergarten tchr., 1995—98; clin. faculty assoc. Brigham Young U., Provo, Utah, 1998—2002; partnership facilitator Brigham Young U./Jordan Sch. Dist., Midvale, Utah, 2002—. Conf. co-chair Univ. Partnership, Sandy, 2005—. Judge State Geography Bee, Lehi, Utah, 1999—. Named Tchr. of Month, Jordan Edn. Assn., 1995; grantee, Jordan Edn. Found., 2005. Mem.: ASCD (assoc.), Internat. Reading Assn. (assoc.), Assn. Childhood Edn. Internat. (assoc.), Phi Delta Kappa (assoc.; constl. conv. rep. 2002—03). Mem. Lds Ch. Avocations: reading, travel, children and youth activities. Home: 675 N 1150 E Lehi UT 84043 Office: Copperview Elem 8449 S 150 W Midvale UT 84047 Home Phone: 801-768-3421; Office Phone: 801-565-7440. Office Fax: 801-302-4912. Personal E-mail: marysunshine73@hotmail.com. E-mail: mary.smith@jordan.k12.ut.us.

SMITH, MAURA ABELN, lawyer, paper company executive; b. Reading, Pa., Oct. 3, 1955; d. Henry Joseph and Lynn (Blashe) Abeln; children: Gwendolyn Casebeer, Karl Casebeer; m. Steven A. Smith, Dec. 18, 1999. AB, Vassar Coll., 1977; M Philosophy, Oxford U., 1979; JD, U. Miami, 1982. Bar: Fla. 1982, Ohio 1999. Assoc. Steel, Hector & Davis, Miami, 1982—87; ptnr. Baker & McKenzie, Miami, 1987-91; gen. counsel GE Co./Plastics, Pittsfield, Mass., 1991—93, v.p., gen. counsel, 1993—98; sr. v.p., gen. counsel, sec. Owens Corning, Toledo, 1998-2000, chief restructuring officer, sr. v.p., gen. counsel, sec., 2000—03, bd. dirs.; sr. v.p., gen. counsel, sec., pub. affairs Internat. Paper, Memphis, 2003—. Rhodes scholar, Oxford, Eng., 1977-79; John M. Olin fellow in law and econs., Olin Found., 1979-82. Mem.: Phi Beta Kappa. Avocations: skiing, horseback riding, tennis, golf. Office: 6400 Poplar Ave Memphis TN 38197 Office Phone: 901-419-3829. E-mail: maura.abelnsmith@ipaper.com.

SMITH, MERRITT ROE, history professor; b. Waverly, NY, Nov. 14, 1940; s. Wilson Niles and Mary Eleanor (Fitzgerald) S.; m. Bronwyn M. Mellquist, Aug. 24, 1974. AB, Georgetown U., 1963; MA, Pa. State U., 1965, PhD, 1971; LHD (hon.), Rensselaer Poly. Inst., 1997. Asst. prof. history Ohio State U., Columbus, 1970-74, assoc. prof., 1974-78; vis. prof. history and sociology of sci. U. Pa., Phila., 1976; prof. history tech. program in sci., tech. and society M.I.T., Cambridge, 1978—, Metcalfe prof. engring. and liberal arts, 1989-92, dir. progam in sci., tech. and society, 1992—96, 2000—02, Leverett and William King Cutten prof., 1993—. Author: Harpers Ferry Armory and the New Technology, 1977, Military Enterprise and Technological Change, 1985, Science, Technology and the Military, 2 vols., 1988, Does Technology Drive History?, 1994, Major Problems in the History of American Technology, 1998, Inventing America, 2002, 2d edit., 2006; mem. editl. bd. Tech. and Culture, 1973-91, Bus. History Rev., 1978-85, MIT Press, 1986-91, Archimedes, 1995—2001. Mem. Mass. Hist. Soc.; bd. advisors MIT Mus. Recipient Cert. of Commendation Am. Assn. State and Local History, 1978, Disting. Tchg. award Ohio State U., 1978, Founders Day award Charles River Mus. Industry, 2003, Arthur C. Smith award MIT, 2006; grantee Ohio State U., 1972, Am. Philos. Soc., 1974, Harvard Bus. Sch., 1974-75, Eleutherian Mills-Hagley Found., 1978-79, Alfred P. Sloan Found., 1994-2002; Guggenheim fellow, 1983-84, Regents fellow Smithsonian Instn., 1984-85. Mem. AAAS, Am. Acad. Arts and Scis., Soc. History Tech. (mem. exec. coun., Dexter Prize com., Da Vinci medal 1994, mus. com., v.p., pres. 1989-91), Orgn. Am. Historians (Frederick Jackson Turner award 1977, Disting. lectr. 2004—), Bus. History Conf., Am. Antiquarian Soc., Newcomen Soc. N.Am., Soc. Indsl. Archeology, History Sci. Soc. (Pfizer award 1978), Phi Kappa Phi, Phi Alpha Theta. Home: 17 Longfellow Rd Newton MA 02462-1505 Office: STS Program MIT 77 Massachusetts Ave Rm E51-185 Cambridge MA 02139 Business E-Mail: roesmith@mit.edu.

SMITH, MICHAEL, academic administrator; b. St. Joseph, Mo., Jan. 30, 1941; s. Walton Joseph and Margaret Dorothy (Chubb) S.; m. Connie Stanton, Oct. 27, 1965; children: Jeffrey, Timothy. AD, Mo. Western Community Coll., 1960; BS, N.E. Mo. State U., 1967; PhD, U. Nebr., 1975. Ins. investigator Retail Credit Co., St. Joseph, Mo., 1963-65; instr. Havana HS, Ill., 1967-68, West Bend High Sch., Iowa, 1968-70, U. Nebr., 1972-75; asst. prof. English Albany Jr. Coll., Ga., 1975-78; chmn. arts and scis., dir. internat. programs U. Minn., Crookston, 1978-80; chief exec. officer, coll. dean N.D. State U., Bottineau, 1980-87; provost, dean of faculty Richard Bland Coll., Coll. William and Mary, 1987-89; chancellor La. State U., Eunice, 1989-95; pres. Our Lady of the Lake Coll., Baton Rouge, 1995—2006. Commr. North Cen. Assn. Colls. and Schs., 1984-, accreditation cons./evaluator, 1982-87, vis. prof. English, U. New Orleans, 1995-98. With U.S. Army, 1960-63. Office: Our Lady of the Lake Coll 7434 Perkins Rd Baton Rouge LA 70808-4374 Home Phone: 225-928-5343; Office Phone: 225-768-1710. Business E-Mail: msmith@ololcollege.edu.

SMITH, (CARL) MICHAEL, lawyer, former federal agency administrator; b. Oklahoma City, Oct. 11, 1944; s. Carl W. Jr. and Nina (Furr) S.; m. Sharon Kay Lewis, June 5, 1971. BA, U. Okla., 1966, JD, 1969. Bar: Okla. 1969, U.S. Dist. Ct. (we., no. and ea. dists.) Okla. 1971, U.S. Ct. Appeals (10th cir.) 1976, U.S. Supreme Ct. 1976. Mem. firm Lawrence, Smith & Harmon, Oklahoma City, 1977-80; pres. Red Rock Exploration, Inc., Oklahoma City, 1980-83; mem. firm Lawrence & Ellis, P.A., Oklahoma City, 1983—95; sec. Okla. Dept. Energy, Oklahoma City, 1995—2002; asst. sec. for fossil energy US Dept. Energy, Washington, 2002—04; of counsel Dunlap, Codding & Rogers, Washington, 2004—. Mem. Blue Ribbon Commn. on Natural Gas, Oklahoma City, 1982; chmn. Okla. Polit. Action Com., Oklahoma City, 1986-90; mem. Okla. Legis. Interim Task Force on Environ. Regulation, Oklahoma City, 1991-92; sec. Okla. Energy Resources Bd., 1992-94; Capt. U.S. Army, 1969-71, Vietnam. Mem. Okla. Ind. Petroleum Assn. (pres. 1994-95). Office: Dunlap Codding & Rogers PC 1601 NW Expressway Ste 1000 Oklahoma City OK 73118 Office Phone: 202-327-5495, 405-607-8600. E-mail: cmike_smith@okpatents.com.

SMITH, MICHAEL D., dean, electrical engineering and computer science professor; m. Chris K. Smith; 2 children. BS, Princeton U., 1983; MS in Elec. Engring., Worcester Polytechnic Inst., 1985; PhD in Elec. Engring., Stanford U., 1993. Rsch. asst. Stanford U., 1986—92; instr. Harvard U., Cambridge, Mass., 1992—93, asst. prof., 1993—97, dir. undergraduate studies engring. scis., 1994—97, assoc. prof., 1997—2000, Gordon McKay prof. computer sci. and elec. engring., 2000—, assoc. dean computer sci. and engring. Sch. Engring. and Applied Scis., 2005—07, dean Faculty Arts and Scis., 2007—. Rschr. Ctr. Rsch. on Computation and Soc.; founder, chief scientist, chmn. Liquid Machines, Lexington, Mass., 2001—. Contbr. articles to profl. jours. Recipient Young Investigator Award, NSF, 1994, Phi Beta Kappa teaching prize. Mem.: IEEE, Assn. Computing Machinery. Office: Harvard U Dean FAS University Hall 5

Cambridge MA 02138 also: Sch Engring and Applied Scis Maxwell-Dworkin Labs, Rm 329 33 Oxford St Cambridge MA 02138 Office Phone: 617-496-5661. Office Fax: 617-496-2908. E-mail: smith@seas.harvard.edu. *

SMITH, MICHAEL JAMES, industrial engineering educator; b. Madison, Wis., May 12, 1945; s. James William and Ruth Gladys (Murphy) S.; m. Patricia Ann Bentley, June 22, 1968; children: Megan Colleen, Melissa Maureen. BA, U. Wis., 1968, MA, 1970, PhD, 1973. Rsch. analyst Wis. Dept. Industry Labor, Madison, 1971-74; rsch. psychologist Nat. Inst. for Occupational Safety and Health, USPHS, Cin., 1974-84; prof. U. Wis., Madison, 1984—. Owner, prin. M.J. Smith Assocs. Inc., Madison, 1991—. Contbr. articles to profl. jours. Mem. APA, Inst. Indsl. Engrs. (sr.), Human Factors Soc., Assn. Computer Machinery, Am. Soc. Testing and Measurement. Avocation: tennis. Home: 6719 Shamrock Glen Cir Middleton WI 53562-1144 Office: U Wis Dept Indsl Engring Human Factors Rsch Lab 1513 University Ave Madison WI 53706-1539 Office Phone: 608-263-6329. Business E-Mail: mjsmith@engr.wisc.edu.

SMITH, MICHAEL PETER, social sciences educator, researcher; b. Dunkirk, NY, Aug. 2, 1942; s. Peter Joseph and Rosalie Barbara (Lipka) S.; m. Patricia Anne Lendway, Aug. 21, 1965. BA magna cum laude, St. Michael's Coll., 1964; MA in Polit. Sci., U. Mass., 1966, PhD in Polit. Sci., 1971. Instr., asst. prof. dept. govt. Dartmouth Coll., Hanover, NH, 1968—71; asst. prof. dept. polit. sci. Boston U., 1971—74; assoc. prof., prof. dept. polit. sci. Tulane U., New Orleans, 1974—86; prof. cmty. studies U. Calif., Davis, 1986—, chmn. dept. applied behavioral scis., 1986—91, chmn. cmty. studies and devel. program, 2001—. Vis. prof. pub. policy U. Calif., Berkeley, 1981, city planning U. N.C., Chapel Hill, 1982, city planning U. Calif., Berkeley, 1985; vis. scholar in govt. U. Essex, Eng., 1979; vis. scholar polit. and social sci. U. Cambridge, Eng., 1982; vis. scholar Inst. Urban and Regional Devel., U. Calif., Berkeley, 1990, 94 Internat. Ctr. for Advanced Studies, NYU, 1998, Ctr. Migration, Policy and Soc., Oxford U., 2005 Author: The City & Social Theory, 1979, City, State and Market, 1988, Transnational Urbanism, 2001; co-author: Restructuring the City, 1983, California's Changing Faces, 1993; editor: Cities in Transformation, 1984, Breaking Chains, 1991, After Modernism, 1992, Marginal Spaces, 1995, Comparative Urban & Community Research, 1986—; co-editor: The Capitalist City, 1987—, The Bubbling Cauldron, 1995, Transnationalism from Below, 1998, City and Nation: Rethinking Place and Identity, 2001, The Human Face of Global Mobility, 2006; mem. editl. bd. Global Networks., 1999—. Office: Dept Human & Cmty Devel Univ Calif Davis CA 95616 Office Phone: 530-752-2243. Business E-Mail: mpsmith@ucdavis.edu.

SMITH, MICHAEL ROBERT, electro-optical engineer, physicist; b. Tela, Honduras, Aug. 24, 1937; s. Ike Morgan and Edith Helen (Hudson) S.; m., div., remarried Lorraine L. Smith, Apr. 26, 2002; children: Stephen, Monica, Meryl. BME, Ga. Inst. Tech., 1959, MS in Nuclear Engring., 1961; PhD, Case Inst. Tech., 1965. Mem. tech. staff Hughes Rsch. Labs., Malibu, Calif., 1965-68; v.p., dir. rsch. Britt Corp., LA, 1968-73; sr. staff engr. Singer/Librascope divsn., Glendale, Calif., 1973-78; pres. Exocor Tech., Newbury Park, Calif., 1978-95; asst. prof., head physics program Calif. Luth. U., Thousand Oaks, 1990-96; design leader LIGO project Calif. Inst. Tech., Pasadena, 1996—. Contbr. articles to profl. jours.; inventor emergency vehicle warning and traffic control sys., emergency vehicle warning sign, flat electro-optic display panel, high power mirror, laser recording film with opaque coating, pulsed gas laser with radiation cooling, infrared laser photocautery device; 8 U.S. patents; 9 fgn. patents. Greek folk dance tchr. Arts Coun., Thousand Oaks, Calif., 1991-97. Mem. IEEE, Laser Electro-Optic Soc. (chair 1995-97), Sigma Xi, Pi Tau Sigma. Republican. Home: 1611 N Roosevelt Ave Pasadena CA 91104-1927 Business E-Mail: smith@ligo.caltech.edu.

SMITH, MICHELLE RENE, elementary school educator; b. Burnet, Tex., Mar. 20, 1967; d. Wayne William and Mildred Martha Green; m. William Lloyd (Skip) Smith, June 10, 1989; children: Madison Paige, Minley Jade. BS, U. Tex., Austin, 1990. Tchr. grade 4-6 gen. edn. and sci. Thrall Ind. Sch. Dist., Tex., 1991—94; tchr. math. 6th grade Chisholm Trail Mid. Sch., Round Rock, 1994—96; tchr. math. 7th grade and algebra 8th grade Thorndale Ind. Sch. Dist., 1996—97; tchr. math. 7th grade Chisholm Trail Mid. Sch., Round Rock, 1997—2000; tchr. math. 7th grade, math. dept. head Leander Mid. Sch., 2000—. Tchr. religious edn. St. Elizabeth's Cath. Ch., Pflugerville, Tex., 2003—, tchr. vacation bible sch., 2004—, St. William's Cath. Ch., Round Rock, 2000—05. Mem.: Assn. Tex. Profl. Educators. Roman Catholic. Avocations: scrapbooks, photography. Home Phone: 512-246-2340.

SMITH, MICHELLE SUN, psychologist; b. Balt., June 9, 1971; d. Nelson Cang and Laura Gamber Sun; m. Michael Timothy Smith, Nov. 22, 1997; children: Nolan Sean, Hailey Elizabeth. PhD, Calif. Sch. of Profl. Psychology, Berkeley, 1998. Lic. psychologist Md., 2001, N.Y., 1999. Staff psychologist, sr. instr. psychiatry U. Rochester, NY, 1999—2001; staff psychologist, coord. eating disorder svcs. Johns Hopkins U. Counseling Ctr., Balt., 2001—03; clin. psychologist MedPsych Assocs., Lutherville, Md., 2003—; asst. prof. U. Md. Dental Sch., Md., 2004—. V.p. program devel. bMed Techs., Rochester, NY, 2001—; cons. Ruxton Orthop. Assocs., Towson, Md., 2004—. Contbr. articles to profl. jours. Recipient Ruth C. Wylie prize in psychology, Goucher Coll., 1993; fellow, Okura Mental Health Leadership Found., 1997. Mem.: APA, Md. Psychol. Assn., Interdisciplinary Coun. of Learning Disorders, Psi Chi. Avocation: autism awareness & early intervention. Office: 2324 West Joppa Rd Ste 220 Lutherville MD 21093 Home Phone: 410-583-2339; Office Phone: 410-583-2623. Business E-Mail: msunsmith@comcast.net.

SMITH, MILAN DALE, JR., federal judge; b. Pendleton, Oreg., May 19, 1942; BA cum laude, Brigham Young U., 1966; JD, U. Chgo., 1969. Bar: Calif. 1970, DC 1972, US Supreme Ct. 1977, US Tax Ct. 1978. Assoc. O'Melveny & Myers, Los Angeles, 1969-72; ptnr. Smith Crane Robinson & Parker LLP (formerly Smith & Hilbig LLP), Torrance, Calif., 1972—2006; cir. judge US Ct. Appeals (9th cir.), 2006—. Pres. Los Angeles State Office Bldg. Authority, 1983-92, Informed Voters League, Torrance, 1975-77; vice chmn. bd. Ettie Lee Homes for Youth, 1973-82, Calif. Fair Employment and Housing Commn., 1987-91; mem. Cabinet of the Interfaith Coalition to Heal L.A., head econ. devel. subcom., 1992-94; bd. trustees Deseret Trust Co. Calif., 2000-06; sec.-treas. Criminal Justice Legal Found., 1996-2005; chair, bd. visitors Sch. Religion, Claremont U., 2005-06. Nat. Honor scholar, 1966-69, U. Chgo. Mem. Brigham Young U. Alumni Assn. (bd. dirs. 1982-86). Office: US Ct Appeals 125 S Grand Ave Pasadena CA 91105-1510 *

SMITH, MOLLY D., theater director; b. Yakima, Wash. d. Kay. BA, Cath. U.; MA in Theatre, Am. U., PhD (hon.), 2001. Founder Perserverance Theatre, Juneau, Alaska, 1979—98; artistic dir. Arena Stage, Washington, 1998—. Creative advisor Sundance Inst. New Plays; lit. advisor Banff Playwright's Colony, Canada; bd. dir. Theatre Comms. Group; panelist Ctr. Internat. Theatre Devel.; spkr. in field; prof. Arts, Music and Theatre Dept. Georgetown U.; judge Susan B. Blackburn Prize. Dir.: (plays) Orpheus Descending, Camelot, An American Daughter, South Pacific, A Moon for the Misbegotten, Agamemnon and His Daughters, Coyote Builds North America, The Great White Hope, All My Sons, Hot 'n' Throbbing, How I Learned to Drive, Cat on a Hot Tin Roof, The Odyssey, The Oedipus Cycle, The Caucasian Chalk Circle, A Streetcar Named Desire, Mother Courage and Her Children, Macbeth, Farther West, The Obscene Bird of Night, Mack and Mabel, 2007; (films) Raven's Blood, Making Contact. Named Artist of Yr., Alaska State Coun. Arts; named one of 100 Most Powerful Women, Washingtonian Mag., 2001; recipient Cmty. Leader award, U. Alaska Southeast. Office: Arena Stage 1101 6th St SW Washington DC 20024 *

SMITH, MORTON ALAN, retired lawyer; b. NYC, Mar. 13, 1931; s. David and Augusta S.; m. Nancy, July 2, 1954 (div. July 1974); children: Robynn, Jeffrey, Richard; m. Jane Saffir, June 10, 1979; children: Michael, Richard. BA, U. Fla., 1953; LLD with honors, U. N.C., 1956. Bar: N.Y. 1957, D.C. 1957. Spl. trial atty. Office Chief Counsel IRS, Phila., 1956-58; spl. asst. U.S. Atty. Dist. N.J., 1957; law clk. to judge U.S. Tax Ct., Washington, 1958-60; assoc. Kaye Scholer, NYC, 1960-62, Saul Silverman, NYC, 1962-67; sr. ptnr. Hall, Dickler, Lawler, Kent & Friedman, NYC, 1967—2000, ret., 2000. Bd. dirs. Eden Park Health Corp., Albany, N.Y. Contbr. articles to profl. jours. V.p. Rye Brook (N.Y.) Bd. Edn., 1968-73; organizer of incorporation of Village of Rye Brook, 1982, now spl. counsel; bd. dirs. Herbert Birch Sch. for Exceptional Children, N.Y.C., Westchester County United Way, 1991; leadership chmn. United Way Campaign, Rye Brook, 1989-91; mem. Westchester County Housing Implementation Commn.; bd. dirs. Eden Park Health Svcs., Albany, N.Y.; pres. Bocaire Home Owners Assn., Boca Raton, Fla. Mem. ABA (tax sec.). Avocations: golf, skiing, tennis, gardening, reading. Personal E-mail: mortsmith@prodigy.net.

SMITH, MORTON EDWARD, ophthalmology educator, dean; b. Balt., Oct. 17, 1934; BS, U. Md., 1956, MD, 1960. Bd. cert. Ophthalmology Bd.; lic. physician Mo., Md., Wis. Rotating intern Denver Gen. Hosp., 1960-61; resident, nat. inst. of neurol. diseases and blindness fellow in opthalmology Washington U. Sch. Medicine-Barnes Hosp., 1961-63; NIH spl. fellow in ophthalmic pathology Armed Forces Inst. of Pathology, Washington, 1964; chief resident, instr. ophthalmology Washington U. Sch. Medicine, St. Louis, 1965-66, instr. ophthalmology, 1966-67, asst. prof. ophthalmology and pathology, 1967-69, assoc. prof. ophthalmology and pathology, 1969-75, prof. ophthalmology and pathology, 1975—, asst. dean, 1978-91, assoc. dean, 1991-96, prof. emeritus, assoc. dean emeritus, 1996—; prof. ophthalmology U. Wis., Madison, 1995-2001. Vis. scholar Eye Inst., Columbia Presbyn. Med. Ctr., N.Y.C., 1966; prof./lectr. Montefiore Hosp., Pitts., 1969, U. Ark., 1970, 77, 80, 82, 84, 86, 88, U. Fla., 1972, 81, U. Tex. and Lackland AFB, San Antonio, 1973, U. Colo., 1974, 82, U. Mo., 1974, 79, 80, 88, So. Ill. U., Springfield, 1974, U. Md., 1975, Montreal (Can.) Gen. Hosp., 1975, U. Wis., 1976, 87, 93, U. Pitts., 1977, 83, 87, U. Iowa, 1977, 87, Cleve. Clinic, 1978, Colo. Ophthalmol. Soc., 1978, Brooke Army Hosp., San Antonio, 1979, Wills Eye Hosp., Phila., 1980, USPHS Hosp., San Francisco, 1981, U. Calif., Davis, 1981, Sinai Hosp., Balt., 1985, 89, 94, U. Calif., San Diego, 1985, Tufts U., Boston, 1985, Cornell U., N.Y.C., 1988, U. Wash., Seattle, 1990, Brown U., Providence, 1990, Vanderbilt U., Nashville, 1991, Duke U., Durham, N.C., 1992; Chandler lectr. Harvard U., 1988; The Lois A. Young-Thomas Meml. lectr. U. Md., 1991; Braley lectr. U. Iowa, 1993; Havener Meml. lectr. Ohio State, 1994. Editor pathology sect.: Perspectives in Ophthalmology, 1977; mem. editl. bd. Ophthalmic Plastic & Reconstructive Surgery, 1986-90; contbr. articles to profl. jours. With USAR M.C., 1958-66. Scholar U. Md., 1958, 59. Fellow Am. Acad. Ophthalmology (ophthalmic pathology com. 1977-83, chmn. ophthalmic com. 1979-83, Honor award for svc. 1981, Sr. Honor award 1992); mem. AMA, Am. Bd. Ophthalmology (diplomate, bd. dirs. 1992—), Assn. for Rsch. in Vision and Ophthalmology (chmn. sect. pathology ann. meeting 1971), Am. Assn. Ophthalmic Pathologists (pres. 1977-80), Assn. Am. Med. Colls. (group med. edn. 1985—), Mo. Med. Assn., Mo. Ophthalmol. Soc., Verhoeff Soc., Theobald Soc., St. Louis Med. Soc., St. Louis Ophthalmol. Soc., Soc. Med. Coll. Dirs. for Continuing Med. Edn., Alpha Omega Alpha (sec.-treas. chpt. 1993-95, councillor 2003—). Home: 1275 Castle Gate Dr Saint Louis MO 63132 Office: Campus Box 8096 660 S Euclid Ave Saint Louis MO 63110-1093 Office Phone: 314-747-5559. Business E-Mail: smithm@vision.wustl.edu.

SMITH, MORTON HOWISON, religious organization administrator, educator; b. Roanoke, Va., Dec. 11, 1923; s. James Brookes and Margaret Morton (Howison) S.; m. Lois Virginia Knopf, July 7, 1925; children: Samuel Warfield, Susanne Rochet Margaret. BA, U. Mich., 1947; BD, Columbia Theol. Sem., 1953; ThM, ThD, Free U., Amsterdam, The Netherlands, 1962. Ordained to ministry Presbyn. Ch., 1954. Pastor Springfield-Roller Presbyn. Chs., Carroll County, Md., 1954; prof. bible Belhaven Coll., Jackson, Miss., 1954-63; guest lectr. Westminster Theol. Sem., Phila., 1963-64; prof. Reformed Theol. Sem., Jackson, 1964-79; stated clk. gen. assembly Presbyn. Ch. in Am., Decatur, Ga., 1973-88; prof. systematic theology Greenville Presbyn. Theol. Sem., 1987—, dean faculty, 1987-98. Moderator gen. assembly Presbyn. Ch. Am., 2000-01; advisor to bd. dirs. Greenville (S.C.) Presbyn. Theol. Sem., 1986-98, bd. dirs.; mem. bd. dirs. Presbyn. Jour., Asheville, N.C., 1965-87; lectr. on theology Republic of So. Africa, June-July, 1988, Riga, Latvia, 1992, Budapest, Hungary, 1994, Prague, Czech Republic, 1994, 95, Trinidad and Tobago, 1995, Zlin, Czech Republic, 1998, 99, on missions, Republic of Korea, June-July, 1989, Munkton, Can., 1998, 99, Recife, Brazil, 1998, 2002, Reformed Sem., St. Petersburg, Russia, New Zealand, 2003. Author: Studies in Southern Presbyterian Theology, 1962, 2d edit. 1987, How Is the Gold Become Dim, 1973, republished 1998, (pamphlet) Reformed Evangelism, 1970, Testimony, 1986, Commentary on the Book of Church Order of the Presbyterian Church in America, 1990, Harmony of the Westminster Confession and Catechisms, 1990, Systematic Theology, 1994; contbr. articles to profl. jours. Trustee Covenant Coll., Lookout Mountain, Tenn., 1982-90. 1st lt. USAAF, 1942-45. Fulbright fellow U.S. Govt., 1958. Mem. N.Am. Presbyn. and Reformed Coun. of Chs. (sec. 1977-92). Presbyterian. Avocations: flying, travel, genealogy. Office: Greenville Presbyn Theol Sem PO Box 690 Taylors SC 29687-0014 Office Phone: 864-322-2717. Personal E-mail: wcflcsc@mtnisp.com.

SMITH, MYRON JOHN, JR., librarian, author; b. Toledo, May 3, 1944; s. Myron John and Marion Oliva (Herbert) S.; 1 son, Myron John III. Student, Coll. Steubenville, 1962; AB, Ashland Coll., 1966; MLS, Western Mich. U., 1967; MA, Shippensburg U., 1969; postgrad., U. Wis., Purdue U.; LittD, Cardinal Newman Coll., 1982. Rsch. librarian G.W. Blunt White Libr., Mystic Seaport, Conn., 1967-68; asst. librarian Western Md. Coll., Westminster, 1969-72; libr. dir. Huntington (Ind.) Pub. Libr., 1972-76; prof. history and libr. sci., dir. librs. Benedum Libr. Salem-Teikyo U.; dir., then assoc. dir. aviation program Salem (W.Va.) Coll., 1976-90; prof. history and libr. sci., libr. dir. Tusculum Coll., Greeneville, Tenn., 1990—. Mem. Am. Com. on History 2d World War, Assn. for Bibliography of History Author: American Naval Bibliography Series, 1972-74, Huntington Centennial Handbook, 1973, The Sophisticated Lady: The Battleship Indiana in World War II, 1973, World War II at Sea: A Bibliography of Sources in English, 1976, (with Robert Webber) Sea Fiction Guide, 1976, The Cloak and Dagger Bibliography, 1976, World War I in the Air, 1977, Air War Chronology 1939-45, 1977, Air War Bibliography Series, 1977—, The Mountain State Battleship: USS West Virginia, 1979, Air War Southeast Asia, 1979, The Soviet Navy, 1941-1978, 1979, The Secret Wars Series, 1980-81, The Soviet Air and Strategic Rocket Forces, 1941-1980, 1981, The Soviet Army, 1941-1980, 1981, Equestrian Studies: The Salem College Guide, 1981, The Cloak and Dagger Fiction Guide: An Annotated Guide to Spy Thrillers, 1981, (with Terry White) 3d edit., 1994, The Mountaineer Battlewagon: USS West Virginia, 1982, The Keystone Battlewagon: USS Pennsylvania, 1983, The Golden State Battlewagon: USS California, 1983, Watergate: A Bibliography, 1983 World War II: Mediterranean and European Theaters, 1984, The United States Navy and Coast Guard, 1946-1983: A Bibliography of English Language Works and 16mm Films, 1984, U.S. Television Network News: A Guide to Sources in English, 1984, Battleships and Battlecruisers, 1884-1984: A Bibliography and Chronology, 1985, Baseball: A Comprehensive Bibliography, 1986, 99th Infantry Division Bibliography, 1986, The Airline Bibliography: The Salem College Guide to Sources on Commercial Aviation, Vol. I, The United States, 1986, Vol. II, Airliners and Foreign Carriers, 1987, Passenger Airliners of the United States, 1926-86: A Pictorial Guide, 1987, rev. edit. through 1991, 1991, 3d rev. edit. through 1995, 4th revised edit., 2002, Brooklyn/Los Angeles Dodgers: A Bibliography, 1987, American Warplane Bibliography, 1989, Volunteer Battlewagon: The U.S.S. Tennessee (BB-43), 1989; editor: Sports Teams and Players Bibliography Series, 1987, Battle and Leaders Bibliography Series, 1988, 100 Years of Opportunity: A Pictorial History of Salem College, 1888-1988, 1988, Pro Football Bio-Bibliography, 1920-1988, 1989, Pearl Harbor, December 7, 1941: An Annotated Bibliography, 1991, Battles of the Coral Sea and Midway, 1942: A Bibliography, 1991, World War II at Sea, 1974-1989: A Bibliography, 1990, Professional Football: The Official Pro Football Hall of Fame Bibliography, 1993, Baseball: A Comprehensive Bibliography-1st Supplement: 1985-1991, 93, The College Football Bibliography, 1994, Glimpses of Tusculum College: A Pictorial History, 1794-1994, 1994, Baseball: A Comprehensive Bibliography-2d Supplement: 1992-1997, 1998, The Airline Encyclopedia, 1909-2000, 2002, The Baseball Bibliography, 2d edit., 2006, Le Roy Fitch: The Civil War Career of a Union River Gunboat Commander, 2007; contbr. articles to various jours. Recipient Nelson Ross award Profl. Football Rsch. Assn., 1993; 1st Am. recipient Richard Franck Gold medal Bibliothek für Zeitgeschichte, Stuttgart, Fed. Rep. Germany, 1981. Mem. ALA, U.S. Naval Inst., U.S. Mil. Inst., U.S. Air Force Found., Assn. Bibliog. of History (pres. 1981-82), Alliance of Librs. in Northeast Tenn. (pres. 1997—), Beta Phi Mu, Phi Alpha Theta. Clubs: Optimist. Office: Tusculum Coll PO Box 5005 Greeneville TN 37743-0001 Home Phone: 423-639-7364; Office Phone: 423-636-7320.

SMITH, N. LINDSEY, lawyer; m. Christine Smith; children: Alex, Emily, Max. BSBA, Bowling Green State U., Ohio; JD, U. Toledo Coll. Law. With legal dept. Nat. City Bank; founder Smith & Condeni, LLP, Cleve., 1980, head estate and bus. planning group. Author: Wealth Management Through Estate Planning. Named one of Top 100 Attys., Worth mag., 2005. Mem.: Soc. Fin. Svcs. Profls. (past pres. Cleve. chpt.). Office: Smith & Condeni LLP 600 Granger Rd 2d Fl Cleveland OH 44131 Office Phone: 216-771-1760. Office Fax: 216-771-3387. E-mail: lindsey@smith-condeni.com.

SMITH, NANCY ANGELYNN, federal agency administrator; b. Nashville, Mar. 28, 1950; d. Russell Monroe and Louise (Stephenson) Smith; m. Richard Christian Egan, Jan. 1, 1999. Student, Vanderbilt U., Nashville, 1966, Am. Internat. Acad. Europe, 1970; BA in Psychology with distinction, Rhodes Coll., Memphis, Tenn., 1972; MS with honors, U. Tenn., Knoxville, 1974; cert. in acctg., U. New Orleans, 1985, U. SC, Aiken, 1987. Contract adminstr. State of Tex. Dept. Health and Human Svcs., Houston, 1976-78; dept. Head Coop. Edn. Program No. Va. C.C., Annandale, 1978-81; revenue agt. IRS Dept. of Treasury, Nashville, 1988-99, mgr., adminstr. IRS, 1999—. Faculty rep. Faculty Senate No. Va. C.C., Annandale, 1979—81; comm. rep. IRS, 2002—. Author: numerous poems; contbr. articles to profl. jours. Vol. Voter Registration program, Denver, 1981—84, Adopt-a-Sch., Nashville, 1993—97, Tenn. State Guard; disaster relief coord. Ky. and Tenn., 1998—99, Red Cross Inst., 1976—78, VITA, 1990—95; vol. Congresswoman Pat Shroeder, Denver, 1981—84, Al Gore for Senate, Nashville, 1987—88, Federica Pena for Mayor, Denver, 1981—; bd. dirs. No. Va. C.C., Annandale, 1978—81. Mem.: DAR, Advancement Individual Minorities, Profl. Mgrs. Assn., Cert. Fraud Examiners Assn., Gamma Beta Phi, Alpha Omicron Pi (chmn. bd. dirs. Colo. chpt.), Omicron Nu (hon.), Phi Kappa Pi (hon.). Avocations: painting, skeet shooting, camping, historical battlefields, collecting edged weapons. Business E-Mail: nancy.smith@irs.gov.

SMITH, NANCY HOHENDORF, sales executive, marketing professional; b. Detroit, Jan. 30, 1943; d. Donald Gerald and Lucille Marie (Kopp) Hohendorf; m. Richard Harold Smith, Aug. 21, 1978 (div. Jan. 1984). BA, U. Detroit, 1965; MA, Wayne State U., 1969. Customer rep. Xerox Corp., Detroit, 1965-67, mktg. rep. Univ. Microfilms subs. Ann Arbor, Mich., 1967-73, mktg. coord., 1973-74, mgr. dir. mktg., 1975-76, mgr. mktg. Can., 1976-77, major account mktg. exec. Hartford, Conn., 1978-79, New Haven, 1979-80, account exec. State of N.Y. NYC, 1981, N.Y. region mgr. customer support Greenwich, Conn., 1982, N.Y. region sales ops. mgr., 1982, State of Ohio account exec. Columbus, 1983, new bus. sales mgr. Dayton, Ohio, 1983, major accounts sales mgr., 1984, info. systems sales and support mgr., quality specialist Detroit, 1985-87, new product launch mgr., ops. quality mgr., 1988, dist. mktg. mgr., 1989-92, major accounts sales mgr., 1992—; graphics arts industry sales mgr., 1998—; sales mgr. corp. accounts Sprint- Nextel Comms., Farmington Hills, Mich., 2005—. Reg. graphic arts industry cons. mgr., 1999. Mem. exec. leadership team Am. Heart Assn. Named to Outstanding Young Women of Am., 1968, Outstanding Bus. Woman, Dayton C. of C., 1984, Women's Inner Circle of Achievement, 1990. Mem. NAFE, Am. Mgmt. Assn., Am. Heart Assn. (mem. exec. leadership team 2005-06), Women's Econ. Club Detroit, Detroit Inst. Arts Founders' Soc., Detroit Hist. Soc., Detroit Hist. Soc., Greater Detroit C. of C. Republican. Roman Catholic. Avocations: interior decorating, reading, music, art. Home: 6462 West Oaks Dr West Bloomfield MI 48324-3269 Home Phone: 248-363-5898; Office Phone: 248-866-0601. Personal E-mail: nancyhsmith@sbcglobal.net.

SMITH, NEIL, former professional sports team executive; b. Toronto, Ont., Can., Jan. 9, 1954; m. Katia Smith. Student, We. Mich. U. Selected NHL amateur draft NY Islanders, with scouting dept., 1980-81; from dir. profl. scouting to dir. farm sys. Detroit Red Wings, 1982; dir. scouting, player procurement, gen. mgr., gov. Adirondack Red Wings (Am. Hockey League); gen. mgr. NY Rangers, 1989-2000, pres., 1992-2000; cons. Anaheim Mighty Ducks, Pitts. Penguins, 2002; gen. mgr. NY Islanders, 2006; cons. Hockey Ops. Dept. Dallas Stars, 2006—. Hockey analyst ESPN, OLN, 2005—06. Bd. dirs. Nat. Child Abuse Prevention Ctr. Named All-Am. Defenseman We. Mich. U., to Hall of Fame, 1991, NHL Exec. Yr. Sporting News. Avocations: raquetball, movies. Office: c/o Dallas Stars 2601 Ave of the Stars Frisco TX 75034

SMITH, NICK H., former congressman, archivist, farmer; b. Addison, Mich., Nov. 5, 1934; s. LeGrand John and Blanche (Nichols) S.; m. Bonnalyn Belle Atwood, Jan. 1, 1960; children: Julianna, Bradley, Elizabeth, Stacia. BA, Mich. State U., 1957; MS, U. Del., 1959. Radio & TV farm editor Sta. WDEL, Wilmington, Del., 1957-59; radio editor Sta. KSWD, Wichita Falls, Tex., 1959-60; capt. intelligence USAF, 1959-61; mem. twp. bd. Somerset Twp., Addison, 1962-68; asst. dep. adminstr. USDA, Washington, 1971—74; state rep. Mich. Ho. of Reps., Lansing, 1978-82; state senator, pres. pro-tem Mich. State Senate, Lansing, 1982-92; mem. U.S. Congress from 7th Mich. dist, 1993—2005, mem. agr., sci., and internat. rels. coms. Mem. budget com. Mich. State Senate, 1993—99, chmn. sci. rsch. com., 1999—2005. Del. Am. Assembly on World Population & Hunger, Washington, 1973; nat. del. on U.S.-Soviet Cooperation and Trade, 1991; deacon Somerset Congl. Ch. Capt. USAF, 1959-61. Fellow Kellogg Found., 1965; named Hon. FFA State Star Farmer, 1987, SCF Conservator of Yr. Hillsdale County, 1988. Mem. Mich. Farm Bur. (bd. dirs.), Jackson C. of C., Mich. State U. Varsity Club, Masons. Republican.

SMITH, NORMAN OBED, retired physical chemist, educator; b. Winnipeg, Man., Can., Jan. 23, 1914; came to U.S., 1950, naturalized, 1958; s. Ernest and Ruth (Kilpatrick) S.; m. Anna Marie O'Connor, July 1, 1944; children: Richard Obed, Graham Michael, Stephen Housley. B.Sc., U. Man., 1935, M.Sc., 1936; PhD, NYU, 1939. Teaching fellow NYU, 1936-39; mem. faculty dept. chemistry U. Man., Winnipeg, 1939-50, asst.

prof., 1946-49, assoc. prof., 1949-50, Fordham U., NYC, 1950-65, prof. chemistry, 1965-84, prof. emeritus, 1984—, chmn. dept., 1974-78; ret., 1984. Sr. phys. chemist Arthur D. Little, Inc., Cambridge, Mass., 1957; indsl. cons. Author: (with others) The Phase Rule and Its Applications, 1951, Chemical Thermodynamics, A Problems Approach, 1967, Elementary Statistical Thermodynamics, A Problems Approach, 1982; contbr. to: Ency. Brit, 1974. Fellow Chem. Inst. Can.; mem. Am. Chem. Soc., Asso. Can. Coll. Organists, Am. Guild Organists (dir. chpt. 1964-66, 79-82, 91-92), Sigma Xi, Phi Lambda Upsilon. Home: 811 E Central Rd Apt 112 Arlington Heights IL 60005-3293

SMITH, NORMAN RANDY, federal judge; b. Logan, Utah, Aug. 11, 1949; s. Norman Busby and Patricia (Mendenhall) S.; m. La Dean Egbert, Jan. 3, 1984. BS magna cum laude, Brigham Young U., 1974, JD, 1977. Bar: Idaho 1977, U.S. Dist. Ct. Idaho 1977, U.S. Ct. Claims 1979, U.S. Tax Ct. 1978, U.S. Ct. Appeals (9th cir.) 1979, U.S. Supreme Ct. 1981. Asst. gen. counsel J.R. Simplot Co., Boise, Idaho, 1977-82; assoc. Merrill & Merrill, Pocatello, Idaho, 1982—84, ptnr., 1984—95; dist. judge Idaho 6th Judicial Dist., 1995—2007, adminstrv. judge, 2004—07; judge US Ct. Appeals (9th cir.), 2007—. Adj. prof., Boise St. U., 1979-81, Idaho State U., 1984- Party chmn. Idaho Rep. Party, 1993-96; county chmn. Bannock County Rep. Party, Pocatello, 1991-93; pres. Idaho State Civic Symphony, Pocatello, 1992-95, 98-99. Recipient George G. Granata award, 2004. Mem. Idaho Dist. Judges Assn. (pres. 1998-2000), Idaho Def. Counsel (pres. 1992-93), Def. Rsch. Inst. (del. Idaho state 1992-94, Exceptional Performance Citation 1993), 6th Dist. Bar Assn. (pres. 1994-95), Rotary (Gate City pres. 1993-94. Idaho Statesman Yr. 2005). Avocations: golf, gardening, work. Office: US Courthouse 801 E Sherman Pocatello ID 83201 Office Phone: 208-478-4140. *

SMITH, NORMAN RAYMOND, academic administrator; b. Toronto, Ont., Can., Oct. 24, 1946; s. William Raymond and Jeanne (Malin) S.; m. Susan Robinson, Dec. 26, 1981; 1 child, Caroline Robinson. BS, Drexel U., 1969, MBA, 1971; EdD, Harvard U., 1984; HLD (hon.) (hon.), Phila. U., 2001, Wagner Coll., 2002. Assoc. dean students Drexel U., Phila., 1971-73; v.p., dean of students, professor Phila. Univ., 1973-78; asst. dean Harvard Grad. Sch. Edn., Cambridge, Mass., 1978-80, John F. Kennedy Sch. Govt., Harvard U., Cambridge, 1980-84; exec. v.p. Moore Coll. Art, Phila., 1984-87; pres., prof. Wagner Coll., SI, NY, 1988—2002, pres. emeritus, 2002—; pres., prof. Richmond, The Am. Internat. U. London, 2002—. Dir. Dime Bancorp; assoc. Harvard U. Philosophy of Edn. Rsch. Ctr., Cambridge, 1987—. Author: Selecting the Right College, 6th edit., 2000. Chair mayor's cabinet transition search City of Boston, 1983-84; trustee N.Y. Coun. of Ind. Colls. and Univs., 1994-97. Lt. U.S. Army, 1969-73. Recipient U. medal Drexel U., 1993, Pres.'s medal NYU, 1994. Mem. Ind. Coll. Fund N.Y. (sec.-treas.), Harvard Club of N.Y.C., Richmond County Country Club. Office: Richmond U Queens Rd Richmond-upon-Thames TW10 6JP England Home: 9 Albert Hall Mansions London SW7 2AN England Office Phone: 020-8332-8246. Business E-Mail: smithn@richmond.ac.uk.

SMITH, NUMA LAMAR, JR., lawyer; b. Rock Hill, SC, Nov. 22, 1915; s. Numa Lamar and Grace (Hanes) S.; m. Mary Catherine Gray, Mar. 24, 1941; children: Patricia Gray (dec.), Elizabeth Hanes, Lamar Douglas. AB summa cum laude, Furman U., 1938; LLB with distinction, Duke U., 1941. Bar: N.Y. 1942, D.C. 1946. Assoc. firm White & Case, NYC, 1941-42, Miller & Chevalier, Washington, 1946-49, partner, 1949-83, counsel, 1983—; bd. visitors, 1973-83. Sr. fellow Duke U. Law Sch., 1979-80 Assoc. editor: Duke Law Jour. 1940-41. Served with U.S. Army, 1942-46; with Judge Adv. Gen. Corps 1944-46. Recipient Gen. Excellence award Furman U., 1938 Fellow Am. Bar Found.; mem. ABA, D.C. Bar Assn., Am. Law Inst., Duke Law Alumni Assn. (pres. 1967-69), Order of Coif, Met. Club (Washington), Burning Tree Club (Bethesda, Md.), Washington Golf Club (Arlington, Va.), The Club at Pelican Bay, Sigma Alpha Epsilon. Baptist. Home: 7515 Pelican Bay Blvd Naples FL 34108-6520

SMITH, O. BRUTON, automotive company executive; Founder Charlotte Motor Speedway, 1959, CEO & dir., 1975—; chmn., CEO Sonic Automotive, Inc., Charlotte, NC, 1997—, Speedway Motor Sports, Inc., Charlotte, 1994—; owner operator Town and Country Ford and various other pvt. bus., Charlotte, NC. Founder Speedway Children's Charities, 1984. Named to, Greater Charlotte Sports Hall of Fame, 2005; recipient Award of Excellence, NASCAR, 1997. Office: Sonic Automotive Inc 6415 Idlewild Rd Ste 109 Charlotte NC 28212 *

SMITH, OLLEN BRUTON, sports association executive; divorced; 4 children. Founder, exec. officer, dir. Lowe's Motor Speedway, Concord, NC, 1959—61, CEO, dir., 1975—; CEO, pres., dir. Atlanta Motor Speedway, 1990—; CEO, chmn. Speedway Motorsports, 1994—; chmn., pres. Bristol Motor Speedway, 1996—, Sears Point Raceway, 1996—, Tex. Motor Speedway, 1996—; owner, operator Town & County Ford, Inc. Named one of Forbes' Richest Americans, 2006. Office: Speedway Motorsports 5555 Concorde Pkwy S Concord NC 28027

SMITH, ORA EVERETT, corporate executive, lawyer; b. Kennett, Mo., Dec. 24, 1947; s. Everett and Thelma May (Johnson) S.; m. Sue Ellen Caldwell, Sept. 3, 1972; children: Everett Eugene, Nathan Thomas. BME and MME, MIT, 1970; JD, Harvard U., 1976. Bar: Mass. 1977, D.C. 1977, U.S. Dist. Ct. Mass. 1977, Calif. 1983, U.S. Dist. Ct. (cen. dist.) Calif. 1983, U.S. Ct. Appeals (9th cir.) 1983. Mgr. engring. U.S. EPA, Cin., 1970-73; atty. New Eng. Telephone, Boston, 1976-77; mng. dir. Gordian Assocs. Inc., Washington, 1977-79; dir. structural materials integrity Rockwell Internat., Thousand Oaks, Calif., 1979-81, dir. physics and chem., 1981-85, dir. external tech. devel., 1985-89; v.p. mktg. Conductus, Inc., Sunnyvale, Calif., 1989-90; pres., CEO Ill. Superconductors Corp., Mt. Prospect, 1990-97, chmn., 1997—; instr. Calif. Inst. of Tech., Pasadena, Calif. Cons. Exec. Office of Pres. of U.S., Washington, 1985—, pres. Sci. and Tech. Campus Corp. Patentee impact sensor and coding apparatus; contbr. articles to profl. jours. Served with USPHS, 1970-72. Adv. com. Ohio's Indsl. Tech. Enterprise. Republican. Office: Calif Inst of Tech Industrial Relations Center 1 90 Pasadena CA 91125 Office Phone: 626-395-4041.

SMITH, ORIN C., retired food products executive; MBA, Harvard U., 1967; BA in Fin., Econ., Acctg. and Statis., U. Wash., 1965. With Touche Ross & Co., 1969—77, 1980—85, State of Wash. Office Mgmt. and Budget, 1977—80, 1985—87, No. Air Freight and Danzas Corp., 1987—90; from v.p., CFO to pres., COO Starbucks, Seattle, 1990—2000, pres., CEO, 2000—05. Bd. dirs. Nike, Inc., Wash. Mutual, Walt Disney Co., 2006—. Bd. dirs. Conservation Internat.; advisory bd. U. of Wash. Sch. Bus.; bd. dirs. U. of Wash. Medicine. Avocations: golf, skiing, reading. Office: Starbucks PO Box 34067 Seattle WA 98124-1067

SMITH, ORIN ROBERT, chemical company executive; b. Newark, Aug. 13, 1935; s. Sydney R. and Gladys Emmett (DeGroff) S.; m. Stephanie M. Bennett-Smith; children: Lindsay, Robin; 1 stepchild, Brendan. BA in Econometrics, Brown U., 1957; MBA in Mgmt., Seton Hall U., 1964; PhD in Econs. (hon.), Centenary Coll., 1991; LLD (hon.), Monmouth Coll., 1994. Various sales and mktg. mgmt. positions Allied Chem. Corp., Morristown, NJ, 1959-69; dir. sales and mktg. Richardson-Merrell Co., Phillipsburg, NJ, 1969-72; with M&T Chems., Greenwich, Conn., 1972-77, pres., 1975-77; with Engelhard Minerals & Chems. Corp., Menlo Park, Edison, NJ, 1977-81, corp. sr. v.p., 1978-81, pres. div. minerals and chems., 1978-81, also bd. dirs., 1979-81, pres., dir. various U.S. subs., 1979-81; exec. v.p., pres. div. minerals and chems. Engelhard Corp., Menlo Park, Edison, 1981-84, bd. dirs., 1981—, pres., CEO, Iselin, NJ, 1984-95, chmn., CEO, 1995—; also bd. dirs. Bd. dirs. Summit Bank Co., The Summit Bancorp, Vulcan Materials Co., PE Corp., Ingersoll-Rand Corp., Engelhard Corp., Mfrs. Alliance. Trustee N.J. State C. of C., Inst. for Tech. Advancement; mem. bd. overseers N.J. Inst. Tech.; trustee Plimoth Plantation; 1st vice chmn. bd. trustees Centenary Coll.; past dir. Minorco, La. Land and Exploration Co.; past trustee Henry R. Kessler Found., Inc.; past chmn. Ind. Coll. Fund N.J.; past dir.-at-large U. Maine Pulp and Paper Found. Lt. (j.g.) USN, 1957-59. Mem. Chem. Mfrs. Assn. (past bd. dirs.), Econ. Club (N.Y.C.), Union League Club (N.Y.C.), Duxbury Yacht Club, New Bedford Yacht Club, N.Y. Yacht Club. Office: Engelhard Corp 101 Wood Ave S Iselin NJ 08830-2703

SMITH, ORVILLE AUVERNE, physiology educator; b. Nogales, Ariz., June 16, 1927; s. Orville Auverne and Bess (Gill) S.; m. Clara Jean Smith; children— Nanette, Marcella. BA in Psychology, U. Ariz., 1949; MA, Mich. State U., 1950, PhD, 1953. Instr. psychology Mich. State U., East Lansing, 1953-54; fellow U. Pa., Phila., 1954-56; trainee dept. physiology and biophysics U. Wash., Seattle, 1956-58, instr. physiology and biophysics, 1958-59, asst. prof., 1959-61, 62-63; asst. dir. Regional Primate Research Ctr., 1962-69, assoc. prof., 1963-67, prof., 1967-97; assoc. dir. Regional Primate Research Center, 1969-71, dir., 1971-88, prof. emeritus, 1997—. Contbr. articles to profl. jours. Mem. Am. Physiol. Soc., Am. Soc. Primatologists (pres. 1977-79), Internat. Congress Physiol. Scis., Am. Assn. Anatomists, AAAS, Pavlovian Soc. N.Am. (pres. 1977-78), Internat. Primatological Soc., AAUP, Neurosci. Soc. Home: 30311 201st Ct SE Kent WA 98042-5920 Office: U Wash Nat Primate Rsch Ctr PO Box 357330 Seattle WA 98195-7330

SMITH, OTIS FITZGERALD, professional sports team executive, former professional basketball player; b. Jacksonville, Fla., Jan. 30, 1964; Grad., Jacksonville U., 1986. Player Denver Nuggets, 1986—87, Golden State Warriors, 1987—89, dir. cmty. rels./Warriors Found., 2000—02, exec. dir. basketball ops., 2002—03; player Orlando Magic, 1989—92, cmty. rels. mgr., 1992—94, dir. player devel., 2003—05, asst. gen. mgr., 2005—06, gen. mgr., 2006—. Founder, bd. dirs. Otis Smith Kids Found., 1989—; v.p. mktg. and cmty. rels. Boys and Girls Club Ctrl. Fla. Office: Orlando Magic 8701 Maitland Summit Blvd Orlando FL 32810 *

SMITH, OZZIE (OSBORNE EARL SMITH), retired professional baseball player; b. Mobile, Ala., Dec. 26, 1954; m. Denise Jackson, Nov. 1, 1980; children: Osborne Earl Jr., Dustin Cameron. Grad., Calif. State Poly. U., San Luis Obispo. Shortstop San Diego Padres Baseball Club, Nat. League, 1977—82, St. Louis Cardinals Baseball Club, Nat. League, 1982—96; baseball analyst St. Louis Cardinals Sta. KPLR, St. Louis, 1997—. Named Member of World Series Championship Team, 1982; named to All-Star Team, Nat. League, 1981—92, 1994, Sporting News, 1982, 1984—87, Baseball Hall of Fame, 2002; recipient Most Valuable Player award, Nat. League Championship Series, 1985, Golden Glove award, 1980—92, Silver Slugger award, 1987. Avocations: jazz, word puzzles, backgammon.

SMITH, PAMELA HYDE, ambassador; b. Tacoma, July 1945; m. Sidney G. Smith (dec.); 2 children. BA in Art History, Wellesley Coll., 1967. Joined US Info. Agy., 1975; asst. & cultural attaché US Embassy, Bucharest, 1976—77; special asst. to USIA Dir., 1977—81; cultural asst. US Embassy, Belgrade, 1982—86; dep. chief Acad. Exch. Program USIA, 1986—91; press attaché US Embassy, Jakarta, 1991—95; dir. Office Geog. Liaison U.S. Info. Agy., 1995—97; pub. affairs officer US Embassy, London, 1997—2001; U.S. amb. to Moldova Dept. State, 2001—.

SMITH, PAMELA ROSEVEAR, air transportation executive; b. Corvallis, Oreg., Nov. 26, 1953; BS, U. Oreg., 1977; MBA, valedictorian, C.W. Post Coll., L.I. U., 2003. V.p. inflight customer svc. Air America, LA, 1984—90, MGM Grand Air, LA, 1990—95; dir. sales Ogden Aviation, New York, 1995—; pres., owner Sader-Smith Mktg., Inc., 1995—; v.p. sales the Am's. Pourshins P/C, NYC, 1998—; v.p. sales, mem. mgmt. bd. Pourshins Inc., NYC, 2004—, bd. dir., corp. sec. Bd. dirs. Pourshins Mgmt., 2004—. Recipient Dean's Award for acad. Excellence, L.I. U., 2003. Mem.: Inflight Food Svc. Assn. (bd. dirs. 1999—), Greater L.I. Running Club, Kappa Alpha Theta (N.Y. Alumni chpt.) (v.p. 1998—99). Avocation: sports, travel, education, cooking, Japanese language. Home and Office: 63 Tooker Ave Oyster Bay NY 11771 Home Phone: 516-624-7083; Office Phone: 516-624-0207. Personal E-mail: pampplc@optonline.net.

SMITH, PATRICIA (PAT) ANN, elementary school educator; b. Wichita, Kans., Dec. 30, 1947; d. Orville Stark Kildow and Jean Robison, Ann Stine Kildow (Stepmother); m. Wilton Ray Smith, Aug. 26, 1967; children: Kevin Ray, Lee Clayton. BA in Edn., Wichita State U., Kans., 1969. Elem. tchr. Derby Pub. Sch., Kans., 1969—70, Broken Arrow Pub. Sch., Okla., 1978—2003. Edn. cons. Houghton Mifflin Pub. Co., Dallas, 2004—. Adv. com. mem. Journey Through the Universe Challenger Ctr., Alexandria, Va., 1998—2005; vol. Tulsa Air and Space Mus., 1997—2006. Named Tchr. of Yr., WalMart, Ea. Okla., 2001; named to book Teachers, by John Yow, 2001, Udvar-Hazy Wall of Honor, Washington, DC, 2005; recipient Unsung Heroes award, Reliastar/No. Life, 2001, Golden Apple award, Broken Arrow Sch. Bd., 2004; grantee, Nat. Geog., 2003; Christa McAuliffe fellow, Okla., 1995, 1998. Mem.: Okla. Ret. Tchrs. Assn., Alpha Delta Kappa (pres. 2006—08). Achievements include Teacher in Space; Ambassador on the Governor's Education Team, OASIS. Personal E-mail: patsmithba@yahoo.com.

SMITH, PATRICIA CRAWFORD, elementary school educator; d. Billy Monroe and Jewel Ann Crawford; m. John William Smith, June 16, 1978; children: Stephanie D'Ann, Whitney Lauren. Degree in elem. edn., Athens State Coll., Ala., 1994; M in elem. edn., U. N.Ala., Florence, 2000, degree in adminstrv. leadership, 2006. Cert. elem. edn. K-6 Ala., 1994. Tchr. Athens City Sch., Ala., 1989—2006, amsti trainer, 2004—06. Named Tchr. of Yr., 2000—01. Mem.: Adminstrv. Leadership. Office: Athens Intermediate Sch 1916 Hwy 72 W Athens AL 35611 Home Phone: 256-233-2513; Office Phone: 256-230-2880.

SMITH, PATRICIA GRACE, federal official; b. Nov. 10, 1947; d. Douglas and Wilhelmina (Griffin) Jones; m. J. Clay Smith, Jr., June 25, 1983; children: Eugene Douglas, Stager Clay, Michelle L., Michael L. BA in English, Tuskegee Inst., 1968; postgrad., Auburn U., 1969-71, Harvard U., 1974, George Washington U., 1983, Fed. Exec. Inst., 1997. Cert. exec. mgmt. tng. devel. assignments Dept. Def., 1986, U.S. Senate Commerce Com., 1987. Instr. Tuskegee Inst., Ala., 1969-71; program mgr. Curber Assocs., Washington, 1971-73; dir. placement Nat. Assn. Broadcasters, Washington, 1973-74, dir. pub. affairs, 1974-77; assoc. prodr. Group W Broadcasting, Balt., 1977, prodr., 1977-78; dir. affiliate rels. and programming Sheridan Broadcasting Network, Crystal City, Va., 1978-80; dep. dir. policy, assoc. mng. dir. pub. info./reference svc. FCC, Washington, 1992-94, acting assoc. mng. dir., pub. info. and reference svcs., 1994—. Chief of staff office assoc. adminstr. for comml. space transp. FAA, U.S. Dept. Transp., 1994-96, dep. assoc. adminstr. for comml. space transp., 1996-97, acting assoc. adminstr., 1997, assoc. adminstr., 1998—. Vice-chmn. Nat. Conf. Black Lawyers Task Force on Comms., Washington, 1975-87; trustee, mem. exec. com., nominating com., youth adv. com. Nat. Urban League, 1976-81; mem. comms. com. Cancer Coordinating Coun., 1977-84; mem. Braintrust Subcom. on Children's Programming, Congl. Black Caucus, 1976—; mem. adv. bd. Black Arts Celebration, 1978-83; mem. NAACP; mem. journalism and comms. adv. coun. Auburn U., 1976-78; mem. Washington Urban League, 1985—; bd. dirs. Black Film Rev., 1989-91; mem. D.C. Commn. on Human Rights, 1986-88, chmn., 1988-91; mem. adv. coun. NIH, 1992-96; mem. bd. advisors The Salvation Army, 1993-2000. Named Outstanding Young Woman of Yr., Washington, 1975, 78; recipient Sustained Superior Performance award FCC, Washington, 1982-95, Disting. Alumnus award Tuskegee U., 1996, C. Alfred Anderson award, 2002. Mem. Women in Comms., Inc. (mem. nat. adv. com.), Broadcasters Club (bd. dirs. 1976-77), Lambda Iota Tau. Democrat. Baptist. Avocations: writing, swimming. Office: DOT/AST 800 Independence Ave SW Rm 331 Washington DC 20591-0001 Office Phone: 202-267-7793.

SMITH, PATRICIA H., library association director; B, Austin Coll., Sherman, Tex.; MLS, U. Tex., Austin. Exec. dir. Tex. Libr. Assn. Mem.: Tex. Libr. Assn. (Libr. of Yr. 1989, Disting. Svc. award 1994), ALA (mem. exec. bd. 2005—, coun. mem., councilor-at-large planning and budget assembly, chair chpt. rels. subcom. on legis. tng., mem. spl. presdl. com. on pub. awareness., com. on committees). Office: Tex Libr Assn 3355 Bee Cave Rd Ste 401 Austin TX 78746-6763 Office Phone: 512-328-1518. Office Fax: 512-328-8852. Business E-Mail: pats@txla.org. *

SMITH, PATRICIA LYNNE, artist; b. Camden, NJ, Nov. 3, 1955; d. Thomas Patrick Connelly and Elizabeth Jean (Swope) Shober; m. William Clarence Smith, Nov. 30, 1973 (div. June 1980); children: Travis, Taryn. BA, Rutgers U., Camden, NJ, 1980; MFA, Rutgers U., New Brunswick, NJ, 1984. Adj. instr. Rutgers U., New Brunswick, NJ, 1983-84, Trenton State Coll., 1989-90. One-woman shows include Piezo Electric Gallery, N.Y.C., 1986, S.O.M.A. Gallery, Berlin, 1994, A.I.R. Gallery, N.Y.C., 1994, St. Peter's Ch., 1994, Croxhapox Gallery, Belgium, 1995, Black and Herron Gallery, N.Y.C., 1996, Studio Five Beekman, 1997, Front Room Gallery, Bklyn., 2006, others, exhibited in group shows at Art Exch. Fair, NYC, 1996—97, Bklyn. Mus. Art, 1997, Cornerhouse, Manchester, Eng., 1997, Gas Works, London, 1997, Gramercy Art Fair, 1997, Rotunda Gallery, 1997, Kunstlerhause, Vienna, 1998, Vassar Coll., Poughkeepsie, N.Y., 1998, Bard Coll., Rheinbeck, N.Y., 1998, Eyewash Gallery, Bklyn., 1994, 1999—2000, Project Space, Toronto, Can., 2001, Sideshow Gallery, Bklyn., 2001, Exit Art, N.Y.C., 2002, Voorkamer, Lier, Belgium, 2002, 2006, Art Ctr. Coll. Design, Pasadena, Calif., 2002, U. Md., College Park, 2003, Solway Jones Gallery, LA, 2003, Carlsbad Mus., N.Mex, 2003, Krasdale Gallery, N.Y., 2004, Stadt Mus., Lier, Belgium, 2004, Stedelijk Mus., Aalst, Belgium, 2004, 2006, Ill. State U., 2004, Gallery 32, London, 2004, Shore Inst. Contemporary Art, Long Branch, N.J., 2005, Pierogi, N.Y., 2005, Galerie In Situ, Aalst, Belgium, 2006, Weatherspoon Art Mus., Greensboro, NC, 2006, Tex. Tech. U., Lubbock, 2007, Ruth Bachofner Gallery, LA, 2007. Recipient Stedman Purchase prize, Rutgers U., 1980; Garden State fellow, 1982—84, Exhbn. grantee, Artist's Space, 1988, 1990. Personal E-mail: smithpl@frontiernet.net.

SMITH, PATRICIA M. (PATTI), state supreme court justice; married; 2 children. BA, Troy State U., 1973; JD, Jones Sch. of Law, 1976. Atty. Bell, Johnson and Medaris; asst. dist. atty. Shelby County, Ala., 1976—80, dist. judge Ala., 1980—2004; assoc. justice Ala. Supreme Ct., 2005—. Organized Shelby County's Children's Policy Council; mem. Governor's Commn. on Crime, Commn. on Future of Juvenile Justice System, Ala. Jud. System Study Commn. on Sentencing; chmn. Task Force on Dependency, Interagency Conference on Youth. Named Judge of the Yr., Nat. Ct. Appointed Special Advocates, 2001. Mem.: Ala. State Bar Assn., Shelby County Bar Assn., Ala. Assn. of Juvenile and Family Ct. Judges, Ala. Assn. of Dist. Ct. Judges. Office: Ala Supreme Ct 300 Dexter Ave Montgomery AL 36104 Office Phone: 205-670-6400. *

SMITH, PATSY JUANITA, financial executive; b. Dallas, Aug. 3, 1939; d. Roland Murl and Ruby Esther (Whiteside) Stephens; m. Jerry Arlin Kerby, June 7, 1957 (div. Nov. 1971); children: Timmy Wayne, Pamela Anita; m. Charles Albert Smith, June 17, 1977. Student, Ins. Inst., Dale Carnegie Sch. Claims adjuster Crum & Forster, Dallas, 1967—77, Atlantic Mut. Co., Dallas, 1978—79, Am. States Ins. Co., Dallas, 1979—81, Trinity Adjusting Co., Dallas, 1981—83; beauty cons. Mary Kay Cosmetics, Dallas, 1980—83, sales dir., 1983—84; loan officer Westco Fin. Svcs., Dallas, 1984—. Precinct chmn. Dem. Party, Dallas, 1981, election judge, 1981, 1982. Named Queen of Recruiting, 1982; recipient Claims Profl. of Yr. award, Ins. Women Dallas, 1998, Ins. Woman of Yr. award, 1999. Mem.: Am. Bus. Womans Assn., Dallas (Tex.) Claims Assn. (pres. 2002—03), Women's Coun. Realtors (state pub. rels. com.), Greater Dallas Bd. Realtors, Mortgage Bankers Assn., Am. Bus. Women Assn. (sec. 1980), Ins. Women of Dallas (pres. 1981—82, 2000—02, Claimswoman of Yr. 1979, 1980, Ins. Woman of Year 1998), Order Blue Goose. Home: 9922 Burnham Dr Dallas TX 75243-2412 E-mail: patjsmith1@sbcglobal.net.

SMITH, PATTI, vocalist, poet, lyricist; b. Chgo., Dec. 30, 1946; m. Fred "Sonic" Smith, Mar. 1, 1980 (dec. Nov. 4, 1994); children: Jesse, Jackson. Albums include Horses, 1975, Radio Ethiopa, 1976, Easter, 1978, Waves, 1979, Dream of Life, 1988, Gone Again, 1996, Peace & Noise, 1997, Gung Ho, 2000, Trampin', 2004, Twelve, 2007; composer (songs) About a Boy, 1996; lyricist, vocalist (Blue Oyster Cult songs) Career of Evil, 1974, Vera Gemini, 1976; author: Seventh Heaven, 1972, Witt, 1973, Ha! Ha! Houdini, 1977, Babel, 1978, Woolgathering, 1992, Early Work, 1995, The Coral Sea, 1996, Patti Smith Complete, 1998, Wild Leaves, 1999, Strange Messenger, 2003, Auguries of Innocence: Poems, 2005; co-author The Night, 1976, (play) Cowboy Mouth, 1971; actor (films) The Rugrats Move (voice only), 1998, The Big Empty, 2003. Named a Comdr., French Order Arts & Letters, 2005; named one of 100 Greatest Women of Rock & Roll, VHI, 1999, 100 Greatest Artists of All Time, Rolling Stone mag., 2004; named to Rock & Roll Hall of Fame, 2007. *

SMITH, PAUL E., lawyer; b. Boulder, Colo., Feb. 21, 1954; Student, Macalester Coll.; BA, U. Colo., 1975; JD cum laude, Harvard U., 1980. Bar: Colo. 1980. Ptnr. Holme, Roberts & Owen, Denver, 1980—99; gen.counsel and exec. v.p. netLibrary Inc.; ptnr. Holme Roberts & Owen, Boulder, Colo., 2003—. Mem. ABA (tax sect.), Colo. Bar Assn., Denver Bar Assn., Boulder Bar Assn. Office: Holme Roberts & Owen 1 Boulder Plaza 1801 13th St Ste 300 Boulder CO 80302-5386 Office Phone: 303-444-5955. Office Fax: 303-866-0200. Business E-Mail: paul.smith@hro.com.

SMITH, PAUL LETTON, JR., geophysicist; b. Columbia, Mo., Dec. 16, 1932; s. Paul Letton and Helen Marie (Doersam) S.; m. Mary Barbara Noel; children: Patrick, Melody, Timothy, Christopher, Anne. BS in Physics, Carnegie Inst. Tech., 1955, MSEE, 1957, PhD in Elec. Engring., 1960. From instr. to asst. prof. Carnegie Inst. Tech., Pitts., 1955-63; sr. engr. Midwest Rsch. Inst., Kansas City, Mo., 1963-66; from rsch. engr. to sr. scientist and group head Inst. Atmospheric Scis., S.D. Sch. Mines and Tech., Rapid City, 1966-81; vis. prof. McGill U., Montreal, Que., Canada, 1969-70; chief scientist Air Weather Svc. USAF, Scott AFB, Ill., 1974-75; dir. Inst. Atmospheric Scis., S.D. Sch. Mines and Tech., Rapid City, 1981-96, prof. emeritus, 1996—. Lectr. Tech. Svc. Corp., Silver Spring, Md., 1972-91; vis. scientist Alberta Rsch. Coun., Edmonton, Can., 1984-85; dir. S.D. Space Grant Consortium, Rapid City, 1991-96; Fulbright lectr. U. Helsinki, 1986; nat. assoc. Nat. Acads., 2004—. Contbr. over 60 articles to profl. jours. Fellow Am. Meteorol. Soc. (Editor's award 1992, Remote Sensing lectr. 2006); mem. IEEE (life, sr.), NRC (assoc.), Weather Modification Assn. (Thunderbird award 1995), Sigma Xi. Home: 2107 9th St Rapid City SD 57701-5315 Office Phone: 605-394-2291. Business E-Mail: paul.smith@sdsmt.edu.

SMITH, PAUL VERGON, JR., retired gas industry executive; b. Lima, Ohio, Apr. 25, 1921; s. Paul Vergon and Aleta Rose (Bowers) S.; m. Alta Fern Chipps, Mar. 2, 1945; children: Douglas, Marsha, Jeffrey, Alison AB, Miami U., Oxford, Ohio, 1942; MS, U. Ill., 1943, PhD, 1945. With Exxon Rsch. & Engring. Co., 1946—66; with Exxon Rsch. & Engring Co., 1972—86, mgr. pub. affairs, 1972—86, mgr. ednl. and profl. soc. rels. Florham Park, NJ, 1981—86; asst. dir. chem. rsch. Esso Petroleum Co., Abingdon, England, 1966—67; dir. chem. rsch. Esso Rsch. S.A., Brussels, 1967—71; mem. adv. bd. Cache, Inc., Austin, Tex., 1979—86; pres. APS Assocs., Westfield, NJ, 1986—90. Bd. dirs., treas. Jets, Inc., Alexandria, Va.; dir. CENTCOM, Ltd.; mem. exec. bd. N.J. Bus./Industry/Sci. Edn. Consortium Patentee in field; contbr. numerous articles to profl. jours., chpts. to books Bd. dirs. United Way Union County, N.J., 1980-86; chmn. rsch. adv. coun. Miami U., 1980-84 Recipient Pres.'s award Am. Assn. Petroleum Geologists, 1955; Spl. award N.J. Sci. Tchrs. Assn., 1985 Mem. AAAS, Am. Chem. Soc. (dir. 1978-86, chmn. bd. 1984-86; Belden award 1984), Am. Soc. Engring. Edn. (dir. 1980-86, v.p. 1980-86), Country Club Naples, Phi Beta Kappa, Sigma Xi, Omicron Delta Kappa, Phi Eta Sigma, Alpha Chi Sigma, Pi Mu Epsilon, Sigma Pi Sigma, Phi Lambda Upsilon Republican. Methodist.

SMITH, PAULA V., library director; Grad., SUNY, Brockport, 1990. Positions including asst. dir., asst. libr. dir. Ctrl. Libr. and Br. Adminstrn. Rochester Pub. Libr. and Monroe County Libr. Sys., NY, interim dir., 2005, dir., 2005—. Mem. adv. com. Rochester Regional Libr. Coun. Mem. adv. bd. Dept. Pub. Adminstrn. SUNY, Brockport. Office: Monroe County Libr Sys 115 South Ave Rochester NY 14604-1896 Office Phone: 585-428-8045. Office Fax: 585-428-8353. E-mail: psmith@libraryweb.org.

SMITH, PETE A., lawyer; b. St. Marys, Ohio, Mar. 29, 1969; BA, U. Cin., 1991; JD, U. Notre Dame, 1994. Bar: Ohio 1994, Ky. 1995. Ptnr. Strauss & Troy, Cin. Pro-bono legal adv. Covington Cmty. Ctr.; mem., Bd. Dirs. Southland Hall Assn. Named one of Ohio's Rising Stars, Super Lawyers, 2006. Mem.: ABA, Ky. Bar Assn., Ohio State Bar Assn., Cin. Bar Assn., Omicron Delta Kappa, Pi Kappa Alpha, Phi Beta Kappa. Office: Strauss & Troy 50 E RiverCenter Blvd Covington KY 41011 Office Phone: 513-621-8900. Office Fax: 513-629-9444.

SMITH, PETER PLYMPTON, former international organization official, former academic administrator, former congressman; b. Boston, Oct. 31, 1945; s. Frederick P. Smith; m. Sarah Giddings; children: Ben, David, Daniel BA magna cum laude, Princeton U., 1968; MAT., Harvard U., 1970, EdD, 1984; D Pub. Svc. (hon.), Norwich U. Asst. to commr. edn. State of Vt., 1969—70; dir. Montpelier (Vt.) Edn. Facility, 1970; founder, 1st pres. Vt. Community Coll., 1970-78; dir. office external programs Vt. State Colls., 1975-76; pres. Appleyard's of Vt., 1979-80; regional mgr. New Eng. Coun. for Advancement Experimental Learning, 1979-80; pres. Hunger Mountain Assocs., Vt., 1980-82; mem. Vt. State Senate, 1981-82; lt. gov. State of Vt., 1983-86; mem.-at-large US Congress from Vt., 1989-91; v.p. Norwich U., Northfield, Vt., 1987-88; dean, Sch. Edn. & Human Devel. George Washington U., 1991—94; pres. Calif. State U., Monterrey Bay, 1994—2005; asst. dir.-gen. for edn. UNESCO, 2005—07. Exec. dir. US Commn. on Responsibilities for Financing Postsecondary Edn., 1991. Author: Your Hidden Credentials: The Value of Learning Outside College, 1982, The Quiet Crisis: How Higher Education Is Failing America, 2004. Bd. dirs. Vt. Pub. Radio; chmn. bd. dirs. Rumney Sch., Middlesex, Vt.; chmn. fund drive United Way, 1980; chmn. Bethany United Ch. of Christ; trustee Washington County Supervisory Union Sch. Dist. Republican.

SMITH, PETER WILLIAM EBBLEWHITE, electrical engineer, educator, research scientist, physicist; b. London, Nov. 3, 1937; m. Jacqueline Marie Mankiewicz, June 18, 1966; children: Christal, Dawn N. BSc, McGill U., Montreal, Que., Can., 1958, MSc, 1961, PhD, 1964. Profl. physicist. Mem. of staff Can. Marconi Co., Mont., 1958-59; mem. tech. staff Bell Labs., Holmdel, NJ, 1963-83; dist. mgr. Bellcore, Red Bank, NJ, 1984-88, div. mgr., 1988-92; prof. elec. and computer engring. U. Toronto, 1992—2003, prof. emeritus, 2003—; exec. dir. Ont. Laser and Lightwave Rsch. Ctr., 1992-95; dir. Nortel Inst. Telecom., 1999—2003. Editor-in-chief IEEE Press Progress in Lasers and Electro-Optics Series, 1987—92, Optics Letters, 1989—95; contbr. over 300 articles to profl. jours., chapters to books. Bd. dirs. Monmouth Arts Found., Red Bank, 1965-82; pres. The Circle for Children Found., 2003—. Recipient Sr. Scientist award NATO, 1979. Fellow IEEE (life, Quantum Electronics award 1986, Third Millennium medal 2000), Optical Soc. Am. (bd. dirs., chmn. bd. editors), Inst. Physics U.K.; mem. IEEE Lasers and Electro-Optics Soc. (pres. 1984). Achievements include first demonstration of waveguide gas laser, nonlinear optical interface; development of hybrid bistable optical devices; 34 patents in field. Office: U Toronto Dept Elec & Computer Engring Toronto ON Canada M5S 3G4 E-mail: peter.smith@utoronto.ca.

SMITH, PHILIP DANIEL, academic administrator, education educator; b. Dayton, Ohio, Dec. 25, 1933; s. Hubert Edgar and Edith (Parker) S.; m. Marilyn Brown, Nov. 25, 1953; children: Carolyn Smith Valentine, Norman Daniel, Stanley Nathan. BS cum laude, Bob Jones U., 1955; MEd, Miami U., Oxford, Ohio, 1956; EdD, Pa. State U., 1964. Dean coll. arts and sci. Bob Jones U., Greenville, SC, 1961-65, registrar, 1965-81, prof. edn., 1956—2005, provost, 1981—2005, provost emeritus, 2005—. Mem. edn. adv. bd. One Touch Systems, Inc., 1995-96; ednl. analyst Bible Colls., Gospel Fellowship Missions Assn., 2007—. Cons. for BJ Help Network, BJ Linc, and BJU Press books Beginnings for Christian Schools, English Skills for Christian Schools, Handwriting for Christian Schools. Pres. Bob Jones U. Alumni Assn., Greenville, 1970-71; mem. coll. parallel adv. com. Tri-County Tech. Coll., Pendleton, S.C., 1973-86. Mem. Assn. Ednl. Communications and Tech. (life mem.; membership coord. profl. assns. 1969-72, vice chair nat. membership com. 1972-73, chair nat. membership com. 1973-75, council del. S.C. chpt. 1972-73, audiovisual instrn. editorial adv. com. 1974-75, del. to Lake Okoboji ednl. media leadership conf. 1972, 74), Assn. Ednl. Communications and Tech. of S.C. (bd. dirs. 1970-75, pres. 1972-73, award for outstanding contbns. and service 1971), Am. Assn. Collegiate Registrars and Admissions Officers, Phi Delta Kappa. Republican. Baptist. Office: Bob Jones U Office Provost Greenville SC 29614-0001 Office Phone: 864-242-5100. Business E-Mail: psmith@bju.edu.

SMITH, PHILIP G., lawyer; b. Louisiana, Mo., Oct. 4, 1946; m. Andrea K. Smith; children: Andrew Gentry, James Lyndon. BS, N.E. Mo. State U., 1968; JD, U. Mo., 1972. Atty. Mem. Rotary Club, Elks, Masons, Mo. Alumni Assn., Mo. State U. Alumnus Assn. Home: PO Box 486 Louisiana MO 63353-0486

SMITH, PHILIP JONES, lawyer; b. York, Pa., May 14, 1941; s. Clark S. and Margaret Ann (Jones) S.; m. Ann F. Johnson, Apr. 21, 1973; 1 child, James M. BA cum laude, Williams Coll., 1963; LLB, U. Va., 1966. Bar: Mass. 1967. Assoc. Ropes & Gray, Boston, 1967-76, ptnr., 1976—. Lectr. Boston U. Sch. of Law, 1984—98; bd. dirs. NAACP Legal Def. and Ednl. Fund, NYC. Contbr. chapters to books, articles to profl. jours. Bd. dirs., pres. Greater Boston Youth Symphony Orch., Boston, 1978-2000; bd. dirs., v.p., pres., treas. Keewaydin Found., Salisbury, Vt., 1980—; bd. dirs., past treas. Project STEP, Boston, 1987-95; overseer, chair facilities com. New Eng. Conservatory, Boston, 1989-95. Fulbright scholar, U. Madrid, 1966—67. Mem.: ABA, Essex County Club, N.Y. Yacht Club, Eastern Yacht Club (sec. 1977—83, bd. dirs. 2001—, rear commodore 2006—), Order of Coif. Home: 35 Harbor Ave Marblehead MA 01945-3636 Office: Ropes & Gray One Internat Pl Boston MA 02110-2624 Office Phone: 617-951-7744. Business E-Mail: p.smith@ropesgray.com.

SMITH, PHILIP MEEK, science administrator, consultant; b. Springfield, Ohio, May 18, 1932; s. Clarence Mitchell S. and Lois Ellen (Meek) Dudley. BS, Ohio State U., 1954, MA, 1955; DSc (hon.), NC State U., 1986. Mem. staff U.S. Nat. Com. for Internat. Geophys. Yr., NAS, 1957-58; program dir. NSF, 1958-63, dir. ops. U.S. Antarctic Rsch. program, 1964-69, dep. head divsn. polar programs, 1970-73, exec. asst. to dir. and sci. advisor to pres., 1974-76; chief gen. sci. br. Office Mgmt. and Budget Exec. Office of Pres., 1973-74; assoc. dir. Office Sci. and Tech. Policy, Exec. Office of Pres., 1976-81; exec. officer NRC-NAS, Washington, 1981-94; ptnr. McGeary and Smith, Washington, 1995—2004; chmn. external adv. com. Nat. Computational Sci. Alliance, 1997—2001, mem., 2002—03; prin. Smith Sci. Policy and Mgmt., Santa Fe, 2004—. Bd. dirs. Aurora Flight Scis. Corp.; adv. cons. bd. U. Ala. Geophys. Inst., 1994—98; adv. bd. Sci.'s Next Wave, 1998—2002; advisor Com. for Econ. Devel., 1997; com. on sci., tech. and health aspects fgn. policy agenda US NRC, 1998—2000, com. on sci. and tech. counterism, 2001—02, mem. com. sci. bases Colo. River Basin water mgmr., 2005—07, mem. com. sci. basis decision making internat. sustainable devel. orgns., 2002—05; chair com. orgn. & strategy Sci. Com. Antarctic Rsch., 1999—2000; co-chair adv. bd. Calif. Inst. Telecom. & Info. Tech., 2000—; mem. US Nat. Com. Internat. Polar Yr., 2003—05; history of geophysics com. Am. Geophys. Union, 2004—; bd. dirs. found. Los Alamos Nat. Lab., 2006—; adv. bd. Lapides Found., 2007—. Author: (with others) The Frozen Future, a Prophetic Report from Antarctica, 1973; contbr. articles to profl. jours. Bd. dirs. Washington Project for Arts, 1983-84, Washington Sculptors Group, 1983-84. 1st lt. U.S. Army, 1955-57. Fellow AAAS, Antarctican Soc.; mem. Cosmos Club (Washington), Am. Alpine Club (Golden, Colo.), Sigma Xi. Office: Smith Sci Policy & Mgmt 767 Acequia Madre 2 Santa Fe NM 87505-2868 Business E-Mail: pmsmith@erols.com.

SMITH, PHILLIPS GUY, banker; b. Orange, NJ, Sept. 15, 1946; s. Phillips Upham and Helen Ottilie (Voderberg) S.; m. Ann Dixon Schickhaus, Dec. 29, 1973; children: Guy Dixon, William Schickhaus, Louisa Upham. B in Engring., Stevens Inst. Tech., Hoboken, NJ; MBA, U. Pa., 1975. Comml. banking rep. The Bank of N.Y., NYC, 1976-78, asst. treas., 1978-79, asst. v.p., 1979-80, v.p., 1980-85, sr. v.p., 1985-93; mng. dir. Internat. Strategy Svcs., Inc., NYC, 1993-2000; prin. Sippican Group LLC, Greenwich, Conn., 2000—. Vestryman Ch. of The Heavenly Rest, N.Y.C., 1983-88, treas., 1985-87; trustee Tabor Acad., Marion, Mass., 1987—, treas., 1991—. Lt. USN, 1970-74, Vietnam. Mem. Racquet and Tennis Club, Down Town Assn., Rockaway Hunting Club, Nantucket Yacht Club. Episcopalian. Home: 9 E 94th St New York NY 10128-0611 Office: Matrix USA LLC 16 E 40th St New York NY 10016 Business E-Mail: psmith@matrixusallc.com.

SMITH, PHYLLIS, actress; b. Lemay, Mo., July 10, 1951; Studied ballet and tap with Majorie Mendolia; B in Elementary Edn., U. Mo., St. Louis. Former St. Louis Cardinals Cheerleader; ballet dancer St. Louis Civic Ballet, The St. Louis Dance Theater; profl. jazz dancer under Raoul Appel; toured the country as a dancer with Able's Baggy Pants Burlesque; toured the country as a dancer and comic skit performer with Mercer Brother's show, Giggles Galore; pre-school tchr. Casting asst. (TV films) A Taste for Killing, 1992, casting assoc. (TV series) Dr. Quinn, Medicine Women, 1993, Spin City, 1996; actor: (TV series) The Office, 2005— (Outstanding Performance by an Ensemble in a Comedy Series, SAG, 2007); (films) I Want Someone to Eat Cheese With, 2006; guest appearances Arrested Development, 2005, Curb Your Enthusiasm, 2005. Mem.: SAG. *

SMITH, QUINCY, Internet company executive; BA in Philosophy, Yale U. Various positions including high tech. corp. fin. divsn. Morgan Stanley & Co., Menlo Park, Calif., 1993—94; sr. dir. investor relations and corp. devel. Netscape, 1995—99; co-founder The Barksdale Group, Menlo Park, Calif., 1999—2002; investment banker Allen & Co.; pres. CBS Interactive CBS Corp., 2006—. Office: CBS 865 Battery St San Francisco CA 94111 *

SMITH, R. GORDON, lawyer; b. Roanoke, Va., May 28, 1938; BA with highest honors, U. Va., 1960; LLB magna cum laude, Harvard U., 1964. Bar: Va. 1964. Law clk. to judge U.S. Ct. Appeals (5th cir.), 1964-65; ptnr. McGuire, Woods, Battle & Boothe, Richmond, Va., 1969—. Exec., legislation editor Harvard Law Rev., 1963-64; bd. dirs. Scott & Stringfellow Fin., Inc., Trigon Healthcare, Inc., Va. C. of C. Fellow Am. Bar Found.; mem. Va. Bar Assn. (pres. 1987-88), Am. Law Inst., Phi Beta Kappa, Omicron Delta Kappa. Office: McGuire Woods 901 E Cary St Richmond VA 23219-4057 Office Phone: 804-775-4347.

SMITH, R. JEFFREY, reporter; b. Milw. s. Robert J. and Eileen Smith; m. Marjorie E. Sun, May 14, 1983. With Sarasota Herald-Tribune, NY, Des Moines Register, Iowa, Milw. Jour., Science mag., Washington, 1979—86; nat. security corr. Washington Post, 1986—98, bur. chief Rome, 1998—2001, nat. news staff reporter Washington, 2001—. Recipient Sci.-in-Soc. Journalism award, Nat. Assn. Sci. Writers, 1982, Pulitzer Prize for investigative reporting, 2006. Office: Washington Post 1150 15th St NW Washington DC 20071

SMITH, RAE, artist; d. Arthur Alfred and Caroline Coletti; m. Robert Kenneth Smith, Feb. 8, 1953; children: Carol Ann Goldstein, Robert K. Jr., Christopher, Cathy Ann Beiter. Tchr. home studio, Yonkers, NY, 1960—86, No. Rochester Art Ctr., Mt. Kisco, NY, 1999—2005, Katonah Art Ctr., NY, 2005—. Exhibitions include Butler Inst. Am. Art, Youngstown, Ohio, Triton Mus. Art, Santa Clara, Calif., Slater Mus., Norwich, Conn., Internat. Mus. Contemporary Masters, San Antonio, Tex., Noyes Mus., Oceanville, NJ, China Mus. Art, Suzhou, Hammond Mus., North Salem, NY. Recipient Audubon Artists Gold medal, Salmagundi Club, NYC, 2001, South Eastern Pastel Soc. award, Nat. Arts Club, NYC, 2002, Jim Lynch award, Pastel Soc. Am., 2003, Art du Pastel En France award, Vernon, 2003, Degas Soc. award, Triton Mus. Art, 2004, Cecelia Cardman Meml. award, Nat. Arts Club, 2005, Great Am. Artworks award, PPCC, Harwich, Mass., 2006. Fellow: Am. Artists Profl. League; mem.: Pastel Soc. Am. (bd. chair, v.p. 1996—), Allied Artists Am. (bd. chair 2002—).

SMITH, RALPH ALEXANDER, cultural and educational policy educator; b. Ellwood City, Pa., June 12, 1929; s. J. V. and B. V. Smith; m. Christiana M. Kolbe, Nov. 16, 1955. AB, Columbia Coll., 1954; MA, Columbia U., 1959, EdD, 1962. Faculty art history and arts edn. Kent (Ohio) State U., 1959-61, Wis. State U., Oshkosh, 1961-63, SUNY, New Paltz, 1963-64; faculty edn. and art edn. U. Ill., Urbana-Champaign, 1964—, prof. cultural and ednl. policy & aesthetic edn., prof. emeritus, 1996—. First Italo DeFrancesca Meml. lectr. Kutztown State U., 1974; Leon Jackman Meml. lectr., Perth, Australia, 85; Dean's lectr. Coll. Fine Arts and Comm., Brigham Young U., 1985; disting. vis. prof. Ohio State U., 1987; sr. scholar Coll. Edn., U. Ill., 1991; Dunbar lectr. Millsaps Coll., 1993; John Landrum Bryant lectr. Harvard U., 1999. Founder, editor: Jour. Aesthetic Edn., 1966—2000; editor: (book) Aesthetics and Criticism in Art Education, 1966, Aesthetic Concepts and Education, 1970, Aesthetics and Problems in Education, 1971, Regaining Educational Leadership, 1975, Cultural Literacy and Arts Education, 1991, Discipline-Based Art Education, 1989; editor: (with Alan Simpson) Aesthetics and Arts Education, 1991; editor: (with Bennett Reimer) The Arts, Education and Aesthetic Knowing, 1992; editor: (with Ronald Berman) Public Policy and the Aesthetic Interest, 1992; editor: General Knowledge and Arts Education, 1994, Excellence II: The Continuing Quest Art Education, 1995, Online Bibliography: Discipline Based Art Education, 1997, Readings in Discipline-Based Art Education: A Literature of Educational Reform, 2000; co-author: Research in the Arts and Aesthetic Education: A Directory of Investigators and Their Fields of Inquiry, 1978, Excellence in Art Education: Ideas and Initiatives, 1987, The Sense of Art: A Study in Aesthetic Education, 1989, Culture and the Arts in Education, 2006; author (with Albert William Levi): (book) Art Education: A Critical Necessity, 1991; contbg. editor: Arts Edn. Policy Rev., 2001—. With Med. Svc. US Army, 1954—57. Recipient spl. merit recognition, Coll. Edn., U. Ill., 1975, Disting. Lectr. Studies in Art Edn. award, 1991. Fellow: Nat. Art Edn. Assn. (Disting., Manuel Barkan Meml. award 1973, Nat. Educator award 2000); mem.: Ill. Art Edn. Assn. (Disting.), Coun. Policy Studies Art Edn. (1st exec. sec. 1978—82). Home: 2909 Heathwood Ct Champaign IL 61822-7659 Office: 360 Education 1310 S 6th St Champaign IL 61820-6925 Business E-Mail: ras@uiuc.edu.

SMITH, RALPH HARRISON, lawyer; b. Albuquerque, Nov. 2, 1951; s. Robert Tatum and Harriet Smith; m. Helen Elizabeth Oakley, July 13, 1974; children: Harrison, William, Robert BA, Washington and Lee U., 1973; MA, Oxford U., 1976; JD, Yale U., 1979. Bar: D.C. 1979, Ala. 1982. Assoc. Convington & Burling, Washington, 1979—82, Cabaniss, Johnston, Gardner, Dumas & O'Neal, Birmingham, Ala., 1982—84; ptnr. Johnston, Barton, Proctor & Powell LLP, Birmingham, 1984—2004; gen. counsel U. Ala. Sys., 2004—. Disting. lectr. law U. Ala. Law Sch., 2005—; pres.'s adv. coun. Birmingham So. Coll., 1987-88; leadership coun. U. Ala., Birmingham, 1988-91, Med. Clinics Bd., Birmingham, 1997; dir. Comm. on Fgn. Rels., Birmingham, 1996-2002; selection com. Rhodes Scholarship, 1982-87, 98—; Ala. sec. Rhodes Scholarship Trust, 2003-04, dist. sec., 2005—; dir. Assn. Am. Rhodes Scholars, 2006—, Trustee Highland's Day Sch., Birmingham, 1985-89; pres. bd. St. Martin's in the Pines Nursing Home, Birmingham, 1990; dir. Ala. Sch. Fine Arts Found., Birmingham, 1993-98, Farrah Law Soc., U. Ala. Law Sch.; mem. Leadership Birmingham, 1988, membership coun., 1998-2001; chancellor Episcopal Diocese of Ala., 2000-2003 Rhodes scholar, 1973. Mem. Birmingham Bar Assn., Tuscaloosa Bar Assn., D.C. Bar Assn., Birmingham C. of C. (trustee 1993-2004), Am. Assn. Rhodes Scholars (dir. 2006—), Rotary Club Birmingham (dir., v.p. 1989-91, 90-91, 2001-02, Paul Harris fellow 2001) Episcopalian. Home: 3519 Country Club Rd Birmingham AL 35213-2826 Office: 1818 U Blvd Tuscaloosa AL 35401 Office Phone: 205-348-8345. Business E-Mail: rsmith@uasystem.ua.edu.

SMITH, RALPH LEE, writer, musician; b. Phila., Nov. 6, 1927; s. Hugh Harold and Barbara (Schatkin) S.; m. Betty H. Smith, Sept. 1954 (div. Jan. 1963); children: David Bruce, Robert Hugh; m. Mary Louise Hollowell, 1971 (div. 1977); m. Shizuko Maruyama, 1977; 1 child, Lisa Koyuki. BA, Swarthmore Coll., Pa., 1951; MEd, U. Va., Charlottesville, 1987. Folk musician on Appalachian dulcimer; recs. include Dulcimer: Old Time and Traditional Music, 1973, Tunes of the Blue Ridge and Great Smoky Mountains, 1983, Across the Blue Ridge, 2005; author: The Story of the Dulcimer, 1986, Appalachian Dulcimer Traditions, 1997, Songs and Tunes of the Wilderness Road, 1999, Folk Songs of Old Kentucky, 2003. Recipient writing awards Columbia U. Grad. Sch. Journalism, U. Mo. Grad. Sch. Journalism, AMA. Home: 1662 Chimney House Rd Reston VA 20190-4302 E-mail: ralphleesmith@comcast.net.

SMITH, RALPH WESLEY, JR., retired federal judge; b. Ghent, NY, July 16, 1936; s. Ralph Wesley and Kathleen S. (Callahan) S.; m. Nancy Ann Fetzer, Dec. 30, 1961 (div. 1981); children: Mark Owen, Tara Denise, Todd Kendall; m. Barbara Anne Milian, Nov. 8, 1982; stepchildren: Kim Highter, Jeffrey Highter, Eric Highter. Student, Sorbonne, U. Paris, Paris, 1954-55; BA, Yale U., 1956; LLB, Albany Law Sch., 1966. Bar: N.Y. 1966, U.S. Dist. Ct. (no. dist.) N.Y. 1966. Assoc. Hinman, Straub Law Firm, Albany, N.Y., 1966-69; chief asst. dist. atty. Albany County, N.Y., 1969-73, dist. atty. N.Y., 1974; regional dir. state nursing home investigation Asst. Atty. Gen., Albany, 1975-77; dir. State Organized Crime Task Force, 1978-82; U.S. magistrate judge U.S. Dist. Ct. (no. dist.) N.Y., Albany, 1982-2001. Judge moot ct. Albany Law Sch., 1983-2001; lectr. N.Y. State Bar Assn., 1985—, Am. Inns of Ct., 1994-99. Capt. USNR, 1957-82, ret. Mem. Fed. Magistrate Judges Assn. (dir. 2d cir. 1992-99), Columbia County Magistrates Assn. Independent. Roman Catholic. Avocations: fishing, bicycling, skiing, sailing, camping. Home: 40 Wequasset Rd Harwich Port MA 02646

SMITH, RAOUL NORMAND, computer science educator; b. West Warwick, RI, May 15, 1938; s. Luke Joseph and Lucienne (Anchambault) S.; m. Mary Frances Hand, Nov. 12, 1966; children: Stephen Edward, Timothy Luke. AB, Brown U., 1963, AM, 1964, PhD, 1968. Instr. Northwestern U., Evanston, Ill., 1967—68, asst. prof., 1968—73, assoc. prof., 1973—80; sr. mem. tech. staff GTE Labs., Waltham, Mass., 1981—83, prin. mem. tech. staff, 1983; prof. Northeastern U., Boston, 1983—2000, dir. grad. schs., 1984—85, dir. rsch., 1985—86, prof. emeritus, 2000—; vis. prof. Jilin U. Tech., Changchun, China, 1985; v.p. China Edn. Corp., 2000—02. Chmn. bd. dirs. Cognitive Computers, Newton, Mass., 1985-87; prin. Raoul N. Smith and Assocs., Cons. Author: Dictionary of Artificial Intelligence, 1989, The Language of Jonathan Fisher, 1985, Probabilistic Performance Models of Language, 1973; co-author: Lexical-Semantic Relations, 1980. Trustee Acton (Mass.) Hist. Soc., 1988-90, dir., 2002-04; mem. AIDS action com., 1985-88. With USAF, 1957-61. Grantee NSF, 1966, 66-67, 71, Am. Philos. Soc., 1974, Am. Coun. of Learned Socs., 1974, Nat. Endowment for the Humanities, 1975, 76-79. Mem. Assn. for Computing Machinery (co-chair spl. interest group on computer and human interaction 1981-85), Union Club. Avocations: antique porcelain, silver and jewelry. Home: 206 Nagog Hill Rd Acton MA 01720-3228 Personal E-mail: raouls500@verizon.net.

SMITH, RAYMOND LEIGH, retired plastic surgeon; b. Norristown, Pa., Sept. 27, 1940; s. Walter Joseph and Pauline C. (Wolfskill) S.; m. Coralynn Elder, Jan. 8, 1966; children: Susan, Elizabeth, Christine. BS, Ursinus Coll., 1962; MD, Temple U., 1966. Diplomate Nat. Bd. Med. Examiners, Am. Bd. Plastic Surgery. Active staff Reading Hosp., Pa., 1976—2005, chief sect. of plastic surgery, 1994-2000, ret. 2005. Mem. Republican Majority Found. Mem. ACS, Am. Soc. Plastic Surgeons, Robert H. Ivy Soc., Am. Assn. Hand Surgery, Northeastern Soc. Plastic Surgeons, Pa. Med. Soc., Lipoplasty Soc. N.Am., Berks County Med. Soc. Lutheran.

SMITH, RAYMOND LLOYD, former university president, consultant; b. Vanceboro, Maine, Jan. 25, 1917; s. Ivan and Genevieve (Gatcomb) S.; m. Beatrice Bennett, Dec. 4, 1943 (dec. Apr. 16, 1998); children: Bennett Charles, Martin Lloyd; m. Rachel Malcolm, March 10, 2002. BS in Mining Engring. cum laude, U. Alaska, 1943; MS in Metall. Engring, U. Pa., 1951, PhD in Metall. Engring, 1953; D.Sc. (hon.), Western Mich. U.; LL.D., No. Mich. U.; D.Eng. (hon.), Mich. Technol. U., S.D. Sch. Mines and Tech. Instr. math. U. Alaska, 1946-47, asst. prof. metallurgy, 1948-49; rsch. assoc. dept. metallurgy U. Pa., 1949-53; sr. rsch. metallurgist Franklin Inst. Labs., Phila., 1953, sect. chief metallurgy, 1954-56, head solid state physics, 1957, tech. dir., 1958-59; prof., head metall. dept. Mich. Technol. U., Houghton, 1959-64, coord. rsch., 1960-64, pres., 1965-79, Am. Soc. Metals, 1979-80, Houghton (Mich.) Daily Mining Gazette, 1979-81, R. L. Smith, Inc. Am. Soc. Metals/The Metallurgical Soc. joint disting. lectr. in materials; lectr. in field. Contbr. numerous articles to metall. sci. jours.; patentee in field. With AUS, 1943—46. Recipient Distinguished Alumnus award U. Alaska, Clair M. Donovan award Mich. Tech. U., D. Robert Yarnall award U. Pa. Engring. Sch.; Outstanding Service award Air Force ROTC; Rotary Paul Harris fellow. Fellow Metall. Soc., AIME (Henry Krumb meml. lectr. 1981), Am. Soc. for Metals (hon.); mem. Scabbard and Blade, Blue Key, Tau Beta Pi, Alpha Sigma Mu (hon. lectr. 1982), Alpha Phi Omega, Phi Kappa Phi, Theta Tau. Home: PO Box 726 Green Valley AZ 85622-0726 Personal E-mail: raysmith726@aol.com. *A sense of humor is one of the important building blocks for that firm sense of balance so necessary to meet the challenges of life. It's like the seasoning of a chef's masterpiece.*

SMITH, RAYMOND THOMAS, anthropology educator; b. Oldham, Lancashire, Eng., Jan. 12, 1925; s. Harry and Margaret (Mulchrone) S.; m. Flora Alexandrina Tong, June 30, 1954; children: Fenela, Colin, Anthony. BA, Cambridge U., Eng., 1950, MA, 1951, PhD, 1954. Sociol. research officer govt., Brit. Guiana, 1951-54; research fellow U. W.I., 1954-59; prof. sociology U. Ghana, 1959-62; sr. lectr. sociology, prof. anthropology U. West Indies, 1962-66; prof. anthropology U. Chgo., 1966-95, prof. emeritus, 1995—, chmn. dept. anthropology, 1975-81, 84-85, 94-95. Vis. prof. U. Calif.-Berkeley, 1957-58, McGill U., Montreal, 1964-65; mem. com. on child devel. rsch. and pub. policy NRC, 1977-80; dir. Caribbean Consortium Grad. Sch., 1985-86. Author: The Negro Family in British Guiana, 1956, British Guiana, 1962, 2d edit., 1980, Kinship and Class In The West Indies, 1988, The Matrifocal Family, 1996; co-author: Class Differences in American Kinship, 1978; editor: Kinship Ideology and Practice in Latin America, 1984; contbr. articles to profl. jours. Co-investigator urban family life project U. Chgo., 1986-90. Served with RAF, 1943-48. Guggenheim fellow, 1983-84 Fellow Am. Anthrop. Assn.; mem. Assn. Social Anthropologists. Office: Univ Chicago Dept Anthropology 1126 E 59th St Chicago IL 60637-1580 Office Phone: 831-471-0471. Business E-Mail: r-smith@uchicago.edu.

SMITH, RAYMOND W., investment banking executive; b. Pitts., 1937; BS, Carnegie-Mellon U., 1959; MBA, U. Pitts., 1969. Budget dir. AT&T, 1976-77; v.p.-regulatory Bell of Pa. and Diamond State Tel., Phila., 1981-83; pres., CEO Bell of Pa. & Diamond State Tel., Phila., 1983-85; vice chmn., CFO, dir. parent co. Bell Atlantic Corp., Phila., 1985-88, pres., COO, 1988, chmn., CEO Phila., 1989-98, Rothschild North America, Inc., NYC, 1999—; founding ptnr. Arlington Capital Partners, 1998—. Bd. dirs., U.S. Airways, CBS Corp., Banneker Technologies; mem. Bus. Roundtable, 1990—; mem. nat. adv. bd. Pvt. Sector Coun., 1990—; mem. James Madison nat. coun. Libr. of Congress, 1990—. Pub. playwright. Mem. Lincoln Ctr., Pres. Commn.-Arts and Humanities, WETA, Carnegie Corp., Carnegie Mellon, Rockham Ventures; trustee, Rockefeller Found., 2006-; With Signal Corps, U.S. Army, 1959-60. Office: Rothschild North Am Inc 1251 Avenue Of The Americas New York NY 10020-1104 also: Arlington Capital Ptnrs Ste 660 600 New Hampshire Ave NW Washington DC 20037

SMITH, REBECCA LYNN, language educator; b. Camp Springs, Md., Oct. 16, 1967; d. D. E. and Edith M. Smith. A in Bus., San Antonio Coll., 1989; BA in English, U. Tex. San Antonio, 2000, M in English, 2003. Supr. Roy Maas' Youth Alternatives, Boerne, Tex., 1993—97. Mem.: Beth Sichma, Alpha Phi, Sigma Tau Delta. Avocations: watercolor painting, travel. Home: 12205 Wilderness Trail San Antonio TX 78233 Office: NW Vista Coll 3535 N Ellison Dr San Antonio TX 78251

SMITH, REGINALD BRIAN FURNESS, retired anesthesiologist, educator; b. Warrington, Eng., Feb. 7, 1931; s. Reginald and Betty (Bell) S.; m. Margarete Groppe, July 18, 1963; children: Corinne, Malcolm. MB, BS, U. London, 1955; DTM and H, Liverpool Sch. Tropical Medicine, 1959. Intern Poole Gen. Hosp., Dorset, England, 1955-56, Wilson Meml. Hosp., Johnson City, NY, 1962-63; resident in anesthesiology Med. Coll. Va., Richmond, 1963-64, U. Pitts., 1964-65, from clin. instr. to prof., 1965-78, acting chmn. dept. anesthesiology, 1977-78; anesthesiologist in chief Presbyn. Univ. Hosp., Pitts., 1976-78; dir. anesthesiology Eye and Ear Hosp., Pitts., 1971-76; prof., chmn. dept. U. Tex. Health Sci. Ctr., San Antonio, 1978-98, anesthesiologist in chief hosps., 1978-98, clin. prof. anesthesiology, 1999—, clin. prof. rehab. medicine, 2003—07, med. dir. hyperbaric medicine and woundcare unit Univ. Hosp., 1993-2000, mem. med. staff Univ. Hosp., 2003—; ret., 2000. Contbg. editor: Internat. Ophthalmology Clinics, 1973, Internat. Anesthesiology Clinics, 1983; contbr. articles to profl. jours. Served to capt. Brit. Army, 1957-59. Fellow ACP, Am. Coll. Anesthesiologists, Am. Coll. Chest Physicians; mem. AMA, Internat. Anesthesia Rsch. Soc., Am. Soc. Anesthesiologists (pres. Western Pa. 1974-75), Tex. Soc. Anesthesiologists, San Antonio Soc. Anesthesiologists (pres. 1990), Tex. Med. Assn., Bexar County Med. Soc. Home: 9 Bristol Green San Antonio TX 78209-1104

SMITH, REX WILLIAM, journalist; b. Danville, Ill., Oct. 19, 1952; s. Ralph William and Lillian Grace (Hart) S.; m. Marion Roach, July 15, 1989. BA cum laude, Trinity U., San Antonio, 1974; MS with highest honors, Columbia U., NYC, 1980. Mng. editor Rensselaer (Ind.) Rep. newspaper, 1974-75; legis. asst. U.S. Rep. Floyd J. Fithian, Washington, 1975-79; reporter, spl. writer Newsday, LI, NY, 1980-87, chief Albany (N.Y.) bur., 1987-91; editor The Record, Troy, NY, 1991-95; mng. editor Times Union, Albany, NY, 1995—2002, editor, v.p., 2002—. Vice chair NY Fair Trial Free Press Conf., 2002—. Contbr. numerous articles to newspapers and mags. Recipient Cmty. Svc. award Rensselaer C. of C., 1975, Media award World Hunger Fund, 1983, Disting. Svc. medal Soc. Profl. Journalists, 1987, Editl. award Common Cause, 1992, Disting. Cmty. Svc. award N.Y. State Pubs. Assn., 1994; Rotary fellow, 1979, Pulitzer Travel fellow Columbia U., 1982; named Citizen of Yr. N.Y. State LWV, 1999. Mem. N.Y. State Assoc. Press Assn. (pres. 1998). Home: 3 Middle Hill Rd Troy NY 12180-6827 Office: Times Union PO Box 15000 Albany NY 12212-5000 Home Phone: 518-266-9424; Office Phone: 518-454-5040. Business E-Mail: rsmith@timesunion.com.

SMITH, RICHARD A., real estate company executive; BS, Columbus State U., Ga.; MS, Troy State U. Various mgmt. positions including corp. dir. risk mgmt., v.p. pers., sr. v.p. human resources, sr. v.p. adminstrn. and mem. oper. com. Days Inns of Am.; exec. v.p. ops. Cendant (formerly HFS Inc.), 1992—96, chmn., CEO real estate svcs. divsn., 1996—2006; vice chmn., pres. Realogy Corp., Parsippany, NJ, 2006—. Mem. policy adv. bd. Joint Ctr. Housing Studies of Harvard U.; bd. trustees Columbus State U. Found.; hon. mem. nat. bd. dirs. Easter Seals. Named one of Real Estate's 25 Most Influential Thought Leaders, Realtor Mag., 2006; recipient Ellis Island Medal of Honor, Nat. Ethnic Coalition of Orgns. Found., Inc., 2000. Office: Realogy Corp 1 Campus Dr Parsippany NJ 07054 Office Phone: 973-407-2000. *

SMITH, RICHARD ALAN, publishing and specialty retailing executive; b. Boston, 1924; married. BS, Harvard U., 1946; LLD (hon.), Boston Coll., 1988. With Smith Mgmt. Co., 1947-61; chmn. bd., CEO Gen. Cinema Corp. (name changed to Harcourt Gen., Inc. 1993), Chestnut Hill, Mass., 1961-91; chmn., CEO Harcourt Gen. Inc., Chestnut Hill, Mass., 1993—2007; chmn. bd., CEO Neiman Marcus, Chestnut Hill, Mass., 1987—2007; chmn., CEO, pres. GC Cos., Inc., Chestnut Hill, Mass., 1993-95, chmn., CEO, 1995—.

SMITH, RICHARD BOWEN, retired national park superintendent; b. Grandville, Mich., Mar. 8, 1938; s. William Jr. and Mary Elizabeth (Bowen) S.; m. Katherine Theresa Short, Sept. 21, 1980. BA in History, Albion Coll., 1960; MA in English, Mich. State U., 1967. Tchr. Grand Rapids (Mich.) Jr. H.S., 1960-66; vol. Peace Corps, Asuncion, Paraguay, 1968-70; ranger Nat. Pk. Svc., Yosemite, Calif., 1971-76, ranger. instr. Grand Canyon, Ariz., 1976-78, ranger, legis. specialist Washington, 1978-80, asst. supt. Everglades, Fla., 1980-83, assoc. regional dir. ops. Phila., 1984-86, supt. Carlsbad Caverns, N.Mex., 1986-88, assoc. regional dir. ops. Santa Fe, 1988-89; assoc. regional dir. resources mgmt. Nat. Park Service, Santa Fe, 1990-94; cons. on protected area mgmt. in L.Am., 1994—; temp. supt. Yellowstone Nat. Pk., 1994—; owner R & K Internat., 1994—2000; assoc. Orgnl. Quality Assocs.., 2000—. Pres. Assn. Nat. Park Rangers, 1977-78; coord. Congress of Internat. Ranger Fedn., San Jose, Costa Rica, 1997, v.p., 1998-2000, pres., 2000-03. Bd. dirs. Yellowstone Assn., 1995-97, Ptnrs. in Parks, 1998-2000. Recipient Meritorious Svc. award Dept. Interior, 1992, Disting. Alumnus award Albion Coll., 2006. Mem. Assn. Nat. Park Rangers (chmn. internat. com. 1997-2000), George Wright Soc. (bd. dirs. 1998—2004), Coalition of Nat. Park Svc. Retirees (exec. coun. 2004—). Home: 2 Roadrunner Trl Placitas NM 87043-9424 E-mail: rsmith0921@earthlink.net.

SMITH, RICHARD C. (DICK), lawyer; b. Jackson, Miss., 1946; BA, Univ. Fla., 1968; JD, Harvard Univ., 1971. Bar: Fla. 1971, US Dist. Ct. (so. dist. Fla.), US Ct. Appeals (5th, 11th cir.). Ptnr., bus. litigation, antitrust & trade regulation practices Shook Hardy & Bacon LLP, Miami, Fla. Editor (legis.): Harvard Jour. on Legislation; editor: partnership & corp. litigation chpt., Southeast Litigation Guide. Mem. Fla. Humanities Council. Served to Lt. JAGC USNR, 1972—75. Mem.: ABA, Assn. Trial Lawyers Am., Acad. Fla. Trial Lawyers, Fla. Bar, Dade County Bar Assn. Office: Shook Hardy & Bacon LLP Suite 2400 Miami Ctr 201 S Biscayne Blvd Miami FL 33131-4332 Office Phone: 305-960-6924. Office Fax: 305-358-7470.

SMITH, RICHARD CHARLES, not-for-profit administrator, educator, consultant, advocate; b. St. Paul, July 30, 1947; s. Arthur George Smith, Edna Alma Smith; m. Joan Rita Oxendine. BA, Calif. State U., San Bernardino, 1976; MBA, U. Calif., Riverside, 1981. Dir. mktg. SCW and Assoc., Riverside, Calif., 1981—84; dir. mktg. and ops. Thomas and Assoc., Riverside, 1984—85; v.p. br. adminstrn. First Fed. Savings and Loan, Ridgecrest, Calif., 1985—90; gen. mgr. KLOA Radio, Ridgecrest, 1990—92; dir. mktg. Ridgecrest Auto Ctr., Ridgecrest, 1992—94; exec. dir. Partnership to Preserve Indep. Living for Srs. and Persons with Disabilities, Riverside, 1994—. Mem. Riverside County C.A.R.E. Team, 2001—; sr. advisor The Beverly Found., 2004—; mem. Am. Soc. on Aging, 2005—; founding mem. Nat. Supplemental Transp. Program Exch.; cons., spkr. in field. Prodr.: (ednl. videos) Health Education Program Series, 2002; contbr. articles to profl. jours. E5 Army, 1966—69, Vietnam. Office: Partnership for Independent Living 6296 Rivercrest Dr Ste K Riverside CA Home Phone: 909-845-4718; Office Phone: 951-867-3800. Personal E-mail: rsmith@vitalco.net.

SMITH, RICHARD F., financial services company executive; BS, Purdue Univ., 1983. Sales rep. Owens Corning, Kans. City, Kans., 1981—83; various mgmt. positions GE, 1983—2005; sales rep. GE Plastics Bus. Group, Itasca, Ill., mktg. mgr., gen. mgr.; pres., CEO GE Capital Modular Space, Malvern, Pa., GE Capital Fleet Services, Eden Prairie, Minn., GE Global Property & Casualty Reinsurance, Overland Park, Kans.; COO GE Ins. Solutions, Overland Park, Kans.; pres., CEO Equifax Inc., Atlanta, 2005, chmn., pres., CEO, 2006—. Office: Equifax Inc 1550 Peachtree St NW Atlanta GA 30309 Mailing: Equifax Inc PO Box 4081 Atlanta GA 30302

SMITH, RICHARD HOWARD, banker; b. Tulare, Calif., Aug. 27, 1927; s. Howard Charles and Sue Elizabeth (Cheyne) S.; B.A., Principia Coll, 1958; LL.B., LaSalle U., 1975; postgrad. Sch. Banking U. Wash., 1970-72; m. Patricia Ann Howery, Mar. 12, 1950 (dec. Sept. 2001); children: Jeffrey Howard, Holly Lee, Gregory Scott, Deborah Elaine; m. Charlene Burruel, Mar. 27, 2004. Prin., Aurora Elementary Sch., Tulare, 1951-53; prin. Desert Sun Sch., Idyllwild, Calif., 1953-55; trust adminstr. trainee Bank of Am., San Diego, 1955-58, asst. trust officer, Ventura, Redlands, Riverside and L.A., 1958-65; asst. trust officer Security Pacific Bank, Fresno, Calif., 1965-68; trust officer, 1968-72, v.p., mgr., 1972-88, Pasadena, 1988-94; v.p. Bank of Am., L.A., 1994-95; ret., 1995; pres. Fiduciary Svcs., Fresno, 1995—; instr. San Bernardino Valley Coll., 1962-, Fresno City Coll., 1977-. With USN, 1945-46. Home: 3222 W Dovewood Ln Fresno CA 93711-2125 Office: Smith Fiduciary Svc 163 7081 N Marks Ave #104 Fresno CA 93711-0232 Office Phone: 559-432-6573.

SMITH, RICHARD J., energy executive; BS in Acctg., Ind. U. and Purdue U.; MBA, U. Indpls. V.p. fin. Energy Svcs. bus. unit Cinergy Corp., Cin., 1996—99, v.p. energy svcs., 1999, pres. Cinergy Resources, Inc., 1999; sr. v.p. transition mgmt. Entergy Corp., 1999—2000, pres. Retail, 2000, group pres. Utility Ops., pres., COO, 2007—. Office: Entergy Corp 639 Loyola Ave New Orleans LA 70113 Office Phone: 504-576-4000. *

SMITH, RICHARD JAMES, retired music educator; b. Baton Rouge, Nov. 28, 1950; s. Jimmie P. and Agnes Mae Smith; m. Lenora Faye McMillon, Mar. 3, 1981 (div. Feb. 28, 1988); m. Dewanna Ann Davis, July 3, 1992 (div. May 2003); m. Elissa Sisk Parks, Oct. 14, 2003; 1 child, James. MusB Edn., La. State U., Baton Rouge, 1972, MusM Edn., 1977, PhD, 1986. Cert. tchr. La. State Dept. Edn., 1972. Band dir. Northside H.S., Atlanta, 1972—73, Redemptorist H.S., Baton Rouge, 1973—74, East Beauregard H.S., DeRidder, La., 1974—77, Hammond H.S., Hammond, La., 1977—78, Silliman Inst., La., 1978—81, Mansfield H.S., Mansfield, La., 1981—83; dir. band and choir Breaux Bridge H.S., Breaux Bridge, La., 1984—85; band dir. Raynaud Mid. Sch., Lake Charles, La., 1985—86, Tallulah H.S., Tallulah, La., 1988—91, Pointe Coupee Ctrl. H.S., LaBarre, La., 1991—94, Glen Oaks H.S., Baton Rouge, 1994—95, Claiborne Acad., Haynesville, La., 1995—97, Jonesboro-Hodge H.S., Jonesboro, La., 1997—98; piano instr. Recreation and Parks Commn., Baton Rouge, 1998—99; band dir. East Iberville H.S., St. Gabriel, La., 1999—2000; piano instr. Recreation and Pks. Commn., Baton Rouge, 2000—. Composer: Symphonic Essay for Band, 1973, March Triumphe, 1974, Go, Ye Trojans, 1975, Adagio for unaccomanpied flute, 1975, Serenade for Unaccomanpied Flute, 1975, Noble Knights, 1976, In Memoriom, 1976, Requiem Mass in D minor, 1977, Fight On!, 1978, Sillman Inst. Alma Mater, 1978, Elegy, 1980, The Silver Star, 1980, Freedom Express, 1982, Marche Royale, 1984, Hail to Liberty, 1986, Hall of Justice, 1986, Freedom and Unity, 1988, InGod We Trust, 1988, Th Blue and the Gold, 1989, River City Grand March, 1989, Beyou-Fest, 1990, A Touch of Tenderness, 1999, The National Game, 2005, The Bride Elect, 2005, Yorktown Centennial March, 2005, The Diplomat, 2005, America First, 2005, The Aviators, 2005, The White Rose, 2005, The Wolverine March, 2005, others; contbr. articles to profl. jour. Mem. Baton Rouge Concert Band, Baton Rouge, 1977—81, Lafayette Concert Band, Lafayette, La., 1984—85, Lake Charles Cmty. Band, Lake Charles, La., 1986—88, North La. Cmty. Band, Monroe, La., 1989—91, Baton Rouge Concert Band, 2001—. Recipient Mem. of All-American Coll. TV Band - La. State U. Marching Band, Chevrolet Corp., 1970, Superior Rating at Dist. Band Festival - Tallulah H.S. Band, La. Music Educators Assn., 1991, Superior Rating at Dist. Choir Festival - Breaux Bridge H.S. Choir, 1985, First Pl. in Mansfield Christmas Parade - Mansfield H.S. Band, Mansfield, LA, Chamber of Commerce, 1981. Mem.: NEA (life), U.S. Achievement Acad. (nat. adv. bd. 1983—2002), La. Bandmasters Assn., La. Music Educators Assn., Music Educators Nat. Conf., La. Educators Assn. (life), Pi Kappa Lambda, Kappa Kappa Psi (life Outstanding pledge 1969). Avocations: travel, reading, music, building 3-d puzzles, miniature golf. Home: 10515 Tallowwood Ave Baker LA 70714 Office: Recreation and Parks Commission 3140 N Sherwood Forest Dr Baton Rouge LA 70814 Office Phone: 225-262-1956. Personal E-mail: rjsmith41@cox.net.

SMITH, RICHARD MILLS, editor-in-chief; b. Detroit, Jan. 12, 1946; s. William Steele Smith and Janet (Mills) Morrison; m. Lee Ann Vanderstoep (div.); children: Scott William, Anna Mills; m. Soon-Young Yoon, Oct. 20, 1978; 1 child, Song-Mee. BA summa cum laude, Albion Coll., 1968; postgrad., Columbia U., 1968—69, MS, 1970; LLD (hon.), Albion Coll., 1993. Reporter Associated Press, NY, 1969; assoc. editor foreign dept. Newsweek, NY, 1970—73, gen. editor nat. affairs dept. NY, 1973—74, editor Asian region, bur. chief Hong Kong Hong Kong, 1974—77; mng. editor Newsweek Internat., NY, 1977—81; asst. mng. editor Newsweek, NYC, 1982, exec. editor, 1983, editor in chief, 1984—, pres., 1991—98, chmn., 1998—. Chmn. Mag. Pub. Am., 1996—97. Trustee Albion Coll; bd. dirs. Cooper-Hewitt Nat. Design Mus., Smithsonian Instn., Harvard AIDS Inst. Recipient Disting. Alumni award, Albion Coll., 1974, Henry Johnson Fisher award, Mag. Pub. of Am., 2001. Mem.: Century Assn., Coun. on Fgn. Rels., Mag. Pubs. Assn. (chmn.), Am. Soc. Mag. Editors (mem. exec. com. 1985—88), Phi Beta Kappa. Office: Newsweek Inc 251 W 57th St New York NY 10019-1802 *

SMITH, RICHEY, manufacturing executive; b. Akron, Ohio, Nov. 11, 1933; s. Thomas William and Martha (Richey) S.; m. Sandra Cosgrave Roe, Nov. 25, 1961; children: Mason Roe, Parker Richey. Grad., Hotchkiss Sch.; BS, U. Va., Charlottesville, 1956. Asst. to pres. Sun Products Corp., Barberton, Ohio, 1960-64, v.p., 1964-67, gen. mgr., dir., 1967-69, chmn., CEO, 1969-76; prin. A.T. Kearney Co., Cleve., 1977-87; chmn., CEO Richey Industries, Inc., Medina, Ohio, 1987—. Bd. dirs. Jaite Packaging, Inc. Exec. com. Gt. Trail coun. Boy Scouts Am.; chmn. capital funds dr. Summit County Planned Parenthood; trustee, found. pres. Old Trail Sch., Barberton Citizens Hosp., Medina County Arts Coun., Akron Regional Devel. Bd.; treas. Friends of Metro Park; found. trustee, vestryman St. Paul's Episcopal Ch.; corp. bd. Cleve. Mus. of Art; bd. govs. The Hotchkiss Sch. Lt. USN, 1957—60, lt. comdr. USNR, 1961—69. Mem. Ohio Commodores, Bluecoats (trustee), Navy League (pres. Akron coun. 1972-73), Young Pres. Orgn., Portage Country Club (bd. dirs.), Mayflower Club, Sawgrass Country Club (Fla.) Farmington Country Club (Charlottesville, Va.), Rotary (trustee Akron 1974-75), Yale Club (N.Y.C.), Rockwell Springs Trout Club, Chi Psi (pres.). Home: 721 Delaware Ave Akron OH 44303-1303 Office: 910 Lake Rd Medina OH 44256-2453 Office Phone: 330-725-4997 x 304. E-mail: rsmith@richeyind.com.

SMITH, RICK, professional sports team executive; b. Sept. 3, 1969; BA, Purdue Univ., Ind., 1992. Asst. strength and conditioning coord. Purdue Univ., 1993—94, defensive backs coach, 1994—95; defensive unit coach Denver Broncos, 1996—99, also pro personnel ops., 1999—2005, asst. gen. mgr., 2006; gen. mgr. Houston Texans, 2006—. Achievements include being NFL's youngest gen. mgr., 2006. Office: Houston Texans Two Reliant Park Houston TX 77054 Office Phone: 832-667-2000.

SMITH, ROBERT BLAKEMAN, lawyer; b. Mt. Vernon, NY, June 18, 1949; s. William Blakeman and Helen Theresa (Curley) S.; m. Laura Lindley Brock, July 18, 1987; children: Morgan Lindley, Justin Pierce. BS, Rensselaer Poly. Inst., 1971, ME, 1973; JD, Boston U., 1976. Bar: N.Y. 1977, U.S. Dist. Ct. (so. and ea. dists.) N.Y. 1977, U.S. Dist. Ct. (no. dist.) N.Y. 1981, U.S. Dist. Ct. Ariz. 1992, U.S. Patent and Trademark Office 1977, U.S. Ct. Appeals (7th cir.) 1979, U.S. Ct. Appeals (fed. cir.) 1982, U.S. Supreme Ct. 1981. Assoc. Brumbaugh, Graves, Donohue & Raymond, NYC, 1976-84, ptnr., 1984-89; of counsel White & Case, NYC, 1989-99, Skadden, Arps, Slate, Meagher & Flom, NYC, 1999—. Lectr. IEEE, N.Y.C., 1983-88, Practising Law Inst., 1990-99. Trustee Delta Phi Found., Ithaca, N.Y., 1978-86, St. Elmo Found., Pearl River, N.Y., 1986—. Mem. N.Y. Intellectual Property Law Assn., Am. Intellectual Property Law Assn. Home: 100 Riverside Dr New York NY 10024-4822 Office: Skadden Arps Slate Meagher & Flom Four Times Sq New York NY 10036-6522 E-mail: Robsmith@SKadden.com.

SMITH, ROBERT BOULWARE, III, vascular surgeon, educator; b. Atlanta, June 15, 1933; s. Robert Boulware Jr. Smith and Mary Eva (Black) Fanning; m. Florence Chance Limehouse, Aug. 22, 1953; children: Victoria Joanne Smith Harkins, Robert Boulware IV, Brian Scott. MD, Emory U., 1957. Diplomate Am. Bd. Surgery. Intern in surgery Columbia Presbyn. Hosp., NYC, 1957-58, resident in surgery, 1960-65; asst. prof. surgery Emory U. Sch. Medicine, Atlanta, 1966-69, assoc. prof., 1969-77, prof., 1977—, head gen. vascular surgery, 1984-98. Chief surg. svc. VA Med. Ctr., Atlanta, 1969-88; assoc. med. dir. Emory U. Hosp., 1993-95, med. dir., 1995-2006. Co-editor: Trauma to the Thorax and Abdomen, 1969, Medical Management of the Surgical Patient, 1982, 4th edit., 2006; contbr. articles to profl. jours.; chpts. to books. Capt. M.C., U.S. Army, 1958-60. Mem. ACS, Am. Surg. Assn., So. Assn. Vascular Surgery (sec. 1986-91, pres. 1992-93), Soc. Vascular Surgery, Assn. VA Surgeons (pres. 1983-84, Disting. Svc. award 1988), Ga. Surg. Soc. (pres. 1992-93), Atlanta Vascular Soc. (pres. 1986-88), Internat. Soc. for Cardiovasc. Surg. (pres. 1996-97). Phi Beta Kappa, Alpha Omega Alpha. Republican. United Methodist. Avocations: music, travel. Office: Emory Univ Hosp 1364 Clifton Rd NE B206 Atlanta GA 30322-1013 Home: 6205 Springhouse Cir Stone Mountain GA 30087-6739 Office Phone: 404-727-3573. Business E-Mail: robert.smith@emoryhealthcare.org.

SMITH, ROBERT CARLISLE, department administrator, welding educator; b. St. Albans, W.Va., Sept. 2, 1939; s. Clarence Mack (stepfather) and Artimitia (Blake) Smith Fowler; m. Janet Lee Koehn, Dec. 28, 1958; children: Teresa Lynn, Stephen Carlisle. BA, Glenville State U., 1984; MSc, Marshall U., 1994. Cert. welding inspector, non-destructive tester. Br. mgr. Va. Welding, Charleston, W.Va., 1963—76; prin. Weld Inspection and Cons., St. Albans, 1976—94; mgr. quality assurance Kanawha Mfg., Charleston, 1988—2003; dept. head, instr. welding W.Va. U., Parkersburg, 1981—2003. Chair edn., adv. com. Mt. Olive Correctional Ctr., W.Va. Contbr. articles. Lt. ROTC 1957-71; committeeman Rep. Party, Kanawha County, 1968-69; former Sun. sch. tchr. Highlawn Baptist Ch.; presenter Nat. Educators Workshop NASA, Langley Space Flight Ctr., 1993. Recipient Disting. West Virginian award Gov. W.Va., 1968, Tchr. of Excellence award Nat. Inst. for Staff and Orgnl. Devel.; named Outstanding Prof. of Yr. W.Va. U. Parkersburg campus, 2005. Mem. Am. Welding Soc. (chmn. 1971-72, program chairperson 1989-90, educator of yr. 1990, 92, 2003-04), Am. Soc. Non-Destructive Testing (membership recruiter 1988), W.Va. Edn. Assn., W.Va. C.C. Assn. Protestant. Avocations: autos, trucks, writing, fishing, banjo. Home: 2302 S Walnut Dr Saint Albans WV 25177-3947 Business E-Mail: carlsmith@mail.wvu.edu.

SMITH, ROBERT EARL, space scientist; b. Indpls., Sept. 13, 1923; s. Harold Bennett and Bernice (McCaslin) S.; m. Elizabeth Lee Usak, Jan. 3, 1947 (dec. 1984); children: Stephanie Lee, Robert Michael, Cynthia Ann, Kelly Andrew; m. Lyla Lee Lewellen, July 1, 1988. BS, Fla. State U., 1959, MS, 1960, U. Mich., 1969, PhD, 1974. Enlisted U.S. Army Air Force, 1943-44; advanced through grades to maj. U.S. Air Force, 1955; airway traffic controller Berlin, 1945; staff weather reconnaissance officer 9th Air Force, 1956; ret., 1963; project scientist Atmospheric Cloud Physics Lab.; dep. chief atmospheric scis. div. NASA/Marshall Space Flight Ctr., Ala., 1963-86; sr. scientific cons. Univs. Space Rsch. Assn., Huntsville, Ala., 1986-87; sr. computer cons. Computer Scis. Corp., Huntsville, 1987-89; chief space sci. and applications div. FWG Associates, Inc., Huntsville, 1989-92; NASA program mgr. Physitron, Inc., Huntsville, 1992-96; sr. computer scientist Computer Scis. Corp., Huntsville, 1996—2002. Mem. AIAA, Pi Mu Epsilon, Sigma Phi Epsilon. Avocation: golf. Home: 125 Westbury Dr SW Huntsville AL 35802-1619 Personal E-mail: r01913smith@bellsouth.net.

SMITH, ROBERT EVERETT, lawyer; b. NYC, Mar. 15, 1936; s. Arthur L. and Augusta (Cohen) S.; m. Emily Lucille Lehman, July 17, 1960; children: Amy, Karen, Victoria. BA, Dartmouth Coll., 1957; LLB, Harvard U., 1960. Bar: N.Y. 1960, U.S. Dist. Ct. (so. dist.) N.Y. 1962, U.S. Ct. Appeals (2d cir.) 1963, U.S. Supreme Ct. 1967, U.S. Dist. Ct. (ea. dist.) N.Y. 1969, U.S. Ct. Appeals (3d cir.) 1982, U.S. Ct. Appeals (9th cir.) 1988. Assoc. Paul, Weiss, Rifkind, Wharton & Garrison, NYC, 1960-65; from assoc. to ptnr. Baar, Bennett & Fullen, NYC, 1965-74; ptnr. Guggenheimer & Untermyer, NYC, 1974-85, Rosenman & Colin LLP, NYC, 1985-98, chmn., 1994-97, counsel, 1998—2002, Katten Muchin Rosenman LLP, NYC, 2002—. With U.S. Army, 1961-64. Mem. ABA, N.Y. State Bar Assn., Assn. of Bar of City of N.Y., Fed. Bar Coun., N.Y. County Lawyers Assn., Internat. Bar Assn., Am. Arbitration Assn. (nat. panel arbitrators), Am. Law Inst. Office: Katten Muchin Rosenman LLP 575 Madison Ave Fl

26 New York NY 10022-2585 Home Phone: 212-744-1208; Office Phone: 212-940-8850. Business E-Mail: robert.smith@kattenlaw.com.

SMITH, ROBERT FREEMAN, history professor; b. Little Rock, May 13, 1930; s. Robert Freeman and Emma Martha Gottlieb (Buerkle) S.; m. Alberta Vester, Feb. 1, 1951 (dec. 1985); children: Robin Ann, Robert Freeman III; m. Charlotte Ann Coleman, Sept. 9, 1985. BA, U. Ark., 1951, MA, 1952; PhD, U. Wis., Madison, 1958. Instr. U. Ark., Fayetteville, 1953; asst. prof. Tex. Luth. Coll., Seguin, 1958-62; assoc. prof. U. R.I., Kingston, 1962-66, U. Conn., Storrs, 1966-69; prof. history U. Toledo, 1969-86, disting. univ. prof., 1986—. Vis. prof. U. Wis., Madison, 1966-67. Author: The United States and Cuba: Business and Diplomacy 1917-1960, 1961 (Tex. Writers' Roundup award 1961), What Happened in Cuba: A Documentary History of U.S.-Cuban Relations, 1963, The United States and Revolutionary Nationalism in Mexico, 1916-1932, 1973 (Ohio Acad. History award 1973), The Era of Caribbean Intervention, 1890-1930, 1981, The Era of Good Neighbors, Cold Warriors, and Hairshirts, 1930-82, 1983, The Caribbean World and the United States: Mixing Rum & Coca-Cola, 1994; contbr. to numerous publs. Retired Col. 7th Hist. Detachment, Ohio Mil. Res. 1st lt. U.S. Army, 1953-55. Knapp fellow in history U. Wis., 1957; Tom L. Evans rsch. fellow Harry S. Truman Libr., Independence, Mo., 1976-77, Mexican Ministry Fgn. Rels. fellow, 1991-92. Mem. Soc. Historians of Am. Fgn. Rels., Soc. Mil. History, U.S. Naval Inst., Ohio Acad. History, So. Hist. Assn., Orgn. Am. Historians, Assn. U.S. Army, State Guard Assn. of U.S., Am. Legion, Masons, Scottish Rite, Shriners, Army Hist. Found., Inst. Land Warfare, Sons of Confederate Vets., Phi Beta Kappa, Phi Alpha Theta. Episcopalian. Avocation: photography. Home: 4110 Dunkirk Rd Toledo OH 43606-2217 Office: U Toledo Dept History Toledo OH 43606

SMITH, ROBERT G., lawyer; b. Washington, Oct. 4, 1943; BA, Johns Hopkins U., 1965; LLB, Harvard U., 1968. Bar: Md. 1969. Ptnr., Environ., Appellate Litigation practices Venable LLP, Balt. & Washington, 1970—. Contbr. articles to profl. jours. Mem. ABA, Assn. Trial Lawyers Am., Def. Rsch. Inst., Air & Waste Mgmt. Assn., Md. C. of C. (Air Quality com.), Md. Bar Assn., Bar Assn. Balt. City. Office: Venable LLP 1800 Mercantile Bank & Trust Bldg 2 Hopkins Plz Baltimore MD 21201 also: Venable LLP 575 7th St NW Washington DC 20004 Office Phone: 410-244-7590, 202-344-4056. Office Fax: 410-244-7742. Business E-Mail: rgsmith@venable.com.

SMITH, ROBERT HUGH, retired engineering construction company executive; b. Wichita, Kans., Dec. 29, 1936; s. Richard Lyon and E. Eileen (O'Neal) S.; m. Melinda Louise Fitch, Sept. 26, 1959 (div. Dec. 1969); children: Robert Blake, Thomas Hugh; m. Margaret Anne Moseley, Dec. 11, 1971; 1 child, Steven Richard. BS, Kans. State U., 1959; MS, U. Kans., 1964, PhD, 1970. Sr. process engr. FMC Corp., Lawrence, Kans., 1959-64; rsch. engr. Phillips Petroleum Co., Bartlesville, Okla., 1964-66; group leader Standard Oil of Ohio, Warrenville Heights, Ohio, 1966-67; sr. rsch. assoc., group leader Atlantic Richfield, Plano, Tex., 1970-80; regional mgr., sr. mgr., sales mgr. Fluor Daniel, Houston and Marlton, NJ, 1980-90; v.p., gen. mgr. Badger Design & Construction, Tampa, Fla., 1990-93; exec. v.p., COO Process divsn. Black & Veatch, Overland Park, 1993-2000; ret., 2000. Patentee in the field; contbr. to profl. jours. Adv. bd. dept. chem. engring, coll. of engring. U. Kans., Lawrence, 1993—; mem. adv. bd. coll. engring. Kans. State U., 1998-2005. Recipient Disting. Svc. award Kans. State U., 1998; named to Engring. Hall of Fame Kans. State U., Chem. and Petroleum Engring. Hall of Fame, U. Kans., 2000. Fellow AIChE (chmn., vice chmn., sec. Dallas chpt. 1962—, exec. bd. Engr. and Cons. Contracting divsn., 1995-97, bd. dirs. 2002-04, career and edn. ops. coun. 2002-03, bd. trustees 2007—, Engr. of Yr. award Dallas chpt. 1980), Phi Lambda Upsilon, Sigma Xi. Avocations: tennis, sailing, skiing, reading. Personal E-mail: bobsmith29@everstkc.net.

SMITH, ROBERT J., JR., real estate executive; b. Rochester, NY, June 1, 1951; s. Robert and Irene (Frisbie) S.; m. Sherry L. Silberman, July 5, 1981; 1 child, Jordan. Student, Ohio U., 1969-73. CPA, Ohio. Gen. mgr. Televac, Inc., Athens, 1975—; CFO, gen. mgr. Practice Mgmt., Inc. (PMI), Cleve., 1988—. Mem. AICPA. E-mail: televac@aol.com.

SMITH, ROBERT JOHN, anthropology educator; b. Essex, Mo., June 27, 1927; s. Will Dan and Fern (Jones) S.; m. Kazuko Sasaki, Aug. 22, 1955. BA summa cum laude, U. Minn., 1949; MA, Cornell U., 1951, PhD, 1953. Engaged in cultural anthrop. field research, N.S., Canada, 1950, Japan, 1951-52, 55, 57-58, Brazil, 1966-67; mem. faculty Cornell U., 1953—, prof. anthropology, 1963-74, Goldwin Smith prof. anthropology, 1974-97, prof. emeritus, 1997—, chmn. dept. Asian studies, 1961-66, chmn. dept. antropology, 1967-71, 76-82, prof. emeritus, 1997—. Vis. prof. anthropology U. Ariz., 1971, U. Hawaii, 1978, Nat. Mus. Ethnology, Osaka, Japan, 1982 Author: (with Cornell) Two Japanese Villages, 1956, (with Cornell, Saito and Maeyama) Japanese and Their Descendants in Brazil, 1967; editor: (with Beardsley) Japanese Culture: Its Development and Characteristics, 1962, Social Organization and the Applications of Anthropology, 1974, Ancestor Worship in Contemporary Japan, 1974, Kurusu: The Price of Progress in a Japanese Village, 1951-75, 1978, (with Wiswell) Women of Suye Mura, 1982, Japanese Society: Tradition, Self and the Social Order, 1983, (with K. Smith) Diary of a Japanese Innkeeper's Daughter, 1984 Served with AUS, 1944-46. Tng. grantee Social Sci. Rsch. Coun., Japan, 1951-52; recipient Individual Exch. award to Japan Inst. Internat. Edn., 1957-58; Fulbright lectr. Tokyo Met. U., 1962-63; NSF rsch. grantee, 1965-67; Japan Found. grantee, 1979; awarded Order of the Rising Sun, Govt. of Japan, 1993. Fellow Assn. Asian Studies (v.p. 1987-88, pres. 1988-89), Soc. Applied Anthropology (editor jour. Human Orgn. 1961-66). Home: 322 Savage Farm Dr Ithaca NY 14850 Business E-Mail: rjs6@cornell.edu.

SMITH, ROBERT LOUIS, construction company executive; b. Parkersburg, W.Va., Apr. 19, 1922; s. Everett Clerc and Janet (Morrison) S.; m. June Irene Odbert, Oct. 25, 1948; children: Peter Clerc, Morrison James, Edna Louise. BS in Civil Engring., Lehigh U., 1944. Design engr. Chrysler Corp., 1944-46; engr. Harrison Constrn. Co., Charleston, W.Va., 1946-47; sr. engr. Creole Petroleum Co., Las Piedras, Venezuela, 1947-55; v.p. Rea Constrn. Co., Charlotte, N.C., 1955-64; exec. v.p. Warren Bros. Co., Cambridge, Mass., 1964-68, pres., 1968-79; also dir.; sr. v.p. Ashland Oil, Inc., Ky., 1974-79; pres. Robert L. Smith & Assos., Lexington, 1979—; pres., dir. Tree Farm Devel. Corp., Cambridge, 1979—. Dir. Panastalto (S.A.), Wilder Constrn. Co., Inc., J.H. Shears Sons, Inc. Fellow ASCE; mem. Nat. Asphalt Pavement Assn. (dir.), Phi Beta Kappa, Tau Beta Pi, Sigma Chi. Republican. Unitarian Universalist. Home and Office: 1010 Waltham St Apt A412 Lexington MA 02421-8065 Home Phone: 781-861-0489; Office Phone: 781-861-0489. Personal E-mail: rlouissmith@comcast.net.

SMITH, R(OBERT) MICHAEL, lawyer; b. Cin., Nov. 25, 1951; s. Barney and Jean (Maloney) S.; m. Leslie Y. Straub. BA in Polit. Sci., U. Cin., 1982; JD, Ohio State U., 1985; MDiv in Bibl. and Theol. studies, So. Bapt. Theol. Sem., 2002. Bar: Ohio 1985, U.S. Dist. Ct. (so. dist.) Ohio 1992, U.S. Supreme Ct. 1992; ordained minister So. Bapt. Ch., 1999. Law clk. to Justice Holmes Ohio Supreme Ct., Columbus, 1985-89; sr. staff atty., referee, editor Ohio Ct. Claims, Columbus, 1989-94. Instr. law Ohio State U., 1985—, instr. continuing edn. courses, 1990—. Incorporator, trustee various non-profit orgns., Cin. and Columbus; pres. So. Bapt. Messianic Fellowship, 1994-97; 2d v.p. Ohio So. Bapt. Conv. Republican. Avocations: target shooting, writing, running, construction. Home: 4325 Kinloch Rd Louisville KY 40207-2853

SMITH, ROBERT MICHAEL, lawyer, mediator, arbitrator, writer; b. Boston, Nov. 4, 1940; s. Sydney and Minnie (Appel) S.; m. Catherine Kersey, Apr. 14, 1981 (dec. 1983); m. Clarissa Redmond, Feb. 11, 1999 (dec. 2001). AB cum laude, Harvard Coll., 1962; diploma, Centro de Estudos de Espanol, Barcelona, 1963; MA in Internat. Affairs, Columbia U., 1964, MS in Journalism with high honors, 1965; JD, Yale U., 1975. Bar: Calif., NY, DC, U.S. Supreme Ct.; barrister Inner Temple, London; solicitor Supreme Ct. of Eng. and Wales; accredited mediator Hong Kong Internat. Arbitration Ctr.; chartered arbitrator, Eng.; registered mediator Ctr. de Mediation et d'Arbitrage Paris. Intern in econ. devel. UN, Geneva, 1964; corr. Time Mag., NYC, 1965-66, The N.Y. Times, Washington, 1968-72, 75-76; atty. Heller, Ehrman, White & McAuliffe, San Francisco, 1976-78; spl. asst. Office of Atty. Gen. of U.S., Washington, 1979-80; dir. Office Pub. Affairs US Dept. Justice, Washington, 1979-80; mem. US delegation U.S. v. Iran Internat. Ct. of Justice, The Hague, 1980; asst. US atty. No. Dist. Calif., San Francisco, 1981-82; counsel, sr. counsel to sr. litigation counsel Bank of Am. NT & SA, San Francisco, 1982-86; disting. vis. fellow Ctr. for Effective Dispute Resolution, London, 2005—, dir. mediation, 2005—. Lectr. FBI Acad., Quantico, Va., 1980, Internat. Bankers Assn. Calif., 1994, Calif. Bankers Assn., 1994, Cmty. Bankers No. Calif., 1994, 95; judge Golden Medallion Broadcast Media awards State Bar Calif., 1985; judge pro tem Mcpl. Ct. City and County of San Francisco, 1989—; conciliator Peninsula Conflict Resolution Ctr.; panelist World Intellectual Property Orgn., Geneva; arbitrator internat. Commercial arbitration ctrs., Vancouver, Cairo, Singapore, Kuala Lumpur, India; CPR Panel of Disting. Neutrals; mem. panel Nat. Assn. for Dispute Resolution; acad. vis. faculty law U. Oxford, 2006-07; sr. common rm. Lincoln Coll. U. Oxford, 2006-07; vis. scholar dept. decision scis. European Inst. Adminstrv. Affairs. Author: Alternative Dispute Resolution for Financial Institutions, 1995, rev. 4th edit., 1998; bd. editors Yale Law Jour., 1974-75; editor Litigation, jour. ABA litigation sect., 1978-81; mem. edit. adv. bd. Bancroft-Whitney, 1991-94; contbr. articles to profl. jours. Bd. dirs. Neighborhood Legal Assistance Found., San Francisco, 1985-87, Nob Hill Assn., San Francisco, 1985-93; bd. dirs., fin. com. St. Francis Found., San Francisco, 1993-94. 1st lt. inf., USAR, 1965-71. Recipient UPI Award for Newswriting, 1958; Harvard Coll. scholar, 1958-62, Fulbright scholar, 1962-63; Columbia U. Internat. fellow, 1964-65. Fellow Internat. Acad. Mediators, Am. Coll. Civil Trial Mediators, Hong Kong Inst. Arbitrators, Chartered Inst. Arbitrators (London); mem. ABA (corp. counsel com. 1986-96, alternative dispute resolution sect. 1994-98), Assn. Atty. Mediators (v.p. No. Calif. chpt. 1995), State Bar of Calif. (pub. affairs com. 1982-85, litigation sect. 1990-96), Bar Assn. of San Francisco (bench-bar media com. 1985-96, alternative dispute resolution com. 1994-98), Assn. Bus. Trial Lawyers No. Calif., Assn. of Former U.S. Attys. No. Dist. Calif., Am. Arbitration Assn. (mem. comml. arbitration panel, No. Calif. adv. coun., mediator Am. Arbitration Ctr. for Mediation), Nat. Assn. Dispute Resolution, The Mediation Soc. (chmn. bd., pres.), Profl. Atty. Mediators, Cmty. Bds. of San Francisco (conciliator), French-Am. C. of C., German-Am. C. of C. West U.S., Harvard Club of San Francisco (bd. dirs. 1986-94, pres. 1992-94), Yale Club of San Francisco (bd. dirs. 1989-94), Soc. Profls. in Dispute Resolution, Columbia U. Alumni Club of No. Calif. (exec. com. 1978-92).

SMITH, ROBERT POWELL, former ambassador, retired foundation administrator; b. Joplin, Mo., Mar. 5, 1929; s. Powell Augusta and Estella (Farris) S.; m. Alice Irene Rountree, Aug. 22, 1953; children: Michael Bryan, Steven Powell, Karen Louise, David Robert. BA, Tex. Christian U., 1954, MA, 1955. Fgn. svc. officer Dept. State, 1955-81; press officer Washington, 1955; vice-consul Lahore, Pakistan, 1956—58; 2d sec. Beirut, 1959-61; consul and prin. officer Enugu, Nigeria, 1962-65; officer-in-charge Ghanaian Affairs, 1966; officer-in-charge Nigerian Affairs, dep. dir. Office West African Affairs, 1967-69; dep. chief of mission, counselor of embassy Pretoria, South Africa, 1970-74; amb. to Malta, 1974-76; amb. to Ghana, 1976-79; amb. to Liberia, 1979-81. Pres. Africa Wildlife Leadership Found., 1981-85. Served with USMCR, 1946-49, 50-52. Decorated Air medal.; recipient Meritorious Honor award State Dept., 1967 Mem. Am. Fgn. Service Assn. Baptist.

SMITH, ROBERT SHERLOCK, state appeals court judge; b. NYC, Aug. 31, 1944; s. Robert and Janet W. (Welt) S.; m. Dian Goldston Smith, Aug. 31, 1969; children: Benjamin Eli, Emlen Matthew, Rosemary Friedman. BA with great distinction, Stanford U., 1965; LLB magna cum laude, Columbia U., 1968. Bar: N.Y. 1968, U.S. Dist. Ct. (so. dist.) N.Y. 1969, U.S. Dist. Ct. (ea. dist.) N.Y. 1977, U.S. Ct. Appeals (2d cir.) 1970, U.S. Ct. Appeals (4th cir.) 1986, U.S. Ct. Appeals (1st cir.) 1988, U.S. Ct. Appeals (7th cir.) 1989, U.S. Ct. Appeals (6th cir.) 1995, U.S. Ct. Appeals (D.C. and 8th cirs.) 1997, U.S. Ct. Appeals (5th cir.) 1999, U.S. Tax Ct. 1974, U.S. Supreme Ct. 1979. Assoc. Paul, Weiss, Rifkind, Wharton & Garrison, NYC, 1968-76, ptnr., 1976—2003; individual practitioner, spl. counsel Kornstein, Veisz, Wexler & Pollard, NYC, 2003—04; assoc. judge NY State Ct. Appeals, NYC, 2004—. Vis. prof. Columbia Law Sch., N.Y.C., 1980-81, lectr. law, 1981-90; adj. Benjamin N. Cardozo Sch. Law, 2006—. Editor-in-chief Columbia Law Review. Mem. ABA, N.Y. State Bar Assn. (vice chair com. ct. adminstrn. 2001-04), Assn. Bar City N.Y. (com. fed. legis. 1981-84, com. on judiciary 1984-87, com. on bicentennial of U.S. Constitution 1988-91), Federalist Soc. N.Y. (pres. lawyers chpt. 1994-2003). Republican. Mem. Reformed Ch. Office: State NY Ct Appeals 20 Eagle St Albany NY 12207-1095 also: 780 Third Ave 18th Fl New York NY 10017 Office Phone: 646-386-3824. Business E-Mail: rssmith@courts.state.ny.us.

SMITH, ROBERT VICTOR, academic administrator, educator; b. Glendale, NY, Feb. 16, 1942; s. Robert Arthur and Marie Marlene (Florence) S. BS in Pharm. Sci., St. John's U., Jamaica, NY, 1963; MS in Pharm. Chemistry, U. Mich., 1964, PhD in Pharm. Chemistry, 1968. Asst. prof., then assoc. prof. U. Iowa, Iowa City, 1968-74; assoc. prof., asst. dir. U. Tex., Austin, 1974-77, area coordinator basic pharmaceutics, 1975-76, assoc. dir. Drug Dynamics Inst., 1977-78, dir. Drug Dynamics Inst., Coll. Pharmacy, 1979-85, James E. Bauerle Centennial prof. Coll. Pharmacy, 1983-85; prof., dean Coll. Pharmacy, Wash. State U., Pullman, 1985-86, vice provost for rsch., dean Grad. Sch., 1987-97; vice provost for rsch. and grad. edn., dean Grad. Sch., U. Conn., Storrs, 1997-2000; provost, vice chancellor acad. affairs U. Ark., Fayetteville, 2000—. Cons. E.R. Squibb, New Brunswick, N.J., 1979-82, Upjohn Co., Kalamazoo, 1982-85; external examiner U. Malaysia, Penang, 1981-82; mem. sci. adv. bd. Biodecision Labs., Pitts., 1985-86; Wash. Exposition Sci. Tech. Found., 1989-90; mem. noms. com. Coun. Grad. Schs., Washington, 1990-91, 96-97; accreditation evaluator Northwest Assn. Schs. and Colls., Seattle, 1991-97; mem. exec. com. grad. deans African-Am. Inst., N.Y., 1992-2000; bd. dirs. Coun. Grad. Schs., 1998, Grad. Record Exam, 1999-2003; exec. sec. U. Ark. 2010 Commn., 2000—; chair Southeastern Conf. Provosts Group, 2003-04. Author: Textbook of Biopharmaceutic Analysis, 1981, Graduate Research: A Guide for Students in the Sciences, 1998, Development and Management of University Research Groups, 1986, The Elements of Great Speechmaking: Adding Drama and Intrigue, 2004, Pedestals, Parapets and Pits: The Joys, Challenges and Failures of Professional Life, 2005, Where You Stand is Where You Sit: An Academic Administrator's Handbook, 2006. Bd. dirs. Wash. Tech. Ctr., 1990-92; exec. sec. 2010 Commn. Grantee NIH, 1974-83; fellow Acad. Pharm. Scis., 1981, Am. Assn. Pharm. Scientists, 1987; recipient Disting. Alumnus award Coll. Pharmacy U. Mich., 1990, Outstanding Svc. award Wash. State U., Grad. and Profl. Student Assn., 1993, 95. Mem. Am. Assn. Colls. Pharmacy (chmn. research and grad. affairs com. 1983-84), U.S. Pharmacopeia (revision com. 1985-90), Acad. Pharm. Scis. (chmn., vice chmn. 1983-85, 90, Presdl. citation 1985), Wash. Rsch. Found. (bd. dirs. 1989-97). Unitarian Universalist. Home: 665 Samara Cir Fayetteville AR 72701-3035 Office: U Ark Adminstrn Bldg Fayetteville AR 72701 Office Phone: 479-575-5459. Business E-Mail: bobsmith@uark.edu.

SMITH, ROBERT W., JR., (JAY), lawyer; b. Balt., Aug. 1, 1951; BS magna cum laude, Univ. Pa., 1973; JD with honors, Univ. Md., 1977. Bar: Md. 1977. Ptnr., chair corp. and securities practice group, mem. exec. com. DLA Piper US LLP, Balt. Bd. trustees McDaniel Coll., Center Stage. Mem.: ABA, Md. State Bar Assn., Order of Coif. Office: DLA Piper US LLP 6225 Smith Ave Baltimore MD 21209-3600 Office Phone: 410-580-4266. Office Fax: 410-580-3266. Business E-Mail: jay.smith@dlapiper.com.

SMITH, ROBERTA, art critic; b. NYC; d. Thomas R. and Eleanor Smith. BA, Grinnell Coll., IA, 1969; ind. study program, Whitney Mus. Am. Art, NYC, 1969. Sr. ed. Art in America, NYC, 1976—80; art critic Village Voice, NYC, 1981—85, NY Times, 1986—. Lectr. in field; guest curator & catalogue essayist Kansas U. Spencer Mus. Art, Lawrence, Kans., 1981; contbr. Arts, Artsforum, Art in America; contbr. to various exhibition catalogues. Author: Rhapsody, 1985; co-author: NY Times Traveler's Guide to International Art Museum Exhibitions, 2005; Illustrator The Stories Huey Tells, 1997. Recipient Frank Jewett Mather award, Coll. Art Assn., 2003; grantee, Natl. Endowment for the Arts, 1975, 1980. Office: NY Times Culture Desk 229 W 43rd St New York NY 10036 Office Phone: 212-556-1345. Office Fax: 212-556-1516.

SMITH, ROBIN ERROL, pediatrician, neurologist, educator; b. Johannesburg, Gaugteng province, South Africa, Dec. 11, 1961; s. Siegmund and Shulamith Smith. MBBch, U. Witwatersrand, South Africa, 1985. Asst. prof. pediat. and neurology Albert Einstein Coll. Medicine, NYC, 2002—; attending physician Schneider Children's Hosp., New Hyde Park. Office: North Shore Long Island Health System 269-01 76th Ave New Hyde Park NY 11040 Home Phone: 516-433-3060; Office Phone: 718-470-3450. Office Fax: 718-343-5826.

SMITH, ROD, professional football player; b. May 15, 1970; Postgrad in econ. & fin., Mo. So. State Coll., postgrad in gen. bus., postgrad in mktg. & mgmt. Wide receiver Denver Broncos, 1994—. Named to NFL Pro-Bowl, 2000—01, 2005. Achievements include being a member of Super Bowl Champion Denver Broncos, 1997, 1998; being the only undrafted NFL reciever to catch over 10,000 yards. Office: Denver Broncos Football Club 13655 Broncos Pky Englewood CO 80112

SMITH, RODGER FIELD, financial executive; b. Milw., Jan. 23, 1941; s. Millard Beale and Alice Catherine (Field) S.; m. Sarah Godfrey, June 19, 1964 (dec. Dec. 1999); children: Rodger F. Jr., Scott G., Reid W. BSChemE, U. Wis., 1964, MBA in Fin. with distinction, 1965. V.p. Allis Chalmers, Milw., 1966-76; mng. dir. Greenwich (Conn.) Assocs., 1976—. Trustee Harbor Funds, Toledo, 1987—; bd. dir. Arlington Capital, London, 1992—; chair dean's adv. bd. U. Wis. Bus. Sch.; mem. Tokeneke Tax Dist. Author articles and spkr. on investing pension funds. Fund raiser United Way, Milw., 1966—76. Mem.: Tokeneke Tax Dist. 1, Bascom Hill Soc., U. Wis. Alumni Assn. (nat. bd. dir. 1994—2000), Wee Burn Country Club (fin. com.), Beta Gamma Sigma, Tau Beta Pi (chmn. trust adv. com. 1986—). Avocations: travel, golf, tennis, coin collecting/numismatics. Office: Greenwich Assocs Office Park Eight Greenwich CT 06831-5195 Office Phone: 203-629-1200. Business E-Mail: rodger@greenwich.com.

SMITH, ROGER WINSTON, retired political theory educator; b. Birmingham, Ala., July 9, 1936; s. Buford Houston and Sarah Louise (Trucks) S.; m. Martha Christin Daniels, Jan. 16, 1960; children: Louisa, David AB magna cum laude, Harvard U., 1958, postgrad. in law, 1958—59; MA in Polit. Sci., U. Calif., Berkeley, 1963, PhD in Polit. Sci., 1971. Teaching assoc. U. Calif.-Berkeley, 1965-66; asst. prof. govt. Coll. William and Mary, Williamsburg, Va., 1967-72, assoc. prof., 1972-80, prof, 1980-2001, prof. emeritus, 2001—. Sr. lectr. politics Glasgow U., 1977-78; lectr. NEH, 1988; cons. Nelson-Hall Pubs., Chgo.; mem. coun. Inst. Internat. Conf. on the Holocaust and Genocide, Jerusalem; chair acad. adv. bd., dir. genocide and human rights univ. program Zoryan Inst., Toronto; v.p. Inst. Study of Genocide, NY. Co-author, editor: Guilt: Man and Society, 1971; co-author: Genocide and the Modern Age, 1987, Genocide, vol. 2, 1991, Bearing Witness to the Holocaust, 1939-89, 1987, The Coming Age of Scarcity, 1998, Pioneers of Genocide Studies, 2002, When Will Genocide Ever End?, 2002, On the Edge of Scarcity, 2002, Race and Ethnic Relations, 15th ann. edit., 2005, Encyclopedia of Genocide and Crimes Against Humanity, 2004; editor: Genocide, 1999; contbg. editor Internet on the Holocaust and Genocide; contbr. articles to profl. jours. Served to 1st lt. U.S. Army, 1960-62, Japan Fellow NSF, 1966, College of William and Mary, 1977 Mem. Am. Polit. Sci. Assn., Internat. Assn. Genocide Scholars (co-founder, v.p., past pres.), Human Rights Watch, PETA. Democrat. Avocations: gardening, walking, opera. Home: 102 Lake Dr Williamsburg VA 23185-3113 Office: Coll William and Mary Dept Govt Williamsburg VA 23187

SMITH, ROGERS MOOD, political scientist, educator; b. Sept. 20, 1953; s. Henry Dale and Betty (Mood) Smith. BA in Polit. Sci., Mich. State U., 1974; MA, Harvard U., 1978, PhD, 1980. Asst. prof. polit. sci. Yale U., New Haven, 1980—85, assoc. prof., 1985—89, Alfred Cowles prof. govt, 1989—2001; Browne Disting. prof. polit. sci. U. Pa., Phila., 2001—. Author: Liberalism and American Constitutional Law, 1985, Citizenship Without Consent, 1985, Stories of Peoplehood, 2003, The Unsteady March, 1999, Civic Ideals, 1997; contbr. articles to profl. jours. Fellow: Am. Acad. Arts & Sci.; mem.: New Eng. Polit. Sci. Assn. (Pres.'s award 1982), Social Sci. History Assn. (Sharlin award), Orgn. Am. Historians (Curie prize), Am. Polit. Sci. Assn. (Greenstone prize, Bunche prize, Easton prize). Avocation: baseball. Office: Univ Pa Dept Political Science 208 S 37th St Philadelphia PA 19104-6215 Home Phone: 610-660-8509; Office Phone: 215-898-7662. E-mail: rogerss@sas.upenn.edu.

SMITH, ROLAND BLAIR, JR., university administrator; b. Washington, Mar. 21, 1946; s. Roland Blair and Annie Louise S.; m. Valerie Peyton, June 16, 1969; children: Rovelle Louise, Roland Blair III. BA, Bowie State U., 1969; MPA, Ind. U., 1976; EdD, Harvard U., 1988. Dir. upward bound Notre Dame (Ind.) U., 1973-83, 86-88, dir. Ctr. for Edn. Opportunity, 1980-83, assoc. prof., 1991-96, dir. urban inst., 1992-96; assoc. provost, adj. prof. edn. and sociology Rice U., Houston, 1996—. Tchg. fellow and grad. asst. Harvard U., 1983-86; exec. asst. to pres. U. Notre Dame, Notre Dame, Ind., 1988-96; 1st v.p., treas. Pvt. Industry Coun., St. Joseph Coun., Ind., 1987-91; cons. Lilly Endowment, Indpls., 1990-91; outside reviewer Nat. Ctr. Edn. Stats, Washington, 1991-92; chmn. bd. dirs. Nat. Assn. Presidential Assts. in Higher Edn., Washington, 1993-94. Contbg. author: (ency.) African- American Education, 1996. Commr. Martin Luther King Fed. Holiday Commn., Washington, 1993-94; trustee YMCA of Michiana, St. Joseph County, Ind.; bd. dirs. NRTS Corp., City of South Bend, Ind., 1993-96, Harvard Alumni Assn. Bd., Cambridge, Mass., 1995—, LifeGift Organ Donation Ctr., 2000—; bd. visitors Bowie State U., 1998-2002; mem. South Bend Elkhart Camp United Negro Coll. Fund; bd. pres. Ctr. faith and Health, 2004—. Recipient Outstanding Achievement award Bowie (Md.) State U., 1985; Named Disting. Alumnus Ind. U., South Bend, Ind., 1983, Nat. Assn. for Equal Opportunity in Higher Edn. (Bowie State U.), 1998. Mem. Am. Assn. Higher Edn. (Black caucus vice chair 1995-97, chair 1997-99, Service award 1998), Am. Conf. Acad. Deans, Phi

Delta Kappa, Kappa Alpha Psi (Achievement award 1986). Democrat. Methodist. Office: Rice U PO Box 1892 - MS #3 Houston TX 77251-1892 Home Phone: 281-997-2778; Office Phone: 713-348-5688. Business E-Mail: rbsmith@rice.edu.

SMITH, RONALD EDWARD, ophthalmologist; b. Walkersville, Md., Oct. 7, 1942; s. Harry Otto and Marjorie Lee Smith; m. Sara Gutelius Watt, Sept. 4, 1965 (div. Oct. 1977); children: Kelly, Matt; m. Suzette Edith Le Blanc, Sept. 6, 1980. BA, Johns Hopkins U., 1964, MD, 1967. Diplomate Am. Bd. Ophthalmology. Intern Johns Hopkins Hosp., Baltimore, Md., 1967—68; resident opthalmology Johns Hopkin's Hosp., Baltimore, Md., 1968—72; asst. prof. U. So. Calif., LA, 1975—78, assoc. prof., 1978—81, prof., 1981—95, prof., chmn. dept. ophthalmology, 1995—. Co-author: Intraocular Inflammation, 1980, Vitrectomy Techniques, 1983, Uveitis: A Clinical Approach, 1986. Lt. comdr. USPHS, 1973—78. Recipient gold medal, Internat. Uveitis Study Group, 1998, Light award, Braille Inst., 1998. Mem.: Am. Acad. Ophthalmology (pres. 1994—95, 1998—, chmn. found. 1998—99). Avocations: golf, skiing, tennis. Office: USC Dept Ophthalmology 2617 E Chapman No 301 Orange CA 92829

SMITH, RONALD FORREST, retired history educator; b. Boone, Iowa, Nov. 26, 1946; s. Forrest Herschel and Eila Bergling Smith; m. Patricia Ann Pietraszek, Apr. 16, 1983; children: Rebecca Ann, Justin Forrest. BA in Polit. Sci., North Ctrl. Coll., Naperville, Ill., 1968; MA in Polit. Sci., U. Ill., Urbana, 1969. History tchr. Chgo. Bd. Edn., 1969—2004; ret., 2004. Owner, dir. Day Camp, Chgo., 1972—78; treas. West Suburban Montessori Sch., Oak Pk., Ill., 1988—90. Author: (book) Man's Inhumanity to Man, 1979, Organized Labor, 1980. Del. Chgo. Tchrs. Union, 1989—2004; corp. sec., bd. mem. United Credit Union, Chgo., 1992—2006. Presbyterian. Avocations: golf, cooking, reading, movies. Home: 536 Selborne Rd Riverside IL 60546

SMITH, RONALD G., music educator; b. Apr. 13, 1954; AB in Music Edn., Marshall U., Huntington, W.Va., 1976; MusM in Music Edn., Ithaca Coll., NY, 1978; D in Musical Arts in Trombone Performance, La. State U., Baton Rouge, 1992. Cert. tchr. NY, 1978. Music tchr. Huntington Christian Acad., 1978—80; music prof., chmn. dept. Pensacola Christian Coll., Fla., 1980—2006; music prof. Piedmont Bapt. Coll., Winston-Salem, NC, 2006—. Presenter in field. Named Tchr. of Yr., Pensacola Christian Coll., 1993. Mem.: Music Educators Nat. Conf., Internat. Trombone Assn. Home: 678 N Payne Rd Winston Salem NC 27127

SMITH, R(ONALD) SCOTT, lawyer; b. Washington, June 30, 1947; s. Joseph Peter Smith and Roberta Ann (Bailey) George; m. Cheryle Rae Coffman, Nov. 15, 1974 (div. July 1977); m. Gloria Jean Haralson, Nov. 30, 1985. BJ, U. Mo., 1970, JD, 1973. Bar: Mo. 1973, US Dist. Ct. (we. dist.) Mo. 1973, US Ct. Appeals (10th cir.) 1990, US Ct. Appeals (8th cir.) 1992, US Dist. Ct. (ea. dist.) Mo. 1996. Field dir. The Mo. Bar, Jefferson City, 1973-75; law clk. to judge Mo. Ct. Appeals (we. dist.), 1975-76; ptnr. Shirkey, Norton & Smith, Kansas City, 1976-77, Jackson & Sherman, P.C. and predecessors, Kansas City, 1977-84, Birmingham & Furry, Kansas City, 1984, Birmingham, Furry & Smith, 1985-92, Birmingham, Furry, Smith & Stubbs, 1992-95, Furry & Smith, P.C., Kansas City, 1996—. Author: (with others) Automobile Accident Handbook, 1984, rev., 1986, Vexatious Refusal and Bad Faith, 1990, Insurance Claims, 1993; editor: The Rights & Responsibilies of Citizenship in a Free Society, 1974, Due Process of Law, 1974, News Headnotes, 1976-84, Young Lawyer, 1977-80; mem. editorial bd. Mo. Bar Jour., 1978-81; (TV series) legal script advisor Lex Singularis, 1973-75; (multimedia) producer, author Freedoms Lost, 1976; producer, playwright (musical-comedy play) Silly in Philly, 1987. Mem. ABA (mem. various coms.), Mo. Bar Assn. (dist. 12 chmn. 1979—, mem. various coms., Disting. Svc. award young lawyers sect. 1978, 79, 80), West Mo. Def. Lawyers Assn., Kansas City Met. Bar Assn. (pres. young lawyers sect. 1981-82, mem. various coms., Disting. Svc. award young lawyers sect. 1982, Leadership award sr. sect. 1985, First Ann. Pres. award sr. sect. 1987), Kansas City Claim Assn., Phi Delta Phi. Democrat. Roman Catholic. Home: 3411 Shady Bend Dr Independence MO 64052-2816 Office Phone: 816-252-0577. Business E-Mail: ssmith@furrysmithlaw.com.

SMITH, RONALD THOMAS, environmental scientist; b. Palmerton, Pa., Feb. 17, 1952; s. Albert Hubert and Jeanne Alice (Kemmerle) S.; m. Jeri Lee Hammond, June 21, 1997; children: Clara Lucy, Curran Troy. BA in English, U. Notre Dame, 1974; MS in Environ. Sci., Ind. U., 1983. Chemist City of Bloomington (Ind.), 1984-91; rsch. sci. Ind. Geol. Survey, Bloomington, 1994—. Sci. advisor and activist McRae & McRae Attys., Bloomington, 1987, People Against the Incinerator, 1988-92, Thousands of People, 1983-87. Environ. activist Citizens Clearinghouse on Hazardous Waste, Arlington, Va., 1987; founder Ind. Voters Party, 1991; pro se litigant Schalk & Smith vs. Lee Thomas, U.S. Ct. Appeals (7th cir.), 1990. Notre Dame scholar, 1970-74; recipient Giraffe Award for Pub. Svc., Giraffe Soc. Am., Everett, Wash., 1992. Mem.: AAAS, Pi Alpha Alpha. Avocations: writing, music, politics, outdoors activities. Office: Ind U Ind Geol Survey 611 N Walnut Grv # S427 Bloomington IN 47405-2208

SMITH, ROWLAND JAMES, educational administrator; b. Johannesburg, Aug. 19, 1938; s. John James and Gladys Spencer (Coldrey) S.; m. Catherine Anne Lane, Sept. 22, 1962; children: Russell Claude, Belinda Claire. BA, U. Natal, 1959, PhD, 1967; MA, Oxford U., Eng., 1967. Lectr. English U. Witwatersrand, Johannesburg, 1963-67; asst. prof. Dalhousie U., Halifax, N.S., Canada, 1967-70, assoc. prof. English, 1970-77, prof., 1977-88, McCulloch prof., 1988-94, chmn. English dept., 1977-83, 85-86, dir. Centre for African Studies, 1976-77, asst. dean arts and scis., 1972-74, dean arts and social scis., 1988-93, provost Coll. Arts and Scis., 1988-89, 90-91, 92-93; vis. prof., rsch. assoc. Multidisciplinary Ctr. Can. Studies, U. Rouen, 1994; prof. Wilfrid Laurier U., Waterloo, 1994—2004, v.p. acad., 1994—2004; prof. English U. Calgary, 2004—, dean humanities, 2004—. Author: Lyric and Polemic: The Literary Personality of Roy Campbell, 1972; editor: Exile and Tradition: Studies in African and Caribbean Literature, 1976, Critical Essays on Nadine Gordimer, 1990, Postcolonizing the Commonwealth: Essays in Literature and Culture, 2000. Bd. govs. Halifax Grammar Sch., 1972-74, Neptune Theatre Found., 1977-78; selection com. IODE Meml. Scholarships for N.S., 1969-71, Rhodes Scholarships N.S., 1972-74; edn. com. Victoria Gen. Hosp., 1986-90; dir. publicity and promotion N.S. Rugby Football Union, 1987-89; chair liaison com. edn. dept. N.S. U., 1990-93; book prize jury Can. Fedn. for Humanities, 1990, regional judge (Can. and the Caribbean) Commonwealth Writers Prize, 1991; chair com. on employment and ednl. equity Coun. Ont. Univs., 1996-99, chair working group on post-diploma degrees, 1999-2001; bd. dirs. Opera Ontario, 2001-04; active Coll. Univ. Consortium Coun., 2000-02; chmn. Ontario Coun. Acad. V.P., 2002-04. Recipient Transvaal Rhodes scholar, 1960; vis. fellow Dalhousie U., 1965-66, vis. scholar Ctr. Canadian Studies U. Western Sydney, Macarthur, New South Wales, 1996; Can. Council leave fellow, 1974-75, research grantee, 1977; grantee Social Scis. and Humanities Research Council of Can., 1978, internat. grantee, 1985, grantee Cultural Personalities Exchange program Assn. Canadian Studies in Australia and New Zealand, 1996, grantee Cultural Personalities Exch. Program, Assn. in Can. Studies in German Speaking Countries, 1997. Mem. Assn. Can. Univ. Tchrs. English (sec.-treas. 1968-70, profl. concern com. 1979-81), Can. Assn. for Commonwealth Lit. and Lang. Studies (exec. mem. 1989-92, pres. 1995-99), Can. Assn. Chmn. English (v.p. 1981-82, pres. 1982-83, exec. mem.-at-large 1985-86), Can. Fedn. Humanities (aid to scholarly publs. com. 1979-85, bd. dirs. 1992-94), MLA (div. chmn. 1984, mem.), Social Scis. and Humanities Rsch. Coun., Can. (chair rsch. grants adjudication com. 1994-96), Can. Rsch. Chairs Program (Coll. Reviewers 2000—), Internat. Coun. for Can. Studies (Can. scholarship and fellowship selection com. 2003-07), Can. Fedn. for the Humanities and Social Scis. (aid to scholarly publs. com. 2004—), Dept. Fgn. Affairs and Internat. Trade (Internat. Scholarships Programs Selection com. 2003-07), Can. Network for Japanese Studies, Prince Takamodo Japan Can. Meml. Fund (mgmt. com. 2007-). Office: Office Dean Humanities Univ Calgary Calgary AB Canada T2N 1N4 Home Phone: 403-283-3504; Office Phone: 403-220-2272. Business E-Mail: rowsmith@ucalgary.ca.

SMITH, ROY (R. SMITH), lawyer; b. 1958; m. Donna Lee Shira, Sept. 9, 1989. AB cum laude, Princeton U., 1980; JD, Columbia U., 1983. Bar: NY 1984. Assoc. Cahill, Gordon & Reindell, 1983—92; atty. Am. Cyanamid Co., 1992—94; sr. atty. Cytec Industries, Inc., West Paterson, NJ, 1994—98, asst. gen. counsel, 1998—2001, v.p., gen. counsel, sec., 2002—. Editor: Columbia Law Review. Office: Cytec Industries Inc Five Garret Mountain Plz West Paterson NJ 07424 Office Phone: 973-357-3100. Office Fax: 973-357-3058. *

SMITH, ROY PHILIP, judge; b. SI, NY, Dec. 29, 1933; s. Philip Aloysius and Virginia (Collins) S.; m. Elizabeth Helen Wink, Jan. 23, 1965; children: Matthew P., Jean E. BA, St. Joseph's Coll., Yonkers, NY, 1956; JD, Fordham U., 1965. Bar: NY. Asst. reg. counsel FAA, NYC, 1966-79; adminstrv. law judge U.S. Dept. Labor, Washington, 1979-83; adminstrv. appeals judge Benefits Rev. Bd., Washington, 1983—, chmn., chief adminstrv. appeals judge, 1988-90. Adj. prof. aviation law Dowling Coll., Oakdale, N.Y., 1972-79; adj. prof. transp. law Adelphi U., Garden City, N.Y., 1975-79; vis. prof. Georgetown U. Law Sch., 1989—. With US Army, 1957—59. Mem.: Fed. Adminstrv. Law Judges Conf. (treas. 1983—84, exec. com. 1982—83), Assn. Bar of City of N.Y. (sec.-treas. aeronautics com. 1978—79), Georgetown U. Libr. Assocs., Friendly Sons of St. Patrick, Edgemoor Club. Avocation: tennis. Home: 6700 Pawtucket Rd Bethesda MD 20817-4836 Office: Benefits Rev Bd 200 Constitution Ave NW Washington DC 20210-0001 Business E-Mail: smith-roy@dol.gov.

SMITH, RUSSELL JACK, diplomat, consultant; b. Jackson, Mich., July 4, 1913; s. Lee C. and Georgia L. (Weed) S.; m. Rosemary Thomson, Sept. 5, 1938; children: Stephen M., Scott T., Christopher G. AB, Miami U., Oxford, Ohio, 1937; PhD, Cornell U., 1941. Asst. instr. English Cornell U., 1937-41; instr. English Williams Coll., 1941-45; with OSS, 1945; asst. prof. English Wells Coll., 1946-47; with CIA, 1947-74, mem. bd. nat. estimates, 1957-62, dir. current intelligence, 1962-66, dep. dir. for intelligence, 1966-71; spl. asst. U.S. Embassy, New Delhi, 1971-74; rsch. cons., 1975—82. Assigned Nat. War Coll., 1951-52, U.S. rep. Brit. Joint Intelligence Com., Far East, Singapore, 1954-56. Author: John Dryden, A Study in Controversy, 1941, The Unknown CIA: My Three Decades with the Agency, 1989, The Little Red House that Jack Built, 2002, Rosemary: A Memoir, 2004, (novels) The Secret War, 1986, The Singapore Chance, 1991, Lodestone, 1993, Whirligig, 1994, Always Afternoon, 1997, Time's Prism, 2000, Downriver, 2001, The Listener, 2002, Lodestar, 2004, Winterset, 2005. Recipient Nat. Civil Svc. League award, 1971, Disting. Intelligence medal CIA, 1974. Mem. Phi Beta Kappa, Phi Delta Theta, Omicron Delta Kappa. Home: 1138 Bellview Rd Mc Lean VA 22102-1104

SMITH, RUSSELL LOUIS, lawyer; b. Atlanta, Sept. 9, 1946; s. Nathan Harry and Edith (Carfield); m. Judith Beth Lavine, June 20, 1971; 1 child, Harris Charles Smith. BA, Vanderbilt U., 1968; JD, U. Ga., 1972. Bar: D.C., 1973, U.S. Supreme Ct., 1977, U.S. Ct. Appeals, (D.C. cir.), 1978. Atty.-advisor U.S. Dept. Treasury, Washington, 1972-76; Washington counsel Consol. Rail Corp., Phila., 1976-82; dir. Office of Automotive Industry Affairs U.S. Dept. Commerce, Washington, 1982-84; minority counsel Com. on Energy and Commerce U.S. Ho. Reps., Washington, 1984-88; assoc. McNair Law Firm, Washington, 1988-89; spl. counsel Govt. Rels. Dept. Willkie Farr & Gallagher LLP, Washington, 1989—. Adj. prof. Georgetown Pub. Policy Inst., Georgetown U. Pres. Adas Israel Hebrew Congregation, Washington, 2005—07. Mem.: Met. Club. Republican. Jewish. Office: Willkie Farr & Gallagher LLP 1875 K Street, NW Washington DC 20006 Home Phone: 202-332-3020; Office Phone: 202-303-1116. Business E-Mail: rsmith@willkie.com.

SMITH, S. KINNIE, JR., lawyer; BA in Econs., Yale U., New Haven, Conn., 1953; JD, U. Wisc. Law Sch., 1956. Ptnr. Sidley & Austin, Chgo., 1964—75; gen. counsel through vice chmn., ANR subsidiary, & sr. v.p. Coastal Corp., 1975—87; pres., vice chair, gen. counsel CMS Energy, Jackson, Mich., 1988—96; counsel Skadden, Arps, Slate, Meagher & Flom, 1996—2002; vice chmn., gen. counsel CMS Energy, Jackson, Mich., 2002—06; sr. counsel Miller, Canfield, Paddock & Stone, P.L.C., Detroit, 2006—. Mem. bd. vis. Univ. Wis. Law Sch. Mem.: ABA, Mich. Bar Assn., Chgo. Bar Assn. Office: Miller Canfield Paddock & Stone Ste 2500 150 W Jefferson Detroit MI 48226-4415 Office Phone: 517-788-1671, 313-496-8477. Office Fax: 517-788-1859, 313-496-8452. E-mail: smithsk@millercanfield.com.

SMITH, SALLYE WRYE, librarian; b. Birmingham, Ala., Nov. 11, 1923; d. William Florin and Margaret (Howard) Wrye; m. Stuart Werner Smith, Sept. 20, 1947 (dec. June 1981); children: Carol Ann, Susan Patricia, Michael Christopher, Julie Lynn, Lori Kathleen. BA, U. Ala., 1945; MA, U. Denver, 1969. Psychometrician U.S. Army, Deshon Gen. Hosp., Butler, Pa., 1945-46, U.S. Vet. Adminstrn. Vocat. Guidance, U. Ala., Tuscaloosa, 1946; clin. psychologist U.S. Army, Walter Reed Gen. Hosp., Washington, 1946-47, U.S. Army, Fitzsimons Gen. Hosp., Denver, 1948, U.S. Vets. Adminstrn., Ft. Logan, Colo., 1948-50; head sci.-engring. libr. U. Denver, Colo., 1969-72; instr., reference libr. Penrose Libr., U. Denver, 1972-80, asst. prof., reference libr., 1980-90, interim dir., 1990-92, asst. prof. emerita, 1992—. Vis. prof. U. Denver Grad. Sch. Libr. Info. Mgmt., 1975-77, 83; info. broker Colo. Rschrs., Denver, 1979—; cons., presenter Indsl. Info. Workshop Inst. Investigaciones Tecnologicas, Bogota, Colombia, 1979, LIPI-DRI-PDIN workshop on R&D mgmt., Jakarta, Indonesia, 1982; mem. BRS User Adv. Bd., Latham, NY, 1983-86. Indexer: Statistical Abstract of Colorado 1976-77, 1977. Recipient Cert. of Recognition, Sigma Xi, U. Denver chpt., 1983. Mem. ALA, Spl. Libr. Assn., Colo. Assn. Librs., Phi Beta Kappa, Beta Phi Mu. Office: Colo Researchers PO Box 22779 Denver CO 80222-0779

SMITH, SAM, columnist, writer; b. Bklyn., Jan. 24, 1948; s. Leon and Betty (Pritzker) S.; m. Kathleen Ellen Rood, Jan. 24, 1976; children: Connor, Hannah-Li. BBA in Acctg., Pace U., NYC, 1970; MA in Journalism, Ball State U., Muncie, Ind., 1974. Acct. Arthur Young & Co., NYC, 1970-72; reporter Ft. Wayne (Ind.) News Sentinal, Ft. Wayne, 1973-76, States News Svc., Washington, 1976-79; press sec. U.S. Senator Lowell Weicker Jr., 1979; writer/reporter Chgo. Tribune, 1979-90, columnist, 1991—. Commentator ESPN Radio. Author: The Jordan Rules, 1991, Second Coming, 1995; co-author: Total Basketball Encyclopedia, 2004, The Perfect Team, 2006; columnist: Hoop Japan msnbc.com; contbr. to publs. With USAR, 1970-76. Named Ball State U. Journalism Alumnus of Yr.; named to Ball State U. Journalism Hall of Fame, 2002; recipient Journalism awards, AP, UPI, Sigma Delta Chi, Sports Local Emmy award, WGN-TV. Mem.: Basketball Writers Assn. (pres. 1998—2005). Office: Chicago Tribune 435 N Michigan Ave Chicago IL 60611-4066 Office Phone: 312-222-5445. Business E-Mail: sasmith@tribune.com.

SMITH, SCOTT A., lawyer; b. Grand Forks, ND, July 17, 1957; married. BA, Stanford U., 1978; JD, U. Calif., Berkeley, 1981. Bar: Wash. 1981, U.S. Ct. Appeals (9th cir) 1982, U.S. Dist. Ct. (Ea. and We. dists.) Wash. Law clk. to Hon. Jerome Farris 9th Cir. U.S. Ct. of Appeals, 1981—82; assoc. Preston, Gates & Ellis, Seattle, 1982—88; ptnr. Short, Cressman & Burgess, Seattle, 1988—2004; prin. Riddell Williams, Seattle, 2004—. Chair Wash. State Access to Justice Bd., Seattle, 2002—04. Recipient Pro Bono award, Wash. State Bar Assn., Allies for Justice award, LEGALS of Wash. Fellow: Am. Bar Found.; mem.: King County Bar Assn. (pres. 1996—97, trustee 1991—97, Helen Geisness award Exemplary Svc.). Office: Riddell Williams Ste 4500 1001 Fourth Ave Plaza Seattle WA 98154 Business E-Mail: SSmith@riddellwilliams.com.

SMITH, SCOTT C., lawyer, legal association administrator; b. Atlanta, Apr. 26, 1960; BA cum laude, Wake Forest U., 1982; JD magna cum laude, Mercer U., 1985. Bar: Ga. 1985. V.p., corp. counsel Genuine Parts Co., Atlanta. Mng. editor Mercer U. Law Rev., 1984-85, mem., 1983-85; contbr. articles to law jours. Capt. U.S. Army, 1985-89. Mem. State Bar Ga., Brainerd Currie Honor Soc., Phi Kappa Phi Office: 2999 Circle 75 Pkwy Atlanta GA 30339-3050 *

SMITH, SCOTT CLYBOURN, publishing executive; b. Evanston, Ill., Sept. 13, 1950; s. E. Sawyer and Jerolanne (Jones) S.; m. Martha Reilly, June 22, 1974; children: Carolyn Baldwin, Thomas Clybourn. BA, Yale U., 1973; M.Mgmt., Northwestern U., 1976. With Northern Trust Co., Chgo., 1973-77, Tribune Co., Chgo., 1977—93, sr. v.p., chief fin. officer, 1989-91, sr. v.p. for devel., 1991-93; pres., pub., CEO Sun Sentinel Co., Ft. Lauderdale, Fla., 1993-97, Chgo. Tribune Co., 1997—2004, interim pres., pub., CEO, 2006—; pres. Tribune Publishing, 2005—. Bd. dirs. McCormick Tribune Found., Chgo. Pub. Edn. Fund, Northwestern Meml. Healthcare, Chgo. Symphony Orch., Nat.-Louis U. Mem.: Newspaper Assn. Am. (chmn. pub. policy com.). Episcopalian. Office: Tribune Co 435 N Michigan Ave Chicago IL 60611-4066 *

SMITH, SELMA MOIDEL, lawyer, composer; b. Warren, Ohio, Apr. 3, 1919; d. Louis and Mary (Oyer) Moidel; 1 child, Mark Lee. Student, UCLA, 1936-39, U. So. Calif. Law School, 1939-41; JD, Pacific Coast U., 1942. Bar: Calif. 1943, U.S. Dist. Ct. 1943, U.S. Supreme Ct. 1958. Gen. practice law; mem. firm Moidel, Moidel, Moidel & Smith, 1943—. Field dir. civilian adv. com. WAC, 1943—45; charter mem. nat. bd. Med. Coll. Pa. (formerly Woman's Med. Coll. Pa.), 1953—, mem. exec. bd., 1976—80, pres., 1980—82, chmn, past pres. com., 1990—92, spkr., honoree 50th anniversary gala, 2003. Author: A Century of Achievement: The National Association of Women Lawyers, 1998, The First Women Members of the ABA, 1999; composer: Espressivo-Four Piano Pieces (orchestral premiere, 1987, performance Nat. Mus. Women in the Arts, 1989), numerous works. Decorated La Orden del Merito Juan Pablo Duarte (Dominican Republic), 1956. Fellow Am. Bar Found. (life); mem. ASCAP, ABA (jr. bar. conf., 1946-52, activities com., 1948-49), Sr. Lawyers divsn. ABA (vice-chair editl. bd. Experience mag. 1997-99, chair arts com. 1998-99, chair editl. bd. Experience Mag. 1999-2001, exec. coun. 1999-2003, Experience mag. adv. bd. 2001—, nominating com. 2003-04, co-chair newsletter 2003-04, chair 2004-05, asst. sec., 2005—, Dist. Svc. award 2003-05), Calif. Supreme Ct. Hist. Soc. (bd. dirs. 2001—, programs and pubs. com., 2004—, State Bar program coord., 2006, founding chair writing competition, 2007), Assn. Learning in Retirement Orgns. in West (pres. 1993-94, exec. com. 1994-95, Disting. Svc. award 1995), Plato Soc. UCLA (discussion leader Constitution Bicentennial Project 1985-87, moderator extension lecture series 1990, Toga editor 1990-93, sec. 1991-92, chmn. colloquium com. 1992-93, Exceptional Leadership award 1994), Euterpe Opera Club (chair auditions 1972, chair awards 1973-75, v.p. 1974-75), Docents L.A. Philharm. (press and pub. rels. 1972-75, cons. coord. 1973-75, v.p. 1973-83, chair Latin Am. Cmty. Rels., Recognition and Honor award, 1978), Calif. Fedn. Music Clubs (chair Am. music 1971-75, conv. chair 1972), Nat. Fedn. Music Clubs (vice-chair Western region 1973-78), Nat. Assn. Composers USA (dir. 1974-79, luncheon chair 1975), Calif. Pres. Coun. (1st v.p.), L.A. Bus. Women's Coun. (pres. 1952), Calif. Bus. Women's Coun. (dir. 1951), Coun. Bar Assns. L.A. County (charter sec. 1950), Inter-Am. Bar Assn., League of Ams. (dir.), Nat. Assn. Women Lawyers (regional dir. western states, Hawaii 1949-51, jud. adminstrn. com. 1960, nat. chair world peace through law com. 1966-67, liaison to ABA Sr. Lawyers Divsn. 1996—, chair bd. elections 1997-98, centennial com. 1997-99, chair com. unauthorized practice of law, social commn. UN, Lifetime Svc. award 1999, honoree annual Selma Moidel Smith law student writing competition 2005—), L.A. Lawyers Club (pub. defenders com. 1951), L.A. Bar Assn. (servicemen's legal aid com. 1944-45, psychopathic ct. com. 1948-53, Outstanding Svc. award 1993), State Bar Calif. (conf. com. on unauthorized practice of medicine 1964, Disting. Svc. award 1993), Women Lawyers Assn. LA (formerly So. Calif. Women Lawyers Assn.)(hon life; pres., 1947, 48, chair law day com. 1966, subject of oral hist. project 1986, 2001), Iota Tau Tau Legal Scholastic Soc. (1st prize 1942, dean L.A. 1947, supreme treas. 1959-62). Home: 5272 Lindley Ave Encino CA 91316-3518

SMITH, SHARMAN BRIDGES, state librarian; b. Lambert, Miss. BS, Miss. U. for Women, Columbus, 1972; MLS, George Peabody Coll., Nashville, 1975. Head libr. Clinton (Miss.) Pub. Libr., 1972-74; asst. dir. Lincoln-Lawrence-Franklin Regional Libr., Brookhaven, Miss., 1975-77, dir., 1977-78; info. svcs. mgr. Miss. Libr. Commn., Jackson, 1978-87, asst. dir. libr. ops., 1987-89, dir. libr. svcs. div., 1989-92; state libr. State Libr. Iowa, Des Moines, 1992—2001; exec. dir. Miss. Libr. Commn., Jackson, Miss., 2001—. Recipient Friend of Edn. award, Iowa Computer Using Educators, 1995, Mem. of Yr. award, Iowa Libr. Assn., 1996. Office: Miss Libr Commn 3881 Eastwood Dr Jackson MS 39211 Office Phone: 601-432-4039. Business E-Mail: sharman@mlc.lib.ms.us.

SMITH, SHARON LOUISE, lawyer, consultant; b. Williamsport, Pa., Apr. 21, 1949; d. Stuart Mallory and Phyllis Virginia (Hartzell) S. Student, Schiller Coll., Heidelberg, Fed. Republic Germany, 1969-70; AB, Grove City Coll., Pa., 1971; MA, Kent State U., Ohio, 1973; JD, Temple U., Phila., 1978. Bar: Pa. 1978, US Dist. Ct. (we. dist.) Pa. 1980, US Ct. Appeals (3rd cir.) 1992. Assoc. Laurel Legal Services, Brookville, Pa., 1980-82; pvt. practice Brookville, 1982—. Cons. Prothonotary, Brookville, 1984-86. Multidisciplinary team for child abuse Jefferson County Child Welfare Dept., Brookville, 1985; bd. dirs. Clarion-Jefferson Cmty. Action, Brookville, 1982, Clearfield-Jefferson Drug and Alcohol Commn., DuBois, Pa., 1983-84, Jefferson County Hist. Soc., 2005-06. Mem. Pa. Bar Assn., Law Alumnae Assn. Temple U., Jefferson County Hist. Soc. Presbyterian. Avocations: swimming, reading. Home: 172 Franklin Ave Brookville PA 15825-1164 Office: 197 Main St Brookville PA 15825 Office Phone: 814-849-6700. Personal E-mail: slsmith1@alltel.net.

SMITH, SHEILA MARIE, lawyer; b. Chgo. d. Donald Thomas and Catherine Ellen (Mariga) Morrison; m. Melvin Smith, Nov. 11, 1989. BSEE, Purdue U., 1981; JD, U. Cin., 1995. Bar: Ohio 1995, U.S. Dist. Ct. (so. dist.) Ohio 1996, U.S. Ct. Appeals (6th cir.) 1996, U.S. Supreme Ct., 1999. Mfg. engr., 1981-92; assoc. Freking & Betz, Cin., 1995-99, ptnr., 2000—. Spkr. in field. Named to Order of Coif U. Cin., 1995. Mem. ABA, Am. Trial Lawyers Assn., Nat. Employment Lawyers Assn., Ohio Employment Lawyers Assn., Cin. Employment Lawyers Assn., Ohio Bar Assn., Cin. Bar Assn. Avocations: golf, travel, cooking. Home: 3345 Legendary Trails Dr Cincinnati OH 45245-3074 Office: Freking & Betz 525 Vine St 6th Fl Cincinnati OH 45202-2139 Home Phone: 513-947-0359; Office Phone: 513-721-1975. E-mail: ssmith@frekingandbetz.com.

SMITH, SHERWOOD HUBBARD, JR., retired electric utilities executive; b. Jacksonville, Fla., Sept. 1, 1934; s. Sherwood Hubbard and Catherine Gertrude (Milliken) S.; m. Eva Hackney Hargrave, July 20, 1957; children: Marlin Hamilton Dohlman, Cameron Hargrave Callaway, Eva Hackney Davis. AB, U. N.C., 1956, JD, 1960; D civil laws, St.

Augustine's Coll., 1988; LDD, Campbell U., 1990; HHD, Francis Marion Coll., 1990. Bar: N.C. 1960. Assoc. Lassiter, Moore & Van Allen, Charlotte, 1960-62; ptnr. Joyner & Howison, Raleigh, 1962-65; assoc. gen. counsel Carolina Power & Light Co., Raleigh, 1965-70, sr. v.p., gen. counsel, 1971-74, exec. v.p., 1974-76, pres., 1976-92, CEO, 1979-96, chmn. bd., 1980-99, chmn. emeritus, 1999—; with Progress Energy Co., 2005—. Former dir. NorTel Network, Northwestern Mut. Life Ins. Co., Wachovia Corp., Durham Corp., Springs, Ind. Trustee Z Smith Reynolds Found., 1978-96, Nat. Humanities Ctr., 1990-93; bd. dirs. NC Citizens Bus. and Industry, chmn., 1985-86; bd. dirs. Rsch. Triangle Found. NC, NC Inst. Medicine; mem. bd. govs. Ctr. Creative Leadership; mem., chmn. Triangle Univs. Ctr. Advanced Studies, 1986—; dir. Franklin St. Ptnrs.; former chmn. bd. trustees, chmn. Rex Hosp.; gov. Boys and Girls Clubs Am. Recipient Nat. Humanitarian award Am. Lung Assn., 1993, Outstanding Leadership award in Mgmt. scis. Am. Soc. Mech. Engrs., 1983, A.E. Finley Disting. Svc. award Greater Raleigh C. of C., 1985, Disting. Citizenship award N.C. Citizens Bus. and Industry, 1997; named to N.C. Bus. Hall of Fame, 1999. Mem.: Greater Raleigh C. of C. (pres. 1979), Phi Beta Kappa. Home: 408 Drummond Dr Raleigh NC 27609-7006 Office: Progress Energy Co PO Box 1551 Raleigh NC 27602-1551

SMITH, SHIRLEY, artist; b. Wichita, Kans., Apr. 17, 1929; d. Harold Marvin and Blanche Carrie (Alexander) S. BFA, Kans. State U., Manhattan, 1951; postgrad., Provincetown Workshop, Mass., 1962-66. One-woman shows include 55 Mercer St. Gallery, NYC, 1973, Wichita Art Mus., Kanas, 1978, Stamford Mus. and Nature Ctr., Conn., 1987, Aaron Gallery, Washington, 1987, 1988, Joan Hodgell Gallery, Sarasota, Fla., 1987, Marianna Kistler Beach Mus. 38 Yr. Retrospective, Kans. State U., 1999—2000, John Jay Gallery, NYC, 2000, Represented in permanent collections Whitney Mus. Am. Art, Phoenix Art Mus., The Aldrich Mus. Contemporary Art, Ridgefield, Conn., Ulrich Mus., Wichita State U., Kans., Everson Mus., Syracuse, NY, U. Calif. Berkeley Art Mus., Marianna Kistler Beach Mus., Kans. State U., Manhattan, Telfair Mus. of Art, Savannah, Ga. Recipient Grumbacher Cash award for mixed media New Eng. Exhbn., Silvermine, Conn., 1967, Acad. Inst. award Am. Acad. Arts and Letters, NYC, 1991, Richard Florsheim Art Funds grantee, 1998, Retrospective Opening grantee, 1999. Mem. Artist Equity. Democrat. Presbyterian. Home: 141 Wooster St New York NY 10012-3163

SMITH, SHIRLEY A., state legislator, state representative; b. 1950; 2 children. AA, Cuyahoga CC; BA, Cleve. State U. Rep. Ohio State Ho. Reps., Columbus, 1998—. Mem. banking, pensions and securities com. Ohio State Ho. Reps., mem. juvenile and family law com., mem. fin. instns., real estate and securities com., ranking minority mem. health com., mem. joint legis. com. on health care oversight. Vice chair Ohio Women's Dem. Caucus; chair region IX exec. com. Nat. Black Caucus of State Legislators; sec. Ohio Legis. Black Caucus; active Cuyahoga County Dem. Del. Mem.: NOW, Ohio Legis. Women's Caucus, Nat. Black Caucus of State Legis., Women in Govt., Emily's List. Democrat. Office: Ohio State House Reps 77 South High Street 10th Floor Columbus OH 43215-6111

SMITH, SIBLEY JUDSON, JR., historic site administrator, educator; b. Alexandria, La., June 26, 1955; s. Sibley Judson and Eunice Lee (Raulins) S.; children: Jacob Lee, Casey Raulins. Student, N.E. La. U., 1973-76; BA in History magna cum laude, Christopher Newport Coll., 1985; MA in Am. Studies, Coll. of William and Mary, 1992. Mus. interpreter Colonial Williamsburg (Va.) Found., 1979-87; coord. of interpretation Hist. Hudson Valley, Inc., Tarrytown, NY, 1987-88; historic site mgr. Philipse Manor Hall State Hist. Site, Yonkers, NY, 1988-91; exec. dir. Hist. Allaire (N.J.) Village, Inc., 1991-97; dir. edn. Vietnam Era Ednl. Ctr., N.J. Vietnam Vets. Meml. N.J. Dept. Mil. and Vet. Affairs, Holmdel, 1997—. Mem. Alpha Chi, Alpha Psi Omega. Avocations: gardening, theater, movies, mus. Office: Vietnam Era Ednl Ctr 1 Memorial Ln PO Box 648 Holmdel NJ 07733-0648 Office Phone: 800-648-8387. Business E-Mail: sjsmith2@njvvmf.org.

SMITH, SIDNEY OSLIN, JR., lawyer; b. Gainesville, Ga., Dec. 30, 1923; s. Sidney Oslin and Isabelle Caroline (Charters) S.; m. Patricia Irwin Horkan, Aug. 4, 1944 (dec. Oct. 19, 2001); children— Charters Smith Wilson, Ellen Smith Andersen, Sidney Oslin III; m. Carolyn S. Reed, Nov. 29, 2004. AB cum laude, Harvard Coll., 1947; LL.B. summa cum laude, U. Ga., 1949. Bar: Ga. 1948. Ptnr. Telford, Wayne & Smith, Gainesville, Ga., 1949-62; asst. solicitor Superior Cts., Northeastern Jud. Cir. Ga., 1951-61, judge, 1962-65, U.S. Dist. Ct. (no. dist.) Ga., 1965-68, chief judge, 1968-74; ptnr. Alston, Miller & Gaines, Atlanta, 1974-82, Alston & Bird, Atlanta, 1982-94, of counsel, 1994—. Chmn. Gainesville Bd. Edn., 1959-62; trustee Brenau Coll., Gainesville, 1974—, chmn., 1976-84; mem. state bd. regents Univ. System of Ga., 1980-87, chmn., 1984-85. Served to capt. U.S. Army, 1943-46, ETO. Fellow ABA, Am. Coll. Trial Lawyers; mem. Am. Law Inst., Am. Judicature Soc., Commerce Club, Chattahoochee Club, Phi Beta Kappa, Phi Kappa Phi, Phi Delta Phi, Phi Delta Theta. Republican. Episcopalian. Home: 3206 Club Pointe Way Gainesville GA 30506-1638 Office: Alston & Bird 1 Atlantic Ctr Atlanta GA 30309-3400 E-mail: smit977@bellsouth.net.

SMITH, SIDNEY RUFUS, JR., linguist, educator; b. Greensboro, NC, Sept. 18, 1931; s. Sidney Rufus and Page (Johnston) S.; m. Vera Pautzsch, Apr. 19, 1969 (div. 1975); children: Stephanie Alice, Eric Brian. BA, Duke U., 1953; PhD, U. N.C., 1965. Asst. prof. U. Conn., Storrs, 1965-66, U. N.C., Chapel Hill, 1966-71, assoc. prof., 1971-79, prof., 1979—, chmn. Germanic langs., 1979-89, 94-97, chmn. linguistics, 1981-84, prof. emeritus, 1997—. Author numerous articles for profl. pubs. Local troop leader Girl Scouts U.S.A. Served to sgt. AUS, 1953-56. Recipient Stephen Freeman award N.E. Conf. Teaching Langs., 1969, cert. of merit Goethe Inst., 1997. Mem.: Am. Assn. Tchrs. German, Soc. Advancement Scandinavian Study. Democrat. Office: U NC Dept Germanic Langs Chapel Hill NC 27599-0001 Business E-Mail: srsmith@email.unc.edu. E-mail: srsmith@mindspring.com.

SMITH, SPENCER BAILEY, engineering and business educator; b. Ottawa, Ont., Can., Jan. 31, 1927; s. Sidney B. and Etta (Bailey) S.; m. Mildred E. Spidell, Dec. 31, 1954 B in Engring., McGill U., 1949; MS, Columbia U., 1950, DSc in Engring., 1958. Adminstrv. engr. Mergenthaler Linotype Co., NYC, 1953-58; ops. research mgr. Raytheon Co., Newton, Mass., 1958-61; ops research mgr. Montgomery Ward & Co., Chgo., 1961-66; assoc. prof., then prof. Ill. Inst. Tech., 1966-96, prof. emeritus, 1996—, chmn. dept. indsl. and systems engring., 1971-77, dir. Stuart Sch. Office of Research, 1977-82. Tchr. TV courses Nat. Tech. U. Author: Computer-Based Production and Inventory Control, 1989; contbr. articles to profl. jours.; patentee on order quantity calculator, 1964. Vol. cons. on sch. redistricting Elem. Sch. Dist., Evanston, Ill., 1972-74 Research grantee Harris Trust and Savs. Bank, 1968-70, Ill. Law Enforcement Commn., 1972-74, U.S. Army C.E., 1981, Am. Prodn. and Inventory Control Soc., 1980 Mem. INFORMS, ASME, Inst. Indsl. Engrs., Univ. Club (Chgo.). Presbyterian. Home: 2530 Lawndale Ave Evanston IL 60201-1158 E-mail: montrosemillennium@comcast.net.

SMITH, SPENCER THOMAS, lawyer; b. NYC, May 3, 1943; s. Spencer H. and Marie K. (Walter) S.; m. Jenny Matilda Anderson, Aug. 15, 1965; children: S. Anders, J. Kirsten. BME, Cooper Union Sch. Engring., 1965; JD, Am. U., 1968. Bar: N.Y. 1969, U.S. Dist. Ct. (ea. and so. dists.) N.Y. 1971, U.S. Ct. Appeals (fed. cir.) 1983. Assoc. Nolte & Nolte, NYC, 1968-70, Nims, Halliday, Whitman, Howes, Collison & Isner, 1970-72; group patent and licensing counsel Litton Industries, Inc., Hartford, 1984-85; sole practice Hartford, 1984-85; sr. group patent atty. Emhart Copr., Farmington, Conn., 1985-89, Black & Decker Corp., Towson, Md., 1989-98; legal counsel Emhart Glass, Enfield, Conn., 1998. Author: Primarily Merely, 1973, Italian System Works Well to Resolve Disputes, 1997. Coach basketball program Farmington Valley YMCA, Simsbury, Conn., 1976-80, Simsbury Youth Soccer Assn., 1976-86. Mem. Licensing Execs. Soc., Greater Hartford C. of C. (mem. high tech. continuing edn. task force 1981-89). Republican. Methodist. Home: 53 Silver Brook Ln North Granby CT 06060-1111 Office: Emhart Glass Rsch Inc 89 Phoenix Ave PO Box 1229 Enfield CT 06082

SMITH, STAN VLADIMIR, economist, finance company executive; b. Rhinelander, Wis., Nov. 16, 1946; s. Valy Zdenek and Sylvia Smith; children: Cara, David. BS in Ops. Research, Cornell U., 1968; MBA, U. Chgo., 1972, PhD in Econs., 1997. Diplomate Am. Bd. Disability Analysts. Lectr. U. Chgo., 1973; economist bd. govs. Fed. Res. System, Washington, 1973-74; staff economist First Nat. Bank of Chgo., 1974; assoc. December Group, Chgo., 1974-77; founding pres. Seaquest Internat., Chgo., 1977-85; mgr., ptnr. Ibbotson Assocs., Chgo., 1981-85; pres. Smith Econ. Group Ltd. divsn. Corp. Fin. Group, Chgo., 1985—. Expert econ. witness in field; adj. prof. DePaul U. Coll. Law, Chgo., 1990. Author: Economic/Hedonic Damages, 1990; founding editor Stocks, Bonds, Bills and Inflation yearbook, 1983-01; editor Jour. Forensic Econs., 1990-01; contbr. articles in field. Founder, exec. dir. Inst. for Value of Life, 1996. Fellow Allied Chem., 1967, John McMullen Trust, 1969; grantee Ford Found., 1972, U.S. Fed. Res., 1973. Fellow: Am. Coll. Forensic Examiners (bd. cert. 1996—); mem.: Soc. Litig. Economists (bd. govs. 1999—), Acad. Econ. and Fin. Experts, Am. Bd. Forensic Examiners, Nat. Future Assn. (arbitrator), Am. Arbitration Assn. (arbitrator 1994—96), Nat. Acad. Econ. Arbitrators (founder 1989—), Nat. Assn. Forensic Econs. (v.p. 2000—03), Am. Fin. Assn., Am. Econ. Assn., Alpha Delta Phi. Office: Smith Econ Group Ltd Ste 600 1165 N Clark St Chicago IL 60610-7861 Office Phone: 312-943-1551. Business E-Mail: stan@smitheconomics.com.

SMITH, STANLEY ROGER, retired professional tennis player; b. Pasadena, Calif., Dec. 14, 1946; s. Charles Kenneth and Rhoda (Widmer) S.; m. Marjory Logan Gengler, Nov. 23, 1974; children: Ramsey Gengler, Trevor Austin, Logan Widmer, Austin Church. BA, U. So. Calif., 1969; L.H.D., Greenville Coll., 1974, Winthrop Coll., NC. Profl. tennis player, 1968—; mem. U.S. Davis Cup Team, 1968-79, 81; adviser Pres.'s Council on Phys. Fitness, 1971-75; chmn. Stan Smith Design, Inc.; dir. coaching USTA. Cons. Sea Pines Plantations, 1971—, Adidas, Landersheim, France, 1971—, Fischer G.m.b.H., Austria, 1980-86, Prince Adv. Staff, 1986—; bd. dirs. Hilton Head br. Citizens & So. Nat. Bank S.C. Writer: nationally syndicated newspaper column Stan Smith's Tennis Tips, 1971—; Author: Inside Tennis, 1974, Stan Smith's Six Tennis Basics, 1974, The Executive Tennis Diary 1975, 1974, Stan Smith's Guide to Better Tennis, 1975, (with Bob Lutz) Modern Doubles, 1975, It's More Than Just a Game, 1977; also video with Arthur Ashe, Vic Braden: Tennis Our Way. Bd. dirs. Greater Los Angeles Big Bros. Am., 1966-71; hon. tennis chmn. Duke's Children's Classic, 1982—; hon. chmn. Am. Festival Fitness and Sport, 1987. Served with AUS, 1970-72. Decorated D.S.M.; named Martini and Rossi Player of Year, 1971, 72; holder 26 U.S. singles and doubles titles, including U.S. Open singles, 1971, U.S. Open doubles, 1968, 74, 78, 80; ranked number one in U.S. doubles, 1968, 69, 1970, 71, 72, 74; number one in U.S. singles, 1969, 71, 72, 73; winner Wimbledon singles title, 1972, 6 World championship tennis titles in 1973, including; World Championship of Tennis Finals in singles, also; Rothman's World Doubles title; ranked world's number one tennis player, 1972, 73; Lebair Sportsmanship Trophy, 1969; Johnston Sportsmanship Trophy, 1968; champion 35 & Over Cir. Singles and Doubles Championships, 1982, 84, 86; named to U.S. Collegiate Hall of Fame, 1984, to Carolina Tennis Hall of Fame, 1986, to Internat. Hall of Fame, 1987. Mem. Assn. Tennis Profls. (dir. 1972-79, 81-83), Men's Internat. Profl. Tennis Council, Athletes in Action, Beta Theta Pi. Clubs: Sea Pines Plantation, Los Angeles Tennis, All England, West Side Tennis, No. Century XXI, Balboa Bay. Republican. Presbyterian. *God has given me certain talents. I feel a great opportunity and responsibility to develop and use these talents to their fullest on and off the tennis courts. I see great potential in our country and especially in our youth today, and I hope to provide some leadership and direction that this youth will need to develop their potential constructively. God has given me a great life so far and I plan to rely on His guidance to take me the rest of the way.*

SMITH, STANTON KINNIE, JR., lawyer; b. Rockford, Ill., Feb. 14, 1931; s. Stanton Kinnie Smith and Elizabeth (Brown) Stanton; m. Mary Beth Sanders, July 11, 1953; children: Stanton E., Kathryn A., Dana. BA, Yale U., 1953; JD, U. Wis., 1956. Bar: Ill. 1956, Mich. 1976. Ptnr. Sidley & Austin Law, Chgo., 1964—84; vice chmn., gen. counsel Am. Natural Resources Co., Detroit, 1975—87; sr. v.p. The Coastal Corp., Houston, 1985—87; vice chmn., gen. counsel CMS Energy Corp., Jackson, Mich., 1987—88, pres., 1988—92, vice chmn., 1992—96, vice chmn., bd. dirs., 2002—05; sr. spl. counsel Skadden, Arps, Slate, Meagher & Flom, NYC, 1996—2002; vice chmn. Trans-Elect, Inc., 2002. Bd. dirs. Clarcor Corp., Mich. Natural Corp., Mich. Nat. Bank. Trustee Founders Soc., Detroit Inst. Arts, Rockford Coll.; devel. bd. mem. Yale U.; trustee Mich. Opera Theatre; bd. advisors U. Wis. Law Sch., Mich. State U., Pub. Utility Inst. Mem.: ABA, Chgo. Bar Assn., Mich. Bar Assn. Office: CMS Energy Corp One Energy Plaza Jackson MI 49201 Business E-Mail: sksmith@cmsenergy.com.

SMITH, STEPHANIE RENAE, middle school educator; b. Atlanta, Apr. 25, 1969; d. Jasper and Dianna H. Smith; 1 child, Kare K. Greene. BS, Tuskegee U., Ala., 1993; MA, Ctrl. Mich. U., Mount Pleasant, 2002; EdS, Argosy U., Sarasota, Fla., 2003, EdD, 2006. Cert. tchr., gifted edn. and reading tchr. Ga. Tchr. grad. sci. lab. Atlanta Pub. Sch. Sys., 1997—99, 8th grade phys. sci. tchr., 1999—2004, after sch. tutor, 2000—, 8th grade earth sci. tchr., 2003—04, tutor 21st century aftersch. program, 2004—05, gifted/challenged tchr. L. Judson Price Mid. Sch., 2004—. Mem. exec. bd. Worthy's Christian Acad.; active sci. instr. Antioch Bapt. Ch. North, Atlanta, tchr. Adult Christian Class. Named Tchr. of Yr., W. L. Parks Mid. Sch., Atlanta, 2001—02. Mem.: NSTA, Ga. Assn. Gifted, Argosy U. Alumni Assn., Central Mich. Alumni Assn., Tuskegee Alumni Assn., Hall of Tolerance, Stopping Hate, Sheriff Assn. Home: 2805 Amber Forest Dr Douglasville GA 30135-7306 Office Phone: 770-842-2291. Personal E-mail: ksrs69@aol.com.

SMITH, STEPHEN ALLEN, mathematician, educator; s. William Francis and Gertrude Elizabeth Smith; m. Karen Ann Jensen, Apr. 27, 2002; children: Gregory, Daniel. BS in Math., U. Cin., 1965; MS in Math., Stevens Inst. Tech., 1967; PhD in Engring.-Econ. Sys., Stanford U., 1972. Rsch. scientist Xerox Rsch. Ctr., Palo Alto, Calif., 1972—82; J.C. Penney prof. Leavey Sch. Bus. Santa Clara U., Calif., 1982—. Prin. Pricing Strategy Assocs., Berkeley, Calif., 1984—95; mem. adv. bd. Spotlight Solutions, Inc., Cin., 1998—2003, StoreSight Sys., Palo Alto, 2000—, Profit Logic, Inc., Cambridge, Mass. Author: New Service Opportunities for Electric Utilities, 1993; mem. editl. bd.: Ops. Rsch. Jour., 1984—2000, Inst. Indsl. Engring., 1997—; contbr. articles to profl. jours. Recipient award for best pub. paper, Jour. Retailing, 1991. Mem.: Inst. Ops. Rsch. and Mgmt. Sci. (chmn. bus. applications 1986—90, sr. editor Mfg. and Svc. Ops. Mgmt. Jour. 2002—). Office: Santa Clara Univ Dept OMIS 500 El Camino Real Santa Clara CA 95053 E-mail: ssmith@scu.edu.

SMITH, STEPHEN GRANT, journalist; b. NYC, Mar. 6, 1949; s. John J. and Nora O.S.; m. Sarah Rowbotham Bedell, May 22, 1982; children: R. Kirk Bedell, Elisabeth DeCou Bedell, David Branson Smith. Student, Deerfield Acad.; BA, U. Pa., 1971. City Hall reporter Daily Hampshire Gazette, Northampton, Mass., 1971-73; spl. assignment reporter Albany Times-Union, 1973-74; dep. regional editor Phila. Inquirer, 1974-76; asst. met. editor Boston Globe, 1976-78; sr. editor Horizon Mag., 1978; staff writer Time Mag., 1978-80, sr. editor, 1980-82, Nation editor, 1982-85, acting asst. mng. editor, 1985-86; exec. editor Newsweek Mag., 1986-91; Washington news editor Knight Ridder newspapers, 1991-94; founding editor Civilization Mag., Washington, 1994-96; editor Nat. Jour., 1996-98, U.S. News and World Report, 1998-2001; exec. v.p. Winner & Assocs., 2001—02; v.p., dir. comm. Brookings Instn., 2003—04; Wash. bur. chief Houston Chronicle, 2004—07; exec. editor Washington Examiner, 2007—. Mem. bd. Nat. Press Found., 2005—. Mem. bd. overseers U. Pa., 2001—; mem. bd. U. Pa. Press, 2005—07. Mem.: Overseas Press Club, Nat. Press Club, U. Pa. Alumni Soc. (exec. com. 1994—2000), World Affairs Coun. Washington, Coun. on Fgn. Rels., Royal St. George's Golf Club, Fourth Estate Golf Soc., Sakonnet Golf Club, Penn Club, White's Club, Beefsteak Club, Chevy Chase Club, Met. Club, Century Club, Brook Club. Office: Washington Examiner 1015 15th St NW Washington DC 20005 Personal E-mail: sgrasmith@gmail.com.

SMITH, STEPHEN MARK, lawyer; b. Newport News, Va., July 1, 1948; s. Joseph and Marian (Sturman) Smith; children: Ryan David, Miles Stephen. BA in Psychology, William & Mary, 1971, JD, 1974. Bar: Va. 1974, N.Y. 1975, D.C. 1975, U.S. Supreme Ct., U.S. Ct. Appeals (2d, D.C., 4th cirs.). Lawyer Rothblatt, Rothblatt, et al., NYC, 1974-76, Joseph Smith Ltd., Hampton, Va., 1976-99; founding mem. Brain Injury Law Ctr. P.C. Mem. com. Va. Beach Dems., 1990—; bd. dirs., coord. Va. state Trial Lawyers Pub. Justice. Mem. AAJ, Am. Bd. Trial Advocates (diplomate), Va. Trial Lawyers Assn. (bd. dirs. 1978—), Brain Injury Assn. Va. (pres. 2007). Avocations: fishing, reading, boating, jogging, golf. Office: Brain Injury Law Center 2100 Kecoughtan Rd Hampton VA 23661 Home: PO Box 829 Virginia Beach VA 23451-0829 Home Phone: 757-362-3266; Office Phone: 757-244-7000. Business E-Mail: ssmith@braininjurylawcenter.com.

SMITH, STEPHEN MARK, music educator; b. Columbia, Mo., Feb. 23, 1954; s. Elmer Lee and Josephine Ann Smith; m. Pamela Layne Snella, July 30, 1978; 1 child, Christopher Stephen. A of Music, Morton Coll., 1974; BS in Music Edn., U. Ill., 1977; M of Spl. Edn., U. North Fla., 1995, postgrad., 2001—02. Cert. tchr. Fla. Dept. Edn., 1988. Commd. ensign USN, 1978, advanced through grades to lt., ret., 1988; music resource tchr. special edn. Duval County Sch. Dist. Music Dept., Jacksonville, Fla., 1988—. Presenter in field. Cubmaster Boy Scouts of Am., Jacksonville, 1988—90, scoutmaster, 1992—93, merit badge counselor, 1994—2002; computer gaming rsch. U. N. Fla., Jacksonville, 2005—07; Runescape player moderator Jacksonville, 2005—; moderator online computer game Runescape, Jagex, London, 2005—. Decorated Sea Svc. Ribbon, Sea Svc. Ribbon First Star, Navy Expeditionary Medal, Pistol Marksman Ribbon, Rifle Marksman Ribbon, Navy Achievement Medal; named Arts Educator of Yr., Cultural Coun., Jacksonville, 1997, Feature Article Educator Teaches in the Key of Success, The Times Union Newspaper, Jacksonville, 1998; recipient cert. of Appreciation, Future Educators Am., 1998, Best Tchg. Practices award, Severely Emotionally Disturbed Network, 2004—06; grantee, U.S. Dept. Edn., 1995, 1996, Duval Pub. Edn. Found., Jacksonville, 1996, 1996, Duval Pub. Edn. Found., 1996, U.S. Dept. Edn., 1997, The Cultural Coun. Greater Jacksonville, 1997, U.S. Dept. Edn., 1998, Duval County Pub. Found., 1998, U.S. Dept. Edn., 1999, Duval Pub. Edn. Found., 1999, The Cultural Coun. of Greater Jacksonville, 1999, Jacksonville Elec. Authority and The Alliance for World Class Edn., 2000, The Alliance for World Class Edn., 2000, Individuals with Disabilities Edn. Act, 2005, Severely Emotionally Disturbed Network, 2004—05, 2004—06. Mem.: Fla. Elem. Music Educators Assn. (state dist. rep. 1990—91), Fla. Music Educators Assn., Appalachian Tr. Assn., The Am. Legion, Pi Lambda Theta, Delta Sigma Pi. Democrat-Npl. Roman Catholic. Avocations: guitar, sailing, camping, computer gaming, flying. Office: Duval County Sch Bd Music Dept 1701 Prudential Dr Jacksonville FL 32207 Personal E-mail: baden@fdn.com.

SMITH, STEVE, professional football player; b. LA, May 12, 1979; Attended, U. Utah. Wide receiver Carolina Panthers, 2001—. Named NFL Comeback Player of the Yr., 2005; named to NFC ProBowl Team, 2005, NFL All-Pro Team, 2005, NFC Pro-Bowl Team, 2007. Office: Carolina Panthers 800 So Mint St Charlotte NC 28202 *

SMITH, STEVEN RAY, law educator; b. Spirit Lake, Iowa, July 8, 1946; s. Byrnard L. and Dorothy V. (Fischbeck) S.; m. Lera Baker, June 15, 1975. BA, Buena Vista Coll., 1968; JD, U. Iowa, 1971, MA, 1971. Bar: Iowa 1971, Ky. 1987, Ohio 1992. From asst. to assoc. dean Sch. Law U. Louisville, 1974-81, acting dean, 1974-75, 76, prof. law, 1971-88, assoc. in medicine Med. Sch., 1983-88; dep. dir/ Assn. Am. Law Schs., 1987-88; dean, prof. law Cleve. State U., 1988-96; pres., dean and prof. Calif. Western Sch. of Law, 1996—. Author: Law, Behavior and Mental Health: Policy and Practice, 1987; contbr. chpts. to books, articles to profl. jours. Trustee U. Louisville, 1980-82, SCRIBES, 1993—; pres. Ky. Congress of Senate Faculty Leaders, 1982-84; bd. trustees Am. Bd. Profl. Psychology, 1994-2001; bd. dirs. Nat. Register of Health Svc. Providers in Psychology, 2002—, San Diego Vol. Lawyers Program, 1998—, Nat. Conflict Resolution Ctr., 2003—; sec., bd. dirs. Assn. for Accreditation of Human Rsch. Protection Programs, 2001—. Recipient Grawemeyer award Innovative Teaching. Metroversity Consortium, 1983. Fellow Ohio State Bar Found., ABA (stds. rev. com. 1991-95, govt. rels. com. 1993-95, joint commn. ABA/Assn. Am. Law Schs. financing of legal edn. 1993-94, 97-98, coun. sect. legal edn. and admission to the bar 1997—, chmn.-elect sect. on legal edn. and admission to the bar 2004-05, chmn. sect. of legal edn. and admissions to the bar 2005-06, bd. govs. San Diego Found. 2006—); mem. APA (pub. mem. ethics com.), Am. Econs. Assn., Assn. Am. Law Schs. (chmn. librs. com., dep. dir. 1987-88, mem. accreditation com. 1993-96, chair accreditation com. 1994-96), Ohio State Bar Assn. (coun. of dels. 1992-96), Order of Coif, City Club of Cleve. (pres. 1994-95). Office: Calif Western Sch Law Office of Dean 225 Cedar St San Diego CA 92101-3046

SMITH, STEVEN SIDNEY, molecular biologist; b. Idaho Falls, Idaho, Feb. 11, 1946; s. Sidney Ervin and Hermie Phyllis (Robertson) Smith; m. Nancy Louise Turner, Dec. 20, 1974. BS, U. Idaho, 1968; PhD, UCLA, 1974. Asst. rsch. scientist Beckman Rsch. Inst. City of Hope Nat. Med. Ctr., Duarte, Calif., 1982-84, staff Cancer Ctr., 1983—, asst. rsch. scientist depts. Thoracic Surgery and Molecular Biology, 1985-87, assoc. rsch. scientist, 1987-95; rsch. scientist City of Hope Nat. Med. Ctr., Duarte, 1995-00, prof. molecular sci., 2000—; dir. dept. cell and tumor biology City of Hope, Duarte, Calif., 1990—2002, assoc. dir. rsch. Prostate Cancer Program, 2003—. Vis. prof. in basic med. scis. Okla. State U., 1995—96; cons. Molecular Biosystems Inc., San Diego, 1981—84, Am. Inst. Biol. Scis., Washington, 1994, Okla. Ctr. for Advancement of Sci. and Tech., 2001—. Editl. bd. mem. Analytical Biochemistry, 1997—2000, exec. editor, 2000—, editl. bd. mem. Inscight Acad. Press., 1998—, Cancer Genomics and Proteomics, 2003; contbr. articles to profl. jours. Named Honors Laureate, Computer World, 2001; fellow Swiss Nat. Sci. Found. fellow, U. Bern, 1974—77, fellow, Scripps Clinic and Rsch. Found., 1978—82, NIH, 1979—81. Mem.: IEEE Computer Soc., Am. Urological Assn., Am. Math. Soc., Am. Chem. Soc., Am. Assn. Cancer Rsch., Am. Soc. Cell Biology, Phi Beta Kappa. Achievements include 5 U.S. patents. Avocations: backpacking, fishing, weightlifting. Office: Kaplan Clin Rsch Lab City of Hope 1500 E Duarte Rd Duarte CA 91010-3011 Home Phone: 323-913-0418; Office Phone: 626-301-8316. Business E-Mail: ssmith@coh.org.

SMITH, S(TEWART) GREGORY, ophthalmologist, inventor, product developer, consultant, author; b. Wyandotte, Mich., Jan. 24, 1953; s. Stewart Gene and Veronica (Latta) S. BA in Econs. with distinction, U. Mich., 1974; MD, Wayne State U., 1978. Diplomate Am. Bd. Ophthalmology, Nat. Bd. Med. Examiners. Intern, Sacred Heart Med. Ctr., Spokane, Wash.,1978; resident in ophthalmology U. Minn., Mpls., 1979-82, fellow cornea and anterior segment surgery, 1982-83; practice medicine specializing in cornea and anterior segment surgery, and ophthalmology Wilmington, Del., 1983—; clin. prof. ophthalmology U. Pa., Hershey Med. Ctr., 1984—; clin. asst. prof. Thomas Jefferson U.; attending surgeon Wills Eye Hosp., Phila., 1995—; mem. sr. faculty 3M Vision Care Dept., Mpls., 1984-90, rsch. cons., 1984, lectr., 1983—, cons. Am. Cyanamid Opthalmic Divsn., 1990-94, Am. Home Product, 1995—; lectr. in field, Korea, Hong Kong, Thailand, Malaysia, Phillipines, France, Spain, Ireland, Portugal, Holland, Denmark, England, Sweden; cons. Am. Home Products, 1995—, cons. Alcon, 1999—; Author: Complications of Intraocular Lenses and Their Management, 1988, Can You Really See Perfectly Again Without Glasses?, 1996; co-author: Vision Without Glasses, 1990, Sight for Life, 1990; contbr. articles to Fly Fisherman Mag. and other profl. publs. Patentee investigational devices and pharmaceutical, tilt control for automotive vehicles. Recipient award for Best Sci. Poster, Contact Lens Assn. of Ophthalmologists, 1980; Best Film award Internat. Congress of Cataract Surgeons, 1985; Grand Prize Am. Soc. Cataract and Refractive Surgeons Film Festival, 1986. Fellow Am. Intraocular Implant Soc., Castroviejo Soc. (Best Paper award 1984), AMA, Eye Bank Assn. Am., Am. Soc. Cataract and Refractive Surgery Internat. Soc. Refractive Surgery, Am. Acad. Ophthalmology (Honor award 1996), Assn. for Rsch. and Vision in Ophthalmology, Internat. Intraocular Implant Club, Wills Eye Hosp. Alumni Soc., European Soc. Cataract and Refracture Soc. Avocations: fly fishing, hunting, saxophone, tennis, skiing. Home: Nine Gates Rd Yorklyn DE 19736 Office: 1100 N Grant Ave Wilmington DE 19805-2671 Home Phone: 302-239-4723; Office Phone: 302-655-3388.

SMITH, STUART ALAN, lawyer; b. NYC, Mar. 16, 1941; s. Sydney S. and Gertrude (Blinder) S.; m. Helaine Levi, Mar. 14, 1982. AB, Columbia Coll., NYC, 1961; LLB, Harvard U., 1964. Bar: N.Y. 1964, U.S. Tax Ct. 1965, U.S. Supreme Ct. 1967, D.C. 1970. Law clk. to chief judge U.S. Tax Ct., Washington, 1964-66; atty. U.S. Dept. Justice Tax Div., Washington, 1966-70; pvt. practice Washington, 1970-73; tax asst. to solicitor gen. U.S. Dept. Justice, Washington, 1973-83; pvt. practice NYC, 1983—. Author: How You Can Get the Most from the New Tax Law, 1982; contbr. articles to law revs. Mem. ABA (chmn. tax sect. subcom.), Assn. of Bar of City of N.Y (fed. taxation com.), Am. Law Inst. (tax adv. group), Univ. Club (N.Y.C., Washington), RAC Club (London). Office: 460 Park Ave New York NY 10022 Office Phone: 212-759-8285.

SMITH, STUART LYON, psychiatrist, corporate financial executive; b. Montreal, Que., Can., May 7, 1938; s. Moe Samuel and Nettie (Krainer) S.; m. Patricia Ann Springate, Jan. 2, 1964; children: Tanya, Craig. BSc, McGill U., 1958, MD, CM, 1962, diploma in psychiatry, 1967; LLD (hon.), Mt. Allison U., 1992, Royal Rds. U., 2000; B.Ap.Sc. (hon.), Humber Coll., 2005. Intern. Montreal Gen. Hosp., 1962-63, resident in psychiatry, 1963-67; from asst. prof. to assoc. prof. medicine McMaster U., Hamilton, Ont., Canada, 1967-75; leader Ont. Liberal Party Ont. Legislature, 1976-82, leader of the opposition, 1977-82; chmn. Sci. Coun. Can., Ottawa, 1982-87; pres. RockCliffe Rsch. and Tech., Inc., 1987—, Philip Utilities Mgmt. Corp., Toronto, Ont., 1994-97. Chmn. com. inquiry Can. U. Edn., 1989—91; chmn. Ensyn Tech. Inc., 1990—; sr. adv. ICF Cons., 2002; chmn. Nat. Round Table on Environment and Economy, Ottawa, 1995—2002; chmn. bd. dirs. Humber Coll., 2002—04, Esna Tech., Inc., 2004—. Decorated knight Nat. Order of Merit (France); McLaughlin travel fellow, 1964-65. Fellow Royal Coll. Physicians and Surgeons of Can. Personal E-mail: smithstuart@rogers.com.

SMITH, STUART SEABORNE, writer, government and union official; b. NYC, Jan. 27, 1930; s. Purcell Leonard and Elizabeth (Wright) S.; m. Birte Moeller Jacobsen, Apr. 27, 1956 (div. 1972); children: Stuart Seaborne, Bjarne Moeller; m. Editha Maria Fuchs, Jan. 3, 1973; children: Cornelia Gerda, Melanie Carla. Student, Princeton U., 1948—51, U. Heidelberg, Germany, 1953—54, U. Madrid, 1954—55, U. Copenhagen, 1955—56. Reporter Balt. Sun, 1957-65, fgn. corr. chief Bonn (Germany) bur., 1965-69, corr. Washington Bur., 1969-70; with ABA, 1970-71, Dept. Justice, Washington, 1971—; exec. dir. Capitol Employees Organizing Group, 1979—; pub. Balt. Banner, 1965. Served with AUS, 1951-53. Recipient Spl. award for meritorious svc. Washington-Balt. Newspaper Guild, 1965, Meritorious Svc. award Dept. Justice, 1985, 87, Sustained Superior Performance award Dept. Justice, 1992, 93. Mem. Am. Fedn. State, County and Mcpl. Employees (pres. coun. 26 1977-80, 87-95, chief steward Local 2830 1975-80, 81-82, pres. 1982—, Meritorious Svc. award Local 2830, 1980). Democrat. Home: 10522 Tyler Ter Potomac MD 20854-4059 Office: Office Of Justice Programs Washington DC 20531-0001 Office Phone: 202-307-0784. Business E-Mail: stuart.smith@usdoj.gov. *I believe in honor and democracy and social justice. I further believe that for the most part we are the ignorant slaves of political and philosophical superstitions, but in the end the truth shall set us free.*

SMITH, SUE FRANCES, newspaper editor; b. Lockhart, Tex., July 4, 1940; d. Monroe John Baylor and Myrtle (Krause) Mueck; m. Michael Vogtel Smith, Apr. 20, 1963 (div. July 1977); 1 child, Jordan Meredith; m. Kirkland Gideon Smith, Apr. 17, 1999. B of Journalism, U. Tex., 1962. Feature writer, photographer Corpus Christi Caller Times, 1962-64; feature writer, editor Chgo. Tribune, 1964-76; features editor Dallas Times Herald, 1976-82; sales assoc. Bumpas Assocs., Dallas, 1982-83; asst. mng. editor for features Denver Post, 1983-84, assoc. editor, 1984-91; asst. mng. editor in charge of Sunday paper Dallas Morning News, 1991-94, asst. mng. editor Lifestyles, 1994-96, dep. mng. editor Lifestyles, 1996—2001, dep. mng. editor recruiting/devel., 2001—. Active Coun. Pres., 1993; juror Pulitzer Prize, 2002, 03. Mem. Am. Assn. Sunday and Feature Editors (pres. 1993), Newspaper Features Coun. (pres. 2002), Tex. AP Mng. Editors (pres. 1999-00, Jack Douglas award disting. svc. 2005, adv. com. conf. 2005, 06), Delta Gamma. Home: 6241 Park Meadow Ln Plano TX 75093-8863 Office: 508 Young St Dallas TX 75202-4893 E-mail: ssmith@dallasnews.com.

SMITH, SURVILLA MARIE, social services administrator, artist, poet; b. Chattanooga, Oct. 17, 1933; d. Charlie and LeGusta (Robinson) Prater; children: Charles, Calvin, Robin. Student, Mass. Bay C.C., Boston, 1965—66, Northeastern U., 1967-79, Mus. Sch. Fine Arts, 1989—91, U. Mass., 1989—96, Simmons Grad. Sch. Mgmt., 1995—97. Exec. sec. The Ecumenical Ctr., Roxbury, Mass., 1965-67, Roxbury Fedn. of Neighborhoods, 1965-68; bus. mgr. Coun. of Elders, Inc., Boston, 1969-72; exec. sec., asst. bookkeeper Edn. Renewal, Inc., Boston, 1972-73; asst. dir. METCO Inter-Dist. Transfer Inc., Roxbury, 1973-75; pupil pers. coord. Met. Coun. for Ednl. Opportunity, Roxbury, 1975-78; with Vis. Nurse Assn. of Boston, 1978-79; sec. Bay State Banner Newspaper, Roxbury, 1980; sr. outreach coord. Mattahunt Community Sch Sr. Outreach, Mattapan, Mass., 1989-95. Founder, chmn., CEO S.P.A.C.E. An Artistic Comty., Inc.; founder., chmn., CEO LED, 1995—. Exhibitions include Steppin Out, Boston, 1993, Treasured Legacy Gallery, 1995, Urban League Ea. Mass., Roxbury, 1997—98, Codman Sq. Br. Libr., Dorchester, Mass., 1997—2002, New Art N.Eng. Libr. Arts Ctr., Newport, N.H., 1997, Dorchester Hist. Soc., 1996, 1997, 1998, Dorchester Art Assn., Boston, 1996, 1997, 1998, Open Studios, South End, Mass., 1998, Roxbury Cmty. Coll. Media Arts Ctr., 1998, Reggie Lewis Ctr., Roxbury, 1998, Rothschild Gallery, Radcliffe Coll., Cambridge, Mass., 1998, Boston City Hall Scollay Sq. Gallery, Boston, 1998, 1999, 2000, Pan African Historical Mus., Springfield, Mass., 1999, Grove Hall Br. Libr., Roxbury, 2000, Egleston Br. Libr., Mass., 2000, Parker Hill Br. Libr., Roxbury, 2000, South End (Mass.) Open Studios, 2000, CVS Windows-The Mall at Grove Hall, Roxbury, 2002, Codman Sq. Br. Libr., Dorchester, 2004—05, CVS Window Porter Sq., Cambridge, 2002—05, Macy's Windows, 2000, 1999, Codman Sq. Libr., Mass., 2004—, North River Cmty. Ch., 2006—, Boston Bus. Assistance Ctr., Roxbury, Mass., 2005—, Represented in permanent collections N.Eng. Zoo, pvt. collections, artwork published, Art New Eng., Art News, ArtsMedia, Art & Antiques; author: (poetry book) Days, Years to Remember: A Collection of Poems, 2003. Active Women's Caucus Art, Boston chpt., Coalition Black Women, Nat. Coun. Negro Women; chmn. health campaign Grove Hall/Franklin Park AARP, Boston, 1990—; vol. Experiment in Internat. Living, Mass., Mattapan/Franklin Park Jubilee Task Force, WGBH, Am. Cancer Soc.; artwork auction donor various orgns. Grantee, New Eng. Found. for the Arts; scholar, U. Mass., Amherst, 1999; Americans for the Arts scholar, 1999. Mem.: PEN N.E., NAACP, Boston Afro-Am. Artists, Nat. Poetry Soc., South End Artists, Mass. Advocates for the Arts, Scis. & Humanities, Dorchester Art Assn., Am. for the Arts, Nat. Writer's Assn., Poetry Soc. Am. Avocations: writing, painting, reading. Home: 4 Wentworth St Dorchester MA 02124-3517 Office Phone: 617-436-1063. E-mail: 1space@gte.net, 1space@verizon.net.

SMITH, SUSAN A., photojournalist; With Nat. Geographic Mag., Washington, 1976—, asst. dir., photography, 1990—. Judge Royal Hort. Soc. Britain in Bloom, 2006, Getty Images 2006 Grants for Editl. Photog. Recipient Nat. Mag. award for Photography, Am. Soc. Mag. Editors, 2007. Office: Asst Dir Photography Nat Geographic Soc 1145 17Th St NW Washington DC 20036-4688 Office Phone: 202-857-7654. Office Fax: 202-429-5755. *

SMITH, SUSAN CARLTON (SUSAN CARLTON SMITH CAVANAGH), artist, illustrator, sculptor; b. Athens, Ga., June 30, 1923; d. Edward Inglis and Hart Wylie Smith; m. George Stanley Terence Cavanagh, Oct. 25, 1977. BS in Zoology, U. Ga., 1947, MFA in Drama, 1961. Sci. illustrator US Pub. Health Communicable Disease Ctr., Atlanta, 1952; artist archeology dept. U. Ga., 1953—, costume designer, speech tchr., drama dept, 1956—61, sci. illustrator biology dept., 1964—65; conservator, asst. curator Med. Ctr. Libr., Duke U., Durham, NC, 1967—90; biological and botanical illustrator Duke U., 1967—90; botanical illustrator U. NC, 1967—90. Lectr. in field. Illustrator Jack & Jill Magazine, 1960—62, (book) Plant Variations and Classification, 1967, Wildflowers of NC, 1968, A Child's Book of Flowers, 1976, A Book of Flowers, 1987, illustrator, text contr. (book) Lady Bug, Lady Bug, 1969 (Top 50 Best Children's Books of Yr., 1969), (Book) Hey Bug!, and Other Poems About Little Things, 1972 (Printers Industries of Am. award), author, illustrator 3 Famous Artists-Naturalists of the Colonial Period, John Abbot, William Bartram, Mark Catesby- A Coloring Book for all Ages, 2002; contbr. to profl. jours.jours.; exhibitions include eleventh Internat. Botanical Congress, Seattle, 1969, Internat. Exhbn. Botanical Art, Johannesburg, South Africa, Second Internat. Exhbn. Twentieth Cent. Botanical Art and Illustration, Carnegie-Mellon U., 1968—69, Duke U. Mus. Art, U. Ga. Mus. Art, Represented in permanent collections Nature Sculptures and Watercolor Miniatures, State Botanical Garden, Ga. Vol. U. NC Botanical Gardens, 1967—89, State Botanical Gardens, Ga., 1989—. Mem.: Trent Soc. History of Med., Duke U., Am. Assn. History of Med., Nat. Soc. Colonial Dames, Jr. Ladies Garden Club, Garden Club Am. (Eloise Payne Lequer medal 1989), Puppeteers of Am., Chi Omega, Phi Kappa Phi. Episcopalian. Avocation: sculpting. Home: 755 Epps Bridge Pkwy #404 Athens GA 30606 Personal E-mail: cavanaghs@bellsouth.net.

SMITH, SUSAN ELIZABETH, guidance director; b. Phila., Mar. 24, 1950; d. E. Burke Hogue and Janet Coffin Hogue Ebert; m. J. Russell Smith, June 17, 1972 (div. June 1989); 1 child, Drew Russell. BS in Elem. Edn., E. Stroudsburg Coll., 1972; MEd in Counseling, U. Okla., 1974, postgrad., 1976-77, Trenton State Coll., 1989-90; EdM in Devel. Disabilities, Rutgers U., 1992, postgrad., 1994—. Cert. elem. tchr., N.C.; cert. elem. tchr., early childhood edn. tchr., guidance and counseling, Okla.; cert. elem. tchr., guidance and counseling, tchr. of handicapped, psychology tchr., supr. instrn., dir. student pers. svcs., N.J. Elem. tchr. Morton Elem. Sch. Onslow County Schs., Jacksonville, NC, 1971-72; instr. U. Isfahan, Iran, 1974-76; guidance counselor Moore (Okla.) Pub. Schs., 1976-77; counselor Johnstone Tng. Ctr. N.J. Divsn. Devel. Disabilities, Bordentown, 1988-90; spl. edn. tchr. Willingboro (N.J.) Schs., 1990-91; guidance counselor Haledon (N.J.) Pub. Schs., 1991-92; spl. edn. adj. tchr. Gateway Sch., Carteret, NJ, 1991-93; guidance counselor Bloomfield (N.J.) Pub. Schs., 1992-94; dir. guidance Somerville (N.J.) Pub. Schs., 1994-95. Adj. prof. in spl. edn. Essex County (N.J.) Coll., 1994; guidance Ft. Lee (N.J.) Schs., 1995-2001; guidance dir. Bogota Schs., N.J., 2001-02, Closter Schs., Closter, N.J., 2002—; cons., seminar and workshop presenter on behavior mgmt., parenting skills, and behavior modification techniques; cons. N.J. Fragile X Assn. Author: Motivational Awards for ESL Students, 1993, Parent Contracts to Improve School Behaviors, 1996; contbr. articles to profl. jours. Leader Boy Scouts Am., Oklahoma City, 1983-87, com. chmn., Redmond, Wash., 1987-88. Recipient Rsch. award ERIC/CAPS, 1992, Svc. award N.J. Fragile X Assn., 1993. Mem. ACA, Am. Sch. Counselor Assn. (grantee 1992), N.J. Counseling Assn., N.J. Sch. Counseling Assn., Assn. for Multicultural Counseling and Devel., AAUW, Assn. for Counselor Edn. and Supervision, N.J. Assn. for Counselor Edn. and Supervision, N.J. Prins. and Suprs. Assn., Nat. Assn. Coll. Admissions Counselors (grantee 1995), Alpha Omicron Pi. Episcopalian. Home: 916 Lincoln Pl Teaneck NJ 07666-2572

SMITH, TAD RANDOLPH, lawyer; b. El Paso, Tex., July 20, 1928; s. Eugene Rufus and Dorothy (Derrick) S.; m. JoAnn Wilson, Aug. 24, 1949; children: Laura Borsch, Derrick, Cameron Ann Compton. LLB, U. Tex., 1951, BBA, 1952. Bar: Tex. 1951. Assoc. firm Kemp, Smith Duncan & Hammond P.C., El Paso, Tex., 1951-52, ptnr., 1952-81, CEO, 1975—98, shareholder, 1981—99; of counsel Kemp Smith, LLP, El Paso, 1999—. Active United Way of El Paso; chmn. El Paso County Reps., 1958-61, Tex. Rep. State Exec. Com., 1961-62; alt. del. Rep. Nat. Conv., 1952, 62, del. 1964, dir. El Paso Elec. Co., 1961-90, State Nat. Bank of El Paso, 1969-90, The Leavell Co., 1970-94; trustee Robert E. and Evelyn McKee Found., 1970-90, Property Trust of Am., 1971-91; mem. devel. bd. U. Tex., El Paso, 1973-81, v.p., 1975, chmn. 1976; dinner treas. Nat. Jewish Hosp. and Rsch. Ctr., 1977, chmn. 1978, presenter of honoree, 1985; bd. dirs. NCCJ 1965-76, chmn. 1965-78; bd. dirs. Southwestern Children's Home, El Paso, 1959-78; trustee Hervey Found., 1990-99, Lydia Patterson Inst., 1994-99 Named Outstanding Young Man, El Paso Jaycees; named to Bd. of Fellows, U. Tex., El Paso, 1997—2001; recipient Humanitarian award, El Paso chpt. NCCJ, 1983. Fellow Am. Bar Found., Tex. Bar Found.; mem. ABA, Tex. Bar Assn., El Paso Bar Assn. (pres. 1971-72), El Paso C. of C. (dir. 1979-82), Sigma Chi. Republican. Methodist. Address: 20 Stratford Hall Cir El Paso TX 79912 Personal E-mail: tadjoann@msn.com.

SMITH, TEFFT WELDON, lawyer; b. Evanston, Ill., Nov. 18, 1946; s. Edward W. and Margery T. (Weldon) S.; m. Nancy Jo Smith, Feb. 25, 1967; children: Lara Andrea, Tefft Weldon II. BA, Brown U., 1968; JD, U. Chgo., 1971. Bar: Ill. 1971, D.C. 2000, U.S. Supreme Ct. 1977. Sr. litigation ptnr. Kirkland & Ellis LLP, Chgo., 1971—, chair, competition and antitrust practice group. Mem. adv. bd. Bur. Nat. Affairs Antitrust and Trade Regulation Reporter; instr. trial advocacy. Contbr. numerous articles on trial practice and antitrust issues to law jours. Mem. ABA (litigation sect., antitrust law sect.), Econ. Club., Univ. Club, Mid-Am. Club, Sea Pines Country Club (Hilton Head, S.C.). Avocations: squash, ferraris, sculpture. Office: 655 15th St NW Washington DC 20005-5701 also: Kirkland & Ellis 200 E Randolph St Fl 54 Chicago IL 60601-6636 Home: 700 New Hampshire Ave NW Washington DC 20037 Office Phone: 202-879-5212. Business E-Mail: tsmith@kirkland.com.

SMITH, THEODORE GLENN, technology educator, researcher; b. Willowbrook, Calif., Oct. 19, 1957; s. Thomas Eugene and Marilyn Glenna Smith; m. Kathleen Ione, May 27, 1978; children: Melissa Lauren, Melanie Kelly. AAS in Electronic Engring., Clark County CC, North Las Vegas, Nev., 1984; BBA magna cum laude, Nat. U., San Diego, 1987; MEd, U. Nev., Las Vegas, 2001; postgrad., Capella, Mpls. Lic. educator Nev., Tex. Electronic technician E.G.& G. Inc. Nev. Test Site, Mercury, 1978—90; tech. instr. Garside Jr. High Sch., Las Vegas, 1992—99; bus., acctg. instr. Clark High Sch., Las Vegas, 1999—2001; computer instr. Bob Miller Mid. Sch., Las Vegas, 2001—02; cons., tutor Nev. Edn. Cons., Las Vegas, 2002—03; online facilitator Clark County Team Acad., Las Vegas, 2003—06; ednl. technologist Trinity Charter Sch., 2006—. Mem. Internat. Surfing Mus., Huntington Beach, Calif., 1972—, Friends of Sea Otter, Monterey, Calif., 1995—. Mem.: Tex. Computer Educator's Assn., Internat. Soc. Tech. Edn. (cons. 2001—), Tex. State Hist. Assn., Alpha Kappa Phi. Republican.

SMITH, THEODORE S., lawyer; b. Summit, NJ, 1955; BArch, Univ. Syracuse, 1978, BS in Mgmt., 1978; JD, Univ. Pa., 1983. Bar: NJ 1983. Law clerk, Hon. Frederick B. Lacey US Dist. Ct., NJ; joined Drinker Biddle & Reath LLP, 1984, ptnr., litig. dept. Florham Park, NJ, co-chair, construction law practice group. Arbitrator Am. Arbitration Assn. Mem.: Am. Inst. Architects (assoc.). Office: Drinker Biddle & Reath LLP 500 Campus Dr Florham Park NJ 07932-1047 Office Phone: 973-549-7210. Office Fax: 973-360-9831. Business E-Mail: theodore.smith@dbr.com.

SMITH, THERESA JOANNE, research scientist, educator; b. Corona, NY, Aug. 22, 1959; d. Felix Adolph and Norma Alberta Smith. BA, CUNY, Flushing, NY, 1982; MS, Tex. Woman's U., Denton, Tex., 1984, PhD, 1988. Lic. practical nurse, NY, 1978. Postdoctoral rsch. assoc. Rutgers, The State U. N.J., Piscataway, 1988—92, rsch. assoc., 1992—96, rsch. asst. prof., 1996—99; asst. prof. U. S.C., Columbia, 1999—2005, assoc. prof., 2005—. Cons. NIH, Ctr. for Sci. Rev., Bethesda, Md., 2001—. Contbr. chapters to books, articles to profl. jours. Named Rschr. of Yr., Coll. Pharmacy, U. S.C., 2002; grantee, Am. Cancer Soc., 1998—2002, NIH, 2002—, 2003—06. Mem.: AAAS, Women in Cancer Rsch., S.C. Alliance for Cancer Chemoprevention, Soc. for Nutrition Edn., Am. Assn. for Cancer Rsch. Democrat. Roman Catholic. Avocations: gardening, travel, fishing. Office: University of South Carolina College of Pharmacy 700 Sumter St Columbia SC 29208 Home Phone: 803-736-9009; Office Phone: 803-777-0857. Office Fax: 803-777-8356. Personal E-mail: tjsmith822@aol.com. Business E-Mail: smithtj@cop.sc.edu.

SMITH, THOMAS A., lawyer, investment company executive; b. Springfield, Ill., Dec. 14, 1956; BA, Wabash Coll., 1978; JD, St. Louis U., 1983, MBA, 1984. Bar: Ill. 1984, Mo. 1985, N.Y. 1990; lic. series 7 Nat. Assn. Securities Dealers, series 24 Nat. Assn. Securities Dealers. Enforcement atty. Ill. Securities Dept., 1984—85; staff atty. divsn. investment mgmt. U.S. SEC, 1986—89; sr. assoc. Wilkie Farr & Gallaghar, 1989—91; asst. gen. counsel Dreyfus Corp., 1991—93, N.Y. Life Ins. Co., NYC, 1994—96, assoc. gen. counsel, 1996—97, v.p., assoc. gen. counsel, 1997—99; exec. v.p., gen. counsel Van Kampen Investments, Inc., 1999—2001; mng. dir., gen. counsel U.S. investment mgmt. Morgan Stanley, NYC, 2001—. Co-author: (book) Regulation of Investment Companies. Office: Morgan Stanley Law Dept 1221 Ave of the Americas 5th Fl New York NY 10020

SMITH, THOMAS EUGENE, investment company executive, financial consultant; b. Brown's Summit, NC, Aug. 23, 1930; s. Howard Cleveland and Annie May (Warren) S.; m. Joan Cretcher Hopkins, Sept. 22, 1948; 1 dau., Vicki Joan. Student, George Washington U., 1948-50, Am. U., 1950-55 (intermittently). Pres., dir. T. Eugene Smith, Inc. investment co. and real estate and fin. cons. co., Falls Church, Va., 1950—; pres. The Potomac Corp., Falls Church, Va., 1960-74; pres., dir. Nat. Bank of Fairfax, Va., 1975-81, dir. Va.; exec. v.p. First & Mchts. Nat. Bank, Richmond, Va., 1981-83; chmn., dir. Decisions and Designs, Inc., McLean, Va., 1983-86; ptnr. Braddock-Ravensworth Ltd. Partnership, 1964—; sec., dir. Port Royal, Inc., 1965—; ptnr. Lee Graham Shopping Ctr., 1969—; chmn., pres., dir. Am. Mobile Home Towns, Inc., holding co., 1969-85; dir., pres. Topsail, Inc., 1983-89; ptnr. Potomac Greens Assn., 1986—. Bd. dirs. Growth Fund of Washington, Am. Funds Tax Exempt Series I, Washington Mut. Investors, M.G. Thalheimer Realty Advisors, Inc.; chmn., bd. dirs. River Capital Corp., Alexandria, Va., 1986-89, J. Webb, Inc., 1986—; acting dir., mgmt. com. Alexandria 20/20, 1988-91, acting dir., 1988-89; pres., dir. Pender Marina Holdings, Inc., 1988—, Pender Land Holdings, Inc., 1990—; adv. bd. CSX Realty, 1992-2003. Bd. dirs. Wolftrap Found., Washington, 1974-84; trustee Sta. WETA-TV, 1978-86; mem. Nat. Capital Planning Commn., Washington, 1980-83, vice chmn., 1981-83; mem. Va. Hwys. and Transp. Commn., Richmond, 1982-86; trustee Ch. Schs., Diocese of Va., 1983-88; mem. Va. Gov.'s Coun. Econ. Advisors, 1985-94, Met. Washington Airports Authority, 1986-94; chmn. Fairfax County Transp. Commn. for the Future, 1988-89; dir. Air and Space Heritage Coun., 1987-90. Mem.: Nat. Assn. Small Bus. Investment Cos. (treas. and bd. dirs. 1962—66), Met. Club (Washington). Democrat. Episcopalian. Office Phone: 703-243-2041. E-mail: tes.mclean@cox.net.

SMITH, THOMAS GORDON, architect; b. Oakland, Calif., Apr. 23, 1948; s. Sheldon Wagers and Margaret (Prendergast) S.; m. Marika Wilson, Dec. 19, 1970; children— Alan, Stuart, Demetra, Andrew, Philip, Duncan. A.B., U. Calif.-Berkeley, 1970, M.Arch., 1975. Lic. architect, Calif. Prin. Thomas Gordon Smith, Architect, Chgo., 1980—; instr. archtl. history Coll. of Marin, Kentfield, Calif., 1976-77; guest instr. archtl. design So. Calif. Inst. Architecture, Santa Monica, 1983; guest lectr., seminar leader Kunstegeschichtlieches Institut der Philipps Universitat, Marburg, W.Ger., 1983; guest tchr. U. Ill., Chgo., UCLA, 1984; assoc. prof. U. Ill., Chgo.; chmn. Sch. Architecture U. Notre Dame, Ind., 1989-98. Exhibited art in shows at Santa Barbara Mus. Art, 1977, Cooper-Hewitt Mus., Chgo. Art Inst., 1980, Louisiana Mus. Modern Art, Copenhagen, 1981, Venice Biennale, 1980, Smith Coll. Mus. Art, 1981, La Jolla Mus. Modern Art, Calif., 1982, Deutsches Architekturmuseum, Frankfurt, W.Ger., 1984; revision of Modern IBM Gallery, N.Y., 1987; author: Classical Architecture: Rule and Invention, 1987, Vitruvias on Architecture, 2003. Bd. dirs. Soc. Cath. Liturgy. U. Calif. grad. fellow, 1974, John K. Branner fellow, 1975, Rome Prize fellow, Am. Acad., 1979; grantee Graham Found. Advanced Study in Fine Arts, 1984, 87, Am. Philos. Soc., 1987. Mem. AIA (Grad. fellow 1973), Soc. Archtl. Historians. Home: 1903 Dorwood Dr South Bend IN 46617-1818 Office: 2025 Edison Rd South Bend IN 46637 E-mail: archtgs@aol.com.

SMITH, THOMAS KENT, retired radiologist; b. Bowling Green, Ohio, Aug. 21, 1934; s. Robert O. and Roslyn Smith; m. Jaleh Saidi, Feb. 1, 1974; children: Jeffrey, Todd, Mark, Blake, Tyler. BS with high honors, U. Cin., 1957; MD, Case Western Res. U., 1961. Intern Nat. Naval Med. Ctr., Bethesda, Md., 1961-62; resident in radiology VA Med. Ctr., Long Beach, Calif., 1965-69; fellow in radiologic pathology Armed Forces Inst. Pathology, Washington, 1968; dir. radiology Harriman Jones Med. Group, Long Beach, 1969-88; fellow in MRI/CT U. Calif., San Francisco, 1988-89; dir. MRI Orange County MRI, Fountain Valley, Calif., 1989-90; chmn. dept. diagnostic imaging Kaiser Permanente Med. Ctr., Honolulu, 1990-2000, dir. MRI, 1994-2000; ret. Mem. adv. bd. Hawaii Permanente Med. Group, Honolulu, 1990—2000; assoc. clin. prof. radiology U. Hawaii, Honolulu,

1990—2000; asst. clin. prof. U. Calif., Irvine, Calif., 1970—88, clin. instr., San Francisco, 1988—89, asst. clin. prof., 1989—99; cons. in radiologic devel. Kaiser Permanente Internat., 1996—98; owner Rubaiyat Vineyard, Sonoma County, Calif. Lt. Med. Corps, Nuc. Submarine Svcs. USN, 1961—65. Named Guide to Am.'s Top Radiologists, 2007. Fellow Am. Coll. Radiology; mem. Hawaii Radiol. Soc. (pres. 1992-93), Radiol. Soc. N.Am., Internat. Soc. Magnetic Resonance in Medicine, Margulis Soc., Alpha Omega Alpha, Sonoma County Grape Growers Assn., Sonoma Valley Vintners and Growers Alliance, Rhone Rangers,. Avocations: fishing, travel, viticulture. Home: Rubaiyat Vineyard 5409 Sonoma Mountain Rd Santa Rosa CA 95404-8884 Fax: 707-544-4117. Personal E-mail: rubaiyatvineyard@aol.com.

SMITH, THOMAS RAMSAUR, JR., lawyer; b. Feb. 12, 1938; AB, Princeton U., 1960; LLB, U. Va., 1963. Assoc. Brown & Wood, NYC, 1963-71, ptnr., 1971-96, mng. ptnr., 1996—2001; ptnr. Sidley Austin Brown & Wood LLP (following merger), NYC, 2001—, vice chmn. mgmt. com., 2001—03, mem. exec. com., 2001—04. Chmn. 2000 Law Firm Appeal Lawyers Alliance for NY. Bd. dir. Legal Aid Soc. Office: Sidley Austin LLP 787 7th Ave New York NY 10019 Office Phone: 212-839-5535. Business E-Mail: tsmith@sidley.com.

SMITH, THOMAS RAYMOND, III, software engineer; b. Phila., Dec. 6, 1946; s. Thomas Raymond and Naomi (Hart) S.; m. Marguerite Anne LeMoyne de Martigny, Sept. 6, 1969; children: Michelle Renée, Heather Anne, Thomas Raymond IV. Student, MIT, 1964-68. Sr. analyst Dabcovich and Co., Lexington, Mass., 1969—71; sr. analyst, prin. Multi-Logic Corp., Burlington, Mass., 1970—73; cons. engr. Digital Equipment Corp. (now Hewlett-Packard Co.), Palo Alto, Calif., 1974—. Co-editor: IEEE Dictionary, 1993; author, co-editor numerous stds. books for Internat. Electrotech. Commn. and IEEE, 1984-93. Mem.: IEEE (chmn. various stds. coms. 1980—96). Home: 36 Toppans Ln Newburyport MA 01950-3843 Office: Hewlett-Packard Co ZK03-3/S01 110 Spit Brook Rd Nashua NH 03062-2711 Business E-Mail: smith@alum.mit.edu.

SMITH, THOMAS SHORE, retired lawyer; b. Rock Springs, Wyo., Dec. 7, 1924; s. Thomas and Anne E. (McTee) S.; m. Jacqueline Emily Krueger, May 25, 1952; children: Carolyn Jane, Karl Thomas, David Shore. BSBA, U. Wyo., 1950, JD, 1959. Bar: U.S. Dist. Ct. Wyo. 1960, U.S. Ct. Appeals (10th cir.) 1960, U.S. Tax Ct. 1969, U.S. Supreme Ct. 1971. Of counsel Brown & Hiser, LLC, Laramie, 1994—2006; ret., 2006. Atty. City of Laramie, 1963-86; instr. mcpl. law U. Wyo., 1987; dir. budget and fin. Govt. of Am. Samoa, 1954-56. Bd. dirs. Bur. Land Mgmt., Rawlins, Wyo., 1984-89, chmn. bd. dirs., 1991-95, Ivinson Hosp. Found., 1994-95, U. Wyo. Found., 1991-99, pres., 1994-95, Am. Nat. Bank, bd. dirs., 1996—. Francis Warren scholar, 1958. Mem Wyo. Bar Assn. (pres. 1984-85), Albany County Bar Assn., Western States Bar Conf. (pres. 1985-86), Elks. Republican. Episcopalian. Avocation: golf. Office: Brown & Hiser LLC PO Box 971 515 E Ivinson Ave Laramie WY 82070-3157

SMITH, TIMOTHY G., telecommunications industry executive; Various mgmt. positions Sun Microsystems, Inc., UUNET Technologies, Inc., Wayport, Inc.; sr. v.p., network systems and infrastructure Vonage Network, Inc., 2005—06, interim pres., 2006, pres., 2006—. Office: Vonage America 23 Main St Holmdel NJ 07733 *

SMITH, TODD A., lawyer; b. Chgo., Aug. 27, 1949; married; 2 children. BSB, U. Kans., 1971; MBA, Northwestern U., 1973; JD, Loyola U., 1976. Bar: Ill. 1976, U.S. Dist. Ct. (no. dist.) Ill. 1980, U.S. Ct. Appeals (7th cir.) 1981, U.S. Supreme Ct. 1980. Asst. Cook County Public Defender, Chgo.; atty. Corboy & Demetrio P.C., Chgo., ptnr., Powers, Rogers, & Smith P.C., Chgo. Adj. prof. law De Paul Coll., 1985—88; mock trial judge, 1978—83; bd. dir. Trial Lawyers Club of Chicago, 1987—; lectr. John Marshall Law Sch., 1985, Loyola U. Sch. Law, 1981—85, 1988; bd. gov Assoc. Trial Lawyers of Am. (ATLA), 1989—, mem. exec. comm., 1998—, treas., 2000—01, sec., 2001—02, v.p., 2002—03, pres. elect, 2003—04, pres., 2004—05; bd. dir. ATLA Endowment, 1999—, ISBA Mutual Insurance Co., 1995—, Ill. Bar Found., 2000—. Assoc. editor: Ill. Trial Lawyers Jour.; contbr. articles to profl. jours. Named Person of the Yr., Chicago Lawyer Mag., 1998; named one of The Best Lawyers in Am., 1997—2004; fellow Internat. Soc. of Barristers, 1996, Am. College of Trial Lawyers, 1996, Am. Bar Found., 1996, Internat. Acad. of Trial Lawyers, 1998, Am. Bd. of Trial Advocates, 1999. Fellow: Am. Coll. Trial Lawyers, Internat. Soc. Barristers, Internat. Acad. Trial Lawyers; mem.: Ill. State Bar Assn. (past pres.). Office: Powers, Rogers, Smith 70 W Madison St 55th Fl Chicago IL 60602

SMITH, TODD P., marketing executive; b. 1968; MBA, U. Iowa, 1996. Worked for Saturn, Daimler Chrysler Corp.; founder, CEO Clear!Blue, Birmingham, Mich., 2000—. Named one of 40 Under 40, Crain's Detroit Bus., 2006. Avocations: music, travel. Office: Clear!Blue 135 North Old Woodward Birmingham MI 48009 Office Phone: 248-644-0800. Office Fax: 248-644-0818.

SMITH, TRINA, academic administrator; b. Rogersville, Ala., Sept. 18, 1971; d. Will Buford and Margaret Cannon Smith. BS, Athens State U., 1993; MS, U. Ala., Huntsville, 2000; M of Accountancy, U. Ala., 2001. Cert. Notary Pub. Br. ops. supr. Union Planters Bank, Athens, Ala., 1994—2000; acct. Calhoun Coll., Decatur, Ala., 2000—. Dir. Habitat for Humanity, Athens, 1994—2000; mem. adv. bd. Dogwood Festival Com., Athens, 1999. Vol. Jr. Achievement, Decatur, Ala., 1997—2000, Care Assurance Sys. for Aging and Homebound, Athens, 1995—99, Found. of Aging, Athens, 1999—2002. Recipient Outstanding Support award, Habitat for Humanity, 1996. Mem.: NAFE, NAACP, Am. Inst. of Cert. Pub. Accts., Nat. Assn. Black Accts., Am. Acctg. Assn., Am. Soc. Women Accts., Nat. Notary Assn., Inst. Mgmt. Accts. Baptist. Avocations: gardening, photography, collecting antiques, investments, outdoor activities. Home: 13708 Dart Cir Athens AL 35611 Office: Calhoun Cmty Coll Hwy 31 S Decatur AL 35609 Personal E-mail: TSmith3671@aol.com.

SMITH, TROY, professional football player; b. Cleve., July 20, 1984; s. Tracy Smith and Kenneth Delaney. BA in Comm., Ohio State U., 2006. Quarterback Balt. Ravens, 2007—. Named Fiesta Bowl MVP, 2006, Big Ten Player Yr., 2006; named to All Big-Ten Conference, 2005—06, Walter Camp All-American Team, 2006; recipient Davey O'Brien award, Davey O'Brien Found., 2006, Walter Camp Player Yr. award, Walter Camp Football Found., 2006, Heisman Meml. Trophy, Heisman Trophy Trust, 2006. Office: Balt Ravens 1 Winning Dr Owings Mills MD 21117 *

SMITH, TROY ALVIN, aerospace research engineer; b. Sylvatus, Va., July 4, 1922; s. Wade Hampton and Augusta Mabel (Lindsey) S.; m. Grace Marie (Peacock) Dees, Nov. 24, 1990. BCE, U. Va., 1948; MS in Engring., U. Mich., 1952, PhD, 1970. Registered profl. engr., Va., Ala. Structural engr. U.S. Army C.E., Norfolk, Va., Wilmington, NC, Washington, 1948-59; chief structural engr. Brown Engring. Co., Inc., Huntsville, Ala., 1959-60; structural rsch. engr. U.S. Army Missile Command, Redstone Arsenal, Ala., 1960-63, aerospace rsch. engr., 1963-80, aerospace rsch. engr., 1980-96; engr. emeritus U.S. Army Aviation and Missile Command, Redstone Arsenal, Ala., 1996—2003, U.S. Army Rsch., Devel., and Engring. Command, Aviation and Missile Rsch., Devel., and Engring. Ctr., Redstone Arsenal, Ala., 2003—. Contbr. articles to profl. jours.; author: 17 major U.S. Army tech. reports on analysis of shells and other structures. With USNR, 1942-46, PTO. Fellow, Dept. Army, 1969. Mem. N.Y. Acad. Scis., Assn. U.S. Army, Elks, Sigma Xi. Achievements include research in procedures for analysis of structures. Avocations: ballroom dancing, bowling, travel, classic automobiles. Home: 2202 Yorkshire SE Decatur AL 35601-3470

SMITH, TUBBY, men's college basketball coach; b. Scotland, Md., June 30, 1951; s. Guffrie & Parthenia Smith; m. Donna Smith; children: Orlando, Shannon, Saul, Brian. BS in Health & Phys. Edn., High Point Coll., 1973. Head basketball coach Gt. Mills (Md.) H.S., 1973-77; head coach Hoke County H.S., Raeford, 1977-79; asst. coach Va. Commonwealth U., 1979-86, U. S.C., 1986-89, Ky. U., 1989-91; head coach U. Tulsa, 1991-95, U. Ga., Athens, 1995-97, U. Ky., Lexington, 1997—2007, U. Minn., Mpls., 2007—. Asst. basketball coach US Men's Nat. Basketball Team, 1999; head coach US Olympic Basketball Team, Sydney, 2000; bd. dirs. Nat. Assn. Basketball Coaches. Founder The Tubby Smith Found., 1987—. Named Jim Phelan Coach of Yr., 2005, Naismith Coll. Coach of Yr., 2003; recipient Henry Iba award, 2003. Coached the U. Ky. to five Southeastern Conf. Titles, 1998-2001, 2003-2004 & 1 NCAA Men's Divsn. I Basketball Championship, 1998. Office: U Minn 205 BFAB 516 15th Ave SE Minneapolis MN 55455 *

SMITH, TURNER TALIAFERRO, JR., lawyer; b. Washington, Dec. 16, 1940; s. Turner Taliaferro and Lois (Fisk) S.; m. Christine H. Perdue; children: Turner T., III, John Webb Tyler. BA magna cum laude, Princeton U., 1962; LLB cum laude, Harvard U., 1968. Bar: Va. 1968, D.C. 1977. Ptnr. Hunton & Williams, Richmond, Va., 1975-2006, sr. counsel, 2007—; tchr. environ. law Washington and Lee U., 1978, Coll. William and Mary, 1979, 80, U. Va. Law Sch., 2005, 06; tchr. internat. environ. law George Mason Law Sch., 2004, tchr. war crimes seminar, 2005, 06. Mem. ABA (chmn. standing com. environ. law 1983, 84, 85, chmn. corp., banking and bus. law sect. com. on environ. controls 1973-80), Va. Bar Assn. Office: Hunton & Williams 1900 K St NW 12 Fl Washington DC 20001 Home Phone: 540-687-6726; Office Phone: 202-955-1692. Business E-Mail: tsmith@hunton.com.

SMITH, V. KERRY, economics professor; b. Jersey City, Mar. 11, 1945; s. Vincent C. and Dorothy E. S.; m. Pauline Anne Taylor, May 10, 1969; children: Timothy, Shelley. AB, Rutgers U., 1966, PhD, 1970. Asst. prof., then assoc. prof. Bowling Green State U., Ohio, 1969-72; rsch. assoc. Resources for Future, Washington, 1971-73; assoc. prof. SUNY, Binghamton, 1973-75, prof., 1975-78; sr. fellow Resources for Future, Washington, 1976-79; prof. U. NC, Chapel Hill, 1979-83; Centennial prof. Vanderbilt U., Nashville, 1983-87; univ. disting. prof. NC State U., 1987-94, univ. disting. prof., dir. Ctr. Environ. and Resource Econ. Policy, 1999—; Arts and Scis. prof. environ. econs. Duke U., 1994-99; W.P. Carey prof. econs. Ariz. State U., Tempe, 2006—. Adviser energy div. Oak Ridge Nat. Lab., 1978-80, U. NC Inst. Environ. Studies, 1980-83; mem. panel NSF, 1981-83, sci. adv. bd. EPA. Author: Monte Carlo Methods, 1973, Technical Change, Relative Prices and Environmental Resource Evaluation, 1974, The Costs of Congestion: An Econometric Analysis of Wilderness Recreation, 1976, Structure and Properties of a Wilderness Travel Simulator: An Application to the Spanish Peaks Area, 1976, The Economic Consequences of Air Pollution, 1976, Scarcity and Growth Reconsidered, 1979, (with others) Explorations in Natural Resource Economics, 1982, (with others) Environmental Policy Under Reagan's Executive Order, 1984, (with W.H. Desvousges) Measuring Water Quality Benefits, 1986, (with others) Environmental Resources and Applied Welfare Economics, 1988, (with R.J. Kopp) Valuing Natural Assets: The Economics of Natural Resource Damage Assessment, Resources for the Future, 1993, Estimating Economic Values for Nature, 1996, (with others) The Smoking Puzzle: Information, Perception and Choices, 2003; editor Advances in Applied Micro Econs. series; contbr. numerous articles to profl. jours. Guggenheim fellow, 1976; grantee Resources for Future, 1970, 73, 74, 86, Fed. Energy Adminstrn. 1975, NY Sea Grant Inst., 1975, Ford Found., 1976, NSF, 1977, 79, 83, Electric Power Rsch. Inst., 1978, Nat. Oceanic and Atmospheric Adminstrn., 1980, Sloan Found., 1981, 86, EPA, 1983-88, NC Sea Grant Program, 1987-93. Russell Sage Found., 1989-91; recipient Frederick V. Waugh medal Am. Agrl. Econ. Assn., 1992. Fellow Am. Agrl. and Econ. Assn., Assn. Environ. and Resource Economists (bd. dirs. 1975-79, v.p. 1979-80, chmn. com. 1982-83, pres. 1985-86, Disting. Svc. award 1989); mem. NAS, Am. Econ. Assn., Econometric Soc., So. Econ. Assn. (exec. com. 1981-83, 1st v.p. 1987, pres.-elect 1988, pres. 1989). Office: Ariz State U PO Box 873806 Tempe AZ 85287-3806

SMITH, VALENE LUCY, anthropologist, educator; b. Spokane, Wash., Feb. 14, 1926; d. Ernest Frank and Lucy (Blachly) S.; m. Edwin Chesteen Golay, June 7, 1970 (dec. June 1980); m. Stanley George McIntyre, Nov. 26, 1983 (dec. Oct. 2000); m. George Addison Posey, Oct. 5, 2005. BA in Geography, U. Calif., 1946, MA in Geography, 1950; PhD in Anthropology, U. Utah, Salt Lake City, 1966. Cert. travel counselor. Prof. earth sci. LA City Coll., 1947-67; prof. anthropology Calif. State U., Chico, 1967—. Cons. World Tourism Orgn., Madrid, 1987. Editor: Hosts and Guests: The Anthrop, 1989, Tourism Alternatives: Potentials and Problems in the Development of Tourism, 1992, Hosts and Guests Revisited, 2001. Mem. Soroptimist Internat., Chico, 1968—; founding pres. Chico Mus. Assn., 1978. Named Fulbright prof., Peshawar, Pakistan, 1953—54; recipient Athena award, US C. of C., 1988. Mem. Internat. Acad. for Study Tourism, Cert. Travel Counselors, Am. Anthrop. Assn., AAUW, Canyon Oaks Country Club, Soroptimists. Republican. Avocations: travel, aviation, photography. Office: U Calif Dept Anthropology Chico CA 95929-0004 Office Phone: 530-891-1155. Business E-Mail: vsmith@csuchico.edu.

SMITH, VERNON G., education educator, state legislator; b. Gary, Ind. BS, Ind. U., 1966, MS, 1969, EdD, 1978; postgrad., Ind.U.-Purdue U., 1986-90. Tchr. Gary Pub. Schs. Systems, 1966-71; resource tchr., 1971-72; asst. prin. Ivanhoe Sch., Gary, 1972-78; prin. Nobel Sch., Gary, 1978-85, Williams Sch., Gary, 1985-92; part-time counselor edn. div. Ind. U. N.W., Gary, 1967-69, adj. lectr., 1987-92, assoc. prof., 1992—; mem. Ind. Ho. of Reps., Indpls., 1990—. Columnist Gary Crusader, 1969-71; speaker Devel. Tng. Inst., 1986—. Author: (with D. McClam) Building Bridges Instead of Walls—History of I.U. Dons, Inc., 1979; also articles. Mem. Gary City Coun., 1972-90; precinct committeeman Gary Dem. Com., 1972-92; founder, chmn. Gary City-wide Festival Com.; bd. dirs. N.W. Ind. Urban League; founder, pres. I.U. Dons, Inc.; past pres. Gary Cmty. Mental Health Bd.; v.p. Gary Common Coun., 1982, 85-87, pres., 1976, 83-84, 88; past mem. bd. dirs. Little League World series; founder, past sponsor Youth Ensuring Solidarity, Young Citizens' League; chmn. Ind. Commn. on Status of Black Males, 1992—; mem. Gov.'s Commn. for Drug-Free Ind., 1990—. Recipient citation in edn. Gary NAACP, 1970, Good Govt. award Gary Jaycees, 1977, Outstanding Svc. award Gary Young Dems., 1979, Businessman of Yr. award Gary Downtown Mchts., 1979, Bd. Dirs. Svcs. award Gary Cmty. Health Ctr., 1982, G.O.I.C. Dr. Leon H. Sullivan award, 1982, Gary Jaycees Youth award, 1983, Info Newspaper Outstanding Citizen of N.W. Ind. and Info. Newspaper's Outstanding Educator award, 1984, Post Tribune Blaine Marz Tap award, 1984, Gary Cmty. Sch. Corp. Speech Dept. Recognition award, 1984, Gary Cmty. Mental Health Ctr.'s 10th Yr. Svc. award, 1985, Roosevelt H.S. Exemplary Svc. award, 1985, Gary Crusader 25th Anniversary award, 1986, Purdue U. Ednl. Opportunity Programs Black History Svc. award, 1986, Educator Par Excellence award Williams Sch., 1987, Black Woman Hall of Fame Found. Success award, 1987, Black Women Hall of Fame Bethune-Tubman-Truth award, 1987, Our Lady of Perpetual Help Ch. Hon. Mem. award, 1987, Gary Educator of Christ Adminstr. Leadership award, 1988, NBC-LEO Appreciation award, 1988, Gary Cmty. Schs. Presenters award, 1991, Mr. G.'s Svc. award, 1991, Appreciation award Ind. Assn. Chiefs Police, 1992, Meth. Hosp., 1992, Bros. Keeper, 1992, Svc. award Ind. Assn. Elem. and Mid. Sch. Prins., 1992, N.W. Ind. Black Expo's Sen. Carolyn Mosby Above and Beyond award, 1995, In the Bethune Tradition award Nat. Coun. Negro Women, 1996, Citizen Yr. award NASW (Ind. chpt.), 1997, 98, Appreciation award Ind. chpt., 1997, Presenters award, Gary Cmty. Sch. Corp. Parent Involvement Program, 1996, Appreciation award, Pitman Square Sch., 1997, 98, 99, Alumni Appreciation award, Froebel High Sch., 1997, 98, 2002, Svc. award, Ind. League Municipal Clerks and Treas., 1998, Facet Excellence in Tchg. award, 1998, Brothers Keeper Appreciation award, 1999, Appreciation award, Lake County Assn. for the Retarded, 1999, New Hope award, 1999, New Hope Men's Day award, 2000; featured cover story Big Brothers Big Sisters Am. Newsletter for Diversity, 2000, Appreciation award, Hoosier Boys Town, 2000, Appreciation award, Gary Reading Coun., 2000, Outstanding Commitment award, Nat. Assn. Social Workers Region I, 2000, Svc. award, Ivanhoe Sch., 2002, Drum Major award, Gary Frontiers, 2002, Majestic Star award, 2002, Appreciation award, City of Lake Station, 2002, New Hope African Am.- Frederic Douglas award, 2003. Mem.: NAACP (life Ovington award 1999), No. Ind. Assn. Black Sch. Educators (founder), Ind. Assn. Sch. Prins., Ind. U. N.W. Alumni Assn. (life Disting. Educator award 1992), Phi Delta Kappa (25 Yr. award (N.W. Ind. chpt.) 1996), Omega Psi Phi (life Omega Man Yr. award 1974, Citizen Yr. award 10th dist. 1989, appreciation award Omicron Rho chpt. 1991, Citizen Yr. award (Alpha Kappa Kappa chpt.) 2003, Man Yr. award (Alpha Kappa Kappa chpt.) 2003). Baptist. Home: PO Box M622 Gary IN 46401-0622 Office: Ind U NW 3400 Broadway # 339 Gary IN 46408-1101 Office Phone: 219-980-7120. Business E-Mail: vesmith@iun.edu.

SMITH, VERNON LOMAX, economist, researcher; b. Wichita, Kans., Jan. 1, 1927; s. Vernon Chessman and Lula Belle (Lomax) S.; m. Candace C. Smith, Mar. 13, 2002. BSEE, Calif. Inst. Tech., 1949; MA in Econs., U. Kans., 1952; PhD in Econs., Harvard U., 1955; D of Mgmt. (hon.), Purdue U., 1990. Asst. prof. econs. Purdue U., West Lafayette, Ind., 1955-58, assoc. prof., 1958-61, prof., 1961-65, Krannert prof., 1965-67; prof. Brown U., Providence, 1967-68, U. Mass., Amherst, 1968-75, U. Ariz., Tucson, 1975—2001, Regents' prof., 1988—2001; prof. econs. & law George Mason U., 2001—. Contbr. articles to profl. jours. Fellow Ctr. for Advanced Study in Behavioral Scis., Stanford, Calif., 1972-73; Sherman Fairchild Disting. Scholar Calif. Inst. Tech., Pasadena, 1973-74; adj. scholar CATO Inst., Washington, 1983—; recipient Nobel prize in econs., 2002. Fellow AAAS, Am. Acad. Arts and Scis., Econometric Soc., Am. Econ. Assn. (Disting. fellow); mem. NAS, Pvt. Enterprise Edn. Assn. (Adam Smith award). Office: George Mason U Interdisc Ctr for Econ Sci 4400 University Blvd MSN 1B2 Fairfax VA 22030-4444 *

SMITH, VERONICA LATTA, real estate company officer; b. Wyandotte, Mich., Jan. 13, 1925; d. Jan August and Helena (Hulak) Latta; m. Stewart Gene Smith, Apr. 12, 1952; children: Stewart Gregory, Patrick Allen, Paul Donald, Alison Veronica Hurley, Alisa Margaret Lyons, Glenn Laurence. BA in Sociology, U. Mich., 1948. Tchr. Coral Gables (Fla.) Pub. Sch. Sys., 1949—50; COO Latta Ins. Agy, Wyandotte, 1950—62; treas. L & S Devel. Co., Grosse Ile, Mich., 1963—84; v.p. Regency Devel., Riverview, Mich., 1984—. Active U. Mich. Bd. Regents, 1985-92, regent emeritus, 1993—; mem. Martha Cook Bd. Govs., U. Mich., pres., 1976-78; del. Rep. County Conv., Grand Rapids, Mich., 1985, 87, 89, 91, 92, 94, 96, Lansing, Mich., 1996, Detroit, 1986, 88, 90, 92, 97; mem. pres. adv. com. Campaign for Mich., 1992-97, mem. campaign steering com., 1992-97. Mem. Mich. Lawyers Aux. (treas. 1975, chmn. 1976, 77, 78, 79), Nat. Assn. Ins. Women (cert.), Faculty Women's Club U. Mich. (hon.), Radrick Farms Golf Club (Ann Arbor), Pres.'s Club U. Mich., Investment Club (pres. 1976, sec. 1974-75, treas. 1975-76), Alpha Kappa Delta. Home: 22225 Balmoral Dr Grosse Ile MI 48138-1403

SMITH, VIN, editor, small business owner, writer; b. Whittier, Calif., May 19, 1944; s. M. Clifford and Anna Eugenia (Hill) S.; m. Marthea Karen Callaham, May 15, 1969 (div. 1979); children: Jayare Smith, Eric Smith; m. Ginger Hammon, Oct. 20, 1984; children: Amy Michelle, Stacey Erin, Kellie Rae. Student, Columbia Sch. Broadcasting, San Francisco, 1967; AA, Cuesta Coll., 1974; grad., Am. Sch. of Piano Tuning, 1978; DD, Ancient Order of the WA, 2004. Sales mgr. Sta. KTAT, Frederick, Okla., 1967-69; announcer KOCY, Oklahoma City, 1969; owner Melmart Markets, San Luis Obispo, Calif., 1971-73, Am. Direct Sales, Grover City, Calif., 1973-79; instr. piano Valley View Acad., Arroyo Grande, Calif., 1977-78, Long Piano Co., San Luis Obispo, 1977-79, piano technician, 1978-79; owner Chocolate Piano, Yreka, Calif., 1979—; instr. piano Makah Indian Tribe, Neah Bay, Wash., 1981-82; sports editor New Words Digest, Bakersfield, Calif., 1988—. Cons., stress evaluator seminar Yreka Stress Therapy Clinic, 1986-87; founder Vinco Distbrs. (formerly Vinco Enhancement Sys.), 1998; chair piano dept. Bogus Sch., 1999-2004, internat. relationship counselor Ask Me com., 2000-03, askdrpiano.com., 2000. Author: (novel) Neon Streets, 2002, Lincoln Park, 2003, Ride the High Waves, 2004, Lucky Pierre's, 2004, The Outrageous Views of Professor Fogelman, 2004, a.k.a. Mandi Wire, 2004, A Bullet for Slade, 2005, Get Mandi Wire, 2005, Jimamon and the Air Kids, 2005; sports columnist New Words Digest, 1987-91; guest columnist Siskiyou Daily News, 1991-94; nat publicist chamber music concerts So. Oreg. State Coll., 1993—; host (TV Show) Vin and Friends, 2003; host, prodr. (nat. broadcast CRN Digital Talk, syndicated on Nat. Radio Network) Vin Smith's Midnight Bookworm, 2005—; contbr. articles to profl. jours. Chmn. heart fund Tillman County Okla., 1968; pub. co-chmn. Siskiyou County No-Prop 174, 1994; campaign worker Ken Jourdan for sheriff, Yreka, 1986; publicity dir. Gene Breceda for supr., 1993-94. Recipient Cert. of Appreciation, Siskiyou County, 1988, Achievement award, 1988, Golden Poet award World of Poetry, 1989, Living Treasure award Siskiyou County, 2003. Mem. Nat. Writers Club (chmn. student com. Yreka chpt. 1988), Author's Guild, Inc., Author's League of Am., Mystery Writers Am., Soc. Children's Book Writers, Jr. C. of C. (sgt.-at-arms Frederick chpt. 1967-69), Kiwanis, Moose. Democrat. Avocations: horse shoe pitching, photography, reading. Home: 710 Knapp St Yreka CA 96097-2343 Office: Chocolate Piano Prodns PO Box 447 Yreka CA 96097-0447 Home Phone: 530-842-3699; Office Phone: 530-842-7672. Business E-Mail: drpiano@earthlink.net.

SMITH, VINCENT MILTON, Feng Shui consultant, educator, writer; b. Barbourville, Ky., Nov. 21, 1940; s. Virgil Milton and Louis (McGalliard) Smith; children: Jessica Todd, Duncan. BA, Harvard U., 1962; LLB, Yale U., 1965. Bar: N.Y. 1966. Assoc. Breed, Abbott & Morgan, NYC, 1965-70, Debevoise & Plimpton, NYC, 1970-75, ptnr., 1975-95; CEO Lang, Winslow & Smith Co., Chatham, NJ, 1995-98; owner VMS Feng Shui Design Co., 1998—, Panergetics, LLC, 2002—. Mem. adv. bd. Chgo. Title Ins. Co., NYC, 1979—2002; vis. Feng Shui prof. Berea (Ky.) Coll., 1999, Williams Coll., Williamstown, Mass., 2001—02; Feng Shui lectr. N.Y. Open Ctr., 1999—; co-founder, chmn. bd. Keen Co., 2000—. Author: Feng Shui: A Practical Guide for Architects and Designers. Trustee Chatham (N.J.) Players, 1967—77, 1987—91, Summit Friends Meeting, Chatham, 1973—99, N.J. Shakespeare Festival, Madison, 1975—80, Playwrights Theatre N.J., 1989—91. Mem.: N.Y. Athletic Club, Harvard Club. Mem. Soc. Of Friends. Personal E-mail: vmsdesign@aol.com. Business E-Mail: vincent.smith@panergetics.com.

SMITH, VIRGINIA ELEANORE, psychologist, educator; b. Bklyn., Aug. 12, 1940; d. Valentine A. and Katherine V. (Angold) Pajer; m. Albert G. Smith, Aug. 12, 1961; children: Daniel, Douglas, Andrew, Katherine, James. BA, Neumann Coll., 1978; MS, Drexel U., 1984; PhD, Union Inst., Cin., 1994; postgrad. clin. tng., Gestalt Therapy Inst. Phila., 1991—. Lic. mental health counselor, Del., Pa. Med. social worker Delaware County Commn. Nursing Svc., Chester, Pa., 1983-84; counselor Manatee County

Mental Health Agy., Bradenton, Fla., 1984-85; pvt. practice Wilmington, Del., 1990—; mental health counselor Correctional Med. Systems, Wilmington, Del., 1990—, AIDS Delaware, Wilmington, 2004—. Adj. prof. Delaware County CC, Media, Pa., 1985—, Widener U., Goldey Beacon Coll., Wilmington, 1987—, Neumann Coll., 2001-; assoc. dir. assessments CATCH, Phila., 1995-2003. Mem. AACD, Am. Sociol. Assn., Mental Health Counselors Assn., Assn. Humanistic Psychologists. Roman Catholic. Avocations: travel, hiking, photography, writing. Home: 830 S Walnut St Kennett Square PA 19348 Personal E-mail: virginiasmith173@comcast.net.

SMITH, VME EDOM (VERNA MAE), social sciences educator, freelance photographer, freelance writer; b. Marshfield, Wis., June 19, 1929; d. Clifton Cedric and Vilia Clarissa (Patefield) Edom; children: Teri Smith Freas, Anthony Thomas. AB in Sociology, U. Mo., 1951; MA in Sociology, George Washington, 1965; PhD in Human Devel., U. Md., 1981. Tchr. Alcohol Safety Action Program Fairfax County, Va., 1973-75; instr. sociology No. Va. C.C., Manassas, 1975-77, asst. prof., 1977-81, assoc. prof., 1981-84, prof., 1984-94, prof. emerita, 1995, coord. coop. edn., 1983-89, Chancellor's Commonwealth prof., 1991-93; adj. faculty Tidewater C.C., 1996—; freelance writer, editor and photographer, 1965—; dir. Clifton and Vi Edom Truth With a Camera (photography workshops), 1994—. Asst. prodr. history of photography program Sta. WETA-TV, Washington, 1965; rsch. and prodn. asst., photographer, publs. editor No. Va. Ednl. TV, Sta. WNVT, 1970—71; cons. migrant divsn. Md. Dept. Edn., Balt., 1977; rschr. photographer Roundabout presch. high sch. series Am. Values Sta. WNVT, 1970—71; documentary photographer Portsmouth (Va.) Redevel. and Housing Authority, 1998—2000; dir. Edom Found. Photojournalism Edn. Author, photographer Middleburg and Nearby, 1988; co-author: Small Town America, 1993; contbr. photographs and articles to various publs. Mem. ednl. adv. com. Head Start, Warrenton, Va. Recipient Emmy, Ohio State Children's Programming award; Fulbright-Hays Rsch. grantee, 1993, Va. Found. Humanities and Pub. Policy grantee, 1997—99. Mem.: Va. Assn. Coop. Edn. (com. mem.). Democrat. E-mail: vme@macs.net.

SMITH, WALTER JOHN, lawyer; b. Omaha, Apr. 19, 1948; s. Walter H. and Margaret A. (Ortman) S.; m. Mary Lou Dreves, June 20, 1970; children: Benjamin, Michael, Jeffrey. JD, Creighton U., 1972; LLM, Harvard U., 1975. Bar: Nebr. 1972, Tex. 1975. Law clk. to Judge E.A. Tamm U.S. Ct. Appeals (D.C. cir.), 1972-73; assoc. Monen, Seidler, McGill, Festerson & Koley, Omaha, 1973-74; mng. ptnr. & mem. exec. com. Baker LLP, Houston, 1975—. Editor (in chief): Creighton Law Rev. Dir. Univ. Houston Law Found., Casa de Amma, Inc., San Juan Capistrano, Calif., Ctrl Houston Inc., Greater Houston Partnership, Fund for Tchrs.; trustee Riverview Sch., Ea. Sandwich, Mass. Sustaining life fellow, Houston Bar Found.; mem. Houston Bar Assn., Coronado Club. Office: Baker & Botts LLP One Shell Plz 910 Louisiana St Houston TX 77002-4995 Office Phone: 713-229-1614. Office Fax: 713-229-7714. Business E-Mail: wsmith@bakerbotts.com.

SMITH, WARREN ALLEN, writer, director, columnist; b. Minburn, Iowa, Oct. 27, 1921; s. Harry Clark and Ruth Marion (Miles) S. BA, U. No. Iowa, Cedar Falls, 1948; MA, Columbia U., NYC, 1949. Chmn. dept. Eng. Bentley Sch., NYC, 1949-54, New Canaan H.S., Conn., 1954-86; founder, pres., chmn. bd. Variety Sound Corp., NYC, 1961-90; pres. Afro-Carib Records, 1971-90, Talent Mgmt., 1982-90, AAA Rec. Studio, 1985-90; founder, pres. Variety Rec. Studio, 1961-96; founder Philosopedia.org, 2005—. Instr. Columbia U., 1961-62. Author: Who's Who in Hell, 2000, Celebrities in Hell, 2002, Cruising the Deuce, 2005, Gossip From Across the Pond, 2005; book rev. editor: The Humanist, 1953—58; editor: (jour.) Taking Stock, 1967—93, Pique, 1990—93, Van Rijn's Pad, 1991, Janestreeter, 1997—98; contbr. book revs. Libr. Jour.; editl. assoc.: Free Inquiry, 1992—2000, columnist: Gay and Lesbian Humanist, 1996—2005, GHQ Humanist, 2005—, syndicated columnist: Manhattan Scene in W.I. newspapers; syndicated columnist Humanist Potpourri in Free Inquiry, 1994—98; drama critic: Brontë Newsletter, 1995—2000, book reviewer: New Humanist, 1997—2000, CD prodr.: Manuel Salazar: Costa Rica's Forgotten Tenor, writer: The Villager, 2002—05. Pres. Taursa Fund, 1971-73; bd. dirs. 31 Jane Street Corp. Treas. Secular Humanist Soc. NY, 1988-93; sec. Jane St. Corp., 1995-97, 98-99; with Jane Street Authors, 2000—; with ACT UP, Hume Soc.; founding mem. Voltaire Soc. Am. With AUS, 1942-46; signer Humanist Manifesto II, 1973, Humanist Manifesto, 2000, Humanist Manifesto III, 2003; mem. 1st Unitarian Ch. Des Moines. Recipient Leavey award Freedoms Found. at Valley Forge, 1985. Mem.: ASCAP, Chel C press (pres. 2004—), NY Soc. Ethical Culture, Bertrand Russell Soc. (bd. dirs. 1973—, v.p. 1977—80), Brit. Humanist Assn., Conn. Edn. Assn., Rationalist Press Assn., Am. Unitarian Assn., Internat. Press Inst., NY Skeptics Soc. (bd. dirs. 1990—94), Asociación Iberoamericana Ético Humanista (hon.), Stonewall Vets. Orgn. (treas. 1998—99), Mensa, Omaha Beach Vets. Assn., Mensa Investment Club (chmn. 1967—2001), Humanist Book Club (pres. 1957—62). Unitarian Universalist. Avocation: teratology. Home and Office: 31 Jane St Apt 10 D New York NY 10014-1980 Personal E-mail: wasm@mac.com.

SMITH, WARREN JAMES, optical scientist, consultant, lecturer, author; b. Rochester, NY, Aug. 17, 1922; s. Warren Abrams and Jessie Madelyn (Forshay) S.; m. Mary Helen Geddes, May 18, 1944 (dec. 1999); children: David Whitney, Barbara Jamie; m. Dung My Luong, Dec. 24, 2000. BS, U. Rochester, 1944; postgrad., U. Calif., Santa Barbara, 1960. Physicist Clinton Engr. Works, Tenn. Eastman Co., Oak Ridge, 1944-46; chief optical engr. Simpson Optical Mfg. Co., Chgo., 1946-59; mgr. optical sect. Raytheon Corp., Santa Barbara, 1959-62; v.p. R & D, Infrared Industries, Santa Barbara, 1962-87; chief scientist Kaiser Electro-Optics, Inc., Carlsbad, Calif., 1987—2005; cons. Rockwell Collins Optronics, Carlsbad, 2005—. Lectr. U. Wis., Madison, 1972—, Genesee Computer Ctr., Rochester, 1982—93, U. Rochester, 1988—92, Sinclair Optics, 1994—2000; cons. in field; expert witness. Author: Modern Lens Design, 1992, 2nd edit., 2004, Practical Optical System Layout, 1997, Modern Optical Engineering, 1966, 4th edit., 2007; editor McGraw-Hill series Optical and Electro-Optical Engineering; contbr. articles to profl. jours. Recipient honored, Tribute Conf., San Diego, 2005. Fellow: Optical Soc. Am. (nat. pres. 1980, organizer, chmn. tech. confs., Fraunhofer medal 2001), Internat. Soc. Optical Engring. (life; nat. pres. 1983, organizer, chmn. tech. confs., Gold medal 1985, Dirs. award 1992), Sigma Chi. Avocations: tennis, sailing. Home: 1165 Countrywood Ln Vista CA 92081-5334 Office: Rockwell Collins Optronics 2752 Loker Ave W Carlsbad CA 92010-6603 Home Phone: 760-727-3253; Office Phone: 760-438-9255 ext. 234. Business E-Mail: wjsmith1@rockwellcollins.com.

SMITH, WAYNE CALVIN, chemical engineer, consultant; b. Beaver, Okla., Mar. 19, 1935; s. Dean C. and Loraine S.; m. Suellyn Joyce Canon, Aug. 18, 1984. BS, Okla. U., 1958, MSChemE, 1964; PhDChemE, Colo. U., 1974. Registered profl. engr., Tex., Okla., Colo.; cert. emergency response specialist. Process engr. Shell Oil Co., Deer Park, Tex., 1958-59; sr. devel. engr. Monsanto, Pensacola, Fla., 1965-66; project leader Phillips Petroleum Co., Bartlesville, Okla., 1967-69; acting chief process control EPA Nat. Enforcement Investigations Ctr., Denver, 1971-78; firm wide mgr. pollution control Dames & Moore, Golden, Colo., 1978-81; regional mgr. Hittman Assocs., Englewood, Colo., 1981-82; pres. Encon Environs Control Svcs., Golden, Colo., 1982-83; chief hazardous waste mgmt. Woodward-Clyde Cons., Englewood, 1983-84; exec. cons. Kellogg Corp., Littleton, Colo., 1984-86; program mgr. Radian Corp., Austin, Tex., 1986-93; prin. engr., program mgr. Tetra Tech, Inc., Oklahoma City, 1993—2003; project mgr. FPM Group Ltd., Midwest City, Okla., 2003—04, ret., 2004—. Contbr. over 30 articles to profl. jours. Capt. USMC, 1959-62. Scholar Magnolia Petroleum Co., 1956-58; fellow Phillips Petroleum Co., 1962-64, Marathon Oil Co., 1966-67, Gulf Oil Co., 1969-71. Mem. AIChE, Am. Arbitration Assn., The Greens Country Club, Sigma Xi. Baptist. Avocations: golf, woodworking. Personal E-mail: wcssjs@sbcglobal.net.

SMITH, WAYNE RICHARD, lawyer; b. Petoskey, Mich., Apr. 30, 1934; s. Wayne Anson and Frances Lynetta (Cooper) S.; m. Carrie J. Swanson, June 13, 1959; children: Stephen, Douglas (dec.), Rebecca. AB, U. Mich., 1956, JD, 1959. Bar: Mich. 1959. Asst. atty. gen. State of Mich., 1960-62; pros. atty. Emmet County (Mich.), 1963-68; dist. judge 90th Jud. Dist., Mich., 1969-72; city atty. City of Petoskey, 1976-98. Trustee North Central Mich. Coll., 1981-98, chmn., 1992-97; trustee/chmn. N. Ctrl. Mich. Coll. Found., 1999—; mem. No. Mich. Community Mental Health Bd., 1972-92, chmn., 1979-81. Mem. Emmet-Charlevoix Bar Assn. (pres. 1967), State Bar Mich., Mich. State Bar Found. Presbyterian. Home and Office: 365 E Main St PO Box 4677 Harbor Springs MI 49740-4677 Office Phone: 231-526-1684.

SMITH, WAYNE THOMAS, healthcare company executive; b. Jan. 29, 1946; BS, Auburn Univ, 1968, MS, 1969; M in hosp. adminstrn., Trinity U.; postgrad., King's Fund Coll. Hosp. Adminstrn. With Trinity Univ, 1971-73, Humana Inc, Louisville, 1973-96, v.p. ctrl. hosp. region, 1978-80, sr. v.p., 1980-85, exec. v.p., 1985-86, pres., COO group health divsn., 1986-96, also bd. dirs.; exec. v.p. Humana Health Care Ops., Louisville, 1991-96; ret. Humana Inc., 1996; pres., CEO, Cmty. Health Sys., Brentwood, Tenn., 1996—, chmn. bd., 2001—. Exec. v.p. health plan ops., bd. dirs. Humana Health Plan, Inc., Louisville; pres. Humana Health Ins. Nev., Inc., Humana Health Plan Fla., Inc., Humana Health Plan Ohio, Inc., Humana Health Chgo. Ins. Co., Humana Kansas City, Inc.; pres., COO Humana Health Plan Tex., Prime Health Mgmt. Svcs.; pres., bd. dirs. HMPK, Inc.; bd. dirs. Praxair, Inc.; chmn. bd. Fedn. Am.'s Hosps. Bd. dirs. Gov.'s Scholars Program, Ky., Actors Theatre of Louisville, Ky. Ctr. for the Arts, The Louisville Orchestra; bd. overseers U. Louisville; mem. exec. com. Greater Louisville Fund for the Arts; past chair bd. dirs. Louisville Collegiate Sch. With U.S. Army, 1969-73, capt., 1973. Mem. Group Health Assn. Am. (bd. dirs.), Health Ins. Assn. Am. (bd. dirs.). Office: Community Health Systems 155 Franklin Rd Ste 400 Brentwood TN 37027-4646 *

SMITH, WENDY HOPE, lawyer; b. NYC, Jan. 19, 1957; d. Morton and Doris Smith. AB, Smith Coll., 1978; JD, Boston U., 1981. Bar: N.J. 1981, U.S. Dist. Ct. 1981, U.S. Ct. Appeals (3d cir.), Supreme Ct. U.S. Law sec. to judge Superior Ct. N.J., Bergen County, 1981-82; assoc. firm Sellar, Richardson, Stuart & Chisholm, Roseland, N.J., 1982-89, ptnr., 1989-97, Sellar Richardson, P.C., 1997-2000, Marshall, Dennehey, Warner, Coleman & Goggin, Roseland, N.J., 2000—. Mem. adv. com. Inst. CLE, 1983—91. Mem. ABA, N.J. Bar Assn., Bergen County Bar Assn., Essex County Bar Assn., Mensa, Smith Coll. Alumnae Assn. (fund rep. 1978-83). Home: 401 Hancock Ct Edgewater NJ 07020-1627 Office: Marshall Dennehey Warner Coleman & Goggin 425 Eagle Rock Ave Ste 302 Roseland NJ 07068 Office Phone: 973-618-4100.

SMITH, WENDY L., foundation executive; b. Chgo., Sept. 12, 1950; d. John Arthur and Dolores Mae (Webb) Rothenberger; m. Alan Richard Smith; children: Angela Fuhs, Erica Smith. Student, Oakton CC, Des Plaines, Ill., 1986, Mundelein Coll., 1990. Purchasing clk. AIT Industries, Skokie, Ill., 1975-76; purchasing agt. MCC Powers, Skokie, 1976-78; office mgr. Spartan Engring., Skokie, 1978-80, Brunswick Corp., Skokie, 1980—; successively sr. sec., coord. indsl. rels., dir. Brunswick Found., Lake Forest, Ill., 1982-89, pres., 1989—. Asst. sec. Brunswick Pub. Charitable Found., Lake Forest, 1989—; mem. adv. com. Found. for Ind. Higher Edn., Stamford, Conn., 1989—, Coun. Better Bus. Burs., Arlington, Va., 1988-90; bd. dirs. Associated Colls. of Ill., 1991—; bd. dirs., mem. trustees com., mem. compensation and benefits com. Donors Forum of Chgo., 1988-93. Bd. dirs. INROADS/Chgo., Inc., 1994—; mem. steering com. Dist. 57 Edn. Found., Mt. Prospect, Ill., 1996—. Recipient Pvt. Sector Initiative Commendation, U.S. Pres., 1987-89. Mem. Donors Forum Chgo. (treas. 1988-91, bd. dirs., mem. exec. com., chairperson audit and fin. com., mem. trustees com. 1992—), Coun. on Founds., Ind. Sector Suburban Contbns. Network (chairperson 1987-89), Women in Philanthropy Corp. Founds. (mem. cmty. rels. com. 1985-87), Chgo. Women in Philanthropy. Avocations: antique restoration, pleasure reading, bowling, golf.

SMITH, WILBUR LAZAR, radiologist, educator; b. Warwick, NY, Oct. 11, 1943; s. Wilbur and Betty (Norris) S.; m. Rebecca Rowlands, June 19, 1965; children: Jason, Daniel, Joanna, Noah, Ethan, Jacob. BA, SUNY, Buffalo, 1965, MD, 1969. Diplomate Am. Bd. Radiology, Am. Bd. Pediat., Am. Bd. Pediatric Radiology. Intern, then resident Buffalo Children's Hosp., 1969-71; resident in pediatric radiology Cin. Gen. and Children's Hosp., 1971-74; asst. prof. pediatrics and radiology Ind. U., Indpls., 1975-78, assoc. prof., 1978-80, acting dir. pediatric radiology, 1979-80; assoc. prof. U. Iowa, Iowa City, 1980-82, prof., 1982—, dir. med. edn. in radiology, 1980-86, vice chmn. dept. radiology, 1986-94, interim head, 1994-96, dir. pediatric radiology, 1980-92; chmn. dept. radiology Henry Ford Health Sys., Detroit, 1998-99; prof. radiology Wayne State U., Detroit, 2000—, chmn. dept. radiology, 2002—; staff radiologist Mich. Children's Hosp., Detroit, 2000—. Vice chmn. radiology for academics Wayne State U., 2001, radiology residency dir., 01, prof., chmn. dept. radiology, 2002—. Assoc. editor Gastrointestinal Imaging in Pediatrics, Acad. Radiology, 1992—, Quar. Rev. Child Abuse, 1998, Radiology 101, co-author, 2d edit. 2004; exec. assoc. editor Acad. Radiology, 1997-2000, assoc. editor, 2000—02; contbr. articles to profl. jours. Vol. soccer coach, 1980-99; physician cons. in child abuse, 1980-; mem. equity adv. com. Iowa City Sch. Bd., 1983-87. With USAR, 1969—77, hon. discharge USAR. Fellow Am. Acad. Pediatrics, Am. Coll. Radiology; mem. AMA, Radiol. Soc. N.Am.(second v.p. 2004-05), Iowa Radiol. Soc. (pres. 1987-88), Assn. Univ. Radiologists (pres. 1995-96, sr. adv. 2001—, Gold medal 2006), Soc. Pediat. Radiology (treas. 1995-98, rep. coun. Acad. Socs. of AAMC 1996-02), Mich. Radiol. Soc. (bd. dirs. 2004—). Mem. Soc. Of Friends. Avocation: photography. Home: 10124 Lasalle Blvd Huntington Woods MI 48070-1162 Office: Detroit Receiving Hosp Dept Radiology (3L8) 4201 St Antoine Detroit MI 48201 Home Phone: 248-582-1521; Office Phone: 313-745-4443. Business E-Mail: wlsmith@med.wayne.edu.

SMITH, WILBURN JACKSON, JR., retired bank executive; b. Charlotte, NC, June 13, 1921; s. Wilburn Jackson and Banna (Oswalt) S.; m. Terry Mosteller, Jan. 4, 1944; children: Kenneth M., M. Scott (dec.), Wilburn Jackson III, Curtis Todd. BS in Acctg., U. NC, 1943; postgrad. in comml. banking, Rutgers U., 1953, postgrad. in investment banking, 1956. With First Union Nat. Bank, Charlotte, 1946-74, exec. v.p., 1960-67, 1st exec. v.p., 1967-74; pres., mng. trustee Cameron-Brown Investment Group, Raleigh, N.C., 1974-78; chmn. loan policy com. N.C. Nat. Bank, Charlotte, 1979-88. Cons. in field. Served with USN, 1943-46. Recipient Citizenship award Charlotte Civitan, 1972. Mem. Robert Morris Assocs., Myers Park Country Club (Charlotte). Baptist. Home: 2222 Selwyn Ave 404 Charlotte NC 28207-2779

SMITH, WILL, actor, rap artist; b. Phila., Sept. 25, 1968; s. Caroline and Willard Smith; m. Sheree Smith, May 9, 1992 (div. 1995); 1 child, Willard III; m. Jada Pinkett Smith, Dec. 31, 1997; children: Jaden Christopher Syre, Willow Camille Reign. Ptnr. Overbrook Entertainment. Albums (as The Fresh Prince with DJ Jazzy Jeff): And in this Corner..., 1989, Homebase, 1991, Rock the House, 1987, He's the DJ, I'm the Rapper, 1988, Code Red, 1993, Big Willie Style, 1997, Willennium, 1999, Maximum Will Smith, 2000, Born to Reign, 2002, Greatest Hits, 2002, Lost and Found, 2005; (singles) Just One of Those Days, 1987, Girls Ain't Nothing But Trouble, 1988, Brank New Funk, 1988, A Nightmare on My Street, 1988, Jazzy's Groove, 1989, I Think I Can Beat Mike Tyson, 1989, Parents Just Don't Understand, (Grammy award for Best Rap Performance, 1989), The Things That U Do, 1991, Summertime, 1991 (Grammy award), Ring My Bell, 1991, I'm Looking for the One (To Be With Me), 1993, Boom! Shake the Room, 1993; Actor: (TV series) The Fresh Prince of Bel-Air, 1990-96, (also exec. prodr. 1994-96), Happily Ever After: Fairy Tales for Every Child (voice), 1995, All of Us, 2003 (also writer, exec. prodr.); (TV appearances) Blossom, 1991, All of Us, 2003; (films) Where the Day Takes You, 1992, Made in America, 1993, Six Degrees of Separation, 1993, Bad Boys, 1995, Independence Day, 1996 (Blockbuster Entertainment award Favorite Actor Sci-Fi), Men In Black, 1997 (MTV Movie awards Best Fight, Best Movie Song, ASCAP award Most Performed Songs for Motion Picture, Blockbuster Entertainment award Favorite Actor Sci-Fi), Welcome to Hollywood, 1998, Enemy of the State, 1998, Wild Wild West, 1999, The Legend of Bagger Vance, 2000, Ali, 2001, Men in Black II, 2002, Bad Boys II, 2003, I, Robot, 2004 (also exec. prodr.), Shark Tale (voice), 2004, Hitch, 2005 (also prodr.), The Pursuit of Happyness, 2006 (also prodr.)(Choice Movie Actor: Drama, Teen Choice Awards, 2007); exec. prodr., Showtime, 2002, The Seat Filler, 2004; prodr. Saving Face, 2004, ATL, 2006. Recipient ShoWest Conv. awards Actor of Yr., 1999, Spl. Internat. Box Office Achievement award 1997, BET award for Best Actor, 2002, Am. Music Award, Favorite Male Artist, 2005; named one of 50 Most Powerful People in Hollywood, 2004-06, 100 Most Influential People, Time Mag., 2006, 100 Most Powerful Celebrities, Forbes.com, 2007 *

SMITH, WILLARD GRANT, psychologist; b. Sidney, NY, June 29, 1934; s. Frank Charles and Myrtle Belle (Empet) S.; m. Ruth Ann Dissly, Sept. 14, 1957; children: Deborah Sue Henri, Cynthia Lynn Koster, Andrea Kay Richards, John Charles. BS, U. Md., 1976; MS, U. Utah, 1978, PhD, 1981. Diplomate Am. Bd. Forensic Examiners, Am. Bd. Psychol. Specialities, Am. Bd. Disability Analysts, cert. forensic cons.; lic. psychologist Utah, cert. sch. psychologist nat. Tchg. asst. dept. ednl. psychology U. Utah; rsch. asst. U. Utah Med. Ctr., 1976-78; rsch. cons. Utah Dept. Edn., 1977; program evaluator Salt Lake City Sch. Dist.; program evaluator, auditor Utah State Bd. Edn., 1978; sch. psychologist Jordan Sch. Dist., Sandy, Utah, 1978-82, tchr., 1979-80; exec. dir. Utah Ind. Living Ctr., Salt Lake City, 1982-83; spl. edn. cons. Southeastern Edn. Svc. Ctr., Price, Utah, 1983-85; sch. psychologist Jordan Sch. Dist., Sandy, Utah, 1985-96; assoc. psychologist Don W. McBride & Assocs., Bountiful, Utah, 1989-91; pvt. practice Sandy, Utah, 1991—. Master sgt. USAF, 1953-76. Decorated Air Force Commendation medal with 2 clusters. Fellow Am. Coll. Forensic Examiners (life); mem. APA, Nat. Assn. Sch. Psychologists, Air Force Assn., Air Force Sgts. Assn., Ret. Enlisted Assn., Am. Legion, VFW, Phi Kappa Phi, Alpha Sigma Lambda. Home: 8955 Quail Hollow Dr Sandy UT 84093-1903 Office Phone: 801-942-5356. E-mail: dr_bill5@msn.com.

SMITH, WILLIAM ASHLEY, lawyer, investment banker, energy executive; b. Birmingham, Ala., Sept. 14, 1944; S. Robert Wesley and Nancy Victoria (Davis) S.; m. Blakeley Dean Dent, Sept. 2, 1967; children: William Ashley, Andrew Lindsey BA, U. Va., 1966; JD, U. Ala., 1969. Bar: Ala 1972. Atty. Sonat, Inc., Birmingham, Ala., 1970-73, asst. sec., 1973-79, asst. v.p., asst. sec., 1979-80, asst. v.p., asst. sec., assoc. gen. counsel, 1980-81, v.p., gen. counsel, sec., 1981-84, v.p., gen. counsel, 1984-87, sr. v.p., gen. counsel, 1987-89, sr. v.p., 1989-91, exec. v.p., 1991-94, exec. v.p., gen. counsel, 1995—99; vice chmn. Sonat Exploration, Birmingham, Ala., 1994-97; exec. v.p. El Paso Corp., 1999—2002; chmn. El Paso Global Gas Group, 2001—02; ptnr. Galway Group, Houston, 2002—. Pres. So. Natural Gas Co., 1989—, chmn., 1991-94. Mem. ABA, Ala. Bar Assn. Episcopalian. Office: Galway Group LP 3050 Post Oak Blvd Ste 1300 Houston TX 77056

SMITH, WILLIAM CHARLES, retired lawyer; b. Batavia, NY, June 9, 1930; s. William F. and Verna B. (Busmire) S.; m. Lucia P. Pierce, July 10, 1954; children: William Charles, Leonard P., Victoria J. BA, U. Buffalo, 1952; LLB, Harvard U., 1955. Bar: Maine 1955, D.C. 1962, Fla. 1995, U.S. Dist. Ct. Maine, 1956, U.S. Tax Ct. 1960, U.S. Ct. Appeals (1st cir.) 1977, U.S. Ct. Claims 1985, U.S. Supreme Ct. 1960. Assoc., Portland, Maine, 1955-57; ptnr. Hutchinson, Pierce, Atwood & Allen, Portland, 1957-59; counsel Office Tax Legis. Counsel, U.S. Treasury Dept., Washington, 1959-61; ptnr. Pierce Atwood, Portland, 1961-96, of counsel, 1996—2005. Exec. com. Fed. Tax Inst., New Eng. Vice chmn. budget com. United Community Services, 1966-68, chmn., 1968-70, nat. budget and consultation com., 1969-71; bd. dirs. Portland Goodwill, Inc., 1967-69, United Way, Inc., 1968-74, 75-80, Portland Widow's Wood Soc., 1962—2005; trustee Portland Regional Opportunity Program, 1967-68, Freyburg Acad., 1976-96, Found. Blood Research, 1979-85. Mem. ABA, Maine Bar Assn., Cumberland County Bar Assn., Am. Law Inst., Am. Coll. Trust and Estate Counsel, Am. Coll. Tax Counsel, Portland Country Club, Mid-Ocean Club (Bermuda), Meadows Country Club (Fla.), Cumerland Club (Maine). Republican. Unitarian Universalist. Personal E-mail: wsmith2@maine.rr.com.

SMITH, WILLIAM HENRY PRESTON, freelance/self-employed writer, editor, former telecommunications industry executive; b. Pleasanton, Tex., Sept. 8, 1924; s. Sidney Newton and Willie Gertrude (Cloyd) S.; m. Frances Dixon, July 1, 1950; children: Juliet, Dixon, David. B.J., U. Tex., 1949. Reporter Dallas Morning News, 1949-52; advt. asst. Dallas Power & Light Co., 1952-55; dir. pub. relations Greater Boston C. of C., 1955-58; with New Eng. Telephone and Telegraph Co., Boston, 1958-86, asst. v.p., 1966-75, corp. sec., 1975-83, dir. pub. relations, 1983-86; free-lance writer Dover, Mass., 1986—. Editor: Bus. Ethics Resource Newsletter. Bd. dirs., v.p. Mass. Soc. for Prevention Cruelty to Children; bd. dirs. Bus. Ethics Found., Urban Dynamics Adv. Coun.; mem. support policies com. United Way Mass; bd. advisors to pres. Andover Newton Theol. Sch. With paratroopers U.S. Army, 1943-46. Decorated Purple Heart, U.S. Army, Bronze Star, U.S. Army. Mem. Am. Soc. Corp. Secs., Friars, Dedham Country and Polo Club, Down Town Club, Wellesley Coll. Club, Sigma Delta Chi, Delta Kappa Epsilon. Republican. Home and Office: 3236 Wingfield Lake Rd Williamsburg VA 23185-7519

SMITH, WILLIAM JAY, author; b. Winnfield, La., Apr. 22, 1918; s. Jay and Georgia (Campster) S.; m. Barbara Howes, Oct. 1, 1947 (div. June 1965); children: David Emerson, Gregory Jay; m. Sonja Haussmann, Sept. 3, 1966. Student, Institut de Touraine, Tours, France, 1938; BA, Washington U., St. Louis, 1939, MA, 1941; postgrad., Columbia U., 1946-47; postgrad. Rhodes scholar, Oxford U., 1947-48; postgrad., U. Florence, Italy, 1948-50; Litt.D., New Eng. Coll., 1973. Asst. in French Washington U., 1939-41; instr. English and French Columbia U., 1946-47; lectr. English Williams Coll., 1951, poet in residence, lectr. English, 1959-64, 66-67; Ford Found. fellow Arena Stage, Washington, 1964-65; writer in residence Hollins Coll., 1965-66, prof. English, 1967, 70-80, prof. emeritus, 1980. Poet laureate Libr. Congress, Washington, 1968-70, hon. cons. in Am. letters, 1970-76; vis. prof., acting chmn., writing divsn. Sch. Arts, Columbia U., 1973, 74-75; mem. staff Salzburg (Austria) Seminar, 1975; mem. jury Nat. Book award, 1962, 70, 75, Neustadt Internat. prize for lit., 1978, Com. of Pegasus Prize for Lit., 1979-98; poet in residence Cathedral St. John the Divine, N.Y., 1985-88. Author: Poems, 1947, Celebration at Dark, 1950, Laughing Time, 1955, Poems, 1947-57, Boy Blue's Book of Beasts, 1957, Puptents and Pebbles: A Nonsense ABC, 1959, Typewriter Town, 1960, The Spectra Hoax, 1961, What Did I See, 1962, Ho for a Hat, 1964, (with Louise Bogan) The Golden Journey; Poems for Young People, 1965, The Tin Can and Other Poems, 1966, If I Had a Boat, 1966, Poems from France, 1967, Mr. Smith and Other Nonsense, 1968, New and Selected Poems, 1970, The Streaks of the Tulip, selected criticism, 1972,

Poems from Italy, 1973, Venice in the Fog, 1975, The Telephone, 1977, Laughing Time, 1980, The Traveler's Tree, New and Selected Poems, 1980, Army Brat, a Memoir, 1980, A Green Place: Modern Poems, 1982, Plain Talk: Epigrams, Epitaphs, Satires, Nonsense, Occasional Concrete and Quotidian Poems, 1988, Ho for a Hat (rev.), 1989, Collected Poems 1939-1989, 1990, Laughing Time: Collected Nonsense, 1990, Birds and Beasts, 1990, Big and Little, 1992 (with Carol Ra) Behind the King's Kitchen: A Roster of Rhyming Riddles, 1992, The Cyclist, 1995 (with Carol Ra) The Sun is Up: A Child's Year of Poems, 1996, The World Below the Window: Poems 1937-1997, 1998, Here is My Heart: Love Poems, 1999, The Cherokee Lottery: A Sequence of Poems, 2000, Around My Room, 2000, The Spectra Hoax (paperback reissue), 2000, The Girl in the Glass: Love Poems, 2002; translator: (with Emanuel Brasil) Brazilian Poetry 1950-80, 1984, (with Ingvar Schousboe) The Pact: My Friendship with Isak Dinesen by Thorkild Bjørnvig, 1983, (with J.S. Holmes) Dutch Interior: Post-War Poetry of the Netherlands and Flanders, 1984, Scirocco by Romualdo Romano, 1951; Poems of a Multimillionaire by Valery Larbaud, 1955, Selected Writings of Jules Laforgue, 1956, Children of the Forest by Elsa Beskow, 1969, Two Plays by Charles Bertin: Christopher Columbus and Don Juan, 1970, The Pirate Book by Lennart Hellsing, 1972, (with Leif Sjöberg) Agadir by Artur Lundkvist, 1979, Moral Tales of Jules Laforgue, 1985, Collected Translations: Italian, French, Spanish, Portuguese, 1985, (with Dana Gioia) Poems from Italy, 1985, (with Leif Sjöberg) Wild Bouquet: Nature Poems by Harry Martinson, 1985, (with Sonja Haussmann Smith) The Madman and the Medusa by Tchicaya U Tam'Si, 1989, Songs of Childhood by Federico Garcia Lorca, 1994, Berlin: The City and the Court, 1996, (with Leif Sjöberg) The Forest of Childhood: Poems from Sweden, 1996, Gyula Illyés: Selected Poems, 1999; editor: Herrick, 1962, Light Verse and Satires by Witter Bynner, 1978, (with F.D. Reeve) An Arrow in the Wall: Selected Poetry and Prose by Andrei Voznesensky, 1986 (one of 16 Best Books of 1986, N.Y. Times), Life Sentence: Selected Poems of Nina Cassian, 1990. Mem. Vt. Ho. of Reps., 1960-62. Served to lt. USNR, 1941-45. Recipient Alumni citation Washington U., 1963; prize Poetry mag., 1945, 64; Henry Bellamann Major award, 1970; Russell Loines award Nat. Inst. Arts and Letters, 1972; Gold medal Labor Hungary 1978; Golden Rose award New Eng. Poetry Club, 1979, médaille de vermeil French Acad., 1991, Pro Cultura Hungarica medal, Hungary, 1993; Nat. Endowment for Arts fellow, 1972, 95; NEH fellow, 1975, 89; Ingram Merrill fellow, 1982; Camargo Found. fellow, 1986, René Vásquez Díaz prize Swedish Acad., 1997. Mem. Am. Acad. Arts and Letters (v.p. for literature 1986-89), Am. Assn. Rhodes Scholars, Acad. Am. Poets, Authors Guild, P.E.N. Clubs: Century. Home: 63 Luther Shaw Rd Cummington MA 01026-9787 Address: 52-56 rue d'Alleray 75015 Paris France

SMITH, WILLIAM RAYMOND, farmer, horse breeder; b. Bowling Green, Ky., June 5, 1932; s. William Raymond and Rose Velta (Biggerstaff) Smith; m. Robin Sommers, July 12, 1954 (div. July 1977); children: Dana Leslie Henning, Lauren Reneé Imgrund; m. Lee Ann McClathchey, Dec. 31, 1994 (div. May 2003). BA in Liberal Arts, U. Chgo., 1953, MA in English, 1959, PhD in History of Culture, 1961. Lic. thoroughbred trainer. Asst. prof. English Pa. State U., Univ. Park, 1961-63, Haverford (Pa.) Coll., 1963-66, Scripps Coll., Claremont, Calif., 1966-67, exec. officer literature divsn., 1966-67; chmn. integrative studies Shimer Coll., Mt. Carroll, Ill., 1967-70; asst. prof. humanities Reed Coll., Portland, 1970-71; prof. history and philosophy U. Pitts., Johnstown, Pa., 1971-98, acad. dean, 1971-72; ret., 1998. Fulbright prof. Am. studies U. Utrecht, Netherlands, 1969—70. Author: History as Argument, 1966, The Rhetoric of American Politics, 1969; co-author: The Colonial Legacy, 1971, Nineteenth Century Literary Criticism, 1986. With US Army, 1955—57. Fellow, Union Rsch. Higher Edn., 1968. Avocation: fox hunting rider. Home: Loghouse Farm 445 Mt Zion Rd Dillsburg PA 17019 Office Phone: 717-432-1554. Personal E-mail: loghousefarm@aol.com.

SMITH, WILLIAM REECE, JR., lawyer; b. Athens, Tenn., Sept. 19, 1925; s. William Reece and Gladys (Moody) S. BS, U. SC, 1946, LLD, 1981; JD, U. Fla., 1949; Rhodes scholar, Oxford U., 1949-52; LLD, U. So. Fla., 1973, Rollins Coll., 1980, U. Fla., 1980, Stetson U., 1985, Nova Southeastern U., 2005; DCL, Central Meth. Coll., 1980, New Eng. Coll., 1980; DHL, Calif. West Sch. Law, 1981; DBA, Tampa Coll., Fla., 1991; LHD, U. So. Fla., 1990. Bar: Fla. 1949. Mem. firm Carlton, Fields, Ward, Emmanuel, Smith and Cutler, Tampa, 1953—, now chmn. emeritus; interim pres. U. So. Fla., 1976-77; city atty. Tampa, 1963-72. Asst. prof. law U. Fla., 1952-53; adj. prof. law Stetson U., 1954-59, 91—; past pres. Fla. Legal Svcs., Inc., Tampa Philharmonic Assn., Fla. Gulf Coast Symphony, Inc. Sec. Fla. Rhodes Scholar Selection Com., 1969-94. Midshipman and ensign USNR, 1943—46. Named Outstanding Young Man of Tampa, 1961; named to Hall of Fame Stetson U. Coll. (inaugural mem.), Tampa Bay Bus. Hall of Fame, 2007; recipient Good Govt. award Fla. Jr. C. of C., 1965, Disting. Am. award Tampa Chpt. Nat. Football Found., 1977, Humanitarian award B'nai B'rith Found., 1977, Pres.'s award Fla. Assn. Retarded Citizens, 1978, Von Briesen award Nat. Legal Aid and Defender Assn., 1980, Brotherhood award NCCJ, 1980, Herbert Harley award Am. Judicature Soc., 1983, Citizen of Yr. award Civitan Club, 1986, Algernon Sydney Sullivan award, U. SC, 1987, Pub. Svc. award Stetson U. Coll. Law, 1990, C.H.I.E.F. award Fla. Ind. Colls. and Univs., 1990, Professionalism award Am. Inns of Ct., 2002. Fellow Am. Coll. Trial Lawyers, Internat. Acad. Trial Lawyers, Fla. Bar Found. (past pres.); mem. ABA (chmn. jr. bar conf. 1960-61, life, ho. dels., sec. 1967-71, pres. 1980-81, Gold medal 1989, Pro Bono Publico award 1994), Am. Bar Found., Am. Bar Endowment, Internat. Soc. Barristers, Am. Law Inst. (mem. coun.), Internat. Bar Assn. (past pres.), Inter-Am. Bar Assn. (mem. exec. coun. 1972-77), Fla. Bar Assn. (pres. 1972-73), Hillsborough County Bar Assn. (pres. 1963), Nat. Conf. Bar Pres. (pres. 1978-79), Greater Tampa C. of C. (pres. 1986-87). Methodist. Home: PO Box 3239 Tampa FL 33601-3239 Office: Carlton Fields Ward Emmanuel Smith & Cutler Corp Ctr 3 10th Flr 4221 W Boy Scout Blvd Tampa FL 33607 Office Phone: 813-223-7000.

SMITH, WILLIAM S., JR., education association administrator; BS in Chemistry, Tex. A&M U., 1970, PhD in Chemistry, 1974. Postdoctoral rschr. U. Calif., Irvine, 1974—77; program mgr. FAA; graduate rsch. Tex. A&M U., 1971—74; phys. scientist FAA, U.S. Dept. Transp., 1977—85; sci. advisor subcom. on space, com. on sci., space and tech. U.S. Ho. of Reps., 1985—88, staff dir. subcom., 1988—94, dep. Dem. chief of staff, 1994—98; v.p. for programs Assn. Univs. for Rsch. in Astronomy, Inc., Washington, 1998—2000, interim pres., 1999—2000, pres., 2000—. Recipient Exceptional Svc. award, NASA, Sci. and Tech. Fellowship award, Dept. Commerce, 1984. Office: AURA Inc Ste 350 1200 New York Ave NW Washington DC 20005 E-mail: wsmith@aura-astronomy.org.

SMITH, YEARDLEY, actress; b. Paris, July 3, 1964; Voice of Lisa Simpson, Maggie Simpson and others The Simpsons, 1989—. Actor: (films) Heaven Help Us, 1985, The Legend of Billie Jean, 1985, Maximum Overdrive, 1986, Three O'Clock High, 1987, Listen to Me, 1989, Zwei Frauen, 1989, City Slickers, 1989, Toys, 1992, Jingle All the Way, 1996, Just Write, 1997, As Good As It Gets, 1997, (voice) We're Back! A Dinosaur's Story, 1993, The Simpsons Movie, 2007,; (TV films) Mom's On Strike, 1984, Tickets, Please, 1988; (TV series) Brothers, 1984, The Tracey Ullman Show, 1987—89, (voice) The Simpsons, 1989—, Herman's Head, 1991, Dharma & Greg, 1997—99, 2001—02, (TV guest appearance) Tales from the Darkside, 1986, Mama's Family, 1986, Mathnet, 1987, Sydney, 1990, Likely Suspects, 1992, Hey Hey, It's Sunday, 1994, Empty Nest, 1994, Smart Guy, 1997, Teen Angel, 1997, Sports Night, 1998, Nash Bridges, 1999, Becker, 2003; (plays) More, 2004, Balancing Act, 2007. Office: The Simpsons c/o Twentieth Television PO Box 900 Beverly Hills CA 90213 *

SMITH, YOLANDA IPPOLITO, law educator, researcher, writer; b. Raleigh, NC, Oct. 12, 1943; d. Luciano and Blanche Ruth Mason Ippolito; m. Ralph Clemens Smith III, May 21, 1999; m. John Jacob Christensen, Nov. 27, 1965 (div.); children: Elizabeth Kristen Christensen, Peter John Christensen. BS, U. Md., College Park, 1965; MA, Norwich U., Northfield, 1981; JD, U. Md., Balt., 1993. Bar: Md. 1993, DC 1995, U.S. Ct. Appeals (4th cir.) 1995, U.S. Dist. Ct. Md. 1995. Bus. franchisee Wicks 'N' Sticks, Gautier, Miss., 1980—82; prof. No. Va. C.C., Alexandria, 1995—. Cons., spkr. in field; adj. faculty No. Va. C.C., 1986—95. Author: Needlepoint Simplified, The Needlepoint Book, rev. edition, Worry-Free Retirement Living: Choosing a Full Service Retirement Community, Bargello Stitchery, Trapunto, Cross Stitchery, Applique and Reverse Applique, The Needlepoint Book, Teach Yourself Needlepoint, Needlepoint: The Third Dimension, The Needlepoint Scraps Book. Home Phone: 703-820-7375.

SMITH, YOUNG MERRITT, JR., lawyer; b. Hickory, NC, July 25, 1944; s. Young Merritt and Christine Ellen (White) S.; m. Louise Garner Price, Sept. 6, 1966 (div. Aug. 1974); 1 child, Patrick Adam; m. Charlie Mae Early, Nov. 19, 1977 (div. May 1985); m. Mary Gayle Jones, June 8, 1985; children: Mary Gaither, Jennifer Gayle. AB, U. N.C., 1966; JD, Duke U., 1969. Bar: N.C. 1969. Pres. The Litchfield Plantation Co., Pawleys Island, S.C., 1969-74, The Figure Eight Island Co., Wilmington, N.C., 1971-74; ptnr. Smith and Smith, Hickory, N.C., 1974-87; lawyer in pvt. practice Hickory, 1987—. Trustee Fund for Peace, N.Y.C., 1970-79, United Health Services N.C., Durham, 1971-73, N.C. Design Found., Raleigh, 1973-76. Mem. N.C. Bar Assn., Delta Kappa Epsilon. Democrat. Episcopalian. Office: Young M Smith Jr Atty PO Drawer 1948 Hickory NC 28603 Home Phone: 828-322-8196; Office Phone: 828-327-4101. E-mail: ysmith@youngsmithlaw.com.

SMITH, YVONNE SMART, advertising executive; b. Asheville, NC; BFA, Auburn U. Asst. art dir. Mademoiselle mag., NYC; art dir. Cargill, Wilson & Acree Advt. divsn. Doyle Dane Bernbach; v.p., assoc. creative dir., assoc. art dir. Chiat/Day Advt., LA, sr. v.p., assoc. creative dir. Venice, Calif., Venice, NYC, London, mng. ptnr., creative dir. LA; prin. Yvonne Smith, Inc. Guest lectr. UCLA, Art Ctr. Coll. Design, LA, U. So. Calif., LA, Art Dirs. Club, Paris; co-chair Internat. Clio Awards, 1999. Subject profl. articles. Recipient One Show awards, N.Y. Art Dirs. Club, Andy awards, Belding awards, award, Art Dirs. Club, Steven Kelly awards, Clio awards, Emmy award, 1998, Silver and Bronze Lions, Cannes Film Festival, 1998. Office: 21344 Rambla Vista Malibu CA 90265-5348

SMITH, ZADIE (SADIE SMITH), writer; b. London, Eng., Oct. 27, 1975; m. Nick Laird, 2004. Grad. in English, Cambridge U., 1997; postgrad., Harvard U. Writer-in-residency Inst. Contemporary Arts; Radcliffe Inst. fellow Harvard U., 2002—03. Author: (novels) White Teeth, 2000 (First Book award, Guardian newspaper, Whitbread First Novel award, Commonwealth Writers prize, Ethnic and Multicultural Media Award, best book/novel, Ethnic and Multicultural Media Award, best female newcomer, James Tait Black Meml. prize for fiction, 2000, WH Smith award, best new talent, 2001, (UK miniseries, 2002; aired on PBS in US), The Autograph Man, 2002 (Wingate Literary prize for fiction, Jewish Quarterly, 2003), On Beauty, 2005 (Orange prize for fiction, 2006, Somerset Maugham award, 2006), (nonfiction) Fail Better, 2006; editor: (anthology) Pieces of Flesh, 2001; author (of introduction): The Burned Children of America, 2003. Named one of 100 Most Influential People, Time Mag., 2006. Mailing: c/o Georgia Garrett AP Watt Ltd 20 John St London WC1N 2DR England also: Hamish Hamilton Ltd c/o Penguin Ltd 80 Strand London WC2R ORL England Office Phone: 20 7405 6774. Office Fax: 20 7831 2154. E-mail: zsmith@literati.net.

SMITH, ZAK, artist; b. Syracuse, NY, July 16, 1976; BFA, Cooper Union, NY, 1994—98; attended, Skowhegan Sch. Painting & Sculpture, Maine, 1999; MFA, Yale U., 1999—2001. One-man shows include 20 Eyes in My Head, Fredericks Freiser Gallery, NY, 2002, Paintings That Look Good and Were Hard to Make, 2003, Hope You Like It, Franklin Art Works, Mpls., 2004, Fredericks Freiser Gallery, NY, 2005, exhibited in group shows at I See You 2, 2001, Comic Release: Negotiating Identity for a New Generation, Carnegie Mellon University, Pitts., 2002, Hello, My Name Is..., 2002, Upstream Gallery, Amsterdam, 2004, Whitney Biennial, Whitney Mus. Am. Art, NY, 2004, Contemporary Mus., Balt., 2004, Feeling Strangely Fine, Estrany De La Mota, Barcelona, Spain, 2005, Represented in permanent collections, Progressive Corporation, Mayfield, OH. Mailing: c/o Fredericks Freiser Gallery 504 West 22nd St New York NY 10011

SMITH, ZANNIE O., retired career officer; b. Columbia, SC, Mar. 27, 1943; BA in History, U. Tampa; M in Bus. Mgmt., Webster U., St. Louis. Enlisted 82d airborne divsn. U.S. Army, 1962, commd. 2d lt., advanced through grades to maj. gen.; chief of staff U.S. Army Res. Command, Atlanta, 1995; asst. divsn. comdr. ops. 10th Mountain Divsn. and Ft. Drum, 1997; dep. comdg. gen., chief of staff I Corps and Ft. Lewis, 1998—2003; ret., 2003. Decorated Def. Superior Meritorious Svc. award, Legion of Merit with 5 oak leaf clusters, Def. Meritorious Svc. medal, Meritorious Svc. medal with 4 oak leaf clusters, Army Commendation medal with 2 oak leaf clusters, Armed Forces Expeditionary medal, four Vietnam Svc. medals, Good Conduct medal, Bronze Star medal with V and 2 oak leaf clusters, Air medal with oak leaf cluster; recipient Combat Infantryman's badge, Ranger Tab, Air Assault badge.

SMITHART-OGLESBY, DEBRA LYNN, food service executive; b. Apr. 24, 1959; BA in Acctg., U. Tex.; MBA, So. Methodist U. Asst. contr. Brinker Internat., Inc., Dallas, 1985—86, contr., 1986—88, v.p., contr., 1988—91, v.p. fin., 1991, exec. v.p., CFO, 1991—97; pres. corp. services, CFO First Am. Autootive Inc., 1997—99; pres. Dekor, Inc., 1999—2000, O/S Partners, 2000—06; chmn. Denny's Corp., Spartanburg, SC, 2006—. Bd. dirs. Brinker Internat., Inc., 1991—97, Denny's Corp., 2003—, Noodles & Co. Office: Dennys Corp 203 E Main St Spartanburg SC 29319

SMITH-EPSTEIN, MARY KATHLEEN, dancer; b. Austin, Tex., Sept. 12, 1940; d. Walter Bentley Jr. and Kathleen Beatrice (Lancaster) Smith; m. Witaly Osins, June 6, 1967 (div. 1975); m. Howard Irwin Epstein, June 20, 1987. Grad. high sch., Dallas. Demi soloist Am. Festival Ballet, European Tour, 1961; prin. dancer HET Nat. Ballet, Amsterdam, Holland, 1962-67; guest artist Berliner Ballet, Berlin, 1964, Ballet De L'Atlantique, Nantes, France, 1967-68, Cologne, Fed. Republic Germany, 1968-70, Ballet Spectacular, Miami, Fla., 1973-74; prin. dancer Opernhaus, Hannover, Fed. Republic Germany, 1968-70, Musiktheater, Gelsenkirchen, Fed. Republic Germany, 1968-71, Ballet Van Vlaanderen, Antwerp, Belgium, 1971-73, Ballet De Wallonie, Charleroi, Belgium, 1973-74, Irish Nat. Ballet, Cork, Ireland, 1975-85, Chgo. Ballet, 1977-78, Ballet Met., Columbus, Ohio, 1978-79; founder, co-dir. Conservatory Classical Dance, Eugene, Oreg., 1989—. Founder N.W. Chamber Ballet, 1988—; artistic dir. 8 Dance Ensemble; guest tchr. Imperial Eleven Ballet, 2000-01, Internat. Ballet Sch., 2000. Choreographer: (ballet) Opus 1, 1978, For Him From Her, 1982, The Catalyst, 1983 (Bursary Irish Arts Council award 1985), Pas De Deux, 1985 (Bursary Irish Arts Council 1985), Logic of the Heart, 1988, Masquerade Suite, 1988, Tango, 1999, Nocturne, 1998, Pro-Fun-Ditties, 1997, No One Knew, 1997; choreographer Ballet N.W., Performing Ensemble Conservatory Classical Dance, 1989—. Treas. Neighborhood Watch, Vida, Oreg., 1988-89, bd. dirs., sec. to pres. Lane Arts Coun., 1993-96; dir. bldg. fund, pres. bd. dirs. Kaygu Dakshang Chuling, 1995—; house dist. chair Lane County Dem. Party, 2005—. Alexandra Danilova scholar, Dallas, 1958. Buddhist. Personal E-mail: khepsteinor@comcast.net.

SMITHER, HOWARD ELBERT, musicologist, educator; b. Pittsburg, Kans., Nov. 15, 1925; s. Elbert S. and Ethel (Schwab) S.; m. Doris J. Arvin (div. 1976); children: Thomas A., Jesse N. Woodsmith; m. Ann M. Woodward. AB magna cum laude, spl. honors in music, Hamline U., 1950; MA in musicology, Cornell U., 1952; postgrad., U. Munich, 1953-54; PhD in musicology, Cornell U., 1960. Instr. Oberlin Coll. and Conservatory of Music, Oberlin, Ohio, 1955-57, asst. prof., 1957-60, U. Kans., Lawrence, 1960-63; assoc. prof. Tulane U., New Orleans, 1963-68, U. N.C., Chapel Hill, 1968-71, prof., 1971-79, dir. grad. studies in music, 1977-79, 83-84, 86-88, James Gordon Hanes prof. humanities in music, 1979-92, James Gordon Hanes prof. emeritus humanities in music, 1992—; John Bird prof. of music U. Wales, Cardiff, 1993-95. Lectr., chmn. panels regional, nat. and internat. meetings, confs., symposiums, 1964-90. Author: A History of the Oratorio, Vol. 1, The Oratorio in the Baroque Era: Italy, Vienna, Paris, 1977 (transl. Italian), Vol. 2, The Oratorio in the Baroque Era: Protestant Germany and England, 1977 (Deems Taylor award ASCAP 1978), Vol. 3 The Oratorio in the Classical Era, 1987, Vol. 4, Oratorio in the 19th and 20th Centuries, 2000; editor Oratorios of the Italian Baroque, 1983—, The Italian Oratorio 1650-1800, Vols. 1-3, 6, 8, 11-13, 16, 18-20, 24-25, 27, 1986-87; Oratorios of the Italian Baroque, 1983—; editor, translator poems in Alfred Einstein's The Italian Madrigal, 1971; music rev. editor Notes, 1967-69; mem. editorial bd. Detroit Monographs in Musicology, 1971-87; chmn. editorial bd. Early Musical Masterworks: Editions and Commentaries, 1978-83; mem. editorial bd. Videodisc Music Series, NEH, 1982-86; contbr. articles to profl. jours. Fellow Cornell U., 1953-54, NEH, Italy, 1972-73, England, 1979-80, Guggenheim, 1984-85; Fulbright sr. rsch. grant in Italy, 1965-66, sr. Fulbright lectr. Moscow State Conservatory, 1990. Mem. Am. Mus. Soc. (hon; chmn. S.E. chpt. 1969-71, mem. coun. 1969-71, 75-77, bd. dirs. 1977-79, pres. 1980-82, del. to Am. Coun. Learned Socs. 1984-88, to Internat. Congress Strasbourg 1982), Music Libr. Assn. (bd. dirs. 1968-70), Soc. for Am. Music, Internat. Assn. Jazz Educators, Internat. Trumpet Guild. Avocations: hiking, jazz trumpet performance.

SMITHER, NICK, automotive executive; b. 1959; Engr. prod. devel., European Divsn. Ford Motor Co., 1980, systems analyst, 1983, mgr. prod. devel., info. tech. integration, So. Am., 1995—2000, sr. v.p., finance sys. teams, exec. dir., global IT, bus. ops., v.p., CIO, 2006—. Office: Ford Motor Co 1 American Way Dearborn MI 48126-2798

SMITHERAM, MARGARET ETHERIDGE, health facility administrator, director; b. Atlanta, Jan. 5, 1938; d. Philip Fitzgerald and Mary Catharine (Dwyer) E.; m. Roy Charles McCracken, May 5, 1975; m. William Bertram Smitheram, Aug. 17, 1985. BA, Emory U., 1960; M in Health Adminstrn., Washington U., St. Louis, 1973. Registered record adminstr., 1960-71; spl. asst. to dir. VA Med. Ctr., Roseburg, Oreg., 1973-74; hosp. adminstrn, specialist VA Central Office, Washington, 1974-75; asst. dir. trainee VA Med. Ctr., Phila., 1976, assoc. dir. Hampton, Va., 1976--80, Buffalo, 1980-81; presdl. exchange exec. Kimberly Clark Corp., Neenah, Wis., 1981-82, Roswell, Ga., 1981-82; dir. VA Med. Ctr., Grand Island, Nebr., 1982-94; interim dir. Grand Island-Hall County Health Dept., 1996-97; instr. Cerritos Coll., 1969-70. Bd. dirs. Project 2M Coordinating Coun., Inc., Grand Island, 1985-87, Hall County Leadership Unlimited, Inc., 1990. Bd. dirs. Grand Island Area United Way, 1987-90 (pres. 1989), Grand Island Concert Assn, 1987-92, Ctrl. Nebr. Goodwill Industries, Inc., 1987-93 (pres. 1991-92). Fellow Am. Coll. Healthcare Execs. (life); mem. rev. bd. State of Nebr. Foster Care, Am. Hosp. Assn., Fed. Exec. Assn. (pres. Grand Island chpt. 1987), Nebr. Hosp. Assn., Grand Island C. of C. (bd. dirs. 1988-92, legis. affairs com 1984-85, priorities com. 1984-85, govtl. affairs com. 1984-88, nominating com. 1991-92, 94-95, audit com. 1992-93, pres. club 1993-94), Rotary Internat. Club #1485 (v.p. 1998-2000, pres. 2000-2001, District 5630 Group Study Exchange Team Leader to South Korea District 3710, 1999, Paul Harris fellow). Home: 221 Trail of the Flowers Georgetown TX 78633

SMITHERMAN, TODD A., psychologist, researcher; BA, Samford U., Ala., 2000; MS, Auburn U., Ala., 2002, PhD, 2006. Clinician Auburn U., Ala., 2000—06; resident U. Miss. Med. Ctr., Jackson, 2005—, postdoctoral psychology fellow, 2005—. Contbr. articles to profl. jours. Charles V. Lair Fellowship Meml. award, Harry Merriwether fellowship. Mem.: APA, Soc. Behavioral Medicine, Assn. Behavioral Cognitive Therapies. Home Phone: 334-559-8633; Office Phone: 601-984-5855.

SMITHEY, DONALD LEON, airport authority director; b. St. Louis, Aug. 31, 1940; children: Kelly, Jill. Student, St. Ambrose Coll., 1962; BS in Bus. Mgmt., So. Ill. U., 1966; postgrad., U. Mo., St. Louis, 1973-74. Asst. ops. dispatcher Ozark Airlines, 1971-72; transp. analyst Olin Corp., 1972-78, cost acct., 1978-80; commr. St. Louis Regional Airport Authority, 1971-80, chmn., 1974-80, airport dir., 1980-83; asst. dir. Cedar Rapids Mcpl. Airport, 1983-85; dir. adminstrn. Omaha Airport Authority, 1985-87, dep. exec. dir., 1987-89, exec. dir., 1989—. With USN Air Res. 1963-66, USN, 1966-68. Mem. Am. Assn. Airport Execs. (Great Lakes chpt.), Airports Coun. Internat., Iowa Airport Exec. Assn. (past pres.), Ill. Pub. Airports Assn. (past v.p.), Exptl. Aircraft Assn., Omaha Rotary Club, Masonic Lodge (Bethalto, Ill.), Tangier Shrine (Omaha), Quiet Birdmen Assn., Silver Wings Fraternity. Office: Omaha Airport Authority 4501 Abbott Dr Omaha NE 68110-2698

SMITHIES, OLIVER, geneticist, educator; b. Halifax, Eng., June 23, 1925; naturalized; PhD in Biochemistry, Oxford U., Eng., 1951; DSc (hon.), U. Chgo., Duke U. Postdoctoral fellow phys. chemistry U. Wis., Madison, 1951—53, from asst. prof. to prof. genetics and med. genetics, 1960—63, Leon J. Cole prof., 1971—80, Hilldale prof., 1980—88; rsch. asst., assoc. Connaught Med. Rsch. Lab., Toronto, Canada, 1953—60; Excellence prof. dept. pathology and lab. medicine U. N.C., Chapel Hill, 1988—. Mem. nat. adv. med. sci. coun. NIH, 1985. Contbr. articles to profl. jours. Recipient William Allen Meml. award, Am. Soc. Human Genetics, 1964, Karl Landsteiner Meml. award, Am. Assn. Blood Banks, 1984, Internat. award, Gairdner Found., 1990, 1993, State of N.C. award, 1994, Alfred P. Sloan Jr. prize, 1994, Hypertension Rsch. award, CIBA, 1996, Cardiovasc./Metabolic Disease Rsch. award, Bristol-Meyers Squibb, 1997, Rsch. Achievement award, AHA, 1998, Albert Lasker award for Med. Rsch., 2001, Max Gardner award, 2002, Wolf prize in medicine, 2003, Prize in Devel. Biology, March of Dimes, 2005; scholar Markle, 1961. Fellow: AAAS; mem.: NAS, Inst. Medicine, Genetics Soc. Am. (v.p. 1974, pres. 1975), Am. Acad. Arts & Sci. Achievements include research in targeted modification of specific genes in living animals. Office: Univ N C Dept Pathology & Lab Med Chapel Hill NC 27599-0001 Office Phone: 919-966-6913. E-mail: oliver.smithies@pathology.unc.edu.

SMITH-MILLER, HENRY HOUCK, architect; b. NYC, Feb. 9, 1942; s. Theodore Roosevelt and Mary Elizabeth (Houck) Smith-Miller. BA, Princeton U., NJ, 1964; BArch, Yale U., New Haven, 1964-65; MArch, U. Pa., 1966. Registered architect, NY, Pa., Md., NC, Calif. Archtl. designer Michael Graves & Peter Eisenman Architects, Princeton, NJ, 1964; architect Richard Meier & Ptnrs., Arch., NYC, 1970-77; ptnr. Rubin & Smith-Miller, Archs., NYC, 1977-81, Smith-Miller & Hawkinson, Archs., NYC, 1981—. Vis. critic architecture U. Va. Sch. Architecture, Charlottesville, 1978-79, Columbia U. Sch. Architecture, NYC, 1981, 84, Harvard U. Grad. Sch. Architecture, Cambridge, Mass., 1987; Thomas Jefferson prof. architecture U. Va. Sch. Architecture, 1989—. Trustee Creative Time,

NYC, 1986—. Recipient Architecture Record awards; Fulbright scholar, 1967-69. Mem. AIA (Design awards NY chpt. 1986, 87, 89, 91, 92, 94), Contemporary Coun. Mus. Modern Art. Democrat. Home and Office: Smith-Miller & Hawkinson Architects 305 Canal St New York NY 10013-2569

SMITHSON, LOWELL LEE, lawyer; b. Kansas City, Mo., Apr. 29, 1930; s. Spurgeon Lee and Lena Louise (Ruddy) S.; m. Rosemary Carol Leitz, Jan. 30, 1960 (div. Sept. 1985); m. Phyllis Galley Westover, June 8, 1986; children: Carol Maria Louise, Katherine Frances Lee. AB in Polit. Sci., U. Mo., Columbia, 1952, JD, 1954. Bar: Mo. 1954, U.S. Dist. Ct. (we. dist.) Mo. 1955, U.S. Supreme Ct. 1986. Ptnr. Smithson & Smithson, Kansas City, 1956-59; assoc. Spencer, Fane, Britt & Browne, Kansas City, 1959-64, ptnr., 1964—. Adj. prof. law U. Mo., Kansas City, 1982. Pres. Kansas City Mental Health Assn., 1963-65; mem. bd. pres. All Souls Unitarian Ch. Kansas City, 1965-67; chmn. com. select dean for law sch. U. Mo., 1983. Btry. Comdr. U.S. Army, 1954-56, Korea. Mem. Kansas City Bar Assn., Lawyers Assn. Kansas City, Assn. Trial Lawyers Am., Western Mo. Def. Lawyers Assn., Fed. Energy Bar Assn., Phi Beta Kappa, Phi Delta Phi. Democrat. Unitarian Ch. Avocations: skiing, reading, painting, swimming, canoeing. Home: 1215 W 65th St Kansas City MO 64113-1803 Office: Spencer Fane Britt & Browne 1000 Walnut 1400 Commerce Bank Bldg Kansas City MO 64106-2140 Office Phone: 816-474-8100. Business E-Mail: lsmithson@spencerfane.com. E-mail: llsmithson@everestkc.net.

SMITH-THOMPSON, PATRICIA ANN, public relations consultant, educator; b. Chgo., June 7, 1933; d. Clarence Richard and Ruth Margaret (Jacobson) Nowack; m. Tyler Thompson, Aug. 2, 1992; children from previous marriage: Deborah, Kurt, Nancy, Janna, Gail, Lori. Student, Cornell U., 1951—52; BA, Centenary Coll., Hackettstown, NJ, 1983. Prodn. asst. Your Hit Parade Batten, Barton, Durstine & Osborne, 1953-54; pvt. practice polit. cons., 1954-66; legal sec., asst. Atty. John C. Cushman, 1966-68; field dep. L.A. County Assessor Office, 1968-69; pub. info. officer L.A. County Probation Dept., 1969-73; dir. consumer rels. Fireman's Fund, San Francisco, 1973-76; spl. projects officer L.A. County Transp. Commn., 1977-78; tchr. Calif. State U., Dominguez Hills, 1979-86. Editor, writer Jet Propulsion Lab., 1979—80; pub. info. dir. L.A. Bd. Pub. Works, 1980—82; pub. info. cons. City of Pasadena, Calif., 1982—84, pub. rels. cons., 1983—90; cmty. affairs cons. Worldport L.A., 1990—92; tchr. Kern County Schs., 2002—. Contbr. articles to profl. jours. Active First United Meth. Ch. Commn. Missions and Social Concerns, 1983—89; bd. dirs. Depot, 1983—87; mem. devel. com. Pasadena Guidance Clinics, 1984—85; pres. Cultural Arts Assn., Bear Valley Springs, 1999—2000, Calif. Press Women, Bay Area, 1975. Recipient Pro award, L.A. Publicity Club, 1978, Outstanding Achievement award, Soc. Consumer Affairs Profls. Bus., 1976, Disting. Alumni award, Centenary Coll., 1992. Mem.: Nat. Assn. Mental Health Info. Officers (3 regional awards 1986), Calif. Press Women (pres. Bay area 1975—76, award 1974, 1978, 1983, 1984, 1985, Cmty. Rels. 1st pl. winner 1986, 1987, 1988, 1989), Nat. Press Women (Calif. chpt. pres. 1975—76, Pub. Rels. award 1986), Pub. Rels. Soc. Am. (accredited mem., consumer program award 1977, 2 awards 1984, Joseph Roos Cmty. Svc. award 1985). Republican. Home and Office: 24145 Jacaranda Dr Tehachapi CA 93561-8309 Office Phone: 661-821-3804.

SMITS, EDWARD JOHN, historian, consultant; b. Freeport, NY, Dec. 11, 1933; s. Karl M. and Jennie (Spring) S.; m. Ruth K. Hall; children: E. John, Robert K., Theodore R. BA, Hofstra U., 1955; MA, NYU, NY, 1959. Curator Nassau County Hist. Mus., East Meadow, NY, 1956-70; dir. Div.sn Mus. Svc. Nassau County, Syosset, NY, 1971-92. Nassau County historian, 1985—; planning coord. Mus. at Mitchel Ctr., 1994-2001; chmn. Nassau County Centennial Com.; CEO, Museums at Mitchel Cradle of Aviation, 2002-04. Author: Long Island Landmarks, 1970, Creation of Nassau County, 1959, Nassau, Suburbia USA, 1974. Trustee Friends for L.I.'s Heritage, Nassau County Hist. Soc.; trustee, past pres. Levittown Libr. Bd. 1st lt. U.S. Army, 1955-56. Fulbright grantee, 1965; recipient Nassau County disting. svc. award, 1970, alumni disting. svc. award Hofstra U., 1970, Achievement award N.Y. State Historians, 2004 Mem. Am. Assn. Mus., Am. Assn. State & Local History. Avocations: book collecting, antique toys, golf. Home: 14 Wavy Ln Wantagh NY 11793-1202 Office Phone: 516-383-1557.

SMITS, HELEN LIDA, medical association administrator, educator; b. Long Beach, Calif., Dec. 3, 1936; d. Theodore Richard Smits and Anna Mary Wells; m. Roger LeCompte, Aug. 28, 1976; 1 child, Theodore. BA with honors, Swarthmore Coll., 1958; MA, Yale U., 1961, MD cum laude, 1967. Intern, asst. resident Hosp. U. Pa., 1967—69; fellow Beth Israel Hosp., Boston, 1969-70; chief resident Hosp. U. Pa., 1970-71; chief med. clinic U. Pa., 1971-75; assoc. adminstr. for patient care svcs. U. Pa. Hosp., 1975-77; v.p. med. affairs Community Health Plan Georgetown U., Washington, 1977; dir. health standards and quality bur. Health Care Financing Adminstrn., HHS, Washington, 1977-80; sr. rsch. assoc. The Urban Inst., Washington, 1980-81; assoc. prof. Yale U. Med. Sch., New Haven, 1981-85; assoc. v.p. for health affairs U. Conn. Health Ctr., Farmington, 1985-87; prof. community medicine U. Conn. Sch. Medicine, Farmington, 1985-93; hosp. dir. John Dempsey Hosp., Farmington, 1987-93; dep. adminstr. Health Care Financing Adminstrn., Washington, 1993-96; pres., chmn. Health Right, Inc., Meriden, Conn., 1996-99; vis. prof. Robert F. Wagner Grad. Sch. Pub. Svc., NYU, 1999—2001. Commr. Joint Com. on Accreditation Hosps., Chgo., 1989-93, chair, 1991-92; mem., co-chair strategic framework bd. Nat. Forum on Health Care Quality Measurement and Reporting, 2000—01; Fulbright lectr. faculty medicine Eduardo Mondlane U., Maputo, Mozambique, 2001-04. Contbr. numerous articles to profl. jours. Bd. dirs. The Ivoryton Playhouse Fedn., Inc., 1990-92, The Connecticut River Mus., 1990-93, Hartford Stage, 1990-93; mem. Dem. Town Com., Essex, Conn., 1982-89; vol. The William J. Clinton Found., Mozambique, 2000-04. Recipient Superior Svc. award HHS, Washington, 1982; Royal Soc. Medicine Found. fellow, London, 1973; Fulbright scholar, 1959-60. Mem. ACP (master, regent 1984-90), Inst. Medicine (vice chmn. com. for evaluation of PEPPAR implementation 2005—), Nat. Acad. Scis., Phi Beta Kappa, Alpha Omega Alpha. Episcopalian. Avocations: sailing, cooking, gardening.

SMITS, JIMMY, actor; b. Bklyn., July 9, 1955; m. Barbara Smits 1981 (div. 1987); 2 children. BA in Theatre, Bklyn. Coll., 1980; MFA, Cornell Univ., 1982. Appearances include Off-Broadway prodns., tours with regional theatres, Anna in the Tropics, 2005; (TV series) Miami Vice, 1984, L.A. Law, 1986-91 (Emmy award Outstanding Actor in Dramatic Series 1990), NYPD Blue, 1994-98, The West Wing, 2004-06 (Outstanding Actor in a TV Series, Nat. Coun. La Raza ALMA award (Am. Latin Media Arts), 2006); (TV movies) Rockabye, 1986, The Highwayman, 1987, Glitz, 1988, The Broken Cord, 1991, Stephen King's The Tommyknockers, 1993, The Cisco Kid, 1994, Solomon & Sheba, 1995, Marshal Law, 1996, (voice) Mother Goose: A Rappin' and Rhymin' Special, 1997, Lackawanna Blues, 2005; (films) Running Scared, 1986, The Believers, 1987, Old Gringo, 1988, Vital Signs, 1989, Fires Within, 1989, Switch, 1990, Gross Misconduct, 1992, The Cisco Kid, 1993, Solomon & Sheba, 1994, My Family, 1994, Marshal Law, 1995, Murder in Mind, 1996, Lesser Prophets, 1997, Bless the Child, 2000, The Million Dollar Hotel, 2000, Price of Glory, 2000, Star Wars: Episode II - Attack of the Clones, 2002, Angel, 2003, Star Wars III - Revenge of the Sith, 2005. Co-founder, mem. bd. dirs. Nat. Hispanic Found. Arts. Avocations: football, basketball, softball, reading. Office: care Sherman Mgmt 1516 S Beverly Dr Apt 304 Los Angeles CA 90035-3059 also: Nat Hispanic Found Arts Waterfront Center 1010 Wisconsin Ave NW Ste 650 Washington DC 20007

SMITS, RONALD FRANCIS, language educator, poet; b. Bayonne, NJ, Dec. 22, 1943; s. Edwin Joseph and Florence Ann Smits; m. Bonnie Lee Brown, June 10, 1970 (div. Mar. 1976); 1 child, Ronald Thomas. AB, Rutgers U., 1966; MS, Ind. State U., 1969; PhD, Ball State U., 1978. Instr. English, Kaskaskia Coll., Centralia, Ill., 1969-74; instr. Ball State U., Muncie, Ind., 1976-78; asst. prof. English, Indiana U. Pa., 1979-92, assoc. prof., 1992-96, prof., 1996—. Contbr. poems to jours. 1st lt. U.S. Army, 1966-68, Vietnam. Doctoral fellow Ball State U., 1974-78; Disting. Faculty Award, Creativ Arts, Indiana U. Pa, 1993; recipient Outstanding Faculty award English Assn. of Pa. State U., 2002. Avocations: walking, nature hikes, nature study, reading. Home: PO Box 466 Ford City PA 16226-0466 Office: Indiana U of Pa Northpointe Campus 167 Northpointe Blvd Freeport PA 16229-2699 Office Phone: 724-294-3300. Business E-Mail: rfsmits@iup.edu.

SMITTLE, NELSON DEAN, military analyst, artist; b. Peebles, Ohio, Sept. 19, 1934; s. Nelson John and Alma Katherine (Green) S.; m. Claire Wiggins, May 5, 1973. BS, BFA, U. Cin., 1962, MA, 1971. Commd. 2d lt. US Army, 1962; staff officer US Army Photo Agy. Pentagon, Washington, 1966; detachment comdr. tactical comms. Vietnam, 1967-68; commn. transferred to USAF, 1970; instr. art U. Cin., 1972; comdr. 907th communications squadron Rickenbacker AFB, Ohio, 1972; dir. ops. fixed communications Air Combat Command Langley AFB, Va., 1982; dir. info. systems AWACS Saudi Arabia, 1984-85; dep. chief of staff standard systems Air Material Command Wright-Patterson AFB, Ohio, 1985; comdr. engrng. installation divsn. Tinker AFB, Okla., 1988; commd. col., ret. USAF, Cin., 1988, 91, ret., 1991; pres. Falcon Techs., Cin., 1991-98; tchr. Princeton City Sch. Dist., Cin., 1992-94; pres. Thumbs Up Aerospace Art, Cin., 1998—; instr. art history Cin. State Tech. & Cmty. Coll., 2000—; mil. analyst 700 WLW AM Radio, Cin., 2001—, WCPO TV, 2003—, WXIX TV, 2001—, WWNC AM Radio, 2006—, WNKU FM Radio, 2006—; lectr. Thumbs Up Am., Ams. at War, 2001—; asst. prof. fine arts Clermont Coll., Batavia, Ohio, 2007—. Lectr. USAF Mus., Ams. at War, 2002—; cons. Air War Coll., Air U., Maxwell AFB, Ala., 1987—, Def. Systems Mgmt. Coll., Ft. Belvoir, Va., 1988—; faculty Cin. Acad. Leadership U. Cin. Coll. Law, 2003—. Author: Army Visual Presentation, 1966 (medal 1966), Famous Moments in Aerospace History, 1997; exhibited in group shows Mus. of Flight, Seattle, 1997, Midland Arts Ctr., Mich., 1997, Wichita Ctr Arts, 1998, Ralice Studio, Cin., 1998, Master Works Exhibit, Cin., 1999, Cin. Mus. Ctr., 1998, Mus. Aviation, Warner Robbins, Ga., 1999, Pub. Libr. Cin., Hamilton County, Ohio, 1999, Cin. Art Club, 2001, Kathy McCoy Design Studio, Batavia, Ohio, 2004, The Miterbox Studio, Cin., 2005; mil. cons. costume dept. Across the Universe, film prodn., 2006; author cover art Jour. of League of World War I Aviation Historians, Jour. WWI Aviation Historians, 1999. Mem. Batavia City Coun., Ohio, 1972; pres. Ohio Buckeye Wing Assn., Columbus, 1973; mem. Air Force Policy Coun., Washington, 1978; congl. campaign mgr., 1993; bd. dirs. Cin. Art Club, 1995-96. Decorated Commendation medal; recipient Meritorious Svc. medal Dept. Def., 1986, 91. Mem.: VFW, DAV, Mil. Officers Assn. Am., Am. Soc. Aviation Artists, Res. Officers Assn., Air Force Assn., Spl. Ops. Warrior Found., 82d Airborne Assn., Aircraft Owners and Pilots Assn., Mil. Order Purple Heart (hon.). Avocations: writing, walking, science fiction. Home and Office: Thumbs Up America 198 Palisades Pointe Cincinnati OH 45238-5653 Office Phone: 513-922-6018. Personal E-mail: deanstargate@aol.com.

SMOAK, LEWIS TYSON, lawyer; b. Orangeburg, SC, Feb. 11, 1944; s. William B. and Louise (Dempsey) S.; m. Elizabeth Adams Babb, July 16, 1966; children: Katherine, Blair, Tyson. BA, Furman U., 1966; JD, U. SC, 1969. Bar: SC 1969, DC 1982. Founder, Ogletree, Deakins, Nash, Smoak and Stewart, Greenville, SC, 1969—. Recipient Ellis Island Medal of Honor, 2006; named one of Best Lawyers in Am., 2006. Fellow Coll. Labor and Employment Lawyers; mem. ABA, Greenville County Bar Assn., SC Bar Assn., DC Bar Assn., Poinsett Club, Greenville Country Club, Wade Hampton Golf Club (Cashiers, NC), Doonbeg (Ireland) Golf Club. Office: 300 N Main St Greenville SC 29601 Office Phone: 864-271-1300.

SMOAK, RANDOLPH DUNCAN, JR., surgeon; b. Bamberg, SC, May 5, 1933; MD, Med. Coll. S.C., 1959. Diplomate Am. Bd. Surgery. Intern Grady Meml. Hosp., Atlanta, 1959-60; resident surgery Med. U. S.C.-Teaching Hosps., 1962-65, resident, tchg. fellow, 1965-66; fellow surgery MD Anderson Cancer Ctr., Houston, 1966-67; surg. staff Orangeburg (S.C.) Calhoun Regional Hosp., 1967-87, emeritus staff, 1987; clin. prof. surgery Med. U. S.C., Charleston, 1987—, U.S.C. Sch. Medicine, Columbia, 86—. Fellow ACS; mem. AMA (pres. 2000-01), So. Med. Assn., Soc. Head and Neck Surgeons, So. Soc. Clin. Surgeons, Soc. Clin. Oncology. Office: 112 Cloister Cove Orangeburg SC 29115 Personal E-mail: randysmoak@earthlink.net. Business E-Mail: smoak@ama-assn.org.

SMOCK, DONALD JOE, real estate analyst, political scientist; s. Joe Clellan and Ruth Esther Smock. BA in Polit. Sci., U. Ctrl. Okla., Edmond, 1990, MA in Urban Affairs, 1993. Rschr. The Nigh Inst. State Govt., Edmond, 1993—94; govt. liaison Elizey Electric Motor Co., 1994—96; govt. affairs dir. Oklahoma City Met. Assn. Realtors, 1997—2002; sr. zoning analyst Zoning-Info. Inc., 2002—06; zoning project mgr. Bock & Clark Corp., 2006. U. Ctrl. Okla. del. to Ctr. Study of Pres. Symposium, Washington, 1993 Charter founder Ronald Reagan Rep. Ctr., 1989; del. State of Okla. Rep. Presdl. Task Force, 1996; mem. Rep. Presdl. Trust, 1996; mem. Mt. Vernon Historical Preservation. Recipient Okla. Rep. Blue Key award, 1984, Presdl. Commn., 1992, Merit cert. Rep. Nat. Com., 1990; named to Ronald Reagon Rep. Ctr. Presdl. Commemorative Honor Roll, 1991; Positive Residential Growth Plan Recognition award, Nat. Assn. Realtors, 2000; recognition for Okla. City Urban Devel. Plan Update, City of Okla., 2000-; by order of President George Bush flag dedicated in name Rotunda of U.S. Capitol, 1990. Mem. Tau Kappa Epsilon (Delta Nu colony inductee, chpt. advisor 1990-92), Fraternity for Life iniductee, David Crain Leadership award 1986, Ed Howell Leadership award 1988-89, Red Carnation Ball dedicated in name 1989-90, 94, Top Alumnus 1990-91), Pi Sigma Alpha. Republican. Mem. Ch. of Christ. Home: PO Box 6323 Edmond OK 73083-6323 Personal E-mail: donaldjsmock@yahoo.com.

SMOCK, RAYMOND WILLIAM, historian; b. Jeffersonville, Ind., Feb. 8, 1941; s. Richard and Lottie (Paciorek) S.; m. Phyllis Lee Chadwick, Feb. 12, 1961 BA, Roosevelt U., Chgo., 1966; PhD, U. Md., College Park, 1974. Rsch. asst. Md. Constl. Conv., Annapolis, 1967-68; lectr. in history U. Md., College Park, 1968-72; co-editor The Booker T. Washington Papers, 14 vols., 1972-83; pres. Instructional Resources Corp., Lanham, Md., 1976-83, Rsch. Materials Corp., College Park, 1982-83, dir., 1982-85; historian, dir. Office for Bicentennial, U.S. Ho. of Reps., Washington, 1983-89, Office of Historian, U.S. Ho. of Reps., Washington, 1989-95. Mem. editl. advisors Md. Historian, College Park, 1971—95; exec. dir. Robert C. Byrd Ctr. for Legis. Studies, Shepherd U., Shepherdstown, W.Va., 2002—. Author: A Talent for Detail: The Photographs of Miss Frances Benjamin Johnston 1889-1910, 1974; co-editor: A Guide to Manuscripts in the Presidential Libraries, 1985, Masters of the House, 1998; editor: Booker T. Washington in Perspective: The Essays of Louis R. Harlan, 1988; author, editor: Landmark Documents on the U.S. Congress, 1998. Ford Found. fellow, 1970; recipient Philip M. Hamer award Soc. Am. Archivists, 1979 Mem. Nat. Coun. Pub. History, Assn. for Documentary Editing (pres. 1983-84), Orgn. Am. Historians, So. Hist. Assn., Soc. History in Fed. Govt. (v.p./pres.-elect 2000—), Assn. Ctrs. for Study of Congress (pres. 2005—), W.Va. Humanities Coun. (bd. mem. 2006—). Avocations: photography, astronomy. E-mail: RaySmock@aol.com, rsmock@shepherd.edu.

SMOCK, TIMOTHY ROBERT, lawyer; b. Richmond, Ind., June 24, 1951; s. Robert Martin and Thelma Elizabeth (Cozad) S.; m. Martha Carolene Middleton, Apr. 4, 1992; children: Andrew Zoller, Alison Pierce. BA, Wittenberg U., Springfield, Ohio, 1973; JD cum laude, Ind. U., Bloomington, Ind., 1977. Bar: Ind. 1977, Ariz. 1979, U.S. Dist. Ct. (so. dist.) Ind. 1977, U.S. Dist. Ct. Ariz. 1979, U.S. Ct. Apeals (7th cir.) 1977, U.S. Ct. Appeals (9th cir.) 1979. Jud. clk. Ct. of Appeals of Ind., Indpls., 1977-79; assoc. Lewis and Roca, Phoenix, 1979-82; assoc./shareholder Gallagher & Kennedy, Phoenix, 1982-89; ptnr. Scult, French, Zwillinger & Smock, Phoenix, 1989-94, Smock and Weinberger, Phoenix, 1994-99, Richards and Smock, Phoenix, 1999—2005, Zwillinger & Georgelos, 2005—. Judge, pro tempore Maricopa County Superior Ct., Phoenix, 1989—; faculty, State Bar Course on Professionalism, Ariz. Supreme Ct./State Bar, Phoenix, 1992—; speaker, Continuing Legal Edn., Maricopa County and Ariz. State Bar, 1988—. Mem. ABA, Ariz. Bar Assn., Maricopa Bar Assn. Office: Zwillinger & Georgelos Ste 600 2425 E Camelback Rd Phoenix AZ 85016 Home Phone: 480-947-9811; Office Phone: 602-224-7888. E-mail: Timothy.Smock@azbar.org.

SMOLANSKY, BETTIE MORETZ, sociology educator; b. Columbia, SC, June 1940; d. Walter Jennings Sr. and Opal (Ledford) Moretz; m. Oles M. Smolansky, Dec. 29, 1966; children: Alexandra Smolansky Zentmeyer, Nicholas Jennings. AB in Sociology, Lenoir-Rhyne Coll., 1962; MA in Sociology, Duke U., 1964; PhD in Sociology, Pa. State U., 1984. From instr. sociology to prof. Moravian Coll., Bethlehem, Pa., 1964—88, prof., 1988—, chmn. Dept. Sociology, 1991—97, 2005—, interim dean faculty, 1998—99, dean acad. affairs, 2000—01. Trustee Moravian Coll., 1977-81, 91-95, sec. presdl. search com., 1996-97; NEH visitor core curriculum workshop Bklyn. Coll., 1985, mem. curriculum evaluation conf. 1988. Co-author: The USSR and Iraq, 1991 (Am. Assn. Advancement of Slavic Studies Marshall Schulman prize 1992), The Lost Equilibrium, 2001. Bd. dirs. Northampton County Area on Aging, Bethlehem, 1984-90, 2003—; vice chair United Way Allocations Panel, Bethlehem, 1984-90; chair YWCA Commn. on Status of Women, Bethlehem, 1992-94; bd. dirs. YWCA of Bethlehem, 1993-97, 98-2002, 1st v.p., 1998-2000, pres., 2001-02. Recipient NDEA fellow, 1962-64, Disting. Alumnus award Lenoir-Rhyne Coll., 1995. Mem. Am. Sociol. Assn., Ea. Sociol. Assn., Lehigh Valley Assn. Acad. Women (pres. 1988-89, Woman of Yr. 1995-96), ODK (advisor 1987-90), AKD (advisor 1991—). Home: 3665 Walt Whitman Ln Bethlehem PA 18017-1553 Office: Moravian Coll Dept Sociology 1200 Main St Bethlehem PA 18018-6650 Office Phone: 610-861-1317. Business E-Mail: mebms01@moravian.edu.

SMOLANSKY, OLES M., retired humanities educator; b. Ukraine, USSR, May 2, 1930; came to U.S. 1950; s. Mykola S. and Irene (Plinto) S.; m. Bettie Moretz, Dec. 29, 1966; children: Alexandra, Nicholas. BA, NYU, 1953; MA, Columbia U., 1955, PhD, 1959. Instr. UCLA, 1960-62; asst. prof. Lehigh U., Bethlehem, Pa., 1963-66, assoc. prof., 1966-70, prof., 1970-85, univ. prof., 1985—2005, emeritus univ. prof., 2005—. Author: The Soviet Union and the Arab East Under Khrushchev, 1974, The USSR and Iraq: The Soviet Quest for Influence, 1991; co-editor: Russia and America: From Rivalry to Reconciliation, 1993, Regional Power Rivalries in the New Eurasia: Russia, Turkey, and Iran, 1995, The Lost Equilibrium: International Relations in the Post-Soviet Era, 2001; contbr. articles to profl. jours. Recipient joint fellowship, Rockefeller Found. and Ford Found., N.Y.C., 1962-63, sr. rsch. joint fellowship, Rsch. Inst. on Communist Affairs and Mid. East Inst., Columbia U., N.Y.C., 1972-73, rsch. fellowship, Ford Found., N.Y.C., 1980-81. Mem. Internat. Studies Assn., Am. Assn. for Advancement of Slavic Studies (Marshall Shulman award 1992), Mid. East Studies Assn., Mid. East Inst. Democrat. Greek-Orthodox. Avocations: music, sports. Home: 3665 Walt Whitman Ln Bethlehem PA 18017-1553 Office: Lehigh U Dept Internat Rels Bethlehem PA 18015 Home Phone: 610-867-6686. Business E-Mail: oms0@lehigh.edu.

SMOLEN, LEE M., lawyer; b. 1960; BS with highest honors, U. Ill., 1982; JD, U. Chgo., 1985. CPA; bar: Ill. 1985. Assoc. real estate group Sidley Austin LLP, 1985—93, ptnr. real estate group, 1993—. Chair Chgo. real estate group Sidley Austin LLP, 2004—, co-chair practice devel. com. Mem.: ABA. Office: One S Dearborn St Chicago IL 60603 Office Phone: 312-853-7823. Office Fax: 312-853-7036. Business E-Mail: lsmolen@sidley.com.

SMOLENSKI, LISABETH ANN, physician; b. Pitts., Oct. 1, 1950; d. Anthony Edward and Betty Jean (Gross) S.; m. William Ward Daniels, May 24, 1980; 1 child, Kathryn Elizabeth. BA, Carlow Coll., Pitts., 1972; MD, Hahnemann U., Phila., 1982. Diplomate Am. Bd. Family Practice. Resident in family practice West Jersey Health Sys., Voorhees, N.J., 1982-85; pvt. practice, Somerville, Tenn., 1985-90, Memphis, 1990—2003; with Spectrum Pain Clinics, Franklin-Nashville, Tenn., 2003—04, Cumberland Back Pain Clinic PC, Cookeville, Tenn., 2005—, Clarksville, Tenn., 2005—. Sec. exec. com. med. staff Meth. Hosp. Somerville, 1988-90. Fellow: Am. Acad. Family Physicians. Republican. Avocation: reading. Office: Cumberland Back Pain Clinic PC 480 Neal St Cookeville TN 38501 also: Cumberland Back Pain Clinic PC 271 Med Park Dr Clarksville TN 37043-6310 Office Phone: 931-520-8104, 931-647-5747.

SMOLENSKY, EUGENE, economics professor; b. Bklyn., Mar. 4, 1932; s. Abraham and Jennie (Miller) S.; m. Natalie Joan Rabinowitz, Aug. 16, 1952; children: Paul, Beth. BA, Bklyn. Coll., 1952; MA, Am. U., 1956; PhD, U. Pa., 1961. Prof. econs. U. Wis., Madison, 1968-88, chmn. dept., 1978-80, 86-88; dir. Inst. for Research on Poverty, U. Wis., 1980-83; dean Grad. Sch. Pub. Policy, U. Calif., Berkeley, 1988-97, prof. pub. policy, 1997—. Author: Public Expenditures, Taxation and the Distribution of Income: The U.S., 1950, 61, 70, 77. Mem. Nat. Acad. Pub. Adminstrn., 1994; mem. com. on child devel. rsch. and pub. policy NAS, Washington, 1982-87, mem. com. on status of women in labor market, 1985-87. With USN, 1952-56. Mem. Am. Econs. Assn. Democrat. Jewish. Avocation: master etching and lithograph collecting. Home: 669 Woodmont Ave Berkeley CA 94708-1233 Office: U Calif Dept Pub Policy 2607 Hearst Ave Berkeley CA 94720-7305 Office Phone: 510-643-3979. Business E-Mail: geno@berkeley.edu.

SMOLEV, TERENCE ELLIOT, lawyer, educator; b. Bklyn., Oct. 5, 1944; s. Lawrence and Shirley (Lebowitz) S.; m. Sherry Gale Rosen, Nov. 24, 1968 (div.); children: Cindy, Scott; m. Phyllis C. Rudko, Oct. 8, 1995. BBA, Hofstra U., 1966; JD, American U., 1969; LLM, NYU, 1974. Bar: NY 1970. Acct. Peat Marwick & Mitchell, NYC, 1969-70; dir. deferred giving Hofstra U., Hempstead, NY, 1971-74; editor Panel Pub., Greenvale, NY, 1970-71; ptnr. Naidich & Smolev, P.C., Bellmore, NY, 1972-92; pvt. practice Mineola, NY, 1992-2000; ptnr. Forchelli, Curto, Schwartz, Mineo, Carlino & Cohn LLP, Mineola, 2000—, ptnr. in charge taxes, trusts and estates, 2000—. Bd. trustees Hofstra U., 1992-2006; adj. prof. Hofstra U., Hempstead, N.Y., 1971—; dist. counsel North Merrick (N.Y.) UFSD, 1975-99; bd. dirs. Gurwin Geriatric Found. Contbr. chapters to books, articles to profl. jours. Mem. Nassau County, NY Dem. Com., 1972-80, mem. jud. screening com., 1992—; mem. IRS Small Bus. Adv. Com., Washington DC, 1975-77; bd. dirs. Arthritis Found. LI, 1995-97, mem Israeli Bond Cabinet LI, 1996-2004; bd. dirs. LI chpt. Anti-Defamation League, Nassau County Micro-Econ. Commn., Nassau County Audit Com.; v.p. NYC Police Mus. Recipient George M. Estabrook award Hofstra U., 1991, Alumni Achievement award Hofstra U., 1993, Cmty. Svc. award Hebrew Acad. Nassau County, 1997; named Senator of Yr., Hofstra U., 1985, Alumnus of Yr., 1996; honoree Diabetes Rsch. Found., 2003. Mem. ABA, N.Y. State Bar Assn., Nassau County Bar Assn., N.Y. State Assn. Sch. Attys. (pres. 1984), Hofstra U. Alumni Senate (pres.

1987-89), Hofstra U. Club (bd. dirs. 1981-95). Avocations: photography, golf. Office: PO Box 31 330 Old Country Rd Ste 301 Mineola NY 11501 Office Phone: 516-248-1700. Business E-Mail: tsmolev@fcsmcc.com.

SMOLIN, LEE, physicist, researcher, writer; b. NYC, June 6, 1955; s. Michael and Pauline (Selman) Smolin. BA, Hampshire Coll., Amherst, Mass., 1975; AM, Harvard U., 1978, PhD in Theoretical Physics, 1979. Mem. Inst. Advanced Study, Princeton, NJ, 1979, 1981—83; postdoctoral physicist Inst. Theoretical Physics, Santa Barbara, Calif., 1980-81; postdoctoral rschr. U. Chgo. Enrico Fermi Inst., 1983—84; asst. prof. Yale U., New Haven, 1984—88; assoc. prof. Syracuse U., NY, 1988-91, prof., 1991—93, Pa. State U., 1993—2001; mem. faculty Perimeter Inst. Theoretical Physics, Waterloo, Ont., Canada, 2001—. Adj. prof. physics dept. U. Waterloo, Canada, 2001—. Contbr. articles to profl. jours.; author: Life of the Cosmos, 1997, Three Roads to Quantum Gravity, 2000, The Trouble with Physics, 2006. Active Clamshell Alliance, 1978; organizer Star Wars Pledge Campaign, 1984-86. Co-recipient First award essay Gravity Rsch. Found., 1985, 2nd award, 1981, 83. Mem. Internat. Soc. Gen. Relativity and Gravitation. Avocations: jazz guitar, sailing, philosophy. Office: Perimeter Inst Theoretical Physics 31 Caroline St N Waterloo ON Canada N2L 2Y5 E-mail: lee@Qgravity.org.

SMOLINSKI, BRYAN, professional hockey player; b. Toledo, Ohio, Dec. 27, 1971; m. Julie Smolinski, July 12. B. Broadcasting, Mich. State U. Center Boston Bruins, 1992-96, Pitts. Penguins, 1996, NY Islanders, 1996—99, LA Kings, 1999—2003, Ottawa Senators, 2003—06, Chgo. Blackhawks, 2006—07, Vancouver Canucks, 2007—. Mem. Team USA, World Cup of Hockey, 1996, 2004. Achievements include being a member of World Cup Champion Team USA, 1996. Office: Vancouver Canucks 800 Griffiths Way Vancouver BC V6B 6G1 Canada *

SMOLLA, RODNEY ALAN, dean, law educator; b. Pueblo, Colo., Mar. 13, 1953; s. Richard Paul and Harriet (Waskowiak) S. BA, Yale U., 1975; JD, Duke U., 1978. Bar: Ill. 1979, U.S. Supreme Ct. 1987. Law clk. to presiding judge U.S. Ct. Appeals, Jackson, Miss., 1978-79; assoc. Mayer, Brown & Pratt, Chgo., 1979-80; asst. prof. De Paul U. Sch. Law, Chgo., 1980-81, U. Ill. Coll. Law, 1981-83; prof. U. Ark. Sch. Law, 1983-87; vis. prof. U. Denver Coll. Law, 1987-88; Arthur B. Hanson prof. constl. law Coll. of William and Mary, Williamsburg, Va., 1988-98, dir. Inst. Bill of Rights Law, 1988-96; dean, George E. Allen prof. U. Richmond Sch. Law, 1998—. Author: Suing the Press: Libel, The Media & Power, 1986 (cert. of merit ABA 1987), Law of Defamation, 1986, Jerry Falwell V. Larry Flynt: The First Amendment on Trial, 1988; (with Banks and Braveman) Constitutional Law: Structure and Rights in Our Federal System, 1991, 3rd edit., 1996, Free Speech in an Open Society, 1992 (William O. Douglas Prize 1993), Smolla and Nimmer on Freedom of Speech, 1994, 3rd edit., 1996, Federal Civil Rights Acts, 1994; editor: A Year in the Life of the Supreme Court, 1995 (ABA Silver Gavel award), Deliberate Intent: A Lawyer Tells the True Story of Murder by the Book, 1999. Fellow, cons. Annenberg Washington Program in Communications, 1987-96; project dir. Annenberg Libel Reform Task Force, 1988-89; reporter Bill of Rights Adv. Com. to the Commn. on the Bicentennial of U.S. Constitution, 1989—. Recipient Recipient Disting. Prof. of Yr. award, U. Ark., 1986, Outstanding Faculty award, Va. State Coun. Higher Edn., 2002. Mem. ABA, Ill. Bar Assn., AAUP (mem. litigation com. 1988—). Office: U Richmond TC Williams Sch of Law Richmond VA 23173 Home: 1848 W Grace St Richmond VA 23220 Office Phone: 804-289-8197. Office Fax: 804-289-8994. E-mail: rsmolla@richmond.edu.

SMOLLER, BRUCE MELVYN, psychiatrist; b. Chgo., Sept. 19, 1944; s. Norman and Beatrice Betty (Janows) Smoller; m. Cosette Nieporent, Aug. 20, 1967; children: Jamie, Lauren. AB, Cornell U., 1965; MD, Tulane U., 1969. Diplomate Am. Bd. Psychiatry and Neurology. Intern Maimonides Med. Ctr., NYC, 1969-70; resident in orthopedic surgery Einstein Med. Ctr., NYC, 1970-73; resident in psychiatry Cornell Med. Ctr., NYC, 1973-76; pvt. practice in psychiatry with emphasis on clin. and rsch. aspects of pain Bethesda, Md., 1976—; chmn. dept. psychiatry Holy Cross Hosp., Silver Spring, Md., 1980-83; assoc. clin. prof. psychiatry George Washington U., 1977-91, clin. prof. psychiatry, 1991—. Cons. NIH, 1979—2001. Co-author: Pain Control: The Bethesda Program; editor: Md. Medicine, The State Med. Soc.'s Jour. With Med. Corps USAR, 1970—78. Mem.: Md. State Med. Soc. (pres.-elect 2006—07), Montgomery County Med. Soc. (pres. 2004—05). Office: 5530 Wisconsin Ave Bethesda MD 20815-4404 Office Phone: 301-951-4466. E-mail: bsmoller@radix.net.

SMOLTZ, JOHN ANDREW, professional baseball player; b. Warren, Mich., May 15, 1967; Draft pick Detroit Tigers, 1985; pitcher Atlanta Braves, 1988—. Named Nat. League Championship Series MVP, 1992, Nat. League Pitcher of Yr., The Sporting News, 1996; named to Nat. League All-Star Team, Maj. League Baseball, 1989, 1992—93, 1996, 2002—03, 2005, 2007; recipient Nat. League Cy Young award, Baseball Writers' Assn. of Am., 1996, Silver Slugger award, 1997, Rolaids Relief award, 2002, Roberto Clemente award, 2005, Lou Gehrig Meml. award, 2005. Achievements include leading the Nat. League in strikeouts, 1992 (215), 1996 (276), wins, 1996 (24), 2006 (16), and saves, 2002 (55). Office: Atlanta Braves Turner Field PO Box 4064 Atlanta GA 30302-4064 *

SMOLYANSKY, JULIE, consumer products company executive; b. Russia; arrived in US, 1976; d. Michael and Ludmila Smolyansky. BA, U. Ill., 1996. Dir. sales and mktg. Lifeway Foods Inc., Morton Grove, Ill., 1997—2002, pres., 2002—, CEO, 2002—, CFO, 2002—, treas., 2002—, dir. Avocation: running. Office: Lifeway Foods Inc 6431 West Oakton Ave Morton Grove IL 60053 *

SMOOKE, MICHAEL G., lawyer; b. LA, Oct. 2, 1945; BA magna cum laude, UCLA, 1967; JD, Harvard U., 1970. Bar: Calif. 1971. Mem. Fulbright & Jaworski L.L.P., LA, ptnr. Lectr. in field. Contbr. articles to profl. jours. Trustee LA County Mus. Art, 1992—; mem. bd. dir. D.A.R.E. Am., Temple Emanuel Beverly Hills Calif.; bd. dir. Jewish Cmty. Found. Named Am. Best Lawyer, one of ten leading real estate lawyers LA, by LA Daily Jour., one of most prominent bus. lawyers LA, by LA Bus. Jour. Mem. ABA (real property, probate and trust law sect.), State Bar Calif., LA County Bar Assn. (real property sect.), Phi Beta Kappa, Omicron Delta Epsilon, Pi Gamma Mu. Note editor Harvard Jour. Legis. 1969-70. Office: Fulbright & Jaworski LLP 555 S Flower St Forty 1st Fl Los Angeles CA 90071 Office Phone: 213-892-9200. Office Fax: 213-892-9494. Business E-Mail: msmooke@fulbright.com.

SMOOT, BURGESS HOWARD, federal official; b. Washington, Mar. 28, 1947; s. James Elias and Frances Galdinia (Hawkins) S.; m. Ann Louise Gordon, Aug. 9, 1982; children: Frederick Hawkins, Chanel Gordon, Ervine Gholston, Shemerrian. Cook Freedmans Hosp., Washington, 1968-70; mail & file clk. Asst. Chief of Staff Intelligence, Washington, 1970-74; adminstrv. asst. logistics Office Joint Chiefs of Staff, Pentagon, Washington, 1974-77, adminstrv. asst. policy & plans, 1977-80. Author: (poetry) Lost in the Beginning. Capt. Neighborhood Watch Group, Fort Washington, Md., 1995-97; presdl. election official, 2000—, primary election judge for Md., 2002, primary and gen. presdl. election judge, 2004; judge for Md. gov., 2002; pres. Sunday Schs. 12rs. through adult Capital Ward, 2002—04, libr., 2004—; judge primary and gen. elections Md., 2006. With U.S. Army, 1965-68, Civil Air Patrol, 1964-65. Decorated Army Commendation medal, Combat Infantry badge, Good Conduct medal, Nat. Def. medal, Vietnam Svc. medal, Vietnam Campaign ribbon, Sharp Shooter's Medal. Mem. Disabled Am. Vets. (comdr., svc. officer, sgt. at arms, hon. guard). Democrat. Mem. Lds Ch. Avocations: baseball, football, wrestling, bowling, pool. Home: 10103 Kathleen Dr Fort Washington MD 20744-2530

SMOOT, DAVID PAUL, finance company executive; b. Guthrie, Okla., Jan. 9, 1947; s. Jerry Edward and Katherine Ann (Doyle) S.; m. Marie Kathleen Stokes, Aug. 6, 1971; children: Aimee, Melissa. Student, Cumberland Coll., 1965—67, Glassboro State Coll., 1967, U. Cin., 1968—69. Regional mgr. Dennison Mfg., Chgo., 1969-77, Wordstream, Chgo., 1978-79; dist. mgr. AM Jacquard, San Francisco, 1979-82; co-founder, v.p. sales Phaser Systems Pub. Co., San Francisco, 1980-82; dir. ctrl. ops. Digital Rsch., Schaumburg, Ill., 1982-85; founder, chmn. bd., CEO Software Funding Internat., Deerfield, Ill., 1985-89, Software Funding Internat. (acquired by The Meridian Group), Deerfield, Ill., 1989; pres. Meridian Software Funding, 1989-92, Am. Indian Svcs. Inc., 1992-95; pres., founder Airborne Remote Mapping, 1995-98, Am. Indian Fin. Svcs. LLC, 1998—; founder, CEO Native Am. Water, LLC, 2002—. Mem. Native Vision program Johns Hopkins U. Hosp., NFL Players Assn. and Nick Lowery Found. Mem. bd. of consult Little City Home for Retarded, Palatine, Ill., 1986; founder, CEO Pro Players Classic Golf Invitational to Benefit Indigenous Youth, 1999—; founding mem. Robert B. Huff Scholarship Found., Chgo.; bd. dirs. Sports Legends Prostate Cancer Found., Phoenix, Ariz.; ptnr. Social Venture Ptnrs. Ariz. Served with U.S. Army, 1969-75. Mem. Assn. Data Processing Svcs. Orgns., Software Pubs. Assn., Syntopicaon XII, IBM PC User's Group (spkr.). Avocations: basketball, sailing, camping, fishing, tennis. Office: Natawa Corp 11 Sundial Cir Ste 19 PO Box 3800 Carefree AZ 85377 Office Phone: 480-595-5506.

SMOOT, FRED, professional football player; b. Jackson, Minn., Apr. 17, 1979; Attended, Miss. State, 2001. Corner back Wash. Redskins, 2001—04, 2007—, Minn. Vikings, 2005—07. Vol. Redskins Relief Fund, Wash., 2001—04. Recipient BJ Blanchard award, 2004, Ed Block Courage award, Redskins, 2003. Office: Wash Redskins 21300 Redskin Park Dr Ashburn VA 20147 *

SMOOT, GEORGE FITZGERALD, III, astrophysicist; b. Yukon, Fla., Feb. 20, 1945; BS in Math and Physics, MIT, 1966, PhD in Physics, 1970. Rsch. physicist MIT, 1970; rsch. physicist, space sciences lab. Univ. Calif., Berkeley, Calif., 1971—, prof. physics, 1994—; rsch. physicist Lawrence Berkeley Lab., 1974—. Team leader, differential microwave radiometer experiment, COBE (Cosmic Background Explorer) satellite; mem. steering group on cosmic background explorer satellite, prin. investigator on isotrophy experiment (NASA), 1975; 80 mem. Mgmt. and Ops. Working Group for Shuttle Astronomy, 1976-80; mem. adv. com. White Mountain Rsch. Station, 1982; mem. superconducting magnet facility for the space station study team, 1985; mem. Ctr. for Particle Astrophysics, U. Calif. Berkeley, 1988; mem. adv. com. Radio Astronomy Lab., 1990. Author: (with Keay Davidson) Wrinkles in Time, 1993; contbr. articles to profl. jours. Recipient Space/Missiles Laurels award Aviation Week & Space Technology, 1992, Popular Sci. award, 1992, Disting. Scientist, ARCS Found., Inc., 1993, Kirby award, 1993, Golden Plate award, 1994, Ernesto Orlando Lawrence award US Dept Energy, 1994; co-recipient Nobel Prize in Physics, Nobel Found., 2006. Mem. Internat. Astron. Union, Am. Phys. Soc. (mem. com. on the safety comml. nuclear reactors, 1974-75), Am. Astron. Soc., Sigma Xi., AAAS. Office: Lawrence Berkeley Nat Lab 1 Cyclotron Rd 5OR5008 Berkeley CA 94720

SMOOT, SKIPI LUNDQUIST, psychologist; b. Aberdeen, Wash., Apr. 10, 1934; d. Warren Duncan and Miriam Stephen (Bishop) Dobbins; m. Harold Richard Lundquist, June 2, 1951 (div. Mar. 1973); children: Kurt Richard, Mark David, Ted Douglas, Blake Donald; m. Edward Lee Smoot, June 14, 1975. BA in Psychology, Coll. of William and Mary, 1978; MA, Pepperdine U., 1980; PhD, Calif. Sch. of Profl., Psychology, San Diego, 1985. Lic. clin. psychologist, Calif.; lic. marriage and family therapist, Calif. Owner, operator McDonald's Restaurants, San Pedro and Torrance, Calif., 1965-76, Williamsburg, Va., 1965-76; psychotherapist Coll. Hosp., Cerritos, Calif., 1979-81, Orange County Child Guidance, Laguna Hills, Calif., 1981-82, Calif. State Police, Costa Mesa, 1982-83, Anaheim, 1983-84; psychologist Orange County Mental Health, Santa Ana, Calif., 1984-85, Psychol. Ctr., Orange and El Toro, Calif., 1985-91; clin. dir. Career Ambitions, Lake Forest, Calif., 1991-98, Psychol. Decisions, Irvine-Laguna Hills, Calif., 1991-94. Psychol. cons. seminars and workshops for bus., Irvine and Laguna Hills, 1991-98. Mem. APA, Calif. Psychol. Assn. Democrat. Avocations: music, travel, rsch. Office: Psychol Decisions Career Ambitions Unltd 10 McLaren Ste D Irvine CA 92618 Office Phone: 949-770-2675. Personal E-mail: skipilsmootphd@cox.net.

SMOREY-GIGER, MARCY, lawyer; Compliance and legal affairs mgr. Wesco Internat. Inc., Pitts., 1999—2002, corp. atty., mgr. compliance programs, 2002—04, corp. counsel, sec., 2004—. Office: Wesco Internat Inc 225 W Station Sq Dr Ste 700 Pittsburgh PA 15219-1122 Office Phone: 412-454-2222. Business E-Mail: msmorey@wesco.com.

SMOTHERMON, REBA MAXINE, elementary school educator; b. Liberal, Kans., July 8, 1933; d. Albert Isaac and Georga Maxine (Long) Shank; m. Wendell Scott Smothermon, Sept. 6, 1953; children: Jennifer Lynn Smothermon Kirby, Wendell Brent Smothermon. BA in Edn., Wichita State U., 1955; MA in Ednl. Psychology and Guidance, U. No. Colo., 1959. Cert. tchr. Kans., Calif., Colo., arthritis instr. Tchr. second grade Unified Sch. Dist. 480/Washington Sch., Liberal, Kans., 1955-57, Adams County Dist. Skyline Vista Sch., Westminster, Colo., 1957-61; elem. tchr. Ventura Unified Santa Ana Sch., Ojai, Calif., 1964-80, Unified Sch. Dist. #480, Southlawn McKinley Schs., Liberal, 1980-95; ret., 1995. Literary coun. mem. Southwest Reading Coun., Liberal, 1985-95. Participant devel. sch. curriculum, 1977-79. Sec. to pres. Evergreen Garden Club, Liberal, 1980-05; youth sponsor, pres. women's group 1st United Meth. Ch., Liberal, 1945—; mem. Liberal Panhellenic, 1980-96; bd. dir., pres. Community Concerts of Liberal, 1987-91; pres. Liberal Woman's Club, 1995—; mem. Kans. Coun. on Travel and Tourism, 2002-05; pres. Book Club I, sec.-treas., tchr. swimming, arthritis support groups. Recipient Lifetime Achievement award, Southwest Daily Times, 2006. Mem. AAUW (pres. local chpt. 1980—, Woman of Yr. 1985, state chmn. internat. rels. com. 1985-90),DAR (regent chaplain 1972-), PEO (various to pres. 1985—), Aurora Club, Ladies' Oriental Shrine N.Am., Delta Kappa Gamma (various to pres. 1981—). Republican. Avocations: music, reading. Home: 830 S Clay F3 PO Box 470 Liberal KS 67905-0470 Personal E-mail: rwsmut@sbcglobal.net.

SMOTHERS, DELORIS RICE, computer career educator; d. Bill Junior and Mamie Ford Rice; m. William Douglas Smothers, June 13, 1998; children: Jemeana Roberson, Knegleshia, Terra, Canderiah. MEd, Ala. A&M U., Normal, 1992—95. Computer & office careers instr. North Ala. Skills Ctr., Huntsville, 1981—2001; cis/oad instr. J. F. Drake State Tech. Coll., Huntsville, 2001—; office sys. mgmt. dept. instr. Ala. A&M U. Recipient Master Tchr. Participant award, Ala. Coll. Sys., 2006. Mem.: Nat. Bus. Edn. Assn., Delta Sigma Theta Sorority, Inc. (life; rec. & corr. sec. 2001—). Home: 6607 Willow Springs Blvd Huntsville AL 35806 Office: J F Drake State Tech Coll 3421 Meridian St N Huntsville AL 35811 Home Phone: 256-864-0137.

SMOTHERS, RONALD, journalist; Reporter New York Times. Panelist NYU Multinational Inst. Am. Studies, 1998. Author: (articles) In Plea Deal a Banker Outlines Money Laundering in Caymans, 1999, Gas Stations Violated Pricing Laws, New Jersey Says, 2005. Office: New York Times Newark Bur 111 Mulberry St Newark NJ 07102 Office Phone: 973-623-3904. Office Fax: 973-802-1877.

SMOTHERS, TOM, actor, singer; b. Feb. 2, 1937; s. Thomas B. and Ruth Smothers; children: Tom, Bo, Riley Rose; m. Marcy Carriker, Sept. 9, 1990. Student, San Jose State Coll. Owner winery, Kenwood, Calif. Nightclub appearances in Reno, Lake Tahoe, Las Vegas, Nev., and various venues in the U.S.; co-star TV situation comedy Smothers Brothers Show, 1965-66, Smothers Brothers Comedy Hour, CBS-TV, 1967-69, 70, weekly variety show The Smothers Brothers Show, NBC-TV, 1975; starred in films The Silver Bears, Get To Know Your Rabbit, A Pleasure Doing Business, Serial, There Goes the Bride, Pandemonium, Speed Zone; starred on Broadway in I Love My Wife, 1978-79; appeared in TV movie Terror at Alcatraz, 1982; starred in Smothers Brothers Spl. and Series, 1988-89. Office: Knave Prodns Ste 107B 6442 Coldwater Canyon Ave North Hollywood CA 91606-1137 Home Phone: 708-748-4550; Office Phone: 818-754-0351. E-mail: SMOBRO1@AOL.COM.

SMOTRICH, DAVID ISADORE, architect; b. Norwich, Conn., Oct. 6, 1933; s. Max Z. and Ida (Babinsky) S.; m. Bernice D. Strachman, Mar. 25, 1956; children: Ross Lawrence, Maura Faye, Hannah. AB, Harvard Coll., 1955, MArch, 1960. Master planning team, Town of Arad, State of Israel, 1961-62; assoc. Platt Assocs., NYC, 1963-65; gen. ptnr. Smotrich & Platt, NYC, 1965-74, Smotrich Platt & Buttrick, NYC, 1975-76, Smotrich & Platt, NYC, 1976-85, David Smotrich & Ptnrs., NYC, 1985—. Cons. to Jerusalem Master Plan Office, Israel Ministry of Housing, 1967. Planning bd. Town of New Castle, N.Y., 1974-81; exec. bd. Road Rev. League, Bedford, N.Y., 1966-70. With AUS, 1955-57. Recipient Bard award, 1969, 85, Archtl. Record award, 1971, 73-75, 78, Design award HUD, 1980. Mem. AIA (Nat. Honor award 1969, N.Y. State Honor awards 1984, 94, Cmty. Design awards 1991, 93, AIA Coll. of Fellows 1993), Assn. Engrs. and Archs. in Israel, Phi Beta Kappa, Harvard Club (N.Y.C.). Home: 7 Mayberry Close Chappaqua NY 10514-1113 Office: David Smotrich & Ptnrs 443 Park Ave S New York NY 10016-7322 Office Phone: 212-889-4045. Personal E-mail: ds@dsmotricharch.com.

SMOUSE, H(ERVEY) RUSSELL, lawyer; b. Oakland, Md., Aug. 13, 1932; s. Hervey Reed and Vernie (Rush) Smouse; m. Creta M. Staley, June 15, 1955; children: Kristin Anne, Randall Forsyth, Gregory Russell. AB, Princeton U., 1955; LLB, U. Md., 1958. Bar: Md. 58, U.S. Tax. Ct. 79, U.S. Ct. Appeals (4th cir.) 60, U.S. Supreme Ct. 74. Atty. Atty. Gen.'s Honors Program, Dept. Justice, Washington, 1958—60; asst. U.S. atty. Dist. Md., 1960—62; assoc. Pierson and Pierson, Balt., 1962—64; atty. B.&O. R.R., Balt., 1964—66; mem. Pierson and Pierson, 1966—69, Clapp, Somerville, Black & Honemann, Balt., 1969—74; pvt. practice Law Offices H. Russell Smouse, 1974—81; mem. Melnicove, Kaufman, Weiner & Smouse, P.A., Balt., 1981—89, chmn. litigation, 1985—89; mem. Whiteford, Taylor & Preston, Balt., 1989—93, chmn. litigation dept., 1989—93; head gen. litigation Law Offices Peter G. Angelos, 1993—; gen. counsel Balt. Orioles, 1993—. Permanent mem. jud. conf. U.S. Ct. Appeals (4th cir.); vice chmn. Legal Aid Bur. Balt. City, 1972—73. Named Best Lawyers in America, 2005—06, 2006—07. Fellow: Am. Coll. Trial Lawyers; mem.: ATLA, ABA, Nat. Assn. R.R. Trial Counsel (exec. com., v.p. ea. region 1986—92), Bar Assn. Balt. City (chmn. grievance com. 1969—70, chmn. judiciary com. and nominating com. 1980, mem. exec. com. 1969—70, 1980, chmn. exec. com. lawyers' com. for ind. judiciary 1989—96), Md. State Bar Assn. (gov. 1981—83), Am. Law Inst. Republican. Presbyterian. Office Phone: 410-649-2000. Business E-Mail: djmiller@lawpga.com.

SMOUSE, PETER E., ecologist, educator; BS in Forestry, U. Calif., Berkeley, 1965; PhD in Genetics, NC State U., Raleigh, 1970. Postdoctoral rschr. zoology U. Tex., Austin, 1970—72; asst. prof. to prof. human genetics U. Mich., 1972—89, prof. biology, 1985—89; prof. II marine and coastal scis. Rutgers U., 1989—96, prof. II ecology, evolution and natural resources, 1996—. Vis. prof. demographic and population genetics U. Tex., 1984—85; assoc. dir. Ctr. Theoretical and Applied Genetics Rutgers U., 1989—96, assoc. dean scis., 1993—95, acting assoc. provost scis., 1993—95, chair ecology, evolution and natural resources, 1997—2001; mem. DNA subcommittee NY State Forensic Commn., 1995—98; vis. scholar Australian Nat. U., 1996—97; mem. adv. com. Columbia Earth Inst., 1998; mem. adv. bd. ecology and evolutionary biology Columbia U., 2001—; mem. adv. bd. Land Inst., 2001—. Contbr. articles to sci. jours.; assoc. editor: Theoretical Population Biology, 1979—82, Evolution, 1987—89, Jour. Heredity, 1990—92, mem. editl. bd.: Internat. Jour. Quantitative Anthropology, 1988—91. Office: Dept Ecology Evolution and Natural Resources Rutgers U Cook Coll 14 Coll Farm Rd New Brunswick NJ 08901-8551 E-mail: smouse@aesop.rutgers.edu.

SMUCKER, RICHARD K., food products executive; m. Emily Delp; 1 child. Grad., Miami U., Ohio; MBA, Wharton Sch. Bus., U. Penn. Pres. The J.M. Smucker Co., 1987—, co-CEO, 2001—. Bd. dirs. The J.M. Smucker Co., Wm. Wrigley Jr., Co., Internat. Multifoods, The Sherwin-Williams Co., Internat. Foodservice Mfr. Assoc.; bd. trustees Cleveland Orchestra, Culinary Inst. Am. Office: 1 Strawberry Ln Orrville OH 44667-1241 *

SMUCKER, TIMOTHY P., food products executive; m. Jennifer Coddington; 3 children. BS Economics, Coll. of Wooster, 1967; MBA Mktg., Wharton Sch. Bus., U Penn, 1969. Chmn. The J.M. Smucker Co., 1984—, co-CEO, 2001—. Bd. dirs. The J.M. Smucker Co., Huntington BancShares, Inc., Dreyer's Grand Ice Cream, Inc., Grocery Mfr. Am., Inc.; bd. trustees Coll. of Wooster; mem. steering com. Heartland Edn. Community. Office: 1 Strawberry Ln Orrville OH 44667-1241 *

SMUKAL, MICHAEL WILLIAM, musician, educator, composer; s. Paul Herbert and Carol Hannen Smukal; children: Michael Adam, Stephen Andrew. BA, MusM, U. Nev., Las Vegas, 1985. Dir. of bands Silvestri Jr. H.S., Clark County Sch. Dist., Las Vegas, 1985—. Composer, arranger Warner Bros. Music Publs., Las Vegas. Music arranger: educational jazz publs. Now Rock, Ye Rested Gentlemen (Editor's Choice, 2004), Song Of The Volga Boatmen, trombonist: with Elvis Presley, 1975—77, Elvis in Concert, CBS TV spl., Spring Tours '77, Elvis Presley, Moody Blue, Elvis Presley, Elvis: A Canadian Tribute, Elvis Presley, Platinum: A Life in Music, Elvis Presley, Elvis in Concert, Elvis Presley, This is Elvis, Elvis Presley, Elvis Aaron Presley. State pres. Nat. Assn. Of Jazz Educators, Las Vegas, Nev., 1984—86. Tech. sgt. USAF, 1971—75, Washington, DC. Named SW Region Disting. Educator of the Yr., Clark County Sch. Dist., 2003—04. Mem.: Internat. Assn. Jazz Educators, Nev. Music Educators Assn., Music Educator's Nat. Conf. Home Phone: 702-896-5186. Personal E-mail: smukal@cox.net.

SMUTNY, ABBY COHEN, lawyer; b. NYC, May 6, 1964; Cert London Sch. Econ. and Polit. Sci.; BA cum laude, Vassar Coll.; cert, Université des Langues et Lettres de Grenoble, 1986; JD, Univ. Chgo. Sch. Law. Bar: NY 1991, DC 1993, US Dist. Ct. (DC). Ptnr. White & Case, Washington. Named one of Litigation's Rising Stars, The Am. Lawyer, 2007. Mem.: Global Arbitration Review (editl. bd 2006—, Leading Lights 45 under 45), Arbitration Internat. (editl. bd. 2006), DC Bar Assn. (chmn. internat. law sect. 1999—2000), Internat. Law Assn., Inst. Transnational Arbitration,

Am. Soc. Internat. Law (chmn. exec. coun. 1999—2002, chmn. exec. com. 2000—02), Internat. Bar Assn., ABA (int. law and practice sect.). Office: White & Case 701 13 St NW Washington DC 20005 Business E-Mail: asmutny@whitecase.com. *

SMUTNY, JOAN FRANKLIN, academic director, educator; b. Chgo. d. Eugene and Mabel (Lind) Franklin; m. Herbert Paul Smutny; 1 child, Cheryl Anne. BS, MA, Northwestern U. Tchr. New Trier H.S., Winnetka, Ill.; mem. faculty, founder, dir. Nat. H.S. Inst. Northwestern U. Sch. Edn., Chgo.; faculty, founder, dir. h.s. workshop critical thinking/edn. Nat. Coll. Edn., Evanston, Ill., exec. dir. h.s. workshops, 1970-75; founder, dir. Woman Power Through Edn. Seminar, 1969-74; dir. Right to Read Seminar in critical reading, 1973-74; dir. seminar gifted h.s. students, 1973; dir. gifted programs for 6th, 7th, 8th graders Evanston pub. schs., 1978-79; dir. gifted programs 1st-8th grade Glenview (Ill.) pub. schs., 1979—. Dir. gifted programs Nat.-Louis U., Evanston, 1980-82, dir. Ctr. for Gifted, 1982—; dir. Bright and Talented Project, 1986—, North Shore Country Day Sch., Winnetka, 1982—; dir. Job Creation Project, 1980-82; dir. New Dimensions for Women, 1973; dir. Thinking for Action in Career Edn. Program 1976-79; dir. TACE, dir. Humanities Program for Verbally Precocious Youth, 1978-79; co-dir., instr. seminars in critical thinking Ill. Family Svc., 1972-75; writer ednl. filmstrips in lang. arts and lit. Soc. Visual Edn., 1970-74; spkrs. bur. Coun. Fgn. Rels., 1968-69; adv. com. edn. professions devel. act U.S. Office Edn., 1969—; state team for gifted, Ill. Office Edn., Office of Gifted, Springfield, Ill., 1977; writer, cons. Radiant Ednl. Corp., 1969-71; cons. ALA, 1969-71, workshop leader and spkr. gifted edn., 1971—; coord. career edn. Nat. Coll.Edn., 1976-78, dir. Project 1987—, dir. Summer Wonders, 1986—, Creative Children's Acad., bd. dirs., Worlds of Wisdom and Wonder, 1978—; dir. Future Tchrs. Am. Seminar in Coll. and Career, 1970-72; cons. rsch. & devel. Ill. Dept. Vocat. Edn., 1973—; evaluation cons. DAVTE, IOE, Springfield, Ill., 1977, mem. Leadership Tng. Inst. Gifted, U.S. Office Edn., 1973-74; dir. workshops for h.s. students; cons., spkr. in field; dir. Gifted Young Writers and Young Writers confs., 1978, 79; dir. Project '92 The White House Conf. on Children and Youth; mem. adv. bd. Educating Able Learners, 1991—; chmn. bd. dirs. Barbereux Sch., Evanston, 1992—; asst. editor, editl. bd. Understanding our Gifted, 1994—. Author: Job Creation: Creative Materials, Activities and Strategies for the Classroom, 1982, A Thoughtful Overview of Gifted Education, 1990, Your Gifted Child—How to Recognize and Develop the Special Talents in Your Child from Birth to Age Seven, 1987, paperback, 1991, Education of the Gifted: Programs and Perspectives, 1990, Teaching Gifted Young Children in the Regular Classroom, 1997, Gifted Girls, 1998, Stand Up For Your Gifted Child, 2001, Gifted Education: Promising Practices, 2003, Differentiated Instruction, 2003, Differentiating For the Young Child, 2004, Differentiating for the Young Child: Teaching Strategies Across the Content Areas, 2004, Acceleration for Gifted Learners, K-5, 2007; editor: The Young Gifted Child: Potential and Promise: An Anthology, 1998, Creativity Series Ablex, 1998—, Underserved Gifted Populations, 2003; contbg. editor: Roper Rev., 1994—; asst. editor: Understanding Our Gifted, 1995—; editor, contbr.: Maturity in Teching; editor: Jour. Ill. Assn. for Gifted, 1995—; mem. adv. bd. Gifted Edn. Press Quar., 1995—; writer: (ednl. filmstrips) The Brothers Grimm, How the West Was Won, Mutiny on the Bounty, Dr. Zhivago, Space Odyssey 2001, Christmas Around the World; contbr. editor numerous books in field; contbr. articles to profl. jours. including Chgo. Parent Mag.; reviewer programs for Gifted and Talented, US Office Edn., 1976-78. Mem. AAUP, Nat. Assn. Gifted Child (nat. membership chmn. 1991—, co-chmn. schs. and programs, co-editor newsletter early childhood divsn., Disting. Svc. award 1996), Nat. Soc. Arts & Letters (nat. bd., 1st and 3d v.p. Evanston chpt. 1990-92), Mortar Bd. Outstanding Educators of Am. 1974, Pi Lambda Theta, Phi Delta Kappa (v.p. Evanston chpt. rsch. chmn. 1990-92). Home: 633 Forest Ave Wilmette IL 60091-1713 Office Phone: 847-901-0173. Personal E-mail: joanfsm@aol.com. *Gifted education is particularly vital in that it discerns the needs of bright, talented children who have an immense amount to contribute to our country and our world. Gifted children are our country's most neglected resource--and most needed. It is my privilege to work in this area, to work with gifted children, their parents and teachers.*

SMYNTEK, JOHN EUGENE, JR., editor; b. Buffalo, Aug. 24, 1950; BA, U. Detroit, 1972. Asst. instr. Mich. State U., East Lansing, 1981; features editor Free Press, Detroit, 1985-92; dir. online svcs. and dir. libr. Free Press Plus, Detroit, 1992-95, spl. features and syndicate editor, 1995—; asst. instr. U. Detroit Mercy, 2000—01. Vis. fellow in journalism Duke U., 1988; profl. student pubs. advisor U. Detroit Mercy, 1992—94; bd. visitors Wayne State U. Coll. Fine, Performing and Comm. Arts, 2001—05. Recipient Fine Arts Reporting award, Detroit Press Club, 1985. Roman Catholic. Office: Detroit Free Press 600 W Fort St Detroit MI 48226-2706 Office Phone: 313-222-5169. Business E-Mail: jsmyntek@freepress.com.

SMYTH, DAVID, writer, editor; b. Buenos Aires, Feb. 7, 1929; came to U.S. 1962, naturalized 1970; s. Currell Hutchinson and Jessie Rodger (Dodds) S.; m. Elli Helene Dusterhoft, Nov. 9, 1968; 1 child, Clifford Dieter. BA, Cambridge U., Eng., 1951, MA, 1967. Tech. writer, copywriter, 1953-55; movie promotion writer, 1956; owner Ace Translation Agy., Buenos Aires, 1957-58; sec. Found. Econ. Edn., 1959; cables editor Buenos Aires Herald, 1960; lexicographer Simon & Schuster English-Spanish Dictionary, 1961; Latin Am. desk editor UPI, NYC, 1962-63, AP, NYC, 1963-73, world svcs. fin. editor, 1973-96; freelance writer, translator, editor, 1997—. Author: You Can Survive Any Financial Disaster, 1977, Worldly Wise Investor, 1988; co-author: The Speculator's Handbook, 1974, Unusual Investments That Could Make You Rich, 1978, No Cost/Low Cost Investing, 1987. Served with Argentine Army, 1952. Mem. N.Y. Fin. Writers Assn. Home: 8 Beechwood Ave Metuchen NJ 08840-2107 E-mail: Currell@aol.com.

SMYTH, DONALD MORGAN, chemistry professor, researcher; b. Bangor, Maine, Mar. 20, 1930; s. John Robert and Selma (Eubanks) S.; m. Elisabeth Luce, Aug. 1, 1951; children: Carolyn, Joanne. BS in Chemistry, U. Maine, 1951; PhD in Inorganic Chemistry, MIT, 1954. Sr. chemist Sprague Electric Co., North Adams, Mass., 1954-58, sect. head, 1958-61, dept. head, 1961-71; assoc. prof. Lehigh U., Bethlehem, Pa., 1971-73, prof., 1973-95, dir. Materials Rsch. Ctr., 1971-92, Paul B. Reinhold prof. materials sci., engring. and chemistry, 1988-95; emeritus, 1995—. Mem. various coms. Lehigh U., 1973-95; mem. materials rsch. adv. com. NSF, 1984-88, chmn., 1985-86, co-chair ad-hoc com. to brief dir., 1986; mem. coun. materials sci. Dept. Energy, 1986-90; presenter in field. Contbr. articles to profl. jours. Recipient Libsch Rsch. award Lehigh U., 1990, Buessem award Dielectrics Rsch. Ctr., Pa. State U., 1991; grantee in field. Fellow Am. Inst. Chemists, Am. Ceramic Soc. (com. edn. electronics divsn. 1974-78, chmn. Lehigh Valley sect. 1978-79, counselor 1982-00, assoc. editor jour. 1988-92, best paper award 1987, 95, Kraner award Lehigh Valley sect. 1990, Sosman lectr. 1996); mem. Am. Chem. Soc., Nat. Acad. Engring., Materials Rsch. Soc., Electrochem. Soc. (various coms., sec. dielectrics and insulation divsn. 1967-69, vice chmn. 1969-70, chmn. 1970-71, rsch. award battery divsn. 1960). Achievements include patents (with others) for Solid-State Battery Cell with Complex Organic Electrolyte Material, Capacitor with Dielectric Film Having Phosphorous-Containing Component Therein, Solid Barrier Electrolyte Incorporating Additive, others; research in defect chemistry and electrical properties of complex oxides. Home: 3429 Mountainview Cir Bethlehem PA 18017-1807 Office: Lehigh Univ Ctr Advanced Material and Nanotech 5 E Packer Ave Bethlehem PA 18015-3102 Home Phone: 610-867-6544; Office Phone: 610-758-3852. Business E-Mail: dms4@lehigh.edu.

SMYTH, JOEL DOUGLAS, newspaper executive; b. Renovo, Pa., Nov. 8, 1941; s. Bernard John and Eva Mae (Stone) S.; m. Madonna Robertson, Nov. 29, 1959; children: Deborah Sue, Susan Kelly, Michael Robertson, Patricia Ann, Rebecca Lee, Jennifer Neilia. Student, Lycoming Coll., 1959. Reporter Del. State News, Dover, 1960-62, news editor, 1962-65, mng. editor, 1965-70, editor, pres., 1970-78; editor Del. Sunday News, 1964-65; pres. Ind. Newspapers, Inc., Dover, 1970-89, chmn., CEO, 1989—. Founding pres. Valley Citizen's League, 1987-90. Recipient writing awards. Mem. AP Mng. Editors Assn. (dir.), Am. Soc. Newspaper Editors, Young Pres.'s Orgn., Sigma Delta Chi. Home: 39833 N 100th St Scottsdale AZ 85262-2975 Office: Independent Newspaper Inc PO Box 70001 Dover DE 19903

SMYTH, JOSEPH PATRICK, retired military officer, physician; b. Norwalk, Conn., Mar. 2, 1933; s. Patrick and Helen (Heffernan) Smyth; m. Ursula Marie Kirwin, Feb. 22, 1961; children: Donna, Jennifer, Joseph. BA, Fairfield U., 1960; MD, Creighton U., 1964. Diplomate Am. Bd. Med. Examiners. Commd. ensign USN, 1963, advanced through grades to rear adm., 1988; intern Phila. Naval Hosp., 1964-65, internal medicine resident, 1965-68, staff physician, 1968-69; internist, chief of medicine U.S. Naval Hosp., DaNang, Vietnam, 1969-70, Orlando, Fla., 1970-76, chief of medicine, exec. officer Yokosuka, Japan, 1976-80, exec. officer Oakland, Calif., 1980-82, comdg. officer, 1984-86, Okinawa, Japan, 1982—84, Naval Med. Command European Region, London, 1986-90; dep. dir. for med. readiness The Joint Staff, Pentagon, Washington, 1990-92; retired US Navy, 1992; med. dir. Volusia County (Fla.) Dept. of Corrections, 1994—2005. Instr. medicine Jefferson Med. Coll., 1966—69; preceptor USN Physician Asst. Program, Orlando, 1971—76; instr. mgmt. course Navy Med. Dept., Washington, 1986; med. coord. entire Gulf War buildup to Joint Chief Staff chmn. Gen. Colin Powell Operation Desert Shield/Storm, Saudi Arabia, 1990—91; med. dir. Volusia County Dept. Corrections, Fla., 1994—2005. Physician Orange County Fla. Alcohol Ctr., Orlando, 1974—76. Decorated Def. Superior Svc. medal, Legion of Merit, Meritorious Svc. medals with 2 oak leaf clusters, Navy Commendation medal with combat V. Mem.: AMA, Orange County Med. Soc., Am. Acad. Physician Execs., Fla. Med. Assn., Am. Acad. Med. Adminstrs. (Levandowski award 1991), Assn. Mil. Surgeons U.S. Republican. Roman Catholic. Home: 400 Sweetwater Blvd Longwood FL 32779-3422

SMYTH, JOSEPH VINCENT, manufacturing executive; b. Belfast, Ireland, July 18, 1919; s. Joseph Leo and Margaret M. (Murray) S.; m. Marie E. Cripe, Mar. 22, 1941; children: Kevin W., Brian J., Ellen M., Vincent P. BS cum laude, U. Notre Dame, 1941. With Arnolt Corp., Warsaw, Ind., 1946-63, exec. v.p., gen. mgr., until 1963; pres., gen. mgr. Hills-McCanna Co., Carpentersville, Ill., 1963-72; pres. Lunkenheimer Co., Cin., 1972-79; v.p. Condec Flow Control Group, Chgo., 1979-82; cons., 1982—. Mem.: K.C. Address: 7656 Spring Bay Cove Orlando FL 32819-7208 Business E-Mail: j.smyth1@cfl.rr.com.

SMYTH, PAUL BURTON, lawyer; b. Phila., Aug. 15, 1949; s. Benjamin Burton and Florence Elizabeth (Tomlinson) S.; m. Denise Elaine Freeland, May 31, 1975. BA, Trinity Coll., 1971; JD, Boston Coll., 1974. Bar: Conn. 1974, D.C. 1975, U.S. Dist. Ct. D.C., 1980, U.S. Supreme Ct., 1985. With Dept. Interior, 1974—. Atty. Office of Hearings and Appeals, Arlington, Va., 1974—76, acting dir., 1993—94, dep. assoc. solicitor for land and water resources, 1995—2007, counselor to solicitor, 2007—; atty. Office of Solicitor, Washington, 1976—82, asst. solicitor for land use and realty, 1982—87, dep. assoc. solicitor for energy and resources, 1987—95; lectr. environ. law George Washington U. Law Sch., Washington, 1997—2001. Editor: Federal Reclamation and Related Laws Annotated, Reclamation Reform Act Compilation, 1982—88; contbr. articles to legal pubs. Bd. dirs. EcoVoce, 1998—; trustee Rocky Mtn. Mineral Law Found., 1999—2001. Mem. ABA (coun. 1991-94, budget officer 1994-98, sec. natural resources, energy and environ. law, exec. editor Nat. Resources and the Environ. 1989-91). Office: Office of Solicitor Dept Interior 18th And C Sts NW Washington DC 20240-0001 Home Phone: 703-683-0322; Office Phone: 202-208-4506. E-mail: paulb.smyth@verizon.net.

SMYTH, RICH, publishing executive; b. Bronx, NY; married; 2 children. BA in Comm., Boston Coll. With Carnation Co. (now Nestle Foods), Dallas, 1985—88; joined So. Living, 1988, nat. sales mgr. NYC, 1996—98, advt. dir., 1998—2000, v.p., 2000—, pub., 2003—. Office: Southern Living PO Box 523 2100 Lakeshore Drive Birmingham AL 35209 Mailing: Southern Living 20th Floor 1271 Ave of Americas New York NY 10020-1391 Office Phone: 888-254-9654, 212-522-1212. Office Fax: 212-522-4199. E-mail: rich_smyth@timeinc.com. *

SMYTH, ROBERY M., lawyer; b. Pitts., Apr. 2, 1969; married; 3 children. BA, Miami U., 1991; JD, U. Cin., 1994. Bar: Ohio 1994, US Dist. Ct. Southern Dist. Ohio 1995. Clerk 1st Dist. Ohio, Ct. of Appeals; ptnr. Drew & Ward, Cin. Named one of Ohio's Rising Stars, Super Lawyers, 2005, 2006. Fellow: Cin. Acad. Leadership for Lawyers; mem.: Ohio State Bar Assn., ABA, Cin. Bar Assn. (sec., Ct. of Appeals Com. 2004—, former co-chair, Young Lawyers Membership Com.). Avocation: genealogy. Office: Drew & Ward Co LPA 1 W Fourth St Ste 2400 Cincinnati OH 45202 Office Phone: 513-621-8210. Office Fax: 513-621-5444.

SMYTH, RYAN, professional hockey player; b. Banff, Alta., Can., Feb. 21, 1976; m. Stacey Smyth. Left wing Edmonton Oilers, 1994—2007, NY Islanders, 2007, Colo. Avalanche, 2007—. Mem. Team Can., Olympic Games, Salt Lake City, 2002, Team Can., World Cup of Hockey, 2004. Achievements include being a member of gold medal Canadian Hockey team, World Junior Championships, 1995, Salt Lake City Olympic Games, 2002; being a member of World Cup Champion Team Canada, 2004. Office: Colo Avalanche Pepsi Ctr 1000 Chopper Cir Denver CO 80204 *

SMYTHE, CHEVES MCCORD, internist, geriatrician, educator, dean; b. May 25, 1924; Student, Yale Coll., 1942—43; MD cum laude, Harvard, 1947. Diplomate Am. Bd. Internal Medicine, Am. Bd. Geriatrics. Intern, asst. resident Harvard Med. Svc., Boston City Hosp., 1947—49, chief resident, 1954—55; resident chest svc. Bellevue, 1949—50; rsch. fellow Presbyn. Hosp., NYC, 1950—52; assoc. medicine Med. Coll. S.C. Sch. Medicine, 1956—58, asst. prof. medicine, 1958—60, assoc. prof. medicine, 1960—66, dean, 1963—65; attending physician Wesley Meml., Cook County North Side VA Hosps., Chgo., 1967—70; with Aga Khan U. Hosp., Karachi, Pakistan, 1990—91; dean faculty health scis., prof. medicine Aga Khan U., Karachi, Pakistan, 1982—85, prof., chmn. dept. medicine, 1990—91; chief Med. Svcs. at LBJ Hosp., Houston, 1991—95; prof. divsn. gen. medicine dept. internal medicine U. Tex. Med. Sch., Houston, 1970—, dean, 1970—75, dean pro tem, 1995—96. Assoc. med. dir. Hermann Hosp., 1996—. Bd. dirs. Assn. Am. Assoc. Med. Colls., Office: U Tex Med Sch 6431 Fannin St 1-108 Houston TX 77030-1501

SMYTHE, WILLIAM RODMAN, physicist, researcher; b. LA, Jan. 6, 1930; s. William Ralph and Helen (Keith) S.; m. Carol Richardson, Nov. 27, 1954 (dec. Dec. 1987); children: Stephanie, Deborah, William Richardson, Reed Terry; m. Judith Brean Travers, Jan. 1, 1989. BS, Calif. Inst. Tech., 1951, MS, 1952, PhD, 1957. Engr. Gen. Electric Microwave Lab., Palo Alto, Calif., 1956-57; asst. prof. U. Colo., 1958-63, assoc. prof., 1963-67, prof., 1967-95, chmn. nuclear physics lab., 1967-69, 81-83, 90-92, prof. emeritus, 1995—. Mem. Am. Phys. Soc. Clubs: Colorado Mountain (Boulder). Achievements include inventing negative ion cyclotron. Home: 2106 Knollwood Dr Boulder CO 80302-4706 E-mail: Rod.Smythe@colorado.edu.

SNADER, JACK ROSS, retired publishing company executive; b. Athens, Ohio, Feb. 25, 1938; s. Daniel Webster and Mae Estella (Miller) S.; m. Sharon Perschnick, Apr. 4, 1959; children: Susan Mae, Brian Ross. BS, U. Ill., 1959. Cert. mgmt. cons. With mktg. Richardson-Merrell, Cin., 1959-65, Xerox Corp., NYC, 1965-67, Sieber & McIntyre, Chgo., 1967-69; pres. Systema Corp., Northbrook, Ill., 1969—; ret. Mem. exec. adv. bd. bus. program Trinity Internat. U. Author Systematic Selling, 1987, The Sales Relationship, 1988. Mem. ASTD, Inst. Mgmt. Cons. Office: Systema Corp 900 Northshore Dr Ste 166 Lake Bluff IL 60044 Office Phone: 847-615-0900.

SNAID, LEON JEFFREY, lawyer; b. Johannesburg, Transvaal, Republic of South Africa, Dec. 24, 1946; came to U.S., 1981; s. Mannie and Hene (Blume) S.; children: Jedd, Nicole. Diploma in Law, U. Witwatersrand, Johannesburg, 1969. Bar: Supreme Ct. Republic South Africa 1971, High Ct. of the Kingdom of Lesotho 1976, Calif. 1982, U.S. Dist. Ct. (so. and ctrl. dists.) Calif. 1982, U.S. Supreme Ct. 1999; cert. immigration law specialist, State Bar Calif. Bd. Legal Specialization. Assoc. Reeders, Teeger & Rosettenstein, Johannesburg, 1972; sole practice Johannesburg, 1973-76; ptnr. Snaid & Snaid, Johannesburg, 1976-81; sole practice San Diego, 1982—. Lectr. legal edn. seminars, San Diego, 1984—. Author (quar. newsletter) Immigration and International Law, The Newcomers Guide to Living in the USA, Easyway USA, The Safe and Smart Guide to living in the USA, Best Business Buddy, The Golden Rules and Strategies of Smart Business. Mem. Am. Immigration Lawyers Assn. (past chmn. CLE San Diego chpt.), San Diego County Bar Assn. (past chmn. immigration com.). Home: 5060 Via Papel San Diego CA 92122-3923 Office: Ste # 211 2727 Camino Del Rio S San Diego CA 92108 Office Phone: 619-725-0797. Business E-Mail: info@snaid.com.

SNAPP, ELIZABETH, librarian, educator; b. Lubbock, Tex., Mar. 31, 1937; d. William James and Louise (Lanham) Mitchell; m. Henry Franklin Snapp, June 1, 1956 (div. Dec. 2001). BA magna cum laude, North Tex. State U., Denton, 1968, MLS, 1969, MA, 1977. Asst. to archivist Archive of New Orleans Jazz Tulane U., 1960-63; catalog libr. Tex. Woman's U., Denton, 1969-71, head acquisitions dept., 1971-74, coord. readers svcs., 1974-77, asst. to dean Grad. Sch., 1977-79, instr. libr. sci., 1977-88, acting Univ. libr., 1979-82, dir. librs., 1982—2002, dir. librs. emeritus, 2002—, univ. historian, 1995—2002; adj. prof. dept. history and govt. Tex. Woman's U., Denton, 2002—; rsch. assoc. Tex. Woman's U. Libr., Denton, 2002—. Chair-elect Tex. Coun. State U. Librs., 1988—90, chmn., 1990—92; adv. com. on libr. formula Coord. Bd. Tex. Coll. and Univ. Sys., 1981—92; Libr. Sys. Act adv. bd. Tex. State Libr. and Archives Commn., 1999—2002; del. OCLC Nat. Users Coun., 1985—87, by-laws com., 1985—86, com. on less-than-full-svcs. networks, 1986—87; trustee AMIGOS Libr. Svcs., 1994—2000, sec. bd. trustees, 1996—97, vice-chmn. bd. trustees, 1997—99, chair bd. trustees, 1999—2000; project dir. NEH consultancy grant on devel. core curriculum for women's studies, 1981—82; chmn. Blue Ribbon com. 1986 Gov.'s Commn. for Women to select 150 outstanding women in Tex. History; project dir. math./sci. anthology project Tex. Found. Women's Resources; co-sponsor Irish Lecture Series, Denton, 1968, 70, 73, 78. Asst. editor Tex. Academe, 1973—76; co-editor: Read All About Her! Texas Women's History: A Working Bibliography, 1995; contbg. author Women in Special Collections, 1984, Special Collections, 1986, book reviewer Libr. Resources and Tech. Svcs., 1973—2002; contbr. articles to profl. jours. Trustee, treas. Adult Day Care of North Tex., 2002—04, v.p., 2004; sec. Denton County Dem. Caucus, 1970. Recipient Ann. Pioneer award, Tex. Woman's U., 1986, Women's Studies Vision award, 1998. Mem.: AAUW (legis. br. chmn. 1973—74, br. v.p. 1975—76, br. pres. 1979—80, state historian 1986—88, treas. 1998—99), ALA (stds. com. 1983—85), AAUP, Tex. Assn. Coll. Tchrs. (pres. Tex. Woman's U. chpt. 1976—77), So. Conf. Brit. Studies, Women's Collecting Group (chmn. ad hoc com. 1984—86), Tex. Hist. Commn. (judge for Farenbach History prize 1990—93), Tex. Libr. Assn. (program com. 1978, Dist. VII chmn. 1985—86, archives and oral history com. 1990—92, co-chair conf. program com. 1994, Tall Texan selection com. 1995—96, treas. exec. bd. 1996—99, Centennial com. 2000—02), AAUW Ednl. Found. (rsch. and awards panel 1990—94), Alliance Higher Edn. (chair coun. libr. dirs. 1993—95), Rotary Internat. (sec. local chpt. 1999—2002), Soroptimist Internat. (pres. Denton chpt. 1986—88), Women's Shakespeare Club (pres. 1967—69), Pi Delta Phi, Alpha Lambda Sigma (pres. 1970—71), Alpha Chi, Beta Phi Mu (pres. chpt. 1976 1978, sec. nat. adv. assembly 1978—79, pres. 1979—80, nat. dir. 1981—83). Methodist. Office: TWU Sta PO Box 424093 Denton TX 76204-4093 Personal E-mail: esnapp@verizon.net. *The idealistic dreams of youth can be translated into making a difference in the work place and in your personal life if you develop a big picture that includes the ideas of individuals of diversity and if you give life your full attention, enthusiasm and courage and give a few your steadfast friendship.*

SNAPP, HARRY FRANKLIN, historian, educator; b. Bryan, Tex., Oct. 15, 1930; s. H.F. and Ethel (Manning) Snapp; m. Elizabeth Mitchell, June 1, 1956 (div. Dec. 20, 2001). BA, Baylor U., 1952, MA, 1953; PhD, Tulane U., 1963. Instr. U. Coll. Tulane U., 1960—62; asst. prof. history Wofford Coll., 1963—64, U. North Tex. (formerly North Tex. State U.), Denton, 1964—69, assoc. prof., 1969—94; dir. Tex. Rsch. Ctr. Biog. Study of Women, Denton, 1995—; pres., dir. Read All About Her Tex. Women's Biographic Ctr., Inc., 1995—. Editor: Brit. Studies Mercury, 1970—84, Tex. Acad., 1973—76; co-editor: Read All About Her! Texas Women's History: A Working Bibliography, 1995, enlarged edit., 1997; author (with others): West Texas Historical Assn. Year Book, 1994, 1996; contbr. articles to profl. jours. Mem. Bridwell Assocs. of So. Meth. U., Friends of Southwestern Art, Am. Com. Irish Studies; mem. adv. com. on acad. freedom and tenure policy, coord. bd. Tex. Coll. and Univ. System. Recipient North Tex. State U. Faculty Rsch. award, 1966, 1967. Mem.: AAUP (pres. North Tex. chpt. 1968—69, pres. Southwestern regional conf. 1971—72, pres. Tex. conf. 1974—76, nat. coun. 1976—86), Butler Soc. (Ireland), Northamptonshire Record Soc., Libr. History Round Table, Libr. Rsch. Round Table, Hist. Assn. (London), Tex. State Hist. Assn., Panhandle-Plains Hist. Soc., West Tex. Hist. Assn. (bd. dirs. 1997—), Am. Hist. Assn., So. Conf. Brit. Studies (sec.-treas. 1969—84), Tulane U. Alumni Assn., Lambda Chi Alpha, Alpha Chi. Democrat. Methodist. Home: 1904 N Lake Trl Denton TX 76201-0602 Office: Read All About Her Tex Women's Biographic Ctr Inc PO Box 424053 Denton TX 76204-4053

SNAPPER, ERNST, mathematics professor; b. The Netherlands, Dec. 2, 1913; came to U.S., 1938, naturalized, 1942; s. Isidore and Henrietta (Van Buuren) S.; m. Ethel Lillian Klein, June 1941; children: John William, James Robert. MA, Princeton U., 1939, PhD, 1941; MA (hon.), Dartmouth Coll., 1964. Instr. Princeton, 1941-45, vis. asso. prof., 1949-50, vis. prof., 1954-55; asst. prof. U. So. Calif., 1945-48, asso. prof., 1948-53, prof., 1953-55; NSF post-doctoral fellow Harvard, 1953-54; Andrew Jackson Buckingham prof. math. Miami U., Oxford, Ohio, 1955-58; prof. math. Ind. U., 1958-63, Dartmouth, 1963—, Benjamin Pierce Cheney prof. math., 1971—79. Mem. Am. Math. Soc., Math. Assn. Am. (pres. Ind. sect. 1962-63, Carl B. Allendoerfer award 1980), Assn. Princeton Grad. Alumni (governing bd.), Soc. for Preservation Bridges of Konigsburg, Phi Beta Kappa (hon.), Pi Mu Epsilon (hon.). Home: PO Box 67 Norwich VT 05055-0067

SNARE, CARL LAWRENCE, JR., retired accountant, financial planner; b. Oct. 25, 1936; s. Carl Lawrence and Lillian Marie (Luoma) Snare. BBA, Northwestern U., 1968; postgrad., San Francisco State U., 1976—77, Roosevelt U.; BS, SUNY, 1995. CPA Calif.; CFP Calif. Asst. sec., contr. Bache Halsey Stuart & Shields Inc. (now Prudential Securities), Chgo.,

1968—73; contr. Innisfree Corp. divsn. Hyatt Corp., Burlingame, Calif., 1973—76; cash mgr. Portland GE, 1976—79; CFO, contr. Vistar Fin. Inc., Marina del Rey, Calif., 1979—82; pres. Snare Properties Co., Long Beach, Calif., 1984—96, Snare Fin. Svcs. Corp., Rialto, Calif., 1985—89, Carl Snare & Assocs., Long Beach; v.p., treas. Carson Estate Co., Rancho Dominguez, Calif., 1988—96; pres., CEO Glenshire Homes, Inc., Phoenix, 1996—98, Glenshire Tech., Boulder, Colo., 1997—99; acct., fin. planner Calif.; ret. Mem.: AICPA, Founder Cash Mgmt. Assn. Home Phone: 217-344-2785. Personal E-mail: carl.snare@lycos.com.

SNAREY, JOHN ROBERT, psychologist, educator; BS, Geneva Coll., Beaver Falls, Pa., 1969; MA, Wheaton Coll., Ill., 1973; EdD, Harvard U., Cambridge, Mass., 1982. Postdoctoral rsch. fellow dept. psychiatry Harvard U., Cambridge, Mass., 1982-84; assoc. rsch. psychologist Wellesley Coll., 1984-85; assoc. prof. human devel. and edn. Northwestern U., Evanston, Ill., 1985-87; prof. human devel. and ethics Sch. Theology and dept. psychology Emory U., Atlanta, 1987—. Mem. senate Emory U., Atlanta, 2001—05, pres., 2003—04. Author: How Fathers Care for the Next Generation, 1993; contbr. articles to profl. jours.; editor: Conflict and Continuity: A History of Ideas on Social Equality and Human Development, 1981, Remembrance of Lawrence Kohlberg, 1988, Race-ing Moral Formation: African Am. Perspectives on Care and Justice, 2004; mem. editl. bd. Harvard Ednl. Rev., 1979—81, Jour. Psychology and Theology, 1986—90, Jour. Moral Edn., 1998—, Am. Ednl. Rsch. Jour., 2001—04, mem. editl. adv. bd. Lawrence Erlbaum Assocs., 1988—90. Recipient Exemplary Dissertation award, Nat. Coun. Social Studies, 1982, Kuhmereker Dissertation award, Assn. Moral Edn., 1983, Outstanding Human Devel. Rsch. award, Am. Ednl. Rsch. Assn., 1988, James D. Moran Book award, Assn. Family and Consumer Sci., 1994, Marie C. Keel, Excellence in Mentoring award, 2003. Fellow: Assn. Moral Edn. (exec. bd. 1986—2007, program chair 1997, treas. 2001—04, pres. 2004—07); mem.: APA, Am. Ednl. Rsch. Assn. (divsn. E exec. bd. 1990—2000, moral devel. and edn. spl. interest group co-chair 1994—96, sec. divsn. E 1997—99, Moral Devel. and Edn. Book award 2006). Office: Emory U Bishops Hall 66 Atlanta GA 30322-0001 Office Phone: 404-727-4185. Business E-Mail: jsnarey@emory.edu.

SNEAD, GEORGE MURRELL, JR., military officer, research scientist, consultant; b. San Diego, Nov. 6, 1922; s. George Murrell and Helen (Olsen) S.; m. Kathleen Hill Dawson, Apr. 26, 1947; children: George Murrell III, James M., William M., John P., Edward W. BS, Va. Mil. Inst., 1943; MS, U. Ill., 1948; PhD, U. Va., 1953. Commd. 2d lt. U.S. Army, 1943, advanced through grades to brig. gen., 1969; with Central Germany campaign 805th Signal Co., Europe, 1945-46; Aleutian sector comdr. Alaska Communication System, 1948-50; sta. at Electronic Warfare Center Ft. Monmouth, N.J. and Ft. Huachuca, Ariz., 1953-56; student U.S. Army Command and Gen. Staff Coll., 1956-57; signal adviser MAAG Vietnam, 1957-58; signal officer Dept. Army, 1958-60; acting dir. research ballistic missile def. Advanced Research Projects Agy., 1960; with U.S. Army Satellite Communications Agy. Ft. Monmouth, 1960-63; student Nat. War Coll., 1963-64; div. signal officer 24th Inf. Div., 1964-65; comdg. officer 7th Signal Group, 1965; dir. Communication /ADP Lab. Ft. Monmouth, 1966-68; exec. asst. chief of staff Communications Electronics, Dept. Army, 1968; dir. army research Dept. Army Washington, 1968-71; dep. comdr. Army Strategic Communications Command, 1971-73; prin. scientist Gen. Research Corp. McLean, Va., 1973-82; pres. Nat. Sci. Ctr. Found., Burke, Va., 1982-84. Chmn. bd. Am. Fed. Savs. & Loan Assn., Lynchburg, Va., 1985-86; sci./bus. cons., 1986—. Active Boy Scouts Am., 1958-68; bd. dirs. Ctrl. Youth Summer Activities, Ft. Monmouth, 1960-63, Arthritis Found., Washington, 1981-84, Lynchburg Symphony, 1990-95; pres. Acad. Music Theatre, Lynchburg, 1985-95; trustee, vice chmn. bd. dirs. Westminster-Canterbury, Lynchburg, 1991-99; trustee Sci. Mus. Va., 1995—; elder Presbyn. Ch., 1986—. Decorated D.S.M., Legion of Merit with two oak leaf clusters, Bronze Star, Air medal, Army Commendation medal with 4 oak leaf clusters. Mem. Assn. U.S. Army, Armed Forces Communications and Electronics Assn. (sec. Washington chpt. 1968-69), Sigma Xi, Kappa Alpha. Office: PO Box 3306 Lynchburg VA 24503-0306 Personal E-mail: g_snead@msn.com.

SNEAD, JAMES ARRINGTON, architect; b. Richmond, Va., June 24, 1950; s. John Elwood and Anna Ruth (Reiche) S. BA, U. N.C., 1972; MArch, Va. Tech. U., 1978. Assoc. CS&D Architects, Balt., 1980-84; v.p., pres. Ziger Hoopes & Snead, Balt., 1984-93; pres. Ziger/Snead Architects, Balt., 1994—. Trustee Gilman Sch., Balt., 1990—, treas., 1998—; mem. adv. bd. Md. Inst. Sch. Continuing Studies, Balt., 1991—, chmn., 1998—. Mem. AIA. Democrat. Presbyterian. Avocations: golf, travel, sailing, skiing. Office: Ziger/Snead Architects 1006 Morton St Baltimore MD 21201-5411

SNEAD, KATHLEEN MARIE, lawyer; b. Steubenville, Ohio, July 1, 1948; d. Donald Lee and Mary Alice (Hobright) O'Dell; m. John Jones Snead, Oct. 14, 1972; 1 child, Megan Marie. BA, Pa. State U., 1970; JD, U. Denver, 1979. Bar: Colo. 1979, U.S. Ct. Appeals (10th cir.) 1980, U.S. Supreme Ct. 1986. Field examiner NLRB, Pitts., 1970-72; freelance photographer Charleston, W.Va., 1973-74; labor relations examiner U.S. Dept. Labor, Denver, 1974-77, labor relations officer, 1978-79; staff atty. Denver & Rio Grande Western R.R., Denver, 1979-81, asst. gen. atty., 1981-84, gen. atty., 1984-92, Southern Pacific Lines, 1992-96, Union Pacific R.R., Denver, 1996-97; pvt. practice Golden, Colo., 1997—. Counsel regulatory & real estate Union Pacific RR Co., 2002—. Mem. Colo. Bar Assn., Colo. Women's Bar Assn., Colo. R.R. Assn. (dir. 1982-84). Avocations: swimming, bicycling, skating, photography. Home: 233 S Devinney St Golden CO 80401-5316 Office: 1331 17th St Ste 406 Denver CO 80202 Office Phone: 303-964-4582. Personal E-mail: kmsnead@up.com.

SNEDAKER, CATHERINE RAUPAGH (KIT SNEDAKER), editor; d. Paul and Charity (Primmer) Raupagh; m. William Brooks; children: Eleanor, Peter William; m. 2d Weldon Snedaker. BA, Duke U. Promotion mgr. Sta. WINR-TV and WNBF-TV, Binghamton, N.Y.; TV editor, feature writer Binghamton Sun, 1960-68; mem. staff, food editor, restaurant critic L.A. Herald Examiner, 1978-80, food and travel editor. Author: The Great Convertibles; editor: The Food Package; guest editor: Mademoiselle mag., 1942; contbr. numerous articles on food and travel to nat. mags. and newspapers. Recipient 3 awards L.A. Press Club, VISTA award, 1979. Democrat. Home: 140 San Vicente Blvd Apt A Santa Monica CA 90402-1533 E-mail: kitsnedaker@verizon.net.

SNEDDON, THOMAS WILLIAM, JR., prosecutor; b. LA, 1941; m. Pam Sneddon. BA, U. Notre Dame, 1963; JD, UCLA, 1966; grad., Nat. Dist. Atty. Sch., U. Houston, 1972, Nat. Homicide Acad., 1977. Dep. dist atty. Santa Barbara County, 1969—77, supr. criminal ops., 1977—82, dist. atty., 1983—. Mem. faculty Santa Barbara Coll. Law, 1989—; chair Com. for Child Support Enforcement, 1991—; advisor Am. Prosecutor's Rsch. Ctr.; pres. Calif. Dist. Atty. Assn., 1989—90; co-chair Nat. Dist. Atty. Child Support Com., Nat. Dist. Atty. Assn. Nat. Com., 1997, v.p., 2000—. Served in US Army, 1967—69. Recipient Leadership award, Calif. Dept. Social Services, 1993, Director's award, Calif. Family Support Coun., 1995, Disting. Faculty award, Nat. Dist. Atty. Coll., 2000. Office: Thomas W Sneddon Jr 1112 Santa Barbara St Santa Barbara CA 93101-2008

SNEDEKER, JOHN HAGGNER, university president; b. Plainfield, NJ, May 30, 1925; s. Alfred H. and Anna Marie (Ward) S.; m. Noreen I. Davey, Dec. 30, 1950; children— John D., Philip A., Patrick W. BS cum laude, N.Y. U., 1951, MA, 1951; Ed.D., Ind. U., 1959. Dir. lab. human devel. U. Mont., 1952-56; cons. psychologist research Purdue U., 1955; assoc. prof., dir. bur. research Ball State U., 1956-61; prof. higher edn., research asso. Ind. U., 1958; prof., dean Western Wash. State U., Bellingham, 1961-62; pres. Western N.Mex. U., Silver City, 1962—. Mem. exec. bd. Internat. Coun. Spl. Edn., 1952-56; Rocky Mountain regional rep. APA, 1953-56; mem. Gov. Wash. Com. Licensing Tchr. Edn., 1961, Wash. State Legislature Rsch. Tech. Com., 1961. Author or co-author rating scales, attitude and opinion measurement devices; contbr. jours. Bd. dirs. Nat. Sci. Fair; trustee N.Mex. Health Found. Served with U.S. Army, 1943-48. Fellow AAAS; mem. Midwest Psychol. Assn., Inter-Am. Soc. Psychology, Am. Ednl. Research Assn., Holland Soc. N.Y. Address: 2200 Pinon St Silver City NM 88061-7735

SNEDIKER, DAVID E., lawyer; b. Chgo., Oct. 2, 1947; BS, U. Notre Dame, 1969; JD, St. John's U., 1975. Bar: N.Y. 1976, Conn. 1983. Ptnr. Paul, Hastings, Janofsky & Walker LLP, Stamford, Conn., mng. ptnr.-Stamford Office. Mem. ABA (com. creditors' rights in real estate financing 1984—, com. land surveys 1985-93, sect. real property, probate, trust law), Pension Real Estate Assn. (govt. affairs com. 1989—), Internat. Assn. Attys. in Corp. Real Estate (bd. dirs. 1991—, vice chmn. 1995—). Office: Paul Hastings Janofsky & Walker 9th Fl 1055 Washington Blvd Fl 9 Stamford CT 06901-2216 Office Phone: 203-961-7401. Office Fax: 203-359-3031. Business E-Mail: davidsnediker@paulhastings.com.

SNEED, JOSEPH TYREE, III, federal judge; b. Calvert, Tex., July 21, 1920; s. Harold Marvin and Cara (Weber) Sneed; m. Madelon Juergens, Mar. 15, 1944 (dec. Dec. 1998); children: Clara Hall, Cara Carleton, Joseph Tyree IV. BBA, Southwestern U., 1941; LLB, U. Tex., Austin, 1947; SJD, Harvard, 1958. Bar: Tex. 1948. From instr. bus. law to prof. U. Tex., Austin, 1947—57, asst. dean, 1949—50; counsel Graves, Dougherty & Greenhill, Austin, 1954—56; prof. law Cornell U., 1957—62; prof. Stanford Law Sch., 1962—71; dean, prof. of law Duke Law Sch., 1971—73; dep. atty. gen. US Justice Dept., 1973; judge US Ct. Appeals (9th cir.), San Francisco, 1973—87, sr. judge, 1987—. Author: The Configurations of Gross Income, 1967, Footprints on the Rocks of the Mountain, 1997; contbr. articles to profl. jours. With USAF, 1942—46. Mem.: ABA, NY Bar Assn., Fed. Bar Assn., Assn. of Am. Law Schs., Am. Jud. Soc., Am. Law Inst. (cons. estate and gift tax project 1960—69), State Bar Tex., Order of Coif. Office: US Ct Appeals PO Box 193939 San Francisco CA 94119-3939 also: US Ct Appeals 9th Cir 95 Seventh St San Francisco CA 94103-1526 *

SNEED, LARRY ALLAN, history professor; b. Vincannes, Ind., Aug. 7, 1948; s. Lawrence Harding and Juanita Mae Sneed; m. Rebecca Bruner Adcock (div.); children: Travis, Shane; m. Barbara Vitale Sneed, June 13, 1995. BS in Hist. Edn., Ind. State U., Terra Houte, 1970; MEd in Hist. Edn., U. Ga., Athens, 1975, EDs in Hist. Edn., 1978. Cert. tchr. 2009. Sci. tchr. New Porterdale Elem. Sch., Covington, Ga., 1972—73; social studies tchr. Newton County High Sch., Covington, 1973—78, North Gwinnett High Sch., Suwanee, Ga., 1978—79, Parkview High Sch., Lilburn, Ga., 1979—2004, Mill Creek High Sch., Hoschton, Ga., 2004—. Home bound tchr. Oakland Ctr., Lawrenceville, Ga., 1987—2000; stadium announcer Parkview High Sch., Lilburn, 1980—2003. Author: No More Silence: An Oral History of the Assassination of President Kennedy, 1998. Guest speaker Kiwanis Club, Lilburn, Calif., 1987, 2001, Rotary Club, Duluth, Ga., 1999, Covington, Ga., 2001. Named Tchr. of Yr., Park View High Sch., 1990; recipient DAR Am. History Tchr. of Yr., Gwinnett County, Ga, 1990—91. Fellow: Dealey Plaza. Republican. Meth. Home: 3010 Clegg Farm Rd Social Circle GA 30025 Office: Mill Creek HS 4400 Braselton Hwy Hoschton GA 30548 Business E-Mail: snee1128@bellsouth.net.

SNEED, PAULA ANN, food products executive; b. Everett, Mass., Nov. 10, 1947; d. Thomas Edwin and F. Mary (Turner) S.; m. Lawrence Paul Bass, Sept. 2, 1978; children: Courtney Jameson. BA, Simmons Coll., 1969; MBA, Harvard U., 1977; D Bus. Adminstrn. (hon.), Johnson & Wales U., 1991. Ednl. supr., femal coord. Outreach Program for Problem Drinkers, 1969-71; dir. plans, program devel. and evaluations Ecumenical Ctr. in Roxbury, Mass., 1971-72; program coord. Boston Sickle Cell Ctr., 1972-75; asst. product mgr. Gen. Food Corp., White Plains, N.Y., 1977-79, assoc. product mgr., 1979-80; product mgr. Gen. Foods Corp., White Plains, N.Y., 1980-82, sr. product mgr., 1982-83, product group mgr., 1983-86, category mgr., 1986-87, v.p. consumer affairs, 1986-90, pres. food svc. div., sr. v.p., 1990-95; sr. v.p. mktg. svcs. Kraft Foods N.Am., 1995, group v.p., pres. e-commerce and mktg. services, 2000—04; sr. v.p. global mktg. resources Kraft Foods Inc., 2004—05, exec. v.p. global mktg. resources & initiatives, 2005—. Mem. bd. dirs. Hercules Inc., 1994-2002, Airgas Inc., 99-, Charles Schwab Corp., 2002-. Bd. dirs. Crispus Attucks Scholarship Fund, Ridgewood, N.J., 1982, Westchester/Fairfield Inroads; trustee Simmons Coll., Teach for Am., Chgo. Children's Museum. Recipient Benevolent Heart award Graham-Windham, 1987, Black Achiever award Harlem YWCA, 1982, MBA of Yr. Harvard Bus. Sch., 1987, Benevolent Heart award Graham Windham Soc., 1987; named MBA of Yr. Harvard Bus. Sch. Black Alumni Orgn., 1987; named one of 100 Top Black Women in Corp. Am. Ebony Mag., 1990, 91, 21 Most Influential African Ams. in Corp. Am., 1991, 97 (One of 40 Most Influential, 1993), Breakthrough 50 Exec. Female Mag., 50 Most Powerful Women Mgrs., 1994, 25 Most Influential Mothers Working Mother Mag., 1998; inducted Acad. Women Achievers N.Y. YWCA, 1990. Mem. AAUW, Exec. Leadership Coun., Chgo. Network, adv. coun. to dean Howard U. Bus. Sch., Nat. Assn. Negro Bus. and Profl. Women, Coalition of 100 Black Women, Soc. Consumer Affairs Profls., Women's Forum. Office: Kraft Foods Inc Three Lakes Dr Northfield IL 60093-2753

SNEED, RICHARD DURWOOD, JR., lawyer; b. New Orleans, May 31, 1946; m. Martha Sue Trimble, Mar. 29, 1968; children: Laurie, Kellie. BA in Econs., U. South Fla., 1968; JD, Stetson U., 1971. Bar: Fla. 1971, U.S. Dist. Ct. (so. dist.) Fla. 1972, U.S. Tax Ct. 1975, U.S. ct. Appeals (5th cir.) 1975, U.S. Supreme Ct. 1975, U.S. Ct. Appeals (11th cir.) 1981, U.S. Dist. Ct. (mid. dist.) Fla. 1990. Assoc. Fee, Parker & Neil, Ft. Pierce, Fla., 1971-73; shareholder Sneed & Messer, P.A., Ft. Pierce, 1973-89; pvt. practice Richard D. Sneed, Jr., P.A., Ft. Pierce, 1989—99. Commr. Ft. Pierce Housing Authority, Ft. Pierce, 1989—; bd. dirs. Learn To Read, Inc.; vice chancellor to Bishop Ctrl. Diocese Fla. Mem.: ATLA, ABA, Ft. Pierce Bar Assn., Fla. Bar (standing com. unlicensed practice law 1986—, probate litigation com., probate law com., cert. real estate lawyer), Exch. Club (pres. Ft. Pierce 1980), Phi Alpha Delta. Episcopalian. Avocations: show horses, flying, vintage sports car racing. Office: Mardi Exec Ctr 1905 25th St S Ste 20604 Fort Pierce FL 34947

SNEED, RONALD ERNEST, retired project engineer, engineering educator; b. Oxford, NC, Nov. 23, 1936; s. Henry Ernest and Jewel Leigh (Hughes) S.; m. Shelba Jean Walters, June 8, 1958; children: Kathy Geneva Grosvenor, Jennie Leigh Berrier. BS in Agrl. Engring., N.C. State U., 1959, PhD in Biol. and Agrl. Engring., 1971. Registered profl. engr., NC; cert. irrigation designer, contractor, landscape irrigation auditor, and irrigation specialist. Sales trainee John Deere Co., 1959-60; ext. specialist NC State U., 1960-62, ext. instr., 1962-69, 70, ext. asst. prof., 1971-75, ext. assoc. prof., 1971-80, prof., 1980-92, prof. emeritus, 1993—; project engr. Agri-Waste Tech., Inc., 1993-2000, Irrigation Consulting, Inc., 1995—; project engr. divsn. soil and water NC Dept. Environment and Natural Resources, 1997-99, project engr. divsn. water quality, 2003—05, Carolina Turkeys, 2004—06, NC Dept. Adminstrn., 2004—05. Maj. gen. U.S. Army, 1960-95, ret. Recipient Outstanding Paper award So. region Am. Soc. Hort. Sci., 1986, 91; Ronald E. Sneed Irrigation Soc., Inc. scholarship established in his honor, 1991. Fellow Am. Soc. Agrl. Engrs. (ednl. aids competition Blue Ribbon 1963-64, 68, 78-79, 85, 89, 91-92, Gunlogson Countryside Engring. award 1992, Outstanding Paper award 1984), The Irrigation Assn. (life tech. mem., Man of Yr. 1981), NC Irrigation Soc., Inc. (Oustanding Contbn. to Irrigation award 1973, former tech. advisor), Soil and Water Conservation Soc., Carolinas Irrigation Assn. (hon.), Res. Officers Assn. (life), Civitan (Civitan of Yr. 1998). Democrat. Baptist. Office: 3405 Malibu Dr Raleigh NC 27607-6505 Office Phone: 919-782-7867. Personal E-mail: rsneed@intrex.net.

SNEERINGER, STEPHEN GEDDES, lawyer; b. Lancaster, Ohio, Mar. 27, 1949; s. Stanley Carlyle and Mary Eleanor (Fry) S.; m. Kristine Karen Serfling, Oct. 6, 1974; children: Mary Rhonda, Robyn Kathleen. BA magna cum laude, Denison U., Granville, Ohio, 1971; JD, Washington U., St. Louis, 1974. Bar: Mo. 1974. Sr. v.p. A.G. Edwards & Sons Inc., St. Louis, 1974—2007. Arbitrator N.Y. Stock Exch., NASD Dispute Resolution, Nat. Futures Assn., Am. Arbitration Assn. Editor: Urban Law Ann., 1973-74; bd. editors Securities Arbitration Commentator. Am. Jurisprudence scholar, 1974. Mem. ABA (dispute resolution sect., arbitration com.), Mo. Bar Assn., Securities Industries Assn. (arbitration com.), Futures Industries Assn., Nat. Assn. Securities Dealers (mem. nat. arbitration and mediation com. 1992-94, 2001-03).

SNEIDER, JOYCE PAPPACHRISTOU, dietician, educator; b. Springfield, Mass., May 15, 1932; d. Hector and Henrietta (Hemerling) Flores; m. Stanley Sneider; children: Dianne, Donna, Paul Jr., Gary. AA, Nassau Community Coll., 1970; BA in Math., Sci. and Home Econs. with honors, Queens Coll., 1973; MA, MS in dietetics/nutrition, NYU, 1976; postgrad., Nova U., 1989—. Cert. tchr., N.Y.C., N.Y., tchr. home econs., health edn., sci., Fla.; lic. dietitian, nutritionist Fla. Tchr. Roslyn High Sch., Elmont Meml. High Sch.; dietitian L.I. (N.Y.) Jewish Hosp.; dietician St. Mary's Hosp.; instr. nutrition Cath. Med. Ctr. Nursing, 1974-76; chief dietician Jamaica (N.Y.) Hosp., 1976-80; tchr. Broward Coutny (Fla.) Bd. Educators, 1981—2000; pvt. practice, 2000—. Adj. prof. Nassau Community Coll., Fla. Internat. U., 1980-81. Contbr. articles to profl. jours. Mem. Am. Dietetics Assn., Am. Home Econs. Assn. (cert.), Fla. Dietetics Assn., Fla. Assn. Computer Educators, Fla. Correctional Edn. Assn., Fla. Assn. Alternative Educators, Phi Beta Kappa, Kappa Delta Pi. E-mail: Joysta@earthlink.net.

SNELL, AUDREY, financial analyst, investment advisor; BA, George Washington Univ.; MBA, Seton Hall Univ. Sr. v.p., mutual fund mgr. SunAmerica Mutual Funds; sr. v.p. equity analyst Brean Murray Carret & Co.; ptnr., sr. rsch. analyst ThinkEquity Partners LLC, San Francisco, 2005—07; v.p., sr. equity analyst banks & fin. services Kaufman Brothers LP, NYC, 2007—. Named one of Best Securities Analysts, Forbes Mag. Office: Kaufman Brothers LP 800 3d Ave New York NY 10022

SNELL, BRUCE M., JR., judge; b. Ida Grove, Iowa, Aug. 18, 1929; s. Bruce M. and Donna (Potter) Snell; m. Anne Snell, Feb. 4, 1956; children: Rebecca, Brad. AB, Grinnell Coll., 1951; JD, U. Iowa, 1956. Bar: Iowa 1956, N.Y. 1958. Law clk. to presiding judge U.S. Dist. Ct. (no. dist.) Iowa, 1956-57; asst. atty. gen., 1961-65; judge Iowa Ct. Appeals, 1976-87; justice Iowa Supreme Ct., Des Moines, 1987—2001, sr. justice, 2001—. Comments editor: Iowa Law Rev. Mem.: ABA, Am. Judicature Soc., Iowa State Bar Assn., Order Coif. Methodist. Home: PO Box 192 Ida Grove IA 51445-0192

SNELL, JENNIFER SUE, school system administrator, psychologist; b. Council Bluffs, Iowa, Oct. 10, 1947; d. Richard William Horrum and Mary Rita Baldwin-Horrum; m. Joel Charles Snell, June 7, 1968; children: Nathan Mikael-Edward, Jason Joel. BS in Elem. Edn. with honors, U. Nebr., Omaha, 1970, MS in Ednl. Psychology with honors, 1974; EdS in Sch. Psychology with honors, U. Iowa, Iowa City, 1980. Cert. Nat. Assn. Sch. Psychologists, prin. U. No. Iowa, 1988. Tchr. grade 2 Blair Cmty. Schs., Nebr., 1970—72; psychol. asst. Edn. Svc. Unit #2, Fremont, 1974—78; sch. psychologist Grant Wood Area Edn. Agy., Cedar Rapids, Iowa, 1980—96, regional adminstr, 1996—. Contbr. articles to profl. jours. Bd. chair Cmty. Empowerment Parent Edn. Consortium, Cedar Rapids, Iowa, 2000; bd. mem. Youth Homes, Iowa City, 2002—, Linn Co. Child Devel. Ctr., Cedar Rapids, 2002—. Mem.: Federated Women's Club, Nat. Assn. Sch. Psychologists. Home: 3105 Allegheny Dr NE Cedar Rapids IA 52402-3315 Office: Grant Wood Area Edn Agy 4050 River Edge Dr NE Cedar Rapids IA 52402 Personal E-mail: snelljennifer47@hotmail.com.

SNELL, LINDA S., internist, educator; b. Salford, Eng., Apr. 24, 1952; BA, U. Alta., 1971, MD, 1975; MHPE, U. Ill., Chgo., 1997. Assoc. dean continuing med. edn. McGill U., Montreal, 1994-2000, dir. divsn. gen. internal medicine, 1994—2004, vice-chair edn. dept. medicine, 2005—; assoc. physician-in-chief McGill U. Health Ctr., Montreal, 2004—. Fellow ACP, Royal Coll. Physicians Can.; mem. Can. Soc. Internal Medicine (pres. 1994-96), Can. Assn. Med. Edn. (treas. 2004-06). Office: McGill U Health Ctr Dept Medicine 687 Pine Ave W Rm M3-07 Montreal PQ Canada H3A 1A1 E-mail: linda.snell@mcgill.ca.

SNELL, MARK A., utilities executive; B in acctg., San Diego State Univ. CPA. Sr. mgr. KPMG Peat Marwick; exec. v.p., CFO World Oil Corp.; CFO, CAO Latham & Watkins; exec. v.p., CFO Dames & Moore, Earth Tech, Long Beach, Calif.; v.p. planning & develop. Sempra Energy, San Diego, 2001; CFO Sempra Global, San Diego, 2001—04, group pres., 2004—06; exec. v.p., CFO Sempra Energy, San Diego, 2006—. Bd. dir. Venoco Inc. Office: Sempra Energy 101 Ash St San Diego CA 92101 *

SNELL, MICHAEL STEVEN, music educator; b. Pocatello, Idaho, Oct. 23, 1961; s. Harold Alfred and Marilyn Elizabeth Snell; m. Molly Ann McAllister, Apr. 11, 1997; children: Megan Marie, Christopher James. MA in Instrnl. Tech., U. Colo., Denver, 1998. Instrumental music tchr. Parker Jr. H.S., Parker, Colo., 1986—96; condr. Colo. Honor Band, Denver, 1990—98; instrumental music dir. ThunderRidge H.S., Highlands Ranch, Colo., 1996—. Exec. sec. Colo. Bandmasters Assn., Denver, 2000—03. Music Tech. grant, Douglas County Edn. Found., 1998. Mem.: Music Educators Nat. Conf., Am. Sch. Band Directors Assn., Colo. Bandmasters Assn (life; exec. sec. 2000—03, Svc. award 2003). Avocations: woodworking, travel, music. Office: ThunderRidge HS 1991 Wildcat Reserve Pkwy Highlands Ranch CO 80129 Home Phone: 303-683-8648; Office Phone: 303-387-2123.

SNELL, PATRICIA POLDERVAART, librarian, consultant; b. Santa Fe, Apr. 11, 1943; d. Arie and Edna Beryl (Kerchmar) Poldervaart; m. Charles Eliot Snell, June 7, 1966. BA in Edn., U. N.M., 1965; MSLS, U. So. Calif., 1966. Asst. edn. libr. U. So. Calif., LA, 1966—68; med. libr. Bedford (Mass.) VA Hosp., 1968—69; asst. law libr. U. Miami, Coral Gables, Fla., 1970—71; acquistions libr. U. N.Mex. Law Sch. Libr., Albuquerque, 1971—72; order libr. Los Angeles County Law Libr., 1972—76, cataloguer, 1976—90; libr. Parks Coll., Albuquerque, 1990—92; records technician Technadyne Engring. Cons. to Sandia Nat. Labs., 1992—93; libr. Tireman Learning Materials Ctr. U. N.Mex., Albuquerque, 1993—96, instr. libr. sci. program Coll. Edn., 1991—; rsch. technician City of Albuquerque, 1996—2006; legal rsch. technician Bernalillo County, 2006—. Ch. libr. Beverly Hills Presbyn. Ch., 1974-90, ch. choir libr., 1976-90. Southwestern Library Assn. scholar, 1965. Mem.: ALA, N.Mex. Libr. Assn., Pi Lambda Theta. Avocations: travel, reading. Office: Law Libr BCMDC 5800 Shelly Rd SW Albuquerque NM 87151 Business E-Mail: psnell@bernco.gov.

SNELL, RICHARD SAXON, anatomist; b. Richmond, Surrey, Eng., May 3, 1925; came to U.S., 1963; s. Claude Saxon and Daisy Lilian S.; m. Maureen Cashin, June 4, 1949; children: Georgina Sara, Nicola Ann,

Melanie Jane, Richard Robin, Charles Edward. MB, BS, Kings Coll., U. London, 1949, PhD, 1955, MD, 1961. House surgeon Sir Cecil P.G. Wakeley, Kings Coll. Hosp. and Belgrave Hosp. for Children, London, 1948-49; lectr. anatomy Kings Coll., U. London, 1949-59, U. Durham, Eng., 1959-63; asst. prof. anatomy and medicine Yale U., 1963-65, assoc. prof., 1965-67, vis. prof. anatomy, 1969; prof., chmn. dept. anatomy N.J. Coll. Medicine and Dentistry, Jersey City, 1967-69; vis. prof. anatomy Harvard U., 1970, 71, 80, 86; prof. anatomy Coll. Medicine, U. Ariz., Tucson, 1970; prof., chmn. dept. anatomy George Washington U. Med. Ctr., Washington, 1972-88, prof. emeritus, 1988—. Author: Clinical Embryology for Medical Students, 1972, 3d edit., 1983, Clinical Anatomy for Medical Students, 1973, 6th edit., 2000, Clinical Anatomy, 7th edit., 2003, Clinical Anatomy By Regions, 8th edit., 2007, Atlas of Normal Radiographic Anatomy, 1976, Atlas of Clinical Anatomy, 1978, Gross Anatomy Dissector, 1978, Clinical Neuroanatomy, 1980, 6th edit., 2006, Student's Aid to Gross Anatomy, 1986, Clinical Anatomy for Anesthesiologists, 1988, Clinical Anatomy of the Eye, 1989, 2d edit., 1997, Gross Anatomy: A Review with Questions and Explanations, 1990, Neuroanatomy: A Review with questions and Explanations, 1992, Clinical Anatomy for Emergency Medicine, 1993, Clinical Neuroanatomy: An Illustrated Review with Questions and Explanations, 3d edit., 2001, Clinical Anatomy: An Illustrated Review with Questions and Explanations, 4th edit., 2003 Clinical Anatomy by Systems, 2006; contbr. articles to med. jours. Med. Rsch. Coun. grantee, 1959; NIH grantee, 1963-65 Mem. Anat. Soc. Gt. Britain, Am. Soc. Anatomists, Alpha Omega Alpha. Home: 518 Boston Post Rd Madison CT 06443-2930

SNELL, STEVEN LAYNE, lawyer, consultant; b. San Fernando, Calif., Nov. 21, 1959; s. Warren Everett and Betty Mae Snell. BA, Johns Hopkins U., Balt., 1982; JD, Northwestern U., Chgo., 1991; LLM, NYU, 1996, JSD, 2004. Registered: NY (Atty.) 1993. Atty. Haight, Gardner, Poor & Havens, NYC, 1991—93, Sonnenschein, Nath & Rosenthal, NYC, 1995—97; legal cons. self employed, Balt., 2001—. Del. Tex. Dem. Conv., Houston, 1988. Mem.: Selden Soc., Maritime Law Assn. the US, ABA Sect. Internat. Law (co-chmn. internat. transp. com. 2004—07). Avocation: travel. Office: 116 W University Pkwy Ste 534 Baltimore MD 21210 Office Phone: 410-243-8678.

SNELLING, BARBARA W., retired state legislator; b. Fall River, Mass., Mar. 22, 1928; d. Frank Taylor and Hazel (Mitchell) Weil; m. Richard Arkwright Snelling, June 14, 1947 (dec. Aug. 1991); children: Jacqueline, Mark, Diane, Andrew. AB magna cum laude, Radcliffe Coll., 1950; D of Pub. Svc. (hon.), Norwich U., 1981; LLD (hon.), Middlebury Coll., 1997; LLD (hon.), St. Michaels Coll., 2002. Pres. Snelling and Kolb, Inc., 1982-95; lt. gov. State of Vt., 1993-97; mem. Vt. Senate, Montpelier, Vt., 1997—99, 2001—02, ret., 2002. Bd. dirs. U.S. Inst. Peace; mem. adv. bd. Westaff Inc. Vt., 1997—. Mem. bd. sch. dirs. Champlain Valley Union HS, 1962—69, chmn., 1962—68, others; mem. Vt. Edn. Adv. Coun., 1968—71, New Eng. Tchr. Edn. Adv. Com., 1968—70, Shelburne Sch. Bd., 1958—73, Vt. Alcohol and Drug Rehab., 1970—73, Vt. State Bd. Edn., 1971—77, Vt. Ednl. Partnerships, 1992—2000, New. Eng. Bd. Dollars for Scholars, 1997—2002, Champlain Valley Area Health Edn. Coun., 1997—2002; bd. dirs. Vt. Cmty. Found., 1986—94, Shelburne Mus., 1988—98, Vt. Program Quality, 1997—2002; trustee Champlain Coll., 1971—74, Radcliffe Coll., 1990—95; v.p. devel. and external affairs U. Vt., 1974—82. Named Vt. Citizen of the Yr., Vt. State C. of C., 2002; recipient Laymen's award, Vt. Edn. Assn., 1965, Fanny G. Shaw award for Disting. Cmty. Svc., Burlington Cmty. Coun., 1972, Hope award, MS Cmty. Champion, 1996, Philanthropy Day award, Nat. Soc. Fundraising Execs., 1997, Susan B. Anthony award, YWCA Vt., 2001, Robert Skiff Cmty. Svc. award, Lake Champlain C. of C., 2002, Vt. Children's Trust Found. award, 2002, Patricia S. Walton award, Vt. Soc. Pub. Adminstrn., 2002, AHEC Bi State Primary Care Assn. award, 2002, Vt. Alzheimer's Assn. award, 2002, Gold heart, Am. Heart Assn., 2002. Office Phone: 802-985-2121. Personal E-mail: ulfkiel@aol.com.

SNELLING, JAMES ANTHONY, biology professor, technologist; b. Omaha, Mar. 30, 1949; s. Lawrence Jack and Tina Maria Snelling; m. Mary Antionette Monico, Feb. 15, 1969; children: Kymberly Dawn Snelling-Donlan, Michelle Marie Dougherty, JoAnn Marie Higgins, Anthony James. BA in Biol. Scis., U. Nebr., Omaha, 1975, MA in Biol. Scis., 1978. Cert. med. technologist Am. Soc. Clin. Pathology, 1989. Med. technologist VA Med. Ctr., Omaha, 1970—2003, Alegent Health MV Hosp., Mo. Valley, Iowa, 2003—. Hospitalman, edn. staff USNR, Omaha, 1968—92; instr. Omaha Coll. Health Careers, 1981—2001; adj. instr. Met. C.C., Omaha, 2003—, Iowa We. C.C., Coun. Bluffs, Iowa, 2003—, Coll. St. Mary, Omaha, 2003—. With med. corps. USNR, 1970—71, Vietnam. Mem.: VFW, Am. Legion. Home: 815 Edgewood Blvd Papillion NE 68046 Home Phone: 402-592-5532. Personal E-mail: jamesandmary2@cox.net.

SNELLING, TROY WAYNE, history educator; b. Excelsior Springs, Mo., 1965; s. Kenneth Wayne and Shirley Louise Snelling. BA in History, Park Coll., 1991, MA in Edn., 1999. History educator Park Hill Sch. Dist., Kans. City, Mo., 1992—, chmn. Dept. Social Studies H.S., 1998—. Bd. dir. Tchg. History Through Reality, Kans. City. Mem.: Orders and Medals Soc. Am., Masons, Phi Alpha Theta. Republican. Episcopalian. Avocations: coin collecting/numismatics, rare books, antiques, trapshooting, vintage cars. Home: 30422 NE 158th Excelsior Springs MO 64024 Office: Park Hill High School 7701 NW Barry Rd Kansas City MO 64153 Personal E-mail: snellingt@hotmail.com.

SNELSON, PAMELA, librarian, association executive, researcher; b. Passaic, NJ, July 2, 1953; d. Eugene H. and Dorothy (Yenason) S. BA, Drew U., 1975, MA, 1980; MLS, Rutgers U., 1976; PhD, Rutgers U. Sch. Info. and Library Studies, 1993. Acquisitions librarian Drew U., Madison, NJ, 1976—77, reference librarian, 1977—78, head periodicals dept., 1978—85, coord. access svcs., 1986—89, asst. dir. automation and public services, 1990—98; coll. librarian Franklin & Marshall Coll., 1998—. Com. mem. N.W. Regional Library Coop., Chester, NJ, 1986-88; cons. William Paterson Coll., Wayne, NJ, 1989. Mem. NJ Library Assn. (sect. pres. 1986-87, Travel grantee 1983), ALA (com. chair 1983-89), Am. Soc. for Info. Sci., Assn. Coll. & Rsch. Libraries (bd. dirs. 2001-05, pres. 2006-07, past pres. 2007-). Avocations: water sports, white water rafting. Office: Franklin & Marshall Coll Library PO Box 3003 Lancaster PA 17604-3003 *

SNIDER, BARRY B., organic chemist; b. Chgo., Jan. 13, 1950; s. Gordon L. and Ruth C. (Tobias) S.; m. Katalin Boros, July 12, 1975; 1 child, Emily L. BS in Chemistry, U. Mich., 1970; PhD, Harvard U., 1973. Postdoctoral fellow Columbia U., NYC, 1973-75; asst. prof. Princeton U., NJ, 1975-81; assoc. prof. Brandeis U., Waltham, Mass., 1981-85, prof., 1985—, chmn. dept. chemistry, 1992-95, Breskin prof. organic chemistry, 1998—. Recipient scholar award Dreyfus Found., 1982; Sloan Found. fellow, 1979; Japan Soc. for Promotion of Sci. fellow, 1999. Mem. Am. Chem. Soc. (Arthur C. Cope scholar 1995), Royal Soc. Chemistry. Office: Brandeis U Dept Chemistry Waltham MA 02454 Home Phone: 617-969-2642; Office Phone: 781-736-2550. E-mail: snider@brandeis.edu.

SNIDER, DARRYL, lawyer; BA, U. Mich., 1971, JD magna cum laude, 1974, PhD in Econ. with highest distinction, 1975. Bar: Calif., U.S. Supreme Ct., Am. Bar Assoc. Adjunct prof. Law Golden Gate Univ., 1977—78, Univ. San Francisco, 1979; atty., shareholder Heller, Ehrman, White, & McAuliffe LLP, Los Angeles, Calif., 1998—. Panel mem. Inst. Con. on Securities Litigation, 1996—97. Mem.: Phi Beta Kappa. Office: Heller Ehrman LLP 333 S Hope St Los Angeles CA 90071-1406 Office Phone: 213-689-7577. Office Fax: 213-614-1868. E-mail: dsnider@hewm.com.

SNIDER, EDWARD MALCOLM, professional sports team executive; b. Washington, Jan. 6, 1933; s. Sol C. and Lillian (Bonas) Snider; m. Christine Snider; children: Craig Alan, Jay Thomas, Lindy Lou, Tina Suzanne, Sarena Lynn, Samuel Everett. BS, U. Md., 1955; LHD (hon.), MCP Hahnemann U., 1985, Thomas Jefferson Hosp., 1999. CPA Md. Maj. stockholder, exec. v.p. Edge Ltd., Washington, 1957—63; v.p. Phila. Eagles Football Club, 1964—67; founder, owner Phila. Flyers Hockey Club, 1967—; chmn. bd. Spectrum Arena (Wachovia Spectrum since 2003), Phila., 1967—; bd. govs. NHL, 1967—. Established Spectacor (now Comcast-Spectacor), 1974, chmn. bd., 1996—; adv. bd. Sol C. Snider Entrepreneurial Ctr., U Pa.; bd. overseers Wharton Sch. U. Pa.; bd. dirs. Inst. Cancer and Blood Diseases, Hahnemann U., Simon Weisenthal Ctr.; bd. trustees Inst. Objectivist Studies. Founder Ed Snider Youth Hockey Found. Co-recipient Lester Patrick Trophy for outstanding svc. to hockey in US, 1980; named Phila.'s greatest sports mover and shaker, Phila. Daily News, 1999; named to Hockey Hall of Fame, 1988, Phila. Flyers Hall of Fame, 1989, Phila. Sports Hall of Fame, Pa. Sports Hall of Fame, Phila. Jewish Sports Hall of Fame; recipient Americanism award, Anti-Defamation League, 1999, Sports Leadership award, Temple U., 2001, William Penn award, Greater Phila. C. of C., 2005, Ellis Island Medal of Honor. Office: Comcast Spectator 3601 S Broad St Philadelphia PA 19148-5250 *

SNIDER, GEORGE RUNYON, JR., retired franchising company executive; b. Huntington, W.Va., Jan. 25, 1941; s. George R. and Marjorie Steuart S.; m. Nora C. Jacobs, Aug. 26, 1988; children: George R. III, Jeremy W. BA, Yale U., New Haven, Conn., 1962. Assoc. dir. pub. affairs Procter & Gamble Co., Cin., 1972-76; dir. pub. rels. BF Goodrich Co., Akron, Ohio, 1977-82; dir. mktg. BF Goodrich Chem. Group, Cleve., 1982-88; dir. mktg. and comms. Walter & Haverfield, Cleve., 1988-92; pres., CEO SRA Internat., Inc., Akron, 1992—2006; ret., 2006. Trustee Old Trail Sch., Bath, Ohio, 1982-88, trustee emeritus, 1989—; trustee, chair audit com. Cuyahoga Valley Scenic R.R., 2006—; advisor Hudson Job Search, 2006-. Named one of 100 Most Influential People in Recruiting Industry, Recruiter Mag., 2002. Mem.: Soc. Cin., Lake Forest Country Club, Rotary Club Hudson (dir. 2007—), New Haven Mory's Assn., Cleve. Club at Key Ctr.

SNIDER, JAMES RHODES, radiologist; b. Pawnee, Okla., May 16, 1931; s. John Henry and Gladys Opal (Rhodes) S.; m. Lynadell Vivion, Dec. 27, 1954; children: Jon, Jan. BS, U. Okla., 1953, MD, 1956. Intern Edward Meyer Meml. Hosp., Buffalo, 1956—57; resident radiology U. Okla. Med. Ctr., 1959—62; radiologist Holt-Krock Clinic and Sparks Regional Med. Ctr., Ft. Smith, Ark., 1962—66; dir. Fairfield Comty. Land Co., Little Rock, 1968—87, Fairfield Comtys., Inc., 1968—87. Assoc. editor: Computerized Tomography, 1976—88. Mem. Ark. Bd. Pub. Welfare, 1969—71; bd. visitors U. Okla.; bd. dirs. U. Okla. Assn., 1967—70, U. Okla. Alumni Devel. Fund, 1970—74. Lt. comdr. USNR, 1957—62. Mem.: AMA, Am. Roentgen Ray Soc., Radiol. Soc. N.Am., Am. Coll. Radiology, Phi Beta Kappa, Alpha Epsilon Delta, Beta Theta Pi. Home: 5814 Cliff Dr Fort Smith AR 72903-3845 Office: 1500 Dodson Ave Fort Smith AR 72901-5128

SNIDER, JEROME GUY, lawyer; b. Mar. 14, 1950; s. Theodore Charles and Minnie Snider; m. Naomi S. Herman, Sept. 20, 1981; children: Benjamin Herman, Todd Nathaniel. AB with highest honors, Rutgers U., 1972; attended, Hebrew U., Jerusalem, 1970—71; JD, U. Pa., 1975. Bar: N.Y. 1976, U.S. Dist. Ct. (so. and ea. dists.) N.Y. 1976, U.S. Dist. Ct. (no. dist.) Calif. 1979, U.S. Dist. Ct. D.C. 1983, U.S. Ct. Appeals (6th cir.) 1984, U.S. Ct. Appeals (D.C. cir.) 1986, U.S. Supreme Ct. 1980. Law clk. to chief judge U.S. Dist. Ct. (so. dist.) N.Y., NYC, 1975—77; assoc. Davis Polk & Wardwell, NYC, 1977—82, ptnr. Washington, 1983—94, NYC, 1994—2006, co-head litig. practice group, 2000—05, gen. counsel, 2006—. Co-author: Corporate Privileged and Confidential Information, Professional Liability in Business and Commercial L:itigation in Federal Courts. Mem.: ABA, Bar Assn. of the City of N.Y. Jewish. Office: Davis Polk & Wardwell 450 Lexington Ave New York NY 10017-3911 Office Phone: 212-450-4060. Office Fax: 212-450-3060. Business E-Mail: jerome.snider@dpw.com, snider@dpw.com.

SNIDER, L. BRITT, federal official; b. Rocky Mount, NC, Jan. 12, 1945; s. Arnold Holmes and Kate Mills (Suiter) S.; m. Virginia Lansford, Aug. 24, 1974; 1 child, Britt Arnold. BA, Davidson Coll., NC, 1966; JD, U. Va., 1969. Counsel judiciary subcom. on constl. rights U.S. Senate, Washington, 1971-75, counsel select com. on intelligence, 1975-76; ptnr. Ketner & Snider, Salisbury, NC, 1976-77; counsel govt. ops. subcom. on govt. info. U.S. Ho. Reps., Washington, 1977; asst. dep. undersec. counterintelligence and security Dept. Def., Washington, 1977-87; minority counsel U.S. Senate Intelligence Com., Washington, 1987-89, gen. counsel, 1989-95, staff dir. commn. on roles and capabilities of U.S. Intelligence Cmty., 1995-96; sr. fellow Ctr. for Study of Intelligence, 1996-97; spl. counsel to dir. CIA, 1997-98, inspector gen., 1998-2001. Staff dir. Commn. to Rev. Security Practices and Procedures Dept. Def., Washington, 1985; adj. prof. Sch. Foreign Svc. Georgetown U., 2005 Served to capt. U.S. Army, 1969-71, Vietnam. Mem.: DC Bar Assn., Va. Bar Assn. Democrat. Episcopalian. Avocations: golf, jogging, reading.

SNIDER, MARIE ANNA, syndicated columnist; b. Croghan, NY, Aug. 9, 1927; d. Nicholas and Dorothy (Moser) Gingerich; m. Howard Mervin, Nov. 27, 1954; children: Vada Marie, Conrad Howard. BS, Goshen Coll., 1949; M in Religious Edn., Mennonite Bibl. Sem., 1957; MS, Kans. State U., 1980. High sch. tchr. Rockway Collegiate, Kitchener, Ont., Can., 1949-53; free-lance writer, 1953-54; pub. rels. Goshen Coll., Ind., 1955-57; free-lance writer, homemaker, 1957-67; info. editor Prairie View, Inc., Newton, Kans., 1967-76, dir., pub. info. & edn., 1976-85, dir. communications, 1985-91; freelance writer, columnist North Newton, 1991—; syndicated columnist "This Side of 60", 1992—. Bd. dirs. Health Systems Agy. of S.E. Kans., 1981-86, v.p., 1986-87; workshop presenter Nat. Coun. of Community Mental Health Ctrs., Atlanta, 1980, N.Y., 1982, 89, Miami, 1987. Editor: Media and Terrorism--The Psychological Impact, 1976; columnist: This Side of 60. Pres. City Council, N Newton, 1977-79, pres. 1980. Recipient 1st Pl. MacEachern award Assn. of Hosp. Pub. Rels., 1981, 1st Pl. Media award Nat. Coun. Community Mental Health Ctrs., 1977, 84, runner-up Pub. Rels. award Nat. Assn. Pvt. Psychiat. Hosps., 1980. Mem. Nat. Soc. Newspaper Columnists. Democrat. Avocations: research on role of women in american comics (speaker and media interviews on this topic), empowerment in aging. Home and Office: PO Box 332 North Newton KS 67117-0332 E-mail: thisside60@aol.com.

SNIDER, ROBERT LARRY, management consultant; b. Muskogee, Okla., Aug. 10, 1932; s. George Robert and Kathryn (Smiser) S.; m. Gerlene Rose Tipton, Nov. 26, 1953; children: Melody Kathryn Porter, Rebecca Lee. BS in Indsl. Engring., U. Houston, 1955, postgrad., 1956, Pomona Coll., 1960. Cert. mgmt. cons. Instr. U. Houston Coll. Engring., 1955-56; sr. indsl. engr. Sheffield Steel Corp., Houston, 1955-59, Kaiser Steel Co., Fontana, Calif., 1959-60; cons. Arthur Young & Co., LA, 1960-61; mgmt. analyst Iranian Oil Exploration & Producing Co., Masjidi-Suliman, Iran, 1961—65; v.p., Dallas office mgr. operating methods divsn. Booz, Allen & Hamilton, Inc., 1966—68, v.p. internat. prodn. and inventory control divsn., 1968—69; prin., gen. cons. practice Peat Marwick Mitchell, CPAs, Houston, 1969-71; exec. v.p. mfg. Sterling Electronics Corp., Houston, 1971-72, COO, pres., 1972-77; CEO, pres. Rapoca Energy Corp., Cin., 1977-79; mng. ptnr., cons. Coopers & Lybrand, Southwest, Houston, 1979-81; mng. dir. S.W. region Korn Ferry Internat., Houston, 1981—83; ptnr.-in-charge Houston Mgmt. Cons. Practice, 1983—91; ptnr. cons. Southwest Enterprise Coopers & Lybrand, Houston, 1991-92, ptnr. S.W. Mfg. Cons. Process Improvement Group, 1992-93, internat. cons. ptnr., 1993-95; mng. ptnr RLS Profl. Svcs. LLC, 1995—; chmn., dir. L&G Snacks, 1997-2000. Chmn. L&G Snacks. Trustee Gene Cragg Caring Forever Found., 1997—99; sr. trustee R. Larry and Gerri R. Snider Native Am. scholarship trust Cullen Coll. Engring., U. Houston, 2004—; sr. trustee Melody Snider, Womens Indsl. Engring. scholarship trust U. Houston, Cullen Coll. Engring., 2006—; past chmn. bd. mem. found. bd. and adminstrv. bd. Chapelwood Meth.Ch.; former mem. adminstrv. bd. Memorial Dr. Meth. Ch., Houston, 1997—99; sr. trustee United Meth. Found. Remainder Trust, 2002—; mem. stewardship com. 1st United Meth. Ch., Conroe, Tex.; deacon, steward, video coord. 1st Christian Ch., Conroe, Tex., 2003—05; past bd. dirs. Houston Jr. Achievement, exec. com.; ret. exec. com. Houston Grand Opera, bd. dirs.; sr. trustee Tipton-Snider Minister Edn. Fund., 1999—; mem. Cullen Coll. Leadership bd. U. Houston, mem. Bridge Builder Soc. Cullen Coll. Engring., 2006—, mem. dean's advisory com. Cullen Coll Engring., 2005—. With C.E. AUS, 1956. Recipient Outstandng Mil. Engr. award Soc. Mil Engrs., 1955; named Disting. Alumni, Cullen Coll. Engring., U. Houston, 1991, named Disting. Indsl. Engring. Alumni, 2005. Mem.: U. Houston Alumni Assn. (life; exec. com. 1985—94, pres. and chmn. bd. 1990—93, past bd. dirs., named to Cir. of Excellence), Phi Kappa Phi, Phi Theta Kappa. Home and Office: 9387 Escondido Dr Willis TX 77318-6621 Personal E-mail: rlarry32@yahoo.com.

SNIDER, SCOTT WILLIAM, civilian military employee; b. Shawnee, Okla., Feb. 17, 1961; s. Grady Max and Bobbie Jean Snider. A in Bus., Seminole Jr. Coll., Okla., 1981; BS, Ctrl. State U., Edmond, Okla., 1984; postgrad., U. Ctrl. Okla. Doorman, usher Jones Theatres, Shawnee, 1976—77; salesman W.R. Jones Co., Shawnee, 1977—80; typist Pottawatomie Ct. House, Shawnee, 1980; civil servant Tinker AFB, Oklahoma City, 1980—. Mem.: Ducks Unlimited. Democrat. Baptist. Avocations: stamp collecting/philately, coin collecting/numismatics, golf, fishing, camping.

SNIDER, STACEY, film company executive; b. Phila., Apr. 29, 1961; m. Gary Jones; children: Katie, Natalie. BA, U. Penn., 1982; JD, U. Calif. LA, 1985. Dir. of devel. Guber-Peters Entertainment Co., 1986—90, exec. v.p., 1990—92; pres. prodn. TriStar Pictures, 1992-96; co-pres. prodn. Universal Pictures, Universal City, Calif., 1996—98, pres. prodn., 1998—99, chmn., CEO, 1999—2006; co-chmn., CEO DreamWorks SKG, Glendale, Calif., 2006—. Bd. dirs. Am. Film Inst. Bd. dirs. Spl. Olympics of So. Calif.; bd. trustees Art Ctr. Coll. of Design, Pasadena, Calif. Named one of 100 Most Powerful Women in Entertainment, Hollywood Reporter, 2005, 2006, Most Powerful Women, Forbes mag., 2005, 50 Most Powerful People in Hollywood, Premiere mag., 2004—05, 100 Most Powerful Women in Bus., Fortune mag., 2005—06, America 's Top Women in Bus.-Game Changers, Pink mag. & Forté Found., 2007; recipient Dorothy and Sherrill C. Corwin Human Rels. Award, Am. Jewish Com., 2003. Office: DreamWorks SKG 1000 Flower St Glendale CA 91201 *

SNIDER, TIMOTHY R., mining executive; BS in Chemistry and Geology, No. Ariz. U., 1979; grad. advanced mgmt. program, U. Pa., 1996. Joined Phelps Dodge Corp., 1970; pres. Phelps Dodge Morenci Inc., Morenci, Ariz.; pres., COO Phelps Dodge Mining Co., Phoenix, 1998—; sr. v.p. Phelps Dodge Corp., Phoenix, 1998, pres., COO, 2003—07; COO Freeport-McMoRan Copper & Gold Inc., Phoenix, 2007—. Office: Freeport McMoRan Copper & Gold Inc 1 N Ctrl Ave Phoenix AZ 85004 *

SNIPES, WESLEY, actor, film producer; b. Orlando, Fla., July 31, 1962; m. April Snipes, 1984 (div. 1990); 1 child, Jelani Asar; m. Nikki Park, Mar. 2003; children: Alimayu Moa-Ton, Iset. Grad., SUNY, Purchase, 1980, D (hon.) in Humanities and Fine Arts. Appeared in Broadway plays Boys of Winter, Execution of Justice, Death and King's Horsemen; (films) Streets of Gold, 1986, Vietnam War Story (ACE award for best actor 1989), Mo'Better Blues, 1989, Major League, 1989, King of New York, 1990, New Jack City, 1991 (NAACP Image award for outstanding actor), Jungle Fever, 1991, The Waterdance, 1992, White Men Can't Jump, 1992, Passenger 57, 1992, Rising Sun, 1993, Demolition Man, 1993, Boiling Point, 1993, Sugar Hill, 1994, Drop Zone, 1994, To Wong Foo, Thanks for Everything, Julie Newmar, 1995, The Money Train, 1995, The Fan, 1996, Murder at 1600, 1997, U.S. Marshals, 1998, One Night Stand, 1998 (Venice Film Festival Volpi Cup award for best actor), Play it to the Bone, 1999, Liberty Stands, 2002, Zigzag, 2002, Unstoppable, 2004, Chaos, 2006; actor, prodr., martial arts choreographer Blade, 1998; actor, prodr. Blade II, 2002, Blade: Trinity, 2004; actor, exec. prodr. Art of War, 2000, Undisputed, 2002; prodr. The Big Hit, 1998, Down in the Delta, 1998, Dr. Ben, 2001; (TV) H.E.L.P., 1990, The Real Malcolm X, 1992, America's Dream, 1996 (NAACP Image award for best actor in a TV movie/series); actor, prodr. (TV) Future Sport, 1998; actor, exec. prodr. Disappearing Acts, 2000; TV guest appearances include The Bernie Mac Show, 2001. Recipient Star on Hollywood Walk of Fame, 1998. *

SNITKOFF, GAIL GOODMAN, immunologist, educator; d. Alvin and Muriel Goodman; m. Louis Steven Snitkoff, June 12, 1976; children: Joshua, Benjamin. PhD, N.Y. State Downstate Med. Ctr., Bklyn., 1974—79. Instr. Union Coll., Schenectady, NY, 1984—86; rsch. asst. prof. Albany Med. Ctr., NY, 1986—91; asst. prof. Albany Coll. Pharmacy, NY, 1991—96, assoc. prof., 1996—. Contbr. articles to profl. jours. Mem. Planned Parenthood, 1980—2005; pres. Schenectady Hadassah, NY, 2003—05; mem. NARAL, 1990—2004; mem., bd. trustees Congregation Gates of Heaven, Schenectady, NY, 1986—92; pres. Schenectady Area Midrasha, NY, 1995—2005. Fellow, NSF, 1979—80, NIH, 1980—82; grantee, 1987—90. Mem.: AAAS (assoc.), N.Y. Acad. Sci. (assoc.), Am. Assn. Microbiology (assoc.), N.Y.C. Ballet Guild (assoc.), Saratoga Performing Arts Ctr. (life), Glass Art Soc. (assoc.), Hadassah (regional v.p. 2006—07), Sigma Xi (assoc.). Jewish. Achievements include patents for immunogenic composites capable of selectively inducing antibody production; research in pharmaceutical compositions employing the same method of selectively inducing antibody production. Avocations: performing arts, contemporary crafts, knitting, reading, travel. Home: 2154 Lynnwood Dr Niskayuna NY 12309 Office: Albany Coll Pharmacy 106 New Scotland Ave Albany NY 12208 Office Phone: 518-694-7227. Business E-Mail: snitkofg@acp.edu.

SNITZER, ELIAS, physicist; b. Lynn, Mass., Feb. 27, 1925; s. Isaac and Jenny (Sussman) Snitzer; m. Shirley Ann Wood, Nov. 22, 1950; children: Sandra, Barbara, Peter, Helen, Louis. BSEE, Tufts U., 1946; MS in Physics, U. Chgo., 1950, PhD, 1953. Rsch. physicist Honeywell Corp., Phila., 1954-56; assoc. prof. Lowell Technol. Inst., Mass., 1956-58; dir. rsch. Am. Optical Co., Southbridge, Mass., 1959-76; mgr. applied physics United Technologies Rsch., East Hartford, Conn., 1977-84; mgr. fiber optics Polaroid, Cambridge, Mass., 1984-88; prof. Rutgers U., 1989-97, prof. emeritus, 1997—. Contbr. articles to profl. jours. With USN, 1943—46. Fellow: Am. Phys. Soc., Ceramic Soc. (Corning Stookey Discovery award 2006), Optical Soc. Am. (John Tyndall award 1994); mem.: IEEE (George Morey award 1971, Quantum Electronics award 1979, Charles Townes award 1991, Otto Schott award 1999, Opto-Electronic Rank prize 2000, LEOS Millenium award 2001), NAE. Democrat. Jewish. Achievements include invention of glass laser; fiber laser amplifier. Home and Office: 78 Ivy Rd Wellesley MA 02482 Office Phone: 781-431-2605. Personal E-mail: snitzer27@yahoo.com.

SNIVELY, DAVID FREDERICK, agricultural products company executive, lawyer; b. Logansport, Ind., Apr. 26, 1954; s. Howard Woodrow Snively and Rebecca S. (Merrell) Hoover; m. Diane Marie Hepper, Aug. 7, 1976; children: Matthew David, Christine Marie, Evan David. BS magna cum laude, Ball State U., 1976; JD magna cum laude, Ind. U., 1979. Bar: Ind. 1979, Mo. 1987, US Dist. Ct. (so. dist. Ind.) 1979, US Ct. Appeals (7th cir.) 1979, US Supreme Ct. 1984. Assoc. Barnes & Thornburg, Indpls., 1979-84; litig. atty. Monsanto Co., St. Louis, 1984-87, asst. litig. counsel, 1987-89, assoc. litig. counsel, 1989-97, asst. gen. counsel litig., dep. gen. counsel, sr. v.p., sec., gen. counsel, 2006—. Note and devel. editor, contbr. Ind. Law Rev., 1978-79. Mem. ABA (co-chair subcommittee on product liability and toxic torts, com. on corp. counsel 1995—), Ind. Bar Assn., Mo. Bar Assn., Lawyers for Civil Justice (bd. dirs. 1990—), Def. Rsch. Inst. (co-chmn. corp. counsel sect.), Phi Delta Phi. Democrat. Roman Catholic. Avocations: marathon running, backpacking, skiing, rollerblading, bicycling. Office: Monsanto Co 800 N Lindbergh Blvd Saint Louis MO 63167-0001 *

SNODDY, CHRIS RAYMOND, athletic trainer; b. Nashville, Nov. 19, 1959; s. Raymond Thomas and Farris (Duke) S. BS, Lipscomb U., 1981; MA, Appalachian State U., 1987. Lic. athletic trainer. Real estate salesperson McKinney & Co., Nashville, 1980-89; head athletic trainer Lipscomb U., Nashville, 1981-91; sr. athletic trainer Ctr. Sports Medicine, Bapt. Hosp., Nashville, 1993—; coord. sports medicine Bapt. Hosp., Nashville, 1997—99, mgr., 1999—2003, dir., 2003—; head athletic trainer Skyline Med. Ctr., 2003—. Dir. sports medicine Pinnacle Rehab., Nashville, 1991-92; cons. sports medicine David Lipscomb H.S., Nashville, 1982-91; adj. faculty Free Will Bapt. Bible Coll., Nashville; cons. Lipscomb U. Sports Medicine. Editor: Where to Go Camping Guide, 1980; contbr. articles to Flying Eagle mag. Recipient Mayor's medallion City of Nashville, 1986, Silver Beaver award Boy Scouts Am., 1995; named Eagle Scout, 1976, Clin. Athletic Trainer of Yr., 1992, 2003, Athletic Trainer of Yr., Southeastern Athletic Trainers Assn., 2005; named to Lipscomb U. Hall of Fame, 2004. Mem. Nat. Athletic Trainers Assn., Tenn. Athletic Trainers Soc. (named to Hall of Fame, 2005). Mem. Ch. of Christ. Lodges: Civitan (bd. dirs. Nashville 1986-87, pres. 1990), Wa-Hi-Nasa (lodge advisor 1995—), Order of Arrow (assoc. advisor Tenn. and Ky. chpts. 1984-87, 2004-05, Founder's award 1976). Avocation: skiing. Home: 315 Bowwood Dr Nashville TN 37217-2301 Office Phone: 615-769-7576.

SNODDY, JAMES ERNEST, education educator; b. Perrysville, Ind., Oct. 6, 1932; s. James Elmer and Edna May (Hayworth) S.; m. Alice Joanne Crowder, Aug. 15, 1954; children: Ryan Anthony, Elise Suzanne. BS, Ind. State U., 1954; MEd, U. Ill., 1961, EdD, 1967. Tchr. Danville (Ill.) Pub. Schs., 1954-57, prin., 1961-64; instr. U. Ill., Champaign, 1965-67; prof. edn. Mich. State U., East Lansing, 1967-72, 78-96, chmn. dept. elem. and spl. edn., 1972-78, ret., 1996, prof. emeritus, 1997—; dir. Program CORK, 1978-82. With U.S. Army, 1955-57. Mem. Am. Assn. for Adult and Continuing Edn., Commn. of Profs. of Adult and Continuing Edn. Methodist. Home: 1926 Creek Lndg Haslett MI 48840-8704 Office: Mich State U 419 Erickson Hall East Lansing MI 48824-1034 Office Phone: 517-339-6548. Business E-Mail: jsnoddy@msu.edu.

SNODGRASS, ROBERT EUGENE, retired psychiatrist; b. Indpls., Feb. 27, 1930; s. William Howard and Della Gladys (Satterly) S.; m. Constance Fusco, Mar. 1, 1958; 1 child, Robert Brent. AB in Anatomy and Physiology, Ind. U., 1952, MD, 1955. Diplomate Am. Bd. Psychiatry and Neurology. Intern Marion County Gen. Hosp., Indpls., 1955-56; resident in psychiatry Ind. U. Med. Ctr., Indpls., 1964-67; pvt. gen. practice Greenwood, Ind., 1958-64; pvt. practice Indpls., 1967-90; staff psychiatrist Madison (Ind.) State Hosp., 1991—2007; ret., 2007. Author: Beloved Madison, 1990; contbr. articles to profl. jours. Mem. Hist. Dist. Bd. Rev., Madison, 1991—. Capt. U.S. Army, 1956-58. Decorated Meritorious Svc. Commendation medal. Fellow Am. Psychiat. Assn.; mem. AMA, Ind. Psychiat. Soc. (past pres.), Jefferson County Hist. Soc. (bd. dirs. 1989—). Avocation: foreign languages. Home: 707 E Main St Madison IN 47250-3650 Personal E-mail: rsnodmd@verizon.net.

SNODGRASS, S. GARY, utilities executive; BBA, Western Ky. U.; MBA, Keller Grad. Sch. Mgmt., Chgo. V.p. human resources USG Corp.; with Exelon Corp., Chgo., 1997—, exec. v.p., chief human resources officer, mem. strategy and policy and ops. mgmt. coms. Author: When Your Career Means Business, Stepping Up - 12 Ways to Rev Up, Revitalize or Renew Your Career, 2007. Recipient Human Resources Leadership award, Hunt-Scanlon Corp., 2004, Colleague of Distinction award, Human Resources Mgmt. Assn. Chgo., 2004. Office: Exelon Corp 10 S Dearborn St 37th Fl PO Box 805398 Chicago IL 60680-5398 Office Phone: 800-483-3220. *

SNOEYINK, VERNON L., civil engineer, educator; BS in Civil Engring., U. Mich., 1984, MS in Sanitary Engring., 1966, PhD in Water Resource Engring., 1968. Asst. prof. sanitary engring. U. Ill., Urbana, 1969-73, from assoc. prof. to prof. environ. engring., 1973—, Ivan Racheff prof. environ. engring., 1989—2004, prof. emeritus, 2005—. Mem.: NAE. Office: U Ill Dept Civil Engring Newmark Civil Engring Lab 205 N Mathews Ave Urbana IL 61801 Home Phone: 217-352-0698. Business E-Mail: snoeyink@uiuc.edu.

SNOKE, DAVID WAYNE, physicist, researcher; b. May 7, 1961; AB magna cum laude, Cornell U., 1983; MS in Physics, U. Ill., 1984, PhD in Physics, 1990. Rsch. asst. Cornell U., Ithaca, N.Y., 1981, teaching asst., 1981-82; rsch. engr. Westinghouse Rsch. & Devel. Ctr., Pitts., 1983; rsch. asst. U. Ill., Urbana, 1984-87, 89-90, univ. fellow, 1987-89; Alexander von Humboldt fellow Max-Planck Inst. for Festkörperforschung, Stuttgart, Germany, 1990-92, guest scientist, 1992; mem. tech. staff Aerospace Corp., LA, 1993-94; asst. prof., dept. physics and astronomy U. Pitts., 1994—2001, assoc. prof., 2001—. Lectr. in field. Contbr. articles to profl. jours. Recipient Early Career award NSF, 1997, Cottrell Scholar award, 1997. Fellow: Am. Phys. Soc., Am. Sci. Affiliation. Office: U Pitts 3941 Ohara St Pittsburgh PA 15260

SNOOK, STOVER HOFFMAN, social sciences educator, researcher; b. Ventnor, NJ, July 28, 1932; s. Stover Garfield and Leah Jane (Hoffman) Snook; m. Marie Melanie Rohrer, June 26, 1954; children: John Stover, Suzanne Marie, Linda Jeanne. BA, Hartwick Coll., 1954; MA, Fordham U., 1960; PhD, Tufts U., 1969. Lic. psychologist Mass., 1973; bd. cert. profl. ergonomist 1993. Staff psychologist Dunlap & Assoc., Stamford, Conn., 1956—62; asst. v.p. Liberty Mut. Ins. Co., Hopkinton, Mass., 1962—97; lectr. Harvard Sch. Pub. Health, Boston, 1974—2006. Com. human factors Nat. Rsch. Coun., Washington, 1984—87; adv. panel rsch. Am. Phys. Therapy Assn., Alexandria, Va., 1996—99; cumulative trauma com. Am. Nat. Stds. Inst., Chgo., 1990—97. Contbr. articles to profl. jours., chapters to books. Recipient Festschrift, Ergonomics, 1999, Kraft Innovation award, Human Factors and Ergonomics Soc., 1997, Extension award, McKenzie Inst. Internat., 2001. Fellow: Internat. Ergonomics Assn., Am. Psychological Soc. (fellow), Ergonomics Soc. (fellow, Ann. Lectr. 1978), Human Factors and Ergonomics Soc. (fellow, Tech. Group award 1992). Democrat. Unitarian. Achievements include development of psychophysical guidelines for manual handling tasks; guidelines for reducing low back pain and disability; incidence and cost data for industrial low back disorders. Avocations: travel, astronomy, history, music. Home: 10472 S E Amberjack Ct Hobe Sound FL 33455

SNOOP DOGG, (CALVIN BROADUS), vocalist, actor; b. Long Beach, Calif., Oct. 20, 1972; s. Beverly Tate; m. Shante Taylor, June 1997; 1 child, Corde Calvin Broadus;children from previous marriage: Cordell Broadus, Cori Broadus. Founder, owner Doggy Style Records, Inc. (formerly DoggHouse Records), 1999—. Musician: (albums) Doggystyle, 1993, Tha Doggfather, 1996, Da Game Is To Be Sold Not To Be Told, 1998, No Limit Top Dogg, 1999, Tha Last Meal, 2000, Doggy Style Allstars: Welcome to Tha House, 2002, Paid Tha Cost to Be da Bo$$, 2002, Soundtrack Raw N Uncut, Vol. 1, 2002, Welcome to Church: Mix Tape, Vol. 1, 2003, R&G - Rhythm and Gangster: The Masterpiece, 2004, Dogg Pound Mix, 2005, Me & My Homies, 2005, Tha Blue Carpet Treatment, 2006, The Chronicalz, Vol. 1: The Mixed Up Album, 2006, (CD singles) Vapors, 1997; actor: (films) Half Baked, 1998, I Got the Hook Up, 1998, Ride, 1998, Caught Up, 1998, Urban Menace, 1999, The Wrecking Crew, 1999, Hot Boyz, 1999, Tha Eastsidaz, 2000, Baby Boy, 2001, Training Day, 2001, Bones, 2001, The Wash, 2001, Crime Partners, 2001, Malibu's Most Wanted (voice), Starsky & Hutch, 2004, Soul Plane, 2004, (voice) Racing Stripes, 2005,: (guest appearance in film) Old School, 2003, (guest appearance in TV show) Just Shoot Me, 2001; author: Tha Doggfather: The Times, Trials, and Hardcore Truths of Snoop Dogg, 1999. Founder Snoop Youth Football League, Calif., 2005. Office: Doggy Style Records 1142 S Diamond Bar Blvd #504 Diamond Bar CA 91765 *

SNORTLAND, HOWARD JEROME, financial consultant; b. Sharon, ND, June 22, 1912; s. Thomas and Aline (Vig) S.; m. Anna Adeline Anderson, Sept. 1, 1940; children: Jan Signe, Kristi Jo, Howard Jay. BA, U. N.D., 1937, MS, 1958. Cashier N.D. Workmen's Compensation Bur., 1937-42, N.D. State Treas.'s Office, 1945-48; with N.D. Dept. Pub. Instrn., Bismarck, 1948-81, supt. pub. instrn., 1977-81; edn. fin. cons., 1981—. Pres. State Econ. Coun., 1978; nat. pres. Com. Ednl. Data Systems, 1965-67 Chmn. Burleigh ARC, 1963-67, bd. dirs., 1946—, vice chmn., 1964—; bd. dirs. Burleigh County Tb Assn., 1950—; stated clk. United Presbyterian Ch., 1942—; pres. N.D. United Christian Campus Fellowship, 1964-67, N.D. Westminster Found., 1963-70; mem. N.D. Synod Coun., 1970—; chmn. United Way Fund, 1983. Served with USAAF, 1942-45. Recipient Summit Conf. award for outstanding pub. svc., 1976. Mem. NEA, N.D. Edn. Assn., N.D. Sch. Bus. Ofcls., N.D. Assn. Adminstrs., Nat. Assn. Adminstrs., N.D. Assn. Ret. Employees (pres. 1987—), Am. Assn. Ret. Persons (vice chmn. N.D. legis. com. 1992-94, chmn. 1994—), Kiwanis, Phi Beta Kappa, Phi Delta Kappa (dir. emeritus).

SNOUFFER, NANCY KENDALL, literature and language educator; b. Long Branch, NJ, Aug. 22, 1941; d. Percival Wallace and Ruby Mae (Braswell) Kendall; m. Eugene Joseph Snouffer, Aug. 27, 1966; 1 child, Kendall Ann. BA in English, Gettysburg Coll., Pa., 1962; MA in English and Journalism, U. N.C., 1964; MS in Edn. and Reading, Western Ill. U., 1974; postgrad., U. Mo., 1976-78. Instr. English U. N.C., Wilmington, 1963-65, Shaw U., Raleigh, N.C., 1965-66; from instr. to asst. prof. English Wright Coll. and Chgo. City Colls., 1967-74; from instr. to asst. prof. reading Western Ill. U., Macomb, 1974-81; prof. comm., lang. and reading Del Mar Coll., Corpus Christi, Tex., 1982—, reading coord., 2001—. Mem. adv. bd. Tex. A&M U., Corpus Christi, 1993—; cons. in field. Author: College Reading Power, 5th edit., 1976-82; assoc. editor jour. Epistle, 1980-83, mem. editorial bd., 1983-85; contbr. articles to profl. jours. Master Tchr. Del Mar, 1986. Grantee Western Ill. U., 1974-81, Del Mar Coll., 1982—, NISSOD Tchg. Excellence award, 1993, Coll. Acad. Support Program Tex. State level Lifetime Achievement award. Mem. Tex. Assn. Developmental Educators, Tex. Coll. Reading Learning Assn. (chair So. membership 1994—, state sec. 1995-97, pres.-elect 1997-98, pres. 1998-99, past pres. 1999-2000, Lifetime Achievement award 2002), Nat. Assn. Devel. Educators (co-chair nat. com., profl. liaison), Internat. Reading Assn., Corpus Christi Literacy Coun. (bd. dirs. 1986-2003, sec. 1988-93, vice-chmn. 1991-92, v.p.-elect 2000-01, chmn. 2001-02), Harbor Playhouse (bd. dirs. 1988, 91-93), Alliance Francaise. Republican. Episcopalian. Avocations: tennis, travel, reading. Home: 4206 Acushnet Dr Corpus Christi TX 78413-2004 Office: Del Mar Coll 101 Baldwin Blvd Corpus Christi TX 78404-3805 E-mail: snouffer@delmar.edu.

SNOW, CHARLES, lawyer; b. Bklyn., May 3, 1932; s. Irving S. and Bessie S.; m. Deanna Friedman, Jan. 15, 1961; children: Lisa C., Amy M. BA, U. Vt., 1954; LLB, Bklyn. Law Sch., 1959. Bar: N.Y. 1959, U.S. Dist. Ct. (ea. and so. dists.) N.Y. 1961, U.S. Ct. Appeals (2d cir.) 1961, U.S. Supreme Ct. 1965. Dep. asst. atty. gen. NY Dept. Law, NYC, 1959—60; asst. US atty. US Dist. Ct. (ea. dist.) NY, Bklyn., 1960—61; asst. regional adminstr. SEC, NYC, 1961—68; ptnr. Wofsey Certilman Haft Snow & Becker, PC, NYC, 1968—77, Snow Becker Krauss, P.C., NYC, 1977—2007, counsel, 2007—. Gen. counsel Securities Traders' Assn. N.Y., 1988—2004. Chmn. Harrison (N.Y.) Planning Bd., 1977-88; mem. New Castle Planning Bd., 1991-97. Mem. N.Y. State Bar Assn. (mem. bus. sect., com. on securities regulation), Securities Traders Assn. N.Y. (hon.). Republican. Jewish. Office: 605 3rd Ave New York NY 10158-0180 Office Phone: 212-455-0300. Personal E-mail: snow.charles@att.net. Business E-Mail: csnow@sbklaw.com.

SNOW, CLAUDE HENRY, JR., information services executive, consultant; b. Lumberton, NC, Feb. 25, 1954; s. Claude Henry and Vada Isabelle (Simpson) S.; m. Sarah Catherine Turnbull, Sept. 26, 1981. BA, U. N.C., 1976, MA, 1978. Communications systems rep. So. Bell Tel. & Tel., Charlotte, N.C., 1978-82; systems mgr. Sykes Datatronics, Atlanta, 1982-83; strategic planning mgr. Lockheed-Ga. Co., Marietta, 1983-86; regional mgr. communications Wang Labs., Atlanta, 1986-88, regional mgr. mktg., mfg., 1989; mgr. Deloitte & Touche, Atlanta, 1989-94; mng. dir. IBM Healthcare Consulting divsn., 1994-2000; exec. dir. IBM Pub. Sector Divsn. Global Svcs., 2000—02; global v.p. health ins. industry Electronic Data Systems, Plano, Tex., 2002—. Mem. U. N.C. Libr. Bd., 1995—; bd. dirs. Ctrs. Disease Control Found., 1999—; bd. visitors U. N.C., Chapel Hill, 2001-06. Mem. SAR, U. NC Alumni Assn. (pres. Atlanta chpt. 1985, mem. adv. bd. 1986-89), Chancellors Club NC. Democrat. Episcopalian. Avocations: golf, Scottish games, historic preservation. Home Phone: 919-960-7990; Office Phone: 919-824-7669. Business E-Mail: claude.snow@eds.com.

SNOW, DASH, photographer; b. NYC, 1981; Exhibited in group shows at Interstate, Nicole Klagsbrun Gallery, 2005, Whitney Biennial: Day before Night, Whitney Mus. Am. Art, 2006, exhibitions include Silence Is The Only True Friend That Shall Never Betray You, Rivington Arms Gallery, NYC, 2006. Mailing: c/o Rivington Arms Gallery 4 E 2nd St 1st Fl New York NY 10003

SNOW, DAVID B., pharmaceutical executive; BS Science and Econs., Bates Coll.; MS Healthcare Admin., Duke U. Sr. vice-pres. Am. Internat. Healthcare, Rockville, Md., 1988—89; pres. and CEO Managed Healthcare Systems, Reston, Va., 1989—93; exec. vice-pres. Oxford Health Plans, Norwalk, Conn.; pres. and CEO WellChoice, New York, NY, 1999—2003; pres., CEO Medco Health Solutions, Franklin Lakes, NJ, 2003, chmn., CEO, 2003—. Office: Medco Health 100 Parsons Pond Franklin Lakes NJ 07417 *

SNOW, GARTH, professional sports team executive, former professional hockey player; b. Wrentham, Mass., July 28, 1969; m. Erica Snow; 1 child, Glenn. Grad., U. Maine, 1993. Goalie U. Maine, 1988—93, Quebec Nordiques, 1993—95, Phila. Flyers, 1995—98, Vancouver Canucks, 1998—2000, Pitts. Penguins, 2000—01, NY Islanders, 2001—06, gen. mgr., 2006—. Named to Second All-Star Team, Hockey East, 1992, 1993, Championship All-Tournament Team, NCAA, 1993. Office: NY Islanders Nassau Veterans Meml Coliseum 1255 Hempstead Turnpike Uniondale NY 11553

SNOW, JACK (JOHN WILLIAM SNOW), investment company executive, former secretary of the treasury; b. Toledo, Aug. 2, 1939; s. William Dean and Catherine (Howard) S.; m. Fredrica Wheeler, June 11, 1964 (div. 1973); children: Bradley, Ian; m. Carolyn Kalk, Aug. 31, 1973; 1 child, Christopher. BA, Kenyon Coll./U. Toledo, 1962; PhD in Economics, U. Va., 1965; LLB, George Washington U., 1967. Asst. prof. econs. U. Md., College Park, 1965-67; assoc. Wheeler & Wheeler, Washington, 1967-72; asst. gen. counsel US Dept. Transp., Washington, 1972-73, dep. asst. sec. for policy, plans and internat. affairs, 1973-74, asst. sec. for govtl. affairs, 1974-75, dep. under sec., 1975-76; adminstr. Nat. Hwy. Traffic Safety Adminstrn., Washington, 1976-77; v.p. govt. affairs Chessie System Inc., Washington, 1977-80; sr. v.p. corp. services CSX Corp., Richmond, Va., 1980-84, exec. v.p., 1984-85; pres., CEO Chessie System R.R.s, Balt., 1985-86, CSX Rail Transport, Jacksonville, Fla., 1986-87, CSX Transp., Jacksonville, Va., 1987-88; pres., COO CSX Corp., Richmond, Va., 1988-89, pres., CEO, 1989-91, chmn., pres., CEO, 1991—2003; sec. US Dept. Treasury, Washington, 2003—06; chmn. Cerberus Capital Mgmt., L.P., NYC, 2006—. Adj. prof. law George Washington U., 1972-75; vis. prof. econs. U. Va., Charlottesville, spring 1977; vis. fellow Am. Enterprises Inst., Washington, spring 1977; bd. dirs. Marathon Oil Corp., 2006-, Verizon Comm. Inc., 2006- Ex officio trustee Nat. Gallery Art. Mem. Va. State Bar. Clubs: Chevy Chase, Metropolitan (Washington); Country of Va. (Richmond). Republican. Episcopalian. Office: Cerberes Capital Mgmt LP 299 Park AVe New York NY 10171 *

SNOW, JAMES BYRON, JR., otolaryngologist, research administrator, educator; b. Oklahoma City, Mar. 12, 1932; s. James B. and Charlotte Louise (Andersen) S.; m. Sallie Lee Ricker, July 16, 1954; children: James B., John Andrew, Sallie Lee Louise. BS, U. Okla., Norman, 1953; MD cum laude, Harvard U., Cambridge, Mass., 1956; MA (hon.), U. Pa., Phila., 1973. Diplomate Am. Bd. Otolaryngology (dir. 1972-90). Intern Johns Hopkins Hosp., Balt., 1956-57; resident Mass. Eye and Ear Infirmary, Boston, 1957-60; prof., head dept. otorhinolaryngology Sch. Medicine U. Okla., Oklahoma City, 1962-72; prof., chmn. dept. otorhinolaryngology and human communication U. Pa., 1972-90; dir. Nat. Inst. on Deafness and Other Comm. Disorders, NIH, Bethesda, Md., 1990-97; convener, corr. Tinnitus Rsch. Consortium, 1998—. Mem. nat. adv. coun. neurol. and communicative disorders and stroke NIH, 1972-76, 82-86; chmn. Nat. Com. Rsch. Neurol. and Communicative Disorders, 1979-80. Editor: Am. Jour. Otolaryngology, 1979-83; Contbr. articles to sci. and profl. jours. Officer, M.C., U.S. Army, 1960-62. Recipient Regents award for superior tchg. U. Okla., 1970, Golden award Internat. Fedn. Otorhinolaryngological Socs., 1989, Disting. Achievement award Deafness Rsch. Found., 1993, Presdl. Meritorious Exec. Rank award, 1994; named to Soc. Scholars Johns Hopkins U., 1991. Fellow Japan Broncho-Esophagological Soc. (hon.), Am. Laryngological Assn. (hon.); mem. ACS (regent 1982-90), AMA (coun. on sci. affairs 1975-86), Soc. Univ. Otolaryngologists (pres. 1975), Am. Acad. Otolaryngology-Head and Neck Surgery, Assn. Acad. Depts. Otolaryngology (pres. 1981-82), Am. Laryngol., Rhinol. and Otol. Soc., Am. Otol. Soc. (merit award 2003), Am. Laryngol. Assn. (editor 1983-89, pres. 1990-91), Am. Broncho-Esophagol. Assn. (editor trans. 1973-77, pres. 1979), Collegium Otorhinolaryngologicum (pres. 2000-02), Phi Beta Kappa, Alpha Omega Alpha. Home: 327 Greenbriar Ln West Grove PA 19390-9490 Personal E-mail: jandssnow@comcast.net.

SNOW, JOEL ALAN, research director; b. Brockton, Mass., Apr. 1, 1937; s. George H. Jr. and Mary W. (Sproul) S.; m. Laetitia Harrer, June 29, 1957 (div. 1983); children: Jonathan E., Nicholas H.; m. Barbara Kashian, Feb. 7, 1992; stepchildren: James, Alexander. BS in Physics, U. N.C., 1958; MA in Physics, Washington U., St. Louis, 1963, PhD in Physics, 1967. Fellow Ctr. Advanced Study U. Ill., Champaign, 1967-68; program dir. for theoretical physics NSF, Washington, 1968-70, head office of interdisciplinary rsch., 1969-71, dep. asst. dir. for sci. and tech., rsch. applications, 1971-74, dir. office of planning and resources mgmt., 1974-76, dir. div. of policy rsch. and analysis, 1976; sr. policy analyst, office of sci. and tech. policy Exec. Office of the Pres., Washington, 1976-77; assoc. dir. for rsch. policy U.S. Dept. Energy, Washington, 1977-81, dir. sci. and tech. affairs, 1981-88; assoc. v.p. for rsch. Argonne Nat. Lab., U. Chgo., 1988-92; dir. Inst. for Phys. Rsch. and Tech. Iowa State U., Ames, 1993-98, prof. elec. and computer engring., 1993—, prof. polit. sci., 1998-2000, exec. assoc. dir. Internat. Inst. Theoret./Applied Physics, 1998—. Rsch. assoc. dept. physics U. Ill., Urbana, 1967-68; instr. physics and electronics U.S. Navy Nulcear Power Shc., New London, Conn., 1958-61; sci. tech. organizer Pres.'s Conf. on Superconductivity, 1987, NSF program rsch. applied to nat. needs, 1971, designer, mgr., founder NSF program interdisciplinary rsch. relevant to problems of society, 1969. Contbr. over 130 articles to mags. and profl. jours. Lt. (j.g.) USN, 1958-61. Recipient Meritorious Svc. award NSF, 1972, Meritorious award William A. Jump Found., 1973, Arthur S. Fleming award Downtown Jaycees, 1974; NSF postdoctoral fellow Ctr. for Advanced Study U. Ill., 1967-68; NSF fellow, 1963-65. Fellow AAAS, Am. Phys. Soc.; mem. IEEE, Am. Chem. Soc., Am. Nuc. Soc., World Future Soc., Sigma Xi, Phi Beta Kappa, Phi Kappa Phi. Achievements include pioneering devel. of federal programs in environment, solar and geothermal energy and energy conservation, sustainable development; fed. programs in technology transfer to industry; developed collaborations between univ., govt. and industry; fostering internat. collaboration in sci., engring. and edn.

SNOW, LURANA S., judge; b. Brooklyn, NY, May 10, 1951; d. Lawrence James and Elizabeth Catherine (Luckso) Schling. AB magna cum laude, Radcliffe Coll., 1972; JD, Harvard Law Sch., 1975; MA in Theology, Barry U., 1998. Bar: Mass. 1975, Fla. 1977, D.C. 1980. Law clk. to Judge Joe Eaton U.S. Dist. Ct., Miami, 1975-77; asst. fed. public defender Miami, 1977-79; asst. U.S. atty. U.S. Dept. of Justice, Ft. Lauderdale, 1980-86; pvt. practice, 1984; magistrate judge U.S. Dist. Ct. (so. dist.) Fla., Ft. Lauderdale, 1986-97; chief magistrate judge US Dist. Ct. (so. dist.) Fla., Ft. Lauderdale, 1997—. With Mass. Gov's. Commn. on Adoption and Foster Care, 1970—1975. Recipient Spl. Achievement award Drug Enforcement Adminstrn., 1981, 84, 86, U.S. Secret Svc., 1984, U.S. Customs, 1984, Bureau of Alcohol, Tobacco and Firearms, 1984, South Fla. Vice Presidential Task Force, 1984. Mem. Fla. Bar Assn., Mass. Bar Assn., DC Bar Assn., Fed. Bar Assn., Fed. Magistrate Judges Assn. Avocations: scuba, skiing, travel, reading, photography. Office: US Courthouse 299 E Broward Blvd Ste 204 Fort Lauderdale FL 33301-1930 Office Phone: 954-769-5460. E-mail: luranasnow@yahoo.com.

SNOW, MARINA, writer; b. Boston, Apr. 9, 1937; d. Charles Ernest Snow and Katherine Alice Townsend; m. Richard DeVere Horton, 1958 (div. 1968); children: Heather Kertchem, James Horton; m. Charles A. Washburn, 1978 (div. 1979). BA, U. Iowa, 1958; MA in Speech Pathology, N.Mex. State U., 1967; MA in Librarianship, San Jose State U., 1976; MA in Theatre Arts, Calif. State U., Sacramento, 1979. Cert. clin. competence Am. Speech and Hearing Assn. Tchr. ESL Inst. Colombo-Americano, Cali, Colombia, 1958-59; tchr. Las Cruces (N.Mex.) Pub. Schs., 1964-66; speech therapist Sutter County Schs., Yuba City, Calif., 1967-72; reference libr. Calif. State U., Sacramento, 1976-95. Author: (novels) The Walking Wounded, 2001 (Best First Novel of 2001-2002 award Bay Area Ind. Pub. Assn., 2001), Look No Further, 2004 (Best Fiction award, Bay Area Ind. Pub. Assn., 2005), (plays) Apricot Coffee, Alkali Flat, (short stories) The Black Iris, 1999, The Masthead, 2006, Artisan: A Journal of Craft; contbr.

articles to profl. jours. Pres. Alkali Flat Neighborhood Assn., Sacramento, 1987—94. Mem.: Calif. Writer's Club, Sacramento Old City Assn. Avocations: theater, historic preservation, gardening.

SNOW, MARLON O., trucking executive, state agency administrator; m. Ann; children. Gen. mgr. spl. commodities Milne Truck Lines, Phoenix, LA, 1970-81; gen. mgr. spl. commodities, sales Motor Cargo, Salt Lake City, 1981-82; owner MST Trucking, Inc., Salt Lake City, 1982—. V.p. Utah Motor Carriers for State of Utah, 1997-98; mem. adv. bd. Zions Bank. Mem. State Bd. Edn., 1994-97, chair, 1995-97; trustee Utah Valley State Coll., 1998; mem. Ho. of Reps., Utah, 1999-2001; bd. regents Bd. Higher Edn. State of Utah, 2001—; bd. dirs. Children's Justice Ctr., State of Utah, 2002-, Riverside Country Club; mem. bd. I.H.C. Hosp. Utah County. Mem. Utah Valley State Coll. Found. (bd. dirs. 1991—), Alpine Sch. Dist. Found. (bd. dirs. 1990-94). Office: 1247 E 430 N Orem UT 84097-5400

SNOW, THEODORE PECK, astrophysics educator; b. Seattle, Jan. 30, 1947; s. Theodore P. and Louise (Wertz) S.; s. Constance M. Snow, Aug. 23, 1969; children: McGregor A., Tyler M., Reilly A. BA, Yale U., 1969; MS, U. Wash., 1970, PhD, 1973. Mem. rsch. staff Princeton (N.J.) U., 1973-77; prof. U. Colo., Boulder, 1977—, dir. Ctr. for Astrophysics and Space Astronomy, 1986-96, dir. Fiske Planetarium, 2000—. Mem. instrument devel. teams for far Ultraviolet Spectroscopic Explorer, 1999—, Cosmic Origins Spectrograph to be installed in Hubble Space Telescope. Author: (textbook) The Dynamic Universe, 1983, 4th edit., 1991, Essentials of the Dynamic Universe 4th edit., 1993 (textbook excellence award Text and Academic Authors Assn. 1994), Physics, 1986, Universe: Origins and Evolution, 1997; contbr. over 200 articles to profl. jours. Fellow Royal Astron. Soc.; mem. Am. Astron. Soc., Astron. Soc. Pacific, Sigma Xi. Achievements include discovery, through observations in ultraviolet visible, and infrared wavelengths, and through laboratory measurement of chemical reactions, of several important processes involving interstellar gas and dust, and their roles in star formation and late stages of stellar evolution. Office: U Colo Ctr Astrophysics Space Astronomy 389 UCB Boulder CO 80309-0389 Business E-Mail: tsnow@casa.colorado.edu.

SNOW, TIFFANY, writer, healer, composer; b. Vista, Calif., 1962; d. Fred Archer and Trisha Ann Wallace; children: Jenni, Sierra, Jesse, Timothy. MS in Theology, Suffield Coll. and Univ., West Hartford, Conn., PhD in Psychology; M in Usui Reiki Sys., Sacred Cir. Spiritual Healing; DD (hon.), World Christianship Ministries, Fresno, Calif. Lic. CE provider, Bd. Registered Nursing, Calif. Healer Divine Wellness Inst., Escondido, Calif., 1999—; pres. Spirit Journey Books, San Diego, 2003—. Inspirational and motivational spkr., tchr. Author: (nonfiction book) Psychic Gifts in the Christian Life - Tools to Connect, The Power of Divine: A Healer's Guide - Tapping into the Miracle (USA Book News Awards 2004 finalist, 2004, Finalist 2004 Reader's Preference Editor's Choice award, 2004, Finalist San Diego Books award, 2004), Forward From the Mind - Distant Healing, Prayer & Remote Viewing, The Holy Frail - The Power of Brokenness: Mending Your Spirit During Trauma, (poetry book) Homesick: A Healer Remembers God - NDE Prayers & Poems of the Mystic Soul, 2006, (nonfiction book) Medical Intuition & Prague in a Quantum World, 2006; songwriter: country music CD Tiffany Snow - Two Wild Horses; composer: (instrumental CD) Indian Desert, Private Island; contbr. articles to jours. and mags., forewards and chpts. to books. Mem.: BMI (songwriter, composer, musician), PMA (pub.), Internat. Assn. Reiki Practitioners (registered tchr. and practitioner 2004), Internat. Assn. Raiki Practitioners, Order of St. Luke the Physician, Publs. Mktg. Assn., Internat. Assn. for Near-Death Studies (corr.), Acad. Religion and Paranormal Studies (life). Office: Divine Wellness Inst PO Box 61 San Marcos CA 92079 Home Phone: 800-535-5474; Office Phone: 800-535-5474. E-mail: adm@tiffanysnow.com.

SNOW, TONY, former White House press secretary, political commentator, analyst; b. Berea, Ky., June 1, 1955; m. Jill Snow, 1987; 3 children. BA in Philosophy, Davidson Coll., NC, 1977; LHD (hon.), Catholic U., 2007. Editl. writer Greensboro Record, 1979, Virginian Pilot, Norfolk, Va., 1981—82; editl. page writer Daily Press in Newport News, 1982—84; dep. editl. page editor Detroit News, 1984—87, nationally syndicated columnist, 1993—2001; editl. page writer Washington Times, 1987—91; columnist USA Today, 1994—2000; with FOX News Channel, 1996—, host FOX News Sunday, 1996—2003, host Tony Snow Show and Weekend Live with Tony Snow, polit. analyst; host Tony Snow Show Fox News Radio; asst. to Pres., press sec. The White House, Washington, 2006—07. Dep. asst. for comm., dir. of speech writing to President George H. W. Bush, 1991—92; dep. asst. for media affairs to President George H. W. Bush, 1991. Tchr. physics and East African geography in Kenya; advocate for the mentally ill and developmentally disabled NC. Avocation: musician with Beats Workin'.

SNOW, TOWER CHARLES, JR., lawyer; b. Boston, Oct. 28, 1947; s. Tower Charles and Margaret (Harper) S. BA in English, Dartmouth Coll., 1969; JD, U. Calif., Berkeley, 1973. Bar: Calif. 1973, US Dist. Ct. (no. dist.) Calif. 1973, US Ct. Appeals (9th cir.) 1973, US Supreme Ct. 1976, US Dist. Ct. (ea. dist.) Calif. 1979, US Ct. Appeals (fed. cir.) 1980, US Ct. Claims 1980, US Ct. Appeals (2d cir.) 1987, NY 1988, US Dist. Ct. (ea. and so. dists.) NY 1988, US Dist. Ct. (ctrl. dist.) Calif. 1989, US Dist. Ct. (no. dist.) Tex. 1995, US Dist. Ct. (so. dist.) Calif. 1996, US Dist. Ct. Ariz. 1996. Ptnr., chmn. litigation dept. Orrick, Herrington & Sutcliffe, San Francisco, 1973-89; ptnr. Shearman & Sterling, San Francisco, 1989-94; ptnr., chmn. securities litigation group, mem. policy com. Brobeck, Phleger & Harrison, LLP, San Francisco, 1995-97; chmn., CEO Brobeck, Phleger & Harrison, San Francisco, 1998—2001; ptnr., mem. Americas Mgmt. Group, Clifford Chance, LLP, 2002—04, cons., 2005—06; ind. cons., 2007—. Arbitrator Nat. Assn. Securities Dealers, Am. Stock Exch., N.Y. Stock Exch., Pacific Coast Stock Exch., Superior Ct. City and County San Francisco, Am. Arbitration Assn.; lectr. in field. Author numerous law handbooks and articles to profl. jours. Mem. San Francisco Mus. Soc., San Francisco Symphony, San Francisco Ballet, San Francisco Opera, Am. Conservatory Theatre. Named Best Lawyer in the U.S. in his Field, Corp. Bd. Member Mag., 2001; named one of 100 Most Influential Lawyers in Am., Nat. Law Jour., 2000, 100 Most Influential Lawyers in Calif., Calif. Law and Bus., 2000, 2002, 100 Most Influential Lawyers in World, Lawyer Mag. (U.K.), 2002, America's Leading Lawyers for Bus., Chambers USA, 2003, 2004, 2005; Rufus Choate scholar, Dartmouth Coll., 1969. Mem. ABA (chmn. subcom. pub. offering litig. 1984-88, co-chair task force on securities arbitration 1988-89, vice chair securities litig. com. 1986-88), Continuing Edn. Bar (bus. law inst. planning com. 1986), Securities Industry Assn., Nat. Inst. Trial Advocacy, San Francisco Bar Assn. (pres. securities litig. sect. 1995). Democrat. Avocations: travel, skiing, running, scuba diving, films. Office Phone: 415-987-5877. Personal E-mail: tower.snow@gmail.com.

SNOW, VANBUREN LOWRY, lawyer; b. Salt Lake City, Aug. 21, 1950; s. Van L. and Alice Grace (Swan) S.; m. Sheryl Lee Crawford, May 12, 1973; children: Christa Lee, John Lowry, Ryan James, Tyler Vanburen, Rebecca Joy, William Devin. BS, Brigham Young U., 1975; JD, Gonzaga U., 1979. Bar: Utah 1979, US Dist. Ct. (Dist. Utah) 1979, US Dist. Ct. (Dist. Ariz.). Pvt. practice, St. George, Utah, 1981-86; sr. ptnr. Snow Jensen & Reece, St. George, Utah, 1986—. Law instr. Weber State Coll., 1987-88, Dixie Coll., St. George, 1985-86. Mem. Utah State Bar (commnr. 1999-2006, pres.-elect 2006-07, pres. 2007-08), Southern Utah Bar Assn. (prse. 1985), Assn. Trial Lawyers Am., Utah Assn. Mcpl. Attys., Comml. Law League Am., Kiwanis (treas. Santa Clara, Utah club, 1984-88). Avocation: sailing. Office: Snow Jensen and Reece PO Box 2747 St George UT 84771 Office Phone: 435-628-3688. Office Fax: 435-628-3275. E-mail: vlsnow@snowjensen.com.

SNOWBARGER, VINCE, former congressman; b. Kankakee, Ill., Sept. 16, 1949; s. Willis Edward and Wahnona Ruth (Horger) S.; m. Carolyn Ruth McMahon, Mar. 25, 1972; children: Jeffrey Edward, Matthew David. BA in History, So. Nazarene U., 1971; MA in Polit. Sci., U. Ill., 1974; JD, U. Kans., 1977. Bar: Kans. 1977, U.S. Dist. Ct. Kans. 1977, Mo. 1987. Instr. Mid-Am. Nazarene Coll., Olathe, Kans., 1973—76; ptnr. Haskin, Hinkle, Slater & Snowbarger, 1977—84, Dietrich, Davis, Dicus et al, 1984—88, Armstrong, Teasdale, Schafly & Davis, Overland Park, 1989—92, Holbrook, Heaven & Fay, P.C., Merriam, 1992—94, Snowbarger & Veatch LLP, Olathe, 1994—96; mem. 105th Congress from 3rd Kans. dist., 1997—99; exec. dir. Kans. Assn. Am. Educators, 2000—01; dep. exec. dir. Pension Benefit Guaranty Corp., Washington, 2002—. Mem. Kans. Legislature, Topeka, 1985-96; majority leader Ho. of Reps., 1993-96; mem. Olathe Planning Commn., 1982-84, Leadership Olalthe; divsn. chmn. United Way, Olathe, 1985-88, chmn. citizen rev. com., 1991-95. Mem. Olathe Area C. of C. (bd. dirs. 1984). Republican. Nazarene. Avocation: politics. Office: 1200 K St NW Washington DC 20005-4026 Home: 12676 Lace Falls Loop Bristow VA 20136-1295 Office Phone: 202-326-4010. Business E-Mail: snowbarger.vince@pbgc.gov.

SNOWDEN, DAVID L., protective services official; BA, Calif. State U., Fullerton. Chief of police, Beverly Hills, Calif. Recipient Am.'s Star award U.S. Marshal's Office, Sherman Block Law Enforcement Profl. of Yr. award Calif. Peace Officers Assn., 2003. Mem. Calif. Police Chiefs Assn. (past pres.), Orange County Chiefs and Sheriffs Assn. (past pres.), L.A. County Chiefs Assn. (past pres.). Office: 464 N Rexford Dr Beverly Hills CA 90210 E-mail: dsnowden@beverlyhills.org.

SNOWDEN, LAWRENCE FONTAINE, retired air transportation executive, retired military officer; b. Charlottesville, Va., Apr. 14, 1921; s. Lawrence Fontaine Snoddy and Beatrice M. (Huffman) S.; m. Martha Roselyn Ham, Nov. 17, 1942; children: John Stephen, Brian Fontaine. Student, Stetson U., 1938-39; BS, U. Va., 1942; MA, Northwestern U., 1950; postgrad., Harvard U., 1968; grad., Indsl. Coll. Armed Forces, 1967. Commd. 2d lt. USMC, 1942, advanced through grades to lt. gen., 1975; comdr. 7th Marine Regt., Vietnam, 1966; ops. officer III Marine Amphibious Force, Vietnam, 1967; asst. dir. personnel Hdqrs. Marine Corps, Washington, 1968-69, dir. systems support group, 1969-70; dir. Marine Corps Devel. Ctr., Quantico, Va., 1970-72; chief of staff U.S. Forces, Japan, 1972-75; U.S. chmn. UN Bd., Japan, 1973-75; chief of staff Hdqrs. U.S. Marine Corps, 1977-79; ret., 1979; v.p. Far East Internat. Service Co. Hughes Aircraft Co., 1979-86, group v.p. Internat. Ground Systems Group Fullerton, Calif., 1986-88; pres. Snowden Internat. Assocs., Tallahassee, Fla., 1988—. Recipient Silver Beaver award Boy Scouts Am., Disting. Eagle Scout award; decorated Disting. Svc. medals (2), Legion of Merit (5), Army Commendation medal, Navy Commendation medal, Purple Heart (2), Cross of Gallantry (3) Vietnam, Second Order of Sacred Treasure Japan) Mem. Marine Corps League, U.S. Navy League, Am. C. of C. in Japan, Am.-Japan Soc., Marine Corps Assn., Econ. Club Fla., Sigma Nu. Clubs: Tokyo.

SNOWDEN, LYNNE, sociologist, educator; BS in Human Resources, U. Del., Newark, 1985, MA in Sociology, 1987, PhD in Sociology, 1990. Vis. prof. Franklin and Marshall U., Lancaster, Pa.; prof. West Chester U., U. N.C., Wilmington. Co-author: Collective Violence, 2000; editor: Terrorism: Readings, Research and Realities, 2004. Mem.: SCJA (bd. dirs. 2000—07), NC Criminal Justice Assn. (chmn. awards 1994—2007, Pres. award 2005). Office: Dept Sociology and Criminal Justice Univ NC Wilmington Wilmington NC 28403-5978 Office Phone: 910-962-3838. Office Fax: 910-962-5978. Business E-Mail: snowdenl@uncw.edu.

SNOWDEN, RUTH O'DELL GILLESPIE, artist; b. Gary, W.Va., Apr. 16, 1926; d. Haynes Thornton and Blanche Beaula (Boling) Gillespie; m. Eugene Louis Snowden, Dec. 21, 1946; children: Wanda Snowden Ballard, Eugene III, Ronald, Marian Snowden Warren, Jeffry. RN, Natharith Coll., 1946; student Sch. Art, Transylvania U., 1983-84, U. Ky., 1985-89. RN. Painter, publicity chmn. Artists's Attic Inc., Lexington, Ky., 1988-89. Exhibited in group shows at U. Ky. Art Mus., Lexington, 1988, 5th Internat. Juried Exhibition Pastels, Nyack, N.Y., 1988, Small Paintings Nat., Ky. Highlands Mus., Ashland, 1988, The Appalachian Cen., U. Ky., 1988, Ft. Wayne (Ind.) Mus. Art, 1986, John Howard Sanden Nat. Artists Seminar, Washington, Nat. Artists' Seminar, Chgo., Huntington (W.Va.) Galleries, Nat. Nursing Art Exhibit, Meth. Med. Cen., Peoria, Ill., Chautauqua Art Assn. Galleries, N.Y., 1990, Central Bank gallery, Chatauqua, 1990, Pastel & Chisel Acad. Fine Arts, 1990, Opera House Gallery, 1990, Sacramento Fine Arts Ctr., 1990, Ariel Gallery, Soho, N.Y., 1990, 91, Sumi-e Soc. Am., Inc., 1993, Watercolor Soc. Ala., 1994; represented in the Director of American Portrait Artists, Am. Portrait Soc., Huntington Harbour, Calif., Audubon Artists Exhibit, N.Y.C., 2003, 2004; numerous local and nat. shows; in pvt. collections. Recipient Assn. Alliance award Am. Frame Co., 1993, Elizabeth Morris Genious award, 2002, Winsor Newton Merchandising award Summie Soc. Am., 2002. Mem. Oil Pastel Assn., Winchester Art Guild, Lexington Art League, Ky. Watercolor Assn. (Bluegrass regional dir. 1988, 89, 90, 91, 92), Ky. Guild Artists and Craftsmen, Inc., Northwest Pastel Soc., Degas Pastel Soc., Pen & Brush Soc. (Perfect Proportion award), Audubon Artists (juried mem.) Avocations: golf, bowling. Home and Studio: 2800 Old Boonesboro Rd Winchester KY 40391-8805 Office Phone: 859-744-6693.

SNOWDEN, III, FRANK MARTIN, history professor; b. Washington, June 22, 1946; s. Frank Martin Snowden, Jr. and Elaine Snowden; m. Margaret McClave, Sept. 4, 1999; children: Claire Brocklehurst, Jessica Lindsay Snowden. BA in Govt., Harvard U., Cambridge, Mass., 1968; BPhil in Politics, Oxford U., England, 1971, DPhil in Politics, 1975. Asst. prof. history Yale U., New Haven, 1975—78, prof. history, 1991—; lectr. history royal holloway coll. U. London, Egham, England, 1978—90, reader history, 1990—91. Author: (book) Violence and Great Estates in the South of Italy: Apulia 1900 - 1922, The Fascist Revolution in Tuscany, 1919-1922, Naples in the Time of Cholera, 1884 - 1911, The Conquest of Malaria: Italy, 1900 - 1962 (Helen and Howard Marraro prize Am. Hist. Assn., 2006); editor: Disastro! Disasters in Italy since 1860. Bd. dirs. Episc. Div. Sch., Cambridge, Mass., 2004—. Fellow, Am. Acad. Rome, 2003; scholar, Nat. Merit Scholarship Commn., 1964—68; Presdl. scholar, US, 1964, Marshall scholarship, Govt. UK, 1968—71. Mem.: Am. Hist. Assn., Phi Beta Kappa. Office: Dept History Yale Univ PO Box 208324 New Haven CT 06520-8324 Business E-Mail: frank.snowden@yale.edu.

SNOWE, OLYMPIA J., senator; b. Augusta, Maine, Feb. 21, 1947; d. George John and Georgia G. Bouchles; m. John McKernan. BA, U. Maine, 1969; LLD (hon.), U. Maine, Orono, 1981, Nasson Coll., 1981, U. Maine, Machias, 1982, Bowdoin Coll., 1982, Colby Coll., 1985; LHD (hon.), Thomas Coll., 1987; LLD (hon.), Suffolk U., 1994; DSc (hon.), Maine Maritime Acad., 1995; LLD (hon.), Colby Coll., 1996, U. New England, 1996; degree (hon.), Harvard U., 1997; LLD (hon.), Bates Coll., 1998. Businesswoman; mem. Maine Ho. of Reps., 1973-76, Maine Senate, 1976-78, 96th-103d Congresses from 2d Maine Dist., 1979-94, mem. budget com., foreign affairs com., com. on aging, 1979-94; co-chair Congl. Caucus for Women's Issues, 1983-94; U.S. senator from Maine, 1995—. Mem. Senate com. armed svcs., 1997-2001, chair, seapower subcom., Senate com. on commerce, sci. and transp., 1995—, chair, oceans and fisheries subcom., Senate Budget com., 1995—, Senate com. small business, 1995—, Senate com. Fgn. Rels., 1995-97; counsel to asst. majority leader, 1997—, House Budget com., 1991-95, House Fgn. Affairs com., 1979-95, House Aging com. 1979-95, Congl. Caucus on Women's Issues 1979-84, co-chair 1983-95; dep. Repub. Whip, 1984-95; dep. Whip, 1996-97; corporator Mechanics Savs. Bank. Recipient Homeric award for adv. of human rights Chian Fedn., 1999, award for "Excelling in Standing up for Choice" Women's Campaign Fund, 1999, Spirit of Enterprise award U.S. Chamber of Commerce, 1997, 99, Woman of Yr. award Glamour Mag., 1998, David and Sherry Huber award for leadership on family planning, women's health issues, Family Planning Assn. of ME, 1998, Golden Bulldog award Watchdogs of the Treasury, Inc., Wash., 1994, 96, 98, Guardian of Small Business award Nat. Fedn. Indep. Bus., Wash., 1994, 96, 98, Responsible Choices award Planned Parenthood of Am., 1998, Spl. honor Nat. Assn. Devel. Orgns., 1998, Disting. Pub. Svc. award Am. Legion, Wash., 1998, Neil W. Allen award Greater Portland Chamber of Commerce, 1997, Legis. award for outstanding svc. to schs. and pub. librs., White Ho. Conf. on Libr. and Info. Svcs. Task Force, Wash., 1997, Pub. Leadership award, Nat. Breast Cancer Coalition, 1997, Magnificent Seven award Bus. & Profl. Women/USA, Wash., 1997, Deborah Morton award Westbrook Coll., Portland, ME, 1997, Golden Gavel award U.S. Senate Leadership, Wash., 1996, Nat. Osteoporosis Assn. award for leadership, Wash., 1996, award for leadership U.S. Distance Learning Assn., Crystal City, Va., 1996, award for leadership United Hellenic Am. Cong., 1995, William H. Natcher Disting. Svc. award Com. for Edn. Funding, 1995, Pub. Svc. award Am. Coll. Obstetricians and Gynecologists, 1995, Nat. Security Leadership award Am. Security Coun., Wash., 1994, Thomas Jefferson award Nat. Am. Wholesale Grocers Assn./Internat. Foodsvc. Distbrs. Assn., 1994, Grace Caucus award Citizens Against Govt. Waste, 1994, Sound Dollar award Free Cong. Found., 1994, Appreciation award Agrl. Stblzn. and Conservation Com. Somerset County chpt., Lifetime Achievement award Am. Hellenic Inst., 1994, Golden Heart award Assn. for Children for Enforcement of Support, ME chpt., 1993, Am. Social Health Assn. award on behalf of women's health issues, 1993, Medal of St. Andrew presented by His All Holiness Dimitrios Ecumenical Patriarch of Constantinople, Wash., 1990, Congrl. Waste Watchers award Coalition to Reform the Davis-Bacon Act, 1990; named to "CQ 50" Congrl. Quarterly Mag., Wash., 1999, Maine Women's Hall of Fame, 1999, Washingtonian Mag. 100 Most Powerful Women, 1997, All Maine Women Honor Soc. U. Maine, 1996, Deficit Reduction Honor Roll Concord Coalition, 1994, Honor Roll for dairy farmer support Associated Milk Prodrs., 1993; named Taxpayer's Hero for preventing govt. waste Citizens Against Govt. Waste, 1997, No Nonsense Am. Women, No Nonsense Coun. on Women's Issues, 1995, Congresswoman of Yr. Nat. Assn. for Transp. Alternatives, 1986; honored by Nat. Coalition for Osteoporosis and Related Bone Diseases, 1999, Edn. and Libr. Networks Coalition, 1997, Am. Assn. Univ. Pres., 1996, Pub. Policy Com. for Hellenic-Am. Women, 1995, Nat. Vietnam Vet. Coalition, 1994; named one of most powerful women, Forbes mag., 2005. Mem.: Philoptochos Soc. Republican. Greek Orthodox. Office: US Senate 154 Russell Senate Bldg Washington DC 20510-1903 E-mail: olympia@snowe.senate.gov. *

SNOWISS, ALVIN L., lawyer; b. Lock Haven, Pa., June 16, 1930; s. Benjamin and Lillian (Kalin) S.; m. Jean Yarnell, Mar. 16, 1973. BA, U. Pa., Phila., 1952, JD, 1955; degree (hon.), Pa. State U., 1998. Bar: Pa. 1956, U.S. Dist. Ct. (mid. dist.) Pa. 1958, U.S. Supreme Ct. 1972. Pvt. practice, Lock Haven, 1955-61; ptnr. Lugg & Snowiss, Lock Haven, 1961—74, Lugg, Snowiss, Steinberg & Faulkner, Lock Haven, 1974-86, Snowiss, Steinberg & Faulkner LLP, Lock Haven, 1987—. Solicitor Clinton County, Lock Haven, 1964-72. Chmn. bd. Lock Haven Hosp. 1986-92, pres., 1982-86; bd. govs. Clinton County Cmty. Found., Lock Haven, 1970-97; chmn. adv. bd. Palmer Mus. Art, State College; v.p. bd. trustees Ross Libr., Lock Haven, 1963-86; mem. exec. com. Pa. Rep. Com., Harrisburg, 1974-80; state committeeman Clinton County Rep. Com., 1967-80. Fellow Am. Coll. Trust and Estate Counsel, Am. Bar Found., Pa. Bar Found. (founding, bd. dirs. 1984-95); mem. Pa. Bar Assn. (zone del. 1976-82, zone gov. 1983-86, treas. 1987-90), Clinton County Bar Assn. (pres. 1975-76), Kiwanis (pres. Lock Haven 1966-67). Republican. Avocations: art history, golf. Home: 414 W Main St Lock Haven PA 17745-1107 Office: 333 N Vesper St Lock Haven PA 17745-1342 Office Phone: 570-748-2961. Personal E-mail: ajsnow16@aol.com.

SNOW-SMITH, JOANNE INLOES, art history educator; b. Balt. d. Henry Williams and Elsie Orrick (Bagley) Snow; m. Robert Porter Smith (dec.); children: Joanne Tyndale Darby, Henry Webster Smith, III (dec.), Constance Elizabeth Bagley, Cynthia Porter Bloom, Robert Porter Smith, Jr.; m. Robert Edward Willstadter (dec.) BA, Goucher Coll.; MA, U. Ariz., 1968; PhD, UCLA, 1976. Prof. Italian Renaissance art history U. Wash., Seattle, 1981—. Program dir. of art history U. Wash. Rome Ctr. in Palazzo Pio, Rome, 1998, 2000, 2002. Author: (book) The Salvator Mundi of Leonardo da Vinci, 1982 (Internat. award 1983), The Primavera of Sandro Botticelli: A Neoplatonic Interpretaion, 1993; contbr. numerous articles to profl. jours. Recipient Rsch. Professorship to study in Oxford and London, U. Wash. Grad. Sch., 1986. Mem. Nat. Soc. Colonial Dames of Am., Renaissance Soc. of Am., Leonardo Soc./U. London, Coll. Art Assn., Seattle Art Mus., Met. Mus. Art, Ashmolean Mus. (Oxford, Eng.). Home: 1414 Shenandoah Dr E Seattle WA 98112-3730 Office: Univ Wash PO Box 353440 Seattle WA 98195-3440 E-mail: jsnowsmi@u.washington.edu.

SNYDER, ALAN CARHART, finance company executive; b. NYC, May 25, 1946; s. John I. and Elfrida (Bendix) S.; m. Mary Burgoyne, Feb. 9, 1974. BS, BA, Georgetown U., 1968; MBA, Harvard U., 1973. Cons. Reynolds Securities, NYC, 1972-73; exec. v.p. Dean Witter Reynolds, NYC, 1975-85; sole proprietor Shinnecock Ptnrs., NYC, 1985-89, mng. ptnr., 1989—; pres., chief oper. officer, bd. dirs. First Exec. Corp., LA, 1990-91; COO, Exec. Life Ins. Co., LA, 1991-93; CEO, Aurora Nat. Life Assurance Co., LA, 1993-94, cons., 1994-95; mng. ptnr. Shinnecock Group L.L.C., LA, 1994—; chmn., CEO, pres. Answer Fin. Inc., LA, 1997—2006. Baker scholar Harvard Bus. Sch., 1973.

SNYDER, ALLEN ROGER, lawyer; b. Washington, Jan. 26, 1946; s. Henry and Sylvia (Oxenburg) S.; m. Susan Port, Aug. 10, 1969; children: Joanna, Carolyn. BA with distinction, George Washington U., 1967; JD magna cum laude, Harvard U., 1971. Bar: D.C. 1973, U.S. Dist. Ct. D.C., Md., U.S. Ct. Appeals (D.C., 4th, 5th, 6th, 8th, 11th cirs.), U.S. Supreme Ct. Temp. assoc. Williams, Connolly & Califano, Washington, 1971; law clk. to assoc. justice J. Harlan U.S. Supreme Ct., 1971, law clk. to assoc. justice W. Rehnquist, 1972; assoc. Hogan & Hartson, Washington, 1972-78, ptnr., 1979—2001; of counsel, 2001—. Mem., then chmn. D.C. Cir. Commn. on Admissions and Grievances, 1984-90, D.C. Ct. Appeals Bd. Profl. Responsibility, 1978-84;mem. D.C. Cir. Adv. Com. on Procedures, 1986-92; mem. com. on pro se litigation U.S. Dist. Ct., 1991-2001. Bd. dirs. Jewish Found. Group Homes, Rockville, Md., 1982-86. Served with USAR, 1968-74. Fellow Am. Acad. of Appellate Lawyers; mem. D.C. Bar Unified (chmn. steering com. div. cts., lawyers and adminstrn. justice 1974-77, long range planning com. 1976, bd. govs. 1977-78), Washington Coun. Lawyers (bd. dirs. 1976-91), Am. Psychiat. Assn. (exec. sec. com. jud. action 1974-77). Office: Hogan & Hartson 555 13th St NW Ste 800E Washington DC 20004-1161 E-mail: ARSnyder@HHLaw.com.

SNYDER, ARNOLD LEE, JR., retired military officer, research director; b. Washington, Oct. 12, 1937; s. Arnold Lee and Frances May (Humbert) S; m. Patricia Dorine Ward, July 6, 1963; children: Heinrick Jason, Sonya Doreen, Ross Nansen. BCE, George Washington U., 1960; MS, U. Colo., 1966; PhD, U. Alaska, 1972. Commd. 2d lt. USAF, 1960; advanced through grades to col., 1981; chief space environ. support sys. devel. sect. Air Force Global Weather Central, Offutt AFB, Nebr., 1972-76; chief ionospheric dynamics br. Geophysics Lab., Hanscom AFB, Mass., 1976-80; test dir. CONUS OTH-B radar system, Columbia Falls AFS, Maine, 1980-81, program dir. Hanscom AFB, 1981-85; dir. Office of Tech. Support, 1985-87; tech. dir. U. Lowell Ctr. Atmospheric Rsch., 1987-89; with The Mitre Corp., 1989-96; pvt. practice, 1996—. Adj. prof. U. Lowell, 1987-89. Contbr. articles to sci. jours. Recipient Legion of Merit, Meritorious Svc. medal with one oak leaf cluster, Commendation medal USAF, R&D award, 1981; Def. Value Engring. award, 1984; Henry Harding scholar, 1955-56. Mem. Am. Geophys. Union, Am. Meteorol. Soc., Air Force Assn., Sigma Xi. Home and Office: PO Box 530 Stockton Springs ME 04981 Home Phone: 207-567-3137. Personal E-mail: palsnyder@aol.com.

SNYDER, ARTHUR, publishing executive; b. Valley Stream, NY, Feb. 6, 1925; s. Arthur and Kathryn (Staubitzer) Snyder; m. Betty Lain Harper, July 8, 1950; children: Susan, Arthur, Betsy, Jack, Heidi, Bonnie. B in Metall. Engring., Cornell U., 1950, MBA, 1952. Mfg. engr. Norton Co., Worcester, Mass., 1952-56, chief acct., 1956-58, asst. contr., 1958-59, mgr. data processing, 1959-61, contr., 1961-65; exec. v.p. A.M. Best Co., Oldwick, NJ, 1965-67, pres., 1968—, chmn., 1971—. Author: (book) Principles of Inventory Control and Managing Capital Expenditures. 1st lt. AUS, 1942—45. Decorated Battlefield Commn., Bronze Star with oak leaf cluster, Purple Heart. Mem.: U.S. Srs. Golf Assn., Cornell Soc. Engrs., Fin. Execs. Inst., Lyford Cay Club (Nassau, Bahamas), Baltusrol Golf Club (Springfield, NJ). Presbyterian. Home: 111 Lloyd Rd Bernardsville NJ 07924-1710 Office: A M Best Company Inc Ambest Rd Oldwick NJ 08858 Office Phone: 908-439-3316. Business E-Mail: snydera2@ambest.com.

SNYDER, ARTHUR E., academic administrator; m. Camille Snyder; children: Melanie, Chris. BA, MBA, Barry U.; EdD, Wilmington Coll. Gen. mgr. AT&T, Fort Lauderdale, Fla.; exec. v.p., chief oper. officer Ensec, Inc., Miami, Fla., Sao Paulo, Brazil; chmn. Dept. Mktg., dean profl./grad. studies Lynn U., Boca Raton, Fla., 1992—2001; dean Tabor Sch. Bus., Dwayne O. Andreas chair exec. mgmt. Millikin U., Decatur, Ill., 2001—03; pres. Indiana Tech., Fort Wayne, 2003—. Chmn. Sister's of Providence Mission Adv. Bd., Downtown Ednl. Partnership. Mem.: Fort Wayne Bus. Forum. Office: Indiana Tech 1600 E Washington Blvd Fort Wayne IN 46803 Office Phone: 260-422-5561.

SNYDER, ARTHUR KRESS, lawyer, restaurant owner; b. LA, Nov. 10, 1932; s. Arthur and Ella Ruth Snyder; m. Mary Frances Neely, Mar. 5, 1953 (div.); children: Neely Arthur, Miles John; m. Michele Maggie Noval, May 14, 1973 (div.); 1 child, Erin-Marisol; m. Delia Wu, Apr. 18, 1981. BA, Pepperdine U., Malibu, Calif., 1953; JD, U. So. Calif., 1958; LLD, Union U., Jackson, Tenn., 1980. Bar: Calif. 1960, US Supreme Ct. 1982, US Ct. Appeals (fed. cir.). Pvt. practice, LA, 1960-67; founder, pres. Arthur K. Snyder Law Corp., LA, 1981-94; pres. Snyder & Assoc., Atty., LA, 1994—. CFO Royal Star Nev., Restaurateurs, 1999—2006; CEO Marisol LLC Restaurateurs Don the Beachcomber Enterprises, 2002—; past instr. LA City Sch., 1965—85. Mem. City Coun., LA, 1967—85. Served to capt. USMC, Korea. Decorated La Tizona de El Cid Compeador Spain, medal Legion of Honor Mex., Hawa Chao Zee You medal China, others. Master: Chaine des Rotisseurs US; mem.: ATLA, ABA, Fed. Cir. Bar Assn., Calif. Bar Assn., LA County Bar Assn., Assn. Roasters of US (table waster), World Film Inst. (chmn. bd. dirs. 1997—2002), Masons. Baptist. Home and Office: Las Vegas Country Club 723 Oakmont Ave #3413 Las Vegas NV 89109 Business E-Mail: artsnyder@alumni.usc.edu.

SNYDER, BARBARA K., pediatrician, educator; MD, George Washington U., 1979. Diplomate in pediatrics and adolescent medicine Am. Bd. Pediatrics. Intern Children's Nat. Med. Ctr., Washington, 1979—80, resident in pediatrics, 1980—82; fellow in adolescent medicine U. Rochester (N.Y.) Sch. Medicine, 1986—88; chief divsn. adolescent medicine, dept. pediatrics Robert Wood Johnson Med. Sch., New Brunswick, NJ, 1990—, assoc. prof., 1994—, dir. eating disorders program, adolescent medicine program, 1990—. Fellow: Am. Soc. Pediats., Soc. Adolescent Medicine; mem.: Acad. for Eating Disorders, N. Am. Soc. for Pediat. and Adolescent Geynecology. Office: U Medicine and Dentistry NJ-Robert Wood Johnson Med Sch Dept Pediats New Brunswick NJ 08903-0019 Office Phone: 732-235-7896.

SNYDER, BARBARA LOU, retired educational association administrator; b. Denison, Iowa, July 13, 1935; d. Alfred Howard and Elsie May Bowen; children: Steven, Terry, Richard, Jonathan. BA, Simpson Coll., 1957; MEd, Mid. Tenn. State U., 1975. Cert. insurance agent TN. Tchr. Huntsville City Schs., Huntsville, Ala., 1966—68, Huntsville Achiev. Sch., 1968—70; resource tchr. Tullahoma City Schs., Tullahoma, Tenn., 1971—95; ins. agent Nat. Health Administr., 1996—2004; lobbyist Tenn. Retired Tchrs. Assn., Nashville, 2001—, assoc. exec. dir. to exec. dir., 2003—04. Legislative chair Tenn Retired Tchrs. Assn., Nashville, 1995—2001. Treas. Tenn. Federation Democratic Women, Nashville, 1997—99, cooresponding sec., 1995—97; convention co-chair 41st Annual Tenn. Federation Democratic Women, Manchester, Tenn., 1998; recording sec. Tenn. Federation Democratic Women, Nashville, 1999—2001; mem. Coffee County Dem. Exec. Com., 1992—, sec., 1998—. Named First Hometown Hero, Tullahoma News, 2001, Mrs. Democrat, Highland Rim Democratic Club, 2000. Mem.: Coffee County Retired Tchrs., Tenn. Retired Tchrs. Assn., Nat. Retired Tchrs. Assn. Democrat. Unitarian. Avocations: reading, gardening, walking, politics. Home: 320 E Fort St Tullahoma TN 37388 Office: Tenn Retired Tchrs Assn 801 Second Ave N Nashville TN 37201 Office Phone: 615-242-8392 x 330. Personal E-mail: bsnyder@cafes.net.

SNYDER, BARBARA ROOK, academic administrator; b. July 23, 1955; BA, Ohio State U., 1976; JD, U. Chgo., 1980. Bar: Ill. 1980. Law clk. for Judge Luther M. Swygert U.S. Ct. Appeals for the Seventh Cir.; with Sidley & Austin, Chgo.; joined law faculty Case Western Res. U., 1983, Ohio State U., Columbus, 1988, assoc. dean for acad. affairs, 2000—01, vice provost for acad. policy and human resources, 2001—03, interim provost, 2003—04, exec. v.p., provost, 2004—07, Joanne W. Murphy/Class of 1965 professorship Moritz Coll. Law; pres. Case Western Reserve U., Cleve., 2007—. Office: Case Western Reserve U Office of Pres 10900 Euclid Ave Cleveland OH 44106-7001 E-mail: barbara.snyder@case.edu. *

SNYDER, BURTON HAROLD, lawyer; b. York, Pa., Nov. 7, 1947; m. Carol A. Oyler. BA in math., Lehigh U., 1969; JD, Harvard U., 1975. Bar: Pa. 1975. Staff counsel Hershey Foods Corp., Hershey, Pa., 1979—82, sr. counsel, 1982—85, ops. dir., gen mgr. for Far East and Middle East Hershey Internat. Ltd., 1985—89, asst. gen. counsel, 1993—2000, v.p., asst. gen. counsel, 2000—02, sr. v.p. pub affairs, gen. counsel, sec., 2002, sr. v.p. internat., gen. counsel, sec., 2002—03, sr. v.p., gen. counsel, sec., 2003—; ptnr. McNees, Wallace & Nurick, Harrisburg, Pa., 1989—93. Mem.: Assn. of Corp. Counsel, ABA. Office: The Hershey Co 100 Crystal A Dr Hershey PA 17033-0810 *

SNYDER, CARL, information technology executive; BS, We. Ill. Univ., 1976. Dir., Global IT Infrastructure & Ops. Tellabs, Naperville, Ill., dir., IT Infrastructure & Ops., 2006—. Named one of Top 25 Chief Tech. Officers, InfoWorld mag., 2007. Office: Tellabs One Tellabs Ctr 1415 W Diehl Rd Naperville IL 60563 Office Phone: 630-798-8800. Office Fax: 630-798-2000.

SNYDER, CAROLINE JEAN, secondary school educator; b. Chgo., Nov. 28, 1964; d. Thomas Allen Crimmins and Dorothy Louise Voss; m. Ronald Snyder, Jan. 27, 1961; 1 child, Clare Rose. Degree, Ill. State U., Normal, 1986. Paralegal Jenner & Block, Chgo., 1992—2002; tchr. Hillcrest HS, Country Club Hills, Ill., 2002—. Home: 7410 160th Pl Tinley Park IL 60477 Office: Hillcrest HS 17401 S Pulaski Rd Country Club Hills IL 60478 Home Phone: 708-429-3484; Office Phone: 708-799-7000. Office Fax: 708-799-0402. Business E-Mail: csnyder@bhsd228.com.

SNYDER, CAROLYN ANN, education educator, librarian, director; b. Elgin, Nebr., Nov. 5, 1942; d. Ralph and Florence Wagner. Student, Nebr. Wesleyan U., 1960—61; BS cum laude, Kearney State Coll., 1964; MS in Librarianship, U. Denver, 1965. Asst. libr. sci. and tech. U. Nebr., Lincoln, 1965—67, asst. pub. svc. libr., 1967—68, 1970—73; from pers. libr. to interim devel. officer Ind. U. Librs., Bloomington, 1973—89, interim dean, 1989—91; adminstrv. army libr. Spl. Svcs. Agy., Europe, 1968—70; dean libr. affairs So. Ill. U., Carbondale, 1991—2000, prof. libr. affairs, 2000—06, dir. found. rels., 2000—06. Team leader Midwest Univs. Consortium for Internat. Activities-World Bank IX project to develop libr. sys. and implement automation U. Indonesia, Jakarta, 1984-86; libr. devel. cons. Inst. Tech. MARA/Midwest Univs. Consortium for Internat. Activities Program in Malaysia, 1985; ofcl. rep. EDUCAUSE, 1996-2000; mem. working group on scholarly comm. Nat. Commn. on Librs. and Info. Sci., 1998-2000. Editor: Library and Other Academic Support Services for Distance Learning, 1997; contbr. chpt. to book and articles to profl. jours. Active Carbondale Pub. Libr. Friends, 1991-, Morris Libr. Friends, 1991—; br. pres. AAUW, Carbondale, 2004-05; bd. dirs. Carbondale Cmty. Arts Bd., 2006-, Carbondale Info. and Telecomm. Commn., 2006-. Cooperative Rsch. grant Coun. on Libr. Resources, Washington, 1984. Mem. ALA (councilor 1985-89, Bogle Internat. Travel award 1988, H.W. Wilson Libr. Staff devel. grant 1981), Libr. Adminstrn./Mgmt. Assn. (pres. 1981-82, numerous others), Com. on Instnl. Coop./Resource Sharing (chair 1987-91), Coalition for Networked Info. (So. Ill. U. at Carbondale rep. 1991-00), Coun. Dirs. State Univ. Librs. in Ill. (chair 1992-93, 99-00), Coun. on Libr. and Info. Resources Digital Leadership Inst. Steering Com. (Assn. Rsch. Librs. rep. 1998-00), Ill. Assn. Coll. and Rsch. Librs. (chair Ill. Bd. Higher Edn. liaison com. 1993-94), Ill. Network (bd. dirs.), Ind. Libr. Assn. (chair coll./univ. divsn. 1982-83), U.S. Grant Assn. (bd. dirs. 1992—), Ill. Libr. Computer Sys. Orgn. (policy coun. 1992-95, 96-00), Nat. Assn. State Univs. and Land-Grant Colls. (commn. on info. tech. and its distance learning and libr. bds. 1994-96), NetIllinois (bd. dirs. 1994-96), OCLC Users Coun. (elected rep. 1995-98), Big 12 Plus Libr. Consortium (chair 1997-98), Nat. Commn. on Librs. and Info. Sci. Working Group on Scholarly Comm., Assn. Rsch. Libr. (vis. program officer 2000-01). Avocations: antiques, theater, movies, reading. Office: So Ill U Ctrl Devel Carbondale IL 62901-6632 Home Phone: 618-457-3689; Office Phone: 618-453-1447.

SNYDER, CHARLES AUBREY, lawyer; b. Bastrop, La., June 19, 1941; s. David and Shirley Blossom (Haas) S.; m. Sharon Rae Veta, Aug. 29, 1963; children: David Veta, Shelby Haas, Claire Frances. BBA, Tulane U., 1963; JD, La. State U., 1966. Bar: La. 1966. Assoc. firm. Milling Benson Woodward, LLP and predecessors, New Orleans, 1966-69, ptnr., 1969—. Bd. dirs. Terre aux Boeufs Land Corp., Kemper and Leila Williams Found., v.p., 2004-07, pres., 2007—. Bd. dirs. New Orleans Speech and Hearing Ctr., pres., 1978-80; bd. dirs. City Pk. Commn., 1991-98, pres., 1995, dir. emeritus, 1999—; bd. dirs. New Orleans Mus. Art, 1996-2002, 04—, v.p., 1998-99, 2007—m sec., 1999-2000. Fellow Am. Bar Found., La. Bar Found.; mem. ABA, La. Bar Assn. (chmn. sect. on corp. and bus. law 1982-83), New Orleans Bar Assn., Am. Law Inst., La. Law Inst. (coun. 2000—), Plimsoll Club, Bienville Club, Beta Gamma Sigma. Home: 74724 River Rd Covington LA 70435-2222 Office Phone: 504-569-7230. E-mail: csnyder@millinglaw.com.

SNYDER, CHARLES ROYCE, sociologist, educator; b. Haverford, Pa., Dec. 28, 1924; BA, Yale U., 1945, MA, 1949, PhD, 1954. Mem. staff Ctr. Alcohol Studies Yale U., 1950-60, asst. prof. sociology, 1956-60; prof. sociology So. Ill. U., Carbondale, 1960-85, chmn. dept., 1964-75, 81-85, prof. emeritus, 1985—. Vis. prof. human genetics Sackler Sch. Medicine, Tel Aviv U., 1980; cons. behavioral scis. tng. com. Nat. Inst. Gen. Med. Scis., NIH, 1962-64; mem. planning com., chmn. program 28th Internat. Congress Alcohol and Alcoholism, 1964. Author: Alcohol and the Jews, 1958; editor: (with D.J. Pittman) Society, Culture and Drinking Patterns, 1962; mem. editl. bd. Quar. Jour. Studies on Alcohol, 1957-83; assoc. editor Sociol. Quar., 1960-63. Mem. theol. commn. United Ch. of Christ, 1964-71; bd. dirs. Ill. Stewardship Alliance, 1990-95. With USNR, WWII. Fellow Am. Sociol. Assn.; mem. Soc. Study Social Problems (v.p. 1963-64, rep. to council Am. Sociol. Assn. 1964-66), Midwest Sociol. Soc. (bd. dirs. 1970-71), AAUP. Home: Apt 1606 8680 E Alameda Ave Denver CO 80247

SNYDER, CLAIR ALLISON, banker; b. Reading, Pa., June 12, 1921; s. Augustus M. and Estella G. (Bright) S.; m. Jean Doris George, June 27, 1948 (dec. Feb. 1997); children: Joan Marie Snyder Ferguson, Jerry George. Student, W.Va. U., 1943-44, U. Mich., 1944-45. With Meridian Bancorp, Inc. and Meridian Bank, Reading, 1938-43, 46-88, exec. v.p., gen. banking, 1973-78, exec. v.p., chmn. credit policy com., 1978-86; pvt. practice fin. cons. Snyder Svcs. Co., Reading, 1987—98. Asst. sec. Bi-Products, Inc., Fairfax, Va. Bd. dirs. Pa. divsn. Am. Cancer Soc., 1965-87, chmn. bd. dirs., 1975-77; chmn. Hope Lodge Com.; chmn. Property Mgmt. Com. With U.S. Army, 1943-46. Recipient Luther Halsey Gulick award Camp Fire Girls, 1966; div. Bronze medal Am. Cancer Soc., also Sword of Hope award Mem. Internat. Soc. for Philosophic Inquiry, Am. Bankers Assn. (cert.), Pa. Bankers Assn. (group chmn. 1972-73), Robert Morris Assocs. (pres. 1972-73), Am. Legion (post comdr. 1948-49), Old Point Golf and Country Club, Moselem Springs Golf Club, Belvedere Plantation Golf and Country Club. Republican. United Church Of Christ. also: 616 Sawgrass Rd Olde Point Hampstead NC 28443 Home: 2000 Cambridge Ave Apt 232 Reading PA 19610-2734 E-mail: rbdynsca@aol.com. *My life has been dedicated to personal achievement, but always with the knowledge that mankind's progress can only occur if each of us is willing to commit some of our efforts and resources to the future.*

SNYDER, DANIEL, professional sports team and communications executive; b. Nov. 23, 1964; m. Tanya Snyder. Founder, chmn., CEO Snyder Communications, Inc. (sold to Havas), 1985—2000; chmn. bd., owner Washington Redskins, 1999—; non-exec. chmn. Six Flags Inc., 2005—; founder, investor Red Zone LLC, 2005—. Bd. dirs. McLeod USA, Ventiv Health; mem., broadcast com. and ventures com. NFL. Bd. dirs. Ctr. for Missing and Exploited Children, Parents in Charge; exec. leadership cabinet Martin Luther King, Jr. Nat. Meml. Found. Project; bd. dirs. Wash. Children's Nat. Med. Ctr.; founder Wash. Redskins Leadership Coun. Mem.: Wash. Bd. Trade, Bus. Executives for Nat. Security. Office: c/o Washington Redskins 21300 Redskin Park Rd Ashburn VA 20147

SNYDER, DARIN W., lawyer; b. Kansas City, Mo., 1963; BA cum laude, Georgetown U., 1985; JD cum laude, U. Chgo., 1988. Bar: Calif. 1988, US Dist. Ct., (Ctrl, No., Ea., and So. Dists. of Calif.), US Ct. of Appeals (Ninth and Fed. Circuits), US Ct. Veterans Appeals. Head O'Melveny & Myers LLP, San Francisco, co-chair patent and tech. litig. practice group, head intellectual property and tech. dept. No. Calif. Divsn. LA. Dir. Bar Assn. San Francisco, Legal Aid Soc. Employment Law Ctr. Bradley Law & Government Fellow, 1987—88. Mem.: Am. Intellectual Property Law Assn., Santa Clara County Bar Assn., ABA (former co-chair intellectual property com., co-chair trade secrets subcommittee litig. sect. 1997—98). Office: O'Melveny & Myers LLP Embarcadero Ctr West 275 Battery St San Francisco CA 94111-3305 Office Phone: 415-984-8846. Office Fax: 415-984-8701. Business E-Mail: dsnyder@omm.com.

SNYDER, DAVID RICHARD, lawyer; b. Kalamazoo, Oct. 9, 1949; s. Richard E. and Margaret L. (Vanderplough) S.; m. Phyllis Alford, Aug. 14, 1971; children: Jason Richard, Carrie Lynn. BA with high honors, Mich. State U., East Lansing, 1971; JD with distinction, Cornell U., Ithaca, NY, 1974. Bar: Calif. 1974. Assoc. Jenkins & Perry, San Diego, 1974-77, ptnr., 1978-83, Aylward, Kintz & Stiska, San Diego, 1983-86, Luce, Forward, Hamilton & Scripps, San Diego, 1986-93, Pillsbury Madison & Sutro LLP, San Diego, 1993—2005; mng. bd. Pillsbury Winthrop LLP, San Diego, 1999—2005, vice chmn., 2004—05; chair bus. dept., ptnr., corp. & securities practice, mem. mng. bd. Pillsbury Winthrop Shaw Pittman LLP, San Diego, 2005—. V.p., dir. San Diego Venture Group, 1989-91; adj. prof. Calif. Western Sch. Law, San Diego, 1982-84; lectr. Calif. Continuing Edn. of Bar, 1983—. Co-author: Drafting Legal Instruments, 1982; editor Cornell Law Rev., 1973-74. Bd. dirs. Boys Club Chula Vista, Calif., 1979-83, San Diego Symphony Orch. Assn., 2006-; pres. Corpus Christi Parish Coun., Bonita, Calif., 1988-90; trustee Children's Hosp. Found., San Diego, 1988-2004, chmn., 1990-92. Mem.: ABA (fed. securities law com. 1987—, chmn. subcom. on ann. rev. fed. securities regulation, dir. corp. dirs. forum), Corp. Dirs. Forum (bd. dirs. 2001—), San Diego County Bar Assn., State Bar Calif., Am. Electronics Assn. (bd. dirs., mem. exec. com. San Diego chpt. 1991—93), Order of Coif, Phi Beta Kappa. Republican. Roman Catholic. Office: Pillsbury Winthrop Shaw Pittman LLP 501 W Broadway Ste 1100 San Diego CA 92101-8298 Office Phone: 619-544-3369. Office Fax: 619-236-1995. Business E-Mail: dave.snyder@pillsburylaw.com.

SNYDER, DAVID WARREN, cardiologist; b. Salt Lake City, Mar. 15, 1949; s. Christopher and Helen (Warren) S.; m. Catherine Ann Turnbull, July 23, 1971; two children. BA, Princeton U., 1971; MD, Duke U., 1975. Diplomate Am. Bd. Internal Medicine. Cardiologist Ochsner Clinic, New Orleans, 1981-89, Cardiol. Cons. La., Metairie, 1989—. Named One of top Doctors La., La. Life mag., 2007. Fellow Am. Coll. Caadiology; mem. Am. Heart Assn., N.Am. Soc. Pacing & Electrophysiology. Office: Cariology Cons La East Jefferson Gen Hosp 4200 Houma Blvd Metairie LA 70006 Office Phone: 504-454-4170. *

SNYDER, DONALD EDWARD, finance company executive; b. Rochester, NY, Nov. 10, 1928; s. Benjamin Orman and Arlien Henrietta (Wing) S.; m. Dorothy Edna Stanke, Oct. 16, 1954; children— Donald Edward, Anne Arlien Snyder Marone, Barbara Lynn Snyder Mitchell, Richard John Snyder. AB, Cornell U., 1950, JD, 1952; postgrad., Ind. U., 1962. Bar: N.Y. 1953. Pvt. practice law, 1953-56; with Eastman Savs. and Loan Assn., 1956-68, pres., 1970-75, chmn. bd., 1979-88; asst. to treas. Eastman Kodak Co., Rochester, 1968-70, gen. credit mgr., 1975-77, with Comptroller's div., 1977-78, asst. treas., 1978-79, treas., 1979-88; chmn. Eastman Kodak Credit Corp., 1985-88; chief exec. officer, chmn. bd., pres. Corp. Officers and Dirs. Assurance Ltd., Hamilton, Bermuda, 1990-93. Bd. dirs. Greater Rochester chpt. Epilepsy Found. Am., 1979-85, Allendale Mut. Ins. Co., 1983-92; bd. dirs. Luth. Ch.-Mo. Synod, 1983-95; vice chmn. bd., chmn. fin. com., mem., chmn. audit com., 1989-95; bd. dirs., mem. exec. com. ACE Ltd., 1985-90, EXEL Ltd., 1985-90, CODA Ltd., 1986-93; mem. investment rev. com. United Way of Greater Rochester, 1979-2000; trustee Seneca Zool. Soc., 1983-90. With USNR, 1946-48. Mem. N.Y. State Bar Assn., Monroe County Bar Assn., Rochester C. of C. (trustee 1980-86), Cornell Club (Rochester), Phi Kappa Tau (nat. fin. advisor, mem. nat. coun. 1988-95, treas., mem. exec. com. Phi Kappa Tau Found. 1991-2002). Home and Office: 14 Hidden Springs Dr Pittsford NY 14534-2897 also: 2700 N AIA Ste 705 Fort Pierce FL 34949

SNYDER, EDWARD ADAMS, dean, economics professor; b. Danville, Pa., July 3, 1953; s. Harry Coolidge and Fay (Adams) S.; m. Kimberly Marie Snyder; children: Alison Marie, Jeffrey Adams, Kevin James. Ba in Econs. and Govt., Colby Coll., 1975; M of Pub. Policy, U. Chgo., 1978, PhD in Econs., 1984. Staff economist Antitrust div. U.S. Dept. Justice, Washington, 1978—82; asst. prof. bus. econs. and pub. policy Sch. Bus. Adminstrn. U. Mich., Ann Arbor, 1982—90, assoc. prof. Sch. Bus. Adminstrn., 1990-94, prof. Sch. Bus. Adminstrn., 1994-98, chair bus. econ. and pub. policy, Sch. Bus. Adminstrn., 1992—95; dean Darden Bus. Sch. U. Va., Charlottesville, 1998—2001; dean U. Chgo. Grad. Sch. Bus., 2001—, prof., 2001—02, George Pratt Shultz prof. economics, 2002—. Rsch. fellow Office for Study of Pub. and Pvt. Instns., U. Mich.; cons. Antitrust div. U.S. Dept. Justice, Chgo., 1982-85, Fed. Home Loan Bank Bd., Washington, 1989; antitrust expert, 1985—; John M. Olin vis. assoc. prof. U. Chgo., 1991-92; dir. William Davidson Inst. Mich. Bus. Sch., 1992-95. Author: Crisis Resolution in the Thrift Industry, 1989; contbr. articles to econ. jours. and law revs., 1985-98. Avocations: foreign policy, sports, sailing. Office: U Chgo Grad Sch of Bus 5807 S Woodlawn Ave Chicago IL 60637 Office Phone: 773-702-1680. E-mail: tsnyder@chicagogsb.edu.

SNYDER, EVAN, cloning and stem cell company administrator, neuroscientist, educator; MD and PhD in Neuroscience, U. Pa., 1981. Resident in pediatrics and neurology Children's Hosp.-Boston; postdoctoral rsch. Harvard Med. Sch., instr. neurology, 1992—96, asst. prof. neurology, 1996—2003; prof., dir. stem cell and regeneration prog. Burnham Inst., La Jolla, Calif., 2003—. Contbr. articles in profl. jours. Office: Burnham Inst Mail Stop 7261 10901 N Torrey Pines Rd La Jolla CA 92037 Office Phone: 858-646-3158. Fax: 858-646-3199; Office Fax: 858-713-6273. Business E-Mail: esnyder@burnham.org. *

SNYDER, GEORGE EDWARD, lawyer; b. Battle Creek, Mich., Feb. 7, 1934; s. Leon R. and Edith (Dullabahn) S.; m. Mary Jane Belt, July 27, 1957 (div. Sept. 23, 1982); children: Sara Lynn, Elizabeth Jane; m. Claudia Gage Brooks, Feb. 25, 1984 BS, Mich. State U., 1957; JD, U. Mich., 1960. Bar: Mich. 1961, U.S. Dist. Ct. (we. and ea. dists.) Mich. 1961. With Gen. Electric Co., 1957-58; asso. firm Miller, Johnson, Snell & Commisky, Grand Rapids, 1960-62, Goodenough & Buesser, Detroit, 1962-66; partner firm Buesser, Buesser, Snyder & Blank, Detroit and Bloomfield Hills, 1966-85, Meyer, Kirk, Snyder & Lynch PLLC, Bloomfield Hills, 1985—. Chmn. bd. dirs. Bill Knapps Mich., Inc., 1998-2000. Chmn. E. Mich. Environ. Action Council, 1974-78; pub. mem. inland lakes and streams rev. com. Mich. Dept. Natural Resources, 1975-76. Served as 2d lt. AUS, 1957. Named one of Best Lawyers in Am., Woodward White, 1992—2007, Mich. Super Lawyers, Law and Politics, 2006—07. Fellow Am. Acad. Matrimonial Lawyers (pres. Mich. chpt. 1991-92), Am. Coll. Family Trial Lawyers, Am. Bar Found., Internat. Acad. Matrimonial Lawyers, Mich. Bar Found; mem. ABA, Am. Judicature Soc., Am. Arbitration Assn. (panel arbitrators), State Bar Mich. (chmn. family law com. 1968-72, mem. rep. assembly 1972-78, chmn. rules and calendar com. 1977-78, mem. family law sect. coun. 1973-76, environ. law sect. coun. 1980-85, prepaid legal svcs. com. 1973-82, com. on judicial selection 1974, com. on specialization 1976-82), Detroit Bar Assn. (chmn. family law com. 1966-68), Oakland County Bar Assn., Delta Upsilon (chmn. trustees, alumni chpt. dep. 1965-70), Tau Beta Pi, Pi Tau Sigma, Phi Eta Sigma. Detroit Athletic Club, Birmingham (Mich.) Athletic Club, Bloomfield Hills Country Club. Episcopalian. Home: 32965 Outland Trl Bingham Farms MI 48025-2555 Office: Meyer Kirk Snyder & Lynch PLLC Ste 100 100 W Long Lake Rd Bloomfield Hills MI 48304-2773 Home Phone: 248-540-1698; Office Phone: 248-647-5111. Business E-Mail: gsnyder@meyerkirk.com.

SNYDER, GRAYDON F., religion educator; b. Peru, Ind., Apr. 30, 1930; s. Clayton Fisher and Irene Elizabeth (Fisher) S.; m. Lois Hannah Horning, June 13, 1953; children: Jonathan Edvard, Anna Christine, Stephen Daniel. BA, Manchester Coll., 1951; MDiv, Bethany Theol. Sem., 1954; ThD, Princeton Theol. Sem., 1961. Asst. prof. Bibl. studies Bethany Theol. Sem., Chgo., 1959—65, prof. Oak Brook, Ill., 1965—79, dean, 1975—86,

Wieand prof. New Testament studies, 1979—88; acad. dean, prof. New Testament Chgo. Theol. Sem., 1986—90, prof. New Testament, 1990—96, adj. prof. New Testament, 1996—99. Mem. accrediting commn. Assn. Theol. Schs., 1976-82. Author: Ante Pacem, 1985, First Corinthians, 1992, Health and Medicine in the Anabaptist Tradition, 1995, Inculturation of the Jesus Tradition, 1999, Irish Jesus, Roman Jesus, 2002, Ante Pacem, rev. edit., 2003, The People are Holy, 2005; mem. editl. bd. Bibl. Rsch., 1965-95, Brethren Life and Thought, 1962-94. Mem. Bd. Edn. # 88, Elmhurst, Ill., 1970-73; chmn. bd. trustees Bethany Hosp., Chgo., 1979-92; del. governing bd. Nat. Coun. Chs., 1986-91. Fellow Westar Inst.; mem. Soc. Bibl. Lit., Chgo. Soc. Bibl. Rsch. (pres. 1969), Studiorum Novi Testamenti Societas. Mem. Ch. of The Brethren. Avocation: early christian art. Home: 5475 S Ridgewood Ct Chicago IL 60615-5314 E-mail: graydonsny@aol.com.

SNYDER, HENRY LEONARD, historian, educator, writer; b. Hayward, Calif., Nov. 3, 1929; s. Henry Runyon and Mary (Rosenberg) S.; m. Janette Marie Hannus, July 21, 1961; children: Michael Jesse, Christopher Henry, David Lyle. BA, U. Calif., Berkeley, 1951, MA, 1960, PhD, 1963. Sr. buyer Dohrmann Comml. Co., San Francisco, 1951—59; instr. to prof. U. Kans., Lawrence, 1963—78, assoc. dean to dean rsch. adminstrn., 1967—78; prof. history, dean arts and scis. La. State U., Baton Rouge, 1979—86; prof. history U. Calif., Riverside, 1986—; dir. Ctr. for Bibliog. Studies, 1989—; dean humanities and social scis. U. Calif., Riverside, 1986; vis. lectr. Bedford Coll., U. London, 1965—66; Fulbright lectr., rsch. scholar U. Hamburg, Germany, 1974; dir. English Short Title Catalogue for N.Am., 1978—. Editor: The Marlborough Godolphin Correspondence, 1975; co-editor: The Scottish Heritage, 1981. Pres. Baton Rouge Opera, 1981-83, Riverside Opera, 1987-90; pres. United Way, Lawrence, 1977; bd. dirs. Arts and Humanities Com., Baton Rouge, 1981-85; Sigmund, Martin, Heller Traveling fellow U. Calif.-Berkeley, 1962-63. Am. Council Learned Soc. sr. fellow, 1969-70 Fellow Royal Hist. Soc. Gt. Brit. Bibliog. Soc. London; mem. Am. Soc. 18th Century Studies (pres. 1980-81), Conf. Brit. Studies (exec. com. 1978-83), Am. Hist. Assn., Internat. Fed. Librs. (chair rarebooks and ms. sect. 1995—). Republican. Congregationalist. Home: 220 Trinity Ave Kensington CA 94708-1139 Office: U Calif Ctr For Bibliog Studies Riverside CA 92521-0154 Office Phone: 951-827-5841. Personal E-mail: hlsnyder@earthlink.net.

SNYDER, JAMES C., JR., lawyer, consumer products company executive; BA, Wake Forest Univ.; JD, George Washington Univ. Bar: Ga., DC, Pa. Ptnr. litigation practice King & Spalding, Atlanta, 1989—2001; corp. counsel Home Depot, Atlanta, 2001—04, v.p. litigation, 2004—06, v.p. litigation & risk mgmt., 2006—, v.p., sec., acting gen. counsel, 2007. Bd. dir. Spl. Olympics, Atlanta. Mem.: ABA, State Bar Ga. Office: Home Depot 2455 Paces Ferry Rd Atlanta GA 30339 *

SNYDER, JAMES EUGENE, JR., lawyer; b. Lexington, NC, June 30, 1945; s. James Eugene and Sarah Frances (Olive) S.; m. Sandra Joyce Craver, June 25, 1966; children: Susan Courtney Snyder Brown, Sandra Elizabeth Snyder Lancaster. Bar: N.C. 1970, U.S. Dist. Ct. (mid. dist.) N.C. 1971, U.S. Ct. Appeals 1978, U.S. Supreme Ct. 1978, U.S. Tax Ct. 1971, U.S. Dist. Ct. (ea. dist.) N.C. 2007. Ptnr. Leonard and Snyder, Lexington, 1970-80; pvt. practice Lexington, 1980—. Mem. N.C. Ho. of Reps., Raleigh, N.C., 1971. Author: (books) Snyder N.C. Corporation Law, 1991, 4th edit., 2003, Snyder N.C. Corporation Law Forms, 1990, 4th edit., 2003, N.C. Automobile Law, 1988, 3d edit., 1999, Take Counsel, 2000, A Lawyer Prayes God's Will for His Clients, 2000, The Saga of Joe Monk, 2000, The Conservative Mind, 2004, Lexical Semantics, 2007. Chmn. Davidson County Rep. Exec. Com., Lexington, 1974; trustee Davidson County C.C., Lexington, 1973-81; candidate U.S. Senate, N.C., 2002; candidate for lt. gov., N.C., 2004. Mem. N.C. Bar Assn. Baptist. Avocations: painting, writing, athletics. Office: 16 W 1st Ave Lexington NC 27292-3304

SNYDER, JAMES M., JR., political science professor, economics professor; BA in Econs., Duke Univ., 1981; PhD, Calif. Inst. Tech., 1985. Asst. prof., dept. econs. Univ. Chgo., 1985—92; assoc. prof., polit. sci. MIT, 1992—97, prof., 1997—98, prof., polit. sci., econs., 1998—2001, Arthur and Ruth Sloan prof. polit. sci., prof. econs., 2001—. STICERD disting. vis. London Sch. Econs., 2003, 04, 06. Recipient Jack Walker award, Am. Polit. Sci. Assn., 2002, Heinz Eulau award, Am. Polit. Sci. Rev., 2003; grantee John Randolph Haynes and Dora Haynes Fellowship, 1984, Alfred P. Sloan Doctoral Dissertation Fellowship, 1984—85, Carnegie Mellon GSIA Postdoctoral Fellowship, 1990—91. Fellow: Am. Acad. Arts & Scis.; mem.: Nat. Bur. Econ. Rsch., Phi Beta Kappa. Office: Dept Polit Sci E53-457 MIT Cambridge MA 02142 Office Phone: 617-253-2669. Business E-Mail: millett@mit.edu. *

SNYDER, JEAN MACLEAN, lawyer; b. Chgo., Jan. 26, 1942; d. Norman Fitzroy and Jessie (Burns) Maclean; m. Joel Martin Snyder, Sept. 4, 1964; children: Jacob Samuel, Noah Scot. BA, U. Chgo., 1963, JD, 1979. Bar: Ill. 1979, U.S. Dist. Ct. (no. dist.) Ill. 1979, U.S. Ct. Appeals (7th cir.) 1981. Ptnr. D'Ancona & Pflaum, Chgo., 1979-92; prin. Law Office of Jean Maclean Snyder, Chgo., 1993-97, 2004—; trial counsel The MacArthur Justice Ctr. U. Chgo. Law Sch., 1997—2004, of counsel, 2004—05. Contbr. articles to profl. jours. Bd. dirs. Citizens Alert, 2005—07. Mem.: Lawyers for the Creative Arts (bd. dirs. 1995—97), ACLU of Ill. (bd. dirs. 1996—99), ABA (mem. coun. on litigation sect. 1989—92, editor-in-chief Litigation mag. 1987—88, co-chair First Amendment and media litigation com. 1995—96, co-chair sect. litigation task force on gender, racial and ethnic bias 1998—2001, standing com. on strategic comms. 1996—2001). Home Phone: 773-285-2245; Office Phone: 773-285-5100. Business E-Mail: jeansnyder@sbcglobal.net.

SNYDER, JED C., foreign affairs specialist; b. Phila., Mar. 24, 1955; s. David and Lynn S. BA, Colby Coll., 1976; MA, U. Chgo., 1978, postgrad., 1978—79. Rsch. asst. U. Chgo., 1979; asst. rschr. Pan Heuristics divsn. R & D Assocs., Marina del Rey, Calif., 1979-80, assoc. rschr., asst. divsn. mgr., 1980-81, cons., 1982-83, Sci. Applications, Inc., 1979-81, Rand Corp., Santa Monica, Calif., 1979-81, Los Alamos (N.Mex.) Nat. Lab., 1984; sr. spl. asst. to dir. Bur. of Politico-Mil. Affairs, Dept. State, Washington, 1981-82; rsch. assoc. Internat. Security Studies Program, Woodrow Wilson Internat. Ctr. for Scholars, Smithsonian Instn., Washington, 1982-84; dep. dir. nat. security studies Hudson Inst., 1984-87; sr. rsch. fellow Nat. Strategy Info. Ctr., 1988-90; mgr. internat. strategic planing MPRI, Inc., 1997-2000; sr. nat. security advisor Dyncorp, 2001—02; sr. analyst CNA Corp., 2002—07; dir. operational net assessment HQ US Naval Forces Europe, 2007—. Cons. Rand Corp., 1983—88; founder, chmn. Washington Strategy Seminar, 1984—90, pres., corp. dir., 1984—93; appointee v.p. Bush's Adv. Task Force on Mid-East, 1987—88; cons. Office of Sec. of Def., 1988—92; apptd. supervisory rsch. prof., sr. fellow and team leader Inst. for Nat. Strategic Studies Nat. Def. U., 1992—97. Contbr. articles to profl. jours. Trustee Kents Hill (Maine) Sch., 1987-92. Comdr. US Naval Forces Europe, Italy. Recipient U.S. Navy award for Superior Civilian Svc., 2005; guest scholar Sch. Advanced Internat. Studies, Johns Hopkins U., 1982-83; fellow U. Chgo., 1979, Inter-Univ. Seminar on Armed Forces and Soc., 1980, MacArthur Sr., 1985-86, Herman Kahn, 1985-86, Smith Richardson, 1987-88, John M. Olin, 1987-88; selected as a Young Am. Leader, Am. Coun. on Fed. Republic of Germany, 1984. Mem. Internat. Inst. for Strategic Studies, Royal United Svcs. Inst., U.S. Naval Inst., Fgn. Policy Rsch. Inst., Coun. on Fgn. Rels. Office: CNA Corporation 1718 M St NW #197 Washington DC 20036-4504 Office Phone: 703-824-2225. Personal E-mail: snyder7@attglobal.net.

SNYDER, JOHN GORVERS, lawyer; b. Boston, June 20, 1960; s. Philip Francis and Sylvia (Gorvers) S.; m. Hinda Mala Simon, July 8, 1984; children: Monica Paige, Kimberly Blaine. BA, Johns Hopkins U., 1982; JD, Cornell U., 1987. Bar: Mass. 1988, U.S. Dist. Ct. Mass. 1989. Assoc. banking law, bus. law and corp. law dept. Craig and Macauley P.C., Boston, 1987—94, ptnr. banking law, bus. law and corp. law dept., 1995—2000; sr. v.p. and gen. coun. Simon Cos., LP, Braintree, Mass., 2000—. Lectr. New England Coll. Fin., 1994-2000. Active Combined Jewish Philanthropies, Boston, 1991—, Anti-Defamation League, Boston, 1993-94, Amherst Coll. Parents Fund, 2004—, Buckingham, Browne and Nichols Sch. Ann. Fund, 1999—. Mem. Mass. Bar Assn., Boston Bar Assn., Phillips Exeter Acad. Alumni Assn., B'nai Brith Realty Lodge, Phi Alpha Delta Internat., Omicron Delta Kappa (Johns Hopkins U. chpt., pres. 1981-82), Delta Upsilon (Johns Hopkins U. chpt.). Avocations: golf, tennis. Home: 7 Laurus Ln Newton Center MA 02459-3138 Address: The Simon Cos LP Attn: John G Snyder SVP 639 Granite St Braintree MA 02184-5366 E-mail: jsnyder@simoncompanies.com.

SNYDER, JOHN HENRY, computer science educator, consultant; b. Wichita, Kans., Mar. 16, 1947; s. Melvin Henry and Cathleen Ann (Collins) S.; m. Patricia Reilly, Mar. 11, 1984; children: Matthew Melvin George, Mark John Joseph. BA in English, Speech and Human Relations, U. Kans., Lawrence, 1970; MS in Computer Edn., Nova Southeastern U., Ft. Lauderdale, Fla., 1984. Cert. tchr. Nev., N.D. Computer sci. tchr. Hyde Park Jr. HS, Las Vegas, Nev., 1981-86, Chapparal HS, Las Vegas, 1986-91, Cimarron Meml. HS, Las Vegas, 1991-94, Advanced Tech. Acad., Las Vegas, Nev., 2004—. Copywriter pub. info. office CCSD, Las Vegas, 1982—84; chmn. gifted children spl. interest group Am. Mensa, 1984; mem. tech. com. Nev. State Network Internet Com., 1994—95; vice chair NW Accreditation Team, 2002—04; cons. Office Supt. Clark County Sch. dist., Las Vegas, 1984, Las Vegas, 85; systems analyst Homes & Narver, 1988; adminstrv. aide EG&G Energy Measurements, Las Vegas, 1989; adj. instr. computer sci., site co-adminstr. Nova U., 1984—93; adj. instr. computer sci. U. Nev., Las Vegas, 1990—, The Meadows Sch., 1991—96; with Nat. State Tchrs. of the Yr., 1993—, 2d v.p., 2001—02, nat. conv. chmn., 2002; nat. coord. Milken Educator States Network, 2000—, Milken Educator Listserve, 2001—. Newsletter editor Nat. State Tchrs. of Yr., 1991-93, nat. newsletter editor, webmaster, 1999—; contbr. articles to profl. jours. Co-chmn. Ednl. Exposition, Las Vegas, 1984; tech. cons. Harry Reid for U.S. Senate, 1986, 92; mem. Nevada 2000 Tech. Subcom., 1993, Nev. State Network Internet Com., 1993-96. With USAF, hon. discharge USAF, 1969. Recipient Innovative Teaching award Bus. Week Mag., 1990, Dolly Parton Chasing Rainbows award, 2003; named Tchr. of Yr., State of Nev., 1989-90, Burger King, 1989-90, U. Nev., Las Vegas, Southland Tchr. of Yr., 1990, Tandy Tech. Scholar, 1991, Nev. Educator of Yr., Milken Family Found., 1992, Nev. Tchr. of Yr. Microsoft Corp./Technology & Learning Mag., 1995; named to Nat. Tchr. Hall of Fame, 2007; Impact Innovator grantee, 1996; McAuliffe fellow, 1994, 97. Mem.: KC (sec., v.p., pres., local lodge newsletter editor), Am. Legion, Phi Delta Kappa (newsletter editor Overall Excellence award 1990), Pi Lambda Theta, Kappa Delta Pi. Democrat. Roman Catholic. Avocations: programming, didjeridu, website construction, virtual reality. Office: Advanced Tech Acad 2501 Vegas Dr Las Vegas NV 89106-1643 Business E-Mail: jhsnyder@interact.ccsd.net.

SNYDER, JOHN JACOB, researcher; b. Harrisburg, Pa., Sept. 21, 1946; s. John Jacob and Evelyn R. (Gutshall) Snyder. BA., Dickinson Coll., 1968; MA., U. of Deleware, 1976. Hist. rsch. Loise Steinman Von Hess Found., Columbia, Pa., 1975—78; cons. arch. hist. Hist. Preservation Trust of Lancaster County, 1978—83, rsch. cons., 1983—. Bd. mem. James Buchanan Found., Lancaster, Pa., 1976—92, Heritage Ctr. Museum, Lancaster, Pa., 1988—97, cons. Montgomery House Restoration, Lancaster, 2004—. Co-author: Clocks of Lancaster County, 1977, Clocks of Berks County, 1995; contbr. articles to jour. Pres. Rock Ford Found., Lancaster, Pa., 1992—94, chmn. Acquisitions com., 1994—. Mem.: Hist. Soc. York County, Hist. Soc. Perry County, Hist. Soc. Lancaster County, Hist. Soc. Chester County, Hist. Soc. Berks County. Republican. Lutheran. Home and Office: PO Box 40 1938 Water St Washington Boro PA 17582 Office Phone: 717-684-6232.

SNYDER, JOHN MICHAEL, lobbyist, public relations executive; b. Kingston, NY; m. Ling-Ling Woo, Jan. 1, 1996. BA, Georgetown U., DC, 1961, MA, 1968. Legis. sec. U.S. Ho. of Reps., Washington, 1964-65; assoc. editor The Am. Rifleman, Washington, 1966-74; chief lobbyist, dir. publs. and pub. affairs Citizens Com. for Right to Keep and Bear Arms, Washington, 1975—; mgr. Telum Assoc. LLC, 2003—. Author: (book) Gun Saint, 2003—; editor: (newsletter) Point Blank, 1974—; editor: (Capitol Hill editor) Gun Week, 1986—. Active Arlington County Rep. Com., 1994-2002. Recipient Grand Knighthood award Order of Michael the Archangel, 1988, Cicero award Nat. Assn. Federally Licensed Firearms Dealers, 1996. Mem. Am. Fedn. Police (nat. v.p. pub. rels. 1989—), Nat. Assn. Chiefs of Police (v.p. pub. affairs 1995—, v.p. Washington Liaison 2000—), Second Amendment Found. (treas. 1986—), St. Gabriel Possenti Soc. Inc. (pres. 1989—), Coun. for Am. (dir.), Asia Soc., Kiwanis Internat., Coun. for Am. (bd. dirs.), Nat. Press Club, Pub. Rels. Soc. Am., Capitol Hill Club, Am. League Lobbyists (hon.). Republican. Roman Catholic. Avocations: swimming, bicycling, reading, movies, theater. Home: PO Box 2844 Arlington VA 22202 Office: Citizens Com Right to Keep and Bear Arms 1250 Connecticut Ave NW Ste 200 Washington DC 20036 Office Phone: 202-326-5259. Personal E-mail: gundean@aol.com.

SNYDER, JOHN MILLARD, travel company executive, educator; b. Chelsea, Mass., Apr. 3, 1946; s. John Henry and Grace (Eby) Snyder; m. Barbara Ripple, Nov. 8, 1969 (div. 1979); 1 child, Logan; m. Glenda Allene Snyder, Sept. 10, 1983; children: Erika, Kimberly. BA, Franklin & Marshall Coll., 1968; MS, Colo. State U., 1974, PhD, 1982; cert., Harvard Sch. Design, 1987. Econ. rsch. assoc. Coll. Natural Resources, Ft. Collins, Colo., 1972-76; econ devel. City Devel. Dept., Kansas City, Mo., 1976-77; v.p. Oblinger Smith Corp., Denver, 1977-79; sr. resource analyst Abt Assocs., Denver, 1979-80; dr. devel. analysis URS Engrs., Denver, 1980-83; pres. Strategic Studies, Inc., Littleton, Colo., 1983—. Pres. Glacier Bay Outfitters, 1990—2001; faculty environ. policy and mgmt. U. Denver, 1990—, dir. environ. policy and mgmt., 1997—2000; co-founder Ecotourism Internat., 1994—; econ. faculty Regis U., 1984—; sr. advisor leisure and hospitality industry bus. rsch. divsn. U. Colo.; sustainable tourism advisor Nat. Geographic Soc. Author: (poems) A Far Off Place, 1995, Best Poems of 1995, 1995, Prospects for Polar Tourism, 2007; contbr. articles to profl. jours. Officer YMCA Guides Program, Littleton, 1984—85; sr. advisor Spl. Family Recreation, Denver, 1985—90; benefactor Le Bal de Ballet, Denver, 1989—; econ. advisor Treas. and Gov. of Colo., Denver, 1979—84. 1st lt. mil. intelligence US Army, 1968—72. Fellow: Explorers Club N.Y.; mem.: Colo. Woodworkers Guild, Denver Zool. Found., Nat. Pks. and Conservation Assn., Fedn. Fly Fishers, Trout Unlimited, Am. Legion, Xi Sigma Pi, Phi Kappa Phi. Office Phone: 303-347-2095.

SNYDER, JON DAVID, dean; b. Portland, Mar. 14, 1953; s. Max M. and Nancy F. Snyder; 1 child, J. B. BA, Wash. State U., 1977, MA, 1980; EdD, Tchrs. Coll., 1992. Assoc. dir. honors program Wash. State U., Pullman, 1979—80; tchr. elem. sch. Vancouver Pub. Schs., Wash., 1977—84; mgr. product Hosts Corp., Vancouver, 1984—87; assoc. dir. rsch. Nat. Ctr. Restructuring Edn., NYC, 1990—92; sr. rschr. Nat. Commn. Tchg., NYC, 1997—2002; dir. tchr. edn. U. Calif., Santa Barbara, 1992—2001; dean Bank St. Coll., NYC, 2001—. Cons. Albertson's Found., Boise, 1997—2000. Author: Makers of Meaning in a Learning Centered School, Dare to Dream, 1996, A Teaching Quality System for Excellence in Equity, 1999. Commr. Calif. Coalition Tchr. Crediting, Sacramento, 1996—2000; cons. Ark. Tchr. Lic. Task Force, Little Rock, 1996, Nat. Assn. State Bds. Edn., Washington, 1992—93. Recipient EPIC award, Internat. Assn. Bus. Comm., 1996; scholar, Wash. State U., Pullman, 1977. Mem.: Nat. Soc. Study Edn., Am. Edn. Rsch. Assn., Phi Delta Kappa. Office: Bank St Coll 610 W 112th St New York NY 10025 Business E-Mail: jsnyder@bankstreet.edu.

SNYDER, JOSEPH JOHN, editor, lecturer, consultant, historian, writer; b. Aug. 27, 1946; s. Joseph John and Amy Josephine (Hamilton) S.; m. Sally Hale Walker, July 4, 1973; children: Lauren Elizabeth, Brian Joseph Seth. BA in Anthropology, George Washington U., 1968; MA in Anthropology, U. N.Mex., 1973. With U.S. CSC, Washington, 1974-77; editor, writer U.S. Nat. Pk. Svc., Harpers Ferry, W.Va., 1977-81; cons. editor Early Man mag., Evanston, Ill., 1978-83; spl. project editor Sea Power Mag., 1986-87, cons. editor, 1987—, Jour. Archaeoastronomy, 1987—. Freelance writer, 1978—; pres. Sta. at Shepherdstown Inc., 1992-2000; pres., chmn. bd. dirs., Atlantic & Pacific High Speed Railway, Inc., 1993—; pres. Duffields-Station Inc., 2003-; lectr. Maya archaeology Norwegian-Caribbean Lines, Miami, Fla., 1982; cons. in field. Author: Kenneth Westcott Jones Transport Menu Collection, 1998, A.D. 2025: Transportation in America, 1998, Musings from a New Manse, 1999, The Phaistos Disc, A Commentary, 1999, Fragments of My Fleece, 2000, 1859: Turning Point of the Modern Era, 2001, Miniatures of American History, 2005; editor: The Only Fight the Cops Could Not Stop, 1998; book rev. assoc. editor: Athena Rev., 1999—; contbr. articles to popular mags. Pres. Tourism Found., Inc., 1996—99; chmn. pks, com. Neighborhood Planning Adv. Group Croydon Pk., Rockville, Md., 1980—81; bd. dir. Agrl. R&D Orgn., 1985—; v.p. bd. dir. Hagerstown (Md.) Roundhouse Mus., 1989—91, Hagerstown-Washington County Conv. and Visitors Bur., 1993—96, sec., 1993—96. With US Army, 1969—71, Vietnam. Decorated Bronze Star. Mem.: Nat. Ry. History Soc., Nat. Geog. Soc. (cons. 1987—), Am. Com. to Advance Study of Petroglyphs and Pictographs (editor), Hakluyt Soc., Coun. Md. Archaeology, Internat. Assn. Torch Clubs, James Rumsey Torch Club (pres. 1997—99, 2003—05), Navy League of U.S. (pres. Frederick-Hagerstown coun. 1993—2006). Democrat. Home: 106 Ashley Dr Shepherdstown WV 25443-9767

SNYDER, LARRY, priest, social services administrator; BA, Ill. Benedictine Coll.; MDiv, St. Paul Sem.; MPA, Hamline U. High sch. tchr. St. Bede Acad., Peru, Ill., Marquette HS, Ottawa, Ill.; ordained priest Archdiocese of St. Paul & Mpls., 1988; assoc. pastor Epiphany Cath. Ch., Coon Rapids, Minn., 1988—90, Nativity of Mary Ch., Bloomington, Minn., 1990—91; asst. to the dir. Cath. Charities of St. Paul & Mpls., 1991—92, assoc. dir., 1992—99, exec. dir., 1999—2005; chaplain Coll. St. Catherine, St. Paul & Mpls.; pres. & CEO Cath. Charities USA, Alexandria, Va., 2005—. Roman Catholic. Office: Cath Charities USA 1731 King St Alexandria VA 22314

SNYDER, LEWIS EMIL, astrophysicist, educator; b. Ft. Wayne, Ind., Nov. 26, 1939; s. Herman Lewis and Bernice (McKee) S.; m. Doris Jean Selma Lautner, June 16, 1962; children: Herman Emil, Catherine Jean. BS, Ind. State U., 1961; MA, So. Ill. U., 1964; PhD, Mich. State U., 1967. Research assoc. Nat. Radio Astronomy Obs., Charlottesville, Va., 1967-69; prof. astronomy dept. U. Va., Charlottesville, 1969-73, 74-75; vis. fellow Joint Inst. for Lab. Astrophysics, U. Colo., Boulder, 1973-74; prof. astronomy dept. U. Ill., Urbana, 1975—2005, prof. emeritus, 2005—, chair astronomy dept., 2002—05. Co-editor: Molecules in the Galactic Environment, 1973; contbr. articles to sci. jours. NASA-Am. Soc. Engring. Edn. summer fellow, 1972, 73; Alexander von Humboldt Found. sr. U.S. scientist award, 1983-84. Mem. AAAS, Am. Phys. Soc., Am. Astron. Soc., Internat. Astron. Union, Union Radio Scientifique Internationale, Alexander von Humboldt Assn. Am. Lutheran. Office: U Ill 1002 W Green St Urbana IL 61801-3074

SNYDER (MACKLEY), LOUISE MARIE, speech pathology/audiology services professional, consultant; d. Gordon Joseph and Audrey Augusta (Garvelman) Mackley. BS, Western Mich. U., 1972; MA, 1972; PhD, Mich. State U., 1993. Cert. tchg. elem. edn., speech pathology Dept. Edn., Mich., 1972, clin. competence Am. Speech-Lang.-Hearing Assn., 1975, myofunctional therapy Inst. Myofunctional Therapy, 1986, pre-primary impaired tchg. endorsement Office of Spl. Edn./Dept. Edn., Mich., 1993, lic. speech-lang. pathology Ind., 1995. Speech-lang. pathologist Port Huron Area Sch. Dist., Mich., 1974—75, Br. Intermediate Sch. Dist., Coldwater, Mich., 1975—, Speech and Lang. Svcs., Coldwater, 1992—; cons. Pines Behavioral Health Svcs., Coldwater, 1993—2003; speech-lang. pathologist Laurels Health Care, Coldwater, 1999—, Sundance Rehab., Angola, Ind., 2000—; instr. Kellogg CC, Battle Creek, 2001—03. Cons. speech pathology Office Spl. Edn.-Dept. Edn., Lansing, 1993—96, Venture Behavioral Health, Battle Creek, 1997—2003. Author: (doctoral dissertation) Contextual Factors in Receptive Vocabulary Development of Three-Year-Old Children in Homogeneous and Heterogeneous Day Care. Pres. Early Bird Exch. Club, Coldwater, Mich., 1997—98, 2000—01, 2004—. Recipient Exchangite of Yr., Early Bird Exch. Club, 1995, 2004, ACE, Am. Speech-Lang.-Hearing Assn., 1996. Mem.: Am. Speech-Lang.-Hearing Assn. (licentiate), Nat. Exch. Club. Avocations: miniature pinschers, Norman Rockwell memorabilia, gardening. Home Phone: 517-279-7410.

SNYDER, MARK JEFFREY, financial planner, actuary; b. Bklyn., May 16, 1947; s. Milton A. and June (Freed) S.; m. Gloria Carol Beskin, May 31, 1969; children: Chad Alan, Heather Lynn. B of Engring. Sci., SUNY, Stony Brook, 1969. CLU, chartered fin. cons., registered fin. planner. Ins. agt. Mass. Mut. Life Ins., Holbrook, N.Y., 1971-79; dist. mgr. Guardian Life Ins. Co., Port Jefferson, N.Y., 1979-81; v.p. pensions Exec. Planners, Ronkonkoma, N.Y., 1981-84; pres. CAS Adv. Services, Inc., Patchogue, N.Y., 1984-93; mng. exec. Integrated Resources Equity Corp., Patchogue, 1986-89, Royal Alliance Assocs., Inc., Patchogue, 1990—; pres. Snyder Fin. Svcs., Patchogue, 1986-91, Snyder Kresh Pension Svcs. Inc., Patchogue, 1989-97, Snyder Kresh Fin. Svcs., Inc., Medford, N.Y., 1990-98, Mark J. Snyder Fin. Svcs., Medford, 1998—. Spkr. in field. Moderator, host Moneywise, Brookhaven Cable TV, Port Jefferson Sta., N.Y., 1987-88; host. WLIM Radio program; contbr. articles to profl. jours. Mem. South Setauket (N.Y.) Civic Assn., 1972—, Three Village Dem. Club, Setauket, 1984—; bd. dirs., pres. Suffolk Estate Planning Coun., 1991-92; chmn. planned giving com. Suffolk County coun. Boy Scouts Am., 1985-87, 93—, mem. exec. bd. 1985—, v.p. 94—, mem. trust com., 1989-98, chmn. Boy Scouts Am. endowment devel. trust com., 1985-87, 93—; v.p. Suffolk County Coun.; pres. SUNY at Stony Brook Alumni Assn., 2000—. Named one of top 300 fin. planners in the country, Worth mag., 1998, top 250, 1999, 2001; named to Rsch. Mag. Advisor Hall of Fame; recipient top 250, Worth mag., 2002. Mem. Soc. Fin. Svcs. Profls.Registered Fin. Planners L.I. (bd. dirs., pres. 1986-87), Pension Forum L.I. (bd. dirs., chmn. pub. rels. 1986-88), Rotary Internat., KP. Democrat. Jewish. Avocations: racquetball, swimming. Office: Royal Alliance Assocs Inc 1731 N Ocean Ave Medford NY 11763-2649 Home Phone: 631-476-4645; Office Phone: 631-289-4224. Business E-Mail: marl@markjsnyder.com.

SNYDER, MARVIN, neuropsychologist; married; 1 child. BA (N.Y. State Regents scholar 1958-62, Meml. award psychology 1962), Bklyn. Coll., 1962; PhD (NDEA fellow 1962-65, USPHS fellow 1965-66, trainee 1966-67), Duke U., 1967. Rsch. psychologist NIMH, 1967—71, Nat. Eye Inst., 1971—72; program dir. neuroscis. Nat. Inst. Drug Abuse, 1974—79, dir. divsn. rsch., 1979—90, dir. Office of Sci. Policy, Edn. and Legislation, 1990—94, acting dep. dir., 1992—93; dir. life scis. rsch. office Fedn. Am. Socs. for Exptl. Biology, 1995—97; pres. Snyder Assocs., 1997—. Mem.

NIH sr. exec. svc. USPHS exec. com. AIDS, 1983-85; mem. Dept. Health and Human Svcs. Orphan Products Bd., 1982-88; mem. The White House Task Force on Drug Abuse Health Issues; co-chmn. Interagy. Com. on Smoking and Health, Interagy. Com. on New Therapies for Pain and Discomfort; exec. sec. Interagy. Com. on Pain and Analgesia, chmn. subcom. on edn. and tng., 1985—; cons. to WHO on drug abuse policy issues, 1985-87, Ctr. Substance Abuse Treatment, 1999-2000, biosensor devel., 2000-02; testifier on drug abuse sci. and policy issues to U.S. Congress; mem. Fed. Coordinating Com. for Sci., Engring. and Technology, Com. on Brain and Behavior, 1990-91. Devel. Guidelines for Protecting Human Subjects in Drug Abuse Studies, 1991; sci. adv. Dynamac Corp., 1999—; adv. bd. Bus.-Higher Edn. Forum, Rsch. Collaboration Initiative, 1999—2001. Author papers and reports on comparative neurology, drug abuse, nutrition, and health and sci. policy. Recipient Devel. of Naltrexone award ADAMHA, 1985, Pub. Svc. award, 1986, Michael Morrison award for excellence in sci. adminstrn. Com. on Problems of Drug Dependence, 1988, Presdl. Meritorious Rank award 1990.

SNYDER, MICHAEL F., telecommunications industry executive; Various positions ADT Security Svcs. Inc., subsidiary of Tyco Internat. Ltd., 1977—97, pres., 1997—2006; CEO Vonage Holdings Corp., 2006—07, bd. dirs., 2006—07. *

SNYDER, NATHAN, entrepreneur, investor; b. Hartford, Conn., Oct. 7, 1934; s. Saul and Betsy (Wand) S.; m. Geraldine Wolff, Dec. 27, 1964; children: Hannah Abigail, Alexander Lowell Wolff. AB, Harvard U., 1956; JD, Columbia U., 1963; postgrad. in bus., NYU, 1967-68. Bar: N.Y. 1963. Assoc. Paul, Weiss, Rifkind, Wharton & Garrison, NYC, 1963-66; v.p., sec. Randolph Computer Corp., Greenwich, Conn., 1966-69, exec. v.p., gen. counsel, bd. dirs., 1969-73; exec. v.p., chief operating officer BanCal Tri-State Corp. (holding co. Bank of Calif.), San Francisco, 1974-76; v.p. acquisitions CBS Inc., NYC, 1976-87; pres. VS & A Communications Ptnrs., NYC, 1987-89, The Snyder Co., New Canaan, Conn., 1989—. Lectr. mgmt. Golden Gate U., San Francisco, 1974-76, Annenberg Sch. Comms., Phila., 1982-87. Editor: Columbia Law Rev., 1962-63. Vol. legal services Office Econ. Opportunity, 1963; bd. dir. S.W. Regional Planning Agy. Served to lt. USNR, 1956-60. Harlan Fiske Stone scholar, 1964-65 Mem. Harvard Club (N.Y.C.), Harvard Club (bd. dirs. Fairfield County). Personal E-mail: naterun7@hotmail.com.

SNYDER, NED, gastroenterologist, medical educator; b. Austin, Tex., Oct. 29, 1944; s. Ned and Beverly Snyder; m. Dorothy Maureen Nelson, Oct. 26, 1968; children: Ned, Andrew Nelson. BA, Yale U., New Haven, Conn., 1966; MD, U. Tex., Galveston, 1970. Diplomate Am. Bd. Internal medicine, 1974, Am. Bd. Internal Medicine, Gastroenterology, 1975. Dir. gastroenterology Providence Health Ctr., Waco, Tex., 1978—2001; pres. Waco Gastroenterology Assocs., 1978—2001; asst. prof. medicine, med. br. U. Tex., Galveston, 1975—78, prof. medicine, chief clin. gastroenterology and hepatology, med. br., 2002—. Hepatology cons. Brooke Gen. Army Hosp., San Antonio, 1976—83; dir. Tex. Nat. Bank, Waco, 1986—97; bd. trustees Providence Health Ctr., Waco, 1986—93; pres. Tex. Acad. Internal Medicine, Austin, 2002—03, U. Tex. Med. Br. Alumni Bd. Trustees, Galveston, 2005—. Contbr. articles to profl. jours. Pres. Tex. Acad. Internal Medicine, Tex., 1999—2003. Fellow: ACP (pres. Tex. chpt. 2002—03, Laurette award 2006, Advocacy award Tex. chpt. 2005), Am. Gastroenterology Assn.; mem.: Mu Delta (Outstanding Resident award 1973), Alpha Omega Alpha. Avocations: ranching, golf, skiing. Home: 1550 Cr 243 Valley Mills TX 76689 Office: Univ Tex Med Br 301 University Galveston TX 77555-0764 Home Phone: 254-945-3351; Office Phone: 409-772-1501. Office Fax: 409-772-4789. Personal E-mail: nedsnyderiii@aol.com. Business E-Mail: nesnyder@utmb.edu.

SNYDER, PETER M., medical educator, medical researcher; BA in Biology summa cum laude, Luther Coll., 1984; MD, U. Iowa, 1989. Diplomate Am. Bd. Internal Medicine, Am. Bd. Cardiovasc. Disease. Resident in internal medicine U. Tex., Dallas, 1989—92; fellow in cardiovasc. diseases Dept. Internal Medicine U. Iowa Hosp. & Clinics, Iowa City, 1992—96, asst. prof. Dept. Internal Medicine, 1996—2000, assoc. prof. internal medicine and physiology and biophysics, 2000—. Contbr. articles to profl. jours. Recipient Clinician Scientist award, 1996, Katz Basic Sci. award, 1998; fellow Student Rsch., U. Iowa, 1985, Student, Am. Heart Assn., 1987—88. Mem.: ACP, Alpha Omega Alpha. Achievements include research in sodium channel structure and function. Office: U Iowa Coll of Medicine Dept Internal Medicine 200 Hawkins Dr Iowa City IA 52242-1009

SNYDER, RICHARD GERALD, research scientist, administrator, educator, consultant; b. Northampton, Mass., Feb. 14, 1928; s. Grant B. and Ruth (Putnam) Snyder; m. Phoebe Jones, Mar. 2, 1949; children: Dorinda, Sherrill, Paul, Jeff, Jon, David. Student, Amherst Coll., 1946-48; BA, U. Ariz., 1956, MA, 1957, PhD, 1959. Diplomate Am. Bd. Forensic Anthropology (dir. 1978-84, 85-91). Tchg. asst. dept. anthropology U. Ariz., Tucson, 1957-58, assoc. rsch. engr. Applied Rsch. Lab., Coll. Engring., 1958-60, mem. staff Ariz. Transp. and Traffic Inst., 1959-60, assoc. prof. sys. engring., 1960; chief phys. anthropology Civil Aeromed. Rsch. Inst. FAA, Oklahoma City, 1960-66, rsch. pilot, 1962-66, intermittent acting chief Protection and Survival Labs., 1963-66; mgr. biomechanics dept. Office Automotive Safety Rsch. Ford Motor Co., Dearborn, Mich., 1966-68, prin. rsch. scientist, 1968; rsch. scientist Hwy. Safety Rsch. Inst. U. Mich., Ann Arbor, 1968—85, assoc. prof. anthropology, 1968-73, head biomed. dept., 1969-84, prof., 1973-85, dir. NASA Ctr. Excellence in Man-Vehicle Sys., 1984-85, named chair, R.G. Snyder disting. univ. prof. indsl. and ops. engring, 2004—. Pres., bd. dirs. George Snively Rsch. Found., 1992—98; assoc. prof. sys. engring. U. Ariz., 1960; adj. assoc. prof. U. Okla., 1963; rsch. assoc. Zoller Lab., U. Chgo., 1964—65, rsch. assoc. dept. anthropology, 1965—67; assoc. prof. Mich. State U., East Lansing, 1967—68; cons. USAF Aerospace Med. Rsch. Labs., NAS, US Dept. Transp., adv. com. Office Naval Rsch. Dept. Navy, numerous others. Assoc. editor Jour. of Comm., 1961—63, cons. editor Jour. Biomechanics, 1967—81, mem. editl. bd. Product Safety News, 1973, adv. bd. Aviation Space and Environ. Medicine, 1980—91, 1994, mem. editl. rev. bd. Stapp Car Crash Jour., 2001—03; contbr. chapters to books, numerous articles to profl. jours. Judge Internat. Sci. Fair, Detroit, 1968; mem. coun. Explorer Scouts, Ann Arbor, 1968—70; bd. dirs. N.Mex. Rsch. Inst., 1996—2000. 1st lt. USAF, 1949—54, Korea. Decorated Disting. Flying Cross, 3 Air Medals; named to Safety and Health Hall of Fame Internat., 1993, Ariz. Aviation Hall of Fame, 1998; recipient Met. Life award, Nat. Safety Coun., 1970, Adm. Luis de Flores Flight Safety award, Flight Safety Found., 1981. Fellow: AAAS, AIAA (assoc.), Soc. Automotive Engrs. (Arch T. Colwell Merit award 1973, Aerospace Congress award 1982, Tech. Contbns. to Air Transport Safety), Am. Acad. Forensic Scis. (T. Dale Stewart award 1992), Royal Anthrop. Inst., Am. Anthrop. Assn., Aerospace Med. Assn. (Harry G. Moseley award 1975, Profl. Excellence award 1978, John Paul Stapp award in Aerospace Biomechanics 1994), Explorers Club; mem.: Aerospace Physiologists Soc., Internat. Soc. Aircraft Safety Investigators, Ariz.-Nev. Acad. Sci., Mach 3 Soc., Order of Daedalians, Sigma Xi, Phi Gamma Delta, Beta Beta Beta. Republican. Congregationalist. Avocations: aviation, aerospace medicine, forensic anthropology. Home: 3720 N Silver Dr Tucson AZ 85749-9709 Office: BioDynamics Internat Tucson AZ 85749

SNYDER, RICK (RICHARD D. SNYDER), computer company executive; BGS with high distinction, Univ. Mich., 1977, MBA with high distinction, 1979, JD, 1982. CPA; bar: Mich. Acct. Coopers & Lybrand, 1982—88, ptnr., 1988—91; exec. v.p. Gateway, Inc., Irvine, Calif., 1991—97, pres. & COO, 1996—97, dir., 1991—97, chmn., 2005—, interim CEO, 2006; pres. Avalon Investments, 1997—2000; founder, CEO, chmn. Ardesta LLC, Ann Arbor, Mich., 2000—. Adj. prof. acctg. U. Mich., 1982—84; dir. Launch Media Inc. Trustee The Henry Ford; bd. mem. U. Mich. Coll. Engring. Nat. Adv. Com.; mem. tech. transfer nat. adv. com. U. Mich.; mem. Gov. e-Mich. Adv. Council; mem. adv. bd. Samuel Zell & Robert H. Lurie Inst. for Entrepreneurial Studies, NanoBus. Alliance; mem. vis. com. Purdue Univ. Sch. Engring.; chmn. Ann Arbor SPARK; mem. The Nature Conservancy, Mich. Chpt. Mem.: Mich. Bar Assn. Office: Gateway Inc 7565 Irvine Center Dr Irvine CA 92618 *

SNYDER, ROBERT ELLIS, retired music educator, minister; b. Columbus, Ohio, June 22, 1930; s. Ellis Emmanuel and Pauline Walker Snyder; m. Paula Schumacher, Aug. 27, 1966; children: Carol Elizabeth, Paul Robert. BA in Music, Capital U., 1952; BDiv, Trinity Luth. Sem., 1956; MusM, U. Colo., 1956; PhD in Choral Conducting and Lit., U. Iowa, 1970. Ordained to ministry Luth. Ch., 1956. Min. Faith Luth. Ch., Detroit, 1956—66; prof. music Ea. Ill. U., Charleston, 1968—95; ret., 1995. Mem.: Am. Choral Dirs. Assn. (nat. treas.). Avocations: golf, tennis, bridge, travel. Home: 114 Longwood Green Ct Aiken SC 29803

SNYDER, ROBERT LYMAN, materials scientist, educator; b. Plattsburgh, NY, June 5, 1941; s. George Michael and Dorothy (Lyman) M.; m. Sheila Nolan, Sept. 1, 1963; children: Robert N., Kristina M. BA, Marist Coll., 1963; PhD, Fordham U., 1968. Postdoctoral fellow NIH U. Pitts., 1968; NRC fellow NASA Elec. Rsch. Ctr., Cambridge, Mass., 1969; asst. prof. ceramic sci. Alfred (N.Y.) U., 1970-77, assoc. prof., 1977-83, prof., 1983-96, dir. Inst. Ceramic Superconductivity, 1987-96; prof., chmn. dept. materials sci. and engring. Ohio State U., Columbus, 1996—2002; prof., chmn. Sch. Materials Scis. and Engring. Ga. Inst. Tech., Atlanta, 2003—. Vis. prof. Lawrence Livermore (Calif.) Lab., 1977, 78, U.S. Nat. Bur. Stds., Gaithersburg, Md., 1980, 81, Siemens AG Ctrl. Rsch. Labs., Munich, 1983, 91; invited prof. U. Rennes, France, 1995. Author: Introduction to X-Ray Powder Diffractometry, 1996; author, editor 8 books; contbr. chpts. to books and over 270 articles to profl. jours. Deputy mayor Village of Alfred, 1973-77; pres. Alfred Vol. Fire Co., 1979-88. Recipient Chancellor's award SUNY, 1980, numerous research grants; named Faculty Exch. scholar SUNY, 1978-96. Fellow Am. Ceramic Soc. (Outstanding Educator award 1999), Am. Soc. Metals (disting.), Internat. Ctr. Diffraction Data (Hanawalt award, 2004); mem. TMS (Leadership award 2002), NAS (U.S. nat. com. on crystallography 1991-95, Codata 2001—), Nat. Inst. Ceramic Engrs., Am. Crystallography Assn. (chmn. applied crystallography div. 1988-92), Materials Rsch. Soc., Ceramic Ednl. Coun., Internat. Ctr. Diffraction Data (bd. dirs. 1986-92, elected chmn. bd. dirs. 1996-2000), Internat. X-ray Analysis Soc. (pres. 2000-2001), Edward Orton Jr. Ceramic Found. (bd. dirs. 1996—), Alfred and Allegany County Fire Assn., Sigma Xi, Phi Kappa Phi. Democrat. Achievements include numerous patents for practical superconductors. Office: Ga Inst Tech Sch Materials Sci and Engring 771 Feist Dr Atlanta GA 30332-0245 Home: 195 14th St NE Ste 1 Atlanta GA 30309-2682 Office Phone: 404-894-2888. Business E-Mail: robert.snyder@mse.gatech.edu.

SNYDER, SOLOMON HALBERT, psychiatrist, pharmacologist; b. Washington, Dec. 26, 1938; s. Samuel Simon and Patricia (Yakerson) S.; m. Elaine Borko, June 10, 1962; children: Judith Rhea, Deborah Lynn. MD cum laude, Georgetown U., 1962; PhD (hon.), Ben Gurion U., 1990; DSc (hon.), Georgetown U., 1986, Northwestern U., 1981, Technion Inst., 2002, Mt. Sinai Med. Sch., 2004, U. Maryland, 2006. Intern Kaiser Found. Hosp., San Francisco, 1962-63; rsch. assoc. NIMH, Bethesda, Md., 1963-65; resident psychiatry Johns Hopkins Hosp., Balt., 1965-68; assoc. prof. psychiatry and pharmacology Johns Hopkins Med. Sch., 1968-70, prof., 1970-77, disting. svc. prof. psychiatry and pharmacology, 1977-80, disting. svc. prof. neurosci., psychiatry, and pharmacology, 1980—, dir. dept. neurosci., 1980—. Wellcome disting. prof. U. Wash., 1999; lectr. in field; lectr. Gross Found., 2005. Author: Uses of Marijuana, 1971, Madness and the Brain, 1973, Opiate Receptor Mechanisms, 1975, The Troubled Mind, 1976, Biologic Aspects of Mental Disorder, 1980, Drugs and the Brain, 1986, Brainstorming, 1989; editor Perspectives in Neuropharmacology, 1971, Frontiers in Catecholamine Research, 1973, Handbook of Psychopharmacology, 1974; contbr. articles to profl. jours. Served with USPHS, 1963-65. Recipient Outstanding Scientist award, Md. Acad. Scis., 1969, John Jacob Abel award, Am. Pharmacology Soc., 1970, A.E. Bennett award, Soc. Biol. Psychiatry, 1970, Gaddum award, Brit. Pharm. Soc., 1974, F.O. Schmitt award in neurosci., MIT, 1974, Rennebohm award, U. Wis., 1976, Stanley Dean award, Am. Coll. Psychiatrists, 1978, Lasker award, 1978, Wolf prize, 1983, Dickson prize, 1983, Sci. Achievement award, AMA, 1985, Ciba-Giegy-Drew award, 1985, Strecker prize, 1986, Edward Sachar Meml. award, Columbia U., 1986, Sense of Smell award, Fragrance Rsch. Found., 1987, J. Allyn Taylor prize, 1990, Pasarow Found. award, 1991, Bower award, Achievement Sci. Franklin Inst., 1991, Joseph Priestley prize, Dickinson Coll., 1992, Baxter award, Am. Assn. Med. Colls., 1995, Bristol-Myers-Squibb Neurosci. prize, 1996, City of Medicine award, 2000, Gerard prize, Soc. Neurosci., 2000, Salmon medal, 2001, Lieber prize, NARSAD, 2001, Disting. lectr., U. Tex., Houston, 2002, Presdl. lectr., Sloan-Kettering Cancer Inst., N.Y., 2002, Goldman-Rakic prize, NARSAD, 2003, Nat. medal sci., US Pres., 2005, Edward Perl award, U. NC, 2007, Albany Prize in Medicine, 2007. Fellow: Am. Philos. Soc., Am. Acad. Arts and Scis., Am. Psychiat. Assn. (Hofheimer award 1972, Disting. Svc. award 1989, Judd Marmor award 2000), Am. Coll. Neuropsychopharmacology (Daniel Efron award 1974); mem.: Inst. Medicine, Am. Pharmacology Soc., Am. Soc. Biol. Chemists, Soc. for Neurosci. (pres. 1979—80, Presdl. lectr. 2000, History of Neurosci. lectr. 2001), Nat. Acad. Scis. (Sarnat prize in mental health 2001). Home: 3801 Canterbury Rd Unit 1102 Baltimore MD 21218-2379 Office: Johns Hopkins U Med Sch Dept Neurosciences 725 N Wolfe St Baltimore MD 21205-2105 Home Phone: 410-889-7379; Office Phone: 410-955-3024. Business E-Mail: ssnyder@jhmi.edu.

SNYDER, VIC, congressman, physician; b. Medford, Oreg., Sept. 27, 1947; m. Betsy Singleton; 1 child, Charles Pennington. BA in Chemistry, Willamette U., 1975; MD, U. Oreg. Health Scis. Ctr., 1979; JD, U. Ark., Little Rock, 1988. Resident family practice U. Ark. Med. Scis., 1979-82; physician family practice Ark., 1982—; mem. Ark. State Senate, 1991-96, US Congress from 2d Ark. dist., 1997—; mem. armed srvc. com., veterans affairs com. Med. missions to Cambodian regufee camps, Thailand, El Salvadoran regufee camps, Honduras, mission hosp., Sierra Leone, Africa, Ethiopian refugee camp, Sudan. With USMC, 1967-69. Democrat. Methodist. Office: US Ho Reps 1330 Longworth Ho Office Bldg Washington DC 20515-0402 also: Dist Office Ste 150 1501 N Univ Little Rock AR 72207 E-mail: snyder.congress@mail.house.gov. *

SNYDER, WILLARD BREIDENTHAL, lawyer; b. Kansas City, Dec. 18, 1940; s. N.E. and Ruth (Breidenthal) S.; m. Lieselotte Dieringer, Nov. 10, 1970 (dec. Nov. 1975); 1 child, Rolf; m. T.J. Sewall, May 17, 1996. BA, U. Kans., 1962, JD, 1965; postgrad., Hague Acad. Internat. Law, The Netherlands, 1965-66, U. Dijon, France, 1966; grad., Command and Gen. Staff Coll., Ft. Leavenworth, Kans., 1977. Bar: Kans. 1965, Mo. 1986, U.S. Tax Ct. 1977, U.S. Ct. Mil. Appeals 1981, U.S. Dist. Ct. Kans. 1965, U.S. Supreme Ct. 1977. Atty., Kansas City, 1970-80, 85—; trust officer, corp. trust officer Security Nat. Bank., Kansas City, 1980-83, corp. sec., 1983—; pres. Real Estate Corp. Inc., Leawood, Kans., 1984—; adv. dir. United Mo. Bank, 1985-90. Bd. dirs. Blue Ridge Bank, mem. trust com. Bank Holding Co., 1991—; German Consul (Hon.) for Kans., Western Mo., 1972—. Mem. Platte Woods City Coun., Mo., 1983—84; bd. govs., past pres. Liberty Meml. Assn.; pres. MacJannett Found., Talloires, France; chmn. Breidenthal-Snyder Found.; nominating and exec. com. Hoover Pres. Libr.; bd. dirs., v.p. Unicorn Theatre, 1998—2004; vice dean Kansas City Consular Corp.; bd. dirs., v.p. FBI Citizens Acad.; bd. dirs., trustee Actors Theater of Kansas City; bd. dirs. Kansas City Metro Crime Commn.; dir. Truman Found., Kansas City; trustee St. Mary Coll., 1998—2001; bd. regents Rockhurst U., trustee; bd. dirs., pres. Navy UDT & SEAL Mus.; dir. and gen. counsel Army Command and GS Found.; bd. dirs., pres. Kansas City Kans. Cmty. Found.; bd. dirs. Don Bosco of Kansas City, Kans., treas. Col. inf. US Army, ret. USAR, ret. Kans. Army N.G. Decorated Bundesverdienst Kreuz IKL BVKam Bandes Bundeswehr Kreuz (silver), Bundeswehr Kreuz (gold) Germany, Legion of Merit, KARNG medal of excellence, Mil. Order of WW award; named to Hon. Order Ky. Cols., OCS Hall of Fame; recipient Golden Honour badge, German Vet. Orgn., Bavaria, 1988. Mem. Mo. Bar Assn., Kansas City Bar Assn., Kansas City Hosp. Attys., Mil. Order of World Wars (chpt. comdr. 1983-84, regional comdr. 1987-91, Patrick Henry award), Nat. Eagle Scout Assn. Avocations: scuba diving, hunting, notgeld collections, cartridge collection. Office: 8014 State Line Rd Ste 203 Shawnee Mission KS 66208-3712 Office Phone: 913-642-5134. Business E-Mail: wbs11@kc.rr.com.

SNYDER, WILLIAM ALBERT, lawyer; b. Elmira, NY, Oct. 19, 1946; s. Arthur F. and Irene M. Snyder; m. Kay Snyder, Jan. 1, 1971; children: Shawn, Kristin. BA, Hobart and William Smith Colls., 1968; JD, U. Fla., 1971; LLM in Estate Planning, U. Miami, Fla., 1996. Bar: Fla. 1971; cert. Fla. Bar Bd. Legal Specialization and Edn. (wills, trust and estates). Assoc. Reasbeck & Fegers, P.A., Hollywood, Fla., 1971-73; pvt. practice atty. Davie, Fla., 1973-82; ptnr. Snyder & Kiar, Davie, 1982-93; pvt. practice atty., 1993; mng. ptnr. Snyder & Snyder, P.A., Davie. Bd. dirs. Broward County Estate Planning Coun., 1980-96, Planned Giving Coun. Broward County, 1995-96; adj. prof. estate planning grad. prog. U. Miami Law Sch. Co-author: Preserving the Legacy of a Family Owned Business: A Psychology of Business Succession and Estate Planning. Mem. Broward County Dem. Exec. Com., 1986; pres. Davie Dem. Club, 1986-88. Capt. USAR, 1971—76. Named a Fla. Super Lawyer, 2006; named one of Top 100 Attys., Worth mag., 2005—06. Mem.: Fla. Bar (mem. wills, trusts and estates law certification com.), Broward County Bar Assn. Office: Snyder & Snyder PA 7931 SW 45th St Davie FL 33328-3011 Office Phone: 954-475-1139 ext. 203. E-mail: bill@snyderlawpa.com. *

SNYDER, WILLIAM BURTON, insurance company executive; b. Clarksburg, W.Va., July 9, 1929; s. William Burton and Mary Catherine (Cornwell) Snyder; m. Georgie Gaye, Oct. 27, 1951 (dec.); children: William Burton, Melissa Ann; m. Sally Marie Snyder, May 17, 2003. BBA in Acctg. cum laude, Tex. Tech U., 1955. With Travelers Ins. Co., 1955-77, v.p., 1970-77; with Govt. Employees Ins. Co., Washington, 1977-93; chmn., pres., CEO GEICO Corp., 1985-93; dir. several small bus., 1993—. Dir. Nat. Capital Area coun. Boy Scouts Am. Capt. USAF, 1950—53. Decorated Air medal. Mem.: Kenwood Country Club (Bethesda, Md.). Republican. Baptist. Personal E-mail: wbs111@aol.com.

SNYDER, WILLIAM W., corporate financial executive; m. Valerie Snyder; 2 children. BSBA, U. Mo., M in Accountancy. CPA. With pub. acctg. Deloitte & Touche; corp. contr. Enterprise Rent-A-Car, 1984—89, asst. v.p. to v.p. corp. acctg., 1989—94, v.p. fleet adminstrn., 1994—95, v.p. info. sys., 1995—98, sr. v.p., chief info. officer, 1998—2002, sr. v.p., CFO, 2002—03, exec. v.p., CFO, 2003—. Office: Enterprise Rent-A-Car 600 Corporate Park Dr Saint Louis MO 63105 *

SNYDERMAN, CARL HENRY, otolaryngologist; b. Ft. Wayne, Ind., Mar. 9, 1956; MD, U. Chgo. Pritzker Sch. Medicine, 1982. Diplomate Am. Bd. Otolaryngology. Resident in gen. surgery West Pa. Hosp., Pitts., 1982-83; resident in otolaryngology Eye Ear Hosp./U. Pitts., 1983-87, fellow, 1987-88; otolaryngologist Montefiore U./Hosp. Pa., Pitts., 1987—, U. Pitts. Med. Ctr., co-director, Ctr. for Cranial Base Surgery; assoc. prof. otolaryngology U. Pitts. Sch. Medicine, prof. otolaryngology and neurological surgery. Lectr. in field. Contbr. articles to peer-reviewed publications. Recipient FIRST award for the study of the role of prostaglandins in head and neck cancer, NIH, Clinical Oncology Career Develop. award, Am. Cancer Soc. Mem. AMA, ACS (pres. southwestern Pa. chpt.), Am. Acad. Otolaryngology-Head and Neck Surgery(mem. com.skull base com., head and neck surgery and oncology com.), Am. Otolaryngology Assn., N.Am. Skull Base Soc. along with collegues, involved with the development of the Expanded Endonasal Transplanum Approach (EEA). Address: Minimally Invasive Neurosurgical Ctr 200 Lothrop St Pittsburgh PA 15213 Office Phone: 412-647-2100, 412-647-6778. *

SNYDERMAN, NANCY, surgeon, medical journalist; m. Doug Snyderman; 3 children. PhD in medicine, U. Nebr. Med. Sch. Cert. otolaryngology U. Pitts., UMDA. Resident in pediatrics and ear, nose, and throat surgery U. Pitts.; dir. head and neck surgery U. Ark. Med. Scis., 1983—87; surgical practice Calif. Pacific Med. Ctr., San Francisco, 1988—; med. corr. Good Morning Am., 1987—2003, 20/20, 1987—2003, ABC News, 1987—2003; v.p. med. affairs corp. staff Johnson & Johnson, 2003—06; chief med. editor NBC News, 2006—. Contbr. to med. jour.; author: Dr. Nancy Snyderman's Guide to Good Health for Women Over Forty, Necessary Journeys, Girl in the Mirror: Raising Adolescent Daughters. Mem.: Am. Acad. of Otolaryngology Head and Neck Surgery (bd. dirs.). Achievements include reporting on med. topics affecting both men and women; traveled and reported extensively from Eastern and Western Europe, Saudi Arabia during Persian Gulf War, Russia, Somalia, Kosovo, Pakistan, and Afghanistan. Office: NBC 30 Rockefeller Plz New York NY 10112

SNYDERMAN, RALPH, medical educator, physician; b. Bklyn., Mar. 13, 1940; 1 child, Theodore Benjamin. BS, Washington Coll., Chestertown, Md., 1961; MD magna cum laude, SUNY, Bklyn., 1965, DSc (hon.) Health Sci. Ctr., 1996. Diplomate Am. Bd. Internal Medicine, Am. Bd. Allergy and Immunology. Intern Duke U. Hosp., Durham, 1965-66, med. resident, 1966-67; public health officer NIH, 1967-72; Howard Hughes med. investigator, asst. prof. medicine and immunology Duke U. Hosp., Durham, N.C., 1972-74, assoc. prof., 1974-77, chief divsn. rheumatology and immunology, 1975-87, prof. medicine and immunology, 1980-87, Frederic M. Hanes prof. medicine and immunology, 1984-87, adj. prof. medicine, 1987-89; surgeon USPHS, NIH, Bethesda, Md., 1967-69; sr. staff fellow Nat. Inst. Dental Rsch., NIH, Bethesda, Md., 1969-70, sr. investigator immunology sect. lab. microbiology and immunology, 1970-72; chief divsn. rheumatology Durham VA Hosp., Bethesda, Md., 1972-75; v.p. med. rsch. and devel. Genentech, Inc., South San Francisco, Calif., 1987-88, sr. v.p. med. rsch. and devel., 1988-89; chancellor for health affairs, dean Sch. Medicine Duke U., Durham, NC, 1989—2004, James B. Duke prof. medicine, 1989—2004; pres., CEO Duke U. Health Sys., Durham, 1998—2004. Howard Hughes med. investigator, Durham, 1972-77; dir. Lab Immune Effector Function, Howard Hughes Med. Inst., Durham, 1977-87; adj. prof. medicine U. Calif., San Francisco, 1987-89. Editor: Contemporary Topics in Immunobiology, 1979, Inflammation: Basic Concepts and Clinical Correlates, 1988, 2nd edit., 1992, Medical Clinics of North America, 1997, Journ. Integrated Med., 1997, Proceedings of Amer. Physician, 1997; contbr. articles to profl. jours. Recipient McLaughlin award, 1978, Alexander von Humboldt award Fed. Republic Germany, 1985, award for lifetime achievements in inflammation rsch. Ciba-Geigy Morris Ziff, 1992, Bonazinga award Soc. for Leukocyte Biology, 1993, Disting. Alumni Achievement award SUNY Bklyn., 1995, Disting. Alumni achievement award Washington Coll., 1995, Disting. Alumni citation, 1996, Lifetime Achievement award Arthritis Found., Eastern Reg., 1997, Lifetime Achievement award Argentine Nat. Acad. Medicine, 1998, others. Mem.: NAS, Am. Acad. Arts and Scis., Soc. for Med. Adminstrs., Assn. Am. Med. Colls. (chair task force on clin. rsch. 1998, chmn. coun. deans 1999—2000, chmn. 2001—02), Am. Coll.

Rheumatology, Assn. Acad. Health Ctrs., Am. Soc. for Biochemistry and Molecular Biology, Assn. Am. Physicians, Am. Fedn. Clin. Rsch., Soc. for Leukocyte Biology, Am. Assn. Cancer Rsch., Am. Acad. Allergy, Am. Soc. Clin. Investigation, Am. Assn. Immunologists, Assn. Am. Physicians (pres. 2003—04), Inst. Medicine, Sigma Xi.

SNYDERS, DIRK JOHAN, electrophysiologist and biophysicist educator; b. Wilrijk, Antwerpen, Belgium, July 18, 1955; arrived in U.S., 1984; s. Godlief Stefaan and Mariette L. Snyders. BS in Med. Sci., U. Antwerp, Belgium, 1976, MD with great honor, 1980. Lic. physician, cert. cardiologist Belgium. Resident then fellow in internal medicine and cardiology Univ. Hosp. Antwerp, 1980—84; postdoctoral fellow U. Calif., San Francisco, 1984—85; instr. medicine Vanderbilt U., Nashville, 1986—87, asst. prof., 1987—95, assoc. prof. medicine and pharmacology, 1995—. With V.I.B. dept. biophysics and pharmacology Antwerp U., 1998—2003; prof. biochemistry U. Antwerp, 1998—, vice-chair dept. biochemistry, 1999—2001, chair dept. biomed. scis., 2001—, prof. biomed. scis., 2001—, vice chair rsch. coun., 2004—. Co-author: The Heart and the Cardiovascular System, 1991; mem. editorial bd. Circulation Rsch.; reviewer Jour. Gen. Physiology, Cardiovascular Rsch., Jour. Molecular and Cellular Cardiology, Molecular Pharmacology, European Jour. Pharmacology, Biophys. Jour., Jour. Biol. Chemistry; contbr. articles to profl. jours. Lt. Med. Svc. Belgian Army, 1987—88. Recipient Specia award Specia NV., Belgium, 1980; hon. fellow Belgian Am. Ednl. Found., NATO rsch. fellow, 1984, med. rsch. fellow Alta. Heritage Found., 1984; rsch. grantee NIH, Am. Heart Assn. Fellow Am. Heart Assn. (basic sci. coun.); mem. AAAS, Biophys. Soc., Soc. Gen. Physiologists, European Working Group (cardiac cellular electropmysiology bd. mem.) Achievements include research on mechanism of action of "specific bradycardiac agents", use-dependent unblocking and voltage clamp validation of modulated receptor theory (cardiac sodium channels and antiarrhythmic agents), electrophysiology and pharmacology of cloned channels molecular localisation of antiarrhythmic drug binding sites, cardiac potassium channels (including human), molecular ion channel structure-function relationships, molecular basis of congenital excitability disorders. Office: Antwerp U Dept Biomed Scis Universiteitsplein 1 T4 2160 Antwerp Belgium Address: Fazantenlaan 6 Antwerp B2610 Belgium Home Phone: 011-32-3-449-4374; Office Phone: 011-32-3-820-2335. E-mail: dirk.snyders@ua.ac.be.

SNYDER-SOWERS, MARY ANNE SARAH, performing arts educator, performing company executive, choreographer; b. Bristol, Tenn., Jan. 26, 1956; d. John Calvin and Pauline June Snyder; m. Lee E. Sowers, June 29, 1991; children: Mark Jason Sowers, Jeffrey Lee Sowers. BA, Va. Intermont Coll., Bristol, 1978; MEd, Milligan Coll., Tenn., 1997. Artistic dir. Bristol Ballet Co., Va., 1978—95; cert. tchr., first dance specialist Johnson City Schs., Tenn., 1995—. Dance grant rev. panelist Tenn. Arts Commn., Nashville, 2005—; prin. dancer Bristol Ballet Co., Va., 1968—82; regional evaluator Southeastern Regional Ballet Assn./Regional Dance Am., Atlanta, 1992—95; facutly mem. ballet dept. Va. Intermont Coll., Bristol, 1978—90; faculty summer arts camp Milligan Coll., 2000—; dir. Hardinge Ballet Ctr./Bristol Sch. Ballet, 1978—95; creative movement and dance specialist, artistic dir. ballet ensemble Mt. View Elem. Sch., Johnson City, 1995—. Dir.: (artisitc director) several ballet cos. Founding bd. mem. A! Mag. For The Arts, Bristol, Va., 1984—86; instr. liturgical dance St. Anne's Cath. Ch., Bristol; assoc. mem., dir. Southeastern Regional Ballet Assn./Regional Dance Am., Atlanta, 1991—95. Grantee, Johnson City Sports Found., 2005—06, Johnson City Area Arts Coun., 2005—06. Mem.: NEA, Tenn. Edn. Assn., Nat. Dance Edn. Orgn., Nat. Dance Edn. Assn. (assoc.), Tenn. Arts Commn. (assoc.; dance grant rev. panelist 2005), Johnson City Edn. Assn. (assoc.; com. chair 1992—2006, negotiating panel 2006). Home: 2859 Carroll Creek Road Johnson City TN 37615 Office: Johnson City Schools/Mountain View Elem 907 King Springs Road Johnson City TN 37601 Home Phone: 423-753-7645; Office Phone: 423-434-5260. Office Fax: 423-434-5596; Home Fax: 423-913-8183. Personal E-mail: maryanne@maryannesowers.com. E-mail: sowersm@jcschools.org.

SNYDMAN, DAVID RICHARD, infectious diseases specialist, educator; b. Phila., Sept. 23, 1946; m. Diane Canter, June 26, 1971; children: Laura Kate, Alexander Julian. BA, Williams Coll., 1968; MD, U. Pa., 1972. Diplomate Am Bd. Infectious Disease, Am. Bd. Internal Medicine. Intern New Eng. Med. Ctr., Boston, 1972-73, resident in medicine, 1973-74; asst. prof. Sch. Medicine Tufts U., Boston, 1979-84, assoc. prof., 1984-90, prof. medicine and pathology, 1990—; hosp. epidemiologist New Eng. Med. Ctr., Boston, 1979-89, 1998—, dir. clin. microbiology, 1987-98, chief divsn. infectious diseases, 1998—. Epidemic intelligence svc. officer CDC, Atlanta, 1974—76. Assoc. editor: Yearbook of Infectious Diseases, 1986-98, Yearbook of Medicine, 2003—; contbr. to 14 books; contbr. over 200 articles to profl. jours. Lt. comdr. USPHS, 1974-76. Grantee NIH, 1982-93, 2004—; recipient U. Pa. A.O.J. Kelly prize, 1972, citation Mass. Dept. Pub. Health, 1994. Fellow ACP, Infectious Disease Soc. (Bristol fellow 1978-79, Ken Kaplan Clinician award Mass. chpt., 2003, Emanuel Wolinsky award 2004); mem. ACP (Tchng. and Rsch. scholar 1979-82), Soc. Hosp. Epidemiologists, Am. Soc. Transplant Physicians, Mass. Infectious Diseases Soc. (Ken Kaplan clinician 2003). Achievements include first description of Lyme arthritis; rsch. in hosp. infections, intravenous catheter-associated infections, transplant-related infectious diseases, antibiotic resistance, sepsis, cytomegalovirus prevention; developer of cytomegalovirus immune globulin. Office: New Eng Med Ctr 750 Washington St Boston MA 02111-1526 Office Phone: 617-636-5788. Business E-Mail: DSnydman@tufts-nemc.org.

SO, YUEN T., neurologist, educator; m. Susan E. So, June 16, 1979; 2 children. BS, Northwestern U., 1974; PhD, Rockefeller U., 1979; MD, Yale U., 1983. Diplomate in Neurology Am. Bd. Psychiatry and Neurology. Asst. prof. neurology U. Calif., San Francisco, 1989—94; assoc. prof. neurology Oreg. Health Scis. U., Portland, 1994—99; prof. neurology Stanford U., Calif., 1999—, dir. neurology clinic, dir. neurology residency program. Contbr. more than 90 papers, chpts., profl. pubs. Named Outstanding Tchr., U. Calif., San Francisco, 1993, Oreg. Health Scis. U., 1998, Stanford U., 1999, AAMC Humanism in Medicine, 2005. Fellow: Am. Assn. Electrodiagnostic Medicine; mem.: Am. Acad. Neurology, Am. Neurol. Assn. (hon.). Office: Stanford U Dept Neurology Stanford U Med Ctr #5235 Stanford CA 94305-5235

SOARIES, DEFOREST B., JR., former state official; m. Donna Soaries; 2 children. Ph.D (hon.), Drew U.; BA, Fordham U.; MDiv, Princeton Theol. Sem.; DMin, United Theol. Sem., Dayton, Monmouth U. Ordained minister Bapt. Ch., 1990. Sr. pastor First Bapt. Ch. of Lincoln Gardens, Somerset, NJ, 1990—; sec. of state State of N.J., Trenton, 1999—2002. Internat. lectr. in field.; founder First Bapt. Cmty. Devel. Corp., Renaissance Cmty. Devel. Credit Union, CDC Properties, Renaissance Employment & Tng. Acad.; faculty Princeton Theol. Sem., Drew U. Theol. Sch., Kean U., Mercer County Coll. Contbr. articles to profl. jours. Vol. Urban League, Newark, Operation PUSH, Chgo.; advocate for at-risk youth; addressee Pres.'s Summit for Am.'s Future in Phila. Office: First Baptist Church of Lincoln Gardens Ste 101-102 630 Franklin Boulevard Somerset NJ 08873

SOAVE, ANTHONY, manufacturing executive; Pres., CEO, founder City Mgmt. Corp., Detroit, 1974—98, Soave Enterprises LLC, Detroit. Dir. Titan Internat., Inc., 1994—. Office: Soave Enterprises LLC 3400 E Lafayette St Detroit MI 48207-4962

SOAVE, ROSEMARY, internist; b. NYC, Jan. 23, 1949; BS, Fordham U., 1970; MD, Cornell Med. Coll., 1976. Diplomate Am. Bd. Internal Medicine, Subspecialty Bd. in Infectious Diseases. Intern, resident N.Y. Hosp., NYC, 1976-79; chief med. resident Meml.-Sloan Kettering Cancer Ctr., NYC, 1979-80; fellow infectious diseases N.Y. Hosp., NYC, 1980-82, asst. prof. medicine, 1982-89, assoc. prof. medicine and pub. health, 1989—. Spkr. in field; mem. Nat. Insts. Allergy and Infectious Diseases-AIDS and Related Diseases Study Sect. Contbr. numerous articles to profl. jours., chpts. to books, reviews and abstracts to profl. jours. Recipient Mary Putnam Jacobi fellowship for rsch., 1981-82, Leopold Schepp Rsch. fellowship, 1983-84, Nat. Found. for Infectious Diseases Young Investigator Matching Grant award, 1984-85; NIH grantee, 1986-89, 83-86, 87-90, 99-00. Fellow ACP, Infectious Diseases Soc. Am.; mem. AAAS, Am. Fedn. Med. Rsch., N.Y. Acad. Scis., Am. Soc. for Microbiology, Harvey Soc., Sigma Xi. Office: NY Presbyn Hosp Weill Cornell Med Ctr Box 125 1300 York Ave New York NY 10021-4805 Office Phone: 212-746-6319.

SOBBOTT, SUSAN, diversified financial services company executive; b. NJ; 2 children. BA, Georgetown Univ.; MBA, Univ. Va. Joined strategic planning group Am. Express, 1990, sr. v.p., gen. mgr. OPEN Lending and Network Devel. group, pres. OPEN small bus. network NYC, 2004—, and global mgmt. team mem. Mentor Women Unlimited; bd. adv. Women's Leadership Exchange. Named one of America's Top Women in Bus.-Game Changers, Pink mag. & Forté Found., 2007; recipient NY Compass award, 2005. Avocations: bicycling, yoga. Office: OPEN Small Bus Network Am Express 200 Vesey New York NY 10281 Office Phone: 212-227-4262. *

SOBEL, ALAN, electrical engineer, physicist; b. NYC, Feb. 23, 1928; s. Edward P. and Rose (Naftalison) S.; m. Marjorie Loebel, June 15, 1952; children: Leslie Ann, Edward Robert. BSEE, Columbia U., 1947, MSEE, 1949; PhD in Physics, Poly. Inst. Bklyn., 1964. Lic. Profl. Engr., N.Y. and Ill. Asst. chief engr. The Electronic Workshop, NYC, 1950-51; head, functional engr. Fairchild Controls Corp., 1951-56; project engr. Skiatron Electronics and TV Corp., 1956-57; sr. rsch. engr. Zenith Radio Corp., Glenview, Ill., 1964-78; v.p. Lucitron inc., Northbrook, Ill., 1978-87, pres., 1987; pvt. practice cons. Evanston, Ill., 1988—; v.p. Machine Vision and Control Internat. Inc., 1994—2003, LightWave Technologies Corp., 2000—. Asst., instr. Poly. Inst. Bklyn.,1957-64; mem. program coms. SID Internat. Symposium, Internat. Display Rsch. Conf., 1970—. Inventor: 14 patents on various display and electron devices; editor Jour. Soc. Info. Display, 1991-99, assoc. editor, 2000—; adv. editor Info. Display Mag., 1991-2003; assoc. editor: IEEE Trans. on Electron Devices, 1970-77; contbr. articles to profl. jours. Mem. Dem. Party of Evanston. NSF fellow, 1959, 60. Fellow Soc. Info. Display (Lewis and Beatrice Winner award 2002); mem. IEEE (sr., life), SPIE, Am. Phys. Soc., Sigma Xi. Democrat. Home and Office: 1307 Beechwood Dr Ann Arbor MI 48103 Office Phone: 847-869-5607. Personal E-mail: as1285@columbia.edu.

SOBEL, BURTON ELIAS, cardiologist, educator; b. NYC, Oct. 21, 1937; s. Lawrence J. and Ruth (Schoen) Sobel; m. Susan Konheim, June 19, 1958; children: Jonathan, Elizabeth. AB, Cornell U., 1958; MD magna cum laude, Harvard U., 1962. Intern Peter Bent Brigham Hosp., Boston, 1962-63, resident, 1963-64, 66-67; clin. asso., cardiology br. NIH, Bethesda, Md., 1964-66, 67-68; asst. prof. medicine U. Calif. at San Diego, La Jolla, 1968-71, asso. prof. medicine, dir. myocardial infarction research unit, dir. coronary care, 1971-73; asso. prof. medicine Barnes Hosp.-Washington U., St. Louis, 1973-75; adj. prof. chemistry Washington U., St. Louis, 1979-94; prof. medicine Barnes Hosp.-Washington U., 1975—, dir. cardiovascular div., 1973—, program dir. specialized ctr. rsch. ischemic heart disease, 1975-89, program dir. specialized ctr. rsch. in coronary and vascular diseases, 1990-94, program dir. principles in cardiovascular rsch., 1975-94; chmn. and E.L. Amidon prof. medicine, prof. biochemistry U. Vt., Burlington, 1994—2005; physician-in-chief Med. Ctr. Hosp. Vt., Burlington, 1994—2005, Fletcher Allen Health Care, Burlington, 1995—2005; prof. medicine, dir. Cardiovasc. Rsch. Inst. U. Vt., Burlington, 2005—. Program dir. Collaborative Clin. Trial Therapy to Protect Ischemic Myocardium Washington U., 1977, prin. investigator Specialized Ctr. of Rsch. in Ischemic Heart Disease, 1975—95, program dir. Principles in Cardiovasc. Rsch., 1975—95, program dir. Nat. Rsch. and Demonstration Ctr. in Ischemic Heart Disease, 1985—95; chmn. cardio renal drugs US Pharmacopeial Conv., 1990—; prin. investigator BARI, II, NIH Fibrinalysis and Coagulation Core U. Vt., 2000; program dir. Cardiovascular Rsch. Inst./ Medtronic Corp./ U. Vt., 2006—, Disting. Rsch. Alliance / Medtronic Corp./ U. Vt., 2006—; bd. dir. Scios Corp., Corvas Corp., Ariad Corp., Bristol Myers Squibb Corp., Fletcher Allen Health Care, New River Pharm., Inc, Nuvelo Corp., Clin. Data, Inc., Intrexon Corp.; scientific adv. bd. CV Therapeutics, Inc.; sci. adv. bd. Epix Med., Inc., New River Pharm., Inc.; chmn. HaptoGuiard, Inc; co-prin. investigator NIH Regional Heart Failure Network Ctr., U. Vt., 2007—. Assoc. med. editor: Heart Bull, 1971—72; editor: Clin. Cardiology, 1971—74; mem. circulation bd. Clin. Guides to Med. Mgmt., 1971—; editor: Coronary Artery Disease, 1989—, Clin. Guides to Med. Mgmt., 1996—, Circulation, 1983—88; cons. editor Circulation; mem. editl. bd.: Circulation Rsch., 1974—, Annals Internal Medicine, 1976—, Am. Jour. Cardiology, 1976—, Cardiology Digest, 1976—77, Jour. Clin. Investigation, 1977—, Jour. Continuing Edn. Cardiology, 1978—, Am. Jour. Physiology: Heart and Circulatory Physiology, 1978—, Cardiology in Elderly, 1991—, Current Med. Lit., —, Churchill Livingstone edtl. adv. bd.: Internat. Seminars Cardiovascular Medicine, 1978—, Cardiology in Rev., 1992—; mem. editl. bd. Internat. Jour. Cardiology, Fibrinolysis, 1986; assoc. editor: Internat. Jour. Cardiology, Fibrinolysis, 1990—, mem. editl. bd.: Current Opinion in Cardiology, —; editor, 1989—; mem. editl. bd. Can. Jour. Cardiology, 1995—, Arteriosclerosis, Thrombosis, and Vascular Biology, 1996—, Clin. Therapeutics, 1996, Clin. Insights in Diabetes, 1999, Heart Disease, 2000, Diabetes Treatment Today, 2000, Am. Jour. Geriatric Cardiology, 2000, Diabetes Care, 2002—, Current Diabetes Revs., 2004—. Served to lt. comdr. USPHS, 1964—68. Recipient Career Rsch. Devel. award, USPHS, 1972, Internat. Recognition award, Heart Rsch. Found., 1981, Disting. Achievement award, Am. Heart Assn. Sci. Couns., 1984, award, Robert J. and Claire Posatow Found., 1988, Va. Heart Ctr., 1991, Drake award, Maine Heart Assn., 1992, E.L. Amidon Excellence in Tchg. award, U. Vt., 2007. Master: ACP, ASIM; fellow: AAAS (councilor 1997—), Am. Coll Angiology, Am. Coll. Cardiology (Disting. Scientist award 1987), Am. Heart Assn. (coun. on basic cardiovasc. scis., clin. coun., circulation and arteriosclerosis, thrombosis and vascular biology, James B. Herrick award 1992, Spl. Recognition award coun. on arteriosclerosis, thrombosis and vascular biology 1999), Molecular Medicine Soc., Royal Soc. Medicine; mem.: Inst. Biomed. Scis. and Tech., Internat. Acad. Cardiovascular Scis., Internat. Soc. Applied Cardiovasc. Biology, Soc. Exptl. Biology and Medicine (councilor 1998—, pres. bd. govs. 2002—, pres.-elect 2005—, pres. 2007—), Assn. Profs. Cardiology (pres.-elect 1992), Internat. Soc. Fibrinolysis and Thrombolysic (councilor), Western Soc. Clin. Rsch., Cardiac Muscle Soc., Am. Physiol. Soc., Assn. Am. Physicians, Am. Soc. Clin. Investigation (councilor, instnl. rep. 1997—), Assn. Univ. Cardiologists, Am. Fedn. Clin. Rsch. (councilor), Alpha Omega Alpha. Avocations: skiing, sailing. Home: 171 Lost Cove Rd Colchester VT 05446-7473 Office: U Vermont Colchester Rsch Facility 208 S Park Dr Colchester VT 05446 Business E-Mail: burton.sobel@uvm.edu.

SOBEL, CLIFFORD M., ambassador; b. 1949; m. Barbara Sobel; 2 children. Student, U. Vt.; BS in Govt., NYU; LLD (hon.), Kean U., 1999. Chmn., pres. SJJ Investment Corp. and CMS Realty Co.; founder, bd. mem. Norcrown Bank of Roseland, NJ, 1985—91; founder, chmn. several cos. that designed, manufactured and imported fixtures in retail environments; chmn. Net2Phone, Inc.; US amb. to the Netherlands US Dept. State, The Hague, Netherlands, 2001—05, US amb. to Brazil Rio de Janeiro, 2006—. Mem. Holocaust Meml. Coun., Washington, 1994—95. Bd. dirs. NJ Performing Arts Ctr.; apptd. by Sec. Def. to bd. visitors Naval Post Grad. Sch., Monterey, Calif., 1993—97; adv. bds. Empower Em. and Rep. Leadership Coun.; del. Rep. Nat. Conv., 1996, 2000; NJ fin. chmn. primary and presdl. campaigns of George W. Bush, 2000; bd. dirs., mem. policy com. Bus. Execs. for Nat. Security; apptd. US Govt. Industry Sector Internat. Trade bd., 1987—89; exec. com. Prosperity NJ, United Jewish Fedn. Metrowest NJ; bd. dirs. Lexington Inst., Arlington, Va.; chmn. bd. overseer Alexis de Tocqueville Instn. Office: DOS Amb 7500 Brasilia Pl Washington DC 20521-7500 *

SOBEL, GERALD, lawyer; BEE, CCNY, 1960; JD, NYU, 1963; MA in Econs., New Sch. Social Rsch., NYC, 1967. Bar: N.Y., U.S. Ct. Appeals (2d and fed. cirs.), U.S. Dist. Ct. (so., ea. and no. dists.) N.Y., U.S. Supreme Ct. Law clerk to Hon. Richard H. Levet U.S. Dist. Ct. (so. dist.) N.Y., NYC, 1964-65; atty., ptnr., sr. litig. ptnr. Kaye, Scholer, Fierman, Hays & Handler, NYC, 1965—. Adj. assoc. prof. Sch. Law NYU; lectr. Columbia Sch. Law, Stanford Sch. Law. Contbr. articles on litigation, patents and antitrust to profl. jours. Fellow: ABA, Am. Intellectual Property Law Assn., Assn. NY Intellectual Property Law; mem.: Fed. Cir. Bar Assn. Office: Kaye Scholer LLP 425 Park Ave New York NY 10022-3506 Office Phone: 212-836-8515. Business E-Mail: gsobel@keyescholar.com.

SOBEL, HOWARD D., dermatologist; b. 1950; MD, Albert Einstein Coll. of Medicine, Bronx, NY, 1973. Cert. in Dermatologic and Cosmetic Surgery. Residency in dermatology and dermatologic surgery Emory U. Sch. Medicine, Atlanta; clin. attending physician in dermatology and dermatologic surgery Lenox Hill Hosp., Beth Israel Hosp., and Cabrini Med. Ctr.; dir. Skin and Spa Cosmetic Surgery Ctr., NY. Editor-in-chief Internat. Jour. of Cosmetic Surgery and Aesthetic Dermatology, appeared on numerous television and radio programs (including: Sally Jesse Raphael Show, Home Show, Good Day NY, CNBC, MSNBC, New York 1, and Channels 2, 4, 5, and 7 News programs). Fellow: Am. Acad. Cosmetic Surgery; mem.: Am. Soc. Laser Surgery, Am. Soc. Hair Restoration Surgery, Am. Soc. Liposuction Surgery, Am. Acad. Dermatological Surgery, Am. Acad. Dermatology. Achievements include helping to pioneer the union of dermaology with cosmetic surgery; the first surgeon in 1986 to perform liposuction using the tumescent solution purely under local anesthesia; founder and chmn. of HDS Labs, the manufacturer if DDF (Doctor's Dermatologic Formula). Avocations: skiing, tennis. Office: Skin and Spa Cosmetic Surgery Ctr 960A Park Ave New York NY 10028 Office Phone: 212-288-0060. E-mail: hdsobel-md@nyc.rr.com.

SOBEL, MARK ESAR, pathologist, researcher; b. NYC, Apr. 14, 1949; s. Abraham David and Selma Etta (Spitzer) S. BA, Brandeis U., 1970; MD, Mt. Sinai Sch. Medicine, NYC, 1975; PhD in Biomed. Scis., CUNY, 1975. Diplomate Nat. Bd. Med. Examiners. Med. intern, clin. fellow in pediatrics Children's Hosp. Med. Ctr./Harvard U. Med. Sch., Boston, 1975-76; rsch. assoc. NIH, Bethesda, Md., 1976-79, 80-83; sr. investigator Nat. Cancer Inst., Bethesda, 1983-92, chief molecular pathology sect., 1992-2001; sr. exec. dir. Am. Soc. Investigative Pathology, Bethesda, 2001—. Vis. scientist Max Planck Inst. for Biochemistry, Martinsried bei Munchen, Germany, 1979-80; dir. Concepts in Molecular Biology course Am. Soc. Investigative Pathology, Rockville, Md., 1987-99. Contbr. more than 100 articles to profl. jours.; patentee in field. Capt. USPHS, 1975-2001. Recipient Commendation medal USPHS, 1989, other awards. Mem. Am. Soc. for Biochemistry and Molecular Biology, Am. Soc. Investigative Pathology (councilor 1995-97, vice pres.-elect 1997-98, v.p. 1998-99, pres. 1999-2000), Assn. for Molecular Pathology (sec.-treas. 1995-97, pres.-elect 1998, pres. 1999), Assn. Accreditation Human Rsch. Protections Programs (bd. dirs. 2001-), Fedn. of Am. Soc. Exptl. Biology Minority Access Rsch. Careers (adv. bd. 2006-), PubMed Ctrl. (Nat. Adv. Com. 2007-), Phi Beta Kappa, Alpha Omega Alpha, Sigma Xi. Jewish. Avocations: classical music, history. Office: Am Soc Investigative Pathology 9650 Rockville Pike Bethesda MD 20814-3993 Business E-Mail: mesobel@asip.org.

SOBEL, NOAM, science educator; BA, MA Psychobiology, Tel Aviv U., 1995; PhD Neurosci., Stanford U., 1999. Asst. prof. Wills Neurosci. Inst. U. Calif., Berkeley, assoc. prof., Wills Neuroscience Inst., asst. prof. Psychology, assoc. prof., Psychology. Contbr. articles to profl. jours. Recipient Moskowitz Jacobs Inc. award, Assn. for Chemoreception Sciences, 2003; fellow, Helen Hay Whitney Found., 2000; Searle Scholar, 2001. Office: U Calif Berkeley Dept Psychology 3210 Tolman Hall Rm G95 Berkeley CA 94720 Office Phone: 510-643-0131, 510-643-0132. Business E-Mail: nsobel@socrates.berkeley.edu. *

SOBEL, ROBERT A., retired orthopedic surgeon; b. Detroit, Feb. 18, 1916; s. David L. Sobel and Sarah Losh; m. Flora Hannah Rosenbaum, Nov. 9, 1941; children: Susan, Daniel, Joel. AB, U. Mich., 1936, MD, 1939. Capt. US Army, 1942—46. Mem.: ACS, Am. Acad. Orthoped. Surgeons. Home: 25800 W Eleven Mile Rd Apt 258 Southfield MI 48034

SOBELL, NINA R., artist; b. Patchogue, NY, May 4, 1947; d. Jack and Helen Ruth (Rosenberg) S.; m. Christopher Rogers Shearer, Sept. 8, 1982 (div. Mar. 1987); 1 child, Jacqueline Corianne. BFA, Temple U., 1969; MFA, Cornell U., 1971. Cert. educator N.Y. Vis. artist Calif. Inst. of the Arts, Valencia, 1975, Sch. of Architecture, London, 1976; vis. lectr. dept. art Reading (Eng.) U., 1976-77; vis. lectr. dept. design & sculpture UCLA, 1979, assoc. prof. electronic imagery, 1984-85; artist-in-residence interactive telecomm. program NYU, NYC, 1991-92, artist-in-residence Ctr. Digital Multimedia, 1994—; instr. video prodn. Sch. Visual Arts, NYC, 1992-93; dir. tech. integration Aux. Svc. High Schs., N.Y.C. Bd. Edn., 1994—. Artist-lectr. Documenta VII, Kassel, Germany, 1977; juror U.S. Film and Video Festival, L.A., 1984; juror media arts divsn. N.Y. State Coun. on the Arts, N.Y.C., 1994; artist-presenter Siggraph, New Orleans, 1996; resident Banff Ctr. for the Arts, 1998-99. Prin. works include installation Interactive Brainwave Drawings, 1974—, interactive installation Videophone Relay, 1977-79; artist/dir. HIV-INFO Interactive Call-In TV Show, Manhattan Pub.-Access Cable, 1992, ParkBench Pub-Access Web Kiosks, 1994—; curriculum designer Online Art Network for At-Risk Youth, N.Y.C. Bd. Edn., 1996; represented in permanent collection Mus. Modern Art, N.Y.C., Whitney Mus. Art Whitney Web Site. Installation/Lecture grantee Found. Art Resources, 1981; Installation grantee N.Y. State Coun. Arts, 1981. Mem. Art and Sci. Collaborations, Inc., Coll. Art Assn., Assn. Ind. Video and Filmmakers, United Fedn. of Tchrs. Democrat. Jewish. Avocations: swimming, cooking, biking, birdwatching, skating.

SOBELLE, RICHARD E., lawyer; b. Cleve., Mar. 18, 1935; BA, Stanford U., 1956, JD, 1960; LLM, U. So. Calif., 1967. Bar: Calif. 1961, U.S. Supreme Ct. 1969. Exec. Tracinda Corp. Mem. ABA (corp., banking and bus. law sect. 1969-95), State Bar Calif. (del. to conf. state bar dels. 1965-77, exec. com. bus. law sect. 1977-78), L.A. County Bar Assn. (exec. coun., jr. barristers 1965-68, exec. com. bus. and corps. sect. 1973-75). Office: Tracinda Corp 150 S Rodeo Dr Ste 250 Beverly Hills CA 90212-2417

SOBERAL, ISABEL M., minister, music educator, social worker; b. Arecibo, PR, Aug. 22, 1940; d. Jesús Soberal and Justina Román; children: Isabel M., Maria T., Ana M., Miguel A. Rodriguez. BA, Catholic U., 1962; MDiv, Evangelical Sem., 1997, MA in Religion, 2001; postgrad., Instituto Teologico Internacional de Puerto Rico, 2002—. Ordained min. Meth. Ch., 2005; LCSW 1963. Social worker Health Dept., PR, 1963—88; handbell choir dir. Samuel Aun Weor handbell choir, PR, 1986—2004; music tchr. Dept. Edn., PR, 1994—2004; pastor United Meth. Ch., Hopkinsville, Ky., 2004—05, Meth. Ch., PR, 2002—04. Hand bell choir dir. Sala Festivales-

Centro Bellas Artes, 2002—04; interpreter Cabinet for Health and Family Svcs. Disability Determination Svcs. Named one of, Musicians Arts Corp., 2003. Mem.: Assn. de Maestros de PR, Am. Guild English Handbell Ringers. Home: 2820 S Virginia St Hopkinsville KY 42240 Office: St John Corona de Vida 2808 S Virginia St Hopkinsville KY 42240 Home Phone: 270-886-8408; Office Phone: 270-886-1049. Office Fax: 270-886-0391. E-mail: isabelm@hesenergy.net, isbsb@aol.com.

SOBERON, PRESENTACION ZABLAN, state bar administrator; b. Cabambangan, Bacolor, Pampanga, Philippines, Feb. 23, 1935; came to U.S., 1977; naturalized, 1984; d. Pioquinto Yalung and Lourdes (David) Zablan; m. Damaso Reyes Soberon, Apr. 2, 1961; children: Shirley, Sherman, Sidney, Sedwin. Office mgmt., stenography, typing cert., East Cen. Colls., Philippines, 1953; profl. sec. diploma, Internat. Corr. Schs., 1971; A in Mgmt. Supervision, Skyline and Diablo Coll., 1979, LaSalle Ext. U., 1980-82; AA, cert. in Mgmt. and Supervision, Diablo Valley Coll. With U.S. Fed. Svc. Naval Base, Subic Bay, Philippines, 22 yrs, clerical, stenography and secretarial postitions, 1955-73, adminstrv. asst., 1973-77; secretarial positions Mt. Zion Hosp. and Med. Ctr., San Francisco, 1977, City Hall, Oakland, Calif., 1978; with State Bar Calif., San Francisco, 1978-79; secretarial positions gen. counsel divsn. and state bar ct. divsn., adminstrv. asst. fin. and ops. divsn., 1979-81; office mgr. sects. and coms. dept., profl. and pub. svcs., 1981-83; appointment adminstr. office of bar rels., 1983-86; adminstr. state bar sects. bus. law sect., estate planning, trust and probate law sect., labor and employment law sect., office of bar rels., 1986-89; adminstr. antitrust and trade regulation law sect., labor and employment law sect., workers' compensation sect., edn. and meeting svcs., 1989-96; adminstr. criminal law sect., 1996—; labor and law employment law sect., 1996—; internat. law sect., 1996—; workers' compensation sect., 1996—; edn. and meeting svcs., 1996-98; ret., 1998. Lectr., min. Our Lady of the Queen of the World Ch.; disc jockey, announcer Radio Sta. DZYZ, DZOR and DWHL, Philippines, 1966-77. Organizer Neighborhood Alert Program, South Catamaran Circle, Pittsburg, Calif., 1979-80. Recipient 13 commendation certs. and outstanding pers. monetary awards U.S. Fed. Svc., 1964-77, 20 Yr. U.S. Fed. Svc. cert., 1975, Nat. 1st prize award Nat. Inner Wheel Clubs Philippines, 1975, Kaiser Vol. Svc. Mem.: NAFE, Am. Soc. Assn. Execs., Our Lady Queen Ch. Filipino Assn., SRF Tigers No. Calif., Castillejos Assn. No. Calif., Olongapo-Subic Bay Assn. Am. (Pitts. rep. 1982—87, bus. mgr. 1988—89, pub. rels. officer 1993—94, bus. mgr. 1997—, bus. mgr. Ulo Ng Apo chpt. 2003—). Roman Catholic. Home: 207 South Catamaran Circle Pittsburg CA 94565-3613 Office: State Bar of Calif 180 Howard St San Francisco CA 94105-1639 Personal E-mail: pzsoberon@comcast.net.

SOBEY, DAVID FRANK, food company executive; b. Stellarton, NS, Can., 1931; s. Frank Hoyse and Irene S.; m. Faye B. Naugle, June 2, 1953; children: Paul David, Janis Irene Hames. D of Commerce (hon.), St. Mary's U., 1991. With Sobeys Inc., Stellarton, 1949—, store mgr., dir. merchandising and advt., v.p., exec. v.p., pres., dep. chmn., chief exec. officer, dir., 1981-85, chmn., 1985—2001, chmn. emeritus, 2001—. Mem. Order of Can., 1996; bd. dirs. Empire Co. Ltd., Sobeys Inc.; chmn. The Sobey Found., Frank H. Sobey Fund for Excellence in Bus. Studies. Bd. dirs. The Sobey Art Found., Boy Scouts Can., Atlantic Salmon Fedn. Named to Canadian Bus. Hall Fame, 2007. Mem.: Abercrombie Golf Club, City Club (New Glasgow), Halifax Club. Office: Sobeys Inc 115 King St Stellarton NS Canada B0K 1S0

SOBEY, DONALD CREIGHTON RAE, real estate developer; b. New Glasgow, NS, Can., Oct. 23, 1934; s. Frank Hoyse and Irene (MacDonald) S.; m. Elizabeth H. Purvis; children: Robert George Creighton, Irene Elizabeth, Kent Richard. B of Commerce, Queen's U.; LLD (hon.), Dalhousie U., 1989. Dir. Alliance Atlantis Corp., 1989—; pres. Empire Co. Ltd., 1969, chmn., 1985—, chmn. emeritus, 2004—; also bd. dirs. Bd. dirs. Sobeys Inc., World Wildlife Found. Gov. Olympic Trust Can.; chair Nat. Gallery Can.; mem. Can. group The Trilateral Commn. Avocations: skiing, tennis, music, art, travel. Office: Empire Co Ltd 115 King ST Stellarton NS Canada B0K 1S0

SOBEY, EDWIN J. C., museum director, oceanographer, consultant; b. Phila., Apr. 7, 1948; s. Edwin J. and Helen (Chapin) S.; m. Barbara Lee, May 9, 1970; children: Ted Wooddall, Andrew Chapin. BS, U. Richmond, 1969; MS, Oreg. State U., 1974, PhD, 1977. Rsch. scientist Sci. Applications, Inc., Boulder, Colo., 1977-79, divsn. mgr., 1979-81; exec. dir. Sci. Mus., West Palm Beach, Fla., 1981-88, Mus. Sci. and History, Jacksonville, Fla., 1988, Nat. Invention Ctr., Akron, Ohio, 1989-92, Fresno Met. Mus., Calif., 1993-95; ednl. cons., 1995—. Exec. dir. A.C. Gilbert's Discovery Village, Salem, Oreg., 1997-99; pres. Northwest Invention Ctr., 1999—; founder Nat. Toy Hall of Fame, 1998; instr. mus. mgmt. U. Wash., 1998-2001. Author: Complete Circuit Training Guide, 1980, Strength Training Book, 1981, The Whole Backpacker's Catalog, 1988, Increasing Your Audience, 1989, Inventing Stuff, 1995, Wrapper Rockets and Trombone Straws-Science at Every Meal, 1996, Car Smarts, 1997, Just Plane Smart, 1998, Young Inventors at Work, 1999, How to Enter and Win an Invention Contest, 1999, Fantastic Flying Fun with Science, 2000, Wacky Water Fun with Science, 2000, Inventing Toys: Kids Having Fun Learning Science, 2001, How to Build Your Own Prize-Winning Robot, 2002, Loco-Motion, 2005, Rocket-Powered Science, 2005, A Field Guild to Roadside Technology, 2006, A Field Guide to Household Technology, 2007; co-author: Aerobic Weight Training Book, 1982; mem. editl. adv. bd. Invent Mag., 1989—92; exec. prodr.: (TV show) Idea Factory, Sta. KFSN-30, 1995—97; co-host (ednl. TV show) Blow the Roof Off, 1992. Alumni v.p. Leadership Palm Beach County; expdn. leader Expdn. Tng. Inst., S.E. Alaska, 1980; mem. U.S. Antarctic Rsch. Program, 1974; founder, bd. dirs. Visually Impaired Sports Program, Boulder, 1978-81; fitness instr. YMCA Boulder, 1977-81; convener 1st Nat. Conf. Sports for the Blind, 1979; bd. dirs. Leadership Palm Beach; vice chmn. County Com. on Artificial Reefs; treas. Leadership Akron Alumni Assn., 1990-91, class pres. Leadership Akron; v.p. Ohio Mus. Assn., 1991-92, pres., 1992-93; bd. dirs. Fla. Mus. Assn., 1988-89; mem. adv. bd. Marine Sci. Inst., 1990—. Lt. USN, 1970-73. Named to Nonfiction Honor List, Voice of Youth Activities, 2003; recipient Disting. award, Akron Coun. Engring. and Scientific Socs., 1992, award, Ohio Ednl. Broadcasting Network Commn., 1994, Congl. award for inventing equitable futures, 2005. Fellow Explorers Club (chair Pacific Midwest chpt. 2002—); mem. Marine Tech. Soc. (sect. chmn. 1982-84), Coral Reef Soc. (chpt. pres. 1982-87), Nat. Inventive Thinking Assn. (bd. dirs. 1989—). Home: 2420 178th Ave NE Redmond WA 98052-5820 Office Phone: 425-861-8685. Personal E-mail: sobey@gte.net.

SOBIESKI, JAROSLAW, aerospace engineer; b. Wilno, Poland, Mar. 11, 1934; came to U.S., 1966; naturalized, 1971. s. Stanislaw and Sabina Sobieszczanski; m. Wanda Dlugosz, Dec. 31, 1958; children: Margaret Ann, Ian Patrick. BS aeros., Tech. U. Warsaw, 1955, MS aeros., 1957, DEng, 1964. Cons. Polish Aircraft Industries, Warsaw, 1957-64; asst. and adj. prof. Tech. U. Warsaw, Warsaw, 1955-64; rsch. assoc. Tech. U. Norway, Trondheim, 1964-66; assoc. prof. St. Louis U., 1966-71; aerospace engr. NASA Langley Rsch. Ctr., Hampton, Va., 1971-89, head rsch. office, 1979-93, chief scientist, 1993—96, multidisciplinary rsch. coord., 1994—2001, mgr. Computational AeroScis. team, 1996—2001, sr. rsch. scientist, 2001—06, disting. rsch. assoc., 2006—. Mem. faculty George Washington U., 1971-2003, U. Va., 1992-99, Va. Poly. Inst., 2004—; pres. and cons. engr. Tech. Analysis Optimization, Inc. Hampton, Va., 1982-02. Co-editor: Structural Optimization jour., 1989-2005; contbr. articles to profl. jours. Recipient Wright Bros. medal, SAE, 2000. Fellow AIAA (mem. tech. com., Nat. Multidisciplinary Design Optimization award 1996); mem. International Soc. for Structural and Multidisciplinary Optimization (founding mem. exec. bd. 1992—2003). Achievements include research in and problem solving for aeronautics, space flight, and high performance computing; multidisciplinary design optimization. Home: 518 Elizabeth Lake Dr Hampton VA 23669-1724 Office: NASA Langley Rsch Ctr MS 188E Hampton VA 23681-0001 Home Phone: 757-851-8690; Office Phone: 757-864-2799. E-mail: jaroslaw.sobieski-1@nasa.gov.

SOBKOWICZ, HANNA MARIA, retired neurologist; b. Warsaw, Jan. 1, 1931; arrived in U.S., 1963; d. Stanislaw and Jadwiga (Ignaczak) S.; m. Jerzy E. Rose, Mar. 12, 1972. BA, Girls State Lyceum, Gilwice, Poland, 1949; M.D, Med. Acad., Warsaw, 1954, PhD, 1962. Intern. 1st Internal Med. Clinic Med. Acad., Warsaw, 1954-55; resident 1st Internal Med. Clinic, Med. Acad., Warsaw, 1955-59, Neurol. Clinic, Med. Acad., 1959, jr. asst., 1959-61, sr. asst., 1961-63; research fellow neurology Mt. Sinai Hosp., NYC, 1963-65; Nat. Multiple Sclerosis Soc. fellow Columbia U., NYC, 1965-66; asst. prof. neurology U. Wis., Madison, 1966-72, assoc. prof., 1972-79, prof., 1979—2006, prof. emerita, 2006—. Contbr. articles to profl. jours. NIH rsch. grantee, 1968—2002. Mem. Internat. Brain Rsch. Orgn., Soc. Neurosci., Internat. Soc. Devel. Neurosci. (editl. bd. 1984—). Office Phone: 608-262-1246. Business E-Mail: hmsobkow@wisc.edu.

SOBLE, MARK RICHARD, lawyer; b. San Francisco, Dec. 25, 1964; life ptnr. Leslye Soble, Nov. 2000. BA with deptl. honors, Stanford U., 1985; JD, U. Mich., 1988. Bar: Calif. 1988, U.S. Dist. Ct. (cen. dist.) Calif. 1988, U.S. Dist. Ct. (ea. dist.) Calif. 1990, U.S. Dist. Ct. (no. and so. dists.) Calif. 2003. Law clk. to chief judge U.S. Dist. Ct. for S.D., Pierre, 1988-89; assoc. Lewis, D'Amato, Brisbois & Bisgaard, LA, 1989-90; counsel enforcement div. Fair Polit. Practices Commn., Sacramento, 1990-96, sr. counsel, 1996—2001; dep. atty. gen. civil div. Office of Calif. Atty. Gen., 2001—. Note editor U. Mich. Jour. Law Reform, 1987-88. Raymond K. Dykema scholar U. Mich. 1987. Mem. State Bar Calif., Sacramento County Bar Assn. (mng. editor Docket 1997, mem.-at-large bar coun. 1998-00). Business E-Mail: mark@4lawyer.net.

SOBOL, ELISE SCHWARCZ, music educator; b. Chgo., June 12, 1951; d. Morton and Harriet Jacobsohn Schwarcz; m. Lawrence Paul Sobol, Aug. 21, 1977 (div. Sept. 1989); children: Marlon I., Aaron L. AA, Simon's Rock Bard Coll., 1971; student, Mannes Coll. Music, 1971—73, Juillard Sch. Music, 1973—74; BA, New Sch. Social Rsch., 1985; MA, Columbia U., 1987. Staff auditorium events, concerts, lectures Met. Mus. Art, 1972-73; sec. to pres. Harry Beall Mgmt. Inc., NYC, 1973-76; sales rep. M.L. Falcone Pub. Rels., NYC, 1976-77; asst. to pres. Jacques Leiser Artist Mgmt., NYC, 1977-78; artist rep. Elise Sobol Mgmt. Inc., South Huntington, NY, 1978-82; dir. early musical devel. program children Calling All Kids, South Huntington, 1981—86; tchr. music Roslyn Mid. Sch., 1987—88, Nassau Boces Divsn. Spl. Edn., 1988—; dir. LI Music Workshop, 1992—. Tchr. young and adult piano students, 1968—; instr. SUNY, Farmingdale, 1993—98; piano adjudicator, NY, 1993—; guest lectr. NYU, NYC, 1999; adj. prof. NYU, Steinhardt Sch. Edn., NYC, 2000—; advisor arts and humanities Internat. Biog. Ctr., Cambridge, England; guest lectr. Hofstra, 2000; adj. faculty C.W. Post Coll. LI U., 2000. Musician: (piano concerts) Chamber Music series at U.S. Mil. Acad., N.Y../N.J. met. area concerts, Disting. Artists series, 2002—03, Met. Area Concerts, 2003, Am. Assn. Univ. Women Commentary and Concerts, 2003; musician: (commentary and concert) A Gentlewoman's Pursuit, AAUW, 2003, concerts in New Zealand, Australia, Eng., Ireland, Can. and U.S.; contbg. author: Spotlight in Making Music with Special Learners, 2004; author, author: An Attitude and Approach for Teaching Music to Special Learners, 2001. Active Nassau Boces Elem. Program PTA, cultural arts coord., 1988—2005. Nominee, NY Senate Women of Distinction Program, 2003; named an Outstanding Am. Tchr., Nat. Honor Roll, 2005—06; recipient Honor award, LI Very Spl. Arts Festival, 1993, Spl. citation, NY State Assembly Ames Elem. Program, 1998, Spl. recognition, Nassau Music Educators Assn., 1999, 1st prize, Dr. Martin Luther King Jr. Performing Arts Competition, 1999—2001, Internat. Peace prize, United Cultural Conv., 2002, citation, Town of Oyster Bay, 2002, award, Ernest Kay Internat. Found., Dublin, 2004. Mem.: AAUP, ASCD, NAFE, Music Educators Nat. Conf., N.Y. State Sch. Music Assn. (chair music spl. learners 1993—). Home: 21 Saxon St Melville NY 11747 Office Phone: 516-662-1250. Business E-Mail: es86@nyu.edu.

SOBOL, ZBIGNIEW W., orthopedist, surgeon; b. Chelmno, Poland, Feb. 25, 1926; arrived in U.S., 1949; s. Wladyslaw and Wanda Caroline Sobol; m. Eve Frances Harvey, Sept. 13, 1956; children: Stefan, Christine, Peter, Andrew. B in Medicine and Surgery, Edinburgh U., Scotland, 1948. Diplomate Am. Bd. Orthopedic Surgery. Intern in surgery Bolton Royal Infirmary, England, 1949; resident in internal medicine Overlook Hosp., Summit, NJ, 1950, resident surgery, 1951; resident orthop. surgery Columbia Presbyn. Med. Ctr. N.Y. Orthop. Hosp., 1952—56; orthopedic surgeon Meml. Hosp., South Bend, Ind., 1962—, St. Joseph Med. Ctr., Mishawaka, Ind., 1962—, chmn. dept. orthopedic surgery, 1991—95. Med. missionary Christian Med. Soc., Jamaica, 1984, Kenya, 1996; hon. cons. Polish hosps., 1986—. Fellow: ACS, Academy Orthopedic Surgeons; mem.: Polish Orthop. and Traumatol. Soc. (hon.). Home: 19072 Summers Dr South Bend IN 46637 Office: 320 W 4th St Mishawaka IN 46544 Office Phone: 574-255-5219.

SOBOLEV, ALEXANDRE ANDREEVICH, physicist; b. Ramenskoye, Russia, June 18, 1952; s. Andrew Puzirev and Anna (Soboleva) Terekhova; m. Yaroslava Stepanovna Schumliakovskaya, Nov. 5, 1975 (div. 1980); 1 child, Yegor; m. Tatiana Arkadievna Silitch, Dec. 19, 1992; 1 child, Maria. MSc, Moscow Inst. Engring. Physics, 1978, PhD, 1990. Rschr. Inst. Physics & Power Engring., Obninsk, Russia. Dep. Obninsk City Coun., 1989-93. Jr. sgr. Soviet Army, 1971-73. Mem.: Obninsk Phys. Soc., Moscow Phys. Soc. Mem. Orthodox Ch. Home Phone: 514-489-3888. Personal E-mail: sobolev9@videotron.ca.

SOBOLEWSKI, JOHN STEPHEN, computer scientist, director, consultant; b. Krakow, Poland, July 14, 1939; came to U.S., 1966; s. Jan Zygmund and Stefania (Zwolinska) S.; m. Helen Skipper, Dec. 17, 1965 (div. July 1969); m. Carole Straith, Apr. 6, 1974; children: Anne-Marie, Elisa, Martin. BE, U. Adelaide, Adelaide, South Australia, 1962, ME, 1966; PhD in Computer Sci., Wash. State U., 1971. Sci. officer Weapons Research Establishment, Salisbury, South Australia, 1964-66; asst. prof. computer sci. Wash. State U., Pullman, 1966-73; dir. research, assoc. prof. U. Wash., Seattle, 1973-80, dir. computer svcs., 1980-88; assoc. v.p. computing U. N.Mex., Albuquerque, 1988—. Cons. govt. and industry, Seattle, 1973—; mem. bd. trustees Fisher Found., Seattle, 1984—. Author: Computers for the Dental Office, 1986; contbr. articles to profl. jours. Served as engr. with Royal Australian Army, 1957-60. Australian govt. scholar, 1954-60, Elec. Res. Bd. scholar CSIRO, Melbourne, Australia, 1961-64. Mem. IEEE, Computer Soc. Roman Catholic. Avocation: mineral collecting. Home: 18422 57th Ave NE Kenmore WA 98028 Personal E-mail: nwminerals@hotmail.com.

SOBONYA, STEPHANIE JEAN N'COLE, mathematics educator; b. Garfield Heights, Ohio, Jan. 30, 1977; d. William Lester, Jr. and Pamela Ann Sobonya. B in Bus. Adminstrn., Kent State U., Ohio, 1999. Lic. Middle Childhood Math/Reading/Lang. Arts Tchr. Ohio, 2005. Human resources specialist Guardsmark, Inc., Independence, Ohio, 1999—2001; human resources coord. Pk. City Solutions, Inc., 2001—03; tchr. math and reading Garfield Heights City Schs., 2005—. Mem.: NEA. Democrat. Roman Catholic. Avocations: travel, cooking, swimming, bicycling, camping. Home: 6300 Greenwood Pkwy #401 Northfield OH 44067 Office: Garfield Heights City Schs 5640 Briarcliff Dr Cleveland OH 44125 Home Phone: 330-468-7981; Office Phone: 216-475-8100.

SOBRATO, JOHN A., construction executive; married; 3 children. Real estate agt., Palo Alto, 1957; founder, prin. Sobrato Devel. Cos., Cupertino, Calif. Trustee U. Santa Clara; vice chmn. Nat. Hispanic U. Named Philanthropist of Yr., NSFRE, 1998; named one of Forbes' Richest Americans, 2006. Office: Sobrato Devel Cos Ste 200 10600 N De Anza Blvd Cupertino CA 95014-2075

SOCHACKI, ANDRZEJ, mechanical engineer, researcher, tourism educator; b. Warsaw, July 26, 1948; came to U.S., 1973; s. Jerzy and Halina (Błażejczyk) S.; married. MS, Warsaw U., 1969; AAS, Maricopa Tech. Coll., Phoenix, 1983; postgrad., Ariz. State U., 1985. Sr. mech. engr. Roger Bus. Products div. Rogers Corp., Mesa, Ariz., 1986-87; sr. mech. design engr. Parker Aerospace Co., Phoenix, 1987-88; sr. project engr. Micro-Rel Inc., Tempe, Ariz., 1988-90; cons., project engr., pres., owner Design & Fabricating Co., Phoenix, 1985-96; founder, pres., chmn. The Vagabond Ctr., Phoenix, 1992; tool engr. Boeing Co., Mesa, Ariz., 1996-98; tchr., lectr. traveling Tourism and Hotels Mgmt. Coll., Warsaw, 1998—. Contbr. articles to profl. jours. Recipient award Medtronic Corp., Phoenix, 1989. Mem. Soc. Mfg. Engrs. (sr.). Roman Catholic. Avocations: piano, research, 6 times travel around the world by car, plane, sailboat, train, and twice by motorcycle. Home and Office: The Vagabond Ctr 3715 E Taylor St Phoenix AZ 85008-6316 Home Phone: 602-244-1293. Personal E-mail: asochacki@yahoo.com.

SOCHEN, JUNE, history professor; b. Chgo., Nov. 26, 1937; d. Sam and Ruth (Finkelstein) S. BA, U. Chgo., 1958; MA, Northwestern U., 1960, PhD, 1967. Project editor Chgo. Superior and Talented Student Project, 1959-60; high sch. tchr. English and history North Shore Country Day Sch., Winnetka, Ill., 1961-64; instr. history Northeastern Ill. U., 1964-67, asst. prof., 1967-69, assoc. prof., 1969-72, prof., 1972—. Author: The New Woman, 1971, Movers and Shakers, 1973, Herstory: A Woman's View of American History, 1975, 2d edit., 1981, Consecrate Every Day: The Public Lives of Jewish American Women, 1981, Enduring Values: Women in Popular Culture, 1987, Cafeteria America: New Identities in Contemporary Life, 1988, Mae West: She Who Laughs Lasts, 1992, From Mae to Madonna: Women Entertainers in 20th Century America, 1999; editor: The New Feminism in 20th Century America, 1972, Women's Comic Visions, 1991; contbr. articles to profl. jours. Nat. Endowment for Humanities grantee, 1971-72 Office: Northeastern Ill U 5500 N Saint Louis Ave Chicago IL 60625-4679 Office Phone: 773-442-5607. Business E-Mail: j-sochen@neiu.edu.

SOCHET, MARY ALLEN, psychotherapist, educator, writer; b. Plattsburgh, NY, Feb. 10, 1938; d. Edwin Elisha and Mary Elizabeth (Thomson) Allen; m. Marvin J. Sochet, 1963; children: Melorra, David. BS in Childhood Edn., SUNY, Plattsburgh, 1958; MA in Human Rels., NYU, 1961, PhD in Human Devel., 1963. Tchr. kindergarten L.I. Pub. Schs., 1958-62; tchr. N.Y.C. Pub. Schs., 1962-64; prof. early childhood edn., child devel. and psychology Bklyn. Coll., 1964-71; program dir., acting exec. dir. Newark Pre-Sch. Coun., 1965-66; psychotherapist N.Y.C. Community Guidance Svc., 1966-78; staff cons. Human Resources Inst., 1966—; pvt. practice psychotherapy NYC, 1966—. Writer, lectr., ednl. cons. and editorial cons. in field. Author: (with Robert Allen) Toward a Caring Community, 1980; contbr. articles on edn., community orgns., peace and mental health to various jours. Founding mem. Community Loft, 1971-74, Neighbor's Network, 1979—; organizing mem. Children's Free Sch., 1969-81; co-chair Perhaps Kids Meeting Kids Can Make a Difference, 1982—. NCCJ fellow, 1961-61; recipient Founder's Day award NYU, 1963. Mem. Am. Psychol. Assn., Soc. Psychol. Study Social Issues, Psychologists for Social Responsibility. Home and Office: 380 Riverside Dr New York NY 10025-1858 Office Phone: 212-662-2327. Business E-Mail: kidsmtgkids@igc.org.

SOCOL, MICHAEL LEE, obstetrician, gynecologist, educator; b. Chgo., Oct. 3, 1949; s. Joseph and Bernice (Bofman) S.; m. Donna Kaner, Dec. 17, 1972. BS, U. Ill., 1970; MD, U. Ill., Chgo., 1974. Diplomate Am. Bd. Ob-Gyn., Am. Bd. Maternal-Fetal Medicine. Resident obstetrics and gynecology U. Ill. Hosp., Chgo., 1974-77; clin. rsch. fellow dept. obstetrics and gynecology L.A. County-U. So. Calif. Med. Ctr., 1977-79; assoc. attending physician Northwestern Meml. Hosp., Chgo., 1980-86, attending physician dept. ob-gyn., 1986—; co-dir. Northwestern Perinatal Ctr., Chgo., 1987—; chief obstetrics Northwestern Meml. Hosp., Chgo., 1987—, dir. maternal-fetal medicine fellowship program, 1987-99, asst. prof. obstetrics and gynecology, 1979-84, assoc. prof., 1984-92, prof., 1992—. Vice chmn. dept. ob-gyn Northwestern Meml. Hosp., Chgo., 1992—. Author: (with others) Clinical Obstetrics and Gynecology, 1982, 1984, Diagnostic Ultrasound Applied to Obstetrics and Gynecology, 1987, Principles and Practice of Medical Therapy in Pregnancy, 1992; peer reviewer Am. Jour. Obstetrics and Gynecology, 1980—, Obstetrics and Gynecology, 1984—; contbr. numerous articles to profl. jours. Fellow Am. Coll. Ob-Gyn., Soc. Maternal-Fetal Medicine, Soc. for Gynecol. Investigation, Am. Gynecol. and Obstet. Soc.; mem. Assn. Profs. Gynecology and Obstetrics. Avocation: marathon running. Office: 333 E Superior St Ste 410 Chicago IL 60611-3015 Office Phone: 312-926-7518.

SOCOLOW, DAVID JACOB, state agency administrator; b. New Haven, Conn., Jan. 31, 1969; s. Robert H. and Elizabeth A. (Sussman) Socolow; m. Erin Marie Spinello, Nov. 20, 1999; 2 children. AB magna cum laude, Harvard U., 1991; MPA, Rutgers U. Phila. fin. coord. U.S. Senator Harris Wofford's campaign, Phila., 1991; N.Y. state fin. dir. Bob Abrams for U.S. Senate, NYC, 1991-92; v.p. Fundraising Mgmt. Group, Washington, 1993-94; dir. Am. Resources Info. Network, Washington, 1995-96; chief staff to Congressman Robert E. Andrews U.S. Ho. of Reps., Washington, 1996—2000; assoc. dir. congressional affairs US Labor Dept., 2001; dir. unemployment ins. NJ Dept. Labor and Workforce Devel., Trenton, NJ, 2002—06, acting commr., 2006, commr., 2006—. Bd. dirs. Ctr. for Environ. Citizenship, Washington, 1995-99; rsch. asst. Clinton-Gore Transition Team, Washington, 1992-93. Democrat. Jewish. Office: NJ Dept Labor and Workforce Devel PO Box 110 Trenton NJ 08625-0110

SOCOLOW, ELIZABETH ANNE, poet, educator, artist, writer; b. NYC, June 15, 1940; d. Ralph Maurice and Frances Irene (Goldberg) Sussman; m. Robert H. Socolow, June 10, 1962 (div. Apr. 1982); children: David Jacob, Seth Louis. BA, Vassar Coll., 1962; MA, Harvard U., 1963, PhD, 1967. Lectr. in English and composition U. Mich., Dearborn, 1993—99; lectr. in English Wayne State U., 1993—99, Lawrence Technol. U., Southfield, Mich., 1994—98; lectr. Bucks County C.C., 1999—2001, Rutgers/Camden at Freehold, 2001—. Poetry editor newsletter Soc. for Lit. and Sci., Athens, Ga., 1989—. Author: Laughing at Gravity: Conversations With Isaac Newton, 1988 (Barnard Women Poets Series prize 1987). Avocations: computer, graphics, cards.

SOCOLOW, ROBERT HARRY, engineering educator, physicist; b. NYC, Dec. 27, 1937; s. A. Walter and Edith (Gutman) S.; m. Elizabeth Anne Sussman, June 10, 1962 (div. Apr. 27, 1982); children: David, Seth; m. Jane Ries Pitt, May 25, 1986; stepchildren: Jennifer, Eric. BA summa cum laude in Physics, Harvard Coll., 1959; MA in Physics, Harvard U., 1961, PhD in Physics, 1964. NSF predoctoral fellow, 1960—64; NSF postdoctoral fellow physics U. Calif. Berkeley and European Ctr. Nuc. Rsch. (CERN), 1964—66; asst. prof. dept. physics Yale U., New Haven, 1966-71; assoc. prof. dept. aerospace and mech. scis., mem. Ctr. Environ. Studies Princeton U., NJ, 1971-77, prof., 1977—79, assoc. dir. Ctr. for Environmental Studies, 1977—78, acting dir. Ctr. for Environmental Studies, 1978—79, prof. dept. mech. and aerospace engring., 1979—, co-dir. Carbon Mitigation Initiative, 2000—. Rsch. assoc. dept. geology and geophysics Yale U., 1971; mem. Inst. Advanced Study Princeton U.,

1971; dir. Princeton U. Ctr. Environ. Studies, 1977—78, acting dir., 1978—79; dir. Princeton U. Ctr. Energy and Environ. Studies, 1979—98; chmn. bd. Am. Coun. Energy Efficient Econ., 1989—93; bd. dirs. Nat. Audubon Soc., 1992—99; mem. environ. sci. adv. com. Environ. Def. Fund, 1999—2001; mem. various com. U.S. Dept. of Energy, 1995—2000; mem. various com. including energy and environmental sys. com., panel on carbon sequestration & com. on alt. and strategies for future hydrogen prod. Nat. Rsch. Council, 1993—2006. Contbr. articles to profl. jours., chapters to books; co-editor: Patient Earth, 1971, Efficient Use of Energy, 1975, Boundaries of Analysis: An Inquiry into the Tocks Island Dam Controversy, 1976, Indsl. Ecology and Global Change, 1994, Environmentally Significant Consumption, 1997; editor: Saving Energy in the Home: Princeton's Expts. at Twin Rivers, 1978; assoc. editor: Ann. Rev. Energy and Environment, 1988—92; editor, 1992—2002; contbg. editor: Environment, 1999—, mem. mng. bd.: Jour. Indsl. Ecology, mem. editl. bd.: Perspectives in Energy, Energy and Bldgs. Named Lifetime Nat. Assoc. of Nat. Acad., 2004; recipient Axelson Johnson Commemorative Lecture award, 2005; grantee John Simon Guggenheim fellowship, 1976—77, German Marshall Fund fellowship, 1976—77. Fellow: Am. Phys. Soc. (Leo Szilard Lectureship award 2003), AAAS. Jewish. E-mail: socolow@princeton.edu. *

SODAL, INGVAR EDMUND, electrical engineer, science administrator; b. Hemne, Norway, Feb. 12, 1934; came to U.S., 1962; s. Ingebrigt L. and Johanna Sodal; m. Sally Rollins; 1 child, Silje M. Degree in elec. engring., Trondheim Tech. Coll., Norway, 1959; BSEE, U. Colo., 1964. Engr. Fjeldseth Engring., Trondheim, 1959-61; rsch. engr. U. Norway, Trondheim, 1961-62, U. Colo. Med. Ctr., Denver, 1964-66, rsch. assoc., 1966-75, instr., lectr., 1975-79; vis. rsch. assoc. dept. engring. U. Colo., Boulder, 1974-75, lectr., 1975-76; asst. prof., div. head. Ohio State U., Columbus, 1979-82, mem. grad. faculty, 1982; pres., chief exec. officer Masstron, Inc., Boulder, Colo., 1983-87; chief scientist Paradygm, Boulder, 1987-89; pres. Pacemark, Inc., Boulder, 1989-90, Med. Physics Colo., Inc., 1991—; ret. Contbr. articles to profl. jours., chpts. to books; holder 6 patents in field. Instr. and/or program coord. in Scandinavian folklore and folk dancing for numerous groups and instns. throughout U.S., Can., and Norway, 1959—. Grantee, NIH, others. Mem. Village Arts Coalition, Sons of Norway. Office: 1550 Moss Rock Pl Boulder CO 80304-1543 E-mail: sodaling@norsk.us, ingvarsodal@netscape.net.

SODANO, SALVATORE F., former stock exchange executive; b. Jan. 17, 1956; m. Anne Sodano; 2 children. BA, Hofstra U., 1977, MBA in Banking and Fin., 1983. Staff acct. Price Waterhouse & Co.; asst. to treas. Morgan Guaranty Internat. Fin. Corp., 1979—83; with Bankers Trust Co., 1983—90, v.p., group head; v.p., dep. controller NY Branch Westpac Banking Corp., 1990—91, v.p., controller, 1991—93, v.p., controller Am. Div., 1993—94, sr. v.p., CFO, 1994—95, sr. v.p., chief mgr., prin. oper. officer, 1995—97; exec. v.p., CFO Nat. Assn. Securities Dealers (NASD), 1997—98, dep. COO, CFO, 1998—2000, vice chmn., 2001—02; acting pres. Am. Stock Exch. LLC, NYC, 1999, chmn., CEO, 1999—2005; dean Frank G. Zarb Sch. Bus. Hofstra U., Hempstead, NY, 2006—. Bd. dirs. Securities Ind. Automation Corp., 1999—2002; bd. trustees Hofstra U., 2001—05, chmn., 2002—05, co-chair endowment com., mem. fin. and devel. coms., mem. dean's exec. coun. Frank G. Zarb Sch. Bus., mem. bus. adv. bd. Merrill Lynch Ctr. for Study of Internat. Fin. Svcs. and Markets, exec.-in-residence. Mem. oversight com. Cath. Health Svcs. of LI; advisor to fin. com. Good Samaritan Hosp.; mem. Chinese Econ. Zone Adv. Bd. Zhongguancun Sci. Park, 2001. Named a Knight, Sovereign Military of Malta, 2003; named Man of Yr., Am. Stock Exch. 5&20 Club, 2001; named to Disting. Post of Knight, Sacred Military Constantinian Order of Saint George, 2001; recipient Alumi Achievement award. Hofstra U., 2000, 100 Black Men Investors Club Performance award, 2002, Spl. Achievement award in Bus., Nat. Italian Am. Found, 2003, Monsignor Thomas J. Hartman Award, Telecare, 2004. Mem.: Econ. Club NY (Ellis Island Medal of Honor award 2000). Office: Hofstra U Frank G Zarb Sch Bus Weller Hall Hempstead NY 11549-1000 Office Phone: 516-463-5678. Office Fax: 516-463-5268. E-mail: Salvatore.F.Sodano@hofstra.edu.

SODDERS, MICHAEL ANDREW, application developer; AA with honors, Tallahassee CC, 2005. Pvt. piano instr., Carrollton, Tex., 1996—2004, Plano, Tallahassee; graphic designer Carrollton, 1997—2000, Plano, Dallas; govt. analyst Fla. Agy. Persons with Disabilities, Tallahassee, 2003—06, application systems programmer, 2006—. Mem.: Am. MENSA, Phi Theta Kappa. Avocations: piano, music. Home Phone: 850-894-1498.

SODERBERG, DALE LEROY, language educator, drama director, producer; b. Warren, Pa., Apr. 24, 1929; s. Leroy Wilbur and Olive Hazel (Colby) S.; m. Marjorie Ann Hamm, Aug. 19, 1951; children: David J., Valli K., W. Mark, Lisa T., Kathi L. BA, Gettysburg Coll., 1951; BD, Luth. Theol. Sem., Gettysburg, Pa., 1954. Cert. secondary English tchr., N.Y., 1968; ordained mins. Luth. Ch., 1954. Pastor Grace Luth. Ch., Clarion, Pa., 1954-57; mission developer, 1st pastor Our Saviour's Luth. Ch., Horseheads, N.Y., 1957-60; dir. Ecclesia Tours (Luth. Fgn. Tours), Horseheads and North Syracuse, N.Y., 1958-67; mgr. Soderberg Travel Svc., Corning, N.Y., 1960-62; pastor St. John's Luth. Ch., Syracuse, N.Y., 1962-66; guest chapel preacher Wittenberg U., Ohio, 1966; tchr. English Ft. Myers (Fla.) High Sch., 1967-68; tchr. English, dir. drama Hamilton (N.Y.) Cen. Sch., 1968-92; retired, 1992; sermon and story writer Ecclesia Svcs., Hamilton, 1984-96. Lay preacher Upstate N.Y. Synod Evang. Luth. Ch. Am., Syracuse, 1968—; advisor student tchrs.at Hamilton Cen. Sch. for Colgate U., Hamilton, 1975-92; clk. Hamilton Stores, Yellowstone Nat. Park, summer 1948, 93. Author: (novels) Pawns, 1980, The Amsterdam Connection, 1999, A Time for Choosing, 2001, Mr. Protestant, 2002, The Winds of Change, 2003, The Manipulators, 2004, Sirocco, 2005, The View from the Pew, 2006, Baladrar, 2007. Dir. tours to Europe, Holy Land and Luth. mission fields in Brit. Guiana, East and West Africa, and India; bd. dirs. Luth. Homes Found., 1993-96; vol. missionary religious edn. tchr. U. of Papua New Guinea, Goroka, spring 1996; mem. Global Missions Team, Upstate N.Y. Synod Evang. Luth. Ch. Am., Syracuse, 1999—; organizer and dir. Bishop's tour to Zimbabwe, 2001. Mem.: N.Y. State Ret. Tchrs. Assn., Hamilton Tchrs. Assn., N.Y. State United Tchrs., Nat. Pk. Conservation Assn., Defenders of Wildlife, Wilderness Soc., World Wildlife Fund, Sierra Club. Democrat. Avocations: travel, photography, home video, creative writing, Hemingway specialization. Home: 1907 Preston Hill Rd Hamilton NY 13346-2321 E-mail: dsoderbe@twcny.rr.com.

SODERBERG, HERMAN ALBERT, minister, educator; b. Bklyn., Dec. 31, 1931; BS in Math. and Physics, Wagner Coll., SI, 1961; MDiv, Drew U., Madison, NJ, 1965, postgrad. Min. United Meth. Ch., NJ, 1962—, NC; instr. Meth. Coll., Fayetteville, NC. Sr. adj. instr. Burlington County Coll., NJ, 1962—; adj. instr. Camden County Coll., NJ, 1962—. With USN, 1951—55. Mem.: ASME, IEEE (life), Am. Chem. Soc., Inst. Radio Engrs., Am. Soc. Testing Materials. Avocations: photography, coin collecting/numismatics, camping, chess, travel. Home: 240-20 Sawtooth Dr Fayetteville NC 28314 Home Phone: 910-860-8382.

SODERBERG, LEIF G., electronics company executive; BA, Harvard Coll.; MS in Mgmt., MIT. Various positions ending with ptnr. McKinsey & Co., Cleveland and Scandinavia, 1978-93; head bus. strategy Land Mobile Products Sector, Network Svcs. Bus. Motorola Inc., 1993-94, v.p., gen. mgr. network Svcs. and Bus. Strategies Group Ill., 1994—98, sr. v.p. Systems Solutions Group Ill., 1998—2000, sr. v.p., gen. mgr., strategy, business development and industry relations, 2000—02, sr. v.p., dir., Motorola's global strategy and corporate development organization, 2002—. Mem. Clearnet's Nominating Com.

SODERBERG, NANCY, former government official, writer; b. San Turce, PR, Mar. 13, 1958; d. Lars Olof and Nancy (MacGilvrey) S. BA in French and Econs., Vanderbilt U., 1980; MS in Fgn. Svc., Georgetown U., 1984. Del. selection asst. Mondale-Ferraro Com., Washington; dep. issues dir. fgn. policy Dukakis for Pres. Com., Boston, 1988; fgn. policy advisor Senator Edward M. Kennedy, Washington, 1985-88, 89-92; fgn. policy dir. Clinton/ Gore Campaign, Little Rock, 1992; dep. asst. dir. transition nat. security Clinton/ Gore Transition, Little Rock, 1992-93; dep. asst. to Pres. for nat. security affairs Nat. Security Coun., Washington, 1993—97; amb. (alt. rep.) UN, NYC, 1997—2001; v.p., dir. NY office Internat Crisis Group, 2001—05; dist. vis. scholar U. North Fla., Jacksonville, 2006—. TV and radio commentator MSNBC; mem. Coun. Fgn. Rels. Author: The Superpower Myth: The Use and Misuse of American Might, 2005. Home: 121 Lantern Wick Pl Ponte Vedra Beach FL 32082 Home Phone: 904-273-2711; Office Phone: 646-591-0912. Personal E-mail: nsoderberg@aol.com.

SODERBERG, PETER H., health products executive; B in engring., Yale Univ. Mgmt. positions Johnson & Johnson, 1968—89; pres. Johnson & Johnson Health Mgmt., 1989—93; group v.p., COO Welch Allyn Inc., Skaneateles Falls, NY, pres., CEO, 2000—06, Hillenbrand Industries Inc., Batesville, Ind., 2006—, Hill-Rom, 2006—. Bd. dir. Greatbatch Inc., AdvaMed. Vice-chmn. Syracuse Symphony Orch., Met. Develop. Authority Ctrl. NY; chmn. CNY Medtech. Office: Hillenbrand Industries Mail Code K71 1069 State Route 46 E Batesville IN 47006-8835 *

SODERBERGH, STEVEN ANDREW, filmmaker; b. Atlanta, Jan. 14, 1963; s. Peter Andrew and Mary Ann (Bernard) S.; m. Elizabeth Jeanne Brantley, Dec. 1, 1989 (div. Oct. 1994). Writer, dir., editor: (films) Sex, Lies, and Videotape, 1989 (Palme d'Or award Cannes Film Festival 1989), King of the Hill, 1993, Schizopolis, 1996, Solaris, 2002; dir., editor: (film) Kafka, 1991, Bubble, 2006; exec. prodr.: (films) Suture, 1994, Good Night and Good Luck, 2005, The Big Empty, 2005 Syriana, 2005, Rumor Has It..., 2005, PU-239, 2006; prodr.: The Daytrippers, 1997, Pleasantville, 1998; dir.: (films) The Underneath, 1995, Gray's Anatomy, 1996, Out of Sight, 1998, The Limey, 1999, Erin Brokovich, 2000, Traffic, 2000, Ocean's Eleven, 2001, Full Frontal, 2002; dir., prodr.: Ocean's Twelve, 2004, Bubble, 2006; writer: (film) Nightwatch, 1998; dir., prodr. (TV series) K St., 2003 Named a WIRED Renegade, WIRED Rave Awards, 2006. Mem. AMPAS, Dirs. Guild Am. Democrat.

SODERLIND, STERLING EUGENE, newspaper industry consultant; b. Rapelje, Mont., Sept. 6, 1926; s. William John and Florence (Longbotham) S.; m. Helen Boyce, Apr. 9, 1955; children: Steven (dec.), Sarah, Lori. BA, U. Mont., 1950; Rhodes Scholar, Oxford U., Eng., 1950-52. Reporter Mpls. Tribune, 1952-55; reporter Wall St. Jour., Chgo., 1955-56, Southeastern bur. chief Jacksonville, Fla., 1956-57, mem. page one editing staff NYC, 1957-65, asst. mng. editor, 1966-70, mng. editor, 1970; econs. editor Dow Jones & Co., Inc., NYC, 1970-77, asst. to pres., 1975-77, v.p., 1977-91; newspaper industry cons., 1992—. Served with USNR, 1944-46. Congregationalist. Home: 58 Wellington Ave Short Hills NJ 07078-3308

SODEY, ANGELA ANN, gifted and talented educator; b. Freeport, Ill., Sept. 26, 1949; d. John Francis and Carolyn Lola McKenna; m. James Carleton Sodey, Sept. 5, 1970; children: Jay Carleton, Christopher John. BA, U. Iowa, Iowa City, 1971; MSE Reading Specialist, Drake U., Des Moines, Iowa, 1978. Tchr. grade 4 Ottumwa (Iowa) Schs., 1971; tchr. grades 5,6 Des Moines Pub. Schs., 1972—75, reading specialist, 1975—77, tchr. grade 3, 1977—79, tchr. grades 4, 5, 6 lang. arts, 1980; kindergarten tchr. Boone (Iowa) Pub. Schs., 1980; tchr. h.s. reading Jefferson County Schs., Denver, 1981—83, elem. talented and gifted tchr. Spencer (Iowa) Pub. Schs., 1984—85, Ft. Madison (Iowa) Pub. Schs., 1985—88, TAG coord., reading coord., 1988—92, tchr. mid. sch. reading, 1992—98, tchr. grade 6, 1998—2004, elem. talented and gifted tchr., 2004—. Bd. dirs. Shining Trail coun. Girl Scouts Am., Burlington, Iowa, 2003—07. Grantee, Wal-Mart, 2004—05. Mem.: Lee County Reading Assn., Iowa Reading Assn. (pres.-elect, pres. 2003—05), Ft. Madison Country Club (bd. dirs. 1994—96), Delta Kappa Gamma (sec. 1992). Independent. Methodist. Avocations: boating, reading, knitting, bicycling, hiking, exercise, travel. Home: 612 Ave G Fort Madison IA 52627

SODHANI, ARVIND, computer company executive; Bachelor's, Master's, U. London; MBA, U. Mich., 1978. Asst. treas. Intel Europe Intel Corp., 1981—84, asst. treas., 1984—88, treas., 1988—90, v.p. and treas., 1990—. Office: 2200 Mission College Blvd Santa Clara CA 95052

SODINI, PETER J., food service executive; b. Jan. 26, 1941; With Fazio's div. of Fisher Foods Inc., 1976-78, Boys Markets Inc., LA, 1978-1990, Buttrey Food & Drug Co., Great Falls, Mo., 1990-91; pres., EDO, Purity Supreme, North Billerica, Mass., 1991-98; pres., CEO Pantry Inc., Sanford, NC, 1998—. Office: Pantry PO Box 1410 Sanford NC 27331-1410

SODOLSKI, JOHN, retired professional society administrator; b. Menasha, Wis., Apr. 11, 1931; s. L.V. and L.W. (Pinkowski) S.; m. C.J. Eppard BS, U. Wis., 1953. Vice pres. Electronic Industries Assn., Washington, 1961-83; pres. U.S. Telephone Assn., Washington, 1983-93; ret., 1993. Served to 1st lt. USMC, 1955 Home: PO Box 1014 Middleburg VA 20118-1014

SODREL, MICHAEL EUGENE, former congressman, small business owner; b. Louisville, Dec. 17, 1945; s. Robert Eugene Sodrel and Nora Baily (Vermillion) Keller, m. Marquita Dean, Nov. 24, 1967; children: Michael Noah, Keesha. Student, Ind. U., Jeffersonville, 1963. Dir. maintenance Sodrel Truck Lines, Inc., Jeffersonville, 1969-72, dir. ops., 1972-74, v.p., 1974-76, exec. v.p., 1976-81, pres., CEO, 1981—2004; mem. US Congress from 9th Ind. dist., 2005—07; mem. sci. com., small bus. com., transp. and infrastructure com. Pres., chief exec. officer, Salem Stage, Inc., Jeffersonville, 1974-2004, The Free Enterprise System, Inc., 1976-2004. Bd. dirs. George Rogers Clark council Boy Scouts Am., New Albany, Ind., 1988—. Served to staff sgt. Nat. Guard US Army, 1966—73. Recipient Spl. Tourism award State of Ind., 1987; named to Hon. Order Ky. Col, 1983. Mem. Nat. Star Route Mail Contractor's Assn. (pres., chmn. bd. 1978-88), Am. Bus. Assn. (bd. dirs. 1987—), So. Ind. C. of C. Clubs: Skal (pres. 1986-87). Lodges: Rotary (pres. 1988—, Paul Harris fellow 1976). Republican. Presbyterian.

SODROSKI, JOSEPH G., medical educator; b. Coaldale, Pa. BS, Allentown Coll., 1976; MD, Jefferson Med. Coll., 1980. Intern in medicine New Eng. Deaconess Hosp., Boston, 1980—81; rsch. fellow in microbiology Dana-Farber Cancer Inst., Sch. Pub. Health Harvard U., Boston, 1981—84, from instr. to assoc. prof. div. human retrovirology Dana-Farber Cancer Inst., 1984—96, prof. div. human retrovirology Dana-Farber Cancer Inst., 1996—97, from instr. assoc. prof. dept. pathology Med. Sch., 1984—96, prof. dept. pathology Med. Sch., 1996—, assoc. prof. dept. cancer biology Sch. Pub. Health, 1992—96, prof. dept. cancer biology Sch. Pub. Health, 1996—97, prof. dept. cancer immunology and AIDS Dana-Farber Cancer Inst., 1997—, prof. dept. immunology and infectious diseases Sch. Pub. Health, 1997—. Chief div. human retrovirology Dana-Farber Cancer Inst. Harvard U., Boston, 1993—97; dir. Ctr. AIDS rsch. Dana-Farbert Inst. Beth Israel Deaconess Med. Ctr./Children's Hosp., Boston, 1994—; mem. sci. adv. bd. Ariel Project for prevention on HIV transmission from mother to infant, 1992—; mem. various coms. confs. in field; mem. external sci. adv. com. div. infectious diseases Mass. Gen. Hosp., 2000; mem. various coms. NIH; mem. sci. adv. bd. Aaron Diamond AIDS Rsch. Ctr. City N.Y., 1989—; mem. sci. adv. bd. Ctr. Human Retrovirology Thomas Jefferson U., 1995. Editor: Jour. Virology, 1993—98; editor: (assoc. editor) AIDS Scis., 1995—; reviewing editor AIDS, 1987—90, Jour. AIDS, 1988— (Howard Temin award for basic sci., 1993), AIDS Rsch. and Human Retroviruses, 1990—, Virology, 1991—, Jour. Virology, 1998—. Recipient David Gottlieb Meml. Lectureship, U. Ill., 1993, Best of What's New award, Popular Sci. mag., 1998, Harvey Lectr., 2005, Retrovirology prize, 2006; fellow, Damon Runyon-Walter Winchell Found., 1982, Am. Found. AIDS Rsch., 1986; grantee, NIH, 1986—2005, Dept. Army, 1987—90, Am. Found. AIDS Rsch., 1987—88; scholar, Leukemia Soc. Am., 1986; postdoctoral fellow, NIH, 1981, Spl. fellow, Leukemia Soc. Am., 1985, Stohlman Meml. scholar, 1991. Mem.: AAAS, Clin. Immunology Soc., Am. Soc. Virology, Am. Soc. Microbiology, Delta Epsilon Sigma, Alpha Omega Alpha, Sigma Xi. Office: Dept Cancer Immunology and AIDS Dana-Farber Cancer Inst 44 Binney St Jimmy Fund Bldg Rm 824 Boston MA 02115 Office Phone: 617-632-3371. Business E-Mail: joseph_sodroski@dfci.harvard.edu.

SOEJIMA, DAISUKE, diversified financial services company executive, economist; b. Tokyo, Jan. 17, 1959; s. Aritoshi and Hiroko Soejima; m. Kiyomi Soejima, Sept. 26, 1987; children: Sayuri, Taiga, Chiaki. BS in Econs., Tokyo U., 1983; MBA, Georgetown U., 1991. Assoc. cons., mgr. coord. Mitsubishi Corp., Tokyo, 1991-95; mgr. Mitsubishi Internat. Corp., Washington, 1995-97, mgr. project and planning NYC, 1997-98, mgr. chem. groups M&A divestitures, 1998-2001; dir. E-Commerce Devel., 1999—2004, unit mgr. investment and devel., 2001—04; pres., CEO Mitsubishi Internat. Food Ingredients Inc., NYC, 2004—, Mitsubishi Food Ingredients (MC) Can., Ltd., 2005—. Sr. rschr. Japan Inst. for Econ. Rsch., Tokyo, 1981—83; founding assoc. Inst. Strategic Leadership, Japan. Grad. adv. bd. Georgetown U. Mem.: Cornell Club, Met. Club, Alpha Mu Alpha, Beta Gamma Sigma. Home: 71 Hoyt St Darien CT 06820-3116 Office: 2160 N Ctrl Rd Ste 400 Fort Lee NJ 07024 also: 5080 Tuttle Crossing Blvd Ste 400 Dublin OH 43016 Office Phone: 201-944-5280. Business E-Mail: daisuke.soejima@mitsubishicorp.com.

SOENEN, MICHAEL J., consumer products company executive; b. 1970; BA, Kalamazoo Coll., 1992. Investment banker Salomon Brothers Inc., 1993—96; assoc. Perry Corp., 1996; pres., CEO FTD.com, 1999—2002; v.p. mktg. FTD Grp. Inc., Downers Grove, Ill., 1997—99, dir. sales and promotions, 1997—99, dir., 2002—04, pres., COO, 2002—04, pres., CEO, 2004—. Mem. Chgo. Gateway Green. Mem.: Young Presidents' Orgn., Econ. Club, Chgo. Club. Office: FTD Group Inc 3113 Woodcreek Dr Downers Grove IL 60515 Office Phone: 630-719-7800. Office Fax: 630-719-6170. *

SOENS, PETER C., real estate company executive; With Avalon Real Estate Agency, NJ; office head Flynn Co., Phila., 1993—2002, ptnr., 1999; prin., co-owner Seligsohn Soens Hess TCN Worldwide, Phila. Named one of 40 Under 40, Phila. Bus. Jour., 2006. Mem.: Bd. Tri-State Real Estate Comml. & Industrial Assn. (pres. elect). Office: Seligsohn Soens Hess Ste 250 1800 John F Kennedy Blvd Philadelphia PA 19103 Office Phone: 215-893-1466. Office Fax: 215-893-1466. E-mail: psoens@sshco.com.

SOERGEL, KONRAD HERMANN, physician; b. Coburg, Germany, July 27, 1929; came to U.S., 1954, naturalized, 1962; s. Konrad Daniel and Erna Henrietta (Schilling) S.; m. Rosina Klara Rudin, June 24, 1955; children: Elizabeth Ann, Karen Theresa, Marilyn Virginia, Kenneth Thomas. MD, U. Erlangen, Germany, 1954, Dr. med., 1958. Intern Bergen Pines County Hosp., Paramus, NJ, 1954-55; resident in pathology West Pa. Hosp., Pitts., 1955-56; rsch. asst. U. Erlangen, Germany, 1956-57; resident in medicine Mass. Meml. Hosp., Boston, 1957-58; fellow in gastroenterology Boston U. Med. Sch., 1958-60, instr., 1960-61; mem. faculty Med. Coll. Wis., Milw., 1961—, prof. medicine, 1969—2002, prof. medicine emeritus, 2003—, prof. physiology, 1993—2002, chief sect. gastroenterology, 1961-93. Chmn. gastroenterology and clin. nutrition study sect. NIH, 1979-80 Contbr. articles to profl. jours., chpts. to books. Recipient Rsch. Career Devel. award USPHS, 1963-72; Alexander von Humboldt Found. sr. fellow, 1973-74 Mem. Am. Gastroenterol. Assn., Am. Soc. Clin. Investigation, Am. Assn. Physicians, German Soc. for Digestive and Metabolic Disorders (hon.), Ger. Soc. Internal Medicine (hon.). Home: 14245 Hillside Rd Elm Grove WI 53122-1677 Office: Med Coll Wis 9200 W Wisconsin Ave Milwaukee WI 53226-3522 Personal E-mail: k.soergel@comcast.net.

SOETEBER, ELLEN, journalist, editor; b. East St. Louis, Ill., June 14, 1950; d. Lyle Potter and Norma Elizabeth (Osborn) S.; m. Richard M. Martins, Mar. 16, 1974. BJ, Northwestern U., 1972. Edn. writer, copy editor Chgo. Today, 1972-74; reporter Chgo. Tribune, 1974-76, asst. met. editor, 1976-84, assoc. met. editor, 1984-86, TV and media editor, 1986, met. editor, 1987-89, assoc. mng. editor for met. news, 1989-91, dep. editor editorial page, 1991-94; mng. editor South Fla. Sun-Sentinel, Ft. Lauderdale, 1994-2001; editor St. Louis Post-Dispatch, 2001—05. Vis. faculty Poynter Inst. Journalism Studies, 2006-; presenter in field. Named to Hall of Achievement, Medill Sch. Journalism, 2003; Journalism fellow, U. Mich., Ann Arbor, 1986—87. Office Phone: 954-522-9287. Personal E-mail: ellsoeteber@aol.com.

SOFAER, ABRAHAM DAVID, lawyer, judge, educator, consultant; b. Bombay, May 6, 1938; arrived in U.S., 1948, naturalized, 1959; m. Marian Bea Scheuer, Oct. 23, 1977; children: Daniel E., Michael J., Helen R., Joseph S., Aaron R., Raphael J. BA in History magna cum laude, Yeshiva Coll., 1962; LLB cum laude, NYU, 1965. Bar: N.Y. 1965, D.C. 1988. Law clk. to Hon. J. Skelly Wright U.S. Ct. Appeals (D.C. cir.), Washington, 1965-66; law clk. to Hon. William J. Brennan Jr. U.S. Supreme Ct., Washington, 1966-67; asst. U.S. atty. U.S. Dist Ct. (so. dist.) N.Y., NYC, 1967-69; prof. law Columbia U., NYC, 1969-79; judge U.S. Dist. Ct. (so. dist.) N.Y., 1979-85; legal advisor U.S. Dept. State, Washington, 1985-90; ptnr. Hughes Hubbard & Reed, Washington, 1991-94; George P. Shultz disting. scholar, sr. fellow Hoover Instn., Stanford U., 1994—. Hearing officer N.Y. Dept. Environ. Conservation, 1975-76. Author: War, Foreign Affairs and Constitutional Power: The Origins, 1976; contbr. articles to legal, polit., fgn. jours.; editor-in-chief: NYU Law Rev, 1964-65. Served with USAF, 1956-59. Root-Tilden scholar NYU, 1965. Mem. ABA, Fed. Bar Assn., N.Y.C. Bar Assn., N.Y. Bar Assn., Am. Law Inst. Jewish. Office: Stanford Univ The Hoover Instn Stanford CA 94305-6010 Office Phone: 650-725-3763. Office Fax: 650-723-2103. Business E-Mail: sofaer@hoover.stanford.edu.

SOFFAR, WILLIAM DOUGLAS, lawyer; b. Houston, Sept. 8, 1944; s. Benjamin and Esther Goldy (Garfinkel) S.; m. Nancy Elise Axelrod, Mar. 29, 1969 (div. Sept. 1989), m. Gail Shinbaum, Jan. 16, 2000; children: Pamela Beth, Stephanie Michelle, Jill Denise. BA, U. Houston, 1966, JD, 1969. Bar: Tex. 1969, U.S. Dist. Ct. (so. dist.) Tex. 1970, U.S. Ct. Appeals (5th cir.) 1974, U.S. Supreme Ct. 1974; cert. mediator in civil law and family law. Atty. examiner U.S. Interstate Commerce Commn., Washington, 1969-70; atty. Law Office of Adolph Uzick, Houston, 1970-72, Walsh & Soffar, Houston, 1972-73; lawyer, sole practice Law Offices of William D. Soffar, Houston, 1973-74; pvt. practice Houston, 1974—. Family law and civil mediator, basic mediation and family mediation trainer Atty.-Mediator's Inst. Bd. dirs. Miller Theater Adv. Coun., Houston, 1985-90, Zina Garrison Found., Houston, 1989-91. Mem. Houston Bar Assn. (bd. dirs., family law sect. mem. 1989-90), Jewish Cmty. Ctr. (health club com. 1971—), Jewish Family Svc. (bd. dirs. 1970-71), Phi Delta Phi. Jewish. Avocations: travel, reading, raquetball. Office: 6575 West Loop S Ste 630 Bellaire TX 77401-3604 Office Phone: 713-664-4344. Personal E-mail: wdsoffar@swbell.net.

SOFMAN, MICHAEL S., dermatologist; b. Newark, Mar. 3, 1959; s. Howard and Harriet Sofman; m. Susan Abano, Sept. 20, 1987; children: Sarah, Andrew. BS in Biology, Georgetown U., Washington, 1981; MD, U. Med. and Dentistry NJ, 1985. Diplomate Am. Bd. Dermatology. Intern U. Pitts., 1985—86; resident SUNY Downtown Med. Ctr., 1986—88, chief resident NY, 1988—89; physician Sobel and Sofman, MD, PA, Hollywood, Fla., 1989—. Fellow: Am. Acad. Dermatology. Office: Sobel and Sofman MD PA 4340 Sheridan St Hollywood FL 33021 Home Phone: 954-236-6642; Office Phone: 954-983-5533.

SOFTNESS, DONALD GABRIEL, marketing professional, manufacturing executive; b. Bklyn. s. Burt H. and Ida (Kaiser) S.; m. Sydell Meyerson; children: Michael, Anita May, Beth. AB, NYU, 1949, MBA, 1959; L.H.D., St. John's U., 1979. Chmn. Softness Group, Inc., NYC, 1960-79; pres. Softness Groupe, NYC, 1979—, SecureVue, Inc., NYC, 1984—. V.p., maj. prin. Radio Stas. WVJ-AM-FM, Newark and NYC; mem. faculty Advt. Week seminars Advt. Age; prodr., promoter Bklyn. Rollathon (skating marathon). Co-author: Cardiologists' Guide to Health and Fitness Through Exercise, 1979; contbr. articles to bus. and trade jours. Patentee in mech. field. Served with USN. Mem. Public Relations Soc. Am., Internat. Radio TV Soc., Am. Coll. Sports Medicine Clubs: N.Y. Yacht. Home and Office: 28 Trues Dr West Islip NY 11795-5139 Office: SecureVue Inc 251 E 51st St New York NY 10022-6534 Office Phone: 212-752-5960. E-mail: don@securevue.net, softdon@aol.com.

SOFTNESS, JOHN, public relations executive; b. Bklyn., Nov. 7, 1930; s. Burt H. and Ida (Kaiser) S.; m. Leona R. Softness (dec.); m. Carol Brady Blades; children: Barney, David, Daniel. BA, U. Miami, 1955. Reporter Miami Herald, 1953; reporter Sta. WTVJ, Miami, Fla., 1954; pub. relations dir. aviation dept. Shell Oil Co., NYC, 1958-60; pres., chief exec. officer The Softness Group, Inc., NYC, 1960-91, chmn., 1992-98; spl. asst. to dean Sch. Bus. U. Miami, 1998-2000; speechwriter Mayor Alex Penelas, Miami-Dale, Fla. Spl. counselor to Bklyn. Borough pres., 1966-76; adj. prof. comm. arts St. John's U., 1981-98; adj. prof. speechwriting U. Miami, 2006; counselor comms. com. N.Y. Heart Assn.; mem. comms. coun. U. Miami. Author: (autobiography) Boy Outta Brooklyn. Dir. Alliance for Ethical Govt., Miami. Served to capt. USAF, 1955-59. Mem. Pub. Rels. Soc. Am., Pride and Alarm (chmn.), Counselors' Acad. Home and Office: 2 Grove Isle Dr Apt 210 Coconut Grove FL 33133-4102 Personal E-mail: softysr@aol.com.

SOGG, WILTON SHERMAN, lawyer; b. Cleve., May 28, 1935; s. Paul P. and Julia (Cahn) S.; m. Saralee Frances Krow, Aug. 12, 1962 (div. July 1975); 1 child, Stephanie; m. Linda Rocker Lehman, Dec. 22, 1979 (div. Dec. 1990); m. Nancy Rosenfield Walsh, June 2, 1991. AB, Dartmouth Coll., 1956; JD, Harvard U., 1959; postgrad., London Grad. Sch. Bus. Studies, 1974-76. Bar: (Ohio) 1960, (Fla) 1970, (U.S. Tax Ct.) 1961, (U.S. Supreme Ct.) 1969. Assoc. Gottfried, Ginsberg, Guren & Merritt, 1960-63, ptnr., 1963-70, Guren, Merritt, Feibel, Sogg & Cohen, Cleve., 1970-84; of counsel Hahn, Loeser, Freedheim, Dean and Wellman, Cleve., 1984-85; ptnr. Hahn Loeser & Parks LLP, Cleve., 1986-2000; of counsel McCarthy, Lebit, Crystal & Liffman Co., Cleve., 2001—. Trustee, pres. Cleve. Jewish News; adj. prof. Cleve. State U. Law Sch., 1960—; lectr. Harvard U. Law Sch., 1978-80. Author: (with Howard M. Rossen) new and rev. vols. of Smith's Review Legal Gems series, 1969—; editor: Harvard Law Rev.; contbr. articles to profl. jours. Trustee Jewish Cmty. Fedn. of Cleve., 1966-72; bd. overseers Cleveland Marshall Coll. Law, Cleve. State U., 1969—, vis. com. Coll. Bus. Adminstrn., 1996-2001, 2003-; mem. U.S. and State of Ohio Holocaust commns.; pres. bd. trustees Ohio Audubon Adv. Bd., 2005—. Fulbright fellow U. London, 1959-60. Mem. Ohio Bar Assn., Fla. Bar Assn., Germany Philatelic Soc., Oakwood Club, Chagrin Valley Hunt, Rowfant Club, Phi Beta Kappa. Home: PO Box 278 Gates Mills OH 44040-0278 Office: McCarthy Lebit Crystal & Liffman 101 W Prospect Ave Ste 1800 Cleveland OH 44115-1088 Home Phone: 440-423-1809; Office Phone: 216-696-1422. Business E-Mail: wss@mccarthylebit.com.

SOGIN, DAVID WARREN, music educator; s. Harold Hymen and Ruth Joy (Reinberg) Sogin; m. Deborah Ann Hanes, Aug. 24, 1980; children: Celia H., Ari K. MusB, La. State U., Baton Rouge, 1972—76; MusM in Edn., N.Tex. State U., Denton, 1976—78; PhD in Music Edn., U. Tex., Austin, 1984—86. Music instr. E.Tex. State U., Commerce, 1978—84; violinist Lexington Philharmonic, Ky., 1986—; assoc. prof. music U. Ky., Lexington, 1986—. Visiting prof. U. Louisville, 1998; spl. rsch. interest grp. chair Music Educators Conf., 2002—06; editl. bd. mem. Internat. Jour. Music Edn., 2004—; rsch. com. mem. Am. String Tchrs. Assn., 2004—. Author: (electronic book & CD) Arts Infused Education in Kentucky, 1998, Orff Research Webliography, 2006; contbr. articles to profl. jours. Para Rabbine Temple Adata Israel, Lexington; bd. mem. Ctrl. Ky. Jewish Fedn., Lexington. Recipient Disting. Participant award, Ky. Music Educators, 2006. Mem.: Am. String Tchrs. Assn., Internat. Soc. Music Edn., Kappa Delta Pi, Phi Kappa Phi (Nat. Honor Soc. Svc. award 2003). Avocations: chess, photography, camping, travel. Office: 105 Fine Arts Blvd Lexington KY 40506

SOGIN, MITCHELL L., biologist, educator; BS in Chemistry and Microbiol., U. Ill., Urbana, 1967, MS in Indsl. Microbiol., 1969, PhD in Microbiol. and Molecular Biology, 1972. NIH postdoctoral fellowship Nat. Jewish Ctr., Denver, 1972—76, sr. staff scientist dept. molecular and cellular biology, 1976—89; asst. prof. dept. biochemistry and biophysics U. Colo. Health Scis. Ctr., 1980—86, assoc. prof. dept. microbiol. rsch., 1987—89; sr. scientist Marine Biol. Lab., Woods Hole, Mass., 1989—, dir. Josephine Bay Paul Ctr. Comparative Molecular Biology and Evolution, 1997—; prof. dept. molecular biology, cell biology and biochemistry Brown U., Providence, 2004—. Assoc. fellow Can. Inst. Advanced Rsch., 1986—99; vis. Miller rsch. prof. U. Calif., Berkeley, 1997—98; sci. adv. Integrated Genomics, Chgo. Contbr. articles to sci. jours.; mem. editl. bd.: Molecular Biology and Evolution, 1994—2000, Jour. Eukaryotic Microbiol., Molecular Phylogenetics and Evolution, Jour. Molecular Evolution, Protist, Environ. Microbiol., Astrobiology. Recipient Stoll Stunkard award, Am. Soc. Parasitologists, 1993. Fellow: Am. Acad. Arts & Scis., Am. Acad. Microbiol., AAAS; mem.: Am. Soc. Cell Biology, Soc. Molecular Biology and Evolution, Internat. Soc. Evolutionary Protozoologists, Soc. Protozoologists, Am. Soc. Microbiol. Office: Josephine Bay Paul Ctr Marine Biol Lab Woods Hole 7 MBL St Woods Hole MA 02543 E-mail: sogin@mbl.edu.

SOH, CHUNGHEE SARAH, anthropology educator; b. Taegu, Korea, May 1, 1947; came to U.S., 1970; d. Sang Yung and Ock Yun (Choi) S.; m. Jerry Dee Boucher. BA in English summa cum laude, Sogang U., 1971; postgrad., U. Calif., Berkeley, 1971; MA in Anthropology, U. Hawaii, 1983, PhD in Anthropology, 1987. Staff instr. English Korean Air Lines, Edn. & Tng. Ctr., Seoul, 1978-79; instr. anthropology Ewha Womans U., Seoul, 1985; post-doctoral assoc. Inst. of Culture and Comm., East-West Ctr., Honolulu, 1987; asst. prof. U. Hawaii, 1990; asst. prof. anthropology Southwest Tex. State U., San Marcos, 1991-94, San Francisco State U., 1994-96, assoc. prof. anthropology, 1996—2006, prof., 2006—. Guest lectr. Chaminade U. Honolulu, 1988; vis. asst. prof. anthropology U. Ariz., 1990-91; adj. prof. Intercultural Inst. Calif., 1996-98; cons. in field. Author: The Chosen Women in Korean Politics: An Anthropological Study, 1991, Women in Korean Politics, 1993; contbr. articles to profl. jour. Bd. dirs. Women Devel. Inst. Internat., 2000—. Grantee East-West Ctr., 1981-87, NSF, 1985-86; fellow Korea Found., 1993, Japan Found., 1997-98, Inst. Social Sci., U. Tokyo, 1997-98, Leiden U. Internat. Inst. for Asian Studies, The Netherlands, 1998, Inst. for Corean-Am. Studies, 1998—; Hoover Inst. scholar, 1996-97, Stanford U. Inst. for Rsch. on Women and Gender scholar, 2000-01; Rsch. and Writing grantee John D. and Catherine T. MacArthur Found., 2000-01. Fellow Am. Anthrop. Assn. (treas. East Asia sect. 2001-03), Inst. for Corean-Am. Studies; mem. Am. Ethnological Soc., Soc. Psychol. Anthropology, Assn. Asian Studies (exec. bd. Com. Women Asian Studies 1995-97), Korean Assn. Womens Studies, Royal Asiatic Soc. Korean Br. Office: San Francisco State U Dept Anthropology 1600 Holloway Ave San Francisco CA 94132-1722 Business E-Mail: soh@sfsu.edu.

SOHLMAN, MICHAEL, foundation administrator; b. Stockholm, 1944; s. Rolf R. and Zinaida (Yarotskaya) S. BA, U. Uppsala, Sweden, 1964, postgrad. in econs. and polit. sci., 1968, U. Stockholm, 1968. Asst. sec. to Commn. Environ. Problems, 1969; with Ministry of Industry, 1972-74; with internat. divsn. Ministry of Fin., 1974-76, with budget dept., 1976, head of planning econ. dept., 1982-84, dir. of budget, 1985-87; fin. counsellor, permanent Swedish del. OECD, 1977-80; with rsch. dept. Social-Dem. Parliamentary Group, 1981-82; under-sec. of state Ministry of Agriculture, 1987-89; under-sec. of state for fgn. affairs Ministry for Fgn. Affairs, 1989-91; exec. dir. Nobel Found., Stockholm, 1992—. Chmn. bd. dirs. Royal Dramatic Theatre, Stockholm, 1993-96; chmn. bd. dirs. Post Pension Fund; bd. dirs. Axel Johnson Internat. Mem. Royal Swedish Acad. Scis., Acad. of Engring. Scis. Office: Nobel Foundation PO Box 5232 102 45 Stockholm Sweden

SOHMER, BERNARD, mathematics professor, administrator; b. NYC, July 16, 1929; s. Sol and Florence (Schonfeld) S.; m. Margot Rosette, July 27, 1952; children: Emily Sohmer Tai, Olivia Sohmer Rosenbaum. BA, NYU, 1949, MS, 1951, PhD, 1958. Lectr. CCNY, NYC, 1952—57; asst. prof. NYU, NYC, 1957—58; faculty CCNY, NYC, 1958—2005, prof. math., 1969—2005, prof. emeritus, 2005—. Founding mem. SEEK program CCNY, NYC, 1964, dean students, 1969—72, v.p. student affairs, 1972—75, chmn. faculty senate, 1977—79, NYC, 1985—91, NYC, 2002—03, chmn. liberal arts and sci. faculty coun., 1979—85, ombudsman, 1991—98, NYC, 2002—03; trustee PSC-CUNY Welfare Fund, 1982—97; pres. Hillel, 1988—2001; sec. U. Faculty Senate CUNY, NYC, 1992—94, vice chair, 1994—98, chair, 1998—2002, ex officio bd. trustees, 1998—2002. Mem. AAAS, AAUP (pres. CCNY chpt. 1966-67, sec. 1977-78), Am. Math. Soc., Math. Assn. Am. (pres. elect NY Met. sect. 1989-90, pres. 1992-93, past pres. 1993-94, gov. 1996-98), Profl. Staff Congress (chair CCNY chpt. 1993-96, exec. coun. 1997-2000). Home: 3345 92nd St Jackson Heights NY 11372-1851 also: 176 E 77th St New York NY 10021 E-mail: bsohmer@earthlink.net.

SOHN, HANSUK, research scientist, educator; b. Seoul, Republic Of Korea; s. Jik-Soo Sohn and Sang-Hee Kim; m. Jeehye Seo; 1 child, Christine Joohee. BS, Sung Kyun Kwan U., Seoul, 1992; MS, U. Iowa, Iowa City, 1995, PhD, 2004. Rsch. assoc. U. Iowa, 2004—05; asst. prof. N.Mex State U., Las Cruces, 2006—. Mem.: Inst. Supply Mgmt., OR Soc., Am. Soc. Engring. Edn., Inst. Indsl. Engrs., Inst. Ops. Rsch. and Mgmt. Scis., Alpha Pi Mu. Office: NMex State U Indsl Engring MSC 4230 Las Cruces NM 88003 Office Phone: 505-646-2957. Office Fax: 505-646-2976. E-mail: hsohn@nmsu.edu.

SOHN, HONG YONG, chemical and metallurgical engineer, educator; b. Kaesung, Kyunggi-Do, Republic of Korea, Aug. 21, 1941; arrived in U.S., 1966; s. Chong Ku and Soon Deuk (Woo) Sohn; m. Victoria Bee Tuan Ngo, Jan. 8, 1971; children: Berkeley Jihoon, Edward Jihyun. BSChemE, Seoul Nat. U., Republic of Korea), 1962; MSChemE, U. NB, Can., 1966; PhD, U. Calif., Berkeley, 1970. Engr. Cheil Sugar Co., Busan, Republic of Korea, 1962-64; rsch. assoc. SUNY, Buffalo, 1971-73; rsch. engr. DuPont Co., Wilmington, Del., 1973-74; prof. metall. engring., adj. prof. chem. engring. U. Utah, Salt Lake City, 1974—. Cons. Lawrence Livermore Nat. Lab., 1976—, Cabot Corp., 1984—, DuPont Co., 1987—, Utah Power and Light Co., 1987—, H. C. Starck, 1997—. Co-author: (book) Gas-Solid Reactions, 1976; co-editor: Rate Processes of Extractive Metallurgy, 1979, Extractive Metallurgy of Refractory Metals, 1980, Advances in Sulfide Smelting, 2 vols., 1983, Recycle and Secondary Recovery of Metals, 1985, Gas-Solid Reactions in Pyrometallurgy, 1986, Flash Reaction Processes, 1988, Metallurgical Processes for the Year 2000 and Beyond, 1988, Metallurgical Processes for the Early Twenty-First Century, 2 vols., 1994, Proceeding of the Julian Szekely Memorial Symposium on Materials Processing, 1997, Value-Addition Metallurgy, 1998, Sulfide Smelting, 2002, Metallurgical and Materials Processing: Principles and Technologies, 3 vols., 2003; contbr. articles to profl. jours. Recipient Fulbright Disting. lectureship, 1983; Camille and Henry Dreyfus Found. Tchr. scholar, 1977, Japan Soc. Promotion Sci. fellow, 1990. Mem.: AIChE, AIME (James Douglas Gold medal 2001), Korean Inst. Chem. Engrs., Korean Acad. Sci. and Tech. (Fellow award 1998), Minerals, Metals and Materials Soc. (past dir., Extractive Metallurgy Lectr. award 1990, Extraction and Processing Sci. award 1990, champion H. Mathewson Gold medal award 1993, Extraction and Processing Sci. award 1994, 1999, 2007, symposium named in his honor). Achievements include patents for process for treating sulfide-bearing ores, continuous solvent extraction with bottom gas injection. Office: U Utah 135 S 1460 E Rm 412 Salt Lake City UT 84112-0114 Office Phone: 801-581-5491. Business E-Mail: hysohn@mines.utah.edu. *Fortunate are those who earn a living by doing what they would rather be doing even if they do not have to do it to earn a living. Material wealth accumulated by doing what one does not enjoy doing is not worth the effort.*

SOHN, JUNGYUL, education educator; b. Seoul, Korea (South), Oct. 11, 1968; s. Dongin Sohn and Youngsoo Kim; m. Soo Kyoung Oh, Jan. 7, 2006. BA with honors, Seoul Nat. U., 1987—91, MA, 1991—93; PhD, U. of Ill., 1996—2002. Rsch. asst. U. Pa., Phila., 1997, U. Ill., Urbana, 1998—2001; rsch. assoc. U. Md., College Park, 2002—04; asst. prof. U. Memphis, 2004—06, Seoul Nat. U., 2006—. Affiliate prof. U. Md., 2004—06; dep. to sec. gen. Internat. Geog. Union, 2007—; mem. adv. bd. BK4 Global and Regional Econ. Analysts Program, 2007—. Mem. editl. bd. Geog. Jour. of Korea, 2003—06, Korean Jour. Regional Sci., 2007—; contbr. articles to profl. jours., chapters to books. Cpl. Korean Army, 1993—95, Gyeonggi Province, Korea. Finalist 16 Competiton Trbout prize in regional sci., 2002; scholar, Woosan Found., 1991—93; Grad. Coll. Conf. Travel grant, U. Ill., 2001, workshop scholar, CSISS, 2004—06. Mem.: Korean Academic Soc. of Indsl. Cluster (mem. editl. bd. jour. 2007—), Regional Sci. Assn. Internat. Avocations: travel, movies, sports. Office: Seoul Nat Univ Dept Geography San 56-1 Sillim-dong Gwanak-gu Seoul 151-746 Republic of Korea Office Phone: 82-2-880-4055. Office Fax: 82-2-876-9498. Business E-Mail: jsohn@snu.ac.kr.

SOHN, MICHAEL N, lawyer; b. May 11, 1940; AB, Columbia Univ, 1960; JD cum laude, Harvard Univ, 1963. Bar: N.Y. 1964, D.C. 1969, US Supreme Ct. 1969. Atty. Gen. Counsel Office, NLRB, Washington, 1964—69; gen. counsel FTC, Washington, 1977—80; chmn. of firm & chmn Policy Com. Arnold & Porter, Washington, 1996—. Mem. exec. com. Regulatory Council of the U.S., 1978—80; mem. council Adminstrv. Conf. of U.S., 1978—83. Office: Arnold & Porter 555 Twelfth St NW Washington DC 20004-1206 Office Phone: 202-942-5005. Office Fax: 202-942-5999. Business E-Mail: michael.sohn@aporter.com.

SOHN, SUNG WON, bank executive; b. 1945; Grad., U. Pitts., Harvard U. Sr. economist President Nixon's Coun. Econ. Advisors, The White House; exec. v.p., chief econ. officer Wells Fargo Banks; pres., CEO Hanmi Fin. Corp., 2005—. Prof. Pa. State U. Sys. Bd. dirs. LA World Affairs Coun., Children's Bur., Claremont Grad Sch. Named most accurate forecaster for We. U.S., Blue Chip Publications, 2002, most accurate economist in U.S., Wall Street Jour., 2006; named one of five most accurate forcasters in U.S., 2001, 100 most influential Minnesotans of 20th century, The Star Tribune; named to Board of Economists, Time mag., 2001. Office: Hanmi Bank 3660 Wilshire Blvd PH-A Los Angeles CA 90010 *

SOIFER, AVIAM, dean, law educator; b. Worcester, Mass., Mar. 18, 1948; married; 2 children. BA cum laude, Yale U., 1969, MA in Urban Studies, 1972, JD, 1972. Bar: Conn. 1974, U.S. Dist. Ct. Conn. 1974, U.S. Supreme Ct. 1994. Law clk. to Judge Jon O. Newman U.S. Dist. Ct. Conn., 1972-73; asst. prof. U. Conn. Sch. Law, 1976-77, assoc. prof., 1977-78, prof., 1978-80, Boston U. Sch. Law, 1980—93, 1998—2003; dean Boston Coll. Law Sch., 1993-98, U. Hawaii, Sch. Law, Honolulu, 2003—. Vis. prof. Boston U. Sch. Law, 1979-80; vis. colleague William S. Richardson Sch. Law, 1999-2000. Author: Law the the Company We Keep, 1995 (Alpha Sigma Nu Nat. Jesuit Book Prize, 1998); contbr. articles to profl. jours. Vice chair Supreme Jud. Ct. Mass. Task Force on Jud. Edn., 1996-2001; mem. steering com. 1st Cir. Task Force on Gender, Race and Ethnicity, 1995-99; trustee New Eng. Med. Ctr., 1997-2002, Cambridge Health Alliance, 2002-03. Recipient Disting. Sr. Rsch. award Boston Coll., 2001-02; named Disting. Scholar Legal Studies Inst., U. Wis., 2001-; Harvard Program in Law and Humanities fellow, 1976-77; Kellog Nat. fellow, 1981-84. Mem. ABA (commn. on coll. and univ. legal studies 1996-2000. Office: William S Richardson Sch Law U Hawaii 2515 Dole St Honolulu HI 96822 Office Phone: 808-956-6343. E-mail: soifer@hawaii.edu.

SOILEAU, MONICA MARIE, economist; d. Freddie George Singleton and Molly Anne Guillory; m. Rolland Soileau, May 13, 1995; children: Hailey Paige, Heather Elaine. Student, U. Phoenix Online, 2000—07. Cert. therapon belief therapist The Therapon Inst., 2007; Christian marriage and family therapist Am. Soc. Christian Therapists, 2007. Operator process unit ConocoPhillips, Westlake, La., 1993—98; optimization economics analyst ConocoPhillips Oil Refinery, Westlake, 1998—. Planning staff ConocoPhillips, Westlake, 1998—. Author: The Forgotten Victims. Vol. The Women's Shelter, Lake Charles, La., 2000—07, ARC, Lake Charles, 2000—07; fund raiser com. & vol. Am. Heart Assn., Lake Charles, 2003—07; vol. and fund raiser Am. Cancer Soc., Lake Charles, 2003—07; loaned exec. United Way, Lake Charles, 2006—07; vol. Partners In Edn., Westlake, 2005—07. Named Outstanding Vol., ConocoPhillips, 2004, 2005, 2006. Home Phone: 337-494-1798; Office Phone: 337-491-5188. Personal E-mail: monica_conoco@yahoo.com.

SOJKA, GARY ALLAN, biologist, educator, academic administrator; b. Cedar Rapids, Iowa, July 15, 1940; s. Marvin F. and Ruth Ann (Waddington) Sojka Green; m. Sandra Kay Smith, Aug 5, 1962; children: Lisa Kay, Dirk Allan. BS, Coe Coll., 1962; MS, Purdue U., 1965, PhD, 1967, DSc (hon.), 2002; DL (hon.), Lycoming Coll., 1995. Rsch. assoc. Ind. U., Bloomington, 1967-69, asst. prof., 1969-73, assoc. prof., 1973-79, prof., 1979-84, assoc. chmn. biology, 1977-79, chmn. biology, 1979-81, dean arts and scis., 1981-84; pres. Bucknell U., Lewisburg, Pa., 1984-95, prof. biology, 1984—2006, prof., pres. emeritus, 2006. Mem. higher edn. commn. Mid. States Assn. Colls. and Schs., 1992-96, chmn. task force on instnl. effectiveness, 1999-2000; chmn. tax policy subcom. Nat. Assn. Ind. Colls. and Univs., 1991-93; mem. study group on internat. edn. Am. Coun. Edn., 1992-94. Mem. So. Ind. Health Sys. Agy., Bedford; vice-chair Am. Livestock Conservancy, 2003—05, chmn. bd., 2005—; chmn. bd. dirs. Stone Belt Coun. Ret. Citizens, Bloomington, 1977—78; mem. nominating com. Ind. Assn. Ret. Citizens, Indpls., 1979; bd. dirs. Geisinger Med. Found., Danville, Pa., 1985—97, 2003—06, mem. regional bd., 1997—2003; chmn. Pa. Assn. Ind. Colls. and Univs., 1989—90; mem. pres.'s commn. NCAA, 1993—95; mem. planning adv. com. Snyder County, Pa., 1996—98, mem. planning commn., 2001—; bd. dirs. Bethesda Found., Lewisburg, 1996—98; trustee, bd. dirs. Am. Livestock Conservancy, 2001—, vice chair, 2003—05, chair bd., 2006—; dir. WITF Public Broadcasting, Harrisburg, bd. trustees, 2003—06; commr. Pa. Gaming Control Bd., 2007; gov. Inst. European Studies, 0989—1994, Citizen for the Future of Pa., 1999—. Recipient Ind. U. Sr. Class Tchg. award, 1975, Frederick B. Lieber award, 1977, Coe Coll. Alumni award of merit, 1982, Gary A. Sojka award Bucknell U., 1992, Cmty. Leadership award Susquahanna Valley Boy Scouts, 1994, Sheepskin award for Disting. Svc. to Higher Edn. Pa. Assn. Colls. and Univs., 2000, ECAC Appreciation award, Bucknell U., 2003, Adam Smith award Econ. Pa., 2003, Disting. Svc. medal Reading (Pa.) Ind. Day Coms., 2004; named to Coe Coll. Athletic Hall of Fame, 1988, Bucknell U. Athletic Hall of Fame, 2006; Gary A. Sojka Pavillion named in his honor, 2003. Mem.: AAAS, Pa. Assn. Coll. and Univs. (interim pres. 1997—98, exec. com., pres., Sheepskin award 1999, Sheepskin award 2000), Phila. Soc. Promotion of Agriculture (pres. elect 2006—07), Am. Coun. Edn. (study group on internat. edn. 1992—94), Nat. Assn. Independent Colls. and Univs. (subcom. chmn. 1991—93), Am. Soc. Biol. Chemists, Am. Acad. Microbiology, Am. Soc. Microbiology, Phi Beta Kappa (hon.; pres. 2007—), Omicron Delta Kappa, Sigma Nu, Sigma Xi. Baptist. Business E-Mail: gsojka@bucknell.edu.

SOKAL, ALLEN MARCEL, lawyer; b. Phila., Dec. 17, 1946; s. Michael Rudolf and Olga (Pories) Sokal; m. Judith Ann Berkowitz, May 25, 1968; children: Michelle Paula, Shira Hermine; m. Sharon Greenfield, Mar. 23, 2003. BSChemE cum laude, U. Pa., 1968; JD, Georgetown U., 1972. Bar: Va. 1973, DC 1974, lic.: US Dist. Ct. (DC Dist.) 1978, US Ct. Appeals (Fed. Cir.) 1982, US Supreme Ct. 1987, registered: US Patent & Trademark Office 1973. Patent examiner US Patent Office, Washington, 1968—73; assoc. Sughrue, Rothwell, Mion, Zinn & Macpeak, Washington, 1973—74; tech. advisor, law clk. to Hon. Jack R. Miller US Ct. Customs & Patent Appeals, Washington, 1974—76; assoc. Finnegan, Henderson, Farabow, Garrett & Dunner LLP, Washington, 1976—82, ptnr., Biotech./Pharm. Practice Group, 1982—, leader, Appellate Sect. Mem. Georgetown Law Jour., 1971—72. Contbr. articles to profl. jours.; spkr. in field. Recipient spl. achievement award, US Patent Office, 1970, 1971, 1972. Mem.: Va. State Bar, Bar Assn. DC, ABA, Assn. Former Ct. Customs & Patent Appeals Law Clks. & Tech. Advisors (sec. 1980), Am. Patent Law Assn. (chmn. current ct. cases subcom., chem. practice com. 1979—81), DC Bar (vice chmn. patent, trademark & copyright divsn. 1983—84, chmn. patent, trademark & copyright divsn. 1984—85), Phi Lambda Upsilon, Tau Beta Pi. Dem. Jewish. Office: Finnegan Henderson Farabow Garrett & Dunner LLP 901 New York Ave NW Washington DC 20001-3315 Office Phone: 202-408-4000. Office Fax: 202-408-4400. Business E-Mail: allen.sokal@finnegan.com.

SOKAL, ROBERT REUVEN, biology professor, writer; b. Vienna, Jan. 13, 1926; came to U.S., 1947, naturalized 1958; s. Siegfried and Klara (Rattner) S.; m. Julie Chen-Chu Yang, Aug. 12, 1948; children: David Jonathan, Hannah Judith. BS in Biology, St. John's U., Shanghai, Republic of China, 1947; PhD in Zoology, U. Chgo., 1952; DSc (hon.), U. Crete, Greece, 1990. From instr. to prof. U. Kans., Lawrence, 1951-69; prof., then leading prof., Disting. prof. SUNY, Stony Brook, 1969-95, dept. chmn., 1980-83, vice provost for rsch. and grad. studies, 1981-82, disting. prof. emeritus, 1995. Fulbright vis. prof. Hebrew/Tel Aviv U., Israel, 1963-64, U. Vienna, Austria, 1977, 78, 84; vis. prof. Inst. Adv. Studies, Oeiras, Portugal, 1971-80; vis. disting. prof. U. Mich., 1975-76; vis. prof. Coll. de France, Paris, 1989. Author: Principles of Numerical Taxonomy, 1963, Biometry, 1969, 3d rev. edit., 1995, Statistical Tables, 1969, 3rd rev. edit. 1995, Introduction to Biostatistics, 1973, 2d rev. edit., 1987, Numerical Taxonomy, 1973; editor Am. Naturalist, 1969-74. Recipient Charles Darwin Lifetime Achievement award in phys. anthropology, 2004; Career investigator NIH, 1964-69; sr. fellow NSF, 1959-60, NATO fellow, 1974, Guggenheim fellow, 1975-76, 84; Ctr. Advanced Study in Behavioral Sci. fellow, 1992-93. Fellow AAAS, Am. Acad. Arts and Scis.; mem. Soc. Study Evolution (pres. 1977), Am. Soc. Naturalists (hon. mem., pres.

1984), The Classification Soc. (pres. 1969-71), Internat. Fedn. Classification Socs. (pres. 1988-89), Nat. Acad. Scis., Linnean Soc. London (fgn.), Soc. Systematic Zoology (hon.), Natural History Mus. (Paris, corr. mem.), B'nai Brith Lodge (pres. 1966). Democrat. Jewish.

SOKLER, BRUCE DOUGLAS, lawyer; b. Newark, May 2, 1949; s. Lester and Aline Irma (Lasner) Sokler; m. Barbara Adele Cunningham, June 1, 1974; children: Sean, Brendan. AB cum laude, Princeton U., 1971; JD, Georgetown U., 1974. Bar: DC 1975, Mass. 1984, US Dist. Ct. (Dist. DC), US Dist. Ct. (Dist. Mass.), US Ct. Appeals (DC Cir.), US Ct. Appeals (2nd Cir.), US Ct. Appeals (8th Cir.), US Supreme Ct. Law clk. to Judge Edward Allen Tamm US Ct. Appeals (DC Cir.), Washington, 1974-75; assoc. Covington & Burling, Washington, 1975-82; ptnr. Mintz, Levin, Lohn, Ferris, Glovsky & Popeo PC, Washington, 1982—, mgr. Fed. Sect. Editor-in-chief Georgetown Law Jour., 1973—74. Mem.: DC Bar Assn., ABA (Antitrust Law Sect., Adminstrv. Litig. Sect.), Fed. Comm. Bar Assn. Office: Mintz Levin Lohn Ferris Glovsky & Popeo PC 701 Pennsylvania Ave NW Washington DC 20004-2608 Office Phone: 202-434-7303. Office Fax: 202-434-7400. Business E-Mail: bdsokler@mintz.com.

SOKOL, DAVID L., energy services provider company executive; b. Omaha, Nebr., 1956; married; children: D.J.(dec.), Kelly. BSCE, U. Nebr., Omaha, 1978; doctorate (hon.), Bellevue U., Nebr. With Citicorp, Henningson, Durham and Richardson, Inc.; pres., CEO, bd. dirs. Ogden Projects, Inc.; pres., CEO Peter Kiewit Energy Company, 1991; chmn., CEO MidAm. Energy Holdings Co. (successor to CalEnergy Co., Inc.), Des Moines, 1991—, pres., from 1991. Co-chmn. for Campaign Nebr., U. Nebr. Found., dir.; mem. Met. Omaha Conv., Sports and Entertainment Authority; bd. dirs. Creighton U., Coll. World Series Omaha, Inc., Omaha Airport Authority, Strategic Command Consultation Co., Joslyn Art Mus., River City Roundup and Rodeo, Nebr. Easter Seal Soc., Mt. Michael Abbey H.S., Archdiocese of Omaha, Girls, Inc., Mid-Am. coun. Boy Scouts Am., Muscular Sclerosis Soc.-Midlands Chpt., United Way Midlands, Edison Electric Inst., Creighton U.; bd. govs. Knights of Ak-Sar-Ben; leadership adv. bd. bd. dir. NCAA; adv. com. arts JFK Ctr.; chmn. Met. Entertainment and Convention Authority Named CEO of Yr., Fin. Times Energy, 2000; recipient Individual Achievement award, Energy Daily, 2001. Mem. Del. Assn. Profl. Engrs., Neb. Soc. Profl. Engrs.; life mem. Horatio Alger Assn. Avocations: hockey, hunting, fishing, running, horseback riding. Office: MidAm Energy Holdings Co 666 Grand Ave PO Box 657 Des Moines IA 50303-0657

SOKOL, JAN D., lawyer; b. NYC, May 27, 1952; BS magna cum laude, Rutgers U., 1974; JD Northwestern Sch. of Law, of Lewis and Clark Coll., 1977. Bar: Oreg. 1978, U.S. Dist. Ct. (dist. Oreg.), U.S. Ct. Appeals (9th cir.) 1981, U.S. Claims Ct. 1982, U.S. Supreme Ct. 1982. Law clerk to Hon. George A. Juba U.S. Dist. Ct. (dist. Oreg.), 1978-79, law clerk to Hon. Gus J. Solomon, 1979-80, law clerk to Hon. James A. Redden, 1980; mng. mem. Stewart, Sokol & Gray, 1994. Case note and comment editor Environmental Law, 1976-77. Mem. ABA (mem. forum com. on the construction industry, fidelity and surety, forest resources com.), Multnomah County.

SOKOL, JENNIFER MARIE, musician, writer; b. Seattle, Wash., Mar. 26, 1958; d. Vilem and Agatha Sokol. BA in violin performance, Ind. U. Founder, first violinist, mgr. Cameo String Quartet. Author: Six Years of Grace: Caregiging Episodes With My Mother, 2007; freelance writer: Cath. Northwest Progress; contbr. articles various profl. jours. Recipient Pres. award for Literary Excellence, Nat. Authors Registry, 2004. Roman Cath. Avocations: reading, ballet, outdoor recreation. Home: 6303 NE 185th St Kenmore WA 98028 Office Phone: 425-485-8380 E-mail: jennifermsokol@aol.com.

SOKOL, LARRY NIDES, lawyer, educator; b. Dayton, Ohio, Sept. 28, 1946; s. Boris Franklin and Kathryn (Konowitch) S.; m. Beverly Butler, Aug. 3, 1975; children: Addie Teller, Maxwell Philip. BA, U. Pa., 1968; JD, Case Western Res. U., 1971. Bar: Oreg. 1972, U.S. Dist Ct. Oreg. 1972, U.S. Ct. Appeals (9th cir.) 1973, U.S. Supreme Ct. 1980. Law clk. chief judge Oreg. Ct. Appeals, Salem, 1971-72; pvt. practice Portland, Oreg., 1972—; prof. law Lewis and Clark Law Sch., Portland. Adj. prof. law sch. environ. litigation Lewis & Clark U., 1984—. Commr. planning City of Lake Oswego, Oreg., 1981-84. Sgt. USAR, 1968-74. Mem. Oreg. State Bar Assn. (chmn. litigation sect. 1983, disciplinary rev. bd. 1982-85), Oreg. Trial Lawyers Assn. Democrat. Jewish. Avocations: running, swimming, squash, model trains, scuba diving. Office: 735 SW 1st Ave Portland OR 97204-3326 Home Phone: 503-635-3785; Office Phone: 503-228-6469. Business E-Mail: lsokol@lpns.com.

SOKOL, ROBERT JAMES, obstetrician, gynecologist, educator; b. Rochester, NY, Nov. 18, 1941; s. Eli and Mildred (Levine) S.; m. Roberta Sue Kahn, July 26, 1964; children: Melissa Anne, Eric Russell, Andrew Ian. BA in Philosophy with highest distinction, U. Rochester, 1963, MD with honors, 1966. Diplomate Am. Bd. Ob-gyn. (assoc. examiner 1984-86), Sub-Bd. Maternal-Fetal Medicine. Intern Barnes Hosp., Washington U., St. Louis, 1966—67, resident in ob-gyn., 1967—70, asst. in ob-gyn., 1966—70, rsch. asst., 1967—68, instr. clin. ob-gyn., 1970; Buswell fellow in maternal fetal medicine Strong Meml. Hosp.-U. Rochester, 1972—73; fellow in maternal-fetal medicine Cleve. Met. Gen. Hosp.-Case Western Res. U., 1974—75, assoc. obstetrician and gynecologist, 1973—83, asst. prof. ob-gyn., 1973—77; asst. program dir. Perinatal Clin. Rsch. Ctr., 1973—78, co-program dir., 1978—82, program dir., 1982—83, acting dir. obstetrics, 1974—75, co-dir., 1977—83, assoc. prof., 1977—81, prof., 1981—83, assoc. dir. dept. ob-gyn., 1981—83; prof. ob-gyn. Wayne State U., Detroit, 1983—2000, dist. prof. ob-gyn., 2000—, chmn. dept. ob-gyn., 1983—89, mem. grad. faculty dept. physiology, 1984—, interim dean Med. Sch., 1988—89, dean, 1989—99, pres. Fund for Med. Rsch. and Edn., 1988—99, interim dir. Applied Genomics Ctr., 2004—; chief ob-gyn. Hutzel Hosp., Detroit, 1983—89; interim chmn. med. bd. Detroit Med. Ctr., 1988—89, chmn. med. bd., 1989—99, sr. v.p. med. affairs, 1992—99, trustee, 1990—99; past pres. med. staff Cuyahoga County Hosps.; mem. profl. adv. bd. Educated Childbirth Inc., 1976—80; dir. C.S. Mott Ctr. for Human Growth and Devel., 1983—89, 1999—. Sr. obstet. cons. Symposia Medicus; cons. Grant Planning Task Force Robert Wood Johnson Found., Nat. Inst. Child Health and Human Devel., Nat. Inst. Alcohol Abuse and Alcoholism, Ctr. for Disease Control, NIH, Health Resources and Svcs. Adminstrn., Nat. Clearinghouse for Alcohol Info., APA; mem. alcohol psychosocial rsch. rev. com. Nat. Inst. Alcohol Abuse and Alcoholism, 1982-86; mem. ob-gyn. adv. panel U.S. Pharmacopial Conv., 1985-90, adv. com. on policy Am. Jour. Ob-gyn., 1999-, internat. adv. bd. Karmanos Cancer Inst., Detroit, Mich., 2002-; mem. clin. rsch. task force Assn. Am. Med. Colls., 1998-2000; mem. WSU Faculty Devel. Coun., 2003—. Mem. internat. editl. bd. Israel Jour. Obstetrics and Gynecology; reviewer med. jours.; mem. editl. bd. Jour. Perinatal Medicine; editor-in-chief Interactions: Programs in Clinical Decision-Making, 1987-90; rschr. computer applications in perinatal medicine, alcohol-related birth defects, perinatal risk and neurobehavioral devel.; contbr. chpts. to books and articles to profl. jours. Mem. Pres.'s leadership coun. U. Rochester, 1976—80, permanent trustee, 1986—; mem. exec. com. bd. trustees Southeast Mich. Ctr. Med. Edn., 1987—2000; chmn. Friends of the Grand Theatre, 2005—; mem. rsch. adv. com. Wayne State U., 2005—; mem. fetal alcohol spectrum disorders prevention adv. com. CDC and Prevention, 2005—07; bd. dirs. Am. U. Caribbean, 2001—, vice chair, 2007—, 2004; trustee Stratford Am., 2004—, pres., 2007—; bd. dirs. Grand Theatre, London, Ont., Canada, 2002—, pres., 2007. Maj. M.C. USAF, 1970—72. Recipient 15 sci. rsch. awards, 1986—, Disting. Svc. award, Wayne State U. Mem.: APHA, ACOG (chmn. steering com. drug and alcohol abuse contract 1986—87, rep. ctr. for disease control & prevention task force 2000—, editor-in-chief ACOG Update 2001—, Outstanding Dist. Svc. Excellence award 2006), NAS (Inst. of Medicine, com. to study fetal alcohol syndrome 1994—96), AMA, Soc. Maternal-Fetal Medicine Found. (found. bd. chmn. 2003—06, award for dedication and leadership 2007), Soc. Physicians Reproductive Choice and Health, World Assn. Perinatal Medicine, Internat. Soc. Computers in Obstetrics, Neonatology, Gynecology (v.p. 1987—89, pres. 1989—92), Soc. for Neuroscis. (Mich. chpt.), Am. Med. Soc. on Alcoholism and Other Drug Dependencies, Am. Gynecol. and Obstet. Soc., Neurobehavioral Teratology Soc., Soc. Perinatal Obstetricians (pres.-elect 1987—88, pres. 1988—89, v.p., Achievement award 1995), Rsch. Soc. Alcoholism, Ctrl. Assn. Obstetricians-Gynecologists (pres.-elect 1997—99, pres. 1999—2000), Detroit Acad. Medicine (pres.-elect 1999—2001, pres. 2001—02), Wayne County Med. Soc., Mich. Med. Soc., Royal Soc. Medicine, Assn. Profs. Ob-gyn., Perinatal Rsch. Soc., Soc. Gynecologic Investigation, Am. Med. Informatics Assn., Chgo. Gynecol. Soc. (hon.), Detroit Physiol. Soc. (hon.), Wayne State U. Acad. Scholars (pres. 2006—07), Alpha Omega Alpha, Sigma Xi, Phi Beta Kappa. Republican. Jewish. Home: 7921 Danbury Dr West Bloomfield MI 48322-3581 Office: Wayne State U CS Mott Ctr for Human Growth and Devel Detroit MI 48201 Home Phone: 248-851-5048; Office Phone: 313-577-1337. Business E-Mail: rsokol@moose.med.wayne.edu. *The drive for academic accomplishment was instilled early in childhood in a home environment which placed value on a multiplicity of interests in science and the arts. My parents taught me what to do. In retrospect, exposure to strong role models-professors of philosophy, pathology, psychiatry and obstetrics-gynecology-takes on increased importance-these individuals showed me how to do it. My family continues to support me in seeking and meeting new challenges. The opportunity to develop and transmit new knowledge sustains a high level of activity. I enjoy what I do.*

SOKOL, RONALD JAY, pediatric gastroenterologist, researcher; b. Chgo., July 18, 1950; s. Max Charles and Edith Sokol; m. Lori Lubman, Aug. 20, 1989; children: Skylar Paul, Jared Todd. BS, U. Ill., 1972; MD, U. Chgo., 1976. Diplomate Am. Bd. Pediat., Am. Bd. Pediatric Gastroenterology. Asst. prof. pediat. U. Colo., Denver, 1983—88; assoc. prof. pediat. U. Colo. Sch. Medicine, Denver, 1989—95, prof. pediat., 1995—, vice chair pediat., 1999—. Program dir. Pediatric Gen. Clin. Rsch. Ctr., Denver, 1998—, head sect. pediat. gastroenterology, hepatology and nutrition, 2006—. Editor: (med. textbook) Liver Disease in Children. Chair children's liver coun. Am. Liver Found., NYC, 1997—2003. Rsch. grantee, NIH, 1985—. Fellow: Am. Acad. Pediat. (nutrition rsch. award 2003); mem.: Am. Pediat. Soc., N. Am. Soc. for Pediat. Gastroenterology, Hepatology and Nutrition (pres. 1996—98), Am. Assn. for Study of Liver Disease, Soc. Pediat. Rsch., Am. Gastroent. Assn. Achievements include patents for antioxidant solution for treatment of cholestatic liver disease and for treatment of non-alcoholic steatohepatitis. Office: Childrens Hosp 1056 E 19th Ave Denver CO 80218 Office Phone: 720-777-6669. Business E-Mail: sokol.ronald@tchden.org.

SOKOLOFF, LOUIS, retired physiologist, neuroscientist; b. Phila., Oct. 14, 1921; married; 2 children. BA, U. Pa., 1943, MD, 1946; MD (hon.), U. Lund, Sweden, 1980; ScD (hon.), Yeshiva U, NY, 1982, U. Glasgow, UK, 1989, Philipps U. Marburg, Germany, 1990; MD (hon.), U. Rome, 1992; ScD (hon.), Georgetown U., Washington, 1992, Mich. State U., Lansing, 1993, U. Pa., Phila., 1997. Intern Phila. Gen. Hosp., 1946-47; rsch. fellow in physiology U. Pa. Grad. Sch. Medicine, 1949-51, instr., then assoc., 1951-56; assoc. chief, then chief sect. cerebral metabolism NIMH, Bethesda, Md., 1953-68, chief lab. cerebral metabolism, 1968—2004, emeritus scientist, 2004—. Chief editor Jour. Neurochemistry, 1974-78. Pvt. 1st class US Army, 1943—46, capt. MC US Army, 1947—49. Recipient F.O. Schmitt medal in neurosci., 1980, Albert Lasker clin. med. research award, 1981, Karl Spencer Lashley award Am. Philos. Soc., 1987, Disting. Grad. award U. Pa., 1987, Nat. Acad. Scis. award in Neurosci., 1988, Georg Charles de Hevesy Nuclear Medicine Pioneer award Soc. Nuclear Medicine, 1988, Mihara Cerebrovascular Disorder Rsch. Promotion award, 1988, Ralph Gerard award Soc. Neuroscience, 1996, Lifetime Achievement award Internat. Soc. Cereb and Mental Health, 1999. Mem. NAS, Inst. Medicine (sr.), Am. Physiol. Soc., Assn. Rsch. Nervous and Mental Diseases, Am. Biophys. Soc., Am. Neurol. Assn., Am. Philos. Soc., Am. Acad. Arts & Sci., Am. Soc. Biol. Chemists, Am. Soc. Neurochemistry, Internat. Soc. Neurochemistry, Internat. Soc. Cereb Blood Flow & Metab. Independent. Jewish. Achievements include development of methods for measurement of cerebral blood flow, metabolism and imaging of local functional activity in the brains of animals and man, and application of this for functional imaging in the brains of animals and man. Office: NIMH/NIH Bldg 49 Rm 1B80 9000 Rockville Pike Bethesda MD 20892-4030 Office Phone: 301-496-1371. Business E-Mail: louissokoloff@mail.nih.gov.

SOKOLOV, RICHARD SAUL, real estate company executive; b. Phila., Dec. 7, 1949; s. Morris and Estelle Rita (Steinberg) S.; m. Susan Barbara Saltzman, Aug. 13, 1972; children: Lisa, Anne, Kate. BA, Pa. State U., 1971; JD, Georgetown U., 1974. Assoc. Weinberg & Green, Balt., 1974-80, ptnr., 1980-82; v.p., gen. counsel The Edward J. DeBartolo Corp., Youngstown, Ohio, 1982-86, sr. v.p. devel., gen. coun., 1986-94; pres., CEO DeBartolo Realty Corp., Youngstown, Ohio, 1994-96; pres., COO Simon DeBartolo Group, Indpls., 1996-98; pres, COO Simon Property Group, Indpls., 1998—. Mem. investment com. Jewish Fedn., Youngstown, 1992—; trustee U. Wis.-Madison Ctr. for Urban Land Econs. Rsch., Youngstown/Mahoning Valley United Way. Alumni fellow Pa. State U., 2000. Mem. Internat. Coun. Shopping Ctrs. (trustee 1994—, chmn. 1998-99), Urban Land Inst. (assoc.). Office: Simon Property Group 115 W Washington St Ste 1465 Indianapolis IN 46204-3464

SOKOLOW, MARVIN JOEL, antiques dealer, appraiser; b. NYC, Apr. 27, 1934; s. Herman Nathan Sokolow and Jane (Allen) Sokolow; m. Mary Elizabeth Verheyen, Apr. 12, 1974; children: David, Karen, Peter, Joanna. BA, CCNY, 1961. Dir. v.p. Rare Art Inc., NYC, 1960—75; antique gallery owner Marvin Sokolow Antique Chinese Art, Winnetka, Ill., 1975—77; mgr. Rare Art II, NYC, 1977—84; antiques dealer, appraiser, cons. Marvin Sokolow Antiques, Bayside, Wis., 1985—. Lectr. in field; cons. in field. Appraiser: (TV series) Antiques Roadshow, 1996—. Vol. group leader U. Settlement Ho., NYC, 1950; vol. field worker Anti-Defamation League, NYC, 1964—65, Bnai Brith, NYC, 1964—65; lender pers. antiques Milw. Art Mus., 2000—04; mem. Regional Telecom. Commn. Milw. County, 2003—; guest appraiser, cons. Hospice of Hills, Harrison, Ark., 2004—. Mem.: Oriental Ceramic Soc. London, Am. Soc. Appraisers (sr.). Avocations: fishing, bicycling, museums, reading.

SOKOLSKY, ROBERT LAWRENCE, journalist; b. Boston, May 18, 1928; s. Henry and Lillian (Gorodetzky) S.; m. Sally-Ann Moss, Aug. 11, 1955; 1 son, Andrew E. AB, Syracuse U., NY, 1950. Reporter Springfield (Mass.) Union, 1950; asst. dir. pub. info. ARC, Syracuse, 1952-54; entertainment editor Syracuse Herald-Jour., 1954-61, Buffalo Courier Express, 1961-72, Phila. Bull., 1972-82; entertainment writer Riverside (Calif.) Press-Enterprise, 1983-2000; syndicated TV columnist Ottaway News Svc., 1988-96, Scripps Howard, 1996-2000; freelance writer, radio commentator pub. radio, 2000—; columnist San Bernardino Sun, 2001—; entertainment editor Inland Empire News Radio, 2001—. Radio show host; freelance writer; guest lectr. Contbr. columns in newspapers, 2001, articles to profl. jours. Bd. dirs. Brush Hollow Civic Assn., Evesham Twp., N.J. Served with U.S. Army, 1950-52. Recipient Sigma Delta Chi award for feature writing, 1950, award for entertainment coverage Twin Counties Press Club, 1984, 87, Lifetime Achievement award Inland Theatre League, 2001. Mem. Am. Newspaper Guild (Page One award for opinion writing), Syracuse Press Club, Greater Buffalo Press Assn., TV Critics Assn., Soc. Profl. Journalists (Excellence in Journalism award 1989, 93), Pen and Pencil Club of Phila., Variety Club. Republican. Jewish. Home and Office: 3080 Saratoga St Riverside CA 92503-5435 Office Phone: 951-785-0798. E-mail: rsokolsky@charter.net.

SOKULSKI, GARY A., lawyer; BSBA, Robert Morris Coll., 1979. CPA Price Waterhouse, 1981—92; joined Reed Smith LLP, Pitts., 1992, now COO, mem. mgmt. com. & exec. com. Mem.: Pitts. Legal Administrators Assn., Pa. Inst. CPAs, Assn. Legal Administrators, Am. Inst. CPAs. Office: Reed Smith LLP 435 Sixth Ave Pittsburgh PA 15219 Office Phone: 412-288-4232. Office Fax: 412-288-3063. Business E-Mail: gsokulski@reedsmith.com.

SOLA, AUGUSTO, pediatrician, educator; m. Marta Rogido; children: Mariana, Carolina, Augusto Jr., Ignacio. BS (Bilingual), Belgrano Day Sch., Buenos Aires, Argentina, 1967; MD, Buenos Aires Nat. U. Sch. of Medicine, Argentina, 1973. Dir. neonatal clin. services U. of Calif., San Francisco, 1991—97, prof. pediat., 1995—97; dir. divsn. of neonatology Cedars-Sinai Med. Ctr., LA, 1997—2001; prof. pediat. U. of Calif., LA, 1997—2001; dir. divsn. of neonatal-perinatal medicine Emory U. Sch. of Medicine, Atlanta, 2001, co-director, devel. progress clinic, 2001—, prof. pediat. and obstetrics,gynecology (tenured), Goddard scholar, 2001—; dir. neonatal rsch., academic affairs Morristown Meml. Hosp., NJ. Prof. pediat., dir. neonatology U. Buenos Aires, 1985—91; dir. neonatal fellowship program Cedars-Sinai Med. Ctr., LA, 1998—2001; cons. Am. Assn. of World Health, 1998—. Author: (book) Cuidados Intensivos Neonatales-Fisiopatologia y Terapeutica, Cuidados Especiales del Feto y Recien Nacido, Fisipatologia y Terapeutica, (manuscript) Jour. of Pediats. Nominee Ten Outstanding Young Profl. of the World, Internat. Jr. Chamber, 1989; recipient E.H. Christopherson award on Internat. Child Health, Am. Acad. of Pediat., 1999. Fellow: Am. Acad. of Pediat.; mem.: AAAS, Am. Acad. of Pediat. Sect. on Internat. Child Health, Soc. of Pediatric Rsch.

SOLA, JURE, electronics executive; BSEE, San Jose State U., 1972. Various mgmt. positions Lika Corp., Stockton, Calif., 1972-80; co-founder, held various mgmt. positions Sanmina Corp. and predecessor, 1980—, pres. & chmn., 1991—2001; co-chmn. Sanmina-SCI, 1999—2002, CEO, 2001—, chmn., 2002—. Recipient Ernst & Young Master Entrepreneur of Yr. award, 2004. Office: Sanmina SCI Corp 2700 N 1st St San Jose CA 95134-2015 *

SOLÁ, VICTORIA M., announcer, writer; b. Englewood, NJ, Nov. 11, 1952; d. Salvador Felix and Hedda Blanc (Westhead) Solá; 1 child, Frank Salvador Solá Grillo. Student, Fairleigh Dickinson U., NJ, 1970—72. Radio host and prodr. jazz WFDU-FM Radio, Teaneck, NJ, 1981—83, jazz dir., 1982—86, radio host and prodr. Latin, 1983—, Latin music dir., 1983—. Contbg. editor Descarga Catalog, NYC, 1996—2002; columnist Latin Beat Mag., Gardena, Calif., 1998, Latin London Mag., 1999; Latin jazz planning com. adv. Smithsonian Inst. Traveling Exhbn. Svc., Washington, 1999—2002, narrator, 2002. Coord. ann. on-air fundraiser for Latin music programming WFDU-FM, Teaneck, NJ, 1983—; participant on-air blood donor drive Bergen Cmty. Regional Blood Ctrs., Paramus, NJ, 1986; vol. fund raiser Operation Rescue North Shore Animal League Am., 2006. Mem.: Internat. Latin Music Hall of Fame (adv. com. 1999—, Spl. Recognition award 2001). Democrat. Avocations: reading, photography, drawing, writing. Office: WFDU-FM 1000 River Rd Teaneck NJ 07666 Office Phone: 201-692-2806 ext. 10. Office Fax: 201-692-2807. E-mail: vickisola1@aol.com.

SOLAN, LAWRENCE MICHAEL, lawyer; b. NYC, May 7, 1952; s. Harold Allen and Shirley (Smith) S.; m. Anita Lois Rush, Mar. 27, 1982; children: Renata, David. BA, Brandeis U., 1974; PhD, U. Mass., 1978; JD, Harvard U., 1982. Bar: N.J. 1982, N.Y. 1984. Law clk. to Hon. Pollock Supreme Ct. NJ, Morristown, 1982-83; assoc. Orans, Elsen & Lupert, NYC, 1983-89, ptnr., 1989-96; assoc. prof. law Bklyn. Law Sch., 1996-2000, prof. law, 2000—, Don Forchelli prof. law, 2004—, assoc. dean academic affairs, 2006—. Bd. dirs. Internat. Acad. Law, Mental Health; vis. assoc. prof. Princeton (NJ) U., 1999—2000, vis. prof., 2002, vis. fellow, 03; vis. prof. Yale Law Sch., 2006. Author: The Language of Judges, 1993, Pronominal Reference, 1983, (with Peter Tiersma), Speaking of Crime: The Language of Criminal Justice, 2005 Mem. Assn. of Bar of City of N.Y., Phi Beta Kappa Home: 163 Ralston Ave South Orange NJ 07079-2344 Office: Bklyn Law Sch 250 Joralemon St Brooklyn NY 11201-3700 Office Phone: 718-780-0357. Business E-Mail: larry.solan@brooklaw.edu.

SOLAND, NORMAN R., corporate lawyer; b. Duluth, Minn., Oct. 17, 1940; m. Carol A. Isaacson, Aug. 29, 1964; children: Kirk, Lisa, Kari, Chad. BA, U. Minn., 1963; JD, Am. Univ., 1972. Bar: Minn. 1973. Analyst CIA, 1963-73; assoc. Thompson, Hessian, Fletcher, McKasy & Soderberg, Thompson, Fletcher, Stone & Morse, 1973-79; corp. counsel Nash-Finch Co., Mpls., 1979-84, asst. sec., counsel, 1984-86, sec., gen counsel, 1986-88, v.p., sec. & gen. counsel, 1988-98, sr. v.p., sec., gen. counsel, 1998—. Mem. ABA, Minn. State Bar Assn., Hennepin County Bar Assn., Am. Corp. Counsel Assn. Office: Nash Finch Co PO Box 355 Minneapolis MN 55440-0355

SOLANO, CARL ANTHONY, lawyer; b. Mar. 26, 1951; s. Nick and Catherine A. (Occhiato) Solano; m. Nancy M. Randazzo, 1989; children: Melanie A., Carla Nicole. BS magna cum laude, U. Scranton, 1973; JD cum laude, Villanova U., 1976. Bar: Pa. 1976, U.S. Dist. Ct. (ea. dist.) Pa. 1978, U.S. Ct. Appeals (3d cir.) 1980, U.S. Ct. Appeals (5th cir.) 1981, U.S. Supreme Ct. 1982, U.S. Ct. Appeals (9th cir.) 1986, U.S. Dist. Ct. (mid. dist.) Pa. 1988, U.S. Ct. Appeals (6th cir.) 1988, U.S. Ct. Appeals (fed. cir.) 1989, U.S. Ct. Appeals (6th cir.) 1988, U.S. Ct. Appeals (7th cir.) 1996. Law clk. Hon. Alfred L. Luongo U.S. Dist. Ct. (ea. dist.) Pa., Phila., 1976—78; assoc. Schnader, Harrison, Segal & Lewis, Phila., 1978—84, ptnr., 1985—. Adj. prof. Villanova U. Sch. Law, 1999—2001. Contbg. author: Federal Appellate Procedure Third Circuit, 1996, MLRC State Survey: Media Libel Law, 1984—, Third Circuit Appellate Practice Manual, 2007. Named Pa. Super Lawyer, 2004—07; named one of Best Lawyers in Am. for Appellate Law, First Amendment Law, 2006, 2007; recipient Legal Achievement award, Burton, 2007. Mem.: ABA, Justinian Soc., St. Thomas More Soc., Phila. Bar Assn. (chair bar news media com. 2003), Pa. Bar Assn. (statutory law com. 1980—95), Am. Law Inst., Order of Coif, Pi Gamma Mu. Roman Catholic. Home: 5 Barrister Ct Haverford PA 19041-1137 Office: Schnader Harrison Segal & Lewis LLP 1600 Market St Ste 3600 Philadelphia PA 19103-7287 Office Phone: 215-751-2202. Business E-Mail: CSolano@Schnader.com.

SOLANO, FRANCIS X., JR., internist; b. Pittston, Pa., Mar. 25, 1954; s. Francis X. and Sarah A. Solano; m. Linette Solano, Mar. 29, 1980; children: Nicole, David, Rachel. BS in Biology, U. Scranton, Pa., 1975; MD, Hahnemann Med. Coll., Phila., 1980. Internist Solano & Kokaces Internal Medicine Assocs., USNC, Pitts., 1997—; resident CMI UPMC, 2000—05, med. dir. Ctr. Quality Improvement and Innovation, 2003—, v.p. PSO, 2005—. Recipient Physician Leadership award, UPMC Health Plan, Physician Innovation award, Aces award, UPMC Health Sys. Fellow: ACP. Office: Solano Kokales & Assocs UPMC 120 Lytton Ave Pittsburgh PA 15213

SOLANO, HENRY L., lawyer; m. Janine Solano; children: Mateo, Amalia, Guadalupe. BS in Mech. Engring., U. Denver; JD, U. Colo.; LLD (hon.), U. Denver. Asst. atty. gen. Human Resources divsn. Colo. Dept. Law, 1977-82; asst. U.S. atty. Dist. Colo., 1982-87; U.S. atty. for Colo. U.S.

Dept. Justice, Denver, 1994-98; solicitor U.S. Dept. Labor, Washington, 1998-2001; ptnr. LeBoeuf, Lamb, Greene & MacRae L.L.P., Denver, 2001—. Exec. dir. Colo. Dept. Instns., 1987-91, Colo. Dept. Regulatory Agys., 1987; acting exec. dir. Colo. Dept. Corrections, 1989-90; chair Cabinet Coun. on Families and Children, 1990-91; mem. adv. com. U.S. Atty. Gen., 1994-95; lectr. Kennedy Sch. Govt. Bd. dirs. Nat. Latino Children's Inst., Nat. Hispana Leadership Inst., Mex.Am. Legal Def. Edn. Fund, Denver Housing Authority, Denver Women's Commn., Colo. Dept. Social Svcs., Colo. Transit Constrn. Authority, Regional Transit Dist. Office: LeBoeuf Lamb Greene & MacRae 125 West 55th St New York NY 10019-5389 Office Phone: 202-986-8056. Business E-Mail: hsolano@llgm.com.

SOLANO, JULIO RAFAEL, priest, educator; b. Barranquilla, Atlantico, Colombia, Sept. 12, 1946; came to U.S., 1971; s. Domingo Rafael Solano and Christine Balderrama. Degree in acctg., Centro Intensificacion Comml., Bogota, Colombia, 1970; BA, St. John Vianney Coll. Sem., Miami, Fla., 1989; MDiv, St. Vincent de Paul Regl. Sem., Boynton Beach, Fla., 1993. Transitional deacon St. Louis Cath. Ch., Miami, 1992—93; asst. pastor St. Elizabeth Cath. Ch., Pompano Beach, Fla., St. Patrick Cath. Ch., Miami Beach, Fla., 1996—98; parochial vicar St. Coleman Cath. Ch., Pompano Beach, 1998—99, St. Elizabeth of Hungary Cath. Ch., Pompano Beach, 1999—2001, St. Vincent Cath. Ch., Margate, Fla., 2001—02; pastor Our Lady Queen of Heaven Cath. Ch., North Lauderdale, Fla., 2002—06, Little Flower Cath. Ch., Hollywood, Fla., 2006—. Tchr. La Salle H.S., Miami, 1996-98; asst. chaplain Serra Club Internat. Pompano Beach, 1994-95. Mem. KC, Assn. Sacerdotes Hispanos. Democrat. Roman Catholic. Avocations: travel, reading, writing, stamps, coins. Office Phone: 954-922-3517. Personal E-mail: frsolano@bellsouth.net.

SOLARO, ROSS JOHN, physiologist, biophysicist; b. Wadsworth, Ohio, Jan. 9, 1942; s. Ross and Lena (Chuppa) S.; m. Kathleen Marie Cole, Sept. 18, 1965; children: Christopher, Elizabeth. BS, U. Cin., 1965; PhD, U. Pitts., 1971. Asst. prof. Med. Coll. Va., Richmond, 1973-77; assoc. prof. pharmacology and physiology U. Cin., 1977-81, prof. pharmacology and cell biophysics, 1981-85, prof. physiology, 1981-88; prof. physiology, head U. Ill., Chgo., 1988—, disting. univ. prof., 1998—. Sec. gen. Internat. Soc. Heart Rsch., 1989-93, sec./treas., 1995-98, pres., 1999, assoc. chair dept. physiology; chmn. exptl. cardiovasc. study sect. NIH, 1990-92; vice-chmn. physiology U. Cin., 1987-88. Editor: Protein Phosphorylation in Heart Muscle, 1986, Handbook of Physiology: The Heart, 2001; co-editor Handbook of Physiology: The Heart, 2001; contbr. articles to profl. jours. including Nature, Jour. Biol. Chemistry, Circulation Rsch. Chmn. rsch. coun. Am. Heart Assn., Met. Chgo., 1990-92. Grantee NIH, 1977—, Fogarty fellow, 1986; Brit. Am. Heart fellow Am. Heart Assn., 1974-75; Sr. Internat. fellow U. Coll. London, 1987. Mem. Am. Physiol. Soc. (chmn. subgroup), Am. Soc. Pharm. Exptl. Therapeutics, Biosphys. Soc. (chmn. subgroup 1983-84). Office: U Ill at Chgo MC901 Physiology & Biophysics 835 S Wolcott Ave Chicago IL 60612-7340 Business E-Mail: solarorj@uic.edu.

SOLARZ, ALAN H., lawyer; BS magna cum laude, SUNY, Albany, 1978; JD cum laude, SUNY, Buffalo, 1983; LLM, NYU, 1987. Bar: NY 1984, US Tax Ct. 1984, US Dist. Ct., So. and Ea. Dists. NY 1992. Ptnr., group co-leader Tax Advice and Controversy Bryan Cave LLP, NYC. Office: Bryan Cave LLP 1290 Ave of the Americas New York NY 10104 Office Phone: 212-541-2075. E-mail: ahsolarz@bryancave.com.

SOLBERG, ELIZABETH TRANSOU, public relations executive; b. Dallas, Aug. 10, 1939; d. Ross W. and Josephine V. (Perkins) Transou; m. Frederick M. Solberg Jr., Mar. 8, 1969; 1 son, Frederick W. BJ, U. Mo., 1961. Reporter Kansas City (Mo.) Star, 1963-70, asst. city editor, 1970-73; reporter spl. events, documentaries Sta. WDAF-TV, Kansas City, Mo., 1973-74; prof. dept. journalism Park Coll., Kansas City, Mo., 1975-76, advisor, 1976-79; mng. ptnr. Fleishman-Hillard Inc., Kansas City, Mo., then exec. v.p., sr. ptnr., gen. mgr. Kansas City br., now regional pres., sr. ptnr.; pres. Fleishman-Hillard/Can., 1994—99. Mem. Kansas City Commn. Planned Indsl. Expansion Authority, 1974-91; bd. dirs. Ferrellgas, Midwest Airlines. Mem. long range planning com. Heart of Am. coun. Boy Scouts Am., 1980-82, bd. dirs., 1986-89; mem. Clay County (Mo.) Devel. Commn., 1979-88; bd. govs. Citizens Assn., 1975—; mem. exec. com. bd. Kansas City Area Devel. Coun., 1989-96, co-chair, 1991-93; trustee Pembroke Hill Sch., 1987-93, U. Kansas City, 1990-2002, exec. com., 1992-2002, Midwest Rsch. Inst., 1995-2002; bd. dirs. Greater Kansas City Cmty. Found. and Affiliated Trusts, 1996-2005, Starlight Theatre, 1996-2002, Union Sta. Bd., 1998-2002, Mo. Devel. Fin. Bd., 2000—, chair, 2003—; regent Rockhurst Coll., 1984-96; active Bus. Coun., Nelson Gallery Found., Nelson-Atkins Mus. Art, 1990—; bd. dirs. Civic Coun. Greater Kansas City, 1992—, chair civic coun., 2003-2005; mem. Jr. League Kansas City. Recipient award for contbn. to mental health Mo. Psychiat. Assn., 1973, Arthur E. Lowell award for excellence in orgn. comm. Kansas City/IABC, 1985, Kansas City Spirit award Gillis Ctr., 1994. Mem. Pub. Rels. Soc. Am. (nat. honors and awards com.—chmn. SilverAnvil com. 1983, Silver Anvil award 1979-82, chair nat. membership com. 1989-91, assembly del.-at-large 1995-96), Counselor's Acad. (exec. com. 1991-92), Mo. C. of C. Pub. Rels. Coun., Greater Kans. City C. of C. (chair 1994-95, bd. exec. com.), River Club, Carriage Club. Office: Fleishman Hillard Inc 2405 Grand Blvd Ste 700 Kansas City MO 64108-2522

SOLBERG, MARY ANN, federal official; Grad., Western Mich. U. Dep. dir. Office Nat. Drug Control Policy Exec. Office of Pres., Washington, 2001—; exec. dir. Coalition of Health Comtys., Troy (Mich.) Cmty. Coalition for Prevention of Drug and Alcohol Abuse; various positions Troy Adult and Cmty. Edn., 1977—91. Mem. adv. com. to develop a nat. prevention sys. Nat. Ctr. for Substance Abuse Prevention; mem. adv. com. Nat. Ad Coun.'s Cmty. Anti-Drug Campaign; mem. Pres.'s Commn. on Drug-Free Cmtys., 1998, co-chairperson. Office: Exec Office of Pres Office Nat Drug Control Policy 750 17th St NW Washington DC 20503

SOLBERG, RONALD LOUIS, investment adviser, portfolio manager; b. Madison, Wis., May 15, 1953; s. Carl Louis and Gladys Irene Evelyn (Oen) S.; m. Anna Maria Teresa Gorgol, May 16, 1983 (div. Aug. 1992); m. Elizabeth Catherine Gillett, Dec. 24, 1996 (div. Oct. 2001). BA in Econs. with honors, U. Wis., 1975; MA, U. Calif., Berkeley, 1977, PhD, 1984. Country risk analyst Wells Fargo Bank, San Francisco, 1978-79; asst. v.p., economist Wells Fargo Ltd., London, 1979-81; cons. RAND Corp., Santa Monica, Calif., 1982-84; acting instr. econs. U. Calif., Berkeley, 1983; 1st v.p., portfolio risk policy mgr. Security Pacific Corp., LA, 1984-92; internat. fin. cons., 1992-94; v.p., fixed-income credit rschr. Pacific Investment Mgmt. Co., 1994-95; mng. dir. head Asian econ. rsch. Chase Manhattan Bank, Hong Kong, 1995-98; acting head of emerging markets securities Asia, Chase Manhattan Asia Ltd., 1996-98; mng. dir., head mkt. and credit rsch. group Tokyo-Mitsubishi Internat. plc, London, 1998—2000; prin. Viking Asset Mgmt., Laguna Beach, Calif., 2001—. Adj. asst. prof. U. So. Calif., L.A., 1985-92. Author: (monograph with G. Grossman) The Soviet Union's Hard-Currency Balance of Payments and Creditworthiness in 1985, 1983; (book) Sovereign Rescheduling: Risk and Portfolio Management, 1988, Country Risk Analysis, 1992; contbr. articles to profl. jours. Research fellow Inst. Internat. Studies, Berkeley, 1982-84. Mem. Am. Econ. Assn., Asia Soc., Nat. Assn. for Bus. Economists, Soc. for Internat. Devel. Avocations: fly fishing, cross country skiing, squash, billiards. Office Phone: 949-291-4643. E-mail: rsolberg@cox.net.

SOLBERG, WINTON UDELL, historian, educator; b. Aberdeen, SD, Jan. 11, 1922; s. Ole Alexander and Bertha Georgia (Tschappat) S.; m. Ruth Constance Walton, Nov. 8, 1952; children: Gail Elizabeth, Andrew Walton, Kristin Ruth. AB magna cum laude, U. S.D., 1943, LHD (hon.), 1987; student, Biarritz Am. U., France, 1946; A.M., Harvard, 1947, PhD, 1954. Instr., then asst. prof. social scis. U.S. Mil. Acad., 1951-54; instr., then asst. prof. history Yale U., 1954-58; fellow Pierson Coll., 1955-58, Morse fellow, 1958; James Wallace prof. history Macalester Coll., 1958-62; vis. prof. U. Ill., 1961-62, assoc. prof. history, 1962, prof., 1967—, chmn. dept. history, 1970-72. Rsch. fellow Ctr. Study History of Liberty in Am., Harvard U., 1962-63; rsch. scholar Henry E. Huntington Library, San Marino, Calif., 1959; dir. Coe Found. Am. Studies Inst., summers 1960-62; lectr., cons. Army War Coll., 1959-62; lectr. U.S. Command and Gen. Staff Sch., 1963-64; Fulbright lectr. Johns Hopkins U. Bologna, 1967-68, Moscow (USSR) State U., 1978, U. Calcutta India, 1993; vis. prof. Konan U., Kobe, Japan, 1981; USIA Lectr., Korea and Malaysia, 1985, Korea, 1992. Author: The Federal Convention and the Formation of the Union of the American States, 1958, The Constitutional Convention and the Formation of the Union, 1990, The University of Illinois, 1867-1894, An Intellectual and Cultural History, 1968, Redeem the Time: The Puritan Sabbath in Early America, 1977, History of American Thought and Culture, 1983, Cotton Mather, The Christian Philosopher, 1994, The University of Illinois, 1894-1904: The Shaping of the University, 2000; also articles. Mem. Ill. Humanities Council, 1973-75; sec. Council on Study of Religion, 1981-85. Maj. inf. AUS, 1943-46, 51-54; lt. col. U.S. Army Res. Recipient Faculty Achievement award Burlington No. Found., 1986, Disting. Teaching award U. Ill. Coll. Liberal Arts and Scis., 1988; NEH sr. fellow, 1974-75; Rsch. grantee NSF, 1981-82 Mem. Am. Hist. Assn., So. Hist. Assn., Orgn. Am. Historians, Am. Studies Assn. (pres. Mid-Am. 1985-86), Am. Soc. Ch. History (pres. 1985-86), AAUP (chpt. pres. 1965-66, mem. council 1969-72, 1st v.p. 1974-76), Phi Beta Kappa. Episcopalian. Home: 8 Lake Park Rd Champaign IL 61822-7101 Office: U Ill History Dept Urbana IL 61801 Office Phone: 217-333-4193. Business E-Mail: wsolberg@uiuc.edu.

SOLBRIG, INGEBORG HILDEGARD, retired literature educator, writer; b. Weissenfels, Germany, July 31, 1923; arrived in U.S., 1961, naturalized, 1966; d. Reinhold J. and Hildegard M. A. (Ferchland) Solbrig. Grad. in chemistry, U. Halle, Germany, 1948; student, Delmar Coll., 1961; BA summa cum laude, San Francisco State U., 1964; postgrad., U. Calif., Berkeley, 1964-65; MA, Stanford U., 1966, PhD in Humanities and German, 1969. Asst. prof. U. R.I., 1969-70, U. Tenn., Chattanooga, 1970-72, U. Ky., Lexington, 1972-75; assoc. prof. German U. Iowa, 1975-81, prof., 1981-93, prof. emerita, 1993—. Domestic and abroad lectr.; former presenter The Light from the East, Coptic Christians/Egypt, 2004. Author: Hammer-Purgstall und Goethe, 1973, Orient-Rezeption, 1996, Orient-Rezeption, Fischer Lexikon Literatur, 1996, 2d edit., 2000, Modulationen von Gold und Licht in Goethes Kunstmärchen, 1997, Momentaufnahmen, 2000, J.G. Herder: Echo of the Cultural Philospher's Ideas in Early African-American Intellectual Writing, 2000, Maria Sibylla Merian..., 2001; main editor: Rilke Heute, Beziehungen und Wirkungen, 1975; editor (and translator): Reinhard Goering: Seeschlacht/Seabattle, 1977; mem. editl. bd.: Kairoer Germanistische Studien, vol. 9 & 10, 1998; contbr. articles to profl. jours., chpts. to books. Mem. Iowa Gov.'s Com. 300th Anniversary German-Am. Rels. 1683-1983, 1983. Named Ky. Col., 1975; recipient Hammer-Purgstall Gold medal, Austria, 1974; fellow, Stanford U., 1965—66, 1968—69, Austrian Ministry Edn., 1968—69; Delta Phi Alpha Deutsche Ehrenverbindung, U. Ky., 1973, Old Gold fellow, Iowa, 1977, Am. Coun. Learned Socs. grantee, German Acad. Exch. Svc. grantee, 1980, Sr. Faculty Rsch. fellow in humanities, 1983, NEH grantee, 1985, May Brodbeck fellow in humanities, 1989, numerous summer faculty rsch. grants. Mem.: MLA (life), Soc. for History Alchemy and Chemistry, Internat. Herder Soc. (founding mem.), Goethe Soc. N.Am., Inc., Can. Soc. 18th Century Studies, Am. Soc. 18th Century Studies, Deutsche Schiller Gesellschaft, Goethe Gesellschaft, Internat. Vereinigung fur Germanische Sprach und Lit. Wiss., Egyptian Soc. Lit. Criticism (hon.), World Peace and Diplomacy Forum (life). Avocations: horseback riding, photography, writing, travel, theology. Home and Office: 1126 Pine St Iowa City IA 52240-5711 *The circumstances of my life took me to many places and cultures. Despite the discord and problems plaguing many parts of this planet, let us not forget that it's the home of the human family, our home. Always remember: Life is, by definition, change.*

SOLDAN, ANGELIKA, political science educator, philosopher; b. Hennigsdorf, Germany, Feb. 10, 1953; d. Hans and Erika Potempa; m. Wolfgang Karl Soldan, May 8, 1987; 1 child, Anja Soldan. MA in Philosophy, Humboldt U., 1975, PhD, 1990, Martin Luther U., Halle-Wittenberg, Germany, 1982. Assoc. prof. philosophy, polit. ethics Humboldt U., Berlin, 1989-91; adj. prof. philosophy, ethics, govt. U. Tex., Brownsville, 1991-98, lectr. social issues and philosophy, 1999—2000, asst. prof., 2000—05, assoc. prof., 2005—. Contbr. articles to profl. jours. Co-founder Gesellschaft für Solidarische Entwicklungszusammenarbeit, 1990. Mem. Am. Philos. Assn., Internat. Fromm Soc., Internat. Nietzsche Soc., Internat. Assn. Women in Philosophy. Office: U Tex Brownsville 80 Fort Brown St Brownsville TX 78520 Office Phone: 956-882-8890. E-mail: angelika.soldan@utb.edu.

SOLE, MICHAEL JOSEPH, cardiologist; b. Timmins, Ont., Can., Mar. 5, 1940; s. Fred and Lillian Sole; m. Susan Karen Samuels, May 26, 1964; children: David Frederick, Leslie Meredith. BSc, U. Toronto, Ont., Can., 1962, MD, 1966. Cert. Coll. Physicians and Surgeons Ont.; diplomate Am. Bd. Internal Medicine. Rotating intern, jr. asst. resident, sr. asst. resident in internal medicine Toronto Gen. Hosp., 1966-69; cardiology fellow Cardiovasc. Rsch. Inst., U. Calif., San Francisco, 1969-71; cardiology fellow Peter Bent Brigham Hosp., Boston, 1971-73, jr. assoc. medicine, 1973-74; rsch. assoc. MIT, Cambridge, 1973-74; instr. medicine Harvard Med. Sch., 1973-74; from asst. to assoc. prof. medicine U. Toronto, 1974-83, prof. medicine and physiology, 1983—, mem. staff inst. med. sci., 1978—, dir. cardiology rsch., 1987-89, dir. centre cardiovasc. rsch., 1989-99, Searle chair cardiovasc. rsch., 1998—; staff cardiologist Toronto Hosp., 1974-89, dir. non-invasive cardiology, 1974-79, dir. cardiology rsch., 1979-89, dir. divsn. cardiology, 1989-98, dir. cardiovasc. program, 1992—97, dir. Peter Munk Cardiac Ctr., 1992-97. Vis. prof. Harvard U., 1975, NIH, Bethesda, Md., 1981, U. B.C., 1982, 91, 92, Capital Med. Sch. and Beijing Hosp., 1985, U. Tokyo, 1992, others; mem. Can. Govt. Task Force Diagnostic Ultrasound, 1976-78; vice-chmn. econs. com. dept. medicine Toronto Gen. Hosp., 1977, chmn., 1978, 79, chmn. emeritus, 1980, mem. various coms., 1981-98, chmn. cardiology rsch. com., 1988-89, mem. cardiovasc. collaborative practice group, 1989-92; rsch. assoc. Ont. Heart Found., 1979-89; assoc. rsch. inst. pediat. Hosp. Sick Children, Toronto, 1979—; mem. med. staff Mt. Sinai Hosp., Toronto, 1979—; mem. adv. bd. Merck Pharms., 1983—, Boots Pharms., 1992-93; mem. Health Rsch. and Devel. Coun., Province of Ont., 1983-86, mem. exec. com., 1984-86; Levesque lectr. Montreal Heart Inst., 1984; mem. cardiovasc. panel Med. Rsch. Coun. Can., 1985-87; mem. heart and blood vessel rsch. adv. com. Toronto Hosp., 1986-89; chmn. cardiovasc. rsch. adv. com. faculty medicine U. Toronto, 1986-87, mem. various coms., 1987—, chmn. rsch. com. dept. medicine, 1987-88, mem. rsch. adv. bd., 1989-97, chair life scis. com., 1990-92, chair decanal promotions com. faculty medicine, 1992-94; mem. exec. com. Centre Cardiovasc. Rsch., 1998-99, chmn. sci. com., 1989-99, mem. exec. com. cardiovasc. clin. rsch. lab., 1992-99, chmn. rsch. com., 1992-99; Pfizer vis. fellow Clin. Rsch. Inst., Montreal, 1988; mem. sr. adv. com. Toronto Western Hosp., 1989-90; Katz vis. prof. U. Chgo., 1989; mem. provincial working group cardiovasc. svcs. Ministry of Health, 1990-91, mem. ctrl. east region cardiovasc. patient care mgmt. group, 1990-91; mem. trial devel. com. diabetes atherosclerosis intervention study WHO and Fournier Pharms., 1991-93, mem. trial exec. com., 1993-2000; mem. Joint Med. Rsch. Coun. Can./Pharm. Mfrs. Assn. Can. Adv. Com. Sci., 1993; mem. organizing coms. various sci. meetings; presenter in field. Mem. editl. bd. Can. Jour. Cardiology, 1988—, Index and Revs. Congestive Heart Failure, 1988-90, Hypertension Can., 1988-90, European Jour. Pharmacology, 1992-96, Cardiosci., 1993, Jour. Heart Failure, 1994—, Circulation, 1996—, Jour. Molecular Medicine, 1996—, Jour. Molecular Cell Cardiology, 1999-2001; mem. internat. editl. bd. Cardiology Digest, 1992—; contbr. chpts. to books and articles to profl. jours.; patentee in field. Recipient Robert Beamish Leadership award, Inst. CV Sci., U. Man., 2001; fellow Ivan Smith Rsch. fellow, U. Toronto, 1964, Hunter fellow, Ont. Heart Found., 1973; grantee Grantee, Heart & Stroke Found. Ont., 1969—, Med. Rsch. Coun. Can., 1982—92, 1994—97; scholar Walter Watkins scholar, U. Toronto, 1962. Fellow Am. Coll. Cardiology (abstract reviewer 1989, 91), Royal Coll. Physicians and Surgeons, Can. Acad. Health Sci.; mem. Am. Soc. Clin. Investigation, Assn. Am. Physicians, Am. Heart Assn. (fellow couns. clin. cardiology, hypertension, circulation and basic sci., mem. exec., basic sci. coun. 1986-89, mem. Katz prize selection com. 1988-90), Can. Inst. Acad. Medicine, Can. Soc. Clin. Investigation, Can. Cardiovasc. Soc. (mem. young investigators award panel 1982-84, mem. student presentation award com. 1988-90, mem. nat. task force cardiovasc. sci. 1992-93, Ann. Rsch. award 1975, Rsch. Achievement award 1989), Heart and Stroke Found. Can. (mem. sci. rev. bd. 1976-79, vice-chmn. 1980-83, chmn. hypertension and cardiovasc. pharmacology panel 1982-83, chmn. molecular biology, biochemistry, pathology panel 1989-90), Can. Med. Assn. (mem. coun. 1982-87), Am. Fedn. Clin. Rsch., Ont. Med. Assn. (alt. del. Toronto Gen. Hosp. bd. 1988-90), Heart and Stroke Found. Ont. (mem. med. rsch. com. 1978-81, bd. dirs. 1986-92, 96—, mem. fin. com. 1986-90, 96-97, mem. corp. rels. com. 1990-92, mem. rsch. policy com. 1991-93, 96-97, chmn. 1997-99, mem. exec. com. 1997-99, nomination com. 1997-99, chmn. 50th anniversary com., mem. audit com., Disting. Rsch. prof. 1989-96, Murray Robertson Meml. lectr. 1989), Internat. Soc. Heart Rsch. (exec. Am. sect. 1979-88, lectr. Latin Am. sect. 1995), Banting Rsch. Found. (hon. sec.-treas. 1979-81), Gairdner Found. (mem. rev. panel 1979-94), Heart Failure Soc. Am. (publs. com. 2000-03, nominating com. 2001-04), Maple Downs Golf and Country Club (Toronto; bd. dirs. 2001-06, exec. bd. 2003-06), Alpha Omega Alpha. Office: Toronto Gen Hosp Eaton 585 University Ave Rm 4N488 Toronto ON Canada M5G 2N2 Office Phone: 416-340-3471. Business E-Mail: michael.sole@uhn.on.ca.

SOLECKI, R. STEFAN, anthropologist, educator; b. Bklyn., Oct. 15, 1917; s. Kazimierz John and Mary (Tarnawski) S.; m. Rose Muriel Lilien, June 24, 1955; children: John Irwin, William Duncan. BSc, CCNY, 1941; MA, Columbia U., NYC, 1950, PhD in Anthropology, 1958. Archaeologist Smithsonian Instn., 1948-54; archaeol. asst. anthropology Columbia U., NYC, 1954-55, mem. faculty, 1959-88, prof. anthropology, 1965-88, prof. emeritus, 1989—, chmn. dept., 1975-78; adj. prof. dept. anthropology Tex. A&M Univ., College Station, 1989—; assoc. curator old world U.S. Nat. Mus., 1957-59. Archael. expdns. to Alaska, 1949, 61, Iraq, 1950-51, 53, 56-57 (field dir.), 60, 78, Sudanese Nubia, 1961, Turkey, 1963, Syria, 1963, 64, 65, 88, 89, Iran, 1968, Lebanon, 1969-73, France, 1975, Ea., Midwestern and Western US; collaborator in archaeology Smithsonian Instn., 1953; cons. UNESCO, 1959. Served with AUS, 1943-45. Fulbright scholar, Iraq, 1952-53; William Bayard Cutting travelling fellow Columbia, 1956-57; Fulbright-Hays faculty research awardee Syria, 1980-81; Fulbright fellow, Iraq, 1988-89. Fellow Am. Anthrop. Assn., Arctic Inst. Am., NY Acad. Scis. (chmn. anthropology sect. 1977-79); mem. NY Archaeol. Assn. (pres. 1960-62), NY Oriental Club (pres. 1965), Profl. Archeologists of NYC (pres. 1980-81), Soc. Archaeology, Am. Schs. Oriental Research (assoc. trustee 1969-71), Prehistoric Soc., Deutsches Archaeologisches Inst., Soc. Préhistorique Français, Archaeol. Inst. Am. (exec. com. 1968-70), Assn. Field Archaeology (pres. 1972-74). Home: 86 Park Pl South Orange NJ 07079-2303 Office: Columbia U Dept Anthropology New York NY 10027

SOLENDER, MICHAEL SAMUEL, lawyer, diversified financial services company executive; b. Chgo., Apr. 14, 1964; s. Stephen and Elsa Solender; m. Holly Renee Fogler, Oct. 23, 1993. BA summa cum laude, Columbia U., NYC, 1986; JD, Yale Law Sch., New Haven, 1989. Bar: NY 1990, DC 1991. Law clk. to Judge Leonard B. Sand US Dist. Ct. (so. dist. NY), 1989—90; assoc. Arnold & Porter, Washington, 1991—97, ptnr., 1997—99, 2001—02; gen. counsel Consumer Product Safety Commn., 2000—01; sr. mng. dir. legal dept. Bear Stearns Cos. Inc., NYC, 2002—04, gen. counsel, sr. mng. dir., 2004—. Recipient Cmty. Svc. award, Urban Justice Ctr., 2005. Mem.: Am. Inn of Ct., Phi Beta Kappa. Office: Bear Stearn Cos Inc 383 Madison Ave New York NY 10179 *

SOLENDER, ROBERT LAWRENCE, retired real estate company executive, retired publishing executive; b. Rochester, NY, Sept. 1, 1923; s. Samuel S. and Catherine (Goldsmith) S.; m. Ellen Van Raalte Karelsen, Nov. 25, 1948; children: Elizabeth, Jefferson, Katherine. BA, Oberlin Coll., 1943. Asst. to pres. Craven & Hedrick, Inc., NYC, 1946-49; with Dallas Times Herald, 1949-75, v.p., advt. dir., 1964-69, v.p., gen. mgr., 1969—71, v.p. sales, 1971—75; dir. NorthPark Nat. Bank, 1973—93; prin. Robert L. Solender & Assocs., Dallas, 1975—; mng. ptnr. The Devonshire Co., Dallas, 1978-95. Interim chmn., CEO, AccuBanc Mortgage Corp., 1992. Trustee SW Med. Found.; bd. dirs. Friends Dallas Pub. Libr.; pres. Dallas Child Guidence Clinic, 1956, Dallas Mental Health Assn., 1959, Hope Cottage Children's Bur., 1973; past bd. dirs. Dallas Theatre Ctr., Child Care Dallas, Tex. Mental Health Assn., Dallas Civic Music Assn., Dallas County United Way, exec. com.; adv. bd. Cmtys. Found. Tex.; assoc. Dallas Mus. Art. Mem.: Masons. Home: 9131 Devonshire Dr Dallas TX 75209-2411

SOLET, MAXWELL DAVID, lawyer; b. Washington, May 15, 1948; s. Leo and Pearl (Rose) S.; m. Joanne Marie Tolksdorf, Sept. 27, 1970; children: David Marc, Paul Jacob. AB, Harvard U., 1970, JD, 1974. Bar: Mass. 1974, U.S. Tax Ct. 1976, U.S. Ct. Claims 1976, U.S. Supreme Ct. 1976. Assoc. Gaston Snow & Ely Bartlett, Boston, 1974-79, Mintz, Levin, Cohn, Ferris, Glovsky & Popeo, P.C., Boston, 1979-82, ptnr., 1982—. Mem. adv. com. tax exempt and gov. entities IRS, 2005—, chmn. adv. com. tax exempt and gov. entities, 2007—. Mem.: ABA, Cambridge Health Alliance (bd. mem. 2005—), Nat. Assn. Bond Lawyers (mem. steering com. bond atty.'s workshop 1992—95, 2007—), Boston Bar Assn. (chmn. tax sect. 1987—89, mem. multidisciplinary practice task force 2000—01, mem. audit com. 2003—), Mass. Bar Assn., Cambridge Hist. Soc. (bd. mem. 1999—2000, sec. 2001—05, v.p. 2005—). Home: 15 Berkeley St Cambridge MA 02138-3409 Office: Mintz Levin Cohn Ferris Glovsky & Popeo PC One Financial Ctr Boston MA 02111 Home Phone: 617-547-3250; Office Phone: 617-348-1739. Business E-Mail: msolet@mintz.com.

SOLEY, ROBERT LAWRENCE, plastic surgeon; b. NYC, Feb. 26, 1935; s. Max and Saide (Leader) S.; m. Judy Wasserman, June 16, 1963; children: John, Jill. BS, Yale U., 1956; MD, NYU, 1959. Diplomate Am. Bd. Surgery, Am. Bd. PLastic Surgery. Intern Bellevue Hosp., NYC, 1955—60; resident in gen. surgery Mt. Sinai Hosp., NYC, 1960—65; resident in plastic surgery Hosp. U. Pa., Phila., 1967—69; practice medicine specializing in plastic surgery White Plains, NY, 1969—. Mem. staff, mem. med. bd. White Plains Hosp., 1985—88, chief sect. plastic surgery, 1988—94. Contbr. articles to profl. jours. Capt. M.C., USAF, 1965-67. Grantee USPHS, 1968-69. Fellow ACS; mem. Am. Soc. Plastic Reconstructive Surgery, Am. Soc. Aesthetic Surgery, N.Y. State Med. Soc. (ho. of dels.), Westchester County Med. Soc. (pres. 1996-97, bd. dirs.), Rotary (bd. dirs. White Plains chpt. 1982-85). Home: 30 Griffin Ave Scarsdale NY 10583-7661 Office: Associated Plastic Surgeons Westchester PC 30 Griffen Ave Scarsdale NY 10583-7661 Personal E-mail: bob@soley.com.

SOLGANIK, MARVIN, real estate executive; b. Chgo., Nov. 7, 1930; s. Harry and Dora (Fastoff) S.; m. Judith Rosenberg, Sept. 11, 1960; children: Randall, Janet, Robert. BBA, Case Western Res. U., 1952. Real estate broker, Cleve., 1950-65, Herbert Laronge Inc., Cleve., 1965-68; sr. v.p. real estate Revco D.S., Inc., Twinsburgh, Ohio, 1968—, corp. dir., 1974—. Adj. prof. Ohio No. U.; guest lectr. Cleve. State U., Case Western Res. U. Sch. Law, Cuyahoga C.C., Ohio No. U., Cleve. Real Estate Bd., CASE Sch. Law. Vol. jewish Welfare Fund, Shaker heights, Ohio; chmn. capital and budget coms. Jewish Fedn.; chmn. Agnon Sch. Bdlg. Com.; bd. dirs. Bellfair-J.C.B.-Home for Emotionally Disturbed Children, Visconsi Cos, Cleve. Inst. Music. Recipient Appreciation award Am. Soc. Real Estate Appraisers, Akron-Cleve. chpt., 1971 Mem. Nat. Assn. Corp. Real Estate Officers, Internat. Council Shopping Ctrs. Office: D S Revco 22925 Holmwood Rd Shaker Heights OH 44122-3005

SOLIDUM, JAMES, finance and insurance executive; b. Honolulu, Mar. 12, 1925; s. Narciso and Sergia (Yabo) S.; m Vickie Mayo, Aug. 14, 1954; children: Arlin James, Nathan Francis, Tobi John, Kamomi Teresa. Student, U. Hawaii, 1949-50; BA, U. Oreg., 1953. CLU. Promotional salesman Tongg Pub. Co., 1953—54; editor Fil-Am. Tribune, 1954—55; master planning technician Fed. Civil Svc., 1955—57; publs. editor Hawaii Sugar Planters Assn., 1957; field agt. Grand Pacific Life Ins. Co., 1957—59, home office asst., 1959—60, supr., 1960—62, asst. v.p., 1962—64; propr. J. Solidum & Assoc., Honolulu, 1964—; pres. Fin. Devel. Inst., 1967—. Contbg. writer Paradise of Pacific Mag., 1957-58, Hawaii Agrl. Mag., 1957-58; gen. ptnr. R.Z. Limited Partnership, 1981—; v.p. Grand Pacific Life Ins. Co., 1983-90; bd. dirs. Hawaii Econ. Devel. Corp., 1982-89; mem. adv. com. Honolulu dist. SBA, 1971-77; bd. advisors Philippine Consulate of Hawaii, 1959. Pres. Keolu Elem. PTA, 1960-62; mem. satisfaction com. Hawaii Visitors Bur., 1963-66; chmn. budget and rev. panel IV, Aloha United Way, 1966-72, bd. dir., 1971-77, 82-88, chmn. bd., 1984; mem. mgmt. svcs. com., 1977, mem. cen. com., 1977-82, chmn. budget and allocations com., 1982-84; chmn. Kamehameha Dist. fin. com. Aloha coun. Boy Scouts Am., 1966; vice chmn. Businessmen's Cancer Crusade, 1965; chmn. Operation Bayanihan, Hawaii Immigration Task Force, 1970; participant Oahu Housing Workshop, State of Hawaii, Hawaii chpt. HUD, 1970; mem. task force on housing and transp. Alternative Econ. Futures for Hawaii, 1973; chmn. Bicentennial Filipiniana, 1976; campaign chmn. State Rep. Rudolph Pacarro, 1964-68; mem. exec. com. Campaign for Reelection U.S. Senator Hiram L. Fong, 1970, Gov. William Quinn for U.S. Senate, 1976; Rep. candidate for Hawaii Ho. of Reps., 1972; mem. Rep. Citizens Task Force on Housing, 1973; trustee St. Louis Alumni Found., 1970—, Kuakini Med. Ctr., 1984-86, Palama Settlement, 1975-82, v.p., 1976, treas., 1980-82; bd. mgrs. Windward YMCA, 1964-67; bd. advisers St. Louis H.S., 1963-64; bd. gov. Goodwill Industries, 1964; bd. dir. Children's Ctr., Inc., 1975-77, Hawaii Multi-Cultural Arts Ctr., 1977-81, treas., 1979; fin. chmn. St. Stephen's Parish Coun., 1974—; bd. dir. St. Louis Fine Arts Ctr., 1985-88; mem. steering com. Conf. Filipino Voter Registrars, 1962. With U.S. Army, 1945-47. Recipient Man of Yr. award Filipino C. of C., 1965, cert. of merit Aloha United Way, 1971, Honor award Wisdom mag., 1974, Outstanding Alumnus honor medal St. Louis HS, 1976, Island Treasure award Cath. Ch. Hawaii, 2003. Mem. Hawaii State C. of C. (bd. dir. 1964-67, chmn. legis. com. 1966-67, v.p. 1970, chmn. election judges 1971, mem. ad hoc com. bus.-youth rels. 1970—), Filipino C. of C. (past pres. 1965, com. chmn.), Am. Soc. CLU, Soc. Fin. Svcs. Profls., Honolulu Assn. Life Underwriters (bd. dir. 1963-66, del. nat. conv. 1967, chmn. life underwriters tng. coun. 1962-67), Hawaii Estate Planning Coun., Hawaii Plantation Indsl. Editors Assn. (sec.-treas. 1957), St. Louis Alumni Assn. (bd. dir., chmn. fin. 1969-75, pres. 1976, treas. 1977—), Phi Kappa Sigma. Republican. Roman Catholic. Home: 2622 Waolani Ave Honolulu HI 96817-1362 Office: 225 Queen St Apt 12-a Honolulu HI 96813-4603

SOLIEMANZADEH, PEYMAN, plastic surgeon, otolaryngologist; s. Manijeh Soliemanzadeh. BS, UCLA, 1995; MD, U. Calif., San Diego, 1999. Diplomate Am. Bd. Otolaryngology-Head and Neck Surgery, 2005. Fellow in facial plastic and reconstructive surgery U. Tex., Houston, 2004—05; dir. facial plastic surgery Aden, Inc, Westlake Village, Calif., 2004—06; co-dir. facial plastic surgery Profiles Beverly Hills, LA, 2006—. Mem.: AMA (assoc.), Am. Acad. Otolaryngology-Head Neck Surgery (assoc.). Jewish.

SOLINGER, JANET W., museum executive; b. Cin., Dec. 20, 1921; d. Fred and Dorothy G. (Gross) Weiland; widowed; children: Dorothy, Regina, Martha. BA, U. Cin., 1943; MA, NYU, 1973; DFA (hon.), Corcoran Coll. of Art, Washington, 1998. Asst. to pres. Hebrew Union Coll., Cin., 1957-60; adminstr. Jewish Mus., NYC, 1961-65; asst. to exec. dir. Finch Coll., NYC, 1965-66; dir. pub. info. and spl. events NYU, 1966-72; dir. Smithsonian resident assoc. program Smithsonian Instn., Washington, 1972-93; v.p. Corcoran Gall. of Art, Washington, 1994—. Lectr. in field. Author: Museums and Universities: New Paths for Continuing Education, 1990, Marketing the Arts, 1992; contbr. articles to profl. jours. Named Washingtonian of Yr., Washingtonian mag., 1984, Outstanding Woman Pioneer in Arts, Smithsonian Archives Am. Art, 2005; recipient decorations, Belgium, 1980, The Netherlands, 1981, Germany, 1982, Gold medal, Smithsonian Inst., 1990, Wash. Woman of the Millenium award, Art Table, 2000, Art Spark award, 2005; Fulbright Fellow, New Zealand, 1992. Mem. AIA (hon.), Washington Archtl. Found. (bd. dirs. 1996-2001), Art Table (bd. dirs. 1994-2000), Faberge Found. (bd. dirs. 1991—), Cosmos Club. Democrat. Jewish. Avocations: golf, bridge, reading, travel. Home: 2801 New Mexico Ave NW Washington DC 20007-3921 Office: Corcoran Gall of Art 500 17th St NW Washington DC 20006-4804 Office Phone: 202-639-1771. Business E-Mail: jsolinger@corcoran.org.

SOLIS, CARLOS, lawyer; b. Managua, Nicaragua, May 15, 1945; came to US, 1952; s. Carlos and Luisa (Serrano) S. BA, U. San Francisco, 1967, JD, 1969. Bar: Calif. 1970, US Dist. Ct. (cen. and no. dists.) Calif. 1970, US Ct. Appeals (9th cir.) 1970, US Dist. Ct. (ea. dist.) Calif. 1972, US Dist. Ct. (so. dist.) Calif. 1973, US Supreme Ct. 1973. Assoc. Kindel & Anderson, LA, 1976, ptnr., 1976—96, Heller Ehrman LLP, 1996—2005; pvt. practice, 2005—. Exec. legal counsel, bd. dirs. internat. student ctr. UCLA, 1976-86, exec. v.p., 1981-86; instr. atty. asst. program UCLA, 1977-79; bd. advisors LA Internat. Trade Devel. Corp., 1981-87; bd. dirs. Pub. Counsel of LA, 2003-05. Assoc. editor U. San Francisco Law Rev., 1968-69; contbr. articles to profl. jours. Bd. dirs. ARC, LA, 1978-93, 95-05, chmn. audit com., 1985-88, bd. advisors, 1993-05; bd. dirs. March of Dimes, LA, 1982-87, LA Pub. Theater Found., 1978-81, Young Musicians Found., 1979-80, Boys and Girls Club East LA, 1986-89; bd. dirs. Am. Diabetes Assn., LA, 1986-93, chmn., 1989-91, bd. dirs. Calif., 1988-93, chmn., 1992-93, mem. nat. minority initiative task force, 1986-92, bd. dirs. Nat., 1993-95; vice chmn. bd. LA United Way, 1982-83, bd. dirs., 1980-03, corp. bd. dirs., 1982-96, treas., 1989-93; pres. LA Open Golf Found., 1979-80. Recipient Alumni award U. San Francisco, 1969, Province award Phi Delta Phi, 1969. Mem. LA Jr. Chamber (pres., chmn. bd. dirs. 1980-81, Most Improved com. award 1975, Dir. of Yr. award 1977, Outstanding Bus. Leader award 1980), Assocs. LA C. of C., LA Area C. of C. (bd. dirs. 1979-80), U. San Francisco Alumni Assn. (pres. San Gabriel Valley chpt. 1976-80), Latin Am. Ctr. Assocs. (pres. 1980-82, bd. advisors 1980-88), Alpha Sigmu Nu, Phi Delta Phi. Avocation: travel. Home: 201 La Vereda Rd Pasadena CA 91105-1227 Personal E-mail: carlossoljs1000@yahoo.com.

SOLIS, HILDA LUCIA, congresswoman, educational administrator; b. LA, Oct. 20, 1957; d. Raul and Juana (Sequiera) S.; m. Sam H. Sayyad, June 26, 1982. BA in Polit. Sci., Calif. State Poly U., 1979; MA in Pub. Adminstrn., U. So. Calif., 1981. Interpreter Immigration and Naturalization Service, Los Angeles, 1977-79; editor in chief Office Hispanic Affairs, The White House, Washington, 1980-81; mgmt. analyst Office Mgmt. and Budget, Washington, 1981-82; field rep. Office Assemblyman Art Torres, LA, 1982; dir. Calif. Student Opportunity and Access, Whittier, 1982—; rep. 57th assembly dist. Calif. State Assembly, Sacramento, 1992-94; mem. Calif. Senate from 24th dist., 1994-2000, U.S. Congress from Calif. 32nd dist., Washington, 2001—; mem. resources com., energy & commerce com., former mem. edn. and workforce com. Cons. South Coast Consortium, L.A., 1986—; mem. South Coast Ednl. Opportunity Pers. Consortium. Bd. dirs. Calif. Commn. on Status of Women, 1993—; corr. pres. Friendly El Monte (Calif.) Dem. Club, 1986—; mem. credentials com. Calif. Dem. Com., 1987-88; trustee Rio Hondo C.C., 1985-92. Recipient Meritorious Svc. award Dept. Def., 1981, Young Careerist award El Monte Bus. and Profl. Women, 1987, Profile in Courage Award John F. Kennedy Libr. Found., 2000; fellow Nat. Edn. Inst., Kellogg Found., 1984-85. Mem. Western Assn. Ednl. Opportunity Pers. (sec. bd. dirs. 1986—), Comision Feminil de Los Angeles (bd. dirs. 1983-84, edn. chmn.), Women of Moose. Democrat. Roman Catholic. Office: 1725 Longworth House Office Bldg Washington DC 20515-0532 also: Ste 211 4401 Santa Anita Ave El Monte CA 91731 *

SOLÍS, MARCO ANTONIO, singer, composer; b. Ario de Rosales, Michoacan, Mexico, Dec. 29, 1959; Co-founder Los Hermanitos Solis, 1962; co-founder, singer & songwriter Los Bukis, 1975—95; solo career, 1995—. Singer: (albums) (with Los Bukis) Falso Amor, 1975, Yo Te Necesito, 1984, Adonde Vas, 1985, Juntos Otra Ves, 1989, Y Para Siempre, 1989, Travez de Tus Ojos, 1991, Me Volvi a Acordarme de Ti, 1991, Si Me Recuerdas, 1991, Quiereme, 1992, Inalcanzable, 1993, Casas de Carton, 1994, Frente a Frente, 1994, Nortenas Y Chicanas, A Donde Vas, 1995, Triste Imaginar, 1995, A Bailar Con, 1996, Romanticos, 1996, (solo albums) Por Amor a Mi Pueblo, 1995, Romanticos de Corazon, 1996, En Pleno Vuelo, 1996, Marco, 1997, Recuerdos, Tristeza y Soledad, 1998, Trovos de Mi Alma, 1999, En Vivo, 2000, Mas de Mi Alma, 2001, En Concierto, 2001, Ty Amor o Tu Desprecio, 2003, Razon de Sobra, 2004, Dos Idolos, 2005; actor: (films) La Coyota, 1987, Como Fui a Enamorarme de Ti, 1991. Recipient Latin Grammy award for Best Regional Mex. Song, 2004, Lifetime Achievement award, Billboard Music Awards, 2005, Super Artist Sales award, Chile, 2006, Male Artist of Yr. award, Premio Lo Nuestra Música Latina, 2006, Spl. Recognition award, 2006, Greatest Hits Album of Yr. award, Billboard Latin Music Awards, 2006, Latin Songwriter of Yr. award, ASCAP, 2007. Office: c/o Elizabeth Sobol Gomez IMG Artists 152 W 57th St 5th Fl New York NY 10019

SOLIS DOYLE, PATTI, political campaign worker; b. Chgo., Aug. 23, 1965; d. Santiago and Alejandrina (Ortega) S. BA in Comm., Northwestern U., 1990. Asst. to treas. City of Chgo., 1989-91; dir. of scheduling for Hilary Rodham Clinton Clinton-Gore Campaign, Little Rock, 1991-92, Clinton Transition Team, Little Rock, 1992-93; spl. asst. to Pres., dir. of scheduling for First Lady The White House, Washington, 1993—2001; campaign asst. Hillary Clinton 2000 Election Campaign, 2000—01; former exec. dir. HILLPAC; campaign mgr. Hillary Clinton 2008 Presidential Campaign, 2006—. Recipient Latinas of Excellence award, Hispanic Mag., 2007. Roman Catholic. First Hispanic woman to lead U.S. presidential campaign. Office: 4420 N Fairfax Dr Arlington VA 22203 *

SOLISH, JONATHAN CRAIG, lawyer; b. Monticello, NY, May 27, 1949; s. David Julius and Gertrude (Hellman) S.; m. Dhana Krushkhov, Dec. 30, 1981; 1 child, Nickolas Brewster. BA, U. Calif., Santa Cruz, 1971; JD, UCLA, 1975. Bar: Calif. 1975, US Dist. Ct. Ctrl. Dist. Calif. 1977, US Ct. Appeals 9th Cir. 1979, US Ct. Appeals Fed. Cir. 1988, US Dist. Ct. So. Dist. Calif. 1988, US Dist. Ct. Ea. Dist. Calif. 1992, US Dist. Ct. No. Dist. Calif. 1993, US Supreme Ct 2000. Ptnr. Solish, Jordan & Wiener, LA, Solish Arbiter & Gehring (merged with Jenkens & Gilchrist), LA; shareholder Jenkens & Gilchrist, P.C., LA, 1997—, firm co-leader franchise & distribution practice group. Assoc. editor Franchise Law Jour., 1992-97, editor-in-chief, 1997-2000; contbr. articles to profl. jours. Mem. LA Olympics Citizens Adv. Com., 1981-84, LA Olympics Cultural and Fine Arts Adv. Com., 1981-84. Mem. ABA (forum com. on franchising 1984-, appellate advocacy com. 1989-, antitrust sect. & subsect. on franchising 1990-, litig. & dispute resolution steering com. 2001-), LA County Bar Assn. (appellate practice 1989-, atty.-client rels. com. 1985-, Pacific Rim com. 1990—, antitrust section 1990—), State Bar Calif. (internat. law sect. 1990-) Office: Jenkens & Gilchrist PC 12100 Wilshire Blvd 15th Fl Los Angeles CA 90025-7120 Office Phone: 310-442-8804. Office Fax: 310-820-8859. Business E-Mail: jsolish@jenkens.com.

SOLIZ, EUSEBIO, military officer; b. San Juan, Tex., Apr. 25, 1979; s. Eusebio and Joangela (Sanchez) Soliz; m. Joangela Sanchez; children: Richard Sanchez, Eusebio, Emma Felicity, Nicholas Sanchez, Michelle Pilar. Enlisted USN, 1997, supr. Ingleside, Tex., 1997—. Decorated Navy Achievement medal. Home: 1011 Espana Dr Portland TX 78374 Home Phone: 512-535-0053. Personal E-mail: soliz53@yahoo.com.

SOLJACIC, MARIN, physicist, educator; b. Zagreb, Croatia, Feb. 7, 1974; arrived in U.S., 1992; s. Ivo and Marija Soljacic; m. Mihaela Papa, Apr. 2, 1976; 1 child, Fran Daniel. BA in Physics, MIT, 1996, BA in Elec. Engring., 1996; PhD, Princeton U., 2000. Pappalardo fellow MIT, Cambridge, Mass., 2000—03, prin. rsch. scientist, 2003—05, asst. prof., 2005—. Cons. OmniGuide Inc., Cambridge, Mass., 2001—; spkr. in field. Contbr. chapters to books, articles to sci. jours. Recipient Adolph Lomb medal, Optical Soc. Am., 2005, TR35 award, Tech. Rev., 2006. Mem.: Phi Beta Kappa. Achievements include 14 patents. Office: MIT Room 6C-419 77 Mass Ave Cambridge MA 02139 Office Phone: 617-253-2467.

SOLKOFF, JEROME IRA, lawyer, educator; b. Rochester, NY, Feb. 15, 1939; s. Samuel and Dorothy (Krovetz) S.; m. Doreen Hurwitz, Aug. 11, 1963; children: Scott Michael, Anne Lynn. BS Sch. Indsl. Rels. and Labor Rels., Cornell U., 1961; JD, U. Buffalo, 1964. Bar: N.Y. 1965, Fla. 1974, U.S. Dist. Ct. (we. dist.) N.Y. 1965; cert. elder law atty., Fla. Bar, Nat. Elder Law, Found. of Nat. Acad. of Elder Law Attys., ABA. Assoc. Nusbaum, Tarricone, Weltman, Bilgore & Silver, Rochester, N.Y., 1964-66, Mousaw, Vigdor, Reeves, Heilbronner & Kroll, Rochester, 1966-70; sr. mcpl. atty. Urban Renewal Agy., Rochester, 1970-73; sole practice Rochester, 1970-73; chief legal counsel Arlen Realty Mgmt., Inc., Miami, Fla., 1973-75; assoc. Britton, Cohen, Kaufman, Benson & Schantz, Miami, 1975-76; chief legal counsel First Mortgage Investors, Miami Beach, Fla., 1976-79; ptnr. Cassel & Cassel, P.A., Miami, 1979-82; sole practice Deerfield Beach, Fla., 1982—. Lectr. on fgn. investment practices in U.S., Eng., 1981-88, Montreal, Que., Can., 1981, estate planning, 1982—, medicaid law and elder law, 1988—. Author: Fundamentals of Foreign Investing in American Real Estate and Businesses, 1981, Checklist of N.Y. Mortgage Foreclosure Procedures, 1970, History of Municipal Employee Unions, 1964, Practice Guide for Florida Elder Law, 1996, National Elder Law Forms Manual, 2005, and yearly supplements. Bd. dirs. Broward Homebound Program, 1990-2001, pres. 1998-99; bd. dirs. Jewish Cmty. Ctrs. of South Broward, Fla., 1979-90, NE Alzheimers Daycare Ctr., Inc., 1990-92; mem. exec. bd. dirs. Broward Alzheimers Assn., 1995—; co-chair Fla. Alzheimers Pub. Policy steering com., 1999-2001. Named Advocate of Yr., Broward County Legal Aid Assn., 2003. Mem. ABA (mem. sects. real property, trust and probate law), Fla. Bar Assn. (sects. real property, trust and probate law, vice-chmn. com. on the elderly 1987-91, lectr. estate planning for the aging and disabled 1989—, founder, chmn. elder law sect. 1994-95, elder law sect., chmn. ethics com. 1998-2000), Nat. Acad. Elder Law Attys., Elder Law Attys., Fla. Acad. Elder Law Attys.

SOLLENDER, JOEL DAVID, management consultant, financial executive, accountant; b. NYC, Nov. 11, 1924; s. Samuel and Flora (Blumenthal) S.; m. Dorothy Leaf, Aug. 6, 1958; children: Jeffrey D., Jonathan L. BS, N.Y. U., 1946. CPA N.Y., 1947. Staff auditor Ernst & Young, NYC, 1946-50; with United Mchts. & Mfrs., Inc., NYC, 1950-86, chief acctg. officer, 1976—, corp. contr., 1977—, sr. v.p., 1980—, mem. exec. mgmt. com. also bd. dirs. subsidiary cos.; assoc. dir. N.Y. Hist. Soc., NYC, 1986—89; mem. adv. coun. to Office of Charities Registration Dept. State, N.Y. State, 1988-89; v.p. fin. Piedmont Industries, NYC, 1989-90; exec. v.p., CFO Earthworm Inc., 1990—92; fin. mgmt. cons.; sr. cons. Internat. Exec. Svc. Corps Agy. for Aid for Internat. Devel., Kazakstan, 1996—. Adv. coun. San Diego State U., 1997—; audit com. San Diego Mus. Art, 1997-2002; fin. com. Globe Theater, 2003-04, audit com., 2004—. With US Army, 1943—45, WW II. Decorated Combat Infantry Badge, Purple Heart with oak leaf cluster, Prisoner of War medal, Bronze Star. Mem. AICPA, N.Y. State Soc. CPAs (chief fin. officer com.), Am. Inst. Corp. Contrs., Rancho Bernardo (Calif.) Men's Club, Bailiwick Club (Greenwich, Conn.), Greenhaven Yacht Club (Rye).

SOLLER, ELAINE RITA, psychologist, artist; b. Phila., Sept. 13, 1933; d. Samuel Jay and Anne Ruth (Fitterman) Klein; m. Alex Soller (div.); children: Marc Steven, Daniel Jay, Cheryl Lynne. BS in Psychology, Wayne State U., Detroit, 1970, MA in Clin. Psychology, PhD in Clin. Psychology, Wayne State U., Detroit, 1978; PsyD, Nova U., Ft. Lauderdale, Fla., 1982. Diplomate Am. Acad. Pain Mgmt., 1990, Am. Bd. Psychol. Specialities, 1997, Am. Bd. Forensic Examiners, 1997. Pvt. practice, Boca Raton, Fla., 1982—84, Southfield, Mich., 1984—92, Ann Arbor, 1993—. Guest lectr. in field. Bd. mem. Dispute Resolution Ctr. Washtenaw County, Ann Arbor, 1998—2004, pres., 2002—04. Fellow: Am. Soc. Clin. Hypnosis (bd. govs., state rep., cert. cons. 1995—); mem.: Mich. Soc. Clin. Hypnosis (past. pres., founder), Assn. Advancement Applied Sports Psychology, Internat. Soc. Hypnosis, NY Acad. Scis. (life), Am. Psychol. Assn., Nat. Assn. Female Execs. Avocations: painting, piano, cello, knitting, poetry.

SOLLERS, JOSEPH SEDWICK, III, lawyer; b. Balt. AB, Princeton Univ., 1977; JD with honors, Univ. Md., 1982. Bar: D.C. 1983. Law clk. Judge Norman P. Ramsey, US Dist Ct. Md.; ptnr., Spec. Matters & Govt. Investigations Practice Group King & Spalding LLP, Washington. Fellow: Am. Col. Trial Lawyers (co-chmn. D.C. subcom., Criminal Litigation com.); mem.: ABA. Office: King & Spalding LLP 1700 Pennsylvania Ave NW Washington DC 20006 Office Phone: 202-626-5612. Office Fax: 202-626-3737. Business E-Mail: wsollers@kslaw.com.

SOLLMAN, GEORGE HENRY, venture capitalist; b. Michigan City, Ind., Nov. 2, 1941; s. Henry Charles and Margaret Elisabeth (Gockel) S.; m. Maureen Tosh, July 12, 1968; children: Jennifer, Erich. Spl. student, MIT, 1965—66; BSEE, Northwestern U., 1964; MSEE, Northeastern U., 1967. Engring. dir. Honeywell Info. Systems, Waltham, Mass., 1964—73; product line mgr. Control Data, Hawthorne, Calif., 1973—76; v.p., gen. mgr. Shugart/Xerox, Sunnyvale, 1976—84; spl. ptnr. Sand Hill Venture Group, Menlo Park, 1984; pres., CEO Centigram Corp., San Jose, 1985—97, AtMotion Inc. (now OpenWave Corp.), Redwood City, Calif., 1997—2000, Arabesque Investments LLC, Atherton, Calif., 2000—; chmn. First Virtual Corp., Redwood Shores, Calif., 2004—, Corticon Techs., San Mateo, Calif., 2000—. Bd. dirs. T-Ventures, Venture Capital arm of Deutsche Telecom, Bonn, Germany, 2001-; chmn. nat. bd. dirs. Am. Elec. Assn.; presdl. nomination Semicondr. Tech. Coun.; co-chmn. Alexis d'Toqueville Soc.; mem. adv. coun. Joint Venture Silicon Valley; chmn. adv. bd. Leavey Sch. Bus., Santa Clara U., 2000-. Patentee in field. Co-chmn. United Way of Santa Clara County; mem. steering com. George Lucas Ednl. Found., Marin County. Home: 242 Polhemus Ave Atherton CA 94027-5439 Office: Arabesque Investments LLC 242 Polhemus Ave Atherton CA 94027-5439 Home Phone: 650-364-9164; Office Phone: 650-365-8186. Personal E-mail: george_sollman@hotmail.com.

SOLLORS, WERNER, literature and language educator; PhD, Freie U., Berlin, 1975. Wissenschaftlicher asst., asst. prof. John F. Kennedy Inst. Freie U., Berlin; from asst. to assoc. prof. English and Comparative Lit. Columbia U.; Henry B. and Anne M. Cabot Prof. English Lit., prof. Afro-Am. studies Harvard U., Cambridge, Mass. Author: Amiri Baraka/LeRoi Joines: The Quest for a Populist Modernism, 1978, Beyond Ethnicity: Consent and Descent in American Culture, Neither Black Nor White Yet Both: Thematic Explorations of Interracial Literature, 1997; contbr. chapters to books Das amerikanische Drama der Gegenwart, 1976, The Harvard Encyclopedia of American Ethnic Groups, 1980, Reconstructing American Literary History, 1986, 1986, Columbia Literary History of the United States, 1988, 1988, Critical Terms for Literary Study, 1990, 1990, Looking Inward, Looking Outward: From the 1920s through the 1940s, 1990, 1990, Nationale und kulturelle Identitat: Studien zur Entwicklung des kollektiven Bewusstseins in der Neuzeit, 1991, Immigrants in Two Democracies: French and American Experience, 1992, Intersecting Boundaries: The Theatre of Adrienne Kennedy, 1992, Il razzismo e le sue storie, 1992, Swedes in America: Intercultural and Interethnic Perspectives on Contemporary Research, 1993, Multiculturalism and the Canon of American Culture, 1993, Configurations de l'ethnicite aux Etats-Unis, 1993, History & Memory in African-American Culture, 1994, Thematics: New Approaches, 1995, Thematics Reconsidered: Essays in Honor of Horst Jr. Daemmrich, 1995, Performances in American Literature and Culture, 1995, New Essays on Henry Roth's Call It Sleep, 1996, Families, 1996, Cultural Difference and the Literary Text, 1996, Beyond Pluralism, 1998, The Sally Hemings-Thomas Jefferson Relationship, 1999, Columbia Companion to 20th Century American Short Fiction, 2001, Dream-Fluted Cane: Essays on Jean Toomes and the Harlem Renaissance, 2001, Not English Only: Redefining "American" in American Studies, 2001, American Studies and Peace, 2001, Mixed-Race Literature, 2001; editor: A Bibliographic Guide to Afro-American Studies, 1972, A Bibliographic Guide to Afro-American Studies Supplement I, 1974; co-editor: Bibliographie amerikanistischer Veröffentlichungen in der DDR bis, 1968, 1976, Varieties of Black Experience at Harvard, 1986, The Invention of Ethnicity, 1989, The Life Stories of Undistinguished Americans as Told by Themselves, 1990, 1999, The Return of Thematic Criticism, 1993, Cane, 1993, Blacks at Harvard: A Documentary History of African-American Experience at Harvard and Radcliffe, 1993, The Black Columbiad: Defining Moments in African-American Literature and Culture, 1994, Theories of Ethnicity: A Classical Reader, 1996, The Promised Land, 1997, Multilingual America: Transnationalism, Ethnicity and the Languages of American Literature, 1998, The Multilingual Anthology of American Literature, 2000, The Norton Critical Edition of Olaudah Equiano, 2000, Interracialism: Black-White Intermarriage in American History, Literature and Law, 2000, The Adrienne Kennedy Reader, 2001, German? American? Literature?: New Directions in German-American Studies, 2002, Interracial Literature: An Anthology of Black-White Contacts in the Old World and the New, 2004, Frank J. Webb: Fiction, Essays and Poetry, 2005, Georges, 2007, The Autobiography of W.E.B. Du Bois, 2007; contbr. articles to profl. jours. Recipient Constance Rourke prize Am. Studies Assn., 1990; John Simon Guggenheim Meml. fellow, Andrew W. Mellon faculty fellow Harvard U., Walter Channing Cabot fellow Harvard U., 1997-98; NEH fellow, 1999-00. Fellow: Am. Acad. of Arts and Scis. Office: Harvard U Barker Center 12 Quincy St Cambridge MA 02138-3804

SOLLS, MARK A., lawyer; b. 1956; married; 3 children. BA in Fin., U. Ill., 1977; JD, So. Ill. U., 1980. Bar: Ill. 1980, Tex. 1982; cert.: mediator. Pvt. practice; v.p., gen. counsel, sec. Pronet, Inc., 1993—97, Dal-Tile Internat., Inc., 1998—2002; exec. v.p., general counsel, sec. Wyndham Internat., Inc., Dallas, 2002—.

SOLLY, RICHARD PETER, music educator; s. Richard Gibson and Jane Ruth Solly. BA, Coll. NJ, 1975, MA, 1976. Cert. tchr. Pa., NJ. Asst. organist Trinity Episcopal Cath., Trenton, NJ, 1975—77; organist, choirmaster, dir. St. Paul's Luth. Ch., Doylestown, Pa., 1972—; tchr. music North Penn Sch. Dist., Lansdale, 1978—. Adj. faculty Bucks County CC, Newtown, Pa., 1977—78; program annotator Bucks County Symphony Orch., Doylestown, 1988—. Composer: The Hymnal, 1982, Hymnal for the Hours, 1989. Recipient Srs. Choice award, North Penn Sch. Dist., 1996, 1997, 1998. Mem.: Organ Hist. Soc., Am. Guild Organists, Kappa Delta Pi. Avocations: travel, baseball, railroading. Home: PO Box 264 Doylestown PA 18901-0264

SOLMAN, JOSEPH, artist; b. Vitebsk, Russia, Jan. 25, 1909; came to U.S. 1912; s. Nathan and Rose (Peskin) S.; m. Ruth Romanofsky (dec. July 1999); children: Paul, Ronni., Nat. Acad. of Design, 1927-30. Easel painter WPA, NYC, 1935-41; pvt. art instr. NYC, 1951-66; art instr. CUNY, NYC, 1967-75; artist NYC, 1935—. One-man shows: Contemporary Arts Gallery, NYC, 1934, ACA Gallery, 1950, 1968, 77, 86; Exhibitions: Retrospective at Phillips Mem. Mus., Washington, 1949, Retrospective at Wichita (Kansas) Mus. of Art, 1984, Robert Brown Contemporary Art, Washington, 1985, Mercury Gallery, Boston and Rockport, Mass., 1995, 96, 98, 99, 2000, 03, 04, 05, 06, Simmons Gallery, San Francisco, 2004, 05; author: books, Joseph Solman, Crown Publishers, 1966, Monotypes of Joseph Solman, Da Capo Press, 1977, Mozartiana, 1990, Joseph Solman, Da Capo Press, 1995; editor-in-chief, Art Front Mag., 1937-38. Recipient of several awards for paintings and portraits including the Nat. Inst. of Arts & Letters, 1961, and 8 prizes from the Nat. Acad. of Design Annuals, 1967-89. Mem. Nat. Acad. of Design (treas. 1979-85, academician, 1974-), Fedn. of Modern Painters & Sculptors (exec. bd. 1968-89); fellow (life) Art Student League.

SOLMER, RICHARD, surgeon; b. South Bend, Ind., Feb. 11, 1947; MD, U. Mich., 1972. Diplomate Am. Bd. Plastic Surgery. Surgical intern Hosp. of the U. Pa., Phila., 1972-73; gen. surgical resident Calif. Hosp. Med. Ctr., LA, 1976-80; plastic surgery resident Allentown (Pa.) Affiliated Hosp., 1980-82; pvt. practice Huntington Beach, and Newport Beach, Calif., 1982—. Fellow Am. Coll. Surgeons; mem. Am. Soc. Plastic Surgeons. Office: 307 Placentia Ave Ste 208 Newport Beach CA 92663-3308 Office Phone: 949-548-0227.

SOLMSSEN, PETER, retired academic administrator; b. Berlin, Nov. 1, 1931; m. Kathleen Mailliard, Dec. 2001. AB, Harvard U., 1952; JD, U. Pa., 1959. Atty. Ballard, Spahr, Andrews & Ingersoll, Phila., 1959-60; with U.S. Fgn. Service, 1961; vice consul Singapore, 1962-63; asst. to under sec. of state, 1963-65; 2d sec. Rio de Janeiro, 1965-67; Cultural attache U.S. Dept. State, Sao Paulo, Brazil, 1967-70; adviser on arts Washington, 1974-80; dep. ambassador at large for cultural affairs, 1981-83; pres. Phila. Coll. Art, 1983-87, U. of the Arts, Phila., 1987-2000. One-man photography exhbns. include: Mus. Art, Sao Paulo. Author and illustrator. Mem.: Philadelphia; Century Assn.

SOLNIT, REBECCA, writer, critic; Author: Secret Exhibition: Six California Artists of the Cold War Era, 1994, Savage Dreams: A Journey into the Landscape Wars of the American West, 1995, A Book of Migrations: Some Passages in Ireland, 1998, Wanderlust: A History of Walking, 2001, As Eve Said to the Serpent: On Landscape, Gender and Art, 2001, Hollow City: The Siege of San Francisco and the Crisis of American Urbanism, 2002, Motion Studies: Time, Space and Eadweard Muybridge, 2003, River of Shadows, 2003 (Nat. Book Critics Circle award, 2004). Grantee Guggenheim Fellowship, NEA Fellowship. Office: c/o Bloomsbury USA 175 5th Ave New York NY 10010

SOLO, JOYCE RUBENSTEIN, volunteer; b. Buffalo, Feb. 14, 1924; d. Jay Harry and Rose (Maisel) Rubenstein; m. Richard D. Solo, Jan. 6, 1946; children: Harry Jay Solo, Eleanor Solo, Sally Solo. BA, Wellesley Coll., 1945. Mem. S.E. Pa. Health Coord. Coun., 1978—84; chair reach to recovery Phila. divsn. Am. Cancer Soc., 1985—87; sec. Sarasota County Health Care Coord. Adv. Coun., Fla., 1993—95; chair sr. adv. com. Sarasota Meml. Hosp., 1996—98; vol. Reach to Recovery Breast Cancer Task Force, Manatee County Am. Cancer Soc.; mem. numerous other health and civic orgn. activities; pres. women's bd. Temple Beth Israel, 1996—98, bd. dirs., 1998—2000; mem. governing bd. Health Systems Agy. S.E. Pa., 1977—86. Mem.: LWV (v.p. Pa. chpt. 1969—73, pres. Phila. 1975—77, pres. Sarasota County 1990—92, healthcare com. chair 1988—90, 1992—), Phi Beta Kappa. Personal E-mail: rjoysolo14@comcast.net.

SOLO, ROBERT ALEXANDER, economist, educator; b. Phila., Aug. 2, 1916; s. Louis C. and Rebecca (Muchnick) S.; m. Roselyn Starr; 1 dau., Tova Maria. BS, Harvard U., 1938; MA, Am. U., 1941; PhD, Cornell U., 1953. Economist fed. and war agys., 1939-41; author, script chief Sta. WCAU-TV, Phila., 1949-50; mem. faculty Rutgers U., New Brunswick, N.J., 1953-55, McGill U., Montreal, Que., Can., 1955-56, CCNY, 1956-58; sr. research economist Princeton U., 1965-66; prof. dept. econs. Mich. State U., East Lansing, 1966-87, prof. emeritus, 1987—; dir. Inst. Internat. Bus. and Devel. Studies, 1966-68. Mem. faculty Johns Hopkins U., Balt., summer 1953, U. Mich., Ann Arbor, summer 1958; lectr. L'Ecole Practique des Hautes Etudes, Sorbonne, Paris, 1964-65; research Institut Recherch Economique et Planification, lectr. U. Grenoble, France, 1972-73; prof. associe U. Paris IV, Dauphine, 1971, 73; cons. NASA, 1965-67, OECD, 1963-65, Commonwealth of P.R., 1959-61, U.S. Dept. Justice, 1994-96; project chmn. Study on Info. Tech., Nat. Conf. Bd., 1969-72; project dir. Nat. Planning Assn., Washington, 1961-63; U.S. del. Yugoslavian Conf. on Transfer of Tech., Belgrade, 1974; mem. Alan T. Waterman award Com., 1976-77; expert witness Dept. Justice, Washington, L.A., 1995-97. Author: Economics and the Public Interest, 1955, Synthetic Rubber: A Case Study in Technological Development under Public Direction, 1959 (reprinted as Across the High Technology Threshold 1980), Economic Organizations and Social Systems, 1967 (reissued 2001), (with Everett Rogers) Inducing Technological Change for Economic Growth and Development, 1973, The Political Authority and the Market System, 1974, Organizing Science for Technology Transfer in Economic Development, 1975, The Positive State, 1981, (with Charles Anderson) Value Judgement and Income Distribution, 1981, Opportunity Knocks: American Economic Policy after Gorbachev, 1991, The Philosophy of Science and Economics, 1991, The Super Power and the Serb, 1998, The Song of Songs: The Harvard Version, 1998, also other books in field; contbr. chpts. to books, articles to profl. jours. Fulbright fellow, 1972-73 Mem. Council European Studies (steering com., exec. com., chmn. research com. 1974-77). Home: 4609 Chippewa Dr Okemos MI 48864-2009 Personal E-mail: solo@mail.msu.edu.

SOLOD, LISA, writer; b. Knoxville, Tenn., Jan. 3, 1956; d. Jay Lawrence and Fredlyn Kovitch Solod; m. John Addison Lambeth, June 23, 1985 (div.); children: Philip Stanhope Lambeth, Grace Amelia Lambeth. AB in Semiotics with honors, Brown U., 1978. Pub. info. officer Mus. Fine Arts, Boston, 1978-79; asst. editor Boston Mag., 1979-80; editor Moviegoer Mag. Whittle Comms., 1980-83; chief advt. copywriter Parsons, Friedman and Cen. Advt. Agy., Boston, 1984-85; pub. rels. dir. So. Va. Coll. for Women, Buena Vista, Va., 1985-86; pub. info. dir. The George C. Marshall Found., Lexington, Va., 1986-88. Instr. expository writing U. R.I., 1984; editl. cons. TeenAge Mag., Cambridge Free Press, The Illustrated, 1983-85; bd. dirs. Project Horizon, 1988-90. Bd. dirs. Montessori Ctr. for Children, Lexington, 1995-99, sec., 1996-98; bd. dirs. Lexington City Sch. Bd., 1997—2001, v.p., 1998—2001; sec. Valley region Va. Sch. Bd. Assn., 1997-98, v.p. Valley region, 1998-99, chmn. Valley region, 1999-2001, bd. dirs. Temple House of Israel, 2004-05, pres. 2006. Recipient 12 fellowships/residencies Va. Ctr. for Creative Arts, Mt. San Angelo, 1989-2004. Democrat. Jewish. Home: 310 Enfield Rd Lexington VA 24450-1756 E-mail: lisa@rockbridge.net.

SOLODKY, HOWARD N., lawyer; b. Buffalo, June 28, 1951; BA in Psychology (hon.), Clark U., 1973; JD cum laude, SUNY, Buffalo, 1976; LLM in Taxation (hon.), George Washington U., 1980. Bar: NY 1977, DC 1980. Jud. clk. appellate divsn. 3rd dept. NY State Supreme Ct., 1976—77; atty. advisor office of chief counsel IRS, Washington, 1977—81; assoc. to ptnr. Melrod, Redman & Gartlan, Washington, 1981—93; prin. David, Hagner, Kuney & Davison, Washington, 1993—98; mem. Womble Carlyle Sandridge & Rice PLLC, Washington, 1998—, chair tax practice group. Office: Womble Carlyle Sandridge & Rice PLLC 7th Fl 1401 Eye St NW Washington DC 20005 Office Phone: 202-857-4424. Office Fax: 202-261-0024. Business E-Mail: hsolodky@wcsr.com.

SOLOFF, LAURA J., academic administrator; BA in English, UCLA. Human resources position Broadway Dept. Stores; dir. career planning & placement Fashion Inst. Design & Merchandising, Calif., campus dir. Calif., regional dir. Calif., dir. student financial svcs. Calif.; dir. human resources & adminstrn. Sony Pictures Entertainment, Culver City, Calif.; mem. Edn. Mgmt. Corp., 1998—; pres. Art Inst. Calif.-Orange County, 2000—03, Art Inst. Calif.-LA, 2003—; regional v.p. Edn. Mgmt. Corp., 2004—. Office: Office Pres Art Institute California LA 2900 31st St Santa Monica CA 90405-3035

SOLOMON, ANDREW P., lawyer; b. Newark, 1953; BA, Brown U., 1975; JD, Harvard U., 1984. Bar: NY 1985. Ptnr. Sullivan & Cromwell, NYC, 1992—, now mng. ptnr. tax group. Mem.: NY State Bar Assn. (tax section exec. com., co-chair, com. of fin. intermediaries). Office: Sullivan & Cromwell LLP 125 Broad St New York NY 10004-2489 also: Sullivan & Cromwell LLP 1 New Fetter Ln London EC4A 1AN England Office Phone: 212-558-4000, 44 20 7959 8900. Office Fax: 212-558-3588. Business E-Mail: solomona@sullcrom.com.

SOLOMON, ANDREW WALLACE, author; b. NYC, Oct. 30, 1963; s. Howard and Carolyn Ruth (Bower) S. BA in English magna cum laude, Yale U., 1985; BA, Jesus Coll., Cambridge U., Cambridge, Eng., 1987, MA in English, 1987. Editl. intern Met. Mus. Art, NYC, 1981, editl. asst., 1982, asst. editor, 1983, editor, 1986; intern dept. old master paintings Sotheby's NY, 1984; galleries corr., contbg. editor Harpers and Queen, London, 1987-91; contbg. editor HG, 1991-93; contbg. writer The NY Times Mag., 1993—2000. Author: The Irony Tower: Soviet Artists in a Time of Glasnost, 1991, A Stone Boat, 1994, The Noonday Demon: An Atlas of Depression, 2001 (Nat. Book award, finalist Pulitzer Prize); contbr. articles to profl. jours. Bd. dirs. World Monuments Fund, Alliance for the Arts, The American Coun. for Cultural Policy, The Victoria and Albert Mus., The Alex Fund, Depression Ctr. of U. Mich., The Worcester (Mass.) Found., Cold Spring Harbor Lab Jesus Coll. Travel grantee, Cambridge U., 1986; Yale Conservation Project fellow for travel, 1985; Brit.-Am. Project fellow; Bogliasco fellow, 1998; recipient Nat. Book award Books for a Better Life, 2001, New Visions award QPB, Ken award Nat. Alliance for Mentally Ill., Charles T. Ruby Loss award, 2002, Silvano Arieti award, 2002, Didi Hirsch Cmty. Svc. award, 2002, Lambda award ALA. Mem. Groucho Club, Oxford & Cambridge Club, Chelsea Arts Club, Century Assn., Nat. Arts Club, Lotos Club, Explorers Club, Coun. on Fgn. Rels., Conservators Coun. of NY Pub. Libr. Democrat.

SOLOMON, ARTHUR CHARLES, pharmacist; b. Gary, Ind., May 30, 1947; s. Laurence A. and Dorothy B. (Klippel) S.; m. Janet Evelyn Irak, Aug. 23, 1969; children: Thomas, Michael, Mark, Jill. BS in Pharmacy, Purdue U., 1970, MS in Clin. Pharmacy, 1972; PharmD. Registered pharmacist; cert. nuclear pharmacist. Clin. prof. pharmacy U. Tex., Austin, 1972-75; v.p. Nuclear Pharmacy, Inc., Atlanta, 1975-83; exec. v.p., COO Diagnostek, Inc., Albuquerque, 1983-95; pres. Health Care Svcs., Inc., 1990-95; exec. v.p., COO Value Rx, Albuquerque, 1995-96; pres. Solomon and Assocs., Albuquerque, 1996-97; pres., CEO, dir. SP Pharms. LLC, Albuquerque, 1997—2001; sr. v.p. Cardinal Health, Albuquerque, 2001—04; COO PharmaFab, Grand Prairie, Tex., 2004—. Adj. prof. U. N.Mex., 1992—. Contbr. articles to profl. jours. Named Disting. Alumnus Purdue U., 1998. Fellow Am. Soc. Cons. Pharmacists, Parental Drug Assn.; mem. Am. Pharm. Assn., Am. Assn. Pharm. Scis., Am. Soc. Hosp. Pharmacy, Nat. Assn. Retail Druggists, Nat. Coun. Prescription Drug Programs, Am. Managed Care Pharmacy Assn. (pres., dir.), Rho Chi, Pi Kappa Phi. Republican. Roman Catholic. Avocations: golf, woodworking, gardening. Home: 6709 Alpine Ln Colleyville TX 76034-7290 Office: ThermaFab 2940 N Hwy 360 Grand Prairie TX 75050 E-mail: asolomon@pharmafab.com.

SOLOMON, BARRY JASON, human services administrator, consultant; b. Boston, May 16, 1934; s. Samuel and Ethel (Fleishman) Solomon; m. C. Priscilla Fugate, June 29, 1958; children: R. Stephen, Jon, Julie Ellen. BS in Biology and Chemistry, Tufts U., Medford, Mass., 1955; MBA in Health Care Adminstrn., Xavier U., Cin., 1960; MPH in Health Care Adminstrn., U. NC, 1989. Chief med. record adminstr. USPHS Hosp., Lexington, Ky., 1956-59; asst. dir. Union Meml. Hosp., Balt., 1960-61; asst. adminstr. James Lawrence Kernan Hosp., Balt., 1961-67; asst. to dean, lectr. health edn. and med. care sects. Yale U. Sch. Medicine, New Haven, 1967-70; dir. health svcs., clin. asst. prof. pharmacy adminstrn. U. RI, Kingston, 1970-76; assoc. dir. for adminstrn. USPHS Hosp., Norfolk, Va., 1976-81; dir., COO, sr. fellow in social medicine Montefiore Hosp., Bronx, NY, 1981-84; assoc. v.p. for med. affairs, mem. exec. coun. of Med. Sch. U. South Fla., Tampa, 1984-89; assoc. prof., acting chmn. dept. comprehensive medicine U. So. Fla., Tampa, 1984-89, assoc. prof. Coll. Pub. Health, 1984-89; cons. in health adminstrn., Columbia, Md., 1989-93; v.p. for acad. affairs North Broward Hosp. Dist., Ft. Lauderdale, Fla., 1993-96; chmn. bd. dirs. Sr. Benefit Ctrs. Am., Inc., 1998-2000. 1st v.p. bd. trustees, CEO Count and Countess de Hoernle Alzheimer's Pavillion, 2000—06, cons. to bd. dirs., 2006—; pres. Villa D'Este Condominium, Inc., 1999—2001; exec. com., nominating com. Vis. Nurse Assn. Tampa Bay, 1987—90; planning com. bd. trustees Hillsborough County Hosp. Authority, 1986—88; profl. affairs com. bd. trustees H. Lee Moffitt Cancer Ctr. and Rsch. Inst., 1986—88; affiliation com. S.W. Fla. Blood Bank, 1988—89; instr. hosp. adminstrn. Xavier U., 1960; course asst., instr. Am. Med. Record Assn., 1962—72; instr. Howard U. Coll. Continuing Edn., Washington, 1993; cons. St. Elizabeth Hosp., Covington, Ky., 1959, City Hosp. Ctr. Elmhurst, 1965, Hall-Brooke Hosp., Westport, Conn., 1968—69, Conn. Mental Health Ctr., New Haven, 1969—70, South County Hosp., Wakefield, RI, 1970—76, Centurion Hosp., Tampa, 1989, Primary Care Svcs., Tampa, 1991, Holland & Knight, Tampa, 1991, NCC Internat., Colchester, England, 1991, F. W. Assocs., Tampa, 1989—92, Decking Design, Norfolk, 1986—93, SMinc., Columbia, 1993, Internat. Flooring & Protective Coatings, Inc., Norfolk, 1993—; sr. cons. Meisel Assocs., Inc., NYC, 1983—; bd. dirs. Care Source, Inc., 2007—; patient safety strategic team North Broward Med. Ctr., 2007—. Contbr. articles to profl. jours. Mem. Nat. Com. Religion and Health, 1982—84; mem., vice chmn. Chariho Sch. Bd., Richmond, RI, 1974—76; mem. Broward Econ. Devel. Coun., Inc.; trustee Montefiore-Mosholu Cmty. Ctr., 1981—84. Lt. USPHS, 1956—59, capt. USPHS, 1976—81. Recipient citation, Suncoast chp. Am. Heart Assn., 1988. Fellow: Am. Coll. Healthcare Execs.; mem.: APHA. Avocation: tennis. Home: 2863 Via Venezia Deerfield Beach FL 33442-8633

SOLOMON, BRUCE MICHAEL, mathematician, educator; b. San Diego, Calif., July 22, 1953; s. Herbert Joel and Elene Gordon Solomon; m. Susan Harriet Swartz, Dec. 27, 1996; children: Naima, Lonica, Leah. BA summa cum laude, UCLA, 1978; PhD, Princeton U., Princeton, NJ, 1982. Assoc. prof. Ind. U., Bloomington, Ind., 1983—. Mem.: Am. Math. Soc. Jewish. Achievements include research in classification of embedded constant mean curvature surfaces in R—3; the absence of skew loops characterizes ellipsoids among compact surfaces in R—3. Office: Indiana University Rawles Hall Bloomington IN 47405 Home Phone: 812-333-8409; Office Phone: 812-855-4900.

SOLOMON, DARLENE J.S., electronics executive; BS, Stanford Univ.; PhD, MIT; grad. exec. develop. program, Stanford Univ. Rsch. & mgmt. positions Hewlett-Packard Laboratories, 1984—99; dir. Life Sciences Technologies Lab. & sr. dir. rsch. & develop. tech. life sciences & chem. analysis Agilent Technologies, Palo Alto, Calif., 1999—2003, v.p. Agilent Labs & chief tech. officer, 2003—. Chair. R&D Calif. Blue Ribbon Task Force on Nanotechnology; mem. adv. bd. NSF Nanobiotechnology Ctr., A-STAR Singapore Econ. Develop., Univ. Calif. Davis, Viterbi Sch. Engring. Univ. So. Calif., Joint Venture Tech. Convergence Consortium, Bay Area Sci. & Innovation Consortium. Named one of Women Worth Watching, Diversity Jour., 2007; named to Women in Tech. Internat. Hall of Fame, 2001; recipient Tribute to Women and Industry award, YWCA, 2004. Achievements include patents in field. Office: Agilent Technologies 395 Page Mill Rd Palo Alto CA 94306 *

SOLOMON, DAVID HARRIS, geriatrician, educator; b. Cambridge, Mass., Mar. 7, 1923; s. Frank and Rose (Roud) Solomon; m. Ronda L. Markson, June 23, 1946; children: Patti Jean Sinaiko, Nancy Ellen. AB, Brown U., 1944; MD, Harvard U., 1946. Intern Peter Bent Brigham Hosp., Boston, 1946—47, resident, 1947—48, 1950—51; fellow endocrinology New Eng. Center Hosp., Boston, 1951—52; faculty UCLA Sch. Medicine, 1952—, prof. medicine, 1966—93, vice chmn. dept. medicine, 1968—71, chmn. dept., 1971—81, assoc. dir. geriatrics, 1982—89; dir. UCLA Ctr. on Aging, 1991—96; prof. emeritus UCLA, 1993—. Chief med. svc. Harbor Gen. Hosp., Torrance, Calif., 1966—71; cons. Wadsworth VA Hosp., LA, 1952—93, Sepulveda VA Hosp., 1971—93; cons. metabolism tng. com. USPHS, 1960—64, endocrinology study sect., 1970—73; cons. RAND Corp., 1997—. Editor: Jour. Am. Geriatric Soc., 1988—93; contbr. numerous articles to profl. jours. Recipient Ollie Randall award, Nat. Coun. on the Aging, 2004. Master: ACP (John Phillips Meml. award 2002); mem.: AAAS, Gerontol. Soc. Am. (Freeman award 1997), Am. Geriatrics Soc. (bd. dir. 1985—93, Milo Leavitt award 1992, Disting. Svc. award 1993, Edward Henderson award 1999, David H. Solomon Disting. Svc. award named in his honor), Am. Fedn. Aging Rsch. (Irving S. Wright award 1990), Western Assn. Physicians (councillor 1972—75, pres. 1983—84), Inst. Medicine Nat. Acad. Sci., Am. Thyroid Assn. (pres. 1973—74, Disting. Svc. award 1986), Endocrine Soc. (Robert H. Williams award 1989), We. Soc. Clin. Rsch. (councillor 1963—65, Mayo Soley award 1986), Am. Soc. Clin. Investigation, Assn. Am. Physicians, UCLA Med. Alumni Assn. (Extraordinary Merit award 2002), Assn. Profs. of Medicine (pres. 1980—81); Alpha Omega Alpha, Sigma Xi, Phi Beta Kappa. Achievements include The Parlow-Solomon Chair on Aging named in his honor at UCLA School of Medicine. Home: 2103 Ridge Dr Los Angeles CA 90049-1153 Home Phone: 310-471-5256; Office Phone: 310-471-5256. Personal E-mail: dsolomon1@earthlink.net.

SOLOMON, EDWARD IRA, chemistry professor, researcher; b. NYC, Oct. 20, 1946; s. Mordecai L. and Sally S. Solomon; m. Darlene Joy Spira, Sept. 15, 1984; children: Mitchell Landau, Paige Elana. BS, Rensselaer Poly. Inst., 1968; PhD, Princeton U., 1972. Rsch. assoc. Princeton U., NJ, 1972-73; postdoctoral fellow H.C. Ørsted Inst., Copenhagen, 1973-74, Calif. Inst. Tech., Pasadena, 1974-75; asst. prof. MIT, Cambridge, Mass., 1975-79, assoc. prof., 1979-81, prof., 1981-82, Stanford U., Calif., 1982-91, Monroe E. Spaght prof. humanities and sci., 1991—, SSRL prof., 2005—. Cons. prof., World Bank lectr. Xiamen U., People's Republic of China, 1984: O.K. Rice lectr. U. NC, 1984, Reilly lectr. U. Notre Dame, 1985; invited prof. U. Paris, 1987; 1st Glen Seaborg lectr. U. Calif., 1990; Frontiers in Chem. Rsch. lectr. Tex. A&M U., 1990; ACS lectr., Argentina, 1992; invited prof. Tokyo Inst. Tech., 1992; Xerox lectr. U. Alta., 1993; lectr. NSC Republic of China, 1993; Leermakers lectr. Wesleyan U., 1994; Amoco lectr. Ind. U., 1995; Kahn lectr. U. N.Mex., 1996, Golden Jubilee invited prof. Tata Inst., India, 1996; Karcher lectr. U. Okla., 1997; Colloquium 3eme Cucle, Switzerland, 1998; FMC lectr. Princeton U., 1998; A.D. Little lectr. MIT, 1998, Nobel Found. lectr. Stockholm U., 2000; invited prof. Tata Inst. Bombay, India, 2000; Crawford lectr. in spectroscopy U. Minn., 2004; McElvain lectr. U. Wis.; Walton lectr. Purdue U., Hill Meml. lectr., Cady lectr., U. Wash.; Kieler Woche lectr., Kiel U., Dawson lectr., U. Ky.; numerous other lectureships. Assoc. editor Inorganic Chemistry, 1985—; mem. editl. adv. bd. Chem. Revs., 1990—, Jour. Inorganic Biochemistry, Chemtracts, Chemistry and Biology, Jour. Biol. Inorganic Chemistry, Coord. Chem. Revs.; mem. editl. bd. Indian Jour. Chemistry, Cen. European Jour. Chemistry, Inorganica Chemica Acta, Metal Based Drugs, Chem. Ctrl. Jour.; contbr. articles to profl. jours. including Jour. Am. Chem. Soc., Inorganic Chemistry, Procs. of NAS, Phys. Rev. Sci. Mem. panels NIH, NSF, Washington; mem. vis. coms. Exxon, U. Calif., Santa Cruz. Recipient Dean award for disting. tchg., 1990, Ramsen award Md. ACS and Johns Hopkins U., 1994, NIH Merit award, 1995, G.W. Wheland medal, U. Chgo., 2001, Frontiers Biol. Chem. award, Max Planck Inst., NIH Merit award, 2002, Centenary medal and lectureship Royal Soc. UK, 2003. Fellow AAAS, NAS, Japan Soc. for Promotion of Sci., Am. Acad. Arts and Scis.; mem. Am. Chem. Soc. (chmn. bioinorganic divsn.), Am. Phys. Soc., Internat. EPR Soc., Soc. Biol. Inorganic Chemistry, Sigma Xi. Achievements include research in structure/function correlations in copper cluster proteins, in electronic structure of the blue copper active site, in spectroscopic definition of the active site in the Cu/ZnO methanol synthesis catalyst, in new spectroscopic probes of non-heme iron enzymes, in excited state potential energy surfaces of inorganic complexes and their contribution to reactivity, on new methods of inorganic spectroscopy; covalency in transition metal complexes. Office: Stanford U Dept Chemistry Roth Way Stanford CA 94305 Office Phone: 650-723-9104. Business E-Mail: edward.solomon@stanford.edu.

SOLOMON, ELINOR HARRIS, economics professor; b. Boston, Feb. 26, 1923; d. Ralph and Linna Harris; m. Richard A. Solomon, Mar. 30, 1957; children: Joan S. Griffin, Robert H., Thomas H. AB, Mt. Holyoke Coll., 1944; MA, Radcliffe U., 1945; PhD, Harvard U., 1948. Jr. economist Fed. Res. Bank Boston, 1945-48; economist Fed. Res. Bd. Govs., Washington, 1949-56; internat. economist U.S. State Dept., Washington, 1957-58; professorial lectr. Am. U., Washington, 1964-66; sr. economist antitrust div. U.S. Dept. Justice, Washington, 1966-82; prof. econs. George Washington U., Washington, 1982—. Econ. cons., Washington, 1982—; expert witness antitrust, fin. networks, electronic funds transfer cases, Washington, 1988—. Author: Virtual Money, 1997; author, editor: Electronic Funds Transfers and Payments, 1987, Electronic Money Flows, 1991; contbr. articles on econs., banking and law to profl. jours. Mem. Am. Econs. Assn., Nat. Economists Club (bd. govs. 1997-98), The Cosmos Club (chmn. program com. 2004-06, bd. mgmt. 2006—, Frontiers of Sci. 2001-04). Home: 6805 Delaware St Chevy Chase MD 20815-4164 Office: George Washington U Dept Econ Washington DC 20052-0001 Personal E-mail: rsolomonhome@earthlink.net.

SOLOMON, ELIZABETH ANN, mathematics educator; d. James Gardner and Deborah Ann Solomon. BS in Interdisciplinary Studies, Baylor U., Waco, Tex., 1999—2003, MS in Curriculum & Instrn., 2004—06. Cert. elem. self-contained grades 1-8 tchr. State Bd. Educator Cert., Tex., 2003, elem. math. tchr. State Bd. Educator Cert., Tex., 2003, gifted & talented grades EC-12 tchr. State Bd. Educator Cert., Tex., 2005. Asst. to dir.

programs, tchr. U. Young People, Baylor U., 2003; math. tchr. Waco Ind. Sch. Dist., 2003—; summer rsch. assoc. Baylor U., 2006. Curriculum writing com. mem. Waco Ind. Sch. Dist., 2006—, textbook selection com. mem., 2006—, campus decision making com. mem., 2006—, leadership cir. mem., 2006—. Mem.: Nat. Coun. Tchrs. Math., Baylor Almuni Assn., Kappa Delta Pi, Kappa Delta (intramural chair 2002—03). Home Phone: 254-733-1927. Business E-Mail: esolomon@wacoisd.org.

SOLOMON, ERIC, federal agency administrator; AB, Princeton U.; JD, U. Va.; LLM, NYU. Ptnr. Drinker Biddle & Reath LLP; tax atty. Cadwalader Wickersham & Taft LLP; ptnr. Ernst & Young LLP; asst. chief counsel (corp.) IRS US Dept. Treasury, dep. asst. sec. regulatory affairs, asst. sec. for tax policy, 2006—. Adj. prof. Georgetown U. Office: US Dept Treasury 1500 Pennsylvania Ave NW Rm 3120 Washington DC 20220 Office Phone: 202-622-0050. Office Fax: 202-622-0605. *

SOLOMON, GAIL ELLEN, physician; b. Bklyn., May 26, 1938; d. Samuel and Estelle (Suffin) S.; m. Harvey Hecht, Oct. 28, 1962; children: Daniel, Jonathan, Elizabeth. AB, Smith Coll., 1958; MD, Albert Einstein Coll. Medicine, 1962. Diplomate Am. Bd. Pediats., Am. Bd. Psychiatry and Neurology (assoc. examiner), Am. Bd. Electroencephalography, Am. Bd. Electroencephalography and Neurophysiology, Am. Bd. Clin. Neurophysiology. Intern in pediat. Bronx Mcpl. Hosp. Ctr., 1962—63, resident in pediat., 1963—64, N.Y. Hosp.-Cornell U. Med. Coll., NYC, 1964—65; NIH vis. fellow in neurology and child neurology Columbia-Presbyn. Med. Ctr., NYC, 1965—68, NIH vis. fellow in clin. neurophysiology and electroenceph.; instr. neurology Columbia U. Coll. of Physicians and Surgeons, NYC, 1968—69, asst. prof. neurology and pediat., 1970—76, assoc. prof. clin. neurology and pediat., 1976—2004, prof. clin. neurology and pediat., 2004—; asst. prof. Cornell U. Med. Coll., 1969—70, prof. clin. neurology and and pediat., 2004—; asst. attending in neurology and pediat. N.Y. Hosp., NYC, 1969—76, dir. electroencephalography, 1969—, assoc. attending in neurology and pediat., 1976—, assoc. attending neurologist in psychiatry, 1983—. Mem. joint com. for stroke facilities NIH; mem. FDA Peripheral and CNS Adv. Com., 1979-83, chmn., 1983, cons., 1983-84; mem. med. audit com. N.Y. Hosp., mem. utilization rev. com.; mem. profl. adv. bd. N.Y. State Epilepsy Assn.; adj. attending physician in neurology Meml.-Sloan Kettering Cancer Ctr., 1982-93; assoc. attending pediatrician Hosp. Spl. Surgery, 1987—; neurology cons. Blythedale Children's Hosp., Valhalla, N.Y., 1991—, Meml.-Sloan Kettering Cancer Ctr., 1993—. Author: (with F. Plum) Clinical Management of Seizures: A Guide for the Physician, 1976, (with Plum and Kutt) 2d edit., 1983; editor: (with Kaufman and Pfeffer) Child and Adolescent Neurology for Psychiatrists, 1992, Neurologic Disorders: Developmental and Behavioral Sequelae, 1999; contbr. articles to profl. jours., chpts. to med. books. Fellow: Am. Acad. Neurology, Am. Acad. Pediats., Am. Electroencephalographic Soc.; mem.: AMA (Physician's Recognition award in Continuing Med. Edn.)), NY State Med. Soc., NY County Med. Soc., Am. Med. Women's Assn., Am. Epilepsy Soc., Am. Acad. Clin. Neurophysiology, Eastern EEG Soc., Am. Med. EEG Assn., Child Neurology Soc., Internat. Child Neurology Assn., Tristate Child Neurology Soc., Assn. for Rsch. in Nervous and Mental Diseases, NY Acad. Sci. Avocations: art, reading, languages, travel. Office: NY Presbyn Hosp Cornell U Med Coll 525 E 68th St New York NY 10021-4870 Home Phone: 914-472-5608.

SOLOMON, GEORGE, physician, military officer; b. Aug. 1, 1959; Attended, Cairo U. Sch. Veterinary Medicine, Egypt, 1979—82; BS in Microbiology, San Diego State U., 1987; MS in Clinical Sci., Calif. State U., Dominguez Hills, 1990; MD, Ross U. Sch. Medicine, Dominica, West Indies, 1994. Diplomate Am. Acad. Antiaging Medicine, 2006, bd. cert. Am. Bd. Family Practice, 1997. Corpsman US Naval Hosp., San Diego, 1982—86, US Navy, 1986—87, clinical lab. scientist Saddleback Hosp., Laguna Hills, Calif., 1988—90; clinical microbiologist Children's Hosp., Kans. City, 1992; resident Family Medicine Residency Program Topeka, 1994—97, chief resident, 1996—97; clinical lab. dir. Family Medicine Residency; pvt. practice Spruce Creek Family Care, Port Orange, Fla., 1997—98; pres. Volusia Family Care PA, Daytona Beach, Fla., 1998—; med. dir. Ageless MediSpa, 2006—. Major USNR, 2000—. Fellow: Am. Acad. Family Practice; mem.: Fla. Acad. Family Practice, Am. Acad. Cosmetic Surgery (assoc.). Office: 1690 Dunlawton Ave Daytona Beach FL 32127

SOLOMON, HENRY, university dean; b. Bronx, NY, Nov. 28, 1926; s. Max and Tillie (Gilerowitz) S.; m. Jacqueline Mona Cohen, May 31, 1953; 1 son, Michael Robert. BA, Bklyn. Coll., 1949; MA, NYU, 1950, PhD, 1960. Rsch. assoc., then sr. staff investigator and dep. prin. investigator Logistics Rsch. Project George Washington U., 1950—66, prof. econs., chmn. dept., 1962—74, 1991—96, dean Grad. Sch. Arts and Scis., 1974—90, prof. and dean emeritus, 1996—. Dep. asst. adminstr. econs., acting asst. adminstr. planning, research and analysis SBA, 1966-67; cons. in field. Assoc. editor: Naval Research Logistics Quar., 1957-90. Served with U.S. Army, 1945-46. Recipient Founder's Day award N.Y. U., 1960 Mem.: Am. Econ. Assn. Home: # 603 5450 Whitley Park Terr Bethesda MD 20814 E-mail: henry20814@aol.com.

SOLOMON, HOWARD, pharmaceutical executive; b. Aug. 12, 1927; s. David and Faye (Gussow) Solomon; m. Carolyn Ruth Bower, Dec. 17, 1961 (dec. 1991); children: Andrew Wallace, David Frederick; m. Sarah Durie Billinghurst, Aug. 27, 2003. BA, CCNY, 1949; LLB, Yale U., New Haven, Conn., 1952. Bar: NY 1952. Atty. Moses & Singer, NYC, 1952-55, Kay Scholer, Fierman Hays & Handler, NYC, 1956-60; pres. Hildred Mgmt. Corp., NYC, 1967-83; dir. Forest Laboratories Inc., NYC, 1964—, CEO, 1977—98, chmn., CEO, 1998—. Dir. Pharmax Ltd., Bexley, Kent., UK, 1979—; bd. trustees NY-Presbyn. Hosp. Bd. dirs. Met. Opera, Lincoln Ctr. for Performing Arts; exec. com. mem., chmn. emeritus NYC Ballet; mem. Sch. AM. Ballet. Mem. NY State Bar Assn., Yale Club, Harmonie Club of NY. Office: Forest Labs Inc 909 3rd Ave New York NY 10022-4731

SOLOMON, JACK AVRUM, JR., lawyer, automotive executive, art dealer; b. Omaha, Oct. 25, 1928; s. John A. and Matilda (Bienstok) S.; m. Josephine J. Kleiman, June 1948 (div. Mar. 1971); children: Debra, Alisa, Michael, Rena; m. Carolyn Summers, Dec. 1973. BS, U. Nebr., 1950, LL.B. cum laude, 1952; LL.M. (Cook fellow), U. Mich., 1953. Bar: Nebr. 1950, Ill. 1951. Practice law, Chgo., 1950—; with firm Stiefel, Greenberg, Burns, Baldridge & Solomon, 1953-66, ptnr., 1958-66, Solomon, Rosenfeld, Elliot & Stiefel, and predecessor, 1966—, sr. ptnr., 1966—. Bd. dirs. Amco Industries, Inc., Chgo., chmn. bd., 1968-69, sec., gen. counsel, 1969-72; sec. Mogen David Wine Corp., Chgo., 1964-71; chmn. bd. Arts and Leisure Corp., 1969-76; pres., chmn. bd. Circle Fine Art Corp., 1968-94; chmn. bd. dirs. S2 Art Group, Ltd., 1996—, Re Society, 1997—, Art of the Movies.com, 1999—; pres. Las Vegas Art Dist., 2002-05; mng. dir. C&J Properties LLC, 2005-, Carjack Properties LLC, 2005—; chmn., CEO Jack Gallary, Inc., 2005— Commr. City of Las Vegas Arts Commn., 2005—; bd. dirs. Boulder Plz. Sculpture Park Found. Mem. Ill., Nebr. bar assns.; mem. Fine Art Pubs. Assn. (pres. 1982—); Mem. Order of Coif. Jewish (pres. temple 1959-61). Club: Nat. Arts (N.Y.C.). Home: 2870 Augusta Las Vegas NV 89109 Office: 1 E Charleston Las Vegas NV 89104 Office Phone: 702-868-7880. Personal E-mail: jsolomon@s2art.com.

SOLOMON, JACK DAVID, investment banker; b. Detroit, July 27, 1930; s. Alexander C. and Anita Ruth Solomon; m. Karla Marie Frantzve, Mar. 26, 2002; children: Jacqueline Cheryl Tal, David Neal, Gregg Harvey, Diana Ruth Rothstein, Moriah Chloé Dee. AA, L.A. City Coll., 1954; BA, L.A. State Coll., 1956, Calif. State Univ., 1958. V.p. JSH Electronics Corp., 1954—60; dir. Harwit Internat. Corp., 1954—60; pres. Fed. Electronics, 1960—66; pres., chmn. Advanced Patent Tech. Corp., 1968—84; pres. Gaming and Tech. Corp., 1976—83, APT Games Inc., 1978—80; co-found., dir. Am. Bank of Commerce, 1978—83; found., chmn. New Age Corp., 1980—94; pres. Genesis investment Corp., 1986—. Dir. Houston Fearless Corp., 1962—65, Western Transistor Corp., 1962—68; chmn. of the bd. dirs. Western Fed. Fin. Corp., 1964—66; dir. Fed. Land and Devel. Corp., 1964—90, Fed. Rsch. and Devel., 1965—83; chmn. of the bd. Advanced Patent tech., 1967—83. Nat. dir. Equal Opportunities Found., 1963—66; sponsor Nat. Hosp. Denever, Colo.; co-founder Israeli Armored Corps Mus.; patron Orr Chadash Orphanage Israel; vice chmn. Calif. Dem. Coun., 1966—70; candidate Calif. State. Sen., 1966; dir. United Jewish Fedn., 1965—67; mem. com. L.A. C. of C.; mem. World Affairs Coun.; mem. of pres. cabinet Am. Israel pub. Affairs Com.; mem. Las Vegas C. of C.; dir. Utah Shakespeareon Festival, 1999—2000. Sgt. USAF, 1948—52, serv. on the Berlin Airlift in Germany. Decorated Medal for Humane Action USAF; recipient Man of the Yr., Southern Calif., 1963, Marshall Medal for Outstanding Social Svc., 1964, Carson White award, 1964, Disting. Svc. award, L.A. Affairs Com., 1966, Disting. Citizen award, City of Montreal, 1966, Meritorious award, Dem. Party, 1966, Ken. Col., 1970, Wall of Honor, Hebrew Univ. of Jerusalem, 1976, Israeli State Med., 1990, Pres. Medal, Suleiman Demirel Pres. of Turkey, 1992. Mem.: Am. Air Mus. in Britian (found. mem.), Armed Forces Commn. and Electronics Assn., Nat. Aeronautics Assn., Internat. Assn. of Bus. and Profl. (hon.), B'nai B'rith, Pres. Club Utah Valley State Coll., Pres. Club Brigham Young Univ., Pres. Club World Jewish Congress (life), 32nd Degree Mason, Scottish Rite (life). Achievements include funded and restored the ancient Zion's Gate and Plaza in Jerusalem; constructed the Colo. Belle Hotel and Casino one of the first of its kind in Laughlin, Nev. Avocation: art. Office Phone: 801-359-3755.

SOLOMON, JOSEPH ALPHOUS, physician; b. Washington, Feb. 21, 1922; s. Albert Henry and Effy Florence (Griffin) Solomon; m. Thelma Elizabeth Hollingsworth, Oct. 4, 1958; children: Jane Elizabeth, Anne Marie, Amy Jo. Degree, U. Richmond, Va., 1942; MD, Med. Coll. Va., Richmond, 1949; Postgrad. in Medicine, Sheltering Arms Hosp., Va., 1951. Bible tchg. Sullivan County Jail, Blountville, Tenn., Maddison House Assisted Living, Kingsport, Tenn.; foreign med. mission Ch., India, 1975—2002. Mayor City of Mackinac Island, Mich., 1968—69. Med. officer USNR, 1943—63. Mem.: Gideons. Republican. Bapt. Avocations: model building, walking, flying. Home: 111 Countryshire Ct Kingsport TN 37663-2809 Personal E-mail: solomontj@juno.com.

SOLOMON, LIBERTINA, retired pharmacist, educator; b. Botosani, Romania, Feb. 5, 1926; d. Harry and Betty Segal; m. Monel Solomon, June 12, 1948; children: Silviu, Aniela. PhD in Biology, U. Bucharest, 1970. Registered pharmacist. Asst. prof. U. Al. L. Cuza, Iasi, Romania, 1949—59, assoc. prof., 1959—72, prof., 1972—89, rschr., 1959—89, chief dept. animal biology, 1975—80; pharmacist asst. Bronx Lebanon Hosp., NYC, 1990—2006. Mem. Com. of According Drs. Degree, Romania, 1975—89. Contbr. more than 80 articles and rsch. papers to profl. jours., chapters to books. Mem.: N.Y. Acad. Sci. Achievements include discovery of 16 new species of gamasida (Acari) and over 160 new species of Romanian fauna; soil and parasitic gamasides. Avocation: travel. Home: 729 W 186 St Apt 2E New York NY 10033

SOLOMON, MARILYN KAY, primary school educator, consultant, small business owner; b. Marshall, Mo., Oct. 16, 1947; d. John W. and Della M. (Dille) S. BS, Ctrl. Mo. State U., 1969; MS, Ind. U., 1974. Cert. in early childhood and nursery sch. edn., Mo., Ind. Tchr. Indpls. Pub. Schs., 1969—74; dir. Singer Learning Ctrs., Indpls., 1974—78, v.p. ECLC Learning Ctrs., Inc., Indpls., 1978—95; pres., CEO, owner Early Learning Ctrs., Inc., Indpls., 1995—; owner, pres., CEO Solomon Antique Restoration, Inc., Indpls., 1996—, The Shoppes at Guilford Junction, 2002—; pres., CEO Woodbridge Group, 1995—. Mem. OJT tng. task force Dept. Labor, Washington; mem. nat. task force for parenting edn. HEW, Washington; cons. to numerous corps. on corp. child care; built 29 child care ctrs. for corps., hosps. and govt. Co-author curricula. Founding bd. dirs. Mid City Pioneer, Indpls., 1977; mem. adv. bd. Enterprise Zone Small Bus. Incubator, Indpls., 1995-2002; founding bd. dirs. Family Support Ctr., Indpls., 1983, pres. bd. dirs., 1985-87; founding mem., co-chair Voices for Children, 1996—2004; mem. White Rivers Gardens State Park, Indpls. Mus. Art, 500 Festival Assn. Recipient Outstanding Leadership award Ind. Conf. on Social Concerns, 1975, 76, 77, Children's Mus. Edn. award, 1974; named to Outstanding Young Women of Am., 1984. Mem. Indpls. Mus. Art, Ind. Lic. Child Care Assn. (v.p. 1992, pres. 1974, 75), State of Ind. Quality and Tng. Coun. (chair 1992), Step Ahead-Marion County (rep. for child care 1992—2005, co-chair educare com. 1999—2005), Ind. Alliance for Better Child Care (bd. dirs. 1992, adv. bd. 1990-95), Pub. Broadcasting (tng. com. 1992-99, child devel. tng. com. 1996-99), Indpls. Zool. Soc. (charter), Order Eastern Star. Office: Early Learning Ctrs Inc 1315 S Sherman Dr Indianapolis IN 46203-2210 E-mail: earlylearn@indy.rr.com.

SOLOMON, MARK RAYMOND, lawyer, educator; b. Pitts., Aug. 23, 1945; s. Louis Isadore and Fern Rhea (Josselson) S. BA, Ohio State U., 1967; MEd, Cleve. State U., 1971; JD with hons., George Washington U., 1973; LLM in Taxation, Georgetown U., 1976. Bar: Ohio, Mich., U.S. Dist. Ct. (ea. dist.) Mich., U.S. Ct. Appeals (6th cir.), U.S. Tax Ct., U.S. Ct. Fed. Claims. Tax law specialist corp. tax br. Nat. Office of IRS, 1973—75; assoc. Butzel, Long, Gust, Klein & Van Zile, Detroit, 1976—78; dir., v.p. Shatzman & Solomon, P.C., Southfield, Mich., 1978—81; prof., chmn. tax/bus. law dept., dir. MS in Taxation Program Walsh Coll., Troy, Mich., 1981—; of counsel in tax matters Meyer, Kirk, Snyder & Lynch, PLLC, Bloomfield Hills, Mich., 1981—. Adj. prof. law U. Detroit, 1977-81. Editor: Cases and Materials on Consolidated Tax Returns, 1978, Cases and Materials on the Application of Legal Principles and Authorities to Federal Tax Law, 1990. Mem.: Mich. Bar Assn., Phi Eta Sigma. Avocation: bridge (life master). Home: 2109 Golfview Dr Apt 102 Troy MI 48084-3926 Office: Meyer Kirk Snyder & Lynch PLLC 100 W Long Lake Rd Ste 100 Bloomfield Hills MI 48304-2773 also: Walsh Coll 3838 Livernois Rd Troy MI 48083-5066 Office Phone: 248-647-5111. Business E-Mail: msolomon@walshcollege.edu.

SOLOMON, MAYNARD ELLIOTT, musicologist, retired recording industry executive; b. NYC, Jan. 5, 1930; s. Benjamin and Dora (Levine) S.; m. Eva Georgiana Tevan, Jan. 22, 1951; children: Mark Jonathan, Nina Stephanie, Maury David. BA, Bklyn. Coll., 1950; postgrad., Columbia U., 1950-51; MusD (hon.), New Eng. Conservatory Music, 2005. Co-founder, co-owner Vanguard Rec. Soc., Inc., NYC, 1950-86; faculty grad. div. CUNY, 1979-81. Vis. prof. SUNY Stony Brook, 1988, Columbia U., N.Y.C., 1990, Harvard U., Cambridge, Mass., 1992, Yale U., New Haven, 1994-95; scholarly advisor Beethoven Archive, Bonn, 1997-2006; faculty grad. divsn. Juilliard Sch., 1998—. Author: Marxism and Art, 1973, Beethoven, 1977 (translated into German, French, Spanish, Portuguese, Japanese, Italian, Bulgarian), Myth, Creativity and Psychoanalysis, 1978, Beethoven's Tagebuch, 1982, Beethoven's Tagebuch, German translation, 1990, Italian translation, 1992, Japanese translation, 2001, Beethoven Essays, 1988, Italian translation, 1998; Mozart: A Life, 1995 (translated into Swedish, Italian, Japanese, German, Portuguese, Hungarian), Late Beethoven, 2003; editor: Joan Baez Songbook, 1964; contbg. editor: Beethoven Forum, Am. Imago; mem. editl. bd. Beethovenhaus edit. Beethoven's Letters; editor: Memories of Beethoven, 1992; prodr. over 100 folk music albums; contbr. articles to profl. jours. Recipient Deems Taylor award ASCAP, 1978, 89, 96, Disting. Vis. award U. Toronto, 1996. Mem. PEN, Am. Musicol. Soc. (bd. dirs. 1984-86, Otto Kinkeldey award 1989, hon. mem. 1999), Authors Guild, N.Y. Inst. for Humanities, Phi Beta Kappa. Home: 1 W 72nd St New York NY 10023-3486 Personal E-mail: maynardsol@aol.com.

SOLOMON, MICHAEL BRUCE, lawyer; b. Chgo., Nov. 8, 1945; s. Arthur J. and Ruth H. (Halpert) S.; m. Tunny Jamri, Dec. 17, 1983. BA, U. Miami, Coral Gables, Fla., 1967, JD, 1970. Bar: Fla. 1970; U.S. Dist. Ct. (so. dist.) Fla. 1972; U.S. Ct. Appeals (5th cir.) 1989, U.S. Ct. Appeals (11th cir.) 1990. Assoc. Theodore M. Trushin P.A., Miami Beach, Fla., 1970-77; ptnr. Klein, Oshinsky & Solomon, Hallandale, Fla., 1978-87; pvt. practice North Miami, Fla., 1988—, 1998—, Hallandale, 1988-98. Spl. asst., pub. defender, Dade County, Fla., 1972-78; ombudsman Dade County pub. defender's office, Miami, 1972. Contbr. article to profl. jour. Mem. So. Dist. Fla. Trial Bar (sec.). Office: 11077 Biscayne Blvd Ph Miami FL 33161-7418 E-mail: mbslaw@netrox.net.

SOLOMON, NEAL EDWARD, management consultant, executive recruiter, social theorist, entrepreneur, author; b. San Diego, Mar. 9, 1960; s. Donald Jay and Roberta Yvonne (Recht) S. BA in Philosophy, Reed Coll., Portland, Oreg., 1981; AM in Philosophy, U. Chgo, 1982. Founder, chmn., CEO Solomon Rsch. LLC, 2004—. Mgmt. cons., 1983—2003. Author: A Turning Point in World History?, 1992, High Performance Venture Characteristics, 1992, Dilemmas of Democracy (3 vols.: A Critique of Liberalism, A Critique of Political Ideology, and The Limits of Social Theory), 1992, The Problem of Modernity, 1993, Theoretical Foundations of Dynamic Macroeconomics, 1993, The Evolution of Philosophy, 1995, Legal Management Theory, 2d edit., 1997, Transformation of the Corporate Law Firm, 1998, others. Democrat. Achievements include inventions regarding electronic commerce, robotics, proteomics, databases, and intelligent systems. E-mail: ulysses@well.com.

SOLOMON, PEARL GOLD, education educator, consultant; d. Joseph and Rose Gold; m. Milton Solomon, Feb. 12, 1950; children: Ellen Heidi Burke, Nancy Whitney Grunwald. BA, Hunter Coll., 1949, MA, 1952; EdD, Columbia U., 1977. Cert. tchr. math. and sci. N.Y. State, sch. dist. adminstr. N.Y. Tchr. elem. edn. and h.s. N.Y.C. schs., 1949—68; tchr. h.s., prin., dir. curriculum Pearl River (N.Y.) Schs., 1968—91; prof. emerita St. Thomas Aquinas Coll., Sparkill, NY, 1991—. Profl. cons. Pk. Ridge Schs., NJ, 2000—05, Edvotek, Inc., 1998—, Columbia U., NYC, 2005—, NYU, NYC, 2005—. Author: (tchrs. text.) The Curriculum Bridge (Outstanding Academic Book. award ALA, 1999), (tchrs. text) No Small Feat, (text) The Math WE Need to Know and Do (Finalist, Book of Yr. Award Am. Assn. of Colls. of Tchr. Edn., 2002), The Assesment Bridge. Founder, dir. Pearl River Comm. Coun., 1975—91. Named Woman of the Yr., Orgn. for Rehab. and Tng., 1979; recipient Cert. Merit, Assembly of State of N.Y., 1987, Disting. Svc. award, County of Rockland, 1987, Liberty Bell award, Rockland County Bar Assn., 1981, Dedication and Contbn. to Cmty. Svc. award, Orangetown Police Dept., 1987. Mem.: Am. Ednl. Rsch. Assn. Office: St Thomas Aquinas Coll Rte 340 Sparkill NY 10976 Office Phone: 845-398-4000. Personal E-mail: pgsolomon@msn.com. E-mail: psolomon@stac.edu.

SOLOMON, PHYLLIS LINDA, social work educator, researcher; b. Hartford, Conn., Dec. 6, 1945; d. Louis Calvin and Annabell Lee (Nitzberg) S. BA in Sociology, Russell Sage Coll., 1968; MA in Sociology, Case Western Res. U., 1970, PhD in Social Welfare, 1978. Lic. social worker Pa. Rsch. assoc. Inst. Urban Studies Cleve. State U., 1970-71; program evaluator Cleve. State Hosp., 1971-74; project dir. Ohio Mental Health and Mental Retardation Rsch. Ctr., Cleve., 1974-75; rsch. assoc. Psychiat. Rsch. Found. of Cleve., 1975; project dir. Ohio Mental Health and Mental Retardation Rsch. Ctr., 1977-78; rsch. assoc. dir., rsch. and mental health planning Fedn. for Cmty. Planning, 1978-88; prof. dept. mental health scis., dir. sect. mental health svcs. and systems rsch. Hahnemann U., Phila., 1988-94; prof. Sch. Social Work U. Pa., Phila., 1994—. Secondary appointment Prof. Social Work in Psychiatry U. Pa. Sch. Medicine, 1994—; adj. prof. dept. psychiatry Allegheny U., 1994—97. Author (with others): Community Services to Discharged Psychiatric Patients, 1984; co-editor: New Developments in Psychiatric Rehabilitation, 1990, Psychiatric Rehabilitation in Practice, 1993, Research Process in the Human Services, 2005; mem. editl. adv. bd. Community Mental Health Jour., 1988—, mem. editl. bd. Jour. Rsch. in Social Work, 1997—2000, Social Work Forum, 1997—, Health and Social Work, 1998—2000, Psychiat. Rehab. Jour., 1999—, Mental Health Svcs. Rsch. Jour., 2001—, Brief Treatment and Crisis Intervention, 2001—, Social Work, 2003—, Am. Psychiat. Rehab. Jour., 2006—; contbr. articles to profl. jours. Trustee Cleve. Rape Crisis Ctr., 1981-84, CIT Mental Health Svcs., Cleve., 1985-88; mem. citizen's adv. bd. Sagamore Hills (Ohio) Children's Psychiat. Hosp., 1984-88; bd. dirs. Plan of Pa., 2004—. Named Evaluator of the Yr., Ohio Program Evaluators Group, 1987; recipient Ann. award Cuyahoga County Cmty. Mental Health Bd., 1988, Armin Loeb award Internat. Assn. Psychosocial Rehab. Svcs., 1999, Outstanding Non-Psychiatrist award Am. Assn. Cmty. Psychiatrists, 2002, Knee/Wittman Outstanding Lifetime Achievement award Nat. Assn. Social Workers Found., 2005. Mem. NASW, U.S. Psychiat. Rehab. Assn., Soc. for Social Work and Rsch. (1st place award for pub. article 1997). Jewish. Home: 205 Governor's Ct Philadelphia PA 19146 Office: U Pa Sch Social Policy & Practice 3701 Locust Walk Philadelphia PA 19104-6214 Business E-Mail: solomonp@sp2.upenn.edu.

SOLOMON, RANDALL LEE, lawyer; b. Dayton, Ohio, June 8, 1948; BA summa cum laude, Wright State U., 1970; JD, Case Western Res. U., 1973. Bar: Ohio 1973, U.S. Dist. Ct. (no. dist.) Ohio 1973, U.S. Ct. Appeals (6th cir.) 1973, U.S. Ct. Appeals (fed. cir.) 1988, U.S. Supreme Ct. 2002. Ptnr. Baker & Hostetler, Cleve. Life mem. Sixth Circuit Jud. Conf., Eighth Dist. Jud. Conf., Ohio; speaker in field. Fellow Am. Coll. Trial Lawyers; mem. ABA (mem. litigation, tort and ins. practice sects.), Ohio State Bar Assn., Cleve. Bar Assn. (chair litig. sect. 1991-92), Nat. Inst. Trial Advocacy (mem. nat. session 1978), Def. Rsch. Inst., Anthony J. Celebrezze Inn. of Ct. (master). Office: Baker & Hostetler LLP 3200 Nat City Ctr 1900 E 9th St Ste 3200 Cleveland OH 44114-3475 Office Phone: 216-861-7327. Business E-Mail: rsolomon@bakerlaw.com.

SOLOMON, RAYMAN LOUIS, dean, law educator; b. Helena, Ark., June 5, 1947; s. David and Miriam (Rayman) S.; m. Carol Avins, Aug. 10, 1975. BA, Wesleyan U., 1968; MA in History, U. Chgo., 1972, JD, 1976, PhD in History, 1986. Bar: Ill. 1976, U.S. Ct. Appeals (7th cir.) 1978, U.S. Ct. Appeals (6th cir.) 1979. Dir. court history project U.S. Ct. Appeals (7th cir.), Chgo., 1976-78; law clk. to presiding judge U.S. Ct. Appeals (6th cir.), Cin., 1978-79; Bigelow fellow instr. U. Chgo. Law Sch., 1979-80; research fellow Am. Bar Found., Chgo., 1980-89, assoc. dir., 1986-89; assoc. dean Northwestern U. Sch. Law, Chgo., 1989—98; prof. law Rutgers U. Sch. Law, Camden, NJ, 1998—, dean, 1998—. Instr. Kent-Ill. Inst. Tech. Coll. Law, Chgo. 1982, Northwestern U., Evanston, Ill. 1986. Author: History of the Seventh Circuit, 1981; editor Am. Bar Found. Research Jour., 1985-87. Bd. dirs. Family Counseling Svc. of Evanston, 1985—, BPI, 1990—. Served with USN, 1969-70. Mem. ABA, Law and Soc. Assn., Selden Soc., Am. Soc. Legal Hist. (bd. dirs. 1985-88). Democrat. Jewish. Office: Rutgers State U Sch Law 217 North Fifth St Camden NJ 08102 Office Phone: 856-225-6191. Office Fax: 856-225-6487. E-mail: raysol@camlaw.rutgers.edu. *

SOLOMON, RICHARD HARVEY, think-tank executive; b. Phila., June 19, 1937; s. Bertram Harvey and Ellen (Harris) S.; m. Anne G. Keatley, Dec. 16, 1991. Student, Harvard U., 1959-63, Yale U., 1961, 63-64; SB, MIT, 1960, PhD, 1966. Tech. photographer, lab. worker Photon, Inc.,

Cambridge, Mass., 1957; rschr. Polaroid Corp., 1959-61; rsch. assoc. Ctr. for Chinese Studies U. Mich., Ann Arbor, Mich., 1966-71, from asst prof. to prof. polit. sci., 1966-71; staff mem. NSC, Washington, 1971-76; head. polit. sci dept. The Rand Corp., Santa Monica, Calif., 1976-86, program dir. Internat. Security Policy Research, 1977-83; mem. Pres.' Commn. on Fgn. Lang. and Internat. Studies Washington, 1978-80; mem. Chief of Naval Ops. exec. panel, 1983—; dir. policy planning staff Dept. of State, Washington, 1986-89, asst. sec. of state for East Asian and Pacific affairs, 1989-92; U.S. ambassador to Philippines, 1992-93; pres. U.S. Inst. of Peace, Washington, 1993—. Author: Mao's Revolution and the Chinese Political Culture, 1999, Chinese Political Negotiating Behavior, 1999, Exiting Indochina, 2000; contbr. articles to profl. jours. Office: US Inst of Peace 1200 17th St NW Ste 200 Washington DC 20036-3011 Office Phone: 202-457-1700. Business E-Mail: usip_requests@usip.org, info@usip.org.

SOLOMON, RISA GREENBERG, clinical social worker, child and family therapist, former entertainment industry executive; b. NYC, June 22, 1948; d. Nathan and Frances (Guttman) Greenberg; m. Philip Howard Solomon, June 21, 1970 (dec. 1994); children: Elycia Beth, Cynthia Gayle. BA, NYU, 1969, MA, 1970, MSSW, 1996. Asst. editor Redbook Mag., NYC, 1969-70; assoc. editor Greenwood Press, Westport, Conn., 1970-71; mng. editor Dushkin Pub., Guilford, Conn., 1971-72; freelance editor Yale U. Press, New Haven, 1972-75; v.p. ops. Videoland, Inc., Dallas, 1980-82; v.p. Video Software Dealers Assn., Cherry Hill, N.J. and Dallas, 1981-83; pres. Videodome Enterprises, Dallas, 1983-94; clin. social worker, child and family therapist pvt. practice, Dallas, 1994—. Cons. Home Rec. Rights Coalition, Washington, 1983—84; spkr. in field of child and adolescent therapy. Bd. dirs. Congregation Anshai Emet, Dallas, 1985-86. Mem. Video Software Dealers Assn. (founder, dir. 1981-82). Democrat. Jewish. Avocations: skiing, travel, tennis, scuba diving. Office: 17103 Preston Rd Ste 100 Dallas TX 75248 Home Phone: 214-369-8961. Personal E-mail: rgs8961@msn.com.

SOLOMON, ROBERT, economist; b. NYC, May 2, 1921; s. Sol and Betty (Brownstone) S.; m. Fern Rice, Sept. 11, 1946 (dec. 2001); children: Carol Ann, Barbara Betty, Anne Eleanor. BA, U. Mich., 1942; MA, Harvard U., 1947, PhD, 1952. With Fed. Res. Bd., 1947-76, assoc. adviser research div., 1963-65, adviser research div., 1965, adviser to bd. govs., 1965-76, dir. div. internat. fin., 1966-72; sr. fellow Brookings Instn., Washington, 1976-80, guest scholar, 1980—. Pres. RS Assos., 1981—2005; vice chmn. deps. of com. of 20 IMF, 1972-74; adj. prof. Am. U., 1962-67; sr. staff economist Coun. Econ. Advisers, 1963-64 Author: The International Monetary System, 1945-81, 1982, Partners in Prosperity, 1991, Money on the Move, 1999, The Transformation of the World Economy, 1999; contbr. articles to profl. jours. 1st lt. USAAF, 1942—45. Decorated D.F.C., Air medal; named Officier Legion of Honor France; recipient Rockefeller Pub. Service award, 1971. Mem. Am. Econ. Assn., Coun. on Fgn. Relations. Clubs: Cosmos (Washington). Home and Office: 8502 W Howell Rd Bethesda MD 20817-6827 Personal E-mail: Rsolo52178@aol.com.

SOLOMON, ROBERT H., lawyer; b. Bklyn., Aug. 23, 1958; s. Murray and Mildred (Teger) S.; m. Felicia Irene Smith, June 30, 1985; children: Zachary, Alexander. BS in Econ cum laude, U. Pa., 1979; JD, Duke U., 1982. Bar: N.Y. 1983, U.S. Supreme Ct., U.S. Ct. Internat. Trade, U.S. Dist. Ct. (ea. & so. dists.) N.Y. Assoc. LeBeouf Lamb Leiby & MacRae, NYC, 1982-84, Wofsey Certilman Haft et al, NYC, 1984-87, Zimmer Victor Schwartz et al, NYC, 1987-89; prin. Robert H. Solomon P.C., Long Beach, 1989—. Arbitrator NY Dist. Ct., Hempstead, 1989—, Supreme Ct. examiner Nassau County, NY, 2005—. Trustee Long Beach Bd. Edn., 1995; bd. dirs. Long Beach Med. Ctr., 2002; pres. Lido Home Civic Assn.; Dem. candidate 4th dist. Nassau County Legis., 2005. David Siegal scholar Duke U., 1980-82, Regents scholar, 1980. Mem. ABA, NY State Bar Assn., Bar Assn. NY, Nassau County Bar Assn., Long Beach Lawyers Assn. (pres. 1995-00), Long Beach C. of C. (v.p. 2000—), Wharton Club, Lions Club Long Beach. Avocation: tennis. Office: 24 E Park Ave Long Beach NY 11561-3504 Personal E-mail: pennduke@aol.com.

SOLOMON, SAMUEL, biochemistry educator, administrator; b. Brest Litovsk, Poland, Dec. 5, 1925; s. Nathan and Rachel (Greenberg) S.; m. Sheila R. Horn, Aug. 11, 1953 (div. 1974); children: David Horn, Peter Horn, Jonathan Simon; m. Augusta M. Vineberg, July 12, 1974. BS with honors, McGill U., 1947, MS, 1951, PhD in Biochemistry, 1953. Rsch. asst. Columbia U., 1953-55, assoc. in biochemistry, 1958-59, asst. prof., 1959-60; assoc. prof. biochemistry and exptl. medicine McGill U., 1960-66, prof., 1967-95, prof. emeritus, 1995—, prof. ob-gyn., 1976-95; dir. endocrine lab. Royal Victoria Hosp., Montreal, Que., 1965-95, dir. research inst., 1982-85; affilate dept. pharmacology U. Sherbrooke, 1995—. Mem. endocrinology and metabolism grants com. Med. Rsch. Coun. Can., 1967-71, regional dir. for Que., 1993-95; vis. prof. endocrinology U. Vt., 1964; cons. in field; Joseph Price orator, 1982, Am. OB-GYN Soc.; mem. steering com. Pharm. Mfg. Assn. Med. Rsch. Coun. Can. Partnership, 1993—; Med. Rsch. Coun. Can. dir. for McGill U., 1993-95. Co-editor: Chemical and Biological Aspects of Steroid Conugation, 1970; mem. editl. bd. Endocrinology, 1962; assoc. editor Can. Jour. Biochemistry, 1967-71, Jour. Med. Primatology, 1971; contbr. articles to profl. jours. Mem. bd. govs. McGill U., 1975-78; mem. steering com. European Study Group on Steroid Hormones, 1974-99, chmn. steering com., 1983-99, chmn. program com., 1990-91; mem. Dubin Commn. on Inquiry Drugs in Athletes, 1988-90. Decorated officer Order of Can. 1997; recipient McLaughlin medal Royal Soc. Can., 1989, Michel Sarrazin prize, 1997. Fellow Chem. Inst. Can., Am. Ob-Gyn. Soc. (hon.), Perinatal Rsch. Soc. Am. (pres. 1976), Soc. Gynecol. Investigation (program chmn. 1980), Endocrine Soc. (publ. com. 1986-89). Home: 239 Kensington Ave 804 Montreal PQ Canada H3Z 2H1 Business E-Mail: samuel.solomon@sympatico.ca.

SOLOMON, SEAN CARL, geophysicist, lab administrator; b. LA, Oct. 24, 1945; BS geophysics, Calif. Inst. Tech., 1966; PhD geophysics, MIT, 1971. From asst. prof. to prof. geophysics MIT, Cambridge, 1972-92; dir. dept. terrestrial magnetism Carnegie Instn. Washington, 1992—. Vis. scientist Lunar Sci. Inst., 1975, Lawrence Livermore Nat. Lab., 1978, Jet Propulsion Lab., 1990—91; guest investigator Woods Hole Oceanographic Inst., 1979—92; vis. faculty Inst. Geophysics and Planetary Physics, dept. earth and space scis. UCLA, 1982—83; Roland and Jane Blumberg vis. prof. planetary scis. U. Tex., Austin, 1988; vis. assoc. divsn. geol. and planetary scis. Calif. Inst. Tech., 1990—91; mem. various groups, teams, coms. NASA, 1974—; earthquake hazards reduction program peer rev. panel U.S. Geol. Survey, 1975, 85; lunar and planetary sci. coun. Univs. Space Rsch. Assn., 1978—80, 1991—93; tech. rev. panel, geophysics rev. panel Dept. Def., 1981—86; chmn. steering com. space sci. working group Assn. Am. Univs., 1987—89; rev. panelist NSF, 1986, 88, 95, 96, 2001, 03, 2006—; chmn. standing com. global seismic network Inc. Rsch. Instns. Seismology, 1988—90; participant numerous oceanographic expeditions, 1967—88. Editor (assoc. editor): Proceedings of the Lunar and Planetary Sci. Conf., 1976, 1978, Jour. Geophys. Rsch., 1976—78, Physics of the Earth and Planetary Interiors, 1977, Eos Transactions of Am. Geophys. Union, 1979—81, Geophys. Rsch. Letters, 1986—88; editor: Tectonophysics, 1981; mem. editl. bd.: Physics and Chemistry of Earth, 1981—85, Astrobiology, 2001—, Earth and Planetary Sci. Letters, 2001—07, mem. editl. com.: Ann. Rev. Earth and Planetary Scis., 1993—97; contbr. articles to profl. jours. Recipient Arthur L. Day prize, NAS, 1999, Public Svc. medal, NASA, 2004, Disting. Alumni award, Calif. Inst. Tech., 2006; fellow Grad., NSF, 1966—68, Postdoctoral, 1971—72, Fannie and John Hertz Found., 1968—71, Alfred P. Sloan Rsch., 1977—81, John Simon Guggenheim Meml., 1982—83. Fellow: AAAS, Geol. Soc. Am. (G.K. Gilbert award 1999), Am. Geophys. Union (pres. elect and pres. 1994—98, pres. planetology sect. 1984—88, chmn. geophys. monograph bd. 1983—84, numerous coms., H.H. Hess medal 2005), Am. Acad. Arts and Scis.; mem.: NAS, Seismol. Soc. Am., Am. Astron. Soc. (divsn. planetary scis.), Tau Beta Pi. Office: Carnegie Instn Dept Terrestrial Magnetism 5241 Broad Branch Rd NW Washington DC 20015-1305 Office Phone: 202-478-8850. E-mail: scs@dtm.ciw.edu.

SOLOMON, STEPHEN L., lawyer; b. NYC, Aug. 15, 1942; s. Sam and Ruth (Goldblum) S.; m. Regina Fisher, Aug. 14, 1969; children: Todd, Lisa. AB, Columbia Coll., 1964; LLB, NYU, 1967. Bar: N.Y. 1967, U.S. Dist. Ct. (so. and ea. dists.) 1969, U.S. Ct. Customs 1970, U.S. Supreme Ct. 1975. Assoc. Burns, Jackson, Summit, NYC, 1969-74; ptnr. Miller, Singer, Michaelson & Raives, NYC, 1974-79; pres. Jarblum, Solomon & Fornari, PC, NYC, 1979-97; ptnr. Rubin Baum LLP, NYC, 1997—2002, Sonnenschein Nath & Rosenthal, NYC, 2002—. Contbr. articles to profl. jours. Active Com. on Philanthropic Orgns., N.Y.C., 1980-83; bd. dirs. Emanu-El Midtown YM/YWHA, N.Y.C., 1979-85, Columbia Coll. Alumni Assn. Mem. Assn. Bar City of N.Y. Democrat. Home: 40 Fifth Ave New York NY 10011-8843 Office: Sonnenschein Nath & Rosenthal LLP 1221 Ave of Americas New York NY 10020 Office Phone: 212-398-5211. Business E-Mail: ssolomon@sonnenschein.com.

SOLOMON, SUSAN, chemist, scientist; d. Leonard Marvin and Alice Solomon. BS in Chemistry, Ill. Inst. Tech., 1977; MS in Chemistry, U. Calif., Berkeley, 1979, PhD in Chemistry, 1981; D (hon.), Tulane U., Williams Coll., SUNY at Stony Brook, Ill. Inst. Tech., U. Colo. Sr. scientist aeronomy lab. NOAA, Boulder, Colo., 1981—88, program leader middle atmosphere group aeronomy lab., 1988—. Adj. faculty U. Colo., 1982—; head project sci. Nat. Ozone Expdn., McMurdo Station, Antarctica, 1986, McMurdo Station, Antarctica, 87; co-chair Intergovernmental Panel on Climate Change. Co-author: Aeronomy of the Middle Atmosphere, 1984; contbr. articles to sci. jours. Named Solomon Glacier and Solomon Saddle in honor of leadership in Antarctic rsch., 1994; named to Hall of Fame, Women in Tech. Inst., 2004; recipient Gold medal, U.S. Dept. Commerce, 1989, Scientist of the Yr. award, 1992, Nat. Medal of Sci., 2000, Arthur S. Flemming awrd, Common Wealth award, Common Wealth Trust, Ozone award, UN Environ. Programme. Fellow: Am. Geophys. Union (J.B. McElwane award 1985), Am. Meteorol. Soc. (Henry G. Houghton award, Carl-Gustaf Rossby award 2000), Royal Meteorol. Soc.; mem.: NAS, European Acad. Scis. (foreign assoc.), French Acad. Scis. (foreign assoc.), US Nat. Acad. Scis., Am. Acad. Arts and Scis. Avocations: creative writing, crafts, scuba diving. Office Phone: 303-497-3483. Business E-Mail: ssolomon@al.noaa.gov.

SOLOMON, TERRI MARCIA, lawyer; b. Passaic, NJ, July 22, 1955; d. Sol and Arlene (Stiskin) S.; m. Howard Michael Topaz, July 4, 1982; children: Richard Harris Topaz, Jonathan Shaun Topaz. BA summa cum laude, U. Mass., 1976; JD, U. Pa., 1979. Bar: NJ 1979, US Dist. Ct. NJ 1979, NY 1980, US Dist. Ct. (so. dist.) NY 1980, US Dist. Ct. (ea. dist.) NY 1980, US Dist. Ct. (no. dist.) NY, 1997, U.S. Ct. Appeals (2d cir.) 1981, US Ct. Appeals (3d cir.) 1981. Assoc. Simpson, Thacher & Bartlett, NYC, 1979-87, counsel, 1988-93; ptnr. Grotta, Glassman & Hoffman, PA, NYC, 1993-96, Littler Mendelson, PC, NYC, 1996—. Fellow Coll. Labor and Employment Attys.; mem. ABA, NY State Bar Assn. (labor employment sect., ADR com.), Assn. Bar of City NY (labor employment sect.). Democrat. Jewish. Office: Littler Mendelson PC 885 Third Ave Ste 1600 New York NY 10022 Home Phone: 212-879-8527; Office Phone: 212-583-9600. Business E-Mail: tsolomon@littler.com.

SOLOMON, WAYNE C., aerospace engineer, educator; BS in Chemistry, U. Idaho, 1956; PhD in Chemistry, U. Oreg., 1963. Staff scientist Air Force Rocket Propulsion, Edwards, Calif., 1963—67; vis. prof. U. Goettingen Inst. Phys. Chemistry, Germany, 1967—69; chief kinetics and thermodynamics Air Force Astronautics Lab., Edwards, 1969—73; dir. high energy laser tech. Bell Aerospace Textron, Wheatfield, NY, 1973—80, dir. advanced tech., 1980—82, progs. dir. prototype laser systems, 1982—86, dir. engrng. for advanced systems, 1987—88; prof. aero. and astronautical engrng. U. Ill. Urbana-Champaign, 1988—, head aero. and astronautical engrng. dept., 1988—99, dir. Ill. Space Grant Consortium, 1991—; pres. CU Aerospace, 1998—. Contbr. articles to sci. jours. Fellow: AIAA. Office: U Ill Dept Aerospace Engrng 306 Talbot Lab 104 S Wright St Urbana IL 61801 Office Phone: 217-244-7646. E-mail: wsolomon@uiuc.edu. *

SOLOMON, WILLIAM TARVER, general construction company executive; b. Dallas, Aug. 11, 1942; s. Marion Bryant and Margaret (Moore) S.; m. Gay Ferguson, Feb. 15, 1964; children— William Tarver Jr., Meredith M. BSCE, So. Meth. U., 1965; MBA, Harvard U., 1967. With Austin Industries, Inc., Dallas, 1967—, chmn., pres., CEO, 1970—; chmn. Austin Comml., Inc., Dallas, Brit. Am. Ins. Co., Dallas; chmn., CEO Austin Industries, Inc., Dallas, now chmn. Bd. dirs. A.H. Belo Corp., Nat. Bank Tex. Past chmn. Dallas Citizens Coun. and Greater Dallas C. of C.; bd. dirs. Baylor U. Med. Ctr. Found., Dallas Mus. Art; trustee Southwestern Med. Found., So. Meth. U. Recipient citation of honor Dallas chpt. AIA, 1985, Humanitarian award NCCJ, Dallas, 1982, Champion of Free Enterprise award Associated Builders and Contractors, 1985, Outstanding Alumni award Southern Meth. U., 1988, Charles Cameron Sprague Cmty. Svc. Award Southwestern Med. Found., 2004, So. Meth. U. Sch. Engrng. Hall of Leaders Disting. Alumni Award, 2005, Linz Award, 2005; inductee Tex. Bus. Hall of Fame, 1996. Mem. ASCE, Young Pres.'s Orgn. (past chmn. Dallas chpt.), Dallas Assembly, Salesmanship Club Dallas, Dallas C. of C. (bd. dirs.). Republican. United Methodist Home: 3830 Windsor Ln Dallas TX 75205-1743 E-mail: bsol@austin-ind.com.

SOLOMONOFF, GALIA, architect; BS magna cum laude in Architecture, CUNY City Coll.; MArch, Columbia U., NYC, 1994. With Office Met. Architecture/Rem Koolhaas, Rotterdam, Germany; project designer Bernard Tschumi Archs., Rafael Vinoly Archs.; prin. OpenOffice, Galia Solomonoff Architecture, NYC. Louis Kahn chair Yale U., New Haven, 2004; adj. asst. prof. architecture Columbia U. Grad. Sch. Architecture; ptnr.-in-charge Dia:Beacon. Office: Solomonoff Architecture Studio 530 W 25th St Rm 409 New York NY 10001 Office Phone: 212-337-3700. Office Fax: 212-337-3730. E-mail: Galia@solomonoff.com. *

SOLOMONS, GUS, JR., (GUSTAVE MARTINEZ), choreographer, dancer, writer; b. Boston; s. Gustave Martinez and Olivia Mae. Student, Boston Conservatory of Music, 1956-59; BArch, MIT, 1961; postgrad., Martha Graham Sch., NYC, 1961-66. Dance soloist Martha Graham Co., NYC, 1964-65, Donald McKayle Co., 1961-64, Merce Cunningham Co., NYC, 1965-68; artistic dir. The Solomons Dance Co., NYC, 1972—; dean, artistic dir. Calif. Inst. of the Arts, Valencia, 1976-78; founder art dir. PARADIGM, 1996—. Vis. artist-in-residence U. Calif., Santa Cruz, Calif. State U., Long Beach, others; dance panelist Nat. Endowment Arts; various other other state art couns., 1983—; assoc. prof. dance numerous colls., univs., including UCLA, Un. Nev.-Las Vegas, Tex. Christian U., York, Simon Fraser, Tisch Sch. Arts, 1994-, prof., 2005-; USIA cons. to Nat. Dance Co., Tanzania, East Africa, 1988, Argentina, 1994. Appearances on TV networks, Sta. WGBH-TV, Boston; choreographr for various univs. and dance cos.; writer dance criticism for Village Voice, Dance Mag., others. Grantee Nat. Endowment for Arts, 1983—, N.Y. State Coun. on the Arts, 1972—; fellow Nat. Endowment for Arts, 1978-80; recipient Master Tchr. award NYU/Tisch, 1996, Bessie award, 2000, Robert A. Muh award for disting. MIT artist/alumnus, 2001, Balasaraswat/Beineke Disting. Tchg. award, 2004. Studio: 889 Broadway New York NY 10003-1212 E-mail: gus.solomonsjr@nyu.edu. *The content of a good dance is the truth about its maker. Performing it is a confession to the audience. The dancer places himself in the position of ultimate vulnerability each time he performs; it is at once cleansing, fulfilling, and courageous.*

SOLOMONS, MARK ELLIOTT, lawyer, art dealer, entrepreneur; b. Buffalo, Mar. 4, 1946; s. Alvin and Trude (Salant) Solomons; m. Jill E Kent, Aug. 20, 1978. BA, U. Rochester, 1967; JD, U. Pa., 1970; LLM, George Washington U., 1973. Staff atty. U.S. Dept. Labor, Washington, 1970-73, counsel coal miners benefits, 1973-77, legis. counsel, 1977-80; prin. Kilcullen Wilson & Kilcullen, Washington, 1980-86; ptnr. Arter and Hadden, Washington, 1986-2001, mem. exec. com., 1989-98; prin. shareholder Greenberg Traurig, Washington, 2001—, nat. co-chair appellate practice group. Guest lectr law and hist SUNY, Stony Brook, 1970—76, Univ Mich, 1977—78, Hobart Col, 1972—76; prin Coun for Excellence in Govt, 1991—; co-owner Frogeye Co; chmn Atlantic Threadworks, 1998—2001; del Atlantic Treaty Asn Gen Assembly, 2000—. Contbr. articles to profl jours. Trustee China Found, 1997—, chair, nominating com., 1997—, v.p., 2003—; mem. US Delegation to Gen. Assembly Atlantic Treaty Assn., 2001—. Master: Am Inn of Ct (counselor 1996—97); mem.: ABA (chair workers compensation and employers liability comt 1987—88, sr. vice chair 1988—2004, vice chair appellate advocacy comt), NY Bar Asn, DC Bar Asn, Fed Bar Asn (chair regulatory reform comt 1988—89). Republican. Office: Greenberg Traurig LLP 800 Connecticut Ave NW Washington DC 20006 Home Phone: 202-483-7209; Office Phone: 202-533-2361. Business E-Mail: solomonsm@gtlaw.com.

SOLOMONS, SETH, marketing executive; b. 1968; Exec. v.p., mktg. dir. Digitas NY, 2007—. Named one of 40 Under 40, Advt. Age, 2007. Office: Digitas NY 355 Park Ave S 3rd Fl New York NY 10010 Office Phone: 212-610-5000. Office Fax: 212-350-7850. *

SOLON, LEONARD R(AYMOND), retired physicist, educator, consultant; b. White Plains, NY, Sept. 11, 1925; s. Morris and Rebecca (Bobrov) S.; m. Charlotte Rothman, June 30, 1946; children: Miriam Solon Weintraub, Matthew Benjamin, Emily Solon Bader. BA, Hamilton Coll., 1947; MSc, Rutgers U., 1949; PhD, NYU, 1960. Cert. Am. Bd. Health Physics. Physicist Nuc. Devel. Assocs., Inc., White Plains, 1950-52; asst. chief, then chief radiation br. AEC, NYC, 1952-60; dir. applied nuc. tech. Tech. Rsch. Group, Inc., Syosset, N.Y., 1960-62; cons. Burns & Roe, NYC, 1962-64, Servo Corp. Am., Hicksville, N.Y., 1962-64; mgr. R&D Del Electronics Corp., Mt. Vernon, N.Y., 1964-67; founder, exec. v.p., tech. dir. Hadron, Inc., Yonkers, N.Y., 1967-75; dir. bur. radiation control N.Y.C. Dept. Health, 1975-91; ret., 1991. Lectr., then adj. assoc. prof. N.Y.U. Inst. Environ. Medicine, 1955-93; environ. & radiol. health cons.; prof. health physics U.S. Mcht. Marine Acad., 1963. Contbr.: Dictionary of American Biography, 1995, The Scribner Encyclopedia of American Lives, vol. 1, 2, 3, 4, 5, 1998-2002; contbr. articles to profl. jours. Served with inf. U.S. Army, 1944-46, ETO. Decorated Combat Inf. badge, Bronze Star. Mem. AAAS, Am. Nuc. Soc., Health Physics Soc., Am. Phys. Soc., N.Y. Acad. Scis., Conf. Radiation Control Program Dirs., Radiol. and Med. Physics Soc. N.Y., Phi Beta Kappa, Sigma Xi. Achievements include co-patentee for laser photocauterizer used in treatment of detached retina; powering lasers using nuclear sources. Office Phone: 631-673-1134.

SOLOSKI, JOHN, journalism and communications educator; AB cum laude, Boston Coll., 1974; MA in journalism, Univ. Iowa, 1976, PhD, 1978. Copy editor, reporter Iowa City Press Citizen, 1977-78; instr. Univ. Iowa, 1977-78, asst. prof. sch. journalism and mass communication, 1978-84, assoc. prof. sch. journalism and mass communication, 1984-85, assoc. prof., head of grad. studies, 1985-92, prof., head of grad. studies, 1992-94, prof., acting dir., 1994-95, prof. sch. of journalism and mass communication, 1995-96, prof., dir. sch. of journalism and mass communication, 1996—, prof. law, 1996—2001; dean Grady Coll. Journalism and Mass Comm. U. Ga., 2001—04, prof. Grady Coll. Journalism and Mass Comm., 2004—. Con. Ottumwa Courier, 1976-77, Iowa City Press-Citizen, 1976-77; speaker in field; vis. prof. Univ. Tech., Sydney, Australia, 1995. Co-author: Reforming Libel Law, 1992, Libel and the Press: Myth and Reality, 1987, Taking Stock: Journalism nad the Publicly Traded Newspaper Company, 2001; contbr. numerous articles to profl. jours.; editor: Journalism and Communication Monographs, 1994—. Recipient Soc. of Profl. Journalists Disting. Svc. award, 1988; numerous rsch. grants. Mem.: Assn. Schs. Journalism and Mass Comm. (pres. 2003—04). Office: Henry W Grady College of Journalism and Mass Communication The University of Georgia Athens GA 30602-3018 Office Phone: 706-542-1704. Business E-Mail: jsoloski@uga.edu.

SOLOTAR, JOAN S., securities analyst; b. Queens, NY, July 30, 1964; d. Eric and Susan (Efros) Rosenbaum; m. Gavin D. Solotar, Nov. 5, 1988; 1 child, Lindsay Jenna. BS, SUNY, Albany, 1986; MBA, NYU, 1991. Rsch. asst. Credit Suisse First Boston, NYC, 1986-89; v.p. equity rsch. Donaldson, Lufkin, Jennette, NYC; assoc. dir. equity rsch. Banc Am. Securities, dir. equity rsch., 2003—07; sr. mng. dir. pub. markets The Blackstone Group, 2007—. Chairperson Rsch. Com. Securities Industry Assn., 2001—02. Office: The Blackstone Group LP 345 Park Ave New York NY 10154

SOLOVY, JEROLD SHERWIN, lawyer; b. Chgo., Apr. 10, 1930; s. David and Ida (Wilensky) S.; m. Kathleen Hart; children: Stephen, Jonathan. BA with honors, U. Mich., 1952; LLB cum laude, Harvard U., 1955. Bar: Ill. 1955, DC 1955. Mem. bd. of editors Harvard Law Review, 1953—55; mem. visiting com. Harvard Law Sch., 1986—92; mem. Harvard Com. U. Resources, 1993—98; assoc. Jenner & Block, Chgo., 1955-63, ptnr., 1963—, chmn., 1991—. Chmn. Spl. Commn. on Adminstrn. Justice in Cook County, 1984-91, Ill. Supreme Ct. Spl. Commn. on Adminstrn. of Justice, 1992-93, Criminal Justice Project of Cook County, 1987-91. Mem. Cook County Jud. Adv. Council, Chgo., 1975-77, 82-89, chmn., 1989-91; trustee U.S. Supreme Ct. Hist. Soc., 1993—. Named one of 100 Most Influential Lawyers, Nat. Law Jour., 1991, 1994, 1997, 2000, 2006, 500 Leading Lawyers in Am., Lawdragon Mag., 2005, 2006, 500 Leading Litigators in Am., 2006; recipient Pro Bono Award, Seventh Cir. Bar Assn., 1993, Professionalism Award, Am. Inns of Ct., 2004, Lifetime Achievement Award, Decalogue Soc. of Lawyers, 2004, John Minor Wisdom Pub. Svc. and Professionalism Award, Am. Bar Assn., 2005. Fellow Am. Coll. Trial Lawyers; mem. ABA, Chgo. Bar Assn., Ill. State Bar. Assn., Am. Law Inst. Clubs: Standard; Lake Shore Country (Chgo.), Phi Eta Sigma, Phi Kappa Phi, Phi Beta Kappa, Pi Sigma Alpha. Office: Jenner & Block 330 N Wabash Avenue Chicago IL 60611-7603 E-mail: jsolovy@jenner.com.

SOLOW, MICHAEL BARRY, lawyer; b. Chgo., Jan. 6, 1959; s. Gilbert and Eunice (Eres) S.; m. Dale Susan Weinbaum, Aug. 21, 1983; children: Corey Francis, Andrew Wenbaum. AB summa cum laude, U. Ill., 1981; JD, Harvard U., 1984. Bar: Ill. 1984, NY 2003, U.S. Dist. Ct. (no. dist.) Ill. 1984, U.S. Dist. Ct. (no. dist.) Tex. 1987, U.S. Dist. Ct. Ariz. 1991, U.S. Dist. Ct. (we. dist.) Mich. 2003, U.S. Dist. Ct. (so. dist.) NY 2004, U.S. Ct. Appeals (7th cir.) 1984, U.S. Ct. Appeals (8th cir.) 1992, U.S. Ct. Appeals (4th cir.) 1993, U.S. Ct. Appeals (6th cir.) 1997, U.S. Supreme Ct. 1993. Law clk. to presiding justice Ill. Supreme Ct., 1984-85; assoc. Hopkins and Sutter, Chgo., 1985-90, ptnr., 1990—2001; ptnr., co-chair Bus. Reorganization and Creditors' Rights Dept., mem. Exec. Com. Kaye Scholer LLP, Chgo., NYC, 2001—. Mem. ABA, Chgo. Bar Assn., Phi Betta Kappa. Office: Kaye Scholer LLP 3 First Nat Plaza, Ste 4100 70 West Madison St Chicago IL 60602 also: 425 Park Ave New York NY 10022 Home Phone: 847-940-7691; Office Phone: 312-583-2310, 212-836-7240. Business E-Mail: msolow@kayescholer.com.

SOLOW, ROBERT MERTON, economist, educator; b. Bklyn., Aug. 23, 1924; s. Milton Henry and Hannah Gertrude (Sarney) Solow; m. Barbara Lewis, Aug. 19, 1945; children: John Lewis, Andrew Robert, Katherine. BA, Harvard U., 1947, MA, 1949, PhD, 1951, DLitt (hon.), 1992; LLD (hon.), U. Chgo., 1967, Brown U., 1972, U. Warwick, 1976, Tulane U., 1983, Dartmouth Coll., 1990, Rensselaer Poly. Inst., 2003, U. Rochester, NY, 2007; DLitt (hon.), Williams Coll., 1974, Lehigh U., 1977, Wesleyan U., 1982, Boston Coll., 1986, Harvard U., 1992, Colgate U., 1990; DSc (hon.), U. Paris, 1975, U. Geneva, 1982, Bryant Coll., 1988; D of Social Sci. (hon.), Yale U., 1976, U. Mass., Boston, 1989; D Social Sci. (hon.), U. Helsinki, 1990, SUNY, Albany, 1991, U. Glasgow, 1992, Rutgers U., 1994; D (hon.), U. Chile, 1992; Conservatoire, Nat. des Arts et Mètiers, Paris, 1994; D in Engring., Colo. Sch. Mines, 1996; postgrad. U. Buenos Aires, 1999; D in Lit. Humanities, NYU, 2000, New School U., 2006. Mem. faculty MIT, 1949—95, prof. econs., 1958—95, inst. prof., 1973—95, prof. emeritus, 1995—; W. Edwards Deming prof. NYU, 1996—97. Sr. economist Coun. Econ. Advisers, 1961—62, cons., 1962—68, RAND Corp., 1952—64; Marshall lectr., fellow commononer Peterhouse Cambridge (Eng.) U., 1963—64; Eastman vis. prof. Oxford U., 1968—69; overseas fellow Churchill Coll., Cambridge; sr. fellow Soc. Fellows, Harvard U., 1975—89; bd. dirs. Boston Fed. Res. Bank, 1975—80, chmn., 1979—80; active President's Commn. on Income Maintenance, 1968—70, President's Com. on Tech., Automation and Econ. Progress, 1964—65, Carnegie Commn. Sci., Tech. and Govts., 1988—93, Nat. Sci. Bd., 1994—2000; found. fellow Russell Sage Found., 2001—. Author (with R. Dorfman, P. Samuelson): Linear Programming and Economic Analysis, 1958; author: Capital Theory and the Rate of Return, 1963, The Sources of Unemployment in the United States, 1964, Growth Theory, 1970, Price Expectations and the Behavior of the Price Level, 1970; author: (with M. Dertouzos, R. Lester) Made in America, 1989; author: The Labor Market as a Social Institution, 1990; author: (with F. Hahn) A Critical Essay on Modern Macroeconomic Theory, 1995; author: Learning from "Learning by Doing", 1997; author: (with J. Taylor) Inflation, Unemployment and Monetary Policy, 1998; author: Monopolistic Competition and Macroeconomic Theory, 1998, Work and Welfare, 1998; editor (with Alan Krueger): The Roaring Nineties, 2002. Bd. dirs., mem. exec. com. Nat. Bur. Econ. Rsch.; trustee Inst. for Advanced Study, Princeton U., 1972—78, Woods Hole Oceanographic Inst., 1988—, Alfred P. Sloan Found., 1992—, Resources for the Future, 1994—2003, Urban Inst., 1994—, German Marshall Fund of U.S., 1994—2002, Ctr. Advanced Study Behavioral Scis., 1982—95, chmn., 1987—95. With US Army, 1942—45. Decorated Bronze Star U.S. Army; recipient David A. Wells prize, Harvard U., 1951, Seidman award in polit. economy, 1983, Nobel prize in Econs., 1987, Nat. Medal of Sci., 2000; fellow, Ctr. Advanced Study Behavioral Scis., 1957—58, Russell Sage Found., 2000—. Fellow: Am. Acad. Arts and Scis., Brit. Acad. (corr.); mem.: NAS (coun. 1977—80, 1995), AAAS (v.p. 1970), Internat. Econ. Assn. (pres. 1999—2002), Econometric Soc. (pres. 1964, exec. com.), Am. Econ. Soc. (exec. com. 1964—66, v.p. 1968, pres. 1979, John Bates Clark medal 1961), Royal Irish Acad. (hon.), Order Pour le Merite (Germany), Acad. dei Lincei, Am. Philos. Soc. Home: 528 Lewis Wharf Boston MA 02110-3920 Office: MIT Dept Econs Cambridge MA 02139

SOLOW, SHELDON L., lawyer; b. Chgo., Sept. 10, 1950; BA with highest honors, U. Ill., 1972; JD, Harvard U., 1975. Bar: Ill. 1975, US Ct. Appeals (7th and 8th cirs.), Customs Ct., US Dist. Ct. (no. dist.) Ill., US Supreme Ct. Mem. Sachnoff & Weaver Ltd., Chgo.; ptnr. Kaye Scholer LLP, Chgo. Faculty mem. Am. Bankers Assn. Nat. Comml. Lending Sch., 1989—, Fed. Res. Bank Examiners Tng. Program, 1990—. Contbr. Mem. panel standing trustees No. Dist. Ill., 1989; trustee Midway Airlines, Inc. Charles Merriam scholar. Mem. ABA (sects. on litigation, corp., bus. and banking law), Chgo. Bar Assn. (mem. bankruptcy and reorganization subcom. 1980—, vice chmn. 1985-86, chmn. 1986-87), Phi Beta Kappa, Phi Kappa Phi, Pi Sigma Alpha. Home: Kaye Scholer LLP 70 W Madison St Ste 4100 3 1st National Plaza Chicago IL 60602 Office Phone: 312-583-2320. Office Fax: 312-583-2360. Business E-Mail: ssolow@kayescholer.com.

SOLOWAY, ALBERT HERMAN, medicinal chemist; b. Worcester, Mass., May 29, 1925; s. Bernard and Mollie (Raphaelson) S.; m. Barbara Berkowicz, Nov. 29, 1953; children: Madeleine Rae, Paul Daniel, Renee Ellen. Student, U.S. Naval Acad., 1945-46; BS, Worcester Poly. Inst., 1948; PhD, U. Rochester, 1951. Postdoctoral fellow Nat. Cancer Inst. at Sloan-Kettering Inst., NYC, 1951-53; research chemist Eastman Kodak Co., Rochester, NY, 1953-56; asst. chemist Mass. Gen. Hosp., Boston, 1956-61, asso. chemist, 1961-73; asso. prof. med. chemistry Northeastern U., Boston, 1966-68, prof. medicinal chemistry, chmn. dept., 1968-71, prof. medicinal chemistry and chemistry, chmn. dept. medicinal chemistry and pharmacology, 1971-74; dean Coll. Pharmacy and Allied Health Professions, 1975-77; dean Coll. Pharmacy Ohio State U., Columbus, 1977-88, prof. medicinal chemistry, 1977-98, Kimberly prof. pharmacy, 1997-2000, dean, prof. emeritus, 1998—. Author rsch. in medicinal chemistry, boron neutron capture therapy of cancer. Recipient Disting. Achievements in Boron Sci. award, Boron USA, 1994. Fellow AAAS, Acad. Pharm. Soc.; mem. AHS (50 Yr. mem.), Am. Chem. Soc., Am. Assn. Coll. Pharmacy, Am. Assn. Cancer Rsch., Torch Club Columbus (pres. 2004-05) Office: Ohio State U 500 W 12th Ave Columbus OH 43210-1214 Business E-Mail: soloway.1@osu.edu.

SOLOWAY, DANIEL MARK, lawyer; b. Buffalo, Jan. 21, 1959; s. Sol Murray and Shirley (Prashker) S.; m. Natalie Ann-Marie Chin, June 10, 1989; children: Rachael Ann, Rebecca Leigh. BA cum laude, SUNY, Buffalo, 1982; JD with honors, Fla. State U., 1985. Bar: Fla. 1985, U.S. Dist. Ct. (no. dist.) Fla. 1985, (mid. dist.) Fla. 1995, (so. dist.) Ala. 1986, U.S. Ct. Appeals (11th cir.) 1985, U.S. Supreme Ct. 1989; bd. cert. in civil trial law, Fla.; cert. Nat. Bd. Trial Advocacy, 1998, civil ct. mediator, 2000. Law clk. Circuit Judge, Tallahassee, 1983-84, Douglass, Davey, Cooper & Coppins, Tallahassee, 1984-85; ptnr. McKenzie & Soloway, Pensacola, Fla., 1985-98; pvt. practice Pensacola, 1998—. Author: Criminal Justice: An Analysis Toward Reform, 1981; contbr. articles to profl. jours.; editor Escambia-Santa Rosa Bar Assn. newsletter, 1989-90, Dry Shoes, Fla. Bar Jour., 1992. Profl. adv. bd. N.W. Fla. Epilepsy Soc., Pensacola, 1989—; speaker on AIDS, State of Fla. Dept. HRS, 1988—; active Escambia County Human Rels. Commn., 1996-98. Recipient Pro Bono Svc. award Escambia-Santa Rosa Bar, 1989-90, Pro Bono Svc. Pres.'s award Fla. Bar, 1990. Mem. Million Dollar Advocates Forum (diplomat), ABA, Assn. Trial Lawyers Am., Escambia-Santa Rosa Bar Assn. (editor newsletter 1989-90), Acad. Fla. Trial Lawyers (speaker 1993—), Nat. Orgn. Social Security Claimants Reps. Democrat. Jewish. Avocation: writing. Office: 901 Scenic Hwy Pensacola FL 32503-6866 Office Phone: 850-435-0555.

SOLOWAY, RICHARD LEWIS, electronics executive; b. Long Branch, NJ, Feb. 27, 1946; Studied, N.Y. Inst. Tech., Old Westbury. V.p. Nat. Alarm Products Co., Farmingdale, NY, 1970—72; co-founder Napco Security Sys. Inc., Amityville, NY, 1972, v.p., 1972—81, sec., treas., 1975—, chmn. bd., 1981—. Named Entrepreneur of Yr. in Mfg., Ernst & Young, 2001. Office: NAPCO Security Sys Inc 333 Bayview Ave Amityville NY 11701-2800 Office Phone: 631-842-9400 x120.

SOLOWEY, CARL, dermatologist, educator; AB, NYU, Bronx, 1953; MD, SUNY, Bklyn., 1957. Diplomate Am. Bd. Dermatology. Intern Kings County Hosp., Bklyn., 1957—58; resident NYU, NYC, 1958—59, 1960—61, Bellevue Hosp., NYC, 1959—60; attending physician Univ. Hosp. Bklyn., 1962—, NY Hosp., Queens, 1962—, LI Jewish Hosp., New Hyde Park, NY, 1962—. Clin. asst. prof. dermatology Med. Sch. SUNY, Bklyn., 1982—. Fellow: ACP, NY Acad. Medicine, Am. Acad. Dermatology. Office: 98-05 63 Rd Rego Park NY 11374

SOLSO, THEODORE M., manufacturing executive; m. Denny; 3 children. BA, DePauw U., 1969; MBA, Harvard U., 1971. Asst. to v.p. personnel Cummins Engine Co., Inc., Columbus, Ind., 1971—72; employment dir. Holset Engring. Co., Ltd. (Cummins' U.K. subs.), Columbus, 1972—74, dir. devel. & tng., 1974—77; exec. dir. personnel Cummins Engine Co., Inc., Columbus, 1977-80; v.p., mng. dir. Holset Engring. Co., Ltd. (Cummins' U.K. subs.), 1980-84; v.p. spl. engine markets Cummins Engine Co., Inc., Columbus, 1984-86, v.p. mktg., 1986-88, v.p., gen. mgr. engine bus., 1988-92, exec. v.p. opers., 1992—94, exec. v.p. & COO, 1994—95, pres. & COO, 1995-00, chmn., CEO, 2000—. Bd. dirs. Ashland, Inc., Cyprus Amax Minerals, Inc. Bd. trustees DePauw U.; bd. advisors U. Mich. Sch. Bus.; past bd. dirs. Heritage Fund Bartholomew County, Ind.; chmn. campaign Bartholomew County United Way; bd. dirs. Otter Creek Golf Course, Columbus, Ind. Mem. Mfrs. Alliance (bd. trustees). Office: Cummins Inc 500 Jackson St Columbus IN 47201 *

SOLTERO-HARRINGTON, LUIS RUBÉN, retired surgeon, educator; b. San Juan, Sept. 4, 1925; s. Augusto Rafael Soltero and Anna Lila Harrington; m. Alice Joyce Carpenter, Apr. 24, 1958; children: Luis Ruben, Kathleen Ann, Susan Joyce, Robert Richard, Sharon Theresa. BS in Agr., U. P.R., Rio Piedras, 1945; BM, MD, Northwestern U., Chgo., 1949. Diplomate Am. Bd. Surgery, Nat. Bc. Med. Examiners, P.R. Rd. Med. Examiners. Intern Michael Reese Hosp., Chgo., 1949-50; resident in gen. surgery Aguadilla (P.R.) Dist. Hosp., 1950-51; resident in gen. surgery, instr. Baylor U. Coll. Medicine and Affiliated Hosps., Houston, 1954-59; resident in gen. surgery Jefferson Davis, VA and M.D. Anderson Hosps., Houston, 1954-57; resident in pediatric, thoracic and cardiovasc. surgery St. Luke's-Tex. Children's Hosp., Houston, 1957-59; asst. prof. surgery U. P.R. Sch. Medicine, 1960-64, assoc. clin. prof., 1972-73, assoc. clin prof., 1973—, in charge devel. heart surgery program, 1960-64, dir. surgery residency tng. program, 1961-64; pvt. practice San Juan, 1959—2003; ret., 2003. Prof. surgery U. del Caribe Sch. Medicine, Cayey, P.R., 1981—; cons. in cardiovasc. and thoracic surgery Med. Examing Bd. P.R., San Juan, 1989; chief thoracic and cardiovasc. surgery Tchrs. Hosp., San Juan, from 1959; dir. surgery residency tng. program Univ. Hosp., Rio Piedras, from 1961; cons. in thoracic and cardiovasc. surgery San Juan City Hosp., 1962—, cons. in surgery, 1964—; cons. in surgery Presbyn. Hosp., 1972—, Mimiya's Hosp., 1987—; cons. in thoracic and cardiovasc. surgery Indsl. Hosp., San Juan, 1975—, Hosp. Met., 1982—, Clinic Fernández García, 1983—; chief surgery Ruiz Arnau Hosp., Bayamon, P.R., 1978—; asst. dir. ICU, Hosp. del Maestro, 1987—; bd. dirs. Rsch. Found. Cardiovasc. Surgery Tex., 1984—, Am. Cancer Soc., 1974; mem. Nat. Adv. Cun. Mended Hearts, Inc., 1969. Author: (textbook) The Management of the Acutely Ill Patient, 2002; contbr. articles to med. jours.; patentee partial occlusion vascular clamp to be used in small blood vessels; inventor respirator for infants based on electronic equipment. Capt., M.C., USAF, 1953-54. Recipient award for outstanding work in cardiovasc. surgery Lions Club, Hato Rey, 1961. Fellow Am. Acad. Pediat., Am. Coll. Legal Medicine (assoc.); mem. AMA (physician recognition award 1986); mem. Denton A. Cooley Cardiovasc. Surg. Soc., Michael E. De Bakey Internat. Cardiovasc. Soc., Pan Am. Med. Assn. (coun. pediatric surgery), P.R. Soc. Cardiology, Am. Heart Assn., P.R. Hear Assn., Phi Chi. Avocations: travel, horticulture, bridge.

SOLTIS, KATHERINE, editor; b. Pitts., Apr. 15, 1950; d. John Andrew and Katherine (Hnidec) Goidich; m. Patrick T. Soltis, July 27, 1973 (div. 1998). BA, Mich. State U., 1972; MA in English/Linguistics, Case Western Res. U., 1982. Part time clk. Case Western Res. U., Cleve., 1974-83; lexicographer Webster's New World Dictionaries, Wiley Pub., Cleve., 1983—. Freelance copy editor. Editor: Webster's New World Vest Pocket Dictionary, 2nd edit., 1994; style guide editor, Webster's New World Desk Dictionary and Style Guide, 2d edit. Trustee Cleve.-Volgograd Ptnr. Cities, 1990-2001; pres. Women Speak Out for Peace & Justice/Women's Internat. League for Peace & Freedom, 1993-95, chair program com., 1995-2001; orgn. rep. Cleve. Coalition Against the Death Penalty, 1981-, chair, 2002-; supporter Ariz. death row inmate, 1981-; mem. Cleve. Pro-Choice Action League, 1996-, Windsong Cleve. Feminist Chorus, 1998-, Ohioans to Stop Executions. Mellon fellow Case Western Res. U. Mem.: Phi Beta Kappa. Soc. Of Friends. Avocations: reading, music, gardening, composting/recycling, foreign travel. Home: 896 Englewood Rd Cleveland Heights OH 44121-2042 Office: Webster's New World Dictionaries 850 Euclid Ave Ste 306 Cleveland OH 44114-3304 Personal E-mail: kssoltis@yahoo.com.

SOLTIS, PAMELA S., botanist, educator; PhD, U. Kans., 1986. Curator molecular systematics & evolutionary genetics Fla. Mus. Natural Hist., Gainesville. Contbr. articles to sci. jours.; assoc. editor: Evolution, Systematic Biology; co-editor: Isozymes in Plant Biology, 1990, Molecular Systematics of Plants II: DNA Sequencing, 1999, Devel. Genetics of the Flower, 2006; co-author: Phylogeny And Evolution Of Angiosperms, 2005. Mem.: Bot. Soc. Am. (pres.-elect 2006—). Office: Fla Mus Natural Hist U Fla PO Box 117800 Gainesville FL 32611 Office Phone: 352-392-1721 ext. 217. E-mail: psoltis@flmnh.ufl.edu. *

SOLTMAN, RONALD P., lawyer; JD cum laude, U. Mich., 1971. Asst. gen. counsel Hosp. Affiliates Internat., Nashville, 1978—81; v.p., asst. gen. counsel Hosp. Corp. Am., 1981—94; sr. v.p., gen. counsel OrNda Health-Corp, 1994—97; exec. v.p., gen. counsel, dir. Vanguard Health Sys., 1997—. Office: Vangard Health Sys 20 Burton Hills Blvd Ste 100 Nashville TN 37215 Office Phone: 615-665-6006.

SOLTYS, JOHN JOSEPH, lawyer; b. Portsmouth, Va., Feb. 4, 1942; children: John J. III, Amy Elaine. BS, USCG Acad., 1963; JD, Willamette U., 1970. Bar: Wash. 1970, U.S. Dist. Ct. (we. and ea. dists.) Wash. 1970. From assoc. to sr. ptnr. Karr, Tuttle, Seattle, 1970-89; shareholder Cozen, O'Connor, Seattle, 1999—. Writer, spkr. in field of product liability, med. malpractice and toxic torts; editor Wash. State Bar Assn. Motor Vehicle Accident Litig. Deskbook, 2000-01; elected super lawyer Wash. State Lt. (j.g.) USCG, 1963-67. Mem. Wash. Def. Trial Lawyers (pres. 1986-87), Fedn. Def. and Corp. Counsel. Avocations: fishing, hunting, gardening. Office: Cozen O'Connor 1201 3rd Ave Ste 5200 Seattle WA 98101-3071 Home Phone: 425-883-2322; Office Phone: 206-340-1000. Business E-Mail: jsoltys@cozen.com.

SOLUM, JOHN HENRY, flutist, educator, author; b. New Richmond, Wis., May 11, 1935; s. Irwin M. and Helen L. (Anderson) S.; m. Millicent Kemp Hunt, July 30, 1960; children: Eric, Andrew. AB, Princeton U., 1957. Concert flutist, 1957—; tchr. Ind. U., Bloomington, 1973, Vassar Coll., Poughkeepsie, NY, 1969-71, 77—, Oberlin (Ohio) Conservatory, 1976. Dir. Bath (Eng.) Summer Sch. Baroque Music, 1979-89; artistic dir. Conn. Early Music Festival, New London, 1982-99; pres. N.Y. Flute Club, 1983-86; mem. music adv. panel NEA, 1990-93; arts adv. panel N.H. Arts Coun., 1995-98. *In addition to his activities related to music, in 1994 Solum began championing the work of the pioneering American modernist artist, James Daugherty (1887-1974). Solum's initiatives have led to special exhibitions of Daugherty's art, lectures, television documentaries, articles, and the recovery and restoration of ten of his large scale murals, including four in Cleveland's State Theater at Playhouse Square and six New Deal murals in Greenwich, Stamford and Darien, Connecticut.* Composer Cadenzas for Mozart's Flute Concertos, 1964; editor flute music; music critic for Notes, Pro Musica, The Consort; author: The Early Flute, 1992; contbg. author: New Grove Dictionary of Musical Instruments, New Grove Dictionary of Music and Musicians; contbr. articles to Mus. Am., Flutist Quar., FLute Talk, Hist. Performance Mag., Woodwind World, Traversieres, Revue de la Société Liégeoise de Musicologie, Pan; flutist throughout N.Am., 1957—, Europe, 1962—, Asia, 1969—, S.Am., 1978—, Russia, 1983—; rec. artist Albany, Arabesque, Boston Skyline, Brunswick, Cambridge, Chesky, Columbia, CRI, Decca Gold Label, EMI, Epiphany, Innova, MCA Westminster, MSR, Philips, RCA, Seraphim, Smithsonian, Vanguard, others. Chmn. Hanoverian Found., 2000—. Recipient Phila. Orch. Youth Contest award, 1957. Mem. Nat. Flute Assn. (treas. 1989-94, Disting. Svc. award 1998), Dolmetsch Found. (bd. dirs.), Galpin Soc., Am. Musical Instrument Soc., Century Assn. (N.Y.). Home: 10 Bobwhite Dr Westport CT 06880-1001 E-mail: jhsolum@optonline.net.

SOLYMOSY, EDMOND SIGMOND ALBERT, marketing professional, retired military officer; b. Budapest, Pest, Hungary, Sept. 3, 1937; came to U.S., 1949; s. Sigmond Ladislas and Gabrielle (Lindelof) S.; m. Mary Ellen Via, Sept. 9, 1961; children: Edmond S.A. Jr., Stephan G., Philip A. BSME, Tex. A&M U., 1960, BBA, 1961, MBA, 1970; postgrad., Mich. U.; 1985, Harvard U., 1991. Commd. 2d lt. U.S. Army, 1961, advanced through grades to gen., 1985; student Nat. Def. U., Washington, 1980-81; comdr. 1st Air Def. Arty. Brigade, Ft. Bliss, Tex., 1981-83; chief of staff U.S. Army Air Def. Ctr., Ft. Bliss, 1983; dir. Human Resources Directorate, Hdqrs. Dept. Army, Washington, 1983-85; dep. comdr. U.S. Army Community and Family Support Ctr., Alexandria, Va., 1985-86; chief of staff U.S. Army I Corps, Ft. Lewis, Wash., 1986-88; chief exec. U.S. Office of Def. Coop., Athens, Greece, 1988-91; ret., 1991; pres. Global Project Mgmt., Houston, 1991—, Am. Southwest Properties Inc., 1993-95, Prime Daniel Asset Mgmt. Corp., 1997-2001; sr. ptnr. Solymosy Investment Assocs., 2000—; owner Bar-O-S Ranch. Advisor Sec. of Army Panel, Washington, 1983-86, Hellenic-Am. C. of C., Athens, 1988-91; bd. dirs. Am. Ikarus Inc., Maxoil Inc., So. Nat. Bank Tex., SNB Bankshares, Tex. A&M U. Rsch. Found., Fin. Literacy Found.; hon. consul Republic of Hungary; chmn. Houston Com. on Fgn. Rels. Author: Continental Economic Alliances, 1981. Sponsor Spl. Olympics, Ft. Lewis, 1986; advisor Mil. Mus., Ft. Lewis, 1986-88; regional v.p. Mediterranean coun. Boy Scouts Am., Athens, 1988-91; mem. devel. com. Tex. A&M U., College Station, 1991, advisor Ctr. for Internat. Bus.; mem. bd. advisors Mosher Inst. for Internat. Policy Studies; mem. Mil. Com., Houston. Decorated D.S.M., Def. D.S.M., Combat Infantryman's Badge, Airborne Parachutist's Badge, Army Ranger, Legion of Merit (3); recipient U.S. and Vietnamese awards for heroism, Greek Disting. Svc. award, 1991. Mem.: VFW, Assn. U.S. Army (Svc. to Soldiers award 1985), Am. Quarter Horse Assn., Armed Forces YMCA (chmn. com. 1982, nat. vol. of yr. award 1983), Am. Palomino Horse Breeders Assn., Internat. Propeller Club (Greece advisor 1989), Kiwanis Club Houston, Hungarian Knights Hospitaller of Order of St. John. Republican. Lutheran. Avocations: sports, jogging, sailing, fishing, hunting. Home: 10150 Dogwood Tr College Station TX 77845-6740 Office: Global Project Mgmt 10150 Dogwood Tr College Station TX 77845 E-mail: essglobal@aol.com.

SOLYOM, ANTAL ENDRE, retired psychiatrist; arrived in US, 1966, naturalized, 1972; s. Antal Solyom and Ilona Molnar; m. Gwen Ellen Cattle, Oct. 30, 1971; 1 child, Alexander Istvan. MD summa cum laude, Med. U. Szeged, Hungary, 1960; PhD in Biochemistry, U. Okla., Norman, 1970; MA in Bioethics, U. Va., Charlottesville, 2003. Diplomate in psychiatry Am. Bd. Psychiatry and Neurology, 1976, in child psychiatry Am. Bd. Psychiatry and Neurology, 1978, cert. in addiction medicine Am. Soc. Addiction Medicine, 1988. Rsch. assoc. dept. pharmacology Rsch. Inst. Pharm. Chemistry, Budapest, Hungary, 1960—64; vis. scientist inst. pharmacology and therapy U. Milano, Italy, 1964—66; postdoctoral fellow Okla. Med. Rsch. Found., Okla. City, 1966—70; rsch. fellow lab. neurochemistry NIH, Bethesda, Md., 1970—72; dir., children's outpatient svc. Detroit Psychiat. Inst., 1975—77; dir. infant study and infant psychiatry program med. sch. U. Mich., Ann Arbor, 1977—85, asst. prof. psychiatry med. sch., 1977—85; asst. prof. psychiatry sch. medicine Wayne State U., 1975—77, co-dir. Eleonore Hutzel recovery ctr. sch. medicine Detroit, 1985—87, assoc. prof. psychiatry sch. medicine, 1985—89; dir. child-adolescent psychiatry edn. Fairlawn Ctr. Child/Adolescent Psychiat. Svcs., Pontiac, Mich., 1987—89; clin. prof. family medicine sch. medicine U. Va., 1989—2002; med. dir. bridges child-adolescent treatment ctr. Centra Health, Inc., Lynchburg, Va., 1989—2002, ret., 2002. Adj. affiliate ctr. biomedical ethics and humanities U. Va. Health Sys., Charlottesville, Va., 2003—; locum tenens psychiatrist Staff Care, Inc., Irving, Tex., 2004—; interim med. dir. child-adolescent psychiatry program Centra Health, Inc., 2004—05. Contbr. more than 40 articles to profl. jours. Fellow: Am. Acad. Child and Adolescent Psychiatry (life); mem.: AMA (life), Mental Health Assn. Ctrl. Va. (bd. dirs. 2002—05), Am. Soc. Bioethics and Humanities, World Fedn. Mental Health, Am. Psychiat. Assn. (life Falk fellow 1973—74). Achievements include research in pharmacological and hormonal regulation of lipid metabolism, particularly the effect of androgens of serum lipoproteins; research on the development and regulation of affects in infants and toddlers; postulated the affect-balance principle to understand the attachment to pecific persons or objects, and conceptualized the disease of addiction as a maladaptive/pathological attachment; proposed special bioethical sonsiderations regarding clinical research in children/adolescents with psychiatric disorders, or in people with decisional impairments needing surrogate decision makers; the ethical challenges to the integrity of physicians regarding financial conflicts of interest in clinical research and in the use of assisted reproductive technologies. Avocations: chess, classical music, travel, reading, swimming. Home: Po Box 3620 Lynchburg VA 24503

SOLZ, HERMANN, plastic surgeon; b. São Paulo, Brazil, May 5, 1952; s. Hermann and Hilde (Sihler) Solz; m. Jeanette Solz, Feb. 29, 1980; children: Sandra, Alex. MD, U. Sul Fluminense, Rio de Janeiro, 1976. Resident in internal medicine Hosp. Matarazzo, São Paulo, 1976; resident in plastic surgery BG Unfallklinik, Ludwigshafen, Germany, 1977—79, Marienhosp. Stuttgart, Germany, 1979—80, St. Markus Krankenhaus, Frankfurt, Germany, 1980; prof. plastic surgery U. Santa Cecilia, Santos, Brazil, 1983—88; plastic surgeon Hosp. Beneficencia Portuguese, Santos, 1983—88; chief plastic surgeon Mannheimer Clinic Plastic Surgery, Germany, 1989—. Fellow: Brazilian Soc. for Plastic Surgery, German Assn. Aesthetic Surgery, German Soc. Plastic Surgery. Avocations: diving, snowboarding, motorsports, languages. Office: Mannheimer Klinik für Plastische Chirurgie Mollstrasse 45 Mannheim D-68165 Germany Office Phone: +49-621-14740/152800. Office Fax: 0621 14849. Business E-Mail: info@beautyclinic.de. E-mail: drsolz@aol.com.

SOMANI, SEEMA, optics scientist; m. Mahesh Somani; children: Anish, Vivek. PhD, Stanford U., Calif., 1998. Sr. scientist Schlumberger Techs., San Jose, Calif., 1999—2001; prin. scientist Advanced Med. Optics, Santa Clara, Calif., 2001—. Office: Advanced Med Optics 3400 Central Expressway Santa Clara CA 95051 Office Phone: 408-773-7353.

SOMASUNDARAN, PONISSERIL, surface and colloid engineering educator; b. Pazhookara, Kerala, India, June 28, 1939; arrived in U.S., 1961; s. Kumara Moolayil and Lakshmikutty (Amma) Pillai; m. Usha N., May 25, 1966; 1 child, Tamara. BS, Kerala U., Trivandrum, India, 1958; BE, Indian Inst. Sci., Bangalore, 1961; MS, U. Calif., Berkeley, 1962, PhD, 1964. Rsch. engr. U. Calif., 1964, Internat. Minerals & Chem. Corp., Skokie, Ill., 1965-67; rsch. chemist R.J. Reynolds Industries, Inc., Winston-Salem, NC, 1967-70; assoc. prof. Columbia U., NYC, 1970-78, prof. mineral engring., 1978-83, La Von Duddleson Krumb prof., 1983-97; dir. NSF Industry U. Coop. Rsch. Ctr. in Novel Surfactants, 1998—; hon. prof. Wuhan Inst. Chem. Tech., 2001—. Chmn. Henry Krumb Sch. Chem. Engring., Materials Sci. and Mining Engring., Columbia U., 1988—97; dir. Langmuir Ctr. for Colloids and Interfaces Columbia U., 1987—; mem. panel NRC; chmn. numerous iainternat. symposia and NSF workshops; mem. adv. panel Bur. Mines Generic Ctr., 1983—91; keynote and plenary lectr. internat. meetings; hon. prof. Ctrl. South U. Tech., China; Brahm

Prakash prof. metallurgy and material sci. Indian Inst. Sci., Bangalore, 1990; hon. rsch. advisor Beijing Gen. Rsch. Inst., 1991—; Henry Krumb lectr. AIME, 1988; cons. in field. Editor: Fine Particles Processing, 1980; editor-in-chief: Encyclopedia of Surface and Colloid Sci.; hon. editor-in-chief Colloids and Surfaces, 1980—; contbr. articles to profl. jours. Pres. Keralasamajam of Greater NY, NYC, 1974-75; bd. dirs. Fedn. Indian Assocs., NYC, 1974-95, Vols. in Svc. to Edn. in India, Hartford, Conn., 1974—; mem. planning bd. Village of Piermont, NY, 1995-2000, mem. zoning bd. appeals, 2000—, mem. citizens adv. com., 2000—. Recipient Disting. Achievement in Engring. award, AINA, 1980, Antoine M. Gaudin award Soc. Mining Engrs.-AIME, 1983, Achievements in Applied Sci. award 2d World Malayalam Conf., 1985, Robert H. Richards award, AIME, 1986, Arthur F. Taggart award Soc. Mining Engrs.-AIME, 1987, honor award Assn. Indian in Am., 1988, VHP award of Excellence, Ellis Island medal of Honor, 1990, Commendations citation State of N.J. Senate, 1991; named Mill Man of Distinction, Soc. Mining Engrs.-AIME, 1983, Disting. Alumnus award Indian Inst. Sci., Bangalore, 1989, Outstanding Contbns. and Achievement award Cultural Festival India, 1991, Recognition award SIAA, 1992, Asian-Am. Heritage award Asian Am. Higher Edn. Coun., 1994, award for outstanding contbn. to sci. and tech. Hudson Valley Malayalee Assn., 2005, AIME Edn. award, 2006. Fellow Russian Acad. Nat. Scis. (fgn.), Chinese Acad. Engring. (fgn.) Indian Nat. Acad. Engring., Instn. Mining and Metallurgy (UK); mem. AICE, NAE, Soc. Mining Engrs. (bd. dirs. 1982-85, Disting. mem. award, also others), Engring. Found. (chmn. bd. 1993-95, chmn. conf. com. 1985-88, bd. exec. com. 1985-88, bd. dirs. 1991—, Frank Aplan award 1992), Am. Chem. Soc., NY Acad. Scis., Russian Acad. Natural Scis. (fgn.), Internat. Assn. Colloid and Surface Scientists (councillor 1989-92), Indian Material Rsch. Soc. (hon.), Sigma Xi. Achievements include patents in field. Office Phone: 212-854-2926. E-mail: ps24@columbia.edu.

SOMER, STANLEY JEROME, lawyer; b. NYC, Oct. 29, 1943; s. David Meyer and Rose (Bleifeld) S.; children: Penny Lynn, Andrew Michael; m. Batia Lebhar, Sept. 13, 1987. BBA in Acctg., Hofstra U., Hempstead, NY, 1966; JD, New York Law Sch., 1969. Bar: NY 1970, US Dist. Ct. (ea. and so. dists.) NY 1972, US Tax Ct. 1983. Assoc. Halpin, Keough & St. John, NYC, 1970-71, Bodenstein & Gumson, NYC, 1971-73; counsel Heatherwood Comm., Hauppauge, NY, 1973-74; ptnr. Somer & Wand, PC, Commack and Smithtown, NY, 1974-88, Somer, Wand & Farrell, Commack and Smithtown, 1989-90; sole practice Commack and Smithtown, 1990-98; ptnr. Somer & Heller LLP, Commack, 1999—. Lectr. NY Law Sch., NYC, 1970-73, Income Property Cons., Huntington, NY, 1976-85. Commiteeman Suffolk Reps., East Northport, NY, 1978. Mem. NY State Bar Assn., Suffolk Bar Assn., Comm. Assoc. Inst., LI Builders Inst. Lodges: Lions (pres. East Northport chpt. 1977-78). Office: Somer & Heller LLP 2171 Jericho Tpke Ste 350 Commack NY 11725-2947 Office Phone: 631-462-2323. Business E-Mail: ssomerandheller@optonline.net.

SOMER-GREIF, PENNY LYNN, lawyer; b. New Hyde Park, NY, Mar. 30, 1970; d. Stanley Jerome and Janice Somer; m. Brian Scott Greif; 1 child, David Joseph Somer Greif. BS, SUNY, Binghamton, 1992; JD, Am. U., 1995. Bar: NJ 1996, NY 1996, DC 2000, Md. 2006. Atty., advisor US SEC, Washington, 1995—2000; assoc. Arnold & Porter LLP, Washington, 2000—06, Ober, Kaler, Grimes & Shriver, Balt., 2006—. Avocations: reading, exercise. Office: Ober Kaler Grimes & Shriver 120 E Baltimore St Baltimore MD 21202-1643 Home Phone: 301-983-1685; Office Phone: 410-347-7341. Business E-Mail: psomergreif@ober.com.

SOMERHALDER, IAN JOSEPH, actor; b. Covington, La., Dec. 8, 1978; Student, William Esper Studio, NYC. Model for Calvin Klein, Dolce & Gabanna, Gucci, Versace, Guess. Actor, prodr. (films) Recess, 2004; actor: (films) Life as a House, 2001, Changing Hearts, 2002, Rules of Attraction, 2002, In Enemy Hands, 2004, The Old Man and the Studio, 2004, Pulse, 2006; (TV films) Anatomy of a Hate Crime, 2001; (TV series) Young Americans, 2000, Smallville, 2004, Lost, 2004—05 (Outstanding Performance by an Ensemble in a Drama Series, Screen Actors Guild award, 2006). Avocations: writing, yoga, horseback riding, snow skiing, water-skiing. Address: care Innovative Artists 1505 Tenth St Santa Monica CA 90401 Mailing: care Innovative Artists 7th Fl 235 Park Ave S New York NY 10003

SOMERHALDER, JOHN W., II, energy executive; m. Rebecca Somerhalder; 4 children. BSCE, Univ. Ariz. Sr. v.p. El Paso Corp., Houston, 1992—96, pres. El Paso Energy Resources Co., 1996, exec. v.p. pipeline group, pres. pipeline group, 2001—05, exec. v.p., 2001—05; pres., CEO AGL Resources Inc., Atlanta, 2006—. Bd. dir., past chmn. Interstate Natural Gas Assn. Am.; bd. dir. Interstate Nat. Gas Assn. Am.; bd. mem. Am. Gas Assn. Bd. mem. Metro Atlanta C. of C., Ga. C. of C. Office: AGL Resources Inc 10 Peachtree Pl Atlanta GA 30309 Mailing: AGL Resources Inc PO Box 4569 Atlanta GA 30302-4569 *

SOMERMAN, MARTHA J., dean, dental educator; m. Norm Schiff. DDS, NYU, 1975; PhD, U. Rochester, 1980. Diplomate Am. Acad. Periodontology. Asst. prof., periodontics and pharmacology Balt. Coll. Dental Surgery, 1984—87, assoc. prof., pharmacology, 1987—91; William K. and Mary Anne Najjar prof., dept. periodontics, prevention and periodontics U. Mich. Sch. Dentistry, 1991—2002, chair dept. periodontics, prevention and geriatrics, 1991—2001, assoc. dean rsch., 2001—02; assoc. prof., pharmacology U. Mich. Med. Sch., 1991—95, prof., pharmacology, 1995—2002; dean U. Wash. Sch. Dentistry, 2002—. Adv. coun. mem. Nat. Inst. of Dental and Craniofacial Rsch. Contbr. articles to profl. jours. Recipient Rsch in Oral Biology Award, Internat. Assn. Dental Rsch., 2005. Fellow: AAAS; mem.: Am. Assn. Dental Rsch. (past pres.). Office: RM D-322 Box 356365 Seattle WA 98195 Office Phone: 206-543-5982. Office Fax: 206-616-2612. Business E-Mail: somerman@u.washington.edu.

SOMERS, ANNE RAMSAY, retired medical educator; b. Memphis, Sept. 9, 1913; d. Henry Ashton and Amanda Vick (Woolfolk) Somers; m. Herman Miles Somers, Aug. 31, 1946; children: Sara Ramsay, Margaret Ramsay. BA, Vassar Coll., 1935; postgrad., U. N.C., 1939—40; DSc (hon.), Med. Coll. Wis., 1975. Ednl. dir. Internat. Ladies Garment Workers Union, 1937—42; labor economist U.S. Dept. Labor, 1943—46; rsch. assoc. Haverford Coll., 1957—63; rsch. assoc. indsl. rels. sect. Princeton U., 1964—84; prof. U. Medicine and Dentistry of N.J.-R. Wood Johnson Med. Sch. (formerly Rutgers Med. Sch.), 1971—84, adj. prof., 1984—2002. Adj. prof. geriat. medicine U. Pa. Sch. Medicine, 1990—2002; mem. Nat. Bd. Med. Examiners, 1983—86; cons. in health econs., health edn., geriats., gerontology, realted areas. Author: Hospital Regulation: The Dilemma of Public Policy, 1969, Health Care in Transition: Directions for the Future, 1971; author: (with H.M. Somers) Workmen's Compensation: The Prevention, Rehabilitation and Financing of Occupational Disability, 1954; author: Medicare and the Hospitals, 1967, Doctors, Patients and Health Insurance, 1961, Health and Health Care: Policies in Perspective, 1971; author: (with N.L. Spears) The Continuing Care Retirement Community: A Significant Option for Long Care?, 1992; editor (with D.R. Fabian): he Geriatric Imperative: An Introduction to Gerontology and Clinical Geriatrics, 1981. Mem. bd. visitors Duke U. Med. Ctr., 1972—77, U. Tex. Health Scis. Ctr., Houston, 1982—86. Named to Health Care Hall of Fame, 1993; recipient Elizur Wright award, Am. Risk and Ins. Assn., 1962. Fellow: Coll. Physicians Phila. (hon.), Am. Coll. Hosp. Adminstrs. (hon.); mem.: Nat. Acad. Social Ins., Inst. Medicine of NAS, Soc. Tchrs. of Family Medicine (hon.). Home: Pennswood Village # C-202 Newtown PA 18940-2401

SOMERS, CLIFFORD LOUIS, lawyer; b. Portland, Maine, Dec. 27, 1940; s. Norman Louis and Adeline Wilhemina (Witzke) Somers; m. Jennie Sierra Somers; children from previous marriage: Alan Mark, Penelope Lee. BA, U. Fla., Gainesville, 1965, JD, 1967. Bar: Fla. 1967, U.S. Ct. Mil. Appeals 1968, U.S. Dist. Ct. (mid. dist.) Fla. 1972, cert.: civil trial lawyer, mediator. Ptnr. Burton, Somers & Reynolds, Tampa, Fla., 1975—77, Miller, McKendree & Somers, Tampa, 1977—85, McKendree & Somers, Tampa, 1985—89, Somers and Morgan, Tampa, 1989—91, Somers and Assocs., Tampa, 1991—99, Barr, Murman, and Tonelli, Tampa, 1999—. Instr law U. Fla, Gainesville, 1967; sec. treas. Chester H. Ferguson-Morris S. White Inn Am. Inns Ct., 1987—89, pres.-elect Chester H. Ferguson-Morris S. White Inn, 1989—90, pres. Chester H. Ferguson-Morris S. White Inn, 1990—91. Contbr. articles to profl. jours. With US Army, 1961—64, Vietnam, capt. JAG US Army, 1968—72, mil. judge JAG US Army, 1971—72. Named one of Best Lawyers in Am., 2007. Mem.: Am. Bd. Trial Attys. (v.p. Tampa chpt 1990—91), Def. Rsch. Inst. (chmn. 2d dist. area west coast 1985—95), Fla. Bar Assn. (chmn. civil procedure rules com 1991—92), Brandon Vets. Post and Park, Am. Legion (comdr. Post 278 1975). Avocations: writing, weightlifting. Office: Barr Murman and Tonelli Ste 1700 201 E Kennedy Blvd Tampa FL 33602-5829 Home: 5700 Mariner St #404 Tampa FL 33609 Office Phone: 813-223-3951. Business E-Mail: csomers@barrmurman.com.

SOMERS, EMMANUEL, retired pathologist; b. Cania, Greece, Jan. 20, 1928; s. Nicholas and Angeliki Psomatakis; m. Katherine Somers; children: Michael, Angela, Nickolas, MaryAnn, Elizabeth. BS, Pub. Coll. Cania, Greece; MD, U. Salonika, Greece, 1955. Diplomate Am. Bd. Pathology, 1964. Intern Hartford Hosp., Conn., 1958—59; pathology resident RI Hosp., Brown U., Providence, 1959—62; fellow surg. pathology Michael Reese Hosp., Chgo., 1962—63, asst. pathologist, 1963—65; assoc. pathologist St. Margaret Hosp., Hammond, Ind., 1965—72, St. Mary's Hosp., Kankakee, Ill., 1972—76, dir. pathology and clin. labs., 1976—80; assoc. med. examiner Med. Examiner Office, Westchester, NY, 1981; dir. pathology and clin. labs. Flushing Hosp. Med. Ctr., NY, 1981—91; ret. 2nd lt. med. corp Greek Army, 1956—58. Fellow: Am. Soc. Clin. Pathologists, Coll. Am. Pathologists; mem.: AMA, Hellenic Med. Soc. NY. Greek Orthodox.

SOMERS, JOHN ARTHUR, insurance company executive; b. Cin., Feb. 24, 1944; s. Arthur Edward and Margaret Mary (Netschke) S.; m. Ann-Christin Ahlander, Dec. 28, 1968; children: Monica Ann, Christina Elizabeth, Mark Edward BS in Econs., Villanova U., 1966; postgrad., Sch. Law, U. Conn., 1966-67; MBA in Fin., U. Conn., 1972. Asst. town mgr. Town of Newington, Conn., 1970-72; v.p. Prudential Ins. Co. Am., Newark, 1972-81; sr. v.p. Tchrs. Ins. & Annuity Assn., NYC, 1981—, exec. v.p., 1996—. Bd. dirs. Cmty. Preservation Corp., Guardian Life. Roman Catholic. Office: Tchrs Ins & Annuity Assn Am 730 3rd Ave New York NY 10017-3206 Home Phone: 732-291-8689; Office Phone: 212-916-4400.

SOMERS, LOUIS ROBERT, retired food company executive; b. Pontiac, Mich., Aug. 8, 1926; s. Jay G. and Maggie (Gee) S.; m. Rynda Horinga, July 28, 1950; children: Linda, Laurie. BS, Mich. State U., 1950. With Kellogg Co., Battle Creek, Mich., 1955-88; controller Kellogg Internat., 1967-70, 72-75; fin. dir. Kellogg Gt. Brit. Ltd., 1970-72; v.p. fin., treas. Kellogg Co., 1975-85, sr. v.p. fin., 1985-88. Trustee Alma Coll., 1982—2001; bd. govs. ARC, 1985—92, chmn. audit com.; bd. dirs. Mich. State U. Devel. Fund, 1983—88.

SOMERS, SUZANNE MARIE (SUZANNE MARIE MAHONEY), actress, writer, singer; b. San Bruno, Calif., Oct. 16, 1946; d. Frank and Marion Mahoney; m. Greg Somers (div.); 1 child; m. Alan Hamel, 1977. Student, Lone Mountain Sch., San Francisco Coll. for Women; studies with Charles Conrad. Owner, founder Suzanne Somers Collection. Sells Somersize products (such as pajamas, clothes, shoes, kitchen appliances, diet and exercise videos and books) on The Home Shopping Network (HSN). Actress: (theater) The Blonde in the Thunderbird, 2004-2005; (films) American Graffiti, 1973, Billy Jack Goes to Washington, 1977, Yesterday's Hero, 1979, Nothing Personal, 1980, Rusty: A Dog's Tale, 1997; (TV films) Sky Heist, 1975, It Happened at Lakewood Manor, 1977, Happily Ever After, 1978, Zuma Beach, 1978, Goodbye Charlie, 1985, Totally Minnie, 1988, Rich Men, Single Women, 1990, Seduced by Evil, 1994, Devil's Food, 1996, Love-Struck, 1997, No Laughing Matter, 1998, The Darklings, 1999; (TV series) Anniversary Game, 1969, High Rollers, 1974, Three's Company, 1977-81, She's the Sheriff, 1987-89, Step by Step, 1991-98; (TV mini-series) Hollywood Wives, 1985; actress, co-exec. prodr.: (films) Exclusive, 1992; host: (TV series) The Suzanne Somers Show, 1994, VH1's 8-Track Flashback, 1995, Candid Camera (co-host), 1997-2000; performer Las Vegas (Nev.) Hilton, MGM Grand, Las Vegas, Sands Hotel, Atlantic City, USO, various TV commls.; author: Touch Me Again, 1973, Keeping Secrets (autobiography), 1988, Suzanne Somers' Eat Great, Lose Weight, 1997, After the Fall: How I Picked Myself Up, Dusted Myself Off and Started All Over Again (autobiography), 1998, Suzanne Somers' Get Skinny on Fabulous Food, 1999, Suzanne Somers 365 Ways to Change Your Life, 1999, Eat, Cheat, and Melt the Fat Away, 2001, The Sexy Years: Discover the Hormone Connection, 2004, Ageless:The Naked Truth about Bioidentical Hormones, 2006. Named Las Vegas Entertainer of Yr., 1986; named an hon. mem., US Military, 2005; recipient Humanitarian award, Nat. Council on Alcoholism, 1992, President's award, Nat. Assoc. of American Drug Counselors, Star on Hollywood Walk of Fame, 2003. *

SOMERVILLE, CHRISTOPHER ROLAND, botanist, educator; b. Oct. 11, 1947; naturalized, US, 1995; BSc in Math., U. Alta., Can., 1974, MSc in Genetics, 1976, PhD in Genetics, 1978; DSc (hon.), Queen's U., 1993, U. Alta., 1997, Wageningen U., 1998. Rsch. assoc. dept. agronomy U. Ill., 1978—81; asst. prof. dept. genetics U. Alta., 1981; assoc. prof. dept. botany and plant pathology Mich. State U., 1982-86, prof., 1986—93; prof. dept. biol. scis. Stanford U., Calif., 1994—; dir. dept. plant biology Carnegie Instn. Washington, Stanford, Calif., 1994. Panel mem. fed. support for soybean rsch. USDA-ARS, 1981; mem. adv. bd. molecular genetics Mass. Gen. Hosp., 1989—92; mem. plant adv. group Cold Spring Harbor Lab., 1990; mem. adv. bd. The Inst. Genomic Rsch., 1992—, Noble Found., 1993—97, Danforth Ctr., 1999—2001; mem. bd. agr. NRC, 1994—96; mem. vis. com. Swedish Found. for Strategic Rsch., 1995, Cornell U. Plant Biology, 1998; mem. President's Adv. Panel on Plant Biodiversity, 1997—98, Alta. Heritage Found., 2000—; vis. prof. U. Glasgow, 1998—; mem. sci. adv. bd. Wellcome Trust, 1999—2001; mem. adv. com. life scis. Cornell U., 2001—; mem. adv. com. U. Wis. Structural Biology Ctr., 2001—; CEO Mendel Biotechnology, 2002—. Contbr. articles to sci. jours.; mem. editl. com.: Photosynthesis Rsch., 1984—87, Plant Physiology, 1985—91, Development, 1986—93, Archives Biochemistry and Biophysics, 1986—2003, Devel. Genetics, 1989—91; editor: The Plant Jour., 1990—94; co-editor: Biochemistry and Molecular Biology of Membrane and Storage Lipids of Plants, 1993, Arabidopsis, 1994, The Arabidopsis Book, 2002; assoc. editor: Ann. Rev. Plant Physiology and Plant Molecular Biology, 1993—97, The Plant Cell, 1995—2000, mem. editl. bd.: Current Biology, 1996—, Procs. NAS, 1997—2000, mem. bd. reviewing editors: Science, 1996—, mem. sr. editl. com.:, 2001—; editor: Current Opinion in Plant Sci., 1997—. Recipient Young Presdl. Investigator award, NSF, 1984, Humboldt Sr. Rsch. award, 1992, Kuhmo award, 2001, Mendel medal, Genetics Soc., 2004. Fellow: AAAS, Royal Soc. London, Royal Soc. Can.; mem.: Internat. Soc. Plant Molecular Biology (bd. mem. 1993—97), Academia Europaea, NAS, Am. Soc. Plant Physiologists (mem. publ. com. 1989—91, Gibbs medal 1993, Schull award 1987). Office: Dept Plant Biology Stanford U Carnegie Instn 260 Panama St Stanford CA 94305-4101 E-mail: crs@stanford.edu.

SOMERVILLE, RICHARD CHAPIN JAMES, atmospheric scientist, educator; b. Washington, May 30, 1941; s. James William and Mollie (Dorf) S.; m. Sylvia Francisca Bal, Sept. 17, 1965; children: Anatol Leon, Alexander Chapin. BS in Meteorology, Pa. State U., 1961; PhD in Meteorology, NYU, 1966. Postdoctoral fellow Nat. Ctr. Atmospheric Rsch., Boulder, Colo., 1966-67; rsch. assoc. geophysical fluid dynamics lab. NOAA, Princeton, NJ, 1967-69; rsch. scientist Courant Inst. Math. Scis., NYC, 1969-71; meteorologist Goddard inst. space studies NASA, NYC, 1971-74; adj. prof. Columbia U., NYU, 1971-74; head numerical weather prediction sect. Nat. Ctr. Atmospheric Rsch., Boulder, 1974-79; prof. meteorology Scripps Inst. Oceanography, U. Calif.-San Diego, La Jolla, 1979—. Author: The Forgiving Air: Understanding Environmental Change, 1996. Fellow: AAAS, Am. Meteorol. Soc.; mem.: Am. Geophys. Union. Office: U Calif San Diego Scripps Inst Oceanography 9500 Gilman Dr Dept 0224 La Jolla CA 92093-0224

SOMES, JOAN MARIE, emergency nurse practitioner; b. St. Paul, Aug. 17, 1952; d. Richard and Jane (Blaiser) Friesen; m. Michael Somes, Nov. 15, 1975. BA in Nursing, Coll. of St. Catherine, St. Paul, 1974; paramedic cert., Inver Hills C.C., Inver Grove Heights, Minn., 1976; MSN, U. Minn., 1989; PhD in Health Adminstrn., Columbia So. U., Orange Beach, Ala., 2002. RN, Minn.; cert. emergency nurse, getiatrics nurse; nat. registered EMT-paramedic; cert. ACLS instr., PALS instr.; cert. TNCC instr.; cert. CATN instr., ENPC instr.; cert. ACLS-EP instr. Paramedic A.L.F. Ambulance, Apple Valley, Minn., 1987-97; charge nurse emergency dept. Divine Redeemer Hosp., South St. Paul, Minn., 1974-94; staff nurse emergency dept. St. Joseph's Hosp., St. Paul, 1994—, emergency dept. educator/staff nurse, 1999—. Instr. numerous local cmty. colls., hosps. and ambulance svcs.; item writer CEN exam., 1994-96, 96-98; edn. specialist Regions Emergency Med. Svcs., 1994—; spkr. in field; co-chair Cornerstones Emergency Nursing Conf., 2000; mem. regional faculty PALS Am. Heart Assn., 2004—; mem. magnet steering com. Health East Hosp. Sys., 2005—; v.p. Emergency Care Instructing LLP, 2006-. Author nursing home study courses; consulting editor Man. of Emergency Dept. and Urgent Care Instrns., 2001--; contbr. articles to profl. jour. Mem. steering com. Minn. Lit. Partnership, 2006—07. Grantee Glaxo Pharm. Co., 1989, Health East Found. 1991, 94, 97, 98, 2006; recipient Mary Piner award Minn. Emergency Nurses Assn. State Coun. 1994-2006 Fellow: Acad. Emergency Nurses; mem.: Vision Coun. for Profl. Devel., Nat. Emergency Nurses Assn. (chair geriatric com. 2003—04, exam item writer com. 2003—, geriat. com. 2005—), Emergency Nurses Assn. (chair state trauma com. 1994—95, sec. treas. Minn. state coun. 1994—95, sec. 1996—98, sec.-treas. Minn. state coun. 1997—2000, pres. Greater Twin Cities chpt. 2001—02, state coun. rep. 2001—03, sec.-treas. Minn. state coun. 2004—07, dir./state coun. liaison Greater Twin Cities chpt., Nurse Competency in Aging award 2005, Deanna Earle award Greater Twin Cities chpt.).

SOMIDE, ADEGBOYEGA ADESINA, financial analyst, state official, educator, writer; arrived in US, 1983; s. Benjamin Emmanuel I. Somide and Esther Akinreti; m. Karen O. Gilpin, Sept. 27, 2003; children: Walton Benjamin children: Joanne O., Jessica T., Denise F. BA, Berea Coll., Ky., 1986; MA, Ea. Ky. U., Richmond, 1987; PhD, U. at Albany SUNY, 2006. Cert. secondary tchr. NY State Edn. Dept., 1992. Tchr. NYC Pub. Schools, 1990—96; rschr. and tchr. U. at Albany SUNY, 1996—2006; sr. fin. and legis. analyst NY State Senate, 2001—; pres., founder Bridge Edn. and Tech. Inst. Contbr. chapters to books, articles to profl. jours. Sunday sch. tchr. First United Meth. Ch., Delmar, NY, 2004—05. Recipient C. Louis Smith award, Berea Coll., 1986; grantee, U. at Albany SUNY, 1998, 1999, 2000, Democracy and Diversity Inst. New Sch. U., 2000. Mem.: Am. Polit. Sci. Assn., Internat. Polit. Sci. Assn., African Studies Assn., Internat. Honor Soc. Social Sci. Avocations: reading, travel, running, international politics. Personal E-mail: somide@yahoo.com.

SOMMA, THOMAS P., art historian, museum director; b. Somerville, NJ, Sept. 8, 1949; s. Thomas P. and Anne Somma; m. Marie A. Dacchille, Dec. 2, 1983. MA, Rutgers U., 1983; BS, Marietta Coll., Ohio, 1972; PhD, U. Del., 1990. Mus. dir. U. Mary Washington, Fredericksburg, Va., 1998—; adj. prof. Georgetown U., Washington, 2001—; asst. prof., mus. dir. Ithaca Coll., 1991—98, instr. semester Washington program, 2001—. Co-project dir. NEH landmarks of Am. History Summer Workshops, Washington, 2004—. Author: (book) The Apotheosis of Democracy (U. of Del. Am. Manuscript Competition Winner, 1992); co-author: The Library of Congress: The Art and Architecture of the Thomas Jefferson Building, Perspectives on American Sculpture before 1925, 2003; co-editor, contbr.: book American Pantheon; contbr. jour. Recipient U. S. Capitol Hist. Soc. fellowship, 1987, 1991. Mem.: Am. Assn. of Mus., Coll. Art Assn. Avocations: chess, literature, travel. Home: 11016 Naples Ct Fredericksburg VA 22407 Office: U of Mary Washington Galleries 1301 College Ave Fredericksburg VA 22401-5358 Home Phone: 540-548-2745; Office Phone: 540-654-1013. Office Fax: 540-654-1171. Business E-Mail: tsomma@umw.edu.

SOMMARUGA, CORNELIO, foundation administrator, diplomat; b. Rome, Dec. 29, 1932; s. Carlo and Anna Maria (Valagussa) S.; m. Ornella Marzorati; 6 children. LLD, U. Zurich, Switzerland, 1957; D of Polit. Affairs (hon.), U. Fribourg, Switzerland, 1985; D in Internat. Rels. (hon.), U. Minho, Portugal, 1989; D of Medicine (hon.), U. Bologna, Italy, 1991; D in Law (hon.), U. Nice, Sophia-Antipolis, France, 1992, Seoul Nat. U., 1992; PhD in Law (hon.), Geneva U., 1997; LHD (hon.), Webster U., St. Louis, 1998. Various diplomatic positions Swiss Confedn.'s Svc., 1960-73; dep. sec. gen. European Free Trade Assn., Geneva, 1973-75; minister plenipotentiary Dept. Pub. Economy, Berne, Switzerland, 1976-77, amb. plenipotentiary, 1977-80, del. Swiss Govt. for Trade Agreements, 1980-83, state sec. external econ. affairs, 1984-86; pres. Internat. Com. Red Cross, Geneva, 1987-99, Assn. Initiatives of Change Internat., Caux, Switzerland, 2002—06. Pres. Geneva Internat. Ctr. for Humanitarian Demining, 2000—. Chmn. bd. Karl Popper Found., Zug, 2000—07; bd. dirs. Found. for Future, 2006—; pres. bd. Found. Internat. Union Against Cancer, Geneva, 2006—. Recipient Presdl. award Tel-Aviv U., 1995, North-South prize Coun. of Europe, 2001, Dr. Jean Mayer Global Citizenship award Tufts U., 2003. Home: 16 chemin Crets-de-Champel CF-1206 Geneva Switzerland Office: GICHD BP 1300 CH-1211 Geneva Switzerland Office Phone: 41 22 906 16 97. Business E-Mail: c.sommaruga@gichd.org.

SOMMER, ALFRED, ophthalmologist, medical educator, researcher; b. NYC, Oct. 2, 1942; s. Joseph and Natalie Sommer; m. Jill Abramson Sommer, Sept. 1, 1963; children: Charles Andrew, Marni Jane. BS summa cum laude, Union Coll., 1963; MD, Harvard U., 1967; MHS in Epidemiology, Johns Hopkins U., 1973. Diplomate Am. Bd. Ophthalmology, Nat. Bd. Med. Examiners. Tchg. fellow in medicine Harvard U. Med. Sch., Boston, 1968—69; dir. Nutritional Blindness Prevention Rsch. Program, Bandung, Indonesia, 1976—79; vis. fellow Inst. Ophthalmology U. London, 1979—80; founding dir., Dana Ctr. for Preventive Ophthalmology Johns Hopkins Med. Insts., Balt., 1980—90; assoc. prof. Johns Hopkins U., Balt., 1981—85, prof. ophthalmology, epidemiology and internat. health, 1985—, dean Johns Hopkins Sch. Hygiene and Pub. Health, 1990—2005, dean emeritus, 2005—. Vis. prof. ophthalmology U. Padjadjaran, Indonesia, 1976—79; cons., advisor Helen Keller Internat., NYC, 1973—; cons., chmn. com. NIH, Bethesda, Md., 1981—; bd. dirs. Internat. Agy. for the Prevention of Blindness, Geneva; cons., com. mem. NAS, Washington, 1989; chmn. program adv. group on blindness prevention WHO, Geneva, 1989—90, com. mem., 1978—90, expert com., 1990—; chmn. steering com. Internat. Vitamin A Cons. Group Micronutrient Forum, Washington, 1975—; pres. Internat. Fedn. of Tissue Banks; chmn. sci. adv. bd. Edna McConnell Clark Found.; mem. Internat. Coun. Ophthalmology; dir.

Becton Dickenson Corp., 1998—, T. Rowe Price Group, 2003—, Internat. Trachoma Initiative Found. of NIH, 2004—, Lasker Found., 2004—; chair expect cmty. health global governance initiative World Econ. Forum; lectr. in field. Author: Epidemiology and Statistics for the Ophthalmologist, 1980, Nutritional Blindness: Xerophthalmia and Keratomalacia, 1982, Vitamin A Deficiency: Health, Survival and Vision, 1995, Detection and Control of Vitamin A Deficiency and Xerophthalmia, 1978, 1982, 1995; chmn. bd. overseers Am. Jours. Epidemiology and Epidemiologic Revs., 1990—2005, also bd. dirs., —; contbr. articles to profl. jours. Recipient Charles A. Dana Found. award for Pioneering Achievement in Health, 1988, Disting. Svc. award for Contbn. to Vision Care, APHA, 1988, E.V. McCollum Internat. Lectureship in Nutrition, Am. Inst. Nutrition, 1988, Second Ann. Am. Coll. Advancement in Medicine Achievement award in Preventative Medicine, 1990, Disting. Contbn. to World Ophthalmology award, Internat. Fedn. Ophthal. Socs., 1990, Smadel award, Infectious Diseases Soc. Am., 1990, Doyne Meml. medal, Oxford, 1995, Albert Lasker award Clin. Rsch., 1997, Helmut Horten Rsch. award, 1997, Gold medal, Singapore Ophthalmology Soc., 1997, Duke Elder Gold medal, Internat. Coun. Ophthalmology, 1998, Prince Mahidol award for contbns. to pub. health, 1998, Bristol-Meyers Nutrition Rsch. award, 2001, Danone Internat. award in nutrition rsch., 2001, Warren Alpert Found. prize, Harvard Med. Sch., 2003, Howe medal, Am. Opthal. Soc., 2003, Pollin prize, Columbia U., 2004, Helen Keller Rsch. Found prize, 2006, Gonin medal, Internat. Coun. Oph., 2007. Mem.: IOM, NAS, Inst. Medicine, Internat. Coun. Ophthalmology, Chgo. Ophthal. Soc., Assn. Schs. of Pub. Health (pres.), Internat. Assn. to Prevent Blindness (bd. dirs. 1978—2005), Nat. Soc. to Prevent Blindness (bd. dirs. 1984—94), Am. Acad. Ophthalmology (chmn. pub. health com. 1982—88, chmn. Quality of Care/Clin. Guidelines 1986—90). Achievements include first to detail and publish epidemiologic approach disaster assessment; nutritional indices predict subsequent mortality in children, surveillance and containment is effective intervention strategy for controlling smallpox; vitamin A deficiency increases childhood mortality and vitamin A supplementation decreases childhood mortality; nerve fiber layer is valuable diagnostic and prognostic sign of early glaucoma; routine preventive services cost-effective in eye disease; clinical guideline development and importance of outcome assessment; research in epidemiologic and public health approaches to ophthalmology, blindness prevention, and improved health and survival. Office: Johns Hopkins U Bloomburg Sch Pub Health 615 N Wolfe St Rm 1041 Baltimore MD 21205-2103 Office Phone: 410-502-4169. Office Fax: 410-502-4167. Business E-Mail: asommer@jhsph.edu.

SOMMER, JAMES KOCH, lawyer; b. Crawfordsville, Ind., June 5, 1932; s. Edwin John and Sophia Kurth (Koch) Sommer; m. Michael Jean Stewart, Feb. 23, 1963; children: John Stewart, Whitney Suzanne. BA, Yale U., 1954; LLB, Harvard U., 1959. Bar: Ind. 1959, U.S. Supreme Ct. 1970. Assoc. Barnes, Hickam, Pantzer & Boyd, Indpls., 1959—62; founding ptnr. and dir. Sommer Barnard (and certain predecessor firms), Indpls., 1962—2003, of counsel, 2003—. Chmn. Indpls. Regulatory Study Commn., 1992—93. Fellow: Indpls. Bar Found. (Disting.); mem.: ABA, Bar Assn. Seventh Fed. Ct., Ind. Bar Assn. Home: 105 Curacao Ln Bonita Springs FL 34134 Office: Sommer Barnard One Indiana Sq Ste 3500 Indianapolis IN 46240 Home Phone: 317-594-9338; Office Phone: 317-713-3500. Business E-Mail: jsommer@sommerbarnard.com.

SOMMER, JAY, writer, literature and language educator; b. Germany, 1927; arrived in US, 1948; m. Shirley Sommer; 1 child. BA, Bklyn. Coll.; MA in Spanish Lang., Lit., Hunter Coll.; MA in Russian, Fordham Univ.; PhD in Comparative Lit., NYU; LHD (hon.), Fontbonne Coll., St. Louis, 2001. Fgn. lang. tchr. New Rochell H.S., NY; ret. Adj. prof., modern lang. Fairfield Univ.; comn. mem. Nat. Comn. on Excellence in Edn., 1983. Author: Journey to the Golden Door. Named Nat. Tchr. of Yr., 1981. Fluent in 10 languages; Holocaust survivor. Mailing: 11 Lakeside Dr New Rochelle NY 10801 *

SOMMER, JEFF, journalist; BA in History with distinction, Cornell U., 1974; MS in Journalism, Columbia U., 1977; MS in Regional Studies-East Asia, Harvard U., 1978. Local reporter The Albany (NY) Knickerbocker News, 1977-79, The Record, Bergen County, NJ, 1979-81, Newsday, 1981-82, Asia bur. chief Beijing, 1983-86, chief corr. Soviet & East European affairs Moscow, 1986-89, fgn. editor, 1989; now sect. editor, Sunday Bus. NY Times. Recipient Hal Boyle award Overseas Press Club, 1985, Knight-Bagehot Fellow Columbia Univ., 2001; edited Pulitzer prize-winning coverage in internat. news, 1992, 93. Office: Sunday Business NY Times 229 W 43rd St New York NY 10036

SOMMER, KENNETH, finance company executive; BA in acctg., Mich. State Univ., 1980. V.p., CFO global ops. & tech. div. Citigroup Inc., CFO, corp. & investment bank, Latin Am.; exec. v.p., chief adminstrv. officer Visa Internat., Foster City, Calif., 2000—06, CEO, 2006—. Mailing: Visa Internat PO Box 8999 San Francisco CA 94128-8999 Office: Visa Internat 900 Metro Ctr Blvd Foster City CA 94404 *

SOMMER, MIRIAM GOLDSTEIN (MIMI G. SOMMER), writer, photographer; b. Springfield, Mass., May 2, 1929; d. Nathan E. and Anna (Ginsberg) Goldstein; children: Babette, Anne. BA, Wells Coll., 1950; rsch. cert., London Sch. Econs., 1953; MS in Art History, So. Conn. State U., 1977. Music dept. adminstr. Yale U., 1963-83; free-lance travel writer, photographer New Haven, 1984—. Mem. Creative Arts Workshop, New Haven, 1960—; mem. New Haven Arts Coun., 1970—, Met. Mus. Art/Yale U. Art Galleries; guest lectr. Journalism dept., So. Conn. State U., 1989-05; mem. Alumna Experiment Internat. Living-World Learning, Bratlelboro, Vt. Contbr. articles to profl. mags. including Colonial Homes mag., Family Fun mag., Touring Am. mag., Coastal Living mag., Conn. mag., Travel Agent mag., Jax Fax Travel Mktg. mag.; also newspapers including NY Times, LA Times, New Haven Register, Hartford Courant, Vineyard Gazette, Norwalk Hour. V.p. Decade Alumni Coun., Williston Northampton Sch., Easthampton, Mass., 1989, co-founder, panelist career day; bd. mem., co-dir. Assn. Handicapped Artists, New Haven, 1989; co-founder Creative Arts Workshop course handicapped artists; commr. and vice-chmn. Cultural Affairs Commn. City of New Haven. Mem. Soc. Profl. Journalists (Excellence in Journalism First Prize Winner 1991 for best mag. spl. supplement feature "Designing Woman, Conn. Mag.), Am. Soc. Journalists and Authors, Soc. Profl. Journalists (Excellence in Journalism, 2002, 1st Pl. and 2nd Pl. Mag. Featured Photo awards competition), Rockport Art Assn. Avocations: pottery, movies, theater, museum. Home: 603 Prospect St New Haven CT 06511-2146 E-mail: miriam.sommer@yale.edu.

SOMMERER, JOHN, accountant, former mayor; b. Mt. Holly, NJ, Oct. 30, 1947; s. John Price and Barbara Elizabeth (Davis) S.; m. Diane Catherine Kuszaj, Aug. 5, 1967; children: James Peter, John Joseph, Paul Andrew, Matthew Thomas. BS, U. Hartford, 1969; MBA, U. Toronto, 1972; postgrad., Columbia U., 1972-74. CPA, Fla., N.J., N.Y. Sr. cons. Deloitte and Touche, NYC, 1974-78; dir. mgmt. info. systems Pantry Pride Enterprises, Ft. Lauderdale, Fla., 1978-82; mng. ptnr. John Sommerer and Co., P.A., Coral Springs, Fla., 1982—; mayor City of Coral Springs, 1994—2004. Treas. Coral Springs Cmty. Chest, 1988-94. Mem. Coral Springs Kiwanis (bd. dirs. 1990, 92, treas. 2004-), Coral Springs C. of C. (pres. 1987, treas. 1986, bd. dirs. 1986-88). Roman Catholic. Home: 9501 NW 44th Pl Coral Springs FL 33065-6602 Office: John Sommerer and Co PA 3300 N University Dr Coral Springs FL 33065-6309 E-mail: cpa@accountant.com.

SOMMERFELD, DAVID WILLIAM, lawyer, educator; b. Detroit, Jan. 21, 1942; s. Henry Anthony and Hilda (Diffley) S.; m. Anne Marlaine Toth, June 27, 1964; children: Catherine, David Jr., Michael, Caroline. BS, U. Detroit, 1963; JD, Detroit Coll., 1967. Trust officer Nat. Bank Detroit, 1963-68; tax supr. Ernst & Ernst, Detroit, 1968-73; ptnr. Monaghan, Campbell, LoPrete & McDonald, Detroit, 1973-77; prof. Detroit Coll., 1977-86; ptnr. Butzel Long, Detroit, 1987—. Lectr. Ind. Soc. CPAs, Indpls., 1980-93, Ohio Soc. CPAs, Columbus, 1987, W.Va. Soc. CPAs, Charleston, 1983-86, 91. Editor Mich. Probate and Trust Law Jour., 1981-83. Fellow Am. Coll. of Trust and Estate Counsel; mem. Mich. Bar Assn., Detroit Bar Assn., Am. Inst. CPA's, Mich. Assn. CPA's, Forest Lake Country Club, Detroit Athletic Club. Roman Catholic. Avocations: bowling, spectator sports, gardening. Office: Butzel Long 41000 Woodward Ave Stoneridge W Bloomfield Hills MI 48304 Business E-Mail: sommerfeld@butzel.com.

SOMMERFELDT, JOHN ROBERT, historian, educator; b. Detroit, Feb. 4, 1933; s. Melvin John and Virginia Zita (Gruenheck) S.; m. Patricia Natalie Levinske, Aug. 25, 1956; children: Ann, James, John, Elizabeth. AB, U. Mich., 1954, AM, 1956, PhD, 1960. Instr. history Stanford U., 1958-59; from instr. to prof. Western Mich. U., 1959-78; prof. history U. Dallas, 1978—, chmn. dept. history, 1984-87, univ. pres., 1978-80. Dir. Medieval Inst., Western Mich. U., 1961-76; exec. dir. Inst. Cistercian Studies, 1973-78; dir. Center Contemplative Studies, 1976-78; pres. Cistercian Publs., 1973-79, chmn. bd., 1976-79. Author: The Spiritual Teachings of Bernard of Clairvaux, 1991, Bernard of Clairvaux On the Life of the Mind, 2004, Bernard of Clairvaux On the Spiritualty of Relationship, 2004, Aelred of Rievaulx: Pursuing Perfect Happiness, 2005, Aelred of Rievaulx On Love and Order in the World and in the Chuch, 2006; editor: Studies in Medieval Culture, 12 vols., 1964-78, Studies in Medieval Cistercian History, II, 1977, Cistercian Ideals and Reality, 1978, Simplicity and Ordinariness, 1980, The Chimaera of His Age: Studies in Bernard of Clairvaux, 1980, Abba: Guides to Wholeness and Holiness, East and West, 1981, Erudition at God's Service, 1987, Bernardus Magister, 1992, Studiosorum Speculum, 1993, Studies in the Theology of St. Thomas Aquinas, 1995. Fulbright scholar, 1954-55; Univ. fellow U. Mich., 1956-57. Mem. Medieval Acad. Am., Am. Hist. Assn., Am. Catholic Hist. Assn., Am. Soc. Ch. History, Phi Beta Kappa, Phi Eta Sigma, Phi Kappa Phi. Republican. Roman Catholic. Home: 2809 Warren Cir Irving TX 75062-8938 Office: U Dallas Dept History Irving TX 75062-4736 Home Phone: 972-255-0608; Office Phone: 972-721-5370. Business E-Mail: jrsommer@udallas.edu.

SOMMERLAD, ROBERT EDWARD, environmental research engineer; b. Jersey City, Aug. 27, 1937; s. Herman Francis and Helen Rita (Joyce) S.; m. Margaret Doreen Breen, Sept. 9, 1961; children: Sharon K., Michael E., Ellen J. BSME, N.J. Inst. Tech., 1960, MSME, 1963, postgrad., 1965. Cert. profl. engr., State of NJ, 1964. Devel. engr., rsch. assoc. Foster Wheeler Energy Corp., Livingston, NJ, 1960-71, head air pollution control sect., 1971-74; v.p. contract ops. Foster Wheeler Devel. Corp., Livingston, 1974-84; pres. Enviresponse Inc., Livingston, 1985-86; dir. bus. devel. Energy and Environ. Rsch. Corp., Edison, NJ, 1987-88; cons., 1988-89; dir. environ. bus. devel. Midwest Rsch. Inst., Falls Church, Va., 1989-90; mgr. combustion tech. Rsch.-Cottrell Cos., 1990-92, cons., 1992-93; mktg. dir. PSI Powerserve, Andover, Mass., 1993-94, cons., program mgr., 1994-95; cons. Gas Rsch. Inst., Chgo., 1995-98, GE Energy and Environ. Rsch. Corp., Gurnee, Ill., 1998—2003; pvt. cons., 2003—; cons. Coll. Lake County, Grays Lake, Ill., 2004—; strategic acct. mgr. Loesche Energy Systems Ltd., 2005—. Mem. coal combustion and applications working group U.S. Dept. Energy U. San Diego, 1981-84. Patentee in field. V.p. Cranford (N.J.) Cmty. Pools Parents Assn., 1975-77, 86-87, pres., 1977-79, 84-89; chmn. N.J. Swimming and Diving Conf., Cranford, 1986-89; v.p. Stonebrook Crossings Homeowners Assn., Gurnee, 1998-2000, pres., 2000—; com. for family aquatic ctr. Gurnee Park Dist., 1996 2002; mem. dept. pub. works com. Village of Gurnee, 2002—; mem. St. Paul the Apostle Choir, 2000-, Parish Pastoral Coun., 2003-. Recipient Outstanding Achievement award Westfield YMCA, 1975. Fellow ASME (mem. rsch. com. indsl. and mcpl. waste 1971—, vice chmn. 1972-74, sec. 1987-91, mem. environ. affairs com. 1982-92, mem. dioxin com. 1985-92, mem. bd. performance test codes 1986-97, chmn. boiler-calorimeter com. 1986-89, numerous com. and conf. chairmanships, Cert. Achievement, Bd. on Codes and Standards, 1997); mem. Air and Waste Mgmt. Assn. (mem. AE-1 com. on particulate and associated acid gases, sec. 1991-94, vice chair 1996), Watchung Amateur Ski Club (mem. exec. bd. 1986-87); diplomate Am. Acad. Environ. Engr. (bd. trustees 2003-). Roman Catholic. Home: 1368 Knottingham Dr Gurnee IL 60031-5632 Office Phone: 847-856-1390.

SOMMERS, GEORGE R., lawyer; b. NYC, Jan. 27, 1955; BA, U. So. Fla., 1975; JD, NYU, 1987. Bar: NJ 1987, US Dist. Ct. NJ 1987, NY 1988, US Dist. Ct. (all dists.) NY 1988, US Ct. Appeals (3d cir.) 1988, US Ct. Appeals (2d cir.) 1989, US Supreme Ct. 1992. Assoc. Sullivan & Cromwell, NYC, 1987-90; pvt. practice lawyer NYC, 1990—. Pres. Bill of Rights Found., NYC, 1994—. Seidler scholar NYU Sch. Law, NYC, 1985. Mem. Hoboken Bar Assn. (pres. 1994). Jewish. Avocations: boxing, chess. Office: 51 Newark St Hoboken NJ 07030-4548 Home Phone: 201-344-3338; Office Phone: 212-709-8389, 201-656-6575.

SOMMERS, JILL E., commissioner; b. Fort Scott, Kans. m. Mike Sommers; 3 children. BA, U. of Kans. Intern Senator Robert J. Dole, Washington DC, 1991—95; legis. aide Clark & Muldoon, P.C., Taggard and Associates; regulatory and legis. affairs Chgo. Mercantile Exch.; policy dir., head of govt. affairs Internat. Swaps and Derivatives Assn., 2005—07; commr. Commodity Futures Trading Commn., 2007—. Office: Commodity Futures Trading Commn Three Lafayette Ctr Washington DC 20581 Office Phone: 202-418-5000. Office Fax: 202-418-5514. E-mail: questions@cftc.gov. *

SOMMERS, MARK, lawyer; b. Chgo., Mar. 29, 1956; BA, Ohio Wesleyan U., 1978; JD, U. Northern Ill., 1982; LLM, U. London, Eng., 1983. Bar: Ill. 1982, NY 1985, Mass. 1985, DC 1989. Ptnr. Finnegan, Henderson, Farabow, Garrett & Dunner LLP, Washington, leader, Trademark & Copyright Sect. Named top 5 trademark attys. in US, Mng. Intellectual Property, top 10 trademark attys. in world. Office: Finnegan Henderson Farabow Garrett & Dunner LLP 901 New York Ave NW Washington DC 20001-3315 Office Phone: 202-408-4000. Office Fax: 202-408-4400. Business E-Mail: mark.sommers@finnegan.com.

SOMMERS, STEPHEN, film director, producer, scriptwriter; b. Indpls. Motion picture dir., writer, prodr. Writer, dir. Catch Me If You Can, 1989, The Adventures of Huck and Finn, 1993, The Jungle Book, 1994, Deep Rising, 1998, The Mummy, 1999; The Mummy Returns, 2001; writer, prodr. Tom and Huck, 1995, The Scorpion King, 2002; writer, prodr., dir., Van Helsing, 2004; prodr. T.V. movie Oliver Twist, 1997; dir. Terror Eyes, 1989; writer Gunmen, 1994. Office: c/o Jim Wiatt William Morris Agy 151 El Camino Dr Beverly Hills CA 90212

SOMMERS, WILLIAM PAUL, management consultant, research and development company executive; b. Detroit, July 22, 1933; s. William August and Mary Elizabeth (Baietto) S.; m. Josephine A. Sommers; children: William F., Clare M., John C. Hughes, Joanna M. Weems, Russell L. Hughes. BSE (scholar), U. Mich., 1955, MSE, 1956, PhD (Riggs fellow, Texaco fellow, Univ. fellow), 1961. Rsch. assoc. U. Mich. Inst. Sci. and Tech., Ann Arbor, 1958-61; chief chem. propulsion space and missile sys. Martin Marietta Corp., Balt., 1956-58, 61-63; v.p. Booz, Allen & Hamilton, Inc., Bethesda, Md., 1963-70, pres. Tech. Mgmt. Group, 1973-79, sr. v.p., 1979-92; exec. v.p. Iameter, Inc., San Mateo, Calif., 1992-94; pres., CEO SRI Internat., Menlo Park, Calif., 1994-98, ret., 1998. Bd. dirs. Gukenheimer Enterprises, H2 Gen. Contbr. articles to profl. jours., also chpt. in book. Pres. Washington chpt. U. Mich. Alumni Club, 1970-71; v.p. Wildwood manor Citizens Assn., 1968-70; chief Adventure Guide program YMCA, 1971-72; bd. visitors Coll. Engring. U. Calif., Davis; mem. nat. adv. bd. Coll. Engring. U. Mich.; mem. conf. bd. Internat. Coun. on Innovation and Tech. Mem.: Wianno Country Club, Nianno Club, Ponte Vedra Lodge and Club, Hyannis Yacht Club, Met. Club (D.C.), Marsh Landing Country Club, Wianno Yacht Club, Ponte Vedra Inn and Club, Pi Tau Sigma, Tau Beta Pi, Sigma Xi. Republican. Roman Catholic. Home (Summer): 49 Warren St Osterville MA 02655 Office Phone: 904-543-1425. Personal E-mail: williamp.sommers@comcast.net.

SOMMESE, ANDREW JOHN, mathematics professor; b. NYC, May 1948; s. Joseph and Frances S.; m. Rebecca Rooze DeBoer, June 7, 1971; children: Rachel, Ruth. BA in Math., Fordham U., 1969; PhD in Math., Princeton U., 1973. Gibbs instr. Yale U., New Haven, 1973-75; asst. prof. Cornell U., Ithaca, NY, 1975-79; assoc. prof. U. Notre Dame, Ind., 1979-83, prof. of math. Ind., 1983—, chair dept. math. Ind., 1988-92, Vincent J. Duncan and Annamarie Micus Duncan chair math. Ind., 1994—, dir. Ctr. Applied Math. Ind., 2005—. Mem. Inst. for Advanced Study, Princeton, N.J., 1975-76; guest prof. U. Bonn, Germany, 1978-79; guest rschr. Max Planck Inst. for Math., Bonn, 1992-93; cons. GM Rsch., Warren, Mich., 1986-97. Editor: Manuscripta Mathematica jour., 1986-93, Advances in Geometry, 2000;mem. editl. bd. Milan Jour. Math., 2002; contbr. articles to profl. publs. Recipient Rsch. award for Sr. U.S. Scientists, Alexander Von Humboldt Found., 1993; A.P. Sloan Found. rsch. fellow, 1979. Mem. Am. Math. Soc., Soc. for Indsl. and Applied Math., Phi Beta Kappa. Office: U Notre Dame Dept Math Notre Dame IN 46556

SOMORJAI, GABOR ARPAD, chemist, educator; b. Budapest, Hungary, May 4, 1935; came to US, 1957, naturalized, 1962. s. Charles and Livia (Ormos) S.; m. Judith Kaldor, Sept. 2, 1957; children: Nicole, John. BS, U. Tech. Scis., Budapest, 1956; PhD, U. Calif., Berkeley, 1960; Dr. Honoris Causa (hon.), Tech. U., Budapest, 1989, U. Pierre et Marie Curie, Paris, 1990, U. Libre Brussels, 1992, U. degli de Ferrara, Italy, 1998, Jozsef Attila U., Szeged, Hungary, 1999, Royal Inst. Tech., Stockholm, 2000; D (hon.), U. Manchester, Eng., 2001. Mem. rsch. staff IBM, Yorktown Heights, NY, 1960-64; dir. Surface Sci. and Catalysis Prog. Lawrence Berkeley Lab., Calif., 1964—; mem. faculty dept. chemistry U. Calif., Berkeley, 1964—, assoc. prof., 1967-72, prof., 1972—, Miller prof., 1978, univ. prof., 2002. Unilever prof. dept. chemistry U. Bristol, Eng., 1972; vis. fellow Emmanuel Coll., Cambridge, Eng., 1989; Baker lectr. Cornell U., Ithaca, NY, 1977; edit. bd. mem. Catalysis Reviews J. Am. Chem. Soc., 2004—; hon. fellow Cardiff U., 2006. Author: Principles of Surface Chemistry, 1972, Chemistry in Two Dimensions, 1981, Introduction to Surface Chemistry and Catalysis, 1994; editor-in-chief Catalysis Letters, 1988—; contbr. articles to profl. jours. Recipient Emmett award Am. Catalysis Soc., 1977, Kokes award Johns Hopkins U., 1976, Albert award Precious Metal Inst., 1986, Sr. Disting. Scientist award Alexander von Humboldt Found., 1989, E.W. Mueller award U. Wis., Chem. Pioneer award Am. Inst. Chemists, 1995, Von Hippel award Materials Rsch. Soc., 1997, Wolf prize in chemistry, Wolf Found., Israel, 1998; Guggenheim fellow, 1969; hon. fellow Cardiff U., 2006. Fellow: AAAS, Am. Phys. Soc. (Langmuir award 2007); mem.: NAS (Irving Langmuir prize in Chem. Physics 2007), Catalysis Soc. N.Am., Am. Chem. Soc. (chmn. colloid and surface chemistry 1981, Surface and Colloid Chemistry award 1981, Peter Debye award 1989, Arthur W. Adamson award 1994, Award for creative rsch. in homogeneous and heterogeneous catalysis 2000, Cotton medal 2002, Remsen award 2006), Hungarian Acad. Scis. (hon. Pauling medal 2000, Nat. Medal of Sci. 2001), Am. Acad. Arts and Scis. Home: 665 San Luis Rd Berkeley CA 94707-1725 Office: U Calif Dept Chemistry D 58 Hildebrand Hl Berkeley CA 94720-0001 E-mail: somorjai@socrates.berkeley.edu. *

SOMSEN, HENRY NORTHROP, retired lawyer; b. New Ulm, Minn., Aug. 12, 1909; s. Henry N. and Meta (Koch) Somsen; m. Anne Elizabeth Duncan, Sept. 12, 1936 (dec.); children: Pennell Anne, Stephen Duncan. BA, U. Minn., 1932, JD, 1934. Bar: Minn. 1934. Pvt. practice law, New Ulm, 1934—85; ptnr. Somsen, Dempsey, Johnson & Somsen, 1934—40, Somen Dempsey & Somsen, 1940—46, Somsen & Somsen, 1946—55; sole practice, 1955—64; ptnr. Somsen & Dempsey, 1965—71, Somsen Dempsey & Schade, 1971—85, of counsel, 1985—. Bd. editors U. Minn. Law Rev., 1932—33. Trustee Minn. State Pks. Found., 1967—77; bd. dirs. Minn. Coun. State Pks., 1956—, pres., 1974—75; bd. dirs., pres. New Ulm Cmty. Concert Assn., 1947—85; bd. dirs. Union Hosp., New Ulm, 1959—77, Highland Homes, Inc., 1970—79, New Ulm Meml. Found., 1958—79, New Ulm Industires Inc., 1952—85, pres., 1968—77; bd. dirs. New Ulm Industires Inc. Found., 1953—85, pres., 1953—83, chmn., 1958—83, Farmers and Mchts. Bank, New Ulm; mem. City Charter Commns., 1940, 1950, 1966, pres., 1966; bd. dirs. Klossner State Bank, Minn., 1947—84, State Bond and Mortgage Co., 1950—80, Am. Arstoone Co., 1955—84, others. Served to capt. JAG US Army, 1943—46. Mem.: ABA, Am. Arbitration Assn. (panel arbitrators 1967, 1985), Am. Judicature Soc., Minn. Bar Assn., Shriners, Masons, Phi Delta Phi, Psi Upsilon. Episcopalian. Home: 211 2d St NW 3-328 Rochester MN 55901-3101

SON, SEUNG HWAN, mathematician, researcher; b. Seoul, Republic of Korea, 1963; s. Kye D. Son. PhD, Univ. Ill., Urbana-Champaign, 1998. Software engr. Lucent Technologies, Boston, 2000—01; asst. prof. Kans. Wesleyan U., Salina, 2001—02, U. Colo., Colo. Springs, 2002—. Mem.: Am. Math. Soc. Achievements include research in Ramanujan's work. Office: Univ Colo 1420 Austin Bluffs Pkwy Colorado Springs CO 80933-7150 Office Phone: 719-262-3515. Office Fax: 719-262-3605. Business E-Mail: sson@uccs.edu.

SON, YOUNG-JIN, medical educator; m. Yoo-Kum Jang Son; children: Jeanie, Annie. PhD, U. Tex., Austin, 1994. Asst. prof. coll. medicine Drexel U., Phila., 2000—. Home: 101 Orchard Ct Blue Bell PA 19422 Office: Drexel Univ Coll Medicine 2900 Queen Ln Philadelphia PA 19129 Home Phone: 215-991-9-8274; Office Phone: 215-991-8471.

SONDAK, ARTHUR, retired management consultant; b. NYC, Oct. 16, 1929; s. Louis and Eva (Dolin) S.; m. Sylvia Mayran, Jan. 17, 1953 (div. 1975); children: Janet, Steven, Donald; m. Susan Altman, Oct. 17, 1999. BBA, Baruch Coll., 1950, MBA, 1958. Employment mgr. Saks Fifth Ave, NYC, 1954-57; wage and salary adminstr. Royal Typewriter Co., NYC, 1957-61; employment mgr. Sperry Rand Corp., NYC, 1961-62; compensation dir., region personnel mgr. Royal Typewriter Co., NYC, 1962-66; mgr. personnel program planning MAI, NYC, 1966-69; personnel dir. ITEL Corp., White Plains, NY, 1969-73; dir. personnel and adminstrn. MAI, NYC, 1973-75; instr. Baruch Coll. Grad. Sch., NYC, 1969-70; prin. Personnel Mgmt. Svcs., Delray Beach, Fla., 1975-99. Editorial adv. bd. AMACOM, N.Y.C., 1986-96; contbr. articles to profl. jours. Adv. bd. Cmty./Advancement Resource Ctr., Middlesex Coll., Edison, 1985-90; career guidance counselor USAF, 1950-54. Avocations: photography, nostalgia, sports, golf. Home: 6320 Crystal View Ln Boynton Beach FL 33437-4041

SONDE, THEODORE IRWIN, lawyer; b. NYC, Jan. 7, 1940; s. Martin and Anne (Greenbaum) S.; m. Susan Kolisch, Sept. 10, 1964; children: Andrea Martine, David Ian. BA, CCNY, 1961; LLB, NYU, 1964; LLM, Georgetown U., 1967. Bar: N.Y. 1964, D.C. 1978, U.S. Supreme Ct. With SEC, Washington, 1964-80, asst. gen. counsel Office Gen. Counsel, 1970-74, assoc. dir. divsn. enforcement, 1974-80; dir. Office Enforcement, FERC, Washington, 1980-81; mem. firm Cole, Corette & Abrutyn, 1982—90, Dechert, Price & Rhodes, 1990—2002, Crowell & Moring, Washington, 2002—04, Hogan & Hartson, Washington, 2005—. Adj. prof.

Georgetown U. Law Sch. 1977-95, George Washington U. Nat. Law Ctr., 1976-82. Contbr. articles to law jours. Office: Hogan & Hartson 555 13th St NW Washington DC 20004 Office Phone: 202-637-3569. Business E-Mail: tsonde@hhlaw.com.

SONDEL, PAUL MARK, pediatric oncologist, educator; b. Milw., Aug. 14, 1950; s. Robert F. and Audrey J. (Dworkus) S.; m. Sherie Ann Katz, Jan. 1, 1973; children: Jesse Adam, Beth Leah, Elana Rose, Jodi Zipporah. BS with honors, U. Wis., Madison, 1971, PhD in Genetics, 1975; MD magna cum laude, Harvard Med. Sch., Boston, 1977. Diplomate Nat. Bd. Med. Examiners, Am. Bd. Pediatrics; lic. physician, Wis. Postdoctoral rsch. fellow Harvard Med. Sch., Boston, 1975-77; intern in pediatrics U. Minn. Hosp., Mpls., 1977-78; resident in pediatris U. Wis. Hosp. and Clinics, Madison, 1978-80; asst. prof. pediatrics, human oncology and genetics U. Wis., Madison, 1980-84, assoc. prof., 1984-86, prof. pediatrics, human oncology and genetics, 1987—, head divsn. pediatric hematology/oncology, program leader, 1990—; assoc. dir. U Wisc. Cancer Ctr., 1996-99, U. Wis. Cancer Ctr., 2006—; vice chair rsch. dept. pediatrics U. Wis., Madison, 2006—. Sub-fellow pediat. oncology; Midwest Children's Cancer Ctr., Milw., 1980; vis. scientist dept. cell biology Weizmann Inst. Sci., Rehovot, Israel, 1987, 2000; chmn. immunology com. Children's Cancer Group 1990-2001; cancer ctr. rev. com. Nat. Cancer Inst., 1997-2000, bd. sci. counselors, 2005— Sr. editor Clin. Cancer Rsch., 1996-99; mem. editl. bd. Jour. Immunology, 1985-87, Jour. Nat. Cancer Inst., 1987—, Jour. Biol. Response Modifiers, 1990—, BLOOD, 1992—, Natural Immunity, 1992—; contbr. articles to Jour. Exptl. Medicine, Jour. Immunology, Cellular Immunology, Immunol. Revs., Med. Pediatric Oncology, Wis. State Med. Jour., Jour. Biol. Response Modifiers, Jour. Pediatrics, Jour. Clin. Oncology, Jour. Clin. Investigation, others State of Wis. Regents scholar, 1968; J.A. and G.L. Hartford Found. fellow, 1981-84. Mem. Am. Assn. Immunologists, Am. Assn. Clin. Histocompatibility Typing, Am. Fedn. Clin. Rsch., Am. Soc. Pediatric Hematology/Oncology, Am. Assn. Cancer Rsch., Am. Soc. Transplant Physicians, Am. Soc. Clin. Oncology, Am. Acad. Pediatrics, Leukemia Soc. Am. (bd. dirs. Wis. chpt. 1987-90 Achievements include patent for Typing Leukocyte Antigens; research on clinical and immunological effects of human recombinant Interleukin-2 and monoclonal antibodies. Home: 1114 Winston Dr Madison WI 53711-3161 Office: U Wis K4/448 Clin Sci Ctr 600 Highland Ave Madison WI 53792-3284 Business E-Mail: pmsondel@humonc.wisc.edu.

SONDERBY, SUSAN PIERSON, federal bankruptcy judge; b. Chgo., May 15, 1947; d. George W. and Shirley L. (Eckstrom) Pierson; m. James A. De Witt, June 14, 1975 (dec. 1978); m. Peter R. Sonderby, Apr. 7, 1990. AA, Joliet Jr. Coll., Joliet, Ill., 1967; BA, U. Ill., 1969; JD, John Marshall Law Sch., 1973. Bar: Ill., 1973; U.S. Dist. Ct. (cen. and so. dists.) Ill., 1978,; U.S. Dist. Ct. (no. dist.) Ill., 1984; U.S. Ct. Appeals (7th Cir.), 1984. Assoc. O'Brien, Garrison, Berard, Kusta, and De Witt, Joliet, Ill., 1973-75, ptnr., 1975-77; asst. atty. gen. consumer protection div., litig. sect. Office of the Atty. Gen., Chgo., 1977-78, asst. atty. gen., chief consumer protection divsn. Springfield, Ill., 1978-83; U.S. trustee (no. dist.) Ill. Chgo., 1983-86; judge U.S. Bankruptcy Ct. (no. dist.) Ill., Chgo., 1986—, chief fed. bankruptcy judge, 1998—2002. Mem. law faculty Fed. Jud. Tng. Ctr., Ill., Practicing Law Inst., Ill., U.S. Dept. Justice, Ill., Nat. Bankruptcy Inst., Ill., Ill. Continuing Edn.; spl. asst. atty. gen., Ill., 1972—78; adj. faculty De Paul U. Coll. Law, Chgo., 1986; past mem. U.S. Trustee adv. com., Ill.; consumer adv. coun. Fed. Res. Bd., Ill.; past sec. of State Fraudulent I.D. com. Dept. of Ins. Task Force on Improper Claims Practices, Ill.; former chair pers. rev. bd., mem. task force race and gender bias, U.S. Dist. Ct.; jud. conf. planning com. 7th Cir. Jud. Conf.; former mem. Civil Justice Reform Act Adv. Com., Adminstrv. Office of the U.S. Cts. Bankruptcy Judges Adv. Group, Ct. Security com., Adminstrv. Office of the U.S. Cts. Budget and Fin. Coun. Contbr. articles to profl. jour. Mem. Fourth Presbyn. Ch., Art Inst. Chgo.; past mem. Westminster Presbyn. Ch., Chgo. Coun. of Fgn. Rels.; past bd. dirs. Land of Lincoln Coun. Girl Scouts U.S.; past mem. individual guarantors com. Goodman Theatre, Chgo.; past chair clubs and orgns. Sangamon County United Way Capital campaign; past bd. dirs., chair house rules com. and legal subcom. Lake Point Tower; past mem. Family Svc. Ctr., Aid to Retarded Citizens, Henson Robinson Zoo. Named Young Career Woman, Bus. and Profl. Women, One of Ten Outstanding Bankruptcy Judges, Turnarounds and Workouts, 2002; named one of 500 Leading Judges in Am., Law Dragon mag., 2006; recipient Spl. Achievement Award, Dept. Justice, 1984, Disting. Svc. Alumni Award, Joliet Jr. Coll., 1987, Disting. Alumni Award, John Marshall Law Sch., 1988, Dir. Award, Exec. Office U.S. Trustee, Leadership Award, Internat. Orgn. Women Exec., Outstanding Svc. to Bench, Am. Bankruptcy Inst., 1990. Master: Abraham Lincoln Marovitz Inn of Ct. (former pres., membership com.); fellow: Am. Coll. Bankruptcy (circuit admissions com.); mem.: ATLA, Comml. Law League Am. (former exec. coun. mem., bankruptcy and insolvency sect., coord. with nat. conf. bankruptcy judges com.), Nat. Conf. Bankruptcy Judges (co-chair ednl. program com. conf. 2001, liaison with bankruptcy rev. commn. com.), Bar Assn. (7th cir.) (former treas., judicial conf. planning com.), Am. Bankruptcy Inst. (bd. dirs. Chgo. chpt.), Fed. Bar Assn., Chgo. Archtl. Found., John Marshall Law Sch. Alumni Assn. (bd. dirs.), Nordic Law Club (past legis. com.), Lawyers Club Chgo. (hon.). Avocations: travel, flying, interior decorating. Office: US Bankruptcy Ct 219 S Dearborn St Ste 638 Chicago IL 60604-1702

SONDHEIM, STEPHEN JOSHUA, composer, librettist, lyricist; b. NYC, Mar. 22, 1930; s. Herbert and Janet (Fox) Sondheim. BA, Williams Coll., 1950. Composer, lyricist. Vis. prof. comtemporary theatre Oxford U., England. Lyricist West Side Story, 1957 (Tony award), Gypsy, 1959, music and lyrics A Funny Thing Happened on the Way to the Forum, 1962, Anyone Can Whistle, 1964, lyricist Do I Hear a Waltz?, 1965, Evening Primrose, 1966, Company, 1970 (Tony award, 1971), Follies, 1971 (Tony award, 1972), A Little Night Music, 1973 (Tony award, 1973), The Frogs, 1974, Pacific Overtures, 1976, Sweeney Todd, 1979 (Tony award, 1979), Merrily We Roll Along, 1981, Sunday in the Park with George, 1984 (Pulitzer prize, 1985), Into the Woods, 1987 (Tony award, 1988), Assassins, 1991, Passion, 1994 (Tony award, 1994), Bounce, 2003, The Frogs, 2004, Chita Rivera: The Dancer's Life, 2005, (incidental music) Girls of Summer, 1956, Invitation to a March, 1961, Twigs, 1971, additional lyrics Candide, 1973, (anthologies) Side by Side by Sondheim, 1976, Marry Me a Little, 1981, You're Gonna Love Tomorrow, 1983, Putting It Together, 1993, (film scores) Stavisky, 1974, Reds, 1981; composer: songs for film Dick Tracy, 1990 (Acad. award); co-author: (films) The Last of Sheila, 1973, Birdcage, 1996, Getting Away with Murder, 1996. Founder Young Playwrights Inc., 1981—. Recipient Creative Arts medal, Brandeis U., 1982, Grammy awards, 1970, 1973, 1975, 1979, 1984, 1988, Kennedy Ctr. Honor for Lifetime Achievement, 1993, Nat. medal of arts, NEA, 1997, Praemium Imperiale, 2000, The Jason Robards award for excellence in theatre, Roundabout Theatre Co., 2005, Golden Plate award, Acad. Achievement, 2005. Mem.: Am. Acad. and Inst. Arts and Letters. *

SONDOCK, RUBY KLESS, retired judge; b. Apr. 26, 1926; d. Herman Lewis and Celia (Juran) Kless; m. Melvin Adolph Sondock, Apr. 22, 1944; children: Marcia Cohen, Sandra Marcus. AA, Cottey Coll., Nevada, Mo., 1944; BS, U. Houston, 1959, LLB, 1961. Bar: Tex. 1961, U.S. Supreme Ct. 1977. Pvt. practice, Houston, 1961-73, 89—; judge Harris County Ct. Domestic Rels. (312th Dist.), 1973-77, 234th Jud. Dist. Ct., Houston, 1977-82, 83-89; justice Tex. Supreme Ct., Austin, 1982; of counsel Weil Gotshal and Manges, 1989-93, Houston Ctr., 1993—. Mem. ABA, Tex. Bar Assn., Houston Bar Assn., Houston Assn. Women Lawyers, Order of Barons, Phi Theta Phi, Kappa Beta Pi, Phi Kappa Phi, Alpha Epsilon Pi. Address: 550 Westcott #220 Houston TX 77007 Office Phone: 713-655-1111. Personal E-mail: sondock@airmail.net.

SONEGO, IAN G., assistant attorney general; b. Louisville, May 27, 1954; s. Angelo and Zella Mae (Causey) S. BA in Polit. Sci. with high honors, U. Louisville, 1976, JD, 1979. Bar: Ky. 1979, U.S. Dist Ct. (ea. dist.) Ky. 1980, U.S. Dist. Ct. (we. dist.) Ky. 1989, U.S. Ct. Appeals (6th cir.) 1989, U.S. Supreme Ct. 1990. Asst. atty. Office Commonwealth's Atty. Pike County, Pikeville, Ky., 1980, sr. asst. atty., 1988-89; assoc. John Paul Runyon Law Firm, Pikeville, 1981-87; asst. atty. gen. Office Atty. Gen., Frankfort, Ky., 1989—. Lectr. criminal law Ky. Bar Assn., Jenny Wiley Park, 1981, Ky. Prosecutors Confs., 1989, 93; mem. Atty. Gen.'s task force child sexual abuse, 1992-94, Nat. Conf. on Domestic Violence, 1996. Contbg. editor Ky. Prosecuter Newsletter, 1991—. Recipient Kesslman award, U. Louisville, 1975, Bd. trustee award, 1979, Outstanding Prosecutor award, Ky. Atty., Award Outstanding Advocacy, Assn. Govt. Attys. in Capital Litigation, 2001. Mem.: Assn. Govt. Attys. in Capital Litig., Ky. Commonwealth's Attys. Assn. (hon.; lectr. 1987, 90, chmn. com. ethics 1984—86, bd. dirs. 1983—85, Spl. award 1987). Office: Office Atty Gen Criminal Appeals Office 1024 Capital Center Dr Frankfort KY 40601-8204 Office Phone: 502-696-5342. E-mail: ian.sonego@ag.ky.gov.

SONEIRA, RAYMOND MARIO, computer company executive, scientist; b. NYC, July 10, 1949; s. Ramon Mario and Amelia (Rodriguez) S.; m. Julia Lobsitz, Feb. 11, 1988; 1 child, Lauren. BA in Physics, Columbia Coll., 1972; PhD in Physics, Princeton U., 1978. Long term mem. Inst. for Advanced Study, Princeton, NJ, 1978-83; prin. investigator, computer sys. rsch. lab. AT&T Bell Labs, Holmdel, NJ, 1983-89; v.p. devel. Cactus Computers, Inc., Rumson, NJ, 1989—99; pres. DisplayMate Techs. Corp., Amherst, NH, 1999—. Cons. engring. and devel. CBS TV Network, N.Y.C., 1967-70. Author: DisplayMate Reference, 1990, DisplayMate Professional Reference, 1992, DisplayMate Multimedia Reference, 1992; contributing editor various computer and video pubs.; contbr. articles to profl. jours. Recipient Best Utility award COMDEX Computer Industry, Atlanta, 1991. Mem. IEEE (sr.), Am. Phys. Soc. (sr.), Soc. Info. Display, Sigma Xi. Achievements include patent in color convergence of color television cameras and monitors; discovery of hierarchial clustering of galaxies and supergalaxies, cosmological and stellar models fro the Hubble Space Telescope, laser range finder using the Parallax Principle; designer of stellar model of the Milky Way galaxy, thermally optimal least-time paths for robots, and mathematical calibration of HPTVs, monitors, projectors and cinemas. Office: DisplayMate Techs Corp PO Box 550 Amherst NH 03031 Office Phone: 603-672-8500. Personal E-mail: whos@soneira.com.

SONETT, JOSHUA ROBERT, medical educator, surgeon; b. 1962; BA cum laude, Duke U., 1984; MD, E. Carolina U., 1988. Cert. Am. Bd. Thoracic Surgeons, Am. Bd. Surgery. Resident gen. surgery U. Mass. Med. Ctr., Worcester, Mass., 1988—93, rsch. fellow cardiothoracic surgery, 1990—91; resident cardiothoracic surgery U. Pitts. Med. Ctr., Pitts., 1993—96; fellow thoracic surgery Sloan-Kettering Meml. Hosp., NYC, 1995—96; asst. prof. surgery U. Md., Balt., 1996—2001, dir. lung transplant program, 1998—2001, co-dir. Photodynamic Therapy Treatment Ctr., 1999—2001, assoc. prof. surgery, 2001, Columbia U., NYC, 2001—; dir. lung transplant program NY Presbyterian Hosp./Columbia U. Med. Ctr., NYC, 2001—, attending surgeon divsn. cardiothoracic surgery, 2001—. Chief thoracic surgery Balt. Veterans Affairs Ctr., Balt., 1996—2001; mem. adv. panel Med. Soc. State of NY Organ Donation. Mem. editl. bd. Jour. Transplantation; contbr. articles to profl. jours. Named one of Best Doctors, NY mag., 2002—04. Mem.: NY Soc. Thoracic Surgery, Am. Coll. Surgeons, Am. Coll. Chest Physicians, Soc. Thoracic Surgeons, So. Thoracic Surg. Assn., Gen. Thoracic Surgery Club, Cardiothoracic Surgery Network. Office: Columbia U 622 W 168th St PH 14 East Rm 104 New York NY 10032 Office Phone: 212-305-8086. Office Fax: 212-342-5382. E-mail: js2106@columbia.edu.

SONFIELD, ROBERT LEON, JR., lawyer; b. Houston, Oct. 28, 1931; s. Robert Leon and Dorothy Harriett (Huber) S.; 1 dau., Sheree. BA, U. Houston, 1956, LLB, JD, 1959; PhD (hon.), U. Eastern Fla., 1962; LLD (hon.), London Inst. Applied Rsch., 1973; cert. fed. taxation, NYU, 1973; cert. securities regulation, Harvard U., 1983. Bar: Tex. 1959, U.S. Supreme Ct. 1959, U.S. Dist. Ct. Tex. 1960, U.S. Tax Ct. 1960, U.S. Ct. Appeals 1960, U.S. Ct. Claims 1974. Mng. dir. Sonfield & Sonfield, Houston, 1959—. Mem. nat. adv. coun. Nat. Fedn. Ind. Bus. Author: Corporate Financing by Sale of Securities to the Public, 1969, Mergers and Acquisitions, 1970, Student Rights, 1971, The Limited Partnership as a Vehicle for Real Estate Investment, 1971, Integration of Partnership Offerings, 1974, The Grantor Trust Rules After The Tax Reform Act of 1986, Incentive Equity Program, Corporate Name Protection Along With Name Registration, A Guide to SEC Corporate Filing, Organizational Professionals' Residual Litigation and Investment Strategy, Comparing California, Delaware and Nevada: Corporate Laws in Light of California Corporations Code Section 2115 and Offering of Unregistered Securities Only to Accredited Investors, Disclosure Policies, Practices and Procedures For Public Companies, Regulation of Franchises, How to Become a Publicly Held Company Via the Registered Distribution of a Percentage of Your Company's Stock to Shareholders, numerous others. Recipient St. John Garwood award, 1957, Frio-Finnegan Outstanding Alumnus award, 1970-71, citation for outstanding contbn. to legal profession, 1971. Mem. Am. Tax Lawyers Assn. (pres.), Lawyers Soc. Houson, Am. Judicature Soc., ABA, Tex. Bar Assn. (dist. com. on admission to state bar, chmn. clients security fund com.), Houston Bar Assn. (com. chmn. coun., tax sect.), Tex. Equal Access to Justice Found., Houston Bar Found., Real Estate Securities and Syndication Inst., Huguenot Soc. of London, Order Stars and Bars, SAR, Sons Confederate Vets., Mil. Order World Wars, Mil. and Hospitaller Order St. Lazarus of Jerusalem, Knightly Assn. St. George the Martyr, Smithsonian Assocs., Houston Heritage Soc., Houston Mus. Fine Arts, Newcomen Soc. N.Am., Phi Delta Phi, Delta Sigma Phi, Met. Club (N.Y.C.), Argyle Club (San Antonio), Houston Club, Houstonian Club. Office: Sonfield & Sonfield 770 S Post Oak Ln Houston TX 77056-6665 Home Phone: 713-850-0918; Office Phone: 713-877-8333. Personal E-mail: robert@sonfield.com.

SONG, DAVID, plastic surgeon, medical educator; b. 1970; MD, UCLA. Cert. Plastic Surgery. Surg. resident Univ. Chgo. Hospitals, plastic surgeon, chief plastic surgeon, 2004—. Spkr. in field; bd. mem. Med. Aid for Children of Latin Am. Contbr. articles to numerous profl. jours. Med. Aid for Children Latin Am. Named one of 40 Under Forty, Crain's Bus. Chgo., 2005. Mem.: Am. Coll. Plastic Surgeons, Am. Coll. Surgeons. Office: Univ Chgo Hosps MC 6035 5841 S Maryland Ave Chicago IL 60637 Office Phone: 773-702-6302. Office Fax: 773-702-1634. E-mail: dsong@surgery.bsd.uchicago.edu. *

SONG, JOHN I., otolaryngologist, surgeon; b. Taegu, Republic Of Korea, Aug. 6, 1965; MD, NYU, NYC, 1991. Diplomate Am. Bd. Otolaryngology, 1998. Clin. asst. prof. U. Pitts. Sch. Medicine, 1997—2000; asst. prof. H. Lee Moffitt Cancer Ctr. and Rsch. Inst., Tampa, Fla., 2000—02; dir. head and neck surgery U. Colo. Sch. Medicine, Denver, 2002—. Fellow: Am. Head and Neck Soc., Am. Assn. Otolaryngology-Head and Neck Surgery. Office: Univ Colo Sch Medicine 4200 E Ninth Ave B-205 Denver CO 80262 Office Phone: 303-315-7988.

SONG, JOSEPH, pathologist, educator; b. Pyong Yang, Korea, May 11, 1927; s. Ha Ju and Hwa Soon (Koh) S.; m. Kumsan Ryu, Apr. 12, 1958; children: Patricia, Michael, Jeff. MD, Seoul U. Sch. Medicine, 1950; MS in Pathology, U. Tenn., Memphis, 1956; MD, U. Ark. Med. Sch., 1965. Diplomate Am. Bd. Pathology. Pathologist in charge State Cancer Detection Survey, Providence, 1956—59; assoc. pathologist Providence Lying-In Hosp., 1958—61; assoc. prof. pathology U. Ark. Med. Ctr., Little Rock, 1961—64; dir. lab. Mercy Hosp., Des Moines, 1965—92, rschr. cancer, 1993—95; clin. prof. pathology Creighton U. Sch. Medicine, Omaha, 1968—95; med. dir. Corning Clin. Labs., Des Moines, 1995—97; ret., 1997. Cons. EPA, Washington, 1975-85; pres. med. staff Mercy Hosp., Des Moines, 1981 Author: (book) The Human Uterus, 1964, Pathology of Sickle Cell Anemia, 1971 (award 1975), Beyond the Horizon, 1995. Elder Winsdor Presbyn. Ch., Des Moines, 1964; com. mem. Aldersgate Meth. Ch., Des Moines, 1995. Major Med. Corps, 1950-52, Korea. Recipient Martin Luther King Med. Achievement award, So. Christian Leadership Conf., Statesmanship award Am. Assn. Med. Adminstrs., Las Vegas, Nev., 1987. Fellow ACP, Coll. Am. Pathologists, Am. Soc. Clin. Pathology, Am. Assn. Cancer Rsch. Methodist. Avocation: classical music. Home: 2345 Park Ave Des Moines IA 50321-1505

SONG, MARK, surgeon, educator; b. Seoul, Republic Of Korea, Feb. 12, 1967; s. Kenneth Kwan-Ho and Estee Jae-Ok Song; m. Donna Ann Daly, Nov. 27, 2004. BA, U. Pa., Phila., 1985—89; MD, SUNY, Bklyn., 1989—93. Diplomate NY, 1993. Asst. prof. surgery SUNY, 2000—; chief divsn. vascular & endovascular surgery LI Coll. Hosp., Bklyn., 2006—. Avocation: golf. Office: LI Coll Hosp 339 Hicks St Brooklyn NY 11201 Business E-Mail: msong@chpnet.ort.

SONG, MI-YEON, education educator, physician; b. Seoul, Republic of Korea, Dec. 21, 1971; d. Young-Ho Song and Jung-Hee Park; m. Sang-Hyun Moon; children: Chai-ho Moon children: Chai-jung Lim, Chai-hyun Lim. MD (Korean Medicine), KyungHee U., Seoul, 1996, PhD, 2001. Diplomate Nat. Cert. Commn. for Accupuncture and Oriental Medicine. Intern KyungHee Med. Ctr., Seoul, 1996—97, resident, 1998—2000; postdoc. fellow Columbia U., NY, 2001—03; instr. Kyung-Hee U., Seoul, 2003—05, asst. prof., 2005—; postdoc. fellow John's Hopkins U., Balt. Contbr. chapters to books. KyungHee Rsch. Fund grantee, KyungHee U., 2003. Mem.: Soc. for Korean Med. Study of Obesity (life), Acad. Oriental Rehab. Medicine (life). Achievements include research in obesity and body composition, complementary and alternative medicine. Home: 7266 Calm Sunset Columbia MD 21046 Office: Kyung Hee U Dept Oriental Rehab Med 1 Hoegi-dong Dongdoemun-gu 13070 Seoul Republic of Korea Personal E-mail: mysong@khmc.or.kr.

SONG, XIAODONG, geophysicist, seismologist; m. Shoumin Liang; children: Thomas W., Angela F. PhD, Calif. Inst. Tech., 1994. Storke-Doherty lectr. Lamont-Doherty Earth Obs. of Columbia U., Palisades, NY, 1996—99; prof. U. Ill., Urbana, 1999—. Named one of Most Important Discoveries in 20th Century, Discover Mag., 2000, Top 100 Sci. Stories of Yr., 2005; recipient Doornbos prize, Internat. Union Geophysics and Geodesy, 1996, Breakthrough of Yr. award, Sci. Mag., 1996, Sci. and Tech. award, Popular Sci. Mag., 1996, Outstanding Young Scientist award, Nat. Natural Sci. Found. China, 1998; Sci. and Tech. Agy. fellow, Rsch. Devel. Corp. Japan, 1997. Mem.: Am. Assn. Advancement Scis., Seismol. Soc. Am., Am. Geophys. Union. Achievements include discovery of the rotation of the Earth's inner core using seismic waves; the Earth's inner core itself is layered with isotropic upper inner core and anisotropic lower inner core; differential inner core rotation using repeated earthquakes. Avocations: travel, reading, swimming. Office: Univ Ill 1301 W Green St 245 NHB Urbana IL 61801 Office Phone: 217-333-1841. Office Fax: 217-244-4996. Business E-Mail: xsong@uiuc.edu.

SONG, XUBIN, mechanical engineer, researcher; b. Yi Wu, China; arrived in US, 1994; s. Sengui Song and Yueqing Hu; m. Rongrong Zhou; 1 child, Justin Jia-Wen. BS in Engring., Nanjing U. Aeronautics and Astronautics, Nanjing, China, 1986; MS in Engring., China Acad. Launch Vehicle Tech., Beijing, China, 1988; MS in Mech. Engring., NC A&T State U., Greensboro, 1996; PhD, Va. Tech. U., 1999. Engr. China Acad. Launch Vehicle Tech., Beijing, 1988—94, MSX Internat., Auburn Hills, Mich., 1999—2000; tech. profl. Visteon Corp, Dearborn, Mich., 2000—04; prin. engr. Eaton Corp, Southfield, Mich., 2004—. Gen. mgr. XYZ Tech. Corp., Canton, Mich., 2003—. Contbr. more than 40 articles to profl. jours. and confs. Mem.: ASME (mem. vehicle design com. 2003—), IEEE, Detroit Chinese Bus. Assn. (sr. bus. mgr. 2001—), Soc. Automotive Engrs. (mem. comml. vehicle powertrain and drivetrain com. 2004—), Phi Kappa Phi. Achievements include seven patents in field; development of torsional vibration control for commercial vehicles; adaptive control for magneto-rheological damper based suspension systems; research in automated optimization design and control of large nonlinear flexible structures; four patents pending; more than ten inventions related to powertrain control under patent application. Office: Eaton Corp 26201 Northwestern Highway Southfield MI 48076 Personal E-mail: xusong@vt.edu. Business E-Mail: xubinsong@eaton.com.

SONG, YONGYI, librarian; b. Shanghai, Dec. 15, 1949; arrived in U.S., 1989; s. Changrui Song and Meiqing Jia; m. Xiaohua Helen Yao, Jan. 1, 1980; 1 child, Xiao. BA, Inst. Shanghai Edn., 1985; MA, U. Colo., 1992; MLS, Ind. U., 1995. Instr. comparative lit. Pa. State U., State College, 1992—93; Chinese bibliographer U. Pitts., 1995—97; sr. libr. East Asian studies/langs. and area studies Dickinson Coll., Carlisle, Pa., 1997—2004; libr. tch. svcs. and collection devel. Calif. State U., LA, 2004—. Author: The Cultural Revolution: A Bibliography, 1966-1996, 1998, The Cultural Revolution and Heterodox Thoughts, 2001, Historical Dictionary of the Chinese Cultural Revolution, 2006; chief editor The Chinese Cultural Revolution Database Online, 2002—06. Recipient 21st Century Nat. Libr. award, Syracuse U. Sch. Info. Studies, NY, 2004; grantee, Chan's Journalism and Culture Found., NYC, 2000; scholar, Pa. Libr. Assn., 2001. Mem.: ALA (Paul Howard award 2005). Office: Calif State U 5151 State Univ Dr Los Angeles CA 90033 Home Phone: 626-300-5906; 626-300-5906; Office Phone: 323-343-4884. Business E-Mail: ysong2@calstatela.edu.

SONG, ZHEN, electrical engineer, researcher; b. Beijing, Mar. 10, 1975; s. Kongzhi Song and Xiaoxia Yan; m. Hong Yan; 1 child, Calla Xueyan. MS, Utah State U., Logan, 2006, PhD, 2007. Cert. IRB tng., Utah State U., 2004, Responsible conduct of rsch., Utah State U., 2004. Rsch. asst. Utah State U., Logan, Utah, 2000—05; intern Siemens Corp. Rsch., Princeton, NJ, 2006—. Contbr. scientific papers to profl. jour. Recipient 2nd Pl. of Smart Dust Challenge, Crossbow Inc., 2005; Dissertation Fellowship, Utah State U., 2005, Rsch. v.p. Fellowship, 2003. Mem.: IEEE (3d pl. student paper/poster award 2007), Assn. Computing Machinery. Achievements include research in wireless sensor network; development of robots. Office: Siemens Corp Rsch 755 Coll Rd E Princeton NJ Home: 1807 Fox Run Dr Plainsboro NJ 08536 Personal E-mail: zhensong@ieee.org.

SONI, JAYSHRI, science educator, director; arrived in U.S., 1989; d. Mangilal and Krishnabai Soni; m. Komal Soni, May 28, 1988; children: Kishen K., Reema K. MSc in Botany, Sagar U., Khandwa, India, 1989, BSc in Biology, 1987; BSc in Edn., Lander U., Greenwood, SC, 1995. Cert. tchr. biology S.C., 1995. Tutor McCormick County Literacy Assn., SC, 1989—95; tchr. sci. Long Cane Acad., McCormick, SC, 1996—98; tchr. math. John de la Howe Sch., McCormick, SC, 2002—04, tchr. sci., 2004—; program dir. Gurukul L.L.C., McCormick, 2005—. Mentor to mid. sch. sci. tchrs. John de la Howe Sch., 2004—. Recipient Presdl. award excellence in tchg. sci., 2006—07; grantee, Am. Aeronautics Assn., 2004-05, Donorschoose.org, 2005-06, 2006—07. Mem.: S.C. State Employees Assn. Home: 4098 Hwy 378 W Mc Cormick SC 29835 Office: John de la Howe Sch Box 154 Hwy 81 Mc Cormick SC 29835 Home

Phone: 864-852-2971; Office Phone: 864-391-2131 110. Home Fax: 864-852-2865. Personal E-mail: ksoni@wctel.net. Business E-Mail: sonij@delahowe.k12.sc.us.

SONNECKEN, EDWIN HERBERT, management consultant; b. New Haven, July 22, 1916; s. Ewald and Pauline (Halfmann) S.; m. Elizabeth Gregory, June 3, 1939; children: William H., Richard G., Paul D. BS, Northwestern U., 1938; MBA, 1940. With Montgomery Ward & Co., Chgo., 1940-42; price adminstr. OPA, Chgo., 1943; mgr. sales B.F. Goodrich Co., Akron, Ohio, 1943-53; dir. planning Ford Motor Co., Dearborn, Mich., 1953-57; pres. Market Planning Corp., NYC, 1957-61; from dir. corp. planning and research to v.p. corp. bus. planning Goodyear Tire & Rubber Co., 1961-80; chmn. Mktg. Sci. Inst., Cambridge, Mass., 1980-84, also trustee, chmn. research policy com.; mgmt. cons., Akron, 1985—. Pres. Akron (Ohio) chpt. Am. Mktg. Assn., 1950, v.p. Detroit chpt., 1955, nat. v.p., dir., 1957, nat. pres., 1964-65, mem. global mktg. coun., 1986—. Pres. YMCA, Akron, 1978; chmn. trustees First Congl. Ch., Akron, 1985, chmn. endowment trust, 1987—. Served with AUS, 1945-46. Mem. Am. Statis. Assn., Am. Assn. Pub. Opinion Research, Nat. Assn. Bus. Economists, Am. Mktg. Assn., Internat. Mktg. Fedn. (pres.), European Soc. for Opinion and Market Research, Beta Gamma Sigma, Portage Country (Akron). Avocation: golf. Home and Office: Apt 333 100 Brookmont Rd Akron OH 44333-3094

SONNEDECKER, GLENN ALLEN, pharmaceutical historian, educator; b. Creston, Ohio, Dec. 11, 1917; s. Ira Elmer and Leta (Linter) S.; m. Cleo Bell, Apr. 3, 1943; 1 child, Stuart Bruce. BS, Ohio State U., 1942, DSc honoris causa, 1964; MS, U Wis., 1950, PhD, 1952; DSc honoris causa, Phila. Coll. Pharmacy and Sci., 1989; PharmD honoris causa, Mass. Coll. Pharmacy, 1974. Lic. pharmacist. Mem. editorial staff Sci. Service, Washington, 1942-43; editor Jour. Am. Pharm. Assn. (practical pharmacy edit.), Washington, 1943-48; asst. prof. U. Wis., 1952-56, asso. prof., 1956-60, prof., 1960-81, Edward Kremers prof., 1981-86; sec. Am. Inst. History of Pharmacy, 1949-57, dir., 1957-73, 81-85, hon. dir. life, chmn. bd., 1988-89; editor-in-chief RPh, 1978-80. Sec., bd. dirs. Friends of Hist. Pharmacy, 1945-49; chmn. Joint Com. on Pharmacy Coll. Librs., 1960-61; US del. Internat. Pharm. Fedn., 1953, 55, 62; US rep. to Mid. East Pharm. Congress, Beirut, 1956; sec. sect. history of pharmacy and biochemistry Pan-Am. Congress Pharmacy and Biochemistry, 1957. Co-author books; contbr. to pharm. and hist. publs. Recipient Edward Kremers award (for writings), 1964, Nat. award Rho Chi, 1967, Schelenz plaquette Internat. Soc. for History of Pharmacy, 1971, Remington honor medal Am. Pharm. Assn., 1972, Urdang medal, 1976, Folch Andreu prize, Spain, 1985, Profile award Am. Found. Pharm. Edn., 1994; Am. Found. fellow, 1948-52, Guggenheim fellow, 1955, Fulbright Rsch. scholar, Germany, 1955-56. Mem. Am. Pharm. Assn. (life; sec. sect. history of pharmacy 1949-50, vice chmn. 1950-51, chmn. 1951-52, rsch. assoc. 1964-65, chmn. joint task force with Acad. Pharm Scis. 1985, hon. chmn. bd. trustees 1985), Internat. Acad. History Pharmacy (1st v.p. 1970-81, pres. 1983-91, hon. pres. 1991—), Am. Assn. History of Medicine (exec. coun. 1966-69), Internat. Gesellschaft fur Geschichte der Pharmazie (exec. bd. 1965-89), hon. mem. socs. for history of pharmacy of Italy, Benelux, pan-Arab, Spain; mem. Sigma Xi, Rho Chi (mem. nat. exec. coun. 1957-59), Phi Delta Chi. Unitarian Universalist. Home: 2030 Chadbourne Ave Madison WI 53726-4047

SONNEMAN, EVE, artist; b. Chgo., 1946; d. Eric O. and Edith S. BFA, U. Ill., 1967; MFA, U. N.Mex., 1969. One-woman shows include Castelli Gallery, N.Y.C., 1976, 78, 80, 82, 84-86, Tex. Gallery, Houston, 1976, 78, 80, 82, 85, Galerie Farideh Cadot, Paris, 1978, 80, 83, François Lambert Gallery, Milan, Italy, 1980, 87, Mpls. Inst. Arts, 1980, La Noveau Musèe, Lyon, France, 1980, Musèe de Toulon, France, 1983, Centre Georges Pompidou, Paris, 1984, Circus Gallery, L.A., 1989, 97, Jones Troyer Fitzpatrick, Washington, 1989, Zabriskie Gallery, N.Y., 1990, Gloria Luria Gallery, Miami, 1990, Grand Central Terminal, N.Y.C., 1991, Charles Cowles Gallery, 1992, Sidney Janis Gallery, N.Y.C., 1996, La Geode Mus., Paris, 1996, Cirrus Gallery, 1997, Bruce Silverstein Gallery, N.Y., 2002, Jadite Gallery, N.Y., 2002, 03, 04, 05, 06, Galeria Turchi, Siena, Italy, 2002, I Space, Chgo., 2005, Mingle Salon, Tokyo, 2005; author: America's Cottage Gardens, 1990, Where Birds Live, 1992; co-author: How To Touch What, 2000; photographs subject of book Real Time, 1976. Grantee Nat. Endowment Arts, 1971, 78, Polaroid Corp., 1978; Cartier fellowship, France, 1989. Address: 446 W 47th St Apt 5C New York NY 10036-2381 Office Phone: 212-582-9375. Personal E-mail: evesonneman@earthlink.net.

SONNEMANN, HARRY, electrical engineer, consultant; b. Munich, Sept. 3, 1924; came to U.S., 1938, naturalized, 1944; s. Leopold and Emmy (Markus) S.; m. Shirley E. Battles, Nov. 25, 1949; children: Carol Jean, Joyce Elaine, Patricia Ann. BS, Poly. Inst. Bklyn., 1954. Research electroence-phalography, 1944-47; asst. to dir. electronics dept. AEC contract, Columbia U., 1947-50; supr. electronics shop Columbia Hudson Labs., 1951-53, head electronics dept., 1954-59; asst. dir. Project Artemis, 1959-64, Project Artemis (Hudson labs.), 1961-64; asst. dir. field engring. Advanced Research Projects Agy., Nuclear Test Detection Office, 1964-67; acting dep. dir. Nuclear Test Detection Office, 1967-68; spl. asst. in electronics to asst. sec. navy for research and devel. Navy Dept., 1968-76, spl. asst. to asst. sec. navy for research and devel., 1976-77; asst. to chief engr. NASA, 1977-78, dep. chief engr., 1978-84, asst. chief engr., 1984-86, cons., 1986—2000; pres. SBC Assocs., McLean, Va., 1988-95. Chmn. Dept. Def. Tactical Satellite Exec. Steering Group, 1968-69, chmn. Dept. Def. nav. satellite exec. steering group, 1969-70, 72-73 Treas. Art League. No. Va., 1967-68; pres. Rotonda Condominium Unit Owners Assn., 1982-84, 97-98, 99-2000. Mem.: Washington Figure Skating (dir. 1968-73, treas. 1969-72), Ice Club of Washington (pres. 1974-76). Home and Office: 7452 Spring Village Dr # 434 Springfield VA 22150-4951 E-mail: hssbc@aol.com.

SONNENBERG, HARDY, data processing executive, researcher, electrical engineer; b. Schoensee, Fed. Republic Germany, Apr. 12, 1939; s. Gustav and Wanda (Neumann) S.; m. Doris Linda Adam, June 20, 1964; children: Kevin, Denise. BS, U. Alta., 1962; MS, Stanford U., 1964, PhD, 1967. Registered profl. engr., Ont. Advanced devel. engr. GTE Sylvania, Mountain View, Calif., 1966-68, engring. specialist, 1968-70, sect. mgr., 1970-73; dir. rsch. Optical Diodes Inc., Palo Alto, Calif., 1973-74; mem. rsch. staff Xerox Rsch. Centre Can., Mississauga, Ont., 1975-78, area mgr., 1978-80, lab. mgr., 1980-86, mgr. rsch. ops., 1986-87, mgr. tech. and engring. systems, 1987-94, v.p. rsch. and tech., 1994-96; pres. Calixo Cons., Freelton, Ont., 1997—. Chmn. indsl. adv. coun. McMaster U., Hamilton, Ont., 1990-93, active, 1987-94. Contbr. articles to profl. jours.; patentee in field. Chmn. bd. dirs. local ch., Hamilton, Ont., 1983-85, 89-93, 98-2002; pres. Sheridan Park Assn., Mississauga, 1988-89; chmn. Conf. Bd. Can. Rsch. Mgrs. Forum, 1991-93. Recipient cert. of recognition for invention NASA, 1973, 74, Achievement award Xerox Corp., 1981, Charles E. Ives Engring. award, 1983. Mem.: IEEE (sr.), Assn. Profl. Engrs. Ont., Am. Phys. Soc., sigma Xi. Avocations: outdoor activities, singing, church participation. Home and Office: 900 Hwy 97 Freelton ON Canada L0R 1K0 E-mail: hsonnenb@ieee.org.

SONNENBLICK, EDMUND HIRAM, medical educator, cardiologist; b. New Haven, Oct. 7, 1932; s. Ira J. and Rosalind (Helfand) S.; m. Linda Bland, Dec. 21, 1954; children: Emily Sonnenblick Offit, Charlotte Sonnenblick Van Doren, Annie E. (dec.). BA, Wesleyan U., Middletown, Conn., 1954; MD, Harvard U., 1958. Diplomate Am. Bd. Internal Medicine. Resident in medicine Presbyn. Hosp., NYC, 1958-60, 62-63; sr. investigator Nat. Heart Inst., Bethesda, Md., 1960-62, 63-68; asst. prof. medicine Harvard Med. Sch., Boston, 1968-70, assoc. prof., 1970-75; co-dir. cardiology Peter Bent Brigham Hosp., Boston, 1968-75, dir. cardiovasc. rsch., 1970-75; Olson prof. medicine, chief carddiology Albert Einstein Coll. Medicine, Bronx, NY, 1975—96, Edmond J. Safra disting. prof. medicine, 1996—, chief emeritus cardiology, 1996—. Vis prof. medicine NY Med. Coll.; assoc. dir. Cardiovasc. Rsch. Inst., Valhalla, NY; editor Progress in Cardiovasc. Diseaess; contbr. over 600 articles to med. jours. Author 15 books and chpts. in books. Trustee Wesleyan U., 1994-97. Sr. surgeon USPHS, 1960-62. Fellow ACP, Am. Coll. Cardiology (Disting. Scientist award 1989), Internat. Soc. for Heart Rsch.; mem. Am. Heart Failure Soc. Am., Am. Hypertension Soc. (co-founder), Am. Coll. Physicians, Am. Assn. Physicians, Century Assn., Am. Soc. Clin. Investigation, Am. Physiol. Soc., Interurban Club, NY Yacht Club, Noroton Yacht Club, Woods Hole Yacht Club. Avocation: sailing. Home: 138 Goodwives River Rd Darien CT 06820-5807 Office: Albert Einstein Coll Medicine Weiler Hosp 1825 Eastchester Rd Bronx NY 10461-2301 Office Phone: 718-904-2932. E-mail: esonnenbli@aol.com.

SONNENFELD, BARRY, director, cinematographer; b. NYC, Apr. 1, 1953; m. Susan Ringo, 1989; 1 child. Grad., NY U., 1978. Cinematographer (films) In Our Water, 1982, Blood Simple, 1984, Compromising Positions, 1985, Three O'Clock High, 1987, Raising Arizona, 1987, Throw Momma from the Train, 1987, Big, 1988, When Harry Met Sally..., 1989, Miller's Crossing, 1990, Misery, 1990, (TV movies) How to Be a Perfect Person In Just Three Days, 1983, Out of Step, 1984 (Emmy award best cinematography 1984), Double Take, 1985, Welcome Home, Bobby, 1986, Classified Love, 1986; dir. (films) The Addams Family (uncredited cameo appearance), 1991, Addams Family Values (also actor), 1993, Get Shorty, 1995 (also exec. prodr., actor), Men In Black, 1997, Maximum Bob (TV series, also exec. prodr.), 1998, Wild Wild West, 1999 (also prodr.), Chippendales, 2000, Men In Black II, 2002 (also actor), R.V., 2006; dir., co-prodr.: For Love or Money, 1993; exec. prodr.: (films) Out of Sight, 1998, Lemony Snicket's A Series of Unfortunate Events, 2004, (TV Series) Fantasy Island, 1998, (TV) Partners, 1999; prodr. (TV Series) Secret Agent Man, 2000 (also creator), The Tick, 2001 (also dir.), Karen Sisco, 2003, (film) The Crew, 2000, Big Trouble, 2002 (also dir.), Ladykillers, 2004. Office: Creative Artists Agy c/o Fred Specktor 9830 Wilshire Blvd Beverly Hills CA 90212 also: United Talent Agency 9560 Wilshire Blvd Fl 5 Beverly Hills CA 90212-2401

SONNENFELD, JEFFREY ALAN, management educator; b. Phila., Apr. 1, 1954; s. Burton David and Rochelle (Galant) S. AB, Harvard Coll., 1976; MBA, Harvard U., 1978, D in Bus. Adminstrn., 1980. Mcht. retail clothing The Heir & Gentry Shop, Hatboro, Pa., 1968—72; pres. Harvard Radio Broadcasting, Cambridge, Mass., 1974—76; mgmt. intern Scott Paper, IBM, Phila., Armonk, 1976—78; adv., tutor Harvard Coll., Cambridge, 1976—80; rsch. asst. Harvard U., Cambridge, 1977—80, asst. prof., 1980—84; assoc. prof. Harvard Bus. Sch., Cambridge, 1984—89; prof. Emory U., Atlanta, 1989, dir. Ctr. Leadership and Career Studies, 1989—97; sr. assoc. dean exec. progs. Sch. Mgmt. Yale U., New Haven, 2001—, Lester Crown prof. mgmt. practice, 2001—. Bd. dirs. Eastgate Pub., NYC, Kloster Cruises Ltd., Miami; founder, pres. Yale Chief Exec. Leadership Inst., 1989-. Author: Corporate Views of the Public Interest: Perceptions of the Forest Products Industry, 1981, Managing Career Systems: Channeling the Flow of Executive Careers, 1984, The Hero's Farewell: What Happens When CEOs Retire, 1988 (best seller 1989), Concepts of Leadership, The International Library of Managment, 1995; co-author: (with R. Gandossy) Leadership and Governance from the Inside Out, 2004, (with Andrew Ward) Firing Back: How Great Leaders Rebound After Career Disasters, 2007; mem. bd. editors Acad. Mgmt. Jour., Acad. Mgmt. Exec., Orgnl. Dynamics, Jour. Occupational Behavior; contbr. articles to profl. jours., chpts. to books. Adv., dir. Am. Assn. Ret. Persons, Washington, 1992; mem. Anti-Defamation League, Washington, 1992, Am. Jewish Com., NYC, 1992; trustee Sacred Heart U. Recipient AT&T-Hawthorne award for Social Sci., 1980, Standout New Mgmt. Book award Bus. Week, 1988. Mem. Acad. Mgmt. (dir., trustee, Outstanding Rsch. in Social Issues award 1981, 84, Award for Best Article, 2005), Kiwanis, Havard Alumni Assn., Harvard Bus. Sch. Club. Democrat. Office: Sch Mgmt Yale U PO Box 208200 New Haven CT 06520-8200 Office Phone: 203-432-5955. E-mail: jeffrey.sonnenfeld@yale.edu. *

SONNENFELD, MARC JAY, lawyer; b. Bryn Mawr, Pa., Sept. 16, 1946; s. Burton David and Rochelle (Galant) S. BA, Swarthmore Coll., 1968; JD, Harvard U., 1971. Bar: Pa. 1971, Mass. 1971, DC 1977, Fla. 1978, US Supreme Ct. 1976. Lectr. Wellesley (Mass.) Coll., 1971-72; law clk. to chief judge U.S. Dist. Ct. (ea. dist.) Pa., Phila., 1972-73; assoc. Ewing & Cohen, Phila., 1973-74, Morgan, Lewis & Bockius, Phila., 1974-78, ptnr., 1978—. Faculty Practising Law Inst., NYC, 2001—04. Dem. committeeman, Phila., 1980-84; chmn. Pa. Lawyers for Dem. Victory, 1988, gen. chmn. ann. fund, 1985-87, bd. trustee Am. Inns of Ct. Found.; mem. bd. mgrs. Swarthmore Coll. (chair audit com.) 1989. Named Am. Leading Lawyers for Bus., Chambers USA, 2003—06, One Of Top 10 Bus. Litig in Phila., The Best Lawyers in Am., 1997—2007, Top Securities Litig., Pa. Super Lawyers, Phila. Mag.; recipient Joseph B. Shane award, Swarthmore Coll. Fellow Am. Coll. Trial Lawyers; mem. ABA, Pa. Bar Assn., Phila. Bar Assn. (exec. com. young lawyers sect. 1976-79, appellate cts. com., fed. cts. com., state civil jud. procedures com., nominating com., chmn. city policy com., chmn. profl. responsibility com. 1985, co-chmn. legis. liaison com. 1987-91, bus. banking and corp. law sect., chair bd. govs. 1986, chmn. 1987, chmn. ann. meeting 1991, asst. treas. 1996, co-chair commerce cost task force 1996-97, bus. Ct. Task Force), Harvard Law Sch. Assn. of Phila. (pres.1987-88), Swarthmore Coll. Annual Fund (bd. mgrs.). Jewish. Avocations: reading, sailing. Office: Morgan Lewis & Bockius 1701 Market St Philadelphia PA 19103-2921 Office Phone: 215-963-5572. Office Fax: 215-963-5001. Business E-Mail: msonnenfeld@morganlewis.com.

SONNENFELDT, HELMUT, former government official, educator, consultant, writer; b. Berlin, Sept. 13, 1926; came to U.S., 1944, naturalized, 1945; s. Walter H. and Gertrud (Liebenthal) S.; m. Marjorie Hecht, Oct. 4, 1953; children: Babette Sonnenfeldt Lubben, Walter H., Stewart H. AB, Johns Hopkins, 1950, MA, 1951. With Dept. State, Washington, 1952-77; formerly dir. Office Rsch. and Analysis for USSR and Eastern Europe, 1965-69; lectr. Sch. Advanced Internat. Studies, Johns Hopkins U., 1958-69, vis. scholar, 1977-78; guest scholar Brookings Instn., Washington, 1978—. Sr. mem. Nat. Security Coun., 1969-74; counselor Dept. State, 1974-77; mem. exec. panel chief ops. USN, 1971—. Former gov. UN Assn. of U.S.; dir. Atlantic Coun. of U.S., World Affairs Coun. Washington; trustee Johns Hopkins U. With AUS, 1945-46. Mem. Coun. on Fgn. Rels. N.Y., Pi Delta Epsilon. Home: 5600 Wisconsin Ave Apt 1505 Chevy Chase MD 20815-4412 Office: Brookings Instn 1775 Massachusetts Ave NW Washington DC 20036-2103 Office Phone: 202-797-6028. Business E-Mail: hsonnenfeldt@brookings.edu.

SONNENSCHEIN, DAVID, music educator, composer, conductor; b. Hamburg, Germany, Nov. 2, 1928; s. Abraham and Elsa Sonnenschein; m. Tamar Gronemann, June 23, 1957; children: Iris, Nurit, Orna. Mus D, Boston U., 1976; MusM, New Eng. Conservatory, Boston, 1968. Dir. Tiberias Conservatory, Tiberias, Israel, 1962—66; music tchr. Reali Sch., Haifa, Israel, 1962—66; instr. Emmanuel Coll., Boston; assoc. prof. music Northeastern U., Boston, chair dept. music, 1993—99. Condr. Chamber Orch., Hamburg, Germany, 1959—62, Hamburg, 1959—61; guest condr. Hamburg Symphony Orch., Hamburg, Germany, 1959—61; condr. Haifa Chamber Choir, Haifa, Israel, 1962—63; assoc. condr. Haifa Symphony Orch., Haifa, Israel; condr. Melrose Symphony Orch., Melrose, Mass., Polymnia Choral Soc., Melrose, Mass., 1971—81; guest condr. Boston Pops Orch., Boston, 1974—79; condr. Northeastern U. Symphony Orch., Boston, 1972—88, Concert Arts Orch., Boston, 1973—84. Author: (music courseware) The Anatomy of Music. Recipient Innovative Excellence in Learning, Tchg. and Tech., Ninth Internat. Conf. on Coll. Tchg., Learning and Tech., 1998; fellow, Brandeis U., 1968—70, Lady Davis, Haifa Technion, 1980—81; scholar, New Eng. Conservatory, 1966—68. Achievements include first to Developer of Music Courseware and Learning Modules for Distance Learning. Avocations: sailing, hiking, cross country skiing. Home: 169 Bonad Rd Chestnut Hill MA 02467 Office: Northeastern University Huntington Ave 373 Ryder Hall Boston MA Personal E-mail: dsonnens@rcn.com.

SONNENSCHEIN, HUGO FREUND, academic administrator, writer, economist, educator; b. NYC, Nov. 14, 1940; s. Leo William and Lillian Silver Sonnenschein; m. Elizabeth Gunn, Aug. 26, 1962; children: Leah, Amy, Rachel. AB, U. Rochester, 1961; MS, Purdue U., 1963, PhD, 1964, PhD (hon.), 1996; PhD (hon.), Tel Aviv U., 1993; D (hon.), U. Autonoma Barcelona, Spain, 1994; PhD (hon.), Lake Forest Coll., 1995, North Ctrl. Coll., 2001, U. Chgo., 2002. Faculty dept. econs. U. Minn., 1964—70, prof., 1968—70; prof. econs. U. Mass., Amherst, 1970—73, Northwestern U., 1973—76, Princeton (N.J.) U., 1976—87, Class of 1926 prof., 1987—88, provost, 1991—93; dean, Thomas S. Gates prof. U. Pa. Sch. Arts & Scis., Phila., 1988—91; pres. U. Chgo., 1993—2000, Hutchinson disting. prof., pres. emeritus, 2000—. Vis. prof. U. Andes, Columbia, 1965, Tel Aviv U., 1972, Hebrew U., 1973, U. Paris, 1978, U. Aix-en-Provence, France, 1978, Stanford U., 1984—85; bd. dirs. Van Kampen Mutual Funds. Editor: Econometrica, 1977—84; mem. editl. bd.: Jour. Econ. Theory, 1972—75, Jour. Math. Econs., 1974—, SIAM Jour., 1976—80; contbr. articles to profl. jours. Trustee U. Rochester, 1992—, U. Chgo., 1993—. Fellow, Social Sci. Rsch. Coun., 1967—68, NSF, 1970—, Ford Found., 1970—71, Guggenheim Found., 1976—77. Fellow: Econometric Soc. (pres. 1988—89), Am. Acad. Arts and Scis.; mem.: NAS, Am. Philos. Soc. Business E-Mail: h-sonnenschein@uchicago.edu.

SONNENSCHEIN, RALPH ROBERT, physiologist; b. Chgo., Aug. 14, 1923; s. Robert and Flora (Kieferstein) S.; m. Patricia W. Niddrie, June 21, 1952; children— David, Lisa, Ann. Student, Swarthmore Coll., 1940—42, U. Chgo., 1942—43; BS, Northwestern U., 1943, BM, MS, Northwestern U., 1946, MD, 1947; PhD, U. Ill., 1950. Research asst. in physiology Northwestern U. Med. Sch., 1944-46; intern Michael Reese Hosp., Chgo., 1946-47; successively research fellow clin. sci., research asst. psychiatry, research asso. psychiatry U. Ill. Med. Sch., Chgo., 1947-51; mem. faculty U. Calif. Med. Sch., Los Angeles, 1951-88, prof. physiology, 1962-88, prof. emeritus, 1988—; liaison scientist Office Naval Research, London, 1971-72. Author papers on pain, innervation of skin, peripheral circulation. Served with AUS, 1943-46. Spl. research fellow USPHS, 1957-58; fellow Swedish Med. Research Council, 1964-65; grantee USAF; grantee Office Naval Research; grantee NIH; grantee NSF. Mem. Am. Physiol. Soc., Microcirculatory Soc., Soc. Exptl. Biology and Medicine, AAAS, Hungarian Physiol. Soc. (hon.). Home: 18212 Kingsport Dr Malibu CA 90265-5636 Office: U Calif Sch Medicine Dept Physiology Los Angeles CA 90095-1751

SONNIER, JOSEPH A., lab administrator, physician; MD, La. State U. Sch. Medicine, 1979. Cert. in Anatomic and Clin. Pathology 1983. Mng. dir. Unipath Ltd.; regional mng. dir., southwest region AmeriPath, pres., 2003—. Office: AmeriPath Inc 7111 Fairway Dr Ste 400 Palm Beach Gardens FL 33410 Office Phone: 561-712-6200.

SONNIER, PATRICIA BENNETT, business management educator; b. Park River, ND, Mar. 25, 1935; d. Benjamin Beekman Bennett and Alice Catherine (Peerboom) Bennett Brenckinridge; m. William McGregor Castellini (dec.); m. Cecil Sherwood Sonnier (dec.); m. Joseph N. Pagano; children: Bruce Bennett Wells (Nabil Subhani), Barbara Lea Ragland. AA, Allan Handcock Coll., Santa Maria, Calif., 1964; BS magna cum laude, U. Great Falls, 1966; MS, U. N.D., 1967, PhD, 1971. Fiscal acct. USIA, Washington, 1954-56; pub. acct. Bremerton, Wash., 1956; statistician USN, Bremerton, Wash., 1957-59; med. svcs. accounts officer USAF, Vandenberg AFB, Calif., 1962-64; instr. bus. adminstrn. Western New Eng. U., 1967—69; vis. prof. econs. Chapman Coll., 1970; vis. prof. U. So. Calif. Sys., Griffith AFB, NY, 1971-72; assoc. prof., dir. adminstrv. mgmt. program Va. State U., 1973-74; assoc. prof. bus. adminstrn. Oreg. State U., Corvallis, 1974-81, prof. mgmt., 1982-90, emeritus prof. mgmt., 1990—, univ. curriculum coord., 1984-86, dir. adminstrv. mgmt. program, 1974-81, pres. Faculty Senate, 1981. Mem. Interinstl. Faculty Senate, 1986-90, pres., 1989-90; exec. dir. Bus. Enterprise Ctr., 1990-92, Enterprise Ctr. LA, Inc., 1992-95; commr. Lafayette Econ. Devel. Authority, 1994-2000, treas., 1995-96, vice chmn., 1996-97, chmn., 1997-98, past chmn., 1998-99, sec., chmn. bldg. com., 1999-2000; cons. process tech. devel. Digital Equipment Corp., 1981. Pres., chmn. bd. dirs. Adminstrv. Orgnl. Svcs., Inc., Corvallis, 1976—83, Dynamic Achivement, Inc., 1983—92; cons. Oregonians in Action, 1990—91, sec., 1999, 2000; cert. adminstrv. mng. pres. TYEE Mobile Home Park, Inc., 1987—92; mem. Leadership LA, 1986; del various convs.; mem. parish coun. St. Patrick's Cath. Ch., 1998—2000, Risen Savior Ch., 2005—06. Fellow: Assn. Bus. Comm. (internat. bd. 1980—86, v.p. Northwest 1981, 2d v.p. 1982—83, 1st v.p. 1983—84, pres. 1984—85); mem.: AAUP (chpt. sec. 1973, chpt. bd. dirs. 1982, pres. Oreg. conf. 1983—85, chpt. bd. dirs. 1984—89, pres. chpt. 1985—86), Corvallis Area C. of C. (v.p. chamber devel. 1987—88, pres. 1988—89, chair bd. 1989—90, Pres.'s award 1986), La. Bus. Incubation Assn. (sec.-treas. 1993—95), Nat. Assn. Tchr. Edn. for Bus. Office Edn. (pres. 1976—77, chair pub. rels. com. 1978—81), Better Bus. Bur. (sec. 1994, treas. 1995, vice-chair 1996, chair 1997, past chair 1998, sec. 1999, chair nominating com. 1999, chair pub. rels., Lafayette Blue Ribbon 1999—2000), Nat. Bus. Edn. Assn., Associated Oreg. Faculties, Am. Vocat. Assn. (nominating com. 1976), Adminstrv. Mgmt. Soc., Assn. Info. Sys. Profls. (chpt. v.p. 1977, chpt. pres. 1978—81), Am. Bus. Women's Assn. (chpt. v.p. 1979, pres. 1980, Top Businesswoman in Nation 1980, Bus. Assoc. of Yr. 1986), Albuquerque Federated Rep. Women (hospitality chair 2003—04, 1st v.p. 2004—), Acadiana Rep. Women (gen. chmn. La. Fedn. Rep. Women's Clubs State Conv. 1997, 1st v.p. 1997—98, pres. 1998—2000, asst. state CAP chmn. 1999—2000, Ahrens for Gov. Com. 2002), Rotary (co-chmn. fundraiser com. 2002), Boys and Girls Club of Corvallis (pres. 1991—92), Lafayette Rotary (cmty. svc. dir. 1993—94, bd. dirs. 1993—2000, treas. 1995—96, sec. 1996—97, v.p. 1997—98, pres. 1998—99, Dist. 6200 Found. award 2000), Rotary of Albuquerque del Norte (silent auction chair 2001—02, dep. dir. internat. svc. com. 2002, dist. 5520 dep. dir. permanent fund, asst. gov. 2003—04, dist. 5520 found. chair 2003—06, dist. 5520 internat. chmn. 2004—06, chmn. Shrimp Fiesta 2005, Dist. 5520 Found. award 2003, 2004, Dist. 5520 Svc. Above Self award 2004—05, Dist. 5520 Found. award 2005, Dist. 5520 Svc. Above Self award 2005—06, Rotarian of Yr. 2006—07, 25 Yr. Perfect Attendance award), Sigma Kappa. Home and Office: Landing at Newport 890 SE Bay Blvd #213 Newport OR 97365

SONNTAG, BERNARD H., agronomist, researcher, public information officer; b. Goodsoil, Sask., Can., June 27, 1940; s. Henry R. and Annie (Heesing) S.; m. Mary L. Ortman, Aug. 10, 1963; children: Calvin, Galen, Courtney Anne. BSA, Sask. U., Saskatoon, 1962, MSc, 1965; PhD, Purdue U., 1971. Economist Agriculture Can., Saskatoon, 1962-66; cons. D.W. Carr & Assoc., Ottawa, Ont., Canada, 1966-68; economist Agriculture Can., Lethbridge, Alta., 1968-79, Saskatoon, 1979-80, dir. rsch. sta. Brandon, Man., 1980-86, Swiftcurrent, Sask., 1986-89, Lethbridge, 1989-95; dir. gen. Prairie Farm Rehab. Adminstrn., Regina, Sask., Canada, 1996-01; pres. Sonntag Agrl. Svcs., Saskatoon, Sask., Canada, 2001—.

Pres. Man. Inst. Agrologists, Brandon, 1984. Recipient Leadership award Bell Can., 1993; named Disting. Agrologist, Alta. Inst. Agrologists, 1995. Fellow Agrl. Inst. Can.; mem. Rotary. Roman Catholic.

SONO, MASAYUKI, architect, artist; b. Kobe, Japan, 1971; MArch, U. Wash., Seattle, 1996, Kobe U., Japan, 1998. Arch. Voorsanger & Assocs., NYC, 1998—2003; prin. arch. Masayuki Sono Archs., NYC, 2003—. Over 60 exhibitions, prin. works include Postcards: The Staten Island Sept. 11th Meml., NY (Merit award, Small Project, NY Constrn. News, 2004), Asia Soc. and Mus. renovation and addition, NYC, U. Va. Art Mus., Charlottesville, LaGuardia Internat. Airport Control Tower, Queens, NY, Aspen Residence, Colo., World Trade Ctr. Site Perimeter Enclosure, NYC, Ashiya Art Gallery, Hyogo, Japan, Shofu-den renovation and addition, Sullivan County, NY. Co-recipient Achievement in the Arts award, Coun. on the Arts & Humanities for Staten Island, 2004. Office: Masayuki Sono Architects 308 Mott St Ste 3F New York NY 10012 E-mail: msono@masasono.com.

SONSINI, LARRY W., lawyer; b. Rome, NY, Feb. 5, 1941; AB, U. Calif., Berkeley, 1963, LLB, 1966; PhD (hon.), Pacific Grad. Sch.of Psychology. Bar: Calif. 1966. Assoc. McCloskey Wilson & Mosher, Palo Alto, 1966—73, ptnr., 1973—78; mng. ptnr., chmn. CEO Wilson, Sonsini, Goodrich & Rosati, Palo Alto, 1978—; prof. securities regulation Boalt Hall Sch. law U. Calif., Berkeley, 1985—. Bd. dirs. N.Y. Stock Exchange (NYSE), 2001—03, Silicon Valley Bancshares, 2003—, Brocade Communications Systems, Inc., Echelon Corp., LSI Logic Corp., Lattice Semiconductor Corp., Pixar, Inc.; chmn. Regulation, Enforcement and Listing Standards Com., Legal Adv. Com., 2003—. Trustee Santa Clara U. Named Bus. Leader of the Yr., Harvard Bus. Sch. Assn. of No. Calif., 2005; named one of Top Ten Lawyers in Bay Area, San Francisco Chronicle, 2003, 100 Most Influential Lawyers, Nat. Law Jour., 2006; recipient Spl. Achievement Award in Commerce and Law, Nat. Italian Am. Found. (NIAF), 2003, Cmty. Svc. Award exemplary leadership, Nat. Conf. Cmty. & Justice, 1993, Visionary Award, Software Devel. Forum, 2000, Dir.'s Award, San Francisco Exploratorium, Boalt Hall Sch. of Law Citation Award, U. Calif., Berkeley, Bus. Hall of Fame Award, Bay Area Coun. Mem.: ABA (com. on fed. regulation securities, subcom. on registration statements), Am. Acad. Arts and Scis., Am. Law Inst. Office: Wilson Sonsini Goodrich & Rosati 650 Page Mill Rd Palo Alto CA 94304-1050 Office Phone: 650-493-9300. Office Fax: 650-493-6811. E-mail: lsonsini@wsgr.com. *

SONSTEBY, CHARLES M., food service executive; Dir. tax, treasury and risk mgmt. depts. Brinker Internat. Inc., Dallas, 1990—94, v.p., treas., 1994—97, sr. v.p. fin., 1997—2001, exec. v.p., CFO, 2001—. Office: 6820 LBJ Fwy Dallas TX 75240

SONTAG, ED, former federal agency administrator; BA in Spl. Edn., SUNY, MA in Elementary Sch. Adminstrn. and Supervision; PhD in Spl. Edn. Adminstrn., Syracuse U. Resident scholar for Wis. Gov. Tommy G. Thompson; deputy asst. sec. US Dept. Interior, 1989—92; prof. U. Wis. - Stevens Point Sch. Edn., 1992—99; senior-level positions Ill. State Bd. Edn., US Dept. Edn., Ind. U., Wis. and NY pub. sch. sys.; dep. chief of staff for mgmt. and ops. US HHS, 2001, asst. sec. adminstrn. and mgmt., 2002. Recipient U. Wis.-Steven Point Vice Chancellor Merit award, Dept. Interior Disting. Safety award. Office: US Dept Health and Human Svcs 200 Independence Ave SW Rm 309 Washington DC 20201

SONTAG, FREDERICK EARL, philosophy educator; b. Long Beach, Calif., Oct. 2, 1924; s. M. Burnett and Cornelia (Nicholson) S.; m. Carol Furth, June 10, 1950; children: Grant Furth, Anne Burnett Karch. BA with great distinction, Stanford U., Calif., 1949; MA, Yale U., New Haven, Conn., 1951, PhD, 1952; LLD (hon.), Coll. Idaho, 1971. Instr. Yale U., 1951-52; asst. prof. philosophy Pomona Coll., Claremont, Calif., 1952-55, assoc. prof., 1955-60, prof., 1970—, Robert C. Denison prof. philosophy, 1972—, chmn. dept. philosophy, 1960-67, 76-77, 1980-84; chmn. coord. com. in philosophy Clarement Grad. Sch. and Univ. Ctr., 1962-65. Vis. prof. Union Theol. Sem., NYC, 1959-60, Collegio de Sant' Anselmo, Rome, 1966-67, U. Copenhagen, 1972; theologian-in-residence Am. Ch. in Paris, 1973; fulbright regional vis. prof., India, East Asia, Pacific areas, 1977-78; nat. adv. coun. Kent Fellowship Program of Danforth Found., 1963-66. Author numerous books, the most recent being; Love Beyond Pain: Mysticism Within Christianity, 1977, Sun Myung Moon and the Unification Church, 1977, also German, Japanese and Korean transl.; (with John K. Roth) God and America's Future, 1977, What Can God Do?, 1979, A Kierkegaard Handbook, 1979, The Elements of Philosophy, 1984, (with John K. Roth) The Questions of Philosophy, 1988, Emotion, 1989, The Return of the Gods, 1989, Willgenstein and the Mystical, 1995, Uncertain Truth, 1995, The Descent of Women, 1997, The Acts of the Trinity, 1997, Truth and Imagination, 1998, 2001: A Spiritual Odyssey, 2001, The Mysterious Presence, 2002, A Kierkegaard Handbook, 2003, American Life, 2006. Pres. bd. dirs. Claremont Family Svc., 1960-64; trustee The Coro Found., LA and San Francisco, 1967-71; bd. dirs., chmn. ways and means com. Pilgrim Place, Claremont, 1970-77. With AUS, 1943-46. Vis. scholar Ctr. for Study Japanese Religions, Kyoto, Japan, spring 1974; vis. fellow East-West Ctr., Honolulu, summer 1974; Wig Disting. prof. award, 1970, 76. Mem. Am. Philos. Assn., Metaphys. Soc. Am. Soc. on Religion in Higher Edn. (Kent fellow 1950-52), Am. Acad. Religion, Phi Beta Kappa. United Ch. Of Christ. Office: Pomona Coll 551 N College Ave Claremont CA 91711-4410

SONTAG, JAMES MITCHELL, oncologist, researcher; b. Denver, Dec. 8, 1939; s. Samuel Henry and Rose Hazel (Silverman) S.; m. Elizabeth Crockett Tunis; children: Ariella, Eythan. BS, Lamar State Coll. Tech., Beaumont, Tex.; MS, U. Ill., 1967; PhD, Weizmann Inst. Sci., Rehovot, Israel, 1971; MPH, Harvard U., 1982. Postdoctoral fellow Damon Runyon Meml. Fund Cancer Rsch., 1971-72; guest worker Nat. Cancer Inst., NIH, Bethesda, Md., 1972-73, staff fellow, 1973-74, exptl. oncologist, 1973-76, mgr. carcinogen bioassay program, 1973-76, asst. to divsn. dir. cancer cause and prevention, 1976-80; exec. sec. Clearinghouse on Environ. Carcinogens, 1976-80, asst. dir. for interagy. affairs Office of Dir., 1980-82, spl. asst. epidemiology and biostatistics program, 1982-96; chief office divsn. ops. & analysis divsn. cancer epidemiology and genetics Nat. Cancer Inst., 1996-99; vol. with grassroots artisians med. mission L.Am., 1999—. Author, editor in field. ESL tchr. 2004-; Served with AUS, 1956-59. Beaumont LWV scholar, 1963-65 Mem. Beta Beta Beta. Personal E-mail: jim18y@msn.com.

SOODIK, LYNN, lawyer; b. Pitts., Aug. 6, 1956; BS with distinction, Pa. State U., 1978; student, Durham U., Eng.; JD, U. Calif. Hastings Coll. Law, San Francisco, 1982. Bar: Calif. 1982, cert.: State Bar Calif. Bd. Legal Specialization (family law) 1988. Prin. Law Offices of Lynn Soodik, P.C., Santa Monica, Calif. Instr., mentor Harriet Buhai Ctr. Family Law, 1990—93. Assoc. articles editor: COMM/ENT, A Jour. of Comm. and Entertainment Law, 1980—82. Mem.: Beverly Hills Bar Assn., LA County Bar Assn. (sec. 1995—96, vice chair 1996—97, chair-elect 1997—98, chair family law sect. 1998—99, mem. exec. com. 1986—99). Office: Law Offices of Lynn Soodik 233 Wilshire Blvd Ste 525 Santa Monica CA 90401-1205 Office Phone: 310-393-8000. Office Fax: 310-394-8182. E-mail: info@lynnsoodik.com. *

SOOHOO, ELENA, strategic planning administrator; b. NYC; BS in Nursing, U. Calif., San Francisco, 1981; MS, Harvard U., 1987. RN, Calif. Rsch. asst. Div. Ambulatory and Community Med. U. Calif., San Francisco, 1976-77; bibliographer Inst. Health Policy Studies U. Calif., San Francisco, 1978; nurse Moffitt Hosp. U. Calif., San Francisco, 1981-82, On Lok Sr. Health Svcs., San Francisco, 1982-83; health policy intern Office Sen. Rosenthal, LA, 1984; health scis. specialist VA, LA, 1985-86; assoc. dir. strategic planning Los Angeles County Dept. Health Svcs., LA, 1992—. Bd. dirs. Bay Area Asian Health Alliance, San Francisco, 1980-84. Mem. planning com. Sta. KRON-TV Health Fair, San Francisco 1979-82; co-chmn. Hop Jok/Chinatown Health Fair, San Francisco 1975-81; mem. Chicanos Health Edn., Berkeley 1977-79; vol. Northbeach Chinatown Family Planning, San Francisco 1974-76, Chinatown Health Fair, N.Y.C. 1971-72; mem. affirmative action com. U. Calif.San Francisco, 1980-81, Harvard U., 1987. Mem. APHA, NAFE, Calif. Assn. Pub. Hosps., Health Fin. Mgmt. Assn., Com. Status Women, So. Calif. Pub. Health Assn., U. Calif.-San Francisco Alumni Assn., Harvard-Radcliffe Club of So. Calif., Sigma Theta Tau. Office: LA County Dept Health Svcs Office Strategic Planning 313 N Figueroa St Ste 701 Los Angeles CA 90012-2602

SOO HOO, TSUNG (BILL) YAO, security studies educator, consultant; s. Yin and Chui Woo Soo Hoo; m. Rachel Ann Cammorato, Nov. 3, 1984; 1 child, Carolyn Yu-yi. PhD, Seton Hall U., 2005. Cert. firearms instr. N.J., 1986. Spl. agt. FBI, West Paterson, NJ, 1970—2001; chair profl. security studies dept. N.J. City U., 2002—. Exec. com. Am. Soc. Indsl. Security, Ltd., Internat., NJ, 2002—. Author: An Alternative Problem-based Collaborative Learning Model and Student Experiences. Mem.: Am. Soc. Indsl. Security (exec. bd. mem. 2005). Office: NJ City U 2039 Kennedy Blvd Rm P216 Jersey City NJ 07305-1597 Home Phone: 201-934-6749; Office Phone: 201-200-3502.

SOON, BOON YI, engineer; b. Singapore, Oct. 18, 1971; s. Ren Joo Soon and Yoke Lan Lee. MS in Electro-Optics, U. Dayton, 1997, MS in Applied Math., 2000, PhD in Electro-Optics, 2002. Optical designer Thales Electro-Optics Pte Ltd, Singapore, 2003—06; sr. transceiver designer Finisar Singapore Pte Ltd, 2006—. Contbr. articles to profl. jours. Charles Buckley scholar, 1993-95, Dayton Area Grad. Studies Inst. scholar, 1998-2002. Mem. Tau Beta Pi, Eta Kappa Nu, Phi Kappa Phi, Pi Mu Epsilon, Golden Key. Avocations: running, surfing the net, movies. Office: Finisar Singapore PTE LTD 10 Ang Mo Kio St 65 05-01/02/03 Techpoint Singapore 569059 Singapore Home Phone: 65-6896-1408. Personal E-mail: boonyi@yahoo.com.

SOON, WILLIE WEI-HOCK, environmental scientist; s. Gim-Chuan Soon and Chiew-See Chua; m. Julia Pham; 1 child, Benjamin Yue-Jian. PhD, U. So. Calif., Los Angeles, 1991. Postdoctoral scientist Harvard-Smithsonian Ctr. Astrophysics, Cambridge, Mass., 1991—97, astrophysicist, 1997—; astronomer Mt. Wilson Obs., Mount Wilson, Calif., 1992—2004; chief scientist Ctr. Sci. and Pub. Policy, Washington, 2003—. Vis. prof. U. Putra, Serdang, Selangor, Malaysia, 1999—2000; sr. rsch. fellow and contbr. techcentralstation.com, Washington, 2001—; chief scientist Ctr. for Sci. and Pub. Policy, Washington, 2003—. Author: (book) The Maunder Minimum and the Variable Sun-Earth Connection; receiving editor New Astronomy, 2002—. Sci. testimony U.S. Senate's Environment and Pub. Works Com., Washington, 2003. Recipient Nuc. and Plasma Sciences Soc. Grad. Scholastic award, IEEE, 1989, Rockwell Dennis Hunt Scholastic prize, U. So. Calif., 1991, award, Smithsonian Instn., 2003, Petr Beckmann award, Doctors for Disaster Preparedness, 2004. Office: Harvard-Smithsonian Ctr Astrophysics 60 Gardent St MS 16 Cambridge MA 02138 Office Phone: 617-495-7488. Office Fax: 617-495-7049. Business E-Mail: wsoon@cfa.harvard.edu.

SOON-SHIONG, PATRICK, pharmaceutical executive; m. Michele Chan; 2 children. MSc, U. Brit. Columbia; MD, U. Witwatersrand. CEO, chmn. bd. VivoRx, Inc., 1994—98; pres., CFO, dir. Am. BioScience, Inc., 1994—; CEO, chmn. bd. Am. Pharm. Partners, Inc. (renamed Abraxis BioScience in 2006), Schaumburg, Ill., 1996—, pres., 2001—. Named one of Forbes' Richest Americans, 2006. Fellow: ACS, Royal Coll. Physicians and Surgeons Can. Achievements include patents in field; invention of cancer treatment Abraxane. Office: Am Pharmaceutical Partners Ste 300 E 1501 E Woodfield Rd Schaumburg IL 60173-5837 *

SOONTHORNPOCT, PUNNEE, biology professor; d. Kimseap Soonthornpoct; m. John G. Barrera, Mar. 9, 1974; 1 child, Robin M. Hattox. BS, La. State U., Baton Rouge, 1966; PhD, Miss. State U., Starkville, 1998. Plant pathologist Ministry Agr., Phnom Penh, Cambodia, 1966—70; instr. Blinn Coll., Bryan Campus, Bryan, Tex.; grad. asst. Miss. State U., Starkville, 1974—74; substitute tchr. Coco Solo H.S., Cristobal Colon, Panama, 1975—77; rsch. technician Tex. A&M Expt. Sta., Weslaco, Tex., 1978—82; rsch. assoc. Tex. A&M U., College Station, 1982—95; grad. asst. Miss. State U., Starkville, 1996—98. Capt. intelligence Cambodian Armyy, 1970—71. Mem.: Blinn PA (pres. 2006—), Coll. Sta. Noon Lion Club (song leader 2006—). Methodist. Home: 702 Esther Blvd Bryan TX 77802 Office: Blinn Coll Biology Dept PO Box 6030 Bryan TX 77805-6030 Office Phone: 979-219-3979. Home Fax: 979-822-6353. E-mail: psoonthornpoct@blinn.edu.

SOORIYAARACHCHI, GAMINI SARATHCHANDRA, oncologist, hematologist, educator; b. Kosgama, Sri Lanka; m. Chandrika Senerath; children: Jasmine, Marcus. MBBS with honors, U. Ceylon, Colombo, Sri Lanka, 1970; diploma in child health, Conjoint Bd. Examiners, London, 1975; diploma in obstetrics, Royal Coll. Ob-Gyn Gt. Britain, 1975; MBA, U. Tenn., Knoxville, 2004. Diplomate Am. Bd. Internal Medicine, Am. Bd. Geriatric Medicine, Am. Bd. Med. Oncology, Am. Bd. Hematology, cert. physician exec. Cert. Commn. Med. Mgmt., 2005. Intern U. Ceylon Tchg. Hosps., 1970-71; sr. house officer Guildford Hosps., England, 1971-73; registrar St. Helens Hosp., England, 1974-75; sr. house officer Royal Marsden Hosp. and Inst. Cancer Rsch., Sutton, England, 1973-74; fellow in med. oncology and hematology U. Wis. Comprehensive Cancer Ctr., Madison, 1975-77; cons. med. oncologist and hematologist Rockford Clinic and Rockford Meml. Hosp., Ill., 1977-83, Oncology Hematology West and Alegent Bergan Mercy Cancer Ctr., Omaha, 1983—; med. dir. Alegent Bergan Mercy Cancer Ctr., Omaha, 1984—; co-dir. bone marrow transplantation program Oncology Hematology West and Alegent Bergan Mercy Med. Ctr., Omaha, 1993—. Asst. clin. prof. medicine U. Ill. Sch. Medicine, Rockford, 1977—83; bd. dirs. Cancer Biotherapy Rsch. Group, Franklin, Tenn.; mem. at-large med. exec. com. Alegent Bergan Mercy Med. Ctr., 2002—03, pres.-elect, vice chmn., 2003—04; pres., chief med. staff Alegent Bergan Mercy Med. Ctr, 2005—; bd. dirs. Missouri Valley Cancer Consortium, Omaha, pres., 1999—2001, prin. investigator, 2006—; assoc. clin. prof. medicine Creighton U. Sch. Medicine, Omaha, 1984—96, clin. prof., 1996—; chmn. prof. edn. Am. Cancer Soc., 1986, Nebr. divsn., 87, bd. dirs. Douglas and Sarpy Counties, Neb., 86, Nebr. divsn., 87; med. dir., founding mem. No. Ill. Hospice Assn., Rockford, 1980—83; mem. exec. com., novel therapeutics com., audit com., ethnic diversity com North Ctrl. Cancer Treatment Group, Mayo Clin., Rochester, Minn.; chmn. Am. Med. Assn. Sec. of Internat. Med. Graduates; alt. rep. AMA Commn. to End Healthcare Disparities. Contbg. author: Cancer Genetics in Women, 1987; contbr. over 60 articles and asbracts to med. jours., including Jour. Clin. Oncology, Blood, Archives Surgery, Jour. Immunotherapy, Cancer Investigation, Annals Pharmacotherapy, Jour. Am. Acad. Dermatology, Jour. Clin. Pathology. Recipient Leadership award (Internat. Med. Grad. Physician), AMA Found., 2006. Fellow ACP, Royal Coll. Physicians (London), Soc. for Biol. Therapy; mem. AMA (alt. del. to House of Dels. 2006-, alt. rep. Commn. to End Healthcare Disparities 2006-), Royal Coll. Surgeons (Eng.), Am. Soc. Clin. Oncology, Am. Soc. Hematology, Am. Soc. for Blood and Marrow Transplantation, Nebr. Med. Assn. Office: Alegent Health Bergan Mercy Cancer Ctr 7710 Mercy Rd Ste 122 Omaha NE 68124-2346

SOOUDI, MATTHEW M., retired surgeon; b. Iran, Oct. 24, 1934; came to U.S., 1962; s. Yahya and Iran (Nicknejad) S.; m. Joyce J. Sooudi, Oct. 2, 1965; 2 children. MD, U. Iran, 1962. Diplomate Am. Bd. Surgery, Am. Bd. Colon and Rectal Surgery, Internat. Bd. Proctology. Intern. Bon Secours Hosp., Grosse Pointe, Mich., 1962-63; resident Grace Hosp., Detroit, 1963-67, Ferguson Clinic, Grand Rapids, Mich., 1967-68; pvt. practice St. Elizabeth Hosp., Tex., Beaumont (Tex.) Med. Hosp., Bapt. Hosp., Tex.; ret., 1996. Fellow ACS, Am. Soc. Colon and Rectal Surgeons, Internat. Assn. Proctologists; mem. AMA, Am. Assn. Phys. Surgeons, So. Med. Assn., Tex. Med. Assn., Tex. Soc. Colon and Rectal Surgeons. Address: 980 Thomas Rd Beaumont TX 77706-4621

SOPANEN, JERI RAINER, photography director; b. Helsinki, Finland, Aug. 14, 1929; arrived in US, 1950; s. Rainer and Helvi Raakel (Salminen) S.; m. Carolyn Maier, 1952 (div. 1956); 1 child, Erik; m. Eileen A. Humeston, 1961 (div. 1980); ptnr. Christine Huneke, 1975 (separated 1991); children: Anya Maarit, Mark; m. Marja Roth, 2000. MusB, Lawrence Coll., 1952; BA, U. So. Calif., 1956. Ind. dir. photography Sopanen Films, Inc., NYC, 1966—. Dir. photography: (films) My Dinner With Andre, 1982, The Gig, 1986, The Luckiest Man in the World, 1989; (documentaries) The Brain, 1986, The Ring of Truth, 1987, The Mind (Emmy award 1989); dir. photography Nova programs, 1991—, Gardens of the World with Audrey Hepburn, 1993. With U.S. Army, 1952-54. Mem. Dirs. Guild Am., Internat. Assn. Theatrical Stage Employees. Democrat. Avocation: cross country skiing. Home and Office: 100 W 89th St Apt 8D New York NY 10024-1936 Office Phone: 212-799-0679. E-mail: jrsopanen@aol.com.

SOPER, JEANNINE, real estate agent; b. NYC, Nov. 24, 1929; d. Antonio Bruno and Marie Kapuscinski; widowed; children: Erik, Wayne. Grad., Scudder Secretarial Coll., 1948, Realtors Inst., 1970. Sec. Std. Brands Inc., NYC, 1948—52, Armstrong Rubber Co., Norwalk, Conn., 1952—53; real estate sales assoc. V, Ducale Real Estate, Norwalk, 1960—63; owner Sopers Real Estate, Norwalk, 1963—66; owner, ptnr. Siegel and Soper, Realtors, Norwalk, 1966—86; realtor, sales mgr. Prudential Real Estate, Norwalk, 1986—91; realtor Wm. Pitt Real Estate, Norwalk, 1991—. Pres. Women's Coun. Realtors, Conn., 1970, Norwalk Bd. Realtors, 1979. Exhibited in group shows at Rowayton Art Ctr., Darien Art Ctr., others. Chmn. Bd. Assessment Appeals, Norwalk, 1989—; pres., treas. Rowayton (Conn.) Art Ctr., 2000—. Mem.: Wilson Cove Yacht Club (life 1st Woman Commodore 1991). Office: Wm Pitt Sothebys Internat Real Estate 162 East Ave Norwalk CT 06851 Office Phone: 203-838-0018. Personal E-mail: jlsoper@optonline.net.

SOPHER, VICKI ELAINE, appraiser; b. Streator, Ill., May 22, 1943; d. Donald Bird and Thelma Elsie (Saxton) Watson; m. Terry Ray Sr., Jan. 20, 1962 (div. July 1982); 1 child, Terry Ray Jr. AA, No. Va. Community Coll., 1973; BA, Am. U., 1976; MS, Bank State Coll. Edn., 1986; Cert., Getty Mus. Mgmt. Inst., 1998. Cert. in appraisal courses George Washington U., 2004. Adminstrv. asst. Decatur & Wilson House, Washington, 1977-81; asst. dir. Decatur House/Nat. Trust for Hist. Preservation, Washington, 1981-84, dir., 1984-95; exec. dir. Hammond-Harwood House Assn., Annapolis, Md., 1996-98; curator Nat. Am. Red Cross, Washington, 1999—2004; pres. Vintage Appraisals, Inc., Tampa, Fla., 2005—. Cons.; founder, pres. Historic House Mus. Met. Washington. Mem. Am. Assn. Mus., Mid-Atlantic Assn. Mus., Am. Assn. State and Local History, Victorian Soc. Am. (bd. dirs.), Am. Soc. Appraisers. Home and Office: Vintage Appraisals 3118 W Wallcraft Ave Tampa FL 33611-1943 Home Phone: 813-902-1986; Office Phone: 815-300-9200. Personal E-mail: vsopher@verizon.net.

SOPHIANOPOULOS, JUDY ANN, environmental scientist; b. Terre Haute, Ind., Feb. 14, 1932; d. Keith and Claribel Symon; m. Alkis J. Sophianopoulos, June 4, 1955; children: Jan Catherine Anderson, Alkis John. BA, Rockford Coll., Ill., 1953; student, La Sorbonne, Paris, 1953-54; MS, Purdue U., 1957, PhD, 1960. Postdoctoral fellow U. Ill., Urbana, 1961; instr. Memphis State U., 1962; tchr. gen. sci. Yeshiva H.S., Atlanta, 1970-71; mass spectrometrist Emory U., Atlanta, 1983-86, sr. rsch. assoc., 1971-83, 86-87, lectr., dir. gen. chem. labs., 1971-87; environ. scientist U.S. EPA, 1987—2005, land disposal restrictions expert, Region 4, 1993—2005; ret., 2005. Contbr. chpt. to book, articles to profl. jours. Tutor Grady H.S., Atlanta, 1991—, Sci. Fair judge, 1993—; vol. McGovern/Shriver Campaign, Atlanta, 1971. Recipient Bronze medal EPA, 1993; Fulbright fellow, 1953. Mem. Am. Assn. for Clin. Chemistry, Am. Chem. Soc., Phi Beta Kappa. Democrat. Episcopalian. Achievements include work on development of theory and procedure for accurate and convenient method for measuring binding of small molecules to proteins; service on team which directed one of largest Superfund site cleanups. Home: 2994 Mccully Dr NE Atlanta GA 30345-3728 Personal E-mail: jsophian@mindspring.com.

SOPP, MARK W., corporate financial executive; B in acctg., New Mex. State Univ., 1987. CPA. CPA Arthur Andersen & Co., 1987—90; sr. acct. through dir. & internat. controller Taylor Made Gold Co., 1990—98; dir. fin. & bus. ops. Titan Systems Corp., 1998—99, v.p. fin. & bus. ops., 1999—2001; sr. v.p., CFO, treas. Titan Corp., 2001—05; exec. v.p., CFO Sci. Applications Internat. Corp., San Diego, 2005—. Office: SAIC 10260 Campus Point Dr San Diego CA 92121 *

SOPRANOS, ORPHEUS JAVARAS, manufacturing executive; b. Evanston, Ill., Oct. 4, 1935; s. James Javaras and Marigoula (Papalexatou) S.; m. Angeline Buches, Dec. 31, 1959; children: Andrew, Katherine. AB, MBA, U. Chgo., 1957. Mgmt. trainee Ford Motor Co., Chgo., 1958-59; with Amsted Industries, Chgo., 1959—, dir. bus. research, 1966-70, treas., 1970-80, v.p., 1980—; pres. Amsted Internat., 1991-93, corp. v.p., 1993-2000, ret. Served with U.S. Army, 1958, 61-62. Mem. Univ. Club (Chgo.), Skokie Country Club.

SORABELLA, PHILIP A., radiologist; m. Elaine E. Franco, Nov. 21, 1945. MD, Columbia P&S, NYC, 1968. Diplomate Am. Bd. Radiology, 1974, Am. Bd. Nuc. Medicine, 1974. Attending radiologist The Valley Hosp., Ridgewood, NJ, 1974—. Lt. US Pub. Health Svc., 1969—71. Office: Radiology Assocs Ridgewood Pa 20 Franklin Turnpike Waldwick NJ 07463 Home Phone: 201-848-5092; Office Phone: 201-447-8210.

SORAJJAKOOL, SIROJ, religious studies educator, psychology professor; b. Bangkok, Nov. 19, 1959; s. Sunti and Srirat Sorajjakool; m. Huiling Lee, Mar. 21, 1982; 1 child, Chanchai. MA in Religion, Andrews U., 1987; MA in Theology, Claremont Sch. Theology, 1997; PhD in Theology and Personality, Claremont Sch. Theology, Calif., 1999. Asst. pastor Ekamai Adventist Ch., Bangkok, 1982—83; assoc. pastor Bangkok Adventist Hosp. Ch., 1983—85; dir. Thailand Adventist Sem., Muak Lek, Saraburi, Thailand, 1987—92; academic dean, Muak Lek Campus Mission Coll., Muak Lek, 1990—92; assoc. dir. Adventist Devel. & Relief Agy., Bangkok, 1992—94; assoc. prof. Loma Linda U., Calif., 1999—2003, program dir., 2000—; rsch. scholar Ctr. Spiritual Life & Wholeness, Loma Linda, 2002—; prof. religion, psychology & counseling Loma Linda U., 2004—. Co-editor: Spirituality, Health, and Wholeness: An Introductory Guide for Healthcare Professionals; contbr. articles to profl. jours. Coord. scholarships for underprivileged elem. sch. students Adventist Devel. & Relief Agy., Chiang Rai, Thailand, 2001—07, coord. gravity fed water sys., 2002—02, coord. scholarships for at-risk girls Chiang Rai, 2003—07. Fellow: Am. Assn. Pastoral Counselors; mem.: Am. Acad. Religion (assoc.; sect. co-chair religion & psychology 2002—05), Soc. Pastoral Theology (assoc.; registrant 2006). D-Conservative. Seventh Day Adventist. Avocations: reading, travel. Office: Loma Linda Univ Rm 228 Griggs Hall Anderson St Loma Linda CA 92350 Business E-Mail: ssorajjakool@llu.edu.

SORAN, Z. OZLEM, medical educator; m. Atilla Soran. MD, Ankara U., Turkey, 1989; MPH, U. Pitts., 2004. Cert. cardiology Turkish Ministry Health, 1996. Chief resident cardiology Dr. MU Tchg. and Rsch. Hosp., Ankara, 1994—95, chief instr., attending cardiologist, 1996—97, attending cardiologist, nterim co-dir. cardiology dept., 1999—2001; instr., post doctoral fellow U. Pitts., Cardiovasc. Inst., 1997—99; asst. prof. medicine U. Pitts., 2001—03, assoc. prof. medicine, assoc. prof. epidemiology/rsch., 2003—. Dir. EECP rsch. lab. U. Pitts., 2001—. Contbr. articles to profl. jours. Named one of Top Forty Rsch., The Astra Zeneca Cardiovasc. Young Investigators' Forum, 2002; recipient Turkey's Best Physician/Scientist award, Anatolian Press Assn., 1999, Mediterranean Press Assn., 2002, Women of Distinction award, Daughters of Ataturk, 2004; grantee HFHC Project, Ctr. for Medicare and Medicaid Svcs., 2001—07; scholar, Turkish Med. Assoc., Internat. Fedn. Med. Students Assn., 1987, Japanese Govt., 1991. Fellow: European Soc. Cardiology, Am. Coll. Cardiology; mem.: AMA (Women Physician Congress), Am. Heart Assn. (clin. cardiology coun.), Turkish Med. Assn., Chamber of Medicine of Ankara, Turkish Cardiology Assn., So. Med. Assn. Office: University of Pittsburgh 200 Lothrop St Presby F-748 Pittsburgh PA 15213 Office Phone: 412-647-4411. Office Fax: 412-647-7005. Business E-Mail: osoran@lycos.com.

SORBER, CHARLES ARTHUR, academic administrator; b. Kingston, Pa., Sept. 12, 1939; s. Merritt Walter and Marjory (Roachford) S.; m. Linda Ellen Babcock, Feb. 20, 1972; children: Kimberly Ann, Kingsley Charles. BS in Sanitary Engring., Pa. State U., 1961, MS in Sanitary Engring., 1966; PhD, U. Tex., 1971. Sanitary engr. U.S. Army, France and Fed. Republic Germany, 1961-65; chief gen. engring. br. U.S. Army Environ Hygiene Agy., Edgewood Arsenal, Md., 1966-69; comdr. U.S. Army Med. Environ. Rsch. Unit, Edgewood Arsenal, Md., 1971-73; dir. environ. quality divsn. U.S. Army Med. Bioengring. R&D Lab., Frederick, Md., 1973-75; asst. dean coll. scis. and math. U. Tex., San Antonio, 1976-77, acting dir. divsn. earth & phys. scis., 1977-80, dir. Ctr. Applied Rsch. & Tech., 1976-80, assoc. dean coll. engring. Austin, 1980-86, L.B. (Preach) Meaders prof., 1985; dean sch. engring. U. Pitts., 1986-93; pres. U. Tex.-Permian Basin, Odessa, 1993-2001; prof. U. Tex., Austin, 2001—; interim vice chancellor for spl. engring. programs U. Tex. Sys., 2002—03; interim pres. U. Tex., Arlington, 2003—04, spl. engring. advisor. Bd. dirs., adv. coun., cons. various cos. and agys. Author, co-author more than 140 papers, book chpts., reports on land application of wastewater and sludges, water and wastewater reuse, water and wastewater disinfection and higher edn. Recipient Disting. Alumnus award Wilkes Coll., 1987, Disting. Grad. award Coll. of Engring., U. Tex., Austin, 1994, Outstanding Engring. Alumnus award Pa. State U., 1994; John A. Focht teach fellow U. Tex.-Austin, 1982. Fellow: ASCE; mem.: NSPE, Coun. Pub. Univ. Presidents and Chancellors (exec. com. Tex. 1994—95, sec.-treas. 1999—2001), Am. Water Works Assn., Am. Soc. Engring. Edn., Water Environ. Fedn. (com. chmn. 1983—85, 1986—89, 1993—96, bd. control 1988—94, v.p. 1990—91, pres.-elect 1991—92, pres. 1992—93, Svc. award 1985, 1989, 1990, 1996), Am. Acad. Environ. Engrs. (trustee 1994—97, 2002—, diplomate, Gordon Maskew Fair award 1993), The U. Tex. Club. Office Phone: 512-322-3776. Business E-Mail: csorber@utsystem.edu.

SORBY, DONALD LLOYD, retired dean; b. Fremont, Nebr., Aug. 12, 1933; s. Lloyd A. and Orpha M. (Simmons) S.; m. Jacquelyn J. Burchard, Nov. 7, 1959; children: Thomas, Sharon. BS in Pharmacy, U. Nebr., 1955; MS, U. Wash., 1958, PhD, 1960. Dir. pharm. services U. Calif., San Francisco, 1970-72; chmn. dept. pharmacy practice Sch. Pharmacy, U. Wash., Seattle, 1972-74; dean Sch. of Pharmacy, U. Mo., Kansas City, 1974-84, Sch. of Pharmacy, U. Pacific, Stockton, Calif., 1984-95, dean emeritus, 1995—. Contbr. articles to profl. jours. Named Disting. Alumnus, U. Nebr. Coll. Pharmacy, 2000. Mem. Am. Pharm. Assn. (Linwood F. Tice award 1995), Am. Assn. Colls. of Pharmacy (pres. 1980-81), Calif. Pharm. Assn., Calif. Soc. Health-Sys. Pharmacists, Sigma Xi, Phi Kappa Phi, Rho Chi. Home: 4362 Yacht Harbor Dr Stockton CA 95204-1126 E-mail: dsorby@att.net.

SORDELLO, STEVE, communications executive; b. 1970; BA in Fin. and Mgmt., Santa Clara U., MBA. Cert. Mgmt. Acct. Various positions in finance and acctg. Syntex Corp., Palo Alto, Calif.; sr. dir., fin. planning Adobe Systems, Inc.; joined Ask Jeeves, Inc., Oakland, Calif., 1999, dir., fin. planning and analysis, 1999—2000, v.p. fin. planning and analysis, 2000, acting CFO, 2000—01, exec. v.p., CFO, 2001—05; CFO TiVo Inc., 2006—. Office: TiVo Inc PO Box 2160 Alviso CA 95002-2160 Office Phone: 510-985-7400. Office Fax: 510-985-7412.

SOREGAROLI, A(RTHUR) E(ARL), mining executive, geologist; b. Jan. 4, 1933; arrived in Can., 1962; s. Arthur Samuel and Margaret Alice S.; m. Rosalie Ann Lawrick, Dec. 22, 1962; children: Carla Jean, Brian Arthur. BSc in Geology, Iowa State U., 1959; MSc in Geology, U. Idaho, 1961; PhD in Geology, U. B.C., Vancouver, Can., 1968. Geologist Idaho Bur. Mines and Geology, Moscow, 1961-62, Noranda Exploration Co. Ltd., Vancouver, 1963-68, chief geologist western dist., 1968-72; asst. prof. geology U. B.C., Vancouver, 1972-74; rsch. scientist Geol. Survey Can., Ottawa, Ont., 1974-76; v.p. exploration Westmin Resources Ltd., Vancouver, 1976-90; chief geoscientist Teck Corp., Vancouver, 1990-98; pres. AES Enterprises, Ltd., Vancouver, 1998—. Dir. Mineral. Record, 1995—, pres., 1999-2001; contbr. papers to sci. lit. Pres. Britannia Beach Hist. Soc. which operates BC Mus. Mining, 1995-03; dir. Pacific Mineral Mus. Soc., 1998-04. With US Army, 1952-54. Fellow Geol. Assn. Can. (Duncan R. Derry Gold medal 1997), Soc. Econ. Geologists (pres. 1985), Geol. Soc. Am.; mem. Prospector and Developers Assn. Can. (life), Assn. Exploration Geochemists (pres. 1989-90), Can. Inst. Mining and Metallurgy (chmn. geology divsn. 1978, Dist. Proficiency Gold medal 1986, Julian Boldly Meml. award 1989, hon. fellow 1990, v.p. Dist. 6 1982-84, Disting. Svc. medal 1991, A.O. Dufresne award 2000, life 2005-), Mineral Assn. Can., Friends of Mineralogy (dir. 1997-00, 03—), Assn. for Mineral Exploration BC (life, Frank Woodside Disting. Svc. award 2004). Avocations: sports, mineral collecting.

SOREL, EDWARD, artist; b. NYC, Mar. 26, 1929; s. Morris and Rebecca (Kleinberg) Schwartz; m. Nancy Caldwell, May 29, 1965; children: Jenny, Katherine; children by previous marriage: Madeline, Leo. Diploma, Cooper Union, 1951; DFA (hon.), Art Inst. Boston, 1998. Co-founder Pushpin Studio, 1953; free-lance artist, 1956—; syndicated Sorel's News Service, 1969-70, King Features. Author, illustrator: Making the World Safe for Hypocrisy, 1972; exhibited in Pushpin Studio retrospective at the Louvre, 1970, other European galleries, 1970-71; exhibited one-man show, Graham Galleries, NYC, 1973, 78, Galerie Bartsch & Chariau, Munich, 1986, Retrospective Exhibition Cooper Union, 1987, Susan Conway Galleries, Washington, 1992, Soc. Illustrators Am. Mus. Illustration, NYC, 1993, Davis and Langdale Galleries, NYC, 1994, 97, 2006, Nat. Portrait Gallery, Washington, 1999; illustrator: Pablo Paints a Picture, 1961, Gwendolyn the Miracle Hen, 1963 (NY Herald Tribune Book award for illustration 1962), What's Good for a Five-Year-Old, 1969, The Duck in the Gun, 1969, Word People, 1970, Magical Storybook, 1972, Superpen, 1978, The Zillionaire's Daughter, 1990, First Encounters, 1994, Unauthorized Portraits, 1997, Johnny on the Spot, 1998, The Saturday Kid, 2000, Literary Lives, 2006; muralist: Waverly Inn, Greenwich Village, NY, 2007; contbr. to Nation, New Yorker, Vanity Fair, American Heritage and Atlantic monthly mags. Recipient awards Soc. Illustrators, Art Dirs. Club N.Y.; Augustus St. Gauden's medal Cooper Union; George Polk award for satiric drawing, 1981; Page One award Newspaper Guild of N.Y. for best editorial cartoon (magazines), 1988, Hamilton King award Soc. Illustrators, 1990, John Singleton Copley medal Smithsonian Instn., 1999, Art Dirs. Hall of Fame, 2001, Karikaturpreis Deutschen Anwaltschaft 2002. Office Phone: 212-665-0698. Office Fax: 212-665-0699. Personal E-mail: edwardsorel@hotmail.com.

SORELL, KITTY JULIA, public relations executive; b. Vienna, Apr. 20, 1937; came to U.S. 1938; d. Bruno Alexander and Ilse (Fischl) Singerman. BA, Syracuse U., 1959. Lic. realtor Real Estate Bd. N.Y. Spl. events coord. Gimbel's, NYC, 1966—69; pub. rels./account exec. Hamra Assocs., NYC, 1969—71; spl. events/pub. rels. dir. Stern Bros., Paramus, NJ, 1972; pub. rels. account exec. Zachary & Front, NYC, 1972—76; dir. pub. rels. RSM&K Advt., NYC, 1976—77; owner Kitty Sorell Pub. Rels., NYC, 1977—; realtor, v.p., assoc. broker Corcoran Group, NYC, 1994—. Reporter Wisdom's Child, 1981-84, The Villager, 1986-88; lectr. in field. Contbg. editor Mktg. Maker mag., 1976. Fundraiser WNET-TV, N.Y.C., 1974-75; vol. pub. rels. Sheridan Sq. Triangle Assn., N.Y.C., 1984-89; pres. bd. dirs. Apt. House Coop., 1991—; bd. dirs. Greenwich Village Alliance, 1994—; mem. Greenwich Village Soc. for Hist. Preservation, 1999—. Mem. Am. Soc. Profl. and Exec. Women, Publicity Club. Democrat. Jewish. Avocations: books, theater. Office: Kitty Sorell Pub Rels 250 W 57th St New York NY 10107 Office Phone: 212-539-4968. E-mail: kjs@corcoran.com.

SORELLE, RUTH DOYLE, writer, journalist; b. Port Arthur, Tex., Oct. 9, 1948; d. Richard Thomas and Ruth Elaine (Droddy) D.; m. Paul Charles SoRelle, Apr. 10, 1970; children: Danielle Amanda, Richard Paul. BJ, U. Tex., 1971; MPH, U. Tex., Houston, 1988. Reporter Port Arthur News, summer 1968, 69, Univ. and Info. Svc., Austin, Tex., 1970-71; med. editor U. Tex. MD Anderson Hosp., Houston, 1973-74; editor Resources Devel. Corp., Houston, 1974-76; med. editor Baylor Coll. Medicine, Houston, 1977-78; copy editor Houston Chronicle, Houston, 1978-79, med. writer, 1979-99; chief sci. editor Baylor Coll., 1999—, editor 2 online newsletters. Instr. U. Houston, 1986, 87, 89; editor websites. Leader Presbyn. Youth Fellowship, Houston, 1989; co-chair Tex. State Strategic Health Partnership. Recipient John P. McGovern award Am. Med. Writers Assn., Community Svc. award Tex. Assoc. Press, 1993, Katie award Dallas Press Club, 1992, 93, Anson Jones award Tex. Med. Assn., 1981, 83, 85, 86, 88, 90, 92, 95, 96, 98, Francis C. Moore award Harris County Med. Assn., 1984-98, Silver Star Tex. award Tex. Hosp. Assn., 1984, 86, 89, 92, Tex. Pub. Health Assn. award, 1981, 89, 90, 91, 94, Houston Area Health Care Coalition's Health Policy Leadership award, 1990, Paul Ellis award Am. Heart Assn., 1988, 95, Nat. Multiple Sclerosis Soc. award for med. writing, 1998, Inernat. Health Reporting award Pan Am Health Orgn., 1998, others. Mem. Am. Med. Writer's Assn. (bd. dirs. southwest chpt. 1994-95), Press Club of Houston (Deadline Coverage award 1984, Investigative Series award 1990, Mag. Feature award 1994). Democrat. Avocations: bicycling, reading, swimming. Business E-Mail: dsorelle@bcm.tmc.edu.

SORELL STEHR, DEBORAH K., lawyer; b. NYC, 1962; m. Mark Stehr; children: Daniel, Julia. AB, Princeton U., 1984; JD, Northwestern U., 1987. Bar: 1987. With Kronish Lieb Weiner & Hellman, O'Sullivan Graev & Karabell; assoc. gen. counsel Nine West Group Inc., 1996—98; gen. counsel Iconix Brand Group, Inc., 1998—, v.p., 1998—99, sr. v.p., 1999—. Office: Iconix Brand Group Inc 215 W 40th St New York NY 10018 Office Phone: 212-730-0030. Office Fax: 212-391-2057.

SOREN, DAVID, archaeologist, educator, writer, filmmaker; b. Phila., Oct. 7. 1946: s. Harry Friedman and Erma Elizabeth (Salamon) Soren; m. Noelle Louise Schattyn, Dec. 22, 1967. BA, Dartmouth Coll., 1968; MA, Harvard U., 1972, PhD, 1973. Cert. Rome Classics Ctr. Curator of coins Fogg Art Mus., Cambridge, Mass., 1972; asst. prof. U. Mo., Columbia, 1972-76, assoc. prof., dept. head, 1976-81; prof. U. Ariz., Tucson, 1982-97, Regents prof., 1997—, dept. head, 1984-89. Guest curator Am. Mus. Natural History, NYC, 1983—90, lectr, 1993—; creator, dir. Kourion Excavations, Cyprus, 1982—89, Portugal, 1983—84, Am. Excavations, Lugnano, Italy, 1988—93; pot cons., field dir. Tunisa Excavations, Chgo. Oriental Inst./Smithsonian Instn., 1973—78; dir. excavations Chianciano, Terme, Italy, 1995—; dir. Orvieto (Italy) Inst. Classical Studies, 2002—; resident in classical archaeology Am. Acad., Rome, 2002. Author: (book) Unreal Reality, 1978, Rise and Fall of Fantasy Film, 1980, Carthage, 1990, Carthage, French edit., 1994, Vera-Ellen: The Magic and the Mystery, 1999, 2d edit., 2003, Lugnano! Excavation of a Roman Villa, 1999, Kourion: Search for a Lost Roman City, 1988, Corpus des Mosaiques de Tunisie, 1972, Corpus des Mosaiques de Tunisie, 3d rev. edit., 1986, Carthage: A Mosaic of Ancient Tunisia, 1987; editor: Excavations at Kourion I, 1987; contbg. editor: Archaeology Mag.; prodr.: (films) Carthage: A Mirage of Antiquity, 1987; creator, guest curator (internt traveling exhbn.) Carhtage: A Mosaic of Ancient Tunisia, 1987—92; editor, founder: Roscius, 1993—95; creative cons. (TV miniseries) Lost Civilizations, 1994; contbr. articles to profl. jours.; prodr.: (documentaries) BBC-TV documentary Malaria and the Fall of Rome, 2002; author: Vera-Ellen: The Magic and the Mystery; 2d edit., 2003; cons.: The History Channel, 2004; cons., on-screen contbr. The Colosseum, History Channel, 2005, Where Did it Come From?, 2006, Where Did It Begin. Named Outstanding Am. Under 40, Esquire Mag., 1985, hon. Italian citizen, Lugnano, Italy, 1989; recipient Cine Golden Eagle, 1980, Angenieux Film award, Indsl. Photography Mag., 1980, Oustanding Am. Under 40 award, C. Johns Hopkins-Britain's Royal Inst. Internat. Affairs, 1985; grantee, NEH, 1979, 1987, Fulbright, Lisbon, 1983. Fellow: Brit. Royal Inst. Internat. Affairs; mem.: Am. Acad. Rome (mem. internat. com. 2003—, bd. dirs. 2003—), Luso-Am. Commn. (citation 1983—84), Archaeol. Inst. Tucson (pres. 1983—86), Am. Sch. Oriental Rsch. (dept. rep. 1981—85), Nat. Geog. Soc. (project dir. 1983—84). Office: U Ariz Dept Classics 371 Mlb Tucson AZ 85721-0001 Office Phone: 520-621-1689. Business E-Mail: soren@u.arizona.edu.

SORENSEN, ALLAN CHRESTEN, service company executive; b. Edson, Alta., Can., Apr. 27, 1938; arrived in U.S., 1962, naturalized, 1965; s. Henry and Vivien A. Sorensen; children: Scott, Jody, Rosey. BS in Pharmacy, Drake U., 1961. Salesman Hoffman LaRoche Pharm. Co., Kitchener, Ont., Canada, 1961-62; salesman Personnel Pool of Am., Inc., Chgo., 1962-63, sales mgr., 1963-67, dir., pres., 1967-89, chief exec. officer, 1978-91, chmn. interim svcs., 1989-97; vice chmn., co-founder Interim Healthcare Inc., Ft. Lauderdale, 1997—2004, pres., CEO, 2004—; dir. Republic Svcs., Inc., Ft. Lauderdale, 1998—. Mem. Am. Staffing Assn. (past pres., bd. dir.), Am. Assn. for Homecare (past chmn., bd. dir.), Broward Workshop. Republican. Home: 333 Sunset Dr #708 Fort Lauderdale FL 33301 Office: Interim Healthcare Inc 1601 Sawgrass Corporate Pkwy Sunrise FL 33323-2827

SORENSEN, ANDREW AARON, academic administrator; b. Pitts., July 20, 1938; s. Albert Aaron and Margaret (Lindquist) S.; m. Donna Ingemie, Aug. 4, 1968; children: Aaron Ashley, Benjamin Samuel. BA, U. Ill., 1959; BDiv, Yale U., 1962, MPh, 1970, PhD, 1971; MPH, U. Mich., 1966. Asst. prof. Cornell U., Ithaca, NY, 1971-73, U. Rochester, NY, 1973-76, assoc. prof. NY, 1976-83; prof., dean U. Mass., Amherst, 1983-86, Johns Hopkins U., Balt., 1986-90, exec. dir. AIDS Inst.; provost, v.p. acad. affairs U. Fla., Gainesville, 1990-96; pres. U. Ala., Tuscaloosa, 1996—2002, U. SC, Columbia, 2002—. Vis. fellow U. Cambridge, 1979—80; pres. bd. Preservation Inst. Nantucket, 1990—96. Author 7 books; chmn. editl. bd. U. Press., Fla., 1990-96; contbr. over 100 articles to profl. jours. Vice-chmn., bd. dirs. Chautauqua Instn., 1996-98; bd. mem. Nat. Sci. Advisory Bd. for Biosecurity, 2005—; mem. Bush Transition Team, 2000-01. U.S. Dept. Edn. fellow Lincoln U., 1966-67, NSF fellow Harvard U., 1975-76; named Amb. of Yr., Greater Columbia C of C. Mem.: So. Univ. Conf. (past pres.), Univ. Rsch. Assn. (trustee), Southeastern Univs. Rsch. Assn. (past chmn. coun. presidents, pres. conf.). Presbyterian. Office: Office of Pres U SC Osborne 206 Columbia SC 29208 Home Phone: 803-777-3104; Office Phone: 803-777-2931. Business E-Mail: sorensen@sc.edu.

SØRENSEN, ERIK, retired diversified financial services company executive; b. Randers, Denmark, July 19, 1944; s. Christen and Erna Sørensen; m. Brigitte Berg; children: Anne Marie, Thomas, Anne Louise, Anne Mette, Anne Sophie. MS in Chemistry, Tech. U. Denmark, 1968; MBA in Internat. Fin., Cph Sch. Econs., 1971. Sr. economist Novo Industri A/S, Bagsvaerd, Denmark, 1970-71, mgr. econs. and planning, 1972-74, v.p. sales and mktg., 1974-80, pres. bioindsl. group, 1980-88; pres. Health Care Grp Novo Nordisk A/S, 1988-1995; pres., CEO Christian Hansen Group, Denmark, 1995—; ret., 2005. Bd. dirs., chmn. ISS A/S. Lt. Danish Army, 1968-70. Office: Chr Hansen Group Bøge Allé 10 2970 Horsholm Denmark

SORENSEN, GILLIAN MARTIN, United Nations official; b. Columbus, Ohio, Mar. 4, 1941; d. John Butlin and Helen (Hickam) Martin; m. Theodore C. Sorensen, June 28, 1969; 1 child, Juliet. BA, Smith Coll., 1963. Commr. N.Y.C. Commn. for UN and Consular Corps, 1978-90; pres. Nat. Conf., 1990-93; undersec gen., spl. advisor for pub. policy UN, NYC, 1993-97, UN asst. sec. gen. for external rels., 1997—2003; sr. advisor UN Found., NYC, 2003—. Del. Dem. Nat. Conv., 1976, 84, 88. Mem.: Acad. Coun. on the UN, Women's Forum, Coun. on Fgn. Rels. Democrat. Office: UN Found 801 Second Ave Ste 404 New York NY 10017 Office Phone: 212-697-3315. Business E-Mail: gsorenson@unfoundation.org.

SORENSEN, HARVEY R., lawyer; b. Chgo., Nov. 3, 1947; s. Harvey T. and Jean Louise (Cline) S.; m. Emily Smith, May 31, 1969 (div. May 1980); children: Abigail, Jeanne, Cornelia; m. Stephanie Sorensen, Dec. 31, 1980; 1 child, Tyler. BA, Beloit Coll., 1969; MSBA, Boston U., 1972; JD cum laude, Northwestern U., 1974. Bar: Wis. 1974, U.S. DISt. Ct. (ea. dist.) Wis. 1974, U.S. Dist. Ct. Kans., U.S. Tax Ct., 1975, U.S. Ct. Claims 2002. Tax acct. Arthur, Young & Co., Chgo., 1974; assoc. Whyte & Hirschboeck, Milw., 1974-75; asst. adj. prof. Wichita (Kans.) State U. Sch. Bus., 1979; ptnr. Foulston & Siefkin, Wichita, 1975—. Bd. dir. Equity Bank N.A., Equity Bankshares, Inc., World Svcs. Group, Inc., chmn., 2005—06. Trustee, vice chmn. Kans. Pub. Telecom. Svc., 1978—97, chmn., 1997—99; bd. dirs. Wichita Downtown Devel. Corp., 1996—2004, chmn., 2001—03; chmn. adv. bd. City of Wichita Self Supporting Mcpl. Improvement Dist., 2001—03; project bus. cons. Jr. Achievement, 1978—93; trustee Wichita Symphony Soc., 1986—96, Wichita Collegiate Sch., 1994—2004, Wichita Sedgewick County Hist. Mus., 1986—89, Wichita Arts Coun., 1979—82; bd. dirs. Goodwill Industries/Easter Seals of Kans. Area, 2001—; bd. cmty. adv. KMUW, 1981—82; co-chmn. Visioneering Wichita, 2004—; commr. City of Eastborough, Kans., 1991—93; treas. St. James Episcopal Ch., 1996—99; bd. dirs. Wichita Greyhound Charities, 1999, Episcopal Social Svcs. Endowment Fund., 2003—. With US Army, 1970—72. Fellow Am. Coll. Tax Counsel; mem. ABA (mem. taxation sect., sec. 2002-, chair bus. coop. and agrl. com. 2005—, chmn. state and local tax com. Lex Mundi 2003-05), Wichita Bar Assn., Kans. Bar Assn. (past sect., v.p., pres. tax. sect. 1984-88), Attys. Family Held Enterprises, Wichita Area C. of C. (bd. dir. 2000—, vice-chmn. 2003—), Rotary. Republican. Episcopalian. Home: 13 Colonial Ct Wichita KS 67207-1056 Office: Foulston Siefkin LLP 1551 N Waterfront Pky Ste 100 Wichita KS 67206-4466 Home Phone: 316-682-9590; Office Phone: 316-291-9774. Business E-Mail: hsorensen@foulston.com

SORENSEN, JOHN B., surgeon; s. Bruce F. and Suzanne B. Sorensen. MD, Temple U., 1986. Cert. surgery Am. Bd. Surgery, 1992, critical care Am. Bd. Surgery, 1995, transplantation surgery U. Pitts., 1993. Dir. transplantation LDS Hosp., Salt Lake City, 1993—2005; chief sect. transplantation dept. surgery U. Utah, Salt Lake City, 2005—. Med. dir. Intermountain Donor Services, Salt Lake City, 2004—. Lt. col. US Army, 2002. Decorated Combat Med. Badge, Bronze Star U.S. Army. Fellow: ACS; mem.: Am. Soc. Transplant Surgeons, Sigma Chi. Mem. Lds Ch. Office: Univ Utah Dept Surgery 30 North 1900 East Salt Lake City UT 84132 Office Phone: 801-585-2816.

SORENSEN, JOHN NOBLE, retired mechanical and nuclear engineer; b. Mpls., Jan. 2, 1934; s. Alfred Noble and Helen Viola (Baker) S.; m. Joan Elizabeth Reiche, Sept. 15, 1954; children: Laura Elizabeth, Nancy Helen, Karen Lynn. BSME, U. N.D., 1955; MSME, U. Pitts., 1958. Cert. engr. Sr. engr. Westinghouse Electric, Pitts., 1955-67; v.p., gen. mgr. NUS Corp., Rockville, Md., 1967-86; v.p., dir. Grove Engring., Inc., Rockville, 1986-93; tech. asst. to commr. NRC, Washington, 1993-97, sr. fellow adv. com. on reactor safeguards, 1997—2001, sr. fellow adv. com. on nuclear waste, 1997—2001, spl. asst. spent fuel project office, 2002—03; prin. cons. Project Enhancement Corp., 2004—. Mem. ASME, NSPE, Am. Nuclear Soc., Sigma Xi. Home: 629 Crocus Dr Rockville MD 20850-2046 Office: Project Enhancement Corporation 20300 Century Blvd Ste 175 Germantown MD 20874-1189 Office Phone: 240-686-3059. Personal E-mail: jsoren5605@aol.com.

SORENSEN, LINDA, lawyer; b. Eureka, Calif., Mar. 3, 1945; BS, U. Wis., 1967; JD, U. Calif., 1976. Bar: Calif. 1976, U.S. Dist. Ct. (no. dist.) Calif. 1976, U.S. Ct. Appeals (9th cir.) 1976, U.S. Dist. Ct. (ea. dist.) Calif. 1977. Assoc., ptnr. Rothschild, Phelan & Mortali, San Francisco, 1976-88; dir. Howard, Rice, Nemerovski, Canady, Falk & Rabkin, San Francisco, 1988-95; shareholder Feldman, Waldman & Kline, P.C., San Francisco, 1997-99; pvt. practice Berkeley, Calif., 1999—; of counsel Stromsheim & Assoc., 2001—. Mem. ABA (mem. subcom. on avoiding powers, bus. bankruptcy com. 1983-95), Bar Assn. of San Francisco (chmn. comml. law and bankruptcy sect. 1984, editor fed. cts. com., no. dist. Calif. digest 1979-82). Office: PO Box 325 Bodega Bay CA 94923 Office Fax: 707-875-9287. Personal E-mail: lindasorensen@earthlink.net.

SORENSEN, MURRAY JIM, lawyer; b. Blackfoot, Idaho, Feb. 10, 1948; s. Murray L. and Lona Mae (Clegg) S.; m. Gay Grimshaw, May 25, 1974; children— Benjamin Jim, Joshua John, Matthew Murray, Daniel Henry, Adam Michael. Student in Political Sci., Brigham Young U., 1965-72; J.D., U. Idaho, 1975. Bar: Idaho 1975, U.S. Dist. Ct. Idaho 1975. Asst. prosecutor Bingham County, Idaho, 1975-77, pub. defender, 1979-82; city atty. City of Blackfoot, 1978-79; ptnr. Blasen & Sorensen Chartered, Blackfoot, 1981—; city atty. City of Basalt, Idaho, 1984—. Chmn. Eastern Idaho Fair Parade, Blackfoot, 1978-79, United Fund, Blackfoot, 1979, Ducks Unltd., Blackfoot, 1983-84; Pres., Idaho 7th Dist. Bar, 1996-97 (v.p. and gen. coun. 1992-94). Named to Outstanding Young Men Am., U.S. Jaycees, 1982. Mem. ABA, Assn. Trial Lawyers Am., Idaho Trial Lawyers Assn., Blackfoot C. of C. (bd. dirs. 1979-80). Mormon. Lodge: Kiwanis (bd. dirs. local lodge 1983-84).

SORENSON, ARNE M., hotel executive; b. Tokyo; BA, Luther Coll., 1980; JD, U. Minn., 1983. Law clk. to Hon. Ellsworth Van Graafeiland U.S. Ct. Appeals (2d cir.), 1983—84; assoc. attorney Latham & Watkins, Washington, 1984—90; ptnr. Latham & Watkins, Washington, 1990—96; sr. v.p. bus. devel. Marriott Internat. Inc., Washington, 1996-98, exec. v.p., CFO, 1998—, pres., continental European lodging, 2003—. Office: Marriott Internat Inc 1 Marriott Dr Washington DC 20058-0001 *

SORENSON, CHRISTOPHER J., lawyer; b. Laramie, Wyo., May 1, 1970; 4 children. BA, Macalester Coll., 1993; JD cum laude, William Mitchell Coll. Law, 1996. Bar: Minn. 1996, US Dist. Ct. (dist. Minn.) 1996, US Dist. Ct. (dist. Colo.) 1996, US Ct. Appeals (1st, 7th, 8th and Fed. cirs.) 1996. Ptnr. Merchant & Gould, P.C., Mpls. Named a Rising Star, Minn. Super Lawyers mag., 2006. Avocation: fishing. Office: Merchant & Gould PC 3200 IDS Ctr 80 S 8th St Minneapolis MN 55402 Office Phone: 612-336-4645. E-mail: csorenson@merchant-gould.com. *

SORENSON, GEORGIA LYNN JONES, political science professor; b. Abilene, Tex., Aug. 23, 1947; d. Wyly King and Olive M. (Sorenson) Jones; 1 child, Suzanna Simmonds Strasburg. BA, Am. U., 1974; MA, Hood Coll., 1976; PhD, U. Md., 1992. Social scientist Nat. Inst. Edn., Washington, 1978-79, U.S. Commn. Civil Rights, Washington, 1976-79; sr. policy analyst The White House, Washington, 1979-80; founder, sr. scholar James MacGregor Burns Acad. Leadership U. Md., College Park, 1980—; d. Adv. mem. W.K. Kellogg Found. Nat Fellows, Battle Creek, Mich., 1996-99; inaugural chair, prof. transformation U.S. Army, U.S. Army War Coll., 2005-06. Co-author: (with James MacGregor Burns) Dead-Center: Clinton-Gore Leadership and the Perils of Moderation, 1999; editor: (with George Goethals and James MacGregor Burns) Encyclopedia of Leadership, 2004, The Quest for a General Theory of Leadership, 2006; contbr. articles to profl. jours. Chair Md. Women's Polit. Caucus, 1991-94; mem. White House Productivity Coun., Washington, 1979; mem. V.P. Youth Employment Task Force, 1979-80. Mem. Am. Polit. Sci. Assn., Internat. Soc. Polit. Psychologists, A.K. Rice Inst. Office: James MacGregor Burns Acad Leadership Univ Md College Park MD 20742-0001 Office Phone: 301-405-6100. Business E-Mail: gsorenson@academy.umd.edu.

SORENSON, GRETCHEN HARTLEY, elementary school educator; b. Muncie, Ind., Dec. 3, 1935; d. James Ross and Lois (Reed) Hartley; m. Ray L. Valour, June 6, 1959 (div. June 1988); 1 child, Virginia; m. George W. Sorenson, June 17, 1988. BFA, Colo. U., 1957; MA in Edn., Ball State U., 1961; cert. elem. edn. administrn., Ariz. State U., 1980. Cert. elem. art, elem. classroom, elem. administrn. Art tchr. Jefferson County (Colo.) Schs., Jefferson County, Colo., 1957-59; tchr. Delaware County Schs., Selma, Ind., 1959-60, Beverly (Mass.) Schs., 1960-61, Delaware County Schs., Muncie, Ind., 1961-66, Park Forest (Ill.) Schs., 1966-68, Scottsdale (Ariz.) Pub. Schs., 1968—95, Trinity Luth. Sch., Fountain Hills, Ariz., 1995—. Trainer of tchrs. Ariz. Bar Found., Phoenix, 1988-93; mem. site-based mgmt. team Laguna Sch., 1990-91. Author: (book) Fifth of Fun, 1986. Mem. ch. bd. Paradise Valley (Ariz.) United Meth. Ch., 1970-74, Desert Hills Presbyn. Ch., Carefree, Ariz., 1975-87, Shepherd Desert Luth. Ch., Scottsdale, 1988—; mem. exec. bd. Luth. Hispanic Ministry; mem. Scottsdale Bicentennial Commn., 1987-90. Recipient Outstanding Young Educator, C. of C., Park Forest, 1968. Mem. Phi Delta Kappa (treas. 1988-91, Outstanding Educator award 1992). Lutheran. Avocations: travel, reading. Home: 15043 E Greene Valley Dr Fountain Hills AZ 85268-1339 E-mail: g2sorenson@att.net.

SORENSON, JAMES LEVOY, research and development company executive; b. Rexburg, Idaho, 1921; m. Beverley Sorenson; 8 children. Pharmaceutical salesman Upjohn Co., 1946—57; co-founder Deseret Pharm., 1957; founder LeVoy's (lingerie bus.), 1960, Sorenson Rsch. Co. (now Abbott Critical Care Sys.), 1962; chmn. Sorenson Devel. Inc. Exec. bd. mem. Nat. Conf. Christians and Jews. Missionary Ch. Jesus Christ Latter-day Saints New Eng. Named one of Forbes' Richest Americans, 1999—, World's Richest People, Forbes mag., 2001—; recipient Giant of Our City award, Salt Lake City, 2006. Achievements include patents for the first computer-based real-time heart monitor, 1975; invention of Sorenson VP-100 videophone, a device which assists the deaf and hard of hearing in communication; disposable surgical mask and the disposable venous catheter. Home: Sorenson Molecular Geneaology Found 2511 SW Temple Salt Lake City UT 84115 *

SORENSON, KENNETH RAYMOND, military officer, chaplain; b. Racine, Wis., Dec. 30, 1961; s. Kenneth Charles and Lois Helen Sorenson; m. Patrice Lynn Hesse, July 2, 1988; children: Joshua David, Hannah Marie, Samuel James, Naomi Ruth. BA in Econs., U. Wis. Parkside, Kenosha, 1984; MDiv, Trinity Internat. U., Deerfield, Ill., 1988, MA in Counseling Psychology, 1999; MS in Marriage and Family Counseling, Tarleton State U., Killeen, Tex., 2006. Lic. minister Evang. Ch. Alliance, Ill., 1989. Maj. US Army, Fort Hood, Tex., 1996—; bn. chaplain 615th Aviation Support Bn. First Cav. Divsn., Fort Hood, 1996—98, 27th Bn. First Cav. Divsn., 1998—99, 1-35 Armor, First Armored Divsn., Baumholder, Germany, 1999—2002; brigade chaplain 2Nd Brigade, First Armored Divsn., 2003—03, 2nd Brigade, First Cav. Divsn., Fort Hood, 2003—05; family life chaplain US Army Garrison, Fort Hood, 2005—. Decorated Bronze Star First Cav. Divsn. Fellow: Am. Assn. Pastoral Counselors; mem.: Am. Assn. Christian Counselors (assoc.). Avocations: reading, fishing, ballroom dancing. Home: 52322-2 Erie Ct Fort Hood TX 76544 Office: Family Life Chaplain Bldg 52024 Fort Hood TX 76544 Home Phone: 254-539-0053; Office Phone: 254-287-6310. Personal E-mail: kenneth.r.sorenson@us.army.mil.

SORENSON, LIANE BETH MCDOWELL, director, state legislator; b. Chgo., Aug. 13, 1947; d. Harold Davidson McDowell and Frances Elanor (Williams) Daisey Van Kleeck; m. Boyd Wayne Sorenson, June 30, 1973; children: Nathan, Matthew, Dana. BS in Edn., U. Del., 1969, M in Counseling with honors, 1986. Tchr. Avon Grove Sch. Dist., West Grove, Pa., 1969-70, Alexis I. duPont Sch. Dist., Wilmington, Del., 1970-73, Barrington (Ill.) Sch. Dist., 1973-75; counseling intern Medill Intensive Learning Ctr.-Christina Sch. Dist., Newark, Del., 1985; counselor Family Violence Shelter CHILD, Inc., Wilmington, 1985, 86-87, dir. parent edn. programs, 1987-88; dir. Office Women's Affairs, exec. dir. Commn. on Status of Women U. Del., Newark, 1988—; mem. Dist. 6 Del. Senate, Dover, 1992—. minority whip. Chair Del. Ho. Edn. Com., 1992—, Adv. Bd. Del. Breast Cancer Coalition, 1998—; commr. Edn. Commn. State Del.; mem. tng. com. Nat. Conf. State Legislatures; mem. Bd. Women's Network Nat. Conf. State Legislatures; mem. joint sunset com. Del. Legislature, Del. House of Reps., 1992-94, Del. Senate, 1994—, Del. Legis. Joint Fin. Com. Del. Legis., 1994—, Coun. State Govts. Toll Fellowship. Presenter papers various meetings & confs. Pres. bd. dirs. Nursing Mothers, Inc., 1980-81; trustee Hockessin Montessori Sch., 1982-84, enrollment chair, 1982-83; trustee Hockessin Pub. Libr., 1982-84, pres. bd., 1982-84; bd. dirs. Del. Coalition for Children, 1986-88; bd. dirs. Children's Bur. Del., 1984-87, sec., 1985-87; pres. Jr. League Wilmington, 1986-87, rsch. coun. v.p., 1985-86; bd. dirs. YWCA New Castle County, 1989-91; pres. Del. Women's Agenda, 1986-88; vice-chair Women's Leadership Ctr., 1992—; mem. Del. Work Family Coalition; bd. dirs. Del. divsn. Am. Cancer Soc., 1993—. Grantee Del. Dept. Svcs. to Children, Youth and Their Families, 1987-88, 1988, State of Del. Gen. Assembly, 1992; recipient Disting. Legis. Svc. award Del. State Bar Assn., 1997, Del Tufo award Delaware Humanities Forum, 1999. Mem.: Hockessin Hist. Soc. (bd. mem. 2000—), Del. Family Law Commn., Del. Alliance for Arts in Edn., Del. Greenway and Trails Coun., Am. Assn. for Higher Edn. (chair women's caucus 1991—92, program chair women's caucus 1990—91, pre-conf. workshop coord. women's caucus 1990 Ann. Conf.), Rotary (charter mem. Hackessin Pike Creek club 1994—). Republican. Methodist. Avocations: camping, hiking. Office: State of Delaware Legislative Hall Rm 210 PO Box 1401 Dover DE 19903-1401

SORENSON, STEPHEN JAY, lawyer; b. Salt Lake City, Aug. 9, 1949; s. Peter Jay and Jeannette (Hanks) S.; m. Corinne Clyde, Jan. 24, 1974; children: Jeannette, Peter, Richard, Michael, Rebecca. Student, Yale U., 1967-69; BA, U. Utah, 1973, JD, 1977. Bar: Utah 1977, U.S. Dist. Ct. Utah 1977, U.S. Ct. Appeals (10th cir.) 1982. Asst. atty. gen. State of Utah, Salt Lake City, 1977-90, chief litig. divsn., 1986-90; asst. US atty. Dist. Utah US Dept. Justice, Salt Lake City, 1990—, chief civil divsn., 1995-98, 2006—, first asst. US atty., 1998—2006, acting US atty., 2006. Mem. Utah Bar Assn. Office: US Atty's Office 185 S State St Ste 300 Salt Lake City UT 84111-1552 Office Phone: 801-325-3218.

SORENSON, STEVEN P., insurance company executive; AB, Harvard Univ.; MBA, Univ. Chgo. Engagement mgr. McKinsey & Co., Chgo., Houston, London; gen. mgr. Progressive Ins. Co.; prod. v.p. Allstate Ins. Co., Northbrook, Ill., 2000—02, v.p., co-leader field ops., 2002—07, sr. v.p. protection distbn., 2007. Office: Allstate Corp 2775 Sanders Rd Northbrook IL 60062 *

SORENSTAM, ANNIKA, professional golfer; b. Stockholm, Oct. 9, 1970; m. David Esch. Student, U. Ariz. With Women's Profl. Golf European Tour, 1992—, LPGA, 1993—, Swedish Nat. Team, 1987-92, Solheim Cup Team, 1994, 96, 98; playing editor Golf Digest, 2006—, Golf for Women, 2006—. Recipient Vare Trophy award, 1998, Espy Awards for Best Female Golfer, ESPN, 1996, 1998, 1999, 2002-2004, Espy Award for Best Female Athlete, 2006; named Rolex Player of Yr., 1995, 97, 98, 2000-2003, Female Athlete of Yr., AP, 2003. Achievements in Tournaments won include: Australian Ladies Open, 1994, U.S. Women's Open, 1995, 96, 2006, Ladies Masters, 1995, 2000, 2002, LPGA Championship, 1997, 2002-2004, Women's British Open, 2003, first woman since 1945 to appear in a PGA Tour event, 2003, inducted into World Golf Hall of Fame, 2003, 61 career LPGA Tour victories, topped $2 million in earnings 2001-2004, only woman in LPGA history to ever go over $2 million in one season. Office: LPGA 100 International Golf Dr Daytona Beach FL 32124-1092

SORGE, KAREN LEE, printing company executive, consultant; b. Warwick, NY, May 27, 1958; d. Wesley Thomas and Margaret Anne (Storms) Kervatt; m. David W. Farquhar, July 16, 1982 (div. Feb. 1990); 1 child: Lauren Nicole; m. Thomas E. Sorge, May 16, 1997; children: Natalie MaKalen Sorge, Ryan Thomas. AS, Roger Williams Coll., 1978, BS cum laude, 1980. Office mgr. Price-Rite Printing Co., Dover, NJ, 1975—76; cons. SBA, Bristol, RI, 1978—80; account exec. P.M. Press Inc., Dallas, 1980—90, sales trainer, 1984—85; v.p. KDF Bus. Forms Inc., Dallas, 1984—90; account exec. Jarvis Press, Dallas, 1990—; pres. Print Trends, Dallas, 1990—. Printer Tex. Aux. Charity Auction Orgn., Dallas, 1985, Cystic Fibrosis, Dallas, 1989—93, Life Enhancement Assn. Programs Found., 1992—, Dallas Soc. Visual Comm., 1992, AIDS Resources Com., Dallas chpt. Cerebral Palsy, 1994, Lloyd-Paxton AIDS Benefit, 1994, Feast for the Eyes Gala-Benefit to Prevent Blindness, 2001, Genesis Women's Shelter, 2002, others. Recipient award, Clampitt Paper Co., Dallas, 1982, P.M. Press Inc., 1983—89, Mead Paper Co., 1985—96, Feast for the Eyes Gala, 2001, Gold award, Adrian Advt., 2004, Silver award, 2005, 2006. Mem. Printing Industry in Am. (recipient Judges Favorite award 1992, Best of Show Hon. Mention award 1994, gold award Best of Tex. 1996), Internat. Assn. Bus. Communicators, Nat. Bus. Forms Assn. Republican. Baptist. Avocation: piano. Home: 2600 Raintree Dr Southlake TX 76092-5536 Office Phone: 817-424-5252. Business E-Mail: printtrends@aol.com.

SORGENFREI, ROBERT L., retired trust company executive; b. Wawaka, Ind., Sept. 25; s. Harold and Flo Sorgenfrei; children: Robert, John. LLB, Ind. U., 1953. Bar: Ind., Calif. Assoc. trust coun. Security Pacific Nat Bank, 1962—75, trust coun., mgr. trust legal divisn., 1975—84; ret., 1984.

SORGER, STEPHAN GUNTHER, marketing professional, educator; b. Washington, Apr. 4, 1959; s. Gunther Urban and Ursula Sorger. BS in Engring., Calif. Poly., San Luis Obispo, 1982; MS in Engring., U. So. Calif., LA, 1985, MBA, 1992. Registered profl. engr., Calif. Sr. engring. mgr. HSQ Tech., South San Francisco, Calif., 1996—98; sr. product mgr. Aspect Comm., San Jose, Calif., 1998—2000; dir. mktg. Facetime Comm., Foster City, Calif., 2000—01; dir. product mgmt. 3Com, Santa Clara, Calif., 2000—01; dir. product mktg. Oracle, Redwood Shores, Calif., 2001—03; dir. product strategy SAP Labs, Palo Alto, Calif., 2004—06; instr. U. Calif., Berkeley, 2003—.

SORGI, LEONARD, lawyer; b. Bklyn., Sept. 4, 1959; BS in Mech. Engring., Polytechnic U., NY, 1982; JD cum laude, NY Law Sch., 1987. Bar: NY 1988, NJ 1988, registered: US Dist. Ct. (So. Dist.) NY 1988, US Dist. Ct. (Ea. Dist.) NY 1988, US Dist. Ct. NJ 1988, US Ct. Appeals Fed. Cir., US Ct. Appeals (11th Cir.), US Patent & Trademark Office. Ptnr., intellectual property dept. Schulte Roth & Zabel LLP, NYC. Contbr. articles to profl. jour.; spkr. in field; editor: NY Law Sch. Law Rev., 1985—86. Mem.: Am. Intellectual Property Lawyers Assn., Licensing Exec. Soc., ABA, NY County Bar Assn., Am. Soc. Mech. Engrs. (chmn. NY Chpt. Govn. Relations Com. 2000—03). Office: Schulte Roth & Zabel LLP 919 Third Ave New York NY 10022 Office Phone: 212-756-2545. Office Fax: 212-593-5955. Business E-Mail: leonard.sorgi@srz.com.

SORIA, SAMUEL SALVADOR, musician; b. Chgo., Apr. 19, 1958; s. Samuel and Rosalie Soria. MusB, Valparaiso U., Ind., 1980; MusM, Northwestern U., Evanston, Ill., 1984. Assoc. organist St. James Episc. Cathedral, Chgo., 1984—88; organist Immaculate Conception Ch., Chgo., 1988—93, Holy Name Cathedral, Chgo., 1993—2002, Cathdral Our Lady Angels, LA, 2002—. Pvt. practice organist. Musician: (CD) Premiere Organ Recording, 2004, Organ Voices, 2005. Recipient 2d prize, J.S. Bach Internat. Competition, Kennedy Ctr., Washington, 1993. Mem.: Conf. Roman Cath. Cathedral Musicians, Am. Guild Organists (prize for improvisation competition 1996). Office: Cathedral of Our Lady of Angels 555 W Temple St Los Angeles CA 90012 Office Phone: 213-680-5200. Business E-Mail: ssoria@olacathedral.org.

SORIANO, ALFONSO GUILLEARD, professional baseball player; b. San Pedro De Macoris, Dominican Republic, Jan. 7, 1976; Player NY Yankees, 1999—2004, Tex. Rangers, 2004—05, Washington Nationals, 2005—06, Chgo. Cubs, 2006—. Named All-Star Game MVP, 2004; named to Am. League All-Star Team, Maj. League Baseball, 2002—05, Nat. League All-Star Team, 2006—07; recipient Silver Slugger award, 2002, 2004—06. Achievements include leading the Am. League in hits (209), runs scored (128), and stolen bases (41), 2002. Office: Chgo Cubs Wrigley Field 1060 W Addison St Chicago IL 60613-4397 *

SORIANO, NANCY MERNIT, editor-in-chief; married; 1 child. Degree in Art History, Bard Coll. Former editor Good Food; former contbg. editor Cosmopolitan, Food & Wine, Brides; joined Country Living, 1982, assoc. decorating editor, home bldg. and arch. editor, exec. editor, 1995—98, editor-in-chief, 1998—. Founder Country Living Restoration Mag., 1996. Design editor (book series) American Country Design, Time Life Books, editor spl. interest publ. Country Living Dream Homes; co-author: (books) Country Living Decorating Style: The New Look of Country, 1999, Country Living Decorating with Baskets: Accents for Every Room, 2000, Country Living Decorating with Candles, 2000, Country Living Handmade Christmas: Decorating Your Tree and Home, 2001, Country Living Handmade Halloween, 2002, Stylish Renovations: Design Ideas for Old and New Houses, 2002. Mem.: Am. Soc. Mag. Editors (bd. dirs.). Office: Hearst Corp Country Living 300 W 57th St New York NY 10019-3788 *

SORKIN, AARON, scriptwriter, television producer, playwright; b. NYC, June 9, 1961; m. Julia Bingham, Apr. 13, 1996 (div. 2006); 1 child, Roxy. Student, SUNY, Purchase; BFA in Musical Theatre, Syracuse U. Creator, prodr. (TV series) Sports Nights, 1998—2000 (Humanitas prize, 1999); creator, writer, exec. prodr.: TV series The West Wing, 1999—2003 (Emmy award for Best for Outstanding Writing in a Drama Series, 2000, 2001, 2002, 2003, Humanitas prize, 2000, 2002, Writer Guild Am. award, 2001, Television Prodr. of the Yr. Producers Guild Am. Golden Laurel award, 2002); creator, writer, exec. prodr. (TV series) Studio 60 on the Sunset Strip, 2006—07; writer: screenplays A Few Good Men, 1992, Malice, 1993; writer: (films) The American President, 1995; writer: Broadway plays A Few Good Men, 1989 (Outer Critics Circle award as Outstanding American Playwright, 1989), Hidden in this Picture, 1990, Making Movies, 1992. Office: Endeavor Talent Agy # 1000 9701 Wilshire Blvd Beverly Hills CA 90212

SORKIN, ALAN LOWELL, economist, educator; b. Decatur, Ill., Nov. 2, 1941; s. Martin and Sally Eileen (Steinberg) S.; m. Sylvia Jean Smardo, Sept. 9, 1967; children: David, Suzanne. BA, Johns Hopkins U., 1963, MA, 1964, PhD, 1966. Rsch. assoc. Brookings Instn., Washington, 1967-69; asst. prof. internat. health and econs. Johns Hopkins U., Balt., 1969-72, assoc. prof. internat. health and econs., 1972-74, adj. prof. dept. internat. health Sch. Hygiene and Pub. Health, 1986—; prof., chmn. dept. econs., 1974—; also adj. prof. preventive and social medicine Med. Sch., U. Md., 1974—. Author: Education, Unemployment and Economic Growth, 1974, Health Economics: An Introduction, 1975, 2d edit., 1983, 3d edit., 1992. The Urban American Indian, 1978, Economic Aspects of Natural Hazards, 1982, Health Care and the Changing Economic Environment, 1986, Monetary and Fiscal Policy and Business Cycles in The Modern Era, 1988, Public Health and Development, 1988, (with others) Female Labor Force and Development, 1990, Nutrition, Food Policy and Development, 1995, (with Irina Farquhar) Economic and Social Aspects of Occupational and environmental Health, 1998, others; contbr. articles to profl. jours. Mem. Am. Econs. Assn., Phi Beta Kappa, Delta Omega. Republican. Lutheran. E-mail: sorkin@umbc2.umbc.edu, asorkin@jhsph.edu Home: 1694 Campbell Rd Forest Hill MD 21050-2342 Office: U Md Dept Econ 5401 Wilkens Ave Baltimore MD 21250-1000 Office Phone: 410-455-2173. Business E-Mail: sorkin@umbc.edu. *Personal relationships are more important than material possessions. Persons with many friends have a sense of well-being that can never be embodied in materialism.*

SORKIN, ANDREW ROSS, reporter, columnist; b. Feb. 19, 1977; BS, Cornell U., 1999. European mergers and acquisitions reporter NY Times, London, 1999—2000, chief mergers and acquisitions reporter, 2000—, columnist SundayBusiness; founding editor DealBook (online financial report published by the Times). Frequent guest appearances on (NBC) Today Show, (PBS) The NewsHour with Jim Leher, (PBS) The Charlie Rose Show, (CNBC) Kudlow & Cramer.(CNBC) Closing Bell, (MSNBC) Abrams Report, (NPR) Talk of Nation, (BBC) World Service and several others. Named one of 30 Most Influential Fin. Journalists in the Nation Under the Age of 30, TJFR/NewsBios; recipient Gerald Loeb award, 2005. Office: NY Times 229 W 43rd St New York NY 10036 Office Phone: 212-556-7395. Office Fax: 212-556-1967. E-mail: sorkin@nytimes.com.

SORKIN, DAVID JAMES, lawyer; b. NYC, June 26, 1959; BA, Williams Coll., 1981; JD, Harvard U., 1984. Bar: NY 1985. Law clk. judge Charles M. Merrill U.S. Ct. Appeals 9th Cir., San Francisco, 1984-85; assoc. Simpson Thacher & Bartlett, NYC, 1985-92, ptnr., 1993—. Office: Simpson Thacher & Bartlett 425 Lexington Ave Fl 15 New York NY 10017-3954 Office Phone: 212-455-3387. Business E-Mail: DSorkin@stblaw.com.

SORKIN, IRA LEE, lawyer; b. NYC, May 30, 1943; s. Nathan and Rosalie (Cohen) S.; m. Ellen M. Sorkin, Aug. 24, 1969; children: Roger David, Peter Neil. BA, Tulane U., 1965; JD, George Washington U., 1968. Trial atty. SEC, NYC, 1968-71, adminstr., 1984-86; asst. U.S. atty. U.S. Atty.'s Office (so. dist.) N.Y., 1971-76, dep. chief, criminal divsn., 1976; ptnr. Squadron Ellenoff Plesent & Lehrer, NYC, 1977-84, Squadron Ellenoff Plesent & Sheinfeld, NYC, 1986—95, Squadron, Ellenoff, Plesent & Sheinfeld LLP, NYC, 1997—2002; chief legal officer Nomura Securities Internat. Inc., NYC, 1995-97; ptnr. Carter, Ledyard & Milburn LLP, NYC, 2002—. Lectr. Nat. Inst. Trial Advocacy, N.Y.C., 1981-91, Securities Industry Assn. Contbr. articles to profl. jours. Tutor inner city students N.Y.C. Sch. Sys., 1996-97. Mem. ABA, N.Y. Coun. Def. Lawyers, Assn. of the Bar for the City of N.Y. Avocations: golf, reading, skiing. Office: Carter Ledyard & Milburn LLP 2 Wall St New York NY 10005 E-mail: sorkin@clm.com.

SORKIN, JENNI, curator, critic; b. Chgo. BFA, Sch. of Art Inst. of Chgo., 1999; MA, Bard Coll., 2002; student PhD program in History of Art, Yale U., 2004—. Former curatorial rsch. asst., project coord. Mus. Contemporary Art, LA; former rsch. asst. Dept. Contemporary Programs and Rsch. Getty Rsch. Inst. Curator (exhibitions include) High Performance: The First Five Years, 1978-1982, Bard Coll., 2002, LA Contemporary Exhibitions, 2003, Judy Chicago: Minimalism, 1965-1973, LewAllen Contemporary, Santa Fe, 2004. Recipient Art Jour. Award for article Envisioning High Performance, Coll. Art Assn., 2004. Mem.: Queer Caucus for Art (co-chair 2004—06). Office: Yale U Hist of Art Dept 56 High St New Haven CT 06520

SORKIN, LAURENCE TRUMAN, lawyer; b. Bklyn., Oct. 20, 1942; s. Sidney and Lilly (Kowensky) S.; m. Joan Carol Ross, June 25, 1972; children: Andrew Ross, Suzanne Ross. AB summa cum laude, Brown U., 1964; LLB, Yale U., 1967; LLM, London Sch. Econs./Polit. Sci., 1968. Law clk. to Judge J. Joseph Smith U.S. Ct. Appeals (2d cir.), 1968-69; assoc. Cahill Gordon & Reindel, NYC, 1969-75, ptnr., 1975—. Vis. lectr. Yale U., 1972, 73; lectr. various profl. orgns.; rsch. asst. to Lester and Bindman for Sook Race and Law in Great Britain, 1972; adj. prof. law Fordham Law Sch., 2007—. Contbr. to State Antitrust Law (Lifland), 1984; author: (with Lifland, Sorkin and Van Cise) Understanding the Antitrust Laws, 1986; mem. bd. editors Antitrust Report, 2004—. Bd. dirs. Legal Aid Soc., N.Y.C., 1988-94, N.Y. Lawyers for Pub. Interest, 1990-93. Fulbright scholar, 1967-68. Mem. ABA (antitrust law sect. 1978—), N.Y. State Bar Assn. (antitrust sect., chmn. com. on legislation 1978-79, sect. sec. 1979-80, chmn. com. on mergers 1987-89, chmn. Clayton Act com. 1989-94, exec. com. 1989-94, comml. and fed. litigation sect. chmn. com. antitrust 1996-98), Assn. Bar City N.Y. (com. trade regulation 1974-77, 95-98, com. on electronic funds transfer 1979-80), Yale Law Sch. Assn. (exec. com. 2000—), Phi Beta Kappa. Office: Cahill Gordon & Reindel 80 Pine St Fl 17 New York NY 10005-1702 Office Phone: 212-701-3209. Business E-Mail: lsorkin@cahill.com.

SORLEY, REBECCA ELLEN, music educator; b. Indpls., June 25, 1964; d. Robert Joe and Carolyn McKinney; m. Darin Scott Sorley, June 7, 1986; children: Allegra Virginia, Alexander Michael, Adam Benjamin. MusB in Piano Performance, Butler U., 1986; MusM in Piano Performance, Ind. U., 1988; ArtsD in Piano Performance, Ball State U., Muncie, Ind., 1996. Adj. instr. Earlham Coll., Richmond, Ind., 1994—96, Ind. U. Sch. Music, Indpls., 1996—97; assoc. prof., dir. ednl. outreach U. Indpls., 1993—, dir. Cmty. Music Ctr., 1999—. Founder Piano Camp U. Indpls., 1994; founder Music Children Concert Series, 1999—; founder, dir. Chamber Music Inst., 2001—; presenter in field. Benefit recitals participant Riley Hosp. Children, Indpls., 2002, Spl. Olympics, Indpls., 2003—, Easter Seals, Indpls., 2005, Indpls. Symphony Orch., 2005, Music Acad. Scholarship, Greenwood, 2005; organist, choir dir. Wallace St. Presbyn. Ch., Indpls., 1991—2001; dir. worhsip and music Ctr. Grove Presbyn. Ch., Greenwood, Ind., 2002—04, dir. Music Acad., 2002—; organist St. Johns United Ch. Christ, 2006—. Grantee, Target Corp., 2002, 2003. Mem.: Indpls. Piano Tchrs. Assn., Internat. Alliance Women in Music, Coll. Music Soc. (campus rep. 2002—), Mu Phi Epsilon (pres. Kappa chpt. 1985—86, pres. alumni chpt. 2001—03). Avocations: running, bicycling, reading. Office: U Indpls Music Dept 1400 E Hanna Ave Indianapolis IN 46227

SOROKOWSKI, ANDREW DENNIS, lawyer, historian; b. Hartford, Conn., Aug. 29, 1950; s. George Wsewolod and Nadia Sorokowski; m. Oksana Bachynska, Mar. 5, 1993. BA, U. Calif., Berkeley, 1972; MA, Harvard U., 1975; JD, Hastings Coll., 1979; PhD, U. London, 1991. Bar: Calif. 1980. Mem. rsch. staff Keston Coll., Kent, U.K., 1984—87; dir. rsch. and documentation Archdiocese of L'viv, Rome, 1989—90; atty. Jaffe, Trutanich, Scatena & Blum, San Francisco, 1990—93; mng. editor, rsch. assoc. Harvard Ukrainian Rsch. Inst., Cambridge, Mass., 1993—97; instr. St. Basil Coll., Stamford, Conn., 1998—99; adj. lectr. U. Mass., Boston, 1999—2000; hist. rsch. specialist U.S. Dept. Justice, Washington, 2000—. Editor: A Millennium of Christian Culture in Ukraine, 1988; co-editor: A Thousand Years of Christianity in Ukraine, 1988. Sec. Shevchenko Sci. Soc., Washington, 2001; bd. dirs. The Washington Group, 2001. Grantee, Internat. Rsch. Exchg. Bd., Poland, 1988. Mem.: Am. Cath. Hist. Assn. (bd. dirs.), Am. Assn. Ukrainian Studies. Office: US Dept Justice ENRD-EDS PO Box 23986 Washington DC 20026-3986

SOROS, GEORGE, pension fund administrator; b. Budapest, Hungary, Aug. 12, 1930; came to US, 1956; s. Tivadar and Elisabeth (Szucs) S.; m. Annaliese Witschak, Sept. 17, 1960 (div. June 1983); children: Robert, Andrea, Jonathan; m. Susan Weber, June 19, 1983 (div.); children: Alexander, Gregory. BS, London Sch. Econs., 1952; LLD (hon.), New Sch. for Social Rsch., 1990; D. Civil Law (hon.), U. Oxford, Eng., 1990; LHD (hon.), Yale U., 1991; degree (hon.), Budapest U. of Economics. Arbitrage trader F.M. Mayer, NYC, 1956-59; analyst Wertheim & Co., NYC, 1959-63; v.p. Arnhold and S. Bleichroeder, NYC, 1963-73; sole proprietor Soros Fund Mgmt., NYC, 1973—; chmn. Soros Fund Mgmt., LLC, NYC, 1996—. Author: The Alchemy of Finance, 1987, 2nd edit., 1994, Opening the Soviet System, 1990, Underwriting Democracy, 1991, Soros on Soros: Staying Ahead of the Curve, 1995, The Crisis of Global Capitalism: Open Society Endangered, 1998, Open Society: Reforming Global Capitalism, 2000, George Soros on Globalization, 2002, The Bubble of America Supremacy: Correcting the Misuse of American Power, 2004, The Age of Fallibility: Consequences of the War on Terror, 2006; contbr. articles to mags. and newspapers Mem. Coun. on Fgn. Rels., NYC, 1988—, Royal Inst. Internat. Affairs, London, 1990—, Bretton Woods Com., Washington, 1989; mem. exec. com. Helsinki Watch, NYC, 1982—; mem. com. Americas Watch, NYC, 1982—; chmn., founding pres. Ctrl. European U., Budapest, 1991; chmn. Open Soc. Fund, 1981, Open Soc. Inst., 1993, founds. in Albania, Belarus, Bosnia and Herzegovina, Bulgaria, Croatia, Czech Republic, Estonia, Georgia, Hungary, Kazakhstan, Kyrgyzstan, Latvia, Lithuania, Macedonia, Moldova, Poland, Romania, Russia, Slovakia, Slovenia, South Africa, Rroma, Ukraine, Yugoslavia. Recipient honor Lawyers Co.for Human Rights, NYC, 1990, Laurea Honoris Causa, U. Bologna, 1995; named one of World's Richest People, Forbes Mag., 1999—, Forbes Richest Americans, 1999—, Named one of New York's Influentials, New York Mag., 2006. Avocations: tennis, skiing, chess, backgammon. Office: Soros Fund Mgmt 888 7th Ave Ste 3300 New York NY 10106-0001 *

SOROSKY, JERI P., academic administrator; b. Chgo. d. Hans S. and Florence J. (Hurwitz) Pakula; m. Gene E. Sorosky; children: Cindi, Dana, Lesli. BA, Roosevelt U., Chgo., 1952; MEd, Fla. Atlantic U., Boca Raton, 1967; EdS, Nova Southeastern U., Ft. Lauderdale, Fla., 1972; EdD, MS, Nova Southeastern U., 1981. Cert. adminstr., supr., media specialist, gifted and elem. educator, Fla. Chairperson Elem. Highland Oaks, North Miami Beach, Fla., 1967-75; mem. faculty gifted program Highland Oaks Gifted Ctr., North Miami Beach, 1975-85; chairperson gifted program Miami (Fla.) Dade C.C., 1985-2000; site adminstr. grad. tchr. edn. program Nova. Southeastern U., Ft. Lauderdale, 1992—2004. Adj. prof. Nova Southeastern U., Ft. Lauderdale, 1979-87, adv. doctoral practicums, 1985-00, cluster coord., 1987-03, admissions com. doctoral programs Tech. and Distance Edn. and Child and Youth Studies, 1996-03, adj. prof. innovative math, 2004-, adj. prof. early childhood, 2004-; chairperson gifted edn. Dade County Schs., Miami, 1990-93; mem. com. State Gifted Task Force, Tallahassee, 1992; presenter in field. Author: GEM Major Module in Gifted Education, 1981, Ideas Unlimited, 1985, Guide for Elementary Educators, 1995, Technology in the Curriculum, 1998; editor: Readings: Gifted Education, 1991, Early Childhood Education, 1982. Project chairperson Kids in Distress, Ft. Lauderdale, 1989. Named Woman of Yr. Bus. Prof. Women, 1985. Mem. Fla. Assn. Gifted (charter, v.p. 1975-97), Nova Southeastern U. Alumni (bd. dirs. 1981-97), AAUW, Phi Delta Kappa (chairperson newsletter 1985-97). Avocations: dance, technology. Office: Nova Southeastern U 1750 NE 167th St North Miami Beach FL 33162-3017 Business E-Mail: jeris@nova.edu.

SORRELL, MICHAEL E., consulting company executive, hospitality executive; b. Pasadena, Calif., Mar. 31, 1945; s. James Hendrick Sorrell and Marie Vivian Bristow. AA, Normandale Coll., Bloomingdale, Minn., 1992; BA, Concordia Coll., St. Paul, 1994. Pres., CEO, owner Daggers/La. Inc., Metairie, 1987-89, Mesa Cons. Svcs./MN/Inc., Mpls., 1989-94, Mesa Cons. Svcs., Inc., Las Vegas, Nev., 1994—; pres., CEO, majority ptnr. S&W Hospitality Group, Inc., Las Vegas, 1999—; ptnr., dir. S.R. Owl Inc., 1999—; chmn., CEO Bristow-Norwich Group Internat., Las Vegas, 2000—. With USAF, 1963-69, USN, 74-89. Mem. VFW, Nat. Assn. Small Bus., Nat. Lic. Beverage Assn., Inst. Mgmt. Cons., Soc. Human Resources Mgmt., Soc. Hospitality Cons., Am. Legion, Fleet Res. Assn., Navy League US, U.S. Naval Inst., Amateur Athletic Union of U.S., Marines' Meml. Club, Victory Svcs. Club. Roman Catholic. Avocations: golf, hiking, tennis. Office: Bristow-Norwich Group Internat 3888 W Sahara Ave Ste 33 Las Vegas NV 89102-0505 Office Phone: 702-364-0989. Business E-Mail: mesaconsultant@aol.com, bristownorwich1@aol.com.

SORRELL, ROZLYN, singer, actress, theater director, educator; b. Bklyn. d. Nathaniel Otis and Cupid Viola (Logan) S. BA in Theatre, CUNY, 1976, MS in Edn., 1985. Cert. tchr. Calif., NY. Tchr. LA Unified Sch. Dist., 1997, Sylvan Learning Ctr., LA, 1998, Westmark Sch., Encino, Calif., 2000, Achievement Sch., Raleigh, NC, 2002, Easter Seals UCP, NC, 2006. Bus. cons., LA, 1989—; voice tchr., LA, 1992—; mem. Albert McNeil Jubilee Singers, LA, 1994—2000. Actress various TV programs, commls., stage prodn. and films, 1986—; soloist Temple of Music and Art, Tucson, 1990, El San Juan (PR) Hotel, 1985, Hour of Power, Glory of Christmas, Glory of Easter, Garden Grove, Calif., 1994—, Miyazaki Civic Culture Hall, Japan, 1996, Anaheim Pond, Calif., 1997, Honolulu Symphony, 1998, Hollywood Bowl, Calif., 1998, Gospel Recording Artist, 2000, Harris Teeter Harvest Festival, Raleigh Conv. Ctr., 2004, Carolina Theatre, Durham, NC, 2005, Spiritual Awakening, WRAL-TV, NC, 2004, Pops in the Park, Regency Theatre, Cary, NC, 2004, 05, 06, African Am. Cultural Ctr., Raleigh, NC, 2004, Greensboro Coliseum, 2005, Progress Energy Ctr. Performing Arts, Meymandi Concert Hall, Raleigh, NC, 2006, 07, NC Fairgrounds, 2006, Raleigh Meml. Auditorium, NC, 2007, Garner Hist. Auditorium, NC, 2007; guest artist, soloist NC Symphony, 2006, 07; soloist NC Theatre Cabaret Night, CMP Gospel Showcase, Dallas Conv. Ctr., 2007; featured soloist Artsplosure Moore Square Park, Raleigh, 2007; dir. Storms of Life, 2005. Mem. AFTRA, SAG, Actors Equity Assn. Avocations: dance, walking, theater, exercise. Office Phone: 866-686-0713. Personal E-mail: rozlyn@rozlynsorrell.com. Business E-Mail: sorrell@sorrell-intl.com.

SORRELL, WILLIAM H., state attorney general; b. Burlington, Vt., Mar. 9, 1947; s. Marshal Thomas and Esther Sorrell; children: McKenzie, Thomas. AB, U. Notre Dame, 1970; JD, Cornell U., 1974. Dep. state's atty. Chittenden County State of Vt., 1975—77, state's atty. Chittenden County, 1977—78, 1989—92; ptnr. McNeil, Murray & Sorrell, 1978—89, sec. adminstrn., 1992—97; atty. gen. State of Vt., 1997—. Pres. United Cerebral Palsy Vt.; sec. Vt. Coalition Handicapped; bd. dirs. Winooski Valley Pk. Dist., Am. Legacy Found. Mem.: Nat. Assn. Attys. Gen. (chmn., past pres.). Democrat. Office: Office Atty Gen 109 State St Montpelier VT 05609-1001 Office Phone: 802-828-3173. Business E-Mail: rhooker@atg.state.vt.us.

SORRELS, RANDALL OWEN, lawyer; b. Va., Dec. 11, 1962; s. Charles Vernon and Marjorie Elaine (Jones) S.; m. Cheryl Ann Casas, June 29, 1985; children: Ashley Michelle, Stephanie Leigh, Darby Nicole, Garrett Ryan. BA in Polit. Sci.and Speech Comm. magna cum laude, Houston Bapt. U., 1984; JD magna cum laude, South Tex. Coll. Law, 1987. Bar: Tex. 1987, US Dist. Ct. (so. dist.) Tex.; bd. cert. in civil trial law and personal injury trial law Tex. Bd. Legal Specialization. Assoc. Fulbright & Jaworski, Houston, 1987-90; ptnr. Abraham, Watkins, Nichols, Sorrels & Friend, Houston, 1990—. Contbr. articles to profl. jours. Named a Super Lawyer, Tex. Monthly, 2003—07; named one of Houston's Top Personal Injury Lawyers, H Tex., 2004—07; recipient Pub. Svc. award, South Tex. Coll. Law Alumni Assn., 2006. Fellow Tex. Bar Found. (trustee 1997-2000, sustaining life), Houston Bar Found., Tex. Bar Found. (sustaining life); mem. ATLA, ABA, Houston Bar Assn. (v.p. 2000-03, dir. 1998-2000, treas. 2003-04, pres.-elect 2004-05, pres. 2005—06), Houston Trial Lawyers Found. (pres. 2000-01), Houston Trial Lawyers Assn. (pres. 1999-2000), Houston Lawyer's Referral Svc. (pres. 2000-01), State Bar Tex. (dir. 1994-97, 2005-, Pres.'s award 2006), Tex. Trial Lawyers Assn. (dir. 1994—), Houston Trial Lawyers Found. (dir. 1998—), Houston Trial Lawyers Assn. (v.p. 1996-98, dir. 1993-96), Am. Bd. Trial Advs. (1997—), Nat. Bd. Trial Advs., Coll. State Bar Tex., Coll. State Bar Tex., Houston Trial Lawyers Found., Houston Bar Assn. (Pres.'s award 2007), Tex. Young Lawyers Assn., Houston Young Lawyers Assn. (named Woodrow B. Seals Outstanding Young Lawyer 1999-2000), Assn. Civil Trial and Appellate Specialists, Million Dollar Advs. Forum, Am. Inns of Ct. Home: 311 Terrace Dr Houston TX 77007-5046 Office: Abraham Watkins Nichols Sorrels & Friend 800 Commerce St Houston TX 77002-1776 Office Phone: 713-222-7211. Business E-Mail: rsorrels@abrahamwatkins.com.

SORRENTINO, MATTHEW JOSEPH, internist, educator; b. Chgo., June 22, 1958; s. Frank and Jeanne (Powers) S.; m. Jeannette B. Martens, June 16, 1984; children: Katrina, Alyssa, Georgina. BS, De Paul U., 1980; MD, U. Chgo., 1984. Intern in internal medicine U. Chgo., 1984-85, resident in internal medicine, 1985-87, fellow in cardiology, 1987-91, chief resident in internal medicine, 1988, asst. prof. medicine, 1991—, dir. clin. programs, 1994—; attending physician in echocardiography U. Chgo. Hosp., 1992—. Named one of Top Cardiologists in Chgo., 2000. Fellow Am. Coll. Cardiology; mem. Am. Heart Assn., Am. Soc. Echocardiography, Am. Soc. Hypertension (designated Specialist in Hypertension, 1999), Alpha Omega Alpha. Office: U Chgo 5841 S Maryland Ave Chicago IL 60637-1463 *

SORSBY, JAMES LARRY, home building company executive; b. Houston, May 31, 1955; s. J.B. Jr. and Viola (Lueckemeyer) S.; m. Terry Prince, July 28, 1984; children: Carson Drew, Cameron Brent. BBA, Stephen F. Austin State U., 1977. Loan officer 1st Mortgage Co. Tex., Houston, 1977-82; pres. The MortgageBanque, Inc., Houston, 1982-88; sr. v.p., treas. Hovnanian Enterprises, Inc., Red Bank, NJ, 1991—96, sr. v.p., CFO, treas., 1996—2000, exec. v.p., CFO, 2000—. Bd. dirs. Am. S.W. Fin. Corp., Phoenix. Office: Hovnanian Enterprises Inc 110 W Front St Red Bank NJ 07701 *

SORSTOKKE, ELLEN KATHLEEN, marketing executive, educator; b. Seattle, Mar. 31, 1954; d. Harold William and Carrol Jean (Russ) Sorstokke. MusB with distinction, U. Ariz., 1976; postgrad., UCLA Extension, 1979-83, L.A. Valley Coll., 1984-85, Juilliard Extension, fall 1987, U. Calif. Berkeley Extension, 1992-93. Pvt. practice music tchr., Tucson, 1975—77, Whiteriver, Ariz., 1977—78, LA, 1980—85, S.I., NYC, 1986—89; music tchr. Eloy (Ariz.) Elem. Schs., 1976-77, Whiteriver (Ariz.) Pub. Schs., 1977-78; svc. writer, asst. svc. mgr. Alfa of Santa Monica, Calif., 1978-79; purchasing agt. Advance Machine Corp., LA, 1979-80; asst. mgr. Atlantic Nuclear Svcs., Gardena, Calif., 1980-81; mgr. Blue Lady's World Music Ctr., LA, 1981-83; instrument specialist Baxter-Northup Music Co., Sherman Oaks, Calif., 1983-85; dir. mktg. Mandolin Bros., Ltd., SI, N.Y., 1985-89; product mgr. Gibson Guitar Corp., Nashville, 1989; sales mgr. Saga Musical Instruments, South San Francisco, Calif., 1990-91, mktg. dir., 1991-95, mktg. analyst, 2002—. Freelance mktg. cons., S.I., Foster City, Atlanta, 1986—; freelance cons. www.fussy-cuts.com, 2002; music cons. 20th Century Fox, L.A., 1984; freelance music copyist and orchestrator, Tucson, L.A., N.Y.C., 1972-89; freelance graphic designer and advt., N.Y.C., S.I., Foster City, Atlanta, 1986—. Contbr. articles to profl. jours. Campaign worker Richard Jones for Supr., Tucson, 1972; mem., program book designer Marina Del Rey-Westchester Symphony Orch., L.A., 1981-83. Scholar U. Ariz., 1973-76, ASCAP scholar UCLA, 1980-81. Mem. Tucson Flute Club (publicity chmn. 1974-75, v.p. 1975-76). Republican. Home Phone: 770-932-5281. Personal E-mail: esorstok@bellsouth.net.

SORSTOKKE, SUSAN EILEEN, systems engineer; b. Seattle, May 2, 1955; d. Harold William and Carrol Jean (Russ) Sorstokke. BS in Systems Engring., U. Ariz., 1976; MBA, U. Wash., Richland, 1983. Warehouse team mgr. Procter and Gamble Paper Products, Modesto, Calif., 1976-78; quality assurance engr. Westinghouse Hanford Co., Richland, Wash., 1978-80, supr. engring. document ctr., 1980-81; mgr. data control and adminstrn. Westinghouse Electric Corp., Madison, Pa., 1981-82, mgr. data control and records mgmt., 1982-84; prin. engr. Westinghouse Elevator Co., Morristown, NJ, 1984-87, region adminstrn. mgr. Arleta, Calif., 1987-90; ops. rsch. analyst Am. Honda Motor Co. Inc., Torrance, Calif., 1990-95; project leader parts sys. Am. Honda Motor Co., Inc., Torrance, Calif., 1995-96, mgr. parts systems and part number adminstrn., 1996-97, mgr. parts systems, 1997-2000, mgr. supply chain mgmt., 2000—02, mgr. process control and regulatory issues, 2002—. Adj. prof. U. LaVerne, Calif., 1991—92; pres. Fussy Cuts Inc., Torrance, Calif., 2000—05. Advisor Jr. Achievement, 1982—83; literacy tutor Westmoreland Literacy Coun., 1983—84; host parent EF Found., Saugus, Calif., 1987—88, Am. Edn. Connection, Saugus, 1988—89, 1991, Aspect Found., 2007—; instr. Excell, LA, 1991—92; mem. Calif. Acad. Math. and Sci., 1996—97; tutor YWCA, 2007. Mem.: Am. Inst. Indsl. Engrs., Soc. Women Engrs., Optomists Charities Inc. (bd. dirs. Acton, Calif. 1991—94). Republican. Methodist. Home: 2567 Plaza Del Amo Unit 205 Torrance CA 90503-8962 Office: Am Honda Motor Co Inc Dept Parts 100 5C 3B 1919 Torrance Blvd Torrance CA 90501-2722 Office Phone: 310-783-2854. Personal E-mail: ssorstokke@msn.com.

SORTE, JOHN FOLLETT, investment firm executive; b. Boston, June 30, 1947; s. Martin Eugene and Elizabeth Foster (Bradley) S.; m. Colleen Sarah Costello, July 28, 1979; children: Bradley Follett, Laura Elizabeth, Kathryn Clare. BAChemE, Rice U., 1969, M in Chem. Engring., 1970; MBA, Harvard U., 1972. Assoc. Shearson Hammill & Co., Inc., NYC, 1972-74; v.p. Shearson Hayden Stone, Inc., NYC, 1974-79; 1st v.p. Shearson Loeb Rhoades, Inc., NYC, 1979-80, Drexel Burnham Lambert, Inc., NYC, 1980-82, mng. dir., 1982-88, exec. v.p., 1989-90, pres., CEO, dir., 1990-92; pres., CEO New Street Capital Corp., NYC, 1992-94; pres. New Street Advisors L.P., NYC, 1994—2001; pres., CEO, dir. Morgan Joseph & Co. Inc., NYC, 2001—. Chmn. NY Media Group, Inc., 1995-2001; bd. dirs. Vail Resorts, Inc. Office: Morgan Joseph & Co Inc 600 Fifth Ave 19th Fl New York NY 10020-2302 E-mail: jsorte@morganjoseph.com.

SORTEBERG, ANN MARIE, education educator; b. Mayville, ND, Sept. 7, 1962; d. Vernon D. Willeson; m. Timothy A. Sorteberg, July 16, 1988. MEd, U. ND, Grand Forks. Head start tchr. Mayville State U., ND, 1992—98, lectr. edn., 1993—98, asst. prof. edn., 1998—. Mem.: ND Assn. Tchr. Educators (historian 2001), Nat. Assn. Edn. Young Children, Delta Kappa Gamma (chpt. pres. 2004—06). Home: 515 153d Ave NE Mayville ND 58257 Office: Mayville State Univ 330 3d St NE Mayville ND 58257 Business E-Mail: ann_sorteberg@mayvillestate.edu.

SORTER, BRUCE WILBUR, federal program administrator, educator, consultant; b. Willoughby, Ohio, Sept. 1, 1931; s. Wilbur David and Margaret Louise (Palmer) S.; m. Martha Ann Weirich, Sept. 2,1960 (div. 1967); 1 child, David Robert. BA, U. Md., 1967; MCP, Howard U., 1969; PhD, U. Md., 1972. Cert. community developer. Commd. USAFR, 1967, advanced through grades to lt. col., 1964; sr. planner, cons. Md. Nat. Capital Park and Planning Com., 1968-71; instr. psychology, sociology Howard and P.G. C.C., Columbia and Largo, Md., 1971-72; cmty. resource devel. dept. Md. Coop. Extension Svc., U. Md., College Park, Md., 1972-92; coord. rural info. ctr. Md. Coop. Ext. Svc., U. Md., College Park, 1989-92; affiliate prof. U. Md., 1985-92, ret., 1996. Ext. advisor USDA Internat. Programs, Washington, 1991-96; co-author, co-dir. Dept. Edn. Coun. Effectiveness Tng. Program, 1979-81; author First County Energy Conservation Plan, Prince George's County, 1978-85. Author, co-author 12 books; contbr. articles to profl. publs., chpts. to books. Developer, dir. teamwork tng. programs U.S. Dept. Edn., U.S. Dept. Agriculture, Brazil, Poland, Nat. Grange, 1972-92; cons. Fed. Power Commn. U.S., 1973-75, State Dept. Natural Resources, Md., 1978-79, Dept. Edn., Brazil, 1981-82, Nat. Grange, 1987, Edn. Ext. Svcs., Poland, 1991-92. Urban Planning fellow Howard U., 1968, Human Devel. fellow U. Md., 1970; recipient Meritorious Svc. award Dept. Def., 1983, Disting. Community Svc. award Md. Community Resource Devel. Assn., 1983, Citation for Outstanding Svc., Ptnrs. of Am., 1983, Excellence in Ednl. Programs award Am. Express, 1984, Project of Yr. award Am. Psychol. Assn., 1976, Award of Yr. Am. Vol. Assn., 1976, Achievement award Nat. Assn. of Counties, 1980, Outstanding Profl. award, U. Md., 2005. Mem. Internat. Cmty. Devel. Soc. (bd. dirs., Achievement award for outstanding contbn. to cmty. devel. 1985, Disting. Svc. award 1990), Md. Cmty. Resource Devel. Assn. (sec.-treas. 1979, pres. 1980, 88-89). Avocations: volunteer work, tennis, sailing, skiing. *Decide where you want to go. Ask yourself, is it worth the cost? If the answer is yes, then go with determination for time is in short supply.*

SORTER, GEORGE HANS, accounting and law educator, consultant; b. Vienna, Dec. 2, 1927; came to U.S., 1938; s. Alfred and Hertha (Kohn) S.; m. Dorienne Lachman, Aug. 18, 1966; children: David, Ivan, Adrienne. Ph.B., U. Chgo., 1953, MBA, 1955, PhD, 1963. C.P.A., N.Y. Instr. U. Chgo., 1955-58, asst. prof., 1959-63, assoc. prof., 1963-65, prof., 1966-74; Vincent C. Ross prof. acctg., prof. of law NYU, 1974—2003, prof. emeritus, 2003—. Arthur Young prof. U. Kans., 1969; Coopers & Lybrand prof. Tuck Sch. Dartmouth Coll., 1982; bd. dirs. NYU Credit Union, 1982-85; dir. Greater N.Y. Savs. Bank, N.Y.C., 1983-97; audit com. City of N.Y., 1985-94. Author: Accounting Theory, 1963, Accounting Thoughts of W.W. Werntz, Boundaries of Accounting Universe, 1978, Relevant Financial Statements, 1978, Financial Accounting: An Events and Cash Flow Approach, 1990, The Mix-Max Co., 1990. Mem. Ill. Sch. Bd. Dist. 233, Flossmoor, 1970-74; bd. dirs. Sch. Emotionally Disturbed Children, Chgo., 1960-74, Renaissance Soc., 1956-74, Found. Acctg. Edn., N.Y.C., 1975-79. Erskine fellow U. Canterbury, 1979 Mem. Am. Acctg. Assn. (v.p 1980-81 Outstanding Acctg. Educator), N.Y. State Soc. C.P.A.s (dir. 1980-82), Am. Inst. C.P.A.s, Fin. Acctg. Standard Adv. Com. Home: 375 S End Ave Apt 15E New York NY 10280 Office: NYU Tisch Hall 40 W 4th St New York NY 10012-1106 Business E-Mail: g.sorter@stern.nyu.edu.

SORTLAND, PAUL ALLAN, lawyer; b. Powers Lake, ND, July 30, 1953; s. Allan Berdette and Eunice Elizabeth (Nystuen) S.; m. Carolyn Faye Anderson, June 23, 1979; children: Joseph Paul, Martha Marie, Nicholas John, Benjamin David. BA, St. Olaf Coll., 1975; JD, U. Minn., 1978. Bar: Minn. 1978, N.D. 1981, U.S. Dist. Ct. Minn. 1979, U.S. Dist. Ct. N.D. 1980, U.S. Ct. Appeals (8th cir.) 1987, U.S. Supreme Ct. 1991. Assoc. Alderson, Ondov, Leonard & Sween, PA, Austin, Minn., 1978-80, Qualley, Larson & Jones, Fargo, N.D., 1980-83; ptnr. Holand, Lochow & Sortland, Fargo, 1983-85; pres. Sortland Law Office, Fargo, 1985-88; ptnr. Messerli & Kramer, Mpls., 1988-92; Sortland Law Office, Mpls., 1993—. Adj. prof. bus. law Moorhead State U., 1987. Mem. ATLA, ND Bar Assn., Minn. Bar Assn. (cert. civil trial specialist), Kiwanis, Million Dollar Advocates Forum, Upper Lake Minnetonka Yacht Club, Gamma Eta Gamma. Lutheran. Home: 120 Quebec Ave S Minneapolis MN 55426-1509 Home Phone: 763-542-1907; Office Phone: 612-375-0400. Business E-Mail: sortland@sortland.com.

SORUM, MATT, drummer; b. Venice Beach, Calif., Nov. 19, 1960; Drummer The Cult, 1988—90, Guns N' Roses, 1990—96, The Cult, 1996—2002, Velvet Revolver, 2002. Musician: (albums) (with The Cult) Sonic Temple, 1989, (with Guns N' Roses) Use Your Illusion I, 1991, Use Your Illusion II, 1991, The Spaghetti Incident?, 1993, (with Slash's Snakepit) It's Five O' Clock Somewhere, 1995, (with Neurotic Outsiders) Neurotic Outsiders, 1996, (with Velvet Revolver) Contraband, 2004, Libertad, 2007, (songs) (with The Cult) Fire Woman, 1989, (with Guns N' Roses) November Rain, 1991 (MTV Video Music awards Best Cinematography, 1992); contbr. (albums) Y Can't Tori Read, 1988, (films) Interview with the Vampire, Grosse Point Blank, The Last Marshal, 1999, Me & Will, 1999, Fish in a Barrel, 2001, Now You Know, 2002, Pauly Shore Is Dead, 2003, Hulk, 2003; actor: (films) Bitter End, 1993, Soundman, 1998. Named Favorite Hard Rock Artist, Am. Music awards, 1992, World's Best Selling Hard Rock Artist of Yr., World Music awards, 1993; named one of 100 Greatest Artists of Hard Rock, VH1, 2001, Sexiest Artists, 2002; recipient Video Vanguard award, MTV Video Music awards, 1992.

SORVINO, MIRA, actress; b. Tenafly, NJ, Sept. 28, 1967; d. Paul Sorvino and Lorraine Davis; m. Christopher Backus, June 11, 2004, children: Mattea Angel, Johnny BA in Asian Studies, Harvard U., 1990. Actor (films) New York Cop, 1993, The Obit Writer, 1993, Barcelone, 1994, Quiz Show, 1994, The Dutch Master, 1994, Mighty Aphrodite, 1995 (Acad. award for Best Supporting Actress), Blue in the Face, 1995, Beautiful Girls, 1996, Tarantella, 1996, Sweet Nothing, 1996, Tales of Erotica, 1996, New York Cop, 1996, Romy and Michele's High School Reunion, 1997, Mimic, 1997 The Replacement Killers, 1998, Too Tired to Die, 1998, Lulu on the Bridge, 1998, Free Money, 1998, Summer of Sam, 1999, At First Sight, 1999, Joan of Arc: The Virgin Warrior, 2000, Triumph of Love, 2001, The Grey Zone, 2001, Wise Girls, 2002, Semana Santa, 2002, Between Strangers, 2002, Gods and Generals, 2003, The Final Cut, 2003; actor, assoc. prodr., Amongst Friends, 1993; actor (TV movies) Parallel Lives, 1994, The Second Greatest Story Ever Told, 1994, Jake's Women, 1996, Norma Jean and Marilyn, 1996, The Great Gatsby, 2001, Human Trafficking, 2005; (TV mini-series) The Buccaneers, 1995, Covert One: The Hades Factor, 2006; (TV appearances) The Guiding Light, 1991, The Swans Crossing, 1992, 1995, Will & Grace, 2003; prodr. (films) Famous, 2000

SOSA, ERNEST, philosopher, educator; b. Cardenas, Cuba, June 17, 1940; s. Ernesto and Maria (Garriga) S.; m. Sara Mercedes, Dec. 21, 1961; children: E. David, Adrian J. BA, U. Miami, 1961; MA, U. Pitts., 1962, PhD, 1964. Instr. U. Western Ont., London, Canada, 1963-64, asst. prof., 1966-67; instr. U. Pitts., 1964; postdoctoral fellow Brown U., Providence, 1964-66, asst. prof. to full prof., 1967-74, chmn. of philosophy, 1970-76, full prof., 1974—, Romeo Elton prof., 1981—. Vis. prof. U. Miami, 1970,

Nat. U. Mexico, 1979, 80, 81, Harvard U., Cambridge, Mass., 1982, U. Salamanca, 1995, 98, Oxford U., 1997; disting. vis. prof. Rutgers U., 1998—; John Locke lectr. Oxford U, 2005; co-chair program com. 20th World Congress of Philosophy, 1998. Author: Knowledge in Perspective, 1991; gen. editor book series, Cambridge Univ. Press, 1990—2002, Blackwell Publishers, 1991—; editor Philosophy and Phenomenol. Rsch.; editor: Nous; contbr. numerous articles to profl. jours. Grantee NSF, 1970-72, Exxon Ednl. Found., 1980-82; recipient Sr. fellowship NEH, 1988-89. Mem. Am. Acad. Arts and Scis., Am. Philos. Assn. (sec.-treas. 1974-82, chair internat. coop. com. 1984-89, ea. divsn. rep. 1995-98, pres. ea. divsn. 2004-05, v.p. ea. divsn. 2003-04 bd. chair 2005—), Am. Coun. Learned Socs./Soviet Acad. Commn., Internat. Fedn. Philos. Soc. (steering com. 1988-98, v.p. 1988-93), Institut Internat. de Philosophie (exec. com. 1993-96). Office: Brown U Dept Philosophy Providence RI 02912-0001 Business E-Mail: sosa@brown.edu.

SOSA, JORGE LUIS, surgeon; s. Eduardo and Elsa Sosa; children: Sarah Elizabeth, Gladys Michelle. MD, U. South Fla., Tampa, 1987. Board Certified in Surgical Critical Care Am. Bd. of Surgery, 1994. Asst. prof. of surgery U. Miami Jackson Meml. Hosp., Fla., 1993—95; trauma attending Delray Hosp., Delray Beach, Fla., 1995—2002; surgeon, pres. Laparoscopic Inst. of South Fla., Hialeah, 1995—. Dir. bariatric surgery Hialeah Hosp., Fla., 2002—05, Palmetto Gen. Hosp., Hialeah, Fla., 2005—. Fellow: Am. Coll. Surgeons; mem.: Am. Soc. for Bariatric Surgery. Conservative. Office: Laparoscopic Inst S Fla 3499 W 4th Ave Ste 201 Hialeah FL 33012 Office Phone: 305-558-0411. Office Fax: 305-863-3802.

SOSA, JOSEPH F., pharmaceutical executive; b. San Juan; BS, Drexel U., 1975. Various positions SmithKline Beecham Pharmaceuticals; mayor Burlington County cmty., Mt. Holly, NJ, 1990—92; rep. 7th legis. dist. NJ Gen. Assembly, 1992—94; dir. Johnson & Johnson, New Brunswick, NJ. Named one of Top 10 Latinos in Healthcare, LatinoLeaders mag., 2004. Office: Johnson & Johnson 1 Johnson & Johnson Plz New Brunswick NJ 08933

SOSA, SAMMY (SAMUEL SOSA), professional baseball player; b. San Pedro de Macoris, Dominican Republic, Nov. 12, 1968; With Tex. Rangers, 1989, Chgo. Cubs, 1992—2004, Balt. Orioles, 2005, Tex. Rangers, 2007—. Selected to N.L All-Star Team, 1995, 98-2002, 2004; led Nat. League in runs, 1998, 2001-2002; led Nat. League in home runs, 2000, 2002; led Nat. League in RBI's 1998, 2001; record for new major league baseball record for homeruns in a single month (21), 1998; single season club record of 35 homeruns at Wrigley Field, 1998; winner Roberto Clemente award for outstanding svc. to cmty. Major League Baseball, 1998. Achievements include hitting HR in most MLB Ballparks (44), 2007; hit 500th career home run, April 4, 2003; hit 600th career home run, June 20, 2007, becoming the 5th player to do so. Office: c/o Tex Rangers 1000 Ballpark Way Arlington TX 76011 *

SOSKIN, WILLIAM H., lawyer, accountant; m. Marian R. Penn; children: Joshua Penn, David Penn. Law, U. of Chgo. Cert. Pub. Accountant, Calif. Pvt. practice atty., Monterey, Calif. Bd. mem. Arkay Found., Carmel, Calif.; trustee Big Sur Land Trust, Carmel, Calif., 2002—05. Recipient AV Rating, Martindale-Hubbell Law Directory, Best Lawyer, The Best Lawyers in Am., Super Lawyer, No. Calif. Super Lawyers; fellow, Am. Coll. of Trust and Estate Counsel. Mem.: Monterey County Bar Assn., Calif. State Bar Assn. Office: Law Offices of William H Soskin 2100 Garden Rd Ste F Monterey CA 93940 Office Phone: 831-649-8006. Office Fax: 831-655-3432.

SOSLAND, KARL Z., lawyer; b. Springfield, Mass., Apr. 3, 1933; s. Saul and Bessie (Shub) S.; m. June L. Sosland, Mar. 31, 1975; children: Daniel, Cynthia, Jayne, Rachel, Elizabeth. BA, U. Conn., 1955; LLB, Columbia U., 1959. Bar: N.J. 1960. Assoc. Robert Gruen, Hackensack, N.J., 1960-64, Gruen & Sosland, Hackensack, N.J., 1964-65, Scangarella and Sosland, Pompton Plains, N.J., 1965-70; pvt. practice Pompton Plains, Paramus, N.J., 1970-97, Hackensack, 1997—. Atty. Bd. Adjustment Norwood (N.J.), 1965-74; mcpl. atty. Pequannock Twp., N.J., 1971-80; judge Mcpl. Ct. Pompton Lakes, 1976-78. Active Fairlawn (N.J.) Bd. Edn., 1964-66; pres. Kinnelon (N.J.) Bd. Edn., 1971. Mem. ABA, N.J. Bar Assn., Morris County Bar Assn., Bergen City Bar Assn. Home: 11 Tecumseh Tr Oakland NJ 07436-2802 Office Phone: 201-337-6730. E-mail: soslawII@aol.com.

SOSNA, MORTON PHILIP, historian, academic administrator; b. Chgo., Apr. 26, 1945; s. Aaron and Rose Sosna; m. Barbara M. Moe, Dec. 17, 1971; children: Rachel Elizabeth Good, Emily Marie. BA, U. Ill., Chgo., 1967; MA, U. Wis., 1967, PhD, 1973. Program officer NEH, Washington, 1973—82; assoc. dir. humanities ctr. Stanford (Calif.) U., 1982—91, lectr. Am. studies, 1983—90; dir. found. rels. Cornell U., Ithaca, NY, 1992—. Vis. asst. prof. history U. Mo., Columbia, 1979—80; lectr. history George Mason U., Fairfax, Va., 1981. Author: In Search of the Silent South: Southern Liberals and the Race Issue, 1977; editor: Reconstructing Individualism: Autonomy, Individuality, and the Self in Western Throught, 2006; editor, contbr.: The Boundaries of Humanity: Humans Animals, Machines, 1990; contbr. articles to profl. publs. (William B. Hesseltine award for best article, 1971). Bd. dirs. Ctr. for Religion, Ethics, and Social Policy, Ithaca, 1993—2000. With USAR, 1969. Fellow, U. Wis., 1968—70. Mem.: So. Hist. Assn. (assoc.), Orgn. Am. Historians (assoc.). Avocations: tennis, basketball. Office: Cornell U 130 E Seneca St Ste 400 Ithaca NY 14850-4353 Office Phone: 607-254-7160. Office Fax: 607-254-7166. Business E-Mail: ms25@cornell.edu.

SOSNICK, STEPHEN HOWARD, economics educator; b. Portland, Oreg., Feb. 24, 1930; s. Benjamin and Natalie (Schmulowitz) S.; m. Galya Chernow, July 14, 1951; children: Beryl, Elika, Randall, Tobin. AB, U. Calif. Berkeley, 1950, PhD, 1954. Inst., Princeton U., NJ, 1954-57; mem. faculty U. Calif., Davis, from 1957, now prof. emeritus, agrl. econs. Author: Hired Hands, 1978; Budget's New Clothes, 1971; also articles.

SOSOKA, JOHN RICHARD, consulting firm executive, engineer; b. LA, Nov. 30, 1929; s. John and Mary (Kovach) S.; m. Audrey T. Trezona, Apr. 26, 1952; children: John Richard Jr., Cathie Ann, Karen Elizabeth. BS in Gen. Engring., UCLA, 1952; MBA, Calif. State U., Long Beach, 1975. Registered mech., elec., fire protection, metallurgy, control systems and civil engr., Calif. Project engr. Stathem Instrument, LA, 1954-55; staff engr. Aerojet Gen., Azusa, Calif., 1955-60; tech. dir. Unitek Corp., Monrovia, Calif., 1960-65; staff engr. TRW Systems, Redondo Beach, Calif., 1965-69; engr. mgr. Allen-Jones Electronics, Gardena, Calif., 1969-70; sect. head City of Long Beach, Calif., 1970-79; pres. Sosoka & Assocs., Los Alamitos, Calif., 1979-90; exec. v.p. Sparvan, Inc., Long Beach, Calif., 1990-91; pres., CEO P2S Engring., Inc., Long Beach, Calif., 1991—2005; ret. Fellow ASHRAE (dir. and regional chair 1990-93, Disting. Svc. award 1988), Inst. Advancement Engring., L.A. Coun. Engrs. and Scientists (Disting. Engr. award); mem. Assn. Energy Engrs. (v.p. 1980-81, Energy Engr. of Yr. award 1985). Republican. Episcopalian. Achievements include patent in Welding. Home: 848 Roxanne Ave Long Beach CA 90815-5013 Personal E-mail: john@sosoka.com.

SOSTARIC, JOE ZELJKO, research scientist; b. Carlton, Victoria, Australia, Aug. 16, 1970; s. Vinko and Milka Sostaric; m. Eri Miyagi, Nov. 30, 2002; 1 child, Emma Jewel. BSc with honors, U. Melbourne, Parkville, Victoria, Australia, 1993, PhD in Sci., 1999. Vis. fellow Nat. Cancer Inst., NIH, Bethesda, Md., 1999—2004; rschr. Ohio State U., Columbus, 2005—. Vis. fellow Fogarty Internat. Ctr., NIH, 1999—2004. Recipient Fellows award for rsch. excellence, Nat. Cancer Inst., NIH, 2004; Spl. Postgraduate studentship, U. Melbourne, 1994—99. Mem.: Soc. Free Radicals in Medicine and Biology, Internat. Soc. Therapeutic Ultrasound, European Soc. Sonochemistry, Am. Chem. Soc. Achievements include patents for methods and compositions for protecting cells from ultrasound mediated cytolysis; discovery of non-cytotoxic concentrations of n-alkyl glucopyranosides completely inhibit cytolysis induced by high intensity ultrasonic waves; dynamic accumulation of surfactants at the gas/solution interface of cavitation bubbles dictate the maximum attainable interfacial concentration; a frequency effect in sonochemistry that was independent of the ultrasound intensity. Office: Ohio State U DHLRI 420 W 12th Ave TMRF 184 Columbus OH 43212 Office Phone: 614-247-5020. Business E-Mail: sostaric.2@osu.edu.

SOSTARICH, MARK EDWARD, lawyer; b. Milw., Apr. 10, 1953; s. Edward Michael and Sophia (Hibler) S.; m. Karen Sue Baranek, June 12, 1976; children: Samantha Nicole, Alex Edward. BA with distinction, U. Wis., Madison, 1975, JD cum laude, 1978. Bar: Wis. 1978, U.S. Dist. Ct. (ea. and we. dists.) Wis. 1978, U.S. Trademark Trial and Appeal Bd. 1995. Assoc. Godfrey & Kahn, Milw., 1978-84, ptnr., 1984-96, Petrie & Stocking SC, Milw., 1997—2004; pvt. practice Elkhorn, 2004—. Editor-in-chief U. Wis. Law Rev., 1978, mem., 1977. Mem. bd. visitors U. Wis., Madison, 1983-88; commr. South Milw. Housing Authority, 1985-86; mem. South Milw. Fire and Police Commn., 1986-92, sec., 1987-91, pres., 1991-92; mem. Wis. Elections Bd., 1987-95, vice chmn., 1990, chmn., 1991; mem. Dem. Nat. Com., 1993, 1995-97; mem. platform and resolutions com. Wis. Dem. Party, 1984-97, 1st vice chmn., 1984, chmn., 1985-97; chmn. Wis. Dem. Party, 1995-97; mem. Assn. State Dem. Chairs, 1993, 95-97; chmn. Milw. County Dem. Party, 1986-97, v.p., 2001, pres., 2001-04; mem., usher, HS Sunday sch. tchr., chmn. organ fundraising com. Trinity Luth. Ch., South Milw.; bd. dirs. Arthritis Found. Wis., 2000-03. Mem.: ABA, Walworth County Bar Assn., 7th Cir. Ct. Appeals Bar Assn., Milw. Bar Assn., Wis. Bar Assn. Avocations: politics, photography, art. Home: 1785 Tamarack St South Milwaukee WI 53172-1048 Office: 6 South Church St Elkhorn WI 53121 Office Phone: 262-723-5041. Personal E-mail: msostarich@charterinternet.com.

SOSTILIO, ROBERT FRANCIS, office equipment marketing consultant; b. Boston, Nov. 17, 1942; s. Natale J. and Louise Sostilio; m. Gail Marie McGuinness, Apr. 17, 1966. Student, U. Maine, 1960—61, Broward Jr. Coll., Ft. Lauderdale, 1967—70, Miami-Dade Jr. Coll., 1979. Product assurance engr. Saxon Copystatics, Miami, Fla., 1970-77; internat. svc. mgr. Saxon Export Corp., Miami, 1977-80; nat. svc. mgr. Cybernet Internat., Warren, N.J., 1980-81; mgr. nat. copier svc. Monroe Systems for Bus., Morris Plains, N.J., 1981-82; nat. OEM mgr. Panasonic Indsl. Co., Secaucus, N.J., 1982-86; assoc. dir. copier rsch. Dataquest, San Jose, Calif., 1987-90; mgr. product program Ricoh Corp., West Caldwell, N.J., 1986-87, dir. copier mktg., 1990-94, dir. strategic planning, 1994-96; group svc. dir. converging digital peripherals Cap Ventures, 1996—2000; pres., CEO Sostilio and Assocs. Internat. Inc., Ocala, Fla., 2002—. Editor: (newsletter) Multifunctionality, 1987, Color Copiers, 1989. Block capt. Meadow Ridge Civic Assn., Basking Ridge, NJ, 1985—87; sgt.-at-arms UNICO Nat., San Jose, 1990. With USN, 1964—67. Roman Catholic. Avocations: woodworking, home remodeling, dog breeding, travel, cooking. Office: Sostilio & Assocs Internat PO Box 830190 Ocala FL 34483 Office Phone: 352-624-2625. E-mail: sostilio@flash.net.

SOSTMAN, DIRK, physician, clinical researcher, medical educator; b. NYC, Nov. 20, 1948; s. Henry and Theodora (Slokker) S.; m. Maria Preka, Sept. 1, 2003; 1 child Erik Alexandros. MD, Yale University, New Haven, 1977. Diplomate Am. Bd. Radiology, Nat. Bd. Med. Examiners. Intern and resident Yale-New Haven Hosp., 1977—82; prof., chair Weill Med. Coll. Cornell U., NYC, 1995—2005, exec. vice dean, 2003—; exec. v.p. The Meth. Hosp., Houston, 2005—; CEO Meth. Physician Orgn., 2006—. Mem. lung scan interpretation panel and nuclear medicine working group Prospective Investigation of Pulmonary Embolism Diagnosis Study, Nat. Heart, Lung and Blood Inst., 1984-88; cons. Fluoromed Pharms, 1988, Am. Cancer Soc., 1992; mem. Duke Comprehensive Cancer Ctr., 1993—; program dir. Duke Winter Imaging Course, 1993-94; vis. prof. U. Pisa, 1993, U. Milan, 1993; dir. Imaging Rsch. Lab. Yale U. Sch. Medicine, 1981-84, dir. MR Imaging, 1983-87; mem. numerous adv. panels. Assoc. editor: Yearbook of Nuclear Medicine, 1984-92; mem. editorial bd.: Investigative Radiology, 1984—, Magnetic Resonance Imaging, 1985—, Jour. Thoracic Imaging, 1985—; manuscript referee; contbr. chpts. to books and numerous articles to profl. jours. Recipient Fales prize Rutgers U., 1972, Dolgan Meml. award Yale U., 1972; Yale U. summer fellowship, 1975, Lamport Biomed. Rsch. award, 1976; Winchester Chest fellow in radiology; grantee in field. Fellow Am. Coll. Chest Physicians, Am. Coll. Radiology; mMem. Fleischner Soc. (George Simon Meml. award 1982, exec. com. 1987-90, mem. Simon award com. 1991—), Soc. MRI (edn. com. 1984-86), Assn. Univ. Radiologists (Pres. 2001, Stauffer award 1988, Stauffer award com. 1983), Radiol. Soc. N.Am., Soc. Thoracic Radiology (founding mem.), Sigma Xi, Phi Beta Kappa, others. leadership in major clinical trials of venous thromboembolism diagnosis. Office: Dunn 200 6565 Fannin St Houston TX 77030 Office Phone: 713-441-2192. Business E-Mail: dsostman@tmh.tmc.edu.

SOTELO, EDUARDO (EL PIOLÍN), radio personality; b. Ocotlán, Jalisco, Mexico, 1971; arrived in US, 1986, permanent resident, 1996; Broadcaster local radio stations, Calif., 1991—2003, KSCA FM101.9, LA, 2003—; with Univision Radio, LA, 2003—. Host (radio shows) Piolín por la Mañana, 2003—. Recipient Marconi Radio award for Spanish Format Personality of Yr., Nat. Assn. Broadcasters, 2006. Achievements include support and organization of demonstrations for immigrants' rights through radio broadcasts. Office: La Nueva #2500 655 N Central Ave Glendale CA 91203 Office Phone: 818-500-4500. Office Fax: 818-500-4550. E-mail: elshowdepiolin@univision.com.

SOTELO-DYNEGA, MARLENE, psychologist; b. Flushing, NY, Sept. 16, 1976; d. Mary and Manuel Sotelo; m. David Dynega, May 26, 2002. BS, Iona Coll., NY, 1998, MA, 2001; D of Psychology, St. John's U., NY, 2002—. Cert. sch. psychologist NY, 2003, Bilingual Ext. (Spanish) Sch. Psychologist NY. Sch. psychologist LMT Sch. for Child Devel., Riverdale, NY, 2001—02; bilingual sch. psychologist Port Chester-Rye Union Free Sch. Dist., Port Chester, NY, 2002—. Mem.: NASP. Office: Thomas A Edison Sch 132 Rectory St Port Chester NY 10573 Office Phone: 914-934-2997. Business E-Mail: marlene.sotelo.dynega@gmail.com.

SOTER, GEORGE NICHOLAS, advertising executive; b. Chgo., May 16, 1924; s. Nicholas A. and Emily (Damascus) S.; m. Effie Hartocollis, Feb. 7, 1949; children: Nicholas, Thomas, Peter. Student, U. Chgo., 1947-51. Writer McCann-Erickson, Chgo., 1951-53; with Needham, Louis & Brorby, Chgo., 1954-62, v.p., creative dir. NYC, 1958-62; v.p., assoc. creative dir. Lennen & Newell Inc., NYC, 1962-67; v.p., co-dir. creative svcs., mgmt. supr. Kenyon & Eckhardt Inc., NYC, 1968-73; exec. v.p., creative dir. Pampuzac-Soter Assocs. Inc., NYC, 1974-76; sr. writer Marsteller Inc., NYC, 1980-82; v.p., creative Lord, Geller, Federico, Einstein, Inc., NYC, 1982-87; sr. v.p., creative dir. Great Scott Advt. Co. Inc., NYC, 1987-93; dir. Soter Advt. & Mktg. Consulting Svcs., NYC, 1993—; copy editor Am. Mgmt. Assn., NYC, 1995—. Founder, pres. Greek Island Ltd., N.Y.C., 1963—86; dir. Interpub. Product Devel. Workshop, N.Y.C., 1967. With U.S. Army, 1943-47, ETO. Home: 468 Riverside Dr # 71 New York NY 10027 Personal E-mail: gsoter@nyc.rr.com.

SOTH, ALEC, photographer; b. 1969; BA, Sarah Lawrence Coll., NY. Prof. photography Mpls. Coll. Art & Design; photographer NY Times Mag., Fortune, Newsweek. One-man shows include The Middle Night, Mpls. Photographer's Gallery, 1993, Art at the Bar, Icebox Gallery, Mpls., 1995—96, Minn. Ctr. Photography, 1998, Portraits (From Here to There), Central Lakes Coll. Gallery, 2001, Sleeping By the Miss., Weitman Gallery of Photography, Wash. U., St. Louis, Mo., 2003, exhibited in group shows at Campus as Place, Photographing Carleton, Carleton Coll. Art Gallery, Minn., 2002, Dog Days, Gallery T, Mpls., 2003, Summer Life, Alice Austen House Mus., Staten Island, NY, 2003, Picturing Bill - Portraits of William Eggleston, John Stinson Fine Arts, New Orleans, 2003, Sao Paulo Biennial, Sao Paul, Brazil, 2004, Whitney Biennial, Whitney Mus. Am. Art, 2004, Represented in permanent collections, San Francisco Mus. Modern Art, LA County Mus. Art, Mus. Fine Arts, Houston, Walker Art Ctr., Mpls., Mpls. Inst. Arts, Odged Mus. Southern Art, New Orleans, Carleton Coll., Minn., ND Mus. Art; author: (book) Sleeping by the Miss., 2004. Recipient Santa Fe Prize Photography, 2003; McKnight Photography Fellowship, 1999, 2004, Jerome Travel & Study Grant, 2001, Minn. State Arts Bd. Grant, 2001, Jerome Grant, 2001. Office: Yossi Milo Gallery 525 W 25th St New York NY 10001-5501 also: Alec Soth Photography 856 Raymond Ave Unit D Saint Paul MN 55114 Office Phone: 651-646-1678. Office Fax: 651-646-2255. E-mail: alec@alecsoth.com.

SOTO, GILBERTO D., music educator; b. Torreon, Mex., May 9, 1961; arrived in U.S., 1983; s. Enrique Soto-Ruiz and Maria Martinez; m. Blanc C. Ramirez, Aug. 23, 1986; children: Daney, Erika. BA in Edn., U. del Noreste, Torreon, 1983; BA in Music, Abilene Christian U., 1986; MusM, U. So. Miss., 1988, PhD in Music Edn., 1995. Music instr. Miss. Coast Coll., 1986—90; prof., chair Laredo C.C., Tex., 1990—2001; assoc. prof., chair Tex. A&M U., Laredo, 2001—05. Tchr. asst. U. So. Miss., Hattiesburg, 1981—90. Co-author: Spotlight on Music, 2005; author: Fiesta De Canciones, 2005. Mem.: Music Educators Nat. Conf., Tex. Music Edn. Assn. Roman Catholic. Home: 8627 Northridge Loop Laredo TX 78045 Office: Tex A&M Univ 5201 Universary Blvd Laredo TX 78041 Office Phone: 956-726-4006.

SOTOMAYOR, ALEXANDER, management consultant; b. NYC, Nov. 3, 1969; s. Enrique and Emiliana Sotomayor. BS in Mgmt., SUNY, Old Westbury, 1996; MBA, U. Phoenix, 2002. Cert. securities ops. profl. Inst. Cert. Bankers, Washington, 2002. Security supr. Virgin Security Svcs., NYC, 1995—98; stock broker trainee Sands Bros. and Co., Ltd., NYC, 1998—99; sales asst. Dreyfus Svc. Corp., NYC, 1999—2001, br. ops. mgr., 2001—06; sales exec. Marcus Evans, NYC, 2006; owner Sotomayer LLC, NYC, 2005—. With Rangers US Army, 1990—94. Decorated Army Achievement medal Dept. Army. Mem.: Am. Mensa, Ranger Rgt. Assn. (life), USA Triathlon, Am. Legion. Roman Catholic. Avocations: triathlon, travel, computers. Home and Office: 98-20 62d Dr Apt 9G Rego Park NY 11374 Office Phone: 718-732-3313. Home Fax: 718-732-3315. Business E-Mail: alexander@sotomayor.net.

SOTOMAYOR, SONIA, federal judge; b. Bronx, June 25, 1954; d. Sonia and Celina (Baez) Sotomayor; m. Kevin Edward Noonan, Aug. 14, 1976 (div. 1983). BA summa cum laude, Princeton U., 1976; JD, Yale U., 1979; LLD honoris causa (hon.), 1999, JD (hon.) honoris causa, 2001. Bar: NY 1980, US Dist. Ct. (ea. and so. dists.) NY 1984. Asst. dist. atty. Office of Dist. Atty. County of NY, NYC, 1979—84; assoc., ptnr. Pavia & Harcourt, NYC, 1984—92; fed. judge US Dist. Ct. (so. dist.) NY, NYC, 1992—98; cir. judge US Ct. Appeals (2d Cir.), NYC, 1998—. Adj. prof. NYU Sch. Law, 1998; lectr. law Columbia Law Sch., 1999. Editor: Yale U. Law Rev., 1979. Mem. State Adv. Panel on Inter-Group Rels., NYC, 1990—92, 1990—91; bd. dirs. P.R. Legal Def. and Edn. Fund, NYC, 1980—92, State of NY Mortgage Agy., NYC, 1987—92, NYC Campaign Fin. Bd., 1988—92. Mem.: ABA, Assn. Hispanic Judges, Am. Philos. Soc., NY Women's Bar Assn., P.R. Bar Assn., Hispanic Bar Assn., Phi Beta Kappa. Office: US Courthouse 40 Foley Sq Rm 401 New York NY 10007 *

SOTOMORA-VON AHN, RICARDO FEDERICO, pediatrician, educator; b. Guatemala City, Guatemala, Oct. 22, 1947; s. Ricardo and Evelyn (von Ahn) S.; m. Eileen Marie Holcomb, May 9, 1990; m. Victoria Monzon, Nov. 26, 1971; children: Marisol, Clarisa, Ricardo III, Charlotte Marie. MD, San Carlos U., 1972; MS in Physiology, U. Minn., 1978. Diplomate Am. Bd. Pediats., Am. Bd. Pediat. Cardiology, Am. Bd. Neonatology-Perinatal Medicine. Rotating intern Gen. Hosp., Guatemala, 1971-72; pediat. intern U. Ark., 1972-73, resident, 1973-75; fellow in pediat. cardiology U. Minn., 1975-78; rsch. assoc. in cardiovasc. pathology United Hosps., St. Paul, 1976; fellow in neonatal-perinatal medicine St. Paul's Children's Hosp., 1977-78, U. Ark., 1981-82; instr. pediats. U. Minn., 1978-79; pediat. cardiologist, unit cardiovasc. surg. Roosevelt Hosp., Guatemala City, 1979-81; asst. prof. pediats. cardiology and neonatology U. Ark., Little Rock, 1981-83; pvt. practice Little Rock, 1983—. Fellow: Am. Coll. Angiology, Am. Coll. Chest Physicians, Am. Coll. Cardiology, Am. Acad. Pediat.; mem.: AAAS, ABA, Soc. Critical Care Medicine, So. Soc. Pediat. Rsch., Ctrl. Ark. Pediat. Soc., Guatemala Coll. Physicians and Surgeons, Soc. Pediat. Echocardiology, Am. Heart Assn., NY Acad. Scis., Ark. Med. Soc., Soc. Genealogists London, Guatemala Acad. Genealogy, Heraldry and Hist. Studies (corr.), The Country Club of Little Rock. Home: 3 River Ridge Ct Little Rock AR 72227-1523 Office: Evergreen Pl 1100 N Univ Ste 142 Little Rock AR 72207 E-mail: rfsotomora@aol.com.

SOTT, JANNY, journalist; BA, Harvard Univ., 1977. Medicine and pub. Health reporter LA Times, 1985—94; reporter NY Times, 1994—. Author: (articles) Life at the Top in America Isn't Just Better, It's Longer (Newswomen's Club of Am. Front Page award, 2005); co-editor: (Book) Portraits: 9/11/01: The Collected Portraits of Grief from The New York Times. Office: The New York Times 229 W 43rd St New York NY 10036 Office Phone: 212-561-1251. Office Fax: 212-556-3690.

SOTTILE, JAMES, lawyer; b. Gainesville, Fla., Sept. 20, 1960; s. James and Judith Sottile; m. Noell Harris; children: James Eliot, David William. BS, U. Fla., Gainesville, 1982; JD, Georgetown U., Washington, 1985. Assoc. Wilmer, Cutler & Pickering, Washington, 1985—87, Nussbaum Owen & Webster, Washington, 1987—89; from assoc. to ptnr. Caplin & Drysdale, Washington, 1989—99; ptnr. Baach Robinson & Lewis, Washington, 1999—2004, Zuckerman Spaeder LLP, Washington, 2004—. Jr. warden St. Alban's Episcopal Ch., Washington, 2007—. Episcopalian. Home: 3508 Cummings Ln Chevy Chase MD 20815 Office: Zuckerman Spaeder LLP 1800 M St NW Washington DC 20036 Home Phone: 301-654-7898; Office Phone: 202-778-1894.

SOTTILE, JOSEPH JAMES, elementary school educator, poet; b. Queens, NY; s. Anthony and Mary Sottile; m. Marilyn Dufford, June 24, 1967; children: Mary Lou, April. AA, Suffolk County CC, Selden, NY, 1964; BS, SUNY, Plattsburgh, 1967; postgrad., SUNY, Brockport, 1971. Tchr. Gates Chili Sch. Dist., Rochester, NY, 1967—2000, tutor out of sch. suspension program, 2001—. Adj. faculty Rochester Inst. Tech., 1980—90; presenter in field. Author: Bathroom Vacation, 1998, Picture Poetry on Parade!, 2004, numerous poems; contbr. articles to popular mags., local newspapers. Mem.: Ret. Tchrs. Orgn. Rochester and Vicinity, Rochester Writers and Books, Rochester Area Children's Writers and Illustrators, Soc. Children's Book Writers and Illustrators. Avocations: bicycling, golf, tennis, racquetball, reading. Personal E-mail: jsottile@frontiernet.net.

SOUDER, MARK EDWARD, congressman; b. Ft. Wayne, Ind., July 18, 1950; s. Edward Getz and Irma (Fahling) S.; m. Diane Kay Zimmer, July 28; children: Brooke Diane, Nathan Elias, Zachary. BS, Ind. U., Ft. Wayne, 1972; MBA, U. Notre Dame, 1974. Mgmt. trainee Crossroads Furniture

Co., Houston, 1974; mktg. mgr. Gabberts Furniture & Studio, Mpls., 1974-76; mktg. mgr., exec. v.p. Souder's Furniture & Studio, Grabill, Ind., 1976-80, pres., 1981-84; econ. devel. liaison for U.S. Rep. Dan Coats, from 1983; mem. U.S. Congress from Ind. 3rd Dist. (formerly 4th), 1995—, Ho. Select Com. on Homeland Security. Mem. edn. and workforce com., govt. reform and oversight com., small bus. com., natural resources com. Publicity chmn. Grabill County Fair, 1977—; advisor Dan Coats for Congress Com., 1980-81; mem. Ind. Area Devel. Coun.; mem. bus. alumni adv. con. Ind. U.-Ft. Wayne. Mem. Midwest Home Furnishings Assn. (dir. 1976-84, past treas., exec. v.p.), Ft. Wayne, Grabill C. of C., Allen County Hist. Soc., Alumni Assn. Ind. U. at Ft. Wayne (dir., past pres.), Alumni Assn. U. Notre Dame. Republican. Mem. Apostolic Christian Ch. Home: 13733 Ridgeview Ct Grabill IN 46741 Office: US Ho Reps 2231 Rayburn Ho Office Bldg Washington DC 20515-1403 Office Phone: 202-225-4436. Office Fax: 202-225-3479. E-mail: souder@mail.house.gov. *

SOUGANIDIS, PANAGIOTIS EMMANUEL, mathematician, educator; s. Emmanuel Souganidis and Stella Michailatsou; m. Thaleia Zariphopoulou-Souganidis, July 14, 1987; children: Ellie Stella, Emmanuel Panagiotis. PhD, U. Wis., Madison, 1983. Asst. prof. Brown U., Providence, 1983—91; prof. U. Wis., Madison, 1991—2000, U. Tex., Austin, 2000—. Recipient Presdl. Young Investigation award, NSF, 1987, Academic prize, Bodossaki Found., 1995; fellow, Sloan Found., 1989. Mem.: Am. Math. Soc. Home Phone: 512-371-3840; Office Phone: 512-471-1754.

SOUHAM, GÉRARD, communications executive; b. Paris, May 30, 1928; s. Lucien and Mary-Françoise (Husson) S.; m. Eliane Meyrat, June 23, 1951; children: Glenn (dec.), Yan, Philip. Diploma, Am. Community Sch., Paris, 1948; cert., Ecole Commerciale de Paris. Chargé de mission State Dept., Europe, 1950-52; pub. info. officer Allied Air Forces NATO, Fontainebleau, 1953-55; chmn. bd., chief exec. officer J. Walter Thompson, Paris, 1955-75, v.p. NYC, 1970-75; prin. S3C Gerard Souham Group Communication Cos., Paris and Lausanne, Switzerland, 1975—, SC3 Gerard Souham Group Communication Cos., NYC, 1979—. Bd. dirs. Am. Overseas Meml., I.T. Fin., AVON, France, Mattel-France; chmn. bd. Turner Prodn. Europe, 1994—98; vice chmn. bd. Avon. Author: Général Souham Comte de l'Empire, 1964, Impressions sur..., 1970, Souham, 1989, Sur les Champs de Bataille de la Révolution et de l'Empire, 1990. Mem. pvt. sector internat. and pub. rels. coms. USIA, 1985; mem. world bd. govs. USO, Washington, 1984, chmn. fundraising com., 1989—, pres., Paris, 1995, bd. dirs. 2000—. Decorated officer Legion of Honor (France); officer Order of Leopold, knight Belgian Crown (Belgium). Mem. Internat. Inst. Strategic Studies London, France, USA (bd. dirs.), Am. Overseas Meml. Assn. (bd. dirs. 1988—), USAF Assn. (life), HM Guards Polo (Windsor, Eng.) (life), Polo de Bagatelle (Paris), NY Athletic, Yacht of Monaco. Roman Catholic. Avocation: collecting fine bindings. Office: Souham Group Comm 500 5th Ave New York NY 10110-0002

SOULE, GEORGE ALAN, literature educator; b. Fargo, ND, Mar. 3, 1930; s. George Alan and Ruth Georgia (Knudsen) S.; m. Carolyn Richards, Nov. 24, 1961; 1 child, Katherine. BA, Carleton Coll., 1951; postgrad., Corpus Christi Coll., Cambridge U., Eng., 1952-53; MA, Yale U., 1956, PhD, 1960. Instr. English lit. Oberlin (Ohio) Coll., 1958-60; asst. prof. U. Wis., Madison, 1960-62; from asst. prof. to prof. Carleton Coll., Northfield, Minn., 1962-95, prof. emeritus, 1995—, chair English dept., 1980—83; tchr. Cannon Valley Elder Collegium, 1998—, vice chair, 2003—05, chair, 2005—07, also bd. dirs. Cons. Ednl. Testing Svc., Princeton, NJ, 1967-84, 94-97; lectr. Wordsworth Winter Sch., Grasmere, UK, 2003-07. Author: Four British Women Novelists: An Annotated and Critical Secondary Biblioigraphy, 1998; editor: Theatre of the Mind, 1974; contbr. articles to profl. jours. Libr. bd. City Northfield, 1997-00; bd. dirs. Northfield Area Found., 2001-02. With US Army, 1954-55. Internat. fellow Rotary, 1952-53, Sterling pre-doctoral fellow Yale U., 1957-58. Mem.: Anthony Powell Soc., The Iris Murdoch Soc., Friends of Dove Cottge, Boswell Soc. of Auchinleck, Johnson Soc. of Lichfield, Mayflower Soc., Oxford and Cambridge Club, Rotary, Phi Beta Kappa. Episcopalian. Avocations: cooking, travel, Jeopardy (Champion Sr. Tournament 1990). Home: 313 Nevada St Northfield MN 55057-2346 Office Phone: 507-646-4322. Fax: 507-645-5099. E-mail: gsoule@charter.net.

SOULE, GEORGE WILLIAM, lawyer; b. Fargo, ND, June 24, 1954; s. Benard B. and Mavis J. (Hogan) S. BA summa cum laude in Econ., Polit., Moorhead State U., 1976; JD magna cum laude, Harvard U., 1979. Bar: Minn. 1979, US Dist. Ct. Minn. 1980, Wis. 1985, US Dist. Ct. Wis. 1988, US Dist. Ct. N. Dakota 1989, US Dist. Ct. (ea.& we.dists.) Wis. 1988. Legal asst. investigator Cahill, Gunhus, Streed, Grinnell, Jeffries & Klinger, Moorhead, 1973-76, law clk., 1977; assoc. Gray, Plant, Mooty, Mooty & Bennett, Mpls., 1979-85; ptnr. Bowman and Brooke, Mpls., 1985—. Bd. visitors Moorhead State U., Minn., 1984—; class agt. Harvard Law Sch. Fund, Mass. 1985, chair Minn. Comm. Jud. Selection 1999-2003. Contbr. articles to profl. jour. Minn. coord. John Anderson for Pres. Campaign, 1979-80; mem. planning com. Midwest Conf. Moderate Reps., Madison, Wis., 1983; cons., writer organizer Tom Heffelfinger for Hennepin County Atty. Campaign, 1986; co-chmn. Lawyers for Durenberger, 1988; issues dir. Kelley for Gov. 19890-90, Legal Aid Soc. Mpls./MSBA Civil Litig. Sect. 1991 -. Recipient Howard Lysne Bus. & Econ. Alumni Achievement award, Moorhead State U., 1993, Professionalism award, Hennepin County Bar Assn., 1997, Atty. of the Yr., Minn. Lawyer, 2000, Super Lawyers, Minn. Law & Politics Mag., 2001—06, Advs. award, Minn. State Bar Assn., 2003, Moorhead Disting. Alumni, Minn. State U., 2005. Mem. ABA 1979-, Minn. State Bar Assn., Hennepin County Bar Assn. 1979-, State Bar Wis., Minn. Def. Lawyers Assn. 1980-, Def. Rsch. and Trial Lawyers Assn., chair & vice-chair Minn. Comm. Jud. Selection., (past pres.) 2004-2006 (bd. dir.) 2006- Minn. Am. Indian Bar Assn. 1994-, Am. Bd. Trial Advs. Office: Bowman & Brooke 150 S 5th St Ste 2600 Minneapolis MN 55402 Office Phone: 612-672-3251. Office Fax: 612-672-3200. Business E-Mail: george.soule@msp.bowmanandbrooke.com.

SOULE, ROBERT GROVE, lawyer; b. Boston, Jan. 12, 1958; s. Augustus W. and Mary R. Soule; m. Maura Kelley, Aug. 21, 1982; children: Courtney K., Katherine W., Zachary A. BA, Harvard U., 1979; JD, Suffolk U., 1983. Bar: Mass. 1983, U.S. Dist. Ct. Mass. 1983. Of counsel First Am. Title Ins. Co., Boston, 1982-85, asst. regional counsel, 1985-87; New Eng. states counsel Minn. Title Ins. Co., Boston, 1987-89; N.E. regional counsel Old Republic Title Ins. Co., Boston, 1989-93; mgr. nat. divsn. Lawyers Title Ins. Corp. (LandAmerica), Boston, 1993—. Contbr. articles to profl. jours., chpts. to books. Mem. Am. Land Title Assn., New Eng. Land Title Assn. (bd. dirs. 1996-2001, pres. 1999-2000), Mass. Conveyancers Assn. (title standards com. 1987—, exec. com. 1989-92), Mass. Bar Assn., Abstract Club. Office: 150 Federal St #200 Boston MA 02110-1713 Fax: 617-619-4848. E-mail: rsoule@landam.com.

SOULER, BENJAMIN KERWI, retired research chemist, pharmacist, consultant; b. Woonsocket, RI, Aug. 8, 1917; s. Harry Nelson and Elizabeth (Kerwin) Souler; m. Cornelia Carruthers, Mar. 26, 2005; m. Priscilla Jepson, Feb. 7, 1942 (dec. Dec. 19, 1947); children: Mary Elizabeth Hardwich, Priscilla Ann Henry. BS, U. RI, Kingston, 1939; MS, U. So. Calif., LA, 1941. Rsch. chemist United Rexall Drug Co., Boston, 1941—46; lab. dir. Am. Home Foods Co., Boston, 1946—47, Elkhart, Ind., 1946—47; sr. rsch. scientist Bristol-Myers Squibb Co., Syracuse, NY, 1947—72; pharmacist cons. various pharmacies Cape Cod, Mass., 1972—86, Orleans Convalescent and Retirement Ctr., Mass., 1986—86; ret. Spkr. in fielf. Candidate US congress NY State Conservative Party, Onadaga County, NY. Pvt. 243rd regiment coastal arty. RI N.G., 1935—38, Woonsocket, pvt. coastal gun crew RI N.G., 1935—38, Ft. Henry G. Wright, Fishers Island, NY, pharmacist's mate USN, 1943—44, lt. comm. cryptographic officer USN, 1944—46, lt. officer courier USN, 1944—46, lt. tng. officer USN, 1952—53. Mem.: DAV, Sampson WWII Sailors, Am. Legion, Bristol Employee's Assn. (pres. 1962), Syracuse Lions Club (pres. 1954). Achievements include patents for war gas (lewisite) decontaminant; highly stable ointment base. Avocations: history, botany, stamp collecting/philately.

SOULTOUKIS, DONNA ZOCCOLA, library director; b. Princeton, NJ, July 28, 1949; d. Peter Joseph and Josephine (Taraschi) Zoccola; m. Dimitrios Athanasios Soultoukis, July 26, 1980. AB, Georgian Ct. Coll., Lakewood, NJ, 1971; cert., Italian U. for Foreigners, Perugia, 1974; MS, Drexel U., 1976. Libr. asst. Geology Libr. Princeton U., 1971-73; libr. Friends Hosp., Phila., 1976-86, dir. libr. svcs., 1986-98; head libr. Temple U., Sch. Podiatric, 1998-99; ref. libr. MCP/Hahnemann U., Phila., 1999-2000; sr. info. scientist Bristol-Myers Squibb Pharm. Rsch. Inst., Hopewell, N.J., N.J., 2000; libr. Our Lady of Lourdes Sch. Nursing, Camden, NJ, 2001—. Cons. Lower Bucks Hosp., Bristol, Pa., 1991-95. Vol. outreach program Old St. Joseph's Ch., Phila., 1992-95, sanctuary min., 1993—, pastoral coun., 1995-98, 2001—05, website adminstr., 2003-07, coord. altar ministers, 2004—, sec. parish coun., 2005—, co-chmn. parish life com., 2006—, mem prayer and spiritualty com., 2007—. Mem. Med. Libr. Assn. (chair mental librs. divsn. 1991-93, chair rsch. com. 1996—), Spl. Librs. Assn. (Phila. chpt. bd. dirs. 1985-88, pres. 1982-84, chmn. long-range planning 1993, mem. adv. bd. 1995-2001, sec. solo divsn. 2000-01, devel. com. 2003-). Avocations: travel, cooking. Home: 290 Cinnabar Ln Yardley PA 19067-5717 Office Phone: 856-757-3722. Business E-Mail: soultoukisd@lourdesnet.org.

SOUPATA, LEA N., human resources specialist; b. NYC; With UPS, Atlanta, 1969—, various positions in human resources and customer service, dist. mgr. NY, 1990—94, mem. mgmt. com. Atlanta, 1995—, v.p. to sr. v.p. human resources. Bd. dirs. UPS. Chair UPS Found.; trustee Annie E. Casey Found.; bd. dirs. Jr. Achievement Ga., St. Basil's Acad. Recipient Human Capital award, Hunt-Scanlon Advisors, 2005. Fellow: Nat. Human Resources Acad.; mem.: Human Resources Policy Assn. (bd. dirs.). Office: UPS 55 Glenlake Pkwy NE Atlanta GA 30328

SOURIAN, PETER, writer, language educator, educator; b. Boston, Apr. 7, 1933; s. Zareh Missak and Zabelle (Bayentz) S.; m. Eve Jeanne Pocquet, Sept. 25, 1971; children: Mark, Delphine. BA, Harvard U., 1955. Lectr. ext. divsn. NYU, NYC, 1963-65; from instr. English to prof. Bard Coll., Annandale-on-Hudson, NY, 1965—75, prof., 1975—, co-dir. Writing Program, 1980—. Faculty New Sch. Social Rsch., NYC, 1975-2000; TV critic Nation mag., NYC, 1975-81; mem. Anahit Prize Com., 1988—; nat. adv. panel George Polk Awards Com., 1979-92. Author: Miri, 1957, The Best and Worst of Times, 1961, The Gate, 1965, (essays and criticism) At The French Embassy in Sofia, 1992; mem. editl. bd. Ararat Quar., 1975—; contbr. articles and fiction to popular mags, profl. jours. and collections. Bd. dirs. Armenian Ctr. Columbia U., N.Y.C., 1988-97; mem. Clemente Course Humanities Adv. Bd., 1999—. With U.S. Army, 1957-59. Recipient Bardian award Bard Coll. Alumni, 2000; Lilly Endowment grant, 1976, Kellogg Found. grant, 1977. Mem. MLA, PEN, Nat. Book Critics Circle, Century Assn. Home: 30 E 70th St New York NY 10021-4942 Office: Bard Coll Annandale on Hudson Annandale On Hudson NY 12504 Office Phone: 845-758-6822.

SOURKES, THEODORE LIONEL, biochemistry professor; b. Montreal, Que., Can., Feb. 21, 1919; s. Irving and Fannie (Golt) S.; m. Shena Rosenblatt, Jan. 17, 1943; children: Barbara, Myra. B.Sc., McGill U., 1939, M.Sc. magna cum laude, 1946; PhD, Cornell U., 1948; D.U. honoris causa, U. Ottawa, Can., 1990. Asst. prof. pharmacology Georgetown U. Med. Sch., 1948-50; research asso. dept. enzyme chemistry Merck Inst. Therapeutic Research, Rahway, NJ, 1950-53; sr. research biochemist Allan Meml. Inst., Montreal, 1953-65; dir. lab. neurochemistry Allan Meml. Inst. Psychiatry, 1965—91; mem. faculty McGill U., Montreal, 1954—, prof. biochemistry, 1965—, prof. psychiatry, assoc. dean of medicine for research Faculty Medicine, 1972-75; prof. pharmacology, 1990—; emeritus, 1991. Mem. Que. Med. Rsch. Coun., 1971-77; sr. fellow Parkinson's Disease Found., N.Y.C., 1963-66. Author: Biochemistry of Mental Disease, 1962, Nobel Prize Winners in Medicine and Physiology, 1901-1965, 1967, Life and Work of J.L.W. Thudichum, 1829-1901, 2003; sect. editor Internat. Jour. of the History of Neuroscis., 1996—. Decorated officer Order of Canada, Venezuelan Order Andrés Bello; laureate of the Wilder Penfield Prix du Que. for Biomed. Sci., 1998. Fellow Royal Soc. Can.; mem. Canadian Biochem. Soc., Pharmacol. Soc. Can., Canadian Coll. Neuropsychopharmacology (Heinz Lehmann award 1982, medal 1990), Am. Soc. Biol. Chemists, Am. Soc. Pharmacology and Exptl. Therapeutics, Am. Soc. Neurochemistry, Internat. Soc. History of Neuroscis. (medal 2001), Internat. Soc. Neurochemistry, Internat. Brain Research Orgn., Sigma Xi. Achievements include research and publs. on drugs for treatment high blood pressure; 1st basic research on methyldopa; elucidation of role of dopamine and other monamines in nervous system; first trials of L-dopa in Parkinson's disease, biochemistry of mental depression, pathways of stress in the nervous system, imaging serotonin in brain, history of biochemistry. Home: 3033 Sherbrooke St W # 303 Montreal PQ Canada H3Z 1A3 Office: McGill U 1033 Pine Ave W Montreal PQ Canada H3A 1A1 E-mail: theodore.sourkes@mcgill.ca.

SOUSANIS, NICK, art web site designer; b. 1973; Tchr., pub. speaking Wayne State U.; co-founder, pub., editor-in-chief Thedetroiter.com, 2002—. Trustee Contemporary Art Inst. Detroit. Named one of 40 Under 40, Crain's Detroit Bus., 2006. Office: Museum of Contemporary Art Detroit 4454 Woodward Ave Detroit MI 48201

SOUSSLOFF, ANDREW D., lawyer; b. Providence, Sept. 21, 1953; s. Dimitri Gregory and Barbara Lucy (Farr) S.; m. Patricia James, June 7, 1986. BA, MA, U. Pa., 1975, JD cum laude, 1979. Bar: NY 1980, Calif. 1987. Assoc. Cadwalader Wickersham & Taft, NYC, 1979-80, Sullivan & Cromwell, NYC, 1981-86, ptnr., 1986—, now co-mng. ptnr. gen. practice group. Mem.: Internat. Bar Assn. (vice-chmn., capital mkts. forum, co-chmn., securities law com. 2000—03). Office: Sullivan & Cromwell 125 Broad St Fl 28 New York NY 10004-2489 Office Phone: 212-558-4000. Office Fax: 212-558-3588. Business E-Mail: soussloffa@sullcrom.com.

SOUTAS-LITTLE, ROBERT WILLIAM, mechanical engineer, educator; b. Oklahoma City, Feb. 25, 1933; s. Harry Glenn and Mary Evelyn (Miller) Little; m. Patricia Soutas, Sept. 3, 1982; children: Deborah, Catherine, Colleen, Jennifer, Karen. BS in Mech. Engring, Duke U., 1955; MS, U. Wis., 1959, PhD, 1962. Design engr. Allis Chalmers Mfg. Co., Milw., 1955-57; instr. mech. engring. Marquette U., 1957-59; instr. U. Wis., Madison, 1959-62, asst. prof., 1962-63, Okla. State U., 1963-65; prof. Mich. State U., 1965—2001, chmn. dept. mech. engring., 1972-77, chmn. dept. biomechanics, 1977-90; dir. biomechanics evaluation lab., 1989—; prof. emeritus Mich. State U., Lansing, 2001—. Cons. A. C. Electronics Co., Ford Motor Co., CBS Research Lab., B. F. Goodrich Co.; lectr. AID, India, 1965 Author: Elasticity, 1973, Engineering Mechanics: Statics, 1999, Engineering Mechanics: Dynamics, 1999; contbr. articles to profl. jours. Vice pres. Okemos (Mich.) Sch. Bd., 1967-72; mem. Meridian Twp. (Mich.) Charter Commn., 1969-70, Meridian Twp. Zoning Bd. Appeals, 1969-71. Recipient award for excellence in instrn. engring. students Western Electric Co., 1970-71, Disting. Faculty award, 1996; NSF grantee, 1964-69, 79, NIH grantee, 1973-75, 79—. Fellow ASME; mem. Soc. Engring. Sci., Am. Soc. Biomechanics, Internat. Soc. Biomechanics, N.Am. Soc. Clin. Gait and Movement Analysis, Sigma Xi, Pi Tau Sigma, Ta Beta Pi. Home: 187 S Highland Dr Leland MI 49654-1143 Office: PO Box 1143 Leland MI 49654-1143 Home Phone: 231-256-7646; Office Phone: 231-256-7646. Business E-Mail: soutas@egr.msu.edu.

SOUTER, DAVID HACKETT, United States supreme court justice; b. Melrose, Mass., Sept. 17, 1939; s. Joseph Alexander and Helen Adams (Hackett) Souter. BA, Harvard U., 1961, LLB, 1966; BA, MA in Jurisprudence, Oxford U., 1989. Bar: N.H. 1967. Assoc. Orr & Reno, Concord, NH, 1966—68, Lowell Ho., Harvard Coll.; asst. atty. gen. State of NH, 1968—71, dep. atty. gen., 1971—76, atty. gen., 1976—78; assoc. justice NH Superior Ct., 1978—83, NH Supreme Ct., 1983—90; judge US Ct. Appeals (1st cir.), NH, 1990; assoc. justice US Supreme Ct., Washington, 1990—. Mem. Maine-NH Interstate Boundary Commn., 1971, NH Police Stds. and Training Coun., 1976—78, NH Jud. Coun., 1976—78, NH Gov.'s Commn. Crime and Delinquency, 1976—78, 1979—83. Trustee Concord Hosp., 1972—85, pres., 1978—84; trustee NH Hist. Soc., 1976—85; v.p., 1980—85; overseer Dartmouth Med. Sch., 1981—87. Rhodes scholar, Magdalen Coll., Oxford U., 1963, Hon. fellow. Master: Gray's Inn (London) (hon.); fellow: Am. Acad. Arts and Scis., Mass. Hist. Soc., Am. Coll. Trial Lawyers (hon.), Am. Bar Found. (hon.); mem.: ABA, Am. Antiquarian Soc., Am. Philos. Soc., Pilgrim Soc. (hon.), New Eng. Hist. Geneal. Soc. (hon.), Merrimack County Bar Assn., Merrimack County Bar Assn., NH Bar Assn., NH Hist. Soc. (v.p. 1980—85, trustee 1976—85), Appalachian Mtn. Club, Phi Beta Kappa. Republican. Episcopalian. Office: US Supreme Ct One First St NE Washington DC 20543 *

SOUTER, PHILIP FRANK, research scientist; Scientist Procter & Gamble Co., Cin. Co-recipient Nat. Inventor of Yr. award, Intellectual Property Owners Edn. Found., 2006. Achievements include development of PuR Purifier of Water Sachets, which are capable of purifying 10 liters of water by pulling contaminants out of non-drinkable water; patents in field. Office: Health Scis Inst Proctor & Gamble Co 1 P&G Plaza Cincinnati OH 45202

SOUTHAM, G(ORDON) HAMILTON, former Canadian government official; b. Ottawa, Ont., Can., Dec. 19, 1916; s. Wilson Mills and Henrietta Alberta (Cargill) S.; m. Jacqueline Lambert-David, Apr. 15, 1940 (div. Mar. 1969); children: Peter, Christopher, Jennifer, Michael; m. Gro Mortensen, May 17, 1969 (div. Jan. 1978); children: Henrietta, Gordon; m. Marion Charpentier, June 26, 1981. BA with honors, Trinity Coll., Toronto, Ont., 1939; postgrad., Christ Ch. Coll., Oxford, Eng., 1939; LLD (hon.), Trent and Carleton Univs.; DCL (hon.), King's Coll. Univ.; DU (hon.), Ottawa U. Reporter The Times, London, 1945-46; editl. writer Ottawa Citizen, 1946-47; with Dept. External Affairs Can., 1948-64, head info. divsn. Ottawa, Canada, 1962-64; amb. Warsaw, 1960-62; founder,. coord. Nat. Arts Centre, Ottawa, 1964—67, dir. gen., 1967-77; spl. advisor to sec. state, 1977-79. Chmn. Ofcl. Residences Coun., 1985-93; founder, chmn. Rideau Canal Mus., 1983; founder, pres. Can. Mediterranean Inst., 1980-86, chmn., 1987; gov. Archaeol. Inst. Am., 1982-88; hon. pres. Can. Classical Assn., 1982-87; chancellor King's Coll. Univ., 1988-95; co-chmn. Task Force on Mil. History Mus., 1990-91; founder, v.p. Can. Battle of Normandy Found., 1992; founder, pres., Valiants Found., 2002. Served with Brit. Army, 1939-40; served to capt. Royal Can. Arty., 1940-45, mentioned in despatches. Decorated officer Order of Can.; award of cultural merit (Poland); Opera of Nat. Arts Ctr. renamed Southam Hall in his honor, 2000. Mem.: Rideau Club (Ottawa). Home: 280 Thorold Rd Ottawa ON Canada K1M 0K2 *"Of those to whom much is given, much is asked".*

SOUTHARD, WILLIAM G., lawyer; b. Toledo, May 6, 1953; s. James Theodore and Dorothy (Fergusson) S.; m. Martha Donelan, Aug. 14, 1976. BA, Williams Coll., 1975; JD, Columbia U., 1978. Bar: U.S. Dist. Ct. Ill. 1979, Mass. 1981, U.S. Dist. Ct. Mass. 1981, U.S. Ct. Appeals (1st cir.) 1985. Assoc. Schiff Hardin & Waite, Chgo., 1978-81, Bingham, Dana & Gould LLP, Boston, 1981-85, ptnr., 1985—2002, dep. chmn. litig., 1994-2000, chmn. litig., 2000—02; ptnr. Bingham McCutchen LLP, 2002—, dep. chair litig., 2002—. Assoc. editor Columbia Jour. Transnat. Law, 1978; contbr. articles to profl. jours. Mem. ABA, ASTM, Boston Bar Assn. Office: Bingham McCutchen LLP 150 Federal St Fl 15 Boston MA 02110-1745 Office Phone: 617-951-8232. Business E-Mail: william.southard@bingham.com.

SOUTHERLAND, HENRY DELEON, JR., retired lawyer, civil engineer; b. Birmingham, Ala., Sept. 8, 1911; s. Henry DeLeon and Edwina (Williams) Southerland; m. Helen Ashe (div.); 1 child, Mary Neill 1 stepchild, Carolyn Wilson Long; m. Louise Harris Wilson, Jan. 22, 1955. Student, Ga. Tech. U., 1929—31; BS, U. Ga., 1934; MS, U. Tenn., 1941; JD, Columbia U., 1948; MA, Samford U., 1983. Registered profl. engr., Tenn., 1942; bar: Ala. 1949. Engring. aide to hydraulic engr. water control planning TVA, Knoxville, Tenn., 1934—48; tax acct. US Steel Corp., Fairfield, Ala., 1948—51, staff asst. land dept., 1951—56, asst. mgr. land dept., 1956—68, mgr. so. lands timber, 1968—71; comml. agt. Birmingham So. RR Co., Fairfield, 1956—71; ret., 1971. Co-author: The Federal Road through Georgia, the Creek Nation, and Alabama, 1806-1836, 1949 (Best non-fiction award Ala. Hist. Assn., Best non-fiction award Ala. Libr. Assn.). Mem. Mountain Brook City Coun., Ala., 1976—80, pres. pro tem, 1980; chmn. planning commn. City of Mountain Brook, 1957—76. Lt. col. US Army, 1946, col. US Army, 1954. Mem.: S.R. (gen. v.p. emeritus), Newcomen Soc., Soc. War of 1812 (past grand marshall), Soc. Colonial Wars (past dep. gov. gen.), St. Andrews Soc. Mid. South (founder), Soc. of Cin. Episcopalian. Avocations: genealogy, gardening, fishing, history. Home and Office: 47 Greenway Rd Mountain Brook AL 35213

SOUTHERLAND, S. DUANE, manufacturing executive; b. Durham, NC, Apr. 24, 1949; s. Sydney Duane and Beatrice Marie (Carver) S.; m. Linda F. Lewis, Jan. 5, 1974, 1 child, S. Duane III. BSE, Duke U., 1971, MS in Engring., 1973, MBA, 1974. Ops. analyst Cooper Group Div. Cooper Industries, Apex, NC, 1974-78, planning analyst Houston, 1978-81, dir. fin. Cooper Electronics Div. Nashua, NH, 1981-83, gen. mgr. Conn. ops. Kirsch Div. Beacon Falls, Conn., 1983-87, pres. Kirsch Div. Sturgis, Mich., 1987-94; pres., CEO Conso Products Co., Union, SC, 1995-98; pres., CEO, dir. Equality Specialties, Inc., NYC, 1999—2001; pres., CEO Conso Products, Union, SC, 2002—, Taos, LLC, Spartanburg, 2005—. Republican. Baptist.

SOUTHERN, DAVID, history professor; b. Great Bend, Kans., Feb. 19, 1938; s. Arnett D. Southern and Maxine Loretto Windon; m. Judith Marie Jarvis (div.); 1 child, Sheri Lee. BA, Alderson-Boraddus Coll., W.Va., 1964; MA, Wake Forest U., NC, 1965; PhD, Emory U., Atlanta, 1971. Instr. N.C. Wesleyan Coll., Rocky Mount, NC, 1965—66; prof. Westminster Coll., Fulton, Md., 1970—2005. Author: The Malignant Heritage: Yankee Progressives and the Negro Question, 1901-1914, 1968, Gunnar Myrdal and Black-White Relations, 1987, John LaFarge and the Limits of Catholic Interracialism, 1911-1963, 1996, The Progressive Era and Race: Reaction and Reform, 1900-1917, 2005; contbr. book revs. to jours., articles to profl. jours. With USAF, 1956—60. Recipient Gustavus Myers award, U. Ark., 1987, 1996; fellow, NEH, 1982—83; Grant, ACLS, APS, CUSHWA. Mem.: So. Hist. Assn., Orgn. Am. Historians. Democrat. Avocations: tennis, basketball, running, gardening, jazz. Home: 116 Merino Canonsburg PA 15317 Personal E-mail: dwsouthern@comcast.net.

SOUTHERN, KIMBERLY ELAINE, art historian, educator; d. Robert James and Ruth Talmadge Sadler; m. David Wayne Southern, June 23, 1994; 1 child, Robert David Sadler. AA, Studio Acad. Comml. Art and Design, Omaha, 1984; BA magna cum laude, U. Nebr., Omaha, 1993; MA,

U. Mass., Amherst, 1997. Dir. advt. Tretiar's Diamond Vogel Paints, Omaha, 1983—85; instr. U. Mass., 1995—96, Holyoke CC, Mass., 1996—97; adj. prof. Montgomery Coll., Rockville, Md., 1998—2006, No. Va. CC, Annandale, 2001—; dir. admissions Md. Coll. Art and Design, Silver Spring, Md., 1998—2000. Admissions Md. Coll. of Art and Design, Silver Spring, Md., 1999—2000; adj. prof. Montgomery Coll., Rockville, Md., 1998—2006. Rsch. asst.: A Concise Dictionary of Art History (by Nancy Frazier), 2000. Recipient Dean's award, U. Nebr., 1993. Mem.: Coll. Art Assn., Smithsonian Instn., Golden Key Nat. Honor Soc., Phi Eta Sigma, Alpha Lambda Delta. Office: No Va CC Extended Learning INst 8333 Little River Turnpike Annandale VA 22003-3796 Personal E-mail: kim.southern@comcast.net.

SOUTHERN, NANCY C., utilities executive; m. Jonathan Asselin; children: Kelly Asselin, Kyle Asselin, Benjamin Asselin. Pres., co-chmn., CEO ATCO Ltd. and Can. Utilities, Calgary, Alba., Canada. Exec. v.p. Spruce Meadows; bd. dirs. Shell Can. Ltd., Akita Drilling Ltd., Sentgraf Enterprises Ltd. Mem. Calgary Econ. Devel. Authority. Named Bus. Woman of Yr., Consumer's Choice Awards, 2005. Office: ATCO Ltd 1600 909 11th Ave SW Calgary AB Canada T2R 1N6

SOUTHERN, ROBERT ALLEN, lawyer; b. Independence, Mo., July 17, 1930; s. James Allen and Josephine (Ragland) S.; m. Cynthia Agnes Drews, May 17, 1952; children: David D., William A., James M., Kathryn S. O'Brien. BS in Polit. Sci., Northwestern U., 1952, LL.B., 1954. Bar: Ill. 1955. Assoc. Mayer, Brown & Platt (now Mayer, Brown, Rowe & Maw), Chgo., 1954-64, ptnr., 1965-96, mng. ptnr., 1978-91, LA, 1991-96; CEO So. Assocs., Grayslake, Ill., 1997—, Chapel Hill, NC, 2004—. Editor in chief Northwestern U. Law Rev., 1953-54. Trustee, v.p., gen. counsel LaRabida Children's Hosp. and Rsch. Ctr., Chgo., 1974-89; trustee Kenilworth (Ill.) Union Ch., 1980-88; pres. Joseph Sears Sch. Bd., 1977-79; trustee Rush U. Med. Ctr., 1983-91, life trustee, 1991—; bd. dirs. Boys and Girls Clubs Chgo., 1986-91; governing mem. Orchestral Assn. Chgo., 1988-93. With U.S. Army, 1955-57. Mem. Chgo. Bar Assn., Lawyers Club Chgo., Order of Coif, Govs. Club (Chapel Hill, N.C.), Chgo. Club. Home: 60116 Davie Chapel Hill NC 27517-8466 Office Phone: 919-969-8292. Personal E-mail: rsouthern@nc.rr.com.

SOUTHGATE, RICHARD W., lawyer, director; b. Chgo., May 6, 1929; m. Anna Fisher Hart, Aug. 25, 1951; children: Richard W., Sarah B., Rebecca W. C., John P. AB cum laude, Harvard U., 1951, LL.B. cum laude, 1954. Bar: Mass. 1954. Assoc. Covington & Burling, Washington, 1956-58; assoc., then ptnr., chmn. policy com. Ropes & Gray, Boston, 1958-94; vol. atty. Greater Boston Legal Svcs., 1995—. Mem. Mass. Commn. on Anti-Takeover Laws; adj. prof. Northeastern U. Sch. Law, Boston, 1996-97. Author: (with Donald W. Glazer) Massachusetts Corporation Law and Practice, 1991. Moderator, Town of Manchester, Mass., 1976-94. Served as sgt. U.S. Army, 1954-56 Mem. Boston Bar Assn., ABA, Mass. Bar Assn. Clubs: Essex County, Somerset; Harvard (Boston). Office: Greater Boston Legal Svcs 197 Friend St Boston MA 02114-1802 Home: 824 Hale St Beverly MA 01915-2214

SOUTHWELL, DONALD G., insurance company executive; Grad., We. Mich. U. Mgmt. positions through pres. ins. & fin. svcs. Prudential Ins. Co. Am., 1974—96; pres. life & health ins. group Unitrin, Inc., Chgo., 1996—99, v.p., 1998—99, sr. v.p., pres. ins. ops., 1999—2002, pres., COO, 2002—06, pres., CEO, 2006—. Bd. dirs. Unitrin, Inc., 2002—. Office: Unitrin Inc One E Wacker Dr Chicago IL 60601 *

SOUTHWICK, CHARLES HENRY, zoologist, educator; b. Wooster, Ohio, Aug. 28, 1928; s. Arthur F. and Faye (Motz) S.; m. Heather Milne Beck, July 12, 1952; children: Steven, Karen. BA, Coll. Wooster, 1949; MS, U. Wis., 1951, PhD, 1953. NIH fellow, 1951-53; asst. prof. biology Hamilton Coll., 1953-54; NSF fellow Oxford U., England, 1954-55; faculty Ohio U., 1955-61; assoc. prof. pathobiology Johns Hopkins Sch. Hygiene and Pub. Health, Balt., 1961-68, prof., 1968-79; assoc. dir. Johns Hopkins Internat. Ctr. for Med. Rsch. and Tng., Calcutta, India, 1964-65; chmn. dept. environ., population and organismic biology U. Colo., Boulder, 1979-82, prof. biology, 1979—, prof. emeritus, 1993—. Rschr. and author publs. on animal social behavior and population dynamics, influences animal social behavior on demographic characteristic mammal populations, primate ecology and behavior, estuarine ecology and environ. quality; mem. primate adv. com. Nat. Acad. Sci.-NRC, 1963-75, com. primate conservation, 1974-75; mem. Gov.'s Sci. Adv. Com. State of Md., 1975-78; mem. com. on rsch. and exploration Nat. Geog. Soc., 1979-2000; mem. adv. bd. Caribbean Primate Rsch. Ctr., 1987-99, Wis. Primate Rsch. Ctr., 1990-98; mem. Integrated Conservation Rsch., 1989-2002; mem. or leader of more than 85 rsch. expdns. on five continents. Editor, author: Primate Social Behavior, 1963, Animal Aggression, 1970, Nonhuman Primates in Biomedical Research, 1975, Ecology and the Quality of Our Environment, 1976, Global Ecology, 1985; Ecology and Behavior of Food-Enhanced Primate Groups, 1988; author: Global Ecology in Human Perspective, 1996. Recipient Fulbright Rsch. award, India, 1959—60, Tchg. Excellence award, U. Colo., 1993. Fellow AAAS, Acad. Zoology, Animal Behavior Soc.; mem. Am. Soc. Zoologists, Ecol. Soc. Am., Am. Soc. Mammalogists, Am. Soc. Primatology (Disting. Primatologist award 1994), Internat. Primatology Soc., Am. Inst. Biol. Scis. Home: 6507 Baseline Rd Boulder CO 80303-3065 Business E-Mail: charles.southwick@colorado.edu.

SOUTHWICK, LESLIE HARBURD, judge, lawyer; b. Edinburg, Tex., Feb. 10, 1950; s. Lloyd M. and Ruth (Tarpley) S.; m. Sharon E. Polasek, Aug. 18, 1973; children: Philip, Catherine. BA cum laude, Rice U., 1972; JD, U. Tex., 1975. Bar: Tex. 1975, Miss. 1977. Law clk. to Hon. John F. Onion Jr. Tex. Ct. Criminal Appeals, Austin, 1975-76; law clk. to Hon. Charles Clark US Ct. Appeals (5th cir.), Jackson, Miss., 1976-77; assoc. Brunini, Grantham, Grower & Hewes, Jackson, 1977-83, ptnr., 1983-89; dep. asst. atty. gen. civil divsn. US Dept. Justice, Washington, 1989—93; judge Miss. Ct. Appeals (Dist. 4), 1995—2006. Adj. prof. Miss. Coll. Sch. Law, Jackson, 1985-89, 98-; mem. Miss. Constn. Study Commn., 1985-86. Author: Presidential Also-Rans and Running Mates, 1984 (ALA Best Reference Book award 1985). Pres. Hinds County Mental Health Assn., Jackson, 1981-82; Miss. campaign mgr. George Bush for Pres., 1980, 88; alternate del. Rep. Nat. Conv., 1984, del., 1988; mem. State Rep. Exec. Com., 1988. Served in USAR, 1992—97 Miss. Army Nat. Guard, 1997—, dep. staff judge advocate US Army, 2004—05, staff judge advocate, 2006. Named Vol. of Yr., Hinds County Mental Health Assn., 1981, 85. Mem. ABA, Miss. Bar Assn. Lodges: Kiwanis. Republican. Roman Catholic. *

SOUTHWICK, PAUL, retired public relations executive; b. West Newton, Mass., Mar. 27, 1920; s. Alfred and Pauline (Winkler) S.; m. Susan Barbara Heider, Feb. 24, 1947; children: Thomas Paul, Peter Alfred, Linda Susan. AB in Econs. cum laude, Harvard Coll., 1943. Coor. AP, Concord, NH, 1947-49; UP UPI, Washington, 1949-57; mem. profl. staff govt. info. subcom. U.S. Ho. Reps., 1957-59; legis. asst., adminstrv. asst. U.S. Senator Long of Hawaii, 1959-62; dep. adminstr. charge accelerated pub. works program Area Redevel. Adminstrn., 1962-63; spl. asst. The White House, 1963-65; spl. asst. for congl. rels. Office of U.S. Sec. Commerce, 1965-67; v.p. Newmyer Assocs., Inc., Washington, 1967-87; ind. cons., 1987-93; ret., 1993. With USNR, 1941-45, PTO. Democrat. Home: 102 Brooksby Village Dr Unit 513 Peabody MA 01960

SOUTHWORTH, ROBERT ALEXANDER, JR., education researcher, educator; b. NYC, Jan. 6, 1959; s. Robert Alexander Southworth, Sr. and Katherine Hobson Southworth; m. Linda Estelle Fischl, Sept. 11, 1994; children: Ekaterina Sophia, Anna Natalya, Robert Alexander III. AB, Dartmouth Coll., 1981; EdM, Tufts U., 1983; EdD, Columbia U. Tchrs. Coll., 1999. Secondary sch. tchg. cert. Mass., 1983, cert. advanced study. Apprentice tchr. Shady Hill Sch., Cambridge, Mass., 1982—83; theater tech dir. Colo. Acad., Denver, 1983—86; asst. dir. Denver Ctr. Performing Arts, 1986—87, Am. Conservatory Theater, San Francisco, 1988—89; asst. rschr. Nat. Ctr. for Restructuring Edn., Schools and Tchg., Teachers Coll., NYC, 1993—96; pres. The SchoolWorks Lab, Inc., NYC, 2002—. Cons. Fenway Mid. Coll. H.S., Boston, 1990—92; adj. prof. Adelphi U. Grad. Sch. Edn., NYC, 1996—99, Bank St. Coll. Edn., NYC, 1998—2002; adj. asst. prof. Teachers Coll. Columbia U., NYC, 1998—2005. Named Bus. Man of Yr., US Congress, 2003. Mem.: Nat. Soc. Study of Edn., Am. Evaluation Assn., Am. Edn. Rsch. Assn., Phi Delta Kappa (v.p. 1997—2000), Kappa Delta Pi. Achievements include research in the positive effect on student scores in Music, ELA and Math due to music; development of a new website to help the public understand school reform; a process to improve teacher learning called Assessment Data Gathering; statewide system of accountability for 84 funded arts partnerships in New York. Home: 340 West 87 St Apt 8A New York NY 10024 Home Phone: 212-580-5209; Office Phone: 212-768-7800. Office Fax: 212-768-8700. Business E-Mail: rasouth@edspeak.org.

SOUTHWORTH, WILLIAM DIXON, retired education educator; b. Union City, Tenn., Dec. 28, 1918; s. Thomas and Gertrude (Dyer) S.; m. Violet Kuehn, July 22, 1944; children: Geoffrey Scott, Linda Jean. PhB, Marquette U., Milw., 1948, MEd, 1950; PhD, NYU, 1961. Tchr., coach La Follette Sch., Milwaukee County, Wis., 1948-51; teaching dist. prin. Grand View Sch., Milwaukee County, 1951-56; supervising dist. prin. Maple Dale Sch., Milwaukee County, 1956-58; bldg. prin. Main St. Sch., Port Washington, NY, 1958-65; asst. supt. for elem. edn. Huntington pub. schs., NY, 1965-67; assoc. prof., acting head dept. adminstrn. and supervision St. John's U., Jamaica, NY, 1967, chmn. dept., 1968-73, prof., 1968-84. Parliamentarian for 35 internat., nat. regional orgns., expert witness, pub. moderator, and workshop leader. Author: Care and Nurture of the Doctoral Candidate, 1968, 74, Q The Story of Captain Quimby Scott, U.S. Navy WWII, 1997, The Art of Successful Meetings, 1997, Murder on the Flagship, 1998, Corpsman!, 1998, Murder Impossible, 2002, The Wonderful World of Words: How to Build and Retain a Superior Vocabulary, 2002, The Sensual Sailor, 2003, Murders in Old Main, 2004; contbr. over 270 articles to ednl. jours., condominium and parliamentary publs. With USN, 1938—44. Lutheran. Home: 411 First Ave N # 811 Saint Petersburg FL 33701 Personal E-mail: vibilfid1@juno.com, williamdrsouthworth@aol.com. *In the conflicting demands of self and society, one must strike a balance by retaining the uniqueness of one's individuality while serving the society that nurtured that uniqueness. It is in the balance thus struck that the complete person evolves self-esteeming, and socially involved.*

SOUTTER, THOMAS DOUGLAS, retired lawyer; b. NYC, Nov. 1, 1934; s. Thomas G. and Hildreth H. (Callanan) S.; m. Virginia Hovenden; children: Alexander D., Christopher A., Hadley H. BA, U. Va., 1955, LL.B., 1962; postgrad., Advanced Mgmt. Program, Harvard U., 1980. Bar: N.Y. 1962, R.I. 1969. Atty. Breed, Abbott & Morgan, NYC, 1962-68; with Textron Inc., Providence, 1968-95, gen. counsel, 1970-95, v.p., 1971-80, sr. v.p., 1980-85, exec. v.p., gen. counsel, 1985-95; cons., 1995-97. Mem. adv. bd. Internat. and Comparative Law Ctr., 1975-95; mem. Assn. Gen. Counsel; bd. dirs. Avco Fin. Svcs., Inc., 1985-95, Paul Revere Corp. 1993-95; trustee New England Legal Found. Nat. chmn. ann. giving campaign U. Va. Law Sch., 1992-94, mem. exec. com. campaign, 1995-2000; former trustee Providence Preservation Soc., Providence Performing Arts Ctr.; mem. U. Va. Arts and Scis. Alumni Coun.; mem. Narragansett coun. Boy Scouts Am. Lt. USNR, 1955-59. Mem. ABA, N.Y. State Bar Assn., R.I. Bar Assn., Internat. Bar Assn. Office: 2 White Birch Ln Barrington RI 02806-4932 E-mail: tdsout@aol.com.

SOUVEROFF, VERNON WILLIAM, JR., corporate financial executive; b. LA, Aug. 12, 1934; s. Vernon William Sr. and Aileen (Young) S.; m. Aileen Patricia Robinson; children: Gail Kathleen, Michael William, Kirk Laron BS in E.E., Stanford U., 1957; postgrad., Ohio State U., 1958-59. With Litton Industries, Beverly Hills, Calif., 1960-75; with ITT Corp., NYC, 1975-87; prin. Bus. Acquisitions and Investments, 1988—; corp. v.p. ITT Corp., NYC, 1983-84, sr. v.p., 1984-87; pres. ITT Gilfillan, 1979-83; group exec. ITT Def. Space Group, 1983-84; CEO ITT Telecom and Electronics N.Am., 1984-86; pres., chief exec. officer ITT Def. Tech. Corp., 1986-87. Mem. U.S. Def. Policy Adv. Com. on Trade, Washington, 1984-88; bd. advisors, investor Venture Resources, Venture Capital, 1988-92; bd. dirs. Elanix, Inc., Formida Holdings Ltd., Australia; chmn. bd. dirs. Formida Software Corp., San Jose, Calif Author books on def. downsizing Served as officer USAF, 1957-60 Recipient Exec. Salute award Los Angeles C. of C., 1981 Mem. IEEE (life), Nat. Contracts Mgmt. Assn., Electronics Industries Assn., Am. Def. Preparedness Assn. (former dir.), Nat. Security Indsl. Assn., Air Force Assn., Navy League, Assn. U.S. Army, Alamo Town Assn. (bd. mem.), S.R. Valley YMCA (chmn.) Presbyterian.

SOVERN, MICHAEL IRA, law educator; b. NYC, Dec. 1, 1931; s. Julius and Lillian (Arnstein) S.; m. Lenore Goodman, Feb. 21, 1952 (div. Apr. 1963); children: Jeffrey Austin, Elizabeth Ann, Douglas Todd; m. Eleanor Leen, Aug. 25, 1963 (div. Feb. 1974); 1 child, Julie Danielle; m. Joan Wit, Mar. 9, 1974 (dec. Sept. 1993); m. Patricia Walsh, Nov. 12, 1995. AB summa cum laude, Columbia U., 1953, LLB (James Ordronaux prize), 1955, LLD (hon.), 1980; PhD (hon.), Tel Aviv U., 1982; LLD (hon.), U. So. Calif., 1989. Bar: N.Y. 1956, U.S. Supreme Ct. 1976. Asst. prof., then assoc. prof. law U. Minn. Law Sch., 1955-58; mem. faculty Columbia Law Sch., 1957—, prof. law, 1960—, Chancellor Kent prof., 1977—, dean Law Sch., 1970-79; chmn. exec. com. faculty Columbia U., 1968-69, provost, exec. v.p., 1979-80, univ. pres., 1980-93, pres. emeritus, 1993. Rsch. dir. Legal Restraints on Racial Discrimination in Employment, Twentieth Century Fund, 1962-66; spl. counsel to gov. N.J., 1974-77; cons. Time Mag., 1965-80; mem. panel of arbitrators N.J. Bd. Mediation, Fed. Mediation and Conciliation Svc.; bd. dirs. Sequa, Asian Cultural Coun., Shubert Orgn., Comcast Corp., Sta. WNET-TV, NAACP Legal Def. Fund, 1976-97, Freedom Forum Newseum; chmn. N.Y.C. Charter Revision Commn., 1982-83; co-chmn. 2d Cir. Commn. on Reduction of Burdens and Costs in Civil Litigation, 1977-80; chmn. Commn. on Integrity in Govt., 1986; pres. Italian Acad. Advanced Studies in Am., 1991-93, Shubert Found., 1996—; chmn. Japan Soc., 1993-2004, hon. chmn., 2004—; chmn. Am. Acad. Rome, 1993-2005, chmn. emeritus, 2005—; chmn. Sotheby's, 2000—; chmn. nat. adv. coun. Freedom Forum Media Studies Ctr., 1993-2001. Author: Legal Restraints on Racial Discrimination in Employment, 1966, Law and Poverty, 1969, Of Boundless Domains, 1994; host Sta. WNET-TV series Leading Questions. Mem. Pulitzer Prize Bd., 1980-93, chmn. pro tem, 1986-87; trustee Kaiser Family Found., 1994-2002, Presdl. Legal Expense Trust, 1994-98; chmn. Sotheby's, 2000. Decorated commendatore Order of Merit (Italy), Order of the Rising Sun, Gold and Silver Star (Japan); recipient Alexander Hamilton medal Columbia Coll., 1993, Citizens Union Civic Leadership award, 1993, Town Hall Friend of the Arts award, 2001, Centennial medal Am. Acad. Rome, 2006. Fellow Am. Acad. Arts and Scis.; mem. ABA, Coun. Fgn. Rels., Assn. Bar City N.Y., Am. Philos. Soc., Am. Arbitration Assn. (panel arbitrators), Am. Law Inst., Econ. Club, Nat. Acad. Arbitrators. Office: Columbia U Sch Law 435 W 116th St New York NY 10027-7297 Office Phone: 212-854-7848. Business E-Mail: mem11@columbia.edu. E-mail: msovern@law.columbia.edu.

SOVIK, EDWARD ANDERS, architect, consultant; b. Honan, China, June 9, 1918; s. Edward Anderson and Anna (Tenwick) S.; m. Genevieve Elaine Hendrickson, June 29, 1946 (dec.); m. Anne Running, Mar. 25, 2001; children: Rolf, Martin, Peter. BA, St. Olaf Coll., Northfield, Minn., 1939; student, Art Students League N.Y., 1939-40, Luther Theol. Sem., 1940—41; MArch, Yale U., New Haven, Conn., 1949; DFA (hon.), Concordia Coll., 1981. Ret. chmn. SMSQ, Architects and predecessors, Northfield, Minn.; prof. art emeritus St. Olaf Coll., Northfield. Lectr. on ch. design at various confs., schs., univs.; participant, planner, del. numerous domestic and fgn. confs. on religion and architecture; mem., officer various profl., religious and pub. bds. and commns. Author: Architecture for Worship; Contbr. numerous articles to mags., anthologies.; works include chs., coll. and univ. bldgs., instns. With USMC, 1942-45; maj. Res. Decorated D.F.C., Purple Heart, Air medals; recipient Diekmann award, N.Am. Acad. Liturgy, 2003. Fellow AIA; mem. AIA Minn. (pres. 1977, Gold medal 1981), Phi Beta Kappa. Democrat. Lutheran. Home: 711 Summit Ave Northfield MN 55057-1568 Personal E-mail: sovik@charter.net.

SOW, DABY, computer scientist, researcher; Mem. rsch. staff IBM, Hawthorne, NY, 2000—. Home Phone: 914-428-3221.

SOWA, ARTUR, mathematician, researcher; b. Poland, Oct. 27, 1965; came to US, 1992; s. Witold and Lucyna Sowa; m. Jolanta Sowa, Aug. 15, 1987; children: Izaak, Oliver. MS in Math., Warsaw U., 1990; PhD in Math., CUNY, 1995. Postdoctoral asst. CUNY, NYC, 1995—97; postdoctoral rsch. assoc. Yale U., New Haven, 1997—2000, lectr., 2000; scientist Pegasus Imaging Corp., Tampa, Fla., 2000—02; online instr. U. Phoenix, 2003—, math. area co-chair, 2006; asst. prof. dept. math. and stats. U. Sask., Saskatoon, Canada, 2007—. Collaborator, nano tech. program Utopia Compression Corp., LA, 2005; CEO, chief scientist Mesoscopia, Inc., 2007—. Contbr. articles to profl. jours. Recipient 1st prize, The Marcinkiewicz Competition, Poland, 1990, Rsch. Associateship award, NRC, 2001. Mem.: IEEE. Achievements include research in mesoscopic description of correlated systems of electrons and the mesoscopic mechanics. Home: 502 8th St E Saskatoon SK Canada S7M 0P8 Personal E-mail: a.sowa@mesoscopia.com.

SOWALD, HEATHER GAY, lawyer; b. Columbus, Ohio, Dec. 26, 1954; d. Martin M. and Beatrice (Kronick) S.; m. Robert Marc Kaplan, June 12, 1977; children: Andrew Scott, Alexis Beth. BA, Case Western Res. U., 1976; JD, Capital U., 1979. Bar: Ohio 1979, U.S. Dist. Ct. (so. dist.) Ohio 1980, U.S. Ct. Appeals (6th cir.) 1981, U.S. Supreme Ct., 1987. Ptnr. Sowald & Sowald, Columbus, 1979-85, Sowald & Daneman, Columbus, 1985-1987, Sowald, Sowald & Mas, Columbus, 1988, Sowald, Sowald & Clouse, Columbus. Hearing officer Cert. Need Rev. Bd. State of Ohio, 1982—, Dept. Adminstrv. Services, 1982—, Dept. Mental Health, 1986—, Dept. Mental Retardation, 1986-88, Dept. Health, 1986-89, Ohio Dept. Liquor Control, 1989—. Bd. dirs. Wilderness Bond, Inc., Franklin County, Ohio, 1982-86, Youth Svcs. Adv. Bd., Franklin County, 1984—, chmn. 1987—, Ohio Bd. of Nursing, 1988—; legal advisor United Way League Against Child Abuse, Franklin County, 1986-87. Mem. Ohio State Bar Assn. (council of dels. 1986, pres. 2004, mem. family law com.), Columbus Bar Assn. (chmn. juvenile law com. 1982-84, chmn. admissions to bar 1984-86, 2005-07, chmn. publications com., 1987-88, chmn. family law com. 1988—, ethics com. 1988—, pres. 1998-99), Franklin County Trial Lawyers Assn. (trustee 1985-88, treas. 1988-89, pres.-elect 1989—, pres. 1989-90), Women Lawyers of Franklin County (pres. 1984-85), Capital U. Law Sch. Alumni Assn. (pres. 1984-86), Ohio Bar Found. (head trustee 2003—), Columbus Bar Found. (head trustee 1999—, mem. grants com. 2007—), Legal Aid Soc. Ctrl. Ohio (head trustee 2006—). Democrat. Jewish. Office: Sowald Sowald & Clouse One Americana 400 S 5th St Ste 101 Columbus OH 43215

SOWANDE, BEVERLY FOLASADE, lawyer, educator; d. Olufela Charles and Mildred Bernice (Marshall) Sowande. BA, CUNY, 1963, MS, 1966; PhD, NYU, 1974; JD, Yeshiva U., 1980. Bar: N.Y., U.S. Dist. Ct. (so. dist., ea. dist.), U.S. Ct. Appeals (2d cir.), U.S. Supreme Ct. Pvt. practice, NYC, 1986—88, 1992—; assoc. counsel Office Gen. Counsel CUNY, 1988—90; 1st dep. gen. counsel Human Resources Adminstrn., NYC, 1990—92. From. lectr. to assoc. prof., dept. academic skills Hunter Coll. CUNY, 1970—92, adj. assoc. prof., women's studies program and dept. polit. sci., 1982—86, NYC, 1995—96, adj. assoc. prof., dept. comm., 1995—96; adj. assoc. prof., consortium for worker edn. City Coll. CUNY, 1987—88; panel mem. departmental disciplinary com. 1st Jud. Dept., 1993—98; presenter in field. Pro bono atty. for indigent and abused women and men Coun. N.Y. Law Assocs. and NYU Law Project for Battered Women, 1986—88; adv. bd. Sanctuary Families Legal Advocacy Ctr., NYC, 1988—90; coord. pro bono domestic violence panel Family Ct. Project, with Victim Svcs. Agy., 1989—93; mem. N.Y.C. Conditional Release Commn., 1989—96; bd. dirs. Lenox Hill Neighborhood Assn., Inc., NYC, 1993—96; trustee Urban Resource Inst., Bklyn., 1994—97, sec. bd. trustees, 1997—98; adv. bd. Rosen Scholars Program, NYC, 1996—97; cert. rape crisis counselor, sexual assault and violence intervention program Mt. Sinai Med. Ctr., NYC, 2004—. Named to Hunter Coll. Hall of Fame, CUNY, 1987; recipient Cert. Appreciation, Urban Women's Retreat, 1991; Univ. Founder's scholar, NYU, 1974, Danforth Found. fellow, 1974. Mem.: N.Y. State Bar Assn. (Pres.'s Pro Bono Svc. award 1989, Merit award 1990), Assn. Bar City of N.Y. (crime victims com. 1992, matrimonial law com. 1992—93, dir. lawyer's com. violence 1994—96, com. profl. responsibility 1997—98), N.Y. Women's Bar Assn. (chair com. battered women 1987—91, coord. pro bono domestic violence project 1987—93, bd. dirs. 1988—92, chair continuing legal edn. com. 1991—94, corr. sec. 1992—93, rec. sec. 1993—94), N.Y. County Lawyers Assn. (com. minorities 1992), Coun. N.Y. Law Assocs. (bd. dirs. 1986—92, chair bd. com. not-for-profit law project 1988—92, Cert. of Appreciation for Pro Bono Activities 1988), Wistarians Alumni Hunter Coll. CUNY (v.p. 1986—88, pres. 1988—90), Alumni Assn. Hunter Coll. CUNY (bd. dirs. 1977—78, sec. 1978—81, 2d v.p. 1981—84, 4th v.p. 1984—87, 2d v.p. 1987—90, chair bylaws revision com. 1987—93, 1st v.p. 1990—93, pres. 1993—96). Personal E-mail: bsowande@aol.com.

SOWDER, FRED ALLEN, foundation administrator, alphabet specialist; b. Cin., July 17, 1940; s. William Franklin and Lucille (Estes) Sowder; m. Sandra Ann Siegman, July 15, 1961 (div. Sept. 1963); 1 child, William. Student, Cin. Sch. Ct. Reporting, 1975; diploma Self-Health Insts., Sch. of Med. Masso-Therapy, 1985; diploma, Cin. Sch. Hypnosis, 1989. Founder World Union Universal Alphabet, Cin., 1981—, Internat. Assn. Sch. Massage, Cin., 1988—. Inventor of hundreds of published and unpublished alphabets and writing systems, including light wave, color and musical tone systems and tactile systems for the blind; author: Sowder Shorthand, 1980, Universal Alphabet: What and Why, 1981, Your Intimacy Quotient: The Symptoms, Causes & Consequences of Intimacy Deprivation, 1996; contbr. numerous articles to mags. State dir. Soc. Separationists, Cin., 1967-70; bd. dirs. ACLU of Ohio, ACLU Found., 1984-89, sec., Cin. chpt., 1984-89. Mem. AAAS, Amnesty Internat., Ohio Com. to Abolish Capital Punishment, No. Ky. Right to Life, Urban Appalachian Coun. Home: PO Box 252 Cincinnati OH 45201-0252 Office: World Union Universal Alphabet PO Box 252 Cincinnati OH 45201-0252

SOWDER, ROBERT ROBERTSON, architect; b. Kansas City, Kans., Dec. 29, 1928; s. James Robert and Agnes (Robertson) S.; m. Joan Goddard, July 26, 1954; 1 dau., Lisa Robertson Lee. BA, U. Wash., 1953; B.Arch., U. Va., 1958; grad. diploma in Architecture, Ecole Des Beaux Arts, Fontainebleau, France, 1952. Designer Architects Collaborative, Boston, 1958-59, Peirce & Pierce (architects), Boston, 1959-63; asso. Fred.

Bassetti & Co. (architects), Seattle, 1963-67; partner Naramore, Bain, Brady & Johanson (architects), Seattle, 1967-81; pres. NBBJ Internat., 1976-81; architect TRA, Seattle, 1981-83; v.p. Daniel, Mann, Johnson & Mendenhall, San Francisco, 1983-93; prin. RRS Consulting, 1993—. Archtl. design critic Boston Archtl. Ctr., 1961-62. Important works include Ridgeway III Dormitories, Bellingham, Wash. (Dept. Housing and Urban Devel. Honor award), Seattle Rapid Transit (HUD Excellence award), Safeco Ins. Co. Home Office Complex, Seattle, King County Stadium, Balt. Conv. Ctr., Oreg. Conv. Ctr., San Francisco (Moscone) Conv. Ctr. Expansion, Honolulu Conv. Ctr., Wilmington (Del.) Conv. Ctr. Mem. Redmond (Wash.) Design Rev. Bd., 1996-2000. Served with CIC U.S. Army, 1954-56. Recipient Premier Prix D'Architecture Ecole Des Beaux Arts, Fontainebleau, 1951, 52, Prix D'Remondet Fontainebleau, 1952 Mem. AIA (emeritus), Internat. Assn. Assembly Mgrs., Seattle Tennis Club, Seattle Rainier Club, Scarab, Sigma Chi. Episcopalian. Home and Office: 17032 NE 135th Ct Redmond WA 98052-1715

SOWELL, LAVEN, retired music educator; b. Wewoka, Okla., Jan. 9, 1933; s. Vestal Laven and Viola Jane Sowell. MusB, U. Okla., 1955; MA, Columbia U., 1964; postgrad., Manhattan Sch. Music, 1956—57, Conservatoire de Musique de Fontainebleu, France, 1966; studied with Clark Snell, Martial Singher, Joseph Benton, John Brownlee, Samuel Margolis, Nadia Boulanger, studied choral conducting with Harry Robert Wilson. Choral condr. Edison H.S., Tulsa, 1961—70; chorus master Tulsa Opera, 1962—94, chorus master emeritus, 1994—; dir. music 1st Presbyn. Ch., Tulsa, 1969—85; prof. music U. Tulsa, 1970—91. Vocal adjudicator various mus. orgns.; tchr. pvt. voice lessons. Co-author: Tulsa Opera Chronicles, 1992; author: My Music Notebook, 2000, With Affection, 2006. Bd. dirs. Tulsa Opera. Recipient Gov.'s Arts award, State of Okla., 1991. Mem.: Tulsa Accredited Music Teacher's Assn., Okla. Music Teacher's Assn. Democrat. Presbyterian. Avocations: travel, reading, opera. Home: 3800 W 71st Apt 2312 Tulsa OK 74132-2153 Office Phone: 918-388-4461.

SOWELL, THOMAS, economist, syndicated columnist; b. Gastonia, NC, June 30, 1930; AB, Harvard U., 1958; A.M., Columbia U., 1959; PhD, U. Chgo., 1968. Economist Dept. Labor, 1961-62; instr. econs. Douglass Coll., Rutgers U., 1962-63; lectr. econs. Howard U., 1963-64; econ. analyst AT&T, 1964-65; asst. prof. Cornell U., 1965-69; assoc. prof. Brandeis U., 1969-70; assoc. prof. econs. UCLA, 1970-74, prof., 1974-80; project dir. Urban Inst., Washington, 1972-74; fellow Center Advanced Study Behavioral Scis., Stanford, Calif., 1976-77; sr. fellow Hoover Instn., 1977, 80—, 1980—. Vis. prof. Amherst Coll., 1977 Author: Ethnic America, 1981, A Conflict of Visions, 1987, Inside American Education, 1993, Race and Culture, 1994, The Vision of the Anointed, 1995, Basic Economics, 2000, Black Rednecks and White Liberals, 2005, On Classical Economics, 2006; contbr. articles to profl. publs, syndicated columnist. Served with USMC, 1951-53. Fellow, Hoover Instn., 1977; sr. fellow, 1980—. Mem. Am. Econ. Assn., Nat. Acad. Edn. Office: Stanford Univ Hoover Instn Stanford CA 94305 also: Creators Syndicate 5777 W Century Blvd Los Angeles CA 90045 Business E-Mail: sowell@stanford.edu.

SOWELL, THORNWELL F. (BIFF), lawyer; b. Wadesboro, NC, Nov. 7, 1950; BA, Clemson Univ., 1973; JD, Univ. SC, 1976. Bar: SC 1976, US Dist. Ct. (SC) 1977, US Ct. Appeals (4th cir. 1977, Fed. cir. 1999), US Ct. Fed. Claims 1992, US Supreme Ct. 1980. Mem., comml. litigation Sowell Gray Stepp & Lafitte LLC, Columbia, SC. Fellow: SC Bar Found.; mem.: ABA, Am. Bd. Trial Advocates, Fedn. Def. & Corp. Counsel, SC Bar (mem. Ho. Del.), Richland County Bar Assn. Office: Sowell Gray Stepp & Lafitte LLC PO Box 11449 1310 Gadsden St Columbia SC 29211 Office Phone: 803-231-7835. Office Fax: 803-231-7885. Business E-Mail: bsowell@sowell.com.

SOWER, VICTOR EDMUND, management educator; b. Roanoke, Va., Sept. 3, 1946; s. Hammond Edmundson and Daphne Muriel (Dymond) S.; m. Judith Lynn Carroll, June 17, 1967; children: Diane C. Sower Fuller, Christopher Hammond. BS in Chemistry, Va. Poly. Inst. and State U., 1968; MBA, Auburn U., Ala., 1980; PhD in Operations Mgmt., U. North Tex., Denton, 1990. Cert. quality engr., Am. Soc. Quality. Process engr. Radford Army Ammunition Plant, Va., 1968—69; mgr. process devel. engring. Ampex Corp., Opelika, Ala., 1971—80; gen. mgr. Tandy Magnetics, Ft. Worth, 1980—87; mfg. cons. Tandy Corp., Ft. Worth, 1987—90; prof. dept. mgmt. and mktg. Sam Houston State U., Huntsville, Tex., 1990—, Piper prof., 2005—. Mem. steering com. Ctr. Bus. and Econ. Rsch., Huntsville, 1990—; cons. various mfg. and svc. orgns. Author: Time Study for the Small Business, 1979, Classic Readings in Operations Management, 1995, An Introduction to Quality Management and Engineering, 1999; mem. editl. rev. bd. Jour. Bus. Strategies, 1990—, Jour. Ops. Mgmt., 1995—; contbr. articles to profl. jours. Mem. dist. com. Bedford area Boy Scouts Am., Tex., 1987-90, dist. advancement chmn., 1988-89. Lt. chem. corps US Army, 1969—71. Decorated Commendation medal US Army; named Piper Prof., Minnie Stevens Piper Found. Tex., 2005; recipient Excellence in Tchg. award, Sam Houston State U., 1996, Excellence in Rsch. award, 2001. Mem. AIChE (sr.), Inst. Supply Mgmt., Am. Chem. Soc., Am. Soc. Quality Control (sr. cert.), Am. Prodn. and Inventory Control Soc., Decision Scis. Inst., Acad. Mgmt Roman Catholic. Office: Sam Houston State U Dept Mgmt and Mktg Huntsville TX 77341-2056 Business E-Mail: sowerv@shsu.edu.

SOWERS, MARILYN RAE, librarian; b. Gary, Ind., Jan. 5, 1943; d. Terzo Paul and Mary Saveria (DeNicola) Amidei; m. George Maxton Sowers, Aug. 27, 1966; children: George, Joseph, John, Michael. AB in History, Ind. U., 1964, MAT in Social Studies, 1966, MLS, 1970. Tchr. Gary Pub. Schs., 1966, libr., 1969-70, MicIntire Pub. Libr., Charlottesville, Va., 1966-69; reference libr. Indpls. Pub. Libr., 1970; asst. libr. Centerville (Ind.) Pub. Libr., 1976-79; interim libr. Ind. U. East, Richmond, Ind., 1978-79; substitute tchr. Richmond (Ind.) Community Schs., 1984-87; media supervisor Union County Sch. Corp., Liberty, Ind., 1987—. Bd. dirs. Ind. Cooperative Libr. Svcs. Authority. Bd. dirs., sec. Wayne Twp. Bd., Richmond, 1985—; mem. Gov.'s Select Commn. for Primary and Secondary Edn., Ind., 1982-84; mem. State Student's Assistance Commn. of Ind., 1988-90. Mem. ALA, NEA, ASCD, Am. Assn. Sch. Librs., Assn. Ind. Media Educators, Ind. State Tchrs. Assn., Assn. Ednl. Comm. and Tech. Avocations: ballroom dancing, camping, running. Office: Union County High Sch 410 Patriot Blvd Liberty IN 47353-1213 Office Phone: 765-458-5136. E-mail: msowers@uc.k12.in.us.

SOWERS, WESLEY HOYT, lawyer, management consultant; b. Whiting, Ind., Aug. 26, 1905; s. Samuel Walter and Bertha E. (Spurrier) S.; m. Gladys Krueger, Jan. 21, 1929; children: Penny (Mrs. David Buxton), Wesley Hoyt Jr. BS, Purdue U., 1926, MS, 1927; JD, DePaul U., 1941; grad., Advanced Mgmt. Program, Harvard, 1960. Bar: Ill. 1940; registered patent atty. and practitioner ICC. Chemist Shell Oil Co., East Chicago, Ind., 1927-29; sales engr. Nat. Lead Co., St. Louis, 1929-31; lab. supr. patent atty. Pure Oil Co., Chgo., 1932-42; v.p. Bay Chem. Co., New Orleans, 1942-50, Frontier Chem. Co., Wichita, Kans., 1950-57; pres. Frontier Chem. div. Vulcan Materials Co., 1957-65; exec. v.p., dir. Vulcan Materials Co., Birmingham, 1958-65; mgmt. counsel, 1965—. Mem. health professions vis. com. Wichita State U. Patentee in field. Past chmn. Met. Planning Commn., Wichita and Sedgwick County, 1958; commr. Kans. Econ. Devel. Bd.; chmn. Kansas Com. for Constitutional Revision, Sedgwick County U.S. Savs. Bonds Sales; past chmn. Kans. Radio Free Europe; past mem. adv. com. Kans. Geol. Survey; mem. Kans. Senate, 1970-81; former mem. engring. adv. council Sch. Engring. and Architecture, Kans. State U.; regent, trustee Wichita State U., HCA/Wesley Med. Ctr., Wichita; bd. dirs. Health Systems Agy. of Southeast Kans., Bd. of Health Sedgwick County, Inst. Logopedics, Quivira council Boy Scouts Am., YMCA, Health Systems Agy. S.E. Kans.; past trustee Midwest Research Inst.; mem. adv. bd. Kans. U. Bus. Sch.; vis. com. Coll. Health Profession, Wichita State U.; chmn. Kans. Health Care Providers Malpractice Commn.; mem. Kans. Health Care Costs Commn., Kans. Health Coordinating Council, Wichita/Sedgwick County Bd. Health; mem. gov.'s adv. commn. Kans. Dept. Health and Environment Mem. AAAS, Kans. C. of C. (past pres., past dir.), Wichita C. of C. (past pres. 1959, past dir., Uncommon Citizen award 1988), Kans. Assn. Commerce and Industry (past pres., dir.), Am. Chem. Soc., AAAS, Smithsonian Assocs., Soc. Chem. Industry, Ill. Bar Assn., Wichita Bar Assn., Phi Delta Theta. Lodges: Rotary. Home and Office: 600 W Arapaho Rd Apt 1034 Richardson TX 75080 Office Phone: 972-907-8857.

SOWMAN, HAROLD GENE, ceramics engineer, researcher; b. Murphysboro, Ill., July 21, 1923; s. Harold Thomas and Thelma (Crombar) S.; m. Gladys May Wright, Dec. 8, 1945; children: Letitia Ann, Daniel Patrick BS in Ceramic Engring., U. Ill., 1948, MS in Ceramic Engring., 1949, PhD in Ceramic Engring., 1951. Assoc. ceramist Titanium Alloy, Niagara Falls, NY, 1951-52; research assoc. Knolls Atomic Power Lab., Gen. Electric Co., Schenectady, 1952-57; various supervisory and mgmt. positions in nuclear materials research and devel. 3M Co., St. Paul, 1957-65, research specialist, 1965-67, sr. research specialist, 1967-70, corp. scientist, 1970-87. Friedberg Meml. lectr. Nat. Inst. Ceramic Engrs., 1988. Contbr. articles to profl. jours. Served to 2d lt. AUS, 1943-46 Recipient Hon. Alumni award for disting. service in engring. U. Ill. Coll. Engring., 1983 Fellow Am. Ceramic Soc. (John Jeppson medal 1985, Samuel Geijsbeek award 1989); mem. Nat. Acad. Engring., Acad. of Ceramics, 3M Carlton Soc., Tau Beta Pi (chpt. Eminent Engr. award 1983). Achievements include patents in field; development of ceramic and nuclear materials. Home: 2275 Harmony Ln #102 Naples FL 34109

SOX, HAROLD CARLETON, JR., physician, educator, editor; b. Palo Alto, Calif., Aug. 18, 1939; s. Harold Carleton and Mary (Griffiths) Sox; m. Carol Helen Hill, Aug. 26, 1962; children: Colin Montgomery, Lara Katherine. BS, Stanford U., 1961; MD cum laude, Harvard U., 1966. Diplomate Am. Bd. Internal Medicine. Intern and resident Mass. Gen. Hosp., Boston, 1966—68; clin. assoc. Nat. Cancer Inst., Bethesda, Md., 1968—70; instr. Dartmouth Med. Sch., Hanover, NH, 1970—73; asst. prof. medicine to prof. clin. medicine Stanford U. Sch. Medicine, Calif., 1973—88; Joseph Huber prof., chmn. dept. medicine Dartmouth Med. Sch., 1988—2001; editor Annals of Internal Medicine ACP, Phila., 2001—. Pretest writing com. Am. Bd. Internal Medicine, 1992—94; panel mem. Nat. Bd. Med. Examiners, Physician Assts. Nat. Certifying Exam., 1973—76; chair com. on priority-setting for health tech. assessment Inst. Medicine, 1990—91, U.S. preventive svcs. task force chair, 1990—95, mem., 1998—2001; chair com. on HIV and U.S. blood supply, 1994—95, vice chmn. com. high value health svcs., 2006—07, mem. complementary and alternative medicine com., 2006—07; chair task force to revise internal medicine residency curriculum Federated Coun. Internal Medicine, 1993—97; chair Inst. Medicine Com. Health Effects Persian Gulf War Svc., 1998—2000, vice-chair First Medicine Com. to Review Evidence to Identify High Value Health Svcs., 2006—; nat. adv. com. generalist physician Scholars Program Robert Wood Johnson Found., 1992—, chmn., nat. adv. com. physician Faculty Scholar Program, 2005—; physician Leaders Nat. Drug Policy, 1997—; founding chair exec. com. Medicare Coverage Adv. Com., 1999—2003; report rev. com. NRC, 2000—05. Author: Medical Decision Making, 1988; editor: Common Diagnostic Tests, 1987, Common Diagnostic Tests, 2d edit., 1990; mem. editl. bd.: Med. Decision Making, 1980—87, Jour. Gen. Internal Medicine, 1985—87, New Eng. Jour. Medicine, 1990—97, cons. assoc. editor: Am. Jour. Medicine, 1988—95, assoc. editor: Sci. Am. Medicine, 1995—2001; contbr. chapters to books, articles to profl. jours. Bd. dirs. Found. Informed Med. Decision Making, 2002—; internat. adv. bd. Clin. Trial Registration Platform program WHO, 2005—. Master: ACP (clin. efficacy assessment subcom. 1985—92, bd. regents 1991—2000, chmn. ednl. policy com. 1994—97, pres. 1998—99); fellow: AAAS, Coll. Physicians Phila. (bd. trustees 2006—), Royal Australasian Coll. Physicians (hon.); mem.: Internat. Com. Med. Jour. Editors, Inst. Medicine Nat. Acads., Assn. Am. Physicians, Soc. Med. Decision Making (trustee 1980—83, pres. 1983—84, 4th Career Achievement award 1998, John Eisenberg award 2007), Soc. Gen. Internal Medicine (coun. 1980—83, Robert J. Glaser Career Achievement award 2000), Alpha Omega Alpha. Home: 232 Philip Pl Philadelphia PA 19106 Office: Am Coll Physicians 190 N Independence Mall W Philadelphia PA 19106-1572 Home Phone: 215-413-3932; Office Phone: 215-351-2620. Personal E-mail: hsox@mail.acponline.org.

SOYER, DAVID, cellist, music educator; b. Phila., Feb. 24, 1923; s. Samson and Esther (Faggin) Soyer; m. Janet Putnam, June 23, 1957; children: Daniel, Jeffrey. Student pub. schs., NYC; DFA (hon.), U. South Fla., 1976, SUNY, 1983. Prof. cello Curtis Inst. Music, 1967; prof. music U. Md.; prof. Manhattan Sch. Music Boston U.; prof. Juilliard Sch. Music, NYC. Musician (cellist): Bach Aria Group, 1948—49, Guilet Quartet, 1949—51, New Music Quartet, 1954—55, Guarneri String Quartet, 1964— (5 Grammy awards for Guarneri Quartet recs.). With USNR, 1942—46. Mem.: Century Assn. Jewish. Home: 6 W 77th St New York NY 10024-5125 Office: Herbert Barrett Mgmt 266 W 37th St Fl 20 New York NY 10018-6648

SOYSTER, MARGARET BLAIR, lawyer; b. Washington, Aug. 5, 1951; d. Peter and Eliza (Shumaker) S. AB magna cum laude, Smith Coll., 1973; JD, U. Va., 1976. Bar: N.Y. 1977, U.S. Dist. Ct. (so. and ea. dists.) N.Y. 1977, U.S. Ct. Appeals (2nd cir.) 1979, U.S. Supreme Ct. 1981, U.S. Ct. Appeals (4th cir.) 1982, U.S. ct. Appeals (11th cir.) 1987, U.S. Ct. Appeals (7th cir.) 1991, U.S. Ct. Appeals (3d cir.) 1992. Assoc. Rogers & Wells, NYC, 1976-84, ptnr., 1984-99, Clifford Chance U.S. LLP, NYC, 2000—. Mem. ABA, Assn. of Bar of City of N.Y., Nat. Assn. Coll. and Univ. Attys., Phi Beta Kappa. Office: Clifford Chance US LLP 31 W 52nd St New York NY 10019 Home Phone: 212-831-9338; Office Phone: 212-878-8479. Business E-Mail: blair.soyster@cliffordchance.com.

SPACE, THEODORE MAXWELL, lawyer; b. Binghamton, NY, Apr. 3, 1938; s. Maxwell Evans and Dorothy Marie (Boone) Space; m. Susan Shultz, Aug. 18, 1962 (div. Apr. 1979); children: William Schuyler, Susanna; m. Martha Collins, Apr. 6, 1991. AB, Harvard U., 1960; LLB, Yale U., 1966. Bar: Conn., 1966, U.S. Dist. Ct. Conn. 1966, U.S. Supreme Ct. 1970, U.S. Tax Ct. 1989, U.S. Ct. Appeals (2nd cir.) 1967, U.S. Ct. Appeals (6th cir.) 1992, U.S. Ct. Appeals (11th cir.) 1994, U.S. Dist. Ct. (ea. dist.) Mich. 1997. Assoc. Shipman & Goodwin LLP, Hartford, Conn., 1966—71, ptnr., 1971—2005, mng. ptnr., 1984—87, adminstv. ptnr., 1988—91, of counsel, 2006—. Mem. Bloomfield (Conn.) Bd. Edn., 1973-85, chmn., 1975-85; treas. Citizens Scholarship Found., Bloomfield, 1971-73, bd. dirs., 1973-91; mem. Bloomfield Human Rels. Commn., 1973-75; mem. Bloomfield Town Dem. Com., 1976-83; corporator Hartford Pub. Libr., 1976—; trustee Conn. Hist. Soc., 1997-2003, mem. libr. com., 1990—, chair, 1993-2000, 06—; chmn. fin. com., coun. mem. Unitarian Soc. Hartford, 1988-91; dir. Old State House Assn., 2003. Lt. (j.g.) USN, 1960-63. Mem. ABA, Conn. Bar Assn. (mem. exec. com. adminstrv. law sect. 1980—), Hartford County Bar Assn., Am. Law Inst., Am. Health Lawyers Assn., Conn. Health Lawyers Assn., Swift's Inn, Hartford Club, 1892 Club. Democrat. Unitarian Universalist. Avocations: reading, classical music. Home: 59 Prospect St Bloomfield CT 06002-3038 Office: Shipman & Goodwin LLP One Constitution Plz Hartford CT 06103-1919

SPACE, ZACK (ZACHARY T. SPACE), congressman; b. Dover, Ohio, Jan. 27, 1961; s. Socrates and Sandra (Gallion) Space; m. Mary Wade, 1988; children: Gina, Nicholas. BA in Polit. Sci., Kenyon Coll., Gambier, Ohio, 1983; JD, Ohio State U., Columbus, 1986. Atty. Space & Space Co., LPA, 1986—, Pub. Defender's Office; spl. counsel to Ohio Attys. Gen. Anthony Celebrezze and Lee Fisher State of Ohio; law dir. City of Dover, Ohio, 2000—06, city atty. Ohio, 2000—06; mem. US Congress from 18th Ohio dist., 2007—, mem. agr. com., transp. & infrastructure com., vets.' affairs com. Mem. St. George Greek Orthodox Ch., Massillon, Ohio. Democrat. Greek Orthodox. Office: 315 Cannon Ho Office Bldg Washington DC 20515 also: 137 E Iron Ave Dover OH 44622 Office Phone: 330-343-2430, 202-225-6265, 330-364-4300. Office Fax: 330-364-2599, 330-364-4330. *

SPACEK, SISSY (MARY ELIZABETH SPACEK), actress; b. Quitman, Tex., Dec. 25, 1949; d. Edwin S. and Virginia S.; m. Jack Fisk, 1974; children: Schuyler Elizabeth, Virginia Madison. Attended, Lee Strasberg Theatrical Inst. Motion picture appearances include Prime Cut, 1972, Badlands, 1974, Carrie, 1976 (Acad. award nomination for best actress 1976), Three Women, 1977 (Best Supporting Actress 1977), Welcome to L.A., 1977, Heartbeat, 1980, Coal Miner's Daughter, 1980 (Acad. award best actress 1980, Golden Globe best actress 1980, Brit. Acad. award nomination best actress 1980, L.A. Film Critics for best actress 1980, Nat. Soc. Film Critics best actress 1980), Raggedy Man (Golden Globe nomination best actress 1981), 1981, Missing, 1982 (Acad. award nomination best actress, Golden Globe nomination best actress 1982, Brit. Acad. award nomination best actress 1982), The River, 1984 (Acad. award nomination best actress), Marie, 1985, Night Mother, 1986, Crimes of the Heart, 1986 (Acad. award nomination best actress, Golden Globe best actress 1986), Violets Are Blue, 1986, JFK, 1991, The Long Walk Home, 1990, Hard Promises, 1992, Trading Mom, 1994, The Grass Harp, 1995, Affliction, 1997, Blast From the Past, 1998, Songs in Ordinary Time, 2000, In the Bedroom, 2001 (Best Actress in Drama Golden Globe 2001, Am. Film Inst. award, Ind. Spirit award, Broadcast Critics award, Chgo. Film Critics award, Fla. Film Critics award, Golden Satellite award, Sundance Film Festival award, Southeastern Film award, N.Y. Film Critics award, L.A. Film Critics award 2001), Last Call, 2002 (nominee Outstanding Supporting Actress in Miniseries or Movie Emmy award) Tuck Everlasting, 2002, A Home at the End of the World, 2004, Nine Lives, 2005, The Ring Two, 2005, Summer Racing: The Race to Cure Breast Cancer, 2005, North Country, 2005, An American Hauntig, 2006; TV movie appearances include Straight Story, 1999, In the Bedroom, 2001 (Acad. award nomination best actress 2001, Brit. Acad. award nomination best actress 2001, Brit. Film Critics Choice award best actress 2001, Sundance Film Festival Spl. prize 2001, Golden Globe best actress 2001, Ind. Spirit award best felmale lead 2001, AFI, Actress of Yr. 2001, L.A. Film Critics best actress 2001, N.Y. Film Critics best actress 2001, SAG nomination best actress 2001, nominee Best Actress Acad. award 2001), The Migrants, 1973, Katherine, 1975, Verna: USO Girl, 1978, A Private Matter, 1992, A Place for Annie, 1994, The Good Old Boys, 1995, Streets of Laredo, 1995, If These Walls Could Talk, 1996, Beyond the Call, 1996, Songs in Ordinary Time, 2000, Midwives (SAG nomination best actress 2001), 2001; guest host TV show Saturday Night Live, 1977; appeared in episode TV show The Waltons. Office: care Creative Artists Agy LLC c/o Steve Tellez 9830 Wilshire Blvd Beverly Hills CA 90212-1804

SPACEY, KEVIN, actor; b. South Orange, NJ, July 26, 1959; s. Thomas and Kathleen Fowler. Student, Juilliard Sch., 1979-81. Actor Old Vic Theatre, England, 2003—, artistic dir., 2004—. Artistic dir. Old Vic Theatre, London, 2003—. Stage appearances include Henry IV, part I, 1981, Barbarians, 1982, Hurlyburly, 1985, Long Days Journey into Night, 1986, National Anthems, 1988, Lost in Yonkers, 1991 (Tony award for Best Featured Actor, 1991, Drama Desk award, 1991), Playland, 1993, The Iceman Cometh, 1997 (Tony award Best Male Performance/Drama 1999), The Philadelphia Story, 2005, Richard II, 2005, A Moon for the Misbegotten, 2007; actor (films) Heartburn, 1986, Working Girl, 1988, Rocket Gibraltar, 1988, Dad, 1989, See No Evil, Hear No Evil, 1989, A Show of Force, 1990, Henry and June, 1990, Glengarry Glen Ross, 1992, Consenting Adults, 1992, Iron Will, 1994, The Ref, 1994, Outbreak, 1995, The Usual Suspects, 1995 (Acad. award for best supporting actor, 1996), Seven, 1995, A Time to Kill, 1996, Looking for Richard, 1996, Midnight in the Garden of Good and Evil, 1997, L.A. Confidential, 1997, Hurlyburly, 1998, The Negotiator, 1998, (voice only) A Bug's Life, 1998, American Beauty, 1999 (Acad. award for best actor, 2000), (voice only) Its Tough to Be a Bug, 1999, Ordinary Decent Criminals, 2000, Pay It Forward, 2000, K-PAX, 2001, The Shipping News. 2001,(voice only)The Tower of Babble, 2001, The Life of David Gale, 2003, Edison, 2005, Superman Returns, 2006; actor, dir., prodr., writer, Beyond the Sea, 2004; actor, prodr. (films) Swimming With Sharks, 1994, The Big Kahuna, 1999, The United States of Leland, 2003; dir. (films) Albino Alligator, 1994; prodr. (films) Triggerstreet.com, 2004, The Sasquatch Dumpling Gang, 2006, Mini's First Time, 2006; exec. prodr. (films) Interstate 88, 2000, Uncle Frank, 2002, Mr. Gibb, 2006; actor (TV series) Wiseguy, 1987-88, Nat. Anthems, 2005; (TV films) The Murder of Mary Phagan, 1988, Fall From Grace, 1990, When You Remember Me, 1990, Darrow, 1991, Doomsday Gun, 1994 Address: William Morris Agy 151 S El Camino Dr Beverly Hills CA 90212-2704 Office: Old Vic The Cut London SE1 8NB England

SPACH, JULE CHRISTIAN, church executive; b. Winston-Salem, NC, Dec. 21, 1923; s. Jule Christian and Margaret Stockton (Coyner) S.; m. Nancy Clendenin, Sept. 18, 1948; children: Nancy Lynn Lane, Margaret Cuningham, Ann Thomerson, Cecelia Welborn, Robert Spach. Student, Va. Mil. Inst., 1942-43; BSChemE, Ga. Inst. Tech., 1949; postgrad., Union Theol. Sem., Richmond, Va., 1951-52, Duke U., 1955-56; MA in Ednl. Adminstrn., U. N.C., Greensboro, 1976; LHD (hon.), Stillman Coll., Tuscaloosa, Ala., 1977; LittD (hon.), Belhaven Coll., Jackson, Miss., 1977; LLD, King Coll., Bristol, Tenn., 1977. Salesman Mengle Corp. subs. Internat. Container Corp., Winston-Salem, 1950-52; from prof. scis., athletic dir. to pres. Quinze de Novembro Coll., Garanhuns, Pernanbuco, Brazil, 1952-64; edn. dir. Cruzada ABC-Recife, Pernanbuco, 1965-70, pres., 1969-70; exec. sec. Parliamentary Christian Leadership, Brasilia, Fed. Dist., Brazil, 1970-73; exec. dir. Presbyn. Mission in Brazil, Campinas, Sao Paulo, 1973-75; moderator Gen. Assembly of Presbyn. Ch. in U.S., Atlanta, 1976-77; exec. dir. Triad United Meth. Home, Inc., Winston-Salem, 1977—. Bd. dirs. First Home Fed. Savs. and Loan. Author: (biography) Every Road Leads Home, 1997. Bd. dirs. Instituto Gammon, Presbyn. Ch. U.S., Forsyth County Coun. on Aging Forsyth County Sr. Svcs. Forsyth County, Covenent Fellowship of Presbyns., William Black Lodge, Synod of N.C., Presbyn. Ch. U.S.A.; bd. visitors Lee's McRae Coll., Montreat Anderson Coll.; mem. cabinet United Way, 1987; chmn. Winston-Salem Forsyth County Coun. on Svcs. to Homeless; chmn. bd. dirs. Sr. Svcs., Inc., Winston-Salem, Missionary Family Counseling Svc. With USAAF, 1943-45, prisoner of war, Poland. Decorated Purple Heart; recipient Jefferson award, 1991; named Hon. Citizen of of Garanhuas, Brazil. Mem. Sertoma Club (3 Svc. awards), Lions, Rotary. Republican. Home: Arbor Acres 1244 Arbor Rd Apt 197 Winston Salem NC 27104-1199 Office: 1240 Arbor Rd Winston Salem NC 27104-1106 Business E-Mail: jspach1@triad.rr.com. *The Christian faith teaches us that the greatest of all gifts is love. This gift comes from God, and it is ours through the presence of His spirit dwelling in us. This love gives man peace within and with his fellow man.*

SPACKMAN, THOMAS JAMES, radiologist; b. Oak Park, Ill., Apr. 24, 1937; s. Thomas Frederick and Louise Mary (Kaiser) Spackman; m. Donna S. Stewart, June 25, 1960; children: Kirsten, Thomas James, Victoria. BA, DePauw U., 1959; MD, Western Res. U., 1964; diploma in bus. studies,

London Sch. Econs., 1987. Intern, then resident in internal medicine Yale-New Haven Med. Ctr., 1964-66, resident in diagnostic radiology, 1966-68, fellow clin. rsch. tng. unit, 1968-69; instr., then asst. prof. radiology Yale U. Med. Sch., New Haven, 1969-74; assoc. prof. U. Pa. Med. Sch., 1974-78; prof. radiology U. Conn. Med. Sch., Farmington, 1978—, head dept., 1978-90; dir. radiology St. Francis Hosp. and Med. Ctr., Hartford, Conn., 1992-93; pres. Elscint, Inc., Hackensack, NJ, 1993-97; sr. v.p. Elscint, Ltd., Haifa, Israel, 1993-97; pres. Spackman Assocs., Vero Beach, Fla., 1997—; chmn. Xicon Technologies LLC, Vero Beach, 1997-98; v.p. physician affairs Quorum Health Resources, 2000—02, Cambio Health Solutions LLC, 2002—05; chmn. Navix Diagnostix, Inc., 2002—; mng. dir. FTI Cabmrio Health Solutions, 2005—. Mem. Conn. Med. Exam. Bd., 1980—86; bd. dirs. Elscint, Inc. Mem. editl. adv. bd. Diagnostic Imaging, 1989—92; contbr. articles to profl. jours., chapters to books. Fellow: Am. Coll. Radiology; mem.: Soc. Pediatric Radiology, Assn. U. Radiolgoists. Business E-Mail: thomas.spackman@fticambiohealth.com.

SPADA, JAMES, writer, photographer, publishing executive; b. S.I., NY, Jan. 23, 1950; s. Joseph Vincent and Mary Ruberto Spada. Student, Wagner Coll., SI, 1968—71, Calif. State U., LA, 1979—80. Pres. Spada Publs., LA; pub. Barbra Quar., LA, 1980-83. Author: Barbra: The First Decade - The Films and Career of Barbra Streisand, 1974, The Films of Robert Redford, 1977, The Spada Report, 1979, Streisand - The Woman and the Legend, 1981, Monroe - Her Life in Pictures, 1982, Judy and Liza, 1983, Hepburn: Her Life in Pictures, 1984, The Divine Bette Midler, 1984, Fonda: Her Life in Pictures, 1985, Shirley and Warren, 1985, Grace: The Secret Lives of a Princess, 1987, Peter Lawford: The Man Who Kept the Secrets, 1991, More than a Woman: An Intimate Biography of Bette Davis, 1993, Streisand: Her Life, 1995, Jackie: Her Life in Pictures, 2000; photographer, pub.: Black & White Men, 2000, Ronald Reagan: His Life in Pictures, 2001, John and Caroline: Their Lives in Pictures, 2001, Edwardian Men, 2004, Julia: Her Life, 2004, The Bush Family, 2004, The Romantic Male Nude, 2007; book packager The 1984 Marilyn Monroe Pin-Up Calendar, 1983, The Telephone Book, 1984, Elizabeth Taylor: A Biography in Photographs, 1984, Bette Davis: A Biography in Photographs, 1985, Natalie Wood: A Biography in Photographs, 1986; one-man shows include Against the Grain Gallery, Cape Cod, 1998, Gallery One, Boston, 2000, Radiant Light Gallery, Portland, Maine, 2001. Democrat. Personal E-mail: jamesspada1@verizon.net.

SPADAFORA, DAVID CHARLES, historian, educator; b. Hamilton, Ohio, June 4, 1951; s. Samuel Charles and Dorothy (Hardy) S.; m. Carolyn Elizabeth Gaugler, Mar. 24, 1973; children: Andrew, Claire. BA, Williams Coll., 1972; PhD, Yale U., 1981; D of Letters (hon.), Lake Forest Coll., 2001. Instr. Simon's Rock Coll., Great Barrington, Mass., 1977-78; lectr. Univ. Conn., West Hartford, 1978-80; research analyst Conn. Gen. Assembly, Hartford, 1980-81; dean of Morse Coll. Yale U., 1982, lectr. in history, 1982—90, dean of Calhoun Coll., 1982-85, assoc. dean of grad. sch., 1985—90; prof. history Lake Forest Coll., Lake Forest, Ill., 1990—, dean of faculty, 1990—93, pres., 1993—2001; pres., libr. Newberry Libr., Chgo., 2005—. Author: The Idea of Progress in Eighteenth-Century Britain, 1990; contbr. articles to profl. jours. Bd. dirs. Yale Coop, New Haven, 1987-90, Recordings for the Blind and Dyslexic Ill. Unit, 1998-2001, Assoc. Colls. of the Midwest, 1993-2001, chmn. 2000-01; bd. dirs. CROYA, Lake Forest, Ill., 1993-2001. Named Alumnus of Yr., Cin. Country Day Sch., 1994; recipient award for Meritorious Svc., Conn. Gen. Assembly, 1981. Fellow: British-Am. Project; mem.: Mid-Am. Club, Phi Beta Kappa. Avocations: golf, tennis.

SPADE, DAVID (DAVID WAYNE SPADE), actor; b. Birmingham, Mich., July 22, 1964; s. Wayne Spade and Judy Todd. BBA, Ariz. State U., 1986. Comml. spokesperson Sierra Mist soda, Capital One credit cards. Cast mem. & writer, Saturday Night Live, 1990; actor (TV series), (voice) Beavis and Butt-Head, 1994-97, Just Shoot Me, 1997-2003, 8 Simple Rules...For Dating My Teenage Daugher, 2004-05, Rules of Engagement, 2007-; (TV host) The Showbiz Show With David Spade, 2005-; appeared in films: Police Academy 4: Citizen on Patrol, 1987, Coneheads, 1993, PCU, 1994, Tommy Boy, 1995, Black Sheep, 1996, A Very Brady Sequel, 1996, Eight Heads in a Duffel Bag, 1997, Senseless, 1998, The Rugrats Movie (voice), 1998, Lost & Found (also writer, exec. prodr.), 1999, Little Nicky, 2000, The Emperor's New Groove (voice), 2000, Joe Dirt, 2001, Dickie Roberts: Former Child Star, 2003, (voice) Racing Stripes, 2005, Grandma's Boy, 2006, The Benchwarmers, 2006; actor, writer, exec. prodr. David Spade: Take the Hit (TV), 1998; exec. prodr. Jerome, 1999; appeared on TV shows The Facts of Life, ALF, The Larry Sanders Show, The Dennis Miller Show, Beavis and Butt-head (voice), The Daily Show, BioRhythm, Comedy Central Roast of Pamela Anderson, 2005. Named to Hollywood Walk of Fame, 2003. *

SPADE, KATE (KATHERINE NOEL SPADE), apparel designer; b. Kansas City, Mo., 1962; m. Andy Spade, 1994. BA in journalism and broadcasting, Arizona State U., 1985. From asst. to accessories editor Mademoiselle mag., 1985—92; co-founder, designer Kate Spade Inc., NYC, 1993—; designer Kate Spade paper and social stationary, 1998—, Kate Spade shoe collection, 1999—, Kate Spade glasses, 2001, Kate Spade beauty, 2002—; co-founder Jack Spade, 1999—, Kate Spade Home, 2002—. Designer (uniforms) Song Airlines (subs. Delta Airlines), 2004. Recipient Perry Ellis award, New Fashion Talent, Coun. Fashion Designers of Am., 1996, Accessory Designer of the Year, 1998, FiFi award for Bath & Body Star of the Year, US Fragrance Found., 2003, FiFi award for Best Fragrance in Ltd. Distribution, U.K. Fragrance Found., 2003, Giants of Design award for Tastemaker, House Beautiful, 2004, Am. Food & Entertaining award for Designer of Yr., Bon Appetit, 2004, Elle Decor Internat. Design award for bedding, 2004. Achievements include stores opening in NYC in 1996, Boston and LA in 1998, and Chgo. and San Francisco in 2000. Office: Kate Spade Inc 48 W 25th St New York NY 10010 *

SPADER, JAMES, actor; b. Boston, Mass., Feb. 7, 1960; s. Jean and Todd Spader; m. Victoria Kheel, 1979; children: Sebastian, Elijah. Student, Phillips Acad., Michael Chekhov Studio. Appeared in pictures Endless Love (debut 1981), The New Kids, 1985, Tuff Turf, 1985, Pretty in Pink, 1986, Mannequin, 1987, Wall Street, 1987, Less Than Zero, 1987, Baby Boom, 1987, Jack's Back, 1988, The Rachel Papers, 1989, Sex, Lies and Videotape (Best actor award Cannes Festival 1989), 1989, Bad Influence, 1990, White Palace, 1990, True Colors, 1991, Storyville, 1992, Bob Roberts, 1992, Music of Chance, 1993, Dream Lover, 1994, Wolf, 1994, Stargate, 1994, Two Days in the Valley, 1996, Crash, 1997, Keys to Tulsa, 1997, Critical Care, 1997, Curtain Call, 1999, Curtain Call, 1999, Supernova, 2000, The Watcher, 2000, Slow Burn, 2000, The Stickup, 2001, Speaking of Sex, 2001, Secretary, 2002, I Witness, 2003, Alien Hunter, 2003; TV movies, Cocaine: One Man's Seduction, 1983, Diner, 1983, A Killer in the Family, 1983, Family Secrets, 1984, Starcrossed, 1985, The Pentagon Papers, 2003; TV series The Family Tree, 1983, The Practice, 2003-2004 (Emmy award Outstanding Lead Actor in a Drama Seriesm, 2004), Boston Legal, 2004- (Emmy award for outstanding lead actor in a drama series, 2005); TV guest appearances Frasier, 1994, Seinfeld, 1997. Office: care Toni Howard/ICM 8942 Wilshire Blvd Beverly Hills CA 90211-1934 *

SPADE-SHENKER, GEORGE LAWRENCE (GEORGE SHENKER), research scientist; b. Sioux City, Iowa, Dec. 14, 1945; s. Walter Charles and LaVancha May (Green) S.; m. Carol Margaret Deaton, Mar. 14, 1966 (div. June 1985); children: Aaron Michael, Margaret. Mem. earthquake study group for China, U.S. Citizen Amb. Programs, 1989. Contbr. articles to profl. jours. Mem. AAAS, Internat. Soc. Philos. Enquiry, Am. Math. Soc., Math. Assn. Am., N.Y. Acad. Scis., Mensa. Avocations: poetry, painting, music. Home and Office: PO Box 2260 Columbia Falls MT 59912-2260

SPAEDER, FRANCIS XAVIER, forensic electrical engineer; s. Leo J. and Frances M. Spaeder; m. Margaret L. Dugas, Aug. 10, 2002; children: Deborah A., Kimberly A. BSEE, Gannon U., Erie, 1964—69. Registered profl. engr., Pa., profl. surveyor, Pa. Lines engr. Alllegheny Power, Greensburg, Pa., 1969—2002; pres. Forensic Engring. Investigations, Greensburg, 1996—. Maj. US Army, 1969—95. Mem.: IEEE (assoc.), Internat. Assn. Arson Investigators (assoc.), PPa. Assn. Arson Investigators (assoc.), Nat. Fire Protection Assn. (assoc.), Am. Acad. Forensic Sci. (assoc.). R-Consevative. Avocations: pistol shooting, hunting, fishing, canoeing. Office: Forensic Engring Investigations 201 Quail Dr Greensburg PA 15601-4727 Office Phone: 724-837-1113.

SPAEDER, ROGER CAMPBELL, lawyer; b. Cleve., Dec. 20, 1943; s. Ferdinand N. and Luceil (Campbell) S.; m. Frances DeSales Sutherland, Sept. 7, 1968; children: Michael, Matthew. BS, Bowling Green U., 1965; JD with honors, George Washington U., 1970. Bar: DC 1971, US Dist. Ct. DC 1971, US Ct. Appeals (DC cir.) 1971, US Ct. Claims 1979, US Dist. Ct. Md. 1984, US Ct. Appeals (2d and 4th cirs.) 1985, US Supreme Ct. 1976. Asst. U.S. atty. D.C., Washington, 1971-76; ptnr. Zuckerman Spaeder LLP, Washington, 1976—. Faculty Atty. Gen. Advocacy Inst., 1974-76, Nat. Inst. Trial Adv., 1978-79; adj. faculty Georgetown U. Law Ctr., 1979-80, Am. U. Ctr. Adminstrn. Justice, 1976-79; lectr. DC Bar Continuing Legal Edn. Programs, 1980-90; Cardozo Prize judge Yale Law Sch., 1992; master Edward Bennett Williams Inn of Ct., 1996—; mem. DC Cir. Jud. Conf., 1991. Contbr. articles to profl. jours. and chpts. to books. Recipient Spl. Achievement award Dept. Justice, 1971. Fellow Am. Coll. Trial Lawyers; Mem. ATLA, ABA (co-chair com. on complex crimes litigation 1989-92, divsn. co-dir. sect. litigation 1992-94), Bar Assn. DC (lectr. Criminal Practice Inst. 1977-80), DC Bar (com. criminal jury instrns. 1972, divsn. cts. lawyers, adminstrn. of justice 1976-78; adv. com. continuing legal edn. 1986), Def. Rsch. Inst., Assn. Plaintiffs' Trial Attys., Nat. Assn. Criminal Def. Lawyers, Omicron Delta Kappa. Home: 7624 Georgetown Pike Mc Lean VA 22102-1412 Office: Zuckerman Spaeder LLP 1800 M St NW Ste 1000 Washington DC 20036-5802 Office Phone: 202-778-1806.

SPAEPEN, FRANS AUGUST, physicist, educator; b. Mechelen, Belgium, Oct. 29, 1948; arrived in U.S., 1971; s. Jozef F. M. and Ursula (Roppe) Spaepen; m. Moniek Steemans, Aug. 21, 1973; children: Geertrui M., Elizabet U., Hendrik J. L. Burgerlijk Metaalkundig Ingenieur, U. Leuven, Belgium, 1971; PhD, Harvard U., 1975. IBM postdoctoral fellow Harvard U., Cambridge, Mass., 1975-77, asst. prof. applied physics, 1977-81, assoc. prof., 1981-83, Gordon McKay prof. applied physics, 1983—2002, Franklin prof. applied physics, 2002—, dir. Materials Rsch. Lab., 1990—98, dir. Rowland Inst., 2002—. Vis. prof. U. Leuven, 1984, 2007, Deutsches Zentrum für Luft-und Raumfahrt-Köln, 2000, Forschungszentrum Jülich, 2001; chmn. Gordon Conf. on Phys. Metallurgy, 1988; NRC com. on solid state scis., 1990—93; NRC com. on condensed matter and materials physics, 1996—98; Krengel lectr. Technion, Israel, 1994; mem. summer rsch. group Los Alamos Nat. Lab., 1986—99; mem. sci. and tech. steering com. Brookhaven Nat. Lab.; chmn. scientific adv. bd. Netherlands Inst. for Metals Rsch.; J.B. Cohen lectr. Northwestern U., 2004. Co-editor: (series) Solid State Physics; mem. editl. bd. Jour. Applied Physics, Applied Physics Letters, 1990—93, 1999—2001, Applied Physics Revs., 1991—97, Phys. Rev., 1994—99, Jour. Non-Crystalline Solids, 1990—94; editor (prin. editor): Jour. Materials Rsch., 2001—; contbr. articles to profl. jours., chpts. to books. Recipient Best Paper award, Acta Metallurgica, 1994, Humboldt award, 1999, R.F. Mehl award, TMS Inst. Metals, 2002, Heyn medal, German Soc. Materials Sci., 2005. Fellow: AIME-The Metall. Soc., Am. Phys. Soc. (chmn. divsn. materials physics 1992); mem.: Max Planck Soc. (external mem.), Vlaamse Academie voor Wetenschappen en Kunsten, Orde van den Prince, Vlaamse Ingenieurs Vereniging, Materials Rsch. Soc. (councillor 1986—88, co-chmn. fall meeting Boston 1990, councillor 1990—92, chmn. program com. 1993—2000, Woody award 1998), Am. Soc. Metals. Office: Harvard Univ Divsn Engring and Applied Scis 29 Oxford St Cambridge MA 02138-2901 Business E-Mail: spaepen@seas.harvard.edu.

SPAETH, EDMUND BENJAMIN, JR., retired lawyer, retired law educator, former judge; b. Washington, June 10, 1920; s. Edmund B. and Lena (Link) S. AB magna cum laude, Harvard U., Cambridge, Mass., 1942; LLB, Harvard U., 1948. Bar: Pa. 1949. Judge Ct. of Common Pleas, Phila., 1964-73, Superior Ct of Pa., 1973-86, pres. judge, 1983-86; of counsel Pepper Hamilton LLP, Phila., 1986—2002. Adj. prof. U. Pa. Law Sch., 1976-97; chair Pennsylvanians for Modern Cts., 1987-2000. Fellow Am. Bar Found. (life); mem. Am. Law Inst. (life), Am. Judicature soc., Order of Coif, Phi Beta Kappa. Home: Cathedral Village Apt L-206 600 E Cathedral Rd Philadelphia PA 19128-1933

SPAETH, GEORGE LINK, ophthalmologist, educator, writer; b. Phila., Mar. 3, 1932; s. Edmund Benjamin and Lena Marie (Link) S.; m. Ann Ward, May 17, 1958; children: Kristin Lea Crowley, George Link Jr., Eric Edmund. BA magna cum laude, Yale U., 1954; MD cum laude, Harvard U., 1959; postgrad., U. Mich., 1960, U. Pa., 1961. Resident surgeon Wills Eye Hosp., Phila., 1961-63, attending surgeon, 1970—, dir. glaucoma svc., 1968—2007, dir. emeritus, 2007—; clin. fellow NIH, Bethesda, Md., 1963-65; instr. U. Pa., Phila., 1965-68; pvt. practice Phila., 1965-68; prof. ophthalmology Temple U. Med. Sch., Phila., 1968-75, Jefferson Med. Coll., Phila., 1975—, Louis Esposito glaucoma rsch. prof., 2000—. Ophthalmologist Chestnut Hill Hosp., Phila., 1975—; attending surgeon, Graduate Hosp.; cons., Bryn Mawr Hosp., Wills Eye Hosp., Hosp. Jefferson Med. Coll. Author: 19 books in ophthalmology, surgery, and med. ethics, 1970—; contbr. over 600 articles to profl. jours.; editor Ophthalmic Surgery jour., 1985-96; editl. editor Ophthalmic Surgery and Lasers; mem. editl. bd. Jour., Ocular Surgery News, Jour. Glaucoma, Jour. Evidence-Based Ophthalmology, Glaucoma Abstracts; manuscript reviewer, New Eng. Jour. Medicine, Med. Letter Drugs and Therapy, others; patentee differometer, tonometer tip cover. Pres. Chestnut Hill Cmty. Assn., Phila., 1970-72; founder, CEO Internat. Soc. Spaeth Fellows, 1975—; trustee, founder, pres. E.B. Spaeth and Glaucoma Svcs. Found., 1978—, Profls. for Nuclear Army Control, 1985-88; tustee, treas. Thomas Skelton Harrison Found., Inc., 1984—; interviewer Yale Alumni Schs. Com., Phila., 1965—; Yale Class coun., 1968—, Yale Assn. Alumni Reps., 1996-2002; trustee Recording for the Blind and Dyslexia, 1996-2002, Internat. Arts-Medicine Assn., Pa. Ballet, 2002—, Bach Festival of Phila., 2002-2005, Squirrel Island Chapel, Maine; curriculum com. Jefferson Med. Coll., 1987-90; institutional review bd. Jefferson Med. Coll., 1990-95; pres. Phila. Glaucoma Inst., 1997—. Lt. comdr. USPHS, 1963-68. NIH grantee, 1968—; recipient Pub. Svc. medal Chestnut Hill Coll., 1972, Sir Stuart Duke Elder Glaucoma award Internat. Glaucoma Soc., 1986, Newberg award Lawyers Alliance for World Security, 1995, Derrick Vail award Internat. Soc. Prevention Blindness, 1996, Trantas award Greek Ophthalmol. Soc., 2000, Frominopolous prize Greek Glaucoma Soc., 2003, Large Flower and Vegetable Garden 1st Pl. award Pa. Horticultural Soc., 2004, Nizankowska award Polish Glaucoma Soc., 2006; named Ophthalmic Visionary, Ocular Surgery News, 2003, Bausch & Lomb, 2005. Fellow Am. Acad. Ophthalmology (chmn. ethics com. San Francisco 1987-95, coun. 1980-93, vice chmn. residency rev. com. Chgo. 1982-88, Sr. honor award 1988, life time achievement award 1999), Am. Assn. Rsch. in Vision and Ophthalmology, Royal Coll. Ophthalmologists U.K., Danish Ophthalmol. Soc., Ind. Soc. of Ophthalmology; mem. Am. Glaucoma Soc. (pres. 1983-85), Coll. Physicians Phila. (sec. 1976-84), Phila. County Med. Soc., Pa. Acad. Ophthalmology (pres. coun.), German Ophthalmol. Congress, Physicians for Social Responsibility (pres. emeritus Phila. chpt.), ACS (bd. govs. emeritus, chmn. emeritus adv. coun. for ophthalmology), Phila. Club, Phila. Cricket Club, Phi Beta Kappa, Alpha Omega Alpha. Democrat. Avocations: composing music, piano, sports, photography, gardening. Office: Wills Eye Hosp 11th Fl 840 Walnut St Philadelphia PA 19107-5109 Home Phone: 215-242-3285; Office Phone: 215-928-3960. Business E-Mail: gspaeth@willseye.org.

SPAETH, JAN MILLS, jury consultant; b. Grinnell, Iowa, July 17, 1951; d. Paul Herbert and Joyce Carol Broadwell; m. Paul Vincent Spaeth, May 26, 1988. BA with honors, U. Wis., Madison, 1973; MA, U. Ariz., 1996; PhD, Calif. Coast U., 1999. Social worker Cass County Dept. Social Svcs., Walker, Minn., 1973—75; dir. rsch. Lakehead Social Planning Coun., Thunder Bay, Ont., Canada, 1975—76; social worker Thunder Bay Social Svcs. Dept., 1976—78; free-lance workshop coord. Duluth, Minn., 1979; freelance litig. cons. Tucson, 1980—. Educator Tucson Free U., 1980, Pima County Jail, Tucson, 1981, Pima County Juvenile Ct. Ctr., Tuscon, 1981; instr. U. Ariz., Tuscon, 1980—94, Pima C.C., Tucson, 1990—94, Cochise C.C., Sierra Vista, Ariz., 1991; supplemental juror questionnaire subcom. Supreme Ct. Ariz., Phoenix, 1995; spkr. in field. Contbr. articles to profl. jours. Recipient Appreciation award, Pima County Juvenile Ct. Ctr., 1982. Mem.: APA, Ariz. Attys. for Criminial Justice, Am. Coll. Forensic Examiners, Am. Soc. Trial Cons. Avocations: hiking, travel, golf, research, writing. Office: Ariz Jury Rsch PO Box 91410 Tucson AZ 85752 Office Phone: 520-297-4131.

SPAETH, KARL HENRY, retired chemicals executive, lawyer; b. Phila., Mar. 12, 1929; s. Edmund Benjamin and Lena Marie (Link) S.; m. Ann Dashiell Wieland, Sept. 14, 1963; children: Karl Henry, Edmund Alexander, Christopher Philip. AB, Haverford Coll., 1951; postgrad., Oxford U., 1955; JD, Harvard U., 1958. Bar: Pa. 1959, U.S. Ct. (ea. dist.) Pa. 1959, U.S. Ct. Appeals (3d cir.) 1959. Assoc. MacCoy, Evans & Lewis, Phila., 1959-62; counsel for fgn. ops. Scott Paper Co., Phila., 1962-69; v.p., corp. sec. Quaker Chem. Corp., Conshohocken, Pa., 1969-95, ret. v.p., 1995, ret. corp. sec., 1998. Bd. dirs. Greater Phila. Devel. Corp., 1991-98; bd. dirs., sec.-treas. Edmund B. Spaeth Clin. Rsch. Found., 1982—; chmn. bd. dirs. Pa. Chem. Industry Coun., 1984-86. Chmn. bd. trustees Quaker Chem. Found., 1982-2003; bd. overseers Univ. Mus., U. Pa., Phila., 1983-89, 90-96; bd. dirs. Opera Co. Phila., 1988-2003; bd. dirs. Chestnut Hill Acad., Phila., 1976-83, pres. 1979-83; mem. Whitemarsh Twp. Bd. Suprs. Pa., 1969-75, chmn., 1972-74; mem. Com. of Seventy, Phila., 1984-96. Comdr. USNR, 1952-55, ret. Mem. Pa. Bar Assn. (chmn. sect. on internat. and comparative law 1980-92), Phila. Com. on Fgn. Rels. (exec. com., sec. 1984-94, chmn. 2001-04), Phila. Club, Phila. Athenaeum, Libr. Co. of Phila., Phila. Cricket Club, Oxford Union Club, Univ. Barge (sec. 1988-94), Mil. Order Fgn. Wars (registrar 1989-91, vice commdr. 1991-93). Republican. Anglican. Home: 2129 Harts Ln Conshohocken PA 19428-2416 E-mail: khspaeth@comcast.net.

SPAETH, NICHOLAS JOHN, lawyer, former state attorney general; b. Mahnomen, Minn., Jan. 27, 1950; m. Cindy Spaeth; children: Gawain Kevin, Carl Wilson, William James, Elizabeth Bedont. AB, Stanford U., 1972, JD, 1977; BA, Oxford U., Eng., 1974. Bar: Minn. 1979, US Dist. Ct. Dist. Minn. 1979, US Ct. Appeals 8th cir. 1979, ND 1980, US Dist. Ct. Dist. ND 1980, US Supreme Ct. 1984, Calif. 1999, US Dist. Ct. Calif. 1999, Mo. 2005. Law clk. US Ct. Appeals 8th cir., Fargo, ND, 1977-78; law clk. to Justice Byron White US Supreme Ct., Washington, 1978-79; atty. pvt. practice, 1979-84; atty. gen. State of ND, Bismarck, 1985—93; ptnr. Dorsey & Whitney, Fargo, ND, 1993-99, Oppenheimer Wolff & Donnelly, Mpls., 1999, Cooley Godward, Palo Alto, Calif., 1999—2000; sr v.p., gen. counsel, sec. GE Employers Reinsurance Corp., Overland Park, Kans., 2000—03, Intuit Inc., Mountain View, Calif., 2003—04; sr. v.p., chief legal officer H&R Block Inc., Kansas City, Mo., 2004—. Adj. prof. law U. Minn., 1980-83. Rhodes scholar, 1972-74. Democrat. Roman Catholic. Office: H&R Block Inc 4400 Main St Kansas City MO 64111 Business E-Mail: nspaeth@hrblock.com. *

SPAFFORD, MICHAEL CHARLES, artist; b. Palm Springs, Calif., Nov. 6, 1935; BA, Pomona Coll., 1959; MA, Harvard U., 1960. Artist-in-residence Dartmouth Coll., 2005. One man shows include Seattle Art Mus., 1982, 86, Reed Coll., 1984, Whtcom county Mus., 1987, U. Puget Sound, Tacoma, Wash., 1973, Tacoma Art Mus., 1975, 86, Utah Mus. Fine Arts, Salt Lake City, 1975, Francine Seders Gallery, Seattle, 1965—, Bellevue Art Mus., 1991, Cheney-Cowles Mus., Spokane, Wash., 1994, Hallie Ford Mus. Art, Willamette U., Salem, Oreg., 1999; exhibited in group shows at Wilcox Gallery, Swarthmore Coll., Pa., 1977, Seattle Art Mus., 1977, 80, 84, Am. Acad. and Inst. Arts and Letters, N.Y.C., 1980, 83, 89, 95, Kobe, Japan, 1981, Eastern Wash. U., 1982, Henry Art Gallery, 1982, 86, Bellevue Art Mus., 1987, 95, Cheney Cowles Mus., 1988, Holter Mus. of Art, Helena, Mont. Recipient Rome Prize Am. Acad. in Rome, 1967-69, award Am. Acad. and Inst. Arts and Letters, 1983, Lifetime Achievement in Arts award Corp. Coun. Arts, Seattle, 1999. Flintridge Found. award for visual artists, 2006; Louis Comfort Tiffany Found. grantee, 1965-66; Neddy fellow, 1996. Address: c/o Francine Seders Gallery 6701 Greenwood Ave N Seattle WA 98103-5225

SPAGNOLETTI, ROBERT JAMES, lawyer, former attorney general; b. 1962; 1 adopted child, Hunter. BS in Mathematics & History, Lafayette Coll., 1984; JD, Georgetown U., 1987. Bar: NJ, NY, Washington, DC. Litig. assoc. Mayor Day Caldwell & Keaton, Houston, Skadden, Arps, Salte, Meagher & Flom, NY & DC; asst. US atty. DC US Dept. Justice, Washington, 1990—2003, chief domestic violence unit, 1995—98, chief sex offence & domestic violence section, 1998—2003; atty. gen. Washington, DC, 2003—06; ptnr. Schertler & Onorato LLP, Washington, 2006—. Prof. law Georgetown U. Law Ctr. Recipient Young Lawyer of Year award, Bar Assn. of DC, 1997, Sullivan Award, Asst. US Atty. Assn., 2002. Democrat. Office: Schertler & Onorato LLP 601 Pennsylvania Ave NW Washington DC 20004 *

SPAGNOLIA, THOMAS NICKOLAS, neurosurgeon, consultant; b. Chgo., Oct. 24, 1949; s. Louis Thomas and Margaret Elaine Spagnolia; m. D'Arcy Adaire Honeycutt, May 15, 1987; children: Alessandra Anise, Christopher Thomas. BA in Biology, U. Mo., St. Louis, 1974, MS, 1980; MD, U. Mo., Columbia, 1983, PhD, 1989. Diplomate Am. Bd. Neurol. Surgery, 1997. Neurosurgeon Bismarck Neurosurgical Assocs., Bismarck, ND, 1997—2005; staff neurosurgeon Med Ctr. One Health Ctr., Bismarck, 2005—. Asst. prof. surgery sch. medicine U. ND, Bismarck, 1997—; assoc. prof. neuroscience U. Mary, Bismarck, 1997—. Named Physician of Yr., Nat. Rep. Congl. Com. Phycicians Adv. Bd., 2003; named one of Best Doctors in Am., 2004, 2005, 2006; recipient Student Leadership award, U. Mo. sch. medicine, Columbia, 1984. Fellow: ACS; mem.: North Am. Spine Soc., Congress of Neurol. Surgeons, Am. Assn. Neurol. Surgeons, Consumer Rsch. Coun. (hon. named one of Am.'s Top Physicians 2004—07). Conservative. Episcopalian. Avocations: singing, firearms collector, music, art, travel. Office: Med Center One 222 North 7th St Bismarck ND 58506-5505 Home Phone: 701-222-2345; Office Phone: 701-323-5422. Personal E-mail: tspagnolia@hotmail.com. Business E-Mail: tspagnolia@mohs.org.

SPAGNOLO, SAMUEL VINCENT, internist, pulmonary specialist, educator; b. Pitts., Sept. 3, 1939; s. Vincent Anthony and Mary Grace (Culotta) S.; children: Samuel, Brad, Gregg; m. Dorcas R. Hardy, Sept. 29, 1996. BA, Washington & Jefferson Coll., 1961; MD, Temple U., 1965. Diplomate Am. Bd. Internal Medicine, Bd. Pulmonary Disease, lic. physician Fla., Calif., Md., D.C., Va., Ariz., Pa., Mass. Sr. resident in medicine VA Med. Ctr., Boston, 1969-70, chief resident in medicine, 1970-71; Harvard Clin.

and Rsch. fellow in pulmonary diseases Mass. Gen. Hosp., Boston, 1971-72; asst. chief med. svc. VA Med. Ctr., Washington, 1972-75, acting chief med. svc., 1975-76, chief pulmonary disease sect., 1976-94, chief of staff, 1998-99, dir. respiratory care and sr. attending in pulmonary diseases, 1999—; instr. in medicine Boston U. Sch. of Medicine, Tufts U. Sch. Medicine, Boston, 1970-71; clin. and rsch. fellow in pulmonary diseases Harvard U. Sch. of Medicine, Mass. Gen. Hosp., Boston, 1971-72; attending physician George Washington U. Med. Ctr., 1972—; clin. asst. prof. medicine Georgetown U., Washington, 1975-77; asst. prof. medicine George Washington U. Sch. of Medicine and Health Scis., Washington, 1972-75, assoc. prof., 1975-81, prof. medicine, 1981—, dir. divsn. pulmonary diseases and allergy, 1978-93; assoc. chmn. dept. medicine George Washington U. Med. Ctr., Washington, 1986-89. Cons. in pulmonary diseases The Washington Hosp. Ctr., Washington, DC, 1977—, Will Rogers Inst., White Plains, NY, 1980—, US Dept. Labor, Washington, 1980—, Walter Reed Army Med. Ctr., Washington, 1987-90; rep. Am. Coll. Chest Physicians to Am. Registry Pathology, Washington, 1981-92; numerous radio tv appearances on Health Oriented Programs; invited lectr. in U.S., Russia, Jordan; chmn., mem. many coms. George Washington U. Sch. of Medicine, George Washington Med. Ctr., VA Med. Ctr., Washington; med. chest cons. in attempted assasination of former Pres. Regan. Author: Clinical Assessment of Patients with Pulmonary Disease, 1986; co-author: (with A.E. Medinger) Handbook of Pulmonary Emergencies, 1986, Handbook of Pulmonary Drug Therapy, 1993, (with Witorsch, P.) Air Pollution and Lung Disease in Adults, 1994; mem. editl. bd. CHEST Jour., 2002-06; mem. editl. bd. Chest, 2006—; contbr. numerous articles to profl jours. including Med. Clin. N.Am., Chest, So. Med. Jour., Am. Jour. Cardiology, Jour. Am. Med. Assn., Clin. Rsch., Am. Rev. Respiratory Disease, Am. Lung Assn. Bull., Clin. Notes on Respiratory Diseases, Jour. Nuclear Medicine, Drug Therapy; presenter abstracts at profl. meetings. Pres., chmn. Found. Vets. Health Care, 1998—. Lt. comdr. USPHS, 1966-68. Decorated cavaliere Order of Merit, Republic of Italy; nominated for Golden Apple award by med. students George Washington Sch. Medicine, Phila., 1977; recipient cert. appreciation D.C. Lung Assn., 1983. Fellow ACP (coun. critical care 1983-85), Am. Coll. Chest Physicians (gov. DC, coun. of govs. 1989-96); mem. Am. Thoracic Soc. (exec. com. DC chpt. 1978, 85, 89, mem. adv. com. Tb control, 1978-84, pres. DC chpt. 1981-83), Nat. Assn. VA Physicians (sec. 1987-89, v.p. 1989-91, pres. 1992-98), Internat. Lung Found. (pres. 1991—). Achievements include first major review of patient outcome during early history of intensive care units; an analysis of mechanisms of hypoxemia in patients with chronic liver disease; first report of Pneumocystis Carinii Pneumonitis in patients with lung cancer; first prospective evaluation of short course therapy reported in U.S. using Isoniazid and Rifampin; first American report using laser through fiberoptic bronchoscope to treat lung cancer; first report to evaluate continuous intravenous morphine to control pain in cancer patients; description of a simple technique to measure the total lung volume non-invasively using the routing chest x-ray. Office: George Washington U 5-425 2150 Pennsylvania Ave NW Washington DC 20037-3201 Office Phone: 202-741-2237. Personal E-mail: drspagnolo@att.net.

SPAGNUOLO, MARIO, physician; b. Naples, Italy, Apr. 14, 1930; s. Vincent Spagnuolo and Ronca Julia; m. Kathryn Birchall, July 10, 1962; children: Mario, Sandra, Peter, Eugene. MD, Naples U., Italy, 1954. Diplomate Am. Bd. Internal Medicine. Instr. of medicine NYU Med. Sch., NYC, 1961—73, asst. prof. to assoc. prof., 1961—73; dir. Irvington House Inst. for Rheumatic Diseases, 1963—70, Juvenile Rheumatoid Arthritis Clinic., Bellevue Hosp., 1966—78; sr. attending St. John's Riverside Hosp., Yonkers, 1974—. Cons. St. Joseph's Hosp., 1982—90; pres. Western Westchester Network Inc.; chief of medicine St. John's Riverside Hosp., 1984—92, chief of staff, 1997—2000, trustee, 1997—. Contbr. over 60 articles in med. textbooks, profl. jours. Named Man of the Yr., Italian Assn. Hosps., 2000. Avocation: painting. Office: 944 N Broadway Ste 201 Yonkers NY 10701 Office Phone: 914-968-5574. E-mail: mariospa@optonline.net.

SPAGNUOLO, MARK MARIO, retired dentist; b. Midland, Mich., July 24, 1928; s. Anthony and Rose Spagnuolo; m. Sarah Frances Novello, Aug. 7, 1954; children: Christina Marie, Anthony Mark, Natalie Louise. BS, Ctrl. Mich. U., Mt. Pleasant, 1951; MS, U. Detroit, 1952, DDS, 1956. Lab. asst. Ctr. Mich. U., 1949—51; instr. U. Detroit, 1951—53; dentist pvt. practice, Ferndale, 1956—57, Lansing, 1959—92; ret., 1992. Pres. Ceatnal Supply Co., Spagnulo Builders, 1982—. Contbr. articles to profl. jours. Co-chair Mich. Com. for Re-election of Nixon, 1972; chmn. Mich. Dentists for Reagan, 1980, 1984; pres. Anthony Apts., 1959—, Park Laynes Gardens Apt., 1993—. Capt. US Dental Corps., 1957—59, cmdr. Army Mobile Dental Svc. Recipient Eagle Scout, 56 merit badges, 3 palms. Fellow: Am. Acad. Gen. Dentistry, Royal Soc. Health, London (pres.); mem.: Nat. Italian-Am. Found., Internat. Platform Assn., Nat. Acupuncture Rsch. Soc., Acad. Gen. Dentistry, Internat. Acad. Orthodontice, Fedn. Dentare Internationale, Assn. Mil. Surgeons US, Mich. Soc. Dentistry Children, Am. Dental Assn. (produced, directed, wrote ednl. film), Mich. Dental Assn., Ctrl. Dist. Dental Soc., Chgo. Dental Soc., Detroit Dist. Dental Soc., Mich. Fedn. Physicians and Dentists (chmn. peer rev. com. 1974—92, bd. dirs. 1975—92, chmn. legis. com. 1975—92, chmn. travel sem. 1976—92), Century Club (founder), Rotary. Republican. Roman Catholic. Home: 1724 Old Mill Rd East Lansing MI 48823

SPAHN, GARY JOSEPH, lawyer; b. NYC, July 23, 1949; s. Harry G. and Mary (Hopkins) S.; m. Lois Luttinger, Aug. 9, 1975; children: Gary J. Jr., Lori J. BA, L.I. U., 1971, MA, 1976; JD, U. Richmond, 1975. Bar: Va. 1975, U.S. Ct. Appeals (4th cir.) 1975, U.S. Supreme Ct. 1980. Law clk. to Hon. Judge Dortch U.S. Dist. Ct. (ea. dist.) Va., Richmond, 1975—77; from assoc. to ptnr. Troutman Sanders LLP (formerly Mays & Valentine), Richmond, 1977—; now ptnr. Troutman Sanders LLP, Richmond, past chmn. products liability and ins. sect. Lectr. in field, 1980—; mem. jud. conf. U.S. Ct. Appeals (4th cir.). Co-author: Virginia Law of Products Liability, 2000 Pres. Southhampton Citizens Assn., Richmond, 1982-85; bd. dirs. Southhampton Recreation Assn., Richmond. 1983, Chesterfield County Crime Solvers. With USAF, 1967-73. Named to Best Lawyers Am. Products Liability, 2007. Mem. ABA (litig. and tort and ins. sects.), Internat. Assn. Def. Counsel (co-chair litig. sect. Products Liability com.), Def. Rsch. Inst., Va. Assn. Def. Attys., Va. Mfrs. Assn., Products Liability Adv. Counsel, Va. Power Boat Assn. (commodore). Avocations: boating, basketball, racquetball, guitar. Office: Troutman Sanders LLP PO Box 1122 1001 Haxall Point Richmond VA 23218-1132 Office Phone: 804-697-1400.

SPAHR, CLINTON S., JR., retired elementary school educator; b. Bayshore, NY, Feb. 3, 1942; s. Clinton Smith and Averil Witona (Courier) S. BS, Hofstra U., 1967, MA, 1972. Tchr. Brentwood (N.Y.) Pub. Schs., 1966-97. Mem. Am. Philatelic Soc., Brentwood Tchrs. Assn., Internat. Soc. World Stamp Collectors. Avocations: collecting stamps, tapes, cds, books. Home: 1408 Sara Cir Port Jefferson Station NY 11776

SPAHR, ELIZABETH, environmental research administrator; b. Warren, Ohio, Nov. 12, 1930; d. Sullivan and Elizabeth (St. Clair) Spahr; children: Gretchen, Carolyn. BS, Case Western Res. U., 1952, MS, 1954, PhD, 1957, MBA, 1973. Sr. rsch. scientist NASA, Cleve., 1956-71; mgr. internat. ops., mgr. spl. projects The Std. Oil Co., Cleve., 1973-86; v.p. strategic planning Ameritrust Corp., Cleve., 1987-92; dir. fin. & adminstrn. AAUW, Washington, 1993-98; CEO Technol. Exec. Inst., 1998—2002; pres. AcromaTech Group, Inc., 1999—2002; assoc. dir. U. Md. Ctr. for Environ. Scis. Horn Point Lab., Cambridge, 2002—. Dir. supply emergency team Internat. Energy Agy., Paris, 1984-86; chair fed. women's program Fed. Exec. Bd., Cleve., 1969-71. Trustee Case Western Res. U., Cleve., 1988-92, chair ann. fund, 1989-93; pres. bd. dirs. Cuyahoga City Hosp. Found., Cleve., 1983-85. Grantee USPHS, 1952-56. Mem. Women in Tech., Arlington C. of C., Strategic Alliance Va. Employers, Strategic Alliance Md. Employers. Office: Univ Md Ctr Environ Sci Horn Point Lab PO Box 775 Cambridge MD 21613-0775 Home: PO Box 352 Trappe MD 21673-0352 E-mail: espahr@hpl.umces.edu.

SPAID, GREGORY P., academic administrator, art educator; b. Mishawaka, Ind. m. Susan R. Spaid. BA in Art, Kenyon Coll., 1969; MFA, Ind. U., 1976. Mem. faculty Berea (Ky.) Coll., 1976—79; prof. art Kenyon Coll., Gambier, Ohio, 1979—, chair art dept., 1984—88, assoc. provost, 1999—2002, acting provost, 2002—03, provost, 2003—. Tchr. summer programs Kenyon Coll., Gambier, Ohio, Santa Fe, Bozeman, Mont., Nantucket Island Sch. Design Art. Photography published in books, The Man Who Created Paradise, 2001, On Nantucket, 2002, Represented in permanent collections Mus. Modern Art, N.Y.C., J. Paul Getty Mus., L.A., Santa Barbara (Calif.) Mus. Art, Smithsonian Instn., Nat. Mus. Am. Art, Washington, Dayton (Ohio) Art Inst., Chase Manhattan Bank, N.Y.C. Fellow Photo Educators fellow, Eastman Kodak, 1993; Individual Artist's fellow, Ohio Arts Coun., 1984, 1986, 1995, 2000, Fulbright Rsch. fellow, Italy, 1987, Profl. Devel. Assistance grantee, Ohio Arts Coun., 1990, Artist Project grantee, 1995. Office: Ransom Hall 21 Kenyon College Gambier OH 43022-9623 *

SPAIN, JAMES DORRIS, JR., biochemist, educator; b. Washington, Feb. 3, 1929; s. James Dorris and Frances (Pitkin) S.; m. Patricia Mann, Oct. 3, 1952; children: James Williamson, Caryn Ann, Mary Alisa. Student, Tulane U., 1947-48; BS, Mich. Technol. U., 1951; MS, Med. Coll. Va., 1953; PhD, Stanford, 1956. Research fellow biochemistry U. Tex.-M.D. Anderson Hosp. and Tumor Inst., 1955-56; assoc. prof. dept. chemistry Mich. Technol. U., Houghton, 1956-62, head dept. biol. scis., 1962-68, prof. biochemistry, 1962-84, prof. emeritus, 1985—. Dir. Ctr. for Instrnl. Computing, Ea. Mich. U., Ypsilanti, 1984-85; vis. prof. Clemson U., S.C., 1985-94; pres. Electronic Homework Sys., Inc., 1994—; cons. Computer Applications in Biology and Chemistry; dir. SUMIT Courseware Devel. Project, 1979-82. Author: Some Computer Programs for Biology, 1970, Biological Simulation Techniques, 1972, Lake Superior Basin Bibliography, 1976, BASIC Computer Models in Biology, 1978, Basic Microcomputer Models in Biology, 1982, Developing Chemical Skills with Computerized Instruction, 1990, Computer Simulation in Biology: A Basic Introduction, 1992, Chemi-Skill-Bildr Electronic Homework System, 1994, ChemSkill Builder for Windows, 1997, ChemSkill Foundations, 1998, Chem Skill Builder/2000, 1999, GOB-ChemSkills, 2002, ChemSkill Builder/3000, 2005; contbr. articles to profl. jours. Chmn. adv. council St. Josephs Hosp. Sch. Nursing, 1967; Trustee, pres. Portage Twp. Sch. Bd., 1968-76; trustee Copper Country Intermediate Sch. Dist., 1975-78. Recipient Faculty Rsch. award, Mich. Technol. U., 1965. Mem. Am. Chem. Soc. (past sect. v.p., chmn.), Rotary, Sigma Xi, Phi Lambda Upsilon. Clubs: Miscowaubik (gov. 1971-74, 79-82), Boscobel Country. Episcopalian. Home: 42498 Lakeshore Dr Chassell MI 49916-9006 also: 129 Leslie Ln Pendleton SC 29670 Home Phone: 800-836-3949. Personal E-mail: jspain.chemskil@prodigy.net.

SPAIN, JAMES WILLIAM, political scientist, writer; b. Chgo., July 22, 1926; s. Patrick Joseph and Mary Ellen (Forristal) S.; m. Edith Burke James, Feb. 21, 1951; children: Patrick, Sikandra, Stephen, William. MA, U. Chgo., 1949; PhD, Columbia U., 1959. Cons. sec. army, 1949—50; with U.S. Fgn. Svc., 1951—53; rschr., lectr. Columbia, 1955—62; mem. policy planning coun. State Dept., 1963—64; dir. Office Rsch. and Analysis for Near East and South Asia, 1964—66; country dir. Pakistan and Afghanistan, 1966—69; charge d'affaires Am. Embassy, Rawapindi, 1969; consul gen. Istanbul, Turkey, 1970-72; minister Am. embassy, Ankara, 1972-74; diplomat-in-residence, vis. prof. history and govt. Fla. State U., Tallahassee, 1974-75; amb. to Tanzania Dar es Salaam, 1975-79; amb., dep. permanent rep. UN, NYC, 1979; amb. to Turkey, Ankara, 1980-81; amb. to Sri Lanka, Colombo, 1985-89; fgn. affairs fellow Carnegie Endowment for Internat. Peace and Rand Corp., Washington, 1982-84; guest resident investor Colombo, Sri Lanka, 1991—. Chmn. Lanka Infrastructure Ltd.; bd. dirs. Hawk Mountain Fed. Express, Ltd.; adj. prof. polit. sci. Am. U., Washington, 1965-67. Author: The Way of the Pathans, 1962, The Pathan Borderland, 1963, American Diplomacy in Turkey, 1984, Pathans of the Latter Day, 1995, Innocents of the Latter Day, 1997, In Those Days: A Diplomat Remembers, 1998, Holding Out in the Eternal City, 2000, The Emperor's Medallion, 2000, The Devils' Mountain, 2000, Digging the Desert, 2000, The Tribsmen's Treasure, 2000, The Monks; Secret, 2000, The Islands' Quota, 2000, Holy Ireland, 2001, Out Beyond, 2002, Innocents, 2002, To Boil a Stew, 2002. Trustee Joseph Frazer Meml. Hosp. With U.S. Army, 1946-47. Fellow Ford Found., 1953-55; recipient Presdl. Exec. award, 1983, Wilbur I. Carr award for Disting. Diplomacy, 1989. Mem. Coun. Fgn. Rels., Washington Inst. Fgn. Affairs, Assn. Diplomatic Studies and Tng., Cosmos Club. Home: Galle Face Ct II # 42 Colombo 3 Sri Lanka Home Phone: 94-11-243-7179; Office Phone: 94-11-243-7179. Personal E-mail: jwspain@sltnet.lk.

SPAIN, MARY ANN, realtor, educator, historian, writer; b. Nashville, May 31, 1950; d. James Ivan Spain and Mary Lou Crocker; m. Don Quitman Reynolds II (div.); m. James Clifford Miller, Oct. 15, 1988 (dec. Aug. 10, 1990). BS, Mid. Tenn. State U., 1972; postgrad., U. Ark., 1982; MAT, Mid. Tenn. State U., 1975, MAT, 1977. Lic. realtor Tenn. Counselor State of Tenn. Dept. Human Svcs., 1972—76; grad. tchg. asst. Mid. Tenn. State U., Murfreesboro, 1974—77; instr. Vol. State C.C., Gallatin, Tenn., 1974—92; grad. tchg. fellow U. Ark., Fayetteville, 1977—82; staff sgt. Chem. Corps, I Corp., 2d Infantry Divsn. U.S. Army, 1983—87; realtor Folk-Jordan Better Homes and Gardens, Nashville, 1987—99; instr. State of Tenn. Real Estate Commn., Nashville, 1995—; realtor Crye-Leike Realtors, Nashville, 1999—. Editor: U.S. Mil. Manuals on Chem. Warfare, Chem. Def., Chem. Ops. Newsletter. Charter mem., founder U.S. Army Nat. Mus., 2004. Decorated Army Commendation medal, Good Conduct medal, Army Achievement medal, Overseas medal; recipient Best Article in State or Local Publ. award, Ark. Hist. Commn., 1981. Mem.: PETA, ASPCA, VFW, Sumner County Realtors Assn. (edn. com. dir., Excellence in Real Estate award 1992—2004, nominee Realtor of Yr. 2003), Tenn. Assn. Realtors, Nat. Assn. Realtors, Women in Mil. Svc. for Am. Meml. Found. (charter), Realtors Polit. Action Group Tenn. Avocations: gardening, fishing, animals, travel, reading. Office: Crye-Leike Realtors 383 Johnny Cash Pky Hendersonville TN 37075 Office Phone: 615-824-8008. E-mail: spainma@realtracs.com.

SPAIN, THOMAS B., retired state supreme court justice; Judge 4th Judicial Cir., Hopkins and Caldwell Counties, 1973—91; justice Ky. Supreme Ct, Frankfort, 1991-95; ret., 1995; of counsel Whitfield & Cox P.S.C. Office: Whitfield & Cox PSC 29 E Center St Madisonville KY 42431-2037 Home Phone: 270-821-4821; Office Phone: 270-821-0656.

SPAINHOUR, J. PATRICK (JAMES PATRICK SPAINHOUR), outsourcing company executive, former apparel executive; b. 1950; married. B, Miss. State Univ., 1972. Positions through v.p. fin. & adminstrn. Kellwood Co., 1972—83; exec. v.p. fin. & ops. Seminole Mfg. Co., 1983; sr. v.p. sourcing Gap Inc., 1988—93; exec. v.p. fin. & ops. Stride Rite Corp., 1993—94; exec. v.p., CFO Donna Karen Co., 1994—96; pres., COO Ann Taylor Stores Corp., 1996, chmn., CEO, 1996—2005; interim chmn., CEO Servicemaster Co., Downers Grove, Ill., 2006, chmn., CEO, 2006—07; CEO Servicemaster Co., Servicemaster lLobal Holdings, Downers Grove, Ill., 2007—. Bd. dir. Tupperware Corp., Circuit City Stores Inc., 2004—, Servicemaster Co., 2005—. Office: Servicemaster Co Ste 600 3250 Lacey Rd Downers Grove IL 60515*

SPAINHOWER, JAMES IVAN, retired college president; b. Stanberry, Mo., Aug. 3, 1928; s. Elmer Enoch and Stella Irene (Cox) S.; m. Joanne Steanson, June 10, 1950; children: Janet Dovell, James Jeffrey. BA, Phillips U., Enid, Okla., 1950, LLD (hon.), 1967; BD, Lexington Theol. Sem., Ky., 1953; MA in Polit. Sci., U. Mo., Columbia, 1967, PhD, 1971, U. Ark., 1954; diploma, U. Pacific Sch. Religion, Berkeley, Calif., 1958; DPA (hon.), Culver-Stockton Coll., 1973; LL.D. (hon.), Maryville Coll., St. Louis, 1976; Litt.D. (hon.), Kirksville Coll. Osteo. Medicine, Mo., 1977; D.H.L. (hon.), Mo. Valley Coll., 1984; LLD (hon.), Eureka Coll., 1989, Lynchburg Coll., 1993. Ordained to ministry Christian Ch. (Disciples of Christ), 1950; pastor chs. in Ark. and Mo., 1953-70; mem. Mo. Ho. of Reps. from, Saline County, 1963-70; pres. Asso. Med. Schs. Mo., Jefferson City, 1970-72; part-time prof. polit. sci. Lincoln U., Jefferson City, 1970-72; treas. State of Mo., 1973-80; pres. Sch. of Ozarks, Point Lookout, Mo., 1981-82, Lindenwood Coll., St. Charles, Mo., 1983-89; pres. divsn. higher edn. Christian Ch. (Disciples of Christ), 1989-93. Author: Pulpit, Pew and Politics, 1979. Chmn. Mo. del. Dem. Nat. Conv., 1976; elected mem. Acad. Squires, 1981; 1st chmn. Mo. Children's Trust Fund, 1984-86. Recipient Mental Health award Mo. Mental Health Assn., 1967, Meritorious Service award St. Louis Globe Dem., 1968, Harry S. Truman award Saline County Young Democrats, 1970, citation of merit Alumni Assn. U. Mo., 1975; named Mo. Lay Educator of Year Mo. chpt. Phi Delta Kappa, 1968 Home and Office: 1616 W Long Blvd Raymore MO 64083 Personal E-mail: jspriny@comcast.net.

SPAKE, MARY BARBARA, music educator; b. Mpls., Apr. 7, 1919; d. Donald Nivison Ferguson and Arline Calista (Folsom); m. Virgil F. Spake, July 2, 1978. BS, U. Minn., 1942, M. Music Edn., 1949. Tchr. Grand Marais (Minn.) Pub. Schs., 1942-43, Litchfield (Minn.) Pub. Schs., 1943-45, Mpls. Pub. Schs., 1945-79, Mpls. Coll. Music, 1949-55, Macalestar Coll., St. Paul, 1950-56; pvt. music tchr. Golden Valley, Minn., 1949—. Asst. choir dir. Cen. Luth. Ch., Mpls., 1946-56; choir dir. Grace U. Luth. Ch., Mpls., 1950-55. Mem. Retired Tchrs. Mpls., Music Educators Nat. Conf., Nat. Assn. Tchrs. of Singing, Sigma Alpha Iota. Avocation: dress making. Home and Office: Apt C227 5800 Saint Croix Ave N Golden Valley MN 55422-4763

SPAKE, REUBEN MICHAEL, mathematics professor, researcher; b. Spokane, Wash., Mar. 20, 1957; s. William Jack and Georgia Geraldine (Christensen) S.; m. Cynthia Spake. BS, U. Calif., Davis, 1978, MA, 1984, PhD, 1986. Mathematician, Edwards AFB, Calif., 1976-79; computer programmer analyst Mgmt. Info. Svcs., Fairfield, Calif., 1979—83; math. teaching asst. U. Calif., Davis, 1983-86; prof. Coll. Charleston, SC, 1987—93; prof. math. Solano CC, Fairfield, Calif., 1993—, Consumnes River Coll., Sacramento, 1994—, San Jacquin Delta Coll., Stockton, Calif., 1994—, Los Medanos Coll., Pitts., 1994—. Pub. power semigroup rsch., 1985—. Recipient Math. Achievement award Bank Am., 1974; Kraft scholar U. Calif., Davis, 1975. Mem. AAAS, SAR, Am. Math. Soc., Math. Assn. Am., NY Acad. Scis., Hereditary Order of First Families Mass., Sons and Daus. of Pilgrims, Sons of the Am. Revolution, Magna Charta Barons, Pi Mu Epsilon, Mu Alpha Theta. Avocations: guitar, music, travel. Office: Solano CC 4000 Suisun Valley Rd Fairfield CA 94534 Personal E-mail: rmspake@yahoo.com.

SPALDING, ANDREW FREEMAN, lawyer; b. Toledo, June 24, 1951; s. Dean and Shirley Louise (Maitland) S.; m. Adele Taylor, May 17, 1980; children: Amy Louise, Adam Freeman, Audrey Wade, Abigail Maitland. BA, U. Calif., Berkeley, 1973; JD, So. Meth. U., 1977. Bar: Tex. 1977, NY 2006, US Dist. Ct. (so., ea. and we. dists.) Tex. 1978, US Ct. Appeals (5th cir.) 1978; bd. cert. civil trial law, personal injury trial law. Assoc. Bracewell & Giuliani, LLP, Houston, 1977-84, ptnr., 1985—. Notes and comments editor So. Meth. U. Law Jour., Dallas, 1976-77. Fellow Tex Bar Found., Houston Bar Found.; mem. State Bar Tex., Houston Bar Assn., Tex. Assn. Def. Counsel, Def. Rsch. Inst., Knights Momus, Krewe Maximilian, Pan Tex. Assembly, Houston Country Club. Office: Bracewell & Giuliani LLP 2300 S Tower Pennzoil Pla 711 Louisiana St Ste 2300 Houston TX 77002-2770 Office Phone: 713-221-1220. Business E-Mail: Andrew.Spalding@bracewellgiuliani.com.

SPALDING, CATHERINE, lawyer; b. Lebanon, Ky. d. Hugh C. and Bernadette (Hill) S. BS in Biology, Spalding U., Louisville, 1970; JD, U. Louisville, 1983. Bar: Ky., U.S. Ct. Appeals (6th cir.), Ct. Vets. Appeals, Fed. Dist. Ct. Pvt. practice law, Louisville, 1983—; asst. county atty. Jefferson County, 1993—2000, family ct. atty., guardian ad litem, 2000—. Editor (book supplement): Kentucky Family Law, 1990. Past bd. dirs. LWV, Portland Mus. Louisville. Mem. ABA, Ky. Bar Assn. (chair family law sect. 1990-91, past newsletter editor, spkr., moderator seminars), Louisville Bar Assn. (chair social security sect. 1992-93), AAUW (past bd. dirs.), DAR (past bd. dirs.) Optimist Club (past bd. dirs.), LWV (past bd. dirs.). Avocation: skiing. Home: 1917 Trevilian Way Louisville KY 40205-2139 Office: 325 W Ormsby Ave Ste 3 Louisville KY 40203-2907

SPALDING, DIANA JOELLE, social worker; d. Richard Sotherin Spalding and Cleah June Finley; children: Nicholas Spalding Early, Marissa Susana Early. BA, U. Colo., Boulder, 1983; MA, Antioch New England Grad. Sch., Keene, NH, 1998. Software engr., Boulder, Colo.; counselor, social worker, psychotherapist, 1985—. Mem. NAACP, So. Poverty Law Ctr., Amnesty Internat., Nature Conservancy; mem. steering com. Boulder Valley Sch. Dist. Parent Coun., 2005—. Buddhism. Avocations: mountain climbing, skiing, bicycling, travel.

SPALDING, JAMES STUART, retired telecommunications industry executive; b. Edinburgh, Nov. 23, 1934; arrived in Can., 1957, permanent resident, 1962; Student, Edinburgh U., 1951-52, Glasgow U., 1953. Gen. mgr., dir. United Corps. Ltd., Montreal, Que., Canada, 1970-72; from pension fund mgr. to exec. v.p. fin. BCE, Inc., Montreal, 1972-90. Mem. Inst. Chartered Accts. Scotland, Order Chartered Accounts Que., Fin. Execs. Inst. Can. (past chmn.), Montreal Soc. Fin. Analysts (past pres.). Home: 126 King St E Brockville ON Canada K6V 1B9 Personal E-mail: stuart231134@aol.com.

SPALDING, WILLIAM R., lawyer, pharmaceutical executive; Sr. ptnr. King & Spalding, LLP, Atlanta, 2001—05; exec. v.p. strategic initiatives Caremark Rx, LLC (formerly Caremark Rx, Inc.), 2005; exec. v.p. strategy and managed care CVS Caremark Corp. Office: CVS Caremark Corp One CVS Dr Woonsocket RI 02895 Office Phone: 401-765-1500. *

SPALTY, EDWARD ROBERT, lawyer; b. New Haven, Oct. 1, 1946; s. Kermit and Elinor Turgeon; m. Suzy Clune; children: Thomas John, Kathleen Tess. BA, Emory U., 1968; JD, Columbia U., 1973. Bar: Mo. 1975, Nebr. 1997, Kans. 1998, Colo. 2003, U.S. Dist. Ct. (we. dist.) Mo. 1975, U.S. Ct. Claims 1977, U.S. Ct. Appeals (8th cir.) 1984, U.S. Ct. Appeals (10th cir.) 1999, U.S. Supreme Ct. 1994, U.S. Dist. Ct. (ea. dist.) Wis. 2004. Assoc. Webster & Sheffield, NYC, 1973-74; mng. ptnr. Armstrong Teasdale LLP, Kansas City, Mo., 1991-2001, ptnr., 1980—. Contbr. articles to profl jours. Chmn. bd. dirs. Mo. Easter Seals, 1990—92; founding mem. Heartland Franchise Assn.; bd. dirs., mem. exec. com. Nat. Easter Seal Soc.; bd. dirs. Mo. Easter Seals, 1984—. With US Army, 1968—70. Named a Superlawyer, Mo., 2006, Kans., 2006; named Best of the Bar, Kans. City Bus. Jour., 2006; named one of Best Lawyers in Am., Chambers USA, 2007—, Woodward White, 1995—; recipient BTI Client Svc. award, Chambers USA, 2007. Mem.: ABA (litigation sect, franchising forum comt), Intern. Rels. Coun. Kansas City, Def. Rsch. Inst., Mo. Orgn. Def. Attys., Lawyers Assn. Kansas City, Kansas City Met. Bar Assn. (chmn antitrust and franchise law comt, co-chair 14th and 16h ann Nat Franchise

Law Inst), Mo. Bar Assn. (civil rules and procedures comt), Lex Mundi (regional vice chair N.Am. dispute resolution, antitrust practice group), German-Am C. of C. (v.p. Kansas City chpt), Nat. Golf Club Kansas City (founder), Phi Delta, Pi Sigma Alpha, Sigma Nu. Home: 13703 NW 73rd St Parkville MO 64152-1120 Office: Armstrong Teasdale LLP 2345 Grand Blvd Ste 2000 Kansas City MO 64108-2617 Office Phone: 816-221-3420. Business E-Mail: espalty@armstrongteasdale.com.

SPALVINS, JANIS GUNARS, steamship company executive; b. Riga, Latvia, May 26, 1936; arrived in Australia, 1949; s. Peter Spalvins and Hilda (Dritmanis) Blumentals; m. Cecily Westall Rymill, Dec. 16, 1961; children: John Rymill and Richard Rymill. B in Econ. Group sec., dir. Camelec Group of Cos., South Australia, 1955-73; asst. gen. mgr. The Adelaide Steamship Co. Ltd., South Australia, 1973-77, chief gen. mgr., dir., 1977-81, mng. dir., 1981-90; dir., chief exec. David Jones Ltd., Australia, 1980, 1988—91; dir. Macmahon Holdings, Ltd., 1987—92; chmn., dir. Galufo Pty. Ltd., 1991—. Fellow Australian Inst. Mgmt., Australian Soc. CPAs, Inst. Chartered Accts., Inst. Dirs., Chartered Inst. Secs., Cruising Yacht of SA, Mt. Osmond Golf Club. Avocations: sailing, tennis, snow and water skiing. Home: 2 Brookside Rd Springfield SA 5061 Australia Office Phone: 618 83792965. Personal E-mail: jgspalvins@bigpond.com.

SPANBOCK, MAURICE SAMUEL, lawyer; b. NYC, Jan. 6, 1924; s. Benjamin and Belle (Ward) S.; m. Marion Rita Heyman, Nov. 21, 1954; children: Jonathan H., Betsy W. BA, Columbia U., NYC, 1944; LLB, Harvard U., 1950. Bar: N.Y. 1950. Ptnr. Carro and Spanbock (name changed to Carro, Spanbock, Kaster et al), NYC, 1952-94; of counsel Kleinberg Kaplan Wolff & Cohen, NYC, 1994—. Trustee Carnegie Coun., NYC, 1980-86, 93-00, chmn. bd., 1987-92, hon. trustee, 2002-; hon. pres. Lincoln Square Synagogue, NYC; sec. Ohr Torah Stone Instns. Israel. Cpl. AUS, 1943-46, ETO. Mem. ABA (chmn. com. on taxation, patent, trademark and copyright law sect. 1979-81), Assn. of Bar of City of N.Y. (com. on copyright 1965-67, art law com. 1977-80, 86-88), Fed. Bar Coun., Nat. Panel Arbitrators, Am. Abitration Assn., Practising Law Inst. (panel on copyrights, 1979). Jewish. Home: 88 Central Park W New York NY 10023-5209 Office: Kleinberg Kaplan Wolff & Cohen 551 5th Ave Fl 18 New York NY 10176-1800 Office Phone: 212-880-9852.

SPANDER, DEBORAH L., lawyer; b. 1969; BA in Polit. Sci. with honors and distinction, Stanford U., 1991; JD, UCLA, 1995. Bar: Calif. 1995. Mgr. bus. and legal affairs BLT Prodn., Inc., LA, 1994—96; assoc. Law Offices of Maidie E. Oliveau, 1996—97; dir. bus. and legal affairs Fox Sports Network, LA, 1998—2001; v.p. bus. and legal affairs Fox Cable Networks Group, LA, 2002—. Guest lectr. UCLA Sch. Law, 1999—2001; adv. bd. mem. Nat. Sports Law Inst., Marquette U. Law Sch. Vol. Friends of Break The Cycle, LA, 1996—. Mem.: Stanford West LA Club, Westcoast Sports Assoc., Women's Entertainment Network, Sports Lawyers Assn. (bd. mem., mem. program com., moderator and spkr. Nat. Conf. 2003—04, spkr. Nat. Conf. 1997—2002). Avocations: tennis, swimming, skiing, travel, cooking.

SPANDORFER, MERLE SUE, artist, educator, writer; b. Balt., Sept. 4, 1934; d. Simon Louis and Bernice P. (Jacobson) S.; m. Lester M. Spandorfer, June 17, 1956; children: Cathy, John. Student, Syracuse U., 1952-54; BS, U. Md., 1956. Mem. faculty Cheltenham (Pa.) Sch. Fine Arts, 1969—; instr. printmaking Tyler Sch. Art Temple U., Phila., 1980-84; faculty Pratt Graphics Ctr., NYC, 1985-86. One woman shows include Richard Feigen Gallery, N.Y.C., 1970, U. Pa., 1974, Phila. Coll. Textiles and Sci., 1977, Ericson Gallery, N.Y.C., 1978, 79, R.I. Sch. Design, 1980, Syracuse U., 1981, Marian Locks Gallery, Phila., 1973, 78, 82, Temple U., 1984, Tyler Sch. Art, 1985, University City Sci. Ctr., 1987, Gov.'s Residence, 1988, Wenninger Graphics Gallery, Provinceton, Mass., 1989, Widener U. Art Mus., 1995, Gloucester County Coll., 1996, Mangel Gallery, 1992, 97, 2000, 03, 06, Cabrini Coll., 1999, Mangel Gallery, 2006, Fireside Gallery, Devon, Pa., 2007; group shows Bklyn. Mus. Art, 1973, San Francisco Mus. Art, 1973, Balt. Mus. Art, 1970, 71, 74, Phila. Mus. Art, 1972, 77, Fundacio Joan Miro. Barcelona, Spain, 1977, Del. Mus. Art, Wilmington, 1978, Carlsberg Glyptotek Mus., Copenhagen, 1980, Moore Coll. Art, Phila., 1982, Tyler Sch. Art, 1983, William Penn Meml. Mus., Harrisburg, Pa., 1984, Ariz. State U., 1985, Tiajin Fine Arts Coll., China, 1986, Beaver Coll., Phila., 1988, The Port of History Mus., Phils., 1987, Sichuan Fine Arts Inst., Chong Qing, China, 1988, Glynn Vivian Mus., Swansea, Wales, 1989, Phila. Mus. Art, 1990, Fgn. Mus., Riga, Latvia, 1995, Woodmere Art Mus., Phila., 1996, Am. Coll., 1997, Cheltenham Ctr. for the Arts, Phila., 1997, Rowan Coll., 1997, Villanova U., 1998, U. Pa., 1999, U. of the Arts, 2001, others; represented in permanent collections Met. Mus. Art, N.Y.C., Whitney Mus. Am. Art, N.Y.C., Paper Mus., Kyoto, Japan, Mus. Modern Art, N.Y.C., The Israel Mus., Balt. Mus. (gov.'s prize and purchase award 1970), Phila. Mus. Art (purchase award 1977), Toyoh Bijutsu Gakko, Tokyo, Library of Congress, Temple U., Colgate U., Reading Mus.; commd. works represented in U. Pa. Inst. Comtemporary Art, 1991; co-author: Making Art Safely, 1993 Recipient award Balt. Mus. Art/Md. Inst. Art, 1971, Govs. prize and Purchase award Balt. Mus. Art, 1970, Outstanding Art Educators award Pa. Art Edn. Assn., 1982, Purchase award Berman Mus., 1995, Artist Equity award, 1996; grantee Pa. Coun. Arts, 1989. Mem. Am. Color Print Soc., Pa. Art Edn. Assn. Jewish. Office: 307 E Gowen Ave Philadelphia PA 19119-1023 Home Phone: 215-379-2813. Personal E-mail: merlespandorfer@comcast.net.

SPANEL, HARRIET, state legislator; b. Audubon, Iowa, Jan. 15, 1939; 3 children. BS in Math., Iowa State U., 1961. Mem. Wash. Ho. of Reps., 1987-93, Wash. Senate, Dist. 40, Olympia, 1993—. Cath. Office: Wash Senate PO Box 40440 Olympia WA 98504-0440

SPANFELLER, JAMES JOHN, JR., publishing executive; b. Phila., Aug. 25, 1956; s. James John Sr. and Patricia Ann (Durkin) S. BA, Union Coll., Schenectedy, NY, 1979. Assoc. pub. Soho News, NYC, 1979-81; dir. Alan Western Communications, NYC, 1981-83; pub. Newsweek on Campus, NYC, 1983-86; nat. sales mgr. Newsweek, NYC, 1986—, sales dir., 1987-89; assoc. pub., sr. v.p. Playboy Mag., 1989-93; pub. Inc. mag., 1993—96, Ziff-Davis Yahoo! Internet Life, 1996—98; v.p. Yahoo! Internet Life, 1998-2000, 1998—2000; pres., CEO Forbes.com, 2001—. Mem. mktg. com. Mag. Pub. Assoc.; bd. dirs. Am. Bus. Media, 2004—. Author: The Fantastic Airplane, 1979. Mem.: N.Y. Athletic. Office Phone: 212-366-8999. Office Fax: 212-366-8801. *

SPANGLER, CLEMMIE DIXON, JR., construction company executive; b. Charlotte, NC, Apr. 5, 1932; s. Clemmie Dixon and Veva C. (Yelton) S.; m. Meredith Jane Riggs, June 25, 1960; children: Anna Wildy, Abigail Riggs. BS, U. N.C., 1954; MBA, Harvard U., 1956; LHD (hon.), Queens Coll., 1985; LLD (hon.), Davidson Coll., 1986, Furman U., 1993; LLD U. N. Carolina (hon.), 2003. Pres. C.D. Spangler Constrn. Co., Charlotte, 1958-86, Golden Eagle Industries, Inc., 1968-86; chmn. bd. Bank of N.C., Raleigh, 1973-82; dir. NCNB Corp., 1983-86; chmn. N.C. Bd. Edn., 1982-86; pres. U. N.C., Chapel Hill, 1986-97; CEO, chmn. C.D. Spangler Constrn. Co., Charlotte, 1997—. Bd. dirs. BellSouth Corp., Atlanta; chmn. bd. dirs. Nat. Gypsum Co., Charlotte. Past deacon Myers Park Bapt. Ch., vice-chmn. Charlotte-Mecklenburg Bd. Edn., Charlotte, 1972-76; past trustee Charlotte Symphony Orch., Crozer Theol. Sem.; past chmn. Charlotte adv. bd. Salvation Army; past bd. dirs. YMCA, Equitable Life Assurance Soc., Jefferson-Pilot Corp.; pres. bd. trustees Mint Mus. Art; bd. dirs. Union Theol. Sem., 1985-90, Assocs. Harvard Bus. Sch.; pres. bd. overseers Harvard Coll., 2003. With U.S. Army, 1956-58. Recipient Liberty Bell award Mecklenburg County Bar Assn., 1985, Alumni Achievement award Harvard Bus. Sch., 1988; named one of Forbes' Richest Americans, 2006. Mem. Assn. Am. Univs., Bus. Higher Edn. Forum, Harvard Club (N.Y.C.), Univ. Club (N.Y.C.), Quail Hollow Country Club (Charlotte). Office: CD Spangler Constrn Co Office of Chmn Box 36007 Charlotte NC 28236-6007

SPANGLER, COLLEEN ANN, marketing professional; b. Toledo, Aug. 14, 1938; d. Irvin Frederick Callahan and Eileen Rose Carey-Callahan; m. Richard Leon Blass (dec.); children: Edie Stacey, Vicki Schramm, Rick Blass; m. Joseph Carl Spangler, Dec. 12, 1977 (dec.); children: Tracy, Scott Splanger. Vol. coord. Lucas County Dem., Toledo, 1986—89; exec. dir. Arcadia Main St. Program, Fla., 1991—93, Arcadia C. of C., 1993—95; promotion dir. Up River Adventure, Nocatee, Fla., 1995—98; mktg. specialist Suncoast Cmty. Blood Bank, Arcadia, 1995—98; mktg. dir. Arcadia Oaks Assisted Living, 1997—2000; mktg. specialist Suncoast Cmty. Blood Bank, Arcadia, 2000—. Mem. DeSoto Home Health Profl. Adv. Com.; adv. coun. mem. DeSoto County Sr. Friendship Ctr.; treas. Voluntary Orgns. Active in Disaster; chair DeSoto County Dem. Exec. Com.; mem. Dem. Nat. Com.; Eucharistic min., parish coun. mem. St. Paul Cath. Ch.; bd. dirs. DeSoto County Econ. Devel. Coun. Mem.: Amvet Aux., Ladies of Moose. Democrat. Roman Catholic. Avocations: reading, needlecrafts, cooking, travel. Home: 1269 SE Tangelo Dr Arcadia FL 34266

SPANGLER, DAVID ROBERT, academic administrator, engineer, educator; b. Flint, Mich., Aug. 17, 1940; s. John Solomon and Margaret Inger (McKinley) S.; m. Sally Jeanne Henry, Aug. 28, 1965; children: Timothy David, Megan Marie. BS, U.S. Mil. Acad., 1962; MS in Engrng., U. Ill., 1966, PhD in Structural Dynamics, 1977. Registered profl. engr. Commd. 2d lt. U.S. Army, 1962, advanced through grades to lt. col., 1979, prof. math. U.S. Mil. Acad. West Point, N.Y., 1968-71, engr. Korea Support Command, 1972-73, dep. dist. engr. C.E. Walla Walla, Wash., 1973-74, research coordinator Def. Nuclear Agy. Washington, 1976-79, bn. comdr. Hawaii, 1979-81, inspector C.E. San Francisco, 1981-82, ret., 1982; prof. engrng. St. Martin's Coll., Lacey, Wash., 1982-84, pres., 1984—. Mem. Nat. Com. for Tunnelling Tech., Washington, 1977-79; cons. Thurston County, Olympia, Wash., 1982-84. Contbr. articles to profl. jours. Bd. dirs. Econ. Devel. Coun., Thurston County, 1985-88, Wash. State Capitol Mus., 1988-91. Decorated Bronze Star with 2 oak leaf clusters, Meritorious Service medal, Def. Nuclear Agy. Joint Service medal. Mem. Soc. Mil. Engrs. (v.p. 1980-81, pres. 1973-74), Nat. Assn. Ind. Colls. and Univs. (bd. dirs. 1992-95, treas. 1994), Ind. Colls. Wash. (bd. dirs.), Assn. Benedictine Colls. and Univs. (pres. 1994-95), Rotary (mem. gov.'s oversight com. on tech. 1996—). Roman Catholic. Avocation: running. Office: St Martins Coll Office of Pres Lacey WA 98503

SPANGLER, DENNIS LEE, physician; b. Akron, Ohio, Nov. 8, 1947; s. Wesley Daniel and Florence Adele (Smith) S.; m. July 7, 1972; children: Mathew Brian, Adam Christopher. BS, U. Akron, 1969; MD, Ohio State Med. Sch., 1973. Diplomate Am. Bd. Pediatrics, Am. Bd. Allergy and Immunology. Intern U. Fla. Med. Sch., Gainesville, 1973-74, resident, 1974-75, fellow allergy and clin. immunology, 1975-77; pvt. practice Atlanta Allergy Clinic, P.A., 1977—; chief med. officer Atlanta Allergy and Asthma Clinic, 1995—. Dir. chronic lung clinic Ga. Bur. Crippled Children, 1984-97; asst. clin. prof. pediatrics Med. Coll. of Ga., 1980-2001; vice chair divsn. of allergy Children's Healthcare of Atlanta, 2000—. Past pres., bd. dirs. midwest branch Ga. Lung Assn., Atlanta, 1981-82, med. adv. com., 1978-97; pres. Fla. Pediatric Alumni Assn., Gainesville, 1985-86. Fellow Am. Acad. Pediatrics, Am. Acad. Allergy and Immunology, Am. Coll. Allergy, Asthma and Immunology (therapeutics com. 1983-88, chmn. drug and anaplylaxis com. 1988-2003, chmn. com. 1987-2004, bd. regents 1996-99), Am. Assn. Cert. Allergists (bd. govs. 1988—, bd. sec. 1997, v.p. 1998, pres. elect 1999, pres. 2000); mem. Am. Thoracic Soc., Ga. Med. Assn., Cobb County Med. Soc., Southeastern Allergy Assn., Cherokee Country Club. Roman Catholic. Avocations: scuba diving, creating stain glass windows. Office: Atlanta Allergy Asthma Clinic 1965 N Park Pl Atlanta GA 30339-2012 Office Phone: 770-952-1071.

SPANGLER, EDRA MILDRED, psychologist; b. Webbville, Ky., Sept. 6, 1941; d. Chester A. and Laura B. (Webb) Sawyer; m. Robert Noel Spangler, Sept. 6, 1959; children: Robert Mark Spangler, Kendra Lynn Lovett. AS in Bus. Adminstrn., Franklin U., 1975; BA in Social Psychology, Park Coll., 1979; MA in Mgmt. and Supervision, Ctrl. Mich. U., 1980; D in Psychology, Wright State U., 1989. Lic. psychologist Ohio, Fla.; diplomate clin. hypnotherapy; diplomate Am. Bd. Psychol. Specialties in Med. Psychology, Forensic Clin. Psychology and Neuropsychology. With adminstrn., mgmt., fin. and computer sys. design various pvt. and govt. orgns., 1958-85; psychology assoc. Stonegate Psychol. Assocs., Columbus, Ohio, 1989-91; dir. pain & stress program The Rehab. Ctr., Columbus, 1991-94; pvt. practice, 1991—; mem. med. staff Riverside Meth. Hosps., Columbus, 1992—; health psychologist Mind/Body Med. Inst., 1993-95; mem. med. staff Grady Meml. Hosp., Delaware, Ohio, 1997—2004. Fellow Biofeedback Cert. Inst. Am., Am. Coll. Forensic Examiners; mem. Ohio Psychol. Assn., Fla. Psychol. Assn., Assn. Applied Psychophysiology and Biofeedback. Avocations: reading, travel, hiking, research in mind/body.

SPANGLER, JOHN L, III, lawyer; b. York, Pa., Jan. 6, 1956; AB, Univ. Ill., 1977; JD, Washington Univ., 1980. Bar: Ga. 1980. Ptnr., head, construction law group Alston & Bird LLP, Atlanta. Editl.bd. Georgia Bar Jour., contbr. Georgia Appellate Practice Handbook. (Amicus Curiae award, Ga. Supreme Ct. for his work, 1986), frequent spkr. on construction law. Mem.: ABA, Atlanta Bar Assn. (chmn., construction law sect. 1994—95). Office: Alston & Bird LLP One Atlantic Plz 1201 W Peachtree St NW Atlanta GA 30309-3424 Office Phone: 404-881-7146. Office Fax: 404-881-7777. Business E-Mail: jspangler@alston.com.

SPANGLER, NITA REIFSCHNEIDER, volunteer; b. Ukiah, Calif., Apr. 17, 1923; d. John Charles and Olga Augusta (Wuertz) Reifschneider; m. Raymond Luper Spangler, Sept. 22, 1946 (dec.); children: Jon Martin, Mary Raymond, Thor Raymond. BA, Univ. Nev., 1944. News reporter Redwood (Calif.) City Tribune, 1944-46, Country Almanac, Woodside, Calif., 1969-77. Mem. bd. dirs. San Mateo (Calif.) County Hist. Assn., 1961-68, pres., 1964-66; founder, 1st pres. Portolá Expedition Bicentennial Found., 1966-70; chmn. San Mateo County Scenic Rds. Com., 1967-76; mem. San Mateo County Hist. Resource Adv.; mem. commn. San Mateo County Parks and Recreation, 1983-97, past chmn.; cons. hwy. aesthetics Cal Trans., 1981-83; mem. sch. coms. Recipient Commendation, County Bd. Suprs., 1968, 1977, 92. Mem. Sierra Club, Western History Assn., Mormon History Assn., Nev. State Hist. Soc. (life), San Mateo County Hist. Assn. (life), Resolution of Thanks 1968, 76, 94), Friends Redwood City, Kappa Alpha Theta. Democrat. Episcopalian. Avocation: historic preservation. Home: 970 Edgewood Rd Redwood City CA 94062-1818

SPANGLER, RONALD LEROY, retired television and aircraft executive, automobile consultant; b. York, Pa., Mar. 5, 1937; s. Ivan L. and Sevilla (Senft) S.; m. Svetlana Gavrilova; children: Kathleen, Ronald Jr., Beth Anne, Pavel. Student, U. Miami, Coral Gables, 1955-59. Radio announcer Sta. WSBA, York, 1955-59; TV prodr. Sta. WBAL-TV, Balt. and NBC TV, 1958-65; pres., chmn. bd. LewRon Television, NYC, Hollywood, Calif., 1965-78, Spanair Inc.; distbr. Rockwell bus. aircraft, 1975-85. Owner Prancing Horse Farm; dealer vintage and modern Ferrari automobiles; racer numerous courses including LeMans, Daytona, Sebring; racer vintage and modern Ferrari automobiles; Ferrari cons. (PBS show) Motorweek; cons. Bentley Motor Cars, Pininfarina S.P.A.; North Am. rep. Pinin Farina Automotive Design, 2005—. Mem. Video Tape Producers Assn. NYC, Rolls Royce Owners Club, Ferrari Clubs Am. and Italia, Mercedes Benz Club Am., Porsche Club Am. Avocation: antique automobile collector. Home: Prancing Horse Farm 3710 Ady Rd Street MD 21154-1432 Office Phone: 410-452-5500. Personal E-mail: PHFarmFerrari@aol.com.

SPANGLER, STANLEY EUGENE, international relations educator; b. Billings, Mont., Apr. 7, 1929; s. John Harold Spangler and Winifred Watt; m. Addie Belle Moore, Sept. 21, 1968; children: John Wayland Spangler, Julia Watt Spangler Garlatz. BA, U. Mont., 1952; MA, Columbia U., 1958; PhD, U. N.C., 1978. Program officer Asia Found., San Francisco, 1960-65; assoc. regional dir. Fgn. Policy Assn., Atlanta, 1965-69; dir. Office Pub. and Internat. Affairs U. N.C. Extension Divsn., Chapel Hill, 1969-73; exec. dir. World Affairs Coun. Boston, 1973-81; internat. program advisor Fletcher Sch. Law and Diplomacy, Medford, Mass., 1983-84; sr. fellow Air Univ. USAF, 1984-89; Sec. of Navy sr. fellow U.S. Naval War Coll., Newport, R.I., 1989-92, sr. fellow, prof. strategy, 1993—. Prof. govt. and fgn. affairs Bentley Coll., Waltham, Mass., 1995—; commr. U.S. Nat. Commn. for UNESCO, Washington, 1976-81; pres. Nat. Coun. World Affairs Orgns., Washington, 1977-80; mem. editl. adv. bd. Fgn. Policy Assn., N.Y.c., 1975-78; exec. mem. Nat. Def. Exec. Res., Washington, 1980-97. Author: Force and Accommodation in World Politics, 1991; contbr. articles to profl. jours. Dir. Curtis-Saval Internat. Ctr., Boston, 1976-81; mem. exec. com., bd. dirs. Ala. World Affairs Coun., Montgomery, 1986-89; bd. dirs. Ctr. for Internat. Visitors, Boston, 1978-81; mem. African studies adv. com. Boston U., 1978-80. Capt. USAF, 1954-56. Johns Hopkins U. fellow, 1952-53; Columbia U. scholar, 1957-58. Mem. AAUP, Am. Polit. Sci. Assn., Boston Com. on Fgn. Rels., Phi Beta Delta. Democrat. Methodist. Avocations: hiking, writing, travel, reading. Home: 17 Kings Way Scituate MA 02066-2609 Business E-Mail: s.spangler@bentley.edu.

SPANIER, GRAHAM BASIL, academic administrator; b. Capetown, South Africa, July 18, 1948; s. Fred and Rosadele (Lurie) Spanier; m. Sandra Kay Whipple, Sept. 11, 1971; children: Brian Lockwood, Hadley Alison. BS, Iowa State U., 1969, MS, 1971, Doctorate (hon.), 2006; PhD, Northwestern U., 1973. Assoc. dean, prof. in charge Pa. State U., University Park, 1973—82, pres., 1995—; vice-provost, prof. SUNY, Stony Brook, 1982—86; provost, v.p. for acad. affairs Oreg. State U., 1986—91; chancellor U. Nebr., Lincoln, 1991—95. Chmn. Presdl. Adv. Group on Info. Tech., 1997—99, Kellogg Commn. on Future of State and Land-Grant Univs., 1997—2000; bd. dirs. Univ. Corp. for Advanced Internet Devel., U.S. Dept. Edn. Commn. on Opportunity in Athletics, 2002—03; host TV and radio programs, 1973—; bd. dirs. Citizens Bank Pa., Jr. Achievement Worldwide; trustee Univs. Rsch. Assn., 2001—05; vice-chmn. Worldwide Univ. Network, 2003—; chair Nat. Security Higher Edn. Adv. Bd., 2005—. Founding editor: Jour. Family Issues. Del. White House Conf. on Families, Washington, 1980; pres., chmn. bd. dirs. Christian Children's Fund, Richmond, Va., 1985—94; bd. dirs. Nat. 4H Coun., 1997—2000. Named Outstanding Young Alumnus, Iowa State U., 1982, Disting. Alumnus, 2005; Woodrow Wilson fellow, 1972. Mem.: Assn. Am. Univs. (com. intellectual property 1997—), Acad. Health Ctrs. (commn. on future of acad. health ctrs. 1996—98), Am. Assn. State Colls. and Univs. (joint commn. on accountability report 1993—95), Nat. Collegiate Athletic Assn. (pres. commn. 1995—97, bd. dirs., exec. com. 1997—2001, divsn. I bd. dirs., chmn. 1998—2001), Am. Coun. on Edn. (commn. on women 1992—95), Nat. Assn. State Univs. and Land Grant Colls. (exec. com. coun. on acad. affairs 1990—91, bd. pres. commn. on info. technologies 1993—99, chmn. 1996—99, bd. dirs. 1997—, chmn. coun. of pres. 1999—2000, bd. chair 2002), Am. Assn. Family and Consumer Scis. (Moran award 1972), Am. Sociol. Assn. (family sect. chmn. 1983—84), Population Assn. Am., Nat. Coun. Family Rels. (pres. 1987—88, Outstanding Grad. Student award 1972), Am. Assn. for Marriage and Family Therapy, Worldwide Univs. Network (vice chair 2003—). Democrat. Avocations: aviation, magic, athletics, public broadcasting. Office: Pa State Univ Office of Pres 201 Old Main University Park PA 16802-1503

SPANJOL, JELENA, finance educator; d. Petar and Svetlana Spanjol; m. Adade A. Deganus, May 1, 2004; 1 child, Mihajlo-Joshua Foali Deganus. PhD, U. Ill., Champaign-Urbana, 2002, BS, 1995. Internat. mktg. coord./bus. devel. mgr. Wolfram Rsch., Champaign, 1996—97; asst. prof. Tex. A&M U., Coll. Sta., 2002—06, U. Ill., Chgo., 2006—. Faculty advisor Am. Mktg. Assn., Tex. A&M U. Student Chpt., 2003—06. Contbr. articles to profl. jours., chapters to books. Grantee Richard D. Irwin fellowship, U. Ill., 2001; Mays Bus. Sch. Summer Rsch. grant, Tex. A&M U., 2004. Mem.: INFORMS, Product Devel. & Mgmt. Assn., Acad. Mgmt., Am. Mktg. Assn. (co-chair mktg. strategy, summer conf. 2007). Office: U Ill Chgo 601 S Morgan St Univ Hall 2214 Chicago IL 60607

SPANN, GEORGE WILLIAM, management consultant; b. Cuthbert, Ga., July 21, 1946; s. Glinn Linwood and Mary Grace (Hiller) S.; m. Laura Jeanne Nason, June 10, 1967; children: Tanya Lynne, Stephen William. BS in Physics with honors, Ga. Inst. Tech., 1968, MS, 1970, MS in Indsl. Mgmt., 1973. Engr. Martin Marietta Corp., Orlando, Fla., 1968-70; rsch. scientist Engring. Exptl. Sta., Ga. Inst. Tech., 1970-75; v.p., dir. Metrics, Inc., mgmt. and engrng. cons., Atlanta, 1973-78, pres., dir., 1978—; v.p., dir. Exec. Data Sys., Inc., 1981—. Mem. Ga. Energy Policy Coun., Ga. Metrication Coun., NASA applications survey group for Landsat follow-on; mem. com. on practical applications of remote sensing from space Space Applications Bd. NRC; market rsch. cons. NOAA, NASA, pvt. cos. Contbr. articles to profl. jours. Regents scholar, 1964. Mem. Am. Soc. Photogrammetry, Urban and Regional Info. Sys. Assn., Atlanta Jaycees, Tau Beta Pi, Phi Kappa Phi, Sigma Pi Sigma. Home: 3475 Clubland Dr Marietta GA 30068-2509 Office: Bldg 14 1640 Powers Ferry Rd SE Marietta GA 30067-5491

SPANO, ROBERT, conductor, music director; b. Conneaut, Ohio, May 7, 1961; Grad., Oberlin Conservatory Music; student, Curtis Inst. Music; D (hon.), Bowling Green State U., 2004. Faculty Oberlin (Ohio) Conservatory of Music, 1989—; asst. condr. Boston Symphony Orch., 1990—93; music dir. Bklyn. Philharm. Orch., 1996—2004; musical dir., Robert Reid Topping chair Atlanta Symphony Orch., Atlanta, 1997—. Faculty mem. Tanglewood Music Ctr., head conducting fellowship program, 1998—2000, dir. of Festival of Contemporary Music, 2003—04; guest condr. Chgo. Symphony Orch., Boston Symphony Orch., Houston Symphony Orch., San Francisco Symphony Orch., Cleve. Orch., L.A. Philharm., Nat. Symphony Orch., Phila. Orch., Royal Opera Covent Gardens, Welsh Nat. Opera, Orch. Filharmonica della Scala, City of Birmingham Symphony. Musician (piano): (chamber concerts) Atlanta Symphony, Brooklyn Philharm, Boston Symphony, Oberlin Conservatory; recordings include Rimsky-Korsakov: Scheherazade and Vaughan Williams: A Sea Symphony, Del Tredici: Paul Revere's Ride and Theofanidis: The Here and Now, Berlioz Requiem, Atlanta Symphony Orch. (Grammy award for Best Choral Performance, 2005), Golijov's Ainadamar: Fountain of Tears (Grammy award for Best Opera Performance, 2007), featured on (TV series) City Arts, PBS, Breakfast with the Arts, A&E, Late Show with David Letterman, CBS, Sunday Morning, (TV special) Sound Choices - Inside the ASO with Monica Kaufman, WSB-TV. Office: Atlanta Symphony Orch 1293 Peachtree St NE Ste 300 Atlanta GA 30309-3552 *

SPANOGLE, ROBERT WILLIAM, marketing and advertising company executive, association administrator; b. Lansing, Mich., Nov. 13, 1942; s. William P. and Mary A. (Lenneman) S.; m. Ruth Ann Long, Jan. 14, 1967; children: John Paul Stephen Donald, Amy Lynn. AA, Lansing C.C., 1969; BA, Mich. State U., 1971; postgrad., U. Pa., 1985. Cons. Nat. League Cities, Washington, 1971-72, Am. Legion, Indpls., 1972-75, dir. membership, 1975-79, exec. dir. Washington, 1975-81, nat. adjutant, 1981—; chmn. HP Direct, Inc., Indpls., 1985—, chmn. exec. com. Washington, 1989—. Mem. individual investors adv. com. N.Y. Stock Exch., N.Y.C., 1989-92. Bd. govs. USO, Washington, 1986-92, Childrens Miracle Network, 2001—; trustee St. Mary of the Woods Coll., Terre Haute, Ind., 1991-2001; treas. Civil War Battle Flags Commn. State of Ind., Indpls., 1994—; sec. 500 Festival Assocs., Indpls., 1985-91; mem. Vet.'s Day Coun., Indpls., 1989; bd. dirs. Indpls. Athletic Club, 1989-93, Crossroads Coun. Boy Scouts Am., 1985-92; civilian aide Sec. Army India, 2003-. With U.S. Army, 1962-65. Recipient Silver Buffalo award, Nat. Council Boy Scouts Am., 2004. Mem. Am. Legion of Mich. (Hon. Comdr. 1985), Kiwanis (exec. com. 1989-92). Roman Catholic. Avocations: golf, hunting, reading. Home: 7420 Killarney Dr Indianapolis IN 46217-5472 Office: Am Legion 700 N Pennsylvania St Indianapolis IN 46204-1129

SPANOS, ALEXANDER GUS, construction and professional sports team executive; b. Stockton, Calif., Sept. 28, 1923; m. Faye Spanos; children: Dean, Dea Spanos Berberian, Alexis Spanos Ruhl, Michael. LLD (hon.), U. Pacific, 1984, Eureka Coll., 1984; DHL (hon.), Wayne State Coll., 2003, Calif. Polytechnic State U., 2004, Anatolia Coll., Thessaloniki, Greece, 2004; HHD (hon.), Hellenic Coll., 2004, Holy Cross Greek Orthodox Sch. Theology, 2004. Chmn. bd. dirs. A.G. Spanos Constrn. Inc., Stockton, Calif., 1960—; chmn. bd. dirs. A.G. Spanos Mgmt. Inc., Stockton, Calif., 1967—, A.G. Spanos Enterprises Inc., Stockton, Calif., 1971—, A.G. Spanos Devel. Inc., Stockton, Calif., 1973—, A.G. Spanos Realty Inc., Stockton, Calif., 1978—, A.G.S. Fin. Corp., Stockton, Calif., 1980—, A.G. Spanos Securities Corp., Stockton, Calif., 1981—, San Diego Chargers, 1984—. Chmn. bd. dirs. AGS Internat. Corp., Stockton, Calif., The Spanos Corp., Stockton, A.G. Spanos Ventures, Stockton, AGS Comms., LLC, Stockton. Former trustee Children's Hosp., San Francisco, San Francisco Fine Arts Mus.; trustee Eisenhower Med. Ctr., Rancho Mirage, Calif., John F. Kennedy Ctr. Performing Arts; hon. regent U. Pacific, Stockton, 1972-82; gov. USO, Washington, 1982—; former gov. Ronald Reagan Presdl. Found.; chmn. U.S. chpt. U.S. Greece bus. coun. Served with USAF, 1942-46. Recipient Albert Gallatin award Zurich-Am. Ins. Co., 1973, Horatio Alger award Horatio Alger Found., 1982, medal of Honor Statue of Liberty-Ellis Islan Found., 1982; named one of Forbes' Richest Americans, 2006. Mem. Am. Hellenic Ednl. Progressive Assn., Calif. C. of C. (bd. dirs. 1980-85). Republican. Greek Orthodox. Avocation: golf. Office: San Diego Chargers Qualcomm Stadium PO Box 609609 San Diego CA 92160-9609 also: A G Spanos Cos 10100 Trinity Pkwy 5th Fl Stockton CA 95219 Business E-Mail: agspr@agspanos.com.

SPANOS, POL DIMITRIOS, engineering educator; b. Messini, Peloponnesus, Greece, Feb. 27, 1950; came to U.S., 1973; s. Dimitrios Constandin Spanos and Aicaterine Polychronis Bonaros; children: Demetri, Eudokia. Diploma in mech. engring., Nat. Tech. U., Athens, 1973; MSCE, Calif. Inst. Tech., 1974, PhD in Applied Mechanics, 1976. Registered profl. engr., Tex., Greece. Rsch. asst. Calif. Inst. Tech., Pasadena, 1973-76, rsch. fellow, 1976-77; from asst. prof. to assoc. prof. U. Tex.-Austin, 1981-84, P.D. Henderson assoc. prof. engring., 1983-84; prof. mech. engring. and civil engring. Rice U., Houston, 1984-88, L.B. Ryon endowed chair in engring., 1988—. Cons. on analytical and numerical applications of theory of dynamics and vibrations, worldwide. Author: Random Vibrations, Probabilistic Offshore Mechanics, Probabilistic Methods in Civil Engineering, Random Vibration and Statistical Linearization, Dynamic Analysis of Non-Linear Structures by the Method of Statistical Quadratization, Stochastic Finite Elements: A Spectral Approach, Computational Stochastic Mechanics, Probabilistic Structural Mechanics: Advances in Structural Reliability Methods, Random Vibrations: A Broad Perspective; contbr. to profl. jour. issues devoted to dynamics and vibrations; mem. editl. bd. 8 jours.; editor-in chief or co-editor 2 primary jours. on mechanics. Recipient European award of sci. N.V. Phillipps Co., Eindhoven, Netherlands, 1969, Presdl. Young Investigator award in earthquake engring. NSF, 1984-89, Cert. merit McDonnell Douglas Astronautics Co., Houston, 1987, G.R. Brown award for superior tchg. Rice U., 1995, 96, Newmark medal for lifetime contbns. to dynamics and vibrations ASCE, 1999; named hon. citizen, Messini, Greece, 2002; inducted into The Acad. of Athens, Greece, 2003. Fellow ASCE, AAM, ASME (participant tech. confs. and coms., Pi Tau Sigma Gold medal 1982, W.L. Huber Civil Engring. Rsch. prize 1989, G.L. Larson Meml. award 1991, Alfred M. Freudenthal medal 1992, Humboldt Rsch. award 1995, Disting. Lectr. 1997—, Newmark medal 1999, Theodore Von Karman medal 2003); mem. NAE, Acad. Athens, Am. Acad. Mechanics, Earthquake Engring. Rsch. Inst., Internat. Assn. for Structural Safety and Reliability (rsch. prize in the area of stochastic dynamics 1997), Hellenic Profl. Soc. (sponsor scholarship com.), A. von Humboldt Assn. Am. (life), Nat. Acad. Engring. Fax: (713) 348-5191. E-mail: spanos@rice.edu.

SPANOVICH, MILAN, retired civil engineer; b. Steubenville, Ohio, Feb. 19, 1929; s. Stanley and Katherine (Komazec) S.; m. Sylvia J. Tomko, Apr. 16, 1971. BS Civil Engring, Carnegie-Mellon U., 1956, MS Civil Engring., 1957. Registered profl. engr., Pa., Ohio, Va., W.Va., Mich., Ky., N.J. Instr. Carnegie-Mellon U., 1957-60; charter assoc., v.p. E. D'Appolonia Assocs., 1957-61; mem. civil engring. staff U. N.Mex., 1961-63; founder, sr. cons. Engring. Mechs., Inc., Pitts., 1963-96. Contbr. articles on soil mechs. to tech. jours.; patentee found. systems. Bd. dirs. Carnegie Mellon U. Andrew Carnegie Soc. Recipient Pitts. Young Civil Engr. of Yr. award, 1969 Fellow ASCE (Pitts. Civl Engr. of the Yr. 1987, chmn. numerous coms.), Am. Cons. Engrs. Council; mem. Cons. Engrs. Council Greater Pitts. (pres. 1972-74), Engring. Soc. Western Pa. (dir. 1972, 77-83), Nat. Soc. Profl. Engrs., Pa. Soc. Profl. Engrs. (pres. Pitts. chpt. 1971, Hornfeck award Pitts. chpt. 1979, state dir. 1976-79, Disting. Service award Pitts. chpt. 1985, Pa. Engr. of the Yr. 1988, Profl. Devel. award 1989, Outstanding Svc. award Pitts. chpt. 1993), ASTM (chmn. task com. on relative density of granular soils 1959-63), Am. Concrete Inst., Hwy. Research Bd., Internat. Soc. Soil Mechs. and Found. Engring., Pitts. Geol. Soc., Am. Arbitration Assn., Profl. Engrs. in Pvt. Practice (chmn. 1970-71), Pitts. Builders Exchange, Soc. Explosives Engrs., Am. Soc. Hwy. Engrs., Carnegie-Mellon U. Alumni Assn. (mem. planning com.), Chi Epsilon Nat. Civil Engring. Honor Soc.

SPARBERG, MARSHALL STUART, gastroenterologist, educator; b. Chgo., May 20, 1936; s. Max Shane and Mildred Rose (Haffron) S.; m. Eve Gaymont Enda, Mar. 15, 1987. BA, Northwestern U., 1957, MD, 1960. Intern Evanston Hosp., Ill., 1960-61; resident in internal medicine Barnes Hosp., St. Louis, 1961-63; fellow U. Chgo., 1963-65; practice medicine specializing in gastroenterolgy Chgo., 1967—; asst. prof. medicine Northwestern U., 1967-72, assoc. prof., 1972-80, prof. medicine, 1980—; instr. Wash. U., St. Louis, 1961-63, U. Chgo., 1963-65. Author: Ileostomy Care, 1969, Primer of Clinical Diagnosis, 1972, Ulcerative Colitis, 1978, Inflammatory Bowel Disease, 1982; contbr. numerous articles to profl. jours. Pres. Fine Arts Music Found., 1974-76, Crohn's Disease and Colitis Found. of Am., pres. Ill. chpt., 1994-97; bd. dirs. Lyric Opera Guild, 1974-94, Chamber Music Soc. North Shore Chgo., 1984—; physician to Chgo. Symphony Orch., 1981-97. With USAF, 1965-67. Named Outstanding Tchr. Northwestern U. Med. Sch., 1972 Mem. AMA, ACP, Am. Gastroent. Assn., Am. Coll. Gastroent. (bd. govs.), Chgo. Med. Soc., Chgo. Soc. Internal Medicine, Chgo. Soc. Gastroenterology (pres.), Chgo. Soc. Gastrointestinal Endoscopy (pres.) Office: 676 N Saint Clair St Ste 1525 Chicago IL 60611-2862 Office Phone: 312-944-7080.

SPARKMAN, BRANDON BUSTER, secondary school educator, consultant, writer; b. Hartselle, Ala., Aug. 2, 1929; s. George Olan and Mary Louise (Jones) S.; m. Wanda Phillips, Sept. 13, 1952; children— Ricky Brandon, Rita Sharon, Robert Lee. BS, U. North Ala., 1952; MA, U. Ala., 1958, EdS, 1961; EdD, Auburn U., Ala., 1970. Tchr., asst. prin. Phllips High Sch., Bear Creek, Ala., 1954-57; prin. Tuscumbia, Ala., 1957-65; asst. supt., 1965-69; ednl. cons. Auburn Center, 1969-70; mem. faculty dept. sch. adminstrn. Auburn U., 1970; asst. supt. for staff personnel devel. Jackson (Miss.) Pub. Schs., 1970-71, supt., 1971-73; sch. supt. Richland County Sch. Dist. 1, Columbia, SC, 1973-75; asst. supt. instruction Hartselle (Ala.) City Schs., 1975-80; supt. Guntersville (Ala.) City Schs., 1980-88; CEO The Right Combination Pub. & Ednl. Svcs. Corp., Guntersville, Ala., 1984-93. Adj. prof. U. Ala., Birmingham, 1998-2000; writer, cons. in field. Sr. author: Blueprint for a Brighter Child, 1973, STEPS (System for Teacher Evaluation of Pre-reading Skills), 1974; co-author: Preparing Your Preschooler for Reading, 1977, Competency Tests for Basic Reading Skills, 1978, Soaring High with Science, 1985, Soaring High with Social Studies, 1985; author: How Well Does Your Child Read, 1979, Writing Composition Made Easy, 1991, Blueprint for Expository Writing, 1993, Reading Skills Competency Tests, 1999; editor: The In-Between Years, 1979; creator: CORE (Program Management Through Computer Systems), 1975; editor, contbg. author: The Advantaged, A Preschool Program for the Disadvantaged, 1969; contbr. articles to profl. jours. Bd. dirs. Morgan County chpt. ARC, United Givers Fund, Colbert-Lauderdale Child Study Center, Sheffield-Tuscumbia Credit Union; bd. govs. Jackson Symphony Orch.; adv. bd. Jackson Mental Health Center. Served with AUS, 1952-54. Recipient Human Relations award Jackson. Mem. Am., Ala assns. sch. adminstrs. (past pres.), Ala. Council Sch. Adminstrn. and Supervision (past pres.), Assn. Supervision and Curriculum Devel., Ala. Assn. Supervision and Curriculum Devel. (past pres.), Florence State U. Alumni Assn. (past pres.) Methodist (ch. sch. tchr., supt., vice chmn. ofcl. bd., chmn. commn. edn.). Home and Office: 2304 Northfield Dr Jasper AL 35504

SPARKMAN, LYLE BRUCE, academic administrator, education educator; b. Springfield, Mo., Sept. 2, 1947; s. Etsyl J. and Rayma LaVern Sparkman; m. Martha Rothrock, Mar. 17, 1984; 1 child, Sarah Anne. BA in English Philosophy, Drury Univ., Springfield, Mo., 1972; MEd Instructional Adminstrn., Univ. Ark., Fayettville, Ark., 1985, EdS Ednl. Specialist, 1999. Cert. tchg., adminstrn. Mo., Ark. News dir. KMTC TV (channel 27), Springfield, Mo., 1973—74; tchr. 3rd grade Kana. City Mo. Schs., Kans. City, South West R-5, Washburn, 1978—83; prin. Rose Bud Elem., Ark., 1984—88, Green Forest Sch., 1988—2002; asst. supt. East newton R.V.I, Granby, Mo., 2002—. Adj. prof. Lindenwood Univ., Granby, 2002—; grant reader USDE Office Migrant Edn, Washington, 2000, Washington, 04; v.p. Crowder Coll. Admin. Adv. Coun., Mo., 2004—06; nat. pilot leader AIM Project Migrant Families, 1997—2002. Co-author: The Heritage of the Ozarks, 1984; prodr.: (plays) The Toby Show, 1972;, performer folk music. Patron Wilson's Creek Nat. Found., Springfield, 1991—2007, Nat. Mil. Pk. Found., Pea Ridge, Ark., 2005—07; pub. info. officer Am. Legion post 163, Neosho, 2005—06. Specialist 5th class US Army, 1969—71. Grantee Documentaries the Past grant, U.S. Dept. Edn., 2005—. Mem.: ASCD, Mo. Archl. Soc. (pres.), Phi Delta Kappa. Southern Baptist. Avocations: archaeology, music, comparative folklore. Home: 1905 Cash St Neosho MO 64850 Office: E Newton R VI 22808 F Hwy 86 Granby MO 64844 Business E-Mail: sparkmanl@mail.enr6.k12.mo.us.

SPARKMAN, ROBIN HAMILTON, editor-in-chief; b. Apr. 29, 1969; d. Nicholas P. and Beatrice S. (Page) Sparkman; m. Howard Zachary Robbins, June 21, 1997. Grad., Wellesley Coll.; MA in Journalism, Columbia U., 1996. Bus. editor MSNBC Online; editor-in-chief Corp. Counsel Magazine. Co-recipient Nat. Editorial Award.

SPARKMAN, STEVEN LEONARD, lawyer; b. Sarasota, Fla., May 30, 1947; s. Simeon Clarence and Ursula (Wahlstrom) S.; m. Terry Jeanne Gibbs, Aug. 23, 1969; children: Joanna Jeanne, Kevin Leonard. BA, Fla. State U., 1969, JD, 1972. Bar: Fla. 1972, U.S. Dist. Ct. (mid. dist.) Fla. 1974, U.S. Ct. Appeals (5th cir.) 1975. Legal rsch. asst. Office Gen. Counsel, Fla. Dept. Revenue, Tallahassee, 1971; legis. intern com. on cmty. affairs Fla. Ho. of Reps., Tallahassee, 1971-72; jud. rsch. aide Fla. 2d Dist. Ct. Appeals, Lakeland, 1972-73; asst. county atty. Hillsborough County, Tampa, Fla., 1973-75; assoc. Carlton, Fields, Ward, Emmanuel, Smith & Cutler, P.A., Tampa, 1975-80, sr. atty., 1980-2001; pvt. practice Plant City, Fla., 2001—. Mem. bd. visitors Fla. State U. Coll. Law, 1994—2000. Trustee Fla. Bapt. Children's Homes, Inc., 2004—; deacon 1st Bapt. Ch., Plant City, 1980—; sec., bd. dirs. Bapt. Towers Plant City, Inc., 1981—84; bd. dirs. Tampa Kiwanis Found., 1997—2000. 1st lt. USAFR, 1973. Mem.: ABA, Plant City Bar Assn. (sec. treas 2003—05, treas. 2005—), Fla. Bar Assn. (exec. coun. local govt. law sect. 1978—79), Kiwanis (bd. dirs. 2003—06, Plant City). Democrat. Office: 102 W Reynolds St Ste 201 Plant City FL 33563 Business E-Mail: sls@sparklaw.com.

SPARKS, BARBARA ANN, adult education educator, educational consultant, researcher; b. Green Bay, Wis., Mar. 1, 1948; d. Donald Robert and Honorine Marion Engebos; children: Chad Paul Grochowski, Rachael Honorine Engebos. BS in Cmty. Edn., U. Wis., Milw., 1977, PhD in Urban Edn., Adult Edn., Adminstrv. Leadership, Sociology, 1995; MEd in Ednl. Adminstrn., Postsecondary Edn., Colo. State U., 1988. Elem. tchr. Rainbow Cmty. Sch., Milw., 1973—76; S.E. ctr. coord., gen. equivalency diploma instr. Multicultural Cmty. HS, Milw., 1976—78; instr., life skills dept. McClain Cmty. HS, Jeffco Schs., Colo., 1978—83; faculty, chair, devel. studies dept. Tech. Edn. Ctr., CC Denver, 1983—86; coord. ednl. outreach, instrnl. svcs. Colo. CC, Occupl. Edn. Sys., 1986—89; dir., office distance learning, divsn. outreach, continuing edn. U. Wis., Milw., 1989—92, adj. faculty, Sch. Edn., 1992—93, departmental rep., vice chancellor academic affairs' tech., instrn. adv. group, 1989—92, campus rep., instrnl. tech. adv. com., 1989—92, student tutor, Learning Resource Ctr., 1990—92, summer faculty instr., 1992; instrnl. design, evaluation specialist, dept. ednl. svcs. Med. Coll. Wis., 1992—93; tech. in edn. specialist Pacific Mountain Network, US Dept. Edn., Star Schs., 1993—94; distance learning, tech. cons., adult sect., adult continuing edn. Colo. Dept. Edn., Aurora Colo. Pub. Schs., 1993—95; distance learning project coord. Western Interstate Commn. Higher Edn., Colo., 1994—96; asst. prof. adult edn., dir. Nebr. Inst. Study Adult Literacy, Tchrs. Coll. U. Nebr., Lincoln, 1996—2000, mem. pers., grad., curriculum coms., faculty mem., dept. vocat. adult edn., 1996—98, co-chair, distance learning work group, 1996—98, dir., dept. vocat., adult edn., Nebr. Inst. Study Adult Literacy, 1996—99, departmental faculty rep., tchrs. coll. equity com., 1997—99, minority student mentor, tchrs. coll. mentor program undergraduate minority students, 1998, adv. faculty mem., vice chancellor's visioning task force extended edn., 1998, chair faculty search com., dept. vocat., adult edn., 1998, program planning leader, 1998—99, faculty rep., tchrs. coll. scholarship com., 1998—2000; asst. prof., program coord. adult edn., dept. adult, cmty. coll. edn., Coll. Humanities, Social Scis. NC State U., Raleigh, 2000—03, affiliate faculty, women's, gender studies program, Coll. Humanities, Social Scis., 2000—03, program planning co-chair, adult edn. rsch. conf. planning com., 2000—02, conf. procs. co-editor, adult edn. rsch. conf. planning com., 2001—02, adult literacy cons., immigrant literacy project, Coll. Humanities and Social Scis., 2002, departmental libr. rep., 2000—03, mem. faculty search coms., dept. adult and CC edn., 2001, curriculum developer, rsch. course, 2001, exec. coun. mem., women's, gender studies, dept. humanities, 2001—03, departmental rep., rsch. com., Coll. Edn., 2001—04, coord., untenured group, Coll. Edn., 2002, coord., family rsch. initiative, dept. adult, CC edn., 2002, rsch. assoc., Evaluation, Rsch., Policy Ctr., 2002, faculty advisor, doctoral seminar, dept. adult, CC edn., 2002—03, rsch. affiliate, cultural context edn. collaboratory, Coll. Edn., 2003; higher edn. cons., 2003—05; evaluation cons., Sch. Edn. U. Colo., Denver, 2005—, adj. faculty, lang., literacy, culture, 2005—, rsch. affiliate, rsch. lab. lang., literacy, 2005—. Chair, legis. com. Colo. Assn. Continuing Adult Edn., 1985—89, exec. bd. dirs., 1986—89, sec., 1989; state coord., gen. equivalency diploma TV project Colo. Dept. Edn., 1986—89; membership com. mem. Nat. U. Telecom. Network, 1989—92; region IV sec., ednl. tech. Nat. U. Continuing Edn. Assn., 1989—93; co-chair, regional conf. Mountain Plains Adult Edn. Assn., Boulder, Colo., 1990; v.p. continuing edn. Wis. Assn. Adult, Continuing Edn., 1990—91, chair, ann. spring conf., 1991, continuing edn. bd. rep., 1992—94; mem. exec. steering com. Midwest Rsch to Practice Conf., 1994—99; co-coord. Third Ann. Women Profs. Adult Edn. Retreat, Homer, Ark., 1999; rsch. assoc. Low Income Women Post-Secondary Edn. Rsch. Network, CUNY, 2000—01; presenter in field; workshop attendee in field. Mem. editl. bd.: Adult Edn. Quar., 1996—2000, Adult Learning, 2001—04, proposal reviewer: Nebr. Dept. Edn., 1997—99, prodr., recorder: compact disc Music of Israel Moreno Santiago y Maximo Zurnigo Gonzales, Boxtop Prodns., 2000, reviewer: ERIC Digests, Clearinghouse Adult, Career Vocat. Edn., 2000; editor (with Q. Geng): (books) Handbook for Culturally Relevant Adult Basic Education (ABE) Teaching and Learning., 2000; author: The struggles of getting an education: Issues of power, culture, and difference for Mexican Americans of the Southwest, 2002; author: (with J. Pettitt, R. Francis, R. Closson, and S. Williams) Proceedings of the 43rd Annual Adult Education Research Conference, 2002; photography book, Photographic documentation of community involvement in historic preservation work, Cornerstones Cmty. Partnerships, 2001, exhibitions include Steamboat Spring Arts Coun. Mem. Show, 2004; guest editor: New Zealand Jour. Adult Learning, 2003, discussant, proposal reader: AERA, Adult Literacy SIG, 2006; contbr. articles, papers, book chpts., monographs in field. Eng. literacy tutor Adult Edn. Ctr., Colo. Springs Sch. Dist., 1993; adult ESL, health care curriculum cons. Asian Cmty. Ctr., Lincoln, 1997; vol. cons. in field, 1997—98; program planning cons. Malone Cmty. Ctr., Lincoln, Nebr., 1998; tech. cons., adult basic edn. program Metro CC, Omaha, 1998; cons. Durham Congregations, Assns., Neighborhoods Jobs_Team, NC, 2002; adult edn. cons., nat. study immigrant settlement rural communities USDA, 2002—03; adult edn. rsch. cons., collaborator, Latino edn. initiative NC CC State Office, Hispanic Affairs Office Gov. NC, 2002—03; vol. Routt County Hist. Preservation, Steamboat Springs, 2003, Steamboat Springs Arts Coun., 2003—04; mem. Spanish, English intercambio conversation group Epilogue Bookstore, Steamboat Springs, 2003; rsch. cons. Steamboat Peace and Justice Ctr., Colo., 2003—, All Families Deserve a Chance Coalition, Denver, 2005—; co-coord. Holistic Health Fair, Steamboat Springs, 2004; adv. bd. mem. Front Range Literacy Action, Colo., 1987—89, Nebr. Appleseed Ctr. Law Pub. Interest, 1998, Multicultural Retention, Student Affairs Dept., S.E. CC, Lincoln, 2000; apptd. coun. mem. State Colo. Literacy Coun., 1987—89; exec. bd. mem. Coords. Adult Literacy, Nebr., 1996—98; bd. mem. Gathering Pl., Lincoln, 1998—99. Recipient Outstanding Leadership award, Colo. Dept. Edn., 1986, Appreciation cert., Colo. Children's Advocacy, 1987, Colo. CC, Occupl. Edn. Sys., 1989, Svc. and Leadership Dedication award, Colo. Assn. Continuing Adult Edn., 1987, Leadership Contbn. award, Colo. Assn. Vocat. Adminstrs., 1987, Diversity Achievement award, Coll. Edn., NC State U., 2001; grant, US Dept. Edn., Adult Basic Edn., Colo. Dept. Edn., 1980, 1986, 1988, Colo. CC, Occupl. Edn. Sys., 1983, Carl Perkins grant, 1986—89, grant, 1988, JTPA Adminstrv. grant, Gov.'s Job Tng. Office, 1986—89, grant, Office Rural Job Tng., 1989, U. Wis., 1990, Colo. Dept. Edn., 1994—95, Nebr. Dept. Edn., 1997, 1998, 1999, U. Nebr., Lincoln, 1997, 1999, 2000, Nat. Inst. Literacy, US Dept. Edn., 1997—2000, Coll. Edn., NC State U., 2003, scholarship, Educators as Developers: Multimedia Prodn., Apple Computer, 1988, Edn. scholarship, Women's Leadership Inst. Colo. CC, Occupl. Edn. Sys., 1989, Edn. Rsch. scholarship, Wis. Assn. Adult, Continuing Edn., 1992. Mem.: Am. Assn. Adult Continuing Edn. (conf. chair, critical theory spl. interest group, commn. profs. 1993, conf. presider 1993, conf. chair, critical theory spl. interest group, commn. profs. 1994, conf. presider 1994, co-chair, rsch. theory spl. interest group session, commn. profs. 2001—02, conf. presider 2001—02, scholarship 1992), Mountain Plains Adult Edn. Assn., Am. Edn. Rsch. Assn.

SPARKS, BENNETT SHER, military officer; b. Pitts., Oct. 10, 1925; s. Julius and Anna K. Sparks; m. Betty Sparks, May 8, 1943 (dec. Nov. 2005); children: Bennett Sher Jr., James Robert, Richard T.(dec.), John N., Julieann, Donna Beth(dec.). Diploma, Naval War Coll., 1973, Armed Forces Staff Coll., 1978, Nat. War Coll., 1978, The Army War Coll., 1988, The Nat. Def. U., The Indsl. Coll. Armed Forces; PhD in Philosophy (hon.), Sampson U., Oxford, Eng., 1986. Lic. aircraft pilot. Enlisted USCG, 1942, commd. ensign, 1955, advanced through grades to rear admiral, 1985, dist. insp. 11th Coast Guard Dist., sr. res. officer Pacific Area San Francisco, sr. res. officer Atlantic Area NYC, comdr. Navy's No. Calif. Maritime Def. Zone San Francisco, civilian aviator; comdr. Navy's Maritime Def. Zone USCG, sector 6, Charleston, SC; ret. USCG, 1993. Aviator Coast and Geodetic Survey, Ala.; chief US Del. to Confedn. Res. Officers (CIOR), NATO Hdqrs., Belgium, 1985-86; internat. sec.-gen. Inter-Allied Confedn. Res. Officers, Brussels, 1992-94. Mem. Calif. Vets. Bd., 1995—, chmn., 1998—99; bd. dirs. Sonoma County Area Agy. of Aging, Calif., 2002—, mem. legis. com., 2002—; bd. dirs. North Bay chpt. Alzheimer's Assn. No. Calif. and Nev., 2002—; bd. dirs. Bank of Hollywood. Decorated Legion of Merit, Coast Guard Commendation medals (2), Coast Guard Achievement medal, The Humanitarian Svc. medal, Arctic Svc. medal, Coast Guard Combat Air Crew Wings with three stars, knight Sovereign Mil. Order Temple of Jerusalem, the NATO Grand Priory, 1983, knight comdr., 1987, Meritorious Svc. medal and the Coast Guard Commmand Ashore Device medal; recipient Navy Disting. Pub. Svc. medal Sec. of Navy, 1983, Coast Guard Disting. Pub. Svc. medal Comdt. of Coast Guard, 1983, 93 (only person in history of Coast Guard to receive 2 awards). Mem. DAV, VFW, Am. Legion, Sonoma County United Vets. Coun., Navy League, Naval Res. Assn., Res. Officers Assn. US (pres. 1982-83, nat. dep. exec. dir., dir. adminstrn. and dir. fin. 1988-91, chmn. bd. trustees, bd. dirs.). Home: 573 Pistachio Pl Windsor CA 95492-8168 Home Fax: 707-838-8662.

SPARKS, BILLY SCHLEY, lawyer; b. Marshall, Mo., Mar. 1, 1923; s. John and Clarinda (Schley) Sparks; m. Dorothy O. Stone, May 14, 1946; children: Stephen Stone, Susan Lee Sparks Raben Taylor, John David. AB, Harvard U., 1945, LLB, 1949. Bar: Mo. 1949. Ptnr. Langworthy, Matz & Linde, Kansas City, Mo., 1949-62, Linde, Thomason, Fairchild, Langworthy, Kohn & Van Dyke, Kansas City, 1962-91; ret., 1991. Mem. Mission (Kans.) Planning Coun., 1954—63, Dist. 100 Sch. Bd., 1964—68, pres., 1967—69; mem. Dist. 512 Sch. Bd., 1969—73, pres., 1971—72; mem. Kans. Civil Svc. Commn., 1975—90; del. Dem. Nat. Conv., 1964; treas. Johnson County Dem. Ctrl. Com., Kans., 1958—64; candidate rep. 10th Dist., Kans., 1956, 3d Dist., Kans., 1962. Lt. USAAF, 1944—46. Mem.: ABA, Nat. Assn. Sch. Bds. (mem. legis. com. 1968—73), Law Assn. Kansas City, Kansas City Bar Assn., Mo. Bar Assn., Kansas City C. of C. (mem. legis. com. 1956—82), Harvard Law Sch. Assn. Mo. (past dir.), Milburn Golf and Country Club, Kansas City (Mo.) Club, Harvard Club (v.p. 1953—54), Am. Legion, St. Andrews Soc. Home and Office: 8517 W 90th Ter Shawnee Mission KS 66212-3053 Office Phone: 913-642-2443.

SPARKS, CHARLES EDWARD, pathologist, educator; b. Peoria, Ill., July 29, 1940; s. William Joseph and Meredith (Pleasants) S.; m. Janet Lindsay Dehoff, Aug. 18, 1977; children: William, Debra, Robert. BS in Biology, MIT, 1963; MD, Thomas Jefferson U., 1968. Diplomate Am. Bd. Pathology, Am. Bd. Clin. Chemistry. Rsch. asst. Mass. Gen. Hosp., Boston, 1963; intern NY Hosp., Cornell Naval Hosp., St. Albans, 1968-69; resident in clin. pathology Hosp. of U. Pa., 1972-75; fellow in cardiopulmonary medicine U. Pa., Phila., 1975-76, asst. instr., 1972-75; fellow in biochemistry Med. Coll. Pa., Phila., 1976-77, instr., 1976-77, asst. to assoc. prof. biochemistry and physiology, 1977-82; assoc. prof. pathology U. Rochester (NY), 1982-88, prof. pathology, 1988—. Advisor med. scientist tng.

program U. Rochester, 1984-92; attending pathologist, dir. clin. chemistry unit Strong Meml. Hosp., 1982—, chair rsc. adv. com., assoc. chair pathology, 1994—, dir. grad. studies in Integrative Biomed. Scis., 1998—. Contbr. articles to profl. jours.; patentee in field. Chairperson Endocrinology VA Merit Rev. Study Sect., 2000—. Lt. comdr. USN, 1969—72. Postdoctoral fellow NIH, 1975-77. Mem. AAAS, Am. Diabetes Assn. (co-chmn. nat. symposium meeting 1988), Acad. Clin. Lab. Physicians and Scientists, Am. Heart Assn. (fellow coun. on arteriosclerosis, mem. nominating com.). Office: Dept Pathology U Rochester 601 Elmwood Ave Rochester NY 14642-0001 Home Phone: 585-381-9549; Office Phone: 585-275-8236.

SPARKS, DALE BOYD, allergist, health facility administrator; b. Springfield, Mo., July 14, 1929; s. Roscoe R. and Ruby V. (Boyd) S.; children: Susan L., Laura A., Lisa M., Jennifer G.; m. Leeanna M. Molcyk Priboy, Apr. 21, 2001. AB, BS, Southwest Mo. State U., 1951; BS in Medicine, U. Mo., 1953; MD, St. Louis U., 1955. Diplomate Am. Bd. Allergy and Immunology. Intern Kansas City (Mo.) Gen. Hosp. U. Med. Ctr., 1955-56; resident U. Mo. Hosp., 1958-60; fellow in allergy and immunology Northwestern U., 1960-61; mem. cons. staff Parkview Cmty. Hosp., 1961—; mem. med. staff Riverside County Regional Med. Ctr., 1961-2000, dir. respiratory therapy, 1968-85, dir. respiratory therapy and diagnostic svcs., 1965—, chmn. dept. medicine, 1978-98, chief med. staff, 1990-98; acting dir., health officer Riverside Pub. Health Dept., 1991-93; ret., 1993. Clin. prof. medicine Loma Linda U. Mem. editl. bd. Immunology and Allergy in Practice, 1980—. Lt. USNR. Fellow ACP (coun. subsplty. socs. 1988—), Am. Coll. Allergy and Immunology (disting., bd. regents 1989-93, pres. 1990-91, chmn. fin. com., treas. 1990-93, recert. com.), Coll. Allergy, Asthma and Immunology; mem. AMA, Am. Lung Assn. (bd. dirs. 1990-95), Am. Heart Assn. (bd. dirs. 1964-70, pres. 1966), Joint Coun. Am. Allergy and Immunology (bd. dirs. 1985-90), Calif. Med. Assn., Calif. Soc. Allergy, Inland Soc. Internal Medicine, Riverside County Med. Assn. (bd. councilors 1980-99, del. CMA 1988-99), Riverside County Found. Med. Care (sec., past pres.). Home and Office: 29368 Big Range Rd Canyon Lake CA 92587 Personal E-mail: dsparksmd@aol.com.

SPARKS, DONALD LEWIS, soil chemistry educator; b. Paris, Ky., June 26, 1953; s. Elmer Johnston and Christine (McKenzie) Sparks; m. Joy Lynn Gooden, Sept. 14, 1984. BS, U. Ky., Lexington, 1975, MS, 1976; PhD, Va. Poly. Inst. and State U., Blacksburg, 1979. Asst. prof. soil chemistry U. Del., Newark, 1979-83, assoc. prof., 1983-87, prof., 1987—, chmn. dept. plant and soil scis., 1989—, disting. prof., 1994—, Francis Alison prof., 1996—, T.A. Baker prof., 2001—02, S. Hallock duPont chair, 2002—. Cons. DuPont Corp., Wilmington, Del., 1981—. Author: Kinetics of Soil Chemical Processes, 1989, Environmental Soil Chemistry, 1995, 2d edit., 2002; editor: Soil Physical Chemistry, 1986, rev. 2d edit. 1998, Rates of Soil Chemical Processes, 1991, Method of Soil Analysis: Chemical Methods, 1996; mem. editl. bd. Am. Jour. Soil Sci. Soc., 1984-93, Geoderma, 1986—, Soil Sci., 1987—, Pedosphere, 1999—, Geochimica Cosmochimica Acta, 1999—, Vadose Zone Jour., 2002—; editor: Advances in Agronomy, 1990—; contbr. over 160 articles and 40 book chpts. to profl. publs. Pres. Torch Club of Del., Newark, 1989—. Recipient U. Dl. Doctoral Advising and Mentoring award. Fellow AAAS, Am. Soc. Agronomy (Environ. Quality Rsch. award, N.E. br. Rsch. award 1986, Francis Alison award 1996), Soil Sci. Soc. of Am. (pres.-elect 1998-99, pres. 1999-00, Soil Sci. Rsch. award 1994, M.L. and Chrystie M. Jackson Soil Sci. award); mem. Internat. Union Soil Sci. (pres.-elect 2000-02, pres. 2002-06), Am. Chem. Soc., Clay Minerals Soc., Geochem. Soc. Mem. Christian Ch. (Disciples Of Christ). Achievements include pioneering application of chemical kinetics to soil systems. Office: U Del Dept Plant and Soil Scis Newark DE 19717-1303 Business E-Mail: dlsparks@udel.edu.

SPARKS, HARVEY VISE, JR., physiologist; b. Flint, Mich., June 22, 1938; s. Harvey Vise and Ellen Louise (Paschall) S.; m. Barbara M. Taylor, Jan. 17, 1969; children— Matthew Taylor, Catherine Elliott, Wendy Sue, Harvey Vise. Student, U. Mich., 1956-59, MD, 1963. Postdoctoral fellow dept. physiology Harvard Med. Sch., Boston and; U. Goteborg, Sweden; instr. U. Mich., 1966-67, asst. prof. physiology, 1967-70, assoc. prof., 1970-74, prof., 1974-78; asst. to dean U. Mich. (Med. Sch.), 1970-71, asst. dean, 1971-72; prof. physiology Mich. State U., East Lansing, 1978—, chmn. dept., 1978-89, vice provost human health programs, 1989-93, univ. disting. prof., 1997—. Fulbright lectr. U. Zimbabwe, 1986-87; vis. prof. U. Zimbabwe, 1995; mem. survey team, liaison com. on med. edn. AMA Am. Assn. Med. Colls.; mem. rev. teams NIH. Author: Casebook of Physiology, 1973, Essentials of Cardiovascular Physiology, 1987; contbr. numerous articles to profl. jours.; editor: (with others) Handbook of Physiology, 1979. Recipient Meritorious Service award Mich. Heart Assn., 1962, Borden award for med. student research, 1963, Merit award NIH, 1988; Mich. Heart Assn. student fellow, 1962-63; John and Mary Markle scholar, 1967-72; USPHS postdoctoral fellow, 1963-66; U. Mich. student research fellow, 1960-61; USPHS grantee, 1963— Fellow Royal Soc. Medicine; mem. AAAS, Am. Physiol. Soc. (pres. 1987-88, editl. bd. Am. Jour. Physiology 1974-88), Microcirculatory Soc., Am. Heart Assn. (coun. on circulation, editl. bd. Circulation Rsch.), Mich. Pub. Health Inst. (bd. dirs. 1989-94), Internat. Union Physiol. Scis. (treas. 1990-97), Coun. Internat. Exch. Scholars (Africa area com. 1988-91), Russian Acad. Sci. (fgn.), Victor Vaughn Soc., Alpha Omega Alpha, Phi Kappa Phi, Phi Zeta. Home: 8122 W Lovejoy Rd Perry MI 48872-8902 Office: Mich State U Dept Physiology East Lansing MI 48824

SPARKS, JACK NORMAN, dean; b. Lebanon, Ind., Dec. 3, 1928; s. Oakley and Geraldine Ruth (Edrington) S.; m. Esther Lois Bowen, Apr. 11, 1953; children: Stephen Michael, Robert Norman, Ruth Ann, Jonathan Russell. BS, Purdue U., 1950; MA, U. Iowa, 1951, PhD, 1960. Tchr. math. Leyden Cmty. H.S., Franklin Park, Ill., 1954—58; rsch. asst. U. Iowa, Iowa City, 1958—60; assoc. prof. applied stats., dir. bur. of rsch. U. No. Colo., Greeley, 1960—65; assoc. prof. ednl. psychology Pa. State U., State College, 1965—68; dir. corr. Campus Crusade for Christ, San Bernardino, Calif., 1968—69; dir. Christian World Liberation Front, Berkeley, Calif., 1969—75; pastor, ch. overseer New Covenant Apostolic Order, Berkeley, 1975—77; dean St. Athanasius Acad. Orthodox Theology, Santa Barbara, Calif., 1977—87, St. Athanasius Coll., Santa Barbara, 1987—93, St. Athanasius Acad. Orthodox Theology, Elk Grove, Calif., 1996—2005, St. John's Orthodox Cathedral, Eagle River, Alaska, 2005—. Cons. Measurement Rsch. Ctr., Iowa City, 1959-60, We. States Small Schs. Project, Greeley, 1962-65, Colo. Coun. Ednl. Rsch., Denver, 1963-65; project dir. Orthodox Study Bible Old Testament, 1998— Author: Letters to Street Christians, 1971, The Mind Benders, 1977, 79, The Resurrection Letters, 1978, The Preaching of the Apostles, 1987, Victory in the Unseen Warfare, 1993; editor: Apostolic Fathers, 1978, 88; gen. editor: The Orthodox Study Bible, 1993, Virtue in the Unseen Warfare, 1995, Prayer in the Unseen Warfare, 1996, Christ Is Our Holiness, 1996, The Coming of the Prince, 1997, Tradition in the Early Church, 1997, The Letters of St. Ignatius, 1998, Faith and Godliness, 1999, Pentecost: A Homily of St. John Chrysostom, 2000, No Graven Image, 2000, The Valley of the Shadow of Death, 2000, Death, Fear of Death, Hope of Resurrection, 2000, Kindling the Fire Within, 2000, How Can Jesus Be Both God and Man, 2001, The Annunciation, 2001, The Bride of Christ, 2001, The Boundless Beauty, 2001, Walking Through the Night, 2001, Out of the Depths, 2002, Redemption and Reconciliation, 2002, A Family Baptized, 2003, Zeal and Patience, 2003, The Biblical Story of Esther, 2006. Trustee Rock Mont Coll., Denver, 1962-77, Thomas Nelson Co., Nashville, 1977-78. 1st lt. U.S. Army, 1952-54 Mem. Am. Sci. Affiliation, Assn. Orthodox Theologians, Conf. on Faith and History, Phi Delta Kappa (pres. Epsilon chpt. 1959-60) Republican. Orthodox Christian. Home: 19042 Monastery Dr Eagle River AK 99577 Home Phone: 907-696-3577; Office Phone: 907-696-2002. Business E-Mail: frjack@saaot.edu.

SPARKS, JANET LINDSAY DEHOFF, pathologist, educator; b. Lawrence, Mass., Sept. 13, 1950; d. Ronald Lee and Barbara Isabelle (Platt) DeHoff; m. Charles Edward Sparks, Aug. 18, 1977; 1 child, Robert. BA in Biology, BS in Med. Tech., U. Pa., 1972, PhD in Pathology, 1980. Cert. med. technologist Am. Soc. Clin. Pathologists. Instr. clin. chemistry U. Pa., Phila., 1974-76; fellow Wistar Inst. Anatomy and Biology, Phila., 1975-80; postdoctoral fellow U. Rochester (N.Y.), 1983-85, scientist, 1985-94, asst. prof. pathology and lab. medicine, 1994-96, assoc. prof. pathology and lab. medicine, 1996—. Cons. NIH, Indpls., 1994-96. Contbr. numerous articles to profl. jours.; patentee in field. Nat. NIDDK RO1 grantee, 1995—. Fellow Coun. on Arteriosclerosis Thrombosis and Vascular Biology; mem. AAAS, Am. Soc. Clin. Pathologists, Am. Diabetes Assn., Am. Heart Assn. (coun. on arteriosclerosis, coun. on clin. cardiology), N.Y. Lipid Club, N.Y. Acad. Scis. Office: U Rochester Dept Pathology 601 Elmwood Ave # 626 Rochester NY 14642-0001 E-mail: janet_sparks@ume.rochester.edu.

SPARKS, JOHN EDWARD, lawyer; b. Rochester, Ind., July 3, 1930; s. Russell Leo and Pauline Anna (Whittenberger) S.; m. Margaret Joan Snyder, Sept. 4, 1954; children: Thomas Edward, William Russell, Kathryn Chapman McCarthy. AB, Ind. U., 1952; LL.B., U. Calif., Berkeley, 1957; postgrad., London Sch. Econs., 1957-58. Bar: Calif. 1958, U.S. Supreme Ct., 1968. Assoc. Brobeck, Phleger & Harrison, San Francisco, 1958-66, ptnr., 1967-95, of counsel, 1996—2003; pvt. practice, 2003—. Adj. prof. law U. San Francisco, 1967-69; pres. Legal Aid Soc. San Francisco, 1978-79, dir., 1971-81. Editor U. Calif. Law Rev., 1956-57. Served to 1st lt. Q.M.C. U.S. Army, 1952-54, Korea. Recipient Wheeler Oak Meritorious award U. Calif., Berkeley, 1986. Fellow Am. Bar Found., Am. Coll. Trial Lawyers; mem. ABA, State Bar Calif., Bar Assn. San Francisco (bd. dirs. 1974-75), Boalt Hall Alumni Assn. (pres. 1983-84). Democrat. Home Phone: 510-524-6106; Office Phone: 510-524-5404. E-mail: jsparks458@aol.com.

SPARKS, JORDIN BRIANNA, singer; b. Staten Island, NY, Dec. 22, 1989; d. Phillippi and Jodi (Weidmann) Sparks. Model for Torrid; toured with Michael W. Smith, 2005, 2006; winner Ariz. Idol competition Fox 10, Phoenix, 2006; contestant & first-place winner American Idol Season 6, 2007; signed to Arista Records/19 Entertainment, 2007—. Actor: (plays) The Wiz, Cinderella, Valley Youth Theatre, Phoenix, 2002; appeared in (TV series) America's Most Talented Kids, 2005, American Idol: The Search for a Superstar, 2007; singer: (albums) For Now, 2003, (singles) This is My Now, 2007. Named Spotlight Overall winner, Gospel Music Assn. Acad., 2004. Achievements include becoming the youngest winner of American Idol. *

SPARKS, KENNETH R., association executive; b. Mar. 26, 1934; BS, Syracuse U., 1956, MS, 1961, PhD, 1964; JD, George Washington U., 1967. Dir. rsch. Voice of Am. USIA, Washington, 1964-67; dep. dir. pub. affairs U.S. Office Econ. Opportunity, Washington, 1967-68, dir., 1968-69; pres. U.S. Cultural and Trade Ctr. Commn., Washington, 1988—90; dep. dir. Fed. City Coun., Washington, 1970-72, exec. v.p., 1972—2004, ret., 2004; dir. Fed. Res. Bank of Richmond, 2004—; pres. Sparks Assocs., 2004—. Adj. faculty Coll. William and Mary Law Sch., 2005—. Mem.: Econ. Club Washington (sec. 1985—2005). Office: PO Box 1202 White Stone VA 22578 Home Phone: 703-451-6806. Personal E-mail: krsparks@aol.com.

SPARKS, MILDRED THOMAS, state agency administrator, educator; b. Montgomery, Ala., Oct. 2, 1942; d. Leon and Annie Lee (Johnson) Thomas; m. John H. Sparks, Aug. 29, 1964; children: Melanie J. Thomas Bosak, Jennifer L. Gerhartz, Regina F. BS, Ala. State U., 1964; MS, Pepperdine U., 1978; postgrad., Claremont Coll., Calif. State U., Boston Coll. Cert. reading specialist, contract mgmt., U. Phoenix, U. Wyo. Tchr. Dayton (Ohio) Schs., 1964-66, Oxon Hill (Md.) Schs., 1966-70; technician Reading Lab. Grambling (La.) State U., 1972; reading lab. aide Calif. City (Calif.) Schs., 1975; reading instr. Cerro Coso So. Outreach, Edwards AFB, Calif., 1976-78; substitute tchr. San Bernardino City Schs., 1979, Aquinas H.S., San Bernardino, 1978-79; reading lab. tchr. San Bernardino H.S., 1979; instr. reading lab. San Bernardino Valley Coll., 1980-81, assoc. prof. reading, dept. head, 1981-86; contract adminstr. Hercules Missile Ordinance and Space Group, Magna, Utah, 1986, Alliant Techsys. (formerly Hercules Missile Ordinance and Space Group), 1987-97; dir. Office of Black Affairs State of Utah, 1997—2000; assoc. prof. Salt Lake CC, Salt Lake City, 2003—. Mem. Pres.'s Diversity Coun. Tchg. Cir. - Courage Teach Salt Lake City (Utah) C.C., 2003—, mem. gen. edn. com. Mem. Black Adv. Coun., Office of Black Affairs, AARP (mem. Utah bd., safety program instr.); presenter workshops, cmty. events; troop vol. Girl Scouts U.S.; vol. The March of Dimes, Am. Heart Assn., Visitation of the Elderly Homebound, Am. Cancer Soc. and Marriage and Family Workshop for Teens, Cath. Cmty. Svcs.; civil rights movement participant Ala. Bus Boycott; mem. minority health adv. bd. Utah Health Dept.; mem. Cath. Women League, Black Caths. Utah, Salt Lake City, African Am. Task Force, Gov.'s Initiative on Family Today, Anti-Discrimination Com.; planning com. United Way Greater Salt Lake, vol.; past pres. Salt Lake Diocesan Pastoral Coun., vol.; mem. Americorp Legacy program, Salt Lake County, Utah State Bd. Aging and Adult Svcs. Mem. Calif Tchrs. Assn., Nat. Coun. Tchrs. English, Assn. Supervision and Curriculum Devel., Western Coll. Reading Assn., Bus. and Profl. Women's Club, Link's, Jack and Jill of Am. Inc., Delta Kappa Gamma, Alpha Kappa Alpha. Roman Catholic (Norton lav lector). Avocations: reading, writing, gardening, cross country skiing. Home: 3790 Becky Cir Salt Lake City UT 84109-3302 Office: Salt Lake CC Coll Devel Edn 4600 S Redwood Rd Salt Lake City UT 84123

SPARKS, NICHOLAS, writer; b. Omaha, Dec. 31, 1965; s. Patrick Michael and Jill Emma Marie (Thoene) Sparks; m. Catherine Sparks, 1989; children: Miles, Ryan, Landon, Lexie, Savannah. BBA with high honors, U. Notre Dame, 1988. Author: (novels) The Notebook, 1996 (Publishers Weekly paperback bestseller list), Message In a Bottle, 1998, A Walk To Remember, 1999, The Rescue, 2000, A Bend in the Road, 2001, Nights in Rodanthe, 2002, The Guardian, 2003, The Wedding, 2003 (Publishers Weekly paperback bestseller list), True Believer, 2005 (Publishers Weekly hardover bestseller), At First Sight, 2005 (Publishers Weekly hardover bestseller), Dear John, 2006; co-author (with Micah Sparks) Three Weeks With My Brother, 2004. Achievements include several weeks on multiple NY Times Best-Seller Lists. *

SPARKS, RAYMOND FREDRICK, protective services official; b. Wichita Falls, Tex., Feb. 16, 1940; s. Carey Frederick and Sybil Louise (David) Sparks; m. Linda Faye Smallwood (div.); 1 child, Thomas Fredrick; m. Bessie Patricia Bostick, Dec. 11, 2006; 1 child, Pat Wayne Bostick. AA, Henderson County Jr. Coll., Athens, Tex., 1960. Cert. EMT Tex.; master firefighter Tex. Firefighter City of Garland Fire Dept., 1972—77, driver engr., paramedic, 1977—81, lt., 1981—84, capt., 1984—91, battalion chief EMS, 1991—97, battalion chief ops., 1997—. Exec. fire officer Nat. Fire Acad., Emmitsburg, Md. With USN, 1961—63. Mem.: Tex. Fire Chiefs Assn. Avocations: hunting, fishing. Office: City of Garland Fire Dept 217 N 5th Garland TX 75040

SPARKS, ROBERT DEAN, medical administrator, gastroenterologist; b. Newton, Iowa, May 6, 1932; s. Albert John and Josephine Emma (Kleinendorst) S.; children: Steven Robert, Ann Louise, John James. BA, U. Iowa, 1955, MD, 1957; D of Humanitarian Svc. (hon.), Creighton U., 1978. Diplomate Am. Bd. Internal Medicine. Intern Charity Hosp. of La., New Orleans, 1957-58, resident in internal medicine, 1958-59, asst. in medicine, 1958-59; fellow in gen. medicine and gastroenterology Tulane U. Sch. Medicine, 1959-62, instr. medicine, 1959-63, asst. prof., 1963-64, assoc. prof., 1964-68, prof., 1968-72, asst. dean, 1964-67, assoc. dean, acting dean, 1967-68, vice dean, 1968-69, dean, 1969-72, chief sect. gastroenterology, 1968-72; chancellor Med. Ctr. U. Nebr., 1972-76, prof. medicine, 1972-76; v.p. U. Nebr. System, 1972-76; health program dir. W.K. Kellogg Found., Battle Creek, Mich., 1976-81, v.p. programming, 1981-82, sr. v.p., 1982, pres., chief programming officer, 1982-86, pres., 1982-88, trustee, 1988, pres. emeritus, cons., 1988-92; pres., CEO, Calif. Med. Assn. Found., Sacramento, 1995-98, sr. assoc., 1998—. Cons. U. Tenn. Health Sci. Ctr., 1988-90, Boston U. Health Policy Inst., 1989-90; mem. sci., compensation and trust rev. coms. Syntex Corp., Palo Alto, Calif., 1987-91, v.p. product safety and compliance, 1991-93; mem. overseers com. to visit Harvard U. Med. and Dental Schs., 1984-90; mem. vis. com. U. Miami Sch. Medicine, 1982-86; assoc. med. dir. for addiction treatment svcs., dir. for edn. and rsch., Battle Creek Adventist Hosp., 1990-91; v.p. Howe-Lewis Internat Inc., Menlo Park, N.Y., 1993-94, cons., 1994-95; mem. adv. coun. to dean Tulane U. Sch. Medicine, 2004—. Mem. editl. bd. Alcoholism Treatment Quar., 1985--; contbr. articles to profl. jours. Bd. dirs. Nat. Coun. on Alcoholism and Drug Dependence, NYC, 1982-93, treas., 1986-88, chmn., 1989-90, past chmn., 1991-92; bd. dirs. Battle Creek Symphony Orch., 1981-88, Lakeview Sch. Dist., Battle Creek, 1979-83, 88-91, Omni Med, 2001-; trustee Monsour Med. Found., Jeannette, Pa., 1976-90, interim pres. 1989, chmn. bd., pres., 1989-90; mem. President's Adv. Bd. on Pvt. Sector Initiatives, Washington, 1986-89; chmn. bd. dirs. Bard Coll. Health Policy and Practice Inst., 1988-96, Consumer Health Info. Rsch. Inst., 1990-95, Chelsea-Arbor Treatment Ctr., 1990-91; bd. dirs. Calhoun County Bd. Health, 1988-91, chmn., 1989-91; mem., bd. dirs. Mental Health and Addictions Found. Mich., Battle Creek, 1991-93; mem. adv. coun. CMA Found., 2004-07; mem. cmty. adv. com., Taser Found., Scottsdale, Ariz., 2005—, bd. dirs. 2006—, chair, 2006—. Recipient Harvard Dental award Harvard U. Sch. Dental Medicine, 1992, Disting. Alumni award for achievement U. Iowa Coll. Medicine, 1998, annual Robert D. Sparks Cmty. Health Leadership Achievement award CMA Found., 1997— Fellow ACP; mem. AMA, Nat. Acad. Scis. Inst. Medicine (com. study of treatment and rehab. svcs. for alcoholism and alcohol abuse, bd. mental health and behavioral medicine), Coun. Mich. Founds. (trustee 1986-88), Assn. Am. Med. Colls. (disting. svc. mem. 1975—), Phi Eta Sigma, Alpha Omega Alpha, Ph Kappa Psi. Republican. Methodist. Avocations: tennis, bridge, reading, travel. Home and Office: 5004 Gresham Dr El Dorado Hills CA 95762-7703 Office Phone: 916-230-0719. Personal E-mail: rdsparksmd1@earthlink.net.

SPARKS, ROBERT RONOLD, JR., lawyer; b. Bklyn., Dec. 4, 1946; s. Robert Ronold Sr. and Marjorie Anne (Boehm) S. BA, Va. Mil. Inst., 1969; JD, U. Va., 1972. Bar: U.S. Dist. Ct. (D.C. cir.) 1979, U.S. Dist. Ct. (ea. dist.) Va. 1979, U.S. Ct. Appeals (2d cir.) 1986, U.S. Ct. Appeals (D.C. cir.) 1975, Va. 1972, U.S. Ct. Appeals (4th cir.) 1982, U.S. Ct. Mil. Appeals 1976, U.S. Tax Ct. 1978, U.S. Supreme Ct. 1981, U.S. Dist. Ct. Md. 1993. From assoc. to ptnr. Sedam & Herge, McLean, Va., 1977-85; ptnr. Herge, Sparks & Christopher, McLean, 1985—2004, Sparks & Craig, McLean, 2005—. Mem. Bd. Regents James Monroe Law Office Mus. and Meml. Library, Fredericksburg, Va., 1983-86; chmn. Fairfax County Electoral Bd., 2006-. Mem. Fairfax County Redevel. and Housing Authority, Fairfax, Va., 1981—82; commr. Fairfax County Indsl. Devel. Authority, 1980—81, Fairfax County Planning Commn., 1983—89; chmn. Fairfax County Electoral Bd., 2006—. Lt. USNR, 1972—77, Philippines. Mem. Va. Bar Assn., D.C. Bar Assn., Rotary (treas., bd. dirs. 1978-80). Roman Catholic.

SPARKS, ROBERT WILLIAM, retired publishing executive; b. Seattle, Dec. 30, 1925; s. James Donald and Gladys (Simmons) S. Student, U. Wash., 1947-50; BA, U. Hawaii, 1954, MA, 1965. Editor, various publs., 1947-64; mng. editor U. Hawaii Press, 1964-66, dir., 1967-87. Cons. East-West Ctr., Jour. Hawaiian History, Japanese and Chinese book pubs., 1987-92; advisor New World Press, Beijing, 1986; mem. adv. bd. to pres. Kamehameha Schs. Author: Seattle, Sitka, San Francisco, 1955, Letters From an Island, 1962, New Endings, 1989, Riding Backwards, 2002; contbr. articles to internat. pub. jours. Served with AUS, 1944-46, PTO. Recipient McInerny editorship, 1953; Pacific House citation Pacific and Asian Affairs Council, 1974 Mem. Assn. Am. Univ. Presses, Assn. Am. Publishers, Internat. Assn. Scholarly Publishers, Soc. for Scholarly Pub., Hawaiian Hist. Soc., Hawaii Found. History and Humanities, Honolulu Acad. Arts, Bishop Mus. Assn. Home: 66 Queen St PH4102 Honolulu HI 96813-4449 Personal E-mail: nihipali@hawaii.rr.com.

SPARKS, SAM, federal judge; b. 1939; BA, U. Tex., 1961, LLB, 1963. Aide Rep. Homer Thornberry, 1963; law clk. to Hon. Homer Thornberry U.S. Dist. Ct. (we. dist.) Tex., 1963-65; assoc. to ptnr., shareholder Hardie, Grambling, Sims & Galatzan (and successor firms), El Paso, Tex., 1965-91; dist. judge U.S. Dist. Ct. (we. dist.) Tex., 1991—. Fellow Am. Coll. Trial Lawyers, Tex. Bar Found. (life); mem. Am. Bd. Trial Advocates (advocate), State Bar Tex Office: US Dist Ct Judge 200 W 8th St Ste 100 Austin TX 78701-2333 Office Phone: 512-916-5230.

SPARKS, THOMAS E., JR., lawyer; b. Little Rock, Jan. 11, 1942; children: Thomas Gunnar, Erik Richard, Andrew Pal. BS, Washington and Lee U., 1963; JD, U. Ark., 1968; LLM, Harvard U., 1970. Bar: Ark. 1968, Calif. 1970. Assoc. Pillsbury Madison & Sutro, San Francisco, 1970-76; ptnr. Pillsbury, Madison & Sutro, San Francisco, 1977-84, Baker & McKenzie, San Francisco, 1984-87, Pillsbury Madison & Sutro, San Francisco, 1987-2000, Pillsbury Winthrop, San Francisco, 2001—. Trustee Grace Cathedral, San Francisco. 1st lt. U.S. Army, 1965. Mem. ABA, Calif. Bar Assn., Calif. Tennis Club (pres. 2000). Office: Pillsbury Winthrop LLP 50 Fremont St San Francisco CA 94105-2230

SPARKS, W. DONALD, II, lawyer; b. Durham, NC, Apr. 16, 1958; BA summa cum laude, Dartmouth Coll., 1980; JD, Yale U., 1983. Bar: Pa. 1983, Del. 1988. Law clk. to Hon. Caleb M. Wright US Dist. Ct. (dist. Del.), 1983—84; atty. Richards, Layton & Finger, P.A., Wilmington, Del. Named one of Top 100 Attys., Worth mag., 2006. Fellow: Am. Coll. Trust and Estate Counsel; mem.: ABA, Del. State Bar Assn., Pa. State Bar Assn. Office: Richards Layton & Finger PA 1 Rodney Sq 920 N King St Wilmington DE 19801 Office Phone: 302-651-7758. Office Fax: 302-498-7758. E-mail: sparks@rlf.com. *

SPARKS, WILLIAM SHERAL, retired librarian; b. Alden Bridge, La., Oct. 30, 1924; s. Fred DeWitt and Truda (Bradford) S.; m. Joy Eleanor Young, Aug. 8, 1947; 1 child, David Frederick. AB, Phillips U., 1946; MDiv, Christian Theol. Sem., 1949; ThM, Iliff Sch. of Theology, 1955, ThD, 1957; MA, U. Denver, 1962. Pastor chs., 1950-60; asst. libr. Kans. Wesleyan U., Salina, 1962-66; dir. libr. and info. svcs. St. Paul Sch. of Theology, Kansas City, Mo., 1966-93, ret., 1993. Horowitz Found. fellow Hebrew Union Coll.-Jewish Inst. of Religion, Cin., 1949-52. Mem. Am. Theol. Libr. Assn.

SPARROW, ALISON KIDDER, painter, sculptor; b. Grosse Pointe, Mich., Feb. 13, 1974; d. Herbert George and Nancy Woodruff Sparrow. BFA, RISD, 1997. Fellow Va. Ctr. for the Creative Arts, Lynchburg, 2002, 2004; artist in residence Mary Anderson Ctr. for the Arts, Mt. St Francis, Ind., 2002—05; Hambidge fellow, 2003; artist in residence Contemporary

Artist Ctr., North Adams, Mass., 2006, Ragdale, Lake Forest, Ill., 2007. Exhibitions include Inst. for Unpopular Culture of San Francisco, Detroit Artists Market, Scarab Club of Detroit, Moore Art Gallery of St. Clair, Nat. Scholastic Hallmark award (Best of Show (Mich. region), Internat. Salon Exhbn. of Small Works, 2002—06, Mike Kelley Selects, 2004, Member Show, 2006, Represented in permanent collections Mary Anderson Ctr., Mt. St. Francis, Ind., Vt. Studio Ctr., Johnson. Tchr. Literacy Volunteers of Am., Detroit, 2000—03; vol. Inst. for Unpopular Culture, San Francisco, 1999—2002, Providence Pub. Schools, 2001, Detroit Inst. of Arts. Recipient Advanced Standing, RISD, 1996; fellow, Woodstock Guild, 2002, 2003, 2006; grantee, Vt. Studio Ctr., 2002, 2004, 2006. Fellow: Scarab Club (assoc.); mem.: Nat. Mus. of Women in the Arts (records stored in archives). Green Party. Protestant. Avocation: writing. Office Phone: 313-300-0971. Personal E-mail: sparrow_alison@yahoo.com.

SPARROW, EPHRAIM MAURICE, mechanical engineering scientist, educator; b. Hartford, Conn., May 27, 1928; s. Charles and Frieda (Gottlieb) S.; m. Ruth May Saltman, Nov. 2, 1952; 1 child, Rachel Bernarr. BS, MIT, 1948, MS, 1949; MA, Harvard Coll., 1950, PhD, 1956; PhD (hon.), U. Brazil, 1967. Heat transfer specialist Raytheon Mfg. Co., 1952-53; rsch. specialist Lewis Rsch. Ctr., NASA, Cleve., 1953-59; prof. mech. engring. U. Minn., 1959—, Inst. prof., 1994—, chmn. fluid dynamics program, 1968-80, Morse alumni disting. tchg. prof., 1980—. Program dir. NSF, 1986-87, dir. chem., biochem. and thermal engring. divsn., 1986-88; vis. prof., chief AID mission U. Brazil, 1966-67; adv. prof. Xi'an Jiaotong U., 1984—; cons. in field, 1960—; pres. 1st Brazilian Symposium on Heat Transfer and Fluid Mechanics, 1966; mem. solar energy panel Fed. Coun. on Sci. and Tech., 1972; U.S. sci. committeeman 5th Internat. Heat Transfer Conf., 1973-74. Author: (with R.D. Cess) Radiation Heat Transfer, 1966, 2nd edit., 1978; editor: Handbook of Numerical Heat Transfer, 1988, Advances in Numerical Heat Transfer, vol. 1, 1997, vol. 2, 2000; hon. mem. editl. bd. Internat. Jour. Heat Mass Transfer, 1964—, Internat. Comm. in Heat Mass Transfer, 1975—; sr. editor Jour. Heat Transfer, 1972-80; editor Series in Computational and Phys. Processes in Mechanics and Thermal Scis., 1980—; chmn. editl. adv. bd. Numerical Heat Transfer, 1978—; contbr. over 560 tech. articles to profl. jours. Recipient Ralph Coates Roe award Am. Soc. Engring. Edn., 1978, Outstanding Teaching award U. Minn., 1985, Fed. Engr. of Yr. award NSF, 1988, Sr. Rsch. award Am. Soc. Engring. Edn., 1989, Horace T. Morse award for outstanding contbns. to undergraduate teaching, 1993, Disting. Tchg. award Acad. Disting. Tchrs., U. Minn., 1997, 99, Donald Q. Kern award, Am. Inst. Chemical Engrs., 1999; named George Hawkins Disting. lectr. Purdue U., 1985. Fellow ASME (Meml. award for outstanding contbn. to sci. heat transfer 1962, Max Jakob award for eminent contbn. 1976, Centennial medal 1980, Disting. Svc. award heat transfer divsn. 1982, Charles Russ Richards Meml. award 1985, Worcester Reed Warner medal 1986, 50th Anniversary award heat transfer divsn. 1988, Disting. lectr. 1986-91, 93-94); mem. NAE, Biomed. Engring. Soc. (faculty advisor 1994—), Sigma Xi (Monie A. Ferst medal for contbn. to rsch. through edn. 1993), Pi Tau Sigma. Home: 2105 West Hoyt Ave Saint Paul MN 55108-1314 Office: U Minn Dept Mech Engring Minneapolis MN 55455-0111 Home Phone: 651-647-0787; Office Phone: 612-625-5502. Business E-Mail: esparrow@umn.edu.

SPARROW, HERBERT GEORGE, III, lawyer, educator; b. Ft. Bragg, NC, May 26, 1936; s. Herbert George and Virginia (Monroe) S.; m. Nancy Woodruff, Mar. 4, 1962; children: Amy Winslow, Edward Harrison, Herbert G. IV, Alison Kidder. AB cum laude, Princeton U., 1958; JD, U. Mich., 1961. Bar: Mich. 1961, Calif. 1964, D.C. 1979, U.S. Ct. Claims 1982, U.S. Tax Ct. 1983, U.S. Ct. Mil. Appeals 1962, U.S. Supreme Ct. 1976. Assoc. Dickinson Wright PLLC, Detroit, 1965-70, ptnr., 1970—. Adj. prof. Detroit Coll. Law, Mich. State U., 1977-99. Author numerous articles environ. law.; speaker in field. Bd. dirs. Family Life Edn. Coun., Grosse Pointe, Mich., 1982-88, Adult Well-Being Svcs., Inc., Detroit, 1995-2001; cons. Adult Well-Being Svcs. Inc., 2001—. Capt. JAGC, U.S. Army, 1962-65. Mem. Mich. Bar Assn. (rep. assembly 1979-85, environ. law sect. coun. 1985-91), Calif. Bar Assn., Detroit Bar Assn., Am. Arbitration Assn. (panel arbitrators 1975—), Mich. State Bar Found. (fellow 1989-93), Environment Law Inst. (former assoc.), Phi Delta Phi (pres. Kent Inn Assn., Ann Arbor 1985-97). Office: Dickinson Wright PLLC 500 Woodward Ave Ste 4000 Detroit MI 48226-3416

SPARROW, JOSHUA D., child psychiatrist; married; 2 children. BA, Wesleyan U.; MD, Yale Med. Sch. Assoc. prof. psychiatry Univ. Marseille Sch. Med., France; asst. prof. psychiatry Harvard Med. Sch., Boston, clin. prof. pediat. emeritus; supr. inpatient psychiatry unit Children's Hospital, Boston, founder Child Devel. Unit; assoc. dir. Brazelton Touchpoints Ctr., dir. spl. initiatives. Cons. Harlem Children's Zone, NYC, Am. Indian Early Head Start Programs, Careplus HMO, NYC; mem. adv. bd. Ready, Set, Learn, 2005—. Co-author (with Dr. T. Berry Brazelton): (NY Times syndicated column) Families Today, 1999—, (books) Touchpoints: Three to Six, 2001, Brazelton Way book series, 2004—; cons. (TV series) Brazelton on Parenting, 2000, Ready, Set, Learn, 2005—, contbr. Family Circle mag., Family & Child mag. Coach girls' soccer team, Brookline, Mass. Office: Children's Hospital Ste 320 1295 Boylston St Boston MA 02215 also: Children's Hospital 300 Longwood Ave Boston MA 02215 also: NY Times Syndication Sales Corp 14th Fl 122 E 42nd St New York NY 10168 Office Phone: 617-355-7639. Office Fax: 617-859-7215, 212-499-3382. E-mail: joshua.sparrow@tch.harvard.edu, nytsyn-families@nytimes.com.

SPARROW, KATHLEEN GAIL, retired secondary school educator; b. Akron, Ohio, Apr. 20, 1948; d. Richard Donald and Eldean Kathryn Kraft Sparrow; m. Philip Heiner Gross, May 5, 1988. BA, Miami U., Oxford, Ohio, 1970; MA, U. Akron, 1974, PhD, 1987. Sci. tchr. Akron Pub. Schs., 1970—92, sci. learning specialist k-12, 1992—2006. Praxis III evaluator Ohio Dept. Edn., Columbus, 2003—; nat. selection com. presdl. awards math. and sci. NSF, Washington, 1998—98; mem. global polymer acad. steering com. U. Akron, 2001—; co-prin. investigator NSF gk-12 grant U. Akron and Akron Pub. Schs., 2001—04; co-prin. investigator NSF comprehensive partnership math. and sci. achievement Akron Pub. Schs., 1996—2001; mem. content rev. com. Ohio graduation test Ohio Dept. Edn., Columbus, 2003—, mem. sci. content rev. com.ohio graduation test, 1999—2000, mem. sci. content standards adv. bd., 2001—02, mem. sci. program model writing com., 2005—; adj. prof. U. Akron, 1994—2005, Ashland U., 1996—. Mem. humane commn. County of Summit, Akron; leadership cir., mem. Humane Soc. Greater Akron, Peninsula. Recipient Nat. Sci. Supr. award, Nat. Sci. Ednl. Leadership Assn., 1999, Disting. award Coun., Akron Coun. Engring. and Sci. Socs., 2001, Friend Sci. award, Sci. Edn. Coun. Ohio, 2001; scholar, Martha Holden Jennings Found., 2002. Mem.: ASCD (assoc.), Nat. Sci. Ednl. Leadership Assn. (assoc.; pres. 2000—01, dir. region E 1996—99, coun. mem. 1999—2001), Nat. Sci. Tchrs. Assn. (assoc.), Phi Delta Kappa (pres. 1987—88, 1996—99, Svc. Key 1989). Independent. Home: 7047 Imperial Beach Cir Delray Beach FL 33446-5632 Home Phone: 561-498-7948. Personal E-mail: ksparrow@adelphia.net.

SPARTZ, ALICE ANNE LENORE, retired retail executive; b. NYC, May 14, 1925; d. John Francis and Alice Philomena (Murray) Rattenbury; m. George Eugene Spartz, Oct. 29, 1949; children: Mary Elizabeth, James, Barbara, Anne, Thomas, William, Michael, John, Matthew, Clare, Robert, Richard. Student, Wright Coll., 1945—47, No. Ill. U., 1950; AA, Triton Coll., 1987. Svc. rep. Ill. Bell Tel., Chgo., 1945-46; stewardess United Airlines, Denver, 1947-49; ret. mgr. Family Life League Resale Shop, Oak Park, Ill., 1987-95; retired, 1995. Mem. Cicero Cmty. Coun., Ill., 1967—69, Pk. Dist. Oak Pk. Com., 1973—74; active Ill. Right to Life Com., Chgo., 1971—2002, Com. Pro-Life Cath., Chgo., 1992—; pres., bd. trustees Trailwood Village Bd., Kingwood, Tex., 2003; bd. dirs. Direct Energy Techs., A Solar Co., Tex.; mem. St. Martha's Roman Cath. Ch.; former bd. dir. Ill. Pro-Life Coalition, Family Life League; vol. canteen worker ARC, Chgo., 1942—45. Mem.: Trailwood Village Cmty. Assn. (trustee 2004). Republican. Roman Catholic. Avocations: travel, sewing, reading, swimming, pro-life activist. Office: 2026 Seven Oaks Dr Kingwood TX 77339

SPATAFORA, MARCELLO, ambassador; b. Innsbruck, Austria, 1941; married; 1 child. Grad. in Internat. Law, U. Pisa, Italy, 1962. With diplomatic corps Italian Ministry Fgn. Affairs, 1964, vice consul Paris, 1968—70, counselor Belgrade, Serbia, 1970—73, counselor, Chargé d'Affaires Beirut, 1975—77, with Office of Sec.-Gen. Rome, 1977—80, amb. to Malaysia, 1980—86, amb. to Malta, 1986—89, chief. Italian del. responsible for organizing Italy's presidency to the European Econ. Cmty., 1989—90, head arms export licensing unit Rome, 1991—93, amb. to Australia, 1993—97, amb. to Albania, 1997—99, gen. dir. multilateral econ. and fin. cooperation Rome, 2000—03, amb., permanent rep. to UN NYC, 2003—. Office: Permanent Mission of Italy to UN 1 United Nations Plz 24th Fl New York NY 10017 Office Phone: 212-486-9191. Office Fax: 212-486-1036.

SPATT, ARTHUR DONALD, federal judge; b. 1925; Student, Ohio State U., 1943-44, 46-47; LLB cum laude, Bklyn. Law Sch., 1949. Assoc. Davidson & Davidson, NYC, 1949, Lane, Winard, Robinson & Schorr, NYC, 1950, Alfred S. Julien, NYC, 1950-52, Florea & Florea, NYC, 1953; pvt. practice NYC, 1953-67, Spatt & Bauman, NYC, 1967-78; justice 10th judicial cir. N.Y. State Supreme Ct., 1979-82; adminstrv. judge Nassau County, 1982-86; assoc. justice appellate div. Second Judicial Dept., 1986-89; dist. judge U.S. Dist. Ct. (ea. dist.) N.Y., Bklyn., 1989-90, Uniondale, NY, 1990-2000, Central Islip, NY, 2000—. Book review editor Bklyn. Law Review, 1948—49. Active Jewish War Vets. With USN, 1944—46. Mem. ABA, Assn. Supreme Ct. Justices State of N.Y., Bar Assn. Nassau County, Jewish Lawyers Assn. Nassau County, Long Beach Lawyers Assn. Office: Long Island Courthouse 1024 Federal Plaza Central Islip NY 11722-4445 Office Phone: 631-712-5620.

SPATT, HARTLEY STEVEN, humanities educator; b. Bklyn., Nov. 21, 1947; s. Milton E. and Blanche S. (Bakstansky) S.; m. Wendy Doroshkin, June 13, 1971; children: Martin, Samantha. BA summa cum laude, Colgate U., 1970; MA, NYU, 1971, Johns Hopkins U., 1973, PhD, 1975. Asst. prof. Towson State U., Balt., 1974-76, SUNY Maritime Coll., Bronx, 1976-81, assoc. prof., 1981-87, prof., 1987—, Disting. Tchg. prof., 2004—, assoc. v.p. for acad. affairs, 1999—2002. Writer, editor A.L. Fierst, Greatneck, N.Y., 1977-80, Reference Works, 1993-2001; bus. mgr. Victorian Studies Bull., N.Y.C., 1983—; writer Chernow Editl. Svcs., N.Y.C., 1985-90. Contbr. articles to Victorian Poetry, Walt Whitman Rev., other profl. jours. NEH fellow, 1979, 82, 86, 2004. Mem. MLA, N.E. Victorian Studies Assn. (chair nominations 1985—), William Morris Soc. U.S. (sec.-treas. 1984—), Phi Beta Kappa. Republican. Jewish. Office: Maritime Coll Suny Bronx NY 10465 Office Phone: 718-409-7250. E-mail: hspatt@sunymaritime.edu.

SPATT, ROBERT EDWARD, lawyer; b. Bklyn., Mar. 26, 1956; s. Milton E. and Blanche S. Spatt; m. Lisa B. Malkin, Aug. 11, 1979; 1 child, Mark Eric. AB, Brown U., 1977; JD magna cum laude, U. Mich., 1980. Bar: N.Y. 1981. Assoc. Simpson Thacher & Bartlett, NYC, 1980-87, ptnr., 1987—. Mem. ABA, N.Y. State Bar Assn., City of N.Y. Bar Assn., Order of Coif. Avocations: photography, boating, reading. Office: Simpson Thacher & Bartlett 425 Lexington Ave New York NY 10017-3954 Office Phone: 212-455-2685. E-mail: RSpatt@stblaw.com.

SPAULDING, DAN, public relations executive; BA, MA, U. Mich. Lt. USN; aide, pub. affairs officer to comdr. Tng. Command U.S. Pacific Fleet, San Diego, 1969-72; news anchor/prodr./reporter Staf. WFRV-TV, Green Bay, Wis., Sta. WEYI-TV, Flint-Saginaw, Mich.; mem. faculty U. Wis., Green Bay; news dir. Sta. KOMU-TV, Columbia, Mo., Sta. WOTV-TV 8; with Seyferth & Assocs., Inc., Grand Rapids, Mich., 1989-94, exec. v.p., 1994—. Active West Mich. Environ. Action Coun. Mem. Pub. Rels. Soc. Am. (accredited). Office: Seyferth Spaulding Tennyson 40 Monroe Center NW, Suite 202 Grand Rapids MI 49503-3003 Business E-Mail: info@seyferthpr.com.

SPAULDING, GEORGE B., state official; b. Washington, Dec. 28, 1952; m. Susan Morse; children: Abigail, Bailey. BA, Antioch Coll., 1975; MEd, U. Vt., 1993. Owner, mgr. radio sta.; operator Black Angus breeding farm; dir. Vt. Acad. Sci. & Tech. Vt. Tech. Coll.; gen. ptnr. Precision Media Inc.; dir., career and workforce develop. Vt. Dept. Edn.; mem. Edn. Commn. States; del. Dem. Nat. Conv., 1988; mem. Vt. Senate, 1985—2000; state treas. State of Vt., 2002—. Adj. instructor Norwich Univ. Mem., past bd. dirs. Cen. Vt. chpt. ARC, United Way; mem. Gov.'s Snowmobile Adv. Coun.; bd. dir. Red Cross, United Way Washington County 4-H Found., Woodbury Coll.; mem. Ctrl. Vt. Adult Basic Edn., Child Care Fund Vt. and Woodbury Coll. Mem. Nat. Assn. Broadcasters, Vt. Assn. Broadcasters, Vt. Angus Assn., Vt. Red Cross, Green Mt. United Way, New Eng. Bd. Higher Ed. Address: 109 State St Montpelier VT 05609 Office Phone: 802-828-2301. Office Fax: 802-828-2772. *

SPAULDING, MAR, retired special education educator; b. Bellevue, Ky., Oct. 16, 1933; d. Mickey and Blanche Harris; m. Stan Lee Spaulding; children: Karla, Julie Underwood, Lisa Williams, Gregory. MA, Ea. Mich. U., 1978; BS, George Mason U., 1973. Cert. educator Emotionally/Neurologically Impaired, Pre-primary Impaired 1978. Head tchr. in nursery sch., Ann Arbor, Mich., 1973—75; intern Ypsilanti State Mental Instn., Mich., 1975—76; tchr. emotionally impaired and pre-primary impaired Monroe County Intermediate Dist., Monroe, Mich., 1978—93. Leader of groups of parents of handicapped children Monroe County Intermediate Sch. Dist., Monroe, Mich., 1978—93, mem. of grant com., 1980—96, tester on child find com., 1979—85. Author: (children's educational book) Kate Lynn's Fantastic Dream, 1999 (Spl. Edn. Tchr. of the Yr. in Monroe County, Mich., 1995), (companion book) Activities to use with Kate Lynn's Fantastic Dream. Includes cognitive, speech and language, fine motor, gross motor and behavioral, emotional skill areas for teachers and parents., 1999. Story lady Head Start, Baker Devel. Ctr., Punta Gorda, Fla., 1996—2002; tutor Continuing Edn. Ctr. and Even Start, Port Charlotte and Punta Gorda, 1996—2003; membership involvement chairperson Peace River Power Squadron, Punta Gorda, 1996—2003; pub. spkr. topics concerning early childhood edn. Early Childhood Edn. Assn. of SW Fla., Punta Gorda, 1999—2003. Recipient Writer's Award, US Power Squadrons, 2001. Mem.: AAUW (Ft. Myers, Fla. chpt.), U.S. Sail and Power Squadrons, Thomas Paine Nat. Hist. Soc., Nat. Honor Soc., Phi Kappa Phi. Liberal. Avocations: travel, sailing, swimming, bicycling, piano. Home: 1536 Islamorada Blvd Punta Gorda FL 33955 Personal E-mail: marstan@nut-n-but.net.

SPAULDING, WALLACE HOLMES, retired federal agency professional; b. Oakland, Calif., Sept. 3, 1928; s. Wallace Holmes and May Gibbons (Alves) S.; m. Dorothy Anne Wollon, Jan. 30, 1960; children: James Wallace, Anne Catherine Bridger. AB, U. Calif., Berkeley, 1950; MA, Johns Hopkins U., 1951; PhD, U. Pa., 1969. Rschr. CIA, McLean, Va., 1952-91; ret., 1991. Author: Is the Comintern Coming Back?, 1998; contbr. chpts. to books and articles to profl. jours. Pres. Fellowship of Concerned Churchmen, McLean, Va., Found. for Christian Theology, Washington; corres. sec. Soc. of Mary, McLean. Col. (ret.) USAR, 1950—81. Decorated Meritorious Svc. medal U.S. Army; Fulbright scholar, The Philippines, 1951-52. Mem.: Phi Beta Kappa, Pan Xenia, Alpha Delta Phi. Avocations: walking, domestic and foreign travel. Home: #917 The Jefferson 900 N Taylor St Arlington VA 22203 Personal E-mail: whsdws@jefres.org.

SPEAKER, SUSAN JANE, lawyer; b. Dallas, Dec. 25, 1946; d. William R. and Jane E. (Aldrich) Turner; m. David C. Speaker, Dec. 21, 1968; children: David Allen, Melissa. BA, U. Ark., 1970, JD, 1985. Bar: Okla. 1985, U.S. Dist. Ct. (no., ea. and we. dists.) Okla. 1985. Assoc. Hall, Estill, Hardwick, Gable, Golden & Nelson, P.C., Tulsa, 1985-91; atty. Resolution Trust Corp., 1991-92; shareholder Speaker & Matthews, P.C., 1992-96; atty. Comml. Fin. Svcs., Inc., Tulsa, 1996-99; exec. dir. properties and concessions Dollar Thrifty Automotive Group, Inc., 1999—. Editor U. Ark. Law Rev., 1983-85. Mem. ABA, ATLA, Okla. Bar Assn., Tulsa Bar Assn., Tulsa Title and Probate Lawyers Assn., Phi Beta Kappa, Delta Theta Phi.

SPEAKMAN, JOSEPH M., retired history professor; b. Phila., May 8, 1940; s. Joseph Aloysius and Dorothy Carney Speakman; m. Karen M. Hudecheck, Aug. 21, 1965. BA, La Salle U., Phila., 1963; MA, Temple U., Phila., 1972; PhD, Temple U., 1976. Prof. history Montgomery County CC, Blue Bell, Pa., 1971—2005, prof. emeritus, 2005—; adj. prof. Villanova U., Pa., Temple U., St. Joseph's U., Phila., La Salle U. Author: (book) At Work in Penn's Woods, 2006; contbr. articles to profl. jours. Mem.: Historical Soc. Penn., Orgn. Am Historians, Am. History Soc. Avocations: piano, baseball, running, hiking. Home: 201 Cobblestone Dr Ardmore PA 19003

SPEAR, ALLAN HENRY, state legislator, historian, educator; b. Michigan City, Ind., June 24, 1937; s. Irving S. and Esther (Lieber) S. BA, Oberlin Coll., 1958, LLD (hon.), 1997; MA, Yale U., 1960, PhD, 1965. Lectr. history U. Minn., Mpls., 1964-65, asst. prof., 1965-67, assoc. prof., 1967-2000; mem. Minn. State Senate, St. Paul, 1973-2000, chmn. jud. com., 1983-93; chmn. crime prevention com., 1993-2000; pres. Minn. State Senate, 1993—2000; vice-chair Minn. Campaign Fin. and Pub. Disclosure Bd., 2001—03. Vis. prof. Carleton Coll., Northfield, Minn., 1970, Stanford U., Palo Alto, Calif., 1970. Author: Black Chicago, 1967. Mem. Internat. Network Gay and Lesbian Ofcls. Avocations: cooking, travel, reading, classical music. Home: 2429 Colfax Ave S Minneapolis MN 55405-2942

SPEAR, HARVEY M., lawyer; b. Providence, May 24, 1922; s. Alfred and Esther S.; m. Ruth Abramson, June 27, 1965; children: Jessica, Elizabeth Rogers. AB, Brown U., 1942; LL.B., Harvard, 1948; MA, George Washington U., 1949, LL.M., 1952, S.JD, 1955. Bar: Mass. 1948, D.C. 1948, N.Y. 1954, U.S. Supreme Ct. 1954; CPA, Md. Asst. U.S. atty. D.C., 1945; legal asst. to chmn., asst. to vice chmn. SEC, 1948—50; spl. asst. to atty. gen. Dept. Justice, 1951—54; pvt. practice law NYC and Washington, 1956—; counsel Cadwalader Wickersham & Taft, NYC, 1996—. Contbr. articles to profl. jours. Mem.: ABA, Assn. of Bar of City of NY. Home: 765 Park Ave New York NY 10021-4254 also: 78 Hither Ln East Hampton NY 11937 Office: One World Fin Ctr New York NY 10281 Business E-Mail: harvey.spear@cwt.com.

SPEAR, JOSEPH E., architect; AA, BArch. Cert. arch., Nat. Coun. Archtl. Registration Bds. Founding sr. prin. Hellmuth Obata & Kassabaum Sport, Kansas City, Mo., 1983—. Prin. works include AT&T Park, San Francisco, Citizens Bank Park, Phila., Oriole Park at Camden Yards (Nat. AIA Honor award), Robert F. Kennedy Stadium, Washington, Jacobs Field, Cleve. (Nat. AIA Honor award). Fellow: AIA. Achievements include the design of 10 major league ballparks. Office: Hellmuth Obata & Kassabaum Sport 300 Wyandotte Ste 300 Kansas City MO 64105 Office Phone: 816-221-1500. Office Fax: 816-221-1578. *

SPEAR, LAURINDA HOPE, architect; m. Bernardo Fort-Brescia. BFA, Brown U., 1972; MArch, Columbia U., 1975. Registered architect, Fla., N.Y.; cert. Nat. Coun. Archtl. Registration. Founding prin. Arquitectonica (ARQ), Miami, Fla., 1977—. Lectr. in field. Prin. works include Pink Ho., Miami, Fla., 1978, The Palace, Miami, 1982 (Honor award Miami chpt. AIA 1982), The Atlantis, Miami, 1982 (Miami chpt. AIA award 1983), The Imperial, Miami, 1983, Casa los Andes (Record Hos. award Archtl. Record 1986), North Dade Justice Ctr., Miami, 1987 (Honor award Miami chpt. AIA 1989), Rio, Atlanta, 1988 (Honor award Miami chpt. AIA 1989), Banco de Credito del Peru, Lima, 1988 (Honor award Miami chpt. AIA 1989), The Ctr. Innovative Tech., Herndon, Va., 1988 (Honor award Va. chpt. AIA 1989, Honor award Miami chpt. 1990, Merit award Fairfax, Va., County Exceptional Design Awards Program 1990), Sawgrass Mills (Merit award Miami chpt. AIA 1990, Honor award Fla. chpt. 1991), Miracle Ctr. (Honor award Miami chpt. AIA 1989), Internat. Swimming Hall of Fame, Ft. Lauderdale, Fla., 1991, Banque de Luxembourg, 1993, Disney All-Star Resorts, Orlando, Fla., 1994, U.S. Embassy, Lima, 1994, USCG Family Housing, Bayamon, P.R., 1994, Altamira Ctr., Caracas, Venezuela, 1994, Festival Walk, Hong Kong, 1998, Miami Fed. Courthouse, Am. Airlines Arena, Miami, 1999, Philips Arena, Atlanta, 1999, Miami Internat. Airport D-E-F Wrap. Mem. beaux arts support group Lowe Art Mus., Miami; bd. dirs. Miami Youth Mus. Recipient Design Awards citation Progressive Architecture, 1975, 80, Rome Prize in Architecture, 1978, Award of Excellence, Atlanta Urban Design Commn., 1989; inductee Interior Design Hall of Fame, 1999. Fellow AIA (Silver medal for design 1998); mem. Internat. Womens Forum, NAD (academician, 1994-). Office: Arquitectonica International Corp 801 Brickell Ave Ste 1100 Miami FL 33131-2945 Office Phone: 305-372-1812. Office Fax: 305-372-1175. Business E-Mail: lspear@arqintl.com.

SPEAR, PETER D., retired academic administrator; BA, Rutgers U., 1966; PhD in Physiol. Psychology, Yale U., 1970. Postdoctoral fellow dept. neurology Stanford U. Sch. Medicine, Calif., 1970—72; asst. prof. psychology Kans. State U., 1972, U. Wis., Madison, 1976—78, assoc. prof., 1978—81, prof., 1981, chair dept. psychology, 1990—94, assoc. dean social sci. Coll. Letters and Sci., 1994—96, provost, vice chancellor for acad. affairs, 2001—05; dean Coll. Arts and Scis. U. Colo., Boulder, 1996—2001; ret., 2005. Co-author: Psychology: Perspectives on Behavior. Business E-Mail: pspear@wisc.edu.

SPEAR, SCOTT LAWRENCE, plastic surgeon; b. Chgo., Aug. 25, 1948; s. Louis and Esther S.; m. Cynthia Staley Spear; children: ALexandra, Geri, Louis. BA (hon.), U. Mich., Ann Arbor, 1968; MD, U. Chgo., 1972. Cert. Mass., 1986, Calif., 1992, Fla., 1990, Washington, 1981—, Md., 1982—, Va., 1982—, Am. Bd. Surgery, Am. Bd. Plastic Surgery, Am. Bd. Med. Examiners. Intern Beth Israel Hosp., Boston, 1972-73; jr. residency San Francisco Gen. Hosp., 1973-74, Beth Israel Hosp., Boston, 1974-75, sr. residency, 1976-78; plastic surgery residency U. Miami, 1978-80; asst. prof. plastic surgery U. Fla., Gainesville, 1980-81, Georgetown U. Sch. Medicine, Washington, 1981-86, assoc. prof. plastic surgery, 1988-90; dir. Georgetown Univ. Hosp. Plastic Surgery training program, 1992—; prof. plastic surgery Georgetown U. Sch. Medicine, Washington, 1990—, and chief, divsn. plastic surgery. Dir. Nat. Capitol Tng. program, Washington, 1992—, Divsn. of Plastic and Reconstructive Surgery, Georgetown U. Sch. Medicine, Washington, 1992—; vis. prof. U., Tex., 1982, U. Fla., 1982, 84, 85, 86, 87, Nat. Naval Med. Ctr., 1983, 85. Author, Surgery of the Breast; sect. editor, Jour. Plastic and Reconstructive Surgery; featured in NY Times, Washington Post, NPR, ABC, NBC, CBS; contbr. more than 225 articles to profl. jours. Named a Top Doctor, Washingtonian mag., 1986-. Mem. ACS, Med. Soc. of D.C., Plastic Surgery Ednl. Found. (past bd. dir.), Am. Cleft Palata Assn., Nat. Capital Soc. of Plastic Surgeons, Am. Soc. of Maxillofacial Surgeons, Am. Soc. of Plastic and Reconstructive Surgeons,

Northeastern Soc. of Plastic and Reconstructive Surgeons (past pres.), Am. Assn. Plastic Surgeons (past pres., bd. dir.), Am. Soc. for Aesthetic Plastic Surgery (past. bd. dir.), Royal and Ancient Soc. Am. Plastic Surgeons (founder, pres.). Has testified before FDA, Congress as expert regarding breast implants. Office: Georgetown Univ Med Ctr Dept Plastic Surgery 1st Fl PHC Bldg 3800 Reservoir Rd NW Washington DC 20007-2113 Office Phone: 202-444-8612, 202-342-2400. E-mail: spears@gunet.georgetown.edu. *

SPEARING, ANTHONY COLIN, English literature educator; b. London, Jan. 31, 1936; came to U.S., 1987; s. Frederick and Gertrude (Calnin) S. MA, Cambridge U., Eng., 1960. W.M. Tapp rsch. fellow Gonville-Caius Coll. Cambridge U., 1959-60, asst. lectr. in English, 1960-64, official fellow Queens' Coll., 1960-87, life fellow, 1987—, dir. studies in English, 1967-85, lectr. in English, 1964-85, reader in medieval English lit., 1985-87; vis. prof. English U. Va., Charlottesville, 1979-80, 84, prof. English, 1987-89, Kenan prof. English, 1989—. William Matthews lectr. Birkbeck Coll., London, 1983—84; invited lectr. numerous colls. and univs. Eng., Europe, Can., U.S.; Lansdowne vis. fellow U. Victoria, 1993; Benjamin Meaker vis. prof. U. Bristol, 2003; Conway lectr. U. Notre Dame, 2007. Author: Criticism and Medieval Poetry, 1964, rev. edit., 1972; (with Maurice Hussey and James Winny) An Introduction to Chaucer, 1965; The Gawain-Poet: A Critical Study, 1970, Chaucer: Troilus and Criseyde, 1976, Medieval Dream-Poetry, 1976, Medieval to Renaissance in English Poetry, 1985, Readings in Medieval Poetry, 1987, The Medieval Poet as Voyeur, 1993, Textual Subjectivity, 2005; editor: The Pardoner's Prologue and Tale (Chaucer), 1965, rev. edit., 1994, The Knight's Tale (Chaucer), 1966, rev. edit., 1995, The Franklin's Prologue and Tale (Chaucer), 1966, rev. edit., 1994; co-editor: (with Elizabeth Spearing) Shakespeare: The Tempest, 1971, Poetry of the Age of Chaucer, 1974, The Reeve's Prologue and Tale (Chaucer), 1979, Julian of Norwich: Revelations of Divine Love, 1998; translator: The Cloud of Unknowing and Other Works, 2001; contbr. numerous articles to profl. jours. Mem. Medieval Acad. Am., Internat. Assn. U. Profs. English, New Chaucer Soc. (trustee 1986-90). Office: Univ Va Dept English 219 Bryan Hall PO Box 400121 Charlottesville VA 22904-4121 Business E-Mail: acs4j@virginia.edu.

SPEARMAN, MAXIE ANN, financial analyst, administrator; b. Piedmont, SC, Sept. 14, 1942; d. J. Mac and Margaret Cecille S. BS, U. SC, 1965; postgrad., Ga. State U., 1985, U. Ga. Acct. Shell Oil Co., Atlanta, 1965-66; internal auditor Sears, Roebuck & Co., Atlanta, 1966-67; acct. Econ. Opportunity Atlanta, Atlanta, 1967-68, City of Atlanta, 1968-78, fin. analyst, 1978-89, sr. fin. analyst planner, 1989—. Investment cons., Atlanta, Conyers, Ga., 1980—. Mem. Rep. Presdl. Task Force, 1985—, U.S. Senatorial Club, Rep. Nat. Com., 1988—, Ga. Rep. Party, 1990—, Atlanta Safety Com., 1985—, Mayor's Spl. Events Task Force, 1990; charter founder Ronald Reagan Rep. Ctr., 1988; del.-at-large Rep. Platform Planning Com., 1992, 94. Recipient safety award Atlanta City Govt., 1990, Presdl. Commn. Exec. Com. of Republican Party award, 1992; Order of Merit award Nat. Rep. Senatorial Com., 1996. Mem. AAUW, NAFE, Am. Mgmt. Assn., Ga. Assn. Med. Victims, Inc. (sec., treas. 1985—), Nat. Trust for Historic Preservation. Methodist. Avocations: writing, tennis, decorating, investing. Home: 1280 Vineyard Dr SE Conyers GA 30013-2466

SPEARMAN, ROBERT WORTHINGTON, lawyer; b. Durham, NC, Jan. 24, 1943; s. Walter and Mary Elizabeth (Dale) S.; m. Patricia Hinds, June 2, 1973; children: Madolyn Marschall, Dorothy Marschall. BA in Polit. Sci., U. N.C., 1965; MA in Philosophy/Econs., Oxford U., 1967; LLB, Yale U., 1970. Bar: NC 1971, DC 1979, U.S. Dist. Ct. (ea., mid. and we. dists. NC), U.S. Ct. Appeals (4th and 5th cirs.), U.S. Supreme Ct. Law clk. to Justice Hugo L. Black U.S. Supreme Ct., Washington, 1971; assoc. Adams, McCullough & Beard, Raleigh, 1971-75, ptnr., 1975—90; ptnr. litig., antitrust & bus. torts practice group leader Parker Poe Adams & Bernstein LLP, Raleigh, 1990—. Adj. prof. Law Sch., U. N.C., Chapel Hill, 1982-83. Vice chmn. corrections planning com. N.C. Crime Control Commn., 1979-81; chmn. Wake County Democratic Com., 1979-81, N.C. Elections Bd., 1981-85. Vice chmn. corrections planning com. N.C. Crime Control Commn., 1979-81; chmn. Wake County Dem. Com., 1979-81, N.C. Elections Bd., 1981-85. Morehead Found. scholar, 1961, Rhodes scholar, 1965; Razor Walker award, 2002, Defender Justice award 2004; named one of Best Lawyers in Am., 2000, 01, 02, 03, 04, 05, 06, 07, Legal Elite, NC, 2003, 04, 05, 06, 07. Fellow Am. Coll. Trial Lawyers (mem. NC State Com. 2003-05); mem. ABA, N.C. Bar Assn. (chmn. comml. litigation com. 1982-83), Phi Beta Kappa. Presbyterian. Office: Parker Poe Adams & Bernstein LLP Ste 1400 150 Fayetteville St PO Box 389 Raleigh NC 27602-0389 Office Phone: 919-828-0564. Office Fax: 919-835-4560. Business E-Mail: bobspearman@parkerpoe.com.

SPEARS, BRITNEY, singer; b. McComb, Miss., Dec. 2, 1981; d. Jamie and Lynne Spears; m. Jason Alexander, Jan. 2, 2004 (annulled Jan. 5, 2004); m. Kevin Federline, Sept. 18, 2004 (div. July 30, 2007); children: Sean Preston, Jayden James stepchildren: Kori, Kaleb. Released signature fragrance Curious Britney Spears, 2004, Britney Spears: Fantasy, 2005, In Control, 2006. Singer: (albums) Baby One More Time, 1999, Oops! I Did It Again, 2000 (Billboard Album artist of the Year, 2000), Britney, 2001, In the Zone, 2003, Britney Spears Greatest Hits: My Prerogative, 2004, B In The Mix, The Remixes, 2005; actor(voice only): (TV films) Hooves of Fire, 1999, Legends of the Lost Tribe, 2002,: (films) Longshot, 2000, Crossroads, 2002, (TV reality show) Britney And Kevin: Chaotic, 2005; guest appearance with husband (reading a top 10 list on The Late Show with David Letterman), 2005; composer: (songs) (for film Drive Me Crazy) You Drive Me Crazy, 1999, (for film Pokémon the First Movie: Mewtwo Strikes Back) Soda Pop, 1999, (for film On The Line) Let Me Be, 2001, (for film Jimmy Neutron: Boy Genius) Intimidated, 2001, (for film Austin Powers in Goldmember) Boys, 2002. Britney Spears Found. Recipient Female Artist of the Year, Billboard, 1999, New Artist of the Year, 1999, Hot Dance Sales Single of Yr. for "Me Against the Music" featuring Madonna, 2004, Choice Music Single "Baby One More Time", Teen Choice award, 1999, Choice Hottie Female & Choice Female Artist, 2000, 2002, Choice Female Artist, 2001, Choice Music Single "Toxic", 2004, Best New Artist, Am. Music Awards, 2000, Grammy for Best Dance Recording for Toxic, 2005. Mailing: Jive Records 137 W 25th St New York NY 10001-7216

SPEARS, DIANE SHIELDS, retired art director, elementary school educator; b. Seattle, May 21, 1942; d. Richard Keene McKinney and Dorothy Jean (Shields) Thacker; m. Howard Truman Spears, Sept. 3, 1977; 1 child, Truman Eugene. BA in Art, English, Edn., Trinity U., 1964; MA in Christian Counseling, San Antonio Theol. Sem., 1986, D of Christian Edn., 1988. Cert. tchr. secondary edn., elem. edn., ednl. supervision, Tex. Instr. ESL Dliel-Geb (Def. Lang. Inst.), San Antonio, 1973-74, Ceta/Ace Bexar County Sch. Bd., San Antonio, 1975-78; tchr. elem. edn., art, music New Covenant Faith Acad., San Antonio, 1983-89; instr. ESL Jewish Family Svc., San Antonio, 1991; from tchr. elem. art to dir. visual arts Edgewood Ind. Sch. Dist., San Antonio, 1992—99; tchr. Pipe Creek Christian Sch., Tex., 2003—06; ret., 2006. Owner, operator Art for Kings, San Antonio, 1985—2004, Spears Art Studio, Inc., 2004—. Illustrator teacher-created materials-lit. activities for young children, 1989-90; author: (art curriculum) Art for Kings, 1987, Spears Art Studio High School Art Survey; editor: (art curriculum) Edgewood Ind. Sch. Dist. Elem. Art Curriculum, 1993-99; exhibited in group shows at Charles and Emma Frye Mus., Seattle, 1966, 68, Centro Cultural Aztlan Galerie Expression, 1998 (Best of Show 1998). Dir. intercessory prayer New Covenant Fellowship, San Antonio, 1980-90. Recipient awards for painting and graphics, San Antonio, 1996-98. Mem.: San Antonio Art Edn. Assn. (1st pl. 1995), Tex. Art Edn. Assn. (1st pl. graphics divsn. 1995), Nat. Mus. for Women in Arts (charter). Republican. Avocations: water-skiing, motorcycle riding, sewing, writing. Home: 264 Mountain Dr Lakehills TX 78063-6725 Office Phone: 830-612-2585. Personal E-mail: spearsartstudio@earthlink.net.

SPEARS, JAE, state legislator; b. Latonia, Ky. d. James and Sylvia (Fox) Marshall; m. Lawrence E. Spears; children: Katherine Spears Cooper, Marsha Spears-Duncan, Lawrence M., James W. Student, U. Ky. Reporter Cin. Post, Cin. Enquirer newspapers; rschr. Stas. WLW-WSAI, Cin.; tchr. Jiya Gakuen Sch., Japan; lectr. U.S. Mil. installations East Anglia, England; del. State of W.Va., Charleston, 1974-80; mem. W.Va. Senate, Charleston, 1980-1993. Mem. vis. com. W.Va. Extension and Continuing Edn., Morgantown, 1993-2000, W.Va. U. Sch. Medicine, 1992—; with state sen., 1980-93; apptd. to Jud. Hearing Bd., 1993-2000. Chmn. adv bd. Sta. WNPB, 1992-94; congl. liaison Am. Pub. TV Stas. and Sta. WNPB-TV, 1992-97; mem. coun. W.Va. Autism Task Force, Huntington, 1981-90; mem. W.Va. exec. bd. Literacy Vols. Am., 1986-90, 94—, pres., 1990-92; mem. Gov.'s State Literacy Coun., 1991-97; bd. dirs. Found. Ind. Colls. W.Va., 1986—; mem. regional adv. com. W.Va. Gov.'s Task Force for Children, Youth and Family, 1989; mem. USS W.Va. Commn., 1989; mem. exec. com. W.Va. Employer Support Group for Guard and Res., 1989, mem. steering com., 1990-92. Decorated Purple Heart (hon.); recipient Susan B. Anthony award NOW, 1982, edn. award Profl. Educators Assn. W.Va., 1986, ann. award W.Va. Assn. Ret. Sch. Employees, 1985, Meritorious Svc. award W.Va. State Vets. Commn., 1984, Vets. Employment and Tng. Svc. award U.S. Dept. Labor, 1984, award W.Va. Vets. Coun., 1984; named Admiral in N.C. Navy, Gov. of N.C., 1982, hon. Brigadier Gen. W.Va. N.G., 1984, One of 11 Women Pioneers of W.Va. Legislature, W.Va. U. Inst. for Pub. Affairs, 1997, Disting. West Virginian, Gov. W.Va., 2005, Comm. award W.Va. Womens Comm., 2006. Mem. DAR, VFW (aux.), Bus. and Profl. Women (Woman of Yr. award 1978), Nat. League Am. Pen Women (Pen Woman of Yr. 1984), Nat. Order Women Legislators, Am. Legion (aux.), Delta Kappa Gamma, Alpha Xi Delta. Democrat. Home and Office: PO Box 98 Shinnston WV 26431 Office Phone: 304-558-0070.

SPEARS, JAMES GRADY, small business owner; b. Port Arthur, Tex., July 20, 1941; s. John Grady and Dorothy Nell (Haney) S. Grad. high sch., Port Arthur. Adminstr. Child Health & Devel. Studies, Oakland, Calif., 1962—69; sales mgr. Sunshine Biscuits Inc., Houston, 1969—75; owner, pres. S.W. Tookie Inc./Tookie's Restaurant, Seabrook, Tex., 1975—. Mem. Greater Houston Conv. and Visitors Bur., Clear Lake Conv. Visitors Bur. With USN, 1959-62. Mem. Tex. Restaurant Assn., Houston Restaurant Assn., Seabrook Assn., Old Seabrook Assn. Republican. Roman Catholic. Avocations: collectibles, fine art, antiques, listening to records, self improvement. Home: 16310 Hickory Knoll Dr Houston TX 77059-5311 Office: SW Tookie Inc/Tookie's Restaurant 1202 Bayport Blvd Seabrook TX 77586-3406

SPEARS, JAMES M(IT), lawyer; b. San Benito, Tex., Dec. 1, 1952; BA, Tex. Tech. Univ., 1975; JD, Univ. Tex., 1978. Bar: Tex. 1978, D.C. 1998. Dep. asst. atty. gen. Lands & Natural Resources div., U.S. Dept. Justice, Washington, 1983—84, Civil div., U.S. Dept. Justice, Washington, 1985—88; gen. counsel FTC, Washington, 1993—94; ptnr. litigation dept. & head antitrust & trade litigation practice group Ropes & Gray, Washington. Contbr. articles to profl. jours. Office: Ropes & Gray One Metro Ctr Suite 900 700 12th St NW Washington DC 20005-3948 Office Phone: 202-508-4681. Office Fax: 202-508-4650. Business E-Mail: mit.spears@ropesgray.com.

SPEARS, LARRY JONELL, lawyer; b. Webb, Miss., Jan. 10, 1953; s. John Spears and Lillian Belle Embrey; m. Treycè L. Gaston, Jan. 14, 1989;children: Lyndzè Rae, Joshua Lawrence. BS, U. Ill., 1976, JD, 1979; MS, So. Ill. U., 1990. Bar: Ill. 1980. Asst. atty gen. Ill. Atty. Gen.'s Office, Murphysboro, 1980-84; asst. pub. defender Jackson County Pub. Defender's Office, Murphysboro, 1985; lectr. Crime Study Ctr., Carbondale, Ill., 1985; sole practice Carbondale, 1985-86; asst. state's atty. Peoria (Ill.) State's Atty. Office, 1986-90, Sangamon County State's Atty. Office, Springfield, Ill., 1990-94; with Student's Legal Svcs. Ill. State U., Normal, 1995—2003; min. Loving Missionary Bapt. Ch., Bloomington, Ill., 2003—; asst. pub. defender McLean County, Ill., 2003—05; assoc. atty. Prior Law Firm, PC, 2005—. Cons. Minority Contractors Assn., Carbondale, 1985; mem. Inmate Advocacy Group, Murphysboro, 1985-86; lectr. Sangamon State U., Springfield, 1990-96. Elijah P. Lovejoy scholar, 1972. Mem. Ill. State Bar Assn., McLean County Bar Assn., Adminstrn. of Justice Assn. (treas. 1984-85), Am. Soc. Criminology (discussant 1984-85), Midwest Criminal Justice Assn., Am. Judicature Soc., LWV, Sphinx Club (Carbondale), Phi Alpha Delta (treas. 1979), Alpha Phi Sigma. Republican. Baptist. Avocations: golf, fishing, songwriting, tennis, volleyball. Home: 1603 E Oakland Ave Bloomington IL 61701-5617 Office: Prior Law Firm PC PO Box 5968 1210 Towanda Ave Bloomington IL 61702-5968 Office Phone: 309-827-4300. Personal E-mail: spearsrain01@aol.com. Business E-Mail: larry.spears@insightbb.com.

SPEARS, LOUISE ELIZABETH, minister, secondary school educator; b. Liberty, Miss., Feb. 2, 1945; d. Willie and Alice Gray Spears; 1 child, Guy Alice. BSc, Alcorn State U., 1966; MSc, Ind. U., 1969; PhD, U. N. Colo., 1975; MDiv, Garrett-Evang. Theol. Sem., 1983. Cert. African Meth. Episcopal Ch., 90. Tchr. Ga. Tchr. Hazlehurst H.S., Hazlehurst, Miss., 1967—68; tchg. asst. Ind. U., Bloomington, Ind., 1968—70; tchr. Ala. State U., Montgomery, Ala., 1970—72, Ky. State U., Frankfort, Ky., 1972—73, Jackson State U., Jackson, Miss., 1975—81; pastor United Meth. Ch., Keosauqua, Iowa, 1983—85, Detroit, 1985—88; tchr. Clarke County Sch. Dist., Athens, Ga., 1998—2004; pastor African Meth. Episcopal Ch., various, Ga., 2000—. Realtor Ga. Real Estate, Atlanta, 1989—92; academic adminstr. Emmanuel Bible Coll., Macon, Ga., 1992—93; substitute tchr. Atlanta Pub. Sch., Atlanta, 1994—98; co-chmn. Augusta Ga. Conf., Augusta, Ga., 2001, mem. stewardship commn.; fin. coord. Reach Out and Touch Club, Inc., 2002—03; mem. Athens-Clarke County Commn. on Disability, 2003; mem. career and tech. edn. exec. adv. bd. Athens-Clarke County Commn. on Disability; mem. career and tech. edn. adv. bd. Tech. Prep Awareness, 2003, mem. sub-com., 03. Co-author: National Poetry Book, 1995; featured cover story: Zebra Mag., 2001. Bd. dir. Reach Out & Touch Club, Inc., Athens, 2001—. Recipient Cmty. Svc. award, Reach Out & Touch Club, Inc., 2000. Mem.: NEA, Reach Out and Touch Club (fin. coord.). Democrat. African Meth. Episcopal. Avocations: reading, travel, writing. Home: 10 Huntington Ln Crawford GA 30630-2333

SPEARS, RONALD DEAN, judge; b. Michigan City, Ind., July 30, 1951; s. Lonnie and Frances Ellen (Benad) Spears; m. Annette Jean Greffe, Dec. 22, 1973; 1 child, Donald Dean. BA, U. Ill., 1974; JD, So. Ill. U., 1977. Bar: Ill. 1977, U.S. Dist. Ct. (ctrl. and so. dists.) Ill. 1977, U.S. Ct. Appeals (7th cir.) 1977, U.S. Supreme Ct. 1983. Law clk. U.S. Dist. Ct., Springfield, Ill., 1977-79; ptnr. Miley, Meyer, Austin, Spears & Romano, P.C., Taylorville, Ill., 1979—93; judge Ill. Cir. Ct., 4th Jud. Cir., Taylorville, 1993—. Atty. City of Taylorville. Col. JAGC, Ill. Army N.G. Mem.: ABA, Ill. Judge's Assn. (bd. govs. 2003—), Lincoln-Douglas Am. Inn of Ct., Christian County Bar Assn. (pres. 1987), Ill. State Bar Assn. (bd. govs. 1997—2002), Toastmasters (pres. 1988), So. Ill. U. Law Sch. Alumni Assn. (pres. 1984), Optimists (pres. 1986, lt. gov. 1986—87). Home: 3501 Lake Dr Taylorville IL 62568-8930 Office: Ill Cir Ct 4th Jud Cir Rm 316 Christian County Courthouse Taylorville IL 62568-2245 Office Phone: 217-824-4810.

SPEARS, SALLY, lawyer; b. San Antonio, Aug. 29, 1938; d. Adrian Anthony and Elizabeth (Wylie) S.; m. Tor Hultgreen, July 15, 1961 (div. Jan. 1983); children: Dagny Elizabeth, Sara Kirsten, Kara Spears. BA, U. Tex., 1960, LLB, 1965. Bar: Tex. 1961, Ill. 1971. Practice law, Stamford, Conn., 1966-67, Chgo., 1970-71, Northbrook, Ill., 1972-73, Toronto, Ont., Canada, 1973-81; assoc. firm Cummings & Lockwood, Stamford, 1966-67, Kirkland & Ellis, Chgo., 1970-71; sr. atty. Allstate Ins. Co., Northbrook, Ill., 1971-73; gen. counsel, sec. Reed Paper Ltd., Reed Ltd., Toronto, 1973-78, Denison Mines Ltd., Toronto, 1978-81; pvt. practice law San Antonio, 1981—. Apptd. by Sec. of Def. to serve on Def. Adv. Com., Women in the Svcs., 1997—99. Author: Call Sign Revlon: The Life and Death of Navy Fighter Pilot Kara Hultgreen, 1998. Mem. Tex. Bar Assn., San Antonio Bar Assn., Bankruptcy Bar Assn., Bexar County Women's Bar Assn., San Antonio Country Club, The Club at Sonterra. Home: 433 Evans Ave San Antonio TX 78209-3725 Office: Ste 106 8151 Broadway San Antonio TX 78209-1938 Home Phone: 210-822-4682; Office Phone: 210-826-7020. Personal E-mail: sespears@swbell.net.

SPECHT, ALICE WILSON, university libraries dean; b. Caracas, Venezuela, Apr. 3, 1948; (parents Am. citizens); d. Ned and Helen (Lockwood) Wilson; m. Joe W. Specht, Dec. 30, 1972; 1 child, Mary Helen. BA, U. Pacific, 1969; MLS, Emory U., 1970; MBA, Hardin-Simmons U., 1983. Libr. social scis. North Tex. State U., Denton, 1971-73; reference libr. Lubbock (Tex.) City and County Libr., 1974-75; system coord. Big Country Libr. System, Abilene, 1975-79; assoc. dir. Hardin-Simmons U., 1981-88, dir. univ. librs., 1988—, dean univ. librs., 2002—. Apptd. Mayor's Task Force Libr. Svcs., 1995-96. Author bibliog. instrn. aids, 1981-90; editor; The College Man, For Pilots Eyes Only. Mem. mayor's task force Abilene Pub. Libr., 1995—96; mem. Libr. Sci. Art. Bd. for Tx. Recipient Boss of Yr., Am. Bus. Women's Assn., 1994. Mem.: ALA, Abilene Libr. Consortium (chair adminstrv. coun. 1990, coord. nat. conf. 1991, 1993, 2002, chair adminstrv. coun. 2006, librart sys. act adv. bd. 2001—), Tex. Libr. Assn. (chair com. 1978—84, sec.-treas. coll. and univ. librs. divsn. 1993—94, legis. com. 1994—), Texshare Ednl. Working Group (chair 1999). Home: 918 Grand Ave Abilene TX 79605-3233 Office: Hardin-Simmons U PO Box 16195 2341 Hickory St Abilene TX 79698-6195 Business E-Mail: aspecht@hsutx.edu.

SPECHT-JARVIS, ROLAND HUBERT, fine arts and humanities educator, dean; b. Dortmund, Germany, Oct. 31, 1954; came to U.S., 1982; s. Otto and Waltraud Specht; m. Shawn Cecilia Jarvis, June 15, 1982; children: Alex Jarvis, Elly Jarvis. Staatsexamen in German and pedagogy, Ruhr U. Bochum, Germany, 1982, Staatsexamen in Law and German, 1982, PhD, 1988. Instr. German St. Cloud (Minn.) State U., 1982-87, asst. prof. German, 1987-89, assoc. prof. German, 1989-92, prof. German, 1992—, dir. Ingolstadt program dept. fgn. langs. and lit., 1984-97, chmn. and dir. dept. fgn. langs., 1988-94, dir. quality enhancement programs State Minn., 1994-97, dean Coll. Fine Arts & Humanities, 1997—. Author: (with H. Walbruck) Deutsch Gestern und Heute, 1986, tchrs. annotated edit., 1986, audio tape program and manual, 1987, workbook, 1987, test series, 1988, Deutsch Aktuell 3 tchrs. edit., 1993, 4th edit. workbook, 1999, Compendium College of Fine Arts and Humanities, 1998, 2000, student edit., 1993, workbook, 1993, tape program manual, 1993, Microsoft Word. Textverarbeitung mit dem Macintosh, 1990, Die Ausbildung des Literarischen Diskurses Friedrich Schlegels zur Zeit der Herausgabe des Athenaeums, 1994, (with Shawn C. Jarvis and Isolde Mueller) Deutsch Aktuell 3, 1998, 5th edit., 2003. V.p., founder Förderverein Ingolstadt-St. Cloud, 1985; bd. dirs. Alexandria-St. Cloud Performing Arts Found., 1997—, St. Cloud State U. Alumni Assn., 1995, Theatre L'Homme Dieu, 1997—, St. Cloud Symphony Orch., 1998-2002, Herberger Coll. Bus., 2000—; mem. coun. Coll. of Arts and Scis., 1995. Mem. St. Cloud Rotary (sec. 1998-99, v.p. 2001-02, pres. 2002-03), Amnesty Internat. Avocations: outdoors, chess, racquetball, motorcycles. Home: 1922 19th Ave SE Saint Cloud MN 56304-2118 Office: St Cloud State Univ 720 4th Ave S Saint Cloud MN 56301-4498 Office Phone: 320-308-3093. E-mail: roland@stcloudstate.edu.

SPECK, EUGENE LEWIS, internist; b. Boston, Dec. 17, 1936; s. Robert A. and Anne (Rosenberg) S.; m. Rachel Shoshana; children: Michael Robert, Keren Sara. AB, Brandeis U., Waltham, Mass., 1958; MS, U. Mass., 1961; PhD, George Washington U., 1966, MD, 1969. Diplomate Am. Bd. Internal Medicine with subspecialty in infectious diseases. Intern N.Y. Hosp.-Cornell, 1969-70; rsch. assoc. NIH, Bethesda, Md., 1970-72; resident Barnes Hosp.-Washington U., 1972-73; instr. medicine Washington U., St. Louis, 1972-73; fellow Strong Meml. Hosp.-U. Rochester, 1973-75; instr. medicine U. Rochester, N.Y., 1973-75, asst. prof. medicine N.Y., 1975-80, U. Nev., Las Vegas, 1980-85, assoc. prof., 1985-95, prof. medicine, 1995—; dir./co-dir. infectious disease unit U. Med. Ctr. of So. Nev., Las Vegas, 1980—; ptnr. Infectious Diseases Consultants, 1983—. Cons. Clark County Health Dept., Las Vegas, 1980—, U. Med. Ctr. So. Nev., Las Vegas, 1980—, Sunrise Hosp., Las Vegas, 1980—, Valley Hosp., Las Vegas, 1980—; Am. coll. physicians gov., State Nev. Contbr. articles to profl. jours., chpts. to books. Recipient Disting. Physician award, State of Nev., 2002. Fellow ACP (elected gov. Nev.); mem. Am. Soc. Microbiology, Infectious Disease Soc. Am., Alpha Omega Alpha. Avocations: tennis, skiing, racquetball. Home: 2228 Chatsworth Ct Henderson NV 89074-5309 Office: Infectious Diseases Cons 3006 S Maryland Pkwy Ste 780 Las Vegas NV 89109-2292 Home Phone: 702-433-1850; Office Phone: 702-737-0740. Personal E-mail: drsduc@aol.com.

SPECK, LAWRENCE W., architect, educator; b. Houston, Apr. 22, 1949; s. H.K. and Esther (Elliot) S.; m. Cynthia Alexander, Jan. 2, 1971 (div. 1988); children: Sloan Garret, Harrison Alexander; m. Amanda Mayhew Dealey, Oct. 3, 1992. BS in Mgmt., MIT, 1971, BS in Art and Design, 1971, MArch, 1972. Registered architect, Mass., Tex. Instr. MIT, Boston, 1972-75; asst. prof. U. Tex., Austin, 1975-79, assoc. prof., 1979-84, prof., 1984—; dean U. Tex. Sch. Arch., Austin, 1993—; prin. Lawrence W. Speck Assocs., Austin, 1975—. Dir. Ctr. Study Am. Architecture U. Tex., Austin; adj. curator architecture Dallas Mus. Art, 1985-87. Editor: Architecture for the Emerging American City, 1985; author: Landmarks of Texas Architecture, 1986; co-editor: New Regionalism, 1987. Bd. dirs. Buell Ctr. Columbia U., N.Y.C., 1985-87. Fulbright Sr. scholar Council for Internat. Exchange Scholars, 1978. Fellow AIA (5 design awards Austin chpt. 1984-87); mem. Tex. Soc. of Architects (3 design awards 1986), Soc. Arch. Historians, Sigma Chi. Avocations: athletics, children's literature.

SPECK, SAMUEL WALLACE, JR., state official; b. Canton, Ohio, Jan. 31, 1937; s. Samuel Wallace Sr. and Lois Ione (Schneider) S.; m. Sharon Jane Anderson, Jan. 20, 1962; children: Samuel Wallace III, Derek Charles. BA, Muskingum Coll., 1959; postgrad., U. Zimbabwe, 1961; MA, Harvard U., 1963, PhD, 1968. Prof. polit. sci. Muskingum Coll., New Concord, Ohio, 1964-83, asst. to pres., 1986-87, exec. v.p., 1987, acting pres., 1987-88, pres., 1988-99; assoc. dir. Fed. Emergency Mgmt. Agy., 1983-86; mem. Ohio Ho. of Reps., 1971-76; state senator from Ohio 20th Dist., 1977-83; dir. Dept. Natural Resources, mem. Gov's cabinet State of Ohio, 1999—2007. Bd. dirs. Camco Fin. Corp., Cambridge, Ohio, Advantage Savs. Bank; pres. Eastern Ohio Devel. Alliance, 1990-92; Fund for Improvement of Postsecondary Edn., 1990-92, chmn. 1991. Contbr. numerous articles on African and Am. govt. and pub. policy. Bd. dirs. Ohio Tuition Trust Authority, 1991-93, Internat. Ctr. for Preservation Wild Animals, 1988-99, Lake Erie Commn., 1999-2007; bd. dirs., chmn. Ohio Water Resources Coun. 1999-2005; mem. Great Lakes Commn., 1999-2007, chmn., 2002-04; mem. Ohio Power Siting Bd., 1999-2007; mem. Ohio Pub. Works Commn., 2003-07; chmn. coun. Great Lakes water mgmt. working group, 2002-05; mem. Ohio Higher Edn. Financing Commn., 2007—. Recipient Outstanding Legislator award VFW/DAV/Am. Legion, Conservation Achievement award State of Ohio, Disting. Svc. award, Nat. Gov. Conf., 2004, Conservation Leadership award, Ohio Nature Conservancy. Republican. Home: 240 Greenbriar Ct Worthington OH 43085-3055

SPECK, WILLIAM T., former physician, health facility administrator; BS, Rutgers U.; MD, Wake Forest U. Sch. Medicine, 1968. Resident Columbia U., NYC, fellow, with dept. pediat. and microbiology; with dept. pediat. Case Western Reserve U., Cleve., prof., dept. pediat., chmn., dir., dept. pediat.; CEO Rainbow Babies and Children's Hosp., Cleve., 1982—92; pres., CEO Presbyn. Hosp. in NYC/Columbia-Presbyn. Med. Ctr., 1992—99; interim dir., CEO Marine Biol. Lab., Woods Hole, Mass., 2000—01, chmn., CEO, 2001—. Bd. trustees Marine Biol. Lab., 1994—; mem. MBL Corp. Office: Marine Biol Lab 7 MBL St Woods Hole MA 02543

SPECKHART, DAWN SEIDNER, bone marrow transplant/leukemia psychologist; b. Miami, Fla., Mar. 8, 1971; d. Jack Edward and Judith Naomi Seidner; m. Michael Alan Speckhart, June 25, 1995; children: Logan Shay, Jordan Elizabeth. BA, Ind. U., 1989—93, MS, 1993—95, PhD, 1995—99. Licensed Psychologist GA, 2000. Clin. psychologist Medlin Treatment Ctr., Stockbridge, Ga., 2000—02; bone marrow transplant/leukemia psychologist Northside Hosp., Atlanta, 2002—. Rsch. psychologist Northside Hosp., Atlanta, 2004—. Mem.: APA, Southeastern Psychol. Assn., Am. Psychosocial Oncology Soc., Alpha Chi Omega (social chair 1991—92, Alumni). Office: Northside Hosp 1000 Johnson Ferry Rd BMT Unit Atlanta GA 30342 Home Phone: 770-641-8699; Office Phone: 404-255-1930. Office Fax: 404-255-1939. E-mail: dawn.speckhart@northside.com.

SPECTER, ARLEN, senator; b. Wichita, Kans., Feb. 12, 1930; s. Harry and Lillie (Shanin) S.; m. Joan L. Levy, June 14, 1953; children: Shanin, Stephen. Student, U. Okla., 1947-48; BA Internat. Rels., U. Pa., 1951; LLB, Yale U., 1956. Asst. counsel Warren Commn., Washington, 1964; magisterial investigator Commn. of Pa., 1965; asst. dist. atty. City of Phila., 1959-63, dist. atty., 1966-74; ptnr. Dechert Price & Rhoads, Phila., 1956-66, 74-80; US senator from Pa., 1981—. Chmn. Senate judiciary com., 2005-, Appropriations Subcom. on Labor, Health and Human Svcs. and Edn. and Related Agys., Subcom. on Agr., Rural Deve. and Related Agys., Subcom. on Transp., Subcom. on Def., Subcom. on Fgn. Opers., Jud. Subcom. on Antitrusts, Bus. Rights, and Competition, Subcom. on Immigration, Subcom. on Terrorism, Tech. and Govt. Info., Govtl. Affairs Subcom. on Internat. Security, Proliferation and Fed. Svcs., Permanent Subcom. on Investigations, Subcom. on Oversight of Govt. Mgmt., Restructuring and D.C.; asst. counsel, Pres. Commn. on the Assassination of President Kennedy (Warren Commn.), 1964; lectr. Temple U. Law Sch., 1972-75, U. Pa. Law Sch., 1968-72 Author: Police Guide to Search and Seizure, Interrogation, and Confession, 1967, (with Charles Robins) Passion for Truth: From Finding JFK's Single Bullet to Questioning Anita Hill to Impeaching Bill Clinton, 2000; contbr. articles to profl. jours. 1st lt. USAF, 1951—53. Recipient Youth Svcs. award B'nai B'rith, 1966; recipient Sons of Italy award, 1968, Community Humanitarian award Bapt. Ch., 1969, man of Yr. award, Temple Beth Ami, 1971, N.E. Cath. High Sch. Outstanding Achievement award, 1973, Congl. award, Am. Soc. of Nephrology, 1998, Legis. of the Year award Nat. Assn. of Alcoholism & Drug Abuse Counselors, 1999, Pub. Policy Leadership award, Am. Cancer Soc., 2000, Spl. Recognition award, Am. Heart Assn., 2003, Lead On! award, Nat. Org. on Disability, 2004. Mem. ABA, Pa. Bar Assn., Phila. Bar Assn., Phi Beta Kappa. Republican. Jewish. Office: US Senate 711 Hart Senate Office Bldg Washington DC 20510-0001 also: District Office Ste 9400 600 Arch St Philadelphia PA 19106 Office Phone: 202-224-4254, 215-597-7200. Office Fax: 202-228-1229, 215-597-0406. *

SPECTER, RICHARD BRUCE, lawyer; b. Phila., Sept. 6, 1952; s. Jacob E. and Marilyn B. (Kron) S.; m. Jill Ossenfort, May 30, 1981; children: Lauren Elizabeth, Lindsey Anne, Allison Lee. BA cum laude, Washington U., St. Louis, 1974; JD, George Washington U., 1977. Bar: Mo. 1977, U.S. Dist. Ct. (ea. and we. dists.) Mo. 1977, U.S. Ct. Appeals (8th cir.) 1977, Ill. 1978, Pa. 1978, U.S. Dist. Ct. (ea. dist.) Ill. 1979, U.S. Ct. Appeals (7th cir.) 1979, Calif. 1984, U.S. Dist. Ct. (cen. dist.) Calif. 1985, U.S. Ct. Appeals (9th cir.) 1986, U.S. Dist. Ct. (so. dist.) Calif. 1987, U.S. Dist. Ct. (no. dist.) Calif. 1988, U.S. Supreme Ct. 1999. Assoc. Coburn, Croft, Shepherd, Herzog & Putzell, St. Louis, 1977-79; ptnr. Herzog, Kral, Burroughs & Specter, St. Louis, 1979-82; exec. v.p. Uniqey Internat., Santa Ana, Calif., 1982-84; pvt. practice LA and Irvine, Calif., 1984-87; ptnr. Corbett, Steelman, & Specter, Irvine, 1987—. Instr. Nat. Law Ctr. George Washington U. 1975; dir. Javo Beverage Co., 2001-. Mem. ABA, Ill. Bar Assn., Mo. Bar Assn., Pa. Bar Assn., Calif. Bar Assn. Jewish. Home: 37 Bull Run Irvine CA 92620-2510 Office: 18200 Von Karman Ave Ste 900 Irvine CA 92612-1086 Office Phone: 949-553-9266. Business E-Mail: rspecter@corbsteel.com.

SPECTOR, ADAM B., investment company executive; BA, Brown U.; MBA, U. Pa. Mng. dir., co-founder Prague office Ameritek Bus. Sys., 1990—91; dir. Internat. Investment Mgmt. Group SEI Investments, 1991—97; mng. dir., dir. mktg., sales and client svcs. Brandywine Global Investment Mgmt. LLC. Named one of 40 Under 40, Phila. Bus. Jour., 2006. Office: Brandywine Global Investment Mgmt, LLC 2929 Arch St, 8th Fl Philadelphia PA 19104 Office Phone: 215-609-3500. Office Fax: 215-609-3501.

SPECTOR, ALFRED ZALMON, computer specialist, educator, consultant; b. Boston, Oct. 14, 1954; s. Asher and Ethel Esther (Karelitz) S. AB in Applied Math, Harvard Coll., 1972-76; PhD in Computer Sci., Stanford U., 1976-81. Asst. prof. Carnegie Mellon U., Pitts., 1981-87, assoc. prof., 1987—, dir. Information Tech. Ctr., 1988; gen. mgr. mktg. and strategy AIM IBM Corp., v.p. svcs. and software IBM Rsch., now v.p. strategy and tech. IBM Software Group Somers, NY. Editor case studies Commn. of Assn. Computing Machinery, N.Y., 1983—; program chmn. Symposium on Operating Systems, Austin, Tex., 1987; chmn. DARPA Reliability Task Force, Washington, 1987—. Contbr. articles to profl. jours. Mem. U.S. Army Sci. Bd., Pentagon, Washington, 1985—. Recipient IBM Faculty Devel. award, IBM, 1984-86. Mem. IEEE (Tsutomu Kanai Award, 2001), AAAS, NAE, Assn. Computing Machinery. Jewish. Avocations: backpacking, piano. Office: Carnegie Mellon U Forbes Ave Pittsburgh PA 15213 also: IBM Software Group Rt 100, Office 2A02 Somers NY 10589 Office Phone: 914-766-1135. Office Fax: 914-766-7170.

SPECTOR, ANITA FROHMANN, retired buyer; b. NYC, Apr. 26, 1943; d. Ira and Minnie (Glazer) Friedman; m. Robert Frohmann, Dec. 24, 1961; 1 child, Edward Frohmann; m. Boris Spector, Apr. 21, 1985; stepchildren: Jeffrey Spector, Lori Spector Krein. BS, Adelphi U., 1984; MA, SUNY, 1992; PhD, Walden U., 1997. Buyer furniture-furnishings Colgate Palmolive Co., NYC, 1983-87, buyer office supplies-forms, 1987-90, buyer fabric care packaging-household surface care packaging, 1990-95, materials sourcing project analyst, 1995-97, oral care buyer point of sale and packaging, 1997—2005; ret., 2005. Mem. Colgate-Palmolive Sys. Applications Products in Data Processing (SAP) core team, 1997—, ergonomics team, 1997—, comml. print team, 2001-02, indirect materials, 2003-05; mem. adv. bd. Adelphi U.; adj. prof. Keller Grad. Sch. Mgmt., DeVry U., 2005-, mem. integrity com., appeals com. Mem. adv. bd. Adelphi U. Named Disting. Alumni Adelphi U. U. Coll., 1998. Mem. AAUW, The Doctorate Assn. N.Y. Educators. Avocations: reading, travel, bicycling, music, interior decorating. Home: 4 Park Ave Apt 16C New York NY 10016-5311 Home Phone: 212-481-7273. Personal E-mail: drantiaspector@aol.com.

SPECTOR, DANIEL EARL, historian, educator; b. Pensacola, Fla., Dec. 19, 1942; s. Joseph and Dorothy Margaret (Givens) S.; m. Esta Gelda Rappaport, Aug. 9, 1964; children: Warren Leigh, Susan Artemis (dec.). BA, George Washington U., 1963; postgrad., U. Fla., 1963-64; MA, U. Tex., 1972, PhD, 1975. Adj. instr. Jacksonville (Ala.) State U., 1975-77; chief skill qualification test br. U.S. Army Mil. Police Sch., Ft. McClellan, Ala., 1975-80; supr. edn. specialist U.S. Army Chem. Sch., Ft. McClellan, 1980-82; chief U.S. Army Chem. Sch. Standardization & Analysis Div., Ft. McClellan, 1982-84; dep. dir. U.S. Army Chem. Sch. Directorate of Tng. & Doctrine, Ft. McClellan, 1984-88; adj. prof. U. Ala., Birmingham, 1986—2001; chem. corps historian U.S. Army Chem. Sch., Ft. McClellan, 1988-94; adj. prof. Troy State U., Ft. Benning, Ga., 2003—05. Accreditation coord. U.S. Army Chem. Sch., Ft. McClellan, 1984-90; accreditation team chief So. Assn. Colls. and Schs., Atlanta, 1985-90; U.S. Army rep. EURO-NATO nuc., biol. and chem. workgroups, 1984-90. Author: Chemical School Annual Historial Reviews, 1988—90; contbr. numerous revs., articles and ency. entries to pubs. Mem. Jacksonville Kiwanis, 1981-92. Alumni scholar George Washington U., 1959-63; NDEA fellow U. Fla., 1963-64, NDFL fellow U. Tex. 1972-73. Mem. Middle Eastern Studies Assn., Middle East Inst., Am. Hist. Assn., Soc. Mil. History, Ala. Assn. Historians, MENSA, Temple Beth-El, Scottish Rite, Hiram Lodge, Ala. Master Gardener, Legion of Honor, Chapel of Four Chaplains, Phi Alpha Theta. Democrat. Jewish. Avocations: gardening, fishing. Home: 1317 7th Ave NE Jacksonville AL 36265-1174 Personal E-mail: drspector@cableone.net.

SPECTOR, DAVID M., lawyer; b. Rock Island, Ill., Dec. 20, 1946; s. Louis and Ruth (Vinikour) S.; m. Laraine Fingold, Jan. 15, 1972; children: Rachel, Laurence. BA, Northwestern U., 1968; JD magna cum laude, U. Mich., 1971. Bar: Ill. 1971, U.S. Dist. Ct. (no. dist.) Ill. 1971, U.S. Ct. Appeals (7th cir.) 1977, U.S. Ct. Appeals (4th cir.) 1984, U.S. Dist. Ct. (cen. dist.) Ill. 1984, U.S. Supreme Ct. 1999, N.Y. 2002, U.S. Ct. Appeals (2d cir.) 2002. Clk. Ill. Supreme Ct., Chgo., 1971-72; ptnr., assoc. Isham, Lincoln & Beale, Chgo., 1972-87; ptnr. Mayer, Brown & Platt, Chgo., 1987-97, Hopkins & Sutter, Chgo., 1997-2001, Schiff, Hardin LLP, Chgo., 2001—. Chmn. ABA Nat. Inst. on Ins. Co. Insolvency, Boston, 1986; co-chmn. ABA Nat. Inst. on Internat. Reins.: Collections and Insolvency, NY, 1988; chmn. ABA Nat. Inst. on Life Ins. Co. Insolvency, Chgo., 1993; spkr. in field. Editor: Law and Practice of Insurance Company Insolvency, 1986, Law and Practice of Life Insurer Insolvency, 1993; co-editor: Law and Practice of International Reinsurance Collections and Insolvency, 1988; contbr. articles to profl. jour. Mem. ABA (chair Nat. Inst. on Life Insurer Insolvency 1993), Chgo. Bar Assn., Lawyer's Club of Chgo. Office: Schiff Hardin LLP 6600 Sears Tower Chicago IL 60606 Home: 1418 N Lake Shore Dr Chicago IL 60610-1642 Office Phone: 312-258-5552. Business E-Mail: dspector@schiffhardin.com.

SPECTOR, ELEANOR RUTH, manufacturing executive; b. NYC, Dec. 2, 1943; d. Sidney and Helen Lebost; m. Mel Alan Spector, Dec. 10, 1966; children: Nancy, Kenneth. BA, Barnard Coll., 1964; postgrad. sch. pub. adminstrn., George Washington U., 1965-67; postgrad sch. edn., Nazareth Coll., 1974. Indsl. investigator N.Y. State Dept. Labor, White Plains, 1964-65; mgmt. intern Navy Dept., Washington, 1965, contract negotiator, 1965-68, contract specialist, 1975-78, contracting officer/br. head, 1978-82, dir. div. cost estimating, 1982-84; dep. asst. sec. def. for procurement Washington, 1984-91; dir. Def. Procurement, Washington, 1991-2000; v.p. contracts Lockheed Martin Corp., Bethesda, Md., 2000—. Advisor Nat. Contract Mgmt. Assn., 1984—, Fed. Contracts Report, 2000—. Recipient Def. Meritoroius Civilian Svc. medal, 1986, 93, 96, Meritorious Svc. Presdl. award, 1989, 94, Disting. Civilian Svc. Presdl. award, 1990, 97, Def. Disting. Civilian Svc. medal, 1991, 94, 2000, Nat. Pub. Svc. award, 1998, Sec. Def. award for Excellence, 1997. Office: Lockheed Martin Corp MP 110 6801 Rockledge Dr Bethesda MD 20817-1877

SPECTOR, GERSHON JERRY, otolaryngologist, educator, researcher; b. Rovno, Poland, Oct. 20, 1937; came to U.S., 1949; naturalized, 1956; m. Patsy Carol Tanenbaum, Aug. 28, 1965. BA, Johns Hopkins U., 1960; MD cum laude, U. Md., 1964. Intern Beth Israel Hosp., Boston, 1964-65; resident in surgery Sinai Hosp., Balt., 1965-66; resident in otolaryngology Mass. Eye and Ear Infirmary, Boston, 1966-69, Peter Bent Brigham Hosp., Boston, 1968-69; teaching fellow in otolaryngology Harvard U. Med. Sch., Boston, 1968-69; assoc. physician Ill. Crippled Children's Svc., Carbondale, 1971; mem. faculty Washington U. Med. Sch., St. Louis, 1971—, assoc. prof. otolaryngology, 1974-76, prof., 1976—; chief dept. otolaryngology St. Louis County Hosp., 1971-77. Mem. staff Washington U. Med. Ctr., Barnes Hosp.; dir. temporal bone bank, 1971-81; guest examiner Am. Bd. Otolaryngology, 1975-77; rsch. cons. neurosci. group, G.D. Searle Pharm. Corp. Mem. editl. bd. Laryngoscope, 1978, editor-in-chief, 1984-94; contbr. articles to med. jours. With U.S. Army, 1969-71. Hancock scholar, 1962. Fellow ACS; mem. AAAS, AMA, Am. Acad. Ophthalmology and Otolaryngology (Honor award 1979), St. Louis Med. Soc., St. Louis County Med. Soc., Am. Coun. Otolarygology, St. Louis Ear, Nose and Throat Club (pres. 1986), So. Med. Assn., Deafness Rsch. Found., Pan. Am. Assn. Otorhinolaryngology and Broncho Esophagology, Am. Soc. Head and Neck Surgery, Soc. Univ. Otolaryngologists, Am. Laryngol., Rhinol. and Otol. Soc. (Edmund Prince Fowler award 1974), Am. Soc. Cell Biology, Electron Microscopy Soc., N.Y. Acad. Scis., Am. Assn. Anatomists, Am. Acad. Facial Plastic and Reconstructive Surgery, Am. Neuro-Otology Soc., Gesellschaft fur Neurootologie und Aequilibrimoetrie A.V., Barany Soc., Am. Radium Soc., Assn. Acad. Surgery, Am. Fedn. Clin. Oncologic Socs., Am Otol. Soc., Acoustical Soc. Am., Soc. for Neurosci., Internat. Skull Base Soc. (founding), Brazilian Skull Base Soc. (hon.), Centurion Club, Alpha Omega Alpha, Psi Chi. Home: 7365 Westmoreland Dr Saint Louis MO 63130-4241 Office: Washington U Med Sch Saint Louis MO 63110 Office Phone: 314-362-7252. Business E-Mail: spectorg@wustl.edu.

SPECTOR, ISRAEL, oncologist; b. Bklyn., May 19, 1937; s. Isidor and Anna Spector; m. Regina McLean, Dec. 17, 1960; children: Adam, Beth Wesch, Chris McPherson. BS, Bklyn. Coll., 1958; MD, Chgo. Med. Sch., 1962. Diplomate Am. Bd. Internal Medicine, 1971, Am. Bd. Hematology, 1976, Am. Bd. Oncology, 1981. Pvt. practice, Wheaton, Md., 1968—2002; oncologist VA Hosp., West Palm Beach, Fla., 2002—04; med. oncologist, hematologist Holy Cross Med. Group, Ft. Lauderdale, Fla., 2005—. Clin. assoc. prof. George Washington U. Sch. Medicine. Surgeon USPHS, 1966—68. USPHS Postdoctoral fellow, 1965—66. Fellow: ACP. Avocation: golf. Office: Holy Cross Med Group 4725 N Federal Hwy Fort Lauderdale FL 33308

SPECTOR, JOHANNA LICHTENBERG, ethnomusicologist, former educator; b. Libau, Latvia; came to U.S., 1947, naturalized, 1954; d. Jacob C. and Anna (Meyer) Lichtenberg; m. Robert Spector, Nov. 20, 1939 (dec. Dec. 1941). DHS, Hebrew Union Coll., 1950; MA, Columbia U., 1960. Rsch. fellow Hebrew U., Jerusalem, 1951-53; faculty Jewish Theol. Sem. Am., NYC, 1954—, dir., founder dept. ethnomusicology, 1962-85, assoc. prof. musicology, 1966-70, Sem. prof., 1970-85, prof. emeritus, 1985—. Author: Ghetto-und Kzlieder, 1947, Samaritan Chant, 1965, Musical Tradition and Innovation in Central Asia, 1966, Bridal Songs from Sana Yemen, 1960, Jewish Music in a Changing World Vol. 1, 2001; documentary films The Samaritans, 1971, Chicago International, 1973, Middle Eastern Music, 1973, About the Jews of India: Cochin, 1976 (Cine Golden Eagle 1979), The Shanwar Telis or Bene Israel of India, 1978 (Cine Golden Eagle 1979), About the Jews of Yemen, A Vanishing Culture, 1986 (Cine Golden Eagle 1986, Blue Ribbon, Am. Film Festival 1986), 2000 Years of Freedom and Honor: The Cochin Jews of India, 1992, Margaret Mead, 1992, Columbus International, 1993; religious and folk recs. number over 10,000; contbr. articles to encys., various jours.; editorial bd. Asian Music. Fellow Am. Anthrop. Assn.; mem. Am. Ethnol. Soc., Am. Musicol. Soc., Internat. Folks Music Coun., World Assn. Jewish Studies, Yivo, Asian Mus. Soc. (v.p. 1964—, pres. 1974-78), Soc. Ethnomusicology (sec.-treas. N.Y.C. chpt. 1960-64). Home: 400 W 119th St New York NY 10027-7125

SPECTOR, JONATHAN, business research organization executive, former dean; B in Math and Econ. cum laude, Wesleyan U., 1978; MBA, Harvard Bus. Sch., 1980. With McKinsey & Co., 1980—86, principal, 1986—92, dir., 1992—2000; CEO Darwin Networks, 2000—04, Seurat Co., 2002—03; chmn., CEO Easy411, Inc., 2003; chmn. bd. The March of Dimes, Mass., 2003—06; vice dean exec. edn. The Wharton Sch., U. Penn., 2004—07; pres., CEO The Conf. Bd. Inc., 2007—. Trustee Wesleyan U., 1996—2002. Office: The Conf Bd Inc 845 Third Ave New York NY 10022 *

SPECTOR, MARTIN WOLF, lawyer; b. Phila., 1938; BA, Pa. State U., 1959; JD, U. Pa., 1962. Bar: Pa. 1962. Judge U.S. Dist. Ct., until 1967; asst. gen. counsel ARA Services, Phila., assoc. gen. counsel, 1969-76, v.p., 1976-83, gen. counsel, 1983—, formerly sr. v.p.; exec. v.p. ARAMARK, Phila., 1985—. Served to lt. USN, 1953-56. Office: ARAMARK 1101 Market St Ste 45 Philadelphia PA 19107-2988

SPECTOR, MELBOURNE LOUIS, retired foreign service officer; b. Pueblo, Colo., May 7, 1918; s. Joseph E. and Dora (Bernstein) S.; m. Louise Vincent, Nov. 23, 1948; 1 son, Stephen David. BA with honors, U. N.Mex., 1941. Intern U.S. Bur. Indian Affairs, 1941, Nat. Inst. Pub. Affairs, 1941; personnel asst. Office Emergency Mgmt., 1941-42; chief classification div. War Relocation Authority, 1942-43, Hdqrs. USAAF, 1943-45; employment officer UNRRA, 1945-46; pvt. employment, 1946-47; personnel officer Dept. State, 1947-49; detail Econ. Coop. Adminstrn., 1948; dep. dir. personnel Econ. Coop. Adminstrn., Marshall Plan, Paris, 1949-51; dep. dir., acting dir. personnel Econ. Coop. Adminstrn., Mut. Security Adminstrn., FOA, 1951-54; asst., dep. dir. Mission to Mexico, ICA, 1954-57, acting dir., 1957-59; chief C. Am., Mex. and Caribbean div. ICA, 1959-61; dir. Office Personnel Mgmt., AID, 1961-62; exec. dir. Bur. Inter-Am. Affairs, Dept. State, 1962-64; commd. consul gen., sec., 1964; counselor for adminstrv. affairs Am. embassy, New Delhi, India, 1964-66; seminarian Sr. Seminar Fgn. Policy, Dept. State, 1966-67; exec. dir. U.S.-Mex. Commn. for Border Devel. and Friendship, 1967-69, Am. Revolution Bicentennial Commn., 1969-71; mem. mgmt., policy and coordination staffs Dept. State, 1971-73; ret., 1973; cons., 1973—. Mem. Fgn. Svc. Grievance Bd., 1976-77; advisor Peace Corps Dir., 1979-80; exec. dir. Am. Consortium for Internat. Pub. Adminstrn., 1980-84, 93-94, dir. Marshall Plan Oral History Project, 1987-97. Mem. Cosmos Club, Am. Soc. Pub. Adminstrn., Pi Kappa Alpha, Phi Kappa Phi. Home: 5111 Connecticut Ave NW # 407 Washington DC 20008-2004

SPECTOR, MICHAEL JOSEPH, agribusiness executive; b. NYC, Feb. 13, 1947; s. Martin Wilson and Dorothy (Miller) S.; m. Margaret Dickson, Sept. 14, 1977. BS in Chemistry, Washington and Lee U., 1968. Rsch. chemist Am. Viscose, Phila., 1968-69; pres. MJS Entertainment Corp., Miami, Fla., 1970-84; also MJS Internat., Inc.; ptnr. Old Town Key West Devel. Ltd., Fla., 1977—2002. Pres. MJS Entertainment of Can., Inc., Toronto, Margo Farms, MJS Prodns., Inc., NYC; chmn., CEO Margo Caribe, Inc., Dorado, PR, 1981—, bd. dir.; pres. Costa Del Norte Devel., Inc., Dorado, 1998—; bd. dir. Goodwill Industries So. Fla., v.p. fin., 1980; bd. dir. Plz. Bank of Miami; hon. Consul Belgium in P.R., U.S. V.I., Turks & Caicos Islands, West Indies, 2000—; dir. Consular Corp. of P.R., 2002, vice-dean, 2003—04, dean, PR, 2004. Internat. judge The Floralies Exhbn., Gent, Belgium, 1995, 2000, 05; knight Sociedad Heraldica Espanola, 2003—. With AUS, 1969-70. Robert E. Lee rsch. grantee Washington and Lee U., 1967-68; named Agri-bus. Exec. of Yr., Govt. of P.R., 1999; knighted Order of King Leopold II, King of Belgium, 2005. Mem. Nat. Assn. Record Merchandisers (dir. Nova divsn., chmn. one-stop distbn. com. 1982-83), Country Music Assn., Dorado Beach Golf and Tennis Club, Bankers Club P.R., Ocean Reef Club (Key Largo, Fla.), Grove Isle Club (Coconut Grove, Fla.). Achievements include patent for synthetic stretching process. Home: Call Box 1370 Dorado PR 00646-1370 Business E-Mail: mspector@margocaribe.com.

SPECTOR, PHIL (HARVEY PHILLIP SPECTOR), record company executive; b. Bronx, NY, Dec. 26, 1939; m. Veronica Bennett, 1968 (div. 1974); children: Gary Phillip and Louis Phillip (twins), Donte Phillip, Nicole and Phillip (twins); m. Rachelle Marie Spector, Apr. 14, 2006. Student, UCLA. Producer with Atlantic Records, 1960-61; founder Philles Records, 1962; now pres. Warner-Spector Records, Inc.; also Mother Bertha Music. Mem. mus. group: Teddy Bears, 1958-59; producer records for Gene Pitney, Ike and Tina Turner, Ben E. King, the Beatles, Righteous Bros., Checkmates, Crystals, Ronettes, John Lennon, George Harrison, The Ramones, Yoko Ono, Leonard Cohen, Dion, Ike & Tina Turner, others; producer album A Concert for Bangladesh (Grammy award); composer songs including You've Lost That Lovin' Feelin' (7 million performances; named most performed song in U.S. broadcasting history 1997), others; appeared in films Tami, Easy Rider; prod., TV documentary film A Giant Stands 5 Ft. 7 In.; prod. film That Was Rock. Named to Rock and Roll Hall of Fame, 1989; named Country Music Song of Yr. Songwriter and Pub. for To Know Him Is To Love Him, 1989; recipient lifetime achievement award U. Calif., Berkeley, 1994, Phila. award Phila. Music Alliance, 1994 (includes star on Phila.'s Walk of Fame), Trustees award (Grammy) NARAS, 2000; inducted into Songwriters Hall of Fame, 1996. Office: c/o Warner-Spector Records Inc 686 S Arroyo Pky Pasadena CA 91105-3233 also: c/o Abkco Music & Records Inc 1700 Broadway New York NY 10019 E-mail: phillesrecords@earthlink.net.

SPECTOR, PHILLIP LOUIS, lawyer; b. LA, July 15, 1950; s. Everett L. Spector and Rebecca (Horn) Newman; m. Carole Sue Lebbin, May 11, 1980; children: Adam, David. Student, U. Birmingham, Eng., 1970—71; BA with highest honors, U. Calif., Santa Barbara, 1972; M in Pub. Policy, Harvard U., 1976, JD magna cum laude, 1976. Bar: Calif. 1976, DC 1978, US Ct. Appeals (DC cir.) 1983, US Supreme Ct. 1983, US Dist. Ct. DC 1985. Law clk. U.S. Ct. Appeals (2d cir.), Brattleboro, Vt., 1976-77; law clk. to U.S. Supreme Ct., 1977-78; assoc. asst. to Pres. U.S., 1978-80; assoc. Verner, Liipfert, Bernhard & McPherson, 1980-83; ptnr. Goldberg & Spector, 1983-92, Paul, Weiss, Rifkind, Wharton & Garrison, Washington, 1992—2005, mng. ptnr. Washington office, 2001—05; exec. v.p., gen. counsel Intelsat Holdings, Ltd., 2005—. Bd. dirs. Global Relief Techs., LLC, WildBlue Comm. Inc., Appleseed Found. Co-author: Communications Law and Practice, 1995, Communications and Techology Alliances: Business and Legal Issues, 1996; contbr. articles to profl. jours. Mem. Coun. on Fgn. Rels., NYC, 1980-85; moot ct. judge Nat. Assn. Attys. Gen., Washington, 1987—; adviser Dem. caucus US House Reps., Washington, 1981-83; speechwriter, podium prodr. Dem. Nat. Convs., NYC, 1980, Phila., 1982, San Francisco, 1984, Atlanta, 1988, NYC, 1992, Chgo., 1996, LA, 2000, Boston, 2004. Recipient Disting. Achievement in Pub. Svc. Medal U. Calif., Santa Barbara, 1981, Close-Up Found. awards Via Satellite Mag., Vol. Recognition award Nat. Assn. Attys. Gen., 1993; named Leading Satellite Specialist in Washington, European Counsel, 2000. Mem. ABA (former chair internat. comm. law com.), Fed. Comms. Bar Assn., Bethesda Country Club, Addison Res. Country Club, Phi Beta Kappa. Jewish. Office: Intelsat 90 Pitts Bay Rd 2d Fl Pembroke HM08 Bermuda Office Phone: 202-944-7340. Business E-Mail: phil.spector@intelsat.com.

SPECTOR, ROBERT DONALD, language educator; b. NYC, Sept. 21, 1922; s. Morris and Helen (Spiegel) S.; m. Eleanor Helen Luskin, Aug. 19, 1945; children: Stephen Brett, Eric Charles. BA, L.I. U., 1948, DHL, 1994; MA, NYU, 1949; PhD, Columbia U., 1962. Instr. L.I. U., Bklyn., 1948-59, asst. prof., 1959-62, asso. prof., 1962-65, prof. English, 1965-94, chmn. senate, 1966-67, 69-70, chmn. dept., 1970-75, dir. humanities and comm. arts, 1975-84, coord. div. of humanities and div. of comms. and performing arts, 1990—, dir. humanities, 1984-90, prof. emeritus, 1993—. Editor, cons. Johnson Reprint Corp., 1967-84 Author: English Literary Periodicals, 1966, Tobias George Smollett, 1968, updated edit., 1989, Pär Lagerkvist, 1973, Arthur Murphy, 1979, Tobias Smollett: A Reference Guide, 1980, The English Gothic, 1983, Backgrounds to Restoration and Eighteenth-Century English Literature, 1989, Political Controversy, 1992, Smollett's Women, 1994, Samuel Johnson and the Essay, 1997, Love Poems & Others, 1998, Mélange a Deux, 1999, Nature's Bounty in Brooklyn, 2000, Poems of Love and Laughter, 2003, New Poems, 2003, All About Love: Poems for Eleanor, 2007; editor: Essays on the Eighteenth Century Novel, 1965, Great British Short Novels, 1970, 9 other vols. English and Am. lit., revs., articles, poetry and song lyrics. Trustee L.I. U., 1969-70; chmn. George Polk Award Com., 1977—. Served with USCGR, 1942-46. Recipient L.I. U. Trustee award for scholarly achievement, 1978, Tristram Walker Metcalfe Alumnus of Year, 1981; Swedish Govt. travel and research grantee, 1966; fellow Huntington Library, 1974; fellow Folger Library, 1975; fellow Newberry Library, 1976 Mem. MLA, Am.-Scandinavian Found. (publs. com. 1962-84), P.E.N., Acad. Am. Poets. Home: 1761 E 26th St Brooklyn NY 11229-2405 Office Phone: 718-448-1115.

SPECTOR, RONNIE See **BENNETT SPECTOR GREENFIELD, VERONICA**

SPECTOR, ROSE, former state supreme court justice; BA, Columbia U.; JD, St. Mary's Sch. Law, 1965. Judge County Ct. at Law 5, 1975-80, 131st Dist. Ct., 1981-92; justice Tex. Supreme Ct., 1993-98; atty. Bickerstaff, Heath, Pollan, Kever & McDaniel, L.L.P., Austin, Tex., 1998—. Office Phone: 512-404-7867.

SPECTOR, WARREN J., former investment company executive; m. Margaret Whitton. Grad., Duke U., Durham, NC. Bd. dirs. Bear Stearns Cos., Inc., 1987—96, 1999—, head mortgage derivative trading unit, 1987, exec. v.p., head fixed income group NYC, 1997—, co-pres., co-COO, 2001—07. Vol. Gift of Life Bone Marrow Registry; chmn. Wall St. divsn. United Jewish Appeal; bd. dirs. NY Shakespeare Festival. Named one of Forty Under Forty, Crain's NY Bus., 1996. Achievements include becoming youngest Life Master in contract bridge, 1974. Avocations: golf, bridge. *

SPEECE, RICHARD EUGENE, civil engineer, educator; b. Marion, Ohio, Aug. 23, 1933; s. Irvin Ward S. and Desta May (Speece); m. Jean Margaret Edscorn, Nov. 15, 1969; children: Eric Jordan, Lincoln Dana. BCE, Fenn. Coll., 1956; M of Engring., Yale U., 1958; PhD, MIT, 1961. Assoc. prof. civil engring. U. Ill., Urbana, 1961-65; prof. N.Mex. State U., 1965-70, U. Tex., Austin, 1970-74; Betz chair prof. environ. engring. Drexel U., Phila., 1974-88; Centennial prof. Vanderbilt U., Nashville, 1988—. Vis. scholar Cambridge (Eng.) U., 1994; cons. to govt., industry. Contbr. articles to profl. jours.; patentee in field. Recipient hon. mention for best paper Trans. Am. Fisheries Soc., 1973, Founders award Assn. Environ. Engrs. Profs., 2005. Mem. ASCE (J. James Cross medal 1983), Assn. Environ. Engring. and Sci. Profs. (disting. lectr. 1978, trustee 1981-83, Disting. Faculty award 1970, Engring. Sci. award 1982, Founders award 2005, 06), Am. Soc. Microbiologists, Water Environ. Fedn. (Harrison Prescott Eddy medal 1966), U.S. ANC (Founders award 1991), Internat. Assn. on Water Pollution Rsch. and Control. Office: Vanderbilt U Dept Civil Engring Nashville TN 37235 Business E-Mail: dick.speece@vanderbilt.edu.

SPEED, CYNTHIA AGNES, retired mathematics professor; d. Carter Coleman and Lillian Jeannette Speed. BA, Calif. State U., Sacramento, 1962; MA, Stanford U., 1967. C.C. Supr. credential Calif., 1980, C.C. Instr. credential Calif., 1973, gen. secondary tchg. credential Calif., 1963. Tchg. asst. in edn. stats. U. of Calif., Berkeley, Calif., 1963; math. instr. Hiram W. Johnson Sr. H.S., Sacramento, 1963—67, John F. Kennedy Sr. H.S., Sacramento, 1967—69; math. lectr. Calif. State U., Sacramento, 1969—69, Calif. Poly. State U., San Luis Obispo, Calif., 1969—71; math. instr. Santa Rosa Jr. Coll., Calif., 1973—73; math. instr. and dept. chair Mendocino Coll., Ukiah, Calif., 1973—2003; ret., 2003. Exec. com. mem. Tech. in the Redwoods Conf., Ukiah, Calif., 1988—89; course descriptors com. mem. Calif. Articulation Number Sys., Sacramento, 1986—88; chairperson, creator, and organizer Math. Contest for Jr. and Sr. H.S. Students in Mendocino and Lake Counties, Ukiah, Calif., 1975—79. Author: (computer program) Technology in the Redwoods Computer Contest Prize Winners, Lake View Water Co. Billing Program, Black Bart Trail Rd. Assn. Dues Assessment Program. Vol. Legal Svcs. Northern Calif., 2007—; mem. East Sacramento Preservation Task Force, 2007—; chairperson Sacred Heart Ch. Ministry to the Homebound, 2006—; v.p. and mem. Lake View Mut. Water Co., Redwood Valley, Calif., 1977—; treas. and mem. Black Bart Trail Rd. Assn., Redwood Valley, Calif., 1977—. Mem.: AAUW, NEA, Cath. Alumni Club Sacramento (treas. 2005—), Calif. Ret. Tchrs. Assn. (treas. 2007—), Calif. Teachers Assn., Nat. Coun. of Teachers of Math., Calif. Math. Coun., Math. Assn. of Am., Calif. Math. Coun., Cmty. Colls. Found. (pres. 2005—), Calif. State U. Sacramento Alumni Assn., Stanford Alumni Assn., Delta Kappa Gamma. Democrat. Roman Catholic. Avocations: piano, swimming, golf, dance, bicycling. Home: 1232 43rd St Sacramento CA 95819 Office: 4949 Black Bart Trail Redwood Valley CA 95470 Office Phone: 707-485-7194. Personal E-mail: sac67449@saclink.csus.edu. Business E-Mail: cspeed@mendocino.edu.

SPEEDIE, MARILYN KAY, microbiologist, educator, dean; b. Salem, Oreg., Nov. 13, 1947; d. Arthur Alexander and Eleanor Ruth (Todd) Wilson; m. Stuart Mitchell Speedie, July 18, 1968; children: Andrea Elizabeth, Christopher Todd. BS Pharm., Purdue U., 1970, PhD, 1973. Asst. prof. Oreg. State U., Corvallis, Oreg., 1973-75; from asst. prof. to prof. dept. chmn. U. Md., Balt., 1975-91, prof. Sch. of Pharmacy, 1991—; dean, prof. U. Minn. Coll. Pharmacy, 1996—. Contbr. articles to profl. jours. Mem.: U.S. Pharmacopoeia, Am. Pharm. Assn., Am. Soc. Health Sys. Pharmacists, Am. Chem. Soc., Am. Assn. Colls. Pharmacy (bd. dirs., pres. 2006—07), Am. Soc. Pharmacognosy (exec. com. 1987—89, 1999—2000), Soc. Indsl. Microbiology, Am. Soc. Microbiology, Rho Chi. Home: 2125 Lower Saint Dennis Rd Saint Paul MN 55116-2804 Office Phone: 612-624-1900. Business E-Mail: speed001@umn.edu.

SPEEGLE, LAURA ANN, elementary school educator; d. James William and Mary Lou Speegle; m. Kimberly Lynn Akers. MA in Edn., Wayne State U., 2003. Cert. tchr. Mich. Educator Detroit Pub. Schs., 1993—. Sch. improvement com. Carl T. Rowan Elem., Detroit, 1994—2001; team leader NASA Explorer Schs., 2005—; sci. adv. com. Mich. Dept. Edn., Lansing, 2004—. Constrn. com. vol. Habitat for Humanity, Detroit, 1998—2005; tutor Macomb (Mich.) Reading Ptnrs., 2001—02. Recipient Educator Achievement award, Booker T. Washington Bus. Assn., 1998; Target Tchr. scholar, Target Inc., 1999, Detroit Urban Systemic Initiative grantee, Detroit Pub. Schs., 1999—2000, Explorer Sch. grantee, NASA, 2005—. Mem.: Nat. Assn. for Edn. of Young Child, Mich. Sci. Tchr. Assn., Courville Girls Running Club (leader 2004—05). Democrat. Avocations: running, volleyball, weightlifting. Office: Detroit Pub Schs Courville Elem 18040 St Aubin Detroit MI 48234 Home Phone: 586-801-5140; Office Phone: 313-866-3000. Office Fax: 313-866-3011; Home Fax: 586-754-4106. Personal E-mail: lauraspeegle@sbcglobal.net.

SPEER, BROWNLOW MAIN, lawyer; b. Delhi, NY, Aug. 24, 1938; s. James Robert and Elizabeth Main Speer; m. Doris Pulver Speer, Jan. 22, 1965; children: James, Andrew(dec.). BA, Haverford Coll., Pa., 1960, Oxford U., Eng., 1962, MA, 1969; JD, Harvard Law Sch., Cambridge, 1970. Bar: Mass. 1970, U.S. Dist. Ct., Dist. Mass. 1971, U.S. Ct. Appeals, 1st Circuit 1974, U.S. Supreme Ct. 1995. Assoc. Palmer & Dodge, Boston, 1970—72; staff atty. Lawyers' Com. for Civil Rights, Boston, 1972—74; dir. of tng. Mass. Defenders Com., Boston, 1974—79, chief appellate atty., 1979—, Com. for Pub. Counsel Svcs., 1984—. Co-author (with Blumenson and Kanstroom): Massachusetts Criminal Practice, 2001; co-author: (with Herrmann) (jour. publ.) Facing the Accuser: Ancient and Medieval Precursors of the Confrontation Clause, 1994; assoc. editor Mass. Law Rev., 2003—. Pres., bd. mgrs. First Parish in Waltham (Mass.) U-U, 1995—97; bd. dirs. Waltham (Mass.) Alliance to Create Housing, 2003—; publicity com. Cmty. Works, Boston, 2003—; mem. Otto M. Stanfield Law Scholarship Com., 2005—. With US Army, 1962—66. Recipient Mass. Super Lawyer, 2005, Kutak-Dodds Defender prize, Nat. Legal Aid and Defender Assn., 2005. Mem.: Am. Acad. Appellate Lawyers, Boston Bar Assn. (mem. coun. 1986—89, John G. Brooks award 1996), ABA, Mass. Bar Assn., Mass. Assn. Criminal Def. Lawyers. Democrat. Unitarian Universalist. Avocations: legal history, language study. Home: 141 Barbara Rd Waltham MA 02453 Office: Com for Pub Coun Svcs 44 Bromfield St Boston MA 02108 Office Fax: 617-988-8485. Business E-Mail: bspeer@publiccounsel.net.

SPEER, DAVID BLAKENEY, b. Sault Ste. Marie, Ont., Apr. 6, 1951; s. Richard Norwood and Mary (Davis) S.; m. Barbara Ann Brugenhemre, June 22, 1974; children: Blake, Sarah. BS in Indsl. Engring., Iowa State U., 1973; MBA, Northwestern U., 1977. Sales engr. Precision Paper, Wheeling, Ind., 1976-78, sales mgr., 1976-78; regional sales mgr. ITW Buildex, Itasca, Ill., 1978-81, nat. sales mktg. mgr., 1981-84, v.p., gen. mgr., 1984-92, ITW Paslode, Lincolnshire, Ill., 1992; group v.p., constrn. products Ill. Tool Works Inc. (ITW), 1994—95, exec. v.p. global constrn. products bus. Glenview, Ill., 1995—2004, exec. v.p. finishing systems bus., 1997—2004, exec. v.p. global Wilsonart laminate bus. unit, 2003—04, pres., 2004—, CEO, 2005—, chmn., 2006—. Bd. dirs. Rockwell Automation, Inc. Mem. adv. bd. Northwestern U. Master of Mgmt. and Mfg. program. Mem. Am. Mgmt. Assn., Am. Mktg. Assn., Am. Soc. Indsl. Engrs., Midwest Indsl. Mfg. Assn. Achievements include brokering historic number of acquisitions within company, 2006. Office: Ill Tool Works Inc 3600 W Lake Ave Glenview IL 60026-1215 Office Phone: 847-724-7500. Office Fax: 847-657-4572. *

SPEER, JACK ATKESON, publisher; b. Wichita, Kans., July 3, 1941; s. Jack Shelley and Shannon C. Speer; m. Judith Ann Fuller, Aug. 5,1967; children: Martin Fuller, Elizabeth Speer Goodwin. BS in Bus. Adminstrn., Kansas. State U., 1966, ML, 1967; postgrad., U. Mo., 1967, U. So. Calif., 1969; IBM Pres.'s Class, Harvard U., 1980. Mem. advt., editorial, mech. staffs Wichita Eagle-Beacon, 1954-64; editorial asst. Emporia (Kans.) Gazette, 1964-65; supr. libr. data processing Kans. State U., Emporia, 1965-67, mgr. data processing ctr. Manhattan, 1967-69; mgr. systems and programming John Wiley Inc.-Becker & Hayes Inc., Bethesda, Md., 1969-72; dir. libr. info. systems Informatics Inc. Info. Systems Group, Rockville, Md., 1972-77; v.p. ops. Arcata Real Estate Data Inc., Miami, Fla., 1977-79; mgr. electronic info. systems Arcata Publs. Group, Norwalk, Conn., 1979-83; v.p. mktg./sales, data imaging group The William Byrd Press, Richmond, Va., 1983-84; sr. v.p. ops. NewsBank Inc., New Canaan, Conn., 1984-85; pres., pub. Buckmaster Pub., Mineral, Va., 1986—. Mem. faculty Cath. U. Am. Libr. Sch., Kans. State U. Libr. Sch.; customer adv. coun. U.S. Postal Svc., 1996—. Author: Amateur Radio Call Directory, 1982—, Buckmaster's Ann. Stockholder Reports, 1986—, Front-Page-News (CD-ROM and Internet), 1989, HamCall (CD-ROM and Internet), 1988—; compiler Libraries and Automation: A Bibliography, 1967, The Living Bible Concordance, 1972. Trustee Jefferson-Madison Regional Libr., 1990-91; commr. Louisa County Planning Commn. 1992-; pres. Louisa County Libr. Found. 2003- Mem. ALA, NRA, Am. Radio Relay League, Nat. Info. Standards Orgn. (CD-ROM com), D.C. Libr. Assn. (pres.), Rotary, Sigma Tau Gamma. Office: Buckmaster Pub 6196 Jefferson Hwy Mineral VA 23117-3425 E-mail: speerj@buck.com.

SPEER, KEVIN PAUL, surgeon; b. Evansville, Ind., June 8, 1959; m. Marcy Carlson Speer, Mar. 24, 1984; children: Casey, Kira. MD, Johns Hopkins U., 1985. Lic. physician N.C., 1992. Assoc. prof. orthopedics Duke U. Med. Ctr., Durham, NC, 1992—2000; pvt. practice Southeastern Orthopedics, Raleigh, NC, 2000—. Fellow, Am. Orthop. Assn., 1992. Fellow: AAOS. Office: Southeastern Orthopedics 3404 Wake Forest Rd Ste 201 Raleigh NC 27609 Business E-Mail: kspeer@nc.rr.com.

SPEER, NANCY GIROUARD, health facility administrator; b. Mankato, Minn., Sept. 14, 1941; d. Jared and Katherine (Schmitt) How; m. Robert L. Girouard, Aug. 29, 1964 (dec. Mar. 1983); children: Robert James Girouard, Mark Jared Girouard; m. David J. Speer, Dec. 21, 1985 (dec. Aug. 1999). BA, Wellesley Coll., 1963; MA in Tchg., Wesleyan U., 1965; cert. mgmt., Smith Coll., 1985. Tchr. secondary sch. Bunnell H.S., Stratford, Conn., 1964-65; tchr., class advisor Lincoln Sch., Providence, 1965-69; substitute tchr. Mankato, 1972-74; pub. info. dir. City of Mankato, 1974-78; univ. editor, dir. pub. affairs forum Mankato State U., 1978-79; comms. mgr. Humphrey Inst., U. Minn., Mpls., 1980-83, dir. external rels., 1983-87, dir. devel. and external rels., 1987-95; dir. devel. Breck Sch., Mpls., 1996-2000; v.p. Abbott Northwestern Hosp., Mpls., 2000—02, Planned Parenthood, Minn., ND, SD, 2002—. Steering com. Minn. Meeting, Mpls., 1990-96. Contbr. articles to mag. and periodicals; photographer for publ. and newspapers. Bd. dir. Minn. Newspaper Found., St. Paul, 1985-91, chair, 1990-91, bd. dir., vice-chair Cabrini House, Mpls., 1993-97; bd. dir., sec. Minn. Ctr. for Book Arts, Mpls., 1990-97; bd. dir. Minn. Landmark Ctr., St. Paul, 1994-2000; dir. Minn. Women's Campaign Fund, Mpls., 1994-2000, co-pres. bd., 1997; vice chair, bd. dir. Loft Lit. Ctr., 2000—; vice-chair Met. Airport Commn., 1999-2003; trustee Lake Forest Acad.; bd. mem. Minn. Advocates Human Rights, Minn. Ctr. for Environ. Advocacy. Bush Leader fellow, 1985-87, Ferry Hall Woman of Distinction, 2006. Avocations: literature, nature, books.

SPEER, RICHARD JOHN, security consultant; b. Oxnard, Calif., Aug. 21, 1958; s. Richard McCord Speer and Betty Jean Wilson. Grad. H.S., Las Vegas, Nev. Enlisted U.S. Army, 1976, advanced through grades to sgt. first class, 1990, infantryman 82nd Airborne Divsn. Ft. Bragg, NC, 1976—81, infantry squad leader, 1981—87, infantry squad leader 4th Infantry Divsn. Ft. Carson, Colo., 1987—88, heavy weapons specialist Spl. Forces Ft. Bragg, 1988—94, project mgr. spl. projects, 1995—98, ret., 1998; ops. support mgr., nuclear security cons. Securitas Security Svcs., NJ, 1998—. Life mem. Rep. Nat. Com., Washington, 1994-, Nat. Rep. Congl. Com., 2003-, Nat. Rep. Senatorial Com., 2003-, Rep. Presdl. Task Force, 2005—. Decorated Army Commendation medal 3rd award U.S. Army, 1984, Meritorious Svcs. medals U.S. Army, 1991, 96, 98. Mem. Heritage Found., N.Am. Hunting Club (life), Am. Legion. Avocation: amateur philatelist. E-mail: rspeersecuritas@aol.com.

SPEER, SUSAN H., bank executive; b. 1941; Sr. v.p., pvt. banking mgr. Zions First Nat. Bank, Salt Lake City, 1997—. Creator pvt. med. svcs. initiative Zions First Nat. Bank. Mem. deferred giving bd. U. Utah, Salt Lake City; mem. adv. coun. Westminster Coll., Salt Lake City. Named one of 25 Women to Watch, US Banker mag., 2006. Mem.: Utah Bankers Assn. (mem. convention com.). Office: Zions First Nat Bank 1 S Main St Salt Lake City UT 84111 *

SPEERS, ROLAND ROOT, II, lawyer; b. Jacksonville, Fla., Oct. 8, 1933; s. Roland Root and Alice (Calkins) S.; m. Florence Briscoe, Dec. 18, 1954; children: Kirsten, Guy, Gina Marie. BA cum laude, UCLA, 1955, JD, 1958. Bar: Calif. 1958, D.C. 1978. Dep. commr. corps. Calif. Dept. Corps., Los Angeles, 1958-59; sec., gen. counsel Suburban Cos., Pomona, Calif., 1959-64; sec. Amcord, Inc., Los Angeles, 1964-66, asst. to pres., 1968, v.p. corp. devel., 1969, v.p., gen. counsel Newport Beach, Calif., 1970, sr. v.p., 1971, exec. v.p., 1972-75, pres., 1975-94; ptnr. Speers, Dana, Teal Balfour & MacDonald, Costa Mesa, Calif., 1977-97. Dir. Logicon, Inc., Torrance, Calif., Twelve Eleven Press, Newport Beach, Calif. Co-author: The Malloy Chronicles: The Hidden Empire, 2003, The Malloy Chronicles: The Rheingold Legacy, 2006, The Malloy Chronicles: The Catalyst, 2006. Trustee Pitzer Coll., Pomona, 1975-80; bd. councillors Center Pub. Affairs U. So. Calif., 1976-81; bd. dirs. Newport Harbor Art Mus., 1977-82; sr. warden St. James Episcopal Ch., 1993; mem rectors counsel St. James Anglican Ch., 2004—. Mem. D.C. Bar Assn., State Bar Assn. Calif., UCLA Alumni Assn., UCLA Law Sch. Alumni Assn., Phi Alpha Delta. Clubs: Big Canyon Country (Newport Beach).

SPEERSTRA, KAREN M., former publishing executive; b. Toledo, July 25, 1940; BA, U. Wis., 1962. Dir. music & art acquisition William C. Brown Pub., Debuke, Ill., 1981-87; tech. pub. dir. Focal Press Digitals Press Newnes & Butterworth Heinemann, Woburn, Mass., 1991-00, ret., 2000—.

SPEESE, MARK E., rental company executive; Student, Western Mich. U. Regional mgr. Thorn Americas, 1979—86; from v.p. N.J. Ops. to chmn., CEO Rent A Center, Plano, Tex., 1986—2001, chmn., CEO, 2001—. Bd. dirs. Rent A Ctr. Office: Rent A Center 5700 Tennyson Pkwy Plano TX 75024 *

SPEICHER, CARL EUGENE, pathologist; b. Carbondale, Pa., Mar. 21, 1933; s. William Joseph and Elizabeth Marcella (Connolly) S.; m. Mary Louise Walsh, June 21, 1958; children: Carl E. Jr., Gregory, Erik. BS in Biology, King's Coll., 1954; MD, U. Pa., 1958; student, Sch. of Aerospace Medicine, Brooks AFB, Tex., 1969. Diplomate Am. Bd. Pathology. Intern U. Pa. Hosp., Phila., 1958-59, resident, 1959-63; chief lab. svcs. USAF Hosp., London, Eng., 1963-66, USAF Med. Ctr. Wright Patterson, Dayton, Ohio, 1966-70; dir. clin. labs. and chmn. dept. pathology Wilford Hall USAF Med. Ctr., San Antonio, 1971-77; prof. dept. pathology Ohio State U., Columbus, 1977—2000, vice chair dept. pathology, 1992—2000, prof. emeritus dept. pathology, 2000—; dir. clin. svcs. Ohio State U. Med. Ctr., Columbus, 1977—2000; dir. clin. lab. Stoneridge Med. Ctr., Ohio State U., 2000—. Co-author: Choosing Effective Laboratory Tests, 1983; author: The Right Test, 1990, 3d edit., 1998. Col. USAF, 1956-77. Decorated Legion of Merit; fellow in med. chemistry SUNY, Syracuse, 1970-71. Mem. AMA, Ohio Soc. Pathologists, Ctrl. Ohio Soc. Pathologists, Am. Assn. for Clin. Chemistry, Assn. Clin. Scientists, Coll. Am. Pathologists, Am. Soc. Clin. Pathologists, Alpha Omega Alpha.

SPEIDEL, JOHN JOSEPH, public health professional, educator; b. Iowa City, Iowa, Sept. 17, 1937; s. Thomas Dennis and Edna (Warweg) Speidel; m. Melissa Jane Webster, Oct. 7, 2001; 1 child from previous marriage, Sabrina Brett. AB cum laude, Harvard U., 1959, MD, 1963, MPH, 1965. Diplomate Nat. Bd. Med. Examiners, Am. Bd. Preventive Medicine. Intern St. Luke's Hosp., NYC, 1963-64; resident N.Y.C. Dept. Health, 1965-67, dep. dir. maternal and infant care project, 1966-67; chief rsch. divsn. Office Population, AID, Dept. of State, Washington, 1969-76, assoc. dir., 1977, dep. dir., acting dir. office, 1978-83; v.p. Population Action Internat. (formerly Population Crisis Com.), 1983-87, pres., 1987-95; program dir. population Hewlett Found., 1995—2003; adj. prof. Bixby Ctr. Reproductive Health Rsch. and Policy U. Calif., San Francisco, 2003—. Lectr. population and family planning Georgetown U., 1973—75. Editor (with others): (book) Female Sterilization, 1971, Hysteroscopic Sterilization, 1974, Intrauterine Devices, 1974, Control of Male Fertility, 1975, Advances in Female Sterilization Technology, 1976, Risks, Benefits and Controversies in Fertility Control, 1978, Reversal of Sterilization, 1978, Pregnancy Termination, 1979, Vaginal Contraception, 1979; contbr. articles to profl. jours. Served to maj. US Army, 1967—69. Recipient Meritorious Unit citiation, Office of Population, 1969—71, Arthur S. Flemming award, Washington Downtown Jaycees, 1972. Mem.: Population Assn. Am., Am. Pub. Health Assn. (Carl S. Shultz award 1982). Office: U Calif San Francisco CRHRP Dept Ob Gyn 3333 California St Ste 335 San Francisco CA 94118 Office Phone: 415-502-3928. Business E-Mail: speidelj@obgyn.ucsf.edu.

SPEIER, JACKIE (KAREN JACQUELINE), lawyer, former state senator; b. San Francisco, May 14, 1950; m. Steven K. Sierra, 1987 (dec. 1994); children: Jackson Kent, Stephanie Katelin. BA, U. Calif., Davis, 1972; JD, U. Calif., 1976. Legal coun., legis. asst. to Rep. Leo J. Ryan US Congress, 1973-78; mem. San Mateo County Bd. Supr., Calif., 1981-86, chairwoman, 1985; mem. Calif. State Assembly, 1986-96, majority whip, 1987-95, mem. health com., judiciary com., fin. & ins. commn., chair consumer protection com., 1991-95; mem. Calif. State Senate from Dist. 8, 1998—2006, chair select com. on govt. oversight, chair select com. on spl. edn., mem. transp. com., appropriations com., edn. com., joint legis. audit com.; of counsel Hanson, Bridgett, Marcus, Viahos, & Rudy LLP, San Francisco, 2007—. Author: This Is Not the Life I Ordered: 50 Ways to Keep Your Head Above Water When Life Keeps Dragging You Down, 2007. Named Legis. of Yr., Met. Transp. Commn., 2004. Democrat. Roman Catholic. Office: Hanson Bridgett Marcus Viahos & Rudy LLP 425 Market St 26th Fl San Francisco CA 94105 E-mail: jspeier@hansonbridgett.com. *

SPEIGHT, JOHN BLAIN, lawyer; b. Cheyenne, Wyo., May 29, 1940; s. Jack B. and Kathryn Elizabeth (Schmidt) S.; m. Sally Karolee Sullivan, Aug. 20, 1960 (div. Apr. 1977); children: Sheryl, Tricia, Jackie; m. Carol Ann McBee, Sept. 16, 1979. BA, U. Wyo., 1962, JD, 1965. Bar: Wyo. 1965. Atty. Standard Oil Calif., 1965-67; asst. atty. gen. State of Wyo., Cheyenne, 1967-69, adminstrv. legal asst. to gov., 1969-71, atty. for reorgn. com., 1969-71; asst. U.S. atty. litigation div. Dist. Wyo., Cheyenne, 1971-72; ptnr. Hanes, Carmichael, Johnson, Gage & Speight, Cheyenne, 1972-75, Hathaway, Speight & Kunz, Cheyenne, 1976—2001, Speight, McCue & Assoc., 2002—. Cons. to sec. interior Dept. Interior, Washington, summer, 1975; mem. Commn. for Uniform State Laws, 1986-90; chmn. Wyo. Jud. Supervisory Commn., 1986-90; bd. dirs. various banks. Chmn. Wyo. Republican. Com., 1973-75; commr. Wyo. Health Care Commn., 2003-; bd. dirs. various civic orgns. Recipient numerous awards for civic activities; named a Top Comml. Litig. Lawyer Am. Registery LLC, 2006; named one of Best Lawyers Am., 1993-2007. Mem. ABA, Wyo. Bar Assn., Laramie County Bar Assn., ATLA, Wyo. Trial Lawyers Assn., Am. Bd. Trial Advs. (diplomate), Young Men's Literary Club. Roman Catholic. Avocations: motorcycle riding, hot air ballooning, skiing. Home: 4021 Snyder Ave Cheyenne WY 82001-1170 Office: PO Box 1709 Cheyenne WY 82003-1709 Office Phone: 307-634-2994. Business E-Mail: jspeight@speightmccue.com.

SPEIR, WILLIAM ARTHUR, JR., critical care physician; b. Macon, Ga., July 18, 1939; s. William Arthur Speir and Esther Marie Garland; m. Mary Hazelton Lehmann, June 8, 1963; 1 child, Mary-Butler S. Mathieson. BS in Chemistry, U. Ga., 1961; MD, Med. Coll. Ga., 1965. Asst. prof. pulmonary medicine Med. Coll. Ga., Augusta, 1971-75, assoc. prof. pulmonary medicine, 1975-80, prof. medicine pulmonary/critical care medicine, 1980-2000, prof. emeritus medicine, 2000—, med. dir. med. ICU, 1977-79, 91-00, chief sect. pulmonary diseases, 1979-92; clin. prof. medicine Mercer U. Sch. Medicine, Macon, Ga., 2000—. Contbr. over 170 articles, abstracts to profl. jours., 4 chpts. to books. Bd. dirs. Augusta Opera

Assn., 1973-80. Lt. comdr., surgeon USPHS, 1966-68. Recipient Pulmonary Acad. award Nat. Heart, Lung and Blood Inst., 1974-79, Order of St. Obscurus award RTH Laennec Assn., 1983; named Ky. Col. Fellow Am. Coll. Chest Physicians (gov. for Ga. 1998-2002, bylaws com. 1993-99, steering com. sect. on respiratory pathophysiology 1984-86, com. undergrad. med. edn. 1976-79, pres. So. chpt. 1980-81, 93-94, Disting. Faculty award 1991), Am. Coll. Critical Care Medicine; mem. Am. Thoracic Soc. (edn. com. 1977-81, councilor-at-large 1980, Disting. Educator award 1972), So. Med. Assn. (chmn. sec. chest diseases 1980-81, 93-94, Paul A. Turner Meml. Lectr. award 1983, 86), Soc. Critical Care Medicine (mem. grad. med. fellowship com. 2004—07), Sovereign Mil. Order Temple Jerusalem (Meritorious Svc. medal 2006), Phi Rho Sigma Med. Soc. Episcopalian. Avocations: painting, writing, cooking, music, gardening. Office Phone: 706-738-7953. Personal E-mail: bandmspeir@comcast.net.

SPEIRN, STERLING K., foundation administrator; married; children: Paolo, Daniel. BA in Polit. Sci., Stanford U., 1970; JD, U. Mich., 1973. Tchr., counselor Univ. Sch., Shaker Heights, Ohio, 1974-76; law clk. to Judge Paul Merlin Office Hearings and Appeals U.S. Dept. Interior, Washington, 1977-78; staff atty. North Ctrl. Legal Assistance Program, Durham, NC, 1979-81; dep. dir. Humboldt Open Door Clinic Cmty. Health Ctr., Arcata, Calif., 1982-85; intern Peninsula Cmty. Found., Burlingame, Calif., 1986; program officer cmty. leagal affairs dept. Apple Computer, Inc., Cupertino, Calif., 1986-90; program officer Peninsula Cmty. Found., San Mateo, Calif., 1990, acting exec. dir., 1991, sr. v.p., 1991-92, pres., CEO, 1992—2005; CEO W.K. Kellogg Found., Battle Creek, Mich., 2006—. Chmn. steering com. Peninsula Grantmakers, San Jose, 1987-90; presenter in field; mem. planning com. Coun. on Founds., Washington, 1991, 92. Founding co-chmn. Peninsula Partnership for Children, Youth and Families, 1994—; bd. dirs. Am. Leadership Forum of Silicon Valley, Driscoll Family Found.; bd. advisors Silicon Valley Cmty. Ventures, Entrepreneurs' Found.; mem. program com. No. Calif. Grantmakers, San Francisco, 1989-90. Fellow Am. Leadership Forum Silicon Valley. Mem. League Calif. Cmty. Founds. (chmn.), Pvt. Industry Coun. San Mateo County. Avocations: hiking, gardening, running, swimming, camping. Office: WK Kellogg Found One Michigan Ave E Battle Creek MI 49017-4012

SPEIRS, DEREK JAMES, diversified financial services company executive; b. Montreal, Que., Can., Dec. 21, 1933; s. James B. and Marie C. (Hunt) S.; m. Carol Alice Cumming, Dec. 8, 1967 (div. Feb. 1989); children: Lara Marie, Gregory Ross, Scott Lawrence Gordon. B. Commerce with honors in Econs., McGill U., 1954, MBA, 1959. Chartered acct., Can., chartered corp. sec. Devel. dir. fine papers, corp. acctg. dir. Domtar, Inc., Montreal, 1970-72, dir. corp. devel., 1976-78, v.p. fin., corp. devel., 1978-89, sr. v.p. fin. and corp. devel., 1989-91; v.p., sec. fin. Consoltex, Montreal, 1972-76, bus. cons., 1991—; pres. Speirs Fin. Inc., Speirs Cons. Inc., Speirs Capital Inc. Mem. Can. Inst. Chartered Accts., Fin. Execs. Inst., C.D. Howe Inst., Lac Marois Country Club, St. James Club, Montreal Amateur Athletic Assn. Avocations: travel, skiing. Home: 365 Stanstead Ave Mont-Royal Montreal PQ Canada H3R 1X5 Office: Ste 1100 2 Pl Alexis Nihon Montreal PQ Canada H3Z 3C1 Office Phone: 514-342-3857. E-mail: speirsco@videotron.ca.

SPEIRS, GREG, artist; Art dir. Grooves Mag., NYC, 1977—79, Changes, Inc., 1980—85. Artwork, Panther Dream Ski for K-2 Corp., 1992, Original Lithuanian Olympic Basketball Jerseys, Am. Eagle Artwork U.S. Olympic Team Bobsleds, 2002, prin. works include for Prince Albert of Monaco Monaco Olympic Bobsled Team. Named to Soc. Illustrators, N.Y., N.Y., 1975, 1976. Achievements include design of first 'Extreme Sports' licensed property character, Scully. Office: No Rules Graphics and Slammin Sports Box #125 Yonkers NY 10710 Office Phone: 800-362-1886. Personal E-mail: skully@skullman.com. E-mail: greg@skullman.com.

SPEIZER, FRANK E., physician, researcher; BA, Stanford U., 1957, MD, 1960. Prof. environ. sci. Harvard Sch. Pub. Health; Edward H. Kass prof. medicine Harvard Med. Sch., mem. environ. epidemiology program dept. environ. health, co-dir. Channing Lab. dept. medicine; sr. physician Brigham & Women's Hosp. Prin. investigator Nurses Health Study, Brigham and Women's Hosp., Harvard Med. Sch. Contbr. articles to profl. jours. Recipient Charles S. Mott prize, 2001. Mem.: Inst. Medicine. Achievements include research in the natural history of respiratory diseases, environmental risks for chronic diseases including risks for cancer and cardiorespiratory diseases. Office: Channing Lab 181 Longwood Ave Boston MA 02115 Business E-Mail: frank.speizer@channing.harvard.edu.

SPEJEWSKI, EUGENE HENRY, physicist, consultant; b. East Chicago, Ind., Sept. 15, 1938; s. Henry Louis and Carrie Jane (Fuss) S.; m. Norma Beverly Seekins, June 8, 1963; children: Maria Suzanne, Beverly Anne, Andrew John, Jeannette Michelle. BS, U. Notre Dame, 1960; PhD, Ind. U., 1966. Research assoc. Ind. U., Bloomington, 1965-67, Princeton U., 1967-69, instr., 1969-71; asst. prof. Oberlin Coll., Ohio, 1971-72; dir. UNISOR, Oak Ridge Assoc. Univs., 1972-85, mgr. SDS program, 1985-86, chmn. spl. projects div., 1986-89; v.p., dir. tng. and mgmt. systems div. Oak Ridge Inst. for Sci. and Edn., 1989-95, v.p., assoc. dir. for edn. and tng. group, 1995-98; cons. Oak Ridge Nat. Lab., 1999—. Vis. prof. physics U. Tenn., Knoxville, 1981-84, adj. prof.; mem., chmn. HHIRF Users Exec. Com., Oak Ridge Nat. Lab., 1982-84; referee U.S. Dept. Energy, various profl. jours. Co-editor: Future Directions in Studies of Nuclei Far from Stability, 1980; contbr. articles to profl. jours. Referee U.S. Soccer Fedn.; bd. dirs. Oak Ridge Community Playhouse, 1985-88, 95—. Mem. AAAS, Am. Phys. Soc., Am. Mgmt. Assn., Oak Ridge Sertoma Club (sec., treas., pres., chair bd. dirs.), Sigma Xi. Office Phone: 865-241-1514. Personal E-mail: spejewskieh@ornl.gov.

SPELFOGEL, EVAN J., lawyer, educator; b. Boston, Jan. 28, 1936; s. Morris R. and Helen S. (Steinberg) S.; m. Beverly Kolenberg; children: Scott, Douglas, Karen. AB, Harvard U., 1956; JD, Columbia U., 1959. Bar: Mass. 1959, N.Y. 1964, U.S. Supreme Ct. 1969. Atty. Office of Solicitor, U.S. Dept. Labor, Washington, Boston, 1959-60, NLRB, Boston, NYC, 1960-64; assoc. Simpson, Thacher & Bartlett, NYC, 1964-69, Dewey, Ballantine, NYC, 1969-77; ptnr. Fellner, Rovins & Gallay, NYC, 1977-80, Summit, Rovins & Feldesman, NYC, 1981-91, Epstein Becker and Green, P.C., NYC, 1991—. Adj. prof. law Baruch Coll., CCNY. Bd. editors Developing Labor Law: The Board, The Courts and the National Labor Relations Act, also co-editor-in-chief Supplements; bd. sr. editors Employee Benefits Law; contbr. articles to profl. jours. Fellow Coll. Labor and Employment Lawyers; mem. ABA (sect. on labor and employment law, exec. coun. 1978-86, co-editor sect. newsletter 1976-92, editl. bd. The Labor Lawyer 1986—, mem. ho. dels. 1987-90, sect. dispute resolution 1992—), FBA (coun. on labor law), N.Y. State Bar Assn. (chmn. labor and employment law sect. 1977-78, exec. coun. 1975—, ho. dels. 1978-79, com. on profl. discipline 1987-90), Assn. of Bar of City of N.Y. (labor com. 1968-71, 87-90, employee benefits com. 1992-96), Indsl. Resl. Rsch. Assn. (sec. N.Y. chpt. 1999-2000, pres. 2000-01), Am. Arbitration Assn. (nat. panel labor arbitrators), Harvard Varsity Club, Phi Alpha Delta. Home: 17 Parkside Dr Great Neck NY 11021-1042 Office: Epstein Becker & Green, PC 250 Park Ave New York NY 10177-0001 Office Phone: 212-351-4539. Business E-Mail: espelfogel@ebglaw.com.

SPELFOGEL, SCOTT DAVID, lawyer; b. Boston, Nov. 27, 1960; s. Evan J. and Beverly (Kolenberg) S. BS, Boston U., 1982; JD, Syracuse U., 1985; LLM, Boston U., 1990. Bar: Mass. 1985, N.Y. 1986, U.S. Dist. Ct. (no. dist.) N.Y. 1986, U.S. Dist. Ct. Mass. 1987; lic. real estate broker, Mass., 1987. Assoc. Jeffrey M. McCrone, P.C., Syracuse, N.Y., 1985-87, Tatarian Law Offices, Boston, 1987-88; asst. gen. counsel The Berkshire Group, Boston, 1988—96, sr. v.p., gen. counsel, 1996—2005, CWCapital LLC, Needham, Mass., 2005—. Mem. ABA, Am. Corp. Counsel Assn., Boston Bar Assn., N.Y. Bar Assn., Mass. Bar Assn. Home: 27 Sentry Hill Rd Sharon MA 02067-1521 Office: CWCapital LLC One Charles River Pl 63 Kendrick St Needham MA 02494 Office Phone: 781-707-9300. Business E-Mail: sspelfogel@cwcapital.com.

SPELKE, ELIZABETH SHILIN, psychology professor; b. NYC, May 28, 1949; d. Alan Shilin and Ruth (Simon) Spelke; m. Elliott M. Blass, Oct. 23, 1988; children: Mae Bridget, Joseph Alan. BA in Soc. Rels., Radcliffe Coll., 1971; PhD in Psychology, Cornell U., 1978; PhD honoris causa, Umeå U., Sweden, 1993, Ecole Pratique des Hautes Etudes, Paris, France, 1999. Asst. prof., dept. psychology U. Pa., 1977—81, assoc. prof., dept. psychology, 1981—86; prof., dept. psychology Cornell U., Ithaca, NY, 1986-96; prof., dept. brain and cognitive sciences MIT, Cambridge, Mass., 1996—2001; prof., dept. psychology Harvard U., Cambridge, 2001—05, co-dir., Mind, Brain and Behavior Inter-faculty Initiative, 2003—, Marshall L. Berkman Prof. Psychology, 2005—. Contbr. articles to profl. sci. jours. Recipient Boyd McCandless Young Scientist Rsch. award, Am. Psychological Assn., 1984, NIH MERIT award, 1993, James McKeen Cattell Fellowship, 1992,, Ipsen Prize in Neuronal Plasticity, 2001; Fulbright-Hays Sr. Rsch. Fellowship, 1983, Guggenheim Meml. fellow, 1988-89, James McKeen Cattell fellow, 1992-93; named one of America's Best in Sci. and Medicine, Time mag., 2001. Fellow AAAS, Am. Psychol. Soc. (William James award, 2000, Disting. Scientific Contribution award, 2000), Soc. Exptl. Psychologists; mem. NAS, Cognitive Neurosci. Soc., Psychonomic Soc., Am. Acad. Arts and Scis., Phi Beta Kappa, Sigma Xi Achievements include research on early development of perception by human infants; rsch. on devel. of reasoning about objects, space, and number by children. Office: Dept Psychology Harvard U 1130 William James Hall 33 Kirkland St Cambridge MA 02138 Office Phone: 617-495-3876. Office Fax: 617-384-7944. E-mail: spelke@wjh.harvard.edu. *

SPELL, DERRICK W., oncologist, educator; MD, La. State U., New Orleans, 1997; BS summa cum laude, Tenn. State U., 1993. Diplomate internal medicine Am. Bd. Internal Medicine, 2000, oncology Am. Bd. Internal Medicine, 2002. Clin. asst. prof. medicine La. State U. Health Scis. Ctr., Baton Rouge, 2002—; physician La. Hematology Oncology Assoc., Baton Rouge, 2004—. Chief hematology and oncology Earl K. Long Med. Ctr. - La. State U. Health Svcs. Ctr., 2002—. Co-chair, health initiatives action team Am. Cancer Soc., Baton Rouge, 2002—04; health svcs. adv. com. E. Baton Rouge Parish Schs., 2005—06; bd. mem. East Baton Rouge Parish Sch. Bd., 2007—; mem. Assn. of Retarded Citizens, Baton Rouge, 2004—06, Hospice Found., Baton Rouge, 2004—05, Children's Charter Sch., Baton Rouge, 2004. T. H. Harris scholarship, State of La., 1989-1993, LA State Bd. of Trustees scholarship, 1989-1993, sholarship, Nat. Honor Soc., 1989, scholarship, Wal-Mart Found., 1989, Cecil Vaughn scholarship in medicine, McNeese State U., 1993, Kushner Meml. scholarship, 1993. Mem.: ACP (assoc.), Am. Soc. Clin. Oncology (assoc.). Achievements include research in use of red blood cell distribution width for colon cancer screening. Office: La Hematology Oncology Assoc 4950 Essen Ln Ste 500 Baton Rouge LA 70809 Office Phone: 225-767-1311. Office Fax: 225-767-1335. Business E-Mail: derricks@marybird.com.

SPELLACY, WILLIAM NELSON, obstetrician, gynecologist, educator; b. St. Paul, May 10, 1934; s. Jack F. and Elmyra L. (Nelson) Spellacy; m. Lynn Larsen; children: Kathleen Ann, Kimberly Joan, William Nelson. BA, U. Minn., 1955, BS, 1956, MD, 1959. Diplomate subsplty. cert. in maternal and fetal medicine Am. Bd. Ob-Gyn. Intern Hennepin County Gen. Hosp., Mpls., 1959—60; resident U. Minn., Mpls., 1960—63; practice medicine specializing in ob-gyn. Mpls., 1963—67, Miami, Fla., 1967—73, Gainesville, Fla., 1973—79, Chgo., 1979—88; prof., dept. head U. Ill. Coll. Medicine, Chgo., 1979—88; dept. chmn. U. So. Fla. Coll. Medicine, Tampa, 1988—2002, prof., 1988—. Prof. dept. ob-gyn. U. Miami, 1967—73; prof., chmn. dept. U. Fla., 1973—79. Contbr. articles to med. jours. Mem.: ACOG, AMA, Inst. Medicine, Ill. Med. Soc., Soc. Perinatal Obstetricians, Ctrl. Assn. Obstetrics and Gynecology, South Atlantic Soc. Obstetrics and Gynecology, Perinatal Rsch. Soc., Am. Diabetes Assn., Assn. Profs. Gynecology and Obstetrics, Am. Fertility Soc., Endocrine Soc., Am. Assn. Obstetricians and Gynecologists, Soc. Gynecol. Investigation, Am. Gynecol. and Obstet. Soc., Am. Gynecol. Soc., Rotary. Episcopalian. Home: 845 Seddon Cove Way Tampa FL 33602-5704 Office: U South Fla Coll Medicine Dept OBGYN 4 Columbia Dr Ste 514 Tampa FL 33606-3589

SPELLER, KERSTIN G. RINTA, psychologist; b. Washington, Nov. 18, 1949; d. Eugene and Saga (Lindberg) Rinta; Thomas Hughes Speller, Sept. 4, 1971; five children. AB, Ohio U., 1971, MS, 1972; PhD, SUNY, Buffalo, 1983. Cert. sch. psychologist. Sch. psychologist Iroquois Ctrl. Schs., Elma, N.Y., 1974-78; cons. psychologist Amherst, N.Y., 1979-84; program dir. Child's Play Preschool Program, Amherst, 1986-95; sch. psychologist Holland (N.Y.) Schs., 1995—2004. Project dir. ISO-9001 GEMCOR, Buffalo, 1993-2004, corp. dir. human rels., 1998-2002. Bd. dirs. Heritage Ctrs. (Assn. Retarded Children), Erie County, N.Y., 1983-2000, govt. affairs com. chair, 1995-2000. Mem. Nat. Assn. Sch. Psychologists, USTA (ea. mgmt. bd., regional v.p. western region 1996-2003, nat. awards com. 1999-2002), Country Club Buffalo, Buffalo Tennis and Squash Club, East Aurora Pony Club, Village Glen Tennis and Fitness Club. Home: 5 Preston Beach Rd Marblehead MA 01945-2005

SPELLER, ROBERT ERNEST BLAKEFIELD, JR., choreographer; b. NYC, Feb. 5, 1936; s. Robert E.B. and Flora Maxine Elliott (Watkins) S. Student, Duke U., 1954-56, NYU, 1958-59, New Sch. for Social Rsch., 1967-68. English lang. sec. Prince Felix Youssoupoff, Paris, 1961—63; v.p. Robert Speller & Sons, Pubs., NYC, 1963—2006, pres., 2006—; coordinator models New Sch. Soc. Rsch., Parsons, NYC, 1972—2001; instr. Baruch Col., NYC, 1980—83; pres. Royalty Rsch. Ctr., 2007—. Choreographer many shows including Toulouse, 1981, The Ritz, 1983, Let's Misbehave, 1985-86; dir. I Died Yesterday, 1983; translator: The Mime (by Jean Dorcy), 1961. Mem. SAG, AFTRA, Actors' Equity Assn. (councillor, 1967-73), Am. Guild Variety Artists, Soc. Stage Dirs. and Choreographers NY, NY Geneal. and Biog. Soc. Episcopal. Home and Office: Robert Speller and Sons 115 E 9th St New York NY 10003-5414 Office Phone: 212-473-0333. Personal E-mail: robertspellerjr@yahoo.com.

SPELLER-BROWN, BARBARA JEAN, pediatric nurse practitioner; b. Windsor, NC, Feb. 8, 1958; d. Thomas Franklin and Esther Lee (Bond) Speller; children: Samuel, Shaun, Shea, Shanele, Samara. BSN, Howard U., 1981; MSN, U. Utah, 1993. Cert. PNP. Charge nurse Rosebud (S.D.) Indian Health Facility, 1981-82, Carl Albert Indian Health Facility, 1982-83; asst. head nurse Pitt County Meml. Hosp., Greenville, N.C., 1984-85; staff nurse St. Bernardine's Hosp., San Bernardino, Calif., 1986, San Bernardino Cmty. Hosp., 1986-87; staff nurse/charge nurse Gorgas Army Hosp., Panama, 1987-90; charge nurse Humana Hosp. Davis North, Layton, Utah, 1990-93; staff nurse Primary Children's Med. Ctr., Salt Lake City, 1990-93; clin. preceptor, PNP Cmty. Health Care Inc., Capital Heights, Md., 1994-95; faculty PNP Our Kids Ctr. Vanderbilt U. Med. Ctr., Nashville, 1995-2000; CPNP pediat. Walter Reed Army Med. Ctr., 2001, Army Med. Ctr., 2001—02; pediat. nurse practitioner hematology/oncology Children's Nat. Med. Ctr., 2002—. Mem. Gospel choir The Word of God Bapt. Ch.; scholarship chairperson Watchcare. 1st lt. USPHS, 1981—83. Named Outstanding Young Woman Am. Delta Sigma Theta. Mem. ANA, Nat. Assn. PNPs, Sigma Theta Tau, Phi Kappa Phi. Home: 11020 Lake Victoria Ln Bowie MD 20720 Personal E-mail: workingmom04@aol.com.

SPELLING, IAN, columnist; b. 1965; BA, SUNY Albany. Writer Albany Student Press, Starlog mag.; freelance columnist NY Times Syndication Sales Corp., 1991—93, syndicated columnist, 1993—. Author: (syndicated columns) Inside Trek & Sci-Fi (title changed to Strange Worlds: Inside Sci-Fi & Fantasy), 1993—. Office: NY Times Syndication Sales Corp 14th Fl 122 E 42nd St New York NY 10168 Office Phone: 212-661-9122. Office Fax: 212-499-3382.

SPELLING, TORI (VICTORIA DAVEY SPELLING), actress; b. LA, May 16, 1973; d. Aaron and Carol Jean Spelling; m. Charlie Shanian, July 3, 2004 (div. Apr. 20, 2006); m. Dean McDermott, May 7, 2006; 1 child, Liam Aaron. Actor: (TV films) Shooting Stars, 1983, The Three Kings, 1987, A Friend to Die For, 1994, Awake to Danger, 1995, Deadly Pursuits, 1996, Co-ed Call Girl, 1996, Mother, May I Sleep with Danger?, 1996, The Alibi, 1997, Way Downtown, 2002, A Carol Christmas, 2003, Hush, 2005, The Family Plan, 2005, Mind Over Murder, 2006; (TV series) Beverly Hills, 90210, 1990—2000, So Downtown, 2003, The Help, 2004, So noTORIous (also co-exec. prodr.), 2006—, Tori & Dean: Inn Love, 2007—; (films) Troop Beverly Hills, 1989, The House of Yes, 1997, Scream 2, 1997, Perpetrators of the Crime, 1998, Trick, 1999, Sol Goode, 2001, Scary Movie 2, 2001, Evil Alien Conquerors, 2002, 50 Ways to Leave Your Lover, 2004, Cthulhu, 2006. Office: c/o United Talent Agy Ste 500 9560 Wilshire Blvd Beverly Hills CA 90212-2401

SPELLINGS, MARGARET LAMONTAGNE, secretary of education; b. Ann Arbor, Mich., Nov. 30, 1957; d. John and Peg Dudar; m. Robert Spellings, 2001; children: Mary, Grace. BA in polit. sci. & jornalism, U. Houston, 1979. Worked for Tex. Gov. William P. Clements; assoc. exec. dir. Tex. Assn. Sch. Bds.; polit. dir. Gov. George W. Bush gubernatorial campaign, Tex., 1994; sr. advisor to Gov. George W. Bush State of Tex., 1994—2000; asst. to Pres. for domestic policy The White House, Washington, 2001—05; sec. US Dept. Edn., Washington, 2005—. Host online interactive forum Ask the White House. Named one of 100 Most Powerful Women in Wash., Washingtonian mag., 2001; recipient Golden Plate award, Acad. Achievement, 2006. Achievements include one of the principal authors of the No Child Left Behind Act, 2001. Office: US Dept Edn 400 Maryland Ave SW Washington DC 20202 *

SPELLMAN, DOUGLAS TOBY, advertising executive; b. Bronx, NY, May 12, 1942; s. Sydney M. and Leah B.S.; m. Ronni I. Epstein, Jan. 16, 1966 (div. Mar. 1985); children: Laurel Nicole, Daren Scott; m. Michelle Ward, Dec. 31, 1986; 1 child, Dallas Ward Spellman. Media buyer Doyle, Dane, Bernbach, Inc., NYC, 1964-66; various postions, 1966-72; media supr. Ogilvy & Mather, Inc., LA, 1972-73; media dir. Vitt Media Internat., Inc., LA, 1973-74; v.p., dir. West Coast ops. Ind. Media Svcs., Inc., LA, 1974-75; owner Douglas T. Spellman, Inc., LA, 1975-77, pres., chmn. bd., 1977-82; pres., COO Douglas T. Spellman Co. div. Ad Mktg., Inc., 1982-85; pres., CEO, chmn. bd. Spellbound Prodns. and Spellman Media divs. Spellbound Comms, 1984-86; gen. ptnr. Faso & Spellman, 1984-86; COO, pres. Yacht Mgmt. Internat., Ltd., 1984-86; v.p. media Snyder, Longino Advt. div. Snyder Advt., 1986-91; advt./media cons., 1986-90; gen. ptnr. Nucleus Nuance, LA, 1987-88, Conv. Photos Unltd., Hawaii, 1988-89; v.p. mktg. Pacific Med. Products, Inc., LA, 1990-91. Media dir. Kennedy-Wilson Inc., LA, 1991-94; dir. media and advt. svcs. Goddard & Claussen/First Tuesday, LA, 1994-97; v.p. advt. and mktg. Cosmetic Tech. Internat., Inc., LA, 1997-98; mng. dir. Med. Mktg. and Advt., LA, 1998-99; dir. media svcs., Publicis Dialog-FusionDM, San Francisco, 1999-2000; mgr. media, promotions and direct mktg. Pleasant Holidays, LLC, LA, 2001—; guest lectr. Sch. Bus. UCLA, 1964-69. Served with USAR N.G., 1964-69. Mem. Aircraft Owner and Pilots Assn., NRA, Calif. Pistol and Rifle Assn., Rolls Royce Owners, Mercedes Benz Am., Aston Martin Owners, Phi Zeta Kappa, Phi Omega Epsilon. Personal E-mail: spellman.doug@att.net.

SPELLMAN, MITCHELL WRIGHT, surgeon, academic administrator, educator; b. Alexandria, La., Dec. 1, 1919; s. Frank Jackson and Altonette Beulah (Mitchell) S.; m. Billie Rita Rhodes, June 27, 1947 (dec.); children: Frank A., Michael A. (dec.), Mitchell A., Maria S. Weaver, Melva A., Mark A., Manly A. (dec.), Rita S. Parks; m. Adrienne Foster Williams, Feb. 14, 2001 (dec. Dec. 2001). AB magna cum laude, Dillard U., 1940, LLD (hon.), 1983; MD, Howard U., 1944; PhD in Surgery, U. Minn., Mpls., 1955; DSc (hon.), Georgetown U., 1974, U. Fla., 1977. Intern Cleve. Met. Gen. Hosp., 1944-45, asst. resident in surgery, 1945-46, Howard U. and Freedmen's Hosp., Washington, 1946-47, chief resident in thoracic surgery, 1947-48, tchg. asst. in physiology, 1948-49, chief resident in surgery, 1949-50, tchg. asst. in surgery, 1950-51; asst. prof. surgery Howard U., 1954-56, assoc. prof., 1956-60, prof., 1960-68; dir. Howard surgery svc. at DC Gen. Hosp., 1961-68; fellow in surgery U. Minn., 1951-54; sr. resident in surgery U. Minn. Med. Sch. and Hosp., 1951—54; dean Charles R. Drew Postgrad. Med. Sch., LA, 1969-77, prof. surgery, 1969-78; asst. dean, prof. surgery Sch. Medicine, UCLA, 1969-78; clin. prof. surgery Sch. Med., U. So. Calif., 1969-78; dean for med. svcs., prof. surgery Harvard Med. Sch., Boston, 1978-90, dean emeritus for med. svcs., 1990—, dean emeritus for internat. projects, 1990—, prof. surgery emeritus, 1990—; dir. internat. exch. programs Harvard Med. Internat., 1995—; exec. v.p. Harvard Med. Ctr., 1978-90. Fellow Ctr. for Advanced Study in Behavioral Scis.; vis. prof. Stanford U., 1975-76; bd. dirs. Kaiser Found. Hosps., Kaiser Found. Health Plan, 1971-89; mem. DC Bd. Examiners in Medicine and Osteopathy, 1955-68; mem. Nat. Rev. Com. for Regional Med. Programs, 1968-70; spl. med. adv. group, nat. surg. cons. VA, 1969-73; mem. Commn. for Study Accreditation of Selected Health Ednl. Programs, 1970-72; chmn. adv. com. br. med. devices Nat. Heart and Lung Inst., 1972; Am. health del. to visit People's Republic of China, 1973; hon. dir. State Mut. Cos., 1990—; mem. com. mandatory retirement in higher edn. NAS/NRC, 1989-91; panel on internat. programs Nat. Libr. Medicine, 1996-97; adv. bd. faculty medicine and health scis. United Arab Emirates U., 2004—. Mem. editl. bd.: Jour. Medicine and Philosophy, 1977-90; contbr. articles on cardiovasc. physiology and surgery, measurement of blood volume, and radiation biology to profl. jours. Past bd. dirs. Sun Valley Forum on Nat. Health; mem. ethics adv. bd. HEW, 1977-81; bd. dirs. Harvard Cmty. Health Plan, 1979-84; former trustee Occidental Coll.; former bd. overseers com. to visit univ. health svc. Harvard, bd. overseers Harvard Cmty. Health Plan, 1984-95; former regent Georgetown U., bd. dirs., 1986-92; former vis. com. U. Mass. Med. Ctr.; mem. bd. visitors UCLA Sch. Medicine; mem. corp. MIT; adv. bd. PEW Scholars Program in Biomed. Scis., 1984-86; bd. dirs. Med. Edn. for South African Blacks, 1985—; adv. bd. United Arab Emirates U. Faculty of Medicine and Health Scis., 2004-. Recipient Disting. Alumnus award Dillard U., 1963, Disting. Postgrad. Achievement award Howard U., 1974, Outstanding Achievement award U. Minn., 1979, Surg. Alumnus of Yr. award U. Minn., 1991, Disting. Support citation Charles R. Drew U. of Medicine, 2002; named U. Minn. Dept. Surgery Alumnus of Yr., 1991; Markle scholar in med. scis., 1954-59; Commonwealth Fund fellow, U. Minn., Mpls., 1955. Mem. AMA, AAAS, AAUP, ACS, Nat. Med. Assn. (William A. Sinkler Surgery award 1968), Soc. Univ. Surgeons, Am. Coll. Cardiology, Am. Surg. Assn., Inst. Medicine of NAS (chmn. program com. 1977-79, governing coun. 1978-80), Nat. Acad. Practice in Medicine, Am. Assn. Sovereign Mil. Order of Malta (Knights and Dames of Malta), Soc. Black Acad. Surgeons, MIT Corp. (life mem. emeritus), Cosmos Club. Roman Catholic. Office: Harvard Med Internat 1135 Tremont St Ste 900 Boston MA 02120 Office Phone: 617-535-6400.

SPELLMAN, THOMAS JOSEPH, JR., lawyer; b. Glen Cove, NY, Nov. 11, 1938; s. Thomas J. and Martha H. (Erwin) S.; m. Margaret Mary Barth, June 23, 1962; children: Thomas Joseph, Kevin M., Maura N. BS, Fordham U., Bronx, NY, 1960, JD, 1965. Bar: NY 1966, US Dist. Ct. (so. and ea.

dist.) NY 1968, US Ct. Appeals (2nd cir.) 1980, US Supreme Ct. 1981. Staff atty. Allstate Ins. Co., NYC, 1966-69; trial atty. Hartford Ins. Co., Hauppauge, NY, 1969-71; ptnr. Wheller & Spellman, Farmingville, NY, 1971-76, Devitt Spellman Barrett, LLP, Smithtown, NY, 1976—. Mem. grievance com. 10th Jud. Dist., Westbury, NY, 1984-92. Trustee Acad. St. Joseph, Brentwood, NY, 2000-04; bd. trustees, exec. com. St. Catherine of Sienna Med. Ctr., Smithtown, NY, 2002—. Capt. USAR, 1960-68. Fellow: NY Bar Found., Am. Bar Found.; mem.: NY Bar State Bar Assn. (ho. of dels. 1989—2005, nominating com. 1992—93, v.p. 1996—98), Suffolk County Bar Assn. (bd. dirs., sec.-treas. v.p. 1982—, pres. 1992—93), Swordfish Club. Westhampton Beach, NY (bd. dirs., sec. 2000—01). Home: 8 Highwoods Ct Saint James NY 11780-9610 Office: Devitt Spellman Barrett LLP 50 Route 111 Ste 314 Smithtown NY 11787-3700 Office Phone: 631-724-8833. Business E-Mail: ingo@devittspellmanlaw.com.

SPELLMAN SWEET, JULIE T., lawyer; b. Orange, Calif., Oct. 11, 1967; BA, Claremont McKenna Coll., 1989; JD, Columbia Univ., 1992. Bar: NY 1993. Assoc. Cravath Swaine & Moore LLP, NYC, 1992—2000, ptnr., corp., 2000—. Bd. trustees Claremont McKenna Coll.; bd. dir. Drew Found. Named a Dealmaker of Yr., The Am. Lawyer mag., 2007; recipient Harlan Fiske Stone Scholar, 1992. Mem.: NY Lawyers for the Pub. Interest, Disability Rights Task Force, Phi Beta Kappa. Fluent in Mandarin Chinese. Office: Cravath Swaine & Moore LLP Worldwide Plz 825 Eighth Ave New York NY 10019-7475 Office Phone: 212-474-1572. Office Fax: 212-474-3700. Business E-Mail: jspellmansweet@cravath.com. *

SPELLMIRE, GEORGE W., lawyer; b. Oak Park, Ill., June 10, 1948; Student, Brown U.; BA, Ohio State U., 1970; JD, De Paul U., 1974. Bar: Ill. 1974, US Dist. Ct. (no. dist.) Ill. 1974, US Tax Ct. 1984, US Ct. Appeals (7th cir.) 1984, US Supreme Ct. 1994. Ptnr. Hinshaw & Culbertson, Chgo., 1982-98, D'Ancona & Pflaum, Chgo., 1998—2003, Spellmire & Sommer, Chgo., 2003—. Author: Attorney Malpractice: Prevention and Defense, 1988, supplemental edit., 1990; co-author: Accounting, Auditing and Financial Malpractice, 1998, supplemental edit., 2000, Accountants' Legal Liability Guide, 1990, Illinois Handbook on Legal Malpractice, 1982, Associates Primer for the Prevention of Malpractice, 1987. Mem. ABA, Am. Coll. Trial Lawyers, Soc. Trial Lawyers, Fed. Trial Bar, Internat. Assn. Def. Counsel (legal malpractice com., def. counsel practice mgmt. com.), Ill. State Bar Assn. Office: 77 W Wacker Dr Ste 4800 Chicago IL 60601-1664 Office Phone: 312-606-8722. Business E-Mail: gws@spellmireSommer.com.

SPELTS, RICHARD JOHN, lawyer; b. Yuma, Colo., July 29, 1939; s. Richard Clark and Barbara Eve (Pletcher) S.; children: Melinda, Meghan, Richard John Jr.; m. Gayle Merves, Nov. 14, 1992. BS cum laude, U. Colo., 1961, JD, 1964. Bar: Colo. 1964, U.S. Dist. Ct. Colo. 1964, U.S. Supreme Ct. 1968, U.S. Ct. Appeals (10th cir.) 1970, U.S. Dist. Ct. (ea. dist.) Mich. 1986. With Ford Motor Internat., Cologne, Germany, 1964-65; legis. counsel to U.S. Senator, 89th and 90th Congresses, 1967-68; minority counsel U.S. Senate Subcom., 90th and 91st Congresses, 1968-70; asst. U.S. atty., 1st asst. U.S. atty. Fed. Dist. of Colo., 1970-77; pvt. practice Denver, 1977-89; risk mgr. sheriff's dept. Jefferson County, Golden, Colo., 1990-91. Selected for Leadership Denver, 1977; recipient cert. for outstanding contbns. in drug law enforcement U.S. Drug Enforcement Adminstrn., 1977, spl. commendation for criminal prosecution U.S. Dept. Justice, 1973, spl. commendation for civil prosecution U.S. Dept. Justice, 1976. Mem. Fed. Bar Assn. (chmn. govt. torts seminar 1980), Colo. Bar Assn. (bd. govs. 1976-78), Denver Bar Assn., Colo. Trial Lawyers Assn., Denver Law Club, Order of Coif. Republican. Methodist. Home and Office: 9715 Sunset Hill Cir Lone Tree CO 80124-6716

SPENCE, ANDREW, artist, painter; b. Bryn Mawr, Pa., Oct. 4, 1947; s. Thomas and Elizabeth Spence; m. Mary Stewart Stoll, June 24, 1977. BFA, Temple U., 1969; MFA, U. Calif., Santa Barbara, 1971. Prof. art Bennington Coll., Vt., 1994—. One-man shows include TransAvant Garde Gallery, Austin, Tex., 1989, Barbara Krakow Gallery, Boston, 1989, Barbara Toll Fine Arts, NYC, 1982-83, 85, 87-88, 90, Compass Rose Gallery, Chgo., 1990, James Corcoran Gallery, LA, 1990, Max. Protetch Gallery, NYC, 1992-93, Barbara Scott Gallery, Miami, 1993, 96, Worcester Art Mus., Mass., 1991, Morris Healy Gallery, NYC, 1996, Art Resources Transfer, NYC, 2000, Edward Thorp Gallery, NYC, 2001, 02, Ulrich Mus. Art, Wichita, Kans., 2005, Edward Thorp Gallery, NYC, 2006; exhibited in group shows including Corcoran Gallery of Art, Washington, 1987, Hirshhorn Mus. and Sculpture Garden, Smithsonian Instn., Washington, 1989, 04, Whitney Mus. Am. Art, NY, 1989, 91-92, Met. Mus. Art, NYC, 1993, Am. Acad. Arts and Letters, NYC, 1994, Wall Street Rising, NYC, 2002, Wayne State U., Detroit, 2004, Andrew Kreps Gallery, NYC, 2006, Lennon Weinberg, NYC, 2007; represented in permanent collections including Addison Gallery Am. Art, Albright Knox Art Gallery, Balt. Mus. Art, Carnegie Mus. Art, Pitts., Cleve. Mus. Art, Cin. Art Mus., Hirshhorn Mus. and Sculpture Garden, Austin Mus. Art, Mus. Modern Art, NY, Met. Mus. Art, NYC, San Diego Mus. Contemporary Art, Walker Art Ctr., Whitney Mus. Am. Art, NYC. Painting grantee Nat. Endowment for Arts, 1987; Guggenheim fellow, 1994.

SPENCE, ANDREW MICHAEL, former dean, finance educator; b. Montclair, NJ, 1943; m. Ann Bennett (div.); children: Graham, Catherine, Marya; m. Monica Spence. BA in Philosophy summa cum laude, Princeton U., 1966; BA, MA in Maths., Oxford U., 1968; PhD in Econs. with honors, Harvard U., 1972. Asst. prof. polit. econ. Kennedy Sch. Govt. Harvard U., Cambridge, Mass., 1971-75, hon. rsch. fellow, 1975—76, vis. prof. econs. dept., 1976-77, prof. econs., 1977-83, prof. bus. adminstrn., 1979-83, George Gund prof. econs. and bus. adminstrn., 1983-86, chmn. bus. econs PhD program, 1981-83, chmn. econs. dept., 1983-84, dean Faculty Arts and Scis., 1984-90; assoc. prof. dept. econs. Stanford U., Calif., 1973-75, Philip H. Knight Prof., dean Grad. Sch. Bus. Calif., 1990-99, Philip H. Knight Prof. Emeritus, prof. mgmt. Calif., 1999—; ptnr. Oak Hill Venture Ptnrs. and Oak Hill Capital Ptnrs., Menlo Park, Calif., 1999—. Bd. dirs. Gen. Mills, Inc., Nike, Inc., Exult Inc., Siebel Syss. Inc., Blue Martini Software, Torstar Corp., ITI Edn.; mem. econs. adv. panel NSF, 1977-79; chmn. Nat. Rsch. Coun. Bd. on Sci., Tech. and Econ., Policy, 1990-97. Author: Market Signaling: Informational Transfer in Hiring and Related Processes, 1974; Co-author: Industrial Organization in an Open Economy, 1980, Competitive Structure in Investment Banking, 1983; past mem. editl. bd. Am. Econs. Rev., Bell. Jour. Econs., Jour. Econ. Theory and Pub. Policy; contbr. over 50 articles to profl. jours. Mem. econs. adv. com. Sloan Found., 1979—. Recipient J.K. Galbraith prize for excellence in tchg., 1978, Nobel prize in econ. scis., 2001, Golden Plate award, Acad. Achievement, 2006; Danforth fellow, 1966, Rhodes scholar, 1966. Fellow Am. Acad. Arts & Scis., 1983-, Econometric Soc.; mem. Am. Econ. Assn. (John Bates Clark medal 1981). Office: Stanford U Grad Sch Bus Bldg 350 Memorial Way Stanford CA 94305-5015 also: Oak Hill Venture Partnership 2775 Sand Hill Rd Ste 220 Menlo Park CA 94025-7085 *

SPENCE, BARBARA E., former publishing company executive; b. Bryn Mawr, Pa., July 8, 1921; d. Geoffrey Strange and Mary (Harrington) Earnshaw; m. Kenneth M. Spence Jr., June 29, 1944; children: Kenneth M. III, Christopher E., Hilary B. Grad. high sch. Movie, radio editor Parade Mag., NYC, 1941-45; with Merchandising Group, NYC, 1946-47; exec. dir. Greenfield Hill Congl. Ch., Fairfield, Conn., 1958-74, dir. religious edn., 1968-74; assoc. Ten Eyck-Emerich Antiques, 1974-76; personnel dir. William Morrow & Co., Inc., NYC, 1976-91; ret., 1991. Chmn. pub. relations, bd. dirs. ARC, 1951-56, Family Service Soc., Fairfield, 1956-57, 61-63; chmn. pub. relations Citizens for Eisenhower, 1952, Fairfield Teens Players, 1968-71; bd. dirs. Fairfield Teens, Inc., 1965-70, Planned Parenthood of Greater Bridgeport, 1969-75, chmn. pub. affairs, 1971-72, chmn. personnel, 1972-73, chpt. vice chmn., 1973-75; pres. steering com. Am. Playwrights Festival Theatre, Inc., Fairfield, 1969-70, v.p., bd. dirs., 1971—; bd. govs. Unquowa Sch., Fairfield, 1963-69; bd. dirs. Fairfield U. Playhouse, 1971-73, Downtown Cabaret Theatre, Bridgeport, 1975-76; bd. missions Southport Congl. Ch., 1998. Mem. AAP (compensation survey com.), Fairfield Women's Exch. (bd. dirs. 1993). Home: 675 Townsend Ave Unit 123 New Haven CT 06512-3175

SPENCE, DAVID WENDEL, application developer; b. Ann Arbor, Mich., Oct. 23, 1951; s. George Baugh and Sarah Frances Spence; m. Mary Beth Charboneau, Jan. 26, 1980; children: Jonathan David, Peter Michael, Sarah Catherine, Benjamin Joseph. BS in Computer Engring., U. Mich., Ann Arbor, 1975. Application programmer Charismatic Renewal Svcs., Ann Arbor, 1975—78; dir. software devel. ADP, Inc., Ann Arbor, 1978—97; sr. staff cons. NetworkTwo Comm. Grp., Ann Arbor, 1997—99; sr. sys. rsch. programmer Merit Network, Inc., Ann Arbor, 1999—2000; product arch. Interlink Networks, Inc., Ann Arbor, 2000—03. Mem.: IEEE, Assn. Computing Machines. Roman Cath. Home: 3259 Bluett Rd Ann Arbor MI 48105-1527 Home Phone: 734-834-6481. Personal E-mail: dspence@computer.org.

SPENCE, DONALD POND, psychologist, psychoanalyst; b. NYC, Feb. 8, 1926; s. Ralph Beckett and Rita (Pond) S.; m. Mary Newbold Cross, June 2, 1951; children: Keith, Sarah, Laura, Katherine. AB, Harvard U., 1949; PhD, Columbia U., 1955. Lic. psychologist, N.Y., N.J. From rsch. asst. to prof. psychology NYU, 1954-74; prof. psychiatry Robert Wood Johnson Med. Sch., Piscataway, NJ, 1974-95; ret., 1995. Vis. prof. psychology Stanford (Calif.) U., 1971-72, Princeton (N.J.) U., 1975-95, Louvain-le-Neuve, Belgium, 1980, William Alanson White Inst., N.Y.C., 1992; mem. personality and cognition rsch. rev. com. NIMH, 1969-73. Author: Narrative Truth and Historical Truth, 1982, The Freudian Metaphor, 1987, The Rhetorical Voice of Psychoanalysis, 1994; mem. editl. bd. Psychoanalysis and Contemporary Thought, Psychol. Inquiry, Theory and Psychology; contbr. articles to profl. jours. With U.S. Army, 1944-46, ETO. Recipient rsch. scientist award NIMH, 1968-74; decorated 2 battle stars. Fellow APA (pres. theoretical and philos. divsn. 1992-93, award disting. theoretical and philos. contbns. to psychology 2004), Am. Psychoanalytic Assn., NY Acad. Sci., Sigma Xi. Democrat. Home: 9 Haslet Ave Princeton NJ 08540-4913 E-mail: dpshaslet@aol.com.

SPENCE, GERRY (GERALD LEONARD SPENCE), lawyer, writer; b. Laramie, Wyo., Jan. 8, 1929; s. Gerald M. and Esther Sophie (Pfleeger) S.; m. Anna Wilson, June 20, 1947; children: Kip, Kerry, Kent, Katy; m. LaNelle Hampton Peterson, Nov. 18, 1969. BSL, U. Wyo., 1949, LLB, 1952, LLD (hon.), 1990. Bar: Wyo. 1952, U.S. Ct. Claims 1952, U.S. Supreme Ct. 1982. Sole practice, Riverton, Wyo., 1952-54; county and pros. atty. Fremont County, Wyo., 1954-62; ptnr. various law firms, Riverton and Casper, Wyo., 1962-78; sr. ptnr. Spence, Moriarity & Schuster, Jackson, Wyo., 1978—2002, Spence, Moriarity & Shockey, 2002—03, Spence Law Firm, 2004—. Founder Trial Lawyers Coll.; lectr. legal orgns. and law schs. Author: (with others) Gunning for Justice, 1982, Of Murder and Madness, 1983, Trial by Fire, 1986, With Justice for None, 1989, From Freedom to Slavery, 1993, How To Argue and Win Every Time, 1995, The Making of a Country Lawyer, 1996, O.J.: The Last Word, 1997, Give Me Liberty, 1998, A Boy's Summer, 2000, Gerry Spence's Wyoming: The Landscapes, 2000, Half Moon and Empty Stars, 2001, Seven Simple Steps to Personal Freedom, 2001, The Smoking Gun, 2003, Win Your Case, 2005, Bloodthirsty Bitches and Pious Pimps of Power: The Rise and Risk of the New Conservative Hate Culture, 2006. Mem. ABA, Wyo. Bar Assn., Wyo. Trial Lawyers Assn., Assn. Trial Lawyers Am., Nat. Assn. Criminal Def. Lawyers Office: The Spence Law Firm LLC PO Box 548 Jackson WY 83001-0548 Office Phone: 307-733-7290. Office Fax: 307-733-5248. Business E-Mail: infointake@spencelawyers.com.

SPENCE, HOWARD TEE DEVON, retired judge, lawyer, consultant, arbitrator, government agency administrator; b. Corinth, Miss., Sept. 29, 1949; s. T. P. and Dorothy M.S.; m. Diane Earl Williams, Feb. 26, 1977 (div. June 1986); children: Derek, Tina, Steven. BA, Mich. State U., 1970, M in Criminal Justice Adminstrn., 1975, M in Labor-Indsl. Relations, 1981, MBA, 1983; JD, U. Mich., 1976, M in Pub. Adminstrn., 1977. Bar: Mich. 1976, U.S. Dist. Ct. (ea. dist.) Mich. 1976, U.S. Ct. Appeals (6th cir.) 1976, U.S. Supreme Ct. 1980, U.S. Dist. Ct. (we. dist.) Mich. 1986; cert. ins. examiner; cert. ct. mediator, Mich. Counselor State Prison of So. Mich., Jackson, 1971-76; personnel adminstr. Mich. Dept. Commerce, Lansing, 1976-77; asst. dir. Mich. Pub. Service Commn., Lansing, 1977-78; dep. ins. commr. Mich. Ins. Bur., Lansing, 1978-92; prin., owner Spence & Assocs., Lansing, 1983—; adminstrv. law judge State of Mich., Lansing, 1992—2002. Arbitrator U.S. Dist. Ct. (we. dist.) Mich., Grand Rapids, 1986, Mich. Employment Rels. Commn., 1992—; mem. Nat. Assn. Securitries Dealers Panel of Neutrals; adj. law prof. Thomas M. Cooley Law Sch., Lansing, 1977-80; adj. instr. Nat. Jud. Coll., Reno, 1993-98; instr. MBA law program West Mich. campus U. Phoenix and online campus, 2003—; presenter in field. Author short stories. Sec., v.p. Ingham County Housing Commn., Okemos, Mich., 1985-90; bd. dirs. Econ. Devel. Corp. City of Lansing, 1981-85. Mem.: NAACP (life), Lansing Black Lawyers Assn., Nat. Arbitration Forum (arbitrator), Am. Arbitration Assn. Panel of Neutrals, Ins. Regulatory Examiners Soc. (bd. dirs., nat. pres. 1990—91), Am. Judges Assn., Wolverine Bar Assn., Black Lawyers Assn., Nat. Assn. Adminstrv. Law Judges, Mich. Assn. Adminstrv. Law Judges (pres. 1998), Assn. Black Judges Mich., Nat. Bar Assn., Mich. Bar Assn. (legal edn. com., mem. adminstrv. law sect. coun.), ABA (editor in chief NCALJ newsletter 1998—99), Blue Key, Kappa Delta Lambda (pres., chmn. bd. dirs., adminstr. Project Alpha, Edn. Found. Inc.), Alpha Phi Alpha. Mem. Ch. of Christ. Club: Renaissance, Economic (Detroit). Home: 1637 Willow Creek Dr Lansing MI 48917-9643 Office Phone: 517-579-0500. Business E-Mail: htspence@spence-associates.com.

SPENCE, JAMES ROBERT, JR., broadcast executive, educator; b. Bronxville, NY, Dec. 20, 1936; s. James Robert and Mary Jeffrey (Grant) Spence; m. Betsy Jo Viener, June 16, 1992. BA, Dartmouth Coll., 1958. Prodn. asst. ABC Sports, Inc. (known as Sports Programs, Inc. through 1966), NYC, 1960-63; asst. to exec. prodr. ABC's Wide World of Sports, 1963-66, coordinating prodr., 1966-70; v.p. program planning ABC Sports, Inc., 1970-78, sr. v.p., 1978-86; pres. Sports TV Internat. Inc., NYC, 1986—2006, exec. prodr., 1986—2006. Adj. assoc. prof. broadcasting NYU Sch. Continuing and Profl. Studies, NYC, 1999—2003; vis. scholar Coll. William and Mary, Williamsburg, Va., 2004—. Author: Up Close and Personal - The Inside Story of Network Television Sports, 1988. With US Army, 1958—60. Mem.: Two Rivers Country Club (Williamsburg, Va.), Westchester Country Club (Rye, NY).

SPENCE, JONATHAN DERMOT, historian, educator; b. Surrey, Eng., Aug. 11, 1936; came to U.S., 1959; s. Dermot Gordon Chesson and Muriel (Crailsham); m. Helen Alexander, Sept. 15, 1962 (div. 1993); children: Colin Chesson, Ian Alexander; m. Chin Annping, Aug. 12, 1993. BA, Cambridge U., Eng., 1959; PhD, Yale U., 1965; L.H.D. (hon.), Knox Coll., 1984, U. New Haven, 1989; DLitt. (hon.), Wheeling Coll., 1985, Chinese U. Hong Kong, 1996, Gettysburg Coll., 1996, Quinnipiac Coll., 1998, Union Coll., 2000, Beloit Coll., 2000, Conn. Coll., 2000; DLitt. (hon.), Oxford U., 2003. Asst. prof. history Yale U., New Haven, 1966-71, prof., 1971—, chmn. dept. history, 1983-90, dir. div. humanities., Sterling prof. history. Wiles lectr. Queens's U., Belfast, 1985; Gauss lectr. Princeton U., 1987; vis. prof. Peking U., 1987; chmn. Council on East Asian Studies; bd. govs. Yale U. Press, 1988—; hon. prof. Nanjing U., 1993, Wuhan U., 1999. Author: Ts'Ao Yin and the K'Ang-Hsi Emperor, 1966, To Change China, 1969, Emperor of China, 1974, The Death of Woman Wang, 1978, The Gate of Heavenly Peace, 1981, The Memory Palace of Matteo Ricci, 1984, The Question of Hu, 1988, The Search for Modern China, 1990, Chinese Roundabout, 1992, God's Chinese Son, 1996, The Chan's Great Continent, 1998, Mao Zedong, 1999, Treason By the Book, 2001; editor: Ch'ing-Shih We'T'I, 1965-73, (with others) From Ming to Ch'ing, 1979; mem. editorial bd. Am. Hist. Rev., 1990-93, Yale Jour. Criticism, 1989, Yale Rev., 1991, China Quar., 1992, Revista Española del Pacifico, 2000. Served with Brit. Army, 1954-56. Recipient John Adison Porter prize, 1965, Christopher award, 1975, Devane teaching medal, 1978, L.A. Times book award, 1982, Vursell prize Am. Acad. and Inst. Arts and Letters, 1983, Comisso prize (Italy), 1987, Gelber prize (Can.), 1990; named to Coun. of Scholars, Libr. of Congress, 1988—; Yale fellow in East Asian Studies, 1962-65, 68-70, Guggenheim fellow, 1979-80, John D. and Catherine T. MacArthur Found. fellow, 1988-93. Fellow Brit. Acad.; mem. Am. Acad. Arts and Scis., Am. Philos. Soc., Am. Hist. Assn. (pres. 2004), Assn. Asian Studies, Order St. Michael and St. George (companion). Home: 691 Forest Rd West Haven CT 06516-7932 Office: Yale U History Dept PO Box 208324 New Haven CT 06520-8324

SPENCE, KENNETH F., III, lawyer, insurance company executive; b. Balt., Apr. 18, 1955; BA summa cum laude, Dickinson Coll., 1977; JD with honors, U. Md., 1982. Bar: Md. 1982, US Fed. Ct. 1982. Mem. litig. dept. Miles & Stockbridge, Balt., 1983—96, ptnr., 1990—96; with USF&G (merged with St. Paul Cos. Inc.), 1996—98; v.p. corp. litig. St. Paul Cos. Inc. (merged with Travelers Property Casualty Corp.), 1998—2004; v.p. legal services divsn., dep. gen. counsel St. Paul Travelers Cos. Inc., 2004, exec. v.p., gen. counsel, 2004—. Mem.: Md. State Bar, Minn. State Bar. Office: St Paul Travelers Companies Inc 385 Washington St Saint Paul MN 55102 *

SPENCE, PAUL HERBERT, librarian; b. Geraldine, Ala., Dec. 25, 1923; s. John Clardy and Leila (Carrell) S.; m. Ruth Schmidt, May 9, 1954 (dec. Aug. 2003); children: John Carrell, Peter Schmidt, Robert McCollough AB, Emory U., 1948, MA, 1956; PhD, U. Ill., 1969. Asst. reference librarian Emory U., Atlanta, 1950-53; periodical reference librarian Air U., Maxwell AFB, 1953-56; dir. library Air Force Inst. of Tech., Wright-Patterson AFB, Ohio, 1957-58; asst. dir. social studies U. Notre Dame, South Bend, Ind., 1959-60, U. Nebr., Lincoln, 1960-63; history and polit. sci. librarian U. Ill., Urbana, 1963-66; assoc. dir. libraries U. Ga., Athens, 1966-70; dir. libraries U. Ala., Birmingham, 1970-84, collection devel. librarian, 1985-89, prof. emeritus, 1989—, libr. cons., 1990—. Bd. dirs. Southeastern Library Network, Atlanta, 1973-75. Served with U.S. Army, 1943-46, ETO Mem. ALA (council mem. 1976-78), Ala. Library Assn. (treas. 1975-76), Southeastern Library Assn. (pres. 1980-82) Democrat. Presbyterian. Home: 614 Warwick Rd Birmingham AL 35209-4426 Office: U Ala at Birmingham 172 Sterne Libr Birmingham AL 35294-0001 Personal E-mail: paulhspence@aol.com. Business E-Mail: pspence@beowulf.mhsl.uab.edu.

SPENCE, ROBERT LEROY, publishing executive; b. Carlisle, Pa., Sept. 13, 1931; s. Leroy Oliver and Esther Helen (Lau) S.; m. Barbara Amelia Hunter, Sept. 1, 1954 (div. Sept. 1978); children— Robert Roy, Bonnie Leigh; m. 2d, Maryanne Elizabeth Yacono, Jan. 10, 1979 BA, Dickinson Coll., 1953; postgrad, Temple U., 1955-57, Rutgers U., 1956, 59-60, U. Pa., 1960. Cert. tchr., N.J. Chmn. dept. math. Haddon Heights High Sch., NJ, 1954-62; sr. editor Silver Burdett Co., Morristown, NJ, 1962-64; editor-in-chief Harcourt Brace Jovanovich, Inc., NYC, 1964-81; v.p., pub. Harper & Row Publishers, Inc., NYC, 1981-85, Scribner Edni. Pubs. div. Macmillan, Inc., NYC, 1985; pres. R&M Spence, Inc., Sparta, NJ, 1985—. Author textbook series: Growth in Mathematics, 1978, Excel in Mathematics, 1989-90, Mathematics Plus: Multicultural Projects, 1993; editor: Financial Planning for The Baby Boomer Client, 2000, 2d edit., 2004, Money Forever, 2002. Mem. Assn. Am. Pubs. (mem. exec. com. 1981-84), Nat. Council Tchrs. Math., Internat. Reading Assn., Am. Numismatic Assn. Avocations: rare coin collecting, coin newsletter author and publisher, artist, writer. Home and Office: 37 Heather Ln Sparta NJ 07871-3538 Personal E-mail: rlsmys@tellurian.net.

SPENCE, ROY MILAM, JR., advertising executive; b. Brownwood, Tex., Oct. 10, 1948; m. Mary Spence; children: Courtney, Ashley, Shay. BA in Govt., U. Tex., 1971. Co-founder GSD&M's Idea City (formerly GSD&M Advt.), Austin, Tex., 1971, pres., 1971—2007, chmn. bd., CEO, 2007—. Mem. devel. bd. U. Tex., Austin, mem. adv. coun. McComb Sch. Bus. Featured in Fortune, The Wall St. Jour., The New York Times, USA Today. Mem. Wal-Mart Lit. Coun. Recipient Disting. Alumnus award, U. Tex., 2004. Office: GSD&M's Idea City 828 W 6th St Austin TX 78703-5420 *

SPENCE, SANDRA, retired trade association administrator; b. McKeesport, Pa., Mar. 25, 1941; d. Cedric Leroy and Suzanne (Haudenshield) S. BA, Allegheny Coll., 1963; MA, Rutgers U., 1964. With Pa. State Govt., Harrisburg, 1964-68, Appalachian Regional Commn., Washington, 1968-75; legis. rep. Nat. Assn. Counties, Washington, 1975-77; fed. rep. Calif. Dept. Transp., Washington, 1977-78; dir. congl. affairs Amtrak, Washington, 1978-81, corp. sec., 1981-83, dir. computer svcs., 1983-84; co-owner Parkhurst-Spence Inc., 1985; owner The Spence Group, 1986-90; v.p. Bostrom Corp., Washington, 1990-92; exec. dir. Soc. Glass and Ceramic Decorators, 1992-2000. Chmn. legis. com. Womens Transp. Seminar, 1977-79, dir., 1982-83, v.p., 1983-84, chmn. edn. com., 1982-83; com. on edn. and tng. Transp. Rsch. Bd., 1982-85; mng. ptnr. Cambio Capital Club, 1996. Contbr. articles to profl. jours. Commnr. DC Commn. for Women, 1983—88, sec., 1983—88; pres. Found. for Work of Laity, 2001—06; coun. mem. Agenda for Del. Women, 2006—; del. Ward III Dem. Com., 1982—90, 1st vice chmn., 1987—88; bd. dir. DC Habitat for Humanity, 1998—2002, chmn. devel. com., 1998—2000, sec., 2000—01, Sussex County Habitat for Humanity, Del., 2003—05, bd. dirs., 2003—06, treas., 2005—06, housing advocate, 2007—; bd. dirs. Del. Housing Coalition, 2007—. Fellow Eagleton Inst. Politics, 1963-64; recipient Achievement award Transp. Seminar, 1982, 83 Mem. LWV (treas. Del. chpt. 2007-), Greater Washington Soc. Assn. Execs. (vice-chair law and legis. com. 1989-90, chmn. 1990-91, chmn. scholarship com. 1992-93, bd. dirs. 1993-96, Rising Star award 1989, Chmn.'s award for Govt. Rels. 1991), Am. Soc. Assn. Execs. (mgmt. cert. 1987), Phi Beta Kappa. Home: 18471 Seashell Blvd Lewes DE 19958 Personal E-mail: sandy_s@juno.com.

SPENCE, SIQUE (MARY STEWART SPENCE), art dealer; b. Balt., Aug. 16, 1946; d. Joseph Adolphus and Nell Orum (Jones) Stoll; m. Ronald A. Kuchta, Nov. 2, 1969 (div. 1975); m. Andrew R. Spence, June 24, 1977. Dir. Galeria del Sol/Fairtree Fine Crafts Inst., Santa Barbara, Calif., 1970-75; asst. to dir. Arco Ctr. for the Visual Arts, LA, 1975-77; registrar Droll/Kolbert Gallery, NYC, 1977-78; gallery asst. Nancy Hoffman Gallery, NYC, 1978-81, dir., 1981—. Office: Nancy Hoffman Gallery 429 W Broadway New York NY 10012-3799 Fax: 212-334-5078.

SPENCE, WILLIAM H., electric power industry executive; BS, Pa. State Univ.; MBA, Bentley Coll. Mgmt. positions through v.p. trading Delmarva Power, 1987—2000; sr. v.p. Conectiv Holdings, 2000—06, Pepco Holdings Inc., 2002—06; exec. v.p., COO PPL Corp., Allentown, Pa., 2006—. Office: PPL Corp 2 N 9th St Allentown PA 18101 *

SPENCER, CAROL BROWN, retired educational association administrator; b. Normal, Ill., Aug. 26, 1936; d. Fred William and Sorado (Gross) B.; m. James Calvin Spencer, Dec. 18, 1965 (div. July 1978); children: James Calvin Jr., Anne Elizabeth. BA English, Calif. State U., LA, 1964,

MA Pub. Adminstrn., 1986. Cert. secondary edn. tchr., Calif. Tchr. English Seneca Vocat. H.S., Buffalo, 1966—70; pub. info. officer City of Pasadena, Calif., 1979—90, City of Mountain View, Calif., 1990—93; exec. dir. Calif. Assn. for Gifted, 1993—98; ret., 1998. Owner PR to Go, 1994— Sec., bd. dirs. Calif. Music Theatre, 1987-90; bd. dirs. Pasadena Beautiful Found., 1984-90, Pasadena Cultural Festival Found., 1983-86, Palo Alto-Stanford Heritage, 1990-93, Mountain View Libr. Found., 1997-98; mayoral appointee Strategic Planning Adv. Com., Pasadena, 1985-86; active Nev. Arts Advocates; trainer Clark County Election Dept., 1997-2007; centennial com. City of Las Vegas, 2004-06 Mem. NOW, DAR, Pub. Rels. Soc. Am., Calif. Assn. Pub. Info. Ofcls. (Paul Clark Achievement award 1986, Mktg. award 1990), City/County Comm. and Mktg. Assn. (bd. dirs. 1988-90, Savvy award for mktg. 1990), Las Vegas Art Mus. Democrat. Episcopalian. Home: 7915 Laurena Ave Las Vegas NV 89147-5064

SPENCER, CHARLES S., anthropologist; BA in Anthropology, Rice U., 1972; MA in Anthropology, U. Mich., 1976, PhD in Anthropology, 1981. Assoc. prof. anthropology U. Conn.; assoc. curator divsn. anthropology Am. Mus. Natural Hist., NYC, 1991—94, chair, curator, 1994—. Adj. assoc. prof. anthropology dept. Columbia U., adj. sr. rsch. scientist Ctr. Environ. Rsch. and Conservation. Contbr. articles to profl. jours., chapters to books. Fellow: Am. Acad. Arts & Scis.; mem.: NAS, AAAS, Soc. Am. Archaeology, Sigma Xi. Office: Divsn Anthropology Am Mus Natural Hist Ctrl Pk West at 79th St New York NY 10024-5192 E-mail: cspencer@amnh.org.

SPENCER, CHERYL L., literature and language educator; BA, Edgewood Coll., 1969; MA in Theater and Drama, U. Wis., Madison, 1993. Cert. tchr. secondary education, English Wis., 1974. Affirmative action asst. officer City of Madison, Wis., 1985—86; English tchr. Madison Met. Sch. Dist., 1969—, English tchr. diploma completion program, 1977—84, English tchr. summer sch., 1975. Sys. strategic planning in tchr. edn. com. U. of Wis., 1989—92; minority student achievement com. Madison Met. Sch. Dist., 1977—79, graduation stds. com., 1999—2000; pres. faculty senate Madison Meml. H.S., 1980—84, scholarship com., 2003—; tchr. edn. rev. panel U. Wis.-Plattville Dept. of Pub. Instrn., State of Wis., Madison, 2003. Producer- organizer, media person (traveling theatre group performances); dir.: (high school play) Plautus' The Captives. Bd. dirs. Urban League of Greater Madison, 1992—94. Recipient Outstanding H.S. Tchr. award, U. of Chgo., 1998. Mem.: Nat. Coun. of Tchrs. of English, Wis. Edn. Assn. Coun. (rep. to state rep. assembly 1977—80), Madison Tchrs. Inc. (bd. dirs., com. chair 1980—94). Office: Madison Memorial High School 201 S Gammon Rd Madison WI 53717 Home Phone: 608-848-5950; Office Phone: 608-663-5990. E-mail: cspencer@madison.k12.wi.us.

SPENCER, CHRISTOPHER S., lawyer, insurance company executive; b. Boston, Mass., Apr. 29, 1946; BA, Beloit Coll., 1969; JD, Univ. Wis., Madison, 1972. Bar: Wis. 1972. V.p., legal Am. Family Ins. Group, Madison, Wis. Office: American Family Insurance Group Legal Dept 6000 American Pkwy Madison WI 53783-0001 Office Phone: 608-249-2111. Office Fax: 608-243-4917. *

SPENCER, DAVID ANTHONY, geologist, researcher, educator; b. London, Nov. 7, 1963; s. Henry William George and Veronica Clair (Bonanno) S. BSc in Geology with honors, U. Exeter, Eng., 1986; Diploma, U. London, 1988, MSc in Structural Geology, 1988; Dr Natural Sci., Swiss Fed. Inst. Tech., Zurich, 1993. Chartered geologist, European geologist. Ins. claims broker Winchester Bowring Ltd., London, 1982-83; platinum exploration geologist Eastern Bushveld Complex, South Africa, 1986-87; rsch. fellow Swiss Fed. Inst. Tech., Zürich, 1988-89, rsch. and tchr. asst., 1989-92, vis. ETH rsch. fellow, 1992-93, vis. rsch. fellow, 1993-94, rsch. fellow in tectonics Zurich, 1994-97; vis. lectr. U. of the Punjab, Lahore, Pakistan, 1995; vis. scientist Tokyo Inst. Tech., Zurich, 1996; rsch. asst. prof., lectr. in structural geology U. Maine, Orono, 1997-98; geologist Saga Petroleum ASA, Norway, 1998—99; project mgr. numerous rsch. projects; founder Spencer Structural Cons., 2000; sr. reservoir geologist Roxar Software Solutions, 2003—. Vis. scientist U. Beijing, 1986; vis. prof. U. of the Punjab, Lahore, 1997—; Himalayan regional coordinating com. Internat. Lithosphere Program, 1992-96, com. tectonic map of Himalaya, 1995; organizer confs. in field; founder, moderator, coord. HimNet, 1994-96; presenter, cons., lectr. in field. Contbr. numerous articles to profl. jours.; European regional editor Himalayan Notes, 1994-97; reviewer numerous internat. jours. in field; assoc. editor The Professional Geologist. Found. gov. Raine's Found. Sch., 2002—; trustee The Raine's Found., 2002—. Sir John Cass Found. scholar, 1987-88, travel award, 1988; recipient travel award Swiss Geol. Soc., 1991, 93, Huber-Kudlich Found., 1992, Swiss Acad. Natural Scis., 1992, Pub. award Staub Fund, 1992, Educational Tng. award Saga Petroleum ASA; rsch. fellow Swiss Nat. Sci. Found., 1994-97; recipient Duke of Edinburgh Gold award, 1987. Fellow Geol. Soc., Royal Geog. Soc., Royal Soc. Arts, Am. Geog. Soc., Geol. Assn. of Can.; mem. AAAS, Inst. Petroleum, Royal Instn. of Gt. Britain, Royal Scottish Geog. Soc. (profl. assoc.), Order of Internat. Fellowship, Internat. Assn. Structural/Tectonic Geologists, Mineral. Soc., European Assn. Geoscientists and Engrs., Soc. for Sedimentary Geology, Geosci. Info. Soc., Computer Oriented Geol. Soc., European Union Geoscis., Am. Geophys. Union, Assn. Geoscientists for Internat. Devel., Geol. Soc Am., Geol. Soc. Switzerland, Geol. Soc. Pakistan, Geol. Soc. Punjab, Geol. Soc. Nepal, Swiss Mineral. and Petrological Soc., Soc. for Mining, Metallurgy and Exploration, Geochem. Soc., Am. Chem. Soc., Petroleum Exploration Soc. of Gt. Britain, Am. Assn. Petroleum Geologists, Nat. Geog. Soc., Assn. Am. Geographers, Can. Assn. Geographers, Brit. Assn. for Advancement of Sci., Sci. Exploration Soc., N.Y. Acad. Scis., Nat. Earth Sci. Tchrs. Assn., Nat. Assn. Geosci. Tchrs., Assn. for Sci. Edn., Himalayan Found., Himalayan Club, Himalayan Explorers Club, Nepal Studies Assn., Internat. Assn. for Ladakh Studies, Integrated Mountain Rsch. Soc., Internat. Mountain Soc., Brit. Mountaineering Coun., Sigma Xi. Avocations: mountain climbing, guitar, long distance walking, sports. Address: PO Box 2827 Reading RE1 9EN England

SPENCER, DAWN JOYCE, advocate; b. St. Louis, Nov. 7, 1938; d. Leslie Sylvan II and Iris Nunn (Burdick) S. AB, Syracuse U., 1964, MA, 1967, MLS, 1995. Cert. secondary education educator, NY, Calif. Exec. sec. to permanent observer Rep. Korea to UN UN, NYC, 1964-65; secondary level social studies tchr. Bd. Edn., Utica, NY, 1966-69; mgr. apt. complex Oakland, Calif., 1969-75; lectr. Fukushima U., Fukushima Med. Coll., Japan, Sakura no Seibo Women's Coll., Kennedy Internat. Coll., 1975-94; dir. Bowerston Pub. Libr., Ohio, 1996—2001; animal advocate Farm Sanctuary, Watkins Glen, NY, 2002—. English fluency instr. to migrant workers NY Dept. Edn., Clinton, summers 1967-68; sr. lectr. Fukushima Women's Coll., 1982-94. Pres. Syracuse-in-Asia, 1962-64; advisor US Mil. Svc. Recruitment, Utica, NY, 1966-69; active Humane Soc. US, Animal Protective League, Oakland, 1969-75, Fukushima Organic Farm Cooperative, 1982-94, Japan Animal Welfare Soc., Tokyo, 1993-94, African Wildlife Found., Am. Rivers, Best Friends Animal Sanctuary, Ctr. Marine Conservation, Defenders of Wildlife, numerous others. Mem. ASPCA, Am. Legal Def. Fund, Greenpeace, Animal Legal Def. Fund, Animal Protection Inst., Ark Trust, Fund for Animals, Humane Soc. US, Humane Soc. Schuyler Co., Last Chance for Animals, Progressive Animal Welfare Soc., People for Ethical Treatment Animals, Farm Sanctuary, In Defense of Animals, United Poultry Concerts, Fund for Animals. Green Party. Avocations: skiing, jazz, computers. Home: 121 Havana Glen Rd Lot 19 Montour Falls NY 14865 Home Phone: 607-535-6703. Personal E-mail: djspence@localnet.com.

SPENCER, DENNIS DEE, medical educator, director; b. Bedford, Iowa, Apr. 1, 1945; s. George and Wilma Spencer; m. Susan S. Spencer; children: Andrea, Joanna; children: Christopher, Kathleen. Grad., Grinnell Coll.; MD, Wash. U., St. Louis, 1971. Intern Barnes Hosp., St. Louis, 1971—72; resident in neurological surgery Yale-New Haven Hosp., 1972—76, assoc. neurosurgeon, 1977—80, attending neurosurgeon, 1980—87; prof. neurosurgery Yale U. Sch. Medicine, 1985—, chief neurosurgery, Nixdorff-German Prof., 1987—97, chmn. dept. neurosurgery, Harvey and Kate Cushing Prof., 1997—, dir. epilepsy program, acting dean, 2003—04. Mem.: Am. Epilepsy Soc. (bd. dirs., Milken Family Found. Clin. Investigator Award 1999), Am. Bd. Neurol. Surgeons (past chair), Am. Assn. Neurol. Surgeons, Soc. Neurol. Surgeons. Achievements include pioneer in sterotaxic cellular replacement therapy for patients with parkinson's desease. Office: Yale Neurosurgery Yale Physicians Bldg 3rd Fl 800 Howard Ave New Haven CT 06519

SPENCER, EDGAR WINSTON, geology educator; b. Monticello, Ark., May 27, 1931; s. Terrel Ford and Allie Belle (Shelton) S.; m. Elizabeth Penn Humphries, Nov. 26, 1958; children: Elizabeth Shawn, Kristen Shannon. Student, Vanderbilt U., Nashville, 1949—50; BS, Wash. and Lee U., Lexington, Va., 1953; PhD, Columbia U., NYC, 1957. Lectr. Hunter Coll., 1954-57; mem. faculty Washington and Lee U., 1957—, prof. geology, head dept., 1962-95, Ruth Parmly prof. Pres. Rockbridge Area Conservation Coun., 1978-79, co-pres. 1992-98; NSF sci. faculty fellow, New Zealand and Australia; dir. grant for humanities and pub. policy on land use planning Va. Found., 1975; dir. grant Petroleum Rsch. Fund, 1981-82; leader field trip Ctrl. Appalachian Mts. Internat. Geol. Congress, 1989. Author: Basic Concepts of Physical Geology, 1962, Basic Concepts of Historical Geology, 1962, Geology: A Survey of Earth Science, 1965, Introduction to the Structure of the Earth, 1969, 3d edit., 1988, The Dynamics of the Earth, 1972, Physical Geology, 1983, Geologic Maps, 1993, 2nd edit., 2000, Geologic Maps of the Buena Vista and Glasgow Quadrangle, Virginia, 2000; co-author: Geologic Map and Report on the Geology of Rockbridge County, Virginia, 2007; author: Earth Science-Understanding Environmental Systems, 2003. Recipient Va. Outstanding Faculty award Va. Coun. of Higher Edn., 1990. Fellow Geol. Soc. Am., AAAS; mem. Am. Assn. Petroleum Geologists (dir. field seminar on fold and thrust belts 1987, 88-91), Am. Inst. Profl. Geologists, Am. Geophys. Union, Nat. Assn. Geology Tchrs., Yellowstone-Bighorn Rsch. Assn., Phi Beta Kappa (hon.), Omicron Delta Kappa (hon.), Sigma Xi. Home: PO Box 1055 Lexington VA 24450-1055 Office Phone: 540-458-8866. E-mail: spencere@wlu.edu.

SPENCER, ELIZABETH, writer; b. Carrollton, Miss., 1921; d. James Luther and Mary James (McCain) S.; m. John Arthur Blackwood Rusher, Sept. 29, 1956. BA, Belhaven Coll., 1942; MA, Vanderbilt U., 1943; LittD (hon.), Southwestern U. at Memphis, 1968; LLD (hon.), Concordia U. at Montreal, 1988; LittD (hon.), U. of the South, 1992; DLitt (hon.), U. NC, Chapel Hill, 1998, Belhaven Coll., 1999. Instr. N.W. Miss. Jr. Coll., 1943-44, Ward-Belmont, Nashville, 1944-45; reporter The Nashville Tennessean, 1945-46; instr. U. Miss., Oxford, 1948-51, 52-53. Vis. prof. Concordia U., Montreal, Que., Can., 1976-81, adj. prof., 1981-86; vis. prof. U. NC, Chapel Hill, 1986-92. Author: Fire in the Morning, 1948, This Crooked Way, 1952, The Voice at the Back Door, 1956, The Light in the Piazza, 1960, Knights and Dragons, 1965, No Place for an Angel, 1967, Ship Island and Other Stories, 1968, The Snare, 1972, The Stories of Elizabeth Spencer, 1981, Marilee, 1981, The Salt Line, 1984, Jack of Diamonds and Other Stories, 1988, (play) For Lease or Sale, 1989, On the Gulf, 1991, The Night Travellers, 1991, (memoir) Landscapes of the Heart, 1998, The Southern Woman, 2001; contbr. short stories to mags. and anthologies. Named to NC Hall of Fame, 2002; recipient Women's Dem. Com. award, 1949, recognition award, Nat. Inst. Arts and Letters, 1952, Richard and Hinda Rosenthal Found. award, Am. Acad. Arts and Letters, 1957, Fortner award for lit., 1998, Award of Merit medal for the short story, 1983, 1st McGraw-Hill Fiction award, 1960, Henry Bellamann award for creative writing, 1968, Salem award for lit., 1992, Dos Passos award for fiction, 1992, NC Gov.'s award for lit., 1994, Corrington award for lit., 1997, Richard Wright award for lit., 1997, award for non-fiction, Miss. Libr. Assn., 1999, Brooks medal, Fellowship of So. Writers, 2001, Thomas Wolfe award for lit., 2002, William Faulkner award for lit. excellence, 2002, Miss. Gov.'s award for excellence in the arts, 2006, Pen/Malamud award for short fiction, 2007; fellow, Guggenheim Found., 1953; Kenyon Rev. fellow in fiction, 1957, Bryn Mawr Coll. Donnelly fellow, 1962, Nat. Endowment for Arts grantee in lit., 1983, Sr. Arts Award grantee, Nat. Endowment for the Arts, 1988. Mem. Am. Acad. Arts and Letters, Fellowship of So. Writers (charter; vice chancellor 1993-97). Home: 402 Longleaf Dr Chapel Hill NC 27517-3042 Office Phone: 919-929-2115. E-mail: elizabeth0222@earthlink.net.

SPENCER, FRANK COLE, medical educator; b. Haskell, Tex., 1925; MD, Vanderbilt U., 1947. Intern Johns Hopkins U., Balt., 1947-48, fellow in surgery, 1947-48, asst. resident in surgery, 1953-54; resident in gen. and cardiothoracic surgery Johns Hopkins Sch. Medicine, Balt., 1954-55; surgeon, outpatient dept. Johns Hopkins Hosp., 1955; resident in surgery Wadsworth VA Ctr. Hosp., 1949—51; asst. prof. surgery Johns Hopkins U., 1955-59, assoc. prof., 1959-61; prof. surgery U. Ky., 1961—66; chmn. dept. surgery, George David Steward prof. surgery NYU, 1966—98, prof. surgery sch. medicine and dir. patient safety. Served to lt. M.C., USN, 1951-53. John and Mary R. Markle scholar in med. sci. Johns Hopkins U., 1956. Office: NYU Sch Medicine HCC 1508 550 1st Ave New York NY 10016

SPENCER, GEORGE HENRY, lawyer; b. Vienna; s. Frank Henry and Lillian (Godin) S.; m. Joan Betty Spencer, Sept. 16, 1956 (dec.); children: Lucy, Margaret, Robert, Nancy; m. Mollie Cole Sabol, Oct. 31, 1987; stepchildren: Jeanne, Marta. BE, Yale U., 1948; JD, Cornell U., 1952. Bar: D.C., N.Y. Examiner U.S. Patent Office, 1952-54; sole practice NYC, Washington, 1954-62; ptnr. Spencer & Frank, Washington, 1962-98, Venable, LLP, Attys. at Law, Washington, 1998—2003; counsel Fitch, Even, Tabin & Flannery, Washington, 2003—06, Dennison, Schultz & MacDonald, Washington, 2007—. Master of bench Prettyman-Leventhal Am. Inn of Ct.; lectr. World Trade Inst. Served to capt. JAGC, U.S. Army, 1956-62. Mem. ABA, Am. Patent Law Assn., Lawyer-Pilots Bar Assn., World Intellectual Property Orgn. (panel of arbitrators and mediators), Cosmos Club (Washington). Avocations: aviation, music, German and French language studies, poetry. Home: 1102 Flor Ln Mc Lean VA 22102-1737 Office: Dennison, Schultz & MacDonald 1727 King St Ste 105 Alexandria VA 22314 Office Phone: 703-837-9600 x17. Personal E-mail: specole@aol.com. Business E-Mail: gspencer@dennisonlaw.com.

SPENCER, HARRISON CLARK, JR., public health administrator, educator; b. Balt., Sept. 22, 1944; s. Harrison Clark, Sr. and Dorothy Margaret (Stokes) Spencer; m. Christine Michel Spencer, Apr. 30, 1977; children: Harrison Clark III, Peter Michel. BA, Haverford Coll., Pa., 1965; MD, Johns Hopkins U., Balt., 1969; MPH, U. Calif., Berkeley, 1972; DTM&H, U. London, 1972. Cert. Calif., 1969. Rsch. med. officer Ctrl. Am. Rsch. U., San Salvador, El Salvador, 1975—77; med. officer CDC, Atlanta, 1977—79, chief, parasitic diseases, 1987—90; sr. lectr., dir. malaria rsch. U. Nairobi Med. Sch., Kenya Med. Rsch. Ctr., 1979—84; sr. med. officer WHO, Geneva, 1984—87; dean Tulane Sch. Pub. Health & Tropical Medicine, New Orleans, 1991—96, London Sch. Hygiene & Tropical Medicine, 1996—2000; pres., CEO Assn. Schools of Pub. Health, Washington, 2000—. Mem. U.K. Gen. Med. Coun., London, 1996—2000. 0.6 USPHS, 1970—91. Recipient Commendation Medal, USPHS, 1984, 1991, Outstanding Svc. Medal, 1989. Fellow: U.K. Acad. Med. Scis., Am. Coll. Preventive Medicine, Am. Coll. Physicians; mem.: Inst. Medicine. Episcopalian. Office: Assn Schs of Pub Health 1101 15th St NW Ste 910 Washington DC 20005 Home: 3700 Massachusetts Ave NW Apt 122 Washington DC 20016-5803 Business E-Mail: hspencer@asph.org.

SPENCER, HERBERT HARRY, structural engineer, researcher, computer analyst; b. Vienna, Jan. 2, 1928; arrived in US, 1953; s. Ingenieur Oskar and Bronia (Steinberger) Schnabel; m. Margot Goldrei (div.); m. Sara Slomka, July 24, 1992. BSc, U. London, 1948; MS, Poly. Inst. Bklyn., 1955; PhD, U. London, 1976. Asst. jr. engr. Tarmac Ltd., Coventry, England, 1944—45, George Wimpey & Co., Coventry, 1945—46, Kershaw & Kaufman, London, 1946—48; engr. William Halcrow & Ptnrs., London, 1948—49, Hydraulic Dept., Nazareth, Israel, 1949—50, Quibuts Eyn Hashofet, Galilee, Israel, 1950—51, Rendel Palmer & Tritton, London, 1951—53; rsch. asst. Poly. Inst. Bklyn., 1953—55; instr. Yale U., New Haven, 1955—56; rsch. asst., lectr. Columbia U., NYC, 1956—59; asst. prof. San Diego State Coll., 1959—61; rsch. assoc. Caltech, Pasedena, Calif., 1961—62; asst. prof. U. So. Calif., LA, 1961—65; sr. scientist Ford Instrument Co., Sperry Gyro, L.I. City, NY, 1965—66, Tech. Rsch. Group, Melville, NY, 1966—67; engr. cons. Spencer Rsch., NYC and London, 1967—77; sr. lectr. Hatfield Poly., England, 1970—77; vis. assoc. prof. U. Pitts., 1976—77; assoc. prof. La. State U., Baton Rouge, 1977—79; vis. rsch. cons. Columbia U., NYC, 1979; asst. prof. Rutgers U., New Brunswick, NJ, 1979—82. Pres. Spencer Sci. Computing, New Brunswick, 1982—; vis. prof. Aero Lab., Technion, Haifa, Israel, 1988, Rutgers U., Piscataway, N.J., 1998-2003 Contbr. articles to profl. jours. Mem. ASCE, ASME, Israeli Soc. Engrs. and Architects, Gesellschaft für Angewandte Mathematik und Mechanik, Structural Rsch. Coun., Mensa, Intertel. Home: 10-8M Landing Ln New Brunswick NJ 08901 Office: Spencer Sci Comp PO Box 4191 Highland Park NJ 08904-4191 Office Phone: 732-246-0499. Business E-Mail: sscc@isp.com.

SPENCER, JAMES R., federal judge; b. 1949; BA magna cum laude (hon.), Clark Coll., 1971; JD, Harvard U., 1974, MDiv, 1985. Staff atty. Atlanta Legal Aid Soc., 1974-75; asst. US atty. Washington, 1978, US Dist. Ct. (Ea. Dist.) Va., 1983, judge, 1986—, chief judge. Adj. prof. law U Va., 1987—. Capt. JAGC US Army, 1975—78, Res. JAGC US Army, 1981—86. Mem.: Old Dominion Bar Assn., Wash. Bar Assn., Richmond Bar Assn., Va. State Bar, State Bar Ga., Nat. Bar Assn., ABA, Sigma Pi Phi, Omega Psi Phi. Office: US Courthouse 401 Courthouse Sq Alexandria VA 22314 Office Phone: 804-916-2250. Office Fax: 276-957-8203.

SPENCER, JAN B., health products executive; b. Rostrup, Germany, 1955; m. Miriam Spencer; 3 children. B in Textile Tech. and Mgmt. Scis., U. Manchester Inst. Sci. and Tech. Comml. sales rep. Kimberly-Clark Corp., Manchester, England, 1979, product mgr. to bus. analyst to bus. mgr., 1980—88, various positions including dir. washroom bus., VSE to UCTAD project mgr. and Scott merger integration mgr., 1988—96, v.p. rsch., devel. & engring. Away From Home, 1996—98, v.p. wiper bus., 1998—2000, v.p. European Ops., Engring., Supply Chain in Profl. sector, 2000—02, pres. Kimberly-Clark Profl. Europe, 2002—03, pres. Kimberly-Clark Profl. N.Am., 2003—04, pres. Kimberly-Clark Profl. North Atlantic, 2004—06, pres. Global Kimberly-Clark Profl., 2006—. Office: Kimberly Clark Corp 1400 Holcomb Bridge Rd Roswell GA 30076 *

SPENCER, JEAN, retired business executive; b. Bklyn., Oct. 26, 1946; d. Frederic R. and Lucy Anne Spencer. BBA cum laude, Adelphi U., 1973, MBA, 1989; MS in Human Nutrition, U. Bridgeport, 1998. Notary public, 1986—. Exec. adminstrv. mgmt. Underwriters Labs., Inc., Melville, NY, 1966—2003, ret., 2003; pres., CEO All Natural Health Corp., Seaford, NY, 1990—2002; ret. Vol., life mem. Nat. Ski Patrol, Colo. Recipient NASTAR Bronze medal, Silver medal. Mem. Am. Coll. Nutrition, Am. Soc. Quality Control, Nat. Nutritional Foods Assn., Nat. Ctr. for Homeopathy. Avocations: skiing, bicycle riding, physical fitness, opera, theater. Office: All Natural Health Inc 3830 Sunrise Hwy Seaford NY 11783-2634 Office Phone: 516-785-5521.

SPENCER, JOHN DANIEL, former mayor; b. White Plains, NY, Nov. 17, 1946; s. Edward and Ann (McGlinchy) Spencer; m. Eileen Looney, May 8, 1971 (div.); children: John, Jr., Jennifer; m. Kathy Spring, 2003; children: Kaitlyn, Patrick, James Grad., Westchester C.C., 1966. Sr. property mgr. Cushman & Wakefield, Inc., 1977-84; v.p. for real estate mgmt. Bankers Trust Co., 1984-91; city councilman City of Yonkers, 1990—95, mayor, 1996—2004. Commr. Human Rights Commn., City of Yonkers, 1983-86; bd. dirs. Northwest Yonkers Civic Assn., 1987-91; pres. North Yonkers Boys and Girls Club, 1987-88, bd. dirs. 1982-84, 87-90; treas. Amackassin Club, 1988-90; counsel Am. Irish Assn. of Westchester; mem. Westchester Irish Com., others. Served in US Army, 1966—69, Vietnam. Decorated Bronze Star, Combat Infantryman's badge; recipient Sen. John E. Flynn Disting. Svc. award, 1987, Ellis Island medal of honors, 1997. Mem. Vietnam Vets. of Am., Am. Legion, VFW. Avocations: golf, reading. *

SPENCER, JOHN HEDLEY, biochemistry educator; b. Stapleford, Eng., Apr. 10, 1933; emigrated to Can., 1956; s. Thomas and Eva (Johnson) S.; m. Magdeliene Vera Kulin, Sept. 16, 1958; children: Robin Anne, David Thomas, Mark Stewart. BSc, U. St. Andrews, Scotland, 1955, BSc with honors, 1956; student, Montreal Cancer Rsch. Soc., 1956-59; PhD, McGill U., 1960. Damon Runyon Meml. Fund postdoctoral fellow Columbia U., NYC, 1959-61; mem. faculty McGill U., Montreal, 1961-78, assoc. prof. biochemistry, 1966-71, prof., 1971-78; prof. biochemistry Queen's U., Kingston, Ont., 1978-98, head biochemistry, 1978-90, prof. emeritus, 1998—. Vis. scientist NICHHD/NIH, Bethesda, Md., 1987-88; vis. prof. U. Montreal, 1992-93. Author: The Physics and Chemistry of DNA and RNA, 1972; co-editor: Planet Earth: Problems and Prospects, 1995. Recipient Ayerst award Can. Biochem. Soc., 1972 Fellow Royal Soc. Can.; mem. Can. Biochem. Soc. (treas. 1966-69, pres. 1979-80), Can. Fedn. Biol. Socs. (pres. 1981-82), Canadians for Health Rsch. (bd. dirs. 2001-06), Biochem. Soc., Am. Soc. Biochemistry and Molecular Biology, Royal Soc. Can., Sigma Xi. Home: 36 Kenwoods Cir Kingston ON Canada K7K 6Y1 E-mail: spencerj@post.queensu.ca.

SPENCER, LARA, television personality, journalist; married, 2000; 1 child. BA in Journalism, Pa. State U. Reporter WDEF-TV, Chattanooga, News 12, LI, NY, WABC, NY Eyewitness News, 1995—99; nat. corr. ABC News' Good Morning Am., 1999—2001, corr., 2001—04; host Antiques Roadshow, WGBH-PBS, 2004—; co-host, NY anchor Paramount TV The Insider, NYC, 2004—. Office: Antiques Roadshow-WGBH 125 Western Ave Allston MA 02134 Studio: Paramount Studios 5555 Melrose Ave Los Angeles CA 90038

SPENCER, LISA ANN, special education educator; d. Jack and Betty Jean Spencer. BS, Bowie State Coll., 1983; M, Howard U., 1989, George Wash. U., 2004. Tchr. PGCPS, Mitchellvile, Md., 1988—90, spl. edn. tchr. Bowie, Md., 1990—97, tech. coord. Hyattsville, Md., 1997—99, regional tech. coord. Oxon Hill, Md., 1999—2004, tng. and support mgr. Upper Marlboro, Md., 2004—. Mem.: NEA, Internat. Soc. Tech. Edn., Assn. Info. Tech. Profls. Democrat. Office Phone: 301-952-6251. Business E-Mail: lspencer@pgcps.org.

SPENCER, LONABELLE (KAPPIE SPENCER), political agency administrator, lobbyist; b. Owatonna, Minn., Aug. 3, 1925; d. Reuben Alvin and Florence Elizabeth (Wells) Kaplan; m. Mark Rodney Spencer, Sept. 14, 1947 (dec. May 1986); children: Gregory Mark, Gary Alan, Carol Ann, Dane Kaplan. BA, Grinnell Coll., 1947. State bd. legis. chair Am. Assn. Univ. Women, Iowa, 1978-82, nat. legis. com. Washington, 1980-83, nat.

bd. legis. chair, 1982-83, nat. legis. and program coms., 1985-89, nat. bd. dir. for women's issues, 1985-89; founder, dir. Nat. Gender Balance Project, Sarasota, Fla., 1988—; bd. dirs., nat. steering com. Nat. Women's Political Caucus, Washington, 1992-97. Lobbyist, cmty. activist state legis. and congress, Fla. Iowa, Washington, 1974—; rep. Fla. women's pol. caucus ERA summit, Washington, 1992—; cons., presenter in field. Author: (manuals) Don't Leave It All to the Experts, 1981, Take An Unratified State to Launch, 1981, I Think We Need a Woman, 1982, It's a Man's World Unless Women Vote, 1983, Woman Power: It's a Capitol Idea, 1995, Gender Balance Project-USA: Politics and Decision Making, 1995, Whose Money Is It Anyway: Wills and Trusts for Women, 1999, Feminists Who Changed America: 1965-1972, 2006. U.S. rep. World Assn. Girl Guides Girl Scouts U.S., Acapulco, Mex., 1965, bd. dirs. Moingona Coun. Girl Scouts U.S., 1965-75; Rep. candidate Iowa Senate, Des Moines, 1976; del. Internat. Fedn. U. Women, Netherlands, New Zealand, Finland, Sweden, 1983, 86, 89,; trustee Grinnell (Iowa) Coll., 1993—; Iowa del. to Nat. Women's Conf., 1977; founder Fla. Women's Consortium, 1989; active People to People Internat.; tour leader Mission in Understanding to Cuba, 2001. Recipient Girl Scout awards Moingona Girl Scout Coun., Des Moines, 1969, 73, 78, Christine Wilson medal for Equality and Justice, Iowa Women's Hall of Fame, Des Moines, 1990; named gift honoree Am. Assn. Univ. Women, Des Moines and Sarasota, Fla. branches, Iowa and Vt. divsns., 1980, 82, 87, 92; named in National Women's Hall of Fame Book of Lives and Legacies, 2002. Mem. AAUW (leader corps, com. mem. 1975—89), UN Fund for Women (UNIFEM), Nat. Assn. Commns. for Women, Vet. Feminists of Am. (Medal of Honor 2000), Women in Senate and House WISH-LIST (founder 1992). Republican. Avocation: travel. E-mail: kappiespencer@webtv.net.

SPENCER, MARGARET GILLIAM, lawyer; b. Spokane, Aug. 30, 1951; d. Jackson Earl and Margaret Kathleen (Hindley) Gilliam; m. John Bernard Spencer, Feb. 21, 1993. BA in Sociology, U. Mont., 1974, MA in Sociology, 1978, JD, 1982. Bar: Mont. 1982, Colo. 1982. Assoc. Holland & Hart, Denver, 1982-84, Roath & Brega, P.C., Denver, 1984-88, shareholder, dir., 1988-89; spl. counsel Brega & Winters, P.C., Denver, 1989; corp. counsel CH2M Hill, Inc., Denver, 1989—. Democrat. Episcopalian. Avocations: skiing, scuba diving. Office: CH2M Hill Inc 9191 S Jamaica St Englewood CO 80112 Business E-Mail: pspencer@ch2m.com.

SPENCER, MELISSA JOHANNA, psychotherapist, special education educator; b. Durham, NC, Sept. 13, 1951; d. Joseph Whitney and Regina Colleen (Barnett) Spencer; m. Charles Ray Barrow, Aug. 21, 1972; children: Matthew R. Barrow, Christine N. Gonzales, Charlotte D. Barrow. Attended, U. Hawaii-Manoa, 1986—88; BA in Psychology, Tex. Tech. U., Lubbock, 1990, MEd in Counseling, 1994, EdD in Counselor Edn., 1999. Lic. profl. counselor NC, 2000, cert. spl. edn. educator 2006. Dir. vols. Rappahannock Coun. Domestic Violence, Fredericksburg, Va., 1999—2000; asst. prof. U. NC-Pembroke, 2000—02; pvt. practice psychotherapy Southeastern Psychol. Svcs., Fairmont, NC, 2002—; tchr. exceptional children with autism Seventy-First HS, Fayetteville, NC, 2003—06, Robeson County Pub. Schs., Lumberton, NC, 2006—. Adv. bd. Substance Abuse & Traumatic Brain Injury Linking Svcs., Fairmont, NC, 2005—06. Recipient Tchg. Excellence award, Jiffy Lube, 2005. Mem.: NEA, Assn. Counselor Edn. and Supervision, Assn. Specialists Group Work, Internat. Assn. Marriage & Family Counselors, Am. Counseling Assn. Office: Southeastern Psychol Svcs 302 N Main Fairmont NC 28340 Personal E-mail: dr_melissajspencer@yahoo.com.

SPENCER, MELVIN JOE, retired health facility administrator, retired lawyer, retired consultant; b. Buffalo Center, Iowa, Jan. 2, 1923; s. Kenos W. and Jennie (Michaelson) S.; m. Dena Joyce Butterfield, Mar. 1, 1952; children: Dennis Norman, Gregory Melvin, Shelly Lynn Spencer Goodnight. AB, U. Mich., 1948, JD, 1950. Bar: Iowa 1950, Mo. 1950, Okla. 1961. Practiced in, Kansas City, Mo., 1950-61, Oklahoma City, 1961—; assoc., then ptnr. Watson, Ess, Marshall & Enggas, 1950-61; ptnr. Miller & Spencer (and predecessor firm), 1961-75, of counsel, 1975-80; adminstr. Deaconess Hosp., 1975-92, cons., 1992-93; ret., 1993. Dir. Union Bank & Trust Co., Oklahoma City, 1977-88, 89-96, adv. dir., 1996-99; dir., sec. Hosp. Casualty Co., 1977-92; dir., treas. VHA Okla., Inc., 1986-92 Assoc. editor Mich. Law Rev., 1949-50. Mcpl. judge City of Roeland Park, Kans., 1952, city coun., 1954; area Rep. precinct chmn., 1968-69; del. Rep. State Conv., 1968, 96; bd. dir. Deaconess Hosp., Oklahoma City, 1966-2005, Christian Counseling Ctr., 1973-75, Witteman Corp., 2005-, Butterfield Meml. Found., 2005—; trustee Okla. Hosp. Assn., 1978-84, chmn. bd. trustees, 1983, trustee Okla. Co. Med. Soc. Found., 2002—; trustee, vice chmn. bd. dir. Ctrl. Coll., McPherson, Kans., 1972-86; trustee Okla. Ambulance Trust, 1984-87; adv. bd. Okla. State U. Tech. Inst., 1980-92; bd. dir. Emergency Med. Svcs. Ctrl. Okla., 1975-78, FMC Ministries, Inc.; const. coun. Free Meth. Ch. World Fellowship, 1975-95; chmn. Free Meth. Found., 1988-99; gen. counsel Free Meth. Ch. N.Am., 1969-95, bd. adminstrn., 1969-99, sec., 1985-95, investment com., 1976-88, chmn. investment com., 1986-88. Capt. USAAF, 1943-46 Named Layman of Yr., Free Meth. Ch. N.Am., 1984; recipient W. Cleveland Rodgers Disting. Svc. award Okla. Hosp. Assn., 1985; fellow Cen. Coll. Acad. of Achievers, 1990. Mem. Okla. Bar Assn., Oklahoma County Bar Assn., Order of Coif, Phi Beta Kappa, Phi Kappa Phi Home: 5910 N Shawnee Ave Oklahoma City OK 73112-1627

SPENCER, MICHAEL C., lawyer; b. Sept. 10, 1951; BA magna cum laude, Yale U., 1973; JD cum laude, Harvard Law Sch., 1976. Bar: N.Y. 1978, Calif. 1978. Law clk. to Hon. William Matthew Byrne, Jr. U.S. Dist. Ct. (cen. dist.) Calif., LA, 1976-77; assoc. atty. Cravath, Swaine & Moore, NYC, 1977-86; assoc. Milberg, Weiss, Bershad, Hynes & Lerach, NYC, 1986—87, ptnr., 1987, Milberg Weiss & Bershad LLP, NYC, 1987—. Office: Milberg Weiss & Bershad LLP 1 Pennsylvania Plz 49th Fl New York NY 10199 Office Phone: 212-946-9450. Office Fax: 212-273-4395. Business E-Mail: mspencer@milbergweiss.com.

SPENCER, REX LEROY, retired secondary school educator; b. Kendallville, Ind., Jan. 29, 1944; s. Richard Donald and Mildred Francis (Fourman) Spencer; m. Diana Carole Land, Nov. 21, 1981; children: Katie Jo, Emily Paige. BS, Defiance Coll., 1966; MA, Ball State U., 1970. Cert. tchr. Ohio. Tchr. Ansonia (Ohio) HS, 1966-80, 1986—2003, Ansonia Mid. Sch., 1982-86; ret., 2003. Instr. Edison CC, Piqua, Ohio, 1983—88, Defiance (Ohio) Coll., 1989—92. Named Outstanding Am. History Tchr., Darke County DAR, 1992. Mem.: NEA, Ohio Coun. Social Studies, Nat. Coun. Social Studies, Ansonia Edn. Assn. (pres. 1976—77, treas. 1991—98), Ohio Edn. Assn., Ohio Ret. Tchrs. Assn. (life), Defiance Coll. Alumni Assn. (bd. dirs. 1976—79, v.p. 1979—80, pres. 1980—82). Methodist. Avocations: golf, bicycling, walking, antiques. Personal E-mail: spencerclan@adelphia.net.

SPENCER, RICHARD PAUL, biochemist, physician, educator; b. NYC, June 7, 1929; s. David E. and Frances (Fried) S.; m. Gwendolyn Enid Williams, Apr. 7, 1956; children: Carolyn Roberts, Jennifer Holt, Priscilla James. AB, Dartmouth Coll., 1951; MD, U. So. Calif., 1954; MA (NSF fellow, Helen Hay Whitney fellow), Harvard U., 1958, PhD, 1961. Intern Beth Israel Hosp., Boston, 1954-55; practice medicine specializing in nuclear medicine; mem. faculty biophysics U. Buffalo, 1961-63; chief radioisotope service VA Hosp., Buffalo, 1961-63; asso. prof. nuclear medicine Yale Sch. Medicine, 1963-68, prof., 1968-74; prof., chmn. dept. nuclear medicine U. Conn. Health Center, 1974-97, prof., vice chmn. Dept. Diagnostic Imaging, 1997—2000, residency dir. nuclear medicine, 2000—. Author: The Intestinal Tract, 1960, (with others) Biophysical Principles, 1965, Radionuclide Studies of the Spleen, 1975, Clinical Focus on Nuclear Medicine, 1977, Handbook of Nuclear Medicine, 1977, Therapy in Nuclear Medicine, 1978, Radiopharmaceuticals: Structure-Activity Relationships, 1981, Interventional Nuclear Medicine, 1984, New Procedures In Nuclear Medicine, 1988; contbr. (with others) articles to profl. jours. Mem. Am. Physiol. Soc., AAAS, Soc. Nuclear Medicine, Biophys. Soc. Achievements include co-discovery of functional asplenia; developed first complete description of relationship of food intake to reproductive success and to longevity in a species. Office: U Conn Health Ctr Farmington CT 06030-2804 Business E-Mail: rspencer@adp.uchc.edu.

SPENCER, RICHARD THOMAS, III, health products executive; b. Oak Park, Ill., Mar. 18, 1936; s. Richard Thomas Spencer Jr. and Lois Anne (Pollock) Spencer; m. Andrea B. Schlickeiser, June 26, 1962; 1 child, Richard Thomas IV. BA, U. Mich., 1959; postgrad., U. Pa., 1976, Stanford U., 1984, Clemson U., 1985. Mktg. group Mobil Oil Co., Detroit, 1962; internat. trade specialist U.S. Dept. Commerce, Detroit, 1963—64; account exec. J. Walter Thompson Co., Detroit, 1965—66; sales mgr. Sarns Inc., Ann Arbor, Mich., 1967—69; v.p. mktg. Cordis Dow Corp., Miami, Fla., 1970—81; pres. mktg. divsn. Cordis Corp., Miami, 1982—87; pres., CEO Uni-Med Internat. Corp., Miami, 1988—2000; exec. v.p., COO, bd. dirs. World Med. Mfg. Corp., Sunrise, Fla., 1995—2000. Bd. dirs. Viacor Corp., Wilmington, Mass., Bioheart, Inc., Weston, Fla., Breeze Med., Inc., Boca Raton, Fla.; cons. in field. Contbr. articles to profl. jours. With CIC US Army, 1959—61. Republican. Avocations: skiing, golf, running, stereo equipment, geopolits. Home and Office: 3641 N 47th Ave Hollywood FL 33021-2211 Home: 811 E Hill Rd North Troy VT 05859 Office Phone: 954-558-3689.

SPENCER, ROGER FELIX, psychiatrist, educator; b. Apr. 19, 1934; came to U.S., 1941; s. Eugene S. Spitzer and Santa Spencer; m. Barbara Ann Houser, Aug. 18, 1958; children: Geoffrey, Jennifer, Rebecca. BS, Yale Coll., 1956; MD, Harvard Med. Sch., 1959. Diplomate Am. Bd. Psychiatry. Intern N.C. Meml. Hosp., Chapel Hill, 1959-60, resident in psychiatry, 1960-63; instr. U. N.C. Sch. Medicine, Chapel Hill, 1963-66, asst. prof., 1966-69, assoc. prof., 1969-76, prof., 1976—. Dir. of liaison and cons., U. N.C., 1967-77, dir. out patient psychiatry, 1977-95. Contbr. articles to profl. jours.;, author short stories. Recipient Career Tchr. award NIMH, 1965-67. Fellow Am. Psychiat. Assn. (life), Am. Psychoanalytic Assn.; mem. N.C. Psychoanalytic Soc. (past pres.), N.C. Psychiat. Assn. (past pres.). Office: UNC Hosps Dept Psychiatry CB 7160 Chapel Hill NC 27599-7160 Home Phone: 919-929-6192; Office Phone: 919-966-5772. Office Fax: 919-843-6102. Business E-Mail: roger_spencer@med.unc.edu.

SPENCER, STEPHANIE, mathematics educator, director; BA in Math., Columbia U., NYC, 1989; MEd in Curriculum & Instrn., Seattle Pacific U., 1998, EdD in Ednl. Leadership, 2003. Tchr. math. Peninsula H.S., Gig Harbor, Wash., 1990—2000, Vashon Island H.S., Wash., 2000—07, dir. curriculum, 2004—07, asst. prin., athletic dir., 2007—. Adj. instr. math. Antioch U., Seattle, 2004—05, coord. math. endorcement, 2005; rsch. asst. C.J. Brown and Assocs., Mill Creek, Wash., 2004—06, project coord., 2005—06. Grantee, Wash. Edn. Leadership Intern Progra, 2000—01, Tchr. Leadership Program, 2002—03. Mem.: Wash. State Math. Coun., Nat. Coun. Tchrs. Math.

SPENCER, WILLIAM EDWIN, retired telecommunications industry executive, engineer; b. Mar. 22, 1926; s. Erwin Blanc and Edith Marie (Peterson) S.; m. Ferne Arlene Nieder, Nov. 14, 1952; children: Elizabeth Ann, Gary William, James Richard, Catherine Sue. Student, U. Kansas City, 1942; AS, Kansas City Jr. Coll., 1945; BSEE, U. Mo., 1948; postgrad., Iowa State U., 1969. Registered profl. engr., Kans. With Southwestern Bell Telephone Co., Kansas City, Mo., 1948-50, Topeka, 1952-61, sr. engr., 1966-69, equipment maintenance engr., 1967-76, engrng. ops. mgr., 1976-79, dist. mgr., 1979—86, ret., 1986. Mem. tech. staff Bell Telephone Labs., N.Y.C., 1961-62, Holmdel, N.J., 1962-66; pres., owner W.E. Spencer Co.; mem. U.S. Senatorial Club, 1985—. Patentee in field. Mem. Rep. Presdl. Task Force, 1984—; supervising judge Shawnee County Election Commn.; trustee, bd. dirs. Brookwood Covenant Ch., also pres. Joy Sr. Group. With AUS, Pentagon, Washington, 1950-52. Recipient Best Kans. Idea award Southwestern Bell Telephone Co., 1972, cert. of appreciation Kans. Miss Teen Pageant, 1984, Rep. Presdl. League of Merit, 1992—. Mem. IEEE, NSPE, Kans. Engrng. Soc., Topeka Engrs. Club (pres.), Telephone Pioneers Assn. (life mem., rep., Sunflower and Heartland chpt., Topeka life mem., coun. pres. and club pres.), Nat. Geog. Soc., Kans. Hist. Soc., Am. Assn. Ret. Persons, U. Mo.-Columbia Alumni Assn., Nat. Travel Club, Topeka Geog. Soc., Active Prime Timer (historian). Republican. Home: 3201 SW Macvicar Ct Topeka KS 66611-1800 Office: 220 SE 6th Ave Topeka KS 66603-3507 Personal E-mail: wespenc@attglobal.net.

SPENCER-FLEMING, JULIA, writer; married; 3 children. Graduate, Ithaca Coll., George Washington Univ.; JD, Univ. Maine. Former atty., Portland, Maine. Author: (novels) In the Bleak Midwinter, 2003 (St. Martin's/Malice Domestic award, 2001, Dilys award, Independent Mystery Booksellers Assn., Agatha, Anthony, Macavity, Barry awards for Best First Novel), A Fountain Filled with Blood, 2004 (Borders Original Voices selection, nominee Barry award for Best Mystery Novel, Deadly Pleasures Mag.), Out of the Deep I Cry, 2004 (St. Martin's Minotaur's lead title, nominee Reviewers' Choice award, Romantic Times Book Club, 2005, nominee Edgar award for Best Mystery, 2004, nominee Anthony award for Best Mystery, 2004), To Darkness and to Death, 2005. Episcopalian.

SPENGLER, DAN MICHAEL, orthopedic surgery educator, surgeon; b. Defiance, Ohio, Feb. 25, 1941; s. Harold A. and Wilhelmina Spengler; m. Cynthia Niswonger; children: Christina, Craig. BS, Baldwin-Wallace Coll., 1962; MD, U. Mich., 1966. Diplomate Am. Bd. Orthopaedic Surgery (bd. dirs. 1988-97). Rotating intern King County Hosp., Seattle, 1966-67; resident in orthopedics U. Mich., Ann Arbor, 1970-73; asst. prof. U. Wash., Seattle, 1974-78, assoc. prof., 1978-83. Author: Low Back Pain, 1982. Bd. dirs. Musculoskeletal Transplant Found.; bd. trustees Jour. of Bone and Joint Surgery, 2004—. Fellow: Am. Acad. Orthopaedic Surgeons; mem.: ACS, Internat. Soc. for Study of Lumbar Pain, Assn. Bone and Joint Surgeons, Am. Bd. Orthopaedic Surgeons (pres. 1993—94), Am. Orthopaedic Assn. (pres. 2003—04), U. Nashville Club. Avocations: flying, golf, running, skiing. Office: Vanderbilt Ortho Inst Med Ctr E S Tower Rm 4200 Nashville TN 37232-8774 Office Phone: 615-343-6364. Business E-Mail: dan.m.spengler@vanderbilt.edu.

SPENGLER, PAUL ALBERT, grants and foundation administrator; b. Buffalo, Feb. 18, 1947; s. Albert Henry and Hazel Mae Spengler; m. Cheryl Ann Spengler, June 22, 1985; stepchildren: Jennifer Ann MacFarlane, Mara Elizabeth Sroczyk. BS, SUNY, Buffalo, 1969, MA, 1973; PhD, U. Del., 1977. Dep. commr. Erie County Dept. Youth Svcs., Buffalo, 1984-87; dir. cmty. svcs. Salvation Army, Buffalo, 1988-93; dir. grants Niagara County C.C., Sanborn, N.Y., 1993-99; dir. found. giving Roswell Pk. Cancer Inst., Buffalo, 2000—. Cons. Edn. Devel. Ctr., Newton, Mass., 1978, Erie C.C., Buffalo, 1999-00, Genesee C.C., Batavia, N.Y., 1999, Adirondack C.C., Queensbury, N.Y., 1999; adj. instr. D'Youville Coll., Buffalo, 1988-90. Author: Yankee Swedish and Italian Acculturization and Economic Mobility in Jamestown New York from 1860 to 1920, 1980; contbr. articles to profl. jours. Sec. standing com. Episcopal Diocese Western N.Y., Buffalo, 1998-2002; vestryman Episcopal Ch. Good Shepherd, Buffalo, 1998—2001, 04-05; mem. legis. commn. homelessness Erie County Legis., Buffalo, 1991-93. N.Y. State Regents scholar, 1965-69; Andelot fellow U. Del., 1973-74, 75-76, 76-77. Democrat. Avocations: reading, gardening, classical music. Home: 26 Groveland St Buffalo NY 14214-1012 Office: Roswell Pk Alliance Elm And Carlton Sts Buffalo NY 14267-0001 Office Phone: 716-845-7719. Business E-Mail: paul.spengler@roswellpark.org.

SPENGLER-MILLER, JANET TAYLOR, retired music educator, choral director; b. Wilmington, Del., Jan. 11, 1941; d. Arthur Holt and Dorothy (Price) Taylor; m. Gary Kenneth Spengler (div. 1990); 1 child, Kristin Spengler Zerbe; m. Richard Stanley Miller, Oct. 15, 2005. BSc in Music Edn., Lebanon Valley Coll., 1963; postgrad., U. N.Mex., 1966—67, Westminster Choir Coll., 1986—89; MSc in Music Edn., Towson State U., 1991. Cert. Orff/Kodaly/Dalcroze music edn. Towson U., music tchr. K-12 Del., nat. tchr. piano Music Tchrs. Nat. Assn. Tchr. music, choral dir. Kennett Jr./Sr. HS, Kennett Square, Pa., 1963—64, Cornwall Elem. Sch., NY, 1964—66; piano instr. Wesley Coll., Dover, Del., 1970—81; tchr. music, choral dir. Caesar Rodney Sch. Dist., Camden, Del., 1981—84; tchr. music William Henry Middle Sch., Dover, 1984—85; tchr. music, choral dir. Seaford Sch. Dist., Del., 1985—2002; ret., 2002. Pres. So. Del. Music Tchrs., Kent County, 1975—80; accompanist, piano recitalist, music workshop presenter, 1987—; mem. edn. bd. Del. Symphony Orch., Wilmington, 2004—. Chair state standards commn. for visual and performing arts Del. Dept. Edn., 1994—97; conductor cmty. chorus Diamond State Chorlaiers, Dover, 1986—92; dir. music Wesley United Meth. Ch., Dover, 1993—. Named State Music Tchr. of Yr., Del. Music Educators, 1990; recipient Jesse Ball duPont Educator award, Del. Symphony Orch., 2002, Lifetime Disting. Svc. award, Del. Music Educators, 2002. Mem.: Del. Music Educators Assn. (pres. 1996—98), Am. Choral Dirs. Assn., Music Tchrs. Nat. Conf. (mem. Ea. Divsn. bd. 1994—2000), Sigma Alpha Iota (pres. chpt. 1962—63, Sword of Honor 1963), Delta Alpha. Republican. United Methodist. Achievements include frequent performer at Delaware All-State Chorus. Personal E-mail: JTMillerMusic@aol.com.

SPENSER, IAN DANIEL, chemistry professor; b. Vienna, June 17, 1924; m. Anita Fuchs, Sept. 5, 1951; children: Helen Ruth, Paul Andrew. BSc with honors, U. Birmingham, Eng., 1948; PhD in Biochemistry, U. London, 1952, DSc in Organic and Biochemistry, 1969; DSc (hon.), McMaster U., 2004. Demonstrator in biochemistry King's Coll., U. London, 1948-52, asst. lectr. in biochemistry Med. Coll. St. Bartholomew's Hosp., 1952-54, lectr., 1954-57; postdoctoral fellow div. pure chemistry NRC Can., Ottawa, Ont., 1953-54; asst. prof. biochemistry McMaster U., Hamilton, Ont., Can., 1957-59, assoc.prof., 1959-64, prof., 1964-68, prof. chemistry, 1968-89, prof. emeritus, 1989—; Akademischer Gast Laboratorium für Organische Chemie/Eidgenössische Technische Hochschule, Zürich, Switzerland, 1971, 89; vis. prof. Inst. Organic Chemistry, Tech. U. Denmark, Lyngby, 1977, Inst. Organische Chemie/Univ. Karlsruhe, Fed. Republic Germany, 1981, Institut für Pharmazeutische Biologie, Universität Bonn, Federal Republic of Germany, 1989. Research in biosynthesis of alkaloids, biosynthesis of vitamin Bl and vitamin B6 Recipient Sr. Scientist award NATO, 1980; recipient Can.-Japan Exchange award, 1982-83, Univ. Club of Hamilton award, 1990. Fellow Royal Soc. Can., Chem. Inst. Can. (John Labatt Ltd. award 1982-83, R.U. Lemieux award 2005), Royal Soc. Chemistry (U.K.); mem. Biochem. Soc., Am. Soc. Biochemistry Molecular Biology, Am. Soc. Pharmacognosy, Phytochem. Soc. N. Am. Office: McMaster U Dept Chemistry Hamilton ON Canada L8S 4M1 Business E-Mail: spenser@mcmaster.ca.

SPERA, DOMINIC GREGORIO, music educator, writer; b. Kenosha, Wis., Apr. 18, 1932; s. Costanzo and Anita Spera; m. Patty Jean Graber, Jan. 22, 1956; children: Gregory Allen, Mark Christopher. MusB in Edn., Ind. U., 1967, MusB in Trumpet, 1967, MusM in Edn., 1968. Bandsman U.S. Army, Fort Sheridan, Ill., 1953—56; profl. musician NYC, 1957—67; dir. of instrumental music U. Jr. and Sr. HS, Bloomington, Ind., 1967—68; prof. of music U. of Wis., Eau Claire, Wis., 1968—77; prof. of music Sch. Music Ind. U., Bloomington, 1977—97, prof. emeritus Sch. Music, 1997—. Profl. trumpet player various TV shows, NYC, 1958—66, Radio City, NYC, 1958—66, City and Roxy Theaters, Bands of Lionel Hampton, Charlie Barnet, Benny Goodman, Tito Puente, Tommy Dorsey Bands, NYC, 1958—66; profl. trumpet player with Burt Bacharach, Johnny Mathis, Henry Mancini, Andy Williams, Frank Sinatra, International Locations, 1966—92. Composer: (songs) more than 100 pub. compositions; author: Blues and the Basics, Making the Changes, 1973, Take the Lead, 1981, Stretching Out, 1985; trumpet soloist and composer (albums) Yamaha Trumpet Series, trumpet soloist, composer, producer Make a Joyful Noise, Chops Don't Fail Me Now; trumpet soloist, composer, producer: albums Dominic Spera Big Band, soloist, condr., edn. dir.: Hawaii Internat. Jazz Festival, 1997—2000, guest soloist, clinician: Jazz Festival, 2003; composer: Dominic Spera Writes for the Brass Quintet, 2005; arranger: CD Dominic Spera Presents the American Popular Songbook for Brass Quintet, 2006. Dir. Eau Claire (Wis.) Jazz Festival, 1968—77; founder, dir. U. Alta. Summer Jazz Camp-, Edmonton, Alberta, Canada, 1979—2002, Bloomington (Ind.) Jazz Festival, 1981—2002. Pvt. first class US Army, 1953—56. Recipient awards, 19 US States, Can., and Australia, 1968—2002, Outstanding Svc. award, Internat. Assn. of Jazz Educators, 1974, 1982; grantee, NEA, 1976. Mem.: Internat. Trumpet Guild (life), Internat. Assn. of Jazz Educators (life), Music Educators Nat. Conf. (life). Achievements include first to publish jazz composition utilizing the 12 tone system of composition introduction and allegro for jazz ensemble and percussion; publish theme and variations for jazz ensemble. Avocations: painting, travel. Home and Office: 3704 Grasstree Ct Bloomington IN 47401 Office Phone: 812-339-3210.

SPERAKIS, NICHOLAS GEORGE, artist; b. NYC, June 8, 1943; s. George and Cathren (Cokatas) S.; m. Yolanda de Carmen Mesa, Feb. 1, 1983. Student, Pratt Inst., 1960, NAD, 1960—61, Art Students League N.Y., Pratt Graphic Art Center, 1961—63. Instr. Sumitt (N.J.) Art Center, 1971, New Sch. Social Research, NYC, 1972—, Fashion Inst. Tech., NYC, 1977—. Exhibited one-man shows at Paul Kessler Gallery, 1963, 64, Provincetown, Mass., Hinckley and Brohel Art Gallery, Washington, 1964, N.Y.C., 1965, Mari Galleries, Woodstock, N.Y., 1966, 67, 68, Larchmont, N.Y., 1967, Eric Schindler Galleries, 1965, Richmond (Va.) Art Gallery, N.Y. U. Student Loeb Center, 1969, L.I. U., 1971, Pratt Inst., 1971, Bienville Gallery, New Orleans, 1972, 74, Pace U., N.Y.C., 1972, Lerner-Heller Gallery, N.Y.C., 1975, 76, Daedal Gallery, Balt., 1976, Reading Mus. Art, (Pa.), 1977, Bklyn. Mus., 1977, Washington Irving Gallery, N.Y.C., 1982, Museo Universitario Del Chopo, Mexico City, 1984, Forum Gallery, N.Y.C., Mus. Contemporary Art, Bogota, The Atler Gallery, Munich, 1989, Galerieverein Blankenese, Hamburg, Fed. Republic Germany, 1988, Galeria Sextante, Bogota, 1989, La Francia, Centro de Arte, Medellin, Colombia, 1989, various woodcut exhbns., Alexander S. Onassis Ctr. N.Y.U., 1995, Claudia Carr Gallery, N.Y.C., 1997-98, The Old Print Shop, N.Y.C., 1998, Stephen Gang Gallery, N.Y.C., 2000, Andrew Edlin Fine Arts, N.Y.C., 2003, others; exhibited group shows, Mercy Hurst Coll., Erie, Pa., 1963, 64, Bklyn. Mus., 1964, 77, Jewish Mus., 1964, Chrysler Mus., 1964, 65, Assoc. Am. Artists Galleries, N.Y.C., 1965, Norfolk (Va.) Mus. Arts Scis., 1965, Long Beach (Calif.) Coll., 1969, Am. Acad. and Nat. Inst. Arts and Letters, 1969, 75, Mid West Mus-Am-Art, 1981, numerous others, print exhbns., France, Italy, Spain, other European Countries, Far East, 1970-71, Lerner-Heller Gallery, 1973, 76, Amherst Coll., 1974, Worcester (Mass.) Mus. Fine Art, 1977, Reading (Pa.) Mus. Art, 1977, Galeria El Museo Santate de Bogota, Colombia, 1992, Mus. Modern Art, Rio de Janeiro, Brazil, 1992, travel Ams., Europe, 1992, Rhino Horn, N.Y.C., 1994, WhiteHall, N.Y.C., 1993, 94, Barnard/Biderman Fine Art, N.Y.C., 1994, 10th Ann. Art Miami 2000, 2000, Siron Studios, N.Y.C., 2001; represented in permanent collections Bklyn. Mus., Walter P. Chrysler Mus., Norfolk, Va., Norfolk Mus. Arts and Scis., N.Y.C. Public Library, Phila. Mus. Fine Arts, Worcester Mus. Fine Art, Flint (Mich.) Art Inst.,

Mus. Modern Art, N.Y.C., U. Conn., Storrs, Amherst Coll., Okla. Fine Arts Center Mus., Am. Acad. and Nat. Inst. Arts and Letters, Detroit Inst. Fine Art, Corcoran Gallery of Art, Midwest Mus. Am. Art, Exeter Acad., Conn., Mus. Modern Art, N.Y.C., print collections Nat. Mus. Am. Art Smithsonian Instn., DeHunter Mus. Art, Chattanooga, Libr. of Congress, Washington, High Mus. Art, Atlanta, Free Libr., Phila., Kunst Mus., Fine Arts Mus. Bern Switzerland, Australian Nat. Gallery, Canberra, Snite Mus. Art, U. Notre Dame, Ind., Bibliotheque Royale Albert/ER, Bruxelles, Belgium, Museo Rayo, Roldanillo, Colombia, Stedelijk Mus., Amsterdam, The Netherlands, Hirshhorn Mus., Washington, Mus. Modern Art Santa Fe de Bogota, Nordjyllands Kunstmus., Aalborg, Denmark, Banco Bozano Simonsen, Rio de Janeiro, Mus. Modern Art, Bogota, Rose Art Mus. Brandeis U., Conn.; organized (with others), Rhino Horn artist group, N.Y.C., 1970. Recipient First Prize Purchase award Mercy Hurst Coll., 1964; Lawrence and Hinda Rosenthal award Am. Acad. and Nat. Inst. Arts and Letters, 1969; Guggenheim graphics fellow, 1970; McDowell Colony summer residency, 1976 Mem. Soc. Am. Graphic Artists. *Art doesn't bring out the voters for candidates X or Z. Art brings forth an experience and enters the knowledge of the viewer, so it helps the individual consider new channels and modes of behavior. One of the reasons there is so much censorship of art is due to the power art has to transform people at the roots not into some action but in a more generalized manner in terms of understanding institutions and traditions for what they really are. I think art changes emotions more than it changes specific ideas.*

SPERATI, CARLETON ANGELO, retired chemist; b. Fergus Falls, Minn., Sept. 1, 1918; s. Carsten Emmanuel S. and Martha Eline Johnson; m. Eloise Morris, June 1, 1941; children: Charles Robert, William Eller, Solveig Sperati Korte. AB, Luther Coll., Decorah. Iowa, 1934—38; MA in Chemistry, U. Ill., Urbana, 1939, PhD in Organic Chemistry, 1941. Lab. asst. Union Oil Calif., San Pedro, Calif., 1940; rsch. chemist E. I. DuPont de Nemours, Inc., Arlington, 1941—50; supr. E. I. DuPont de Nemours & Co., Wilmington, Del., 1952—55; sr. supr. E. I. DuPont de Nemours & Co, 1955—60, rsch. assoc., 1960—69; rsch. fellow E. I. DuPont de Nemours & Co., Parkersburg, W.Va.; cons. E. I. DuPont de Nemours & Co, 1979—98; C. Paul Stocker prof. of engring. (first appointee to the position) Ohio U., Athens, Ohio, 1979—81, Stocker adj. prof. of chem. engring., 1981—. Cmn. U.S.A. tech. adv. group tech. com. 37 on terminology Internat. Orgn. Standardization, Geneva, 1989—98; presenter in field. Contbr. articles to profl. jours. Fellow: ASTM Internat. (Frank W. Reinhart award in terminology 1991, Award of Merit 1998); mem.: Am. Chem. Soc. (life Best Paper of Yr. 1986). Lutheran. Achievements include patents in field. Avocations: music, travel, reading, white water canoeing, skiing. Home: 23 Mustang Acres Parkersburg WV 26104-8040 Office Phone: 304-485-2374. Personal E-mail: pka00099@mail.wvnet.edu.

SPERBER, ALAN B., urologist; s. Fred and Liselotte Sperber; m. Elizabeth Ann Pinck, June 6, 1982. BA, NYU, NYC, 1963, MD, 1967. Diplomate Am. Bd. Urology, 1977. Surg. intern Albert Einstein Coll. Medicine, Bronx, 1967—68, surg. resident, 1968—69; urology resident NYU Med. Ctr., 1971—75; attending physician Bellevue Hosp., 1975—78; asst. attending urologist NYU Med. Ctr., 1978—; clin. assoc. prof. urology NYU Sch. Medicine, 1992—. Contbr. articles to profl. jours. Maj. US Army, 1969—71, Vietnam. Fellow: ACS; mem.: Am. Urol. Assn. Avocations: classical music, skiing, hiking, sports, reading.

SPERBER, DANIEL, physicist; b. Vienna, May 8, 1930; came to U.S., 1955, naturalized, 1967; s. Emanuel and Nelly (Lieberman) S.; m. Ora Yuval, Nov. 29, 1963; 1 son, Ron Emanuel. M.Sc., Hebrew U., 1954; PhD, Princeton U., 1960. Tng. and rsch. asst. Israel Inst. Tech., Haifa, 1954-55, Princeton U., 1955-60; sr. scientist, rsch. adviser Ill. Inst. Tech. Rsch. Inst., Chgo., 1960-67; assoc. prof. physics Ill. Inst. Tech., 1964-67, Rensselaer Poly. Inst., Troy, NY, 1967-72, prof., 1972—. Nordita prof. Niels Bohr Inst., Copenhagen, 1973-74, NATO research fellow, vis., prof., 1974-77; vis. prof. G.S.I., Darmstadt, Fed. Republic Germany, 1983; sr. Fulbright research scholar, Saha Inst. Nuclear Physics, Calcutta, India, 1987-88. Contbr. over 100 sci. papers to profl. jours. Served to capt. Israeli Army, 1948-51. Fellow Am. Phys. Soc.; mem. Israel Phys. Soc., N.Y. Acad. Scis., Sigma Xi. Jewish. Home: 1 Taylor Ln Troy NY 12180-7162 Office: Rensselaer Poly Inst 110 8th St Dept Physics Troy NY 12180-3522 Business E-Mail: sperbd@rpi.edu. *My goals are to further an understanding of nature by basic research in nuclear theory and to introduce a new generation to this research.*

SPERELAKIS, NICHOLAS, SR., retired physiology and biophysics educator, researcher; b. Joliet, Ill., Mar. 3, 1930; s. James and Aristea (Kayaidakis) S.; m. Dolores Martinis, Jan. 28, 1960; children: Nicholas Jr., Mark (dec.), Christine, Sophia, Thomas, Anthony. BS in Chemistry, U. Ill., 1951, MS in Physiology, 1955, PhD in Physiology, 1957. Cert. in electronics, radio and radar US Navy & Marine Corps Electronics Sch., 1952. Tchg. asst. U. Ill., Urbana, 1954-57; instr. Case Western Res. U., Cleve., 1957-59, asst. prof., 1959-66, assoc. prof., 1966; prof. U. Va., Charlottesville, 1966-83; Joseph Eichberg prof. physiology Coll. Medicine U. Cin., 1983-96, chmn. dept., 1983-93, Eichberg prof. emeritus, 1996—. Cons. NPS Pharm., Inc., Salt Lake City, 1988-95, Carter Wallace, Inc. Cranbury, N.J., 1988-91; vis. prof. U. St. Andrews, Scotland, 1972-73, U. San Luis Potosi, Mex., 1986, U. Athens, Greece, 1994; Rosenblueth prof. Centro de Investigacion y Avanzades, Mex., 1972; mem. sci. adv. com. several internat. meetings, editl. bds. numerous sci. jours. Co-editor: Handbook of Physiology: Heart, 1979; editor: Physiology and Pathophysiology of the Heart, 1984, 2d edit., 1988, 3rd edit., 1994, 4th edit., 2000, Calcium Antagonists: Mechanisms of Action on Cardiac Muscle and Vascular Smooth Muscle, 1984, Cell Interactions and Gap Junctions, vols. I and II, 1989, Frontiers in Smooth Muscle Research, 1990, Ion Channels in Vascular Smooth Muscle and Endothelial Cells, 1991, Essentials of Physiology, 1993, 2d edit., 1996, Cell Physiology Source Book, 1995 (Outstanding Acad. Book, Choice Am. Libr. Assn. 1996, 98), 3d edit., 2001, Electrogenesis of Biopotentials, 1995; assoc. editor Circulation Rsch., 1970-75, 75-80, Molecular Cellular Cardiology; regional editor Current Drug Targets, 2000-02; contbr. more than 500 articles to profl. jours. Lectr. Project Hope, Peru, 1962. Sgt. USMC, 1951—53, Korean War, with USMCR, 1953—59. Recipient Disting. Alumnus award Rockdale (Ill.) Pub. Schs., 1958, Rsch. Excellence award Am. Heart Assn. Ohio, 1995, Visionary award Am. Heart Assn., S.W. Ohio, 1996; U. Cin. Grad. fellow, 1989; NIH grantee, 1959-99. Mem. IEEE, Engring. in Medicine and Biology, Am. Physiol. Soc. (chair steering com. sect. 1981-82), Biophys. Soc. (coun. 1990-93), Am. Soc. Pharmacology and Exptl. Therapeutics, Internat. Soc. Heart Rsch. (coun. 1980-89, 92-98), Am. Hellenic Ednl. Progressive Assn. (pres. Charlottesville chpt. 1980-82), Ohio Physiol. Soc. (pres. 1990-91), Phi Kappa Phi. Independent. Greek Orthodox. Avocations: ancient Greek coins, stamp collecting/philately. Personal E-mail: nicksperel@aol.com.

SPERGEL, DAVID NATHANIEL, astrophysicist, educator; b. Rochester, NY, Mar. 25, 1961; s. Martin S. and Rochelle S. (Leffert) S.; m. Laura H. Kahn, Aug. 26, 1990; children: Julian J., Sarah E., Joshua. AB summa cum laude in Astronomy, Princeton U., NJ, 1982; AM in Astronomy, Harvard U., 1984, PhD in Astronomy, 1985. Postdoctoral fellow Harvard U., 1986; long-term mem. Inst. Advanced Study, Princeton, 1986—88, W.M. Keck disting. vis. prof. astrophysics, 2000—01; asst. prof. Princeton U., 1987—92, assoc. prof., 1992—97, prof., 1996—, Charles Young prof. astronomy on Class of 1897 Found., chair dept. astrophysy. scis., assoc. faculty mem. dept. physics, assoc. faculty mem. mech. and aerospace engring.; fellow Princeton Ctr. Theoretical Physics. Mem. sci. adv. bd. Hayden Planetarium, 1994—97; vis. assoc. prof. dept. astronomy U. Md., 1995; mem. adv. bd. Inst. Theoretical Physics Exec. Com., 1996—2000, chair adv. bd., 1998—99; chair origins subcommittee NASA, 2003—04, mem. space sci. adv. coun., 2003—04, chair sci. adv. coun., 2005—06, chair astrophysics subcommittee, 2005—07. Contbr. articles to sci. jours. Recipient Presdl. Young Investigator award NSF, 1988-93, Bart Bok prize Astron. Soc. Australia, 1994; Alfred P. Sloan Rsch. fellow, 1988-92. Mem.: NAS, Internat. Astron. Union, Am. Phys. Soc., Am. Astron. Soc. (Helen B. Warner prize 1994), Phi Beta Kappa. Office: Princeton U Peyton Hall Rm 113 Princeton NJ 08544 Office Phone: 609-258-3589. Office Fax: 609-258-8226. E-mail: dns@astro.princeton.edu. *

SPERGEL, IRVING ABRAHAM, social worker, researcher; b. NYC, Jan. 17, 1924; s. Julius and Frieda Mann Spergel; m. Bertha Jampel Spergel, June 27, 1949 (dec. Nov. 1989); children: Barry Alexander, Mark Jonathan, Daniel Jeremy; m. Annot Mary McGiffin, Oct. 5, 1996. BSS, CCNY, 1946; MA, Columbia U., NYC, 1948, PhD in Social Work, 1960; MSW, U. Ill., 1952. Program asst. YM-YWHA, Wilmington, Del., 1948—49; gang worker, supr. NYC, 1950, 1952; ct. rep. Youth Bd., NYC, 1954, 1958, 1960; dir. Neighbors United St. Club project Lenox Hill Neighborhood House, NYC, 1954—57; from asst. to assoc. prof. U. Chgo., 1960—66, prof., 1967—92, George Herbert Jones prof., 1993—2002, George Herbert Jones prof. emeritus, 2002—. UN youth adv. Hong Kong Govt., 1970—71; external examiner social work Chung Chi Coll., 1978—97; cons. Hong Kong Coun. Social Svc., 1978—97; cons., rschr. in field. Author: Racketville, Slumtown, Haulberg, 1964, Street Gang Work, 1966, Community Problem Solving, 1969, The Youth Gang Problem: A Community Approach, 1995, Reducing Youth Gang Violence, 2007. Mem. Ill. Gov.'s Commn. on Gangs, 1995—96, Nat. Youth Gang Adv. Com., Boys and Girls Clubs Am., 1989—91; mem. acad. adv. com. Ill. Criminal Justice Info. Authority, 1989—. With US Army, 1943—46, ETO. Grantee, Ford Found., 1960, NIMH, 1960—61, US Dept. Justice, 1987—2003. Jewish. Office: U Chgo Sch Social Svc Adminstrn 969 E 60th St Chicago IL 60637 Office Phone: 773-702-1134. Business E-Mail: iasperge@uchicago.edu.

SPERGEL, JONATHAN MICHAEL, pediatrician, allergist, immunologist, researcher; married. MD, PhD, Mt. Sinai Sch. Medicine, NYC, 1992. Diplomate Am. Bd. Pediatrics, Am. Bd. Allergy and Immunology. Asst. prof. U. Pa. Sch. Medicine, Phila., 1998—. Chief allergy Children's Hosp. Phila., 2006—. Contbr. articles to profl. jours. Fellow: Am. Acad. Allergy, Asthma and Immunology, Am. Acad. Pediatrics, Am. Coll. Allergy. Office: Children's Hosp Phila 34th St and Civic Ctr Blvd Philadelphia PA 18977

SPERLING, ALLAN GEORGE, lawyer; b. NYC, Dec. 10, 1942; s. Saul and Gertrude (Lober) Sperling; m. Susan Kelz, 1965 (div. 2001); children: Matthew Laurence, Stuart Kelz, Jane Kendra; m. Ferne Goldberg, 2001. AB, Columbia U., 1964; LLB, Yale U., 1967. Bar: N.Y. 1969, U.S. Ct. Appeals (2d cir.) 1975. Law clk. to Hon. William H. Timbers U.S. Dist Ct., New Haven, 1967-68; assoc. Cleary, Gottlieb, Steen & Hamilton, NYC, 1968-75, ptnr., 1976—. Editor Yale Law Jour. Bd. dirs. Vol. Lawyers for the Arts, 1998—, Merce Cunningham Dance Found., NYC, 1985-98, 2000—, chmn. bd., 1992-98; chmn. bd. Rye (NY) Arts Ctr. Inc., 1985-88, bd. dirs., 1990-94; bd. dirs. Friends of the Neuberger Mus. Art, Purchase, NY, 1989-2004, chmn. bd., 1997-2000. Mem.: N.Y. State Bar Assn., Phi Beta Kappa, Order of the Coif. Home: 2 Fifth Ave New York NY 10011 Office: Cleary Gottlieb Steen & Hamilton 1 Liberty Plz Fl 43 New York NY 10006-1470 Office Phone: 212-225-2260. Office Fax: 212-225-3999. Business E-Mail: asperling@cgsh.com.

SPERLING, GEORGE, psychologist, educator; s. Otto and Melitta Sperling BS in Math., U. Mich., 1955; MA in Psychology, Columbia U., 1956; PhD in Psychology, Harvard U., 1959. Rsch. asst. in biophysics Brookhaven Nat. Labs., Upton, NY, summer 1955, rsch. asst. in psychology Harvard U., Cambridge, Mass., 1957-59; mem. tech. rsch. staff Acoustical and Behavioral Rsch. Ctr., AT&T Bell Labs., Murray Hill, NJ, 1958-86; prof. psychology and neural sci. NYU, NYC, 1970-92; disting. prof. cognitive scis., neurobiology and behavior U. Calif., Irvine, 1992—. Instr. psychology Washington Sq. Coll., NYU, 1962-63; vis. assoc. prof. psychology Duke U., spring 1964; adj. assoc. prof. psychology Columbia U., 1964-65; acting assoc. prof. psychology UCLA, 1967-68; hon. rsch. assoc. Univ. Coll., U. London, 1969-70; vis. prof. psychology U. Western Australia, Perth, 1972, U. Wash., Seattle, 1977; vis. scholar Stanford (Calif.) U., 1984; mem. sci. adv. bd. USAF, 1988-92. Recipient Meritorious Civilian Svc. medal USAF, 1993; Gomberg scholar U. Mich., 1953-54; Guggenheim fellow, 1969-70, APS fellow. Fellow: APA (Disting. Sci. Contbn. award 1988), AAAS, Am. Psychol. Soc. (William James fellow), Optical Soc. Am. (Tillyer award 2002), Am. Acad. Arts and Sci.; mem.: NAS, Internat. Neural Network Soc. (founding mem., mem. governing bd. 1987—91, Helmholtz award 2004), Soc. Math. Psychology (exec. bd. 1979—85, chmn. 1983—84), Soc. Exptl. Psychologists (Warren medal 1996), Psychonomic Soc., Soc. Computers in Psychology (steering com. 1974—78), Eastern Psychol. Assn. (bd. dirs. 1982—85), Ann. Interdisciplinary Conf. (organizer 1975—, founder), Assn. Rsch. in Vision and Ophthalmology, Sigma Xi, Phi Beta Kappa. Office: U Calif SS Plz A Dept Cognitive Scis Irvine CA 92697-5100 E-mail: sperling@uci.edu.

SPERLING, GODFREY, JR., retired journalist; b. Long Beach, Calif., Sept. 25, 1915; s. Godfrey and Ida (Bailey) Sperling; m. Betty Louise Feldmann, June 22, 1942; children: Mary McAuliffe, John Godfrey. BS, U. Ill., 1937; JD, U. Okla., 1940. Bar: Ill. 1940. Pvt. practice, Urbana, Ill.; reporter Champaign-Urbana News-Gazette, 1940-41; mem. staff Christian Sci. Monitor, 1946—2005, Midwest bur. chief, 1957-62, N.Y. bur. chief, 1962-65, news mgr., asst. chief Washington bur., 1965-73, nat. polit. corr., 1970-83, chief Washington Bur., 1973-83, sr. Washington columnist, 1971—2005; ret. Served to maj. USAF, 1941—46, col. USAF Res., 1960—. Recipient Alumni Achievement award, U. Ill., 1987, Spl. citation, Nat. Press Found. for unique contbns. to Am. journalism, 1994; fellow, Woodrow Wilson Found., 1976—; Sperling Journalism fellow, U. Ill., 2003. Mem.: Fort Myer Officers Club, Overseas Writers Club (Washington), Nat. Press Club (Washington), White House Press Corr. Assn., Congl. Press Corr. Assn., Mass. Bar Assn., Ill. Bar Assn., Okla. Bar Assn., Sperling Breakfast Group (host 1966—2001), Cosmos Club (Washington), Gridiron Club Washington (pres. 1991), Sigma Delta Chi. Christian Scientist. Home: 8101 Connecticut Ave Apt N500 Chevy Chase MD 20815-2827

SPERLING, IRENE R., publishing executive; Asst. mktg. coord. seminars and trade shows Security World Publ., 1979—80; asst. show mgr. Cahners Expn. Group Kitchen and Bath and Office Product Shows, 1980—83, co-pub., 1983—86, v.p. sales and mktg., 1986—2000, publ., 2000—; publisher Tradeshow Week, LA, 2000—02; v.p. spl. projects and internat. sales Trade Show Exec. Mag., 2003—05, v.p., assoc. pub., 2005—.

SPERLING, JOHN GLEN, education company executive, educator; b. Willow Springs, Mo., Jan. 9, 1921; s. Leon Birchfield and Lena (McNama) S.; m. Virginia Vandergrift, June 1951 (div. 1965); 1 child, Peter Vandegrift. BA, Reed Coll., 1948; MA, U. Calif., 1952; PhD, U. Cambridge, Eng., 1955. Mem. faculty Northern Ill. U.; instr. U. Md., Europe, 1955-57; asst. professor Ohio State U., Columbus, 1957—61; prof. Humanities San Jose (Calif.) State U., 1961—73, dir., Right to Read Project, dir., NSF Cooperative Coll.-Sch. Sci. Prog in Econ.; pres. Inst. Profl. Devel., San Jose, 1972-76; founder, pres. U. Phoenix, 1976-80; founder, dir. Apollo Group Inc., Phoenix, 1973—, pres., 1973—98, CEO, 1973—2001, chmn. bd. dir., 1973—2004, acting exec. chmn., 2006—. Author: The South Sea Company, 1964, Great Depressions: 1837, 1893, and 1929, 1966, Against All Odds, 1989; co-author: (with Peter Dixon) War Finance 1698-1714, (with Suzanne Helburn) Economic Concepts and Institutions, 1974, Industry Performance, 1974, National Economic Policies, 1974, Social and Economic Priorities, 1974, Communist Economics, 1974, Third World Economics, 1974, (with Robert Tucker) For Profit Higher Education: Developing a World Class Workforce, 1997; contbr. articles to profl. jours. including Hist. Jour., Econ. History Rev., Bull. NASSP, Rule Mag., among others. Cons. Combating Juvenile Delinquency, Sunnyvale, Calif., 1972-75. Recipient Ehrman Studentship, Kings Coll., Cambridge U., 1953-55, Acad. Freedom award Calif. Fedn. Tchrs., L.A., 1988; named of Forbes Richest Americans, 2006. Mem. Arizona Club. Democrat. Founder the U. Phoenix, which has established itself as a leading provider of higher education programs for working adults by focusing on servicing the needs of the working adult; Primary investor in Genetic Savings and Clone, Inc., "Missyplicity Project" (cloned dog) and "Operation CC" (cloned cat that was created was called CopyCat), made first sale: a cloned male kitten, for $50,000 in December, 2004; latest quest: to research, develop, and sell the new science of longevity; opponent of drug prohibition and is actively financing initiatives to legalize medical marijuana in the US. Office: Apollo Group Inc 4615 E Elwood St Phoenix AZ 85040-1958 Office Phone: 480-921-5394.

SPERLING, NORMAN, editor; b. Washington, Mar. 19, 1947; s. Frederick and Katherine (Goloboff) Sperling; children: Lumin E., Mason. BA, Mich. State U., East Lansing, 1974; MA, U. Calif., Berkeley, 1987. Planetarium dir. Princeton Day Sch., NJ, 1970—76; asst. editor Sky & Telescope Mag., Cambridge, Mass., 1976—81; sci. editor AltaVista.com, Palo Alto, Calif., 2000; lectr. Sonoma State U., Rohnert Park, Calif., 1984—99; planetarium coord. Chabot Obs. and Sci. Ctr., Oakland, Calif., 1992—96; extension instr. U. Calif., Berkeley, 1987—; editor, publ. Jour. Irreproducible Results, San Mateo, Calif., 2004—. Cons. Edmund Scientific Co., Barrington, NJ, 1975—84; expert witness astronomy, 1985—; study assoc. AAAS Project Liberal Edn. & Sci., 1988—89. Author: What Your Astronomy Textbook Won't Tell You, 2002, Any Parent's Recipe for Great Baseball, 2007. Vice chair Bay Area Skeptics, San Francisco, 1991—. Recipient Nat. Svc. award, Western Amateur Astronomers, 1991, Spec. award, Astronomical Assn. Northern Calif., 1989. Fellow: Internat. Planetarium Soc.; mem.: Nat. Assn. Sci. Writers. Achievements include invention of Astroscan telescope; leader, astronomer solar eclipse expeditions: NC 1970, Quebec 1972, Mauritania 1973. Tanzania 1980, Baja Calif. 1991. Avocation: baseball. Office: Jour Irreproducible Results 413 Poinsettia Ave San Mateo CA 94403 Business E-Mail: nsperling@california.com.

SPERLING, REISA A., neurologist, researcher; MD, Harvard U., 1991. Cert. Neurology, 1996. Intern Brigham and Women's Hosp., Boston, 1992, now neurologist; chief resident Longwood Residency Program, Boston; fellowship Harvard Longwood Neurology Training Program, Boston, 1997; dir. Therapeutic Trials in Alzheimer's Disease, staff physician Memory Disorders Unit Brigham Behavioral Neurology Group, Boston. Fellow Harvard/MIT Clin. Investigator Training Program; grantee Am. Acad. Neurology Clin. Rsch. Training Fellowship. Office: Brigham Behavioral Neurology Group 221 Longwood Ave Boston MA 02115 Office Phone: 617-732-8060. Office Fax: 617-738-9122. E-mail: rasperling@bics.bwh.harvard.edu. *

SPERLING, SHELDON J., prosecutor; m. Marvetta Sperling; 2 children. BA, Northeastern State Coll., 1971; JD, U. Tulsa, 1979. Pvt. practice, Tulsa, 1979—82; asst. dist. atty. Okla. Dist. Atty.'s Office, 1983—85; asst. US atty. (ea. dist.) Okla. US Dept. Justice, 1985—89, 1st asst. US atty., criminal chief, 1989—2000, US atty. (ea. dist.) Okla., 2000—. Mem. Tulsa County Bar Assn., 1979—82, Am. Bar Assn., 1979—86, Okla. Dist. Atty.'s Assn., 1983—85, Nat. Dist. Atty.'s Assn., 1984, Nat. Assn. Asst. US Attorneys, 1994—2001, exec. dir., regional dir., del. Recipient Special Commendations, FBI Dir. William S. Sessions, 1993, FBI Dir. Louis J. Freech, 1998, FBI Dir. Robert S. Mueller III, 2002, Dept. Justice Dir. award, 1994. Mem.: Bar of Northern Dist. Okla., Bar of Eastern Dist. Okla., Phi Rho Pi, Rho Theta Sigma, Delta Theta Phi. Office: US Attys Office 1200 W Okmulgee St Muskogee OK 74401 *

SPERO, BARRY MELVIN, retired health facility administrator; b. Richmond, Va., July 13, 1937; s. Stanley Leo and Jean (Marmorstein) Spero; m. Merle Burns, May 29, 1960; children: Amy, Robin, Melissa. BA, U. Richmond, 1959; MHA, Med. Coll. Va., 1961. Asst. adminstr. Bapt. Hosp., Nashville, 1963-66, adminstrv. dir., 1966-68; v.p., dir. hosp. adminstrn. Hosp. Affiliates, Inc., Nashville, 1968-71; exec. dir. Bon Secours Hosp., Grosse Pointe, Mich., 1971-77; pres. The Mt. Sinai Med. Ctr., Cleve., 1977-85; pres., pres. NeWell Health Care System Newton-Wellesley Hosp., 1985-90; pres. Maimonides Med. Ctr., Bklyn., 1990-95; pres., CEO Masonicare, Wallingford, Conn., 1995—2005; ret., 2005. Mem. pers. practice com. Combined Jewish Philantropies; chmn. United Way West Suburban Hosp. divsn.; regional bd. mem. Bay Bank Middlesex; mem. Perpetual Benevolent Fund Com., Blue Print 2000, Commonwealth Mass.; bd. dirs. Premier Health Alliance, chmn., 1981—84; bd. dirs. Premier Preferred Care, Healthfirst; trustee Villa Maria Nursing Ctr./Bon Secours Hosp., 1974—94, chmn., bd. dirs., 1988—94; bd. dirs. Conn. Assn. Not-for-Profit Providers for the Aging, League Vol. Hosps. and Homes, 1991—95, chmn.-elect, 1992—95; mem. State of Ohio Gov.'s Commn. on Health Care Cost, 1984—85; various coms. Coun. Tchg. Hosps., 1992—95; treas. Vol. Hosps. Am., Mass., 1986—90; chmn. hosp. adv. com. Blue Cross N.E. Ohio, 1983—85; trustee Med. Instrumentation Sys., 1978—84; bd. dirs. Am. Assn. Homes and Svcs. for the Aging, 1998—; adv. bd. Gateway Cmty. Coll. Fellow: Am. Coll. Healthcare Execs.; mem.: Greater New Haven C. of C. (bd. dirs.), Ohio Hosp. Assn. (bd. trustees 1981—85, exec. coun.), Mass. Hosp. Assn. (com. on health sys. 1986—90, bd. trustees 1987—90, com. on Medicare payment for outpatient svcs. 1989—90), Met. Boston Hosp. Coun. (chmn. 1988—90), New Eng. Healthcare Assembly (Blue Ribbon com. 1985—90), Greater Cleve. Hosp. Assn. (bd. trustees 1981—85, exec. coun.), Greater N.Y. Hosp. Assn. (bd. govs. 1992—94), Am. Assn. Homes Svcs. Aging (bd. dirs. 1997—,), Conn. Hosp. Assn. (bd. dirs. 1997—2000), Coun. Tchg. Hosps. (various coms. 1992—94), Am. Hosp. Assn. (com. on Medicare payment for outpatient svcs. 1989—90). Jewish. Avocation: Avocations: golf, tennis, scuba diving. Home: 112 Acadia Dr Poinciana FL 34759

SPERO, JOAN EDELMAN, foundation administrator; b. Davenport, Iowa, Oct. 2, 1944; d. Samuel and Sylvia (Halpern) Edelman; m. C. Michael Spero, Nov. 9, 1969; children: Jason, Benjamin. Student, L'Inst. d'Etudes Politiques, Paris, 1964-65; BA in Internat. Rels. with honors, U. Wis., 1966; MA, Columbia U., 1968, PhD, 1973; LLD (hon.), Amherst Coll., 1997. Asst. prof. Columbia U., NYC, 1973-79; amb. of U.S. to UN Econ. and Social Coun., NYC, 1980-81; v.p. Am. Express Co., NYC, 1981-83, sr. v.p. internat. corp. affairs, 1983-89; treas., sr. v.p., 1989-91; exec. v.p. corp. affairs and communications Am. Express Co., 1991-93; under sec. for econ., bus. and agrl. affairs Dept. of State, Washington, 1993-97; pres. Doris Duke Charitable Found., NYC, 1997—. Vis. scholar Fed. Res. Bank NY, 1976—77; bd. dirs. IBM Corp., 1st Data Corp.; hon. trustee The Brookings Inst. Author: The Politics of International Economic Relations, 6th edit., 2003, The Failure of the Franklin National Bank, 1980; contbr. articles to profl. jours. Trustee Wis. Alumni Rsch. Found., 1997—, Columbia U., 1998; trustee emeritus Amherst Coll.; mem. Coun. Am. Ambs. Named to Acad. Women Achievers, YWCA, 1983; named Fin. Woman of Yr., Fin. Women's Assn., 1990; recipient George Washington U. Disting. Statesperson award, 1994; Woodrow Wilson fellow. Mem. Am. Acad. Diplomacy, Found. Execs. Group, Coun. on Fgn. Rels. (bd. dirs.), Am. Philos. Soc., Phi Beta Kappa. Democrat. Jewish. Avocations: writing, swimming. Office: Doris Duke Charitable Found 650 5th Ave 19th Fl New York NY 10019-6108 Office Phone: 212-974-7000.

SPERO, MORTON BERTRAM, retired lawyer; b. NYC, Dec. 6, 1920; s. Adolph and Julia (Strasburger) S.; m. Louise Thacker, May 1, 1943 (dec. Dec. 2003); children: Donald S., Carol S. Flynn. BA, U. Va., 1942, LLB, 1946. Bar: Va. 1946, U.S. Dist. Ct. (ea. dist.) Va., U.S. Ct. Appeals (4th cir.), U.S. Supreme Ct. 1961. Mem. legal staff NLRB, Washington, 1946-48; pvt. practice Petersburg, Va., 1948—2001; sr. ptnr. Spero & Levinson, Petersburg, 1970-75, Spero & Diehl, Petersburg, 1975-85; ret., 2001. Chmn. The Community Bank, Petersburg, 1976-79, dir., 1976-91. Chmn. United Fund Drive, 1960, bd. dirs., 1999-2003; pres. Dist. IV Petersburg Coun. Social Welfare, Southside Sheltered Workshop, 1965, pres. Congregation B'rith Achim, 1973. Lt. USNR, 1942-45, WWII. Recipient Outstanding Mem. award Petersburg chpt. B'nai B'rith, 1966; Svc. to Law Enforcement award Petersburg Police Dept., 1965. Fellow Am. Acad. Matrimonial Lawyers; mem. Va. Bar Assn., Petersburg Bar Assn. (pres. 1981-82), Va. State Bar (coun. 1981-84, chmn. criminal law sect. 1972, chmn. family law sect. 1979, bd. dirs. litigation sect. 1983-86, Lifetime Achievement award for family law sect. 1995), Va. Trial Lawyers Assn. (v.p. 1972), Civitan Club (hon.), Rotary, Elks (exalted ruler 1968). Democrat. Jewish. Home: 9706 Bunker Ct Petersburg VA 23805-9125

SPERONE, KENNETH J., transportation executive; s. Joseph Nicholas and Thelma Margaret Sperone; m. Terri Jo Ebert; 1 child, Nicholas. BS in Mgmt., Ind. Wesleyan U., 2001; MS in Mgmt., IIT, 2003. Wood pattern maker Allen Pattern Works, Ft. Wayne, 1975—79, Std. Pattern, Ft. Wayne, 1979—98, Internat. Truck & Engine, Ft. Wayne, 1998—2000, mgr. rapid prototype lab., 2000—. Mem.: Soc. Manf. Engrs. (mem. panel experts 2005). Avocations: golf, collecting diecasts cars. Office: Internat Truck and Engine 2911 Meyer Rd Fort Wayne IN 46803

SPEROS, JAMES DEMITRIOS, advertising executive; b. NYC, Jan. 15, 1954; s. George and Liberty (Stikardis) S.; m. Noreen Mary McKenna, Oct. 29, 1977; children: Keri Melissa, Lindsay Ann. BBA, Bernard M. Baruch Coll., 1976; postgrad., Duke U., 1987. Media planner Benton and Bowles, NYC, 1976; asst. media dir. SSC and B, NYC, 1976-78; group media supr. N.W. Ayer, NYC, 1978-79; advt. dir. AT&T, 1979—98; chief mktg. officer Ernst & Young LLP, 1998—2006; sr. v.p., chief mktg. officer Marsh & McLennan Companies., Inc., NYC, 2006—. Chmn. Assn. Nat. Advertisers, 2002—04. Recipient Print Powerhouse award Inside Print Mag., 1986, Communicator of the Yr. award Bus. Wire, 2001; named one of 100 Best and Brightest Ad Clients Advt. Age mag., 1986; named to the Am. Advertising Fedn. Hall of Achievement, 1993 Mem. Mktg. Media Edn., Assn. of Nat. Advertisers (chmn. print com. 1986-89, mgmt. com. 1989—), Consumer Audit Adv. Com. (BPA 1987-88). Greek Orthodox. Republican. Avocations: caligraphy, playing guitar, platform tennis, pen collection. Office: Marsh & McLennan Companies Inc 1166 Ave Americas New York NY 10036

SPERRY, LEN THOMAS, psychiatrist and preventive medicine educator; b. Milw., Dec. 1, 1943; s. Leonard V. and Wanda R. (Sadowski) S.; m. Patricia L. Garcia, June 11, 1977; children: Tracey, Christen, L. Timothy, Steven, Jonathon. BA, St. Mary's U. Minn., Winona, Minn., 1966; PhD, Northwestern U., 1970; MD, Am. U., Caribbean, 1981; D in Ministry, Barry U., 2001. Diplomate Am. Bd. Profl. Psychology, Am. Bd. Psychiatry and Neurology, Am. Bd. Preventive Medicine. Asst. prof. Marquette U., Milw., 1971-74; assoc. prof. U. Wis., Milw., 1974-75, U.S. Internat. U., San Diego, 1976-78; resident in psychiatry and preventive medicine Med. Coll. Wis., Milw., 1982-85; fellow in behavioral medicine U. Wis. Med. Sch., Milw., 1984-85; assoc. prof. psychiatry, preventive medicine Med. Coll. Wis., Milw., 1986-92, prof., 1992-2000, prof. cmty. and family medicine, 1998-2000, vice chair dept. psychiatry, 1997-2000, clin. prof. psychiatry, 2000—; prof. health adminstrn., prof. psychology Barry U., Miami Shores, Fla., 2000—02, dir. doctoral program in counseling, 2003; prof., dir. doctoral program in counseling Fla. Atlantic U., 2003—. Author: Learning Performance and Individual Differences, 1972, Contract Counseling, 1974, You Can Make It Happen: Self-Actualization and Organization, 1977, Together Experience, 1978, Aderian Counseling and Psychotherapy, 1987, Psychiatric Case Formulations, 1992, Psychopathology and Psychotherapy, 1993, 2d edit., 1996, Psychiatric Consultation in the Workplace, 1993, Handbook of Diagnosis and Treatment of DSM-IV Personality Disorders, 1995, Psychopharmacology and Psychotherapy, 1995, Treatment Outcomes in Psychotherapy and Psychiatric Interventions, 1996, Aging in the 21st Century, 1996, Family Therapy: Ensuring Treatment Efficacy, 1997, The Disordered Couple, 1997, The Intimate Couple, 1998, Brief Therapy Strategies with Individuals and Couples, 2000, Ministry and Community, 2000, Integrative and Biopsychosocial Therapies, 2000, Spirituality in Clinical Practice, 2001, Transforming Self and Community, 2002, Effective Leader, 2002, Becoming an Effective Therapist, 2003, Becoming an Effective Health Care Manager, 2003, Sex, Priestly Ministry and the Church, 2003, Executive Coaching, 2004, Spiritually-Oriented Psychotherapy, 2005, Couple and Family Assessment, 2005, Health Promotion and Health Counseling, Couples Therapy (2d edit.), 2005, Family Therapy Techniques, 2005, Cognitive Behavior Therapy of DSM-TR Pesonality Disorders, 2006, Psychological Treatment of Chronic Illness, 2006, The Ethical and Professional Practice of Counseling and Psychotherapy, 2007, Dictionary of Ethical and Legal Terms and Issues; contbr. articles to profl. jours. Bd. dirs. Am. Coun. on Sci. and Health, Nat. Acad. for Certified Family Therapists, St. Camillus Health Ctr., 1996-2000, Cath. Health Svcs., 2001—; cons. dir. Staff Devel. Am. Appraisal Assn., Milw., 1972-76. Northwestern U. fellow, 1969, Med. Coll. Wis. grantee, 1981. Fellow APA (Harry Levinson award 1998), Am. Psychiat. Assn. (chair com. on psychiatry in workplace 1998—,disting. fellow 1998-2001), Am. Coll. Preventive Medicine, Am. Coll. Psychiatrists, Am. Bd. Profl. Psychology, Am. Bd. Psychiatry and Neurology, Acad. Orgnl. and Occupational Psychiatry (v.p. 1993-96, Alan McLean lifetime achievement award 2000), Group for Advancement of Psychiatry, Coalition for Family Diagnosis. Avocations: reading, racquet sports, music. Office: Fla Atlantic U 777 Glades Rd Boca Raton FL 33431 Business E-Mail: lsperry@fau.edu.

SPERZEL, GEORGE E., JR., former personal care industry executive; b. 1951; BS in Bus. Adminstrn./Mgmt., U. Louisville, 1977. With General Electric Co., 1977-93; v.p., CFO Andrew Jergens Co., Cin., 1993-2000, Kao Am. Inc., Wilmington, Del., 1995-2000; svp and CFO Alliant Exchange, Inc., 2000—. Office: Alliant Food Service 9933 Woods Dr Skokie IL 60077-1057

SPETH, GERALD LENNUS, educational consultant, management consultant; b. Logan, Utah, July 14, 1934; s. Fredrick William and Elizabeth LaVern (Nuttall) Speth; m. Dora Goff, Aug. 11, 1955; children: Camille, Michael Gerald, Mark Alan, Janell, Doreen. BS, Utah State U., 1956; MBA, Ind. U., 1969; EdD, Ball State U., 1988. Auditor Ernst & Ernst, Salt Lake City, 1956, 58-59; officer 1st and 2d lt. U.S. Army, 1956-58, officer capt. to col., 1959-82; contr. Columbia Club, Indpls., 1982-83; sr. v.p. Allied Fidelity Corp., Indpls., 1983-85; adj. faculty Ind. Cen. U., Indpls., 1982-85; prof., dir. grad. bus. progs. U. Indpls., 1985—2001, prof. emeritus, 2001—. Cons. in field. Counselor in stake presidency, bishop, area welfare dir., mission pres., high councilor LDS Ch., 1965—. Decorated Legion of Merit, Bronze Star medal. Mem.: U.S. Govt. Accts. Assn., Am. Soc. Mil. Comptrs., Delta Mu Delta, Kappa Delta Psi, Alpha Kappa Psi, Sigma Iota Epsilon, Beta Gamma Sigma. Home: 8337 Goldfinch Cir Indianapolis IN 46256-1629 Office: U Indpls 1400 E Hanna Ave Indianapolis IN 46227-3630 Business E-Mail: speth@uindy.edu. E-mail: dgspeth@sbcglobal.net.

SPETH, JAMES GUSTAVE, dean, environmental studies educator, lawyer; b. Orangeburg, SC, Mar. 4, 1942; s. James Gustave and Amelia St. Clair (Albergotti) S.; m. Caroline Cameron Council, July 3, 1965; children: Catherine Council, James Gustave, Charles Council. BA summa cum laude, Yale U., 1964, LLB, 1969; MLitt, Oxford U., 1966; LLD (hon.), Clark U., 1995; MSE (hon.), Coll. of the Atlantic, 2001; LLD (hon.), Vt. Law Sch., 2005. Bar: D.C. 1969. Law clk. to Justice Hugo L. Black U.S. Supreme Ct., 1969-70; sr. staff atty. Natural Resources Def. Council, Washington, 1970-77; mem. Council Environ. Quality, Washington, 1977-79, chmn., 1979-81; prof. law Georgetown U. Law Ctr., Washington, 1981-82; pres. World Resources Inst., Washington, 1982-93; adminstr. UN Devel. Program, NYC, 1993-99; dean, prof. Yale Sch. Forestry and Environ. Studies Yale U., 1999—. Founded World Resources Inst.; organized Western Hemisphere Dialogue environ. and devel., 1990; chaired U.S. Task Force internat. devel. and environ. security. Contbr. articles to profl. jours.; speaker in field. Bd. dirs. World Resources Inst., Nat. Resources Def. Coun., Woods Hole Rsch. Ctr., Keystone Ctr., Leadership award 1994. Recipient Resources Def. award Nat. Wildlife Fedn., 1976, Barbara Swain award of honor Nat. Resources Coun. Am., 1992, Environ. Law Inst. Lifetime Achievement award, 1999, Blue Planet prize, 2002; named to Global 500 Honor Role UN Environ. Program, 1988; Rhodes scholar, 1964-66. Mem. Coun. on Fgn. Rels. (N.Y.C.). Episcopalian. Home: 88 Mulberry Farms Rd Guilford CT 06437-3215 E-mail: gus.speth@yale.edu.

SPEVACK, MARVIN, language educator; b. NYC, Dec. 17, 1927; s. Nathan and Miriam (Propper) S.; m. Helga Husmann, May 28, 1962; 1 child, Edmund Daniel (dec.). BA, CCNY, 1948; MA, Harvard U., 1950, PhD, 1953. Instr. English CCNY, 1955-61; asst. prof. City Coll. N.Y., 1961-63; prof. English, U. Muenster, Germany, 1963-89, dir. English seminar, 1964-89, dir. Inst. Erasmianum, 1974-89; Fulbright lectr. U. Münster, Germany, 1961-62. Vis. prof. U. Munich, 1962-63, NYU, summer 1966, Harvard U., summer 1973, U. N.Mex., 1985-86, Bowling Green State U., fall 1989; fellow Folger Shakespeare Libr., 1970, 98; hon. rsch. fellow Univ. Coll., London, 1980-81, 94—; vis. fellow Wolfson Coll., Cambridge (Eng.) U., 1984; scholar-in-residence Ctr. for Renaissance and Baroque Studies, U. Md., spring 1989; vis. rsch. fellow Inst. for Advanced Studies in Humanities, U. Edinburgh, Scotland, 1991. Author: Harvard Concordance to Shakespeare, 1973, A Complete and Systematic Concordance to the Works of Shakespeare, 9 vols., 1968-80, Robert Burton, Philosophaster, 1984, Shakespeare: The second, Third, and Fourth Folios, 1985, New Cambridge Julius Caesar, 1988, Shakespeare-Text, Language and Criticism: Essays in Honor of Marvin Spevack, 1988, New Variorum Antony and Cleopatra, 1990, A Shakespeare Thesaurus, 1993, James Orchard Halliwell- Phillipps: A Classified Bibliography, 1997, A Victorian Chronicle: The Diary of Henrietta Halliwell-Phillipps, 1999, James Orchard Halliwell-Phillipps: The Life and Works of the Shakespearean Scholar and Bookman, 2001, Isaac D'Israeli on Books: Pre-Victorian Essays on the History of Literature, 2004, Curiosities Revisited: The Works of Isaac D'Israeli, 2007; also articles and editions. Served with AUS, 1953-55. Guggenheim fellow, 1973-74, Andrew W. Mellon Found. fellow Huntington Libr., 1992, Ctr. for Book fellow Brit. Libr., London, 1994-95. Mem. MLA, Internat. Assn. Univ. Profs. English, Internat. Shakespeare Assn., The Bibliog. Soc., Deutsche Shakespeare Gesellschaft W., Shakespeare Assn., Soc. Textual Scholarship, Harvard Club (N.Y.C.), Harvard of Rhein-Ruhr Club (Germany), Phi Beta Kappa. Home: 14 Potstiege 48161 Münster Germany Office: 12-20 Johannisstrasse 48143 Münster Germany

SPEVAK, ERIC SCOTT, lawyer; b. Syracuse, NY, Feb. 28, 1959; s. Mannie and Sylvia Spevak. BA cum laude, Hobart Coll., 1981; JD, Villanova U. Sch. Law, 1984. Bar: Pa. 1984, NJ 1984. Assoc. Archer & Greiner, P.C., Haddonfield, NJ, 1984-86; ptnr. Gerstein, Cohen Kurtzman & Spevak, P.A., Haddonfield, NJ, 1986-90, Adinolfi & Spevak, P.A., Haddonfield, NJ, 1990—. Instr. NJ Inst. for CLE, 1995—; mem. NJ Dist. IV Ethics Com., 2002-; co-host The Law and You, 1994-1999; cert. divorce mediator, South Jersey Mediation Ctr.; lectr. ATLA, Am. Acad. Matrimonial Lawyers; legal commentator NBC Today Show, CNN, MSNBC News, Fox News with Paula Zahn, ABC Sunday Morning with Wally Kennedy, CNN's The Point with Greta Van Susteran, MSNBC's Hardball with Chris Matthews, Court TV's Catherine Cryer Live, CNN Headline News. Contbr. articles to profl. jours. Head coach Cherry Hill Lightening Boys Soccer, 1997—2001; mgr. Syracuse Sky Chiefs World Series Little League Champions, CHALL, 1999; coach South Jersey Maccabi Girls Soccer, Richmond, 2000, Miami, 2001; chairperson Cherry Hill Twp. Com. Recreation and Veteran's Affairs, 2005; appointed NJ WWII commr., 2006; mayor's liaison vet. affairs Cherry Hill Twp. Named NJ Super Lawyer, NJ Monthly Mag., 2005, 2006, 2007, Citizen of Yr., Jewish War Vets. USA, Dept. NJ, Inc., 2005, Hon. Comdr., Fort Dix NJ, 2006—; named one of Ten Leading Divorce Attys. in So. NJ, Digital Press Internat., 2005, Listed Atty. 10 Leaders, 2005, 2006, 2007; recipient Commendation medal, NJ, 2006, Meritorious Svc. medal, 2006, Patrick Henry award, Nat. Guard Assn. US, 2006, Cert. of Appreciation for meritorious pub. svc., NJ Supreme Ct., 2006. Mem.: NJ State Family Law Assn. (exec. com. 1995), Haddonfield Bus. and Profl. Assn. (solicitor/bd. mem. 2000—01), Burlington County Bar Assn. (mem. family law com. bd. dirs. 1993—95, matrimonial early settlement panelist, lectr.), NJ Bar Assn. (mem. family law exec. com. 1994—95), South Jersey Family Law Assn. Inns of Ct. (vice chmn. 1995—2002, v.p. 1997—), Camden County Bar Assn. (trustee 1988—92, co-chairperson family law com. 1989—94, bd. trustees 1989—94, chmn. family law com. 1989—94, co-chair 1999, co-chairperson family law com. 1999—2002, co-chair 2000, bd. trustees 2001—04, sec. 2002—03, chairperson family law com. 2002—, treas. 2003—04, second v.p. 2004—05, first v.p. 2005—06, Blue Ribbon panelist, lectr., pres. 2007—). Avocations: soccer coach, baseball coach, basketball official. Office: Adinolfi & Spevak PA 4 Kings Hwy E Haddonfield NJ 08033-2002

SPEYER, JAMES L., oncologist; b. Flushing, NY, July 26, 1948; MD, Johns Hopkins U., 1974. Cert. Internal Medicine 1977, Hematology 1978, Med. Oncology 1979. Intern NY Presbyn. Hosp., NYC, 1974—75, resident in medicine, 1975—76, resident in hematology, 1976—77; fellow Nat. Cancer Inst., Bethesda, Md., 1977—79; assoc. dir. clin. affairs NYU Cancer Inst., NYC, 1998—, assoc. dir. clin. and hosp. ops., 2003—; prof. clin. medicine NYU, NYC, 1980—, prof. medicine, 2002—. Office: NYU Cancer Inst 160 E 34th St New York NY 10016-6402 Office Phone: 212-731-5432. Business E-Mail: james.speyer@nyumc.org.

SPEYER, JASON LEE, aeronautical engineer, educator; b. Boston, Apr. 30, 1938; s. Joseph Louis and Ruth Sylvia (Steinmetz) S.; m. Barbara Joan Sachs, Sept. 11, 1966; children— Gil, Gavriel, Rakhel, Joseph BS, MIT, 1960; MS, Harvard U., 1964, PhD, 1968. Registered profl. engr., Tex. Engr. Boeing Co., Seattle, 1960-61; sr. engr. Raytheon Co., Bedford, Mass., 1961-68; sr. analyst Analytical Mechanics Assocs., Inc., Cambridge, Mass., 1968-70; mem. research staff Charles Stark Draper Lab., Cambridge, Mass., 1970-76; Harry H. Power prof. engrng. U. Tex., Austin, 1976-90; prof. engrng. UCLA, 1990—. Lectr. MIT, 1971-76; vis. scientist Weizmann Inst. Sci., 1972-73; Lady Davis prof. Technion, Haifa, Israel, 1983; Hunsaker vis. prof. aeros. and astronautics MIT, 1989-90. Recipient Hocott Disting. Engrng. Rsch. award Coll. Engrng., U. Tex., 1985, Exceptional Civil Svc. award USAF, 1991; Raytheon fellow, 1963-67; Hugh L. Dryden lectureship Am. Inst. of Aeronautics and Astronautics, 1995 Fellow IEEE (bd. govs. Control Sys. Soc. 1982—, assoc. editor Transaction on Automatic Control), AIAA (Mechanics and Control of Flight award 1985, Dryden lectureship in rsch. 1995, assoc. editor Jour. Spacecraft and Rockets, Jour. Guidance and Control), NAE. Home: 11358 Chalon Rd Los Angeles CA 90049-1721 Office: UCLA Dept Mech Aerospace Engring 420 Westwood Plz # 951597 Los Angeles CA 90095-8357

SPEYER, JERRY I., real estate company executive; b. June 23, 1940; m. Lynne Tishman (div.); 3 children; m. Katherine G. Farley, 1991; 1 child. BA, Columbia Coll., 1962; MBA, Columbia U., 1964. Co-founder, pres., CEO Tishman Speyer Properties, NYC, 1978—. Dep. chair Federal Reserve Bank of NY, chmn., 2007—; chmn. emeritus Columbia U., Real Estate Board of NY; bd. mem. Siemens AG, Yankees Global Enterprises, Real Estate Roundtable, Urban Land Inst.; mem. Council on Foreign Relations. Vice chmn. Museum of Modern Art, NYC, NY Presbyterian Hospital; co-chair NYC Partnership. Named one of Top 200 Collectors, ARTnews Mag., 2004, 2005, 2006. Mem.: Economic Club of NY. Avocation: Collector of Contemporary Art. Office: Tishmanspeyer Properties 45 Rockefeller Plz Fl 12 New York NY 10111-1299 Office Phone: 212-715-0300. *

SPEZIALE, RICHARD SALVATORE, financial executive; b. NYC, Jan. 27, 1957; s. Vito Anthony and Sally Ann (Buccheri) S.; m. Linda Candida Scro, May 31, 1986; children: Derek Joseph, Chiara Rose, Deanna Caterina. BSBA, L.I. U., 1983, MBA, 1988. Account exec. Dreyfus Corp., Garden City, NY, 1983-85; fin. advisor Home Life, Hauppauge, NY, 1985-86; br. chief SEC, NYC, 1986-91; 1st v.p., dept. mgr. Prudential Securities, NYC, 1991-94; mng. dir. Citigroup Markets and Banking, NYC, 1994—. Instr. NYU, N.Y.C., 1989-91, Securities Tng. Corp., N.Y.C., 1989-91. Cpl. U.S. Army, 1975-78. Mem. Securities Industry Assn. (mem. capital com. 1994-03), Bond Market Assn. (mem. capital com. 1995-2003). Avocations: diving, bicycling, weightlifting. Home: 143 Tahlulah Ln West Islip NY 11795-5219 Office: Citigroup Markets and Banking 388 Greenwich St New York NY 10013-2339

SPEZZA, JASON, professional hockey player; b. Mississauga, Ont., Can., June 13, 1983; Center Binghamton Senators (Am. Hockey League), 2002—03, 2004—05, Ottawa Senators, 2002—. Named to All-Rookie Team, Am. Hockey League, 2003, First All-Star Team, 2005; recipient John B. Sollenberger Trophy, 2005, Les Cunningham Plaque, 2005. Office: Ottawa Senators Scotiabank Place 1000 Palladium Dr Kanata ON K2V 1A5 Canada *

SPHIRE, RAYMOND DANIEL, anesthesiologist, educator; b. Detroit, Feb. 12, 1927; s. Samuel Raymond and Nora Mae (Allen) S.; m. Joan Lois Baker, Sept. 5, 1953; children: Suzanne M., Raymond Daniel, Catherine J. BS, U. Detroit, 1948; MD, Loyola U., Chgo., 1952. Diplomate Am. Bd. Anesthesiology. Intern Grace Hosp., Detroit, 1952-53; resident Harvard Anesthesia Lab.-Mass. Gen. Hosp., 1953-55; attending anesthesiologist Grace Hosp., Detroit, 1955-72, dir. dept. inhalation therapy, 1968-70; sr. attending anesthesiologist, dir. dept., dir. dept. respiratory therapy Detroit-Macomb Hosps. Assn., 1970—, trustee, 1978—, chief of staff, 1980—. Clin. asst. prof. Wayne State U. Sch. Medicine, 1967—; clin. prof. respiratory therapy Macomb Community Coll., Mount Clemens, Mich., 1971—; examiner Am. Registry Respiratory Therapists, 1972—; insp. Joint Rev. Com. Respiratory Therapy Edn., 1972— Co-author: Operative Neurosurgery, 1970, First Aid Guide for the Small Business or Industry, 1978 With AUS, 1944-45; 1st lt. M.C., USAF, 1952 Fellow Am. Coll. Anesthesiologists, Am. Coll. Chest Physicians; mem. AMA, Am. Soc. Anesthesiologists, Wayne County Soc. Anesthesiologists (pres. 1967-69), Am. Assn. Respiratory Therapists, Soc. Critical Care Medicine, Country Club of Detroit, Grosse Pointe Club, Cumberland Club (Portland, Maine), Severance Lodge. Roman Catholic. Home and Office: 36 Sunningdale Dr Grosse Pointe Shores MI 48236

SPICE, DENNIS DEAN, financial consultant; b. Rochester, Ind., Feb. 7, 1950; s. Donnelly Dean and Lorene (Rhodes) S.; m. Linda Kay Buehler, Oct. 1, 1971; children: Kristie Lorene, Danielle Deanne. AA, SUNY, Albany, 1974; BA, Ea. Ill. U., Charleston, 1978; MBA, U. Ill., Urbana, 1985. Employee benefits mgr. Ea. Ill. U., Charleston, 1977-80; disbursements officer State U. Retirement Sys., Champaign, Ill., 1980-81, asst. dir. adminstrn., 1981-85, assoc. exec. dir., 1985-90, exec. dir., 1991-95; pres., chmn. Instnl. Advisors, Ltd., Champaign, 1995—; dir. corp. rels. U. Ill Fire Svc. Inst., Champaign, 2006—. Mng. mem., founding ptnr. Open Prairie Ventures, Champaign, 1997—2006; mem. Sch. Tech. Ea. Ill. U., Charleston; bd. dirs. credit union U. Ill.; adv. bd. Riler North Cap. Mgmt., Inc. Staff sgt. USMC, 1968-77, Vietnam. Paul Harris fellow. Mem.: Champaign West Rotary Club. Office: Institutional Advisors Ltd 5008 W Bluebill Rd Ste 200 Champaign IL 61822 Business E-Mail: dspice@ia-ltd.com.

SPICER, BEVERLY WHITE, writer, photojournalist, artist; m. Christopher Hanes Spicer, 1969 (div. 1976). BA in Physiol. Psychology, Converse Coll., 1969; MS in Arch., U. Tex., 2000. Rschr. U. Va., Charlotteville, 1969—71; asst. to pub. Tex. Monthly Mag., Austin, 1976—77; freelance photojournalist, 1978—. Author: The Ka'Bah: Rhythms of Culture, Faith and Physiology, 2004; co-author: Open Ceilings: Women of Power Outside The Paradigm, 1994; columnist, editor, digital journalist (online photojournalism mag.). Vol. Seton Hosp., Austin, 1990—94. Grantee, NIH, 1982, Mike Hogg grant, U. Tex., 1999. Mem.: AIA (assoc.). Avocations: swimming, walking, movies, music, kundalini yoga. Home: 4705 Eilers Ave Austin TX 78751

SPICER, HAROLD OTIS, retired English language educator, communications educator; b. Gosport, Ind., Dec. 10, 1921; s. Otis R. and Hattie Grace (Wampler) S.; m. Hilda Jane Templeton, June 21, 1946 (dec. Nov. 1994); children: Sherry Lynne (dec. May 1987), Sylvia Jean, Stephen Michael, Zachary Ian. BA, DePauw U., 1947, MA, 1949; PhD, Ind. U., 1962. Instr. English DePauw U., Greencastle, Ind., 1947-49, asst. prof. English, 1957-63; from instr. to prof. English We. Ill. U., Macomb, 1949-57; adj. prof. English Ind. U., Indpls., 1960-63; assoc. prof. to prof. English Ind. State U., Terre Haute, 1963-85; ret., 1985. Sec. Main Street, Greencastle, 1993-95. Author: Covered Bridges of Putnam County, 1989, Organizational Handbook for Council on Aging, 1989 (Ameritech Tchr. Vol. award, 1989), James Whitcomb Riley: Hoosier Poet, 1993; co-author: DePauw: Pictorial History, 1987; editor: Ten O'Clock News, a museum newsletter, 2003—05; author, narrator, interviewer: 20th Century Golden Memories, 2001—02. Pres. Ret. Tchrs. Putnam County, Greencastle, 1988-90, 2005-06, Putnam County Coun. on Aging, 1990-96 (Man of Yr. award 1994); bd. dirs. Heritage Preservation Soc., Greencastle, 1993—, Putnam County Found., 1995-02, sec., 2000-03; pres. West Ctrl. Ind. Area Agy. on Aging, 2000, 06; coach DePauw U. team Gen. Electric Co. Coll. Bowl Program, 1962, coach Ind. State U. team, 1963. Recipient Danforth Tchr. grant, 1959, Man of Yr. award Area 7 Agy. on Aging West Ctrl. Ind. Econ. Devel. Dist., Terre Haute, 1994; named Older Hoosier of Yr. Ind. Gov.'s Conf., Indpls., 1994, RSVP Vol. of Yr., 1995, Ameritech Vol. Tchr. of Yr., 1989, Martin H. Miller Vol. of Yr. award Ind. Family and Social Svcs. Adminstrn., 1999, Outstanding Leadership award in area/agy. on aging Ind. Assn. Area Agys. on Aging, 2000. Mem.: VFW (life), Am. Assn. Ret. Persons (pres. Putnam County chpt. 1995—96, 1999—2002, 2005—06), Kiwanis Club Greencastle, West Ctrl. Ind. Civil War Roundtable (v.p. 1998—2000), Greencastle C. of C. (bd. dirs. 1995—99, Putnam County Citizen of Yr. 1996), Am. Legion. Avocations: music, writing, travel. Home: PO Box 892 Greencastle IN 46135-0892 Personal E-mail: h.spicer@insightbb.com.

SPICER, HOLT VANDERCOOK, retired theater educator; b. Pasadena, Calif., Feb. 1, 1928; s. John Lovely and Dorothy Eleanor (Clause) S.; m. Marion Arel Gibson, Aug. 16, 1952; children: Mary Ellen, Susan Leah, Laura Alice, John Millard. BA, U. Redlands, 1952, MA, 1957; PhD, U. Okla., 1964. From instr. speech and theatre to prof. S.W. Mo. State Coll., 1952-93, emeritus prof., 1993—, head dept. speech and theatre, 1967-71, dean Sch. Arts and Humanities, 1971-85. Chmn. Dist. 4 Nat. Debate Tournament Com., 1955, 58, 64, 68 Vestryman Episcopalian Ch.,

1981—85, 1998—2001; bd. dirs. Springfield (Mo.) Cmty. Ctr., 1981—. Named Debate Coach of Decade U.S. Air Force Acad., 1965, Holt V. Spicer Debate Forum, 1988; recipient Alumni Achievement award in Speech and Debate U. Redlands, 1991, Alumni award of appreciation S.W. Mo. State U., 1996; team won CEDA Nat. Debate championship, 1992. Mem.: AAUP, Am. Forensic Assn., Speech Communication Assn. Episcopalian. Home: 2232 E Langston St Springfield MO 65804-2646 E-mail: holtspicer9@mchsi.com.

SPICER, JOHN AUSTIN, physicist; b. Rock Springs, W.Va., Sept. 25, 1930; s. Ernest Marvin and Ruth (Stevens) S.; m. Erika Gruendig, 1959; children: Cynthia, Michael, Marilynn. BS, U. Wyoming, 1956, MS, 1957; PhD, U. Freiburg, Germany, 1962. Mathematician Geotech. Corp., Laramie, Wyo., 1956-57; physicist Goodyear Aerospace Corp., Litchfield, Ariz., 1962-63; head engr. Aeroject Gen. Corp., Azusa, Calif., 1963-64; mathematical analyst North Am. Aviation Info. Systems Div., Downey, Calif., 1973-76; program mgr. Chrysler Space Systems Div., New Orleans, La., 1966-68; sr. research mathematician U. Dayton Research Inst., Ohio, 1968-70; ops. research analyst U. McCall Printing Corp. Systems Dept., Dayton, 1970-71; mathematician Systems Dyamics Br. AF Flight Dynamics La., 1971-72; physicist Radar and Microwave Tech. Br. Af Avionics lab., 1972-74, Analysis and Evaluation Br. AF Avionics Lab., 1974-89; physicist tech group, target recognition br. AF Avionics Lab., Dayton, Ohio, 1989-98. Contbr. articles on neural networks, wavelets and fractal methodology to profl. jours.; presenter in field. Achievements include inventing "exact stability," which is a numerical integration routine that yields a dead beat response, that is, always stable and controllable, reaches equilibrium in minimum time, and is always stable. Office: WL/AACR Bldg 620 Dayton OH 45433-7001 Home: PO Box 323 Loveland OH 45140-0323

SPICER, RONALD L., financial services educator; b. Louisville, Jan. 21, 1949; s. Robert Joseph and Ann (Stafford) S.; m. Joan E. Vining, Dec. 20, 1969 (div. June 1988); children: Jennifer Joan Spicer McMullen, Ronald Geoffrey; m. JoAnn F. Snyder, Feb. 18, 1989; 1 child, Veronica Michelle. BS in Psychology and Sociology, Carroll Coll., 1971; MA in Orgn. Mgmt., U. Phoenix, 1997; MBA in Bus., Regis U., 1999; PhD in orgn. and mgmt., Capella U., 2006. CPCU, CLU, CHFC, ARM. V.p. sales Alexander & Alexander, Atlanta, 1982-88; exec. v.p. Powell and Co., Atlanta, 1988-89; v.p. sales Corroon and Black, Balt., 1989-90; broker, owner Profl. Ins. Brokers, York, Pa., 1990-93; sr. account exec. Hilb, Rogal and Hamilton, Denver, 1993-95; ins. program coord. Pikes Peak C.C., Colorado Springs, 1995-97; pres., CEO Peak Profl. Svcs., Inc., Colorado Springs, 1997—, owner, 1997—; dir. edn. Colo. Tech. U., Denver, 1997—. Adv. com. Ins. Inst. of Am., Malvern, Pa., 1995—; mem. next generation com., Life and Health Ins. Edn. Assn., N.Y.C., 1996-97. Author: (book) Colorado P&C PreLicense Course, 1998, Colorado Life and Health Pre-License Course, 1999; contbr. articles to profl. jours. Mem. Soc. CPCU (Pikes Peak chpt. pres. 1998-99, pres. 1999-2000), Soc. Fin. Svc. Profls. (Pikes Peak chpt. pres. 2000-01), Optimist (pres. Uptown Club 1979-81), Masons. Republican. Episcopal. Lutheran. Avocations: skiing, camping, scuba diving. Office: Peak Profl Svcs Inc 953 Bayfield Way Colorado Springs CO 80906 Office Phone: 303-362-2981. Business E-Mail: rspicer@coloradotech.edu.

SPICER, S(AMUEL) GARY, lawyer, writer, educator; b. Dickson, Tenn., Jan. 8, 1942; s. Clark and E. Maybelle (Hogin) S.; children: Victoria, S. Gary Jr., Matthew, Katy, Mark, David. BA, Adrian Coll., 1964; MBA, Wayne State U., 1965; JD, Detroit Coll. Law, 1969; LLD (hon.), Adrian Coll., 2002. Bar: Mich. 1969, Tenn. 1969. With pers. dept. GM Truck & Coach, Detroit, 1964-66; with trust dept. Nat. Bank Detroit, 1966-69; acct. Price Waterhouse & Co., Detroit, 1969-71; propr. Law Firm of S. Gary Spicer, Detroit, 1971—. Adj. prof. law, sports and entertainment Mich. State U., Lansing, 2002—; adj. prof. law, sports U. Detroit, 2006—. Author: Surviving Success, 1990. Co-chmn. endowment com. Adrian (Mich.) Coll., 1982-94, Don and Dolly Smith Found., Detroit, 1981—; trustee Grosse Pointe Acad., 1983-95, Joseph Sloan Bonsall and Mary Ann Bonsall Found., 1988—, Don Baylor Found., 1995—, JoAnne Nicolay Found., 1996—, Richard A. and Donna L. Sterban Found., 1997—, Pam Lewis Found, 1997—, Detroit Sch. Arts, 2004—; Detroit Tigers Players Home Clubhouse Scholarship Fund, Doris and Don Duchene, Sr. Found., Mary I. McLeod Found.; former elder, treas., Fort St. Presbyn. Ch.; memorabilia cons. Ernie Harwell Libr. Sports. With USAR, 1965-71 Recipient Young Alumni Achievement award Adrian Coll. Alumni Assn., 1987; named to Athletic Hall of Fame, Adrian Coll., 1996. Mem. Detroit Athletic Club Avocations: Russian literature, squash. Office Phone: 313-884-9700. Personal E-mail: sgspicer@aol.com.

SPIEGEL, ALLEN MICHAEL, dean, internist; b. Lundsberg, Germany, May 18, 1946; BA summa cum laude, Columbia U., 1967; MD cum laude, Harvard U., 1971. Intern and resident in internal medicine Mass. Gen. Hosp., Boston, 1971—73; mem. Endocrinology Rsch. Tng. Program Nat. Inst. Diabetes and Digestive and Kidney Disease, NIH, 1973—76, sr. investigator Metabolic Diseases Branch, 1977—84, chief molecular pathophysiology sect. Metabolic Diseases Br., 1985—; chief Metabolic Diseases Br., 1988, sci. dir., 1990—99, dir., 1999—2006; dean Albert Einstein Coll. Medicine Yeshiva U., 2006—. Recipient Jacobaeus Prize, Novo Nordisk Insulin Found., 1990, Komrower Meml. Lecture Award, Soc. for the Study of Inborn Errors of Metabolism, 1996, Edwin B. Astwood Lecture Award, Endocrine Soc., 1998. Mem.: Inst. Medicine, Assn. Am. Physicians, Am. Soc. Clin. Investigation. Office: Albert Einstein Coll Medicine Jack and Pearl Resnick Campus 1300 Morris Park Ave Bronx NY 10461

SPIEGEL, ANDREA, marketing executive; Mktg. and advt. mgr. Avis Rent A Car; dir. mktg. Virgin Atlantic Airways; v.p. mktg. Cunard Line; owner AKS Comms.; mktg. cons. Virgin USA; chief mktg. officer JetBlue Airways, Forest Hills, NY, 2005—. Office: JetBlue Airways 118-29 Queens Blvd Forest Hills NY 11375

SPIEGEL, DANIEL LEONARD, lawyer; b. Balt., Sept. 5, 1945; s. William and Anna (Stiffman) S.; m. Marianne Albertson; 1 child, Anna. BA magna cum laude, Washington U., St. Louis, 1967; MPA, Harvard U., 1969; JD, Georgetown U., Washington, 1979. Legis. asst. to Sen. Alan Cranston U.S. Senate, Washington, 1969-76, legis. asst. to Sen. Hubert Humphrey, 1971—76; spl. asst. to Sec. Cyrus Vance US Dept. State, Washington, 1977-78, mem. policy planning staff, 1978-79; ptnr. Akin Gump Strauss Hauer & Feld LLP, Washington, 1983—93, dir. internat. practice, 1991-93, ptnr., pub. law & policy, mem. mgmt. com., 1996—; vice chmn. AG Global Solutions (joint venture between Akin Gump and First Internat. Resources Inc.); amb., permanent rep. US Mission to UN, Geneva, 1993-96. Sr. advisor Clinton-Gore transition Dept. of State, Washington, 1992-93. Office: Akin Gump Strauss Hauer & Feld LLP Ste 400 1333 New Hampshire Ave NW Washington DC 20036-1532 Office Phone: 202-887-4000. Office Fax: 202-887-4288. Business E-Mail: dspiegel@akingump.com.

SPIEGEL, ELWYN, advertising executive, art director; b. NYC, Apr. 26, 1926; s. Morris and Rose Ann (Nemetzky) S.; m. Doris Kay, Apr. 25, 1954 (dec.); children: Elizabeth Ann Simendinger, Susan Gail Ambrose, Laura Faith Ciecierski. BSEE, N.C. State U., 1945; BS in Econs., Columbia U., 1950. Pres. Ad Infinitum, Inc., Hackensack, NJ, 1954-63; exec. v.p. Alden Advt. Agy., NYC, 1964-81; pres. Spiegel/Labatt-Simon, Inc., NYC, 1981-88, Compris, Inc., NYC, 1989-96, Elwyn Spiegel & Ptnrs., NYC, 1996—. Cons. in field. Creative dir. TV commls. including Colorforms, 1976 (Clio award, 1976), creative dir. (mag.) Russell Fabrics, 1981; author: Get a New Life, The Jackknife Gypsies, The Hollow Island, 2007, The Shadow People, 2007, Ferry to Uskudar, 2007. Judge, Clio Awards, N.Y.C., 1975. Recipient Silver award, Neographics 1977, Addy (4), Am. Advt. Fedn., 1977-80, Desi (8), Graphics Design USA, 1981-82, Clio (3), Clio Adv. Bd., 1981. Mem. Nat. Trust for Hist. Preservation, Kiwanis (pres. 1954-55), Alpha Delta Sigma. Avocations: photography, music, sports cars, literature, writing. Address: 41 Park Ave New York NY 10016-3400 Home Phone: 212-696-0831; Office Phone: 212-490-1991. Business E-Mail: espiegel@ix.netcom.com.

SPIEGEL, HERBERT, psychiatrist, educator; b. McKeesport, Pa., June 29, 1914; s. Samuel and Lena (Mendlowitz) S.; m. Natalie Shainess, Apr. 24, 1944 (div. Apr. 1965); children: David, Ann; m. Marcia Greenleaf, Jan. 29, 1989. BS, U. Md., 1936, MD, 1939. Diplomate Am. Bd. Psychiatry. Intern St. Francis Hosp., Pitts., 1939-40; resident in psychiatry St. Elizabeth's Hosp., Washington, 1940-42; practice medicine specializing in psychiatry NYC, 1946—; attending psychiatrist Columbia-Presbyn. Hosp., NYC, 1960—; faculty psychiatry Columbia U. Coll. Physicians and Surgeons, 1960—. Adj. prof. psychology John Jay Coll. Criminal Justice, CUNY, 1983-; mem. faculty Sch. Mil. Neuropsychiatry, Mason Gen. Hosp., Brentwood, N.Y., 1944-46. Author: (with A. Kardiner) War Stress and Neurotic Illness, 1947, (with D. Spiegel) Trance and Treatment: Clinical Uses of Hypnosis, 1978, 2d edit., 2004; subject of book: (by Donald S. Connery) The Inner Source: Exploring Hypnosis with Herbert Spiegel, M.D.; mem. edit. bd.: Preventive Medicine, 1972; Contbr. articles to profl. jours. Profl. advisory com. Am. Health Found.; pub. edn. com., smoking and health com. N.Y.C. div. Am. Cancer Soc.; adv. com. Nat. Aid to Visually Handicapped. Served with M.C. AUS, 1942-46. Decorated Purple Heart. Fellow Am. Psychiat. Assn., Am. Coll. Psychiatrists, Am. Soc. Clin. Hypnosis, Am. Acad. Psychoanalysis, Internat. Soc. Clin. and Exptl. Hypnosis, William A. White Psychoanalytic Soc., N.Y. Acad. Medicine, N.Y. Acad. Scis.; mem. Am. Orthopsychiat. Assn., Am. Psychosomatic Soc., AAAS, AMA, N.Y. County Med. Soc. Office: 19 E 88th St New York NY 10128-0557 Home Phone: 212-860-8540; Office Phone: 212-534-8877.

SPIEGEL, HERMAN D.J., architecture and structural engineering educator; b. Boston, Dec. 31, 1924; s. Harry and Annie (Gittleman) S.; m. Sally Peery, June 2, 1957; children: Robert Stewart, William Steven. BS in Arch., RISD, 1953; M Structural Engring., Yale U., 1955. Registered profl. engr., Calif., Mass., R.I., D.C., Ky., Md., Va., Conn. Dean Sch. Arch. Yale U., New Haven, 1971—76, from instr. archtl. engring. to prof. emeritus, 1955—93, prof. emeritus arch. engring., 1992—; founder, prin. Spiegel Zamecnik & Shah Cons. Structural Engrs., New Haven, 1956—, Washington, 1971—. Lectr. in field. With U.S. Army, 1943-46, WW II, ETO and PTO. Recipient Alumni Gold medal, RISD, 1972. Fellow ASCE, Yale Eng. and Sci. Soc.; mem. AIA (hon.), ASTM, Amigos de Gaudi (hon.), Assn. Collegiate Schs. Arch., Am. Concrete Inst., Am. Inst. Steel Constrn., Conn. Soc. Architects (hon.), Conn. bldg. Congress, Yale Engring. Soc., Army and Navy Club of Washington, Mory's Assn. Inc., Yale Club of N.Y.C., Yale Club of New Haven. Office Phone: 203-245-7446.

SPIEGEL, JAYSON LESLIE, lawyer, educator, professional society administrator; b. NYC, Mar. 1, 1959; s. Jack and Frieda Rhoda (Michaelson) S.; m. Deborah Marie Scott, Nov. 1, 1986; children: Kyle Reid, Alicia Jean. AB, Georgetown U., 1980; JD, U. Va., 1983; postgrad., USMC Command and Staff Coll., 1991, Army Command and Gen. Staff Coll., 1996; MS in Strategic Studies, US Army War Coll., Carlisle, Pa., 2006. Bar: Md. 1984, D.C. 1985, U.S. Ct. Appeals (D.C. cir.) 1986, U.S. Ct. Mil. Appeals 1987, U.S. Ct. Appeals (4th cir.) 1987, U.S. Supreme Ct. 1988, U.S. Ct. Claims 1990. Law clk. to assoc. judge Md. Ct. Appeals, Balt., 1983—84; assoc. Jordan, Coyne, Savits & Lopata, Washington, 1985—91, ptnr., 1991—94; dep. asst. sec. U.S. Army, 1994—99, acting asst. sec., 1997—98; exec. dir. Res. Officers Assn., 1999—2003; sr. nat. def. counsel Ball Janik, LLP, 2003—05; prin. tech. dir. General Dynamics Info. Tech. (and predecessor corp.), 2005—. Lectr. law and transfusion medicine NIH, 1989, 91-94. Contbr. articles to profl. jours. Mem. recreation adv. bd. Montgomery County, Md., 1989-93. With USAR, 1981—, Desert Shield/Desert Storm, 1990-91. Mem.: ABA (young lawyers mem. com. on law and nat. security, vice chair internat. criminal law com. 1991—94), Conf. of Def. Assn. (Can.), Nat. Def. Indsl. Assn., Md. Bar Assn., D.C. Bar Assn. (founder, chmn. com. on law and nat. security 0197—1994, Com. Chmn. of Yr. 1988, 1991), U.S. C. of C. (com. of 100 assn. execs. 2000—03), Mil. Coalition (bd. dirs. 1999—2003), Res. Officers Assn. (life), Army and Navy club. Avocations: running, tennis. Office Phone: 202-292-1856. Personal E-mail: jayson.spiegel@gdit.com. Business E-Mail: jspiegel@anteon.com.

SPIEGEL, JERROLD BRUCE, lawyer; b. NYC, Apr. 11, 1949; s. Seymour S. and Estelle (Minsky) S.; m. Helene Susan Cohen, Mar. 3, 1972; children: Dana Sean, Amy Barrett, Evan Tyler. BS, Queens Coll., 1970; JD cum laude, NYU, 1973. Bar: NY 1974. Assoc. Austrian, Lance & Stewart, NYC, 1973-75, Gordon Hurwitz Butowsky Baker Weitzen & Shalov, NYC, 1975-79; ptnr. Shapiro Spiegel Garfunkel & Driggin, NYC, 1979-86, Frankfurt Kurnit Klein & Selz P.C., NYC, 1986—. Editor: Ann. Survey Am. Law, 1972—73. Mem. ABA (corp. law sect.), Order of the Coif, Omicron Delta Epsilon. Office: Frankfurt Kurnit Klein & Selz PC 488 Madison Ave Fl 9 New York NY 10022-5754 Office Phone: 212-826-5543. Business E-Mail: jspiegel@fkks.com.

SPIEGEL, JOAN ELIZABETH, anesthesiologist, educator; b. Buffalo, May 4, 1967; d. David Isaac and Sally Bogolub Fand; m. Jeffrey Howard Spiegel, Apr. 9, 1995 (div. May 2002); 1 child, Jacob Harris. BS, MIT, Cambridge, Mass., 1990; MD, U. Mich., Ann Arbor, 1995. Diplomate Am. Bd. Anesthesiology, Am. Bd. Internal Medicine. Clinician Beth Israel Deaconess Med. Ctr., Boston, 2002—, dir. post anesthesia care unit, 2003—. Course dir. surg. airway mgmt. Surg. Ctr. Beth Israel Deaconess Med. Ctr., Boston; instr. Harvard Med. Sch., Boston, 2002—; cons. MedaCorp Consulting, Boston, 2006—. Author, editor: Anesthesia: Key Words Defined, 2006, cons. editor: Med. Sci. Monitor, 2005—; contbr. articles to profl. jours. Recipient Rsch. award, STARR Found. of MIT, 1990, Am. Heart Saver award, Am. Heart Assn., 2002; grantee, Portex, Inc., 2003. Mem.: Am. Soc. Anesthesiologists. Achievements include patents pending for endotracheal tube pressure device. Avocations: bicycling, gardening, inventing. Office: BIDMC Dept Anesthesia 330 Brookline Ave ST-308 Boston MA 02215 Business E-Mail: jspiegel@bidnc.harvard.edu.

SPIEGEL, LAWRENCE HOWARD, advertising executive; b. NYC, Oct. 9, 1942; s. Melvin Arthur and Rose (Black) S.; m. Christy Mansfield; children from previous marriage: Robert, David. BA, NYU, 1963. Print buyer William Esty Co., NYC, 1964-65, broadcast buyer, 1965-66; media planner Batten, Barton, Durstine & Osborn, Inc., NYC, 1966-67, media supr., 1967-68, assoc. media dir., 1969-72, v.p., 1972-74; media group head Jack Tinker & Ptnrs., NYC, 1968-69; v.p. Tracy-Locke, Dallas, 1974-80, sr. v.p., 1980-84, exec. v.p., 1984-89; prin. The Richards Group, Dallas, 1989—. Pres. Tex. Coun. Advt., 1991-97, Leading Agy. Network, 1997—; dir. Dream Fund, 1999—; charter mem. broadband video adv. bd. AOL. Guest editor Mktg. and Media Decision mag., June 1982. Mem. Dallas Cable Bd., 1983-86; chmn. mktg. com. U. Tex., Dallas, 1984-89; pres. Cable Access Dallas, Inc., 1985-86; trustee Dallas Symphony Assn., 1978—; bd. dirs. Equest Inc., 1991-92, DREAM Fund, 1999—. Staff sergeant US Army. Recipient Excellence award, Am. Women in Radio and TV, 2006. Mem. Assn. Broadcasting Execs. Tex. (pres. 1975-76), Am. Women in Radio and TV, Inc. (bd. dirs. 1992-93), Dallas Ad League. Republican. Avocations: skiing, sailing. Office: The Richards Group 8750 N Central Expy Ste 1200 Dallas TX 75231-6436 Office Phone: 214-891-5843. Business E-Mail: Larry_Spiegel@richards.com.

SPIEGEL, LINDA F., lawyer; b. Bronx, NY, Mar. 13, 1953; d. Rubin E. and Edna (Zucker) S.; m. Paul Duboff, June 12, 1983; 1 child, Joshua Michael. AB, Columbia U., 1974; JD, Boston U., 1978. Bar: N.J. 1978, U.S. Dist. Ct. N.J. 1978, N.Y. 1980, U.S. Dist. Ct. (so. and ea. dists.) N.Y. 1980, U.S. Supreme Ct. 1982. Tax editor Prentice Hall, Englewood, N.J., 1978; pvt. practice, Hackensack, N.J., 1978-83, 88—; assoc. Friedman, Carney & Wilson, Newark, 1983-84; pvt. practice New Milford, N.J., 1984-85; assoc. LaFianza and Strull, Hackensack, 1985-87, ptnr., 1987-88. Instr. Inst. Legal Asst. and Paralegal Tng., Mahwah, NJ, 1978—81; chair Bergen County Youth Svcs. Commn., 2003—04. Spkr. Boy Scouts Am., Bergen, N.J., 1980; atty.-acct. divsn. United Jewish Cmty., River Edge, N.J., 1978—; trustee Women's Am. Orgn. Rehab. through Tng., 1987-88; chmn. Jean Robertson Women Lawyers Scholarship Found., Inc., 1987-94. Mem. ABA, Am. Arbitration Assn. (comml. and constrn. arbitator 1989—), N.J. Women Lawyers Assn., N.J. State Bar Assn., Bergen County Bar Assn. (trustee 1989-94, editor-in-chief Bergen Barrister 1991-94), Women Lawyers in Bergen County (pres. 1987-89, editor-in-chief newsletter 2003—), B'nai Brith. Democrat. Avocations: theater, tennis, swimming, square and country dancing. Office: 79 Main St Ste 1 Hackensack NJ 07601-7126 Office Phone: 201-489-1001. E-mail: lfsesq@aol.com. *Notable cases include: A.L. vs. P.A., 213 N.J. Super 391, 1986, cert. den 107, J.J. 110, 1987.*

SPIEGEL, MELVIN, retired biology professor; s. Philip Edward and Sadie (Friedman) S.; m. Evelyn Sclufer, Apr. 16, 1955; children: Judith Ellen, Rebecca Ann. BS, U. Ill., 1948; PhD, U. Rochester, 1952; MA (hon.), Dartmouth Coll. Research fellow U. Rochester, 1952-53, Calif. Inst. Tech., 1953-55, 64-65; asst. prof. Colby Coll., 1955-59; mem. faculty Dartmouth Coll., Hanover, NH, 1959—, prof. biology, 1966-93; prof. emeritus Dartmouth Coll, Hanover, NH; chmn. dept. biol. scis. Dartmouth Coll., Hanover, NH, 1972-74. Summer investigator Marine Biol. Lab., Woods Hole, Mass., 1954—; sr. rsch. biologist U. Calif.-San Diego, 1970-71; vis. prof. biochemistry Nat. Inst. Med. Rsch., Mill Hill, London, 1971; vis. prof. Biocenter, U. Basel, 1979-82, 85; Wilson Meml. lectr. U. N.C., 1975; program dir. developmental biology NSF, 1975-76; mem. cell biology study sect. NIH, 1966-70 Editl. bd.: Biol. Bull., 1966-70, 71-75, Cell Differentiation, 1979-88; contbr. articles to profl. jours. Trustee Marine Biol. Lab. Corp.; mem. exec. com., trustee Marine Biol. Lab., 1976-80. Fellow AAAS; mem. Am. Soc. Cell Biology, Am. Soc. Devel. Biology, Internat. Soc. Devel. Biologists (sec.-treas. 1977-81, bd. dirs. 1981-85). Home Phone: 603-643-4353. E-mail: melvin.spiegel@dartmouth.edu.

SPIEGEL, PHYLLIS, public relations consultant, journalist; b. Bronx, NY; d. Bernard and Lillian (Horowitz) Finkelberg; m. Stanley Spiegel, Sept. 20, 1959 (div. 1981); children: Mark, Adam. BA, NYU. Feature writer various newspapers, pubs., 1960's-70's; dir. pub. rels. Mort Barish Assocs., Princeton, NJ, 1975-80; account exec. pub. rels. Keyes Martin, Springfield, NJ, 1980-84; pres. Phyllis Spiegel Assocs., Plainsboro, NJ, 1984—. Pub. rels. dir., founder Red Oak Coop. Nursery Sch., Middletown, N.J., 1960's, Matawan (N.J.) Student Enrichment Program, 1960s-70s; pub. rels. cons., event organizer New Philharm. of N.J., Morristown, 1991-93; mem. Child Placement Rev. Bd. of Family Ct., Mercer County, N.J., 1994-98. Recipient Commendation from Gov. N.J. for U. Med. and Dentistry of N.J. campaign, 1983, Commendation for N.J. Pharm. Assn. campaign Pub. Rels. News Assn., 1979. Mem.: Soc. Humanistic Judaism (bd. dir. 1983—85). Avocations: film and theatre, classical music, reading, travel, walks. Office: Phyllis Spiegel Assocs PO Box 243 Plainsboro NJ 08536-0243

SPIEGEL, SIEGMUND, architect; b. Gera, Germany, Nov. 13, 1919; came to US, 1938, naturalized, 1941. s. Jakob and Sara (Precker) S.; m. Ruth Josias, Apr. 13, 1945; children: Sandra Renee, Deborah Joan. Student, Coll. City NY, 1939—40, Columbia U., NYC, 1945—50; DHL (hon.), Hofstra U., Hempstead, NY, 1993. Registered arch., NY, NJ, Mass., Md., Va., Pa., Conn., Ga., Vt., Tenn., NH, Fla.; lic. profl. planner, NJ. Draftsman Mayer & Whittlesey, Archs., NYC, 1941-47, office mgr., 1947-55; pvt. practice arch. East Meadow, N.Y., 1956—. Author: The Spiegel Plan; contbr. articles to Progressive Arch.; prin. works include Syosset Hosp., NY, 1962, Reliance Fed. Savs. and Loan Assn. Bank, Queens, NY, 1961, Louden Hall Psychiat. Hosp., 1963, Human Resources Sch., Albertson, NY, 1964, Nassau Ctr. for Emotionally Disturbed Children, 1968, Harbor Club Apt., Babylon, NY, 1968, Reliance Fed. Bank, Albertson, 1967, North Isle Club and Apt. Cmty., Coram, NY, 1972, County Fed. Savs. & Loan Assn., Commack, NY, 1972, Birchwood Glen Apt. Cmty., Holtsville, NY, 1972, Bayside Fed. Savs. & Loan Bank Plaza, Patchogue, NY, 1973, L.E. Woodward Sch. for Emotionally Disturbed Children, Freeport, NY, 1974, Birchwood Sagamore Hills, Blue Ridge and Bretton Woods Condominium Cmtys., Coram, NY, 1975, Maple Arms Condos, Westbury, NY, 1982, Dept. Pub. Works, Freeport, NY, Nuc. Molecular Resonance Bldg., 1983. Served with AUS, 1941-45, ETO. Decorated Purple Heart, Bronze Star, Croix de Guerre with palme (Belgium); recipient grand prize for instnl. bldgs. (for Syosset Hosp.), LI Assn., 1963, grand prize Human Resources Sch., 1966, grand prize Stony Brook Profl. Bldg., 1966, Beautification award, Town Hempstead, NY, 1969, Archi award for Harbour Club Apts., LI Assn., 1970, for Birchwood Blue Ridge Condominiums, 1974, Dr. Martin Luther King Jr. award Nassau County, 1986, Louise E. Yavner award NY State Bd. Regents, 1992; fellow Acad. Mktg. Sci., LI U., 1971. Mem. AIA, N.Y. State Assn. Archs., East Meadow C. of C. (pres. 1966), Kiwanis Club. Home and Office: Carlton Terr 6-D 10245 Collins Ave Bal Harbour FL 33154-1407 Personal E-mail: sigaia@aol.com.

SPIEGELBERG, EMMA JO, business education educator, academic administrator; b. Mt. View, Wyo., Nov. 22, 1936; d. Joseph Clyde and Dorcas (Reese) Hatch; m. James Walter Spiegelberg, June 22, 1957; children: William L., Emory Walter, Joseph John. BA with honors, U. Wyo., 1958, MEd, 1985; EdD, Boston U., 1990. Tchr. bus. edn. Laramie H.S., Wyo., 1960—61, 1965—93, adminstr., 1993—97; prin. McCormick Jr. H.S., Cheyenne, 1997—2002; exec. dir. Wyo. Assn. Secondary Sch. Prins., 2001—. Author: Branigan's Accounting Simulation, 1986, London & Co. II, 1993; co-author: Glencoe Computerized Accounting, 1993, 2d edit., 1995, Microcomputer Accounting: Daceasy, 1994, Microcomputer Accounting: Peachtree, 1994, 3d edit., 2000, Microcomputer Accounting: Accpac, 1994, Computerized Accounting with Peachtree, 1995, 2000, 02. Bd. dir. Cathedral Home for Children, Laramie, 1967-70, 72—, pres., 1985-88, Laramie Plains Mus., 1970-79. Named Wyo. Bus. Tchr. of Yr., 1982, Wyo. Asst. Prin. of Yr., 1997. Mem.: NASSP, NEA, Wyo. Assn. Secondary Sch. Prins. (sec., treas. 1997—2001), Albany County Edn. Assn. (sec. 1970—71), Wyo. Edn. Assn., Wyo. Bus. Edn. Assn. (pres. 1979—80, Hall of Fame 2004), Internat. Soc. Bus. Edn. (rep. Mt. Plains chpt. 2006—07), Mt. Plains Bus. Edn. Assn. (Wyo. rep. to bd. dirs. 1982—85, pres. 1987—88, Sec. Tchr. of Yr. 1991, Leadership award 1992), Nat. Bus. Edn. Assn. (bd. dir. 1987—88, 1991—96, Sec. Tchr. of Yr. 1991), Wyo. Vocat. Assn. (exec. bd. 1978—80, pres. 1981—82, exec. sec. 1986—89, Outstanding Contbns. to Vocat. Edn. award 1983, Tchr. of Yr. 1985), Am. Vocat. Assn. (policy com. region V 1984—87, region V Tchr. of Yr. 1986), U. Wyo. Alumni Assn. (bd. dir. 1985—90, pres. 1988—89), Laramie C. of C. (bd. dir. 1985—88), Zonta (v.p. 2002—03, pres. 2003—04, dist. 12 parliamentarian 2004—06, bd. dirs. 2007—), Delta Pi Epsilon, Pi Lambda Theta, Chi Omega, Alpha Delta Kappa (state pres. 1978—82), Phi Delta Kappa, Kappa Delta Pi. Episcopalian. Home: 3301 Grays Gable Rd Laramie WY 82072-5031 Office Phone: 307-745-5468. Personal E-mail: jwejspiegelberg@aol.com.

SPIEGELBERG, HARRY LESTER, retired paper company executive; b. New London, Wis., Apr. 24, 1936; s. Harry Henry and Gladys Louise (Kalt) Spiegelberg; m. Bonnie Faye Ludden, Jan. 23, 1960; children: Susan Faye Spiegelberg Schuldes, Sharon Louise Spiegelberg Kozlowski, Stephen Harry, Scott Charles. BSChemE, U. Wis., 1959; MS, Inst. Paper Chemistry, Appleton, Wis., 1963, PhD, 1966; MBA, U. Chgo., 1980. Tchg. asst. U. Wis. Coll. Engring., Madison, 1957-59; engr. Kimberly-Clark Corp., Neenah, Wis., 1959-61, rsch. scientist, 1965-68, mgr. new concepts, 1968-73, dir. R & D, 1973-84, v.p. consumer tissue rsch., 1985-92, v.p. tech. and patent strategy, 1992-93, v.p. tech. transfer, 1993-96; ret., 1996. Mem., past chmn. indsl. liaison coun. Coll. Engring., 1987—93; founder, chmn. Paper Industry Internat. Hall of Fame; past pres. Ctr. Project Inc. Paper industry bus. columnist:; contbr. chapters to books; patentee in nonwovens and tissue fields. Mem. U. Wis. Found. Capt. C.E. USAR, 1959—67. Recipient Disting. Svc. citation, U. Wis., 1986, Disting. Alumni award, 2007. Congregationalist. Avocations: bicycling, backpacking, kayaking, antique farm equipment. Home: 3624 S Barker Ln Appleton WI 54915-7038 E-mail: hspiegel@new.rr.com.

SPIEGELMAN, ART, writer, cartoonist; b. Stockholm, Feb. 15, 1948; s. Wladek and Anzia (Zylberberg) S.; m. Francoise Mouly, July 12, 1977; children: Nadja, Dashiell. Student, Harpur Coll. (now SUNY), Binghamton, NY. Creative cons., artist, designer, editor, writer Topps Chewing Gum, Inc., Bklyn., 1966-88; editor Douglas Comix, 1972; contbg. editor Arcade, the Comics Revue, 1975-76; founding editor Raw, 1980—; artist, contbg. editor New Yorker, 1992—2003. Instr. San Francisco Acad. Art, 1974-75, N.Y. Sch. Visual Arts, 1979-87. Author, illustrator: The Complete Mr. Infinity, 1970, The Viper Vicar of Vice, Villainy, and Vickedness, 1972, Ace Hole, Midge Detective, 1974, The Language of Comics, 1974, Breakdowns: From Maus to Now: An Anthology of Strips, 1977, Work and Turn, 1979, Every Day Has Its Dog, 1979, Two-Fisted Painters Action Adventure, 1980, Maus: A Survivor's Tale, 1986 (Joel M. Cavior award for Jewish Writing 1986, Nat. Book Critics Cir. nomination 1986, Pulitzer prize 1992), Maus, Part Two, 1992 (Nat. Book Critics Cir. nomination 1992, Pulitzer prize 1992), Open Me.I'm a Dog!, 1997; (with J.M. March) The Wild Party, 1994, Kisses from New York; (with F. Mouly) Read Yourself Raw, 1987, In the Shadow of No Towers, 2004 (named one of the 100 Notable Books of 2004, NY Times Book Review); contbr. The Apex Treasury of Underground Comics, 1974; compiling editor (with B. Schneider) Whole Grains: A Book of Quotations, 1972; creator (with composer Phillip Johnston) Drawn to Death: A Three Panel Opera, Am. Repertory Theatre Co., Cambridge, Mass.; editor (comic series) Little Lit; exhbns. include N.Y. Cultural Ctr., Inst. Contemporary Art, London, Seibu Gallery, Tokyo, Mus. Modern Art, N.Y.C., 1991, Galerie St. Etienne, N.Y.C., 1992, Ft. Lauderdale Mus. Art, 1993; creator Wacky Packages, Garbage Pail Kids and other novelties; contbr. to numerous underground comics. Recipient Playboy Editorial award for best comic strip, 1982, Yellow Kid award for best comic strip author, 1982, Regional Design award Print mag., 1983, 84, 85, Inkpot award San Diego Comics Conv., 1987, Stripschappening award for best fgn. comics album, 1987, Alpha Art award Angoulerne, France, 1993; Named one of Time Mag. 100 Most Influential People, 2005. Office: c/o The Steven Barclay Agency 321 Pleasant St Petaluma CA 94952-2648 Office Phone: 888-965-7323.

SPIEGLER, JOSEPH ANDREW, lawyer; b. LI, NY, Apr. 4, 1968; BA magna cum laude, NYU, 1990; JD, U. Notre Dame, 1994. Bar: Ill. 1994, US Dist. Ct. (no. dist. Ill.). Ptnr. Winston & Strawn, Chgo., 1994—2007, Much Shelist, Chgo., 2007—. Office: Much Shelist 191 N Wacker Dr Chicago IL 60606-1615 Office Phone: 312-521-2765. Business E-Mail: jspiegler@muchshelist.com.

SPIELBERG, STEPHEN PAUL, dean, educator; b. 1945; m. Laurel A. Spielberg. AB, Princeton U., 1966; PhD in pharmacology, U. Chgo., 1971; MD, U. Chgo. Pritzker Sch. Medicine, 1973. Pediat. resident Children's Hosp. Med. Ctr., Boston, 1974—75; instr. to asst. prof. pediat. & pharmacology Johns Hopkins U. Sch. Medicine, 1971—81; assoc. prof. to prof. pediat. & pharmacology U. Toronto, 1981—92, dir. Ctr. for Drug Safety Rsch., 1988—92; sr. scientist rsch. inst. Hosp. for Sick Children, Toronto, established & headed div. pediat. clin. pharmacology and toxicology, 1987—92; exec. dir. exploratory biochemical toxicology and clin. and regulatory develop. Merck Labs., 1992—97; v.p. pediat. drug develop. Johnson & Johnson Pharm. Rsch. & Develop., Titusville, NJ, 1997—2003, established dept. of pediat. drug develop.; v.p. health affairs Dartmouth Coll., 2003—; dean & prof. pediat. and pharmacology and taxicology Dartmouth Med. Sch., 2003—. Adj. prof. pediat., medicine and pharmacology Thomas Jefferson U.; adj. prof. pediat. Robert Wood Johnson Med. Sch.; mem. adv. bd. PediaLink; mem. Fed. Adv. Com., Nat. Children's Study, Nat. Inst. of Child Health and Human Develop.; chair Pediat. Task Force, Pharm. Rsch. and Mfr. of Am.; bd. dirs. Found. for NIH; mem. panel on ethics and pediat. clin. trials Inst. Medicine; mem. pediat. adv. subcom. FDA; mem. sci. adv. bd. Elizabeth Glaser Pediat. Rsch. Network. Recipient Rawls-Palmer Award, Am. Soc. for Clin. Pharmacology and Therapeutics, 1992, Werner Kalow Award for Pharmacogenetics and Drug Safety, 1995, William B. Abrams Award and Lectureship, FDA & Am. Soc. for Clin. Pharmacology and Therapeutics, 2001, Exceptional Service Award, Pharm. Rsch. and Mfr. of Am., 2003. Fellow: Nat. Inst. of Child Health and Human Develop. Office: Dartmouth Med Sch 1 Rope Ferry Rd Hanover NH 03755

SPIELBERG, STEVEN (ALLAN), film director, producer; b. Cin., Dec. 18, 1946; m. Amy Irving, Nov. 27, 1985 (div. Feb. 2, 1989); 1 child: Max Samuel; m. Kate Capshaw Oct. 12, 1991; children: Theo (adopted), Sasha, Sawyer, Mikaela (adopted), Destry, Jessica (stepchild). BA, Calif. State U., Long Beach; D of creative arts (hon.), Brandeis U., 1986; DHL (hon.), Yale U., 2002. Founder Amblin Entertainment, 1984—; co-founder (with Jeffrey Katzenberg & David Geffen), ptnr. DreamWorks SKG, Universal City, 1994—. Co-founder DreamWorks SKG, 1995—2005; co-creator of concept, story and design of new game franchises EA Games, LA, 2005—. Dir.: (films) The Last Gun, 1959, Jaws, 1975, 1941, 1979, Raiders of the Lost Ark, 1981 (Acad. Award nomination for best dir., 1982), Indiana Jones and the Temple of Doom, 1984, Indiana Jones and the Last Crusade, 1989, Hook, 1991, Jurassic Park, 1993, The Lost World: Jurassic Park, 1997, Minority Report, 2002, War of the Worlds, 2005; (TV films) Columbo: Murder by the Book, 1971, Duel, 1971, Something Evil, 1972, Savage, 1973, (episodes for TV series) The Name of the Game, 1968, Marcus Welby, M.D., 1969, Night Gallery, 1970, The Psychiatrist, 1971, Owen Marshall: Counselor at Law, 1971; exec. prodr.: (films) I Wanna Hold Your Hand, 1978, Used Cars, 1980, Continental Divide, 1981, Gremlins, 1984, Back to the Future, 1985, Young Sherlock Holmes, 1985, The Money Pit, 1986, An American Tail, 1986, Innerspace, 1987, *batteries not included, 1987, Who Framed Roger Rabbit, 1988, The Land Before Time, 1988, Tummy Trouble, 1989, Dad, 1989, Back to the Future Part II, 1989, Joe Versus the Volcano, 1990, Yume, 1990, Back to the Future Part III, 1990, Roller Coaster Rabbit, 1990, Gremlins 2: The New Batch, 1990, Arachnophobia, 1990, Trail Mix-Up, 1993, We're Back! A Dinosaur's Story, 1993, I'm Mad, 1994, The Flinstones, 1994, Casper, 1995, Balto, 1995, Twister, 1996, The Lost Children of Berlin, 1997, Men in Black, 1997, Deep Impact, 1998, The Mask of Zorro, 1998, The Last Days, 1998, The Haunting, 1999, Eyes of the Holocaust, 2000, Jurassic Park III, 2001, Price for Peace, 2002, Men in Black II, 2002, The Legend of Zorro, 2005, Monster House, 2006, Disturbia, 2007, Transformers, 2007; (TV films) Class of '61, 1993, Survivors of the Holocaust, 1996, Shooting War, 2000, Semper Fi, 2001, We Stand Alone Together, 2001, Burma Bridge Busters, 2003, Dan Finnerty & the Dan Band: I Am Women, 2005; (TV miniseries) Band of Brothers, 2001 (Emmy for outstanding miniseries, 2002), Broken Silence, 2002, Taken, 2002 (Emmy for outstanding miniseries, 2003), Into the West, 2005; (TV series) The Plucky Duck Show, 1992, Family Dog, 1992, SeaQuest DSV, 1993—96, ER, 1994, Pinky and the Brain, 1995—98, Freakazoid!, 1995—97, Toonsylvania, 1998—2000, Pinky, Elmyra & the Brain, 1998, On the Lot, 2007; prodr.: (films) An American Tail: Fievel Goes West, 1991; writer (films) Ace Eli and Rodger of the Skies, 1973, dir., prodr. E.T. the Extra-Terrestrial, 1982 (Acad. Award nomination for best dir., 1983, Acad. Award nomination for best picture, 1983), Twilight Zone: The Movie, 1983, The Color Purple, 1985 (Acad. Award nomination for best picture, 1986), Empire of the Sun, 1987, Always, 1989, Schindler's List, 1993 (Acad. Award for best dir., 1994, Acad. Award for best picture, 1994, Golden Globe for best dir., 1994), Amistad, 1997, Saving Private Ryan, 1998 (Acad. Award for best dir., 1999, Acad. Award nomination for best picture, 1999, Golden Globe for best dir., 1999, Disting. Pub. Svc. Award USN, 1999), Catch Me If You Can, 2002, The Terminal, 2004, Munich, 2005, dir., writer Fighter Squad, 1961, Escape to Nowhere, 1961, Firelight, 1964, Slipstream, 1967, Amblin', 1968, The Sugarland Express, 1974, Close Encounters of the Third Kind, 1977 (Acad. Award nomination for best dir., 1978); prodr.: (films) Memoirs of a Geisha, 2005, Flags of Our Fathers, 2006, Letters from Iwo Jima, 2006; prodr., writer (films) Poltergeist, 1982, exec. prodr., writer The Goonies, 1985, (TV series) Amazing Stories, 1985—87, Tiny Toon Adventures, 1990—92, Animaniacs, 1993—98, dir., prodr., writer Artificial Intelligence: AI, 2001, asst. dir. action scenes (films) Star Wars III: Revenge of the Sith, 2005. Mem. adv. bd. Sci. Fiction Mus. and Hall of Fame. Recipient Man of Yr. award Hasty Pudding Theater, Harvard U., 1983, Outstanding Directorial Achievement award for feature films Dirs. Guild Am., 1985, Film award Brit. Acad. Film and TV Arts, 1986, Irving Thalberg Mem. award Acad. Motion Picture Arts and Scis., 1987, Golden Lion award for career achievement Venice Film Festival, 1993, Life Achievement award Am. Film Inst., 1995, John Huston award Artists Rights Found., 1995, Kennedy Ctr. Honor, John F. Kennedy Center for Performing Arts, 2006; named Entertainment Weekly's Most Powerful Person in Entertainment, 1997, Lifetime Achievement award, Dir. Guild Am., 2000; named one of 50 Most Powerful People in Hollywood Premiere mag., 2004-06, Forbes' Richest Americans, 1999—, World's Richest People, Forbes mag. 2001—, 100 Top Celebrities, Forbes mag., 2001—, 100 Most Powerful Celebrities, 2007; knighted Order of British Empire, 2001. Fellow Brit. Acad. Film and TV Arts. Achievements include winning film contest with 40-minute war movie, Escape to Nowhere, at age 13; made film Firelight at age 16, and made 5 films while in coll.; became TV dir. at Universal Pictures at age 20. Office: Creative Artists Agy 9830 Wilshire Blvd Beverly Hills CA 90212-1804 *

SPIELBERGER, CHARLES DONALD, psychologist, educator; b. Atlanta, Mar. 28, 1927; s. A.R. and Eleanor (Wachman) S.; m. Carol Lee, June 4, 1971. BS, Ga. Inst. Tech., 1949; BA, U. Iowa, 1951, MA, 1953, PhD, 1954. Asst. prof. med. psychology Duke U., Durham, N.C., 1955-58, from asst. prof. to assoc. prof. psychology, 1955-63; prof. psychology Vanderbilt U., Nashville, 1963-66; tng. specialist in psychology NIMH, Bethesda, Md., 1965-67; prof. psychology, dir. clin. training program Fla. State U., Tallahassee, 1967-72; prof. psychology U. South Fla., Tampa, 1972—85, dir. clin. tng., 1972—78, disting. univ. rsch. prof., 1985—. Fellow Netherlands Inst. for Advanced Study, Wassenaar, 1979-80, 85-86; cons. FAA, NIMH, VA, USAF, others. Author: Anxiety and Behavior, 1966, Understanding Stress and Anxiety, 1979, Anxiety in Sports, 1989, Test Anxiety: Theory, Assessment and Treatment, 1995; editor: Stress and Anxiety Series, 1975; editor: (gen.) Centennial Psychology Series, 1979—; editor: (in-chief) Encyclopedia of Applied Psychology, 2004—. Named Disting. scholar U. South Fla., 1973, Disting. Sci. Contbr., Fla. Psychol. Assn., 1977, 88, Outstanding Faculty Rschr., U. South Fla., 1985. Fellow APA (pres. 1991-92, nat. treas. 1987-90, nat. coun. v.p. 1994-99, 2001-, pres. divsn. clin. psychology 1989, pres. divsn. cmty. psychol. 1975-76, pres. divsn. internat. psychol., 2002, Disting. Sci. Contbr. to Cmty. Psychology 1982, Disting. Sci. and Prof. Contbr. Clin. Psychology 1989, Disting. Contbr. Edn. Psychology 1992, Disting. Contbr. Profl. Practice 1993, APA/APF Gold Medal Disting. Contbr., 2003, Disting. Contbr. Internat. Psychology, 2005 pres. divsn. media psychol., 2005); mem. Southeastern Psychol. Assn. (pres. 1975-76), Soc. for Personality Assessment (pres. 1986-89, Disting. Sci. Contbr. 1990), Nat. Coun. Sci. Soc. Presidents (chair 1996-2000), Internat. Stress Mgmt. Assn. (pres. 1992-2000), Internat. Coun. Psychologists (pres. 1986-87), Internat. Assn. Applied Psychology (pres. 1998-2002, Wundt James Disting. Contbr. award), Stars & Anxiety Rsch. Soc. (pres. 1980-84), Psi Chi (nat. pres. 1980-83). Home: 11313 Carrollwood Dr Tampa FL 33618-3703 Office: U South Fla Dept Psychology Tampa FL 33620 Business E-Mail: spielber@cas.usf.edu.

SPIELER, EMILY A., dean, law educator; AB, Radcliffe Coll., Harvard U., 1969; JD, Yale U., 1973. Ptnr. Women's Law Collective, Cambridge, Mass.; spl. asst. atty. gen. Mass. Dept. Pub. Health's Lead Poisoning Prevention Div.; commr. W.Va. Workers' Compensation Fund; first dep. atty. gen. for civil rights Govt. W.Va., mem. Human Rights Commn.; Hale J. and Roscoe P. Posten Prof. Law W.Va. U., 1990—2002; dean Northeastern U. Sch. Law, 2002—. Com. mem. U.S. Department of Energy, Nat. Inst. Occupl. Safety and Health. Contbr. articles to law jours. Recipient Fulbright award, 2001, Martin Luther King Jr. Advocacy of Justice Award. Mem.: NAS, Nat. Acad. Soc. Insurance. Office: Northeastern U Sch Law 120 Knowles Ctr 400 Huntington Ave Boston MA 02115 Home Phone: 617-739-3960; Office Phone: 617-373-3307. Office Fax: 617-373-8793. Business E-Mail: e.spieler@neu.edu.

SPIELER, RICHARD EARL, oceanographer, educator; b. Washington, Mar. 11, 1942; s. Ernst Henry Spieler and Gladys Gnegy; m. Janice Schact (div.); children: Lara L., Lisel R. BA, U. Md., 1963; BS, Ark. State U., 1970, MS, 1971; PhD, La. State U., 1975. Curator fishies Milw. Pub. Mus., 1975—91; assoc. prof. Nova S.E. U., Ft. Lauderdale, Fla., 1991—96, prof., 1996—, dir. Guy Harvey Rsch. Inst., 1999—2002, dir. acad. programs, 2006—. Cons. fish ecology, physiology, 1991—. Contbr. articles to profl. jours. Lt. col. USAFR, 1963—92. Avocations: sailing, scuba diving, reading, hiking. Office: Nova Southeastern Univ Oceangraphic Ctr 8000 N Ocean Dr Dania Beach FL 33004 Office Phone: 954-262-3613.

SPIELMAN, RICHARD SAUL, genetics educator; b. NYC, Feb. 25, 1946; s. Ralph and Beatrice C. (Kramer) S.; m. Vivian G. Cheung. AB, Harvard Coll., 1967; PhD, U. Mich., 1971. Rsch. assoc. U. Mich., Ann Arbor, 1971-74; from asst. prof. to prof. U. Pa., Phila., 1974—. Office: U Pa Sch Medicine Dept Genetics 415 Curie Blvd Philadelphia PA 19104-4218

SPIELVOGEL, SIDNEY MEYER, investment banker; b. NYC, July 14, 1925; s. Hyman and Rae (Mandel) S.; m. Beverly Anne Gold, Dec. 18, 1960; 1 son, Peter James. BSS., CCNY, 1944; A.M., Harvard U., Cambridge, Mass., 1946, MBA, 1949. Economist Treasury Dept., Washington, 1946-47; assoc. dept. mgr. Alexander's Dept. Stores, 1949-53; asst. to mdse. mgr., dept. mgr. Bloomingdale's Dept. Store, 1953-56; with Prudential-Bache Securities Inc., 1956-88, 1st v.p., 1971-75, sr. v.p., 1975-85, mng. dir., 1986-88. Dir. MoneyMart Assets Inc., 1976-96, pres., 1981-87; lectr. Hunter Coll., N.Y.C., 1963-68, The New Sch., 1993-96. Bd. dirs. Emanu-el Midtown YM-YWHA, N.Y.C., 1975-91; mem. Harvard Grad. Soc. Coun., 1983-88, 89-92, 94—, chmn., 1985-87. Recipient Outstanding Svc. award, Harvard Alumni Assn., 2006. Mem. Harvard Club (N.Y.C.), Harvard Bus. Sch. Club (N.Y.C.), World Trade Center Club (N.Y.C.), Phi Beta Kappa. Home: 245 E 19th St New York NY 10003-2639 Office: Corp Capital Cons Inc 730 Fifth Ave New York NY 10019

SPIERER, ROBERT, family practice physician; b. S.I., NY, June 26, 1945; s. Efram and Regina (Stern) Spierer; m. Marilyn J Borak, July 7, 1968; children: Sharon, Henry, Eric. BA, Columbia U., 1967; MD, Albert Einstein Coll. Medicine, 1971. Diplomate Am Bd. Family Medicine, Am. Bd. Pediatrics, Am. Bd. Emergency Medicine, Am. Bd. Internal Medicine, cert. added qualification in geriatrics Am. Bd. Internal Medicine. Intern Montefiore Med. Ctr., Bronx, NY, 1971-72, resident in pediatrics, 1972-73, 1975-76; resident in internal medicine U. Medicine and Dentistry of N.J., Newark, 1976-77; physician Edison (N.J.) Med. Group, 1977-98, Monroe Medical Group, 1999—. With USPHS, 1973—75. Office: Monroe Med Group 369 Applegarth Rd Monroe Township NJ 08831-3732 Office Phone: 609-395-1900.

SPIERINGS, EGILIUS LEONARDUS HENDRICUS, pharmacologist, neurologist, headache specialist, clinical trialist; b. Helmond, The Netherlands, Aug. 16, 1953; came to U.S., 1986; s. Egilius L.H. and Johanna A. (Schellekens) S.; m. Maria K.B. Zarska, Dec. 27, 1976; children: Sven E.J., Natalia M.K. BS cum laude, Erasmus U., Rotterdam, The Netherlands, 1974, MD, 1978, PhD in Experimental Pharmacology, 1980. Registered in medicine, cert. in neurology The Netherlands; lic. physician Mass. Intern in neurosurgery Univ. Hosp., Rotterdam, Netherlands, 1980-81, resident in neurology, 1982—84; fellow in headache mgmt. Headache Rsch. Found., Boston, 1981-82; resident in psychiatry Hippolytus Hosp., Delft, Netherlands, 1985; asst. prof. neurology Tufts U. Sch. Medicine, Boston, 1986-90; dir. Headache Rsch. Found., 1986—89, John R. Graham Headache Ctr., 1987—90; dir. headache sect. dept. neurology Brigham & Women's Hosp., 1990—94, dir. headache rsch. dept. neurology, 1994—96; dir. Boston Clin. Rsch. Ctr., Wellesley Hills, 1996—2003, Medvadis Rsch. Corp., 2003—; chief sci. officer H. Capnia, Inc., 2004—. Lectr. neurology Harvard Med. Sch., 1990-99, assoc. clin. prof. neurology, 1999—; spkr. in field. Author: The Pathophysiology of the Migraine Attack, 1980, Migraine, 1986, Migraine Questions & Answers, 1995, 2d edit., 2001, Management of Migraine, 1996, Headache, 1998; co-author: Hoofdpijn, 1984; sect. editor Office Practice of Neurology, 1996, 2003; editor: De Pathogenese van Migraine, 1982; contbr. numerous articles to profl. jours. and chpts. to books, over 40 radio and TV appearances. Edn. dir. Headache Coop. New Eng., 1991-2003. Fellow Am. Assn. Study of Headache (bd. dirs. 1991-93); mem. Netherlands Migraine Found. (bd. dirs. 1980-85), Netherlands Soc. Migraine Patients (bd. dirs. 1982-86), Internat. Headache Soc. (bd. dirs. 1985-86, assoc. editor Cephalagia, 1986-89). Home: 24 Algonquian Dr Natick MA 01760-6095 Office: 25 Walnut St Ste 400 Wellesley Hills MA 02481 Office Phone: 781-431-1113. Business E-Mail: spierings@medvadis.com.

SPIERKEL, GREGORY M., information technology executive; b. 1957; BA, Carleton U., Ottawa, Can.; MBA, Georgetown U.; attended, Advanced Manufacturing Program at INSEAD, Fontainbleau, France. Mng. dir. Mitel Telecom, United Kingdom, 1986—89; gen. mgr. Mitel Far East Ltd., Hong Kong, 1989—90; pres., CEO, N. Am. Mitel Inc., Reston, Va., 1992—96, v.p., global sales and marketing Canada, 1996—97; sr. v.p., pres. Ingram Micro Inc., Santa Ana, Calif., 1997—99; pres. Ingram Micro Asia-Pacific, 1997—99; exec. v.p. Ingram Micro Inc., 1999—2004, officer, 1997—; pres. Ingram Micro Europe, 1999—2004, Ingram Micro Inc., 2004—05, CEO, 2005—. Bd. mem. Sch. Bus., U. Calif., Irvine. Office: Ingram Micro Inc 1600 E St Andrew Pl Santa Ana CA 92705-4931 Office Phone: 714-566-1000. Office Fax: 714-566-7900. *

SPIERS, RONALD IAN, diplomat; b. Orange, NJ, July 9, 1925; s. Thomas Hoskins and Blanca (De Ponthier) S.; m. Patience Baker, June 11, 1949; children: Deborah Wood, Peter, Martha, Sarah. BA, Dartmouth Coll., 1948; M in Pub. Affairs, Princeton U., 1950. With AEC, 1950-54; officer-in-charge disarmament and arms control Dept. State, Washington, 1955-61, dir. NATO affairs, 1962-66; polit. counselor Am. Embassy, London, 1966-69; asst. sec. for Politico-Mil. Affairs U.S. Dept. State, 1969-73; amb. to Bahamas, Am. Embassy, Nassau, 1973-74, dep. chief of mission London, 1974-77; U.S. permanent rep. to CENTO Coun., 1977-79; amb. to Turkey, Am. Embassy, Ankara, 1977-80; asst. sec. for intelligence and rsch., mem. U.S. Intelligence Bd. U.S. Dept. State, Washington, 1980-81; amb. to Pakistan, Am. Embassy, Islamabad, 1981-83; under-sec. for mgmt. U.S. Dept. State, 1983-89; under-sec. gen. for polit. affairs UN, NYC, 1989-92; internat. affairs cons. Dept. State, 1992—. Career ambassador U.S. Fgn. Svc., 1984. Served to lt. (j.g.) USN, 1943-46, PTO. Woodrow Wilson fellow Princeton U., 1948. Fellow Nat. Acad. of Pub. Adminstrn.; mem. Am. Fgn. Svc. Assn., Internat. Inst. Strategic Studies, Coun. on Fgn. Rels., Am. Acad. of Diplomacy, Washington Inst. Fgn. Affairs. Home: 1320 Middletown Rd South Londonderry VT 05155-9145 E-mail: rispiers@comcast.net.

SPIERS-LOPEZ, PERNILLE (PERNILLE LOPEZ), consumer products company executive; b. Denmark; arrived in US, 1984; m. Jason Lopez, 1989; 2 children. With Door Store, Coral Gables, Fla., Stor (purchased by IKEA); sales mgr. West Coast stores IKEA, 1991—93, store mgr. Pitts., 1993—97, head, human resources, 1997—2003; pres. IKEA N. Am., Plymouth Meeting, Pa., 2001—. Bd. trustees Save the Children. Named one of America's Top Women in Bus.-Game Changers, Pink mag. & Forté Found., 2007; recipient Nat. Working Parent award, Terri Lynne Lokoff Child Care Found., 2005. Office: IKEA N America Plymouth Commons 496 W Germantown Pike Plymouth Meeting PA 19462 Office Phone: 800-434-4532. *

SPIES, FRANK STADLER, lawyer; b. Adrian, Mich., Aug. 7, 1939; s. Charles F. and Lucille M. (Stadler) S.; m. Lynette K. Wells, July 25, 1964; children: Anne, Jane, Charles. BBA, U. Mich., 1961, LLB, 1964. Bar: Mich. 1964, U.S. Dist. Ct. (we. dist.) Mich. 1964, U.S. Ct. Appeals (6th cir.) 1971. Assoc. Schmidt, Smith, Howlett & Halliday, Grand Rapids, Mich., 1964-66; asst. city atty. City of Grand Rapids, 1966-69, U.S. Dept. Justice, Grand Rapids, 1969-77; U.S. atty. Western Dist. Mich., Grand Rapids, 1974-77; pvt. practice Grand Rapids, 1977-81, 84-97; assoc. Kaufman, Payton & Kallas, Grand Rapids, 1981-84; ptnr. Bensinger, Cotant & Menkes, Grand Rapids, 1997—. Instr. bus. law Davenport Coll., Grand Rapids, 1967-68, Grand Valley State U., Grand Rapids, 1978-79. Recipient Dirs. Honor award, U.S. Secret Svc., 1977. Mem. ABA, Grand Rapids Bar Assn., Nat. Assn. Former U.S. Attys., Grand Rapids East Rotary, Republican. Presbyterian. Home: 2122 Tenway Dr SE Grand Rapids MI 49506-4526 Office: 3152 Peregrine Dr NE Ste 210 Grand Rapids MI 49525 Home Phone: 616-949-7716; Office Phone: 616-365-9600. E-mail: fspies@bcma.net.

SPIES, JAMES B., radiologist, educator; MD, Georgetown U., DC, 1980. Diplomate in vascular and interventional radiology Am. Bd. Radiology, 2005. Prof. Dept. Radiology Georgetown U., 2004—, chmn. Dept. Radiology, 2004—. Maj. USAF, 1985—89. Fellow: Am. Coll. Radiology, Soc. Interventional Radiology (chmn. found. 2005—). Achievements include research in uterine fibroid embolization, uterine fibroids. Office: Georgetown University Hospital 3800 Reservoir Rd NW CG 201 Washington DC 20007-2113 Office Phone: 202-444-3450.

SPIES, KAREN BORNEMANN, writer, educational consultant; b. Renton, Wash., Sept. 5, 1949; d. William Edward and Aina Jeanette (Johnson) Bornemann; m. Allan Roy Spies, July 18, 1970; children: Karsten, Astrid. BA, Calif. Luth. U., 1970; MEd, U. Wash., 1974. Vice prin., tchr. Lake Washington Sch. Dist., Kirkland, 1971—79; tchr. various pub. schs. NJ, 1979—82; tchr. kindergarten Mt. Park Sch., Lake Oswego, Oreg., 1982—84; writer, seminar leader, cons. Wash., 1984—87. Lectr. Arapahoe C.C., Littleton, 1988-98; ski instr. various locations, 1974—; curriculum writer Augsburg-Fortress Pubs.; lectr. in field. Author: Family

Activities for the Christmas Season, 1988, Denver, 1988, Raffi: The Children's Voice, 1989, Visiting in the Global Village, Vol. I, 1990, Vol. II, 1991, Vol. III, 1992, Vol. IV, 1993, Vol. V, 1994, Everything You Need to Know About Grieving, 1990, Competitiveness, 1991, Barbara Bush, 1991, George Bush, 1991, Everything You Need to Know About Incest, 1992, Our National Holidays, 1992, Our Money, 1992, The American Family: Can It Survive?, 1993, Everything You Need to Know About Diet Fads, 1993, Our Folk Heroes, 1994, Earthquakes, 1994, Our Presidency, 1994, Isolation vs. Intervention, 1995, Buffalo Bill Cody: Western Legend, 1998, Franklin D. Roosevelt, 1999, John F. Kennedy, 1999, Heroes in Greek Mythology, 2002, The Iliad and Odyssey in Greek Mythology, 2002, Pan Am Flight 103: Terrorism over Lockerbie, 2003. Bd. Regents Calif. Luth. Univ.; organist Wooden Cross Luth. Ch., 1977—79; bd. dirs. Parent Pathways. Recipient Notable Social Studies Trade Books for Young People, 2000; Title III grantee, 1974. Mem. AAUW, Soc. Children's Book Writers and Illustrators, Mensa, Profl. Ski Instrs. Am., Colo. Authors' League, Pi Lambda Theta. Republican. Lutheran. Avocations: tennis, reading, sewing, skiing, golf. Personal E-mail: buddyspies@msn.com.

SPIES, LEON FRED, lawyer; b. Blue Grass, Iowa, Oct. 8, 1950; s. Fred William and Alma Lois (Lineburg) S.; m. Janet Rae Peterson, July 15, 1979; children: Caitlin, Allison. BBA with distinction, U. Iowa, 1972, JD with distinction, 1975. Bar: Iowa 1975, U.S. Dist. Ct. (no. and so. dists.) Iowa 1975, U.S. Ct. Appeals 1975, U.S. Supreme Ct. 1987, U.S. Dist. Ct. (cen. dist.) Ill. 2000. Assoc. Heintz & Mellon, Iowa City, 1975-76; ptnr. Mellon & Spies, Iowa City, 1976—. Magistrate jud. dept. State of Iowa, 1978-83; instr. trial advocacy U. Iowa Coll. Law, 1996—. Bd. chmn. Johnson County Red Cross, Iowa City, 1982-84; bd. dirs. Big Bros./ Big Sisters, Johnson County, Iowa, 1985-89. Master: Am. Inns of Ct. (pres. Dean Mason Ladd Inn 1995—96); fellow: Am. Coll. Trial Lawyers, Iowa Acad. Trial Lawyers; mem.: ATLA, ABA, Am. Judicature Soc., Assn. Trial Lawyers Iowa, Iowa Bar Assn., Nat. Assn. Criminal Def. Lawyers. Democrat. Methodist. Home: 2349 Kent Ct NE Iowa City IA 52240-9633 Office: Mellon & Spies Ste 411 102 S Clinton St Iowa City IA 52240-4024 Personal E-mail: spieslegal@aol.com.

SPIEVACK, ALAN R., research and development company executive, surgeon; AB, Kenyon Coll., Ohio, 1955; MD, Harvard Med. Sch., 1959. Cert. Gen. Surgery. Tng. gen. surgery Boston City Hosp., 1965; rsch. and teaching fellowships Harvard U. and Am. Heart Assn., 1962—67; faculty mem. to asst. clin. prof. surgery Harvard Med. Sch., 1965—2000, taught and practiced surgery Boston and Cambridge, Mass.; founder Acell, Inc., 1999, v.p., dir. technology. Maxwell E. Power prize Scholar in Biology, Fulbright Scholarship. Fellow: Am. Coll. Surgeons; mem.: Mass. Med. Soc., Boston Surgical Soc. Achievements include several US patents in regenerative medicine. Office: ACell Inc 10555 Guilford Rd Ste 113 Jessup MD 20794 Office Phone: 800-826-2926. Office Fax: 410-715-4511. *

SPIGARELLI, JAMES L., science administrator; BA in Chemistry, MS in Chemistry, PhD in Chemistry, Kans. State Coll. Various positions Midwest Rsch. Inst., Kansas City, Mo., 1961—78, v.p., 1978—91, sr. v.p., 1991—97, exec. v.p., 1997—98, COO, 1998—99, pres., CEO, 1999—. Bd. dirs. Sci. City at Union Sta., Kansas City Mus., KCCatalyst, Brush Creek Cmty. Ptnrs., Sci. Pioneers; founding bd. mem. Kansas City Area Life Sci. Inst., Inc., 2000; trustee Univ. Mo.-KC, Avila Coll., Rockhurst Univ. R&D task force Kansas City Area Life Scis. Inst., 1999; trustee U. Mo., Kansas city, Avila Coll., Rockhurst U.; bd. dirs. Kansas City Area Life Scis. Inst., 2000. Lt. Chemical Corps US Army, Rocky Mt. Arsenal. Named Tech. Leader of Yr., Silicon Prairie Tech. Assn., 2000; recipient Meritorious Achievement award, Pitts. State U., 1993. Fellow: Coll. Arts and Scis. Alumni, Kans. State U. Office: Midwest Rsch Inst 425 Volker Blvd Kansas City MO 64110

SPIHLMANN, KRIS ANN, mathematics educator; b. Breese, Ill., Oct. 2, 1980; d. Steven Norbert and Kimberly Jo Spihlmann. BS in Edn., SE Mo. State U., Cape Girardeau, 2002; MS in Ednl. Adminstrn., Ea. Ill. U., Charleston, 2005. Cert. secondary math. and gen. sci. tchr., ednl. adminstr. Ill. Math. tchr. Carlyle Cmty. Unit Dist., Ill., 2002—, chmn. math. dept. Carlyle HS, 2003—, cheerleading coach, 2003—; math. tchr. Kaskaskia Coll., Centralia, Ill., 2003—06. Presenter in field. Mem.: Ill. Coun. Tchrs. Math., Nat. Coun. Tchrs. Math. Home: 331 South St Carlyle IL 62231 Office: Carlyle HS 1461 12th St Carlyle IL 62231

SPIKES, JESSE J., lawyer; b. McDonough, Ga., May 17, 1950; BA in English magna cum laude with highest honors, Dartmouth Coll., 1968-72; BA in Philosophy and Politics, Oxford U., Eng., 1974; JD, Harvard U., 1977. Bar: Ga. 1977, D.C. 1981. Gov.'s intern Ga. Intern Program, Atlanta, 1972; freelance constrn. worker Atlanta, 1973; assoc. planner office of planning Dept. Human Resources, Atlanta, 1974; law clk. Alston, Miller & Gaines, Atlanta, 1975, assoc., 1977-78; law clk. Smith, Cohen, Ringel, Kohler & Martin, Atlanta, 1976, Heller, Ehrman, White & McAuliffe, San Francisco, 1976; law clk. to Hon. Damon J. Keith U.S. Ct. Appeals, Sixth Cir., Detroit, 1978-79; assoc. Long, Aldridge, Heiner, Stevens & Sumner, Atlanta, 1979-80; gen. counsel Atlanta Life Ins. Co., 1980-81; legal adviser Al Bahrain Arab African Bank, Manama, Bahrain, 1981-85; ptnr. Long, Aldridge & Norman, Atlanta, 1986, McKenna Long & Aldridge LLP, Atlanta. Bd. dir. Atlanta Life Fin. Grp., John H. Harland Co. Chmn. Fulton County Bd. Registration and Elections; gen. counsel Young Working for Ga. Campaign Com.; bd. dirs. Atlanta Organizing Com., Underground Festival, Inc., Atlanta Symphony Orch. League; bd. trustees Agnes Scott Coll.; v.p. Strike Out Found.; active Brit.-Am. Conf. for Successor Generation, 1988, Leadership Atlanta, Class of '88, bd. children's Health-care Atlanta Found., Metro Atlanta C. of C. Rufus Choate scholar Dartmouth Coll., 1971; Rhodes scholar Oxford U., 1972; Earl Warren scholar Harvard U., 1974. Mem. ABA (standing com. lawyer competence), Nat. Bar Assn., State Bar Ga., DC Bar, NFL Players Assn., NBA Players Assn., 100 Black Men Atlanta, Inc., Phi Beta Kappa, Atlanta Bar Assn., Gate City Bar Assn. Office: McKenna Long & Aldridge LLP 303 W Peachtree St NE Ste 5300 Atlanta GA 30308-3503 Office Phone: 404-527-4140. Office Fax: 404-527-4198. Business E-Mail: jspikes@mckennalong.com.

SPIKES, PATRICIA WHITE, medical technologist; b. Houston, Nov. 30, 1951; d. Albert Carr and Willie Mae (Sneed) White; m. Herbert Charles Pete, May 24, 1980 (div.); 1 dau., Sheatri Denise; m. John Ray Spikes, Sept. 7, 1991; 1 child, John Ray II. BS Tex. Christian U., Ft. Worth, 1974. Med. technologist, edn. coordinator Riverside Gen. Hosp., Houston, 1974-76; chief lab. technologist Almeda Med. Lab., Houston, 1976-80; med. technologist Jefferson Davis Hosp., Harris County Hosp. Dist., Houston, 1980—, Lyndon B. Johnson Hosp., Harris City Hosp. Dist. Founder Coalition of Pre-Sch. Dirs., 1982—; dir. Parents Calling Parents, Houston, 1980—; and 3d v.p. Vols. in Pub. Sch. Adv. Bd., Houston, 1981, 2d v.p., 1983, pres. 1986-89, v.p. tng. chair, 1990-92, v.p. community coalitions, 1993; mem. Tex. State Bd. for Vols. in Pub. Sch., 1982—, sec., 1988—, 1st v.p., 1985, pres., 1986, sec. 1987—; chairperson Bucks for Belts Coalition for Sch. Bus Seat Belts, 1985; chair awards com. Salute to Sch. Vols.; mem. Mayor's Task Force on Edn., Houston, Mayor's Com. on Child Abuse Prevention; panelist Regional IV Svc. Ctr. State Seminar; mem. adv. bd. Blueridge Health Dept., Attucks Community Coll.; pres. Reynolds Elem. Parent Tchr. Orgn., 1982, treas., 1984; sec. Pershing Middle Sch., PTO, 1985, Class of 1969 Worthing High Sch. Reunion; candidate for Houston Ind. Sch. Dist. Bd. Edn., 1989; pres. Kings Row Child Care Parent Tchrs. Orgn., 1978; mem. Nat. Sch. Vol. Program 1982—, Mo. City Space; panelist Houston Area Black Sch. Educators, 1987; bd. dirs. Women in Action, 1984-85; mediator Dispute Resolution Ctr., 1984—, Women of Vision, Chs. Interested in Premature Parentage; city wide adv. com. Houston Ind. Sch. Dist., 1988; edn. adv. com. Family Life; pres. adv. com. Inner City 4-H, 1989—; chmn. adult leaders adv. bd. Harris County 4-H, 1989-91, treas. 1890 program, 1991-93; chmn. Northeast Adolescent Program, 1990-92; computer maintenance adv. com. Reagan High Sch., 1988—; chair Salute to Sch. Vols., 1984-86; speaker career day Houston Ind. Sch. Dist., 1989—; chmn. adv. bd. Sunnyside Multi-Svc. Ctr./Health Ctr., 1991—; mem. steering com. Tex. Cancer Coun., 1992—; spkr., active Teen Health Symposium Prairie View Adminstrn. 1980 4-H Program, 1992, 93; coord. baby buddy program Sunnyside Clinic City of Houston Health Dept., 1989—; mem. S.E. br. adv. bd. ARC, 2000-, chair, 2004-06, membership com. Greater Houston coun., 2004-; mem. membership com. Nat. Healthy Start Assn., 1974—; consortium chmn. Sunny Futures Healthy Start Program, Houston, 1998-2003; coord. Girls Rite of Passage, 2000-02; chmn. Prairie View A&M Coll. Coop. Extension Project H.O.P.E., 2001—; cons. Families Under Urban and Social Attack Non Profit Devel., 2002—; CEO, founder S&J Literary Works, 2003, Rewriting the Script Through Connections, 2005; mem. Syphilis Elimination Adv. Task Force, 2003—; chair Syphilis Elimination Bd., ARC, 2004-06; mem. program svcs. com.; mem. Sunnyside Pride, 2005; mem. Healthy Minority Marriage Initiative, 2006; mem. City of Houston HIV/AIDS Task Force, 2003—; workshop trainer Families Under Urban and Social Attack, 2004—; presenter, cons., spkr. in field. Recipient Vols. in Pub. Sch. Spl. Service cert., 1984; recipient numerous certs. of appreciation. Mem. NAACP, Delta Sigma Theta. Recipient Cert. of Appreciation, Vols. Am., 1980, Vols. in Pub. Schs., 1986, 87, Houston Ind. Sch. Dist., 1981, 82, 83, pres.' award Vols. in Pub. Schs., 1986-95; Outstanding Service award Reynolds Sch., 1982, cert. recognition Training Tchrs. and Adminstrs. Parent Involvment, 1986, Kay On-going Edn. Ctr., Pershing Mid. Schs., 1987, Neighborhood Ctrs. Crystal House Cmty. Svc. award, 2005, Vol. award Prairie View A&M U. project H.O.P.E. Democrat. Baptist. Mem. Top Ladies of Distinction. Home: 3134 Sunbeam St Houston TX 77051-3526 Personal E-mail: pspikes30@aol.com.

SPIKES, TAKEO, professional football player; b. Sandersville, Ga, Dec. 17, 1976; Student, Auburn U., 1995—97. Linebacker Cin. Bengals, 1998—2002, Buffalo Bills, 2003—07, Phila. Eagles, 2007—. Named to Nat. Football Conf. (NFC) Pro-Bowl Team, 2003—04. Office: Phila Eagles 1 NovaCare Way Philadelphia PA 19145 *

SPIKOL, EILEEN, artist; b. Sarasota, Fla. 1 child, Hannah. BA in Fine Arts, Fordham U., 1975; MFA in Sculpture, City Coll., NYC, 1977. Supr. reproduction studio Am. Mus. Natural History, NYC, 1971-78; tchr. painting and drawing grades 7-12 Fieldston Sch., Riverdale, N.Y., 1977-79; tchr. molding, casting, patina workshop Children's Mus. Manhattan, NYC, 1979-80; tchr. art spl. edn. Sch. Visual Arts, NYC, 1982; tchr. drawing, painting, sculpture, printmaking Studio in a Sch., NYC, 1987-90; instr. Bronx (N.Y.) Mus. Arts, 1990-91. Tchr. sculpture Md. Ctr. Arts Goucher Coll., Towson, 1986; adj. prof. art edn., spl. edn. Bkyln. (N.Y.) Coll., 1979-85, field supr.; adj. prof. fine arts St. Johns U., Queens, N.Y., 1991-93; artist in residence Found. Michel Karolyi, Vence, France, 1989, Domiciliary Care Program for Homeless Vets., St. Albans (N.Y.) VA Ctr., 1997—; adj. prof. in art edn., spl. edn. Nat. History N.Y.C., 1979-85; lectr. in field. One woman exhbns. include Soho 20 Gallery, N.Y.C., 1974, 75, 77, 78, Maples Gallery Fairleigh Dickinson U., Teaneck, N.J., 1980, 84, Islip Art Mus., E. Islip, N.Y., 1986, Bronx (N.Y.) Mus. Arts, 1988; group exbhns. include One Hundred Acres Gallery, N.Y.C., 1972, Aldrich Mus., Ridgefield, Conn., 1974, New Britain (Conn.) Mus., 1974, Hera Gallery, Wakefield, R.I., 1976, Bronx (N.Y.) Mus. Arts, 1979, 1980, Landmark Gallery, N.Y.C., 1979, Nobe' Gallery, N.Y.C., 1979, Walnut St. Galleries, Phila., 1979, Blaffer Gallery U. Houston, 1980, Mus. Natural History, N.Y.C., 1982, The Fine Arts Ctr. SUNY, Stony Brook, 1982, Fed. Plz., N.Y.C., 1982, Freedman Gallery Albright Coll., Reading, Pa., 1982, The New Mus., N.Y.C., 1984, Henry Street Settlement, N.Y.C., 1986, Artspace Gallery, New Haven, Conn., 1992, Leopold-Hoesch-Mus., Duren, Ger., 1992, B4A Gallery, N.Y.C., 1993; featured in Arts Mag., Soho Weekly News, Womanart, The Nation, The Village Voice, Coll. Art Jour., N.Y. Times, Newsday, New Haven Register. Home: 175 W 72nd St New York NY 10023-3203

SPILIOTES, NICHOLAS JAMES, lawyer; b. Blue Point, NY, Nov. 1, 1955; s. James Nicholas and Constance (Greven) S.; m. Lauren Talner, June 3, 1984; children: Alexander, Ariana. BA, Williams Coll., 1977; MIA, Columbia U., 1979, JD, 1985. Bar: N.Y., 1985, D.C. 1989. Jr. staff mem. NSC, Washington, 1979-81; special asst. Office of the U.S. Rep., U.S. Mission to the UN, NYC, 1981; research assoc. Ctr. Strategic and Internat. Studies, Washington, 1981-82; assoc. Morrison & Foerster, Washington, 1988-92, ptnr., 1992—, mng. ptnr. ops., 1997—2000, exec. com., bus. dept. chmn., 2004—, leader project fin. & devel. practice group, 2001—04. Mem. ABA (vice chmn. African law com. 1991-93), Am. Hist. Assn. Democrat. Office: Morrison & Foerster 2000 Pennsylvania Ave NW Washington DC 20006-1812 Office Phone: 202-887-1579. Business E-Mail: nspiliotes@mofo.com.

SPILKER, LINDA JOYCE, aerospace scientist; b. Mpls., Apr. 26, 1955; d. Arthur Elzear and Bonnie Joy (Jansen) Bies; m. John Leonard Horn, Jr., July 31, 1976 (div.); children: Jennifer, Jessica; m. Thomas Richard Spilker, 1997. BA in Physics, Calif. State U., Fullerton, 1977; MS in Physics, Calif. State U., LA, 1983; PhD in Geophysics and Space Physics, UCLA, 1992. Rep. Voyager Infrared Radiometer and Spectrometer expt. Jet Propulsion Lab., Pasadena, Calif., 1977-90, sci. assoc. Voyager Photopolarimeter, 1984-90, sc. assoc. Voyager Infrared Radiometer and Spectrometer, 1988-90, study scientist Cassini asst., 1988-90, co-investigator Cassini Composite Infrared Spectrometer, 1990—, dep. project scientist Cassini mission, 1990—, prin. investigator planetary geology and geophysics, 1993—. Mem. planetary sci. data steering group NASA, Washington, 1991-95, adv. coun. for planetary data sys. ring node, Moffett Field, Calif., 1990—. Contbr. chpt. Van Nostrand Encyclopedia of Planetary Science, 1994; contbr. jour. articles Icarus. Pres. North San Gabriel Valley Dem. Club, Monrovia, Calif., 1992-94. Named one of Hottest 25 in Orange County, Orange County Metro mag., 2004; named to Hall of Fame, Placentia-Yorba Linda Unified Sch. Dist., 1998—99; recipient Exceptional Svc. medal, NASA, 1990, Sci. Achievement award, 1992, Disting. Alumna award, Calif. State U., L.A., 1996, Calif. State U., Fullerton, 2005. Mem. AAAS, AAUW, Divsn. of Planetary Sci. Democrat. Presbyterian. Avocations: hiking, astronomical observing, piano, jogging. Home: 457 Granite Ave Monrovia CA 91016-2324 Office: Jet Propulsion Lab MS 230-205 4800 Oak Grove Dr Pasadena CA 91109-8001 Business E-Mail: Linda.J.Spilker@jpl.nasa.gov.

SPILLANE, DENNIS KEVIN, lawyer; b. NYC, Sept. 15, 1953; s. Denis Joseph and Mary Kate (Sullivan) S. BA magna cum laude, Manhattan Coll., 1974; JD, N.Y. Law Sch., 1978; MS in Taxation, Pace U., 1986, post-masters cert. in bus., 1992. Bar: N.Y. 1979, U.S. Dist. Ct. (ea. and so. dists.) N.Y. 1979, U.S. Tax Ct. 1986, D.C. 1988, U.S. Ct. Appeals (2d cir.) 1988, U.S. Supreme Ct. 1988, Conn. 1989. Asst. dist. atty. Borough of Bronx, NYC, 1978-85; prin. atty. N.Y. State Tax Dept., NYC, 1985-87; supervising atty. Office of Profl. Discipline, N.Y. State Edn. Dept., 1987—. Prof. law and taxation Pace U., 1987—. Contbr. articles to profl. jours. Mem. Conn. Bar Assn, N.Y. State Bar Assn., D.C. Bar Assn. Conservative. Roman Catholic. Office: NY State Edn Dept 475 Park Ave S Front 3 New York NY 10016-6901 Business E-Mail: dspillan@mail.nysed.gov.

SPILLANE, MARY CATHERINE, television producer; b. S.I., NY, Nov. 30, 1956; d. Joseph Bernard and Mary Catherine (Minoque) Spillane. BA, U. Hartford, 1978. Exec. sec. CBS Evening News, NYC, 1978-80, asst. to prodr., 1980; weekend prodr./E.N.G. coord. Sta. KTVI-TV, St. Louis, 1981-82, spl. projects prodr., 1982-83, asst. news dir., 1983-86; assoc. prodr. CBS News, Detroit, 1986, NYC, 1986-87, sr. prodr., 1987-89, Washington, 1989-93, prodr., 1993-99, CBS Weekend News, London, 1999—2006, CBS Evening News, London, 2006—. Avocations: reading, travel, cooking, gardening. Office: CBS News 1st Fl Bldg 10 Chiswick Park Chiswick High Rd London W4 5X5 England Home Phone: 44 208 400 5547; Office Phone: 44 207 887 3000. E-mail: msx@cbsnews.com.

SPILLER, EBERHARD ADOLF, physicist, researcher; b. Halbendorf, Ger., Apr. 16, 1933; came to U.S., 1968; s. Walter Richard and Ruth Elfriede Spiller; children: Michael, Bettina. Diploma, U. Frankfurt, Ger., 1960, PhD, 1964. With U. Frankfurt, 1960-68; physicist IBM Research Center, Yorktown Heights, NY, 1968-93; emeritus physicist IBM, 1993-97; owner Spiller X-Ray Optics, 1996—. Guest prof. Tech. U. Denmark, 1994—95, U. Ctrl. Fla., 1996; vis. scientist European Synchrotron Radiation Facility Nat. Inst. Stds. and Tech., 1996—97; vis. scientist Lawrence Livermore Lab., Calif., 1997—. Author: Soft X-Ray Optics, 1994. Fellow AAAS, Am. Optical Soc., Photo-Optic Instrumentation Soc.; mem. German Phys. Soc. Achievements include research in solid state physics, laser and coherence optics, nonlinear optics, thin films, soft x-rays, x-ray microscopy, lithography; inventor multilayer x-ray optics, x-ray astronomy, x-ray lithography. Office: Lawrence Livermore Nat Lab MS-L210 Livermore CA 94551 Office Phone: 925-423-4938. E-mail: spiller@llnl.gov.

SPILLERS, WILLIAM RUSSELL, civil engineering educator; b. Fresno, Calif., Aug. 4, 1934; s. William Horton and Marguerite Ester (Johnson) S.; m. Priscilla Watson, Sept. 10, 1960 (div. 1981); children: Sarah, William, Lars; m. Sandra Lynn Newsome, July 15, 1983 (div. 1995); m. Joy Bechard, Mar. 13, 2000. Student, Fresno State Coll., 1951-53; BS, U. Calif., Berkeley, 1955, MS, 1956; PhD, Columbia U., 1961. Registered profl. engr., N.Y., N.J. Structural engr. John Blume Assocs., San Francisco, 1956-57; teaching asst. Columbia U., NYC, 1957-61, prof. civil engring. and engring. mechanics, 1961-76; prof. civil engring. Rensellaer Poly. Inst., Troy, NY, 1976-90; prof., chmn. civil and environ. engring. N.J. Inst. Tech., Newark, 1990—, disting. prof. civil and environ. engring., 1995—. Cons. Weidlinger Assoc., N.Y.C., 1957-76, Geiger Berger Assoc., N.Y.C., 1957-76, DeLeuw Oh Eocha, Manchester, Eng., 1974, Parsons Hawaii, L.A., 1983, Horst Berger Ptnrs., N.Y.C., 1980; organizer NSF workshop on design theory, Troy, N.Y., 1988. Author: Automated Structural Analysis, 1972, Iterative Structural Design, 1975, Intro Structures, 1985; (with R. Levy) Analysis of Geometrically Nonlinear Structures, 1995, 2d edit., 2003, Introduction to Structures, 2002; editor 4 books including Design Theory, 1988; contbr. over 140 articles to profl. jours. Named Educator of Yr. award, Cons. Engrs. Coun. N.J., 1998; NSF fellow, 1976, Guggenheim fellow, 1968. Mem. ASCE (numerous coms., chmn. exec. com. TCCP, 1987), Internat. Assn. Bridge & Structural Engrs. Democrat. Achievements include contribution to the development of fabric structures; initiated the science of design theory; participated in development of applications of digital computers to large structural systems. Home: 7 Oak Ave West Orange NJ 07052-2409 Office: NJ Inst Tech Dept Civil & Environ Engring Newark NJ 07102 Office Phone: 973-596-2479. E-mail: spillers@njit.edu.

SPILLETT, ROXANNE, social services administrator; 1 son, Keith. BA in Edn., SUNY; postgrad., St. Lawrence U., Hunter Coll., NYC. Tchr., curriculum writer NY State Schs., 1971-73; program specialist Girl Scouts USA, 1973; dir. nat. health project Boys & Girls Clubs Am., Atlanta, 1978-79, dir. program svcs., 1979-91, asst. nat. dir. program svcs., 1991-1995, v.p. N.E. regional office, 1995, acting pres., 1995-96, pres., 1996—. Vice chair bd. dirs. Nat. Assembly of Health and Human Svc. Orgns. Office: Boys & Girls Clubs Am 1275 W Peachtree St NE Atlanta GA 30309-3404

SPILLIAS, KENNETH GEORGE, lawyer; b. Steubenville, Ohio, Nov. 8, 1949; s. George and Angeline (Bouyoucas) S.; m. Monica Mary Saumweber, May 10, 1975; children: Geoffrey David, Alicia Anne, Stephanie Marie BA, Pa. State U., 1971; JD magna cum laude, U. Pitts., 1974. Bar: Pa. 1974, Fla. 1978, U.S. Supreme Ct. 1978, U.S. Ct. Appeals (2d, 3d, 4th, 5th, 6th cirs.) 1975, (11th cir.) 1981, U.S. Dist. Ct. (mid. dist.) Fla. 1979, U.S. Dist. Ct. (so. dist.) Fla. 1978. Trial atty. U.S. Dept. Justice, Washington, 1974—76; asst. dist. atty. Dist. Atty. Allegheny County, Pitts., 1976—78; asst. atty. gen. Fla. Dept. Legal Affairs, West Palm Beach, 1978—79; ptnr. Spillias & Mitchell, West Palm Beach, 1979—82, Considine & Spillias, West Palm Beach, 1982—83, Schneider, Maxwell, Spillias et al, West Palm Beach, 1984—86, Wolf, Block, Schorr et al, West Palm Beach, 1986—88, Shapiro & Bregman, West Palm Beach, 1988—91; of counsel Greenberg, Traurig et al, West Palm Beach, 1991; pvt. practice West Palm Beach, 1991—97; ptnr. Lewis, Longman & Walker, P.A., West Palm Beach, 1997—. Instr. bus. law Coll. of Palm Beaches, West Palm Beach, 1980-81; lectr. in field County commr. Bd. County Commrs., Palm Beach County, 1982-86; co-founder, mem. Children's Svcs. Coun., Palm Beach County, 1986-91; steering com. Fla. Atlantic U. Inst. Govt., Boca Raton, 1983-94; bd. dirs. The Literacy Coalition Palm Beach County, West Palm Beach, 1990-00, health and human svcs. Fla. Dist. IX, 1995-98, Ctr. Family Svc., West Palm Beach, 1992-96, Palm Beach County Coun. Arts, 1987-88; mem. West Palm Beach Planning Bd., 1997—, chmn., 2001—; mem. policy coun. Fla. Inst. Govt., Tallahassee, 1985-86; fund raising chmn. United Cerebral Palsy Telethon, West Palm Beach, 1984-85; judge Palm Beach Post Pathfinders Awards, 1992-98; bd. dirs. South Fla. Fair, Palm Beach County Film and TV Commn., chmn. 2005—, Bob Carter's Actors Workshop and Repertory Theater, Econ. Coun. Palm Beach County, 2005—. Recipient Cmty. Svc. award Downtown Civitan Club, West Palm Beach, 1983, Man of Day award United Cerebral Palsy, 1986, Spl. Honoree award Palm Beach County Child Advocacy Bd., 1986, Children's Trust award Exch. Club/Dick Webber Ctr. for Prevention Child Abuse, 1991, Up and Comers award in Law, South Fla. Bus. Jour./Price Waterhouse, 1988, Achievement award Nat. Assn. Counties, 1986, Employment Law award Palm Beach County Legal Aid Soc., 2002; named to Outstanding Young Men Am., U.S. Jaycees, 1975, 84 Mem. ABA, Palm Beach County Bar Assn. (appellate practice com. 1990—), Am. Hellenic Ednl. Progressive Assn. (pres. 2001-02), Fla. Bar Assn. (appellate advocacy and city, county and local govt. sects.), Order of Coif, Kiwanis. Avocations: sports, writing, theater, reading, music. Home: 147 Gregory Rd West Palm Beach FL 33405-5029 Office: Ste 1000 1700 Palm Beach Lakes Blvd West Palm Beach FL 33401-2006 Office Phone: 561-640-0820. Business E-Mail: kspillias@llw-law.com.

SPILLMAN, JANE SHADEL, curator, writer, researcher; b. Huntsville, Ala., Apr. 30, 1942; d. Marvin and Elizabeth (Russell) Shadel; m. Don Lewis Spillman, Feb. 18, 1973 (dec. Jan. 1999); children: K. Elizabeth, Samuel Shadel. AB, Vassar Coll., 1964; MA, Cooperstown Grad. Program, 1965. Rsch. asst. Corning (N.Y.) Mus. Glass, 1965-70, asst. curator, 1971-73, assoc. curator Am. glass, 1974-77, curator, 1978—, head of curatorial dept., 1994-99, dep. dir. collections, 1999—2004. Cons. The White House Curator's Office, Washington, 1987-90, other museums. Author: Complete Cut and Engraved Glass of Corning, 1979, rev. edit., 1997, Knopf Collectors Guide to Glass, Vol. 1, 1982, Vol. 2, 1983, White House Glassware, 1989, Masterpieces of American Glass, 1990, The American Cut Glass Industry: T.G. Hawkes and His Competitors, 1996, European Cut Glass Furnishings for Eastern Palaces, 2006, also 6 other books, numerous articles; editor The Glass Club Bull., 1999—. Mem. Am. Assn. Mus. (chair curators com. 1989-93), Nat. Early Am. Glass Club (bd. dirs. 1989-95), Glass Circle of London, Internat. Assn. for the History of Glass (gen. sec. 2003—). Office: Corning Mus Glass 1 Museum Way Corning NY 14830-2253

SPILLMAN, ROBERT ARNOLD, architect; b. Bethlehem, Pa., May 21, 1931; s. Otto Henry and Ruth Meredith (Miller) S.; m. Cidney Jane Brandon, July 7, 1956; children: Catherine, Sarah, Peter. BArch, Cornell U., 1954. Registered arch., Pa., N.J. Archtl. designer Office Douglass Orr, New Haven, 1956-58; ptnr. Lovelace & Spillman, Archs., Bethlehem, 1959-70; sr. ptnr. Spillman Farmer Archs., Bethlehem, 1971-82; pres. Spillman Farmer Shoemaker Pell Whildin, P.C., Bethlehem, 1983—96, sr. prin., 1997—. Trustee Laros Found., Bethlehem, 1970-2007; pres. Bethlehem Libr. Bd., 1970-74, United Way Northampton and Warren Counties, 1979-81, Lehigh River Found. Lehigh Valley Indsl. Parks bd., 1985-96, pres., 1996-2001; chmn. Bethlehem Bd. Hist. Archtl. Rev., 1961-82; mem. pres.'s coun. Lehigh Valley Partnership, 2001—; bd. dirs. KidsPeace, 2003—; Olympic torchbearer, 1996. 1st lt. USAF, 1954-56. Fellow AIA (pres. Ea. Pa. chpt. 1969-70); mem. Pa. Soc. Archs. (disting. bldg. awards 1971, 76, 78, 94, 2001, 02, 04, 05, 06), Soc. Coll. and Univ. Planners, Bay Head Yacht Club (N.J.) (rear commodore 1985-87, vice commodore 1999-2001, commodore 2001-03). Democrat. Episcopalian. Office: Spillman Farmer Shoemaker Pell Whildin 1 W Broad St Bethlehem PA 18018-5704 Business E-Mail: rspillman@spillmanfarmer.com.

SPILMAN, JANET LYNNE, special education educator; b. Marysville, Calif., Nov. 29, 1957; d. Mary Elizabeth and James Maurice Spilman. BA in Hist. and Polit. Sci., Jamestown Coll., ND, 1980; BS in Spl. Edn., Moorhead State U., Minn., 1983; MEd, U. La Verne, Calif., 2004. Specialist Instrn. Credential: Learning Handicapped Commn. on Tchr. Credentialing, Calif., 1989, Single Subject Tchg. Credential: Soc.Sci. Commn. on Tchr. Credentialing, Calif., 1989, Resource Specialist Cert. Commn. on Tchr. Credentialing, Calif., 2000, Nat. Cert. In Assistive Tech. Calif. State U. Northridge, 2000. Case mgr., behavior analyst Fraser Hall, Inc, Fargo, ND, 1983—85; spl. edn. tchr. Yuma Union H.S. Dist. - Kofa H.S., Yuma, Ariz., 1985—89; job coord. Job Tng. Partnership Act - Summer Youth Program, 1986—88; tchr. (govt.) Yuma Union H.S. Dist., Migrant Edn. Dept., Yuma, Ariz., 1987—89; resource specialist Live Oak Unified Sch. Dist., Calif., 1989—94; ind. living instr. Cmty. Resource Svcs., Marysville, Calif., 1994—96; spl. day class tchr., emotionally disturbed program Milhous Sch., Inc., Sacramento, 1996—97; resource specialist Wash. Unified Sch. Dist., West Sacramento, Calif., 1997—2002, Sacramento City Unified Sch. Dist., Sacramento, 2002—. Mem.: ASCD, Vocat. Evaluation and Work Adjustment Assn., Nat. Rehab. Assn., Assn. for Children and Adults with Learning Disabilities, Coun. for Children with Behavioral Disorders, Calif. Assn. for Resource Specialists, Phi Delta Kappa, Assn. Calif. Sch. Adminstrs., Am. Assn. Sch. Adminstrs., Prader Willi Assn., Coun. For Exceptional Children. Avocations: working cattle, packing (horse and burro), hiking, photography, gardening, horseback riding. Home: 9524 North Butte Rd Live Oak CA 95953 Home Phone: 916-275-7799. Personal E-mail: spilman-rsp@comcast.net.

SPILMAN, ROBERT HENKEL, furniture company executive; b. Knoxville, Tenn., Sept. 27, 1927; s. Robert Redd and Lila (Henkel) S.; m. Jane Bassett, Apr. 2, 1955; children: Robert Henkel Jr., Virginia Perrin, Vance Henkel. BS, N.C. State U., 1950. With Cannon Mills, 1950-57; with Bassett Table Co., Va., 1957-60; dir. Bassett Furniture Industries Inc., 1960—97, exec. v.p., 1966, pres., 1966-89, CEO, 1979—97, chmn., 1982—97, ret., 1997. Bd. dir. Internat. Home Furnishing Ctr., High Point, N.C.; adv. bd. Liberty Mut. Ins. Co Trustee Va. Found. Ind. Colls.; bd. dir. Blue Ridge Airport Authority. Lt. U.S. Army, WWII and Korea. Named Humanitarian of Yr., City of Hope, 1982; named to Furniture Hall of Fame, 2005; recipient Best CEO Home Furnishing Industry award, Wall Street Transcript, 1981, 1982. Mem. Am. Furniture Mfrs. Assn. (James T. Ryan award 1984), Nat. Furniture Mfrs. Assn. (bd. dir., past pres.), Furniture Factories Mktg. Assn. (past chmn., bd. dirs.), Va. Mfrs. Assn. (past dir. exec. com.), Bassett Country Club, Commonwealth Club, Kinloch Golf Club, Linville Golf Club, Grandfather Golf and Country Club (Linville, N.C.), The Country Club Va., Olde Farm (Bristol, Va.). Episcopalian. Avocation: fishing. Office: Spilman Properties PO Box 880 Bassett VA 24055 Personal E-mail: bspilman@sitestar.net.

SPINA, ANTHONY FERDINAND, lawyer; b. Chgo., Aug. 15, 1937; s. John Dominic and Nancy Maria (Ponzio) S.; m. Anita Phyllis De Orio, Jan. 28, 1961; children: Nancy M. Spina Okal, John D., Catherine M. Spina Samatas, Maria J. Spina Samatas, Felicia M. Spina DiGiovanni. BS in Social Sci., Loyola U., Chgo., 1959; JD, DePaul U., Chgo., 1962. Bar: Ill. 1962; US Supreme Ct. 2005. Assoc. Epton, Scott, McCarthy & Bohling, Chgo., 1962-64; pvt. practice Elmwood Park, Ill., 1964-71; pres. Anthony & Spina, PC, 1971-84; arbitrator Circuit Ct. of Cook County, 1990—98; pres. Spina, McGuire & Okal, PC, Elmwood Park, 1985—. Codifier Rosemont Village Ordinances, 1971, Elmwood Park Bldg. Code, 1975, Leyden Twp. Codified Ordinances, 1987. Mem. Elmwood Pk. Bldg. Code Planning Commn. Bd. Appeals; bd. dirs. Sheridan Carrol Charitable Works Fund, 1994—; atty. Leyden Twp., Ill., 1969—89, Village of Rosemont, Ill., 1971; counsel for Pres. and dir. Cook County Twp. Ofcls. Ill., 1975—96; counsel for exec. dir. Ill. State Assn. Twp. Ofcls., 1975—96; counsel Elmwood Park Village Bd., 1967—89, Norwood Park St. Lighting Dist., 1988—, various Cook County Twps. including DuPage, 1980—82, Maine, 1981—97, Norwood Park, 1982—, Wayne, 1982—84, Berwyn Twp., 1997—99, Hanover Twp., 1997, Cook County Hwy. Commrs. Traffic Fine Litigation, 1974—96, 1999—2001, Hanover Twp. Mental Health Bd., 1991—2002, Glen Edens Assn., 1994—99, Berwyn Twp. Mental Health Bd., 1997—2002. Recipient Lacodaire medal Deans Key Loyola U., Loyola U. Housing awards, 1965, 71, 76; Appreciation award Cook County Twp. Ofcls., B. Scidmore award Ill. Twp. Attys. Assn., 2002. Mem. ABA, Ill. Bar Assn., Chgo. Bar Assn., West Suburban Bar Assn. Cook County (past chmn. unauthorized practice law sect.), Am. Judicature Soc., Justinian Soc. Lawyers, Ill. State Twp. Attys. Assn. (past v.p., pres. 1982-86, dir. 1996-99, dir. emeritus 1999—, B. Scidmore award 2002), Nat. Inst. Town and Twp. Attys. (past v.p., pres. 1993-95, Ill. del.), Montclare/Leyden C. of C., Edgebrook C. of C. (past bd. dirs.), Nat. Assn. Italian Am. Lawyers, Nat. Italian Am. Bar Assn., Joint Civic Com. Chgo. (exec. com.), World Bocce Assn. (dir. 1994--), St. Rocco Soc. Simbario, KC (scribe, trustee, past Grand Knight, bldg. corp. dir. 1967-99), Calabresi in Am. Orgn. (bd. dirs. 1991—), Fra Noi Ethnic Publ. (dir. 1995—), Blue Key, Delta Theta Phi, Tau Kappa Epsilon, Pi Gamma Mu. Roman Catholic. Office: 7610 W North Ave Elmwood Park IL 60707-4100 Office Phone: 708-453-2800. Business E-Mail: aspina@smolaw.com.

SPINA, DOUGLAS JOHN, priest, educator; b. Providence, Apr. 27, 1949; s. Angelo and Gilda (Petrucci) Spina. BA, Our Lady of Providence Sem. Coll., Warwick, RI, 1971, Cath. U., Louvain, Belgium, 1973, MA, 1974, MA in Moral and Religious Scis., 1975, PhD, 1979. Ordained Roman Cath. priest, Diocese Providence, 1976. Instr. Italian grammar and lit. Ursuline Convent Sch., Tildonc, Belgium, 1972—75; assoc. pastor St. Clement Ch., Warwick, RI, 1976—78, St. Mary's Ch., Newport, RI, 1979—81; Catholic chaplain Roger Williams U., Bristol, RI, 1979—81; instr. religion Our Lady of Providence Prep. Sem., Providence, 1981—82; from asst. to assoc. prof. religious studies Salve Regina U., Newport, RI, 1982—87; assoc. pastor St. Joan of Arc Ch., Cumberland, RI, 1987—90; chaplain, adj. prof. Bryant Coll., Smithfield, RI, 1990—96; pastor St. Anthony's Ch., Woonsocket, RI, 1992—97; adj. prof. religious studies Calif. State U., Long Beach, Calif., 1996—97; pastor Our Lady of Grace Ch., Johnston, RI, 1997—2004; chaplain Johnston Police Dept., 1998—2004, Johnston Fire Dept., 1999—2004, KC, North Providence, RI, 2001—; chaplain RI chpt. Am. Guild Organists, 2003—; pastor St. Martha's Ch., East Providence, RI, 2004—. Mem. nat. bd. dirs. Nat. Religious Studies/Theology Honor Soc., NYC, 1986—88; mem. Humanities Forum of R.I., 1986; bd. dirs. Lucy's Hearth, Middletown, RI, 1986—87; mem. Bishop's Task Force on AIDS, Roman Cath. Diocese, Providence, 1988—89. Author: (plays) Could've Been, 1988 (First Place award R.I. Cable TV Video Prodn. Competition Ednl., Instrn. Category., 1989), (Book) Reaching Across the Table: Meditations on the Journey towards Common Ground, 2001; contbr. articles short stories, poetry to various publications. Recipient Citation, Mayor, Cranston, R.I., 1976, Citation, Key to City, Mayor of Warwick, R.I., 1978, Citation, Mayor of Woonsocket, R.I., 1992, R.I. State Senate, 2001, R.I. Gov.'s Office, 2001, Mayor, Johnston, R.I., 2001, Mayor East Providence, 2006. Mem.: Coll. Theology Soc., Cath. Campus Ministry Assn., R.I. Philos. Soc., Cath. Theol. Soc. Am. Avocation: collector Victorian period. Home and Office: St Marthas Rectory 2595 Pawtucket Ave East Providence RI 02914 Home Phone: 401-434-4060; Office Phone: 401-434-4060. Personal E-mail: Bd0521111@aol.com.

SPINA, FRANCIS X., state supreme court justice; b. Pittsfield, Mass., Nov. 13, 1946; m. Sally O'Donnell; 2 children. BA, Amherst Coll.; JD, Boston Coll. Law Sch. With Western Mass. Legal Services, 1972—74; asst. city solicitor Pittsfield Law Dept., 1975—77; second asst. dist. atty. Berkshire County Dist. Attorney's Office, Mass., 1979—83; atty. Reder, Whalen, and Spina, 1983—87, Katz, Lapointe, and Spina, 1987—93; judge Mass. Superior Ct., 1993-97, Appeals Ct., Pittsfield, 1997-99; assoc. justice Mass. Supreme Jud. Ct., Boston, 1999—. Mem. Mass. Standing Com. on Pro Bono Legal Services. Mem.: Boston Bar Assn., Mass. Bar Assn. Office: Supreme Judicial Court 1 Pemberton Sq Ste 2-500 Boston MA 02108-1717 *

SPINDEL, ROBERT CHARLES, electrical engineering educator; b. NYC, Sept. 5, 1944; s. Morris Tayson and Isabel (Glazer) S.; m. Barbara June Sullivan, June 12, 1966; children: Jennifer Susan, Miranda Ellen BSEE, Cooper Union, 1965; MS, Yale U., 1966, MPhil, 1968, PhD, 1971. Postdoctoral fellow Woods Hole Oceanographic Instn., Mass., 1971-72, asst. scientist Mass., 1972-76, assoc. scientist Mass., 1976-82, sr. scientist Mass., 1982-87, chmn. dept. ocean engring. Mass., 1982-87; dir. applied physics lab. U. Wash., Seattle, 1987—. Mem. naval studies bd. NRC, 1987-99; mem. Naval Rsch. Adv. Com., 1998—. Contbr. articles to profl. jours.; patentee on underwater nav. Recipient A.B. Wood medal Brit. Inst. Acoustics, 1981, Gano Dunn medal The Cooper Union, 1989, Ocean Engr. Soc. Tech. Achievement award, 1990. Fellow IEEE (assoc. editor jour. 1982—), Acoustical Soc. Am., Marine Tech. Soc. (pres. elect 1991-93, pres. 1993-95), Oceanography Soc. (Munk award 2001). Independent. Jewish. Avocations: auto restoration, hiking. Home: 14859 SE 51st St Bellevue WA 98006-3515 Office: U Wash Applied Physics Lab 1013 NE 40th St Seattle WA 98105-6606 E-mail: spindel@APL.Washington.edu.

SPINDLER, GEORGE DEARBORN, anthropologist, educator, writer; b. Stevens Point, Wis., Feb. 28, 1920; s. Frank Nicholas and Winifred (Hatch) S.; m. Louise Schaubel, May 29, 1942 (dec. Feb. 1997); 1 dau., Sue Carol Spindler Coleman. BS, Central State Tchrs. Coll., Wis., 1940; MA, U. Wis., 1947; PhD, U. Calif. at Los Angeles, 1952. Tchr. sch. in Wis., 1940-42; rsch. assoc. Stanford U., 1950-51, mem. faculty, 1951—85, prof. anthropology and edn., 1960-78, exec. head dept., 1963-67, 84; ret., 1985. Cons. editor Holt, Rinehart & Winston, 1965-91, Harcourt, 1991-99, Wadsworth-Thomson, 2002-; vis. prof. U. Wis., 1979-85, U. Calif., Santa Barbara, 1986-91, Harvard U., 1999. Author: Menomini Acculturation, 1955, (with A. Beals and L. Spindler) Culture in Process, 1967, rev. edit., 1973, Transmission of American Culture, 1959, (with L. Spindler) Dreamers Without Power, 1971, rev. edit., 1984, Burgbach: Urbanization and Identity in a German Village, 1973, (with Louise Spindler) The American Cultural Dialogue and its Transmission, 1990, (with Lorie Hammond) Innovations in Educational Ethnography, 2006; editor: Education and Anthropology, 1955, (with Louise Spindler) Case Studies in Cultural Anthropology, 1960—, Am. Anthropologist, 1962-66, Methods in Cultural Anthropology, 1965-71, Case Studies in Education and Culture, 1966-72, Basic Units in Anthropology, 1970, (with Janice Stockard) Globalization and Urbanization in Fifteen Cultures-Born in One World, Living in Another, 2006; editor, contbr.: Education and Culture, 1963, Being An Anthropologist, 1970, Education and Cultural Process, 1974, rev. edit., 1987, 97, The Making of Psychological Anthropology, 1978, 2nd edit., 1994, Doing the Ethnography of Schooling, 1982, Interpretive Ethnography of Schooling at Home and Abroad, 1987, Pathways to Cultural Awareness: Cultural Therapy with Students and Teachers, 1994, Fifty Years of Anthropology and Education: A Spindler Anthology, 2000. Pres. Peninsula Sch. Bd., Menlo Park, Calif., 1954-56. Served with AUS, 1942-45. Recipient Lloyd W. Dinkelspeil award Stanford U., 1978, Disting. Svc. award Soc. Internat. Diplomacy and Third World Anthropologists, 1984, Disting. Career Contbn. award Com. on Role and Status of Minorities, Am. Edn. Rsch. Assn., Nat. Acad. Edn., 1994, Father of Ednl. Ethnography award Nat. Ednl. Ethnography Conf., 2000, George and Louise Spindler Excellence award Stanford U., 2001; fellow Ctr. Advanced Study of Behavioral Scis., 1956-57; subject of Vol. 17 Psychoanalytic Study of Soc. essays, 1992. Fellow Am. Anthrop. Assn.; mem. Southwestern Anthrop. Assn. (pres. 1962-63), Coun. for Anthropology and Edn. (pres. 1982, George and Louise Spindler award for outstanding contbns. to ednl. anthropology 1987, disting. Scholar award 1998), Nat. Acad. Edn. Office: Ethnographics 1247 Alice St Davis CA 95616-2174 Personal E-mail: geospinner@aol.com. *My major aims as a professional observer and interpreter of human behavior are to acquire knowledge by research and disseminate understanding to others by teaching, writing, and editing. As a person I try to keep love, work, play in balanced relationship to each other, and strive for tolerance at least, and hopefully appreciation for others who are different than myself.*

SPINDLER, GEORGE S., lawyer, retired oil industry executive; BCE, Ga. Inst. Tech., 1961; JD, DePaul U., 1966. Bar: Ill. 1966. Asst. gen. counsel, patents and licensing Amoco Corp., Chgo., 1979-81, gen. mgr. info. svcs., 1981-85, v.p. planning and adminstrn., 1985-87, assoc. gen. counsel, 1987-88, dep. gen. counsel, 1988-89, v.p., gen. counsel, 1989-92, sr. v.p., gen. counsel, 1992-95, sr. v.p. law and corporate affairs, 1995-99; ret., 1999. Dir. Methode Electronics Inc, 2004—. Office: Methodde Electronics 7401 W Wilson Ave Chicago IL 60706

SPINDLER, JAMES ANDREW, not-for-profit executive; b. Morgantown, W.Va., Oct. 20, 1950; s. Garold Ralph and Elizabeth (Carroll) Spindler; m. Ann Bailie Trautman; children: Emma Carroll, Eliza Bailie children: James Andrew, Jr. AB, Harvard Coll., Cambridge, Mass., 1972; MPA, Princeton U., 1975, PhD, 1983. Bus. fellow The Brookings Instn., Washington, 1980—82; v.p. Continental Ill. Nat. Bank., Chgo., 1984—85, Fed. Res. Bank of N.Y., NYC, 1985—89, sr. v.p., 1989—93; mng. dir. Fin. Svcs. Vol. Corps, NYC, 1993—95, exec. dir., 1995—2005, pres., CEO, 2005—. Mem. Basle Com. on Banking Supervision, Switzerland, 1991—93, G10 Com. on Payment and Settlement Sys., Basle, 1991—93; prin. investigator Russia Initiative Project of the Carnegie Corp. of NY, NYC, 2000—01; mem. bd. dirs. Dubai Fin. Svc. Authority, United Arab Emirates, 2004—. Author: The Politics of International Credit: Private Finance and Foreign Policy in Germany and Japan, 1984, (Op-Ed Pieces) International Herald Tribune, San Francisco Chronicle, and The Jakarta Post, 2001. Recipient Medal of Svc. for assistance in developing Russian fin. mkts., Ctrl. Bank of Russia and the Russian Finance Ministry, 1996. Mem.: Bretton Woods Com., Am. Coun. on Germany, Coun. on Fgn. Rels. Presbyterian. Avocations: classical music, travel, running. Office: Financial Services Volunteer Corps 800 3d Ave 11th Fl New York NY 10022 Office Phone: 212-771-1412. Business E-Mail: jspindler@fsvc.org.

SPINDLER, JUDITH TARLETON, elementary school educator; b. Dayton, Tenn., Mar. 4, 1932; d. Frank Willson and Julia Elizabeth (Venable) S. BS in Edn., Longwood Coll., 1953; MA in Edn., Va. Commonwealth U., 1976. Tchr. Oceana, King's Grant Sch., Virginia Beach, Va., 1953-66, Ginter Park Elem. Sch., Richmond, Va., 1966-67, Bon Air Elem. Sch., Chesterfield County, Va., 1967-87; ret., 1987. Founder, Web of Hope, 2006, St. Mary's Knitters, 2006. Recipient 86 ribbons for 1st, 2nd and 3rd pl. awards various knitting competitions, 5 Best in Show awards rosette competition, including blue ribbons State Fair Va., 1998, 6 ribbons Best in Show rosette Chesterfield County Fair, 1998, 2 Best in Show Chesterfield County Fair, 1 Best in Show State Fair of Va., 3 Blue ribbons Chesterfield County Fair, 2000, 2 Red Ribbons, 1 White Ribbon Va. State Fair, 2000, 3 Blue ribbons Chesterfield County Fair, 2 Red ribbons, 1 White ribbon 1 Blue, 5 in Va. State Fair, 2002, 1 Blue ribbon, 1 Red Ribbon, 3 Blue ribbons State Fair Va., 2004, 2 blue ribbons, 2 red ribbons State Fair Va., 2006; Humanitarian award ARC. Mem. NEA, Va. Edn. Assn., Knitting Guild Am. (qualified tchr.), Knit Wit Guild (founding mem.), West End Web of Hope and St. Mary's Knitters. Avocations: knitting, reading, travel. Home: 10201 Navarre Ct Richmond VA 23238-5543

SPINDLER, PAUL, communications executive, consultant; b. Chgo., May 2, 1931; s. Isaac Edward and Sophie (Stein) Spindler; m. Gail Klynn; children from previous marriage: Kevin, Makayla, Sydney, Jeffrey. BA in Journalism, Temple U., 1952. Reporter Akron Beacon Jour., Akron, Ohio, 1955-58, San Francisco Examiner, 1958-59; editor Santa Clara (Calif.) Daily Jour., 1959-63; dir. pub. affairs Litton Industries, Inc., Beverly Hills, Calif., 1963-68; dir. pub. relations Internat. Industries, Beverly Hills, 1968-70; pres. Paul Spindler & Co., LA, 1970-75; exec. v.p. Manning Selvage & Lee, Inc., NYC, 1975-85; pres. The Spindler Co., LA, 1985-87; pres. Western div. GCI Group, LA, 1987-91; pres. GCI Spindler, LA, 1991-96; chmn. Bristol Retail Solutions, Inc., Newport Beach, Calif., 1996-98; pres. Paul Spindler Co., LA, 1998—. Bd. dirs. Phoenix House Calif.; bd. visitors, Temple U. Sch. Comm. and Theatre; co-pres., dir., The Partnership Scholars, 2004—. Bd. dirs. Bright Future Adoption Found. Cpl. US Army, 1952—54. Mem. Mountain Gate Country Club (L.A.). Democrat. Jewish. Office: Paul Spindler Co 1901 Ave of the Stars 2nd Flr Los Angeles CA 90067 Office Phone: 310-286-0102. Business E-Mail: paul@spindlercompany.com.

SPINELLO, IRENE M., internist; m. Barry Joseph Spinello, Nov. 13, 1993; 1 child, Nina. Critical care physician Kern Med. Ctr., Bakersfield, Calif., 2002—. Dir. ICU Kern Med. Ctr., 2003—. Contbr. articles to profl. jours. Master: Am. Coll. Ethical Physicians; fellow: Am. Bd. Hosp. Physicians, Am. Coll. Chest Physicians; mem.: Soc. Critical Care Medicine. Conservative. Achievements include design of intensivist-led ICU model; development of airway workshop; vascular access workshop; rhythm recognition workshop; ACLS workshop. Avocations: British history, WWII history, gardening. Office: Kern Medical Center/UCLA 1830 Flower St Bakersfield CA 93305 Home Phone: 661-872-0690; Office Phone: 661-326-2000. Office Fax: 661-326-2950. E-mail: spinelloi@kernmedctr.com.

SPINETTA, JEAN-CYRIL, airline executive; b. Paris, Oct. 4, 1943; s. Adrien Spinetta and Antoinette Brignoli; m. Nicole Ricquebourg, Nov. 22, 1969; children: Eric, Isabelle, Cécile, Adrien. Student, Paris Law Sch.; diploma, Inst. Internat. Politics, Paris; graduate, Ecole Nationale d'Administration. Ctrl. adminstrv. attache, 1969-70; nat. adminstr. Paris Higher Edn. Secondary Schs., 1970-72; bur. chief dept. investments and planning Nat. Edn. Ministry, 1972-76; spl. prosecutor State Coun. Govt., 1976-78; sec. gen. French Govt., 1978-81; info. svc. chief Prime Min. of France, 1981-83; dir. colls. Ministry Nat. Edn., 1983-84; cabinet dir. Min. Labour, Employment and Profl. Devel., 1984-86; inspector gen. Nat. Edn. Adminstrn., 1986-88; cabinet dir. Min. Social Affairs and Employment, Min. Overseas Transport, 1988-90; chair, CEO Air Inter, 1990-93; indsl. advisor Presidency of the Republic, 1994-95; adminstr. to 1st mission pub. svc. relevant to govt., 1995; chmn., CEO Air France, 1997—; CEO Air France-KLM Group, 2004—. Decorated officer Legion of Honor, officer Nat. Order of Merit (France), Officier des Palmes Académiques, Nat. Edn. Ministry. Mem.: IATA (chmn. 2004), Assn. European Airlines (pres. 2001). Avocations: tennis, skiing. Office: Air France 125 W 55th St New York NY 10019-5369 also: 45 Rue de Paris 95747 Roissy France Office Phone: 33-1-41-56-61-69. Office Fax: 33-1-41-56-61-59.

SPINKA, WILLIAM J., art educator; b. Bridgeport, Conn., Oct. 3, 1920; s. Jacob J. Spinka and Anna M. Syrotiak; m. Valerie A. Lauten, June 19, 1943; children: Kenneth W., Caryl V. BS in Edn., CCNY, 1942, MS in Edn., 1945. Tchr., phys. edn. dir. Birch Wathen Sch., NYC, 1942—44; instr. engring. USMcht. Marine Acad., Kings Point, 1944—45; instr. art CCNY, 1946—60, asst. prof. art, 1961—66, assoc. prof., 1967—81, prof., 1981—85, prof. emeritus, 1986, archtl. design rsch. projects, 1986—. Ednl. affiliate Am. Soc. Interior Design, NYC, 1976—88; profl. mem. Nat. Soc. Interior Designers, 1960—75; sculptor; painter. Exhibitions include Salmagundi Club, Nat. Arts Club, Nat. Acad., NY, 1976—99, Corcoran Gallery, 1946, Lever House Gallery, 1986—95, one-man shows include Canton Artists Guild, Conn., 1979, works pub. in mags. Ensign US Maritime Svc., 1944—46. Mem.: Audubon Artists Inc. (v.p. sculpture 1987—93, sr. v.p. 1994—98, Gold medal of honor 1988, Silver medal of honor 1992). Avocations: construction, landscape design, athletics. Home: 4658 Grosvenor Ave Bronx NY 10471

SPINNER, LEE LOUIS, accountant; b. Hillsboro, Ill., Nov. 9, 1948; s. John Louis and Clara Mae (Brown) Spinner; m. Rosemary T. Dean, Mar. 2, 2002. BS in Acctg., U. Ill., 1971, MAS in Acctg., 1972; MS in Taxation, DePaul U., 1983. CPA, Ill. Sr. tax acct. Ernst & Young, Chgo., 1972-78; dir. tax returns and audits Sunbeam Corp., Chgo., 1978-82; dir. tax compliance Sara Lee Corp., Chgo., 1982-83; mgr. tax compliance AM Internat., Inc., Chgo., 1983-85; mgr. taxes Household Mfg., Inc., Prospect Heights, Ill., 1985-89; mgr. internat. taxes Pittway Corp., Chgo., 1990-2000; dir. taxes Methode Electronics, Inc., Harwood Heights, Ill., 2000—. Instr. tax tng. program Ernst & Young, 1975-78; tax advisor Sta. WIND, Call Your Acct., Chgo., 1977-78. Sec. Grant Park Accts. Softball League, Chgo., 1976-77. Mem. AICPA, Ill. CPA Soc., U. Ill. Alumni Assn. (bd. assoc., audit com. 1997—), Top Social Athletic Club, Moose, KC. Democrat. Roman Catholic. Home: 435 W Wilshire Dr Palatine IL 60067-4788

SPINNER, STEVEN L., food products executive; With AFI Foodservice Distributors Performance Food Group, Richmond, Va., 1985—89; v.p. AFI Foodservice Distributors, 1989—97, pres., 1997—2000; regional pres. Broadline div. Performance Food Group, Richmond, Va., 2000—01, pres. Broadline div., 2001—02, sr. v.p., CEO Broadline div., 2002—05, pres., COO, 2005—06, pres., CEO, 2006—. Office: Performance Food Group 12500 West Creek Pkwy Richmond VA 23238 *

SPINNEY, CAROLL, entertainer, educator; b. Waltham, Mass., Dec. 26, 1933; s. Chester and Margaret Spinney; m. Janice Spinney (div. 1971); children: Jessica, Melissa, Ben; m. Debra Grilray. Studied Comml. Art, Art Inst. Boston; LHD (hon.), Villanova U., 2004. Lectr. in field; orch. condr. various cities. Illustrator, full time puppeteer Bozo's Big Top, 1960, performed Big Bird and Oscar (TV series) Sesame Street, 1969— (Lifetime Acheivement award, Daytime Emmy Awards, 2006); author (with J. Milligan): The Wisdom of Big Bird (and the Dark Genius of Oscar the Grouch): Lessons Learned From a Life in Feathers; actor: (films) Follow That Bird. Served USAF, Las Vegas. Recipient 6 Emmy awards, 2 Grammy awards, Star on the Hollywood Walk of Fame, Living Legend award, Library of Congress, 2000. Achievements include performing in the White House for all the First Ladies since Nixon. Office: Sesame Street One Lincoln Plaza New York NY 10023

SPINOWITZ, ALAN LEE, dermatologist; b. Oceanside, NY, Feb. 21, 1955; s. Seymour and Gilda; m. Randi Gail Schwartz; children: David, Sam, Jake. BA, Hofstra U., Hempstead, NY, 1977; MD, SUNY, Bklyn., 1981. Dermatologist pvt. practice, Garden City, NY, 1987—. Office: 877 Stewart Ave Garden City NY 11530

SPINRAD, RICHARD WILLIAM, federal agency administrator, oceanographer; b. NYC, Apr. 6, 1954; s. Leonard William and Thelma (Zipkin) S.; m. Alanna Wynn Thompson, June 1, 1980; 1 child, Gary Brian. BA, Johns Hopkins U., 1975; MS in Phys. Oceanography, Oreg. State U., 1978, PhD in Marine Geology, 1982. Rsch. asst. Oreg. State U., Corvallis, 1975-82; rsch. scientist Bigelow Lab. for Ocean Sci., West Boothbay Harbor, Maine, 1982-86, prin. investigator, 1986—94; pres. Sea Tech., Inc., Corvallis, 1986-87; program mgr. optical oceanography Office of Naval Research, Arlington, Va., 1987-89; div. dir. Office of Naval Rsch., Arlington, Va., 1989-94; dir. Consortium for Oceanographic Rsch. & Edn. (CORE), 1994—99; tech. dir. Oceanographer of the Navy, 1999—2003; asst. adminstr., Nat. Ocean Svc. Nat. Oceanic and Atmospheric Adminstrn., Washington, 2003—05, asst. adminstr., Office of Oceanic and Atmospheric Rsch., 2005—. Adj. faculty George Mason U., 1994-97, U.S. Naval Acad., 1997-99; trustee Bigelow Lab. for Ocean Scis., 1995-; led develop. Nat. Ocean Sciences Bowl for HS Students, CORE; US permanent rep., Intergovernmental Oceanographic Commn., UNESCO, 2004-; co-chair, White House Joint Subcommittee on Ocean Sci. and Tech. Editor-in-chief: Oceanography; co-author with Admiral James D. Watkins, Oceans 2000: Bridging the Millennia; contbr. sci. articles to profl. jours. Recipient Disting. Civilian Svc. award, Dept. Navy, 2003, Presdl. Rank award. Mem. NAS, AAAS, Am. Soc. Limnology and Oceanography, Am. Geophys. Union, Oceanography Soc., Optical Soc. Am. (Johns Hopkins U. Schs. com.), Oceanography Soc. (coun. 1994-97, pres.-elect), Am. Meteorological Soc., Navy Leaque Democrat. Jewish. Avocations: banjo, outdoor activities, woodworking. Office: NOAA Office of Oceanic and Atmospheric Rsch 1315 East-West Hwy Silver Spring MD 20910 Office Phone: 301-713-2458. Office Fax: 301-713-0163. *

SPINRAD, ROBERT JOSEPH, computer scientist; b. NYC, Mar. 20, 1932; s. Sidney and Isabel (Reiff) S.; m. Verna Winderman, June 27, 1954; children: Susan Irene, Paul Reiff. BS, Columbia U., 1953, MS (Bridgham fellow), 1954; PhD (Whitney fellow), MIT, 1963. Registered profl. engr., N.Y. Project engr. Bulova Research & Devel. Lab., NYC, 1953-55; sr. scientist Brookhaven Nat. Lab., Upton, NY, 1955-68; v.p. Sci. Data Systems, Santa Monica, Calif., 1968-69; v.p. programming Xerox Corp., El Segundo, Calif., 1969-71, dir. info. scis., 1971-76, v.p. systems devel., 1976-78, v.p. research Palo Alto Rsch. Ctr., 1978-83, dir. systems tech., 1983-87, dir. corp. tech., 1987-92, v.p. tech. analysis and devel., 1992-94, v.p. technology strategy, 1994-98; ret.; cons. in field, Palo Alto, Calif., 1998—. Contbr. articles to profl. jours. Fellow Am. Acad. Arts & Scis.; mem. Nat. Acad. Engring., Calif. Coun. on Sci. and Tech., Sigma Xi, Tau Beta Pi. Achievements include patents in field. E-mail: robert@spinrad.com.

SPIRA, MELVIN, plastic surgeon; b. Chgo., July 3, 1925; s. Samuel and Jessie (Tivin) S.; m. Rita Silver, Nov. 27, 1952; children— Mary Ann, Joel Bennett, Pamela Beth Student, Wright Jr. Coll, Chgo., 1942-43, Franklin and Marshall Coll., Lancaster, Pa., 1943-44; DDS, Northwestern U., 1947, MSD, 1951; MD, Med. Coll. of Ga., 1956. Diplomate Am. Bd. Plastic Surgery (chmn. 1984-85). Intern Duke U. Hosp., Durham, NC, 1956-57, jr. asst. resident, 1958-59, asst. resident, 1959-60; resident Jefferson Davis Hosp, Houston, 1960-61, asst. in surgery and plastic surgery; sr. attending physician Ben Taub Gen. Hosp, Houston, attending physician, Tex. Children's Hosp., Houston, St. Lukes Episcopal Hosp., Houston; prof. Baylor Coll. Medicine, Houston, past head divsn. plastic surgery. Past chmn. Am. Bd. Plastic Surgery. Served with USN, 1943-45, 48-50 Fellow ACS; mem. Houston Surg. Soc., Am. Soc. Maxillofacial Surgeons (pres. 1974-75), Am. Soc. Plastic and Reconstructive Surgeons, Harris County Med. Soc., Plastic Surgery Research Council, So. Med. Assn., Tex. Med. Assn., Am. Trauma Soc., G.V. Black Soc., Internat. Soc. for Burn Injuries, Am. Burn Assn., Am. Cleft Palate Assn., Am. Assn. Plastic Surgeons (pres. 1992-93), Acad. Plastic Surgery Forum, Internat. Soc. Reconstructive Microsurgery, Tex. Surg. Soc., Michael E. DeBakey Internat. Cardiovascular Soc., Baron Hardy Soc., Am. Soc. for Aesthetic Plastic Surgery, Alpha Omega Alpha, Sigma Xi Avocations: skiing, photography, painting, tennis, golf. Office: Baylor College Of Medicine Div Of Plas 1709 Dryden Rd Ste 1600 Houston TX 77030-2414 Personal E-mail: rmspira@comcast.net.

SPIRA, PATRICIA GOODSITT, retired association executive; b. Milw. d. Lawrence Manfred and Ruth Pauline (Miller) Goodsitt; m. Marvin Alfred Spira, July 12, 1952; children: David, James, Ann, Ellen. BA in History, U. Wis., Milw., 1967. Dir. group sales Swan Theatre and Supper Club, Milw., 1962-63; mgr. box office Performing Arts Ctr., Milw., 1969-80; dir. devel. St. Louis Conservatory and Schs., 1980-81; pres. The Internat. Ticketing Assn., NYC, 1981—2002; ret., 2002. Tchr. Creative Dramatics, Milw., 1962-66; adv. coun. Town Hall, N.Y.C., 1989—; bd. dirs. Theatre and Dance Co., N.Y.C., 1986-89. Bd. dirs. Milw. Chamber Music Soc., 1974-80, Soc. Preservation Profl. Touring Entertainment History, 1998; bd. dirs. Sledgehammer Theatre, 2003-, mng. dir., 2004-; chair bd. dirs. Great Am. Children's Theatre, 1977-80. Mem. Am. Soc. Assn. Execs. (cert.). Avocations: reading, travel, theater. Home: 645 Front St unit 607 San Diego CA 92101 Office Phone: 619-544-1484. Personal E-mail: pspira@cox.net. Business E-Mail: pspira@sledgehammer.org.

SPIRO, HERBERT JOHN, political scientist, ambassador; b. Hamburg, Germany, Sept. 7, 1924; came to U.S., 1938, naturalized, 1944; s. Albert John and Marianne (Stiefel) S.; m. Elizabeth Anna Petersen, June 7, 1958 (div.); children: Peter John, Alexander Charles Stiefel; m. Marion Ballin, July 22, 1985. Student, San Antonio Jr. Coll., 1942-43; AB summa cum laude, Harvard U., 1949, MA, 1950, PhD, 1953; MA (hon.), U. Pa., 1971. Adminstrv. asst. U.S. War Dept., Vienna, 1945-46; mem. faculty Harvard U., Cambridge, Mass., 1950-61, asst. prof., 1957-61; assoc. prof. polit. sci. Amherst (Mass.) Coll., 1961-65; prof. polit. sci. U. Pa., Phila., 1965-73; mem. policy planning staff Dept. State, Washington, 1970-75; ambassador to Cameroon, 1975-77; amb. to Equatorial Guinea, 1975-76; fellow Woodrow Wilson Internat. Ctr. for Scholars, Smithsonian Instn., Washington, 1978; vis. prof. polit. sci. Def. Intelligence Sch., Washington, 1979-80; univ. prof. polit. sci. John F. Kennedy Inst. for N.Am. Studies, Free U. Berlin, 1980-89. Fulbright sr. rsch. prof. U. Coll. Rhodesia and Nyasaland, 1959-60; cons. Brit. Commn. to Rev. Constn., Fedn. Rhodesia and Nyasaland, 1960, Japanese Commn. on Revision Constn., 1962; vis. assoc. prof. U. Chgo., 1961, Stanford (Calif.) U., 1963; chmn. Asian and African Studies program, Amherst-Smith-Mt. Holyoke Colls., U. Mass., 1964-65; vis. prof. internat. affairs Woodrow Wilson Sch., Princeton (NJ) U., 1966; adv. coun. polit. sci. Haverford Coll., 1966-71; affiliated with Nuffield Coll., Oxford (Eng.) U., 1967-68; resident scholar Rockefeller Found. Study Ctr., Bellagio, Italy, 1968, 78; vis. prof. govt., guest scholar Ctr. for Internat. Affairs, Harvard U., 1983; vis. scholar U. Tex., Austin, 1984-89; life mem. Brit. studies faculty seminar U. Tex., Austin, 1983—; rschr. Lyndon Baines Johnson Presdl. Libr., 1985-86; fellow Aspen (Colo.) Inst. Humanistic Studies, 1986; adj. prof. govt. U. Tex., Austin, 1989-91; participant internat scholarly and diplomatic confs.; founder Brackenridge H.S.-Wilhelm Gymnasium Exchange; lectr. in field. Author: Politics of German Codetermination, 1958, (with others) Patterns of Government, 1958, 2d edit., 1962, Government by Constitution, 1959, Politics in Africa, 1962, 2d edit., 1975, Five African States, 1963, World Politics: The Global System, 1966, (with others) Authority, Nomos I, 1958, Responsibility, Nomos III, 1960, Privacy Nomos XIII, 1971, Why Federations Fail, 1968, Responsibility in Government, 1969, The Dialectic of Representation 1619-1969, 1969, Politics as the Master Science: From Plato to Mao, 1970 (with others), Theory and Politics, 1971 (with others), Between Sovereignty and Integration, 1974, A New Foreign Policy Consensus?, 1979, (with others) The Legacy of the Constitution, 1987, (with others) Anti-Americanism, 1988; editor, contbr.: (with others) Africa: The Primacy of Politics, 1966, Patterns of African Development, 1967, 'Privatization' of U.S. Foreign Relations, 1995; contbr.: World Book Ency., Ency. Britannica, Intern. Ency. of the Social Scis.; host Spiro's Conversations, Austin Community TV, 1992-97, San Antonio TimeWarner Access TV channel 20, 1999-2006; contbr. articles to profl. jours. Del. Tex. State Rep. Conv., 1990-92; precinct chmn. Travis County; Rep. cand. for Tex. Ho. of Reps., 1991, U.S. House of Reps., 1992, 94, U.S. Senate, 1993. Decorated Bronze Star medal with oak leaf cluster, Purple Heart; grand officer Legion of Valor Cameroon, 1977; recipient Detur prize Harvard Coll., 1948, Bowdoin prize, 1952; John Harvard scholar, 1949-51, Holzer scholar, 1949-51; Guggenheim fellow, 1959-60, Social Sci. Research Council faculty fellow, 1962, 67-68, Rockefeller Found. fellow, 1958, Sheldon travelling fellow Harvard U., also Fulbright fellow, 1953-54; Moody grantee Lyndon Baines Johnson Found., 1985. Fellow Assn. for Diplomatic Studies; mem. African Studies Assn., Am. Polit. Sci. Assn. (coun. 1968-70, chmn. election com. 1969), Internat. Polit. Sci. Assn., Am. Soc. Polit. and Legal Philosophy, Coun. Fgn. Rels., Coun. Am. Ambs., Am. Fgn. Svc. Assn., Mil. Order Purple Heart, San Antonio World Affairs Coun., Harvard Alumni Assn. (apptd. regional dir. Tex. 1994-97), San Antonio Coll. Alumni Assn. (dir. 1999—, Disting. Former Student award 2000), Wissenschaftliche Gesellschaft Berlin, Signet Soc., Harvard U. Faculty Club, Harvard Club (N.Y.C., del. to Tex.), Harvard Club Berlin (pres. 1985-89), Harvard Club Austin (pres. 1990-92), Harvard Club San Antonio, Phi Beta Kappa. Republican. Address: Apt 713 1 Towers Park Ln San Antonio TX 78209-6423 Personal E-mail: octospiro@sbcglobal.net.

SPIRO, ROBERT HARRY, JR., foundation and business executive, educator; b. Asheville, Dec. 5, 1920; s. Robert Harry and Eoline Peterson (Shaw) S.; m. Juanita T. Henderson, June 25, 2006; children by previous marriage: Robert Timothy, Elizabeth Susan, James Monroe. BS, Wheaton Coll., Ill., 1941; postgrad. Navy Supply Sch., Harvard U., 1943; postgrad., U. N.C., 1945-46; PhD, U. Edinburgh, Scotland, 1950; student, Union Theol. Sem., summers 1951-53; postdoctoral, Duke U., summer 1956; ScD (hon.), Fla. Inst. Tech. Assoc. prof. King Coll., Bristol, Tenn., 1946-50; prof. history Miss. Coll., 1950-57; pres. Blue Ridge Assembly, Black Mountain, NC, 1957-60; dean Coll. Liberal Arts Mercer U., prof. history, 1960-64; pres. Jacksonville U., Fla., 1964-79; under sec. of Army, 1980-81; cons. to bus., 1981-84, 86-99; nat. exec. dir. Res. Officers Assn. U.S., 1984-86; chmn. RHS Imprinted Products Inc., 1988-99; past bd. mgrs. Voyager Variable Annuity of Fla., 1972-79. V.p. Am. Security Coun. Found., 1991—99, chmn., 2002—; pres. Nat. Security Caucus Found., 1997—2002; past pres. Fla. Assn. Colls. and Univs.; mem., past chmn. Ind. Colls. and Univs., 1964—79, chmn, 1967; sec.-treas. Assn. Urban Univs., 1968—76; past mem. Fla.-Columbia Ptnrs.; gen. chmn. Jacksonville Sesquicentennial Commn., 1970—72; mem. N.C. Tricentennial Commn., 1959—65; past mem. adv. coun. Robert A. Taft Inst. Govt., Inst. Internat. Edn. Editor (with D.F. Winkler and J.C. Reilly Jr.) Destroyer Squadron Two From Leyte Gulf Through Okinawa, 2002; contbr. articles to profl. publs. and encys. Trustee Southwestern Bapt. Theol. Sem., 1968—78; chmn. bd. Bapt. Coll. and Sem., Washington, 1989—2001. Ensign to lt. USNR, 1941—45, PTO, ret. rear adm. USNR, 1978. Decorated Palmes Academique (France); recipient Disting. Civilian Svc. award, Dept. of Army, 1981, Disting. Alumnus award, Navy Supply Corps Sch., 2000, Disting. Svc. award, Mil. Order Carabao, 2005. Mem. Navy League U.S. (former pres. Jacksonville coun.), Naval Res. Assn. (nat. adv. coun.), Res. Officers Assn. U.S. Naval Inst., Am. Legion, Kiwanis (pres. Clinton, Miss. 1956-57; pres. Georgetown, D.C. Club 1991-92), Phi Delta Kappa, Alpha Kappa Psi, Phi Alpha Theta, Phi Kappa Phi. Home: 904 Cherokee Rd Charlotte NC 28207 *Esse Quam Videre "To Be Rather than to Seem" is an eloquent apothegm I learned in high school Latin classes. For me it has been a demanding goal for daily living, a worthy aspiration for each task in life and a challenging vision of what I wish and ought to be.*

SPISAK, JOHN FRANCIS, corporation executive; b. Cleve., Mar. 27, 1950; s. Ernest Lawrence and Adele Marie (Chipko) S.; m. Barbara Ann Heisman, June 10, 1972; children: John Stefan, Theresa Rose. BS in Chemistry, Purdue U., 1972, BS in Biology with honors, 1972. Rsch. engr. Anaconda Minerals, Tucson, 1972-79; chief metallurgist Fed. Am. Uranium, Riverton, Wyo., 1979-80; v.p. ops. Anschutz Mining Corp., Denver, 1980-87; chmn. bd. dirs. Warrenton Refining (subs. of Anschutz Corp.), Denver, 1987-89; dir., owner BE&K/Terranext, Inc., Denver, 1989—; pres. Continental Supply, Woodland, Calif., 2003—; pres., CEO Precision Assessment Tech. Corp., Lone Tree, 2006—. Mem. Western States-U.S. Senate Coalition for Superfund Reform; CEO, Am. Purification Corp., Newport Beach, Calif., 1998-02, pres. Prosonic Corp., Marietta, Ohio, 2002-03; CEO, Exegesis, 2005-, mgmt. cons., exec. coach, 2003-06. Contbr. articles to profl. publs.; patentee sequential flotation of sulfide ores. Named One of Fifty Colo. Top Bus. Leaders, Colo. Assn. Commerce and Industry. Mem. AIME, Soc. Mining, Metallurgy and Exploration, Nat. Assn. Environ. Mgrs. (co-founder, bd. dirs. Washington chpt., co-chmn. govt. liaison and advocacy com.), Denver Petroleum Club, Elks. Republican. Roman Catholic. Avocations: classical piano, bicycling, model railroads. Home: 9384 Oakbrush Way Lone Tree CO 80124-3070 Office: Precision Assessment Tech Corp 10475 Park Meadows Dr Ste 600 Lone Tree CO 80124 Office Phone: 720-279-2392. Personal E-mail: tnxtceo@aol.com. Business E-Mail: john.spisak@precisiontecha.com.

SPITALERI, VERNON ROSARIO, newspaper publisher, manufacturing company executive; b. Pelham, NY, Aug. 2, 1922; s. Rosario S. and Martha (Landerer) S.; m. Marjorie A. Ferrar, Oct. 14, 1952; children: Marc, Eric, Kris, Lynn. BS, Carnegie Mellon U., 1942. Mgr. mech. dept. Am. Newspaper Pubs. Assn., NYC, 1946-53; rsch. dir., gen. adminstr. Miami Herald and Knight Newspapers (Fla.), 1953-57; chmn. bd., pres. Sta-Hi Corp., Newport Beach, Calif., 1957-74; v.p. Republic Corp., 1974-76, Sun Chem. Corp., 1976-79. Chmn. bd. Sta-Hi Color Service, Sta-Hi Europe, Brussels, Concrete Floats-Huntington Engring. Corp., Huntington Beach, Calif., Kamalloy Alloys Corp.; editor, pub. Laguna Beach (Calif.) News-Post, 1967-81; pres. Laguna Pub. Co., Nat. Newspaper Found.; dir. Suburban Newspapers Am.; chmn. bd. Victory Profl. Products, Mango Surfware. Pres. Boys Club, Laguna Beach; mem. citizens adv. com. Laguna Beach; pres. Laguna Beach Libr. Bd., Laguna Playhouse, Laguna Coord. Coun.; bd. dirs. Sta-Hi Found.; dir. Opera Pacific, Festival of Arts. Lt. comdr. USNR, 1942-46. Decorated Purple Heart. Mem. Am. Mgmt. Assn., Nat. Newspaper Assn. (dir.), Calif. Newspaper Pubs. Assn. (dir.), Laguna Beach C. of C. (bd. dirs.), Dana Point Yacht Club, Alpha Tau Omega. Republican.

SPITZ, BARBARA SALOMON, artist; b. Chgo., Jan. 8, 1926; d. Fred B. and Sadie (Lorch) Salomon; m. Lawrence S. Spitz, Mar. 19, 1949; children— Thomas R., Linda J., Joanne L. Student, Art Inst. Chgo., 1942—43, R.I. Sch. Design, 1945; AB, Brown U., 1947. One-woman exhbns. include Benjamin Galleries, Chgo., 1971, 73, Kunsthaus Buhler, Stuttgart, Germany, 1973, Van Straaten Gallery, Chgo., 1976, 80, Elca London Studio, Montreal, Que., Can., 1977, Loyola U. Chgo., 1988, Schneider, Bluhm, Loeb gallery, Chgo., 1993, Newport Beach Pub. Lib., 2002, The Ctr. Gallery, 1994; group exhibitions include Am. Acad. Arts and Letters, Library of Congress traveling print exhbn., Tokyo Cen. Mus. Arts, Nat. Acad. Design, NYC, Pratt Graphic Ctr., Honolulu Acad. Arts, Wadsworth Atheneum, Nat. Aperture, 1986—, Laguna Art Mus., others; represented in permanent collections Phila. Mus. Art, DeCordova Mus., Okla. Art Ctr., Milw. Art Ctr., Los Angeles County Mus. Art, Art Inst. Chgo., Portland Mus. Art, Wadsworth Atheneum, med. arts programs UCLA, Block Mus./Northwestern U., Smart Mus./U. Chgo. Vice-chmn. Chgo. area Brown U. Bicentennial Drive; treas. Hearing and Speech Rehab. Ctr., Michael Reese Hosp., 1960; fine arts patron bd. Newport Harbor Art Mus. Mem. Print Club Phila., Boston Printmakers, Arts Club of Chgo., Soc. Am. Graphic Artists. Address: 1106 Somerset Ln Newport Beach CA 92660-5629 E-mail: bsslss@mac.com.

SPITZ, HUGO MAX, retired lawyer; b. Richmond, Va., Aug. 17, 1927; s. Jacob Gustav and Clara (Herzfeld) S.; m. Barbara Steinberg, June 22, 1952; children: Jack Gray, Jill Ann Levy, Sally Vinikoff. AA, U. Fla., 1948, BLaws, 1951, JD, 1967. Bar: Fla. 1951, S.C. 1955, U.S. Dist. Ct. (so. dist.) Fla. 1951, U.S. Dist. Ct. (ea. dist.) S.C. 1956, U.S. Ct. Appeals (4th cir.) 1957. Asst. atty. gen. State of Fla., Tallahassee, 1951; assoc. Williams, Salomon & Katz, Miami, Fla., 1951-54, Steinberg & Levkoff, Charleston, SC, 1954-57; sr. ptnr. The Steinberg Law Firm L.L.P., Charleston, 1957-2001; ret., 2001. Lectr. S.C. Trial Lawyers Assn., Columbia, 1958—, S.C. U. Sch. Law, Columbia, 1975, S.C. Bar Assn., 1955—; assoc. mcpl. judge Charleston, 1972-74, chief mcpl. judge, 1974-76; commr. Charleston County Substance Abuse Commn., 1976-79; bd. govs. S.C. Patient's Compensation Fund, Columbia, 1978-97; adv. mem., atty. S.C. Legis. Coun. for Worker's Compensation; chmn. bd. dirs. Franklin C. Fetter Health Ctr., Charleston, 1977-78; mem. S.C. Appellate Def. Commn., 1985-86; founding sponsor Civil Justice Found., 1986—; bd. pres. Charleston Jewish Fedn., 1990-91, pres., 1991-92. Pres. Synagogue Emanu-El, 1969-71. With USN, 1945-46. Recipient Order of Silver Crescent, Gov. SC, 2001, Cmty. Achievement award, 1993. Fellow S.C. Bar Assn., U. S.C. Ednl. Found.; mem. ABA, Civil Justice Found., S.C. Law Inst., S.C. Trial Lawyers Assn. (founder and pres. 1985-86, Disting. Svc. award 2001), S.C. Claimants' Attys. for Workers Compensation (hon. life bd. mem., founder, exec. com. 1986), S.C. Workers Compensation Ednl. Assn. (life, bd. dirs. 1978-98), S.C. Law Inst., Am. Judicature Soc., Trial Lawyers Am. (mem. pres. coun. 1986-87, stalwart 2001), Nat. Rehab. Assn., Nat. Orgn. Social Security Claimants' Reps. S.C. Bar (chmn. trial and appellate sect. 1982-83, ho. of dels. 1984-85), So. Assn. Workmen's Compensation Adminstrs., Nat. Inst. for Trial Advocacy (com. chmn. 1985), Hebrew Benevolent Soc. (life, pres. 1974-75), Jewish Cmty. Ctr. (Charleston) (v.p. 1972-74), Hebrew Orphan Soc. (life, pres. 2000-01), B'nai B'rith, Elks (life). Democrat. Home: 337 Confederate Cir Charleston SC 29407-7430 Personal E-mail: hspitz@comcast.net.

SPITZ, MARK, Olympic athlete; b. Modesto, Calif., Feb. 10, 1950; m. Suzy Weiner; 2 children. BS, Ind. U, 1972. Mem. U.S. swimming team Olympic Games, 1968, 72, guest TV swimming commentator. Former owner Beverly Hills Real Estate Co. Author: (novels) The Mark Spitz complete book of swimming, 1976, Seven Golds: Mark Spitz Own Story, 1987. Inducted as Honor Swimmer to Internat. Swimming Hall of Fame, 1977; Sullivan award for top athlete in any sport AAU, 1971; named World Swimmer of Yr., 1969, 1971, 1972. won total of 9 Olympic Gold medals, 4x100m freestyle, 4x200m freestyle, 1968, 1972, 100m freestyle, 200m freestyle, 100m butterfly, 200m butterfly, 4x100m medley, 1972; only Olympian in history to win 7 Gold medals (all World Records) in a single Olympics, Munich Olympic Games, 1972, Silver Medal, 100m butterfly, Bronze Medal, 100m freestyle, Mexico City Olympic Games, 1968, 5 Gold medals Pan-Am. Games, 1967, held 32 world records, 1967-1972; 4 times Champion NCAA, 1969-72.

SPITZ, SEYMOUR JAMES, JR., retired fragrance company executive; b. Milw., Nov. 17, 1921; s. Seymour James and Marie (Spinette) S.; m. Elizabeth Taylor Parks, Feb. 7, 1948 (div. Aug. 1967); children: William Taylor, Elizabeth Seymour, Anne Bellin; m. Ellen C. Flynn, July 25, 1969; 1 dau., Ellen Christina. SB, MIT, 1943. With Newport Industries div. Heyden Newport Chem. Corp., Pensacola, Fla., 1946-65; asst. chief engr., 1955-57; asst. v.p., 1957-58; v.p. Newport Industries div. Heyden Newport Chem. Corp., 1959-60, exec. v.p., 1960-61, pres., 1961-65; v.p. parent co. Heyden Newport Chem. Corp., 1962-65, became group v.p., 1965; exec. v.p. Heyden Newport Chem. Corp. (renamed Tenneco Chems., Inc.), 1966; pres. Tenneco Chems., Inc., 1967-69; sr. v.p. parent co. Tenneco Inc.; pres. and dir. Internat. Flavors & Fragrances Inc., NYC, 1970-85. Mem. MIT Corp. Devel. Com., 1977-86; trustee Spence Sch., 1982-88, Savannah (Ga.) Symphony, 1990-95, 98, Telfair Mus. Art, Savannah, 1993-96; MBA adv. bd. Ga. Southern U., 1998—. USN ENS-LCDR, 1943-46. Mem. Univ. Club (N.Y.C.), Larchmont Yacht Club (N.Y., trustee 1986-89), Landings Club, Oglethorpe Club (Savannah, bd. dirs. 1995-99). Home: 6 Brandenberry Rd Savannah GA 31411-2201 E-mail: sjstennis@bellsouth.net.

SPITZBERG, IRVING JOSEPH, JR., lawyer; b. Little Rock, Feb. 9, 1942; s. Irving Joseph and Marie Bettye (Seeman) S.; m. Roberta Frances Alprin, Aug. 21, 1966 (div. 1988); children: Edward Storm, David Adam; m. Virginia V. Thorndike, Dec. 24, 1988. BA, Columbia U., 1964; B.Phil., Oxford U., 1966; JD, Yale U., 1969. Bar: Calif. 1969, DC 1985, Va. 1995. Asst. prof. Pitzer Coll., Claremont, Calif., 1969-71; fellow Inst. Current World Affairs, NYC, 1971-74; vis. lectr. Brown U., Providence, 1973; assoc prof. SUNY, Buffalo, 1974-80, dean of coll., 1974-78; gen. sec. AAUP, Washington, 1980-84; exec. dir. Coun. for Liberal Learning of Assn. Am. Colls., Washington, 1985-89; pres. The Knowledge Co., Fairfax, Va., 1985-2001; ptnr. Spitzberg & Drew, Washington, 1990-92; of counsel Spirer & Goldberg, Washington, 1993—; pvt. practice, 1993—. Coord. Alvan Ikoku Coll., Nigeria, 1979-80; cons. Bd. Adult Edn., Kenya, 1973-74, Philander Smith Coll., Little Rock, 1978-80; co-dir. nat. study on campus life for Carnegie Found. for Advancement Teaching, 1989-90. Author and editor: Exchange of Expertise, 1978, Universities and the New International Order, 1979, Universities and the International Exchange of Knowledge, 1980; author: Campus Programs on Leadership, 1986, Racial Politics in Little Rock, 1987; co-author: (with Berdahl and Moodie), Quality and Access in Higher Education, 1991, (with Virginia Thorndike) Creating Community on College Campuses, 1992; polit. columnist Prince William Times, 2001-02. Founder Coalition for Ednl. Excellence, Western NY, 1978-80, Advocates for the Rural Crescent, Va., 1999-2002, Coun. Liberal Learning; founding mem. Alliance for Leadership Devel., Washington, 1985; counsel GASP, Pomona, Calif., 1969-71; Dem. Committeeman, Erie County, NY, 1978-80; founding pres. Internat. Found. for St. Catherine's Coll., Oxford, 1986-91; v.p. Sparks-Glencoe Cmty. Coun., 2004-05; pres. North County Preservation, Inc., 2004—; chair Internat. Quranic Ctr., 2006—. Nat. winner Westinghouse Sci. Talent Search, 1960; Kellett scholar Trustees of Columbia U., 1964-66. Mem. Am. Immigration Lawyers Assn., Nat. Acad. Elder Law Attys., Washington Ethical Soc. (adj. leader 2002—), Ethical Culture Soc., Columbia Club, Yale Club (Washington), Rotary Internat. Jewish. Avocation: the internet. Personal E-mail: ijs@aol.com.

SPITZE, GLENYS SMITH, retired teacher and counselor; b. Rozel, Kans., May 20, 1919; d. Harry H. and Mary Louisa (Mishler) Smith; m. LeRoy A. Spitze, Dec. 31, 1942 (dec. Nov. 1995); children: Randall LeRoy, Kevin Lance, Kimett Alvin, Terril Christian, Shawn Smith; 1 fosterchild, Theo Ritz-Spitze. Cert. tchg., U. Kans., Lawrence, 1939; AA, San Jose City Coll., Calif., 1963; BA in Psychology, San Jose State U., 1965, MA in Child Devel., 1968. Cert. tchr., counselor, Calif. Elem. sch. tchr. Topeka County Schs., Richland, Kans., 1939-40, Kinsley Pub. Schs., Kans., 1940-42; presch. substitute tchr. AAUW Kindergarten, Newark, Ohio, 1945—46; presch. tchr. Meth. Ch. Facility, Campbell, Calif., 1956-58; guest lectr. Govt. Sch. Social Work, Colombo, Sri Lanka, 1965-66; instr. man-woman relationship San Jose State Free U., 1966-67; child devel. lab. psychol. examiner Child Labs San Jose State U., 1967-68; pvt. informal practice tchr., counselor, cons. San Jose, Kailua-Kona, Hawaii. Vocal music dir. grades 1-3 Southside Sch., 1940-41; 6th dist. Calif. Congress Parent-Tchrs. Social Welfare dir., officer 6th dist. com. Calif. Coun. on Crime and Delinquency, San Jose, 1956-62; mem. kindergarten com. AAUW, Newark, Ohio, 1945-46; coord. Sangha Symposium, Asian Philosophy Club, San Jose State U., 1964-65; lectr. in field. Contbr. articles, poems to profl. publs. Hon. del. Gov. Brown's Conf. on Prevention of Juvenile Delinquency, Sacramento, 1963; co-organizer Post Polio Support Group, Kailua-Kona, HI, 2000. Mem.: Psi Chi. Avocations: writing, reading, swimming, snorkeling, anthropology. Home: 78-6800 Alii Dr KKSRC 5-103 Kailua Kona HI 96740-4421 Home (Summer): 311 E Bowman Woodland Park CO 80863 also: PO Gen Delivery Woodland Park CO 80863 Home Phone: 719-687-1306. Personal E-mail: gmglenys@webtv.net.

SPITZE, ROBERT GEORGE FREDERICK, agricultural studies educator; b. Berryville, Ark., Oct. 12, 1922; s. Wesley Henry and Nora Catherine (Stullken) Spitze; m. Hazel Cleo Taylor, Mar. 4, 1944; children: Glenna Dean, Ken Rollin. Student, Columbia U., 1944; BS (Sears Roebuck nat. fellow), U. Ark., 1947; PhD (Knapp research fellow), U. Wis., 1954. Instr. U. Wis., Madison, 1950; asst. prof. to prof. U. Tenn., Knoxville, 1951-60; prof. agrl. econs. U. Ill., Urbana, 1960-93. Vis. prof. Wye Coll., U. London, 1967-68; vis. research prof. policy U.S. Dept. Agr., Washington, 1975; vis. lectr. various univs., U.S. and Eng.; cons. Fed. Intermediate Credit Bank, 1958-59, Ill. Gen. Assembly Commn. on Revenue, 1963, Tex. A&M U., 1970, Am. Farm Bur. Fedn., Chgo., 1971, Ill. Gov.'s Commn. on Farm Income, 1972, Nat. Agrl. Research Policy Adv. Com., 1975, U.S. Dept. Agr. Econs. Research Service, 1976, Wharton Econometric Forecasting Inc., 1977, Nat. Rural Center, Washington, 1979-80, Nat. Public Policy Com., 1980, Okla. State U., 1986; mem. Ill. Gov.'s Council Econ. Advisers, 1974-76 Co-author: Food and Agricultural Policy, Economics and Politics, 1994; co-editor Policy Rsch. Notes, 1975-92, Food, Agriculture, and Rural Policy into the Twenty-first Century, 1994; editor: Agricultural and Food Policy: Issues and Alternatives for the 1990s, 1990; contbr. articles to profl. jours., chpts. to books Lt. USNR, 1943—47. Recipient Funk recognition award, 1973, Excellence in Teaching award U. Ill., 1977, Outstanding Agr. Coll. Alumni award U. Ark., 1994; co-recipient Outstanding Philanthropist Award Nat. Agrl. Alumni Devel. Assn., 2004 Mem. AAAS, Am. Econ. Assn., Am. Agrl. Econs. Assn. (Disting. Policy award 1981, Disting. Teaching award 1972, travel study grantee to France 1964), Internat. Assn. Agrl. Econs., Agrl. Econs. Soc. (U.K.), AAUP, Blue Key, Sigma Xi, Omicron Delta Kappa, Gamma Sigma Delta, Phi Eta Sigma, Alpha Zeta, Phi Sigma Office: U Ill Dept Agr Econ 1301 W Gregory Dr Dept Agr Urbana IL 61801-9015

SPITZER, ADRIAN, pediatrician, educator; b. Bucharest, Rumania, Dec. 21, 1927; came to U.S., 1963, naturalized, 1968; s. Osias and Sophia S. S.; m. Carole Zelter, Oct. 31, 1951; 1 son, Vlad. BS, Matei Basarab Lyceum, Bucharest, 1946; MD, Med. Sch. Bucharest, 1952. Diplomate: Am. Bd. Pediat., Am. Bd. Pediats./Nephrology. Intern White Plains (N.Y.) Hosp., 1964; resident Hosp. Med. Coll. Pa., 1965-66; postdoctoral fellow pediatric nephrology Albert Einstein Coll. Medicine, 1966-67; postdoctoral fellow in renal physiology Cornell U. Med. Sch., 1967-68; practice medicine specializing in pediatric nephrology Bronx, NY, 1968—; asst. prof. pediatrics Albert Einstein Coll. Medicine, 1968-72, assoc. prof., 1972-76, prof., 1976—, dir. div. nephrology, 1973-99; mem. staff Bronx Mcpl. Hosp. Ctr., Hosp. Albert Einstein Coll. Medicine/Montefore Med. Ctr.; mem. Medicine B Study sect.-NIH, 1976-80. Prof. C. Donders rotating chmn. U. Utrecht, The Netherlands, 1990-91; Christiansen vis. fellow St. Catherine's Coll.; vis. fellow dept. biochemistry Oxford U., 1981-82; coord. Internat. Study Kidney Disease in Children; chmn. organizing com. 1st-7th Internat. Workshop on Devel. Renal Physiology, 1980-98, pres., 2001; mem. renal adv. com. N.Y.C. Dept. Health; sci. adv. bd. rsch. and grant com. Nat. Kidney Found., 1982; chmn. pediatric nephrology bd. Am. Bd. Pediat., 1982-83. Mem. editorial bd.: Pediatric Nephrology, Seminars in Nephrology; assoc. editor: Pediatric Renal Disease, 1979, 2d edit., 1992; editor: The Kidney Development, 1982. NIH spl fellow, 1967; John E. Fogarty Sr. Internat. fellow, 1981-82; grantee NIH, N.Y. State Health Research Council, Nat. Kidney Found.; recipient Bela Schick medal for extraordinary achievements in acad. and clin. pediatrics; The Scientific Advancement award of the Internat. Pediatr. Nephrol. Assn. Mem.: Intersoc. Coun. for Kidney and Urinary Tract Rsch. (sec.-treas. 1984—89), Am. Pediat. Soc., Am. Acad. Pediat. (Henry L. Barnett award 2005), Soc. Pediatric Rsch., Am. Physiol. Soc., Am. Fedn. Clin. Rsch., Am. Soc. Pediatric Nephrology (coun. 1977—80, pres. 1981—82, Founder's award 2006), Am. Soc. Nephrology (com. on govtl. rels. 1999—2001). Office: Albert Einstein Coll Medicine Montefiore Med Ctr 111 E 210th St Bronx NY 10467-2401 Office Phone: 718-655-1120. Business E-mail: spitzer@aecom.yu.edu.

SPITZER, CARY REDFORD, avionics consultant, electrical engineer; b. New Hope, Va., July 31, 1937; s. Clyde Burke and Marion Jeanette (Redford) S.; m. Carrie Laura Ruth Logan, June 18, 1960; 1 child, Stiegel Logan. BSEE, Va. Poly. Inst. & State U., 1959; MS in Engring. Mgmt., George Washington U., 1970. Rsch. engr., engring. mgr. Langley Rsch Ctr., NASA, Hampton, Va., 1962-94; founder, pres. AvioniCon, Inc., 1993—. Lectr. UCLA, 1989—, George Washington U., 1994. Author: Viking Orbiter Views of Mars, 1981, Digital Avionics Systems, 1987, 2d edit., 1993, Avionics Handbook, 2000, Digital Avionics Handbook, 2007; contbr. articles to sci. publs. 1st lt. USAF, 1959-62. Recipient Volare award Airline Avionics Inst., 1988; named Va. Peninsula Engr. of Yr., 1993; recipient Digital Avionics award Am. Inst. of Aeronautics and Astronautics, 1994; nominated Collier Trophy, 1991. Fellow: IEEE (Centennial medal 1984, Millennium medal 2000), AIAA (assoc.); mem.: Aerospace and Electronic Systems Soc. of IEEE (pres. 1973—74, editor-in-chief Trans. 1996—99, chmn. IEEE-USA aerospace policy com. 1997—2000), Exch. Club (pres. Williamsburg 1985). Methodist. Avocations: kite flying, car mechanics. Home and Office: 3409 Foxridge Rd Williamsburg VA 23188-2499 Home Phone: 757-229-8296; Office Phone: 757-221-8031.

SPITZER, DANIEL E., neurosurgeon; b. NYC; s. Bernard and Anne Spitzer; m. Heidi Litt; children: Zachary, Rachel. BA, Princeton U., NJ, 1979; MD, NYU, 1983. Diplomate Am. Bd. Neurosurgery, 1992. Resident in neurosurgery Albert Einstein/Montefiore Hosp., Bronx, NY, 1989; neurosurgeon Hudson Valley Neurosurgery, Suffern, NY, 1989—. Patentee in field. Named Physician of Yr., Nyack Hosp., NY, 2003. Avocations: aviation, photography, scuba diving, tennis, skiing. Office Phone: 845-368-0286.

SPITZER, ELIOT LAURENCE, governor, former state attorney general; b. Bronx, June 10, 1959; s. Bernard and Anne Spitzer; m. Silda A. Wall, Oct. 17, 1987; children: Elyssa, Sarabeth, Jenna. BA, Princeton U., 1981; JD, Harvard U., 1984. Law clk. to Hon. Robert W. Sweet US Dist. Ct. (so. dist.) NY, NYC, 1984—85; assoc. Paul, Weiss, Rifkind, Wharton & Garrison, 1985—86, Skadden Arps Slate Meagher & Flom, 1992—94; ptnr. Constantine & Ptnrs., NYC, 1994—98; asst. dist. atty. NYC, 1986—92, chief, Labor Racketeering unit, 1991—92; atty. gen. State of NY, Albany, 1999—2007, gov., 2007—. Analyst, commentator on nat. news programs including NBC's Today Show, CNN's Burden of Proof, CNBC, Court TV; pro bono counsel N.Y. State Commn. for the Study of Youth Crime and Violence, 1993—94. Editor: Harvard Law Rev.; contbr. articles in leading newspapers and legal jours. Founder Ctr. for Cmty. Interest. Named Crusader of the Yr., TIME mag., 2002; named one of The World's Most Influential People, 2005; recipient Paul H. Douglas Ethics in Govt. award, U. Ill., 2004, Jacob J. Javits Pub. Svc. award, Am. Psychiatric Assn., 2005. Democrat. Jewish. Avocations: running, tennis. Office: Office of Gov State Capitol Albany NY 12224 *

SPITZER, HUGH D., lawyer; b. Seattle, Feb. 14, 1949; s. George Frederick and Dorothy Lea (Davidson) S.; m. Ann Scales, Oct. 14, 1983; children: Johanna Spitzer, Claudia Spitzer, Jenny Spitzer. BA, Yale U., 1970; JD, U. Wash., 1974; LLM, U. Calif., 1982. Bar: Wash. 1974, U.S. Dist. Ct. (ea. and we. dists.) Wash. 1975, U.S. Ct. Appeals (9th and D.C. cirs.) 1975, U.S. Supreme Ct. 1980. Program analyst N.Y.C. Health and Hosp. Corp., 1970-71; labor lawyer Hafer, Cassidy & Price, Seattle, 1974-76; legis. asst. Seattle City Coun., 1976-77; legal counsel to mayor City of Seattle, 1977-81; mcpl. bond lawyer Foster Pepper & Shefelman, PLLC, Seattle, 1982—. Affiliate prof. sch. law U. Wash. Contbr. articles to profl. jours. Chair Seattle Law Income Housing Levy Oversight com., 1988-96, Wash. State Affordable Housing Adv. Bd., 2000—; vice chair Puget Sound Water Quality Authority Wash. State, 1989-96, State Tax Structure Com., 2001-02. Mem. Nat. Assn. Bond Lawyers, Am. Judicature Soc. (mem. exec. com. Coun. on Pub. Legal Edn.). Democrat. Avocations: piano, hiking, skiing. Office: Foster Pepper & Shefelman PLLC 1111 3rd Ave Bldg Ste 3400 Seattle WA 98101-3292 Office Phone: 206-447-8965. E-mail: spith@foster.com.

SPITZER, JOHN BRUMBACK, lawyer; b. Toledo, Mar. 6, 1918; s. Lyman and Blanche (Brumback) S.; m. Lucy Ohlinger, May 10, 1941 (dec. Oct. 13, 1971); children: John B., Molly (Mrs. Edmund Frost), Lyman, Adelbert L.; m. Vondah D. Thornbury, July 3, 1972 (dec. Nov. 2001); stepchildren: Vondah, Barbara, James R. Thornbury. Grad., Phillips Andover Acad., 1935; BA, Yale U., 1939, LLB, 1947. Bar: Ohio 1947. Law clk. to U.S. Supreme Ct. Justice Stanley Reed, 1947-48; ptnr. Marshall, Melhorn, Cole, Hummer & Spitzer, Toledo, 1955-86, Hummer & Spitzer, Toledo, 1986-89; with Hummer Legal Svcs. Corp., 1990—2002; ptnr. Spitzer and Hummer, 1990—. Pres. Spitzer Paper Box Co., 1955-63; v.p. Spitzer Bldg. Co., 1960-91, pres. 1992—. Pres. Toledo Symphony Orch., 1956-58, v.p., sec., 1958-86, trustee, 1986—. Maj. AUS, World War II. Mem.: Belmont Country Club. Congregationalist. Home: 29620 Gleneagles Rd Perrysburg OH 43551-3530 Office: Spitzer Bldg Co Rm 430 Spitzer Bldg 520 Madison Ave Toledo OH 43604 Office Phone: 419-255-1440. Personal E-mail: info@winelandlegal.com.

SPITZER, LOIS NANCY, language educator; b. Roslyn, NY, Oct. 6, 1958; d. Bernard and Ann (Poster) Yellin; m. Lee B. Spitzer, Aug. 20, 1977; children: Joshua, Larisa. BA, Calif. State U., Fullerton, 1979; MEd, RI Coll., Providence, 1983; EdD, Boston U., 1989. Instr. English as 2d lang. Project Personal/Indochnese Refugee Assistance Program, Providence, 1981, Genesis Sch. Indochinese Adults, Providence, 1983—84; asst. prof. English as 2d lang. Mans Landing C.C., NJ, 1988—94; sr. lect. English as 2d lang. U. Nebr., Lincoln, 1994—2003; tchr. English as 2d lang. Pemberton Twp. Pub. Schs., NJ, 2004—06; tchr. English as 2d lang., dept. chair Riverside Pub. Schs., NJ, 2006—. Presenter in field. Author: Journeying with Joshua: Reflections on Raising an Autistic Child for Parents, Teachers and Friends, 2005; contbr. articles to profl. jours. Mem.: NJ TESOL, TESOL. Baptist. Home: 10 Bentwood Dr Bordentown NJ 08505

SPITZER, MARC LEE, commissioner, former state legislator; b. Pitts., Sept. 12, 1957; s. Richard A. and Edith (Brodie) S., m. Jacque, one child. BA in History and Polit. Sci. summa cum laude, Dickinson Coll., 1979; JD cum laude, U. Mich., 1982. Bar: Ariz. 1982, U.S. Dist. Ct. Ariz. 1982, U.S. Tax Ct. 1982, U.S. Ct. Appeals (9th cir.) 1985. Dir. KPMG Peat Marwick, Phoenix, 1982—; mem. Ariz. State Senate, Phoenix, 1992—2000, majority leader, 1997—2000; commr. Ariz. Corp. Commn., Phoenix, 2000—06, chmn., 2003—05; commr. Fed. Energy Regulatory Commn., Washington, 2006—. Bd. dirs. Ariz. Acad., 1990; mem. devel. com. Dickinson Coll., 1985-86; dir. Arizonans for Cultural Devel.; vice-chmn. Ariz. 18th Dist., 1986—; alternate del. 1988 Rep. Nat. Conv. GOP; legal counsel Ariz. Rep. Party. Recipient awards for legis. svc. from 32 non-profit orgns. Mem. ABA (vice-chmn., tax legis. sect.), State Bar Ariz. (cert. specialist taxation), Ariz. Tax Research Found. (bd. dirs. 1984—), Ariz. Tax Research Assn., Maricopa County Bar Assn., Phoenix 100 Rotary, Heritage Found., Ariz. Club, Phi Beta Kappa, Sigma Alpha Epsilon. Jewish. Avocations: fishing, prospecting, classical music, racquetball. Office: Fed Energy Regulatory Commn 888 First St NE Washington DC 20426

SPITZER, MATTHEW LAURENCE, law educator; b. LA, June 23, 1952; s. William George and Jeanette Dorothy S.; m. Jean Fuksman, July 8, 1973; 1 child, Amanda Elizabeth. BA in Math., UCLA, 1973; JD, U. So. Calif., 1977; PhD in Social Scis., Calif. Inst. Tech., 1979. Assoc. Nossaman, Guthner, Knox & Elliott, LA, 1977—79; asst. prof. Northwestern U., Chgo., 1979—81; William T. Dalessi prof. law U. So. Calif., LA, 1987—2000, assoc. prof., 1981—84, prof., 1984—, dir. law and rational choice programs, 1990—2000, co-dir. Ctr. Comms. Law and Policy, 1998—, dean, Carl Mason Franklin prof. law, 2000—06, Robert C. Packard Trustee Prof. Law, 2006—; prof. law and social scis. Calif. Inst. Tech., Pasadena, 1992—2000, 2006—. Vis. prof. law U. Chgo., 1996, Stanford U., Calif., 1997, NYU, 2007; mem. organizing com. Telecoms. Policy Rsch. Conf., Washington, 1991-94. Author: Seven Dirty Words and Six Other Stories, 1986; co-author: (with T. Hazlett) Public Policy Toward Cable Television, 1997. Recipient (shared with Elizabeth Hoffman) Ronald H. Coase prize U. Chgo., 1986. Mem.: Am. Law and Econs. Assn. (bd. dirs. 1997—2000). Avocations: paperweight collecting, audiophile. Office: U So Calif Gould Law School Los Angeles CA 90089-0071 Home Phone: 323-550-8609; Office Phone: 213-740-6473.

SPITZER, MATTHEW LAWRENCE, retired retail store executive; b. Pitts., June 20, 1929; s. Martin and Ruth G. S.; children: Mark, Edward, Eric, Joseph. Student, U. Buffalo, 1948-50. Lic. airline transport pilot. Product line mgr. Gen. Dynamics, Rochester, NY, 1962-67; dir. contracts Friden divsn. Singer, San Leandro, Calif., 1968-69; asst. v.p. Talcott Computer Leasing, San Francisco, 1970-71; pres. Spitzer Music Mgmt. Co., Hayward, Calif., 1972-95, Spitzer Helicopter Leasing Co., Hayward, 1991—2006. Chmn. bd. Leo's Audio and Music Techs., Oakland, Calif. Mem. Masons, Mensa. Personal E-mail: mspitz6685@aol.com.

SPITZER, MORTON EDWARD, management consultant; b. NYC, Jan. 3, 1937; s. Henry Lawrence and Martha (Michel) S.; m. Nancy Dinetz, Oct. 10, 1965; children: Matthew, Douglas. BA, Bklyn. Coll., 1957; MS, N.C. State U., 1959; PhD, N.Y. U., 1964. Dir./mgr. planning and analysis The Prudential Ins. Co. Am., Newark, 1964-74, v.p. S.W. ops. Houston, 1975-79, v.p. ordinary agys. Newark, 1979-87, pres. North Ctrl. ops. Mpls., 1988, sr. v.p. dist. agys. Newark, 1989, Woodland Hills, Calif., 1990-91; COO Liberty Life Assurance Co. Boston, Dover, NH, 1992—2002, ret., 2002. Bd. dirs. Liberty Life Assurance Co., Boston, Liberty Assignment Co., Liberty Life Distbrs. LLC, Liberty Life Securities LLC, BARCO Lto, Barbados, Limra Internat., N.Am. Life and Health of N.Y.; bd. govs. ACLI Forum 500; bd. dirs. N. Am. Co., NY, N.Am. Life and Health Ins. Co. N.Y., Vetinsurance Internat. Co-author: The Law and Personnel Testing, 1971. Bd. dirs. Nat. Soc. to Prevent Blindness, N.J., 1986-89, nat. bd. dirs., Chgo., 1989. Mem. APA, Am. Psychol. Soc., Ea. Psychol. Assn., Sigma Xi. Avocations: tennis, art. Home: 449 E Deering Rd Deering NH 03244

SPITZER, ROBERT J., academic administrator; BBA, Gonzaga U.; MPhil, St. Louis U.; STB, Gregorian U., Rome; ThM, Weston Sch. Theology, Cambridge, Mass.; PhD in Philosophy, Cath. U. of Am. Tchr. Georgetown U., 1984-90, Seattle U., 1978-80, 90-98; pres. Gonzaga U., 1998—. Co-founder U. Faculty for Life; founder, adv. Life Principles. Office: Gonzaga U 502 E Boone Ave Spokane WA 99258-0001 *

SPITZER, TOBA, rabbi; MDiv, Reconstructionist Rabinnical Coll., 1997. Rabbi Congregation Dorshei Tzedek, West Newton, Mass. Named one of The Top 50 Rabbis in America, Newsweek Mag., 2007. Office: Congregation Dorshei Tzedek 60 Highland St West Newton MA 02465 Office Phone: 617-965-0330.

SPITZLI, DONALD HAWKES, JR., lawyer; b. Newark, Mar. 19, 1934; s. Donald Hawkes and Beatrice (Banister) S.; children: Donald Hawkes III, Peter Gilbert, Seth Armstrong. AB, Dartmouth Coll., 1956; LLB, U. Va., 1963. Bar: Va. 1963. Assoc. Willcox, Savage, Lawrence, Dickson & Spindle, Norfolk, Va., 1964-67, 68-70, ptnr., 1971-77; atty. Eastman Kodak Co., Rochester, N.Y., 1967-68; pres. Marine Hydraulics Internat., Inc., Chesapeake, Va., 1978-80; sole practice Virginia Beach, Va., 1980—. Owner Chieftain Motor Inn, Hanover, N.H., 1980-87. Comdr. USNR, 1956-70. Episcopalian. Office: 4460 Corporation Ln Ste 180 Virginia Beach VA 23462 Home Phone: 757-426-2012; Office Phone: 757-499-1191. Personal E-mail: airbuzzard24@aol.com.

SPITZNAGEL, JOHN KEITH, retired microbiologist, immunologist, physician; b. Peoria, Ill., Apr. 11, 1923; s. Elmer Florian and Anna S. (Kolb) S.; m. Anne Moulton Sirch, Feb. 2, 1947; children: John, Jean, Margaret, Elizabeth, Paul. BA, Columbia U., 1943, MD, 1946. Diplomate Nat. Bd. Med. Examiners, Am. Bd. Internal Medicine. Intern Johns Hopkins Hosp., Balt., 1946-47; resident in internal medicine Barnes Hosp., St. Louis, 1949-51; vis. investigator Rockefeller Inst., NYC, 1952-53, Nat. Inst. Med. Research, London, 1967-68; mem. faculty U. N.C., Chapel Hill, 1957-79, prof. microbiology and infectious diseases, prof. medicine, 1957-79; cons. N.C. Meml. Hosp., Chapel Hill, 1974-79; ad hoc adviser NIH, 1971—; prof. microbiology and immunology, chmn. dept. Emory U., Atlanta, 1979-93, prof. emeritus microbiology and immunology, 1993—, assoc. dean rsch., 1997-98; attending physician, vol. and co-founder Good Samaritan Health and Wellness Ctr., Jasper, Ga., 2002—, chmn. exec. bd., CEO, 2004—06. Mem. study sect. bacteriology and mycology NIH, 1975-79, 85-89, chmn., 1977-79. Editor: Infection and Immunity, 1970-80, Jour. Immunology, 1973-80, Jour. Reticuloendothelial Soc, 1973-80. Served with M.C. AUS, 1947-57. Recipient Research Career Devel. award USPHS, 1957-67, Disting. Service award Sch. Medicine U. N.C., Chapel Hill, 1987; USPHS postdoctoral fellow, 1968; USPHS and AEC grantee; lectureship named in his honor, Spitznagel Lectureship on Host Antimicrobial Def., Emory U., 1998. Fellow ACP, Infectious Disease Soc.; mem. AAAS (life), Am. Soc. Microbiology (div. group councilor 1977-79), Am. Assn. Immunologists, Reticuloendothelial Soc. (pres. 1982), Infectious Disease Soc., So. Soc. Clin. Rsch., Assn. Am. Med. Sch. Microbiology and Immunology Chmn. (pres. 1990-91), Sigma Xi. Achievements include research on cell biology of human neutrophil polymorphonuclear leukocytes, and oxygen ind. mechanisms of antimicrobial phagocytoses; first to demonstrate cationic antimicrobial proteins of polymorphonuclear leukocytes granules; co-discoverer of a cationic protein of polymorph granules with antimicrobial action and a powerful attractant for mononuclear phagocytes. Home: 95 Starcross Ln # 20804 Jasper GA 30143-7883 Office: 1510 Clifton Rd NE Atlanta GA 30322-4218 E-mail: spitzna@mac.com.

SPIVAK, ALVIN A., retired public relations executive; b. Phila., Nov. 30, 1927; s. Herman and Bella (Haimovitz) S.; m. Martha Barry, Dec. 21, 1964; 1 dau., Denise. BS, Temple U., 1949. With I.N.S., 1949-58, Senate reporter, also mem. gen. staff Washington, 1951-58; with U.P.I., 1958-67, White House reporter, 1960-67; pub. affairs dir. Nat. Adv. Commn. on Civil Disorders, 1967-68, Democratic Nat. Com., 1968-70; corp. pub. affairs dir. Gen. Dynamics Corp., 1970-94, ret., 1994. Served with USAAF, 1946-47. Mem. Mil. Order of Carabao, Nat. Press Club, Beta Gamma Sigma. Home: 5726 W 1st Sq SW Vero Beach FL 32968-2256

SPIVAK, JOAN CAROL, communications executive; b. Phila., May 12, 1950; d. Jack and Evelyn Lee (Copelman) S.; m. John D. Goldman, May 17, 1980; children: Jesse, Marcus. AB, Barnard Coll., 1972; M of Health Scis., Johns Hopkins U., 1980. Freelance writer, NYC, 1980-84; project dir. Impact Med. Communication, NYC, 1984-87; exec. v.p., gen. mgr. health and sci. strategies Edelman Worldwide, NYC, 1987—2002; pres. Prime Medica, Inc., 2002—07; cons., 2007—. Co-author: (pamphlet) Lead: New Perspectives on an Old Problem, 1978; contbr. The Book of Health, 1981, articles to profl. jours. Bd. dirs. May O'Donnell Dance Co., N.Y.C., 1983-85, Chamber Ballet U.S.A., N.Y.C., 1985-87, Nat. Child Labor Commn., 1991-2000, Cases, 1995-2001, Learning Through an Expanded Arts Program, 2004—. Mem. N.Y. Acad. Sci. Democrat. Jewish. Avocations: pottery, boating. Personal E-mail: joan.spivak@gmail.com.

SPIVAK, KENIN MATHEW, personal care industry executive; b. NYC, May 14, 1957; s. Edwin Howard and Charlotte S. AB, Columbia U., 1977, MBA, JD, Columbia U., 1980. V.p. Merrill Lynch Capital Markets, 1985-88; COO, MGM/UA Comm. Co., 1988-90; pres. Island World Group, 1991-94; co-chmn., exec. com. Premiere Radio Network, LA, 1995-97; chmn. Knowledge Exch., LA, 1995-97; pres., CEO, Archon Comm., Inc., LA, 1995-97; vice chmn. John Paul Mitchell Systems, Beverly Hills, Calif., 1994—; chmn. Aquarius Holdings, Inc., LA, 1997-2000; chmn., CEO, Telemac Corp., 1998—; chmn. Paul Mitchell Advanced Edn. Inc., Costa Mesa, Calif., 2003—. Editor: Knowledge Exchange Business Encyclopedia. Office: 6701 Center Dr W Ste 700 Los Angeles CA 90045-1565 Home: 139 N Clark Dr West Hollywood CA 90048-3072

SPIVAK, LEONARD A., lawyer; b. N.Y.C., July 11, 1943; s. Jack and Esther (Peckolick) S.; children: Kate, Allison, Jon, Gabrielle. B.A. with honors, SUNY-Stony Brook, 1964; LLB cum laude, Columbia U., 1967. Bar: N.Y. 1967, U.S. Dist. Ct. (so. and ea. dists.) N.Y., US Ct. Appeals (2d, 3d, 5th, 7th, 9th and 10th cirs.), U.S. Supreme Ct. Assoc., Gilbert, Segal & Young, N.Y.C., 1967-68; assoc. Cahill, Gordon & Reindel LLP, N.Y.C., 1968-75, ptnr., 1975—. Bd. dirs. Stony Brook Found., Raby Peck Found. Mem. Alumni Assn. SUNY-Stony Brook (past pres.). Democrat. Office: Cahill Gordon & Reindel LLP 80 Pine St Fl 17 New York NY 10005-1790 E-mail: LSpivak@cahill.com.

SPIVAK, MARK R., lawyer; b. NYC, Nov. 5, 1958; BA magna cum laude, Muhlenberg Coll., 1980; JD, Georgetown U., 1983. Bar: NJ 1983, DC 1984. Ptnr., co-head Bus. & Internat. Sect. Vinson & Elkins LLP, Washington, DC. Assoc. editor The Tax Lawyer, 1982—83. Office: Vinson & Elkins LLP Willard Office Bldg 1455 Pennsylvania Ave, Ste 600 Washington DC 20004 Office Phone: 202-639-6664. E-mail: mspivak@velaw.com.

SPIVEY, BRUCE E., ophthalmologist, educator, health facility administrator; b. Cedar Rapids, Iowa, Aug. 29, 1934; s. William Loranzy and Grace Loretta (Barber) S.; children: Lisa, Eric; m. Patti Amanda Birge, Dec. 20, 1987. BA, Coe Coll., 1956; MD, U. Iowa, 1959, MS, 1964; MEd, U. Ill., 1969; DSc (hon.), Coe Coll., 1978. Diplomate Am. Bd. Ophthalmology (fellow, bd. dirs. 1975-83, chmn. oral exam 1976-81). Asst. prof. U. Iowa Coll. Medicine, Iowa City, 1966, assoc. prof., 1968—71; dean Sch. Med. Scis. U. Pacific, San Francisco, 1971—76; prof., chmn. dept. ophthalmology Pacific Med. Ctr. (now Calif. Pacific Med. Ctr.), San Francisco, 1971—87; pres., CEO, dir. Calif. Pacific Med. Ctr., San Francisco, 1976—91; exec. v.p., CEO Am. Acad. Ophthalmology, San Francisco, 1977—93; pres., CEO Calif. Healthcare Sys., Bay area, 1986—92; CEO Northwestern Healthcare Network, Chgo., 1992—97, Columbia Cornell Care, NYC, 1997—2000, Columbia Cornell Network Physicians, NYC, 1998—2000. Bd. dirs. Reliance Group Holdings Inc., NYC; trustee, bd. dirs., sec. bd. MedEx, Balt., 1999—; v.p. Am. Bd. Med. Spltys., 1978—80, pres., 1980—82, Coun. Med. Splty. Socs., 2000—02, dep. exec. v.p.,

2002—; chmn. bd. dirs. Vol. Hosps. of Am.-No. Calif., 1985—87, nat. bd. dirs., 1991—96; nat. adv. coun. NEI/NIH, 1987—92; spl. med. adv. group Dept. Vets Affairs, 1987—93; trustee, bd. dirs., sec. bd. Ophthal. Mut. Ins. Co., 1988—; trustee, sec. bd. PrimeSight, San Francisco, 1996—99; bd. dirs., chmn. MedBiquitous, Balt., 2001—. Contbr. over 115 articles to profl. jours.; inventor instruments for eye surgery. Bd. dirs. Pacific Vision Found., San Francisco, 1978—, U.S.-China Ednl. Inst., 1979—; trustee Coe Coll., 1985—, Found. AAO, 1981—, Internat. Coun. Ophthalmology, 1985—, Helen Keller Internat., 1999—; trustee Medbiquitous, 2000-07, chmn, 2001—06. Served to capt. U.S. Army, 1964-66. Decorated Bronze Star; recipient Emile Javal Gold medal Internat. Contact Lens Council, San Francisco, 1982, Gradle medal Pan-Am. Assn. Ophthalmol., Disting. Alumni award U. Iowa, 2003, others. Fellow ACS, Am. Acad. Ophthalmology (Disting. Svc. award 1972, Sr. Honor award 1986, Guest of Honor 1996, Lifetime Achievement award, 2002); mem. AMA, Am. Ophthal. Soc. (Howe medal 1993, bd. dirs. 1986-91, pres. 1994-95), Academia Ophthal. Internat. (Bernardo Streiff Gold medal 2002), Soc. Med. Adminstrs. (pres. 1999-2001), Internat. Congress Ophthalmology (sec.-gen. 1978-82), Internat. Coun. Ophthalmology (sec.-gen. 1994—2006, trustee 1986—, pres. 2006—, Jules Francois Gold medal 2006, Sir John Wilson award 2007), Pacific-Union Club, Chevy Chase Club, Knickerbocker Club, Cosmos Club. Presbyterian. Office: 945 Green St San Francisco CA 94133 Business E-Mail: bruce@spivey.org.

SPIVEY, CHRISTINA ALEASE, social worker, researcher; b. Augusta, Ga., Aug. 7, 1977; d. Harry Allen and Linda Agnes Spivey. BA, Am. U., Washington, 1998; MA, U. Chgo., 2001; PhD, U. Ga., Athens, 2004. LCSW Ga., 2002. Data mgmt. specialist U. Ga., Coll. Pharmacy, Augusta, 2006—07; rsch. coord. U. Ariz., Coll. Pharmacy, Tucson, 2006—. Contbr. articles to profl. jours. Jeanne C. Marsh scholar, U. Chgo., Sch. Social Svc. Adminstrn., 2000—01. Mem.: Golden Key. Home Phone: 520-615-7814. Personal E-mail: caspivey@juno.com.

SPIVEY, DONALD, history professor; AB in History, U. Ill., Urbana-Champaign, 1971, MA in History, 1972; PhD in History, U. Calif., Davis, 1976. Rsch. asst. dept. elem. edn. U. Ill., 1971—72; tchg. asst. dept. history U. Calif., Davis, 1972—74, lectr. in history, 1975—76; music instr. Sacramento, 1972—74; asst. prof. history Wright State U., Dayton, Ohio, 1976—79; assoc. prof. history U. Conn., 1979—85, prof. history, 1985—93, dir. grad. studies dept. history, 1987—89, founding dir. Inst. African-Am. Studies, 1989—93; prof. history U. Miami, Coral Gables, Fla., 1993—, chair dept. history, 1993—98, assoc. dir. Ctr. for Rsch. on Sport in Soc., 1997—. Vis. asst. prof. history U. Mich., Ann Arbor, 1978—79; presenter in field; mem. exec. v.p. and provost search com. U. Miami, 2004—; co-dir. African-Am. History Summer Inst. for Miami-Dade Tchrs., 1999—2004; mem. exec. bd. Ctr. for Rsch. on Sport in Soc., 1998—; chair Prologue Hist. Soc.; hist. advisor Dade County African-Am. Tchrs. for Curriculum Reform. Author: Schooling for the New Slavery: Black Industrial Education, 1868-1915, 1978, The Politics of Miseducation: The Booker Washington Institute of Liberia, 1929-1984, 1986, Fire From the Soul: A History of the African-American Struggle, 2003; contbg. editor: Union and the Black Musician: The Narrative of William Everett Samuels and Chicago Local 208, 1984, Sport in America: New Historical Perspectives, 1985; contbr. articles to profl. jours., chapters to books. Developer, host Grooving in the Grove Jazz Series; mem. Historic Overtown Restoration Comm.; mem., host Miami Com. to Select Outstanding Local History Tchr.; bd. dirs. Wolfson Media History Ctr., 1993—94. Recipient Tchg. cert. of appreciation, Omega Psi Phi, 1997, cert. of appreciation, Dade County Sch. Bd., Fla., 1997, Twelve Good Men Cmty. Svc. award, Ronald McDonald Ho., Miami, 1998, Excellence in Tchg. award, U. Miami, 2002. Mem.: Conn. Acad. Arts and Scis., Phi Beta Kappa, Phi Kappa Phi. Office: Dept History U Miami PO Box 248107 Coral Gables FL 33124-4662

SPIVEY, TED RAY, language educator; b. Fort Pierce, Fla., July 1, 1927; s. Theodore Roosevelt and Etty Pearl (Sumner) S.; m. Julia Brannon Douglass, June 30, 1962; children— Mary Leta Cashin, John Andrew. AB, Emory U., 1949; MA, U. Minn., 1951, PhD, 1954. Reporter Greenville Reporter, SC, 1949-50; instr. Emory U., Atlanta, 1954-56; mem. faculty Ga. State U., Atlanta, 1956-89, assoc. prof. English, 1960-64, prof., 1964-89, Regents' prof., 1984-89, emeritus, 1989—. Author: (with Kenneth M. England) A Manual of Style, 1960, The Renewed Quest, 1969, The Coming of the New Man, 1971, The Journey Beyond Tragedy, 1980, Revival: Southern Writers in the Modern City, 1986, The Writer as Shaman: The Pilgrimages of Conrad Aiken and Walker Percy, 1986, To Die in Atlanta: Poems of the Civil War and After, 1987, Beyond Modernism: Toward a New Myth Criticism, 1988, A City Observed: Poems of the New Age, 1988, (with Arthur Waterman) Conrad Aiken: A Priest of Consciousness, 1989, Flannery O'Connor: The Woman, The Thinker, the Visionary, 1995, Airport: America Rediscovered, 1997, Time's Stop in Savannah: Conrad Aiken's Inner Journey, 1997, Bridges of Light: Four Poets of the Golden Isles, 2001. Served with USN, 1945-46. Urban Life Center grantee, 1977-80. Mem. So. Atlantic MLA, Brittany Club. Democrat. Episcopalian. Home: 104 Plemmons Dr Saint Simons Island GA 31522-9767

SPLANE, RICHARD BEVERLEY, social work educator; b. Calgary, Alta., Can., Sept. 25, 1916; s. Alfred William and Clara Jane (Allyn) S.; m. Verna Marie Huffman, Feb. 22, 1971. BA, McMaster U., 1940, LLD (hon.), 1990; cert. social sci. and adminstrn., London Sch. Econs., 1947; MA, U. Toronto, 1948, MSW, 1951, PhD, 1961, LLD (hon.), 2005, Wilfrid Laurier U., 1988, U. B.C., 1996. Exec. dir. Children's Aid Soc., Cornwall, Ont., Canada, 1948—50; with Health and Welfare Can., Ottawa, 1952—72, exec. asst. to dep. min. nat. welfare, 1959—60, dir. unemployment assistance, 1960—62, dir. gen. welfare assistance and svcs., 1960—70, asst. dep. min. social allowances and svcs., 1970—72; vis. prof. U. Alta., Edmonton, 1972—73; prof. social policy Sch. Social Work, U. B.C., Vancouver, 1973—82. Cons. Govt. Can., Govt. Alta., UNICEF. Author: The Development of Social Welfare in Ontario, 1965; (with Verna Huffman Splane) Chief Nursing Officers in National Ministries of Health, 1994, 75 Years of Community Service to Canada: Canadian Council on Social Development, 1920-1995, George Davidson Social Policy and Public Policy Exemplar, 2003 Served with RCAF, 1942-45. Recipient Centennial medal Govt. Can., 1967, Charles E. Hendry award U. Toronto, 1981, Commemorative medal for 125th anniversary of Confedn. of Can., 1992, Disting. Svc. award Internat. Coun. on Social Welfare, 1996, Queen's Golden Jubilee medal, 2002. Mem. Can. Assn. Social Workers (Outstanding Nat. Svc. award 1985, Touzel award 2002, Queens Golden medal 2002), Can. Inst. Pub. Adminstrn., Can. Hist. Assn., Can. Coun. on Social Devel. (Lifetime Achievement award 1995), Internat. Assn. Schs. Social Work, Internat. Confs. Social Devel. (prof. emeritus U. BC 1991-06), World Federalists Can., UN Assn. Can. (bd. dirs. Vancouver br.), Vancouver Club, Officer Order Can. Mem. United Ch. Can. E-mail: splane@interchange.ca.

SPLETE, ALLEN PETERJOHN, educational association administrator, educator; b. Carthage, NY, June 24, 1938; s. Howard Henry and Minnie Bertha (Peterjohn) S.; m. Marilyn Lois Detweiler, June 18, 1966; children: Heidi, Michael. BA, St. Lawrence U., 1960; MA with distinction, Colgate U., 1962; PhD, Syracuse U., 1968; LHD, Campbellsville Coll., 1990; LLD, Davis and Elkins Coll., 1990; LHD, Mt. Union Coll., 1992, St. Thomas Aquinas Coll., 1992, U. Indpls., 1994, Juniata Coll., 1994, Hastings Coll., 1994; EdD, Marywood Coll., 1995; LHD, Holy Family Coll., 1996, Wesley Coll., 1996, Bluffton Coll., 2003; LHD (hon.), Millikin U., 2007. Adminstrv. asst. to v.p. acad. affairs Syracuse U., NY, 1965—68, assoc. dean, exec. asst. to provost, 1968—70; v.p. for acad. planning St. Lawrence U., Canton, NY, 1970-82; pres. Westminster Coll., New Wilmington, Pa., 1982-85; exec. v.p. Coun. Ind. Colls., Washington, 1985-86, pres., 1986-2000; dir., pres. Consulting Svc., 2002—05; pres. emeritus Coun. Ind. Colls., Washington, 2000—. Dir. Nat. Prepaid Tuition Plan, 1988-91; cons. York Coll., Pa., 1974; planning and rsch. com. NY State Com. on Ind. Colls. and Univs., 1975-82; statewide higher edn. adv. com. NY State Senate Com. on Higher Edn., 1979-82; nat. adv. bd. Flaming Rainbow U., 1989-96; adv. bd. Assn. Gov. Bds. Presdl. Search Consultation Svc., 1987-94, Academic Search Consultation Svc., 1989—, mem. Harvard Sem. for new pres. adv. bd., 1990—; bd. dirs. Tchr. Edn. Accreditation Coun., 1998—2006, chair, 2001—06, chair emeritus 2006-; oversight and rev. com. leadership and orgnl. devel. program United Negro Coll. Fund, 1991-96, SCT adv. coun., 1996-2001; adv. bd. Eric Nat., 1996-03, Boyer Ctr. for Advanced Studies, 1998-2005; UAW/Ford U. Help Steering Com., 1997-01; exec. bd. Project Pericles, 1999-05 (nat. adv. bd. 2005-), CIC Pres. Consulting Svc., 2003-05, designated Fulbright Senior Specialist 2006-. Co-author: Frederic Remington-Selected Letters, 1988, A Good Place To Work: Sourcebook for the Academic Workplace, 1991, Presidential Transitions in Private Colleges, 2005; editor: (with others) Confs. on Adirondack Park, 1972-82, Can.-Am. Relations, 1974-75, Presidential Essays — Success Stories, 2000; contbr. articles to profl. jours. Chmn. planning bd. Village of Canton, 1974-81; elder Neelsville Presbyn. Ch., 1986-89; trustee Adirondack Conservancy, Wilsboro, NY, 1980-82; trustee Millikin U., 2000-06; mem. adv. bd. Sage Scholars, 2000-06, mem. nat. bd., 2006-. Served to 1st lt. US Army, 1960-62. Recipient Alumni citation, St. Lawrence U., 1987, Algernon Sydney Sullivan award, 1997, CIC Acad. Leadership award, 2000, Henry D. Paley award, Nat. Assn. Ind. Colls. and Univs., 2001, Partnership award, Assn. Presbyn. Colls. and Univs., 2000; grantee, John Ben Snow Found., 1981. Mem. Pa. Assn. Colls and Univs. (govt. rels. com. 1983-85), Mid. States Assn. (team chmn. com. on higher edn. 1976-78, 81), Assn. Am. Colls. (project rev. cons. 1981-82), Soc. Educators and Scholars (bd. editors), Assn. Am. Colls. (pres. adv. com. 1977-78, reviewer Quill project 1978-79), St. Lawrence County Hist. Assn. (pres. 1977-82), Frederic Remington Mus. Assn., Beta Theta Pi (v.p. 1980-83). Republican. Avocations: sports, gardening, travel, poetry, classical music. Home: 10821 Longmeadow Dr Damascus MD 20872-2240 Office: Coun Ind Colls 1 Dupont Cir NW Ste 320 Washington DC 20036-1137 Office Phone: 301-253-1274. Personal E-mail: amsplete@yahoo.com.

SPLINTER, MICHAEL R., manufacturing executive; BEE, U. Wis., Madison, 1972, MEE, 1974. Gen. mgr., exec. v.p. Intel Corp., Santa Clara, Calif., 1984—96; v.p. and asst. Gen. mgr. Tech. and Mfg. Group, Intel Corp., Santa Clara, Calif., 1996—98, v.p. and Gen. mgr., 1998—99, sr. v.p. and Gen. mgr., 1999—2001, exec. v.p. and Gen. mgr., 2001, exec. v.p. and dir., Sales and Mktg. group, 2001—03; pres. and CEO Applied Materials, Inc., Santa Clara, Calif., 2003—. Mem. Computer Sys. Policy Project; bd. dir. Semiconductor Equipment and Materials Intern., Silicon Valley Leadership Group. Named to, Jr. Achievement Hall of Fame; recipient Intern. Partnership Award, Calif.-Israel C. of C., Disting. Alumni Award, U. Wis. Mem.: Governors' Coun. of World Econ. Forum, Applied Materials (bd. dir. 2003). Office: Applied Materials Inc 3050 Bowers Ave Santa Clara CA 95054 *

SPLINTER, WILLIAM ELDON, agricultural engineering educator; b. North Platte, Nebr., Nov. 24, 1925; s. William John and Minnie (Calhoun) Splinter; m. Eleanor Love Peterson, Jan. 10, 1952 (dec. Jan. 1999); children: Kathryn Love, William John, Karen Ann, Robert Marvin; m. Elizabeth Butters Calhoun, Feb. 9, 2002. BS in Agrl. Engring., U. Nebr., 1950; MS in Agrl. Engring., Mich. State U., 1951, PhD in Agrl. Engring., 1955. Instr. agrl. engring. Mich. State U., East Lansing, 1953-54; assoc. prof. biology and agrl. engring. N.C. State U., Raleigh, 1954-60, prof. biology and agrl. engring., 1960-68; head agrl. engring. dept. U. Nebr., Lincoln, 1968—88, vice chancellor rsch., 1988—93; interim dean Coll. Engring. & Tech. U., 1994—95, 2001—02; interim dir. Nebr. State Mus., 2002—. Cons. engr.; exec. bd. Am. Assn. Engring. Socs.; hon. prof. Shengyang (People's Republic of China) Agrl. U. Contbr. articles to tech. jours.; patentee in field. Vol. dir. L.F. Larsen Tractor Mus. Served with USNR, 1946-51. Recipient Massey Ferguson Gold medal, 1978, John Deere Gold medal, 1995, Disting. Svc. award Kiwanis, 1994, George Howard-Loiuse Pound award, 2001; named to Nebr. Hall of Agrl. Achievement; named Disting. Alumni, U. Nebr., Lincoln, 2000, Mich. State U., 2005; named U. Nebr. Splinter Rsch. Lab. in his honor, 2004. Fellow AAAS, NSPE, Am. Soc. Agrl. Engrs. (pres., adminstrv. council, found. pres., Presdl. citation 1999); mem. Nat. Acad. Engring., Soc. Automotive Engrs., Am. Soc. Engring. Edn., Sigma Xi, Sigma Tau, Sigma Pi Sigma, Pi Mu Epsilon, Gamma Sigma Delta, Phi Kappa Phi, Beta Sigma Psi. Home: 4801 Bridle Ln Lincoln NE 68516-3436 Office: U Nebr Lincoln PO Box 830833 Lincoln NE 68583-0833 Office Phone: 402-472-8389. Business E-Mail: wsplinter1@unl.edu.

SPLITT, DAVID ALAN, lawyer, writer; b. Ripon, Wis., Nov. 28, 1945; s. Orville Sylvester and Joyce Eileen (Anson) S.; m. Martha Ann Corson, Mar. 19, 1966; children: Amy Emmeline, Sarah Daisy. BA in English, Va. Poly. Inst. and State U., 1966; JD, Am. U., 1971. Bar: D.C. 1971, U.S. Supreme Ct. 1981. Tchr. Bowie (Md.) H.S., 1966-68; freelance journalist and photographer Washington, 1968-70; ptnr. Christensen, Splitt & King, Washington, 1971-74; gen. counsel D.C. Bd. Edn., 1974-79; dir. documents Washington, 1979—82; of counsel Stein, Miller, Brodsky & Beerman, Washington, 1983-84; pvt. practice Washington, 1985—2000; sr. v.p., mng. counsel Affiliated Computer Svc., Inc., 2001—. Gen. counsel D.C. Sch. Law, 1988-96, adj. prof. law, 1995-97, U. D.C., 1991-96; spl. asst. city adminstr. for fin. mgmt. systems, dir. city computer ctr., Washington, 1980-81. Dir., vice chmn. Choral Arts Soc. of Washington, 1974-84, chmn., 1984-85; dir., v.p. Traditional Music Documentation Project, Washington. Author: Post-Conviction Relief for Federal Prisoners, 1973, The Resolution of Detainers for Federal and State Prisoners, 1971; editor: Inquiry and Analysis, 1977-79, Becoming a Better Board Member, 1982, D.C. Rulemaking Handbook and Publications Style Manual, 1983, D.C. Produrement Regulations, 1987, A Guide to Procurement Law in the District, 1998; columnist: The Exec. Educator, 1978-96, eSch. News Law and Ethics, 1997—; editor, The Corporate Counselor, 2001-; editor, Policy Bytes, 2002-. Recipient Outstanding Svc. awards D.C. Govt., 1976, 78, 79, Mayor's Disting. Pub. Svc. award, 1983. Mem. ABA, Inter-Am. Bar Assn., Computer Law Assn., Aircraft Owners and Pilots Assn., Exptl. Aircraft Assn., Lawyer-Pilots Bar Assn., Am. Radio League, (licensee amateur extra class). Republican. Home: 6111 Utah Ave NW Washington DC 20015-2461 Office Phone: 240-686-2915. E-mail: david.splitt@acs-inc.com.

SPLITTSTOESSER, WALTER EMIL, botanist, educator; b. Claremont, Minn., Aug. 27, 1937; s. Waldemar Theodore and Opal Mae (Young) S.; m. Shirley Anne O'Connor, July 2, 1960; children: Pamela, Sheryl, Riley. BS with distinction (univ. fellow), U. Minn., 1958; MS, S.D. State U., 1960; PhD, Purdue U., 1963. Plant breeder U. Minn., 1956-58; weed scientist S.D. State U., 1958-60; plant physiologist Purdue U., 1960-63, Shell Oil Co., Modesto, Calif., 1963-64; biochemist U. Calif., Davis, 1964-65; mem. faculty U. Ill., Urbana, 1965-97, prof. plant physiology, 1974-97, head vegetable crops div., 1972-82. Vis. prof., biotechnologist Univ. Coll., Dublin, Ireland, 1987; vis. prof. Univ. Coll., London, 1972, La Trobe U., Melbourne, Australia, 1995; biologist Parkland Coll., Champaign, Ill., 1974; vis. rsch. assoc. Rothamsted Exptl. Sta., Herpenden, England, 1980; disting. vis. prof. Nagoya (Japan) U., 1982. Author: Vegetable Growing Handbook, 1979, 3d edit., 1990; contbr. articles to profl. jours.; rev. editor: Analytical Biochemistry, 1969-78, NSF, 1978-79; others. Recipient J.H. Gourley award Am. Fruit Grower-Am. Soc. Hort. Sci., 1974, Outstanding Grad. Educator award, 1990; NIH fellow, 1964-65. Fellow Am. Soc. Hort. Sci. (rev. editor jour. 1969-98), Japanese Soc. Promotion of Sci.; mem. Am. Soc. Hort. Sci., Plant Growth Reg. Soc. Am., Sigma Xi (pres. 1990-91), Alpha Zeta, Gamma Sigma Delta, Delta Theta Sigma, Phi Kappa Phi. Home: 2006 Cureton Dr Urbana IL 61801-6226 Personal E-mail: splittst@uiuc.edu.

SPOCK, MICHAEL, museum administrator; b. NYC, Jan. 25, 1933; s. Benjamin McLane and Jane Davenport (Cheney) Spock; m. Judith TenEyck Wood, Apr. 30, 1955; children: Daniel Wood, Peter Ford, Susannah Cheney. BS in Biology, Antioch Coll., 1959; postgrad., Harvard U., 1961—62. Staff mem. Dayton Mus. Natural Hist., Ohio, 1955—58; ptnr. Spock Art, Yellow Springs, Ohio, 1957—61; exhibit technician Ohio State Mus., Columbus, 1959—60; inst. Dept. Biology Antioch Coll., 1959—61; dir. Children's Mus., Boston, 1962—85; v.p. pub. programs Field Mus. Natural Hist., Chgo., 1986; inst. Harvard U. Grad. Sch. Edn.; pres. Cultural Edn. Collaborative, Boston; rsch. fellow Chapin Hill Ctr. for Children, U. Chgo. Trustee Met. Cultural Alliance, Boston, Computer Mus. Recipient John Cotton Dana award leadership in mus. edn.; Osher Fellowship, Exploratorium, San Francisco. Fellow: AAAS; mem.: New England Mus. Assn., Internat. Coun. Mus., Am. Assn. Youth Museums (pres., Great Friend to Kids award), Am. Assn. Museums (sec. 1979—80, v.p. 1977—79, 1986, coun. mem. 1971—89, named to Centennial Honor Roll 2006, Disting. Svc. award). Office: Chapin Hill Ctr for Children Univ Chicago 1313 E 60th St Chicago IL 60637 Office Phone: 773-256-5188. E-mail: mspock@chapinhall.org. *

SPODAK, MICHAEL KENNETH, forensic psychiatrist; b. Bklyn., Nov. 5, 1944; s. Harry and Betty (Rahn) S.; children: Lisa Beth, Brett David. BS, Union Coll., 1966; MD, SUNY-Syracuse, 1970. Diplomate: Nat. Bd. Med. Examiners, Am. Bd. Neurology and Psychiatry. Intern Mary Imogene Bassett Hosp., Cooperstown, NY, 1970-71; resident John Hopkins Hosp., Balt., 1974-77; practice medicine specializing in civil and criminal forensic psychiatry Towson, Md., 1977—; chief dept. psychiatry Balt. County Gen. Hosp., Randallstown, 1978-85; mem. staff Clifton T. Perkins Hosp. Ctr., Jessup, Md., 1977-92; clin. asst. prof. psychiatry U. Md. Hosp., Balt., 1983-97; psychiat. cons. Bur. Disability Ins., Social Security Adminstrn., Workmen's compensation Commn., Balt., 1981—; dir. community forensic services Mental Hygiene Adminstrn., Md., 1982-92; faculty Nat. Jud. Coll., 1988—. Mem. Md. Task Force on Somatic Therapies Contbr. numerous articles on forensic psychiatry to profl. jours., chpt. to book. Served with M.C. USN, 1972-74. Mem. Am. Acad. Psychiatry and Law, Am. Psychiat. Assn., Md. Psychiat. Soc. (chmn. peer rev. com. 2001), Md. Med. Soc. (chmn. occupational health com. 1983-90), Baltimore County Med. Soc. Office: 26 W Pennsylvania Ave Towson MD 21204-5001 Office Phone: 410-337-0343. E-mail: mkspodak@yahoo.com.

SPODEK, BERNARD, early childhood educator; b. Bklyn., Sept. 17, 1931; s. David and Esther (Lebenbaum) S.; m. Prudence Debb, June 21, 1957; children: Esther Yin-ling, Jonathan Chou. BA, Bklyn. Coll., 1952; MA, Columbia U., 1955, EdD, 1962. Cert. early childhood edn. tchr., N.Y. Tchr. Beth Hayeled Sch., NYC, 1952-56, N.Y. City Pub. Schs., Bklyn., 1956-57, Early Childhood Ctr., Bklyn. Coll., 1957-60; asst. prof. elem. edn. U. Wis.-Milw., 1961-65; assoc. prof. early childhood edn. U. Ill., Champaign, 1965-68, prof. dept. curriculum and instrn., 1968-97, dir. dept. grad. programs, 1986-87, chair dept., 1987-89, dir. hons. program, Coll. Edn., 1984-86, mem. faculty Bur. Ednl. Rsch., 1981-85, prof. emeritus, 1997—; adv. prof. Hong Kong Inst. of Edn., 1999-2001. Dir. insts. Nat. Def. Edn. Act, 1965-67, dir. experienced tchr. fellowship program, 1967-69, co-dir. program for tchr. trainers in early childhood edn., 1969-74; vis. prof. Western Wash. State U., 1974, U. Wis., Madison, 1980, Kobe Shinwa Women's U., Japan, 2004, 07; vis. scholar Sch. Early Childhood Studies, Brisbane (Australia) Coll. Advanced Edn., Delissa Inst. Early Childhood Studies, S. Australia Coll. Advanced Edn., 1985, Beijing Normal U., Nanjing Normal U., East China Normal U., Shangai, People's Republic China, 1986; rsch. fellow Kobe U., Japan, 1996; adj. prof. Queensland (Australia) U. Tech., 2000. Author or co-author: (with others) A Black Studies Curriculum for Early Childhood Education, 1972, 2d edit., 1976, Teaching in the Early Years, 1972, 3d edit., 1985, Early Childhood Education, 1973, Studies in Open Education, 1975 (Japanese trans.), Early Childhood Education: Issues and Perspectives, 1977, (with Nir-Janiv and Steg) International Perspectives on Early Childhood Education, 1982 (Hebrew trans.), with Saracho and Lee (Mainstreaming Young Children, 1984, (with Saracho and Davis) Foundations of Early Childhood Education, 1987, 2d edit. (Japanese trans.), 1991, Right from the Start, 1994 (Chinese, Portuguese and Korean translations), Dealing with Individual Differences in the Early Childhood Classroom, 1994; editor: Handbook of Research in Early Childhood Education, 1982, rev. edit., 2005, Today's Kindergarten, 1986; (with Saracho and Peters) Professionalism and the Early Childhood Practitioner, 1988; (with Saracho) Early Childhood Teacher Education, 1990, Issues in Early Childhood Curriculum, 1991, Educationally Appropriate Kindergarten Practices, 1991, Issues in Childcare, 1992, Handbook of Research on the Education of Young Children (Portuguese tranls.), 1993, Language and Literacy in Early Childhood Education, 1993, Issues in Early Childhood Educational Evaluation and Assessment, 1996, Multiple Perspectives on Play in Early Childhood Education, 1998, Contemporary Perspectives in Early Childhood Curriculum, 2002, Contemporary Perspectives on Literacy in Early Childhood Education, 2002, Contemporary Perspectives on Play in Early Childhood Education, 2003, Studying Teachers in Early Childhood Settings, 2003, Contemporary Perspectives on Language Policy and Literacy Instruction, 2004, Contemporary Perspectives on Families, Communities, and Schools for Young Children, 2005, International Perspectives on Research in Early Childhood Education, 2005, Handbook of Research on the Education of Young Children, 2d edit., 2006, Contemporary Perspectives on Socialization and Social Development in Early Childhood Education, 2007, Contemporary Perspectives on Social Learning in Early Childhood Education, 2007; (with Safford and Saracho) Early Childhood Special Education, 1994; (with Garcia, McLaughlin & Saracho) Meeting the Challenge of Cultural and Linguistic Diversity, 1995; (with Saracho and Pellegrini) Issues in Early Childhood Educational Research, 1998, others; series editor Yearbook in Early Childhood Education, early childhood edn. publs., 1990-00; series co-editor: Contemporary Perspectives in Early Childhood Education, 2002—; guest editor Studies in Ednl. Evaluation, 1982, Early Education and Child Development, 1995; also contbr. chpts to books, articles to profl. jours. Mem. Am. Ednl. Rsch. Assn. (chair early childhood and child devel. spl. interest group 1983-84, publs. com. 1984-86), Nat. Assn. Edn. Young Children (sec. 1965-68, bd. govs. 1968-72, pres. 1976-78, editl. adv. bd. 1972-76, book rev. editor, 1972-74, cons. editor, 1985-87 Young Children jour., tchr. edn. commn. 1981-88, chair commn. on appropriate edn. 4-5 yr. old children, 1984-85, cons. editor Early Childhood Rsch. Quar. 1987-90), Nat. Soc. for Study of Edn. (1972 yearbook com., Asia-Pacific edn. rev.), Pacific Early Childhood Edn. Rsch. Assn. (pres. 2000—). Office: Univ Ill Dept Curriculum & Instrn 1310 S 6th St Champaign IL 61820-6925 Home Phone: 217-352-1482. Business E-Mail: b-spodek@uiuc.edu.

SPOERI, RANDALL KEITH, healthcare company executive; b. Cleve., June 12, 1946; s. Theodore Warren and Marion (Barrick) S.; m. Kathleen Loma Bryden Hayes, Aug. 31, 1968 (div. Mar. 1981); 1 child, Jennifer Anne; m. Deborah Jean Hammett, June 20, 1981 (div. Nov. 1998); 1 child, Jason Randall; m. Laura Joan Lenhardt, Apr. 24, 1999. BS, Calif. Polytech. State U., 1968; MS, Tex. A&M U., 1970, PhD, 1976. Math. statistician U.S. Bur. of the Census, Suitland, Md., 1976-80; assoc. prof. U.S. Naval Acad., Annapolis, 1980-83; assoc. exec. dir. Am. Statis. Assn., Alexandria, Va., 1983-88; sr. corp. statistician Humana, Inc., Louisville, 1988-92; chief program coord. info. branch Health Care Fin. Adminstrn., Balt., 1993; asst.

v.p. Nat. Com. for Quality Assurance, Washington, 1994-95; adminstrv. v.p. health care analysis NYLCare Health Plans, Inc., NYC, 1995-98; v.p. med. and quality informatics HIP Health Plans, NYC, 1998—2004; dir. Health Analytics, Cerner Corp., Kans. City, Mo., 2005—. Author: Quantitative Methods In Quality Management, 1991; contbr. articles to profl. jours. Mem. adv. com. Health Care Fin. Adminstrn., Balt., 1990-92, bur. dir. citation, 1993, adv. bd. Juran Inst., Wilton, Conn., 1995-98. 1st lt. U.S. Army, 1970-72. Recipient Svc. award Am. Statis. Assoc., Alexandria, 1994. Fellow AAAS, Am. Soc. for Quality (health care divsn. chair 1995-96); mem. Am. Statis Assn., Inst. Indsl. Engring., Inst. for Ops. Rsch. and the Mgmt. Scis. Avocations: sports, music. Home: 148 Top Of The World Way Green Brook NJ 08812-1839

SPOERRY, ROBERT F., manufacturing executive; B Mech. Engring., Fed. Inst. Tech., Zurich Switzerland; MBA, Univ. Chgo. Mgmt. positions with Mettler-Toledo Internat., 1983—87, head. indsl. & retail (Europe), 1987—93, pres., CEO, 1993—98, chmn., pres., CEO, 1998—. Bd. dir. Phonak Group. Bd. dir. Swiss-Am. C. of C. Office: Mettler-Toledo Internat 1900 Polaris Pkwy Columbus OH 43240 Office Phone: 614-438-4511. *

SPOFFORD, GEORGE EDSON, IV, lawyer; b. Savannah, Aug. 9, 1960; s. George Edson III and Nancy Kaye Spofford; m. Anita T. Tallaksen, June 26, 1982; children: Avery Lauren, George Edson V. BA cum laude, Auburn U., Ala., 1982; JD, Emory U., Atlanta, 1985. Bar: Ga. Bar Assn. 1985, Fla. Bar Assn. 1986, Ala. Bar Assn. 1989, cert.: US Dist. Ct. of Appeals Mid. Dist. of Fla. 1989, US Ct. of Appeals Fed. Circuit 1992, Fla. Bar (Circuit Ct. Mediator) 2003, US Dist. Ct. of Appeals No. Dist. of Fla. 2004, Bd. Cert. Constrn. Law Specialist: Fla. Supreme Ct. 2005. Corp. counsel Misener Marine Constrn., Inc., Tampa, 1985—87; atty. Cummings Lawrence & Vezina, PA, Ft. Lauderdale, 1987—92; owner S&E Contractors, Inc., Clearwater, Fla., 1992—95; shareholder Glenn Rasmussen Fogarty & Hooker, PA, Tampa, 1996—. Gen. counsel Underground Utility Contractors Fla., Orlando, 1999—. Pres., bd. dirs. Hyde Pk. Preservation, Inc., Tampa. Mem.: Tampa Yacht and Country Club (fleet capt. 2005—06). Conservative. Baptist. Avocations: fly fishing, diving, boating. Office: Glenn Rasmussen Fogarty & Hooker PA 100 S Ashley Dr Ste 1300 Tampa FL 33601 Home Phone: 813-229-3333; Office Phone: 813-229-3333. Office Fax: 813-229-5946.

SPOFFORD, SALLY (SALLY HYSLOP), artist; b. NYC, Aug. 20, 1929; d. George Hall and Esther (McNaull) Hyslop; m. Gavin Spofford, Mar. 11, 1950 (dec. Jan. 1976); children: Lizabeth Spofford Smith, Leslie Spofford Russell. Student, The China Inst., NYC, 1949, The Art Students League, 1950; BA with high honors, Swarthmore Coll., 1952. Instr. Somerset Art Assn., Peapack, N.J., 1978-95, Hunterdon Mus. Art, Clinton, N.J., 1985—; adv. bd., lectr. Apollo Muses, Inc., Gladstone, N.J.; trustee Artshowcase, Inc. One-woman shows include Riverside Studio, Pottersville, NJ, 1985, Morris Mus., Morristown, NJ 1989, Schering-Plough Gallery, Madison, NJ, 1989, Phoenix Gallery, NYC, 1990, Robin Hutchins Gallery, Maplewood, NJ, 1992, Berlex Labs. Corp. Office, Wayne, NJ, 1992, Hunterdon Mus. Art, Clinton, 1993, 2003, Newark Acad., Livingston, NJ, 1997, Simon Gallery, Morristown, 2004, 2007; exhibited in group shows at Hickory, NC Mus., 1983, Purdue U., 1983, Monmouth, NJ, 1984, Nabisco Brands Gallery, East Hanover, NJ, 1985, 89, Hunterdon Mus. Art, 1988, 93, 99, Schering-Plough Gallery, Madison, 1988, Morris Mus., Morristown, 1989, Montclair, NJ State U., 1995, Williams Gallery, Princeton, NJ, 1997, Monmouth Mus., Lincroft, NJ, 1998, Newark Acad., Livingston, 2000, Bristol-Myers Squibb Gallery, Princeton, NJ, 2005; represented in permanent collections NJ State Mus., Trenton, Newark Mus., Morris Mus., Morristown. Painting residency fellow Vt. Studio Ctr., 1992. Mem. Assoc. Artists N.J. (pres. 1985-87), N.J. Watercolor Soc., Federated Art Assns. of N.J. (panel mem. 1985, demonstrator 1991). Home: PO Box 443 Bernardsville NJ 07924-0443 Office Phone: 908-766-1219.

SPOGLI, RONALD P., ambassador; m. Georgia Beth Caudle; 2 children. AB in Hist., Stanford U., Calif., 1970; MBA, Harvard U., 1975. V.p. corp. fin. dept. Dean Witter Reynolds, Inc., LA, 1978—82, mng. dir. investment banking divsn.; ptnr. Freeman Spogli & Co., LA, 1983—; US amb. to Italy US Dept. State, Rome, 2005—. Lead rschr. Stanford U. Labor Migration Project, Milan. Bd. dirs. (presdl. appointee) J. William Fulbright Fgn. Scholarship Bd., 2002—. Recipient J. William Fulbright Fgn. Scholarship, 2002. Address: American Embassy Rome Italy Via Vittorio Veneto 119/A-00187 Rome Italy Office: American Embassy Rome Italy PSC 59 Box 100 F APO AE 09624 Italy also: DOS Amb 9500 Rome Pl Washington DC 20521-9500 Office Phone: 39-06-46741. Office Fax: 39-06-488-2672. E-mail: webteam@usembassy.it. *

SPOHN, HERBERT EMIL, psychologist; b. Berlin, June 10, 1923; s. Herbert F. and Bertha S.; m. Billie M. Powell, July 28, 1973; children: Jessica, Madeleine. BSS., CCNY, 1949; PhD, Columbia U., 1955. Research psychologist VA Hosp., Montrose, NY, 1955-60, chief research sect., 1960-64; sr. research psychologist Menninger Found., Topeka, 1965-80, dir. hosp. research, 1979-94, dir. research dept., 1981-94; ret., prof. emeritus for rsch., 1994—. Mem. mental health small grant com. NIMH, 1972-76, mem. treatment assessment rev. com., 1983-86, chmn. 1986-87. Author: (with Gardner Murphy) Encounter with Reality, 1968; assoc. editor: Schizophrenia Bull, 1970-87, 91—; contbr. articles to profl. jours. Served with AUS, World War II. USPHS grantee, 1964— Fellow Am. Psychopath. Assn.; mem. AAAS, N.Y. Acad. Sci., Soc. Psychopath. Research, Phi Beta Kappa, Sigma Xi. Office: 1906 SW Village Dr Topeka KS 66604-3714 E-mail: hspohn@prodigy.net.

SPOHN, NOR RAE, computer company executive; married; 2 children. BS in Computer Sci., Iowa State U., 1980; MEE, Stanford U. R&D engr. Hewlett-Packard Co., 1980, R&D mgr. LaserJet Divsn., 1998—2002, v.p., gen. mgr. Personal LaserJet Solutions, 2002—07, sr. v.p. LaserJet Printing Bus., 2007—. Mem. Gov.'s Sci. & Tech. Adv. Coun., Idaho, 2006—. Chair Idaho Sci., Math. and Tech. Coalition; bd. mem. Treasure Vallet Math. & Sci. Ctr.; bd. adv. Sch. Engring. Boise State U. Named to WITI Hall of Fame, Women in Tech. Internat., 2006. Office: Hewlett Packard Co Personal LaserJet Solutions Divsn 3000 Hanover St Palo Alto CA 94304-1185 *

SPOHN, WILLIAM GIDEON, JR., mathematician, retired musician; b. Lancaster, Pa., Mar. 8, 1923; s. William Gideon and Inza Mae (Huber) S.; m. Alice Liane Bailey, Sept. 13, 1946 (div.); children: Susan Jeannine Grochowina (dec.), William Gideon III (dec.), Peter Jonathan, Kathleen Anne Precht, Mary Louise; m. Evelyn Walsh Moreland, June 15, 1963 (div. Oct. 1978); m. Claire Louise Burgstahler, Dec. 19, 1987 (div. Sept. 1999). BA, St. Johns Coll., 1947; MA, U. Calif., Berkeley, 1950; PhD, U. Pa., 1962. Instr. math. Temple U., Phila., 1952-54, U. Del., Newark, 1954-56; mathematician Aberdeen Proving Ground, Md., 1954-55; instr. math. Bowling Green (Ohio) State U., 1956-59; mathematician, sr. staff Johns Hopkins U. Applied Physics Lab., Laurel, Md., 1959-84; singer, prodr. Spohn Music Co., Columbia, Md., 1981-99. Contbr. articles to profl. jours. Served to lt. USNR, 1943-46, PTO. Johns Hopkins U. Applied Physics Lab. fellow, 1966-67. Mem. Math. Assn. Am. Home: 1 Heritage Farm Dr Mount Airy MD 21771-5783

SPOHR, EARL CLYDE, retired investment advisor, military officer; b. Washington, Jan. 15, 1931; s. Earl Clyde and Helen Ruth Spohr; m. Gloria Sue Crabtree, June 19, 1962. Diploma, Cal-Aero Tech. Inst., Calif., 1951. Aircraft maintenance USAF, 1950—69, advisor air nat. guard, 1964—68, aircraft maintenance supt. Vietnam, 1968—69, sr. enlisted advisor Rhine Main AFB, Germany, 1969—74, aircraft maintenance supt. March AFB, Calif., 1974—75, Thule AFB, Greenland, 1975—76, sr. enlisted advisor Ramstein AFB, Germany, 1976—79, Malstrom AFB, Mont., 1979—81; ret. Chmn. Ill. Am. Diabetes Assn., 1986—89; dir. Iowa Found. for Health Care, Iowa, 1988—; pres. Ill. Found. for Quality Health Care, 2003—. Pres. Co. Hist. Soc., Mt. Vernon, Ill., 1986—87; pres., exec. dir. ARC, Jefferson Co., Ill., 1984—86; pres. Crossroads Cmty. Hosp. Aux., Mt. Vernon, Ill., 2005—; v.p. Jefferson Co. C. of C., 1985—88; com. chmn. Crosswalk Cmty. Action Agy., 1987—; state legislative chmn. AARP, Ill., 1984—87. Comdr. sgt. USAF, 1950—81. Recipient Purple Cross, Masonic Bodies, 1988. Mem.: Air Force Assn., Internat. Soc. Phil. Rsch., MENSA. Republican. Avocations: travel, reading, volunteering. Home: 108 Mockingbird Ln Woodlawn IL 62898 Office: Ill Found for Quality Health Care 2625 Butterfield Rd Oak Brook IL 60521

SPOKANE, ROBERT BRUCE, biophysical chemist; b. Cleve., Aug. 5, 1952; s. Herbert Norman and Marjorie Ellen (Firsten) S.; m. Linda Carol Wright, June 20, 1976; children: Lea, Hannah, Tara. BS in Chemistry, Ohio U., 1975; MS in Biophys. Chemistry, U. Colo., 1978, PhD in Biophys. Chemistry, 1981. Cert. full cave diver. Tchg. asst. dept. chemistry U. Colo., Boulder, 1975-77, rsch. asst. dept. chemistry, 1977-81; staff scientist Procter & Gamble Co., Cin., 1981-84; rsch. scientist dept. neurophysiology Children's Hosp., Cin., 1984-90; sr. scientist, product mgr. YSI Co., Yellow Springs, Ohio, 1990—. Cons. Synthetic Blood Internat., Yellow Springs, 1992. Contbr. articles to profl. jours. Rescuer, treas. Boulder Emergency Squad, 1980; rescue diver Kitty Hawk Scuba, Dayton, Ohio, 1992. Recipient Merck Index award Ohio U., 1975. Mem. Am. Chem. Soc., N.Y. Acad. Sci., Am. Physiol. Soc., Nat. Speleological Soc. (cave diving sect.), Sigma Xi. Achievements include research in implantable glucose sensors; oxygen tonometer for peritoneal oxygen measurements; interferant removal system for biosensors for methanol, ethanol, glutamate, and glutamine, optical carbon dioxide sensor, water chemistry in submerged caves. Home: 1715 Garry Dr Bellbrook OH 45305-1362 Office: YSI Co 1725 Brannum Ln Yellow Springs OH 45387-1107 Office Phone: 937-767-7241. Business E-Mail: rspokane@ysi.com.

SPOLAN, HARMON SAMUEL, lawyer; b. Phila., Dec. 12, 1935; s. Jay and Edythe (Greenberg) S.; m. Betty Jane Evnitz, Mar. 30, 1958; children: Michael, Suzanne. AB, Temple U., 1957, LLB, 1959; postgrad., Oxford U., 1966. Bar: Pa. 1960. Ptnr. Ravetz & Shuchman, Phila., 1960-68, Blair & Co., NYC, 1968-72; v.p. Butcher & Singer, Phila., 1972-74; pres. Capital First Corp., Phila., 1974-75, State Nat. Bank, Rockville, Md., 1975-78, Jefferson Bank, Phila., 1978-99; pres., bd. dirs. JeffBanks, Inc., Phila., 1986-99; sr. mem. Cozen O'Connor, Phila., 1999—2007, of counsel, 2007—. Lectr. law U. Pa., Phila., 1964-68. Author: Federal Aids to Financing, 1970; contbr. articles to profl. jours. Former chmn. bd. Huntingdon Hosp., Willow Grove, Pa., 1982—89; bd. dirs. YMHA, Phila., 1978—95, Anti-Defamation League, 1982. Named Man of Yr., Nat. Assn. Women Bus. Owners, 1978, Disting. Alumnus, Central H.S., 1975. Mem. ABA, Phila. Bar Assn. Democrat. Jewish. Office: 1900 Market St Philadelphia PA 19103-3527 Home Phone: 215-985-0260. Business E-Mail: hspolan@cozen.com.

SPONG, JOHN SHELBY, retired bishop, writer, columnist; b. Charlotte, NC, June 16, 1931; s. John Shelby and Doolie Boyce (Griffith) S.; m. Joan Lydia Ketner, Sept. 5, 1952 (dec. 1988); children: Ellen Elizabeth, Mary Katharine, Jaquelin Ketner; m. Christine Mary Bridger, Jan. 1, 1990. AB, U. N.C., 1952; M.Div., Va. Theol. Sem., 1955; D.D., St. Paul's Coll., 1976, Va. Theol. Sem., 1977; DHL (hon.), Muhlenburg Coll., 1998, Holmes Inst. Chgo., 2003, Lehigh U., 2006, U. NC, 2006. Ordained to ministry Episcopal Ch., 1955, bishop, 1976; rector St. Joseph's Ch., Durham, NC, 1955-57, Calvary Ch., Tarboro, NC, 1957-65, St. John's Ch., Lynchburg, Va., 1965-69, St. Paul's Ch., Richmond, Va., 1969-76; bishop Diocese of Newark, 1976-2000, ret., 2000. Mem. governing body Nat. Episc. Ch., 1973-76; vis. lectr., Harvard U. Div. Sch., 2000, U. Pacific, Stockton, Calif., 2003; mem. faculty Grad. Theol. Union, Berkeley, Calif., 1997, 99, 2001, 03, 05, 07. Author: Honest Prayer, 1973, This Hebrew Lord, 1974, Dialogue--In Search of Jewish-Christian Understanding, 1975, Christpower, 1976, The Living Commandments, 1977, The Easter Moment, 1980, Into the Whirlwind: The Future of the Church, 1983, Beyond Moralism, 1986, Survival and Consciousness, 1987, Living in Sin? A Bishop Rethinks Human Sexuality, 1988, Rescuing the Bible from Fundamentalism--A Biship Rethinks the Meaning of Scripture, 1991, Born of a Woman, 1992, Resurrection: Myth or Reality?, 1994, Liberating the Gospels, Reading the Bible with Jewish Eyes, 1996, Why Christianity Must Change or Die, 1998, Here I Stand: My Struggle for a Christianity of Integrity, Love and Equality, 2000, A New Christianity for a New World, 2001, The Sins of Scripture-Exploring the Bible's Texts of Hate to Discover The God of Love, 2005, Jesus for Non Religious, 2007; columnist Beliefnet.com, 2000—02, Waterfront Media, 2002—. Elected Quartercentury Scholar Emmanuel Coll., Cambridge, Eng., 1992, named Humanist of Yr., 1999, William Belden Noble lectr. Harvard U., 2000. Mem.: Rotary. Episcopalian. Home: 24 Puddingstone Rd Morris Plains NJ 07950-1114

SPONSLER, GEORGE CURTIS, III, science administrator, lawyer; b. Collingswood, NJ, Dec. 2, 1927; s. George Curtis and Mary Grace (Hollinberger) S.; m. Bridget Ruth Butcher, Sept. 3, 1955; children: Freda Grace, Naomi Margaret Bride, Curtis Alexander. BS in Engring. Physics, Princeton U., 1949, MA, 1951, PhD, 1952; JD, George Washington U., 1981. Bar: Md. 1981, D.C. 1982, U.S. Ct. Appeals (4th cir.) 1982, U.S. Ct. Appeals (fed. cir.) 1984. U.S. Supreme Ct. 1986. With Lincoln Lab., MIT, 1952-56; liaison officer Office Naval Research, London, 1956-58, head spl. projects br. Washington, 1958-59; sr. scientist Hoffman Sci. Center, Santa Barbara, Calif., 1959-60; chief sci., dir. tech. analysis and ops. research U.S. Navy Bur. Ships, 1960-63; dir. advanced planning, fed. systems div. IBM, 1963-66, dir. center exploratory studies, 1966-68; exec. sec. div. engring. Nat. Acad. Sci.-NRC, 1968-70; pres. Law Math. and Tech. Inc., 1970—2002; semi-ret. On leave, Congl. fellow U.S. Senate, Washington, 1987-88; mem. adv. com. to Office Emergency Planning, Nat. Acad. Sci., 1967-72, chmn. subcom. automation, 1966-68, mem. joint adv. com. on electromagnetic pulse, 1970-74; cons. Exec. Office of Pres., 1971-73 Contbr.: Tech. Innovation, Harper Ency. of Sci.; author articles in field. Fellow AAAS (electorate nominating com. 1980-83, chmn.-elect sect. X, 1983-84, chmn. 1984-85, mem. coun. 1985-86), Am. Physics Soc.; mem. IEEE (life, sr., chmn. subcom. on privacy of communications and info. policy com. 1982-85, aerospace R&D policy com. 1990-92), Phi Beta Kappa, Sigma Xi. Democrat. Episcopalian. Personal E-mail: sponsler@worldnet.att.net.

SPONZILLI, EDWARD GEORGE, lawyer; b. Newark, Mar. 30, 1948; s. Edward James and Dorothy Maria (Murillo) Sponzilli. BA in History with high honors, Rutgers U., 1971, JD, 1975; summer diploma, Cath. Inst. of Paris, 1971; MA, Columbia U., 1972. Bar: N.J. 1975, U.S. Dist. Ct. N.J. 1975, U.S. Ct. Appeals (3d cir.) 1976, U.S. Supreme Ct. 1979, D.C. 1979, N.Y. 1981, U.S. Ct. Appeals (2d cir.) 1992, U.S. Dist. Ct. (so. dist.) N.Y. 1991, U.S. Dist. Ct. (ea. dist.) N.Y. 1991. Law clk. to judge U.S. Dist. Ct. NJ, Newark, 1975—77; assoc. Pitney, Hardin & Kipp, Morristown, NJ, 1975—81, Dunn, Pashman, Sponzilli, Swick & Finnerty (formerly Cummins, Dunn & Pashman), Hackensack, NJ, 1982—, ptnr., 1984—95, Norris, McLaughlin & Marcus, P.A., 1995—. Co-adj. prof. Rutgers U., New Brunswick, NJ, 1980—81, 1994, 98, mcpl. pros., 1981—, mem. Jessup Internat. Law Moot Ct. Team, 1975, coach Mock Trial Team, 1994—97; counsel Judo of NJ Inc., Cranford, 1983—; judge law sch. moot ct. competition Seton Hall, 1977—79, 1981, 81, 86; cert. civil trial atty. NJ Supreme Ct., 1997—; mem. faculty Nat. Inst. Trial Advocacy, 1995—; faculty N.J. Atty. Gens. Trial Advocacy Inst., 2002—. Contbr. articles to profl. jours. Active Rutgers U. Found., 1987—; bench bar media com. NJ Supreme Ct., 2007—. Named Superlawyer, NJ Mag., 2005—07; recipient Nancy Higgenson Dorr award, Rutgers U., 1971, Disting. Svc. award, Animals Need You-Kindness Corp., NJ, 1981, Client Protection award, NJ Supreme Ct. Fund for Client Protection, 1999; Henry Rutgers scholar. Master: Am. Inns of Ct (pres. 2000—01); mem.: ATLA, ABA (trial practice com. of litigation sect.), Assn. Fed. Bar NJ, NJ Mcpl. Prosecutors Assn., NJ Criminal Def. Assn., NJ State Ct. (mediator, fed. arbitrator), Nat. Assn. Coll. and Univ. Attys., NJ Def. Assn., Middlesex County Bar Assn., Essex County Bar Assn., Bergen County Bar Assn., Trial Attys. NJ (trustee 1987—), NJ Trial Lawyers Assn., NJ State Bar Assn. (higher edn. com.), Columbia Grad. Faculties Alumni Assn., Rutgers U. Law Sch. Alumni Assn. (nominating com. 1982, program dir. 1982, treas. 1991—92, sec. 1992—93, v.p. 1993—94, pres. 1994—95, exec. counsel, alumni fedn. rep.), Scarlet R Round Table Alumni Assn., Phi Alpha Delta, Kappa Sigma (sec. 1978—79, alumnus advisor 1978—99, v.p. 1979—82, pres. 1982—86, dist. grand master 1986—2000, pres. 1994—2001, chmn. nat. legal comm. 1995—97, trustee Gamma Upsilon chpt., Steven Alonso Jackson award 1999), Phi Beta Kappa. Home: 37 Brookside Ave Caldwell NJ 07006-5603 Office: Norris McLaughlin & Marcus PA 721 Rt 202-206 PO Box 1018 Somerville NJ 08876-1018 Office Phone: 908-252-4166. Business E-Mail: egsponzilli@nmmlaw.com.

SPOONER, DAVID M., federal agency administrator, lawyer; BA, U. Va., 1991; JD, Coll. William and Mary, 1994. Legal counsel to Rep. Wes Cooley US Ho. of Reps, Washington, comm. dir. Com. on Agr., assoc. Com. on Rules; adminstrv. asst. Office of Rep. Sue Myrick, US Ho. of Reps, Washington, press sec., legis. dir.; transition coord. Office of US Trade Rep. Exec. Office of the Pres., Washington, spl. textile negotiator Office of US Trade Rep., 2002—05; asst. sec. import adminstrn. Internat. Trade Adminstrn. US Dept. Commerce, Washington, 2005—.

SPOONHOUR, JAMES MICHAEL, lawyer; b. San Antonio, Mar. 24, 1946; s. Robert W. and Marie C. S.; m. Terri Walker; children: Taylor, Erin, Whitney, Michael. BA, U. Nebr., 1968, MA, 1970; JD, Georgetown U., 1974. Bar: Fla. 1974, U.S. Dist. Ct. (mid. dist.) Fla. 1974. Assoc. Lowndes, Piersol, Drosdick & Doster, Orlando, Fla., 1974-76; asst. prof. law Loyola U., New Orleans, 1976-77; ptnr. Lowndes, Drosdick, Doster, Kantor & Reed, P.A., Orlando, 1977—. Lectr. on eminent domain and property taxes. Contbr. articles to profl. jours. Bd. dirs. Vis. Nurse Assn., Orlando, 1979-89, Croquet Found. Am., 2001, Friends Casa Feliz, 2005—; chmn. sch. bd. The First Acad., Orlando, 1986-89. With USAF, 1970-72. Mem. ABA, Assn. Eminent Domain Profls., Fla. Bar, Orange County Bar Assn. Republican. Office: Lowndes Drosdick Doster Kantor & Reed PA 215 N Eola Dr Orlando FL 32801-2095 Home Phone: 407-474-1383; Office Phone: 407-418-6300. Business E-Mail: james.spoonhour@lowndes-law.com.

SPOOR, RHYS, dentist; Grad., U. Wash., 1983. With Aesthetic & Restorative Dentistry, Seattle. Fellow: Pierre Fauchard Acad., Acad. Gen. Dentistry; mem.: Am. Acad. Cosmetic Dentistry. Office: Aesthetic & Restorative Dentistry 701 5th Ave Ste 4660 Seattle WA 98104 Office Phone: 206-682-8200. E-mail: info@rhysspoor.com.

SPOOR, WILLIAM HOWARD, food products executive; b. Pueblo, Colo., Jan. 16, 1923; s. Charles Hinchman and Doris Field (Slaughter) S.; m. Janet Spain, Sept. 23, 1950; children: Melanie G., Cynthia F., William Lincoln. BA, Dartmouth Coll., 1949; postgrad., Denver U., 1949, Stanford U., 1965. Asst. sales mgr. N.Y. Export divsn. Pillsbury Co., 1949-53; mgr. N.Y. office Pillsbury Co., 1953-62, v.p. export divsn. Mpls., 1962-68, v.p., gen. mgr. internat. ops., 1968-73, CEO, 1973-85, also bd. dirs., chmn. exec. com., 1987, pres., CEO, 1988, past chmn. bd. dirs. Bd. dirs. Coleman Co. Mem. regional export expansion coun. Dept. Commerce, 1966-74; bd. dirs. exec. Coun. Fgn. Diplomats, 1976-78; mem. bd. visitors Nelson A. Rockefeller Ctr., Dartmouth Coll., 1992-95; Minn. Orchestral Assn., United Negro Coll. Fund, 1973-75; chmn. Capitol City Renaissance Task Force, 1985; trustee Mpls. Found., 1985-92; mem. sr. campaign cabinet Carlson Com. U. Minn., 1985; mem. corps. rels. com. Nature Conservancy, 1985; mem. Nat. Cambodia Crisis Com., pres. pvt. sector Dept. Transp. task force, 1982, pres. pvt. sector survey on cost control, 1983; chmn. YWCA Tribute to Womwn in Internat. Industry. 2d lt. inf. U.S. Army, 1943-46. Recipient Golden Plate award, Am. Acad. Achievement, Disting. Bus. Leadership award, St. Cloud State U., Miss. Valley World Trade award, Outstanding Achievement award, Dartmouth Coll., Horatio Alger award, 1986, Medal of Merit, U.S. Savs. Bond Program; honored with William H. Spoor Dialogues on Leadership, Dartmouth Coll., honored Fair Player Minn. Women's Polit. Caucus, 1989. Mem.: Nat. Fgn. Trade Coun., Grocery Mfrs. Am. (treas. 1973—84), Minn. Bus. Partnership, Minn. Hist. Soc. (mem. exec. com. 1983, bd. dirs.), Mpls. Club (bd. govs. 1985, pres. 1986), Old Baldy Club, Woodhill Country Club, River Club NYC, The Country Club Salt Lake City, Alta Club, Phi Beta Kappa. Home: 1173 Oak Forest Rd Salt Lake City UT 84103 Office: 4900 IDS Ctr Minneapolis MN 55402 Office Phone: 612-330-4621.

SPORE, KEITH KENT, newspaper executive; b. Milw., May 29, 1942; s. G. Keith and Evelyn A. (Morgan) S.; divorced; children: Bradley, Julie, Justine; m. Kathy Stokebrand. BS in Journalism, U. Wis., Milw., 1967. City editor Milw. Sentinel, 1977-81; asst. mng. editor/news Milw. Jour. Sentinel, 1981-89, mng. editor, 1989-91, editor, 1991-95, editl. page editor, 1995, pres., 1995—, pub., 1996—. Author: (novels) The Hell Masters, 1977, Death of a Scavenger, 1980. With U.S. Army, 1961-64. Recipient Freedom of Info. award Soc. Profl. Journalists, 1995; named Mass Comms. Alumnus of Yr., U. Wis.-Milw., 1994. Mem. Greater Milw. Com. Office: Milw Jour Sentinel PO Box 661 Milwaukee WI 53201-0661 E-mail: kspore@onwis.com.

SPORLEDER, THOMAS LYNN, economist, researcher; b. Perrysburg, Ohio, Apr. 2, 1942; s. John Loren Sporleder, Ruth Cordelia Westrick; m. Marjorie Jean Stout; children: Thomas James, Candace Lynn. BS, Ohio State U., 1964, MS, 1965, PhD, 1968. Mgr. Agrl. Grading Sta. Campbell Soup Co., Napoleon, Ohio, 1961—64; prof. agrl. econs. Tex. A&M U., College Station, 1968—89; prof. agribus., income enhancement endowed chair Ohio State U., Columbus, 1989—. Vis. scholar USDA, Washington, 1974—75; rsch. economist Office Tech. Assessment, U.S. Congress, Washington, 1976—77; bd. dirs. Internat. Food and Agribusiness Mgmt. Assn., Washington, Heartland Agdeavor Assn., Columbus. Contbr. articles to profl. jours. Mem.: Am. Agrl. Econs. Assn. (pres. agribus. econs. and mgmt. sect. 2002—03). Roman Catholic. Office: Ohio State Univ 2120 Fyffe Rd Columbus OH 43210-1066 Home: 15025 Harbor Point Dr E Thornville OH 43076-8040 Office Phone: 614-292-0286. Business E-Mail: sporleder.1@osu.edu.

SPORN, AARON ADOLPH, physician, educator; b. NYC, Nov. 5, 1953; s. Herbert and Eunice (Aron) S.; m. Beverly Sporn; children: Hunter, Melanie. BS, SUNY, Stony Brook, 1974; MD, Columbia U., 1978. Diplomate Am. Bd. Orthopaedic Surgery. Intern. gen. surgery Roosevelt Hosp., NYC, 1978-79, resident gen. surgery, 1979-80; resident, chief resident in orthopaedic surgery NYU and Bellevue Hosp., NYC, 1980-83; fellow Midwest Inst. for Orthopaedics, Cin., 1983-84; v.p. medical affairs Inst. for Medicine in Sports, Trenton, NJ, 1984-85; clin. sr. instr. Hahnemann U. Med. Sch., Phila., 1986—; 1991clin. instr. Rutgers U. Med. Sch., New Brunswick, NJ, 1986—91; chief, dept. orthopaedic surgery Robert Wood Johnson U. Hosp. at Hamilton, 1994—2004, vice chmn., dept. surgery, 1993-95, chmn. dept. surgery, 1995—98. Vis. clin. fellow Columbia U., N.Y.C., 1978-80, teaching asst. NYU, N.Y.C., 1982-83; com. mem. Arthroscopy Bd. N.Am. Exam Com., 1989-90; cons. N.J. State Police, Trenton, 1987-92; fundraising com. orthopaedics wing Hamilton Hosp.,

Trenton, 1989. Contbr. articles to profl. jours. Ind. Rsch. Project grantee NIMH, 1975, 88. Fellow Am. Acad. Orthopaedic Surgery, Arthroscopy Bd. N.Am.; mem. Phi Beta Kappa. Office: Med Arts Bldg 8 Quakerbridge Plz Hamilton NJ 08619-1255

SPORN, MICHAEL V., producer, director; b. NYC, Apr. 23, 1946; s. Mario and Amy (Young) Rosco. BFA, N.Y. Inst. Tech., 1967. Asst. dir. Hubley Studio, NYC, 1972-76; supr., coord. R. Williams Animation, NYC, 1976-77; asst. dir. R.O. Blechman Prodns., NYC, 1977-79; founder, owner, dir. Michael Sporn Animation Inc., NYC, 1980—. Prodr., dir.: Doctor DeSoto, 1984 (Oscar nomination 1985), Abel's Island, 1988 (Emmy nomination 1988), Red Shoes, Dancing Frog, Ira Sleeps Over, dir.: The Man Who Walked Between the Towers, 2005 (Am. Libr. Assn. Carnegie Medal, 2006), 30 other animated films. Recipient Ace awards Acad. Cable Arts, 1990-92. Mem. ASIFA East (bd. dirs. 1974—, 23 awards 1972—), Acad. Motion Picture Arts and Scis. Office: Michael Sporn Animation Inc 35 Bedford St New York NY 10014 Office Phone: 212-242-0647.

SPORTY, LAWRENCE DOUGLAS, psychiatrist; b. June 17, 1943; BA in Chemistry and Biology, Queens Coll., CUNY, 1964; MD, SUNY, Bklyn., 1968. Diplomate Am. Bd. Psychiatry and Neurology. Attending psychiatrist SUNY, Bklyn., 1972—74; adminstrv. and clin. dir. South Beach Psychol. Ctr., NY, 1972—74, chief of svc. NY, 1974—75; asst. clin. prof. SUNY-Downstate Med. Ctr., Bklyn., 1975—76; med. dir. Met. State Hosp., Norwalk, Calif., 1978—79; assoc. prof. clin. psychiatry U. So. Calif., LA, 1978—79, chief adult in-patient svcs., 1979; acting chmn. dept. psychiatry U. Calif.-Irvine Med. Ctr., Orange, 1979—82, vice chmn. clin. svcs., 1982—87; assoc. clin. prof., 1979, clin. prof., 1979—83, prof. clin. psychiatry, 1983—. Cons., lectr. in field. Contbr. articles to profl. jours. Fellow: Am. Psychiat. Assn. (disting. life); mem.: So. Calif. Psychiat. Soc. (exec. coun. 1982—84), Alpha Omega Alpha. Office: 2021 E 4th St Ste 118 Santa Ana CA 92705 Office Phone: 714-285-0870.

SPOTNITZ, ALAN JEFFREY, cardiothoracic surgeon; b. NYC, May 31, 1944; s. Hyman and Miriam (Berkman) S. BA, Harvard U., 1966; MD, Columbia U., 1970. Intern gen. surgery Beth Israel Hosp., Boston, 1970-71; rsch. fellow Columbia U., NYC, 1973-74; resident gen. surgery Beth Israel Hosp., Boston, 1971-75; thoracic resident thoracic surgery Presbyn., NYC, 1978-79; assoc. prof. clin. surgery Robert Wood Johnson Med. Sch., New Brunswick, NJ, 1982—87, chief sect. cardiac surgery, 1988—2001. Dir. surg. clerkship program Robert Wood Johnson Med. Sch., New Brunswick, 1982—, assoc. dir. thoracic surgery residency program U. Medicine and Dentistry N.J., 1991-2001. Author: (with others) Homograft Valve Durability: Host or Donor Influence, Heart Vessels, 1990; contbr. articles to profl. jours. Maj. USAF, 1975—77. Office: Robert Wood Johnson Med Sch 125 Paterson St New Brunswick NJ 08901 Home Phone: 732-828-2217; Office Phone: 908-235-7805. Business E-Mail: spotnitz@umdnj.edu.

SPOTO, CARL ALEXANDER, JR., history educator; b. Saranac Lake, NY, Mar. 14, 1972; s. Katherine Schaffer; m. Sarah Jean Cudzilo, July 5, 2003; 1 child, Grace Katherine. BA, SUNY Cortland; M, Nazareth Coll. of Rochester. Cert. tchr. NY State. Tchr. Honeoye Falls-Lima CSD, NY, 1994—96, Midlakes CSD, Clifton Springs, NY, 1996—. Coach Midlakes H.S., Clifton Springs. Mem.: NYS Coun. for the Social Studies (corr.). Democrat. Home: 8 Larkspur Lane Fairport NY 14450 Office: Midlakes HS 1554 State Route 488 Clifton Springs NY 14432 Home Phone: 585-377-4809; Office Phone: 315-548-6300. Business E-Mail: cspoto@midlakes.org.

SPOTTSWOOD, LYDIA CAROL, nurse, health facility administrator; b. NYC, May 6, 1951; d. Rudolph Messerschmidt and Eleanor Schlesinger; m. Paul Gregory Spottswood, Feb. 17, 1989; children: Mark Philip, Jayne Alexander, Erin Lenore. BS in Nursing, U. Va., Charlottesville, 1972. RN Va., Colo., D.C. Head nurse operating room U. Va. Hosp., Charlottesville, Va., 1974—77; nurse Children's Hosp., Washington, 1978—79, Wurzburg Army Med. Hosp., Germany, 1979—80; mem. city coun. City of Kenosha, Wis., 1990—98; dir. New Start Cmty. Health Ctr. (now Kenosha Cmty. Health Ctr.), Wis., 1994—95; mem. bd. U. Wis. Benevolent Found., 2000—. State and regional bd. mem. Area Health Edn. Ctr. Sys., Wis., 1996—2000; columnist Kenosha News, Wis., 2001—02. Past chair 1st Dist. Dem. Party Wis., congl. cand., 1996—98; mem. First Presbyn. Ch., Kenosha, Wis. Recipient Congl. Svc. Recognition award, Rep. Peter Barca, 1996, Svc. award, Kenosha County Med. Soc., 1996; grantee, HHS, 1994. Avocations: skiing, horseback riding, interior decorating, travel.

SPRAGGINS, JOHNNIE DAVID, sociology and cultural studies educator; b. Opelika, Ala., Oct. 13, 1954; s. John David and Alma Jean McCormick Spraggins; 1 child, Jada Ruth. BA, Auburn U., 1978, MA, 1988, U. Mich., 1993, PhD, 1995. Rsch. assoc. Auburn U., 1981-90; prof. Madonna U., U. Mich.-Ann Arbor, 1990—96; prof. sociology Asian divsn. U. Md., Tokyo, 1996—99; prof. Randolph-Macon Coll., Ashland, Va., 1999—2001; asst. prof. Our Lady of the Lake U., San Antonio, 2001—06; mem. faculty dept. sociology U. Tex., San Antonio, 2006—. Advisor Woman's Studies Coun., Randolph-Macon Coll., 1999—; vis. asst. prof. SUNY, Geneseo; vis. asst. prof. Asian divsn. U. Md., Sagamihara-shi, Japan; prof. Kitasato U., Sagamihara-shi, Kanagawa-ken, 1996-98. Contbr. articles to profl. jours. Mem. Ctr. for Rsch. on Social Orgn., Am. Sociological Assn., Soc. Applied Sociology. Democrat. Buddhist. Avocations: gardening, travel. E-mail: johnnie.spraggins@utsa.edu.

SPRAGUE, ANN LOUISE, aerospace scientist; b. Bellfonte, Pa., Feb. 25, 1946; d. David Carpenter and Opal (Wheat) S.; m. Donald M. Hunten, 1995. BA Geology, Syracuse U., 1969; MA, Boston U., 1980; PhD, U. Ariz., 1990. Tchr. sci. Selinsgrove Mid. Sch., 1970—79; space scientist Lunar and Planetary Lab. U. Ariz., Tucson, 1990—. Mem. Lunar and Planetary Exploration com. NRC, 2000— Contbg. author: Caloris Basin: An Enhanced Source for Potassium in Mercury's Atmosphere, 1990, Sulfur at Mercury, Elemental at the Poles and Sulfides in the Regolith, 1995, Water Brought In to Jupiter's Atmosphere by Fragments R and W of Comet SL-9, 1996, Distribution and Abundance of Sodium in Mercury's Atmosphere, 1985-1988, 1997, Exploring Mercury: The Iron Planet, 2003; editl. bd. ICARUS Mem. AAAS, Internat. Astron. Union, Am. Astron. Soc. (com. divsn. planetary scis.), Am. Geophys. Union Office: U Ariz Lunar & Planetary Lab Tucson AZ 85721-0001 Business E-Mail: sprague@lpl.arizona.edu.

SPRAGUE, CHARLES W., lawyer, finance company executive; b. Orange, NJ, Nov. 14, 1949; BA cum laude, Yale U., 1971; MBA, JD, NYU, 1975. Bar: NY 1976, DC 1993, Wis. Atty. Sullivan & Cromwell, 1975—83, Reboul MacMurray, 1983—92, Sprague & Coultas, 1992—94; exec. v.p., gen. counsel, sec. Fiserv, Inc., Brookfield, Wis., 1994—, chief admin. officer, 1999—. Mem.: ABA, Wis. State Bar Assn., DC Bar Assn., Internat. Bar Assn. Office: Fiserv Inc PO Box 979 255 Fiserv Dr Brookfield WI 53045 Office Phone: 262-879-5000.

SPRAGUE, EDWARD AUCHINCLOSS, retired professional society administrator, economist; b. NYC, Oct. 9, 1932; s. Irvin Auchincloss and Maude Browning (Fisher) S.; m. Patricia Ivy Cannon, Apr. 27, 1957; children: James Edward, Elizabeth Mary, Jennifer Ann. BA, Princeton U., 1954; MA, NYU, 1961. Rsch. analyst N.J. State C. of C., Newark, 1957-59; assoc. economist F.W. Dodge Corp., NYC, 1959-62; economist Lehman Bros., NYC, 1962-67; v.p. Nat. Assn. Mfrs., NYC and Washington, 1967-77; dir. tax policy The Tax Found., Washington, 1977-82, sr. v.p., 1985-89; exec. dir. Tax Exec. Inst., 1982-85; v.p., exec. dir. The Tax Coun., 1979-82, 86-91, cons., 1991-92, Employers Coun. on Flexible Compensation, Washington, 1992-93; ret., 1993. Editor: Building Business, 1961-62; jour. The Tax Executive, 1983-85. With U.S. Army, 1955-57. Republican. Home: 2850 Prism Ct Lusby MD 20657

SPRAGUE, JOHN LOUIS, management consultant; b. Boston, 1930; s. Robert Chapman and Florence Antoinette (van Zelm) S.; m. Mary-Jane Whitney, June 19, 1952; children: John Louis, William Whitney, Catherine van Zelm, David Hyatt. AB, Princeton, 1952; PhD, Stanford, 1959. With Sprague Electric Co., North Adams, Mass., 1959-87, co-dir. engrng. labs., sr. v.p. engrng., 1964-65, v.p. research and devel., 1965-66, sr. v.p. semi-condr. div., 1967-76, pres., 1976-87, chief exec. officer, 1981-87; pres. John L. Sprague Assocs. Inc., 1988—2003; self-employed, 2003—. Bd. dirs. MRA Labs., Inc., Calif. Micro Devices. Chmn. Williamstown United Fund-ARC Campaign, 1961; trustee Pine Cobble Sch., 1978, Middlesex Sch., 1994-96. Lt. (j.g.) USNR, 1952-55. Mem. IEEE, Electrochem. Soc., Am. Chem. Soc., Sci. Research Soc. Am., Confrerie des Chevaliers du Tastevin, Confrerie de la Chaine des Rotisseurs, Princeton Club (N.Y.C.), Sigma Xi, Phi Lambda Upsilon. Home: 175 Bee Hill Rd Williamstown MA 01267-2703 Office Phone: 413-743-9454. E-mail: beehilljon@aol.com.

SPRAGUE, MARY GABRIELLE, lawyer; b. Phila., Oct. 7, 1957; AB summa cum laude, Harvard U., 1979; JD, Yale U., 1983. Bar: Colo. 1984, D.C. 1992. Law clk. to Hon. Jim R. Carrigan US Dist. Ct. Colo., 1984-85; law clk. to Hon. Byron R. White US Supreme Ct., Washington, 1986-87; ptnr. Arnold & Porter, Washington. Mem. Phi Beta Kappa. Office: Arnold & Porter 555 12th St NW Washington DC 20004-1206 Office Phone: 202-942-5773. Office Fax: 202-942-5999. E-mail: Mary.Gay.Sprague@aporter.com.

SPRAGUE, PETER JULIAN, software company executive, lecturer; b. Detroit, Apr. 29, 1939; s. Julian K. and Helene (Coughlin) S.; m. Tjasa Krofta, Dec. 19, 1959; children: Carl, Steven, Kevin, Michael. Student, Yale U., 1961, MIT, 1961, Columbia U., 1962-66. Chmn. Wave Sys., Inc.; bd. dirs. Enlighten Software Inc. Bd. dirs. vwink.com, Inc. Trustee Strang Clinic. Mem. Yale Club. Office: Wave Systems Corp 1 Penn Plz Ste 2420 New York NY 10119

SPRAGUE, RAYMOND, music educator; b. Yonkers, NY, Nov. 28, 1947; s. Raymond Arthur and Rosemary (Lockwood) S.; m. Kathleen Jane Turner, May 30, 1981. BA in Music, Williams Coll., Williamstown, Mass., 1969; MMus, U.N.Mex., 1973; DMA, U. Colo., 1979. Tchr. cert. music/choral-gen. k-12 Ind., 1985. Instr. Albuquerque Acad., 1969-71; grad. asst. U. N.Mex., Aubuquerque, 1972-73; instr., grad. asst. U. Colo., Boulder, 1973-77; dir. music King of Glory Luth. Ch., Arvada, Colo., 1974-77; asst. prof., dir. choral activities St. Mary's Coll., South Bend, Ind., 1977-84; assoc. prof., dir. choral activities U. New Orleans, 1985-95, prof., 1995—99; dir. music St. Charles Ave. Bapt. Ch., New Orleans, 1986-91; artistic dir., conductor La. Vocal Arts Chorale, New Orleans, 1992—99; prof. and dir. choral activities Davidson (NC) Coll., 1999—, chmn. music dept., 2000—06. Clinician, adjudicator, guest conductor high sch. and colls. Musical debut Carnegie Hall, 1999, Return Engagement, 2006; Mus. and book reviewer The Choral Jour., 1977—; editor Treble Choir Music, 1985—; articles to profl. jours. Mem. Am. Choral Dirs. Assn. (state pres. La. chpt. 1989, state pres. Ind. choral dirs. 1983), Chorus Am., Coll. Music Soc. Episcopalian. Avocations: hiking, camping, fishing, golf, sports. Office: Davidson Coll Dept Music Davidson NC 28035 Office Phone: 704-894-2591. Business E-Mail: rasprague@davidson.edu.

SPRAGUE, RICHARD A., lawyer; b. Balt., Sept. 22, 1925; s. George Sidney and Marian (Barsel) S.; divorced; children: Thomas Andrew, Barbara Anne. BS, Temple U., 1949; LLB, U. Pa., 1953. Bar: Pa., 1954, NY, 2002, U.S. Dist. Ct. (ea. dist.) Pa., 1971, U.S. Ct. Appeals (Fed. cir.), U.S. Supreme Ct., 2003. Asst. vol. defender Defender Assn., Phila., 1954—57; asst. dist. atty. Dist. Atty.'s Office, Phila., 1958—65, 1st asst. dist. atty., 1966—74; counsel Berger & Montague, Phila., 1975—79; sr. ptnr. Sprague & Sprague, Phila., 1979—; pres. judge ct. of jud. discipline Commonwealth Pa. Former chief counsel Select Com. on Assassinations, U.S. Ho. of Reps.; spl. prosecutor for Washington County, Pa., 1970-85, for Delaware County, Pa., 1971-74, for Phila. County dist. atty., 2000-; spl. asst. to U.S. atty. gen., 1973-74; spl. counsel to Pa. Supreme Ct. Jud. Inquiry and Rev. Bd., 1981-83; spl. investigator for Allegheny County, Pa., 1999—; vol. defender Defender's Assn. Phila.; lectr. Temple U. Sch. Law, Phila., 1972-; mem. faculty ATLA; mem. Phila. Criminal Justice Coordinating Commn., U.S. Senate Jud. Nominating Commn.; former treas. Phila. Regional Planning Coun. Gov.'s Justice Commn.; bd. dirs. Biotech. Found., Inc. With USN, 1943-45, WWII. Mem. ABA (antitrust law sect., criminal justice sect.), Pa. Bar Assn., Phila. Bar Assn. (bd. govs. 1971-74), Nat. Dist. Attys. Assn., Assn. Trial Lawyers Am. Office: Sprague & Sprague 135 S 19th St Ste 400 Philadelphia PA 19103-4912

SPRAGUE, WILLIAM DOUGLAS, lawyer; b. Houston, Dec. 23, 1941; s. William Douglas and Helen (Mims) S.; m. Marilyn Wells, Aug. 7, 1965; children: William Douglas III, Anne W., Robert L. BS, U. Wis., 1964; JD, Harvard U., 1967. Bar: Mich. 1972, Ind. 1978, Pa. 1991. Assoc. Reinhart, Boerner, Van Deuren, Norris & Rieselbach, Milw., 1967-71; lawyer Ford Motor Credit Co., Dearborn, Mich., 1971-77; various legal positions to sr. v.p. adminstrn. AMAX Coal Co., Indpls., 1977-87; assoc. gen. counsel Alumax Inc., San Mateo, Calif., 1987-88; v.p., gen. counsel Lukens Inc., Coatesville, Pa., 1988; v.p., gen. counsel, sec. AmeriSource; sr. v.p., gen. counsel, sec. AmerisourceBergen (from merger of Bergen Brunswig and AmeriSource Health), Valley Forge, Pa., 2001—05, sr. v.p., gen. counsel, 2005—. Chmn. bd. dirs. United Way Chester County, Exton, Pa., 1992-94. Mem. ABA, Phi Kappa Phi, Phi Eta Sigma. Avocations: golf, bridge. Office: AmerisourceBergen PO Box 959 Valley Forge PA 19482 Office Phone: 610-727-7159. *

SPRANG, MILTON LEROY, obstetrician, gynecologist, educator; b. Chgo., Jan. 15, 1944; s. Eugene and Carmella (Bruno) S.; m. Sandra Lee Karabelas, July 16, 1966; children: David, Christina, Michael. Student, St. Mary's Coll., 1962-65; MD, Loyola U., 1969. Diplomate Am. Bd. Ob-gyn; Nat. Bd. Med. Examiners; CME accreditation. Intern St. Francis Hosp., Evanston, Ill., 1969-70, resident, 1972-75, sr. attending physician, 1985—; assoc. attending phsycian Evanston Hosp., 1975-79, attending physician, 1980-84, sr. attending physician, 1985—, v.p. med. staff, 1990-91, pres.-elect, 1991-92, pres., 1992-93; also bd. dirs., 1991-94; sec. exec. com. Evanston Hosp., 1993-94; chmn. ob-gyn Cook County Grad. Sch. Medicine, Chgo., 1983-91. Instr. Northwestern U. Med. Sch., Chgo., 1975-78, asst. prof., 1984-95, assoc. prof., 1995-04, prof., 2004—; pres. Northwestern Healthcare Network Physician Leadership, 1994; lectr. acad. and civic groups Ob-Gyn. Nat. Ctr. Advanced Med. Edn., 1991—; bd. dirs. Ill. Found. Med. Rev.; bd. trustees Ill. State Ins. Svcs., 1992—, chair, 1998-00, chair rates and res., 2002—; bd. govs. Ill. State Med. Inter-Inst. Exch., 1987-92; adv. bd. practicing physicians Sec. Health and Human Svc. and Ctr. for Medicare Svcs., 2005—, Ctrs. Medicare and Medicaid. Editor: Profl. Staff News, 1992-93; chmn. editorial bd. Jour. Chgo. Medicine, 1986-91; contbr. articles to profl. jours. Bd. dirs. Am. Cancer Soc., chmn. profl. edn. com. North Shore unit, 1982-85; bd. dirs. Chgo. Community Info. Network, 1994-95; mem. Nat. Rep. Congrl. Com., 1981—, Ill. Med. Polit. Action Com.; bd. advisors Nat. Youth Leadership Forum on Medicine, Chgo., 1998—; trustee Midwest Ctr. Women's Healthcare, 2002—, pres., 2002—; adv. patients and med. profession. With USN, 1970-72. Fellow: ACOG (chmn. Ill. sect. 1975—76), ACS, Inst. Medicine Chgo.; mem.: AMA (com. to select pub. mem. 2003—, Physician Recognition award 1977, 1980, 1983), Gt. Lakes States Coalition of Dels. to AMA (chmn. 2003—), Orgn. State Med. Assn. Presidents (steering com. 2003—06, sec. 2006—, v.p. 2007), Chgo. Found. Med. Care (med. care evaluation and edn. com. 1980—83, nominating com. 1980—84, practice guidelines com. 1984), Ednl. and Scientific Found. (bd. dirs. 1994—98), Chgo. Med. Soc. (adv. com. advt. stds. 1978—84, physician's rev. com. 1980—85, trustee ins. bd. 1982—, nominating com. 1985—, treas. 1986—89, chmn. fin. com. 1986—89, trustee 1986—92, sec. 1989—90, pres.-elect 1990—91, chmn. bd. trustees 1990—91, pres. 1991—92, chmn. ethical rels. com. 1994—), Ill. Med. Soc. (del. to AMA 1987—, govt. affairs com. 1988—, chmn. reference com. 1989, chmn. fin. com. 1992—94, sec.-treas. 1994—96, chmn. bd. trustees 1996—98, chmn. bylaws com. 1998—99, pres. 2000—01), Physician Benefit Trust (chmn. fin. com. 1993—2004, chmn. 2004—, adv. coun. 2005—). Roman Catholic. Avocations: reading, swimming. Home: 4442 Concord Ln Skokie IL 60076-2606 Office: AGSO 1000 Central St Evanston IL 60201-1777 Home Phone: 847-677-5890; Office Phone: 847-869-3300. E-mail: sprangml@aol.com.

SPRANSY, JOSEPH WILLIAM, corporate lawyer; b. Durham, NC, July 17, 1946; s. George Brower and Marion Elizabeth (Dibble) S.; m. Lillian Drew Darden, Aug. 8, 1970; children: Katherine Leigh, Joseph William II. AB in Math., King Coll., Bristol, Tenn., 1968; JD, U. N.C., 1973. Bar: Ala. 1973, US Dist. Ct. (no. dist.) Ala. 1973, US Ct. Appeals (5th cir.) 1976, US Supreme Ct. 1980, US Ct. Appeals (11th cir.) 1981. Math. tchr. Castlewood HS, Va., 1968—70; program dir. Camp Monroe, Laurel Hill, NC, 1968-70; assoc. Bradley, Arant, Rose & White, Birmingham, Ala., 1973-79; corp. counsel US Pipe and Foundry Co., 1979—2003, v.p., 1999—2003; pvt. practice, 2003—. Vice moderator Birmingham Presbytery, Presbyn. Ch. USA, 1986, moderator, 1987; elder Mountain Brook Presbyn. Ch., 1982-84, 1986-88, 91-94, 98-2000; asst. scoutmaster, Boy Scouts Am., 1994-2006, troop 320 com. chair, 1994-97. Mem. ABA, Ala. State Bar Assn. (chair labor and employment sect. 1992-93, chair bus. law sect. 1999-2000), Birmingham Bar Assn. (chair mem. com. 1997-2003), Assn. Corp. Counsel in Am. (bd. dirs. Ala. chpt. 1985-91, 1998-2003, sec.-treas. 2002), U. NC Alumni Assn. (pres. Ala. chpt. 1983-84, 95), Phi Alpha Delta. Clubs: Birmingham Sailing, Birmingham Tip Off Club (bd. dirs. 1992-96), Ruffner Mountain Nature Ctr. (bd. dirs. 2004—, treas. 2005-06, sec. 2007—, exec. com.). Avocations: woodworking, sailing. Home: 4000 Hunters Ln Birmingham AL 35243-5820 Office: Law Office Joseph W Spransy PO Box 430093 Birmingham AL 35243 Office Phone: 205-930-9800. Business E-Mail: jwspransy@spransylaw.com.

SPRATLAN, LEWIS, composer, educator; b. Miami, Sept. 5, 1940; m. Melinda Spratlan. BA, Yale U., 1962, MusM, 1965. Faculty mem. Pa. State U., 1967—70, Amherst Coll., Mass., 1970—, prof. music. Mass., 1980—, chmn. music dept. Mass., 1977—94. Composer: Missa Brevis, 1965, Cantate Domine, 1968, Serenade for 6 instruments, 1970, Moonsong, 1970, Two Pieces for orch., 1971, Woodwind quintet, 1971, Fantasy, 1973, Ben Jonson Songs, 1974, Coils for ensemble, 1980, String Quartet, 1982, When Crows Gather, 1986, Hung Monophonies, 1990, Night Music, 1991, In Memorian, 1993, A Barred Owl, 1994, Concertino, 1994, Psalm 42, 1996, Apollo and Daphne Variations, Vocalise with Duck, 1998, Sojourner, 2000, Life is a Dream, 2000 (Pulitzer prize for music, 2000), Mayflies, 2000, Of Time and the Seasons, 2001, Peeves, 2001, (chamber opera) Earthrise, 2002, Zoom, 2003, The Manatees at Blue Springs, 2003, Streaming, 2004, Mega-Ditty, 2004, Piccolosophy, 2005, Wonderer, 2005, Shadow, 2006. Guggenheim fellowship, NEA fellowship, Mass. Artists Found. fellowship, MacDowell fellowship. Office: Music Dept Amherst Coll PO Box 5000 Amherst MA 01002-5000 Business E-Mail: mlspratlan@amherst.edu.

SPRATT, JOHN MCKEE, JR., congressman, lawyer; b. Charlotte, NC, Nov. 1, 1942; s. John McKee and Jane Love (Bratton) Spratt; m. Jane Stacy, May 31, 1968; children: Susan Elizabeth, Sarah Stacy, Catherine Bratton. AB, Davidson Coll., 1964; MA, Corpus Christi Coll., Oxford U., 1966; LL.B., Yale U., 1969. Ops. analyst Office of Asst. Sec. Def., 1969-71; ptnr. Spratt, McKeown & Spratt, York, SC, 1971-82; pres. Spratt Ins. Agy., Ft. Mill, SC, 1973-82, Bank of Ft. Mill, SC, 1973-82; mem. US Congress from 5th SC dist., 1983—, chmn. budget com., mem. armed svcs. com. Chmn. bd. visitors Winthrop Coll., 1976; bd. dirs. Piedmont Legal Svcs., Inc., 1978-82; bd. visitors Davidson Coll., 1978-80; chmn. bd. trustees Divine Saviour Hosp., York, 1980-82 Positions up to capt. JAGC US Army, 1969—71. Decorated Meritorious Svc. medal. Mem. SC Bar Assn. (ho. dels.), ABA. Democrat. Presbyterian. Office: US Ho Reps 1401 Longworth Ho Office Bldg Washington DC 20515-4005 Office Phone: 202-225-5501. *

SPRATT, RANDALL N., health products executive; BS in Biology, U. Utah. Exec. positions to COO Advanced Lab. Systems; chief process officer McKesson Provider Technologies, Alpharetta, Ga.; exec. v.p. chief info. officer McKesson Corp., San Francisco, 2005—. Office: McKesson Corpn 1 Post St San Francisco CA 94104

SPRAY, PAUL ELLSWORTH, retired surgeon; b. Wilkinsburg, Pa., Apr. 9, 1921; s. Lester E. and Phoebe Gertrude (Hull) S.; m. Mary Louise Conover, Nov. 28, 1943; children: David C., Thomas L., Mary Lynn (Mrs. Thomas Branham). BS, U. Pitts., 1942; MD, George Washington U., Washington, DC, 1944; MS, U. Minn., 1950. Diplomate Am. Bd. Orthop. Surgery. Intern U.S. Marine Hosp., SI, 1944-45; resident Mayo Found., Rochester, Minn., 1945-46, 48-50; practice medicine specializing in orthop. surgery Oak Ridge, Tenn., 1950-98; ret., 1998; vol. physician Knoxville Interfaith Clinic, 1998—. Mem. active staff Oak Ridge Hosp., 1950-98, hon. staff, 98-2000, 01—, mem. staff, 2000-01; courtesy staff Harriman Hosp., Tenn., ret., 1998; vol. vis. cons. CARE Medico, Jordan, 1959, Nigeria, 1962, 65, Algeria, 1963, Afghanistan, 1970, Bangladesh, 1975, 77, 79, Peru, 1980, U. Ghana, 1982; AMA vol. physician, Vietnam, 1967, 72; vis. assoc. prof. U. Nairobi, 1973; mem. tchg. team Internat. Coll. Surgeons to Peru, 1979, 84; vis. prof. orthop. surgery U. Khartoum, 1976; hon. prof. San Luis Gonzaga U., Ica, Peru, 1979; AmDoc vol. cons. U. Biafra Tchg. Hosp., 1969; vis. prof. Mayo Clinic, 1988; sec. orthops. overseas divsn. CARE Medico, 1971-76, sec. Medico adv. bd., 1974-76, vice chmn., 1976, chmn., 1977-79, v.p. CARE, Inc., 1977-79, pub. mem. CARE bd. dirs., 1980-90, mem. bd. overseers, 1991-99; chmn. Orthops. Overseas, Inc., 1982-86, treas., 1986-88, emeritus mem., 1994; mem. U.S. organizing com. 1st Internat. Acad. Symposium on Orthops., Tianjin, China, 1983; mem. CUPP Internat. Adv. Coun., 1986-99; invited guest spkr. Japan Orthop. Assn., 1994; mem. curriculum com. Oak Ridge Inst. Continual Learning, 1999-2007; bd. dirs. MMC Oak Ridge Found., chmn., 2003-04, emeritus, 2007. Mem. editl. bd. Contemporary Orthopedics, 1984-96. Pres. Anderson County Health Coun., 1976—77, v.p., 1975, hon. bd. dirs.; pres. health commn. Coun. So. Mountains, 1958—65, sec., bd. dirs., 1965—66; Tenn. pres. UN Assn., 1966—67; vice-chmn. bd. Camelot Care Ctr., Tenn., 1979—82, chmn. Tenn., 1982—86; hon. mem. World Orthopedic Concern, 1990; with del. to Vietnam People to People, citizen amb. to Vietnam, 1993; del. to Oak Ridge's Sister City, Obninsk, Russia Obninsk, Russia, 1993; trustee Vietnam Am. Scholarship Fund, 1992—95; Rotary vol. orthopaedic surgeon Kikuyu Hosp. Rehab. Ctr. of East Africa Presbyn. Ch., 1998; vol. Habitat for Humanity, 2004; bd. dirs. Meth. Hosp. Oak Ridge Found., 2000—, chmn., 2003—04, emeritus, 2007; bd. dirs. Hope of East Tenn., 2002—06, Clinch Valley Home Health Assn., 2005—. Named to Anderson County Hall of Fame for Philanthropy, 2007; recipient Svc. to Mankind award, Serotoma, 1967, Humanitarian award, Lions Club, 1968, Freedom Citation, Sertoma, 1978, award, Amb. Goodwill Lions Club, 1979, Medico Disting. Svc. award, 1990, 1st Ann. Vocat. Svc. award, Oak Ridge Rotary, 1979, Tech. Comm. award, East Tenn. chpt. Soc. for Tech. Comm., 1983, Individual Achievement award, Meth. Med. Ctr. of

Oak Ridge, 1991, Humanitarian award, Orthopaedics Overseas, 1992, Biographic Exhibit recognition, Mus. Appalachia Hall of Fame, Norris, Tenn.; fellow Melvin Jones fellow, Lions Club, 1993. Fellow ACS, Internat. Coll. Surgeons (Tenn. regent 1976-80, bd. councilors 1980-84, hon. chmn. bd. trustees 1981-83, trustee 1983-84, v.p. US sect. 1982-83, mem. surg. teams com. 1983-90, Humanitarian award 1992); mem. AMA (Humanitarian Svc. award 1967, 72), Sociètè International Chirugie Orthopèdique et de Traumuatologie, So. Orthop. Assn., Western Pacific Orthop. Assn., Am. Fracture Assn., Am. Acad. Orthop. Surgeons (mem. com. on injuries 1980-86), Tenn. Med. Assn. (com. on emergency med. svcs. 1978-97), Peru Acad. Surgery (corr.), Peruvian Soc. Orthop. Surgery and Traumatology (corr.), Clin. Orthop. Soc., Mid-Am. Orthop. Soc., Rotary Club (Oak Ridge chpt., chmn. cmty. and world svc. com. 2000-04, Paul Harris fellow). Home: 507 Delaware Ave Oak Ridge TN 37830-3902 Home Fax: 865-483-8657. Personal E-mail: spray507@aol.com.

SPRAYREGEN, JAMES H.M., diversified financial services company executive, lawyer; b. Dec. 2, 1959; BA cum laude, U. Mich., 1982; JD cum laude, U. Ill., 1985. Bar: Ill. 1985, NY 1985, US Dist. Ct. (no. dist. Ill.) 1985, US Dist. Ct. (ea. dist. Wis.) 1988, US Dist. Ct. (so. & ea. dists. NY) 1992, US Dist. Ct. (we. dist Mich.) 1992, US Dist Ct. (dist. Ariz.) 1992, US Dist. Ct. (dist. Del.) 1992. Atty. Lord, Bissell & Brook, 1985—89, Rudnick & Wolfe, 1989—90; ptnr., mem. firm mgmt. com. Kirkland & Ellis, LLP, Chgo., 1990—2006; mng. dir. investment banking divsn. The Goldman Sachs Group, Inc., NYC, 2006—. Co-chmn. Internat. Com. Am. Bankruptcy Inst., bd. dir.; Chicago region bd. dir. Anti-Defamation League; vice chmn. Chicago region Am. Com. Weizman Inst. Sci. Named Top Debtor Lawyer by active assignments, Deal's Bankruptcy Insider newsletter, 2004; named one of 12 Dealmakers of Yr., Am. Lawyer, 2004, 45 Under Forty: Rising Stars Pvt. Bar, 2003. Mem.: Seventh Circuit Bar Assn. (Ill. chmn. Comml. Bankruptcy Law & Procedure), Chicago Bar Assn., Ill. Bar Assn., Comml. Law League Am., ABA. Office: The Goldman Sachs Group Inc 85 Broad St New York NY 10004 *

SPRECHER, CHRISTINA M., lawyer; b. Wabash, Ind., Apr. 1, 1970; BA, Ind. U., Bloomington, 1992; JD, Valparaiso U. Sch. Law, 1995. Bar: Ohio 1996. Ptnr. Frost Brown Todd LLC, Cin. Mem., Bd. Trustees, Exec. Com. Cin. Ballet; pres. BRAVO!. Named one of Ohio's Rising Stars, Super Lawyers, 2006; recipient Inspiring Fine Arts Vol. award, Inspire Mag., 2006. Mem.: Internat. Coun. Shopping Centers, Moot Ct. Soc., ABA (mem., Probate and Trust Law Sect.), Ohio State Bar Assn., Cin. Bar Assn. Office: Frost Brown Todd LLC 2200 PNC Ctr 201 E Fifth St Cincinnati OH 45202-4182 Office Phone: 513-651-6800. Office Fax: 513-651-6981.

SPRECHER, JEFFREY C., commodities exchange executive; b. 1955; BSChemE, U. Wis., Madison; MBA, Pepperdine U., Malibu, Calif. Pres. Western Power Grp., Inc.; owner Continental Power Exch., 1997—2000; founder, CEO Intercontinental Exch., Atlanta, 2000—, chmn. bd., 2002—. Mem. bd. dirs. New York Bd. of Trade, 2007—. Named a Top Entrepreneur, Bus. Week mag., 2002; named one of five finalists, CEO of the Year, Marketwatch, 2006. Mem.: U.S. Commodity Futures Trading Commn. Global Market Adv. Com., Energy Security Leadership Coun. Office: Intercontinental Exch 2100 RiverEdge Pky Ste 500 Atlanta GA 30328 *

SPRECHER, KEVIN S., lawyer; b. Willingboro, NJ, Feb. 24, 1968; BS Indsl. Engring., Purdue U., 1992; JD, Valparaiso U., 1995. Bar: Ohio 1995, US Ct. of Appeals Fed. Cir. 1995, registered: US Patent and Trademark Office. Ptnr. Frost Brown Todd LLC, Cin. Mem. Purdue U. President's Coun. Named one of Ohio's Rising Stars, Super Lawyers, 2006. Mem.: Ohio State Bar Assn., Cin. Bar Assn., Cin. Intellectual Property Law Assn., Am. Intellectual Property Law Assn., Inst. Indsl. Engineers, ABA, Purdue Club of Cin. Office: Frost Brown Todd LLC 2200 PNC Ctr 201 E Fifth St Cincinnati OH 45202-4182 Office Phone: 513-651-6121. Office Fax: 513-651-6981.

SPRECHER, BARON WILLIAM GUNTHER, pianist, composer, conductor, diplomat; b. Saarbrucken, Germany, Jan. 20, 1924; arrived in U.S., 1952; s. Wolf and Karoline (Jung) Sprecher; m. Blossom Tag, Aug. 6, 1952. Studied piano with Prof. Wittels, Tel Aviv; studied piano with Madame Vengerova, NYC; studied composition with Paul Ben-Haim, Tel Aviv, studied conducting with Georg Singer; degree (hon.), Inst. Vocal Arts, 1957; D in Philosophy Music (hon.), World U. Roundtable, 1988; Mus D (hon.), London Inst. Applied Rsch., 1991, DFA, HHD, London Inst. Applied Rsch., 1993; Mus D (hon.), Australian Inst. Coord. Rsch., 1991; diploma, Gran Premio Am., 1990, Paladino del Tricolore, 1990; D Musicology, Somerset U.; D Music (hon.), Atlantic Southeastern U.; Diploma, Acad. Argentina de Diplomacia; Assoc. (hon.), Inst. Affairs Internat., Paris, 1993; DD (hon.), The Christian Congregation; rerum politicarum LittD (hon.), U. Aeterna Lucina Vitama, 1991; LittD (hon.), Eng., 1994; PhD (hon.), Germany, 1994. Korrepetitor Israel Folk Opera, Tel-Aviv, 1940-43; piano soloist Israel Philharm. Orch., Tel-Aviv, 1946-48; music dir. Temple Anshe Chesed, NYC, 1966—69, Temple Sholom, Greenwich, Conn., 1976—82; pres., music dir. Bronx Philharm., NYC, 1971-83; music dir. Sta. WEVD, NYC, 1969-85; asst. pianist accompanying Lotte Lenya, Richard Tucker, Jan Peerce, Itzhak Perlman, Jan Kiepura, Ilona Massey; prof. Inst. Hautes Etudes Economiques et Sociales. Rsch. prof. Alliance Universelle Paix Connaissance, Paris, 1991; prof. Haute Ecole de Recherche, Inst. des Hautes Etudes Economiques et Sociales; mem. coun. Inst. de Documentation et D'Etudes Europeennes; dep. mem., diplomat Internat. State Parliament; dep. mem. assembly Internat. Parliament for Safety and Peace. Composer: (song book) Yinglish, piano soloist 1st performance of Gershwin's Concerto in F in Israel; composer Piano Sonata, 1945, Jerusalem Concerto for Piano and Orch., 1967, (TV) Great is Thy Faith, 1970; pianist-condr. 24 record albums; mem. The First Piano Quartet (Acad. award nomination, Peabody award). Consul Sovereign State Aeterna Lucina for State and City of NY; comdr. fgn. rels. Island Du Caricom, 1995; diplomat World Jewish Congress; senator Coun. of States for Protection of Life and Human Rights, Palermo, Italy; del. at large Rep. Presdl. Task Force, nat. rep. senatorial com.; active Nat. Com. to Preserve Social Security and Medicare, Ctr. for Am. Values, Sr. Coalition, Common Cause; founding sponsor Disabled Vets. Life Meml. Gold Medal Merit Soc., Washington, 2004; Reagan Presdl. Libr. supporter USS Ronald Reagan, Air Force One. Decorated noble knight Noble House of Amena, knight order Knight Templars of Jerusalem, knight comdr. Lofsensis Ursinius Order, baron Order of Bohemian Crown, comdr. Order of Golden Lance (Australia), Capt. Légion de L'Aigle Mer, Baron of Montsalvat, knight Holy Grail, count San Ciriaco, comdr. fgn. rels. Island du Caricom, 1995, Sen Maison Internat. Des Intellectuels, Sen European Parliament, Internat. Parliament for Safety and Peace, diplomat World Jewish Congress, Laird-Lord of Camster, Caithness, Scotland, 1995; recipient Diplomatic medal Internat. Parliament for Safety and Peace, 1995, Gold Cross of Honour, Albert Schweitzer Soc. Austria, Albert Einstein medal, Circulo Nobiliario Caballeros U., 1992, Swan Knight (Chevalier du Cygne), Order of the Swan, Congl. Order of Merit, 2006; named Knight of Yr., Internat. Writers and Artists Assn., 1995; recipient Medal of Merit, Rep. Presdl. Task Force, 1998, Noble Conquistador, Internat. Chivalric Order of the Knights of Justice, Music and Humanity award, 2003, Hall of Fame Music and Humanity award ABI, 2003, Disting. Leader Gold medal, 2003, Rep. Senatorial Gold medal of Freedom, 2004; Ronald Reagan Ranch Trailblazer, Name on Freedom Wall, Rep. Presidential Task Force (Life), name on Wall of Freedom, Rep. Ctr., Washington, Cert. of Appreciation, Pres. Bush and V.P. Dick Cheney, others. Fellow United Writers' Assn. India; mem. ASCAP, Maison Internat. des Intellectuels, Internat. Parliament for Safety and Peace, World Parliament Confedn. of Chivalry (Grand Coun.), World Acad. Assn. of the Universe (life), Bronx Philharm. Symphony Soc., Inc. (founder, pres.), Internat. Platform Assn., Am. Fedn. Musicians, Robert Stolz Soc. Gt. Britain, World Univ. Roundtable (trustee, founder), Internat. Cultural Corr. Inst., Circulo Nobiliario de los Caballeros Universales (grandmaster U.S.), Lègion de L'Aigle de Mer (capt.), USA United Srs. Assn. Inc., Order the Templars (knight, count San Ciriaco). Avocations: walking, music, coin collecting/numismatics, antique coptic ethiopian crosses.

SPRENGER, GORDON M., hospital administrator; b. Albert Lea, Minn., Apr. 30, 1937; Bachelors degree, St. Olaf Coll., 1959; masters degree, U. Minn., 1961. Registrar USAF Hosp., Hamilton AFB, Calif., 1961-64; with St. Luke's Hosp., Milw., 1964-67, Northwestern Hosp., Mpls., 1967-71; exec. v.p. Abbott-Northwestern Hosp., Mpls., 1971-75, pres. ceo., 1975-88, LifeSpan, 1982-92; exec. ofcr HealthSpan, 1992-94; chief exec. ofcr Allina Health, 1994—. Prof. U. Minn., 1976—; acad. lectureship; preceptor. Mem. ACHE and AHA; Affiliated Hosp. Srvs: Past Sec. Bd mem., 1971-74; Council of Community Hosp., chair. 1980-81; Governor's Task Force on Nursing, 1981; Health Political Action Comm. of Minn., chair. 1981; Minn. Hosp. Assoc. Governmntl Relations Comm., chair. 1979, bd mem, 1978-81, exec. comm. treas., 1981; chair. elect, Minn. Hosp. Assoc., 1982; MMI Cos bd mem, currently vice chair., preceptor and faculty mem., U of Minn. Hosp. and Health Care Admin., 1982 bd of Minnehaha Acad.; disting. alumnus, St. Olaf Coll., mem. bd of regents; Voluntary Hosp. of Amer., past chair., mem. Medtronics, Inc., bd of dirs., 1991-; mem. St. Paul Cos., bd of dirs. Office: Allina Health System 5601 Smetana Dr PO Box 9310 Minneapolis MN 55440-9310 Home: 6244 Ridge Rd Chanhassen MN 55317-9438

SPRIESER, JUDITH A., former software company executive; BA in Linguistics, Northwestern U., MBA in Fin. CPA, Ill., 1982. Comml. banker Harris Bank, Chgo., 1974-81; dir. treasury ops. Esmark, 1981-84; asst. treas. internat. Nalco Chem. Co., 1984-87; asst. treas. corp. fin. Sara Lee Corp., 1987-90; sr. v.p., CFO Sara Lee Bakery N.Am., 1990-93, pres., CEO, 1993-94; sr. v.p., CFO Sara Lee Corp., 1994-99, CEO, Foods and Food Svc., 2000-2001; CEO Transora, Chgo., 2001—05. Bd. dirs. USG Corp., Reckitt Benckiser, Allstate Corp., 1999-, Kohl's Corp., 2003-, CBS Corp., 2005- Bd. dirs. Hinsdale Hosp. Found.; trustee Northwestern U. Mem. AICPA, Chgo. Network, Young Pres. Orgn., Chgo. coun. Fgn. Rels., Econ. Club, Conf. Bd. Coun. Fin. Execs. Mailing: Bd Dir Allstate Corp 2775 Sanders Rd Northbrook IL 60062-6127

SPRIESTERSBACH, DUANE CARYL, academic administrator, speech pathology/audiology services professional, educator; b. Pine Island, Minn., Sept. 5, 1916; s. Merle Lee and Esther Lucille (Stucky) Spriestersbach; m. Bette Rae Bartell, Aug. 31, 1946; children: Michael Lee, Ann. BEd, Winona State Tchrs. Coll., 1939; MA, U. Iowa, 1940, PhD, 1948. Asst. dir. pers. rels. Pacific Portland Cement Co., San Francisco, 1946-47; prof. speech pathology U. Iowa, Iowa City, 1948-89, prof. emeritus, 1989—, dean. Grad. Coll., v.p. ednl. devel. and rsch., 1965-89, v. pres. and dean emeritus, 1989—, acting pres., 1981-82; v.p. ops. Breakthrough, Inc., Oakdale, Iowa, 1993-94; freelance cons., 1994—2006. Com. mem. Nat. Inst. Neurol. Disease and Blindness; chmn. dental tng. com. Nat. Inst. Dental Rsch., 1967—72, chmn. spl. grants rev., 1978—82; chmn. bd. dirs. Midwest Univs. Cons. Internat. Activities, Columbus, 1978—87. Author: (book) Psychosocial Aspects of Cleft Palate, 1973; author: (with others) Diagnostic Methods in Speech Pathology, 1978; co-editor: Cleft Palate and Communication, 1968, Diagnosis in Speech Language Pathology, rev. edit., 1999, The Way It Was: The University of Iowa 1964-1989, 1999. Pres. Iowa City Cmty. Theater, 1964, 1977, 1983. Served to lt. col. US Army, 1941—46, ETO. Decorated Bronze Star; fellow Nat. Inst. Dental Rsch., 1971. Fellow: AAAS; mem.: Midwestern Assn. Grad. Schs. (chmn. 1979—80), Am. Cleft Palate Assn. (pres. 1961—62, disting. svc. award), Am. Speech and Hearing Assn. (pres. 1965, honor award), Assn. Grad. Schs. (pres. 1979—80), Cosmos Clug (Washington), Mortar Bd., Sigma Xi. Home: 2 Longview Knoll NE Iowa City IA 52240-9148 Office: Univ Iowa M212 Oakdale Hall Iowa City IA 52242-5000 Home Phone: 319-351-8756; Office Phone: 319-335-4012. Business E-Mail: duane-spriestersbach@uiowa.edu.

SPRIGGS, DAVID RANDALL, healthcare administrator, educator; b. Chgo., May 12, 1950; s. Randall and Mary Spriggs; m. Nancy J. Gerlach, Jan. 22, 1973. BS, U. Wis., 1973, MD, 1977. Cert. Am. Bd. Internal Medicine; lic., N.Y. Fellow Dana Farber Cancer Inst., Boston, 1982-85; from instr. to assst. prof. Harvard U., Boston, 1985-89; asst. prof. U. Wis., Madison, 1989-93; mem., chief devel. chemotherapy, Winthrop Rockefeller chair med. oncology Meml. Sloan-Kettering Cancer Ctr., NYC, 1993—. Sr. editor: (jour.) Clin. Cancer Rsch., 1996. Grantee Nat. Cancer Inst., 1994—. Mem. AAAS, Am. Assn. for Cancer Rsch., Am. Soc. Clin. Oncology. Avocations: golf, science fiction. Office: Meml Sloan Kettering Hosp 1275 York Ave New York NY 10021-6094 Home Phone: 212-717-6438; Office Phone: 212-639-2203.

SPRIGGS, RICHARD MOORE, ceramics engineer, science administrator, researcher; b. Washington, Pa., May 8, 1931; s. Lucian Alexander and Kathryn (Aber) S.; m. Patricia Anne Blaney, Aug. 1, 1953 (dec. 2002); children: Carolyn Elizabeth Spriggs Muchna, Richard Moore, Alan David; m. Brenda L. Ferrier, May 5, 2005. BS in Ceramics, Pa. State U., 1952; MS in Ceramic Engring., U. Ill., 1956, PhD, 1958. Sr. research engr. Ferro Corp., Cleve., 1958-59; sr. staff scientist, group leader, ceramics rsch. AVCO Corp., Wilmington, Mass., 1959-64; assoc. prof. metall. engring. Lehigh U., Bethlehem, Pa., 1964-67, prof. metallurgy and materials sci. and engring., 1967-80, adminstrv. asst. to pres., 1970-71, asst. v.p. for adminstrn., 1971-72, v.p. for adminstrn., 1972-78, dir. phys. ceramics lab., 1964-70, assoc. dir. Materials Research Ctr., 1964-70; vis. sr. staff assoc. Nat. Materials Adv. Bd. NRC, Washington, 1979-80, sr. staff officer, staff scientist, 1980-87, staff dir. bd. on assessment of NBS programs, 1984-87; J.F. McMahon prof. ceramic engring., dir. NYS Ctr. Advanced Ceramic Tech. N.Y. State Coll. Ceramics, Alfred (N.Y.) U., 1987-97, dir. office of sponsored programs, 1988-97, prof. emeritus, 1997—. Affiliate staff scientist Pacific Northwest Lab., 1994—. Contbr. articles to profl. pubs. Co-patentee in field Pres., bd. dirs. YMCA, Bethlehem, Pa., 1978-79. Served to lt. USNR, 1952-56 Fellow Armco Steel Corp., 1956-58, Am. Coun. on Edn., 1970-71; Centennial fellow Coll. Earth and Mineral Scis., Pa. State U., 1996, Alumni Achievement award, 1999, 30th Ann. SHS Medal of Honor, 1997, Disting. Engring. Alumnus awrd U. Ill., 1988. Fellow: Brit. Inst. Materials, Ceramic Soc. Japan (Centennial medal 1991), Am. Ceramic Soc. (trustee pension trust fund 1979—84, pres. 1984—85, coord. programs and meetings 1991—92, Ross Coffin Purdy award 1965, Hobard M. Kraner award Lehigh Valley sect. 1980, Orton lectr. 1988, McMahon lectr. 1988, Mueller lectr. 1996, Albert Victor Bleininger award Pitts. sect. 2000, disting. life); mem.: Serbian Acad. Scis. and Arts (fgn.), Ceramic Assn. N.Y. (sec.-treas. 1988—99), Fed. Materials Socs. (trustee 1978—84), Materials Rsch. Soc., Materials Rsch. Soc. Japan (hon.), World Acad. Ceramics (trustee 1988—96, 2006—), Brit. Ceramic Soc., Ceramic Ednl. Coun., Nat. Inst. Ceramic Engrs., Internat. Inst. for Sci. of Sintering, Rotary (dir. 1982—87, pres. 1985—86). Office Phone: 607-587-8557. Personal E-mail: rmspriggs@excite.com.

SPRINCE, LEILA JOY, retired librarian; b. Toronto, Ont., Can., July 10, 1936; came to U.S., 1981; d. Harry and Anna Helen Caller; children: Alan Rosenthal, Joel Rosenthal; m. Arnold Joel Sprince, Feb. 16, 1982 BA, U. Toronto, 1957, B of Edn., 1962; MA, U. South Fla., 1987. Cert. tchr., Ont. Ballet dancer Volkoff Can. Ballet, Toronto, 1953-54; tchr. h.s. North York Bd. Edn., Toronto, 1958-60; libr. Broward County Libr. Sys., Plantation, Fla., 1987-88, 91-93, Margate, Fla., 1988-91, head youth svcs. Coconut Creek, Fla., 1996—2001; ret., 2001. Advisor Omnigraphics Pub., Detroit, 1993—; cons. Gale/U*X*L* Pubs., N.Y.C., 1996—; state facilitator summer programs State Libr. Fla., 1993. Contbr. articles to profl. jours. Mem. nat. children and youth membership orgns. outreach com. ALA/ALSC, 2001—; mem. adv. bd. Broward County Libr., 2006—. Mem. ALA (Best Books for Young Adult Cmty. spkr. 1989, 90), Fla. Libr. Assn. (spkr.), B'nai B'rith Women (fin. sec. 1983, pres. 1984, 85), Phi Kappa Phi, Beta Phi Mu. Democrat. Jewish. Avocations: music/dance, computers, travel, history. Home Phone: 954-741-3288. Personal E-mail: ajsprince@aol.com.

SPRING, BONNIE JOAN, preventive medicine educator; b. Hackensack, NJ, Oct. 9, 1949; d. John Edwin and Sonja Joan (Litwinowich) S. BA, Bucknell U., 1971; MA, Harvard U., 1975, PhD, 1977. Diplomate Am. Bd. Health Psychology, Am. Bd. Profl. Psychology; lic. psychologist, Mass., Ill. Rsch. scientist Biometrics Rsch., NYC, 1975-78; instr. psychology Harvard U., Cambridge, Mass., 1977, asst. prof., 1977-82, assoc. prof., 1982-84; prof. psychology Tex. Tech U., Lubbock, 1984-88, dir. clin. tng., 1986-88; prof. U. Health Scis.-Chgo. Med. Sch., 1988-98, U. Ill., Chgo., 1998—2005; prof. preventive medicine, dir. behavioral medicine, co-dir. cancer prevention Feinberg Sch. Medicine, Northwestern U., Chgo., 2005—. Lectr. psychiatry Columbia Coll. Physicians and Surgeons, NYC, 1979-86; vis. lectr. nutrition MIT, Cambridge, 1979-80; staff psychologist Mass. Mental Health, Boston, 1981-84; rsch. assoc. prof. psychiatry U. Md. Med. Sch., Balt., 1984-90. Author: Psychology, 1988; editor: Attentin in Schizophrenia, 1979, Psychopharmacology, 1986-95; mem. editl. bd. Jour. Social and Clin. Psychology, 1985—, Psychopharmacology, 1995-2000, Jour. Cons. and Clin. Psychology, 1996—; contbr. articles to profl. jours. Mem. com. on status of women Harvard U., 1979-81; panel mem. com. on nat. needs for behavioral rsch. pers. Inst. Medicine, NAS, Washington, 1984086; panel mem. nat. plan for rsch. on schizophrenia NIMH, 1987; mem. behavioral medicine study sect. NIH, 1994-98. Nutrition grantee Ctr. for Brain Scis., 1980-81, Ford Found., 1981-82, VA, 1989—, schizophrenia grantee NIMH, 1980-84, grantee NIH, 1995—. Fellow APA; mem. Am. Psychol. Soc., Soc. for Behavioral Medicine (pres. 2007-), Am. Coll. Neuropsychopharmacology. Avocations: travel, running. Office: Northwestern U Dept Preventive Medicine 680 N Lakeshore Dr Ste 1220 Chicago IL 60611 Office Phone: 312-908-2293. Business E-Mail: bspring@northwestern.edu.

SPRING, CARL CHAFFEE, JR., writer; b. LA, Nov. 17, 1936; s. Carl C. Spring, Sr. and Emilie Temple Spring; m. Alice Waters, Oct. 7, 1967 (dec. July 24, 2007). BA, Calif. State U., LA, 1960, MA, 1968. Writer, news editor, LA, 1960—68; med. writer, sr. editor Audio-Digest Found., Glendale, Calif., 1968—. Melvin Jones fellow, 2002, 2006. Mem.: Am. Med. Writers Assn. (v.p. 1973—74), Lions Club (editor of bull. 1994—, program chmn. 1994—, LA Internat., pres. 2004—05), Bay Cities Shrine Club (pres. 2001—02). Republican. Episcopalian. Avocations: beach walks, swimming, travel, meteorology. Home: 3490 Wade St Los Angeles CA 90066 Office: Audio-Digest Found 1577 E Chevy Chase Dr Glendale CA 91206 Office Phone: 818-240-7500. Personal E-mail: ccspring55@earthlink.net.

SPRING, KATHLEEN, writer; b. Mich. d. Edward and Mary Broilo; m. Samuel Taylor (div. 1984); 1 child, Justin; m. Paul Riethmeier (div. 1991) AD summa cum laude, Oakland C.C., 1990; BA cum laude, Wayne State U., 1993. Cert. holistic health profl. Adminstr. comm. dept. Wayne State U., Detroit, 1990-95; stringer The Daily Tribune, Royal Oak, Mich., 1992-98; writer, photographer Spring Times, Detroit, 1992-98; pub. rels. mktg., editor Fanclub Found. for Arts, Southfield, Mich., 1993-98; writer, tchr. Spring Times, Lyons, Colo., 1998—; travel cons. holistic svcs. Rocky Mt. Retreats, 1998—; dir. Integrated Healers Assn., Boulder, Colo., 2004—05. Founder E. Pk. Tea Time Readers, 2004—07; co-founder LIPS Poetry, 2006—07. Author: Small Towns, Detroits Crown, 1997, WRITERS Birthing of Creative Writing and Capturing Random Memories, 2002; dir., author, exec. prodr.: (documentaries) Sandstone Quarry History: Our Stones Gather Moss, 2001; Lyons Geology, 2002; Come Stay Awhile, 2003. Vol. PBS-Detroit, 1982-95. Named Journalist of Yr., Wayne State U., 1992; scholar numerous acad. scholarships. Mem.: Colo. Press Women (8 journalism awards 2007), Denver Film Soc., Colo. Authors League, Film and Video Assn., Women in Comm., Soc. Profl. Journalists (1st v.p. 1993—98, Howard Dubin Outstanding Pro Chpt. Mem. 1996, Cir. of Excellence-Newsletter 1996). Avocations: travel, books, films, photography. Office: Spring Times PO Box 512 Lyons CO 80540-0512

SPRING, MICHAEL, editor, writer; b. NYC, Oct. 14, 1941; s. Sol and Muriel (Roth) S.; m. Marjorie Hornblower Bauer, Mar. 1965 (div. 1980); children: Declan, Evan; m. Janis Abrahms, 1993. BA, Haverford Coll., Pa., 1964; MA, Columbia U., NYC, 1970. Reporter Bergen Record, Hackensack, NJ, 1969-71; editor Scholastic Inc., NYC, 1971-87; editorial dir. Fodor's Travel Publs., 1987-94, v.p., 1989-94; pub. Macmillan Travel, NYC, 1994-99; pub. Frommer's Travel Guides John Wiley & Sons, NYC, 1999—2001; pub. Wiley Travel, 2001—. Broadcaster, writer WNCN-FM, N.Y.C., 1983-84. Author: Great Weekend Escape Book, 1982, 4th rev. edit. 1990, Student's Guide to Julius Caesar, 1984; editor: American Way of Working, 1980, 50 vol. Barron's Book Notes series, 1984, Scholastic Literature Anthologies, 4 vols., 1985, 87, Great European Itineraries, 1987, Touring Europe, 1990, 3d edit. 1994; contbg. editor Conde Nast's Traveler, 1987—; travel expert CNN Travel Show, 1991-94, WCBS Radio daily travel show, 1998—. Democrat. Jewish. Home: 20 Country Rd Westport CT 06880-2525 Office: John Wiley & Sons 111 River St Hoboken NJ 07030-5774 Home Phone: 203-227-4771; Office Phone: 201-748-5662. Business E-Mail: mspring@wiley.com.

SPRINGER, DAVID WILLIAM, dean, social sciences educator; b. NYC, Sept. 1, 1968; s. Paul David and Elizabeth Springer; m. Sarah Eagle Smith, Dec. 8, 2001; 1 child, Aidan David. BA, Fla. State U., 1990, MSW, 1992, PhD, 1997. LCSW Tex., ACSW. Clin. social worker Univ. Behavioral Ctr., Orlando, Fla., 1992—94; rsch. assoc. Fla. State U., Tallahassee, 1994—97; asst. prof. U. Tex., Austin, 1997—2000, assoc. prof., 2000—02, assoc. dean, 2002—, assoc. dean, disting. tchg. prof., 2005—. Author: Substance Abuse Treatment for Criminal Offenders, 2003, Handbook of Forensic Mental Health with Victims and Offenders, 2007. Fundraiser Leukemia and Lymphoma Soc., Austin, 2000; bd. dirs. Austin Child Guidance Ctr., 1998—2003, Great Wall China Adoption, 2007—. Named to Acad. Disting. Tchrs., U. Tex. at Austin, 2005, Who'w Who in Social Scis. Higher Edn., 2004; recipient Outstanding Grad. Tchg. award, U. Tex. at Austin, 2003. Mem.: NASW, Tex. Assn. Social Work Deans and Dirs. (pres. 2005—07), Coun. Social Work Edn., Soc. Social Work and Rsch. Democrat. Avocations: guitar, photography, camping, hiking, surfing. Office: U Tex at Austin Sch Social Work Austin TX 78712 Office Phone: 512-471-0512. Office Fax: 512-471-7268. Business E-Mail: dwspringer@mail.utexas.edu, dswspringer@mail.utexas.edu.

SPRINGER, DOUGLAS HYDE, retired food products executive, lawyer; b. Englewood, NJ, Jan. 31, 1927; s. Arthur Hyde and Melicent Katherine (Messenger) S.; m. Virginia Helen Chouinard, Nov. 23, 1949; children: Susan Compton, Debora Lee. Student, Wesleyan U., 1944-45; AB, Yale U., 1947; LLB, Columbia U., 1950. Bar: N.Y. 1950. Atty. Port of N.Y. Authority, 1950-52; legal counsel Worthington Corp., Harrison, N.J., 1953-61, asst. sec., 1956-61; asst. counsel Campbell Soup Co., Camden, N.J., 1961-65, asst. sec., 1965, spl. assignments, 1966, dir. spl. studies, corp. planning, 1966-69, dir. corp. planning frozen foods, 1969-70, asst. treas., 1970-71, treas., 1971-73, v.p. fin. planning, 1973-75, v.p., controller, 1975-78, v.p., treas., 1978-88, v.p. investment mgmt., 1988-90. Trustee Meml. Health Alliance, 1981—99; trustee, treas. Virtua Health Hosp., 2000—06, Virtua Health Found., 2003—; mem. adv. bd. Pa. Liberty Mut. Ins. Co., 1971—88; Ea. regional adv. bd. Arkwright-Boston Mfrs. Mut. Ins.

Co., 1985—90; exec. sec. Gov.'s Interstate Adv. Com., 1966; asst. to mem. Pres.'s Commn. on Postal Orgn., 1967—68; spl. asst. to chmn. South Jersey Port Corp., 1969—71; mem. NJ Econ. Devel. Coun., 1972—76; mem. adv. coun. Tax Found., 1980—89. Trustee Nat. Food Processors Assn. Retirement Plan and Trust Indenture Fund, 1976—89, Perkins Ctr. for Arts, 1979—88, Ind. Coll. Fund NJ, 1982—88, The Estaugh, 2004—; mem. exec. bd., v.p. fin. Camden County coun. Boy Scouts Am., 1978—90; bd. dirs. YMCA of Burlington County, 1995—2007, sec., 2000—07, Yale Alumni Fund, 1996—2002, exec. com., 1998—2002. With USNR, 1944—46. Mem. Nat. Assn. Corp. Treas. (bd. dirs. 1982-88), Phila. Treas. Club, Internat. Bus. Forum (bd. dirs. 1980-88), Phi Nu Theta, Phi Delta Phi, N.J. Soc. Pa. (pres. 1992-93, treas. 1994—). Clubs: Yale (Phila., N.Y.C.); Nassau (Princeton, N.J.), Laurel Creek (Mt. Laurel, N.J.), Y's Men's Club (v.p., 1992-94, pres., 1994-95). Home: 670 Medford Leas Medford NJ 08055

SPRINGER, FLOYD LADEAN, architect; b. Goodrich, ND, Feb. 1, 1922; s. George Roy Springer and Louise Baumbach; m. Dorothy Mae Shepard (dec. Sept. 1995); children: Debra Louise, Tami June. Student, U. Denver, 1948-51; BS in Archtl. Engring., U. Colo., 1952; postgrad., U. Wash., 1953-54, U. Utah, Portland, Oreg., 1980. Apprentice to arch. Gilbert R. Horton AIA, 1946-48; job capt. Robert Hall and Ira Cummings, Archs., 1956-57; mem. archtl. staff Austin Co., 1964, Naramore, Bain, Brady and Johanson, 1965, Roland Terry and Assocs., 1967, John Graham & Co., 1967-68; mem. various archtl. firms Wash. and Alaska, 1952-69; prin. Floyd Springer/Arch., Seattle, 1969—. Arch. numerous pvt. comml. and residential projects, 1969—; corp. mem., emeritus Am. Inst. of Arch. Contbr. articles to profl. jours. Cpl. inf. U.S. Army, 1941-44, PTO. Decorated Silver Star. Mem.: AIA (emeritus), Pacesetters Club, Masons. Presbyterian. Avocations: photography, ballroom dancing, leaded art glass, painting, writing. Home and Office: 18548 60th Ave NE Kenmore WA 98028-8725

SPRINGER, GEORGE STEPHEN, mechanical engineering educator; b. Budapest, Hungary, Dec. 12, 1933; came to U.S., 1959; s. Joseph and Susan (Grausz) S.; m. Susan Martha Flory, Sept. 15, 1963; children: Elizabeth Anne, Mary Katherine. B in Engring., U. Sydney, Australia, 1959; M in Engring., Yale U., 1960, MSc in Engring., 1961, PhD, 1962; D (hon.), Tech. U. Budapest, 2000, U. Sydney, 2007. Registered profl. engr., Mass. Asst. prof. mech. engring. MIT, Cambridge, 1962-67; prof. mech. engring. U. Mich., Ann Arbor, 1967-83; Paul Pigott prof. Stanford (Calif.) U., 1983—, chmn. dept. aeronautics and astronautics, 1990—2001. Author: Erosion by Liquid Impact, 1975; co-author, co-editor 14 books; contbr. over 200 articles to scholarly and profl. jours. Recipient Pub. Svc. Group Achievement award, NASA, 1988, Medal of Excellence in Composite Materials U. Del., 1999. Fellow AIAA (Engr. of Yr. 1995, Structures Structural Dynamics and Materials award 2000), ASME (Worcester Reed Warner medal 1994), Soc. Advancement Materials and Process Engring. (Delmonte award 1991); mem. Am. Phys. Soc., Soc. Automotive Engrs. (Ralph Teetor award 1978), NAE, Hungarian Nat. Acad. Sci. (fgn. mem.), Am. Soc. Composites (Outstanding Rschr. award 1997). Achievements include patents in field. Office: Stanford U Dept Aeronautics & Astronautics Stanford CA 94305 Office Phone: 650-723-4135. Business E-Mail: gspringer@stanford.edu.

SPRINGER, JEFFREY ALAN, lawyer; b. Denver, Feb. 26, 1950; s. Stanley and Sylvia (Miner) S.; m. Amy Mandel, Nov. 11 1995; children: Cydney Erin, Samantha Libby, Jackson Stanley, Harrison Louis. AB, Princeton U., 1972; JD, U. Colo., 1975. Bar: Colo. 1975, U.S. Dist. Ct. Colo. 1975, U.S. Ct. Appeals (10th cir.) 1975, U.S. Supreme Ct. 1978, U.S. Ct. Appeals (8th cir.) 1986. Assoc. Gerash & Springer, Denver, 1975-79; sole practice Denver, 1979-81; pres. Springer and Steinberg, P.C., Denver, 1981—. Mem. com. on mcpl. ct. rules Supreme Ct. Colo., 1985-86; mem. standing criminal justice act com. U.S. Dist. Ct., 1994-96. Mem. ABA, ATLA, Colo. Trial Lawyers Assn. (bd. dirs. 1988-90), Colo. Criminal Def. Bar (bd. dirs. 1985-86, 87-88, pres. 1988-89). Office Phone: 303-861-2800. E-mail: law@springer-and-steinberg.com.

SPRINGER, JERRY (GERALD NORMAN SPRINGER), television talk show host, radio personality; b. London, Feb. 13, 1944; BA in Polit. Sci., Tulane U.; JD, Northwestern U., 1968. Presdl. campaign aide Sen. Robert F. Kennedy; elected mem. at large Cin. Coun., 1971-77; elected mayor Cin., 1977; polit. reporter, commentator WLWT-TV, Cin., 1982-84, anchor, mng. editor, 1984-93; host The Jerry Springer Show, 1991—, Springer on the Radio, Air Am. Radio, 2005—06. Author Ringmaster, 1998; video collection Jerry Springer: Too Hot for TV; actor: (films) A Fair to Remember, 1998, Citizen Verdict, 2003, The Defender, 2004, (TV films) Since You've Been Gone, 1998, Talking to Americans, 2001; actor, prodr.: (films) Ringmaster, 1998; performer, Dancing With the Stars, 2006; host America's Got Talent, 2007-. On-site reporter Cin. Reaches Out; mem. adv. bd. Audrey Hepburn Hollywood for Children Fund; co-host Stars Across America Muscular Dystrophy Labor Day Telethon; v.p. bd. Nat. Muscular Dystrophy Assn.; founder scholarship fund Kellman Sch., Chgo. Recipient 7 Emmy awards for nightly news commentaries; named Best Anchor Cin. Mag. 5 times. Achievements include top rated daytime talk show series in the U.S. Office: Jerry Springer Show 454 N Columbus Dr Fl 2 Chicago IL 60611-5514 also: Air America Radio 641 Avenue Of The Americas Fl 4 New York NY 10011-2038 *

SPRINGER, LINDA M., federal official; BS, Ursinus Coll., 1977. Staff assoc. Coopers and Lybrand, 1977—79; actuary Penn Mut. Life Ins. Co., Phila., 1979—86, exec. asst. to pres., 1986—87, asst. v.p. & prod. mgr., 1987—90, v.p. & prod. mgr., 1990—92; actuary Provident Mut. Life Ins. Co., Berwyn, Pa., 1992—95, asst. v.p. & actuary, 1995—96, v.p. and contr., 1996—2000, sr. v.p. & contr., 2001—02; counselor to the dep. dir. for mgmt. Office Fed. Fin. Mgmt., Office Mgmt. & Budget, Washington, 2002—03, contr., 2003—05; dir. US Office Pers. Mgmt., Washington, 2005—. Avocations: golf, gardening, cello. Office: US Office Pers Mgmt Theodore Roosevelt Fed Bldg 1900 E St NW Rm 5A09 Washington DC 20415 *

SPRINGER, MARLENE, retired academic administrator; b. Murfreesboro, Tenn., Nov. 16, 1937; d. Foster V. and Josephine Jones; children: Ann Springer, Rebecca Springer. BA in English and Bus. Adminstrn., Centre Coll., 1959; MA in Am. Lit., Ind. U., 1963, PhD in English Lit., 1969. Chair English dept. U. Mo., Kansas City, 1980-81, acting assoc. dean grad. sch., 1982; Am. Coun. of Edn. Adminstrn. fellow U. Kans., Lawrence, 1982-83; dean grad. sch. U. Mo., Kansas City, 1983-84, assoc. vice chancellor acad. affairs & grad. studies, 1985-89; vice chancellor acad. affairs East Carolina U., Greenville, NC, 1989-94; pres. Coll. Staten Island, CUNY, 1994—2007. Author: Edith Wharton and Kate Chopin: A Reference Guide, 1976; What Manner of Woman: Essays, 1977, Thomas Hardy's Use of Allusion, 1983, Plains Woman: The Diary of Martha Farnsworth, 1986 (Choice award 1986), Ethan Frome: A Nightmare of Need, 1993. Huntington Libr. fellow, 1988. Mem.: Coun. Grad. Schs. (chair 1986—88), Assn. Tchr. Educators (chair 1992), Acad. Leadership Acad. (exec. com. 1992—94), Am. Assn. State Colls. and Univs., Am. Coun. on Edn. (profl. devel. com. 1991—, invited participant Nat. Forum 1984, bd. dirs. 2001—). *

SPRINGER, PAUL DAVID, lawyer, film company executive; b. NYC, Apr. 27, 1942; s. William W. and Alma (Markowitz) S.; m. Mariann Frankfurt, Aug. 16, 1964; children: Rob, Will. BA, U. Bridgeport, 1963; JD, Bklyn. Law Sch., 1967. Bar: N.Y. 1968, U.S. Dist. Ct. (so. and ea. dists.) N.Y. 1968, U.S. Ct. Appeals (2d cir.) 1970, U.S. Supreme Ct. 1973, Calif. 1989. Assoc. Johnson & Tannenbaum, NYC, 1968—70; assoc. counsel Columbia Pictures, NYC, 1970, Paramount Pictures, NYC, 1970—79, v.p., theatrical distbn. counsel, 1979—85, sr. v.p., chief resident counsel East Coast, 1985—87, sr. v.p., asst. gen. counsel LA, 1987—. Bar: N.Y. 1968, U.S. Dist. Ct. (so. and ea. dists.) N.Y. 1968, U.S. Ct. Appeals (2d cir.) 1970, U.S. Supreme Ct. 1973, Calif. 1989. Trustee West Cunningham Park Civic Assn., Fresh Meadows, N.Y., 1978—. Mem. ABA, Assn. of Bar of City of N.Y., L.A. Copyright Soc., Acad. Motion Picture Arts and Scis., Motion Picture Pioneers. Office Phone: 323-956-8408. Business E-Mail: paul_springer@paramount.com.

SPRINGER, ROBERT DALE, retired air force officer, consultant, lecturer; b. Millheim, Pa., Jan. 17, 1933; s. Simon Peter and Ruth Olive (McCool); m. Bonnie Joan Brubaker, Aug. 30, 1953; children: Robert Dale Jr., Debra K. Springer Miller, Curtis A., Michele L. Becker, Tania. BA in Social Sci., George Washington U., 1964, MS in Internat. Affairs, 1969. Cert. command pilot. Commd. 2d lt. USAF; advanced through grades to lt. gen.; comdr. 435th Tactical Airlift Wing, Rhein-Main Air Base, Federal Republic Germany, 1978-80, 322d Airlift Divsn., Ramstein Air Base, Federal Republic Germany, 1980-81, Air Force Manpower and Pers. Ctr., Randolph AFB, Tex., 1982-84, 21 A.F., McGuire AFB, NJ, 1984-85; insp. gen. USAF, Washington, 1985-87; with DCS-pers. Mil. Airlift Command, Scott AFB, Ill., 1981-82, vice comdr.-in-chief, 1987-88; ret., 1988; pres. bsone, Inc., 1999—, NovaLogic Sys., 1999—. Media cons., lectr., 1989—; dir. Air Force Commissary Svc., San Antonio, 1982-84, Army-Air Force Exch. Svc., Dallas, 1982-84; chmn. bd. dirs. Air Force Welfare Bd., San Antonio, 1982-84; mem. adv. bd. First Bank; bd. dirs. NovaLogic, Inc. Founding exec. dir Air Force Meml. Found., 1992-96, pres. 1996-98, vice chmn., 1998—; trustee Aerospace Edn. Found., 1992-94, The Falcon Found., 1996—; dir. NC Military Found., 2006-. Mem. Air Force Assn. (Presdl. Citation 1984), Airlift-Tanker Assn. (life mem., sr. v.p. 1989-94), Arnold Air Soc. (exec. dir. 1990-93, trustee 1993-2001), Ret. Officers Assn. (life), Daedalians (life), Masons (33 deg.). Lutheran. Avocations: golf, reading. Personal E-mail: bsone@nc.rr.com.

SPRINGER, SALLY PEARL, university administrator; b. Bklyn., Mar. 19, 1947; d. Nathaniel Margulies and Fanny (Schoen) S.; m. Hakon Hope; children: Erik Jacob Hope, Mollie Liv Hope. BS, Bklyn. Coll., 1967; PhD, Stanford U., 1971. Postdoctoral fellow Stanford U. Med. Sch., Calif., 1971-73; asst. prof. SUNY, Stony Brook, 1973-78, assoc. provost, 1981-85, assoc. prof., 1978-87; exec. asst. to chancellor U. Calif., Davis, 1987-92, asst. chancellor, 1982-2001, assoc. chancellor, 2001—. Author: (with others) Left Brain, Right Brain, 1981 (Am. Psychol. Found. Disting. Contbr. award 1981), 5th rev. edit., 1998, How to Succeed in College, 1982, Admission Matters: What Students and Parents Need to Know About Getting Into College, 2005; contbr. articles to profl. jours Mem. Internat. Neuropsychol. Soc., Psychonomic Soc. Office: Univ Calif Office Chancellor Davis CA 95616 Home Phone: 530-756-3990; Office Phone: 530-752-2068. Business E-Mail: spspringer@ucdavis.edu.

SPRINGER, TIMOTHY ALAN, health researcher, immunology educator; b. Ft. Benning, Ga., Feb. 23, 1948; BA in Biochemistry, U. Calif., Berkeley, 1971; PhD in Biochemistry & Molecular Biology, Harvard U., 1976. NIH rsch. fellow U. Cambridge (Eng.)/MRC Lab. Molecular Biology, 1976-77; asst. prof. Med. Sch., Harvard U., 1977-83, assoc. prof., 1983-89, Latham family prof., 1989—. Chief lab. membrane immunochemistry Dana-Farber Cancer Inst., Boston, 1981-88; v.p. Ctr. Blood Rsch. Inst. Biomed. Rsch., Boston, 1988—; organizer Juan March Found. Workshop, Madrid, 1991. Assoc. editor Jour. Immunology, 1981-85; adv. editor Jour. Exptl. Medicine, 1981-85; mem. editl. bd. Hybridoma, 1981-, Jour. Clin. Immunology, 1988-92, Cellular Immunology, 1988-93, Cell Regulation, 1989-92, New Biologist, 1989—; contbr. numerous articles to profl. jours. NIH grantee, 1988, basic Rsch. prize, Am. Heart Assn., 1993, William B. Coley Medal for Disting. Rsch. in Fundamental Immunology, Cancer Rsch. Inst., 1995, Marie T. Bonazinga award for Excellence in Leukocyte Biology Rsch, Society for Leukocyte Biology, 1995, Crafoord prize, 2004. Mem. Am. Assn. Immunologists, Reticuloendothelial Soc. (membership chair 1986—, chair 1989), Am. Soc. Biol. Chemists, Am. Assn. Immunologists (block chmn. macrophages and natural killer cells 1985-86), Am. Assn. Pathologists, Nat. Acad. Scis. (chair biophysics and computational biology sect. 29 2004-), Am. Acad. Arts and Sciences, Phi Beta Kappa. Office: Ctr for Blood Rsch Inst for Biomedical Rsch Harvard Med Sch Warren Alpert Bldg Rm251 200 Longwood Ave Boston MA 02115 Office Fax: 617-278-3200, 617-278-3232. Business E-Mail: springer@cbr.med.harvard.edu.

SPRINGER, WILMA MARIE, retired elementary school educator; b. Goshen, Ind., Jan. 13, 1933; d. Noah A. and Laura D. (Miller) Kaufman; m. Walter Frederick Springer, May 25, 1957; children: Anita Daniel, Timothy, Mark. BA, Goshen Coll., 1956; MS, Bradley U., 1960. Tchr. Topeka Elem. Sch., Ind., 1956—57, Metamora Grade Sch., Ill., 1957—59, Bellflower Unified Sch. Dist., Calif., 1960—61, 1968—2001, Lindstrom Elem. Sch., 1970—89, Jefferson Elem. Sch., Bellflower, 1989—92, Woodruff Elem., 1992—93, Williams Elem. Sch., Lakewood, Calif., 1993—96, Baxter Elem. Sch., Bellflower, 1996—2001; ret., 2001. Chmn. gifted and talented edn. Lindstrom Elem. Sch., Lakewood, 1986—89, Jefferson Elem. Sch., Bellflower, 1989—91, Baxter Elem., 1996—2001; stage mgr. Hour of Power TV Crystal Cathedral, 1983—; mem. program quality rev. team State of Calif., 1989—91; mem. adv. bd. Weekly Reader, 1989—96. Contbr. articles to profl. jours. Active sch. bd. campaign, 1984, Bellflower City Coun., 1988, state senator and assemblyman campaigns, 1986-87; petition circulator various state initiatives, 1987-88; bd. dirs. Women's Ministries of Crystal Cathedral, Garden Grove, Calif., 1978-88; educator del. People to People Ambassadors Program, South Africa, 2003, Russia, 2004. Instructional Improvement Program grantee State of Calif., 1986-87; recipient Recognition award Regional Ednl. TV Adv. Coun., 1986, Cathedral Star award Women's Ministries of Crystal Cathedral, 1985. Mem.: AAUW, NEA (del. nat. conv. 1986, 1987, 1990, 1992, 1993, 1994, 1995), Calif. Tchrs. Assn. (del. 1986, 1994), Bellflower Edn. Assn. (elem. dir. 1986—88, treas. 1988—89, v.p. 1989—91, pres. 1991—95), Toastmasters (Founder's Dist. Gov. 2001—02, Disting. Toastmaster, Disting. Dist.), Delta Kappa Gamma. Republican. Mem. Reformed Churches of Am. Avocations: quilting, painting. Home: 3180 Marna Ave Long Beach CA 90808-3246 Personal E-mail: wmspr@aol.com.

SPRINGFIELD, JAMES FRANCIS, retired lawyer, banker; b. Memphis, Nov. 5, 1929; s. C.L. and Mildred (White) S.; m. Shirley Burdick, June 1, 1951 (div.); children: Sidney, Susan, James Francis; m. Nancy Hardwick Ragan, Feb. 8, 1987 (dec. Jan. 1988); m. Donna Thomas Moore, Feb. 22, 1989. BA with distinction in econs., Rhodes Coll., 1951; LLB, U. Memphis, 1960. Bar: Tenn. 1960. With Union Planters Nat. Bank, Memphis, 1951-94, exec. v.p., sr. trust officer, head trust dept., 1968-85, gen. counsel, sec. bd., 1985-94; sec. bd., exec. v.p., gen. counsel Union Planters Corp., 1985-94; ret., 1994. Adv. bd. Memphis Alzheimer's Assn., 1999-2001; president's coun. Rhodes Coll., Memphis, chmn., 1991-92, internat. chmn. ann. fund, 1995-96; chmn. bd. trustees So. Coll. Optometry, 1978-80; trustee Plough Found., Memphis Conf. United Meth. Ch. Fund., 1978-85, U. Tenn. Med. Units Found., 1975-82, MidSouth Pub. Comm. Found., 1985-87, 98-2007, sec. bd., 2002-07; chmn. fin. com. Hutchinson Sch.; sec. bd. trustees Vision Edn. Found., 1977-78; bd. regents Tenn. Trust Sch., chmn., 1977; mem. pres.'s adv. coun. Lambuth Coll., 1982-85; exec. bd. Chickasaw coun. Boy Scouts Am., 1983-87; bd. visitors Memphis State U. Cecil C. Humphreys Sch. Law, treas. Balmoral Civic Club, 1967-68; pres., bd. dir. Village of Bailey Station Homeowners Assn., Inc., 2000-01; dir. Shoreline Towers Condominium Assn. Inc., 2004-06. Lt. (j.g.) USNR, 1951-54. Mem. Tenn. Bar Assn. (chmn. interprofl. rels. com. 1976), Memphis and Shelby County Bar assn. (chmn. moral fitness com. 1972), Tenn. Bankers Assn. (chmn. legis.com. trust div. 1976-77, treas. 1972-73, pres. 1976-77, bd. dir. 1976-77), Bank Adminstrn. Inst. (chmn. trust commn. 1981-82), Estate Planning Coun. Memphis (pres. 1973-74), Sigma Nu (div. comdr. 1967-68, treas., bd. dir. House Corp. 1966-81), Omicron Delta Kappa (Rhodes Coll. chpt., pres. ODK Assocs. 2002-03). Republican. Home: 1692 Village Ridge Rd Collierville TN 38017-9793 Personal E-mail: jimmyspringfield@msn.com.

SPRINGFIELD, SANYA A., federal agency administrator; BS in zoology, Howard U., PhD in physiology and biophysics. Fellow Dept. Pharmacology Robert Wood Johnson Sch. Medicine, Piscataway, NJ; asst. prof. to assoc. prof. Dept. Biology CCNY, 1985—95; program dir. Divsn. Integrative Biology and Neurosiences NSF; participant NIH Grants Assoc. Program; sci. rev. adminstr. Grants Rev. Br. Nat. Cancer Inst., dir. Comprehensive Minority Biomedical Br., 1999—, acting dir. Ctr. to Reduce Cancer Health Disparities. Office: Comprehensive Minority Biomedical Br Nat Cancer Inst 6116 Executive Blvd Ste 7028 Bethesda MD 20892-8350 also: Ctr to Reduce Cancer Health Disparities Nat Cancer Inst 6116 Executive Blvd Ste 602 MSC 8341 Bethesda MD 20892 Office Phone: 301-496-7344. Office Fax: 301-402-4551. E-mail: springfs@mail.nih.gov.

SPRINGSTEEN, BRUCE (BRUCE FREDERICK JOSEPH SPRINGSTEEN), musician, singer; b. Freehold, NJ, Sept. 23, 1949; s. Douglas and Adele Springsteen; m. Julianne Phillips, May 13, 1985 (div. 1989); m. Patti Scialfa, June 8, 1991; children: Evan James, Jessica Rae, Sam Ryan. Student, Ocean County CC, 1967. Playing & performing with The E-Street Band, 1972—89, 1999—. Musician: (albums) Greetings from Asbury Park, 1973, The Wild, The Innocent and the E-Street Shuffle, 1973, Born to Run, 1975 (Gold Record award, 1975), Darkness on the Edge of Town, 1978, The River, 1980, Nebraska, 1982, Born in the U.S.A., 1984 (Best Pop/Rock Album of Yr., Downbeat Readers Poll, 1984), Bruce Springsteen and the E-Street Band Live/1975-85, 1986, Tunnel of Love, 1987, Chimes of Freedom, 1988, Human Touch, 1992, Lucky Town, 1992, Bruce Springsteen's Greatest Hits, 1995, The Ghost of Tom Joad, 1995, In Concert/MTV Unplugged, 1997, Tracks, 1998, 18 Tracks, 1999, Live in New York City, 2001, The Rising, 2002 (Grammy award best male rock vocal performance, 2003, Grammy award best rock song, 2003, Grammy award best rock album, 2003), The Essential Bruce Springsteen, 2003, Devils and Dust, 2005 (Grammy award, Best Solo Rock Vocal Performance, 2006), Born to Run: 30th Anniversary 3 Disc Set, 2005, Bruce Springsteen & The E-Street Band: Hammersmith Odeon, London '75, 2006, We Shall Overcome: The Pete Seeger Sessions, 2006 (Grammy award, Best Traditional Folk Album, 2007), The Classic Interviews, 2006, Live in Dublin, 2007, Magic, 2007; composer: (songs) Growing Up, Blinded By the Light, Sprit in the Night, Rosalita (Come Out Tonight), 1973, Born to Run, Thunder Road, Tenth Avenue Freeze Out, Jungleland, 1975, Badlands, Prove It All Night, The Promised Land, 1978, The River, Hungry Heart, Out in the Street, 1980, Atlantic City, 1982, Dancing in the Dark, Born in the USA, Cover Me, I'm On Fire, Glory Days, My Hometown, 1984, Brilliant Disguise, Tunnel of Love, 1987, Human Touch, Better Days, 1992, Streets of Philadelphia, 1994 (Golden Globe award for Best Original Song in a Film, 1994, Acad. award for best original song in a film, 1994, MTV Best Video from a Film award, 1994, Grammy, Song of Yr., 1994), Secret Garden, 1995, Dead Man Walking, 1996 (Acad. award nominee for best original song in a film, 1996), The Rising, Lonesome Day, Waitin' on a Sunny Day, Mary's Place, 2002; appears on: albums Rumble Doll with Patti Scialfa, 1993, The Wind with Warren Zevon, 2003 (Grammy award, Best Rock Performance By A Duo Or Group With Vocal for song "Disorder in the House", 2003); exec. prodr.: Wings for Wheels: The Making of Born to Run, 2005 (Grammy award for Best Long Form Music Video, 2007). Recipient Grammy award for best male rock vocalist, 1984, 1987, 1994. Achievements include being inducted into Rock and Roll Hall of Fame, 1999. Office: c/o Barbara Carr Creative Artists Agy LLC 2000 Ave of the Stars Los Angeles CA 90067 Office Phone: 424-288-2000. *

SPRINKEL, BERYL WAYNE, economist, consultant; b. Richmond, Mo., Nov. 20, 1923; s. Clarence and Emma (Schooley) S.; m. Lory Kiefer, Aug. 29, 1993; children: Gary L., Kevin G. Student, N.W. Mo. State U., 1941-43, U. Oreg., 1943-44; BS, U. Mo., 1947; MBA, U. Chgo., 1948, PhD, 1952; LHD (hon.), DePaul U., 1975; LLD (hon.), St. Michael's Coll., 1981, U. Mo., 1985, U. Rochester, 1985, Govs. State U., 1988, U. Nebr., 1988; Doctor of Pub. Adminstrn., Marion Coll., 1988. Instr. econs. and fin. U. Mo., Columbia, 1948-49, U. Chgo., 1950-52; with Harris Trust & Savs. Bank, Chgo., 1952-81, v.p., economist, 1960-68, dir. rsch., 1963-69, sr. v.p., 1968-74, economist, 1968-81, exec. v.p., economist, 1974-81; undersec. monetary affairs Dept. Treasury, Washington, 1981-85; chmn. Coun. Econ. Advisers, The White House, Washington, 1985-89, mem. Pres.'s Cabinet, 1987-89; pvt. cons. economist, 1989—. Cons. Fed. Res. Bd., 1955-59, Bur. of Census, 1962-70, Joint Econ. Com. U.S. Congress, 1958, 62, 67, 71, Ho. of Reps. Banking and Currency Com., 1963, Senate Banking Com., 1975; econ. adv. bd. to sec. commerce, 1967-69; bd. economists Time mag., 1968-80. Author: Money and Stock Prices, 1964, Money and Markets-A Monetarist View, 1971; co-author: Winning with Money, 1977 Pres. Homewood-Flossmoor (Ill.) Community High Sch., 1959-60. With AUS, 1943-45. Recipient Hamilton Bolton award Fin. Analysts Assn., 1968, Alexander Hamilton award U.S. Treasury, 1985, Disting. Alumnus award U. Chgo., 1986, Disting. Alumnus award U. Mo., 2000. Fellow Nat. Assn. Bus. Economists; mem. Nat. Assn. Bus. Economists, Beta Gamma Sigma. Home (Winter): 16625 Waters Edge Fort Myers FL 33908 Home Phone: 239-482-7593. Personal E-mail: sprinkelec@comcast.net.

SPRINKLE, MARTHA CLARE, elementary school educator; b. Tehachapi, Calif., Oct. 17, 1944; d. William Foote and Mildred Sprinkle; BA, U. Calif., Santa Barbara, 1966; MA in Orgn. Mgmt., U. Phoenix, 2000. Cert. tchr. Calif., water aerobics instr. 1986. Tchr. Muroc Unified Sch. Dist., Edwards, Calif., 1966—71, Elk Hills Sch., Tupman, Calif., 1971—79, Tehachapi Valley Recreation and Pks., 1979—2007, So. Kern Unified Sch., Rosamond, Calif., 1984—2003. Planning commr. City of Tehachapi, Calif., 1984—2007. Home: PO Box 149 Tehachapi CA 93581 E-mail: mcsprink@sbcglobal.net.

SPRINKLE, ROBERT LEE, JR., podiatrist; b. Winston-Salem, NC, July 13, 1932; s. Robert Lee and Elton Elizabeth Sprinkle; children: Robert III, Karen, Ralph, Richard, Roy, Randy, Drouin; m. Nancy House Dixon. Student, Salem Coll., 1952; BS, Ohio Coll. Podiatry, 1956; DPM, Pa. Coll. Podiatry, 1970. Diplomate Am. Bd. Disability Analysts, Am. Coun. Cert. Podiatric Phys. and Surgeons, Sr. Acad. Ambulatory Podiatric Surgeons. Pvt. practice, Winston-Salem, 1957—. Chmn. N.C. Bd. Podiatry Examiners, 1968-74; clin. assoc. prof. Dr. William M. School Coll. Podiatric Medicine; researcher reconstructive surgery human foot and ankle; bd. dirs. Cmty. Gen. Hosp. Found., Thomasville, N.C.; bd. dirs. Am. Coun. Cert. Podiatric Phys. and Surgeons. Chmn. Mayor's Com. on Hiring the Handicapped, 1963-64; commr. Old Hickory Coun., Boy Scouts Am., 1970-71, v.p., 1973-74, Silver Beaver award, 1969, mem. adv. bd. Old North State Coun.; pres. St. Leo's Parochial Sch. PTA, 1969-70; dir. Halfway House, 1965-66; chmn. Bishop McGuiness PTA, 1976. Recipient St. George medal Charlotte Diocese, Roman Cath. Ch., 1971; Schering grantee, 1972-74. Mem. APHA, Am. Podiatric Med. Assn. (life mem.), N.C. Podiatry Assn. (past pres., Podiatrist of Yr. 1976), Piedmont Podiatry Assn., Acad. Ambulatory Podiatric Surgeons (life mem.), Internat. Analgesia Soc., Forsyth Country Club, Colonial Country Club, Twin City Club, KC (4th degree), SAR (life; N.C. state registrar, past pres. Bethabara chpt., N.C. state pres. 2002—, mem. George Washington Found.), SCV, NRA (life), Rotary (Paul Harris fellow, dist. gov. 1976-77), St. Andrew's Soc.,

Sons of the Revolution (life; state chpt. sec. pres. NCSSR). Republican. Roman Catholic. Home: 10 Mock St Thomasville NC 27360-4622 Office: ABC Family Foot and Ankle Clinic PO Box 366 17 W Main St Thomasville NC 27360-3934 Office Phone: 336-472-2757. Business E-Mail: foot1@northstate.net.

SPRINKLE, SHANNON M., lawyer; b. Columbus, Oh., May 19, 1977; BA, Univ. Fla., 1998; JD, Tulane Law Sch., 2001. Bar: Ga. 2001. Assoc. atty. Carlock, Copeland, Semler & Stair, LLP, Atlanta. Spkr. in field. Contbr. articles to numerous profl. jours. Named Rising Star, Ga. Super-Lawyer Mag., 2006. Mem.: ABA (Tort Trial and Insurance Practice Section, Officers & Directors Liability Com.), Atlanta Bar Assn., Ga. Defense Lawyers Assn. Office: Carlock Copeland 2600 Marquis Two Tower 285 Peachtree Ctr Ave Atlanta GA 30303-1235

SPRINKLE, WILLIAM MELVIN, acoustical engineer, engineering executive; b. Washington, Sept. 2, 1945; s. Melvin Cline and Gladys Virginia (Miller) S.; div.; children: Timothy William, Allison Anne; m. Theresa Torregrossa Ellis, June, 2004. BS in Chemistry, Randolph-Macon Coll., Ashland, Va., 1967; M in Engring. Adminstrn., Va. Poly. Inst. & State U., 1990. Registered profl. engr., Va. Sr. cons. Sprinkle & Assocs., Kensington, Md., 1973-76; audio systems engr. Robertshaw Controls Co., Richmond, Va., 1976-80; sr. engr. TDFB-Engrs. & Archs., Richmond, 1980-85; property mgmt. officer Signet Bank, Richmond, 1985-87; asst. dir. engring. Va. Dept. Corrections, Richmond, 1987—. Mem. summer adj. faculty Eastman Sch. Music, Rochester, NY, 1974-83. Editor newsletter Richmond Area Bicycling Assn., 1993-94; contbr. Time Saver Standards for Architectural Design Data, 1982. Eagle scoutmaster Boy Scouts Am., 1970-72, unit commr., 1990-92; bd. assocs. Randolph Macon Coll., 2005-. Mem. Acoustical Soc. Am., Pi Delta Epsilon (v.p.). Baptist. Office: Dept of Corrections 6900 Atmore Dr Richmond VA 23225-5646

SPRINTHALL, NORMAN ARTHUR, psychology educator; b. Attleboro, Mass., Aug. 19, 1931; s. William Archie and Edith Jarvis (Clark) S.; m. Barbara Weller (div. 1974); children: Douglas, Jane, Carolyn; m. Lois May Thies. AB magna cum laude, Brown U., 1954, MA, 1959; EdD, Harvard U., 1963. Dir. fin. aid Brown U., 1955-60; asst. prof., then asso. prof. psychology, program chmn. counseling Harvard U., 1963-72; mem. faculty U. Minn., Mpls., 1972-82, prof. ednl. psychology, 1973-82, program chmn. counseling, 1972-74; prof. psychology, head counselor edn. program N.C. State U., Raleigh, 1982-87, prof., counselor, 1987-95, prof. emeritus, 1995—. Co-dir. Ethical Reasoning Project in Pub. Adminstrn., U.S. and Poland, 1993-95, Russia, 1998-99. Author: Educational Psychology: Readings, 1969, Guidance for Human Growth, 1971, Educational Psychology: A Developmental Approach, 7th edit., 1998, Value Development as the Aim of Education, 2d edit., 1981, Adolescent Psychology: A Developmental View, 1984, 2d rev. edit., 1988, 3d edit., 1995; co-author: Stewart-Sprinthall Management Survey (SSMS) Ethics and Public Administration, others; mem. editl. bd. profl. jours. Bd. dirs. Josephson Inst. Advancement of Ethics, 1986-90, mem. bd. advisors Character Counts Coalition, 1994—2004. Co-recipient Kuhmerker Career Rsch. award, Assn. for Moral Educator, 2005. Fellow APA (Disting. Sr. Contbr. award); mem. Phi Beta Kappa. Office Phone: 910-278-7839. E-mail: nlsprint@earthlink.net.

SPRITZER, RALPH SIMON, lawyer, educator; b. NYC, Apr. 27, 1917; s. Harry and Stella (Theuman) S.; m. Lorraine Nelson, Dec. 23, 1950; children: Ronald, Pamela. BS, Columbia U., 1937, LL.B., 1940. Bar: N.Y. bar 1941, U.S. Supreme Ct. bar 1950. Atty. Office Alien Property, Dept. Justice, 1946-51; anti-trust div. Dept. Justice, 1951-54, Office Solicitor Gen., 1954-61; gen. counsel FPC, 1961-62; 1st asst. to solicitor gen. U.S., 1962-68; prof. law U. Pa., Phila., 1968-86, Ariz. State U., Tempe, 1986—; gen. counsel AAUP, 1983-84. Adj. prof. law George Wasington U., 1967; cons. Adminstrv. Conf. U.S., Ford Found., Pa. Gov.'s Justice Commn. Served with AUS, 1941-46. Recipient Superior Service award Dept. Justice, 1960; Tom C. Clark award Fed. Bar. Assn., 1968 Mem. Am. Law Inst. Home: 1024 E Gemini Dr Tempe AZ 85283-3004 Office: Ariz State Univ Coll Law Tempe AZ 85287 Office Phone: 480-965-7419.

SPRIZZO, JOHN EMILIO, federal judge; b. Bklyn., Dec. 23, 1934; s. Vincent James and Esther Nancy S.; children: Ann Esther, Johna Emily, Matthew John. BA summa cum laude, St. John's U., Jamaica, NY, 1956; LLB summa cum laude, St. John's U., 1959. Bar: N.Y. 1960. Atty. U.S. Dept. Justice, 1959-63; asst. U.S. atty. so. dist. N.Y. Dept. Justice, NYC, 1963-68, chief appellate atty., 1965-66, asst. chief criminal div., 1966-68; assoc. prof. Fordham U. Law Sch., NYC, 1968-72; ptnr. Curtis, Mallet-Prevost, NYC, 1972-81; judge U.S. Dist. Ct. (So. Dist.), NY, 1981—2000, sr. judge NY, 2000—. Cons. Nat. Com. for Reform of Criminal Laws, N.Y.C., 1971-72; mem. Knapp Commn., 1971-72; assoc. atty. Com. of Ct. on Judiciary, N.Y.C., 1971-72 Co-contbr. articles to profl. law revs. Mem. ABA, D.C. Bar Assn., Assn. of Bar of City of N.Y. Office: US Dist Ct US Courthouse 500 Pearl St Rm 1350 New York NY 10007-1502

SPROAT, EDWARD F., III, (WARD SPROAT), federal agency administrator; b. Sept. 12, 1951; With Gas Cooled Reactor Assocs., La Jolla, Calif.; mgr.-nuc. group bus. unit, mgr. projects Limerick Engring. Station PECO Energy, sect. mgr. computer engring., mgr. elec. engring. nuc. generation br., dir. quality mgmt. Phila. Electric, 1991—94, dir. engring. PECO Nuc., dir. engring and maintenance Limerick Nuc. Generating Station, dir. strategic programs PECO Nuc.; v.p. internat. projects Exelon Generation, bd. dirs., COO Board of Pebble Bed Modular Reactor Pty. Ltd. South Africa, 2002; mng. ptnr. McNeill, Sproat & Assocs., LLC, Berwyn, Pa.; dir. Office Civilian Radioactive Waste Mgmt. US Dept. Energy, Washington, 2006—. Office: US Dept Energy 1000 Independence Ave SW Washington DC 20585

SPROAT, RUTH C., retired director, consultant; b. Lake Forest, Ill., Aug. 22, 1930; d. Christian Peter and Anna Elsa Christensen; m. Robert M. Volpe (div.); m. John Gerald Sproat, Mar. 18, 1967; 1 stepchild, Barbara Jeanne. BA in History, Lake Forest Coll., 1952; MA in History, Northwestern U., 1962. Registrar, admissions counselor Lake Forest Coll., 1948—68, dir. alumni affairs, 1972—74; dir. Master's Degree Program, asst. to pres. Lake Forest Coll. Grad. Sch. Mgmt., 1968—70, asst. to pres., 1971—72; dir. higher edn. SC Ednl. TV Network, Columbia, 1974—80, asst. dir. programming, exec. prodr., prodr., 1980—82, dir. higher edn., project dir., prodr., exec. prodr., 1982—87, asst. to pres. for devel. Satellite Ednl. Resources Consortium, 1988—92, exec. staff, dir. planning, grants and rsch., project dir., exec. prodr., 1992—97, cons. and asst. to pres., 2000—02; dir. devel. U. SC, Columbia, 1997—99; ret., 2002; cons. in field, 2002—. V.p. S.C. chpt. Am. Women in Radio and TV, 1983; co-prodr. with Am. Film Inst. Am. TV and Video Festival, India, 1985, prodr., presenter, India, 1986—91. Project dir., grant writer: (PBS TV series) Voices and Visions; U.S. project dir. Spaceship Earth; coordinating prodr. Cinematic Eye (Day Time Emmy award). Mentor to devel. staff Columbia Mus. Art, 2002. Recipient Alumni Disting. Svc. citation, Lake Forest Coll., 1987. Mem.: Hist. Columbia Found., Ill. Assn. Coll. Registrars and Admissions Officers (hon.; pres. 1965), Am. Assn. Collegiate Registrars and Admissions Officers (hon.; sec. 1966—68), Riverbanks Zoo Soc., Friends of U. S.C. Sch. Music (sec. 2001—03, dir. publicity for ann. fundraiser 2002—03, 2003—04, v.p. 2005—), State Mus. S.C., Sierra Club. Democrat. Avocations: gardening, writing, photography, travel. Home: 1686 Woodlake Dr Columbia SC 29206 E-mail: rcsproat@sc.rr.com.

SPROGER, CHARLES EDMUND, retired lawyer; b. Chgo., Feb. 18, 1933; s. William and Minnette (Weiss) Sproger. BA (David Himmelblau scholar), Northwestern U., 1954, JD, 1957. Bar: Ill. 1957. Assoc. Ehrlich & Cohn, 1958-63, Ehrlich, Bundesen, Friedman & Ross, 1963-72; partner Ehrlich, Bundesen, Broecker & Sproger, 1972-77; pvt. practice, 1977—2000; ret., 2000. Mem. adv. com. curriculum Ill. Inst. Continuing Legal Edn., Chgo., 1976—90; v.p. Mediation Coun. of Ill., 1986-87; arbitration panelist for Cir. Ct. Cook County, 1990—. Editor: Family Lawyer, 1962-63; contbr. articles to legal publs. Mediator Pastoral Psychotherapy Inst., 1982-86, vol. Coun. for Jewish Elderly, Chgo., 2002-. Recipient Vol. of Yr. award, Coun. for Jewish Elderly, 2004. Fellow Am. Acad. Matrimonial Lawyers (bd. examiners 1972-86, chmn. Law Day U.S.A. 1975); mem. ABA, Ill. Bar Assn. (chmn. coun. family law 1970-71), Chgo. Bar Assn. (matrimonial law com. 1958-2000), Am. Arbitration Assn. (divorce mediation com. 1983-92), Decalogue Soc., U. Mich. Club Chgo. (pres. 1988-89, bd. dirs. 1987-2004), Phi Alpha Delta. Address: 2800 W Birchwood Ave Chicago IL 60645-1218

SPROLE, FRANK ARNOTT, retired pharmaceutical executive, lawyer; b. Bklyn., Sept. 13, 1918; s. Frank Newland and Eleanor Arnott (Greenberg) S.; m. Sarah Louise Knapp, Sept. 23, 1944; children: Wendy Sprole Bangs, Frank J., Anne Sprole Mauk, Jonathan K., Sarah Sprole Obregon. BA, Yale U., 1942; LLB, Columbia U., 1949. Bar: N.Y. 1949. Assoc. firm Winthrop Stimson, Putnam & Roberts, NYC, 1949-50; atty. Bristol-Myers Co., NYC, 1950-52, asst. sec., 1952-55, sec., 1955-67, v.p., 1965-73, sr. v.p., 1973-77, vice-chmn. bd., 1977-84; ret., 1984. Officer Proprietary Assn., Washington, 1978-84; dir., officer Knapp Fund, N.Y.C., 1960-93. Pres. bd. trustees Hotchkiss Sch., Lakeville, Conn., 1980-85; trustee Internat. Inst. Rural Reconstrn., N.Y.C., and Manila, 1983-87. Lt. comdr. USNR, 1942-45, PTO. Mem. Assn. of Bar of City of N.Y., Yale Club of N.Y.C., Wee Burn Country Club, Bohemian Club, John's Island Club, Riomar Country Club, Oak Harbor Club. Republican. Episcopalian. Home: 394 Mansfield Ave Darien CT 06820-2112

SPROLES, KEVIN, entrepreneur, Internet company executive; b. 1983; Founder & CEO Volusion, Inc., Simi Valley, Calif., 1999—. Named one of Best Entrepreneurs Under 25, BusinessWeek, 2006. Office: Volusion Inc 1736 Erringer Rd Simi Valley CA 93065 Office Phone: 800-646-3517. Office Fax: 805-435-7476.

SPROTT, DAVID ARTHUR, statistician, educator, psychologist, educator; b. Toronto, Ont., Can., May 31, 1930; s. Arthur Frederick and Dorothy (Barry) S.; m. Muriel Doris Vogel; children: Anne, Jane. BA, U. Toronto, 1952, MA, 1953, PhD, 1955. Rsch. asst. Galton Lab., London, 1955-56; biogeneticist, clin. tchr. dept. psychiatry U. Toronto, 1956-58; assoc. prof. stats. U. Waterloo, Ont., 1958-61, prof. Ont., 1961-96, disting. prof. emeritus, 1996—, prof. psychology Ont., 1964-96, dean math. Ont., 1966-72, chmn. dept. stats. Ont., 1966-75; prof. Centro de Investigacion en Matematicas, Guanajuato, Mex., 1993—. Vis. prof. various univs. and colls. Author: Statistical Inference in Science, Springer Series in Statistics, 2000; contbr. numerous articles to profl. jours. Recipient Gold medal Statis. Soc. Can., 1988. Fellow Am. Statis. Assn., Inst. Math. Stats., Royal Soc. Can., Royal Photog. Soc.; mem. Internat. Statis. Inst., Statis. Soc. Can. (hon.). Avocations: photography, wine making. Office: Dept Stats and Actuarial Sci U Waterloo Math Faculty Waterloo ON Canada N2L 3G1

SPROTT, JAMES D., lawyer; b. Auburn, Ind., Mar. 13, 1949; BA, Hendrix Coll., 1970; JD, So. Methodist U., 1973. Bar: Ark. 1973, US Ct. Appeals (8th Cir.), US Dist. Ct. (We. Dist. Ark.), US Dist. Ct. (Ea. Dist. Ark.). Ptnr. Sprott & Golden, Harrison, Ark., 2005—. Mem.: Ark. Bar Found. Inc. (pres. 1998—99), Ark. Trial Lawyers Assn., Ark. Bar Assn. (chmn. bd. gov. 2002—03, pres.-elect 2005—06, pres. 2006—07), ABA, Boone County Bar Assn. Office: Sprott & Golden 502 N Walnut Harrison AR 72601 Office Phone: 870-741-3633. Office Fax: 870-741-5479.

SPROTT, RICHARD LAWRENCE, foundation administrator, researcher; b. Tampa, Fla., Aug. 9, 1940; s. Joseph Albert and Marie Marguerite (Goaper) S.; m. Margaret Ann Weidel, June 19, 1965; children: Lynn Marie, Deborah Ann. Student, Franklin and Marshall Coll., 1958—60; BA, U. N.C., 1962, MA in Psychology, 1964, PhD in Psychology, 1965. Asst. prof. Oakland U., Rochester, Mich., 1967-69; assoc. staff scientist Jackson Lab., Bar Barbor, Maine, 1969-71, staff scientist, 1971-80; health scientist adminstr. Divsn. Rsch. Resources, NIH, Bethesda, Md., 1980-81; br. chief Nat. Inst. on Aging, Bethesda, 1981-84, assoc. dir., 1984-98; exec. dir. Ellison Med. Found., Bethesda, 1998—. Editor: Hormonal Correlates of Behavior, 1975, Age, Learning Ability and Intelligence, 1980; mem. editl. bd. Exptl. Aging Rsch. Jour., 1978-; contbr. articles to profl. jours. Mem. Bar Harbor Town Coun., 1975-79, chmn., 1978-79; mem. bd. appeals Town of Bar Harbor, 1972-75, mem. warrant com., 1972-75. NIH fellow, 1965-67; NIH grantee, 1969-79; recipient Kent award Gerontologic Soc. Am., 1997. Fellow Am. Psychol. Assn., Gerontol. Soc. Am.; mem. Behavior Genetics Assn. (membership chmn. 1979), Am. Acad. Behavioral Medicine, Am. Fedn. Aging Rsch. Home: 11514 Regency Dr Potomac MD 20854-3733 Office: Ellison Med Found 4710 Bethesda Ave Ste 204 Bethesda MD 20814-5226 Home Phone: 301-299-6805; Office Phone: 301-657-1830. Business E-Mail: rsprott@ellisonfoundation.org.

SPROUL, GAYLE CHATILO, lawyer; b. Phila., Dec. 13, 1954; d. Norman and Roslyn Chatilo; m. Edward William Sproul, May 25, 1980; children: Sophia, Molly. AB, Rutgers U., New Brunswick, NJ, 1975; M in Journalism, Temple U., Phila., 1980; JD, Villanova Law Sch., Pa., 1983. Law clk. Judge John P. Fullam, U.S. Dist. Ct., E.D. Pa., Phila., 1983—85; assoc. Schnader Harrison Segal and Lewis, Phila., 1985—89; of counsel Dechert LLP, Phila., 1997—2003; gen. atty. NBC, NYC, 1989—96; ptnr. Levine Sullivan Koch & Schulz, Phila., 2003—. Pres. Pa. Freedom Info. Coalition, Harrisburg, Pa., 2006—; editor MLRC Bull., NYC, 1997—2001; mem. MLRC Pub.Com., NYC, 2005—. Office: Levine Sullivan Koch & Schulz LLP 2112 Walnut St Third Fl Philadelphia PA 19103 Office Phone: 215-988-9778.

SPROUL, HARVEY LEONARD, lawyer; b. Williamsburg, Ky., Oct. 8, 1933; s. Harvey Lafayette and Ruth (Renfro) S.; m. Sylvia Ann Moulton, May 31, 1958; children: Daniel Harvey, Susan Rebecca Sproul Brown, Jane Anne Sproul Luttrell, Lyda Bentley Sproul Beane. BSBA, U. Tenn., 1955, JD, 1957. Bar: Tenn. 1957, U.S. Dist. Ct. (ea. dist.) Tenn. 1957, U.S. Supreme Ct. 1960, U.S. Ct. Appeals (6th cir.) 1972. Assoc. Dannel & Fowler, Lenoir City, Tenn., 1961-62; ptnr. Dannel & Sproul, Lenoir City, 1962-65; judge County of Loudon, Tenn., 1966-74; ptnr. Sproul & Harvey, Lenoir City, 1979-82, Sproul & Hinton, Lenoir City, 1988—. Prin. Harvey L. Sproul, Lenoir City, 1974-79, 82-88; vice-chair Tenn. Adv. Comm. for Local Planning, 1971-74; atty. Lenoir Bd. Edn., 1980-90; county atty. Loudon County, 1982-2007; staff judge adv. 125th ARCOM/USAR, Nashville, 1986-89. Pres. Lenoir City Jaycees, 1966-67, Lenoir City Rotary, 1970, Lenoir City C. of C., 1980-82, Loudon County C. of C., 1993, bd. dirs., 1988-; organizing chmn. East Tenn. Devel. Dist., 1966-68, Tellico Planning Coun., 1966-74, Loudon County Visitors Bur., 1989-91, Knoxville HS Alumni Assn., 1993-95; bd. dirs. Loudon County Econ. Devel. Agy., 1990-, Nine Countries One Vision, 2000-05, Good Samaritan Ctr., 2003-05, Loudon County Edn. Found., 2005-, Loudon County United Way, 2006-; bd. trustees Roane State CC, 2001-. Ret. col. JAGC USAR. Recipient Robert E. Gonia Regional Leadership award, 2002; named one of Outstanding Young Men in Am., Lenoir City Jaycees, 1962; named Tenn.'s Outstanding Young Man, Tenn. Jaycees, 1967, Man of Yr., Loudon County C. of C., 1989. Mem. ABA, Tenn. Bar Assn., Tenn. County Attys. Assn. (pres. 1997-98), Loudon County Bar Assn., Tenn. Coun. Sch. Bd. Attys. (v.p.), Tenn. County Judges Assn. (v.p. 1972-74), Omicron Delta Kappa, Kappa Sigma, Phi Delta Phi, Delta Sigma Phi. Democrat. Methodist. Avocations: tennis, jogging. Office: Sproul & Hinton 205 E Broadway St Lenoir City TN 37771-2911 Personal E-mail: hlsproul@charter.net.

SPROUL, JOHN ALLAN, retired utilities executive; b. Oakland, Calif., Mar. 28, 1924; s. Robert Gordon and Ida Amelia (Wittschen) S.; m. Marjorie Ann Hauck, June 20, 1945; children: John Allan, Malcolm J., Richard O., Catherine E. AB, U. Calif., Berkeley, 1947, LL.B., 1949. Bar: Calif. 1950. Atty. Pacific Gas & Electric Co., San Francisco, 1949-52, 56-62, sr. atty., 1962-70, asst. gen. counsel, 1970-71, v.p. gas supply, 1971-76, sr. v.p., 1976-77, exec. v.p., 1977-89; ret.; gen. counsel Pacific Gas Transmission Co., 1970-73, v.p., 1973-79, chmn. bd., 1979-89, also bd. dirs. Atty. Johnson & Stanton, San Francisco, 1952-56. Bd. dirs. emeritus Hastings Coll. Law. Served to 1st lt. USAAF, 1943-46. Mem. Calif. Bar Assn. (inactive), Pacific Coast Gas Assn., Pacific-Union Club, Orinda Country Club. Home: 8413 Buckingham Dr El Cerrito CA 94530-2531 Office: Pacific Gas & Electric Co Mail Code B26 PO Box 770000 San Francisco CA 94177-0001 also: Pacific Gas & Electric Co 77 Beale St Rm 2680 San Francisco CA 94105-1814 Office Phone: 415-973-2693. Office Fax: 415-973-8808. Personal E-mail: johnsproul@comcast.net.

SPROULE, JAMES MICHAEL, communications educator, writer; b. Dayton, Ohio, Feb. 8, 1949; s. John Harper and Katherine Veronica Sproule; m. Betty Ann Mathis, Mar. 3, 1973; children: John Harold, Kevin William. BA, MA, Ohio State U., Columbus, 1971, PhD, 1973. Asst. prof. U. of Tex. of Permian Basin, Odessa, 1973—77; assoc. prof. Ind. U. S.E., New Albany, 1977—86; vis. lectr. U. of Calif., Berkeley, 1986—87; prof. San Jose (Calif.) State U., 1987—2001; prof., dir. Bowling Green (Ohio) State U., 2001—04; prof. St. Louis U., 2004—. Author: (book) The Rhetoric of Western Thought, Propaganda and Democracy, Channels of Propaganda, Speechmaking, Communication Today, Argument: Language and Its Influence. Recipient Golden Anniversary Monograph award, Nat. Comm. Assn., 1988; fellow, NEH, 1983. Mem.: Western States Comm. Assn., Internat. Soc. for the History of Rhetoric, Author's Guild, Nat. Comm. Assn. (pres. 2007). Home: 3655 Flora Pl Saint Louis MO 63110-3703 Office: St Louis Univ Saint Louis MO 63108 Home Phone: 314-772-8141. Business E-Mail: sproulej@slu.edu.

SPROULE, MICHAEL E., insurance company executive; b. Toronto, Can. m. Doreen Sproule; 3 children. BA in Math, Physics, U. Toronto, MBA in Fin., Mktg. Cons. Tillinghast; various positions MetLife; former sr. v.p., CFO Alper Holdings USA, Inc., NYC; exec. v.p., CFO AmerUs Group; sr. v.p. New York Life, 1999—2001, 2002—03, acting CFO, 2001, CFO, 2002—, exec. v.p., 2003—. Fellow: Soc. Actuaries; mem.: Am. Acad. Actuaries. Office: New York Life 51 Madison Ave New York NY 10010 *

SPROULL, ROBERT FLETCHER, research and development company executive; b. Ithaca, NY, June 6, 1947; s. Robert L. and Mary L. Sproull; m. Lee Sonastine, June 26, 1971; 1 child, Katherine. AB in Physics, Harvard U., 1968; MS in Computer Sci., Stanford U., 1970, PhD in Computer Sci., 1977. Mem. rsch. staff Xerox Palo Alto Rsch. Ctr., 1973—77; asst. prof. Carnegie Mellon U., Pitts., 1977-80, assoc. prof., 1980-83; v.p. Sutherland, Sproull & Assoc., Pitts., 1980-90, Sun Microsystems Lab., Burlington, Mass., 1990—2006, fellow, 1990—, interim dir., 2000—06, dir., 2006—. Venture ptnr. Advanced Tech. Ventures, 1981—; mem. tech. adv. coun. R. F. Donnelley & Sons, Chgo., 1981—89; mem. adv. com. NSF, Washington, 1990—97; bd. dirs. Alphatech, Inc., 2000—04. Co-author: (book) Principles of Interactive Computer Graphics, 1979, Logical Effort: Designing Fast CMOS Circuits (The Morgan Kaufmann Series in Computer Architecture and Design). Mem. sci. adv. bd. USAF, 1997—99. Sr. asst. health svcs. officer USPHS, 1970—72. Fellow: Am. Acad. Arts & Scis.; mem.: AAAS, NAE (councillor 2006—). Achievements include patents in field. Office: SUN Microsysystem Lab ubur02-311 1 Network Dr Burlington MA 01803-2757 Home Phone: 617-964-7793; Office Phone: 781-442-0353. Personal E-mail: bob.sproull@sun.com.

SPROULL, ROBERT LAMB, retired academic administrator, physicist, director; b. Lacon, Ill., Aug. 16, 1918; s. John Steele and Chloe Velma (Lamb) S.; m. Mary Louise Knickerbocker, June 27, 1942; children: Robert F., Nancy M. Sproull Highbarger. AB, Cornell U., 1940, PhD, 1943; LLD (hon.), Nazareth Coll., 1983; DMusic (hon.), New Eng. Conservatory, 1997. Research physicist RCA labs., 1943-46; faculty Cornell U., 1946-63, 65-68, prof. physics, 1956-63, dir. lab. atomic and solid state physics, 1959-60, dir. materials sci. center, 1960-63, v.p. for acad. affairs, 1965-68; dir. Advanced Research Projects Agy., Dept. Def., Washington, 1963-65; v.p., provost U. Rochester, NY, 1968-70, pres., 1970-84, pres. emeritus, 1984—. Prin. physicist Oak Ridge Nat. Lab., 1952; physicist European Rsch. Assoc., Brussels, 1958-59; lectr. NATO, 1958-59; pres. Environ. Literacy Coun., 1997-99, chmn. 1999—; past bd. dirs., John Wiley & Sons, Charles River Labs., United Technols. Corp., Xerox Corp., Bausch & Lomb; mem. sci. adv. com. GM Corp., 1971-80, chmn., 1973-80; mem. Def. Sci. Bd., 1966-70, chmn., 1968-70; mem. Naval Rsch. Adv. Com., 1974-76, Sloan Commn. Higher Edn., 1977-79, N.Y. Regents Commn. Higher Edn., 1992-93. Author: Modern Physics, 1956, A Scientist's Tools for Business, 1997; Editor: Jour. Applied Physics, 1954-57. Trustee Deep Springs Coll., 1967—75, 1983—87, Cornell U., 1972—77. Ctr. for Advanced Study in Behavioral Scis. fellow, 1973; Meritorious Civilian Svc. medal Sec. of Def., 1970. Fellow Am. Acad. Arts and Scis.; mem. Telluride Assn. (pres. 1945-47), Inst. of Def. Analysis (trustee 1984-92). Home: 6 Eliot Circle Pittsford NY 14534 Personal E-mail: lambspr@aol.com.

SPRUILL, W. MURRAY, lawyer; b. Columbia, NC, Mar. 24, 1954; BS in Biology, E. Carolina U., 1976; PhD in Genetics, Molecular Biology, NC State U., 1981; JD, George Washington U., 1992. Bar: Va. 1992, NC 1996, registered: US Patent and Trademark Off. Sr. atty. Ciba-Geigy Corp.; patent examiner US Patent and Trademark Office, Washington; ptnr., chmn., biotech., pharmaceutical patent group, Research Triangle Alston & Bird LLP, Raleigh, NC. Frequent lectr. and author on biotech. and pharmaceutical patent law. Office: Alston & Bird LLP Ste 600 3201 Beechleaf Ct Raleigh NC 27604-1062 Office Phone: 919-862-2202. Office Fax: 919-862-2260. Business E-Mail: murray.spruill@alston.com.

SPRUNG, ARNOLD, lawyer; b. NYC, Apr. 18, 1926; s. David L. and Anna (Stork) S.; m. Audrey Ann Caire; children: Louise, John, Thomas, Doran, D'Wayne. AB, Darmuth Coll., 1947; JD, Columbia U., 1950. Bar: N.Y. 1950, U.S. Dist. Ct. (so. dist.) N.Y. 1950, U.S. Patent Office 1952, U.S. Dist. Ct. (we. dist.) N.Y. 1954, U.S. Ct. Appeals (2d cir.) 1958, U.S. Ct. Customs and Patent Appeals 1958, U.S. Dist. Ct. (ea. dist.) N.Y. 1962, U.S. Dist. Ct. (no. dist.) Tex. 1971, U.S. Supreme Ct. 1971, and others. Sr. ptnr. Sprung, Kramer, Schaefer & Briscoe, Westchester, N.Y., 1950—. Lt. USN, 1943-46, PTO. Mem. ABA, N.Y. Intellectual Property Assn. Avocations: skiing, wind surfing, racquetball, biking, tennis. E-mail: asprung@aol.com.

SPRUNGER, KEITH L., historian, educator; b. Berne, Ind., Mar. 16, 1935; s. Arley and Lillian (Mettler) S.; m. Aldine Mary Slagell, June 13, 1959; children: David, Mary, Philip. BA, Wheaton Coll., 1957; MA, U. Ill., 1958, PhD, 1963. Tchr. Berne (Ind.) High Sch., 1958-60; Oswald H. Wedel prof. history Bethel Coll., N. Newton, Kans., 1963—2001. Author: Dutch Puritanism, 1982, The Learned Doctor William Ames, 1972, Voices

Against War, 1973, Auction Catalogue of The Library of William Ames, 1988, Trumpets From The Tower, 1994, Campus, Congregation, and Community, 1997. Mem. Newton Historic Preservation Commn.; bd. dirs. Germantown Mennonite Historic Trust. Recipient Harbison award Danforth Found., 1972; fellow Social Sci. Rsch. Coun., 1969, Am. Coun. Learned Soc. fellow, 1976, Huntington Libr. fellow, 1982, 90; grantee Am. Philos. Soc., 1967, 1969, 83, The Netherlands Orgn. for Advancement of Pure Rsch., 1983. Fellow Pilgrim Soc.; mem. AAUP, Am. Hist. Assn., Am. Soc. Ch. History (coun. 1974-76), Conf. on Faith and History, Dutch Mennonite Hist. Cir. Mennonite. Avocation: book and postcard collecting. Home: 2412 Clg Ave North Newton KS 67117 Office: Bethel Coll 300 E 27th St North Newton KS 67117 Office Phone: 316-283-2500. Business E-Mail: sprunger@bethelks.edu.

SPRY, DONALD FRANCIS, II, lawyer; b. Bethlehem, Pa., Nov. 17, 1947; s. Donald Francis and Carol Annette (Bolger) S.; m. Mary Frances, June 20, 1981; stepchildren: Michael Matlaga, Michelle Fehnel. BA, Moravian Coll., 1969; JD, U. Pitts., 1972. Bar: Pa. 1972, U.S. Dist. Ct. (ea. dist.) Pa. 1975. Assoc. Law Offices of Edmund P. Turtzo, Bangor, Pa., 1973—76; ptnr. Turtzo, Spry, Powlette & Sbrocchi, P.C., Bangor, 1976—83, Turtzo, Spry, Powlette, Sbrocchi & Faul, P.C., Bangor and Stroudsburg, Pa., 1983—90, Turtzo, Spry, Sbrocchi, Faul & LaBarre, P.C., Bangor and Stroudsburg, 1990—2000; mem. King, Spry, Herman, Freund & Faul, LLC, Bethlehem, 2001—. Capt. USAR, 1979-80. Mem. ABA (family law sect.), Pa. Bar Assn. (chmn. family law sect. edn. law com.) Northampton County Bar Assn. (family law com.), North County Bar Assn. (pres.-elect 1989, pres. 1990), Pa. Sch. Bds. Assn., Nat. Sch. Bds. Assn., ACLU, Edn. Law Assn., Pomfret Club. Republican. Methodist. Office: King Spry Herman Freund & Faul LLC 1 W Broad St Bethlehem PA 18018 Home Phone: 610-691-1215; Office Phone: 610-332-0390. Business E-Mail: dfs@kingspry.com.

SPUDICH, JAMES A., biology professor; b. Collinsville, Ill., Jan. 7, 1942; married, 1964; 2 children. BS, U. Ill., 1963; PhD in Biochemistry, Stanford U., 1968. Asst. prof. biochemistry U. Calif., San Francisco, 1971-74, assoc. prof., 1974-76; prof. structural biology, biochemistry and devel. biology Stanford U. Sch. Medicine, 1977—92. Editor: Annual Rev. Cell Biology, 1987-1998. Recipient Lewis S. Rosentiel award for disting. work in basic med. rsch., 1996, Repligen Corp. award, 1997. Mem. Am. Soc. Cell Biologists (pres. 1989), Nat. Acad. of Sci., 1991, Am. Acad. of Arts and Scis., 1997. Achievements include research in molecular basis of cytokinesis amoeboid movement and other forms of cell motility. Office: Stanford U Sch Medicine Dept Biochemistry Stanford Med Ctr Beckman Ctr B400 Stanford CA 94305-5307

SPUDICH, JOHN LEE, biochemist, molecular biologist, chemistry professor; PhD, Univ. Calif., Berkeley. Jane Coffin Childs Postdoctoral Fellow Harvard Univ.; prof., dept. biochemistry, molecular biology, microbiology and molecular genetics Univ. Tex. Houston Med. Sch., 1991—, and Robert A. Welch disting. chair in chemistry, 2002—, also dir., Ctr. for Membrane Biology, 2002—. Recipient Merit award, Nat. Inst. Gen. Med. Sci., NIH, 2003. Fellow: Am. Acad. Arts & Scis.; mem.: Am. Soc. Photobiology (past. pres.). Office: UT Houston Med Sch PO Box 20708 Houston TX 77225 Office Phone: 713-500-5473. Office Fax: 713-500-0545. Business E-Mail: John.L.Spudich@uth.tmc.edu. *

SPURGEON, DENNIS RAY, federal agency administrator, former manufacturing executive; b. Lake City, Iowa, Oct. 21, 1943; s. Merle Donald and Dorothy (Gidel) S.; m. Carrol Ann Malanoski, Feb. 19, 1966; children: Dennis Jr., Scott, Kimberly. BS, U.S. Naval Acad., 1965; SM in Nuclear Engring., MIT, 1969. Regional mgr. Gen. Atomic Co., Washington, 1973-75, exec. asst. to pres. San Diego, 1975-76; asst. dir. U.S. Energy Rsch. and Devel. Adminstrn., Washington, 1976-77; v.p. UNC Naval Products Div., Montville, Conn., 1977-78; pres. UNC Nuclear Industries, Richland, Wash., 1978-80; group v.p. UNC Inc., Falls Church, Va., 1980-85; chmn., CEO Swift Group LLC, Potomac, Md.; exec. v.p., COO USEC, Inc., 2001—03; asst. sec. for nuclear energy US Dept. Energy, Washington, 2006—. Chmn. Normco Contractors Inc., Morgan City, La., 1985—, NGS Enterprises Inc., Morgan City, 1985—. With USN, 1965-73. Office: US Dept Energy Forrestal Bldg 1000 Independence Ave SW Washington DC 20585

SPURGEON, EDWARD DUTCHER, lawyer, educator, foundation administrator; b. Newton, NJ, June 2, 1939; s. Dorsett Larew and Mary (Dutcher) S.; m. Carol Jean Forbes, June 17, 1963; children: Michael Larew, Stephen Edward. AB, Princeton U., 1961; LLB, Stanford U., 1964; LLM in Taxation, NYU, 1968. Bar: Calif. 1965. Assoc. atty. Stammer McKnight et al, Fresno, Calif., 1964-67, Paul Hastings Janofsky and Walker, LA, 1968-70, ptnr., 1971-80; prof. law U. Utah Coll. Law, Salt Lake City, 1980-90, Wm. H. Leary prof. law and policy, 1990-93, assoc. dean acad. affairs Coll. Law, 1982-83, dean Coll. Law, 1983-90, clin. prof., 2002—; dean Sch. Law U. Ga., Athens, 1993-98, prof., 1993—2002; ptnr. Moyle & Draper, Salt Lake City, 2000—03, of counsel, 2003—05. Vis. prof. law NYU, 1985, Univ. Coll. London, fall 1990, Stanford U. Law Sch., spring 1991, dist. vis. prof. law UOP-McGeorge Sch. of Law, 2003-; ex-officio mem. Utah State Bar Commn., 1984-90. Co-author: Federal Taxation of Trusts, Grantors and Beneficiaries, 1st edit., 1978, 2d edit., 1989, 3d edit., 1997. Mem. Utah Gov.'s Task Force Officers and Dirs. Liability Ins., 1985-87, Utah Dist. Ct. Reorgn. Commn., 1986-87, Justice in 21st Century Commn., Utah, 1989-91; bd. visitors, exec. com. Stanford U. Law Sch., 1988-93; pres., dir. Albert and Elaine Borchard Found., 1983—; exec. dir. Borchard Found. Ctr. on Law and Aging, 1998—; dir. Nat. Sr. Citizens Law Ctr., 1999—, pres., 2002-2005. Mem. ABA (Commn. on Legal Problems of the Elderly 1991-95, spl. advisor 1995-2003), Am. Bar Found.

SPURGEON, KENNETH R., history professor; b. Wichita, Kans., Jan. 28, 1964; s. R. L. and Donna V. Spurgeon; m. Amy D. Spurgeon, Jan. 20, 1996; children: Lauren S., Rebecca B., Sarah J., Jonathan G. BA in History, Wichita State U., Kans., 1997, MA in History, 2002. Dir. humanities, social and behavioral scis. Cowley Coll., Arkansas City, Kans., 2002—, instr. history and govt., 1999—. Exec. dir. Lone Chimney Films, Wichita, 2006—. Prodr. and writer: (documentaries) Touched by Fire: Bleeding Kansas. Home: 1804 N Columbine Andover KS 67002 Office: Cowley College 4501 E 47th St South Wichita KS 67210 Home Phone: 316-733-6752; Office Phone: 316-554-2758.

SPURLOCK, MORGAN, television producer, film producer; b. Parkersburg, W.Va., Nov. 7, 1970; m. Alexandra Jamieson, May 3, 2006. BFA, NYU, 1993. Prodr.: (TV series) I Bet You Will, 2002; exec. prodr.: 30 Days, 2005—; (films) Class Act, 2006; prodr., dir., writer: Super Size Me, 2004; actor: Drive-Thru, 2006; author: (book) Don't Eat This Book: Fast Food and the Supersizing of America, 2006. Mem.: ACLU.

SPURRIER, STEVE(N) (ORR), college football coach; b. Miami Beach, Apr. 20, 1945; m. Jerrie Spurrier. Quarterback San Francisco 49'ers, 1967-75, Tampa Bay Buccaneers, 1976; head coach Tampa Bay Bandits, USFL, 1983—85, Duke U., 1987—90, U. Fla., Gainesville, 1990—2002, Wash. Redskins, 2002—03, U. South Carolina, Columbia, 2004—. Winner Heisman Trophy, U. Fla., 1966. Office: Rex Enright Athletic Center 1300 Rosewood Drive Columbia SC 29208

SPYERS-DURAN, PETER, librarian, educator; b. Budapest, Hungary, Jan. 26, 1932; came to U.S., 1956, naturalized, 1964; s. Alfred and Maria (Almasi-Balogh) S-D; m. Jane F. Cumber, Mar. 21, 1964; children: Kimberly, Hilary, Peter. Certificate, Free U. Budapest, 1955; MA in L.S, U. Chgo., 1960; Ed.D., Nova S Ea. U., 1975. Profl. asst. libr. adminstrn. div. ALA, Chgo., 1961-62; assoc. dir. librs., assoc. prof. U. Wis., 1962-67; dir. librs., prof. Western Mich. U., 1967-70; dir. librs., prof. libr. sci. Fla. Atlantic U., 1970-76; dir. libr. Calif. State U., Long Beach, 1976-83; prof. libr. and info. sci., dir. libr. Wayne State U., Detroit, 1983-86, dean, prof. libr. and info. sci. program, 1986-95, dean and prof. emeritus, 1995—; cons. Spyers-Duran Assocs., 1995—; acting univ. libr. Nova Southeastern U., Ft. Lauderdale, Fla., 1996-97. Vis. prof. State U. N.Y. at Geneseo, summers 1969-70; cons. publs., libr. and info. scis.-related enterprises; chmn. bd. internat. confs., 1970—. Author: Moving Library Materials, 1965, Public Libraries - A Comparative Survey of Basic Fringe Benefits, 1967; editor: Approval and Gathering Plans in Academic Libraries, 1969, Advances in Understanding Approval Plans in Academic Libraries, 1970, Economics of Approval Plans in Research Libraries, 1972, Management Problems in Serials Work, 1973, Prediction of Resource Needs, 1975, Requiem for the Card Catalog: Management Issues in Automated Cataloging, 1979, Shaping Library Collections for the 1980's, 1981, Austerity Management in Academic Libraries, 1984, Financing Information Systems, 1985, Issues in Academic Libraries, 1985; mem. editorial bd. Jour. of Library Adminstration, 1989-95. Mem. Kalamazoo County Library Bd., 1969-70; Bd. dirs. United Fund. Reciient G. Flint Purdy award for outstanding contbns. Wayne State U., 1999. Mem. ALA, Mich. Libr. Assn., Internat. Fed. Libr. Assns., Assn. Info. Sci., Fla. Libr. Assn., Calif. Libr. Assn., Fla. Assn. Community Colls., Boca Raton C. of C., U. Chgo. Grad. Libr. Sch. Alumni Club (pres. 1973-75), Solinet Mich. Libr. Consortium (founder charter bd. mem. 1973—, bd. dirs. 1973-76), Detroit Area Libr. Network (pres. bd. dirs. 1985-95), Mich. Ctr. for Book (pres. 1988-89), Am. Soc. Info. Sci., Assn. Libr. and Info. Sci. Edn., Sago Point Homeowners Assn. (pres., bd. dirs. 2001-05), Bayou Club Cmty. Assn. (pres., bd. dirs. 2005—). Home: 7295 Maidencane Ct Largo FL 33777-4900 Office: Wayne State Univ Librs Detroit MI 48202 Business E-Mail: spyers-duran@wayne.edu, ae8249@wayne.edu.

SPYKER, LEOLA EDITH, missionary; b. Wallace, Mich., Mar. 15, 1925; d. Oscar Eugene Anderson and Edith Ragnhild Nelson; m. George Spyker, Feb. 16, 1951 (div. June 1967); children: Marilyn Joy, John George, Thomas Oscar, Sandra Lee. AA, N. Park U., Chgo., 1944; BA, Bob Jones U., Greenville, SC, 1947; postgrad. in Counseling, Seattle Pacific U., Seattle, Wash., 1969—70. Cert. in ESL Upton Coll., Pasadena, Calif., 1961, in French and Italian, Academia Uruapan, Michoacan, Mex. 1965, in Secondary Edn. Mich., Wis., Wash., Tex. Instr. King's Garden Sch., Seattle, 1969—71; lectr. Seminario El Calvario, El Carmen, Nuevo Leon, Mexico, 1971—74, 1977—80; lectr. in missionary outreach, anthropology, history, comparative religions Inst. Misionera Morelia, Michoacan, 1983—92; prof. U. Michoacan, Uruapan, Michoacan, Mexico, 1975—77, Mexico, 1982—84. Founder, dir. Casa Hogar La Esperanza, Uruapan, Michoacán, Mexico; conf. spkr. Vida Abundante, Morelia, Mexico, 1980—2003; coord. student groups to Honduras, Cuba, Nicaragua and Spain, 1995, 99, 2002; Spanish translator internat. conf. for Billy Graham, Amsterdam, 1996; worker refugee rehab. and outreach, Honduras, Nicaragua, 84, Honduras, Nicaragua, 86. Contbr. 40 articles to mission publs. Avocations: painting, travel, reading, ornithology. Home: PO Box 2050 2021 Harvey Dr Mcallen TX 78501 Office Phone: 956-682-6774. Personal E-mail: leolas@juno.com.

SQUATRITO, DOMINIC J., judge; BA, Wesleyan U., 1961; JD, Yale U., 1965. Sr. judge US Dist. Ct. Conn., 1994—. Fulbright scholar, U. Florence, Italy, 1962. Office: US Dist Court 450 Main St 1st Fl Ste 108 Hartford CT 06103-3010 Office Phone: 860-240-3873.

SQUERI, STEPHEN, diversified financial services company executive; BS, MBA, Manhattan Coll. Cons. Arthur Andersen & Co., 1981—85; mgmt. positions Am. Express, NYC, 1985—2000, pres. establishment services, U.S. & Canada, 2000—01, pres. global comml. card group, 2002—05, exec. v.p., CIO, 2005—. Office: Am Express Am Express Tower World Fin Ctr 200 Vesey St New York NY 10285 *

SQUIBB, SAMUEL DEXTER, chemistry professor; b. Limestone, Tenn., June 20, 1931; s. Benjamin Bowman and Lou Pearl S.; m. JoAnn Kyker, Dec. 15, 1951; children: Sandra Lavanne, Kevin Dexter. BS, E. Tenn. State U., 1952; PhD, U. Fla., 1956. Assoc. prof., dir. chemistry Western Carolina U., Cullowhee, NC, 1956-60; asst. prof., dir. chemistry Eckerd Coll., St. Petersburg, Fla., 1960-63, asso. prof., 1963-64; prof. chemistry U. N.C., Asheville, 1964-94, prof. emeritus, 1994—, chmn. dept., 1964-94. Vis. prof. U. NC, Chapel Hill, 1976-81, 83-87, 92-95, Clemson U., SC, 1982; cons. So. Assn. Colls. and Schs., State of W.Va. Author: Experimental Organic Chemistry, 1972, Understanding Chemistry One, 1979, rev. 1990, Two, 1981, rev. 1991, Three, 1981, rev. 1992, Four, 1981, rev. 1992, Five, 1981, rev. 1989, Six, 1984, Chemistry One, 1976, rev. 1987, Two, 1980, rev. 1990, Experimental Chemistry One, 1976, rev. 1988, Two, 1981, rev. 1991; contbr. articles to profl. jours. Mem. Grose United Meth. Ch. Disting. Tchr. award U. N.C.-Asheville, 1983; S.D. Squibb Disting. Chemistry Lectureship U. N.C., Asheville, established 1997; named to We. Carolina Fedn. Square and Round Dancing Hall of Fame, 2001; recipient Pres.'s Svc. award, Folk, Round and Square Dancing Fedn. N.C., 2001. Fellow Am. Inst. Chemists (life, nat. publs. bd. 1988-92); mem. Am. Chem. Soc. (Charles H. Stone award Carolina Piedmont sect. 1979, Disting. Chemist award Western Carolinas sect. 1993, chmn. Tampa Bay subsect. 1963, Western Carolina sect. 1981, editor Periodic News Western Carolina sect. 1980-2007), NC Inst. Chemists (pres. 1977-79, sec. 1975-77, 85-91, Disting. Chemist award 1986), Skyland Twirlers Square Dance Club, Silver Spurs Advanced Square Dance Club, Jerry's Kids Advanced Square Dance Club, Skylarks Round Dance Club, Phi Beta Kappa.

SQUIER, DAVID LOUIS, manufacturing executive; b. Buffalo, Oct. 30, 1945; s. Clayton L. and Ruth H. Squier; m. Sue Sampson, Aug. 12, 1967; children: Jennifer, Allison. BS in Mech. Engring., Lehigh U., 1967; MBA, Wharton Sch., U. Pa., 1971. With mfg. mgmt. program GE, various cities, 1967-70; mgr. corp. planning Howmet Corp., Greenwich, Conn., 1971-73, mgr. corp. and bus. planning Muskegon, Mich., 1973-75, plant mgr. Hampton, Va., 1976-78, gen. mgr. Wichita Falls, Tex., 1979-82, v.p. Greenwich, 1983-87, sr. v.p., 1987-89, exec. v.p., 1989-91, COO, 1991-92, pres., CEO, 1992-2000, also bd. dirs., advisor, 2000—. Mem. rev. and prioritization bd. Iacocca Inst., Bethlehem, Pa., 1990—. Office: Howmet Corp 1 Misco Dr C Whitehall MI 49461-1755

SQUIER, JACK LESLIE, sculptor, retired art educator; b. Dixon, Ill., Feb. 27, 1927; s. Leslie Lee and Ruth (Barnes) S.; m. Jane Bugg, June 9, 1950. Student, Oberlin Coll., Ohio, 1945—46; BS, Ind. U., Bloomington, 1950; M.F.A., Cornell U., Ithaca, NY, 1952. Instr. Cornell U., 1952, asst. prof. art, 1958—61, assoc. prof., 1961—65, prof. art, 1965—2005, prof. emeritus, 2005—. Designer Howatt Pottery Co., N.Y.C., 1953; account exec. Jamian Advt. Co., N.Y.C., 1954-58; asst. prof. U. Calif., Berkeley, 1960; mem. Internat. Assn. Art, UNESCO, 1964-72, mem. exec. com., 1966-69, v.p., 1969-72 One-man shows include Alan Gallery, N.Y.C., 1956, 59, 62, 64, White Mus., Cornell U., 1959, 68, Instituto de Arte Contemporaneo, Lima, Peru, 1963, Landau-Alan Gallery, N.Y.C., 1966, 69, Herbert F. Johnson Mus., Cornell Univ. (retospective of work, 1953-93); exhibited in group shows at Mus. Modern Art, N.Y.C., 1957, Whitney Mus., N.Y.C., 1952, 54, 56, 58, 62, 67, 78, Hirshhorn Mus., Washington, 1978, Mus. Fine Arts, Boston, 1958, Chgo. Art Inst., 1960, Brussel's Worlds Fair, 1956, competition, Auschwitz, Poland, 1957, Albright-Knox Mus., Buffalo, 1968, Claude Bernard Gallery, Paris, 1957, Hanover Gallery, London, 1958; represented in permanent collections Mus. Modern Art, N.Y.C., Whitney Mus. Art, Hirshhorn Mus., Instituto de Arte Contemporaneo, Everson Mus., Syracuse, N.Y., Stanford U. Mus., St. Lawrence U. Mus., SUNY at Potsdam, Ithaca Coll., Johnson Mus. at Cornell U., Houston Mus., Hamilton Coll. Mus., Hood Mus.-Dartmouth (N.H.) U., Castellani Mus., Niagara U., N.Y., Fogg Mus., Harvard U., Cambridge; bronze garden piece at Fogg Mus./Harvard U., Conn. Conservancy; retrospective exhbn. Herbert F. Johnson Mus. Cornell U., 1993; work pub. in various, books, mags., newspapers, slide collections, catalogs. Served with AC USN, 1945-47. Home: 6217 Celadon Cir Palm Beach Gardens FL 33418

SQUIRE, ALEXANDER, management consultant; b. Dumfrieshire, Scotland, Sept. 29, 1917; s. Frederick John and Lillian (Ferguson) S.; m. Isabelle L. Kerr, June 23, 1945; children: Jonathan, David, Deborah, Stephen, Philip, Martha, Timothy, Rebecca, Elizabeth. BS, MIT, 1939. Research metallurgist Handy and Harman, Fairfield, Conn., 1939-41; devel. metallurgist Sullivan Machinery Co., Michigan City, Ind., 1941-42; head powder metallurgy br. Watertown Arsenal Lab., Mass., 1942-45; mgr. metall. devel. Westinghouse Electric Corp., Pitts., 1945-50; project mgr. Bettis Atomic Power Lab., Pitts., 1950-62; gen. mgr. plant apparatus div. Westinghouse, 1962-69; dir. purchases and traffic Westinghouse Electric Corp., 1969-71; pres. Westinghouse Hanford Co., Richland, Wash., 1971-79; bus. cons. Richland, 1979-80; dep. mng. dir. Wash. Public Power Supply System, 1980-85, cons., 1985—. Mem. Nat. Acad. Engring., Am. Nuclear Soc., Am. Soc. Metals, AIME, Am. Def. Preparedness Assn. Address: Pittsboro Christian Village 1825 East St Pittsboro NC 27312

SQUIRE, ANNE MARGUERITE, retired humanities educator; b. Amherstburg, Ont., Can., Oct. 17, 1920; d. Alexander Samuel and Coral Marguerite Park; m. William Robert Squire, June 24, 1943; children: Frances, Laura, Margaret. BA, Carleton U., Ottawa, 1972, BA with honors, 1974, MA, 1975; LLD (hon.), Carleton U., 1988; DD (hon.), United Theol. Coll., 1979, Queen's U., 1985. Cert. tchr., Ont. Adj. prof. Carleton U., 1975-82; sec. div. ministry personnel and edn. United Ch. Can., Toronto, 1982-85, moderator, 1986-88; ret., 1988. Author curriculum materials, 1959—; contbr. articles to profl. jours. Mem. bd. mgmt. St. Andrew's Coll., Saskatoon, Sask., 1982, Queens Theol. Coll., Kingston, Ont., 1999-2005; founding mem. Muslim-Christian Dialogue Group; patron MultiFaith Housing Initiative; hon. advisor Can. Ctr. for Progressive Christianity. Recipient Senate medal Carleton U., 1972. Mem. Can. Research Inst. for Advancement Women, Delta Kappa Gamma (pres. 1978-79). Mem. United Ch. Can. Office: 731 Weston Dr Ottawa ON Canada K1G 1W1 E-mail: a.squire@sympatico.ca.

SQUIRE, DANIEL HARRIS, lawyer; b. Huntington, NY, Apr. 14, 1954; BA summa cum laude, Yale U., 1976; JD magna cum laude, Harvard U., 1980. Bar: DC 1980, US Ct. Appeals (DC, fed., 1st, 2nd, 4th, 8th and 10th cir.), US Ct. Internat. Trade, US Ct. Fed. Claims, US Dist. Ct. DC, Fed. dist. cts. nationwide, Superior Ct. DC. Assoc. Wald, Harkrader & Ross, Washington, 1980-85; ptnr. Skadden, Arps, Slate, Meagher & Flom, Wash., 1985—, Wilmer Cutler Pickering Hale and Dorr LLP, Wash., DC. Co-author: Hazardous Waste Regulation Handbook, 1985; contbr. chpts. to manuals, articles to law jours. Mem.: Phi Beta Kappa. Office: Wilmer Cutler Pickering Hale and Dorr LLP 1875 Pennsylvania Ave NW Washington DC 20006 Office Phone: 202-663-6000. Office Fax: 202-663-6363. Business E-Mail: daniel.squire@wilmerhale.com.

SQUIRE, LARRY RYAN, neuroscientist, psychologist, educator; b. Cherokee, Iowa, May 4, 1941; s. Harold Walter and Jean (Ryan) S.; children: Ryan, Luke. BA, Oberlin Coll., 1963; PhD in Psychology, MIT, 1968; postgrad., Albert Einstein Med. Coll., 1968-70. With U. Calif. San Diego (UCSD), 1970—, prof., 1981—; rsch. career scientist VA Med. Ctr., San Diego, 1980—; mem. faculty U. Calif. Irvine Ctr. Neurobiology of Learning & Memory, 1981—. Lectr. in field. Editor, author: Memory and Brain, 1987; co-author: Memory: From Mind to Molecules, 1999; editor Behavioral Neuroscience, 1990-95; mem. editl. adv. bd. numerous profl. jours.; contbr. articles to profl. jours., chpts. to books. Recipient Charles A. Dana Award for Pioneering Achievements in Health and Education, 1993, Disting. Sci. Contbn. award APA, Lashley prize Am. Philosophical Soc., McGovern award AAAS; William James fellow Am. Psychol. Soc. Mem. Nat. Acad. Scis., Am. Acad. Arts and Scis., Soc. Neurosci. (pres. 1994), Am. Philos. Soc., Inst. Medicine. Office: UCSD SDVAMC 3350 La Jolla Village Dr San Diego CA 92161 Office Fax: 858-552-7457. E-mail: lsquire@ucsd.edu.

SQUIRE, WALTER CHARLES, lawyer; b. NYC, Aug. 5, 1945; s. Sidney and Helen (Friedman) S.; m. Sara Jane Abamson; children: Harrison, Russell, Zachary, Andrew. BA, Yale U., 1967; JD, Columbia U., 1971. Bar: N.Y. 1971, U.S. Dist. Ct. (so. and ea. dists.) N.Y. 1975, U.S. Ct. Appeals (2d cir.) 1974, U.S. Supreme Ct. 1977. Ptnr. Jones Hirsch Connors & Bull P.C., NYC, 1986-98, Jacobson, Mermelstein & Squire, LLP, NYC, 1998—; prin. Squire & Co., LLC, NYC, 1998—. Bd. govs. Arthritis Found. N.Y., Inc., 1993-99; bd. dirs. MedicAlert Found., N.Y., 1990-99. Mem. ABA, N.Y. State Bar Assn., Assn. of Bar of City of N.Y., Internat. Bar Assn., Licensing Execs. Soc., Chartered Inst. Arbitrators (London), Am. Arbitration Assn. (arbitrator 1975-2000, mediator 1993—), Am. Acad. Hosp. Attys., Risk Ins. Mgmt. Soc. (lectr. 1983-84), AIDA Reinsurance & Ins. Arbitration Soc. (cert.). Office: Jacobson Mermelstein et al 52 Vanderbilt Ave New York NY 10017-3808 Office Phone: 212-697-1420.

SQUIRES, ARTHUR MORTON, chemical engineer, educator; b. Neodesha, Kans., Mar. 21, 1916; s. Charles Loren and Vera Amber (Moore) S. AB with distinction in Chemistry, U. Mo., 1938; PhD, Cornell U., 1947. Design engr. M.W. Kellogg Co., NYC, 1942-46; asst. dir. process devel. Hydrocarbon Research, Inc., NYC, 1946-51, dir. process devel., 1951-59; cons. chem. process industries NYC, 1959-67; prof. chem. engring. CUNY, 1967-74, disting. prof., 1974-76, chmn. dept. chem. engring., 1970-73; Vilbrandt prof. chem. engring. Va. Poly. Inst. and State U., Blacksburg, 1976-82, disting. prof., 1978-86, disting. prof. emeritus, 1986—. Author: The Tender Ship, 1986; editor: (with D.A. Berkowitz) Power Generation and Environmental Change, 1971; contbr. articles to profl. jours.; patentee in field Mem. N.Y. Pro Musica, 1953-60 Fellow Am. Acad. Arts and Scis., AAAS; mem. ASME, NAE, AIChE (inst. lectr.), Am. Chem. Soc. (Henry H. Storch award 1973), Internat. Soc. for Human Ethology, Human Behavior and Evolution Soc., Sigma Xi, Tau Beta Pi Avocation: performing medieval and renaissance music. Home: 2710 Quincy Ct Blacksburg VA 24060-4124 Office: Va Poly Inst and State U Dept Chem Engring Blacksburg VA 24061 Home Phone: 540-951-8369. Business E-Mail: verasqu@vt.edu.

SQUIRES, JAMES A., rail transportation executive; Atty. Norfolk So. Corp., Va., 1992, sr. gen. counsel, 2002—03, v.p. law, 2003—04, sr. v.p. law, 2004—06, sr. v.p. fin. planning, 2006—07, exec. v.p. fin., 2007—, CFO, 2007—. Office: Norfolk So Corp Three Commercial Pl Norfolk VA 23510-2191 Office Phone: 757-629-2680. *

SQUIRES, JAMES RALPH, development company executive; b. Jan. 2, 1940; s. William Guilford and Ruby Alice (Whittington) S.; m. Ann Newton, Apr. 17, 1965; children: Samuel Guilford, James Drew. Student, pub. schs., Charlotte, NC. With Squires Constrn. Co., 1959-62; pres. SBS Builders, Inc., Charlotte, 1968-70, Ralph Squires Homes, Charlotte, 1970-88, Squires & Assocs., Realtors, 1975-88. Bd. dirs., mem. exec. com. Park Meridian Bank, 1991, Dover Mortgage, First Landmark; chmn. Squires Enterprises, Inc. Mem. Charlotte Tree Commn., 1977; bd. dirs. Athletic Found. U. N.C., Charlotte, 1979-84, Better Bus. Bur., 1983, MMAES Inn, 1983-87, Charlotte Symphony; pub. mem. N.C. State Bar,

1980-85; pres. Metrolina Home Owners, 1982, bd. dirs., 1983; bd. govs. Polit. Action Com. for Bldg. Industry; mem. bd. visitors Mercy Hosp., Charlotte, 1986; bd. dirs. Mercy Hosp. Found., chmn., 1993—; chmn. new bldg. fund United Cerebral Palsy; mem. exec. coun. Mecklenburg County coun. Boy Scouts Am., 1986-90; mem. exec. coun. Muscular Dystrophy Assn., Charlotte, 1987; mem. N.C. Wildlife Resources Commn., 1995-98 bd. dirs. Harris YMCA, N.C. March of Dimes, 1997. Recipient Profile award N.C. Blue Cross/Blue Shield, 1974, Albert Gallatin merit cert., 1974; named Charlotte Builder of Yr., 1977. Mem. Nat. Homebuilders Assn., N.C. Homebuilders Assn. (v.p. 1975), Charlotte Homebuilders Assn. (pres. 1974), Charlotte Bd. Realtors, Carolina Ambs., Quail Hollow Country Club, Old North State Country Club, Grandfather Golf and Country Club, Brays Island Plantation. Republican. Baptist. Home: 6828 Phillips Place Ct Charlotte NC 28210-2715

SQUIRES, JOHN, publishing executive; b. Pocatelllo, Idaho; BA, U. Washington, 1981. Asst. circulation director People Mag., 1989—92; consumer mktg. dir. Entertainment Weekly & Sports Ilustrated Mag., 1992—96; pres. Entertainment Weekly Mag., 1998—2002; sr. v.p. consumer mktg. Time Inc., NYC, 1996—98, exec. v.p., 2002—04, pres., sports & leisure group, 2004—05, co-COO, 2005, exec. v.p. Sports Illus. Named to Direct Mktg. Assn. Circulation Coun. Circulation Hall of Fame, 2003. Office: Sports Illustrated 1271 Avenue of the Americas New York NY 10020-1300 *

SQUIRES, KELLEY ELIZABETH, music educator; b. Wheaton, Ill., June 1, 1973; d. David Guild and Mary Ann Squires. BSc, U. of Ill., 1993—99; MusM, U. of Conn., 2002—04. Teaching Credential Calif., 2004. Choral music dir./chairperson Workman Arts and Entertainment Acad., City of Industry, Calif., 2004—05; vocal music dir. Wellesley HS, Mass., 2002—04; vocal music dir./cheerleading coach Ottumwa HS, Iowa, 1999—2002, Beckman Jr/Sr HS, Dyersville, Iowa, 1996—99; choral mus. dir. Rancho Cucamonga HS, Calif., 2005—. Actress, choreographer, dir. Ottumwa Cmty. Players, Ottumwa, Iowa, 2000—02; freelance choreographer, 1991—; vocalist, actress, dancer, 1980—; cheerleading pep coach Rancho Cucamonga HS, 2005—. Mem. Visual and Performing Arts Taskforce, Hacienda La Puente, Calif., 2004—05; vocalist and runner Susan G. Komen Breast Cancer Orgn., Ottumwa, Iowa, 1999—2002; choir mem. First Evang. Free Ch. of Fullerton, Calif., 2004—05; vocalist Brookridge Cmty. Ch., Bradford, Mass., 2002—04. Presdl. scholarship, Culver-Stockton Coll., 1991—93. Mem.: Internat. Jazz Educators Assn., So. Calif. Vocal Assn., Music Educators Nat. Conf., Am. Choral Directors Assn., Wellesley Cmty. Players, Grand Opera Ho., Ottumwa Cmty. Players, Sigma Alpha Iota, Alpha Xi Delta Frat. (v.p., social chmn., song leader, and chaplain 1991—96). Independent. Christian/Protestant. Avocations: singing, swimming, cooking, travel, dance. Office: Rancho Cucamonga HS 11801 Lark Dr Rancho Cucamonga CA 91701 Home: 10950 Church St Apt 2022 Rancho Cucamonga CA 91730-8079 Personal E-mail: kelleysquires@yahoo.com. E-mail: kelley_squires@cjuhsd.k12.ca.us.

SQUIRES, NANCY, psychology professor; PhD, U. Calif., San Diego, 1972. Prof. biopsychology SUNY, Stony Brook, chairperson Dept. Psychology. Office: Dept Psychology SUNY Stony Brook Psychology B154 Stony Brook NY 11794 Office Phone: 631-632-7808. E-mail: nancy.squires@stonybrook.edu.

SQUIRES, RICHARD FELT, research scientist; b. Sparta, Mich., Jan. 15, 1933; s. Monas Nathan and Dorothy Lois (Felt) S.; m. Else Saederup, 1 child, Iben. BS, Mich. State U., 1958; postgrad., Calif. Inst. Tech., 1958-61. Rsch. biochemist Pasadena Found. for Med. Rsch., 1961-62; chief biochemistry sect. rsch. dept. A/S Ferrosan, Soeborg, Denmark, 1963-78; neurochemistry group leader CNS Biology sect. Lederle Labs. div. Am. Cyanamid Co., Pearl River, NY, 1978-79; prin. rsch. scientist The Nathan S. Kline Inst. for Psychiat. Rsch., Orangeburg, NY, 1979-2000, ret., 2000. Contbr. over 85 articles to profl. jours.; patentee in field. Nat. Inst. Neurol. and Communication Disorders and Stroke grantee, 1981-84. Mem. Soc. Neurosci., Collegium Internat. Neuro-Psychopharmacologicum, Internat. Soc. Neurochemistry, Am. Soc. Neurochemistry, Am. Soc. Biochemistry and Molecular Biology, Am. Soc. Pharmacology and Exptl. Therapeutics. Home: 861 Laugenour Ct Woodland CA 95776-4911 Personal E-mail: else_dick@hotmail.com.

SQUIRES, WILLIAM ALLEN, distribution company executive; b. Springfield, Mass., May 30, 1949; s. Robert P. and Irma Ruth (Alpert) Squires; m. Nancy Faye Weiner, Nov. 15, 1981; children: Maxine Rhea, Sarah Jill, Michelle Anne. BA, U. Pa., 1971; postgrad., Temple U., 1971-74. Cert. CPR, first aid instr. ARC. V.p. Esquire Gas Products Co., Enfield, Conn., 1972-87, pres., 1987—. Mem. assoc. bd. Enfield Nat. Bank, Enfield, Conn., 1989—91. Singer: Spl. Olympic World Games Opening Ceremony, 1995, Makhela Choral Group; soloist for nat. anthem: numerous minor league and coll. sports events. Mem. local emergency planning com. Town of Enfield, 1988—; bd. dirs. Jewish Family Svc. Greater Springfield, Mass., 1983—86, Goodwill Industries Springfield-Hartford Area, Inc., 1997—2003; life mem. Friends of Storrowton; torchbearer Olympic Torch Relay, 1996; mem. distbn. com. Springfield Jewish Endowment Found., 2006; bd. dirs. Congregation Kodimoh; mem. Kodimoh Brotherhood, v.p., 2001—02; mem. we. Mass. athletic recruiting com. U. Pa., chmn. we. Mass. athletic recruiting com., 1974—2005, mem. We. Mass. Secondary Sch. Com., chmn. We. Mass. Secondary Sch. com., 1974—84, mem. N.E. regional adv. bd., bd. assoc. alumni trustees. Finalist Family Bus. of Yr. award, U. Conn. Sch. Bus., 2003. Mem.: U. Pa. Alumni Assn. (pres. We. Mass. Club 1974—2005, pres. We. New Eng. Club 1975—2005, v.p. class of 1971 1981—2006), Nat. Wildlife Fedn. (life), Nat. Audubon Soc. (life), Enfield Rotary Club (pres. 1982—83), Rotary Internat. (dist. sec. 1984—85, dist. gov.'s area rep. 1995—96, Paul Harris fellow 1988, 2000), Delta Upsilon Alumni (treas. U. Mass. chpt. 1979—82). Jewish. Home: 33 Willow Cir Longmeadow MA 01106-2152 Office: Esquire Gas Products Co PO Box 281 156 Spring St Enfield CT 06082-3431

SQUIRES, WILLIAM RANDOLPH, III, lawyer; b. Providence, Sept. 6, 1947; s. William Randolph and Mary Louise (Gress) S.; m. Elisabeth Dale McAnulty, June 23, 1984; children: Shannon, William R. IV, Mayre Elisabeth, James Robert. BA in Econs., Stanford U., 1969; JD, U. Tex., 1972. Bar: Wash. 1973, U.S. Dist. Ct. (we. dist.) Wash. 1973, U.S. Dist. Ct. (ea. dist.) Wash. 1976, U.S. Ct. Appeals (9th cir.) 1976, U.S. Supreme Ct. 1976, U.S. Ct. Fed. Claims 1982. Assoc. Oles, Morrison, Rinker, Stanislaw & Ashbaugh, Seattle, 1973-78; ptnr., chmn. litig. group Davis Wright Tremaine, Seattle, 1978-97; mem. Summit Law Group, Seattle, 1997—2007, chmn., 2005—07; of counsel Corr Cronin Michelson Baumgardner & Preece, Seattle, 2007—. Fellow Am. Coll. Trial Lawyers; mem. ABA, Internat. Bar Assn., Wash. State Bar Assn., King County Bar Assn., Wash. Athletic Club, Rainier Club (Seattle). Episcopalian. Home: 5554 NE Penrith Rd Seattle WA 98105-2845 Office: Corr Cronin Michelson Baumgardner and Preece 1001 Fourth Ave Ste 3900 Seattle WA 98154 Home Phone: 206-524-8634; Office Phone: 206-652-8658. Business E-Mail: rsquires@corrcronin.com.

SQUYRES, STEVEN WELDON, astronomy educator, planetary geology researcher; b. Woodbury, NJ, Jan. 9, 1956; m. Mary Squyres; children: Katie, Nicole. BA in Geology, Cornell U., 1978, PhD in Planetary Sci., 1981. Assoc. Voyager imaging sci. team, 1978—81; radar investigator Magellan mission to Venus; mem. Mars Observer gamma-ray spectrometer flight investigation team; co-investigator Russian Mars '96 Mission; assoc. NRC, Ames Rsch. Ctr., NASA, 1981—86; assoc. prof. dept. astronomy Cornell U., 1986, Goldwin Smith prof. astronomy; mem. Planetary Geol. Working Group, NASA, 1982—; scientific principal investigator Mars Exploration Rover Project, twin rovers, Spirit and Opportunity; co-investigator Mars Express Mission, Mars Reconnaissance Orbiter's High Resolution Imaging Science Experiment; mem. Gamma-Ray Spectrometer Flight Investigation Team, Mars Odyssey mission; mem. imaging team Cassini mission to Saturn. Chair space sci. adv. com. NASA, mem. adv. coun. Author: Roving Mars: Spirit, Opportunity, and the Exploration of the Red Planet, 2005; contbr. articles to profl. jours. Recipient Harold C. Urey prize, 1987, Carl Sagan award, Am. Astronomical Soc., 2004, Rave Award in Science, WIRED, 2005, Benjamin Franklin medal in Earth and Environ. Sci., Franklin Inst., 2007. Fellow World Tech. Network (World Tech. Network award (Space), 2005); mem. AAAS, Am. Geophys. Union. Office: Cornell U 428 Space Sciences Bldg Ithaca NY 14853 Office Phone: 607-255-3508. E-mail: squyres@astro.cornell.edu. *

SREEBNY, LEO M., oral biology and pathology professor; b. NYC, Jan. 8, 1922; s. Morris and Lillie (Bogdanoff) S.; m. Mathilda H. Sternfeld, Mar. 9, 1945; children: Oren, Daniel. BA, U. Ill., 1942, D.D.S., 1945, MS, 1950, PhD, 1954; MD (hon.), Semmelweis Med. U., 2001. With dept. periodontics U. Ill., 1948-57, asso. prof., 1956-57; asso. prof., chmn. dept. oral biology U. Wash., Seattle, 1957-60, prof., 1960-75; dir. U. Wash. (Center for Research Oral Biology), 1967-75; dean Sch. Dental Medicine, SUNY-Stony Brook, 1975-79, prof. dept. oral biology and pathology, 1979—. Cons. VA Hosp., Seattle, 1960—; mem. dental study sect. NIH, 1964-68, chmn., 1967-68; mem. com. on sci. policy Nat. Acad. Sci., 1973-74; mem. med. adv. coun. Internat. Conf. on Integrative Medicine, 1998-99. Author: (with Julia Meyer) Secretory Mechanisms in Salivary Glands, 1963, The Salivary System, 1987, (with I. Van der Waal) Diseases of the Salivary Glands, 1997; contbr. numerous articles to sci., biol. jours. Mem. med. adv. bd. Sjogren's Syndrome Found., 1997, bd. govs. 1998—. Served with AUS, 1942-45; with USNR, 1946-48. Recipient Internat. Assn. for Dental Research Sci. award, 1969; Silver medal for contbns. to dental sci. and art City of Paris, 1979; Salivary Research Group Award, 1987. Mem. Fedn. Dentaire Internat. (chmn. sci. assembly com. 1973—, rep. UN Conf. on Youth 1983-84), Internat. Assn. Dental Research (bd. govs. 1981), Fedn. Dentaire Internat. (list of honor 1988), Am. Assn. Dental Research, ADA. Home: 35 Gnarled Hollow Rd East Setauket NY 11733-2929 Office: SUNY Stony Brook Sch Dental Medicine Stony Brook NY 11794-0001 E-mail: lsreebny@usa.net.

SREENIVASAN, KATEPALLI RAJU, mechanical engineer, educator; b. Kolar, India, Sept. 30, 1947; married 1980; 2 children. BE, Bangalore U., 1968; ME, Indian Inst. Sci., 1970, PhD in Aero. Engring., 1975. JRD Tata fellow Indian Inst. Sci., 1972-74, project asst., 1974-75; fellow U. Sydney, Australia, 1975, U. Newcastle, 1976-77; rsch. assoc. Johns Hopkins U., Balt., 1977-79; asst. prof. to assoc. prof. Yale U., New Haven, 1982-85, prof. mech. engring., 1985—2002, Harold W. Cheel prof. mech. engring., 1988—2002, prof. physics, 1990—2002, prof. applied physics, 1993—2002; Disting. Univ. prof., dir. Inst. Phys. Sci. and Tech., U. Md., College Park, 2002—; Abdus Salam hon. prof., dir. Internat. Ctr. Theoretical Physics, Trieste, Italy. Vis. scientist Indian Inst. Sci., 1979, vis. prof., 1982, Calif. Inst. Tech., Pasadena, 1986, Rockefeller U., 1989, Jawaharlala Nehru Ctr. Advancement Sci. Studies, 1992, chmn. mech. engring. dept., 1987-92; vis. prof. DFVLR, Gottingen, Germany, 1983; mem. Inst. Advanced Study, Princeton, NJ, 1995. Contbr. articles to Physics World and other profl. jours. Recipient Narayana Gold medal Indian Inst. Sci., 1975, Disting. Alumnus award, 1992; Humboldt Found. fellow, 1983, Guggenheim fellow, 1989. Fellow AAAS, ASME, Am. Phys. Soc. (Otto Laporte award 1995), AIAA (assoc.), Am. Acad. Arts and Scis., Third World Acad. Scis. (Engring. Sci. medal 2003), Conn. Acad. Arts and Scis.; mem. NAS, NAE, Am. Math. Soc., Conn. Acad. Sci. and Engring., Sigma Xi. Achievements include research in origin and dynamics of turbulence; control of turbulent flows; chaotic dynamics; fractals. Office: U Md 4211 Computer & Space Scis Bldg College Park MD 20742-2431 Office Phone: 39-040-224-0250, 301-405-4878. E-mail: krs@ictp.trieste.it, sreeni@umd.edu. *

SRERE, BENSON M(ORTIMER), communications executive, consultant; b. Rock Island, Ill., Aug. 13, 1928; s. Jacob H. and Margaret (Weinstein) S.; m. Betty Ann Cerruti, June 20, 1957; children: David Benson, Anne Michele, Peter John. BA magna cum laude, U. So. Calif., 1949. Newsman U.P., LA, 1948-56; assoc. editor Good Housekeeping mag., NYC, 1956-59, sr. editor, 1959-67, asst. mng. editor, dir. spl. publs. div., 1967-68, mng. editor, 1968-72, exec. editor, v.p., 1972-75, v.p., editorial dir., 1975-76; v.p., gen. mgr. King Features Syndicate, 1976-81; v.p. Hearst Metrotone News, 1976-81; exec. asst. to pres. Hearst Corp., 1981—, v.p., 1983-94. Dir. Hearst/ABC Video Svcs., Hearst/ABC Viacom Entertainment Svcs., A&E Cable Network, Lifetime Cable Network, 1980-94. Trustee Optometric Center of NY Found., 1978-79. Served with U.S. Army, 1950-52. Mem. Soc. Profl. Journalists, Phi Beta Kappa, Phi Kappa Phi, Phi Eta Sigma. Home: 11 Lafayette Ct Greenwich CT 06830-5324

SRIDHARAN, SUGANDHI, neurologist; d. Suppiah and Rani Sinnatamby; m. Mailvaganam Sridharan, Mar. 18, 1999. MBBS, North Colombo Med. Coll., Ragama, Sri Lanka, 1994. Intern Coney Island Hosp., Bklyn., 2000—01; resident North Shore U. Hosp., Manhasset, NY, 2001—04; neurologist Kalamazoo Neurology P.C., 2005—. Fellow, North Shore U. Hosp., 2004—05. Fellow: Am. Assn. Neuromuscular and Electrodiagnostic Medicine; mem.: Am. Acad. Neurology. Office: Kalamazoo Neurology PC 1541 Gull Rd Ste 100 Kalamazoo MI 49048 Home Phone: 269-344-0734; Office Phone: 269-381-7380. Office Fax: 269-381-1608. Personal E-mail: sugandhisri@msn.com.

SRINIVASAGUPTA, DEEPAK, chemical engineer, researcher; s. Ranganayaki Sanji and Srinivasa Gupta Aravela. Bachelor of Tech. with honors, Indian Inst. Tech., Kharagpur, West Bengal, 1998; MS, Washington U., St. Louis, 2001, DSc, 2002. Cert. in lab. safety, U. South Fla., Tampa, 2003, in cleanroom safety, U. South Fla., Tampa, 2003, in high pressure gas cylinder safety, U. South Fla., Tampa, 2003, in personal protection equipment, U. South Fla., Tampa, 2003, in hazard comm., U. South Fla., Tampa, 2004, in workers compensation for suprs., U. South Fla., Tampa, 2004, in solid edge fundamentals, Pella Corp., 2005. Engr. Bhoruka Gases Ltd., Bangalore, Karnataka, India, 1997; testing engr. Aspen Tech. Inc., Cambridge, Mass., 2000; grad. rsch. and tchg. asst. Wash. U., Saint Louis, Mo., 1998—2002; post-doctoral rsch. assoc. U. South Fla., Tampa, 2003—04, vis. rsch. asst. prof., 2004; sr. composite process engr. Pella Corp., Murray, Ky., 2004—. Lectr. in field. Author: (literary column) International Policy for the 21st Century, Do Appearances Matter, Judicial Activism: Self-serving and Ill-thought?; contbr. articles to profl. jours. Mentor Upward Bound, Murray, Ky., 2005; webmaster Grad. Professsional Coun., Wash. U., Saint Louis, Mo., 1999—2000; web designer Dept. Chem. Engring., Wash. U., Saint Louis, 1999—2000. Recipient Best Hall Coun. Mem. award, Indian Inst. Tech., 1995-1996, Prem Internat. Award, AVOPA, 1998; fellow, Dept. Chem. Engring., Wash. U., 1998-2000, Boeing McDonnell Found., Wash. U., 2000-2002; Nat. Talent Search Scholarship, Govt. of India, 1992-1998. Mem.: Am. Chem. Soc., IEEE, AIChE (AIChE Process Devel. Division's Student Paper Award 2004), Am. Radio Relay League, World Wildlife Fund, Murray State U. Amateur Radio Club (assoc.), Mensa, Tau Beta Pi, Sigma Xi (life). Achievements include invention of time-stamped model predictive control algorithm; research in sensor fault detection. Home Phone: 270-753-4387; Office Phone: 270-767-2676. E-mail: deepu134@gmail.com.

SRINIVASAN, AMIA P., Philosophy scholar; b. Bahrain; BS in Philosophy, Yale Univ., 2007; PhD student in Philosophy, Oxford Univ., 2007—. Dem. ward chair New Haven. Recipient 2nd Place prize, Elie Wiesel Prize in Ethics Essay Contest; Rhodes Scholar. Achievements include being founder of Yale Philosophy Rev.; winning nat. and Yale prizes for work in ethics, philosophy, and lit. *

SRINIVASAN, ASHOK, radiologist; s. Natarajan and Vijayalakshmi Srinivasan; m. Prachi Agarwal. MBBS, Madras Med. Coll., Chennai, 1998; MD, All India Inst. Med. Scis., New Delhi, 2003. Diplomate Nat. Bd. of Medicine, India, 2002. Clin. fellow in neuroradiology U. Ottawa, Ont., Canada, 2003—05; clin. lectr. in radiology U. Mich. Health Sys., Ann Arbor, 2005—06, asst. prof. radiology, 2006—. Mem.: Radiol. Soc. N.Am. Achievements include research in predictive value of MRI in patients with multiple sclerosis. Office: University of Michigan Health System 1500 E Medical Center Dr Ann Arbor MI 48109 Home Phone: 734-397-0415; Office Phone: 734-936-8825. Business E-Mail: ashoks@med.umich.edu.

SRINIVASAN, HEMA, mathematics professor, researcher; d. M.R. and Vedavalli Srinivasan; m. Steven D. Cutkosky; 2 children. BSc with honors, South Indian Edn. Coll., Bombay, 1978; MS, Ind. U., Bloomington, Ind., 1982; PhD, Brandeis U., Waltham, Mass., 1986. Vis. instr. Mich. State U., East Lansing, 1986—88; rsch. asst. prof. Purdue U., West Lafayette, 1988—89; asst. prof. U. Mo., Columbia, 1989—93, assoc. prof., 1993—97, prof., 1997—. Gen. mem. Math. Scis. Rsch. Inst., Berkeley, Calif., 2002; vis. fellow Chennai Math. Inst., India, 1991; vis. prof. Northwestern U., Boston, 2000—00. Editor: (book) Commutative Algebra and Algebraic Geometry, Contemporary Math., 2005. Recipient Ghia Math. prize, Bombay U., 1978; fellow, IBM, 1984—86; Nat. Sci. Talent scholar, Nat. Coun. Edn. Rsch. and Tng., India, 1975—80, Rsch. grants, Nat. Sceince Found., 1989—2000. Mem.: Assn. Women Math. Office: Univ Mo Department of Mathematics Columbia MO 65211 Office Phone: 573-882-1452. Office Fax: 573-882-1869. Business E-Mail: srinivasanh@missouri.edu.

SRINIVASAN, PURUSHOTHAMAN, electrical engineer, researcher; s. Srinivasan Vengadabalagurumoorthy and Vijayalakshmi Srinivasan. BS in Electronics and Comm. Engring., Pondichary U., India; PhD, IMEC/N.J. Inst. Tech., 2007. Sr. design engr. Whirlpool Corp., St. Joseph, Mich., 1999—2002; rschr. N.J. Inst. Tech., University Heights, 2002—07; sr. device engr. Contour Semicondrs., Billerica, Mass., 2007—. Cons. InPHot Inc., Princeton, NJ, 2004. Contbr. articles to profl. jours. Recipient Recognition, Whirlpool Corp., 2001, Electronic Design Ctr. Excellence award, 2001, Best Innovator, 2002; grantee, N.J. Inst. Tech., 2003—, U. Md., 2003; Hashimoto fellow, N.J. Inst. Tech., 2005—06, Internat. scholar, Interuniversity Microelectronics Ctr., 2004—05. Mem.: IEEE, Electrochem. Soc. (Travel grantee 2003, 2004, 2005). Achievements include research in High-k dielectrics. Home: 7 Hardwood Dr Billerica MA 01862 Personal E-mail: purushothaman@ieee.org.

SRINIVASAN, RANGASWAMY, chemical physicist; b. Madras, India, Feb. 28, 1929; came to U.S., 1953; s. K. Rangaswamy. BSc with honors, Madras U., India, 1949; PhD, U. So. Calif., 1956. Mgr., rsch. T.J. Watson Rsch. Ctr. IBM, Yorktown Heights, NY, 1961-90; chief exec. officer UV Tech Assocs., Ossining, NY, 1990—. Vis. rsch. prof. chemistry Ohio State U., Columbus, 1966-67, Wellman Lab., Mass. Gen. Hosp., Boston, 1987-89, Columbia-Presbyn. Med. Ctr., N.Y.C., 1984-90. Editor: (books) Organic Photochemical Syntheses, Vol. 1., 1972, Vol. 2, 1976; contbr. over 200 articles to profl. jours. Guggenheim fellow, 1966; recipient award for creative invention Am. Chem. Soc., 1997, Essalen award for chemistry in the pub. interest, 1997. Fellow AAAS, Am. Physical Soc. (Biol. Physics prize 1998), NY Acad. Scis., Am. Soc. Laser Medicine and Surgery; mem. NAE (Inventor's Hall of Fame 2002), Am. Inst. Physics (Indsl. Applications prize 2003), Optical Soc. Am. (Wood prize 2004). Achievements include invention of Ablative Photodecomposition, a laser technique for removal of microscopic thickness of organic matter such as plastics (of use in microelectronics) or tissue (of use in LASIK eye surgery).

SRINIVASAN, VENKATARAMAN, marketing and management educator; b. Pudukkottai, Tamil Nadu, India, June 5, 1944; came to U.S., 1968; s. Annaswamy and Jambagalakshmi Venkataraman; m. Sitalakshmi Subrahmanyam, June 30, 1972; children: Ramesh, Mahesh. B Tech., Indian Inst. Tech., Madras, India, 1966; MS, Carnegie-Mellon U., 1970, PhD, 1971. Asst. engr. Larsen & Toubro, Bombay, 1966-68; asst. prof. mgmt. and mktg. U. Rochester, NY, 1971-73, assoc. prof. NY, 1973-74, Stanford (Calif.) U., 1974-76, prof., 1976-82, dir. PhD program in bus., 1982-85, Ernest C. Arbuckle prof. mktg. and mgmt. sci., 1982—2003, Adams disting. prof. mgmt., 2003—; mktg. area coord. Stanford U., 1976—78, 1988—93, 2000—03. Mem. bd. acad. trustees Mktg. Sci. Inst., 2004—; cons. in field. Mem. editl. bd. Jour. Mktg. Rsch., 1988—, Mktg. Sci., 1980—, Mgmt. Sci., 1974-91; contbr. articles to profl. jours. Mem. Am. Mktg. Assn., Inst. Ops. Rsch./Mgmt. Scis. Hindu. Avocation: classical music.

SRIRAM, S., educator; b. Neyveli, Tamil Nadu, India, Nov. 3, 1973; s. Saroja Raghavan; m. Priya Rajagopal, Mar. 6, 2003. PhD, Purdue U., West Lafayette, Ind., 2004. Asst. prof. SUNY, Binghamton, 2004—05, U. Conn., Storrs, 2005—. Home: 36 westview Ave Shewsbury MA 01545 Office: Univ Conn Sch Bus 2100 Hillside Rd Storrs Mansfield CT 06269 Home Phone: 508-842-2421; Office Phone: 860-486-9351. Business E-Mail: ssriram@business.uconn.edu.

SRIRANGARAJAN, SESHAN, electrical engineer, researcher; arrived in US, 2001; s. Srirangarajan H.R. and Vathsala Srirangarajan. B of Engring. in Electronics, U. Mumbai, India, 2001; MSEE, U. Minn., Mpls., 2005, postgrad. in electrical engring., 2001—. Tchg. asst. U. Minn., 2002—04, rsch. asst., 2004—; intern Honeywell Internat., Mpls., 2005—06; grad. instr. dept. elec. and computer engring. U. Minn., Mpls., 2007—. Recipient Cert. Appreciation award, Royal Commonwealth Soc., 1995, Outstanding Tchg. Asst. award, U. Minn., 2002—04, Technical award, Honeywell Tech. Ctr., 2006; grantee Golden Jubilee Scholarship, Tata Chem. Found., 2001. Mem.: IEEE. Hindu. Achievements include patents pending for installation procedure for anchor location information in people and asset localization. Home: 921 24th Ave S Apt # 7 Minneapolis MN 55406 Office: U Minn 200 Union St SE 4-174 EE/CSci Bldg Minneapolis MN 55455 Office Fax: 612-625-4583; Home Fax: 612-625-4583. Business E-Mail: seshan@umn.edu.

SRIVASTAVA, PUNEET, engineering educator, researcher; s. Virendra Kumar and Shail Srivastava; m. Priya Srivastava, Dec. 1997. BTech, Allahabad Agrl. Inst., India, 1992; MS in Biol. and Agrl. Engring., U. Ark., Fayetteville, 1995; PhD in Agrl. and Biol. Engring., Pa. State U., University Park, 1999. Asst. curator Patrick Ctr. Environ. Rsch. Acad. Natural Scis., Phila., 2001—04; asst. prof. Auburn U., Ala., 2004—. Office: Auburn Univ 200 Corley Bldg Auburn AL 36849

SRIVASTAVA, SANJEEV KUMAR, electrical engineer, researcher; b. Gorakhpur, Uttar Pradesh, India, Jan. 27, 1976; s. Sant and Saroj Srivastava; m. Ankita Saxena. BS in Engring., Madan Mohan Malviya Engring. Coll., Gorakhpur, India, 1993—97; MS in Tech., Indian Inst. Tech. Delhi, 1997—99; PhD, Tex. A&M U., Coll. Station, 2000—03. Exec. project engr. Secure Meters Ltd., New Delhi, 1999—2000; asst. scholar sci. Ctr. Advanced Power Sys., Tallahassee, 2003—. Presenter in field. Mem.: IEEE (v.p. various socs. 2002—03), Alumni Assn. Indian Inst. Tech. Delhi, Power Engring. Soc., Instn. Engring. & Tech. Achievements include research in probabilistic assessment of damage caused due to a weapon hit; incorporating probability in electrical power system reconfiguration process; agent based reconfiguration of power systems; intelligent systems applications to power systems. Office: Ctr Advanced Power Sys 2000 Levy Ave Tallahassee FL 32310 Business E-Mail: sanjeev@ieee.org.

SROCK, MARLENE, elementary school educator; b. Wells, Minn., 1951; BS in Elem Edn., Saint Cloud State Univ., 1973; MS in Elem Edn., Minot State Univ. Named ND Tchr. of Yr., 2007. Office: Bel Air Elem Sch 501 25 St NW Minot ND 58703 Business E-Mail: m.srock@sendit.nodak.edu.

SROKA, JOHN WALTER, trade association executive; b. Perth Amboy, NJ, July 24, 1946; s. John and Mary (Teliszewski) S.; m. Paula J. Devitt, Aug. 17, 1968; children: Amanda, Alexandra. BA in Psychology, Fairleigh Dickinson U., 1968, postgrad., 1968-69; postgrad. in law, Am. U., 1972-73. Asst. exec. dir. Associated Gen. Contractors of Am., Washington, 1973-87; exec. v.p. Nat. Assn. Sheet Metal and Air Conditioning Contractors, Chantilly, Va., 1987—. Sgt. U.S. Army, 1969-71. Mem. Am. Soc. Assn. Execs. Roman Catholic. Office: SMACNA 4201 Lafayette Center Dr Chantilly VA 20151-1219 Office Phone: 703-803-2980. Business E-Mail: jsroka@smacna.org.

SRONCE, ASHLEY RANDALL, comedian, writer; b. Asheville, NC, Feb. 19, 1975; BA in Philosophy, U. NC, Chapel Hill, 1997. Photoboater Nantahala Outdoor Ctr., Bryson City, NC, 1999—2002; comedienne, actress, writer, lounge pianist NYC, 2001—; editor Pennypress, Norwalk, Conn., 2003—06. Adventure travel photographer Nantahala Outdoor Ctr., Nepal, 1999—2001. Volunteer, Kibo Art Gallery - Murals; author (artist): (blog) The Scuttlebutt Grunt. Mem.: Am. MENSA (life). Achievements include invention of dog leash. Home Phone: 917-531-7933. Personal E-mail: ashleysronce@gmail.com.

SRULOWITZ, MARVIN, lawyer; BA, AA, Yeshiva U., 1969; JD, NYU, 1972. Bar: N.Y. 1973, U.S. Dist. Ct. (ea. and so. dists.) N.Y. 1973, U.S. Ct. Appeals (2d cir.) 1974, U.S. Ct. Internat. Trade 1976, U.S. Supreme Ct. 1976. Assoc. Delson & Gordon, NYC, 1972-77, Mayer Nussbaum Katz & Baker, P.C., NYC, 1977-80; sole practice NYC, 1981—. Mem. New York County Lawyers Assn., Am. Arbitration Assn. Office: 16 E 34th St 16th Fl New York NY 10016-4359 Office Phone: 212-686-1224. Office Fax: 212-532-3206. Business E-Mail: marvinlaw@aol.com.

STAAB, DIANE D., lawyer; BA, CUNY Hunter Coll., 1977; JD, Yeshiva U., 1980. Bar: N.Y. 1981. Assoc. atty. Hall, McNicol, Hamilton & Clark, 1980-84, Patterson, Belknap, Webb & Tyler, 1984-87; corp. counsel Internat. Paper Co., 1987—95; v.p., gen. counsel, corp. ethics/environ. compliance officer Ariz. Chem., Panama City, 1996—2001; gen. counsel Internat. Paper Europe, 2001—. Mem. ABA (mem. bus. law sect. fed. ref. of securities com. 1988-2001, vice-chmn. com. on corp. & bus. legis. subcom. on corp. governance 1992-98), Assn. of the Bar of the City of N.Y. (mem. spl. com. on election law 1987-89, mem. corp. law com. 1989-92, sec. com. on corp. law dept. 1992-93). Office: Internat Paper 400 Atlantic St Stamford CT 06921 Office Phone: 32 02 774 1254.

STAAB, THOMAS ROBERT, consumer product company financial executive; b. Beaver Falls, Pa., Apr. 23, 1942; s. Henry Louis and Margaret Constance (Clarke) S.; m. Angela Maria Simon, Aug. 6, 1965; children: Thomas II, Jennifer, Thea. BBA, U. Pitts., 1964, MBA, 1965. CPA, Pa. Sr. audit mgr. Price Waterhouse & Co., Pitts., 1970-77; practice fellow Fin. Acctg. Standards Bd., Stamford, Conn., 1978-80; dir. corp. acctg. and taxes Fieldcrest Cannon Inc., Eden, NC, 1981-84, asst. contr., 1985, contr., 1986-91, v.p. fin., 1992-93, CFO, 1994-97; bd. dirs., sr. v.p., CFO Lorillard Inc., Greensboro, NC, 1998—. Served to lt. USN, 1966-70. Mem. AICPA, Pa. Inst. CPAs. Republican. Roman Catholic. Home: 3726 NC # 65 Reidsville NC 27320 Office: Lorillard Inc PO Box 10529 714 Green Valley Rd Greensboro NC 27404-0529

STAAL, ERIC, professional hockey player; b. Thunder Bay, Ont., Can., Oct. 29, 1984; Center Carolina Hurricanes, 2003—. Player NHL YoungStars Game, 2004. Achievements include being a member of Stanley Cup Champion Carolina Hurricanes, 2006. Office: Carolina Hurricanes RBC Ctr2 1400 Edwards Mill Rd Raleigh NC 27607

STAATS, ARTHUR W., psychology professor; b. Jan. 17, 1924; BA in Psychology, UCLA, 1949, MA in Psychology, 1953, PhD in Gen. Exptl. and Clin. Psychology, 1956. Psychologist UCLA Counseling Ctr., Los Angeles, 1950-53; clin. trainee VA Hosps., Los Angeles, 1953-55; instr. psychology Ariz. State U., Tempe, 1955-56, asst. prof., 1956-58, assoc. prof., 1958-60, prof., 1960-64; NSF faculty fellow U. London, 1961-62; vis. prof. U. Calif., Berkeley, 1964-65; prof. ednl. psychology and research U. Wis. Research and Devel. Ctr. Cognitive Learning, Madison, 1965-67; vis. prof. U. Hawaii, Honolulu, 1966-67, prof. psychology and ednl. psychology, 1967—. Author Complex Human Behavior, 1963, Learning, Language and Cognition, 1968, Child Learning, Intelligence, and Personality: A Behavioral Interaction Approach, 1971, Social Behaviorism, 1975, Psychology's Crisis of Disunity: Philosophy and Method for a Unified Science, 1983, Behavior and Personality: Psychological Behaviorism, 1996; editor Human Learning, 1964, Current Issues in Theoretical Psychology, 1987, Annals of Theoretical Psychology, Vol. 5, 1987; contbr. over 80 articles to profl. jours. and 61 chpts. to books; editl. bd. 9 Am. and internat. jours. Named in his honor, Arthur W. Staats Unifying Psychology lectr. (annually). Fellow AAAS, Am. Psychol. Soc., APA (gen. psychology divsn., exptl. psychology divsn., devel. psychology divsn., personality and social psychology divs., clin. psychology divsn., ednl. psychology divsn., theoretical and philos. psychology divsn., exptl. analysis of behavior divsn.); mem. Sociedad Interamericana de Psicologia, Psychonomic Soc., Assn. Latinoamericana del Analisis y Modificacion del Comportamiento, Soc. for Exptl. Social Psychology. Home: 1460 Kamole St Honolulu HI 96821-1422 Office: U Hawaii Dept Psychology Honolulu HI 96822 Office Phone: 808-377-3195. Business E-Mail: staats@aloha.com.

STAATS, DEAN ROY, retired reinsurance executive; b. Somerville, NJ, Sept. 18, 1924; s. Roy Theodore and Mabel Ellen (Rhodes) S.; m. Marilyn Ann Hockenbury, 1947 (div. 1956; 1 child, Barry Clinton; m. Marilyn Lee Truitt, Dec. 16, 1961 B.Sc., Brown U., 1946, MA, 1948. Asst. actuary N.Am. Reassurance Co., NYC, 1959-67, data processing officer, 1967-69, v.p., actuary, 1969-71, sr. v.p., 1971-84, exec. v.p., 1984-86; pres., dir. NARe Life Mgmt. Co., NYC, 1985-86; rep. Life Ins. Guaranty Corp, 1977-86; U.S. mgr. Can. Reassurance Co., 1984-86; cons. actuary, 1986-89. Served to lt. (j.g.), USN, 1943-46, PTO Fellow Soc. Actuaries; mem. Am. Acad. Actuaries N.Y. Jr. Actuaries Club (pres. 1960-61), Soc. Actuaries (reins. adminstrn. com. 1984-85) Clubs: Anchor and Saber (pres. 1959-60). Republican. Avocations: art, tennis, gardening, travel. Home and Office: 3 Post Run Newtown Square PA 19073-3014 Home Phone: 610-356-5236; Office Phone: 610-356-5236.

STAATS, THOMAS ELWYN, neuropsychologist; s. Percy Anderson and Julia (Bourmorck) S.; m. Debra R.; children: Lauren Malu, Kara Kristyn, Stacy Rhnea, Ronald Derek. BA cum laude, Emory U., 1970; MA, U. Ala., 1972, PhD, 1974; postgrad., U. Tex., Tyler, 1992. Diplomate Am. Bd. Profl. Disability Cons.; lic. psychologist. Dir., chief psychologist Caddo Parish Diagnostic Ctr., Shreveport, La., 1974-81; exec. dir. Doctors Psychol. Ctr., Shreveport, 1979-91, Comprehensive Assessments, 1991—. Cons. to Charter Forest Hosp., 1989-2000, Shreveport Impairment and Disability Evaluation Ctr., 1993—; clin. assoc. prof. psychology La. State U., Shreveport, 1977-1990; clin. assoc. prof. psychiatry La. State U. Sch. Medicine, Shreveport, 1980-92, 2003—; neuropsychol. cons. to dept. psychiatry, 1992-2002; mem. faculty Am. Acad. Disability Evaluating Physicians, 1986—, Health South Impairment Evaluation Lectr. Series, 1998—. Author: Manual for the Stress Vector Analysis Test Series, 1983, The Doctors Guide to Instant Stress Relief, 1987, Stress Management and Relaxation Training System Handbook; contbr. articles to profl. jours. and popular mags. Mem. Gov.'s Com. of 1000, La., 1979. Recipient AADEP award, 1991; Grad. Rsch. Coun. fellow, 1974. Fellow Am. Inst. Stress; mem. APA, Nat. Acad. Neuropsychology, Nat. Register of Health Svc. Providers. Episcopalian. Avocations: scuba diving, gun collecting, camping, boating, paintball competition. Home: 4 Beaux Rivages Dr Shreveport LA 71106 Office: Comprehensive Assessments Inc 4300 Youree Dr Ste 200 Shreveport LA 71105 Office Phone: 318-424-2354. Personal E-mail: drtomstaats@bellsouth.net.

STABENOW, DEBORAH ANN, senator, former congresswoman; b. Gladwin, Mich., Apr. 29, 1950; d. Robert Lee and Anna Merle (Hallmark) Greer; m. Tom Athans; children: Todd Dennis, Michelle Deborah. BS magna cum laude, Mich. State U., 1972, MSW magna cum laude, 1975. With spl. svcs. Lansing (Mich.) Sch. Dist., 1972-73; county commr. Ingham County, Mason, Mich., 1975-78; state rep. State of Mich., Lansing, 1979—91, state senator, 1991—94; mem. 103rd-106th Congress from Mich. 8th dist. U.S. Ho. Reps., 1997—2001; US Senator from Mich., 2001—. Founder Ingham County Women's Commn.; co-founder Council Against Domestic Assault. Recipient Service to Children award Council for Prevention of Child Abuse and Neglect, 1983, Disting. Service to Mich. Families award Mich. Council Family Relations, 1983, Outstanding Leadership award Nat. Council Community Mental Health Ctrs., 1983, Snyder-Kok award Mental Health Assn. Mich., Awareness Leader of Yr. award Awareness Communications Team Developmentally Disabled, 1984, Communicator of Yr. award Woman in Communications, 1984, Lawmaker of Yr. award Nat. Child Support Enforcement Assn., 1985, Disting. Service award Lansing Jaycees, 1985, Disting. Service in Govt. award Retarded Citizens of Mich., 1986, Cmty. award Mich. Mental Health, 1988, Boxing Glove award Nat. Com. to Preserve Social Security and Medicare, 1999, Home Health Hero Nat. Assn. for Home Care, 1999, Friend of Farm Bur. Mich. Farm Bur., 1999, Leadership award Nat. Coun. of Space Grant Dirs., 1998, Outstanding Achievement Nat. Farmers Union, 1998, Legislator of Yr. award Nat. Multiple Sclerosis Soc., 1992, Assn. for Children's Mental Health, 1991, Mich. Assn. of Vol. Adminstrs., 1989, Citizens Alliance to Uphold Spl. Edn., 1989, Recognition award State 4-H Alumni, 1991, Public. Elected Ofcl. award Nat. Assn. Social Workers, 2004, Congressional Support for Sci. award Inst. Food Technologists, 2004, Cmty. Health Defender award Nat. Assn. Cmty. Health Centers, 2005; named One of Ten Outstanding Young Ams. Jaycees, 1986. Mem. NAACP, Nat. Assn. Social Workers, Lansing Regional C. of C., Delta Kappa Gamma. Democrat. Meth. Office: US Senate 702 Hart Senate Office Bldg Washington DC 20510 also: District Office Ste 100 221 W Lake Lansing Rd East Lansing MI 48823-8661 Office Phone: 202-224-4822, 517-203-1760. Office Fax: 202-228-0325, 517-203-1778. E-mail: senator@stabenow.senate.gov. *

STABILE, BRUCE EDWARD, surgeon; b. Monterey Park, California, Apr. 14, 1944; s. Edward Emilio and Angela (Cramandozzi) S.; m. Caroline Graston, Sept. 18, 1967; children: Jessica, Drew. BA, UCLA, 1966; MD, U. Calif., San Francisco, 1970. Diplomate Am. Bd. Surgery. From assoc. prof. to prof. vice chmn. dept. surgery Sch. Medicine U. Calif., San Diego, 1985—93; from asst. prof. to assoc. prof. Sch. Medicine UCLA, 1977—85, vice chmn. dept. surgery Sch. Medicine, 1993—. Chmn. dept. surgery Harbor UCLA Med. Ctr., Torrance, 1993—, acting med. dir., 1997-98; interim assoc. dean UCLA Sch. Medicine, 1997-98; med. expert Med. Bd. Calif., 1980—; bd. dirs. Am. Bd. Surgery, 1998-2004. Mem. editl. bd.: Jour. Surg. Rsch., 1993—97, Archives of Surgery, 1991—2004. Fellow ACS (gov. 2001—, pres. So. Calif. chpt. 2005-06), Am. Surg. Assn.; mem. Soc. Univ. Surgeons, Assn. Acad. Surgery, Am. Gastroenterol. Assn., San Diego Soc. Gen. Surgeons (pres. 1992-93), L.A. Surg. Soc. (pres. 2000-01), Pacific Coast Surg. Assn. (pres. 2007—). Office: Harbor U Calif at L A Med Ctr 1000 W Carson St Torrance CA 90502-2004 Office Phone: 310-222-2701. Business E-Mail: bstabile@ucla.edu.

STABILE, PATRICE CHRISTINE, mathematics educator; b. Bronx, Aug. 19, 1956; d. Herman and Dolores Hansen; m. Stephen Lawrence Stabile, Aug. 11, 1979; children: Kristen Patrice, Robert Lawrence. BA, Iona Coll., New Rochelle, NY, 1978; MA, We. Conn. State U., Danbury, 2006. Math tchr. Msgr. Scanlan H.S., Bronx, NY, 1978—84, Wappingers Jr. H.S., Wappingers Falls, NY, 2001—. Substitute tchr. Wappingers Ctrl. Sch. Dist., NY, 1998—2001. Pres. Oak Grove PTA, Poughkeepsie, NY, 1993—97; cheerleading coach Wappingers Pop Warner, Wappingers Falls, NY, 2001—06, Wappingers Jr. High, 2006—. Named Rotary Club Tchr. of the Yr., Rotary Club, 2005. Home: 66 Helen Dr Wappingers Falls NY 12590 Office: Wappingers Junior High School 30 Major Macdonald Way Wappingers Falls NY 12590-3740 Home Phone: 845-297-0936; Office Phone: 845-298-5200. Office Fax: 845-298-5156. Personal E-mail: btm819@msn.com.

STABLER, LEWIS VASTINE, JR., lawyer; b. Greenville, Ala., Nov. 5, 1936; s. Lewis Vastine and Dorothy Daisy Stabler; m. Monteray Scott, Sept. 5, 1958; children: Dorothy Monteray Scott, Andrew Vastine, Monteray Scott Smith, Margaret Langston. BA, Vanderbilt U., 1958; JD with distinction, U. Mich., 1961. Bar: Ala. 1961. Assoc. Cabaniss & Johnston, Birmingham, Ala., 1961-67; assoc. prof. law U. Ala., 1967-70; ptnr. Cabaniss, Johnston, Gardner, Dumas & O'Neal (and predecessor firms), Birmingham, 1970-91, Walston, Stabler, Wells, Anderson and Bains, Birmingham, 1991-97; pvt. practice, Birmingham, 1997—. Mem. com. of 100 Candler Sch. Theology, Emory U. Bd. editors: Mich. Law Rev, 1960-61. Fellow Am. Bar Found. (life); mem. Am. Law Inst. (life), Ala. Law Inst. (mem. coun., dir. 1968-70), ABA, Ala. Bar Assn., NASD (arbitrator), Birmingham Bar Assn., Am. Judicature Soc., Am. Assn. R.R. Trial Counsel, Order of Coif. Methodist (cert. lay speaker). Clubs: Country of Birmingham, Rotary. Home: 3538 Victoria Rd Birmingham AL 35223-1404 Office: PO Box 53-1161 Birmingham AL 35253-1161 Office Phone: 205-970-4990. Personal E-mail: vstabler@gmail.com.

STABLER, RUSSEL W., insurance agent; b. Williamsport, Pa., Oct. 25, 1948; s. Hiram Clifford Stabler and Rebbeca Nmi Holmes. BS in Edn., U. ND, Grand Forks, 1992. Security specialist supr. USAF, 1964—87; security supr. ASP Moorhead, Fargo, ND, 1989—97; tchr. Amidon, ND, 1992; owner ND Notary Pub., Fargo, 1998—, Tiger Leader Field Inspection Svc., Fargo, 2001—. Avocations: reading, stamp collecting/philately, needlecrafts, model building.

STABY, DOROTHY LOUISE, elementary school educator; b. Washington, July 26, 1932; d. Charles Pemberton and Eleanor (Thompson) Sheffield; m. Jack Bradford Staby, Oct. 27, 1956; children: John Bradford, Robert Stanford, Mary Katherine. BS in Edn. with honors, James Madison U., 1954; MA, State U. Iowa, 1955; postgrad., Columbia U., 1957, Bklyn. Coll., 1957, SUNY, New Paltz, 1962, SUNY, Binghamton, 1993. Cert. elem., health and phys. edn. tchr., N.Y. Tchr. phys. edn. Garden City (N.Y.) High Sch., 1955-58; substitute tchr.1st-12th grades Amityville Sch., Capaigue Sch., Massapeque Sch., LI, N.Y., 1958-63; tchr. 1st and 2d grades St. Patricks Elem. Sch., Owego, N.Y., 1969-70; tchr. 5th grade Glenwood Elem. Sch., Vestal, N.Y., 1970-83; tchr. 2d grade Clayton Ave. Elem. Sch., Vestal, NY, 1983—97. Head, counselor Coll. Settlement Farm Camp, Willow Grove, Pa., 1954-55; instr. Iowa City Recreation Dept., 1955; counselor Garden City Recreation Dept., 1956-57, Country Day Camp, Plainedge, N.Y., 1960-62; tchr. computer Vestal Schs., 1983-87, Vestal Recreation Dept., Vestal, 1989-90, health tchr. Vestal H.S., 1988. Reading vol. Clayton Ave Elem. Sch., 1997—. State U. Iowa scholar, 1954-55. Mem. NEA, AAUW, N.Y. Edn. Assn., Vestal Ret. Tchrs. Assn. Democrat. Methodist. Avocations: computers, reading, sports. Home: PO Box 475 Little Meadows PA 18830-0475 E-mail: jds56@cableracer.com.

STACEY, JAMES ALLEN, retired judge; b. Norwalk, Ohio, Dec. 26, 1925; s. James Calvin and Glenna (Cleveland) S.; m. Marlyn Frederick, Aug. 21, 1948; children: James A. Jr., Libble M. Romigh, Lorrie Stacey Singler, David F., CamAllison Shenigo, Tricia Stacey Berger. Student, Bucknell U., 1943—44, Ohio Wesleyan U., 1944—46, U. N.C., 1944—45; JD, Cleveland-Marshall Law Sch., 1951. Bar: Ohio 1952, U.S. Dist. Ct. (no. dist.) Ohio 1955. Ptnr. McGory & Stacey, Sandusky, Ohio, 1954—56; assoc. Steinemann & Zieher, Sandusky, Ohio, 1956—60; ptnr. Work, Stacey & Moyer, 1960—67; judge Sandusky Mcpl. Ct., 1967—95, ret., 1995. Mem. Ohio State Traffic Law Com., 1969-95, chmn., 1978-82. Mem. Sandusky Jaycees, 1952-62, Erie-Ottawa Mental Health Bd., 1968-87, Ex-Offenders for Help Bd., 1975-81; bd. dirs. Camp Fire Girls, 1956-60, L.E.A.D.S., 1984-86, Sandusky C. of C., 1984-86. Served with USNR, 1943-46. Mem. Ohio State Bar Assn., Ohio Mcpl. Judges Assn. (exec. bd. 1970-80), Am. Judicature Soc., Am. Judges Assn., Erie County Bar Assn., Amvets, Beta Theta Pi, Sandusky Exch. Club (bd. dirs. 1999-2004), Car Coddlers Ohio (life mem.), Am. Legion, Elks, Eagles Club. Republican. Presbyterian. Home: 1407 Julianne Cir Sandusky OH 44870-7032

STACEY, JAMES HENRY, writer, columnist; b. Chgo., July 26, 1935; s. John James and Mary (Hollister) S.; m. Lelia West, Feb. 4, 1956 (div. Mar. 1978); children: Nicole, Michelle; m. Carol Ann Levenson, Apr. 26, 1980. BA, Grinnell Coll., 1957; MA, San Francisco State U., 1960. Asst. editor Bus. Week, Chgo., 1966-68; lectr. Northwestern U., Evanston, Ill., 1968-71; writer, devel. officer U. Chgo., 1972-76; nat. affairs editor Am. Med. News, Chgo., 1976-83, sci. news editor, 1983-86, dir. media rels., 1986-99; freelance writer Chgo., 1999—. Author: Inside the New Temple, 1993, A Wounded Name, 2001, The Medicine Men, 2006; co-author: Severed Trust, 2001; contbr. articles to mags. Avocations: theater, travel, literature. Home: Apt 3006 260 E Chestnut St Chicago IL 60611-2464 Personal E-mail: j.stacey@rcn.com.

STACEY, TRUMAN, journalist, consultant; b. Port Arthur, Tex., Dec. 8, 1916; s. James Harrison and Billie (Davis) S.; m. Dorothy Mary Piboin, May 25, 1963 (dec.); m. Norma Elaine Trahan, Feb. 2, 1980 (dec.). B in Philosophy, U. Detroit, 1946, MA, 1954. Reporter Beaumont (Tex.) Enterprise, 1937-42, Oklahoma City Daily Oklahoman, 1943-44, Detroit Free Press, 1944-45; dir. pub. rels. U. Detroit, 1945-49; reporter Washington Times Herald, 1949-50; sports editor Lake Charles (La.) Am. Press, 1950-60, editor-in-chief, 1961-82; dir. communications Diocese Lake Charles, 1982-90, pres. Coun. of Cath. Men, 1990-92. Author: Louisiana's French Heritage, 1990, The Church Visible, 2000. Mem. Calcasieu Parish Family Svc. Agy., La., 1979-82; coord. SW La. Citizens for Ednl. Freedom, 1968-70; bd. dirs. La. Coun. Music and Performing Arts, 1967-79, Calcasieu Citizens for Decency, 1967-69, Lake Charles Symphony Orch., 1967-69. Sgt. U.S. Army, 1942-43; mem. Mayor's Armed Forces Commn., 2003—. Decorated chevalier Order of Merit France; named to La. Sports Writers Hall of Fame, 1982, Columbian Hall of Fame, 1987; recipient Merit award, Sociedad Española de La., 1978, Silver Antelope award, Boy Scouts Am., 1979, George Washington medal of Honor, Freedom Found., 1980, Faith and Freedom award, Religious Heritage Am., Inc., 1980, Harry J. O'Haire Meml. award, Serra Internat., 1987, John Donahue award, Serra Internat. Found., 2003, Pilgrim's Shell award, Latin Patriarch Jerusalem, 1988, Nat. Silver Merit medal, Knights of Peter Claver, 1992, Gold medal of merit, 2003, Stephen T. Victory Meml. award, La. Bar Assn, 1992, Past State Deputies award, La. K.C, 1994, Spes Mundi-O'Connell award, Internat. Cath. Com. on Scouting, 2000, Donald Millet Meml. award, S.W. La. Hist. Assn., 2001, Silver St. George emblem, Nat. Cath. Com. on Scouting, 2002, Silver medal of Merit, Sacred Mil. Constantinian Order St. George, 2002, Bishop Charles Pascal Greco Lifetime Achievement award, KC, 2004, St. Christopher emblem, Tex. KC, 2005. Mem.: NCCJ (Brotherhood award 1975), La. Press Assn. (bd. dirs. 1976—79), S.W. La. Hist. Assn. (pres. 2000—02), Inst. de la Maison Royale de France, Lake Charles C. of C. (Man of Yr. 1971), Am. Soc. Newspaper Editors, AP Mng. Editors Assn., La.-Miss. AP Assn. (pres. 1962—63, Merit citation 30 Yrs. Cmty. Svc. 1980), La. Sports Writers Assn., Order St. Lazarus of Jerusalem (officer 2002, Grand Cross award 2006). Avocations: reading, classical music, stamp collecting/philately. Home: 1802 2nd Ave Lake Charles LA 70601-6432

STACEY, WESTON MONROE, JR., nuclear engineer, physicist, educator; b. Birmingham, Ala., July 23, 1937; s. Weston Monroe and Dorothy (Toole) S.; m. Penny Smith; children: Helen Lee, Weston Monroe III, Lucia Katherine. BS in Physics, Ga. Inst. Tech., 1959, MS in Nuc. Sci., 1963; PhD in Nuc. Engring., MIT, 1966. Nuc. engr. Knolls Atomic Power Lab., Schenectady, NY, 1962-64, 66-69; assoc. dir. applied physics divsn. and dir. fusion program Argonne Nat. Lab., Chgo., 1969-77; Callaway Regents prof. Ga. Inst. Tech., Atlanta, 1977—. Author: Modal Approximation in Reactor Physics, 1967, Space-Time Nuclear Reactor Kinetics, 1969, Variational Methods in Nuclear Reactor Physics, 1972, Fusion Plasma Analysis, 1981, Fusion, 1984, Nuclear Reactor Physics, 2001, 2d edit., 2007, Fusion Plasma Physics, 2005; contbr. articles to profl. jours. Recipient Cert. Appreciation Dept. Energy, 1981, 88, Disting. Assoc. award Dept. Energy, 1990, Rsch. award Sigma Xi, 1998. Fellow: Am. Nuc. Soc. (bd. dirs. 1974—77, Outstanding Achievement award 1981, 1996, Seaborg medal 2001, Wigner award 2003), Am. Phys. Soc.; mem.: AAAS, Am. Soc. Engring. Edn. Office: Ga Inst Tech Nuclear Engring Dept 0425 Atlanta GA 30332-0425 Office Phone: 404-894-3714. Business E-Mail: weston.stacey@nre.gatech.edu.

STACHEL, JOHN JAY, physicist, researcher; b. NYC, Mar. 29, 1928; s. Jacob Abraham and Bertha Z. Stachel; m. Evelyn Lenore Wassermann, Feb. 8, 1953; children: Robert, Laura, Deborah. BS, CCNY, 1956; MS, Stevens Inst. Tech., 1959, PhD, 1962. Instr. physics Lehigh U., Bethlehem, Pa., 1959-61; instr. physics U. Pitts., 1961-62, research assoc., 1962-64; asst. prof. physics Boston U., 1964-69, assoc. prof., 1969-72, prof., 1972-96; dir. Ctr. for Einstein Studies, Boston U., 1985—, prof. emeritus, 1996—. Vis. rsch. assoc. Inst. Theoretical Physics, Warsaw, 1962; vis. prof. King's Coll., U. London, 1970-71, U. Paris, 1990-91, Max Planck Inst. History of Sci., Berlin, 1994—, Calif. Inst. Tech., 1998; vis. sr. rsch. fellow Dept. Physics, Princeton U., 1977-84; rsch. assoc. U. Calif., Berkeley, 1994; master mind lectr. British Acad., 2005; lectr. Smithsonian Inst. Ann. Dibner Lecture, 2005, Wartofsky Meml. Lecture, City U. NY, 2005. Author: Einstein from B to Z, 2002; editor: Selected Papers Leon Rosenfeld, 1979, Foundations of Space-Time Theories, 1977, Einstein Studies, 1989—, Collected Papers of Albert Einstein, 1977-88, Einstein's Miraculous Year, 1998, 2d edit., 2005. Office: Boston U Ctr Enstein Studies 745 Commonwealth Ave Rm 505 Boston MA 02215-1401 Home Phone: 617-734-9684. Business E-Mail: stachel@bu.edu.

STACK, EDWARD W., retail executive; Mdse. mgr., store mgr., pres. Dick's Sporting Goods Inc., Pitts., 1977—84, chmn., CEO, 1984—. Office: Dick's Sporting Goods Inc RIDC Park W 300 Industry Dr Pittsburgh PA 15275 *

STACK, FRANK HUNTINGTON, painter, retired art educator; b. Houston, Oct. 31, 1937; s. Maurice Z. and Norma Rose (Huntington) S.; m. Mildred Roberta Powell, June 12, 1959; children: Joan Elaine, Robert Huntington. BFA, U. Tex., 1959; postgrad., Sch. Art Inst. Chgo., 1960-61; MA, U. Wyo., 1963. Assoc. art editor Houston Chronicle, 1959-60; instr. U. Mo., Columbia, 1963-69, prof. art, 1969-95, Catherine P. Middlebush prof. humanities, 1995-2000, prof. emeritus, 2000—. Mem. regional adv. bd. Mo. Arts Coun., Columbia, 1979-80; mem. exec. bd. U. Mo. Art and Archaeology Mus., Columbia, 1981-84; chmn. art dept. U. Mo., Columbia, 1981-83; mem. pers. com. U. Mo. Columbia Arts and Sci. Coll., Columbia, 1976-80; vis. artist W.Va. Arts Coun. and Exxon, Shepherd Coll., Shepherdstown, W.Va., 1983. Artist, author: (cartoons) The New Adventures of Jesus, 1963-95, (book of cartoons) Dorman's Doggie, 1990; illustrator artist: (graphic novel) Our Cancer Year, 1994 (Best Graphic Novel Harvey award 1995), Naked Glory: erotic art of Frank Stack. 1997; artist traveling exhibit Watercolors by Frank Stack, 1977-79; editor: (collection of comic strips) Alley Oop, 3 vols. 1946-47, 47-48, 48-49, 1990, 93, 95 (nominated Best Reprint 1991, 94, 96), Alley Oop mag., 1997—; mem. dv. bd. Jour. Cartoon and Comic Art, 1984—; contbg. writer The Comics Jour., 1989—. Mem. mus. rev. bd. U. Mo., 4 campus sys., Columbia, 1989. With US Army, 1960—62. Recipient Rsch. Grants, U. Mo. Rsch. Coun., Columbia, 1969, 85, 93, 98, Gov.'s Arts awards Artist of Yr. Mo. Arts Coun., St. Louis, 1986. Mem. Kans. Watercolor Soc. (awards 1992, 96), Columbia Art League (adv. bd. 1978-82), Mo. Watercolor Soc. (award 2003). Avocations: historical research, art history, newspaper comics of 1930's and 40's, collector of master prints. Home: 409 Thilly Ave Columbia MO 65203-3458 Personal E-mail: frankstack@gmail.com.

STACK, GEOFFREY LAWRENCE, real estate developer; b. Trinidad, Brit. West Indies, Sept. 16, 1943; s. Gerald Francis and V. Louise (Bell) S.; m. Victoria Hammack, 1970 (div. 1986); 1 child, Kathryn; m. Nancy J. Haarer, Apr. 19, 1987; children: Alexandra, Natalie. BA, Georgetown U., 1965; MBA, U. Pa., 1972. Dir. acquisitions J.H. Snyder Co., LA, 1972-75; from project mgr. to exec. v.p. Richards West, Newport Beach, Calif., 1975-77; pres. Regis Homes Corp., Newport Beach, 1977-93; mng. dir. Sares-Regis Group, Irvine, Calif., 1993—. Bd. dirs. Arral & Ptnrs., Hong Kong, Calif. Housing Coun., Sacramento, Tejon Ranch Co. Chmn. bd. dirs. Nat. Multihousing Coun., 1987—; trustee Urban Land Inst., Marine Corps Scholarship Found., 2005. Capt. USMC, 1967—70. Decorated 2 Bronze Stars, 21 Air medals, Navy Commendation medal, Purple Heart. Mem. Young Pres. Orgn., Big Canyon Country Club, Pacific Club, Olympic Club, Calif. Club. Democrat. Roman Catholic. Office: SARES REGIS Group 18802 Bardeen Ave Irvine CA 92612-1521 Office Phone: 949-756-5959. Business E-Mail: jstack@sares-regis.com.

STACK, GEORGE JOSEPH, philosopher, writer; b. NYC; m. Mary K. Di Maria, 1997; children: Diane, Christopher, stepchildren: Jena, Shelley. BA, Pace U., 1960; MA, Pa. State U., 1962, PhD, 1964. Instr. humanities Pa. State U., 1962-63; instr. philosophy L.I. U., 1963-64, asst. prof., 1964-67, SUNY, Brockport, 1967-68, asso. prof., 1968-70, prof., chmn., 1970-77, 1985—94, prof., 1994—95, prof. emeritus, 1995—, also advisor Center for Philosophic Exchange, 1970-82. Author: Berkeley's Analysis of Perception, 1970, reprinted, 1991, On Kierkegaard: Philosophical Fragments, 1976, Kierkegaard's Existential Ethics, 1977;: 2d edit., 1992, Japanese transl., 1985, Sartre's Philosophy of Social Existence, 1978, reprinted, 1992, Lange and Nietzsche, 1983, Japanese translation, 2006, Nietzsche and Emerson, 1992, Nietzche's Anthropic Circle, 2005; contbg. author Nietzsche and Modern German Thought, 1991, Emerson/Nietzsche, 1998, The Emerson Enigma, 2003; contbg. author: Ralph Waldo Emerson Bicentenary Appraisals, 2006; contbr. numerous articles and reviews to profl. jours. Office: PO Box 92 Grapevine TX 76099-0092

STACK, JIM, professional sports team executive; Grad., Northwestern U., 1983. Draft pick Houston Rockets, 1983; profl. basketball player Belgium, Israel and France, 1983—88; scout Chgo. Bulls, 1988—89, spl. asst. to v.p. basketball ops., 1989—96, asst. v.p. basketball ops., 1996—2000; asst. coach Ind. Pacers, 2000—03; advanced scout NY Knicks, 2003—04; gen. mgr. Minn. Timberwolves, 2004—. Office: Minn Timberwolves 600 First Ave N Minneapolis MN 55403 *

STACK, KEVIN J., lawyer; b. NYC, Aug. 12, 1951; BA cum laude, UCLA, 1973; JD cum laude, Loyola U., LA, 1976. Bar: Calif. 1976, U.S. Dist. Ct. (ctrl. dist.) Calif. 1977. Ptnr. Knapp, Petersen & Clarke, Glendale, Calif., 1984—. Office: Knapp Petersen & Clarke 500 N Brand Blvd Fl 20 Glendale CA 91203-1923

STACK, MAY ELIZABETH, retired library director; b. Jackson, Miss., Nov. 10, 1940; d. James William and Irene Thelma (Baldwin) Garrett; m. Richard Gardiner, Apr. 15, 1962; children: Elinor, Harley David. BS, Miss. State Coll. for Women, 1962; MBA, Western New Eng. Coll., 1981; MLS, So. Conn. State U., 1989. Clk. Western New Eng. Coll., Springfield, Mass., 1965-66, acquisitions staff, 1966-72, cataloger, 1972-84, asst. dir., 1984-89, acting dir., 1989-90, dir., 1990—2005. Chair Ctrl./Western Mass. Automated Resource Sharing Collection Devel. Com., Paxton, Mass., 1993-95, exec. bd., 1993-96. Mem. East Longmeadow (Mass.) Hist. Soc., 1989-92. Mem. ALA, Mass. Libr. Assn., Assn. Coll. and Rsch. Librs., Libr. and Mgmt. Assn., Libr. Info. and Technology Assn. Methodist. Avocations: horseback riding, show dogs. Office: Western New Eng Coll D'Amour Libr 1215 Wilbraham Rd Springfield MA 01119-2612 Business E-Mail: mstack@wnec.edu.

STACK, PAUL FRANCIS, lawyer; b. Chgo., July 21, 1946; s. Frank Louis and Dorothy Louise Stack; m. Nea Waterman, July 8, 1972; children: Nea Elizabeth, Sera Waterman. BS, U. Ariz., 1968; JD, Georgetown U., 1971. Bar: Ill. 1971, U.S. Ct. Claims 1975, U.S. Tax Ct. 1974, U.S. Ct. Internat. Trade 1977, U.S. Supreme Ct. 1975. Law clk. U.S. Dist. Ct., Chgo., 1971-72; asst. U.S. atty. No. Dist. Ill., Chgo., 1972-75; mng. dir. Stack & Filpi, Chgo., 1976—. Bd. dirs. Riverside (Ill.) Pub. Libr., 1977-83, Suburban Libr. Sys., Burr Ridge, Ill., 1979-82; mem. Mayor's ad hoc adv. com. on Ctrl. Libr., Chgo., Ill., 1987-88; mem. bd. edn. Twp. H.S. Dist. 208, Riverside, Ill., 1989-97; pres. Village of Riverside, Ill., 1997-2001; mem. exec. com. Chgo. Area Transp. Study, 1999-2001. Mem. Chgo. Zool. Soc. (gov. 1980—, planned giving adv. com. 1996-99), Chgo. Bar Assn., Union League Club of Chgo. (bd. dirs. 1986-89). Home: 238 N Delaplaine Rd Riverside IL 60546-2035 Office: 140 S Dearborn St Ste 411 Chicago IL 60603-5201

STACK, ROBERT B., lawyer; b. Feb. 9, 1955; MA, NYU, 1980; MSFS, Georgetown Univ., 1984, JD magna cum laude, 1984. Bar: NY 1987, DC 1988. Law clk. Judge Thomas A. Flannery, US Dist. Ct. (DC dist.), Justice Potter Stewart, US Supreme Ct., 1985; ptnr., co-chmn. Tax dept. Wilmer Cutler Pickering Hale & Dorr, Washington. Editor (in chief): Georgetown Law Jour. Mem.: US Council on Internat. Bus. (mem. Tax com.), Internat. Fiscal Assn. Office: Wilmer Cutler Pickering Hale & Dorr 1899 Pennsylvania Ave NW Washington DC 20006 Mailing: Wilmer Cutler Pickering Hale & Dorr 2445 M St NW Washington DC 20037 Office Phone: 202-663-6272. Office Fax: 202-663-6363. Business E-Mail: robert.stack@wilmerhale.com.

STACK, STEPHEN S., manufacturing executive; b. DuPont, Pa., Apr. 25, 1934; s. Steve and Sophie (Baranowski) Stasenko; m. Lois Sims Agnew, May 25, 1996. BSME, Case Western Res. U., 1956; postgrad., Syracuse Univ. registered profl engr., Ill. Mech. engr. Kaiser Aluminum, Erie, Pa., 1956-58; instr. Gannon Univ., Erie, Pa., 1958-60, Syracuse U., NY, 1960-61; engrg. supr. A.O. Smith Corp., Erie and Los Angeles, 1961-66; gen. mgr. Am. Elec. Fusion, Chgo., 1966-67; mgr.new products Maremont Corp., Chgo., 1967-69; dir. market planning Gulf and Western Ind., Bellwood, Ill., 1969-71; mgmt. and fin. cons. Stack & Assocs., Chgo., 1971-76; founder, pres. Seamcraft, Inc., Chgo., 1976—. Mem. Ill. Legis. Small Bus. Conf., 1980, Gov.'s Small Bus. Adv. Commn., 1984-94, Ill. State House Conf. on Small Bus., 1984, 86, 99; chmn. West Cell Svcs., 1988-2000; chmn., founder Bridge Pers. Svcs. Corp., 1989—; vice pres., founder Ind. Bus. Assn. Ill., 1993-94; small bus. adv. coun. Fed. Res. Bank Chgo., 1989-91, Nat. Fedn. Ind. Bus., 1980—, mem. Ill. State. Leadership Coun. 1999-, del. White House Conf. on Small Bus., 1986, Nat. Small Bus. Attitudes Rsch. Panel, 1987-, pres. Chgo. Marine Heritage Soc., 1999—, mem. Navy League of US, 1991—, del. Congl. Small Bus. Summit, 1998, 2000, 02, 04, 06; with Ill. Small Bus. Leadership Coun., 2000—. Treas. Sem. Townhouse Assn., 1993-94; active Lincoln Park Conservation Assn., Sheffield Neighbors Assn.; mem. adv. coun., DePaul U. Coll. Commerce, 2000—. Recipient Am. Legion award, 1948, Case Western Res. U. Honor key, 1956, Eagle Scout award, 1949. Mem. Ill. Mfrs. Assn. (bd. dirs. 1986-98, vice chmn. 1995-98), Small Mfrs. Action Couns. (vice chmn. 1986-87, chmn. 1988-89), Mfrs. Polit. Action Com. (exec. com. 1987-98, vice chmn. 1993-95, chmn. 1995-98), Am. Mgmt. Assn., Pres. Assn., Blue Key, Beta Theta Pi, Theta Thau, Pi Delta Epsilon. Chgo. Yacht Club, East Bank Club, Fullerton Tennis Club (pres. 1971-79, treas. 1979-83, bd. dirs. 1983-86), Lake Shore Ski Club (v.p. 1982, 91), Lincoln Park Tennis Assn. Patentee in liquid control and metering fields. Office: 932 W Dakin St Chicago IL 60613-2922

STACKELBERG, JOHN RODERICK, history professor; b. Munich, May 8, 1935; came to U.S., 1946; s. Curt Freiherr and Ellen (Biddle) von Stackelberg; m. Steffi Heuss, Oct. 10, 1965 (div. Apr. 1983); m. Sally Winkle, Mar. 30, 1991; children: Katherine Ellen, Nicholas Olaf, Emmet Winkle. AB, Harvard U., 1956; MA, U. Vt., 1972; PhD, U. Mass., 1974. Reading instr. Baldridge Reading Svcs., Greenwich, Conn., 1957-62; lang. tchr. Hartnackschule, Berlin, 1963-67; English and social studies tchr. Lake Region Union High Sch., Orleans, Vt., 1967-70; lectr. history San Diego State U., 1974-76; asst. prof. history U. Oreg., Eugene, 1976-77, U. S.D., Vermillion, 1977-78, Gonzaga U., Spokane, Wash., 1978-81, assoc. prof. history, 1981-88, prof. history, 1988—, Powers prof. of humanities, 1997—. Author: Idealism Debased, 1981, Hitler's Germany: Origins, Interpretations, Legacies, 1999, (with Sally A. Winkle) The Nazi Germany Sourcebook: An Anthology of Texts, 2002; contbr. articles to profl. jours. Pres. Spokane chpt. UN Assn., 1986-90. With U.S. Army, 1958-60. Leadership Devel. fellow Ford Found., 1969-70. Avocations: chess, tennis. Home: 530 W 24th Ave Spokane WA 99203 Office: Gonzaga U Dept History Spokane WA 99258-0001 Office Phone: 509-747-2077. Personal E-mail: rodstackelberg@comcast.net.

STACKHOUSE, JERRY, professional basketball player; b. Kinston, NC, Nov. 5, 1974; Student, N.C. U., 1997. Basketball player Phila. 76ers, 1995—98, Det. Pistons, 1997—2002, Washington Wizards, 2002—04, Dallas Mavericks, 2004—. Named to NBA All-Rookie Team, 1995—96, NBA All-Star Game, 2000, 2001. Office: c/o Dallas Mavericks The Pavillion 2909 Taylor St Dallas TX 75226

STACKHOUSE, JOHN EWELL HARBOUR, judge; b. NYC, Apr. 3, 1939; s. George B. Stackhouse and Adeline Harbour; m. Linda Starlin, June 22, 1965 (div. Jan. 1983); children: Daniel A.H., Laura Ruth; m. Joan L. Beranbaum, May 19, 1985; 1 child, Ross H.S. BA in English, The Citadel, Charleston, SC, 1960; LLB, St. Johns U., Bklyn., 1966. Bar: NY 1970, US Dist. Ct. (so. dist.) NY 1973. Judge Supreme Ct. N.Y. County, NYC. Counsel bd. ethics City NY, 1970—71. Contbr. articles to profl. jours. First lt. US Army, 1961—63. Recipient Pub. Svc. award, Legal Aid Soc. NY, 1998, Diversity Champion award, NY City Bar Assn., 2007. Mem.: Assn. Bar NY (mem. com., mem. task force women in cts.). Office: Supreme Ct NY 80 Centre St New York NY 10013-4390 Office Phone: 646-386-3751. Business E-Mail: jstackito@courts.state.ny.us.

STACKHOUSE, MAX LYNN, religious studies educator; b. Ft. Wayne, Ind., July 29, 1935; s. C. Dale and Naomi Elizabeth (Graham) S.; m. N. Jean Hostetler, Aug. 19, 1959; children: Dale Emil, David Graham, Sara Elizabeth. BA, De Pauw U., Greencastle, Ind., 1957, LHD (hon.), 1995; cert., Nijenrode U., Breukelen, The Netherlands, 1958; MDiv, Harvard U., Cambridge, Mass., 1961, PhD, 1965; DLitt (hon.), DePauw U., 1996. Ordained to ministry United Ch. of Christ, 1961. Lectr. Harvard Divinity Sch., Cambridge, Mass., 1964-66; asst. prof. Andover-Newton Theol. Sch., Mass., 1966-69, assoc. prof. Mass., 1969-73, prof. Mass., 1973-78, Herbert Gezork prof. Mass., 1978-93; Stephen Colwell prof. Princeton Theol. Sem., NJ, 1993—2004, Rimmer and Ruth de Vries prof. theology and pub. life NJ, 2004—06, prof. emeritus, 2007—. Federick disting. vis. prof. De Pauw U., 2007, vis. prof. United Theol. Coll., Bangalore, India, 1973, 76, 82, 87, 00, Pacific Theol. Coll., Suva, Fiji, 1982, Das Sprachenkonvikt, East Berlin, 1983; pres. joint doctoral program Boston Coll. and Andover Newton Theol. Sch., 1988-89, chmn. rels. and soc. dept., 1975-93; dir. Kuyper Ctr. Pub. Theology, 1994-06; pres. Berkshire Inst. Theology and Arts, 1991—. Author: Creeds, Society and Human Rights, 1984, Public Theology and Political Economy, 1987, Apologia, 1988 (Best Booklist Internat. Bull. Missiology 1988), On Moral Business, 1994, Christian Ethics in a Global Era, 1996, Covenant and Commitments, 1998, God and Globalization, vol. 1, 2000, vol. 2, 2001, vol. 3, 2002; author, editor 22 books; mem. editl. bd. Jour. Religious Ethics, Christian Century, Jour. Polit. Theology; contbr. articles to profl. jours. Investigation team Am. Com. Human Rights, Philippines, 1984; pres. James Luther Adams Found., 1987-93; exec. sec. Am. Com. Higher Edn. in India, 1986-91. Rsch. grantee Ctr. for Urban Studies, Harvard U., 1965-66, Assn. Theol. Schs., 1986-87, Lilly Endowment, Indpls., 1989, 91, Pew Charitable Trusts, 1993, 98; recipient Outstanding Alumnus award DePauw U., 1988. Fellow Soc. Sci. Study Religion (bd. dirs. 1980-84), Soc. Values in Higher Edn.; mem. NAACP, Amnesty Internat. (pres.-elect 2007), Am. Theol. Assn. (v.p. then pres. elect, 2007), Soc. Christian Ethics (past pres., past exec. sec.), Stockbridge Club. Democrat.

STACKPOLE, KERRY CLIFFORD, association executive; b. Putnam, Conn., Feb. 24, 1955; s. Howard Thompson Stackpole and Shyrlee Gladys Burr; m. Miriam Weisberg, July 29, 1984. MEd, Cambridge Coll., 1983. Gen. mgr. E.J. Ardon Co., Boston, 1978-82; ops. mgr. Fotobeam/Brookside, Waltham, Mass., 1982-83; assoc. dir. Printing Industries of New Eng., Natick, Mass., 1983—, v.p., 1989-91; exec. dir. Smaller Bus. Assn. New Eng.; Waltham, Mass., 1991-93; pres., CEO The Assn. for Work Process Improvement, Inc., 1993-97, Electronic Messaging Assn., 1997—2000; chmn. CEO Neoterica Ptnrs., LLP, McLean, Va., 2000—. Bd. dirs. Mass. Cert. Devel. Corp., EC Inst., Denver, Conv. Industry Coun.; mem. U.S. C. of C. Com. of 100, 2000-02. Recipient HIRE Trust Fund award Graphic Arts Employers of Am., 1987, 2000. Fellow Am. Soc. Assn. Execs. (cert., mem. ann. meeting adv. com. 1996-97, mem. edn. com., 1996-99, chmn., exec. mgmt. sect. coun., 1997-98, bd. dirs., 1997-98, mem. key industries assn. com. 2000—); mem. Assocs. Advance Am. Com. (chmn. 1999-2000), New Eng. Soc. Assn. Execs. (committeeman 1983-84, membership devel. com. 1989-91, chmn. edn. com. 1991-93, bd. dirs. 1991—, treas.-sec. 1994-95, chmn.-elect 1995, chmn. bd. dirs. 1996-1997, immediate past chmn. 1997-98, Ralph Louis Towne award 1986). Avocations: reading, cross country skiing, ocean kayaking, jazz music buff. Office: Neoterica Ptnrs LLP PO Box 7763 Mc Lean VA 22106 Personal E-mail: kstackpole@neoterica.com.

STACOM, TARA IRENE, real estate company executive; d. Matthew J. and Claire P. Stacom; m. Paul Allan Nussbaum, June 8, 1985. BS in Fin., Lehigh U., Pa., 1980. Broker to exec. v.p. Cushman & Wakefield, Inc., NYC, 1980—2005, bd. dirs., 2003—, vice chmn., 2005—. Mem. ethics com. Real Estate Bd. NY, bd. dirs. comml. brokerage divsn.; bd. dirs. WX (NY Women Execs. in Real Estate), 2004—; dir. Realty Found. NY, 2004—. Dir.'s Cir. mem. Girls, Inc.; bd. trustees Lehigh U., Pa. Achievements include becoming Cushman & Wakefield's top-producing broker in 2004, the first woman to accomplish this at the company. Office: Cushman & Wakefield 51 W 52nd St New York NY 10019-6178 Office Phone: 212-841-7843. E-mail: tara.stacom@cushwake.com. *

STACY, BILL WAYNE, academic administrator; b. Bristol, Va., July 26, 1938; s. Charles Frank and Louise Nelson (Altwater) S.; m. Sue Varnon; children: Mark, Sara, James. BSEd., S.E. Mo. State U., 1960; MS, So. Ill. U., 1965, PhD, 1968. Tchr. Malden High Sch., Mo., 1960-64; faculty Southeast Mo. State U., Cape Girardeau, 1967-89, dean Grad. Sch., 1976-79, interim pres., 1979, pres., 1980-89, Calif. State U., San Marcos, 1989-97; chancellor U. Tenn., Chattanooga, 1997—2004; headmaster Baylor Sch., Chattanooga, 2004—. Bd. dirs. River Valley Ptnrs. Bd. dirs. United Way; mem. Allied Arts Bd. Mem. Am. Assn. Higer Edn., Chattanooga C. of C. (bd. dirs.). Presbyterian. Office: Baylor Sch PO Box 1337 Chattanooga TN 37401 *

STACY, DENNIS WILLIAM, architect; b. Council Bluffs, Iowa, Sept. 22, 1945; s. William L. and Mildred Glee (Carlsen) S.; m. Judy Annette Long, Dec. 28, 1968; 1 child: Stephanie. BArch, Iowa State U., 1969; postgrad., U. Nebr., 1972. Registered arch., Iowa, Tex., Colo., Mo., Nat. Coun. Architectural Registration Bds. Cert.; registered interior designer Tex. Designer Troy & Stalder Archs., Omaha, 1967, Archs. Assocs., Des Moines, 1968-69, Logsdon & Voelter Archs., Temple, Tex., 1970; project arch. Roger Schutte & Assocs., Omaha, 1972-73; arch., assoc. Robert H. Burgin & Assocs., Council Bluffs, 1973-75, Neil Astle & Assocs., Omaha, 1975-78; owner, prin. Dennis W. Stacy, AIA, Arch., Glenwood, Iowa, 1978-81; pres. Stacy Archs., Inc., Dallas, 1981—2001, Stacy Archtl. Studio, PLLC, 2002—. Mem. organizing com. symposium Tex. A&M U., 1991—2006. Archtl. works include: Davies Amphitheater, 1980, Addison Nat. Bank Bldg., 1985, Villa Roma, 1988, C.U. Performing Arts Ctr., 1989, Mercedes-Benz Distbn. Ctr., 1987, Dallas Chpt. AIA Offices, 1990, Janadria Festival Arena, 1994, Physicians Consultants Clinic, 1994, Horizon Pain Mgmt. Ctr., 1995, Rheumatology Assoc. Clinic, 1996, Addison Nat. Br. Bank, 1996, Cummins So. Plains Distbn., Fabrication and Corp. Offices Ctr., 1998, Arthur Murray Dance Studios, 2001, 06, Tatum Residence, 2001, Big Glee Office Plz., 2006; co-author Guide to Dallas Architecture, 1999, History of the Dallas Chapter of the American Institute of Architects, 2007. Mem. City of Dallas Urban Design Adv. Com., 1992-96, chmn., 1995-96; dir. Greater Dallas Planning Coun., 1997-05; chmn. Glenwood Zoning Bd. Adjustment, 1979-81; chmn. Mills County Plant Iowa Program, 1979-81; mem. S.W. Iowa Citizen's Adv. Com., Iowa State Dept. Transp., 1977-81; regional screening chmn. Am. Field Svc. Internat./Intercultural Programs, 1974-79, Iowa-Nebr. rep., 1978-80. With U.S. Army, 1969-71. Decorated Nat. Def. Svc. medal, Vietnam Svc. medal, Vietnam Campaign medal, Army Commendation medal, Disting. Alumnus Design Achievement award Iowa State U., 1999. Fellow AIA (chmn. nat. conv. 2000, Iowa Design Honor award 1981, Dallas AIA commendation awards 1990, 92, 95-98, Citation of Honor award 1991-92, 2001, Dallas Design awards 1991, 96-97, Tex. Design Honor award 1992, Dallas AIA Firm of Yr. award 1992, Nat. Presdl. Citation 2000, Dallas commr. design 1991, chmn. Dallas design awards 1992, pres. Dallas AIA 1996), Tex. Soc. Archs. (environ. resource com. 1994-95, chmn., Tex. arch. pub. com., 1992-98, chmn. 1997, 98), Nat. Coun. Archtl. Registration Bds., Iowa State U. Adv. Coun. (1997-2000, 05-07, chmn. 1999-2000), Am. Legion, Masons. Home and Office: 4148 Cobblers Ln Dallas TX 75287-6725 Office Phone: 972-250-1909. Personal E-mail: dstacyarch@aol.com.

STACY, ZACHARY AARON, pharmacist; s. Bruce Alan and Cynthia Ann Stacy; m. Tracy LouAnn Young, Sept. 6, 2003. B in Chemistry, Blackburn Coll., Carlinville, Ill., 1997, B in Biology, 1997; M in Chemistry, So. Ill. U., Edwardsville, 1999; B of Pharmacy, St. Louis Coll. Pharmacy, 2003, PharmD, 2003. Asst. prof. pharmacy practice St. Louis Coll. Pharmacy, St. Louis, 2004—. Recipient Excellence in Clin. Tchg. award, St. Louis Coll. Pharmacy, 2005. Mem.: Ill. Pharmacist Assn. (assoc.), Am. Pharmacist Assn. (assoc.), Metro-East Pharmacist Assn. (assoc.; bd. mem. 2005—06), Am. Soc. of Health-System Pharmacists (assoc.), Gateway Coll. Clin. Pharmacy (assoc.; pres. 2004—07), Am. Coll. Clin. Pharmacy (assoc.). Office: St Louis Coll Pharmacy 4588 Parkview Pl Saint Louis MO 63110 Home Phone: 618-288-2234; Office Phone: 314-446-8536. Office Fax: 314-446-8500. Business E-Mail: zstacy@stlcop.edu.

STADDON, JOHN ERIC RAYNER, psychology professor, neurobiology professor, zoology professor; b. Grayshott, Hampshire, Eng. came to U.S., 1960; s. Leonard John and Dulce Norine (Rayner) S.; m. Lucinda Paris. BSc, Univ. Coll., London, 1960; PhD, Harvard U., 1964; D honoris causa, U. Charl de Gaulle, Lille III, 2006. Asst. prof. psychology U. Toronto, Ont., Canada, 1964-67; from asst. prof. to prof. Duke U., Durham, NC, 1967-72, prof., 1972-83, J.B. Duke prof. psychology, prof. neurobiology and biology, 1983—. Author: Adaptive Behavior and Learning, 1983, The New Behaviorism, 2001, Adaptive Dynamics, 2001; editor Behavioural Processes, 1979-2001, Behavior and Philosophy, 1993-2004; mem. editl. bd. Jour. Exptl. Analysis of Behavior, 1979-82. Recipient von Humboldt prize, 1985. Fellow AAAS, N.Y. Acad. Scis., Soc. Exptl. Psychologists; mem. Phi Beta Kappa (hon.), Sigma Xi. Avocations: history, philosophy of science, public policy. Office: Duke U Dept Psychology and Neurosci PO Box 91050 Durham NC 27708 Business E-Mail: staddon@psych.duke.edu.

STADE, GEORGE GUSTAV, humanities educator; b. NYC, Nov. 25, 1933; s. Kurt Herman and Eva Bergit (Aronson) S.; m. Dorothy Louise Fletcher, Dec. 16, 1957; children: Bjorn, Eric, Nancy, Kirsten. BA, St. Lawrence U., 1955; MA, Columbia U., 1958, PhD, 1965. Tchr. Collegiate Sch., NYC, 1957-58; instr. Bernard Baruch Sch. Bus., NYC, 1958-59, Bklyn. Poly. Inst., 1959-60, Rutgers U.-Newark, 1960-62, Columbia U., NYC, 1962, asst. prof., 1965, assoc. prof., 1968, prof. English, 1971—. Cons. in field. Author: Robert Graves, 1967, Confessions of a Lady-Killer, 1979, Sex and Violence, a Love Story, 2005, Love is War, 2006; editor: European Writers, Selected Letters of E.E. Cummings, 1968, Six Modern British Writers, 1974, Six Contemporary British Writers, 1976, European Writers: Selected Authors, 1992, British Writers Supplement II, 1992, British Writers Supplement III, 1995, British Writers Supplement IV, 1997; cons. editl. dir.: Barnes and Nobles Classics; contbr. articles to profl. jours. Mem. PEN, NY Book Critics Circle, Popular Culture Assn., MLA Home: 430 W 116th St New York NY 10027-7220 Office: Columbia U 604 Philosophy Hall New York NY 10027 Home Phone: 212-866-3180; Office Phone: 212-854-6410. Business E-Mail: ggs3@columbia.edu.

STADELMAN, WILLIAM RALPH, chemicals executive; b. Ont., Can., July 18, 1919; s. John Joseph and Lillian (Trachsell) S.; m. Jean MacLaren, Nov. 2, 1951; 1 child, Mary Laren. BASc, U. Toronto, 1941; MBA, U. Pa., 1949. Chief process engr. Can. Synthetic Rubber, Ltd., 1943-47; lectr. mktg. U. Pa., 1948-49; asst. to mgr. Pa. Salt Mfg. Co., 1950; sec.-treas. Ont. Research Found., Mississauga, 1950-64, pres., 1964-84, WRS Associates, 1984—; dir., sr. exec. Inst. Chem. Sci. and Tech., 1985-89. Dir. Med. Tech. Investment Corp. Fellow World Acad. Art and Sci.; mem. Assn. Profl. Engrs. Ont., Innovation Mgmt. Assn. Can., Bd. Trade Met. Toronto, Club of Rome, Caledon Ski Club.

STADELMANN, WAYNE KARL, plastic surgeon; b. Milw., Wis., July 17, 1964; MD (with honors), U. Chgo.-Pritzker Sch. Medicine, 1990. Cert. Am. Bd. Plastic Surgery. Intern, gen. surgery U. Chgo. Hosp. & Clinics, 1990—91, resident, gen. surgery, 1991—94; resident, plastic surgery South Fla. Coll. Medicine, Tampa, Fla., 1994—97; joined staff Concord Hosp., NH, 2003—, New London Hosp., 2005—; private practice Stadelmann

Plastic Surgery, PC, NH. Named one of Top Doctor, NH Mag. Mem.: Phi Beta Kappa. Office: Stadelmann Plastic Surgery PC 248 Pleasant St Ste 201 Pillsbury Bldg Concord NH 03301 Office Phone: 603-224-5200. Office Fax: 603-224-5091. *

STADLER, BRIAN M., lawyer; b. Far Rockaway, NY, July 9, 1965; BS summa cum laude, U. Pa. Wharton Sch., 1987; JD, Columbia Law Sch., 1990. Bar: NY 1991. Assoc. Simpson Thacher & Bartlett LLP, NYC, 1990—98, ptnr., 1998—. Named a Dealmaker of Yr., Am. Lawyer mag., 2007; Harlan Fiske Stone scholar, 1989—90. Office: Simpson Thacher & Bartlett LLP 425 Lexington Ave New York NY 10017-3954 Office Phone: 212-455-3765. Office Fax: 212-455-2502. *

STADLER, GERALD P., transportation executive; b. 1937; married. Student, Loyola U. Chmn. S&M Moving Sys., Santa Fe, Calif.; sec. United Van Lines, Fenton, Mo., 1982—84, vice chmn., 1984—2001, also bd. dirs., 1978—, chmn., 2001—; chmn., CEO UniGroup Inc., 2001—. Mem.: American Moving Storage Assn. (bd. dirs.). Office: United Van Lines Inc 1 United Dr Fenton MO 63026-2578

STADLER, SELISE MCNEILL, laboratory and x-ray technician; b. Portsmouth, Va., Dec. 27, 1960; d. William M. and Jorja Lee (Rigg) Gaidos; m. Stephen Michael McNeill, Feb. 29, 1988 (div. July 1993); 1 child, Stephen Michael Jr.; m. David Robert Stadler, June 15, 1996. Cert. chiropractic asst., Practice Mgmt. Assn., 1983; student, Tarrant County Coll., 2000—01. Cert. limited radiologic technologist, instr. cert. World Modeling Assn. Chiropractic asst. Dr. Brad Hayes, D.C., Tulsa, Okla., 1982-84; adminstrv. asst. Dr. Wallace Gauntner, M.D., Pitts., 1984, sec., 1985-87; traffic mgr., office mgr. WVBS-AM/FM, Wilmington, NC, 1985-87; med. asst. Dr. J. Bailey Bland, D.C., Wilmington, 1988-90; therapy/radiology supr. Dr. Roy L. Creasy Jr., D.C., Wilmington, 1990-91; med. asst., radiologist Westside Clinic, Dallas, 1991-94; model, exec. instr. Aleksaundra's Prodns., Ft. Worth, 1994-96; med. asst., radiologist Dr. Wayne R. English Jr., D.O., Ft. Worth, 1994-2000; lab/x-ray technician, med. asst. Care Now, Ft. Worth, 2001—02; x-ray/bone scan technician Kaner Med. Group, Bedford, Tex., 2001—02; med. asst., x-ray tech. Premier Orthopedics, Dr. Craig Saunders, MD and Dr. Marvin Van Hal, MD, 2002—07; X-ray tech., med. asst. HEB Bone & Joint, Dr. Daniel Foster & Dr. Frank Swords, 2007—. Author published poetry. Vol. Holy Family Cath. Ch., Ft. Worth, 1997-99. Recipient Employee Excellence award, Aleksaundra's Prodns., 1996. Mem. Tex. Soc. Radiologic Technologists (cert. in CPR and automated external defibrillation program), Am. Soc. Radiologic Technologists, Fort Worth Astronomy Club. Episcopalian. Avocations: scuba diving, horseback riding, horse breeding, tennis, rollerblading. Home Phone: 817-238-9317; Office Phone: 817-267-4492. E-mail: selise@charter.net.

STADNICAR, JOSEPH WILLIAM, lawyer; b. Corpus Christi, Tex., Oct. 30, 1963; s. Edward and Carrie Louise (Garris) Stadnicar. BBA, John Carroll U., 1986; MBA, Ohio State U., 1989, JD, 1990. Bar: Ohio 1990. Assoc. Gerald E. Schlafman Co., Fairborn, Ohio, 1991—95; pvt. practice Beavercreek, Ohio, 1995—97. Asst. pros. atty. City of Fairborn, 1990—95; pros. atty. City of Beavercreek, 1990—2001; assoc. Hammond & Stier Law Office, Beavercreek, 1996—98; ptnr. Hammond, Stire and Stadnicar, Beavercreek, 1998—. Trustee Family Violence Prevention Ctr. of Greene County, Xenia, Ohio, 1995—, Am. Heart Assn., Miami Valley, Ohio, 1996—. Mem.: ABA, Greene County Bar Assn., Ohio Bar Assn., Fairborn C. of C., Beavercreek C. of C., Rotary. Avocations: fishing, camping. Office: 3834 Dayton Xenia Rd Beavercreek OH 45432-2833 E-mail: jstadnicar@beavercreeklaw.com.

STADTHER, MICHAEL JON, entrepreneur, writer, publisher; b. Mobile, Ala. m. Helen Demetrios. BS in Math., Tulane U., 1973. Software developer, NYC; prin. GDK Systems Inc., NYC; co-owner, pres. The Frustum Group, White Plains, 1991—96; now owner publ. co. Treasure Trove Inc., Pound Ridge, NY. Author, illustrator, publisher A Treasure's Trove: A Fairy Tale About Real Treasure for Parents and Children of All Ages, 2004, A Treasure's Trove Puzzle Book Companion, 2004. Trustee Caramoor Ctr. for the Arts, Katonah, NY; supporter Music Conservatory of Westchester, White Plains, NY. Office: Treasure Trove Inc 161 Cherry St New Canaan CT 06840

STADTHERR, MARK A., chemical engineer, educator; b. Austin, Minn. BChE in Chem. Engring., U. Minn., Mpls., 1972; PhD in Chem. Engring., U. Wis., Madison, 1976. Faculty U. Ill., Urbana-Champaign, 1976-95; chem. engring. faculty U. Notre Dame, Ind., 1996—. Lectr. in field. Contbr. articles to profl. jours. Recipient Xerox award for engring. rsch., 1982, Computing in Chem. Engring. award AIChE, 1998; named GTE Emerging scholar lectr. U. Notre Dame, 1986. Mem.: ASEE, SIAM, ACS, AICHE (chair Computing and Sys. Tech. Divsn. 2002—03). Achievements include research on advanced computational strategies for process engineering, application of interval analysis to chemical engineering problems, environmentally conscious process design, ecological modeling. Office: Dept Chem Engring Univ Notre Dame Notre Dame IN 46556 Business E-Mail: markst@nd.edu.

STADTLER, WALTER EDWARD, diplomat; b. NYC, Apr. 4, 1936; s. Walter Henry and Paula (Nagl) S.; m. Maida Maria Macdonald, Mar. 4, 1937; children: Fiona, Walter Jr., Catriona. Student, Sorbonne U., Paris, 1955-56; AB, Fordham U., 1957; postgrad., Columbia U., 1957-58. With Dept. State, 1962—94; vice consul Am. Consulate, Southampton, Eng., 1962-63; third sec. Am. Embassy, London, 1963-64, econ. officer, second sec. Bonn, Fed. Republic of Germany, 1966-69; personnel officer Dept. State, Washington, 1966-69; second sec. Am. Embassy, Pretoria, South Africa, 1969-72, charge' d'affaires then dep. chief of mission, 1982-85, first sec. Addis Ababa, Ethiopia, 1972-75, Stockholm, 1975-78; European affairs advisor U.S. Mission UN, NYC, 1978; mem. Royal Coll. Def. Studies, London, 1979; counselor Am. Embassy, Bonn, Fed. Republic of Germany, 1980-82; mem. Sr. Seminar, Washington, 1985-86; ambassador Am. Embassy, Cotonou, Benin, 1986-90; v.p. Nat. Def. U., Ft. McNair; sr. fellow Office of the Sec. of Def., 1992—94; U.S. mem. Internat. Def. Adv. Bd. for the Baltic Republics, 1995—2000; prof. and dir., program on peacekeeping policy George Mason U., Fairfax, Va., 1995—2000; bd. chair Geodata Systems, Inc., 1999—. Bd. mem. Nat. Def. U. Found., Coop. Housing Found.; mem. Coun. on Standards for Internat. Edn. Travel; councillor Atlantic Coun. of the U.S. Served to capt. U.S. Army, 1958-62. Mem. Am. Fgn. Service Assn., Army and Navy Club. Roman Catholic. Avocations: music, travel, fgn. policy and polit. mil. hist. Office: 7063 Wyndale St NW Washington DC 20015-1428 Home Phone: 202-364-5208; Office Phone: 202-363-9894. E-mail: walter.stadtler@digicola.com.

STADTMAN, EARL REECE, biochemist, researcher; b. Carrizozo, N.Mex., Nov. 15, 1919; s. Walter William and Minnie Ethyl (Reece) Stadtman; m. Thressa Campbell, Oct. 19, 1943. BS, U. Calif., Berkeley, 1942, PhD, 1949. With Alcan Hwy. survey Pub. Rds. Adminstrn., 1942—43; rsch. asst. U. Calif., Berkeley, 1938—49, sr. lab. technican, 1949; AEC fellow Mass. Gen. Hosp., Boston, 1949—50; chemist lab. cellular physiology Nat. Heart Inst., 1950—58, chief enzyme sect., 1958—62, section chief lab. biochemistry, 1962—. Biochemist Max Planck Inst., Munich, Pasteur Inst., Paris, 1959—60; faculty dept. microbiology U. Md.; prof. biochemistry grad. program dept. biology Johns Hopkins U.; adv. com. Life Scis. Rsch. Office, Am. Fedn. Biol. Sci., 1974—77; chmn. dept. biochemistry Found. Advanced Edn. Scis., 1966—68; biochem. study sect. rsch. grants NIH, 1959—63; Julius Schultz Meml. vis. prof. U. Miami, 2002. Editor: Jour. Biol. Chemistry, 1960—65, Current Topics in Cellular Regulation, 1968—, Circulation Rsch., 1968—70; exec. editor: Archives Biochemistry and Biophysics, 1960—2001, Life Scis., 1973—75, Procs. NAS, 1975—81, Trends in Biochem. Rsch., 1975—78; mem. editl. bd. Biochemistry, 1969—76, 1981—. Recipient medallion, Soc. de Chemie Biologique, 1955, U. Pisa, 1966, Presdl. Rank award as Disting. Sr. Exec., 1981, Rsch. award, Am. Aging Assn., 1992, Lifetime Achievement and Mentoring award, NIH, 1998, Sci. and Humanity prize, Oxygen Club Calif., 2002, Trevor Slater award, Soc. for Free Rabical Rsch., 2002. Mem.: NAS (award in microbiology 1970), Washington Acad. Scis. (award biol. chemistry 1957, Nat. medal sci. 1979, meritorious exec. award 1980, Robert A. Welch award in chemistry 1991, Paul Glenn award in aging 1993, Lifetime Achievement award 2007), Am. Soc. Microbiology, Am. Acad. Arts and Scis., Am. Soc. Biol. Chemists (publs. com. 1966—70, coun. 1974—77, pres. 1983—, Merck award 1983), Am. Chem. Soc. (exec. com. biol. div 1959—64, chmn. div. 1963—64, Paul Lewis Lab. award in enzyme chemistry 1952, Hillebrand award 1969), Washington Oxygen Club. Office: Nat Heart and Lung Inst 9000 Rockville Pike Bethesda MD 20892-0001 Home Phone: 301-869-1747; Office Phone: 301-496-4096. Business E-Mail: erstadtman@nih.gov.

STADTMAN, THRESSA CAMPBELL, biochemist; b. Sterling, NY, Feb. 12, 1920; d. Earl and Bessie (Waldron) Campbell; m. Earl Reece Stadtman, Oct. 19, 1943. BS, Cornell U., 1940, MS, 1942; PhD, U. Calif., Berkeley, 1949. Rsch. assoc. U. Calif., Berkeley, 1942-47, Harvard U. Med. Sch., Boston, 1949-50; biochemist Nat. Heart, Lung and Blood Inst. NIH, USPHS, HHS, Bethesda, Md., 1950—. Mem. Burroughs-Wellcome Fund Toxicology Adv. Commn., 1994-97; pres. Internat. Soc. Vitamins and Related BioFactors, 1998-2001. Editor Jour. Biol. Chemistry, Archives Biochemistry and Biophysics, Molecular and Cellular Biochemistry; editor-in-chief Bio Factors, 1991-95; contbr. articles on amino acid metabolism, methane biosynthesis, vitamin B12 biochemistry, selenium biochemistry to profl. jours. Helen Haye Whitney fellow Oxford U., Eng., 1954-55; Rockefeller Found. grantee U. Munich, 1959-60; recipient Rose award, 1987, Klaus Schwarz medal, 1988, Life Achievement Women in Sci. award L'Oreal-UNESCO, 2000, Bertrand medal and prize Assn. European Trace Elements and Metals in Biology and Medicine, Venice, 2001. Mem. NAS, Am. Soc. Microbiology, Biochem. Soc., Soc. Am. Biochemists, Am. Chem. Soc., Am. Acad. Arts and Scis., Sigma Delta Epsilon (hon.). Home: 16907 Redland Rd Derwood MD 20855-1954 Office Phone: 301-496-3002. Business E-Mail: tc.stadtman@nih.gov.

STADTMUELLER, CLAIRE LOUISE, soprano, performing arts educator; 1 child, Alexis Wyrofsky. MusB, New Eng. Conservatory, Boston, 1981; MusM, U. of R.I., 2004. Soloist Carnegie Hall, NYC, 1998—2007; vis. lectr. Assumption Coll., Worcester, Mass., 2004—. Singer (creator of concept): (cd) Sweet Peace. Avocation: practioner of reconnective healing. Home: 963 Seven Mile Rd Hope RI 02831 Home Phone: 401-823-4843. Personal E-mail: cstadtmueller@earthlink.net.

STAEHELIN, LUCAS ANDREW, cell biology professor; b. Sydney, Feb. 10, 1939; came to U.S., 1969; s. Lucas Eduard and Isobel (Malloch) S.; m. Margrit Weibel, Sept. 17, 1965; children: Daniel Thomas, Philip Roland, Marcel Felix. Dipl. Natw., Swiss Fed. Inst. Tech., Zurich, 1963, PhD in Biology, 1966. Research scientist N.Z. Dept. Sci. and Indsl. Research, 1966-69; research fellow in cell biology Harvard U., Cambridge, Mass., 1969-70; asst. prof. cell biology U. Colo., Boulder, 1970-73, assoc. prof., 1973-79, prof., 1979—. Vis. prof. U. Freiburg, 1978, Swiss Fed. Inst. Tech., 1984, 92, U. Melbourne, Australia, 1998; mem. cellular biology and physiology study sect. NIH, Bethesda, Md., 1980-84, mem. DOE panel on rsch. directions for the energy bioscis., 1988, 92; mem. NSF adv. panel for cellular orgn., 1994-96; mem. plant biology panel NASA. Editl. bd. Jour. Cell Biology, 1977-81, European Jour. Cell Biology, 1981-90, Plant Physiology, 1986-92, Plant Jour., 1991-97, Biology of the Cell, 1996-99, Planta, 2003—, Current Opion in Plant Biology, 2003—; editor: (with C.J. Antzen) Encyclopedia of Plant Physiology, Vol. 19, Photosynthesis III, 1986; contbr. numerous articles to sci. jours. Recipient Humboldt award Humboldt Found., 1978, Sci. Tchr. award U. Colo., 1984, Outstanding Faculty award U. Colo.-Boulder Parents Assn., 2001, Highly Cited Rschr. ISI, 2004, Haselkorn Scholar award, U. Chgo., 2006; grantee NIH, 1971-, USDA, 1994-, NASA, 1997-; hon. sr. fellow U. Melbourne, Australia, 1998, Am. Assn. Adv. Sci., 2004. Mem. AAAS, Am. Soc. Cell Biology, Am. Soc. Plant Physiology, German Acad. Natural Scis. Leopoldina. Home: 2855 Dover Dr Boulder CO 80305-5305 Office: Dept Molecular Cell U Colo 347 UCB Boulder CO 80309-0347 Home Phone: 303-494-8742; Office Phone: 303-492-8843. E-mail: staeheli@colorado.edu.

STAEHLE, ROBERT L., foundation executive; b. Rochester, NY, Apr. 22, 1955; s. Henry Carl and Isabel Montgomery S. BS in Aero. and Astronautic Engring., Purdue U., 1977. Prin. investigator Skylab Expt. ED-31 (bacteria aboard Skylab), NASA/Marshall Space Flight Center, Huntsville, Ala., 1972-74, student trainee engring., 1974-77; sci. observation analyst Caltech/Jet Propulsion Lab., Pasadena, Calif., 1977-78, engr. advanced projects group, 1978-83, mem. tech. staff system integration sect. of Space Sta., 1983-87, mem. tech. staff and space sta., user ops. team leader, 1987-88; from tech. mgr. to dep. mgr.various positions Jet Propulsion Lab., Pasadena, Calif., 1988—2004, dep. mgr. Space Experiments Sys. Sect., 2004—. Prin. founder, pres. World Space Found., South Pasadena, Calif., 1979—; founding dir. So. Calif. Space Bus. Roundtable, 1987-95; bd. dirs. Altadena Foothills Conservancy, 2000—. Co-author: Project Solar Sail; New Am. Libr., 1990; contbr. articles to profl. jours. Mem. Cmty. Leaders Adv. Bd. for Irvine Scholars, Occidental Coll., L.A., 1996-97; bd. dirs. Caltech Y, 1987-93. Nat. Space Club Goddard scholar, 1977; Charles A. Lindbergh Fund grantee, 1986. Fellow Brit. Interplanetary Soc.; mem. Tau Beta Pi, Sigma Gamma Tau. Avocations: photography, hiking, mountain biking. Office: Jet Propulsion Lab Pasadena CA 91109 Business E-Mail: robert.l.staehle@jpl.nasa.gov.

STAEHR, JONATHAN EDWARD, lawyer; b. Auburn, NY, Mar. 17, 1971; s. Jean Marie and Joseph Paul Staehr; m. Jennifer Ann Hemming, Oct. 2, 2004. BS, Cornell U., Ithaca, NY, 1995; JD, SUNY, Buffalo, 2001. Bar: NY 2002. Ptnr. Hemming & Staehr, PC, Cheektowaga, NY, 2006—. Mem.: Erie County Bar Assn. (assoc.). Home: 60 Valley Brook Ln East Amherst NY 14051 Office: Hemming & Staehr PC 3725 Genesee St Ste 1 Cheektowaga NY 14051 Home Phone: 917-842-6278; Office Phone: 716-631-7250. Office Fax: 716-631-7258; Home Fax: 716-631-7258. Business E-Mail: jstaehr@adelphia.net.

STAELIN, DAVID HUDSON, electrical engineering educator, consultant; b. Toledo, May 25, 1938; s. Carl Gustav and Margaret E. (Hudson) S.; m. Ellen Mahoney, June 16, 1962; children: Carl H., Katharine E., Paul H. SB, MIT, 1960, SM, 1961, ScD in Elec. Engring., 1965. Instr. elec. engring. MIT, Cambridge, 1965, asst. prof., 1965—69, assoc. prof., 1969—76, prof., 1976—, asst. dir. Lincoln Lab. Lexington, 1990—2001. Vis. asst. scientist Nat. Radio Astronomy Obs., Charlottesville, Va., 1968-69; cons. Jet Propulsion Lab., Pasadena, Calif., 1969, Wellesley, Mass., 1965—; dir. Environ. Rsch. and Tech., Inc., Concord, Mass., 1969-78; co-founder, chmn. PictureTel Corp., Peabody, Mass., 1984-87; mem. com. on radio frequency requirements for rsch., NAS, Washington, 1980-86, chmn. 1983-86; chmn. advanced microwave sounder working group NASA, Washington, 1981-82, mem. space applications adv. com., 1983-86; mem. adv. com. info. tech. Pres. U.S., Washington, D.C., 2003-05. Co-author: Made in America, 1989, Electromagnetic Waves, 1994; contbr. articles to profl. jours. Fellow: IEEE, AAAS; mem.: Am. Geophys. Union, Am. Meteorl. Soc., Internat. Union for Radio Sci. Achievements include patents for grinding and polishing sheet glass, display of dynamic images, ribbon-beam cathode ray tube. Office: MIT Rm 26-341 Cambridge MA 02139

STAELIN, EARL HUDSON, lawyer; b. Toledo, Apr. 24, 1940; s. Carl Gustav and Margaret E. (Hudson) S.; m. Carol Jane Keeney, Mar. 24, 1973 (div. 1995); 1 child, Vijay Hudson. BA, Yale U., 1962; LLB, U. Mich., 1966. Bar: Ohio 1966, Tex. 1998, Tex. 1982, US Dist. Ct. (we. dist.) Tex. 1988, Colo. 2004, US Ct. Appeals (5th cir.) 1994, Colo. 1998. Assoc. atty. Marshall, Melhorn, Toledo, 1966-69; pvt. practice Toledo, 1969; lectr. law U. Toledo Coll. Law, 1971-72; staff atty. Toledo Legal Aid Soc., 1969-71, dir., 1971-76, sr. staff atty., 1977-81; pvt. practice cons. nutrition Austin, Tex., 1981—82, Denver, 2001—05; staff atty. City of Austin Law Dept., 1982-86; pvt. practice Law Ofcs. of Earl H. Staelin, Austin and Aurora, Colo., 1986—2004; ptnr. Onsager Staelin & Guyerson LLC, Denver, 2004—. Presenter in field. Contbr. articles to profl. jours. Pres. Toledo Coun. on World Affairs, 1971-76; co-organizer Conferences on Nutrition and Crime, Austin, 1982, San Antonio, 1983. Mem. Colo. Bar Assn., State Bar Tex., Humanists Colo. (bd. mem. 2001-, pres. 2007-). Democrat. Unitarian Universalist. Office: Ste 1401 1873 S Bellaire St Denver CO 80222 Mailing: 7982 S Cedar St Littleton CO 80120 Office Phone: 303-512-1123. E-mail: estaelin@comcast.net.

STAELIN, RICHARD, business administration educator; b. Larchmont, NY, Aug. 3, 1939; s. Richard Carl and Dorothy (Potts) S.; m. Julie Ann Fischer, Aug. 24, 1963; children: Adam, Kate. BSME, U. Mich., 1961, BS in Math., 1962, MBA, 1963, PhD, 1969. Market planner IBM, Harrison, NY, 1963-66; prof. Carnegie-Mellon U., Pitts., 1969-82; Edward and Rose Donnell prof. Duke U., Durham, NC, 1982—, assoc. dean faculty affairs, 1982-91, assoc. dean exec. edn., 2000—02, dep. dean, 2002—04; exec. dir. Teradata CRM Ctr., 2004—; mng. dir. GEMBA, 1995-97; exec. dir. Mktg. Sci. Inst., Cambridge, Mass., 1991-93. Vis. prof. Australian Grad. Sch., Kensington, 1980—81. Author: Consumer Protection Legislation and the U.S. Food Industry, 1980; mem. editl. bd. Jour. Mktg. Rsch., 1974-82, Jour. Consumer Rsch., 1976-87; area editor Mktg. Sci., 1983-88; editor-in-chief Mktg. Sci., 1995-97. Mem. Pitts. Exec. Bd.; treas. Pitts. Arts and Crafts Ctr., 1976-79; bd. dirs. Dispute Settlement Ctr., Chapel Hill, NC, Bio Electronics, Frederick, Md., 2005—; bd. vis. drama dept. Duke U., 1990-96. Recipient Best Mktg. Paper award Inst. Mgmt. Sci., 1985, NCNB Faculty award 1990, AMA/Irwin Disting. Mktg. Educators award, 1996, O'Dell award JMR, 1998, Manyard award; HEW grantee, 1972-74, NSF grantee, 1973-79. Mem.: Ill. State Med. Soc. (pres. elect 2006—), INFORMS, Assn. Consumer Rsch., Am. Mktg. Assn. (Converse award 2000). Office: Fuqua Sch of Bus Science Dr Rm 339 Durham NC 27706-2597 Home Phone: 919-382-9977; Office Phone: 919-660-7824. E-mail: rick@staelin.com.

STAFF, JACK ROBERT, international economist, author, monk; b. 1946; s. Robert J. and Harriet G. (Karber) S.; m. Martha Lee Coleman, 1976 (div. 1994); children: Adrian, Marika. Student Wilhelms Universität, W.Ger., 1966; BA, Kalamazoo Coll., 1968; postgrad. Ateneo de Manila Univ., Philippines, 1969; MBA, Am. Mgmt. Assn., 1970; MPA, Harvard U., 1990; DDiv, Universal Life Monastery, 2002. Ordained Taoist-Christian monk DaQin Lineage, 2002. Sr. cons. George Odiorne Assocs., Ann Arbor, Mich., 1972-74; assoc. cons. Hutchings Orgn., Palo Alto, Calif., 1974-75; sr. mgmt. cons. E.H. White & Co., Inc., San Francisco, 1975-78; pres. The Wavelink Orgn., Honolulu, 1978-94; internat. economist dept. fin. econ. Coll. Bus. Adminstrn U. Hawaii, 1991-94; consulting analyst State of Hawaii, Honolulu, 1979-94; pres. Wakashan Consulting, Livingston, Mont., 1994-95; econs. prof. Mont. State U., Bozeman, 1995-97; pres. Cyberesults.com, 1996-98; dir., chief economist Zona Rsch. Inc., Redwood City, Calif., 1998-2001; pres. J.R. Staff & Co., 2001—; rsch. mgr. Inst. Philippine Culture, Manila, 1969; sector adviser U.S. Dept. State, Washington, 1978; fiscal project mgr. U. Hawaii, Honolulu, 1980; vis. lectr. Pacific Asian Mgmt. Inst., 1981; coordinator Pacific Devel. Program East-West Ctr., Honolulu, 1981; mem. staff Prime Minister's Disaster Relief Com., Fiji, 1981; mem. adv. staff Kahauale'a Geothermal Energy Project, 1982-83; mem. Gov.'s Adv. Com. on Criminal Justice Info. Systems, 1984; vis. lectr. Inst. Econ. Devel. and Policy, East-West Ctr., Honolulu, 1992; mem. state innovations task force Nat. Govs. Assn, 1992. Author: Political Aspects of Modernization: Buddhist Experiences in Southeast Asia, 1968, Assessment of International Health Manpower Planning, 3 vols., 1978-80; Consolidated Fiscal Procedures in Education, 1981, Trades and Tradeoffs: Strategic Policy Operants in Public-Private Partnerships, 1990, Bioregionalism as a Public Policy Operant, 1992, Learning to Wave, 2002, Caring to Live, 2003, Reunions with Bliss, 2004; co-author: MBO Systems Manual, 1974; National Manpower Utilization Study, 1976. Dep. dir. Anchorage Econ. Opportunity Agy., Alaska, 1971-72; diplomatic liaison Coll. Fgn. Study Program, W.Ger., 1966. Served with USAFR, 1970-72. Hughes Meml. scholar Kalamazoo Coll., 1965-68; invited scholar Internat. Negotiations Workshop Harvard Law Sch., 1990. InterPacific fellow, 1989-90; recipient Rewick award, McManns award Harvard U. Sch. Govt., 1989-90, Internat. Peace award Beyond War Found., 1987, Outstanding Prof. award U. Hawaii Coll. Bus., 1993; named to Movers and Shakers of Silicon Valley List, San Jose Mercury-News, 2001. Home and Office: PO Box 2445 Sandpoint ID 83864 E-mail: j_r_staff@yahoo.com.

STAFF, JOEL V., energy executive; b. 1944; BA, U. Tex., Austin, 1967; MBA, Tex. A&M U., Kingsville, 1971. Various fin. and gen. mgmt. positions Baker Hughes, Inc., 1976—93; chmn., pres., CEO Nat.-Oilwell, Inc., 1993—2001, exec. chmn., 2001—02; chmn., CEO Reliant Energy, Inc., Houston, 2003—07, non-exec. chmn., 2007—. Bd. dirs. Reliant Energy, Inc., 2002—, Nat. Oilwell, Inc., Ensco Internat., Inc.; adv. dir. King Chapman & Broussard; devel. bd. U. Tex. Health Sci. Ctr., Houston. Adv. dir. Boys and Girls Club, Houston. Office: Reliant Energy Exec Offices PO Box 2286 Houston TX 77252-2286 *

STAFF, VIRGIL CLINTON, retired history educator; b. South Haven, Minn., Apr. 2, 1928; s. Herman Theodore Staff and Eva Mae Holm; m. Katie Velma LaVada Falkner. BA, Atlantic Union Coll., 1951; MA, U. Calif., Berkeley, 1954. Cert. gen. secondary Calif. Mgr. Blue Chip Co., Richmond, 1957, Alta Employment Agy., Oakland, Calif., 1957—58; staff James Lick Sch., San Francisco, 1958—68; instr. Am. history Balboa H.S., San Francisco, 1968—89; ret., 1989. Author: D-Day on the Western Pacific, 1982; contbr. articles to profl. jours. With US Army, 1954—56. Mem.: Am. Hist. Assn., Mutual UFO Network (state sect. dir. 1980—90, dir. No. Calif. chpt. 1990—99, dir. We. Region 1999—, bd. dirs. 1999—), Feather River Rail Soc., Pacific Locomotive Assn., Railway and Locomotive Hist. Soc., Calif. State Sheriffs' Assn. (assoc.), Lexington Group, Friends of Cal History Dept., Bay Area Electric RR Assn., Am. Legion. Avocation: philately. Home: 1700 Sonoma Ave Berkeley CA 94707 Personal E-mail: sbx120@earthlink.net.

STAFFELDT, DARLENE MARIA PREBLE, library director; b. Great Falls, Mont. d. Ardith and Lowell Preble; m. Bill Staffeldt; children: Carla, Dora. MLS, U. Wash. With State Libr. Mont., Helena, 1976—, reference libr., libr. devel. cons., dir. info. resources, dir. statewide libr. resources, state libr., 2004—. Recipient Gov.'s award for Excellence, 1993, Sheila Cates Libr. of Yr. award, Mont. Libr. Assn., 1999. Office: Montana State Libr PO Box 201800 Helena MT 59620-1800 Office Phone: 406-444-3115. Office Fax: 406-444-0266. E-mail: dstaffeldt@mt.gov. *

STAFFIER, PAMELA MOORMAN, psychologist; b. Passaic, NJ, Dec. 7, 1942; d. Wynant Clair and Jeannette Frances (Rentzsch) Moorman; m.

John Staffier, Jr., Apr. 5, 1975; children: M. Anthony, C. Matthew. BA, Bucknell U., 1964; MA in Psychology, Assumption Coll., Worcester, Mass., 1970, CAGS, 1977; PhD, Union Inst., 1978. Psychologist Westboro (Mass.) State Hosp., 1965, prin. psychologist, asst. to supt., 1973—76; rsch. psychologist Wrentham (Mass.) State Sch., 1966, Cushing Hosp., Framingham, Mass., 1967; prin. psychologist, asst. to supt. Grafton (Mass.) State Hosp., 1967—72; dir. Staffier Clinic, 1978—; psychologist Moriarty Mental Health Clinic. Cons. in field. Mem.: APA (assoc.), Nat. Register Health Svc. Providers Psychology, Mass. Psychol. Assn., Am. Psychol. Practitioners Assn. (founding mem.). Achievements include research in state hospital closings; biochemical basis of schizophrenia. Home: 68 Adams St Westborough MA 01581 Office: 57 E Main St Westborough MA 01581-1464 Office Phone: 508-366-0406. Personal E-mail: johnstaffier@charter.net.

STAFFIERI, VICTOR A., energy executive; BA, Yale U., 1977; JD, Fordham U., 1980. From atty. to gen. counsel L.I. Lighting Co., Hicksville, NY, 1980-92; sr. v.p., gen. counsel, corp. sec. LG&E Energy Corp., Louisville, 1992, sr. v.p. pub. policy, gen. counsel, 1992-93, pres. Louisville Gas and Electric Co., 1993-97, pres. distbn. svcs. divsn., 1995-97, CFO, 1997-99, pres., COO, 1999—2001, chmn., CEO, 2001—. Bd. trustees Bellarmine Coll., 1995—; co-chair Jefferson County-Louisville Area C. of C. Family Bus. Partnership, 1996-97; bd. dirs. Ky. Country Day, 1996—, Metro United Way, 1998—. Mem. Louisville Area C. of C. (bd. dirs. 1994-97). Office: LG&E Energy Corp Dept Corp Comm 220 W Main St Louisville KY 40202

STAFFORD, ARTHUR CHARLES, medical association administrator; b. Cleve., May 10, 1947; s. Charles Arthur and Florence Mildred (Hovey) S.; m. Patricia Anne Cz, Dec. 20, 1991. BS, Kent State U., 1977; MBA, Lake Erie Coll., 1984. Med. tech. VA, Cleve., 1977-81, supr. med. tech., 1981-97; lab. mgr. Univ. Hosps. Health System Meml. Hosp. of Geneva, Ohio, 1998-99; instr. Lake Erie Coll., Painesville, Ohio, 1980-82; mgr. customer svc. Giant Eagle Supermarket, Madison, Ohio, 2001—02; instr. Cuyahoga C.C., Cleve., 1988-91, 2003—; customer svc. Progressive Ins. Co., Mayfield Heights, 2004—. Pres. Kent State U. Veterans Assn., 1974, mem. Kent State U Budget Review Com., 1975. Contbr. articles to profl. jour. Mem. Am. Legion, 1974, VFW, 1973. With USN, 1968-72. Mem.: Rock and Roll Hall of Fame, Founders Club. Republican. Avocations: genealogy, computers, antiques, chess, cooking. Home: 2193 Chimney Ridge Dr Madison OH 44057-2588 E-mail: czstafford@ncweb.com.

STAFFORD, C. STEWART, educational consultant, educator; b. Bluefield, W.Va., Aug. 25, 1939; s. John Roy Stafford and Virginia Walker O'Rourke Stafford. BA, Flora MacDonald Coll. Cert. Teacher NC Dept. of Pub. Instrn., 1961. Tchr. Robeson County Pub. Schs., Lumberton, NC, 1961—66; tchr. of gifted/talented Cumberland County Pub. Schs., Fayetteville, NC, 1963—75, asst. prin., 1967—75, coord. of fed. project, 1975—78, resouce tchr. for gifted/talented, 1979—83; vice chmn. adv. com. NC State Bd. Edns. Title IV, 1976—80; resource tchr. for gifted/talented Ft. Bragg Dependents Schs., NC, 1983—99; acting dir. career develop. program Ft. Bragg Schs., 1986, ednl. technologist, 1999—. Cons. and trainer NC Dept. Pub. Instrn., Raleigh, NC, 1967—90; US rep. World Confederation Profl. Tchrs., 1977; pres., nc assn. of educators NC Assn. Educators, 1978—79; trainer NC Tchr. Acad., Durham, 1994—. Contbr. booklet, training manual. Adv. dir. North Carolina State Bd. Educations, 1977—82. Recipient Outstanding Tchr. Yr., NC Assn. Gifted and Talented, 1986, Spl. Services award, NC Assn. of Educators, 1974 - 1983, Disting. Svc., Nat. Edn. Assns. First Am. Caucus, 1977. Mem.: NEA (life), Assn. Supervision and Curriculum Develop., Phi Delta Kappa (assoc.), ASCD (assoc.), NC Assn. for the Gifted,Talented (life), NC Assn. of Educators (life). Achievements include research in Mainstreaming the Gifted and Talented: Grades 7-12; Integrating Schools in the 1960s; Effective Instructional Methods for Gifted/Talented Students; Construction of the North Carolina Association of Educators State Headquarters. Avocations: reading, travel. Home: P O Box 53024 Fayetteville NC 28305-3024 Office: Fort Bragg Schs P O Box 70089 Fort Bragg NC 28307-0089 Home Phone: 910-485-3579; Office Phone: 910-436-4666 222.

STAFFORD, DONALD GENE, chemistry professor; b. Valliant, Okla., Oct. 9, 1930; s. Otto Lewis and Rose Lavelle (Osterdock) S.; m. Jane Wright, July 5, 1951; children: Michael Royce, Robert Gene, Joel Dan. BS, U. Okla., 1957, PhD, 1969; MS, Okla. State U., 1961. Prof. sci. edn. East Cen. U., Ada, Okla., 1961-73, prof. chemistry, 1973—. Adj. prof. U. Okla., Norman, 1970—. Author: The Improvement of Science in Oklahoma (7-12), 1970, Guidelines and Successful Practices in Elementary Edn, 1970, Wings for a Dinosaur, 1972, Early Childhood Resource Book, 1972, Teaching Science in the Elementary School, 1973, 3d edit., 1979, Teaching Science in the Secondary School, 1973, Research, Teaching, and Learning with the Piaget Model, 1976, Investigations in Physical Science, 1976, The Learning Science Program K-6 (7 children's books and 7 tchr.'s guides), 1976, TOP, The Oklahoma Project, Chemistry, 1987, The Learning Cycle, 1988, The Lost City of Balee, A Novel for Young Teenagers, 2000, Don's Rhymes, A Book of Poetry, 2000. Served with AUS, 1948-53. Mem. Am. Chem. Soc., Nat. Sci. Tchrs. Assn., Okla. Sci. Tchrs. (pres. 1973-74, 78-79), Sigma Xi. Home: 2202 Fullview Dr Ada OK 74820-4436 Home Phone: 580-332-9246. Personal E-mail: donjane@cableone.net.

STAFFORD, FRANK P., economist, educator; b. 1962; married; 3 children. BA, Northwestern U., 1962; MBA, U. Chgo., 1964, PhD, 1968. Asst. prof. econs. U. Mich., Ann Arbor, 1966—71, assoc. prof., 1971—73, 1974—75, prof., 1978—, chmn., 1980—83. Spl. asst. for econ. affairs Office Asst. Sec. Policy, Eval. and Rsch. Dept. Labor, Washington, 1975—76, mem. small grants panel, 1978—80; vis. assoc. prof. Stanford U., 1973—74; vis. prof. U. Saarlands, Saarbruken, Germany, 1986; vis. scholar Worklife Study Ctr., Stockholm, 1988; rschr. Indsl. Inst. for Econ. and Social Rsch., Stockholm, 1979, Stockholm, 84. Editor (with F. Thomas Juster): Americans' Use of Time, 1982; bd. editors: Am. Econ. Rev., 1976—78; contbr. articles to profl. jours. Home: 3535 Daleview Dr Ann Arbor MI 48105-9686 Business E-Mail: fstaffor@umich.edu.

STAFFORD, FRANK PETER, JR., economics professor, consultant; b. Chgo., Sept. 17, 1940; s. Frank Peter and Ida Gustava (Tormala) S.; m. Lilian Elisabeth Lundin, Aug. 8, 1964; children: Craig Peter, Jennifer Elisabeth, Christine Anna BA, Northwestern U., 1962; MBA, U. Chgo., 1964, PhD, 1968. Asst. prof. econs. U. Mich., 1966-71, assoc. prof., 1971-73, 74-75, prof., 1976—, chmn. dept. econs., 1980—, rsch. scientist Inst. Social Rsch., 1995—, chair budget study com., 1995—, assoc. dir. Inst. for Social Rsch., 2000—. Vis. assoc. prof. Grad. Sch. Bus.-Stanford U., 1973-74; spl. asst. for econ. affairs U.S. Dept. Labor, Washington, 1975-76; vis. prof. dept. econs. U. Saarlandes, Fed. Republic Germany, 1986; faculty rsch. assoc. Inst. Social Rsch., Ann Arbor, 1979—; vis. scholar Indsl. Inst. for Econs. and Social Rsch., Stockholm, 1979, 83, 90, Worklife Study Ctr., Stockholm, 1988, 90; Tinbergen Found. prof. U. Amsterdam, 1992, 94; panel mem. Social Sci. Rsch. Coun., N.Y.C., 1979—; rsch. assoc. Nat. Bur. Econ. Rsch., Cambridge, Mass., 1983—; prof. econs. Tinbsrgne Found. U. Amsterdam, 1992; vis. scholar U. Stockholm, 1994. Author, editor: Time Use Goods and Well Being, 1986, Studies in Labor Market Behavior: Sweden and the United States, 1981; mem. editorial bd.: Am. Econ. Rev., 1976-78; contbr. articles to profl. jours. Dir. Panel Study of Income Dynamics, 1995—. Grantee NSF, 1973, 80, 95—, 2002—, NICHD, 1995—, Nat. Ins. on Aging, 1999—. Mem. Am. Econs. Assn. Home: 3535 Daleview Dr Ann Arbor MI 48105-9686 Office: U Mich Dept Econs Lorch Hall Rm 312 Ann Arbor MI 48105 Office Phone: 734-936-0323. Business E-Mail: fstaffor@umich.edu.

STAFFORD, J. FRANCIS CARDINAL, Cardinal; b. Balt., July 26, 1932; s. F. Emmett and Mary Dorothy Stafford. Student, Loyola Coll., Balt., 1950—52; BA, St. Mary's Sem., Balt., 1954; STB, STL, Gregorian U., Rome, 1958; MSW, Cath. U., 1964; postgrad., Rutgers U., 1963, St. Mary's Sem. and Univ., Balt., 1973—75. Spiritual moderator Ladies of Charity Ch., Balt., 1966—76; spiritual moderator Soc. St. Vincent de Paul, Balt., 1965—76; urban vicar Archdiocese of Balt., 1966—76, monsignor, 1970, vicar gen., auxiliary bishop, 1976—82; bishop Diocese of Memphis, 1982—86; archbishop Archdiocese of Denver, 1986—96; pres. Pontifical Coun. Laity, 1996—2003; elevated to cardinal, 1998—; mem. Major Penitentiary, Apostolic Penitentiary, 2003—. Archdiocesan liaison Md. Cath. Conf., Balt., 1975—78; Oriental Orthodox/Roman Cath. cons. Nat. Cath. Conf. Bishops, 1977—85, com. on doctrine, 1978—82, chmn. ecumenical and interreligious affairs com., 1987—90; co-chmn. bilateral dialogue Roman Cath./World Meth. Coun., 1977—86; co-chmn. U.S. Roman Cath.-Luth. Dialogue, 1986—; chmn. Bishops' com. marriage and family life U.S. Cath. Conf., 1978—84; mem. gen. Synod Bishops, Vatican City, 1980. Contbr. articles to profl. jours. Trustee Good Samaritan Hosp., Balt., 1973—77, Cath. U. Am., 1990—, Blue Cross of Md., Inc., 1973—76, Balt. Urban Coalition, 1970—75; trustee, chmn. St. Thomas Theol. Sem., 1987—; bd. dirs. Assn. Cath. Charities, Balt., 1966—76, U. Md. Sch. Social Work and Planning, 1973—76. Recipient Father Kelly Alumni award, Loyola H.S., 1978, Alumni Laureate, Loyola Coll., 1979. Mem.: Oriental Orthodox Roman Cath. Consultation, World Meth. Conf. Roman Cath. Dialogue (co-chmn. 1977—86), Congregation for Doctrine of Faith, Luth. Roman Cath. Dialogue, Nat. Conf. Cath. Bishops. Office: Major Penitentiary Apostolic Penitentiary 00120 Vatican City Italy Home Phone: 3906 69887203; Office Phone: 0669887625. Business E-Mail: vati877@apostpnt.va.

STAFFORD, JAMES FRANCIS, cardinal; Ordained priest, Balt., 1957; aux. bishop, 1976; bishop Memphis, 1982—86; archibishop Denver, 1986—96; pres. Pontifical Coun. for Laity, Vatican, 1996—; elevated to cardinal, 1998; Major Penitentiary Apostolic Penitentiary, Vatican City, 2003—. Office: Tribunale della Penitenzieria Apostolica Palazzo della Cancelleria 00120 Vatican City Italy Office Phone: 390669887625.

STAFFORD, REBECCA, retired academic administrator, sociologist, consultant; b. Topeka, July 9, 1936; d. Frank C. and Anne Elizabeth (Larrick) S.; m. Willard Van Hazel. AB magna cum laude, Radcliffe Coll., 1958, MA, 1961; PhD, Harvard U., 1964. Sociology lectr., dept. social rels. Sch. Edn., Harvard U., Cambridge, Mass., 1964-70, mem. vis. com. bd. overseers, 1973-79; assoc. prof. sociology U. Nev., Reno, 1970-74, prof., 1973-80, chmn. dept. sociology, 1974-77, dean Coll. Arts and Scis., 1977-80; pres. Bemidji (Minn.) State U., 1980-82; exec. v.p., prof. sociology Colo. State U., Ft. Collins, 1982-83; pres. Chatham Coll., Pitts., 1983-91, prof. sociology, 1992-93; pres. Monmouth U., West Long Branch, NJ, 1993—2003. Cons. higher edn., 1992—, U.S. Internat. U. on Acad. Planning, 1992-94, USDA, 1992-93, Integra Bank, 1992-93, Millsaps Coll, Jackson, Miss., 1991, U. Pitts. Med. Sch., 1992-93; co-dir. acad. leadership inst. Carnegie Mellon U., 1991-93, U. Tenn., Knoxville, 1992-93; vis. scholar dept. sociology Harvard U., 1991; mem. faculty coll. mgmt. program. Carnegie Mellon U., Pitts., 1984-93; cons. adult devel. grant Harvard U. Health Svcs., Cambridge, 1979, rsch. sociologist, 1964-69; dir. ednl. enrichment project Harvard Sch. Edn., 1966-67, 69-70. Mem. editl. bd. Sociometry, 1974-77, Sociol. Focus., 1974-77; contbr. articles to profl. jours.; presenter papers at profl. confs. Trustee Monmouth Med. Ctr., 1993—, Winchester-Thurston Sch., Pitts., 1986-91, Montefiore Hosp., Pitts., 1990-93; trustee Presbyn.-Univ. Hosp., Pitts., 1984-93, exec. planning com., 1986-89, fin. com., 1989-93; pres. Pitts. Coun. Higher Edn., 1990; mem. Found. Ind. Colls. Inc. Pa., 1984-91, sec., 1986; mem. Colo. Commn. Higher Edn. Task Force on Quality, 1981; mem. adv. bd. Animal Rescue League, Pitts., 1989-93; founder Bemidji Area Women's Network, Minn., 1980-82; mem. intergovtl. planning steering com. Bemidji, 1980-82; mem. cmty. rels. com. Girl Scouts Southwestern Pa., 1983-86; mem. brotherhood dinner coun. Nat. Conf. Christians and Jews, 1985; mem. hon. centennial com. Pa. Sch. Blind Children, Pitts., 1986; mem. citizens sponsoring com. Allegheny Conf. Cmty. Devel., Pitts., 1983-91; mem. five state regional bd. First Union Nat. Bank, 1996—; bd. dirs. Pitts. Symphony, 1984-93, First Fidelity Bank, N.A., N.J., 1993-95, Integra Bank, Pitts., 1987-97, Urban League, Pitts., 1984-87, Women's Ctr., Ft. Collins, Colo., 1982-83, Coun. Colls. Arts and Scis., 1978-81; chmn. Harvard U. Grad. Soc. Coun., 1987-93. Recipient McCurdy-Rinkle prize for rsch. Eastern Psychiat. Assn., 1970; named Woman of Yr. in Edn., City of Pitts., 1986, Vectors/Pitts., 1987, Woman of Yr. in Edn., YWCA Tribute to Women, 1989, Women of Distinction award Muscular Dystrophy Assn., 1999, Women of Leadership award Monmouth County Girl Scouts Am., 1995, Woman of Achievement in Edn. award Monmouth County Adv. Commn. on Status of Women, 1994, Salute to Policymakers award Exec. Women in N.J., 1994; grantee Am. Coun. Edn. Inst. Acad. Deans, 1979, Inst. Ednl. Mgmt., Harvard U., 1984. Mem. Assn. Ind. Colls. and Univs. of N.J. (v.p. 1999—, sec. 1998-99, treas. 1994-98, pres. northeastern conf. 1995-99, bd. dirs. 1993—), Am. Coun. on Edn., Assn. Am. Colls., Soc. for Coll. and Univ. Planning (mem. instl. decision making and resource planning acad. 1994—), Ind. Coll. Fund (treas. 1995-96, bd. dirs. 1993—), Nat. Coun. Family Rels., Harvard U. Alumni Assn. (bd. dirs. 1985-87), Phi Beta Kappa, Phi Kappa Phi. Business E-Mail: Becky@monmouth.edu.

STAFFORD, WILLIAM FRANKLIN, veterinarian, educator; b. Loudon, Tenn., Mar. 18, 1955; s. Gene Franklin and Martha Catherine Stafford; m. Jody Ann Rudd, Sept. 1, 1979; children: William Brent, Emily Ann. DVM, U. Tenn., Knoxville, 1980. Cert. secondary edn. tchr. Veterinarian Bilderback Animal Clinic, Sweetwater, Tenn., 1980—85; farmer Loudon, 1982—2004; tchr. Loudon H.S., 2005—. Deacon and master min. Stockton Valley Bapt. Ch., Loudon, 2000—. Named New Tchr. of Yr., London County Edn. Found., 2005—06; named one of Young Dairymen, Dairymen, Inc., 1990. Mem.: Lions. Home: 1622 Stafford Rd Loudon TN 37774 Fax: 865-458-4536. Personal E-mail: volvolvolv@aol.com.

STAFFORD, WILLIAM HENRY, JR., federal judge; b. Masury, Ohio, May 11, 1931; s. William Henry and Frieda Gertrude (Nau) S.; m. Nancy Marie Helman, July 11, 1959; children: William Henry III, Donald Helman, David Harrold. BS, Temple U., 1953, LL.B., 1956; JD, 1968. Bar: Fla. 1961, U.S. Ct. Appeals (5th cir.) 1969, U.S. Supreme Ct. 1970. Assoc. firm Robinson & Roark, Pensacola, 1961-64; individual practice law Pensacola, 1964-67; state atty., 1967-69; U.S. atty., 1969-75; U.S. dist. judge U.S. Dist. Ct. for No. Dist. Fla., Tallahassee, 1975—, chief judge, 1981-93, sr. judge, 1996—. Fgn. Intelligence Surveillance Ct., 1996—2003. Instr. Pensacola Jr. Coll., 1964, 68; mem. judicial council U.S. Ct. Appeals (11th cir.), 1986-89; apptd. com. on intercircuit assignments, 1987-92, subcom. on fed. jurisdiction, 1983-87; adj. prof. Fla. State U. Coll. Law, 1992-97. Lt. (j.g.) USN, 1957-60. Mem. Fla. Bar (mem. numerous coms., bench/bar commn. 1991-92, bench/bar implementation commn. 1993), Dist. Judges Assn. 11th Cir. (pres. 1984-85), State Fed. Judicial Council Fla., William H. Stafford Am. Inn Ct., Tallahassee Bar Assn., Tallahassee Inn (founding pres. 1989-91), Mason (33d degree), Sigma Phi Epsilon, Phi Delta Phi. Republican. Episcopalian. Office Phone: 850-521-3617.

STAGE, THOMAS BENTON, psychiatrist; b. Marietta, Ohio, July 23, 1926; s. John Douglas and Grace (Shawhan) S.; m. Doris Jeane Weinstock, Dec. 22, 1951; children: Samuel Ray, Amy Elizabeth, James Robert; m. Alicia Anderson Marsh, June 7, 1993. BA cum laude, Marietta Coll., 1949; MD, Ohio State U., 1952. Diplomate: Am. Bd. Psychiatry and Neurology. Intern Detroit Receiving Hosp., 1952-53; psychiat. resident, fellow Menninger Sch. Psychiatry, Topeka, 1953-56; sect. chief, chief psychiatry VA Hosp., Topeka, 1956-62, adminstr. Sheridan, Wyo., 1962-66, dir. Salem, Va., 1967-72; dep. asst. chief med. dir. for ambulatory care VA Central Office, Washington, 1972-74; dir. No. Va. Mental Health Inst., Falls Church, 1974-78; asst. commr. for mental health State of Va., Richmond, 1978-79; dir. clin. svcs. Fairfax-Falls Ch. Cmty. Svcs. Bd., Vienna, Va., 1979-82, psychiat. cons. for med. affairs, 1982-99, med. dir. Fairfax, 1999—2002, cons. quality improvements, 2002—. Instr. Menninger Sch. Psychiatry, 1958-62, U. Wyo. Sch. Nursing, 1963-66; assoc. prof. U. Va. Med. Sch., 1972-74; cons. surveyor Joint Commn. on Accreditation of Hosps., 1976-2004; cons. Crow-No. Cheyenne USPHS Hosp., 1963-66, Ala. Dept. Mental Health (Wyatt Com.), 1986-91; psychiatric cons. on accreditation Commonwealth of Va. Dept. Mental Health, Mental Retardation and Substance Abuse, 1982-2002; mem. Comprehensive Mental Health Ctr. Com., 1968-73, Gov.'s Adv. Commn. on Mental Health, 1971-74; chmn. Drug Abuse Rehab. Com., 1970-73; cons. adminstrv. psychiatry NIMH, 1975-78; chmn. steering com. Asso. Faculties Program Community Psychiatry, Washington, 1975-77; mem. State Health Coordinating Coun., 1976-89. Contbr. articles to profl. jours. Served wtih USNR, 1944-46, PTO. Fellow Am. Psychiat. Assn. (life, disting.); mem. Am. Assn. Psychiat. Adminstrs., Washington Psychiat. Soc., Psychiat. Soc. Va., Am. Assn. Community Psychiatrists. Home: 11410 Hollow Timber Way Reston VA 20194-1906 Office: Fairfax-Falls Ch Cmty Svcs Bd 12011 Government Center Pkwy Fairfax VA 22035-1100

STAGEBERG, ROGER V., lawyer; B in Math. with distinction, U. Minn., 1963, JD cum laude, 1966; MA in History and Theology, Luther Seminary, 2006. Assoc. Mackall, Crounse & Moore, Mpls., 1966-70, ptnr., 1970-86; shareholder and officer Lommen, Abdo, Cole, King & Stageberg, P.A., Mpls., 1986—. Co-chmn. joint legal svcs. funding com. Minn. Supreme Ct., 1995-96. Mem. U. Minn. Law Rev. Bd. dirs. Mpls. Legal Aid Soc., 1970-2003, treas., 1973, pres., 1977, dir. of fund, 1980—, chmn. of fund, 1998-2000; chmn. bd. trustees Colonial Ch. of Edina, 1975, chmn. congregation, 1976, pres. found., 1978; officer, trustee Mpls. Found, 1983-88. Mem. Minn. State Bar Assn. (numerous offices and coms., pres. 1994), Hennepin County Bar Assn. (chmn. securities law sect. 1979, chmn. attys. referral svc. com. 1980, sec. 1980, treas. 1981, pres. 1983), Order of Coif. Office: Lommen Abdo Cole King & Stageberg PA 80 S 8th St Ste 2000 Minneapolis MN 55402-2119 Home Phone: 612-378-3001; Office Phone: 612-336-9335. Business E-Mail: roger@lommen.com.

STAGER, DONALD K., retired construction company executive; Chmn., pres., CEO Dillingham Constrn. Holdings Inc., Pleasanton, Calif., 1982-99; with Guy F. Atkinson Co., 1952—82; ret., 1999. Recipient, Roebling award Am. Soc. of Civil Engineers, 1995, Golden Beaver award for Mgmt Beavers, Inc., 1998. Office: 957 Wapato Way Manson WA 98831-9595

STAGER, JOHN C., information scientist, educator; b. Johnstown, Pa., June 28, 1955; s. John A. and Lillian R. Stager; m. Joanne F. Burke, Nov. 1, 1986; children: Jessica, Cassidy Boyd. AA, Riverside C.C., 1995; BA in Environ. Studies, U. Redlands, 2000, M in Mgmt., 2001; MS in Mgmt. of Info. Systems, Claremont Grad. U., 2004, PhD in Mgmt. of Info. Systems, 2007. Programmer US Nat. Bank, Johnstown, Pa., 1974—77, Carnegie Mellon U., Pitts., 1976—77; programmer analyst North Am. Van Lines, Ft. Wayne, Ind., 1977; sr. programmer Philips Industries Inc., Dayton, Ohio, 1977—79; programmer, analyst Kaufman and Broad, LA, 1979; sr. computer analyst/dba Beckman Instruments Inc., Brea, Calif., 1979—80; sr. staff cons. Yourdon, Inc., NYC, 1980—81; sr. computer analyst/dba Beckman Instuments, Brea, Calif., 1981—82; data adminstr. Shiley Inc., Irvine, Calif., 1982—83; account systems engr. IBM, LA, 1983—84; systems mgr. Colonial Ins. Co., Anaheim, Calif., 1984—86; sr. cons. Carter, Hawley, Hale Stores, Anaheim, Calif., 1986—89; database adminstr. No. Ariz. U., Flagstaff, Ariz., 1989—90; pres./prin. cons. Acorn Design Consultants, Inc., Norco, Calif., 1999—2006; sr. cons. Compuware, Irvine, Calif., 1990—2004; adj. prof. U. Redlands, Calif., 2004—06, Chapman U., Orange, Calif., 2005—06; dir. sys. devel. Pemco Technologies, Seattle, 2006—. Author: (book chapter) Geographical Information Systems in Business; contbr. articles to prof. jours. Fellow, Claremont Grad. U., Sch. Info. Sci., 2002—04; Whitehead Leadership Soc. fellow, U. Redlands, 2000. Mem.: Western History Assn., Am. Soc. Environ. History, Western Social Sci. Assn. (sect. coord. geography 2004—06), Assn. Am. Geographers, Assn. Info. Systems. Home Phone: 425-377-0203. Personal E-mail: jcstager@earthlink.net.

STAGG, CLYDE LAWRENCE, lawyer; b. St. Petersburg, Fla., May 22, 1935; s. Milton Gurr and Clyda Montese (Lawrence) S.; m. Betsy Barron, Aug. 22, 1959; children: Sharon, Brian, Lauren, Stephen. BSJ, U. Fla., Gainesville, 1956, LLB, 1959. Bar: Fla. 1959, US Dist. Ct. (mid. dist.) Fla. 1959, US Ct. Appeals (5th cir.) 1969, US Supreme Ct. 1971, US Ct. Appeals (11th cir.) 1987. Assoc. Shackleford, Farrior, Tampa, Fla., 1959-60; asst. solicitor Hillsborough County Solicitor's Office, Tampa, 1960-61; chief asst. state atty. State Atty.'s Office, Tampa, 1963-64, asst. state atty., 1961-63; ptnr. Whitaker, Mann & Stagg, Tampa, Knight, Jones, Whitaker & Germany, Tampa, 1965-67, Holland & Knight, Tampa, 1968-74, 80-86, Stichter, Stagg, Hoyt, et al, Tampa, 1974-79, Stagg, Hardy, Ferguson, Murnaghan & Mathews P.A., Tampa, 1986-93, Akerman, Senterfitt & Eidson P.A., Tampa, 1993—2006; pvt. practice Tampa, 2006—. Bd. dirs. Fla. Lawyers Mut. Ins. Co., 1987- Mem., sec. Hillsborough Area Regional Transit Authority, Tampa, 1979—85; mem., sec., vice chmn., chmn. Tampa Sports Authority, 1985—89; spl. counsel US Senator Bob Graham, 1988; mem. nat. conf. of commrs. Uniform State Laws, 1996—2005; bd. dirs. United Way Greater Tampa, Inc., Tampa, 1988—91, Fla. Blood Svcs., Inc., Tampa, 1989—, chmn., 2003—07. Named one of Legal Elite, Fla. Trend mag., 2004, 2007. Mem. ABA, Am. Bar Found. (life), Fla. Bar (bd. govs. 1974-75), Hillsborough County Bar Assn. (pres. 1970-71, Outstanding Lawyer award 1998), Fla. Bar Found. (life); Am. Bd. Trial Advocates, Greater Tampa C. of C. (bd. dirs. 1988-91), Am. Inn Ct. (master emeritus of bench). Home: 3303 W San Nicholas St Tampa FL 33629-7034 Office: 401 E Jackson St Ste 1700 Tampa FL 33602 Office Phone: 813-223-3130. Personal E-mail: staggadr@verizon.net.

STAGG, LOUIS CHARLES, English language and literature educator; b. Jan. 3, 1933; s. Louis Anatol and Gladys (Andrews) S.; m. Mary Casner, June 5, 1959; children: Robert Charles, Helen Marie. BA in English, La. Coll., Pineville, 1955; MA in English, U. Ark., Fayetteville, 1957, PhD in English, 1963. Tchg. asst. English U. Ark., 1955-59; asst. prof. William Jewell Coll., 1959-60; instr. Stephen F. Austin State U., 1960-62; asst. prof. Memphis State U. (now U. Memphis), 1962-69, assoc. prof., 1969-77, prof. English lang. and lit., 1977-98, prof. emeritus, 1998—, dir. grad. studies in English, 1985-88, dir. English Drama Players, 1968-92, dir. undergrad. advising for English, 1970-80, 88-91, chair policies and procedures com. for English, 1983-95, cons. for 2001 program. Chmn. acad. policies com. Memphis State U. Senate, 1981-82, 88-90, 93-96, exec. com. senate, 1987-91, 93-96, parliamentarian of senate, 1987-88, 90-91, 94-96, humanities rep. budget adv. com. dean Coll. Arts and Scis., 1992-93, adv. bd. Acad. Exch. Quar., 1997-2000, steering com., chair of schedules, originator Alliance Creative Theatre, Edn. and Rsch. series, 1986, 89-90, 92, 94, 96, 98; cons. NEH, 1975-76, 78, Ohio State U. Press, 1985-86, U. Jordan, Amman, 1985; chair policies and procedures subdivsn. Eng. dept. so. assn. colls., schs. self study, steering com. 1992-93; cons. Memphis State U. Learning Media-Ctrs. catalogue Shakespeare holdings, 1992-93, rev., 1993-95. Author: (with J. Lasley Dameron) Poe's Critical Vocabulary, 1966; author series: Index to the Figurative Language of John Webster's Tragedies, 1967, of Ben Jonson's Tragedies, 1967, of Thomas Heywood's Tragedies, 1967, of George Champman's Tragedies, 1970, of Thomas Middleton's Tragedies, 1970, of Cyril Tourneur's Tragedies, 2d edit., all 7 under title Index to the Figurative Language of the Tragedies of Shakespeare's Chief 17th Century Contemporaries, 1977, 3d edit., 1982, Index to the Figurative Language of the Tragedies of Shakespeare's Chief 18th Century Contemporaries, 1984; contbr. to Great Writers of the English Language Dramatists, 1979, 87; circulation editor Interpretations, 1976-80, Libraries of the World Series for U. Memphis Libr. Jour. (series 1-11); contbr. articles to profl. jours. Mem. Memphis Oratorio Soc. Chorus, 1969-92, diction coach, 1987; active Memphis Symphony Chorus, 1993-04, newsletter com., 1999-00; active Memphis in May Sunset Symphony Choir, 1996, Martin Luther King Tribute Concert Choir, 1995-96, 99-04, City of Memphis Faure Requiem Concert, 2001, Memphis Symphony Chorus and Orch. prodn. Rolling Requiem for 9/11/02; lay reader Episcopal Ch.; program chair Friends of Univ. Librs., 2000-02, v.p., 2002-03, pres. 2003—05, exec. coun., 2005—, vice chmn. pub. programs, 2005—; mem. at large exec. com. U. Memphis Assn. Retirees, 2003-06. Grantee NEH, 1967, Memphis State U., 1965, Travel grant to U.S. Libr. Congress, 1971. Mem. MLA (life), So. Humanities Coun. (sec.-treas. 1974-76, exec. com. 1976-83, 94-96, chmn. coun. 1993-94, chmn. sect. humanities in pluralistic soc. 1984, ad hoc com. on crisis in tchg. humanities 1977, chmn. local arrangements for convs. 1975, 94, chmn. sect. on Thomas Hardy 1996), Tenn. Philol. Assn. (pres. 1976-77, exec. com. 1977, local arrangements chmn. 1965, 69, 75, 87, chmn. Shakespeare sect. 1996, local arrangements com. for Memphis conv. for 2009), Marlowe Soc. Am. (book reviewer 1984, 86-88, 93), Am. Soc. for Theatre Rsch., Samuel Beckett Soc., Conf. on Christianity and Lit., South Cen. Conf. on Christianity and Lit. Soc. for Study of Works of Harold Pinter (life, asst. constn. revision 1988, asst. with planning 1992, treas. 1994-98, exec. com. 1994-98), Ark. Philol. Assn., Shakespeare Assn. Am. (local arrangements host com. 1985), Stratford-upon-Avon Shakespeare Festival (Eng.), Eugene O'Neill Soc., Alliance for Creative Theatre, Edn. and Rsch. (chmn. schedules com., originator of proposal 1986, 89-90, 92, 94, 96, 98, cons. residency S.E. Mo. State U. 1997), Internat. Shakespeare Assn., Am. Soc. Theatre Rsch., Internat. Soc. Theatre Rsch., Medieval and Renaissance Drama Soc., Renaissance Soc. Am., South Cen. Renaissance Conf. (life, chmn. nominations 1976, exec. com. 1978-80, program com. 1981-83, chmn. sect. Shakespeare 1981, 85, 95, 99, 2002-04, chair non dramatic lit., 2005, chair Renaissance drama sect. 2006, chair Renaissance drama sect. 2007, chair renaissance poetry sect., chair politics in history and drama 2007, 16th Century lit. 1982, chmn. local arrangements 1983, symposium on humanism 1984, chmn. Shakespeare on film and the tchg. Brit. drama 1986, chmn. music in Shakespeare's plays, 1987, chmn. sect. Thematic Approaches to Tudor/Stuart Drama 1988, chmn. sect. Medieval Influences on Renaissance drama 1993, chmn. Shakespeare's Villains: Stage and Page 1995, Adaptions of Renaissance Drama 1993, chmn. local arrangements for conv. 1990, chmn. spl. session 1989, 95, Shakespeare II sect. 1996, chair Renaissance Drama Sect. 1999, 01, chmn. Performing Rennaissance Drama 2001), South Cen. MLA (life, assoc. editor for English, South Cen. Bull. 1982-84, nominations com. 1985-86, 95-96, book reviewer South Cen. Rev. 1983, 85-86, sec. English I.B. Renaissance, 1986, chair, 1987, sec. spl. sect. Renaissance Drama, 1988, chair Shakespeare's Tragicomedies and tragi-comic romances, 1989, co-chair local arrangements, 1999, chair panel on renaissance drama criticism 1995, sec. renaissance drama sect. 1997, sect. chmn. 1998, mem. com. Conv., Memphis, 1999, 2007, sec. renaissance non-dramatic lit. 2005, local arrangements com. Memphis 2007 conv.), South Atlantic MLA, South Ctrl. Coll. English Assn. (sec.-treas. 1980-81, v.p. 1981-82, pres. 1982-83, exec. com. 1983-90, co-host 1982, com. constitution revision 1989), Coll. English Assn., Internat. Patristic Medieval and Renaissance Conf. (sect. chmn. Medieval drama 1977, chair Shakespeare session 1994, chmn. Renaissance drama section 1995, chmn. 17th century Brit. lit. sect. 1996, chmn. Milton sect. 1996), Am. Theatre Assn. (chmn. sect. combining Brit. lit. and theatre in teaching of drama 1983, chmn. Shakespeare sect. 1994), Marlowe Soc. Am., Eugene O'Neill Soc., Stratford Can. Shakespeare Festival, AAUP (sec. treas. Memphis State U. chpt. 1982-86, v.p. 1986-88, pres. 1988-90), Memphis Met. Area Assn. of Phi Beta Kappa (pres. memphis alumni assn. 1985-88, spl. panel Soc. and New Scholarship at 37th triennial coun. 1994), Memphis Alumni Assn. of Phi Beta Kappa, Humanities Tenn., Alpha Chi. Democrat. Home: 5219 Mason Rd Memphis TN 38117-2104 Personal E-mail: mlcshake@aol.com.

STAGGERS, KERMIT LEMOYNE, II, history and political science professor, state legislator, municipal official; b. Washington, Pa., Nov. 2, 1947; s. Kermit LeMoyne and Christine Ruby (Scherich) S.; m. June Ann Wenda, Aug. 22, 1970; children: Ayn Kristen Staggers Bird, Kyle Lee Staggers. BS, U. Idaho, 1969, MA, 1975; PhD, Claremont Grad. U., 1986. Instr. history Troy (Ala.) State U., 1975-76, U. Idaho, Moscow, 1977, Northwestern Coll., Orange City, Iowa, 1979-80, Coll. Lake County, Grayslake, Ill., 1981-82; lectr. history Chapman Univ., Orange, Calif., 1979, U. Md.-Europe, Heidelberg, Germany, 1988-89; vis. instr. history Trinity Internat. U., Deerfield, Ill., 1980; adj. instr. history U. St. Francis, Joliet, Ill., 1982; prof. history and polit. sci. U. Sioux Falls (S.D.), 1982—; mem. S.D. Senate, Pierre, 1995—2002, Sioux Falls City Coun., 2002—. Lectr. Diplomatic Acad. Ukrainian Fgn. Ministry and Nat. U. Kiev-Mohyla Acad., 2001; expert analyst on polit. and social issues for local radio and TV. Contbr. articles to profl. jours. Chair Senate Transp. Com., 1997-99; bd. dirs. Siouxland Heritage Museums, Sioux Falls, 2006—. Capt. USAF, 1970-76. Recipient Guardian Small Bus. award Nat. Fedn. Ind. Bus., 1996; Malone Faculty fellow, 1993. Mem. Orgn. Am. Historians, Great Plains Polit. Sci Assn. (pres. 2000-01), Federalist Soc., Fulbright Assn., Hist. Soc., Kiwanis, Phi Alpha Theta, Phi Kappa Phi. Republican. Avocations: book collecting, travel. Home: 616 E Wiswall Pl Sioux Falls SD 57105-2030 Office: U Sioux Falls Dept History/Polit Sci 1101 W 22nd St Sioux Falls SD 57105-1699 Office Phone: 605-331-6754. Business E-Mail: kermit.staggers@usiouxfalls.edu.

STAGGERS, MARY E., minister; b. Rocky Mount, NC, Sept. 28, 1923; d. John and Emma Jane White; m. Calvin Staggers, Jr., May 18, 1938; children: Luther, Gervis, Earlie Mae, Curtis, Herbert, Betty Joann, Yvonne. BA, Coll. New Rochelle, 1983; M in Profl. Studies, N.Y. Theol. Sem., 1985; M in Humanities, Ctr. Humanities N.Y., 1985; D of Theology of Bible, Internat. Sem. Fla., 1990; DD, Balt. Coll. Bible, 1988. Pastor Holy Redeemer Bapt. Ch., Bklyn., 1961—. Family therapist Beth Israel Hosp., NYC, 1980—98; min. N.Y.C. World's Fair. Author: It's Seed Time, 1999, The Spirit Supercedes Nature, 2003. Liaison N.Y.C. Cmty. Bd. Dist. 16; v.p. Women's Nat. Evang. and Missionary Conf., 1996—2001; pres. World Conf. Gospel Explosion, 1994—, United Ladies Ministers Counsel, 1978—99; pres. Ea. N.Y. br. Women's Nat. Evang. and Missionary Conf., 1997—2001; pres. Mother's Bd. Cedar Grove Bapt. Ch., 1940—51. Mem.: N.Y.C. Clergy Conf., Ea. Bapt. Conf., So. Bapt. Conf., Nat. Bapt. Conf. Democrat. Avocations: cooking, reading, writing. Office Phone: 718-816-5181.

STAGGS, THOMAS O., entertainment company executive; Mgr. strategic planning Walt Disney Co., Burbank, Calif., 1990—94, v.p. planning & development, 1995—97, exec. v.p., CFO, 1998—99, sr. exec. v.p., CFO, 2000—. Office: Walt Disney Co 500 S Buena Vista St Burbank CA 91521-0006 Office Phone: 818-560-1000. *

STAGINNUS, ULF, pharmaceutical executive, health economist; b. Eilenburg, Germany, Dec. 27, 1970; s. Lothar Fritz and Hermine Staginnus; m. Libia Marina Naranjo Cruzatty, Aug. 11, 2004; 1 child, Julien Staginnus Naranjo. MS in Econs. with hon., U. Bayreuth, Germany, 1996, degree in pharm. mktg. and strategic mgmt. Cons., health econs. & outcomes rsch. HealthEcon Ltd., Basel, Switzerland, 1997—98; sr. mgr. health econs., new product devel. Glaxo Smith Kline Biologicals, Brussels, 1998—2001; assoc. dir. global health econs. and competitive intelligence Baxter Healthcare, Madrid, 2001—04; sr. mgr. worldwide outcomes rsch. Pfizer Inc., NYC, 2004—05; mng. dir., ptnr. European Health Econs., Madrid, 2005—06; assoc. dir. outcomes rsch. Bristol-Myers Squibb, Madrid, 2006—. Mem. editl. bd.: Spanish Jour. Health Econs.; contbr. chapters to books, articles to profl. jours. Mem.: Internat. Soc. of Pharmacoeconomics & Outcomes Rsch. Office Phone: 34 638029 982. Personal E-mail: ustaginnus@hotmail.com. Business E-Mail: ulf.staginnus@bms.com.

STAGLIN, GAREN KENT, computer company executive, venture capitalist; b. Lincoln, Nebr., Dec. 22, 1944; s. Ramon and Darlene (Guilliams) S.; m. Sharalyn King, June 8, 1968; children: Brandon Kent, Shannon King. BS in Engring. with honors, UCLA, 1966; MBA, Stanford U., 1968. Assoc. Carr Mgmt. Co., NYC, 1971-75; v.p. Crocker Nat. Bank, San Francisco, 1975-76; dir. fin. Itel Corp., San Francisco, 1976-77, pres. ins. services divsn., 1977-79; corp. v.p., gen. mgr. ADP Automotive Svcs. Group, San Ramon, Calif., 1978-91; chmn., CEO Safelite Glass Corp., Columbus, Ohio, 1991-97, chmn., 1998-2000; owner Staglin Family Vineyard, Rutherford, Calif., 1985—; pres., CEO eOne Global L.L.C., Napa, Calif., 2000—05; sr. advisor FT Ventures, San Francisco, 2005—. Bd. dir. Certive Corp., Specialized Bicycle Corp., Global Document Solutions, Inc., Solera, Inc., ExL Svcs., Inc., Kestrel Wireless, Free Run Techs. Bd. dir. Peralta Hosp. Cancer Inst., 1977-78, Berkeley Reportory Theatre, 1979-85; trustee Justin Sienna HS, Napa, Calif., 1995-20; chmn. major gifts program East Bay region Stanford U., Calif., 1989-92; mem. adv. bd. Stanford Bus. Sch., 1995-2000; judge Cambridge Bus. Sch., 2004-; chmn. 75th anniversary campaign Stanford Grad. Sch. Bus., 1998-00; capital campaign UCLA Coll. Letters Sci., 2004-; pres. bd. trustees Am. Ctr. Wine, Food and Arts, Napa, Calif., 1998-03; pres. Rutherford Charitable Orgn., 1994-. Lt. USN, 1968—71. Recipient Gold Spike award, Stanford U., 2000, Honors Fellow award, UCLA, 2006. Mem. Stanford Assocs. (bd. govs. 1985-92), World Pres. Orgn., Internat. Inst. Soc. (bd. govs. 1985-92), Nappa Valley Vintners Assn. Democrat. Lutheran. Home: PO Box 680 1570 Bella Oaks Ln Rutherford CA 94573 Office Phone: 707-280-5374. Business E-Mail: garen.stagline@solerainc.com.

STAHELI, KORY D., law librarian; BA, Brigham Young U., 1984, JD, 1987, MLIS, 1991. Atty. Snow, Nuffer, Engstrom & Drake, St. George, Utah, 1987—90; reference libr. Brigham Young U. Law Library, Provo, Utah, 1990—91, head of reference svcs., 1991—95, assoc. dir. pub. svc. Howard W. Hunter Law Libr., 1995—98, assoc. dir. collection devel. and faculty outreach, 2004—05, dir., 2005—; assoc. dir., head pub. svcs. Wiener-Rogers Law Libr., U. Nev., Las Vegas, 1998—2004, interim dir., 2002. Spkr. in field. Contbr. articles to profl. jours. Mem.: Am. Assn. Law Libs. Office: Howard W Hunter Law Lib 256 JRCB PO Box 28000 Provo UT 84602-8000 Office Phone: 801-422-9223. E-mail: stahelik@lawgate.byu.edu. *

STAHL, CRAIG L., lawyer; b. Riverside, NJ, Jan. 14, 1959; s. George W. Stahl III and Judy R. (Collins) Stahl; m. Donna J. Jacobs, Aug. 18, 1984; 1 child, Bryan T. AB cum laude, Princeton U., 1981; JD, So. Meth. U., 1984. Bar: Tex. 1984, admitted to practice: US Dist. Ct. (No. Dist.) Tex., US Dist. Ct. (So. Dist.) Tex., US Dist. Ct. (We. Dist.) Tex., US Dist. Ct. (Ea. Dist.) Tex., US Ct. Appeals (5th Cir.). Assoc. Bracewell & Patterson, Houston, 1984—, Sifford & Pezzulli, Dallas, 1986; ptnr., Energy Litig. Andrews Kurth LLP, The Woodlands, Tex. Elected mem., Rep. Com. Burlington County, NJ, 1979—81. Mem.: Tex. Bar Found., Houston Bar Found., State Bar Tex., Houston Young Lawyers Assn., Houston Bar Assn., ABA, NJ Assn. Soccer Coaches (All-State award 1977). Republican. Methodist. Avocations: jogging, golf, soccer, tennis. Office: Andrews Kurth LLP 10001 Woodloch Forest Dr Ste 200 The Woodlands TX 77380 Office Phone: 713-220-4834. Office Fax: 713-238-7478. Business E-Mail: cstahl@andrewskurth.com.

STAHL, FRANK LUDWIG, civil engineer; b. Fuerth, Germany; came to U.S., 1946, naturalized, 1949; s. Leo E. and Anna (Regensburger) S.; m. Edith Cosmann, Aug. 31, 1947; children: David, Robert. BSCE, Tech. Inst. Zurich, Switzerland, 1945. With Ammann & Whitney, Cons. Engrs., NYC, 1946-93, project engr., 1955-67, assoc., 1968-76, sr. assoc., 1977-81, chief engr. Transp. div., 1982-93; pvt. cons., 1994—. Expert in field. Prin. works include Verrazano-Narrows Bridge, Throgs Neck Bridge, Walt Whitman Bridge, improvements to Golden Gate Bridge, rehab. of Williamsburg Bridge, N.Y.C., Royal Gorge Bridge, Colo., Interstate-10 Deck Tunnel, Phoenix; author: Cable Corrosion in Bridges and Other Structures; co-author: Golden Gate Bridge, Report of the Chief Engineer to the Board of Directors, Vol. II; contbr. articles to profl. jours. on bridge design and constrn. Recipient Gold award The James F. Lincoln Arc Welding Found., 1986, John A. Roebling medal Internat. Bridge Conf., 1992. Fellow ASCE (Thomas Fitch Rowland prize 1967, Innovation in Civil Engring. award of mert 1983, Metro. Civil Engr. of Yr. award 1987, Roebling award 1990), ASTM (vice chmn. com. A-1 on steel, stainless steel and related alloys 1978-83, chmn. steel reinforce-subcom. 1971-82, award of merit 1982); mem. Am. Inst. Steel Constrn. (Prize Bridge award 1986), Engring. Found. (rsch. coun. on structural connections), Internat. Assn. Bridge and Structural Engring., Internat. Bridge Tunnel and Turnpike Assn. Home: 20911 28th Rd Flushing NY 11360-2412 Personal E-mail: bridgfrank@aol.com.

STAHL, JACK LELAND, real estate company executive; b. Lincoln, Ill., June 28, 1934; s. Edwin R. and Edna M. (Burns) S.; m. Carol Anne Townsend, June 23, 1956; children: Cheryl, Nancy, Kellea BS in Edn., U. N.Mex., 1957. Tchr. Albuquerque Pub. Schs., 1956-59; pres. House Finders, Inc., Albuquerque, 1959-65; v.p. N.Mex. Savs. & Loan Assn., Albuquerque, 1965-67; chmn. bd. Hooten-Stahl, Inc., Albuquerque, 1967-77; mem. N.Mex. Ho. of Reps., 1969-70; pres. The Jack Stahl Co., Albuquerque, 1977—; mem. N.Mex. Senate, 1981-86; lt. gov. State of N.Mex., 1987-90. Mem. exec. bd. Gr. S.W. Coun. Boy Scouts Am, 1982-89; bd. dirs. BBB N. Mex., 1968-82, pres. 1975-76; trustee Univ Heights. Hosp.,1980-85; vice chmn. N. Mex. Bd. Fin., 1987-90, N. Mex. Cmty. Devel. Coun., 1987-90; bd. dirs. Ctr. for Entrepreneurship and Econ. Devel., 1994-96; mem. Gov.'s Bus. Adv. Coun., 1995-97. Named Realtor of Yr., Albuquerque Bd. Realtors, 1972. Mem. Nat. Assn. Realtors, Nat. Homebuilders Assn., N.Mex. Amigos, 20-30 Club (pres. 1963-64), Rotary. Republican. Methodist. Office: 1911 Wyoming Blvd NE Albuquerque NM 87112-2865 Office Phone: 505-292-6635.

STAHL, JAMES F., engineer; Grad. in Civil Engring., Loyola Marymount U., 1965. Chief engr., gen. mgr. County Sanitation Dists. LA County, Whittier, Calif., 2000—07; ret., 2007. Mem.: NAE. Office: County Sanitation Dists LA County 1955 Workman Mill Rd Whittier CA 90601 Office Phone: 562-908-4288 ext. 2301. Office Fax: 562-695-6139. *

STAHL, JOHN ALAN, psychometrician; b. Washington, Nov. 19, 1946; s. Wilbur Edward and Marian Joan Stahl; m. Christie Jane Chandler, Dec. 30, 1981; children: Heather, Samuel. BS, U. Md., College Park, 1969, BA, 1978; MA, George Washington U., Washington, 1981; PhD, Northwestern U., Evanston, Ill., 1989. Mgr. evaluation and rsch. Am. Soc. Clin. Pathologists; mgr. test devel. and rsch. Nat. Assn. Pharmacy, Niles, Ill., 1993—94; sr. psychometrician Promissor Inc., Evanston, 1995—. Vis. asst. prof. U. Ill., Chgo., 2006; presenter in field. Contbr. articles to profl. jours. Capt. US Army, 1969—75. Mem.: Nat. Coun. Measurement in Edn., Am. Ednl. Rsch. Assn. Methodist.

STAHL, LADDIE L., engineering company executive; b. Terre Haute, Ind., Dec. 23, 1921; s. Edgar Allen and Martha (Llewellyn) S.; m. Thelma Mae Beasley, Dec. 11, 1942; children: Stephanie, Laddie L., Craig. BSCE, Purdue U., 1942; MS in Engring., Johns Hopkins U., 1950. With GE, 1954-90, mgr. planning and resources, electronics sci. and engring., corp. research and devel. Schenectady, NY, 1974-76, mgr. electronics systems programs ops., elec. sci. and engring., 1976-84, mgr. spl. programs and project devel. operation, 1984-90; dir. tech. transfer program Data Storage Systems Ctr. Carnegie Mellon U., Pitts., 1990—. Chmn. adv. group U.S. Army Electronics Command, 1971-74; mem. U.S. Army Sci. Bd., 1978-87; cons. in field. Contbr. articles to profl. publs. Mem. alumni bd. dirs. Purdue U., 1979-82. Served with U.S. Army, 1942-54, ETO; maj. gen. Res. (ret.), 1954-77. Decorated D.S.M., Legion of Merit. Mem. AIAA (sr.), IEEE (life), Am. Def. Preparedness Assn., Army and Navy Club (Washington), Tau Beta Pi, Chi Epsilon. Home: 29 Fairway Ln Rexford NY 12148-1213 Office: Carnegie Mellon U Data Storage Sys Ctr ECE Dept 5000 Forbes Ave Pittsburgh PA 15213-3815 Office Phone: 518-399-0451. Personal E-mail: lstahl2@nycap.rr.com.

STAHL, MADONNA, retired judge; b. Robinson, Ill., Sept. 26, 1928; d. Lawrence Joy and Inez Lucille (Kennedy) S.; children: Khushro Ghandhi, Rustom Ghandhi, Behram Ghandhi. BS, U. Ill., 1950; JD, Albany Law Sch., 1973. Bar: N.Y. 1974, U.S. Dist. Ct. (no. dist.) N.Y. 1974, U.S. Ct. Appeals (2nd cir.) 1975, U.S. Supreme Ct. 1978. Atty. trainee N.Y. State Dept. Commerce, Albany, 1973-74; atty. Legal Aid Soc., Albany, 1974-76; ptnr. Powers, Stahl & Somers (and predecessor firms), 1976-89; part-time judge Albany City Ct., 1984-89, full-time judge, 1990-97; ret., 1997. Mem. com. on character and fitness N.Y. State Supreme Ct. A.D. 3d Dept., Albany, 1980-86; jud. hearing officer State of N.Y., 1997-2000. Lobbyist Com. for Progressive Legislation, Schenectady, 1968-70. Mem. Women's Bar Assn. State N.Y. (Capital dist. pres. 1983-84). Democrat. Unitarian Universalist. E-mail: judge_stahl@yahoo.com.

STAHL, NANETTE, librarian, biblicist; b. Brooklyn, NY, July 23, 1941; d. David and Hannah Stahl; m. William W. Hallo, Oct. 18, 1998. BA, Brooklyn Coll., Brooklyn, NY, 1964; MLIS, Pratt Univ., Brooklyn, NY, 1966; PhD, Univ. Calif., Berkeley, Calif., 1993. Judaica Bibliographer Univ. Calif., Sch. of Law, Berkeley, Calif., 1970—80; head libr. Bureau of Jewish Edn., San Francisco, 1980—89; Judaica curator Yale Univ. Libr., New Haven, 1993—. Author: Law and Liminality in the Bible, 1996; editor: (book) Sholem Asch Reconsidered, 2004. Mem.: Assn. Jewish Studies, Assn. of Jewish Libr. Office: Yale Univ Libr Box 208240 130 Wall St New Haven CT 06520

STAHL, NICK, actor; b. Harlingen, Tex., Dec. 5, 1979; Actor: (TV miniseries) Seasons of Love, 1999; (TV series) Carnivàle, 2003—05; (TV films) Stranger at My Door, 1991, Woman with a Past, 1992, Incident in a Small Town, 1994, Blue River, 1995, My Son Is Innocent, 1996, Wasted, 2002; (films) The Man Without a Face, 1993, Safe Passage, 1994, Tall Tale, 1995, Eye of God, 1997, Disturbing Behavior, 1998, Soundman, 1998, The Thin Red Line, 1998, All Forgotten, 2000, Sunset Strip, 2000, In the Bedroom, 2001, The Sleepy Time Gal, 2001, Bully, 2001, Taboo, 2002, Bookies, 2003, Terminator 3: Rise of the Machines, 2003, Twist, 2003, Sin City, 2005.

STAHL, NORMAN A., literature and language professor, department chairman; b. San Francisco, Apr. 21, 1949; AA, City Coll. San Francisco, 1969; BA, San Francisco State U., 1971, MA, 1976; PhD, U. Pitts., 1983. Rsch. assoc. U. Pitts., 1980-82; asst. prof. divsn. devel. studies Ga. State U., Atlanta, 1982-87; assoc. prof. dept. curriculum & instrn. No. Ill. U., DeKalb, 1987-93, prof., chair dept. curriculum & instrn., 1994-99, chair dept. literacy edn., 1999—. Author: Teaching Developmental Reading, 2003; contbr. articles to profl. jours. Pres. DeKalb Edn. Found., 1999—2001. Recipient Disting. Rsch. award Coll. Reading and Learning Assn., 1990, NY. Coll. Learning Skills Assn., 1996; Am. Coun. Devel. Edn. Assns. fellow, 2006. Mem. Coll. Reading Assn. (pres. 1991-92, treas. 1985-88), Internat. Reading Assn. (pres. history reading spl. interest group 1992-94), Am. Reading Forum (chair bd. dirs. 1996-97), Nat. Reading Conf. (historian 1998-2003, bd. dir. 2003-05, v.p. 2005-06, pres. elect 2006—). Office: No Ill U Dept Literacy Edn Dekalb IL 60115 Office Phone: 815-753-9032. Business E-Mail: stahl@niu.edu.

STAHL, NORMAN H., judge; b. Manchester, NH, 1931; BA, Tufts U., 1952; LLB, Harvard U., 1955. Law clk. to Hon. John V. Spalding Mass. Supreme Ct., 1955—56; assoc. Devine, Millimet, Stahl & Branch, Manchester, NH, 1956—59, ptnr., 1959—90; dist. judge US Dist. Ct. (NH dist.), 1990—92; cir. judge US Ct. Appeals (1st cir.), Concord, NH, 1992—. Del to Rep. Nat. Conv., 1988. Mem.: N.H. Bar Assn. Office: US Courthouse Ste 8730 1 Courthouse Way Boston MA 02210 *

STAHL, RICHARD SHELDON, surgeon; b. Chattanooga, Tenn., Dec. 8, 1950; s. Paul and Alena S. BA in Physics, Emory U., 1972; MD, Vanderbilt U., 1976; MBA, U. New Haven, 1994. Diplomate Nat. Bd. Med. Examiners, Am. Bd. Surgery, Am. Bd. Plastic Surgery. Intern, asst. resident dept. surgery Yale U. Sch. Medicine, New Haven, 1976-80, chief resident, 1980-81; resident plastic and reconstructive surgery Emory U. Sch. Medicine, 1981-82, chief resident, 1982-83; instr. surgery Yale U. Sch. Medicine, 1980-81, asst. prof. plastic surgery, 1983-89, assoc. prof. plastic surgery, 1989-90, assoc. clin. prof. plastic surgery, 1991-95, clin. prof. plastic surgery, 1995—, attending physician Yale Vascular Ctr., 1986-90, chmn. telemedicine com., 1998—; attending physician dept. surgery Yale-New Haven Hosp., 1980-81, 83—, asst. med. dir. surgery emergency svcs., 1983-90, attending physician surg. ICU, 1986-88, dir. internat. ops. dept. surgery, 1995—, assoc. chief dept. surgery, 1994—; attending physician Hosp. St. Raphael, 1983—, West Haven VA Hosp., 1983—; ptnr., pvt. practice Thoracic Healing Solutions, Guilford, Conn. Founding co-dir. Yale Breast Care Ctr., 1989-90; cons. physicians assoc. surg. residency program Yale U.-Norwalk Hosp., 1978-81; resident surgeon Hospital Albert Schweitzer, Deschapelles, Haiti, 1980; med. mgmt. cons. Yale-New Haven Health Sys., 1997-98; program dir. of clin. telemedicine of NASA Comml. Space Ctr. at yale, 1997—; spkr. in field. Sports reporter The Chattanooga Times, 1967-69; contbr. over 40 articles to profl. jours. Pres. Kingswood Homeowner's Assn., 1987-93; mem. Charter Oak Bassett Hound Club, 1981—. Recipient Rsch. grant Charles W. Ohse Fund, Rsch. grant Smith Kline and French Labs., Rsch. grant Kendall Co.; named one of Top Doctors in NY Met. area, NY mag., 2007, Redbook, McCall's. Fellow Am. Coll. Surgeons (mem. Conn. chpt.); mem. APHA, AMA, Am. Assn. Plastic Surgeons, Am. Soc. Plastic and Reconstructive Surgeons, Am. Coll. Physician Execs., Am. Coll. Med. Quality, Am. Burn Assn., Soc. for Critical Care Medicine, New Eng. Soc. Plastic and Reconstructive Surgeons (v.p. 1998-99), New Haven County Med. Soc., Conn. Soc. Am. Bd. Surgeons, Conn. State Med. Soc., Sigma Xi. Office: Yale New Haven Hosp Assoc Chief Dept Surg CB228 20 York St New Haven CT 06504 also: Thoracic Healing Solutions 5 Durham Rd Guilford CT 06437 Office Phone: 203-458-4440. *

STAHL, WILLIAM MARTIN, retired surgeon; b. Danbury, Conn., Nov. 6, 1922; s. William Martin and Isabel Sara Stahl; m. Patricia Ann Maloney, Aug. 8, 1988; m. Betty Barrett, May 6, 1944 (div. June 3, 1966); children: Matyas Sebastian, William Martin, Elizabet Cordelia, Katherine Anne, Sarah Elizabeth, Jonathan Barrett, Elizabeth Parkinson; m. Alice Miller, June 12, 1968 (dec. Aug. 12, 1986). BA, Dartmouth Coll., Hanover, NH, 1943; MD, Harvard U., Boston, Mass., 1946. Diplomate Am. Bd. of Surgery, 1956, cert. critical care Coll. Critical Care Medicine, 1987. Intern Mary Hitchcock Meml. Hosp., Hanover, NH, 1946—47; gen. practice medicine Danbury, Conn., 1947—51; surg. resident Bellevue Hosp., NYC, 1953—57; pvt. practice surgery Danbury, 1957—62; chief of surgery Danbury Hosp., 1960—62; assoc. prof. surgery Coll. Medicine U. Vt., Burlington, Vt., 1962—66; prof. surgery NYU, NYC, 1966—77, NY Med. Coll., Valhalla, NY, 1977—97, ret., 1997. Dir. surgery Met. Hosp., NYC,

1977—82, Lincoln Med. and Mental Health Ctr., NYC, 1980—97. Contbr. 19 chpts. to books, over 175 articles to profl. jours. Capt. med. corps. US Army, 1951—52. Home: 145 Rockland Avenue Larchmont NY 10538 Home Phone: 914-834-2969. Personal E-mail: mdreedman@aol.com.

STAHLMAN, MILDRED THORNTON, pediatrician, pathologist, educator, researcher; b. Nashville, July 31, 1922; d. James Geddes and Mildred (Thornton) Stahlman. AB, Vanderbilt U., 1943, MD, 1946; MD (hon.), U. Goteborg, Sweden, 1973, U. Nancy, France, 1982. Diplomate Am. Bd. Pediat., Am. Bd. Neonatology. Intern Boston Children's Hosp., 1947—48; resident Vanderbilt Univ. Hosp., 1948—49; fellow Royal Caroline Inst. Medicine, Sweden, 1949—50; cardiac resident La Rabida Sanitarium, Chgo., 1951; instr. pediat. Vanderbilt U., Nashville, 1951—58, instr. physiology, 1954—60, asst. prof. pediat., 1959—64, asst. prof. physiology, 1960—62, assoc. prof. pediat., 1964—70, prof., 1970—, prof. pathology, 1982—, Harvie Branscomb Disting. prof., 1984, dir. divsn. neonatology, 1961—89, prof. pediat. and pathology. Editor: Respiratory Distress Syndromes, 1989; contbr. over 175 articles to profl. publs., chpts. to books. Recipient Apgar award, Am. Acad. Pediat., 1987; grantee NIH, 1954—. Mem.: AAAS, Inst. Medicine NAS, Royal Swedish Acad. Scis., So. Soc. Pediatric Rsch. (pres. 1961—62), Am. Physiology Soc., Soc. Pediatric Rsch., Am. Pediatric Soc. (pres. 1984, John Howland award 1996). Episcopalian. Home: 538 Beech Creek Rd S Brentwood TN 37027-3421 Office: Vanderbilt Univ Med Ctr 2215 B Garland Ave 1125 MRB IV LH Nashville TN 37232-0656 E-mail: mildred.stahlman@vanderbilt.edu.

STAHR, BETH A., librarian; b. Elmhurst, Ill., June 13, 1951; d. John H. Pohlmann and Mary Anne Price; m. Charles Ward Stahr, Aug. 25, 1973; children: Margaret L., Andrew J. BS Engring., Purdue U., 1973; MLS, Syracuse U., 1999. Environ. specialist Owens Corning Fiberglas, Toledo, 1973—78; genealogical rschr. pvt. practice, Wausau, Wis., 1988—98; libr. Southeastern La. U., Hammond, La., 1999—, asst. prof., 2000—06, assoc. prof., 2006—. V.p., trustee Wis. Genealogical Coun., 1992—98; treas., trustee Assn. Profl. Genealogists, Washington, 1994—95, Bd. Cert. Genealogists, Washington, 1998—, pres., 2004—05. Vol. Birch Trails coun. Girl Scouts Am., Tomahawk, Wis., 1980—91; v.p., trustee La. Genealogical and Hist. Soc., La., 2001—. Mem.: ALA, La. Geneal. and Hist. Soc. (v.p. 2001—05), ACRL, Phi Kappa Phi. Episcopalian. Home: 55 Dogwood Ln Covington LA 70435 E-mail: bstahr@selu.edu.

STAHR, CELIA SUZANNE, art historian, educator; d. Carl Wolfgang and Illene Louise Stahr; m. Gary Allen Lee, May 21, 2000; 1 child, Mei Lin Miriam Lee-Stahr. BA, San Francisco State U., 1980, MA, 1989; PhD, U. Iowa, Iowa City, 1997. Adj. prof. San Francisco State U., 1997—2007, Sonoma State U., Cotati, Calif., 1998—99, Coll. Marin, Calif., 1999—2000, Calif. Coll. Arts, Oakland, 1999—2003, San Francisco Art Inst., 2004—05, U. San Francisco XARTS, 2004—. Affiliated scholar Inst. for Women & Gender, Stanford U., 2000—02; presenter in field. Contbr. essays to books, articles to profl. pubs. Vol. Women's Resource & Action Ctr., Iowa City, 1991—95; active Women Against Racism, 1994—95; vol. Rape Victim Advocacy, Iowa City, 1995. Grantee Schumacher scholarship, U. Iowa, 1996, Seashore Dissertation fellowship, 1996, USA Rsch. grant, 1996. Mem.: Coll. Art Assn. Avocations: tai chi, salsa dance. Office: The U San Francisco XARTS 2130 Fulto St San Francisco CA 94117-1080 Personal E-mail: CeliaStahr@aol.com.

STAHR, CURTIS BRENT, photographer, art association administrator, educator; b. West Union, Iowa; s. Freman H. and Lucile M. (Schreiner) S. AA, Ellsworth Coll., 1966; BFA, Peru State Coll., Nebr., 1968. Cert. tchr., Iowa, Colo., Ariz. Art dir. Iowa Falls (Iowa) High Sch., 1968-70, Wiley (Colo.) Schs., 1971-72, Judson Sch., Scottsdale, Ariz., 1973-79; freelance graphic artist, photographer and mktg. dir., 1979-88; prof. photography, photography dir. Des Moines Area C.C., 1988—; art dir. Homestead Assn., Des Moines, 1993-98. Bd. dirs. Homestead Corp., Alpha Inst., Unoged Corp., v.p., 1999; v.p. Young Masters Photographic Art Collection, 1998—; pres. Interpretive Photography, 1999; art dir. Starland Design Band Group, 1979-86, graphic effects dept. Bischoff's, 1987-88; photographic dir. ednl. exchange trip to China. Exhibited in 16 one-man art shows, in 34 invited/juried art shows; represented in numerous pvt. collections; photographer numerous field trips including migration of Am. eagle from Alaska to Fla., all 99 Iowa County Courthouses, Yellowstone Nat. Park, Grand Teton Nat. Park, Waterton-Glacier Internat. Peace Park (U.S. and Can.), Isle Royale Nat. Park, Grand Canyon Nat. Park, Denali Nat. Park, Arctic Nat. Park & Preserve, Canyon de Chelly Nat. Monument, Rainbow Bridge Nat. Monument, Devils Tower Nat. Monument, Effigy Mounts Nat. Monument, Yosemite Nat. Park, Sequoia Nat. Park, Kings Canyon Nat. Park, Japser Nat. Park (Can.), Glacier Nat. Park (Can.), Banff (Can.) Nat. Park, Terra Nova Nat. Park (Newfoundland), Boundary Waters Canoe Area Wilderness, Quetico Provincial Park, Can., North Magnetic Pole, Can., Canyonlands (Utah), Auyuittuq Nat. Park Res., Can., Ellesmere Island Nat. Park Res, Can. Yoho Nat. Park, Can., Kootenay Nat. Park, Can., Angel Falls, Venezuela, Machu Picchu, Peru, Atacama Desert, Chile, Queen Charlotte Islands, Can.,Nahanni Nat. Pk. Res., Yukom, Lake Titicac, Bolivia and Peru, North Baffin Nat. Pk., Baffin Islands, Can., Hells Canyon, U.S.A., Sand Hills, Nebr., U.S.A., Seeley-Swan Valley, Mont., U.S.A., Iwavik Nat. Pk., Yukon Ter.; numerous cross country trips to U.S., Can., Mex., Cen. Am., S.Am., Yukon Territory and Arctic Cir. Speaker Ariz.-Calif. Lecture Series, 1982-84; chairperson art evaluation com. State of Iowa, 1970; bd. dirs. Ariz. Arts Festival, 1974-79, Muscular Dystrophy Assn. Fund Drive, Ariz., 1982-85. Recipient 14 purchase awards. Democrat. Office: Des Moines Area CC 2006 S Ankeny Blvd Ankeny IA 50021-8995

STAINBACK, SUSAN BRAY, retired education educator; b. Balt., May 22, 1947; d. William Devaugh and Cleo Margaret (Selig) Bray. BS, Radford Coll., 1968; MEd, U. Va., 1970, EdD, 1973. Tchr. Albemarle County Schs., Crozet, Va., 1968-70; edn. specialist Hope Haven Children's Hosp., Jacksonville, Fla., 1973-74; prof. edn. U. No. Iowa, Cedar Falls, 1974—98, prof. emeritus, 1998—; Matthew J. Gujlielmo Endowed Chair dept. spl. edn. Calif. State U., LA, 1988-89. Co-author: Establishing a Token Economy in the Classroom, 1973, Classroom Discipline: A Positive Approach, 1974, Educating Students with Severe Maladaptive Behavior, 1980, The Severely Motorically Impaired Child: A Handbook for Classroom Teachers, 1980, Teaching Eating Skills, 1982, Integration of Students with Severe Handicaps into Regular Schools, 1985, Qualitative Research, 1988, How to Help Your Child Succeed in School, 1988, Making the Grade, 1989. Home: 8616 Rippling Waters Rd Blairsville GA 30512-8015

STAINES, DAVID MCKENZIE, language educator; b. Toronto, Aug. 8, 1946; s. Ralph McKenzie and Mary Rita (Hayes) S. BA, U. Toronto, 1967; AM, Harvard U., 1968, PhD, 1973. Asst. prof. English Harvard U., Cambridge, Mass., 1973-78, vis. assoc. prof., summers 1980, 82; assoc. prof. English U. Ottawa, Ont., 1978-85, prof. Ont., 1985—, vice-dean faculty of Arts Ont., 1994-95, dean faculty of arts Ont., 1995—2003. Author: Tennyson's Camelot, 1982, Beyond the Provinces: Literary Canada at Century's End, 1995; contbr. articles to profl. jours.; editor: The Canadian Imagination, 1977, The Forty-ninth and Other Parallels, 1986, Margaret Laurence: Critical Reflections, 2001, The Letters of Stephen Leacock, 2006; editor Jour. Can. Poetry, 1984—; gen. editor New Can. Libr., 1988—; translator The Complete Romances of Chrétien de Troyes, 1990; co-editor Elements of Literature, 1987, 90, 04, The Short Story in English, 1991, Northrop Frye on Canada, 2003, Marshall McLuhan's Understanding Me, 2003. Recipient Lorne Pierce medal, 1998; Ind. study fellow NEH, London, 1977-78, fellow Huntington Libr., San Marino, Calif., 1979. Fellow Royal Soc. Can.; mem. Medieval Acad. Am. (chmn. com. on ctrs. and regional assn. 1981-87), MLA, Internat. Arthurian Soc., Assn. Can. Univ. Tchrs. English. Roman Catholic. Avocations: theater, bridge. Home: 222 Clemow Ave Ottawa ON Canada K1S 2B6 Business E-Mail: dstaines@uottawa.ca.

STAINES, GAIL M., university librarian; BA, MLS, U. Buffalo, PhD in Higher Edn. Adminstrn. Assoc. prof. Niagara CC, Sanborn, NY, 1988—98; exec. dir. Western NY Libr. Resources Coun., 1998—2006; univ. libr. Saint Louis U., Mo., 2006—. Vis. prof. School of Informatics, SUNY, Buffalo, 1990—. Reviewer Jour. Libr. Adminstrn. and Mgmt. Named one of Movers and Shakers, Libr. Jour., 2004. Mem.: ALA, NY Libr. Assn., Libr. Adminstrn. and Mgmt. Assn., Assn. Coll. and Rsch. Librs., Beta Phi Mu. Office: Saint Louis U Pius XII Meml Libr 3650 Lindell Blvd Saint Louis MO 63108 Office Phone: 314-977-3120. E-mail: gstaines@slu.edu. *

STAINES, MAVIS AVRIL, performing company executive; b. Cowansville, Que., Can., Apr. 9, 1954; d. David Russell and Betty (Knott) S.; m. Jyrki Virsunen, Feb. 4, 1988. Student, Nat. Ballet Sch., 1968-73, 81-83. Dancer Nat. Ballet of Can., 1973-78, 1st soloist, 1975-78; dancer Dutch Nat. Ballet, 1978-81; artistic dir. The Nat. Ballet Sch., Toronto, Ont., Canada, 1989—. Mem. artistic staff Nat. Ballet Sch., 1982; assoc. artistic dir., 1984; juror Prix de Lausanne, Switzerland, 1993, 94, 95, pres. jury 1998, 99; guest spkr., 1997; presenter Prix de Lausanne Internat. Symposium, 1997; mem. task force on classicl ballet tng. DANCE/USA, Phila., 1994; pres. Prix de Lausanne, 1998, 99; artistic pres. designate, 2001; artistic pres., 2001-; bd. dirs. Kala Nidhi Fine Arts of Can. Recipient Toronto Arts award for performing arts, 1998, Can.'s Most Powerful Women: Top 100 award Women's Exec. Network, 2006. Office: The Nat Ballet Sch 400 Jarvis St Toronto ON Canada M4Y 2G6 Business E-Mail: mavis-assist@nbs-enb.ca.

STAINROOK, HARRY RICHARD, photographer, retired bank executive; b. Phila., Jan. 11, 1937; s. Millward M. and Janet Stainrook; m. Judith Anne, May 21, 1966; children: Jennifer, Eric. BA, Rutgers U., 1970. Mgr. bank ops. First Pa. Bank, Phila., 1956-61, asst. v.p. br. dept., 1964-73, v.p., mgr. London office, 1973-75, v.p. internat. dept., 1975-78, sr. v.p. comml. group, 1978-81, exec. v.p., trust and investments, 1981-85; exec. v.p. trust and investments Mfrs. and Traders Trust Co., Buffalo, 1985-97, ret., 1997; prin., owner Harry Stainrook, Ltd., NYC, 2006—. Exhibitions include Art Dialogue Gallery, Buffalo, 2006; photographer (exhibitions) Art Dialogue Gallery, Buffalo, 2007; exhibitions include Collectors Gallery, Albright Knox Art Mus., Buffalo, 2007. Past chmn., bd. dirs. Greater Buffalo Opera Co.; past pres. Buffalo Philharm. Orch., Acad. Vocal Arts, Phila. With US Army, 1961—64. Mem. Western NY Artists Group, World Future Soc., Inst. Noetic Scis., Saturn Club. Lutheran. Home: 150 Columbus Ave Apt 4A New York NY 10023-5964 Office Phone: 646-228-7290. Personal E-mail: hstainrook@nyc.rr.com.

STAIR, THOMAS OSBORNE, physician, educator; b. Richmond, Va., Jan. 10, 1950; s. Frederick Rogers Jr. and Martha (Osborne) S.; m. Lucy Caldwell, Dec. 28, 1973; children: Rebecca Caldwell, Peter Caldwell. AB, U. N.C., 1971; MD, Harvard U., 1975. Diplomate Am. Bd. Emergency Medicine (examiner 1982-88). Residency dir. emergency dept. Georgetown U. Sch. Medicine, Washington, 1979-85, asst. dir. emergency dept., 1979-89, asst. dean for continuing med. edn., 1985-89, chair dept. emergency medicine, 1989-95; prof. U. Md., Balt., 1995-98; assoc. prof. Harvard Med. Sch., 1998—; attending emergency physician Brigham and Women's Hosp., Boston, 1998—. Co-author: Common Simple Emergencies, 1985, Emergency Medicine, 1997, Minor Emergencies, 1999. Recipient Excellence in Teaching award Emergency Medicine Residents Assn., 1986. Fellow Am. Coll. Emergency Physicians; mem. Soc. Acad. Emergency Medicine, Am. Med. Informatics Assn. Home: 46 Woodcliff Rd Newton MA 02461-1825 Office: 75 Francis St Boston MA 02115-6110 Home Phone: 617-928-3375; Office Phone: 617-732-5640. Business E-Mail: tstair@partners.org.

STAIR, WILSON ALFRED, JR., urban designer, landscape architect; b. St. Louis, Feb. 9, 1946; s. Wilson Alfred Stair and Teresa Kathleen Donahoe; m. Jan Hanson, Nov. 1, 1968. BS in Environ. Design, U. Okla., 1973, BArch, MArch, U. Okla., 1974. Registered landscape arch., Ariz., N.Mex., Fla., S.C. Urban designer divsn. urban redevelopment City of St. Petersburg, Fla., 1976—81; design dir., project mgr. D.V. Preiser Designs, Inc., Tampa, 1982-83; project mgr. H.L. Yoh Co., Inc., 1983-86; urban design mgr. urban design divsn. City of Tampa, 1986—. Mem. Livable Roadways Com., Tampa, 1992—; design rev. com. Fla. Dept. Transp., Tampa, 1992—; bd. dirs. Mayor's Beautification Program, Tampa. Project designer Janus Landing, 1981, Tampa Downtown Riverwalk, 1989, CBD Streetscape. Staff sgt. USAF, 1966-70. Recipient Recognition award for ednl. contbn. to dept. landscape arch. U. Fla., 1992. Mem. Am. Soc. Landscape Archs., Tau Sigma Delta. Democrat. Methodist. Avocations: martial arts, motorcycling, hiking, watercolor painting. Home: Unit 206 782 Village Lake Ter N Saint Petersburg FL 33716-3146 Office: City Tampa Growth Mgmt and Devel Svcs Dept 306 E Jackson St Tampa FL 33602-5223 Office Phone: 813-274-8402. Personal E-mail: wilson.stair@tampagov.net.

STAIRS, DENIS WINFIELD, political science professor, department chairman; b. Halifax, NS, Can., Sept. 6, 1939; s. Henry Gerald and Freda (Winfield) S.; m. Valerie Downing Street, Aug. 10, 1963 (div. Dec. 1986); children: Robert Woodliffe, Christopher Winfield; m. Jennifer Smith, July 18, 1987. BA, Dalhousie U., 1961, Oxford U., 1964, MA, 1968; PhD, U. Toronto, 1969. Asst. prof. dept. polit. sci. Dalhousie U., 1966-70, assoc. prof., 1970-75, dir. Centre Fgn. Policy Studies, 1971-75, prof. polit. sci., 1975—, McCulloch prof., 1995—2005, chmn. dept., 1980-85, v.p. acad. and rsch., 1988-93; prof. emeritus, 2005—. Bd. dirs. Atlantic Coun. Can., 1979—, Inst. Rsch. Pub. Policy, 1989-97, 98-06; mem. coun. Social Sci. and Humanities Rsch. Coun. Can., 1981-87; mem. rsch. coun. Can. Inst. Advanced Rsch., 1986-97; bd. dirs. Orgn. for Study of Nat. History of Can., 1995-98; bd. vis. Can. Forces Coll., 2002—, chair, 2006—; fellow, mem. adv. com. Can. Def. and Fgn. Affairs Inst., 2002—. Author: The Diplomacy of Constraint: Canada, the Korean War, and the United States, 1974; editl. bd. Internat. Jour., 1997—. Rhodes scholar, 1961; J.W. Dafoe postgrad. fellow internat. studies, 1965-66; Can. Coun. leave fellow, 1972-73; Social Scis. and Humanities Rsch. Coun. Can. leave fellow, 1979-80; recipient Disting. Writing award, Marcel Cadieux, 2000, 2003. Fellow Royal Soc. Can., Order of Can. (officer 2006-); mem. Can. Polit. Sci. Assn. (pres.), Can. Inst. Internat. Affairs, Internat. Studies Assn. Clubs; Royal N.S. Yacht Squadron. Office: Dalhousie U Dept Polit Sci Halifax NS Canada B3H 4H6 Office Phone: 902-494-2396.

STAIVISKY, JEANNE LOUISE, counselor, alcohol/drug abuse services professional; b. Hughesville, Pa., Dec. 30, 1947; d. Charolotte Bowen and John Staivisky. AA in Psychology, Palm Beach Jr. Coll., 1981; BS in Gen. Psychology, Nova U., 1984, M in Sci. in Counseling Psychology, 1987. Lic. profl. counselor Ill., 2003, nat. cert. psychologist Psychology Profl. Bd., 2000, lic. mental health counselor Ind., 1999, cert. Nat. Bd. Cert. Counselors, 1996, Am. Acad. Health Providers Addictive Disorders, 1995. Program mgr., counselor Hugs Not Drugs Treatment Program, Boca Raton, Fla., 1987—87; clin. supr., counselor The Starting Pl., Hollywood, Fla., 1987—89; counselor, clin. supr. Adolescent Substance Abuse Counseling Svc., Kaiserslautern and Hanau, Army Military Bases, Germany, 1987—89, clin. supr., counselor Kaiserslauter and Hanau, 1989—97, counselor, acting clin. supr. Camp Zama, 1997—2002, counselor Schofield Barracks/Wahiawa, Hawaii, 2002—05, County Substance Abuse Program, Ft. Campbal, Ky., 2005—. Cons. Crisis Intervention Team, Kaiserslauter; sponsor Teen Peer Facilitator Programs, Kaiserslautern; chair Character Edn. Program in Schools, Camp Zama, Japan, 2000—02; team mem. Camp Zama HS Crisis Intervention Team, 1997—2002; yean mem. WMS Crisis Intervention Team Wheeler Army Airfield Middle School, 2002—; youth 2 youth group Youth 2 Youth Internat. Group Camp Zama, 1998—2002; sponsor S.A.D.D., Kaiserslautern and Camp Zama, 1987—2002; chairperson Jorney Into Adulthood for Teens Risk, 1996—97; sponsor ASACS Role Model Club, Wheeler Army Air Base/WMS, Hawaii, 2002—05; sponsor educating parents teen issues Teen Panel, Schofiield Barracks/Wahiawa, 2002—05; counselor Army Substance Abuse Program, counselor psychol. series 180 GS-11, 2005—. Author: Looking For The Pot of Gold at The End of The Rainbow, poems; contbr. articles to profl. jours. Sponsoring mem. So. Law Poverty-Wall of Tolerance Civil Rights, Alabama, Ga., 2004—07. Mem.: APA, Nat. Assn. Master Psychologists, Nat. Alcohol and Drug Abuse Counselors, Tenn. Alcohol and Drug Abuse Counselors, Am. Mental Health Cousnelors, Am. Assn. Counseling. Achievements include 1990 letter of Commendation from Gerneral Crosbie E. Saint; SAIC 1990 Environmental Achievement Award for Single Superior Performance; 1997 415th Base Support Battalion Community Coin; SAIC 2000 Founders Award; Y2Y group nominated to represnt the Army in the first DoD Youth Alcohol and Drug Awareness Program Award; 2002 Legendary Service Award for the Army Military Community in Hawaii. Avocations: needlecrafts, stamp'in up-making cards, designing clothes, collecting poreclain dolls from all over the world. Home: 226 Cullom Way Clarksville TN 37043 Personal E-mail: jeanne123047@yahoo.com.

STAKE, PETER, artist, educator; BFA, Ariz. State U.; MFA, Calif. State U., Long Beach. Chmn. art & art hist. dept. Skidmore Coll., Saratoga Springs, Calif. Exhibitions include, Ctr. Art & Design, U. Wales Inst. Bd. trustees Hyde Collection. Office: Skidmore College- Art Dept 815 North Broadway Sasselin 200 Saratoga Springs NY 12866 Office Phone: 518-580-5032. E-mail: pskake@skidmore.edu.

STAKER, ROBERT JACKSON, retired judge; b. Kermit, W.Va., Feb. 14, 1925; s. Frederick George and Nada (Frazier) S.; m. Sue Blankenship Poore, July 16, 1955; 1 child, Donald Seth; 1 stepson, John Timothy Poore. Student, Marshall U., Huntington, W.Va., W.Va. U., Morgantown, U. Ky., Lexington; LL.B, W.Va. U., 1952. Bar: W.Va. 1952. Practiced in Williamson, 1952-68; judge Mingo County Circuit Ct., Williamson, 1969-79; U.S. dist. judge So. Dist. W.Va., Huntington, 1979-95, sr. U.S. dist. judge, 1995—2005. Served with USN, 1943-46. Democrat. Presbyterian. Personal E-mail: robert_staker@wvsd.uscourts.gov.

STALCUP, JOE ALAN, retired lawyer, dean; b. Hooker, Okla., Feb. 13, 1931; s. Herbert I. and Ruby (Gantt) S.; m. Nancy Jo Vaughn, Sept. 3, 1950; children: Melinda, Sondra Jo, Cheri Ann. BBA cum laude, So. Methodist U., 1951, JD magna cum laude, 1959, M.Th. magna cum laude, 1978. Bar: Tex. 1959. Tchr. Dallas Ind. Sch. Dist., 1951-57; assoc. atty. firm Locke, Purnell, Boren, Laney & Neely, Dallas, 1959-66; assoc. atty., partner firm Geary, Brice & Lewis, Dallas, 1966-67; founder, sr. partner firm Stalcup, Johnson, Meyers & Miller (and predecessor firm), Dallas, 1968-75; dean Sch. Theology for the Laity, 1978—80, prof., 1992—96, 2003—06. Pres. Dallas County Young Democrats, 1952-54; Bd. dirs., mem. exec. com. N. Tex. Christian Communications Commn., 1972-78; bd. dirs., v.p. Greater Dallas Council Chs., 1972-75; bd. dirs., chmn. Christian Ch. Found., 1976-84, 86-91, Christian Bd. Publ., 1991-98. Mem. ABA, Tex. Bar Assn., Dallas Bar Assn., Am. Judicature Soc., Phi Alpha Delta. Mem. Disciples of Christ (minister). Home and Office: 7528 Benedict Dr Dallas TX 75214-1903

STALEY, ALVIN, artist, educator; b. Phila., Jan. 27, 1955; s. Albert Mungo and Elease Staley; m. Bretta Reed, Feb. 1, 1977; children: Altroy Willie, Kizzi Alicia Staley Gibson. BA, Claflin U., Orangeburg, SC, 1976; MFA, Am. U., DC, 1981. Instr. art Morris Coll., Orangeburg, SC, 1984—85; chmn. Dept. Art Claflin U., Orangeburg, 1985—87; artist-in-residence Orangeburg-Wilkinson H.S., 1987—. Coord. visual arts, instr. Orangeburg-Calhoun Consortium for Arts, 1989—2004; instr. drawing Gov.'s Sch. for Arts and Humanities, Greenville, SC, 1988—2003; adj. prof. art Claflin U. Exhibitions include Annual Oil Painters Open Invitational, Nat. Bank SC, 2002 (First Pl. Best in Show award, 2002), 2006, SC State Fair, 2003 (Best in Show award, 2003), Burwell Gallery, Spartanburg, SC, 2004, Spartanburg County Mus., Columbia, SC, 2004, Piccolo Spoleto Art Festival, Charleston, SC, 2005 (Second Pl. award), 2006 (Second Pl. award), Arthur Rose Mus., Orangeburg, SC, 2006, Hofp Gallery, Columbia, SC, 2006. Nominee Distinguished Tchrs. in Arts, Coca Cola Co., 2004, 2005; recipient Star Tchr. award, Time Warner Cable, 2005. Mem.: Nat. Art Edn. Assn. Home: 153 Harvey lane Orangeburg SC 29118 Office: Orangeburg-Wilkinson High 601 Bruin Parkway Orangeburg SC 29118 Home Phone: 803-534-4727; Office Phone: 803-516-6062. Personal E-mail: as577@aol.com.

STALEY, DAWN MICHELLE, professional basketball player; b. Phila., May 4, 1970; d. Estelle. Grad., U. Va., 1992. Profl. basketball player Brazil, France, Italy, Spain, Richmond Rage, ABL, 1996—98, Charlotte Sting, WNBA, 1999—; head women's basketball coach Temple U., 2000—. Mem. USA Basketball Teams, 1989—. Founder Dawn Staley Found. Named USA Basketball Female Athlete of Yr., 1994, MVP, Goodwill Games, 1994, Phila. Big Five Coach of Yr., 2002, Atlantic 10 Coach of Yr., 2004; named to First Team All-ABL, 1997, WNBA All-Star Team, 2001, 2002, 2003; recipient Spectrum Award, ARC, 1998, Entrepreneurial Spirit Award, WNBA, 1999, Sportsmanship Award, 1999. Achievements include being a member of US Women's Basketball gold medal team, Atlanta, 1996; being a member of US Women's Basketball gold medal team, Sydney Olympics, 2000; being a member of US Women's Basketball Team, Athens Olympics, 2004; having her number retired at U. Va; being the first women in professional basketball history to record 1,000 career assists; serving as Olympic Flag bearer, Athens Olympic Games, 2004. Office: 100 Hive Dr Charlotte NC 28208-7707

STALEY, GREG, retail executive; Former pres., CEO Toys 'R' Us, USA; former dir., consultant KB Toy Stores, now pres., CEO, 2005—. Office: KB Toys 100 West St Pittsfield MA 01201

STALEY, HENRY MUELLER, manufacturing executive; b. Decatur, Ill., June 3, 1932; s. Augustus Eugene, Jr. and Lenore (Mueller) S.; m. Violet Lucas, Feb. 4, 1955; children— Mark Eugene, Grant Spencer. Grad., Governor Dummer Acad., 1950; BS in Psychology, Northwestern U., 1954, MBA in Finance, 1956. Salesman Field Enterprises, Chgo., 1953; salesman A.E. Staley Mfg. Co., 1951, mgmt. trainee, 1956-57, ins. mgr., 1957-59, asst. treas., 1959-65, treas., asst. sec., 1965-73, v.p., treas., asst. sec., 1973-77, v.p. bus. and econ. analysis, 1977-87, also dir., 1969-85; pvt. investor Decatur, 1987—. Dir. Staley Continental, Inc., 1985-88. Crusade chmn. Macon County unit Am. Cancer Soc., 1964-65, mem. bd. dirs., 1965-71, vice chmn. bd., 1965-66, chmn. bd., 1966-69; bd. dirs. United Way Decatur and Macon County, 1972-74; mem. adv. council Millikin U., 1968-91, chmn. adv. coun., 1970-71; mem. Decatur Meml. Hosp. Devel. Council, 1969-71, mem. finan. com., bd. dirs., 1970-79, mem. long-range planning com., 1976-77, mem. devel. and community relations com., 1977-78. Mem. Decatur C. of C. (dir. 1967-72), Sigma Nu, Decatur Country.Club. Home and Office: 276 N Park Pl Decatur IL 62522-1952

STALEY, JAMES E., bank executive; Officer J.P. Morgan Chase & Co., head Pvt. Bank, mng. dir. to CEO asset & wealth mgmt., mem. exec. com., 2001—. Office: JP Morgan Chase & Co 270 Park Ave New York NY 10017-2070

STALEY, KENNETH BERNARD, civil engineer; b. Dec. 31, 1948; s. Kinzy and Bernice Florence (Williams) S.; m. Sheila Ruth Keeys, Apr. 26, 1975; children: Tabbatha, Christina, Harrison. ThM, Villanova U., 1971, MA, 1976, DD, 1978. Registerd profl. engr.; ordained to ministry Bapt. Ch., 1978. Cost estimator Joseph A. McCollum Inc., Marlton, N.J., 1967-69; expeditor R. V. Rulon Inc., Riverton, N.J., 1971; field engr. United Engrs., Phila., 1971-72; civil engr., v.p., dir. Kinzy Staley & Sons, Inc., Phila., 1972—. Vol. Aid Sickle Cell Anemia, 1974, Mendenhall Ministries, Miss.; asst. pastor Christian Stronghold Bapt. Ch., Phila., 1978—; bd. dirs. Christian R&D, Phila., Germantown Cmty. Devel., Phila.; bd. advisors Manna Bible Inst., Phila.; trustee Ctr. Urban Theol. Studies, Conservative Bapt. Sem., Phila. Prison Sys. Mem. Nat. Soc. Profl. Engrs., Assn. Cost Engrs., Am. Arbitration Assn., Am. Ceramic Soc., Am. Concrete Inst., Phila. Engrs. Club, Alpha Phi Alpha. Democrat. Home: 1130 Lakeside Ave Philadelphia PA 19126-2308 Office: Covenant Cons Group PO Box 698 Bala Cynwyd PA 19004-0698

STALEY, LYNN, literature educator; b. Madisonville, Ky., Dec. 24, 1947; d. James Mulford and Florine (Hurt) Staley. AB, U. Ky., 1969; MA, PhD, Princeton U., 1973. Grad. asst. Princeton (N.J.) U., 1971-73; instr. English Colgate U., Hamilton, NY, 1974-75, from asst. to assoc. prof., 1975-86, prof., 1986—. Author: The Voice of the Gawain-Poet, 1984, The Shepheardes Calendar: An Introduction, 1990, Margery Kempe's Dissenting Fictions, 1994; author: (with David Aers) The Powers of the Holy: Religion, Politics and Gender in, 1996;, 1996; editor: The Book of Margery Kempe, 1996; translator, 2001, Dictionary of the Middle Ages, 2004, Languages of Power in the Age of Richard II, 2005; contbr. articles to profl. jours. NEH fellow, 2003—04, Guggenheim fellow, 2003—04. Mem. MLA, Medieval Acad. Am., Renaissance Soc. Am., New Chaucer Soc., Spenser Soc. Office: Colgate U Dept English 13 Oak Dr Dept English Hamilton NY 13346-1383 Office Phone: 315-228-7667. Business E-Mail: lstaley@mail.colgate.edu.

STALEY, THOMAS FABIAN, language professional, academic administrator; b. Pitts., Aug. 13, 1935; s. Fabian Richard and Mary (McNulty) S.; m. Carolyn O'Brien, Sept. 3; children: Thomas Fabian, Caroline Ann, Mary Elizabeth, Timothy X. AB, BS, Regis Coll., 1957; MA, U. Tulsa, 1958; PhD, U. Pitts., 1962; D.H.L., Regis Coll. Asst. prof. English Rollins Coll., 1961-62; mem. faculty U. Tulsa, 1962-88, prof. English, 1969-88, dean Grad. Sch., 1969, dean Coll. Arts and Scis., 1981-83, provost, v.p. acad. affairs, 1983-88, McFarlin prof. modern lit., 1988; prof. English, dir. Ransom Humanities Rsch. Ctr. U. Tex., Austin, 1988—, Chancellor's Centennial prof. of the Book, 1989—92, Harry Huntt Ransom chair liberal arts, 1992—. Fulbright prof., Italy, 1966-67; Fulbright lectr., 1971; Danforth assoc., 1962-67; chmn. Internat. James Joyce Symposium; dir. Grad. Inst. Modern Letters, 1970-81. Author: James Joyce Today, 1966, James Joyce's Portrait of the Artist, 1968, Italo Svevo: Essays on His Work, 1969, (with H.J. Mooney) The Shapeless God: Essays on the Modern Novel, 1968, (with B. Benstock) Approaches to Ulysses: Ten Essays, 1970, Approaches to Joyce's Portrait: Ten Essays, Jean Rhys: A Critical Study; editor: Il Punto Su Joyce, 1973, Dorothy Richardson, Ulysses: Fifty Years, 1974, Twentieth-Century Women Novelists, 1982, British Novelists, 1890-1929, Traditionalists, Dictionary of Lit. Biography, Vols. 34, 36, 70, 77, An Annotated Critical Bibliography of James Joyce, 1989, Joyce Studies: An Annual edit., 1990-2003, Studies in Modern Literature Series, 1990—, Reflections on James Joyce: Stuart Gilbert's Paris Journal, 1993, Writing the Lives of Writers, 1998, James Joyce Quar., 1963-89; adv. editor Twentieth-Century Lit., 1966—, Jean Rhys Rev., 1986—; bd. dirs. Eighteenth-Century Short Title Catalogue/North America, 1990; mem. editl. bd. Tulsa Studies in Women's Literature, Jour. Modern Lit., 1989—, Mailer Rev., 2007—; contbr. articles to profl. jours. Bd. dirs. Tulsa Arts Coun., 1969-76, NCCJ, 1979—, Christopher Isherwood Found.; pres. James Joyce Found., 1968-72; chmn. bd. Undercroft Montessori Sch., 1968-70, Marquette Sch., 1969-70; bd. dirs. Cascia Hall Prep. Sch.; chmn. disting. authors com. Tulsa Libr. Trust, 1984; mem. bd. commrs. Tulsa City-County Libr., chmn., 1980-82; mem. adv. coun. Tex. Inst. for Humanities; trustee Regis U., 1992—; bd. dirs. Libr. of Am., 1994—, Harlick Trust, 1994—; mem. symposium com. Lyndon Baines Johnson Presdl. Libr., 1993—; mem. AFI Dallas Internat. Film Festival Bd., 2006—. Recipient Am. Council Learned Socs. award, 1969, 80 Mem. MLA, Internat. Assn. Univ. Profs. English, Anglo-Irish Studies Assn., Am. Com. for Irish Studies, Assn. Internat. de Bibliophilie, James Joyce Soc., Hopkins Soc., Tex. Philos. Soc. (bd. dirs. 1991—), Internat. James Joyce Found. (hon. trustee), LBJ Centennial Hist. Soc., US Tennis Assn., Tulsa Tennis Club, Westwood Country Club, The Athenaeum Club (London), Grolier Club (N.Y.), Edgecomb Tennis Club (Kennebunk, Maine), Tarry House, Phi Beta Kappa. Business E-Mail: TFS@mail.utexas.edu.

STALEY, WARREN R., agricultural products and diversified services company executive; b. Springfield, Ill., May 14, 1942; BS in Elec. Engring., Kans. State U., 1965; MS in Bus. Adminstrn., Cornell U., 1967. With Cargill, Inc., Mpls., 1969—, gen. mgr., European corn milling bus., 1978—82, gen. mgr., Argentine ops., 1983—87, pres. for N.Am. and Latin Am., to 1998, pres., COO, 1998—2000, CEO, 1999—, chmn., 2000—. Bd. dirs., Cargill, Inc., 1995-, U.S. Bancorp, 1999-, Target Corp., 2001-; apptd. mem. President's Export Coun. (PEC), 2003, chmn. Cargill Found. Bd. dirs. Greater Twin Cities United Way, Minn. Pvt. Coll. Coun. Office: Cargill Inc 15407 McGinty Rd, W Wayzata MN 55391 *

STALKER, JACQUELINE D'AOUST, academic administrator, educator; b. Penetang, Ont., Can., Oct. 16, 1933; d. Phillip and Rose (Eaton) D'Aoust; m. Robert Stalker; children: Patricia, Lynn, Roberta. Teaching cert., U. Ottawa, 1952; tchr. music, Royal Toronto Conservatory Music, 1952; teaching cert., Lakeshore Tchrs. Coll., 1958; BEd with honors, U. Manitoba, 1977, MEd, 1979; EdD, Nova U., 1985. Cert. tchr. Ont., Man., Can. Adminstr., tchr., prin. various schs., Ont. and Que., 1952-65; area commr. Girl Guides of Can., throughout Europe, 1965-69; administr., tchr. Algonquin Community Coll., Ottawa, Ont., 1970-74; tchr., program devel. Frontenac County Bd. Edn., Kingston, Ont., 1974-75; lectr., faculty advisor dept. curriculum, edn. U. Man., Can., 1977-79; lectr. U. Winnipeg, Man., Can., 1977-79; cons. colls. div. Man. Dept. Edn., 1980-81, sr. cons. programming br., 1981-84, sr. cons. post secondary, adult and continuing edn. div., 1985-88, dir. post secondary career devel. br. and adult and continuing edn. br., 1989; asst. prof. higher edn., coord. grad. program in higher edn. U. Man., 1989-92, assoc. prof., coord. grad. program in higher edn., 1992-95. Cons. lectures, seminars, workshops throughout Can. Contbr. articles to profl. jours.; mng. editor Can. Jour. of Higher Edn., 1989-93. Mem. U. Man. Senate, 1976-81, 86-89, bd. govs., 1979-82; Can. rep. Internat. Youth Conf., Garmisch, Fed. Republic of Germany, 1968; vol. Can. Cancer Soc.; mem. Assn. RN Accreditation Coun., 1980-85; chair Child Care Accreditation Com., Man., 1983-90; chair Task Force Post-Secondary Accessibility, Man., 1983; vol. United Way Planning and Allocations; provincial dir., mem. nat. bd. Can. Congress for Learning Opportunities for Women. Recipient award for enhancing the Outreach activities of the univ. U. Man., 1994. Mem. Can. Soc. Study Higher Edn., Man. Tchrs. Soc., U. Man. Alumni Assn., Women's Legal Edn. and Action Fund.

STALL, ALAN DAVID, packaging company executive; b. Moose Jaw, Sask., Can., June 14, 1951; arrived in US, 1982; s. Joel and Evelyn (Schwartz) S.; m. Carol I. Johnston; children: Jeffrey, Jennifer, Michael, Timothy. BSME, U. Sask., 1973; MBA, Lewis U., 1986. Registered profl. engr., Ont. Devel. engr. DuPont Can., North Bay, Ont., 1973-76; project engr. Union Carbide Corp. Can., Lindsay, 1976-79, engring. mgr., 1979-82; mgr. shirring rsch. Union Carbide Corp., Chgo., 1982-85; dir. engring. tech. Viskase Corp., Chgo., 1985-90, v.p. engring., 1990-95; gen. mgr. Kuko Corp., Gross-Gerau, Germany, 1995-98; pres. Films Casings Tech. Inc., Woodridge, Ill., 1996—; gen. mgr. Alfacel Inc., Woodridge, 1998—; v.p. Teepak de Mex., 2003—; CEO Stratek Plastics, Wallingford, Conn., 2006—. Patentee breathable plastic, shirring apparatus, sausage stuffing machine, cellulose casings, cellulose regeneration. Rotary bus. exchange fellow, London, 1982. Mem. Engring. Inst. Can., Can. Soc. Mech. Engrs., Soc. Plastics Engrs., Assn. Profl. Engrs., Ont., Am. Mensa, Can. Club Chgo. Home: 23W540 James Way Naperville IL 60540-9552 Office: FCT Inc PO Box 5415 Woodridge IL 60517-0415 Personal E-mail: astall@msn.com.

STALL, RICHARD J., JR., lawyer; b. Covington, Ky., July 5, 1941; BS with distinction, Purdue U., Lafayette, Ind., 1963; JD, Stanford U., Calif., 1966. Bar: Calif., U.S. Supreme Ct., U.S. Dist. Ct. (ctrl. dist.), U.S. Ct. Appeals (9th cir.). Assoc. Lawler, Felix & Hall (now Arter & Hadden), LA, 1966-70; ptnr. pvt. practice, LA, 1971-93; prin. Law Office of Richard J. Stall, Jr., et al, LA, 1994—. Contbg. author: Ins. Jour. Mem.: ABA, Culver-Marina Bar Assn. (past pres., dir.), Santa Monica Bar Assn., Nat. Assn. Railroad Trial Counsel, L.A. County Bar Assn., Calif. State Bar Assn. (real estate sect.), Beverly Hills Bar Assn. (real estate sect.), Assn. Bus. Trial Lawyers, Am. Arbitration Assn., Lion's Club (past pres.), Tau Beta Pi, Sigma Chi (Delta Delta Chpt. past pres.). Office: Law Office Richard J Stall Jr Ste 200 10507 W Pico Blvd Los Angeles CA 90064-2319 E-mail: rstall@picolaw.com.

STALL, WILLIAM READ, retired newswriter; b. Phila., Feb. 21, 1937; s. Sidney Joseph and Helen (Read) S.; m. Carolee Ramsey, July, 1961 (div. 1979); children: Tracy Stall Roll, Erica Stall Wiggins; m. Anne Elizabeth Baker, Dec. 8, 1979. BS, U. Wyo., 1959. Reporter Laramie (Wyo.) Boomerang, 1956-59, Associated Press, Cheyenne, Wyo., 1960-63, corres. Reno, 1963-66, bur. chief, polit. writer Sacramento, 1966-74; press sec. Edmund G. Brown Jr., Sacramento, 1975-76; staff writer, asst. met. editor, corres. L.A. Times, 1976-81, editorial writer, 1984-90, polit. writer, 1990-96, editl. writer, 1997—2006; bur. chief Hartford Courant, Washington, 1981-84; ret., 2006. Sr. lectr. journalism dept. U. So. Calif., 1985-94. With U.S. Air N.G., 1960-67. Named Disting. Alumni, U. Wyo., 2005; recipient Pulitzer prize for editl. writing, 2004. Mem. Am. Alpine Club (dir. 1992-98). Episcopalian. Avocations: rock climbing, mountain climbing, sailing. Personal E-mail: billstall@aol.com.

STALLER, JOHN EDWARD, archaeologist, anthropologist, educator; b. Grosseraming, Austria, Jan. 28, 1951; s. John Staller and Elizabeth; m. Margaret Mary Tentler, Jan. 20, 1973. BA, Roosevelt U., Chgo., 1981; MA, So. Meth. U., Dallas, 1990, PhD, 1994. Rsch. assoc. The Field Mus., Chgo., 1999—. Bd. dirs. Fulbright Assn., Chgo., 1999—; adj. prof. Loyola U., Chgo., 1996, Roosevelt U., 2000; vis. asst. prof. U. Ill., Chgo., 1999—2000; vis. faculty in Summer Inst. MIT Workshop, 2001; vis. lectr. Northeastern Ill. U., 2003; vis. asst. prof. U. Ky., 2005—06. Editor (senior editor): Histories of Maize: Multidisciplinary Approaches to the Prehistory, Biogeography, Domestication, and Evolution of Maize; contbr. articles to profl. jours. Fulbright scholar, 1988—89, 1989, 2007. Mem.: World Archtl. Congress, Soc. Am. Archaeology, Fulbright Assn., Inst. Andean Studies, Am. Anthrop. Assn. Office: The Field Museum Dept of Anthropology 1400 S Lake Shore Dr Chicago IL 60605

STALLINGS, CHARLES HENRY, retired physicist; b. Durham, NC, Dec. 28, 1941; s. Henry Harroll and Dorothy (Powers) S.; m. Elizabeth Bright, Sept. 4, 1965; children: Deborah, Sharon. BS, N.C. State U., 1963, MS, 1964; PhD, U. Wis., 1970. Sr. physicist Physics Internat. Co. (now Maxwell Physics Internat.), San Leandro, Calif., 1970-73, dep. dept. mgr., 1974-76, dept. mgr., 1976-79, dir. satellite x-ray test facility office, 1979-81, dir. bus. devel., 1981-83, v.p., dir. rsch. devel., v.p., gen. mgr., 1983—2001; ret., 2001. Contbr. articles to tech. jours. Mem. Gen. Plan Rev. Com., Pleasanton, Calif., 1983. Mem. Am. Phys. Soc., IEEE (mem. pulsed power sci. and tech. com. 1996—, chmn. 12th internat. pulsed power conf. 1999). Home: 3608 Fieldview Ct Pleasanton CA 94588

STALLINGS, FRANK, JR., realtor, director; b. Concord, NC, Aug. 21, 1954; s. Frank and Theresa Ann Stallings BS in Indsl. Engring., N.C. State U., 1976; MS in Adminstrn., George Washington U., 1979. Lic. real estate agt. Tex. Jr. indsl. engr. Naval Air Rework Facility, Norfolk, Va., 1974—75; indsl. engr. Babcock & Wilcox, Lynchburg, Va., 1977—79; sr. prin. engr. NCR Corp., Columbia, SC, 1979—82; mgr. indsl. engring. Mars Electronics, Ltd., Reading, England, 1987—88; liaison between European/U.S. mfg. divsn., sr. indsl. engr. M&M/MARS, Inc., Waco, Tex., 1982—84, mgr. quality assurance, 1984—87, mgr. indsl. engring., 1988—96, inbound logistics mgr., 1996—97; mng. prin. Oracle Corp., 1998—2001, practice mgr., 2001; mgmt. cons., 2001—05; dir. indsl. engring. Minyards, Inc., 2005—. Coach Heart of Tex. Soccer League, Waco, 1985-87; Sunday sch. tchr. Columbus Ave. Bapt. Ch., Waco, 1988-97, mem. Missions com., 1991-96, Bapt. Youth leader, 1990-97, mem. ch. singles coun., 1989-91; Sunday sch. tchr. First Bapt. Hartsville (S.C.) Ch., 1998-2000; exec. mem. singles coun. Waco Bapt. Assn.; counselor Royal Ambs., 1990-96; children's leader Bible Study Fellowship, 1995-97; v.p. DFW Aquatic Plant Club, 2006-; dir. Chaucer Estates Howmeowners Assn., 2006-. Mem. Inst. Indsl. Engrs. (sr.), Am. Soc. Quality Control, Am. Prodn. and Inventory Control Socl., Am. Radio Relay League, Project Mgmt. Inst. (cert.), Radio Amateurs Civil Emergency Svcs., Amateur Radio Emergency Svcs., Ten-10 Internat. Amateur Radio Network, Waco Amateur TV Soc. (bd. dirs. 1995-96), Appalachian Trail Soc. (life). Democrat. Avocations: camping, boating, running, bicycling, radio operator. Home: PO Box 89 Argyle TX 76226-0089 Business E-Mail: frank@stallings.com.

STALLINGS, (CHARLES) NORMAN, lawyer; b. Tampa, Fla., Apr. 3, 1914; s. Otto Pyromus and Minnie Henderson (Mitchell) S.; m. Mary Phillips Powell, Feb. 6, 1943 (dec. 1999); children: Charles Norman, Jean Katherine (dec.), Mary Anne. AB, U. Fla., 1935; JD, Harvard U., 1938, LL.M., 1940. Bar: Mo. 1939, Fla. 1940, D.C. 1941, Ga. 1946. Asso. firm Ryland, Stinson, Mag & Thomson, Kansas City, Mo., 1938-39, Sutherland, Tuttle & Brennan, Washington, 1940-41, Atlanta, 1946-49; mem. firm Shackleford, Farrior, Stallings & Evans, Tampa, Fla., 1949-84, of counsel, 1984—2002, Gray & Robinson, 2003—. Vice chmn. Hillsborough County (Fla.) Aviation Authority, 1955-61. Served to lt. col. U.S. Army, 1941-46, ETO. Decorated Bronze Star; Croix de Guerre avec Palma, Belgium. Fellow Am. Coll. Trial Lawyers; mem. ABA, Hillsborough County Bar Assn. (past pres.), Fla. Bar (past gov.), Univ. Club (past pres.), Tampa Yacht and Country Club (past gov.), Ye Mystic Krewe of Gasparilla (past capt. and king), Phi Delta Phi, Kappa Alpha. Republican. Episcopalian. Home: 3501 Bayshore Blvd Apt 805 Tampa FL 33629 Office: PO Box 3324 Tampa FL 33601-3324

STALLINGS, RONALD DENIS, lawyer; b. Evansville, Ind., Feb. 22, 1943; s. Denis and Gertrude (Tong) S.; m. Vicki Lee Chandler, Aug. 21, 1965; children: Courtnay, Claire, Ryan. B in Indsl. Engring., Ga. Inst. Tech., 1965; LLB, U. Va., 1968. Bar: Ga. 1968. Assoc. Powell, Goldstein, Frazer & Murphy LLP, Atlanta, 1968—75, ptnr., 1976—2000, co-counsel, 2001—05; sr. v.p., gen. counsel, corp. sec. Reliance Trust Co., Atlanta, 2001—. Co-author: Georgia Corporate Forms, 1988. Mem. ABA, Ga. Bar Assn., Atlanta Bar Assn., Nat. Assn. Bond Lawyers, Am. Soc. Corp. Secs., Phoenix Soc. Atlanta (trustee 1987-93). Roman Catholic. Home: 4601 Polo Ln NW Atlanta GA 30339-5345 Office: Reliance Trust Co 500 Northpark Ste 400 1100 Abernathy Rd NE Atlanta GA 30328-5646 Business E-Mail: rstallings@relico.com.

STALLINGS, VIRGINIA A., pediatric gastroenterologist; BS, Auburn U.; MS, Cornell U.; MD, U. Ala. Cert. pediatrics, clin. nutrition. Pediat. resident U. Va.; nutrition fellow Hosp. for Sick Children, Toronto; prof. pediatrics U. Pa. Sch. Med., Phila.; with Children's Hosp. Phila., 1985, attending physician, div. gastroenterology & nutrition, chief of nutrition sect., prof. pediatrics, Jean Cortner Endowed Chair in Pediat. Gastroenetology, dir. Nutrition Ctr., dep. dir. Joseph Stokes Rsch. Inst. Mem.: APA, Inst. Medicine (chair food & nutrition bd. 1999). Office: Children's Hosp of Philadelphia 34th St & Civic Ctr Blvd Philadelphia PA 19104

STALLMAN, DONALD LEE, environmental executive; b. Rochester, NY, Feb. 20, 1930; s. William F. and Clara Elizabeth (Boulle) S.; m. Dolores Anita Putney, Nov. 8, 1958; stepchildren: Nancy, Terri, Jeff. Student, Hobart Coll., Geneva, NY, 1948-49, U. Rochester, 1953-54. V.p. Kolstad Assocs., Inc., Rochester, NY, 1954—2002; pres. Water Treatment Assocs., Latham, NY, 1975—, KB Fabrications, Latham, 1977—. Chmn. bd. Water Treatment Assocs.; vice chmn. bd. KB Fabrications; adv. bd., pres. Bruner Corp., Milw., 1982-83. Designer Chock-o-Lette Spl. Aircraft Wheel Chock, 1978, Water Treatment Skid for Oil Field Applications, 1980; inventor in field. Cons. Capital Dist. Planning Commn., Albany, 1980-81. With U.S. Army, 1951-53. Decorated Bronze Star medal, Silver Star medal, Purple Hearts (2). Mem. Am. Soc. Plumbing Engrs., Quiet Birdman Soc., Sigma Chi. Republican. Roman Catholic. Avocations: flying, boating, golf. Office: Water Treatment Assocs PO Box 367 Latham NY 12110-0367 Home: 16 Hillcrest Rd Latham NY 12110-4133 Office Phone: 518-785-5654. Personal E-mail: alboff@aol.com.

STALLMAN, RICHARD MATTHEW, software developer; b. NYC, 1953; BA in Physics, Harvard U., 1974; PhD (hon.), Royal Inst. Tech., Stockholm, 1996, U. Glasgow, 2001, Free U. Brussels, 2003, U. Nacional de Salta, Argentina, 2004. Software developer MIT, Cambridge, 1971-83. Chief GNUisance, GNU Project, 1984—; founder, pres. Free Software Found., Boston, 1985—; hon. prof. Universidad Nacional de Ingeniería de Perú, 2003. Author: Free Software, Free Society, 2002; (software) EMACS, 1975, GNU EMACS, 1984, GNU C Compiler, 1988, GNU General Public License, 1989, GNU GPL Version 3, 2007. Bd. dirs. League Programming Freedom, 1989-95, pres., 1989-92. Recipient Grace Hopper award Assn. Computing, 1990, MacArthur prize fellowship MacArthur Found., 1990, Pioneer award Electronic Frontier Found., 1998, Yuri Rubinski Insight Found. award, 1999, Takeda prize for social/econ. betterment, 2001, Fondazione Pistoletto prize, 2005, Extremadura Free Knowledge prize, 2007. Mem.: NAE, Am. Acad. Arts and Scis. Avocations: Balkan folk dance, Balinese and Javanese Gamelan music, reading. Office: Free Software Found 51 Franklin St 5th Fl Boston MA 02111 Office Phone: 617-542-5942.

STALLONE, GEORGE R., neurophysiologist; b. Camden, NJ, Aug. 22, 1963; s. George Ralph and Rose Marie Anne Stallone. BS in Zoology, U. Md., 1989; D of Chiropractic, We. States Chirpractic Coll., 1994; postgrad. in clin. neurology, Logan Coll. Chiropractic, 1998. Cert. intraoperative neurophysiologic monitoring. Resident Triad Family Health, Hanover, Pa., 1995—96; intern Banister Chiropractic, Jacksonville, Fla., 1996—97; chiropractor pvt. practice, Nephi, Utah, 1998—2003; intraoperative neurophysiologist Teaneck, NJ, 2004—. Instr., rschr. Triad Family Health, 1995—96; rschr., lectr. Mind/Body Inst., Jacksonville, 1996—97. Sec. Ch. Men's Group, Mona, Utah, 2000—01. Mem.: Am. Soc. Electrophysiologists, Masons. Avocations: flying, scuba diving, skiing, martial arts. E-mail: stallone@nebonet.com.

STALLONE, SYLVESTER ENZIO, actor, film director, scriptwriter; b. NYC, July 6, 1946; s. Frank and Jacquline (Labofish) S.; m. Sasha Czack, Dec. 28, 1974 (div. Feb. 14, 1985); children: Sage, Seth; m. Brigitte Nielsen, Dec. 15, 1985 (div. July 13, 1987); m. Jennifer Flavin, May 17, 1997; children: Sophia, Sistine, Scarlet. Student, Am. Coll. of Switzerland, 1965-67, U. Miami, 1967-69. Formerly, usher, fish salesman, horse trainer, delicatessen worker, truck driver, bouncer, zoo attendant, short order cook, pizza demonstrator, phys. edn. tchr., motel supt., bookstore detective Appeared in motion pictures No Place to Hide, 1970, The Party at Kitty and Stud's, 1970, Lords of Flatbush, 1973, The Prisoner of Second Avenue, 1975, Capone, 1974, Farewell, My Lovely, 1975, Death Race 2000, 1975, Cannonball, 1976, Rocky, 1976, (Oscar for Best Picture 1976, Golden Globe award for best picture 1976, Donatello award for best actor in Europe 1976, Christopher Religious award 1976, Bell Ringer award Scholastic Mag. 1976, Nat. Theatre Owners award 1976) F.I.S.T, 1978, Paradise Alley, 1978, Rocky II, 1979, Nighthawks, 1981, Victory, 1981, Rocky III, 1982, First Blood, 1982, Rhinestone, 1984, Rambo: First Blood Part II, 1985, Rocky IV, 1985, Cobra, 1986, Over the Top, 1987, Rambo III, 1988, Lock Up, 1989, Tango and Cash, 1989, Rocky V, 1990, Oscar, 1991, Stop! Or My Mom Will Shoot, 1992, Cliffhanger, 1993, Demolition Man, 1993, The Specialist, 1994, Judge Dredd, 1995, Assassins, 1995, Firestorm, 1996, Daylight, 1996, Copland, 1997, An Alan Smithee Film: Burn Hollywood Burn, 1998, Antz (voice only), 1998, Get Carter, 2000, Driven (also prod.), 2001, D-Tox, 2002, Avenging Angelo, 2002, My Little Hollywood, 2002, Taxi 3, 2003, Shade, 2003, Spy Kids 3-D: Game Over, 2003, Rocky Balboa, 2006; dir. film Paradise Alley, 1978, Rocky II, 1979, Nighthawks, 1981, Rocky III, 1982, Staying Alive (also prodr.), 1983, Rocky IV, 1985; author: The Lords of Flatbush, 1974, Rocky, 1976, F.I.S.T., 1978, Paradise Alley, 1977, The Rocky Scrapbook, 1977, Rocky II, 1979, Rocky III, 1982, First Blood, 1982, Staying Alive, 1983, Rhinestone (screenplay), 1984, Rambo: First Blood Part II, 1985, Rocky IV, 1985, Cobra, 1986, Over the Top, 1987, Rambo III, 1988, Rocky V, 1990, Cliffhanger (screenplay), 1993, Driven (screenplay), 2001, Rocky Balboa, 2006; exec. prodr.: Heart of a Champion: The Ray Mancini Story, 1985, Rocky Balboa, 2006; exec. prodr., host (TV Series) The Contender, 2005. Recipient Star of the Year award 1977, named Show West actor of the year 1979, Artistic Achievement award Nat. Italian Am. Found., 1991, Order of Arts and Letters, French Ministry, 1992, Caesar award for Career Achievement, 1992. Mem. Screen Actors Guild, Writers Guild, Stuntmans Assn. (hon.), Dirs. Guild. Achievements include being nominated for two Oscars (acting and writing) in same year (1976); occurred for only 3d time in history. *Once in one's life, for one mortal moment, one must make a grab for immortality; if not, one has not lived.* *

STALLSMITH, BECKI LAUGHLIN, music educator; d. Homer and Linda Jo Laughlin; m. John Allen Stallsmith, July 11, 1987; children: Nellie Camille, Benjamin Alexander. MusB in Edn., U. Kans., Lawrence, 1989. Cert. tchr. Kindermusik Internat., 2007. Music asst. Shelton State C.C., Tuscaloosa, Ala., 1990—96; music educator Bevill State C.C., Jasper, Ala., 1996—. Bd. dirs. Literacy Coun. Ctrl. Ala., Birmingham, Ala. Bd. dirs. Walker County Literacy Coun., Jasper, 1996; coord. Reading is Fundamental, Jasper, 2005. Named Vol. of Yr., Walker County Literacy Coun., 2005; grantee, Walker Area Cmty. Found., 2003. Mem.: Kiwanis (assoc.). Home: 7819 Old Tuscaloosa Road Parrish AL 35580 Office: Bevill State Cmty Coll 1411 Indiana Ave Jasper AL 35501 Home Phone: 205-686-9437; Office Phone: 205-387-0511. Business E-Mail: bstallsmith@bscc.edu.

STALLWORTH, STANLEY B., lawyer; b. 1963; BS summa cum laude, Ala. Agrl. and Mech. U., 1985; JD, U. Wis., 1990. Bar: Ala. 1990, Ill. 1990, Wis. 1990. Joined Sidley Austin Brown & Wood, Chgo., 1990—, now ptnr. real estate practice, and co-chmn. com. on racial and ethnic diversity. Articles editor Univ. Wis. Multi-Cultural Law Jour., 1989—90. Bd. trustees Univ. Wis. Law Alumni Assn.; chmn. bd. trustees Chgo. Acad. for Arts. Mem.: Chgo. Coun. of Lawyers (bd. dir.), Nat. Bar Assn., ABA, Cook

County Bar Assn. (past mem. exec. bd. dir.). Office: Sidley Austin Brown & Wood LLP Bank One Plz 10 S Dearborn St Chicago IL 60603 Office Phone: 312-853-4715. Office Fax: 312-853-7036. Business E-Mail: sstallworth@sidley.com.

STALNAKER, JUDITH ANN, education educator; b. San Diego, Sept. 3, 1942; d. Harold Willard and Dorothy Ione (Maxwell) Growcock; m. Archie LaVern Stalnaker, Aug. 31, 1963; children: Dena Lyn Garcia, Keri Leigh Hale. BA, teaching credential, Calif. State U., San Diego, 1973; MA, reading specialist credential, San Diego State U., 1985. Cert. tchr., reading specialist. Tchr. El Centro Sch. Dist., Calif., 1976—98; prof. San Diego State U., Calexico, Calif., 1987—89; ret. Presenter critical thinking skills, Imperial County, Calif., 1986, El Centro, 1986, English/lang. arts framework, El Centro, 1989. Mem. Young Democrats, San Diego, 1962-63; mem. McKinley Sch. PTA, 1969-75, pres., 1971-72. Mem. AAUW, Imperial County Reading Coun. (v.p. 1988-89), Internat. Reading Assn., Lang. Arts Leadership Team, Jr. Women's 10,000 Club (pres. 1971-72), Calif. Fedn. Women's Clubs (jr. mem. De Anza dist., v.p. 1972-73, Calif. Jr. Citizen of Yr. 1972), Del Rio Ladies Golf Assn. (officer, 1998-02, Pres. Cup winner, 2005), B.P.O Elks El Centro (officer, 1999-02, chmn., vet. affairs nat. hon., 2003). Lutheran. Avocations: world travel, reading, golf.

STALOFF, ARNOLD FRED, financial services executive; b. Dover, NJ, Dec. 12, 1944; s. William and Ida (Greenberg) S.; m. Sharon Marcia Teplitsky, June 10, 1967; children: Kimberly, Lindsay. BBA, U. Miami, 1967. Statistician U.S. Census Bur., Washington, 1967-68; fin. analyst SEC, Washington, 1968-71; sr. v.p. Phila. Stock Exch., 1971-78; v.p. Securities Industry Automation Corp., NYC, 1978-80; pres. Fin. Automation Corp., Phila., 1980-83, Phila. Bd. Trade, 1983-89; pres., CEO Commodity Exch., Inc. (COMEX), NYC, 1989-90; CEO Bloom Staloff Corp., Phila., 1991—2003; chmn. SFB Market Sys., Inc., 2005—07. Bd. dirs. Lehman Bros. Fin. Products, Inc.; bd. govs. Phila. Stock Exch., 1991-97. Bd. dirs. Variety Club for Handicapped Children, Phila., 1987-92; mem. adv. bd. Phila. Internat. Airport, 1988—; mem. U. Miami Pres.'s Cir. Mem. Nat. Futures Assn. (bd. dirs. 1987-90). Avocations: fly fishing, golf, skiing. Office Phone: 856-853-1800. Business E-Mail: staloff@staloff.com.

STAM, DAVID HARRY, librarian; b. Paterson, NJ, July 11, 1935; s. Jacob and Deana B. (Bowman) S.; m. Deirdre Corcoran, May 15, 1963; children: Julian, Wendell, Kathryn. AB, Wheaton Coll., 1955; postgrad., New Coll., U. Edinburgh, 1955-56; MLS, Rutgers U., 1962; postgrad., CUNY, 1963-64; PhD, Northwestern U., 1978. Asst. editor library publs., reference librarian, manuscript cataloguer New York Pub. Library, 1959-64; librarian Marlboro (Vt.) Coll., 1964-67; head tech. services dept. Newberry Library, Chgo., 1967-71, assoc. librarian, 1969-73; librarian Milton S. Eisenhower Library, Johns Hopkins U., Balt., 1973-78; Andrew W. Mellon dir. rsch. libraries N.Y. Pub. Library, NYC, 1978-86; Univ. librarian Syracuse U., 1986-98, Univ. librarian emeritus, 1998—, sr. scholar, history dept., 1998—. Trustee Gladys K. Delmas Found. Author: Wordsworthian Criticism, 1974, International Dictionary of Library Histories, 2001; co-author (with Rissa Yachnin): Turgenev in English: A Checklist of Works by and about Him, 1960; co-author: (with Deirdre C. Stam) Books on Ice, 2005; contbr. articles to profl. jours. Bd. dirs. Chamber Music Am. Served with USNR, 1956-58. Brit. Acad. Overseas fellow, 1975, Brit. Libr. fellow, 1995-96. Mem.: Am. Antiquarian Soc., Am. Hist. Assn., Keats-Shelley Assn. Am. (bd. dirs.), Grolier Club (N.Y.C.), Princeton Club N.Y. Office: Syracuse U History Dept Eggers Hall Syracuse NY 13244 E-mail: dhstam@syr.edu.

STAM, HEIDI, lawyer; b. 1956; BA, Tufts U.; JD, Am. U.; LLM, Harvard Law Sch. Pvt. practice; mem. SEC, 1987—97, sr. adv. to dir., chief of staff, asst. chief counsel, assoc. dir. legal and disclosure issues, Investment Mgmt. Divsn.; prin.-in-charge securities regulations The Vanguard Group, 1997—2006, gen. counsel, 2005—, sec., 2005—, mng. dir., 2006—. Office: The Vanguard Group Inc PO Box 2600 Valley Forge PA 19482-2600

ST-AMAND, PIERRE, geophysicist; b. Tacoma, Wash., Feb. 4, 1920; s. Cyrias Z. and Mable (Berg) St. A.; m. Marie Pöss, Dec. 5, 1945; children: Gene, Barbara, Denali, David. BS in Physics, U. Alaska, 1948; MS in Geophysics, Calif. Inst. Tech., 1951, PhD in Geophysics and Geology, 1953; Dr. honoris causa, U. De Los Altos, Tepatitlan, Mex., 1992. Asst. dir. Geophys. Lab., U. Alaska, also head ionospheric and seismologic investigations, 1946-49; physicist U.S. Naval Ordnance Test Sta., China Lake, Calif., 1950-54, head optics br., 1955-58; head earth and planetary sci. div. U.S. Ordnance Test Sta., 1961-78, cons. to tech. dir., head spl. projects office, 1978-88; fgn. service with ICA as prof. geol. and geophys. Sch. Earth Scis., U. Chile, 1958-60; originator theory rotational displacement Pacific Ocean Basin. Pres. Saint-Amand Sci. Services; adj. prof. McKay Sch. Mines, U. Nev., U. N.D.; v.p., dir. Covillea Corp.; v.p., dir. tech. Muetal Corp.; cons. World Bank, Calif. Div. Water Resources, Am. Potash & Chem. Co., OAS; mem. U.S. Army airways comms. sys., Alaska and Can., 1942-46; cons. Mexican, Chilean, Argentine, Philipines, Can., Rhodesian govts.; mem. Calif. Gov.'s Com. Geol. Hazards; mem. com. magnetic instruments Internat. Union Geodesy and Geophys., 1954-59, Disaster Preparation Commn. for L.A.; charter mem. Sr. Exec. Svc.; led drought relief expdns., India, The Philippines, Mex., Okinawa, Japan; rep. fed. emergency com. for LA (Calif.), USN. Adv. bd. GeoScience News; contbr. 100 articles to scientific jours. Chmn. bd. dirs. Ridgecrest Regional Hosp.; chmn. bd. dirs. Indian Wells Valley Airport Dist.; pres., dir. Indian Wells Valley Water Dist.; v.p. bd. dirs. Kern County Acad. Decathlon; mem. water resources bd. Kern County. Decorated knight Mark Twain, Mark Twain Jour.; recipient cert. of merit OSRD, 1945, cert. of merit USAAF, 1946, letter of commendation USAAF, 1948, Spl. award Philippine Air Force, 1969, Diploma de Honor Sociedad Geologica de Chile, Disting. Civilian Svc. medal USN, 1968, L.T.E. Thompson medal, 1973, Thunderbird award Weather Modification Assn., 1974, Disting. Pub. Svc. award Fed. Exec. Inst., 1976, Meritorious Svc. medal USN, 1988, Disting. Alumnus award U. Alaska, 1990; Fulbright rsch. fellow France, 1954-55. Fellow AAAS, Geol. Soc. Am., Earthquake Engr. Rsch. Inst.; mem. Am. Geophys. Union, Weather Modification Assn., Am. Seismol. Soc., Sister Cities (Ridgecrest-Tepatitlan) Assn. (pres.), Rotary (past pres., Paul Harris fellow), Footprinters Internat. (mem. grand bd., pres.), Sigma Xi. Achievements include patents in photometric instrument, weather and ordnance devices, pvt. pilot multi-engine-instruments; identified Denali: Fairweather Faults in Alaska and Canada, Atacama Fault in Chile. Home and Office: 1748 W Las Flores Ave Ridgecrest CA 93555-8635 Office Phone: 760-375-0481. Personal E-mail: st-amand@ridgecrest.ca.us.

STAMAS, STEPHEN, not-for-profit administrator; b. Salem, Mass., Apr. 26, 1931; s. Theodore and Georgia (Fotopulos) S.; m. Elaine Heidi Zervas, Apr. 24, 1955; children: Heidi, Theodore. AB, Harvard, 1953, PhD, 1957; B.Phil. (Rhodes scholar), Oxford U., 1955. Budget examiner Bur. Budget, Washington, 1957-59; loan officer Devel. Loan Fund, Washington, 1959-60; mgr. internat. divsn. treasurer's dept. Standard Oil Co. (NJ), NYC, 1960-63, dep. European fin. rep. London, 1963-64, chief economist NYC, 1969-70, dep. mgr. pub. affairs dept., 1971; govt. rels. mgr. Esso Europe, 1964-67; petroleum planning mgr. Esso Internat., 1967-68; dep. asst. sec. for fin. policy Dept. Commerce, Washington, 1968-69; v.p., pub. affairs Exxon Corp., NYC, 1973-86; pres. Wallace Funds, NYC, 1986-87, NY Philharm., 1984-89, chmn., 1989-96. Trustee, pres. Am. Ditchley Found.; trustee emeritus Rockefeller U.; chmn. Am. Assembly, Columbia U., Marlboro Sch. Music; mem. bd. overseers Harvard Coll., 1979-85; bd. dirs. NY Philharm.-Symphony Soc.; bd. dirs. emeritus Lincoln Ctr. for the Performing Arts; bd. dirs. The Greenwall Found., Seacor SMIT, Inc.; co-chmn. Am. Trust for Brit. Libr. Fellow Am. Acad. Arts & Scis.; mem. Am. Assocs. Royal Acad., Coun. Fgn. Rels., Acad. Polit. Sci., Am. Coun. on Germany, Scarsdale Golf Club (NY), Phi Beta Kappa. Clubs: Harvard (NYC), Century Assn. (NYC), Manursing Island (Rye, NY). Home: 325 Evandale Rd Scarsdale NY 10583-1505 E-mail: astolatz@aol.com. *

STAMATAKIS, CAROL MARIE, lawyer, former state legislator; m. Michael Shklar. BA, Ohio State U., 1982; JD, Case Western Res., 1985. Bar: N.H. 1985, U.S. Dist. Ct. N.H. 1985. Atty. Elliott, Jasper & Stamatakis, Newport, NH, 1990-93; state rep. N.H. State Legislature, 1988-94; atty. State of N.H., Concord, 1994—. Instr. Am. Inst. Banking, Claremont, 1987-88, 91-92, 95. Treas., mem. Town of Lempster N.H. Conservation Commn., 1987—; town chair N.H. Dem. Party, 1987—. Mem. N.H. Bar Assn., Sierra Club, Upper Valley Group (former vice chair and solid waste chair). Avocations: drawing, painting. Home: PO Box 807 Newport NH 03773-0807

STAMATY, MARK ALAN, cartoonist, writer, artist; b. Bklyn., Aug. 1, 1947; s. Stanley and Clara Gee Stamaty. B.F.A., The Cooper Union, 1969. Mem. faculty Parson's Sch. Design, NYC, 1977-81. Author-illustrator: (children's books) Who Needs Donuts?, 1973 (Bklyn. Art Books For Children award 1974), Small in the Saddle, 1975, Minnie Maloney & Macaroni, 1976, Where's My Hippopotamus?, 1977, Too Many Time Machines, 1999, Alia's Mission, 2004, (comic strip collections) Macdoodle St., 1981, Washingtoon, 1983; cartoonist: Macdoodle St. Village Voice newspaper, 1978-79, Carrrttoooonnn, Village Voice newspaper, 1980-81, (Washington Post and syndication) Washingtoon, 1981-94, Boox, N.Y. Times Book Review, 2001—; polit. cartoonist TIME mag., 1994-96, Doodlennium, 1996-98; contbr.: The New Yorker mag., 1992—, Slate Mag., 1996—; illustrator various publs., including: (children's book) Yellow Yellow, 1971, (Bklyn. Art Books for Children award); cartoon coverage of Milan fashion show for GQ Mag., 2000—. Recipient Purchase award, N.J. State Mus., 1969, Gold medal, Soc. Illustrators, 1974, Silver medal, 2005, Gold medal cert., 2005, Forte Dei Marmi, Museo-Premio Satira Politica, 2005, Augustus Saint Gaudens award for art, Cooper Union, 2007. Mem. PEN Am. Ctr. Avocations: impersonating Elvis Presley, softball, swimming. Office Phone: 212-396-0744. E-mail: markstamaty@earthlink.net.

STAMBAUGH, ARMSTRONG A., JR., restaurant and hotel executive; b. Cleve., Nov. 1, 1920; s. Armstrong Alexander and Beatrice (Snyder) S.; m. Janet Turley Marting, July 26, 1943 (div. 1958); children: Susan Reed (Mrs. Roy H. Beaton, Jr.), Sally Russell (Mrs. Michael H. Huber), Elizabeth Renshaw (Mrs. Michael C. Warr); m. Aagot Hinrichsen Cain, June 10, 1972. BA, Dartmouth Coll., 1942; Indsl. Adminstr., Harvard U., 1943, MBA, 1946. Research asst., then instr. bus. adminstrn. Harvard Grad. Sch. Bus. Adminstrn., 1946-48; with Gulf Oil Corp., 1948-66, coord. sales devel. mktg. hdqrs. Houston, 1962-63, v.p. Eastern marketing region Phila., 1963-66; exec. v.p. adminstrn. Howard Johnson Co., Inc., 1966-70, exec. v.p. ops. and adminstrn., 1970-79, exec. v.p., asst. to pres., 1979-81, dir., 1969-81; operator, developer food and lodging facilities, 1981-98. Pres. trustees Fox Chapel Country Day Sch., Pitts., 1955-57; div. vice chmn. Boston United Fund, 1961; bd. dirs. Houston Internat. Trade and Travel Fair, 1962-63, World Affairs Coun. Phila., 1964-65; dir. Phila. C. of C., 1964, 65, 66; bd. overseers Hanover Inn, Dartmouth Coll., 1979-85, chmn., 1984-85; trustee Old Sturbridge Village, Mass., 1979-01. Served to lt. (j.g.) USNR, 1943-46. Mem. Pine Valley Golf Club (N.J.), Weston Golf Club (Mass.), Edgartown Golf Club (Mass.), Boston Skating Club, Vineyard Haven Yacht Club (Mass.), Paradise Valley Country Club (Ariz.), Delta Tau Delta. Home and Office: 5 Blossom Ln Weston MA 02493-1103 Personal E-mail: aastam@flash.net.

STAMBAUGH, JOHN EDGAR, oncologist, hematologist, educator, pharmacologist; b. Everrett, Pa., Apr. 30, 1940; s. John Edgar and Rhoda Irene (Becker) Stambaugh; m. Shirley Louise Fultz, June 24, 1961; 4 children. BS in Chemistry cum laude, Dickinson Coll., Carlisle, Pa., 1962; MD, Jefferson Med. Coll., 1966, PhD, 1968. Intern Thomas Jefferson U. Hosp., Phila., 1968-69, resident, 1968-69; oncology fellow Jefferson Med. Coll., 1970-72, instr. pharmacology, 1969-70, asst. prof., 1970-74, assoc. prof., 1974-82, prof., 1982—. Pvt. practice med. oncology, hematology and cancer pain, Woodbury, NJ; staff physician Underwood Meml. Hosp., Woodbury, 1972—2004, West Jersey Hosp., 1973—. Contbr. articles to profl. jours. Fellow: Am. Soc. Pain Mgmt., Am. Acad. Pain Mgmt., Am. Coll. Clin. Pharmacology; mem.: Am. Assn. Clin. Rsch., Am. Pain Soc., Internat. Assn. for Study of Pain, Am. Assn. for Cancer Rsch., Am. Soc. Clin. Oncology, Am. Soc. for Pharmacology and Exptl. Therapeutics, Camden County Med. Soc., Gloucester County Med. Soc., NJ Med. Soc. (del.), Am. Soc. Clin. Pharmacology, AMA, ABA, Sigma Xi. Office: 17 W Red Bank Ave Ste 101 Woodbury NJ 08096-1630 Office Phone: 856-848-9292. Personal E-mail: oncohem@verizon.net.

STAMBAUGH, LARRY G., financial consultant; b. Topeka, Feb. 1, 1947; s. Merle J. and Eileen M. (Denslow) S.; m. Sallie M. Underwood, Jan. 18, 1969 (div. Oct. 1981); children: Matt, Julie; m. Suzanne Van Slyke, May 14, 1982 (div. Oct. 2006); children: Todd, Scott, Andy. BBA, Washburn U., 1969. CPA, Kans. Mgr. KPMG Peat, Marwick, Mitchell Co., Kansas City, Mo., 1969-76; co-owner Automotive Investment & Devel. Co., Olathe, Kans., 1976-82; chief fin. officer CNB Fin. Corp., Kansas City, Kans., 1983-90, ABC Labs., Columbia, Mo., 1990, pres., chief exec. officer, 1990-92; chmn., pres., CEO Maxim Pharms., San Diego, 1993—2006; prin. Apercu Cons., 2006—. Bd. dirs. BioCom; mem. adv. bd. U. Calif. San Diego Rady Sch. Bus. Chmn. bd. dirs. Forum for Corp. Dirs., 1996-99. Recipient Dir. of Yr. award, Forum for Corp. Dirs., 2002, 2006. Mem. Am. Mgmt. Assn., Nat. Assn. Corp. Dirs. Avocations: photography, golf. Home: 645 Front St 314 San Diego CA 92101 Office Phone: 619-955-8204. Personal E-mail: lgstambaugh@gmail.com.

STAMBERG, SUSAN LEVITT, radio personality; b. Newark, Sept. 7, 1938; d. Robert I. and Anne (Rosenberg) Levitt; m. Louis Collins Stamberg, Apr. 14, 1962; 1 child, Joshua Collins BA, Barnard Coll. 1959; DHL (hon.), Gettysburg Coll., 1982, Dartmouth Coll., 1984, Knox Coll., U. N.H., SUNY, Brockport. Editorial asst. Daedalus, Cambridge, Mass., 1960-62; editorial asst. The New Republic, Washington, 1962-63; host, producer, mgr., program dir. Sta. WAMU-FM, Washington, 1963-69; host All Things Considered Washington, 1971-86; host Weekend Edition Nat Pub. Radio, Washington, 1987-89; spl. corr. Nat. Pub. Radio, 1990—. Bd. dirs. AIA, Washington, 1983-85, PEN/Faulkner Fiction Award Found., 1985—. Author: Every Night at Five, 1982, The Wedding Cake in the Middle of the Road, 1992, Talk: NPR's Susan Stamberg Considers All Things, 1993. Recipient Honor award Ohio U., 1977, Edward R. Murrow award Corp. for Pub. Broadcasting, 1980; named Woman of Yr., Barnard Coll., 1984; fellow Silliman Coll. Yale U., 1984—; inducted Broadcasting Hall of Fame, 1994, Radio Hall of Fame, 1996. Avocations: drawing, piano, knitting. Office: Nat Pub Radio 635 Massachusetts Ave NW Washington DC 20001-3753 Office Phone: 202-513-2000.

ŠTAMBUK, NIKOLA, research scientist; b. Varaždin, Croatia, Mar. 25, 1959; s. Ranko and Vjera (Mrakovčić) Š.; m. Ana Lazić, Nov. 12, 1988; children: Albert, Danijel. MD, Zagreb U., Croatia, 1984, MS, 1988; PhD, Inst. Med. Rsch. Occup. Health, Zagreb, 1991. Intern Sisters of Mercy Clin. Hosp., Zagreb, 1984-85; resident Railway Health Ctr., Zagreb, 1986-88; postdoctoral fellow Mc Gill U., Montreal, Can., 1991-92; rschr. Rugjer Bošković Inst., Zagreb, 1994—. Sci. com. Internat. Conf. on Math. and Computer Modelling and Sci. Computing, Berkeley, Calif., 1993, Boston, 1995, Washington, 1997. Contbr. articles to profl. jours. Mem. Internat. Assn. for Math. and Computer Modelling, Internat. Ocular Inflammation Soc., Internat. Soc. for Thymology and Immunotherapy. Achievements include the discovery of necklace model, I Ching and horseshoe map representation of the genetic code (SCA procedure), rsch. in models of artificial barriers constrn., protein transfer and molecular recognition, computer-aided drug design, compartmental volume-pressure relationships. Office Phone: +3851 4680 193. E-mail: stambuk@irb.hr.

STAMELMAN, RICHARD HOWARD, French and humanities educator; b. Newark, Mar. 7, 1942; s. Louis Robert and Golda (Senzer) S.; children: Emily, Gibson, Jeremy White. BA, Hamilton Coll.; PhD, Duke U. Asst. prof. French and humanities Wesleyan U., Middletown, Conn., 1967-74, assoc. prof., 1974-79, prof., 1979-93, William R. Kenan Jr. prof. humanities, 1983-92, dean humanities, 1986-89, dir. Ctr. for the Humanities, 1976-82, dir. humanities devel., 1982-85; dir. Weston Ctr. for Fgn. Langs., Lits. and Cultures Williams Coll., Williamstown, Mass., 1992-97, prof. Romance langs., comp. lit., 1992—2007; chmn. dept. French and Italian U. Colo., Boulder, 1991-92; vis. prof. comp. lit. Dartmouth Coll., 2007—. Organizer study group Ecrire le Livre: Autour d'Edmond Jabès, Cerisy-la-Salle, France, 1987; co-dir. Edouard Morot-Sir Summer Inst. for French Cultural Studies, Hanover, NH, 1994. Author: The Drama of Self in Guillaume Apollinaire's Alcools, 1976, Claude Garache: Prints, 1965-85, 1985, Lost Beyond Telling: Representations of Death and Absence in Modern French Poetry, 1990, Perfume: Joy, Obsession, Scandal, Sin A Cultural History of Frangrance from 1750 to the Present, 2006; editor: Contemporary French Poetry, Studies in 20th Century Literature, 1989, Ecrire le Livre: Autour d'Edmond Jabès, 1989, Italian transl., 1991, French Poetry since the War, L'Esprit Créateur, 1992; editor, prin. translator: The Lure and the Truth of Painting, Selected Essays by Yves Bonnefoy, 1995; translator: The Grapes of Zeuxis and Other Fables by Yves Bonnefoy, 1987, Once More the Grapes of Zeuxis by Yves Bonnefoy, 1989, The Last Grapes of Zeuxis by Yves Bonnefoy, 1993, Transmorphoses by Yves Bonnefoy, 1998; mem. editl. bd. French Forum; contbr. articles to profl. jours. Recipient Chevalier dans l'ordre des Palmes Académiques award French Govt., 1993; NEH fellow, 1973, John Simon Guggenheim Meml. Found. fellow, 1999; Am. Council Learned Socs. grantee, 1983 Mem. MLA (regional del. 1987-90, mem. program com. 1996-99), Societe Francaise des Parfumeurs. Home: PO Box 1624 Norwich VT 05055 Business E-Mail: richard.h.stamelman@dartmouth.edu.

STAMEY, DERRICK, management consultant; b. Asheville, NC, Nov. 3, 1970; M in Project Mgmt., Western Carolina U., Cullowhee NC, 1997. Sr. project mgr. IKON Office Solutions, Charlotte, NC, 2002—05; exec. prodr. BRMP, Asheville, NC, 2006—06. Home: 13416 McCoy Rd Huntersville NC 28078 Personal E-mail: jondstamey@yahoo.com.

STAMEY, THOMAS ALEXANDER, urologist, educator; b. Rutherfordton, NC, Apr. 26, 1928; s. Owen and Virginia (Link) S.; m. Kathryn Simmons Dec. 1, 1973; children: Fred M., Charline, Thomas A. III, Allison, Theron. BA, Vanderbilt U., 1948; MD, Johns Hopkins U., 1952. Diplomate Am. Bd. Urology. Intern, then resident Johns Hopkins Hosp., 1952-56; asst. prof. urology Johns Hopkins U. Sch. Medicine, Balt., 1958-60, assoc. prof., 1960-61; assoc. prof., chmn. divsn. urology Stanford (Calif.) U., 1961-64, assoc. prof., 1964-90, prof., 1991—, chmn. dept., 1964-95. Author: Renovascular Hypertension, 1967, Pathogenesis and Treatment of Urinary Tract Infections, 1980, Urinalysis and Urinary Sediment: A Practical Guide for the Health Science Professional, 1985; editor: Campbell's Urology, edits. 4-6, 1978-92, Monographs in Urology, 1980-99. Capt. M.C., USAF, 1956-58. Recipient Sheen award ACS, 1990, Ferdinand C. Valentine award N.Y. Acad. Medicine, 1991. Mem. Am. Urol. Assn. (Ramon Guiteras award 1995, John K. Lattimer award 2000, Eugene Fuller Triennial Prostate award 2001), Am. Surg. Assn. (sr.), Inst. Medicine of NAS. Avocations: fishing, astronomy. Office: Stanford U Med Ctr Dept Urology S 287 300 Pasteur Dr Stanford CA 94305-5118 Home Phone: 650-851-3100. Business E-Mail: tstamey@stanford.edu.

STAMLER, JEREMIAH, physician, educator; b. NYC, Oct. 27, 1919; s. George and Rose (Baras) S.; m. Rose Steinberg, 1942; 1 son, Paul J. AB, Columbia U., NYC, 1940; MD, SUNY, Bklyn., 1943. Cert. specialist in clin. nutrition. Intern L.I. Coll. Medicine div. Kings County Hosp., Bklyn., 1944, fellow pathology, 1947; research fellow cardiovascular dept. Med. Research Inst., Michael Reese Hosp., Chgo., 1948, research assoc., 1949-55, asst. dir. dept., 1955-58; established investigator Am. Heart Assn., 1952-58; dir. heart disease control program Chgo. Bd. Health, 1958-74, dir. chronic disease control div., 1961-63, dir. div. adult health and aging, 1963-74; assoc. dept. medicine Northwestern U. Feinberg Sch. Medicine, Evanston, Ill., 1958-59, asst. prof. dept. medicine, 1959-65, assoc. prof., dept. medicine, 1965-71, prof., dept. community health and preventive medicine, 1972—90, chair, dept. cmty. health and preventative medicine, 1972—86, Harry W. Dingman prof. cardiology, 1973—90, prof. emeritus, 1990—; attending physician Northwestern Meml. Hosp., 1973-89, chmn., dept. cmty. health and preventative medicine, 1973—85; exec. dir. Chgo. Health Research Found., 1963-72, bd. dirs., 1972—. Cons. medicine St. Joseph Hosp., Chgo., 1964—, Rush-Presbyn.-St. Luke's Hosp., Chgo., 1966—; professorial lectr. dept. medicine Pritzker Sch. Medicine, U. Chgo., 1970—; vis. prof. internal medicine Rush. Presbyn.-St. Luke's Med. Center, 1972—. Author: (with L. N. Katz) Experimental Atherosclerosis, 1953, (with others) Nutrition and Atherosclerosis, 1958, (with A. Blakeslee) Your Heart Has Nine Lives-Nine Steps to Heart Health, 1963, (with others) Epidemiology of Hypertension, 1967, Lectures on Preventive Cardiology, 1967, (with A. Blakeslee) Four Keys to a Healthy Heart, 1976; fgn. cons., editoral cons.: Heartbeat; editor and mem. editl. bd. of major jours.; contbr. articles to profl. jours. Served to capt. AUS, 1944-46. Recipient Howard W. Blakeslee award, 1964, Albert and Mary Lasker Med. Journalism award, 1965, Conrad Elvehjem award Wis. Med. Soc., 1967, (with others) Albert Lasker Spl. Service award, 1980, Donald Reid medal, Joint Com. London Sch. Hygiene and Tropical Medicine and Royal Coll. Physicians, 1988, John Jay award Columbia College, N.Y., 1990, Nat. Cholesterol award, First Nat. Cholesterol Conf., James D. Bruce Meml. award for Disting. Contributions in Preventative Medicine, Am. Coll. Physicians, others; named to Ctr. for Sci. in the Pub. Interest's Nutrition Hall of Fame. Fellow Am. Coll. Cardiology (Disting. Svc. award 1985), Am. Pub. Health Assn. (John M. Snow award 1986), AAAS; mem. Am. Fedn. Clin. Research, Am. Heart Assn. (bd. dirs., past vice-chmn. exec. com., fellow coun. arteriosclerosis, chmn. council on epidemiology and prevention, award for outstanding efforts in heart rsch., 1964, award of merit, 1967, Svc. award, 1980-81, Disting. Rsch. Achievement award 1981, Achievement award 1987, Gold Heart award, 1992, Gold Heart award from Chgo. Affiliate), Am. Physiol. Soc., Am. Soc. Clin. Investigation, Am. Soc. Clin. Nutrition, Am. Soc. Study Arteriosclerosis (past bd. dirs., past chmn. program com., past sec.-treas.), Am., Chgo. diabetes assns., Assn. Tchrs. Preventive Medicine, Am. Soc. Clin. Nutrition, Assn. Clin. Scientists, Middle States Pub. Health Assn., Central Soc. Clin. Research, Chgo. Heart Assn. (Coeur d'Or award 1979), Ill. Pub. Health Assn. (mem. exec. com.), Ill. Acad. Scis., Diabetes Assn. Greater Chgo. (dir.), Soc. Exptl. Biology and Medicine (sec. Ill. chpt.), Am. Inst. Nutrition, Chgo. Nutrition Assn., Chgo. Acad. Scis., Internat. Soc. and Fedn. Cardiology (chmn. sci. bd., council on epidemiology and prevention, mem. exec. com.), Inst. Medicine Chgo. (Coleman award 1987), Phi Beta Kappa. Office: 680 N Lake Shore Dr Apt 1102 Chicago IL 60611-4480 also: Northwestern U Feinberg Sch Medicine Dept Preventative Medicine 680 N Lake Shore Dr Ste 1102 Chicago IL 60611 *

STAMM, ALAN, lawyer; b. Galesburg, Ill., Nov. 22, 1931; s. Gustave Frederick and Miriam (Simon) S.; m. Shelley Lynn Ramage, Mar. 19, 1978; 1 child, Lucinda Anne. Student, Universidad Nacional de Mex., summer 1950; AB, Yale U., 1952; JD, Harvard U., 1957. Bar: Calif. 1957, U.S. Supreme Ct. 1963. Assoc. Thelen Reid & Priest, LLP (formerly

Thelen, Marrin, Johnson & Bridges), San Francisco, 1957-60; staff atty. Litton Industries Inc., Beverly Hills, Calif., 1960-66, asst. sec., 1963-66; sec., gen. counsel Internat. Rectifier Corp., LA, 1966-69, v.p., 1968-69; v.p., gen. counsel Republic Corp., LA, 1969-71, bd. dirs., 1970-71; v.p., gen. counsel Sat. Rev. Industries, NYC, 1971-72, Mattel Inc., Hawthorne, Calif., 1972-74, staff cons., 1974-75; of counsel Long & Levit, LA, 1975-82, O'Donnell & Gordon, LA, 1983-87, Hedges, Powe & Caldwell, LA, 1988-90; pvt. practice LA, 1990—. Judge pro tem Mcpl. Ct. LA Jud. Dist., 1977—, LA Superior Ct. 1989—; arbitrator Nat. Assn. Securities Dealers, 1981—, NYSE, 1994-. Founding trustee Ctr. for Law in Pub. Interest; former trustee Marlborough Sch., LA; former mem. bd. govs. Century City Hosp., LA; counsel bus. and profl. com. LA Philharm.; former bd. dirs. Yale Alumni Fund. Lt. j.g. USNR, 1952—54, ret. lt. comdr. USNR. Mem. ABA, State Bar of Calif., LA Bar Assn., Harvard Law Sch. Assn., LA County Art Mus., Am. Arbitration Assn. (nat. panel arbitrators 1968—), NAACP, Sierra Club, Nat. Assn. Yale Alumni (former bd. govs.), Yale Club of So. Calif. (former dir.), Harvard Club of So. Calif., Phi Beta Kappa. Home: 422 Denslow Ave Los Angeles CA 90049-3507 Office: 1950 Pelham Ave Unit 1 Los Angeles CA 90025-5835

STAMM, BARBARA MARIE ANDERSON, elementary school educator, interior designer; b. Oakland, Calif., June 11, 1937; d. Reuben Anders Anderson and Helen Frances (Westphal) Sjogren-Anderson; m. George F. Stamm, July 26, 1959; children: George Anders, Anne-Marie. AA, U. Calif., Berkeley, 1957, BA, 1959. Tchr. Antioch Unified Sch. Dist., Calif., 1959—62, 1966—68, 1976—95; interior designer San Francisco Bay Area, 1975—. Author: (classroom trial) People v. Mission Mouse, 1987; dir.: (choral reading) T.S. Eliot's Cats, 1992. Pres. Delta Meml. Hosp. Aux., Antioch, 1970; bd. trustees Delta Meml. Hosp. Bd., Antioch, 1973; v.p. Citizens for Responsible Active Waterfront Design and Devel., Antioch, 1987. Republican. Lutheran. Avocations: travel, gardening, reading, cooking. Home: 501 B St Antioch CA 94509-1202 Personal E-mail: bstamm501@aol.com.

STAMM, CAROL ANN, obstetrician, gynecologist; b. Denver, Aug. 8, 1959; d. Robert L. and Mary Ellen Stamm. BA in Biology cum laude, U. Colo., 1981, cert. in elem. tchg., 1985; MD with honors, U. Colo., Denver, 1991. Diplomate Am. Bd. Ob-Gyn. Bilingual elem. tchr. Denver Pub. Schs., 1986—87; intern in ob-gyn U. Colo. Sch. Medicine, Denver, 1991—92, resident in ob-gyn, 1992—95, asst. prof., 1997—2003; staff ob-gyn, asst. prof. Denver Health Med. Ctr., 1995—2003; dir. women's health rotation Colo. Health Found. (formerly High St. Primary Care Clinic), Denver, 2003—, asst. prof. clin. medicine, 2003—, dir. women's svcs., 2004—. Mem. Patient and Family Edn. Work Group, 1996—97; mem. ob-gyn edn. com. U. Colo. Health Scis. Ctr., 1997—2003; dir. ob-gyn Grand Rounds, 1997—2001; provider design team Lifetime Clin. Record Project, 1998—2001; alt. mem. Colo. Multiple Instl. Rev. Bd., 1998—2003; presenter in field. Co-author: (book) Management of High-Risk Pregnancy, 4th edit., 1999, Medical Care of the Pregnant Patient, 2000, The Female Athlete, 2002, Contemporary Therapy in Obstetrics and Gynecology, 2002; contbr. articles to profl. jours.; peer reviewer Jour. Obstetrics and Gynecology, 1999—, Am. Jour. Obstetrics and Gynecology, 1999—. Recipient Richard Whitehead award, Phi Rho Sigma, 1989; grantee, March of Dimes, 2000—01; Trust fellow, Am. Cancer Soc. Brooks, 1988, Acad. Enrichment grantee, U. Colo. Health Scis. Ctr., 1993—95, NIH subcontract grantee, U. Pitts., 2000—03, NIH grantee, IBBEX, 2002. Fellow: ACOG (History fellow 2006); mem.: N.Am. Menopause Soc, Golden Key, Phi Beta Kappa (mem. mortar bd.). Avocations: reading, running, pilates, symphony, opera. Home: 155 S Jackson St Unit C Denver CO 80209 Office: Colorado Health Found 1801 High St Denver CO 80218 Office Phone: 303-869-2158. Business E-Mail: cstamm@health1.org.

STAMM, JOHN WILLIAM RANDOLPH, dentist, educator; b. Germany, Nov. 3, 1942; naturalized, Can., naturalized, US; married; 2 children. DDS, U. Alta., Can., 1967; DDPH, U. Toronto, Can., 1969, MScD, 1971. Diplomate Am. Bd. Dental Pub. Health. Dental dir. Baffin region Nat. Health & Welfare, 1967; pvt. dental practice Fort Saskatchewan, Alta., 1968; rsch. asst. & biometrics Sch. Hygiene & Faculty Dentistry U. Toronto, 1968—71; asst. prof. Faculty Dentistry McGill U., 1971—74, assoc. prof., 1974—80, chmn., 1974—84, prof., 1980—84; dir. Dental Rsch. Ctr. U. N.C., 1985—89; prof. U. N.C. Sch. Dentistry, 1985—, asst. dean, 1985—89, dean, 1989—2005. Vis. prof. U. Riyadh, Saudi Arabia, 1980; mem. expert adv. panel oral health WHO, 1984—90; mem. study sect. oral biology and medicine NIH, 1988—90; cons. Que. Min. Social Affairs, 1974—76, Alta. Health Unit Assn., 1977—79, Can. Electrolytic Zinc, 1978—82, Can. Dental Assn., 1980, Am. Fund Dental Health, 1980—83, Dental Health St. Regis Indians, N.Y. State Dept. Health, 1980; pres. Can. Div. of the Internat. Assn. for Rsch., 1984. Mem. editl. bd. Jour. Dental Edn., 1980—83, Jour. Cmty. Dentistry and Oral Epidemiology, 1988—, Oral Diseases, 1994, assoc. editor Caries Rsch., 1995—; contbr. articles to profl. jours. Grantee, Ont. Dept. Health, 1969, McGill U., 1973, Que. Health Sci. Rsch. Coun., 1973, Min. Social Affairs Que., 1972—74, Nat. Inst. Dental Rsch., 1976—78, 1985, Med. Rsch. Coun., 1981—84, Nat. Health and Welfare, 1982—85, NIH, 1985—, Robert Wood Johnson Found., 1986—91. Fellow: AAAS, Am. Assn. for the Advancement for the Sci., Japanese Soc. for Promotion of Sci., Acad. Dentistry Internat., Royal Coll. Dentists of Can. (chief examiner 1980—82), Internat. Coll. Dentists, Am. Coll. Dentists; mem.: Internat. Assn. Dental Rsch. (treas. 1997—2001), Can. Soc. Pub. Health Dentists (pres. 1979—81), Can. Dental Assn., Am. Assn. Dental Rsch., Am. Assn. Pub. Health Dentists, Am. Assn. Dental Schs., Omicron Kappa Upsilon. Office: U NC Sch Dentistry Cb 7450 105 Dental Research Center Chapel Hill NC 27599-7450 Office Phone: 919-966-3415.

STAMOOLIS, JAMES JOHN, academic administrator, educator; s. James Peter and Evangeline K. Stamoolis; m. Evelyn Carol Nilsson, June 3, 1967; children: John James, Joel James, Joshua James. BS in Indsl. Engring., Lehigh U., 1967; MDiv, Trinity Evang. Div. Sch., Deerfield, Ill., 1970, ThM, 1971; ThD, U. Stellenbosch, South Africa, 1980. Ordained to ministry Bapt. Gen. Conf., 1977. Regional dir. Students Christian Assn. of South Africa, Cape Town, Cape Province, 1978—80; theol. sec. Internat. Fellowship of Evang. Students, London, 1981—89; grad. dean Wheaton Coll., Ill., 1989—98; exec. dir. theol. commn. World Evang. Fellowship, Wheaton, Ill., 1998—2001; pres./CEO, Wycliffe Seed Co., Santa Ana, Calif., 2002—02; pres. Mgmt. Cons. Assocs., Wheaton, Ill., 2003—05; sr. v.p. for acad. affairs, dean of Coll. and Grad. Sch., Trinity Internat. U., Deerfield, Ill., 2005—07. Trustee No. Bapt. Theol. Sem., Lombard, Ill., 1997—2006. Author: (book) Eastern Orthodox Mission Theology Today; editor: Three Views on Eastern Orthodoxy and Evangelicalism; contbr. articles to profl. jours. Mem.: Am. Acad. of Religion, Internat. Assn. of Mission Studies, Am. Soc. of Missiology (pres. 2000—01).

STAMOS, JOHN, actor; b. Orange County, Calif., Aug. 19, 1963; s. Bill and Loretta Stamos; m. Rebecca Romijn, Sept. 19, 1998 (div. Mar. 1, 2005). Drummer with various bands. Actor: (TV series) General Hospital, 1982-84 (Emmy award, 2 Soap Opera Digest awards), Dreams, 1984, You Again?, 1986-87, Full House, 1987-95, ER, 2006 (TV movies) Daughter of the Streets, 1990, Captive, 1991, The Disappearance of Christina, 1993, Fatal Vows: The Alexandra O'Hara Story, 1996, A Match Made in Heaven, 1997, Sealed with a Kiss, 1999, How to Marry a Billionaire: A Christmas Tale, 2000, Fortunate Son, 2000, The Reagans, 2003, Wedding Wars, 2006; (films) Never Too Young to Die, 1986, Born to Ride, 1991, Private Parts, 1998, The Marriage Fool, 1998, Dropping Out, 2000, Party Monster, 2003, I Am Stamos, 2004; actor, assoc. prodr. (films) My Best Friend's Wife, 2001, actor, prodr. (TV series) Theives, Jake in Progress, 2005; exec. prodr. (TV series) Virgin Chronicles, 2002, (TV films) The Beach Boys: An American Family, 2000; TV appearances include Hangin' with Mr. Cooper, 1992, Tales from the Crypt, 1993, Step by Step, 1994, Baywatch, 1995, Clone High, 2003, Friends, 2003. Recipient Youth in Film award. Mem. AFTRA, Child Help U.S.A. (nat. spokesperson). Office: William Morris Agy care Les Stollman 151 El Camino Dr Beverly Hills CA 90212-2775 *

STAMP, FREDERICK PFARR, JR., federal judge; b. Wheeling, W.Va., July 24, 1934; s. Frederick P. Sr. and Louise (Aul) S.; m. Joan A. Corson, Sept. 20, 1975; children: Frederick Andrew, Joan Elizabeth. BA, Washington and Lee U., 1956; LLB, U. Richmond, 1959, LLD (hon.), 2006. Bar: W.Va. 1959, Va. 1959, Pa. 1986, U.S. Supreme Ct. 1973, U.S. Ct. Appeals (4th cir.) 1962, U.S. Dist. Ct. (no. dist.) W.Va. 1960, U.S. Dist. Ct. (so. dist.) W.Va. 1975, U.S. Dist. Ct. (we. dist.) Pa., U.S. Tax Ct. 1973, W.Va. Supreme Ct. Appeals 1966, Va. Supreme Ct. Appeals 1959. Assoc., then ptnr. Schrader, Stamp, Byrd, Byrum & Companion and predecessor firms, Wheeling, 1960-90; judge US Dist. Ct. (no. dist.) W.Va., Wheeling, 1990-94, 2001—06, chief judge, 1994—2001, sr. judge, 2006—. Mem. ho. of dels. W.Va. Legislature, Charleston, 1966-70. Mem. W.Va. Bd. Regents, Charleston, 1970-77; trustee Linsly Sch., Wheeling, 1977—, U. Richmond, 1997—. Fellow Am. Bar Found., Am. Coll. Trial Lawyers; mem. W.Va. Bar Assn. (pres. 1981-82), W.Va. Commn. on Uniform State Laws, Nat. Conf. Commrs. on Uniform State Laws. Office: US Dist Ct PO Box 791 12th and Chapline Sts Wheeling WV 26003

STAMPER, EWA SZUMOTALSKA, psychologist; b. Warsaw, Sept. 8, 1954; came to U.S., 1984; d. Tadeusz and Regina S.Szumotalska MA in Clin. Psychology, U. Warsaw, Poland, 1978; PhD in Psychology, New Sch. U., NYC, 1992. Staff therapist Marital Therapy Counseling Ctr., Warsaw, 1978—79, Ctr. for Psychotherapy and Personality Growth, Warsaw, 1978—80; sr. staff therapist Lab. for Psychoedn. Polish Psychol. Assn., Warsaw, 1981—85; postgrad. affiliate Washington Sq. Inst. for Psychotherapy, NYC, 1990—92; police psychologist Honolulu Police Dept., 1993—98; pvt. practice, Honolulu, 1994—. With Tng. Ctr. for Family Therapy, Warsaw, 1976—78, Stuyvesant Poly., NYC, 1988—89, North Ctrl. Bronx (N.Y.) Hosp., 1988—89, Yale Psychiat. Inst., 1989—90, Castle Med. Ctr., Kailua, Hawaii, 1993—94; co-chmn. Crystal Methampetamine Forum, Honolulu, 1996—99. Mem. APA, Am. Acad. Experts in Traumatic Stress, Hawaii Psychol. Assn. (clin. divsn. rep. 1998-99, coord. for Disaster Response Network 2005—). Avocations: horseback riding, raising German Shorthaired Pointers and Siamese cats, gardening, fiction and poetry writing, running. Office: 30 Aulike St Ste 308 Kailua HI 96734 Office Phone: 808-261-5555. Personal E-mail: ewastamper@aol.com.

STAMPER, JOHN W., architecture educator, academic administrator; b. Mishawaka, Ind., Dec. 18, 1950; s. Clay V. and Hazel M. Stamper; m. Erika Pistorius, June 28, 1986; 1 child, Alessandra Marie. Mar., U. Ill., Champaign-Urbana, 1973—75; MA, Williams Coll., Williamstown, Mass., 1975—77; PhD, Northwestern U., Evanston, Ill., 1981—85. Lic. architect, Ill., 1981. Assoc. prof. U. Notre Dame, Ind., 1984—, assoc. dean, 2004—. Author: (scholarly books) The Architecture of Roman Temples: The Republic to the Middle Empire, Chicago's North Michigan Avenue: Planning and Development, 1900-1930. Com. mem. Mayor's Civic Alliance, South Bend, Ind., 2003—06. Grantee Fontainebleau Traveling Fellowship, U. Ill., Dept. Architecture, 1974. Mem.: AIA, Soc. Archtl. Historians. Democrat-Npl. Roman Catholic. Achievements include proposing a radically new reconstruction of the Temple of Capitoline Jupiter in Rome. Avocations: travel, photography. Home: 228 N Esther St South Bend IN 46617 Office: Univ Notre Dame Sch Architecture Notre Dame IN 46556 Home Phone: 574-251-0724. Office Fax: 574-631-8486; Home Fax: 574-631-8486. Business E-Mail: stamper.1@nd.edu.

STAMPER, NORMAN H., protective services official; BS, MS in Criminal Justice Adminstrn., San Diego State U.; PhD in Leadership and Human Behavior, U.S. Internat. U. Chief of police Seattle Police Dept., 1994—. Exec. dir. Mayor Pete Wilson's Crime Control Commn.; apptd. (by U.S. Atty. Gen. and Sec. Health and Human Svcs.) Adv. Coun. Violence Against Women; mem. adv. panel on Excessive Force by Police, Police Exec. Rsch. Forum, Major Cities Chiefs; mem. steering com. Seattle Equal Justice Coalition; co-chair Ptnr's. in Pub. Edn's. Urban Scholar's Program; mem. bd. dirs. Leadership Tomorrow; trustee Ctr. for Ethical Leadership. Author: Removing Managerial Barriers to Effective Police Leadership, 1992; tchnical adv. Municipal Police Administration, 1992. Named to Alumni Hall of Fame Boys and Girls Club of Am.; recipient Katharine M. Bullitt award for Leadership Ptnrs. in Pub. Edn. Mem. Internat. Assn. Chiefs of Police. Office: Seattle Police PO Box 34986 Seattle WA 98124-4986

STAMPER, ROBERT LEWIS, ophthalmologist, educator; b. NYC, July 27, 1939; m. Naomi T. Belson, June 23, 1963; children: Juliet, Marjorie, Alison. BA, Cornell U., 1961; MD, SUNY-Downstate, 1965. Diplomate Am. Bd. Ophthalmology (assoc. examiner 1976-92, bd. dirs. 1992-99). Intern Mt. Sinai Hosp., NYC, 1965-66; resident in ophthalmology Washington U.-Barnes Hosp., St. Louis, 1968-71; Nat. Eye Inst.-NIH fellow dept. ophthalmology Washington U., St. Louis, 1971-72, from instr. ophthalmology to asst. prof. dept. ophthalmology, 1971-72; asst. prof. dept. ophthalmology Pacific Presbyn. Med. Ctr., San Francisco, 1972-76, assoc. prof. ophthalmology, 1976-87; chmn. dept. ophthalmology Calif. Pacific Med. Ctr. (formerly Pacific Presbyn. Med. Ctr.), San Francisco, 1987-96; vice-chmn. dept. ophthalmology U. Calif., San Francisco, 1999—2003, prof. clin. ophthalmology, dir. glaucoma, 1999—. Asst. opthalmologist Barnes Hosp., St. Louis, 1971-72, Harkness Hosp., San Francisco, 1973-74; dir. ophthalmic photography and fluorescin angiography, dept. ophthalmology Washington U., St. Louis, 1969-72; dir. resident tng. Pacific Presbyn. Med. Ctr., 1972-89, dir. glaucoma svc., vice-chmn. dept. ophthalmology, 1974-87; chief ophthalmology svc. Highland Hosp., Oakland, Calif., 1974-76; clin. instr. dept. ophthalmology U. Calif., San Francisco, 1974-77, prof. clin. ophthalmology, 1998—; clin. asst. prof. ophthalmology U. Calif., Berkeley, 1974-78, asst. clin. prof. ophthalmology, 1978-85; sr. rsch. assoc. Smith-Kettlewell Inst. Visual Scis., San Francisco, 1972-89; project co-dir. ophthalmic curriculum for med. students Nat. Libr. Medicine, 1973-75; commr. Joint Commn. on Allied Health Pers. in Ophthalmology, 1975-87, bd. dirs., 1978-88, sec., 1980, v.p., 1982-83, pres., 1984-85; provisional asst. chief dept. ophthalmology Mt. Zion Hosp., San Francisco, 1976-87, assoc. chief dept. ophthalmology, 1982-86; ophthalmic cons. Ft. Ord, Calif., 1976-1984, Oakland Naval Hosp., 1978-83; instr. Stanford U., Calif., 1977—; glaucoma cons. U. Calif., Davis, 1978-84; vis. lectr. dept. ophthalmology Hadassah Hebrew U. Med. Ctr., Jerusalem, 1978, Oxford U. Eye Hosp., Eng., 1986; ind. med. examiner State of Calif., 1979—; mem. appeals hearing panel Accreditation Coun. for Grad. Med. Edn., 1986-93, mem. residency rev. com. for ophthalmology, 1993-98; mem. provisional courtesy staff Peralta Hosp., Oakland, 1988-92; mem. ophthalmic devices adv. panel USFDA, 1989-92; presenter, lectr. in field. Co-author: Update in Glaucoma, 2004, 2d edit., 2006; editor Ophthalmology Clinics of North Am., 1988-2004, 06; mem. editl. adv. com. Ophthalmology, 1982-89, mem. editl. bd., 1983-94; co-author: Becker and Shaffer's Diagnosis and Management of the Glaucomas, 7th edit., 1999; co-editor Essentials in Ophthalmology: Glaucoma, 2007; contbr. articles to profl. jours. Chmn. bd. Agy. Jewish Edn., Oakland, 1986-89; bd. dirs. Jewish Fedn. Greater East Bay, Oakland, 1992-94; bd. dirs. Found. Glaucoma Rsch.; mem. glaucoma adv. com. Nat. Soc. to Prevent Blindness, 1981-2004; mem. Am. Diabetes Assn. Surgeon USPHS, 1966-68. Recipient Self-Instrnl. Material in Ophthalmology award Nat. Soc. for Performance and Instrn., 1975, Honor award Am. Acad. Ophthalmology, 1982, Sr. Honor award, 1992, Statesmanship award Joint Commn. on Allied Health Pers. in Ophthalmology, 1989, Disting. Alumnus award Wash. U. Sch. Medicine, 2004; named Troutman Master Tchr. in Ophthalmology, 2000; Regents scholar NY State, 1961, scholar NY State, 1965; Blalock fellow UCLA Sch. Medicine, 1961, Fight for Sight fellow Dept. Ophthalmology NY Hosp. and Cornell Med. Ctr., 1962, 63, 64. Fellow Am. Acad. Ophthalmology and Otolaryngology (rep. to joint commn. on allied health pers., faculty home study course sect. X, chmn. sect. VIII 1983-85, bd. councilors, editl. adv. com. Opthalmology jour. 1982-89, editl. bd. Ophthalmology jour. 1983-94, and many others), ACS; mem. AMA (Physician's Recognition award 1989), Am. Ophthalmologic Soc., Assn. for Rsch. in Vision and Ophthalmology, Calif. Med. Assn. (asst. sec. sect. ophthalmology, chmn., sci. bd. rep. adv. panel on ophthalmology 1985-91), Nat. Soc. Prevent Blindness (mem. glaucoma adv. com. 1981-2004), No. Calif. Soc. Prevent Blindness (bd. dirs. 1986—, pres.-elect 2006—), Calif. Assn. Ophthalmology, Pan Am. Ophthal. (bd. dirs. 1992—), Soc., NY Acad. Scis., Las Vegas Ophthal. Soc. (hon.), Am. Glaucoma Soc. (v.p. 1997-99, pres. 1999-2000), Glaucoma Rsch. Found. (bd. dirs.). Office: Dept Opht UCSF Med Ctr 8 Koret Way San Francisco CA 94143-0730 Office Phone: 415-476-3717. Business E-Mail: stamperr@vision.ucsf.edu.

STAMPFER, MEIR JONATHAN, epidemiologist, nutritionist, educator; b. Lincoln, Nebr., Mar. 1, 1950; s. Joshua and Goldie Stampfer; m. Claire Diane Blum, Dec. 30, 1975; children: Samuel, Eliane, Orly. AB, Columbia Coll., 1973; MD, NYU, 1977; MPH, Harvard U., 1980, DPH, 1985. Diplomate Am. Bd. Med. Examiners. Instr. medicine Harvard Med. Sch., Boston, 1982-85, asst. prof. medicine, 1985-88; assoc. prof. Harvard Sch. Pub. Health, Boston, 1988-93, prof. nutrition and epidemiology, 1993—, chair Dept. Epidemiology, 2000—; assoc. physician Brigham & Women's Hosp., Boston, 1982-92; physician Brigham and Women's Hosp., Boston, 1992—. Lectr. in field. Contbr. numerous articles to profl. jours. Recipient Nat. Rsch. Svc. award NIH, 1977-82; NIH grantee, 1982—. Fellow Am. Heart Assn., Am. Coll. Nutrition; mem. Internat. Soc. Cardiology, Soc. Epidemiologic Rsch. Democrat. Jewish. Office: Dept Epidemiology Kresge Bldg, 9th Fl 677 Huntington Ave Boston MA 02115 also: Channing Lab 181 Longwood Ave Boston MA 02115-5804 Office Phone: 617-432-6477. Office Fax: 617-566-7805. Business E-Mail: mstampfe@hsph.harvard.edu.

STAMPKE, STUART REH, physicist, researcher; b. Burbank, Calif., Apr. 20, 1950; BS in Physics summa cum laude, Calif. State U., Northridge, 1973; PhD in Physics, Calif. Inst. Tech., Pasadena, 1982. Rsch. fellow in physics Calif. Inst. Tech., Pasadena, 1982; rsch. assoc. Mich. State U., East Lansing, 1982-86; scientist I Superconducting Super Collider Lab., Waxahachie, Tex., 1989-94; sr. scientist Aura Sys., Inc., El Segundo, Calif., 1996—2003. From vis. asst. prof. to vis. assoc. prof. U. Notre Dame, Ind., 1986-88; mem. part-time faculty Calif. State U., Northridge, 1994-96. Contbr. articles to profl. jours. on particle physics, detectors, and accelerator physics. Mem. IEEE, Am. Phys. Soc., Am. Solar Energy Soc. E-mail: s.stampke@ieee.org.

STAMSTA, JEAN F., artist; b. Sheboygan, Wis., Nov. 2, 1936; d. Herbert R. and Lucile Caroline (Malwitz) Nagel; m. Duane R. Stamsta, Aug. 18, 1956; children: Marc, David. BS, BA, U. Wis., 1958. Guest curator Milw. Art Mus., 1986; resident artist Leighton Artist Colony, Banff, Alta., Can., 1987. One-woman shows include Am. Craft Mus., N.Y.C., 1971, Winona (Minn.) State U., 1986, Lawrence U., Appleton, Wis., 1990, Walkers Point Ctr. Arts, Milw., 1990, U. Wis. Ctr., Sheboygan, 1998, Wis. Luth. Coll., Milw., 1999, Carroll Coll., Waukesha, Wis., 2006, exhibited in group shows at Cleve. Mus. Art, 1977, Milw. Art Mus., 1986, 1988, Nat. Air and Space Mus., Smithsonian Instn., Washington, 1986, Madison (Wis.) Art Ctr., 1987, 1990, Paper Press Gallery, Chgo., 1988, North Arts Ctr., Atlanta, 1990, Dairy Barn Cultural Arts Ctr., Athens, Ohio, 1991, Paper Arts Festival, Appleton, 1992, Fine Arts Mus., Budapest, Hungary, 1992, Tilburg Textile Mus., Netherlands, 1993, U. Wis. Union Gallery, 1994, Holland Area Arts Coun. Gallery, U. Mich., Ann Arbor, 1996, Charles Allis Art Mus., Milw., 1996, Bergstrom-Mahler Mus., Neenah, Wis., 1998, West Bend Mus. Art, Wis., 2000, Three Rivers Arts Festival, Pitts., 2001, U. Wis. Alumni Assn., Milw., 2002, Racine (Wis.) Art Mus., 2003, 2005, Rochester Art Ctr., 2004. Fellow Craftsman fellow, NEA, 1974. Avocations: swimming, travel. Home: 9313 Center Oak Rd Hartland WI 53029 E-mail: jstamsta@aol.com.

STANALAJCZO, GREG CHARLES, computer company executive; b. 1959; Degree, Oakland U. With CDI Computer Svc., Inc., Troy, Mich., 1986-95, pres., 1993-95; exec. v.p., COO, co-owner Trillium Teamologies, Inc., Royal Oak, Mich., 1996—; pres., owner Stano Enterprises, LLC, Stano Transp. Svcs., LLC, Stano Electronics & Tech., LLC; owner, ptnr. Sullivan Investment Group, 3rd St. Properties; ptnr. Heritage Pewter LLC; founder, pres. Trillium Charities, Inc.; owner, pres. Stano Electronics and Tech., LLC; co-owner, sec. and v.p. i-mdo.USA, Inc.; COO, co-owner, co-founder i-mob USA, Inc. Office: Trillium Teamologies Inc 219 S Main St Ste 300 Royal Oak MI 48067-2611 Office Phone: 248-584-2080. E-mail: greg_stano@compuserve.com.

STANBRIDGE, BRYAN SCOTT, music educator, composer; s. Richard Scott and Maribeth Kay Stanbridge. MusB in Performance, Ea. Mich. U., Ypsilanti, 2003; MusM in Performance, Bowling Green State U., Ohio, 2006, MusM in Composition, 2006. Dir. percussion Riverview HS, Mich., 1999—2001, Chelsea HS, Mich., 2000—02, Edsel Ford HS, Dearborn, Mich., 2001—; asst. dir. marching band North Farmington HS, Farmington Hills, Mich., 2001—03. Musician: Andrea Reinkemeier's Through Leaves, Frederic Rzewski's Wails. Pres. Winterset Ter. Condo. Assn., Toledo, 2005—06. Regent scholar, Ea. Mich. U., 1999—2003. Mem.: Am. Fedn. Musicians, Percussive Arts Soc., Coll. Music Soc., Am. Composers Forum, Golden Key, Phi Kappa Phi. Democrat. Roman Catholic. Avocations: bicycling, hiking, golf. Home Phone: 419-754-3319; Office Phone: 419-372-8610. Personal E-mail: sorcerer@geocities.com.

STANBRIDGE, ERIC JOHN, biology professor; b. London, May 28, 1942; came to U.S., 1965; BS, Brunel U., 1964; PhD, Stanford U., 1971. Rsch. asst. Wistar Inst., Phila., 1965—67; mem. sci. staff Nat. Inst. Med. Research, London, 1968-69; research assoc. med. microbiology Stanford (Calif.) U., 1972-73, instr. med. microbiology, 1973-75; asst. prof., dept. microbiology U. Calif., Irvine, 1975-78, assoc. prof., dept. microbiology, 1978-82, prof., dept. microbiology and molecular genetics, 1982—, disting. prof., dept. microbiology and molecular genetics, 2002—. Chmn. Gordon Conf. Cancer Biology, 1985; advisor Office of Tech. Assessment, 1986; co-organizer UCLA-Triton Bioscis. Symposium, 1986; mem. external adv. bd., U. Calif. San Francisco Comprehensive Cancer Ctr., 2000-; bd. sci. advisors, Norwegian Inst. Gene Ecology, 2002-; coll. reviewers, Can. Rsch. Chairs Program, 2003-;lectr. in the field. Editorial bd. mem. Microbiol. Revs., 1985-, In Vitro, 1987-, J. Cellular Biochemistry, 1990-, Oncology Rsch., 1992-, Geno Methods, 1993-, Cancer Rsch. Ency., 1999-, Cancer Letters, 1998-; assoc. editor Cancer Research, 1985-, J. Cellular Physiology, 1989-, Molecular and Cellular Differentation, 1992-, Cancer Sci. (Japan), 2004-; contbr. articles to profl. jours. and chpts. to books; 4 US patents in the field. Fellow Leukemia Soc., 1976-1978, Internat. Union Against Cancer, 1979, Eleanor Roosevelt Internat., 1983-84, Am. Acad. Microbiology, 1986, AAAS, 1993; recipient Research Career Devel. award, NIH, 1978-83, NIH Merit award, 1987-96, Phi Kappa Phi Biology Colloquium award, Oregon State U., 1988; named one of Outstanding Young Men of Am., Jaycees, 1979. Mem. AAAS, NY Acad. Scis., Internat. Orgn. Mycoplasmologists, Am. Soc. Microbiology, Sigma Xi, Tissue Culture Assn., Internat. Orgn. Mycolplasmologist, Am. Assn. for Cancer Rsch., Internat. Soc. for Differentiation, UICC Acad. Fellows Office: U Calif Irvine B235/B210 Med Sciences Mail Code 4025 Irvine CA 92697-4025 Office Phone: 949-824-7042, 949-824-5259. Office Fax: 949-824-8598. Business E-Mail: ejstanbr@uci.edu.

STANBURY, JOHN BRUTON, retired pharmacologist, educator; b. Clinton, NC, May 15, 1915; s. Walter A. and Zula (Bruton) S.; m. Jean F. Cook, Jan. 6, 1945; children: John Bruton, Martha Jean, Sarah Katherine, David McNeill, Pamela Cook. AB, Duke U., Durham, NC, 1935; MD, Harvard U., Cambridge, Mass., 1939; Doctor honoris causa, U. Leiden, Netherlands, 1975, U. Pisa, Italy, 1994, U. Cuyo, Argentina, 2005. House officer Mass. Gen. Hosp., 1940-41, asst. resident, 1946, chief med. resident, 1948, mem. med. staff, 1949—; research fellow pharmacology Harvard Med. Sch., 1947; vis. prof. medicine U. Leiden, 1955; prof. exptl. medicine MIT, Cambridge, 1966-80, emeritus, 1980—. Cons. Pan Am. Health Orgn., WHO, UNICEF, U.S. AEC. Author: Endemic Goiter: The adaptation of man to iodine deficiency, 1954, Metabolic Basis of Inherited Disease, 5th edit., 1984, The Thyroid and Its Diseases, 5th edit., 1984, Endemic Goiter, 1969, Human Development and the Thyroid, 1972, Endemic Goiter and Endemic Cretinism, 1980, Prevention and Control of Iodine Deficiency Disorders, 1987, A Constant Ferment, 1991, The Damaged Brain of Iodine Deficiency, 1994, The Inborn Errors of the Thyroid System, 1994, Iodine in Pregnancy, 1998, The Iodine Trail, 2007. Served from lt. (j.g.) to comdr. USNR, 1941-45. Decorated gran oficial Ordenar Hipoloitio Unanue (Peru); recipient Delmar S. Fahrney medal Franklin Inst., 1993, Prince Mahidol award, Thailand, 1994. Mem. Am. Assn. Physicians, Soc. Clin. Investigation, Am. Thyroid Assn. (pres. 1969), Am. Acad. Arts and Scis., Endocrine Soc., Endocrine Socs. Finland, Colombia, Peru, Ecuador and Argentina, Internat. Coun. for Control of Iodine Deficiency Disorders (chair emeritus). Democrat. Episcopalian.

STANCATO, FRANKLIN ANTHONY, psychology professor; b. Mar. 18, 1930; MA, U. Denver, 1957; PhD, U. Notre Dame, South Bend, Ind., 1969. Tchr. Whidefield HS, Colorado Springs, 1957—64; psychology prof. Ctrl. Mich. U., Mt. Pleasant, 1968—. Mem.: Am. Edn. Rsch. Assn., Nat. Soc. Study Edn. Home: 568 Hiawatha Dr Mount Pleasant MI 48858 Office: Ctrl Mich U 315 Ronan Hall Mount Pleasant MI 48858

STANCELL, ARNOLD FRANCIS, chemical engineering educator, retired oil industry executive; b. NYC, Nov. 16, 1936; s. Francis and Maria (Lucas) S.; m. Constance Newton, Apr. 21, 1973; 1 child, Christine BChemE magna cum laude, CCNY, 1958; ScD, MIT, Cambridge, 1962. Registered profl. engr., NY. Rsch. scientist, rsch. mgr. Mobil Oil Corp., Edison, NJ, 1962—72, chem. planning assoc., mgr. NYC, 1973—75, v.p. chem. divsn. Macedon, NY, 1976—79, mgr. corp. planning NYC, 1980—81, regional exec. mktg. and refining London, 1982—84, planning v.p. mktg. and refining NYC, 1985—86, v.p. U.S. exploration and prodn. Fairfax, Va., 1987—88, v.p. internat. exploration and producing, 1989—93; prof. chem. engring. Ga. Inst. Tech., Atlanta, 1994—2001, endowed chair prof. chem. engring., 2001—. Vis. prof. MIT, Cambridge, 1970, 1998, adv. bd., 1976—; adv. bd. CCNY, 1990—, Carnegie Mellon U., 1999— Contbg. author: Polymer Science and Materials, 1971; contbr. articles to Jour. Applied Polymer Sci., AIChE Symposia Series, Jour. Macromolecular Sci. Recipient Profl. Achievement award, Nat. Orgn. Black Chemists and Chem. Engrs., 1975, Career Achievement award CCNY, 1993. Fellow AIChE (Chem. Engring. Practice award 1997); mem. Nat. Acad. Engring., Tau Beta Pi. Achievements include research in mgmt. and growth of domestic and internat. businesses in chemicals, oil and natural gas; patents for petrochemical and polymer processes and plasma processes at surfaces. Business E-Mail: arnold.stancell@chbe.gatech.edu.

STANCEU, TIMOTHY CHARLES, federal judge; b. Canton, Ohio, July 31, 1951; s. Charles and Marian Kathryn (Coman) S. AB, Colgate U., 1973; JD, Georgetown U., 1979. Bar: D.C. 1980, U.S. Ct. Appeals (fed. cir.) 1991, U.S. Ct. Internat. Trade, 1991. Environ. protection specialist U.S. EPA, Washington, 1974-82; spl. asst. to asst sec. U.S. Dept. Treasury, Washington, 1982-85, dep. dir. Office Trade and Tariff Affairs, 1985-89; atty. Hogan & Hartson, Washington, 1990—2003; judge US Ct. Internat. Trade, NYC, 2003—. Mem. Nat. Assn. Fgn. Trade Zones (dir. 1992—). Republican. Office: US Ct Internat Trade One Federal Plz New York NY 10278-0001 *

STANCILL, JAMES MCNEILL, finance educator, consultant; b. Orange, NJ, July 30, 1932; s. James Sr. and Anne Jeanne (Sauter) S.; m. Catherine Jackson, Sept. 25, 1954; children: Martha A., Mary C., Christine E. AB, George Wash. U., Washington, DC, 1954, MBA, 1957; PhD in Fin. and Econs., U. Pa., Phila., 1965. Buyer Melpar Inc., Falls Church, Va., 1954-59; instr., adminstrv. officer U. Pa., Phila., 1959-64; prof. fin. U. So. Calif., LA, 1964—. Prin. Stancill & Assocs., Pasadena, Calif., 1964—, The McNeill Bush Co. Ltd.; chmn. S.W. Products Co., 1991—97. Author: Management of Working Capital, 1970, Entrepreneurial Finance: for New and Emerging Businesses, 2004; contbr. numerous articles to Harvard Bus. Rev., 1977—. Avocations: genealogy, sailing, travel. Office: U So Calif Marshall Sch Bus Los Angeles CA 90089-1427 Business E-Mail: stancill@marshall.usc.edu.

STANCZAK, JULIAN, artist, educator; b. Borownica, Poland, Nov. 5, 1928; came to U.S., 1950, naturalized, 1957; s. Victor and Elizabeth (Cwynar) S.; m. Barbara M. Meerpohl, June 10, 1963; children: Danuta M., Christopher. B.F.A., Cleve. Inst. Art., 1954; M.F.A., Yale U., 1956. Tchr. Art Acad. Cin., 1957-64, Cleve. Inst. Art, 1965—. One-man shows include Dayton Art Inst., 1964, Martha Jackson Gallery, N.Y.C., 1964, 65, 68, 71, 72, 75, 77, 79, Miami U., Oxford, Ohio, 1965, Feingarten Galleries, Los Angeles, 1966, Kent State U., 1968, Dartmouth, 1968, Akron (Ohio) Art Inst., 1969, Cleve. Inst. Art, 1971, London Arts Gallery, 1971, Cin. Art Mus., 1972, 80, Corcoran Gallery Art, Washington, 1972, Canton (Ohio) Art Inst., 1974, Pollack Gallery, Toronto, 1975, Ohio State U., 1976, IMF and CARE, Washington, 1978, Butler Inst. Am. Art, Youngstown, Ohio, 1980, Nat. Mus., Warsaw, Poland, 1981, Alice Simsar Gallery, Ann Arbor, Mich., 1982, 88, New Gallery, Cleve., 1983, Charles Foley Gallery, Columbus, Ohio, 1984, 88, Walker Gallery, Chgo., 1986, Carl Solway Gallery, Cin., Jane Haslem Gallery, Washington, 1986, Standard Oil Co. Hdqrs., Cleve., 1987, Alice Simsar Gallery, Ann Arbor, Mich., Boca Raton Mus. Art, Fla., 1989, Carl Solway Gallery, Cin., Charles Foley Gallery, Columbus, Ohio, Ctr. for Contemporary Art, Cleve., 1990; one man retrospective David Anderson Gallery, Buffalo, N.Y., Dennos Mus-.,Traverse City, Mich., Butler Inst. of Am. Art., Youngstown, Ohio, 2000, /Columbus Mus. of Art, 2001, Ashville Mus. of Art, N.,C., 2001, Lowe Art Mus Univ. Miami, Fla., 2001; many others; exhibited in group shows: Mus. Modern Art, N.Y.C., 1965, Albright Knox Art Gallery, Buffalo, 1965, 68, Detroit Art Inst., 1965, Larry Alrich Mus., 1965, U. Ill., 1965, Gallery Moos, Toronto, 1965, Kranert Art Mus., Urbana, Ill., 1965, San Francisco Mus. Art, 1965, Flint (Mich.) Inst. Art, 1966, Carnegie Inst., Pitts., 1967, Japan Cultural Forum, 1967, Smithsonian Instn., Washington, 1967, 69, 85, Dept. State, Washington, 1968, Cin. Art Mus., 1968, 83, Del. Art Ctr., 1970, Seibu, Tokyo, 1971, Mansfield (Ohio) Art Ctr., 1973, Butler Art Inst., Youngstown, Ohio, 1973, Minn. Art Mus., Mpls., 1973, Akron Art Inst., 1975, Indpls. Mus. Art, 1976, Bklyn. Mus. Art, 1976, 80, Cleve. Mus. Art, 1976, 77, 83, Memphis Acad. Art, 1981, Nat. Gallery Art, 1981, 85, Hirshhorn Mus. Art, 1981, Montclair Art Mus., N.J., 1982, Art Acad. Cin., 1986, Embassies Travelling Exhbn., Madrid, 1987, Warsaw, Poland, 1991; represented in permanent collections: Nat. Mus. Am. Art, Albright Knox Art Gallery, Larry Aldrich Mus., Mus. Modern Art, Dayton Art Inst., Hirshhorn Mus., Washington, Butler Inst. Am. Art, Youngstown, Ohio, Rufino Tomajo Mus., Mex., Cleve. Art Assn., Milw. Art Inst., Canton (Ohio) Art Inst., USIA, N.Y.C., Balt. Mus. Art, San Francisco Mus. Art, Herron Mus. Art, Indpls., Okla. Art Ctr., Oklahoma City, Pa. Acad. Fine Arts, Phila., Carnegie Inst., Pitts., Cleve. Mus. Art, Cin. Art Mus., Tulsa Mus. Fine Arts, Columbus (Ohio) Art Mus., Akron Art Inst., Corcoran Art Mus., Nat. Gallery, Washington, Lowe Art Mus., Coral Gables, Fla., Contemporary Art Mus., Houston, Winnipeg Fine Arts Ctr., Man., Can., Dracket Fine Art Collection, Cin., Kalamazoo Inst. Arts, Worcester Art Mus., Phoenix Art Mus., Indpls. Mus. Art, Wasserman Devel. Corp., Cambridge, Dartmouth Coll., Hanover, N.H., Etzold Sammlung, Cologne, Fed. Republic Germany, Johnson & Johnson Fine Art Collection, Conn., Nelson Rockefeller Collection, N.Y., Chase Manhattan Bank, N.Y., Mus. Fine Arts, Los Angeles, Newport Harbor Mus., Newport Beach, Calif., N.Y. State U. at Buffalo; mus. collections include Aldrich Mus. Comtemporary Art, ridgefield, Conn., Akron Art Inst., Ohio, Asheville Mus. Art, Asheville, N.C., Albright Knox Art Gallery, Buffalo, Ball State U. Mus. Art, Muncie, Ind., Balt. Mus. Art, Boca Raton, Fla., Butler Inst. Am. Art, Youngstown, Ohio, Canton Art Inst., Ohio, Carnegie Inst., Pitts., Mus. Modern Art; others; represented in permanent collections at Air Products & Chems., Alcoa, Am. greetings, Cleve., Ameritrust Bank, Cleve., David Anderson Collection, Buffalo, Am. Republic Ins. Co., Des Moines, Atlantic ridgefield Com., N.Y., The Art Collection First Nat. Bank Chgo., Balt. Gas & Electric, Balt., Bank N.Y.; others; monographs include Gene Baro Corcoran Gallery Art, Washington, Rudolf Arnheim, Harry Rand, Robert Bertholf, Poetry and Rare Book Collection, SUNY Buffalo, 20 Tectronic Images and Poetry Barbara Stanczak Clev., (color and form Vibrations of Geometrical Space) Dennos Mus. ctr. Northwestern Mich. Coll., Traverse City, Mich. Recipient 1st prize Dayton Art Inst., 1964; recipient Butler Inst. Am. Art award, 1966, Cleve. Fine Arts prize, 1970, Ohio Arts Council award, 1972, Best of Show award Internat. Platform Assn., 1973-76 Mem. Abstract Artists Am., Internat. Platform Assn. Achievements include being a pioneer in optical art. Address: 6229 Cabrini Ln Seven Hills OH 44131-2848 Business E-Mail: bstanczak@gate.cia.edu.

STANDARD, KENNETH G., lawyer; b. Sept. 4, 1936; AB, Harvard Coll., 1958, LLB, 1962; LLM, NYU, 1971. Bar: US Ct. Appeals (2nd Cir.), US Dist. Ct. (Ea. Dist. NY), US Dist. Ct. (So. Dist. NY). Former v.p. and sr. counsel products divsn. Bristol-Myers Co.; dir. Office Legal Svcs. NYC Sch. Sys., 1985—89; asst/ gen. counsel labor rels. Environ. and Benefits Plans ConEd, NYC, 1989—2000; spl. counsel labor and employment practice group Morgan Lewis & Bockius LLP, 2000—04; ptnr. Epstein Becker & Green PC, 2004—. Named one of 100 Most Powerful Minority Bus. Leaders in N.Y., Crain's N.Y. Bus., 2003. Mem.: ABA, NYC Bar Assn., NY State Bar Assn. (pres. 2004), Harvard Club (v.p. 1997—99, pres. 1999—2002). Office: Epstein Becker & Green PC 250 Park Ave New York NY 10177 Office Phone: 212-351-4670. Office Fax: 212-661-0989. E-mail: kstandard@ebglaw.com.

STANDIFORD, HAROLD C., medical educator; b. Aberdeen, Md., Aug. 25, 1938; MD, U. Md. Sch. Medicine, 1964. Cert. Internal Medicine, Infectious Diseases. Intern, medicine U. Md. Hosp., Balt., 1964—65, resident, medicine, 1965—66; resident, infectious diseases U. Wash. Hosp., Seattle, 1966—67; fellow U. Wash. Sch. Medicine, Seattle, 1967—69; prof. medicine, divsn. infectious diseases U. Md. Sch. Medicine, dir., Infection Control and Antimicrobial Effectiveness, Divsn. Infectious Diseases. Hosp. appointment Balt. VA Med. Ctr., Mich. Contbr. articles to profl. jours. Office: Divsn Infectious Diseases Infection Control & Antimicrobial Effectiveness Suite 400 29 South Greene St Baltimore MD 21201 Address: Baltmore V21 Med Ctr 10 S Greene St Baltimore MD 21201

STANDIFORD, RONALD DAWSON, minister, educator; b. Balt., July 2, 1949; s. Howard William and Rosalie Burton Standiford; m. Darby Shaver, Sept. 7, 1985; children: Leah Dawson, Emily Ashmore. BA in Polit. Sci., Am. U., 1971; MA in Religion, Westminster Sem., 1979, MDiv, 1980. Ordained minister Presbyn. Ch. Am., 1981. Law clk. Law Office Saunders M. Almond, Jr., Towson, Md., 1974—77; assoc. pastor Timonium (Md.) Presbyn. Ch., 1981—88; pastor Redeemer Presbyn. Ch., Kingsville, Md., 1988—. Program com. Md. Hist. Soc., Baltimore, Md., 1989—92; adj. faculty Redeemer Classical Christian Sch., Kingsville, Md., 1996—, founder, 1996; pres. Beachmont Christian Camp, 1984—94; rhetoric tchr. Redeemer Classical Christian Sch., Kingsville, Md., 1996—. Co-author: Villages; Baltimore County, MD, 1994; exhibitions include various local shows, 1990. Mem. campaign com. Md. Ho. Dels., 1994, 1998. Recipient award, Am. U., 1971. Achievements include first to founder, 1st K-12 classical christian school in Maryland. Avocations: gardening, racquetball, tennis. Home: Beachmont Farm 6415 Mt Vista Road Kingsville MD 21087 Home Phone: 410-592-4830; Office Phone: 410-592-9625. Personal E-mail: classicdadman@yahoo.com.

STANDISH, JOHN SPENCER, textile manufacturing company executive; b. Albany, NY, Apr. 17, 1925; s. John Carver and Florence (Spencer) S.; m. Elaine Joan Ritchie, Oct. 20, 1962 (div. 1984); children: John Carver, Christine Louise; m. Patricia Hunter, Nov. 9, 1985. BS, MIT, 1945. Asst. to prodn. mgr. Forstmann Woolen Co., Passaic, NJ, 1945-52; various positions Albany Internat. Corp., 1952-72, v.p., 1972-74, exec. v.p., 1974-76, vice chmn., 1976-84, chmn., 1984-98, also bd. dirs., 1958-98, chmn. emeritus, 1998—. Bd. dirs. Albany chpt. ARC, 1966-92, chpt. chmn., 1971-74, bd. govs., Washington, 1980-86; bd. dirs. United Way Northeastern N.Y., Albany, 1980-97, pres., 1984-85; trustee Albany Med. Coll. and Ctr., 1984-93, Siena Coll., Loudonville, N.Y., 1987-2003; chmn. U. Albany Fund, 1982-87, 89-92; pres. U. Albany Found., 1992-98. Sgt. U.S. Army, 1946-47. Mem.: Ft. Orange Club, Schuyler Meadows Country Club, John's Island Club (Fla.). Republican. Episcopalian. Avocations: bridge, tennis, golf. Home: 395 Llwyd's Ln Vero Beach FL 32963

STANDISH, WILLIAM LLOYD, judge; b. Pitts., Feb. 16, 1930; s. William Lloyd and Eleanor (McCargo) S.; m. Marguerite Oliver, June 12, 1963; children: Baird M., N. Graham, James H., Constance S. BA, Yale U., 1953; LLB, U. Va., 1956. Bar: Pa. 1957, U.S. Supreme Ct. 1967. Assoc. Reed, Smith, Shaw & McClay, Pitts., 1957—63, ptnr., 1963—80; judge Ct. Common Pleas Allegheny County, Pitts., 1980—87, U.S. Dist. Ct. (we. dist.) Pa., Pitts., 1987—. Solicitor Edgeworth Borough Sch. Dist., 1963-66. Bd. dirs. Sewickley (Pa.) Cmty. Ctr., 1981-83, Staunton Farms Found., mem., 1984-2002, trustee, 1984-92; corporator Sewickley Cemetery, 1971-87; trustee Mary and Alexander Laughlin Children's Ctr., 1972-90, Leukemia Soc. Am., 1978-80, We. Pa. chpt., 1972-80, We. Pa. Sch. Deaf, 1983—, YMCA of Sewickley, 1996—; bd. dirs. Pitts. Theol. Sem., 2001—. Recipient Pres. award, Leukemia Soc. Am., 1980. Mem. ABA, Pa. Bar Assn., Allegheny County Bar Assn., Am. Judicature Soc., Acad. Trial Lawyers Allegheny County (treas. 1977-78, bd. dirs. 1979-80), Am. Inn of Ct. (Pitts. chpt. 1993—). Office: US Dist Ct 6170 US Post Office & Ct House 700 Grant St Pittsburgh PA 15219-1906 Office Phone: 412-208-7430. Business E-Mail: Judge_William_Standish@pawd.uscourts.gov.

STANDLEY, JOHN T., food market executive; married; 2 children. BS in Acctg., Pepperdine U. Audit mgr. retail and fin. industry groups Arthur Andersen LLP, LA; v.p. fin. Food 4 Less Supermarkets, Inc., Compton, Calif., 1991—94; sr. v.p. admin. Smith's Food & Drug, Salt Lake City; CFO Smitty's Supervalu Inc., Phoenix; sr. v.p., CFO Ralphs Grocery Co., 1996—98, Fred Meyer, Inc., Portland, Oreg., 1998—99; exec. v.p., CFO Fleming Co. Inc., Oklahoma City, 1999, Rite Aid Corp., Camp Hill, Pa., 1999—2002, sr. exec. v.p., chief adminstrv. officer, 2002, CFO, 2003—05; CEO Pathmark Stores, Inc., 2005—. Office: Pathmark Stores Inc 200 Milik St Carteret NJ 07008 *

STANEK, JIM, actor; b. Cranberry, Pa., Aug. 15, 1971; m. Beth Stanek; 3 children. BA, Carnegie Mellon U., 1994. Actor: (Broadway plays) Indiscretions, 1995, A Funny Thing Happened on the Way to the Forum, 1996, The Rivals, 2004, Little Women, 2005, Lestat, 2006; (plays) Captain Courageous, The Musical, 1999, Saturday Night, 2000, Thoroughly Modern Millie, 2000, Let's Face It, 2001, The 3hree Musketeers, 2001, The Good Companions, 2001, Chrysalis, 2001, Cyrano de Bergerac, 2001, Damn Yankees, 2002, The Threepenny Opera, 2003, Oh Boy!, 2003, Best Foot Forward, 2004, My Fair Lady, 2004, I Love You, You're Perfect, Now Change, 2005, Slut, 2005, Jacques Brel is Alive and Well and Living in Paris, 2006; (TV series) The Adversaries, 1998, Guiding Light, 2005. *

STANFIELD, BRENT B., federal agency administrator; BS in Biol. Sciences, U. Calif., Irvine, 1973; PhD in Neurobiology, Washington U., St. Louis, 1978. Post-doctoral trainee Washington U., St. Louis, Salk Inst. for Biol. Studies, mem. faculty Devel. Neurobiology Lab., 1981; dir. unit on devel. neuroanatomy Lab. Neurophysiology NIMH, 1987—96, acting dep. dir. Divsn. Intramural Rsch., 1996—97, dir. Office Sci. Policy and Program Planning, 1998—2000; dep. dir. Ctr. Sci. Rev., NIH, 2000—03, acting dir., 2003—05; dir. Divsn. Extramural Activities Nat. Inst. Diabetes and Digestive and Kidney Diseases, NIH, 2005—. Asst. adj. prof. dept. neurosciences U. Calif. Sch. Medicine, San Diego, 1982. Office: Nat Inst Diabetes and Digestive and Kidney Diseases 2 Democracy Plz Rm 715 6707 Democracy Blvd Bethesda MD 20892 Office Phone: 301-594-8843. Office Fax: 301-480-3965. E-mail: stanfbr@niddk.nih.gov.

STANFIELD, CHARLES FREEMAN, chemist; s. William Thomas and Elizabeth Stanfield; m. Susan Lois Stanfield, Sept. 1, 1979; 1 child, Ashleigh Joy. BS in Chemistry, Ga. Inst. Tech., 1979; PhD, U. Ariz., Tucson, 1987. Postdoctoral staff Hoffmann-LaRoche; with Biogen-Idec, Genosys Biotechnologies, MedImmune, DSM Pharms., mgr. analytical devel. Greenville, NC, 2000—. Vol. Winterville Stormwater Adv. Com., NC, 2007—, Greenville Homeless Shelter, 2007—. Recipient Pres.'s award, DSM Pharms., 2003; grantee, 2007—. Mem.: Am. Chem. Soc. Office: DSM Pharms 5900 NW Greenville Blvd Bldg 8 Greenville NC 27834 Business E-Mail: freeman.stanfield@dsm.com.

STANFILL, DENNIS CAROTHERS, corporate financial executive; b. Centerville, Tenn., Apr. 1, 1927; s. Sam Broome and Hattie (Carothers) S.; m. Therese Olivieri, June 29, 1951; children: Francesca, Sara, Dennis Carothers. BS, U.S. Naval Acad., 1949; MA (Rhodes scholar), Oxford U., 1953; LHD (hon.), U. S.C. Corporate finance specialist Lehman Bros., NYC, 1959-65; v.p. finance Times Mirror Co., Los Angeles, 1965-69; exec. v.p. 20th Century-Fox Film Corp., 1969-71, pres., 1971, chmn. bd., chief exec. officer, 1971-81; pres. Stanfill, Bowen & Co., 1981-90; chmn. bd. dirs., chief exec. officer AME, Inc., 1990-91; co-chmn., co-CEO Metro-Goldwyn-Mayer, Inc., 1992-93; sr. advisor Credit Lyonnais, 1993-95; pres. Dennis Stanfill Co., 1995—. Trustee Calif. Inst. Tech. Served to lt. USN, 1949-59; politico-mil. policy div. Office Chief Naval Ops., 1956-59.

STANFORD, CHARLOTTE A., humanities educator; BA in Latin & Humanities with honors, Brigham Young U., Provo, Utah, 1993; MA in Medieval Studies, U. Conn., Storrs, 1996; PhD in Art History, Pa. State U., University Park, 2003. Art instr. Pa. State U., 1998—2002; asst. prof. art Shippensburg U., 2001; asst. prof. humanities Brigham Young U., 2003—. Presenter in field, 1999—; grad. council mem., advisor Outdoor Adventure Club Brigham Young U., 2004—; lectr. in field, 2005. Contbg. photographer (CD-Rom) Strasbourg Found. Oeuvre Notre-Dame, 2005; contbr. articles to profl. jours. Recipient Honorable Mention award for essay contest, Brigham Young U., 2006; grantee Hyslop grant for rsch. travel, Pa. State U., 2001, Kennedy Internat. Ctr. Travel grant, Brigham Young U., 2005, Scott Opler fellowship, Soc. Architectural Historians, 2005; Faculty Travel grant, Brigham Young U., 2004, Ctr. European Studies Travel grant, 2006.

STANFORD, EDWARD JOSEPH, gynecologist; b. LA, Feb. 22, 1957; m. Kathleen J. Jones, Mar. 16, 1987; children: Paul Christopher, Drew Kathleen. BS in Sports Medicine, Pepperdine U., Malibu, Calif., 1979; MS in Kinesiology, U. Calif., LA, 1981; MD, Med. Coll. Pa., Phila., 1985. Dir. Ctr. Advanced Pelvic Surgery, Belleville, Ill., 1998—; pres. KESCO, Inc, Centralia, 2003—. Office: Center for Advanced Pelvic Surgery PC 4550 Memorial Dr Belleville IL 62220 Office Phone: 618-233-0370.

STANFORD, HENRY KING, college president; b. Atlanta, Apr. 22, 1916; s. Henry King and Annie Belle (Callaway) S.; m. Laurie Ruth King, Sept. 19, 1936; children: Henry, Lowry, Rhoda, Peyton. AB, Emory U., 1936, MA, 1940, LLD, 1961; postgrad., U. Heidelberg, Germany, 1936—37; MS in Govt. Mgmt., U. Denver, 1943, LLD, 1962; PhD, NYU, 1949; DCL, Jacksonville U., Fla., 1963; LLD, Loyola U., New Orleans, 1968, U. Akron, Kyung Hee U., Seoul, Korea, 1968, Rollins Coll., 1977, Barry Coll., 1979; DHL, U. Tampa, 1969; DLitt, U. R.I., 1970, U. Chile, Santiago, 1980; D in Higher Edn., U. Miami, 1981; DHL, Birmingham-So. Coll., 1987. Instr. Emory U., 1937-40; asst. prof. Ga. Inst. Tech., 1940-41; instr. NYU, 1943-46; prof. pub. adminstrn., also dir. sch. pub. adminstrn. U. Denver, 1946-48; pres. Ga. Southwestern Coll., Americus, 1948-50; dir. U. Ctr. in Ga., 1950-52; asst. chancellor U. Sys. of Ga., 1952-53; pres. Ga. State Coll. for Women, Milledgeville, 1953-56; chief of party NYU-Internat. Cooperation Adminstrn. Contract, Ankara, Turkey, 1956-57; pres. Birmingham-So. Coll., 1957-62, U. Miami, Fla., 1962-81, pres. emeritus, 1981—; interim pres. U. Ga., 1986-87, pres. emeritus, 1987—. Rsch. asst. Tax Found., N.Y.C., 1943-44; staff N.A.M. com. exec., 1944-46; chmn. Fed. Res. Bank Atlanta, 1969, 72. Trustee Knight Found., 1982-97; vice chmn. Invest-in-Am., 1984-86, chmn. 1986-87; chmn. Dade County Cmty. Rels. Bd., 1969-71; bd. visitors Air U., Maxwell AFB, Ala., 1963-66; trustee Caribbean Resources Devel. Found., 1978-85, pres., 1978-83, chmn., 1983-84; chmn. Jimmy Carter Hist. Site Adv. Commn., 1990-2001. Decorated Star of Africa medal Liberia, 1971; officer Order of Merit Fed. Republic of Germany, 1972; recipient Eleanor Roosevelt-Israel Humanitarian award, 1965, Outstanding Civilian Svc. award U.S. Army, 1966, Silver Medallion Fla. Region NCCJ, 1968, Ga. Region, 1987, Disting. Svc. award Ga. Coll., 1979, hon. alumnus, 1996, C.H.I.E.F. award Ind. Colls. and Univs. Fla., 1983, Sibley award Ga. Mil. Coll., 1991, Emory medal, 1991, Adrian Dominican Ednl. Leadership award Barry U., 1991, Atlanta Boys' High Alumnus award, 1992, James Blair Humanitarian award Americus, 1993, Westmeyer award pub. svc. NYU, 1993. Mem. So. Assn. Colls. and Schs. (chmn. commn. colls. 1960-62, pres. 1972-73), Nat. Assn. Ind. Colls. and Univs. (dir. 1976-80), Assn. Caribbean Univs. and Rsch. Insts. (v.p. 1965-79), Golden Key Honor Soc. (bd. dirs. 1982-91), Internat. Assn. Univ. Pres. (exec. com. 1977-81), Delta Phi Alpha, Phi Beta Kappa, Omicron Delta Kappa, Phi Sigma Iota, Alpha Kappa Psi, Phi Mu Alpha, Phi Kappa Phi, Rotary Club (pres. Americus club 1984-85). Methodist. Office: PO Box 1065 Americus GA 31709-1065 Home Phone: 229-924-1303. E-mail: hksumuga@bellsouth.net. *The greatest literary influence on my life has been Goethe's Faust, Part I. Reading it in the original German as a college student, I was struck immediately with the demands Faust made of himself in concluding the contract with Mephistopheles: he would lose his soul if he ever chose a "bed of ease," succumbed to flattery, opted for pleasure alone, or said to any one moment, "Linger awhile; you are so nice!" In other words, whenever he ceased striving, he was lost.*

STANFORD, (FRANCES) JANE HERRING, dean, management consultant, educator, writer; b. Lockhart, Tex., Dec. 17, 1939; d. John William and Frances Argyra (Cheatham) Jr.; m. Rube V. Stanford; children: (Steven) Scott, Lisa Ann. BS, Texas A&M U., Kingsville; MS in Counseling, Texas A&M U., Corpus Christi; MBA, Texas A&M U., Kingsville; PhD in Orgn. Theory and Strategic Mgmt., U. North Tex. Tchg. fellow U. North Tex., Denton; prof. bus. policy and strategic mgmt., pres. faculty senate Texas A&M U., Kingsville, 1990—, grad. rsch. advisor, MBA/MPA program, Coll. Bus., 1992-98, 2004—, asst. v.p. Acad. Affairs, 1997—99, ret., 1999, vis. assoc. prof. mgmt. Corpus Christi, Tex., 2000—04, Kingsville, 2004—07, interim dean, Coll. Bus. Adminstrn., 2007—, chair dept. mgmt. and mktg. Coll. Bus., 1993—97, current mem. grad. faculty, Coll. Bus. grad. rsch. advisor; mgmt. cons. Strategic Mgmt. Solutions, Inc.,

1999—. Chair univ. assessment, budgeting and planning com. Tex. A&M U., 1997—98; internat. lectr. strategic mgmt. within internat. context, Colombia, Argentina; workshop leader and participant in acad. issues. Author: Building Competitiveness: U.S. Expatriate Management Strategies in Mexico, 1995; contbr. articles to profl. jours. and conf. procs. Named Leadership Corpus Christi Class of XXX, 2001—02; fellow Sys. Chancellor's fellow in leadership in higher edn. program, Tex. A&M U., 1997. Mem.: Univ. Grad. Faculty, Soc. Advancement Mgmt., Acad. Mgmt., Inst. Mgmt. Cons., Strategic Mgmt. Soc., Delta Signa Pi, Kappa Delta Pi (life). Presbyterian. Avocations: book collecting, photography, travel. Home: 13526 Carlos Fifth Ct Corpus Christi TX 78418 Office: Tex A&M Univ Kingsville TX 78363 Office Phone: 361-593-3802. Personal E-mail: jhstanford@aol.com.

STANFORD, JOSEPH STEPHEN, diplomat, lawyer, educator; b. Montreal, Que., Can., May 7, 1934; s. Walter Albert and Geraldine (O'Loghlin) S.; m. Agnes Mabelle Walker, Nov. 16, 1957; children: Kevin, Karen, Michael. BA, U. Montreal, 1953; LLB, U. Alta., Edmonton, Can., 1956. Bar: Alta. 1957; called to Queen's Counsel 1984. Mem. Greenan, Cooney & Stanford, Calgary, Alta., Canada, 1957-60; joined Fgn. Svc., Dept. External Affairs, Govt. of Can., 1960; amb. to Israel Tel Aviv, 1979-82; also Can. high commr. to Cyprus; asst. dep. min. for Africa and Mid. East Dept. External Affairs, Ottawa, Ont., 1983-85, asst. dep. min. for Europe, 1985-87, assoc. undersec. of state for external affairs, 1987-88; dep. solicitor gen. Govt. of Can., Ottawa, 1988-93; ret., 1994; sr fellow, conflict mgr. Canadian Center Mgmt. Devel., Ottawa, 1993-96; assoc., bd. dirs. Conflict Mgmt. Group, Cambridge, Mass., 1994—97, 2002—04, chmn. bd. dirs., 1997-99, Cons. Conflict Mgmt. Group, Cambridge, Mass., 1994—97. Contbr. articles on internat. law, fgn. investment and conflict resolution to profl. jours. Roman Catholic. Avocations: canoeing, skiing. Home: 58 Amberwood Cres Ottawa ON Canada K2E 7C3 Home Phone: 613-226-2334; Office Phone: 613-226-1328. Personal E-mail: joseph.stanford066@sympatico.ca.

STANG, ARNOLD, actor, writer, film director; b. NYC, Sept. 28, 1928; s. Harold Louis and Anna (Chest) S.; m. JoAnne Taggart, Sept. 21, 1949; children: David Donald, Deborah Jane Stang-Healy. Ind. actor, dir., writer, NYC, 1936—. Actor: (Broadway prodns.) Front Page, A Funny Thing Happened On the Way to the Forum, Wallflower, All in Favor, (TV shows) Bonanza, Ed Sullivan Show, McHale's Navy, Bewitched, Milton Berle Show, Jack Benny Show, Jackie Gleason Show, Top Cat, Emergency, Robert Klein Show, Playhouse 90, Frank Sinatra Spls., Bob Hope Spls., What's My Line, Bill Cosby Show, Tales From The Dark Side, numerous others, (stock theatrical prodns.) Don't Drink the Water, Death Knocks, Charley's Aunt, Finian's Rainbow, Three Men on a Horse, The Gazebo, Wish You Were Here, Pajama Game, Let 'Em Eat Cake, Anything Goes, Luv, Tobacco Road, Play It Again, Sam, Annie Get Your Gun, (starring film roles) Double for Della, Arnold the Benedict, Honorable Myrtle, The Expectant Father, Dondi, The Wonderful World of the Brothers Grimm, The Aristocats, Hello Down There, Alakazam the Great, The Man With the Golden Arm, The Cottonwood, Hercules in New York, Skidoo, My Sister Eileen, Seven Days Leave, Let's Go Steady, It's A Mad, Mad, Mad World, Dennis the Menace, numerous featured roles; rec. artist numerous albums including Winnie & Baby Pooh, Winnie the Pooh, Peter and the Wolf, Arnold Stang Meets Gus Edwards, Beezy the Sneezy Bee, The Hippy Hippo, Chester the Chimp, Further Adventures of Harry the Horse. Mem. Screen Actors Guild, Acad. Motion Picture Arts and Scis., Actors Equity Assn., AFTRA. Clubs: Players (N.Y.C.). Avocations: gardening, poetry, carpentry, social work. Office: 257 Park Ave S 9th Fl New York NY 10010

STANG, PETER JOHN, organic chemist; b. Nûrnberg, Germany, Nov. 17, 1941; came to U.S., 1956; s. John Stang and Margaret Stang Pollman; m. Christine Schirmer, 1969; children: Antonia, Alexandra. BS, DePaul U., Chgo., 1963; PhD, U. Calif., Berkeley, 1966; degree (hon.), Moscow State Lomonossov U., 1992, Russian Acad. Scis., 1992. Instr. Princeton (N.J.) U., 1967-68; from asst. to assoc. prof. U. Utah, Salt Lake City, 1969-79, prof., 1979-92, Disting. prof. chemistry, 1992—. Co-author: Organic Spectroscopy, 1971; author: (with others) Vinyl Cations, 1979; editor: (with F. Diederich) Modern Acetylene Chemistry, 1995, Metal Catalyzed Cross Coupling Reactions, 1998, (with Z. Rappaport) Dicoordinated Carbocations, 1997; editor-in-chief Jour. Organic Chemsitry, 2000-01; contbr. numerous articles to sci. publs. Recipient Humboldt-Forschungspreis, 1977; JSPS fellow, 1985; Fulbright-Hays sr. scholar, 1988. Fellow AAAS; mem. NAS, Am. Acad. Arts and Scis., Am. Chem. Soc. (assoc. editor jour. 1982-99, editor 2002-, award for Creative Rsch. and Applications of Iodine Chemistry, 2007), Chinese Acad. Scis. (fgn. mem.). Office: U Utah Dept Chemistry 315 South 1400 East Salt Lake City UT 84112-0850 Office Phone: 801-581-8329. E-mail: stang@chemistry.utah.edu.

STANG, ROLF KRISTIAN, vocalist, educator, actor, advertising executive, writer; b. Rockford, Ill., Sept. 19, 1939; s. Trygve Ingvald and Kirsten (Anfinsen-Kristiansen) S. BA, Augustana Coll., 1961; MA, Columbia U., 1963; performance/repertoire cert., opera div., Musikhochschule, Hamburg, Germany, 1964. Vocal soloist Christoph-Weber-Barock Ensemble, Hamburg, 1965-67; German and music faculty Coll. of White Plains, N.Y., 1968-73; sec. Internat. Percy Grainger Soc., White Plains, N.Y., 1974-79, pres., 1979—. Music critic Norway Times, NYC, 1970—; advt. exec. The Frank Vos Co AS/VP, 1973-83; lectr., recital Songs of Frederick Delius, Cambridge U., 1984—; multimedia lectr. on career of Wagnerian singer Kirsten Flagstad, 1995—; lectr. on English composer Frederick Delius, 1966—. Translator Songs of Grieg, Collected Works of Grieg, 1993; composer (for solo voice, chorus and orch.) Backward Tracings--A Tallahassee Triptych, 1974; (for soprano, chorus and orch.) Train Window Thoughts; (for chorus/6 instruments) Hymns in Praise of Night/Nietzschean Nocturnes; Lied/Romanse Art Song and opera rep. (Am., English, German, Norwegian, Swedish) 1968—; concert vocalist numerous states and countries, 1963—; author, actor touring with one-man play on Norwegian composer Edvard Grieg, US, Norway, Eng., 1993—; Millennium characterization of Viking-age voyager Icelander Leif Eriksson, 2000—; touring as Danish author Hans Christian Andersen, 1994—, as Askeladden telling Norwegian fairytales and singing traditional songs, 1995—; author one-man show, portrayer Henrik Ibsen--The Quiet Eye of the Hurrican, 2006—. Vol. Cath. Ctr. for Deaf, N.Y.C., 1975-79, Children to the Beach program, N.Y.C., 1978-83, Reaching Out to the Homeless, N.Y.C., 1988—. Decorated knight (Norway), St. Olav medal King Harald V of Norway, 1997; named to Scandinavian-Am. Hall of Fame, 1998; recipient Leif Eriksson citation, 2000. Mem. SAG, Am. Choral Dirs. Assn. (life), Nordmanns Forbundet/Norsemen's Fedn. (hon., life), Delius Assn. of Fla. (life), Delius Soc. of Great Britain, Sons of Norway Internat., Delius Soc. of Phila. (life), Am.-Scandinavian Soc. of N.Y., Soc. for Advancement of Scandinavian Studies (life), Edvard Grieg Soc. Great Britain (hon., life). Lutheran. Avocations: furniture making, carpentry, gardening, promoting Nordic culture and music. Home: The Monks Cell 29 W 65th St New York NY 10023-6630 E-mail: rolf_k_stang@hotmail.com.

STANGE, JAMES HENRY, architect; b. Davenport, Iowa, May 25, 1930; s. Henry Claus and Norma (Ballhorn) S.; m. Mary Suanne Peterson, Dec. 12, 1954; children: Wade Weston, Drew Dayton, Grant Owen. BArch, Iowa State U., 1954. Registered architect, Iowa, Nebr., Kans., Mo., Okla. Designer Davis & Wilson, Lincoln, Nebr., 1954-62, v.p., 1962-68; v.p., sec. Davis, Fenton, Stange, Darling, Lincoln, Nebr., 1977-92, pres., 1976—93, chmn., 1978—94. Mem. State Bd. Examiners for Engrs. and Architects, 1989-92, chmn. region V NCARB, 1991. Prin. works include Dorsey Labs., 1960, East H.S., Lincoln, 1966, Lincoln Gen. Hosp., 1967, Lincoln Airport Terminal, Sq. D Mfg. Plant, Lincoln, Bryan Meml. Hosp. (masterplans and additions), 1970, 80, 90, Bryan Ambulatory Care Ctr. Med. Office Bldg., Same Day Surgery Conf. Ctr., Parking Garage, 1993-95, Nebr. Wesleyan Theatre, Lincoln, Hasting (Nebr.) YMCA, various structures U. Nebr., Lincoln, ctr. and br. offices Am. Charter Fed. Savs. & Loan, S.E. H.S. (addition), 1984, U. Nebr. Animal Sci. Bldg., 1987, Beadle Ctr., UNL, 1991, Carriage Park Parking Garage, 1995. V.p. Nebr. Jazz Orch., 1995, 2000—, pres., 1997, Nebr. Art Assn., 1996—99; deacon 1st Presbyn. Ch., 1960, chmn. bd. trustees, 1968—90, elder, 1972—87, 1997—99, chmn. property com., 1998—2000, found. bd. trustees, 2005—; bd. dirs. Capitol Assn. Retarded Citizens, 1968—72, 1994—, pres., 1970; chmn. United Way Campaign, 1986, chmn. bd., 1988; chmn. endowment com. Bryan Hosp. Found., 1988—90; bd. dirs. Delta Dental, 1987—92, Downtown Lincoln Assn., 1985—94, mem. steering com., 1989; mem. mayor's com. Study Downtown Redevel., 1989, pub. bldg. commn., masterplan rev. com., 1994; bd. dirs. Bryan LBN Found.; pres. Lincoln Ctr. Assn., 1979. Recipient Honor award Conf. on Religious Architecture-First Plymouth Ch. Addition, 1969, also numerous state and nat. awards from archtl. orgns.; inducted into Hall of Fame, Iowa H.S. Athletic Assn., 2001. Mem. AIA (Nebr. bd. dirs. 1964-65, treas. 1965, sec. 1966, v.p. 1967, pres. Nebr. 1968, mem. com. on architecture for health 1980-94, Regional Design award 1976, 88, 96), Am. Assn. Health Planners, Interfaith Forum on Religion, Art, Architecture, Lincoln C. of C. (bd. dirs. 1982), Exec. Club (pres. 1972), Crucible Club, 12 Club, Hillcrest Country Club (pres. 1977), Lincoln U. Club (sec. 1992, bd. dirs. 1991-97, pres. 1995, 96, teammates mentor 2000—). Avocations: travel, photography, golf. Home: 3545 Calvert St Lincoln NE 68506-5744 Office: Davis Design 211 N 14th St Lincoln NE 68508-1616 Personal E-mail: jh3545@aol.com.

STANGE, SHARON (SHERRI), science educator; d. Edwin and Thelma Lowry; life ptnr. Donald Domenigoni; children: Brian, Karla Sluis. AA, Mt. San Jacinto Coll., 1972—77; BSc, U. of Calif., 1978—81; M, LaVerne U., 1995—96. Teaching Credential Calif. State U., San Bernardino, 1982. Tchg. asst. Kiddie Korners Preschool, Hemet, Calif., 1972—74; biology lab asst. Mt. San Jacinto Coll., San Jacinto, Calif., 1973—82; sci. tchr. San Jacinto Unified Sch. Dist., Calif., 1982—; sub. tchr. Hemet Unified Sch. Dist., Calif., 1979—82; environ. sci. tchr. Mt. San Jacinto Coll., 1989—90. Mentor tchr. San Jacinto Unified Sch. Dist., 1998—, green schools coord., 2004—; profl. affairs/scholarship chair Delta Kappa Gamma/Gamma Theta chpt., 1999—; scholarship chair Gene Lombard Meml. Scholarship, 2001—; sci. club advisor Monte Vista and North Mountain Mid. Sch., San Jacinto, 1982—98; cheerleading advisor Monte Vista Mid. Sch., San Jacinto, 1984—92; sci. fair coord. Monte Vista Mid. Sch./North Mountain Mid. Sch., San Jacinto, 1982—2001; sci. dept. chair Monte Vista and North Mountain Mid. Sch., San Jacinto, 1982—. Co-founder Valley Youth Task Force, Hemet/San Jacinto, Calif., 1991—93; leader Neighborhood Watch, Hemet/San Jacinto, 1991—98; mem. PTA, Hemet/San Jacinto, 1973—2005, Friends of the No. San Jacinto Valley, 1995—2005. Recipient Calif. Environ. Edn. award, State of Calif., 1995, Inland Empire Environ. Educator of the Yr., Calif. State U. San Bernardino, 1994, Outstanding Biology Achievement, Mt. San Jacinto Coll., 1976, Environ. Edn. award, Nat. Audubon Soc., 1991, We Honor Ours award, Calif. Teachers Assn., 1992, 1994; Audubon Naturalist grant, Hemet Valley Women's Club, 1995. Mem.: NSTA, San Jacinto Teachers Assn./CTA/NEA (pres., v.p., site rep, San Gorgonia coun. rep 1983—2005), Mt. San Jacinto Coll. Alumni Assn. (life; v.p.), Living Desert Assn., Nat. Audubon Soc./San Bernardino Valley chpt. (v.p./edn. chair/idyllwild christmas bird count compiler 1980—2005). Avocations: fishing, camping, travel, birdwatching. Office: North Mountain Middle Sch 1202 E 7th St San Jacinto CA 92583 Home Phone: 951-925-4007; Office Phone: 951-487-7797.

STANGEL, PHILIP DAVID, secondary school educator, band instructor; s. Benjamin Wencil and Beverly Ann Stangel; m. Mary Lee Egger, Apr. 12, 1959; children: David, Matthew. MusB Edn., St. Norbert Coll., De Pere, Wis., 1979. Cert. instrumental music edn. Wis., 1979. Grades 7 - 9 band instr. Green Bay (Wis.) Pub. Schools, 1979—80; grades 5 - 12 band instr. Freedom (Wis.) Area Pub. Schools, 1980—99; grades 9 - 12 band instr. / woodwind emphasis Pulaski (Wis.) Cmty. Schools, 1999—. Recipient Teachers are Tops award, NBC Channel 26, 1998—99. Mem.: NEA, Green Bay City Band, Nat. Band Assn., N.Am. Saxophone Alliance, Am. Fedn. Musicians, Music Educators Nat. Conf., Wis. Band Masters Assn. (pres. 1997—98), Harley Owners Group, Nat. Railroad Mus. Democrat. Roman Catholic. Avocations: tour guide, bicycling, reading, performing. Office: Pulaski High Sch 1040 South Saint Augustine Street Pulaski WI 54162 E-mail: pdstangel@pulaski.k12.wi.us.

STANGER, ILA, editor-in-chief; b. NYC; d. Jack Simon and Shirley Ruth (Nadelson) S. BA, Bklyn. Coll., 1961. Feature and travel editor Harpers Bazaar, NYC, 1969-75; exec. editor Travel and Leisure mag., NYC, 1975-85; editor in chief Food and Wine Mag., NYC, 1985-89, Travel and Leisure mag., NYC, 1990-93; mng. editor More mag., NYC, 1993—. Writer on arts, features and travel. Mem. Am. Soc. Mag. Editors Office: More Magazine 375 Lexington New York NY 10017 Office Phone: 212-499-1766. Business E-Mail: ila.stanger@meredith.com.

STANGER, JOHN GOODMAN, literature and language professor, archivist; b. Chgo., 1940; s. Julius John and Rosamond Fixmer Stanger; m. Carol Jean Lenling, June 27, 1965; children: John, Jeanne, Jennifer. BA, Ill. Coll., Jacksonville, 1961; diploma, Atlanta Law Coll., 1964; MA, Concordia U., River Forest, Ill., 1967. Cert. tchr. grades 13-14 Ill. Tchr. English and history Sch. Dist. 89, Maywood, Ill., 1966—2000; instr. English Triton Coll., River Grove, 1968—77; instr. reading Concordia U., River Forest, 1977—79, instr. English, 1999, Morton Coll., Cicero, 2000—01, Wright Coll., Chgo., 2000—01; prof. English Elmhurst Coll., 2001—. History fair sponsor Melrose Pk. Sch., Ill., 1990—2000, supr. student tchrs. history, 1986—97, sponsor sch. newspaper, 1975—91. Editor: English: Argumentation, 2003, English Composition I, 2004, Prominent Pen Pals, 2005, English, 2006; author: Argumentation II, 2006, Writing Across the Curriculum, 2007; guest columnist: Wednesday Jour. Mem. econ. com. Village of Oak Park, Ill., 1983; archivist Grace Luth. Ch., River Forest, 2005—; mem. reunion planning com. Oak Park-River Forest H.S., 2005—. Capt. Ill. Nat. Guard, 1964—65. Mem.: ROMEOS, Soc. Am. Archivists, Kappa Delta Pi, Alpha Phi Sigma, Pi Gamma Mu, Phi Alpha Theta. Lutheran. Avocations: reading, sports, writing. Office: Elmhurst Coll 190 Prospect Ave Elmhurst IL 60126-3296 Home: 727 Gunderson Ave Oak Park IL 60304 Office Phone: 630-617-3475. Business E-Mail: stangerj@elmhurst.edu.

STANGL, PETER E., transportation executive; BA, MA, Univ. Conn. With Met. Transp. Authority, NY, 1980—95; pres. Metro North Railroad, NY, 1983—91; chmn., CEO Met. Transp. Authority, NY, 1991—95; pres. Bombardier Transit Corp., 1995—2000, Bombardier Transp. US, 2000—03; non-exec. chmn. Laidlaw Internat., Naperville, Ill., 2003—. Past vice chmn. Am. Public Transit Assn. Office: Laidlaw International Ste 400 55 Shuman Blvd Naperville IL 60563 *

STANHAUS, JAMES STEVEN, lawyer; b. Evergreen Park, Ill., Oct. 22, 1945; s. Wilfrid Xavier and Mary (Komanecky) S.; m. Naomi Evelyn Miller, June 27, 1971; 1 child, Heather. AB magna cum laude, Georgetown U., 1966; JD magna cum laude, Harvard U., 1970. Bar: Ill. 1970, U.S. Dist. Ct. (no. dist.) Ill. 1970. Assoc. Mayer, Brown, Rowe & Maw LLP, Chgo., 1971-76, ptnr., 1977—2005, sr. counsel, 2005—. Mem. ABA, Ill. Bar Assn., Chgo. Bar Assn., Chgo. Coun. Lawyers, Chgo. Estate Planning Coun., Met. Club, Riverpark Club (Chgo.), Phi Beta Kappa. Avocations: computers, tennis, racquetball. Office: Mayer Brown Rowe & Maw LLP 71 S Wacker Dr Ste 3300 Chicago IL 60606-4637 Office Phone: 312-701-7135. Business E-Mail: jstanhaus@mayerbrownrowe.com.

STANISH, CHARLES, anthropologist, educator; BA, Pa. State U., 1979; AM, U. Chgo., 1983, PhD, 1985. Postdoctoral rsch. fellow, vis. asst. prof. dept. anthropology U. Ill., Chgo., 1986—87; asst. curator dept. anthropology Field Mus. Natural Hist., 1988—92, assoc. curator, 1993—97; assoc. prof. dept. anthropology UCLA, 1998—2000, prof., 2001—, interim dir. Cotsen Inst. Archaeology, 2001—03, dir. Cotsen Inst. Archaeology, 2003—; rsch. assoc. dept. anthropology LA County Mus. Natural Hist., 2001—. Adj. assoc. prof. grad. coll. dept. anthropology U. Ill., Chgo., 1988—97; adj. prof. dept. anthropology U. Chgo., 1990—97; vice chair dept. anthropology Field Mus. Natural Hist., 1993—95, chair, 1995—97. Contbr. articles to profl. jours., chapters to books; co-editor: Ecology, Settlement and Hist. in the Osmore Drainage, 1989, Archaeol. Rsch. on the Islands of the Sun and Moon, Lake Titicaca Bolivia: Final Results from the Proyecto Tiksi Kjarka, 2004; author: Ancient Andean Polit. Economy, 1992, Ancient Titicaca: The Evolution of Complex Soc. in Southern Peru and Northern Bolivia, 2003; co-author: Archaeol. Rsch. at the Site of Tumatumani Juli, Peru, 1994, Archaeol. Survey in the Juli-Desaguadero Area, Lake Titicaca Basin, Peru, 1997, Ritual and Pilgrimage in the Ancient Andes. The Islands of the Sun and Moon, 2001; mem. editl. bd.: Latin Am. Antiquity, 1998—. Fellow: Am. Acad. Arts & Scis. Office: Dept Anthropology UCLA 341 Haines Hall Los Angeles CA 90095-7553 E-mail: stanish@anthro.ucla.edu.

STANISLAO, JOSEPH, engineering educator, consultant; b. Manchester, Conn., Nov. 21, 1928; s. Eduardo and Rose (Zaccaro) S.; m. Bettie Chloe Carter, Sept. 6, 1960. BS, Tex. Tech. U., Lubbock, 1957; MS, Pa. State U., Univ. Park, 1959; DSc in Industrial Engring, Columbia U., NYC, 1970. Registered profl. engr., Mass., Mont. Asst. engr. Naval Ordnance Research, University Park, Pa., 1958-59; asst. prof. N.C. State U., Raleigh, 1959-61; dir. rsch. Darlington Fabrics Corp., Pawtucket, RI, 1961-62; from asst. prof. to prof. U. R.I., Kingston, 1962-71; prof., chmn. dept. Cleve. State U., 1971-75; prof., dean N.D. State U., Fargo, 1975-94, acting v.p. agrl. affairs, 1983-85, asst. to pres., 1983—, dir. Engring. Computer Ctr., 1984—, prof. emeritus indsl. engring. and mgmt. Fargo, 1994—; pres. XOX Corp., 1984-90; chmn. bd., CEO ATSCO, 1989-94, chief engr., 1993—; prof. emeritus N.D. State U., 1994. Adj. prof. Mont. State U., 1994—, dir. indsl. and mgmt. engring. program, 1996—, mfg. rsch., sponsored by Nat. Sci. Found. 1997—; pres., CEO J&B Inc., 1996—2006; v.p., co-owner, bd. dirs. D.T.&J., Inc., Fargo, N.D., 1999-2006, London, 1999—; v.p. engring. Roll-A-Ramp, Rolla-A-Latter, and Rolla-A-conveyor, 2000-05; cons. to healthcare sys., 1999-2005. Contbr. chpts. to books, articles to profl. jours. Served to sgt. USMC, 1948-51. Recipient Sigma Xi award, 1968; Order of the Iron Ring award N.D. State U., 1972, Econ. Devel. award, 1991; named Best Tchr., Alpha Pi Mu, 2005; USAF recognition award, 1979, ROTC appreciation award, 1982. Mem. Am. Inst. Indsl. Engrs. (sr.; v.p. 1964-65), ASME, Order of the Engr., Am. Soc. Engring. Edn. (campus coord. 1979-81), Acad. Indsl. Engrs. Tex. Tech U., Lions, Elks, Am. Legion, Phi Kappa Phi, Tau Beta Pi (advisor 1978-79). Roman Catholic. Achievements include patents for pump apparatus, pump fluid housing, roll-conveyer, and handicap loading dock; roll-a-ramp; invention of Telescopic Sliding Ramp, Thermal-Brick. Avocations: pool, billiards. Home: 8 Park Plaza Dr Bozeman MT 59715-9343 Office: Mont State U M&IE Dept 304 Roberts Hall Bozeman MT 59717-3800 Office Phone: 406-994-5943. Personal E-mail: bstanislao2314@msn.com. Business E-Mail: jstanslo@ie.montana.edu.

STANKEVITZ, DIANE LYNN, athletic trainer; b. West Covina, Calif., May 7, 1963; d. Richard Joseph Stankevitz and Geraldine Ann Vezzuso. BS, UCLA, 1996; MS, Calif. State U., Long Beach, 1998. Cert. athletic trainer Nat. Athletic Trainer's Assn., 2000, strength and conditioning specialist NSCA, 1999, MT L.A. County Dept. of Health, 1998. Athletic trainer East L.A. Coll., Monterey Park, Calif., 2000—, instr., 2000—, Rio Hondo Coll., Whittier, Calif., 2001—. Prodr.(stand-up comedienne): (comedy) The Comedy Train. Scholarship fundraiser The Comedy Train, West Covina, Calif., 2001. Recipient Faculty Appreciation award, Student Body of Rio Hondo Coll., 2004. Mem.: Nat. Strength and Conditioning Assn. (assoc.), Nat. Athletic Trainer's Assn. (assoc.), Phi Kappa Phi (life). Home: 1818 Sam Diego St West Covina CA 91790 Office: East Los Angeles College 1301 Avenida Cesar Chavez Monterey Park CA 91754 Home Phone: 626-833-5763; Office Phone: 323-265-8611. Office Fax: 323-265-8909. E-mail: distanky@hotmail.com.

STANKEY, JOHN T., information technology executive; m. Shari Stankey; 3 children. B finance, Loyola Marymount Univ., 1985; MBA, UCLA, 1991. Exec. dir. advanced comm. network, local wholesale ops. Pacific Bell, 1985—98; v.p. industry markets SBC Comm. Inc., 1998—2000, pres. industry markets, 2000—02, pres., CEO SBC Southwestern Bell, 2002—03, sr. exec. v.p., chief tech. officer, 2003—06, AT&T Inc., 2006—. Named one of Premier 100 IT Leaders, Computerworld, 2006, Top 25 Chief Tech. Officers, InfoWorld mag., 2006. Office: AT&T Inc 175 E Houston St San Antonio TX 78205

STANKIEWICZ, JAMES A., otolaryngologist; b. Chgo., Ill., Oct. 30, 1948; Attended, U. Chgo., Ill., 1966—70, MD, 1974. Cert. Otolaryngology. Resident, basic surgery U. Chgo., Ill., 1974—75, resident, otolaryngology Ill., 1975—78; team physician Ill. HS, 1975—76; otolaryngology cons., student and employee health clinic U. Chgo., 1976—78; lectr. U. Chgo. Med. Sch., 1977—78; otology clerk Pub. Health Svc., 1977; asst. chief otology US Navy-Navy Regional Med. Ctr., Oakland, Calif., 1978—79, otolaryngology staff, chief otology, 1979—80; clin. assoc., dept otolaryngology U. Calif., San Francisco, 1979—80; asst. prof., dept. otolaryngology-head and neck surgery Loyola U. Med. Ctr., Stritch Sch. Medicine, 1980—85, assoc. prof.-tenure, dept. otolaryngology-head and neck surgery, 1986—90, prof., dept. otolaryngology-head and neck surgery, 1990—, vice-chmn., dept. otolaryngology-head and neck surgery, 1987—, chmn. dept. otolaryngology-head and neck surgery, 2005, attending physician-full time, dept. otolaryngology-head and neck surgery, 1980—; attending physician, dept. otolaryngology-head and neck surgery, cons. Hines Veterans Hosp., Hines, Ill., 1980—; attending physician (courtesy staff) Children's Meml. Hosp. Chgo., Ill., 1984—; residency program dir., dept. otolaryngology-head and neck surgery Stritch Sch. Medicine, 1995—. Co-dir., Loyola U. Health Sys. Nasal Sinus Ctr.; cert. occupational hearing conservationist, 1977—; presenter in field. Contbr. chapters to books, articles to profl. jours.; mem. editl. bd. Operative Techniques in Head and Neck Surgery, Sinus Newsletter, Vanderbilt U., Ear, Nose, Throat Jour., St. Louis, Mo., Otolaryngology-Head and Neck Surgery, 2005—, mem. internat. editl. bd., 2004—07, reviewer for several profl. jours. Fellow: Am. Coll. Surgeons, Am. Acad. Otolaryngology-Head and Neck Surgery (Honors award, New Orleans, La. 1989, First Place Poster President's award, San Diego, Calif. 1990); mem.: Am. Acad. Otolaryngology Allergy, Sinus and Allergy Health Partnership, Soc. Univ. Otolaryngologists-Head and Neck Surgeons, Parmly Hearing Inst.-Loyola U., Am. Cleft Palate-Craniofacial Assn., Am. Rhinologic Soc. (chmn., CME com. 1994—2005, cons. 1995—96, bd. dir. 1998—2001, 2005—06, 2nd v.p. 2005—06, 1st v.p. 2007—), Am. Broncho-Esophagological Assn., Am. Acad. Pediatrics-Specialty Divsn., Pan American Head and Neck Soc., Pacific Coast Oto-Ophthalmological Soc., Chgo. Laryngological and Otological Soc. (pres. 1994—95), Ill. State Med. Soc., Chgo. Med. Soc., AMA. Office: Loyola U Med Ctr Stritch Sch Medicine 2160 S First Ave Maywood IL 60153 Office Phone: 708-216-9183. Office Fax: 708-216-3835, 708-216-4834.

STANLEY, ALESSANDRA, critic; Corr. NY Times, Moscow, co-chief Moscow bur., chief Rome bur., chief TV critic NYC. Office: NY Times Culture Desk 229 W 43rd St New York NY 10036 Office Phone: 212-556-8892. Office Fax: 212-556-1516.

STANLEY, BRIAN JORDAN, lawyer; b. Duncan, Okla., Sept. 10, 1954; s. Elmer E. and Betty Sue Stanley; m. Ruth Anne Lynn Stanley, Apr. 6, 1979 (div. Mar. 1989); children: Lindsey Jordan, Brent Alan; m. Francine Michelle La Valle, Oct. 18, 1996. BA in Polit. Sci., U. Okla., 1979; JD with honors, Oklahoma City U., 1985. Bar: (Okla.) 1985, (U.S. Dist. Ct. (we. dist.) Okla.); cert. comml. investment mem. Sports writer The Norman (Okla.) Transcript, 1979-80; oil and gas landman Milt McCullough, Oklahoma City, 1980-81; trust officer Liberty Nat. Bank & Trust, Oklahoma City, 1981-83; atty. Michael P. Rogalin, Oklahoma City, 1985-86, William H. Mattoon, Norman, 1986-87, Fed. Deposit Ins. Corp., Oklahoma City, 1987, Reed, Shadid & Pipes, Oklahoma City, 1987-88, Mosburg, Sears, Kunzman & Bollinger, Oklahoma City, 1988; v.p., corp. gen. counsel, bd. dirs. The Hefner Co., Inc., Oklahoma City, 1989—. Contbr. articles to profl. jours. Mem.: NRA, Mensa. Libertarian. Roman Catholic. Avocations: politics, music. Office: The Hefner Co Inc PO Box 2177 Oklahoma City OK 73101-2177 Home Phone: 405-321-2069; Office Phone: 405-236-4404. Business E-Mail: bstanley@hefnerco.com.

STANLEY, (MALCHAN) CRAIG, school system administrator, consultant, psychologist, researcher; b. Boston, Nov. 19, 1948; s. Harry Eugene and Ruth (Shultz) S.; 1 child, Jessica. BA in Psychology, Antioch Coll., Yellow Springs, Oh., 1971; MEd, Boston State Coll., 1975; EdD, Boston Coll., 1992. Counselor Fernald Sch., Waltham, Mass., 1970-71, psychologist, 1975; tchr. Boston Pub. Schs., 1972-74; sch. psychologist EdCo, Inc., Brookline, Mass., 1975-76, Greater Lawrence Ednl. Collaborative, Lawrence, Mass., 1976-77, exec. dir., 1977—2004; ret., 2004; ednl. cons., 2004—. Sec. adv. commn. Mass. Dept. Edn., 1981-84; treas. Mass. Orgn. Ednl. Collaboratives, 1988-93, pres., 1993-95. Chmn. Greater Lawrence Interagy. Task Force, 1980—83; clk. Middleton Planning Bd., 1991—96; trustee Middleton Congl. Ch., 2001—04. Recipient Ednl. Excellence award, Pioneer Inst., 2003, E. Robert Stephens Rsch. award, AESA, 2003. Mem.: USCG Aux., Assn. Ednl. Svc. Agys. (exec. coun. 1997—2000). Home: 19 Gates Rd Middleton MA 01949-1924 Office Phone: 978-777-4775. E-mail: craig77@comcast.net.

STANLEY, DANIEL RAYMOND, SR., federal agency administrator; b. Kansas City, Kans., Sept. 29, 1951; s. Winfield Scott and Irene May (Flint) S.; m. Kay Carrol Armstead, Jan. 4, 1970; children: Elizabeth Kay, Daniel Raymond Jr. Student, U. Kans., 1970-73; BS in Nuclear Tech., SUNY, Albany, 1979. Enlisted USN, 1973, advanced through grades to lt., weapons officer, 1980-83; officer Office Joint Chiefs of Staff, Washington, 1983-85; resigned, 1985; mgr. strategic and space systems Washington Studies and Analysis Group, Arlington, Va., 1985-87; mgr. bus. planning McDonnell Douglas Corp., St. Louis, 1987; adminstrv. asst. Office of Senator Robert J. Dole, Kans.; commr. Postal Rate Commn., 1996—2000; prin. dep. asst. sec., manpower, reserve affairs, Dept. Army, US Dept. Def., dep. asst. sec., Senate affairs, prin. dep. asst. sec., legis. affairs, acting asst. sec. legis. affairs, 2005, asst. sec., legis. affairs, 2005—. Contbr. articles to profl. jours. Mem., analyst Stanton Group, Washington, 1986, Dole for Pres. Def. Policy, Washington, 1987; cubmaster Boy Scouts Am., Springfield, Va., 1987. Mem. Assn. of Army, Armed Forces Communication and Electronics Assn., Submarine League. Clubs: Army-Navy Country (Arlington). Avocation: golf. Office: Asst Sec Legis Affairs Rm 3E966 Dept Defense 1300 Defense Pentagon Washington DC 20301-1300 Office Phone: 703-697-6210.

STANLEY, DAVID JOHN, research and development company executive; b. Camp Lejeune, NC, Mar. 8, 1951; s. Herbert Nelson Stanley and Mildred Bennet Davis; m. Judy Jennifer Mattie, June 13, 1998 (div. Nov. 28, 2006); children: Kristin E. Patrie, Caralissa Caprice, Jennifer M. Chambers, Siteris Olyssa Mattie-Stanley. Attended, Aberdeen High Sch., Md., 1970. Cert. explosive ordnance disposal US Army, 1971. Cons. Ordnance Cons., Pueblo, 1991; ammunition insp. Dir. Logistics, 1991—93, logistics, 1994—96; mil. logistics instr. B & T Svcs., Fort Carson, Colo., 1999—2005; pres., CEO, founder Pikes Peak Cargo Secure, Inc., Colo. Springs, 2002—; exec. v.p., founder Invention Venture, Inc., Denver, 2005—. Chief warrant officer three US Army, 1970—91, Many Locations. Decorated MSM, ARCOM, NDSM, Overseas, EOD, German Silver EIC US Army. Mem.: Rocky Mt. Inventors Assn. (assoc.). Independent. Bapt. Achievements include patents for cargo tie-down system; patents pending for cargo securement devices; trademark variable all terrain tiedown systems; development of shelter systems for the military; container systems for the military. Avocations: travel, reading. Office: Pikes Peak Cargo Secure Inc 4740 Forge Rd Ste 112 Colorado Springs CO 80907 Home Phone: 719-243-2986; Office Phone: 719-579-0476. Office Fax: 719-538-5935; Home Fax: 719-538-5935. Personal E-mail: vatts@comcast.net. Business E-Mail: david.stanley@ppcsinc.com.

STANLEY, DEIRDRE, lawyer; b. Huntsville, Ala. BA, Duke U.; JD, Harvard U., 1989. With Cravath, Swaine & Moore, NYC and London, 1990—97; assoc. gen. counsel, head mergers and acquisitions group GTE Corp., 1997—99; dep. gen. counsel USA Networks, Inc. (now InterActive Corp.), 1999—2002; sr. v.p., gen. counsel The Thomson Corp., 2002—. Office: The Thomson Corp Toronto-Dominion Bank Tower 66 Wellington St W Toronto Canada M5K 1A1

STANLEY, DUFFY B., architect, planner; b. Midland, Tex., Feb. 14, 1923; s. Benjamin M. and Mary L. (White) S.; m. Irene M. Muller, July 31, 1948; children: Sheila, Lars, Brock, Sonya, Sharon. BArch, Tex. A&M U., 1948; diploma (hon.), U. Autonoma de Cd. Juarez, Mex., 1977. Registered architect, Tex., N.Mex.; cert. Nat. Coun. Archtl. Registration Bds. Draftsman, designer J.J. Black, Architect, Midland, 1948-51; job capt. Carroll & Daeuble Architects, El Paso, Tex., 1951-57; pvt. practice El Paso, 1957—. Lectr. in field. Author: Open Space in the El Paso Region, 1970. Vice chmn. Citizens Environ. Coun. of El Paso, 1972—73; chmn. GARC com. West Tex. Coun. Govts., El Paso, 1977; chmn. El Paso County Hist. Commn., 1978, Zoning Bd. of Adjustment, El Paso, 1959—70; mem. Open Space Com., El Paso, 1970—71; bd. dirs. Mission Heritage Assn. of El Paso, 1977—84. Capt. US Army, 1943—46, ETO. Decorated Combat Inf. badge, Bronze Star, Silver Star; recipient Caudill award, Tex. Assn. Sch. Bds. and AIA Tex., 1996. Fellow AIA (chpt. pres. 1964, Design award 1995, Service to Profession award 1991, Lifetime Achievement award El Paso chpt. 2004). Avocations: reading, family. Office: 303 Texas Ave Ste 704 El Paso TX 79901-1452

STANLEY, E. RICHARD, biomedical researcher; b. Sydney, NSW, Australia, Sept. 26, 1944; came to US 1977; s. Neville Fenton and Muriel (MacDonald) S.; m. Pamela Mary Fetherstonhaugh, Feb. 6, 1970; children: Damian Alexander, Robert Fenton. BSc with honors, U. Western Australia, 1967; PhD in Med. Biology, U. Melbourne, Australia, 1970. Mem. sr. sci. staff Ont. Cancer Inst., Toronto, 1972-77; lectr. dept. medicine and biophysics U. Toronto, 1972-73, asst. prof., 1973-77; asst. prof. dept. microbiol. and Immunology, cell biology Albert Einstein Coll. Medicine, Bronx, 1977-79, assoc. prof., 1979-84, prof., 1984-87, Renee and Robert A. Belfer prof. devel. biology, chair dept. devel. and molecular biology, 1987—. Cons. Cetus Corpn., Emeryville, Calif., 1983; sci. adv. bd. Internat. Coun. for Coordination Cancer Rsch., NYC, 1989. Contbr. articles to profl. jours. Named to Roll of Honor, Internat. Union Against Cancer; recipient Scholar award, Leukemia Soc. Am., 1977, Irma T. Hirschl Career Scientist award, 1983, Marie T. Bonazinga Rsch. award, Soc. Leukocyte Biology, 1989, Method to Extend Rsch. in Time (MERIT) award, NIH, 1989, 2002, E. Donnall Thomas prize, Am. Soc. Hematology, 2006. Achievements include isolation and characterisation of growth factor, colony stimulating factor-1 and its receptor; cloning CSF-1 gene; establishment of the biological importance of CSF-1 in regulation of white cell production and placental function. Office: Dept Devel and Molecular Biology Albert Einstein Coll Med 1300 Morris Park Ave Bronx NY 10461-1926 E-mail: rstanley@aecom.yu.edu.

STANLEY, EDWARD ALEXANDER, geologist, paleontologist, researcher, retired director, forensic specialist; b. NYC, Apr. 7, 1929; s. Frank and Elizabeth (Wolf) S.; m. Elizabeth Ann Allison, June 7, 1958; children: Karen (dec.), Scott. BS, Rutgers U., 1954; MS, Pa. State U., 1956, PhD, 1960. Rsch. geologist Amoco Petroleum Co., Tulsa, Okla., 1960-62; prof. U. Del., 1962-64, U. Ga., 1964-77; assoc. dean rsch., chmn. geology dept. Indiana (Pa.) U., 1977-81; supr. biostratigraphy Phillips Petroleum Co., Bartlesvill, Okla., 1981-86; dir., comdg. officer NYC Police Dept. Crime Lab., 1986—94; pvt. practice, 1994—. Cons. in field. Contbr. articles to profl. jours. Served to sgt. U.S. Army Air Corps/USAF, 1947—50. Grantee NSF, 1965-68, 74, Rsch. grant Office Water Resources, 1965-68; NAS exch. prof. Soviet Union, 1968-69, 73; invited guest Moscow Police Dept. Forensic Labs., 1990; invited speaker FBI Internat. Symposium on Forensic Trace Evidence, 1991, 98; recipient Commemorative medal of the lab. Dept. Botany, Jozsef Attilla U., Szeged, Hungary, 2000, Millenium medal, 2000. Fellow: AAAS, Geol. Soc. Am.; mem.: Am. Soc. Crime Lab. Dirs., Am. Acad. Forensic Sci., Am. Assn. Petroleum Geologists, Sigma Xi. Presbyterian. Avocations: photography, music, firearms. Home: 578 Myrtle Ct Harrisburg PA 17112-2255 Personal E-mail: eas.aquila7@verizon.net.

STANLEY, ELIOT HUNGERFORD, small business owner, writer, lawyer; b. Baton Rouge, Jan. 4, 1942; s. Allan John Stanley and Ruth Ristine Moore; m. Julia Frances Adams, Aug. 29, 1981. BA in History, Harvard U., 1963; JD, George Washington U., 1972. Legis. asst. U.S. Sen. Fred Harris, Washington, 1964—65; mem. congl. liaison staff Office of Sec. HUD, Washington, 1965—66; staff dir. Hon. Chet Holifield, Washington, 1967—69; assoc. dir. Citizens Advocate Ctr., Washington, 1970—72; acting regional counsel U.S. Commn. Civil Rights, NYC, 1973—76, legal cons. Washington, 1977—81; owner, CEO New Eng. Antigenics, Portland, Maine, 1982—2003; cons., 2003—. Mem. Gov. of Maine's Trade Mission to Brazil and Argentina, 1997; mem. seminar on def. and nat. security Brookings Inst., Washington, 1967; mem. advance staff Hubert Humphrey Campaign for Pres., 1968. Author: (short stories) River Coffee and Five Others, 1995; editor: The Jewel (by Rockwell Kent), 1990 (1st pl. graphic arts award, 91); author: Nat. Report on Police Practices, U.S. Commn. on Civil Rights, 1981. Commr. Portland Civil Svc. Commn., 2003—05; mem. Maine Regulatory Fairness Bd., 2006—; speech writer Sargent Shriver Campaign for V.P. U.S., 1972. Recipient Disting. Svc. award, U.S. Commn. on Civil Rights, 1975. Mem.: Linnaean Soc. N.Y., Baxter Soc. Maine (founder, 1st pres.), Caxton Club of Chgo., Book Club of Calif. Democrat. Unitarian. Avocations: lecturing, book arts, ornithology, natural history. Office: PO Box 1822 Portland ME 04104 Office Phone: 207-773-2597. Personal E-mail: jaes15@maine.rr.com.

STANLEY, ELLEN MAY, historian, consultant; b. Dighton, Kans., Feb. 3, 1921; d. Delmar Orange and Lena May (Bobb) Durr; m. Max Neal Stanley, Nov. 5, 1939; children: Ann Y. Stanley Epps, Janet M. Stanley Horsky, Gail L. Stanley Peck, Kenneth D., Neal M., Mary E. Stanley McEniry. BA in English and Journalism, Ft. Hays State U., Kans., 1972, MA in History, 1984. Pvt. practice local/state historian, cons., writer local history, Dighton, 1973—; cons. genealogy, 1980—. Vice chmn. State Preservation Bd. Rev., Kans., 1980-87; area rep. Kans. State Mus. Assn., 1978-84. Author: Early Lane County History: 12,000 B.C.–A.D. 1884, 1993 (Cert. of Commendation, Am. Assn. for State and Local History, 1994), Cowboy Josh: Adventures of a Real Cowboy, 1996, Early Lane County Development, 1993, Golden Age, Great Depression and Dust Bowl, 2001 (Ferguson Kans. History Book award Kans. Author Club, 2002); contbr. articles to profl. jours. Precinct woman com. Alamota Township, Kans., 1962-86; mem. Dem. State Affirmative Action Com., 1975. Recipient hon. mention for photography Ann. Christian Arts Festival, 1974, Artist of Month award Dane G. Hansen Mus., 1975. Mem. Kans. State Hist. Soc. (pres. 1990-91), Lane County Hist. Soc. (sec. 1970-78). Methodist. Avocations: fossil hunting, walking, photography, antiques. Home: 100 N 4th Dighton KS 67839 Office: 110 E Pearl St Dighton KS 67839

STANLEY, GWEN G., elementary school educator; b. Abbington, Pa., Feb. 11, 1954; d. Richard A. and Doris K. Guba; m. Ray L. Stanley, June 6, 1976; children: R. L., Sarah Rae. BA, Maryville Coll., 1977; MA in Edn., Ga. State U., 2002, D of Edn., 2003. Nat. Bd. Cert. Tchr. US, 2001, cert. asst. tchr. 2005. Libr. educator Whittier County Schs., Calif., 1976—79; tchr. Montessori Sch. of Ligonier, Ligonier, Pa., 1981—83, Ligonier Bd. of Edn., 1985—88, Perston Ridge Monetssori Sch., Alpharetta, Ga., 1990—92, Forsyth County Bd. of Edn., Cumming, Ga., 1992—, Ga. State U., Atlanta, 2004—. Presentor Internat. Reading Assn., Reno, 2003—04; standards and benchmarks contbr. Forsyth County Schs., Ga., 2000—01. Contbr. seminar on literacy. Recipient Tchr. of Yr., 2002. Office: Forsyth County Schs 1670 James Burgess Rd Suwanee GA 30024 Home Phone: 770-475-2153; Office Phone: 770-888-7511. Personal E-mail: gstanley@forsyth.k12.ga.us.

STANLEY, HARRY EUGENE, physicist, researcher; b. Norman, Okla., Mar. 28, 1941; s. Harry Eugene and Ruth S.; m. Idahlia (Dessauer), June 2, 1967 (dec. Mar. 2003); children: Jannah, Michael, Rachel. BA in Physics, Wesleyan U., 1962; postgrad., U. Cologne, Germany, 1962—63; PhD in Physics, Harvard U., 1967; PhD (hon.), Bar Ilan U., Ramat Gan, Israel, 1994, Roland Eötvös U., Budapest, Hungary, 1997, U. Liege, 2001, U. Dortmund, 2001, U. Wroclaw, 2004. NSF pre-doctoral rsch. fellow Harvard U., Mass., 1963—67; mem. staff Lincoln lab. MIT, Cambridge, 1967—68, asst. prof. physics, 1969—71, assoc. prof., 1971—73; Miller rsch. fellow U. Calif., Berkeley, 1968—69; Hermann von Helmholtz assoc. prof. health sci. and tech. Health Sci. and Tech. Program Harvard U., MIT, 1973—76; vis. prof. Osaka U., Japan, 1975; prof. physics, physiology Sch. Medicine, dir. ctr. polymer studies Boston U., 1976. Joliot-Curie vis. prof. Ecole Superieure de Physique et Chimie, Paris, 1979; vis. prof. Peking U., 1981, Seoul Nat. U., 1982; hon. prof. U. Pavia; 30th Ann. Saha Meml. Lecture, 1992; Sigma Xi nat. lectr., 2002-03; dir. NATO Advanced Study Inst., Cargese, Corisca, 1985, 88, 90, IUPAP Internat. Conf. on Thermodynamics and Statis. Mechanics, 1986, Enrico Fermi Sch., Varenna, Italy, 1996, 2003, Gordon Rsch. Conf. on Water and Aqueous Solutions, 1998, NATO advanced rsch. workshop, 1999, 2001; cons. Sandia Nat. Lab., 1983-94, Dowell Schlumberger Co., 1982-92, Elscint Co., 1983-85; nat. co-chmn. Com. of Concerned Scientists, 1974-76; Disting. prof. U. Paris, 2004. Author: Introduction to Phase Transitions and Critical Phenomena, 1971, From Newton to Mandelbrot: A Primer in Theoretical Physics, 1990, Fractal Forms, 1991, Fractal Concepts in Surface Growth, 1995, Cours de physique, 1999, Introduction to Econophysics: Correlations and Complexity in Finance, 2000; editor: Biomedical Physics and Biomaterials Science, 1972, Cooperative Phenomena Near Phase Transitions, 1973, On Growth and Form: Fractal and Non-Fractal Patterns in Physics, 1985, Statis. Physics, 1986, Random Fluctuation and Pattern Growth, 1988, Correlations and Connectivity: Geometric Aspects of Physics, Chemistry and Biology, 1990, Fractals in Science, 1994, Disordered Materials and Interfaces, 1996, Physics of Complex Systems, 1997, Statis. Mechanics in the Physical Biological and Social Sciences, 1997, Application of Statis. Mechanics to Practical Problems, 1999, Structure and Function of Biological Systems under Extreme Conditions, 2002, Statis. Physics, 2000, Statis. Mechanics: From Rigorous Results to Applications, 2000, Scaling in Disordered Systems, 2002, New Kinds of Phase Transitions, 2002; editor Physica A., 1988—. Recipient Choice award, Am. Assn. Book Pubs., 1972, Macdonald award, 1986, Venture Rsch. award, Brit. Petroleum, 1989, Mass. Prof. of Yr. award, Coun. Advancement and Support of Edn., 1992, Floyd K. Richtmyer prize, 1997, Turnbull prize, 1998, Memory Ride prize, 2001, NSF Disting. Tchr. Scholar prize, 2001, Nicholson medal, 2003, Boltzmann medal, 2004, Teresiana medal, 2004; Nat. Merit scholar, Wesleyan U., 1962, Fulbright scholar, U. Cologne, 1962—63, John Simon Guggenheim Meml. fellow, 1979—80. Fellow AAAS, NAS, Am. Phys. Soc. (chmn. New Eng. sect. 1982-83, Centennial lectr. 1999); mem. NAS (non-linear sci. panel), Hungarian Phys. Soc. (hon.), Brazilian Acad. Sci. (hon.). Home: 50 Metacomet Rd Waban MA 02468-1465 Office: Boston U Ctr for Polymer Studies Boston MA 02215 Office Phone: 617-353-2617. Business E-Mail: hes@bu.edu. *The greatest joy of my prof. life is to share in the excitement of learning something new, however minor about the workings of nature. The greatest joy of my personal life is to be able to imagine that I've done my very best to meet the needs of my family and my co-workers. The greatest obstacle to happiness is the persistent feeling that it is impossible to find that tortuous path whereby both joys may occasionally be experienced.*

STANLEY, HEIDI, bank executive; Grad., Wash. State U., 1979. With IBM, San Francisco, Tucson; joined Sterling Savings Bank, Spokane, Wash., 1985, exec. v.p. Corp. Adminstrn., vice chair, COO, 2003—. Vice chmn. Am.'s Cmty. Banker's Membership Com.; mem. Govt. Affairs Steering Com.; bd. govs. WSU Found., chmn. planning com. Named one of 25 Most Powerful Women in Banking, US Banker, 2006. Mem.: Spokane C. of C. (bd. mem.). Office: Sterling Savings Bank 111 N Wall St Spokane WA 99201 *

STANLEY, HELEN CAMILLE, composer, musician; b. Tampa, Fla. d. Edward and Lucy Gage (Crehore) S.; widowed; 1 child, Helen Marjorie. MusB, Cin. Conservatory Music, 1951; MusM, Fla. State U., 1954; BS, Muskingum Coll., 1961. Instr. music and fine arts Jacksonville (Fla.) U., 1962-67; instr. music in communications Jones Coll., Jacksonville, 1965-66; composer, condr. St. Paul's by-the-Sea, Jacksonville Beach, Fla., 1976; composer-in-residence, pianist Fla. Contemporary Ensemble, Jacksonville, 1986; ind. composer, lectr., pianist, 1963—. Cons. Beaches Fine Arts Series, Neptune Beach, Fla., 1973—. Composer Rhapsody for Electronic Tape and Orchestra, 1972 (Composition Commn. award), Allegro, Passacaglia, Sonata for trombone and piano, various instrumental and vocal works, Evocation I for piano; orchestral works on CD include: Fanfare for Orchestra (Warsaw Nat. Philharmonic Orch. and Owensboro Symphony), 1994, Passacaglia (St. Petersburg Philharmonic), Concerto Romantico, Prague, 1997, Fanfare for Orchestra (All American Celebration by Owensboro Symphony), 1999; composer website theme music The Living Music Found.; composer Dorian Diversion in Functional Chromaticism, 2003, Phrygiana for Piano, 2005, Concerto Romantico, 2006. Mem. Soc. Mayflower Descs., 1987—. Recipient Pogner Music Composition award, Cin., 1950, C. Hugo Ensemble Composition award, Cin., 1951, Anthem Descant award St. Paul's by-the-Sea, 1980, Art Ventures Fund award, 1992, Jacksonville Cmty. Found. award, 1994; named Outstanding Achievements Classical Music, Jacksonville, 1997. Mem. ASCAP, Am. Music Ctr., Am. Keyboard Artists, Performing Arts Directory, Pi Kappa Lambda. Avocations: art, walking, dance. Address: 1768 Emory Cir S Jacksonville FL 32207-7707 Home and Studio: Aladdin Farm 12047 Aladdin Rd Jacksonville FL 32223-3201 Office Phone: 904-268-5475. E-mail: hscomposer@aol.com.

STANLEY, HUGH MONROE, JR., lawyer; b. Ft. Lewis, Wash., Oct. 25, 1944; s. Hugh Monroe Sr. and Rita (McHugh) S.; m. Patricia Page, Aug. 17, 1968; children: Allison Michelle, Matthew Monroe, Trevor Marshall. BA magna cum laude, U. Dayton, 1966; JD, Georgetown U., 1969. Bar: Ohio 1969, U.S. Ct. Appeals (6th cir.) 1983, U.S. Supreme Ct. 1979. Assoc. Arter & Hadden, Cleve., 1969-76, ptnr., 1976—2003, chmn. litigation dept., 1983-96; ptnr. Tucker Ellis & West LLP, 2003—. Fellow Am. Bar Found., Bar Assn. Greater Cleve., Am. Coll. Trial Lawyers, Internat. Acad. Trial Lawyers, Internat. Soc. Barristers, Nat. Assn. R.R. Trial Counsel; mem. ABA, Fed. Bar Assn., Def. Rsch. Inst., Cleve. Assn. Civil Trial Attys., Ohio Assn. Civil Trial Attys. Republican. Roman Catholic. Avocation: reading. Office: Tucker Ellis & West 1150 Huntington Bldg 925 Euclid Ave Ste 1100 Cleveland OH 44115-1475 Home Phone: 440-338-6920; Office Phone: 216-696-3934. Business E-Mail: hstanley@tuckerellis.com.

STANLEY, JASON, education educator; b. Syracuse, NY, Oct. 12, 1969; s. Manfred Intrator and Sara Stanley, Mary Breya Stanley (Stepmother) and William Rivera (Stepfather); m. Njeri Thande, Aug. 18, 2001. BA, SUNY at Stony Brook, 1990; PhD, MIT, Cambridge, 1995. Lectr. U. Coll., Oxford, England; asst. prof. philosophy Cornell U., Ithaca, NY, 1995—2000; assoc. prof. philosophy U. Mich., Ann Arbor, 2000—04; prof. dept. philosophy Rutgers U., New Brunswick, NJ, 2004—. Author: Knowledge and Practical Interests, 2005, Language in Context, 2007; editor: Stanford Encyclopedia of Philosophy, 2002—; mem. editl. bd. Philosopher's Imprint, 2002—, assoc. editor Nous, 2004—. Recipient H. Lee Dennison Valedictorian, SUNY at Stony Brook, 1990; Vis. Fellow, New Coll., Oxford U., 2003, Australian Nat. U., 2003. Jewish. Avocation: blogging. Office: Rutgers U Dep Philosophy 26 Nichol Rd New Brunswick NJ 08901 Office Phone: 732-932-9861. Personal E-mail: jasoncs@rci.rutgers.edu.

STANLEY, JEAN-DANIEL, geological oceanographer; b. Metz, France, Apr. 14, 1934; came to US, 1941, naturalized, 1946; s. Paul Emile and Madeleine (Simon) Streisguth; m. Adrienne N. Ellis, Mar. 5, 1988; children: Marc Michel, Eric Paul, Brian Northrop, Natalie Anne, Susan N. B.Sc., Cornell U., 1956; M.Sc., Brown U., 1958; D.Sc., U. Grenoble, France, 1961. Rsch. geologist French Petroleum Inst., Paris, 1958-61; asst. to dir. US Waterways Expt. Sta., Vicksburg, Miss., 1961-63; asst. prof. geology Ottawa U., Ont., Canada, 1963-64; rsch. assoc. prof. Dalhousie U., Halifax, NS, Canada, 1964-66; sr. scientist, oceanographer, dir. Geoarchaeology-Global Change Program, NMNH Smithsonian Instn., Washington, 1966—; adj. prof. U. Québec, 1992—2001. Cons. to govts. Mediterranean countries; sci. expert Internat. Ct. Justice, 1981—. Editor: New Concepts of Continental Margin Sedimentation, 1969, Mediterranean Sea: A Natural Sedimentation Laboratory, 1972, Marine Sediment Transport and Environmental Management, 1976, Sedimentation in Submarine Canyons, Fans and Trenches, 1978, The Shelfbreak: A Critical Interface on Continental Margins, 1983, Geological Evolution of the Mediterranean Basin, 1985, Nile Delta, A Geological Excursion, 1997; contbr. chpts to books, articles to profl. jours. Bd. dirs. Geoarchaeology and World Deltas Programs. Served to capt. C.E., US Army, 1961-63. Recipient médaille Alpes Maritimes, France, 1976, F.P. Shepard medal Soc. for Sedimentary Geology, 1990, Gold Trident medal Italian Acad., 1998; named Hon. Prof., East China U., 1995; grantee in field. Fellow Geol. Soc. Am., AAAS, Geol. Soc. Belgium; mem. Internat. Assn. Sedimentologists, Am. Assn. Petroleum Geologists, Soc. Econ. Paleontologists and Mineralogists, Geol. Soc. Washington, Cosmos Club (Washington), Sigma Xi. Clubs: Cosmos (Washington). Office: Smithsonian Instn E205 Nl Mus Natural History Washington DC 20013-7012 Business E-Mail: stanleyd@si.edu.

STANLEY, MARGARET KING, performing arts association administrator; b. San Antonio, Dec. 11, 1929; d. Creston Alexander and Margaret (Haymore) King; children: Torrey Margaret, Jean Cullen. Student, Mary Baldwin Coll., 1948-50; BA, U. Tex., Austin, 1952; MA, U. Incarnate Word, 1959. Cert. elem. tchr. Tex. Elem. tchr. San Antonio Ind. Sch. Dist., 1953-54, 55-56, Arlington County Schs., Va., 1954-55, Ft. Sam Houston Schs., San Antonio, 1956—58; art and art history tchr. St. Pius X Sch., San Antonio, 1959-60; originator, founding chairwoman Student Music Fair, San Antonio, 1963; English tchr. Trinity U., 1963-65; designer-mfr., owner CrisStan Clothes, Inc., San Antonio, 1967-73; founder, exec. dir. San

Antonio Performing Arts Assn., 1976-92; founding chmn. Joffrey Workshop, San Antonio, 1979; radio host On Stage with Margaret Stanley Sta. KTRU-FM, San Antonio, 1983-98. Founder CrisStan Clothes, MKS Designs. Orginator with the Joffrey Ballet Jamboree, 1984. Mem. Met. Opera Nat. Coun., 1969—80; founder Arts Coun. San Antonio, 1962, v.p., 1975; pres. San Antonio Symphony League, 1971—74; v.p., founder San Antonio Opera Guild, 1974—, pres., 2002—05; bd. govs. Artists Alliance San Antonio, 1982; founder San Antonio Early Music Festival, 1990—92; artistic advisor, dir. presentation, dir. devel. San Antonio Symphony, 1992—94; founding organizer Musica San Antonio, 1997—98; v.p. Instnl. Devel. Carver Cultural Ctr., 1998—2000; adv. bd. Hertzberg Circus Collection, San Antonio Dance Umbrella, Houston Early Music, Morgan-Scott Ballet, Hot Springs Mus. Festival; pres. Univ. Roundtable, 1995—97. Named to Women's Hall of Fame, San Antonio, 1984, Disting. Alumnae, St. Mary's Hall, 1990; recipient Outstanding Tchr. award, Arlington County Sch. Dist., 1954, Emily Smith award for outstanding alumni, Mary Baldwin Coll., 1973, Today's Woman award, San Antonio Light Newspaper, 1980, Woman of the Yr. in Arts award, San Antonio Express News, 1983, Erasmus medal, Dutch Consulate, 1992, Mary Baldwin Sesquicentennial medallion, 1992, Opera Guild Founder's award, 2000, Vol. Achievement award, Opera Vols. Internat., 2005, Music Support award, Cactus Pear Festival, 2006; Tchg. fellow, Trinity U., San Antonio, 1964—66. Mem.: S.W. Performing Arts Presenters (chmn. 1988—92), Battle Flowers Assn., Jr. League San Antonio (Vol. Extraodinaire 2001), Women in Comm. (Headliner award 1982), Assn. Performing Arts Presenters (award for commn.of Jamboree 1984), Internat. Soc. for Performing Arts (hon.; regional rep. 1982—85, bd. dirs. 1991—97). Avocations: travel, reading, cooking, music, dance.

STANLEY, PETER WILLIAM, former academic administrator; b. Bronxville, NY, Feb. 17, 1940; s. Arnold and Mildred Jeanette (Pattison) Stanley; m. Mary-Jane Cullen Cosgrove, Sept. 2, 1978; 1 child, Laura. BA magna cum laude, Harvard U., 1962, MA, 1964, PhD, 1970; LHD (hon.), Occidental Coll., 1994, Rhodes Coll., 2001. Asst. prof. history U. Ill., Chgo., 1970—72, Harvard U., 1972—78, lectr. history, 1978—79; dean of coll. Carleton Coll., Northfield, Minn., 1979—84; program officer in charge edn. and culture program Ford Found., 1984—87, dir. edn. and culture program, 1987—91; pres. Pomona Coll., Claremont, Calif., 1991—2003, pres. emeritus, 2003—; v.p. Isaacson, Miller, Boston, 2004—. Lectr. Fgn. Service Inst., Arlington, Va., 1977—89. Author: A Nation in the Making: The Philippines and the United States, 1974; co-author: Sentimental Imperialists: The American Experience in East Asia, 1981; editor: Reappraising an Empire: New Perspectives on Philippine-American History, 1984; contbr. articles to profl. jours. Trustee The Coll. Bd., 1991—99, vice-chmn., 1993—94, chmn., 1994—96, Barnard Coll., 2000—06; humanities and scis. coun. Stanford U., 1986—2002; nat. adv. coun. Nat. Fgn. Lang. Ctr., 1991—2002; bd. dirs. The James Irvine Found., 1997—2006, chmn., 2003—06; bd. dirs. The Pacific Basin Inst., 1998—, chmn., 1998—2003; bd. dirs. The Hitachi Found., 1993—2000, Assn. Am. Colls. and Univs., 1995—2001, vice-chmn., 1998—99, chmn., 1999—2000; bd. fellows Claremont Grad. U. and Claremont U. Consortium, 1991—2003; bd. overseers Nat. Bd. Ednl. Testing and Pub. Policy, 2000—. Fellow Frank Knox Meml. fellow, Harvard U., 1962—63, Charles Warren Ctr. for Studies in Am. History fellow, 1975—76. Mem.: Coun. on Fgn. Rels., Assn. Asian Studies, Am. Hist. Assn., Phi Beta Kappa. Home: 65 Knollwood Dr Old Saybrook CT 06475 Office: Pomona Coll Pres Office Claremont CA 91711-6301

STANLEY, RALPH, bluegrass musician; b. Stratton, Va., Feb. 25, 1927; Founder (with Carter Stanley) band, Stanley Bros. and Clinch Mountain Boys, 1946, albums include: Old Country Church, Hills of Home, Old Home Place, The Stanley Sound Around The World, Plays Requests, A Man and His Music, I Want to Preach the Gospel, Cry From the Cross, Let Me Rest on Peaceful Mountain, Banjo in the Hills, Best of Bluegrass, Folk Song Festival, In Person, 1983, Collector's Edition Vols. 1-6, Long Journey Home, Rank Strangers, Clinch Mountain Country, Together for the Last Time; appeared at Royal Albert Hall, London, 1966. Recipient Living Legend award Lib. Congress, 2000, Nat. Medal Arts Nat. Endowment Arts, 2006; grammy nominations, Best Country Vocal Collaboration for Miner's Prayer" (with Dwight Yoakam), 1994, Best Bluegrass Album, Clinch Mountain Country, 1999, Best Bluegrass Album, I Feel Like Singing Today with Jim Lauderdale, others. *

STANLEY, RICHARD HOLT, consulting engineer; b. Muscatine, Iowa, Oct. 20, 1932; s. Claude Maxwell and Elizabeth Mabel (Holthues) S.; m. Mary Jo Kennedy, Dec. 20, 1953; children: Lynne Elizabeth, Sarah Catherine, Joseph Holt. BSEE, BSME, Iowa State U., 1955; MS in Sanitary Engring., U. Iowa, 1963. Registered profl. engr., Iowa. With Stanley Cons. Inc., Muscatine, Iowa, 1955—, pres., 1971-87, chmn., 1984—. Vice chmn. HNI Corp., 1979-05; chmn Nat. Constrn. Industry Coun., 1978, Com. Fed. Procurement Archtl.-Engring. Svcs., 1979; pres. Ea. Iowa CC, Bettendorf, 1966-68; mem. indsl. adv. coun. Iowa State U. Coll. Engring., Ames, 1969-97, chmn., 1979-81; bd. dirs. Stanley Cons. Inc., Muscatine, Iowa. Contbr. articles to profl. jours. Bd. dirs. N.E.-Midwest Inst., 1989-95, treas., 1991-93, chmn., 1993-95; bd. dirs. Stanley Found., 1956—, pres., 1984—, chmn., 1995—; bd. dirs. Muscatine Health Support Found., pres., 1984—; bd. dirs. Muscatine United Way, 1969-75, Iowa State U. Meml. Union, 1968-83, U. Dubuque, Iowa, 1977-93, Inst. Social and Econ. Devel., 1992-2001, Unity Healthcare, 1999-2005, chmn. 1999-2002; bd. govs. Iowa State U. Found., 1982-96. Recipient Young Alumnus award Iowa State U. Alumni Assn., 1966, Disting. Svc. award Muscatine Jaycees, 1967, Profl. Achievement citation Coll. Engring., Iowa State U., 1977, Anson Marston medal Iowa State U., 1991, Harry S. Truman disting. svc. award Am. Assn. C.C., 1998; Disting. Alumni Achievement award U. Iowa Alumni Assn., 1999, award for Citizen Diplomacy, Nat. Coun. for Internat. Visitors, 2000, Hoover medal, 2001, Order of Knoll Cardinal and Gold award Iowa State U., 2004; named Sr. Engr. of Yr., Joint Engring. Com. Quint Cities, 1973; named to Disting. Engring. Alumni Acad., U. Iowa, 1998; named to Muscatine H.S. Hall of Honor, 2000. Fellow ASCE, Am. Cons. Engrs. Cos. (chmn. 1976-77, Cmty. Svc. award 1997, Disting. Award of Merit 1998), Iowa Acad. Sci.; mem. IEEE (sr.), ASME, Am. Soc. Engring. Edn., Nat. Soc. Profl. Engrs., Cons. Engrs. Coun. Iowa (pres. 1967), Iowa Engring. Soc. (pres. 1973-74, John Dunlap-Sherman Woodward award 1967, Disting. Svc. award 1980, Voice of Engr. award 1987, Herbert Hoover Centennial award 1989), Muscatine C. of C. (pres. 1972-73), C. of C. of U.S. (constrn. action coun. 1976-91), Rotary, Tau Beta Pi, Phi Kappa Phi, Pi Tau Sigma, Eta Kappa Nu. Presbyterian (elder). Home: 516 Hogan Ct Muscatine IA 52761-2740 Office: Stanley Cons Inc Stanley Bldg Muscatine IA 52761

STANLEY, RICHARD P., mathematics professor; b. NYC, June 23, 1944; s. Alan and Shirley (Silver) S.; m. Doris S. Skulsky, July 4, 1971; children: Kenneth, Sharon. BS, Calif. Inst. Technology, 1966; PhD, Harvard U., 1971. Math. instr. MIT, Cambridge, Mass., 1970-71; Miller research fellow Miller Inst., Berkeley, Calif., 1971-73; asst. prof. applied math. MIT, Cambridge, 1973-75, assoc. prof. applied math., 1975-79, prof. applied math., 1979-2000, Norman Levinson prof. applied math., 2000—. Cons. in field. Author: Combinatorics and Commutative Algebra, 1983, 2d edit., 1996, Enumerative Combinatorics, Vol. 1, 1986, Vol. 2, 1999. Recipient SIAM Polya Prize Soc. Indsl. and Applied Math., Guggenheim Fellowship, Guggenheim Found., 1983-84, Steele prize for math. exposition, 2001, Rolf Schock prize in math Royal Swedish Acad. Scis., 2003. Fellow Am. Acad. Arts and Scis.; mem. Nat. Acad. Scis., Am. Math. Soc., Math. Assn. Am. Office: MIT Dept Math 2-375 77 Massachusetts Ave Cambridge MA 02139-4307 E-mail: rstan@math.mit.edu.

STANLEY, SCOTT, JR., editor; b. Kansas City, July 11, 1938; s. Winfield Scott and Irene Mae (Flint) S.; m. Janice Johns, Aug. 30, 1959 (dec. July 1992); children: Leslie, Scott, Margaret; m. Cynthia Ward, Dec. 30, 1995; 1 child, Elizabeth. BA, Earlham Coll., 1960. Mng. editor Am. Opinion mag., Boston, 1961-85; editor Rev. of The News mag., Boston, 1965-85; editor-in-chief Conservative Digest, Washington, 1985-88, Am. Press Internat., Washington, 1987—; pres. USA Tech., 1991-92; mng. editor Nutrition and Healing, 1994-2000; dep. editor Insight on the News, Washington, 1995—2005. Mem. nat. bd. dirs. Young Ams. for Freedom, 1960-62; public speaker and univ. lectr., 1962— Keynote speaker Am. Party Nat. Conv., 1976; pres. Ams. Legal Def. Fund, 1977—; bd. govs. Council for Nat. Policy, 1981—; bd. dirs. Free Congress Polit. Action Com., 1985-88, Conservative Caucus Found., 2006—; pres. Scott Stanley Real Estate Trust, 1988— Recipient award of merit Young Ams. for Freedom, Freedom award Nat. Congress for Freedom. Mem.: Nat. Press Club. Episcopalian. Personal E-mail: cwardstanley@cox.net.

STANLEY, SHERRY A., lawyer; b. Buffalo, Oct. 17, 1955; d. Arthur A. and Irene S. Stanley. BA, U. West Fla., 1975; JD, U. Fla., 1978. Bar: Fla. 1978. Assoc. Mahoney, Hadlow & Adams, Miami, Fla., 1978-80; ptnr. Steel, Hector & Davis, Miami, 1980-87, Weil, Gotshal & Manges, Miami, 1987-92; sr. counsel Barnett Banks, Inc., Miami, 1992-94; ptnr. Coll, Davidson, Carter, Smith, Salter & Barkett, P.A./Shook, Hardy Bacon, Miami, Fla., 1994—2000; exec. v.p., gen. counsel Greenstreet Ptnrs., 2001—; dir. Semeo Energy, Inc., 2004—05. Dir. SEMCO Energy, Inc., 2004—05. Mem.: Fla. Bar, Order of Coif, Phi Theta Kappa. Republican. Roman Catholic. Office: 2601 S Bayshore Dr Ste 800 Miami FL 33133 Home Phone: 305-667-9394; Office Phone: 305-858-8119. Business E-Mail: sas@greenstreetpartners.com.

STANLEY, STEVEN MITCHELL, paleontologist, educator; b. Detroit, Nov. 2, 1941; s. William Thomas and Mildred Elizabeth (Baker) S.; m. E. Ellen Reynolds, Dec. 28, 2005. AB with highest honors, Princeton U., 1963; PhD, Yale U., 1968. Asst. prof. U. Rochester, 1967-69; asst. prof. paleobiology Johns Hopkins U., 1969-71, assoc. prof., 1971-74, prof., 1974—2005, chmn. dept. Earth and planetary Scis., 1987-88, chmn. MS program in environ. scis. and policy; rsch. prof. U. Hawaii, 2005. Assoc. in rsch. Smithsonian Instn., 1972—; mem. bd. earth scis. NRC, 1985—, vice chmn., 1988, mem. bd. earth scis. resources, 1988-88, com. on solid earth scis., exec. and steering com., 1988, 2004—, com. on geoscis., environ. and resources, 1990-96. Author: Relation of Shell Form to Life Habits in the Bivalvia, 1970, (with D.M. Raup) Principles of Paleontology, 1971, Macroevolution: Pattern and Process, 1979, The New Evolutionary Timetable: Fossils, Genes, and the Origin of species, 1981, Earth and Life Through Time, 1986, Extinction, 1987, Exploring Earth and Life Through Time, 1992, Children of the Ice Age: How a Global Catastrophe Allowed Humans to Evolve, 1996, Earth System History, 1999; mem. editl. bd. Am. Jour. Sci., 1975—, Paleobiology, 1975-82, 88—, Evolutionary Theory, 1973—. Recipient Outstanding Paper award Jour. Paleontology, 1968, Allan C. Davis medal Md. Acad. Scis., 1973, Outstanding Tech. Paper award Washington Geol. Soc., 1986, Bownocker medal Ohio State U., 1997; Guggenheim fellow, 1981 Fellow NAS (Mary Clark Thompson Medal, 2006), Am. Acad. Arts and Scis., Geol. Soc. Am. (chmn. Penrose com. 1978, councilor 2002—); mem. Paleontol. Soc. (councilor 1976-77, sr. councilor 1991-93, pres. 1993-94, Charles Schuchert award 1977, medal 2007), Soc. for Study Evolution (councilor 1982-84), Am. Geophys. Union (pub. affairs com.), Paleontol. Rsch. Inst., Am. Geol. Inst. (mem. exec. com. 1996-99, pres. 2001—), Nat. Assn. Geosci. Tchrs. (James H. Shea award, 2004). Business E-Mail: stevenst@hawaii.edu.

STANLEY, TIM, information technology executive; BS in Engring., U. Wash.; degree in Internat. Bus. and Tech. Mgmt., Thunderbird U., Ariz. State U. With Intel Corp., Optima/KPMG, Innova Tech, Kimberly-Clark Corp.; v.p. info. sys. Nat. Airlines, chief info. officer; ptnr. USWeb (now marchFIRST); v.p., info. tech. devel. Harrah's Entertainment, Las Vegas, 2001—03, sr. v.p., chief info. officer, 2003—. With USAF. Named one of the Top 25 Unsung Heroes of the Internet, Interactive Week Mag., Top 25 Chief Tech. Officers, InfoWorld mag., 2006. Office: Harrahs Entertainment Inc One Harrahs Ct Las Vegas NV 89119 *

STANO, SISTER DIANA, academic administrator; AB, Ursuline Coll.; PhD, Ohio State U. Prof. edn. Ursuline Coll., Pepper Pike, Ohio, chair edn. dept., dir. grad. program in non-pub. sch. adminstrn., dir. master's degree program, dean of grad. studies, dir. of instl. rsch., pres., 1996—. Bd. trustees Coll. of New Rochelle; sec. bd. trustees Ohio Found. Ind. Coll.; cons. in field. Recipient YWCA Women of Profl. Excellence award, No. Ohio Live Rainmaker in Edn. award. Mem.: In Counsel With Women, Exec. Women's Leadership Forum. Office: Ursuline Coll 2550 Lander Rd Pepper Pike OH 44124-4398

STANOS, STEVEN PETER, JR., osteopath; b. May 31, 1968; DO, Nova Southeastern U., Miami, Fla., 1995. Cert. Am. Bd. Phys. Medicine and Rehab., 2000. Intern Chgo. Osteo. Hosps. & Med. Ctrs./Midwestern U., 1995—96; phys. medicine and rehab. resident Rehab. Inst. Chgo./Northwestern U. Med. Sch., 1996—99, J. Frankel pain fellow, 1999—2000; med. dir. Chronic Pain Care Ctr. Rehab. Inst. Chgo., 2002—. Co-chmn. Am. Acad. Phys. Medicine and Rehab. Pain Task Force. Contbr. chapters to books; mem. editl. bd.: Pain News, featured: magazines Rehab Management, 2005. Office: Chronic Pain Care Ctr Rehab Inst Chgo 1030 N Clark St Ste 320 Chicago IL 60610 Office Phone: 312-238-7800. Office Fax: 312-238-7801.

STANSBERRY, JAMES WESLEY, air force officer; b. Grafton, W.Va., Dec. 29, 1927; s. William Adrian and Phyllis Gay (Robinson) S.; m. Audrey Mildred Heinz, May 7, 1950; children: Nora G., Amy G. Stansberry Goodhand, Lisa Porten. BS, U.S. Mil. Acad., 1949; MBA with hons., Air Force Inst. Tech., 1956. Advanced through grades from pvt. to lt. gen. USAF; chief prodn. (Kawasaki Gifu Contract Facility), Gifu, Japan, 1956-57; dep. asst. to Sec. of Def. for atomic energy Washington, 1970-71; dep. dir. procurement policy U.S. Air Force, 1972-73; dep. chief staff contracting and mfg. (Hdqrs. Air Force Systems Command), Andrews AFB, Md., 1977-81; comdr. Electronic Systems Div. Hanscom AFB, Mass., 1981-84; pres. Stansberry Assocs. Inc., 1984—. Bd. dirs. Griffon Corp., Kidde Techs., Inc., Triton. Decorated DSM with oak leaf cluster, Legion of Merit with oak leaf cluster; named Disting. grad. Lancaster (N.Y.) H.S., award, Wall St. Jour., 1956, Mervin E. Gross award, USAF, 1956. Mem.: Order of Sword. Methodist. Home: 1117 Vera Cruz Ct Virginia Beach VA 23454 Office Phone: 757-716-2804. Personal E-mail: us49@aol.com. *The real secrets are enthusiasm, competence and good luck; and it helps immensely to marry a good woman. Work and persistence define us, accomodating various levels of talent and intelligence. Work and persistence prevail, buttressed by discipline and determination, and perhaps supported by a good sense of humor.*

STANSELL, LELAND EDWIN, JR., lawyer, mediator, educator; b. Central, SC, July 13, 1934; s. Leland Edwin and Hettie Katherine (Hollis) S.; children: James Leland, Susan. BS, Fla. So. Coll., 1957; LLB, U. Miami, Fla., 1961, JD, 1968. Bar: Fla. 1961; cert. civil mediator Fla. Supreme Ct., U.S. Dist. Ct. Fla. Assoc. Wicker & Smith, Miami, 1961-62, ptnr., 1962-75; pvt. practice, Miami, 1975-99, Leland E. Stansell, Jr., P.A., Miami, 1995—. Chmn. Appellate Jud. Nominating Com., Dade County (Fla.), 1983-87; mem. adv. com. Am. Arbitration Assn., 1975-90. Served with U.S. Army, 1957. Mem. ABA (ho. of dels. 1982-86), Fla. Bar (bd. govs. 1966-70, 70-80), Dade County Bar Assn. (dir. 1969-72, exec. com. 1974-75, pres. 1975-76), U. Miami Law Alumni Assn. (dir., officer, pres. 1968-69), Fla. Criminal Def. Attys. Assn. (treas. 1964-66), Am. Judicature Soc., Am. Bd. Trial Advs., Internat. Assn. Def. Counsel, Fla. Acad. Profl. Mediators, Fedn. Ins. Counsel, Miami Beach Rod and Reel Club (pres.), Coral Reef Yacht Club, Miami City Club, Ocean Reef Yacht Club, Delta Theta Phi (pres. Miami alumni chpt. 1966, regional dir. 1968. Office: 19 W Flagler St Miami FL 33130-4400

STANSELL, RONALD BRUCE, retired investment banker; b. Hammond, Ind., Apr. 9, 1945; s. Herman Bruce and Helen Rose Stansell; m. Kathie Van Atta, Oct. 2, 1976; children: Kelsey, Kymberlie. BA, Wittenberg U., 1967; MA, Miami U., Oxford, Ohio, 1969. Investment officer First Nat. Bank, Chgo., 1969-73; mgr. investments Chrysler Corp., Detroit, 1973; asst. v.p. A.G. Becker, Chgo., 1973-76; v.p. Blyth Eastman Dillon, Chgo., 1976-79, Dean Witter Reynolds Inc., Chgo., 1979-82, First Boston Corp., 1982-88; sr. v.p. Prudential-Bache Securities, Chgo., 1988-90; ptnr. William Blair & Co., 1991-99; pres. Oakmont of Carolina, 1999—2001. Mem. Mettawa (Ill.) Zoning Bd., 1978-80; treas. Village of Mettawa, 1977-78, trustee, 1980-91. With USMCR, 1968-74. Mem. Bond Club Chgo., Investment Analyst Soc., Fixed Income Group, Grandfather Golf Club, Forest Creek Golf Club, Belfair Golf Club, Berkeley Hall Club, Old Chatham Club, Diamond Creek Golf Club, Univ. Club.

STANSFIELD, CHARLES W., educational administrator; m. Charlene Rivera, Sept. 6, 1989. BA in Spanish, Fla. State U., 1968, MA in Fgn. Lang. Edn., 1969, MS in Teaching English as Second Lang., 1970, PhD in Fgn. and Second Lang. Edn., 1973. Tchr. English, Centro Colombo-Americano, Bogota, Colombia, 1966; 2jr. high sch. tchr. Spanish Fla. State U. Demonstration Sch., 1968-69; instr. Spanish, U. Colo., Boulder, 1970-73, asst. prof., 1973-80, assoc. prof., 1980-81; assoc. program dir. lang. programs Ednl. Testing Svc., Princeton, NJ, 1981-86; dir. fgn. lang. edn. and testing div. Ctr. for Applied Linguistics, Washington, 1986-94, dir. ERIC Clearinghouse Lang. and Linguistics, 1986-94; pres. Second Lang. Testing, Inc., Bethesda, Md., 1994—. Dir. Peace Corps Tng. Ctr., Managua, Nicaragua, 1978; mem. exec. com. Joint Nat. Com. Langs., 1988—93; conf. coord. Interagy. Lang. Roundtable Invitational Symposium Lang. Aptitude Testing, Rosslyn, Va., 1988; mem. adv. bd. Nat. Fgn. Lang. Resources Ctr. U. Hawaii, 1991—93; presenter in field. Author: Cuademo de ejercicios, 1976, rev. edit., 1981; author: (with others) Multiple-Choice Items and the Test of English as a Foreign Language, 1988; co-author: Manual de laboratorio, 2d rev. edit., 1981, The Test of Spoken English as a Measure of Communicative Ability in the Health Professions, Validation and Standard Setting, 1983; co-editor: Second Languag Proficiency Assessment: Current Issues, 1988, Language Aptitude Reconsidered, 1990; contbr. articles to profl. jours. Named Outstanding Alumnus, Fla. State U., 1994; Colo. Congress Fgn. Lang. Tchrs. scholar, 1981. Mem.: Colo. Tchrs. English Spkrs. Other Langs. (Gladys Doty award 1987), Washington Area Tchrs. English Spkrs. Other Langs., Tchrs. English Spkrs. Other Langs., Internat. Lang. Testing Assn. (pres. 1992—93), Nat. Coun. Measurement Edn., Nat. Assn. Bilingual Edn., Internat. Assn. Applied Linguistics, Am. Ednl. Rsch. Assn., Am. Coun. Tchg. Fgn. Langs. (Paul Pinsleur award 1984), Am. Assn. Tchrs. Spanish and Portuguese (life). Office: 6135 Executive Blvd Rockville MD 20852-3437 Office Phone: 301-231-6046. Business E-Mail: cstansfield@2LTI.com.

STANSKY, PETER DAVID LYMAN, historian, writer, retired professor; b. NYC, Jan. 18, 1932; s. Lyman and Ruth (Macow) Stansky. BA, Yale U., 1953, King's Coll., Cambridge U., Eng., 1955, MA, 1959; PhD, Harvard U., 1961; DL (hon.), Wittenberg U., 1984. Tchg. fellow history and lit. Harvard U., 1957-61, from instr. to asst. prof. history, 1961-68; assoc. prof. Stanford (Calif.) U., 1968-73, prof., 1973-74, Frances and Charles Field prof., 1974—2004, Frances and Charles Field prof. emeritus, 2004—, chmn. dept. history, 1975-78, 79-82, 89-90, assoc. dean humanities and scis., 1985-88. Chmn. publs. com. Conf. Brit. Studies, 1970—78, vis. fellow Wesleyan Ctr. Humanities, Middletown, 1972; pres. Pacific Coast Conf. Brit. Studies, 1974—76, N.Am. Conf. Brit. Studies, 1983—85; vis. fellow All Soul's Coll. Oxford (Eng.) U., 1979, vis. fellow St. Catherine's Coll., 83. Author: Ambitions and Strategies, 1964, England Since 1867, 1973, Gladstone, 1979, William Morris, 1983, Redesigning the World, 1985, On or About December 1910, 1996, Another Book that Never Was, 1998, From William Morris to Sergeant Pepper, 1999, Sassoon: The Worlds of Philip and Sybil, 2003, The First Day of the Blitz, 2007; co-author: Journey to the Frontier, 1966, The Unknown Orwell, 1972, Orwell: The Transformation, 1979, London's Burning, 1994. Guggenheim fellow, 1966—67, 1973—74, Am. Coun. Learned Socs. fellow, 1978—79, NEH fellow, 1983, 1998—99, Royal Hist. Soc. fellow, Ctr. Advanced Study Behavioral Scis., 1988—89. Fellow: Am. Acad. Arts and Scis. (coun. 1994—98, 2002—05); mem.: AAUP, Century Assn., William Morris Soc., Victorian Soc., Conf. Brit. Studies, Am. Hist. Assn. Home: 375 Pinehill Rd Hillsborough CA 94010-6612 Office: Stanford U Dept History Stanford CA 94305-2024 Office Phone: 650-723-2663. Business E-Mail: stansky@stanford.edu.

STANTON, AMY, marketing executive; BA; M in Mktg., U. Pa. Account dir. Bartle Bogle Hegarty, NYC; dir. mktg. & comm. NYC2012; chief mktg. officer, sr. v.p. Martha Stewart Living Omnimedia, 2005—. Office: Martha Stewart Living Omnimedia 11 W 42nd St New York NY 10036 Office Phone: 212-827-8000.

STANTON, DONALD SHELDON, retired academic administrator; b. Balt., June 8, 1932; s. Kenneth Gladstone and Dorothy Erma (Hetrick) S.; m. Barbara Mae Hoot, June 25, 1955; children: Dale Richard, Debra Carol, Diane Karen. AB, Western Md. Coll., 1953; Litt.D., Oglethorpe U., 1999; LLD, Western Md. Coll., 1981; MDiv magna cum laude, Wesley Theol. Sem., 1956; MA, Am. U., 1960; Ed.D., U. Va., 1965; L.H.D., Columbia Coll., 1979; Litt.D., Albion Coll., 1983. Ordained to ministry United Methodist Ch., 1956; pastor Balt. and Va. confs. United Meth. Ch., 1953-59; dir. Richmond (Va.) Area Wesley Found., 1959-63; chaplain, dean of students Greensboro Coll., 1963-65; chaplain Wofford Coll., 1965-69; dir. office coll. services United Meth. Div. Higher Edn., Nashville, 1969-75; v.p. for devel. Wesleyan Coll., 1975-78; pres. Adrian Coll., 1978-88, Oglethorpe U., Atlanta, 1988-99, pres. emeritus, 1999—; interim pres. Haywood Cmty. Coll., 2005—06. Adminstr., prof. European internat. ednl. programs, summers 1960, 69-71, 73; chmn. pres.'s assn. Mich. Intercollegiate Athletic Assn., 1986-87. Contbr. articles, revs. to profl. publs. in U.S., Japan, Argentina, chpts. to books; editor: Faculty Forum, 1972-74; bass-baritone soloist. Bd. dirs. Toledo Symphony, 1980-83, Lewanee County Jr. Achievement, 1980-83, Found. Ind. Higher Edn., 1996-99, Nat. Conf. for Cmty. and Justice, Atlanta Region, Atlanta Area coun. Boy Scouts Am.; chair bd. trustees U. Ctr. Ga., 1994-96; chair So. Collegiate Athletic Conf., 1994-95. Adminstrn. bldg. at Adrian Coll. named in honor of Stanton and his wife, 1988. Mem. Am. Assn. Univ. Adminstrs. (bd. dirs. 1990-93), Ga. Assn. Colls. (pres. 1992), Soc. Wesley (Disting. Alumni Recognition award 1988), Ga. Found. for Ind. Colls. (vice chair 1992), Nat. Assn. Ind. Colls. and Univs. (past mem. pub. rels. com.), Assn. Pvt. Colls. and Univs. Ga. (treas. 1996-97), Rotary, Omicron Delta Kappa, Order of Omega, Tau Kappa Epsilon, Psi Chi, Phi Eta Sigma. Home: 312 Tillman Rd Lake Junaluska NC 28745-9779 Personal E-mail: stantons2@earthlink.net.

STANTON, HARRY DEAN, actor; b. West Irvine, Ky., July 14, 1926; Actor: (films) Tomahawk Trail, 1957, The Proud Rebel, 1958, Pork Chop Hill, 1959, A Dog's Best Friend, 1959, Cool Hand Luke, 1967, Kelly's Heroes, 1970, Two-Lane Blacktop, 1971, Pat Garrett and Billy the Kid, 1971, Dillinger, 1973, Zandy's Bride, 1974, The Godfather, Part II, 1974, Rancho Deluxe, 1974, Farewell, My Lovely, 1975, The Missouri Breaks, 1976, 92 in the Shade, 1976, Renaldo and Clara, 1977, Straight Time, 1977, The Rose, 1979, Wise Blood, 1979, Alien, 1979, Deathwatch, 1979, The

Black Marble, 1980, UFOria, 1980, Private Benjamin, 1980, Escape from New York, 1981, Young Doctors in Love, 1982, One From the Heart, 1982, Tough Enough, 1983, Christine, 1983, Repo Man, 1984, The Bear, 1984, Red Dawn, 1984, Paris, Texas, 1984, One Magic Christmas, 1985, Pretty in Pink, 1986, Fool for Love, 1986, The Last Temptation of Christ, 1988, Dream A Little Dream, 1989, Twister, 1989, The Fourth War, 1990, Wild at Heart, 1990, Man Trouble, 1992, Twin Peaks: Fire Walk With Me, 1992, Cent et une nuits, 1995, Never Talk to Strangers, 1995, Midnight Blue, 1996, Down Periscope, 1996, Ben Johnson: Third Cowboy on the Right, 1996, She's So Lovely, 1997, Fire Down Below, 1997, The Mighty, 1998, Ballad of the Nightingale, 1998, Fear and Loathing in Las Vegas, 1998, The Straight Story, 1999, The Green Mile, 1999, The Man Who Cried, 2000, The Pledge, 2001 Ginostra, 2002, Chrystal, 2004, The Wendell Baker Story, 2005, Alien Autopsy, 2006, You, Me, and Dupree, 2006, Inland Empire, 2006, Alpha Dog, 2007, The Good Life, 2007; (TV films) Flatbed Annie and Sweetie Pie: Lady Truckers, 1979, I Want to Live, 1983, Payoff, 1992, Hostages, 1993, Hotel Room, 1993, (mini-series) Dead Man's Walk, 1996; (TV series) Big Love, 2006- Mem. Screen Actors Guild. Office: Bresler Kelly & Assocs 11500 W Olympic Blvd Ste 510 Los Angeles CA 90064-1578 *

STANTON, JOHN JEFFREY, editor, director, journalist, government agency administrator, educator; b. Wichita Falls, Tex., July 19, 1956; s. John Joseph Jr. and Joan (Marley) S.; m. Scylla Maria Silva, Jan. 6, 1981; 1 child, Damien Kristian. BS in Pub. Adminstrn. and Bus. Adminstrn., Nichols Coll., 1978; M in Pub. Adminstrn., U. Detroit, 1980. Rsch. asst. Am. Enterprise Inst., Washington, 1977; rep. aide R.I. Ho. of Reps., Providence, 1977-78; mng. editor Am. Politics, Washington, 1982, assoc. editor, 1983, corp. advisor, 1984, sr. editor, 1985-87; editor, govt. programs mgr. ENTEK, Alexandria, Va., 1988-90; govt. programs dir., cons. Tuckerman Group, Springfield, Va., 1991; analyst, writer Nat. Security Issues, Arlington, Va., 1991—; program dir. TeleStrategies, McLean, Va., 1991-93; Washington corr., mem. editl. bd. Tech. Transfer Jour., 1994-98; editor Tech. Transfer Newsletter; asst. to pres., info. transfer specialist Am. Def. Preparedness Assn., Arlington, 1994-97; contbg. writer Nat. Def. Mag., 1996—; adminstrn. dir. Nat. Def. Indsl. Assn., Arlington, 1997—2004; Washington corr. Australian Def. Mag., 1998-99; editor Voice of the Indsl. Base NDIA, 1998—2000; tchr., adminstr. St. Stephens & Agnes, 2005—; rsch. assoc. Rsch. Inst. for European and Am. Studies, 2006—; mem. Triangle Inst. for Security Studies, 2007—. Creator, co-host (radio) Power Breakfast, Sta. WNTR, Washington, 1987, Am. Politics Radio, 1987; commentator WAMU-NPR, WBAL, KPFA, Am. Talk Live, NYC, Radio 101, Croatia, Radio Adelaide, KCMO, Kansas City, WNTR, WAMU, WBAC, Balt.; campaign mgr. Madsen for Congress, 8th dist., Va., 2004; polit.-mil. analyst CBS News, CNN, ABC, 2001—. Co-author: America's Nightmare, 2003; author: A Power But Not Super, 2004, Talking Politics with God and the Devil in Washington, DC, 2007; contbr. articles to profl. jours., popular mags. Polit. campaign cons. to Glenn Tenney, 1992—; commr. Arlington Little League Baseball, 1993, coach 1997—; mentor Arlington County Ct. Sys., 1997; varsity football coach Wakefield H.S., Arlington, Va., 1998-2002, St. Stephen's Agnes, 2003—. Recipient Doers Honoree The Washington Times, 1988. Avocation: coaching youth sports programs. Personal E-mail: cioran123@yahoo.com. Business E-Mail: jstanton@sssas.org.

STANTON, JOHN W., communications executive; b. Seattle; BA in Polit. Sci., Whitman Coll.; MBA, Harvard U. Chmn., CEO Western Wireless (now Alltel Corp.), Bellevue, Wash., 1992—2005; chmn. Telocator, 1986—95; chmn., CEO VoiceStream Wireless, 1992—2002; cons. cellular and long-distance bus.; v.p. McCaw Comms., 1983; exec. v.p., COO McCaw Cellular, 1985—88, vice-chmn., 1988—91; dir. McCaw and LIN Broadcasting, 1991—94; co-founder Stanton Comms., 1988; founder, chmn., CEO (now Western Wireless) Pacific N.W. Cellular, 1992; dir. Columbia Sportswear Co., 1997—. Bd. dirs. Advanced Digital Info. Corp., Columbia Sportswear, Pacific Sci. Ctr.; trustee Whitman Coll. Mem.: Cellular Telecomms. Industry Assn. (chmn. emeritus). Office: c/o Columbia Sportswear 14375 NW Science Park Drive Portland OR 97229

STANTON, JULIA A., lawyer; b. Torrance, Calif., Feb. 14, 1968; BA, Pomona Coll., 1990; JD, Loyola law Sch., 1993. Bar: Calif. 1993, US Dist. Ct. Ctrl. Calif. Ptnr., family law practice Brandmeyer & Stanton, Long Beach, Calif. Named a Rising Star, So. Calif. Super Lawyers, 2006. Mem.: State Bar Calif., LA County Bar Assn., Women Lawyers Assn. LA, South Bay Bar Assn. Office: Brandmeyer & Stanton Ste 1940 1 World Trade Ctr Long Beach CA 90802 Office Phone: 562-499-2131. Office Fax: 562-499-2132.

STANTON, KATHRYN, retail executive; b. Nov. 29, 1954; BS in Acctg., U. Ill., 1976; MBA, U. Chgo., 1996. CPA, Ill. From auditor to mgr. Arthur Anderson, Chgo., 1976-81, mgr., 1981-86; from controller to v.p. finance, CFO Follett Corp., Chgo., River Grove, Ill., 1986-97, v.p. finance, CFO River Grove, Ill., 1997—. Bd. dirs. Mus. Sci. and Industry, Chgo. Mem. Am. Inst. CPAs, Financial Exec. Inst., Ill. CPA Soc., Chgo. Council Foreign Rels. Office: Follett Corp 2233 N West St River Grove IL 60171-1895 Fax: 708-452-9347.

STANTON, LOUIS LEE, federal judge; b. NYC, Oct. 1, 1927; s. Louis Lee and Helen Parsons (La Fétra) S.; m. Berit Eleonora Rask; children: L. Lee, Susan Helen Benedict, Gordon R., Fredrik S. BA, Yale U., 1950; JD, U. Va., 1955. Assoc. Davis Polk Wardwell Sunderland & Kiendl, NYC, 1955-66, Carter, Ledyard & Milburn, NYC, 1966-67, ptnr., 1967-85; judge U.S. Dist. Ct. (So. Dist.), NY, 1985—96, sr. judge NY, 1996—. Served to 1st lt. USMCR, 1950-52. Fellow Am. Coll. Trial Lawyers, N.Y. Bar Found.; mem. Va. Bar Assn. Office Phone: 212-805-0252.

STANTON, M(ORRIS) DUNCAN, psychologist, researcher, dean; b. Lockport, NY; *Forebears came from England, Scotland, Wales, the Netherlands, France, Ireland, Germany, and Lithuania. Ancestors include a country doctor, several clergy, Canada's first female medical school graduate, a civil engineer who helped build the Panama Canal, artists, teachers, writers, an attorney, two superintendents of schools, and a registered nurse. Related to: Sir Francis Drake, President Grover Cleveland, Alexander Graham Bell, Lincoln's Secretary of War Edwin M. Stanton, and Elizabeth Cady Stanton's husband, New York anti-slavery journalist, attorney and political lecturer Henry Stanton.* BA in Psychology, Alfred U., 1962; MA in Clin. Psychology, George Washington U., 1964; PhD in Clin. and Cmty. Psychology, U. Md., 1968. Lic. psychologist NY, Ky., bd. cert. diplomate in clin. psychology Am. Bd. Profl. Psychology, bd. cert. diplomate in family psychology Am. Bd. Profl. Psychology, approved supr. Am. Assn. Marriage Family Therapy, cert. in treatment of alcohol and other psychoactive substance abuse disorders APA. Commd. 2d lt. US Army, 1962, advanced through grades to capt., 1966, chief psychologist 98th med. deetachment Ft. Dix, NJ and Ft. Meade, Md., 1968—71, dir. psychology tng. Walter Reed Gen. Hosp. Washington, 1971—72; chief psychologist 98th Med. Detachment (Vietnam), Ft. Meade, Md., 1968—71; intern Walter Reed Gen. Hosp., Washington, 1966—67; lectr. U. Md., 1969—72; from asst. prof. to assoc. prof. psychology in psychiatry U. Pa. Sch. Medicine, Phila., 1972—83; assoc. clin. dir. Penn Psychiatry Phila. Gen. Hosp., 1972—74; dir., addicts and families prog. Phila. Child Guidance Clinic, 1974—83; dir., family therapy tng. program Drug Dependence Treatment Ctr., Phila. VA Med. Ctr., 1974—79; faculty mem. family therapy tng. ctr. Phila. Child Guidance Clinic, 1977—83; tchg. faculty Family Inst. of Phila., 1977—83; instr. Wilmington Med. Ctr., Del., 1978—79; dir., rsch. Phila. Child Guidance Clinic, Pa., 1982—83; prof., psychiatry (psychology) U. Rochester Sch. Medicine and Dentistry, 1983—97; dir., div. family programs, dept. psychiatry U. Rochester Med. Ctr., 1983—93; dir., rsch., div. family programs, dept. of psychiatry U. of Rochester Med. Ctr., 1993—97; prof., dean Sch. Profl. Psychology and Social Work Spalding U., Louisville, 1997—99, v.p., acad. rsch., 1999, prof. emeritus psychology, 1999—. Vis. scholar Fulbright Found., USIA, Argentina, 1991; cons. White House Office of Drug Abuse Policy, 1977—81, USIA, 1987—96, Inst. Medicine Nat. Acad. Scis., 1988, 1991—92; chair, mem. various rev. comms., task forces, site visit teams NIDA, NIMH, NIAAA, 1975—; mem. 16 editl. bds., including Am. Jour. Drug Alcohol Abuse, Family Process, Psychosocial Stress, 1980—; bd Family Process Press, NYC, 1982—99; spkr., presenter invited lectrs., workshops in 27 countries. *Conducted an anonymous survey of drug use among 2,372 Army personnel in Vietnam which, via testimony before the U.S. Senate Special Subcommittee on Alcoholism and Narcotics, received considerable attention in the national media. Consultant/advisory board member to over 90 government agencies, universities, medical centers, and organizations across five continents. Published reviews of the outcome studies on family and couples therapy for drug abuse (meta-analysis, 1997), and the methods for getting reluctant substance abusers to enter treatment or self-help (2004). Author of a recent, brief, and at times humorous book on how America can cure its health care system.* Contbr. more than 150 works to sci., profl. publs.; author: monographs and books in field, 1977—. Mem. dept. def. task group on alcoholism The Pentagon, Washington, 1971—72; ad hoc com. mem. special action office on drug abuse policy The White House, Washington, 1974; mem. advisory group family therapy prevention rsch. project Nat. Inst. Drug Abuse, 1981—82; chair, moderator family rsch. conf. Alcohol, Drug Abuse and Mental Health Adminstrn., 1981; cons. Family Health Plan, 1985—88; cons., sponsor, supr. Fulbright Commn., 1987—92. Decorated Bronze Star Medal; recipient Plaque of Appreciation, Found. for Parents in Action (Argentina), 1991, Shield of Police of Salta Province (Argentina), 1991, Cert. of Appreciation for Svc. on Mayor's Drug, Alcohol Planning Com., City of Louisville, 1998; grantee, NIH (NIDA/NIAAA), 1974—84, 1995—; Ann. Disting. fellow, Pikes Peak Mental Health Ctr., 1980. Fellow: APA (Pres. Citation 2001), Acad. Family Psychology, Nat. Coun. Family Rels. (Award Appreciation for dedication to the enhancement of family life 1988, Recognition cert. for longstanding svc. 1988, Legacy Circle award 1999), Am. Assoc. Marriage and Family Therapy (Outstanding Rsch. Contbn. in Marital and Family Therapy 1980, Cumulative Contbn. Family Therapy Rsch. award 2003, Ky. Divsn. award of Appreciation 2004); mem.: Internat. Family Therapy Assn., Am. Family Therapy Acad. (chair alcohol and drug interest group 1982—87, Disting. Contbn. Family Systems Rsch. 1997), Associacion Sistemica de Buenos Aires (hon.), South African Inst. Marital and Family Therapy (hon.). Office: The Morton Center 1028 Barret Ave Louisville KY 40204

STANTON, PAMELA FREEMAN, interior designer, writer; b. Jacksonville, Tex., July 18, 1941; d. William Thomas and Ruth Ethel (Branton) Freeman; m. Karl F. Edmonds, Jr., Jan. 28, 1961 (div. 1966); m. Charles Calvin Stanton, Sept. 1, 1973; 1 child, Julie Anne. AA in Bus., Kilgore Coll., 1961. Design cons., Denver, Boston and Salem, Oreg., 1963-69; exec. sec. Alexander: Alexander of Tex. Inc., Dallas, 1967-69; interior designer Milmac Furniture, Dallas, 1969-73, Homestead House, Denver, 1973-76; case aide counselor Eliot Cmty. Mental Health Ctr., Concord, Mass., 1980-82; pres., owner Stancom Designs, Virginia Beach, Va., 1990-2000; interior designer Willis Furniture Co., 2000—. Author: I Am That I Am, 1994 (Best Book of Yr. N.Am. Bookdealers Exch., 1995). Recipient Cert. of Appreciation for vol. work Emerson Hosp., Concord, 1981; named Internat. Writer of Yr., 2003. Mem.: Interior Design Soc. (assoc.). Republican. Avocations: collecting art, travel, gardening, theatre-plays, entertaining. Home and Office: 4401 Leatherwood Dr Virginia Beach VA 23462-5704 Office Phone: 757-499-3432.

STANTON, PATRICK MICHAEL, lawyer; b. Phila., Sept. 8, 1947; s. Edward Joseph and Helen Marie (Coghlan) S.; m. Kathleen Ann Fama, Aug. 22, 1970; children: Cheryl Marie, Susan Elizabeth. BS in History, St. Joseph's U., 1969; JD, U. Va., 1972; MBA, Fairleigh Dickinson, 1984. Bar: Ohio 1972 (inactive), N.J. 1982, N.Y. 1985, U.S. Dist. Ct. (so. dist.) Ohio 1972, U.S. Dist. Ct. (ea. dist.) N.J. 1982, U.S. Dist. Ct. (so. dist.) N.Y. 1984. Assoc. Taft, Stettinius & Hollister, Cin., 1972—80; labor counsel Union Camp Corp., Wayne, NJ, 1980—83; dir. labor rels., equal employment opportunity programs W.R. Grace & Co., NYC, 1983—86; of counsel Shanley & Fisher, P.C., Morristown, NJ, 1986—89, ptnr., chmn. labor and employment group, 1989—95; dir. Stanton, Hughes, Diana, Cerra, Mariani & Margello, P.C., Morristown, 1995—2003; atty., shareholder Ogletree, Deakins, Nash, Smoak & Stewart, P.C., Morristown, 2004—. Adj. prof. bus. law Fairleigh Dickinson U. 1984-92; pres. Sidney Reitman employment law Am. Inn. Ct., 1997-2001. Pres., bd. dirs. N.Y. State Adv. Coun. on Employment Law, Inc., N.Y.C., 1985-86. DuPont scholar U. Va., 1970. Mem. ABA, N.J. State Bar Assn. (exec. com. labor employment law sect. 1989—, rec. sec. 1995-97, treas. 1997-99, 2d vice chair 1999-2001, 1st vice chair 2001-03, chair 2003-05, immediate past chmn. 2005—), Phi Alpha Theta, Delta Mu Delta. Roman Catholic. Home: 292 Forest Ave Glen Ridge NJ 07028-1808 Office: Ogletree Deakins Nash Smoak & Stewart PC 10 Madison Ave Ste 402 Morristown NJ 07960-7303 Home Phone: 973-746-4762; Office Phone: 973-656-1600. Office Fax: 973-656-1611. Business E-Mail: patrick.stanton@ogletreedeakins.com.

STANTON, R. THOMAS, lawyer; b. Moline, Ill., 1943; BA, Knox Coll., 1965; postgrad., Harvard U., 1966—67; JD, Northwestern U., 1969. Bar: Ohio 1969, N.Y. 1982. Mng. ptnr. Squire Sanders & Dempsey LLP, chmn. Cleve., 1990—, chmn., mgmt. com. Bd. editors Northwestern U. Law Review, 1969. Bd. chair Leadership Cleve., Univ. Circle, Inc.; trustee The Musical Arts Assn./The Cleve. Orchestra, Ohio Bus. Roundtable; mem. law bd. Northwestern Univ.; mem. Dean's Adv. Coun. Case Western Reserve Law Sch. Mem. Order of Coif. (chmn. mgmt. com.). Office: Squire Sanders & Dempsey LLP 4900 Key Tower 127 Public Sq Cleveland OH 44114-1304 Office Phone: 216-479-8728. Fax: 216-479-8780. Business E-Mail: rstanton@ssd.com.

STANTON, ROBERT ALAN, orthopaedic surgeon; b. NYC, June 28, 1946; s. Jay and Shirley (Rader) S.; m. Debby Ellen Beach, June 16, 1973; 1 child, Jim. BA, Williams Coll., 1968; MD, Coll. Physicians and Surgeons, 1972. Intern Columbia-Presbyn. Med. Ctr., NYC, 1972-73, resident in surgery, 1973-74; resident in orthopaedics Yale U., 1974-77; pres., dir. Orthopaedic Specialty Group, P.C., Fairfield, Conn., 1981—; clin. instr., orthopaedics, rehabilitation Yale Univ. Med. Sch. Chmn. Alumni Fund of Williams Coll., Williamstown, Mass., 1993-96; bd. dirs. Bridgeport Hosp. Found., 1988-95; bd. investors Bridgeport Hosp., 1995—. Edward John Noble Found. fellow Columbia U., 1969-70. Fellow ACS, Am. Acad. Orthop. Surgeons; mem. Am. Orthop. Soc. Sports Medicine, Arthrascopy Assn. N.Am., nternat. Soc. for Arthroscopy, Knee Surgery and Orthop. Sports Medicine, Williams Club N.Y., Nantucket Yacht Club, Fairfield County Hunt Club (pres.), Internat. Polo Club (Palm Beach). Avocations: skiing, polo, tennis, running, gardening. Office: Orthopaedic Specialty Group PC 75 Kings Highway Cutoff Fairfield CT 06824-5340 Office Phone: 203-337-2600. *

STANTON, ROBERT JAMES, JR., geologist, educator; b. LA, June 17, 1931; s. Robert James and Audrey (Franke) S.; m. Patricia Ann Burns, Sept. 13, 1953; children: John, Carol. BS, Calif. Inst. Tech., 1953, PhD, 1960; MA, Harvard U., 1956. Research geologist Shell Devel. Co., Houston, 1959-67; mem. faculty Tex. A&M U., 1967—, prof. geology, 1972-86, Ray C. Fish prof. geology, 1986-98, head dept., 1979-83, prof. geology emeritus, 1998—. Vis. prof. U. Nuremburg-Erlangen, Germany, 1984; rsch. assoc. invertebrate paleontology Natural History Mus. L.A. County. Co-author: Paleoecology: Principles and Applications, 1981, 2d edit., 1990. Served with AUS, 1953-55. Fellow Geol. Soc. Am.; mem. Internat. Paleontol. Union, Paleontol. Soc., Paleontol. Research Inst., Soc. Econ. Paleontologists and Mineralogists (Outstanding Paper award 1970), Sigma Xi, Tau Beta Pi. Home: 2297 Valleyfield Ave Thousand Oaks CA 91360 Office: Nat Hist Mus LA County Dept Invertebrate Paleontol 900 Exposition Blvd Los Angeles CA 90007 Home Phone: 805-493-1517. Business E-Mail: robertstanton@adelphia.net.

STANTON, ROBERT JOHN, JR., retired language educator, writer; b. NYC, July 7, 1942; s. Robert John Stanton and Mary McGinty; m. Felicia Lena Giancola, Nov. 15, 1959; children: Robert III, Sharon. BA, Hofstra U., 1970; MA, U. Mass., Amherst, 1972, postgrad., 1974-79. Instr. English Flagler Coll., St. Augustine, Fla., 1972-74; tchg. asst. U. Mass., Amherst, 1974-77, lectr. in rhetoric, 1979-81; English tchr. Bishop Kenny H.S., Jacksonville, Fla., 1982-83, Duval County Pub. Schs., Jacksonville, 1984-87; asst. prof. English Jacksonville U., 1987-91, assoc. prof. English, 1992—2006, chmn. divsn. humanities, 1993-97; ret., 2006. Author: Seventeen British Novelists, 1978, Gore Vidal, 1978, Truman Capote, 1980, Views From A Window: Conversations with Gore Vidal, 1980; (poems) Collected Word Paintings, 2000; co-author: Beneath Mad River Mansion, 1992, Noah's Orbella, 1994, The Devil's Rood, 1996, Dangerous Words, 2003. Mem. ACLU, Fla. Assn. Depts. English (pres. 1996), Swift River Hist. Soc. Democrat. Avocations: astronomy, reading, writing, observing the universe.

STANTON, ROGER D., lawyer; b. Oct. 4, 1938; s. George W. and Helen V. (Peterson) S.; m. Judith L. Duncan, Jan. 27, 1962; children: Jeffrey B., Brady D. (dec.), Todd A. AB, U. Kans., 1960, JD, 1963. Bar: Kans. 1963, U.S. Dist. Ct. Kans. 1963, U.S. Ct. Appeals (10th cir.) 1972, U.S. Supreme Ct. 1973. Assoc. Stanley, Schroeder, Weeks, Thomas & Lysaught, Kansas City, 1963—68; ptnr. Weeks, Thomas & Lysaught, Kansas City, 1969—81, also bd. dirs., chmn. exec. com., 1981-82; ptnr. Stinson, Mag & Fizzell, Kansas City, 1983-96, chmn. products practice group, also bd. dirs., 1993-95; ptnr. litig. practice Berkowitz Stanton Brandt Williams & Shaw LLP, Prairie Village, Kans., 1997—2005; pvt. practice Overland Pk., Kans., 2005—. Chmn. bd. editors Jour. Kans. Bar Assn., 1975-83; contbr. articles to profl. jours. Active Boy Scouts Am., 1973-79; pres. YMCA Youth Football Club, 1980-82; co-chmn. Civil Justice Reform Act com. Dist. of Kans., 1991-95; bd. dirs. Kans. Appleseed Found., 2000—. Fellow: Am. Coll. Trial Lawyers (state SRSC Com. 1983—88, state chmn. 1984—86, state SRSC Com. 2001—02); mem.: Hist. Soc. Tenth Cir. (bd.dirs. 2005—), Earl O'Conner Inn of Ct. (founding mem. 1991—), Kans. Assn. Def. Counsel (pres. 1977—78), Johnson County Bar Assn. (chmn. bench, bd. dirs. bar com., bd. dirs.), Johnson County Bar Found. (pres., trustee), Kans. Bar Assn. (Pres.'s award 1982), Def. Rsch. Inst. (state co-chmn. 1979—90, Exceptional Performance award 1979), Internat. Assn. Def. Counsel, U. Kans. Kansas City Alumni (bd. dirs. 2001—), U. Kans. Sch. Law Alumni Assn. (bd. dirs. 1975—76, 1985—86), Phi Delta Phi. Office: Ste 500 Bldg 51 9393 W 110th St Overland Park KS 66210 Office Phone: 913-451-6958. Business E-Mail: rstanton@stanton-law.com.

STANTON, RONALD P., export company executive; b. 1928; Grad., City College of NY; PhD (hon.), Yeshiva U., 1982. Chmn. Transammonia, Inc., NYC, 1965—. Mem. bd. of trustees Yeshiva U., New York, 1976—, vice chmn bd. of trustees, 1992—2002, chmn. bd. of trustees, 2002—; bd. mem. Lincoln Center, New York, NY Presbyterian Hospital, New York; chmn. Ministerial Commt. Office: Transammonia Inc 350 Park Ave New York NY 10022

STANTON, SYLVIA DOUCET, artist, gallery owner; b. New Orleans, Sept. 21, 1935; d. Clifton Leo Sr. and Maria Delbert (Alfonso Swiber) Doucet; m. Robert Elmer Stanton, Jan. 3, 1953; children: Robert, Sylvia, Barbara, Richard, Laura, Cheri. Grad. high sch., New Orleans, 1952. Real estate agt. Century 21, Slidell, La., 1982-88; ptnr. Doucet's Jewelry, Slidell, 1969-82; owner Plantation Antiques, Slidell, 1974-88, Magnolia Plantation, Slidell, 1988-97, Doucet-Stanton Ltd., Slidell, 1988-97, Gallery at Milbrook, Picayune, Miss., 2001—05; co-owner Lott Stanton Gallery, Jackson, Miss., 2006—. Appraiser jewelry, antiques, real estate, 1969—; artist, painter, 1950—. Exhibited in group shows at Montserrat Gallery, N.Y.C., Abita Gallery, Abita Springs, La., The Gallery at Millbrook, Picayune, Miss., Serenity Gallery, Bay St. Louis, Miss., Sterling Art Gallery, New Orleans, Represented in permanent collections Montserrat Salon, NY. Founder Le cotillion, Slidell, 1975; founding chmn. Pres. Coun. of Le Cotillion, 1987. Recieved title of nobility Countess De Miron Delbert, Greece, 1988. Mem.: Allied Artists of Am., New Orleans Art Assn., Inner Wheel (dist chmn. 6840 1990—91, founding pres. Slidell 1989), World Trade Ctr., Albuquerque Art League, Bayou Liberty Garden Club (sec. 1988—), Picayune Garden Club, Ozone Camellia Club. Republican. Roman Catholic. Avocations: art, antiques, gardening, interior decorating. Home: 615 E Lakeshore Dr Carriere MS 39426 Office: Lott Stanton Gallery 1800 N State St Jackson MS 39202 Home Phone: 601-798-0002. Personal E-mail: stanfam2@bellsouth.net.

STANTON, WILLIAM ANTHONY, diplomat; b. Jersey City, Jan. 17, 1947; s. Harold Arthur Stanton and Armen Katherine Kharajian; m. Karen Clark Stanton, Sept. 14, 1984; children: Katherine Ruth, Elizabeth Armen. BA, Fordham U., 1968; MA, U. N.C., 1970, PhD, 1978. Fgn. svc. officer, 1978—; consular Embassy Beirut, 1979—81; staff asst. Sec. NE S Asian Affairs, 1982—83; polit. officer U.S. Embassy, Beijing, 1987-90; sr. tng. Hoover Instn., Stanford, Calif., 1990-91; polit.-mil. affairs officer U.S. Embassy, Islamabad, Pakistan, 1991-93; spl. asst. for East Asian affairs Office Under Sec. for Polit. Affairs, U.S. Dept. State, Washington, 1993-94; dep. dir. office Chinese and Mongolian affairs U.S. Dept. State, Washington, 1994-95; min. counselor for polit. affairs U.S. Embassy, Beijing, 1995-98; sr. seminar U.S. Dept. State, Washington, 1998-99, dir. Office of UN Polit. Affairs, 1999-2001, dir. Office of Egyptian and No. African Affairs, 2001—03; dep. chief of mission, US Embassy in Canberra US Dept. State, Washington, 2003, chargé d'affaires ad interim, US Embassy in Canberra, 2005—06; dep. chief of mission US Embassy, Seoul, Republic of Korea, 2006—. Mem. Am. Fgn. Svc. Assn., Phi Beta Kappa. Office: US Embassy Seoul Unit Number 15550 APO AP 96205-5550 E-mail: stantonwa@state.gov.

STANTON, WILLIAM F., retired elementary school educator, retail executive; b. Chgo., June 30, 1950; s. Robert Crawford and Margaret Virginia Stanton. BA, MacMurray Coll., 1978; MA, U. Ill., 1983. Tchr. grade 6 Glen Oaks Sch., Hickory Hills, Ill., 1977—81; tchr. grades 3, 4, 6 Knox Elem. Sch., Chandler, Ariz., 1981—2005; retail supr. J.C. Penney, Mesa, Ariz., 1991—. Mem. oversight com. SANTAN Credit Union, Chandler, 1995—. Mem.: ASCD, NEA, Ariz. Geog. Alliance, Internat. Reading Assn. Avocations: travel, reading, photography.

STANTON, WILLIAM JOHN, JR., marketing educator, author; b. Chgo., Dec. 15, 1919; s. William John and Winifred (McGann) S.; m. Imma Mair, Sept. 14, 1978; children by previous marriage: Kathleen Louise, William John III. BS, Ill. Inst. Tech., 1940; MBA, Northwestern U., 1941, PhD, 1948; D (hon.), Cath. U. Santo Domingo, Dominican Republic, 2003. Mgmt. trainee Sears Roebuck & Co., 1940-41; instr. U. Ala., 1941-44; auditor Olan Mills Portrait Studios, Chattanooga, 1944-46; asst. prof., asso. prof. U. Wash., 1948-55; prof. U. Colo., Boulder, 1955-90; prof. emeritus, 1990—; head mktg. dept. U. Colo., 1955-71, acting dean, 1963-64; assoc. dean U. Colo. (Sch. Bus.), 1964-67; ret. Author: Economic Aspects of Recreation in Alaska, 1953; author: (with others) Challenge of Business, 1975; author: (with M. Etzel and B. Walker) Marketing, 14th edit., 2007, Marketing, Spanish, Chinese, Portuguese, Indonesian and Korean transl., 2003; author: (with R. Varaldo) Italian edit., 2d edit., 1989;

author: (with others) South African edit., 1992; author: (with M.S. Sommers and J.G. Barnes) Canadian edit., Fundamentals of Marketing, 11th edit., 2004; author: (with K. Miller and R. Layton) Australian edit., 4th edit., 2000; author: (with Rosann Spiro and G.A. Rich) Management of a Sales Force, 12th edit., Spanish, Portuguese, Chinese, and Russian transl., 2007; contbr. articles to profl. jour. Mem. Am. Mktg. Assn., Mktg. Educators Assn., Beta Gamma Sigma. Roman Catholic. Home: 1445 Sierra Dr Boulder CO 80302-7846

STANTON-HICKS, MICHAEL D'ARCY, anesthesiologist, pain medicine specialist; b. Adelaide, Australia, June 3, 1931; arrived in U.S., 1972; s. Cedric Stanton-Hicks and Florence (Haggett) Perrin; m. Kristina Litsmark, Aug. 4, 1969 (div. Aug. 1984); children: Erik Michael, Leif Neal; m. Ursula Koch, Aug. 27, 1985. MB, BChir, Adelaide U., 1962; Dr. med., U. Dusseldorf, 1984. Bd. equivalent Am. Bd. Anesthesiology; diplomate Am. Bd. Pain Medicine, Interventional Pain Practice, 2002. Intern Queen Elizabeth Hosp., Adelaide, 1961-62, tutor, staff anesthesiologist, 1970-72; resident Royal Postgrad. Med. Sch., London and Lasarettet Köping, 1966-68; asst. dir. anesthesiology intensive care Södersjükhuset, Stockholm, 1968-69; instr. anesthesiology U. Wash. Med. Sch., Seattle, 1969-70, asst. prof., 1972-75; prof., chmn. dept. U. Mass. Med. Sch., Worcester, 1975-83; prof. U. Colo. Health Scis. Ctr., Denver, 1983-86, vice chmn. dept., 1983-85, acting chmn., 1985-86; prof., dir. pain clinic and rsch. Johannes Gutenberg U., Mainz, Germany, 1986-88, prof., 1986—97; dir. pain mgmt. ctr. Cleve. Clinic Found., 1988-98, vice chmn. pain mgmt. and rsch. divsn. anesthesia, 1998—; prof. Lerner Coll. Medicine, Case Western Res. U., Cleve., 2004—. Med. examiner Indsl. Commn. Ohio; mem. Ohio Pain Adv. Com., Dept. Health; mem. liaison com. med. bd. Ohio Pain Com.; advisor Am. Acad. Disability Evaluating Physicians, 2000-02; appt. to gov.'s task force on compassionate care, Dept. of Health, Ohio; bd. dirs. World Inst. Pain; sci. advisor Reflex Sympathetic Dystrophy Assn., 2006. Author, editor Regional Anesthesia: Advances and Selected Topics, 1978, (with Boas) Chronic Low Back Pain, 1982; author, editor: (with Wilson and Harden) CRPS: Current Diagnosis and Therapy, 2005; co-author: (with Raj and Nolte) Illustrated Manual of Regional Anesthesia, 1988 (Most Beautiful Book of Yr. award Frankfurt, Fed. Republic Germany Pubs. Book Conv., 1989), (with Janig and Boas) Reflex Sympathetic Dystrophy, 1989, (with Janig) Reflex Sympathetic Dystrophy: A Reappraisal, 1996; author: Pain and Sympathetic Nervous System, 1989; exec. editor Pain Practice Jour., 2001—, sect. editor Complex Regional Pain Syndrome, 2002, mem. editl. bd. Pain Physician, 2002—. Squadron leader res. Royal Australian Air Force, 1962-65. Named Scientist of Yr. Am. Herschel Soc., 1991-92; recipient Disting. Scientist award Reflex Sympathetic Dystrophy Assn., 2002, Disting. Svc. award European Soc. Regional Anesthesia, 2003, Lifetime Achievement award, Am. Soc. Interventional Pain Physicians, 2007; Australian Univs. Commn. mature age scholar, 1953-60. Fellow Royal Coll. Surgeons (faculty anesthetists), Royal Coll. Anesthetists, Am. Acad. Pain Medicine, Interventional Pain Practice; mem. Internat. Assn. Study Pain (chmn. spl. interest group pain and sympathetic nervous sys. 1990—), World Inst. Pain (bd. dirs. 1995—), Am. Soc. Regional Anesthesia (bd. dirs. 1979-91, pres. 1989-90, Disting. Svc. award, 1998), Assn. Anesthetists Gt. Britain and Ireland, Ohio State Med. Assn., Cleve. Acad. Medicine, Am. Acad. Med. Infrared Imaging (bd. dirs. 1991-95, pres. 1994-95, William Hobbins Rsch. award 1993), Am. Acad. Disability Evaluating Physicians (adv. com. mem. complex regional pain syndrome 2000—02), Am. Pain Soc., Am. Acad. Pain Medicine, Am. Neuromodulation Soc. (pres. 1994-98, bd. dirs. 1998-2000), Reflex Sympathetic Dystrophy Assn. (sci. adv. bd. 2000-05), Am. Soc. Interventional Pain Practice (Lifetime Achievement award 2007), Army-Navy-Air Force Club. Republican. Anglican. Avocations: skiing, photography, travel, flying. Home: 11405 Clearfield Lane Chardon OH 44024 Office: Cleve Clinic Found 9500 Euclid Ave Cleveland OH 44195-0001 Office Phone: 216-445-9559. Business E-Mail: stantom@ccf.org.

STANUTZ, DONALD J., chemicals executive; Various sr. positions Texaco Chem. Co.; with Huntsman Corp., 1994—, exec. v.p. polyurethanes, PO and performance chems., 1999—2000, exec. v.p. global sales and mktg., 2000—01, exec. v.p., COO Huntsman LLC, 2001—04, divsn. pres. performance products, 2004—. Office: Huntsman Corp 500 Huntsman Way Salt Lake City UT 84108 Office Phone: 801-584-5700. *

STAPLES, GEORGE MCDADE, federal agency administrator, former ambassador; b. 1947; m. Jo Ann; 1 child, Catherine. BA, U. So. Calif., 1970; MS, Ctrl. Mich. U. With U.S. Fgn. Svc., El Salvador, Uruguay, Equatorial Guinea, Bahamas, Zimbabwe, 1961-81, sr. Turkey desk officer Bur. European Affairs Washington, sr. watch officer State's Ops. Ctr., dep. chief of mission Bahrain; US amb. to Rwanda US Dept. State, Kigali, Rwanda, 1999—2001, US amb. to Equatorial Guinea & Cameroon, 2001—04; nat. security affairs fellow Hoover Instn., Stanford U., 1995-96; polit. advisor to Supreme Allied Comdr. NATO, Brussels, 2004—06; dir. US Fgn. Svc. US Dept. State, Washington, 2006—, dir. human resources, 2006—. Officer USAF, 1970-78. Office: US Dept State Harry S Truman Bldg 2201 C St NW Rm 6218 Washington DC 20520 E-mail: rwandaamb@yahoo.com.

STAPLES, HEIDI L, poet, writer; b. Dade County, Fla., Dec. 12, 1971; d. Jeaniene Eddye Cole and Robert Wesley Kitchen; m. John V. Staples, May 16, 2004. PhD in English Lit. and Creative Writing, U. Ga., 2003. Edn. assoc. Planned Parenthood, Syracuse, 1994—95; writing instr. Syracuse U., 1996—98; tefl instr. The Lang. Ho., Prague, Czech Republic, 1998—99; asst. to the editors Ga. Rev., Athens, 2002—03; writing instr. U. Ga., 2002—03; part-time faculty Syracuse U., NY, 2003—. Co-founder and co-editor Parakeet, Syracuse, NY, 2003—05; asst. editor Verse, Athens, Ga., 2001—03; asst. coord. Helen Lanier Speaker's Series, Chaired Series of the UGA English Dept., Athens, Ga., 2001—03; asst. editor Salt Hill, Syracuse, 1997—98, poetry editor, 1995—97. Founder and moderator Grad. Student Reading Series, Athens, Ga., 2002—03; judge Ga. Scholastic Assn., Athens, Ga., 2001; mentor Syracuse Mentor and Youth in Learning Program, 1995—98; hotline counselor Athens Rape Crisis Line, Ga., 1992—93. Scholar Grad. Sch. scholarship, Syracuse U., 1995—98; Grad. assistantship, U. of Ga., 2002—03, Tchg. assistantship, 2000—02, Summer Rsch. grant, Syracuse U., 1996, fellowship, 1995—96. Mem.: PEN, Assoc. Writing Programs. D-Liberal. Avocations: baking, piano, canoeing. Home: 115 Roosevelt Avenue Syracuse NY 13210 Office: Syracuse Univ 240 Hbc Syracuse NY 13210 Home Phone: 315-472-9710; Office Phone: 315-443-9314. Personal E-mail: hlkitche@syr.edu.

STAPLES, LYLE NEWTON, lawyer; b. Radford, Va., Feb. 16, 1945; s. Lester Lyle and Velma Jean (King) S.; m. Christie Mercedes Carr, Feb. 1, 1971; children: Scott Andrew, John Randolph, Brian Matthew, Melissa Ann. BA, U. Md., 1967, JD, 1972; LLM in Taxation, Georgetown U., 1977. Bar: Md. 1973, U.S. Supreme Ct. 1978, U.S. Tax Ct. 1981, U.S. Dist. Ct. Md. 1981, U.S. Ct. Appeals (4th cir.) 1981. Tax law specialist IRS, Washington, 1972-77; assoc. Hessey & Hessey, Balt., 1978-82, Rosenstock, Burgee & Welty, Frederick, Md., 1982-84; sole practice Hampstead, Md., 1984-91; mem. firm Johnson, Parker & Hess, Westminster, Md., 1991-96; pvt. practice Westminster, 1996—. Vis. asst. prof. Towson (Md.) State U., 1981—82. Treas., bd. dirs. Literacy Coun. of Carroll County, Inc., 1993-98. Served with U.S. Army, 1968-69, Vietnam. Mem. ABA, Md. Bar Assn., Fin. Planning Assn., Carroll County C. of C. Democrat. Methodist. Home: 813 Clearview Ave Hampstead MD 21074-2325 Office: Ste 210 79 E Main St Westminster MD 21157-5026 Office Phone: 410-840-2000. E-mail: lstaples@infionline.net.

STAPLETON, BEVERLY COOPER, aerospace executive; b. Birmingham, Ala., June 4, 1933; d. Herston MacAger and Virginia (Averyt) Cooper; m. John Parker Stapleton, Aug. 31, 1959 (div. July 1981); children: Lisa Karen, Lawrence Cooper BBA magna cum laude, U. Miami, 1954; MA, U. Ala., 1960. Tchr. Miami Beach H.S. Dade County Pub. Schs., Fla., 1956—59; mem. behavior R & D program U. Ala., Tuscaloosa, 1959—61; contracts adminstr. Houghton Mifflin Co., Palo Alto, Calif., 1974—78; Calif. sales rep. Prentice-Hall Inc., San Jose, 1978; contract adminstr., cost analyst United Techs., Sunnyvale, Calif., 1978—82; mgr. contract adminstrn. Echo Sci. Corp., Mountain View, Calif., 1982; contracts mgr. Lockheed Martin Corp. Missiles & Space, Sunnyvale, 1982—98; ret., 1998. Instr. master's program in contracts and material mgmt. St. Mary's Coll., Moraga, Calif., 1984—86; mem. adv. bd. grad. program in contracts and acquisition mgmt. Golden Gate U., San Francisco, 1984—85; contracts mgr. Hubble Space Telescope Program, 1983—85. Fellow polit. sci. U. Ala., 1954-55; recipient Women of Achievement award Santa Clara County Commn. on Status of Women, 1985 Fellow Nat. Contract Mgmt. Assn. (cert., pres. San Francisco area chpt. 1984-85, nat. coun. fellows 1983—, nat. exec. com. 1986-88, nat. bd. dirs. 1985-86, 97-98, nat. v.p. 1987-88), Mgmt. Assn. (treas. Chem. Systems divsn., 1981), Beta Gamma Sigma, Delta Delta Delta Democrat. Presbyterian. Home: 3728 Rhoda Dr San Jose CA 95117-3421

STAPLETON, COREY, financial planner; b. Seattle, Sept. 17, 1967; BS, U.S. Naval Acad., 1992; MA, Temple U., 1995. Commd. officer USN, 1986, advanced through grades, 1997; fin. planner Prudential Ind. Fin. Svcs., 1997—. Mem. Midland Empire Pachyderm Club, 1998—; campaign aide Bob Dole for Pres. Campaign, 1996; campaign mgr. Norm Mills, Mont. State House Dist. 19, 1998; chair Yellowstone County Young Reps., 1999-2000. Mem. Am. Legion, Billings C. of C., Rotary. Office: 2015 Eastridge Dr Billings MT 59102-7904 E-mail: stapletonct@aol.com.

STAPLETON, CRAIG ROBERTS, ambassador; b. Kansas City, Mo. m. Dorothy Walker, 1971; children: Walker, Wendy Reyes. BA magna cum laude, Harvard U., 1967, MBA. Real estate exec., pres. Marsh and McLennan Real Estate Advs., Inc., NYC, 1982—2001; US amb. to Czech Republic US Dept. State, Prague, 2001—03, US amb. to France Paris, 2005—. Ptnr. with George W. Bush Tex. Rangers Baseball Team, 1989—98; chmn. Conn. State Re-Election Campaign George W. Bush, 2004; bd. dirs. Allegheny Properties, Metro PCS, TB Woods and Winston Ptnrs. Former bd. dirs. Peace Corps; pres. Vaclav Havel Found.; trustee Brunswick Sch., Greenwich, Conn.; vis. com., other coms. Harvard U. Recipient Jan Masaryk Medal for Svc. to Czech Republic. Office: DOS Amb 9200 Paris Pl Washington DC 20521 *

STAPLETON, HARVEY JAMES, physics professor; b. Kalamazoo, Dec. 22, 1934; s. Herbert James and Viola Delia (Early) S.; m. Joan Eilleen Sylvander, June 22, 1957; children: Patricia Lynne, Susan Joan, Jeffrey Denis. BS, U. Mich., 1957; PhD, U. Calif., Berkeley, 1961. Faculty physics U. Ill., Urbana, 1961—, prof., 1969-95, prof. emeritus, 1995—, assoc. dean Grad. Coll., 1980-95, assoc. vice chancellor for rsch., 1987-95; interim dean Grad. Coll., 1992; interim vice chancellor for rsch. U. Ill., 1992. Alfred P. Sloan fellow, 1962-64 Contbr. articles to profl. jours. Fellow Am. Phys. Soc.; mem. Phi Beta Kappa, Sigma Xi, Phi Sigma Kappa, Phi Kappa Phi, Phi Eta Sigma. Roman Catholic. Home: 3806 Gulf Of Mexico Dr Unit 310 Longboat Key FL 34228-2733 Personal E-mail: hjstapleton@earthlink.net.

STAPLETON, JAMES FRANCIS, lawyer; b. Bridgeport, Conn., June 30, 1932; s. James M. and Lucy V. (Moran) S.; m. Margaret M. Daly, July 13, 1957; children: James F., Mark T., Paul and Kathleen. BSS, Fairfield U., 1954; LLB, Boston Coll., 1957; LLM, Georgetown U., 1958. Bar: Conn. 1957, U.S. Dist. Ct. (ea. and so. dists.) N.Y. 1979, U.S. Ct. Appeals (2d cir.) 1966, U.S. Dist. Ct. Conn. 1961, Mass. 1957, U.S. Supreme Ct. 1965. Atty., Appellate Sect., Antitrust Divsn. U.S. Dept. Justice, 1957-58; assoc., ptnr. Marsh, Day & Calhoun, Bridgeport, 1958-73; city atty. City of Bridgeport, 1971-73; legis. counsel Conn. Bankers Assn., 1971-73; judge Conn. Superior Ct., 1973-78; chmn. Criminal Justice Commn. State of Conn., 1991-95; ptnr. Day, Berry & Howard, Stamford, Conn., 1978—2002, of coun., 2003—. Active Bridgeport Bd. Edn., 1960—69. Fellow Am. Bar Found., Am. Coll. Trial Lawyers (chmn. state com. 1994-96, regent 1996-2000); mem. ABA (ho. of dels. 1984-88), Am. Bd. Trial Advocates, Conn. Bar Assn. (bd. govs., ho. of dels., v.p., pres.), Fed. Bar Coun. Found. for 2d Cir. (v.p., chmn.). Home: 6 Winding Way Trumbull CT 06611 Office: Day Pitney LLP One Audubon St New Haven CT 06511 Personal E-mail: jfstapleton@daypitney.com.

STAPLETON, JAMES HALL, retired statistician, educator; b. Royal Oak, Mich., Feb. 8, 1931; s. James Leo and Dorothy May (Hall) S.; m. Alicia M. Brown, Apr. 3, 1963; children: James, Lara, Sara. BA, Eastern Mich. U., 1952; MS, Purdue U., 1954, PhD, 1957. Statistician Gen. Electric Co., 1957-58; asst. prof. stats. and probability Mich. State U., East Lansing, 1958-63, assoc. prof., 1963-72, prof., 1972—2007, chmn. dept., 1968-75, grad. dir., 1987—2006. Cons. Gen. Telephone Co. of Ind.; vis. prof. U. Philippines, 1978-79 Mem. USS-Mich. Swim Com., AAU, 1976-84, chmn., 1976-78; mem. Mich. AAU Exec. Bd., 1976-81. NSF fellow, 1966-67 Mem. Inst. Math. Stats., Am. Statis. Assn. Office: Mich State U Dept Statistics East Lansing MI 48823 Office Phone: 517-355-9678. E-mail: stapleton@stt.msu.edu, staplet5@aol.com.

STAPLETON, JAMES JOHN, marketing executive, writer; b. San Jose, Calif., Oct. 29, 1962; s. Stephen Jerome Stapleton and Frances Renard; m. Kim Vojvodich; children: Jeffrey, Christopher. BS, Santa Clara U., Calif., 1984. Mktg. dir. Ireland, San Filippo, San Jose, Calif., 1985—95; dir. bus. devel. Grant Thornton, San Jose, 1991—92; dir. tech. mktg. Arthur Andersen, San Jose, 1996—98; global dir. mktg., computers and networking PricewaterhouseCoopers, San Jose, 1998—2003, global dir. knowledge mgmt. TICE, 2003—05; chief mktg. officer Fenwick & West, Mountain View, Calif., 2005—. Author: Developing a CPA Practice: A Comprehensive Guide to Building a Successful Accounting Firm, Executive's Guide to Knowledge Management: The Last Competitive Advantage; author, pub. (mag.) Profl. Svcs. Mktg. Report. Active St. Christopher's Ch., San Jose, 1991—. Roman Catholic. Avocations: writing, golf, volleyball. Home: 1323 Dale Ave San Jose CA 95125 Office: Fenwick & West 801 California St Mountain View CA 94041 Home Phone: 408-624-7846; Office Phone: 650-335-7641. Office Fax: 650-938-5200. Business E-Mail: jstapleton@fenwick.com.

STAPLETON, JEAN (JEANNE MURRAY), actress; b. NYC, Jan. 19, 1923; d. Joseph E. and Marie (Stapleton) Murray; m. William H. Putch (dec.); 2 children. Student, Hunter Coll., NYC, Am. Apprentice Theatre, Am. Actors Co., Am. Theatre Wing; studied with Harold Clurman; LHD (hon.), Emerson Coll.; degree (hon.), Hood Coll., Monmouth Coll. Opera debut in Candide with Balt. Opera Co.; appeared in The Italian Lesson with Balt. Opera; first N.Y. stage role in The Corn is Green, Equity Library Theatre; starred as mother in Am. Gothic, Circle-in-the-Sq.; Broadway debut with Judith Anderson In The Summer House; also appeared on Broadway in Damn Yankees, Bells Are Ringing, Juno, Rhinoceros and Funny Girl, Arsenic & Old Lace, Bwax & On Tour; first major break in comic ingenue role as Myrtle Mae with Frank Fay in Harvey on-tour; played with nat. tour of Come Back, Little Sheba starring Shirley Booth; starred in tour of Morning's at Seven, The Show-Off, Daisy Mayme; (Films) Damn Yankees, 1958, Bells Are Ringin, 1960, Something Wild, 1961, Up the Down Staircase, 1967, Cold Turkey, 1971, Klute, 1971, The Buddy System, 1984, Michael, 1996, You've Got Mail, 1998, Pursuit of Happiness, 2001; (TV series) All in the Family, 1968-79, Archie Bunker's Place, 1979, Beakman's World, 1995-96; (TV Films) Tail Gunner Joe, 1977, You Can't Take It With You, 1979, Aunt Mary, 1979, Angel Dusted, 1981, Isabel's Choice, 1981, Eleanor, First Lady of the World, 1982, Something Afoot, 1984, A Matter of Sex, 1984, Grown-Ups, 1985, Dead Man's Folly, 1986, Tender Places, 1987, Mother Goose Rock 'n' Rhyme, 1990, Fire in the Dark, 1991, The Habitation of Dragons, 1992, The Parallax Garden, 1993, Ghost Mom, 1993, Lily Dale, 1996, Chance of a Lifetime, 1998, Baby, 2000, Like Mother Like Son: The Strange Story of Sante and Kenny Kimes, 2001; (guest appearances) Robert Montgomery Presents, 1952, Women with a Past, 1954, The Phileo TV Playhouse, Dr. Kildare, 1961, Dennis the Menace, 1962, The Nurses, 1962, The Defenders, 1962, Car 54, Where Are You?, 1962, Studio One, Naked City, 1963, Armstrong Circle Theatre, Jackie Gleason Show, The Eleventh Hour, 1963, Route 55, 1963, My Three Sons, 1964, The Patty Duke Show, 1965, Scarecrow and Mrs. King, 1984, Faerie Tale Theatre, 1983, 1985, The Love Boat, 1986, Shelley Duvall's Bedtime Stories, 1992, Ray Bradbury Theatre, Grace Under Fire, 1994 (Emmy nomination), Caroline in the City, 1995, Murphy Brown, 1996, Everybody Loves Raymond, 1996, Style and Substance, 1998, Touched by an Angel, 2000; performances include The Matchmaker at A.C.T., San Francisco, Trying Times Shakespeare Co. D.C., 1994, Night Seasons, Signature Theatre N.Y., 1994, Blithe Spirit, Costa Mesa, Calif., Mrs. Piggle-Wiggle on Showtime, stepmother in N.Y.C. Opera's Cinderella, 1995, On Tour: Eleanor: Her Secret Journey, 1998-99, Indian Ink by Tom Stoppard, A.C.T., Geary Theater, San Francisco, 1999, The Habitation of Dragon's on TNT, Roads to Home, Night Seasons, The Birthday Party, Mountain Language, Classic Stage Co., N.Y.C., The Death of Papa, Hartford Stage, 1999, Eleanor: Her Secret Journey, Coconut Grove Playhouse, Miami, Fla., 1999, Canon Theatre, L.A., Royal Poinciana, Palm Beach, Fla., Spreckles Theatre, San Diego, Paramount Theatre, Austin, Tex., Marines Meml. Theatre, San Francisco, 2000, Smithsonian Inst., Washington, 2000, Hartford (Conn.) Stage, 2000, Syracuse (N.Y.) Stage, 2000; CD-Rom Grandma Ollie's Morphabet Soup, 1996. U.S. commr. to Internat. Woman's Yr. Commn. and Nat. Conf. Women, Houston, 1977; bd. dirs. Women's Rsch. and Edn. Inst.; trustee Actors' Fund Am. Recipient Emmy award for best performance in comedy series All in the Family 1970-71, 71-72, 78, Golden Globe awards Hollywood Fgn. Press Assn. 1972, 73, Obie award, 1990, Cable Ace award. Mem. AFTRA, SAG, Actors Equity Assn. Office: care Bauman & Assocs 5757 Wilshire Blvd Los Angeles CA 90036-3635

STAPLETON, JEAN, journalism educator; b. Albuquerque, June 24, 1942; d. James L. and Mary (Behrman) S.; m. John Clegg, Apr. 15, 1965 (dec. Sept. 1972); m. Richard Bright, Jan. 13, 1973 (div. 1985); children: Lynn, Paul Bright; m. William Walter Farran, Nov. 9, 1996. BA, U. N.Mex., 1964; MS in Journalism, Northwestern U., 1968. Reporter Glenview (Ill.) Announcements, 1967-68, Angeles Mesa News Advertiser, LA, 1968-69, City News Svc., Radio News West, LA, 1969-71; press sec. polit. campaign, 1972; instr. journalism East L.A. Coll., 1973-75, prof., dept. chair, 1975—. Author: Equal Marriage, 1975, Equal Dating, 1979. Recipient Lifetime Achievement award, Journalism Edn. Coalition, 2006. Mem. NOW (pres. LA chpt. 1973-74), Soc. Profl. Journalists, LA Poets and Writers Collective. Democrat. Methodist. Home: 3232 Philo St Los Angeles CA 90064-4719 Office: East LA Coll 1301 Avenida Cesar Chavez Monterey Park CA 91754-6001 Office Phone: 323-265-8875. Business E-Mail: staplej@elac.edu.

STAPLETON, KATHARINE HALL (KATIE STAPLETON), commentator, writer; m. Benjamin Franklin Stapleton; children: Benjamin Franklin III, Craig Roberts, Katharine Hall. BA, Vassar Coll., 1941. Prodr., writer, host Cooking with Katie Sta. KOA, 1979—89. Author: Denver Delicious, 1980, 3d edit., 1983, High Notes, 1985. Chmn. women's divsn. United Fund, 1955-56, founder, chmn. Denver Debutante Ball, 1955, 56, hon. chmn. Nat. Travelers Aid Assn., 1952-56 95-; commr. Denver Centennial Authority, 1958-60; trustee Washington Cathedral, regional v.p., 1967-73; trustee Colo. Women's Coll., 1975-80; sole trustee Harmes C. Fishback Found., 1989-; hon. chmn. Le Bal à Versailles, 2000-07, Rocky Mountain Planned Parenthood Campaign, 2007. Decorated Chevalier de L'Etoile Noire (France), comdr. Chevalier de Tastevin; recipient People-to-People citations, 1960, 66, Beautiful Activist award, Colo.-Wyo. Restaurant Assn. award, 1981, Humanitarian of Yr. award Arthritis Found., 1995, Arts award Colo. Symphony, 1998; Outstanding Vol. Fundraiser, Nat. Philanthropy Day, 1995, Outstanding Alumna, Barstow Sch., 2003, Girl Scout award, 2006. Mem. Denver Country Club. Republican. Episcopalian. Home: 8 Village Rd Cherry Hills Village CO 80113-4908 E-mail: kties8@aol.com.

STAPLETON, MARYLYN ALECIA, diplomat; b. St. Thomas, V.I., Sept. 25, 1936; d. Lambert George and Aletha C. (Callendar) John; m. Frank Stapleton, Oct. 22, 1967 (div. Apr. 1983); 1 child, Linda E. Student, Washington Bus. Inst., 1959. Reservations agt. Caribair Airlines, St. Thomas, 1954-56; sales clk. Macy's Dept. Store, NYC, 1956-57, Gift Shop, NYC, 1957-63; supr. Ea. Airlines, Inc., NYC and St. Thomas, 1964-86; travel cons. Caribbean Travel Agy., St. Thomas, 1986-87; asst. commr. Dept. Licensing and Consumer Affairs, Govt. of V.I., St. Thomas, 1987-95, dep. of planning and natural resources, 1995—, small bus. tech. assistance program coord., 1995—; state exec. dir. Internat. Assn. Plumbing Mech. Officials, 1999—; environ. program mgr. Dept. Planning and Natural Resources, 2004. Owner, pres. Stapleton Enterprises, St. Thomas, 1989—. Pub. rels. officer Nevis Benevolent Soc., St. Thomas, 1966-85; state chair Dem. party V.I., 1986—, dist. chair, 1984-86; small bus. ombudsman Clean Air Act of 1990, 1998—. Recipient Legis. Resolution V.I. Legislature, St. Thomas, 1986. Mem. Internat. Assn. Plumbing and Mech. Ofcls., Nat. Assn. Plumbing, Heating and Cooling Contrs., St. Thomas/St. John Plumbing Assn. (pres. 1995—), St. Thomas Lioness Club (treas. 1985-86, pagent chair 1986-87, pres. 1987-88, mem. chair 1988-89, Melvin Jones fellow 1989), Lions Club of Charlotte Amalie (bd. dirs.). Democrat. Anglican. Home: 148-87 Est Annas Retreat PO Box 303739 St Thomas VI 00803-3739 Office: Democratic Party of Virgin Islns PO Box 3739 Saint Thomas Charlotte Amalie VI 00801 Office Phone: 340-774-3320.

STAPLETON, PATRICIA JEAN, elementary school educator; b. Springfield, Ill., May 27, 1950; d. John Patrick and Velma Rae Stapleton. BS in Edn., Ill. State U., Normal, 1974, MS, 1982. Mem. staff Milner Libr., Ill. State U., Normal; phys. edn. tchr. Kaskaskia Edn. Ctr., Kaskaskia Spl. Edn. Dist., Centralia, Ill., 1984—86, Ea. Ill. Area Spl. Edn., Charleston, Ill., 1987—. Named Vol. of Yr., Spl. Olympics and Recreation, 1982; recipient Teddy Ann Lovellette award for svc. Mem.: NEA, Ill. Edn. Assn., Ill. Assn. Health, Phys. Edn. and Recreation, Ill. Edn. Assn. (Teddy Ann Lovellette award for svc.). Roman Catholic. Avocations: camping, photography, reading, travel. Home: 442 County Rd 425 N Sigel IL 62462

STAPLETON, WALTER KING, federal judge; b. Cuthbert, Ga., June 2, 1934; s. Theodore Newton and Elizabeth Grantland (King) Stapleton; m. Georgianna Duross Stapleton; children: Russell K., Theodore N., Teryl J. BA, Princeton, 1956; LLB, Harvard, 1959; LLM, U. Va., 1984. Bar: Del. Assoc. Morris, Nichols, Arsht & Tunnell, Wilmington, Del., 1959—65; dep. atty. gen. State of Del., 1963—64; ptnr. Morris, Nichols, Arsht & Tunnell, 1966—70; judge US Dist. Ct., Wilmington, Del., 1970—85, chief judge, 1983—85; judge US Ct. Appeals (3d cir.), 1985—99, sr. judge, 1999—. Mem. Jud. Conf. US, 1984—85. Bd. dirs. Am. Bapt. Chs., 1978. Mem.: ABA, Del. Bar Assn., Am. Jud. Soc. Baptist. Office: US Ct Appeals Lockbox 33 5323 Fedl Bldg 844 N King St Wilmington DE 19801-3519 *

STAPP, DAN ERNEST, retired lawyer, utilities executive; b. New Orleans, July 1, 1934; s. James Frank Stapp Jr. and Marguerite Edna (Joubert) Stapp; m. Barbara Allan Wilmot, June 10, 1961; children:

Marguerite Wilmot(dec.), Mary Darby, Paul Wilmot(dec.), James Andrew. BBA, Loyola U., New Orleans, 1955, LL.B., 1957. Bar: La. 1957. With New Orleans Pub. Service Inc., 1958-68, asst. to v.p., 1965-68; with Entergy Svcs. (formerly MSU System Svcs. Inc.), New Orleans, 1968-92; v.p., sec., asst. treas. Entergy Svcs., 1968-80, sr. v.p., 1980-92. Sec. System Fuels, Inc., New Orleans, 1972-92, Entergy Corp. (formerly Middle South Utilities, Inc.), New Orleans, 1974-92, Systems Entergy Resources, Inc., Jackson, Miss., 1974-91, Electec, Inc., 1984-91, Entergy Ops., Inc., 1990-91, Entergy Power, Inc., 1990-92. Trustee Mercy Hosp., New Orleans, 1973-80, pres., 1975, chmn. bd. devel., 1971-72; mem. pres.'s coun. Loyola U., 1975-85, chmn., 1980-82; adv. coun. Coll. Bus. Adminstrn., 1969-70; mem. adv. bd. Asso. Cath. Charities, 1979-82; gen. chmn. United Way Greater New Orleans, 1978, trustee, 1978-84; mem. exec. bd. New Orleans Area coun. Boy Scouts Am., 1980-85, pres., 1984-85. 2d lt. AUS, 1957. Mem. ABA, La. Bar Assn., New Orleans Country Club, Country Club La., Blue Key (past chpt. pres.), Alpha Sigma Nu, Delta Theta Phi. Republican. Roman Catholic. Home: 19415 Kelly Wood Ct Baton Rouge LA 70809

STAPRANS, ARMAND, electronics executive; b. Riga, Latvia, Feb. 28, 1931; s. Theodore and Elvira (Ulmanis) S.; m. Vija Spalvins, Sept. 25, 1955; children: Silvija, Armin, Erik. Student, Willamette U., 1949-52; BSEE, U. Calif., Berkeley, 1954, MSEE, 1955, PhDEE, 1959. Rsch. asst. dept. elec. engring. U. Calif., 1955-57; engr. microwave tube div. Varian Assocs., Palo Alto, Calif., 1957-60, engring. mgr., 1960-68, ops. mgr., 1978-78, 86-89, chief engr., 1978-86, gen. mgr. coupled cavity tube divsn., 1989-92, v.p., 1990-95; gen. mgr. microwave power tube products, 1992-95; pres. microwave power tube products divsn. Comms. and Power Inds., Palo Alto, Calif., 1995-98; mgmt. cons., 1999—. Contbr. articles to profl. jours., chpt. to book; patentee microwave tubes field. Fellow IEEE (electron device adminstrv. com. 1983-88). Home: 445 Knoll Dr Los Altos CA 94024-4732 Office: Comm & Power Inds M S B 100 Microwave Power Tube Prod Divsn PO Box 50750 Palo Alto CA 94303-0665 Home Phone: 650-948-9521.

STAR, ALEXANDER, chemist, educator; b. Almaty, Kazakhstan, May 8, 1971; s. Victor Star and Regina Koritny-Star; m. Angela Goldman, Aug. 13, 1992; children: David, Michelle. BSc in Chemistry, Tel Aviv U., 1994, PhD in Chemistry, 2000. Postdoctoral assoc. UCLA, Calif., 2002; sr. scientist Nanomix Inc., Emeryville, Calif., 2002—05; asst. prof. U. of Pitts., Pitts., 2005—. Cons. Nanomix Inc., Emeryville, Calif., 2005—07. Contbr. articles to profl. jours. Recipient Intel award, Intel, 1998; fellow Buchmann Doctoral fellow, Buchmann Fund, 1996—99; grantee, NSF, 2003—04, 2007—, DOE, 2003, EPA, 2003; scholar Schwarz Meml. Grad. scholar, Schwarz Fund, 1997. Mem.: Israel Chem. Soc., Materials Rsch. Soc., Am. Chem. Soc. Achievements include patents for carbon nanotube sensors; research in chemistry of carbon nanotubes; development of industrial gas nantechnological sensors; invention of medical breath and bio-nanoelectronic sensors; patents pending for fabrication of nanosensor arrays. Office: University of Pittsburgh 219 Parkman Ave Pittsburgh PA 15260 Home Phone: 412-521-0414; Office Phone: 412-624-6493. Office Fax: 412-624-4027. Business E-Mail: astar@pitt.edu.

STARACE, ANTHONY FRANCIS, theoretical atomic physicist; b. NYC, July 24, 1945; s. Louis J. and Ione A. (Liva) S.; m. Katherine Anne Fritz, June 25, 1968; children: Alexander Fritz, Anne Katherine. AB cum laude, Columbia Coll., 1966; MS, U. Chgo., 1967, PhD, 1971. Rsch. assoc. Imperial Coll., London, 1971-72; asst. prof. dept. physics and astronomy U. Nebr., Lincoln, 1973-75, assoc. prof., 1975-81, prof., 1981—, chmn., 1984-95, assoc. dean for sci. rsch., 2000—01, George Holmes Univ. prof., 2001—. Adv. bd. Inst. Theoretical Atomic and Molecular Physics Harvard-Smithsonian Ctr. Astrophysics, 1993-96, chmn., 1994-95; vis. fellow Harvard-Smithsonian Inst. Theoretical Atomic and Molecular Physics, Cambridge, Mass., 1995-96; sci. adv. com. Advanced Light Source Lawrence Berkeley Nat. Lab., 2001-05; sci. adv. bd. Max Planck Inst. Physics of Complex Sys., Dresden, Germany, 2007—. Author: Theory of Atomic Photoionization, 1982; assoc. editor Revs. of Modern Physics, 1996-2006; mem. editl. bd. Phys. Rev. A, 1993-98. Rsch. fellow Albert-Ludwigs U., Freiburg, Germany, 1979-80, Alexander von Humboldt fellow, 1979-80, Alfred P. Sloan Found. fellow, 1975-79; Vis. fellow Joint Inst. for Lab. Astrophysics U. Colo., Boulder, 1992-93; recipient Outstanding Rsch. and Creative Activity award U. Nebr. Sys., 2005. Fellow Am. Phys. Soc. (chmn. div. atomic molecular and optical physics 1990-91), AAAS, mem. Sigma Xi (pres., 2003-04). Achievements include research in theoretical atomic physics; few-body dynamics, properties of atoms in strong external fields, coherent control of atomic processes, intense laser interactions with atoms and quantum information. Office: U Nebr Dept Physics and Astronomy 116 Brace Lab Lincoln NE 68588-0111 Office Phone: 402-472-2795. E-mail: astarace1@unl.edu.

STARBIRD, MICHAEL, mathematics professor; BA, Pomona Coll.; PhD in Math., Univ. Wis., Madison. With U. Tex., Austin, 1974—, assoc. dean, Coll. Natural Sciences, 1989—97, univ. disting. tchg. prof., dept. math., prof. math., mem., Acad. Disting. Teachers. Vis. position Inst. for Advanced Study, Princeton, NJ, Univ. Calif., San Diego, Jet Propulsion Lab.; conducts video courses in calculus, statistics and probability The Teaching Co.; presenter in field; tchr. of mini-courses for Math. Assn. Am. and NSF. Co-author (with Edward Burger): The Heart of Mathematics: An Invitation to Effective Thinking, 2000 (Robert W. Hamilton Book award, 2002), Coincidences, Chaos, and All That Math Jazz:Making Light of Weighty Ideas, 2005. Recipient Minnie Stevens Piper Professorship, Jean Holloway award for Tchg. Excellence, President's Associates Tchg. Excellence award; Friar Soc. Centennial Tchg. Fellowship. Mem.: Am. Math. Soc. (mem. nat. edn. com., member-at-large for the coun., mem., com. on edn., mem., math. and edn. reform bd.), Math. Assn. Am. (mem. nat. edn. com., mem., com. on the undergraduate program in math., Deborah and Franklin Tepper Haimo award for Disting. Coll. or Univ. Tchg. Math. 2007). Office: Dept Math Univ Tex Austin RLM 11 122 Austin TX 78712 Office Phone: 512-471-5156. Office Fax: 512-471-9038. Business E-Mail: starbird@math.utexas.edu. *

STARCHER, LARRY VICTOR, state supreme court justice; b. Rocksdale, W.Va., Sept. 25, 1942; m. Rebecca Wiles; children: Mollianne, Victor, Amy. AB cum laude, W.Va. U., 1964, JD, 1967. Bar: W.Va. 1967. Judge and chief judge W.Va. Ct. (17th jud. cir.), 1977—96; justice W.Va. Supreme Ct. Appeals, 1997—, chief justice, 1999, 2003. Pvt. practice, Morgantown, 1976—; dir. North Ctrl. W.Va. Legal Aid Soc., 1969-76; former instr. law, pub. adminstrn., and history W.Va. U.; contract adminstr. W.Va. U., 1966-67, asst. to v.p., 1967-69. Editor W.Va. Law Rev.; contbr. articles to profl. jours. Mem. City Coun. Morgantown, 1971-72; mem. W.Va. Martin Luther King, Jr. Holiday Commn. Fellow Harvard U., summer 1978. Mem. ATLA, Am. Correctional Assn., W.Va. Jud. Assn., W.Va. State Bar, Monongalia County Bar Assn., Kanawha County Bar Assn., Conf. Chief Justices, Beta Theta Pi, Phi Delta Phi, Phi Alpha Theta, Pi Sigma Alpha. Avocations: carpentry, gardening. Office: Supreme Ct Appeals State Capitol Rm E 307 Charleston WV 25305 Office Phone: 304-558-2604. Business E-Mail: larrystarcher@courtswv.org.

STARCK, CHRISTIAN WALTER, retired judge, law educator; b. Breslau, Germany, Jan. 9, 1937; s. Walter and Ruth (Hubrich) S.; m. Brigitte Edelmann, Aug. 31, 1965; children: Annette, Johannes, Marie-Christine. Student, U. Kiel, 1957, U. Freiburg, 1958-59; Dr. iur., U. Würzburg, 1963, Habil., 1969. Clk. Fed. Constl. Ct., 1964-67; govt. ofcl., 1968-69; lectr. U. Würzburg, 1969-71; prof. pub. law U. Göttingen, Germany, 1971; prof. emeritus, 2005—; rector U. Göttingen, 1976-77; judge Constl. Ct. Lower Saxony, Germany, 1991—2006. Vis. prof. U. Paris-Sorbonne, 1987, U. Nanjing, 1989; mem. TV bd. Zweites Deutsches Fernsehen, 1978-92; pres. TV bd. ARTE, 1991-2000. Author: Der Gesetzesbegriff des Grundgesetzes, 1970, Spanish edit., 1979, Das Bundesverfassungsgericht im politischen Prozess, 1976, Japanese edit., 1978, Der demokratische Verfassungsstaat, 1995, La Constitution, cadre et mesure du droit, 1994, Praxis der Verfassungs auslegung, 1994, vol. II, 2006, Grundgesetz Kommentar, 5th edit., 3 vols., 2005, Freiheit und Institutionen, 2002; editor: Studien und Materialien zur Verfassungsgerichtsbarkeit, 1973—; co-editor: Juristenzeitung, 1978—2006; contbr. over 300 articles to law jours. and festschriften, —. Fellow, Inst. for Advanced Study, Berlin, 1990—91. Mem. Internat. Assn. Constl. Law (exec. com. 1981-2004, hon. pres. 2004-), Acad. Scis. Göttingen, Assn. German Profs. Pub. Law (exec. com. 1988-89, pres. 1998-99), German Assn. Comparative Law (exec. com. 1986-), Soc. Juris Publici Europaei (pres. 2003-07, hon. pres. 2007-). Home: Schlegelweg 10 D-37075 Göttingen Germany Personal E-mail: c.starck@gwdg.de.

STARER, BRIAN DOUGLAS, lawyer; b. Utica, NY, 1945; BS, U.S. Merchant Marine Acad., 1967; JD, Union U., 1972. Bar: NY 1972, US Dist. Ct. (no., so. and ea. dists.) NY, US Ct. Appeals (2nd, 3rd and 5th cirs.) 1973, US Ct. Appeals (9th cir.) 1976, US Supreme Ct. 1977, US Ct. Internat. Trade 1977, US Ct. Customs and Patent Appeals 1980. Mem. Haight Gardner Holland & Knight, NYC; ptnr., maritime law, dir., mem. mgmt. com. Holland & Knight, NYC, 1997—. Mng. editor Albany Law Rev., 1971-72; contbr. articles to profl. jours. Named to Internat. Maritime Hall of Fame, 2002. Mem. ABA, Maritime Law Assn. US, Internat. Bar Assn., NY State Bar Assn. Office: Holland & Knight 195 Broadway Fl 24 New York NY 10007-3189 Office Phone: 212-513-3200. Business E-Mail: brian.starer@hklaw.com.

STARFIELD, BARBARA HELEN, pediatrician, educator; b. Bklyn., Dec. 18, 1932; d. Martin and Eva (Illions) Starfield; m. Neil A. Holtzman, June 12, 1955; children: Robert, Jon, Steven, Deborah. AB, Swarthmore Coll., 1954; MD, SUNY, 1959; MPH, Johns Hopkins U., 1963. Tchg. asst. in anatomy Downstate Med. Ctr., NYC, 1955—57; intern in pediat. Johns Hopkins U., 1959—60, resident, 1960—62, dir. pediatric med. care clinic, 1963—66, dir. cmty. staff comprehensive child care project, 1966—67, dir. pediatric clin. scholars program, 1971—76, prof. health policy, joint appointment in pediat., 1975—, disting. univ. prof., 1994—. Mem. Nat. Com. Vital Stats., 1994—2002; cons. DHHS; mem. nat. adv. coun. Agy. for Health Care Policy and Rsch., 1990—94; adv. subcom. on Health Systems and Svcs. Rsch. Pan Am. Health Orgn., 1988—92, 1995—; cons. Health Care Fin. Adminstrn., 1980—. Editl. bd. Med. Care, 1977—79, Pediat., 1977—82, Internat. Jour. Health Svcs., 1978—, Med. Care Rev., 1980—84, Health Svc. Rsch., 1996—, assoc. editor Ann. Rev. Pub. Health, 1996—2001; contbr. articles to profl. jours. Recipient Dave Luckman Meml. award, 1958, HEW Career Devel. award, 1970—75, Disting. Investigator award, Assn. Health Svcs. Rsch., 1995, 1st Primary Care Achievement award, Pew Charitable Trust Fund, 1994, 1st Ann. Rsch. award, Ambulatory Pediatric Assn., 1990, Baxter prize, 2004. Fellow: Am. Acad. Pediat.; mem.: APHA (Martha May Eliot award 1995), Internat. Soc. for Equity in Health (pres. 2000—02), Ambulatory Pediatric Assn. (pres. 1980), Internat. Epidemiologic Assn., Soc. Pediatric Rsch., Inst. Medicine of NAS (governing coun. 1981—83), Alpha Omega Alpha, Sigma Xi. Office: Johns Hopkins Sch Hygiene 624 N Broadway Baltimore MD 21205-1900 Business E-Mail: bstarfie@jhsph.edu.

STARGATT, BRUCE M., lawyer; b. NYC, July 8, 1930; s. Sydney S. and Janet (Feldman) S.; m. Barbara Hirschfeld, Aug. 21, 1954; children: Linda, Daniel, Deborah. AB, U. Vt., 1951; LLB, Yale U., 1954. Bar: Del. 1955, N.Y. 1955, D.C. 1956. Assoc. Arnold Fortas & Porter, Washington, 1954; ptnr. Young, Conaway, Stargatt & Taylor, Wilmington, Del., 1956—, now of counsel. Lawyer chmn. Del. Appellate Ct. Handbook comm., 1984—95; chmn. Del. Supreme Ct. Rules Lawyers Adv. Comm., 1986—93. 1st Lt. USAF, 1954—56. Recipient Herbert Harley award Am. Judicature Soc., 1993. Fellow Am. Bar Found., Am. Coll. Trial Lawyers; mem. ABA (ho. of dels., bd. gov. 2003-2006), Am. Law Inst., Del. State Bar Assn. (pres. 1981-82, 1st State Disting. Svc. award 1992), Del. Bar Found. (pres. 1995-2000). Office: Young Conaway Stargatt & Taylor 17th Fl 1000 West St PO Box 391 Wilmington DE 19899-0391

STARING, GRAYDON SHAW, lawyer; b. Deansboro, NY, Apr. 9, 1923; s. William Luther and Eleanor Mary (Shaw) S.; m. Joyce Lydia Allum-Poon, Sept. 1, 1949; children: Diana Hilary Agnes, Christopher Paul Norman. AB, Hamilton Coll., 1947; JD, U. Calif., Berkeley, 1951. Bar: Calif. 1952, U.S. Supreme Ct. 1958. Atty. Office Gen. Counsel, Navy Dept., San Francisco, 1952-53; atty. admiralty and shipping sect. U.S. Dept. Justice, San Francisco, 1953-60; assoc. Lillick & Charles (now Nixon Peabody), San Francisco, 1960-64, ptnr., 1965—88, of counsel, 1989—. Titulary mem. Internat. Maritime Com.; bd. dirs. Marine Exch. at San Francisco, 1984-88, pres. 1986-88; instr. pub. speaking Hamilton Coll., 1947-48; adj. prof. Hastings Coll. Law, 1996-97, Boalt Hall, U. Calif., 1999. Author: Law of Reinsurance, 1993; assoc. editor Am. Maritime Cases, 1966-92, editor, 1992—; contbr. articles to legal jours. Mem. San Francisco Lawyers Com. for Urban Affairs, 1972-90; bd. dirs. Legal Aid Soc., San Francisco, 1974-90, v.p., 1975-80, pres., 1980-82. With USN, 1943-46, comdr. USNR. Fellow Am. Bar Found., Am. Coll. Trial Lawyers; mem. ABA (chmn. maritime ins. com. 1975-76, mem. standing com. admiralty law 1976-82, 86-90, chmn. 1990, ho. dels. 1986-90), Fed. Bar Assn. (pres. San Francisco chpt. 1968), Bar Assn. San Francisco (sec. 1972, treas. 1973), Calif. Acad. Appellate Lawyers, Maritime Law Assn. U.S. (exec. com. 1977-88, v.p. 1980-84, pres. 1984-86), Brit.-Am. C. of C. (bd. dirs. 1987-2001), City Club San Francisco, Tulane Admiralty Inst. (permanent adv. bd.), Assocs. Maritime Mus. Libr. (dir. 1990-2001, pres. 1992-94). Office: Nixon Peabody LLP 1 Embarcadero Ctr Fl 18 San Francisco CA 94111-3900 Home Phone: 510-540-7722; Office Phone: 415-984-8310. Personal E-mail: Starlaw@att.net. Business E-Mail: gstaring@nixonpeabody.com. *"How small, of all that human hearts endure,/That part which laws or kings can cause or cure!".*

STARK, ALBERT MAXWELL, lawyer; b. Trenton, NJ, May 3, 1939; m. Ellen Stark, Nov. 20, 1966; children: Jared, Rachel. BA, Darmouth Coll., Hanover, NH, 1960; LLD, U. Pa., Phila., 1963. Bar: N.J. 1964. Asst. to gov. of N.J., 1964; asst. atty. City of Trenton, 1965-66; asst. prosecutor Mercer County, N.J., 1967-68. Author: Beyond the Bar - Challenges in the Life of a Lawyer, 2002, A War Against Terror Through My Eyes, 2006; host radio programs Lawline, WHWH, 1985—95, In the Pub. Interest, WIMG, 1996—95. Recipient Humanitarian award Thomas A. Edison State Coll., 2000, award Trial Attys. of N.J., 2000. Mem. ABA, N.J. Bar Assn., Mercer County Bar Assn., Mercer County C. of C. (Citizen of Yr. 1994), Rotary Internat. (Fred Harris fellow 1996). Avocations: writing, tennis, skiing. Office: Stark & Stark 993 Lenox Dr Lawrenceville NJ 08648-2316 Office Phone: 609-896-9060.

STARK, BRUCE GUNSTEN, artist; b. Queens, NY, Feb. 17, 1933; s. Richard M. and Karen (Gunsten) S.; m. Joan Patricia Lauer, Nov. 19, 1960; children: Robert, Ronald. Student, Sch. Visual Arts, NYC, 1955-58. Artist, cartoonist NY Daily News, NYC, 1961—82. One-man shows Art Inst., Pitts., 1968, U. Kutztown, Pa., 1970, N.Y. Bank for Savs., N.Y.C., 1971; group shows Nat. Art Mus. Sport, N.Y.C., 1971; represented in permanent collections Everett Dirksen Library, L.D. Johnson Library, Baseball Hall Fame, Cooperstown, N.Y., Basketball Hall Fame, Mass. Served with USN, 1952-54. Recipient Nat. Cartoonist Soc.'s Rueben Catagory awards for sports, 1966, 75, spl. features, 1968; Page One award for best sports cartoon, 1970, 73 N.Y.C., 71; 3d, 4th, 6th prizes Internat. Salon de Caricatures Montreal, 1966, 68, 69; Most Outstanding Achievement award Sch. Visual Arts, 1982 Achievements include having original cartoons requested by Pres. Nixon, Johnson; 1st color cartoon appearing on front page of N.Y. Daily News. Home: 3139 Stonewater Dr Lakeland FL 33803-2572 *My goals, ideas, principles and standards of conduct are all helpfully outlined for me by God in His holy word— the Bible. I really need no other source. Whatever success has come to me, I think, is because of this, and what God has done for me, through His Son, Jesus Christ.*

STARK, DENNIS EDWIN, private investor, retired bank executive; b. Springfield, Ill., Dec. 24, 1937; s. Edwin C. and Ida (Fentem) S. BS, Ill. Wesleyan U., 1959; Sanxay fellow practical ethics, Princeton U., 1959-60; MBA, Harvard U., 1962. Adminstrv. asst. to chmn. bd. Industrial Valley Bank, Phila., 1962-64; fin. analyst E.I. DuPont de Nemours, Wilmington, Del., 1964-65; asst. treas. Old Stone Bank, Providence, 1965-68, treas., 1968-71; sr. v.p., treas., sec. Old Stone Bank and Old Stone Corp., Providence, 1971-76; exec. v.p., chief fin. officer Old Stone Corp., Old Stone Bank, 1976-86, Dime Bank, NYC, 1986-88; ptnr. Bank Mgmt. Ptnrs., NYC, 1988-90; sr. v.p., CFO, corp. sec. Cen Fed Bank, Pasadena, Calif., 1990-92; exec. v.p., CFO, corp. sec. Ea. Bank, Lynn, Mass., 1992-96; ptnr. Fin. Mgmt. Ptnrs., Pawtucket, RI, 1996-99; v.p. bus. and fin., CFO U. R.I., Kingston, 1999—2003; bank dir., exec. v.p., CFO, corp. sec. Ind. Bank, East Greenwich, RI, 2003—05; ret., 2005. Bd. dirs., chmn. fin. com. Preservation Soc. Pawtucket; trustee, chmn. Preserve R.I.; mem. Diocesan Coun. Episcopal Diocese; mem. audit com. RISD; Elizabeth Johnson Pawtuckt Rsch. Libr.; Friends of the Brown Librs.; vestry, treas. St. Martins Episcopal Ch., Providence; dep. to gen. conv. Episcopal Ch. USA, mem. exec. coun., mem. investment com.; bd. dirs. exec. com. and fin. com., chmn.strategic planning com. R.I. Philharm.; bd. dirs. R.I. Hist. Soc., mem. facilities com.; bd. trustees Mus. Primitive Art and Culture, Chorus of Westerly. Mem. Fin. Execs. Inst., Harvard Bus. Sch. Assn. of R.I., Acacia (co-founder Ill. Wesleyan U. chpt.), Providence Art Club, Hope Club, Univ. Club (R.I.), Harvard Club (N.Y.C.), Agawam Hunt, Dunes Club, Brown Faculty Club, U. R.I. Univ. Club (treas.). Republican. Episcopalian. Avocations: stamp collecting/philately, coin collecting/numismatics. Home (Summer): 41 Courtway St Narragansett RI 02882-3610 E-mail: destark@cox.net.

STARK, DIANA, public relations executive; b. NYC, July 01; d. Benjamin and Sara (Zelasny) S. BA, Hunter Coll. Promotion mgr. TV Guide mag., NYC, 1950-61, Show Bus. Illustrated, NYC, 1961-62; broadcast specialist Young & Rubicam, NYC, 1962-69; pres. Stark Comms. Inc., NYC, 1969-76; pub. svc. publicity account exec. Y & R E, NYC, 1976-77; pres. Stark Comms. Internat., NYC, 1978—. Pub. rels. workshop leader Chgo. Econ. Devel. Corp., 1973-76; cons. to Asahi Shimbun for English Language Newsletter. 1991-92, columnist Host mag., 1960-65; writer, producer programs for women's TV shows, 1962—. Book developer Ellis Island: The First Experience With Liberty, 1991. Coord. We Have Arrived, Portraits at Ellis Island, Augustus Sherman Photographs, 1902-24. Mem. NATAS (trustee 1974-78, publicity com., chmn., chpt. gov. 1972-76, 82-86, 87-91, editor N.Y. TV Directory 1987-90). Home Phone: 212-582-5619; Office Phone: 212-582-5619. Office Fax: 212-765-3670. Business E-Mail: dstarkny@aol.com.

STARK, FORTNEY HILLMAN (PETE STARK), congressman; b. Milw., Nov. 11, 1931; s. Fortney Hillman Sr. and Dorothy M. (Mueller) S.; children: Jeffrey Peter, Beatrice Ann, Thekla Brumder, Sarah Gallun, Fortney Hillman Stark III; m. Deborah Roderick; children: Hannah Marie, Andrew Peter. BS In Engring., MIT, 1953; MBA, U. Calif. Berkeley, 1960. Teaching asst. MIT, Cambridge, 1953-54; prin. Skaife & Co., Berkeley, Calif., 1957-61; founder Beacon Savs. & Loan Assn., Antioch, Calif., 1961; pres., founder Security Nat. Bank, Walnut Creek, Calif., 1963-72; mem. U.S. Congress from 13th (formerly 9th) Calif. dist., 1973—; mem. ways and means com., formerly chmn., now ranking minority mem. health subcom.; mem. joint econ. com. Bd. dirs. ACLU, 1971, Common Cause, 1971, Starr King Sch.; del. Dem. State Cen. Com.; trustee Calif. Dem. Coun. Capt. USAF, 1955-57. Mem. Delta Kappa Epsilon. Democrat. Unitarian. Office: US Ho Reps 239 Cannon Ho Office Bldg Washington DC 20515-0513 *

STARK, HAROLD MEAD, mathematics educator; b. LA, Aug. 6, 1939; s. James Asher and Pearl (Kelso) S. BS, Calif. Tech. U., 1961; MA, U. Calif., Berkeley, 1963, PhD, 1964. Mem. faculty U. Mich., Ann Arbor, 1964-66, 67-68, Dearborn, 1966-67, MIT, Cambridge, Mass., 1969-90; mem. faculty, dept. math. U. Calif.-San Diego, La Jolla, 1980—, chair math. dept., 1990-94. Bd. trustees Math. Scis. Rsch. Inst., Berkeley, 1989-94. Mem. Am. Math. Soc. (nominating com. 1982-85, coun. 1987-90), NAS. Office: U Calif San Diego Math Dept 0112 9500 Gilman Dr La Jolla CA 92093-0112 *

STARK, JOAN SCISM, education educator; b. Hudson, NY, Jan. 6, 1937; d. Ormonde F. and Myrtle Margaret (Kirkey) S.; m. William L. Stark, June 28, 1958 (dec.); children: Eugene William, Susan Elizabeth, Linda Anne, Ellen Scism; m. Malcolm A. Lowther, Jan. 31, 1981. BS, Syracuse U., 1957; MA (Hoadly fellow), Columbia U., 1960; Ed.D., SUNY, Albany, 1971. Tchr. Ossining (N.Y.) High Sch., 1957-59; free-lance editor Holt, Rinehart & Winston, Harcourt, Brace & World, 1960-70; lectr. Ulster County Community Coll., Stone Ridge, NY, 1968-70; asst. dean Goucher Coll., Balt., 1970-73, assoc. dean, 1973-74; assoc. prof., chmn. dept. higher postsecondary edn. Syracuse (N.Y.) U., 1974-78; dean Sch. Edn. U. Mich., Ann Arbor, 1978-83, prof., 1983-2001, prof. and dean emeritus, 2001—; dir. Nat. Ctr. for Improving Postsecondary Teaching and Learning, 1986—91. Editor: Rev. of Higher Edn., 1991-96; contbr. articles to various publs. Leader Girl Scouts U.S.A., Cub Scouts Am.; coach girls Little League; dist. officer PTA, intermittently, 1968-80; mem. adv. com. Gerald R. Ford Library, U. Mich., 1980-83; trustee Kalamazoo Coll., 1979-85; mem. exec. com. Inst. Social Research, U. Mich., 1979-81; bd. dirs. Mich. Assn. Colls. Tchr. Edn., 1979-81. Mem. Am. Assn. for Higher Edn., Am. Ednl. Rsch. Assn. (Div. J. Rsch. award 1998), Assn. Study Higher Edn. (dir. 1977-79, v.p. 1983, pres. 1984, Rsch. Achievement award 1992, svc. award 1998, Disting. Career award 1999), Assn. Innovation Higher Edn. (nat. chmn. 1974-75), Assn. Instl. Rsch. (disting. mem., Sidney Suslow award 1999), Assn. Colls. and Schs. Edn. State Univs. and Land Grant Colls. (dir. 1981-83), Acctg. Edn. Change Commn., Phi Beta Kappa, Phi Kappa Phi, Sigma Pi Sigma, Eta Pi Upsilon, Lambda Sigma Sigma, Phi Delta Kappa, Pi Lambda Theta.

STARK, LARRY A., state agency administrator; BA in Hist., Ohio Wesleyan U.; JD, W.Va. U. Exec. v.p. Milton Tri-County Bank; v.p. investor rels. Key Centurion Bankshares; various positions Banc One W.Va.; commr., chairperson W.Va. Divsn. Banking, 2001—. Office: WVa Divsn Banking State Capitol Complex Bldg 3 Rm 311 1900 Kanawha Blvd E Charleston WV 25305-0240 Office Phone: 304-558-2294. Office Fax: 304-558-0442. E-mail: lstark@wvdob.org.

STARK, LE A., JR., music educator; b. Houston, Jan. 3, 1931; s. Levi Alvin, Sr. and Sarah (Vining) Stark. MusB, N. Tex. U., 1953; MusM, Sam Houston U., 1983. Permanent tchr. cert. Tex. Tutor Dr. Isabel Scionti Studio, Denton, Tex., 1951—54; pvt. piano tchr. Houston, 1954—; head piano dept. Houston Bapt. U., 1969—72; instr. piano & music theory San Jacinto Jr. Coll., Houston, 1972—74; instr. piano, music theory & history U. Houston, 1974—96. Founder Houston Music Tchr.'s Forum, 1961. Mem. Ecumneical Coun. Religious Music, Houston, 1955—57. With US Army, 1954—56. Mem.: Phi Mu Alpha (life), Pi Kappa Lambda (life). Independent. Avocations: gardening, travel, reading, history.

STARK, MARTIN J., management consultant; b. NYC, May 29, 1941; s. Nathan and Lola (Belmont) S.; m. Shigemi Matsumoto, Apr. 27, 1967. AA, Glendale Coll., 1960; BA, Calif. State U., 1966; postgrad., San Fernando Valley Coll. Law, 1967—70. Sys. analyst Indsl. Electronic Engrs., Van Nuys, Calif., 1969—71, sales mgr., 1971—73; sales rep. Columbia Artists Mgmt., Inc., NYC, 1973—78, sales mgr., 1978—79, v.p. bus. affairs, mgr. data processing, 1979—82; dir. corp. affairs Kolmar-Luth Entertainment, Inc., NYC, 1982—84; pres. Oryx & Corp., NYC, 1984—85; exec. v.p. Asco Aerospace Products, Inc., El Segundo, Calif., 1985—87, Internat. Engine Parts, Inc., Chatsworth, Calif., 1987—92; pres. Stark & Assocs., Northridge, Calif., 1985—91; owner Mail Boxes Etc., 1992—. Lectr. Calif. State U., Long Beach, U. So. Calif.; cons. City of N.Y., Memory Data Software, IEPO, Inc.; advisor Thornton Protégé Program Thornton Sch. Music U. So. Calif.; bd. dirs. Holy Cross Hosp.; mentor Thornton Sch. Music, U. So. Calif. Mem.: Calabas C. of C., Classical Singer's Assn., Delta Upsilon. Avocations: sports cars, antiques, travel. Home: 18342 Chatham Ln Northridge CA 91326-3603 Office: 23679 Calabasas Rd Calabasas CA 91302-1502 Office Phone: 818-591-1086. E-mail: mbe1047@aol.com.

STARK, NELLIE MAY, forester, ecologist, educator; b. Norwich, Conn., Nov. 20, 1933; d. Theodore Benjamin and Dorothy Josephine (Pendleton) Beetham; m. Oscar Elder Stark, Oct. 1962 (dec.). BA, Conn. Coll., 1956; AM, Duke U., 1958, PhD, 1962. Botanist Exptl. Sta., U.S. Forest Svc., Old Strawberry, Calif., 1958-66; botanist, ecologist Desert Rsch. Inst., Reno, 1966-72; prof. forest ecology Sch. Forestry, U. Mont., Missoula, 1972-92; pvt. cons. Philomath, Oreg. Pres. Camas Analytical Lab., Inc., Missoula, 1987—92. Author: Will Your Family Survive the 21st Century, 1997, Memories of Wren, Oregon, 1998, So You Want to Build a Little Log Cabin in the Woods, 2002, Thirteen Days of Christmas, 2005; contbr. articles to profl. jours. Named Disting. Dau. Norwich, Conn., 1985; recipient Conn. award Conn. Coll., 1986, 54 grants. Mem. Ecol. Soc. Am. (chair ethics com. 1974, 76), Soc. Am. Foresters (taskforce 1987-88).

STARK, PATRICIA ANN, psychologist; b. Ames, Iowa, Apr. 21, 1937; d. Keith C. and Mary L. (Johnston) Moore. BS, So. Ill. U., Edwardsville, 1970, MS, 1972; PhD, St. Louis U., 1976. Counselor to alcoholics Bapt. Rescue Mission, East St. Louis, Ill., 1969; rschr. alcoholics Gateway Rehab. Ctr., East St. Louis, 1972; psychologist intern Henry-Stark Counties Spl. Edn. Dist. and Galesburg State Rsch. Hosp., Ill., 1972—73; instr. Lewis and Clark C.C., Godfrey, Ill., 1973—76, asst. prof., 1976—84, assoc. prof., 1994, coord. child care svcs., 1974—84; mem. staff dept. psychiatry Meml. Hosp., St. Elizabeth's Hosp., 1979—2001; supr. students interns, 1974—94. Dir. child and family svc. Collinsville Counseling Ctr., 1977-82; clin. dir., owner Empas-Complete Family Psychol. and Hypnosis Svcs., Collinsville, 1982—; cons. cmty. agys., 1974—; mem. adv. bd. Madison County Coun. on Alcoholism and Drug Dependency, 1977-80. Mem. APA, Ill. Psychol. Assn., Midwestern Psychol. Assn., Am. Soc. Clin. Hypnosis, Internat. Soc. Hypnosis. Office: 2802 Maryville Rd Maryville IL 62062 Office Phone: 618-345-6632.

STARK, RICHARD **See WESTLAKE, DONALD**

STARK, RICHARD BOIES, surgeon, artist; b. Conrad, Iowa, Mar. 31, 1915; s. Eugene and Hazel (Carson) S.; m. Judy Thornton, Oct. 31, 1967 AB, Stanford U., 1936; postgrad., U. Heidelberg, 1936—37; MD, Cornell U., 1941. Diplomate Am. Bd. Plastic Surgery (pres. 1967-68). Intern Peter Bent Brigham Hosp., Boston, 1941-42; asst. resident surgery Childrens Hosp., Boston, 1942; plastic surgeon Northington Gen. Hosp., Ala., 1945-46, Percy Jones Gen. Hosp., Mich., 1946; postwar fellow anatomy and embryology Stanford U., 1946-47; from asst. resident to resident in head and neck surgery VA Hosp., Bronx, NY, 1947-50; asst. resident, resident surgery, plastic, head and neck and gen. surgery N.Y. Hosp., NY, 1947-50; instr. surgery Cornell U., 1950-52, asst. prof., 1952-55, assoc. prof., 1955; asst. attending surgeon N.Y. Hosp., 1950-55; asst. prof. surgery Columbia U., 1955-58, assoc. prof., 1958-73, prof. clin. surgery, 1973—; assoc. attending surgeon St. Luke's Hosp., NYC, 1955-58, founding attending surgeon dept. plastic surgery, 1958—; founder dept. plastic surgery, 1955. Cons. Walter Reed Med. Ctr., 1970-77 Author: Plastic Surgery at the New York Hospital 100 Years Ago, 1952, (textbooks) Plastic Surgery, 1962, Cleft Palate, 1968, Aesthetic Plastic Surgery, 1980, Total Facial Reconstruction, 1985, Plastic Surgery of the Head and Neck, 1986; founding editor: Annals Plastic Surgery, 1978-81; assoc. editor: Plastic Reconstructive Surgery, 1977-82; contbr. 51 chpts. to books, more than 210 articles to profl. jours.; 25 one-man art shows, 1946—; rep. in permanent art exhibits, NY Hosp., St. Lukes Hosp., Army Med. Mus. Chmn. Medico Adv. Bd., 1976-77; mem., v.p. CARE Bd.; v.p. Wellborn Found., N.Y.C. Served to maj. M.C., AUS, 1943-46. Decorated Bronze Star (U.S.); Medal of Honor (2) (Vietnam); cavallero Order of San Carlos (Colombia), Dieffenbach medal (Berlin), Gold medal Nat. Inst. Social Scis.; named Disting. Alumnus, St. Lukes-Roosevelt Hosp. Fellow ACS; mem. Am. Assn. Plastic Surgeons, Am. Soc. Plastic and Reconstructive Surgery (pres. 1966, Spl. Achievement award), Found. Am. Soc. Plastic and Reconstructive Surgery (pres. 1961-65), Am. Surg. Assn., Soc. Univ. Surgeons, French Soc. Plastic Surgeons, Brasilian Soc. Plastic Surgeons, Colombian Soc. Plastic Surgeons, Argentina Soc. Plastic Surgeons, Brit. Assn. Plastic Surgery, Peruvian Acad. Surgeons, N.Y. Surg. Soc., N.Y. Acad. Medicine (pres. Friends Rare Book Room), Plastic and Reconstructive Surgery (sec., pres. 1966), N.Y. State Med. Soc. (pres., sec., med. history), N.Y. Regional Soc. Plastic and Reconstructive Surgery (pres. 1064-65), Halsted Soc. (pres. 1973-74), James IV Assn. Surgeons, Am. Soc. Aesthetic Plastic Surgery (pres. 1974-75), Nat. Arts Club (exhibiting mem.), Century Club (profl. artist), Artist Fellowship, Lotos Club. Home: 3744 SE Old St Lucie Blvd Stuart FL 34996

STARK, ROBERT J., lawyer; b. Middletown, NY, July 16, 1970; s. Jeffrey and Patricia Stark. BA, Lafayette Coll., Easton, Pa., 1992; JD, Vanderbilt U., Nashville, Tenn., 1995. Bar: N.J. 1995, N.Y. 1996, U.S. Dist. Ct. NJ. 1995, U.S. Dist. Ct. (So. Dist.) N.Y. 1996, U.S. Dist. Ct. (Ea. Dist.) N.Y. 1996. Panelist and bankruptcy confs. Contbr. articles to law jours. Recipient Jessup Internat. Moot Ct. Team, Vanderbilt U. Law Sch., 1994-1995; scholar McKnight-Black Scholarship, Lafayette Coll., 1992. Mem.: Turnaround Mgmt. Assn., Bar Assn. of City of N.Y. E-mail: rstark@akingump.com.

STARK, ROBERT MARTIN, mathematician, civil engineer, educator; b. NYC, Feb. 6, 1930; s. Alexander and Julia (Gross) S.; m. Carol LaSage, Jan. 13, 1955 (dec. Mar. 1988); children: Bradley R., Timothy D., Steven M., Candice B. AB, Johns Hopkins U., 1951; MA, U. Mich., 1952; PhD, U. Del., 1965. Rsch. scientist Bausch and Lomb, Rochester, NY, 1955; instr. Rochester Inst. Tech., 1956-57; asst. dean engring., asst. prof. math. Cleve. State U., 1957-62; instr. U. Del., 1962-64, asst. prof. civil and environ. engring., math. scis., 1964-68, assoc. prof., 1968-76, prof., 1976—2002, prof. emeritus, 2002—; pres., cons. applied sci. R.M. Stark & Co., Inc., 2003—. Vis. assoc. prof. MIT, 1972—73; chmn. grad. program in ops. rsch.; cons. in field. Author: (with R.L. Nicholls) Mathematical Foundations for Design: Civil Engineering Systems, 1972, reprinted 2005, (with R.H. Mayer, Jr.) Quantitative Construction Management: Uses of Linear Optimization, 1983, (with R. Engelbrecht-Wiggans and M. Shubik) Auctioning, Bidding and Contracting, 1983, (with C. Sloyer, et al) Contemporary Applied Mathematics Series, 1987, Mathagrams, 1996. Mem. Del. Heritage Commn., 1990—, treas., 2005—; bd. dirs. Generations Home Care, Inc., 1989—, Wilmington Sr. Ctr., 1994—2006, Meals on Wheels, Del., 1990—2003; bd. dirs., v.p. White Clay Watershed Assn., 1992—97; mem. cmty. adv. bd. WHYY Pub. Broadcasting Corp., 2002—; bd. dirs. U. Mich., Del., 2002—. Recipient Outstanding Alumnus award, U. Del. Dept. Civil and Environ. Engring., 1999; grantee, Office Naval Rsch., 1974—81, NSF, 1969—70, U.S. Army Rsch. Office, 1966—68. Mem. AAAS, ASCE, Nat. Coun. Tchrs. Math., Inst. Mgmt. Sci., Ops. Rsch. Soc. Am., Phila. Ops. Rsch. Soc. (pres. 1970), U. Del. Assn. Ret. Faculty (pres. 2004—), Del. Acad. Sci. (bd. dirs. 1990—, pres. 1994-96, 2005-), Ft. Del. Soc., (bd. dirs., 2006—), English Speaking Union (bd. dirs. 2007-), Rotary Club Wilmington.

STARK, S. DANIEL, JR., casino and gaming resort company executive; b. Port Hueneme, Calif., Mar. 26, 1953; s. S. Daniel and Eloise Marie (Fisher) S.; m. Pauline Laube Finley, June 7, 1997; 1 child, Kaitlyn Elizabeth. BS, Calif. Poly. U., Pomona, 1981; cert. in exec. mgmt., Claremont Grad. U., 1989, MA in Mgmt., 1992. Driver-guide San Diego Wild Animal Pk./Zool. Soc. San Diego, Escondido, Calif., 1974—76; attractions host Disneyland divsn. The Walt Disney Co., Anaheim, Calif., 1976—80, mgmt. intern, 1981, supr. ops., 0981—1982, area supr. ops., dept. mgr., 1982—87; mgmt. cons. S.D. Stark, Jr., Las Vegas, 1985—2000; dir. mktg. Ramada Express Hotel & Casino, Laughlin, Nev., 1988—89; exec. dir. San Bernardino Conv. and Visitors Bur., Calif., 1989—98; pres., CEO Panama City Beach Conv. & Visitors Bur., 1998—99; exec. dir. Bay County Tourist Devel. Coun., Fla., 1998—99; dir. corp. mktg. Boyd Gaming Corp., Las Vegas, 1999—2005, v.p. corp. mktg., 2006—. Part-time instr. mgmt. and mktg. So. Calif. campus U. Phoenix, 1997-98, Nev. campus, 1999—, area chair for mktg., 2001-04; cons. Hemmeter Devel. Corp., Honolulu, 1985, Calif. Authority Racing Fairs, Sacramento, 1987-88, USIA for Latvian Ministry Transp., tourism divsn., 1992, U.S. Bur. Land Mgmt., tourism mgmt. project U. Alaska Sch. Mgmt.; adj. prof. Sch. Bus. and Pub. Admisntrn., Calif. State U., San Bernardino, 1992-93 Bd. dirs. Leadership So. Calif., 1993-98, grad. pub. affairs tng., 1993; congl. appointee del. White House Conf. on Travel and Tourism, 1995; mem. regional econ. strategies consortium So. Calif. Assn. Govts., 1996-98; mem. Visit Fla. Mktg. Com., 1998-99; bd. dirs. Fla. Assn. Conv. and Visitors Burs., 1998-99, Speedway Childrens Charities Las Vegas Chpt., 1999—, treas., 2000-01, chmn., 2001-2002; v.p. Cops Helping Kids, 2002-2003, pres., 2003-04; mem. spl. events com. Las Vegas Centennial Commn.; bd. trustees Crime Stoppers of Nev., Inc., 2004—. Recipient recipient World Champion Trail Horse award Am. Jr. Quarter Horse Assn., 1972, resolution Calif. Assembly, 1989, 98, San Bernardino County Bd. Suprs., 1989, City of San Bernardino Mayor and Coun., 1989, 98, Calif. Senate, 1989, 98, Calif. Tourism award for Best Spl. Event-Rt. 66 Rendezvous, 1997, Rt. 66 Rendezvous Founder's award San Bernardino Conv. and Visitors Bur., 2004; selected as one of 1991 Up and Coming Young Bus. Leaders in San Bernardino County; named one of Inland Empire Bus. All Stars, 1991. Mem. U.S. Equestrian Fedn. (life), Am. Quarter Horse Assn (life), Assn. Travel Mktg. Execs., Internat. Assn. Conv. and Visitors Burs. (cert. comm., conv. mktg., tourism mktg.), Pub. Rels. Soc. Am. (bd. dirs. Calif. Inland Empire chpt. 1990-95, Polaris award 1997), Calif. and Nev. Festivals and Events Assn. (pres. 1997-98, bd. dirs. 1994-98, 2002—), Inland Empire Tourism Coun. (bd. dirs. 1996-98, exec. com. 1996-98, treas. 1997-98), Calif. Travel Industry Assn., Tourism Assn. So. Calif. (bd. dirs. 1990-95, vice chair 1992-95), Western Assn. Convs. and Vis. Bur. (chmn. Calif. coun. 1992-94), E Clampus Vitus Inc. (bd. proctors 2005—, sec. 2006-07, v.p. 2007—), FarmHouse Fraternity (internat. bd. dirs. 1986-94, v.p. 1990-92, Snyder Alumni award 1984). Avocations: boating, fishing, films, equestrian competition. Office: Boyd Gaming Corp 6465 S Rainbow Blvd Las Vegas NV 89118-3215 Personal E-mail: sdsjr@aol.com.

STARKE, HAROLD EUGENE, JR., lawyer; b. Richmond, Va., Aug. 1, 1944; BA, Randolph-Macon Coll., Ashland, Va., 1967; JD, U. Richmond, 1971; LLM in Taxation, NYU, 1973. Bar: Va. 1971, DC 1981. Ptnr. Troutman Sanders LLP, Richmond. Editor U. Richmond Law Rev., 1970-71. Bd. trustees Randolph-Macon Coll., 1983-85, 95-97, 99—. Fellow Am. Coll. Tax Counsel, Am. Bar Found.; mem. ABA (taxation sect.), Va. State Bar (chmn. taxation sect. 1985-86), DC Bar, Richmond Estate Planning Coun., McNeill Honor Soc., Phi Delta Phi. Office: Troutman Sanders LLP Troutman Sanders Bldg 1001 Haxall Point PO Box 1122 Richmond VA 23218-1122 Office Phone: 804-697-1287.

STARKEY, BOB (ROBERT G. STARKEY), women's college basketball coach; b. Sept. 7, 1959; m. Sherie Hayslett. Asst. coach Winfield HS, W.Va. Coll., 1984—87, Poca HS, W.Va.; asst. coach women's basketball Marshall U., Huntington, W.Va., 1988—89; asst. coach men's basketball La. State U., 1990—96, adminstrv. asst. men's and women's basketball, 1996—97, asst. coach women's basketball, 1998—2007, acting head coach women's basketball, 2007, assoc. head coach, 2007—. Office: La State U Womens Basketball Athletics Dept PO Box 25095 Baton Rouge LA 70894-5095 Office Phone: 225-578-6643. E-mail: rstarke@lsu.edu. *

STARKEY, CLIFF, musician; b. Phila., Pa., Mar. 19, 1963; Recording artist Capitol Records; mem. Emeril Live Band, 1997—, The Groovemasters. Composer: (songs) Phila. Conv. Bd. promotional video; musician: (music video projects) NFL Studios. Achievements include touring with the Three Degrees, the Temptations, and Pieces of a Dream. Office Phone: 323-462-6252.

STARKEY, JERRY L., real estate developer; BBA, N. Tex. State Univ., Denton; JD, Tex. Tech. Univ., Lubbock. Bar: Tex. Pres., secy. Fla. Design Communities, 1994—2005; pres., sec. Ashton Care Sys. Inc., 1996—98; pres., COO Watermark Communities LP (WCI), Bonita Springs, Fla., 1998—2005, pres., CEO, 2005—. Bd. trustees Fla. Gulf Coast Univ., 2001—. Office: WCI 24301 Walden Ctr Dr Bonita Springs FL 34134 *

STARKEY, RICHARD **See STARR, RINGO**

STARKEY, RUSSELL BRUCE, JR., energy executive; b. Lumberport, W.Va., July 20, 1942; s. Russell Bruce and Dorotha Mable (Field) S.; m. Joan McClellan, May 27, 1966; children: Christine, Pamela, Joanne. BS, Miami U., Oxford, Ohio, 1964; grad. student, U. New Haven, 1972—73, N.C. State U., 1974—75; postgrad., U.S. Navy Schs., 1964—66, postgrad., 1968. From sr. engr., nuc. generation sect. to prin. engr. Carolina Power & Light Co., Raleigh, NC, 1973—75; supr. quality assurance, supt. tech. and adminstrn. Brunswick Steam Electric Plant, Southport, NC, 1975—77; plant mgr. H. B. Robinson Steam Electric Plant, Hartsville, SC, 1977—83; mgr. environ. svcs. Carolina Power & Light Co., Raleigh, 1984—85, mgr. nuc. safety and environ. svcs. dept., 1985—88; mgr. Brunswick Nuc. Project Dept., 1988—89, v.p., 1989—92, v.p. Nuc. Svc. Dept., 1992—93; exec. v.p. energy mgmt. divsn. Hesco, Inc., 1993; from dir. indsl. electrotech. lab. to v.p. gen. tech. mgr. Advanced Energy Corp., 1993—97; cons. U.S. Enrichment Corp., Paducah, Ky., 1997—98, tng. mgr., 1998—2001, plant gen. mgr., 2001—05, v.p. ops., 2005—. With USN, 1964-73. Named Hon. Ky. Col. Mem.: Am. Nuc. Soc. Home: 6613 Belle Chase Ct Gaithersburg MD 20882 Office: 6903 Rockledge Dr Bethesda MD 20817

STARKEY, THOMAS D., surgeon; b. Dallas, Dec. 2, 1954; s. Claude Maurice and Betty Lulu (Bobo) Flores. BA, Tex. Tech. U., 1977; MD, U. Tex. Southwestern, Dallas, 1982. Diplomate Am. Bd. Surgery, Am. Bd. Thoracic Surgery. Surgery intern U. Mich. Hosps., Ann Arbor, 1982-83, surgery resident, 1983-88, resident, cardiovascular and thoracic surgery, 1988-90, thoracic surgery fellow, 1990; cardiopulmonary transplantation fellow Stanford U., 1991; cardiothoracic surgeon St. Thomas Hosp., Nashville, 1991—, Cardiovascular Surgery Assocs., Nashville, 1991—; also bd. dirs. Dir. heart transplant program St. Thomas Hosp., 1992—. Contbr. (with others) articles to profl. jours. Fellow ACS, Am. Coll. Cardiology; mem. AMA, Soc. Thoracic Surgeons, So. Thoracic Surg. Assn., United Network of Organ Sharing, Nashville Acad. Medicine, Tenn. Med. Assn., Internat. Soc. for Heart & Lung Transplantation, Am. Soc. for Artificial Internal Organs, Nashville Surg. Soc., Frederick A. Coller Surg. Soc., John Alexander Soc. Avocations: flying, sailing. Office: Cardiovascular Surgery Associates Pc 4230 Harding Pike Ste 450 Nashville TN 37205-6048

STARKMAN, GARY LEE, lawyer; b. Chgo., Sept. 2, 1946; s. Oscar and Sara (Ordman) Starkman. AB, U. Ill., 1968; JD cum laude, Northwestern U., 1971. Bar: Ill. 1971, U.S. Dist. Ct. (no. dist.) Ill. 1972, U.S. Ct. Appeals (7th cir.) 1972, U.S. Supreme Ct. 1974, Trial Bar U.S. Dist. Ct. (no. dist.) Ill. 1982, U.S. Ct. Appeals (3d cir.) 1984, U.S. Ct. Appeals (D.C. cir.) 1984. Asst. U.S. Atty. No. Dist. Ill., 1971-75; gen. counsel, dir. rsch. Citizens for Thompson Campaign Com., 1975-77; counsel to Gov. of Ill., 1977-81; admissions com. U.S. Dist. Ct. (no. dist.) Ill., 1982-90; ptnr. Ross & Hardies, Chgo., 1990—2003, McGuire Woods LLP, Chgo., 2003—. Co-author: (textbook) Cases and Comments on Criminal Procedure, 1974, 6th edit., 2003; contbr. articles to profl. jours.; reviewer in field. Chmn. state agys. divsn. Jewish United Fund Met. Chgo., 1978-81; chmn. Ill. Racing Bd., 1991-96; bd. dirs. Internat. Assn. Racing Commn., 1992-94; cmty. adv. bd. Jr. League Chgo., 1979-83. Named one of Ten Outstanding Young Citizens, Chgo. Jr. C. of C., 1978; recipient John Marshall award for appellate litigation, Atty. Gen. U.S., 1974, Nat. Svc. award, Tau Epsilon Pi, 1968. Mem.: ABA (litigation sect.), Chgo. Bar Assn. (constl. law com.), Decalogue Soc., Northwestern U. Law Alumni Assn. Office: McGuire Woods LLP 77 W Walker Dr Ste 4100 Chicago IL 60601-1681 Home Phone: 773-929-4422; Office Phone: 312-750-2788. Business E-Mail: gstarkman@mcguirewoods.com.

STARKS, DANIEL J., medical technology and services executive; BA, Shimer Coll., Waukegan, Ill.; JD magna cum laude, U. Minn. Law Sch., 1979. Comml. litigation atty. Nichols, Starks, Carruthers and Kaster, 1979—85; gen. counsel to pres., CEO Daig Corp. (bought by St. Jude Medical Inc.), 1985—96; pres., CEO, Daig Corp. St. Jude Medical Inc., St. Paul, 1996—98, dir., 1996—, pres., CEO Cardiac Rhythm Mgmt. div., 1998—2001, pres., COO, 2001—04, chmn., pres., CEO, 2004—. Bd. dir. Urologix Inc. Office: St Jude Medical Inc 1 Lillehei Plz Saint Paul MN 55117-9913 *

STARKS, DORIS N., retired nursing educator, administrator; b. Conecuh County, Ala., July 30, 1937; m. Wilbert L. Starks Sr., Dec. 25, 1961; children: Wilbert L. Jr., Garrick Edward. BS in Nursing, Tuskegee U., 1958; MS in Nursing, The Cath. U. of Am., 1965; PhD, Union Grad. Sch., 1978. Lic. nurse, Md. Staff nurse VA Hosp. Ctr., Tuskegee, Ala., 1958-61, insvc. edn. instr., 1965-66; staff nurse Washington Hosp. Ctr., 1963-65; asst. prof. med./surg. nursing Tuskegee U., 1966-68; prof. Community Coll. Balt, 1968, asst. chair dept. nursing, 1980-84, chair, 1984-86, chair dept. nursing and health scis., 1986-89, dir. nursing program, 1989; asst. dean, prof. nursing div. Coppin State Coll., Balt., 1990-91, dean nursing, div. nursing, 1991-98; ret., 1998. Item writer Nat. State Bd. Exam. Test Pool. Author bi-weekly health issues column Christian World, 1976-77. Mem. adv. coun. on vocat. edn. City of Balt. 1nd lt. US Army Nurse Corps., 1959-62. Recipient plaque and commendation Tuskegee Inst. Alumni Assn., 1983, Leadership in Nursing award Md. Found. for Nursing, 1994, Strong Blacks in Health Care award, Balt., 1995; honoree Black Nurses Assn., 1984; inducted Tuskegee U. Sch. Nursing Hall of Fame, 1992. Fellow Am. Acad. Nursing; mem. ANA, Tuskegee U. Nurses Alumni Assn. (Balt. met. area chpt.), Nat. Coalition of 100 Black Women, Alpha Kappa Alpha, Sigma Theta Tau, Chi Eta Phi. Home: 318 Bullskin St Charles Town WV 25414

STARKS, FRED WILLIAM, chemicals executive; b. Millford, Ill., Aug. 16, 1921; s. Otis Earl and Evelyn Viola Starks; m. Minnie Jane Reynolds, Sept. 4, 1946; children: David F., Steven J., Daniel J. BS, U. Ill., 1943, MS, 1947; PhD, U. Nebr., 1950. Supr. US Rubber Co., Torrance, Calif., 1943—44, DuPont, Niagara Falls, NY, 1950—57; pres. Starks Assocs., Inc., Buffalo, 1957—89, chmn., 1989—. Spl. lectr. U. Buffalo, 1959—63. Lt. (j.g.) USNR, 1944—46. Avery fellow, 1948—49, USPHS fellow, 1949—50. Mem.: Am. Inst. Chemists, NY Acad. Sci., Am. Chem. Soc., Chemists Club, Buffalo Club, Cosmos, Sigma Xi. Achievements include patents in field. Office: Starks Assocs Inc 1280 Niagara St Buffalo NY 14213-1592

STARKWEATHER, FREDERICK THOMAS, retired data processing executive; b. Sioux City, Iowa, Feb. 24, 1933; s. Fred Ervin and Gertrude Faye (Madden) S.; m. Margot Glassen, Nov. 19, 1959; children: Thomas Frederick, Jerry Russell, Michael Glassen. BA in Math. and Physics, U. Nebr., Omaha, 1955. Mathematician Flight Determination Lab., White Sands Missile Range, N.Mex., 1955-56; supervisory mathematician Analysis & Computation, White Sands Missile Range, 1956-81; chief data scis. divsn. Nat. Range Ops., White Sands Missile Range, 1981—93; co-owner B and T Managed Care, LLC, 2001—; owner The Spotlight Restaurant, 2002—. Nat. coun. rep. Am. Def. Preparedness Assn., Washington, 1980-93; pres. White Sands Pioneer Group, White Sands Missile Range, 1983-86; bd. dirs. Assn. U.S. Army, Washington. Author hist. and geneal. books; contbr. book revs. and articles to newspapers and mags. Chmn. El Paso (Tex.) City Planning Commn., 1980-84; bd. dirs. El Paso County Hist. Soc., 1983-87; mem. El Paso County Hist. Commn., 1983-2000. With USAR, 1955-63. Recipient Profl. Secs. Internat. Exec. of Yr. award, 1987, Conquistador award City of El Paso, 1980; named Disting. Alumnus U. Nebr., Omaha, 1985; named to Hon. Order of St. Barbara U.S. Field Arty. Assn., 1988; cited for svcs. to mankind El Paso chpt. Sertoma, 1985. Mem. Fed. Mgrs. Assn. (bd. dirs.), Freedom Found. at Valley Forge (pres. El Paso chpt., George Washington Hon. medal 1982), El Paso C. of C. (assoc. dir. 1984-92, bd. dirs.), Toastmasters (dist. gov. 1970-71), Masons, Tau Kappa Epsilon (Hall of Fame 1986). Avocations: coin collecting/numismatics, genealogy, books, weaponry.

STARKWEATHER, GARY KEITH, optical engineer, computer company executive; b. Lansing, Mich., Jan. 9, 1938; married; 2 children. BS in Physics, Mich. State U., 1960; MS in Optics, U. Rochester, 1966. Optical engr. Bausch & Lomb, Inc., Rochester, NY, 1962-64; sr. engr. optical systems Xerox Corp., Rochester, NY, 1964-68, rsch. fellow, 1975-78, sr. fellow Palo Alto, Calif., 1978-88; fellow advanced tech. group Apple Computer, Inc., Cupertino, Calif., 1988—97; architect, rschr. Microsoft Corp., Redmond, Wash., 1997—. Instr. optics Monroe C.C., 1968-69. Recipient Johann Gutenberg prize Soc. Info. Display, 1987, Sci. and Tech. Acad. award for input scanning of film images, 1995. Mem. NAE, Optical Soc. Am. (David Richardson medal 1991), Soc. Photog. Inst. Engrs. Achievements include Achievements include research in optics and electronics and their specific system interaction, involving display and hard copy image systems; invention of the laser printer.

STARLING, JAMES RALPH, surgeon, educator; b. Madison, Wis., Feb. 9, 1943; MD, U. Rochester, 1969. Cert. in surgery, recert. Intern U. Va., 1969-70, resident, 1970-72, U. N.C., 1972-75; with U. Wis. Clin. Sci. Ctr., Madison. Prof. surgery U. Wis. Mem. AAAS, Am. Surg. Assn., CSS, Soc. Univ. Surgeons.

STARNER, DON EDWARD, radiologist, educator; b. Zanesville, Ohio, June 28, 1959; s. Larry and Sara Ann Starner; 1 child, Ryan. BS, The Ohio State U., 1982. Cert. Radiographer Am. Registry of Radiologic Technologists, 1982, Quality Mgmt. Radiographer Am. Registry of Radiologic Technologists, 2002, lic. Radiologic Technologist Fla. Dept. Health, 1988.

X-ray technologist The Ohio State U. Hospitals, Columbus, Ohio, 1982—88; from clin. instr. to program dir. West Boca Med. Ctr. Sch. of Radiography, Boca Raton, Fla., 1988—91, program dir., 1991—96; dir. of clin. radiography edn. Indian River CC, Ft. Pierce, Fla., 1996—. Contbr. chapters to books Web-Based Training, 2001; actor: (films) Brubaker, 1980. Mem.: AAUP, Fla. Assn. of C.C., Am. Soc. of Radiologic Technologists, Am. Registry of Radiologic Technologists. Home: 6717 NW Dorothy St Port Saint Lucie FL 34983 Office: Indian River Community College 3209 Virginia Ave Fort Pierce FL 34981

STARNES, EARL MAXWELL, retired urban and regional planner, architect, educator; b. Winter Haven, Fla., Sept. 14, 1926; s. Thomas Lowe and Kathryn Maxwell (Gates) Starnes; m. Dorothy Jean Prather, Aug. 21, 1949; children: Tom, Will, Janet, Patricia. Student, Fla. So. Coll., 1946—48; BArch cum laude, U. Fla., 1951; MS in Urban and Regional Planning, Fla. State U., 1973, PhD, 1977. Registered arch., Fla. Assoc. Courtney Stewart, Ft. Lauderdale, Fla., 1951-52, William Bigoney, Ft. Lauderdale, 1952-53, William T. Vaughn, Ft. Lauderdale, 1953, Alfred B. Parker, Miami, Fla., 1953-55, Rufus Nims, Miami, 1955-57; ptnr. Starnes & Rentscher, Miami, 1957-63, Starnes, Rentscher & Assocs., Miami, 1963-71; dir. divsn. mass transp. Fla. Dept. Transp., Tallahassee, 1971-72; dir. divsn. state planning Fla. Dept. Adminstrn., 1972-75; engaged in rsch. and cons. svc. Tallahassee, 1975; prof., chmn. urban and regional planning Coll. Architecture U. Fla., Gainesville, 1976-88, prof. urban and regional plan coord., doctoral studies, 1989-93, prof. emeritus, 1993—. Instr. architecture U. Miami, 1953; adj. asst. prof. dept. urban and regional planning Coll. Social Scis., Fla. State U., 1971—74; mem. adv. panel B8-15 Nat. Coop. Hwy. Rsch. Program, Transp. Rsch. Bd., NRC-Nat. Acad. Scis., 1974—; mem. adv. bd. Pub. Tech., Inc., 1974—; mem. N. Ctrl. Fla. Regional Planning Com., 1980—85, Fla. Substate Dist. Com., 1985—87; co-chmn. Joint Liaison Com. Divsn. Responsibility Urban Svcs., Dade County, Fla., 1965—71; chmn. joint policy com. U. Miami-Dade County Jackson Med. Ctr., 1966—71; chmn. Cape Fla. State Pk. Adv. Coun., 1966—69, Dade County Landscape Ordinance Study Com., 1967—70, S. Fla. Everglades Area Planning Coun., 1969—71; vis. lectr. Calif. Poly. State U., San Luis Obispo, 1988—89; cons. Urban Planning Fla. and Caribbean. Prin. works include 1st Unitarian Ch., Miami; co-author: Growth Management, 1992, Rural Sustainability in America, 1996; co-author: (with Richard Rubino) History of Planning in Florida, 2007; contbr. articles to profl. jours., chapters to books. Active Nat. Task Force Natural Resources and Land Use Info. and Tech., 1973—74, Cape Fla. Acquisition Com., 1966, South Dade Mental Health Soc., 1967—68, Dade County Downtown Govtl. Ctr. Com., 1967—71, Miami Downtown Devel. Authority, 1970, Gov.'s Task Force Resource Mgmt., 1971—72, Fla. Gov.'s Commn. Property Rights, 1993—94, Fla. Greenway's Commn., 1991—93, Fla. Greenway Coordinating Coun., 1998—99; bd. dirs., chmn. retirement and compensation com. State Assn. County Commrs., 1968—71; mem. Alachua County Budget Study Com., 1978, Fla. Land Use Adv. Com. Phosphate Lands, 1978—80, Suwanee River Water Mgmt. Bd., 1982—87, 1991—98, chmn., 1987—88, Fla. Inst. Phosphate Rsch., 1984—87; bd. dirs. 1000 Friends Fla., 1986—2003; mem. gov.'s adv. commn. coastal mgmt., 1997; county commr. Dist. 7 Dade County, 1964—71; vice mayor, 1964, 1968. With USCG, 1944—46. Fellow: AIA (urban design com. 1976—80), Assn. Collegiate Schs. Planning (bd. dirs. 1986—88), Nat. Inst. Bldg. Scis. (steering com. for rsch. 1979—80), Am. Inst. Cert. Planners, Gargoyle Soc.; mem.: Phi Kappa Phi. Democrat. Unitarian Universalist. Office: PO Box 234 Cedar Key FL 32625-0234 Personal E-mail: estarnes@inetw2.net.

STARNES, SOFIA MOLINA, writer, editor; b. Manila, Philippines, Dec. 10, 1952; arrived in US, 1986, naturalized, 1989; d. Antonio M. Molina and Carmen Gómez-Arnau; m. William H. Starnes, Jr., Mar. 4, 1986. B in English Philology, U. Complutense, Madrid, Spain, M in English Philology, 1976. Tchr. English Colegio Manzanares, Madrid, 1970—72, Colegio Rodríguez Sopeña, Madrid, 1973—83, Centro Profesional Sopeña, Madrid, 1980—84, head studies, 1982—84; instr. English Berlitz Sch. Langs., Madrid, 1984—86; free-lance writer and manuscript editor Williamsburg, Va., 1986—. Assoc. editor Eve's Legacy, NYC, 1987—89; poetry columnist Christianity and the Arts (on-line), Chgo., 1999—2001; jury panel mem. Va. Commn. Arts, Richmond, 2001; manuscript editor Creative Writing Critiques, Williamsburg, Va., 1995—; poetry judge Christopher Newport U. Writers Conf., Newport News, Va.; poetry editor Anglican Theol. Rev., 2007—. Author: over 120 poems. Liturgical min. St. Bede Cath. Ch., Williamsburg. Recipient Rainer Maria Rilke Poetry award, 1997, Aldrich Poetry award, 2001, Editor's prize, 2001, Marlboro Poetry award, 2002, Honor Book award, Libr. Va., 2003, prize, Conf. Christianity and Lit. Poetry, 2004; Poetry fellowship, Va. Commn. for Arts, 2000. Mem.: Acad. Am. Poets, Poetry Soc. Va. (poetry judge), Va. Writers Club (2d v.p. 1997—98, poetry judge 2005, Outstanding Poetry Achievement award 2006), Ut Prosim Soc., Va. Tech. Roman Catholic. Avocations: travel, needlecrafts, creative cuisine. Home: 4951 Burnley Dr Williamsburg VA 23188-8806 Home Fax: 757-564-3468. Personal E-mail: smstarnes@widomaker.com.

STARNES, WILLIAM HERBERT, JR., chemist, educator; b. Knoxville, Tenn., Dec. 2, 1934; s. William Herbert and Edna Margaret (Osborne) Starnes; m. Maria Sofia Molina, Mar. 4, 1986. BS with honors, Va. Poly. Inst., Blacksburg, 1955; PhD, Ga. Inst. Tech., Atlanta, 1960. Rsch. chemist Esso Rsch. & Engring. Co., Baytown, Tex., 1960—62, sr. rsch. chemist, 1962—64, polymer additives sect. head, 1964—65, rsch. specialist, 1965—67, rsch. assoc., 1967—71; instr. and rsch. assoc. dept. chemistry U. Tex., Austin, 1971—73; mem. tech. staff AT&T Bell Labs., Murray Hill, NJ, 1973—85; prof. chemistry Poly. U., Bklyn., 1985—89, head dept. chemistry and life scis., 1985—88, assoc. dir. polymer durability ctr., 1987—89; Floyd Dewey Gottwald Sr. prof. chemistry Coll. William and Mary, Williamsburg, Va., 1989—2006, Floyd Dewey Gottwald Sr. prof. chemistry emeritus, 2006—, prof. applied sci., 1990—2006. Invited lectr. several fgn. countries and U.S.; ofcl. guest USSR Acad. Scis., 1990, Russian Acad. Scis., 1992; disting. vis. prof. Beijing Inst. Tech., 1996; vis. scientist Tex. Acad. Scis., 1964—67; mem. bd. doctoral thesis examiners Indian Inst. Tech., New Delhi, 1988, McGill U., Montreal, 1989, MacQuarie U., Sydney, 1991, McMaster U., Hamilton, Canada, 1994; panelist, reviewer NSF Acad. Rsch. Facilities Modernization Program, 1990; channel program mentor U. Cairo, 1994—95; mem. opinion leader panel Wall St. Jour., 1995—; charter mem. dept. chemistry adv. coun. Va. Poly. Inst. and State U., 1998—; sci. advisor European Multinational Environ. Rsch. Project on PVC in Soil and Landfills, 1995—99; cons. numerous indsl. cos., govtl. and pvt. agys.; course dir. continuing edn. Editor-in-chief: Jour. Vinyl and Additive Tech., 1998—, mem. adv. bd., bd. reviewers: Jour. Vinyl Tech., 1981—83, mem. editl. bd.: Jour. Chem. and Biochem. Kinetics, 1992—, Polymer Degradation and Stability, 1997—, Internat. Jour. Coatings Sci., 2001—, The Chemist, 2003—; contbr. chapters to books, articles to profl. jours. Named honoree Plastics History and Artifacts Program, Plastics Pioneers Assn., 2001; recipient Profl. Progress award, Soc. Profl. Chemists and Engrs., 1968, Disting. Tech. Staff award, AT&T Bell Labs., 1982, Polymer Sci. Pioneer award, Polymer News, 1988, Honor Scroll award, N.J. Inst. Chemists, 1989, Excellence in Innovation award, Hampton Rds. Tech. Coun., 2004; fellow, NSF, 1958—60; grantee, 1989—, Nat. Bur. Stds. Ctr. Fire Rsch., Internat. Copper Rsch. Assn., Va. Ctr. Innovative Tech., GenCorp Found., several indsl. cos. Fellow: AAAS (Project 2061 1985—86, chmn. chemistry subpanel 1985—86, mem. panel on phys. scis. and engring. 1985—86), Soc. Plastics Engrs. (thesis advisor nat. award of vinyl plastics divsn. 1996, 1998, nat. publs. com. 1998—2001, 2006—, Best Student Paper Advisor nat. award vinyl plastics divsn. 2007, hon. grantee), NY Acad. Scis., Am. Inst. Chemists (life); mem.: Soc. Chem. Industry, Va. Acad. Sci., Am. Chem. Soc. (bd. dirs. southeastern Tex. sect. 1970, spkrs. bur. divsn. polymer chemistry 1976—, mem.-at-large exec. com. Va. sect. 1995), N.Am. Thermal Analysis Soc., Ut Prosim Soc. Va. Tech., Phi Lambda Upsilon (pres. Va. Poly. Inst. chpt. 1954—55), Sigma Xi (M. A. Ferst award Ga. Inst. Tech. chpt. 1960), Phi Kappa Phi (life). Achievements include patents in field; invention of ester thiol stabilization technology for poly(vinyl chloride); research in degradation, stabilization, flammability, microstructures and polymerization mechanisms of synthetic polymers, especially poly(vinyl chloride); free radical chemistry; carbon-13 nuclear magnetic resonance and organic synthesis; subspecialities include organic chemistry, polymer chemistry. Office: Coll William and Mary Dept Chemistry PO Box 8795 Williamsburg VA 23187-8795 Business E-Mail: whstar@wm.edu.

STAROSELSKY, ALEXANDER, mechanical engineer, materials scientist; 3 children. MSc, Moscow Inst. Electronics and Math., 1989; ScD, Russian Acad. Sci., Moscow, 1991; PhD, MIT, 1997. Vis. scientist Courant Inst. of Math. Scis., NYU, 1993; staff scientist United Techs. Rsch. Ctr., East Hartford, Conn., 1997—2004, Pratt and Whitney, 2004—. Adj. prof. Hartford U., Conn., 1998—. Contbr. articles to profl. jours. Grantee, Office of Naval Rsch., 2001—03, USAF, 2006—. Fellow: NY. Acad. Sci.; mem.: ASME, Soc. for Computational Engring. and Sci. Achievements include research in fracture thermal-mechanical fatigue, mechanics of advanced alloys; large deformation plasticity; surfactant assisted fracture; acoustics, vibration; mass transport in non-saturated porous media. Office: Pratt and Whitney 400 Main St MS 165-16 East Hartford CT 06108 Home Phone: 860-674-8002; Office Phone: 860-565-2751. Personal E-mail: starosel@alum.mit.edu.

STAROSTIN, ALEKSANDR B., nuclear scientist, researcher; b. Vladimirovka, Russia, Jan. 27, 1967; arrived in US, 1998; s. Boris I. and Elena F. Starostin; m. Natalia V. Nilova, Mar. 28, 1991; 1 child, Anastassia A. MS in Nuc. Physics, Petersburg Tech. U., St.Petersburg, Russia, 1992; PhD in Particle Physics, Petersburg Nuc. Physics Inst., Gatchina, Russia, 2001. Sr. rsch. scientist Petersburg Nuc. Physics Inst., Gatchina, Russia, 1992—98; rschr. U. Calif., LA, 1998—. Fellow, Govt. of Russian Fedn., 1997—98. Office: Univ California Box 951547 Los Angeles CA 90095-1547 Office Phone: 310-825-2259. Business E-Mail: starost@ucla.edu.

STAROSTINA, NATASHA, research scientist; arrived in US, 1998, arrived in US, 1998; d. Vladimir Nilov and Valentina Nilova; m. Aleksandr Starostina; 1 child, Anastasia. BS in Physics, Leningrad Poly. Inst., St. Petersburg, Russia, MS in Engring., 1994. Staff rsch. assoc. UCLA, 1999—2002; atomic force microscopy scientist Pacific Nanotechnology Inc., Irvine, Calif., 2002—. Office: Pacific Nanotechnology 17981 Sky Park Cir Ste J Irvine CA 92614 Office Phone: 949-253-8813. Office Fax: 949-253-8816. Business E-Mail: nstarostina2003@yahoo.com.

STARR, DAVID, editor, publisher; b. NYC, Aug. 1, 1922; s. Aaron and Helen (Simon) S.; m. Marjorie Giffen, Aug. 3, 1943; children: Pamela, Peter. BA, Queens Coll., 1942. Reporter, rewriteman L.I. Daily Press, 1942-50; exec. editor Nassau Daily Rev. Star, 1950-53; asst. editor Newark Star-Ledger, 1954-56; asso. editor L.I. Press, 1953-54, 56-62, mng. editor, 1962-69, editor, 1969-77; sr. editor Newhouse Newspapers, 1971—; pub. Springfield Republican, 1977-99, pres., 1999—. Pres. Springfield Ctrl., Inc., 1978-88, chmn., 1989-95. Trustee Nassau C.C., SUNY, 1959-66; bd. dirs. Springfield Libr. and Mus. Assn., chmn., 1988-90; mem. Mass. Cultural Coun., 1980—; bd. dirs. Am. Arts Alliance, 1988-92, chmn., 1989-92. Mem. Am. Soc. Newspaper Editors, Am. Newspaper Pubs. Assn. Office: The Republican Co 1860 Main St Springfield MA 01103-1000 E-mail: dstarr@repub.com.

STARR, EDWARD H., JR., lawyer; b. Greenwich, Conn., 1953; BA cum laude, Duke Univ., 1975; JD, Univ. Richmond, 1975. Bar: Va. 1979. Ptnr., tort liability, product liability, insurance coverage Troutman Sanders LLP, Richmond, Va. Editor: Va. Insurance Law Digest, 1992—. Mem.: ABA, Va. Assn. Def. Attys., Fedn. Def. & Corp. Counsel, Va. Bar Assn., Richmond Bar Assn., Def. Rsch. Inst. Office: Troutman Sanders LLP Bank Am Ctr 1111 E Main St PO Box 1122 Richmond VA 23218-1122 Office Phone: 804-697-1268. Office Fax: 804-698-5137. Business E-Mail: ed.starr@trtoutmansanders.com.

STARR, FRANCIS, physics professor; BS with honors, Carnegie Mellon U., Pitts., 1990—93; MA, PhD, Boston U., 1994—99. Asst. prof. physics Wesleyan U., Middletown, Conn., 2003—; dept. dir. ctr. theoretical & computational physics NIST, Gaithersburg, Md. Contbr. articles to profl. jours. Office: Wesleyan Univ Dept Physics 265 Church St Middletown CT 06459

STARR, ISIDORE, law educator; b. Bklyn., Nov. 24, 1911; BA, CCNY, 1932; LLB, St. John's U., Jamaica, NY, 1936; MA, Columbia U., 1939; JSD, Bklyn. Law Sch., 1942; PhD, New Sch. Social Rsch., 1957. Bar: NY 1937. Tchr. various high schs., NYC, 1934-61; from assoc. prof. to prof. edn. Queen's Coll., 1961-75, prof. emeritus, 1975—. Dir. Inst. on Law-Related Edn., Lincoln-Filene Ctr., Tufts U., 1963, Law Studies Inst., NYC, 1974; adv. on Our Living Bill of Rights Film Series (6 films) Ency. Brit. Ednl. Corp.; mem. Ariz. Ctr. for Law-Related Edn.; coun. on pub. legal edn. State of Wash., 2001—; cons. in field. Author: The Lost Generation of Prince Edward County, 1968, The Gideon Case, 1968, The Feiner Case, 1968, The Mapp Case, 1968, The Supreme Court and Contemporary Issues, 1968, Human Rights in the United States, 1969, The American Judicial System, 1972, The Idea of Liberty, 1978, Justice: Due Process of Law, 1981; co-editor Living American Documents, 1971, (with John Hope Franklin) The Negro in 20th Century America, 1967. Bd. dirs. Phi Alpha Delta Juvenile Justice Program, 1981—. 1st lt. U.S. Army, 1943-46. John Hay fellow, 1952-53; recipient Army Commendation medal, 1946, Outstanding Citizen award Philip Morris Cos., 1992. Mem. ABA (hon. chair adv. commn. on Youth Edn. for Citizenship, Isidore Starr award for Spl. Achievment in Law Studies, Leon Jaworski award 1989), Nat. Coun. Social Studies (past pres.), Washington Coun. Pub. Legal Edn., Phi Beta Kappa, Phi Alpha Delta (cert. of appreciation 1981). Home: 12501 Greenwood Ave N Apt C406 Seattle WA 98133-8000

STARR, JEFFREY, lawyer, bank executive; BA, Muhlenberg Coll, 1983; JD, Touro Coll., 1986. Bar: Calif. 1987, N.Y. 1988. Sr. v.p., gen. counsel North Fork Bancorp, Inc, 1987—. Mem.: N.Y. Bankers Assn. Office: North Fork Bancorp 275 Broadhollow Rd Melville NY 11747 Office Phone: 631-844-1470. E-mail: jstarr@nfb.com.

STARR, JUDSON WILMARTH, lawyer; b. Boulder, Colo., July 18, 1945; s. Wilmarth Holt and Eva Jones Starr; 1 child, Alexander. BA, Washington and Jefferson Coll., 1968; JD, Georgetown U., 1975. Bar: D.C. 1975, Va. 1978. Staff Office of the Adminstr. U.S. EPA, Washington, 1972—73; asst. editor Environ. Law Inst., Washington, 1973—75; assoc. Price Grove, Washington, 1975—78; dir. environ. crimes unit Dept. Justice, Washington, 1982—87, chief environ. crimes sect., 1987—88; ptnr., Environ., Corp. Def. & White Collar practices Venable LLP, Washington, 1988—. Adv. mem. U.S. Sentencing Commn. on Corp. Sentencing; co-chair Ann. Am. Law Inst.-ABA Conf. on Environ. Crimes; chair Environ. Crimes Subcom. Bus.; mem. adv. bd. Corp. Counsel Inst., Georgetown Univ.; mem. adv. panel criminal law Am. Law Inst. of ABA. Contbr. articles to profl. jours.; editor: Georgetown Rev. Law & Pub. Interest; co-author: Environmental Crimes Deskbook, 1995, Environmental Criminal Liability: Avoiding & Defending Enforcement Actions, 1995; author: The Knock on the Door: Preparing for and Responding to a Criminal Investigation, 1999. Founding mem., pres. Bethesda (Md.)/Chevy Chase Baseball League, 1995—99. Capt. US Army, 1968—70. Decorated Bronze Star; named a Top Washington Lawyer, Washingtonian Mag., 2004; named one of Nation's Top White Collar Crime Experts, Nat. Law Jour., Corp. Counsel's Best Lawyers, Criminal Def. Law, 2004; named to Best Lawyers in Am., 2003—04, 2005—06. Mem.: Barristers. Avocations: baseball, golf, sailing. Office: Venable LLP 575 7th St NW Washington DC 20004 Office Phone: 202-344-4886. Office Fax: 202-344-8300. Business E-Mail: jwstarr@venable.com.

STARR, KENNETH See STARR, MAURICE

STARR, KENNETH WINSTON, dean, lawyer; b. Vernon, Tex., July 21, 1946; s. W. D. and Vannie Maude (Trimble) Starr; m. Alice Jean Mendell, Aug. 23, 1970; children: Randall Postley, Carolyn Marie, Cynthia Anne. BA, George Washington U., 1968; MA, Brown U., 1969; JD, Duke U., 1973; LLD (hon.), Hampden Sydney Coll., 1992, Shenandoah U., 1993, John Marshall Coll. Law, 1993, Pepperdine U., 1996. Bar: Calif. 1973, D.C. 1979, Va. 1979. Law clk. to Judge David Dyer U.S. Ct. Appeals (5th cir.), Miami, Fla., 1973—74; assoc. Gibson, Dunn & Crutcher, Los Angeles, 1974—75; law clk. to Chief Justice Warren E. Burger U.S. Supreme Ct., Washington, 1975—77; assoc., ptnr. Gibson, Dunn & Crutcher, Washington, 1977—81; counselor to atty gen. of U.S. Dept. Justice, Washington, 1981—83; judge U.S. Ct. Appeals (D.C. circuit), Washington, 1983—89; solicitor gen. US Dept. Justice, Washington, 1989—93; ptnr. Kirkland & Ellis LLP, Washington, 1993—2005, of counsel LA, 2005—; ind. counsel for Whitewater, 1994—99; Duane and Kelly Roberts Dean and Dean, prof. law Pepperdine U. Sch. of Law, Malibu, Calif., 2004—. Author: First Among Equals: The Supreme Court in American Life, 2002; contbr. articles to legal jours. Legal advisor CAB transition team office of pres.-elect, 1980—81, SEC transition team, 1980—81; bd. adv. Duke Law Jour. Named one of 75 Best Lawyers In Washington, Washingtonian survey mag., 2002; recipient Disting. Alumni awards, George Washington U., Duke U., Atty. Gen.'s award for disting. svc., 1993, Am. Values award, U.S. Indsl. Coun. Ednl. Found., 1993. Fellow: Am. Bar Found. (jud. fellows com., jud. conf. com. on bicentennial of U.S. constn.); mem.: ABA, Am. Inns of Court, Va. Bar Assn., D.C. Bar Assn., Calif. Bar Assn., Supreme Ct. Hist. Soc., Inst. Jud. Adminstrn. (pres.), Am. Judicature Soc., Am. Law Inst., Phi Delta Phi (Hughes chpt. Man of Yr. 1973), Order of Coif. Republican. Office: Pepperdine U Sch of Law 24255 Pacific Coast Hwy Malibu CA 90263 Fax: 310-506-4266. Business E-Mail: ken.starr@pepperdine.edu.

STARR, KEVIN, librarian, educator; b. San Francisco, Sept. 3, 1940; m. Sheila Gordon, June 10, 1963; children: Marian, Jessica. BA, U. San Francisco, 1962; MA, Harvard U., 1965, PhD, 1969; MLS, U. Calif., Berkeley, 1974; postgrad., Ch. Div. Sch. Pacific, Berkeley, 1983-84. From asst. to assoc. prof. Am. lit. Harvard U., Cambridge, Mass., 1969-74; city libr. San Francisco, 1973-76; prin. Kevin Starr Assocs., San Francisco, 1983-85; prof. comm. arts U. San Francisco, 1981-89; prof. Sch. Planning and Devel. U. So. Calif., 1989—98, univ. prof., 1998—; state libr. Calif., 1994—2004; state libr. emeritus, 2004—. Allston Burr sr. tutor Eliot House Harvard U., Cambridge, 1970-73; cons. Beyl and Boyd, Inc., San Francisco, 1979-83; sr. cons. Hill and Knowlton USA, San Francisco, 1983-84; vis. assoc. prof. English U. Calif., Berkely, 1974, vis. lectr. polit. sci., 1976, lectr. librarianship, 1978; adj. prof. humanities San Francisco State U., 1975-76; Regent's lectr. polit. sci. U. Calif., Riverside, 1977; adj. prof. English Santa Clara (Calif.) U., 1977-78; vis. prof. history U. Calif., Davis, 1985-86; vis. scholar, media fellow Hoover Inst., 1986-88; vis. fellow Ctr. Humanistic Studies, Claremont McKenna Coll., 1987; faculty master Embassy Residential Coll., 1990-94. Sr. editor New West Mag., 1977; vatican corr. Hearst Newspapers, Rome, 1978; columnist Examiner, San Francisco, 1977-83; contbng. editor L.A. Times, 1994—; contbr. articles to profl. jours., chpts. to books; auth. Americans and the California Dream, 1850-1915, 1973, Inventing the Dream: California Through the Progressive Era, 1985, Material Dreams: Southern California Through the 1920s, 1990, Endangered Dreams: The Great Depression in California, 1996, The Dream Endures: California Enters the 1940s, 1997, Embattled Dreams: California in War and Peace, 1940-1950, 2002, Coast of Dreams: California on the Edge, 1990-2003, 2004, California: A History, 2005. Exec. aide to mayor San Francisco, 1973; bd. trustees Am. Issues Forum, 1975-76, Calif. Hist. Soc., 1992—; co-chmn. sister city com., San Francisco and Sydney, Australia, 1981-86; advisor Jr. League San Francisco, 1982-84; canidate San Francisco Bd. Suprs., 1984; councilor Am. Antiquarian Soc., 1996—; mem. Calif. Coun. Humanities, 1996—; regent Cathedral St. Mary Assumption, San Francisco, 1996—. Lt. German Army, 1962-64. Recipient Nat. Humanities Medal, NEH, 2006. Mem.: Calif. Historical Soc., Calif. Coun. Humanities, Am. Antiquarian Soc. Office: Univ So Calif SOS 175 Los Angeles CA 90089 *

STARR, MARTIN KENNETH, management educator; b. NYC, May 21, 1927; s. Harry and Melanie (Krauss) S.; m. Polly Exner, Apr. 3, 1955; children: Christopher Herschel, Loren Michael. BS, MIT, 1948; MS, Columbia U., 1951, PhD, 1953. Ptnr., dir. M.K. Starr Assocs., 1956-61; prof. mgmt. sci. Columbia U., NYC, 1961-96, dir. Ctr. for the Study of Ops., 1980-95, dir. Ctr. for Enterprise Mgmt., 1995-96, vice dean Grad. Sch. Bus., 1974-75; Disting. prof. ops. mgmt. Crummer Grad. Sch. Bus. Rollins Coll., Winter Park, Fla., 1996—2003, prof. emeritus, 2003—, dir. Ctr. for Enterprise Mgmt., 1996—2001; prof. emeritus Columbia U., 1996—. Lectr. in field; cons. in field. Author: (with David W. Miller) The Structure of Human Decisions, 1967, (with David W. Miller) Inventory Control-Theory and Practice, 1972, Product Design and Decision Theory, 1963, (with David W. Miller) Executive Decisions and Operations Research, 2d edit., 1969, Systems Management of Operations, 1971, Management: A Modern Approach, 1971, Production Management: Systems and Synthesis, 2d edit., 1972, (with Irving Stein) The Practice of Management Science, 1976, Operations Management, 1978, (with David G. Dannebring) Management Science: An Introduction, 1981, (with Earl K. Bowen) Statistics for Business and Economics, 1982, (with Marion Sobol) Statistics for Business and Economics: An Action Learning Approach, 1983, Managing Production and Operations, 1989, Global Corporate Alliances and the Competitive Edge, 1991, (with Marion Sobol) Introduction to Statistics for Executives, 1993, Operations Management: A Systems Approach, 1996, CD-text rev., 2000, Production and Operations Management, 2004, Foundations of Production and Operations Management, 2006; editor: Executive Readings in Management Science, 1965, (with Milan Zeleny) Multiple Criteria Decision Making, 1977, Global Competitiveness: Getting the U.S. Back on Track, 1988; editor-in-chief Mgmt. Sci., 1967-82; mem. editl. bd. Behavioral Sci., 1970—, Internat. Jour. Flexible Mfg. Sys., 1989—; mem. editl. adv. bd. Jour. Ops. Mgmt., 1983—; editl. adviser Operational Rsch. Quar., 1970-85; cons. editor: Columbia Jour. World Business: Focus: Decision Making, fall, 1977, Quantitative Methods in Mgmt.; contbr. articles to profl. jours. Fellow Inst. for Ops. Rsch. and the Mgmt. Scis., Inst. Mgmt. Scis. (pres. 1974-75), Prodn. and Ops. Mgmt. Soc. (pres.-elect 1994—, pres. 1995, past pres., bd. dirs. 1996—, chair Coun. of Pres. 1999—); mem. Beta Gamma Sigma. Achievements include having an annual award named in his honor by the Production and Operations Management Society. Home: 100 S Interlachen Ave #304 Winter Park FL 32789-4450 Office: Rollins Coll 120 Crummer Grad Sch Bus Winter Park FL 32789 Office Phone: 407-383-4264. Business E-Mail: mstarr@cfl.rr.com. *The ability to manage complex systems, to maximize societal benefits under conditions of safety and security, has become the most pressing requirement in the decade 2006-2015. Remarkable growth of strong systems interdependencies has occurred since 2000. Global connectivity through the Internet is altering established patterns for living and doing business. Management science using the systems approach combines art and logic with advancing computer-linked technology to rationalize* *transitions to achieve social benefit. Perhaps a new name is needed to describe this effort. By whatever name it is called, the impact of systems-oriented management science will determine the character of the 21st century and will, in turn, be changed by it.*

STARR, MAURICE KENNETH (KENNETH STARR), museum director; b. Libertytown, Md., Apr. 28, 1922; s. Maurice Scott and Nellie Gray (Fisher) S.; m. Betty Jane Leslie, Dec. 23, 1943; children: Leslie Gray, Maurice Winfield (dec.) BA, Duke U., 1945; MA, Yale U., 1947, PhD, 1957. Prin. Tsingtao Am. Sch., Republic of China, 1947-49; grad. asst. Peabody Mus., Yale U., New Haven, 1951-53; curator Asiatic archeology and ethnology Field Mus. of Natural History, Chicago, 1953-70, research assoc., 1970—; dir. Milw. Pub. Mus., 1970-88; mem. rev. panel NSF, Washington, 1977, program dir. informal sci. edn., 1988—. Lectr. U. Chgo., 1958-73; mem. adv. council Nat. Mus. Act, Washington, 1978-80, 81-82; mem. mus. program policy panel Nat. Endowment for Arts, Washington, 1981-84; collections panel, 1983-84, advancement panel, 1985; mem. adv. com. Eleutherian Mills-Hagley Found., Wilmington, Del., 1982-85; mem. nat. adv. bd. Fernbank Mus. Natural History, 1985—. Author monograph: Ch'eng-tzu-yai: the Black Pottery Culture Site at Lung-shan-chen in Li'ch'eng-hsien, Shantung Province, 1956; co-author: Catalogue of Chinese Rubbings from Field Museum, 1981; also numerous articles, bulls., revs. on China and museums. Bd. dirs. Riveredge Nature Ctr., Newburg, Wis., 1972-78 Recipient Vocat. Service award Milw. Rotary Club, 1982, Adminstr. award Milw. Art Commn., 1988; Sterling jr. fellow in anthropology Yale U., 1952, Sterling sr. fellow in anthropology, 1953; grantee Wenner-Gren Found., 1956, 74, Am. Council Learned Socs.-Social Sci. Research Council, Field Mus. Natural History, Taiwan, 1960 Fellow Wis. Acad. Scis., Arts and Letters (chair fellows selection com. 1988-90); mem. Am. Assn. Mus. (numerous positions, including mem. council 1975-82, mem. exec. com. 1975-82, v.p. 1975-78, pres. 1978-79, 79-80, mem. accreditation commn., 1982-88, profl. standards and practices com. 1982-87, ethics task force 1987—, governance task force 1988-90, chmn. drafting com. Museums for a New Century 1981-84; named to Centennial Honor Roll, 2006), Assn. Sci. Mus. Dirs. (exec. com. 1973-78, pres. 1974-75, 75-76), Assn. Sci.-Tech. Ctrs. (bd. dirs. 1975-77, chmn. research com. 1975), Midwest Mus. Conf. (chmn. fin. com. 1976-77, v.p. at large 1976-77, pres. 1974-75, 75-76, Disting. Svc. award 1979, hon. life mem. 1988), Wis. Fedn. of Mus. (hon. life 1987), Phi Beta Kappa, Sigma Xi *

STARR, MICHAEL, lawyer; b. NYC, July 20, 1948; s. Harry and Gertrude (Spitz) S.; m. Marsha Talan, Sept. 5,1982; children: Rachel Talan, Garret Matthew. BA summa cum laude, SUNY, Binghamton, 1970; PhD in Philosophy, U. Mich., 1976; JD, Yale U., New Haven, Conn., 1979. Bar: NY 1980, US Dist. Ct. (so. and ea. dists.) NY 1981, US Ct. Appeals (DC cir.) 1980, US Ct. Appeals (2d cir.) 2000, US Supreme Ct. 1986. Law clk. to judge Abner J. Mikva US Ct. Appeals (DC cir.), Washington, 1979—80; assoc. Kaye, Scholer, Fierman, Hays & Handler, NYC, 1980—88; of counsel Parker, Chapin, Flattau & Klimpl LLP, NYC, 1988—97; ptnr. Hogan & Hartson LLP, NYC, 1997—. Bd. arbitrators Nat. Assn. Securities Dealers, 1995-03; mem. human resources com. NYC Partnership & C. of C., 1990-98; bd. dirs. Ct. Apptd. Spl. Advs., NYC, 1982-2000; mediator US Ct. (ea. dist.) NY, 1992—. Editor Yale Law Jour., 1978-79; editl. bd. Employment Law Strategist, The Corporate Counsellor; employment law columnist Nat. Law Jour., 1998—; contbr. articles to profl. publs. Woodrow Wilson fellow, 1970. Fellow Coll. Labor and Employment Lawyers; mem. ABA (labor and employment law sect., internat. labor law com.), Internat. Soc. Labor Law, Fed. Bar Coun., Assn. of Bar of City of NY (US in global economy select com. 1995-00, labor and employment law com. 1989-92, civil rights com. 1985-88, children and the law com. 1984-85), Coun. NY Law Assocs. (bd. dirs. 1982-86), Second Cir. Pro Bono Panel Civil Appeals. Office: Hogan & Hartson LLP 875 3rd Ave New York NY 10022-6225 Home Phone: 212-249-5021; Office Phone: 212-918-3000. Business E-Mail: mstarr@hhlaw.com.

STARR, PAUL ELLIOT, sociologist, educator, editor, writer; b. NYC, May 12, 1949; s. Saul and Sarah Marion (Buzen) S.; m. Sandra Lurie Stein, Apr. 12, 1981 (dec.); m. Ann Baynes Coiro, June 9, 2000. BA, Columbia U., 1970; PhD, Harvard U., 1978. Jr. fellow Harvard Soc. Fellows, 1975-78; asst. prof. Harvard U., Cambridge, Mass., 1978-82, assoc. prof., 1982-85; prof. sociology Princeton (NJ) U., 1985—, Stuart Prof. Comm., Pub. Affairs, Woodrow Wilson Sch.; founder, co-editor The Am. Prospect. Author: The Discarded Army: Veterans After Vietnam, 1974, The Social Transformation of American Medicine, 1983 (C. Wright Mills award 1983, Pulitzer prize for nonfiction 1984, Bancroft award 1984), The Logic of Health-Care Reform, 1992, The Creation of the Media: Political Origins of Modern Communications, 2004 (Goldsmith Book prize 2005), Freedom's Power: The True Force of Liberalism, 2007. Guggenheim Found. fellow, 1981-82. Democrat. Office: Dept of Sociology Wallace Hall Princeton U Princeton NJ 08544-1010

STARR, RINGO (RICHARD STARKEY), musician, actor; b. Liverpool, Eng., July 7, 1940; s. Richard and Elsie (Gleave) Starkey; m. Maureen Cox, Feb. 11, 1965 (div. 1975); children: Zak, Jason, Lee; m. Barbara Bach, Apr. 27, 1981. Drummer Ed Clayton Skiffle Group, 1959; drummer & singer Rory Storm's Hurricanes, 1959—62, The Beatles, 1962—69; solo performer, 1970—. Formed Pumpkinhead Records (with Mark Hudson). Musician: (albums) (with The Beatles) Please, Please Me, 1963, With the Beatles, 1963, Meet the Beatles, 1964, Beatles for Sale, 1964, A Hard Day's Night, 1964 (Grammy award best performance by a group, 1964, Grammy award best new artists, 1964), Help!, 1965, Yesterday & Today, 1966, Rubber Soul, 1966, Revolver, 1966, Sergeant Pepper's Lonely Hearts Club Band, 1967 (Grammy award album of the yr., 1967, Grammy award best contemporary album, 1967), Magical Mystery Tour, 1967, The Beatles (The White Album), 1968, Yellow Submarine, 1968, Abbey Road, 1969, Let It Be, 1970 (Grammy award best original score, 1970), Beatles Anthology, 1995 (Grammy award best long form music video, 1996, Grammy awards best pop performance & best short form music video for Free As A Bird single, 1996); film appearances (with The Beatles) A Hard Day's Night, 1964, Help!, 1965, Yellow Submarine (voice), 1968, Let It Be (also co-exec. prodr.), 1970, TV film appearances Magical Mystery Tour (also co-prodr., co-dir.), 1967; musician: (solo albums) Sentimental Journey, 1970, Beaucoups of Blues, 1970, Ringo, 1973, Goodnight Vienna, 1974, Blast from Your Past, 1975, Ringo's Rotogravure, 1976, Ringo the Fourth, 1977, Scouse the Mouse, 1977, Bad Boy, 1978, Stop and Smell the Roses, 1981, Old Wave, 1983, Starr Struck, 1989, Time Takes Time, 1992, Vertical Man, 1998, I Wanna Be Santa Claus, 1999, Ringo Rama, 2003, Tour 2003, Choose Love, 2005, Ringo Starr & Friends, 2006, (with All-Starr Band) Ringo Starr and His All-Starr Band, 1989, Ringo Starr and His All-Starr Band: Live From Montreux, 1992, Ringo Starr and His Third All-Starr Band, 1997, Ringo & His New All-Starr Band, 2002; musician: (with George Harrison, Ravi Shankar and others) (albums) The Concert For Bangla Desh, 1972 (Grammy award album of the yr., 1972); actor: (films) Candy, 1968, The Magic Christian, 1969, Commonwealth, 1970, 200 Motels, 1971, Blindman (also known as Il Cieco and Il Pistolero Cieco), 1972, That'll Be the Day, 1974, Lisztomania, 1975, Sextette, 1978, Caveman, 1981, Give My Regards to Broad Street, 1984, To the North of Katmandu, 1986; actor, prodr., dir. (films) Born to Boogie, 1972, actor, prodr. Son of Dracula, 1974; actor: (TV films) Ringo, 1978, The Cooler, 1982, Princess Daisy, 1983, Alice in Wonderland, 1985, Shining Time Station Christmas: 'Tis a Gift, 1990; (TV series) Thomas the Tank Engine & Friends (voice), 1985—91, Shining Time Station, 1990—91. Decorated Order Brit. Empire; inducted with The Beatles into Rock and Roll Hall of Fame, 1988. Office: c/o KOCH Entertainment 22 Harbor Park Dr Port Washington NY 11050

STARR, ROSS MARC, economist, educator; b. Oak Ridge, Nov. 14, 1945; s. Chauncey and Doris E. S.; m. Susan S. Strauss, July 2, 1967; children: Daniel, Diana. BS, Stanford U., 1966, PhD, 1972. Cons. Rand Corp., summers 1966, 67, Western Mgmt. Sci. Inst., Grad. Sch. Mgmt., UCLA, summers 1967, 71; Cowles Found. staff rsch. economist Yale U., New Haven, 1970, faculty, 1970-74, assoc. prof. econs., 1974, U. Calif., Davis, 1975-76, prof. econs., 1976-80, San Diego, 1980—, chmn. dept., 1987-90. Vis. lectr. London Sch. Econs., 1973-74, Peoples U. China, Beijing, 1987; vis. scholar U. Calif., Berkeley, 1978-80, vis. prof., 1997; vis. prof. European U. Inst. Florence, Italy, 2007. Author: General Equilibrium Theory: An Introduction, 1997; co-editor: Essays in Honor of Kenneth J. Arrow, 1986: v.1, Social Choice and Public Decision Making, v.2, Equilibrium Analysis, v.3, Uncertainty, Information and Communication; editor: Gen. Equilibrium Models of Monetary Economies, 1989; contbr. articles to profl. jours. NDEA fellow, 1966-69, Yale jr. faculty fellow, 1973-74, Guggenheim fellow, 1978-79; NSF grant, 1979-81, 83-85. Office: U Calif San Diego Dept Econs 0508 9500 Gilman Dr La Jolla CA 92093-0508 Home Phone: 858-455-1630; Office Phone: 858-534-3879. Business E-Mail: rstarr@ucsd.edu.

STARR, STEPHEN, restaurant owner; Grad., Temple U., 1977. Owner Grand Mom Minnie's, Phila.; owner cabaret, comedy club Stars, Phila.; owner Ripley Music Hall, Phila., The Concert Co. (acquired by Electric Factory Concerts in 1990), Phila., Shake, Burger and Roll, Phila., The Bank, Phila., Cafe Republic, Phila.; founder, owner Starr Restaurant Org., Phila., 1995—, Continental Restaurant and Martini Bar, Phila., 1995—, Buddakan, Phila., Tangerine, Phila., Pod, Phila., Alma de Cuba, Phila., Morimoto, Phila., Jones, Phila., Angelina, Phila., El Vez, Phila., Striped Bass, Phila., Washington Square, Phila., Barclay Prime, Phila., Morimoto, NYC, 2006—, Buddakan, NYC, 2006—. Named Restaurateur of the Year, Bon Appetit mag., 2005. Office: Starr Restaurant Org 134 Market St Philadelphia PA 19106

STARR, STEVEN DAWSON, photographer; b. Albuquerque, Sept. 6, 1944; s. Richard Vernon and Carol (Harley) S.; m. Marilynne Sue Anderson, Aug. 6, 1965; 1 child, Stephen Richard. Student, Antioch Coll., 1962-63, Bethel Coll., 1963-64; BA, San Jose State Coll., 1967. Photographer San Jose Mercury-News, Calif., 1966-67; photographer, picture editor A.P., 1968-73; audiovisual producer Starr Productions, Inc., Coral Gables, Fla., 1974-85; photographer Picture Group Agy., 1986-88, Saba Press, NYC, 1988—2000, Corbis, 2000—. Recipient Pulitzer prize for spot news photography, 1970, Nat. Headliners award, 1970, George Polk Meml. award, 1970, Pictures of Year hon. mention, 1970 Office: Corbis 902 Broadway 4th Fl New York NY 10010 E-mail: steve@stevestarr.com.

STARRETT, FREDERICK KENT, lawyer; b. Lincoln, Nebr., May 23, 1947; s. Clyde Frederick and Helen Virginia (Meyers) Starrett; m. Linda Lee Jensen, Jan. 19, 1969; children: Courtney, Kathryn, Scott. BA, U. Nebr., 1969; JD, Creighton U., 1976. Bar: Nebr 1976, Kans 1977, US Dist Ct Nebr 1976, US Dist Ct Kans 1977, US Ct Appeals (8th and 10th cirs) 1983, Mo 1987, US Dist Ct (we dit) Mo 1987, US Supreme Ct 1993. Pvt. practice law, Gt. Bend, Kans., 1976-77, Topeka, 1977-86; with Miller, Bash & Starrett, P.C., Kans. City, Mo., 1986-90; ptnr. Lathrop Norquist & Miller, 1990-91, Lathrop and Norquist, Overland Pk., Kans., 1991-95, Lathrop & Gage L.C., Overland Pk., Kans., 1996—. Judicial nominating commr 10th Judicial Dist, 2000—04. Lt (jg) USNR, 1969—72. Named one of, Mo./Kans. Super Lawyers, 2006. Mem.: ABA, Kans. Assn. of Defense Counsel, Mo. Orgn. Def. Lawyers, Def. Rsch. Inst. (state rep. Kans. 1998—2001, bd. dirs. 2002—05), Am. Bd. Trial Advs. (pres. Kans. chpt. 1997), Kans. Bar Assn. (pres. litig. sect. 1985—86), Civitan Club (pres. 1985—86, Disting. Pres. award 1985—86). Democrat. Presbyterian. Avocations: aviation, scuba diving, sailing. Office: Lathrop & Gage LC 10851 Mastin Blvd Bldg 82 Ste 1000 Shawnee Mission KS 66210-1669 Home Phone: 913-469-8271; Office Phone: 913-451-5140. Business E-Mail: fstarrett@lathropgage.com.

STARRETT, LUCINDA, lawyer; b. Washington, June 21, 1957; BA magna cum laude, Princeton U., 1979; student, U. Nigeria, Nsukka, 1980-84; JD cum laude, U. Pa., 1984. Bar: Calif. 1986. Law clerk to Hon. Dorothy W. Nelson U.S. Ct. Appeals (9th cir), 1984-85; ptnr. Latham & Watkins, LA, 1991—. Chief comment editor Jour. Capital Markets and Securities Regulation, 1983. Mem. bd. alternative dispute resolution Western Justice Ctr. Fulbright scholar, Nigeria, 1980—81. Mem. ABA, L.A. County Bar Assn. Office: Latham & Watkins 633 W 5th St Ste 4000 Los Angeles CA 90071-2005 E-mail: cindy.starrett@lw.com.

STARR KINS, GLORIA, public relations executive, writer, photojournalist, writer, editor; b. Feb. 23, 1927; Soc. editor ITALAMERICAN mag., NYC, 1957-60, Privilege mag., Canada, The Tatler, London; doyen UN Corr. Assn., 1957—2006; UN corr. Sta. WQXR, NYC, 1957—; assoc. prodr. Sandy Lesberg Show Sta. WOR, NYC, 1960-64; coord. "Open Mind" NBC-TV, NYC, 1960-64; dep. to Charlie Van Rensselaer, society columnist Jour. Am., NYC, 1960-64; founding editor, UN corres. N.Y. Voice, NYC, 1960-85; editor soc. and diplomatic The Diplomatist mag., London, 1960-85; editor UN soc. and diplomatic Saturday Eve. Post, Holiday, Status mag., London, 1968-73; US/London editor The New Horizon; sr. editor Diplomatic World Bull., 1990-96; internat. soc. editor Washington Internat. UN-Consular Corps, 1995—; pres. Kins Grop Ltd.; USA/UN bur. chief, editor-in-chief Soc. and Diplomatic Rev.; soc. and diplomatic editor Jewish Post; chief editor, head NY office Curtis Pub.; mng. dir. USA Imphotismus, Berlin, UBM Rec. Co., Berlin; chairperson media divsn. Obs. Cultural and Audiovisual Communication-Info. Poverty Program. Bd. dirs. N.J. World Trade Coun., NJ, Paul Robeson Found., Harmonia Opera Co., Japan; vice chmn. Earth Access com.; mem. I.C.C.C., CORE Govt. Liaison and Protocol. Exec. com. U.S. com. for refugees UN, 1986, bd. dirs. NGO, 1986; bd. dirs. UNICEF, 1978—, founding mem. Manhattan chpt., 1978—; bd. mem. internat. affairs The SNAP Student Found., Rochester, NY. Named Comdr., Order of St. Stanislas, 2002, Dame of the Sovereign Mil. Order of the Temple of Jerusalem, 2002; recipient honor, Dalai Lama for vol. work on Tibetan freedom, 1963, Nat. Honor of Merit, Pres. Alfredo Stroesner of Paraguay, 1959—60, Humanitarian award, Internat. Coun. for Caring Cmtys., 2001. Mem. Lansdowne Club (London), Islamic Coun. Europe (founding mem. London, rep. US), Islamic Heritage Soc., Nat. Com. in Am. Fgn. Policy Inc., Rep. Club (N.Y.C.). Office: The Kins Group Ltd 131 E 66th St New York NY 10021-6129 Office Phone: 212-628-1743. Fax: 212-288-6848. Personal E-mail: kinsgroup@aol.com.

STARRS, ELIZABETH ANNE, lawyer; b. Detroit, Jan. 1, 1954; d. John Richard and Mabel Angeline (Gilchrist) S. BA, U. Mich., 1975; JD, Suffolk U., 1980. Bar: Mass. 1980, Colo. 1983, U.S. Dist. Ct. Mass. 1981, U.S. Ct. Appeals (1st. cir.) 1981, Colo. 1983, U.S. Dist. Ct. Colo. 1983, U.S. Ct. Appeals (10th cir.) 1983. Assoc. Denner & Benjoya P.C., Boston, 1980—83, Kennedy & Christopher P.C., Denver, 1983—86, shareholder, 1986—2003, pres., 1994—2000; ptnr. Starrs Mihm & Caschette LLP, Denver, 2003—. Mem. jud. nominating commn. 2d Jud. Dist., Colo., 2000—05; adj. prof. U. Denver, 2000—05. Troop leader Girl Scouts U.S., Denver, 1984-85; pres. Colo. Women's Bar Assn. Found., 1992-94 Fellow Internat. Acad. Trial Lawyers, Am. Coll. Trial Lawyers., Am. Bar Found., Colo. Bar Found.; mem. Colo. Bar Assn. (litig. coun. 1989-96, chair 1993-94, profl. liability chair 1991-93, pres., 2006-07), Denver Bar Assn. (trustee 2001-04, pres. 2002-03), Colo. Women's Bar Assn. (bd. dirs. 1984-85, v.p. 1989-90), U.S. Dist. Ct. Colo. (com. conduct 1997-2003), Am. Bd. Trial Advs. (adv. mem., exec. coun. Colo. chpt. 2004—, pres. 2007), Faculty Fed. Advs. Office: Starrs Mihm & Caschette LLP 707 17th Ste 2600 Denver CO 80202 Home Phone: 303-355-9876; Office Phone: 303-592-5900. Business E-Mail: estarrs@starrslaw.com.

STARRY, DONN ALBERT, retired aerospace corporate executive, retired military officer; b. NYC, May 31, 1925; s. Don Albert and Edith (Sortor) S.; m. Leatrice Hope Gibbs, June 15, 1948; children: Michael, Paul, Melissa, Melanie. BS, U.S. Mil. Acad., 1948; MS in Internat. Affairs, George Washington U., 1966. Commd. 2d lt. U.S. Army, 1948, advanced through grades to gen., 1977; svc. in Europe, Korea and Vietnam; comdr. 11th armored cavalry rgt. Vietnam, Cambodia, 1969-70; assigned Dept. Army Staff, 1970-72; comdr. Armor Center and Ft. Knox, Ky., 1973-76, V Corps, Europe, 1976-77; comdr. Tng. and Doctrine Command Ft. Monroe, Va., 1977-81; comdr. in chief U.S. Readiness Command, 1981-83, ret., 1983; v.p. mission analysis and tech. affairs Ford Aerospace and Communications Corp., Detroit, 1983-84, v.p., gen. mgr. space missions group, 1984-86; exec. v.p. Ford Aerospace Corp., Arlington, Va., 1987-90; spl. asst. to pres. BDM Internat., McLean, Va., 1988-90. Chmn. bd. Maxwell Techs. Inc., San Diego, 1995-97, Universal Voltronics, Brookfield, Conn., 1998-2007; author, lectr., counselor to govt. and industry. Mem. Def. Sci. Bd., 1985—93, Order of Aaron and Hur, Friends of Fifth of May; mem. bd. Eisenhower Found., 1995—; chmn. bd. U.S. Cavalry Meml. Found., 1995—2003; mem. bd. Army Hist. Found., 2000—; mem. Army Sci. Bd., 2002—. Decorated Def. D.S.M., Army D.S.M. with oak leaf cluster, Silver Star, Bronze Star with V, Soldier's medal, Purple Heart, Legion of Merit with 2 oak leaf clusters, French Ordre Nationale du Merite, German Knight Commdr.'s Cross of Order of Merit with Badge and Star, Disting. Flying Cross, Air Medal with 9 oak leaf clusters; named to U.S. Army Ft. Leavenworth Command and Gen. Staff Coll. Hall of Fame, 1993; recipient Gold medal The Order of St. George; named to Joint Forces Staff Coll. Hall of Fame, 2006, Internat. Comdrs. Wall, The Armor Ctr., Ft. Knox, 2006. Mem.: Assn. U.S. Army, U.S. Armor Assn. Episcopalian. Address: 3003 Downing St Williamsburg VA 23185 Personal E-mail: dastarry@cox.net.

STARSHAK, JAMES L., lawyer; b. Chgo., Feb. 3, 1945; s. Norbert Phillip and Enda (Reiter) S.; m. Susanne M. Smith, Oct. 25, 1969; children: Lesle M., Phillip E. BBA, U. Notre Dame, 1966, JD, 1969. Bar: Ill. 1969, Hawaii 1972, U.S. Dist. Ct. (no. dist.) Ill., U.S. Tax Ct., U.S. Supreme Ct. Atty. estate tax IRS, Chgo., 1969-71, Honolulu, 1971-77; ptnr. Steiner & Starshak, Honolulu, 1971-79; assoc. Conahan & Conahan, Honolulu, 1979-86; ptnr. Carlsmith, Ball et al, Honolulu, 1986—. Office: Carlsmith Ball Pacific Tower 22d Fl 1001 Bishop St Honolulu HI 96813-3429

STARYK, STEVEN SAM, violinist, concertmaster, educator; b. Toronto, Ont., Can., Apr. 28, 1932; s. Peter and Mary Staryk; m. Ida Elisabeth Busch, May 17, 1963; 1 child, Natalie. Student, Royal Conservatory of Music, Toronto, 1942-48, Harbord Collegiate Inst., 1945-48; LittD (hon.), York U., Toronto, 1980. Soloist, concertmaster CBC-Radio Can., Toronto, 1951-55, Royal Philharmonic Orch., London, 1956-59; 1st concertmaster, tchr. Concertgebouw Orch. and Amsterdam Conservatory, 1960-63; concertmaster Chgo. Symphony Orch., 1963-67; prof. of violin Oberlin (Ohio) Coll. Conservatory, 1968-72, Acad. of Music, Vancouver, B.C., Canada, 1972-75, Royal Conservatory of Music, Toronto, 1975-87; concertmaster Toronto Symphony, 1982-87; prof. of violin, chair string div. U. Wash. Sch. Music, Seattle, 1987-97, prof. emeritus, 1997—. Faculty music U. Toronto, 1980-87; vis. prof. U. Victoria, 1972, U. Ottawa, 1975, Northwestern U., 1965-66; founding mem. Quartet Can., 1975-80. Soloist, recitalist, N.Am., Europe and the Far East; recording artist on EMI-HMV, CBC, Everest, Orion, other labels; biography (by Thane Lewis) Fiddling with Life, 2000. Recipient 2 Arts awards Can. Coun., Ottawa, 1968, 75, Queen's Silver Jubilee medal Govt. of Can., Toronto, Shevchenko medal, Winnipeg, Man., Can.; biography "Fiddling with Life" by T. Lewis and S. Staryk, 2002. Home: 12068 E Bella Vista Cir Scottsdale AZ 85259-6034 Office: U Wash Sch Music Mail Stop DN-10 PO Box 353450 Seattle WA 98195-3450

STARZINGER, VINCENT EVANS, political scientist, educator; b. Des Moines, Jan. 12, 1929; s. Vincent and Genevieve (Evans) Starzinger; m. Mildred Hippee Hill, June 16, 1953; children: Page Hill, Evans. AB summa cum laude, Harvard U., 1950, LLB, 1954, PhD, 1959; AM (hon.), Dartmouth Coll., 1968. Bar: Iowa 1954. Practice with firm Bannister, Carpenter, Ahlers & Cooney, Des Moines, 1954; tchg. fellow, instr. govt. Harvard U., 1957—60; mem. faculty dept. govt. Dartmouth U., 1960—94, chmn. dept. govt., 1972—77, 1983—85, Joel Parker prof. law polit. sci., 1976—94, prof. emeritus, 1994—. Author: Middlingness: Juste Millieu Political Theory in England and France, 1815-48, 1965, republished as The Politics of the Center, 1991; contbr. articles to profl. jours. With US Army, 1955—56. Recipient award, Am. Philos. Soc.; fellow, Earhart Found., 1970—71; Sheldon Traveling fellow, 1950—51, Social Sci. Rsch. Coun. fellow, 1958—59, Faculty fellow, Dartmouth U., 1963—64. Mem.: ABA, Iowa Bar Assn., Am. Polit. Sci. Assn., Cambridge (Mass.) Boat Club, Am. Alpine Club, Phi Beta Kappa. Home: Elm St Norwich VT 05055 Office: PO Box 981 Hanover NH 03755-0981 Office Phone: 603-643-6016.

STASEK, LORRAINE ANNE, elementary school educator; b. East Chgo., Ind., July 12, 1932; m. Charles R. Stasek; children: Diane, Charles R., John Charles, Ruthanne. AA in Social Work, 1976; BA in Sociology, Calumet Coll., 1978, BS in Elem. Edn., 1980; BA in Theology, Cal Coll., 1984; M Elem. Edn., Purdue U., Hammond, Ind., 1990. Lic. life elem. tchr., Ind. Substitute tchr. East Chicago Pub. Sch. System, Ind.; tchr. Ind. Harbor Cath. Elem. Sch., East Chicago. Task force Grand Cal, bd. pres., citizen of yr. award. Leadership roles Roman Cath. Ch.; mem. Citizens in Action, Operation Hope Inc.(pres.). Recipient Silver Beaver medal Boy Scouts Am., St. Anne medal Cath. Diocese of Gary, Vol. in Action award State of Ind., Hoosier Environ. Coun. award. Mem.: ASCD, NSTA, Coalition for a Clean Environment.

STASH, SUSAN MICHELE, critical care nurse; b. Inglewood, Calif., Mar. 28, 1965; d. Michael Paul and JoAnn Patricia (Margan) S. BSN, Westminster Coll., Salt Lake City, 1987. RN, Calif.; cert. med.-surg. nurse ANCC. Staff nurse gen. surg. unit St. Joseph Hosp., Orange, Calif., 1987-91; staff nurse gen. med. surg. unit Castle Med. Ctr., Kailua, Hawaii, 1992-94; staff nurse renal/pulmonary/telemetry unit Mary Washington Hosp., Fredericksburg, Va., 1994-95; intermediate med. care unit staff nurse Onslow Meml. Hosp., Jacksonville, NC, 1995-97; staff nurse progressive care unit Swedish Med. Ctr., Englewood, Colo., 1998—; staff nurse subacute ICU Hoag Meml. Hosp. Presbyn., Newport Beach, Calif., 1999—. Mem. ANA, AACN, Am. Assn. Cert. Nurses, Sigma Theta Tau.

STASHOWER, DANIEL MEYER, writer; b. Cleve., Sept. 21, 1960; s. David L. and Sally (Weiss) S.; m. Alison Corbett, May 18, 1996. BA, Northwestern U., 1982; MFA, Columbia U., 1984. Magician, 1978—; author, 1986—. Author: The Ectoplasmic Man, 1985, Elephants in the Distance, 1989, Teller of Tales: The Life of Arthur Conan Doyle, 1999 (Edgar Allan Poe award Mystery Writers Am., 2000), The Dime Museum Murders, 1999, The Floating Lady Murder, 2000, The Houdini Specter, 2001, The Boy Genius and the Mogul, 2002, The Beautiful Cigar Girl, 2006. Raymond Chandler Fulbright fellow, 1992-93. Business E-Mail: daniel@stashower.com.

STASIO, MARILYN LOUISE, columnist; b. Boston, Aug. 20, 1943; d. Joseph Louis and Margaret Martha (Crivello) S.; m. Richard Joseph Hummler, Apr. 24, 1971 (dec. Oct. 1990). BA, Regis Coll., 1964; MA, Columbia U., 1966. Theater critic CUE Mag., NYC, 1968-78; columnist Penthouse, NYC, 1975-80, Politicks, NYC, 1977-78; theater critic The Trib, NYC, 1978, After Dark, NYC, 1981-82, Entertainment Weekly, NYC,

1988-90, NY Post, NYC, 1978-88; book critic NY Times, NYC, 1988—, mystery reviewer. Adj. theater prof. NYU, The New Sch.; teaching residencies Va. Tech., Emerson Coll.; vis. lectr. Carnegie Mellon, Columbia U., Hunter, Bennington Coll., SUNY (Buffalo and Albany), Howard U., Mich. U., U. Ala., Dallas Theater Ctr.; seminar participant Leage Profl. Theater Women, 1993, Naples Lit. Seminar, 1991, Key West Lit. Seminar, 1988, Conn. Libr. Coun. Seminar, 1986, ATA Conf.: Women in Can. Theater, Montreal, 1985, World Affairs Conf. at Boulder U., 1984. Co-author: "Showtune" Memoir with Jerry Herman, 1996; author: The Lily Room, Broadway's Beautiful Losers. Mem.: Am. Soc. Journalists and Authors, Nat. Writers Union, Authors Guild, Lit. Mgrs. and Dramaturgs of the Americas, NY Drama Critics Cir., Nat. Book Critics Cir. Democrat. Office: NY Times 229 West 43rd St New York NY 10036

STASSEN, JOHN HENRY, lawyer; b. Joliet, Ill., Mar. 22, 1943; s. John H. and Florence C. (McCarthy) S.; m. Sara A. Gaw, July 6, 1968; children: John C., David A. BS, Northwestern U., 1965, JD, Harvard U., 1968. Bar: Ill. 1968. Assoc. Kirkland & Ellis, LLP, Chgo., 1968, 73-76, ptnr. 1977—. Contbr. articles to legal jours. Mem. bd. govs. Northwestern U. Libr., chmn., 2003-07; bd. dirs. Landmark Preservation Coun. Ill., chmn., 2001-03. Lt. comdr., JAGC, USNR, 1969-72. Mem. ABA (past chmn. com. on futures regulation), Ill. Bar Assn., Chgo. Bar Assn., Phila. Soc., Mid America Club. Office: Kirkland & Ellis 200 E Randolph St Ste 5900 Chicago IL 60601-6436 Home: 16346 Timber Ln New Buffalo MI 49117 Office Phone: 312-861-2238. Business E-Mail: jstassen@kirkland.com.

STASSINOPOULOS, ARIANNA See **HUFFINGTON, ARIANNA**

STASTNY, JOHN ANTON, real estate executive; b. Chgo., June 30, 1921; s. Joseph and Bozena (Brezina) S.; m. Elizabeth Regina Ossowski, Jan. 2, 1943; children: Mary Elizabeth, John Bernard. Grad. high sch., Chgo. Owner, pres. Stastny Builders, Berwyn, Ill., 1945—; founder, pres. John A. Stastny & Co., Inc., Berwyn, 1954—, Care Ctr. Profls. Inc., Berwyn, 1961-95, Fairfax Health Care Ctr., Berwyn, Ill., 1975-95; chmn. bd. Fairview Health Care Ctr., LaGrange Park, Ill., 1983-95. Pres., adv. bd. Fed. Nat. Mortgage Assn., Washington, 1971-73; chmn. bd. Fed. Home Loan Bank, Chgo., 1972-78. Contbr. articles to profl. jours.; co-founder (tech. jour.): Compendium of Multi-Family Housing, 1965. Bd. dirs. Avery Coonley Sch., Downers Grove, Ill., 1956-60, MacNeal Meml. Hosp., Berwyn, 1978-95; founding gov. West Towns Cmty. Nursing Svc., Berwyn, 1968, Washington Sq. retirement housing, Hinsdale, Ill., 1986; elected del. Cmty. Caucus, Hinsdale, 1955. With U.S. Army, 1942-43. Named Presdl. Appointee Constrn. Industry Collective Bargaining Com., Washington, 1969-71, advisor to U.S. Del. to Econ. Commn. for Europe, U.S. State Dept., Geneva, Switzerland, 1971; named to Housing Hall of Fame, Washington, 1980. Mem. Chgo. Home Builders Assn. (life mem., bd. dirs., pres. 1964-65, Award of Merit 1961), Nat. Assn. Home Builders (life bd. dirs., pres. 1971, numerous disting. service awards 1965-78), Nat. Housing Ctr. (gov., chmn. 1974), Lambda Alpha Internat. (Key award 1964). Clubs: Edgewood Valley Country (LaGrange, Ill.). Republican. Avocations: fishing, golf. Home: 3231 Golfside Dr Naples FL 34110-7006

STASZESKY, FRANCIS MYRON, electric power industry executive, consultant; b. Wilmington, Del., Apr. 16, 1918; s. Frank J. and Ruth (Jones) S.; m. Barbara F. Kearney, May 30, 1943; children: Francis Myron, John B., Barbara J., Faith A., Paul D. BSME, MIT, 1943; MSME, Mass. Inst. Tech., 1943. Mech. engr. Union Oil Co. Calif., LA, 1943-45; with E.I. duPont de Nemours Co., Wilmington, Del., 1946-48; joined Boston Edison Co., 1948, supervising engr. design and constrn., 1948-57, supt. engring. and constrn. dept., 1957-64, v.p., asst. to pres., 1964-67, exec. v.p., 1967-79, pres., chief operating officer, 1979-83; cons., 1983—; dir. Boston Edison Co., 1968-83. Fellow ASME (life); mem. IEEE (sr., life), Nat. Acad. Engring., Engring. Soc. New Eng. (pres. 1961-62). Address: 60 Champlain Cir Plymouth MA 02360

STATES, J. CHRISTOPHER, molecular biology educator, researcher; b. Albany, NY, Oct. 22, 1952; s. Jonathon C. and Ninfa F. (Scorzari) S.; m. Germaine Russo, Apr. 26, 1980; children: Gregory, Vanessa. BS Biochemistry, SUNY, Buffalo, 1974; PhD Pathology and Molecular Biology, Albany Med. Coll., 1980. Rsch. asst. Albany Med. Coll., 1974-75; postdoctoral fellow U. Calgary, Alberta, Can., 1980-84; rsch. scholar Children's Hosp. Rsch. Found., Cin., 1984-86, asst. prof., 1986-88, Wayne State U., Detroit, 1988-97, assoc. prof., 1997—. Reviewer Nat. Sci. and Engring. Rsch. Coun., Ottawa, Can., 1993; program dir. rsch. apprentice program, Wayne State U., 1989—; reviewer Toxicology and Applied Pharmacology, 1994—, DNA and Cell Biology, 1993—, Biotechs., 1996—, Drug Metabolism & Disposition, 1996—. Contbr. articles to profl. jours.; patentee in field. Recipient N.Y. State Regents scholarship, 1970-74, postdoctoral fellowship Alberta Heritage Med. Rsch. Found., Edmonton, Can., 1980-84; rsch. grantee Nat. Cancer Inst., Bethesda, Md., 1988-94, Nat. Inst. Environ. Health Scis., Research Triangle Park, 1997—. Mem. Internat. Soc. for Study of Xenobiotics. Office: Wayne State U 2727 2nd Ave Detroit MI 48201-2671

STATHAM, JASON, actor; b. London, Sept. 12, 1972; Former Olympic diver British Nat. Diving Team. Actor: (films) Lock, Stock and Two Smoking Barrels, 1998, Snatch, 2000, Turn It Up, 2000, Ghosts of Mars, 2001, The One, 2001, Mean Machine, 2001, The Transporter, 2002, The Italian Job, 2003, Collateral, 2004, Cellular, 2004, Transporter II, 2005, London, 2005, Revolver, 2005, Chaos, 2006, The Pink Panther, 2006, Crank, 2006, War, 2007. Office: Creative Artists Agy 9830 Wilshire Blvd Beverly Hills CA 90212 *

STATHIS, NICHOLAS JOHN, lawyer; b. Calchi, Greece, Feb. 27, 1924; Republican. s. John and Sylvia (Koutsonouris) S. Student, Columbia U., 1942-43, 44-48, AB, 1946, JD, 1948. Bar: NY 1949. Assoc. James Maxwell Fassett, NYC, 1948—50; asst. counsel to spl. com. to investigate organized crime in interstate commerce U.S. Senate, Washington, 1951; trial atty. Fidelity & Casualty Co., NYC, 1952; law sec. to Harold R. Medina Judge U.S. Ct. Appeals (2d cir.), NYC, 1952—54; spl. dep. atty. gen. N.Y. State Election Frauds Bur., Dept. Law, NYC, 1956; assoc. Watson, Leavenworth, Kelton & Taggart, NYC, 1954—60, ptnr., 1961—81, Hopgood, Calimafde, Kalil, Blaustein & Judlowe, NYC, 1981—84, Botein, Hays & Sklar, NYC, 1984—89; of counsel White & Case, NYC, 1989—93; corp. coun., dir. intellectual property Aphton Corp., NYC, 1993—. Lectr. Practising Law Inst., N.Y.C., 1968-69. Contbr. articles to profl. jours. on trademarks. Pres., exec. dir., chmn., bd. dirs. Found. Classic Theatre and Acad., 1973—; bd. dirs. Concert Artists Guild, 1974-91, Pirandello Soc., 1976—, Bklyn. Philharm. Orch., 1986-91, Orpheon, Inc., 1986-98, Friends of Young Musicians, 1998—. With AUS, 1943-44. Mem. ABA, Assn. of Bar of City of N.Y., N.Y. State Bar Assn., Fed. Bar Coun., Am. Intellectual Property Law Assn., N.Y. Intellectual Property Law Assn. Greek Orthodox. Office: 515 Madison Ave Ste 2511 New York NY 10022-5403

STATHOPOULOS, PETER, internist; b. Hackensack, NJ, Mar. 24, 1952; s. Anastasios and Vasiliki S.; m. Diane Menichella. MD, U. Thessaloniki, 1981. Diplomate Am. Bd. Internal Medicine. Intern St. Vincent's Med. Ctr., SI, 1981-82, resident in internal medicine, 1982-84, attending physician, 1985—. Office: 856 Castleton Ave Staten Island NY 10310-1809 Office Phone: 718-720-6300.

STATHOS, LIFTERIA K., retired educational association administrator; b. Hartford, Conn. d. Peter Karlames and Nota Politis; Student, Hart Sch. Music Hillyer Coll. (now U. Hartford), Conn., 1950—60; AA with honors, Tunxis CC, Farmington, Conn., 1971; BA, BS, Ctrl. Conn. State U., New Britain, 1980, MA, 1982; PhD, U. Conn., Storrs, 1984. Edn. sec. Bur. Pupil Pers. and Spl. Edn. Svcs., State Dept. Edn., Hartford, 1959—69, edn. acct., 1969—80, edn. adminstr., 1980—89. Co-chmn. St. George Ch. Libr., New Britain; New Britain Gen. Hosp. Aux.; mem. planning com. Hospice of Greater New Britain; founder ch. libr. St. George Ch., New Britain, 1993—; mem. Organized Srs. St. George Ch.-Still Going Strong, 1985—. Mem.: AAUW, Daus. Penelope (life), New Britain Indsl. Mus., Ladies Philoptochos Soc. (bd. dirs., former pres., v.p., sec., treas.), New Britain Mus. Am. Art, Coll. Club New Britain (mem. scholarship com. 1989). Republican. Greek Orthodox. Avocations: piano, stamp collecting/philately, gardening, cooking, reading. Home: 40 Knollwood Dr New Britain CT 06052-1123

STATHOS, MARGARET MORELAND, musician; b. Salem, Mass., Sept. 13, 1925; d. Philip Atkins Moreland and Madeline Allen Prescott; m. Charles Anthony Stathos, Dec. 12, 1964; children: Philip Moreland, Stephanie Prescott. Diploma in Piano, New England Conservatory Music, Boston, 1946; BA in Musicology, Boston U., 1949; postgrad., Hochschule Music, Berlin, Germany, 1957—58, Hochschule Music, Munich, Germany, 1961—64, Music Konservatorium I, Bern, Switzerland, 1958; studied with, Bruce Hungerford, Ambach, Germany, 1961—64. Mem. faculty Longy Sch. Music, Cambridge, Mass., 1954—57; specialist early Am. music Concord Mus., Mass., 1982—90; pvt. practice instr. music Lincoln, Mass., 1985—. Bd. dirs. Lincoln Arts Coun., Boston; lectr. in field. Musician: Lordly and Dame Concert Mgmt., 1952—57; author: A History of Compassion, 2000, (biographies) American National Biography, 2000. Recipient award, German Acad. Austauschienst, 1957—59; grantee, Minuteman Nat. Pk., 1978—80. Mem.: Am. Anti-Vivisection Soc., Am. Assn. State and Local History, Emerson Soc., Thoreau Soc., Assn. Hungerford Archives (bd. dirs. 1990—). Avocations: transcendentalism, animal rights advocacy. Home: 69 Todd Pond Rd Lincoln MA 01773 Office Phone: 781-259-9173. Personal E-mail: pmstathos@aol.com.

STATLER, IRVING CARL, aerospace engineer; b. Buffalo, Nov. 23, 1923; s. Samuel William and Sarah (Strauss) S.; m. Renee Roll, Aug. 23, 1953; children: William Scott, Thomas Stuart BS in Aero. Engring., U. Mich., 1945, BS in Engring. Math., 1945; PhD, Calif. Inst. Tech., 1956. Research engr. flight research dept. Cornell Aero. Lab., Inc., Buffalo, 1946-53, prin. engr. flight research dept., 1956-57, asst. head aeromechanics dept., 1957-63, head applied mechanics dept., 1963-70, sr. staff scientist aeroscis. div., 1970-71; research scientist U.S. Army Air Mobility Research and Devel. Lab., Moffett Field, Calif., 1971-73, dir. Aeromechanics Lab., 1973-85, dir. AGARD, 1985-88; sr. staff scientist NASA Ames Rsch. Ctr., 1988-92, chief Human Factors Rsch. Divsn., 1992—. Research scientist research analysis group Jet Propulsion Lab., Pasadena, Calif., 1953-55; chmn. flight mechanics panel adv. group aerospace research and devel. NATO, 1974-76; lectr. U. Buffalo, Millard-Fillmore Coll., Buffalo, 1957-58 Served with USAAF, 1945-46 Fellow AIAA (Internat. Cooperation in Space Sci. medal 1992), AAAS, German Aerospace Soc., Royal Aero Soc.; mem. Am. Helicopter Soc., Sigma Xi. Home: 1362 Cuernavaca Circulo Mountain View CA 94040-3571 Office: NASA Ames Rsch Ctr MS 262-4 Moffett Field CA 94035 Home Phone: 650-966-1364; Office Phone: 650-690-6003. E-mail: irving.c.statler@nasa.gov.

STAUB, AUGUST WILLIAM, theater producer, educator; b. New Orleans, Oct. 9, 1931; s. August Harry and Laurel (Elfer) S.; m. Patricia Gebhardt, Nov. 22, 1952; 1 child, Laurel Melicent. BA, La. State U., 1952, MA, 1956, PhD, 1960. Instr., tech. dir. La. State U., 1955; instr. Ea. Mich. U., 1956-58; assoc. dir. Dunes Summer Theatre, Michigan City, Ind., summers 1957-60; asst. prof., assoc. dir. univ. theatre U. Fla., 1960-64; assoc. prof. U. New Orleans, 1964-66, prof., chmn. dept. drama and communications, 1966-76; prof., head drama dept. U. Ga., 1976-95, prof. emeritus, 1996—. Exec. producer Jekyll Island Mus. Comedy Festival, 1984-88, Highlands (N.C.) Playhouse, 1989-2000, Ga. Repertory Theatre, 1991-95; staff dir. Theatre in the Square, Marietta, Ga., 1996—; exec. sec. Theatres of La.; v.p. New Orleans Internat. Jazz Festival, 1967-69; pres. S.W. Theatre Conf., 1973-74. Author: Lysistrata, 1968, The Social Climber, 1969, A Small Bare Space, 1970, Introduction to Theatrical Arts, 1971, Creating Theatre, 1973, Varieties of Theatrical Arts, 1980, 83, 94; gen. editor: Artists and Ideas in the Theatre (Peter Lang), 1989—2006; assoc. editor Speech Tchr., 1966-68, So. Speech Comm. Jour., 1974-77, Quar. Jour. Speech, 1977-79. Bd. dirs. Friends Ga. Mus., Athens, Ga. Symphony, Coun. Arts for Children, New Orleans, New Orleans Ctr. Creative Arts, Athens Arts. Commn., Ga. Alliance Arts Edn. Lt. AUS, 1952-54. Recipient Creativity in Rsch. medallion U. Ga., 1987, Disting. Svc. award S.W. Theater Conf., 1985; La. State U. Found. Disting. Faculty fellow, 1970-71. Fellow Coll. of Fellows of Am. Theatre (bd. dirs. 1999-2001), Coll. of Fellows of the S.W. Theatre Assn.; mem. Am. Theatre Assn. (pres. 1985-86, bd. dirs.), Univ. and Coll. Theatre Assn. (pres. 1974-75), Nat. Assn. Schs. Theatre (pres. 1981-83), Univ. Resident Theatre Assn. (bd. dirs. 1976-79), Inst. European Theatre, Nat. Theatre Conf., Am. Soc. Theatre Rsch., Internat. Fedn. Theatre Rsch., Soc. Lit., Sci. and Arts Home: 190 Ravenwood Ct Athens GA 30605-3340 Personal E-mail: pastaub@bellsouth.net. *How good it is to be able to spend a lifetime doing what one loves to do.*

STAUB, CAROL ANNE, artist; b. Milford, Del., Jan. 30, 1948; d. Charles Edward and Isabelle Gill; m. William Edward Staub, July 23, 1977; children: William Knapp, Denise Casalino. Instr., Port St. Lucie, Fla., 2003, Elliott Mus., Stuart, Fla., 2004, 05, 06, 07, Somerset Art Assn., Bedminster, NJ, 2006, 07. One-woman shows include Town of South Palm Beach, Fla., 2005, Mark's In The Park, Boca Raton, Fla., 2007, Represented in permanent collections U. Fla., Ft. Pierce, Fla., Elliott Mus. Art, Stuart, Fla., Arcolle, Sergines, France, Museo De Collage, Mexico, Assn. Promotion Social Artetica, Rome, Italy, Country Arts Found., Ingram, Tex., Real Tart Gallery, Taranaki, New Zealand; contbr. articles to newspapers; numerous group shows including most recently, exhibited in group shows at Somerset Art Assn., Pluckemin, NJ, 2006, Cornell Mus. Art, Delray Beach, Fla., 2006, Vero Beach Mus. Art, Fla., 2006, Morris Pub. Libr., Whippany, NJ, 2006, Elliott Mus., Stuart, Fla., 2006, 2007, Coral Springs Mus. Art, Fla., 2007, Boca Raton Mus. Art Artist's Guild, Boca Raton, Fla., 2007, Vero Beach Mus. Art, Fla., 2007, Cornell Mus. Art, Delray Beach, Fla., 2007, Anniston Mus. Nat. History, Ala., 2007, A.E. Backus Mus., Ft. Pierce, Fla., 2007, Somerset Art Assn., Pluckemin, NJ, 2007. Finalist, The Artist's Mag., 2002, Artist's Mag., 2006; recipient Merit award, A.E. Bean Backus Mus., 2005, award, Nat. Collage Soc., 2005, Best in Show award, Somerset Art Assn., 2006, Ana Drobnies award, San Diego Watercolor Soc., 2004, East West Arts Frames award, 2005, numerous others, hon. mention, Best Abstract Design award, Creative Catalyst Productions, 2006. Mem.: Watercolor Soc. Ala. (assoc. past pres. award 2006), San Diego Watercolor Soc. (assoc. Ana Drobnies award 2004, East West Arts and Frames award 2005), The Fla. Watercolor Soc. (assoc.), The Palm Beach Watercolor Soc., Fla. (assoc.), Exptl. Artists Am. (assoc.), The Nat. Watercolor Soc. (assoc.), The Nat. Collage Soc. (assoc. award 2005, cash award 2006), The Am. Watercolor Soc. (assoc.), The Internat. Soc. Exptl. Artists (assoc. Am. Frame award 2006), Allied Artists Am. (assoc.), Vero Beach Mus. Art Artist's Guild (life), NJ Watercolor Soc. (life Excellence award 2005, Beall Rodgers Meml. award 2005, Nicholas Reale Meml. award 2006), Women In The Visual Arts (life), Garden State Watercolor Soc. (life Am. Frame award 2005), Internat. Soc. Acrylic Painters (life Savoir-Faire award 2006), The Nat. Assn. Women Artists (life; bd. dirs., treas. Fla. chpt., merit award 2005), The Boca Raton Mus. Art Artists Guild (life). Avocations: cooking, golf, bowling, reading, photography. Home (Winter): 10316 Crosby Place Port Saint Lucie FL 34986 Home (Summer): 531 Elizabeth Ave Somerset NJ 08873 Home Phone: 772-466-4386. Home Fax: 772-466-2982. Personal E-mail: carolcando@aol.com.

STAUB, W. ARTHUR, health care products executive; b. Detroit, Dec. 25, 1923; s. Edward Elmer and Emma Josephine (Fleury) S.; m. Alla Elizabeth Edwards, June 26, 1948; children: James Randall, Sally Ann, David Scott. BS, Dartmouth Coll., 1944; MD, Temple U., 1947. Intern Muhlenberg Hosp., Plainfield, NJ, 1947-48; resident in pediatrics Abington (Pa.) Meml. Hosp., 1950-51; practice medicine specializing in pediatrics Westfield (N.J.) Med. Group, 1948-63; assoc. med. dir. Ciba Pharm. Co., Summit, NJ, 1963-66; med. dir., v.p. life sci. div. Becton-Dickinson and Co., Rutherford, NJ, 1966-70; v.p. med. affairs C. R. Bard Co., Murray Hill, NJ, 1970-88, also bd. dirs. Bd. dirs. Crestmont Fed. Savs. and Loan Assn., Edison, N.J., Colonial Trust Nat. Bank, North Palm Beach, Fla.; cons. Children's Specialized Hosp., Westfield, 1948-88, Overlook Hosp., Summit, 1948-88. Contbr. articles to profl. jours. Deacon Presbyn. Ch., Westfield, 1959—. Ensign USNR, 1944—50, to capt. USAF, 1950—53. Fellow Am. Coll. Physician Execs.; mem. AAAS, Assn. Advancement Med. Instrumentation, Health Industry Mfrs. Assn. (chmn. med. and sci. steering com.). Clubs: Echo Lake Country (Westfield) (bd. trustees 1984-88); Lost Tree (North Palm Beach, Fla., bd. govs. 1989-94, sec. 1989-94); Skytop (Pa.). Republican. Presbyterian. Avocations: golf, physical fitness, reading, sailing, travel. Home: 3330 Devonshire Way Palm Beach Gardens FL 33418 E-mail: DoctorWAS@aol.com.

STAUBACH, ROGER THOMAS, real estate executive, former professional football player; b. Cin., Feb. 5, 1942; s. Robert Joseph and Elizabeth (Smyth) S.; m. Marianne Jeanne Hoobler, Sept. 4, 1965; children: Jennifer Anne, Michelle Elizabeth, Stephanie Marie, Jeffrey, Amy Lynn. Student, Roswell Mil. Inst., N.Mex., 1960-61; BS, US Naval Acad., 1965. Quarterback Dallas Cowboy Football Team, 1969-79; former announcer CBS Football.; pres. Holloway-Staubach Co. (name now Staubach Co.), 1980-92; chmn., CEO, pres. Staubach Co., Dallas, 1993—. Author: First Down, Lifetime to Go, 1974, Time Enough to Win, 1981. Bd. dirs. Halliburton Co., Gibson Greetings, Salvation Army; active Pres. Coun. on Phys. Fitness, 1981-83. Served as Lt. USNR, 1965—69. Recipient Heisman Trophy, 1963, Teddy Roosevelt award Nat Collegiate Athletic Assn., Spirit of Entrepreneurship award North Tex. Entrepreneurs Found., 2005, Spirit of Generations award Sr. Source Dallas, Torch of Conscience award Am Jewish Congress, Congressional Medal of Honor Patriot award, 2006; played Pro Bowl, 1971, 76, 78; inducted into Nat. Football League Hall of Fame, 1985, Tex. Bus. Hall of Fame; named Corp. Services Exec. of Yr. Comml. Property News, Disting. Grad. US Naval Acad., Tex. Legend Galleria C. of C. Mem. Fellowship of Christian Athletes. Roman Catholic. Office: Staubach Co 15601 Dallas Parkway Ste 400 Addison TX 75001 *

STAUBER-JOHNSON, ELIZABETH JANE, retired elementary school educator; b. Duluth, Minn., Apr. 7, 1950; d. Edward James and Kathleen Mary (LeBlanc) Stauber; m. A(lden) Ronald Johnson, July 26, 1975; children: Todd Alden, Heidi Ann, Dean Edward, Shane Ronald. BS summa cum laude, Coll. St. Scholastica, 1972; MEd summa cum laude, U. Minn., Duluth, 1982; PhD in Curriculum/Instrn. Elem. Math. Edn., U. Minn., 1996. Cert. tchr., Minn. Tchr. Ind. Sch. Dist. 709/Duluth Pub. Schs., 1972-88; tchr. elem. math. Nettleton Math./Sci./Computer Magnet Sch., Duluth, 1988-93; asst. prof. math. edn. U. Wis., Superior, 1993-97; ret., 1997. Pres. Equine Allies, Inc., 2004—; trainer Success Understanding Math. Project, Des Moines, gender-ethnic excellence student achievement GESA, 1991—; instr. tchr. Family Math., Mpls., 1988—; mem. project for reforming and improving math. edn. com. Minn. Dept. Edn., math. framework team, 1992—; com. mem. Gov.'s Nat. Sci. Found. Statewide Systemic Initiative, 1991—, Coll. of St. Scholastica Ctr. for Promotion of Underrepresented in Sci., 1990—; desegregation adv. com. Duluth Schs., 1987—; initiative com. Gov.'s Nat. Sci. Found.; team mem. Minn. Dept. Edn. Math. Frameworks; presenter in field Trustee Coll. St. Scholastica, Duluth, chair acad. affairs; bd. dirs. Marshal Coll. Prep. Sch., 2003—, v.p., 2004—; pres. Equine Ailies, Inc., 2004—; bd. dirs. MArshall Sch., Duluth, 2004—, v.p., 2005—. Mem. Minn. Coun. Tchrs. Math., Nat. Assn. Tchrs. Math., Minn. Reading Assn., Arrowhead Reading Coun. (bd. dirs. 1984—, pres. 1988-89), Assn. Childhood Edn. (pres. Duluth chpt. 1980-81, state bd. dirs. 1982-83), Phi Kappa Phi, Alpha Delta Kappa (pres. 1982-84), Phi Delta Kappa. Avocations: reading, children's pop-up books, orchid collecting/growing, showing and breeding quarter horses. Home: 2400 Minnesota Ave Duluth MN 55802-2518

STAUBITZ, ARTHUR FREDERICK, retired lawyer, health products executive; b. Omaha, Mar. 14, 1939; s. Herbert Frederick Staubitz and Barbara Eileen (Dallas) Alderson; m. Linda Medora Miller, Aug. 18, 1962; children: Michael, Melissa, Peter. AB cum laude, Wesleyan U., Middletown, Conn., 1961; JD cum laude, U. Pa., 1964. Bar: Ill. 1964, U.S. Dist. Ct. (no. dist.) Ill. 1964, U.S. Ct. Appeals (7th cir.) 1964, Pa. 1972. Assoc. Sidley & Austin, Chgo., 1964-71; sr. internat. atty., asst. gen. counsel, dir. Japanese ops. Sperry Univac, Blue Bell, Pa., 1971-78; from asst. to assoc. to dep. gen. counsel Baxter Internat. Inc., Deerfield, Ill., 1978—85, v.p., dep. gen. counsel, 1985—90; v.p. Baxter Diagnostics, 1990—91; sr. v.p., sec., gen. counsel Amgen, Inc., Thousand Oaks, Calif., 1991—92; v.p., gen. mgr. Ventures Group Baxter World Trade Corp., Deerfield, Ill., 1992—93; v.p., sec., gen. counsel Baxter Internat. Inc., Deerfield, 1993, sr. v.p., gen. counsel, 1993—97, sr. v.p. portfolio strategy, 1997—98; ret., 1998. Mem. Planning Commn., Springfield Twp., Montgomery County, Pa., 1973-74, mem. Zoning Hearing Bd., 1974-78; bd. dirs. Twp. H.S. Dist. 113, Deerfield and Highland Park, Ill., 1983-91, pres., 1989-91; trustee Food and Drug Law Inst., 1991-92, 93-96, Carthage Coll., Kenosha, Wis., 1996—, exec. com., 1999—; bd. dirs. Music of the Baroque, 1994-2001, vice-chmn.; mem. adv. bd. Ariz. Cancer Ctr. Episcopalian. Home: 6251 E Placita Aspecto Tucson AZ 85750 Office Phone: 520-529-2331. Personal E-mail: staubitz@msn.com.

STAUBUS, GEORGE JOSEPH, finance educator; b. Brunswick, Mo., Apr. 26, 1926; s. George Washington and Florence Lidwina (Pittman) S.; m. Sarah Mayer, Apr. 11, 1949; children: Lindsay, Martin, Paul, Janette. BS, U. Mo., 1947; MBA, U. Chgo., 1949, PhD, 1954. C.P.A., Ill. Instr. U. Buffalo, 1947-49, U. Chgo., 1950-52; asst. prof. then prof. acctg. U. Calif.-Berkeley, from 1952, now Michael N. Chetkovich prof. emeritus. Vis. prof. NYU, 1965, London Bus. Sch., 1966-67, U. Kans., 1969-70; Erskine lectr. U. Canterbury, New Zealand, 1972, 91. Author: A Theory of Accounting to Investors, 1961, Activity Costing and Input-Output Accounting, 1971, Making Accounting Decisions, 1977, An Accounting Concept of Revenue, 1980, Activity Costing for Decisions, 1988, Economic Influences on the Development of Accounting in Firms, 1996, The Decision-Usefulness Theory of Accounting: A Limited History, 2000. Served with USN, 1944-46. Recipient Disting. prof. Calif. Soc. C.P.A.s, 1981 Mem. Am. Acctg. Assn. (disting. internat. lectr. 1982), AICPA, Fin. Execs. Inst. Office: UC Berkeley Haas Sch Bus Berkeley CA 94720-0001

STAUDENMEIER, WILLIAM JOHN, JR., academic administrator, dean, sociology professor; b. Wilmington, Del., Oct. 28, 1950; s. William John and Virginia Arlene Staudenmeier; m. Elizabeth Robin Medina, May 28, 1978; children: William Francis, Thomas Maxim. BS, U.S. Mil. Acad., West Point, NY, 1972; MA in Mgmt. and Human Rels., Webster Coll., St. Louis, Mo., 1978; PhD in Sociology, Washington U., St. Louis, Mo., 1985. Chief drug and alcohol edn. and rehab. Travis AFB, Fairfield, Calif., 1972—75; chief drug/alcohol abuse control Clark AFB, Angeles, Philippines, 1975—76, Hdqs. Mil. Airlift Command, Scott AFB, Ill., 1976—78; acting asst. prof. sociology Drake U., Des Moines, 1985—87; asst. prof.

sociology Eureka Coll., Ill., 1987—90, assoc. prof. sociology, 1990—95, prof. sociology, 1995—, v.p. acad. affairs, dean, 2005—06. Divsn. chair social scis. and bus. divsn. Eureka Coll., 1991—94; manuscript referee jours., 1987—2005; instr. cmty. orgn. sect. Nat. Alcoholism Tng. Program for Profls., St. Louis, 1976—78; cons. and instr. alcohol studies cert. program, employee assistance program Continuing Edn. Washington U., St. Louis, 1980—84; cons. Harbor Ho., St. Louis, 1983—84; cons. employee assistance edn. and rsch. program Sch. of Indsl. and Labor Rels., Cornell U., Ithaca, NY, 1987; cons. medicalization of substance abuse treatment in the workplace Inst. for Behavioral Rsch., U. of Ga., Athens, 1987; faculty rep. to bd. of trustees Eureka Coll., 1988—90, chair coll. strategic planning, 1989—91, founder, dir., faculty colloquia series, 1988—94; vis. scientist U. Edinburgh, 1994; vis. fellow Sch. Indsl. and Labor Rels., Cornell U., NY, 1992. V.p. Eureka Area United Way, 1989—91; charter chpt. faculty adviser Eureka Coll. Nat. Charter Campus Chpt. of Habitat for Humanity, 1988—92; bd. dirs. Solano County Mental Health Adv. Bd., Vallejo, Calif., 1974—75. Capt. USAF, 1972—78. Named pioneering EAP practioner for oral history project, Prof. Harrison M. Trice, Cornell U., 1987, Dean's Lectr., Office of the Dean, Eureka Coll., 1988, 1995; recipient PhD tuition scholarship, Washington U., 1980—85, Helen B. Cleaver Disting. Tchg. award, Eureka Coll., 1989—90; fellow, Nat. Inst. on Alcohol Abuse and Alcoholism, 1979—80. Mem.: Kettil Bruun Soc. for Social and Epidemiol. Rsch. on Alcohol, Midwest Sociol. Soc. (soc. bd. of dirs. 2004—06, sec. 1999—2001), Ill. Sociol. Assn. (governing bd. 1995—2001, pres. 1998—99), Alpha Chi (life). Achievements include helping pioneer early social actions drug/alcohol education/rehabilitation in the USAF. Avocations: hiking, reading, chess, soccer. Office: Eureka Coll 300 E College Ave Eureka IL 61530 Office Phone: 309-467-6301.

STAUDERMAN, ALBERT PHILIP, JR., media production consultant; b. Englewood, NJ, Dec. 14, 1936; s. Albert Philip Stauderman and Martha Louise (Dodd) Williamson; m. Helen MacKenzie Layton, Dec. 27, 1958; children: Elizabeth, Sarah, Edward (Ted). BSc, Syracuse U., 1958. Audio-visual prodn. supr. Luth. Ch. in Am., Phila., 1960-64; TV comml. prodn. supr. Procter & Gamble, Cin., 1964-71, assoc. mgr., 1971-82; dir. advt. prodn. Richardson-Vicks, Wilton, Conn., 1982-85; chmn., CEO Bird Bonette Stauderman Inc., Westport, Conn., 1985—; co-chmn., dir. Bird Bonette Stauderman Europe Ltd., London, 1996-2000, chmn., dir., 2000—, founder Sao Paulo, Brazil, 2001—, Sydney, 2006—. Pres. Dikaia Found., Inc., 1995—2001. Author: TV Commercial Production Cost Trends, 1985, 2d. edit., 1986; writer, dir. various pub. svc. TV Commls., 1970-82; actor Golden Age TV programs, 1949-56. Commr. Wilton (Conn.) various land use Commns., 1988—; founding pres. Syracuse U. Newhouse Sch. Alumni Assn., 1985—87; pres. congregation and coun. St. Michael's Luth. Ch., New Canaan, Conn., 1999—2001. Recipient Alumni Svc. award Syracuse U., 1981. Mem. Sprite Island Yacht Club (chmn. race com. 1993-98), Minute Man Yacht Club, Sloane Club (London), Williams Club (NYC), Delta Upsilon. Republican. Office Phone: 203-454-8781.

STAUDERMAN, BRUCE FORD, advertising executive, writer; b. Jersey City, Mar. 17, 1919; b. Herbert Henry and Helen Ann (Jacobus) S.; m. Claude Outhier, Mar. 23; 1946. Student, Syracuse U., 1936-38, TV Workshop, NYC, 1949-50, Sch. TV Technique, 1950. V.p. TV, radio, films Meldrum & Fewsmith, Inc., Cleve., 1954-62, exec. v.p., chmn. plans bd., exec. creative dir., 1973-79; v.p., creative dir. Ogilvy & Mather, NYC, 1962-69, Kenyon & Eckhardt, Inc., NYC, 1979-83, Barnhart & Co., Denver, 1983-84; pres. Stauderman Advt., 1984—; v.p., creative dir. Mktg. Resources Group, 1985-88. Dir. TV, Intermarco-Elvinger (advt. co.), Paris, 1969-73; TV cons. gov., Ohio, 1958; mem. coun., judge C.L.I.O. Festival, 1960—; chmn. Paris jury, 1969-73; jury mem. Internat. Advt. Film Festival, Cannes, Venice, 1976— Author: The England Book, 2006; radio, TV program writer: House of Mystery, The Big Story, Columbia Workshop, 1946-51; writer, producer, dir., WXEL-TV, Cleve., 1951-54. Mem. men's com. Cleve. Playhouse, 1958-62; chmn. TV com. Cleve. United Fund, 1958-59. Served from pvt. to 2d lt. AUS, 1941-46; to 1st lt. N.G. Essex Troop AUS, 1948-50. Mem. Am. Assn. Advt. Agys. (TV and radio adminstrs. com. 1958-62), Am. Fedn. TV and Radio Artists, Naval Club (London). Home: 8647 Falcon Green Dr West Palm Beach FL 33412-1576 E-mail: bfswriter@aol.com.

STAUDOHAR, PAUL DAVID, economics professor, labor arbitrator; b. Duluth, Minn., Dec. 3, 1940; s. Matthew Paul Staudohar and Patricia Constance Landell. BA, U. Minn., 1962; MBA, U. So. Calif., LA, 1966, MA, 1968, PhD, 1969. Adminstrv. officer United Calif. Bank, LA, 1964—66; instr. econ. U. So. Calif., LA, 1967—69; asst. prof. bus. adminstrn. Calif. State U., Hayward, 1969—72, assoc. prof. bus. adminstrn., 1972, prof. bus. adminstrn., 1977—2007, prof. emeritus, 2007—. Pres. Internat. Assn. of Sports Economists, France, 1999—2002; bd. editors Jour. of Individual Employment Rights, 1992—; co-founder Jour. of Sports Econs., bd. editors, 2000—. Author: Labor Econ. and Indsl. Rels., 1994, Playing for Dollars, 1996; author, editor: Diamond Mines: Baseball and Labor, 2000, More Sports Best Short Stories, 2004, The Best Dog Stories, 2007, mem. edit. bd.: Wolters Kluwer Law & Bus., 2007—. Recipient disting. svc. award, Omicron Delta Epsilon, 1981. Mem.: Am. Arbitration Assn., Am. Econ. Assn., Nat. Acad. Arbitrators, Beta Gamma Sigma (hon.). Office: Calif State U East Bay 25800 Carlos Bee Blvd Hayward CA 94542 Office Phone: 510-885-3080.

STAUFFER, ERIC P., lawyer; b. Tucson, Feb. 1, 1948; s. Robert D. and Jeanne E. (Catlin) S.; m. Jane F. Snyder, Aug. 2, 1969; children: Curtis Austen, Marcus Elias, Laura Afton. BA, New Coll. of Fla., 1969; JD, Yale U., 1972. Bar: Ariz. 1972, Maine 1974, D.C. 1979. Spl. asst. to gov., fed. state coord. State of Maine, 1973-75; Maine alt. New England Regional Commn., 1973-75; gen. counsel Maine State Housing Auth., 1976-77; adminstrv. asst. to chmn. Dem. Nat. Com., 1977-78; mem. Preti, Flaherty, Beliveau & Pachios, PLLP, Portland, Maine, 1978—. Bd. dirs. Jr. Achievement Maine, Inc., 1995-98; pres. Goodwill Industries No. New Eng., 1981-82, bd. dirs., 1979-93, 1999-2005. Fellow Am. Coll. Mortgage Attys.; mem. Am. Health Lawyers Assn., Maine State Bar Assn., Ariz. State Bar, DC Bar, Maine Real Estate Devel. Assn. (bd. dirs. 1991—, Pub. Svc. award 1992, Founder's award 2002, Vol. of Yr. 2007), Maine Bar Found. (bd. dirs. 2007—). Office: Preti Flaherty Beliveau & Pachios PLLP PO Box 9546 One City Ctr Portland ME 04112-9546 Home Phone: 207-774-2461; Office Phone: 207-791-3000. Business E-Mail: estauffe@preti.com.

STAUFFER, GEORGE B., dean, musician, historian, consultant; b. Hershey, Pa., Feb. 18, 1947; s. Howard Hamilton and Elizabeth Boyer Stauffer; 1 child, Matthew. BA, Dartmouth Coll., Hanover, NH, 1969; MA, Bryn Mawr Coll., Pa., 1971; PhD, Columbia U., NYC, 1978. Adj. asst. prof. Yeshiva U., NYC, 1978—79; asst. to prof. music CUNY, NYC, 1979—2000; dean, prof. music Mason Gross Sch. Arts, Rutgers U., New Brunswick, NJ, 2000—. U. organist, chapel music dir. Columbia U., 1977—99; bd. trustees Keewaydin Found., Salisbury, Vt., 1981—2000. Author: (books) The Organ Preludes of J.S. Bach, 1980, Bach: The Mass in B-Minor, 1997; co-author: Organ Technique: Modern & Early, 2002; editor: J.S. Bach as Organist, 1986, The World Of Baroque Music, 2006; gen. editor: Yale Music Masterworks Series, 2002—. Fellowship, Guggenheim Found., NYC, 1985—86, Fulbright Commn., DC, 1999—2000, Am. Coun. Learned Societies, NYC, 1999—2000. Mem.: Coll. Music Soc., Am. Bach Soc. (adv. bd. mem. 2000—, pres. 1996—2000), Am. Musicological Soc. Avocation: canoeing. Home: 1050 George St 16M New Brunswick NJ 08901 Office: Office of Dean Mason Gross Sch 33 Livingston Ave New Brunswick NJ 08901 Office Phone: 732-932-9360. Business E-Mail: stauffer@masongross.rutgers.edu.

STAUFFER, JOHN WILLIAM, cultural historian; b. Lincoln, Nebr. s. William Albert and Jean Stanley Stauffer; m. Deborah Cunningham; 1 child, Erik Isaiah. MALS in Humanities, Wesleyan U., 1991; MA in Am. Studies, Purdue U., 1993; PhD in Am. Studies, Yale U., 1999. Asst. prof. Harvard U., Cambridge, Mass., 1999-2001, assoc. prof., 2001—03, prof., 2003—. Spkr. in field. Author: The Black Hearts of Men, 2002 (Frederick Douglass Book prize 2002, Lincoln prize, 2d pl. winner, 2003), The Meteor of War: The John Brown Story, 2004; editor: My Bondage and My Freedom, 2003, The Works of James McCune Smith, 2006, Prophets of Protest, 2006, The Problem of Evil, 2007. Newhouse fellow in writing Yale U., 1996-97, Rsch. fellow, 1994-95, History and Am. Studies Rsch. fellow, 1996, Charlotte Newcombe fellow Woodrow Wilson Nat. Fellowship Found., 1997-98; grantee NEH, 1999; recipient Ralph Henry Gabriel prize, 1999, Jan Thaddeus Tchg. award Harvard U., 2002, Frederick Douglass Book prize, 2002, Avery Craven prize, 2003, Lincoln prize, 2003, Everett Mendelsohn Excellence in Mentoring award, 2005. Mem. Soc. for Values in Higher Edn., Orgn. of Am. Historians (presenter 1998), Am. Studies Assn. (Ralph Henry Gabriel prize 1999), Daguerreian Soc., Phi Kappa Phi. Avocations: photography, tennis, ballet, dance (jazz). Office: Harvard U Dept English Barker Ctr 12 Quincy St Cambridge MA 02138-3804 Home: 1 Amory Pl Cambridge MA 02139 Home Phone: 617-642-7108; Office Phone: 617-864-4508. Business E-Mail: stauffer@fas.harvard.edu.

STAUFFER, SCOTT WILLIAM, lawyer, accountant; b. Oshkosh, Wis., Aug. 17, 1954; s. Robert Edward and Shirley Lydia (Wrasse) S.; m. Debralee Bowland, Nov. 14, 1987. BBA in Acctg., U. Wis., 1975; JD, U. Denver, 1979. Bar: Colo. 1979; CPA, Colo. Tax acct. Arthur Andersen & Co., Denver, 1979-82; tax mgr. Gary-Williams Oil, Englewood, Colo., 1982-85; pvt. practice Aurora, Colo., 1986—. Active Colo. Chorale, Denver, 1977—, pres., 1984-85, 92-93 Mem. ABA, AICPA, Colo. Bar Assn. (multidisciplinary practice taskforce 2000-02, ethics com. 1997-99, exec. coun. solo and small firm sect. 2002-, chair 2004-05), Denver Bar Assn. (chmn. law office mgmt. com. 1993-95, chmn. intraprofl. com. 1997-04), Colo. Soc. CPA (chmn. fed. tax com. 1994-96, bd. dirs. 2000-02), Am. Assn. Atty.-CPA., Denver Tax Assn. (chair 2003), Bethany Luth. Ch. Found. (pres. 2002-04). Lutheran. Avocations: singing, golf, travel, reading, computer. Home: 8147 W Frost Pl Littleton CO 80128-4325 Office: 2851 S Parker Rd Ste 720 Aurora CO 80014-2728 Office Phone: 303-337-2323. Business E-Mail: sstauffer@staufferlawcpa.com.

STAUFFER, THOMAS GEORGE, retired hotel executive; b. Akron, Ohio, Mar. 4, 1932; s. Caldwell E. and Rose C. (Ortscheidt) S.; m. Lois Campsey, June 18, 1960. BS, Case Western Res. U., 1954. Cert. hotel adminstr. Pres. Renaissance Hotels Internat. (Ams.), 1954-98; ret., 1998. Trustee Cleve. Bot. Garden. Recipient Legion of Honor, Order of DeMolay. Mem. Am. Hotel and Motel Assn., Urban Land Inst., Nat. Restaurant Assn. (past dir.), Rolling Rock Club, Lakewood Country Club, Masons, Scottish Rite, Sigma Chi (Significant Sigma Chi). Home: 19 Warwick Ln Cleveland OH 44116-2305 Personal E-mail: lcstgs@aol.com.

STAUFFER, THOMAS MICHAEL, university president; b. Harrisburg, Pa., Dec. 5, 1941; s. John Nisley and Louise Lee Stauffer; children: Amity Juliet, Courtney Amanda, Winston Thomas; life ptnr. Susie Heller. BA cum laude, Wittenberg U., Ohio, 1963; Cert. in E. European Politics, Freie U. Berlin, 1964; MA, PhD, U. Denver, 1973; Doctorate (hon.), Jackson State U., 2002. Asst. dean Keene State Coll., 1971—72; dir. office leadership devel., v.p., external rels. Am. Coun. on Edn., 1972—82; pres., prof. pub. policy U. Houston-Clear Lake, 1982—91; spl. asst. to adminstr. NASA, 1991—92; pres., prof. pub. policy and internat. rels. Golden Gate U., 1992—99; CEO Mgmt. Cons. Internat., 1985—2006, Young Pres. Orgn. Internat., 1999—2001, Family Bus. Internat. Consultation, 2001—06; exec. dir. Lincoln Ctr. for Ethics in Internat. Mgmt.; prof. global bus. Thunderbird Sch. Global Mgmt., 2003—05; pres., CEO, prof. mgmt. Am. U. Afghanistan, 2006—. Exec. sec. Fedn. Assn. of Acad. Health Care Profls.; chmn. task force Am. Coun. Edn.; exec. dir. Bus. Higher Edn. Forum, Nat. Com. Higher Edn. Issues, 1975—82; mem. bd. trustees Am. U. Afghanistan; bd. dirs. Am. U. Afghanistan Found. Exec. editor Ednl. Record and Higher Edn. and Nat. Affairs; contbr. chpts. to books and articles to profl. jours. and newspapers. Chair Challenger Ctr. for Space Sci. Edn.; chair nat. bd. Ctr. for Advanced Space Studies; com. advanced tech. Tex. Econ. Devel.; chmn. com. advanced tech. Houston Com. on Econ. Diversification Planning, Houston World Trade Ctr. Task Force, Clear Lake Area Econ. Devel. Found.; co-chair Tex. Sci. and Tech. Coun.; pres. St. John Hosp.; co-chair San Francisco World Trade Assn.; chair San Francisco Consortium on Higher Edn., San Francisco Mayor's Blue Ribbon Com. on Econ. Devel.; mem. steering com. Silicon Valley Mfrs. Group; bd. dirs. San Francisco C. of C., San Francisco YMCA, Acad. of Art U., Chefs for Humanity. Recipient Disting. Alumni award Grad. Sch. Internat. Studies U. Denver, 1989, Tex. Senate Resolution of Commendation, 1991, Challenger Ctr. Nat. award, 1990, ACE Fellow Anniversary award, 1990, 05, Leadership HS Do the Right Thing award, 1998; Am. Coun. on Edn. fellow in acad. adminstrn., 1971-72, Ford Found. and Social Sci. Found. fellow, 1963-68, sr. fellow Am. Leadership Forum. Home: 3080 Coombsville Rd Napa CA 94558 Office: 1806 Green St San Francisco CA 94123 Office Phone: 415-516-8767. Business E-Mail: auafpresident@gmail.com.

STAUFFER, VALERIE VILAS, civic volunteer; b. NYC, Aug. 29, 1935; d. Frank Jay and Kathleen Vilas Brown; m. John Eugene Stauffer, June 5, 1956; children: Jill Stauffer Cobbs, Karen Stauffer Murphy, John Christian, Peter Eugene. BA, Wellesley Coll., Mass., 1956; MA, Manhattanville Coll., Purchase, NY, 2007. V.p. Stauffer Tech., Greenwich, Conn., 1985—. Contbr. Greenwich Rev. mag.; editor: Quality Assurance of Food, 1988, Round Hill Association Newsletter, 1991—92; mng. editor: Inkwell mag., 2004—. Chmn. dist. 7 Rep. Town Meeting, Greenwich, Conn., 1984—, chmn. social svcs. com., 1997; chmn. Friends of Greenwich Libr., 1997—99; trustee, exec. com., sec. bd. trustees Greenwich Libr., 1999—. Mem. Greenwich Hist. Soc. (bd. dirs. 2007-), Greenwich Garden Club (pres. 1999-2001). Home: 6 Pecksland Rd Greenwich CT 06831-3738 Office: Stauffer Tech 6 Pecksland Rd Greenwich CT 06831-3738 Personal E-mail: stauftek@aol.com.

STAUNTON, IMELDA (IMELDA MARY PHILOMENA BERNADETTE STAUNTON), actress; b. London, Jan. 9, 1956; d. Joseph and Bridie (McNicolas) Staunton; m. Jim Carter, 1985; 1 child. Grad., Royal Acad. Dramatic Art. Actress (TV series) The Singing Detective, 1986, Thompson, 1988, Izzy, 1990, Up the Garden Path, 1990, Muriel Spry, 1993, If You See God, Tell Him, 1993, Stella Phelps, 1995, Is It Legal?, 1995, Mrs. Twit, 2003, Let's Write a Story, 2003, (films) Comrades, 1987, They Never Sleep, 1990, Antonia and Jane, 1991, Peter's Friends, 1992, Much Ado About Nothing, 1993, Deadly Advice, 1993, Sense and Sensibility, 1995, Twelth Night: Or What You Will, 1996, Remember Me?, 1997, Shakespeare in Love, 1998, Rat, 2000, Another Life, 2001, Crush, 2001, Ready, 2002, The Virgin of Liverpool, 2003, Bright Young Things, 2003, Blackball, 2003, I'll Be There, 2003, Vera Drake, 2004 (Coppa Volpi award, Venice Film Festival, 2004, Gold Lion award, Venice Film Festival, 2004, Best Actress, NY Film Critic Circle award, 2004, Los Angeles Film Critics Assn. award, 2004, Washington, DC Film Critics, 2004), 3 & 3, 2005, Nanny McPhee, 2005, 3 & 3, 2005, Freedom Writers, 2007, (TV) A Sleeping Life, 1989, Yellowbacks, 1990, The Englishman's Wife, 1990, The Heat of the Day, 1990, A Masculine Ending, 1992, Don't Leave Me This Way, 1993, Woodcock, 1994, Mole's Christmas, 1994, Citizen X, 1995, The Adventures of Mole, 1995, David Copperfield, 1999, Murder, 2002, Cambridge Spies, 2003, Fingersmith, 2005, A Midsummer Night's Dream, 2005, My Family and Other Animals, 2005, The Wind in the Willows, 2006, (TV miniseries) Look at the State We're In, 1995, Cambridge Spies, 2003;, performer repertory productions, (stage appearances) Guys and Dolls, 1982, 1996, The Beggar's Opera, 1985, A Chorus of Disapproval, 1985 (Laurence Olivier award, Soc. of West End Theatre, Best Supporting Actress, 1985, London Critics Circle award, Best Supporting Actress, 1985, Laurence Olivier award, 1986), The Corn is Green, 1985 (Laurence Olivier award, 1986), The Wizard of Oz, 1986, Fair Maid of the West, 1986, Uncle Vanya, 1988 (Plays and Players London Theatre Critics award, Best Supporting Actress, 1988), Into the Woods, 1990 (Olivier award, Best Actress in a Musical, 1991), Phoenix, 1990 (Laurence Olivier award, Best Actress in a Musical, 1990); voice The Snow Queen's Revenge, 1996, The Ugly Duckling, 1997, The Canterbury Tales, 1998, The Chicken Run, 2000, Jack and the Beanstalk, 2000, guest appearances (TV) A Sleeping Life, 1989, Charity, 1993, "Local Government," Look at the State We're In!, 1995, A Bit of Fry and Laurie, 1995, Midsomer Murders, 1999, Incubus, 2003. Assoc. mem. Royal Acad. Dramatic Art. Address: Peters Fraser & Dunlap Ltd Drury House 34-43 Russell St London WC2B 5HA England Office Phone: 44 (0) 207 344 1041. Office Fax: 44 (0) 207 836 9543. *

STAVELY, KEITH WILLIAMS FITZGERALD, librarian; b. New Brunswick, NJ, May 13, 1942; s. Homer Eaton and Elizabeth (Williams) S.; m. Kathleen Fitzgerald, Aug. 19, 1978; 1 child, Jonathan Keith. BA, Yale U., 1964, PhD, 1969; MLS, Simmons Coll., 1980. Asst. prof. English Boston U., 1969—74, Ohio State U., 1990—91; lectr. English Boston Coll., 1975—80; adult svcs. libr. Watertown Free Pub. Libr., Mass., 1979—89, br. libr., 1984—89, head adult svcs., 1989—90; reference libr. Somerville Pub. Libr., Mass., 1991—92; asst. adminstr. Fall River Pub. Libr., Mass., 1992—99, adminstr., 1999—. Author: Puritan Legacies: Paradise Lost and the New England Tradition, 1630-1890, 1987, paperback edit., 1990, The Politics of Milton's Prose Style, 1975; co-author: Family Man: What Men Feel About Their Wives, Their Children, Their Parents, and Themselves, 1978, America's Founding Food: The Story of New England Cooking, 2004; contbr. articles and revs. to profl. publs. Fellow Fulbright Found., India, 1964-65, Am. Coun. Learned Socs., 1988-89, John Simon Guggenheim Meml. Found., 1989. Mem. MLA (Prize for Ind. Scholars 1987), ALA, Mass. Libr. Assn., Phi Beta Kappa. E-mail: kstavely@sailsinc.org, kstavely@cox.net.

STAVERT, ALEXANDER BRUCE, archbishop; b. Montreal, Apr. 1, 1940; s. R. Ewart and Kathleen H. (Rosamond) S.; m. Diana Greig, June 26, 1982; children: Kathleen, Rosamond, Timothy. Student, Lower Can. Coll., Montreal, 1957; BA, Bishop's U., 1961; STB, U. Toronto, Ont., Can., 1964, ThM, 1976, DD (hon.), 1986; DCL (hon.), Bishop's U., 2007. Ordained to ministry Anglican Ch. as deacon, 1964, as priest, 1965. With Mission of Schefferville, Que., 1964-69; fellow, tutor in div. Trinity Coll., U. Toronto, 1969-70, chaplain, 1970-76; with St. Clement's Mission East, St. Paul's River, Que., 1976-81; chaplain Champlain Regional Coll., Bishop's U., 1981-84; dean, rector St. Alban's Cathedral, Prince Albert, Sask., Canada, 1984-91; consecrated bishop Anglican Diocese of Que., Quebec, 1991—; metropolitan Province of Can., 2004—; archbishop Quebec, 2004—. Address: Diocese of Que 31 rue des Jardins Quebec City PQ Canada G1R 4L6 Office Phone: 418-692-3858. Business E-Mail: archbishop@quebec.anglican.ca.

STAVES, SUSAN, humanities educator; b. NYC, Oct. 5, 1942; d. Henry Tracy and Margaret Staves. AB, U. Chgo., 1963; MA, U. Va., 1964, PhD, 1967. Woodrow Wilson intern Bennett Coll., Greensboro, NC, 1965-66; from asst. prof. to prof. Brandeis U., Waltham, Mass., 1967-93, Paul Proswimmer prof. of Humanities, 1993—2001, dept. chair, 1986-89, 95-98, prof. emerita, 2001—. Clark prof. UCLA, 1989—90. Author: Players' Scepters: Fictions of Authority in the Restoration, 1979, Married Women's Separate Property in England, 1660-1833, 1990, A Literary History of Women's Writing in Britain, 2006, Studies on Voltaire and the 18th Century, (essays) Fetter'd or Free?: Collected Essays on 18th Century Women Novelists, 1986, History, Gender, and 18th Century Literature, 1994, Woman and Political Writing, 1998, Enchanted Ground: Reimagining John Dryden, 2004, Cambridge Companion to Aphra Behn, 2004, Women and Material Culture, 1660-1830, 2007; co-author (with John Brewer): Early Modern Conceptions of Property, 1994; co-editor (with Cynthia Ricciardi): Elizabeth Griffith's Delicate Distress, 1997; contbr. articles to profl. jours. Mem. ACLU, 1967—; assoc. mem. Belmont Dem. Town Com., Belmont, Mass. Woodrow Wilson fellow, 1963—64, Woodrow Wilson Dissertation fellow, 1966—67, Harvard Liberal Arts fellow, 1980—81, John Simon Guggenheim fellow, 1981—82, Emeritus fellow, Andrew W. Mellon Found., 2005—06. Mem.: AAUP, MLA (exec. com. divsn. on late 18th century English lit. 1984—86), Am. Soc. for 18th Century Studies (exec. bd. 1987—90). Episcopalian. Avocations: hiking, harpsichord. Office: Brandeis U Dept English MS 023 Waltham MA 02454 Home Phone: 617-489-1095; Office Phone: 781-736-2161. Business E-Mail: staves@brandeis.edu.

STAVIG, MARK LUTHER, language educator; b. Northfield, Minn., Jan. 20, 1935; s. Lawrence Melvin and Cora (Hjertaas) S.; m. Donna Mae Ring, July 3, 1957; children— Anne Ragnhild, Thomas Edward, Rolf Lawrence BA, Augustana Coll., 1956, Oxford U., 1958, MA, 1962; PhD, Princeton U., 1961. Instr. to asst. prof. English U. Wis., Madison, 1961-68; from assoc. prof. to prof. English Colo. Coll., Colorado Springs, 1968—2001; ret., 2001—. Author: John Ford and the Traditional Moral Order, 1968, The Forms of Things Unknown: Renaissance Metaphor in Romeo and Juliet and A Midsummer Night's Dream, 1995; editor: Ford, 'Tis Pity She's a Whore, 1966. Fellow Danforth Found., 1956-61, Woodrow Wilson Found., 1956-57; Fulbright scholar Oxford U., 1956-58 Mem.: Shakespeare Assn. Am. Democrat. Home: 1409 Wood Ave Colorado Springs CO 80907-7348

STAVIG, RICHARD THORSON, retired literature educator; b. Tacoma, May 14, 1927; s. Lawrence Melvin Stavig and Cora Hjertaas; m. LaVonne Josephine Engebretson, Aug. 13, 1950; children: Jofrid, Kaia. BA, Augustana Coll., Sioux Falls, SD, 1950; MA, Princeton U., NJ, 1953, PhD, 1955. Asst. prof. English Washington and Jefferson Coll., Washington, Pa., 1953—55; assoc. prof. English Kalamazoo Coll., 1955—92, prof. English, dir. fgn. study, 1958—74; ret., 1992. With USN, 1945—46. Named Fulbright prof., Heidelberg U., Germany, 1958—59. Home: 2415 Highpointe Dr Kalamazoo MI 49008-2074

STAVISKY, TOBY ANN, state legislator; b. NYC; m. Leonard Stavisky, 1964 (dec. 1999); 1 child, Evan. BA, Syracuse U.; Grad. Degree, Hunter Coll., Queens Coll. Social studies tchr. N.Y.C. Pub. High Schs.; dist. mgr. N.E. Queens 1980 Census; mem. N.Y. Senate from 16th Dist., Albany, 1999—, asst. minority whip, 2003—. Mem. legis. coms. fin., transp., tourism, recreation and sports devel. N.Y. State Sen. 16th Dist., ranking minority mem. higher edn. com., mem. aging com., mem. civil svc. and pensions com., mem. edn. com. Founder North Flushing Sr. Ctr., bd. dirs.; trustee Whitestone Hebrew Ctr. Named Worthy Woman of Forest Hills; recipient Claire Shulman award, Top 10 Women in Bus., 2004, award, Neurol. Impaired Brain Injured Children, 2002, Counseling, Admissions and Fin. Aid Legis. Consortium, 2003, Flushing C. of C. and Bus. Assn., Taiwanese Assn. Am., CUNY, Korean-Am. Assn. Flushing. Democrat. Office: Rm 504 Legislative Office Bldg Albany NY 12247 also: 14436 Willets Point Blvd Flushing NY 11357-3411 Office Phone: 718-445-0004. Business E-Mail: stavisky@senate.state.ny.us.

STAVITSKY, ABRAM BENJAMIN, immunologist, educator; b. Newark, May 14, 1919; s. Nathan and Ida (Novak) S.; m. Ruth Bernice Okney, Dec. 6, 1942; children: Ellen Barbara, Gail Beth. AB, U. Mich., 1939, MS, 1940; PhD, U. Minn., 1943; VMD, U. Pa., 1946. Research fellow Calif. Inst. Tech., 1946-47; faculty Case Western Res. U., 1947—, prof. microbiology, 1962—, prof. molecular biology and microbiology, 1983-89, emeritus, 1989; mem. expert com. immunochemistry WHO, 1963-83; mem. microbiology fellowship com. NIH, 1963-66; mem. microbiology test com. Nat. Bd. Med. Examiners, 1970-73; chmn. microbiology test com. Nat. Bd. Podiatry Examiners, 1978-82; adj. staff in pathobiology Lerner Rsch. Inst., Cleve. Clinic Found., 2006—. Mem. editl. bd. Jour. Immunological Methods, 1979-88, Immunopharmacology, 1983-96. Vice pres. Ludlow Community Assn., 1964-66. Fellow AAAS; mem. Am. Assn. Immunologists, Am. Soc. Microbiology, Sigma Xi. Home: 14604 Onaway Rd Shaker Heights OH 44120-2845 Office: 2119 Abington Rd Cleveland OH 44106-2333 Home Phone: 216-752-8631. Business E-Mail: abs7@case.edu.

STAVOLE, JANET M., librarian, director; b. Cleve., Nov. 25, 1949; d. Frank A and Gertrude E Stavole. BA, Kent State U., 1972, MLS, 1972—77. Children's libr. Kent Free Libr., Ohio, 1973—78, Main Children's Rm. Akron-Summit County Pub. Libr., Akron, Ohio, 1979—85; br. mgr. & early childhood libr. Nordonia Hills Br. Akron-Summit County Pub. Libr., Northfield Ctr., Ohio, 1985—. Pres. Akron-Summit County Pub. Libr. Staff Assn., 1984—85. Mem.: Ohio Libr. Coun. Avocations: reading, gardening, art. Office: Akron-Summit County Pub Libr 9458 Olde Eight Rd Northfield OH 44067 Office Phone: 330-467-8595. Office Fax: 330-467-4332. E-mail: jstavole@akronlibrary.org.

STAVRIDIS, JIM (JAMES GEORGE STAVRIDIS), career military officer; b. West Palm Beach, Fla., Feb. 15, 1955; s. Paul George and Shirley Anne Stavridis; m. Laura Elizabeth Hall, May 28, 1981; children: Christina Anne, Julia Elizabeth. BS, U.S. Naval Acad., Annapolis, Md., 1972; PhD, Tufts U., 1983, MA in Law and Diplomacy, 1984; Disting. grad., Nat. War Coll., 1992. Commd. ensign USN, advanced through grades to adm., 2006; commdg. officer USS Barry, Norfolk, Va., 1993—96; comdr. Destroyer Squadron 21, San Diego, 1997—98; exec. asst. to sec. USN, Washington, 1998—2000, dir. navy ops. group, 2000—02; comdr. USS Enterprise Carrier Strike Group, 2002—04, Cruiser Destroyer Group 12, Mayport, Fla., 2002—04; sr. mil. asst. to sec. US Dept. Def., Washington, 2004—06; comdr. US So. Command, Miami, 2006—. Author: Division Officer's Guide, Watch Officer's Guide, Command at Sea; contbr. articles to profl. jours. Decorated Def. Superior Svc. medal, Legion of Merit, Meritorious Svc. medal, Navy Commendation medal, Navy Achievement medal; recipient Adm. Arleigh Burke award, Newport Navy League award, John Paul Jones award for Inspirational Leadership, Navy League. Home: 3501 Granada Blvd Coral Gables FL 33134 Office: US So Command 3511 NW 91st Ave Miami FL 33172 Business E-Mail: n00@ccdg12.navy.mil.

STAVROPOULOS, ROSE MARY GRANT, community activist, volunteer; b. Decatur, Ill. d. Walter Edwin and Ora Lenore (Kepler) Grant; m. Stan Stavropoulos; children: Becky Ann Stavropoulos Betian, Stephanie Diane. BS, Ea. Ill. U. Cert. elem. edn. Tchr. 2nd grade Garfield Sch., Decatur; bd. dirs. Wilmot Sch. Bd. PTA, Deerfield, Moraine Girl Scout Coun., Deerfield, also bd. dirs.; chmn. Human Rels. Commn., Deerfield; mem. sr. citizen adv. com. Deerfield Park Dist.; pres. Lake County (Ill.) LWV; chmn. Deerfield Village Caucus; pres. Caring For Others, Inc., Deerfield, Deerfield Area LWV; bd. mem., pres. Deerfield Area United Way, pres. Mem. Deerfield Village Caucus Adv. Coun. Recipient Deerfield Human Rels. Humanitarian award, Lerner Life's Citizen of Month. Mem. Deerfield Area Hist. Soc., Highland Park Hosp. Aux, Legacy at Bryant Ranch Home Assn. (bd. dirs., treas., sec.), Delta Zeta. Home: 23959 Sanctuary Pkwy Yorba Linda CA 92887 Personal E-mail: jjjjgrandma@aol.com.

STAVROPOULOS, WILLIAM S., retired chemical company executive; b. Bridgehampton, NY, May 12, 1939; m. Linda Stavropoulos; children: S. William, Angela D. BS in Pharm. Chemistry, Fordham U.; PhD in Medicinal Chemistry, U. Washington; LLD (hon.), Northwood U., 1998. Rsch. chemist in pharm. rsch. Dow Chem. Co., Midland, Mich., 1967, rsch. chemist for diagnostics product rsch., 1970, rsch. mgr. diagnostics product rsch., 1973, bus. mgr. diagnostics product rsch., 1976, bus. mgr. polyolefins, 1977, dir. mktg. plastics dept., 1979; comml. v.p. Dow Chem. Co. Latin Am., Coral Gables, Fla., 1980; pres. Dow Latin Am., 1984; comml. v.p., basics and hydrocarbons Dow Chem. Co. U.S.A., Midland, Mich., 1985-87, group v.p., 1987-90; pres. Dow U.S.A., 1990; v.p. The Dow Chem. Co., 1990, sr. v.p., 1991, pres., CO0, 1993—95, CEO, 1995—2000, 2002—04, chmn., 2001—06. Bd. dirs. Dow Corning Corp., The Dow Chem. Co., Marion Merrel Dow Inc., BellSouth Corp., Chem. Financial Corp., Maersk Inc., NCR Corp.; trustee, Fidelity Group of Funds; bd. Am Enterprise Inst. Public Policy Rsch.; CEO Essex Chem Corp, 1988-92. Recipient Ellis Island Medal of Honor, 1998, Man of the Year award, Hellenic Am. C. of C., 2000, Palladium Medal award, Societe de Chimie Industrielle, 2001, Annual Bus. Mgmt. award, Society of Plastic Engineers, 2003. Mem.: Society of Chem. Industry (Chem. Industry Medal award 2003). *

STAWICKI, JOSEPH JOHN, JR., marketing executive; b. New Haven, Nov. 27, 1944; s. Joseph J. Sr. and Tonya (Bolash) S.; m. Barbara Jean Schneider, Jan. 19, 1968; children: Laura, Kevin, Dennis. BS, St. Joseph Coll., 1966; MBA, No. Ill. U., 1968. Investment adminstr. Phoenix Equity Planning Corp., Hartford, Conn., 1971—74; asst. prof. Ctrl. Conn. State U., New Britain, 1975—81; trade officer New Eng. Trade Assistance Ctr., Boston, 1981—83; dir. ops. Multimate Internat. Corp., East Hartford, Conn., 1983—84; pres. Mercor Resources Corp., Winsted, Conn., 1985—, also bd. dirs.; pres. Stawicki Realty, Winsted, 1988—. Mem. Wyantenuck Country Club, Elks, Sigma Iota Epsilon. Roman Catholic. Home: PO Box 416 Winsted CT 06098-0416 Office: Mercor Resources Corp 135 W Wakefield Blvd Winsted CT 06098-2929 Personal E-mail: joseph.stawicki@snet.net.

STAWNYCHY, ZORIANA MARIA, financial executive; b. NYC, May 31, 1953; d. Walter and Eugenia (Hanusczcak) Salak; m. Yuri Andrij Stawnychy, Oct. 26, 1985. BA, Fordham U., 1975. Cert. fin. planner, registered investment advisor. Fin. planner Cigna, NYC, 1978—83, 1985—90; mgr. Bruce Raines Assocs., NYC, 1983—84; sr. fin. counselor Ind. Fin. Services, White Plains, NY, 1984—85; owner Stawnychy Fin. Svcs., Inc., Butler, NJ, 1991—. Mem. Fin. Planning Assn. Avocation: tennis.

STAY, BARBARA, zoologist, educator; b. Cleve., Aug. 31, 1926; d. Theron David and Florence (Finley) S. AB, Vassar Coll., 1947; MA, Radcliffe Coll., 1949, PhD, 1953. Entomologist Army Research Center, Natick, Mass., 1954-60; vis. asst. prof. Pomona Coll., 1960; asst. prof. biology U. Pa., 1961-67; asso. prof. zoology U. Iowa, Iowa City, 1967-77, prof., 1977—. Fulbright fellow to Australia, 1953; Lalor fellow Harvard U., 1960 Fellow AAAS, Entomol. Soc. Am.; mem. Soc. Comparative and Integrative Biology, Am. Inst. Biol. Scis., Am. Soc. Cell Biology, Iowa Acad. Scis., Sigma Xi. Office: Univ Iowa Dept Biology Iowa City IA 52242 Home Phone: 319-351-5036. E-mail: barbara-stay@uiowa.edu.

STAYIN, RANDOLPH JOHN, lawyer; b. Cin., Oct. 30, 1942; s. Jack and Viola (Tomin) S.; children: Gregory S., Todd R., Elizabeth J. BA, Dartmouth Coll., 1964; JD, U. Cin., 1967. Bar: Ohio 1967, U.S. Dist. Ct. (so. dist.) Ohio 1968, U.S. Dist. Ct. D.C. 1977, U.S. Ct. Appeals (6th cir.) 1968, U.S. Ct. Appeals (fed. cir.) 1986, U.S. Supreme Ct. 1974, U.S. Ct. Appeals (D.C. cir.) 1976, U.S. Ct. Internat. Trade, 1985. Assoc. Frost & Jacobs, Cin., 1967-72; exec. asst., dir. of legislation U.S. Sen. Robert Taft, Jr., Washington, 1973-74, chief of staff, 1975-76; assoc. Taft, Stettinius & Hollister, Washington, 1977, ptnr., 1978-88, Barnes & Thornburg, Washington, 1988—. Mem. adv. coun. U.S. and FGN. Comml. Svc., U.S. Dept. Commerce. Chmn., mem. numerous coms., chmn., worker campaigns for local politicians Rep. Party state and local orgns.; mem. Citizens to Save WCET-TV, 1967-72, Fine Arts Fund, 1970-72, Cancer Soc., 1970-72; chmn. agy. rels. com. Hamilton County Mental Health and Mental Retardation Bd., 1969-71, vice chmn., 1971, chmn., 1971-72; v.p. Recreation Commn., City of Cin., 1970-72; mem. funds mgmt. com. Westwood 1st Presbyn. Ch., 1968, v.p., 1969, pres., 1970, trustee, 1970, elder, 1971-72; bd. dirs. Evans Mill Pond Owners Assn., v.p., 1986, pres., 1987; chmn. Washington Nat. Cathedral Fund Com., mem. devel. com.; co-chair 1907 Soc. Mem.: ABA (sect. on internat. law and practice, vice chmn-.com.on nat. legislation 1977—79, internat. sect., anti-trust sect.), D. C. Bar Assn. (com. on internat. law), Internat. Bar Assn., Am. Soc. Assn. Execs. (legal sect., internat. sect.). Avocations: theater, tennis, skiing, travel, boating. Office: Barnes & Thornburg 750 17th St NW Ste 900 Washington DC 20006-2225 Office Phone: 202-289-1313.

STAYTON, JAMES MICHAEL, music educator; b. Phila., Mar. 1, 1975; s. Norman J. and Mary J. Stayton; m. Catherine A. Padovano, July 20, 2002. BA in Music, Fla. Atlantic U., 2001—01, MA in Music, 2005. Dir. music ministry Our Lady Queen of Heaven Ch., North Lauderdale, Fla., 1994—2002; dir. omusic ministry St. Pius X Ch., Ft. Lauderdale, Fla., 2002—; music tchr. St. Helen Sch., Lauderdale Lakes, Fla., 1996—2001; tchr., dir. choral activities Cardinal Gibbons H.S., Ft. Lauderdale, 2003—. Composer choral art songs and contemporary music. Mem.: Am. Guild Organists, Am. Choral Dir.'s Assn., Nat. Cath. Educator's Assn., Fla. Music Educator's Assn., Music Educator's Nat. Conv., Sigma Alpha Mu (pres., edn. chmn. 1996—99, Brother of the Yr. 1998). Roman Catholic. Avocations: golf, travel, cooking. Office: Cardinal Gibbons HS 2900 NE 47th St Fort Lauderdale FL 33308 Home Phone: 561-306-6281; Office Phone: 954-491-2900. Office Fax: 954-772-1025. Personal E-mail: stayton@cghsfl.org.

STAYTON, THOMAS GEORGE, lawyer; b. Rochester, Minn., May 1, 1948; m. Barbara Joan Feck, Aug. 8, 1970; children: Ryan, Megan. BS, Miami U., Oxford, Ohio, 1970; JD, U. Mich., 1973. Bar: Ind. 1973, U.S. Dist. Ct. (so. dist.) Ind. 1973, U.S. Ct. Appeals (7th cir.) 1977. Ptnr. Baker & Daniels, Indpls., 1973—. Sustaining mem. Product Liability Adv. Coun. Recipient Sagamore of the Wabash Gov. of Ind., 1988. Mem. ABA, Ind. State Bar Assn., Indpls. Bar Assn. Office: Baker & Daniels 300 N Meridian St Ste 2700 Indianapolis IN 46204-1782 Home Phone: 317-733-0516; Office Phone: 317-237-1260. E-mail: tstayton@bakerd.com.

STAYTON, WILLIAM RALPH, psychologist, educator; b. Kelso, Wash., Dec. 25, 1933; s. Ralph Willard and Marguerite (Hunter) S.; m. Kathleen Boucher, Sept. 4, 1954; children: Mark, John, Cheryl, Paul. BA, U. Redlands, 1956; MDiv, Andover Newton Theol. Sem., 1960; ThD, Boston U., 1967; PhD, Inst. Advanced Study of Human Sexuality, 2002. Ordained to ministry Am. Bapt. Ch., 1959. Assoc. min. 1st Bapt. Ch. in Newton, Mass., 1956-61; min. 1st Bapt. Ch., Gloucester, Mass., 1961-68; chaplain New Eng. Bapt. Hosp., Boston, 1968-71; asst. prof. U. Pa. Sch. Medicine, Phila., 1971—78; adj. assoc. prof. U. Pa. Grad. Sch. Edn., Phila., lectr., faculty, 1982—2004; asst. prof. Jefferson Med. Coll./Thomas Jefferson U., 1978-83; marriage and family therapist Wm R. Stayton & Assocs., Ltd., P.C., Phila., 1978—. Mem. faculty La Salle U., Phila., 1983-2002; prof. and coord., human sexuality program Widener U., Chester, Pa., 1999-2006, prof./scholar-in-residence, 2006—; exec. dir. Ctr. for Sexuality and Religion, 2006—. Editor spl. issue Topics in Clin. Nursing, 1980; contbr. articles to profl. jours., chpts. to books. Pres. Cmty. Svcs. for Human Growth, Paoli, Pa., 1989-91, bd. dirs., 1981-97. Named Man of Yr., B'nai B'rith, Gloucester, Mass., 1968; recipient Outstanding Svc. award Community Svcs. for Human Growth, 1990, Richard J. Cross award U. Medicine and Dentistry N.J., 1997, Dean's award Sch Human Svc. Professions Widener U., 2002, Tchr. Excellence award Kappa Delta Pi, 2006. Mem. APA, Am. Assn. Marriage and Family Therapists, Am. Assn. Sex Educators, Counselors and Therapists (bd. dirs. 1982-86, 88-90, 2005—, chmn. dist. VI 1982-86, pres. 1996-98, Outstanding Svc. award 1978-87, Disting. Svc. award 2000, Profl. Standard of Excellence award 2006), Sex Info. and Edn. Coun. U.S. (pres. 1985-87, sec. 1990-92), Soc. for Sci. Study Sex (chmn. ann. meeting 1983), Pa. Assn. Marriage and Family Therapists (continuing edn. com. 1985-90), Planned Parenthood Southeastern Pa. (bd. dirs. 1999—2006, 1st vice chmn. 2001-04, chmn. 2004-06), Phi Kappa Phi. Democrat. Home: 81 Andover Ct Wayne PA 19087-5616 Office: 987 Old Eagle School Rd Ste 719 Wayne PA 19087-1708 Home Phone: 610-647-9616; Office Phone: 610-971-0700. Personal E-mail: wmstayton@cs.com.

STEAD, EDWARD BENJAMIN, lawyer; b. 1947; s. Charles Edward and Shirley J. Stead; m. Henrietta Wright, Mar. 16, 1996. BA, St. Lawrence U., 1969; JD, St. John's U., NYC, 1973. Bar: NY 1974, Ill. 1975, Mass. 1986, Calif. 1990. Corp. lawyer IBM Corp., 1973-85; sr. v.p., gen. counsel, sec. Culinet Software, Inc., 1985-88; v.p., gen. counsel Apple Computer, Inc., Cupertino, Calif., 1989—95, sec., 1993-95, sr. v.p., gen. counsel, 1995—97; exec. v.p., gen. counsel Blockbuster, Inc., Dallas, 1997—2006. Mem. Am. Corp. Counsel Assn. (dir. 1987-88), Santa Clara County Bar Assn. (law found., dir.). *

STEAD, JAMES JOSEPH, JR., securities company executive; b. Chgo., Sept. 13, 1930; s. James Joseph and Irene (Jennings) S.; m. Edith Pearson, Feb. 13, 1954; children: James, Diane, Robert, Caroline. BS, DePaul U., 1957, MBA, 1959. Asst. sec. C. F. Childs & Co., Chgo., 1957-62; exec. v.p., sec. Koenig, Keating & Stead, Inc., Chgo., 1962-66; 2d v.p., mgr. midwest mcpl. bond dept. Hayden, Stone Inc., Chgo., 1966-69; sr. v.p., nat. sales mgr. Ill. Co. Inc., 1969-70; mgr. instl. sales dept. Reynolds and Co., Chgo., 1970-72; partner Edwards & Hanly, 1972-74; v.p., instnl. sales mgr. Paine, Webber, Jackson & Curtis, 1974-76; v.p., regional instl. sales mgr. Reynolds Securities, Inc., 1976-78; sr. v.p., regional mgr. Oppenheimer & Co., Inc., 1978-88; sr. v.p., regional mgr. fixed income Tucker Anthony, 1988—; instr. Mcpl. Bond Sch., Chgo., 1967—. With AUS, 1951-53. Mem. Security Traders Assn. Chgo., Nat. Security Traders Assn., Am. Mgmt. Assn., Mcpl. Fin. Forum Washington. Clubs: Execs., Union League, Mcpl. Bond, Bond (Chgo.); Olympia Fields Country (Ill.); Wall Street (N.Y.C.). Home: 1005 Hickory Ridge Ct Frankfort IL 60423-2114 Office: 1 S Wacker Dr Chicago IL 60606-4614 Office Phone: 312-853-2820 ext. 118.

STEAD, WILLIAM WALLACE, medical educator, researcher, department chairman; b. Durham, NC, Aug. 23, 1948; s. Eugene Anson Jr. and Evelyn Emogene S.; m. Janet Louise Mackey, Aug. 13, 1977; 1 child, Elizabeth Mackey. BA in Chemistry, Duke U., 1970, MD, 1973. Diplomate Am. Bd. Internal Medicine, Am. Bd. Nephrology. Intern in medicine Duke U., Durham, 1973, resident in medicine, 1974, fellow in nephrology, 1975-76, assoc. medicine, 1977-80, asst. prof. medicine, 1980-83, assoc. prof. medicine, 1984-90; prof. medicine and biomed. informatics Vanderbilt U., Nashville, 1991—, assoc. vice chancellor health affairs, chief info. officer, 1991, dir. Informatics Ctr., 1991, univ. info. arch., 1999—2000, chmn. Vanderbilt Ctr. Better Health, 2002—. Dir. HealthStream, Inc., Nashville, 1998—; mem. com. nat. quality report on health care delivery Inst. Medicine Nat. Acads., Washington, 2000-01, com. rapid advance demonstration projects, 2002, computer sci. and telecom. bd. Nat. Rsch. Coun., 2002-; bd. regents Nat. Libr. Medicine, Bethesda, 2001-05; mem. commn. systemic interoperability, 2004-05. Editor in chief: Jour. Am. Med. Informatics Assn., 1993-2002; editor: Proceedings of Eleventh Annual Symposium on Computer Applications in Medical Care, 1987. Recipient Healthcare Pioneer award Computers in Healthcare, 1991; grant of fast track provision of IAIMS Nat. Libr. Medicine, 1995-99. Fellow Am. Coll. Med. Informatics (founding fellow), Am. Inst. Med. and Biol. Engring. (founding fellow); mem. Am. Med. Informatics Assn. (bd. dirs. 1999—, pres.'s award 1997), Inst. Medicine of NAS, Engle Soc., Sigma Xi, Alpha Omega Alpha. Office: Vanderbilt U Med Ctre 3401 West End Ave Ste 290 Vanderbilt Campus Mail Stop 8670 Nashville TN 37203-6866 Business E-Mail: bill.stead@vanderbilt.edu.

STEAD LEE, POLLY JAE See LEE, PALI

STEADMAN, DAVID ROSSLYN AYTON, corporate financial executive, director; b. Wembley, Eng., June 7, 1937; came to U.S., 1980; s. Eric and Iris Sina (Smith) S.; m. Beryl Ellen Giles, Jan. 5, 1963 (div.); children: Michael, Christopher, Timothy; m. Sharon Ruatto, Apr. 9, 2001 B.Sc. in Engring. with honors, City U., London, 1960. Mng. dir. Cossor Electronics, Harlow, England, 1974-78; chmn. EMI med. Electronics, London, 1978-80; pres. Raytheon Data Systems, Norwood Mass., 1980—84, Raytheon Ventures, Lexington, 1985-87; chmn., CEO GCA Corp., Andover, Mass., 1987-88; pres. Atlantic Mgmt. Assocs., Inc., Bedford, NH, 1988—; chmn. Brookwood Cos., Inc., 1989—2007, Visibility, Inc., 1996-2000, CEO, 1999-2000; chmn. Visaer, Inc., 2000—05, Telequip Corp., 2000—06. Chmn. Tech/Ops-Sevcon, Inc.; bd. dirs. Aavid Thermal Techs., Inc., Sterling Constrn. Co. Inc. Fellow Instn. Elec. Engrs. (U.K.); mem. Inst. Mgmt. (U.K.; companion), Inst. Mech. Engrs. (U.K.). Avocations: music, sailing. Office: Atlantic Mgmt Assocs Inc PO Box 10670 Bedford NH 03110 Personal E-mail: drsteadman@aol.com.

STEADMAN, DAVID WILTON, retired museum director, deacon; b. Honolulu, Oct. 24, 1936; s. Alva Edgar and Martha (Cooke) S.; m. Kathleen Carroll Reilly, Aug. 1, 1964; children: Alexander Carroll, Kate Montague. BA, Harvard U., Cambridge, Mass., 1960, MAT., 1961; MA, U. Calif.-Berkeley, 1966; PhD, Princeton U., NJ, 1974; M Theol. Studies, Ch. Divinity Sch. of Pacific, 2002. Ordained deacon Episcopal Ch., 2004. Lectr. Frick Collection, NYC, 1970-71; asst. dir., acting dir., assoc. dir. Princeton U. Art Mus., 1971-73; dir. galleries Claremont Colls., Calif., 1974-80; art cons. Archtl. Digest, LA, 1974-77; rsch. curator Norton Simon Mus., Pasadena, Calif., 1977-80; dir. Chrysler Mus., Norfolk, Va., 1980-89, Toledo Mus. Art, Ohio, 1989-99; ret., 2000. Author: Graphic Art of Francisco Goya, 1975, Works on Paper 1900-1960, 1977, Abraham van Diepenbeeck, 1982. Trustee Phillips Collection, Washington, Norton Simon Mus., Pasadena. Chester Dale fellow Nat. Gallery Art, Washington, 1969-70 Episcopalian. Personal E-mail: punto31157@aol.com.

STEADMAN, JOHN MONTAGUE, judge; b. Honolulu, Aug. 8, 1930; s. Alva Edgar and Martha (Cooke) S.; m. Alison Storer Lunt, Apr. 8, 1961; children: Catharine N., Juliette M., Eric C. Grad., Phillips Acad., Andover, Mass., 1948; BA summa cum laude, Yale U., 1952; LLB magna cum laude, Harvard U., 1955. Bar: D.C. 1955, Calif. 1956, U.S. Supreme Ct. 1964, Hawaii 1977. Assoc. Pillsbury, Madison & Sutro, San Francisco, 1956-63; atty. US Dept. Justice, 1963-64; dep. under sec. for internat. affairs US Army, 1964-65; spl. asst. to sec. & dep. sec. US Dept. Def., 1965-68; gen. counsel USAF, 1968-70; vis. prof. law U. Pa. Law Sch., 1970-72; prof. law Georgetown U. Law Ctr., Washington, 1972-85, assoc. dean, 1979-84; assoc. judge DC Ct. Appeals, 1985—2004, sr. judge, 2004—. Instr. Lincoln Law Sch., San Francisco, 1961-62, San Francisco Law Sch., 1962-63; vis. prof. U. Mich. Sch. Law, 1976, U. Hawaii Sch. Law, 1977; of counsel firm Pillsbury, Madison & Sutro, Washington, 1979-85 Editor: Harvard Law Rev, 1953-55. Sinclair-Kennedy Traveling fellow, 1955-56 Mem. Am. Law Inst., Cosmos Club, Phi Beta Kappa, Delta Sigma Rho, Zeta Psi. Episcopalian. Office: DC Ct Appeals 500 Indiana Ave NW Washington DC 20001-2131 Office Phone: 202-879-2765. Business E-Mail: jsteadman@dcca.state.dc.us.

STEAMER, ROBERT JULIUS, political science professor; b. Rochester, NY, Oct. 14, 1920; s. William August and Lotte (Becker) S.; m. Jean Worden, Apr. 12, 1947; children: Gregg Robert, James Worden. BA in Social Sci., Bucknell U., 1947; MA in Polit. Sci., U. Va., 1952; PhD, Cornell U., 1954; postgrad. law, Oxford U., Eng., 1968-69. Asst. prof. Oglethorpe U., 1952-55, U. Mass., 1955-56; assoc. prof. La. State U., 1956-62; prof. polit. sci., chmn. dept. Lake Forest (Ill.) Coll., 1962-72; prof. U. Mass., Boston, 1972-88, dean Coll. II, 1974-76, vice chancellor for acad. affairs, provost, 1976-79. Vis. summer prof. Tulane U., 1958, Cornell U., 1960, UCLA, 1965; staff cons. La. sect. U.S. Commn. Civil Rights, 1961 Author: The Constitution: Cases and Comments, 1959, The Supreme Court in Crisis, 1971, The Supreme Court: Constitutional Revision and the New Strict Constructionism, 1973, Chief Justice: Leadership and the Supreme Court, 1986; sr. co-author: American Constitutional Law: Cases and Commentary, 1991; contbr. articles to profl. jours. Served with USAAF, 1942-46. Recipient Gt. Tchr. award Lake Forest Coll., 1965; Lilly Found. Research award, 1967; Major Research award Project 87, 1981; hon. research fellow U. Exeter, Eng., 1981 Mem. Am. Polit. Sci. Assn., Midwest Polit. Sci. Assn. (v.p. 1970-71), New Eng. Polit. Sci. Assn. (pres. 1979-80) Home: 1 Sinclair Dr Apt 101 Pittsford NY 14534-1735 Office Phone: 585-248-1388.

STEANS, PHILLIP MICHAEL, lawyer; b. Oak Park, Ill., May 23, 1943; s. William B. and Evelyn A. Steans; m. Randi R. Solberg, Sept. 17, 1966; children: Erik, Joshua, Molly. BA summa cum laude, Ripon Coll., Wis., 1965; JD, U. Chgo., 1968. Bar: Wis. 1968, Ill. 1968, U.S. Dist. Ct. (we. dist.) Wis. 1968. Ptnr. Solberg & Steans, Menomonie, Wis., 1968-85; mng. ptnr. Steans, Skinner, Schofield & Higley, Menomonie, 1985-91; shareholder Bakke-Norman, S.C., Menomonie, 1991-94; pres. Phillip M. Steans, S.C., Menomonie, 1994—. Dist. atty. Dunn County, Wis., Menomonie, 1969-74; asst. city atty. City of Menomonie, 1969-86; asst. family ct. commr. Dunn County, 1993. NCAA scholar, 1965. Mem. Nat. Bd. Trial Advocacy (civil and criminal sect.). Avocations: racquetball, reading, cooking. Home: E5745 708th Ave Menomonie WI 54751-5515 Office: 393 Red Cedar St Ste 6 Menomonie WI 54751-2267 Home Phone: 715-235-3273; Office Phone: 715-235-5550. Business E-Mail: psteans@steanslaw.com.

STEARLEY, ROBERT JAY, retired packaging company executive; b. Brazil, Ind., Sept. 6, 1929; s. Melvin George and Hila Mona (Bolin) S.; m. Helen Louise Dellacca, Nov. 25, 1950; children: Rhonda Jo, Robert Thomas. BS in Mech. Engring., Rose Hulman Inst. Tech., 1957; postgrad., Harvard U., 1979. Gen. mgr. Poly Tech Corp., Mpls., 1961-63; gen. mgr. plastics Gt. Plains Bag Corp., Stamford, Conn., 1963-66, v.p., 1966-71, v.p. ops., 1971-75, pres., 1975-84, dir., 1966-84; v.p. Jefferson Smurfit Corp., Alton, Ill., 1984—. Mem. Paper Shipping Sack Mfg. Assn. (dir. 1980-82), Am. Legion Clubs: Norwood Hills Country (St. Louis). Lodges: Elks. Republican. Methodist. Home: 2 Country Estates Pl Saint Louis MO 63131-3411

STEARNS, CLIFFORD BUNDY, congressman, diversified financial services company executive; b. Washington, Apr. 16, 1941; s. Clifford Robert and Emily Elizabeth (Newlin) Stearns; m. Joan Bette Moore, 1973; children: Douglas Moore, Clifford Bundy Jr., Scott Newlin. BSEE, George Washington U., 1963. Mgr. Control Data Sys., Inc., LA, 1967-69; sr. contract adminstr. CBS, Inc., Stamford, Conn., 1969; account exec. Kutola Advt. Agy., Greenwich, Conn., 1970-71, Images 70/Wilson Haight Welch, Inc., Greenwich, 1971-72; motel owner Hatfield, Mass., 1972-77; pres., motel mgr. Stearns House, Inc., Silver Springs, Fla., 1972—88; mem. U.S. Congress from 6th Fla. dist., 1989—, mem. vets. affairs com., mem. energy and commerce com., chmn. subcom., commerce, trade, consumer protection chmn., others. Broker Silver Springs (Fla.) Real Estate, 1981—88. Bd. dirs. Boys Club Ocala, 1980—84; trustee, vice chmn. Monroe Regional Hosp., Ocala, Fla., 1984—89; pres. Toastmaster Club, LA, 1962. Capt. USAF, 1963—67. Mem.: Marion County Motel Assn. (pres. 1979), Fla.

Assn. Realtors, Am. Assn. Realtors, Fla. Hotel/Motel Assn., Am. Hotel/Motel Assn., Marion C. of C. (bd. dirs. 1987—), Kiwanis (pres. Ocala club 1984). Republican. Presbyterian. Avocations: basketball, swimming, computers. Office: US House of Reps 2370 Rayburn House Office Bldg Washington DC 20515-0906 also: 115 SE 25th Ave Ocala FL 34471-9179 *

STEARNS, FRANK WARREN, lawyer; b. Washington, July 20, 1949; s. Robert Maynard and Ermyntrude (Vaiden) S.; m. Judith Anne Ketcheson, Sept. 7, 1974; children: Frank W. Jr., Brian S., Joe G. BA, Washington & Lee, 1971; JD with honors, George Washington U., 1974. Bar: Washington DC 1975, Va. 1980, Supreme Ct. Va., U.S. Dist. Ct. (DC 1975, ea. dist. Va.), U.S. Ct. Appeals (DC cir. 1975, 4th cir. 1985), U.S. Supreme Ct. Law clk. Superior Ct. D.C., Washington, 1974-75; asst. corp. counsel Office of the Corp. Counsel, Washington, 1975-79; asst. county atty. County Atty's Office, Fairfax County, Va., 1979-80; mng. ptnr. Wilkes Artis P.C., Fairfax, Va., 1984-2001; ptnr., Real Estate, State & Local Govt., Communications practices Venable LLP, Vienna, Va., 2001—. Bd. dirs. No. Va. Bldg. Industry Assn., 1987-94; trustee Greater Washington Bd. Trade-P.A.C., 1987-2003; chmn. tech. adv. com. NVBIA, Loudoun, Va., 1986-90, mem. Econ. Devel. Commn. Arlington County, Va. Coun. Excellence in Govt., Washington, 1989—98; Commr. Arlington County Econ. Devel. Commn., Arlington, Va., 1987—91. Mem. ABA, Va. State Bar Assn., Va. Trial Lawyers Assn., DC Bar Assn., Fairfax County Bar Assn., Barristers, Counsellors, Fairfax C. of C. (PAC trustee 2003—). Avocations: tennis, golf. Office: Venable LLP Ste 300 8010 Towers Crescent Dr Vienna VA 22182 Office Phone: 703-760-1956. Office Fax: 703-821-8949. Business E-Mail: fwstearns@venable.com.

STEARNS, MILTON SPRAGUE, JR., financial executive; b. NYC, June 3, 1923; s. Milton Sprague and Katherine (Stieglitz) S.; m. Virginia McCormick; children: Virginia Parker Stearns King, John Brackett (dec.), Barbara Ellison Stearns Terry, Kathryn Trowbridge Stearns Sergio, Elizabeth Sprague (dec.). Grad., Phillips Exeter Acad., 1942; BS cum laude, Harvard U., 1946, MBA, 1948. With The Fidelity Bank, Phila., 1948-72, group v.p. nat. lending div.; pres. Charter Fin. Co., Radnor, Pa., 1972—2005, Main Line Adult Day Ctr., 1997-99; chmn., chief exec. officer Judson Infrared, Inc., 1976-87. Ret. trustee Franklin Inst., Bryn Mawr Presbyn. Ch., pres. 1993-95. Served with USNR, WWII; lt. (j.g.) Res. ret. Mem. Robert Morris Assoc. (pres. Phila. chpt. 1961-62), Spee Club Cambridge, Mass., Merion Golf Club, Merion Cricket Club, Phila. Skating and Humane Soc., Delray Beach (Fla.) Club, Country Club Fla., Gulfstream Bath and Tennis Club, Pine Tree Golf Club, The Little Club. Home: 43 Righters Mill Rd Gladwyne PA 19035-1548 Office: Villa 53 1400 Waverly Rd Gladwyne PA 19035 Personal E-mail: msscharter@aol.com.

STEARNS, NEELE EDWARD, JR., investment company executive; b. Chgo., Apr. 2, 1936; s. Neele Edward Sr. and Grace (Kessler) S.; m. Bonnie Ann Evans; children: Katherine Stearns Sprenger, Kendra Stearns Drozd. BA magna cum laude, Carleton Coll., 1958; MBA with distinction, Harvard U., 1960. Audit staff Arthur Andersen Co., 1962-66, audit mgr., 1966-67; asst. gen. mgr. internat. divsn. Imperial-Eastman Corp., 1967-68; asst. treas. Allied Products Corp., 1968-69, treas., 1969-72; v.p. Henry Crown (Ill.) and Co., 1972-75, v.p., controller, 1975-79; exec. v.p., COO Henry Crown and Co., 1979—86; pres., CEO, CC Industries, Inc., Chgo., 1986-95; chmn. exec. com. Barnes Internat., Inc., Northbrook, Ill., 1996-99; chmn. Wallace Computer Svcs., Inc., 2000, Fin. Investments Corp., Chgo., 2001—. Bd. dir. Click Commerce, Inc. Trustee Evanston Northwestern Healthcare; bd. dir. Presbyn. Homes. Mem. Comml. Club Chgo., Econ. Club Chgo., Country Club Fla., Chgo. Club, Old Elm Club, Skokie Country Club, Phi Beta Kappa. Office: Fin Investments Corp 405 N Wabash River Plz 2E Chicago IL 60611 Office Phone: 312-494-4513. Business E-Mail: nstearns@fic-sff.com.

STEARNS, PETER NATHANIEL, history professor, academic administrator; b. London, Mar. 3, 1936; (parents Am. citizens); s. Raymond P. and Elizabeth (Scott); children: Duncan, Deborah; m. Carol Zisowitz, Mar. 26, 1978 (div. 1999); children: Clio Elizabeth, Cordelia Raymond. AB, Harvard U., 1957, MA, 1959, PhD, 1963. From instr. to assoc. prof. U. Chgo., 1962-65; prof., chmn. history dept. Rutgers U., New Brunswick, NJ, 1965-74; Heinz prof. history Carnegie Mellon U., Pitts., 1974—, chmn. dept. history, 1986-92, dean Coll. Humanities and Social Scis., 1992-2000; provost George Mason U., 2000—. Co-dir. Pitts. Ctr. for Social History, 1986-92; chmn. acad. adv. coun. NYC Coll. Bd., 1982-85; chmn. Pacesetter World History commn., Coll. Bd., 1992-95, Coll. Bd. Advanced Placement World History, 1997-2006; adv. bd. Liberal Edn., 2001— Author: The Working Classes and the Rise of Socialism, 1971, European Society in Upheaval: Social History since 1800, 1967, Swedish transl., rev. edit., 1975, 3rd edit., 1991, Priest and Revolutionary: Lamennais and the Dilemma of French Catholicism, 1967, Polish tranl., 1967, Modern Europe 1789-1914, 1969, Revolutionary Syndicalism and French Labor: a cause without rebels, 1971; author: (with Harvey Mitchell) Workers and Protest: The European Labor Movement, The Working Classes and the Rise of Socialism, 1890—1914; author: The European Experience since 1815, 1972, 1848: The Revolutionary Tide in Europe, 1974, (publ. in England) The Revolutions of 1848, Lives of Labor: Work in Maturing Industrial Society, 1975, German tranl., 1975, Old Age in European Society, 1977, Face of Europe, 1977, Paths to Authority: Toward the Formation of Middle Class Consciousness, 1978, Be A Man! Males in Modern Society, 1979, rev. edit., 1990; author: (with Linda Rosenzweig) Themes in Modern Social History, 1985; author: (with Carol Stearns) Anger: The Struggle for Emotional Control in America's History, 1986; author: World History: Patterns of Change and Continuity, 1987, 6th edit., 2006; author: (with others) Makers of Modern Europe, 1987;: rev. edit., 1994;; author: (with others) Documents in World History, Vol.1: The Great Tradition and Vol. 2: The Modern Centuries, 1987; author: Life and Society in the West, The Modern Centuries, 1987, Expanding the Past: A Reader in Social History, 1988, Life and Society in the West, The Modern Centuries, 1988; author: (with C. Stearns) Emotion and Social Change, Toward a New Psychohistory, 1988; author: (with Andrew Barnes) Social History and Issues in Consciousness and Cognition, 1989; author: Jealousy: Evolution of an Emotion in American History, 1989, Interpreting the Industrial Revolution, 1991; author: (with Michael Adas and Stuart Schwartz) World Civilizations, 1991, 4th edit., 2003; author: Meaning Over Memory: Issues in Humanities Education, 1993, The Industrial Revolution in World History, 1993, 3rd edit., 2006, Swedish tranl., American Cool: Developing a 20th Century Emotional Style, 1994, Turbulent Passage: A Global History of the 20th Century, 1994, rev. edit., 2003, 3rd edit., 2005; author: (with Ron Harre) Discursive Psychology in Practice, 1995; author: Millenium III, Century XXI, 1996; author: (with Hinshaw) Encyclopedia of the Industrial Revolution, 1996, with Hinshaw: rev. edit., 1998;; author: Fat History: Bodies and Beauty in the West, 1997, rev. edit., 2002, Schools and Students in Industrial Society: Japan and the West, 1997, History in Documents, 1998; author: (with Lewis) Emotional History of the U.S., 1998; author: World History in Documents: and Comparative Analysis in World History, 1998, Battleground of Desire: The Struggle for Self-Control in Modern America, 1999, Experiencing World History, 2000, Teaching, Learning and Knowing History, 2000, Gender in World History, 2000, Consumerism in World History, 2001;: rev. edit., 2006;; author: (with Brindle) Facing Up to Management Faddism, 2001; author: Cultures in Motion, 2001, Anxious Parents: History of Modern American Child Rearing, 2003, Western Civilization in World History, 2003, A Day in the Life, 2005, Behavioral History, 2005, Childhood in World History, 2005, Global Outrage: Evolution and Impact of World Opinion, 2005, American Fear, 2006, Revolutions in Sorrow, 2007, Revolutions in Sorrow: American Death in Comparative Perspective, 2007; editor: Century for Debate, 1969, The Impact of the Industrial Revolution, 1972; editor: (with Walkowitz) Workers in the Industrial Revolution, 1974; editor: The Other Side of Western Civilization, 1979, rev. edit., 1984, 4th edit., 1991, The Rise of Modern Women, 1977; author (with S. Gosch): Travel in Premodern World History, 2007; editor (with Michael Weber): The Spencers of Amberson Avenue: A Turn-of-the-Century Memoir, 1983; editor: (with Van Tassel) Old Age in a Bureaucratic Society, 1986; editor: Encyclopedia World History, 2000, Encyclopedia of European Social History, 1999; editor in chief Jour. Social History, 1967—, mng. editor, 1967—; contbg. editor: History of Emotions, Thinking History, 2004; contbr. articles to prof. jours. Bd. dirs. Ctr. for Arts and Culture, 2005—; pres. Toynbee Soc., 2007—. Guggenheim Found. fellow, 1973-74; NEH grantee, 1981-84, 86, 90, Rockefeller Found. grantee, 1982-83. Fellow Internat. Soc. for Rsch. on Emotion; mem. Am. Hist. Soc. (v.p. 1995-98), World History Assn., Am. Hist. Assn. (v.p., head teaching div. 1995-98), Nat. Bd. Profl. Tchg. Standards. Democrat. Avocations: racquet sports, travel. Home: 7750 Wyckland Ct Clifton VA 20124 Office: George Mason Univ Fairfax VA 22030 Office Phone: 703-993-8776. Business E-Mail: pstearns@gmu.edu.

STEARNS, RICHARD GAYLORE, judge; b. LA, June 27, 1944; s. Gaylore Rhodes and Jeannetta Viola (Hofheinz) S.; m. Patricia Ann McElligott, Dec. 21, 1975. BA, Stanford U., 1968; MLitt, Oxford U., Eng., 1971; JD, Harvard U., 1976. Bar: Mass. Dep. campaign mgr. McGovern for Pres., Washington, 1970-72; spl. asst. U.S. Senate, Washington, 1972-73; asst. dist. atty. Norfolk County, Dedham, 1976-79, 80-82; del. dir. Kennedy for Pres., Washington, 1979-80; asst. U.S. atty. U.S. Dept. Justice, Boston, 1982-90; assoc. justice Superior Ct. Mass., Boston, 1990-94; U.S. dist. judge U.S. Dist. Ct. Mass., Boston, 1994—. Author: Massachusetts Criminal Law: A Prosecutor's Guide, 24st edit., 2004. Trustee Vincent Meml. Hosp., Boston. Rhodes scholar, 1968. Mem. ABA, Mass. Bar Assn., Phi Beta Kappa. Office: US Courthouse 1 Courthouse Way Ste 7130 Boston MA 02210-3009

STEARNS, ROBERT LELAND, curator; b. LA, Aug. 28, 1947; s. Edward Van Buren and Harriett Ann (Hauck) S.; m. Sheri Roseanne Lucas, Oct. 2, 1982 (div. 1994); children: Marissa Hauck, Caroline Lucas. Student, U. Calif., San Diego, 1965-68, BFA, 1970; student, Calif. Poly. State U., San Luis Obispo, 1968. Asst. dir. Paula Cooper Gallery, NYC, 1970-72; prodn. asst. Avalanche Mag., NYC, 1972; dir. Kitchen Ctr. for Video/Music, NYC, 1972-77, Contemporary Arts Ctr., Cin., 1977-82; dir. performing arts Walker Art Ctr., Mpls., 1982-88; dir. Wexner Ctr. for Arts, Columbus, Ohio, 1988-92; mem. Wexner Ctr. Found., Columbus, 1990-92; dir. Stearns & Assocs./Contemporary Exhbn. Svcs., Columbus, Ohio, 1992—2000; sr. prgm. dir. Arts Midwest, Mpls., 1998—2005; cons. curator Franklin Park Conservatory, Columbus, Ohio, 2005—. Adj. prof. dept. art, assoc. dean Coll. Art, Ohio State U., Columbus, 1988-92; lectr. Sch. of the Art Inst. Chgo., 2002; cons. McKnight Found., St. Paul, 1978, Jerome Found., 1978-79; chmn. Artists TV Workshop, N.Y.C., 1976-77; bd. dirs., chmn. Minn. Dance Alliance, Mpls., 1983-88; bd. dirs. Haleakala, Inc., N.Y.C.; mem. various panels Nat. Endowment for Arts, Washington, 1977-91; mem. pub. arts policy Greater Columbus Arts Coun., 1988-90; adv. coun. Bklyn. Acad. Music, 1982-84, Houston Grand Opera, 1991-93; fundraising cons. Art for Life Columbus AIDS Task Force, 2000-; mem. Advocacy Com. Ballet Met, Columbus, 2003-. Author, editor: Robert Wilson: Theater of Images, 1980, Photography and Beyond in Japan, 1995; author: Mexico Now: Point of Departure, 1997, Robert Wilson: Scenografie e Installazioni, 1997, Illusions of Eden: Visions of the American Heartland, 2000, Aspirations: Toward a Future in the Middle East, 2001, The View from Here: Recent Pictures from Central Europe and the American Midwest, 2002, Russel Wright: Living with Good Design, 2006; editor: Dimensions of Black, 1970; exec. editor: Breakthroughs: Avant Garde Art in Europe and America 1950-1990, 1991; author and editor numerous catalogues. Mem. gov.'s residence com. State of Ohio, 2004—. Decorated chevalier Order of Arts and Letters (France); Travel grantee Jerome Found., 1986, Japan Found., 1991, Can. Cultural Ministry, 2004. Office Phone: 614-288-7150. E-mail: arts2020@aol.com.

STEARNS, SHEILA MACDONALD, academic administrator; b. Ft. Snelling, Minn., Aug. 30, 1946; d. Alexander Colin and Marie Kristine (Peterson) MacD.; m. Hal Stearns, June 22, 1968; children: Scott, Malin. BA, Univ. Mont., Missoula, 1968, MA, 1969, EdD, 1983. English and history tchr. Wiesbaden (Germany) Jr. High Sch., 1969-72; libr. media specialist Missoula Pub. Schs., 1975-77; dir. alumni rels. Univ. Mont., Missoula, 1983-87, v.p. univ. rels., 1987-93; chancellor Univ. Mont. Western, Dillon, 1993—99; pres. Wayne State Coll., Mich., 1999—2003; commr. higher ed. State of Mont., Helena, 2003—. Contbr. articles to profl. publs. Chair gov. bd. dirs. St. Patrick Hosp., Missoula, 1991-93; mem. Mayor's Adv. Bd., Missoula; nat. chair NAIA Coun. of Pres., 1996-97; chair NAIA Gender Equity com. Mem. Missoula C. of C. (v.p. exec. com.), Rotary (bd. dirs.) Alpha Phi (Chi chpt.), Phi Delta Kappa. Roman Catholic. Avocations: golf, reading, writing. Office: Commissioner Of Higher Education 46 N Last Chance Gulch St Helena MT 59601-4122 Office Phone: 406-444-0311. *

STEARNS, STEPHEN JEROLD, history professor, writer; b. Boston, Dec. 24, 1935; s. Maurice and Minna Stiller Stearns; m. Anna Brennen (div. Apr. 1973); 1 child, Lisa Deborah Stearns Deal; m. Lee Jeffries Whedon (dec. May 1992); stepchildren: Samuel Whedon, Matthew Whedon, Joss Whedon. BA, Harvard Coll., 1957; MA, Columbia U., 1959; PhD, U. Calif., Berkeley, 1967. Tchg. asst. U. Calif., Berkeley, 1964—65; asst. prof. history dept. Vassar Coll., Poughkeepsie, NY, 1965—67, Richmond Coll., SI, 1967—72; assoc. prof. Coll. S.I., 1972—. Adj. assoc. prof. Columbia Tchrs. Coll., N.Y.C., 1986. Editor, author introduction: (books) Great Illusion (N. Angell), 1970, In Savage Times (L. Woolf), 1970, International Government (L. Woolf), 1971, Paris (L. Hart), 1972. Fulbright grantee U.S. Edn. Commn. U.K., 1962-63, 63-64. Mem. Am. Hist. Assn., Conf. on Brit. Studies. Democrat. Jewish. Home: 895 W End Ave New York NY 10025-3500 Office: Coll of S I CUNY 2800 Victory Blvd Staten Island NY 10314-6609 Office Phone: 718-982-2873.

STEARNS, STEWART WARREN, charitable association executive; b. Denver, Apr. 8, 1947; s. Vinton H. and Marjorie L. (Tedro) S.; m. Marjorie L. Fuller, Jan. 25, 1969; children: Theresa Lyn, Gregory Robert. BS, Ea. N.Mex. U., 1970; MA, No. Ill. U., 1973; postgrad., SUNY, Albany, 1974—. Mng. editor Studies in Linguistics, DeKalb, Ill., 1972-73; instr. No. Ill. U., DeKalb, 1972-73; cons. AID, Guatemala, 1973-74; instr. Skidmore Coll., Saratoga Springs, N.Y., 1975; OAS fellow Guatemala, 1976-77; asst. dir. Chaves County Cmty. Action Program, Roswell, N.Mex., 1977-78; exec. dir. United Way Chaves County, Roswell, 1978-83, Levi Strauss Found., Dallas, 1983-85, Cmty. Trust Met. Tarrant County, Ft. Worth, 1985-88; pres., CEO, Cmty. Found., Sarasota County, 1989—. NDEA fellow, Dallas, 1970-71. Office Phone: 941-955-3000. Business E-Mail: stewart@cfsarasota.org.

STEARNS, SUSAN TRACEY, lighting design company executive, lawyer; b. Seattle, Oct. 28, 1957; d. Arthur Thomas and Roberta Jane (Arrowood) S.; m. Ross Alan De Alessi, Aug. 11, 1990; 1 child, Chase Arthur. AA, Stephens Coll., 1977, BA, 1979; JD, U. Wash., Seattle, 1990. Bar: Calif. 1990, U.S. Ct. Appeals (9th cir.) 1990, U.S. Dist. Ct. (no. dist.) Calif 1990, U.S. Dist. Ct. (we. dist.) Wash. 1991, Wash. 1991. TV news prodr. KOMO, Seattle, 1980-86; atty. Brobeck, Phleger & Harrison, San Francisco, 1990-92; pres. Ross De Alessi Lighting Design, Seattle, 1993—. Author periodicals in field. Alumnae Assn. Coun. Stephens Coll., Columbia, Mo., 1995—. Named Nat. Order of Barristers, U. Washington, Seattle, 1990. Mem. ABA (mem. state labor and employment law subcom.), Wash. State Bar Assn. (mem. bench-bar-press com.), State Bar Calif., King County Bar Assn., Bar Assn.San Francisco, Wash. Athletic Club. Avocations: travel, dance. Office: Ross De Alessi Lighting Des 2330 Magnolia Blvd W Seattle WA 98199-3813

STEARNS, TIMOTHY P., biology professor, geneticist; BS in Genetics, Cornell U.; PhD in Biology, MIT. Postdoc. fellow Stanford U., Palo Alto, Calif., faculty, 1993—, assoc. prof. dept. biol. sci.; assoc. prof. dept. genetics Stanford U. Sch. Medicine, Palo Alto. Rsch. prof. Howard Hughes Med. Inst., 2002—. Howard Hughes Med. Inst. grantee, 2002. Office: Biol Sci Lokey 136 Stanford Univ Stanford CA 94305-5020 Office Phone: 650-752-6934. Office Fax: 650-724-9945. Business E-Mail: stearns@stanford.edu.

STEBBINS, DONALD J., car parts manufacturing company executive; BS in Fin., Miami U., Ohio; MBA, U. Mich. With Citibank, Bankers Trust Co.; v.p., treas., asst. sec. Lear Corp., Southfield, Mich., 1992, sr. v.p., CFO, treas., 1997, pres., COO Americas, pres., COO Europe, Asia and Africa; pres., COO Visteon Corp., 2005—. Office: Visteon Corp One Village Center Dr Belleville MI 48111 *

STEBBINS, HENRY BLANCHARD, lawyer; b. Hartford, Conn., June 14, 1951; s. Herbert Bellows and Katherine (Reynolds) S.; m. Alison Finney, May 30, 1976; children: Duncan Finney, Martha Reynolds, H. Benjamin. BA cum laude, U. N.H., 1973; JD, Boston U., 1976. Bar: N.H. 1976, U.S. Dist. Ct. N.H. 1976. Assoc. Sheehan, Phinney, Bass & Green, Manchester, NH, 1976—80, ptnr., 1980—97, mgmt. com., 1994—97; sr. ptnr. Stebbins Lazos & Van Der Beken, Manchester, 1997—. Trustee Manchester Boys and Girls Club, 1983-2003; chmn. Vocat. Partnership Found., 1986-91; bd. dirs. Brookside Ch. Nursery Sch., 1984-90, Leadership N.H., 1994-95; bd. dirs. United Way Greater Manchester, 1986-95, chmn., 1990-92; mem. N.H. Rep. State com., 1995-99, N.H. Rep. Fin. Com., 1995-97, N.H. legal counsel Dole for Pres. Campaign; mem. fin. com. George W. Bush Presdl. Campaign; bd. dirs., legal counsel, mem. exec. com. Manchester C. of C., 1997-2001; hon. co-chair bus. adv. coun. Rep. Nat. Com., 2002-03. Named N.H. Businessman of Yr., 2003. Mem. ABA, N.H. Bar Assn., Manchester Bar Assn. (pres. 1982-83), Assn. Bank Holding Cos. (lawyers div. 1985-93), Rissa Club. Office: 66 Hanover St Manchester NH 03101-2230 Office Phone: 603-672-3700. E-mail: hstebbins@slvlaw.com.

STEBBINS, PAUL H., energy executive; b. 1965; 3 children. BA Govt., Georgetown Univ., 1979. Bunker broker Gary Bunkering Services, Inc.; with Trans-Tec Services, 1985, World Fuel Services Corp., 1995—, sr. vice-pres, 1995—97, exec. vice-pres., 1997—2000, pres. and COO, 2000—02, chmn. and CEO, 2002—. Planning coord. Internat. Energy Corp. Office: World Fuel Services Ste 400 9800 NW 41st St Miami FL 33178 *

STEBBINS, ROBERT ALAN, sociology educator; b. Rhinelander, Wis., June 22, 1938; s. William Nelson and Dorothy May (Guy) S.; m. Karin Yvonne Olson, Jan. 11, 1964; children: Paul, Lisa, Christi. BA, Macalester Coll., 1961; MA, U. Minn., 1962, PhD, 1964. Assoc. prof. Presbyterian Coll., Clinton, SC, 1964-65; assoc. prof.to prof. Meml. U. Nfld., St. John's, Canada, 1965-73; prof. U. Tex.-Arlington, 1973-76; prof. sociology U. Calgary, Alta., Canada, 1976-99, faculty prof. social scis. Alta., 2000—, dept. head Alta., 1976-82; head dept. sociology and anthropology Meml. U. Nfld., 1968-71. Author: Commitment to Deviance, 1971, The Disorderly Classroom: Its Physical and Temporal Conditions, 1974, Teachers and Meaning, 1975, Amateurs, 1979, The Magician, 1984, Sociology: The Study of Society, 2d edit., 1990, Canadian Football: The View from the Helmet, 1987, Deviance: Tolerable Differences, 1988, The Laugh-Makers: Stand-Up Comedy as Art, Business, and Life-Style, 1990, Amateurs, Professionals and Serious Leisure, 1992; co-editor: Fieldwork Experience, 1980, The Sociology of Deviance, 1982, Experiencing Fieldwork, 1991, Career, Culture, and Social Psychology in a Variety Art, 1993, Predicaments: Moral Difficulty in Everyday Life, 1993, The Franco-Calgarians: French Language, Leisure and Linguistic Lifestyle in an Anglophone City, 1994, The Connoisseur's New Orleans, 1995, The Barbershop Singer: Inside the Social World of a Musical Hobby, 1996, Tolerable Differences: Living with Deviance, 2d edit., 1996; After Work: The Search for an Optimal Leisure Lifestyle, 1998, The Urban Francophone Volunteer: Searching for Personal Meaning and Community Growth in a Linguistic Minority, 1998, The French Enigma: Survival and Development of Canada's Francophone Societies, 2000, Exploratory Research in the Social Sciences, 2001, New Directions in the Theory and Research of Serions Leisure, 2001, The Organizational Basis of Leisure Participation: A Motivational Exploration, 2002, Francophonie et langue dans un monde diverse en évolution: contacts interlinguistiques socioculturels, 2003, Volunteering as Leisure/Leisure as Volunteering: An International Assessment, 2004, Between Work and Leisure: A Study of the Common Ground of Two Separate Worlds, 2004, Challenging Mountain Nature: Risk, Motive, and Lifestyle in Three Hobbyist Sports, 2005, Serious Leisure: A Perspective for our Own Time, 2006, A Dictionary of Nonprofit Terms and Concepts, 2006. Pres. St. John's Orch., 1967-68; mem. Dallas Civic Symphony, 1973-76, Orch. Soc. of Calgary, 1978-97. Can. Coun. Sabbatical Leave fellow, 1972-72, Calgary Inst. for Humanities fellow, 1987-88, Killam resident fellow, 1990; NEH summer stipend, 1976; Acad. Leisure Scis. fellow, 1996—, Royal Soc. Can. fellow, 1999—. Mem. Leisure Studies Assn., Can. Sociology and Anthropology Assn. (pres. 1988-89), Internat. Sociol. Assn., Assn. for Can. Studies, World Leisure and Recreation Assn. (bd. dirs. 1997-2002), Social Sci. Fedn. Can. (pres. 1991-92), Can. Assn. for Leisure Studies (v.p. 1993-96). Home: 144 Edgemont Estates Dr NW Calgary AB Canada T3A 2M3 Office: U Calgary Dept Sociology 2500 University Dr NW Calgary AB Canada T2N 1N4 Office Phone: 403-220-5827. E-mail: stebbins@ucalgary.ca.

STEBEL, MICHAEL DAVID, marketing professional, consultant; b. NYC, June 8, 1953; s. Bernard and Arlene Stebel; m. Beth Roberts, Mar. 5, 2006; children: Jacob Alan, Meryl Ann. BA, Hofstra U., Hempstead, NY, 1976. Dir. mktg. AT&T Global Info. Solutions, Hauppauge, NY, 1992—94; exec. v.p. corp. strategy Boundless Technologies, Hauppauge, 1994—99; pres. Boca Rsch., Boca Raton, Fla., 1999—2001; chief mktg. officer Ener1, Inc., Boca Raton, 2001—03; CEO TVR Comm., Woodside, NY, 2003—06; pres. Nexentra Tech. Mktg., LLC, Delray Beach, Fla., 2006—. Cons. in field. Named to Pres.'s Club, AT&T Global Info. Solutions, 1994. Mem.: Nat. Assn. Photoshop Profls., Am. Mktg. Assn. Home Phone: 561-252-1081. Office Phone: 561-252-1081. Office Fax: 954-697-0306. Business E-Mail: mike@nexentra.com.

STEC, JOHN ZYGMUNT, retired real estate company officer; b. Stalowawola, Poland, Jan. 21, 1925; Came to U.S.A. 1947. s. Valenty and Maria (Madej) S. m. Wanda G. Baca, Oct. 13, 1956; children: David, Maria, Monica. Student, Poland, 1941-44, Kent State U., Ohio, 1965-66, student, 1966-67. Cert. Master of Corporate Real Estate. With The Singer Co., Cleve., 1952-54, dis. mgr., 1954-60, sales supr., 1960-67, dir. real estate Detroit and Chgo., 1967-73; v.p. Fabri Center of Am., Beachwood, Ohio, 1973—; sr. v.p. real estate Fabri-Centers of Am., Inc., Beachwood, Ohio, 1987—2005, spl. counsel to pres., 2005—; ret., 2005. Cons. in field. With U.S. Army, 1950-52. Mem. Nat. Assoc. of Corporate Real Estate (speaker, organizer 1974-77, audit Com. 1977-79, bd. dirs. 1970-82, Outstanding Achievement award 1982). Chagrin Valley Club. Repulican. Roman Catholic. Avocations: swimming, hiking, reading. Home: 725 Sagewood Dr Chagrin Falls OH 44023-6733 Office: Coventry Investment Real Estate Advisors 8401 Chagrin Rd Ste 1 Chagrin Falls OH 44023 Office Phone: 216-789-2278. Business E-Mail:

jstec@coventryadvisors.com. *Personal philosophy: Think success and you'll be successful. Perseverence of any goal leads to achievement. Learning is knowledge. Knowledge is the most powerful key that leads to greatness and opens any door.*

STECCATO, CARL L., lawyer; b. Bronx, NY, Mar. 18, 1954; BA, York Coll., CUNY; JD, NY Law Sch., 1985. Bar: NY 1987, NJ 1987, US Dist. Ct. So., Ea., No. & We. Districts NY. Ptnr. Wilson, Elser, Moskowitz, Edelman & Dicker LLP, White Plains, NYC. Mem.: ABA (torts & ins. practice sect.), Am. Corp. Counsel Assn. (portfolio mem.), Assn. of the Bar of the City of NY, NY State Bar Assn. (ins. sect.), Nat. Fire Protection Assn., Am. Boat & Yacht Coun. Office: Wilson Elser Moskowitz Edelman & Dicker LLP 3 Gannett Dr White Plains NY 10604 Office Phone: 914-323-7000 ext. 4269. Office Fax: 914-323-7001. Business E-Mail: steccatoc@wemed.com.

STECHER, ESTA E., lawyer, investment company executive; b. Mpls., Apr. 3, 1957; BA summa cum laude, U. Minn., 1979; JD, Columbia U., 1982. Bar: N.Y. 1983. Ptnr. Sullivan & Cromwell, 1982—94; gen. counsel, mng. dir. Tax dept. Goldman, Sachs & Co., NYC, 1994—2000, gen. counsel, co-head legal dept., 2000—. Trustee Columbia Univ. Mem.: ABA, Assn. Bar City of New York, N.Y. Bar Assn. Office: Goldman Sachs and Co Legal Dept 1 New York Plz 37th Fl New York NY 10004 Office Phone: 212-902-3490. Office Fax: 212-902-3876.

STECHER, JOE W., prosecutor; b. Fremont, Nebr., 1952; BA, Wayne State Coll., 1974; JD, U. Nebr. Coll. Law, 1984. County atty. Dodge County, Nebr., 1999—2002; asst. US atty. Dist. Nebr. US Dept. Justice, 2002—06, acting US atty., 2006—07, US atty., 2007—. Dir. Neb. County Attorney's Assn., 1996—2002. Recipient Dir. award, US Atty's Office Nebr., 2005. Office: US Atty First Nat Bank Bldg 1620 Dodge St Ste 1400 Omaha NE 68102 *

STECHER, KENNETH W., financial corporation executive; With Inter-Ocean Life Ins. Co. (acquired by Cin. Fin. Corp.); joined Cin. Fin. Corp., 1973—, sr. v.p., treas., co. sec., 1997—, CFO, 2001—. Office: 6200 S Gilmore Rd Fairfield OH 45014-5141

STECHER, PAULINE, painter, educator; b. Bklyn. d. Helen Solomon; m. Bernard Stecher, Aug. 20, 1950; children: Martin Alan, David Joseph. Attended, pvt. studio instrn. with Paul Puzinas, NYC, 1961—63. Oil painting instr., Bellerose, Bellerose Village, Little Neck, New Hyde Park, NY, 1965—85. Judge, lecture demonstrator American Pen Women, Floral Park Art League, Flushing Art League, Ind. Art Soc., Island Art Guild, Rockville Ctr. Art Club, Tri-County Artists, Queens Alliance Artists, Suburban Art League, 1978—. Exhibitions include Newington-Cropsey Found. Gallery Art, Hastings-on-Hudson, NY, Westchester County Ctr., NY, Salmagundi Club, NYC, Nat. Arts Club, Nassau County Mus. Art, Roslyn, NY, various galleries, Long Island's East End, Boca Raton and Naples, Fla.; painting reproduced in Literary Cyclist by Prof. James E. Starrs, 1997; contbr. articles and paintings to Grumbacher's Palette Talk magazine, 1983, as featured tchr., 1987, in cover, 1990. Fellow: Hudson Valley Art Assn. (Isabel Steinschneider Meml. award 1991, First prize Dumond Meml. award Best Light and Atmospheric Effect 1998, Spradling Meml. award 2000, Georgie Read Barton Meml. award 2002, First place Still-life Jane Peterson Meml. award 2004), Am. Artists Profl. League (bd. dirs. 1985—2002, Dirs. award 1991, John R. Grabach Meml. award 1994, Helen De Cozen award 1997, Pres.'s award 1998, 2001, Raymond Chow Meml. award 2006); mem.: Nat. Art League (Gold medal 1973), Art. League Nassau County (Coun. Am. Artists Soc. Painting award 1993). Avocation: painting. Home: 80-30 250th St Bellerose NY 11426 Personal E-mail: pauline.stecher@worldnet.att.net.

STECKLER, LARRY, publishing executive, writer; b. Bklyn., Nov. 3, 1933; s. Morris and Ida (Beekman) S.; m. Catherine Coccozza, June 6, 1959 (div. June 1999); children: Gail Denise, Glenn Eric, Kerri Lynn, Adria Lauren; m. Lorraine Mary Rubsamen, Oct. 16, 1999. Student, CCNY, 1951; degree in Grad. Realtor's Inst., Parkstate Inst., 2007. Lic. realtor Ariz., 2005, cert. E-Pro Nat. Assn. Realtors. Assoc. editor Radio-Electronics mag., NYC, 1957-62, editor, 1967-85; pub., editor-in-chief Radio Electronics mag., NYC, 1985-92; electronics editor Popular Mechanics mag., NYC, 1962-65; assoc. editor Electronic Products mag., Garden City, NY, 1965-67, Electro-Tech., 1967; editl. dir. Merchandising 2-Way Radio mag., NYC, 1975-77; v.p., dir. Gernsback Publs., NYC, 1975-84, pres., dir., 1984—2003; pub., editl. dir. Spl. Projects mag., 1980-84, Radio-Electronics Ann., 1982-84; pub., editor-in-chief Hands-On Electronics, 1984-88, Computer Digest, 1985-90, Experimenters Handbook, 1986-96, Modern Short Stories, 1987-90, Video/Stereo Digest, 1989-91, Popular Electronics Mag., 1988-99, GIZMO, 1988-99, Hobbyists Handbook, 1989-96, Sci. Probe! mag., 1989-93, StoryMasters, 1989—2001, Electronics Shopper, 1990-99, Electronics Market Ctr., 1991-99, Electronics Now Mag., 1992-99, Radio Craft, 1993-96, Poptronix Handbook, 1996—2003; pres. Claggk, Inc., 1986—2003, Silicon Chip, 1993-94, Sci. Probe Inc., 1989-93, Poptronix Inc., 1997—2005, Ariz., 2005—; realtor Long Realty Co., Tucson, 2005—. Mem. electronics adv. bd. Bd. Coop. Ednl. Svcs., Nassau County, NY, 1975—77; pres. Electronics Industry Hall of Fame, 1985—2001; bd. dirs. Pub. Hall of Fame, 1987—89. Pub., editor-in-chief Poptronics, 2000-03, Poptronics Shopper, 2000-03, PC Tech, 2000-03; co-editor The Shofar, 1998-2002; contbr. articles to profl. jours., popular mags.; author Hugo Gernsback, A Man Well Ahead of His Time, 2007. Bd. dirs. Nassau County coun. Camp Fire Girls, 1971-72; 1st v.p. bd. dirs. Temple Beth Am, Las Vegas, 1998-2002 pres. 2001-02; apptd. bd. adjusters, Marana, Ariz., 2005—; apptd. sec.-treas. Dove Mt. Civic Assn., Marana, 2005—; appt. adv. bd. Citizens Park, Marana, 2007—, chair, 2007—. With U.S. Army, 1953-56. Recipient Coop. award Nat. Alliance TV and Electronic Svcs. Assns., 1974, 75; inducted into Electronics Industry Hall of Fame, 1985; ISCET Gov's. award, 1998, FESA Pres. award, 1998. Mem.: IEEE, LA Press, Soc. Profl. Journalists, Internat. Performing Magicians (exec. dir.), Internat. Underwater Explorers Soc., Am. Mgmt. Assn., Nat. Electronics Sales and Svc. Dealers Assn. (rec. sec. NY State 1976—78, treas. 1991—94, Man of Yr. award 1975, 1985, M.L. Finneyberg Excellence award 1994), Internat. Soc. Cert. electronic Technicians (chmn. 1974—76, 1979—81, dir.-at-large 1991—93, rep. to NESDA bd. 1991—93, chmn. 1993—95, Region 9 dir. 1995—97, chmn. 1999—2001, Chmn.'s award 1985), Am. Soc. Bus. Press Editors (sr.), Radio Club Am. Home: 12317 N Fallen Shadows Dr Marana AZ 85653 Office: Long Realty Co 12080 N Dove Mountain Blvd Ste 100 Marana AZ 85653 Home Phone: 520-572-8144; Office Phone: 520-918-5761. Personal E-mail: lartronics@aol.com, larrysteckler@aol.com. *Do not be afraid to try the unaccepted. Do not be afraid to do the undesirable. Do what you enjoy...do it well...and after it is done...never regret having done it...only regret what you have not yet done.*

STECKLER, PHYLLIS BETTY, business and publishing consultant; b. NYC; d. Irwin H. and Bertha (Fellner) Schwartzbard; m. Stuart J. Steckler; children: Randall, Sharon Steckler-Slotky. BA, Hunter Coll.; MA, NYU. Editl. dir. R.R. Bowker Co., NYC, Crowell Collier Macmillan Info. Pub. Co., NYC, Holt Rinehart & Winston Info. Systems, NYC; pres., CEO Oryx Press, Scottsdale, Ariz., 1973-76, Phoenix, 1976—2000, Zephyr Info., Phoenix, 2001—; publ. cons., 2001—. Adj. prof. mktg. scholarly publs. Grad. History dept., Ariz. State U., Tempe; mem. dean's coun. Coll. of Extended Edn., Ariz. State U., Phoenix; mem. adv. coun. Republic Bank Ariz., NA. Past chmn. Info. Industry Assn.; past chair Ariz. Ctr. for the Book; past pres. Contemporary Forum of Phoenix Art Mus.; founding mem. Nat. Edn. Network, U.S. Dept. Edn.; past pres. Friends of the Libr., U.S.A.; mem. Ariz. Women's Forum; bd. dirs. Ariz. region Com. for the Weizmann Inst. Sci.; mem. order coun. Republic Bank, Ariz. Recipient Women Who Make a Difference award The Internat. Women's Forum, 1995, Excellence in Pub. award Ariz. Book Pub. Assn., 1997, The Pub. History Program Ariz. State U. Founding Friend award, 2000; elected to Hunter Coll. Hall of Fame. Mem.: ALA, Ariz. Libr. Assn., Univ. Club of Phoenix. Home and Office: 6446 N 28th St Phoenix AZ 85016-8946 Home Phone: 602-955-4288. E-mail: pbs.zephyr@cox.net.

STECKO, PAUL T., packaging company executive; With Internat. Paper Co.; pres., CEO Tenneco Packing, 1993-96, COO, 1997-98, pres., COO, 1998-99; CEO, chmn. bd. Packaging Corp. of Am., Lake Forest, Ill., 1999—. Bd. dirs. Tenneco, Am. Forest and Paper Assn., State Farm Mut. Ins. Co. Office: Packaging Corp of Am 1900 W Field Ct Lake Forest IL 60045-4828 *

STECKROAT, PATRICIA A., special education educator; b. Bristol, Pa., July 27, 1970; d. James J. and Joann D. Klein; m. Thomas F. Steckroat, June 20, 1998; children: Payton, Ryan. BS, Millersville U., 1992; M, Arcadia U., 1998; postgrad., Gwynedd Mercy Coll., 2006. Cert. adminstr. Learning support tchr. Pennsbury H.S., Fairless Hills, Pa., 1994—2003, reading specialist, 2003—. Spl. edn. chmn. Pennsbury H.S., 2000—. Avocations: reading, travel. Office: Pennsbury Sch Dist 608 S Olds Blvd Fairless Hills PA 19030

STEDMAN, RICHARD RALPH, retired lawyer; b. Columbus, Ohio, July 18, 1936; s. Ralph Dale and Kathleen (Smith) S.; m. Elizabeth Ann Witschey, Dec. 18, 1965; children: Gretchen Kathleen, Richard Ralph II, Patrick Christopher Raymond. BBA, Ohio State U., 1958, JD, 1964. Bar: Ohio 1964; CPA, Ohio. Staff acct. Price Waterhouse & Co., Columbus, 1958-60; salesman Royal McBee Co., Columbus, 1960; assoc. Vorys, Sater, Seymour & Pease, Columbus, 1964-69, ptnr., 1970-99. Contbr. articles to profl. jours. Trustee Found. Cath. Diocese of Columbus, 1985-2000; trustee Ohio Dominican Coll., 1990-96, St. Charles Prep. Sch., 1990—, Edward Orton, Jr. Ceramic Found., 1994—. Merson fellow Ohio State U., 1963-64. Mem. Athletic Club Columbus, Columbus Club, Brookside Golf and Country Club, Zanesfield Rod and Gun Club, Equestrian Order of Knights Holy Sepulchre of Jerusalem, Order of St. Gregory the Great. Republican. Avocations: golf, fishing, photography.

STEED, THERESA JEAN, manufacturing executive; b. Grapeland, Tex., Mar. 10, 1932; d. Robert Tresband and Alma Inez (Denson) Bobbitt; m. Jarvis Lacy Steed, July 8, 1950; children: Judy Karen, Pamela Kay, Kim Lacy. Grad., Elliott Bus. Sch., Houston, 1949; BMus. Edn., So. Coll. Fine Arts, Houston, 1956; postgrad., U. Tex., 1961, Sul Ross U., Alpine, Tex., 1962, U. Wis., 1962; M Rhymes (hon.), Duke U., 1961. Exec. sec. various cos., Houston, 1950—57; tchr. elem. sch. Rosenburg Ind. Sch. Dist., Tex., 1957—58; tchr. kindergarten/music edn. Sonora Ind. Sch. Dist., Tex., 1959—65; tchr. elem. sch. Houston Ind. Sch. Dist., 1965—67, Conroe Ind. Sch. Dist., Tex., 1968—70; co-founder, co-owner Steed Tile & Mfg. Co., Conroe, 1965—. Author: Audio-Visual Curriculums for Music Education: Kindergarten Through Eighth Grade, 1962 Mem. Dem. Nat. Com., Washington, 1993—, Dem. Senatorial Campaign Com., Washington, 1996—, Nat. Senatorial Com., 2000-07. Recipient Presdl. Letter of Commendation, Pres. Lyndon B. Johnson, 1968—70. Mem.: Soverign Order Knights of Justice (UK), Am.'s Nat. World War II Mus. (charter), Order Ea. Star (assoc. matron 1963), Nat. Women's History Mus. (charter), Nat. Trust for Hist. Preservation, Women in Constrn. (charter) (reporter 1970—75, publicity chmn.), Nat. Federated Music Clubs Am., Pilot Club, Delta Kappa Gamma (publicity chmn. 1962—65). Methodist. Avocations: cooking, gardening, politicking. Home: 452 Lexington Ct Conroe TX 77302-3050 Personal E-mail: quechick007@yahoo.com.

STEEFEL, DAVID SIMON, lawyer; b. Mpls., June 27, 1951; s. Lawrence D. Jr. and Marion (Charlson) S.; m. Mary Ann Moody, May 24, 1981; children: Emily, Daniel, Katherine. BA, Carleton Coll., 1973; JD, U. Colo., 1978. Bar: Colo. 1978, U.S. Dist. Ct. Colo. 1978, U.S. Ct. Appeals (10th cir.) 1978. Assoc. Gorsuch, Kirgis, Denver, 1978-80, Holme Roberts & Owen, Denver, 1980-84, ptnr., 1984—, litig. practice group leader, 1999—. Instr. U. Colo. Law Sch., Boulder, 1978, 91. Home: 1300 Green Oaks Dr Littleton CO 80121-1331 Office: Holme Roberts & Owen 1700 Lincoln St Ste 4100 Denver CO 80203-4541 Home Phone: 303-347-2913; Office Phone: 303-866-0348. Business E-Mail: david.steefel@hro.com.

STEEG, MOISE S., JR., lawyer; b. New Orleans, July 25, 1916; s. Moise S. and Carrie (Gutmann) S.; m. Marion B., Sept. 14, 1943 (dec.); children: Barbara Steeg Midlo, Marion, Robert M.; m. Melba Law, Nov. 29, 1969. LLB, Tulane U., 1937. Bar: La. 1937, U.S. Dist. Ct. (ea. dist.) La. 1939, U.S. Ct. Appeals (5th cir.) 1946, U.S. Supreme Ct. 1950, U.S. Ct. Appeals (11th cir.) 1981. Practice, New Orleans, 1937—; assoc. Rittenberg & Rittenberg, 1937-38; sole practice, 1938-46; founder Gertler & Steeg, 1946-48, Steeg & Morrison, 1948-50, Marcus & Steeg, 1950-54, Steeg & Shushan, 1954-71; sr. ptnr. The Steeg Law Firm, LLC, 1972—. Bd. dirs. Loyola U., chmn., 1979—, mem. search com. for dean Coll. Law; chmn., founder New Orleans Hist. Dist. and Landmarks Com.; bd. dirs. chmn. bd. New Orleans Mus. Art, 1980; bd. overseers Hebrew Union Coll.; bd. dirs. Delgado Jr. Coll., New Orleans Symphony; founder, dir. New Orleans Ednl. and Rsch. Corp.; bd. dirs. Louise Davis Sch. for Retarded Children, Touro Infirmary, 1963-69; mem. Ochsner Found. Hosp. Bd., 1985—; bd. visitors Trinity Episcopal Sch., 1989—; organizer, sec. New Orleans Bus. Coun., 1986; pres. Temple Sinai, 1966-67; chmn. Anti-Defamation League, Jewish Cmty. Ctr., chmn. Aquarium Drive, Aquarium of Ams.; local counsel Nat. Dem. Party, 1966. Served to capt. USAF, 1942-46. Recipient Brotherhood Award, NCCJ, 1980, Disting. Alumnus award Tulane Law Sch., 1991, Isidore Newman Sch., Svc. award Newcomb Coll. Soc., Cmty. Svc. award New Orleans Bar Assn. Times-Picayune Loving Cup, 2004, Contbn. to Arts award Mayor, 2004; Mem. Paul Tulane Honor Soc. Home: One River Place 3 Poydras St New Orleans LA 70130-1665 Office: 201 Saint Charles Ave Ste 3201 New Orleans LA 70170-1032 Office Phone: 504-582-1199. Business E-Mail: msteeg@steeglaw.com.

STEEL, DANIELLE FERNANDE, author; b. NYC, Aug. 14, 1947; d. John and Norma Schuelein-Steel; 9 children. Student, Parsons Sch. Design, 1963, NYU, 1963-67. Vice pres. pub. relations and new bus. Supergirls Ltd., NYC, 1968-71; copywriter Grey Advt., San Francisco, 1973-74; founder Steel Gallery of Contemporary Art, San Francisco, 2003—. Author: (novels) Going Home, 1973, Passion's Promise, 1977, Now and Forever, 1978, The Promise, 1978, Season of Passion, 1980, Summers End, 1980, To Love Again, 1981, Remembrance, 1981, Once in a Lifetime, 1981, The Ring, 1981, Palomino, 1981, To Love Again, 1981, Remembrance, 1981, Loving, 1981, Once In A Lifetime, 1982, Crossings, 1982, A Perfect Stranger, 1982, Thurston House, 1983, Changes, 1983, Full Circle, 1984, Family Album, 1985, Secrets, 1985, Wanderlust, 1986, Fine Things, 1987, Kaleidoscope, 1987, Zoya, 1988, Star, 1988, Daddy, 1989, Message from Nam, 1990, Heartbeat, 1991, No Greater Love, 1991, Jewels, 1992, Mixed Blessings, 1992, Vanished, 1993, Accident, 1994, The Gift, 1994, Wings, 1994, Lightning, 1995, Five Days in Paris, 1995, Malice, 1996, Silent Honor, 1997, The Ranch, 1998, Special Delivery, 1997, The Ghost, 1997, The Long Road Home, 1998, The Klone And I, 1998, His Bright Light, 1998, Mirror Image, 1998, Bittersweet, 1999, Granny Dan, 1999, Irresistible Forces, 1999, The Wedding, 2000, The House on Hope Street, 2000, Journey, 2000, Lone Eagle, 2001, Leap of Faith, 2001, The Kiss, 2001, The Cottage, 2002, Sunset in St. Tropez, 2002, Answered Prayers, 2002, Dating Game, 2003, Johnny Angel, 2003, Safe Harbour, 2003, Ransom, 2004, Second Chance, 2004, Echoes, 2004, Impossible, 2005, Miracle, 2005, Toxic Bachelors, 2005, The House, 2006, Coming Out, 2006, Bungalow Two, 2006, H.R.H., 2006, Sisters, 2007; (children's books) Martha's Best Friend, Martha's New School, Martha's New Daddy, Max's New Daddy, Max and The Babysitter, Max's Daddy Goes To The Hospital; contbr. poetry to mags., including Cosmopolitan, McCall's, Ladies Home Jour., Good Housekeeping. Chevalier of the Disting. Order of Arts & Letters, France, 2002. Home: PO Box 1637 New York NY 10156-1637 Office: care Dell Publishing 1540 Broadway New York NY 10036-4039

STEEL, DUNCAN GREGORY, engineering educator; b. Cleve., Jan. 11, 1951; s. Robert John and Mildred (Graham) S.; children: Adam, Benjamin. BA, U. N.C., 1972; MS, U. Mich., 1973-75, PhD, 1976. Physicist Exxon Rsch. and Engring., Linden, NJ, 1977-78, Hughes Rsch. Labs., Malibu, Calif., 1975-85; prof. U. Mich., Ann Arbor, 1985—; sr. rsch. scientist Inst. Gerontology Sch. Medicine, U. Mich., Ann Arbor, 1986—, sr. rsch. scientist biophys. rsch. divsn., 1992—, area chair optical scis., dir. optical scis. lab., 1989—, dir. biophysics, Robert J. Hiller prof., 2005—, Peter S. Fuss prof., 2001—05. Topical editor Jour. Optical Soc., Washington, 1986—92. Contbr. articles to profl. jours. Guggenheim fellow, 1999. Fellow IEEE, Optical Soc. Am., Am. Phys. Soc. Achievements include development of first phase conjugate laser; first high resolution nonlinear laser spectroscopy of semiconductor heterostructures; research in of collision induced resonances in atoms; low noise (below the standard quantum limit) room temperature semiconductor lasers; of first demonstration of coherence optical control and wave function engineering in quantum dots; of first demonstration of wave function engineering; first deimonstration quantum entanglement in a single quantum dot; demonstration of in vitro tryptophan phosphorescence for studies of protein structure in solution; discovery of of structural annealing in proteins during protein folding. Office: U Mich Physics Dept 500 E University Ave Ann Arbor MI 48109-1120 Home: 11516 Waters Rd Chelsea MI 48118-9615 Home Phone: 734-433-9034. Business E-Mail: dst@umich.edu.

STEEL, MICHAEL J., lawyer; b. Marysville, Calif., May 9, 1955; BA, Univ. Calif., Davis, 1977; JD, Univ. Calif., Hastings, 1982. Bar: Calif. 1982. Ptnr., co-leader Environ. Litigation practice Pillsbury Winthrop Shaw Pittman, San Francisco. Office: Pillsbury Winthrop Shaw Pittman 50 Fremont St San Francisco CA 94105 Office Phone: 415-983-7320. Office Fax: 415-983-1200. Business E-Mail: michael.steel@pillsburylaw.com.

STEEL, PHILIP S., manufacturing executive; b. Phila., Nov. 1, 1934; s. Robert Wenzing and Beryl (Vanhorn) S.; m. Joan Crawford, June 1, 1979; children: Philip, Amy, Eric, Robert. BArch, Pa. State U., 1957; MArch, U. Calif., Berkeley, 1963. Registered architect, Fla., Maine, Pa., N.J.; Nat. Coun. Archs. Registration Bd. cert. Prin. Philip Steel & Assoc., AIA, West Chester, Pa., 1964-75, Palm Beach, Fla., 1975-88, Ft. Pierce, Fla., 1988—. Past mem. Fla. State Bd. Bldg. Codes and Stds. Works exhibited in group shows McBridge Gallery, Annapolis, Md., Patricia Cloutier Art Gallery, Tequesta, Fla., Arnold Art Store, Newport, R.I., Admiralty Gallery, Vero Beach, Fla., Geary Gallery, Darien, Conn. Chmn. Landmark Commn. for Palm Beach, Fla.; chmn. Under Oaks Show and Fla. Competitive, Ctr. for the Arts, Vero Beach; bd. mem. Cultural Affairs Coun. St. Lucie County; mem. St. Lucie County Seaport Adv. Commn., St. Lucie County U. Task Force. Lt. comdr. USNR, 1957-59. Recipient Disting. Bldg. award Pa. Soc. Architects, 1969, 1st honor award, 1971, Internat. Torchburner award Am. Hotel and Motel Assn., 1985, 2nd place watercolor Backus Gallery, Ft. Pierce, Fla., 1994, 1st place watercolor Backus Gallery, Ft. Pierce, 1995, 96, Sanford Studio award N.E. Water Color Soc.'s Ann. Nat. Exbhn., Kent Art Assn., 1996, 2d place award St. Lucie County Profl. Arts League Regional Exhbn., 1997, Silver Brush award Fla. Watercolor Soc., Melvin Gallery, Lakeland, Fla., 1997. Mem. AIA (pres. Palm Beach chpt., state dir. Indian River chpt.), Pa. Soc. AIA (past state dir., past pres.), Rotary Club Palm Beach. Avocations: sailing, music, tennis. Office: 2030 Harbortown Dr Fort Pierce FL 34946-1438 Office Phone: 561-465-8322. E-mail: philstreal@bellsouth.net.

STEEL, ROBERT K., federal agency administrator, former diversified financial services company executive; b. Aug. 3, 1951; married; 3 children. BA in History & Polit. Sci., Duke U., 1973; MBA, U. Chgo., 1984. Joined Goldman Sachs Group, Inc., 1976, head equities divsn. Europe NYC, 1988—94, head instnl. equities U.S., 1994—98, co-head equities divsn., 1998—2001, head equities divsn., 2001—02, vice chmn., 2002—04, adv. dir., non-exec. chmn., securities divsn., 2004—06; sr. fellow, Ctr. Bus. & Govt. John F. Kennedy Sch. Govt., Harvard U., Cambridge, Mass., 2004—06; under sec. for domestic fin. US Dept. Treasury, Washington, 2006—. Chmn. The After School Corp., 2004—. Vice chmn. bd. trustees Duke U.; chmn. Duke U. Mgmt. Co. Mem.: NYSE (mem. various coms.), Securities Industry Assn. (bd. dirs.). Office: US Dept Treasury 1500 Pennsylvania Ave NW Washington DC 20220

STEEL, VIRGINIA (GINNY), university librarian; BA, U. Rochester; MLS, U. Chgo. Libr. Ariz. State U. Librs., Tempe; head Social Scis. and Humanities Libr., head Access Svcs. Dept., acting asst. univ. libr. pub. svcs. U. Calif., San Diego, 1988—97; assoc. dir. pub. svcs. MIT, Cambridge, 1997—2001; dir. librs. Wash. State U., Pullman, 2001—05; univ. libr. U. Calif., Santa Cruz, 2005—. Mem.: Greater Western Libr. Alliance Inc. Office: U Calif Santa Cruz Univ Libr 320 McHenry Libr 1156 High St Santa Cruz CA 95064 Office Phone: 831-459-2076. E-mail: vsteel@ucsc.edu. *

STEELBERG, CHAD, broadcast advertising company executive; Attended, U. So. Calif. Co-founder, chief tech. officer, CEO AdForce (acquired by CMGI), 1995—99; co-founder, chief tech. officer, CEO, chmn. Winfire (purchased by Broadband Digital Group), 1999—2000; CEO Broadband Digital Group, 2000—; chmn., CEO dMarc Broadcasting, Inc. (purchased by Google), Newport Beach, Calif., 2002—06. Spkr. in field. Recipient Smithsonian award for develop. of the best tech. in information services, 2000. Office: dMarc Broadcasting Inc 537 Newport Ctr Ste 355 Newport Beach CA 92660

STEELBERG, RYAN, broadcasting advertising company executive; Co-founder, head sales and mktg. AdForce (acquired by CMGI), 1995—99; founder, CEO 2CAN Media (AdSmart) (acquired by CMGI, 1999; co-founder, dir. Winfire (purchased by Broadband Digital Group), 1999—2000; pres. Broadband Digital Group, 2000—, dMarc Broadcasting, Inc. (purchased by Google), Newport Beach, Calif., 2002—06. Finalist Entrepreneur of Yr., Ernst & Young, 2000; named one of 50 Most Influential Businesspeople, Orange County Bus. Jour. Office: dMarc Broadcasting Inc 537 Newport Ctr Ste 355 Newport Beach CA 92660

STEELE, ALISON, lawyer; b. St. Petersburg, Fla., Aug. 29, 1962; d. Alton Edward and Charlotte Hollar Steele. BA, Stetson U., DeLand, Fla., 1984; JD, Stetson U., 1987. Bar: Fla. 1987, US Dist. Ct. (mid. dist.) Fla., US Dist. Ct. (no. dist.) Fla., US Dist. Ct. (so. dist.) Fla., US Ct. Appeals (11th cir.), US Supreme Ct. Assoc. Rahdert, Acosta & Dickson, P.A., St. Petersburg, Fla., 1987—88; law clk. Magistrate Judge Thomas Wilson, Tampa, Fla., 1988—90; ptnr. Rahdert, Steele, Bole & Reynolds, P.A., St. Petersburg, 1990—. Office: Rahdert Steele Bole & Reynolds PA 535 Central Ave Saint Petersburg FL 33701 Office Phone: 727-823-4191.

STEELE, ANA MERCEDES, retired federal agency administrator; b. Jan. 18, 1939; d. Sydney and Mercedes (Hernandez) S.; m. John Hunter Clark, June 2, 1979. AB magna cum laude, Marywood Coll., 1958. Actress, 1959-64; sec. Nat. Endowment for Arts, Washington, 1965-67, dir. budget and rsch., 1968-75, dir. planning, 1976-78, dir. program coordination, sr. exec. svc., 1979-81, assoc. dep. chmn. programs, dir. program coordination, 1982-93, acting chmn., acting sr. dep. chmn., 1993, sr. dep. chmn., sr. exec. svc., 1993-96, dep. chmn. mgmt. and budget, sr. exec. svc., 1996-98; ret., 1998. Guest lectr. George Washington U., 1987; trustee Marywood Coll., 1989-96, Marywood U., 1997-98. Author, editor report: History of the National Council on the Arts and National Endowment for the Arts During the Johnson Administration, 1968; editor: Museums USA (Fed. Design Coun. award of Excellence 1975), 1974, National Endowment Arts, 1965-85: A Brief Chronology of Federal Involvement in the Arts, 1985. Former reader Rec. for the Blind, N.Y.C.; former tutor Future for Jimmy, Washington; judge Helen Hayes Awards, 2003-06. Named Disting. Grad. in Field of Arts, Marywood Coll., 1976; recipient Sustained Superior Performance award Nat. Endowment for Arts, 1980, Disting. Svc. award, 1983-85, 89, 92, 96, Presdl. medal Marywood U., 2000; named to Disting. Alumnae Hall of Fame, Ursuline Acad., 2001. Mem. Actors' Equity Assn., Screen Actors Guild, Delta Epsilon Sigma, Kappa Gamma Pi. Home: 2475 Virginia Ave NW Apt 604 Washington DC 20037-2639

STEELE, (MARGARET) ANITA MARTIN, law librarian, law educator; b. Haines City, Fla., Dec. 30, 1927; d. Emmett Edward and Esther Majulia (Phifer) Martin; m. Thomas Dinsmore Steele, June 10, 1947 (div. 1969); children: Linda Frances, Roger Dinsmore, Thomas Garrick, Carolyn Ann; m. James E. Beaver, Mar. 1980 (dec. Feb. 1996). BA, Radcliffe Coll., 1948; JD, U. Va., 1971; M in Law Librarianship, U. Wash., 1972. Asst. prof. law U. Puget Sound, Tacoma, 1972—74, assoc. prof. law, 1974—79, prof. law, 1979—94, dir. law libr., 1972—94; prof. law, dir. law libr. Seattle U., Tacoma, 1994—98, prof. law emeritus, 1998—. Author: (book) Martin and Carmichael Descendants in Ga., 1811-1994, 1994; contbr. articles to profl. jours.; mem. editorial adv. bds.: various law book pubs. Treas. Congl. Campaign Orgn., Tacoma, 1978, 1980; mem. adv. bd. Clover Pk. Vocat.-Tech. Sch., Tacoma, 1980—82. Mem.: DAR, Collectors' Cir. of Art Mus. Va., Colonial Dames XVII Century. Libertarian. Home: 4434 Pheasant Ridge Rd Condo # 303 Roanoke VA 24014-5280 E-mail: ams145@cox.net.

STEELE, CARL LAVERN, academic administrator; b. Patoka, Ill., Aug. 22, 1934; s. Boyd Alfa and Effie Jane (Corson) S.; m. Lula Irene Saliba, June 11, 1961; children: Jeffrey Van, Gregory Michael, Douglas Alan. BEd, So. Ill. U., 1956, MEd, 1960; MLS, No. Ill. U., 1971. Tchr. Shawneetown (Ill.) Community High. Sch., 1956-57; GED instr. U.S. Army, Ft. Hood, Tex. and Ulm, Fed. Republic of Germany, 1957-59; tchr. Forrest-Strawn-Wing Unit Dist., Forrest, Ill., 1959-61, Richwoods Community High Sch., Peoria, Ill., 1961-66; asst. dir. instructional materials Sauk Valley Coll., Dixon, Ill., 1966-68; dir. Ednl. Resources Ctr., Rock Valley Coll., Rockford, Ill., 1968-93; ret., 1993. Part-time traffic safety instr. Rock Valley Coll., 1992—2006. Asst. World Record sec. Nat. Fresh Water Fishing Hall of Fame, Hayward, Wisc., 1977-79. Served with U.S. Army, 1957-59. Mem. ALA, Assn. Ednl. Communications and Technology, Ill. Assn. Ednl. Communications and Technology (conv. chmn. 1976), No. Ill. Media Assn. (conv. chmn.), Learning Resource Commn. ICCCA (chmn. 1981). Democrat. Presbyterian. Avocations: fishing, travel, reading, woodworking, gardening. Home: 5758 Weymouth Dr Rockford IL 61114-5569 Personal E-mail: lsteele@steele.com.

STEELE, CHARLES, JR., civil rights association executive, former state legislator; b. Tuscaloosa, Ala., Aug. 3, 1946; m. Cathelean Annette; children: LeKeisha, Charla. Student, Miss. Valley State, Oakland U.; BA, Am. Internat. U.; LHD (hon.), Stillman Coll.; Ph.D (hon.), Am. Internat. U. Co-owner Van Hoose and Steele Funeral Home; former mem. Tuscaloosa City Coun.; senator Ala. State Senate, Montgomery, 1995—2004; pres., CEO SCLC, Atlanta, 2004—. Mem. Local Legis. No. 1 Com., Fiscal Responsibility and Accountability Com., Fin. and Taxation Gen. Fund Com., Fin. and Taxation Edn. Com., Agr. and Forestry Com., Health and Human Resources Com., Oil and Gas subcom. Commerce, Transp., and Utilities Com., Indsl. Devel. and Recruitment Com., Small Bus. and Rural Devel. Com., Constitution, Campaign Fin., Ethics, and Elections Com., Postsecondary and Higher Edn. subcom. Edn. Com., Law Enforcement and Victims Rights subcom., Violence in Schs. subcom. Judiciary Com.; chairperson Rural Devel. subcom. Small Bus. and Rural Devel. Com., Mental Health subcom. Health and Human Resources Com. Named one of Most Influential Black Americans, Ebony mag., 2006. Mem. Nat. Assn. Funeral Dirs. and Morticians, Ala. Funeral Dirs. and Morticians Assn. Democrat. Baptist. Avocations: walking, reading. Office: SCLC PO Box 89128 Atlanta GA 30312

STEELE, CHARLES GLEN, retired accountant; b. Faulkton, SD, July 24, 1925; s. Clifford D. and Emily O. (Hanson) S.; m. Shirley June Ferguson, Nov. 9, 1947; children: Richard Alan (dec.), Deborah Ann Steele Most (dec.). BBA, Golden Gate U., San Francisco, 1951, MBA, 1962. With Deloitte Haskins & Sells, 1951-86, partner, 1963-86, partner charge Chgo. office, 1973-76, partner charge personnel and adminstrn. NYC, 1976-78, chmn., chief exec. officer, 1978-86. Instr. evening program Golden Gate U., 1952-58. Served with USNR, 1943-48, aircraft carrier fighter pilot, 1946-48. Recipient Elijah Watts Sells Gold medal for highest grade in U.S. for C.P.A. exam., 1951 Mem. AICPA. Home and Office: 5 Stonecrest Circle Rancho Mirage CA 92270

STEELE, CLAUDE MASON, psychology professor; b. Chgo., Jan. 1, 1946; s. Shelby and Ruth (Hootman) S.; m. Aug. 27, 1967; children: Jory, Claude Benjamin. BA in Psychology, Hiram Coll., 1967; MA in Social Psychology, Ohio State U., 1969, PhD in Social Psychology, minor in Statistical Psychology, 1971; PhD (hon.), Yale U., 2002, Princeton U., 2003. Asst. prof. U. Utah, Salt Lake City, 1971-73; from asst. to prof. U. Washington, Seattle, 1978-87, prof. psychology, 1985—87; prof. U. Mich., Ann Arbor, 1987-91, rsch. scientist Inst. Social Rsch., 1989—91; prof. psychology Stanford U., Calif., 1991—, fellow Ctr. Advanced Study in Behavioral Sciences, 1994—95, chmn. Dept. Psychology, 1997—2000, Lucie Stern prof. social sciences, 1997—, co-dir. Ctr. Comparative Studies in Race and Ethnicity, 1999—2002, dir. Ctr. Comparative Studies in Race and Ethnicity, 2002—. Mem. psychosocial rsch. study sect. Nat. Inst. Alcohol Abuse and Alcoholism, 1984—88; mem. rev. panel and mental health rsch. edn. rev. panel Nat. Inst. Mental Health, 1979—83. Assoc. editor Personality and Social Psychology Bull., 1984—87, consulting editor Jour. of Social Issues, 1983—90, Jour. Personality and Social Psychology, 1990—, Attitudes and Social Cognition, 1990—, Psychol. Rev., 1990—, Motivation and Emotion, 1990—, Basic and Applied Social Psychology, 1990—, Jour. Exptl. Social Psychology, 1990—. Mem. King County Alcoholism and Drug Abuse Adminstrv. Bd., 1980—85. Recipient numerous rsch. grants. Mem. Soc. Exptl. Social Psychology (sec.-treas. 1987-88, chmn. 1988-89), Am. Psychol. Soc. (bd. dirs. 1991-96), Am. Psychol. Assn. (William James Fellow award for disting. sci. career contribution, 2000, Disting. Sci. Contribution award, 1998, Sr. Award Disting. Contributions to Psychology in Pub. Interest, 1998), Soc. Personality and Social Psychology (pres. 2002-03) (Donald Campbell award, 2001), Am. Acad. Arts and Sciences, Nat. Acad. Edn., NAS Home: 562 Junipero Serra Blvd Stanford CA 94305-8442 Office: Stanford U Dept Psychology Jordan Hall Bldg 420 Stanford CA 94305 Office Phone: 650-725-9849. Office Fax: 650-725-5699.

STEELE, ERNEST CLYDE, retired insurance company executive; b. Corbin, Ky., May 11, 1925; s. J. Fred and Leona (McFarland) S.; m. Cora Jones, June 17, 1944 (dec. Nov. 1988); children: Gerald R., David. P.; m. Helen LeCoultre, July 7, 1990 (dec. Jan. 2007). BS with honors, U. Ky., 1948, MS, 1950. Asst. actuary Peninsular Life Ins. Co., Jacksonville, Fla., 1950-54; actuary Pioneer Life & Casualty Co., Gadsden, Ala., 1955; v.p., actuary Guaranty Savs. Life Ins. Co., Montgomery, Ala., 1956-57; exec. v.p., actuary Am. Investment Life Ins. Co., Nashville, 1958-59; pres., actuary Appalachian Nat. Life Ins. Co., Knoxville, Tenn., 1959-67; sr. v.p., chief investment officer, ops. analyst Coastal States Life Ins. Co., Atlanta, 1968-71, exec. v.p., dir., 1971-74, pres., dir., 1974-79; pres. Occidental Life Ins. Co. of N.C., 1979-85, chmn., 1986-88; pres., dir. Peninsular Life Ins. Co., 1981-83, chmn., 1986-88; exec. v.p. investments MCM Corp., 1985-88; ret., 1988. Past pres. Ga. Assn. Life Inst. Cos., 1976-77. Past pres. Gt. Smoky Mountain Coun. Boy Scouts Am., 1965—66. Served to 2d lt. US Army, 1943—45. Fellow Life Mgmt. Inst.; mem. Life Office Mgmt. Assn. (past chmn. bd.), Am. Coun. Life Ins. (past dir.), U. Ky. Alumni Assn. (past bd. dirs.), Am. Acad. Actuaries, Pi Mu Epsilon. Republican. Baptist. Home: 103 Newell Village Cir Seymour TN 37865-5931 Personal E-mail: erneststeele@bellsouth.net. *My success in life is measured by the success of those with whom I have been associated.*

STEELE, HOWARD LOUCKS, economic development consultant, author; b. Pitts., Jan. 27, 1929; s. Howard Bennington and Ruby Alberta (Loucks) S.; m. Sally E. Funk, June 6, 1952 (div. 1977); children: John F., David A., Patricia A.; m. Jane R. Cornelius, July 30, 1977 (div. 1996); 1 child, Jennifer L.; m. Elaine Haddock, Aug. 23, 1997. BS, Washington and Lee U., 1950; MS, Pa. State U., 1952; PhD, U. Ky., 1962. Sales mgr. Greenville (Pa.) Dairy Co., 1952-56; owner H.L. Steele Bulk Milk Hauling, Greenville, 1955-60; asst. prof. Clemson (S.C.) U., 1956-57, assoc. prof., 1957-64, Ohio State U., Columbus, 1964-71; with Fgn. Agrl. Svc./Internat. Coop. and Devel. U.S., Dept. Agr., Washington, 1971-97; ret.; econ. devel. cons., 1997—. Project mgr. AID, Guatemala, 1976-77, Bolivia, 1977-80, Honduras, 1980-82, Sri Lanka, 1982-84, Bur. L.Am. and Caribbean USAID, Washington, 1984-88, office of the dir. tech. assistance divsn., 1988-90, with office of dep. adminstr., 1990-97; USDA liaison officer Inter-Am. Inst. Coop. in Agr., 1993-97; instr. U. Md., College Park, 1974-76; vis. prof. U. Sao Paulo, Piracicaba, Brazil, 1964-66; ptnr. Kingwood Acres Farm, Rockwood, Pa., 1966-98. Author: Commercializacao Agricola, 1971, A 200 Year History of Some Descendents of the Pioneer James Steel of Castleblaney, Ireland and Mt. Pleasant, Pennsylvania, 1994, Your Tax Dollars at Work (I'd Rather Have Gone Business Class!), 1998, Food Soldier, 2002, Food Soldier: Fighting the Cold War With Bushels and Bales, 2005; contbr. articles to profl. jours. Recipient Nat. Forensic Union award; named One of Outstanding Young Men U.S., U.S. Jaycees, 1965; cert. of merit Dept. Agr., 1975, 92. Mem.: SAR, Masons, Internat. Assn. Agrl. Economists, Am. Agrl. Econs. Assn., Shriners, Sigma Nu, Gamma Sigma Delta. Home: 5204 Holden St Fairfax VA 22032-3418 Office Phone: 703-978-4066. Personal E-mail: ehsteele@cox.net.

STEELE, JAMES EUGENE, retired school system administrator; b. South Norfolk, Va. s. James Edward and Blanche Eugenia (Munden) S. BS in Music Edn., Coll. William and Mary (now Old Dominion U.), Norfolk, Va., 1961; MEd in Ednl. Adminstrn. and Supervision, Temple U., Phila., 1972; EdD in Ednl. Adminstrn., Nova U., Ft. Lauderdale, Fla., 1976. Cert. tchr., Va. Piccoloist Va. Symphony Orch., 1951-73; dir. choral music Hampton City Schs., Va., 1960-65, supr. music, 1965—2003; ret., 2003. Guest flute soloist Music Tchrs. Assn., Great Britain, 1962. Dir. fine arts divsn. Hampton Assn. Arts Humanities, 1967—. Mem. NEA, Va. Edn. Assn., Hampton Edn. Assn., Va. Assn. Sch. Execs., Hampton Instrnl. Suprs. Assn., Tidewater Regional Suprs., Va. Assn. Sch. Curriculum Devel., Va. Music Suprs. Assn., Va. Music Educators Assn., Music Educators Nat. Conf., Va. Choral Dirs. Assn., Va. Band and Orch. Dirs. Assn., Va. String Tchrs. Assn. Home: 132 Fayton Ave Norfolk VA 23505-4428

STEELE, JAMES HARLAN, retired veterinarian; b. Chgo., Apr. 3, 1913; s. James Hahn and Lydia (Nordquist) S.; m. Aina Oberg, 1941 (dec. 1969); children: James Harlan, David, Michael; m. Maria-Brigitte Meyer. DVM, Mich. State Coll., 1941; MPH, Harvard U., 1942. With USPHS, 1943-71; advancing through grades to asst. surgeon gen. for vet. affairs and chief vet. officer; chief vet. pub. health activities Communicable Disease Center, Atlanta, 1947-71; prof. environ. health U. Tex. Sch. Pub. Health, Houston, 1971-83, prof. emeritus, 1983—. Cons. WHO, 1950-2005, Pan-Am. Health Orgn., 1945—, FAO, UN, 1960; vis. prof. Tex. A&M U., 1976—, all univ. prof., 1981-82; spkr. in field. Author: (with J. Arthur Myer) Bovine Tuberculosis Control in Man and Animals, 1969, 95, (with Charles Thoen), Mycobacterium Bovis Infections, revised edit., 2005, (with James Steele) Hendrik Stafseth and Public Health Veterinarians Ole Stalheim, 2005; editor-in-chief CRC Zoonoses Handbooks, 1979-84, cons. editor, 1994, 8 vols. transl. into Russian and Farsi, Bacterial & Viral Zoonoses, 2 vols. rev. by Beran; mem. editl. cons. bd. APHA Control Communicable Disease, 1960-2000, Merck Vet. Manual, 1955-2005; contbr. articles to profl. jours. and sects. to books on food hygiene and irradiation. Recipient Carlos Finlay medal Cuba Acad. Sci., 1952, Mich. State U. Centennial award, 1955, Mich. State U. Alumni award, 1958, USPHS Order of Merit, 1963, Karl F. Meyer Gold Head Cane award, 1966, Disting. Svc. award USPHS, 1971, Mich. State U. Coll. Vet. Medicine award, 1972, hon. mem. Epidemic Intelligence Svc., 1975, James Law lectr. Cornell U., 1983, Centennial award U. Pa., 1984, Am. Vet. Med. Assn. Internat. Vet. award, 1984, Pub. Svc. award, 1993; James H. Steele Vet. Pub. Health award World Vet. Epidemiology Soc., 1975, Disting. Svc. award Am. Vet. History Soc., 1995, James H. Steele award Ctr. for Disease Control, 1998, Disting. Alumni award Mich. State U., 2001, Calvin Schwabe Lifetime Achievement award, 2005, James McCallam award Mil. Surgeons, 2005, Surgeon Gen.'s medallion USPHS, 2005, Abraham Horowitz award, Pan American Edn. Health Org., Wash., 2006; named James H. Steele ann. lectr. in his honor U. Tex. Health Sci. Ctr., 1993, James H. Steele Epidemiology Professorship in his honor, 1996, James Steele Diseases in Nature, Tex. Health Dept., Austin, 2007. Fellow APHA (emeritus, 1984; Bronfman award 1971, Centennial award 1972), Am. Coll. Epidemiology (founding fellow); mem. Am. Soc. Tropical Medicine (emeritus), Am. Coll. Vet. Preventive Medicine (founder, hon. diploma 1983, Pres.'s award 1994), Nat. Acad. Health Practiioners, World Vet. Epidemiology Soc. (founder, pres. 1971), Am. Vet. Epidemiology Soc. (pres. 1968-88), World Vet. Assn. (hon.), Philippines Vet. Med. Assn. (hon.), Peru Vet. Med. Assn. (hon.), Hellenic Vet. Soc. (Athens Greece, hon. diploma, 1977), U.S. Animal Health Assn. (life), U.S.-Mex. Pub. Health Assn. (hon., life, Border award 2003), Mil. Surgeons Assn. (hon. life), Infectious Disease Soc. Am. (emeritus), XXI World Vet. Congress (Moscow, hon. diploma 1979), German Health Svc. (hon. diploma, 1988, Order of Merit 1993), Harvard U. Alumni Assn. (Alumni award 1998), Alpha Psi. Episcopalian. Home: 10722 Riverview Houston TX 77042-1121 Personal E-mail: drjameshsteele@houston.rr.com. *I have believed firmly throughout my career that I should share my knowledge and expertise with my fellow man, be he American or citizen of the world. Those of us who are more fortunate to be endowed with intellectual advantages have an even greater responsibility to share.*

STEELE, JOHN HYSLOP, marine scientist, oceanographic institute administrator; b. Edinburgh, Nov. 15, 1926; s. Adam and Annie H.; m. Margaret Evelyn Travis, Mar. 2, 1956; 1 son, Hugh. B.Sc., Univ. Coll., London U., 1946, D.Sc., 1964. Marine scientist Marine Lab., Aberdeen, Scotland, 1951-66, sr. prin. sci. officer, 1966-73, dep. dir., 1973-77; dir. Woods Hole Oceanographic Instn., Mass., 1977-89, pres. Mass., 1986-91. Mem. NAS/NRC Ocean Sci. Bd., 1978-88, chmn., 1986-88; mem. rsch. and exploration com. Nat. Geog. Soc.; mem. Arctic Rsch. Commn., 1988-92; trustee U. Corp. Atmospheric Rsch., 1987-91, Bermuda Biol. Sta., R.W. Johnson Found.; del. Internat. Coun. Exploration Sea; hon. prof. U. Aberdeen. Author: The Structure of Marine Ecosystems, 1974; Contbr. articles to profl. jours. Served with Brit. Royal Air Force, 1947-49. Recipient Alexander Agassiz medal Nat. Acad. Sci., 1973 Fellow Royal Soc. London, AAAS, Royal Soc. Edinburgh, Am. Acad. Arts and Scis. Home: PO Box 25 Woods Hole MA 02543-0025 Office: Woods Hole Oceanographic Inst Woods Hole MA 02543 E-mail: jsteele@whoi.edu.

STEELE, JUDITH MCCONNELL, writer; b. Lamar, Colo., Oct. 5, 1945; d. Taylor and Elva June (Buchtel) McC.; m. Richard M. Steele, Nov. 14, 1975. BA, Cornell Coll., 1967; MA, Northwestern U., 1972. Vol. Peace Corps, Sergipe, Brazil, 1968-70; translator office Project Hope, Rio Grande do Norte, Brazil, 1972; reporter, columnist The Idaho Statesman, Boise, 1978-93; freelance writer fiction, poetry Boise, 1993—. Chair young writers competition IJA Prodns., Boise, 1994, project dir. Fine Line Press, 2007-. Author: Stories From Home, 1989, More Stories From Home, 1993, (anthology) Family, 1998, Woven on the Wind, 2001; collaborative work with Sun Valley Ctr. Arts, 1999, Balance Dance Co., 2003, Dance Forum, 2003; group exhibits with Chris Binion, 1998-99; poetry duet, 2000-2002. Mem. Snake River Writers, Log Cabin Literary Ctr., Acad. Am. Poets.

STEELE, KAREN DORN, journalist; b. Portland, Oreg., Oct. 27, 1943; d. Ronald and Margaret Elizabeth (Cates) Moxness; m. Charles Stuart Dorn, Oct. 30, 1965 (div. Oct. 1982); children: Trilby Constance Elizabeth Dorn, Blythe Estella Dorn; m. Richard Donald Steele, July 4, 1983. BA, Stanford U., 1965; MA, U. Calif., Berkeley, 1967. Prodr. Sta. KSPS-TV, Spokane, Wash., 1970—72, dir. news and pub. affairs, 1972—82; reporter Spokesman-Rev., Spokane, 1982—87, environ./spl. projects reporter, 1987—2005, investigative reporter, 2005—. Contbr. articles to sci. publs. (Olive Br. award NYU Ctr. War, Peace & The Media, 1989). Bd. dirs. Women Helping Women, Spokane, 1994; trustee St. George's Sch., Spokane, 1988-92. Mid-career fellow Stanford Knight Fellowship Program, 1986-87, Arms Control fellow Ctr. for Internat. Security and Arms Control, Stanford U., 1986-87; Japan Travel grant Japan Press Found., Tokyo, 1987, Rsch. grantee John D. and Catherine T. MacArthur Found., 1992; recipient Gerald Loeb award Anderson Sch. Mgmt. UCLA, 1995, George Polk award L.I. U., 1995, William Stokes award U. Mo., 1988, Nat. Headliner award, Excellence in Legal Journalism award Wash. State Bar Assn., 2000, Payne award U. Oreg., 2006; named to State Hall of Journalistic Achievement, Wash. State U., Pullman, 1995. Unitarian Universalist. Office: Spokesman Review 999 W Riverside Ave Spokane WA 99210-2160 Home Phone: 509-536-6259; Office Phone: 509-459-5462. Business E-Mail: karend@spokesman.com.

STEELE, KENNETH FRANKLIN, JR., hydrologist; b. Statesville, NC, Jan. 16, 1944; s. Kenneth Franklin and Ruth Virginia (Wilhelm) Steele; m. Sheila Kay Stumpf, Sept. 3, 1966 (dec.); children: Krista Robin, Celisa Anne; m. Beth Vaughan-Wrobel, Sept. 24, 2005. BS in Chemistry, U. N.C., 1966, PhD in Geology, 1971. Registered profl. geologist, Ark., registered hydrogeologist. From instr. to assoc. prof. geology U. Ark., Fayetteville, 1970-83, dir. Ark. Water Resources Ctr., 1988—2001, prof., 1983—. Mem. State Bd. Registration for Profl. Geologists, 1992-96, 2000-2004, chmn., 1996, 2002-03, vice chmn., 2001-02; cons. in field. Contbr. numerous articles to profl. jour., chpts. to books; editor: Animal Waste and the Land-Water Interface. Mem. Internat. Order St. Luke the Physician. Summer faculty fellow Oak Ridge Associated Univ., 1981, 83, 85. Mem. Nat. Ground-Water Assn., Internat. Assn. Hydrologists, Am. Inst Hydrology, Assn. Applied Geochemists, Soc. Environ. Geology & Health, Geol. Soc. Am. (regional bd. dir. 1980-82, 84-86), Am. Water Resources Assn. (bd. dirs. 1991-94), Ark. Ground Water Assn. (bd. dir. 1988-90, 93-95, v.p. 1991, pres. 1992), Nat. Assn. Water Inst. Dirs. (counselor 1990-93), Nat. Inst. Water Resources (bd. dir. 1998-2001). Achievements include research on the importance of rainstorms on ground and surface water chemistry in karstic terrain, nitrate and pesticide contamination of ground water, and evolution of ground water chemistry with emphasis on iron and arsenic. Office: U Ark Dept Geoscis 113 Ozark Hall U Ark Fayetteville AR 72701-4040 Home: PO Box 1065 Fayetteville AR 72702 Office Phone: 479-575-7937. Business E-Mail: ksteele@uark.edu.

STEELE, MICHAEL S., former lieutenant governor; b. Oct. 19, 1958; m. Andrea Steele; children: Michael, Drew. Grad., Johns Hopkins U.; JD, Georgetown U., 1991; student, Augustinian Friars Sem. Pvt. law practice; assoc. internat. law firm Cleary, Gottlieb, Steen & Hamilton, Wash., DC, 1991—97; chmn. Republcian Ctrl. Com. for Prince George's County, Md., 1994—2000; cand. Md. State Comptroller, 1998; chmn. Md. Republican Party, 2000—02; lt. gov. State of Md., Annapolis, 2003—07. Advisor to campaigns of fellow politicians; treas., advisor Michele Dyson for Congress, 1994. Host (hour long radio program) WOLB 1010AM, Balt., Md., appeared (numerous radio and TV programs including) Politically Incorrect with Bill Maher, Metro Talk, That Show With Those Black Guys, The Joe Madison Show, Extra, Capitol Sunday, BET Tonight; contbr. columns in newspapers including The Washington Times, The Washington Post, The Baltimore Sun, The Jour. Newspapers. Bd. visitors U.S. Naval Acad., 2002; commr. Nat. Fed. Election Reform Commn.; mem. St. Mary's Cath. Ch., Landover Hills, Md. Named Md. State Republican Man of Yr., Man. of Yr., Ch. cmty., 1998. Mem.: NAACP (served blue ribbon panel on election reform, bd. dirs. hospice of nat. capital area, Prince George's County chpt.), Johns Hopkins U. (bd. trustees), Johns Hopkins Soc. Black Alumni, Term Limits Coalition (chmn. 2000), Truth iN Taxation Com. (hon. co-chmn. 1996), Republican Nat. Convention Phila., Pa. (del. 2000), Republican Nat. Convention San Diego, Calif. (alt. del. 1996), Md. State Minority Outreach Task Force (chmn. 1995—97), Md. State Republican Party Victory Campaigns, Prince George's County Md. Black Republican Coun., Republican Nat. Com. (mem. exec. com.), Knights of Columbus. Republican. Catholic. *

STEELE, MILDRED ROMEDAHL, educator; b. Boone, Iowa, Jan. 13, 1924; d. Joe and Gladys Madeline (Bonebright/Cree) Romedahl; m. Otto Scott Steele Jr., Sept. 4, 1947; children: Martha Steele Knepper, John Joseph, Timothy Scott. BA, Simpson Coll., 1946; MA, Drake U., 1968; Edn. Specialist, U. Iowa, 1973, PhD, 1982. Instr. Des Moines Area Community Coll., Ankeny, 1972-73, Drake U., Des Moines, 1973, 77; coord. communication Cen. Coll., Pella, Iowa, 1977-90, emerita asst. prof. of English, 1990. Lectr. Iowa Humanities Bd., 1991—; lectr. in field. Co-author: 101 Voices and Guide, 1973; editor: An Iowa Soldier in World War I, 1993, 15 volumes Romedahl Family History (CD), 1996, 3 volumes Steele Family History, 2005; author numerous poems and contbr. numerous articles to profl. jours. Chmn. Higher Edn. and Campus Ministry, Iowa, 1984-88; vice chmn. adminstrv. coun. Pella United Meth. Ch., 1988—, chmn. bd. trustees, 1990-92, cons. to bldg. com.; bd. dirs., bd. fellows Sch. Religion U. Iowa, 1986-88. Recipient Alumni Achievement award Simpson Coll., 1991, Stars in Our Crown award, 1992. Mem. AAUW, Nat. Assn. Devel. Edn. (nat. sec. 1988-90, chmn. 1987-88, exec. bd., Outstanding Svc. award 1988, Nat. Rsch. award 1986, 95), Nat. Simpson Coll. Alumni Bd., Pi Lambda Theta, Sigma Tau Delta, Delta Delta Delta. Democrat. Home and Office: Vriendschap Village 2604 Fifield Rd Apt A103 Pella IA 50219

STEELE, MYRON THOMAS, state supreme court chief justice; b. Taunton, Mass., July 28, 1945; s. Myron Thetus and Coleen Amelia (Polk) Steele; m. Beverly June Heaps, Feb. 4, 1967; children: Clayton Carter, Jenness Farnham. BA, U. Va., 1967, JD, 1970. Bar: Va. 1970, Del. 1970, U.S. Dist. Ct. Del. 1970, U.S. Ct. Appeals (3d cir.) 1974. Assoc. Prickett, Ward, Burt & Sanders, Dover, Del., 1970, 1973, ptnr., 1974; dep. atty. gen. State of Del., 1971—72; v.p., dir. Prickett, Jones, Elliott, Kristol & Schnee, Dover, 1974—88; assoc. judge Superior Ct., 1988—90, res. judge, 1990—94; vice chancellor Ct. Chancery, Del., 1994—2000; justice Del. Supreme Ct., 2000—, chief justice, 2004—. Mem. exec. com. Del. Democratic State Com., 1974—88; bd. dirs. Childrens Bur. Del., Del. News Coun.; chmn. Consumer Affairs Bd., 1974—88, Ctrl. Del. Health Care Corp., 1990—93. Served to 1st. lt. US Army, 1970, col. ret. Del. N.G.,

1974—97. Mem.: ABA (mem. jud. liaison comml. and bus. litig. com., bus. sect.), Del-Vets, Commn. on Ct. 2000 (Del.), Kent County Bar Assn. (past pres.), Va. State Bar, Del. Bar Assn. (past v.p.), Kiwanis (past pres.), Rehoboth Beach Country Club, Wilmington Club, Masons. Episcopalian. Office: Del Supreme Ct Carvel State Office Bldg 820 N French St Fl 11 Wilmington DE 19801 *

STEELE, PATRICIA ANN, librarian, dean; b. Columbus, Ohio, Mar. 28, 1943; d. Gerald Henry and June Eileen (McCullough) Costlow; m. Charles Nolan Steele, Aug. 31, 1963; children: Kelly Colleen, Ryan Charles. AB in English, Ind. U., 1966, MLS, 1981. Cert. tchr., Mich. Tchr. Chippewa Valley Schs., Mt. Clemens, Mich., 1966-67; br. head, extension asst. Lansing Pub. Library, Mich., 1967-74; head librarian, Atomic Energy Commn. plant research lab. Mich. State U., East Lansing, 1969-73; head librarian, Health, Physical Edn. and Recreation Library Ind. U., Bloomington, 1979-81, head librarian sch. of library and info. sci., 1981, exec. assoc. dean, head customer and access svcs., coord. academic info. and customer svc., Ruth Lilly interim dean of univ. libraries, 2005—. Chmn. faculty council ednl. task force on pornography Ind. U., 1985—; cons., specialist conspectus Research Libraries Group, 1985-86. Editor Library Sci. Nat. Newsletter, 1984-86; columnist Library Bookshelf, 1981—, InULA Innuendo, 1984—. Mem. ALA (vice chmn. library sci. librarians discussion group 1984-86), Ind. Library Assn. (chmn. exec. com. div. on women 1983-86), Ind. U. Librarian's Assn., Stone Hills Area Library Sci. Authority. Avocations: swimming, jogging, hiking. Office: Herman B Wells Libr Ind U 1320 E Tenth St Bloomington IN 47405 *

STEELE, RICHARD J., management consultant; b. Elkhart, Ind., Sept. 27, 1925; s. Cornelius H. and Harriett (Poel) S.; m. Shirley P. Ballard, Sept. 28, 2001; children: Barbara, Cheryl, Patricia, Thomas, Richard Jr., Marjorie, Gregory, Susan, Kathleen. SB, MIT, 1946; MBA, Ind. U., 1949. Cert. mgmt. cons. V.p. Fry Cons.'s, Inc., Chgo., 1950-70; pres. Richard Steele Cons.'s, Inc., Columbia, Md., 1978-96; group v.p. Macro Systems, Inc., Silver Spring, Md., 1972-78; sr. v.p. Birch & Davis Assocs., Inc., Silver Spring, 1979-94. Counselor Nat. Health Coun., N.Y.C., 1971-94. Author: (with others) Determinants of HMO Success, 1988. Trustee Village of Riverwoods, Ill., 1967. Lt. USNR, 1943-75, WWII, Korea. Recipient Award of Merit Am. Heart Assn., 1974. Mem. Inst. Mgmt. Cons. Unitarian Universalist. Home and Office: 712 Eagle View Cir Tallahassee FL 32311-1209 Business E-Mail: rjsteele@alum.mit.edu.

STEELE, RODNEY REDFEARN, judge; b. Selma, Ala., May 22, 1930; s. C. Parker and Miriam Lera (Redfearn) S.; m. Frances Marion Blair, Aug. 1, 1964; children: Marion Scott, Claudia Redfearn, Parker Blair. AB, U. Ala., 1950, MA, 1951; LLB, U. Mich., 1954. Bar: Ala. 1954, U.S. Dist. Ct. (mid. dist.) Ala. 1959, U.S. Ct. Appeals (5th cir., now 11th cir.) 1981. Law clk. Ala. Ct. Appeals, 1956-57; assoc. Knabe & Nachman, Montgomery, Ala., 1957-61; asst. U.S. atty. Dept. Justice, Montgomery, 1961-66; staff atty. So. Bell T&T Co., Atlanta, 1966-67; judge U.S. Bankruptcy Ct., Mid. dist. Ala., Montgomery, 1967—, chief judge, 1985-99; ret., 1999—. Served with U.S. Army, 1954-56, Korea. Mem. ABA, Ala. State Bar, Montgomery County Bar Assn. Democrat. Episcopalian. Home: 1227 Magnolia Curv Montgomery AL 36106-2136

STEELE, SHELBY, writer, educator; b. Chgo., 1946; s. Shelby Sr. and Ruth S. Grad., Coe Loll., 1968; M in Sociology, So. Ill. U., 1971; PhD in English, U. Utah, 1974. Prof. dept English Calif. State U., San Jose; rsch. fellow Hoover Instn., Stanford, Calif. Author: The Content of Our Character: A New Vision of Race in America, 1991 (Nat. Book Critics Circle award 1991), A Dream Deferred: The Second Betrayal of Black Freedom in America, 1998, (TV documentary) Seven Days in Bensonhurst (Emmy award, San Francisco Film Festival award); contbr. essays to profl. jours. Mem.: Ctr. for New Am. Cmty. at Manhattan Inst. (nat. bd.), Univ. Accreditation Assn., Am. Acad. Liberal Edn. (nat. bd.), Nat. Assn. Scholars. Office: Hoover Inst Pub Affairs Stanford Univ Stanford CA 94305-6010

STEELE, SHIRLEY SUE, retired special resource educator; b. Shelbyville, Tenn., Apr. 10, 1939; d. Clarence Sr. and Laura Ocie (Marr) McCullough; m. James Harold Levi Steele, June 23, 1957; children: Tonya Sue, Michaele Ann. BS magna cum laude, U. Tenn., 1973. Cert. spl. edn. tchr., Tenn. Spl. resource tchr. Chattanooga City Schs., ret.; tchr. spl. edn. Orange Grove Ctr., Chattanooga. Bd. dirs. Scouting for Spl. Citizens, Freedom Found.; leader Explorers Club for the Retarded. Mem. Alpha Soc. (tchr. Sunday sch. autistic children), Kappa Delta Pi. Home: 5720 Laurel Ridge Rd Chattanooga TN 37416-1050 Personal E-mail: shirstill@aol.com.

STEELE-GOETEMANN, JUDITH ANN, artist, educator, art gallery owner; b. Gloucester, Mass., June 11, 1935; d. Owen Eldred Steele and Elizabeth Verna Lawson; m. Gordon George Goetemann, Dec. 27, 1958; children: Elisabeth, David, Mark, Christopher. AA, Sullins Coll., Bristol, Va., 1955; student, Boston Mus. Sch., 1956, Romano Sch. Art, Gloucester, 1954—55, Evanston Arts Ctr., Chgo., 1966—69; BA in Art and Secondary Edn., Coll. St. Benedict, St. Joseph, Minn., 1974. Instr. spl. art labs. Kennedy Sch., St. Joseph, Minn., 1972—73, tchr. grades 1-3, 1974—75; tchr. grades 9-12 Apollo H.S., St. Cloud, 1976—77; co-dir. European studies St. John's U., St. Joseph, 1983, 1988, 1989, Upper Mid-West Assn. Ind. Colls., St. Paul, 1983, 1984, 1988, 1990. Adj. prof. art Coll. St. Benedict, St. Joseph, 1980—90, St. Johns U., Colleqeville, Minn.; lectr. in field. One-woman shows include St. John's U., 1976, 1989, Blaisdell Pl., Mpls., 1982, Coll. St. Benedict, 1984, 1991, Meridian Hotel, Boston, 1988, Hammond Castle, Gloucester, 1989, U. St. Thomas, 1995, exhibited in group shows at Marshall Field and Co. Gallery, Chgo., 1976, U. Minn., St. Paul, 1977, Augsburg Coll., 1978, Bergen County Mus., NJ, 1980, North Hennepin C.C., Bklyn. Pk., Minn., 1981—82, Women's Art Regional Minn., Mpls., 1982, BFM Gallery, NYC, 1983, 1985, Gallery 702, St. Cloud, 1993, Coll. St. Benedict/St. John's U., 1993, Rockport Art Assn., Mass., 1994 (Excellence in Watercolor award), Nat. Weavers Symposium, Mpls., 1994, exhibitions include Am. Craft Coun., Rhinebeck, NY, 1978, 1980, Notre Dame U., South Bend, Ind., 2005, Bryan Gallery, Rocky, Mass., 2005, 2006, Rocky Neck, 2005, Gloucester Stage Co., 2006, Mus. Fine Arts, Boston, 2007, Sullins Coll., Bristol, Va., Boston Mus. Sch., others. Critic Oddessy of the Mind, St. Cloud, 1996—98; critic, juror various schs. and assns., 1976—2000. Recipient Cerino Meml. prize, 1996, Harriet Wengenroth award, 1996, Cereno Meml. prize, 1997, G.O. Davis award, 1998, W.J. Hibbard Meml. award, 1999, Marguerite Pearson Gold medal, 2006. Mem.: Cape Ann Artisans, Soc. Encouragement of Arts (charter mem.), Rocky Neck Art Colony. Democrat. Roman Catholic. Office: Goetemann Gallery 37 Rocky Neck Ave Gloucester MA 01930 Office Phone: 978-281-6128. Personal E-mail: goetemann.gallery@verizon.net.

STEELMAN, SARA GERLING, retired art association administrator; b. Wichita, Kans., Apr. 24, 1946; d. Paul Henry and Amy (Gessner) Gerling; m. John Henry Steelman; 1 child, Amy. BS in Zoology, U. Chgo., 1967; PhD in Behavior Genetics, Stanford U., 1976. Instr. dept. psychology No. Ill. U., DeKalb, 1974-75; instr. Fullerton (Calif.) Jr. Coll., 1976-80; postdoctoral fellow dept. psychobiology U. Calif., Irvine, 1976-80; asst. prof. dept. biology Skidmore Coll., Saratoga Springs, NY, 1980-83; staff writer Saratogian, Saratoga Springs, 1983-86; contbg. writer Indiana Gazette, 1987-93; elected mem. Pa. Ho. of Reps., Harrisburg, 1991—2002; adminstr. Indiana Arts Coun., Indiana, Pa., 2002—06; ret. Contbr. articles to sci. publs. Asst. treas. Ind. Libr. Bd.; co-chair com. women in politics Pitts. Inst. Politics, 1993—2002; bd. dirs. Adagio Health. Rsch. fellow, Nat. Inst. Aging, 1979—80. Mem.: LWV, AAUW (Notable Woman 1991), Common Cause (state chairperson), Century Club (treas.). Democrat. Avocations: gardening, music, horseback riding.

STEEN, JOHN, health policy company executive, consultant; b. Bklyn., Dec. 14, 1941; m. Carol Nolde, June 3, 1978 (div. Nov. 2001); 1 child, Thoa Flaherty; m. Karen Kauffeld, June 20, 2004. BA, NYU, 1962, MA, 1964, PhD, 1965. Cert. of Need. Asst. dir. Health Systems Agy. of N.Y.C., 1976-86; mgr. C.O.N./planning Munns & Dobbins, CPAs, Scarsdale, N.Y., 1986-92; exec. dir. Essex & Union Adv. Bd. for Health Planning, Inc., South Orange, N.J., 1992-95; rsch. asst. prof. Seton Hall U., South Orange, 1992-95; dir. regulatory compliance State Health Planning Agy., Atlanta, 1996-97; prin. John Steen & Assocs., Meadville, Pa., 2004—. Vis. prof., lectr 8 colls. and univs.; pres. Am. Health Planning Assn., 2006-07. Contbr. articles to profl. jours. Mem. health task force Cmty. Coun. of Greater N.Y., 1971-74, chmn. state health issues com., 1974-76; chmn. project rev. com. Comprehensive Health Planning Agy. of N.Y.C., 1974-76; officer, chmn. health and hosps. com. Cmty. Bd. #2, Staten Island, N.Y., 1973-76; chmn. landmarks com. Borough Coun., Mountain Lakes, N.J., 1984-92, borough historian, 1993-97; bd. dirs. Morris County Trust for Historic Preservation, Morristown, 1998-2000. Mem. APHA, Am. Health Planning Assn. (bd. dirs., chair pub. policy), Am. Coll. Med. Quality, Mensa. Office: John Steen & Assocs 18254 Southwood Dr Meadville PA 16335-9292 Home Phone: 814-333-3742. E-mail: jwsteen@expedient.net.

STEEN, JOHN THOMAS, JR., lawyer; b. San Antonio, Dec. 27, 1949; s. John Thomas and Nell (Donnell) S.; m. Ida Louise Clement, May 12, 1979; children: John T. III, Ida Louise Larkin, James Higbie Clement. AB cum laude, Princeton U., NJ, 1971; JD, U. Tex., 1974; Honor grad., US Army Mil. Police Sch., 1974. Bar: Tex. 1974, US Dist. Ct. (we. dist.) Tex. 1976, US Ct. Appeals (5th cir.) 1989. Assoc. Matthews & Branscomb, San Antonio, 1977—82; ptnr. Soules, Cliffe & Reed, San Antonio, 1982—83; sr. v.p., gen. counsel, dir. Commerce Savs. Assn., San Antonio, 1983—88; pvt. practice San Antonio, 1988—. Trustee San Antonio Acad., 1976-81, 87-93, chmn. bd., 1989-91, adv. coun., 1991—; v.p. Bexar County Easter Seal Soc., San Antonio, 1976-77; trustee, vice-chmn. San Antonio C.C. Dist., 1977-82; bd. dirs. Tex. Easter Seal Soc., Dallas, 1977-80, San Antonio Rsch. and Planning Coun., 1978-81, Cmty. Guidance Ctr., 1983-84, Accord Med. Found., 1987-92; vice-chmn. Leadership San Antonio, 1978-79; dir. Fiesta San Antonio Commn., 1982-83, 93-96, 98-2001, 2003—, v.p., 2004-06, pres. 2007—; commr. Bexar County, San Antonio, 1982, Tex. Commn. on Economy and Efficiency in State Govt., 1985-89; adv. bd. Freeman Coliseum, 1985-91, chmn. bd. 1990-91; pres. San Antonio Performing Arts Assn., 1984-85; trustee World Affairs Coun. San Antonio, 1982—, chmn. bd., 1984-86; trustee United Way, San Antonio, 1985-92, Tex. Cavaliers Charitable Found., 1994-97, 2003-05, Austin Coll., 1996-2001; bd. dirs. Houston Livestock Show and Rodeo; adv. bd. U. Tex., San Antonio, 1987—, exec. com. chancellor's coun. U. Tex. Sys., 2005—, active Pan-Tex. Assembly, 1985-2002; commr. Tex. Alcoholic Beverage Commn., 1998—, chmn., 2002—; exec. com. Rep. Eagles, 2000-01; hon. dir. San Antonio Livestock Exposition, Inc.; bd. dirs. Fiesta Commn. Charitable Corp., 2004—, chmn. and pres., 2007-08. 1st lt. USAR. Named Chevalier Confrérie de Chevaliers du Tastevin, Sous-Commanderie de So. Tex., 1994—. Fellow San Antonio Bar Found., Tex. Bar Found. (life); mem. Tex. Bar Assn., San Antonio Acad. Alumni Assn. (pres. 1976-77), Ivy Club (Princeton, NJ), San Antonio German Club (pres. 1982-83), Order of Alamo, Tex. Cavaliers (bd. dirs. 1989-92, 94-97, comdr. 1994-95, King Antonio LXXIV 1996-97, Kings coun. 1997—, vice chmn. 2003-04, chmn. 2004-05), San Antonio Country Club (bd. govs. 1990-93, v.p. 1992-93), Argyle Club, Conopus Club (bd. dirs. 1989-90), Princeton Club San Antonio and South Tex. (pres. 1980-81), Maclean Soc. at Princeton U., Sons of the Republic of Tex. (life), Phi Delta Phi. Republican. Home: 601 Garraty Rd San Antonio TX 78209-6148 Office: 300 Convent St Ste 2440 San Antonio TX 78205-3722 Office Phone: 210-224-7700.

STEEN, LOWELL HARRISON, retired physician; b. Kenosha, Wis., Nov. 27, 1923; s. Joseph Arthur and Camilla Marie (Henriksen) S.; m. Cheryl Ann Rectanus, Nov. 20, 1969; children: Linda C., Laura A., Lowell Harrison Jr., Heather J., Kirsten M. BS, Ind. U., Bloomington, 1945; MD, Ind. U., 1948. Intern Mercy Hosp.-Loyola U. Clinics, Chgo., 1948-49; resident in internal medicine VA Hosp., Hines, Ill., 1950-53; pvt. practice Highland, Ind., 1953—; ret., 1999. Pres., CEO Whiting Clinic, 1960-85; mem. hon. staff St. Catherine Hosp., East Chicago, Ind.; hon. staff Cmty. Hosp., Munster, Ind.; bd. commrs. Joint Commn. Accreditation of Hosps. With M.C., AUS, 1949-50, 55-56 Recipient Disting. Alumni Svc. award Ind. U., 1983 Fellow ACP; mem. AMA (trustee 1975, chmn. bd. trustees 1979-81), Ind. Med. Assn. (pres. 1970, chmn. bd. 1968-70), World Med. Assn. (dir. 1978-82, chmn. 1981-82, del. world assembly), Ind. Soc. Internal Medicine (pres. 1963), Am. Soc. Internal Medicine (Disting. Internist award 1981), Lake County Med. Soc., Ind. U. Sch. Medicine Alumni Assn. (pres. 1989-90, Disting. Alumnus award 1981). Presbyterian. Home: 8800 Parkway Dr Highland IN 46322-1520 Personal E-mail: candlsteen@comcast.net.

STEEN, LYNN ARTHUR, mathematician, educator; b. Chgo., Jan. 1, 1941; s. Sigvart J. and Margery (Mayer) S.; m. Mary Elizabeth Frost, July 7, 1940; children: Margaret, Catherine. BA, Luther Coll., 1961; PhD, MIT, 1965; DSc (hon.), Luther Coll., 1986, Wittenberg U., 1991, Concordia Coll., Minn., 1996. Prof. math. St. Olaf Coll., Northfield, Minn., 1965—. Vis. scholar Inst. Mittag-Leffler, Djursholm, Sweden, 1970-71; writing fellow Conf. Bd. Math. Sci., Washington, 1974-75; exec. dir. Math. Sci. Edn. Bd., Washington, 1992-95; spl. asst. to provost St. Olaf Coll. Author: Counterexamples in Topology, 1970, Everybody Counts, 1989; editor: Mathematics Today, 1978, On the Shoulders of Giants, 1990, Math. Mag., 1976-80, Why Numbers Count, 1997, Mathematics and Democracy, 2001, Achieving Quantitative Literacy, 2004, Math and Biology 2010, 2005; contbg. editor: Sci. News, 1976-82. NSF Sci. faculty fellow, 1970-71, Danforth Found. grad. fellow, 1961-65. Fellow AAAS (sec. math. sect. 1982-88); mem. Am. Math. Soc., Math. Assn. Am. (pres. 1985-86, Disting. Svc. award 1992), Coun. Sci. Soc. Pres. (chmn. 1989), Sigma Xi (Bd. Dirs. Spl. award 1989). Home: 716 Saint Olaf Ave Northfield MN 55057-1523 Office: St Olaf Coll Dept of Math Northfield MN 55057 E-mail: steen@stolaf.edu.

STEEN, PAUL JOSEPH, retired broadcasting executive; b. Williston, ND, July 4, 1932; s. Ernest B. and Inez (Ingebrigtson) S.; m. Judith Smith; children— Michael M., Melanie. BA, Pacific Luth. U., 1954; MS, Syracuse U., 1957. Producer, dir. Sta. KNTV, San Jose, Calif., 1957-58, Sta. KVIE, Sacramento, 1958-60; asst. prof. telecommunications Pacific Luth. U., Tacoma, 1960-67; dir. ops. Sta. KPBS San Diego State U., 1967-74; gen. mgr., 1974-93; prof. telecommunications and film, 1974-93; dir. univ. telecommunications. Co-chmn. Office of New Tech. Initiatives. Dir. (tel. program) Troubled Waters (winner Nat. Ednl. TV award of excellence 1970). With AUS. Named Danforth Assoc. Mem. Pacific Mountain Network (bd. dirs., chmn., bd. of govs. award 1993), NATAS, Assn. Calif. Pub. TV Stas. (pres.), San Diego County Sr. Golf Assn. (past pres.), Pi Kappa Delta. Home: 6068 Caminito De La Taza San Diego CA 92120-5323 Business E-Mail: psteen@mail.sdsu.edu.

STEENBERGH, TIMOTHY ALLEN, psychology professor; b. Ypsilanti, Mich., Feb. 12, 1971; s. Jack Omar and Elaine Joy Steenbergh; m. Tracey Michelle Steenbergh; children: Jackson Lon, Molley Dee. PhD, U. Memphis, 2001. Cert. health svc. povider psychology Ind., 2004. Clin. health psychology fellow Mich. State U., Genesys Regional Med. Ctr., Grand Blanc, 2001—03; asst. prof. psychology Ind. Wesleyan U., Marion, 2003—06, assoc. prof. psychology, 2006—, dir. Lilly student rsch. initiative, 2005—07. Author: (book) Problem and Pathological Gambling. Mem., contbr. Coll. Wesleyan Ch., Marion, 2003—07. Scholar, Ind. Wesleyan U. Lilly Scholar Coun., 2005—06; Hinds Rsch.fellow, Ind. Weslyean U., 2006—08. Mem.: Assn. Advancement of Behavioral and Cognitive Therapies (assoc.). Achievements include development of gambler's beliefs questionnaire. Office: Dept Psychology Indiana Wesleyan Univ 4201 S Washington Marion IN 46953 Office Phone: 765-677-1991.

STEEN-HINDERLIE, DIANE EVELYN, social worker, musician; b. Duluth, Minn., June 13, 1947; d. Julian Sem and Evelyn Synnove (Helgaas) Steen; m. John Peter Hinderlie, June 27, 1971 (div. Sept. 1987); children: Peder Donald, Erik Steen; m. John Richard Olson, July 21, 1989. BA in Asian Studies/Social Psychology cum laude, St. Olaf Coll., 1969; postgrad., U. Minn. and other instns., 1991, Hamline U., 1989—91. Lic. social worker, Minn.; cert. music tchr. Music Tchrs. Nat. Assn. Social worker child care licensing Hennepin County Welfare Dept., Mpls., 1970—73; mem. clergy team exch. program Luth. World Fedn., Göppingen, Germany, 1973—77; mem. clergy team, music dir. Jubilation Singers Bethel Luth. Ch., Rochester, Minn., 1978—83; mem. clergy team, music dir. youth choir First Luth. Ch., St. Louis Park, Minn., 1983—86; adminstr. Family Child Care facility, St. Louis Park, 1986—90; faculty, tchr. Stenson Suzuki Studios and Home Studio, St. Louis Park, 1988—92; small group leader, tchr. vol. Mt. Olive Ch., Children's Hosp., Mpls., 1993, 1996—98; workshop and children's ministry Augsburg Coll. Youth and Family Inst., Trinity Cong., 1998—; founding dir. Fair Pay Inst., Mpls., 1995—; trainer United for a Fair Economy, 1997—. Founder orgn. and curriculum Early Childhood Orgn. for Edn. with Singing, 1993—, co-leader German-Am. youth group exch., 1979-82; co-founder Family DayCare Cert. Program and Babygarten (B-12 edn.) classes, 1970-73; bd. dirs. Midwest Coun., Nat. Peace Inst. Found., Grinnell, Iowa, 1991; presenter in field.; root causes of violence action team Initiative for Violence-Free Families, 4th Jud. Dist. Minn., 1997—; cons. Concordia Lang. Villages, 2005—. Author: (tng. manual) Mother Tongue Singing/Voice Method, 1988, (study packet) School Start Time/Teen Sleep Deprivation, 1996-97, A+=Baby Church School, 2002; rec. artist, mem. ensemble record/cassettes Nowell Sing We, 1986; performer Nordic Am. Psalmodikon Forbundet, 1997—. Vol. People of Faith Peacemakers, Feminists in Faith/ReImagining and Jewish Cmty. Rels. Coun., 1992-2003, Muslim-Christian Rels. Coun., Joint Religious Legis. Coalition, Bread for the World; founder People for Reforming Early Start Time for Teens Orgn., Mpls., 1993—; mem. steering com. Progressive Cmty. and FairVote, Minn., 1994-99; local host youth com. NAACP Conv., Mpls., 1995; vol. Common Cause, St. Paul and Washington; charter mem. US Holocaust Mus., 1993; co-founder antitorture com. Women Against Mil. Madness, 2005. Recipient appreciation plaque Christian Boy/Girl Scouts Germany; Svc. pin Am. Luth. Ch. Women; listed in Minn. Profiles, Minn. Hist. Soc. A Tribute to Outstanding Minn. Women by Marilyn Chelstrom, 2001; named Asset Builder of Month, St. Louis Park Children First Initiative, 1997; named to Honor Roll, Mendota Mdewakanton Dakota Cmty., 1999. Mem.: MADD, Minn. Music Tchrs. Assn. (first early childhood music chair 2001—03), Assn. Pre- and Perinatal Psychology and Health, Wash. Nat. Cathedral, Soc. for Psychol. Studies of Social Issues, Interfaith Alliance Minn., Nat. Luth. Choir Acad., Suzuki Assn. Americas (study area co-organizer, editl. adviser), Internat. Suzuki Assn., Nat. Assn. Tchrs. Singing and VoiceCare Network, UN Assn., Sojourner Project, Inc., Am.'s Jr. Miss. Coun., Germanic-Am. Inst., Nat. Peace Found., Amnesty Internat., Minn. Parenting Assn., Ctr. for Victims of Torture, World Wildlife Fund, Sons of Norway (lodge trustee 1991—), Phi Beta Kappa, Am. Mensa. Green. Lutheran. Avocations: reading, political activism, concerts, travel, memory albums. Office: Fair Pay Inst PO Box 16031 Minneapolis MN 55416-0031

STEENLAND, DOUGLAS M., air transportation executive; married; 2 children. BA in History, Calvin Coll.; JD, George Washington U., 1976. Sr. ptnr. Verner, Liipfert, Bernhard, McPherson and Hand, Washington; v.p., dep. gen. counsel Northwest Airlines Corp., Eagan, Minn., 1991—94, sr. v.p., gen. counsel Minn., 1994—98, exec. v.p., gen. counsel and alliances Minn., 1998—99, exec. v.p., chief corp. officer Minn., 1999—2001, pres. Minn., 2001—, CEO, 2004—, also bd. dirs. Minn., 2001—. Mem. bd. dirs. MAIR Holdings, Inc., The Guthrie Theater, The Minn. Symphony Orch.; mem. Super Bowl XL-Detroit 2006 Host Com. Office: Northwest Airlines Corp 2700 Lone Oak Pkwy Eagan MN 55121 Office Phone: 612-726-2111. *

STEENSGAARD, ANTHONY HARVEY, federal agency administrator; b. Rapid City, SD, Mar. 21, 1963; s. Harvey Hans and Dorothy Lorraine (Hansen) S. Student, Ft. Mead Vocat. Inst., 1974—75, U. SD, 1978—80, Anchorage CC, 1983—84; BSCE, U. Alaska, 1985; student, Northwestern U., 1986; AAS in Indsl. Security, CC Air Force, 1989; BS in Criminal Justice, Wayland U., 1989; MS in Computer Systems Engring., U. Calif., San Diego, 1996; LLD in Criminal Law, U. Trinity Coll., 2000, PhD in Computer Engring., 2000; BSc in Criminal Psychology, Rusland Coll., 2003. Lic. pilot, amateur radio operator; cert. hostage negotiator FBI, FBI Nat. Acad., Va., 1987; Fed. Air Marshal Sch., FAA; cert. Instr. Am. Soc. Protection Profls., 1986—, fed. emergency mgmt. agy. level III incident comdr., security specialist, 2001—, info. security specialist, intelligence and surveillance profl., 2001—; cons. US Navy Fighter Weapons Sch., 1994-98. Bookseller B. Dalton Bookseller, Rapid City, 1978—81, Anchorage, 1981—83; warehouseman Sears, Roebuck & Co., Anchorage, 1983—85; air res. technician Alaska Air N.G., Anchorage, 1985—88; agt., draftsman, engring. cons., asst. intelligence officer US Border Patrol, El Centro, Calif., 1988—; mil. liaison Def.-Law Enforcement Assistance Program, 2004; spl. agt. Dept. Homeland Security, 2004—. Fed. counter terrorism cons., 2001—; fed. info. warfare cons., 2001—; computer cons., 1994-2000; computer criminal investigator, 1999—; CEO Totalwarfare-.com webzine, 1997—; founding assoc. Amazon.com.; technical support working group, technical support officer Dept. Homeland Security, 2002—; intelligence officer US Coast Guard Auxiliary, 2003—; founding mem. US Dept. Homeland Security, 2003. Author: Unit Security Manager's Guide Book, 1988. Vol. Spl. Olympics, Rapid City, 1981; navigator, observer Civil Air Patrol, Anchorage, 1981; mentor Municipality Anchorage Sch. Dist., 1983—84; mem. Alaska Peace Officer's Assn., 1986—89, Calif. Law Enforcement Officers Assn., 1989—96; sr. pilot Civil Air Patrol, Rapid City, 1996, pub. affairs officer, 1996—98, aerospace edn. officer, 1998—2000, wing dir. aerospace edn., 2000—04; aviator, aircraft navigator US Coast Guard Aux., 2003—; vol. US Senator George McGovern's Campaign, Rapid City, 1980, Senator Tom Daschle's Campaign, Rapid City, 1980. With USNR, 1980—81, with USMCR, 1981—85, with USAF, 1985—98, with Operation Desert Shield, 1990, with Operation Desert Storm, 1991, with Operation Provide Comfort, 1991, with Operation Liberty Shield, 2002, with Operation Enduring Freedom, 2001—03, with USAR, 2001—05. Recipient Hon. Sci. award Bausch and Lomb, 1984, commendation State of Alaska, 1987, 2d commendation, 1988, Brigadier Gen. Charles E. Yeager Aerospace Achievement award, 2000, Blanchard trophy, 1990, Afghanistan royal Oder Almara el Ala, 2003. Fellow N.Am. Acad. Arts and Sci.; mem. DAV (life), Am. Chem. Soc., US Cavalry Assn. (heritage mem.), HTML Writer's Guild, Am. Legion, Air Force Assn., VFW, Fraternal Order Eagles, SD Sheriff's Assn., Fraternal Order of Police, Nat. Border Patrol Coun., Virtual Geog. League, WWII Meml. Soc. (charter mem.), US Naval Inst., US Coast Guard Inst., Nat. D-Day Mus. Found., Nat. WWII Mus. (founding mem.), Adventurer's Club. Avocations: reading, flight simulations, aviation, history, wargaming. Office: US Border Patrol Dept Homeland Security 31 Hopkins Plz 7th Fl Baltimore MD 21201 Personal E-mail: ahsteensgaard@juno.com.

STEENSLAND, RONALD PAUL, librarian; b. Dothan, Ala., Dec. 16, 1946; s. Maurice John and Claire Folkes S.; m. Nancy Hollister, Dec. 20, 1970; 1 child, Ronald Paul. BA, Fla. State U., 1969, MS, 1970; postgrad.,

Miami U., Ohio, 1972, U. Md., 1980, US Army War Coll., 1995. Dir. Davidson County Pub. Libr., Lexington, N.C., 1970-73, Hidalgo County Libr. System, McAllen, Tex., 1973-76, Los Alamos County Libr., 1976-77, Lexington Pub. Libr., 1977—2003, Bay County Libr. Friends of Libr., 2003—. Chmn. John Cotton Dana Library Public Relations Awards, 1977 Treas. Hildago County chpt. ARC, 1975. Served as co. comdr., bn. comdr., brigade comdr., asst. divsn. comdr., col., US Army, USAR, 1969-2005. Recipient Service award United Way. Mem. ALA, Res. Officers Assn. (sec.-treas. chpt. 100), Assn. U.S. Army (sec. Bluegrass chpt.), U.S. Chess Fedn., Southeastern Library Assn., Ky. Library Assn., Lexington C. of C., Alpha Tau Omega. Clubs: Lafayette, Pres.'s, Lexington Chess, Rotary. Baptist. Office: Lexington Pub Libr 140 E Main St Lexington KY 40507-1318 Personal E-mail: ron2085@yahoo.com.

STEEPLES, DOUGLAS WAYNE, retired university dean, consultant, researcher; b. Great Bend, Kans, Mar. 30, 1935; s. Marion Wayne and Dorothy Augusta (King) S.; children from previous marriage: Donald Bruce, John Douglas, Sheila Margaret; m. Christine Marie MacKinnes, Dec. 8, 1990. BA summa cum laude, U. Redlands, 1957; MA, U.N.C., 1958, PhD, 1961; cert., Inst. Ednl. Mgmt., Harvard U., 1981. Asst. prof. history Calir. State U., North Ridge, 1961—64; prof. history Earlham Coll., Richmond, Ind., 1963-80; acad. v.p. Wartburg Coll., Waverly, Iowa, 1979-80; exec. v.p. Westminster Coll., Salt Lake City, 1980-83; provost Ohio U., Delaware, Ohio, 1983-85, acting pres., winter 1984; dean Coll. Liberal and Fine Arts, U. So. Colo., Pueblo, Colo., 1985-89; v.p. for acad. affairs Aurora U., Ill., 1989—93, v.p. acad. planning, 1993—94; dean, prof. history Coll. Liberal Arts, Mercer U., Macon, Ga., 1994-2000, ret., 2000; proctor, participant clin. practice program Mercer U. Med. Sch., Macon, 2005—. Cons. higher edn. mgmt.; cons., reader advanced placement program Ednl. Testing Svc., Princeton, NJ, 1976-93; cons., evaluator North Ctrl. Assn. Sch. and Coll., Chgo., 1985-1994; mem. Accreditation Rev. Commn., 1992-94; bd. dirs. Western Ind. Coll. Fund, Salt Lake City, 1980-83; bd. dirs. Am. Conf. Acad. Deans, 1995-2000, sec.-treas., 1998-99; trustee Econ. and Bus. Hist. Soc., 1995-2000, pres., 1998-99; bd. dirs. Associated New Am. Colls., 1994-00. Editor, contbg. author: Institutional Revival: Case Histories, 1986, Successful Strategic Planning Case Studies, 1989, Mng. Change in Higher Ed., 1990, Treasure from the Painted Hills: Calico Calif., 1882-1907, 1999; (with David O. Whitten) Democracy in Desperation: The Depression in the 1890s, 1998 (Choice Mag. Acad. Book of Yr. award); editor John Randolph Spears, Illustrated Sketches of Death Valley, 2000, Advocate for Am. Enterprise: William Buck Dana and the Commercial and Fin. Chronicle, 1865-1910, 2001; assoc. editor Bus. Libr. Rev., 1996-2001; occational columnist for Macon Telegraph; contbr. over 50 articles to profl. jours.; contbr. 100 book revs. Adv. bd. Pueblo Symphony Orch., 1987—89; allocations com. United Way, Richmond, 1976—79, Pueblo, 1988—89, Aurora, 1990—94; vol. in svc., spl. cons. to pres. Ho-Chunk Wis. Winnebago Nation, 2001; mem. Mayor's Commn. on Restoration of Ft. Hawkins, Macon, Ga., 1997—; pipe maj. Mercer U. Pipes and Drums, 2002—06, pipe sgt., 2006—; chmn. com. Eagle Scouts, scoutmaster, dist. scout committeeman, neighborhood commr. wood badge; pres. Luth. Inter-parish Coun., Richmond, 1975—78; bd. dir. Soc. for Use and Preservation of Resources, Richmond, 1976—79. Scholar U. Redlands, Calif., 1953-57; Danforth fellow, 1957-61; Woodrow Wilson fellow, 1957-58; Found. for Econ. Edn. fellow in bus., 1963; Am. Philos. Soc. grantee, 1966 Mem. Am. Hist. Assn., Orgn. Am. Hist., So. Hist. Assn., Soc. for Values in Higher Edn., Sierra Club, Rotary (bd. dirs. 1983-84), Palaver Club, Phi Beta Kappa (senator united chpt. 1973-79, sec.-treas. mid-Ga. alumni assoc. 1996-2000, pres. 2003-04), Omicron Delta Kappa, Phi Kappa Phi. Republican. Avocations: mountain climbing, running, bagpiping. Office: 656 River North Blvd Macon GA 31211-6340 Office Phone: 478-750-1051. E-mail: steeplesmcn@aol.com.

STEER, JOHN RICHARD, lawyer; b. Greenwood, SC, Sept. 9, 1949; s. Robert Lindley and Evelyn (Patterson) S.; m. Mary-Lynne Server, July 29, 1979; children: Meredith, Derrison. BS, Clemson U., 1971, MS, 1975; JD, U. S.C., 1978. Bar: SC 1979, US Ct. Appeals (4th cir.) 1982, US Ct. Appeals (5th and DC cirs.) 1988, US Ct. Mil. Appeals 1989, US Supreme Ct. 1988, US Ct. Appeals (1st cir.) 2000. Instr., regional specialist Clemson (SC) U. Extension Svc., 1973; legis. asst. US Senator Strom Thurmond, Washington, 1974-76, state office staff asst. Columbia, SC, 1976-79, legis. dir. Washington, 1979-85, adminstrv. asst., 1985-86; chief dep. gen. counsel US Sentencing Commn., Washington, 1986-87, gen. counsel, 1987—99, mem., vice chair, 1999—. Contbr. articles to law rev. Active Springfield United Meth. Ch., Va. Mem. Clemson U. DC Area Alumni Assn. Home: 8413 Lake Crest Ter Fairfax Station VA 22039-2678 Office: US Sentencing Commn 1 Columbus Cir NE Ste 2-500 Washington DC 20002-8040 Home Phone: 703-690-3321; Office Phone: 202-502-4500, 202-502-4592. Business E-Mail: jsteer@ussc.gov.

STEER, REGINALD DAVID, lawyer; b. NYC, July 16, 1945; s. Joseph D. and Rozica (Yusim) S.; m. Marianne Spizzy, July 22, 1983; children: Derek B., Trevor A. BA, U. Minn., 1966, JD, 1969. Bar: Minn. 1969, Calif. 1973, U.S. Dist. Ct. (no., ea. so. and ctrl. dists.) Calif., U.S. Ct. Mil. Appeals 1969, U.S. Ct. Appeals (9th cir.), U.S. Ct. Appeals (11th cir.), U.S. Supreme Ct. 1981, U.S. Ct. Internat. Trade, 1994. Ptnr. Akin Gump Strauss Hauer & Feld, LLP, San Francisco. Capt. US Army, 1969—73. Fellow Am. Coll. Trial Lawyers; mem. ABA (antitrust and litigation sects.), San Francisco (Calif.) Bar Assn. Office: Akin Gump Strauss Hauer & Feld LLP 580 California St Ste 1500 San Francisco CA 94104 Home Phone: 415-665-9037; Office Phone: 415-765-9520. E-mail: rsteer@akingump.com.

STEERE, ALLEN CARUTHERS, JR., physician, educator; b. Apr. 11, 1943; m. Margaret Mercer, 1969; children: Allen Caruthers III, Margaret Hamilton, Samuel Mercer, John Summers. BA, Columbia U., 1965, MD, 1969; DSc. (hon.), Indiana U., 1992, SUNY, 1997; M (hon.), Harvard Med. Sch., 2002. Diplomate Am. Bd. Internal Medicine; lic. rheumatologist, N.Y., Ga., Ct., Mass. Intern St. Luke's Hosp., NYC, 1969-70, asst., sr. resident, 1970-72, chief resident, instr. medicine, 1972-73; chief resident, instr. medicine Coll. Physicians and Surgeons Columbia U., NYC, 1972-73; clin. fellow in rheumatology Yale U., New Haven, 1975-77, asst. prof. medicine, epidemiology and pub. health, 1977-81, assoc. prof. medicine, 1981-87; prof. medicine, chief rheumatology and immunology New Eng. Med. Ctr. Tufts U., Boston, 1987—2002, Natalie V. & Milton O. Zucker prof. rheumatology/immunology, 1998—2002; prof. medicine Harvard Med. Sch., Boston, 2002—; dir. rheumatology Mass. Gen. Hosp., 2002—06, dir. clin. rsch. in rheumatology, 2006—. With USPHS, 1973-75. Recipient Citation for Elucidation of Lyme disease, Infectious Diseases Soc. Am., 1984, Ciba-Geigy Rheumatology prize, Internat. League Against Rheumatism, 1985, award for discovery of Lyme disease, Nat. Inst. Arthritis and Musculoskeletal Skin Diseases, 1988, Richard and Hinda Rosenthal award, ACP, 1990, Joseph Mather Smith prize, Coll. Physicians and Surgeons, Columbia U., 1990, Zucker Faculty prize, Tufts U., 1990, award for studies Lyme disease, Nat. Health Coun., 1990, Lee C. Howley Sr. prize, Arthritis Found., 1993, Gold medal, Albert Sabin Vaccine Inst., 1998, Astute Clinician award, NIH, 1999, award, Am. Lyme Disease Found., 2000, Columbia Coll. of Phys. and Surgeon's Alumni award for Disting. Acad. Accomplishment, 2001. Mem. Am. Soc. Clin. Investigation, Am. Fedn. Clin. Rsch., Am. Coll. Rheumatology (Howard and Martha Holley rsch. prize in rheumatology 1995), Assn. Am. Physicians, Clin. Immunology Soc. Office: Mass Gen Hosp 55 Fruit St CNY 149/8301 Boston MA 02114

STEERE, WILLIAM CAMPBELL, JR., pharmaceutical executive; b. Ann Arbor, Mich., June 17, 1936; s. William Campbell and Dorothy (Osborne) S.; m. Lynda Gay Powers, Jan. 29, 1957; children: William, Mark, Christopher. BS, Stanford U., 1959. Sales rep. Pfizer & Co., Modesto, Calif., 1970-72; v.p., dir. ops. Pfizer Labs, NYC, 1982-84; sr. v.p., dir. ops. Pfizer Pharms., NYC, 1982-84, exec. v.p., 1984-86, pres., 1986-91; pres., CEO Pfizer Inc., 1991-92, CEO, 1991—2000, chmn., 1992—2001, chmn. emeritus, 2001—. Bd. dirs. NYU Med. Ctr., Health Mgmt. Assocs. (HMA), Met Life, Dow Jones. Bd. dirs. N.Y. Bot. Garden; bd. overseers Meml. Sloan-Kettering Cancer Ctr. Mem. Bus. Coun. (bd. dirs.), Univ. Club, N.Y. Yacht Club. Avocations: sailing, skiing. Office: Pfizer Inc 235 E 42nd St New York NY 10017-5755 Office Phone: 212-573-3116. Office Fax: 212-573-2200.

STEFANESCU, DORU MICHAEL, metallurgical engineer, educator; b. Sibiu, Romania, Nov. 15, 1942; arrived in US, 1980; s. Claudiu and Augusta Veturia Stefanescu; m. Pamela Gayle Stefanescu; children: Alina Augusta Coryell, Carla Christina. Dipl.Ing., U. Polit., Bucharest, 1965; D in Engring., U. Politehnica, Bucharest, 1972; D (hon.), Tech. U., Cluj-Napoca, Romania, 1998, U. Transylvania, Brasov, Romania, 2001. Vis. prof. U. Wis., Madison, 1980; prof. of metall. engring. The U. Ala., Tuscaloosa, Ala., 1984—87, disting. prof., 1987—2005, dir. solidification lab., 1987—2005, cudworth prof. engring., 2002—05, prof. emeritus, 2005—; prof. Ohio State U., Columbus, 2005—. Vis. prof. Inst. Nat. Polytechnique de Toulouse, France, 2002. Author: Science and Engineering of Casting Solidification, 2002; editor: ASM Handbook Vol 15 - Casting, 1992; contbr. over 350 scientific papers. Recipient Merit award, Am. Foundrymen's Soc., 2000. Fellow: Am. Soc. Metals Internat. Office: The Ohio State U 137 Fontana Lab 116 W 19th Ave Columbus OH 43210 Office Phone: 614-292-5629.

STEFANI, GWEN (GWEN RENEE STEAFANI), singer; b. Anaheim, Calif., Oct. 3, 1969; d. Dennis and Patti Stefani; m. Gavin McGregor Rossdale, Sept. 14, 2002; 1 child, Kingston James McGregor. Student, Calif. State U., Fullerton. Singer No Doubt, 1986—. Designer, creator fashion line L.A.M.B. (Love. Angel. Music. Baby.), 2004—; launched toy doll line (8 dolls) Love. Angel. Music. Baby. Fashion Dolls, 2006. Singer: (albums with No Doubt) No Doubt, 1992, Tragic Kingdom, 1995, Beacon Street Collection, 1995, Collector's Orange Crate, 1997, Return of Saturn, 2000, Rock Steady, 2001 (Grammy awards: Best Pop Performance By A Duo Or Group With Vocal for song "Hey Baby", 2002, Best Pop Performance By A Duo Or Group With Vocal for song "Underneath it All", 2003), The Singles 1992-2003, 2004, Everything In Time, 2005, (solo albums) Love, Angel, Music, Baby, 2004, The Sweet Escape, 2006, (songs) Just A Girl, Spiderwebs, Don't Speak, 1995, Simple Kind of Life, 2000, Hella Good, Hey Baby, Underneath It All, 2001, It's My Life, 2003 (MTV Video Music award Best Group Video, 2004, MTV Video Music award Best Pop Video, 2004), Hollaback Girl, 2005 (Billboard awards, Digital Song of Yr., 2005), (with Moby) South Side, 1999, (with eve) Let Me Blow Your Mind, 2001 (Grammy award, Best Rap/Song Collaboration, 2001); actor: (films) Zoolander, 2001, The Aviator, 2004, (voice only): (TV appearances) King of the Hill, 2001, (TV guest appearances) Saturday Night Live, 1996, 2001, Mad TV, 2000, Dawson's Creek, 2002. Recipient Best Choreography In a Video for Hollaback Girl, MTV Video Music Awards, 2005, Best Art Direction In a Video for What You Waiting For?, Favorite Female Artist, Am. Music Awards, 2005, New Artist of Yr., Billboard Music Awards, 2005, Best-Selling New Female Artist, World Music Awards, 2005. *

STEFANICK, MARCIA LYNN, medical educator, researcher; d. John Edward and Doris Marie Stefanick; m. Robert Neil Horowitz. BA in Biology, U. Pa., Phila., 1974; PhD in Physiology, Stanford U., 1982. Rsch. asst. Oreg. Regional Primate Rsch. Ctr., Beaverton, 1974—75; rsch. asst., physiology dept. Stanford U., Calif., 1975—76, sr. rsch. scientist Stanford Ctr. for Rsch. in Disease Prevention, 1987—97, assoc. prof. medicine, 1997—2003, prof. medicine, 2003—. Chair, steering and exec. com. Women's Healthy Initiative, 1998; prin., co-prin. investigator numerous rsch. trials and studies. Contbr. articles to profl. jours. Democrat. Avocations: hiking, running. Office: Stanford U Hoover Pavilion N229 211 Quarry Rd Stanford CA 94305 Home Phone: 650-968-8171; Office Phone: 650-725-5041.

STEFANO, TONI AMANDA, voice educator; b. Bedford, Ohio, June 11, 1970; d. Patrick Paul and Charlotte France Stefano; m. Matthew G. Hartman; 1 child, Alexander Hartman. MusB, U. Akron, Ohio, 1995; MusM, Peabody Conservatory Music, Balt., 2000. Voice tchr. McDonogh Sch., Reisterstown, Md., 2000. Singer: Anne Truelove, The Rake's Progress, Countess Maria Luisa, With Blood, With Ink, Julia Herriton, Where Angels Fear to Head, Despina, Cosi fan Tutti, Lucy, The Telephone, Lauretta, Gianni Schicchi, Papagena, Die Zauberflote, Christine, The Crucible. Office: Till The Fat Lady Sings LLC 7 Bensmill Ct Reisterstown MD 21136

STEFANON, ANTHONY, lawyer; b. Bellefonte, Pa., Sept. 6, 1949; s. Severino and Dorothy (Albright) S.; m. Elizabeth Jo Windsor, Nov. 22, 1969; children: Dyon, Justin. BS in Aerospace Engring., Pa. State U., 1971; JD, Dickinson U., 1977. Bar: Pa. 1977, US Dist. Ct. (mid. dist.) Pa. 1977, US Ct. Appeals (3rd cir.) 1991. Assoc. Myers & Potteiger, Harrisburg, Pa., 1977-79; ptnr. Myers, Potteiger & Stefanon, Harrisburg, Pa., 1979-82; assoc. Thomas & Thomas, Harrisburg, Pa., 1982-85; ptnr. Stefanon & Lappas, Harrisburg, Pa., 1985-88; pvt. practice Harrisburg, Pa., 1988—. Mem. Am. Assn. Justice, Pa. Trial Lawyers Assn., Pa. Bar Assn., Dauphin County Bar Assn. Avocations: squash, auto racing, restorations. Office: 407 N Front St Harrisburg PA 17101-1221 Office Phone: 717-232-0511. Personal E-mail: tonystefanon@verizon.net.

STEFANOV, IVANKA, music educator; d. Miodrag and Jozefa Zivkovic; m. Petar Stefanov; 1 child, Emi. B, Acad. of Musical Art, 1967—71. Treas. Jr. Friday Morning Musicale Club, Tampa, Fla., 1997—2004. Ch. pianist and choir dir. Presbyn. Ch. of Seffner, Seffner, Fla., 1992—98. Recipient Honor Roll, Nat. Guild of Piano Tchr., 2004. Mem.: Nat. Guild of Piano Teachers (assoc.), Nat. Fedn. of Musical Clubs (assoc.), Music Tchr. Nat. Assn (assoc.). Home: 9005 Bana Villa Ct Tampa FL 33635 Home Phone: 813-885-5414.

STEFANOV, STEFAN MINEV, mathematics professor, researcher; b. Sevlievo, Bulgaria, Aug. 8, 1964; s. Minio Stefanov and Nedka Marinova (Kadieva) Minevi. BS, Sofia U., Bulgaria, 1988, MEd, MS, Sofia U., Bulgaria, 1989, PhD in Ops. Rsch., 1991, DSc in Math., 1996. Asst. prof. Neofit Rilski U., Blagoevgrad, Bulgaria, 1991-96, assoc. prof., 1996-97, prof., 1997—. Extraordinary prof. and rsch. fellow U. Limerick, Ireland, spring 1998; mem. rsch. group in math. inequalities and applications, Melbourne, Aus.; editor: Jour. of Inequalities in Pure and Applied Mathematics, Melbourne. Contbr. numerous articles on math. programming and numerical analysis to profl. jours., textbooks and monographs; reviewer many internat. math. jours. Mem. Nat. Acad. Syndicate, Bulgaria, 1992—. Recipient medal Ministry of Edn., Bulgaria, 1982, contbg. to science, engring. and computer science for the monograph Separable Programming, Open Soc. Fund, 2001. Fellow Nat. Acad. Scis.; mem. Royal London Math. Soc., European Math. Soc., Am. Math. Soc. (reviewer, editor Math. Revs. Jour. 1997—), Math. Programming Soc. Phila., Soc. Indsl. and Applied Math., Union Bulgarian Mathematicians, Union Bulgarian Scientists (contbn. award 1996, 98), Activity Group on Optimization Phila., Ops. Rsch. Soc. Bulgaria, Can. Math. Soc., Can. Applied and Indsl. Math. Soc. Avocations: history, philosophy, fiction, fine arts. Home: 4 Ilio Vlaev Str 5400 Sevlievo Bulgaria Office: Neofit Rilski U 66 Ivan Mihailov Str 2700 Blagoevgrad Bulgaria Home Phone: ++359 675 34729. E-mail: stefm@aix.swu.bg.

STEFANOVIC, MARGARETA, science educator; d. Predrag and Branislava Stefanovic. MS in Elec. Engring., U. So. Calif., LA, 2002, PhD in elec. Engring., 2005. Post doctoral rschr. U. So. Calif., 2005; asst. prof. U. Wyo., Laramie, 2005—. Contbr. articles to profl. jours. Charles L. Powell engring. doctoral fellowship, U. So. Calif., 2000—04. Mem.: IEEE. Achievements include research in control systems. Office: U of Wyo Dept 3295 1000 E University Ave Laramie WY 82071 Home Phone: 307-742-6282; Office Phone: 307-766-6780. Business E-Mail: mstefano@uwyo.edu.

STEFANOVIC, VICTOR R., electrical engineer, consultant; b. Belgrade, Yugoslavia, Aug. 2, 1940; arrived in US, 1979; s. Ratimir and Milica Mihailovic Stefanovic; m. Dragana Kotarlic Stefanovic, July 16, 2003. MSc, McGill U., 1969, PhD, 1975. Prof. Concordia U., Montreal, Canada, 1969—79, U. Mo., Columbia, Mo., 1979—81; mgr. motion control Gen. Electric, Charlottesville, Va., 1981—85; v.p., gen. mgr. electronic sys. divsn. Electro-Craft, Mpls., 1985—86; v.p., mgr. engring. Electronic Speed Control divsn. Emerson Electric, St. Louis, 1986—89; dir. drives divsn. Vickers, Milan, 1989—92; cons. V-S Drives, Afton, Va., 1992—. Adj. prof. U. Bologna, Italy, 1990, U. Torino, Italy, 1991—92, Va. Tech., Blacksburg, 1995—; invited keynote spkr. Several Profl. Conf. Contbr. articles to tech. publs. Fellow: Inst. Elec. and Electronic Engring. Achievements include patents in field; one international patent. Avocations: sailing, skiing, tennis. Home and Office: 8540 Taylor Creek Rd Afton VA 22920

STEFANSKI, EDWARD, professional sports team executive; m. Karen Stefanski; children: Edward Jr., Kevin, Matthew, David. Grad., U. Pa., 1976. Pres. Preferred Mortgages Corp.; head basketball coach Monsignor Bonner HS, Drexel Hill, Pa., 1979—83; color analyst Big Five Basketball, 1979—90; Atlantic 10 color analyst ESPN, 1988—99; dir. scouting NJ Nets, 1999—2003, sr. v.p. basketball ops., 2003—04, gen. mgr., 2004—. Office: NJ Nets 390 Murray Hill Pky East Rutherford NJ 07073 *

STEFANYSHYN-PIPER, HEIDEMARIE M., astronaut; b. St. Paul, Minn., Feb. 7, 1963; d. Michael and Adelheid Stefanyshyn; m. Glenn A. Piper; 1 child. BS in Mech. Engring., MIT, 1984, MS in Mech. Engring., 1985. Tng. as Navy basic diving officer and salvage officer Naval Diving and Salvage Tng. Ctr., Panama City, Fla.; several tours of duty as an engring. duty officer in area of ship repair and maintenance; underwater ship husbandry ops. officer for the supr. of salvage and diving Naval Sea Systems Command; astronaut, mission specialist NASA Johnson Space Ctr., 1996—. Crew mem., will perform spacewalks Space Shuttle Atlantis (STS-115), 2006. Recipient Meritorious Svc. medal, Navy Commendation medal (2), Navy Achievement medal (2). Mem.: Am. Soc. Mech. Engineers. Avocations: scuba diving, swimming, running, rollerblading, ice skating. Office: Astronaut Office CB NASA Lyndon B Johnson Space Ctr Houston TX 77058

STEFFAN, JUDY MAE, medical/surgical nurse; b. Beatrice, Nebr., Apr. 6, 1949; d. Wilke J. and Mary Elizabeth (Shultz) Duitsman; m. William Arthur Steffan, Apr. 22, 1967; 1 child, Rodney Alan. RN, Lincoln Gen. Hosp. Sch. Nursing, 1973. Nurse Beatrice (Nebr.) Cmty. Hosp., 1973—80, Luth. Hosp., Beatice, 1980—83; pvt. duty nurse various nursing agencies, Omaha. Bus. adviser to Frank Sinatra; polit. advisor to Sen. Ted Kennedy, 1988—96, Pres. Bill Clinton, 1992—96. Author: A Presidential Story, 1996. Mem. St. Joseph's Cath. Ch., Beatrice. Recipient Bausch and Lomb Honoary Sci. award, 1966. Democrat. Roman Catholic. Achievements include discovery of re-creation and the partitioning effect. Avocations: piano, reading. Home: 420 N 86th St Lincoln NE 68505 Office Phone: 402-488-7776.

STEFFE, CYNTHIA, fashion designer; m. Richard Roberts. Grad., Parsons Sch. of Design, 1981. Asst. to Donna Karan and Louis Dell'Olio Anne Klein & Co., 1981—83; designed sportswear line Spitalnick & Co., 1983—88; prin., owner Cynthia Steffe Collection, 1988—. Francess & Rita, Cynthia's Closet. Featured as one of the "New Majors" Women's Wear Daily, one of "Fifty Most Beautiful People" People Mag. Avocations: auctions, tennis, gardening. Office: 550 7th Ave Fl 21 New York NY 10018-3203

STEFFEL, VERN JOHN, JR., lawyer; b. Chgo., July 10, 1950; s. Vern John and Adeline T. (Safranski) S.; m. Cynthia Louise Corkum, Aug. 4, 1973; children: Corkum L., Gabrielle M. BS, Western Mich. U., 1972; postgrad., U. Notre Dame, London, summer 1974; JD, Ohio No. U., 1975. Bar: Mich. 1975, U.S. Dist. Ct. (ea. and we. dists.) Mich. 1980. Assoc. Allen, Worth & Hatch, Battle Creek, Mich., 1975-78; sole practice Battle Creek, 1978-85; sr. ptnr. Steffel & Steffel, Battle Creek, 1985—. Bd. dirs. Steffel Design Studio, Battle Creek. Editor Ohio No. U. Law Review, 1974. Bd. dirs. Y-Ctr. Battle Creek, 1984-98, pres. 1990-93; bd. dirs. Sherman Lake YMCA Outdoor Ctr., 1998—, chair, 2003-05. Mem. ABA, Assn. Trial Lawyers Am., Comml. Law League Am., Mich. Bar Assn., Mich. Trial Lawyers Assn., Calhoun County Bar Assn. Roman Catholic. Avocations: marathons, skiing, swimming. Home: 564 Breezy Bluff St Battle Creek MI 49015-3576 Office: 332 Columbia Ave E Ste A Battle Creek MI 49015-4411 Office Phone: 269-962-3545. Business E-Mail: vsteffel@steffellaw.com.

STEFFEN, LLOYD HOWARD, minister, religious studies educator; b. Racine, Wis., Nov. 27, 1951; s. Howard C. and Ruth L. (Rode) S.; m. Emmajane S. Finney, Feb. 14, 1981; children: Nathan, Samuel, William. BA, New Coll., 1973; MA, Andover Newton Theol. Sch., 1978; MDiv, Yale U., 1978; PhD, Brown U., 1984. Ordained to ministry United Ch. of Christ, 1983. Chaplain Northland Coll., Ashland, Wis., 1983-90, assoc. prof., 1982-90, Lehigh U., Bethlehem, Pa., 1990-97, chaplain, 1990—, prof., 1997—; co-dir. Mellon Global Citizenship, 2003—04; chair dept. religion studies Lehigh U., Bethlehem, Pa., 2000—06. Mem. theol. com. Wis. Conf. United Ch. of Christ, Madison, 1985—87; mem. div. ch. and ministry NW assn. Wis. Conf., Eau Claire, 1987—90; mem. ecumenical commn. Penn N.E. Conf., 1994—96; mem. Common Ground, Bethlehem, Pa., 1994—97, chair, 1995—97; mem. ch. and ministry com. Pa. Northeast Conf., 1997—2000; mem. ethics com. St. Luke's Hosp., Bethlehem, Pa., 1998—; mem., sec., vice chair, bd. dirs. Religious Coalition for Reproductive Choice, 2002—; non-govtl. orgn. rep. UN, 2002—, sec., 2005—; 10th Curtis Lectr. Sacred Heart Univ., 1999; Frederick C. Wood Lectr. Cornell U., 2002; mem. instl. rev. bd. Haverford Coll., 2005—; bd. dirs. Justice Witness Ministries, United Ch. Christ. Author: Self-Deception and the Common Life, 1986, Life/Choice: The Theory of Just Abortion, 1994, Abortion: A Reader, 1996, Executing Justice: The Moral Meaning of the Death Penalty, 1998, 2d edit., 2006, The Demonic Turn: The Power of Religion to Inspire or Restrain Violence, 2003, Holy War, Just War: Exploring the Moral Meaning of Religious Violence, 2007; contbr. articles to profl. jours. Town supr. Town of La Pointe, Wis., 1984-87; bd. dirs. Justice Witness Ministries, United Ch. of Christ, 2006—. Recipient 1st Pilgrim Press Church and Soc. Book award, 2001, NEH Inst. award, Harvard U., 1988, East-West Ctr., 1995; fellow, Brown U., 1982; faculty devel. grant, Northland Coll., 1986, faculty devel. grantee, 1990, Lehigh U., 1994, 1998, 2003, Travel grant, Ford Found., 2004, Mellon Global Citizenship grant, Japan, 2003. Mem. Soc. Christian Ethics, Am. Acad. Religion, Assocs. for Religion and Intellectual Life, Assn. for Coordination of Univ. Religious Affairs. Home: 1349 Woodland Cir Bethlehem PA 18017-1636 Office: Lehigh U Johnson Hall # 36 Bethlehem PA 18015 Office Phone: 610-758-3877. Business E-Mail: lhs1@lehigh.edu.

STEFFENS, ANNIE LAURIE, sign language educator, interpreter; b. NYC; d. Robert William and Irene Marie (Hoecker) S. Cert., U. Ariz., Tucson, NYU, Gallaudet U., DC. Cert. sign lang. interpreter, sign lang. educator. Sign language interpreter high sch., Brattleboro, Vt., Longmeadow, Mass.; tchr. sign language pvt. sch., Putney, Vt., Main Street Arts, Saxtons River, Vt., Cmty. Coll., Greenfield, Mass., Cheshire Hosp., Keene, NH, YMCA, Keene, Brattleboro Sr. Ctr., Brattleboro Recreation Ctr.; pvt. practice. Developer new program using Am. sign lang., 1995—; mem. sign lang. choir Gallaudet U., NYU; poetry educator Main Street Arts; mem. new Am. Sign Lang. program Grace Cottage Hosp., Townsend, Vt., 1996; developer, designer Am. Sign Lang. Mentorship, 1997—, Am. Sign Lang. Linguistics program, 1998—. Author: (poem) Down Peaceful Paths. Advocate Women's Shelter, Brattleboro; counselor Vt. respite care project Mental Health of Southeastern Vt., Brattleboro. Named Am. Sign Language Tchr. of Excellence, 1998; recipient Bronze medal for excellence in Am. sign lang., 1999, Angel award, 2000. Mem. Nat. Assn. Deaf, Sign Instrs. Guidance Network. Avocations: signing to music, dance, singing, poetry, painting abstract designs. Home: 14 Spruce St Brattleboro VT 05301-2716

STEFFENS, BRIAN DOUGLAS, elementary school educator, music director; b. Elizabeth, NJ, Mar. 25, 1958; s. Herbert Gustave and Billie Virginia Steffens; m. Kyle Marie Gullery, July 14, 1984; children: Daryl Ginger, Jaimeson Douglas. MusB Edn. magna cum laude, SUNY, 1980; MusM Edn., Ithaca Coll., 1984. Cert. elem., secondary tchr. Va. Dir. band Madrid-Waddinton Sr. H.S., NY, 1981—82, Monroe-Woodbury Sr. H.S., Central Valley, NY, 1984—87, Langley H.S., McLean, Va., 1987—2000, Farmwell Sta. Mid. Sch., Ashburn, Va., 2000—02, River Bend Mid. Sch., Sterling, Va., 2002—. Composer: Sunrise on the River's Bend. Moderator, bd. deacons Ashburn Presbyn. Ch., Va., 2003—05. Named Tchr. of Yr., Langley H.S., 1996; recipient Music Dept. Blue Ribbon, Va. Music Educators Assn., 2005, 2006. Mem.: Music Educators Nat. Conf. (licentiate). Presbyterian. Office: River Bend Mid Sch 46240 Algonkian Pkwy Sterling VA 20165 Home: 42733 Explorer Dr Brambleton VA 20148 Home Phone: 703-430-8434; Office Phone: 703-444-7574. Office Fax: 703-444-7578. Personal E-mail: bksteffens@aol.com. Business E-Mail: bsteffen@loudoun.k12.va.us.

STEFFER, ROBERT WESLEY, clergyman; b. Spokane, Wash., June 24, 1934; s. Harold Wesley and Kathryne (Trumble) S.; m. Diane DeMoisey, Aug. 19, 1960; children: Erika Kirsten, Beauregard Gregory Robert. BA, Whitworth Coll., 1956; BD, Lexington Theol. Sem., 1959; MA, Ind. U., 1966, PhD, 1967. Ordained to ministry Christian Ch. (Disciples of Christ), 1959. Civilian dir. religious edn. U.S. Army Armor Ctr., Ft. Knox, Ky., 1960-64; assoc. regional min. Christian Ch. (Disciples of Christ), Oklahoma City, 1967-71; prof. Phillips U., Enid, Okla., 1971-76; fraternal worker div. overseas ministries Christian Ch. (Disciples of Christ), Barrow-in-Furness, Cumbria, Eng., 1976-79; Lilly vis. prof. religious edn. Christian Theol. Sem., Indpls., 1979-81; dir. edn. for mission Christian Ch. (Disciples of Christ), Indpls., 1981-87; exec. regional min. Christian Ch. (Disciples of Christ) in Can., Guelph, Ont., 1987-97; interim sr. minister Eureka (Ill.) Christian Ch., 1997-98; curator Cane Ridge Hist. Preservation Project, 1998—. Sec. Coll. Chs. of Christ in Can., Guelph, 1987-97. Editor Cane Ridge Bull., 1999—; contbr. articles to religious publs. and ency. Col., chaplain USAR ret., 1964—. Lilly Found. fellow in adult edn. Ind. U., 1964-66. Mem. Disciples of Christ Hist. Soc. (life, trustee 1990-94), Religious Edn. Assn. (bd. dirs. 1994-97), Conf. Regional Mins. and Moderators (2nd v.p.), Ch. Fin. Coun. (bd. dirs. 1995-96, exec. com. 1995), Phi Delta Kappa, Theta Phi. Democrat. Avocations: gardening, reading, travel, music. Office: PO Box 26 Paris KY 40362-0026 Mailing: PO Box 5226 Paris KY 40362-5226 Office Phone: 859-987-5350. E-mail: canerdgmtg@aol.com.

STEFFEY, LELA, state legislator, banker; b. Idaho Falls, Idaho, Aug. 8, 1928; d. Orawell and Mary Ethel (Owen) Gardner; m. Carl A. Hendershott, Jr., Apr. 16, 1949 (div. 1961); children: Barry G. Hendershott, Bradley Carl Hendershott, Barton P. Hendershott; m. Warren D. Steffey, July 13, 1973; children: Dean, Wayne, Luann, Scott, Susan. Grad., Am. Inst. Banking, 1972. With Pacific Tel. & Tel., San Diego, 1948—49, Bank of Am., San Diego, 1949—52, escrow officer, mgr. consumer loans, 1961—63; with Gen. Dynamics/Astro, San Diego, 1960—61; real estate agt. Steffey Realty, Mesa, Ariz., 1978—. Mem. Ariz. Ho. of Reps, Phoenix, 1982—86, vice-chmn. banking and ins. com., 1982—86, house appropriations, judiciary, counties and municipalities coms., 1986—90, chmn. counties and municipalities com., 1987—90, chmn. transp., 1991—, multi-state hwy. transp. commn., 1993—94. Founder Citizens Com. Against Domestic Abuse; chmn. adv. bd. Mesa Mus., 1981—83; precinct com., dep. registrar Legis. Dist. 29, 1978—; pres. Mesa (Ariz.) Rep. Women, 1980; del. to Rep. Nat. Conv., Dallas, 1984; bd. dirs. Mesa Cmty. Coun., 1985—, Ariz. Hist. Soc., Ariz., Ariz. Life Found., Aide to Women Ctr. Mem.: Am. Legis. Exchange Coun., Ariz. Fedn. Rep. Women (bd. dirs.), Nat. Fedn. Rep. Women, Nat. Order Women Legislators (v.p. 1987—88, pres. 1989—90), Ariz. Assn. of Women (bd. dirs.), Am. Mothers Assn., Pi Beta Phi. Mem. Ch. Lds Ch. Office: Ariz Ho of Reps 1700 W Washington St Phoenix AZ 85007-2812

STEFFY, MARION NANCY, state agency administrator; b. Fairport Harbor, Ohio, Sept. 23, 1937; d. Felix and Anna (Kosaber) Jackopin; 1 child, Christopher C. BA, Ohio State U., 1959; postgrad., Butler U., 1962-65, Ind. U., 1983. Exec. sec. Franklin County Mental Health Assn., Columbus, Ohio, 1959-61; caseworker Marion County Dept. Pub. Welfare, Indpls., 1961-63, supr., 1963-66, asst. chief supr., 1966-73; dir. divsn. pub. assistance Ind. Dept. Pub. Welfare, Indpls., 1973-77, asst. adminstr., 1977-85; regional adminstr. Adminstrn. Children and Families Ill. Dept. Health and Human Svcs., Chgo., 1985-98; nat. dir. Performance Initiative, 1998—. Lectr. Ball State U., Lockyear Coll., Ind. U. Grad. Sch. Social Work; mem. Ind. Devel. Disabilities Coun., 1979-81, Ind. Cmty. Svcs. Adv. Coun., 1978-81; Ind. Child Support Adv. Coun., 1976-82, Welfare Svc. League, 1968—; chmn. rules com. Ind. Health Facilities Coun., 1974-81; chmn. Lawrence Twp. Roundtable, 1983—; dir. Palette and Chisel Acad. Fine Arts, 2003. Mem. Nat. Assn. State Pub. Welfare Adminstrs., Am. Pub. Welfare Assn., Network of Women in Bus. Roman Catholic.

STEGALL, MARK D., surgeon, medical educator; b. Lubbock, Tex., June 24, 1957; BA, Harvard Coll., 1979; postgrad., Trinity Coll., Oxford (Eng.), 1979; MD, Columbia U., 1984. Diplomate Am. Bd. Surgery. Resident in surgery Presbyn. Hosp., NYC, 1984-91; post-doctoral rsch. scientist Columbia U., NYC, 1987-89; fellow in transplantation U. Wis., Madison, 1991-93; asst. prof. surgery, dir. pancreas and islet transplantation U. Colo., Denver, 1993-98; dir. kidney and pancreas transplantation surgery Mayo Clinic, Rochester, Minn., 1998—, chmn. divsn. transplantation surgery, 2002—; assoc. prof. surgery Mayo Med. Sch., Rochester, 1998—. Post-Doctoral Rsch. fellow N.Y. State Diabetes Fund, 1987-88; recipient NIH-NIAID Individual Nat. Rsch. Svc. award, 1988-89, Upjohn prize N.Y. State Transplantation Soc., 1988. Mem. Am. Soc. Transplant Surgeons (Upjohn award 1989, Ortho Faculty Devel. award 1995), Soc. Univ. Surgeons, Assn. Acad. Surgery. Office: Mayo Clinic Campus Box C-318 200 1st St SW Rochester MN 55905-0002

STEGENGA, JAMES JAY, bank examiner; b. Berea, Ky., May 1, 1954; s. Preston Jay and Marcia J Stegenga. BA, Hope Coll., Holland, Mich., 1976; MA, U. So. Calif., LA, 1978; MBA, San Diego State U., 1982. Cert. regulatory compliance mgr. Inst. Cert. Bankers, Washington, 1999, bank examiner FDIC, 1990. Asst. examiner FDIC, Seattle, 1986—88, bank examiner Sacramento, 1990—98, sr. bank compliance examiner Grand Rapids, Mich., 1998—. Mem.: Inst. Cert. Bankers (licentiate), Mensa. Mem. Reformed Church In America.

STEGER, CHARLES WILLIAM, academic administrator; b. Richmond, Va., June 16, 1947; s. Charles William and Virginia Belle (Garrett) S.; m. Janet Grey Baird, Sept. 13, 1969; children: Christopher B., David C. BArch, Va. Poly. Inst. & State U., 1970, MArch, 1971, PhD, 1978. Registered architect, Va. Project planner, architect Wiley & Wilson Inc., Lynchburg, Va., 1971-72, mgr. urban planning dept., 1973-74; dir. Environ. Design Consortium Inc., Blacksburg, Va., 1974-85; inst. grad. urban design program Coll. Architecture and Urban Studies, Va. Poly. Inst. and State U., Blacksburg, 1974-76, chmn. grad. urban design program, 1976-81; dean Coll. Architecture and Urban Studies, Va. Poly. Inst. and State U., Blacksburg, 1981-93; acting v.p. for pub. svc. Va. Poly. Inst. and State U., Blacksburg, 1990-93, v.p. for devel. and univ. rels., 1993-99; pres. Va. Tech. U., 2000—. Bd. dirs. Va. Found. Architecture, Richmond, Innovative Tech. Authority; mem. Gov.'s Secure Va. Tech. Initiative, 2001-02; mem. Gov.'s Va. Preparedness and Security Panel, 2001-02; bd. mem. Va. Advanced Shipbuilding and Carrier Integration Ctr., 2001-. Contbr. articles to jours. in field. Bd. dirs. Hollins Coll., Roanoke, Va., 1987-96, Boswil Found., Switzerland, 1986—, Ctr. in the Square, Roanoke, 1993-99; v.p. Va. Tech. Found., Inc., 1993-99; adv. coun. Va. Ctr. on Rural Devel., 1992—; commr. Govs. Commn. on Population Growth and Devel., Richmond, 1989-94; pres. Endowment Found. for We. Va. Found. for Arts and Scis. Fellow AIA (bd. dirs. ACSA Health Facilities Rsch. Program, Washington 1989—, ACSA Coun. on Arch. Rsch., 1987—); mem. Am. Planning Assn., Am. Inst. Cert. Planners, Commonwealth Club (Richmond, Va.), Shenandoah Club (Roanoke, Va.). Avocations: cattle farming, golf, canoeing. Office: Va Tech (0131) Office of Pres 210 Burruss Hall Blacksburg VA 24061 Office Phone: 540-231-6231.

STEGER, EDWARD HERMAN, retired chemist; b. New Orleans, Dec. 11, 1936; s. Herman Christoph and Katherine (Walther) S.; m. Amy Patricia Duvall, July 29, 1960; children: David B., Sandra E. BS, Tulane U., 1958. Analytical chemist Atlantic Rsch. Corp., Gainesville, Va., 1960-64, head control lab., 1964—2004, ret., 2004. Presenter at profl. confs. Contbr. articles to Fine Particle Soc. Jour. Lt. USNR, 1958—60. Mem.: NY Acad. Scis., Am. Chem. Soc., Alpha Chi Sigma, Phi Eta Sigma, Phi Beta Kappa. Baptist. Home: 4311 Alta Vista Dr Fairfax VA 22030-5302

STEGER, RALPH JAMES, chemist; b. Meridian, Okla., Jan. 24, 1940; s. Daniel Bose and Opal Creola (Brothers) S. BS in Chemistry and Math., Langston U., 1962. Cartographer Aeronautical Chart and Info. Ctr. ACIC USAF, St. Louis, 1962-63; lab. technician Sigma Chem. Co., St. Louis, 1963; phys. scientist U.S. Army Chem. Corps, Edgewood Arsenal, Md., 1963-65; rsch. chemist Chem. Rsch., Devel. and Engring. Ctr. SMCCR Rsch. Lab., Analytical Div., Aberdeen Proving Ground, Md., 1965-86; chemist Chem. Rsch., Devel. and Engring. Ctr. SMCCR-Detection, Detection Technology, Aberdeen Proving Ground, 1986-97. Adv. com. Garrison Gents, Balt., 1980—; ACOR monitoring govt. contracts, Balt., 1987—. Contbr. articles to profl. jours. Mem. AAAS, N.Y. Acad. Sci., Okla. Hist. Soc. Office: CBDCOM-RTE Aberdeen Proving Ground MD 21010-5423 Personal E-mail: rjsteger@erols.com.

STEGMAYER, JOSEPH HENRY, housing industry executive; b. Teaneck, NJ, Jan. 4, 1951; s. Arthur Harry and Alicia (Ward) S.; m. Delene Russell. BS in Fin., U. Louisville, 1973. Spl. projects Worthington Industries Inc., Columbus, Ohio, 1973-75, dir. investor rels., 1975-77, dir. corp. rels., 1977-80, v.p. corp. devel., 1980-82, v.p., CFO, treas., 1982-93, also bd. dirs.; pres., vice chmn. Clayton Homes, Inc., Knoxville, Tenn., 1985—98, also bd. dirs.; pres. retail & CFO Champion Enterprises, Inc., Auburn Hills, Mich., 1998-2000; chmn., CEO Centex Mfg. Housing Group, Dallas, 2000—03; chmn., pres., CEO Cavco Industries, 2003—. Editor: We've Only Scratched the Surface, 1981. Chmn. YMCA, Columbus, 1981-83; pres. and chmn. Columbus Zoo, 1987-93; bd. dirs. Muskingum Coll., 1984-93, Knoxville Zoo, Found. of Diocese of Columbus, United Way Knoxville; chmn. Ronald McDonald House, Columbus; mem. chancellor's assocs. bd. U. Tenn.; dir. Desert Voices Oral Learning Ctr.; mem. provost's bd. Ariz. State U. Named Citizen of Yr., Columbus Jaycees, 1984; recipient Outstanding Achievement in Fin. award Phi Beta Kappa, 1984. Roman Catholic. Avocations: scuba diving, travel, investing. Office: CAVCO 1001 N Central Ave Phoenix AZ 85004 Office Phone: 602-256-6263.

STEGMULLER, AGNES LEONORE, physical education educator; b. Phila., Jan. 24, 1923; d. George August and Agnes B. Stegmuller. BS in Edn., Temple U., Phila., 1945, MS in Edn., 1948; postgrad., Sorbonne U., Paris, 1954, Brigham Young U., Laie, Hawaii, Pa. State U. From tchr. to dept. head health and phys. edn. Sch. Dist. Phila., 1946—93; adj. prof. Temple U., Phila., 1993—. Pres. Dist. I Track Offcls., Abington, Pa., 2004—06. Vol. Spl. Olympics, Phila., March of Dimes, Pa.; mem. U.S. Women's Basketball Olympic Com., 1978—79; pres. Temple U. Coll. Health, Physical Edn., Recreation and Dance Alumni, 1998—99. Named Agnes L. Stegmuller scholarship in her honor, Temple U., 1994; named to Temple U. Hall of Fame, 1989, Pa. Sports Hall of Fame, 1999, Pa. Lacrosse Hall of Fame, 2002; recipient Steoher award, Phila. Sch. Dist., 1986, Coach of Yr., Women's Sports Fedn., 1988, Pathfinder award, Am. Alliance Health, Physical Edn., Recreation and Dance, 1990, Conwell award, Temple U., 2000, Meritorious Svc. award, Pa. Interscholastic Athletic Assn., 2004. Mem.: AAHPERD (Pa. liason), Pa. AAHPERD (v.p. 1988—92, girls sports chmn.), Delta Phi Kappa, Phi Delta Kappa. Home: 27 Jeffrey Rd Aldan PA 19018

STEH, BILL DRAGO, neuropsychologist; b. San Pedro, Calif., Oct. 22, 1971; s. Drago and Ann Steh; m. Kristi Lynn Wagner Steh, July 10, 1999; 1 child, Derek James Drago. BS in Biol. Psychology, U. Calif., 1993; PhD in Clin. Psychology/Neuropsychology, Calif. Sch. Profl. Psychology, 2000. Lic. psychologist Calif., 2002. Assoc., pvt. practice Neuroscience Associates, Inc., LA, 2001—; assoc. dir. clin. svcs. med. psychology assessment ctr. UCLA-Neuropsychatric Inst. and Hosp., 2003—. Adj. prof. Pepperdine U., Grad. Sch. Edn. and Psychology, Culver City, Calif., 2003—. Fellow, UCLA, Neuropsychiatric Inst. and Hosp., 2000—02; scholar, Calif. Sch. Profl. Psychology, Fresno, 1993—97. Mem.: APA, Internat. Neuropsychological Soc., Nat. Acad. Neuropsychology, Psi Chi. Avocations: baseball, exercise, weightlifting, music, backgammon. Office: UCLA-Neuropsychiatric Inst 760 Westwood Plz C8-734 Los Angeles CA 90095 Home Phone: 310-645-1778; Office Phone: 310-794-5300. E-mail: bsteh@mednet.ucla.edu.

STEHLE, EDWARD RAYMOND, secondary education educator, school system administrator; b. Pitts., May 30, 1942; s. Edward August and Mary Josephine (Veverka) S.; m. Alberta McConnell; 1 child, Christian Dollison (dec.). BA, U. Pitts., 1964; MA, Columbia U., 1966, doctoral student, 1966-68. Instr. European history C.W. Post Coll., Long Island U., Greenville, NY, 1967—68, Middlebury Coll., Vt., 1968-69; history master The Lawrenceville Sch., NJ, 1969—, dir. day students, 1978—83, asst. dir. coll. counseling, 1983—88, chmn. history dept., 1988—94; asst. dir. The NJ Scholars Program, Lawrenceville, 1981, dir., 1982—91, chmn. bd., 1988—96, bd. dirs., 1988—. Cons. U. Del. Sea Grant Coll., Newark, 1981-82; cons. on history of migrations Statue of Liberty-Ellis Island Found., NYC, 1985-88; mem. selection com. Morris County Summer Opportunities for Tchrs. Program, Morristown, NJ, 1985-86; trustee Craftsbury Chamber Players, Greensboro, Vt., 1985-89; N.E.H. Coun. for Basic Edn. fellowship ind. study in the humanities, 1997. Co-author: A Guide to Programming in Basic Plus, 1975; contbr. Harper's Encyclopedia of the Modern World, 1972. Vice pres. Assoc. Mems., Ch. of Christ, Greensboro, 1974-76, pres., 1976-78. Vis. scholar Cambridge U., Eng., 1996. Mem. Am. Hist. Assn., Nassau Club (Princeton, NJ), Mountainview Country Club (Greensboro, Vt.), N. Am. Conf. British Studies. Democrat. Episcopalian. Avocation: painting. Home: 2810 Main St Lawrenceville NJ 08648-1017 Office: The Lawrenceville Sch Main St Lawrenceville NJ 08620-2310 Office Phone: 609-620-6080. Business E-Mail: estehle@lawrenceville.org.

STEHMAN, FREDERICK BATES, gynecologic oncologist, educator; b. Washington, July 20, 1946; s. Vernon Andrew and Elizabeth Coats (Bates) S.; m. Helen Sellinger, July 17, 1971; children: Christine Renee, Eileen Patricia, Andrea Kathleen, Lara Michelle. AB, U. Mich., 1968, MD, 1972. Diplomate Am. Bd. Ob-gyn. Resident in ob-gyn. U. Kans. Med. Ctr., Kansas City, 1972-75, resident in surgery, 1975-77; fellow in gynecol. oncology UCLA, 1977-79; asst. prof., attending staff Ind. U. Med. Ctr., Indpls., 1979-83, assoc. prof., 1983-87, prof., 1987—, chief gynecol. oncology, 1984-88, interim chmn., 1992-94, chair 1994—; chief ob-gyn service Wishard Meml. Hosp., Indpls., 1987-95. Author: (with B.J. Masterson and R.P. Carter) Gynecologic Oncology for Medical Students, 1975; also articles. Nat. Cancer Inst. grantee, 1981-89. Fellow Am. Coll. Obstetricians and Gynecologists, ACS (chpt. dir. 1984-92); mem. AMA, Am. Soc. Clin. Oncology, Am. Cancer Soc., Am. Gynecology and Obstetrics Soc., Ind. Med. Assn., Assn. Profs. Gynecology and Obstetrics, Central Assn. Obstetricians and Gynecologists, Gynecol. Oncology Group, K.E. Krantz Soc., Marion County Med. Soc., Soc. Gynecol. Oncologists, Western Assn. Gynecol. Oncologists, Phi Chi. Office: Ind U Med Ctr 550 University Blvd # 2440 Indianapolis IN 46202-5149

STEIB, JAMES TERRY, bishop; b. May 17, 1940; Ordained priest Roman Cath. Ch., 1967. Titular bishop, Fallaba, 1983; aux. bishop St. Louis, 1983; consecrated bishop, 1984; bishop Diocese of Memphis, 1993—. Address: Diocese of Memphis PO Box 341669 Memphis TN 38184-1669

STEICHEN, RANDALL R., lawyer; b. 1952; BA cum laude, Northwestern Coll., 1976; JD with distinction, Univ. Iowa, 1980. Bar: Iowa 1981, Colo. 1982, Wash. 1989. Law clerk, Hon. Louis W. Schultz Iowa Supreme Ct., 1980—82; ptnr., trial practice group Dorsey & Whitney LLP, Seattle, and co-chair, construction and design law group. Arbitrator Am. Arbitration Assn. Mng. editor Iowa Law Rev., 1979—80, lectr., writer in field. Named a Super Lawyer, Wash. Law & Politics, 2003. Mem.: ABA, Associated Builders and Contractors of Western Wash. (v.p., bd. dir.), Ct. Fed. Claims Bar Assn., Board of Contract Appeals Bar Assn., Seattle-King County Bar Assn., Wash. State Bar Assn. Office: Dorsey & Whitney LLP Ste 3400 US Bank Ctr 1420 Fifth Ave Seattle WA 98101-4010 Office Phone: 206-903-8857. Office Fax: 206-903-8820. Business E-Mail: steichen.randall@dorsey.com.

STEIDEL, CHARLES C., astronomy educator; b. Ithaca, NY, Oct. 14, 1962; married. AB in Astrophysy. Scis., Princeton U., NJ, 1984; PhD in Astronomy, Calif. Inst. Tech., Pasadena, 1990. Parisot fellow U. Calif., Berkeley, 1989—90, Hubble fellow, 1990—93; asst. prof. physics MIT, Cambridge, Mass., 1993—95; asst. prof. astronomy Calif. Inst. Tech., 1995—97, assoc. prof., 1997—98, prof., 1998—. Mem. telescope allocation com. Cerro Tololo Inter-Am. Obs., 1994—97; mem. sci. steering com. Keck Obs., 1996—2003, co-chair sci. steering com., 1997—2003; mem. Hubble space telescope second decade com., 1998—99; mem. external sci. rev. panel Next Generation Space Telescope, 1998—99; mem. space scis. origins sub-com. NASA, 1998—2000; chair sci. working grp. Calif. Extremely Large Telescope, 1999—2002, co-chair steering com., 2000—02; mem. Hubble fellowship selection com., 2000; chair sci. adv. com. Thirty Meter Telescope (formerly Calif. Extremely Large Telescope), 2003—. Contbr. articles to sci. jours. Recipient Young Investigator award, NSF, 1994—99, Helen B. Warner prize, Am. Astron. Soc., 1997; fellow Alfred P. Sloan Found., 1994—96, David and Lucile Packard Found., 1997—2002, MacArthur Found., 2002. Mem.: NAS (US/Japan Frontiers in Sci. organizing com. 1997—98). Office: Calif Inst Tech Dept Astronomy 1201 E Calif Blvd Pasadena CA 91125-0001 Home: 230 S Arroyo Blvd Pasadena CA 91105

STEIDLEY, JUAN DWAYNE, lawyer, judge; b. Claremore, Okla., Mar. 8, 1959; s. J.D. and Gwendolyn Ann (Barnes) S.; m. Teresa Ann Brim, July 31, 1987; 1 child, Terrence. BA, Okla. State U., 1981; JD, Tulsa U., 1984. Bar: Okla. 1985. Judge, 1999—. Mem. Ho. of Rep. Okla. Ho. of Reps., Oklahoma City, 1986-98; past chmn. Sequoyah Dist. Boy Scouts Am. Methodist. Home: 2710 Highwood Ct Claremore OK 74017-4872 Office: Rogers County Court House 219 S Miss Divs II Claremore OK 74017

STEIER, AUDREY KELLER, music educator; b. Newark; d. Solomon Charles and Tillie (Tomarin) Keller; m. Herbert Steier (dec.); children: Marcy Byer, Lisa Moore, David. BS in Music Edn., NYU, 1956; Hebrew cert. and religious edn., Hebrew Union Coll. Jewish Inst. Religion. Music tchr. Elizabeth Bd. Edn., NJ, 1956—57; religious sch. music tchr. Temple B'Nai Jesurun, Short Hills, NJ, 1957—80, pre-sch. dir., 1966—91, youth group adv., 1980—82; pre-sch. dir. Temple Has Shalom, Warren, NJ, 1992—97. Cons. Various Pre-Sch., Essex County, 1990. Mem.: Nat. Coun. Jewish Women (life; v.p. 1980—93). Avocations: knitting, needlecrafts, travel, reading. Home: 4200 Cleveland Lane Rockaway NJ 07866

STEIGBIGEL, ROY THEODORE, epidemiologist, educator, research scientist; b. Bklyn., Nov. 23, 1941; s. Samuel and Lillian I. (Parker) S.; m. Julia Ann Enterline, June 10, 1967 (div. 1983), children: Keith D., Glenn N.; m. Sidonie Ann Morrison, Oct. 15, 1985; 1 child, Andrew M. BA, Carleton Coll., 1962; MD, U. Rochester, 1966. Diplomate Am. Bd. Internal Medicine, Am. Bd. Infectious Disease. Resident U. Rochester, NY, 1966-68, Stanford U., Palo Alto, Calif., 1970-71, fellow, 1971-73; from asst. to assoc. prof. U. Rochester, NY, 1973-83; prof. SUNY, Stony Brook, 1983—. Mem. adv. bd. infectious disease U.S. Pharmacopea, Rockville, Md., 1980—; mem. adv. panels NIH, Bethesda, Md., 1985-87. Contbr. over 15 chpts. to books and over 100 articles to profl. jours. Served in USPHS, 1968-70. Fellow NIH, 1971-73, grantee, 1985—. Fellow ACP, Infectious Disease Soc. Am. Office: SUNY Stony Brook Sch Medicine Hsc T 15 080 Stony Brook NY 11794-8153 Office Phone: 631-444-3490. Business E-Mail: roy.steigbigel@stonybrook.edu.

STEIGER, PAUL ERNEST, editor, journalist; b. NYC, Aug. 15, 1942; s. Ernest and Mary Agnes (Walsh) Steiger; m. Heidi Brine, Nov. 23, 1985 (div.); children: Isabelle Amanda, William Ernest; m. Wendy Brandes, July 22, 2001; children from previous marriage: Erika Maren, Laura Arlene. BA in economics, Yale U., 1964. Staff reporter Wall Street Jour., San Francisco, 1966-68, asst. mng. editor NYC, 1983-85, dep. mng. editor, 1985—91, mng. editor, 1991—2007, v.p., 1992—2007, editor-at-large, 2007—; staff writer LA Times, 1968-71, econ. corr. Washington, DC bur., 1971-78, bus. editor LA, 1978-83. Mem. Pulitzer Prize Bd., 1999—2007; rep., Dow Jones SmartMoney Bd., Wall Street Journal Mag., SmartMoney.com. Co-author: (book) The 70's Crash and How to Survive It, 1970. Chmn. Com. to Protect Journalists, 2005—. Recipient G.M. Loeb Award, UCLA, 1971, 1974, 1978, John Hancock Award, 1971, George Beveridge Editor of Yr. Award, Nat. Press Found., 2001, Leadership Award, Am. Soc. Newspaper Editors, 2002, Lifetime Achievement, John E. Anderson Sch. Mgmt., UCLA, 2002, Columbia Journalism Award, Columbia U. Sch. Journalism,

2002, Decade of Excellence Award, World Leadership Forum, 2005, Mo. Honor medal, Mo. Sch. Journalism, 2005; Poynter Fellow, Yale U., 2001—02. Office: Wall Street Journal Dow Jones & Co Inc 200 Liberty St New York NY 10281-1003 *

STEIGERWALD, LOUIS JOHN, III, corporate executive; b. Syracuse, NY, Dec. 24, 1953; s. Louis John Jr. and Virginia (Irving) S.; m. Mary Rescorl, May 31, 1980; children: Amy Elizabeth, Louis John IV. BS, St. Lawrence U., 1976. Salesperson Cathedral Candle Co., Syracuse, 1976-80, v.p., 1980-2001, pres., 2001—, also bd. dirs. Account exec. United Way Ctrl. NY, Syracuse, 1982-83, sect. chmn., 1984-85; active Boy Scouts Am., 1992-2003. Mem. Nat. Ch. Goods Assn. (bd. dirs. 1990-2000, pres. 1997, 98), Nat. Candle Assn. (bd. dirs. 1989-99, 2005—), Ea. Ch. Goods Guild, Onondaga Hist. Assn. (bd. dirs. 2004—). Avocations: golf, tennis, woodworking, skiing, music. Office: Cathedral Candle Co 510 Kirkpatrick St Syracuse NY 13208-2100

STEIKER, CAROL S., law educator; b. Phila., May 31, 1961; AB in History and Lit., Harvard-Radcliffe, 1982; JD, Harvard U., 1986. Bar: NY 1987, DC 1988. Law clk. to Judge J. Skelly Wright US Ct. Appeals DC Cir.; law clk. to Justice Thurgood Marshall US Supreme Ct.; asst. prof. law Harvard Law Sch., Cambridge, Mass., 1992—98, prof., 1998—, assoc. dean academic affairs, 1998—2001. Office: Harvard Law Sch 1563 Massachusetts Ave Cambridge MA 02138 Office Phone: 617-496-5457. Office Fax: 617-496-5156. Business E-Mail: steiker@law.harvard.edu.

STEIL, GEORGE KENNETH, SR., lawyer; b. Darlington, Wis., Dec. 16, 1924; s. George John and Laura (Donahoe) S.; m. Mavis Elaine Andrews, May 24, 1947; children: George Kenneth, John R., MIchelle Steil Bryski, Marcelaine Steil-Zimmermann. Student, Platteville State Tchrs. Coll., 1942-43; JD, U. Wis., Madison, 1950. Bar: Wis. 1950, U.S. Tax Ct. 1971, U.S. Dist. Ct. (western dist.) Wis. 1950. Assoc. J. G. McWilliams, Janesville, 1950-53; ptnr. McWilliams and Steil, Janesville, 1954-60, Brennan, Steil, Basting & MacDougall, Janesville, 1960-72; pres. Brennan, Steil & Basting (S.C., and predecessor), Janesville, 1972—. Lectr. law U. Wis., 1974; bd. dirs. Acuity Ins. Co., Sheboygan, Wis.; mem. fin. coun. Roman Cath. Diocese of Madison; mem. Wis. Supreme Ct. Bd. Atty. Profl. Responsibility, 1982-87, chmn., 1984-87; chmn. gov.'s adv. coun. jud. selection State of Wis., 1987-92; chmn. Wis. Lottery Bd., 1987-90. Bd. dirs. St. Coletta Sch. for Exceptional Children, Jefferson, Wis., 1972-76, 78-84, 86-89, chmn., 1982-83; bd. regents U. Wis., 1990-97, pres., 1992-94; bd. dirs. U. Wis. Hosp. Authority, 1996—2004, chmn., 2002-04; bd. dirs., chair U. Wis. Med. Found., 1996-99. Recipient Disting. Svc. award U. Wis. Law Alumni, 1991, Cath. Leadership awrd Diocese of Madison, 1998; named Knight of St. Gregory, Pope John Paul II, 1997. Fellow Am. Bar Found. (life), Am. Coll. Trust and Estate Counsel; mem. ABA, Jamesville Area C. of C. (pres. 1970-71), State Bar Wis. (pres. 1977-78), Wis. Bar Found. (bd. dirs. 1976-2003, Charles L. Goldberg Disting. Svc. award 1990). Roman Catholic. Home: 2818 Cambridge Ct Janesville WI 53548-2797 Office: PO Box 1148 1 E Milwaukee St Janesville WI 53545 Home Phone: 608-754-7119; Office Phone: 608-756-4141. Business E-Mail: gsteilsr@brennansteil.com.

STEIMAN, H. ROBERT, dean, dental educator; BS, ND State U., 1964; MS, Wayne State U., 1967, PhD in physiology, 1969; DDS, U. Detroit, 1973; MS in endodontics, Ind. U., 1979. Diplomate Am. Bd. Endodontics. Chmn. dept. physiology, dept. basic scis. U. Detroit-Mercy Sch. Dentistry, named chmn. dept. endodontics, 1980, interim dean, 2000—01, dean, 2001—. Office: 8200 W Outer Dr Box 98 Detroit MI 48219 Office Phone: 313-494-6621. Office Fax: 313-484-6627. Business E-Mail: steimanr@udmercy.edu.

STEIN, ADAM MATTHEW, military officer; b. West Palm Beach, Fla., Feb. 12, 1983; s. Lewis Michael and Bonita Robins Stein. BA in Polit. Sci., Duquesne U., Pitts., 2005; MBA, U. Pitts., 2007—. Sr. fin. svcs. cons. PNC Bank, Pitts., 2004—05; commd. USN, Pitts., 2005—. Pres. student exec. bd. Katz Bus. Sch. U. Pitts., 2006—. Navy Postgrad. scholar, USN, 2005. Democrat. Avocations: travel, reading, jogging, sports. Home: Apt 1702 1420 Centre Ave Pittsburgh PA 15219 Office Phone: 412-722-9643. Personal E-mail: amstein@gmail.com.

STEIN, ALLAN MARK, lawyer; b. Montreal, Quebec, Can., Oct. 18, 1951; came to U.S., 1977; s. Boris and Beatrice (Fishman) S. B in Commerce, Sir George Williams, 1972; BA, Loyola, Montreal, 1973; B in Civil Law, McGill U., 1976, LLB, 1976; JD, Nova U., 1979. Bar: Fla. 1979, U.S. Dist. Ct. (so. dist.) Fla. 1979, U.S. Ct. Appeals (5th cir.) 1980, U.S. Ct. Appeals (11th cir.) 1983, U.S. Dist. Ct. Ariz. 1993. Assoc. Law Offices of Paul Landy Beiley, Miami, Fla., 1980, Heitner & Rosenfeld, Miami, 1980-85, Rosenfeld & Stein, Miami, 1985-90, Rosenfeld, Stein & Sugarman, Miami, 1990-94, Rosenfeld & Stein P.A., Miami, 1994—. Mem. North Dade Bar Assn. (bd. dirs. 1985-90). Republican. Jewish. Avocations: photography, history. Office: 18260 NE 19th Ave Ste 202 Miami FL 33162-1632 Office Phone: 305-940-8080. Business E-Mail: allanstein@aol.com.

STEIN, ARLAND THOMAS, lawyer; b. Pitts., Nov. 19, 1938; s. Thomas Edward and Josephine Cecelia (Kiedaisch) Stein; m. Helen Marie Horin, Aug. 14, 1965; children: Thomas Arland, John Andrew, Christian Michael. BS in Engring. Sci., Purdue U., 1961, postgraduate student, 1960-62; LLB, U. Va., 1965. Bar: Pa. 1965, Ohio 1966, US Patent Office 1967, US Supreme Ct. 1969. Assoc. Blenko, Leonard & Buell, Pitts., 1965-71; ptnr. Yeager, Stein & Wettach, Pitts., 1971-74; Reed Smith Shaw & McClay, Pitts., 1974-1999, Barnes & Thornburg, Indianapolis, 1999-2005, Hahn, Loeser and Parks, 2005-. Mem. ABA, Allegheny County Bar Assn., Am. Patent Law Assn., Pitts. Patent Law Assn., Lic. Execs. Soc., Tau Beta Pi, Omicron Delta Kappa (charter, Purdue chpt.), Rose Ade Found., life mem. Rep. Lutheran. Clubs: Masons, KT, Duquesne Club, Columbia Club. Office: Hahn Loeser and Parks 65 E State St Ste 1400 Columbus OH 43215 Office Phone: 614-233-5104. E-mail: astein@hahnlaw.com.

STEIN, BARRY EDWARD, medical educator; BA, CUNY, Queens, 1966, MA, 1969; PhD, CUNY, 1971. Prof. dept. physiology Med. Coll. Va.-Va. Commonwealth U., Richmond, 1982-94, affil. prof., 1994—; prof., chair dept. neurobiology and anatomy Wake Forest U Sch. Medicine, Winston-Salem, NC, 1994—. Bd. trustees The Gwendolyn Hardy Williams and Oliver Williams Found., Inc., 1992—; lectr. in field. Co-author: The Merging of the Senses, 1993; contbr. chpts. to books including The Cognitive Neurosciences, 1995, 99, Electrophysiology of Vision, 1991, The Development of Intersensory Perception: Comparative Perspectives, 1994, others; co-editor: The Handbook of Multisensory Processes, 2004; mem. editl. bd. Jour. Cognitive Neuroscience, The Behavioral and Brain Sciences; contbr. numerous articles to profl. pubs. including Jour. Neurophysiology, Jour. Neurosci., Sci., Jour. Comparative Neurology, others. Home: 1825 Georgia Ave Winston Salem NC 27104-3101 Office: Wake Forest Sch Medicine Med Ctr Blvd Winston Salem NC 27157-0001 Business E-Mail: bestein@wfubmc.edu.

STEIN, BEN(JAMIN) (JEREMY), television personality, writer, lawyer, economist; b. Washington, Nov. 25, 1944; s. Herbert and Mildred (Fishman) S.; m. Alexandra Denman, June 22, 1968 (div. 1974); m. Alexandra Denman, 1977; 1 child, Thomas. BA, Columbia U., 1966; LLB, Yale U., 1970. Bar: Conn. Trial lawyer FTC, Washington, 1970-72; speech writer The White House, Washington, 1973-74; columnist Wall St. Jour., NYC, 1974-76; writer, commentator, columnist LA Herald-Examiner, 1978-87; TV personality Win Ben Stein's Money, Comedy Ctrl., 1997—; host Turn Ben Stein On Comedy Ctrl., 1999—2001. Fin. cons. LAACO, Inc., LA; contbg. editor Am. Spectator, 1980—; law and econs. tchr. Pepperdine, Malibu, 1992—; adj. prof. Am. U., Washington, U. Calif. Santa Cruz; spokesperson Clear Eyes eye drops. Author: On The Brink, 1977, The View from Sunset Boulevard, 1978, DREEMZ, 1978, Moneypower, 1980, 'Ludes, 1981, Financial Passages, 1986, A License to Steal, 1992, Tommy and Me, 1999, How To Ruin Your Life, 2002, How to Ruin Your Love Life, 2003, How to Ruin Your Financial Life, 2004, (with Phil DeMuth) You Can Time the Market!, 2003, Can America Survive? The Rage of the Left, the Truth, and What to Do about It, 2004, Yes, You Can Be a Successful Income Investor: Reaching for Yield in Today's Market, 2005, (with Philip De Muth) Mechanical and Electrical Equipment for Buildings, 1999; author numerous articles on leveraged buy-outs and other fin. frauds for Barrons, 1984—; syndicated columnist King Features Syndicate; regular columnist LA Mag., NY Mag., E! Online, N.Y. Times (Everybody's Money) SundayBusiness; contbr. Wash. Post, Wall St. Jour.; guest speaker on fin. Fox News Channel; co-creater: (TV series) Fernwood Tonight; actor: (films) The Wild Life, 1984, Ferris Bueller's Day Off, 1986 (ranked as one of 50 most famous scenes in Am. films), Planes, Trains, and Automobiles, 1987, Ghostbusters II, 1989, Soapdish, 1991, Honeymoon in Vegas, 1992, Dennis the Menace, 1993, My Girl 2, 1994, North, 1994, The Mask, 1994, Richie Rich, 1994, Miami Rhapsody, 1995, Casper, 1995; (TV series) The Wonder Years, 1988-91, (voice) Animaniacs, 1993, (voice) Freakazoid, 1995, (voice) Earthworm Jim, 1995, (voice) The Mask, 1995, (voice) Bruno the Kid, 1996, (voice) The Secret Files of the SpyDogs, 1998; (TV films) Mastergate, 1992, The Day My Parents Ran Away, 1993, (voice) Santa vs. the Snowman, 1997, Breakfast with Einstein, 1998; exec. prodr. Turn Ben Stein On, 1999; host: (TV series) Win Ben Stein's Money, 1997-2002 (Daytime Emmy award Outstanding Game Show Host, 1999); TV appearances include Charles in Charge, 1987, 88, 90, MacGyver, 1991, Melrose Place, 1993, Full House, 1993, Hearts Afire, 1993, 94, Tales from the Crypt, 1995, Lois & Clark: The New Adventures of Superman, 1995, Married...With Children, 1995, The Marshal, 1995, (voice) Duckman, 1996, 97, Seinfeld, 1997, Murphy Brown, 1997, Muppets Tonight!, 1998, (voice) Rugrats, 1998, The Drew Carey Show, 2001, (voice) The Adventures of Jimmy Neutron: Boy Genius, 2002, (voice) Family Guy, 2003, (voice) The Fairly Odd Parents, 2004; contbr. CBS TV News Mem. Writers Guild Am., Screen Actors' Guild, Am. Fedn. TV and Radio Actors, Yale Club NYC, Friars, LA Athletic Club, Calif. Yacht Club, Morningside Country Club. Republican. Jewish. Office: 8787 Shoreham Dr West Hollywood CA 90069-2231 Office Phone: 310-652-9406. Personal E-mail: benstein@aol.com.

STEIN, BERNARD ALVIN, retail executive, consultant; b. Winnipeg, Can., June 4, 1923; s. Herman Louis and Rebecca (Harris) S.; m. Dorothy Lock, Jan. 1, 1942; 1 dau., Marilynn Stein Lakein. Vice-pres. food drug div. Giant Food, Inc., Washington, 1951-69; v.p., gen. mgr. Read Drug Stores, Balt., 1969-70; pres. Scotty Stores div. Sav-A-Stop, Jacksonville, Fla., 1970-71; pres., gen. mgr. Liberal Markets, Dayton, Ohio, 1971-72; pres. Pueblo Supermarkets, San Juan, P.R., 1972-74, Hills Supermarkets, Brentwood, NY, 1974-75, Allied Supermarkets, Detroit, 1976-78, Chatham Supermarkets, Detroit, 1978-81; CEO Network Assocs., Chgo., 1981-92; bus. cons. Balt., 1992—; pres. Jewelery Markdowns, Inc., 2003—. Pres. Jewelry website business, 2003—. Mem. Presdl. Com. for Emergency Food Controls, 1969; mem. scholarship com. Am. Indian Edn. Found., 2004—. Served with USAAF, 1943-45. Decorated Air medal. Home: 7902 Brynmor Ct # 104 Pikesville MD 21208-4351 Office Phone: 410-486-3099. Personal E-mail: bernie230@comcast.net. E-mail: jewelrymd@comcast.net.

STEIN, BERNARD L., journalist; b. Cleve. m. Marguerite Adams; 1 child, Anna. BA in Lit., Columbia U., 1963; postgrad., U. Calif., Berkeley, 1964—66; DHL (hon.), Manhattan Coll., 1999. Editor Riverdale Press, 1978—2005, co-pub., 1980—. Mem. team of scholars editing Mark Twain's writing for pub. U. Calif. Press; James H. Ottaway Disting. vis. prof. SUNY, New Paltz, NY, 2002; prof. journalism Hunter Coll. CUNY, 2005—. Named Writer of the Yr., N.Y. Press Assn., 1986; recipient First Amendment award, Soc. Profl. Journalists, 1989, Pulitzer Prize for editl. writing, 1998. Office: c/o Riverdale Press 6155 Broadway Bronx NY 10471-3136 Office Phone: 718-543-6065. Business E-Mail: bstein@riverdalepress.com.

STEIN, BRADLEY DANIEL, child and adolescent psychiatrist, researcher; b. Pitts., Dec. 13, 1964; s. Richard Marvin Stein and Elsa Audrey Beckerman; m. Allison Suzanne Liss, Feb. 3, 1996; children: Rachel Leia, Devon Andrew, Dylan Michael. BA, Georgetown U., Washington, DC, 1986; MD, U. Pitts., 1990, MPH, 1996, MPH, 1997; PhD, RAND Grad. Sch., Santa Monica, Calif., 2002. Lic. Adult Psychiatry Am. Bd. Psychiatry and Neurology, 1997. Asst. prof. psychiatry Western Psychiat. Inst. and Clinic, U. Pitts., 1996—97, assoc. prof. psychiatry, 2005—; Robert Wood Johnson clin. scholar UCLA, 1997—99; health svcs. rsch. RAND Corp., Santa Monica, 1997—; asst. prof. rsch. psychiatry, divsn. child psychiatry U. So. Calif., LA, 1999—2005; sr. dir. rsch., evaluation and outcomes Cmty. Care Behavioral Health Orgn., Pitts., 2005—. Psychiat. cons. Internat. Rescue Com., Bosnia-Herzegovina and Croatia, 1994; consulting psychiatrist LA Unified Sch. Dist. Mental Health Svcs. Unit, 1997—2006; assoc. dir. mental and behavioral health RAND Ctr. for Domestic and Internat. Health Security, Santa Monica, 2003—05. Mem.: Am. Acad. Child and Adolescent Psychiatry (Norbert and Charlotte Rieger Svc. Program award for Excellence 2006). Avocations: soccer, travel, reading. Office: Cmty Care Behavioral Health 112 Washington Pl Ste 700 Pittsburgh PA 15219 Home Phone: 412-422-1554; Office Phone: 412-454-8633.

STEIN, CHRIS, musician; b. Bklyn., Jan. 5, 1950; m. Barbara Sicuranza, 1999; 1 child, Akira. Co-founder, guitarist Blondie, 1974—82, 1997—. Musician: (albums) Blondie, 1976, Plastic Letters, 1977, Parallel Lines, 1978, Eat to the Beat, 1979, Autoamerican, 1980, The Hunter, 1982, No Exit, 1999, Livid, 2000, The Curse of Blondie, 2004, Live, 2004, Best Live, 2005. Named to Rock and Roll Hall of Fame, 2006. Office: c/o 10th St Entertainment Ste G410 700 San Vicente Blvd West Hollywood CA 90069

STEIN, DANIEL ALAN, lawyer; b. Washington, Mar. 9, 1955; s. Edward Seymour and Ann Rose Stein; m. Sharon McCloe, Oct. 18, 1986; children: Claire, Corrieanne. BA, Ind. U., 1977; JD, Cath. U. Am., 1984. Bar: D.C. 1984, U.S. Dist. Ct. D.C. 1985, U.S. Ct. Appeals (D.C. cir.) 1987, U.S. Tax Ct. 1987, Md. 2002, U.S. Dist. Ct. Md. 2003. Profl. staff mem. select com. on narcotics abuse and control U.S. Ho. of Reps., Washington, 1977—81; pvt. practice Washington, 1984—89; exec. dir. Immigration Reform Law Inst., Washington, 1986—88, Fedn. for Am. Immigration Reform, Washington, 1982—86, 1989—2004, pres., 2004—. Mem. Capitol Hill Club, Nat. Press Club. Republican. Avocations: trombone, american history, western civilization, jazz, antique books. Office: Fedn for Am Immigration Reform 1666 Connecticut Ave NW Ste 400 Washington DC 20009-1039 Office Phone: 202-328-7004.

STEIN, DAVID ERIC, physicist, defense analyst, futurist, retired military officer; b. Jacksonville, Fla., Jan. 13, 1950; s. Stanley Wolfe and Dorothy Jean (Lilley) S. BS with high honors, U. Fla., 1971, postgrad., 1971-72, MS in Physics, 1977; grad., Air Command and Staff Coll., 1982, Naval War Coll., 1995, Air War Coll., 1996. Instr. dept. physics U. Fla., Gainesville, 1971-74, NSF rsch. asst., 1974-76; 1st lt. US Army, 1977—79; capt. USAF, 1979—87; transferred to USAF Reserve, 1987, maj., 1989—94, lt. col., 1994—99; with USAF HQ Air Force Systems Command, Andrews AFB, Md., 1992, Air Force Sci. adv. bd., 1994-95; project engr. advanced surveillance concepts Rome Air Devel. Ctr., 1979-81; field engr. radar systems test and evaluation Rome Air Devel. Ctr. and MIT Lincoln Lab., 1981-83; radar data and imagery analyst 6585th Test Group, Holloman AFB, N.Mex., 1983-87; elec. engr. specialist LTV Aircraft Products Group, 1987-90; fellow engr. Westinghouse Electric Corp., 1990-91; ops. rsch. analyst CSCI, 1992-94, Office of Asst. Sec. of Air Force, 1995, 96-97, Joint Staff, 1996, 98-99, Army Digitization Office, 1999-2000, CACI, 2000—03, Northrop Grumman Info. Tech., 2003—. Part-time coll. faculty, 1982-84; short course instr. radar techs. George Washington U., 1991-97; adv. assoc. editor NATO Advanced Rsch. Workshop, Bad Windsheim, Germany, 1988; cons., 1994—. Editor-in-chief Applied Computational Electromagnetics Soc. Jour., 1987-93, FUTUREtakes, 2003-; assoc. sci. editor: Frontier Perspectives, 2000—; contbr. articles to profl. jours.; patentee in field. Recipient Disting. Svc. award Applied Computational Electromagnetics Soc., 1994; fellow Alpha Found.'s Inst. for Advanced Study; J. Hillis Miller Meml. scholar U. Fla., Ford Found. fellow. Mem. Am. Phys. Soc., Am. Assn. Physics Tchrs., World Affairs Coun., World Future Soc., Army-Navy Club, Philos. Soc. Washington, Fla. Blue Key, Phi Beta Kappa, Sigma Pi Sigma, Omicron Delta Kappa, Phi Kappa Phi. Achievements include identification of new atmospheric refractivity effects on low-altitude radar propagation, extended quantum-mech. computational technique to electromagnetic scattering, co-pioneered new acquisition sizing methodology for next-generation fighter aircraft; co-authored section of Defense Critical Technologies Plan for the Executive Office of the President; key advisor to Air Force Requirements Oversight Council; mem. U.S. delegation to NATO Y2K integrated process team; identified non-Y2K compliant NATO command and control systems and possible impact to interconnected U.S. systems; identified systems acquisition implications of alternative geostrategic futures, asymmetric-capable adversaries, new concepts in warfare, futuristic techs; co-pioneered modeling and simulation as a technology investment planning tool for an uncertain and rapidly changing national security environment. Home: PO Box 169 Linthicum Heights MD 21090-0169 Home Phone: 410-385-3315; Office Phone: 202-452-5592. Home Fax: 410-385-3315. Personal E-mail: futuretakes@cs.com.

STEIN, DAVID FRED, investment company executive; b. NYC, May 17, 1940; s. William Howard and Phoebe Louise (Hockstader) S.; m. Susan Vail Berresford, June 17, 1963 (div. 1970); 1 child, Jeremy Vail; m. Ellen Gail Cohen, Sept. 16, 1973; children: Katharine Ellen, Nicholas David. BA, Harvard U., 1962; MBA, Harvard Grad. Sch. Bus. Adminstrn., 1965. Assoc. Bache & Co., NYC, 1965-68; assoc., then gen. ptnr. Kuhn Loeb & Co., NYC, 1969-77; mng. dir. Lehman Brothers Kuhn Loeb, NYC, 1977-83, Shearson Lehman Am. Express, NYC, 1983-86; sr. exec. v.p., dir. Am. Express Bank, NYC, 1986-87; mng. dir. Shearson Lehman Hutton, NYC, 1987-89; mng. dir., mem. exec. com. The Stamford Co., NYC, 1989-90; mng. dir. J & W Seligman & Co., NYC, 1990-96, vice chmn., 1997—; co-chmn. Seligman Henderson Co., NYC, 1991-98. Bd. dirs. Griffin Land & Nurseries Inc. Trustee P.R. Traveling Theatre, NYC, 1970-72, Altro Health and Rehab. Ctr., Bronx, NY, 1975-82, Montefiore Med. Ctr., Bronx, 1990—, Montefiore Health Svcs., 2006—, Our Lady of Mercy Hosp., 2006—, Children's Aid Soc., 2000—; trustee Blythedale Children's Hosp., Valhalla, NY, 1977-2001, hon. trustee, 2001—; trustee Riverdale Country Sch., Bronx, 1988-2000, chmn. bd. trustees, 1997-2000, trustee emeritus, 2005—; active Coun. on Fgn. Rels. With U.S. Army, 1962-63. Mem. Nat. Assn. Security Dealers (internat. com. 1970-85), Century Country Club (Purchase, N.Y.), River Club (NYC), Harvard Club (NYC), Edgartown (Mass.) Yacht Club, Mill Reef Club (Antigua, Brit. V.I.), Chappaquiddick Beach Club (Edgartown), Reading Room Club (Edgartown). Democrat. Avocations: reading, sailing, bicycling, fishing. Home: 875 Park Ave New York NY 10021-0341 Office: J & W Seligman 100 Park Ave Fl 8 New York NY 10017-5516

STEIN, ELEANOR BANKOFF, retired judge; b. NYC, Jan. 24, 1923; d. Jacob and Sarah Rashkin Bankoff; m. Frank S. Stein, May 27, 1947; children: Robert B., Joan Jenkins, William M. Student, Barnard Coll., 1940—42; BS in Econ., Columbia U., NYC, 1944; LLB, N.Y. U., NYC, 1949; grad., Ind. Jud. Coll., 1986. Bar: N.Y. 1950, Ind. 1976, U.S. Supreme Ct. 1980. Atty. Hillis & Button, Kokomo, Ind., 1975—76, Paul Hillis, 1976—78, Bayliff, Harrigan, 1978—80; judge Howard County Ct., 1981—89; ret., 1989. Co-referee Howard County Juvenile Ct., Kokomo, 1976—78. Mem. Rep. Women's Assn. Kokomo, 1980—; bd. dir. Kokomo Human Rels. Commn., Ind., 1967—70, Howard County Legal Aid Soc., 1976—80; bd. advisors St. Joseph Hosp., 1979—2000; bd. dir. Howard County Children's Ctr., 1993—98. Mem.: ABA, Howard County Bar Assn., Ind. Bar Assn., Nat. Assn. Women Judges, Ind. Jud. Assn., Am. Judicature Soc., Kokomo Country Club. Jewish. Home: 3204 Tally Ho Dr Kokomo IN 46902 Personal E-mail: eleanorbstein@aol.com.

STEIN, ELIAS M., mathematician, educator; b. Antwerp, Belgium, Jan. 13, 1931; arrived in US, 1941; s. Elkan and Chana (Goldman) S.; m. Elly Intrator, Mar. 21, 1959; children— Jeremy, Karen AB, U. Chgo., 1951, MA, 1953, PhD, 1955; degree (hon.), Peking U., 1988, U. Chgo., 1992. Instr. MIT, Cambridge, 1956-58; asst. prof., then assoc. prof. U. Chgo., 1958-63; mem. Inst. for Advanced Study, Princeton, N.J., 1962-63, 1984-85; prof. dept. math. Princeton U., N.J., 1963—, chmn. dept. math. N.J., 1968-70, N.J., 1985-87. Author: Singular Integrals and Differentiability Properties of Functions, 1970 (Am. Math. Soc. Steele prize 1984), Topics in Harmonic Analysis Related to the Littlewood-Paley Theory; co-author: (with G. Weiss) Introduction to Fourier Analysis on Euclidean Spaces, Harmonic Analysis, 1993; contbr. articles to profl. jours. NSF fellow, 1955-56, sr. post-doctoral fellow, 1962-63, 71-72; Sloan Found. fellow, 1961-63; Guggenheim Found. fellow, 1976-77, 1984-85, Wolf prize in math., Wolf Found., Israel, 1999, Nat. Medal of Sci., 2002. Mem. NAS, Am. Acad. Arts and Scis., Am. Math. Soc., Swedish Acad. of Scis. (Schock prize 1993). Home: 132 Dodds Ln Princeton NJ 08540-4106 Office: Princeton U Dept Math 802 Fine Hall Washintgon Rd Princeton NJ 08544-0001 Office Phone: 609-258-6463. Business E-Mail: stein@math.princeton.edu.

STEIN, ELLEN GAIL, information technology manager; b. NYC, May 19, 1951; d. Manuel W. and Bella (Skutel) Stein. BA, SUNY, Stony Brook, 1972; M of Urban Planning, Hunter Coll., 1976; cert. program execs. state/local govt., Harvard U., 1985. Sr. rsch. assoc. Nassau Suffolk (N.Y.) Regional Med. Program, 1976-77; sr. planner N.Y.C. Dept. Correction, 1977—79; group leader criminal justice Mayor's Office, Dept. Ops., 1979—81, dep. asst. dir. citywide spl. projects, 1981, dir. citywide audit implementation, 1981—84; adminstr. Bur. Supplied N.Y.C. Bd. Edn., NYC, 1984—90; mgmt. cons. Project Provide Hope, Russia, Citizen's Budget Commn., 1990-94; pres., CEO FEDVentures Inc., 1994-99; assoc. commnr. office first dep. commr. N.Y.C. Dept. Tech. and Telecomm., 1999—. Mem. Nat. Assn. Purchasing Mgmt., Am. Women Econ. Devel., Ctrl. Women's Focus, Gov.'s Procurement Coun. (N.Y.), Human Svcs. Coun. (contracting com.). Office: 75 Park Pl Fl 9 New York NY 10007-2146 Office Phone: 212-788-2345. Personal E-mail: egstein@hotmail.com. Business E-Mail: estein@doitt.nyc.gov.

STEIN, ELLIOT, JR., business executive; b. St. Louis, Jan. 31, 1949; s. Elliot and Mary Ann (Bleiweiss) S.; m. Pamela Sztybel, Oct. 4, 1997. BA, Claremont McKenna Coll., 1971. Assoc. Lehman Bros., NYC, 1972-79; chmn. Caribbean Internat. News Corp., San Juan, 1985—; ptnr. Commonwealth Capital Ptnrs., NYC, 1988—. Bd. dirs. Apollo Investment Corp., VTG Holdings, Inc., Cloud Solutions LLC; adv. bd. Investigative Group Internat., 1998—. Trustee Claremont Grad. U., 1980—, New Sch. U., 1990—; bd. councillors Annenberg Sch. Comm., U. So. Calif., 1998—. Democrat. Office: Commonwealth Capital Ptnrs 509 Madison Ave Ste 604 New York NY 10022

STEIN, ERIC, retired law educator; b. Holice, Czechoslovakia, July 8, 1913; arrived in US, 1940, naturalized, 1943; s. Zikmund and Hermina (Zalud) Stein; m. Virginia Elizabeth Rhine, July 30, 1955. JUD, Charles U., Prague, Czechoslovakia, 1937; JD, U. Mich., 1942; Dr. honoris causa, Vrije U., Brussels, 1978, U. Libre, 1979, West-Bohemian U., Pilsen, Czech Republic, 1997. Bar: Ill. 1946, DC 1953. Practiced law, Prague, 1937; with State Dept., 1946-55; acting dep. dir. Office UN Polit. Affairs, 1955; mem. faculty U. Mich. Law Sch., Ann Arbor, 1956, prof. internat. law and orgn., 1958-76, Hessel E. Yntema prof. law, 1976-83, emeritus prof., 1983—; co-dir. internat. legal studies, 1958-76; dir., 1976-81. Vis. prof. Stanford Law Sch., 1956, 77, Law Faculties, Stockholm, Uppsala, Lund, Sweden, 1969, Inst. Advanced Legal Studies U. London, London, 1975, U. Ariz., 1991, 92; lectr. Hague Acad. Internat. Law, 1971; vis. lectr. European U. Inst., Florence, Italy, 1983, Jean Monnet prof., 91; vis. lectr. Acad. European Law, Beijing, 1986, Shanghai, 90, U. Tokyo, Kyoto, 1986, Coll. Europe, Madrid, 1988, Bruges, Paris, Heidelberg, Germany; Henry Morris lectr Kent Coll. Law, Chgo., 1992; Jeanne Kiewit Taylor disting. vis. lectr. U. Ariz., 1993; adviser US del. UN Gen. Assembly, 1947—55; mem. adv. panel, cons. Bur. European Affairs, State Dept., 1966—73; cons. US rep. for trade negotiations, 1979; vice chmn. com. Atlantic studies Atlantic Inst., 1966—68; mem. adv. coun. Inst. European Studies Free U., Brussels, 1965—70; mem. US Com. Legal Edn. Exch. with China, 1983—91; lectr. Acad. European Law, Florence, 1990. Author (with others): American Enterprise in the European Common Market-A Legal Profile, vols I, II, 1960; author: (with H. K. Jacobson) Diplomats, Scientists and Politicians: The United States and the Nuclear Test Ban Negotiations, 1966 (U. Mich. Press Best Book of Yr. award); author: Harmonization of European Company Law: National Reform and Transnational Coordination, 1971, Impact of New Weapons Technology on International Law-Selected Aspects, 1971, Un Nuovo Diritto per l'Europa, 1991, Czecho/Slovakia: Ethnic Conflict, Constitutional Fissure, Negotiated Breakup, 1997, Czech translation, 2000, Thoughts from a Bridge: A Retrospective of Writings on New Europe and American Federalism, 2000 (U. Mich. Press Best Book of Yr. award); editor (with Peter Hay): Law and Institutions in the Atlantic Area, Readings, Cases and Problems, 1987; editor: (with Peter Hay and Michel Waelbrock) European Community Law and Institutions in Perspective, 1976; co-author, co-editor: Courts and Free Markets-Perspectives from the United States and Europe, 1982; bd. editors Am. Jour. Internat. Law, 1965—, mem. adv. bd. Common Market Law Rev., 1964—, Legal Issues of European Integration, 1974—, Rivista di Diritto Europeo, 1978—, Columbia Jour. E. European Law, 1994—, Columbia Jour. European Law, 1994—; contbr. articles to profl. jours. Mem. Internat. Com. Revision Czechoslovak Constn., 1990—92. With US Army, 1943—46. Decorated Bronze Star, Order Italian Crown, Italian Mil. Cross; named Hon. Citizen of Hometown Holice, Czech. Republic, 2001; recipient Lifetime Achievement medal, Am. Soc. Comparative Law, 2004, Lifetime Contbn. prize, European Union Studies Assn., 2005, First Degree Outstanding Scholarly Achievement medal, Pres. Czech. Republic, 2001, Gold medal, Charles U., Prague, 2005; fellow, Inst. Advanced Study, Berlin, 1984—85; Gugenheim fellow, 1962—63, Social Sci. Rsch. Coun. grantee, Rockefeller Found. scholar-in-residence, 1965, 1973, Alexander von Humboldt Stiftung grantee, 1982, Rsch. grantee, IREX, 1995. Mem.: ABA (co-chmn. European law com. 1982, mem. coun. sect. internat. law and practice 1983—84), Internat. Acad. Comparative Law, Brit. Inst. Internat. and Comparative Law, Am. Soc. Internat. Law (exec. coun. 1954—57, bd. rev. and devel. 1965—67, 1970—75, hon. v.p. 1982—2000), European Studies Assn., Coun. Fgn. Rels., Internat. Law Assn. Home: 2649 Heather Way Ann Arbor MI 48104-2850 Office Phone: 734-764-0541. E-mail: steine@umich.edu.

STEIN, FLORENCE TAUB, retired social worker; b. Bklyn. d. Isidor and Mary Marcus Taub; m. Milton Stein, June 23, 1949 (dec.); children: Susan D., Joseph L. BA in Social Work, NY U., NYC, 1938; MS, Columbia U. Sch. Social Work, NYC, 1941. ACSW. Social worker Bklyn. Jewish Hosp., 1941—44, social work supr., 1944—46, Grace New Haven Hosp., 1946—48; social work cons. NY Dept. Health, NYC, 1948—51; dir. dept. social work Kingsbrook Hosp., Bklyn., 1951—55; assoc. dir. social work Maimonides Hosp., Bklyn., 1964—67; cons. staff edn. Mt. Sinai Hosp., NYC, 1967—69; asst. prof. social work Mt. Sinai Sch. Medicine, NYC, 1968—69; asst. dir. to assoc. dir. dept. social work Roosevelt Hosp., NYC, 1969—78; dir. dept. social work St. Luke's Roosevelt Hosp., NYC, 1978—82; social work cons. Columbia U. Sch. Social Work, NYC, 1982—87. Chair pers. practices, merger com. Jewish Family Svcs. South Middlesex County, East Brunswick, 1986—2006, bd. mem., 1986—2006, Jewish Family Social Soc. Svcs., Edison, 2006—, Jewish Family and Vocat. Svcs. Middlesex County, 2006—. Editor conf. proceedings; contbr. articles to profl. jours. Commr. Office on Aging Monroe Twp., NJ, 1997—; pres. Monroe Twp. Hadassah, NJ, 1988—90, Sisterhood Rossmoor Jewish Congregation; v.p. Southern NJ Region Hadassah, Neptune, 2001—03; bd. mem. Cancer Care, NYC, 1982. Named Citizen of Yr., Kiwanis, 1991; recipient Outstanding Leadership as Pres., Met. NY Soc. Hosp. Social Work Dirs., 1978, honors as chair merger com., Jewish Family and Vocational Svcs., 2006, proclamation, NJ State Senate and Gen. Assembly, 2006. Mem.: Soc. Social Work, Leadership in Health Care (pres. 1978), Nat. Assn. Social Workers (life). Democrat. Jewish. Avocations: bridge, dance, shuffleboard, reading. Home: 604 A Tilton Way Monroe Township NJ 08831-2002

STEIN, FRANKLIN JOSEPH, language educator; b. Eau Claire, Wis., Mar. 26, 1945; s. Herbert Charles Stein and Gwenn Marie Lassek. BS in Secondary Edn., U. Wis., Eau Claire, 1968; BS in Computer Sci., Coleman Coll., La Mesa, Calif., 1989, MIS in Info. Sys., 1995. Cert. tchr. Wis., Thailand, TESOL/TEFL LC Coaching Sch., Calif., 2007. Biology, sci., Spanish tchr. Stanley-Boyd HS, Stanley, Wis., 1968-71; salesman Jerry's Hammond Organ & Piano Studios, Eau Claire, Wis., 1971—72; dept. mgr. Day Music Co., Eau Claire, 1973—74; store mgr. Tropic Waters Pet Store, Eau Claire, 1975-76, Thearle Music Co., San Diego, 1977—82; 6th grade tchr. St. Paul's Luth. Sch., Pacific Beach, Calif., 1977-78; profl. theatre organist Organ Power Pizza Restaurants, San Diego, 1977-85; store mgr. Organ Stop Inc., San Diego, 1982—89; computer programmer analyst Health Examinetics, Rancho Bernardo, Calif., 1989-91; clin. computer systems specialist SHARP Health Care, San Diego, 1991—97; systems programmer/clin. analyst U. Calif., San Diego, 1997—2002; counselor emotionally disturbed youth New Alternatives, Inc. Comprehensive Adolescent Treatment Ctr., San Diego, 2003—04; tchr. English Thailand, 2007—. Profl. musician, 1965—. Author: Technician's Manual of Thermography, 1987, IDXrad User's Manual & Annual Updates, 1991-97; editor: Manual of Thermography, 1988. Music dir., organist Airman Meml. Chapel US Marine Corps Air Sta., Miramar, Calif., 1996—2007; sponsor PLAN USA/Childreach, 2000—. Recipient Silver medal Piano Performance Wis. Music Educators, 1962, 63, Cert. of Merit for Excellence in Sci., Wis. Jr. Acad. of Sci., 1963. Democrat. Buddhist. Avocation: classical music. Home and Office: 10227 Kamwood Pl San Diego CA 92126-5139 Personal E-mail: fjstein@msn.com.

STEIN, GARY S., retired judge, lawyer; b. Newark, June 13, 1933; s. Morris J. and Mollie (Goldfarb) S.; married, July 1, 1956; children— Jill, Carrie, Michael, Terri, Jo; m. Et Tilchin, July 1, 1956 AB, Duke U., 1954, LL.B. with distinction, 1956; D.H.L. (hon.), N.J. Inst. Tech., 1985. Bar: D.C. 1956, Ohio 1957, N.Y. 1958, N.J. 1963. Research asst. U.S. Senate AntiTrust and Monopoly Subcom., Washington, 1955; assoc. Kramer, Marx, Greenlee & Backus, NYC, 1956-65; sole practice Paramus, NJ, 1966-72; ptnr. Stein & Kurland, Esquires, Paramus, NJ, 1972-82; dir. Gov.'s Office of Policy and Planning, Trenton, NJ, 1982-85; assoc. justice Supreme Ct. N.J., Hackensack, 1985—2002, ret., 2002; counsel Pashman Stein, Hackensack, 2002—. Mcpl. atty., Paramus, 1967-71; counsel N.J. Election Law Revision Commn., 1970; atty. Bd. Adjustment, Teaneck, N.J., 1973-82 Mem. editl. bd. Duke Law Jour., 1954-56, assoc. editor, 1955-56. Mem. Dist. Ethics Com. for Bergen County, N.J., 1977-80, chmn. 1981. Served with U.S. Army, 1957-58, 61-62 Mem. ABA, N.J. State Bar Assn. (com. on state legislation 1973-79, chmn. 1973-76, jud. selection com. 1976-81, Constl. amendment com. 1977-79, court modernization com. 1976-79), Bergen County Bar Assn., Order of Coif. Jewish. Avocation: tennis. Office: Pashman Stein Ct Plaza South 21 Main St Hackensack NJ 07601 Office Phone: 201-488-8200. Business E-Mail: gstein@pashmanstein.com.

STEIN, GEORGE HENRY, historian, educator, administrator; b. Vienna, May 18, 1934; came to U.S., 1939, naturalized, 1948. m. Dorothy Ann Lahm, Nov. 22, 1963; 1 child, Kenneth. BA with honors (State Regents scholar), Bklyn. Coll., 1959; MA in History (Regents fellow), Columbia U., 1960, PhD in History (Pres.'s fellow), 1964. Lectr. history City Coll., CUNY, 1962-63; instr. dept. history Columbia U., NYC, 1963-65, asst. prof., 1965-66; assoc. prof. dept. history SUNY-Binghamton, 1966-70, prof., 1970-73, disting. teaching prof., 1973-98, emeritus, 1998—, vice chmn. grad. affairs, 1974-76, v.p. acad. affairs, 1976-87, provost, 1985-87, acting pres., 1986-87. Manuscript evaluator and cons. to numerous publishers, 1964—. Author: The Waffen SS: Hitler's Elite Guard at War, 1939-45, 1966, paperback edit., 1984 (transl. into German, 1967, French, 1967, Spanish, 1973, Portuguese, 1970, Japanese, 2002, Finnish, 2004); contbr. articles on modern European history to scholarly publs.; editor: Hitler, 1968; contbr. book revs. to hist. jours. Served with USAF, 1953-57. NEH fellow, 1970-71 Mem. Am. Hist. Assn. (mem. conf. group on cen. European history, conf. group for use of psychology in history), Acad. Polit. Sci., Assn. of Contemporary Historians, Am. Assn. Higher Edn., Nat. Assn. State Univs. and Land Grant Colls. (mem. council acad. affairs 1976-87), Am. Counc. Edn. (exec. com. nat. coun. chief acad. officers 1983-85), Com. Internat. d'Histoire de la Deuxieme Guerre Mondiale, WWII Studies Assn. Office: SUNY Dept History Binghamton NY 13902-6000 Home: 395 Savage Farm Dr Ithaca NY 14850

STEIN, GRANT T., lawyer; b. Chgo., Aug. 4, 1956; BBA cum laude, Emory Univ., 1978; JD cum laude, Univ. Ga., 1981. Bar: Ga. 1981. Law clk., Hon. W. Homer Drake US Bankruptcy Ct. (no. dist.), Georgia; ptnr., head, Bankruptcy, Reorganization and Workouts Group Alston & Bird, LLP, Atlanta. Exec. com. Emory Univ. Bd. Visitors. Fellow: Am. Coll. Bankruptcy; mem.: Southeastern Bankruptcy Law Inst. (dir.), Assn. of Insolvency and Restructuring Advisors (dir., v.p.). Office: Alston & Bird LLP One Atlantic Ctr 1201 W Peachtree St NW Atlanta GA 30309-3424 Office Phone: 404-881-7285. Office Fax: 404-881-7777. Business E-Mail: gstein@alston.com.

STEIN, HOWARD S., retired banker; b. NYC, Dec. 27, 1939; s. J. Zachary and Adele (Epstein) S. BA, U. Mich., 1961; MBA, Harvard U., 1963. Mem. treas.'s staff Gen. Motors Corp., NYC, 1963-69; dep. dir., dir. fiscal ops. Human Resources Adminstrn., City of N.Y., 1969-71, dep. adminstr., 1972-74, 1st dep. adminstr., 1974-78; asst. commr. Manpower and Career Devel. Agy., NYC, 1971-72; dep. commr. rent and housing maintenance Housing and Devel. Adminstrn., City of N.Y., 1972; v.p. Citicorp Credit Services Inc., NYC, 1979-86; sr. v.p. Citicorp Retail Services Inc., NYC, 1986-87; exec. dir. Landmark Mut. Funds Group of Citibank, N.A., NYC, 1987-88; v.p. br. banking sect. devel. div. Citibank NA, 1989-91, sr. credit officer worldwide securities svcs. div. Fin. Instns. Group NYC, 1991-94; group risk mgr. Global Transaction Svcs., NYC, 1995—2001, head operational risk mgmt., emerging markets and transaction svcs., 2002—03; mng. dir., head operational risk mgmt. Global Corp. and Investment Bank, 2003—04; ret., 2004; treas., bd. dirs. Applecore Ptnrs. (formerly Ptnrs. of '63), 1999—; sr. advisor Fortent (formerly Searchpace Corp.), 2005—; chmn. adv. com. Risk Bus., 2006—. Lectr. human resources policy Nova U., Ft. Lauderdale, Fla., 1973-74; field instr. adminstrn. specialization NYU Sch. Social Work, 1976-77; mem. risk mgmt. com. Participants Trust Co., 1995-99. Past Bd. dirs., chmn. program com. Vol. Urban Cons. Group, Inc.; past chmn. bd. dirs. Nova Inst; past treas., past pres., bd. dirs. Child Study Assn. Am./Wel-Met, Inc., 1963-85; past treas., bd. dirs. Career Center for Social Services Greater N.Y., Inc.; past treas., past pres. bd. dirs. Cavalier King Charles Spaniel Club U.S.A., Inc.; past bd. dirs., past sec. Child Welfare Info. Services; treas., bd. dirs., chmn. fin. com. WNYC Radio; bd. dirs. Senate Residence Owners Inc., New Goddard-Riverside Housing Devel. Fund Co., N.Y.C. Health and Hosps., Corp., 1976,; past bd. dirs. Homes for the Homeless; past mem. corp. Children's Mus., Boston; bd. dirs., treas., chair fin. com. Goddard Riverside Neighborhood House; trustee, chair fin. com. Pratt Inst.; treas., bd. dirs. Applecore Ptnrs., 1999—; past mem. Dept. Disciplinary com. Supreme Ct. State N.Y. Appellate Divsn. 1st Jud. Dept.; past mem. corp. adv. com. U. Mich., Coll. Lit., Sci and the Arts, treas.; bd. dirs. The Childrens' Cause for Cancer Advocacy, 2003—; mem. risk mgmt. adv. com., Fin. Svcs. Vol. Corp, 2006—. Mem.: Risk Mgmt. Assn. (co-chmn. operational risk coun. 2002—03, chair 2004, past mem. bd. and exec. com.), Inst. Internat. Fin. (mem. working group on operational risk 2001—04), Harvard (N.Y.C., past mem. admissions com.). Home: 1158 5th Ave New York NY 10029-6917 Office Phone: 212-378-1415. Personal E-mail: owardstein@aol.com.

STEIN, JACOB, computer programmer, analyst; b. NYC, Aug. 20, 1960; s. John H. Kliever and Ann DuBois; m. Sara Wallach, Aug. 18, 1981 (div. 1991); m. Miriam Tichomirov, Oct. 4, 1994; children: Samson, Abigail and Hannah (twins). Student, Kazon Ish Rabbinical Inst., 1981-86; cert. programmer, Cope Inst., 1988. Programmer Eastern Systems, Bklyn., 1988-90, Presidential Life, Nyack, N.Y., 1990-94, Group Health Inc., NYC, 1995—. Mem. Mensa. Republican. Jewish. Avocations: talmudic research, theological writing, hiking, genealogy. Office: Group Health Inc 9th Ave New York NY 10001 Home: 15 Sherri Ln Spring Valley NY 10977-1309 Office Phone: 212-615-0667. Business E-Mail: jstein@ghi.com.

STEIN, JAMES ERIC, pediatric surgeon; b. NYC, Mar. 25, 1959; children: Stephanie, Dylan. Bachelor's degree, Brown U., Providence, RI, 1981; MD, Tufts U. Sch. Medicine, Boston, 1986. Cert. Surgery, 1995, Pediatric Surgery, 1998. Intern, dept. surgery Tufts-New England Med. Ctr., 1986—87, resident, dept. surgery, 1987—89, 1991—92, chief surgical resident; rsch. fellow, pediatric surgery Boston Children's Hosp., 1989—91; pediatric surgery fellow Royal Children's Hosp., Melborne, Australia, 1993—94, Babies and Children's Hosp., NYC, 1994—96; attending pediatric surgeon, divsn. surgery Children's Hosp., LA, 1996—, dir., Extra Corporeal Membrane Oxygenation program, mem., cancer com.; attending pediatric surgeon Huntington Meml. Hosp., Pasadena, Calif., 1996, Pomona Valley, Calif., 1996; asst. prof. surgery Keck Sch. Medicine, U. So. Calif., 1996—. Contbr. articles to peer-reviewed publications. Office: Childrens Hosp LA 4650 Sunset Blvd Los Angeles CA 90027 Office Phone: 323-669-2991. E-mail: jstein@chla.usc.edu.

STEIN, JAMES HOWARD, medical educator, researcher; b. Milw., Wis., Aug. 17, 1964; Bachelor's degree with honors, U. Wis.; MD, Yale U., 1990. Diplomate Am. Bd. Echocardiography in Comprehensive Adult Echocardiography, cert. Internal Medicine, 1993, Cardiovascular Disease, 1997. Intern, internal medicine U. Chgo. Pritzker Sch. Med. Ctr., 1990—91, resident, cardiology, 1991—93; fellow in cardiology Rush-Presbyterian-St. Luke Med. Ctr., Chgo., 1994—96; assoc. prof. cardiovascular medicine U. Wis. Med. Sch., Madison, Wis., 1996—. Dir., atherosclerosis imaging rsch. program U. Wis.; assoc. dir., preventative cardiology program U. Wis. Hosp. and Clinics, dir., vascular health screening program, dir., preventive cardiology; dir. Outpatient Cardiovascular Medicine Svcs.; assoc. dir. Adult Echocardiography Lab.; mem. Complications of HIV Therapy Subcommittee Rsch. Adv. Com., Adult AIDS Clin. Trial Group Divsn. AIDS, Nat. Inst. Allergy and Infectious Diseases; ad hoc reviewer for two NIH study sessions. Co-author: Am. Soc. Echocardiography Recommendations for Use Echocardiography in Clinical Trials; contbr. articles to peer-reviewed jours. Named one of Top Docs in Cardiology, Madison Mag. Fellow: Am. Coll. Cardiology (co-chmn. ann. scientific sessions 2006, rep. to Nat. Cholesterol Edn. program, mem. clin. expert and consensus documents task force, W. Proctor Harvey Young Tchr. award for Excellence in Tchg.); mem.: ACP, Am. Soc. Echocardiography (mem. Carotid IMT task force), Am. Heart Assn., Alpha Omega Alpha. Office: Sect Cardiovascular Medicine U Wis Med Sch G7/341 CSC 600 Highland Avenue H6-315 MC 3248 Madison WI 53792-3248 Office Phone: 608-263-9648. Office Fax: 608-263-0405. Business E-Mail: jhs@medicine.wisc.edu. *

STEIN, JANE WALLISON, lawyer; b. Mar. 23, 1947; AB, Barnard Coll., 1968; MA, NYU, 1969; JD magna cum laude, Bklyn. Law Sch., 1974. Bar: NY 1975. Ptnr., co-leader Project Fin. practice Pillsbury Wiinthrop Shaw Pittman, NYC. Editor (in chief): Bklyn. Law Rev. Mem.: Nat. Assn. Bond Lawyers, NY State Bar Assn., Assn. Bar City of NY (chmn. com. on Project Fin. 2002—). Office: Pillsbury Winthrop Shaw Pittman 1540 Broadway New York NY 10036 Office Phone: 212-858-1225. Office Fax: 212-858-1500. Business E-Mail: jane.stein@pillsburylaw.com.

STEIN, JOHN C., lawyer; b. Flint, Mich., May 8, 1939; s. Joseph Aloyosius and Gertrude (Carlin) S.; m. Dorothea Ruel, Nov. 20, 1965; children: John Jr., Christian, Peter, Thea. BA, U. San Francisco, 1963; JD, U. Calif. Hastings, San Francisco, 1966; cert., Mil. Justice Sch., Newport, RI, 1968. Bar: Calif. 1966, U.S. Dist. Ct. (no., ctrl. and so. dists.) Calif. 1969. Dep. city atty. City of San Francisco, Office of City Atty., 1969-71; with The Boccardo Law Firm, San Jose, Calif., 1971—, mng. ptnr., 1981-99. Judge pro tem San Francisco County Superior Ct., 1978—, Santa Clara County Superior Ct., 1981—; lectr. U. Santa Clara Law Sch., 1985—, Hastings Coll. of Law, U. C. San Francisco. Bd. dirs. Katherine Delmar Burke Sch. Girls, San Francisco, 1988-92, Planning Orgn. for The Richmond, San Francisco, 1985-88. Capt. USMC, 1966-69. Fellow Am. Coll. Trial Lawyers; mem. ATLA, Consumer Attys. of Calif. (Trial Lawyer of Yr. San Jose), Am. Bd. Trial Advocates. Democrat. Roman Catholic. Avocations: golf, skiing, scuba diving. Office: Boccardo Law Firm 111 W Saint John St Ste 400 San Jose CA 95113-1107 Office Phone: 408-298-5678. Business E-Mail: jstein@boccardo.com.

STEIN, JUDITH, history professor; b. Bklyn., Apr. 17, 1940; d. George and Anne Stein. PhD, Yale U., New Haven, Conn., 1968. Prof. history CUNY, 1968—. Disting. chair US history Moscow State U., 2006. Author: (book) World of Marcus Garvey and Running Steel, Running America; editor: Internat. Labor and Working Class History, 1990—; contbr. columns in newspapers, articles to profl. jours. Fellow, NEH, 1980, Am. Coun. Learned Socs., 1992; grantee, Fund Labor Studies, 1990—91, Gerald Ford Presdl. Libr., 2002. Mem.: Orgn. Am. Historians (assoc. Japan Residency award 2001), Am. Hist. Assn. (assoc.; chmn. Wesley Logan com. 2000—03). Office: Graduate Ctr CUNY 365 Fifth Ave New York NY 10016 Home Phone: 212-866-6608; Office Phone: 212-817-8434. Business E-Mail: jstein@gc.cuny.edu.

STEIN, KARL N., plastic and reconstructive surgeon; b. Phila., July 1, 1940; BA in Chemistry, Temple U., 1962, MD, 1966. Diplomate Am. Bd. Plastic Surgery. Intern U. Pa. Grad. Hosp., 1966-67; resident in surgery Abington Meml. Hosp., 1967-68, SUNY Up-State Med. Ctr., 1970-71, instr. in surgery, 1970—; resident in plastic surgery Hosp. Albert Einstein Coll. Medicine, Bronx Mcpl. Hosp. Ctr., 1971-74, asst. instr. plastic surgery and hand surgery, 1974; pvt. practice in plastic surgery, 1974—. Surgeon Sherman Oaks (Calif.) Burn Ctr., 1975—; cons. L.A. Dept. Water and Power; med. legal expert for burns and plastic surgery; med. legal cons. Author (patent) Treatment of Tar Burns, 1980. Capt. USAF, 1969-71. Fellow Am. Coll. Surgeons; mem. AMA, Am. Soc. Plastic and Reconstructive Surgeons, Am. Burn Assn., Am. Soc. Aesthetic Plastic Surgery, Calif. Soc. Plastic Surgeons, Calif. Med. Assn., L.A. County Med. Assn. Office: PO Box 220340 Newhall CA 91322-0340 Office Phone: 661-255-5451.

STEIN, KEITH LANCE, health system administrator; Diploma, Rensselaer Poly. Inst.; MD, Albany Med. Coll., 1980. Diplomate in anesthesiology and critical care medicine Am. Bd. Anesthesiology. Intern, resident, fellow U. Mass. Med. Ctr., 1980—85; chief med. officer, sr. v.p. Bapt. Health, Jacksonville, Fla., 1999—. Fellow: Am. Coll. Chest Physicians, Am. Coll. Critical Care Medicine. Office: Bapt Health 800 Prudential Dr Jacksonville FL 32207 Office Phone: 904-202-2938. E-mail: keith.steinmd@bmcjax.com.

STEIN, KIRA D., psychiatrist; d. David H. and Vivien Y. Burt; m. Michel R. Stein, Aug. 18, 1996. BA in Polit. Sci., UCLA, 1991; Post-Baccalaureate Premedical Cert., Bryn Mawr Coll., Pa., 1993; MD, U. Rochester, NYC, 1997. Bd. cert. psychiatry Am. Bd. Psychiatry and Neurology, 2003, registered Drug Enforcement Agy., 1999, cert. in cognitive behavioral therapy UCLA Anxiety Disorders Clinic, 2000, in interpersonal psychotherapy UCLA Interpersonal Psychotherapy Clinic, 2001. Intern internal medicine Huntington Meml. Hosp., LA, 1997—98; resident adult psychiatry program UCLA Neuropsychiatric Inst., 1998—2001; pvt. practice Kira Stein, MD, APC, Sherman Oaks, Calif., 2001—; clin. instr. UCLA Neuropsychiatric Inst., David Geffen Sch. Medicine, 2001—. Contbr. chapters to books, articles to profl. jours. Mem.: So. Calif. Psychiat. Soc., Calif. Psychiat. Assn., Am. Psychiat. Assn. Avocations: travel, camping, hiking, swimming, theater. Office: Ste 410 15300 Ventura Blvd Sherman Oaks CA 91403 Home Phone: 818-990-5901; Office Phone: 818-990-5901.

STEIN, LAURA, lawyer, consumer products company executive; b. 1961; children: Amanda, Christopher. BA, Dartmouth Coll., 1983; JD, Harvard Law Sch., 1987; MA, Dartmouth Coll. Bar: Calif., 1987. Tracsactional corp. lawyer Morrison & Foerster, San Francisco; asst. gen. counsel, regulatory affairs The Clorox Co., Oakland, Calif., 1992—99, sr. v.p., gen. counsel, 2005—, H.J. Heinz Co., Pittsburgh, Pa., 2000—05. Dir. Franklin Resources, Inc. Mem.: Am. Soc. Corp. Sect., ABA (chmn. Commn. on Domestic Violence), Assn. Corp. Counsel (treas., mem. exec. com.), Calif. State Bar. Office: Clorox Co 1221 Broadway Oakland CA 94612-1888 *

STEIN, LAURENCE JAY, lawyer; b. West Hartford, Conn., Mar. 20, 1961; s. Milton and Selma (Roth) S.; m. Miriam Beth Siegel, Aug. 17, 1986. AB magna cum laude, Harvard Coll., 1982; JD, Stanford U., 1985. Bar: Ill. 1986, Calif. 1999. Clk. to Chief Judge Walter J. Cummings U.S. Ct. Appeals (7th cir.), Chgo., 1985-86; assoc. Latham & Watkins, Chgo., 1986-92, partner, 1993-97, LA, 1997—, global chmn. Tax Dept., 2000—. Recipient Urban A. Sontheimer award Stanford U., 1985, John Harvard Scholarships, Harvard Coll., 1979-82. Mem. ABA, Calif. Bar Assn., Order of the Coif, Phi Beta Kappa Avocation: golf. Office: Latham & Watkins 633 W 5th St # 4000 Los Angeles CA 90071-2005

STEIN, LAWRENCE A., lawyer; b. Balt., Mar. 18, 1965; s. Hersh and Ellen (Hart) S.; m. Diane Wells, June 23, 1991; children: Joshua A., Julie E. AB, U. Chgo., 1988; JD, No. Ill. U., 1993. Bar: Ill. 1993, U.S. Dist. Ct. (no. dist.) Ill. 1993, U.S. Dist. Ct. Md. 1994, U.S. Dist. Ct. (we. and ea. dists.) Wis. 2001, U.S. Ct. Appeals (7th cir.) 1993, Md. 1994, U.S. Supreme Ct. 1997. Shareholder Huck Bouma PC, Wheaton, Ill., 1993—. Advisor Prairie State Legal Svcs., Carol Stream, Ill., 1993—. Commr. Glen Ellyn Architecture Review Commn., 1994-97; pres. Friends of the No. Ill. U.

Librs., 2003-04; mem. Law Sch. Alumni Coun., No. Ill. U., 2003—; sec. Glen Ellyn Libr. Found., Ill., 2006-07; trustee Glen Ellyn Pub. Libr., 2007—. Recipient Am. Jurisprudence award for excellence in appellate advocacy Lawyers Coop., 1991. Mem.: ABA, Am. Inns Ct., Ill. State Bar Assn., DuPage County Bar Assn., U. Chgo. Club of Met. Chgo. (bd. dirs. 2003—04), Phi Delta Phi. Republican. Jewish. Home: 300 Lorraine St Glen Ellyn IL 60137-5632 Office: Huck Bouma PC 1755 S Naperville Rd Wheaton IL 60187-8144 Office Phone: 630-221-1755. Business E-Mail: lstein@huckbouma.com.

STEIN, LAWRENCE V., lawyer; b. Newark, Feb. 10, 1950; AB cum laude, Columbia Coll., 1971; MA, Cornell U., 1974; JD magna cum laude, U. Pa. Law Sch., 1976. Atty. Arnold & Porter, 1976—84, ptnr., 1984—92; sr. v.p., gen. counsel, sec. Genetics Inst., 1992—97; sr. v.p., chief legal counsel Wyeth-Ayerst Global Pharms. and Genetics Inst., 1997—2001; sr. vp., dep. gen. counsel Wyeth, 2001—03, sr. v.p., gen. counsel Madison, NJ, 2003—. Comment editor U. Penn Law Rev., 1975—76. Avocation: golf. Office: Wyeth 5 Giralda Farms Madison NJ 07940-0874 Office Phone: 973-660-6138. E-mail: steinl@wyeth.com.

STEIN, MARK RODGER, allergist; b. Phila., Apr. 24, 1943; s. Eli and Norma Stein; m. Phyllis Feinstein, Dec. 27, 1964; children: Amy Lynn, Philip Warren. BA, LaSalle Coll., Phila., 1964; MD, Jefferson Med. Coll., Phila., 1968. Diplomate Nat. Bd. Med. Examiners, Am. Bd. Internal Medicine, Am. Bd. Allergy and Immunology. Intern Abington Meml. Hosp., Pa., 1968-69; resident internal medicine Letterman Army Med. Ctr., San Francisco, 1972-75; fellow allergy and clin. immunology Fitzsimons Army Med. Ctr., Denver, 1975-77; pvt. practice West Palm Beach, Fla., 1979—. Asst. prof. depts. medicine and pediatrics Uniformed Svcs. U. Health Scis. Sch. Medicine, Bethesda, Md., 1978—79; clin. asst. prof. dept. internal medicine U. South Fla. Coll. Medicine, Tampa, 1979—83, Tampa, 1997—2000; clin. care cons. Clin. Ctr., NIH, Bethesda, 1978—79; mem. active staff Good Samaritan Hosp., West Palm Beach, Fla., chief svc. dept. allergy, 1990—98, chief svc. allergy, 2001—; chief dept. allergy St. Mary's Hosp., West Palm Beach, 1985—98; mem. active staff Palm Beach Gardens Med Ctr.; chief allergy svc. Intracostal Health Sys., 2000—01. Editor Gastroesophageal Reflux Disease and Airway Disease, 1999; contbr. articles to profl. jours. Trustee Am. Lung Assn., West Palm Beach, 1984-93, 95-2007. Fellow ACP, Am. Acad. Allergy, Asthma and Immunology, Am. Coll. Allergy, Asthma and Immunology (chmn. geriat. com. 1988-90), Am. Assn. Cert. Allergists, Am. Coll. Chest Physicians; mem. Am. Thoracic Soc., Mil. Allergists, Fla. Med. Assn., Palm Beach County Med. Assn., Asthma and Allergy Found. Am., Fla. Allergy and Immunology Soc. (pres. 1987-88), Southeastern Allergy Assn. Jewish. Avocations: tennis, golf. Office: 840 Us Highway 1 North Palm Beach FL 33408-3830 Home Phone: 561-622-2728; Office Phone: 561-626-2006. Personal E-mail: latallergy@aol.com.

STEIN, MARVIN, psychiatrist, historian; b. St. Louis, Dec. 8, 1923; s. Samuel G. and Dora (Kline) S.; m. Ann Hackman, May 5, 1950; children: Leslie, David, Lisa. BS, MD, Washington U., St. Louis, 1949; grad., Phila. Psychoanalytic Inst., 1959. Intern St. Louis City Hosp., 1949-50; asst. resident in psychiatry Barnes Hosp., St. Louis, 1950-51; fellow in psychiatry Hosp. U. Pa., 1953-55; asst. prof., then assoc. prof. psychiatry U. Pa. Med. Sch., 1956-63; prof. psychiatry Cornell U. Med. Sch., NYC, 1963-66; prof., chmn. dept. psychiatry SUNY Downstate Med. Ctr., Bklyn., 1966-71; chmn. dept. psychiatry Mt. Sinai Sch. Medicine, NYC, 1971-87, Esther and Joseph Klingenstein prof., 1971-94, Esther and Joseph Klingenstein prof. emeritus, 1994—. Mem. fellowships rev. panel NIMH, 1961-64, chmn. mental health extramural rsch. adv. com., 1968-71, chmn. rev. com. Mental Health Aspects of AIDS, 1988-90; mem. rsch. adv. com. VA, 1965-68, mem. rsch. svc. merit rev. bd. in behavioral sci., 1972-75; chmn. Mental Health Rsch. Career Award Com., 1963-67; chmn. bd. dirs. Founds. Fund for Rsch. in Psychiatry, 1967-70; mem. behavioral medicine study sect. NIH, 1981-83, geriatric rev. com., 1986-88. Contbr. articles on brain and behavior and immune function and history of psychiatry to med. and history jours. USPHS postdoctoral fellow, 1951-53; mental health career investigator, 1956-61; sr. fellow grantee, 1961-63. Mem. Am. Psychiat. Assn. (chmn. rsch. coun. 1981-84), N.Y. Acad. Medicine (Salmon com. 1984—), Alpha Omega Alpha. Home: 5700 Arlington Ave Bronx NY 10471-1503 Office: Mt Sinai Sch Medicine 1 Gustave L Levy Pl New York NY 10029-6500 Business E-Mail: marvin.stein@mssm.edu.

STEIN, MELVIN A., accountant; b. NYC, Sept. 7, 1932; s. William H. and Lillian (Goldberg) S.; m. Barbara Blumencranz, Dec. 17, 1955 (dec.); children: Susan, Karen; m. Marie Sacco, Nov. 1, 1992. BS, NYU, 1953. Pvt. practice acctg., Jericho, NY, 1961-75; pres. Stein & Stein, P.C., Hicksville, 1975-81, Stein, Stein & Feit, P.C., 1982—. Bd. dir. Stern Sch. Bus. N.Y. U., treas. bd. dir., 1991—92, v.p. bd. dir., 1995—, alumni bd. dir., mem. dean adv. coun., 2002—, pres. exec. forum, 2002—, dir. entrepreneurship conf., 2000—. Recipient NYU Alumni Meritorious Svc. award, 2005. Mem. AICPA, N.Y. State Soc. CPAs, N.J. Soc. CPAs, C.W. Post Tax Inst., NYU Club, Princeton Club, The Exec. Forum (pres.). Jewish. Home: 7 Ingleside Ln White Plains NY 10605-5009 Office: 1 Frederick Pl Hicksville NY 11801-4205 also: Buccaneer Mall St Thomas VI 00801 Office Phone: 516-938-2100. Personal E-mail: cpa35@aol.com.

STEIN, MILTON MICHAEL, retired lawyer; b. NYC, Sept. 18, 1936; s. Isidore and Sadie (Lefkowitz) S.; m. Jacqueline Martin, June 17, 1962; children: April, Alicia. AB, Columbia U., NYC, 1958, LLB, 1961. Bar: N.Y. 1962, Pa. 1971, U.S. Supreme Ct. 1971. Asst. dist. atty. N.Y. County, 1962-67; sr. counsel Nat. Commn. for Reform of Fed. Criminal Law, Washington, 1967-70; asst. dist. atty., chief of appeals City of Phila., 1970-73; asst. dir. Nat. Wire Tapping Commn., Washington, 1973-75; dir. D.C. Law Revision, Washington, 1975-77; spl. asst. HUD, Washington, 1977-79; asst. gen. counsel U.S. Commodity Futures Trading Commn., Washington, 1979-83; v.p. N.Y. Futures Exch., NYC, 1983-89, N.Y. Stock Exch., NYC, 1989—2005; ret., 2005; arbitrator, 2005—; adjudication com. COMEX, MYMEX, 2006—. Democrat. Jewish. Home: Hudson House PO Box 286 Ardsley On Hudson NY 10503-0286 Personal E-mail: thejamis@aol.com.

STEIN, PAUL DAVID, cardiologist; b. Cin., Apr. 13, 1934; s. Simon and Sadie (Friedman) S.; m. Janet Louise Tucker, Aug. 14, 1966; children: Simon, Douglas, Rebecca. BS, U. Cin., 1955, MD, 1959. Intern Jewish Hosp., Cin., 1959-60, med. resident, 1961-62, Gorgas Hosp., C.Z., 1960-61; fellow in cardiology U. Cin., 1962-63, Mt. Sinai Hosp., NYC, 1963-64; rsch. fellow Harvard Med. Sch., Boston, 1964-66; asst. dir. cardiac catheterization lab. Baylor U. Med. Ctr., Dallas, 1966-67; asst. prof. medicine Creighton U., Omaha, 1967-69; assoc. prof. medicine U. Okla., Oklahoma City, 1969-73; prof. rsch. medicine U. Okla. Coll. Medicine, Oklahoma City, 1973-76; dir. cardiovascular rsch. Henry Ford Hosp., Detroit, 1976-94, med. dir. cardiovascular rehab., 1994-2000; dir. rsch. St. Joseph Mercy Oakland Hosp., Pontiac, Mich., 2000—04, dir. rsch. edn., 2005—; Henry Ford prof. medicine Case Western Res. U., Cleve., 1994—2000; prof. medicine Wayne State U., Detroit, 2003—. Adj. prof. physics Oakland U., Rochester, Mich., 1985— Author: A Physical and Physiological Basis for the Interpretation of Cardiac Ausculation: Evaluations Based Primarily on Second Sound and Ejection Murmurs, 1981, Pulmonary Embolism, 1996, 2d edit., 2007; contbr. articles to profl. jours. Coun. on Clin. Cardiology fellow Am. Heart Assn., 1971, Coun. on Circulation fellow, 1972. Recipient Lifetime Achievement award, Am. Heart Assn., Mich. chpt., 2002. Master Am. Coll. Chest Physicians (pres. 1993); fellow ACP (Laureate award, Mich. chpt. 2003), ASME, Am. Coll. Cardiology. Office Phone: 248-858-6772. Office Fax: 248-858-3244. Business E-Mail: steinp@trinity-health.org.

STEIN, PAULA JEAN ANNE BARTON, hotel real estate company executive, real estate broker; b. Chgo., July 29, 1929; m. Marshall L. Stein; children: Guy G., George L.; guardian of Bradley Stein, Gregory Stein. BA, Lake Forest Coll., Ill., 1951; postgrad., Roosevelt U., Chgo., 1955—77, UCLA, 1978—79. Adminstrv. asst. publicity Kefauver for Pres., Chgo., 1951; adminstrv. asst. Wells Orgns., Chgo., 1952; rschr., writer Employers Assn. Am., Chgo., 1951-52; writer Woodworking Jobbers Assn., Chgo., 1953; cons. LA, 1978-80; pres., broker Steinvest, Inc., Chgo., 1980—; freelance writer, 1996—. Cons., hotels Nat. Diversified Svcs., Inc., Chgo., 1990—, Beach Hotel, Inc., Monterey, Calif., IBA Women's Adv. Bd., 1999; advocate for learning disorder solutions. Script for first TV bus. prog. on WGN-TV, 1951-52. Mem. Ragdale Found., Lake Forest, Ill. IBA fellow, 1990. Mem. World Future Soc. (profl.), Sisters in Crime, Mystery Writers, So. Poverty Law Ctr., others. Avocations: painting, writing. Home and Office: Steinvest Inc 2291 Hybernia Dr Highland Park IL 60035-5509 Home Phone: 847-748-8348. Office Fax: 847-748-8349. Personal E-mail: steinvest@msn.com.

STEIN, ROBERT A., writer, educator, military officer; b. Duluth, Minn., Aug. 5, 1933; s. A. A. and Grace (Wichterman) Stein; m. Betty Lou Pavlik, 1955; children: Robert Jr., David K., Steven J. BS in Commerce, U. Iowa, 1956; degree with hons. in Academic Instr. Sch., USAF, 1966; MA in Counselor Edn., U. Iowa, 1968, MA in Writing, 1986; degree with honors, Indsl. Coll. Armed Forces, 1973. Cert. tchr. Iowa, profl. counselor. Commd. 2d lt. USAF, 1956, advanced through grades to col., 1977, pilot trainee Goodfellow AFB, Tex., 1957, pilot 345th Squadron Sewart AFB, Tenn., 1957—61, instr. pilot 1602nd Wing Chateauroux AB, France, 1961—64; asst. prof. aerospace studies U. Iowa, Iowa City, 1964-66, assoc. prof., 1966-68, prof., 1975-77; dir., safety and security U. Iowa Hosps./Clinics, Iowa City, 1977-85; mem. faculty divsn. writing Kirkwood CC, Iowa City, Cedar Rapids, 1984-89; writer, tchr. Iowa City, 1985—. Writer, tchr. Iowa City/Johnson County Sr. Citizens Ctr., 1994—; sports announcer U. Iowa. Author: (novels) Apollyon: A Novel, 1985, The Chase, 1988, The Black Samaritan, 1997, 2d edit., 2000, The Vengeance Equation, 2000, hardcover edit., 2001, Death Defied (Internat. Lit. award, 1988); co-author: (screenplays) WGAW-Registered, 2001. Decorated Bronze Star; named to, Iowa Athletics Hall of Fame, 2002; recipient Outstanding Faculty award, U. Iowa, 1968. Mem.: Authors League Am., Authors Guild, Mil. Affairs Assn. (charter), Air Force Assn. (life), Nat. Iowa Varsity Club (exec. bd., pres. 2002—03, Lifetime Achievement award 1999), Nat. Iowa Lettermen's Club (past pres.), Rotary (Paul Harris fellow), Daedalians, Phi Delta Kappa. Avocations: flying, travel, reading, swimming. Home and Office: 2020 Ridgeway Dr Iowa City IA 52245-3238

STEIN, ROBERT ALAN, electronics executive; b. Chgo., Oct. 18, 1930; s. Manfred and Mildred (Rosenfield) S.; m. Frances Roslyn Berger, Dec. 25, 1960; 1 dau., Marcia Beth. BA, U. Chgo., 1950, MBA, 1953. C.P.A., Ill. Sr. auditor Scovell, Wellington & Co., Chgo., 1955—63; supr. corp. acctg. Mack Trucks, Inc., Montvale, NJ, 1963—65; v.p. fin., treas. Lionel Corp., NYC, 1965—82; pres. ITI Electronics, Inc., Livingston, NJ, 1982—. With US Army, 1953—55. Mem. Am. Inst. CPAs. Personal E-mail: itielect@aol.com.

STEIN, ROBERT ALLEN, lawyer, educator, former legal association administrator; b. Mpls., Sept. 16, 1938; s. Lawrence E. and Agnes T. (Brynildson) S.; m. Sandra H. Stein; children: Linda Stein Routh, Laura Stein Conrad, Karin Stein O'Boyle. BS in Law, U. Minn., 1960, JD summa cum laude, 1961; LLD (hon.), Uppsala U., Sweden, 1993. Bar: Wis. 1961, Minn. 1967. Assoc. Foley, Sammond & Lardner, Milw., 1961-64; prof. U. Minn. Law Sch., Mpls., 1964-77, dean, 1979-94, Everett Fraser prof. law, 2006—; assoc. dean U. Minn., 1976-77, v.p. adminstrn. and planning, 1978-80, faculty rep. men's intercollegiate athletics, 1981-94; of counsel Mullin, Weinberg & Daly, PA, Mpls., 1970-80, Gray, Plant, Mooty, Mooty & Bennett, Mpls., 1980-94, 2006—. Vis. prof. UCLA, 1969-70, U. Chgo., 1975-76; commr. Uniform State Laws Commn. Minn., 1973—; v.p. Nat. Uniform Laws Com., 1991-93, exec. comm., 1991—, sec., 1997—; acad. fellow Am. Coll. Trusts and Estates Counsel, 1975—; vis. scholar Am. Bar Found., Chgo., 1975-76; trustee Gt. No. Iron Ore Properties, 1982—, Uniform Laws Found., 1992—; advisor Restatement of Law Second, Property, 1977—, Restatement of Law Trusts (Prudent Investor Rule), 1989-90, Restatement of Law Third, Trusts, 1993—; chmn. bd. dirs. Ednl. Credit Mgmt. Corp., 1993—; bd. dirs. Fiduciary Counselling Inc. Author: Stein on Probate, 1976, 3d edit., 1995, How to Study Law and Take Law Exams, 1996, Estate Planning Under the Tax Reform Act of 1976, 2d edit, 1978, In Pursuit of Excellence: A History of the University of Minnesota Law School, 1980, contbr. articles to profl. jours. Founding bd. dirs. Park Ridge Ctr., 1985-95; co-chair Gov.'s Task Force on Ctr. for Treatment of Torture Victims, 1985, bd. dirs., 1985-87. Fellow Am. Bar Found (bd. dirs. 1987-94), Am. Coll. Tax Counsel; mem. ABA (coun. sect. of legal edn. and admission to bar 1986-91, vice chairperson 1991-92, chair-elect 1992-93, chair 1993-94, exec. dir. 1994-2006), Internat. Acad. Estate and Trust Law (academician), Internat. Bar Assn. (profl. and pub. interest divsn. sec. 2004-06, vice chair 2006—), Am. Judicature Soc. (bd. dirs. 1984-88), Am. Law Inst. (coun. mem. 1987—, exec. com. 1993—), Minn. Bar Assn. (bd. govs. 1979-94, exec. coun., probate and trust law sect. 1973-77), Hennepin County Bar Assn., U. Minn. Alumni Assn. (nat. pres. 2005-06). Office: U Minn Law Sch 229 19th Ave S Minneapolis MN 55455 Home Phone: 763-545-1701; Office Phone: 612-625-3047. Business E-Mail: stein@umn.edu.

STEIN, ROBERT BENJAMIN, biomedical researcher, physician; b. Buffalo, Oct. 28, 1950; s. Frank and Eleanor (Bankoff) S.; m. Marcia Joan Lieberman, Aug. 10, 1975 (div.); children: Rebecca Anne, Joshua David; m. Sophia Anne Rose, Dec. 29, 1989 (div.); children: Susan Claire, Stephanie Michelle; m. Faye Elizabeth Sutherland, Aug. 12, 2000. BS, Ind. U., 1972; MD, PhD, Duke U., 1979. Diplomate Am. Bd. Anatomic and Clin. Pathology. House staff Duke U. Med. Ctr., Durham, N.C., 1980-83; sr. rsch. fellow Dept Virus and Cell Biology Merck Sharp & Dohme Rsch. Labs, West Point, Pa., 1983-87, assoc. dir. molecular and cardiovascular pharmacology, 1987-89, sr. dir., head dept. pharmacology, 1989-90; v.p. rsch. Ligand Pharms., Inc., San Diego, 1990-92, v.p. rsch. and preclin. devel., 1992-93, sr. v.p., CSO, 1993-96; exec. v.p., rsch. and preclin. devel. DuPont Merck, Wilmington, Del., 1996-98; exec. v.p. rsch. and preclin. DuPont Pharms., Wilmington, 1998—. Contbr. articles to profl. jours., chpts. to books. Ins. Med. scholar, 1977-79; James B. Duke scholar, 1976-78; Lang Med. Pub. award, 1979; NIH grantee, 1974-75. Fellow Am. Soc. Clin. Pathologists, N.Y. Acad. Scis., Am. Physiol. Soc., AAAS, Sigma Xi, Phi Beta Kappa, Alpha Omega Alpha. Avocations: piano, history, literature. E-mail: Robert.B.Stein@dupontpharma.com.

STEIN, RONALD J., lawyer; b. NYC, 1935; AB, Columbia U., 1956; LLB cum laude, Harvard U., 1959; LLM, Georgetown U., 1962. Bar: NY 1959, DC 1959, Fla. 1975. Adminstrv. ptnr., labor, employment practice area Stroock & Stroock & Lavan LLP, NYC. Bd. dir. City Parks Found., NYC, 92nd St. YMCA, NYC. Bd. of editors Harvard Law Rev., 1958—59. Mem.: NY State Bar Assn., Assn. Bar City NY. Office: Stroock & Stroock & Lavan LLP 180 Maiden Ln New York NY 10038-4982 Office Phone: 212-806-6018. Office Fax: 212-806-6006. Business E-Mail: rstein@stoock.com.

STEIN, RUTH ELIZABETH KLEIN, physician; b. NYC, Nov. 2, 1941; d. Theodore and Mimi (Foges) Klein; m. H. David Stein, June 9, 1963; children: Lynn Andrea Stein Melnick, Sharon Lisa, Deborah Michelle. AB, Barnard Coll., NYC, 1962; MD, Albert Einstein Coll. Medicine, Bronx, NY, 1966. Diplomate Am. Bd. Pediat., Devel. Behavioral Pediat. Intern, then resident Bronx Mcpl. Hosp. Ctr., 1966—68; sr. resident, fellow; 1968instr. dept. pediats. George Washington U., Washington, 1968—70; with Albert Einstein Coll. of Medicine, Bronx, 1970—77, assoc. prof. pediats., 1977—83, prof., 1983—; vice-chmn. dept. pediats. Albert Einstein Coll., 1992—2002, dir. office of acad. affairs, dept. pediats., 1997—2002; pediatrician-in-chief, dir. pediats. Jacobi Med. Ctr. (formerly Bronx Mcpl. Hosp. Ctr.), 1992—97. Vis. prof. pub. health dept. epidemiology Yale U. Sch. Medicine, New Haven, 1986-87; scholar-in-residence United Hosp. Fund, NY, 1995-97; dir., prin. investigator Preventive Intervention Rsch. Ctr. for Child Health, NY, 1983-94, Nat. Child Health Assessment Planning Project, NY, Behavioral Pediatric Tng. Program, NY; dir. gen. pediatrics Pediat. Divsn., NY, 1992-97; apptd. to Montefiore Med. Ctr., North Ctrl. Bronx Hosp., Jacobi Med. Ctr.; bd. dirs. Ctr. for Child Health Rsch. of Am. Acad. Pediatrics, mem. exec. com., 1999-2004; co-chmn. com. on evaluation of child health 2002-04, NRC/Inst. Medicine, 1999-2005; bd. sci. advisors Nat. Inst. Arthritis and Musculoskelatal and Skin Diseases, 2005—; bd. sci. counselors Nat. Ctr. Health Stats. of CDC, 2006—. Editor: Caring for Children with Chronic Illness: Issues and Strategies, 1989, Health Care for Children: What's Right, What's Wrong, What's Next, 1997; mem. editorial bd. Jour. Behavioral and Devel. Pediatrics, 1993-2006, Ambulatory Pediatrics, 1998-2005; contbr. articles to profl. jours. Fellow Am. Acad. Pediats.; mem. APHA, Am. Pediatric Soc., Soc. for Pediat. Rsch., Ambulatory Pediat. Assn. (bd. dirs. 1982-89, pres. 1987-88, rsch. award 1995, Ray Helfer award 1999), NY Acad. Medicine (chmn. NY forum on child health 2001-05), Soc. for Devel. and Behavioral Pediats., Alpha Omega Alpha. Jewish. Home: 91 Larchmont Ave Larchmont NY 10538-3748 Office: Albert Einstein Coll Med Montefiore Med Ctr Dept Pediat 111 E 210 St Bronx NY 10467-2804 Office Phone: 718-920-7932. Business E-Mail: rstein@aecom.yu.edu.

STEIN, SAM LEE, lawyer; b. Cherokee, Okla., Nov. 19, 1958; s. Leroy Clark and Rosevelyn Edith (Peterson) Stein; m. Kelly Lee Pelter, Dec. 27, 1980; children: Patrick Leroy, Kelsy Lee. BS in Agr., Okla. State U., 1981; JD with honors, U. Okla., 1987. Bar: Okla. 1987, U.S. Dist. Ct. (we. dist.) Okla. 1987, U.S. Dist. Ct. (no. dist.) Tex. 1987, Tex. 1988, U.S. Dist. Ct. (we. dist.) Tex. 1989, U.S. Ct. Appeals (5th cir.) 1993, cert.: Tex. Bd. Legal Specialization (civil trial and consumer and comml. lawl) 1994. Assoc. Morris, Moore, Dalrymple, et. al., Amarillo, Tex., 1987—89, Templeton & Garner, PC, Amarillo, 1989—90; shareholder Garner, Stone & Lovell, Amarillo, 1990—94; mng. shareholder Garner, Lovell & Stein, PC, Amarillo, 1994—97; prin. Garner & Stein, LLP, Cherokee, Okla., 1997—2001, Garner, Stein & Dean, LLP, Cherokee, 2001—04, Whittenburg, Whittenburg, Garner & Stein, P.C., Cherokee, 2004—. Asst. scoutmaster Troop 335 Boy Scouts Am., Cherokee, 1997—, bd. dirs. Cimarron Coun. Enid, Okla., 1999—. Recipient Profl. Responsibility award, U. Okla., 1987. Mem.: ATLA, ABA, Okla. Trial Lawyers Assn., Okla. Bar Assn., State Bar Tex. Office: Whittenburg Whittenburg Garner & Stein PC 305 S Grand Cherokee OK 73728 Home Phone: 580-596-2830; Office Phone: 580-596-3000. E-mail: sstein@akslc.net.

STEIN, SANDRA LOU, educational psychology professor; b. Freeport, Ill., Oct. 6, 1942; d. William Kenneth and Marien Elizabeth Stein. BS, U. Wis., Madison, 1964; MS Edn., No. Ill. U., 1967, EdD, 1969. Tchr. English Rockford Sch. Dist., Ill., 1964—65; tchr. Russian Jefferson County Sch. Dist., Lakewood, Colo., 1965—66; asst. prof. edn. U. S.C., Columbia, 1969—71, No. Ill. U., DeKalb, 1971—72, Rider U., Lawrenceville, NJ, 1972—75, assoc. prof. edn., 1975—81; prof. edn. Rider Coll., Lawrenceville, 1981—2007, dept. chair, 1983—91, 2003—07; ret., 2007. Cons. on measurement and evaluation, women's edn., 1973— Contbr. articles to ednl. publs Deacon Presbyn. Ch. Lawrenceville, 1984—87. Recipient Disting. Tchg. award Rider Coll. and Lindback Found., 1981 Mem. APA, AAUP (chpt. pres. 2000-01, negotiating team 2002, Outstanding Achievement award Rider Coll. chpt. 1988), Am. Ednl. Rsch. Assn., Phi Delta Kappa (chpt. pres. 1986-87, Svc. Key award 1991, faculty advisor 1994—99) Home: 70 Wiltshire Dr Lawrenceville NJ 08648-2585 E-mail: stein@rider.edu.

STEIN, SANDRA THERESE, pharmacist; b. Milw., Sept. 21, 1935; d. Harland Wheaton Stein and Sylvia Therese Perla. BS, U. Wis., Madison, 1960; PhD in Neotarian Philosophy, 1977, D of Nutripathy, 1988; LLB, Lasalle U., Chgo., 1991; D of Pharmacy, Broadmore U., Belize, 2000. Registered pharmacist Wis. Pharmacist mgr. Enterprise Pharmacy, Milw., 1968—83; pharmacy staff VA Hosp., North Chgo., 1983—88; pharmacist-in-charge Sentry Drugs, Milw., 1988—94, Durg Emporium, Greenfield, Wis., 1994—98; pharmacy staff Kohls Pharmacy, Milw., 1998—2003; relief pharmacist RPH On The Go, Milw., 1994—. Cons. Health Foods, Milw., 2000—. Avocations: reading, writing, movies, computers.

STEIN, SHERYL E., lawyer; b. Bklyn., Apr. 20, 1952; BA cum laude, Univ. Miami, 1974; JD, Southwestern Univ., 1978. Bar: Calif. 1979. Ptnr., office mng. ptnr., leader office Corp. & Securities practice sect. Pillsbury Winthrop Shaw Pittman, LA. Mem.: LA County Bar Found. (bd. mem.), LA County Bar Assn., Org. Women Exec. Office: Pillsbury Winthrop Shaw Pittman Suite 2800 725 S Figueroa St Los Angeles CA 90017 Office Phone: 213-488-7194. Office Fax: 213-629-1033. Business E-Mail: sheryl.stein@pillsburylaw.com.

STEIN, SOL, publishing executive, writer; b. Chgo, Oct. 13, 1926; s. Louis and Zelda (Zam) S.; m. Patricia Day, Mar. 31, 1962 (div. Oct. 1997); children: Kevin David, Jeffrey Lewelyn, Leland Dana, Robert Bruce, Andrew Charles, David Day, Elizabeth Day; m. Edith Tennenbaum Shapiro, Nov. 25, 2000. BSS, CCNY, 1948; MA, Columbia U., 1949, postgrad., 1949-51. Lectr. social studies CCNY, 1948-51; sr. editor, ideological adv. staff Voice of Am., US State Dept., 1951-53; exec. dir. Am. Com. for Cultural Freedom, 1953—56; gen. editor, originator Beacon Press Paperbacks, Boston, 1954—; mng. editor Rsch. Inst. Am., 1956—58; cons. to pres. Harcourt, Brace, Jovanovich, NYC, 1958-59; exec. v.p. The Mid-Century Book Soc., NYC, 1959-62; pres., editor in chief Stein and Day Pubs., Briarcliff Manor, NY, 1962-89; pres. The Colophon Corp., Scarborough, NY, 1983-95, The WritePro Corp., 1989—2001, The Stein Software Corp., 1993—. Lectr., playwright Columbia U., 1958-60, Dialogue for Writers, Pub., U. Calif., Irvine, 1990-93; treas. The Forensic Found., N.Y.C., 1959-62; founding mem. Playwrights Group, The Actors Studio, 1957. Author: (plays) The Illegitimist, 1953 (1st prize Dramatists Alliance), A Shadow of My Enemy, 1957, (novels) The Husband, 1969, The Magician, 1971, Living Room, 1974, The Childkeeper, 1975, Other People, 1979, The Resort, 1980, The Touch of Treason, 1985, A Deniable Man, 1989, The Best Revenge, 1991 (computer software) WritePro, The Stein Creative Writing Program, 1989—, FirstAid for Writers, 1991, FictionMaster, 1993, WritePro for Business, 1996; (non-fiction) A Feast for Lawyers, 1989, Stein on Writing, 1995, How to Grow a Novel, 1999, (with James Baldwin) Native Sons, 2004; also articles, revs. poetry. Mem. exec. com. Am. Friends of Captive Nations. Served to 1st lt. AUS, 1945-47. Fellow Yaddo Found., 1952, MacDowell Colony, 1952-56. Recipient Disting. Instr. award U. Calif. at Irvine, 1992. Mem. New Dramatists Com. (coun. mem.), Internat. Brotherhood Magicians (hon. life), Writers Guild Am. East, Authors Guild, Phi Beta Kappa. Avocations: tennis, inventing computer software programs. Office: 277 E South Broadway Tarrytown NY 10591-5334 Personal E-mail: solstein@aol.com.

STEIN, STEPHEN, lawyer; b. Bklyn., Oct. 22, 1943; s. Alex and Rachel (Osbrach) S.; m. Susan Helane Cooper, Dec. 23, 1965; children: Sharyn, David. AB, NYU, 1964; JD, Bklyn. Law Sch., 1967. Bar: NY 1967, US Dist. Ct. (so. dist.) NY 1967, US Ct. Appeals (3rd cir.) 1973, Nev. 1974, US Ct. Appeals (9th cir.) 1974, US Supreme Ct. 1974, US Ct. Appeals (5th cir.) 1975, US Ct. Appeals (4th cir.) 1976, US Ct. Appeals (8th and 11th cirs.) 1982, US Ct. Appeals (6th cir.) 1987. Spl. atty. criminal div. US Dept.

Justice, Phila., 1971-74; ptnr. Goodman, Stein & Chesnoff, Las Vegas, Nev., 1974—92, Stein & Rojas, Las Vegas, Nev. Pres. Temple Beth Am, Las Vegas, 1985-87. Lt. comdr. JAGC, USN, 1968-71. Named one of Best Criminal Defense Attys., Las Vegas Review-Jour., 1999. Mem. Nev. Trial Lawyers Assn. (bd. dirs. 1986-87). Democrat. Office: Stein & Rojas 520 S 4th St Las Vegas NV 89101 Office Phone: 702-384-5563. *

STEIN, STEPHEN WILLIAM, lawyer; b. NYC, Apr. 12, 1937; s. Melvin S. and Cornelia (Jacobowitz) S.; m. Judith N., Jan. 22, 1966. AB, Princeton U., 1959; LLB, Columbia U., 1962; LLM, NYU, 1963. Bar: NY 1962. Assoc. White & Case, NYC, 1963-67; atty. advisor U.S. Agy. Internat. Devel., Washington, 1967-69, regional legal advisor Mission to India New Delhi, 1969-71, asst. gen. counsel Washington, 1971-73; assoc. ptnr. Delson & Gordon, NYC, 1973-87; ptnr. Kelley Drye & Warren, NYC, 1987—. U.S. exec. com. Indonesian Trade, Tourism & Investment Promotion Program, 1990-92; mem. U.S.-Indonesia Trade & Investment Adv. Com., 1989-92; vis. instr. Internat. Devel. Law Inst., 1993; lectr. Internat. Law Inst., Washington, 1984, 85; spkr. in field. Mem. ABA (mem. sect. internat. law, co-chair African law com. 1999-2002), Assn. Bar of City of N.Y. (mem. com. project fin. 1997-2003, mem. com. Asian affairs 1992—2004, former mem. others), Am. Indonesian C. of C. (bd. dirs. 1986—, pres. 1989-96). Home: 320 Central Park W New York NY 10025-7659 Office: Kelley Drye & Warren 101 Park Ave New York NY 10178-0062 Office Phone: 212-808-7794. Business E-Mail: sstein@kelleydrye.com.

STEIN, THOMAS HENRY, social sciences educator; b. Elmhurst, Ill., May 17, 1949; s. Peter Leonard and Marion Edith (Zirbel) S.; m. Alberta Piazza, July 10, 1971; 1 child, Heather. BA in Polit. Sci., Loyola U., Chgo., 1971; postgrad., Loyola U., 1972-76; MS in Edn., Pacific Western U., 1988, PhD in Edn., 1989. Cert. tchr., Ill. Budget analyst, dean global studies divsn. U.S. Dept. Def., Gt. Lakes Naval Sta., Ill., 1971—72; global studies dean, tchr. social sci., coach bowling, softball Mother Guerin High Sch., River Grove, Ill., 1972—; tchr. Highland Park (Ill.) High Sch., 1981-84. Instr. Franklin Park (Ill.) Park Dist., 1977—; tchr. Triton Coll., River Grove, 1990-91; evaluator Chgo. Met. History Fair, 1980-89; faculty adviser Scholastic, Inc., N.Y.C., 1990—; dir. Students Against Animal Cruelty, River Grove, 1991—; moderator Nat. Honor Soc., 1993—; adj. faculty St. Mary's U., 2003--. With Ill. N.G., 1971-77. Recipient Outstanding Achievement award Am. Express/Assn. Am. Geographers, 1989, Heart of the Sch. award for Peace and Justice, Archdiocese of Chgo. Fellow Acad. Polit. Sci.; mem. ASCD, Nat. Coun. Social Studies, Nat. Hist. Soc., Ctr. Study of the Presidency, Nat. Cath. Edn. Assn., Orgn. History Tchrs., Am. Polit. Sci. Assn. Democrat. Roman Catholic. Home: 3601 Emerson St Franklin Park IL 60131-1713 Office: Guerin Coll Prep HS 8001 W Belmont Ave River Grove IL 60171-1096 Office Phone: 708-453-6233 ext 91. Business E-Mail: tstein@guerinprep.org.

STEIN, ZENA A., retired epidemiologist, educator; b. Durban, South Africa, July 7, 1922; married; 3 children. BA in History, U. Capetown, 1941, MA in History with honors, 1942; MB, BChir, U. Witwatersrand, 1950, DSc (hon.), 1993. Med. officer Alexandra Health Ctr. & U. Clinic, Johannesburg, 1952—55; registrar psychiatry Shenley Mental Hosp., England, 1956; rsch. assoc. Dept. Social & Preventive Medicine U. Manchester, 1959—62, sr. rsch. fellow Mental Health Rsch. Fund, Dept. Social & Preventive Medicine, 1959—62, rsch. fellow, Medical Rsch. Coun., Dept. Social & Preventive Medicine, 1962—65; rsch. assoc. Assn. for Aid Crippled Children, NYC, 1965—66; assoc. prof. epidemiology Columbia U. Sch. Pub. Health, NYC, 1966—73, prof. pub. health epidemiology, 1973—92, prof. pub. health epidemiology, Gertrude H. Sergievsky Ctr., 1977—, assoc. dir. rsch. and acad. affairs, 1986—; dir. epidemiology of brain disorders rsch. dept. NY State Psychiat. Inst., NYC, 1968—98, co-dir. HIV Ctr. for Clin. and Behavioral Studies, 1987—; co-dir. HIV Ctr. for Clin. and Behavioral Studies, NY State Psychiatric Inst. Columbia U., NYC, 1987—, prof. psychiatry dept. psychiatry, 1991—92, acting chair divsn. epidemiology, sch. pub. health, 1993—95, prof. emerita dept. epidemiology & psychiatry, sch. pub. health, 1993—. Cons. Pan Am. Health Orgn., 1972, WHO, 1978, 83, 86, 91, UNICEF, South African Med. Rsch. Coun., 1992-93, Robert Wood Johnson Found., 1993-94; vis. prof. U. Sydney, 1975, Nat. Inst. Mental Health, Lima, Peru, 1988, Inst. Sukperiore de Sanita, Rome, 1989; hon. prof. Nat. Sch. Pub. Health, Madrid, Spain, 1999; co-dir. Africa Ctr. Population Studies & Reproductive Health, Mtubatuba, South Africa, 1999; spkr. in field. Co-editor: (with Hatch, M.) Reproduction at the Workplace, 1986, (with M. Wright, J. Scandlyn) Women's Health and Apartheid: The Health of Women and Children and the Future of Progressive Health Care in Southern Africa, 1988, (with A. Zwi) Action on AIDS in Southern Africa: Maputo Conference on Health in Transition in Southern Africa, 1990; co-author: (with Kline, J.) Conception to Birth: Epidemiology of Prenatal Development, 1989; editl. bd. Am. Journal of Public Health, Genetic Epidemiology, Teratogenesis, Carcinogenesis & Mutagenesis, Reproductive Toxicology, American Journal of Human Genetics; contbr. chpts. to books and articles to profl. jours. Lt. South African Defense Force, 1943—45. Recipient Physicians & Surgeons Disting. Svc. award, Coll. Physicians & Surgeons, Columbia U., 1994, 75th Jubilee medal, U. Witwatersrand Med. Sch., 1997, Tribute to Zena Stein award, Internat. Conf. Microbicides Organizing Com., 2002; grantee Fogarty Ctr., NIMH. Mem.: NAS, NIMH (mem. study sects.), Joint Commn. Internat. Aspects Mental Retardation, Am. Soc. Human Genetics, Am. Epidemiological Soc., Soc. Study of Social Biology, Soc. Life History Rsch. Psychiatric Epidemiology, Internat. Epidemiological Assn., Soc. Epidemiologic Rsch., Am. Pub. Health Assn. (Wade Hampton Frost award & lecture 1992, John Snow award 1999), Am. Assn. Mental Deficiency, Inst. Medicine (sr. mem. 1998), Nat. Inst. Child Health & Human Devel., Nat. Inst. Occupl. Safety & Health, Nat. Inst. Environ. Health Scis. Office: HIV Ctr NY State Psychiat Inst 722 W 168th St New York NY 10032-2603 Business E-Mail: zas2@columbia.edu.

STEINAGLE, MARTIN GENE, contractor, paralegal, poet, writer; b. Buffalo, Aug. 27, 1951; s. Raymond George and Dorothy Jean (Martin) Steinagle. Cert.: So. Career Inst., Boca Raton, Fla. (paralegal) 1987; comml. art illustrated design Wesport, Conn., 1971, electromechanicl Tech. Advanced Tng. Ctr., Kenmore, N.Y., 1983, firearms N. Am. Sch. of Firearms, Scranton, Pa., 1982. Carpenter Barden Homes, Middleport, NY, 1974—77; grademan Lockport Excavating Inc., Lockport, NY, 1978—81; illustrator Thencan, Lockport, NY, 1985—2002; owner New Day Constrn., Lockport, NY, 1988—. Author: Everyday, But Not Common Poems and Quotes, 2001, More, but Not Common Poems and Quotes, 2004, Common Poems and Quotes to Read, 2005, (songs) Please, Why, 1974, Every Bus on the Street, 1974, (poem) Love is Two, 1982, You're Like a Candle, 1973. Mem.: Improved Order of Red Men, Loyal Order of Moose. Democrat. Judaic Christian. Avocations: art, reading, writing, music, computers. Home and Office: 284 Willow St Apt 24 Lockport NY 14094

STEINBACH, HAROLD I., lawyer; b. Bronx, NY, Aug. 31, 1956; s. Aaron and Phyllis (Feldfeber) S.; m. Beryl Joy Schwartz, Mar. 14, 1982; children: Sarah Brandl, Rachel Beth, Avi Michael. BA, SUNY, Binghamton, 1978; JD, NYU, 1981. Bar: N.Y. 1982, N.J. 1983, U.S. Dist. Ct. (so. dist.) N.Y. 1982. Assoc. Flemming, Zulack & Williamson, NYC, 1981-83; assoc., then ptnr. Kleinberg, Kaplan, Wolff & Cohen, P.C., NYC, 1983-2000; ptnr. Parker Duryee Rosoff & Haft, PC, NYC, 2000—01, Steinbach & Assocs., Hackensack, NJ, 2002—, NYC, 2000—01. Trustee Jewish Braille Inst. Am., Inc., 1992-2004. Mem.: N.Y. State Bar Assn. (bus. law and property law sects.), Phi Beta Kappa. Jewish. Home: 665 Ogden Ave Teaneck NJ 07666-2203 Office: 1 Univ Plz Ste 412 Hackensack NJ 07601 Office Phone: 201-525-1990. E-mail: harold@steinbachesq.com.

STEINBACH, LYNNE SUSAN, radiologist, educator; b. San Francisco, Dec. 28, 1953; d. Howard Lynne and Ilse (Rosengarten) S.; m. Eric Franklin Tepper, Aug. 14, 1977; 1 child, Mark Evan. Student, Vassar Coll.; BA, Stanford U., 1975; MD, Med. Coll. Pa., 1979. Cert. Am. Bd. Radiology, 1983. Intern Coll. Medicine and Dentistry N.J., Newark, 1979—80; resident radiology N.Y. Hosp.-Cornell Med. Ctr., NYC, 1980—83; fellow musculoskeletal radiology Hosp. Spl. Surgery Cornell Med. Ctr., NYC, 1983—84; asst. prof. radiology U. Calif., San Francisco, 1984—92, assoc. prof., 1992—98, prof., 1998—. Chief musculoskeletal imaging U. Calif. San Francisco. Editor 4 books; contbr. articles 130 on radiology, chpts. on musculoskeletal radiology to profl. publs. Fellow Am. Coll. Radiology; mem. Internat. Skeletal Soc. (mem.-at-large 2002-03, asst. sec. 2003-04, bd. dirs., 2006-, Pres. medal, 1996), Internat. Soc. Mag. Res. Med. (bd. dirs., 2007), San Francisco Radiol. Soc. (sec. treas. 1994, pres. 1996), Radiol. Soc. N.Am., Am. Assn. Women Radiologists (mem.-at-large 1987-88, sec. 1989-91, v.p. 1991-92, pres.-elect 1992-93, pres. 1993-94), Am. Roentgen Ray Soc., Assn. U. Radiologists, Soc. Skeletal Radiology. Avocations: swimming, travel, music, art. Home Phone: 415-388-7840. E-mail: lynne.steinbach@radiology.ucsf.edu.

STEINBACH, MEREDITH LYNN, writer, educator; b. Ames, Iowa, Mar. 18, 1949; d. Christopher Gene and Joy Janice (Johnson) Steinbach; m. Charles Ossian Hartman, May 5, 1979 (div. Dec. 1991); 1 child Zachary Steinbach Hartman BGS, U. Iowa, 1973, MFA, 1976. Teaching fellow U. Iowa, Iowa City, 1975-76; writer in residence Antioch Coll., Yellow Springs, Ohio, 1976-77; lectr. in fiction Northwestern U., Evanston, Ill., 1977-79; vis. asst. prof. U. Washington, 1979-82; Bunting fellow Harvard-Radcliffe, Cambridge, Mass., 1982-83; asst., assoc. prof. Brown U., Providence, R.I., 1983-97, prof. English, 1997—. Author: Zara, 1982, Here Lies the Water, 1990, Reliable Light, 1990, The Birth of the World As We Know It, Or, Teiresias, 1996, In the Realm of Which There Is No Sign, 1995. Recipient Pushcart prize Best of the Small Presses, 1976, R.I. award for Excellence in Lit., R.I. Coun. on Arts, 1986-87, O'Henry award for short story, 1990, creative writing fellow in fiction Nat. Endowment for Arts, 1978; Travel grant Thomas J. Watson Inst. for Internat. Study, France and Greece, 1993-94. Mem.: PEN, Assoc. Writing Programs, Amnesty Internat. Office: Brown U Dept of English Grad Program Literary Arts Box 1923 Providence RI 02912 E-mail: Meredith_Steinbach@Brown.edu.

STEINBAUGH, ROBERT P., management and finance educator; b. Mineral City, Ohio, Aug. 25, 1927; s. Paul W. and Blanche (Lechner) Steinbaugh; m. Carolyn Ann Gates, Nov. 24, 1967. BS, Ohio State U., 1950, MA, 1952, PhD, 1957. Instr. Miami U., Oxford, Ohio, 1953-55, Ohio State U., Columbus, 1955-57; asst. prof. mgmt. and fin. Ind. State U., Terre Haute, 1957-60, assoc. prof., 1960-63, prof. bus. adminstrn., 1963—. Mem. Acad. Mgmt., Am. Mgmt. Assn., Ohio State Alumni Assn., Beta Gamma Sigma, Delta Sigma Pi, Delta Pi Epsilon, Phi Delta Kappa, Phi Kappa Phi. Lodges: Rotary. Republican. Episcopalian. Home: 675 Woodlawn Ct Terre Haute IN 47803-4253

STEINBAUM, BERNICE, art dealer; b. Flushing, NY, Jan. 3, 1941; d. Julius Dov and Sarah (Lasker) Aptowitz; m. Harold Steinbaum; children: Jeremy, Sarah, Carrie. BA, Queens Coll., 1961; MA, Hofstra U., 1965; PhD in Art Edn., Columbia U., 1977. Tchr. Iowa Pub. Sch. System; assoc. prof. Drake U., Iowa; prof. Hofstra U., NYC; gallery dir. Bernice Steinbaum Gallery, NYC. Curator numerous exhbns. and traveling mus. shows; speaker in field; juror numerous art shows. Host: Art Time with Mrs. Steinbaum, Iowa; contbr. articles to profl. publs., mags., and newspapers; author: The Rocker, 1992. Named Woman of Yr. NOW, 1988. Office: Bernice Steinbaum Gallery 3550 N Miami Ave Miami FL 33127-3112 Office Phone: 305-573-2700. Personal E-mail: bernicepla@bellsouth.net.

STEINBAUM, ROBERT S., publishing executive, lawyer; b. Englewood, NJ, Oct. 13, 1951; s. Paul S. and Esther R. (Rosenberg) S.; m. Rosemary Konner, May 26, 1982; children: Marshall, Elliot. BA, Yale U., 1973; JD, Georgetown U., 1976. Bar: D.C. 1976, N.J. 1980, N.Y. 1982. Atty. Cole & Groner P.C., Washington, 1976—79; asst. U.S. atty. U.S. Atty.'s Office, Newark, 1979—84; atty. Scarpone & Edelson, Newark, 1984—87; pub. N.J. Law Jour., Newark, 1987—. Trustee N.J. Jewish News, Whippany, 1990-95, 96—, pres., 2002-04, Blood Ctr. N.J., East Orange, 1987-93, Leadership N.J., 1990; trustee Leadership Newark, 1997—, United Jewish Cmtys. MetroWest, N.J., 2002—, N.J. Vol. Lawyers for Arts, 2004—. Office: NJ Law Jour PO Box 20081 238 Mulberry St Newark NJ 07101-6081 Business E-Mail: rsteinbaum@alm.com.

STEINBERG, ALAN WOLFE, investment company executive; b. Bklyn., Oct. 26, 1927; s. Benjamin F. and Gertrude (Wolfe) S.; m. Suzanne Nichols, Oct. 12, 1958; children: Carol Albanese, Laura Frohman, Benjamin T. AB with honors and spl. distinction in math, Columbia U., 1947, MS, 1950. Indsl. engr. USDA, Washington, 1948—50; ops. rschr. Port N.Y. Authority, 1950—55; prof. engring. NYU, 1956—63; pres. Am. Computing Ctrs., NYC, 1962—66; v.p., dir. TBS Computer Ctrs., NYC, 1967—76; mng. ptnr. Alan W. Steinberg Partnership, NYC and Coral Gables, 1974—. Contbr. articles to profl. jours. Nat. advisor automation United Jewish Appeal, N.Y.C., 1965-75; trustee Fla. Nature Conservancy, Winter Park, 1990—, treas., 1990-2004; bd. dirs., treas. Fla. Audubon Soc., Casselberry, 1984-95, Defenders of Wildlife, Washington, 1985-95, chmn. bd. dirs. 1995-98, treas., 2000—; 1st v.p. Tropical Audubon Soc., South Miami, 1983-93; trustee Stiltsville Trust, Miami, 2004—. Recipient Chmn.'s award Fla. Audubon Soc., 1989, 93; funded named scholarship Columbia Coll. Fellow Fairchild Tropical Garden; mem. Columbia Coll. Alumni Assn. (bd. dirs. 1992-93), Phi Beta Kappa. Home: 5522 Riviera Dr Coral Gables FL 33146-2747 Office: 1501 Venera Ave Ste 205 Coral Gables FL 33146-3052 Home Phone: 305-667-1153. Personal E-mail: SteinbergX@aol.com.

STEINBERG, ANDREW B., federal agency administrator, lawyer; b. 1958; m. Roxann Steinberg; 2 children. BA magna cum laude, Princeton U., 1980; JD cum laude, Harvard Law Sch., 1984. Jud. law clk. to Hon. Richard A. Gadbois, Jr. US Dist. Ct., Calif.; assoc. Gibson, Dunn and Crutcher LLP, 1986—90; assoc. gen. counsel & sr. atty. for antitrust Am. Airlines, Inc., 1990—96; sr. v.p. to exec. v.p., gen. counsel, and sec. Sabre, Inc., 1996—2000; exec. v.p. adminstrn., gen. counsel & corp. sec. Travelocity.com, Inc., 2000—02; v.p., gen. counsel & corp. sec. Church & Dwight Co., Inc., 2002—03; chief counsel FAA, Washington, 2003—06; asst. sec. for aviation & internat. affairs US Dept Transp, Washington, 2006—. Office: US Dept Transp 400 Seventh St SW Rm 10232 Washington DC 20590 *

STEINBERG, ARTHUR IRWIN, periodontist, educator; b. Pitts., Sept. 16, 1935; s. Ben and Sylvia (Jacobs) S.; m. Barbara Fay Ehrenkranz, May 23, 1959; chldren: Sharon Jill, Mindy Ruth, Michael Eli. BS in Microbiology, U. Pitts., 1957, postgrad. in Radiobiology, 1959, DMD cum laude, 1963; diploma in Periodontology-Immunology, Harvard U., Cambridge, Mass., 1966. Asst. prof. periodontology SUNY, Buffalo, 1966-67; assoc. prof. periodontology Temple U., Phila., 1967-68, assoc. prof. grad. periodontology, 1968-70; attending periodontist Phoenixville Hosp., Pa., 1971—95; clin. assoc. prof. U. Pa. Sch. Dental Medicine, 1981—2002, clin. prof. gen. restorative dentistry, 2002—, clin. prof. periodontics, 2007—. Mem. infections control com., by-laws com., religious affairs com., 1977—, credentials com., 1982—; mem. staff Suburban Gen. Hosp. Norristown, Pa., 1971-80, Phoenixville Hosp., 1968-95; asst. prof. periodontics U. Pa., 1973-82, clin. assoc. prof., 1982-2002, clin. prof. gen. restorative dentistry, 2000—, admissions interviewer Sch. Dental Medicine, 2002—; lectr. continuing edn., off-campus program U. Pitts., 1973-93; Fulbright-Hays lectr. Nat. U. Ireland, Cork, 1970-71; vis. prof. Cork Dental Sch. and Hosp., 1971—; lectr. Periodontology Soc. Madrid, 1980, 5th Region Soc. Periodontology Viña Del Mar, Chile, 1985; dentist in pediatrics Charlestown Boys Club, Mass., 1965-66; spkr. Periodontists Conv., Chgo., 1966, NJ Coll. Medicine and Dentistry, Conn. Dental Assn., 1967, U. Ind. Schs. Dentistry and Medicine, Phila. Ann. Dental Sci. Session, 1969, NJ Dental Assn., 1970, Wilmington chpt. Sigma Epsilon Delta, 1974, Lehigh Valley Dental Soc.m 1974, Inst. Medicine, Bucharest, Romania, 1976, Irish Dental Assn., 1992, other confs., and convs.; participant Project Head Start, Childrens Hosp., Boston, 1966; mem. fund-raising subcom. Harvard U. Sch. Dental Medicine, 1980—; mem. faculty U. Pitts., 1988-93; commencement spkr. U. Pa. Sch. Dental Medicine, 1988, Harcum Coll. Dental Hygiene Program, 1994-95, C.C. of Phila. Dental Hygiene Program, 2002; presenter Phila. County Dental Soc., Ann. Meeting Liberty Dental Conf., 1988, 90, Acad. Gen. Dentistry Ann. Meeting, 1988; judge divsn. medicine and healthcare Del. Valley Sci. Fair, 1997; clin. prof. gen. restorative dentistry U. Pa., 2002; admissions interviewer U. Pa. Sch. Dental Medicine, 2002—. Contbg. author: The Fulbright Experience, 1987, Dentistry and the Allergic Patient, 1973; contbr. numerous articles to profl. jours. Named to Phoenixville Hosp. Hall of Honor, 1996; USPHS fellow; reipient Dean J.L.T. Appleton Excellence in CLin. Tchg. award U. Pa., 2003. Fellow Acad. Dentistry Internat., Internat. Acad. Dental Studies, Am. Coll. Dentists, Coll. Physicians Phila., Pierre Fouchard Acad.; mem. AMA, AAUP, Harvard Dental Alumni Assn., Harvard Odontological Soc., Fulbright Assn., Nat. Fulbright Alumni Assn. (a founder 1976, v.p.fin. affairs 1976-79), Am. Acad. Periodontology (ins. com. 1969, hosp. care com. 1973-74, continuing edn. spkr. 1976 conv., 1983 conv., nominating com. chmn. Pa. region to exec. coun. 1975, nat. clin. affairs com. 1984), Am. Coll. Clin. Pharmacology, Northea. Soc. Periodontists, Acad. Stomatology Phila., Phila. Acad. Scis., Sigma Xi, Omicron Kappa Upsilon (life, pres. 2004—), Psi Omega (dep. councillor Zeta chpt. 1977-79, 2004—), Masons (32 degree Shriner), Legion Honor Chapel Four Chaplains, Rotary (dir. 1973-76, chmn. found. com., chmn. internat. svc. 1974-76), B'nai B'rith, Hadassah (assoc. mem.), Harvard of Phila., 25 Yr. Club U. Pa., Area Study (pres. 1976-77), Am. Soc. Ret. Dentists, Omicron Kappa Upsilon (sec./treas. chpt. 2005-06). Home and Office: 1681 Pheasant Ln Norristown PA 19403-3331 Office Phone: 215-898-3268. Business E-Mail: arthurst@pobox.upenn.edu.

STEINBERG, ARTHUR JAY, lawyer; b. Bklyn., Sept. 25, 1955; s. Eugene and Estelle (Bzezensky) S.; m. Ninette Zavelson, Oct. 19, 1980; children: Jaclyn, Lauren, Alyx. BA in Econs. cum laude, Columbia Coll., 1976; JD, NYU, 1979. Bar: NY 1980, US Dist. Ct. (so., ea. and no. dists.) NY, US Cir. Ct. (2d cir.) 1986, US Cir. Ct. (4th cir.) 1991. With Kaye, Scholer LLP, NYC, 1979-87, ptnr., 1988—. Recipient Order of the Coif. Mem. ABA, Am. Banks Inst., NYC Bar Assn. Democrat. Jewish. Office: Kaye Scholer LLP 425 Park Ave New York NY 10022-3506 Office Phone: 212-836-8564. E-mail: asteinberg@kayescholer.com.

STEINBERG, DANIEL, preventive medicine physician, educator; b. Windsor, Ont., Can., July 21, 1922; came to US, 1922. s. Maxwell Robert and Bess (Krupp) S.; m. Sara Murdock, Nov. 30, 1946 (dec. July 1986); children: Jonathan Henry, Ann Ballard, David Ethan; m. Mary Ellen Stratthaus, Aug. 11, 1991; 1 stepchild: Katrin Seifert. BS with highest distinction, Wayne State U., Detroit, 1941, MD with highest distinction, 1944; PhD with distinction, Harvard U., Boston, 1951; MD (hon.), U. Gothenburg, Sweden, 1991. Intern Boston City Hosp., 1944-45; physician Detroit Receiving Hosp., 1945-46; instr. physiology Boston U. Sch. Medicine, 1947-48; joined USPHS, 1951, med. dir., 1959; research staff lab. cellular physiology and metabolism Nat. Heart Inst., 1951-53, chief sect. metabolism, 1956-61, chief of lab. metabolism, 1962-68; lectr. grad. program NIH, 1955, mem. sci. adv. com. ednl. activities, 1955-61, com. chmn., 1955-60; mem. metabolism study sect. USPHS, 1959-61; chmn. heart and lung research rev. com. B Nat. Heart, Lung and Blood Inst., 1977-79; vis. scientist Carlsberg Labs., Copenhagen, 1952-53, Nat. Inst. Med. Research, London, 1960-61, Rockefeller U., 1981; pres. Lipid Research Inc., 1961-64, adv. bd., 1964-73; prof. medicine Sch. Medicine, U. Calif., San Diego, 1968—. Former editor Jour. Lipid Research; mem. editorial bd. Jour Clin. Investigation, 1969-74, Jour. Biol. Chemistry, 1980-84, Arteriosclerosis, 1980—; exec. editor Analytical Biochemistry, 1978-80; contbr. articles to profl. jours. Bd. dirs. Found. Advanced Edn. in Scis., 1959-68, pres., 1956-62, 65-67. Served to capt. M.C. AUS, World War II. Fellow, Am. Cancer Soc., 1950—51. Mem. Nat. Acad. Scis., AAAS, Am. Acad. Arts and Scis., Am. Heart Assn. (mem. exec. com. coun. on arteriosclerosis 1960-63, 65-73, chmn. coun. arteriosclerosis 1967-69), Fedn. Am. Scientists (exec. com. 1957-58), Am. Soc. Biol. Chemists, Am. Soc. Clin. Investigation, Assn. Am. Physicians, Am. Fedn. Clin. Rsch., Inst. Medicine, European Atherosclerosis Discussion Group, Alpha Omega Alpha. Home: 7742 Whitefield Pl La Jolla CA 92037-3810 Office: U Calif San Diego Dept Medicine 9500 Gilman Dr La Jolla CA 92093-0682 Home Phone: 858-454-0597; Office Phone: 858-534-0569. Personal E-mail: dsteinb1@san.rr.com. Business E-Mail: dsteinberg@ucsd.edu.

STEINBERG, DAVID ISAAC, social sciences educator, consultant; b. Cambridge, Mass., Nov. 26, 1928; s. Naaman and Miriam (Goldberg) S.; m. Isabel Maxwell, 1951 (div. 1962); 1 child, Christopher; m. Ann Myongsook Lee, May 15, 1964; children: Alexander L., Eric D. BA, Dartmouth Coll., 1950; MA, Harvard U., 1955; DLitt (hon.), Sungkunkwan U., Seoul, Republic of Korea. Analyst Nat. Security Coun., Washington, 1951-53; program officer Asia Found., NYC, 1956-58, asst. rep. Burma, 1958-62, Hong Kong, 1962-63, rep. Republic of Korea, 1963-68, Washington, 1968-69; cons., sr. fgn. svc. officer AID, Washington and Bangkok (Thailand), 1969-86; ret., 1986; pres. Mansfield Ctr. for Pacific Affairs, Helena, Mont., 1986-87, Sr. Resources Internat., 1989-94; disting. prof. Korea Studies Georgetown U., Washington, 1990-94; rep. The Asia Found., Seoul, Republic of Korea, 1994-97; dir. Asian studies Sch. Fgn. Svc. Georgetown U., Washington, 1997—, Disting. prof. and dir. Asian studies, 1997—. Pvt. cons., Washington, 1987—, World Bank, 1987—, Woodrow Wilson Ctr. for Scholars of the Smithsonian Instn., Dept. of State and the Agy. for Internat. Devel., the Can. Internat. Devel. Agy., Devel. Assocs., Inc., and others; founding mem. Burma Studies Found., De Kalb, Ill., 1987. Author: Burma's Road Toward Development, 1981, Burma, 1982, The Republic of Korea Economic Transformation and Social Change, 1988, The Future of Burma, 1990, Burma: The State of Myanmar, 2001, Stone Mirror: Reflections on Contemporary Korea, 2003, Turmoil in Burma: Contested Legitimacies in Myanmar, 2006; co-editor Georgetown Southeast Asia Survey 2002-05. 1st lt. U.S. Army, 1953-55. Fellow Lingnan U., Canton, China, 1948, Dartmouth Coll., 1950; named Disting. Prof. of Korea Studies, Georgetown U. Mem. Assn. Asian Studies, Oriental Ceramic Soc., Asia Devel. Roundtable (chmn. 1984-86, 87—), Siam Soc., Royal Asiatic Soc. (life Korea br.), Burma Rsch. Soc. (life), Asia Soc. (cons. 1988—), Cosmos Club, Royal Bangkok (Thailand) Sports Club. Home: 6207 Goodview St Bethesda MD 20817-6101 Office: Georgetown U Sch Fgn Svc Washington DC 20057 Home Phone: 301-263-0339; Office Phone: 202-687-0251. Business E-Mail: steinbdi@georgetownuniversity.edu.

STEINBERG, DAVID JOEL, academic administrator, historian, educator; b. NYC, Apr. 5, 1937; s. Milton and Edith (Alpert) S.; m. Sally Levitt (div. Dec., 1986); children: Noah, Jonah; m. Joan Diamond, Aug. 28, 1987. BA magna cum laude, Harvard U., 1959, MA, 1963, PhD, 1964; LittD, Kyung Hee U., Seoul, Korea, 1989; LLD (hon), Keimyung U., Daegu, Korea. Prof. history U. Mich., 1964-73; exec. asst. to pres. Brandeis U., Waltham, Mass., 1973-77, v.p., univ. sec., 1977-83; pres. L.I. U., Brookville, NY, 1985—. Testified before Com. on Fgn. Affairs, U.S. Ho. of Reps., Fgn. Affairs Com. of U.S. Senate; cons. The Ford Found., UN Fund for Population Activities. Author: Philippine Collaboration in World War II, 1967 (Univ. Press award, 1969), The Philippines: A Singular and a Plural Place, 1982, 1987, Asia in Western and World History: A Guide for Tchg., 1993; co-author: The Emergence of Modern Southeast Asia: A New History, 2004, Religion and Religiosity in the Philippines and Indonesia: Essays on State, Society and Public Creeds, 2005. Chmn. Commn. Ind. Colls. and Univs.; past pres. Cambridge (Mass.) Ctr. for Adult Edn., chmn. L.I. Group; bd. trustee Nat. Commn. Coop. Edn. English Speaking Union Exch. scholar, Malvern Coll., NDEA scholar, Fulbright Found. exch. scholar. Mem. Coun. Fgn. Rels., Assn. Asian Studies (chmn. fin. com.), Harvard Club (N.Y.C.), Century Club (N.Y.C.). Democrat. Jewish. Office: LI Univ Off Pres 700 Northern Blvd Greenvale NY 11548-1320 Business E-Mail: pres@liu.edu.

STEINBERG, DONALD R., lawyer; b. 1962; BSE magna cum laude, Princeton Univ., 1984; JD cum laude, Harvard Univ., 1988. Bar: Mass. 1988, U.S. Patent & Trademark Office. Ptnr., vice chmn. Intellectual Property dept. Wilmer Cutler Pickering Hale & Dorr, Boston, 1994—. Adj. faculty mem. New Eng. Sch. Law. Mem.: Intellectual Property Owners Assn. (mem. Trademark Law Com.), Phi Beta Kappa. Office: Wilmer Cutler Pickering Hale & Dorr 60 State St Boston MA 02109 Office Phone: 617-526-6453. Office Fax: 617-526-5000. Business E-Mail: donald.steinberg@wilmerhale.com.

STEINBERG, HOWARD, chemical company executive, consultant; b. Chgo., Aug. 23, 1926; s. Leo and Hattie (Seskind) Steinberg; m. Eve Taubman, Feb. 10, 1946; children: Lisa Beth Leonard, Gary Robert, Erik Jon. BS, U. Ill., Urbana, 1946—48; PhD, UCLA, 1948—51. Rsch. chemist Aerojet Gen. Corp., Azusa, Calif., 1952—52; rsch. assoc. UCLA, 1952—53; collaborator USDA, Pasadena, Calif., 1953—54; mgr. organic rsch. U.S. Borax Rsch. Corp., Anaheim, Calif., 1954—58, asst. dir., 1958—59, assoc. dir., 1959—61, dir. chem. rsch., 1961—63, v.p., 1963—69, pres., 1969—90; v.p. US Borax and Chem. Corp., LA, 1969—90, dir., 1973—90, cons., 1990—92; dir. Ireco Chem. Co., Salt Lake City, 1970—75. Author: (book) Organoboron Chemistry; co-author (book (treatise); editor: (books) Progress in Boron Chemistry; contbr. numerous research papers; numerous US and foreign patents in field of organoboron chemistry. Mem. Sci. and Engring. Adv. Coun., Calif. State Univ., Fullerton, 1964—90; dir. Orange County Cultural Groups Found., Fullerton, Calif., 1970—71. Pre-aviation cadet Air Corp US Army, 1945—45. Named to Am. Men Sci., Adv. Com. apptd. by the NAS, 1961, Leading Men in the USA, 1965; AEC Fellow, UCLA, 1950—51, AEC Postdoctoral Fellow, MIT, 1951—52. Mem.: AIME, Am. Chem. Soc., Brit. Chem. Soc., Indsl. Rsch. Inst., Soc. Chem. Industry, Phi Lambda Upsilon, Pi Mu Epsilon, Sigma Xi. Achievements include researcher and coauthor with Professor Donald J. Cram in the first two papers of his seminal work (Host-Guest chemistry) leading to his 1987 Nobel Prize in Chemistry. Avocations: woodworking, golf, fiction writing. Home and Office: 16 Corte Sevilla San Clemente CA 92673 Office Phone: 949-661-9009.

STEINBERG, HOWARD ELI, lawyer, diversified financial services company executive; b. NYC, Nov. 19, 1944; s. Herman and Anne Steinberg; m. Judith Ann Schucart, Jan. 28, 1968; children: Henry Robert, Kathryn Jill. AB, U. Pa., 1965; JD, Georgetown U., 1969. Bar: N.Y. 1970, U.S. Dist. Ct. (so. and ea. dists.) N.Y. 1973, U.S. Ct. Appeals (2d cir.) 1976. Assoc. Dewey, Ballantine, Bushby, Palmer & Wood, NYC, 1969-76, ptnr., 1977-83; exec. v.p., gen. counsel Reliance Group Holdings, Inc., NYC, 1983-2000, exec. v.p., chief corp. ops., 2000—01; exec. v.p., gen. counsel Prudential Securities, Inc., NYC, 2001—03, Prudential Equity Group, NYC, 2003—05; ptnr. McDermott Will & Emery LLP, NYC, 2005—. Chmn. N.Y. State Thruway Authority, 1996—99; dep. chmn. L.I. Power Authority, 1999—. Editor: Georgetown Law Jour., 1968—69. Bd. dirs. Puerto Rican Legal Def. and Edn. Fund, Inc., 1993—95, Sheltering Arms Children's Svc., 1997—2005; bd. overseers U. Pa. Sch. Arts and Scis., 1989—2002; bd. regents Georgetown U., 1999—2005. Capt. JAGC USAR, 1972—74. Mem.: ABA, Securities Industry Assn. (co-chair, mem. fed. regulation com. 2001—05, mem. exec. com. compliance and legal divsn. 2001—05), Assn. Bar City of N.Y. (mem. com. scurities regulation 1984—87, mem. com. corp. law 1987—90, mem. com. fed. legis. 1990—93, chair ad hoc com. Senate Confirmation Process 1991—92), N.Y. State Bar Assn., Univ Club. Office: McDermott Will Emery 340 Madison Ave New York NY 10017 Office Phone: 212-547-5415. Business E-Mail: hsteinberg@mwe.com.

STEINBERG, JEFFREY MARK, obstetrician, gynecologist, medical researcher; b. Phila., Oct. 7, 1953; BS, UCLA, 1973; MD, U. Guadalajara, Mex., 1977; MS, U. Saskatchewan, Can., 1978. Diplomate Am. Bd. Ob-Gyn, Am. Bd. Med. Reproductive Endocrinology. Advanced infertility tng. Bourne Hall Clinic, Cambridge U., England; intern, obstetrics and gynecology U. Saskatchewan. Regina, 1977—78; resident, endocrinology Rush Presbyterian St. Lukes Hosp., Chgo., 1979—81; dir. InVitro Fertilization program Northridge Hosp. Med. Ctr., Calif., 1981-83; dir. fertility InVitro Fertilization program Glendale Adventist Med. Ctr., Calif., 1986; fellow reproductive endocrinology and infertility U. Calif.-San Diego, La Jolla, 1986—88; med. dir. Fertility Inst. (LA, Calif. and Las Vegas, Nev.), 1986—. Hosp. appt. Northridge Hosp. Med. Ctr., Calif.; hosp. appt., dept. reproductive medicine U. Calif. San Diego. Contbr. articles to profl. jours.; featured on 60 Minutes and several other news programs and documentaries in the field of infertility and related disorders. NIH grantee, 1986. Fellow Am. Coll. Obstetricians and Gynelcologists; mem. Am. Fertility Soc., Am. Assn. Gynecologic Lapnrascopists, Pacific Coast Fertility Soc. Avocations: music, recording and sound engring. Office Phone: 818-776-8700.

STEINBERG, JONATHAN S., cardiologist, educator; BA, Queens Coll., 1976; MD, Mt. Sinai Sch. Medicine, 1980. Diplomate Am. Bd. Internal Medicine with subspecialty cardiovasc. disease and clin. electrophysiology. Resident NYU Med Ctr., chief resident NY VA, 1981-84; fellow critical cardiology George Washington U. Med. Ctr., 1984-86; fellow electrophysiology Columbia Presbyn. Hosp., 1986-88; chief divsn. cardiology, dir. arrhythmia svc. St. Luke's-Roosevelt Hosp. Ctr. Prof. medicine Columbia U., Coll. Physicians and Surgeons. Office: St Lukes-Roosevelt Hosp Ctr 1111 Amsterdam Ave New York NY 10025-1716 Fax: 212-523-3915.

STEINBERG, LAURA, lawyer; b. Phila., Feb. 3, 1948; d. Leonard and Pearl (Zeid) S.; children; Seth, Adam, Bree. BA magna cum laude with honors, Bryn Mawr Coll., 1968; JD cum laude, Harvard U., 1972. Bar: Mass. 1972, U.S. Dist. Ct. Mass. 1972, U.S. Dist. Ct. R.I. 1974, U.S. Ct. Appeals (1st cir.) 1973, U.S. Ct. Appeals (10th and D.C. cirs.) 1986, U.S. Ct. Appeals (4th cir.) 1988, U.S. Claims Ct. 1979, U.S. Supreme Ct. 1988. Assoc. Sullivan & Worcester, Boston, 1972-79, ptnr., 1979—, mem. mgmt. com., 1988-2000, head litigation dept., 1987—99, chair complex bus. fiduciary litigation group, 2004—. Dir. Greater Boston Legal Svcs., 1987-90. Bd. dirs. Law Firm Resources Project, Boston, 1980-86, Lawyers Com. for Civil Rights Under Law, 1998—; pres. Peirce Extended Day Program, Inc., West Newton, Mass., 1983-86. Spl. career fellow U. Calif., Berkeley, 1968-69; Fulbright scholar, 1968. Mem. Boston Bar Assn. (vice-chmn. litigation sect. 1992-94, chmn. 1994-95). Avocations: reading, tennis. Office: Sullivan & Worcester LLP One Post Office Sq Ste 2100 Boston MA 02109-2129 Office Phone: 617-338-2800. E-mail: lsteinberg@sandw.com.

STEINBERG, LAWRENCE EDWARD, lawyer; b. Dallas, Nov. 25, 1935; s. Oscar J. and Pearl L. (Soloman) S.; children: Adam Joseph, Ilana Sara, Oliver David. BBA, U. Tex., 1958; JD, So. Meth. U., 1960. Bar: Tex. 1960. Since practiced in, Dallas; ptnr. firm Steinberg Soloman & Meer, 1971-88, Johnson & Steinberg, Dallas, 1988-93; chmn., CEO Eagle Equity, Inc., Dallas, 1991—; of counsel Jenkins & Gilchrist, Dallas, 1993—98. Active Urban Rehab. Stds. Bd., Dallas, 1975-76; adv. com. affirmative action program Dallas Ind. Sch. Dist., 1974-76; regional bd. chmn. Anti-Defamation League of B'nai Brith, 1974-77, nat. exec. com., 1977—, nat. law com., 1974-87; trustee Edna Gladney Home, 1975-92; v.p., trustee Shelton Sch., 1987-90; trustee Temple Emanu-El, 1992-94, Dallas Jewish Cmty. Found., 1990-2001, 2005—; pres. U. Tex. Hillel Found., 2001-2003, mem. exec. com., 2001—; bd. dirs. Jewish Fedn. Greater Dallas, 1984-87, 91-94, Dallas Coun. on World Affairs, 1998—, Stephen Wise, Acad., 1998-2002, Dallas Holocaust Ctr., 1998—, Jewish Inst. Nat. Securities Affairs, 1999—, Dallas Furniture Found., 2003—; v.p. Am. Jewish Commn., 2003—; regional bd. chmn. Am. Israel Pub. Affairs Com., 1997-2001, nat. exec. com., 1998—; mem. Dallas Com. Fgn. Rels. 2d lt. U.S. Army, 1959-60. Mem. Columbian Club, Masons, Shriners, Zeta Beta Tau, Phi Delta Phi, Beta Gamma Sigma, Pi Tau Pi (nat. pres. 1964-66). Home: 10131 Hollow Way Rd Dallas TX 75229-6634 Office: 5430 LBJ Fwy Ste 1575 Dallas TX 75240

STEINBERG, LEIGH WILLIAM, sports agent; b. LA, 1949; m. Lucy Steinberg; 3 children. BA in Polit. Sci., UCLA, 1970; JD, U. Calif., Berkeley, 1973. Founder, ptnr. Steinberg, Moorad & Dunn, 1975—99; CEO Assante Sports Mgmt. Group, 1999—2003; founder, ptnr. Steinberg, Tollner & Moon, Newport Beach, Calif., 2003—. Co-author (with Michael D'Orso): Winning with Integrity: Getting What You Want Without Selling Your Soul, 1998. Office: 660 Newport Ctr Dr Ste 1000 Newport Beach CA 92660

STEINBERG, LEO, art historian, educator; b. Moscow, July 9, 1920; arrived in U.S., 1945; s. Isaac N. and Anna (Esselson) S. PhD, NYU Inst Fine Arts, 1960; PhD (hon.), Phila. Coll. Art, 1981, Parsons Sch. Design, 1986, Mass. Coll. Art, 1987, Bowdoin Coll., 1995, Columbia U., 2004, Harvard U., 2006. Freelance writer, translator, life-drawing instr. Parsons Sch. Design; assoc. prof. art history Hunter Coll., CUNY, NYC, 1962—66, prof., 1966-75; prof. Grad. Ctr. CUNY, 1969-75, co-founder art history dept., 1972; Benjamin Franklin prof. art. history U. Pa., Phila., 1975-91, prof. emeritus, 1991—. A.W. Mellon lectr. in Fine Arts, Nat. Gallery Art, Washington, D.C., 1981-82; Gauss Lectures, Princeton U., NJ, 1985; Charles Eliot Norton lectr. Harvard U., Cambridge, Mass., 1995-96; Meyer Schapiro Chair, Columbia U., N.Y., 1991; spkr. in field. Author: Jasper Johns, 1963, Other Criteria: Confrontations with Twentieth-century Art, 1972, 2d edit., 2007, Michelangelo's Last Paintings, the Conversion of St. Paul and the Crucifixion of St. Peter in the Cappella Paolina, Vatican Palace, 1975, Borromini's San Carlo alle Quattro Fontane: A Study in Multiple Form and Architectural Symbolism, 1977, The Sexuality of Christ in Renaissance Art and in Modern Oblivion, 1983, 2nd revised and enlarged edit., 1996, Encounters with Rauschenberg, 1999, Leonardo's Incessant Last Supper, 2001. Recipient award in lit. Am. Acad. and Inst. Arts and Letters, 1983; fellow Am. Acad. Arts and Scis., 1978, Univ. Coll., London U., 1979, MacArthur Found., 1986; resident scholar, Am. Acad. in Rome, Getty Ctr. for History of Art and the Humanities, Santa Monica, Calif. Mem. Coll. Art Assn. Am. (bd. mem., 1969-71, recipient Frank Jewett Mather award for Distinction in Criticism, 1956, 84, Disting. Scholar award 2002). Home: 165 W 66th St New York NY 10023-6508

STEINBERG, MARTY, lawyer; b. Balt., May 13, 1945; BS cum laude in Pharmacy, U. Pitts., 1968; JD cum laude, Ohio State U., 1971. Bar: Ohio 1971, Fla. 1974; U.S. Supreme Ct. 1981; Registered Pharmacist Ohio 1968. Atty. U.S. Dept. Justice, Washington, Miami, 1972-78, atty. in charge N.Y. regional offices Washington, 1978-79; chief counsel, permanent subcommittee on investigations U.S. Senate, Washington, 1979-82; ptnr. Holland & Knight, Miami, Fla.; mng. ptnr., litig., intellectual property, antitrust Hunton & Williams LLP, Miami, 1999—. Inst. Canisius Coll. Buffalo, N.Y. 1978-79, SUNY Buffalo 1978-79, Am. U. Washington D.C. 1980-81. Contbr. articles to profl. jours. Bd. dirs. Miami Citizens Against Crime. Recipient Am. Jurisprudence award. Mem. ABA, Fla. Bar Assn., Ohio State Bar Assn., Am. Law Inst. (chmn. civic justice adv. com.), Fellow, Am. Coll. Trial Lawyers, Am. Bar Found., Am. Pharm. Assn., Am. Assn. Corporate Counsel. Office: Hunton & Williams LLP 1111 Brickell Ave Miami FL 33131 Office Phone: 305-810-2500. Office Fax: 305-810-2460. Business E-Mail: msteinberg@hunton.com.

STEINBERG, MEYER, chemical engineer; b. Phila., July 10, 1924; s. Jacob Louis and Freda Leah S.; m. Ruth Margot Elias, Dec. 24, 1950; children: David Martin, Jay Louis. BSChemE, Cooper Union, 1944; MSChemE, Bklyn. Poly. Inst., 1949. Registered profl. engr. N.Y. Jr. chem. engr. Manhattan dist., Kellex Corp., Oak Ridge, Los Alamos, 1944-46; asst. chem. engr. Deutsch & Loonam, 1947-50; chem. engr. Guggenheim Brothers, Mineola, NY, 1950-57; head process sci. div. Brookhaven Nat. Lab., Upton, NY, 1957—. Expert in fossil and nuclear energy; v.p. HCE LLC on coal conversion energy and environment. Author: (with Martin Hallman) Carbon Dioxide Greenhouse Gas Mitigation Technologies, 1999; contbr. articles to profl. jours. Served with AUS, 1944-46. Recipient IR-100 award, 1970; Wasson award Am. Concrete Inst., 1972, Engr. of Year award, 1985, Ind. award Quest, 1985, Greenman award, Internat. Energy Agy., London UK, IEA Greenhouse Program, 1996. Fellow Am. Nuclear Soc., Am. Inst. Chem. Engrs. (dir. L.I. sect.); mem. Am. Chem. Soc., AAAS, Am. Concrete Inst., Inst. Assos. Hydrogen Energy, Sigma Xi. Democrat. Jewish. Achievements include research on nuclear and fossil energy. Home: 15 Alderfield Ln Melville NY 11747-1724 Office: Brookhaven Nat Lab Upton NY 11973 Office Phone: 631-427-0768. Office Fax: 631-427-0590. Personal E-mail: mrsteinb@optonline.net.

STEINBERG, MICHAEL, music critic, educator; b. Breslau, Germany, Oct. 4, 1928; came to U.S., 1943, naturalized, 1950; s. Siegfried and Margarethe (Cohn) S.; m. Jane Bonacker, July 26, 1953 (div. 1983); children: Peter Sebastian, Adam Gregory; m. Jorja Fleezanis, July, 1983. AB, Princeton U., 1949, M.F.A., 1951; Mus. D. (hon.), New Eng. Conservatory Music, 1966. Free-lance writer, 1952—; head history dept. Manhattan Sch. Music, NYC, 1957-64; music critic Boston Globe, 1964-76; dir. publs. Boston Symphony Orch., 1976-79; artistic adviser San Francisco Symphony, 1979-89, program annotator, lectr., 1989-99; artistic adviser Minn. Orch., 1989-92; artistic dir. Minn. Sommerfest, 1990-92; program annotator, lectr. N.Y. Philharmonic, 1995-2000. Vis. mem. faculty Hunter Coll., 1954, U. Sask. (Can.), 1959, Smith Coll., 1964, Brandeis U., 1964-65; faculty New Eng. Conservatory Music, 1968-71, Wellesley Coll., 1971-72, Brandeis U., 1971-72, Mass. Inst. Tech., 1973; disting. vis. prof. McMaster U., Hamilton, Ont., 1982; U. Mo., 2006; cons. NEH, Nat. Endowment for Arts, Mass. Council of Arts and Humanities, Calif. Arts Council, Rockefeller Found.; free-lance writer, lectr. Author: The Symphony: A Listener's Guide, 1995, The Concerto: A Listener's Guide, 1998, Choral Masterworks: A Listener's Guide, 2005, (with Larry Rothe) For the Love of Music, 2006. Served with U.S. Army, 1955-57. Recipient Sang prize for criticism in arts, 1969; citation for Excellence in Criticism Am. Guild Organists, 1972. Mem. Am, Internat. musicological socs. Home: 750 2d St South # 701 Minneapolis MN 55401-2375 Home Phone: 612-332-0236. Personal E-mail: fleeberg@earthlink.net.

STEINBERG, MILTON, retired educational association administrator; b. Cornwall, NY, Apr. 3, 1941; s. Samuel Lewis Steinberg, Anna Ethel Steinberg; m. Francine Steinberg (div.); children: Daniel B., Rachel T. Rubenstein; m. Rimma Steinberg, Sept. 14, 1986; stepchildren: Marina Harary, Galina Ziegler. BA in Psychology, UCLA, 1963; MS in Adminstrv. Scis., City U., London, 1968. Sales rep. Gen. Tng. Svc., NYC, 1969—70; caseworker City of NY, Bronx, 1970—71; state vet. counselor NY State, Spring Valley, 1971—; ret., 2005. Vol. Congressman Benjamin A. Gilman campaign, Rockland County, NY, 1991—2002; sec. B'nai Jeshurun Synagogue, Monsey, NY, 1987—. Specialist 4th class US Army, 1963—65. Recipient Cert. of Honor, Town of Ramapo, N.Y., 1995, Cert. of Humanitarianism, 1993, 1995, Cert. of Appreciation, Rockland County Am. Legion, 1997, 2000. Mem.: DAV (life), Nat. Mus. Am. Jewish Mil. History, Vietnam Vets. Am., Am. Legion (county svc. officer, post svc. officer), Jewish War Vets. (state svc. officer, post svc. officer, nat. svc. officer, Cert. Appreciation 1999, 2001, Cert. Merit 1995). Republican. Jewish. Avocations: travel, gardening, reading, photography, music. Office: Bur Vets Edn 116 West 32nd St 5th Fl New York NY 10001 E-mail: amerivet@hotmail.com.

STEINBERG, MORTON M., lawyer; b. Chgo, Feb. 13, 1945; m. Miriam C. Bernstein, Aug. 25, 1974; children: Adam Michael, Shira Judith. AB with honors, U. Ill., 1967; JD, Northwestern U., 1971. Bar: Ill. 1971, DC 1994, Colo. 1995, NY, 2003, US Dist. Ct. (no. dist.) Ill. 1971, US Dist. Ct. Colo. 1998, US Ct. Appeals (7th cir.) 1971, US Supreme Ct. 1974. Assoc. Caffarelli & Wiczer, Chgo., 1971-73, Arnstein, Gluck, Lehr, Barron & Milligan, Chgo., 1974-76, ptnr., 1977-86, DLA Piper US LLP (and predecessor firms), 1986—. Spkr. in field. Sr. editor Jour. Criminal Law and Criminology, Northwestern U., 1969-71. Chmn. Chgo. region Leaders Tng. Fellowship, 1962-63; bd. dirs. Camp Ramah Wis., Inc., Chgo., 1974—, sr. v.p., 1992-94, pres. 1994-2003, chmn. bd. trustees, 2003-; bd. dirs., pres. Ramah Day Camp, Inc., Chgo., 2001-03; bd. dirs., v.p. Camp Ramah Wis. Endowment Corp., 1993-2003, pres. 2003-; bd. dirs. North Suburban Synagogue Beth-El, Highland Park, Ill., 1978—, corp. sec., 1983-87, pres., 1989-91, chmn. bd. trustees, 1991-93, trustee, 1991—; mem. Nat. Ramah Commn., Jewish Theol. Sem., 1987—, v.p., 1994-2003, pres., 2003-2007; mem. bd. overseers Albert A. List Coll., 2004—; mem. leadership coun. Conservative Judaism, 2004-2007; bd. dirs. MERCAZ USA 2006-, Found. Conservative Judaism in Israel, 1985-90; Midwest region bd. dirs. United Synagogue of Conservative Judaism, 1989-91, 94-2003; mem. editor's cir. Jewish Forward Newspaper, 1997-2000; trustee Am. Jewish Hist. Soc., 1998—; charter mem. US Holocaust Meml. Mus., 1992; pro bono counsel Frank Lloyd Wright Preservation Trust, Oak Park, Ill., 1996—; elected del. from US to 35th World Zionist Congress, Jerusalem, 2006; bd. govs. State Israel Bonds, 2007-. With 801st Gen. Hosp. USAR, 1969—75. Recipient Youth Leadership award Nat. Fedn. Jewish Men's Clubs, NYC, 1963; Merit cert. US Dist. Ct. Fed. Defender Program, Chgo., 1969; named Ill. Super Lawyer, Chgo. Mag., 2005-07. Mem. ABA, DC Bar, NY State Bar Assn., Ill. State Bar Assn., Chgo. Bar Assn., Profl. Assn. Diving Instrs. (cert. scuba open water diver 2005), Standard Club. Jewish. Home: 1320 Lincoln Ave S Highland Park IL 60035-3459 Office: DLA Piper US LLP Ste 1900 203 N La Salle St Chicago IL 60601-1225

STEINBERG, ROBERT PHILIP, lawyer; b. Danville, Ill., Apr. 4, 1931; s. Frederick Philip and Beulah Iona (Olmsted) S.; m. Doris Elizabeth Blank, May 10, 1958; children: Susan Elizabeth, Mary Louise. BA, DePauw U., 1953; LLB, N.Y. U., 1956. Bar: N.Y. 1956, Pa. 1959. Assoc. Shearman & Sterling, NYC, 1956, Drinker Biddle & Reath, Phila., 1958-65, ptnr., 1965-97, chmn., 1992-94, of counsel, 1997-98; ptnr. Commons & Commons LLP, Phila., 1998—2004, of counsel, 2004—. V.p. Germantown Hist. Soc., Phila., 1991-95, The Phila. Theatre Co., 1992-96; pres. E. Falls Cmty. Coun., 1997-2000. Mem. Phila. Bar Assn. (treas. 1970-72). Home: 3906 W Netherfield Rd Philadelphia PA 19129-1014 Office: Commons & Commons LLP 6377 Germantown Ave Philadelphia PA 19144 Office Phone: 215-849-4400. E-mail: psteinberg@commonslaw.com.

STEINBERG, ROY BENNETT, television producer, director, educator; b. NYC, Mar. 24, 1951; s. Seymour and Flora Joyce (Matthews) S.; m. Marlena Lustik, Sept. 8, 1984, 1 child, Alexa Catherine. BA, Tufts U., 1973; MFA, Yale U., 1978. Guest artist various univs., 1978-87; dir. Circle Repertory Co. Lab., NYC, 1985-90; artistic dir. John Michael Kohler Arts Ctr., Sheboygan, Wis., 1988; prodr. Guiding Light, CBS-TV, NYC, 1990-98; dir. One Life To Live, 1999; prodr., dir. Days of Our Lives, NBC; prof. Muhlenberg Coll., 1999—. Freelance drama coach, N.Y.C., 1978—; script cons. Circle Repertory Co. Lab., N.Y.C., 1985-90; casting dir. Theatre Matrix, N.Y.C., 1981-83; adv. bd. Sch. Film & TV, N.Y.C., 1995—. Actor: (play) Wings, 1979 (Tony nomination 1979), (TV spl.) The Wall, 1980, (soap opera) Another World, 1985, (film) The Man Who Envied Women, 1986; dir. (play) Private Lives, 1987, Absent Friends, 1987, Broadway Bound, 1988, The Miser, 1989, The Learned Ladies, 1989, The Marriage Fool, 1989, Othello, 1989, Children, 1996, Blithe Spirit, 1997, Intuition, 1997. Five Towns Music & Art Found. scholar, 1969, 4 Emmy nominations, 1990-93. Mem. AFTRA (nat. del. 1988), Actors Equity Assn. (dep.), Soc. Stage Dirs. and Choreographers, Dirs. Guild Am., Screen Actors Guild. Avocations: travel, cooking, movies, sports, reading. Home: 3821 Berry Drive Studio City CA 91604 Office Phone: 818-840-2816. Business E-Mail: rsteinberg@dool.net.

STEINBERG, RUBIN, retired art educator, artist; b. Chgo., May 31, 1934; s. Louis Steinberg and Tanya Zelmanov; m. Marcia Kay Mann, 1960. B in Edn., Chgo. Tchrs. Coll., 1957; M in Edn., Roosevelt U., 1961; MFA, Art Inst. Chgo., 1968. Art tchr. Curie HS for the Performing and Creative Arts, Chgo., 1960—95. One-man shows include Bernard Horwich Jewish Cmty. Ctr., Chgo., 4 Arts Assocs., Evanston, Ill., One Ill. Ctr., Chgo., Monroe Gallery, Oak Park Libr., Park Forest Art Ctr., Northbrook Racquet Club # 2, Deerfield HS, Mayer Kaplan Jewish Cmty. Ctr., Skokie, Ill., Krochs & Brentanos, Chgo., Bonwit Teller, Suburban Fine Arts Ctr., Highland Park, Ill., A.R.C. Gallery, Chgo., Chgo. Cultural Ctr., Renaissance Ct., exhibited in group shows at Chgo. Soc. Artists Retrospective, 1983, Mus. Sci. and Industry, Chgo., Ill. State Mus., Springfield, So. Ohio Mus., Portsmouth, 1982, Oakbrook Invitational Crafts Exhbn., 1979—80, 1987—91, North Shore Art League, 1979, Chgo. Soc. Artists, 1977—, Am. Jewish Artists Club Exhbns., 1970—, Midwest Craft Festival, —, North Shore Art League, 1974—, 1978—, 1986, Art Inst. Chgo., 1968, 1973 (Mcpl. Art League award, 1973), Suburban Fine Arts Festeival, Highland Park (award for excellence, 1973), Old Orchard Art Festival, North Shore Art League, 1971—96, Gold Coast Assn., 1967—89, Mcpl. Art League (award for excellence, 1990), Blue Moon Gallery, Skokie, 1996, 2000, Balzekas Mus., Chgo., 1996, Loyola U., 1997, Taipei Fine Arts Mus., Taiwan, 1999, Time Life Bldg., Chgo., 1999, Spertus Mus., Represented in permanent collections So. Ohio Mus., Ill. State Mus., Spertus Mus. Judaica, Kraziai Mus. Contemporary Art, Lithuania, Sudler & Co., Chgo., McDonald's Corp., Oakbrook, Ill., Continental Bank, Chgo., Borg Warner, JJ Barrett, Inc. Comm., Slotowski Sausage Co., Malow Cordage Corp., Mt. Prospect, Ill., Morgan, Madison Steel Co., Skokie, Dance Fashions, Chgo., Aval Corp., P&R Mfg. Co., Lyric Opera Chgo., Peat, Marwick & Mitchell, Accts., Chgo., Marshall Field's Home Store, Schaumburg, Ill., Binney & Smith Co., Easton, Pa., Sanford Co., Bellwood, Ill., Sakura of Am., Hayward, Calif., Emily Oaks Nature Ctr., Skokie. Served with US Army, 1958—60. Address: 3127 W Jerome St Chicago IL 60645

STEINBERG, RUSSELL, composer, secondary education educator; BA summa cum laude, UCLA, 1981; MusM with honors, New Eng. Conservatory, Boston, 1983; PhD in Music, Harvard U., 1987. Postdoctoral tchg. asst. Harvard U., Cambridge, Mass., 1988-90; orch. dir. Temple Emanuel, Beverly Hills, Calif., 1990-93; composer-in-residence Music Festival Goucher Coll., Balt., 1993; dir. Music Media Lab. and prof. ext. sch. UCLA, 1993, vis. asst. prof. music theory and composition, 1991-93; pres. Five-One Prodns., Ltd., 1995; dir. music Milken Cmty. H.S. Prof. composition and music appreciation Extension Sch., 1993—. Solo compositions include Small Rain, Periods of Luminance, Tonal Whispers, Sequoia Sonata, ichroisms, Atonal Variations (all for piano), White Crane Study,

Latigo Lides Canticles, Double Stop Etude (all for violin), Five Preludes (for guitar); duo compositions include Flute Sonata, Six Duos for Violin, Fantasy for Flute and Piano, Classic Berlin; trios include Fanfares for Three Trumpets, Rings of Saturn, Piano Trio; quartets include String quartet, Woodwind Quartet, Change of Heart, also others; film scores include You Are What You Eat, 1993, Paper Flowers (documentary), 1993, Class (comedy-variety pilot), 1992, Fatal Charm (feature-length psychodrama), 1991, Dressage Freestyle music, 1991, Amber Waves (documentary), 1990, others; author: (CD-Rom) Richard Strauss: Three Tone Poems, 1992, Microsoft's Multimedia Strauss, 1994; orchestral compositions include Symphony No. 1 City Strains, 1998; contbr. articles to profl. jours.; commns. include Sheridon Stokes, Flute Sonata, 1993, Endre Granat and Alex Horvath, Violin Duos, 1992, Aspen Ctr. for Advanced Composition, City Strains, 1993, others. Recipient Disting. teaching award Harvard U., 1987, 1st prize New World String Quartet Competition, 1987; Aspen fellow, 1992, 93, MacDowell fellow, 1991, Cummington Cmty. of the Arts fellow, 1985; ASCAP grantee for young composers, 1987. Mem. Musicians Union Local 47, Coll. Music Soc., Am. Music Ctr., Harvard Group for New Music (founding mem.), NuClassix Inc. (founding mem.), Nat. Assn. Composers (2nd prize 1984, 86), Phi Beta Kappa, Phi Kappa Lambda.

STEINBERG, RUSSELL MAX, behavioral pediatrician, educator; b. Salinas, Calif., Aug. 18, 1941; s. Martin and Eve S. AB in Zoology, UCLA, 1963, MA in Zoology and Endocrinology, 1964, PhD in Zoology and Endocrinology with distinction, 1969; MD, Med. Coll. Ohio, Toledo, 1972. Diplomate Nat. Bd. Med. Examiners. Intern in pediatrics Affiliated Hosps. U. Calif., Irvine, 1972-73, resident in pediatrics Affiliated Hosps., 1973-74; chief resident in pediatrics then mem. staff Childrens Hosp. of Orange County and U. Calif. Ivine Affiliated Hosps.; fellow in behavioral pediatrics and learning disabilities UCLA, 1975-76; behavioral pediatrician Childrens Med. Group, Anaheim, Calif., 1976-79; physician in child devel. program Fairview Devel. Ctr., Costa Mesa, 1979-81, physician behavior adjustment program, 1981—2004, chief med. staff, 1985, 1994—95; asst. clin. prof. pediatrics U. Calif., Irvine, 1990-94. Adj. asst. prof. zoology UCLA, 1969, instr. pediatrics, 1976; adj. asst. prof. pharmacy, U. Toledo, 1970-71; vis. lectr. Tchr. Edn. U. Calif., Irvine, 1980-93; lectr. and presenter in field. Contbr. articles to profl. jours. Rsch. fellow Ford Found., 1966, US Pub. Health Svc., 1965-69. Mem. Am. Acad. Pediatrics (assoc.), Soc. Devel. and Behavioral Pediatrics, Orange County Pediatric Soc., Sigma Xi.

STEINBERG, SALME ELIZABETH HARJU, academic administrator, historian; b. NYC; d. Johan Edward and Jenny Lydia (Peltonen) Harju; m. Michael Stephen Steinberg, Sept. 15, 1963; children: William, Katharine Lovisa. BA, Hunter Coll., 1960; MA, CCNY, 1962; PhD, Johns Hopkins U., 1971. Lectr. history Goucher Coll., Towson, Md., 1971—72; asst. prof. history Northwestern U., Evanston, Ill., 1972—75; prof. Northeastern Ill. U., Chgo., 1975—83, chmn. dept., 1983—87, assoc. provost then acting provost, 1987—92, provost, v.p. for acad. affairs, 1992—95, pres., 1995—. Author: Reformer in the Marketplace: Edward W. Bok and The Ladies' Home Journal, 1979; contbr. articles to profl. jours. Named to, Hunter Coll. Hall of Fame, 1997; recipient 14th Ann. award Appreciation, Asian Am. Coalition Chgo., 1997; grantee, Danforth Found., 1967—68. Episcopalian. Avocations: opera, theater. Office: Northeastern Ill U Office of President 5500 N Saint Louis Ave Chicago IL 60625-4679

STEINBERG, WILLIAM MARK, physician; b. NYC, Apr. 16, 1945; s. Louis and Florence (Weisberger) S.; m. Leah Stern, 1970; 3 children. BA, Columbia Coll., 1966; MD, NYU, 1970. Intern Kings County/Downstate, NYC, 1970-71; resident in medicine Boston U., 1973-74, U. Conn., Hartford, 1974-75; fellow in gastroenterology U. Fla., Gainesville, 1976-79; asst. prof. gastroenterology George Washington U., Washington, 1979-83, assoc. prof. medicine, 1983-90, prof. gastroenterology, 1990—. Dir. William M. Steinberg bd. rev., Balt., 1999—. Fellow ACP, Am. Coll. Gastroenterology; mem. Am. Pancreatic Assn. (pres. 1995-96), Am. Gastroent. Assn. Achievements include research in diagnosis and therapy of pancreatic disorders. Office: 1201 Seven Locks Rd Ste 111 Rockville MD 20854

STEINBERGER, JACK, physicist, researcher; b. Bad Kissingen, Germany, May 25, 1921; came to U.S., 1935; s. Ludwig Lazarus and Berta (May) S.; m. Joan Beauregard, 1943, (div. 1962); children: Joseph, Richard Ned; m. Cynthia Eva Alff; children: Julia Karen, John Paul. BS in Chemistry, U. Chgo., 1942, PhD in Physics, 1948; degree (hon.), Ill. Inst. Tech., 1989, U. Glasgow, 1990, Dortmund U., 1990, Columbia U., 1990, U. Autonoma de Barcelona, Spain, 1992, U. Blaise Pascal, Clermont-Ferrand, France, 1995, U. Würzburg, 1997. Mem. Inst. for Advanced Study, Princeton, NJ, 1948-49; asst. U. Calif., Berkeley, 1949-50; prof. Columbia U., NYC, 1950-68, Higgins prof., 1968-72; staff mem. European Orgn. for Nuclear Research, Geneva, 1968-86, dir., 1969-72; prof. physics Scuola Normale, Pisa, Italy, 1986—. Pfc. U.S. Army, 1943-46. Co-recipient Nobel prize in physics, 1988; recipient Nat. Medal of Sci., 1988, Mateuzzi medal Societa Italiane delle Scienze, 1991; fellow Guggenheim Found., Sloan Found. Mem. Am. Acad. Arts and Scis., Heidelberg Acad. Scis., Academia Europea, Academia Nationale dei Lincei. Avocations: tennis, sailing. Home: 25 Chemin des Merles CH 1213 Onex Switzerland Office: European Ctr for Nuclear Rsch CH 1211 Geneva 23 Switzerland E-mail: jack.steinberger@cern.ch.

STEINBRENNER, GEORGE MICHAEL, III, professional baseball team and shipbuilding company executive; b. Rocky River, Ohio, July 4, 1930; s. Henry G. and Rita (Haley) Steinbrenner; m. Elizabeth Joan Zieg, May 12, 1956; children: Henry G. III, Jennifer Lynn, Jessica Joan, Harold Zeig. BA, Williams Coll., 1952; postgrad., Ohio State U., 1954—55. Asst. football coach Northwestern U., 1955, Purdue U., 1956—57; treas. Kinsman Transit Co., Cleve., 1957—63; pres. Kinsman Marine Transit Co., Cleve., 1963—67, dir., 1965; pres., chmn. bd. Am. Ship Bldg. Co., Cleve., 1967—78, chmn. bd., 1978—; prin. owner NY Yankees, Bronx, 1973—90, 1993—, limited ptnr., 1990—93; owner Bay Harbor Inn, Tampa, Fla., 1988—. Bd. dirs. Gt. Lakes Internat. Corp., Gt. Lakes Assocs., Cin. Sheet Metal & Roofing Co., Nashville Bridge Co., Nederlander-Steinbrenner Prodns. Chmn. Olympic Overview Commn.; v.p. US Olympic Com., 1989; mem. Cleve. Little Hoover Com., group chmn., 1966; chmn. Cleve. Urban Coalition; vice chmn. Greater Cleve. Growth Corp., Greater Cleve. Jr. Olympic Found.; founder Silver Shield Found., NYC. 1st lt. USAF, 1952—54. Named Outstanding Young Man of Yr., Ohio Jr. C. of C., 1960, Cleve. Jr. C. of C., 1960, Chief Town Crier, Cleve., 1968, Man of Yr., Cleve. Press Club, 1968; recipient General Douglas MacArthur award, US Olympic Com., 2002, New Yorker of Yr. Mem.: Greater Cleve. Growth Assn. (bd. dirs.). Avocation: owns racehorse Bellamy Road trained by Nick Zito. Office: NY Yankees Yankee Stadium E 161st St & River Ave Bronx NY 10451 *

STEINDLER, MARTIN JOSEPH, chemist; b. Vienna, Jan. 3, 1928; came to U.S., 1938; s. J.P. and M.G. S.; m. Joan Long, Aug. 16, 1952; children: M.H., T.P. PhB, U. Chgo., 1947, BS, 1948, MS, 1949, PhD, 1952. Chemist Argonne (Ill.) Nat. Lab., 1953-74, sr. chemist, 1974—, assoc. dir. div. chem. engring., 1978-84, dir. chem. tech. div., 1984-93, sr. tech. advisor, 1993—. Mem. adv. com. on nuclear waste NRC, Washington, 1988-96, chmn. 1995; adminstrv. judge ASLBP, 1973-90. Contbr. articles to profl. publs.; patentee in field. Pres. Matteson-Park Forest (Ill.) Sch. Bd., 1959-78. Recipient Disting. Performance medal U. Chgo., 1992, Meritorious Svc. award for Scientific Excellence, U.S. NRC, 1996, Lawroski award, ANL Chem. Tech. Divsn., 2002. Mem. AAAS, Am. Nuclear Soc., Am. Inst. Chem. Engrs. (Robert E. Wilson award 1990). Office: Argonne Nat Lab 9700 Cass Ave Argonne IL 60439-4803

STEINDLER, WALTER G., retired lawyer; b. NYC, Dec. 2, 1927; s. Mortimer B. and Ray (Feingold) S.; m. Carol A. Halpin, June 28, 1969; children: Michael, Morty, Melissa, Amy, Ellen. BA, Queens Coll., 1950; JD, NYU, 1953. Bar: N.Y. 1953, U.S. Supreme Ct. 1965, U.S. Dist. Ct. (ea. dist.) N.Y. 1972, U.S. Dist. Ct. (so. dist.) 1974, U.S. Ct. Appeals (2d cir.) 1974. Ptnr. Borden Skidell Fleck & Steindler, Jamaica, NY, 1955-62; pvt. practice law Babylon, NY, 1962-67; town atty. Town of Babylon, 1967-69; asst. county atty. Suffolk County, NY, 1970-71; ptnr. Sarisohn, Carner, Steindler, Lebow, Braun & Castrovinci, Commack, NY, 1976-93; ret., 1993. Capt., judge adv. 2d area command N.Y. Guard, N.Y.C., 1965-70; guardian ad litem 20th Jud. Cir. Lee County, Fla., 1995-98. With US Army, 1946—47. Mem.: Free Sons Israel (pres. 1953), Masons. Office: 350 Veterans Memorial Hwy Commack NY 11725-4330 Office Phone: 631-543-7667. Personal E-mail: wgscas@charter.net.

STEINEM, GLORIA, writer, editor, advocate; b. Toledo, Mar. 25, 1934; d. Leo and Ruth (Nuneviller) S.; granddaughter of suffragette Pauline Steinem; m. David Bale, Sept. 3, 2000 (dec. Dec. 30, 2003); step-son Christian Bale. BA in Govt., magna cum laude (hon.), Smith Coll., 1956; postgrad. (Chester Bowles Asian fellow), India, 1957-58; D. Human Justice, Simmons Coll., 1973, PhD (hon.). Co-dir., dir. edn1. found. Ind. Rsch. Svc., Cambridge, Mass. and NYC, 1959-60; contbg. editor Glamour Mag., NYC, 1962-69; co-founder, contbg. editor New York Mag., 1968-72; feminist lectr., 1969—; co-founder, editor Ms. Mag., 1971-87, columnist, 1980-87, cons. editor, 1987—. Active various civil rights and peace campaigns including United Farmworkers, Vietnam War Tax Protest, Com. for the Legal Def. of Angela Davis (treas., 1971-72); active polit. campaigns of Adlai Stevenson, Robert Kennedy, Eugene McCarthy, Shirley Chisholm, George McGovern; Co-founder, bd. dirs. Women's Action Alliance, 1970-2001, (now Feminist Majority Found.); co-founder, convenor, mem. nat. adv. com. Nat. Women's Polit. Caucus, 1971; co-founder, pres. bd. dirs. Ms. Found. for Women, 1972-1990; founding mem. Coalition of Labor Union Women, 1974, Pres. Voters for Choice, 1979; mem. Internat. Women's Year Commn., 1977, pres. Choice USA, co-founder, chmn. Liberty Media for Women, 1998 (current owner and operator Ms. mag); editorial cons., Conde Nast Publications, 1962-69, Curtis Publishing, 1964-65, Random House Publishing, 1988-, McCall Publishing. Author: The Thousand Indias, 1957, The Beach Book, 1963, Wonder Woman, 1972, Outrageous Acts and Everyday Rebellions, 1982, Marilyn: Norma Jeane, 1986, Revolution from Within: A Book of Self-Esteem, 1992; contbg. corr. NBC Today Show, 1987—88; author: Moving Beyond Words: Age, Rage, Sex, Power, Money, Muscles - Breaking the Boundaries of Gender, 1994; contbr. to various anthologies. Named Woman of Yr., McCall's mag., 1972; named to Nat. Women's Hall of Fame, 1993; recipient Penney-Missouri Journalism award, 1970, Award for Journalism, Gov. Ohio, 1972, Bill of Rights award, ACLU of So. Calif., 1975, Mo. Honor Medal for Disting. Svc. in Journalism, U. Mo. Sch. Journalism, 2005; Woodrow Wilson Internat. Ctr. for Scholars Fellow, 1977. Mem.: Author's Guild, Soc. Mag. Writers, Nat. Press Club, AFTRA, NOW, Phi Beta Kappa. Coined phrase "reproductive freedom" during 1972 nat. abortion debate. Office: MS Magazine 433 S Beverly Dr Beverly Hills CA 90212-4401 also: Choice USA 712 Hershey Ave Monterey Park CA 91755-1473

STEINER, DAVID M., dean; BA, MA, Oxford U.; PhD, Harvard U. Assoc. prof. Sch. Edn. Boston U., chmn. Edn. Policy; dir. Arts Edn. Nat. Endowment of Arts, Washington, DC, 2004—05; dean Sch. Edn. Hunter Coll., CUNY, NYC, 2005—. Vis. prof. Cambridge U.; sr. rsch. assoc. Mass. State Edn. Policy. Contbr. articles to profl. jours. Mem.: Clare Hall Coll. (life). Office: Hunter Coll Sch Edn Rm W1000 695 Park Avenue New York NY 10021 Office Phone: 212-772-4622, 212-772-4621. E-mail: David.Steiner@hunter.cuny.edu.

STEINER, DAVID MILLER, lawyer; b. Phoenix, Apr. 9, 1958; s. Paul Miller and Nan (Adamson) S. BA, Columbia U., 1980; MALD, Tufts U., 1985; JD, Cornell U., 1988; M of Internat. and Pub. Affairs, Columbia U., 1989; LLM in Taxation, NYU, 1993. Bar: N.Y. 1988. English tchr. Peace Corps, Tahoua, Niger, 1980-82; law clk. to Judge Jane Restani U.S. Ct. Internat. Trade, NYC, 1989-91; law clk. to Judge Reynaldo Garza U.S. Ct. Appeals (5th cir.), Brownsville, Tex., 1991-92; assoc. Wasserman, Schneider and Babb, 1993-95; with N.Y.C. Law Dept. Office of the Corp. Counsel, 1995—2002, U.S. Dept. Justice, Washington, 2002—. Mem. ABA, N.Y. County Lawyers Assn. (com. on taxation), Univ. Club, Cornell Club, Meridian Soc., Linden Cir., Young New Yorkers for the Philharm, Young Friends of Save Venice. Avocations: ballroom dancing, backgammon, running. Home: 2298 17th St NW # 3 Washington DC 20009- Office: US Dept Justice Tax Divsn PO Box 55 Ben Franklin Sta Washington DC 20044- E-mail: sirius_001@yahoo.com.

STEINER, DAVID P., waste management executive; BS in Acctg., La. State U., Baton Rouge, 1982; JD with honors, UCLA, 1986. Assoc. Gibson, Dunn & Crutcher, San Jose; ptnr. Phelps Dunbar, New Orleans; v.p., dep. gen. counsel Waste Mgmt., Inc., Houston, 2000—01, sr. v.p., gen. counsel, corp. sec., 2001—03, exec. v.p., CFO, 2003—04, CEO, 2004—. Mem.: ABA, Calif. Bar Assn., La. Bar Assn. Office: Waste Mgmt Inc 1001 Fannin St Ste 4000 Houston TX 77002 Office Phone: 713-512-6200. *

STEINER, DONALD FREDERICK, biochemist, physician, educator; b. Lima, Ohio, July 15, 1930; s. Willis A. and Katherine (Hoegner) S. BS in Chemistry and Zoology, U. Cin., 1952; MS in Biochemistry, U. Chgo., 1956, MD, 1956; D Med. Sci. (hon.), U. Umea, 1973, U. Ill., 1984, Technische Hochschule, Aachen, 1993, U. Uppsala, 1993, Mt. Sinai Sch. Medicine, NYC, 1998. Intern King County Hosp., Seattle, 1956-57; USPHS postdoctoral research fellow, asst. medicine U. Wash. Med. Sch., 1957-60; mem. faculty med. sch. U. Chgo., 1960—, chmn. dept. biochemistry, 1973-79, A.N. Pritzker prof. biochemistry, molecular biology and medicine, 1985—, sr. investigator Howard Hughes Med. Inst., 1986—. Jacobaeus lectr., Oslo, 1970; Luft lectr., Stockholm, 1984. Co-editor: The Endocrine Pancreas, 1972, discoverer proinsulin. Recipient Gairdner award Toronto, 1971, Hans Christian Hagedorn medal Steensen Meml. Hosp., Copenhagen, 1970, Lilly award, 1969, Ernst Oppenheimer award, 1970, Diaz-Cristobal award Internat. Diabetes Fedn., 1973, Banting medal Am. Diabetes Assn., 1976, Banting medal Brit. Diabetes Assn., 1981, Passano award, 1979, Wolf prize in medicine, 1985, Frederick Conrad Koch award Endocrine Soc., 1990. Mem. AAAS, Nat. Acad. Scis., Am. Soc. Biochemists and Molecular Biologists, Am. Philos. Soc., Am. Diabetes Assn. (50th Anniversary medallion 1972, Albert Renold award 2007), European Assn. Study Diabetes (hon.), Am. Acad. Arts and Scis., Am. Philos. Soc., Sigma Xi, Alpha Omega Alpha. Home: 2626 N Lakeview Ave Apt 2508 Chicago IL 60614-1821 Business E-Mail: dfsteine@midway.uchicago.edu.

STEINER, ELIZABETH, philosopher, psychologist, educator; b. St. Louis, Jan. 30, 1925; d. Anton Steiner and Walburga Rustige; m. George S. Maccia, Feb. 10, 1947. BS in Zoology, St. Louis U., 1946; grad. studies in zoology, U. Kans., 1947; MEd in Biology and Edn., U. Mo., 1949; MA in Philosophy and Psychology, U. Manitoba, Can., 1954; PhD in Philosophy, U. So. Calif., 1957. Tchg. asst. gen. chemistry and gen. zoology St. Louis U., 1945—46; instr. zoology U. Kans., 1947; tchr. phys. and biol. scis. Kanawha HS, Iowa, 1949—50; tchr.anatomy and microbiology LA City Coll., 1950—52; tchr. phys. and biol. scis. LA Sr. HS, 1951—52; instr. philosophy U. Manitoba, 1953—54; lectr. philosophy U. So. Calif., 1956—57; asst. prof. philosophy Marietta Coll., Ohio, 1957—60; prof. philosophy of edn. Ohio State U., 1961—66; prof. philosophy U. Southwestern La., 1966—67; prof. philosophy of edn. and rsch. methodology Ind. U., Bloomington, 1967—90, prof. women's studies, 1973—90, honors prof., 1985—90, prof. emeritus, 1990—. Chemist Atlas Powder Co., Weldon Springs, Mo., 1943, Scullen Steel Co., St. Louis, 1947—48; microbiologist Wood Treating Chem. Co., St. Louis, 1947—48; vis. prof. grad. studies Ohio State U., 1959, rsch. assoc., 1960—61; vis. prof. psychology of edn. U. BC, Canada, 1960; vis. prof. philosophy of edn. UCLA, 1963; vis. prof. postgrad. studies Nat. U. Mex., Mexico City, 1981; Fulbright prof. philosophy of edn. Fed. U. Rio de Janeiro, 1981; vis. prof. U. Warsaw, U. Zagreb, Croatia, Hungarian Acad. Scis. Inst. Sociology, Czechoslovak Acad. Scis., 1984; rsch. coord. inst. child devel. and family life Ohio State U., 1960—61, co-dir. ednl. theory ctr., 1962—66, co-dir. social studies curriculum ctr., 1963—66; dir. ednl. inquiry methodology program Ind. U., 1973—76, dir. grad. studies activities, hist. philos. and comparative studies of edn., 1976—78, dir. nat. sci. found. project, 1979, dir. grad. studies and philosophy of edn., 1981—90; dir. overseas study program Hangzhou U., China, 1988; presenter in field. Contbr. numerous articles to profl. jours. Achievements include logical analysis of education as a field of study and so introduction of educology as its designation; application of logic as a critical tool in decision-making about the morality of human behavior; psychological analysis of the female professorial workspace in the US and throughout the world; development of women studies as part of the university curriculum.

STEINER, GEORGE (FRANCIS STEINER), author, educator; b. Paris, Apr. 23, 1929; s. Frederick George and Elsie (Franzos) S.; m. Zara Shakow, 1955; children: David Milton, Deborah Tarn. BA, U. Chgo., 1949; MA, Harvard U., 1950; PhD, Oxford U., 1955; DLitt (hon.), Trinity Coll., Dublin, 1996; LittD (hon.), Louvain U., 1980, Mount Holyoke Coll., 1983, Durham U., 1995; D honoris causa, U. Bristol, 1989; DLitt (hon.), U. Glasgow, 1990, U. Liége, 1990, U. Ulster, 1993, U. Durham, 1995, Kenyon Coll., 1996, U. Rome, 1998, U. Sorbonne, 1998, U. Salamanca, 2002, U. London, 2006, U. Bologna, 2006. Mem. staff Economist, London, 1952-56; mem. staff Inst. Advanced Study Princeton (N.Y.) U., NJ, 1956-58, Gauss lectr. NJ, 1959-60; Massey lectr., 1974; First Lord Weidenfeld prof. Comp. Lit. Oxford U., 1994—; Charles Eliot Norton prof. poetry Harvard U., 2001—. Cons. and lectr. in field; Maurice lectr. U. London, 1984, Leslie Stephen lectr. Cambridge U., 1985, W.P. Ker lectr. U. Glasgow, 1986; lectr. Page-Barbour Lectures U. Va., 1987, Gifford lectr., 1990; vis. prof. Coll. France, 1992; First Lord Weidenfeld vis. prof. comparative lit., Oxford U., 1994—. Author: Tolstoy or Dostoevsky, 1958, The Death of Tragedy, 1960, Anno Domini, 1964, Language and Silence, 1967, Extraterritorial, 1971, In Bluebeard's Castle, 1971, The Sporting Scene: White Knights in Reykjavik, 1973, After Babel, 1975 (adapted for TV as The Tongues of Men, 1977), Heidegger, 1978, On Difficulty and Other Essays, 1978, The Portage to San Cristobal of A.H., 1981, Antigones, 1984, George Steiner: A Reader, 1984, Real Presences, 1989, Proofs and Three Parables, 1992, Homer in English, 1996, No Passion Spent, 1996, The Deeps of the Sea, 1996, Errata, An Examined Life, 1997, Grammars of Creation, 2001, Lessons of the Masters, 2003; editor: The Penguin Book of Modern Verse Translation, 1966, Homer: A Collection of Critical Essays (with Robert Flagles), 1962. Decorated chevalier de la Legion d'Honneur (France); Churchill Coll. fellow, 1961—; Hon. Royal Academician (London), Commandeur dans l'Ordre des Arts et des Lettres (Paris); hon. fellow Balliol Coll., Oxford, Eng., 1995, St. Anne's Coll., Oxford; Fulbright prof., 1958-69; recipient O. Henry Short Story award, 1958, Guggenheim fellowship, 1971-72, Zabel award Nat. Inst. Arts and Letters, U.S., 1970, King Albert medal Royal Belgian Acad., 1982, P.E.N. Internat. Fiction prize, 1993; Faulkner Fiction grantee P.E.N., 1983; Le Prix du Souvenir, 1974, Truman Capite Lifetime award for Lit., 1999, Prince of Asturias prize in humanities, 2001, Ludwig-Börne prize, Germany, 2003; named Hon. Royal Academician, London. Fellow British Acad.; mem. Am. Acad. Arts and Scis. (hon.), English Assn. (pres. 1975), German Acad. Lit. (corr.). Office: Churchill Coll Cambridge England

STEINER, HEINZ, science professor, researcher; b. Birrwil, Aargau, Switzerland, July 1, 1956; Diploma, Swiss Fed. Inst. Tech., Zuerich, 1980; PhD, U. Duesseldorf, Germany, 1989. Postdoctoral rschr. NIMH, Bethesda, Md., 1990—95; rsch. asst. prof. U. Tenn. Coll. Medicine, Memphis, 1995—2000; assoc. prof. molecular and cellular pharmacology Rosalind Franklin U. Medicine & Sci./Chgo. Med. Sch., North Chgo., 2000—. Rsch. grant, NIH, 1998—. Office Phone: 847-578-8679. Business E-Mail: heinz.steiner@rosalindfranklin.edu.

STEINER, HENRY JACOB, law and human rights educator; b. Mt. Vernon, NY, June 14, 1930; s. Meier and Bluma (Henigson) S.; m. Pamela Pomerance, Aug. 1, 1982; stepchildren: Duff, Jacoba. BA magna cum laude, Harvard U., 1951, MA, 1955, LLB magna cum laude, 1955. Bar: N.Y. 1956, Mass. 1963. Law clk. to Hon. John M. Harlan U.S. Supreme Ct., 1957-58; assoc. Sullivan and Cromwell, NYC, 1958-62; asst. prof. sch. law Harvard U., Cambridge, Mass., 1962-65, prof., 1965—, Jeremiah Smith Jr. prof. law, 1986—2005; prof. emeritus, 2005—. Founder, dir. Law Sch. Human Rights Program, 1984—2005; chair univ. com. on human rights studies Harvard U., 1994—2002; bd. dirs. U. Middle East project, 1996—99, chair bd. dirs., 2000—07; vis. prof. Yale U., 1972—73, Stanford U., 1965; cons. AID, 1962—64, Ford Found., 1966—69. Co-author: (textbook) Transnational Legal Problems, 4th edit., 1994, Tort and Accident Law, 2d edit., 1989, International Human Rights in Context: Law, Politics, Morals, 3d edit., 2007; author: Moral Argument and Social Vision in the Courts, 1987, Diverse Partners: Non-Governmental Organizations in the Human Rights Movement, 1991; former devels. editor Harvard Law Rev.; contbr. articles to profl. jours. Office: Harvard U Law Sch Cambridge MA 02138 Home: 28 Madison St Cambridge MA 02138 Business E-Mail: hsteiner@law.harvard.edu.

STEINER, HERBERT MAX, physics professor; b. Goeppingen, Germany, Dec. 8, 1927; came to U.S., 1939, naturalized, 1944; s. Albert and Martha (Epstein) S. BS, U. Calif., Berkeley, 1951, PhD, 1956. Physicist Lawrence Berkeley Lab., Berkeley, Calif., 1956—; mem. faculty U. Calif., Berkeley, 1958—, prof. physics, 1966-2000, prof. emeritus, 2000—, William H. McAdams prof. physics, chmn. dept., 1992-95; vis. scientist European Center Nuclear Research, 1960-61, 64, 68-69, 82-83, Max Planck Inst. Physics and Astrophysics, Munich, 1976-77; vis. prof. Japanese Soc. Promotion Sci., 1978. Vis. prof. physics U. Paris, 1989-90; vis. scientist Deutsches Electron Synchrotron Lab., 1995-96. Author articles in field. Served with AUS, 1946-47. Recipient Sr. Am. Scientist award Alexander von Humboldt Found., 1976-77; Guggenheim fellow, 1960-61 Fellow Am. Phys. Soc. Office: U Calif Berkeley Dept Physics 7300 Berkeley CA 94720-0001 Home Phone: 510-527-8692; Office Phone: 510-486-6805. Business E-Mail: steiner@lbl.gov.

STEINER, JEFFREY JOSEF, manufacturing executive; b. Vienna, Apr. 3, 1937; came to U.S., 1958; s. Beno and Paula (Bornstein) S.; m. Claude Angel, Apr. 11, 1957 (div. 1972); children: Eric, Natalia, Thierry; m. Linda Schaller, Mar. 6, 1976 (div. June 1983); children: Benjamin, Alexandra. Student textile design, U. London, 1956; student textile mfg., Bradford Inst. Tech., London, 1957; HHD (hon.), Yeshiva U., 1996. Mgmt. trainee Metals and Controls div. Tex. Instruments, Attleborough, Mass., 1958-59, mgr. internat., 1959-60, pres. Argentina, Brazil, Mex., Switzerland, France, 1960-66, Burlington Tapis, Paris, 1967-72; chmn., pres. Cedec S.A. Engring. Co., Paris, 1973-84; chmn., CEO Fairchild Corp., NYC, 1985—, Banner Aerospace, 1993—. Bd. dirs. Copley Fund, Fall River, Mass. Trustee Montefiore Med. Ctr., NYC; bd. dirs. Israel Mus., Yeshiva U. Bus. Sch. Decorated Knight of Arts (France), knight Indsl. Merit of France, chevalier de L'Ordre des Arts et des Lettres, 1990, chevalier de L'order National du Merite (France), commandatore de la Republica (Italy); recipient mayor's medal City of Paris, 1990; named one of Top 200 Collectors, ARTnews Mag., 2004, 05, 06. Mem. City Athletic Club, Racing Club, Polo Club. Jewish. Avocations: tennis, sailing, collector of Impressionism, modern & contemporary art. Office: The Fairchild Corp 110 E 59th St New York NY 10022 Home Phone: 212-410-9200; Office Phone: 212-308-6700. E-mail: jsteiner@fairchild.com.

STEINER, JOHN MICHAEL, sociologist, educator; b. Prague, Czech Republic, Aug. 3, 1925; arrived in US, 1953; s. Kurt John and Ilse (Ornstein) Steiner; 1 child, Ingmar Michael Augustus. BA, U. Melbourne, 1952; MA, U. Mo., 1955; PhD, U. Freiburg, 1968. Liaison officer United Relief and Rehab. Adminstrn. Mission, Prague, 1946—48; immigration officer Dept. Immigration, Canberra, Melbourne, Australia, 1949—52; indsl. therapist Hosp. No. 1, Fulton, Mo., 1955—56; lectr. speech U. Calif., Berkeley, 1956—59; rsch. social psychologist USAF, Wright-Patterson AFB, Ohio, 1959—61; rsch. assoc. Inst. World Civilization, Freiburg, Germany, 1963—64; vis. asst. prof. Dept. Criminology, 1964—65; prof. sociology Sonoma State U., Rohnert Park, Calif., 1968—92, sr. scholar in residence, 1993—, prof. emeritus, 1992—. Founding dir. Sonoma State Holocaust Studies Ctr., 1984—92. Author: Power Politics and Social Change in National Socialist Germany, 1975; author: (with Joel E. Dimsdale) Survivors, Victims, and Perpetrators Essays on the Nazi Holocaust, 1980; author: Craig, Haney, Curtis Banks and Philip Zimbardo, Das Stanford Gefängnis Experiment, 1984; contbr. articles to profl. jours., books, chpts. to books on polit. crime. Co-founder, v.p. Ams. Dem. Action, Berkeley, 1960. Recipient Disting. cross Svc. and Valor, Czech Republic, 1948, cert. recognition, Calif. State Assembly, 1994, Order of Merit, Pres. Germany, 2002; fellow, Fulbright Found., 1974—75, 1981—82; Alexander von Humboldt rsch. fellow, U. Freiburg, 1964—67, 1990. Mem.: Fulbright Assn., Czechoslovak Acad. Arts and Scis., Acad. Criminal Justice Scis., Alexander von Humbodt Assn., Am. Sociol. Assn., Alpha Pi Zeta. Democrat. Achievements include research in authoritarian personality based on SS (Nazi) perpetrators; role margin as the site of moral and social intelligence; case of Germany and national socialism; Hitler's exemptions from the Nuremberg Racial Laws; genocide, Holocaust and perpetrator studies on price-tag switching. Avocations: art, antiques, swimming, photography. Home: 65 Sotelo Way Novato CA 94945 Office: Sonoma State U Dept Sociology Rohnert Park CA 94928 Business E-Mail: john.steiner@sonoma.edu.

STEINER, PAUL ANDREW, retired insurance executive; b. Woodburn, Ind., Feb. 17, 1929; s. Eli Gerig and Emma Mae (Yaggy) Steiner; m. Ruth Edna Henry, Sept. 1, 1950; children: Mark, Nancy, Jonathan, David. AB, Taylor U., 1950. CPCU. Owner feed and grain, lumber and constrn. firms, Bluffton, Ohio, 1951-64; home office rep. Brotherhood Mut. Ins. Co., Ft. Wayne, Ind., 1964-65, dir. claims, 1966-71, v.p., treas., 1968-71, pres., 1971-94, chmn. bd., 1974-2000. Trustee emeritus Taylor U.; past chmn. Summit Christian Coll.; past pres. Ft. Wayne Rescue Mission; past sec. William Taylor Found., bd. dirs. Mem.: Soc. CPCU (past nat. ethics com., past pres. No. Ind. chpt.), Mut. Ins. Cos. Assn. Ind. (past pres.), Conf. Casualty Ins. Cos. (past pres.), DEVCO Mut. Assn. (past chmn.), Nat. Assn. Mut. Ins. Cos. (past chmn. bd., Merit award 1973), Christian Bus. Men's Com. Ft. Wayne, Nat. Assn. Evangs. (past treas., Layman of Yr. 1977), Am. Bible Soc. (sr. trustee), Ft. Wayne Rotary Club (past pres.). Republican. Mem. Fellowship Of Evangelical Churches. Home: 1825 Florida Dr Fort Wayne IN 46805-5036

STEINER, ROBERT ALAN, neuroendocrinologist, educator; b. Chgo., Mar. 9, 1947; s. Alan Dale and Elizabeth Ann (Smith); m. Sally Jean Hewett, Mar. 19, 1983. BA, U. Pacific, 1969; PhD in Physiology, Oreg. Health & Sci. U., 1975. Sr. fellow Regional Primate Rsch. Ctr. U. Wash., Seattle, 1974—78, asst. prof. ob-gyn., physiology and biophysics, 1978—83, assoc. prof., 1983, prof. Adj. prof. biology U. Wash. Contbr. articles to profl. jours.; mem. editl. bd.: Biology of Reproduction, 1986—90, Endocrinology, 1986—90, 1994—98, 2001—04, Am. Jour. Physiology, 1993—98, Neuroendocrinology, 2000—; editor: Molecular and Cellular Neurosciences, 1991—94. Recipient Nat. Human Growth Found. award, 1977; grantee, Nat. Inst. Child Health and Human Devel., 1978—. Mem.: Soc. Behavioral Neuroendocrinology, Internat. Soc. Neuroendocrinology, Internat. Neuropeptide Soc., Am. Physiol. Soc., Soc. Study Reproduction, AAAS, Soc. Neuroscience, Endocrine Soc. Democrat. Office: Dept Physiology and Biophysics U Wash Box 357290 Seattle WA 98195-7290 E-mail: steiner@u.washington.edu.

STEINER, ROBERT FRANK, biochemist; b. Manila, Philippines, Sept. 29, 1926; came to U.S., 1933; s. Frank and Clara Nell (Weems) S.; m. Ethel Mae Fisher, Nov. 3, 1956; children: Victoria, Laura. AB, Princeton U., 1947; PhD, Harvard U., 1950. Chemist Naval Med. Research Inst., Bethesda, Md., 1950-70, chief lab. phys. biochemistry, 1965-70; prof. chemistry U. Md., Balt., 1970—, chmn. dept. chemistry, 1974—; prof. emeritus, 1996—; dir. grad. program in biochemistry U. Md., Balt., 1985. Biophysics study sect. NIH, 1976. Author: Life Chemistry, 1968, Excited States of Proteins and Nucleic Acids, 1971, The Chemistry of Living Systems, 1981, Excited States of Biopolymers, 1983, A Pilot's Tale and Other Stories, 1998, The Decoy and Other Stories, 1999, The Student Pilot and Other Stories, 2000, The Beauty Contest and Other Stories, 2002, Dreamtime, 2004; editor Jour. Biophys. Chemistry, 1972—, Jour. Fluorescence, 1991; contbr. over 160 articles to profl. jours. Served with AUS, 1945-47. Recipient Superior Civilian Achievement award Dept. Def., 1966; NSF rsch. grantee, 1971-77, NIH, 1973-93. Fellow Washington Acad. Sci., Japan Soc. for Promotion Sci.; mem. Am. Soc. Biol. Chemists. Clubs: Princeton (Washington). Achievements include development of fluorescence techniques for studying proteins. Home: 2609 Turf Valley Rd Ellicott City MD 21042-2021 Office: 5401 Wilkens Ave Baltimore MD 21250-1000 Office Phone: 410-465-0987. Personal E-mail: xuzw63A@aol.com.

STEINER, ROBERT LISLE, retired language educator; b. Tehran, Iran, May 21, 1921; s. Robert Lisle and Lois (Foresman) S.; m. Margaret S. Sherrard, June 4, 1944; children: Patricia Jean, Robert Lisle III, William Sherrard, John Scott. BA, Wooster Coll., Ohio; MA, Columbia U., 1948. Cons. Commn. Chs. on Internat. Affairs, 1948-49; cultural attache Am. embassy, Iran, 1950-52; educationist U.S. Office Edn., 1952-54; program dir. Am. Friends of Mid. East, 1954-59; v.p. Vershire Co., Vt., 1959-62; dir. Peace Corps, Kabul, Afghanistan, 1962-66; regional dir. North Africa, Near East and South Asia, 1966-69; dir. Washington office Devel. & Resources Corp., 1969-70; dir. Ctr. for Cross-Cultural Tng. and Rsch., adviser to univ. pres. on internat. affairs U. Hawaii, Honolulu, 1971-72; dir., gen. mgr. Hawaii Pub. Broadcasting Authority, 1972-73; exec. dir. N.J. Edn. Consortium, Princeton, 1973-78; pres. InterLink Lang. Ctrs., Princeton, 1979-91, chmn., 1992—. Tchr. U. Kansas City, Mo., 1957, Bradford (Vt.) Acad., 1961; poultry cons. Mid. East Tech. U., Ankara, Turkey, 1963. Councilman, v.p. Shanks Village Assn., Orangeburg, N.Y., 1948; chmn. Kabul Sch. Bd., 1965. Served as pilot USNR, 1943-46. Mem. Princeton Mid. East Soc. (sec. 1986-88, treas. 1993-95). Democrat. Presbyterian. Home: 1898 Villa Ct Lancaster PA 17603-2386 Office: Interlink Lang Ctrs 1898 Villa Ct Lancaster PA 17603-2386

STEINER, ROGER JACOB, linguistics educator, writer, researcher; b. South Byron, Wis., Mar. 27, 1924; s. Jakob Robert and Alice Mildred (Cowles) S.; m. Ida Kathryn Posey, Aug. 7, 1954 (dec. May 1992); children: David Posey, Andrew Posey, Anthony Wright. BA cum laude, Franklin & Marshall Coll., 1945; MDiv, Union Theol. Sem., 1947; MA, U. Pa., 1958, PhD, 1963. Ordained to ministry, Meth. Ch., 1947. Clergyman United Meth. Ch., NY, Wis., Pa., 1945-61; lectr. U. Bordeaux, France, 1961-63; instr. dept. langs. & lit. U. Del., Newark, 1963-64, asst. prof., 1964-71, assoc. prof., 1971-80, prof., 1980-85, dept. linguistics U. Del., Newark, 1985-96, prof. emeritus, 1998—. Cons. Charles Scribner's Sons, N.Y.C., 1972-75, Larousse, N.Y.C., 1981-84, Houghton-Mifflin, Boston, 1981-84, Macmillan, 1994-99. Author: Two Centuries of Spanish and English Bilingual Lexicography (1590-1800), 1970, New College French and English Dictionary, 1972, 3d edit., 2004; editor: Simon & Schuster's International Spanish Dictionary, 2d edit., 1997, Cuyás Spanish and English Dictionary, 3d edit., 1999, New College Spanish and English Dictionary, 3d edit., 2003; contbr. articles to profl. jours., chpts. to books. Recipient fellowship Am. Philos. Soc., Phila., 1971, Lilly Found., Phila., 1979-81. Mem. MLA (founder lexicography group 1974-75, chmn. 1976, 77, 80, 85), Dictionary Soc. N.Am., Phi Beta Kappa (pres. chpt. 1975-76). Republican. Avocation: languages. Office: U Del Dept Linguistics Newark DE 19716-2551 Personal E-mail: jakobjoos@comcast.net.

STEINER, RUTH, musicologist, educator; b. Oak Park, Ill., Feb. 2, 1931; d. Eugene and Ruth Piette; children: Jonathan, Miriam. BA, Wellesley Coll., Mass., 1952; MA, U. Calif., Berkeley, 1958; PhD, Cath. U. of Am., Washington, DC, 1964. Prof. of music Cath. U. of Am., Washington, 1966—2000; ret., 2000. Author: (book) Studies in Gregorian Chant, 1999; contbr. articles to profl. jours. Grant, Nat. Endowment for the Humanities, 1989, 1992, 1994, 1982, 1985, 1988. Mem.: Am. Musicological Soc. (sec. 1984—89), Medieval Acad. of Am. Home: 6624 Barnaby St NW Washington DC 20015

STEINER, STUART, college president; b. Balt., July 24, 1937; s. Louis and Lillian (Block) S.; m. Rosalie Weiner, Sept. 12, 1962; children: Lisa, Susan, David, Robyn. AA, Balt. Jr. Coll., 1957; BS, U. Md., 1959; grad. cert., Fla. State U., 1962; MSW., U. Pa., 1963; JD, U. Balt., 1967; MA, Tchrs. Coll., Columbia U., 1972; EdD, Columbia U., 1987. Caseworker, then supr. and dir. juvenile ct. services Balt. Dept. Social Services, 1960-64; dir. info. and referral ctr. Health and Welfare Coun. Met. Balt., 1964; dir. admissions and placement Harford Jr. Coll., Bel Air, Md., 1965-67; dean of students Genesee Community Coll., Batavia, NY, 1967-68, dean of coll., 1968-75, pres., 1975—. Pres. SUNY West, acting dep. to chancellor for community colls., 1985, pres. of assn. Pres. of Pub. Community Colls., 1987-89; acting pres. Fashion Inst. Tech., N.Y.C., 1997-98; CEO Ednl. Found. Fashion Industries, 1997-98; bd. dirs. Workforce Investment Bd.; commr. Commn. of Higher Edn., Mid. States Assn., 1999—. Contbr. chpts. to art books and articles to profl. jours. Bd. dirs. St. Jerome Hosp., Genesee County Community Chest, campaign chmn.; bd. dirs. Health Sci. Agy., Western N.Y.; trustee Villa Maria Coll.; trustee, v.p. N.Y. Chiropractic Coll.; bd. dirs. St. Jerome Hosp., Genesee Mercy Healthcare, United Meml. Med Ctr.; pres. Genesee County United Way, Community Coll. of Balt. Hall of Fame. Sigma Delta scholar U. Md., 1958-59, Heuisler scholar U. Balt. Law Sch., 1960-61, Kellogg fellow, 1971-72; recipient CEO award Assn. of C.C. Trustees (N.E. region) 1997. Mem. Pvt. Indsl. Coun. (bd. dirs. 1983-2000, workforce investment bd. 2000-02). Home: 33 Woodcrest Dr Batavia NY 14020-2721 Office: Genesee Community Coll 1 College Rd Batavia NY 14020-9703 Office Phone: 585-345-6812. E-mail: ssteiner@genesee.edu.

STEINER, UWE, language educator; PhD, Free U., Berlin, 1987, Habilitation, 1998—98. Wiss. mitarbeiter Free U., Berlin, 1984—89, wiss. asst., 1990—97; assoc. prof. Rice U., Houston, 2001—. Contbr. articles to profl. jours. Mem.: MLA, Am. Assn. Tchrs. German, Internat. Assn. Germanic Studies, Am. Soc. Eighteenth Century Studies, Deutscher Hochschulverband, Deutscher Germanistenverband. Office: Rice Univ Dept German PO Box 1892 Houston TX 77251-1892 Office Phone: 713-348-3243. Office Fax: 713-348-4863.

STEINETZ, BERNARD GEORGE, JR., endocrinologist; b. Germantown, Pa., May 30, 1927; s. Bernard George Sr. and Hazel Scott (Jefferds) S.; m. Jane Rutledge Nash, June 17, 1949; children: Scott Jefferds, Ann Rutledge Steinetz Barton. AB, Princeton U., 1950, PhD, Rutgers U., 1954. Sr. scientist Warner-Chilcott Co., Morris Plains, NJ, 1954-58; sr. rsch. assoc. Warner-Lambert Rsch. Inst., Morris Plains, 1958-67; head reprod. endocrinology CIBA Pharm. Co., Summit, NJ, 1967-71; mgr. cartilage rsch. and endocrinology CIBA-Geigy Corp., Ardsley, NY, 1971-84; rsch. assoc. prof. Lab. Exptl. Medicine and Surgery in Primates NYU Med. Ctr., Tuxedo, 1984—, rsch. prof., 1991—; prof. environ. medicine Nelson Inst. Environ. Medicine NYU Sch. Medicine, Tuxedo, 1997—. Co-investigator NIMH-NIH, 2002—, Morris Animal Found., 2002—; prin. investigator Philip Morris Found., 2003—. Contbr. articles to profl. jours. Mem. Drug Utilization Rev. Coun. of the State of N.J., Trenton, 1977-86. CIBA Rsch. fellow CIBA Pharm. Co., 1968; grantee March of Dimes, 1987-89, 95-97, Morris Animal Found., 1987-93, NIH (NICHHD) 1994-98, Cancer Rsch. Found. Am., 1999-2002, Philip Morris Found., 2003—. Fellow: N.Y. Acad. Scis. (mem. conf. orgn. com. 1968—70, keynote spkr. internat. conf. 2000, 2004); mem.: AAAS, Orthopaedic Rsch. Soc., Soc. Study of Reproduction, Am. Physiol. Soc., Endocrine Soc. Achievements include patents for method of determining pregnancy in dogs which has now been applied to cats and several endangered species. Home: 9 Sherwood Dr Mountain Lakes NJ 07046-2122 Office: NYU Sch Med Nelson Inst Eviron Medicine 57 Old Forge Rd Tuxedo Park NY 10987-5007 Office Phone: 845-731-3517. Business E-Mail: steinetz@env.med.nyu.edu.

STEINFELD, JEFFREY IRWIN, chemistry professor, educator, writer; b. Bklyn., July 2, 1940; s. Paul and Ann (Ravin) S. B.Sc., MIT, 1962; PhD, Harvard U., 1965. Postdoctoral fellow U. Sheffield, Yorkshire, England, 1965-66; asst. prof. chemistry MIT, Cambridge, 1966-70, assoc. prof., 1970-79, prof., 1980—. Author: Molecules & Radiation, 1974; co-author: Chemical Kinetics and Dynamics, 1989, 2d edit., 1999; editor: Laser and Coherence Spectroscopy, 1977, Laser-Induced Chemical Processes, 1981; co-editor: Spectrochimica Acta, 1983-98; contbr. articles to profl. jours. Treas. Ward 2 Democratic Com., Cambridge, 1972-73 NSF fellow Harvard U., Cambridge, 1962-65; NSF fellow Sheffield U., 1965-66; Alfred P. Sloan Found. research fellow MIT, 1969-71; Guggenheim fellow, 1972-73 Fellow Am. Phys. Soc.; mem. AAAS, Union Concerned Scientists, Fedn. Am. Scientists, Sigma Xi, Phi Lambda Upsilon. Jewish. Office: MIT Room 2-221 Cambridge MA 02139

STEINFELD, MANFRED, furniture manufacturing executive; b. Josbach, Germany, Apr. 29, 1924; s. Abraham and Paula (Katten) Steinfeld; m. Fern Goldman, Nov. 13, 1949; children: Michael, Paul, Jill. Student, U. Ill., 1942; BS in Commerce, Roosevelt U., 1948, LLH (hon.), 1997. Rsch. analyst State of Ill., 1948-50; v.p. Shelby Williams Industries, Inc., Chgo., 1954-63, pres., 1964-72, chmn. bd., 1973-96, chmn. exec. com., 1996—99. Bd. dirs. Amalgamated Trust & Savs. Bank; founder Daniel Paul Chairs LLC, 2004. Mem. adv. bd. Sch. Human Ecology U. Tenn., 1981—87, devel. coun., 1982—87; mem. adv. bd. dept. interior design Fla. Internat. U., 1981—85; life trustee Roosevelt U., Chgo.; past pres. Roosevelt U. Bus. Sch. Alumni Coun.; hon. governing mem. Art Inst. Chgo., mem. com. 20th century decorative art, endowed gallery on 20th century deocrative art, 1984; established Manfred Steinfeld Sch. Hospitality Mgmt. Roosevelt U., 1988; endowed Fern and Manfred Steinfeld Chair Judaic Studies, U. Tenn., Knoxville, 1995; endowed Danny Cunniff Leukemia Rsch. Lab., Hadassah Hosp., Jerusalem; endowed profl. chair Weitzman Inst., Rehovot, Israel, 1993; mem. U. Tenn. Devel. Coun., 1985—2005; nat. vice chmn. Jewish United Fund, 1988—94, bd. dirs., 1987, 1997; chmn. bd. dirs. Jewish Fedn. Chgo., 1988—2000. Staff sgt. AUS, 1942—45, 1st lt. AUS, 1950—52. Decorated Bronze Star, Purple Heart; named Small Bus. Man of Yr., Ctrl. Region, 1967, Vol. of Yr., U. Tenn., 1998; recipient Horatio Alger award of disting. Ams., 1981, Outstanding Bus. Leader award, Northwood Inst., 1983, Lifetime Achievement award, Hospitality Design Mag., 1999, Julius Rosenwald award, 2000. Mem.: Horatio Alger Assn., Bocaire Country Club (Boca Raton, Fla.), Bryn Mawr Country Club (Chgo.), Std. Club (Chgo.), Beta Gamma Sigma. Home: 1300 N Lake Shore Dr Apt 34D Chicago IL 60610-5165 Personal E-mail: manfern@aol.com.

STEINFELD, PHILIP SHELDON, pediatrician; b. Bronx, Mar. 4, 1932; s. Samuel and Sarah (Frishman) S.; m. Ruth L. Hyman, Aug., 1961 (div. June 1977); children: Andrea, Melissa, David; m. Sherry Lynn Rubinroit, Jan. 15, 1978; 1 child, Sara. BS, Queens Coll., 1953; MD, U. Basle, Switzerland, 1960. Diplomate Am. Bd. Pediatrics. Rotating intern Kings County Hosp. Ctr., Bklyn., 1960-61; resident pediatrics Mt. Sinai Hosp., NYC, 1961-63, jr. clin. asst. pediatrics, 1963-65, sr. clin. asst., 1965-68; attending pediatrician L.I. Jewish Hosp., 1968—, North Shore Univ. Hosp., 1970—; clin. instr. pediatrics Cornell U., NYC, 1986-90, clin. asst. prof. pediatrics, 1991—. Mem. adv. bd. TEMPO, Woodmere, N.Y., 1975-92, Five Town Adolescent Ctr., Woodmere, 1975-93. Fellow Am. Acad. Pediatrics. Office: 1573 Broadway Hewlett NY 11557-1428 Home Phone: 516-374-6356; Office Phone: 516-374-3322. Business E-Mail: philsteinfeld@pol.net.

STEINFINK, HUGO, chemical engineering professor; b. Vienna, May 22, 1924; s. Mendel and Malwina (Fiderer) S.; m. Cele Intrator, Mar. 21, 1948; children: Dan E., Susan D. BS, CCNY, 1947; MS, Columbia U., 1948; PhD, Bklyn. Poly. Inst., 1954. Rsch. chemist Shell Devel. Co., Houston, 1948-51, 53-60; T. Brockett Hudson prof. chem. engring. U. Tex., Austin, 1960-2000, prof. emeritus, 2000. Contbr. articles to profl. jours. With AUS, 1944-46. Fellow Am. Mineral Soc.; mem. AIChE, Am. Chem. Soc., Am. Crystallographic Assn. (pres.-elect 1994, pres. 1995, past pres. 1996), Materials Rsch. Soc., Phi Beta Kappa, Sigma Xi, Phi Lambda Epsilon. Home: 3811 Walnut Clay Dr Austin TX 78731-4011 Office Phone: 512-471-5233. E-mail: steinfink@che.utexas.edu.

STEINGASS, SUSAN R., lawyer; b. Cambridge, Mass., Dec. 18, 1941; BA in English Lit., Denison U., 1963; MA in English Lit. with honors, Northwestern U., 1965; JD with honors, U. Wis., 1976. Bar: Wis. 1976, US Dist. Ct. Wis. 1976. Instr. dept. English La. State U., 1965—66, Calif. State Coll., LA, 1966—68, U. Wis., Stevens Point, 1968—72; law clk. Hon. Nathan S. Heffernan Wis. Supreme Ct., 1976—77; ptnr. Stafford, Rosenbaum, Reiser and Hansen, 1977—85; judge Dane County Cir. Ct., Wis., 1985—93; ptnr. Habush, Habush & Rottier, S.C., Madison, Wis., 1993—. Lectr. civil procedure, environ. law, evidence, trial advocacy Law Sch., U. Wis., 1981—, dir. comm. and advocacy programs, 2003—; instr. Nat. Inst. for Trial Advocacy, 1987—, trustee, 2002—; instr. Nat. Jud. Coll., 1993—. Note and comment editor Wis. Law Rev., 1974-76; co-editor: Wisconsin Civil Procedure Before Trial, 1994, The Wisconsin Rules of Evidence: A Courtroom Handbook, 1998—. Chair Wis. Equal Justice Task Force, 1989—91, Wis. Sentencing Commn., 2003—; mem., chair Wis. Jud. Selection Com., 2003—. Recipient Disting. Svc. award Am. Assn. Mediators, 1991, Presdl. award of excellence State Bar Wis., 2000; named Wis. Trial Judge of Yr. Am. Bd. Trial Advocates, 1992. Fellow Wis. Bar Found.; mem. ATLA, ABA (ho. dels. 2000—06), Am. Bar Found., Am. Law Inst., Wis. Bar Assn. (pres. 1998-99), Wis. Law Alumni Assn. (bd. dirs., pres. 2001-05), Wis. Acad. Trial Lawyers, Wis. Equal Justice Fund (pres. 2000-05), Wis. Trust Account Found. (bd. dirs. 1999), Order of the Coif (Marygold Melli Achievement award 2001). Office: Habush Habush Davis & Rottier SC 150 E Gilman St Ste 2000 Madison WI 53703-1481 also: Univ Wis Law School 975 Bascom Mall Madison WI 53706 Business E-Mail: ssteingass@habush.com.

STEINGLASS, PETER JOSEPH, psychiatrist, educator; b. NYC, Mar. 1, 1939; s. Sam and Bella Sarah (Bernstein) S.; m. Abbe Stahl, July 1, 1962; children: Matthew Aaron, Joanna Eowyn. AB, Union Coll., 1960; MD, Harvard U., 1965. Diplomate Am. Bd. Psychiatry and Neurology. Head clin. rsch. program Nat. Inst. Alcohol Abuse and Alcoholism, Washington, 1971-74; asst. prof. psychiatry George Washington U., Washington, 1974-77, assoc. prof. psychiatry, 1977-81, prof. psychiatry and behavioral sci., 1981-90; exec. dir. Ackerman Inst. for the Family, NYC, 1990—2004, pres., CEO, 2004—05, pres. emeritus, 2005—. Vis. prof. psychiatry Hebrew U., Jerusalem, 1981-82; clin. prof. psychiatry Cornell U. Med. Coll., 1993—. Author: The Alcoholic Family, 1987; contbr. articles to sci. publs. Lt. comdr. USPHS, 1969-71. Fellow Am. Psychiat. Assn., Am. Assn. Marriage and Family Therapy (cumulative contbn. award 1992), Assn. Clin. Psychosocial Rsch.; mem. Am. Family Therapy Acad. (charter, bd. dirs. 1987-89, v.p. 1989-91, Disting. Contbn. award 1987), Aesculapian Soc., Phi Beta Kappa. Democrat. Jewish. Avocations: photography, classical music. Office: Ackerman Inst for the Family 149 E 78th St New York NY 10021-0405 Office Phone: 212-481-1860. Business E-Mail: psteinglass@ackerman.org.

STEINHAFEL, GREGG W., retail executive; BBA, Carroll Coll., 1977; MBA, Northwestern Univ., 1979. With Target Corp., Mpls., 1979—, sr. v.p., gen. mdse. mgr., 1987—94, exec. v.p. merchandising, 1994—99, pres. Target Stores, 1999—. Mem. bd. dir. Toro Co. Dir. Walker Art Ctr. Office: Target Corp 1000 Nicollet Mall Minneapolis MN 55403-2467 *

STEINHARDT, MICHAEL H., diversified financial services company executive; b. Bklyn., 1940; s. Sol Frank Steinhardt; m. Judy Steinhardt; children: Jacob, Joshua, Kira. BS, U. Pa. Wharton Sch. Fin., 1960. Rsch. assoc.; staff writer; securities analyst; founding ptnr. Steinhardt Ptnrs. L.P., 1967—95; mng. mem. Steinhardt Mgmt. LLC, 1996—. Author: No Bull: My Life In and Out of the Markets, 2001. Chmn. Jewish Life Network/Steinhardt Found., NYC, 1994—, Jewish Media Renaissance, Birthright Israel; trustee & chmn. investment com. NYU, 1995—; trustee Brandeis U., Bklyn. Bot. Garden, Wildlife Conservation Soc., Mus. Jewish Heritage; mem. vis. com., dept. Greek & Roman art Met. Mus. Art, NYC. Named one of Top 200 Collectors, ARTnews Mag., 2003—06; recipient Medallion, U. Albany, 2004. Jewish. Avocation: collector of classical antiquities & modern art, especially drawings. Mailing: Jewish Life Network 10th Fl 6 E 39th St New York NY 10016

STEINHARDT, RALPH GUSTAV, III, law educator; b. Bethlehem, Pa., July 28, 1954; s. Ralph Gustav Jr. and Mary Etzler (Hawks) S.; m. Donna Scarboro, Oct. 23, 1982; children: Ruth Jackson Steinhardt, Ralph Gustav IV. BA summa cum laude, Bowdoin Coll., 1976; JD, Harvard U., 1980. Bar: D.C. 1980, U.S. Dist. Ct. D.C. 1981, U.S. Ct. Appeals (D.C. and 9th cirs.) 1983, U.S. Supreme Ct. 1984. Assoc. Patton Boggs & Blow, Washington, 1980-85; prof. law Nat. Law Ctr. George Wash. U., Wash., 1985; assoc. dean Elliott Sch. Internat. Affairs George Wash. U., Wash., DC, prof. law & Internat. Affairs. Co-dir. Oxford-GW Summer Inst. in Internat. Human Rights Law, 1994—; litig. adv. Internat. Human Rights Law Grp., Wash., 1985—; mem. coun. advs. UN High Commr. for Refugees, Washington, 1987—, vis. fulbright prof. law U. Coll.Galway Ireland. Contbg. author: Testimonial Privileges, 1983, World Justice? U.S. Courts and International Human Rights, 1991, United Nations Legal Order, 1994; contbr. articles to profl. jours. Pro bono counsel in field; bd. dirs. Hancock Point (Maine) Village Improvement Soc., 1988-92. Recipient Pro Bono Atty. award Internat. Human Rights Law Group, 1987; finalist for Trial Lawyer of Yr., 1989; Henry Luce Found. scholar, 1976-77; Fulbright scholar Faculty of Law, Univ. Coll., Galway, Ireland, 1995-96. Mem. Am. Soc. Internat. Law (exec. com. 1994), Phi Beta Kappa. Mem. Soc. Of Friends. Avocations: musical composition, sailing. Office: Elliott Sch Internat Affairs George Wash U Lerner Hall B421 2000 H St N W Washington DC 20052 Office Phone: 202-994-5739. Office Fax: 202-994-9817. Business E-Mail: rstein@law.gwu.edu.

STEINHART, JESSICA, lawyer; BA, U. Mich., Ann Arbor, 1992; JD, Fordham U., NYC, 1996. Tax assoc. Coopers & Lybrand LLC, NYC, 1996—98; assoc. Greenberg Traurig LLC, NYC, 1998—2000; sr. counsel Pfizer Inc., NYC, 2000—02; asst. gen. counsel Sanofi-Aventis, Bridgewater, NJ, 2002—. Contbr. articles to profl. jours. Recipient Archibald Murray Pub. Svc. award, Fordham U. Sch. Law, 1993—96. Mem.: N.J. Assn.Corp.

Counsel, N.Y. State Bar Assn., Phi Psi. Office: Sanofi-Aventis 55A-515A 55 Corporate Dr PO Box 5925 Bridgewater NJ 08807 Office Phone: 908-981-4939.

STEINHAUER, GILLIAN, lawyer; b. Aylesbury, Bucks, Eng., Oct. 6, 1938; d. Eric Frederick and Maisie Kathleen (Yeates) Pearson; m. Bruce William Steinhauer, Jan. 2, 1960; children: Alison (Humphrey) Eric, John, Elspeth. AB cum laude, Bryn Mawr Coll., Pa., 1959; JD cum laude, U. Mich., 1976. Bar: Tenn. 1998, U.S. Dist. Ct. (ea. dist.) Mich. 1976, U.S. Ct. Appeals (6th cir.) 1982. From assoc. to sr. ptnr. Miller, Canfield, Paddock & Stone, Detroit, 1976-92; dir. Commonwealth of Mass. Workers' Compensation Litigation Unit, Boston, 1992—2002; atty. U.S. Postal Svc., 2002—. Chancellor Cath. Ch. St. Paul, Detroit, 1976-83, 91; pres. bd. trustees Cath. Cmty. Svcs. Inc., 1989-92; bd. dirs. Spaulding for Children, 1991-92, Davenport House, 1992-96, chair 1995-96, vestry mem. St. Michael's Ch., Marblehead, Mass., 1994-97; chpt. mem. St. Mary's Cathedral, Memphis, 2005—. Mem. Mich. State Bar Found. (life), Fed. Jud. Conf. 6th Cir. (life). Home: 4010 S Galloway Dr Memphis TN 38111-6842

STEINHAUER, SHERRI, professional golfer; b. Madison, Wis., Dec. 27, 1962; Student, U. Tex. Mem. Futures Tour, LPGA Tour, 1986—; mem. US Team Solheim Cup, 1994, 1998, 2000. Achievements include winning LPGA Tour events including du Maurier Ltd. Classic, 1992, Sprint Championship, 1994, Weetabix Women's British Open, 1998, 99, Japan Airlines Big Apple Classic, 1999, Sybase Classic Presented by Lincoln Mercury, Women's British Open, 2006, State Farm Classic, 2007; 4 LPGA career holes-in-one. Office: c/o LPGA 100 Internat Golf Dr Daytona Beach FL 32124-1092

STEINHAUS, JOHN EDWARD, retired anesthesiologist, educator; b. Omaha, Feb. 23, 1917; s. Emil F. and Pearl (Haynie) S.; m. Mila Jean Pinkerton, Feb. 21, 1943; children: Kathryn, Carolyn, Barbara, William, Elizabeth. BA, U. Neb., Lincoln, 1940, MA, 1941; MD, U. Wis., Madison, 1945, PhD, 1950. Diplomate Am. Bd. Anesthesiologists. Pvt. practice specializing in anesthesiology, Madison, Wis., 1951-58, Atlanta, 1958—; faculty U. Wis., 1951-58; mem. faculty Emory U., Atlanta, 1958—, prof. anesthesiology, 1959-87, prof. emeritus, 1987—, chmn. dept., 1959-85; chief anesthesiology service Grady Meml. Hosp., 1959-77, Emory U. Hosp., 1958-85; ret., 1987. Author: Medical Care Divided; contbr. articles to profl. jours. Past pres. Anesthesia Found. Mem. Am. Soc. Anesthesiologists (past pres., Disting. Service award 1982), So. Soc. Anesthesiologists (past pres.), AMA, AAAS, Assn. U. Anesthetists (past pres.), Anesthesiology History Assn. (past pres.), Soc. Pharm. Exptl. Therapeutics, Phi Beta Kappa, Sigma Xi, Alpha Omega Alpha. Home and Office: 836 Castle Falls Dr NE Atlanta GA 30329-4114 Personal E-mail: jsteinh@emory.edu.

STEINHAUSER, JOHN WILLIAM, retired lawyer; b. Akron, Ohio, June 25, 1924; s. John Hugo and Francis Lillian (Pearson) S.; m. Patricia E. Mooney, Dec.1, 1956; children: John, Christian, Mark, Sharon. BSBA, Ohio State U., 1949; JD, U. Mich., 1950. Bar: Mich. 1950, Colo. 1972. Atty., dir. L.Am., dir. export sales, gen mgr. Africa-Far E. Chrysler Corp., dir. Chrysler Internat., dir. Africa-Far East, 1950-71; atty. Denver, 1971—; founder, dir., pres. Pearson Energy Corp., 1977—. Founder, chmn. Sharon Energy, Ltd., Denver, 1980, also dir., 1980-97. Active Colo. Rep. Com.; sponsor Denver Symphony; pres. John and Patricia Steinhauser Found. With USNR, 1943—46. Mem. ABA, SAR, Colo. Bar Assn., Mich. Bar Assn., Soc. Internat. Law, Rocky Mountain Mineral Law Found., Cherry Hills Country Club, Royal Poinciana Golf Club, Rotary. Home: 46 Charlou Cir Englewood CO 80111-1103 Personal E-mail: johnsteinhauser@comcast.net.

STEINHOFF, RAYMOND O(AKLEY), consulting geologist; b. Hart, Mich., Apr. 22, 1925; m. Anne M. Steinhoff, 1952; 1 child, Kirk O. BS, MS, So. Meth. U., 1948; PhD in Geology, Tex. A&M, 1965. Instr. geology Tex. A&M U., Coll. Sta., Tex., 1948-51; geologist Atlantic Rich., Wichita, Kans., 1951-53, Humble Oil and Refining Co., New Orleans, 1953-57; asst. prof. geology Tulane U., New Orleans, 1957-65, assoc. prof., 1965-70, chmn. dept., 1969-70; prof. and dept. head geology Stephen F. Austin State U., Nacogdoches, Tex., 1970-78; divsn. geologist Buttes, New Orleans, 1978-79; cons. geologist Graham, New Orleans, 1979-83. Cons. Trinexco, New Orleans, 1964-69. Sgt. US Army, 1944—46, WWII, 1st lt. USAF, 1952—53, Korea. Mem. Am. Assn. Petroleum Geologists (emeritus), New Orleans Geol. Soc. (emeritus), Phi Kappa Phi (emeritus).

STEINHORN, IRWIN HARRY, lawyer, educator, corporate financial executive; b. Dallas, Aug. 13, 1940; s. Raymond and Libby L. (Miller) Steinhorn; m. Deborah Kelley Steinhorn, Apr. 7, 2002; 1 child, Leslie Robin. BBA, U. Tex., 1961, LLB, 1964. Bar: Tex. 1964, U.S. Dist. Ct. (no. dist.) Tex. 1965, Okla. 1970, U.S. Dist. Ct. (we. dist.) Okla. 1972. Assoc. Oster & Kaufman, Dallas, 1964-67; ptnr. Parness, McQuire & Lewis, Dallas, 1967-70; sr. v.p., gen. counsel LSB Industries, Inc., Oklahoma City, 1970-87; v.p., gen. counsel USPCI, Inc., Oklahoma City, 1987-88; ptnr. Hastie & Steinhorn, Oklahoma City, 1988-95; mem., officer, dir. Conner & Winters, Oklahoma City, 1995—. Adj. prof. law Oklahoma City U. Sch. Law, 1979—; lectr. in field. Mem. adv. com. Okla. Securities Commn., 1986—; mem. exec. adv. bd. Oklahoma City U. Sch. Law, 2000—; bd. dirs. Okla. Venture Forum, 2000—. Served to capt. USAR, 1964-70. Mem.: ABA, Com. to Revise Okla. Bus. Corp. Act, Okla. Bar Assn. (bus. assn. sect., sec., treas. 1986—87, chmn. 1988—89), Tex. Bar Assn., Rotary, Phi Alpha Delta. Republican. Jewish. Home: 224 NW 18th St Oklahoma City OK 73103 Office: Conner & Winters One Leadership Sq 211 N Robinson Ave Ste 1700 Oklahoma City OK 73102-7136 Home Phone: 405-524-5621; Office Phone: 405-272-5711. Business E-Mail: isteinhorn@cwlaw.com.

STEINHORN, ROBIN H., neonatologist, educator; b. Akron, Ohio, June 12, 1956; d. Paul Henry and Marion Robinson Heise; m. David Marc Steinhorn; children: Rachel, Benjamin. BS, U. Akron, 1976; MD, Washington U., 1980. Bd. cert. pediat. Am. Bd. Pediat., bd. cert. neonatal-perinatal medicine. Neonatologist Children's Hosp. Buffalo, 1991—99; chief neonatology Children's Meml. Hosp., Chgo., 1999—; intern Wash. U., St. Louis, 1980—81; resident, fellow U. Minn., 1982—88. Assoc. prof. pediat. SUNY, Buffalo, 1991—99; prof. pediat. Northwestern U., Chgo., 1999—2002, Raymond and Hazel Speck Berry chair neonatology, 2002—. Editor: (book) Extracorporeal Cardiopulmonary Support in Critical Care, 2000; contbr. articles to profl. jours. Grantee, NIH, 1995—. Fellow: Am. Heart Assn. (leadership coun. 2004—, Established Investigator award 1998); mem.: Am. Pediat. Sco., Soc. for Pediat. Rsch., Am. Thoracic Soc., Am. Acad. Pediat. Achievements include innovations in treatment of newborn pulmonary hypertension. Office: Childrens Meml Hosp Neonatology #45 2300 Childrens Plaza Chicago IL 60614 Office Phone: 773-880-4142. Business E-Mail: r-steinhorn@northwestern.edu.

STEINHUBL, STEVEN RUDOLF, cardiologist, educator; b. Newark, Aug. 22, 1959; m. Monica Steinhubl; children: Gavin, Lisa. MS in Physiology, Georgetown U., Washington, DC, 1984; BS in Chem. Engring., Purdue U., West Lafayette, Ind., 1981; MD cum laude, St. Louis U. Sch. Medicine, 1988. Diplomate Am. Bd. Internal Medicine, Cardiovascular Disease, 1997, Interventional Cardiology, 1999, lic. Calif., NC, Commonwealth of Ky. Rsch. engring. summers Mallinckrodt, Inc., 1978—80; process engr., synthetic chem. divsn. Eastman Kodak Co., 1981—83; resident, internal medicine David Grant USAF Med. Ctr. in conjunction with U. Calif., Davis Sch. Medicine, Travis AFB, Calif., 1988—91; staff internist, asst. chief internal medicine, chief cardiopulmonary lab 3rd Air Force Med. Ctr., Elmendorf AFB, Alaska, 1992—94; staff cardiologist 59th Med. Wing, Lackland AFB, Tex., 1998—2002; staff cardiologist, asst. prof. medicine, Uniformed Svcs. U. Health Scis. Wilford Hall Air Force Med. Ctr., 1998—2002, dir., cardiovascular rsch., dir. coronary critical care unit, dir. cardiac catheterization lab.; fellow, cardiology Cleve. Clinic Found., Cleve., 1994—97, fellow, interventional cardiology, 1997—98; staff inteventional cardiologist, assoc. prof. medicine, assoc. dir. cardiac catherization lab. U. NC, 2002—04; assoc. prof. medicine U. Ky. Coll. Medicine Cardiovascular Rsch. Ctr., 2004—, dir., cardiovascular edn. & clin. rsch., 2004—, dir., cardiology fellowship program, 2004—, staff interventional cardiologist, 2004—. Cons. Accumetrics, Sanofi-Aventis, Bristol Myers Squibb; prin. investigator for funded projects; invited lectr. in field. Mem. editl. bd. Acute Coronary Syndromes (also co-editor-in-chief), Am. Heart Jour., Jour. Am. Coll. Cardiology, theheart.org; contbr. chapters to books; editl. assitance and peer reviewer Am. Heart Jour., Am. Jour. Cardiology, Am Jour. Medicine, Arteriosclerosis, Thrombosis and Vascular Biology, Atherosclerosis, Coronary Artery Disease, Circulation, European Heart Jour., Heart, Jour. Am. Coll. Cardiology, AMA, Jour. Thrombosis and Haemostasis, Jour. Thrombosis and Thrombolysis, Mayo Clinic Proceedings, Nature Medicine, Thrombosis and Haemostatis. Decorated Meritorious Svc. Medal with Oak Leaf Clusters; named one of Best Physicians in Am., 2005; Chief Cardiology Fellow, 1995—97, Clin. Rsch. award, 1998, Health Professions Scholarship Program, 1985—88. Mem.: Order of Pythagoras, Gimlet, Alpha Sigma Nu, Alpha Omega Alpha, Phi Eta Sigma, Omicron Delta Kappa. Office: U Ky Coll Medicine Cardiovascular Rsch Ctr 326 Charles T Wethington Bldg 900 S Limestone St Lexington KY 40536-0200 Office Phone: 859-323-8040, 859-323-5479. Office Fax: 859-323-6475. Business E-Mail: srstei2@email.uky.edu, steinhubl@uky.edu. *

STEINMAN, LISA MALINOWSKI, English literature educator, writer; b. Willimantic, Conn., Apr. 8, 1950; d. Zenon Stanislaus and Shirley Belle Malinowski; m. James A. Steinman, Apr. 1968 (div. 1980); m. James L. Shugrue, July 23, 1984. BA, Cornell U., 1971, MFA, 1973, PhD, 1976. Asst. prof. English Reed Coll., Portland, Oreg., 1976-82, assoc. prof., 1982-90, prof., 1990—, Kenan prof. English lit. and humanities, 1993—. Cons. NEH, Washington, 1984—85. Author: Lost Poems, 1976, Made in America, 1987, All That Comes to Light, 1989, A Book of Other Days, 1992, Ordinary Songs, 1996, Masters of Repetition, 1998, Carslaw's Sequences, 2003, Invitation to Poetry, 2007; editor: Hubbub Mag., 1983—; mem. editl. bd. Williams Rev., 1991—, Stevens Jour., 1994—; contbr. articles to profl. jours. Fellow Danforth Found., 1971-75, NEH, 1983, 96, 2006, Oreg. Arts Commn., 1983, Nat. Endowment for Arts, 1984; Rockefeller Found. scholar, 1987-88; recipient Pablo Neruda award, 1987, Oreg. Inst. Lit. Arts award, 1993. Mem. MLA (appt. adv. com. publ. 2006—), Poets and Writers, PEN (N.W. chpt., co-founder, officer 1989-93). Home: 5344 SE 38th Ave Portland OR 97202-4208 Office: Reed Coll Dept English 3203 SE Woodstock Blvd Portland OR 97202-8138 Business E-Mail: lisa.steinman@reed.edu.

STEINMANN, JOHN COLBURN, architect; b. Monroe, Wis., Oct. 24, 1941; s. John Wilbur and Irene Marie (Steil) S.; m. Susan Koslosky, Aug. 12, 1978 (div. July 1989); m. Genevieve Sim, Aug. 29, 1998. BArch, U. Ill., 1964; postgrad., Ill. Inst. Tech., 1970-71. Registered architect, Wash., Oreg., Calif., N.Mex., Ariz., Utah, Alaska, Wis., Ill., Hawaii. Project designer C.F. Murphy Assocs., Chgo., 1968-71, Steinmann Architects, Monticello, Wis., 1971-73; design chief, chief project architect State of Alaska, Juneau, 1973-78; project designer Mithun Assos., architects, Bellevue, Wash., 1978-80; owner, prin. John C. Steinmann Assos., Architect, Kirkland, Wash., 1980-94; supr. head facilities sect. divsn. fin. Dept. Edn. State of Alaska, Juneau, 1994-96; docs. mgr. Loschky Marquardt and Nesholm, Architects, Seattle, 1996-98; project mgr. Dept. Gen. Adminstrn. Divsn. Engring. and Archtl. Svsc., State of Wash., Olympia, 1998-99; project mgr. URS Architects, Seattle, 2000—04, RIM Architects, Honolulu, 2005—. Bd. dirs. Storytell Internat.; lectr. Ill. Inst. Tech., 1971-72. Prin. works include Grant Park Music Bowl, Chgo., 1971, Menomonee Falls (Wis.) Med. Clinic, 1972, Hidden Valley Office Bldg., Bellevue, 1978, Kezner Office Bldg., Bellevue, 1979, The Pines at Sunriver, Oreg., 1980, also Phase II, 1984, Phase III, 1986, The Pines at Sunriver Lodge Bldg., 1986, 2d and Lenora highrise, Seattle, 1981, Bob Hope Cardiovascular Rsch. Inst. lab animal facility, Seattle, 1982, Wash. Ct., Bellevue, 1982, Anchorage Bus. Pk., 1982, Garden Townhouses, Anchorage, 1983, Vacation Internationale, Ltd. Corp. Hdqs., Bellevue, 1983, Vallarta Torres III, Puerto Vallarta, Mex., 1987, Torres Mazatlan (Mex.) II, 1988, Canterwood Townhouses, Gig Harbor Wash., 1988, Inn at Ceres (Calif.), 1989, Woodard Creek Inn, Olympia, Wash., 1989, Northgate Corp. Ctr., Seattle, 1990, Icicle Creek Hotel and Restaurant, Leavenworth, Wash., 1990, Bellingham (Wash.), Market Pl., 1990, Boeing Hot Gas Test Facility, Renton, Wash., 1991, Boeing Longacres Customer Svc. Tng. Ctr. Support Facilities, Renton, 1992, Boeing Comml. Airplane Group Hdqs., Renton, 1996, U. Wash./Cascade C.C., Bothell, 1999, Wash. State U., Pullman, Wash., Sea-Tac Airport Comm. Control Ctr., Seattle, 2000, McCarty, Internet Cafe and Residence Hall Renovation, U. Wash., Seattle, 2001, K'ima Med. Ctr. Dental Clinic, Hoopa, Calif., 2001, Sea-Tac Airport Flight Info. Mgmt. Sys., 2002; 600 Bed student housing, classroom, parking mixed use project, U. Idaho, Moscow, The Vegetable Bin, Seattle, 2004, Kona Coffee and Tea Plantation Visitors Ctr., Hawaii, 2006, Misawa Family Housing, Misawa, Japan, 2007; also pvt. residences. Served to 1st lt. C.E., USAR, 1964-66, Vietnam. Decorated Bronze Star. Mem. AIA, Am. Mgmt. Assn., Nat. Coun. Archtl. Registration Bds., U. Wash. Yacht Club, Columbia Athletic Club, Alpha Rho Chi. Republican. Roman Catholic. Address: 4316 106th Pl NE Kirkland WA 98033-7919 Mailing: PO Box 2041 Honolulu HI 96805

STEINMETZ, DAVID CURTIS, religious studies educator; b. Columbus, Ohio, June 12, 1936; s. Walter Curtis and Lucy Margaret (Binderbasen) S.; m. Virginia Ruth Verploegh, June 20, 1959; children: Claire Elise, Matthew Eliot. BA (hon.), Wheaton Coll., Wheaton, IL, 1954—58; BD (hon.), Drew U., Madison, NJ, 1958—61; ThD, Harvard U., Cambridge, MA, 1961—66. Ordained to ministry United Meth. Ch., 1959. Asst. and assoc. prof. Lancaster Theol. Sem., Lancaster, Pa., 1966—71; Amos Ragan Kearns prof. of the history of christianity Duke U., Durham, NC. Vis. prof. Harvard U., 1977; adv. coun. Interpretation, Richmond, Va., 1979-84, 87-92. Author: Misericordia dei, 1968, Reformers in the Wings, 1971, Luther and Staupitz, 1980, Luther in Context, 1986, Calvin in Context, 1995; editor Oxford Studies in Historical Theology; mem. editorial bd. Archiv für Reformationsgeschichte, 1977-93, Duke U. Monographs in Medieval and Renaissance Studies, 1972-98, Brill Studies in Medieval and Reformation Thought, Leiden, Netherlands, 1981-99. Pres. Am. Friends of the Herzog Aug. Libr., St. Louis, Mo., 1996—2002; mem., governing bd. Meeter Ctr. for Calvin Studies, Grand Rapids, Mich., 1993—99; pub. The Labytrinth Press, Durham, NC, 1981—95. Named Scholar-Tchr. of Yr. Duke U., 1986; Rockefeller doctoral fellow Rockefeller Found., 1964-66, faculty fellow Assn. Theol. Schs., 1970, 77-78, Guggenheim fellow Guggenheim Found., 1977-78, NEH summer fellow, 1990. Mem. Medieval Acad. Am., Am. Soc. Ch. History (pres. 1985), Renaissance Soc. Am., Soc. for Reformation Rsch., Am. Friends of the Herzog August Bibliothek (founding pres.). United Methodist. Achievements include research in History of Biblical Interpretation in Reformation Europe. Office: Duke University The Divinity School Durham NC 27708-0967 Personal E-mail: dsteinmetz@nc.rr.com. E-mail: steinmtz@acpub.duke.edu.

STEINMETZ, RICHARD BIRD, JR., lawyer; b. Orange, NJ, Mar. 27, 1929; s. Richard Bird and Charlotte (Quinby) S.; m. Merriam Holly Miller, June 9, 1956; children: Richard Blair, Jonathan Bird, Edward Quinby. BA, Yale U., New Haven, Conn., 1950; JD, Harvard U., Cambridge, Mass., 1955. Bar: NY 1955. Assoc. Chadbourne and Parke, NYC, 1955-59; with Anaconda Co., NYC, 1959-79, v.p., gen. counsel, 1971-79; v.p. Colt Industries Inc., NYC, 1979-82; v.p., gen. counsel Pittston Co., Greenwich, Conn., 1982-84; exec. v.p. Case, Pomeroy and Co., NYC, 1984-94. Bd. dirs. Case, Pomeroy and Co. Served to capt. USMC, 1950-52. Mem. ABA, Assn. of Gen. Counsel. Republican. Episcopalian. Home: 275C Park St New Canaan CT 06840-5739

STEINMEYER, ROBERT JAY, retired lawyer; b. Aug. 10, 1921; s. William F. and Willie (Davis) Steinmeyer; m. Susie (Levicki), Dec. 23, 1948; children: William Bruce, James Jay, Sharon Sue. BS, U. Nebr., 1943; post grad., Albany Law Sch., 1947—48; LLB, George Washington U., 1949. Bar: D.C. 1950, Calif. 1958. Devel. engr. G.E. Co., Schenectady, NY, 1943—46, patent atty., 1947—53, patent counsel, 1953—57, Beckman Instruments, Inc., Fullerton, Calif., 1957—63, resident counsel, 1963—71, v.p., legal, 1971—85, dir., 1984—85; sole practice Fullerton, Calif., 1985—86; of counsel Karon, Morrison, and Savikas Ltd., Fullerton, Calif., 1986—88; ret., 1988. Mem.: ABA, Assn. Corp. Patent Counsel (pres. 1975—76), Am. Patent Law Assn., Pi Mu Epsilon, Sigma Tau, Order of Coif. Home: 813 Morningside Dr Fullerton CA 92835 Personal E-mail: steinfull21@gmail.com.

STEINMILLER, JANET L., literature and language educator; b. Pitts., June 11, 1954; d. Eunice C Kravec and Louis W Steinmiller; children: Justin D Ingala, Kevin D Ingala. MLS, U. Pitts., 1998. Professional Certificate Commonwealth of Pa., 1998. Tchr. English grades 9 - 12 Booker Wash. Inst. Tech., Kakata, Liberia, 1976—77; tchr. English and Reading grades 7 - 12 Forest Area Sch. Dist., Tionesta, Pa., 1978—81; libr. elem.,mid. sch., tchr. English and Reading S.A. Escuela Campo Alegre, Caracas, Venezuela, 1981—. Presenter (conference paper) The Plagiarism Problem, Dancing with Databases (Cert. of Achievement, 2003). Recipient Hon. Membership in the Nat. Honor Soc., Araguaney Chpt. of Escuela Campo Alegre, 1991—. Home Phone: 412-787-7609.

STEINMILLER, JOHN F., professional sports team executive; b. Mt. Prospect, Ill. m. Corinne Steinmiller; children: John Henry, Mary Kate. V.p. bus. ops. Milw. Bucks, 1977—. Bd. dirs. Midwest Athletes Against Childhood Cancer Fund, Metro Milw. YMCA; chmn. Milw. Conv. and Visitors Bur. VISIT Milw.; mem. Greater Milw. Com. Recipient Contardi Commitment award Midwest Athletes Against Childhood Cancer Fund, 1991, Vol. of Yr. award YMCA, 1996. Office: Milw Bucks 1001 N Fourth St Milwaukee WI 53203-1314 Office Phone: 414-227-0500. E-mail: jsteinmiller@milwaukeebucks.com. *

STEINSMITH, WILLIAM, internist, research scientist; b. NYC, July 31, 1933; s. David Steinsmith and Dorothy Burtoff. BS, U. Calif., San Francisco, 1965, MD, 1968. Lic. physician and surgeon Calif. Med. Bd., Va. Bd. Medicine. Freelance polit. journalist, 1960—; postdoctoral scholar in pharmacology and pharmacokinetics dept. pharmacology U. Calif.-San Francisco, 1969—74; pvt. practice internist San Francisco, 1970—2004; asst. chief of medicine St. Joseph's Hosp., San Francisco, 1973—76; ind. rsch. in math. biology, 1974—; med. staff internist Veterans Home of Calif., Yountville, Calif., 1989—91. Author: (polit. history/analysis) Lenin, Inter-Imperialism, and National-Colonial Revolution, 1979. Recipient Owen D. Young Prize in Internat. Rels., U. Calif.- Berkeley, 1963. Mem.: San Francisco Med. Soc./U. Calif.-San Francisco Health Care Fedn. (bd. trustees, exec. com. 1973—75). Home and Office: 2418 20th Ave Apt 202 San Francisco CA 94116 Personal E-mail: bbhaywood@aol.com.

STEINWURTZEL, RICHARD A., lawyer; b. Newark, Jan. 1, 1950; BA cum laude, Union Coll., 1972; JD with honors, George Washington U., 1975. Bar: D.C. 1975. Ptnr. Fried, Frank, Harris, Shriver & Jacobson, Washington. Mem. ABA (sect. corp., banking and bus. law), N.Y. State Bar Assn., D.C. Bar, Securities Industry Assn. (mem. legal and compliance divsn. 1985—). Office: Fried Frank Harris Shriver & Jacobson 1001 Pennsylvania Ave NW Washington DC 20004-2505

STEIR, MICHAEL S., real estate company executive; BA in Economics, U. NC, Chapel Hill. Broker Huberth & Peters, NY; joined Studley, NYC, 1984, chmn. and CEO, exec. com. Bd. mem. Film soc. Lincoln Ctr., Mus. of City NY, Realty Found. NY, Ave. of Americas Found., Hamptons Internat. Film Festival. Recipient Most Ingenious Deal of Yr. award, 1984. Office: Studley 300 Park Ave 3rd Floor New York NY 10022 Office Phone: 212-326-1096. *

STEITZ, JOAN ARGETSINGER, biochemistry professor; b. Mpls., Jan. 26, 1941; d. Glenn D. and Elaine (Magnusson) Argetsinger; m. Thomas A. Steitz, Aug. 20, 1966; 1 child, Jon. BS, Antioch Coll., 1963; PhD, Harvard U., 1967; DSc (hon.), Lawrence U., Appleton, Wis., 1981, Rochester U. Sch. Medicine, 1984, Mt. Sinai Sch. Medicine, 1989, Bates Coll., 1990, Trinity Coll., 1992, Harvard U., 1992, Brandeis U., 2002, Brown U., 2003, Princeton U., 2003, Watson Sch. Biol. Sciences, Cold Spring Harbor Lab., 2004. NSF postdoctoral fellow, Andorra, 1967—69; Jane Coffin Childs Meml. Fund Fellow, Divsn. Cell Biology Med. Rsch. Coun. Lab. Molecular Biology, Cambridge, England, 1967—70; asst. prof. molecular biophysics and biochemistry Yale U., New Haven, 1970-74, assoc. prof., molecular biophysics and biochemistry, 1974-78, prof., molecular biophysics and biochemistry, 1978—92, Henry Ford II prof. molecular biophysics and biochemistry, 1992—98, chmn. dept. molecular biophysics and biochemistry, 1996—99, dir. molecular genetics program Boyer Ctr. Molecular Medicine, Sterling prof. molecular biophysics and biochemistry, 1998—. Josiah Macy Scholar Max Planck Inst. fur Biophysikalische Chemie (Göttingen), Germany and Med. Coun. Ctr., Lab. of Molecular Biology, Cambridge, England, 1976—77; Fairchild Disting. Fellow Calif. Inst. Technology, Pasadena, Calif., 1984—85; investigator Howard Hughes Med. Inst, Yale Univ., 1986—; scientific dir. Jane Coffin Child Fund for Med. Rsch., 1991—2002; dir., molecular genetics program Boyer Center for Molecular Medicine; mem. vis. com. for biology divsn. Caltech, Calif. Inst. Technology, 1999—; mem. basic sciences scientific adv. bd. Fred Hutchinson Cancer Ctr., 2001—; mem. scientific adv. bd., biology divsn. Molecular Biology Dept., Princeton Univ., Max Planck Inst. for Biophysical Chemistry (Göttingen), 1999—; mem. Lasker Awards Jury, 2001—, Jury for L'Oréal UNESCO award, 2001—; mem. scientific adv. com. Sci. Found. Ireland, 2002—. Mem. editl. bd. Genes and Development, 1994—, assoc. editor RNA, 1994—, bd. reviewing editors Science, 2004—. Bd. overseers Harvard Univ., 2003—. Co-recipient (with Thomas R. Cech) Warren Triennial Prize, Mass. Gen. Hosp., 1989; named Fritz Lipmann Lectr., Am. Soc. for Biochemistry and Molecular Biology, 1989, 11th Ann. Keith Porter Lectr. on Cell Biology, Am. Soc. for Cell Biology, 1992; recipient Young Scientist award, Passano Found., 1975, Eli Lilly Award in Biol. Chemistry, 1976, U.S. Steel Found. Award in Molecular Biology, 1982, Lee Hawley, Sr. Award for Arthritis Rsch., 1983, Nat. Medal Sci., 1986, Radcliffe Grad. Soc. Medal for Disting. Achievement, 1987, Dickson Prize for Sci., Carnegie-Mellon U., 1988, Christopher Columbus Discovery Award in Biomed. Rsch., 1992, Rebecca Rice award for Disting. Achievement, Antioch Coll. Alumni Assn., 1993, Weizmann Women and Sci. Award, 1994, City of Medicine Award, 1996, Disting. Svc. award, Miami Bio/Technology Winter Symposium, 1996, Novartis Drew Award in Biomed. Rsch., 1999, UNESCO-L'Oreal Women in Sci. Award, 2001, Lewis S. Rosenstiel for Distinguished Work in Basic Medical Rsch. Award, 2002, FASEB Excellence in Sci. Award, 2003, Howard Taylor Ricketts Award, U. Chgo., 2004, Caledonian Rsch. Found. Prize Lectureship, Royal Soc. Edinburgh, 2004, The RNA Soc. Lifetime Achievement Award, 2004, Gairdner award for achievement in med. rsch., Gairdner Found., 2006. Fellow: AAAS, Am. Acad. Microbiology; mem.: NAS, Inst. Medicine, Academia Europaea, Japanese Biochemical Soc. (hon.), European Molecular Biology Orgn. (assoc.), Conn. Acad. Sciences and Engring., Am. Philos. Soc., Am. Acad. Arts and Sciences. Office Phone: 203-737-4418. Business E-Mail: joan.steitz@yale.edu.

STELCK, CHARLES RICHARD, geology educator; b. Edmonton, Alta., Can., May 20, 1917; s. Robert Ferdinand and Florella Maud (Stanbury) S.; m. Frances Gertrude McDowell, Apr. 24, 1945; children: David, Brian, Leland, John (dec.). BSc, U. Alta., 1937, MSc, 1941, DSc (hon.), 2003; PhD, Stanford U., 1951. Registered profl. geologist Alta. Field geologist B.C. Dept. Mines, Victoria, Canada, 1939-41, Canol Project, Norman Wells, N.W.T., Canada, 1941-43, Imperial Oil Co., Calgary, Alta., 1943-49; from lectr. to prof. emeritus geology U. Alta., Edmonton, 1946—. Contbr. numerous articles principally on biostratigraphy of Cretaceous to sci. publs. Decorated officer Order of Can.; recipient Disting. Educator award Am. Assn. Petroleum Geologists, 2001, Queen's Golden Jubilee medal, 2002, Alberta Centenial medal, 2005; named to Can. Petroleum Hall Fame, 2005. Fellow Royal Soc. Can.; mem. Assn. Profl. Engrs., Geologists and Geophysicists Alta. (Centennial award 1979), Geol. Assn. Can. (Logan medal 1982), Geol. Soc. Am., Can. Soc. Petroleum Geologists (Douglas medal 1994, Stanley Slipper gold medal 2002), Order of Can. (officer 1997). Conservative. Office: U Alta Dept Earth & Atmospheric Scis Edmonton AB Canada T6G 2E3

STELLA, FRANK PHILIP, artist; b. Malden, Mass., May 12, 1936; s. Frank and Constance Aida (Santonelli) S.; m. Barbara Rose, 1961 (div.); children: Rachel, Michael, Laura; m. Harriet McGurk, 1978; children: Peter, Patrick. AB in History, Princeton U., 1958, DFA (hon.), 1984; degree (hon.), Mpls. Coll. Art Design, 1974, Brandeis U., 1985, Dartmouth Coll., 1985. Represented by Leo Castelli Gallery, 1959; artist-in-residence Dartmouth Coll., 1963; instr. Brandeis U., 1969; Charles Eliot Norton prof. poetry Harvard U., Cambridge, Mass., 1983. Lectr. Pratt Inst., Bklyn., 1960, Yale U., 1965, Cornell U., 1965, Seattle Art Mus., 1967, Detroit Inst. Arts, 1967, Art Inst. Chgo., 1968, 85, Bezalel Acad. Arts and Design, Jerusalem, 1981, Whitney Mus., Mus. Fine Art, Boston, 1982, San Antonio Art Inst., 1983, Harvard U., 1983-84, Musee Nat. d'Art Moderne, Paris, 1984, Coun. for U.S. and Italy, N.Y., 1984, Frick Collection, N.Y., 1985, Dartmouth Coll., 1985; instr. art U. Saskatchewan, 1967, Brandeis U., 1968; vis. critic dept. art, Cornell U., 1965. One-man shows Leo Castelli Gallery, N.Y.C., 1960, 62, 64, 66, 69, 73, 75, 79, 82, Galerie Lawrence, Paris, 1961, 64, Ferus Gallery, L.A., 1963, 65, Kasmin Ltd., London, 1964, 66, 68, M. Knoedler & Co., 1976, 81, 85, David Mirvish Gallery, London, 1966, Pasadena (Calif.) Art Mus., 1966, Seattle Art Mus., 1967, Galerie Bischofsberger, Zurich, Switzerland, 1967, Gallery Modern Art, Washington, 1968, Irving Blum Gallery, L.A., 1968, 69, 71, 73, Mus. Modern Art, N.Y.C., 1970, 1987 (restrospective); touring show Stella, since 1970, 1978, Galerie Daniel Templon, Paris, 1975, Andre Emmerich, Zurich, 1976, Galerie M Bochum, Fed. Republic Germany, 1977, Mus. Modern Art, Oxford, Eng., 1977, Galerie Valeur, Nagoya, Japan, 1978, 79, Getler/Pall Gallery, N.Y.C., 1980, Akira Ikeda Gallery, Nagoya, Japan, 1980, 81, 82, 83, 85, 86, 87, 88, 89, Koh Gallery, Tokyo, 1980, Knoedler Gallery, 1977, 80, 82, 85, 87, Galerie Hans Strelow, Dusseldorf, Fed. Republic Germany, 1981-82, 87, Mus. Modern Art, San Francisco, 1983, Inst. Contemporary Arts, London, 1985, Greenberg Gallery, St. Louis, 1985-86, Laumeier Sculpture Pk., St. Louis, 1986, Gagosian Gallery, N.Y.C., 1987, Nat. Mus. Art, Osaka, Japan, 1988, Staatsgalerie Stuttgart, Fed. Republic Germany, 1988-89, Kawamura Mem. Museum of Art, Japan, 1991; numerous group shows throughout U.S., Europe, 1959—, including 37th Corcoran Gallery Art Bienniale, Washington, 1981; included in permanent collections, Bernard Jacobson Gallery, London, Addison Gallery Am. Art, Phillips Acad., Andover, Mass., Art Gallery Ont., Toronto, Can., Balt. Mus., Rose Art Mus., Brandeis U., Waltham, Mass., Bklyn. Mus., List Art Ctr., Brown U., Providence, Cleve. Art Mus., Contemporary Art Mus., Houston, Dallas Mus. Fine Art, Denver Mus. Art, Des Moines Art Ctr., 1st Nat. Bank Houston, Fogg Art Mus., Boston, Guggenheim Mus., High Mus., Atlanta, Hirshhorn Mus. and Sculpture Garden, Washington, Ind. U. Art Mus., Bloomington, Inst. Contemporary Art, Phila., Jacksonville (Fla.) Art Mus. Inc., Kitakyushu (Japan) Mcpl. Mus., Kunstmuseum, Basel, Switzerland, Stedelijk Mus., Amsterdam, Art Inst., Chgo., Detroit Inst. Art, L.A. County Mus. Art, Walker Art Center, Mpls., Mus. Modern Art, N.Y.C., San Francisco Mus. Art, Whitney Mus. Am. Art, N.Y.C., Albright-Knox Gallery, Buffalo, La. Mus., Humlebaek, Denmark, Met. Mus. Art, N.Y.C., Milw. Art Ctr., Mpls. Inst. Arts, Modern Art Mus. Ft. Worth, Moderna Museet, Stockholm, Musee Nat. d'Art moderne, Paris, Mus. Bochum, Fed. Republic Germany, Mus. Boymans von Beuningen, Rotterdam, The Netherlands, Mus. Contemporary Art, Chgo., Mus. Contemporary Art, L.A., Mus. Fine Arts, Houston, Nagoaka (Japan) Mus. Art, Smithsonian Instn., Washington, Nat. Gallery Art, Washington, Nationalgalerie, Berlin, Nat. Mus. Am. Art, Washington, Nelson-Atkins Mus. Art, Kansas City, Mo., Phila. Mus., Phillips Collection, Washington, Portland (Oreg.) Ctr. Visual Arts, St. Louis Art Mus., Seattle Art Mus., Seibu Art Mus., Tate Gallery, London, Toledo Mus. Art, Vancouver (B.C.) Art Mus., Can., Wadsworth Atheneum, Hartford, Conn., Wallraf-Richartz Mus., Cologne, Fed. Republic Germany; author: Frank Stella: Illustrations after El Lissitzky's Had Gadya 1982-84, 1985, Working Space, 1986; work subject of numerous monographs and publs.; subject of film Frank Stella at the Fogg 1984, 1985. Bd. dirs. Coun. for U.S. and Italy. Recipient 1st prize Tokyo Internat. Biennale, 1967, Claude M. Fuess award Phillips Acad., 1979, Skowhegan Medal for Painting, 1981, Mayor's Award of Honor Mayor of N.Y.C., 1982, Award of Am. Art Pa. Acad. Fine Arts, 1985, Creative Arts award Brandeis U., 1968; hon. fellow Bezalel Acad. Arts and Design, 1981, Am. Acad. Arts and Letters, 1982-83. Fellow Soc. Fellows (NYU). Office: Bernard Jacobson Gallery 6 Cork St London W1S 3EE England

STELLA, JOHN ANTHONY, financial executive; b. Jessup, Pa., Feb. 3, 1938; s. John Anthony and Alda (Parri) S.; m. Aurelia M. Arre, Feb. 20, 1965; children: John C., Matthew A., Krista R. BS, U. Detroit, 1960; MBA, NYU, 1965. Bus. evaluation cons. Allied Chem. Co., NYC, 1965-70; treas. Spinnerin Yarn Co., Hackensack, NJ, 1970-72, Penn-Dixie Cement Corp., NYC, 1972-74; v.p. finance Halecrest Co., 1974-76; treas. Rsch.-Cottrell, 1976-84, v.p., contr./treas., 1984-88; pres. John A. Stella & Assocs., Plainfield, NJ, 1988-91; sr. v.p. Investment Support Systems, Inc., Bloomfield, NJ, 1991-95. Pres. State Tax Auditing and Rsch., Inc., Bethlehem, 1993—. Served with AUS, 1960. Office: State Tax Auditing & Rsch Inc 1775 Arden Ln Bethlehem PA 18015-5829

STELLA, MARIE VITA, retired engineer, consultant, homeland and information security; b. Bklyn., Mar. 27, 1943; d. Joseph Domenico and Maria (Savino) Stella. BA, CCNY, 1965—70; MS, U. Colo., 1980. Cert. info. sys. security profl. Cons. IBM, White Plains, NY, 1980—82; telecommunication engr. Port Authority of NY and NJ, NYC, 1982—84; dep. dir. govt. systems Network Mgmt., Fairfax, Va., 1984—85; lead engr., group leader MITRE Corp, McLean, Va., 1985—90; dep. dir. Network Strategies, Fairfax, Va., 1990—91; lead security engr. FAA, Washington, 1991—2005; sr. rsch. fellow Ctr. For Tech. and Nat. Security Policy, Nat. Def. U., Washington, 2003—04; ret., 2005. Cons. in field. Vol. Ct. Apptd. Spl. Adv. (CASA), Spotsylvania, Va., 1998—2004. Home Phone: 804-744-1420. Personal E-mail: mvstella_99@yahoo.com.

STELLA, VALENTINO JOHN, chemistry professor; b. Melbourne, Victoria, Australia, Oct. 27, 1946; came to U.S., 1968; s. Giobatta and Mary Katherine (Sartori) S.; m. Mary Elizabeth Roeder, Aug. 16, 1969; children: Catherine Marie, Anne Elizabeth, Elise Valentina. B of Pharmacy, Victorian Coll. Pharmacy, Melbourne, 1967; PhD, U. Kans., 1971. Lic. pharmacist, Victoria. Pharmacist Bendigo (Victoria) Base Hosp., 1967-68; asst. prof. Coll. Pharmacy U. Ill., Chgo., 1971-73; from asst. prof. to assoc. prof. to prof. Sch. Pharmacy U. Kans., Lawrence, 1973-90, Univ. disting. prof., 1990—. Dir. Ctr. for Drug Delivery Rsch.; cons. to 15 pharm. cos., U.S. Japan, Europe. Co-author: Chemical Stability of Pharmaceuticals, 2d edit., 1986; co-editor: Prodrugs as Novel Drug Delivery Systems, 1976, Directed Drug Delivery, 1985, Lymphatic Transport of Drugs, 1992; author numerous papers, revs., abstracts. Fellow AAAS, Am. Assn. Pharm. Scientists, Am. Acad. Pharm. Scientists. Roman Catholic. Achievements include 16 U.S. patents; rsch. in application of phys./organic chemistry to the solution of pharm. problems. Office: U Kans West Campus Dept Pharm Chemistry 2095 Constant Ave Lawrence KS 66047-3729 Home: 1135 W Campus Rd Lawrence KS 66044-3115

STELLAR, ARTHUR WAYNE, school system administrator; b. Columbus, Ohio, Apr. 12, 1947; s. Fredrick and Bonnie Jean (Clark) S. BS, Ohio U., 1969, MA, 1970, PhD, 1973. Tchr. Athens City Schs., Ohio, 1969-71; curriculum coord., tchr. Belpre City Schs., Ohio, 1971-72; prin. elem. schs., head tchr. learning disabilities South-Western City Schs., Grove City, Ohio, 1972-76; dir. elem. edn. Beverly Pub. Schs., Mass., 1976-78; coord. spl. projects and systemwide planning Montgomery County Pub. Schs., Rockville, Md., 1978-80; asst. supt. Shaker Heights, Ohio, 1980-83; supt. schs. Mercer County Pub. Schs., Princeton, W.Va., 1983-85, Oklahoma City Pub. Schs., 1985-92, Cobb County, Ga., 1992-93, Kingston Sch. Dist., NY, 1996—2001; dep. supt. Boston Pub. Schs., 1993-95, acting supt., 1995-96; pres., CEO High/Scope Ednl. Rsch. Found., Ypsilanti, Mich., 2001—03; v.p., chief edn. officer Renaissance Learning, Madison, Wis., 2003—04; sr. assoc. Proact Search, Inc., Milw., 2004—; rep. Docufide, Inc., LA, 2004—05, also adv. bd. dirs., 2004—05; supt. Taunton Pub. Schs., Mass., 2005—. Mem. ednl. adv. bd. Tchrs. Support Network, 2004—; adj. prof. Lesley Coll., Cambridge, Mass., 1976-78; adj. faculty Harvard U., 1992-93; assoc. Sch. Match, Ohio, 2004—. Author: Educational Planning for Educational Success, Effective Schools Research: Practice and Promise; editor: Effective Instructional Management; cons. editor, book rev. editor Jour. Ednl. Pub. Rels.; mem. editl. bd. Jour. Curriculum & Supervision, Reading Today's Youth; contbr. articles to profl. jours. Mem. Urban Ctr. Ednl. Adv. Bd., US Dept. Edn. Urban Supt. Network, Coun. Great City Schs. Bd., Urban Edn. Clearing House Adv. com., U. Okla. Adminstrn. cert. program com., Cmty. Literacy Coun. Bd.; chmn. bd. dirs. Langston U.; bd. dirs. Oklahoma County chpt. ARC, Jr. Achievement Greater Oklahoma City Bd., Okla. State Fair Bd., Horace Mann League, 1993—, v.p. 2000-01, pres.-elect, 2001-02, pres. 2002-03, past pres. 2003-04, mem. found. com., 2003-05; v.p. Last Frontier Coun. Bd., v.p. NY State PTA, 1996-2000, Kingston chpt. Rip Van Winkle Coun.; v.p. Boy Scouts Am., 1996-2001, membership chmn., 1996-97; exec. bd. Nat. Dropout Prevention Ctr. Network, 1998—, chmn., 2003-05; curriculum com. NY State Coun. Sch. Supts., 1996-2001; bd. dirs. Friends Historic Kingston, 1996-2001, Friends Senate House, Kingston, 1996-2001, Project Contemporary Competitiveness Inc., 2005—. Named a Friend, Horace Mann League, 2006; named to Linden McKinley H.S. Acad. Hall of Fame, 2003; recipient Silver Beaver award, Boy Scouts Am., 1990, Amb. award, Horace Mann League, 1995—2007; fellow, Charles Kettering Found. IDEA, 1976, 1978, 1980, NEH, Danforth Found., 1987—88. Mem. ASCD (life, exec. coun., pres. 1994-95, rev. coun. 1997-2002), Mich. ASCD, Mass. ASCD, Ohio ASCD, Okla. ASCD (Publ. award 1989), NY ASCD, Wis. ASCD, Internat. Soc. Ednl. Planning, Internat. Reading Assn. (govt. rels. com. 2003-04), Nat. Soc. Study Edn., Nat. Planning Assn., Nat. Assn. Gifted Children (life), Nat. Assn. Edn. Young Children (life), Nat. Coun. Tchrs. English (life), Music Educators Nat. Conf. (life), Nat. Orgn. Legal Problems Edn., Nat. Policy Bd. Ednl. Adminstrn., Am. Assn. Sch. Adminstrs. (life, Leadership for Learning award 1991, Dr. Effie Jones Humanitarian award 2007), Coll. Bd. Advanced Placement Spl. Recognition award 1991, Nat. Assn. Elem. Sch. Prins. (life), Am. Edn. Fin. Assn., Nat. Assn. Edn. Young Children (life), Nat. Sch. Pub. Rels. Assn. (Honor award 1991), Am. Mus. Natural Hist. (assoc.), Mass. Assn. for Sch. Supts., Mass. Assn. for Edn. of Young Children, Harvard U. Roundtable of Supts., Mass. Urban Supts., Nat. Sch. Pub. Rels. Assn., Taunton Area C. of C., World Coun. Curriculum and Instrn. (life, bd. dirs. N.Am. chpt. 1996-2000, pres. 2000-02), Coun. Basic Edn., Ohio Assn. Elem. Sch. Adminstrs., Buckeye Assn. Sch. Adminstrs., Ohio U. Coll. Edn. (disting. alumnus award 1991), Okla. Assn. Sch. Adminstrs., Mass. Assn. Sch. Adminstrs., Okla. Coalition Pub. Edn., Okla. Commn. Ednl. Leadership, Urban Area Supts. (Okla. br.), Ohio U. Alumni Assn. (nat. dir. 1975-78, pres. Ctrl. Ohio chpt. 1975-76, pres. Mass. chpt. 1976-78, life mem. trustees acad.), World Future Soc. (life) Greater Oklahoma City C. of C. (bd. dirs.), Okla. Heritage Assn., Heritage Hills Assn. (bd. dirs.), Victorian Soc. (New England chpt.), Nat. Eagle Scout Assn. (life), Aerospace Found. (hon. bd. dirs.), PLATO, Learning, Inc. (bd. dirs. 2000-03), Tchrs. Support Network (adv. bd. dirs. 2004—), Am. Bus. Card Club, Coca Cola Collectors Club, Internat. Club, Mgmt. Consortium (bd. advisors),Fulbright Alumni Assn. (life), Tau Kappa Epsilon Alumni Assn. (regional officer Mass. 1976-78, named Alumni Nat. Hall of Fame 1986, Nat. Alumnus of Yr. 1993, Excellence in Edn. award 1993), Kappa Delta Pi (life; advisor Ctrl. Okla. chpt., nat. publs. com.), Phi Delta Kappa (life). Methodist. Office Phone: 508-821-1201. Business E-Mail: astellar@tauntonschools.org.

STELLATO, LOUIS EUGENE, lawyer; b. Bethlehem, Pa., 1950; BBA, U. Tex., 1972; JD, U. Pitts., 1977; LLM, Temple U., 1979. Bar: PA. 1977. With Touche Ross & Co., 1979-81; with tax dept. Sherwin-Williams Co., 1981-87, sr. corp. counsel, 1987-90, asst. secy., corp. dir. taxes, 1990-91, v.p., gen. counsel, sec., 1991—. Office: Sherwin Williams Co 101 Prospect Ave NW Cleveland OH 44115-1075 Office Phone: 216-566-2000. *

STELLE, KELLOGG SHEFFIELD, physicist; b. Washington, Mar. 11, 1948; s. Charles Clarkson and Jane Elizabeth (Kellogg) S. AB, Harvard Coll., 1970; PhD, Brandeis U., 1977. Field observer Bartol Research Found., South Pole, Antarctica, 1970-72; lectr. math. King's Coll., U. London, Eng., 1977-78; sci. assoc. Cern, Geneva, 1980-81, 87, 97-98; rsch. fellow Imperial Coll., London, 1978-80, advanced fellow, 1982-87, lectr. then reader, 1987-95, prof. physics, 1995—, head theoretical physics group, 2002—. Mem. Inst. for Advanced Study, Princeton, N.J., 1986; vis. fellow Ecole Normale Supérieure, Paris, 1981-82; program dir. Inst. Henri Poincaré, Paris, 2000. Editor Classical and Quantum Gravity, 1984-93; contbr. articles to profl. jours. Recipient Rsch. award, Alexander Von Humboldt Found., 2006. Fellow Inst. of Physics, Am. Phys. Soc.; mem. AAAS, Fedn. Am. Scientists. Office: Blackett Lab Imperial Coll Prince Consort Rd London SW7 2AZ England

STELLMACHER, JON MICHAEL, corporate financial executive; b. Green Bay, Wis., Feb. 25, 1956; s. Leroy Frederick and Helen Mae (Koss) S.; m. Rebecca Jean Hein, Aug. 20, 1976; children: James Michael, Paul Frederick, Abigail Joy. BBA with distinction, U. Wis., 1978. Underwriting clk. State Life Insur. Fund, Madison, Wis., 1977-78; actuarial student Aid Assn. for Luths., Appleton, Wis., 1978-79, actuarial asst., 1979-83, asst. actuary, 1983-85, assoc. actuary, 1985-87, 2nd v.p., actuary, 1987—97, v.p., 1997—99, sr. v.p., 1999—2002; exec. v.p. Thrivent Fin. for Luths., Appleton, 2002—05, exec. v.p., chief adminstrv. officer, 2005—. Chpt. reviewer Health Ins. Textbook, Soc. Actuaries, 1984-85; chmn. actuaries sect. Health Workshop Nat. Fraternal Congress Am., 1986, 88; mem. actuarial adv. com. Wis. Health Ins. Risk Sharing Pool, 1987—92; co-chmn. workshop, spring meeting Soc. Actuaries, 1989, 91, Loma Ins. Comm., 1999-2000. Acting pres., v.p. coun. 1st English Luth. Ch., Appleton, 1984; mission interpreter Am. Luth. Ch., Appleton area, 1985-87, Sunday Sch. tchr., 1984-2006, stewardship com., 1981-90, social concerns com. 1991-94, Elderly Housing Task Force, 1990-91, Benevolence Task Force, 1994; co-chair Capital Appeal, 2000; asst. den leader Cub Scouts, Boy Scouts Am., Appleton, 1989-91; asst. coach Appleton Soccer Club, 1990-93, Odyssey of the Mind, 1990-93; coach Appleton Park and Recreation Dept., 1990-98; vice chmn. Arthur Krempin Sch. Music and Art, 2003-04; bd. dirs. Appleton Boychoir, 1994—, pres., 1999—; bd. dirs. Appleton Med. Ctr. Found., 2000—, sec., 2001—; bd. dirs. United Way Fox Cities, 2001—, co-chmn. campaign com., 2002, vice-chair, 2006, chair, 2007; mem. sr. adv. bd. Jr. Achievement, 2001—; bd. dirs. YMCA of the Fox Cities, 2002—, vice-chair, 2006-07, co-chair capital campaign, 2006-07; bd. dirs. Fox Cities Performing Arts Ctr., 2003—, ThedaCare, 2006—, Wis. Mfrs. and Commerce, 2006—; mem. Theda Care Quality Coun., 2003—, Cmty. Health Action Team, 2005—; co-chair Emergency Shelter Endowment Campaign, 2005-06; bd. regents Luther Coll., 2007—. Fellow Soc. Actuaries; mem. Am. Acad. Actuaries. Office: Thrivent Fin for Luths 4321 N Ballard Rd Appleton WI 54919 Home: 3124 E Sandpiper Ln Appleton WI 54913-7771 Office Phone: 920-628-2002. Business E-Mail: jon.stellmacher@thrivent.com.

STELLUTO, SHARON RENEE, apparel designer, painter; b. West Trenton, NJ, Apr. 17, 1981; d. Joseph Fernando and Barbara Ann Stelluto. BFA, SUNY, New Paltz, 2003. Asst. to profl. artist Andrew Braitman Art Studio, Charlotte, NC, 1995—98; server, barista, hostess Xando's Coffee, Bar, Bryn Mawr, Pa., 1999—2000; display designer, sales assoc. Illuminations, King of Prussia, Pa., 2001—01; sales assoc. Health and Nutrition Ctr., New Paltz, 2002—02; customer svc. rep. Certa Pro Painters, Oaks, Pa., 2003—03; handbag designer, office mgr., pub. rels. Debbie Brooks Designs, Gardiner, NY, 2003—04; asst. designer of handbags, quality supr., office mgr. L'egent Internat., Newburgh, NY, 2004. Fashion vendor Accessories Show at Jacob Javitts Ctr., Manhattan, NY, 2004—04; invitation Internat. Biennial of Contemporary Art, Ferrara, Italy, 2004—04. Official 2004 olympics pop art, Splash To Victory, one-woman shows include Living Seed Gallery, exhibitions include Samual Dorsky Mus., Backstage Studio Productions, Kingston Libr., online art exhibit, www.projekt30.com. Avocations: steel welder, piano, hiking, oil painting. Home Phone: 845-255-3797. Personal E-mail: sstelluto@yahoo.com.

STELLWAGEN, ROBERT HARWOOD, biochemistry professor; s. Harwood John and Alma Dorothy S.; m. Joanne Kovacs, June 15, 1963; children: Robert Harwood, Alise Anne. AB, Harvard U., 1963; PhD, U. Calif., Berkeley, 1968. Staff fellow NIH, Bethesda, Md., 1968-69; postdoctoral scholar U. Calif., San Francisco, 1969-70; asst. prof. biochemistry, molecular biology U. So. Calif., LA, 1970-74, assoc. prof., 1974-80, prof., 1980—, chmn. dept., 1981-86, vice chmn. dept., 1993—2006. Vis. scientist Nat. Inst. for Med. Rsch., Mill Hill, Eng., 1979. Contbr. articles to profl. jours. Recipient Henderson prize Harvard U., 1963; NSF fellow, 1963-67; NIH grantee, 1971-84. Mem. Sierra Club, Phi Beta Kappa. Democrat. Office: U So Calif Keck Sch Medicine 1333 San Pablo St Los Angeles CA 90089-9151 Home Phone: 805-532-9986; Office Phone: 323-442-1149. Business E-Mail: stellwag@usc.edu.

STELPSTRA, WILLIAM JOHN, minister; b. Paterson, NJ, Nov. 1, 1934; s. Duke and Nellie (Stapert) S.; m. Anna Rizkovsky, Sept. 6, 1958; 1 child, Linda Mae. BA, Alma White Coll., 1957; B. of Religion, Zarephath Bible Sem., 1958. Ordained to ministry Pillar of Fire Ch., 1954. Pastor Pillar of Fire Ch., Little Falls, N.J., 1956-60; evangelist Wesleyan Meth. Ch., 1960-64; founder, dir. Bethel Children's Home, Paterson, N.J., 1964-71, Bethel Ranch Rehab. for Men, West Milford, N.J., 1971—; founder, pres. World for Christ Crusade, Inc., N.J., Fla., 1960—, dir. fgn. missions Haiti, Ghana, India, 1980—; adminstr. Fellowship House, Bloomfield, N.J., 1979—, Bright Side Manor, Teaneck, N.J., 1978—. Mem. Ocean Grove C. of C. Republican. Wesleyan Ch. Avocations: painting with oils, swimming, boating, travel, gardening. Home: 1005 Union Valley Rd West Milford NJ 07480-1220 Office Phone: 973-728-3267. Personal E-mail: revstelpstra@aol.com.

STELTZLEN, JANELLE HICKS, lawyer; b. Atlanta, Sept. 18, 1937; d. William Duard and Mary Evelyn (Embrey) Hicks; divorced; children: Gerald William III, Christa Diane. BS, Okla. State U., 1958; MS, Kans. State U., 1961; JD, U. Tulsa, 1981. Bar: Okla. 1981, U.S. Dist. Ct. (no., ea. and we. dists.) Okla. 1981, U.S. Tax Ct. 1982, U.S. Ct. Claims 1982, U.S. Ct. Appeals (10th cir.) 1983, U.S. Ct. Appeals (Fed. cir.) 1984, U.S. Supreme Ct. 1986; lic. real estate broker. Pvt. practice, Tulsa, 1981-97. Lectr. Coll. of DuPage, Glen Ellyn, Ill., 1976, Tulsa Jr. Coll., 1981-88; dietitian, Tulsa; res. dep. for Tulsa County Sheriff's Office; 2d dep., legal Tulsa County Clk., 1997-2000. Christian counselor 1st United Meth. Ch., Tulsa, 1986—, coord. legal counseling ministry, 1985—, lay pastor, 1987—; mem. Tulsa County Bd. Equalization and Excise Tax Bd., 1989-90; mem. Leadership Tulsa XX, 1993—; recipient of Leadership Tulsa Paragon award, 1996; bd. dirs. Sister Cities Tulsa/San Luis Potosi, 1988—, South Peoria Neighborhood Connection Found., 1991—, pres., 1995-96; active Tulsa County Tax Oversight Com., 1994—, Tulsa Home Rule Charter Com., 1994—. Recipient Okla. Sr. Olympics medal. Mem. Okla. Bar Assn., Tulsa County Bar Assn., Vol. Lawyers Assn. (bd. dirs.), Am. Dietetic Assn., Tulsa Dist. Dietetic Assn., Kiwanis Internat., Mensa, DAR, Delta Zeta. Republican. Avocations: swimming, scuba diving, jogging, bicycling, reading. Home: 6636 S Jamestown Pl Tulsa OK 74136-2615

STELWAGON, JENNIFER COOPER, psychiatrist; b. Valdosta, Ga., Jan. 18, 1973; d. Michael Thomas and Margaret Ann (Sorensen) Cooper; m. William Mantz Stelwagon, Apr. 28, 2007. BA magna cum laude, DePauw U., Greencastle, Ind., 1995; MD, Johns Hopkins U., Balt., 1999. Lic. physician NY, diplomate Am. Bd. Psychiatry and Neurology, Am. Bd. Addiction Psychiatry. Resident in psychiatry NY Presbyn. Hosp./Weill Cornell Med. Ctr./Payne Whitney Clinic, NYC, 1999—2003; fellow in addiction psychiatry Weill Med. Coll. of Cornell U., NYC, 2003—04; staff psychiatrist Bridge Back to Life, NYC, 2004—05; pvt. practice psychiatry NYC, 2004—; med. dir. drug treatment Exponents, NYC, 2004—07. Clin. instr. psychiatry Weill Med. Coll. of Cornell U., 2006—. Named Career Directions Resident of the Yr., Pfizer Inc., 2002; recipient Alumni award for resident tchg., Payne Whitney Clinic, 2003. Mem.: Am. Acad. Addiction Psychiatry, Am. Psychiat. Assn. Avocations: skiing, scuba diving. Office: 239 E 73d St Ste 1W-A New York NY 10021

STELZENMULLER, CYRIL VAUGHN, lawyer; b. Fairfield, Ala., Jan. 25, 1928; s. James Grey and Helen (Brennan) S.; m. Jeannette Faye Wood, Mar. 19, 1965; 1 child, James Wood. BA, Cornell U., 1950, LLB with distinction, 1952. Bar: Ala. 1952, U.S. Dist. Ct. (no. dist.) Ala. 1955, U.S. Ct. Appeals (5th cir.) 1955, U.S. Ct. Appeals (D.C. cir.) 1973, U.S. Ct. Appeals (6th cir.) 1975, U.S. Supreme Ct. 1980, U.S. Ct. Appeals (11th cir.) 1982. Law clk. to judge U.S. Ct. Appeals (5th cir.), New Orleans, 1954-55; assoc. Burr & Forman, Birmingham, Ala., 1955-64, ptnr., 1964—. Contbr. articles to law rev. Col. ANG. Mem. Order of Coif, Phi Beta Kappa. Avocation: stained glass. Home: 3537 Victoria Rd Birmingham AL 35223-1403 Office: Burr & Forman LLP Ste 3000 Southtrust Tower Birmingham AL 35203-3204

STELZER, IRWIN MARK, economist; b. NYC, May 22, 1932; s. Abraham and Fanny (Dolgins) S.; m. Marian Faris Stuntz, 1981. BA cum laude, NYU, 1951, MA, 1952; PhD, Cornell U., 1954. Fin. analyst Econometric Inst., 1952; tchg. fellow Cornell U., 1953-54; instr. U. Conn., 1954-55; rschr. Twentieth Century Fund, 1953-55; economist W.J. Levy, Inc., 1955-56; sr. cons., v.p. Boni, Watkins, Jason & Co., Inc., 1956-61; rschr. Brookings Instn., 1956-57; pres. Nat. Econ. Rsch. Assocs., Inc., 1961-85, I.M. Stelzer Assocs. Inc., 1986—; dir. Energy and Environmental Ctr., Harvard U., 1987-90. Dir. econ. policy studies Am. Enterprise Inst., 1990-98; bd. dirs. Econs. Policy Inst., Oxford U.; dir. econ. policy studies Hudson Inst., 1998—; adv. coun. Electric Power Rsch. Inst.; adv. com. revision of rules of practice and procedure FERC; chmn. com. on adequate power supply FPC; bd. dirs. The Energy Adv. Group of the Keystone Ctr; mng. dir. Rothschild, Inc.; mem. trade and environment policy adv. com. US Trade Rep.; vis. fellow Nuffield Coll., Oxford U.; sr. rsch. fellow Smith Inst.; adv. bd. Am. Antitrust Inst.; lectr. in field. Author: Selected Antitrust Cases: Landmark Decisions, 1955, The Antitrust Laws: A Primer, 1993, 4th edit., 2001, Neoconservatism, 2004, The NEOCON Reader, 2004; econ. columnist The Sunday Times, London, 1986—; contbg. editor The Weekly Standard; columnist Courier Mail, Australia; contbr. articles to econs. field. Mem. Mayor's Energy Policy Adv. Group for NYC; adv. panel Pres.'s Nat. Commn. for Rev. of Antitrust Laws and Procedures; mem. Gov.'s Adv. Panel on Telecom., bd. governing trustees Am. Ballet Theatre; bd. dirs. U.S. Nat. Com., World Energy Conf., Regulatory Policy Inst., Oxford U.; mem. Fed. Energy Regulatory Com. Task Force on Pipeline Competition; pres. appointee advisor to U.S. Trade Rep. Mem. Am. Econ. Assn., Reform Club, Cosmos Club, Phi Beta Kappa. Home: PO Box 1008 Aspen CO 81612-1008 Office: 1150 17th St NW Ste 502 Washington DC 20036 Home Phone: 202-797-9292. Personal E-mail: stelzer@aol.com.

STELZER, PATRICIA JACOBS, retired secondary school educator; b. Springfield, Ohio, Sept. 7, 1936; d. George Kenneth and Beatrice Snook Jacobs; m. James Glea Stelzer, May 12, 1956; children: Michael G., Samantha S. Moehn, James Todd. BS in Edn., Wright State U., 1973, MA in History, 1997. Reporter, features writer, columnist Springfield News-Sun, 1962—65; social studies tchr. Schaefer Jr. H.S., Springfield, 1975—77, 1978—81, South H.S., Springfield, 1977—78, 1981—2000; ret., 2000; chmn. social studies dept. South H.S., Springfield, 1991—2000. Adj. prof. history Clark State C.C., Springfield, 2001—; cons. Ohio test scholastic achievement State of Ohio Dept. Edn., Columbus, 1985—87; participant cert. assessment pilot program social studies program Nat. Bd. Profl. Tchg. Stds., 1998. Author (book): Dangerous Research, By George!, Deadly Research By George!. Pres. Springfield Civic Theater, 1984—85; performer, mem. pub. rels. com. Music-Stage Theater, Springfield, 1964—68, 1975; dir., choreographer Northwestern H.S. and South H.S., Springfield, 1977—91; advt. dir. Choral Arts Springfield, 2004—05. Lutheran. Avocations: golf, travel, theater, writing. Home: 6541 Troy Rd Springfield OH 45502 Office: Clark State CC 570 E Leffel Ln Springfield OH 45501

STELZIG, SAMUEL FREDERIC, retired secondary school educator; b. Brainard, Minn. s. Roy Frederic and Marguerito M. Stelzig; m. Joyce Stelzig, Aug. 26, 1967; children: Scott Frederic, Kimberly Elain. BS in Indsl. Arts, Winona State U., Minn., 1963, MS in Indsl. Arts, 1967. Cert. tchr. Minn. Tchr. indsl. tech. North HS, North St. Paul, Minn.; ret., 2000. Author numerous poems. Bd. dirs. Cerebrial Palsy Minn. Recipient Dist. Merit award, Boy Scouts Am., Minn. Mem.: Masons, Scottish Rite, Shriners. Democrat. Jewish. Home: 1240 Ferndale St N Saint Paul MN 55119

STELZNER, PAUL BURKE, textile company executive; b. Iowa City, Iowa, Jan. 1, 1935; s. Glenn W. and Ruth (Schroder) S.; m. Martha Jane Schneeberger, Aug. 23, 1958; children: Martha Elizabeth Beuke and Barrie Jane Lubbering. BS, Muskingum Coll., 1960; postgrad., Akron U., 1961-65. Tech. dir. Buckeye Fabric Finishing Co., Coshocton, Ohio, 1963-74; sec., sales mgr. Excello Fabric Finishers Inc., Coshocton, 1966-74; gen. mgr. Mineral Fiber Mfg. Corp., Coshocton, 1974-76, dir., 1998—2007; v.p., gen. mgr. Kellwood Co. Recreation Group, 1976-85; v.p. Am. Recreation Products, Inc., New Haven, Mo., 1985-88; v.p., gen. mgr. John Boyle & Co., Statesville, NC, 1989-93, pres., CEO, 1993—2005, dir., 1999—2007. Bd. dirs. Indsl. Fabrics Found., 1998-2002. Served with USN, 1953-57. Mem. Indsl. Fabrics Assn. Internat. (dir. 1973-74, 82-88, 94-99). Presbyterian. Home: 843 Scenic Ridge Dr Washington MO 63090

STEM, CARL HERBERT, business educator; b. Eagleville, Tenn., Jan. 30, 1935; s. Marion Ogilvie and Sara Elizabeth (Jones) Stem; m. Linda Marlene Wheeler, Dec. 28, 1963; children: Anna Elizabeth, Susan Kathleen, John Carl, David Leslie. *Great-great-great-great-grandfather Jacob Stem — of Pennsylvania Dutch ancestry — migrated from the Philadelphia region after the Revolutionary War to Granville County, N.C., where there is still a farming village named Stem. In the 1830s several sons migrated to Middle Tennessee. Great-great-grandfather John Richard Stem was a lieutenant in the 55th (McKoins) Tennessee Infantry (CSA). Great-grandfather Marion Luther Stem was the first to "leave the farm", owning general merchandise stores. Grandfather Charles R. Stem practiced country dentistry for more than 50 years. Father Marion Ogilvie Stem died at the age of 28 in 1941.* BA, Vanderbilt U., Nashville, 1957; AM (Woodrow Wilson fellow, Harvard scholar), Harvard U., Cambridge, Mass., 1960, PhD, 1969. Internat. fin. economist, bd. govs. Fed. Res. System, Washington, 1963—70; from assoc. prof. to prof. econs. Tex. Tech. U., Lubbock, 1970—75; from assoc. prof. to prof. internat. fin. Tex. Tech U., Lubbock, 1970—2001; prof. emeritus Tex. Tech. U., Lubbock, 2001—; from chmn. fin., adminstr. grad. programs, exec. assoc. dean to dean Tex. Tech U. Coll. Bus. Adminstrn., Lubbock, 1971—97, dean emeritus, 1997—. Sr. econ. adviser Office Fgn. Direct Investments, U.S. Dept. Commerce, Washington, 1973-74; cons. US Dept. Treasury, 1974-75; mem. faculty Grad. Sch. Credit and Fin. Mgmt., Lake Success, NY, 1974-87; adj. scholar Am. Enterprise Inst. Pub. Policy Rsch., Washington, 1974-88; treas. Mission Jour., Inc., 1969-88. Editor (with Makin and Logue): Eurocurrencies and The International Monetary System; contbr. articles to profl. jours. Trustee St. Mary Plains Hosp., Lubbock, Tex., 1987-92, chmn., 1992; v.p. Tex. Coun. Collegiate Edn. Bus., 1977-78, pres., 1978-79; mem. acad. adv. bd. United Arab Emirates U., Al Ain, 1996-03; mem. Coun. on Podiat. Med. Edn., Washington, 1998—; bd. visitors Abilene Christian U., 1998—; elder Broadway Ch. of Christ, Lubbock, 2001-04, Ch. of Christ, Overland, Kans., 2007—; elder Overland Pk. Ch. Christ, Kans., 2007—. Capt. Security Agy. AUS, 1961-62. Fulbright scholar, U. Reading, Eng., 1957—58. Fellow Phi Beta Kappa; mem. Southwestern Bus. Adminstrn. Assn. (pres. 1982-83), Nat. Assn. for Bus. Econs., So. Bus. Adminstrn. Assn. (v.p. 1985-86, pres. 1986-87), Lubbock Econ. Coun. (pres. 1973), Am. Assembly Collegiate Schs. Bus. (stds. com. 1981-84, bd. dirs. 1993-96), Lubbock Club (pres. 1986-87), Omicron Delta Kappa, Phi Kappa Phi, Beta Gamma Sigma, Tau Kappa Alpha, Phi Beta Kappa. Avocations: genealogy, history. Home: 12508 W 123rd St Overland Park KS 66213 Personal E-mail: cstem@sbcglobal.net. *Most important to me are the ever timely values of our Judeo-Christian heritage- faith in God and a deep appreciation for the inherent value of man. These values have underpinned my aspirations and sustained me through disappointments. They have generated the perseverance and continual hope so vital to me as I have worked for self-growth and to make a contribution to the institutions and people with which I have been associated in various periods of my life.*

STEMBRIDGE, JOHN REESE, mathematics professor; PhD in combinatorics and algebra, MIT, 1985. Prof. math. Univ. Mich., Ann Arbor. Grantee Guggenheim Fellowship, 2000. Achievements include being one of 18 top mathematicians and computer scientists (Atlas of Lie Groups Project) from the US to successfully map E8, one of the largest and most complicated structures in mathematics. Office: 4854 East Hall Math Dept Univ Mich 525 E Univ Ave Ann Arbor MI 48103-1043 Office Phone: 734-936-1790. Office Fax: 734-936-0937. Business E-Mail: jrs@umich.edu. *

STEMERMAN, DAVID H., radiologist; b. Elmira, NY, Aug. 2, 1966; BA, Emory U., 1988; MD, Boston U., 1992. Diplomate Nat. Bd. Med. Examiners; bd. cert. Am. Bd. Radiology. Intern Mass. Gen. Hosp., Boston, 1992-93; resident Temple U., Phila., 1993-97; fellow NYU, NYC, 1997-98; assoc. radiologist Abington (Pa.) Meml. Hosp., 1998-99, St. Joseph's Med. Ctr., 1999—2000, St. Barnabas Hosp., 2000—01; pres. GDS Imaging PC, Larchmont, NY, 2001—. Office Fax: 914-722-9409.

STEMMLER, EDWARD JOSEPH, physician, retired health facility administrator, dean; b. Phila., Feb. 15, 1929; s. Edward C. and Josephine (Heitzmann) Stemmler; m. Joan C. Koster, Dec. 27, 1958; children: Elizabeth, Margaret, Edward C., Catherine, Joan. BA, La Salle Coll., Phila., 1950, ScD (hon.), 1983; MD, U. Pa., 1960; ScD (hon.), Ursinus Coll., 1977, Phila. Coll. Pharmacy and Sci., 1989; LHD (hon.), Rush U., 1986, Med. Coll. Pa., 1994; ScD (hon.), SUNY, Syracuse, 1994; ScD, Georgetown U., 1998. Diplomate Am. Bd. Internal Medicine. Intern U. Pa. Hosp., 1960—61, resident in internal medicine, 1961—63, fellow in cardiology, 1963—64, chief med. resident, 1964—65, chief med. outpatient dept., 1966—67; chief of medicine U. Pa. Med. Svc., VA Hosp., Phila., 1967—73; deans com. VA Hosp., 1974—88; instr. medicine grad. divsn. medicine U. Pa., 1964—66, NIH postdoctoral rsch. trainee, dept. physiology, grad. divsn. medicine, 1965—67, assoc. in medicine grad. divsn. medicine, 1966—67; assoc. in physiology Grad. Div. Medicine, 1967—72, from asst. prof. medicine to prof., 1967—91, Robert G. Dunlop prof., 1981—91, prof. emeritus, 1991—; assoc. dean Univ. Hosp. Sch. Medicine, 1973, assoc. dean student affairs, 1973—75, from acting dean to dean, 1974—88, dean emeritus, 1989—; exec. v.p. U. Pa. Med. Ctr., 1986—89, Assn. Am. Med. Colls., 1990—94, sr. adv. to pres., 1994—95. Nominating and ad hoc governance coms. Nat. Bd. Med. Examiners, 1985, exec. com., 1986—99, vice-chmn., 1987—89, treas., 1989—91, chmn., 1991—95; ednl. policy com. Nat. Fund for Med. Edn., 1975—77; deans com. VA Hosp., 1974—89; chmn. Pa. Deans Com., 1976—87, Mid-Ea. Regional Med. Libr. Svcs., 1978—81; adv. com. dept. medicine U. Ala., Birmingham, 1985—89; vis. com. Tufts U. Sch. Medicine, 1990—94, Med. U. S.C., 1990—99, U. Calif., Davis, 1993—. Contbr. articles to profl. jours. Trustee Dorothy Rider Pool Healthcare Trust, 1991—2000, Ursinus Coll., 1991—2006, Wintergreen Nature Found., 1996—2001, Saw Cmty. Found., 2000—04, AHC Cmty. Found., 2002—; mem. oper. bd. U. Va. Med. Ctr., 2004—. Recipient Frederick A. Packard award, 1960, Albert Einstein Med. Ctr. staff award, 1960, Roche award, 1960, Disting. Svc. award, Nat. Bd. Med. Examiners, 1999. Master: ACP (treas., chmn. investment com. 1975—80, Laureate award Ea. Pa. region 1986, Disting. Svc. award); mem.: AMA, Am. Clin. and Climatological Soc. (pres. 1997—98), Coll. of Physicians of Phila. (bd. censors, coun. 1979—85, coun. 1990—92), Assn. Am. Med. Colls. (ad hoc external exam. rev. com. 1980—82, exec. coun., coun. of deans adminstrv. bd. 1980—85, chmn. 1983—85, nat. chmn.-elect 1985—86, chmn. assembly 1986—87), Inst. Medicine, Alpha Omega Alpha. Republican. Mem. Christian Ch. Home: RR 1 Box 676 Roseland VA 22967-9209 Personal E-mail: ejstemmler@aol.com.

STEMPEL, ERNEST EDWARD, insurance executive; b. NYC, May 10, 1916; s. Frederick Christian and Leah Lillian S.; m. Phyllis Brooks (dec. Mar. 1993); children: Diana Brooks Bergquist, Calvin Pinkcomb, Neil Frederick, Robert Russell. AB, Manhattan Coll., 1938; LL.B., Fordham U., 1946; LL.M., NYU, 1949, D.J.S., 1951; LL.D. (hon.), Manhattan Coll., 1986. Bar: N.Y. 1946. With Am. Internat. Underwriters Corp., NYC, 1938-53; v.p., dir. Am. Internat. Co. Ltd., Hamilton, Bermuda, 1953-63, chmn. bd., from 1963; ret. Chmn., dir. Am. Internat. Assurance Co. (Bermuda) Ltd., Am. Internat. Reins. Co. Ltd., Bermuda, Philippine Am. Life Ins. Co., Manila, Australian Am. Assurance Co., Ltd., Am. Internat. Assurance Co., Ltd., Hong Kong, AIG Life Ins. Co., Del. Am. Life Ins. Co., Wilmington, Del., Am. Internat. Life Assurance Co. of N.Y.; pres., dir. Starr Internat. Co. Inc.; sr. advisor Am. Internat. Group Inc.; dir. C.V. Starr & Co. Inc., N.Y.C., Am. Life Ins. Co., Wilmington, Seguros Interamericana (S.A.), Mexico, Mt. Mansfield Co., Inc., Stowe, Vt., Seguros Venezuela (C.A.), Caracas, dir. Am. Internat. Underwriters (Latin Am.), Inc., Bermuda, Am. Internat. Underwriters Mediterranean, Inc., Bermuda, Pacific Union Assurance Co., Calif., Underwriters Adjustment Co., Panama. Served to lt. (s.g.) USNR, 1942-46. Named one of Forbes' Richest Americans, 2006. Mem. Am. Bar Assn., N.Y. State Bar. Clubs: Marco Polo (N.Y.C.), Royal Bermuda Yacht (Bermuda), Mid-Ocean (Bermuda), Coral Beach & Tennis Club (Bermuda), Riddell's Bay Golf and Country (Bermuda). Office: Am Internat Co Ltd Am Internt Bldg Richmond Rd Pembroke HM 08 Bermuda

STEMPEL, GUIDO HERMANN, III, journalism educator; b. Bloomington, Ind., Aug. 13, 1928; s. Guido Hermann Jr. and Alice Margaret (Menninger) S.; m. Anne Elliott, Aug. 30, 1952; children: Ralph Warren, Carl William, Jane Louise. Student, Carnegie Tech., 1945-46; AB in Journalism, Ind. U., 1949, AM in Journalism, 1951; PhD in Mass Communication, U. Wis., 1954. Sports editor Frankfort (Ind.) Times, 1949-50; instr., asst. prof. Sch. Journalism, Pa. State U., University Park, 1955-57; from assoc. prof. to prof. Dept. Journalism, Cen. Mich. U., Mt. Pleasant, 1957-65; assoc. prof. Sch. Journalism, Ohio U., Athens, 1965-68, prof., 1968-82, Disting. prof., 1982—96, Disting. prof. emeritus, 1996—, dir., 1972-79, dir. Scripps Survey Rsch. Ctr., 2002—07. Rsch. cons. Ohio Newspaper Assn., Columbus, 1985—; chmn. rsch. com. Coll. Media Advisors, 1963-69, 79-84; adv. bd. dept. comm. arts U. West Fla., 1987-00; survey coord. Scripps Howard News Svc., 1992—. Co-author: The Media in the 1984 and 1988 Presidential Campaigns, 1991; assoc. editor, Newspaper Rsch. Jour., 1992-2001; co-editor Web Jour. of Mass Comm. Rsch., 1997—; editor, co-author: The Practice of Political Communication, 1994; co-editor, co-author: Research Methods in Mass Communications, 1981, 2d edit., 1989, The Media in the 1984 and 1988 Presidential Campaigns, 1991, Historical Dictionary of Political Communication in the United States, 1999, Mass Communication Research and Theory, 2003; author: Media and Politics in America, 2003; editor: Journalism Quar., 1972-89; sr. rsch. editor Newspaper Research Jour., 2000—; contbr. articles to profl. jours. Mem. bd. visitors Def. Info. Sch., Ft. Meade, 1985-96. Named to Ctrl. Mich. Journalism Hall of Fame, 2004; recipient Chancellor's award, U. Wis., 1977, Francis Asbury award, West Ohio Meth. Conf., 2004, Harold C. Nelson award, U. Wis., 2004. Mem. Assn. for Edn. in Journalism and Mass Comm. (chmn. rsch. com. 1968-71; Eleanor Blum award 1989, Trayes Tchr. of Yr. 1997, Disting. Svc. award 1999, award for excellence in contbns. to journalism 2005, Paul Deutschmann award for excellence in rsch. 2007), Soc. Profl. Journalists, Rotary (pres. Athens unit 1984-85). Democrat. Methodist. Home: 7 Lamar Dr Athens OH 45701-3730 Office: Ohio Univ Sch of Journalism Athens OH 45701 Business E-Mail: stempel@ohio.edu.

STEMPEL, JOHN DALLAS, international studies educator; b. Easton, Pa., July 26, 1938; s. John Emmert and Mary Roberts (Farmer) S.; m. Nancy A. Dean, Feb. 11, 1961 (div. Jan. 1990); m. Susan Hodgetts, May 18, 1991; children: Amy, Alix, Jill. AB cum laude, Princeton U., 1960; MA with distinction, U. Calif., Berkeley, 1963, PhD, 1965. Jr. officer U.S. Embassy U.S. Fgn. Svc., Conakry, Guinea, 1966, acting dep. chief mission U.S. Embassy Bujumbura, Burundi, 1966-68, watch officer State Dept. Ops. Ctr. Washington, 1968-70, staff asst. to dep. sec. state, 1968-70, Ghana desk officer, 1970-72, polit.-econ. officer U.S. Embassy Lusaka, Zambia, 1972-74, from sr. internal polit. reporter to dep. chief sect. to acting polit. counselor U.S. Embassy Tehran, Iran, 1975-79; diplomat-in-residence, mem. faculty U.S. Naval Acad., Annapolis, Md., 1979-81; dir. ops. ctr. Dept. State U.S. Fgn. Svc., Washington, 1981-83, dir. Office Near East and South Asian Affairs Bur. Internat. Security Affairs Dept. Def., 1983-84; spl. asst. Persian Gulf affairs U.S. Dept. State, Washington, 1984-85; consul gen. U.S. Fgn. Svc., Madras, India, 1985-88; prof. internat. studies, assoc. dir. Patterson Sch. Diplomacy and Internat. Commerce U. Ky., Lexington, 1988-93, prof. internat. studies, dir. Patterson Sch. Diplomacy, 1993—2003, sr. prof. internat. studies Patterson Sch. Diplomacy, 2003—. Adj. prof. George Washington U., Washington, 1968-72, 80-85, Am. U., Washington, 1975; prof. Regional Coop. and Devel. Coll., Tehran, 1975-78; rsch. assoc. Mershon Ctr. Ohio State U., 1972; Mary Moody Northen chair prof. Va. Mil. Inst., 2005. Author: Inside the Iranian Revolution, 1981, Faith, Diplomacy and the International System, 2000; (monograph) Theory and Practice in Foreign Affairs: Why Two Worlds Seldom Meet, 1972; contbr. articles to profl. jours. With USN, 1960-62, lt. USNR, 1962-70. Mem. Internat. Studies Assn., N.Y. Coun. on Fgn. Rels. (mem. U.S. Dept. Commerce Export Coun. Ky.). Avocations: tennis, reading, railroads, philosophy. Office: U Ky Patterson Sch Diplomacy Patterson Tower Rm 455 Lexington KY 40506-0027 Home Phone: 859-255-5356; Office Phone: 859-257-4666.

STEMPER, BRIAN D., biomedical engineer, educator; b. Fond du Lac, Wis., Oct. 30, 1974; s. Gerald A. and Judith M. Stemper; m. Julie M Rumpf, June 28, 2003. BS in Biomed. Engring., Milw. Sch. Engring., 1998; PhD, Marquette U., Milw., 2004. Biomed. rschr. Milw. Sch. Engring. Rapid Prototyping Ctr., 1996—98; tchg. asst. Marquette U., Milw., 1998—2000, rsch. asst., 2000—03; rsch. engr. dept. neurosurgery Med. Coll. Wis., Milw., 2003—04, asst. prof. dept. neurosurgery, 2004—. Author: articles in peer-reviewed jours. Bd. mem. Rocky Mountain Bioengring. Symposium, Inc. Recipient Best of Session, Rocky Mountain Bioengring. Symposium, 2000, Best Paper by a Young Rschr., Internat. IRCOBI Conf. Biomechanics of Impact, 2004. Mem.: Soc. Automotive Engrs., Assn. for the Advancement of Automotive Medicine, ASME, Cervical Spine Rsch. Soc. R-Consevative. Roman Catholic. Office: Med Coll of Wis 9200 W Wisconsin Ave Milwaukee WI 53226 Office Phone: 414-384-2000 41525. Business E-Mail: stemps@mcw.edu.

STEMPIEN, JOSEPH JEFFREY, music educator; b. Lewistown, Pa., Aug. 13, 1952; s. Joseph Victor and Thelma Elizabeth Stempien; m. Eleanor Jane Lurwick, Nov. 22, 1975; children: Heather Lynne, Aimee Leigh. MusM in Music Edn., Ithaca Coll., NYC, 1983. Instrumental music tchr. Penn Yan Mid. Sch., Penn Yan, NY, 1978—, Hobart & William Smith Colls., Geneva, NY, 1989—; band dir. Keuka Coll., Keuka Park, NY, 2002—; choral and band dir. Penn Yan United Meth. Ch., Penn Yan, NY, 1992—; prin. trumpet Orch. of the So. Fingers Lakes, Corning-Elmira, NY, 1982—; trumpet player So. Tier All Star Jazz Band, Finger Lakes Area, NY, 1990—; mechanic Marbles Automotive, Penn Yan, NY, 2002—. Condr. Penn Yan Area Cmty. Band, Penn Yan, NY, 1991—2004. Mem.: ITG (assoc.), NYSSMA (assoc.), MENC (assoc.), Kappa Kappa Psi (life), Phi Mu Alpha (life). Home: 519 Assembly Ave PO Box 475 Keuka Park NY 14478 Office: Penn Yan Central School District 515 Liberty St Penn Yan NY 14527 Home Phone: 315-536-8402; Office Phone: 315-536-3366. Personal E-mail: stempien@usadatanet.net.

STEMPLER, JACK LEON, aerospace executive; b. Newark, Oct. 30, 1920; s. Morris and Ida (Friedman) S.; m. J. Adelaide Williams, Oct. 28, 1950; children: Mark N., Sandra J., Carrie B. BA, Montclair State U., NJ, 1943; LL.B., Cornell U., 1948. Bar: NY 1949, DC 1949. Atty. com. uniform code mil. justice Dept. Def., 1948-49, atty. adviser legis. div., 1949-50; asst. counsel Munitions Bd., 1950-53; counsel Armed Forces Housing Agy., 1952-54, Advanced Research Projects Agy., 1958-65; asst. gen. counsel logistics Dept. Def., 1953-65, asst. to sec. def. for legislative affairs, 1965-70; gen. counsel Dept. Air Force, 1970-77; asst. to sec. of def. for legis. affairs, 1977-81; v.p. legis. affairs LTV Aerospace, Washington, 1982-92; ret., 1992. Cons. in field. Served to 1st lt. USMCR, 1942-46, PTO. Recipient Outstanding Civilian Performance award Dept. Def., 1959, Distinguished Civilian Service award, 1965, Distinguished Civilian Service award with palm, 1969, with 2d bronze palm, 1970; Exceptional Civilian Service award USAF, 1973, 75, 77; awarded Presdl. rank of Disting. Exec., 1980; recipient Disting. Public Service award Dept. Def., 1981 Mem. Fed. Bar Assn., D.C. Bar Assn., Cornell Law Sch. Assn. Home: 4701 Newcomb Pl Alexandria VA 22304-1506

STENBERG, CARL W., III, public administration educator, dean; b. Pitts., July 8, 1943; s. Carl W. and Mildred (Baggs) S.; m. Kirstin D. Thompson; children: Erik Anders, Kerry Cathryn, Kaameran Baird. BA, Allegheny Coll., 1965; MPA, SUNY, Albany, 1966, PhD, 1970. Research asst. NY State Div. Budget, Albany, 1967; analyst, then sr. analyst US Adv. Commn. on Intergovtl. Relations, Washington, 1968-77, asst. dir. for policy implementation, 1977-83, acting exec. dir., 1982; exec. dir. Council of State Govts., Lexington, Ky., 1983-89; prof., dir. Weldon Cooper Ctr. for Pub. Svc. U. Va., Charlottesville, 1989-95, Disting. prof. pub. svc., 1991-95; prof., dean Yale Gordon Coll. Liberal Arts U. Balt., 1995—2003; prof. Sch. Govt. U. NC, Chapel Hill, 2003—, dir., pub. adminstrn. program, 2006—. Mem. Am. Part Program USIA, 1987; adj. prof. George Washington U., 1971, 81, Am. U., 1972-80, 82, U. Md., 1976, U. So. Calif., 1984-87; v.p. Bureaucrat Inc., Washington, 1973-77, mng. editor, 1973-77. Feature editor Pub. Mgmt. Forum Pub. Adminstrn. Rev., 1977-83, editor U. of Va. newsletter, 1994-95; co-editor-in-chief The Regionalist, 1997-2002. Pres. Reston Home Owners' Assn., Va., 1973-74; mem. U.S. del. Ad Hoc Group on Urban Problems, OECD, 1980-82. Vivien Stewart vis. fellow Cambridge U., Eng., 1980; recipient Disting. Alumni award Polit. Sci. Dept. Rockefeller Coll., 1985. Fellow: Nat. Acad. Pub. Adminstrn. (chair bd. dirs. 2002—04); mem.: Va. Alliance for Pub. Svc. (pres. 1991—92), Am. Soc. Pub. Adminstrn. (pres. 1990—91, Marshall E. Dimock award, Louis Brownlow award, Donald Stone award). Home: 301 Madera Ln Chapel Hill NC 27517-8356 Office: U NC Sch Govt CB # 3330 Knapp Bldg Chapel Hill NC 27599-3330 Office Phone: 919-962-2377. E-mail: stenberg@sog.unc.edu.

STENBERG, DONALD B., lawyer; b. David City, Nebr., Sept. 30, 1948; s. Eugene A. and Alice (Kasal) Stenberg; m. Susan K. Hoegemeyer, June 9, 1971; children: Julie A., Donald B. Jr., Joseph L., Abby E. BA, U. Nebr., 1970; MBA, Harvard U., 1974, JD cum laude, 1974. Bar: Nebr. 1974, U.S. Dist. Ct. Nebr. 1974, U.S. Ct. Appeals (fed. cir.) 1984, U.S. Ct. Claims 1989, U.S. Ct. Appeals (8th cir.) 1989, U.S. Supreme Ct. 1991. Assoc. Barlow, Watson & Johnson, Lincoln, Nebr., 1974—75; ptnr. Stenberg and Stenberg, Lincoln, 1976—78; legal counsel Gov. of Nebr., Lincoln, 1979—82; sr. prin. Erickson & Sederstrom, Lincoln, 1983—85, of counsel, 2003—; pvt. practice Lincoln, 1985—90; atty. gen. State of Nebr., Lincoln, 1991—2002. Mem.: Phi Beta Kappa. Republican. Office: Erickson & Sederstrom Regency Westpointe 10330 Regency Pkwy Dr Ste 100 Omaha NE 68114-3761 Office Phone: 402-397-7120. Business E-Mail: donstenberg@eslaw.com.

STENBIT, JOHN PAUL, former federal agency administrator; b. Oakland, Calif., June 1, 1940; s. Paul Charles and Antoinette (Ingulia) S.; m. Albertine Heederik, Aug. 19, 1966; children: Elisabeth Francesca, Antine Elaine. BS, Calif. Inst. Tech., 1961, MS, 1962; postgrad., Stanford U., 1981. Rsch. fellow Technische Hogesch., Eindhoven, The Netherlands, 1962-63, 65-67; engr. Aerospace Corp., El Segundo, Calif., 1962-68; prin. dep. dir. Office of Sec. US Dept. Def., Washington, 1973-77; engr. TRW, Redondo Beach, Calif., 1968—73, Fairfax, Va., 1977—2001; asst. sec. def. networks & info. integration (formerly command, control, comm. & intelligence) US Dept. Def., Washington, 2001—04. Mem. adv. bd. Dir. Naval Intelligence, Washington, 1982-91; mem. sci. adv. group Def. Communications Agy., Arlington, Va., 1989—; bd. dirs., Cogent Systems, 2004-, Loral Space & Communications Inc., 2006-; cons. Def. Sci. Bd., Washington. Chmn. Internat. Children's Festival, Fairfax, 1991-92. Recipient medal for outstanding pub. svc. Sec. Def., 1977; Fulbright fellow, The Netherlands, 1962-63, Aerospace Corp., The Netherlands, 1965-67. Mem.

NAE, AIAA, Security Affairs Support Assn. (bd. dirs. 1990—), Electronic Industries Assn. (bd. dirs. 1991—), Armed Forces Communications and Electronics Assn., Va. Bus. Coun., Korean-Am. Bus. Coun., Met. Club (Washington). Republican.

STENCHEVER, MORTON ALBERT, obstetrician, gynecologist; b. Paterson, NJ, Jan. 25, 1931; s. Harold and Lena (Suresky) Stenchever; m. Diane Bilsky, June 19, 1955 (dec. 1999); children: Michael A., Marc R., Douglas A.; m. Luba Kane, Sept. 8, 2001. AB, NYU, 1951; MD, U. Buffalo, 1956. Diplomate Am. Bd. Ob-gyn., 1965. Intern Mt. Sinai Hosp., 1956-57; resident obstetrics and gynecology Columbia-Presbyn. Med. Center, NYC, 1957-60; asst. prof., Oglebey research fellow Case-Western Res. U., Cleve., 1962-66, asso. prof. dept. reproductive biology, 1967-70, dir. Tissue Culture Lab., 1965-70, coordinator Phase II Med. Sch. program, 1969-70; prof., chmn. dept. obstetrics-gynecology U. Utah Med. Sch., Salt Lake City, 1970-77; prof. ob-gyn. U. Wash. Sch. Medicine, Seattle, 1977-98; prof. emeritus, 1998—; chmn. dept. U. Wash. Sch. Medicine, Seattle, 1977-96. Chmn. test com. for ob-gyn. Nat. Bd. Med. Examiners, 1979-82; cons. in urogynecology Fedn. Internat. for Gynecology & Obstetrics, 1998—. Author: Labor: Workbook in Obstetrics, 1968, Labor: Workbook in Obstetrics, 2d edit., 1993, Human Sexual Behavior: A Workbook in Reproductive Biology, 1970, Human Cytogenics: A Workbook in Reproductive Biology, 1973, Introductory Gynecology: A Workbook in Reproductive Biology, 1974; co-author: Comprehensive Gynecology, 1987, Comprehensive Gynecology, 4th edit., 2001, Caring for the Older Woman, 1991, Health Care for the Older Woman, 1996, Office Gynecology, 1992, Office Gynecology, 2d edit., 1996, Good Health, Great Sex After 40: A Woman's Guide, 1997; sr. editor: Atlas of Gynecology, 5 vols., 1997—99, assoc. editor: Ob-Gyn., 1986—2001, Ob-Gyn. Survey; editor: Clinical Updates in Women's Health Care, 2001—, ACOG Clin. Review, 2001—; mem. editl. bd.: Western Jour. Medicine; contbr. articles to profl. jours. Served to capt. USAF, 1960-62. Fellow Am. Coll. Obstetricians and Gynecologists (com. on residency edn. 1974-80, learning resource commn. 1980-86, vice chmn. 1982-83, chmn. prolog self-assessment program 1982-86, vice chair com. health care for the underserved women 1995-97), Am. Assn. Obstetricians and Gynecologists, Am. Gynecol. Soc., Am. Gyencol. and Obstetrical Soc., Pacific Coast Ob-Gyn. Soc.; mem. AAAS, AMA, Am. Bd. Ob-Gyn. (bd. dir. 1988-2004, v.p. 1990-92, treas. 1992-96, chmn. 1996-98, mem. resident rev. com. 1993-97, chmn. divsn. female pelvic medicine/reconstructive surgery), Assn. Profs. Gynecology and Obstetrics (chmn. steering com. teaching methods in ob-gyn. 1970-79, v.p. 1975-76, pres. 1983-84, v.p. Found. 1986-87, pres. Found. 1987-91), Pacific N.W. Ob-Gyn. Soc., Wash. State Med. Assn., Seattle Gynec. Soc. (v.p. 1981, pres.-elect 1982, pres. 1982-83), Am. Soc. Human Genetics, Ctrl. Assn. Ob-Gyn., Soc. Gynecologic Investigation, Wash. State Obstet. Soc., Tissue Culture Assn., N.Y. Acad. Sci., Utah Ob-Gyn. Soc., Utah Med. Assn., Teratology Soc., Am. Fertility Soc., Internat. Pelvic Floor Dysfunction Soc. Home: 8301 SE 83rd St Mercer Island WA 98040-5644 Office: Ob-Gyn 130 Knickerson St Ste 211 Seattle WA 98109 Office Phone: 206-286-1775. Business E-Mail: mstenchever@acog.org.

STENDAHL, BRITA KRISTINA, humanities and social studies educator; b. Stockholm, Jan. 10, 1925; came to U.S., 1954; d. Johan Victor and Ingeborg (Normann) Johnsson; m. Krister Stendahl, Sept. 7, 1946; children: Johan, Anna, Dan. Cand. Theology, Uppsala U., Sweden, 1949, cand. Philosophy, 1954, PhD (hon.), 1981. Hist. and lit. tchr. Gymnasium, Uppsala, Sweden, 1949-54; hist. and lit. tchr. extension program Harvard U., Cambridge, Mass., 1956-59, hist. and lit. tchr. freshman program, 1964-74; hist. and lit. tchr. seminar program Radcliffe Coll., Cambridge, 1976-84; cultural sec. Ch. of Sweden, Stockholm, 1984-88. Mem. Govt. Coun. for Coord. and Planning of Rsch., Stockholm, 1985-88. Author: (monographs) Søren Kierkegaard, 1976, The Force of Tradition, 1984, The Education of a Self-Made Woman, Fredrika Bremer, 1801-1865, 1994, (autobiography) Sabbatical Reflections, 1978; contbr. Multicultural Writers from Antiquity to 1945, 2002; book reviewer:, translator Swedish drama and poetry. Co-chair Fellowship in Israel for Arab-Jewish Youth, Boston, 1972-84, 88-95; bd. dirs. The Abraham Fund, N.Y.C., 1996-2006. Bunting fellow, Radcliffe Coll., Cambridge, Mass., 1961-63; assoc. fellow Henry A. Murray Ctr. at Radcliffe, 1981-82; recipient Myron B. Bloy award The Assn. for Religion and Intellectual Life, 1993. Mem. Arstasallskapet for Fredika Bremer-Studier (first chmn. 1985—89). Democrat. Lutheran. Avocations: walking, Tai Chi.

STENEHJEM, WAYNE KEVIN, state attorney general, lawyer; b. Mohall, ND, Feb. 5, 1953; s. Martin Edward and Marguerite Mae (Peg) (McMaster) Stenehjem; m. Tama Lou Smith, June 16, 1978 (div. Apr. 1984); 1 child, Andrew; m. Beth D. Bakke, June 30, 1995. AA, Bismarck Jr. Coll., ND, 1972; BA, U. ND, 1974, JD, 1977. Bar: N.D. 1977. Ptnr. Kuchera & Stenehjem, Grand Forks, ND, 1977—2000; spl. asst. atty. gen. State of ND, 1983—87, atty. gen., 2000—; mem. ND Indsl. Commn., 2001—; chair RAGA, 2001—02; mem. ND Ho. Reps., 1976—80, ND State Senate, 1980—2000, pres. pro tempore, 1998—99; bd. Univ. and Sch. Lands, 2001—. Chmn. Senate Com. on Social Svcs., 1985—86, Senate Com. on Judiciary, 1995—2000, Interim Legis. Judiciary Com., 1995—2000, Legis. Coun., 1995—2000; mem. Nat. Conf. Commrs. on Uniform State Laws, 1995—2000, Gov.'s Com. on Juvenile Justice. Bd. dirs. No. Lights coun. Boy Scouts Am., 2005—; chmn. Dist. 42 Reps., Grand Forks, 1986—88; bd. dirs. Christus Rex Luth. Ch., pres., 1985—86; bd. dirs. no. lights coun. Boy Scouts Am., 2005—; bd. dirs. ND Spl. Olympics, 1985—89, Bismarck Mandan Big Bros. Big Sisters, 2001—. Named Champion of People's Right to Know, Sigma Delta Chi, 1979, ND Friend of Psych., ND Psychol. Assn., 1990, Outstanding Young Man of ND, Jaycees, 1985; recipient Excellence in County Govt. award, ND Assn. Counties, 1991, Love Without Fear award, Bismarck Abused Adult Resource Ctr., 2003, Lone Eagle award, ND Peace Officers Assn., 2005, Public Svc. award, Lignite Energy Coun., 2005. Mem.: Grand Forks County Bar Assn., N.D. State Bar Assn. (Legis. Svc. award 1995). Republican. Home: 1216 Crestview Ln Bismarck ND 58501 Office: Office of the Atty Gen State Capitol Bldg 600 E Boulevard Ave Bismarck ND 58505-0040

STENGEL, RICHARD, editor; b. NYC, May 2, 1955; m. Mary Pfaff; 2 children. BA magna cum laude, Princeton U., 1977; student in English and History, Christ Church Oxford U., 1981. Staff writer Time Mag., NYC, 1981—83, assoc. ed., 1984—88, sr. writer, essayist, contbr., 1989—, mng. ed. Time.com, 2000, culture ed., nat. ed., mng. ed., 2006—; pres., CEO Nat. Constitution Ctr., Phila., 2004—06. Ferris prof. journalism, instr. course Politics and the Press Princeton U., 1998—99; senior adviser, chief speechwriter presidential candidate Bill Bradley, 1999. Author: January Sun: One Day, Three Lives, a South African Town, 1990; author: (with Nelson Mandela) Long Walk to Freedom, 1993; author: You're Too Kind: A Brief History of Flattery, 2000; co-prodr.: (documentaries) Mandela, 1995; writer (articles) The New Yorker, The New Republic, NY Times, and many other publications, TV commentator MSNBC, CNN. Rhodes Scholar. Office: Time Mag One Time Warner Ctr New York NY 10019-8016

STENGEL, ROBERT FRANK, engineering and applied science educator; b. Orange, NJ, Sept. 1, 1938; s. Frank John and Ruth Emma (Geidel) S.; m. Margaret Robertson Ewing, Apr. 8, 1961; children: Brooke Alexandra, Christopher Ewing. SB, MIT, 1960; MS in Engring., Princeton U., 1965, MA, 1966, PhD, 1968. Aerospace technologist NASA, Wallops Island, Va., 1960-63; tech. staff group leader C.S. Draper Lab., Cambridge, Mass., 1968-73, Analytic Scis. Corp., Reading, Mass., 1973-77; assoc. prof. Princeton (N.J.) U., 1977-82, prof. engring. and applied sci., 1982—, assoc. dean engring., 1994-97. Cons. GM, Warren, Mich., 1985-94; mem. com. strategic tech. U.S. Army NRC, 1989-92; vice chmn. Congl. Aero. Adv. Com., Washington, 1986-89; mem. com. on trans-atmospheric vehicles USAF Sci. Adv. Bd., 1984-85; mem. com. on low altitude wind shear and its hazard to aviation Nat. Rsch. Coun., 1983, Navy Theater Missile Defense com. NRC, 2000-01. Author: Stochastic Optimal Control: Theory and Application, 1986, reprinted as Optimal Control and Estimation, 1994, Flight Dynamics, 2004; N.Am. editor Cambridge Aerospace Series, 1993—98; contbr. over 200 tech. papers to profl. publs.; patentee wind probing device. Lt. USAF, 1960—63. Recipient Apollo Achievement award NASA, 1969, Cert. of Commendation, MIT, 1969, Excellence in Aviation award FAA, 1997, John R. Ragazzini Edn. award, AACC, 2002. Fellow IEEE, AIAA (Mechanics and Control of Flight award 2000); mem. Inst. Advanced Study. Home: 329 Prospect Ave Princeton NJ 08540-5330 Office: Princeton U D202 Engineering Quadrangle Princeton NJ 08544-0001 Office Phone: 609-258-5103. Office Fax: 609-258-6109. Business E-Mail: stengel@princeton.edu.

STENGEL, RONALD FRANCIS, management consultant; b. Lock Haven, Pa., Oct. 18, 1947; s. Elmer S. and Elizabeth (Heivley) S.; m. Margaret Linda Dezack, Aug. 23, 1969. BSME, U. Pa., 1969, MBA, 1976. Mfg. engr. Control Data Corp., Valley Forge, Pa., 1969-70; mgr. mfg. svcs. Knoll Internat., East Greenville, Pa., 1970-75; ptnr. mgmt. cons. Touche Ross & Co., Phila., 1976-85; pres. RF Stengel & Co. Inc., Valley Forge, 1985—. Office Phone: 610-296-8950.

STENGRIM, LAURA ANN, political scientist, researcher; b. Fargo, ND, Feb. 27, 1979; d. Glen Roland and Shirley Ann Stengrim. BA in English cum laude, St. John's U., St. Joseph, Minn., 2000; MA in Writing Studies & English, U. Ill., Urbana, 2003. Tchg. asst. U. Ill., Urbana, 2001, asst. course dir., 2004—06, grad. asst. chancellor's civic commitment task force, 2006—; rsch. intern Carter Ctr., Atlanta, 2005. Invited panelist Democratizing Edn. Liberty Tree Found., Madison, Wis., 2005; keynote spkr. Ga. Communication Assn., Toccoa Falls, 2006. Co-author: Globalization & Empire: The U.S. Invasion of Iraq, Free Markets, and the Twilight of Democracy; author: America Unbound; writer, mem. editl. bd. Pub. i, 2002. Organizer, adv. Gt. Campus, CARE3, Champaign, Ill., 2006. Recipient Outstanding Acad. Article, U. Ill., 2006. Mem.: So. Poverty Law Ctr., Nat. Communication Assn., Grad. Employees Orgn. (steward 2003). Dfl. Home Phone: 217-778-8138.

STENHOUSE, EVERETT RAY, clergy administrator; b. Minco, Okla., May 15, 1931; s. George E. and Jessie Loraine (Dean) S.; m. Alice Irene English, Aug. 22, 1948; children: Brenda Jones, Judy Lundberg, Stephen, Andrew. Student, U. Calif. Berkeley, U. Athens, 1969-71. Ordained to ministry Assemblies of God, 1955. Pastor Wayside Chapel, Bakersfield, Calif., 1955-59, Bethel Temple, Bakersfield, 1960-63; dist. dir. youth So. Calif. Dist. Assemblies of God, Costa Mesa, Calif., 1963-67; assoc. pastor 1st Assembly of God, San Diego, 1968-69; missionary Assemblies of God Fgn. Missions, Athens, Greece, 1969-73; pastor Bethany Ch., Alhambra, Calif., 1974-79; supt. So. Calif. Dist., Assemblies of God, Costa Mesa, 1979-85; asst. gen. supt. Gen. Coun. Assemblies of God, Springfield, Mo., 1986-94. Bd. adminstrn. Nat. Assn. Evangs., Wheaton, Ill., 1986-94, Pentecostal Fellowship of No. Am., Ont., Can., 1986-94; chmn., bd. dirs. Assemblies of God Theol. Sem., Springfield, 1991-94, Ministers Benefit Assn., Springfield, 1986-94; bd. mem. Evangel U., 1986-94. Contbr. articles to various mags. Mem. Assemblies Of God Ch. Home: 77696 Westbrook Ct Palm Desert CA 92211-0416 Personal E-mail: erevev@aol.com.

STENITZER, GEORGE IGNATIUS, corporate communications specialist; b. Granite City, Ill., June 30, 1956; s. George Ignatius and Beatrice Marie (Cuenca) S.; m. Donna Dwyer, Jan. 16, 1982; children: Jody Bea, Jonathan Jacob. BA in English, Quincy Coll., 1977. Editor Alton (Ill.) Citizen, 1978-80; writer Sverdrup Corp., St. Louis, 1980-84; advt. mgr. Consol. Aluminum, St. Louis, 1984-85; mgr. advt. Southwestern Bell Telecom, St. Louis, 1985-90; corp. mgr. news rels. Southwestern Bell Corp., St. Louis, 1990-94; dir. corp. positioning Ameritech Corp., Chgo., 1994-99; v.p. corp. comm. R.R. Donnelley & Sons, Chgo., 1999-2000, Tellabs, Chgo., 2000—. Mem.: Bus. Mktg. Assn. (dir. Chgo. chpt. 2001—03, exec. v.p. 2002—03, pres. 2003—04), Pub. Rels. Soc. Am. (dir. Chgo. chpt. 2000—04), Nat. Investor Rels. Inst. (dir. Chgo. chpt. 2000—01), Bus. Profl. Advt. Assn. (treas. 1985—87, v.p. profl. devel. 1987—88, pres. 1988—89, pub. The St. Louis Bus. Profl. Advt. Assn. Communicator 1989—90). Roman Catholic. Personal E-mail: geo4747@yahoo.com. Business E-Mail: george.stenitzer@tellabs.com.

STENNER, ROBERT DAVID, environmental and health research engineer, toxicologist; b. Fennimore, Wis., Mar. 12, 1946; s. Arno F. and Edna M. (Mill) S.; m. Vicki S. Muller, June 12, 1965; children: James Brian, Heidi Diane. BS in Power Mechanics with honors, U. Wis., Menomonie, 1970; MS in Nuc. Engring., Idaho State U., 1981; PhD in Toxicology, Wash. State U., 1996. Environ. engr., emergency response-oil spills Gaston County Air Pollution Control, Gastonia, NC, 1973-77; environ. engring. specialist environ. divsn. State of Idaho, Pocatello, 1977-81; chem. and radiation protection engr. Pacific Gas and Electric Co., San Francisco, Eureka, Calif., 1981-84; rsch. engr. sci. III, IV and V Battelle N.W. Labs., Richland, Wash., 1984—. Mem. audit team Assurance Program for Remedial Action, Dept. of Energy, Washington, 1984-86; risk assessment rep. Environ. Mgmt. Ops. Cons. Selection Team, Richland, 1988-89; mem. chem. protection initiative team Battelle N.W. Labs., 1989-90, point of contact-Life Sci. Ctr., 1993—; mem. tech. team Ctr. for Risk Excellence, Dept. Energy, 1998—; pres., chmn. bd. SEA, Inc., 1999—; tech. lead Exposure to Dose-Environ. Health Initiative; mem. tech. bd., 1999; adj. prof. environ. sci. and regional planning Wash. State U. Contbr. articles to profl. jours. Sec. Lions Club, Bessemer City, N.C., 1974-77; youth program counselor United Meth. Chs., numerous cities, 1973-95; vol. ARC, Kennewick, Wash., 1989; chmn. bd. dirs. Pacific N.W. Cross Connection Youth Mission; bd. mem. Ingalls Creek Enrichment Ctr.; HazMat team leader DHS Regional Tech. Integration Initiative Seattle and Cin. regions, DHS EP&R Stds. Devel. Recipient Merit award Menomonie Area C. of C., 1970. Mem. ASTM (chair E47.05 and E54.02 homeland security-emergency preparedness subcom.), Soc. Toxicology, Pacific N.W. Assn. Toxicologists, Soc. Risk Analysis. Avocations: outdoor recreation, european sports car restoration, travel, music. Home: 1238 Glenwood Ct Richland WA 99352-9404 Office: Battelle NW Labs PO Box 999 Richland WA 99352-0999 Office Phone: 509-375-2916. Business E-Mail: robert.stenner@pnl.gov.

STENNETT, WILLIAM CLINTON (CLINT STENNETT), television station executive, state legislator; b. Winona, Minn., Oct. 1, 1956; s. William Jessie and Carole Lee Stennett. BA in Journalism, Idaho State U., 1979. Gen. mgr. Wood River Jour., Hailey, Idaho, 1979-85, pres., pub., 1985-87; pres. Sta. KSVT-TV, Ketchum, Idaho, Sta. KSKI-FM, Sun Valley, Idaho; mem. Idaho Ho. of Reps., Boise, 1990-94; mem., minority leader Idaho Senate, Dist. 25, Boise, 1996—. Named Legislator of Yr., Idaho Soil Conservation Dists., 1994, Idaho Wildlife Found., 1996, Idaho Assn. Recyclers, 2002, Idaho Profl. Firefighters Assn., 2002; recipient Gen. Excellence award, Idaho Newspaper Assn., 1985, 1986—87. Mem.: Idaho Broadcasters (bd. dirs.), Ketchum Sun Valley C. of C. (bd. dirs. 1990—95), Rotary. Democrat. Office Phone: 208-332-1000.

STENT, ANGELA E., political scientist, educator, director; b. London, Feb. 24, 1947; arrived in U.S., 1970; d. Ronald Walter and Gabriele Stent; m. Daniel H. Yergin, Aug. 10, 1975; children: Alexander Yergin, Rebecca Yergin. BA in Econs. and History with honors, Cambridge U., Eng., 1969; MSc with distinction, London Sch. Econs., 1970; AM in Soviet Studies, Harvard U., 1972, PhD in Govt., 1977. Assoc. prof. dept. govt. Georgetown U., Washington, 1983—, prof. dept. govt. and Sch. Fgn. Svc., 1998—, dir. Ctr. for Eurasian, Russian and East European Studies, 2001—; nat. intelligence officer for Russia and Eurasia, Nat. Intelligence Coun., Washington, 2004—05. Sr. policy advisor Office Policy Planning U.S. Dept. State, Washington, 1999—2001; adv. bd. mem. U.S.-Russia Bus. Coun., Women in Internat. Security, Am. Inst. for Contemporary German Studies. Author: From Embargo to Ostpolitik, 1981, Russia and Germany Reborn, 1999; contbr. articles to profl. jours. Mem.: Coun. Fg. Rels. N.Y., Cosmos Club. Office: Ctr for Eurasian Russian and East European Studies Georgetown Univ Washington DC 20057

STENT, GUNTHER SIEGMUND, molecular biologist, educator; b. Berlin, Mar. 28, 1924; came to U.S., 1940, naturalized, 1945; s. George and Elizabeth (Karfunkelstein) S.; m. Inga Loftsdottir, Oct. 27, 1951; 1 son, Stefan Loftur. BS, U. Ill., 1945, PhD, 1948; DSc (hon.), York U., 1984. Research asst. U. Ill., 1945-48; research fellow Calif. Inst. Tech., 1948-50, U. Copenhagen, Denmark, 1950-51, Pasteur Inst., Paris, France, 1951-52; asst. research biochemist U. Calif., Berkeley, 1952-56, faculty, 1956—, prof. molecular biology, 1959-94; prof. emeritus, 1994—; prof. arts and scis. U. Calif., 1967-68, chmn. molecular biology, 1980-86, chmn. molecular and cell biology, 1987-92, dir. virus lab., 1980-86. Document analyst U.S. Field Info. Agy. Tech., 1946-47; mem. genetics panel NIH, 1959-64, NSF, 1965-68; fellow Inst. Advanced Studies, Berlin, 1985-90. Author: Papers On Bacterial Viruses, 2d edit., 1966, Molecular Biology of Bacterial Viruses, 1963, Phage and the Origin of Molecular Biology, 1966, The Coming of the Golden Age, 1969, Function and Formation of Neural Systems, 1977, Morality as a Biological Phenomenon, 1978, Paradoxes of Progress, 1978, Molecular Genetics, 2d edit., 1978, Nazis, Women and Molecular Biology, 1998, Paradoxes of Free Will, 2002; mem. editl. bd. Jour. Molecular Biology, 1965-68, Genetics, 1963-68, Zeitschrift für Vererbungslehre, 1962-68, Ann. Revs. Genetics, 1965-69, Ann. Revs. Microbiology, 1966-70, Jour. Neurosci., 1988-96; contbr. aricles to profl. jours. Merck fellow NRC, 1948-54; sr. fellow NSF, 1960-61; Guggenheim fellow, 1969-70; Fogarty Resident scholar NIH, 1990-92. Mem. NAS, Am. Acad. Arts and Scis., Soc. Neurosci., Am. Philos. Soc., Acad. Scis. and Lit. of Mainz (Germany), European Acad. Scis. and Arts. Home: 145 Purdue Ave Kensington CA 94708-1032 Office Phone: 510-642-5214. Business E-Mail: stent@berkeley.edu.

STENT, TERRY, pilot, art collector; m. Margaret Stent. BA, Yale Univ., 1961; MBA, Harvard Univ., 1968. Pilot Delta Air Lines, 1970—97. Dir. Callanwolde Fine Arts Ctr., Atlanta, 1983—86; mem. bd. commr. & Art Forum Smithsonian Am. Art Mus., Washington, chmn. bd. commr., 1999—2003; mem. Art Collectors group High Mus. Art, Atlanta, 1993—, dir., 1997—, chmn. collections com., 1999—2001, bd. chmn., 2001—. Fighter pilot USS Coral Sea USN, Vietnam. Decorated nine Air Combat medals; named one of Top 200 Collectors, ARTnews Mag., 2004. Avocation: collector of 19th & 20th century art, especially Hudson River School, Ashcan School & American Realism. Mailing: High Museum of Art 1280 Peachtree St NE Atlanta GA 30309

STENWICK, MICHAEL WILLIAM, retired internist, geriatrician, consultant; b. Red Wing, Minn., Nov. 12, 1941; s. Vincent Ferdinand and Geraldine Frances (Veith) S.; m. Judith Ann Nelson, June 10, 1961; children: Scott Michael, Gregg William. BS cum laude, Hamline U., 1963; MD, U. Minn., 1969. Diplomate Am. Bd. Internal Medicine. Fellow dept. pharmacology U. Minn., Mpls., 1966-68; intern in internal medicine Northwestern Hosp., Mpls., 1969-70, resident in internal medicine, 1970-73; sr. internist internal medicine sect. Bloomington Lake Clinic, Mpls., 1973—2000; ret., 2000. Bd. dirs. Bloomington Lake Clinic, Mpls., pres. 1977, v.p. 1989-97, fin. com., 1987—, chmn. properties, 1984—, chmn. trustees profit sharing; med. adviser Kimberly Quality Care, St. Paul, 1990-94; internal medicine cons. Fairview Multiple Sclerosis Ctr. and Rehab. Unit, Mpls., 1986-91; informal adviser internal medicine sect. Minn. Relative Value Index, Mpls., 1971; mem. task force Riverside Med. Ctr., Mpls., 1988-91, chmn. critical care com., 1986-91, reviewer quality assurance subcom., 1989-90. Contbr. articles to profl. jours. Mem., co-organizer, 1st pres. Cyrus Barnum Soc., U. Minn. Med. Sch., Mpls.; bd. dirs. Signal Inn Beach and Racquetball Club, Sanibel Island, Fla., 1983-84, 89-98, Signal Inn Condominium Assn., Sanibel Island, 1983-84, 89-98; co-emcee Nursing Talent Show, Northwestern Hosp., Mpls., 1969; 1st med. dir. Beltrami Health Ctr., Mpls., 1970-72. Recipient scholarship Charles and Alora Allis Found., 1960-63, Walter Kenyon award, 1963, grant U. Minn., 1963; named to Wall Honor, Red Wing HS, 2005. Fellow ACP; mem. AMA, Am. Soc. Internal Medicine, Minn. Med. Assn., Hennepin County Med. Assn., Mpls. Soc. Internal Medicine, Minn. Acad. Medicine. Republican. Lutheran. Achievements include research in drug specificity that could be defined even in an alkylating agent; providing evidence for an active role of the choroid plexus in distributing and concentrating morphine in the brain. Office: Bloomington Lake Clinic 3017 Bloomington Ave Minneapolis MN 55407-1771

STENZEL, MARY FRANCIS, social worker; b. Milw., Apr. 9, 1960; d. Joseph Edward and Betty Josephine (Andracki) Gronowski; m. Paul Anthony Stenzel, Oct. 17, 1997. BSW, Marian Coll., 1982; MBA, Cardinal Stritch Coll. U., 1992. Geriatric social worker various nursing homes, Milw., 1984—86; youth care specialist Child and Adolescent Treatment Ctr., Milw. County, 1988—94. Pres. Milw. Area Self Help, W. Milw., 1997—. Cpl. USMC, 1976—80. Mem.: Brain Injury Assn. (mem. Brain Injury Support Group). Roman Catholic. Avocations: crafts, gardening, scrapbooks, woodworking. Home: 3115 W Plaza Dr Franklin WI 53132 Office Phone: 414-761-3186.

STEP, EUGENE LEE, retired pharmaceutical executive; b. Sioux City, Iowa, Feb. 19, 1929; s. Harry and Ann (Keiser) S.; m. Hannah Scheuermann, Dec. 27, 1953; children: Steven Harry, Michael David, Jonathan Allen. BA in Econs., U. Nebr., 1951; MS in Acctg. and Fin., U. Ill., 1952. With Eli Lilly Internat. Corp., London and Paris, 1964-69, dir. Elanco Internat. Indpls., 1969-70, v.p. marketing, 1970-72, v.p. Europe, 1972; v.p. mktg. Eli Lilly and Co., Indpls., 1972-73, pres. pharm. div., 1973-86, exec. v.p., 1986—. Bd. dirs. Cell-Genesys. 1st lt. U.S. Army, 1953-56. Mem. Pharm. Mfrs. Assn. (bd. dirs. 1980-92, chmn. 1989-90), Internat. Pharm. Mfrs. Assn. (pres. 1991-92). Home: PO Box 8997 Rancho Santa Fe CA 92067-8997 Office Phone: 858-759-8958.

STEPAK, ASA MARTIN, writer, linguist; b. Bklyn., Nov. 23, 1950; s. Louis and Anna (Leyter) S. BA cum laude, NYU, 1973. Author: Southern Rhapsody, 1995, Southern Heritage Potpourri, 1995, Southern Heritage Revisited: A Compendium of Behind the Scene E-mail's, 2000, Music: Primordial Birdsong, 2001, Linguistics: Oral Metaphor Construct, Knowledge Inheritance, 2002, Fundamental Basis of Sentence Competency and Word Order, 2003, Symbiotic Competiveness, 2003, A Recipe for Peace, 2003-04, Frequency Value Grammar, 2004, Entropy as a Formal Method, 2005.

STEPAN, FRANK QUINN, chemicals executive; b. Chgo., Oct. 24, 1937; s. Alfred Charles and Mary Louise (Quinn) S.; m. Jean Finn, Aug. 23, 1958; children: Jeanne, Frank Quinn, Todd, Jennifer, Lisa, Colleen, Alfred, Richard. AB, U. Notre Dame, 1959; MBA, U. Chgo., 1963. Salesman Indsl. Chems. div. Stepan Chem. Co., Northfield, Ill., 1961-63, mgr. internat. dept., 1964-66, v.p. corporate planning, 1967-69, v.p., gen. mgr., 1970-73, pres., 1973-84; pres., chmn., CEO Stepan Co., Northfield, Ill., 1984-99, chmn., CEO, 1999—2005, chmn., 2006—. Bd. dirs. Am. Chemistry Coun. Mem. liberal arts coun. Notre Dame U., South Bend, Ind.,

1972—; bd. dirs. Big Shoulders, Chgo. 1st lt. AUS, 1959-61. Mem. Soap and Detergent Assn. (bd. dirs., exec. com., chmn.), Ill. Bus. Roundtable (policy com., sec.), Econ. Club Chgo., Exmoor Country Club, Bob O'Link Golf Club, Everglades Club, Sailfish Club Fla. Home: 200 Linden St Winnetka IL 60093-3862 Office: Stepan Co Edens & Winnetka Rds Northfield IL 60093

STEPAN, FRANK QUINN, JR., (F. QUINN STEPAN JR.), chemical company executive; b. 1960; married; 3 children. BA, U. Notre Dame, 1982; MBA, U. Chgo., 1988. With Monsanto Co., 1983—87, Stepan Co., Northfield, Ill., 1987—, v.p., gen. mgr. Surfactant dept., pres., 1999—2005, CEO, 2005—. Dir. Follett Corp.; bd. dirs. Am. Chem Coun. Office: Stepan Co 22 W Frontage Rd Northfield IL 60093 Office Phone: 847-446-7500, 847-501-2100.

STEPANEK, JOHN, emergency physician; b. Seoul, Republic of Korea, Sept. 13, 1964; s. Edward and Shirley Stepanek; m. Shahandeh Nael. Assoc. in Arts, Tulsa Jr. Coll., 1990; BS, Northeastern State U., Tahlequah, Okla., 1993; D in Osteo. Medicine, Okla. State U., Tulsa, 2001. Emergency med. resident Integris SW Med. Ctr., Oklahoma City, 2002—05; emergency med. physician Morningstar Emergency Physicians, Claremore, Okla., 2005—06; asst. clin. prof. emergency medicine Okla. State U. Med. Ctr., Tulsa, 2006—. Staff sgt. USAF, 1984—88, Turkey and Germany. Mem.: Am. Coll. Emergency Physicians. Personal E-mail: step741@hotmail.com.

STEPANEK, JOSEPH EDWARD, real estate developer, consultant; b. Ellinwood, Kans., Oct. 29, 1917; s. Joseph August and Leona Mae (Wilson) S.; m. Antoinette Farnham, June 10, 1942; children: Joseph F., James B., Antoinette L., Debra L. BSChemE, U. Colo., 1939; DEng in Chem. Engring., Yale U., 1942. Registered profl. engr., Colo. Engr. Stearns-Roger Mfg., Denver, 1939-45; from asst. to assoc. prof. U. Colo., Boulder, 1945-47; from cons. to dir. UN, various countries, 1947-73; cons. internat. indsl devel., U.S.-China bus. relations Boulder, 1973—. Bd. dirs. 12 corps., 1973—. Author 3 books on indsl. devel.; contbr. 50 articles to profl. jours. Exec. dir. Boulder Tomorrow, 1965-67. Recipient Yale Engring. award Yale Engring. Assn., 1957, Norlin award U. Colo. 1978, Annual award India League of Am., 1982. Mem. AAAS. Democrat. Unitarian Universalist. Avocation: ranching. Home: 11679 Gold Hill Rd Boulder CO 80302-9789 Personal E-mail: jestepanek@worldnet.att.net.

ŠTĚPÁNEK, PETR, computer science educator; b. Pardubice, Czech Republic, Jan. 24, 1943; s. Otakar and Ludmila (Brabcová) Š.; m. Olga Burešová, Dec. 19, 1970; children: Kateřina Barbora. Promovany matematik, Charles U., Prague, 1965, RNDr, 1968, postgrad., 1973, DSc in Logic, 1991. Asst. prof. computer sci. Charles U., Prague, 1965-87, assoc. prof., 1987-98, prof., 1998—, head dept. theoretical computer sci. and math. logic, 2000—. Free-lance cons., Prague, 1992—. Author: Mathematical Logic Set Theory, 1982. Mem. Fed. Assembly, Prague, 1992; chmn. Dist. Orgn. Civic Dem. Party, Prague, 1993-95. Rsch. grantee Ministry Edn., Prague, 1993, Czech Grant Agy., Prague, 1996—. Mem. Am. Math. Soc., Assn. Symbolic Logic, Assn. Logic Programming (hon.), Info. Soc. (Czech forum 2000—). Mem. Civic Democratic party. Office Phone: 420 221 914 243. Business E-Mail: stepanek@ktilm.mff.cuni.cz.

STEPANIAN, STEVEN ARVID, II, lawyer, financial consultant; b. Charleroi, Pa., Apr. 15, 1935; s. Steven A. and Edithmarion M. (McElligott) Stepanian; m. Pamela S. Abbey, Feb. 15, 1979. AB magna cum laude, U. Pitts., 1957; LLB, Harvard U., 1963. Bar: Pa. 1964, U.S. Supreme Ct. 1967. Assoc. Reed Smith, 1963—69, ptnr., 1970—78; pvt. practice Pitts., 1978—; ptnr., gen. counsel Marine Magnesium Co., 1988—, US Windforce, 1998—; gen. counsel Strategic Market Resources LLC, 2004—. Dir. NFL Alumni, 1982—89. Lt. USAF, 1957—69, maj. USAF, 1968—69. Mem.: ABA (chair sports law com.), Pa. Athletic Assn., Pa. Bar Assn., Univ. Club (past pres.), Duquesne Club. Democrat. Roman Catholic. Home: 123 Millstone Ln Pittsburgh PA 15238-1623 Office: Gateway Towers Ste 4-G 320 Fr Duquesne Blvd Pittsburgh PA 15222-1103 Home Phone: 412-968-7777; Office Phone: 412-281-0555. Business E-Mail: sastepanian@comcast.net.

STEPANSKI, ANTHONY FRANCIS, JR., computer company executive; b. Jersey City, June 29, 1941; s. Anthony Francis and Gertrude Stepanski; m. Jane Ellen Schuler, Sept. 5, 1965; children: Matthew A.W., Melinda Kate BA in Physics, Clark U., 1963. Sales rep. IBM Corp., NYC, 1964-68; from sales rep. to sr. v.p. AGS Computers, Inc., Mountainside, NJ, 1968—82, exec. v.p., 1982-93, bd. dirs.; pres., CEO AGS Info. Services, Inc., 1986-93; CEO Origin Tech., N.A. (subs. Origin BV/Amsterdam, Netherlands), 1994—97; mng. dir. Melmatt Ptnrs., LLP, 1998—2000, 2004—; CEO, bd. mem. IZODIA, plc, London, 2001—02. Trustee Clark U., Worcester, Mass., 1987-99, Children's Specialized Hosp. Found., Mountainside, 1989-96; bd. dirs. Westchester Artificial Kidney Ctr., Valhalla, N.Y., 1982-97, Westfield Symphony Orch., N.J., 1983-96. Served with USAR, 1964-70.

STEPHAN, ALEXANDER FRIEDRICH, German language and literature educator; b. Lüdenscheid, Fed. Republic Germany, Aug. 16, 1946; arrived in US, 1968; s. Eberhard and Ingeborg (Hörnig) S.; m. Halina Konopacka, Dec. 15, 1969; 1 child, Michael. MA, U. Mich., 1969; PhD, Princeton U., 1973. Instr. German Princeton (NJ) U., 1972-73; from asst. prof. to prof. German UCLA, 1973-85; prof. German U. Fla., Gainesville, 1985-2000, chmn., 1985-93; prof. German, Ohio Eminent scholar, sr. fellow Mershon Ctr., Ohio State U., 2000—. Author: Christa Wolf, 1976, Die deutsche Exilliteratur, 1979, Christa Wolf (Forschungsbericht), 1981, Max Frisch, 1983, Anna Seghers im Exil, 1993, Im Visier des FBI, 1995, paperback edit. 1998, English transl. Communazis, 2000, Anna Seghers: Das siebte Kreuz. Welt und Wirkung eines Romans, 1997; editor: Peter Weiss: Die Ästhetik des Widerstands, 1983, 3d edit., 1990, Exil. Literatur und die Künste, 1990, Exil-Studien, 1993—, Christa Wolf: The Author's Dimension, 1993, 2d edit., 1995, Themes and Structures, 1997, Uwe Johnson: Speculations about Jakob and Other Writings, 2000, Early 20th Century German Fiction, 2003, Anna Seghers, Die Entscheidung, 2003, Americanism and Anti-Americanism. The German Encounter with American Culture after 1945, 2004, Exile and Otherness: New Approaches to the Experience of the Nazi Refugees, 2005, The Americanization of Europe: Culture, Diplomacy, and Anti-Americanism After 1945, 2006; co-editor: Studies in GDR Culture and Society, 1981—90, Schreiben im Exil, 1985, The New Sufferings of Young Werther and Other Stories from the GDR, 1997, Rot=Braun? Brecht Dialog, 2000, Nationalsozialismus und Stalinismus bei Brecht und Zeitgenossen, 2000, Jeans, Rock und Vietnam. Amerikanische Kultur in der DDR, 2002, Refuge and Reality: Feuchtwanger and the European Emigres in California, 2005, Das Amerika der Autoren von Kafka bis, 2006, America On My Mind, 2006; co-prodr.: (TV films) Im Visier des FBI, 1995, Das FBI und Marlene Dietrich, 2000, Das FBI und Brechts Telephon, 2002, Exilanten und das OSS, 2002, Thomas Mann und der CIA, 2002. Grantee, NEH, 1974, 1984, 1997, Am. Coun. Learned Socs., 1976, 1977, 1984, Am. Philos. Soc., 1979, 1981, 1992, Humboldt Found., 1988, 1994, 1998—99, 2002—03, Guggenheim Found., 1989, German Acad. Exch. Svcs., 1993, 1997, Feuchtwanger Meml. Libr., 1998, Weichmann Stiftung, 1998, Transcoop/AvH, 2002—04; Fulbright Sr. Specialist, 2005—. Mem.: German PEN, German Assn. for Am. Studies, German Studies Assn., Internat. Anna Seghers Soc., Soc. Exile Studies. Office: Ohio State U Dept Germanic Lang Lit 498 Hagerty Columbus OH 43210-1340 Office Phone: 614-247-6068. Business E-Mail: stephan.30@osu.edu.

STEPHAN, JOHN JASON, historian, educator; b. Chgo., Mar. 8, 1941; s. John Walter and Ruth (Walgreen) S.; m. Barbara Ann Brooks, June 22, 1963. BA, Harvard U., 1963, MA, 1964; PhD, U. London, 1969. Rsch. assoc. Social Sci. Ctr., Waseda U., Tokyo, 1969—70; mem. faculty U. Hawaii, Honolulu, 1970—, prof. history, 1977—2001, emeritus prof. history, 2001—, chmn. East Asian studies program, 1973—74, dir. program on Soviet Union in Pacific-Asia region, 1986—88. Rsch. prof. Japan Found.; fellow U. Hokkaido, 1976-77; vis. prof. Inst. of Far East, Moscow, 1982, Inst. Econ. Rsch., Khabarovsk, USSR, 1982-83, Stanford U., 1986, Kennan Inst. for Advanced Studies, 1987; adj. rsch. assoc. East-West Ctr., 1988-92; Sanwa disting. lectr. Tufts U. Fletcher Sch. Law and Diplomacy, 1989. Author: Sakhalin: A History, 1971, The Kuril Islands: Russo-Japanese Frontier in the Pacific, 1974, The Russian Fascists, 1978, Hawaii Under the Rising Sun, 1984, Soviet-American Horizons on the Pacific, 1986, The Russian Far East, 1994. Sr. assoc. mem. St. Antony's Coll., Oxford (Eng.) U., 1977; Bd. dirs. Library Internat. Relations, Chgo., 1976-87; Hawaii rep. U.S.-Japan Friendship Commn., 1980-83. Recipient Kenneth W. Baldridge prize Hawaii chpt. Phi Alpha Theta, 1996; Fulbright fellow, 1967-68; Asia Found. grantee, 1974. Mem. AAUP, Am. Hist. Assn., Am. Assn. Advancement Slavic Studies, Assn. Asian Studies, Authors Guild, Internat. House of Japan, Can. Hist. Assn. Home: 4334 Round Top Dr Honolulu HI 96822-5021 Office: U Hawaii Dept History 2530 Dole St Honolulu HI 96822-2303 Office Phone: 808-956-9600. Business E-Mail: stephan@hawaii.edu.

STEPHAN, KENNETH C., state supreme court justice; b. Omaha, Oct. 8, 1946; m. Sharon Ross, Apr. 19, 1969; 3 children. BA, U. Nebr., 1968, JD with high distinction, 1972. Bar: Nebr. Atty. pvt. practice, 1973-97; judge Nebr. Supreme Ct., Lincoln, 1997—. With US Army, 1969—71. Mem.: Am. Coll. Trial Lawyers (jud. fellow). Office: Nebr Supreme Ct State Capitol Bldg Rm 2211 PO Box 98910 Lincoln NE 68509-8910 Office Phone: 402-471-3737. Business E-Mail: kstephan@nsc.state.ne.us.

STEPHANI, NANCY JEAN, social worker, journalist; b. Garden City, Mich., Feb. 19, 1955; d. Ernest Helmut Schulz and Margaret Mary Fowler Thompson; m. Edward Jeffrey Stephani, Aug. 29, 1975; children: Edward J., Margaret J., James E. AA, Northwood Inst., Midland, Mich., 1975; student in theology, Boston Coll., 1991; BS summa cum laude, Lourdes Coll., Sylvania, Ohio, 1992; MSW, Ohio State U., 1995. Lic. ind. social worker; cert. cognitive behavioral therapist, master addictions counselor. Profl. facilitator Parents United, Findlay, Ohio, 1989-94; contbg. writer Cath. Chronicle, Toledo, 1988-95; mem. ministry formation faculty Cath. Diocese of Toledo, 1992-96; crisis intervention specialist John C. Hutson Ctr., 1994-98; contbg. writer Sunset Gazette, Findlay, Ohio, 1996-98; mgr. Century Health Svcs., Findlay, Ohio, 1998, dir. emergency mental health svcs., 1998—, co-chair strategic planning action team, 1999-00; prof., field coord. MSW program Ohio State U., Lima, 2000—. Social work clinician Family Svc. Hancock County, coord. clin. svcs. Family Svc., 1997—98, Blanchard Valley Home Health Social Svc.; trustee, bd. dirs. Hope House for Homeless, Findlay, 1990—99, v.p., 1996—97, pres., 1997—99; mem. Hancock County Cluster on Elderly; v.p., pres. parish coun. St. Michael Parish, Findlay, 1985—89, adult edn. coord., 1986—93, mem. strategic plan core com., 1989—91; program planning com. Family Life Conf., Cath. Diocese, 1994—95, mem. accreditation com. ministry formation dept.; profl. facilitator Hope Plus Program through Hancock County Common Pleas Ct., 1996—; coord. critical incident stress mgmt. team Hancock County, 1997—; profl. facilitator Hancock County Survivors of Suicide group, 1997—2000; coord. Hancock County Survivors of Suicide Group, 1997—; field instr. dept. social work U. Findlay, Ohio, 1996—, mem. social work adv. coun., 1998—, adj. faculty, 2003—; field instr. Capital U., Bowling Green State U., Heidelberg U., 1997—98; mem. adj. faculty Owens Tech. Coll., Findlay; trustee City Mission, 2000—04; co-program coord., field edn. coord. MSW program Ohio State U., Lima, 2001—; profl. facilitator Persons Affected by a Loved one's Suicide, 2002—. Founder Food Coop., MPBA, Findlay, 1981; founding mem. Chopin Hall, Findlay, 1983; mem. Hancock County AIDS Task Force, 1994-98; strategic planning com. mem., co-chair goal setting com. Findlay Pub. Schs., 1994, steering com., Call to Action Northwest Ohio, 1997—; trustee City Mission, 1999—; clin. dir. Hancock County CISM Team; mem. Red Cross Disaster Svcs. Team; mem. BURHC Pandemic Flue Preparedness Com., 2006—; mem. Ohio State U.-Lima campus disaster team, pandemic flu preparedness com., 2006—. Nat. Inst. Food Svcs. grantee, 1974; Diocese of Toledo grantee, 1991; Ohio State U. Coll. Social Work grantee, 1994. Mem. NOW, NASW (ethics com. Ohio 1997—, v.p. bd. trustees 2000-02, nat. com. on nominations and leadership 2001—, region VII rep. nat. leadership identification com. 2001-04, treas.-elect 2003—, program planning com., Social Worker of Yr. Region 1, 2000), AAUW (legis. chair Findlay chpt.), Internat. Critical Incident Stress Found., Am. Assn. on Child Abuse, Transpsychol. Assn., Friends of Creation Spirituality, Cognitive/Behavioral Profl. Soc., Call to Action, Pax Christi, Women in Ch. Leadership, Green Cross (clin. mem.). Avocations: jogging, hiking, cooking, travel. Home: 2615 Goldenrod Ln Findlay OH 45840-1025 Office Phone: 419-422-3711. Personal E-mail: NancyStephani@hotmail.com.

STEPHANIC, BARBARA JEAN, art historian, writer, curator, researcher; b. LA, Sept. 1, 1937; d. Frank Cecil (Stepfather) and Ethel Louise Jones; m. Jeffery Lynn Stephanic, May 4, 1985; children: Deborah Louise Arnold, Lorraine Marie Ward, Charles Frank Ward. AA, Antelope Valley Coll., Lancaster, Calif., 1978; BA, George Washington U., Washington, 1981, MA, 1985; PhD, U. Md., College Park, 1997. Art history lectr. Montgomery Coll., Rockville, Md., 1986—87, No. Va. C.C., Alexandria, 1987—90; assoc. prof. art history Charles County C.C., La Plata, Md., 1990—97; prof. art history Coll. So. Md., La Plata, 1997—. Art history lectr. Georgetown U., Washington, 1990—97; curator Fine Arts Ctr. Gallery Coll. So. Md., La Plata, 1993—; adj. prof. Parsons Sch. Design and Smithsonian Instn., Washington, 1993—2000; study abroad lectr. Coll. So. Md., La Plata, 2003—; faculty cons. Ednl. Testing Svc., Princeton, NJ, 1993—2004; adj. prof. Am. U., Washington, 1995—96; academic advisor Parsons Sch. Design, Washington, 1996—97; mem. art adv. bd. U. Md. U. Coll., Adelphi, 2003—, vice chmn. art adv. bd., 2006—; guest lectr. in field. Contbr. exhibition catalogue; author: (exhibition catalogue) The Graphic Work of Joseph Pennell From the Permanent Collection of The George Washington University; contbr. exhibition catalogue; author: (exhibition catalogue) Dialogue in Color and Form: The Art of Joseph Holston, Dynamic Spaces: Abstract Form Within and Beyond the Landscape: Painting, Collage, and Assemblage by Larry Chappelear, Color in Freedom: Journey Along the Underground Railroad, Paintings and Graphics by Joseph Holston. Founding mem. Nat. Mus. Am. Indian, Washington, 2000—06; mentor Literacy Coun. No. Va., Alexandria, Va., 1998—2000; mem. Sewell-Belmont Ho., Washington, 2005—06. Recipient Faculty Svc. award, Coll. So. Md., 1996, 1999, Faculty Excellence award, Faculty Senate, Coll. So. Md., 1999, Nat. Inst. for Staff and Orgnl. Devel., C.C. Leadership Program, 2000; Outstanding Scholar in the Field of Humanities, Antelope Valley Coll., 1978, Outstanding Scholar, Alliance Francaises, 1978, Faculty Devel. grantee, Coll. So. Md., 2004, 2006. Mem.: Nat. Assn. U. Women, Assn. Historians Am. Art, Assn. Faculty for Advancement C.C. Tchg., Am. Studies Assn., Coll. Art Assn., C.C. Profs. Art and Art History (treas. 1999—2000), George Wash. U. Alumni (life), Literacy Coun. Am., Alliance Francaises (Outstanding Scholarship 1978), Phi Delta Gamma (Beta chpt., Scholastic Achievement award 1983, 1986). Office: College Southern Maryland 8730 Mitchell Rd La Plata MD 20646 Home Phone: 703-329-1658; Office Phone: 301-934-7860. Business E-Mail: barbaras@csmd.edu.

STEPHANOPOULOS, GEORGE ROBERT, political reporter, former federal official; b. Fall River, Mass., Feb. 10, 1961; s. Robert and Nikki C. Stephanopolous; m. Alexandra Wentworth, Nov. 20, 2001; children: Elliott Anastasia, Harper Andrea. BA in Polit. Sci. summa cum laude, Columbia U., 1982; MA in Theology, Oxford U., 1986. Adminstrv. asst. to Rep. Edward Feighan US Congress, Washington; dep. comm. dir. Dukakis/Bentsen campaign, 1988; exec. floor mgr. to House Majority leader Dick Gephardt US Congress, Washington; dir. comm. Clinton/Gore campaign, Little Rock, 1992, The White House, Washington, 1992—96, sr. adv. to the Pres. for policy & strategy, 1993-96; vis. prof. polit. sci. Columbia U., NYC, 1997; contbr. & corr. ABC News, 1997—, chief Washington corr., 2005—; host This Week with George Stephanopoulos, 2002—. Author: All Too Human: A Political Education, 1999. Recipient Medal of Excellence, Columbia U., 1993; Rhodes Scholar, Oxford U. Mem.: Phi Beta Kappa. Democrat. Greek Orthodox. Address: 1717 DeSales St NW Washington DC 20036 *

STEPHEN, JOHN ERLE, lawyer, consultant; b. Eagle Lake, Tex., Sept. 24, 1918; s. John Earnest and Vida Thrall (Klein) S.; m. Gloria Yzaguirre, May 16, 1942; children: Vida Leslie Stephen Renzi, John Lauro Kurt. LLB, JD, U. Tex., 1941; postdoctoral, Northwestern U., 1942, U.S. Naval Acad. Postgrad. Sch., Annapolis, 1944; cert. in internat. law, U.S. Naval War Coll., Newport, RI, 1945; cert. in advanced internat. law, U.S. Naval War Coll., 1967. Bar: Tex. 1946, FCC 1946, US Ct. Appeals (DC cir.) 1949, US Dept. Treasury 1947, US Tax Ct. 1953, US Supreme Ct. 1955, US Dist. Ct. DC 1956, US Ct. Appeals (2d cir.) 1959, Wash. 1963, Ohio, 1964, US Ct. Appeals (7th cir.) 1964, US Dist. Ct. (so. dist.) NY 1964, Ind. 1968, US Dist. Ct. (so. dist.) Fla. 1969, DC 1972, US Dist. Ct. (no. dist.) Ill. 1974, US Dist. Ct. (we. dist.) Wash. 1975, Mich. 1981, US Dist. Ct. (we. dist.) Mich. 1981, US Dist. Ct. (so. dist.) Tex. 1981. News editor Tex. Broadcasting Sys., 1937; grad. asst., instr. radio-TV broadcasting, co-founder Radio House U. Tex., 1938—41; dir. news and spl. events Capital Broadcasting Co., Inc. Sta. KTBC, Austin, Tex., 1941; gen. mgr., corp. counsel Sta. KOPY, Houston, 1946; gen. atty., exec. asst. to pres. Tex. Star Broadcasting Co. and affiliated cos., Houston, 1947-50; ptnr. Hofheinz & Stephen, Houston, 1950—56; sr. v.p., gen. counsel TV Broadcasting Co. of Houston, Tex. Radio Corp., Gulf Coast Network, 1953—56; spl. counsel, exec. asst. Mayor, City of Houston, 1953—57; spl. counsel Houston C. of C., 1953—57; sr. v.p., gen. counsel Air Transp. Assn. Am., Washington, 1958-70; v.p., gen. counsel Amway Corp. and affiliated cos. (now Alticor, Inc.), Ada, Mich., 1971-82; counsellor, cons. Austin, Tex., 1983—. Radio, TV adv. Jack Wrather Prodns. Inc., Dallas, 1946—50, Beverly Hills, 1948—54, Mercury Films, Hollywood, Calif., 1948—52; chief protocol City of Houston, 1953—56; advisor Chancellors and Consulates Gen. of Mex., San Antonio, Houston, New Orleans, Washington, 1956—66, Aero. Radio, Inc., 1956—66, Zenith Pictures, Santauroe, PR, 1967—69, Mobil Internat. Oil Co., South Am., 1971—72, US Econ. Stabilization Agy., 1972—75, co-chmn. industry task-force on term-limit pricing, 1972—75; chair, counsel aerospace industries joint com. navigable airspace worldwide Internat. Air Transport Assn., Montreal, London, 1961—72; appointed legal advisor US Interagy. Group on Internat. Aviation, Washington, 1958—69; exec. com. global airlines supersonic/high-capacity jets insurer Soc. Préparatoire pour Air Transport Ins., S.A., Zurich, 1967—70; atty. Gen. Creighton W. Abrams Jr., Comdr. US Mil. Assistance Command, Vietnam, Saigon/Washington, 1970—71; adv. bd. Jour. Air Law and Commerce, 1966—72; vis. lectr. Harvard Bus. Sch., Pacific Agribus. Conf., Southwestern Legal Found., Inter-Am. Aviation Law Conf., Inst. Aerospace Law, Indsl. Coll. of Armed Forces, Assn. of Bar City of NY, Chgo. Bar. Assn., Internat. Assn. Ins. Coun., Am. Women in Radio & TV, Radcliffe Coll., U. Houston; apptd. by Pres. of US legal advisor, del. US Diplomatic Dels. to Internat. Treaty Confs., Paris, London, Rome, Tokyo, Madrid, Bermuda, Guadalajara, Dakar, 1958—69, Internat. Air-Rte. Dels. to UK, France, Spain, Portugal, Belgium, The Netherlands, Japan, Rep. of Korea, Mex., Australia, Argentina, Soviet Union, and Brazil, 1958—69; legal advisor, del. US dels. to UN Specialized Orgns. Montreal, Geneva, Paris, Rome, 1964—71; US rep. Internat. Conf. on Aircraft Disturbance and Sonic Boom, London, 1966; hon. faculty, vis. lectr. sch. of law, sch. of bus. U. Miami, 1968—72; accredited corr. UN, NATO, Rep. and Dem. Nat. Convs.; exec. officer USNR Pub. Affairs Co. 8-7, 1950—57; cons. Edison Electric Inst. Task Force Nuc. Property Ins., 1972. Assoc. editor Air Laws and Treaties of the World (3 vols.), US editor Yearbook of Air and Space Law. Chief comm. and transp. group Harris County/Houston CD, 1952-56; chmn. legal com. Nat. Aircraft Noise Abatement Coun., Washington; mem. adv. bd. Mus. Fine Arts Houston, 1953-57, Battelle Meml. Inst., 1962-66; bd. dirs. Contemporary Arts Assn. and Mus., Houston, 1952-57; mem. exec. com. Tex. Transp. Inst., 1964-72; apptd. conferee Global Strategy Conf., US Naval War Coll., 1958. Comdr. USNR, ret. PTO and S.E. Asia, 1941-46, mem. staff Supreme Allied Comdr. Atlantic NATO, 1954, ret. res. Recipient Jesse L. Lasky award RKO Pictures-CBS, Hollywood, Calif., 1939, H.J. Lutcher Stark prize U. Tex., 1939, 40, Walter Mack award PepsiCo, U. Tex., 1941, Internat. Rels. award Nouvelle Caledonie, Noumea, New Caledonia, 1943, Best US Pub. Svc. Broadcasts award CCNY, 1946, Arthur Freed award Freed Herseman Corp., 1946, First-FM (West) award Frequency Modulation Assn., Washington, 1947, Tex. State Network award mobile coverage Nat. Presdl. Convs., Phila., 1948, Chgo., 1952, Trusonic Wireless Microphone award Acad. Motion Picture Arts & Scis., Beverly Hills, 1951, L.Am. Free Trade Assn. Air Cargo award, Mexico City, 1953, Frank White award, Mutual Broadcasting Sys., NY, 1953, H.M.S. SHEFFIELD citation Brit. Royal Navy U.S. Cruise, 1954, C.R. Smith Aviation Devel. award Am. Airlines, NY, 1955, Universal Internat./Interstate Theaters world premiere ceremonial award, Houston, 1955, award Latin Am. Freetrade Assn., Caracas, 1955, KLM Royal Dutch Airlines Super-Constellation Transatlantic award, Washington, 1956, Capt. Eddie Rickenbacker Air Transport Advancement award Eastern Air Lines, NY, 1956, Padre Alvarez award Boys Town Chorale Internat. Tour, Canavati Industries, Monterrey, 1957, Allied Rod & Gun Club Triple Crown trophy, Gander, Nfld., 1958, Iron Duke award No. Va. Lit. Soc., Arlington, 1962, Scandinavian Airlines Sys. Transpolar US-Africa Route, Johannesburg, 1967, Pres.'s Outstanding commendation internat. law U.S. Naval War Coll., Newport, 1967, IBM Corp. Exec. Computer Concepts prize, San Jose, Calif., 1976, M.Y. ENTERPRISE Cruise award Peter Island, Brit. V.I., 1978, Martha's Vineyard, Nantucket, 1979, Glacier Bay Cruise award M.V. MALIBU, Sitka, Alaska, 1980, 50 yr. Meritorious Practice award State Bar Tex., 1996. Mem.: ARC (lifeguards-water safety examiner), ABA (chmn. coun. sect. pub. utility, comms. and transp. law, standing com. on aero. law, chmn. sect. adminstrv. law aviation com.), FBA (DC chpt., exec. com. transp. coun., comm. coun.), Avatar Lit. Soc. (pres.), State Bar Mich. (emeritus), DC Bar, Houston Bar Assn., Am. Law Inst. (advisor Restatement (2d) of Torts), World Peace Through Law Ctr. Geneva (chmn. internat. aviation law com., advisor world air piracy and hijacking treaties), Fed. Comm. Bar Assn. (frequency modulation broadcasting com., tall-TV towers com.), Assn. ICC Practitioners, Am. Judicature Soc., Washington Fgn. Law Soc. (vis. lectr. 1967—68), Naval Submarine League, Venezuelan Air and Space Law Soc. (hon.), Japanese Air Law Soc. (hon.), Naval War Coll. Found., USS Pres. Adams Assn. (hon.), USS St. Paul (CA-73) Assn. (life), Tex. Navy (Admiral), Flying Col., Internat. Club (Washington), Houston Polo Club, Lake Shore Club (Chgo.), Saddle and Cycle Club (Chgo.), Breakfast Club (Houston), Boca Raton Beach and Tennis Club (Fla.), Lago Vista Polo Club (hon.), Execs. Club (Houston), Del Coronado Beach and Tennis Club (Calif.), Nat. Aviation Club (Washington), Order Ky. Cols., Phi Eta Sigma, Delta Sigma Rho (pres. Tex. chpt. 1940). Home: 6904 Ligustrum Cv Austin TX 78750-8352 Personal E-mail: johnerle_stephen@yahoo.com.

STEPHEN, TSE, artist, educator; b. Hong Kong, Oct. 20, 1938; arrived in US, 1959; s. Kwan-Yeung Tse and So-Kwan Chu; m. May Kam, Mar. 23, 2973; 1 child, Lisa. BFA, Washburn U., Topeka, Kans., 1965; MFA, U. Idaho, Moscow, 1967. Prof. emeritus Big Bend Coll., Moses Lake, Wash., 1966—96. One-man shows include U. Idaho Mus. Art, 1966, U. Oreg. Mus. Art, 1977, Kristen Gallery, 1977, 1978, 1980, 1982, 1985, Spokane C.C., 1978, Whatcom Mus. Hist. Art, 1980, Wash. State U., 1983, Prichard Art Gallery, U. Idaho, 1986, 30 group shows. Mem.: Asian Art Coun. E-mail: stephenstse@msn.com.

STEPHENS, BART NELSON, former foreign service officer; b. Norfolk, Va., May 29, 1922; s. Bart Dannelly and Lura Lee (Cannon) S.; m. Barrett Krausz, Jan. 7, 1950; children: Tracey Rainier, Schuyler Barrett, Holly Cannon, Sinah Kendall Lee. AB, Duke, 1943; grad., USNR Midshipman Sch., Notre Dame, 1944; AM, Harvard, 1947. Divisional asst. Greece-Turkey-Iran sect., pub. affairs overseas program staff Dept. State, 1948-49; asst. pub. affairs officer Thessaloniki, Greece, 1950; asst. info. officer Athens, 1950-51; pub. affairs officer Patras, Greece, 1951-54 and, Thessaloniki, 1954; dir. Amerika Haus, Nuernberg, Germany, 1955-59; mem. cultural council City of Nuernberg, 1958-59; mgmt. analyst USIA, Washington, 1959-61; cultural attache Am. Embassy, Warsaw, Poland, 1963-65; dir. Am. Cultural Center, Saigon, Vietnam, 1967-68; 1st sec., regional projects officer Am. Embassy, Vienna, Austria, 1968-70; consul, pub. affairs officer Am. consulate gen. Stuttgart, Germany, 1970-73; area coordinator (Europe) USIA, Washington, 1973, seminar-conf. Programming officer, 1973-74; dep. dir. Office Internat. Arts Affairs, Dept. State, 1974-76; counselor cultural affairs officer Am. Embassy, Bangkok, 1977-82; counselor Sr. Fgn. Service. Contbr. articles to profl. jours. Vice chmn., bd. dirs. Thailand-U.S. Ednl. Found., 1977-82; bd. dirs. John F. Kennedy Found., Thailand, 1977-82, John E. Peurifoy Found., 1979-82, Lynchburg Symphony Orch., 1992-93; exec. sec. Eisenhower Exch. Fellowship Selection Com., Thailand, 1977-82; mem. winter forums com. Sweet Briar Coll., 1990-96. Lt. (j.g.) USNR, 1944-46, PTO. Decorated Bronze Star with combat V, Purple Heart.; recipient Meritorious Svc. award USIA, 1956, medal for civilian service in Vietnam, 1968, Civilian award U.S. European Command, 1973. Mem. Am. Fgn. Svc. Assn., Soc. Lees of Va., Siam Soc., Phi Beta Kappa, Omicron Delta Kappa, Phi Eta Sigma, Pi Kappa Phi. Home: 501 V E S Rd Apt C210 Lynchburg VA 24503 *Personal responsibility should be an essential principle for all of us, in the family, job and community. My 34 years in the U.S. Foreign Service gave me a wonderfully stimulating and rewarding career and a profound belief: the diplomatic service is America's first line of defense.*

STEPHENS, BOBBY GENE, college administrator, consultant; b. Glendale, SC, Mar. 8, 1935; s. Dewey and Bertha Cordelia (Mott) S.; m. Sandra Elizabeth White, June 27, 1957; children: Elaine, Ward, Todd, Adam. BS, Wofford Coll., Spartanburg, SC, 1957; MS, Clemson U., SC, 1961, PhD, 1964; LHD, MacMurray Coll., Jacksonville, Ill., 1987. Textile chemist Reeves Bros., Fairforest, SC, 1957-58; grad. asst. Clemson U., 1960-63; instr. chemistry Wofford Coll., Spartanburg, SC, 1963-64, asst. prof., 1964-67, assoc. prof., 1967-72, prof., v.p. acad. affairs, 1972-80; pres. MacMurray Coll., Jacksonville, Ill., 1980-86; v.p. research and enrollment Wofford Coll., Spartanburg, SC, 1986-91, v.p. sci. and tech., 1991—, prof. chemistry emeritus, 2000—. Project dir. Howard Hughes Med. Inst., 1992—; pres. BGS Cons.; cons. in field Contbr. articles to sci. jours.; inventor extractions with propylene carbonate, 1975; producer: TV series The Psychology of Interpersonal Behavior, 1974. Co-chmn. Daniel Morgan Restoration Com., 1986-88; vice chmn. Spartanburg County Pollution Control Authority, 1970-74; bd. dirs. SC Lung Assn., Spartanburg, 1970-75; sect. maj. United Way, 1975-77; chair SC State Libr. Bd., 2004—. 1st lt. US Army, 1958-60. Recipient Jefferson award SC Acad. Sci., 1969; recipient 1st prize graphics div. 2d Edit. Art Contest, 1971, 2d and 3d prizes Lawson's Fork Creek Photography Contest, 1978, Alumni Disting. Svc. award Wofford Coll., 2001; USPHS grantee; NSF grantee Mem. Am. Chem. Soc. (chair Western Carolinas sect. 2003), Nat. Assn. Gifted Children, Assn. Ednl. Communications and Tech., Phi Beta Kappa. Methodist. Home: 460 S Fairview Ave Spartanburg SC 29302 Office: Wofford College 429 N Church St Spartanburg SC 29303-3663 Office Phone: 864-573-8844. Personal E-mail: bgsphd@bellsouth.net. Business E-Mail: stephensbg@wofford.edu.

STEPHENS, DEBORAH LYNN, health company executive; b. Newton, Iowa, May 30, 1952; d. Clarence Harry and Nancy Elizabeth (Gass) Wright; m. David K. Brender, Dec. 18, 1971 (div.); m. Michael E. Stephens, May 21, 1988 (div.). BS, U. Iowa, 1974; postgrad., U. Wis., Milw., 1978-80, U. Calif., Berkeley, 1987. Asst. to dean of fin. U. Iowa Coll. Medicine, Iowa City, 1975-77; contract audit acct. Miller Brewing Co., Milw., 1977-79; asst. contr. Unicare Health Facilities, Milw., 1979-81; v.p. fin. Sacred Heart Rehab. Hosp., Milw., 1981-84; COO, exec. v.p. Sacred Heart Rehab. Hosp., Med. Rehab. Inst., Milw., 1984-88; CEO, prin. founding mem., chmn. bd. Behavioral Health Sys., Birmingham, Ala., 1989—, also bd. dirs. Cons. on rehab., fin., multi-corp. planning and zero-base budgeting 1988; founding mem. Am. Rehab. Network, Inc., Washington, 1986-87; mem. oral exam. bd. City of Milw., 1984-86, Jefferson County, Ala., 1995; mem. prospective payment adv. com. HHS, Washington, 1986; nat. presenter on zero-base budgeting, corp. reorgns., managed care, and planning. Contbr. articles to profl. jours. Mem. healthcare cost containment com. Bus. Coun. Ala., Rotary Club of Birmingham. Named one of Top 5 Thriving Bus. Women in Birmingham, Bus. to Bus., 1995, one of Top 78 nat. Entrepreneurs, Entrepreneur mag., 1996; featured in Healthwatch, Open Minds, Entrepreneur mag., Birmingham Post Herald, Birmingham News. Mem. Hosp. Fin. Mgmt. Assn. (governing bd. 1981-88), Nat. Forensic League (life), Nat. Assn. Accts., Nat. Assn. Rehab. Facilities (prospective payment adv. bd. 1986-88, com. on med. oriented facilities 1983-88), Ga. Managed Care Assn. (bd. dirs. 1995), Birmingham C. of C. (Small Bus. Person of Yr. award 1995), Venture Club, Kappa Kappa Gamma. Avocations: dance, skiing, jogging, travel, reading. Office: Behavioral Health Systems 2 Metroplex Dr Ste 500 Birmingham AL 35209-6812 Office Phone: 205-879-1150. E-mail: deborahlstephens@aol.com, dstephens@bhs-inc.com.

STEPHENS, DONALD R(ICHARDS), investor; b. San Francisco, June 28, 1938; s. Donald Lewis and Anona Marie (O'Leary) S.; m. Christina Brinkman, Sept. 11, 1971 (div. 1996); m. Patricia Hamilton, Oct. 21, 2000; children: Lane B., Justin H., Nicholas W., Adam H. BS, U. So. Calif., 1961; JD, Hastings Coll., 1969. Pres. Campodonico & Stephens, San Francisco, 1963-65; pres., owner Union Investment Co., San Francisco, 1966-69; assoc. Law Offices of Louis O. Kelso, 1969-72; pres. D.R. Stephens & Co., San Francisco, 1972—; mng. ptnr. Stephens & Stephens, San Francisco, 1999—. Chmn., bd. dirs., CEO Bank of San Francisco Co., 1978-91; chmn., bd. dirs. N.Am. Trust REIT; bd. dirs. Am. Inst. for Fgn. Study, Charles Schwab Family of Funds Inc. Bd. dirs. Bay Area Coun.; trustee St. Francis Meml. Hosp., San Francisco, 1976-82; mem. policy adv. bd. U. Calif., 1985—. Mem. Urban Land Inst., World Bus. Coun., Bohemian Club, Reserve Palm Desert, Napa Valley Reserve. Republican. Presbyterian. Avocations: tennis, bridge. Office Phone: 415-781-8000. Business E-Mail: info@drstephens.net, drstephens@drstephens.com.

STEPHENS, EDWARD CARL, communications educator, writer; b. LA, July 27, 1924; s. Carl Edward and Helen Mildred (Kerner) S.; children: Edward, Sarah, Matthew. AB, Occidental Coll., 1947; MS, Northwestern U., 1955. Advt. exec. Dancer-Fitzgerald-Sample Inc., NYC, 1955-64; prof. Medill Sch. Journalism, Northwestern U., Evanston, Ill., 1964-76; prof., chmn. dept. advt. S.I. Newhouse Sch. Pub. Communications, Syracuse U., NY, 1976-80, dean, 1980—89; prof. comms. S.I. Newhouse Sch. Pub. Comms. Syracuse U., 1990-92, prof. emeritus, 1992—. Cons. Foote, Cone & Belding Communications Author: (novels) A Twist of Lemon, 1958, One More Summer, 1960, Blow Negative!, 1962, Roman Joy, 1965, A Turn in the Dark Wood, 1968, The Submariner, 1974, (nonfiction) Submarines, 1960. Mem. George Polk Awards Com. With USN, 1943-46, 1950-53. Capt. USNR (ret.). Decorated Purple Heart Mem. Am. Acad. Advt. (pres. 1976-77), Assn. Edn. Journalism and Mass Communication, The Army and Navy Club, Authors League, Century Club of Syracuse, Alpha Tau Omega. Episcopalian. Personal E-mail: stephens@dreamscape.com.

STEPHENS, ELISA, college president; d. Richard A. Stephens; married; 1 child. BA, Vassar Coll.; JD, U. San Francisco, 1985. Law clk. San Francisco Superior Ct., Calif., 1985—86; in-house counsel Cellular Holdings, Inc., 1987—88, Acad. of Art Coll., San Francisco, 1989—92, pres., 1992—. Contbg. editor Barclays Law Publishers, 1986—88. Bd. dirs. Am. Red Cross Bay Area Chpt., San Francisco Lyric Opera. Mem.: Royal Soc. Arts, Assn. Rewards for Coll. Scientists, Nob Hill Assn. (pres. 2003—05), San Francisco Jr. League, San Francisco Rotary Club, Univ. Club, Met. Club, San Francisco City Club, Young Pres. Orgn., Calif. Bar Assn. Office: 79 New Montgomery St 6th Fl San Francisco CA 94105-3410 *

STEPHENS, JACK EDWARD, civil engineer, consultant; b. Eaton, Ohio, Aug. 17, 1923; s. Harry M. and Mary Elizabeth (Galloway) S.; m. Virginia May Ives, June 19, 1948; children: Jay Edward, Jerry Edward, Jill Louise, Jana Lynn. BS in Engring., U. Conn., Storrs, 1947; MS in Engring., Purdue U., West Lafayette, Ind., 1955, PhD, 1959. Registered profl. engr., Conn. Jr. hwy. engr. Conn. Dept. Hwys., New Haven, 1949-50; instr. U. Conn., Storrs, 1947-48, asst. prof., then assoc. prof. civil engring., 1950-62, prof. civil engring., 1962-88, head civil engring. dept., 1965-72, prof. emeritus, 1989—, dir. Conn. Advanced Pavement Lab., 1995—2004; sr. rsch. advisor Conn. Advanced Pavement Lab., 2004—. Soils cons. A.J. Macchi Engrs., Hartford, Conn., 1958-65; pavement cons. Conn. Dept. Hwys., Hartford, 1962-63, Consumers Union Auto Test Facility, Colchester, Conn., 1991—; prin. Jack E. Stephens Soil and Materials Test Lab., Storrs, 1958—. Contbr. jour. articles to Procs. Assn. Asphalt Paving Tech., Transp. Rsch. Bd., others. Cpl. U.S. Army, 1943-46, ETO. Named to Acad. Disting. Engrs. and Hall of Fame, U. Conn. Sch. Engring., 2007; recipient citation for tchg. excellence, Western Electric Fund, Washington, 1974; fellow Automobile Safety Found., Washington, 1958—59. Mem. ASCE (life, B. Wright award Conn. sect. 1989), NSPE, AAUP, Assn. Asphalt Paving Tech. (life), Conn. Acad. Sci. and Engring. (chmn. transp. com. 1984-94), Conn. Soc. Profl. Engrs., Am. Rd. and Transp. Builders Assn., Transp. Rsch. Bd., Am. Assn. Engring. Edn., Am. Soc. for Photogrammetry and Remote Sensing, Sigma Xi. Office: U Conn Transp Inst Box U-202 Storrs Mansfield CT 06269-5202 Office Phone: 860-429-7600. E-mail: jack.stephens@uconn.edu.

STEPHENS, JAMES LINTON, mechanical engineer; b. Stamford, Conn., Nov. 1, 1956; s. James Regis and Beatrice Helen (Johnson) S.; children: Mark Linton, Jaimee Lee, Matthew James. BS in Mech. Engring., BS in Biomed. Engring., Northwestern U., Evanston, Ill., 1980; profl. devel. degree in engring., U. Wis., Madison, 2001; MBA with distinction, U. Wis., Parkside, 2003. Registered profl. engr., Wis. Mfg. engr. Parker Hannifin Corp., Des Plaines, Ill., 1980-81, St. Mary's, Ohio, 1981-84; mfg. engr. Ohmeda divsn. BOC Group, Madison, Wis., 1984-91, sr. mfg. engr. Ohmeda divsn., 1991-95; sr. engr., project mgr. CNH Am., LLC, Racine, Wis., 1995—. Mem. steering com. for engring. profl. devel. program U. Wis., Madison, 1994; mem. alumni bd. dirs. U. Wis., Parkside. Ill. State scholar, 1975. Mem. Soc. Mfg. Engrs. (treas. Madison chpt. 1984-85, 2d vice chmn. 1985-86, 1st vice chmn. 1986-87, chmn. 1987-88, certification chmn. 1988—, fundraiser 1987—, seminar and workshop leader 1987—, Chmn. plaque 1988, machining tech. assn. bd. advisors 1996-98, chmn. machining and material removal tech. cmty. 2006—), U. Wis. Alumni Assn. (bd. dirs. 2006—), Beta Gamma Sigma. Avocations: swimming, tennis, reading, running, skiing. Office: CNH Am LLC 7000 Durand Ave Racine WI 53406

STEPHENS, JAMES T. (J.T. STEPEHENS), publishing executive; b. 1939; married. BA in Bus. Adminstrn., Yale U., 1961; MBA, Harvard U., 1964. With Ebsco Industries Inc., Birmingham, Ala., 1961—, asst. v.p., 1966-67, v.p., 1967-70, exec. v.p., 1970—71, pres., also bd. dirs., 1971—2005, chmn. Office: EBSCO Industries Inc 5724 Highway 280 E Birmingham AL 35242-6818 also: PO Box 1943 Birmingham AL 35201-1943

STEPHENS, JAY B., lawyer, defense equipment manufacturing company executive; b. Akron, Iowa, Nov. 5, 1946; s. Lyle R. and Marie (Borchers) S. BA magna cum laude, Harvard U., 1968, JD cum laude, 1973. Bar: DC 1973, US Supreme Ct., 1979. Assoc. Wilmer, Cutler & Pickering, Washington, 1973-74; asst. spl. prosecutor Watergate Spl. Prosecution Force, Washington, 1974-75; assoc. gen. counsel Overseas Pvt. Investment Corp., Washington, 1976-77; asst. US atty. US Dept. Justice, Washington, 1977-81, spl. counsel to asst. atty. gen., 1981-83, dep. assoc. atty. gen., 1983-85, assoc. dep. atty. gen., 1985-86, US atty. DC Dist., 1988-93; dep. counsel to Pres. The White House, Washington, 1986-88; ptnr. Pillsbury, Madison & Sutro, Washington, 1993-97; v.p. and dep. gen. counsel Honeywell, Morristown, NJ, 1997—2001; assoc. atty. gen. US Dept. Justice, Washington, 2001—02; sr. v.p., gen. counsel, sec. Raytheon Co., Lexington, Mass., 2002—. Dir. Nat. Legal Ctr. for Pub. Interest, New Eng. Legal Found. Contbr. articles to profl. jours. Knox fellow Oxford, Eng., 1968-69. Mem. DC Bar Assn., Asst. US Atty. Assn., Nat. Assn. Former US Attys. (dir.), Federalist Soc., Coun. Fgn. Rels., Supreme Ct. Hist. Soc., Phi Beta Kappa. Republican. Presbyterian. Office: Raytheon Co 870 Winter St Waltham MA 02451 Office Phone: 781-522-5096. Office Fax: 781-522-6471. *

STEPHENS, JERRY WAYNE, librarian, director; b. Birmingham, Ala., Sept. 10, 1949; s. William Larkin and Odell (Kerr) S.; m. Lisa Brown, June 2, 1972; children: Jeramy Wayne, Elizabeth Ashley, John Larkin BS in Acctg., U. Ala.-Birmingham, 1974, MBA, 1976; M.L.S., U. Ala., 1977, PhD in Adminstrn. Higher Edn., 1982. Svc. mgr. Hammond Organ Studios, Birmingham, 1973-74; acct. Mervyn Sterne Libr., U. Ala., Birmingham, 1974-75, asst. to dir., 1975-76, asst. dir., 1976-85, libr., dir., 1985—; interim fiscal officer Univ. Coll. U. Ala., Birmingham, 1982, interim asst. v.p. for acad. affairs, 1989-91. Vice chmn. Network Acad. Librs., 1985-86, 95-96, chmn., 1986-88, 96, 2000-01; cons. Birmingham Pub. Libr., 1977—; cons. Southeastern Libr. Assn., Atlanta, 1979-80; bd. dirs. Southeastern Libr. Network, treas., 1992-93, chmn., 1993-94; mem. user's coun. Online Computer Libr. Ctr., 1997—, pres.-elect, 2000-01, pres., 2001-2002, bd. trustees, 2002—. Contbr. articles to profl. publs. Sponsored exec. United Way, Birmingham, 1978, sr. exec., 1982; foster parent Dept. Pensions and Securities, Birmingham, 1982-83; elder Homewood Cumberland Presbyn. Ch., Birmingham, 1982-84, 88-90. With USN, 1972-73 Named one of Outstanding Young Men Am., U.S. Jaycees, 1978, 79 Mem. ALA, SE Libr. Assn., Ala. Libr. Assn. (treas. 1977-78), Am. Mgmt. Assn. Avocations: camping, softball. Office: U Ala-Birmingham Mervyn H Sterne Libr 1530 3d Ave South Birmingham AL 35294-0014 Office Phone: 205-934-6360. E-mail: jerry@beowulf.mhsl.uab.edu, jerryw@uab.edu.

STEPHENS, JOE ALAN, investigative reporter; b. Mariemont, Ohio, July 26, 1959; s. Ken and Wilma (Vanover) S. Student, De Pauw U., 1977-78; BA in English, Miami U., Oxford, Ohio, 1981. Editor-in-chief Clermont Sun, Batavia, Ohio, 1981-83; investigative reporter State Jour.-Register, Springfield, Ill., 1983-87; investigative & spl. projects reporter Kansas City (Mo.) Star, 1987—99; spl. projects desk reporter Washington Post, 1999—. Co-recipient George Polk award for fgn. reporting, 2006; recipient George Polk award for polit. reporting, 1994, Fred Moen Sweepstakes award Mo. Assoc. Press Mng. Editors Assn., Columbia, 1994, Pub. Svc. award Kansas City Soc. Profl. Journalists, 1993. Mem. Investigative Reporters and Editors. Office: Washington Post 1150 15th St NW Washington DC 20071-0070 Home: # Lwr 1523 T St NW Washington DC 20009-3909 Office Phone: 202-334-6723. Office Fax: 202-334-6581. E-mail: stephensj@washpost.com.

STEPHENS, JOHN CHARLES, audiologist, educator; b. Ithaca, NY, Aug. 19, 1950; s. Clarence Fredrick and Janet Pauline Stephens. MS, Ithaca Coll., 1983. Cert. audiologist Am. Speech, Lang. and Hearing Assn., 1983. Dir. audiology clinic, clin. prof. Ithaca Coll., Ithaca, NY, 1983—. Cons. The Racker Ctr., Ithaca, 1985—95. Fin. officer Hiefer Internat., 1994—. Named Friend of Yr., Ithaca Spl. Children's Ctr., 1991. Office: Ithaca Coll Rt 96B Ithaca NY 14850 Home Phone: 607-274-3714. Business E-Mail: jstephens@ithaca.edu.

STEPHENS, LAURENCE DAVID, JR., linguist, investor, oil industry executive; b. Dallas, July 26, 1947; s. Laurence D. Sr. and Amy Belle (Schickram) S.; m. Susan Leigh Foutz, Apr. 16, 1988; 1 child, Laurence David III. MA, Stanford U., 1972, PhD, 1976. Cert. minerals mgr. Nat. Assn. Royalty Owners, 2003. Vis. fellow Yale U., New Haven, summer 1979; rsch. fellow U. SC, Columbia, 1980; asst. prof. U. NC, Chapel Hill, 1982-88, assoc. prof., 1989—; pres. Colgate Mgmt. Co., Inc., Dallas, 1997—; gen. ptnr. Moorman, Schickram & Stephens, Ltd., Dallas, 1997—; mgr. Stephens Resources, LLC, 2004—; v.p., mgr. 4025 Colgate LLC, 2004—05, 3712 Wentwood, LLC, 2004—05. Co-author: Two Studies in Latin Phonology, 1977, Language and Metre, 1984, The Prosody of Greek Speech, 1994, Discontinuous Syntax, 1999, Latin Word-Order: Structured Meaning and Information, 2006; editor ann. vol. L'Année Philologique, 1987-92; contbr. numerous articles to profl. jours. Mem. University Park Cmty. League, Park Cities Hist. Soc., Nat. Trust for Hist. Preservation, Washington, 1989—, The Dallas Symphony Assn. Ann. Fund, Metro. Opera Guild, N.Y.C., 1992—, Wythe County VA Hist. Soc., 1998—. Grantee L'Année Philologique, NEH, 1987-89, 89-91, 91-93. Mem. Am. Philol. Assn., Greek and Latin Linguistic Assn. (chmn. 1987-92), N.Y. Acad. Scis., Indogermanische Gesellschaft, Internat. Soc. Bibliographie Classique, Arabian Horse Assn., Nat. Assn. Royalty Owners, Sigma Xi. Achievements include discovery of language universal regularities concerning labiovelar phonemes, laws of palatalization, the law of catathesis in Greek (pitch lowering), and grammatical, semantic, pragmatic (information structure) regularities of discontinuous constituency and nonconfigurational syntactic structures in Greek and Latin; co-developer of Justeson-Stephens probability distribution for cognates between unrelated languages, Justeson-Stephens probability distribution of the numbers of vowels, consonants, and total phonological inventory size in the languages of the world; research on the law of the quantitative form of diachronic polysemy growth, semantic universals of aspect and modality, universals of writing systems and their evolution. Home: 2785 Turnpike Rd Lexington VA 24450 also: 3319 Greenbrier Dr Dallas TX 75225 Office: 30 Crossing Ln Ste 204 Lexington VA 24450 Office Phone: 540-463-3146. Personal E-mail: lsteph8694@aol.com.

STEPHENS, LEE-ANN WILLIAMS, elementary school educator, educator; b. Cleve., July 9, 1962; d. Joseph Ernest Williams and Joan Lee (Campbell) Warren; m. Terry Brian Stephens, Sept. 21, 1985. BA in Internat. Studies, Miami U., 1984; postgrad., U. Mex., 1984; BS in Elem. Edn., U. Minn., 1989. Cert. elem. tchr., Minn. Asst. adult probation officer Alliance (Ohio) Mcpl. Courthouse, 1982-83; assoc. buyer Dayton Hudson Dept. Store Co., Mpls., 1985-88; elem. tchr. Dowling Pub. Sch., Mpls., 1989; now tchr. Park Spanish Immersion Sch., Minn. Math tutor African Am. Acad. for Accelerated Learning, Mpls., 1989—; coord. Mpls. Council Chs. Tutoring Program, 1988-89. Named Minn. Tchr. of Yr., 2007. Mem. ASCD, Nat. Coun. Tchrs. Math. Avocations: aerobics, bowling, reading. Office: Park Spanish Immersion Sch 6300 Walker St Minneapolis MN 55416 *

STEPHENS, LOREN M., publishing executive, writer; b. NYC, Mar. 8, 1944; d. Seymour and Carol Meyer; m. Dana Miyoshi; 1 child, Joshua. BA, Cornell U., Ithaca, NY, 1965; MA in Internat. Affairs, Columbia U., NYC, 1967. Editor Houghton Mifflin, Boston, 1969—71; assoc. Berg & Co./Mortgage Banker, Boston, 1971—73, sr. v.p., 1973—80; asst. v.p. Nat. Med. Enterprises, LA, 1980—82; prin. Stephens & Hyde, LA, 1982—84, One Step Prodns., Studio City, 1984—97; asst. devel. officer Anti Defamation League, LA, 1990—94, dir. devel., 1994—2000, dir. planned giving & endowments, 2000—05; dir. devel. U. Judaism, 2005—06. Pres. Write Wisdom, Inc.; founder, owner Provenance Press, 2000—. Exec. prodr.: (documentaries) Legacy of the Hollywood Black List, 1985 (Cine Gold Eagle, 1985), Sojourner Truth: Ain't I a Woman, 1987 (Golden Apple, 1987), Los Pastores (Cine Gold Eagle, 1997). Alice Stetton Fellow, Columbia U., 1966, 1967. Avocations: skiing, hiking, teaching writing classes. Home: 847 S Bundy Dr Los Angeles CA 90049 Office Phone: 310-820-2052. Business E-Mail: loren@writewisdom.com.

STEPHENS, MICHAEL, library and information scientist, educator; BA in Telecommunications and Film, Ind. U., 1987, MLS, 1995; PhD in Info. Sci., U. N. Tex., Denton, 2007. Asst. mgr. audio visual services St. Joseph's County Pub. Libr., South Bend, Ind., 1991—94, libr. adult reference and info. services, 1994—97, mgr. audio visual services, 1997, networked rsch. trainer, 1997—2001, mgr. networked resources devel. and tng., 2001—04, spl. projects libr., 2004—06; adj. faculty Ind. U. Sch. Libr. and Info. Sci., River Forest, 1997—2006, Dominican U. Grad. Sch. Libr. and Info. Sci., River Forest, 2005—06, instr., 2006—. Cons. implementing weblogs and instant messaging Darien Libr., Conn., 2005; cons. implementing weblogs in libraries Purdue U. Libraries, W. Lafayette, Ind., 2005; mem. organizing com. Internet Librarian Conf., 2003—, Internet Librarian Internat. Conf., 2005—. Named one of the Movers and Shakers, Libr. Jour., 2005. Mem.: Pub. Libr. Assn., Ind. Libr. Fedn., Am. Soc. Info. Sci. and Tech., ALA. Office: Grad Sch Libr and Info Sci Dominican Univ 7900 W Division River Forest IL 60305 Office Phone: 708-524-6603. Office Fax: 574-621-8000. Personal E-mail: mstephens7@mac.com. Business E-Mail: mstephens@dom.edu.

STEPHENS, NORRIS LYNN, school librarian; b. Charleroi, Pa., Dec. 14, 1930; BFA, Carnegie-Mellon U., 1954, MFA, 1957; M in Sacred Music, Union Theol. Sem., NY, 1956; MLS, U. Pitts., 1966, PhD, 1968. Sales clk. Wagner-Bund Music Co., Pitts., 1957—62; assoc. organist E. Liberty Presbyn. Ch., Pitts., 1962—83, First Bapt. Ch., Pitts., 1983—98. Sr. libr. U. Pitts., 1966—98, adj. asst. prof., 1972—82. Co-author: Collected Editions, Historical Series and Sets-Monuments of Music, 1997; contbr. chapters to books, articles to profl. pubs. Grantee, NEH, 1984. Mem.: Am. Guild Organists, Am. Musicological Soc. (chpt. chair 1982—84), Internat. Music Libr. Assn., Music Libr. Assn. (chpt. chair 1982—84), Bibl. Archaeol. Soc., Charles Avison Soc. Avocations: gardening, model railroading, stamp collecting/philately, coin collecting/numismatics.

STEPHENS, NORVAL BLAIR, JR., marketing consultant; b. Chgo., Nov. 20, 1928; s. Norval Blair and Ethel Margaret (Lewis) S.; m. Diane Forst, Sept. 29, 1951; children: Jill E., John G., Sandra J. (dec.), Katherine B., James N. BA, DePauw U., 1951; MBA, U. Chgo., 1959. Asst. to v.p. ops. Walgreen Drug Co., Chgo., 1953-56; with Needham, Harper Worldwide (formerly Needham, Harper & Steers), Chgo., 1956-86, v.p., 1964-70, sr. v.p., 1970-72, exec. v.p. internat., 1972-74, exec. v.p., mng. dir. NYC, 1974-75; exec. v.p. Chgo. office Needham, Harper & Steers, 1975-82, exec. v.p. internat., 1982-86; also dir.; pres. Deltacom, NYC, 1971-76; pres. Norval Stephens Co., 1987—2000; exec. dir. Internat. Comms. Agy. Network, 1988-98; founder, dir., pres. Barrington Area Cmty. Found.,

1998—. Trustee DePauw U., 1979—. Recipient Rector award DePauw U., 1976, Old Gold Goblet award for outstanding svc. DePauw U., 1994, Outstanding Greek Vol. award N.Am. Interfraternity Conf., 2001, Carol Beese award Barrington Area C. of C., 2004; named Young Man of Yr., Arlington Heights Jaycees, 1964, Barrington Area Citizen of Yr., 1999; named to Sr. Hall of Fame, Barrington, Ill., 2002. Mem. DePauw Alumni Assn. (pres. 1977-79), Phi Beta Kappa, Delta Tau Delta (bd. dirs. edn. found. 1987—, vice chmn. 1994-95, chmn. 1995—, 2d v.p. Arch chpt. 1988-90, 1st v.p. 1990-92, pres. 1992-94). Republican. Methodist. Home: 3400 Garlands Lane Barrington IL 60010 Personal E-mail: norval@norvalstephens.com. *I view my life not as a passage but a daily renewing challenge: to be better; to be a better father, husband, brother, son; to return each day an honest day's work; to bear witness to my beliefs and my faith; to serve my fellowman. I seek a whole life and a life of rewarding parts, each a lesson and an experience.*

STEPHENS, OTIS HAMMOND, JR., political science professor, law educator; b. East Point, Ga., Sept. 20, 1936; s. Otis Hammond and Mary Margaret (Fisher) S.; m. Linda Duren, June 18, 1960 (dec. July 1988); children: Ann S. Henderson, Carol S. Frazier; m. Mary Torpey Ballard, Oct. 21, 1989. AB cum laude, U. Ga., 1957, MA, 1958; PhD, Johns Hopkins U., 1963; JD with high honors, U. Tenn., 1983. Bar: Tenn. 1984. Grad. rsch. asst. U. Ga., 1957-58; jr. instr. Johns Hopkins U., 1959-61; asst. prof. to prof. Ga. So. Coll., 1962-67; assoc. prof. U. Tenn., Knoxville, 1967-71, prof., 1971—, Lindsay young prof., 1981-82, alumni disting. svc. prof. polit. sci., 1983—, acting head dept., 1986-88; Russell Sage Found. resident in law and social sci. Harvard Law Sch., 1975-76; assoc. dean Coll. of Arts and Scis. Univ. Tenn., 1996—2000; resident scholar of Constitutional Law Coll. Law, Univ. Tenn., 2000—. Lectr. U.S. Govt. Mgmt. Devel. Ctr., 1972-96; panel mem., chmn. various assns. Author: The Supreme Court and Confessions of Guilt, 1973; co-author: (with Gregory J. Rathjen) The Supreme Court and the Allocation of Constitutional Power, 1980; (with John M. Scheb, II) American Constitutional Law: Essays and Cases, 1988, American Constitutional Law, 1993, 3d edit., 2003, (with Richard A. Glenn) Unreasonable Searches and Seizures: Rights and Liberties Under the Law, 2006; contbr. articles to profl. jours., chpts. to books. Pres. Nat. Accreditation Coun. for Agys. Serving the Blind and Visually Handicapped, 1979-83; pres. Am. Coun. of Blind, 1987-89; trustee Am. Found. for Blind, 1987-99, exec. com., 1992-99; mem. Gov.'s Adv.Com. on Fair Employment Opportunity, State of Tenn., 1987-95. Ford Found. pub. affairs grantee, 1961, faculty rsch. grantee summers 1968, 69, 70, 74, 91, Coll. of Law, 2003, 04; recipient Migel medal Am. Found. Blind, 2001; grad. fellow Am. Found. Blind, 1962, Johns Hopkins U., 1958-62; liberal arts fellow law and polit. sci. Harvard Law Sch., 1975-76; recipient Acad. Achievement award Recording for the Blind, Inc., 1962, Alumni Assn. Outstanding Teaching award U. Tenn., 1977, 84, L.R. Hesler award, 1998-99, Macebearer, 2001-02. Mem. AAUP (pres. U. Tenn. chpt. 1985-86), ABA, Am. Polit. Sci. Assn. (exec. coun. pub. law sect. 1990-92), Tenn. Polit. Sci. Assn. (pres. 1991-92), So. Polit. Sci. Assn., Tenn. Bar Assn., Knoxville Bar Assn., Phi Beta Kappa (pres. Epsilon of Tenn. chpt. 1981-82), Golden Key, Order of Coif, Omicron Delta Kappa, Phi Kappa Phi, Pi Sigma Alpha. Home: 1141 Southgate Rd Knoxville TN 37919-7647 Office: U Tenn Coll of Law Ste 377 1505 W Cumberland Ave Knoxville TN 37996

STEPHENS, RALPH RENNE, massage therapy educator; b. Vinton, Iowa, Apr. 19, 1948; s. E.O. and Carrie D. S.; m. Sara Ann Beckley. BS in Indsl. Edn., Iowa State U., 1971; Natural Therapeutics Splst., N.Mex. Sch. Natural Therapeutics, 1986. Lic. massage therapist Iowa, N.Mex., massage therapy instr. N.Mex., cert. therapeutic massage and bodywork Nat. Cert. Bd. Therapeutic Massage and Bodywork, St. John method neuromuscular therapy. Pvt. practice Helping Hands Body Therapy Ctr., Iowa City, 1986-92; staff instr. Carlson Coll. Massage Therapy, Cedar Rapids, Iowa, 1987-92; instr. St. John Neuromuscular Therapy Seminars, 1991-99; pvt. practice Ralph Stephens Seminars, Cedar Rapids, 1992—; mem. tchg. staff Himalayan Inst. Yoga Sci. and Philosophy of U.S.A., Honesdale, Pa., 2001—. Dir. sports massage Iowa City Annual Hospice Road Race Com., 1986-88; cons., sys. engr., equipment supplier to workshop and seminar presenters Helping Hands Audio/Video, 1989-94; chairperson Iowa Bd. Examiners Massage Therapy, Des Moines, 1995-2000; sec. Iowa Bd. Examiners Massage Therapy, Des Moines, 1992-95; presenter in field. Author: Massage Therapy Principles and Practice, 1999, 2d edit., 2003, Therapeutic Chair Massage, 2005; contbr. articles to profl. jours.; prodr. videos Seated Therapeutic Massage, Vol. 1, Back and Neck, 1995, Vol. 2, Shoulder, 1996, Vol. 3, Forearm, Wrist and Hand, 1996, Feel Great Hands on Health Series (4 tapes) Feel Great Every Day, Posture Yourself and Move Right, Massage Made Easy, Stretching that Works, 1998, Event Sports Massage, 1998, Side-Lying Therapeutic Massage, 1999, Therapeutic Sports Massage for the Lower Extremity, 1999, Anatomy of the Lower Extremity, 1999, Medical Massage for the Cervical Region, 2001, Medical Massage for the Lumbar Region, 2002, Golf-Flexology, 2003, Medical Massage for the Abdominal Wall, 2006; monthly editl. columnist Massage Today, 2000-, quar. columnist Up Close and Personal Newsletter, 2002-. Trustee Am. Massage Therapy Assn. Found., 1990-93, 95-96; chairperson Walford (Iowa) Disaster Preparedness Com., 1999. Mem. Am. Massage Therapy Assn. (cert. sports massage therapist, registered massage therapist cert., organizer, chair Iowa sports massage team 1986-88, 1st v.p., convention coord. Iowa chpt. 1988-89, edn. chair Iowa chpt. 1988-89, pres. Iowa chpt. 1989, ctrl. dist. rep. nat. bd. dirs. 1990-93, media spokesperson nat. media rels. team 1991-96, nat. nominating com. 1994, mem.-at-large nat. bd. dirs. 1995-96, nat. nominating commn. 1998-99, Disting. Nat. Officer award 1993, 96, Meritorious award Iowa chpt. 1997, Nat. Meritorious award 1997), Himalayan Inst. Yoga Sci. and Philosophy, tchg. staff, 2000. Independent. Avocations: golf, yoga, meditation. Home: PO Box 8267 Cedar Rapids IA 52408-8267 Office: Ralph Stephens Seminars LLC PO Box 8267 Cedar Rapids IA 52408-8267 Office Phone: 319-350-1590. Business E-Mail: ralph@ralphstephens.com.

STEPHENS, RICHARD, aerospace transportation executive; BS in Math., U. So. Calif., 1974; MS in Computer Sci., Calif. State U., Fullerton, 1984. V.p., gen. mgr. Integrated Def. Sys. Homeland Security and Svcs. Boeing Co., Chgo., sr. v.p. Internal Svcs., pres. Shared Svcs. Grp., sr. v.p. Human Resources and Adminstrn., 2005—; mem. Boeing Exec. Coun. Vice chmn. Orange County Bus. Coun.; mem. Pvt. Sector Sr. Adv. Com. Dept. Homeland Security, 2003—; mem. Sec. of Edn.'s Commn. on Future of Edn., 2005. Officer USMC. Recipient Profl. of Yr. Award, Am. Indian Sci. & Engring. Soc., 2004, Gold. Silver Knight and Excellence in Leadership awards, Nat. Mgmt. Assn. Fellow: AIAA; mem.: Pala Band of Mission Indians (chmn. 1988—89). Office: Boeing Co 100 N Riverside Chicago IL 60606-1596 Office Phone: 312-544-2000. *

STEPHENS, ROBERT DAVID, environmental engineering executive; b. La Follette, Tenn., Nov. 8, 1949; s. Robert Oscar and Billie Jean (Maples) S.; m. Donna Jean Reece, July 11, 1970 (div. Apr. 1984), m. Mary Nasca, Sept. 2004; children: Jaclyn-Marie Svetlana, Robert Igor. BA in Biology, Berea Coll., Ky., 1971; postgrad., U. Cin., 1973-74. Cert. environ. assessor Fla., environ. trainer, registered environ. mgr., lic. environ. profl. Environ. specialist Ky. Dept. Health, Ludlow, 1971-74; project mgr. Pedco Environ. Specialists, Cin., 1974-77; environ. control mgr. Mobil Chem. Corp., Richmond, Va., 1978-84; v.p. Environ. Analysis Corp., Richmond, 1984-85; mgr. Environ. Rsch. and Tech. Group GSX Corp., Greensboro, N.C., 1985-86; mgr. regulatory affairs and cmty. rels. Internat. Tech. Corp., Knoxville, Tenn., 1986-88, mgr. environ. studies Tampa, Fla., 1988-90; gen. mgr. First Environment, Inc., Tampa, 1990-91; co-owner Bruder Stephens, Inc., Tampa, 1991—2004; pres. Environ. Evaluations Inc., 2004—. Faculty Fla. C. of C. Environ. Seminars, 1988—; adj. faculty U. Fla. Treeo Ctr., U. South Fla. Coll. Pub. Health; expert witness in environ. mgmt., sampling and analysis, environ. risk, indoor air quality, mold and mildew. Contbr. articles to profl. jours. Co-founder Berea Cmty. Theater, 1970; bd. dirs. So. Waste Info. Exch., Inc., 1998-2004. Mem. Fla. Bar Assn. (assoc., environ and land use sect.), Fla. Environ. Assessors Assn. (pres. 1996-97, bd. dirs. 1993—), Internat. Soc. Tech. & Environ. Profls. (exec. dir.), Va. Orchid Soc. (pres. 1980-85, del. World Orchid Congress, Miami 1984), Ridge Orchid Soc., Tampa Club (bd. dirs. 1999-2002), Outback Bowl (bd. dirs. 2001—). Republican. Avocations: horticulture, guitar. Home: PO Box 145 Mango FL 33550-0145 Office: 717 W Wheeler Rd Brandon FL 33510 Office Phone: 813-684-8049. Business E-Mail: robert@environmentalevaluations.com.

STEPHENS, SCOTT, art educator; BFA in Painting, Wash. U., St. Louis; studied grad. work, U. Chgo.; MFA, U. Ala. Prof. fine art Montevallo U., 1983—. Exhibitions include Montgomery Mus. Fine Art, U. Montevallo, residencies, Centrum vor Grafiek Frans Masereel in Kasterlee, Belgium, Tamarind Summer Workshop in Traditional Lithography. Named U.S. Prof. Yr. State Ala., Carnegie Found. Advancement of Teaching, 2006; fellow So. Arts Fedn., NEA, Ala. State Coun. Arts. Office: Dept Arts U Montevallo Montevallo AL 35115

STEPHENS, SHAND SCOTT, lawyer; b. Pasadena, Calif., Mar. 25, 1949; s. Elmer Shand and Gladys Joy (Baker) S.; m. Marcia Pizzo, July 25, 1982 (div. Dec. 1985); m. Kieran Candy, Feb. 6, 1999; children: Sofia, Shannon, Shand BA, Yale U., 1971; JD, U. Calif., San Francisco, 1975. Bar: Calif. 1975, U.S. Dist. Ct. (no., so., ea. and cen. dists.) Calif. 1975, U.S. Ct. Appeals (8th, 9th, 11th cir.) 1975. Assoc. Bronson, Bronson & McKinnon, San Francisco, 1978-82, ptnr., 1982—93; counsel Aon Corp., Nat. Litigation, 1993—2004; ptnr. DLA Piper Rudnick Gray Cary US, LLP, 2004—. Gen. counsel San Francisco State U. Found., 1987-93; gen. counsel Westamerica Bank, San Rafael, Calif., 1987-93; bd. dirs. Russian Art Found., Kydsncars. Named No. Calif. Super Lawyer, 2005, So. Bay Area Best Lawyer, 2005; recipient Calif. Lawyer of Yr. award, 1998. Mem. ABA, Calif. Bar Assn., Order of Coif. Avocations: american civil war history and archaeology, skiing, tennis. Home Phone: 415-435-2606; Office Phone: 415-615-6028. Business E-Mail: shand.stephens@dlapiper.com.

STEPHENS, SIDNEY DEE, human resources specialist, retired chemical manufacturing company executive; b. St. Joseph, Mo., Apr. 26, 1945; s. Lindsay Caldwell and Edith May (Thompson) S.; m. Ellen Marie Boeh, June 15, 1968 (div. 1973); m. Elizabeth Ann Harris, Sept. 22, 1973; 1 child, Laura Nicole. BS, Mo. Western State U., 1971; MA, U. Houston, 1980; advanced cert. employment law, Inst. Applied Mgmt. and Law, 1998. Cert. Stephen Covey programs facilitator, 1997. Assoc. urban planner Met. Planning Commn., St. Joseph, 1967-71; prodn. acctg. assoc. Quaker Oats Co., St. Joseph, 1971-72, office mgr., pers. rep. Rosemont, Ill., 1972-73, employee and cmty. rels. mgr. New Brunswick, NJ, 1973-75, Pasadena, Tex., 1975-80; mgmt. cons., Houston, 1981—; regional mgr. human resources Syngenta Crop Protection Inc., 2001—, ret., 2004—; pvt. advisor fin. adminstrn. Ross Estates Investments, Ltd., Houston, 2004—; pvt. mgmt. cons. Stephens & Stephens Ltd., 2006—. Contbr. articles to profl. jours. With USNR, 1963-65. Mem. ASTD, Nat. Soc. for Human Resources Mgmt., Houston Human Resources Mgmt. Assn. (cmty. and govtl. affairs com. 1984-85, 85-86). Republican. Methodist. Home and Office: 16446 Longvale Dr Houston TX 77059-5420 Office Phone: 281-488-8330. Fax: 281-488-8912. E-mail: elsid45@aol.com.

STEPHENS, STEVE ARNOLD, real estate broker; b. Irby, Cheshire, Eng., May 25, 1945; came to U.S., 1983; s. Harold Dennis George and Hilda Leonora (Howell) S.; m. Lynn Williams, Apr. 14, 1983. Student, Manchester U., Eng., 1967-69. Lic. pvt. detective, Ill.; cert. comml. investment. From cadet to detective Cheshire Police, England, 1961-69; acting detective sgt. Merseyside Police, England, 1969-75; acting sgt. Hampshire Police, England, 1975-77; retail store owner Horsham, West Sussex, Eng., 1977-79; pvt. detective Carratu Internat., London, 1979-83, D.A.C. Stephens, Aurora, Ill., 1983-86; broker Coldwell Banker Comml.-Primus Realty, Oswego, Ill., 1986-98; broker, owner Stephens Comml. Real Estate, Aurora, Ill., 1998—. Bd. dirs. Aurora Crimestoppers, pres., 1995-96. Recipient Rep. Legion of Merit award, Rep. Order of Merit award. Mem. Nat. Assn. Realtors (CCIM), CCIM Inst. (cert., bd. dirs. Ill. CCIM chpt. 1992-97, sec.-treas. 1994, v.p. 1995, pres. 1996, v.p. region 7 1999-2001, nat. bd. dirs. 1999-2005), No. Ill. Comml. Assn. Realtors (dir. 1995-97), Soc. Indsl. and Office Realtors (SIOR), Internat. Assn. Chiefs Police, Ill. Assn. Realtors, Greater Aurora C. of C. (Small Bus. of Yr. award 2006). Avocations: travel, literature, golf. Home: 7 Saddlewood Ct Sugar Grove IL 60554 Office: 518 N Lake St Aurora IL 60506-3105 Office Phone: 630-906-9900. *Work hard. Tell the truth and shame the Devil!.*

STEPHENS, THEODORE REED, lawyer; b. Sept. 22, 1966; BA in History, Princeton U., 1988; JD, Stanford U., 1991. Bar: Pa. 1992, DC 1993. Law clk. to Hon. Clifford Scott Green US Dist. Ct. Ea. Dist. Pa.; trial atty. civil fraud sect., civil divsn. US Dept. Justice, 1995—2003; ptnr., litig. & bus. regulation practice Sonnenschein Nath & Rosenthal LLP, Washington, 2003—. Recipient Spl. Commendation Award, US Dept. Justice, 2002. Mem.: ABA (health law sect.), Am. Inns of Ct. (Edward Bennett Williams Chpt.), Am. Health Lawyers Assn., DC Bar Assn.

STEPHENS, THOMAS G., automotive executive; BS in Mech. Engring., U. Mich., 1971. With GM, Mich., 1969—; exptl. engr., staff project engr. GM Cadillac Motor Car Divsn., Detroit, 1971—80, supr. product engring., 1980—82, staff engr. emission, transmissions, 1982—85; sr. staff engr. transmission, powertrain controls GM Buick-Oldsmobile-Cadillac Powertrain Divsn., 1985—88; plant mgr. GM Buick-Oldsmobile-Cadillac Powertrain Livonia Engine Plant, 1988—90; dir. engring. GM Engine Divsn., 1990—91; dir. engine engring. GM Powertrain, 1991—93, engring. ops. gen. mgr. Pontiac, 1993—94; v.p. GM, Detroit, 1994; v.p., group dir. engring. ops. GM Truck Group., 1996—2000; v.p. vehicle integration GM, 2001; group. v.p. GM Powertrain, 2001—. Mem.: NAE, U. Mich. Nat. Adv. Coun., Detroit Sci. Ctr. (bd. trustees). *

STEPHENS, THOMAS M(ARON), education educator; b. Youngstown, Ohio, June 15, 1931; s. Thomas and Mary (Hanna) S.; m. Evelyn Kleshock, July 1, 1955. BS, Youngstown Coll., 1955; MEd, Kent State U., 1957; EdD, U. Pitts., 1966. Lic. psychologist, Ohio. Tchr. Warren (Ohio) public schs., 1955-57, Niles (Ohio) public schs., 1957-58; psychologist Montgomery County, Ohio, 1958-60; dir. gifted edn. Ohio Dept. Edn., Columbus, 1960-66; assoc. prof. edn. U. Pitts., 1966-70; prof. edn. Ohio State U., 1970—, chmn. dept. exceptional children, 1972-82, chmn. dept. human services edn., 1982-87, assoc. dean Coll. Edn., 1987-92, prof., 1987-92, prof. emeritus, 1992—; clin. prof. edn. U. Dayton, Ohio, 1993—; exec. dir. Sch. Study Coun. Ohio, Columbus, 1993—. Mem. Higher Edn. Consortium for Spl. Edn., chmn., 1976-77; pub., pres. Cedars Press, Inc. Author: Directive Teaching of Children with Learning and Behavioral Handicaps, 2d edit, 1976, Implementing Behavioral Approaches in Elementary and Secondary Schools, 1975, Teaching Skills to Children with Learning and Behavioral Disorders, 1977, Teaching Children Basic Skills: A Curriculum Handbook, 1978, 2d edit., 1983, Social Skills In The Classroom, 1978, 2d edit., 1991, Teaching Mainstreamed Students, 1982, 2d edit., 1988, Social Behavior Assessment Scale, 1991; dir.: Jour. Sch. Psychology, 1965-75, 80—; exec. editor: The Directive Tchr.; assoc. editor: Spl. Edn. and Tchr. Edn., Techniques, Behavioral Disorders, Spl. Edn. and Remedial Edn.; contbr. articles to profl. jours. Named to Ohio State U. Coll. of Edn. Hall of Fame, 1999; U.S. Office of Edn. fellow, 1964-65. Mem. APA, NASP (charter), State Dirs. for Gifted (pres. 1962-63), Coun. for Exceptional Children (gov., Tchr. Educator of Yr. tchr. edn. divsn. 1985), Coun. Children with Behavioral Disorders (pres. 1972-73). Home: 551 E Cooke Rd Columbus OH 43214-2813 Office: Sch Study Coun of Ohio 2080 Citygate Dr Columbus OH 43219 Office Phone: 614-785-0481. Business E-Mail: tstephens@ssco.org.

STEPHENS, WILLIAM THEODORE, lawyer; b. Balt., Mar. 31, 1922; s. William A. and Mildred (Griffin) S.; m. Arlene Alice Lesti, June 2, 1958; children: William Theodore Jr., Renée Adena. Grad., Balt. City Coll., 1941; student, U. Md., 1946-47; AB, JD, George Washington U., 1950, postgrad., 1951. Bar: D.C. 1951, Md. 1950, Va. 1959. Assoc. J.L. Green, Washington, 1950-51; with J.M. Cooper, Washington, 1952-54; sr. ptnr. Stephens Law Firm, Washington, 1955—. Gen. counsel Exotech, Inc., Gaithersburg, Md.; prin. owner BARBCO, Inc., Va., Fairfax Raquet Club; gen. counsel various nat. corps. and assns. Author: Rental Contracts - Contracts for the Rental of Personal Property, 2000. 1st lt. AUS, 1941-45. Mem. ABA, D.C. Bar Assn. (sect. taxation 1959—, sect. corps, banking and bus. law 1960—), Bar Assn. D.C. (sec. taxation 1959-68), XVI Corps Assn. (pres. 1967), Commonwealth Club, Univ. Club, Capitol Hill Club, Army-Navy Country Club, Regency Sport and Health Club, Jockey Club, LaCosta Country Club, Racquet Club Internat., Kappa Alpha (preceptor, ct. of honor, James Ward Wood Province 1988-91), Delta Theta Phi. also: 881 Ocean Dr Key Biscayne FL 33149-2609 Home: 785 Crandon Blvd #1804 Key Biscayne FL 33149-2591 E-mail: wmstephens@adeplia.net.

STEPHENS, WILLIAM THOMAS, forest products manufacturing company executive; b. Crossett, Ark. married. BS, U. Ark., 1965, MS, 1966. CEO Riverwood Corp., 1982—85; chmn., pres., CEO Manville Corp., Denver, 1986—96; pres., CEO MacMillan Bloedel Ltd., 1997—99; chmn., CEO Boise Cascade Holdings, Boise, Idaho, 2004—. Office: Boise Cascade PO Box 50 1111 W Jefferson St Boise ID 83728 *

STEPHENSON, ALAN CLEMENTS, lawyer; b. Wilmington, NC, Nov. 7, 1944; s. Abram Clements and Ruth (Smith) Stephenson; m. Shannon Kennedy; children from previous marriage: Edward Taylor, Anne Baldwin. AB in Hist., U. N.C., 1967; JD, U. Va., 1970. Bar: NY 1971. Assoc. Cravath, Swaine & Moore, NYC, 1970-78, ptnr., 1978-88; mng. dir. Wasserstein, Perella and Co. Inc., NYC, 1988-92; ptnr., corp. Cravath, Swaine & Moore LLP, NYC, 1992—. Mem. external adv. bd. undergrad. honors program U. N.C., 1998—. Trustee Cold Spring Harbor Lab., 2003-. Morehead scholar, John M. Morehead Found., 1963. Mem.: NY State Bar Assn., Assn. of Bar of City of NY, Brook Club, Union Club, Farmington Country Club, Meadow Brook Club, Links Club, Phi Beta Kappa. Office: Cravath Swaine & Moore LLP 825 8th Ave 47th Fl New York NY 10019-7475 Office Phone: 212-474-1400. Office Fax: 212-474-3700. Business E-Mail: astephenson@cravath.com.

STEPHENSON, ARTHUR EMMET, JR., investment company executive; b. Bastrop, La., Aug. 29, 1945; s. Arthur Emmet and Edith Louise Stephenson; m. Toni Lyn Edwards, June 17, 1967; 1 child, Tessa. BS in Fin. magna cum laude, La. State U., 1967; MBA (Ralph Thomas Sayles fellow), Harvard U., 1969. Chartered fin. analyst. Adminstrv. aide to U.S. Sen. Russell Long of La., Washington, 1966; security analyst Fidelity Funds, Boston, 1968; chmn. bd., pres. Stephenson & Co., Denver; sr. ptnr. Stephenson Ventures; founder, chmn. Gen. Comm., Inc., Denver; founder, chmn. bd. dirs. StarTek, Inc.; 1987—2006. Bd. dirs. Danaher Corp.; founder Charter Bank and Trust, chmn., 1980—91; mem. adv. bd. First Berkshire Fund, 1984—2002, Capital Resources Ptnrs., L.P., 1987—2004; former pub. Law Enforcement Product News, Colo. Book, Pub. Safety Product News, 1990—98, Denver mag., Denver Bus. mag.; bd. dean's adv. Bus. Sch. Harvard U., 2006—. Del. White House conf., 1980; past. nat. trustee Nat. Symphony Orch., John F. Kennedy Ctr. Performing Arts, 1995—98; past mem. nat. steering com. Norman Rockwell Mus., Stockbridge, Mass.; past mem. Colo. Small bus. Coun.; past mem. assocs. coun. Templeton Coll., Oxford (Eng.) U. Named to Hall of Distinction, Coll. Bus. Adminstrn., La. State U., 1999, La. State U., 2006; recipient Hall of Fame award, Inc. mag., 1994, Albert Einstein Tech. medal, 1999. Mem.: Young Pres. Orgn. (chpt. chmn. 1992—93), Colo. Investment Advisors Assn. (treas., bd. dirs. 1975—76), World Pres.'s Orgn., Chief Execs. Orgn., Harvard U. Bus. Sch. Assn. (internat. pres. 1987—88), So. Calif. Harvard Bus. Sch. Club, Jonathan Club (L.A.), Annabel's (London), Colo. Harvard Bus. Sch. Club (pres. 1980—81, chmn. 1981—82), Thunderbird Country Club (Rancho Mirage, Calif.), Delta Sigma Pi, Kappa Sigma, Beta Gamma Sigma, Phi Kappa Phi, Omicron Delta Kappa. Office: 400 Nevada Way Boulder City NV 89005

STEPHENSON, CLARENCE DAVID, historian, educator, writer, researcher; b. East Mahoning Twp., Pa., Mar. 24, 1919; s. David Elias Stephenson and Grace Marcella Sutor; m. Marcella Helen Manner, June 3, 1945; children: Grace, Richard, Nancy, Alice. BS in Edn., Indiana State Tchrs. Coll., Pa., 1941; M of Letters and History, U. Pitts., 1948. Tchr. Brackenridge Jr. H.S., Allegheny County, Pa., 1941—42; substitute tchr. Westinghouse H.S., Allegheny County, 1946; tchr. Springdale Jr. H.S., Allegheny County, 1946—47; advisor history and edn. Pa. Dept. Pub. Instrn., Harrisburg, Pa., 1956—60; case worker Indiana County Pub. Assistance Office, 1964—77; ret. Editor: The Clymer Cherryhill Story, 1953, Indiana County History, 5 vols., 1978—95; author, editor (numerous leaflets and pamphlets). Major donor to various orgns.; chmn. Com. Save John Sutton Hall, Indiana U., Indiana, 1995, Marion Ctr. Bicentennial Com., 1976; ofcl. historian Indiana County, 2003. With US Army, 1942—45. Recipient Rsch. award, Ho. Reps., Pa., 2002, Distinction medal, Ind. U., Pa., 2002. Mem.: Pa. Canal Soc. (founder, charter mem. 1966—), Hist. Geneal. Soc. Indiana County, Pa. Soc. NYC, Marion Ctr. Area Lions Club (charter mem., pres. 1970—), Phi Delta Kappa (Outstandint Alumni award 1982). Presbyterian. Avocations: reading, writing, genealogy, stamp collecting/philately, photography.

STEPHENSON, EDWARD, psychology professor; b. Black River, Jamaica, W.I., Jan. 17, 1958; s. Leandro Stephenson and Merle Ivadne Ireland. BA, Queens Coll., 1979; PhD, U. Calif., 1987. Assoc. prof. Fla. Meml. U., 1997—. Mem.: Assn. Black Psychol., Am. Psychol. Assn. Office Phone: 305-623-1404. Personal E-mail: estephen@fmuniv.edu. E-mail: edward4@bellsouth.net.

STEPHENSON, HERMAN HOWARD, retired banker; b. Wichita, Kans., July 15, 1929; s. Herman Horace and Edith May (Wayland) S.; m. Virginia Anne Ross, Dec. 24, 1950, (dec. Sept. 2004); children: Ross Wayland, Neal Bevan, Jann Edith. BA, U. Mich., 1950; JD with distinction, U. Mo., Kansas City, 1958, LLD (hon.), 1993. Bar: Kans. 1958. With City Nat. Bank, Kansas City, Mo., 1952-54, City Bond & Mortgage Co., Kansas City, 1954-59, Bank of Hawaii, Honolulu, 1959-94, CEO, 1989-94, ret. chmn., 1994—. Bd. dirs. Friends of Cancer Rsch. Ctr. Hawaii. With US Army, 1950—52. Mem.: Pacific Forum/CSIS (bd. govs.), Navy League U.S., Waialae Country Club, Oahu Country Club, Eagle Bend Country Club, Rotary, Pi Eta Sigma, Kappa Sigma.

STEPHENSON, HUGH EDWARD, JR., retired surgeon; b. Columbia, Mo., June 1, 1922; s. Hugh Edward and Doris (Pryor) S.; m. Sarah Norfleet Dickinson, Aug. 15, 1964; children— Hugh Edward III, Ann Dunlop. AB, BS, U. Mo., 1943; MD, Washington U., St. Louis, 1945. Diplomate Am. Bd. Surgery, Am. Bd. Thoracic Surgery. Mem. faculty U. Mo. Sch. Medicine, Columbia, 1953—; prof. surgery U. Mo. Hugh E. Stephenson Jr. Dept. Surgery, Columbia, 1956—, chmn. dept. surgery, 1956—60, chief div. gen. surgery, 1976—87, chief staff, 1982—94; John Growdon Disting. prof. surgery emeritus U. Mo. Sch. Medicine, Columbia, 1987—, interim dean, 1988—89, assoc. dean, 1989—92, dist. prof. surgery emeritus, 1993;

curator U. Mo. System, 1996—. Pres. bd. curators U. Mo., 2000; Markle scholar acad. medicine, 1954-60. Author: Immediate Care of the Acutely Ill and Injured, 2d edit, 1974, Cardiac Arrest and Resuscitation, 4th edit., 1975, The Kicks That Count; Contbr. articles to profl. jours. Named one of Outstanding Young Men of Nation, Nat. Jr. C. of C., 1956, James IV Surg. Traveler Gt. Britain, 1962, Dist. Faculty award, 1989. Mem. ACS, AMA (del., chmn. coun. on med. edn. 1994-95, co-chmn. liaison com. on med. edn. 1995, pres. surgical caucus 1996), Vascular Surgery Soc., Soc. Thoracic Surgeons, So. Thoracic Surgery Assn., So. Med. Assn. (coun., pres. 2001), Mo. Med. Assn. (chmn. jud. coun. 1986—, v.p. 1986-87), Beta Theta Pi (trustees, pres. gen. frat. 1978-81). Baptist. Home: 5 Danforth Cir Columbia MO 65201-3509 Office: University of Missouri Hugh E Stephenson Jr Dept Surgery 1 Hospital Dr Columbia MO 65201-5276 Home Phone: 573-442-3834; Office Phone: 573-882-5645.

STEPHENSON, JOHN HUGHBANKS, artist, retired art educator; b. Waterloo, Iowa, Oct. 27, 1929; s. James Weaver and Della Hughbanks Stephenson; m. Susanne Groves Stephenson, Sept. 2, 1961; 1 child, Tara Jo. BA in Edn., U. No. Iowa, Cedar Falls, 1952; MFA, Cranbrook Acad. Art, Bloomfield Hills, Mich., 1958; DA, Grand Valley State U., Allendale, Mich., 1992. Prof. emeritus Sch. Art and Design, Ann Arbor, Mich., 1959—, Catherine B. Heller disting. prof., 1990—95, interim dean, 1991—93. Juror Maj. Exhbn., Washington, 1965, Mich. Coun. for Arts, Detroit, 1986—90, Ill. Coun. Staff sgt. USAF, 1952—55. Grantee, Asian Cultural Coun., 1962—63, Nat. Endowment for the Arts, 1986—87. Mem.: Internat. Acad. Ceramics. Avocation: gardening.

STEPHENSON, LARRY KIRK, geography educator, financial planner; b. Seattle, Sept. 22, 1944; s. Norman Eugene and Virginia Dare (Frost) S.; m. Margery Alsever, Aug. 15, 1992 (dec. Sept. 2006); children: Matthew Alan, Leah Anela. BS, Ariz. State U., 1966, MA, 1971; PhD, U. Cin., 1973. Manpower rsch. analyst Employment Security Commn. of Ariz., 1969-70; asst. prof. geography U. Hawaii, Hilo, 1973-76, assoc. prof., 1976-78, chmn. dept. geography, 1975-77; planner Ariz. Dept. Health Svcs., Phoenix, 1978-84; strategic planner City of Glendale, Ariz., 1984-92; pub. health analyst Gila River Indian Cmmty., Ariz., 1992-98, econ. devel. planner, 1998—2005; exec. dir. Eastern Ariz. Counties Orgn., 2006—. Vis. lectr. dept. geography Ariz. State U., 1978, adj. assoc. prof., 1979—; vis. assoc. prof. dept. geography, area devel. and urban planning U. Ariz., 1978; faculty U. Phoenix, 1979—; adj. prof. Golden Gate U., 1981—, Coll. St. Francis, 1982—; ptnr. Urban Rsch. Assocs., Phoenix, 1981—; faculty Troy State U., 1990—; governing bd. Gila County CC Dist., Ariz., 2004—. Author: Statistics for Health Managers, 1981; co-author: Student Study Guide and Instructor's Manual to accompany Geography: A Modern Synthesis, 4 edits., 1975-83; editor: Kohala keia: Collected Expressions of a Community, 1977; contbr. articles to profl. jours., chpts. to textbooks. Active. Hawaii Island Health Planning Coun., 1974-78, Glendale Cmty. Colls. Pres.'s Coun., 1986-92. With U.S. Army, 1966-68. NDEA fellow 1971-72. Mem. Am. Inst. Cert. Planners, Am Planning Assn., Assn. Am. Geographers, Ariz. Planning Assn. (pres. 1987—), S.W. Profl. Geog. Assn., Lambda Alpha. Unitarian Universalist. Home: HC 4 Box 28K Payson AZ 85541 Office: PO Box 2010 Payson AZ 85547 Office Phone: 928-972-5378. Personal E-mail: lstephe739@aol.com.

STEPHENSON, MASON WILLIAMS, lawyer; b. Atlanta, May 29, 1946; s. Donald Grier and Katherine Mason (Williams) S.; m. Linda Frances Partee, June 13, 1970; children: Andrew Mason, Walter Martin. AB cum laude, Davidson Coll., 1968; JD, U. Chgo., 1971. Bar: Ga. 1971, U.S. Dist. Ct. (no. dist.) Ga. 1985. Assoc. Alston, Miller & Gaines, Atlanta, 1971-76, ptnr., 1976-77, Trotter, Bondurant, Griffin, Miller & Hishon, Atlanta, 1977-82, Bondurant, Miller, Hishon & Stephenson, Atlanta, 1982-85, King & Spalding, LLP, Atlanta, 1985—, mng. ptnr. Atlanta office, 2001—. Fin. com. Atlanta Olympic Organizing Com., 1988—90. Mem. ABA (sect. bus. law, real property, probate and trust sect.), Am. Coll. Real Estate Lawyers, State Bar Ga. (exec. com., real property law sect. 1989-97, chair intangible rec. tax com. 1994-97), Atlanta Bar Assn. (chair real estate sect. 1981-82), Causeway Club, Capital City Club, Phi Beta Kappa, Phi Delta Phi. Avocations: boating, skiing, jogging. Office: King & Spalding LLP 1180 Peachtree St Atlanta GA 30309 Office Phone: 404-572-4600. Office Fax: 404-572-5100. Business E-Mail: mstephenson@kslaw.com.

STEPHENSON, PATRICIA ANN, public health researcher, educator; b. Washington, July 21, 1954; arrived in Sweden, 1990; d. Stanley Edwin and Mary Virginia (Brenneman) S.; m. Marsden Grigg Wagner, Dec. 14, 1990. BS, Calif. State U., Hayward, 1979; ScD, Johns Hopkins U., 1986. RN. Asst. prof. Sch. Pub. Health U. Wash., Seattle, 1986-90, adj. asst. prof. Sch. Nursing, 1987-90; sr. rschr. Ctr. for Pub. Health Rsch., Karlstad, Sweden, 1990-94; cons. health policy analyst, ops. rschr. Copenhagen, 1990-97; sr. advisor health and research USAID, Washington, 1998—. Vis. assoc. prof. Sch. Pub. Health U. Mich., Ann Arbor, 1995-96; cons. WHO, 1989, UNICEF, 1990—, World Bank, 1995-96. Mng. editor, co-founder European Jour. Pub. Health, 1991-94; author, editor: Tough Choices - InVitro Fertilization and the New Reproductive Technologies, 1993; contbr. articles to profl. publs. Women's health policy fellow John D. and Catherine T. MacArthur Found., 1995; recipient Commendation for work in fertility U.K. Parliament/House of Commons, 1989. Mem. APHA, Global Health Council, Delta Omega. Avocations: equestrian sports, dog agility training. Home: 123 Sherman Ave Takoma Park MD 20912 E-mail: pstephenson@usaid.gov.

STEPHENSON, RANDALL L., telecommunications industry executive; b. Okla. City, Apr. 22, 1960; m. Lenise H. Stephenson. BS in Acctg., Ctrl. State U., Edmond, Okla., 1982; MS in Acctg., U. Okla., Norman. With Southwestern Bell Tel. Co., Oklahoma City, 1982, area mgr. corp. taxes, 1986—91, dist. mgr. fin. analysis, 1991—92; dir. fin. SBC Internat. SBC Comm., Inc., Mexico City, 1992—96, contr. San Antonio, 1996—97, v.p., contr., 1997, sr. exec. v.p., CFO, 2001—04; chmn. Cingular Wireless LLC, 2003—04; COO SBC Comm., Inc., 2004—05, AT&T Inc. (merger of SBC Comm. & AT&T Corp.), San Antonio, 2005—07, chmn., CEO, 2007—. Bd. dirs. Cingular Wireless LLC, 2001—06, AT&T Inc., 2005—, Emerson Electric, 2006—; mem. audit com. H.E. Butt Grocery Co. Mem. nat. exec. bd. Boy Scouts Am.; mem. exec. com., audit com. United Way San Antonio; bd. mem. San Antonio Met. Missions Bd. Named one of 50 Who Matter Now, Business 2.0, 2007. Mem.: Okla. Soc. CPAs. Office: AT&T Inc 175 E Houston St PO Box 2933 San Antonio TX 78299-2933 *

STEPHENSON, RICHARD ISMERT, lawyer; b. Augusta, Kans., Oct. 13, 1937; s. Paul Noble and Dorothy May (Ismert) S.; m. Mary Lynn Bryden, July 2, 1967 (div. 1973); 1 child, Richard William; m. Linda Cox, Apr. 5, 1976. BA, U. Kans., 1958; JD, U. Mich., 1965. Bar: Kans. 1965, U.S. Dist. Ct. Kans. 1965, U.S. Ct. Appeals (10th cir.) 1965. Assoc. Fleeson, Gooing, Coulson & Kitch, Wichita, Kans., 1965-72, ptnr., 1973-95; gen. counsel RAGE Inc. and Affiliated Cos., Wichita, 1995—. Lt. (j.g.) USNR, 1959-62. Recipient Hilden Gibson award, U. Kans., 1958. Mem. ABA (forum on franchising), Def. Rsch. Inst., Internat. Assn. Def. Counsel, Kans. Bar Assn., Wichita Bar Assn., Wichita Country Club, Pi Sigma Alpha, Beta Theta Pi. Avocations: golf, fishing. Home: 9203 Killarney Wichita KS 67206-4027 Office: RAGE Inc 1313 N Webb Rd Ste 200 Wichita KS 67206-4077 Office Phone: 316-634-1888. Business E-Mail: dick@rage-inc.com.

STEPHENSON, ROSCOE BOLAR, JR., state supreme court justice; b. Covington, Va., Feb. 22, 1922; AB, Washington and Lee U., 1943, JD, 1947, LL.D. (hon.), 1983. Bar: Va. 1947. Ptnr. Stephenson & Stephenson, Covington, 1947-52; commonwealth's atty. Alleghany County, Va., 1952-64; ptnr. Stephenson, Kostel, Watson, Carson and Snyder, Covington, 1964-73; judge 25th Jud. Cir. Ct. Commonwealth Va., Covington, 1973-81; justice Va. Supreme Ct., Richmond, 1981-97, sr. justice, 1997—. Recipient Covington Citizen of Yr. award, 1973, Outstanding Alumni award Covington H.S., 1973, Disting. Alumnus award Washington and Lee U., 1997. Fellow Am. Coll. Trial Lawyers; mem. Va. State Bar (council 1969-73), Va. Bar Assn., Va. Trial Lawyers Assn., Order of Coif, Omicron Delta Kappa. Home: North Ridge Hot Springs VA 24445 Office: Va Supreme Ct 214 W Main St PO Box 198 Covington VA 24426-0198 also: Va Supreme Court Supreme Court Bldg 100 N 9th St Richmond VA 23219-2335 Office Phone: 540-962-6601.

STEPHENSON, SHERRY MADELINE, trade economist; d. Joe Harrell and Bettie Beasley Stephenson; children: Matthew Hector Travis, Corinne Louise Madeline. MA, NYU, 1976; PhD, Grad. Inst. Internat. Studies, Geneva, 1987. Trade specialist UNCTAD, Geneva, 1978—80; trade specialist Gen. Agreement Tariffs and Trade GATT, Geneva, 1980—82; prin. adminstr. Trade Directorate OECD, Paris, 1983—91; advisor Ministry of Trade, Jakarta, Indonesia, 1992—95; prin. trade specialist Trade Unit OAS, Washington, 1995—2000, dep. dir. for trade, 2000—05, dir. dept. trade and competitiveness, 2006—. Cons. Pacific Econ. Cooperation Coun., Singapore, 1993—2000, Asian Devel. Bank, Manila, 1993—96, World Bank, Washington, 1995—97, USAID, 1997—2000. Editor: (academic books) Services Trade in the Western Hemisphere, 2000, Services Trade Liberalization and Facilitation, 2002. Mem.: European Inst., Internat. Trade and Fin. Assn., Pacific Econ. Cooperation Coun., Inter-American Dialogue, Cosmos Club. Office: Orgn Am States 1889 F St NW Washington DC 20006 Office Phone: 202-458-3342. Business E-Mail: sstephenson@oas.org.

STEPHENSON, THOMAS A., publishing executive; b. SD; BS, Northern State U., Aberdeen, SD; MBA, U. Minn. With Knight Ridder Newspapers, 1975—97; sr. v.p. ops. & adminstrn. San Antonio Express-News, Tex., 1997, exec. v.p. & gen. mgr. Tex., pres. & pub. Tex., 2006—. Bd. mem. San Antonio United Way, San Antonio Econ. Devel. Found. Mem.: Tex. Daily Newspaper Assn. (legis. affairs com.). Office: San Antonio Express-News 301 Ave E San Antonio TX 78205 Office Phone: 210-250-3000. *

STEPHENSON, TONI EDWARDS, publishing executive, investment company executive, communications executive; b. Bastrop, La., July 23, 1945; d. Sidney Crawford and Grace Erleene Little; m. Arthur Emmet Stephenson Jr., June 17, 1967; 1 child, Tessa Lyn. Grad. owner/pres. mgmt. program, Harvard Bus. Sch. Pres., dir. Gen. Comm., Inc., Denver; sr. v.p., founder Stephenson & Co., Denver, 1971—; ptnr. Stephenson Properties, Stephenson Ventures. Past. pres. Children's Hosp. Assn. Vols.; past troop leader Girl Scouts Am.; past dir. Anchor Ctr. for Blind Children; dir. bd. dean's advisors Harvard U. Bus. Sch.; past dir. The Children's Hosp., St. Joseph's Hosp., Cherry Creek H.S. Parent Tchr. Conf. Orgn. Mem. Harvard Bus. Sch. Club Colo., DAR, Delta Gamma, Annabel's (London), Thunderbird Country Club.

STEPHENSON, VIVIAN M., former retail executive; B Math., NYU; MBA, U. Havana; PhD (hon.), Mills Coll., Oakland. Mgmt. positions Rand Info. Sys., Occidental Petroleum Corp., Assoc. Credit Burs. Svcs., Inc.; dir. info. sys. devel. Mervyn's, 1989-90, v.p. MIS, 1990-94, sr. v.p., 1994-95; sr. v.p., chief info. officer Dayton Hudson Corp., Mpls., 1995-2000; exec. v.p., chief info. officer Target Corp., Mpls., —2000; ret., 2000. Bd. dirs. MobiNetrix Sys. Inc.; mem. info. sys. customer adv. coun. IBM; mem. Tandem Americas Customer Coun; chmn. bd. dir. Mills Coll. Chair bd. dirs. San Francisco AIDS Found.; mem. Nat. Retail Fedn. Info. Sys. Bd. Mem. Calif. C. of C. Office: Target Corp 1000 Nicollet Mall Minneapolis MN 55403-2467

STEPNER, DONALD LEON, lawyer; b. Boston, Apr. 23, 1939; s. Neil and Sadie (Adelman) S.; m. Beth Klass, Aug. 14, 1965 (div. Dec. 1985); children: David, Jeff. AA, Wentworth Inst., Boston, 1958; BA, Ky. Wesleyan Coll., 1963; JD, U. Ky., 1966. Bar: Ky. 1966, U.S. Dist. Ct. Ky. 1966, U.S. Ct. Appeals (6th cir.) 1966, U.S. Supreme Ct. 1971. Assoc. Charles Adams, Covington, Ky., 1966-69; ptnr. Adams, Stepner, Woltermann & Dusing, Covington, 1969—. Pres. Ky. State Ethics Com. Bd. dirs. Boys Club. Recipient Human Rels. award NCCJ, 1986. Fellow Am. Coll. Trial Lawyers; mem. ABA (ho. delegates 2000-), Ky. Bar Assn. (pres. 1999-2000), No. Ky. Bar Assn., Ky. Def. Rsch. Inst., Kenton County Bar Assn. (pres. 1973-74, Merit award 1973, Gavel award 1973), US Soccer Fedn. (cert. referee, pres. 1980-85), Ky. HS Referees Assn., No. Ky. Soccer Assn. (ofcl. pres. 1980—). Avocations: golf, jogging, bicycling. Office: Adams Stepner Woltermann & Dusing PO Box 861 Covington KY 41012-0861

STEPNER, MICHAEL JAY, architect; b. Chgo., Aug. 7, 1940; s. Lester Harry and Florence (Addison) S.; m. Rosemary Reiser, Apr. 2, 1965; children: Rachel, Jessica, Adam, Joshua, Rebekah. Student, U. Minn., 1961-62; BArch, U. Ill., 1964; postgrad., U. Calif., Berkeley, 1971, U.S. Navy Engring. Schs., 1965-66. Registered architect, Calif. Urban designer, planner Crosstown Assocs., Chgo., 1968-71; urban designer, planner planning dept. City of San Diego, 1971-81, asst. planning dir., 1981-88, acting planning dir., 1987-88, city architect, 1988-92, asst. to city mgr., spl. projects coord., 1992-94, city urban design coord., 1984—97; pvt. practice The Stepner Design Group, San Diego; dean New Sch. Arch. and Design, 1997—2001. Vis. critic in urban design U. Ill, Chgo., 1970-71, San Diego State U. Grad. Sch. Planning and Pub. Adminstrn., Urban Design & Site Planning Inst., 1974-85; lectr. Urban Conservation Grad. Sch. History, U. San Diego, 1978, 81, 82, 84; asst. prof., lectr., design critic New Sch. Arch. and Design, San Diego City U., 1988—, prof. arch. and urban design; faculty assoc. for transp. and land use planning Lincoln Inst. Land Policy, Cambridge, Mass., 1993—; former mem. hist. bldg. code bd. State of Calif.; peer profl. Federal Govt. Design Excellence Program, 2002-04; mem., dir. Community Planning and Design Ctr., San Diego, 1971-74; mem. faculty New Sch. Arch. and Design.; mem. post licensure competency task force Calif. Archtl. Registration Bd. Bd. dirs. Citizens Coordinate for Century III, 1991—; mem. Regional Urban Design Assistance Team, Seattle, Washington, and Liverpool, Eng.; past bd. dirs. Californians for Preservation Action; mem. Congress for the New Urbanism; mem. Calif. State Bd. Arch. Exams, 1999; peer profl. Fed. Ct. Fed. Design Excellence Program, 2002-04. Recipient Leadership in Planning award New Sch. Architecture, 1992, Gaslamp Pioneer award San Diego Gaslamp Quarter Found., 1993, Ellen and Roger Revelle award Citizens Coordinate for Century III, 1993. Fellow AIA (co-chair housing assistance team City of Washincton, 1990, bd. dirs. San Diego chpt. 1976-78, 94-95, 97—, pres-elect 2001, mem. nat. urban design com., past mem. Calif. coun., hist. preservation-urban conservation com., urban design commr. San Diego chpt. 1975-76, Spl. award for Excellence in Govt. 1983), Am. Inst. Cert. Planners, Inst. for Urban Design; mem. Am. Planning Assn. (Disting. Leadership award Calif. chpt. 1991), San Diego Fed. Courthouse Design Team (selection panel), Urban Land Inst., Lambda Alpha. Home: 4260 Hortensia St San Diego CA 92103-1105 Office: 3620 30th St Ste B San Diego CA 92104 Office Phone: 619-234-2112. Business E-Mail: stepner1@pacbell.net.

STEPONAITIS, VINCAS PETRAS, archaeologist, anthropologist, educator; b. Boston, Aug. 10, 1953; s. Vincas and Elena (Povydis) S.; m. Laurie Cameron, Dec. 31, 1976; children: Elena Anne, Lillian Kazimiera. AB in Anthropology magna cum laude, Harvard U., 1974; MA in Anthropology, U. Mich., 1975, PhD in Anthropology, 1980. From lectr. to assoc. prof. dept. anthropology SUNY, Binghamton, 1979-87; assoc. prof. U. N.C., Chapel Hill, 1988-94, prof., 1995—, dir. Rsch. Labs. Archaeology, 1988—. Guest worker Nat. Bur. Stds., 1979; adj. lectr. dept. anthropology SUNY, Binghamton, 1979; lectr. and presenter in field. Author: Ceramics, Chronology, and Community Patterns, An Archaeological Study at Moundville, 1983, Archaeology of the Moundville Chiefdom, 1998, (CD-Rom) Excavating Occaneechi Town, 1998; editor Southeastern Archaeology, 1984-87; regional editor Investigations in Am. Archaeology, 1987-91; mem. editl. bd. Prehistory Press, 1990-97, Southern Cultures, 1992—, Am. Archaeology, 1996-2000; contbr. articles to profl. jours. Smithsonian Instn. fellow, 1978-79; grantee NSF, 1978-80, 83, 89-92, 94, 2000, 05, IMLS, 2003, Wenner-Gren Found., 1981, 86-88, Nat. Geographic Soc., 1987-88, Z. Smith Reynolds Found., 1992-94, Alcoa Found. 2005. Fellow Am. Anthrop. Assn.; mem. Soc. Am. Archaeology (Presdl. Recognition award 1993-94, exec. com. 1983-84, treas. 1992-94, pres. 1997-99), Archaeological Conservancy (bd. dirs. 2000—, chmn. 2003—), Ctr. for Maya Rsch. (bd. dirs. 2002-), Southeastern Archaeol. Conf. (editor 1984-87, pres. 1990-92), N.C. Archaeol. Soc. (exec. sec. 1988-91, sec. 1991-96), N.C. Archaeol. Coun. (exec. com. 1988-92), Archaeol. Soc. S.C., Ala. Archaeol. Soc., Miss. Archaeol. Soc., La. Archaeol. Soc. Office: U NC Rsch Labs Archaeology Alumni Bldg Cb 3120 Chapel Hill NC 27599-3120

STEPP, JAMES MICHAEL, finance company executive; b. Huntington, W.Va., Apr. 26, 1944; s. James Dial and Helen (Shelton) S.; m. Lillian Arlene Radeker, Jan. 3, 1970; children: James Michael, Scott Adams, John Radeker. BS, U.S. Mil. Acad., 1966; MBA, Stanford U., 1972. Commd. lt. C.E. U.S. Army, 1966, advanced through grades to capt., 1968, served in Vietnam, resigned, 1970; asst. v.p. Bank of Am., San Francisco, 1972-75, v.p. NYC, 1975-81; v.p., treas. Fotomat Corp., Wilton, Conn., 1981-83, Emhart Corp., Hartford, Conn., 1983-89; pres. Am. Corp. Fin. Group Inc., West Hartford, 1989-92; exec. v.p., CFO Purolator Products Co., Tulsa, Okla., 1992—, bd. dirs. Adv. dir. Conn. Nat. Bank, 1986-92. Bd. dirs. Jr. Achievement, North Cen. Conn., 1986-92. Decorated Silver Star, Bronze Star, Purple Heart, Army Commendation medal, Air medal. Mem. Fin. Execs. Inst., Stanford Bus. Sch. Alumni Assn., West Point Soc. of N.Y. Republican. Episcopalian. Avocations: tennis, fishing, jogging, golf. Home: 7021 Old Dairy Ln Charlotte NC 28211-3562

STEPS, BARBARA JILL, lawyer; b. Springfield, Mo., June 19, 1945; d. Louis Edward and Margaret Pearl (Stiver) Bredeman; m. Robert William Steps, Dec. 21, 1968; children: Rebecca Harper, Aaron Andrew, Jessica Anne. BA in Psychology, St. Louis U., 1966; JD, U. Mo., 1969; MBA, U. Conn., 1983. Atty. Ralston Purina Co., St. Louis, 1969; law clerk U.S. Dist. Ct., St. Louis, 1969-72; assoc. Stone, Keck & Staser, Evansville, Ind., 1973-75, Cline & Callahan, Indpls., 1975-77, Law Office, Herbert V. Camp, Ridgefield, Conn., 1978-81; from comml. counsel to corp. counsel, sec. Framatome Connectors USA, Inc. (now FCI USA, Inc.), Fairfield, Conn., 1981-93; v.p., counsel, sec. FCI USA, Inc. (formerly Framatome Connectors USA, Inc.), Etters, Pa., 1993—2002, sr. v.p. adminstrn., counsel, sec., 2002—. Mem.: ABA, Am. Corp. Counsel Assn. Home: 23 Emlyn Ln Mechanicsburg PA 17055-8017 Office: FCI USA Inc 825 Old Trail Rd Etters PA 17319-9392

STEPTER, CHARLES RAYMOND, JR., lawyer; b. Dallas, Aug. 29, 1945; s. Charles Raymond Sr. and Eugenia Belle (Baise) S.; m. Marie Lanneau, June 28, 1970; A.B., Mercer U., 1970; J.D., Stetson U., 1973. Bar: Fla. 1973, U.S. Dist. Ct. (mid. dist.) Fla. 1973, U.S. Supreme Ct. 1977, U.S. Dist. Ct. (no. and so. dists.) Fla. 1981, U.S. Ct. Appeals (11th cir.) 1981, U.S. Tax Ct. Dep. clerk Cir. Ct., Orange County, Fla., 1971. Assoc. Fishback, Davis, Dominick & Simonet, Orlando, Fla., 1973-74, law clerk, 1973-74; ptnr., 1974-78; ptnr. Fishback, Davis, Dominick & Bennett, Orlando, 1978-82; ptnr. Fishback, Davis, Dominick & Simonet, and Fishback, Davis, Dominick & Bennett, 1974-81; of counsel Zinkow, Kosto & Rotella and Kosto & Rotella, PA, 1982-86; bd. dirs. Fla. Legal Services, Inc.; pvt. practice, 1986-89; ptnr. Fishback, Dominick, Bennett, Stepter, Ardaman, Ahlers & Bonus, 1990-; gen. counsel Nat. Auto Auction Assn., 1986-; rsch. asst. Prof. Harry W. Haden. Exec. dir. Stetson Law Rev. Bd. dirs. Orange County Legal Aid Soc., Orlando, treas., 1979—, pres., 1982-83. Served with U.S. Army, 1968-70, 199th Light Infantry Brigade, Vietnam. Mem. ABA, Fla. Bar (chmn. delivery legal services com. 1984—, ex-officio mem. commn. access to legal system), Acad. Fla. Trial Lawyers, Orange County Bar Assn. (vice chmn. remember the kids com., student intern legal aid soc. 1972), Phi Alpha Delta (Marshall). Home: 1833 Lake Grove Ln Orlando FL 32806-7838 Office: Fishback Dominick Bennett Stepter Ardaman Ahlers & Bonus LLP 170 E Washington St Orlando FL 32801-2397

STEPTOE, MARY LOU, lawyer; b. Washington, July 15, 1949; d. Philip Pendleton and Irene (Hellen) S.; m. Peter E. Carson, Sept. 1986; children: Elizabeth Maud, Julia Grace. BA, Occidental Coll., 1971; JD, U. Va., 1974. Bar: Va., 1974, Supreme Ct., 1987, D.C. 1996. Staff atty., Bur. of Competition FTC, Washington, 1974-79, atty. advisor to commr., 1979-86, exec. asst. to chmn., 1988-89, assoc. dir., Bur. of Competition, 1989-90, dep. dir., 1990-92, acting dir., 1992-95, dep. dir., 1995-96; ptnr. Skadden Arps Slate Meagher & Flom LLP, Washington. Office Phone: 202-371-7020. Business E-Mail: msteptoe@skadden.com.

STEPTOE, SONJA, journalist; b. Lutcher, La., June 16, 1960; d. Eldridge Willie and Rosa Jane Steptoe. BA in Econs., U. Mo., 1982, B in Journalism, 1982; JD, Duke U. Law Sch., 1985. Staff reporter Wall St. Jour., NYC, 1985—90; sr. editor Sports Illustrated, NYC, 1990—2001, People Mag., NYC, 2001—02; nat. corr. CNN Sports, NYC, 1999—2001; corr. HBO Sports, 1995—2001; sr. corr. Time Mag., LA, 2002—06, deputy news dir., 2006—. Editl. adv. bd. U. Mo. Alumni Mag., Columbia, Mo., 1991—96; alumni bd. Duke U. Law Sch., Durham, NC, 1996—98; mem. U. Mo. Strategic Develop. Bd., 1988—. Co-author: (book) Guide to Women's Golf, 1993, A Kind of Grace" The Autobiography of the World's Greatest Female Athlete, 1997. Bd. mem. Alvin Ailey Dance Sch., NYC, 2001—02, Assoc. Black Charities, NYC, 1989—97. Recipient Emmy award, Nat. Assn. TV Arts and Sci., 1998, Nat. Headliner award, Press Club of Atlantic City, 1999, Disting. Alumni award, U. Mo., Duke Law Sch. Young Alumni award, 1994, 2000. Mem.: ABA.

STERBA, JEFFRY E., energy executive; BA in Econ. summa cum laude, Washington Univ., St. Louis; post-grad study in Econ., Washington Univ., Univ. N.Mex. Various positions PNM (subs. PNM Resources), Albuquerque, 1977—98; exec. v.p. USEC, Md., 1998—2000; pres. PNM (subs. PNM Resources), Albuquerque, 2000; chmn., pres., CEO PNM Resources, Albuquerque, 2000—. Chmn. Edison Elec. Inst., 2007—, Elec. Power Rsch. Inst. Former campaign chmn. United Way Ctrl. N. Mex.; mem. Gov. Bus. Adv. Coun.; bd. dir. US C. of C.; co-chmn. Albuquerque Econ. Forum. Mem.: Mortar Board, Omicron Delta Kappa. Office: PNM Resources Alvarado Sq Albuquerque NM 87158-0001 Office Phone: 505-241-2700. Office Fax: 505-241-2367. *

STERBENZ, JAMES PHILIP GUENTHER, computer network scientist; s. Bertram L. Jr. and Lois Sterbenz; m. Kristine L.G. Sterbenz; 1 child, Katarina. BSEE, BSCS, ABEcon, Wash. U., 1981, MS, 1986, DSc, 1991. Adv. engr., scientist IBM Rsch., Milford, Conn., 1991—94, Hawthorne, NY, 1991—94; prin. MTS GTE Labs., Waltham, Mass., 1994—99; sr. network scientist BBN Technologies, Cambridge, Mass., 1999—2003, mgr. mobile wireless and active networking, 1999—2002; assoc. prof. Dept. Elec. Engring. and Computer Sci. U. Kans., 2005—. Chair Internat. Working Conf. on Active Networks, 2002, 03; vis. rsch. scientist U. Mass., Amherst, 2003-05; vis. prof. computing Lancaster (Eng.) U., 2003—; program chair Internat. Workshop Self-Organizing Sys., 2006, mem. steering com., 2006—. Author: High Speed Networking, 2001; editor Protocols for High Speed Networks, 1999-2001, Active Networks, 2002;

mem. editl. bd. IEEE Network, Computer Networks, 1999—, Jour. Comm. and Networks, 2000—. Mem.: IEEE (sr.; chmn. ComSoc TCGN 1994—99, steering com. 1999—, chmn. program hot interconnects 2004, gen. chmn. 2005—06, mem. steering com. 2006—), Korean Inst. Computer Sci., Instn. Elec. Engrs. U.K., Inst. Elec., Info. and Comm. Engrs., Protocols for High-Speed Networks (keynote address 1994, program chair 1999, steering com. chair 2000—), Internat. Fedn. Info. Processing Soc., Interplanetary Chpt. Internet Soc., Assn. Computing Machinery (vice chair SIGCOMM 99 conf.). Avocation: railway signaling. Home and Office: PO Box 4050 Lawrence KS 66046-1050 Home Phone: 508-944-3067. Business E-Mail: jpgs@sterbenz.org.

STERIN, STEVEN M., chemicals executive; m. Ellen Sterin; 2 children. BBA, Univ. Tex., Austin, 1995, M in acctg., 1995. CPA Tex., NC. Tax acct. Price Waterhouse; fin. mgmt. positions through v.p. fin. Reichold Inc., 1997—2003; dir. fin., contr. chem. bus. Celanese Corp., Dallas, 2003—05, v.p., corp. contr., 2005—07, sr. v.p., CFO, 2007—. Office: Celanese Corp 1601 W LBJ Freeway Dallas TX 75234 *

STERLING, ANNE D., library association executive; Mem. UN Assn., World Affairs Coun., UN Non-govtl. Orgn. Conf.; pres. Harford County Sch. Bd., Md. Mem.: Va. Women's Network (past chair), League of Women Voters - Va. (first v.p., Richmond Met. area 1998—, bd. dirs. 2005—), Assn. Library Trustees and Advocates (pres. 2006—07), ALA. Office: County of Henrico Public Library 1001 N Laburnum Ave Richmond VA 23223 Office Phone: 804-304-4142. Office Fax: 804-285-9133. E-mail: nimbleleap@aol.com.

STERLING, ARTHUR JAMES, retired legal assistant; b. Pineville, La., July 27, 1944; s. Leon Henry and Dorothy Mae Sterling; children: Hope, Monique, Heather. AA in Bus. Adminstrn., Compton CC, Calif., 1986; student in psychology, U. Southern Calif., LA, 1988—89; AA in Bus. Paralegal, Cerritos CC, Norwalk, Calif., 1994; PhD in Counseling, Progressive Univeral Life Ch., Sacramento, 2000. With U.S. Naval Weapons Sta., Seal Beach, Calif., 1979-83, Norwalk Superior Ct., 1991; law clk.; guidance counselor, 2000—02; ret., 2006. Dave Holt Meml scholar, K.T. Skula meml. scholar, Johnson Controls, Inc. Fund scholar, Amy Welch Meml. scholar. Mem. Soc. for Advancement of Mgmt. (pres.), Phi Beta Lambda (pres.), Associated Student Body (senator, pres.), The Oxford Club, The Highlander Club. Democrat. Avocations: computers, cooking, reading. Home: 4216 Carlin Ave #C Lynwood CA 90262-5278 Office Phone: 310-631-8774. Personal E-mail: drdoodlebug06@yahoo.com.

STERLING, DONALD T., real estate mogul, professional sports team owner; b. Chgo., 1934; m. Shelly Stein, 1957; 3 children. BA, Calif. State U., LA; JD, Southwestern U. Sch. Law, LA. Owner NBA LA (formerly San Diego) Clippers, 1981—, chmn. bd. Bd. govs. NBA. Founder Donald T. Sterling Charitable Foundation. Office: LA Clippers Staples Ctr 1111 S Figueroa St Ste 1100 Los Angeles CA 90015 *

STERLING, KEIR BROOKS, historian, educator; b. NYC, Jan. 30, 1934; s. Henry Somers and Louise Noel (de Wetter) S.; m. Anne Cox Diller, Apr. 3, 1961; children: Duncan Diller, Warner Strong, Theodore Craig. BS, Columbia U., 1961, MA, 1963, profl. diploma, 1965, PhD, 1973. Asst. to dean Sch. Gen. Studies Columbia U., NYC, 1959-65; rsch. grantee England, 1965-66; instr. history Pace U., NYC and Pleasantville, NY, 1966-71, from asst. prof. to assoc. prof., 1971-77, adj. prof., 1977-83; ordnance br. historian U.S. Army Ordnance Ctr. and Sch., Aberdeen Proving Ground, Md., 1983-94, Ft. Lee, Va., 1994-98; historian U.S. Army Combined Arms Support Command, Ft. Lee, 1998—. Lectr. gen. counseling Bklyn. Coll., CUNY, 1967-68; asst. acad. dean, adj. asst. prof. history, coord. Am. studies program, dir. summer session Marymount Coll., Tarrytown, N.Y., 1968-71; asst. dean Rockland C.C., SUNY, Suffern, 1971-73; vis. prof. Mercy Coll., Westchester C.C., King's Coll., Nyack Coll., U. Wis., 1971, 75, 78-80, 83, Harford (Md.) C.C., 1987-94; adj. instr. Army Logistics Mgmt. Coll., Ft. Lee, 1995—; co-project dir. Am. Ornithologists Union Centennial Hist., Project, 1976-89; cons. Arno Press, Inc., 1973-78, Coun. State Colls. of N.J., 1984-85, NSF, 1983—, Am. Trust for Brit. Libr., 1986-89; active Columbia U. Seminar on History and Philosophy of Sci., 1976-83; archivist, historian mem. steering com. sect. mammalogy Internat. Union Biol. Scis., 1985—2007; judge Ann. Nat. History Day Competition U. Md., 1993-; chair historian/archivist com. Internat. Fedn. Mammalogy, 2007—; grant reviewer Tchg. Am. History Program U.S. Dept. Edn., 2003-. Author: Last of the Naturalists: The Career of C. Hart Merriam, 1974, 77; editor: Notes on the Animals of North America (B.S. Barton), 1974; assoc. editor: Am. Nat. Biog., 1989-98; editor, contbr.: Natural Sciences in America, 1974, 68 vols., 1974, Biologists and Their World, 1978, 77 vols.; gen. editor, contbr.: The International History of Mammalogy, 1987—; sr. editor, contbr. (with R. Harmond, G. Cevasco, and L. Hammond) Biographical Dictionary of American and Canadian Naturalists and Environmentalists, 1997; contbg. author: Ground Warfare: An International Encyclopedia, 2002, Dictionary of Am. History, 3d edit., 2003, Encyclopedia of World Environmental History, 2003; editor, contbr. to numerous works in history, Am. natural scis., and Am. mil. history. With US Army, 1954—56. Grantee Theodore Roosevelt Meml. Fund, Am. Mus. Natural History, 1967, Nat. Geog. Soc., 1977, NSF/Am. Soc. Mammalogists, 1978, Pace U., 1980, 81, NSF, 1981-82, IREX, 1982; recipient Editor's Quill Award, Internat. Assn. of Torch Clubs, 2003. Mem.: History of Sci. Soc., Orgn. Am. Historians, Am. Hist. Assn., Assn. Bibliography of History (mem. coun. 1994—), Am. Soc. Environ. History (sec., mem. governing bd., editor newsletter), Am. Ornithologists Union (co-chmn. centennial hist. com., mem. archives com., grantee 1976, 1977), Am. Soc. Mammalogists (mem. archives com., mem. 75th ann. com.), Phi Delta Kappa, Sigma Tau Delta, Phi Alpha Theta. Democrat. Episcopalian. Home: 7104 Wheeler Rd Richmond VA 23229-6939 Office: 3901 A Ave Room 119 Fort Lee VA 23801-1807 Office Phone: 804-734-0082. Business E-Mail: keir.sterling@us.army.mil. E-mail: kbs1934@cs.com.

STERLING, RAYMOND LESLIE, civil engineering educator, researcher, consultant; b. London, Apr. 19, 1949; came to U.S., 1966; s. Richard Howard and Joan Valeria (Skinner) S.; m. Linda Lee Lundquist, Aug. 8, 1970 (div. Sept. 1982); children: Paul, Juliet, Erika; m. Janet Marie Kjera, Aug. 20, 1983; 1 child, Zoey. B in Civil and Structural Engring. with 1st class honors, U. Sheffield, Eng., 1970; MS in Geol. Engring., U. Minn., 1975, PhDCE, 1977. Registered civil engr., Minn.; chartered structural engr., Eng. Engr. trainee Met. Water Bd., London, 1968; civil engr. Egil Wefald and Assocs., Cons. Engrs., Mpls., 1969-71; structural engr. Husband and Co., Cons. Engrs., Eng., 1971-73; rsch. asst. U. Minn., Mpls., 1973-77, dir. Underground Space Ctr., 1977-95, asst. prof. dept. civil and mineral engring., 1977-83, assoc. prof., 1983-95; project. coord., structural engr. Setter, Leach and Lindstrom, Inc., Mpls., 1976-77; prin. cons. Itasca Cons. Group, Inc., Mpls., 1981-94; prof. civil engring. La. Tech. U., Ruston, 1995—, dir. Trenchless Tech. Ctr., 1995—. Vice-chmn. U.S. Nat. com. on tunneling tech. NRC, NAS, 1990-91, chmn. 1992-94, com. on infrastructure, 1991-93, bd. infrastructure and the constructed environment, 1994-96; acting co-dir. Minn. Cold Climate Bldg. Rsch. Ctr. U. Minn., 1987-89, co-dir. Bldg. Energy Rsch. Ctr., 1986, speaker's bur., other u. coms.; energy adv. com. Legis. Com. on Minn. Resources, 1989-95; com. on moisture control in bldgs. U.S. Bldg. Thermal Envelope Coordinating Coun., 1985-86; program planning com. on bldg. founds. U.S. Dept. Energy, 1985-95; adv. bd. for energy efficient residence demonstration project Nat. Assn. Home Builders, 1980; mem. Gov's. Exxon Oil Overcharge Adv. Task Force, 1986, Mpls. Energy Future Com., 1980-81, Scientist's Inst. for Pub. Info., N.Y.; cons. U.S. Army Corps. Engrs., UN, N.Y., Opus Corp., Mpls., Dames & Moore Internat., London, City of Mpls., Larson Engring., White Bear, Minn., Pilsbury Co., Mpls., Colgate Divsn. Sch., Rochester, N.Y., others; adv. prof. Chongqing Jianzhu U., Sichuan, People's Republic China, 1985—; vis. rschr. Nat. Inst. Pollution and Resources MITI, Japan, 1991; vis. prof. U. Mo., Rolla, 1979; Shimizu prof. civil and mineral engring., U. Minn., 1988-95; adv. prof. Tongji U., Shanghai, 1996—; mem. eminent speaker program Instn. Engrs., Australia, 1993; hon. prof. Changsha Rwy. U., China, 1998—, Xian U. Arch. and Tech., China, 1999; lectr., presenter in field. Author: Earth Sheltered Housing Design: Guidelines, Examples and References, 1978, transl. into Chinese, French, Spanish and Russian, 2d. edit., 1985, (with others) Earth Sheltered Community Design: The Design of Energy-Efficient Residential Communities, 1980 (award for Best Book in Architecture and Urban Planning Profl. and Scholarly div. Assn. Am. Pubs. 1981), transl. into Spanish, 1981, Underground Building Design, 1983, translated into Japanese and Russian, others, Building Foundation Handbook, 1988, Underground Space Design, 1993, others; editor: (with others) Key Questions in Rock Mechanics: Proc. 29th U.S. Symposium on Rock Mechanics, 1988; contbr. articles to profl. jours. including Jour. Agrl. Engring., Internat. Jour. Rock Mechanics and Mining Scis., Exptl. Mechanics, many others. Named Most Valuable Profl., Gulf Coast Trenchless Assn., 1999; recipient Young Engr. of Yr. award, Minn. Fedn. Engring. Soc., 1982, Applied Rsch. award in rock mechanics, NRC, 1993, elected fgn. mem., Acad. Engring. of Russian Fedn., 1993, Person of Yr. award, Trenchless Tech. mag., 2001, Engring. Faculty Professionalism award, La. Engring. Found., 2005; grantee Shimizu Constrn. Co., 1987—93, Nat. Assn. Homebuilders, 1989, U.S. Dept. Energy, 1989—90, NSF, 1991, Minn. Dept. Transp., 1991, ASHRAE, 1991—92, many others. Fellow: Am. Soc. Civil Engrs. (bd. dirs. 1985—92, pres. Minn. sect. 1990—91, Young Civil Engr. of Yr. award 1982, Stephen D. Bechtel Pipeline Engring. award 2003), Royal Soc. Arts, Mfrs. & Commerce, Inst. Structural Engrs., Instn. Civil Engrs.; mem.: NSPE, Internat. Soc. Trenchless Tech. (vice chmn. 1999—2002, chmn. 2002—05), N. Am. Soc. Trenchless Tech. (bd. dirs. 1996—, treas. 1997, internat. rep. 1998—, vice chmn. 1999, chmn. 2000), Internat. Tunneling Assn. (coordinating editor jour. 1986—95, co-sr. editor 1996—, animateur working group on direct/indirect advantages of underground structures 1997—2000), Am. Underground Constrn. Assn. (Award of Distinction 2000). Achievements include research in underground construction, underground space utilization, trenchless technology, rock mechanics, and energy use in buildings. Office: Trenchless Technology Ctr Louisiana Tech U PO Box 10348 Ruston LA 71272-0046 Office Phone: 318-257-4072. Business E-Mail: sterling@latech.edu.

STERLING, RICHARD LEROY, English and foreign language educator; b. Atlantic City, Feb. 18, 1941; s. Richard Leroy and Anne (Bass) S. BA, Am. U., 1968; MA, Cath. U., 1971; PhD, Howard U., 1990. Head Start tchr. DC Pub. Schs., summer 1968, tchr. French and English, adult and continuing edn., 1969-71, 76-83; instr. French Howard U., Washington, 1973-76, grad. tchg. asst., 1983-85, instr., lectr. in French, 1985-89; tchr. English Cmty.-Based Orgns., DC Pub. Schs., 1989-91; asst. prof. French and English Bowie (Md.) State U., 1991-97, assoc. prof. French, 1997—, dir. modern langs. program, 1997—. Tchr. summer enrichment program for gifted children Sch. Edn., Howard U., summers 1985, 86; tchr. ESL, DC Pub. Schs., summer, 1989, 94; asst. coord. Humanities Immersion Program, Project Access for H.S. Students, Bowie State U., summer 1997-98; vice-chmn. World Centennial Conf.; French, Am. and Planetary Dimensions of Saint-John Perse, U. DC, 1987; mem. adv. coun. Northeast Conf. Tchg. Fgn. Langs; NAACP-ACT-SO competition humanities judge 1997-2000; adj. assoc. prof. English, Southeastern U., Washington, summer 1998—; judge DC Pub. Schs. World Langs. Festival, 2001; presenter, book reviewer in field. Author: The Prose Works of Saint-John Perse: Towards an Understanding of His Poetry, 1994; contbg. editor MaComere Rev., 2003—; contbr. articles to profl. jours. Active Assn. Democratique des Francais a L.Etranger, 1988—, Senegal friendship com. Office Cmty. and Ethnic Affairs, Prince George's County Govt., Md., 1993-94, Inst. for Haitian Cultural and Sci. Affairs, 1992-94, local arrangements com. Conf. Coll. Composition and Communication, Washington, 1995, Friends of the Corcoran, 1999; membership com. and outreach com. St. John's Ch., Washington, 1993, ch. growth com., 1995. With U.S. Army, 1964-66. Mem. MLA, Coll. Lang. Assn., Mid. Atlantic Writers Assn. (chmn. essay contest com. 1995-2000, bd. dirs. 2000—), Samuel Beckett Soc., Societe des Professeurs Francais et Francophones d'Amerique, Zora Neale Hurston Soc., Am. Assn. Tchrs. French (sec.-treas. Washington chpt. 1986-90), Nat. Cathedral Assn., Md. Fgn. Lang. Assn. (bd. dirs. 1997-2001, 2003—), Coun. Internat. d'Etudes Francophones, Friends DC Superior Ct. (bd. dirs. 1996—), Univ. Club (Washington), Md. Fgn. Lang. Assn. (bd. dirs., 1997-2001, 03-06), Oxford Round Table (presenter), Pi Delta Phi, Sigma Tau Delta. Democrat. Episcopalian. Avocations: classical music, history, travel. Office: Bowie State U Dept English & Modern Langs Bowie MD 20715 Business E-Mail: rsterling@bowiestate.edu.

STERLING, ROBERT LEE, JR., investment company executive; b. Cleve., June 12, 1933; s. Robert Lee and Kathryn (Durell) S.; children from previous marriage: Robert Livingston, William Lee, Cameron Platt; m. Joyce Lanier Milner, June 4, 1994. Student, U. Edinburgh, Scotland, 1955; BA, Brown U., Providence, 1956; MBA, Columbia U., NYC, 1962. Corp. rsch. analyst Morgan Guaranty Trust, NYC, 1962-63; asst. comptr. Western Hemisphere CPC Internat., NYC, 1963—76; v.p. White, Weld & Co., Inc., NYC, 1976—78, Merrill Lynch Asset Mgmt., 1978-80, Wood, Struthers & Winthrop Mgmt. Corp., NYC, 1980-83; sr. v.p. Shearson Lehman Bros. Asset Mgmt., 1983-88; v.p., sr. portfolio mgr. Chase Manhattan Bank, 1988-93; exec. v.p., sr. portfolio mgr. Melhado, Flynn & Assocs., Inc., NYC, 1993—; mng. ptnr. Winthrop Asset Mgmt., 1995—. Mem. adv. bd. Mus. Modern Art, Oxford U., Eng.; trustee Soc. of the Four Arts, Palm Beach, Preservation Soc., Palm Beach, Game Coservancy, U.S. Mem. New Eng. Soc. (past pres., J.P. Morgan medal), St. Nicholas Soc., Pilgrims, NY State Soc. of Cin. (past pres.), St. Andrew's Soc., Univ. Club, Everglades Club, Bath and Tennis Club, Bathing Corp., Anabell's, Meadow Club, Alpha Delta Phi, Alpha Kappa Psi. Home: 200 Regent Park Palm Beach FL 33480 Office: Melhado Flynn & Assocs Inc 530 5th Ave New York NY 10036-5101 Office Phone: 800-333-3610.

STERLING, THOMAS W., metal products executive; B in Civil Engring., Vanderbilt U., Nashville; law degree, Samford U., Birmingham, Ala. Bar: Ala., Pa. Mgmt. trainee Fairfield Works US Steel, Ala., 1969, various positions in oper., pers. svcs. and comml. depts., 1969—75, asst. mgr. equal employment opportunity Employee Rels. Dept. Pitts., 1975, various employee rels. positions, v.p. employee rels., 1986, v.p. employee benefits, 1996, sr. v.p. human resources, 2003—04, sr. v.p. human resources & bus. svcs., 2004—07, sr. v.p. adminstrn., 2007—; v.p. labor rels., steel and related resources US Steel Group USX Corp., 1984—86; pres. Transtar, Inc. (now subs. of US Steel), 2000—03. US Steel rep. on bd. dirs. Maglev, Inc. Pres., bd. dirs. Greater Pitts. Coun. of Boy Scouts of Am.; bd. trustees Robert Morris U., Moon Twp., Pa.; chmn. bd. dirs. U. Pitts. Med. Ctr. Braddock; bd. dirs. U. Pitts. Med. Ctr. McKeesport, Heritage Health Found. Office: US Steel 600 Grant St Pittsburgh PA 15219-2800 Office Phone: 412-433-1121. *

STERN, (SOL) ALAN, science administrator, astrophysicist, researcher; b. New Orleans, Nov. 22, 1957; s. Leonard Arthur and Joel Strauss (Sugar) S.; m. Carole Ann Jones, Aug. 5, 1982; children: Sarah L., Kate E., Jordan. BS, U. Tex., 1978, MS in Aerospace Engring., 1980, BA, 1981, MS in Planetary Atmospheres, 1981; PhD in Astrophysics and Planetary Sci., U. Colo., 1989. Engr. NASA Johnson Space Ctr., Houston, 1979-80; systems engr. Martin Marietta Aerospace, Denver, 1982-83; spacecraft / instrument engr. Lab. for Atmospheric and Space Physics U. Colo., Boulder, 1983-86, rsch. assoc., 1989—90, asst. dir. Office of Space Sci. and Tech., 1986—87, asst. to v.p. for rsch., 1987—88, rsch. fellow Ctr. for Space & Geosciences Policy, 1989—91, rsch. assoc. Ctr. for Astrophysics and Space Astronomy, 1990—91, prof. adj. Astrophysical and Planetary Scis. Dept., 2002—; prin. scientist Space Science Dept. S.W. Rsch. Inst., 1991-92, sect. mgr., 1992—97, dept. dir., 1998—2005, exec. dir. Space Sci. and Engring. Div., 2004—07; assoc. adminstr. sci. mission directorate NASA, 2007—. Mem. lunar exploration sci. working group NASA, 1992—, discovery program sci. working group, 1989—90, chmn. Neptune/Pluto outer planet sci. working group, 1994—, project scientist Spartan-Halle spacecraft mission; prin. investigator Alice UV spectrometer in ESA/NASA Rosetta mission, Lunar Recon Orbiter Lyman-Alpha Mapping (LAMP) Experiment, Ralph Imager/IR Spectrometer on New Horizons, Alice UV Spectrometer on New Horizons, New Horizons Pluto-Kuiper Belt Mission. Author: The U.S. Space Program After Challenger, 1987, Pluto and Charon, 1997, The Exploration of Pluto, 1997, The Search for Extra-Solar Earthlike Planet: Techniques and Technology, 1997, The Exploration of Pluto, 1997, Pluto and Charion, 1997, Our Worlds, 1998, Our Universe, 2000, Worlds Beyond: The Thrill of Planetary Exploration as told by Leading Experts, 2003; editor: Geophysical Research Letters Spl. Issues on Pluto and the Moon, 1989, 91, (U. Ariz. space sci. series volume) Pluto and Cluster; contbr. numerous articles to profl. jours. Named one of he World's Most Influential People, TIME Mag., 2007; recipient Martin Marietta New Design Innovation Award, 1983, Solar Max Repair Mission Recognition Award, 1984, Hale-Bopp Sounding Rocket Campaign Group Achievement Award, NASA, 1998, New Millennium Deep Space-1 Mission Group Achievement Award, 2002, Rosetta Group Achievement Award, 2005; grad. fellow, Colo. Commn. on Higher Edn., 1988—89. Mem. AAAS, AIAA, Internat. Astron. Union, Am. Astron. Soc., Am. Geophys. Union, Aircraft Owners and Pilots Assn. Avocations: flying, scuba diving, photography, skiing, hiking, gardening, writing. Office: Sci Mission Directorate NASA 300 E St SW Washington DC 20546-0001 Office Phone: 303-546-9670, 202-358-3889. E-mail: astern@swri.edu, alan.stern@nasa.gov. *

STERN, ANDREW L. (ANDY STERN), labor union administrator; b. West Orange, NJ, 1950; BA in Edn. & Urban Planning, U. Pa., 1971. State social svc. worker, mem. Local 668 Svc. Employees Internat. Union (SEIU), 1973—80, mem. internat. exec. bd. Wash., DC, 1980—, org. field svc. programs, 1984—96, internat. pres., 1996—. Bd. dirs. AFL-CIO Housing and Bldg. Investment Trust, Medicare Rights Ctr., Aspen Inst., Broad Found., Inst. of Medicine. Author: (novels) A Country That Works, 2006. Bd. dir. Rock the Vote; chmn. Ctr. for Cmty. and Corp. Ethics. Mem.: Am. Hosp. Assn. (commn. on workforce for hosps. and health systems.), Nat. Acad. Social Ins. (bd. dir.). Office: Svc Employees Internat Union 1313 L St NW Washington DC 20005-4101 *

STERN, ANDREW MILTON, public relations executive; b. Cleve., Mar. 22, 1949; s. Sidney Harrison Stern, Jr. and Sue (Friedlander) Miller; m. Sabina R. Bobzin, Feb. 28, 1971; children: David Patrick, Eric Thomas. BA, U. Del., 1970. Press sec. to mayor City of Wilmington, Del., 1970-73; dir. pub. affairs Wilmington Med. Ctr., 1973-75; staff asst. to pres. The White House, Washington, 1975-77; dir. pub. relations and advt. Wylain, Inc., Dallas, 1977-80; sr. v.p. Assocs. Corp. N.Am., Dallas, 1980-82; chmn., chief exec. officer Sunwest Communications, Inc., Dallas, 1982—. Founder, dir. Dallas Nat. Bank. Chmn. Med. City Dallas Hosp., Dallas County Hist. Found. Mem. Pub. Rels. Soc. Am., North Dallas C. of C. (past chmn.). Clubs: Salesmanship, Prestonwood, Press (Dallas). Republican. Jewish. Home: 5916 Club Oaks Dr Dallas TX 75248-1124 Office: Sunwest Communications Inc 5420 Lyndon B Johnson Pwy 1475 Dallas TX 75240-6265

STERN, ARTHUR PAUL, electronics executive; b. Budapest, Hungary, July 20, 1925; arrived in U.S., 1951; s. Leon and Bertha (Frankfurter) Stern; m. Edith M. Samuel; children: Daniel, Claude, Jacqueline. Diploma in Elec. Engring., Swiss Fed. Inst. Tech., Zurich, 1948; MSEE, Syracuse U., NY, 1956. Mgr. electronic devices and applications lab. GE, Syracuse, NY, 1957-61; dir. engring. Martin Marietta Corp., Balt., 1961-64; dir. ops. Bunker Ramo Corp., Canoga Park, Calif., 1964-66; v.p., gen. mgr. advanced products divsn. Magnavox, Torrance, Calif., 1966-79; pres. Magnavox Advanced Products and Systems Co., Torrance, 1980-90; vice chmn., bd. dirs. Magnavox Electronic Systems Co., Ft. Wayne, Ind., 1987—90; pres. Ea. Beverly Hills Corp., 1991—. Instr. GE Bus. Mgmt., 1955—57; non-resident staff mem. MIT, 1956—59; pres. Calif.-Israel C. of C., 1994—98, chmn. bd. dirs., 1998—2000; bd. dirs. Jewish Coun. Pub. Affairs, 1996—2002; mem. governing coun. Am.-Jewish Congress, 1997—98; v.p. Progressive Jewish Alliance, 1999—2004. Co-author: (book) Transistor Circuit Engineering, 1957, Handbook of Automation, Computation and Control, 1961; contbr. articles to profl. jours. Mem. adv. bd. dept. elec. engring. U. Calif., Santa Barbara, 1980—92; mem. Sch. Engring. Adv. and Devel. Coun. Calif. State U., Long Beach, 1985—90; chmn. bd. dirs. Calif. Humanitarian Found. for Holocaust Survivors, 2000—06; regional chair, bd. dirs. Ams. for Peace Now, 2002—; bd. dirs. So. Calif. Ams. for Dem. Action, 2000—; chmn. engring. divsn. United Jewish Appeal, Syracuse, 1955—57; bd. dirs. Bur. Jewish Edn., LA, 1995—, chmn. investment com., 2000—05; vice-chmn. Jewish Cmty. Rels. Com. of Jewish Fedn. of L.A., 1998—2003; bd. dirs. Jewish Fedn. Greater L.A., 2003—05. Recipient Justice-Tzedek award, Labor Zionist Alliance, 2001, Educating for Life award, Bur. Jewish Edn., 2004. Fellow: IEEE (pres. 1975, bd. dirs., officer 1970—77, guest editor spl. issue IEEE Trans. on Circuit Theory 1956, invited guest editor spl. issue Procs. IEEE on Integrated Electronics 1964, Centennial medal 1984, Millennium medal 2000, Haraden Pratt award 2001), AAAS; mem.: Sigma Xi, Eta Kappa Nu Assn. (eminent mem.). Achievements include patents in field. Personal E-mail: apstern@att.net.

STERN, BRIAN E., printing company executive; b. London, Nov. 8, 1947; B in History, U. East Anglia, Norwich, Eng., 1969; MBA, Harvard U., 1973. Sales position Rank Xerox Ltd. (now Xerox Europe) Xerox Corp., London, 1969, with Stamford, Conn., 1976—, head corp. bus. strategy, 1992—94, pres. personal document products divsn., pres. office document products group, pres. Xerox Tech. Enterprises, corp. v.p. Stamford, Conn., 1993—95, sr. v.p., 1995—, pres. supplies bus. group, 2001—04, sr. v.p. Fuji Xerox Ops., 2004—; with Boston Consulting Group. Bd. dirs. HNI Corp., 1998—. Office: Xerox Corp 800 Long Ridge Rd Stamford CT 06904 Office Phone: 203-968-3000. *

STERN, CARL LEONARD, retired news correspondent, federal official, educator; b. NYC, Aug. 7, 1937; s. Hugo and Frances (Taft) S.; m. Joy Elizabeth Nathan, Nov. 27, 1960; children: Lawrence, Theodore. AB, Columbia U., 1958, MS, 1959; JD, Cleve. State U., 1966, JD (hon.), 1975, New Eng. Coll. Law, 1977. Bar: Ohio 1966, DC 1968, US Supreme Ct. 1969. Law corr. NBC News, Washington, 1967—93; dir. Office of Pub. Affairs U.S. Dept. Justice, Washington, 1993—96; Shapiro Prof. of Media and Pub. Affairs George Washington U., 1996—. Mem. editl. stds. rev. com. Pub. Broadcasting Svc., 2005; lectr. Nat. Jud. Coll.; adj. prof. George Washington U., Stanford U. Editl. bd. The Dist. Lawyer Mem. Dept. Transp. Task Force on Assistance to Families in Aviation Disasters, 1997; mem. nat. adv. coun., Cleve. Marshall Law Sch.; bd. dir. Hist. Soc., DC Cir. Recipient Peabody award, 1974, Emmy award, 1974, Gavel award, 1969, 74, Headliner Club award, 1991, Edmond J. Randloph award US Dept. Justice. Mem. ABA (vice chmn. criminal justice sect. com. on criminal justice and media, gov., forum com. on comm. law, working group intelligence requirements and criminal code reform, standing com. on strategic comm.), AFTRA (nat. exec. bd. 1984-86, first v.p. Washington, Balt. chpt. 1985-87) Home: 2956 Davenport St NW Washington DC 20008

Office: George Washington U #400 805 21st St NW Washington DC 20052 Home Phone: 202-362-0181; Office Phone: 202-994-1464. Personal E-mail: sterncarl@aol.com. Business E-Mail: cstern@gwu.edu.

STERN, CARL WILLIAM, JR., management consultant; b. San Francisco, Mar. 31, 1946; s. Carl William and Marjorie Aline (Gunst) S.; m. Karen Jaffe, Sept. 7, 1966 (div. Mar. 1972); 1 child, David; m. Holly Drick Hayes, Mar. 21, 1985; children: Kenneth, Matthew. BA, Harvard U., 1968; MBA, Stanford U., 1974. Cons. Boston Cons. Group, Inc., Menlo Park, Calif., 1974-77, mgr., 1977-78, London, 1978-80, v.p. Chgo., 1980-87, sr. v.p., 1987-97, pres., CEO, 1998—2003, co-chmn. bd., 2004—. Lt. USNR, 1968-71. Office: Boston Consulting Group Inc 200 S Wacker Dr Ste 2700 Chicago IL 60606-5846

STERN, COLIN D., lawyer, retail executive; b. Johannesburg, Dec. 3, 1948; BA, U. Witwatersrand, South Africa, 1970; LL.B. cum laude, U. Witwatersrand, 1971; LL.M., Harvard U., 1978; LL.M. in Taxation, Temple U., 1984. Bar: Transvaal, South Africa 1974, Pa. 1979, U.S. Dist. Ct. (ea. dist.) Pa. 1979. Assoc. Morgan, Lewis & Bockius, 1978-80; assoc., ptnr. Cohen, Shapiro, Polisher, Shiekman & Cohen, 1980-89; exec. v.p., gen. counsel Charming Shoppes, Inc., Bensalem, Pa., 1991—. Mem. ABA, Pa. Bar Assn., Phila. Bar Assn. Office: Charming Shoppes Inc 450 Winks Ln Bensalem PA 19020-5993 *

STERN, DAVID JOEL, national basketball association commissioner; b. NYC, Sept. 22, 1942; s. William and Anna (Bronstein) Stern; m. Dianne Bock, Nov. 27, 1963; children: Andrew, Eric. BA, Rutgers U., 1963; LLB, Columbia U., 1966. Bar: N.Y. 1963. Assoc. Proskauer Rose Goetz & Mendelsohn, NYC, 1966—74, ptnr., 1974—78; gen. counsel NBA, NYC, 1978—80, exec. v.p. bus. & legal affairs, 1980—84, commr., 1984—. Mem. Martin Luther King Jr. Fed. Holiday Commn., 1988—; White House Conf. for a Drug-Free Am., 1988; bd. dirs. NAACP, 1990—93; trustee Beth Israel Med. Ctr., 1985—, Rutgers U. Found., 1987—, Columbia U., 1992—. Named to Internat. Jewish Sports Hall of Fame, 1998. Mem.: ABA, Assn. Bar City NY (chmn. com. on entertainment and sports 1983—86), NY State Bar Assn. Achievements include assisting in creation of NBA Entertainment Divsn. Office: NBA Olympic Tower 645 5th Ave Fl 10 New York NY 10022-5986 *

STERN, DAVID MARK, dean, educator; b. Great Neck, NY; s. Robert and Florence Stern; m. Kathleen Shirley Stern; children: Eric David, Alan Robert. BS, Yale U., 1973; MD, Harvard U., 1978. Mem. faculty Coll. Physicians and Surgeons, Columbia U., NYC, 1983—2002, named Gerald & Janet Carrus Prof. of Surg. Sci., 1998, dir. Ctr. Vascular and Lung Pathobiology, dir. Juvenile Diabetes Rsch. Ctr.; dean sch. medicine, sr. v.p. clin. activities Med. Coll. Ga., Augusta, 2002—05, prof. medicine, physiology and grad. studies, 2002—05; Christian R. Holmes prof. medicine U. Cincinnati, 2005—, dean Coll. Medicine, 2005—. Mem.: Am. Assn. Physicians, Am. Soc. Clin. Investigation. Office: Univ Cincinnati Coll Medicine 231 Albert Sabin Way PO Box 670552 Cincinnati OH 45267-0552 Office Phone: 513-558-7334. Business E-Mail: dstern@mail.mcg.edu. E-mail: david.stern@uc.edu.

STERN, DONALD ALLAN, lawyer; b. NYC, Apr. 13, 1954; s. Robert and Florence S.; m. Antje Mewes, Sept. 14, 1989; children: Elizabeth, Robert. AB, Harvard U., 1976, JD, 1980. Assoc. Cleary, Gottlieb, Steen & Hamilton, NYC, 1980-88, ptnr., 1989—. Corp. trustee Jackson Lab., Bar Harbor, Maine, 1986-90, governing trustee, 1990—, chmn. bd., chmn. exec. com., chmn. compensation com., 2001-06, life trustee, 2006—; unit commr. Boy Scouts Am., Nassau County, N.Y., 1992—; commr.-at-large Village of Thomaston, 1998—. Office: Cleary Gottlieb Steen & Hamilton 1 Liberty Plz Fl 38 New York NY 10006-1470 Office Phone: 212-225-2640. E-mail: dstern@cgsh.com.

STERN, DONALD KENNETH, lawyer; BA, Hobart Coll., 1966; JD, Georgetown U., 1969; LLM, U. Pa., 1973. Intern Dist. Atty.'s Office, Mineola, NY, 1967, Citizen's Adv. Ctr., Washington, 1968; staff atty. Defender Assn. Phila., Cmty. Legal Svcs., Phila., 1969-71; adj. prof. law, supervising atty. Boston Coll. Law Sch., Boston Coll. Legal Assistance Bur., 1971-73, asst. prof. law, dir. clin. programs, supervising atty., 1973-75; asst. atty. gen., dir. atty. gen. clin. program, Mass. Atty. Gen.'s Office, Boston Coll. Law Sch., 1975-77, asst. prof. law, dir. atty. gen. clin. program, spl. asst. atty. gen., 1977-78, asst. atty. gen., dir. atty. gen. clin. program, 1978-79; chief govt. bur. Mass. Atty. Gen.'s Office, 1979-82; assoc. Hale and Dorr, Boston, 1982-85, jr. ptnr., 1985-87, sr. ptnr., 1987, 91-93, of counsel, 1990-91; chief legal counsel to Gov. Mass., 1987-90; U.S. atty. Dist. Mass., 1993—2001; ptnr. Bingham McCutchen, LLP, 2001—; lectr. Harvard Law Sch., 2002—05. Office: Bingham McCutchen LLP 150 Federal St Boston MA 02210-1726 Office Phone: 617-951-8250. E-mail: donald.stern@bingham.com.

STERN, EDWARD ABRAHAM, physics professor; b. Detroit, Sept. 19, 1930; s. Jacob Munich and Rose (Kravitz) S.; m. Sylvia Rita Sidell, Oct. 30, 1955; children: Hilary, Shari, Miri. BS, Calif. Tech., 1951, PhD, 1955. Post-doctoral fellow Calif. Tech., Pasadena, 1955-57; asst. prof. U. Md., College Park, 1957-61, assoc. prof., 1961-64, prof., 1964-65, U. Wash., Seattle, 1965—2000, emeritus, 2000—. Contbr. over 200 articles to profl. jours.; editor; three books. Recipient B. Warren award Am. Crystallography Assn., 1979, Outstanding Achievement award Internat. XAFS Soc., 2000; named Guggenheim fellow, Cambridge, Eng., 1963-64, NSF Sr. Post-doctoral fellow, Haifa, Israel, 1970-71, Fulbright fellow, Jerusalem, Israel, 1985-86. Fellow AAAS, Am. Physical Soc. Achievements include patent for x-ray focusing device; development of x-ray absorption fine structure technique; research on surface plasmons, nonlinear reflection from surfaces, electronic properties of alloys, structural phase transition; named Father of EXAFS. Office: U Wash Dept Physics PO Box 351560 Seattle WA 98195-1560 Home Phone: 206-525-2771; Office Phone: 206-543-2023. Business E-Mail: stern@phys.washington.edu.

STERN, ELIZABETH ESPIN, lawyer; b. Prince Georges County, Md., June 21, 1961; d. Cesar A. and M. Cecilia (Salvador) E.; m. Michael L. Stern, May 16, 1992; children: Alexander, David. BA magna cum laude, U. Va., 1983; JD, U. Va. Sch. Law, 1986. Bar: Va. 1986, U.S. Dist. Ct. (Ea. Dist.) Va., D.C. 1988, Supreme Ct. Va., U.S. Ct. Appeals, D.C. Cir. Ptnr. comml. immigration Pillsbury Winthrop Shaw Pittman LLP (formerly Shaw Pittman LLP), Washington, 1986—2005, ptnr. & head bus. immigration practice group, 2005; ptnr., head global migration and exec. transfers Baker & McKenzie LLP, Washington, 2005—. Spkr. in field. Named one of Top 30 lawyers in Washington, Washingtonian Mag., 2004, Top 10 Immigration Lawyers in DC, Legal Times, 2006, DC Super Lawyers, 2007; recipient Martin Preis award, Vol. Bar Assn. D.C., 1992. Fellow: ABA, Bar Assn. D.C. (chair immigration com.); mem.: U.S. C. of C., Internat. Sects. Am. Immigration Lawyers Assn., Soc. for Human Resources Mgmt., Immigration Tech. Assn. Am., D.C. Bar Assn. (internat. sec. 1986—, chair young lawyers sect. 1992—93, del. to ABA, Young Lawyer of Yr. 1994), Va. Bar Assn., Am. Immigration Lawyers Assn., Washington Internat. Trade Assn. Republican. Avocation: journalism. Office: Baker & McKenzie LLP 815 Connecticut Ave NW Washington DC 20006-4078 Office Phone: 202-452-7000. Business E-Mail: elizabeth.e.stern@bakernet.com.

STERN, ERIC L., lawyer; b. Dec. 2, 1956; m. Jacqueline S. Stern. BA, Brandeis U., 1978; JD, Boston Coll. Law Sch., 1981. Bar: Pa. 1981, Mass. 1987. Ptnr. Morgan, Lewis & Bockius LLP, Phila., leader firmwide real estate practice. Mem.: Internat. Coun. Shopping Ctrs., Internat. Assn. Attys. and Execs. Corp. Real Estate, Phila. Region Nat. Assn. Indsl. and Office Properties, Samuel Zell and Robert Lurie Real Estate Ctr.-Wharton Sch. U. Pa., Am. Coll. Real Estate Lawyers. Office: Morgan Lewis & Bockius LLP 1701 Market St Philadelphia PA 19103 Office Phone: 215-963-5178. Office Fax: 215-963-5001. Business E-Mail: estern@morganlewis.com.

STERN, FRITZ RICHARD, historian, educator; b. Breslau, Germany, Feb. 2, 1926; came to U.S., 1938, naturalized, 1947; s. Rudolf A. and Catherine (Brieger) S.; m. Margaret J. Bassett, Oct. 11, 1947 (div. 1992); children: Frederick P., Katherine Stern Brennan; m. Elisabeth Niebuhr Sifton, Jan. 1, 1996. BA, Columbia U., 1946, MA, 1948, PhD, 1953; DLitt (hon.), Oxford U., 1985; LLD (hon.), New Sch. for Social Rsch., 1997, Columbia U., 1998; LLD (hon.), U. Wroclaw, 2002. Lectr., instr. Columbia U., 1946-51, faculty, 1953—, prof. history, 1963—, Seth Low prof. history, 1967-92, univ. prof., 1992-96, provost, 1980-83; acting asst. prof. Cornell U., 1951-53; univ. prof. emeritus Columbia U., 1997—; tchr. Free U. Berlin, 1954, Yale U., 1963; permanent vis. prof. U. Konstanz, West Germany, 1966—; sr. adviser U.S. Embassy, Bonn, 1993-94. Élie Halévy prof. U. Paris, spring 1979; Phi Beta Kappa vis. scholar, 1979-80; Tanner lectr. Yale, 1993. Author: The Politics of Cultural Despair, 1961, The Failure of Illiberalism-Essays in the Political Culture of Modern Germany, 1972, rev. edit., 1992, Gold and Iron: Bismarck, Bleichroeder and the Bldg. of the German Empire, 1977 (recipient Lionel Trilling award Columbia U.), Dreams and Delusions: The Drama of German History, 1987, rev. edit. 1999, Einstein's German World, 1999; editor: The Varieties of History, 1956, 71, (with L. Krieger) The Responsibility of Power, 1967; mem. editorial bd. Foreign Affairs, 1978-92; contbr. articles to profl. jours.; reviewer Fgn. Affairs, 1963-95. Trustee German Marshall Fund, 1981-99, Aspen Inst. of Berlin, 1983—; senator Deutsche Nationalstiftung, 1994—; mem. Trilateral Commn., 1983-90. Decorated Officer's Cross Order of Merit Fed. Republic of Germany; fellow Center Advanced Behavioral Scis., 1957-58; fellow Social Sci. Research Council, 1960-61; fellow Am. Council Learned Socs., 1966-67; fellow Netherlands Inst. Advanced Study, 1972-73; mem. Nuffield Coll., Oxford, 1966-67, Inst. Advanced Study Princeton, 1969-70; Guggenheim fellow, 1969-70; Ford Found. grantee, 1976-77; vis. scholar Russell Sage Found., 1989, spring 1993; recipient Leopold-Lucas-prize Evang. Faculty U. Tübingen, 1984, Peace prize German Book Trade Frankfurt Book Fair, 1999, Bruno Snell medal U. Hamburg, 2002, Leo Baeck medal, NY, 2004, Nationalpreis, Berlin, 2005. Mem. Am. Hist. Assn., AAAS, Am. Philos. Soc., Coun. Fgn. Rels., Deutsche Akademie für Sprache und Dichtung (corr.), Berlin Brandenburgische Akademie der Wissenschaften (corr.), Orden Pour le Mérite, Germany, Phi Beta Kappa (senator-at-large 1973-78). Clubs: Century (N.Y.C.). Home: 15 Claremont Ave New York NY 10027-6802 E-mail: fs20@columbia.edu.

STERN, GARY HILTON, bank executive; b. San Luis Obispo, Calif., Nov. 3, 1944; s. Robert Earl and Joy Merdis (Shimon) S.; m. Mary Katherine Nelson, Aug. 17, 1969; children: Matthew Stuart, Meredith Faulkner. AB, Washington U., St. Louis, 1967; MA, Rice U., 1970, PhD, 1972. Economist Fed. Res. Bank of N.Y., NYC, 1970-73, mgr. domestic research, 1973-77; mgr. fixed income research Loeb Rhoades, Hornblower, NYC, 1977-78; sr. economist A.G. Shilling & Co., NYC, 1978-81; sr. v.p. Fed. Res. Bank Mpls., 1982-85, CFO, 1983, pres., CEO, 1985—. Adj. assoc. prof. NYU, 1980-82; adj. asst. prof. Columbia U., 1976-79 Author: In the Name of Money, 1980. Trustee West Side Montessori Sch., N.Y.C., 1978-79; bd. dirs. Nat. Coun. Econ. Edn., N.W. Area Found., Carlson Sch. Mgmt. U. Minn.; bd. trustees Hamline U., Mpls. Coll. Art and Design. NDEA scholar, 1969-70; Bache & Co. scholar, 1963-67; univ. scholar Washington U.-St. Louis, 1964-67, Rice U.-Houston, 1967-70 Mem.: Mpls. Club (treas.). Office: Fed Res Bank Mpls 90 Hennepin Ave Minneapolis MN 55401 Office Phone: 612-204-5000. *

STERN, GEOFFREY, lawyer; b. Columbus, Ohio, Nov. 29, 1942; s. Leonard J. and Anastasia (Percin) S.; m. Barbara Shnider; children: Emily Staheli, Elizabeth Leskowyak; stepchildren: Courtney, Jennifer, Brian Feuer. Student, Williams Coll., 1960-63; BA cum laude, Ohio State U., 1965, JD summa cum laude, 1968. Bar: Ohio 1968. Assoc. Alexander, Ebinger, Holschuh & Fisher, Columbus, Ohio, 1968-72; ptnr. Folkerth, Calhoun, Webster & O'Brien, Columbus, Ohio, 1972-80, Arter & Hadden, Columbus, Ohio, 1980-93; disciplinary counsel Supreme Ct. of Ohio, 1993-97; counsel Kegler, Brown, Hill & Ritter, Columbus, 1997-2000, dir., 2000—. Nat. coordinating counsel for asbestos litigation Combustion Engrng. Inc. and Basic, Inc., 1985-93; lectr. on legal ethics and profl. responsibility; mem. Spl. Commn. to Review Ohio Ethics Rules, 1995-98, Spl. Commn. on Legal Edn., 1995-98; mem. symposium on ethics and Chinese legal sys., Shanghai, 1998; keynote spkr. Faith and Law Symposium, 1999; spl. investigator Bd. Commrs. Character and Fitness Ohio Supreme Ct., 1998. Sr. editor Ohio State Law Jour., 1967-68. Pres. Bexley (Ohio) City Coun., 1977-80, mem., 1973-80, mem. Bexley Civil Svc. Commn., 1983-85; v.p., trustee Creative Living, Columbus, 1981-89, Ohio Citizens Com. for Arts, Columbus, 1982-88; mem. Nat. Def. Com. on Asbestos in Bldgs. Litigation, 1986-92; pub. mem. Ohio Optical Dispensers Bd., Columbus, 1978-82. Recipient Am. Jurisprudence Evidence award Ohio State U. Coll. Law, 1967. Fellow Am. Bar Found., Columbus Bar Found., Ohio State Bar Found.; mem. Ohio State Bar Assn. (com. on legal ethics and profl. conduct, sec. 1981-90, vice chmn. 1990-92, chmn. 1992-93), Columbus Bar Assn. (profl. ethics com. 1975-86, 90-93, Liberty Bell award for Cmty. and Profl. Svc. 1998), Order of Coif, Phi Beta Kappa, Pi Sigma Alpha. Home: 278 Crossing Crk N Columbus OH 43230-6108 Office: Kegler Brown Hill & Ritter 65 E State St Ste 1800 Columbus OH 43215-4213 Office Phone: 614-462-5400. Business E-Mail: gstern@keglerbrown.com.

STERN, GERALD MANN, lawyer; b. Chgo., Apr. 5, 1937; s. Lloyd and Fannye (Wener) S.; m. Linda Stone, Dec. 20, 1969; children: Eric, Jesse, Maia. BS in Econs., U. Pa., 1958; LL.B. cum laude, Harvard, 1961. Bar: D.C. 1961, Calif. 1991, U.S. Supreme Ct. 1971. Trial atty. civil rights div. U.S. Dept. Justice, 1961-64; assoc. firm Arnold & Porter, Washington, 1964-68, ptnr., 1969-76; founding ptnr. Rogovin, Stern & Huge, Washington, 1976-81; exec. v.p., sr. gen. counsel Occidental Petroleum Corp., LA, 1981—92; spl. counsel fin. instn. fraud and health care fraud U.S. Dept. Justice, Washington, 1993-95; intl. legal cons. pvt. practice, Washington, 1995—; cons. Antitrust divsn. U.S. Dept. Justice, 1998—2001. Bd. dirs. Oceania Cruises, Inc., Miami, Fla., Pitzer Coll., Claremont, Calif. Author: The Buffalo Creek Disaster, 1976; co-author: Southern Justice, 1965, Outside the Law, 1997. Trustee Facing History and Ourselves, 1996. Home and Office: 3322 Newark St NW Washington DC 20008-3330 Office Phone: 202-253-2257, 202-362-2078. Fax: 202-364-2595. E-mail: GMS37@aol.com.

STERN, HAL, information technology executive; BS, Princeton U., NJ. Mem. rsch. staff massive memory project Princeton U.; mem. tech. staff Polygen Corp.; with Sun Microsystems, Inc., Santa Clara, Calif., 1991—, chief technologist NE US sales area, chief tech. officer Sun ONE (iPlanet) infrastructure products, chief arch. Sun profl. svcs., chief tech. officer Sun svcs., v.p., chief tech. officer software, 2005, sr. v.p. systems engrng. Author: Managing NFS and NIS; contbg. editor: SunWorld Mag.; mem. editl. staff, adv. bd. JavaWorld mag. Office: Sun Microsystems Inc 4150 Network Cir Santa Clara CA 95054 Office Phone: 650-960-1300. *

STERN, HERBERT JAY, lawyer; b. NYC, Nov. 8, 1936; s. Samuel and Sophie (Berkowitz) S.; children: Jason Andrew and Jordan Ezekiel (twins), Samuel Abraham, Sarah Kathrine. BA, Hobart Coll., 1958; JD (Ford Found. scholar), U. Chgo., 1961; LL.D. (hon.), Seton Hall Law Sch., 1973, Hobart Coll., 1974; L.H.D. (hon.), Newark State Coll., 1973; D.C.L. (hon.), Bloomfield Coll., 1973; Litt.D. (hon.), Montclair State Coll., 1973. Bar: N.Y. 1961, N.J. 1971. Asst. dist. atty., New York County, 1962-65; trial atty. organized crime and racketeering sect. Dept. of Justice, 1965-69; chief asst. U.S. atty. Dist. of N.J., Newark, 1969-70, U.S. atty., 1971-74, U.S. dist. judge, 1974-87; ptnr. Stern & Kilcullen, Roseland, NJ, 1990—. Adv. com. U. Chgo. Law Sch. Author: Judgment in Berlin, 1984 (Valley Forge award Freedoms Found. 1984, Torch of Learning award Am. Friends of Hebrew U. 1987), Trying Cases to Win, Vol. I, 1991, Vol. II, 1992, Vol. III, 1993, Vol. IV, 1995; co-author: Trying Cases to Win, Anatomy of A Trial, 1999, Trying Cases to Win: Evidence Weapons for Winning, Vol. I, 2000, Vol. II, 2003, Vol. III, 2004; subject of book Tiger in the Court, 1973. Trustee Hobart and William Smith Colls. Named One of America's 10 Outstanding Young Men U.S. Jr. C. of C., 1971; Swartzer scholar U. Chgo. Law Sch., 1985; recipient Dean's Club award U. Akron Sch. Law, 1986, medal of excellence Hobart Coll., 1990, Citizen's award N.J. Acad. Medicine, 1997. Fellow ABA, Am. Law Inst. (Clarence Darrow award), Internat. Platform Assn.; mem. ABA, N.J. Bar Assn., Fed. Bar Assn. (past pres. Newark chpt., recipient William J. Brennan, Jr. award 1987), Essex County Bar Assn., Am. Judicature Soc., Phi Alpha Delta. Achievements include being subject of book Tiger in the Court, 1973. Office: 75 Livingston Ave Roseland NJ 07068-3701 E-mail: dpenna@sgklaw.com.

STERN, HOWARD ALLAN, radio personality, television show host; b. Jackson Heights, NY, Jan. 12, 1954; s. Ben and Rae S.; m. Alison Berns, 1978 (div. 2001); children: Emily, Debra, Ashley Jade. BA in Comm., Boston U., 1976. Disc jockey Sta. WRNW, Briarcliff Manor, NY, 1976-78, Sta. WCCC, Hartford, Conn., 1978-79, Sta. WWWW, Detroit, 1979-80, Sta. WWDC, Washington, 1980-82, Sta. WNBC, NYC, 1982-85, Sta. WXRK, NYC, 1985—2005, numerous other markets, 1986—2005; disc jockey Howard Stern Show Sirius Satellite Radio, 2006—. Author: Private Parts, 1993, Miss America, 1995; TV shows include The Howard Stern Show (WOR-TV), 1990-92, The Howard Stern Interview (E!), 1992-93, The Howard Stern Show (E!), 1994-2005, Howard Stern on Demand, 2005-; actor (films) Private Parts, 1997; writer, exec. prodr., voice Doomsday, 2000; writer, exec. prodr. (TV series) Son of the Beach, 2000-02; recordings include 50 Ways To Rank Your Mother, 1982, Crucified by the FCC, 1991; pay-per-view spls./videos include: Howard Stern's Négligé and Underpants Party, U.S. Open Sores, Butt Bongo Fiesta, The Miss Howard Stern New Year's Eve Pageant. Libertarian candidate for gov. State of NY, 1994. Rest Stop on I-295 in NJ named in his honor, 1995, recipient Rave Awards, Wired Renegade, WIRED, 2005; named one of 100 Most Influential People, Time Mag., 2006 Office: care Don Buchwald & Associates 10 E 44th St New York NY 10017-3601

STERN, JAMES ANDREW, investment banker; b. NYC, Oct. 1, 1950; s. Arthur and Lenore (Oppenheimer) S.; m. Jane Yusem, April 13, 1975; children: Peter, David. BS, Tufts U., 1972; MBA, Harvard U., 1974. Assoc. Lehman Bros. Inc., NYC, 1974-79, v.p., 1979-82, mng. dir., 1982-94; chmn. The Cypress Group, NYC, 1994—. Bd. dirs. Lear Corp., Southfield, Mich., Affinia Group Inc., Medpointe Inc. Trustee Tufts U., Medford, Mass., 1982-, chmm. bd. trustees 2003-, Jewish Mus., N.Y.C.; bd. dirs. Cystic Fibrosis Found. Mem. Quaker Ridge Golf Club (Scarsdale, NY), Beach Point Club (Mamaroneck, NY). Avocations: golf, reading. Office: The Cypress Group Inc 65 E 55th St New York NY 10022-3219 Office Phone: 212-705-0151. Business E-Mail: jstern@cypressgp.com.

STERN, JEAN, museum director; b. Casablanca, Morocco, Mar. 28, 1946; arrived in U.S., 1955, naturalized, 1962; s. Frederic and Sultana Stern; m. Linda Susan Stern, Jan. 18, 2004; m. Carol Elizabeth Adams (div.); children: Carrie Dona, Hannah Marie. BA History, Calif. State, Northridge, Calif., 1968; MA Art History, Calif. State, San Diego, Calif., 1972; post graduate, UCLA, LA. Instr. San Diego State Univ., San Diego, 1974—76; instr. art history Mesa Coll., San Diego, 1976; dir. Petersen Galleries, Beverly Hills, Calif., 1978—91; exec. dir. The Irvine Mus., Irvine, Calif., 1992—. Guest curator San Diego Mus. of Art, San Diego, 1976. Co-author: Enchanted Isle, 2003, California, This Golden Land, 2001; contbr. essays, articles pub. numerous to profl. jour. Mem.: Am. Assn. Mus., Calif. Art Club (Man of the Yr. 1998). Avocation: coin collecting/numismatics. Office: The Irvine Mus 18881 Von Karman #100 Irvine CA 92612 Office Phone: 949-476-0294.

STERN, JOAN NAOMI, lawyer; b. Phila., Mar. 7, 1944; d. Clarence J. and Diana D. (Goldberg) S. BA, U. Pa., 1965; JD, Temple U., 1977. Bar: Pa. 1977. Assoc. Blank Rome LLP, Phila., 1977—83, ptnr., 1983—, co-chair pub. fin. group, 1983-92, chair pub. fin. group, 1993, chair pub. fin. dept., 1994—. Cons. counsel Phila. Charter Commn., 1993-94. Contbr. articles to profl. jours. Mem. Sch. Dist. Task Force on Regulatory Reform, Phila., 1987, Tax Policy and Budget Com., Phila., 1989, Phila. Mayor's Fiscal Adv. Com., 1990; chair Sch. Dist. of Phila. Task Force on Alt. Financing Strategies, 1995; bd. mgrs. Moore Coll. Art and Design, Phila., 1993—, vice chair bd. trustees, 1995-, bd. mgrs., 1995—; bd. dirs. Police Athletic League, Phila., 1994—, Urban Tree Connection, 2000—; trustee The Franklin Inst., 2004—, Thomas Skelton Harrison Found., 2006—; bd. dirs. Am. Jewish Congress, 1995—, Jewish Fedn. of Greater Phila., 2000—. Fellow Am. Bar Found. (life); mem. ABA, Nat. Assn. Bond Lawyers, Phila. Bar Assn., Phila. Bar Assn. (chmn. mcpl. govt. com. 1983-97), Pa. Assn. Bond Lawyers. Office: Blank Rome LLP One Logan Square Philadelphia PA 19103-6998 Office Phone: 215-569-5526. E-mail: stern@blankrome.com.

STERN, JOSEPH A., lawyer; b. Cleve., Dec. 7, 1949; s. Arthur J. and Thelma (Arnold) S. BA, Yale U., 1972, JD, 1976. Assoc. Winthrop Stimson, NYC, 1976-79, Fried Frank Harris Shriver & Jacobson, NYC, London, 1979-84, ptnr., 1984—2005; gen. counsel, exec. v.p., corp. sec. Dow Jones & Co., 2005—. Chmn., dir. Mex. Am. Legal Defense and Edn. Fund, L.A., 1991-95; dir. Am. Friend Chamber Music of Europe, N.Y.C., 1986—. Mem. ABA, City Bar N.Y., Am. Law Inst.

STERN, JOSEPH SMITH, JR., former footwear manufacturing company executive; b. Cin., Mar. 31, 1918; s. Joseph S. and Miriam (Haas) S.; m. Mary Stern, June 14, 1942; children: Peter Joseph, William Frederick, Peggy Ann Graeter. AB, Harvard U., 1940, MBA, 1943; HHD (hon.), Xavier U., 1988; DSc (hon.), U. Cin., 1998. With R. H. Macy & Co., NYC, 1940-41; with U.S. Shoe Corp., Cin., 1941-68, v.p., 1951-65, pres., 1965-66, chmn. bd., chief exec. officer, 1966, chmn. exec. com., 1966-68, dir., 1956-70. Prof. bus. policy emeritus U. Cin. Pres. bd. trustees Cin. and Hamilton County Pub. Libr.; chmn. Cin. Bicentennial Com., Greater Cin. Tall Stacks Commn.; trustee Cin. Music Hall Assn., Cin. Hist. Soc., Children's Hosp. Med. Center, Cin. Symphony Orch., Cin Country Day Sch., 1956-72, Family Svc., Cin., 1964-82; trustee, pres. Cin. Mus. Festival Assn.; pres. bd. trustees Children's Convalescent Hosp., Cin., 1972-75; bd. overseers vis. com. univ. libr. Harvard U. Served to lt. USNR, 1943-46. Recipient Disting. Community Svc. award NCCJ, 1986, Great Living Cincinnatian award Cin. C. of C., 1989, Disting. Svc. award U. Cin. Coll. Bus., 1992. Mem. Am. Footwear Industries Assn. (life; dir.) Jewish (past pres. temple). Clubs: Literary (Cin.), Harvard (Cin.) (pres. 1965), Queen City (Cin.), Queen City Optimists, Harvard (N.Y.C.). Home: 3 Grandin Pl Cincinnati OH 45208-3402

STERN, JUDITH SCHNEIDER, nutritionist, researcher, educator; b. Bklyn. d. Sidney and Lillian (Rosen) Schneider; m. Richard C. Stern; 1 child, Daniel Arthur. BS, Cornell U., 1964; MS, Harvard U. Sch. Pub. Health, 1966, ScD, 1970. Rsch. asst., dept. food sci. and nutrition MIT, Cambridge, 1964—65; rsch. assoc. dept. human behavior and metabolism The Rockefeller U., NYC, 1968—72, asst. prof. dept. human behavior and metabolism, 1972—74; contbg. editor Vogue Mag., Conde Nast Publs.,

NYC, 1974; asst. prof. nutrition U. Calif., Davis, 1975—77, assoc. prof. dept. nutrition, 1977—82, dir. food intake lab. group, 1980—2001, prof. dept. nutrition, 1982—, prof. divsn. endocrinology, clin. nutrition and vascular biology, 1988—, disting. prof., 2003—. Mem. editl. bd. Internat. Jour. Obesity, 1976-85, Appetite, 1990, Obesity Rsch., 1993—2002, Nutrition Today, 1999—. Bd. sci. advisors Am. Coun. Sci. and Health, 1980—; mem. U.S. Dept. Agr. Dietary Guidelines Adv. Com., 1983—85; mem. obesity task force NIDDK, 1996—2002, AAAS; mem. expert com. U.S. Pharmacopeia Bioavailability and Nutrient Absorption, 2000—03; mem. adv. bd. USDA Nat. Agrl. Rsch. Ext., Edn. and Econs., 2000—03. Recipient Sec.'s Honor award USDA, 2004; NIH tng. grantee, 1979-2006. Fellow Am. Heart Assn.; mem. Am. Soc. Clin. Nutrition (pres. 1995-96), Am. Dietetic Assn., Am. Diabetes Assn., Am. Obesity Assn. (co-founder, v.p. 1995-), N.Am. Assn. for Study of Obesity (pres. 1992-93), Inst. Medicine of NAS, Inst. Food Technologists, Am. Soc. Nutrition Sci. (chair pub. info. com. 1992-94), Sigma Xi, Delta Omega. Office: U Calif Dept Nutrition 1 Shields Ave Davis CA 95616-5271 Home Phone: 530-297-5550; Office Phone: 530-752-6575. Business E-Mail: jsstern@ucdavis.edu.

STERN, JULIAN NATHANIEL, lawyer, pharmaceutical executive; b. NYC, Oct. 13, 1924; s. Mark James and Celia (Bluestone) Stern; m. Dorothy Bennett, Oct. 15, 1956; children: John Hiram, Michael Vaughn. BS, NYU, NYC, 1946; LLB, Yale U., New Haven, 1949. Bar: NY 1950, DC 1951, Calif. 1956. Ptnr. Heller Ehrman LLP, Menlo Park, Calif., 1960—2006; chmn. bd. dirs. Pherin Pharm. Inc., Redwood City, Calif., 2004—. Bd. dirs., corp. sec. FibroGen, Inc., South San Francisco, Calif., 1993—, DepoMed, Inc., Menlo Park, Calif., 1996—, Roxro Pharm., Inc., Menlo Park, 2001—. Contbr. articles to legal jours.; revising editor: Mertens Law of Taxation, 1955—56. Trustee Am. Cancer Soc., Calif., 1966—, chmn. Calif., 1988—89; pres. Alta Bates Hosp. Found., Berkeley, Calif., 1985—86; trustee, treas. U. Calif. Mus., Berkeley, 1970—72; trustee Gasser Found., 1993—; pres., trustee Williams Found., 2001—; chmn. Fedn. Dem. Clubs, Contra Costa, Calif., 1966—68. With US Army, 1943—46, ETO. Recipient St. George medal, Am. Cancer Soc., 1990. Avocation: tennis. Office: Heller Ehrman LLP 275 Middlefield Rd Menlo Park CA 94025 Office Phone: 650-324-7039.

STERN, KENNETH P., broadcast executive; b. 1963; BA, Haverford Coll.; JD, Yale U. Mgmt. and legal cons. Radio Free Europe/Radio Liberty, Munich and Prague; dep. gen. counsel Clinton/Gore Campaign, 1996; chief counsel 53rd Presdl. Inaugural Com.; sr. adv., cons. to dir., dir. affiliate rels., rsch. & media training US Internat. Broadcasting Bur., Washington, 1996—99; exec. v.p. Nat. Pub. Radio (NPR), 1999—, CEO, 2006—. Recipient Harold Kurzman Prize in Polit. Sci. Mem.: Phi Beta Kappa. Office: NPR 635 Massachusetts Ave, NW Washington DC 20001 Office Phone: 202-513-2000. Office Fax: 202-513-3329.

STERN, LEO G., lawyer; b. Mpls., Apr. 10, 1945; s. Philip J. and June I. (Monasch) S.; m. Christine E. Lamb, June 29, 1968; children: Alison M., Zachary A. BA, U. Calif., Davis, 1967; JD cum laude, U. Minn., 1970. Bar: Minn. 1970, U.S. Dist. Ct. Minn. 1971, Calif. 1971, U.S. Ct. Appeals (6th, 7th and 8th cirs.) 1985, U.S. Supreme Ct. 1993, Wis. 1999; cert. mediator and arbitrator, Minn. Ptnr. Cox, King & Stern, Mpls., 1970-77, Wright, West & Diessner, Mpls., 1977-84, Fredrikson & Byron, P.A., Mpls., 1984—. Mem. Minn. Bar Assn. (governing coun. environ. and natural resources law sect. 1989-95, governing coun. litig. sect. 1995-99), Am. Arbitration Assn. (arbitrator, mediator), Nat. Arbitration Forum, Nat. Assn. Securities Dealers, Internat. Inst. Conflict Prevention and Resolution. Avocations: sailing, jogging. Home: 206 Central Ave S Wayzata MN 55391-1818 Office: Fredrikson & Byron PA 4000 US Bank Plz 200 S 6th St Minneapolis MN 55402 Home Phone: 952-476-2461; Office Phone: 612-492-7061. Business E-Mail: lstern@fredlaw.com.

STERN, LEONARD NORMAN, real estate developer, former pet supply manufacturing company executive; b. NYC, Mar. 28, 1938; s. Max and Hilda (Lowenthal) Stern; m. Judith Stern (div.); children: Emanuel Theodore, Edward Julius, Andrea Caroline; m. Allison Maher, 1987. BS cum laude, NYU, 1956, MBA, 1957; DHL (hon.), Yeshiva U., 1985; LLD (hon.), Fairleigh Dickinson, 1995. Formerly pres., dir., now chmn., CEO Hartz Group, Inc., 1959—, sold pet div., 1999; chmn., CEO Hartz Mountain Industries Inc., 1966—; founder Stern Pub., 1986—99; owner 667 Madison Ave., NYC, Tribeca Grand Hotel, NYC, SoHo Grand Hotel, NYC, Harmon Cove, Secaucus, NJ, Lincoln Harbor, Weehawken, NJ, Colgate Ctr., Jersey City, Journal Square, Jersey City. Mem. adv. bd. Chem. Bank, NYC, 1970-; active real estate constrn., devel. Bd. dirs. Manhattan Day Sch., Jewish Ctr., NYC; founder Albert Einstein Coll. Medicine, 1958; mem. NYC Holocaust Meml. Commn.; founder Homes for the Homeless, 1986-; trustee NYU, 1976-1996, former chmn. fin. com. Named Graduate and Undergraduate Schs. of Bus. The Leonard N. Stern Sch. Bus., NYU, 1984; named one of Forbes' Richest Americans, 1999—, World's Richest People, Forbes mag., 2001—; recipient Albert Gallatin medal, NYU. Office: Hartz Group 667 Madison Ave 26th Floor New York NY 10021 *

STERN, LOUIS WILLIAM, marketing educator, consultant; b. Boston, Sept. 19, 1935; s. Berthold Summerfield Stern and Gladys (Koch) Cohen; m. Rhona L. Grant; children: Beth Ida, Deborah Lynn. AB, Harvard U., 1957; MBA in Mktg, U. Pa., 1959; PhD in Mktg, Northwestern U., 1962. Mem. staff bus. research and consumer mktg. sects. Arthur D. Little, Inc., Cambridge, Mass., 1961-63; from asst. prof. bus. orgn. to prof. Ohio State U., Columbus, Ohio, 1963—70, prof. mktg., 1970—73; from prof. mktg. to A. Montgomery Ward prof. mktg. Northwestern U., 1973—83, John D. Gray disting. prof. mktg., 1983—2001, John D. Gray disting. prof. emeritus mktg., 2001—; on leave as exec. dir. Mktg. Sci. Inst., Cambridge, Mass., 1983-85; Thomas Henry Carroll Ford Found. vis. prof. Harvard U. Grad. Sch. Bus. Adminstrn., 1984-85; Dorinda and Mark Winkelman Disting. Scholar sr. fellow, co-dir. Jay H. Baker Retailing Initiative, The Wharton Sch., U. Pa., 2004—06; mem. bd. trustees Williston Northhampton Sch., Easthampton, Mass. Mem. staff Nat. Commn. on Food Mktg., Washington, 1965-66; vis. assoc. prof. bus. adminstrn. U. Calif., Berkeley, 1969-70; guest lectr. York U., U. Minn., U. Ky., UCLA, Ohio State U., U. N.C., Duke U., U. Wis., U. Pitts., U. Chgo., MIT, U. Mich., U. Pa., Cornell U., U. Mo., Norwegian Sch. Econs. and Bus. Adminstrn.; faculty assoc. Hernstein Inst., Vienna, Austria, 1976-77, Mgmt. Centre Europe, 1988-96; faculty assoc. Gemini Cons. Inc., Montvale, N.J., 1977-96, mem. midwest adv. bd., 1989-94; Xerox rsch. prof. Northwestern U., 1981-82; cons. to FTC, 1973, 80; vis. scholar U. Calif., Berkeley, 1997-2001; mem. faculty adv. bd. CSC Index, 1997-98; co-dir. Jay H. Baker Retailing Initiative Wharton Sch., U. Pa., 2004. Author: Distribution Channels: Behavioral Dimensions, 1969, (with Frederick D. Sturdivant and others) Managerial Analysis in Marketing, 1970, Perspectives in Marketing Management, 1971, (with John R. Grabner, Jr.) Competition in the Marketplace, 1970, (with Anne T. Coughlan, Erin Anderson and Adel I. El-Ansary) Marketing Channels, 6th edit., 2001, (with Thomas L. Eovaldi) Legal Aspects of Marketing Strategy: Antitrust and Consumer Protection Issues, 1984; (with Adel I. El-Ansary and James R. Brown) Management in Marketing Channels, 1989; mem. editl. bd. Jour. Mktg. Rsch., 1976-82, Jour. Mktg., 1979-83, Mktg. Letters, 1988-94; contbr. articles to profl. jours. Mem. exec. com. Northwest Area Coun. on Human Rels., Columbus, 1971—72. Rsch. grantee Ohio State U., 1964-73, Mktg. Sci. Inst., 1976-77, 88-90, 92-94; recipient Harold H. Maynard award best article Jour. Mktg., 1980, Kellogg's Spl. Lifetime Achievement Award for Tchg. Excellence, 1999; named Mktg. Educator of Yr. Sales and Mktg. Execs. Internat., 1989, also Chgo. chpt. 1990, Outstanding Profl. of Yr. award, 1992, and named One of Top 6 Profs. in Kellogg Sch., Northwestern U., Grad. Mgmt. Assocs., 1984-94, (named 6 times Outstanding Prof. Exec. Masters Program), One of Top 12 Tchrs. in U.S., U.S. Bus. Schs., Bus. Week; named Dorinda and Mark Winkelman Disting. scholar, Sr. fellow Wharton Sch., U. Pa., 2004. Mem. AAUP, Am. Mktg. Assn. (mem. program com. educators conf. 1971, chmn. com. 1978, Paul D. Converse award 1986, Richard D. Irwin Disting. Mktg. Educator of Yr. 1994), Hellenic Inst. Mktg. (hon.), Beta Gamma Sigma. Home: Apt 1401 800 Elgin Rd Evanston IL 60201-5629 Office: Northwestern U Kellogg Sch Mgmt Dept Mktg Evanston IL 60208-2001 Home Phone: 847-866-8952; Office Phone: 847-491-2718. Business E-Mail: lwstern@kellogg.northwestern.edu.

STERN, MARCUS A., journalist; b. Washington; Grad., UCLA. With San Pedro News-Pilot, Calif., States News Svc., Washington; with Washington Bur. Copley News Svc., 1983—, news editor, Washington bur., 2000—. Recipient Eugene Katz award, Ctr. Immigration Studies, 1998, Edgar A. Poe award, White House Corrs. Assn., 2006, George Polk award for polit. reporting, 2006, Pulitzer Prize for nat. reporting, 2006. Office: Copley News Svc Washington Bur 1100 Nat Press Bldg Washington DC 20045 Business E-Mail: marcus.stern@copleydc.com.

STERN, MARGARET BASSETT, retired special education educator, author; b. Bklyn., June 6, 1920; d. Preston Rogers and Jeanne (Mordorf) Bassett; m. Fritz R. Stern Oct. 11, 1947 (div. Dec. 1992); children: Frederick Preston, Katherine Stern Brennan. BA, Wellesley Coll., 1942; MEd, Bank Street Coll. Edn., NYC, 1943, MEd, 1974. Propr. Castle Sch., NYC, 1944-51; dir. Mothers' Coop. Nursery Sch., Ithaca, N.Y., 1952-54; tchr. sci. and math. The Brearley Sch., NYC, 1956-57. Cons., lectr. Head Start, Tuskegee, Ala., 1964; cons. in math. The Gateway Sch., N.Y.C., 1967-90; spl. lectr. Columbia U. Tchrs. Coll., N.Y.C., 1990-94; condr. workshops in Eng., 1960-88. Author: (with Catherine Stern and Toni Gould) Structural Reading Program, Workbooks and Teachers Guides A through E, 1963, 3d edit., 1978, Structural Arithmetic Workbooks and Teachers Guides Grades 1-3, 1965, 2d edit., 1966, (with Stern) Children Discover Arithmetic, 1971, (with Gould) Spotlight on Phonics, Four Workbooks and Teachers Guides, 1980, Sound/Symbol Activities and Decoding Activities, 1980, 2d edit., 1994; Experimenting with Numbers, 1988, 2004, Structural Arithmetic, 1-3, 1992, 2006. Recipient award, Orton Dyslexia Soc. N.Y., 1989, Bank St. Coll. Edn., 1998. Mem.: Nat. Coun. Tchrs. Math., Internat. Dyslexia Assn. Home: 3204 River Crescent Dr Annapolis MD 21401 Personal E-mail: structuralarith@aol.com.

STERN, MARIANA CARLA, epidemiologist, educator; d. Jorge E. Stern and Graciela B. Orlando de Stern; m. Hans Jochen Schenk, May 25, 2001; children: Toviel B. Schenk, Eliam G. Schenk. Licenciatura en Ciencias Biologicas, U. Buenos Aires, 1992; PhD, U. Texas, Houston, 1997. Grad. rsch. asst., sci. pk. rsch. divsn. M.D. Anderson Cancer Ctr., Smithville, Tex., 1992—97; vis. fellow Nat. Inst. Environ. Health Scis., Research Triangle Park, NC, 1997—2001; asst. prof. preventive medicine U. So. Calif., LA, 2001—. Recipient Rsch. Career Devel. award, Stop Cancer Found., 2001—04; grantee Rsch. grant, Wright Found., 2002, 2005, Rsch. award, Prostate Cancer Found., 2007. Mem.: Am. Assn. Cancer Rsch. Office: Univ So Calif 1441 Eastlake Ave Los Angeles CA 90089 Business E-Mail: stern_m@ccnt.usc.edu.

STERN, MARILYN, photographer, editor, writer; b. Detroit, Nov. 8, 1953; d. Julian and Phyllis Stern. BA, Brown U., 1976. Photographer's asst., NYC, 1976-82; freelance photographer, 1976—; freelance writer, 1985—; picture editor Across the Board mag., NYC, 1990-96; faculty Internat. Ctr. of Photography, 2001, NYU, 2004—. Photographer, organizer: (book) Masked Culture: The Greenwich Village Halloween Parade, 1994; author, photographer: Kval! Die Walfänger der Lofoten, 1990; solo exhbns. Profil Gallery, Bratislava, 2001, Scandinavia House, N.Y.C., 2003; several group exhbns., 1976--; represented in permanent collection Detroit Inst. Arts, also numerous pvt. collections. Travel Study grantee Royal Norwegian Consulate to Norway in the U.S., 1987, Am.-Scandinavian Found., 1986. E-mail: mstern@sternphoto.com.

STERN, MARILYN JEAN, special education educator; b. Akron, Ohio, Oct. 7, 1937; d. Walter Keith Pallage and Betty Jane Freeman-Pallage; m. Robert Stern, June 14, 1974 (dec.); children: John Daily, Anne Tunney, Jane Henault, Andrew Daily. BS in Elem. Edn., U. Akron, 1961, MS in Spl. Edn., 1978. Cert. in tchg. Ohio, 1974, Penn., 1963, in tchg. spl. edn. 1978. Tchr. Phila. Sch. Dist., 1963—64; spl. edn. tchr. Summit County Bd. Mental Health, Tallmadge, Ohio, 1974—78, Girard Sch. Dist., Pa., 1978—2004; spl. edn. Learning Disabilities tchr. NW Tri-County Intermediate Unit, Girard, 1978—88, county computer advisor edn. Erie County, Pa., 1988—90, ret., 2004. Computer cons. NW Tri-County Intermediate Unit, 1985—90; vol. reading tutor Neighborhood Network Program, Erie County, 2004—; presenter in field; leader spl. programs 4th grade level. Mem. Lake Erie Ballet Bd., Erie, Pa., 1980—92; polit. action chair Girard Fedn. Tchrs., 2000—04; past pres. Erie Reading Coun.; nominating chmn. Local Ridge Coun., act 48 hours chairperson, spl. projects chair; reader Erie Zoo. Mem.: Keystone State Reading Assn. (exec. bd. mem. 2003—), Internat. Reading Assn. (chair 2000—, del. to conf. 2005), Reading Tchrs. Orgn. (pres. 2003—05). Presbyterian. Avocations: reading, gardening, quilting, fiber arts, quilting. Home: 1420 Lord Rd Fairview PA 16415

STERN, MARVIN, history professor; b. Bronx, NY; s. Ben Stern. BA, MA, PhD, Brandeis U.; MA, Harvard U., Yale U. Assoc. prof. history Lawrence Technol. U., Southfield, Mich., 1994—. Author: Thorns and Briars, 1991; contbr. articles to profl. jours. Pvt. 1st class US Army. Vis. fellow, Cambridge U., Oxford U. Mem.: Cambridge Soc., Oxford U. Soc., Oxford Union, Harvard Club, Oxford and Cambridge Club. Office: Lawrence Technol Univ 21000 W Ten Mile Rd Southfield MI 48075

STERN, MITCHELL, broadcast executive; B, U. Pa., 1976; MBA, U. Chgo., 1978. With CBS TV Stas. Divsn., 1978—86, dir. planning and adminstrn. WCBS-TV NYC, dir. planning and adminstrn. WBBM-TV Chgo., fin. analyst corp. office; v.p., CFO Fox TV Stas., LA, 1986—90, v.p., sta. mgr. KTTV-Fox 11, 1990—92, sr. v.p., 1990—92, exec. v.p., COO, 1992—93, pres., COO, 1993—98, chmn., CEO, 1998—2003, Twentieth TV, LA, 1998—2003; CEO DirecTV, 2003—05. Office: Fox TV Stas Inc 205 E 67th St New York NY 10021

STERN, MORT(IMER) P(HILLIP), communications educator, editor, reporter, consultant; b. New Haven, Conn., Feb. 20, 1926; s. Bernard and Louise Eleanor (Spiro) S.; m. Patricia Ruth Freeman, Jan. 10, 1946; children: Susan C., Margaret L. AB, U. Ark., 1947; MS, Columbia U., NYC, 1949; postgrad., Harvard U., Cambridge, Mass., 1954—55; PhD, U. Denver, 1969. Reporter S.W.-Am., Ft. Smith, Ark., 1946-47; night bur. mgr. UPI, Little Rock, 1947-48; reporter, polit. writer, state editor Ark. Gazette, Little Rock, 1949-51; reporter, rewrite man Denver Post, 1951-53, night city editor, 1953-54, asst. editor Rocky Mountain Empire sect., 1955-56, mng. editor, 1956-58, assoc. editor, 1958, editl. page editor, 1958-65, asst. to pub., 1965-70, editl. page editor, 1971-73; dean Sch. Pub. Comm. U. Ala., 1973-74; dean Sch. Journalism U. Colo., Boulder, 1974-77; lectr. journalism U. Denver, 1953-54, adj. prof., 1970, exec. dir. pub. affairs, 1977-78, exec. asst. to chancellor, 1978-84; prof., chmn. dept. journalism and mass communication U. No. Colo., Greeley, 1985-90; pres. P. Paty & Co., Georgetown, Colo., 1989—. Atwood prof. journalism U. Alaska, Anchorage, 1981-82. With USAAF, 1944-45. Mem. Georgetown Bd. of Selectmen, 1997-99; mem. Georgetown Bd. Adjustment, 2001-07. Nieman fellow Harvard U., 1954-55; named Disting. Alumnus dept. journalism U. Ark., 1999; inducted to Fulbright Coll. Alumni Acad. U. Ark., 1999. Mem.: Georgetown Libr. Assn. (v.p. 1999, pres. 2001—04, bd. dirs.), Phi Beta Kappa, Sigma Delta Chi, Omicron Delta Kappa. Baptist. Home: PO Box 549 Georgetown CO 80444-0549

STERN, NOAH J., lawyer; b. Albany, NY, Apr. 26, 1971; BA, U. Calif. Berkeley, 1993; MA, Ind. U. Bloomington, 1996; JD, NY U. Sch. Law, 1999. Bar: Ohio 1999, US Tax Ct. Assoc. Dinsmore & Shohl LLP, Cin. Mem., Bd. Trustee Adath Israel Synagogue. Named one of Ohio's Rising Stars, Super Lawyers, 2006. Mem.: Ohio State Bar Assn., Cin. Bar Assn. Office: Dinsmore & Shohl LLP 255 E Fifth St Ste 1900 Cincinnati OH 45202-4700 Office Phone: 513-977-8460. Office Fax: 513-977-8141.

STERN, PAULA, international trade consultant; b. Chgo., Mar. 31, 1945; d. Lloyd and Fan (Wener) Stern; m. Paul A. London; children: Gabriel Stern London, Genevieve Stern London. BA, Goucher Coll., 1967; MA in Middle Eastern Studies, Harvard U., 1969; MA in Internat. Affairs, Fletcher Sch. of Law and Diplomacy, 1970, MA in Law and Diplomacy, 1970, PhD, 1976; D Comml. Sci. (hon.), Babson Coll., 1985; LLD (hon.), Goucher Coll., 1985. From legis. asst. to sr. legis. asst. to U.S. Sen. Gaylord Nelson U.S. Senate, Washington, 1972—74, 1976; guest scholar Brookings Inst., Washington, 1975-76; policy analyst Pres. Carter-V.P. Mondale Transition Team, Washington, 1977-78; internat. affairs fellow Council on Fgn. Rels., Washington, 1977-78; commr. Internat. Trade Commn., Washington, 1978-87, chair, 1984-86; sr. assoc. Carnegie Endowment for Internat. Peace, Washington, 1986-88; sr. fellow Program Policy Inst., 1994—95. Howard W. Aikire chmn. internat. bus. and econs. Hamline U., 1994—2000; chairwoman The Stern Group, Inc., 1988—; bd. dirs. Avaya, Inc., Avon Products, Inc., Hasbro, Inc.; mem., sr. advisor U.S. trade policy coun. Competition Policy Inst., 1991—93; sr. fellow Progressive Policy Inst., 1994—95; pub. vice chairwoman Atlantic Coun. U.S.; trustee Com. Econ. Devel.; mem. Inter-Am. Dialogue, Coun. Fgn. Rels.; mem. high level adv. group Global Subsidies Initiative Project; past co-chair Internat. Competition Adv. Com.; antitrust divsn. U.S. Dept. Justice; past chmn. US Export-Import Bank; past mem. U.S. Pres. Adv. Com. on Trade Policy and Negotiation; bd. dirs. Carnegie Coun. Ethics and Internat. Affairs. Author: Water's Edge--Domestic Politics and the Making of American Foreign Policy, 1979; contbg. author newspapers; contbr. articles to profl. jours. Recipient Journalism award, Alicia Patterson Fund, 1971, Joseph Papp Award for Racial Harmony, Found. Ethnic Understanding, 2004. Democrat. Jewish. Avocations: sculpting, tennis, dance. Office: 3314 Ross Pl NW Washington DC 20008-3332 Home Phone: 202-966-7893; Office Phone: 202-966-7894. Business E-Mail: pstern@sterngroup.biz.

STERN, PETER, communications executive; b. 1972; m. Sue Stern; 3 children. BA, Harvard U., 1994; law degree, Yale Law Sch., 1997. Assoc. prin. McKinsey & Co.; v.p., Strategic Initiatives Time Warner Inc.; sr. v.p., Strategic Planning Time Warner Cable, 2004—05, exec. v.p., Product Mgmt., 2005—. V.p., Bd. Dirs. Stamford Symphony Orch. Named one of 40 Executives Under 40, Multichannel News, 2006. Office: Time Warner Cable One Time Warner Ctr New York NY 10019

STERN, RICHARD DAVID, investment company executive; b. New Rochelle, NY, Nov. 5, 1936; s. Leo and Grace Marjorie S.; m. Phyllis Marlene Edelstein, Nov. 20, 1966; children: Marjorie Anne, Andrew Howard. AB, Princeton U., 1958; MBA, Harvard U., 1962. CFA. 1st v.p. Newburger, Loeb & Co., NYC, 1962-74, also bd. dirs., 1969-74; sr. investment officer Ctrl. Trust Co. (now known as PNC Bank), Cin., 1974—76, owner bus. valuation cons. co., 1976—78; v.p. Gt. Western Bank & Trust Co. (now Wells Fargo Bank), Phoenix, 1978-84; pres. Stern, Ludke & Co. (now Stellar Capital Mgmt. LLC.), Phoenix, 1984—, mng. mem., 2000—. Co-author: Air Cushion Vehicles, 1962. Trustee endowment trust Phoenix Chamber Music Soc., 1982-91; v.p., 1986-90, bd. dirs., 1982-91, 93-94; pres. Cen. Ariz. chpt. Arthritis Found., 1982-84, chmn. planned giving com., 1986-91, mem. nat. planned giving com., 1987-89; chmn. endowments and trusts com. Temple Beth Israel, Phoenix, 1980-83; dir., investment com. Endowment Found., Temple Solel, Paradise Valley, 1990-92; pres. Am. Jewish Com., Phoenix, 1983-84, bd. dirs., 1980-84, adv. bd., 1985-2005; bd. dirs. Asian Arts Coun., Phoenix Art Mus., 1987-93, v.p., 1989-90, pres., 1990-92; trustee Ariz. Theatre Co., 1990-97, mem. regional nominating com., 1995-97, chmn., 1995-96, asst. treas., 1996-97; grants award panelist Phoenix Office of Arts and Culture, 2002, 05. Mem. CFA Inst., Phoenix CFA Soc. (chmn. profl. conduct com. 1980-83, membership com. 1990-91, bd. dirs.), Anti-Defamation League (dir. Ctrl. Ariz. chpt. 1986—, exec. bd. 1989—, chair nominating com. 1990-94, 2001—, chair bd. devel. 1993-94, treas. 1994-2004, assoc. nat. commr. 1998—), Princeton Alumni Assn. No. Ariz. (alumni schs. com. 1992—, v.p. 2005—), Univ. Club Phoenix (bd. dirs. 1990-92, fin. com. 1990-91), Harvard Bus. Sch. Club Ariz. (bd. dirs. 1991—, pres. 1993-95), Clearwater Hills Improvement Assn. (dir. 2002-, sec. 2006-). Republican. Home: 7547 N Lakeside Ln Paradise Valley AZ 85253-2857 Office: 2200 E Camelback Rd Ste 130 Phoenix AZ 85016-3455 Business E-Mail: rstern@stellarmgt.com.

STERN, RICHARD GUSTAVE, writer; b. NYC, Feb. 25, 1928; s. Henry George and Marion (Veit) S.; m. Gay Clark, Mar. 14, 1950 (div. Feb. 1972); children: Christopher Holmes, Kate Macomber, Andrew Henry, Nicholas Clark; m. Alane Rollings, Aug. 9, 1985. BA, U. N.C., 1947; MA, Harvard U., 1950; PhD, State U. Iowa, 1954. Mem. faculty U. Chgo., 1955—, prof. English, 1965—, Helen Regenstein prof. English, 1990—2002, prof. emeritus, 2002. Author: Golk, 1960, Europe and Up and Down with Baggish and Schreiber, 1961, In Any Case, 1962, Teeth, Dying and Other Matters, 1964, Stitch, 1965, 1968: A Short Novel, An Urban Idyll, Five Stories and Two Trade Notes, 1970, The Books in Fred Hampton's Apartment, 1973, Other Men's Daughters, 1973, Natural Shocks, 1978, Packages, 1980, The Invention of the Real, 1982, A Father's Words, 1986, The Position of the Body, 1986, Noble Rot: Stories, 1949-88, 1989 (book of yr. award Chgo. Sun-Times 1990), Shares and Other Fictions, 1992, One Person and Another, 1993, A Sistermony, 1995 (Heartland award, nonfiction book of year), Pacific Tremors, 2001, What Is What Was, 2002, Almonds to the Zhoof: The Collected Stories of Richard Stern, 2005; editor: Honey and Wax, 1966. Recipient Longwood Found. award, 1960, Friends of Lit. award, 1963, fiction award Nat. Inst. Arts and Letters, 1968; Nat. Coun. Arts and Humanities fellow, 1967-68, Carl Sandburg award for fiction, 1979, Arts Coun. awards, 1979, 81, Am. Acad. and Inst. of Arts and Letters medal of Merit for Novel, 1985; Rockefeller fellow, 1965, Guggenheim fellow, 1973-74. Fellow Ctr. Advanced Studies in the Behavioral Scis.; mem. Am. Acad. Arts and Scis. Business E-Mail: rstern@uchicago.edu.

STERN, ROBERT, psychiatrist; b. Aug. 12, 1928; BS, Swiss Fed. Inst. Tech., Zurich, 1951; MS, Yale U., 1953, PhD, 1956; MD, Case Western Res. U., 1966. Diplomate Am. Bd. Psychiatry and Neurology; lic. physician, Conn. Asst. prof. chemistry Wesleyan U., Middletown, Conn., 1957—58, Conn. Coll., New London, 1959-60; supr. bio-organic chem. rsch. Arthur D. Little, Inc., Cambridge, Mass., 1960-62; vis. fellow medicine Mass. Gen. Hosp., 1964; rsch. assoc. biol. chemistry Harvard Med. sch., Boston, 1964, tchg. fellow psychiatry, 1967-68; intern medicine King County Hosp./U. Wash., Seattle, 1966-67; resident in psychiatry McLean Hosp., Belmont, Mass., 1967-68; jr./sr. asst. resident internal medicine Yale-New Haven Hosp., 1968-70, clin. fellow medicine, 1970-71; postdoctoral fellow psychiatry Yale U. Sch. Medicine, 1971-73, asst. clin. prof. psychiatry, 1974-86, assoc. clin. prof. psychiatry, 1986—; pvt. practice New Haven, 1973—. Cons. Child Guidance clinic of Southeastern Conn., New London, 1973-82; cons. CHAMPUS peer reviewer Qualidigm, Inc., Middletown, 1994—; lectr. in field. Contbr. articles to profl. jours. Fellow Am. Psychiat. Assn. (Disting. life fellow); mem. New Haven Individual Practice Assn. (co-chmn. psychiatry panel 1985-98, quality assurance com. 1989-98, bd. dirs. 1986-89), Conn. Psychiatry Soc. (councilor-at-large 2001—06, councilor 2000-01, pres. New

Haven/Middlesex chpt. 1999-2000, treas. 1996-99). Conn. State Med. Soc., New Haven County Med. Assn., New Haven pvt. practice com. 1995—. Office: 340 Whitney Ave New Haven CT 06511-2317 Office Phone: 203-562-9110.

STERN, ROBERT ARTHUR MORTON, architect, educator, writer; b. NYC, May 23, 1939; s. Sidney S. and Sonya (Cohen) S.; m. Lynn G. Solinger, May 22, 1966 (div. 1977); 1 child, Nicholas S.G. BA, Columbia U., 1960; MArch, Yale U., 1965. Registered architect, Calif., Colo., Conn., Fla., Hawaii, Ill., Ind., Maine, Mass., Mich., N.H., N.J., Ohio, S.C., Tex., N.Y., D.C., Ga. Program dir. Archtl. League N.Y., 1965-66; designer Office Richard Meier, Architect, NYC, 1966; cons. Small Parks Program, Dept. Parks, NYC, 1966-70; urban designer, asst. to asst. adminstr. housing and devel. adminstrn. NYC, 1967-70; ptnr. Robert A.M. Stern & John S. Hagmann, Architects, NYC, 1969-77; prin. Robert A.M. Stern, Architects, 1977-89, sr. ptnr., 1989—. Bd. dirs. Walt Disney Co.; cons. Eye on New York TV documentary, CBS-TV, 1966-67; mem. architecture com. Whitney Mus. Am. Art, 1970-76, adv. commn., archtl. sect. Venice Biennale, 1980; lectr. architecture Columbia U., 1970-72, asst. prof. 1973-77, assoc. prof., 1977-82, prof. 1982—; vis. fellow Inst. for Architecture and Urban Studies, 1974-76, trustee, 1983-85; dir. Temple Hoyne Buell Ctr. for Study Am. Architecture, 1984-88, dir. Hist. Preservation Program, 1991-98; vis. lectr. Yale U., 1972, 73; vis. critic R.I. Sch. Design, 1976, U. Pa., 1977, N.C. State U., Raleigh, 1978; William Henry Bishop vis. prof. architecture Yale U., fall 1978; editorial cons. Archtl. History Found., 1979-83; dean Yale Sch. Arch., 1998—; J.M. Hoppin prof. arch., 2000—. Author: New Directions in American Architecture, 1969, rev. edit., 1977, George Howe: Toward a Modern American Architecture, 1975, (with Deborah Nevins) The Architect's Eye, 1979, (with John M. Massengale) The Anglo-American Suburb, 1981, (with Thomas Catalano) Raymond Hood, 1982, East Hamptons Heritage, 1982, (with John M. Massengale and Gregory Gilmartin) New York 1900, 1983, Pride of Place, 1986, (with Gregory Gilmartin and Thomas Mellins) New York 1930, 1987, (with Raymond Gastil) Modern Classicism, 1988, The House That Bob Built, 1991, The American Houses of Robert A.M. Stern, 1991, (with Thomas Mellins and David Fishman) New York 1960, 1995, (with Thomas Mellins and David Fishman) New York 1880, 1999. Mem. N.Y.C. Mayor's Task Force on Urban Design, 1966-67, architects selection com. N.Y. Conv. Ctr., 1979; trustee Am. Fedn. Arts, 1967-79, Inst. for Architecture and Urban Studies, 1983-85; v.p. Cunningham Dance Found., 1969-73; bd. dirs. Preservation League N.Y., 1984—, Historic Landmarks Preservation Ctr., 1995—; trustee Nat. Bldg. Mus., 1999—, Trust for Historic Preservation, 2000—. Recipient numerous awards for archtl. works including Nat. Hon. awards of AIA, 1980, 85, 90, John Jay award Columbia Coll., 1991. Fellow Am. Acad. Arts & Scis., AIA (bd. dirs. N.Y. chpt. 1976-78, Disting. archtl. award N.Y. chpt. 1982, 84, 85, 87, medal of honor 1984), Soc. Archtl. Historians (bd. dirs. 1975-78), Archtl. League N.Y. (pres. 1973-77, exec. com. 1977—), N.Y. State Assn. Architects (excellence in design cert. 1985), Am. Architecture Found. (bd. regents 1989-91), Skidmore, Owings and Merrill Found. (bd. dirs. 1984-90), Chgo. Inst. for Architecture and Urbanism (bd. dirs. 1990-93), Century Assn., Coffee House Club. Office: 460 W 34th St Fl 18 New York NY 10001-2320 *

STERN, ROBERT C., pediatrician, medical educator; b. NYC, Dec. 13, 1938; s. Samuel and Lily S. BA, Drew U., Madison, NJ, 1959; MD, Albert Einstein Coll. Medicine, 1963. Diplomate Nat. Bd. Med. Examiners, Am. Bd. Pediat., Am. Bd. Pediatric Pulmonology. Intern pediat. U. Hosps. Cleve., Babies and Childrens Hosp. Divsn., 1963-64, jr. asst. resident pediat., 1964-65; sr. asst. resident pediat. Bronx Mcpl. Hosp. Ctr., NYC, 1965-66; fellow cystic fibrosis/pediat. pulmonary diseases Case Western Res. U. Sch. Medicine, Cleve., 1968-70; sr. instr. pediat. Case Western Res. U., Cleve., 1970-71, asst. prof., 1971-77, assoc. prof., 1977-83, prof., 1983—. Cons. Cystic Fibrosis Founds. various countries, 1990—, various pharm. and med. tech. cos., 1990—. Author: Treatment of Hospitalized Cystic Fibrosis Patients, 1998, Treatment of Cystic Fibrosis, 2000; contbr. numerous chpts. to Nelson's Textbook of Pediatrics, 1979—, also over 100 articles to med. jours. Pres., CEO, Children's Lung Found., Cleve., 1983—. Capt. USAF, 1966-68. Recipient David Stuckert award Cystic Fibrosis Rsch. Inst., San Francisco, 1997. Mem. Am. Thoracic Soc., Soc. Pediat. Rsch. Achievements include introduction of heparin lock for intermittent administration of intravenous drugs; research in cystic fibrosis. Home: 2300 Overlook Rd Apt 406 Cleveland Heights OH 44106-2391 Office: Univ Hosp Cleve 11100 Euclid Ave Cleveland OH 44106-1736 Personal E-mail: rcs1@prodigy.net.

STERN, ROBERT D., publishing executive; b. NYC, Sept. 30, 1929; s. Morris and Jean (Gordon) S.; m. Natalie Greenberg, Sept. 5, 1952 (div. 1978); children: Mitchell, Bradley; m. Roslyne Paige, June 5, 1978. BA, Syracuse U., 1950; JD, NYU, 1953, LLM, 1958. Bar: N.Y. 1955, U.S. Dist. Ct. (D.C. cir.) 1953, U.S. Supreme Ct. 1967. Ptnr. Fink, Weinberger, Levin & Gottschalk, NYC, 1957-59, 1957—72; chmn. Rudor Consol. Industries, 1972—99, Dance Mag., Inc., 1985—2001, AGC/Sedgwick Inc., Princeton, NJ, 1990—2001. Bd. dirs. Ctr. for Graphic Comms. Mgmt. and Tech., NYU, N.Y.C., 1979—; chmn. bd. dirs. AGC Sedgwick, Princeton, N.J., Rudor Consol. Ind. Inc.; pub. Stern's Performing Arts Directory, 1989-98. Bd. dirs. YMCA, N.Y.C., 1987-90 Mem. ABA, N.Y. State Bar Assn., Sheldrake Yacht Club (Mamaroneck, N.Y.), Birchwood Country Club (Westport, Conn.). Avocations: tennis, skiing, sailing. Home: 2 Imperial Lndg Westport CT 06880-4934 Office Phone: 203-454-0752.

STERN, ROBERT MORRIS, gastroenterologist, psychologist, researcher; b. NYC, June 18, 1937; s. Irving Dan and Nellie (Wachstetter) S.; m. Wilma Olch, June 19, 1960; children: Jessica Leigh, Alison Rachel. AB, Franklin and Marshall Coll., 1958; MS, Tufts U., 1960; PhD, Ind. U., 1963. Research assoc. dept. psychology Ind. U., 1963-65; asst. prof. psychology Pa. State U., 1965-68, assoc. prof., 1968-73, prof., 1973—2005, emeritus, 2005—, disting. prof., 1992—2005, head dept., 1978-87. Author (with W.J. Ray): Biofeedback, 1977; author: (with W.J. Ray and C.M. Davis) Psychophysiological Recording, 1980; author: (with K.L. Koch) Electrogastrography, 1985; author: (with W.J. Ray and K.S. Quigley) Psychophysiological Recording, 2nd edit., 2001; author: (with K.L. Koch) Handbook of Electrogastrography, 2004; contbr. articles. Recipient Nat. Media award Am. Psychol. Found., 1978 Mem. Am. Psychol. Soc., Aerospace Med. Assn., Soc. Psychophysiol. Rsch., Am. Gastroent. Assn., Internat. EGG Soc., Functional Brain-Gut Rsch. Assn., Internat. Brain-Gut Soc. Home: 1360 Greenwood Cir State College PA 16803-3232 Office: Pa State U 512 Moore Bldg University Park PA 16802-3105 Office Phone: 814-865-1712. Business E-Mail: RS3@psu.edu.

STERN, ROBIN LAURI, medical physicist; b. Urbana, Ill., Mar. 12, 1959; d. Morris Stern and Myrna (Tanzer) Stern Longenecker; m. Donald Neil Bittner, May 20, 1989. BA in Physics and German Studies, Rice U., 1981; MS in Physics, U. Mich., 1983, PhD in Physics, 1987. Rsch. assoc. Duke U., Durham, N.C., 1987-89; postdoctoral rsch. fellow U. Mich., Ann Arbor, 1989-91; asst. prof. U. Calif.-Davis, San Francisco, 1992-98; assoc. prof. U. Calif., Davis, 1998—2004, prof., 2004—. Cons. Scanditronix, Inc., Livonia, Mich., 1991. Contbr. articles to jours. Rev. of Sci. Instruments, Magnetic Resonance Imaging, Med. Physics. Argonne Nat. Lab. grantee, 1985-86; Nat. Merit scholar, 1977-81. Fellow Am. Assn. Physicists in Medicine; mem. Am. Soc. Therapeutic Radiology and Oncology, Sigma Pi Sigma, Phi Beta Kappa. E-mail: robin.stern@ucdc.udavis.edu.

STERN, ROSLYNE PAIGE, magazine publisher; b. Chgo., May 26, 1926; d. Benjamin Gross and Clara (Sniderman) Roer; m. William E. Weber, May 3, 1944 (div. Mar. 1956); m. Richard S. Paige, June 28, 1958 (div. Apr. 1978); children: Sandra Weber Porr, Barbara Paige Kaplan, Elizabeth Paige (dec.); m. Robert D. Stern, June 5, 1978. Cert., U. Chgo., 1945. Profl. model, singer, 1947-53; account exec. Interstate United, Chgo., 1955-58; sales mgr. Getting To Know You Internat., Great Neck, NY, 1963-71, exec. v.p., 1971-78; pub. After Dark Mag., NYC, 1978-82; assoc. pub. Dance Mag., NYC, 1978-85, pres., pub., 1985—2001, pres. emeritus, 2001—. Bd. dirs. Rudor Consol. Industries, Inc., N.Y.C., AGC/Sedgwick, Inc., Princeton, N.J. Founding pres. Dance Mag. Found., NYC, 1984-86 chair Dance Mag. awards, 1986-2004; life mem. nat. women's com. Brandeis U., Waltham, Mass., 1958—; bd. dirs. Westport Arts Ctr.; The Internation Com. for Dance Libr. of Israel. Recipient Disting. Svc. award Dance Notation Bur., 1996, Am. Coll. Dance Festival award, 1998, Pres.'s award Dance Masters of Am., Inc., 1998, Documents of Dance award Dance Library of Israel, 1999. Mem. Pub. Relations Soc. Am., LWV, Am. Theatre Wing, Nat. Arts Club. Democrat. Jewish. Avocations: dance, theater, opera, visual arts, travel. Home: 2 Imperial Lndg Westport CT 06880-4934 Office: 1930 Broadway Ste 25C New York NY 10023 Office Phone: 212-724-4909. Personal E-mail: sterndance@aol.com.

STERN, SAMUEL ALAN, lawyer; b. Phila., Jan. 21, 1929; AB, U. Pa., 1949; LLB, Harvard U., 1952. Bar: Mass. 1952, D.C. 1958. Ptnr. Wilmer, Cutler & Pickering, Washington, 1962-88, Dickstein, Shapiro & Morin, Washington, 1988-92, Hills, Stern & Morley LLP, Washington, 1999—; pvt. practice law and bus. Washington and St. Petersburg, Russia, 1992-94, Washington, 1997-98; counsel Rogers & Wells, Washington, NYC, 1994-97. Vis. prof. law Harvard Law Sch., Cambridge, Mass., 1976; dir. Internat. Law Inst. Georgetown U., 1971—2004, adj. prof. law, 1979—92; asst. counsel Warren Commn., 1964; cons. UN, 1984—96; bd. dirs. Warp Network Corp., Verihealth Internat., Pan-Asia Pictures, Beijing, VeriPay, Target World Ltd., Commonwealth Shore Power, China Alarm Holdings LTD, Global Dataguard Inc., Precipia, Inc.; lectr. profl. confs. on project fin., privatization, cross-border investment and alternative dispute resolution; arbitrator internat. comml. disputes. Contbr. articles to legal jours. Mem. ABA, Am. Law Inst., Internat. Bar Assn., D.C. Bar Assn. Home: 210 Lee Ct Alexandria VA 22314 Office: 1120 20th St NW North Bldg 2d Fl Washington DC 20036 Office Phone: 202-822-1638. Business E-Mail: sastern@hillsandstern.com.

STERN, SANDOR, film director, writer; b. Timmins, Ont., Can., July 13, 1936; s. Stephen Mendel and Ann (Gurevitch) S.; m. Marlene Greenstein, May 19, 1957 (div. 1976); children: Shawn, Mark, Adam, Jamie; m. Kandy Lea Cave, Jan. 26, 1980; children: Lauren, Seth. BA, U. Toronto, 1957, MD, 1961. Intern New Mount Sinai Hosp., Toronto, 1961-62; physician Toronto, Can., 1962-68; writer LA, 1968—; dir., 1974—. Writer (films) The Amityville Horror, 1978, Fastbreak, 1979 (NAACP Image award); writer, dir. (film) Pin, 1988, (TV films) Web of Deceit, 1990, Deception: A Mother's Secret, 1991, Dangerous Pursuit, 1989, John and Yoko, 1985, Muggable Mary: Street Cop, 1982, (TV miniseries) Woman on the Run: The Lawrencia Bembeneck Story, 1992-93; dir. (TV films) Glitz, 1988, Passions, 1984, Heart of a Child, 1993, The Stranger Beside Me, 1995, Gridlock, 1995, Badge of Betrayal, 1996, In My Sister's Shadow, 1997; co-writer, dir. (TV films) Jericho Fever, 1992, Duplicates, 1992, A Child's Cry for Help, 1994, (episodes for TV shows) Touched by an Angel, 1997, 98, 99, Promised Land, 1997, 98, 99, Early Edition, 2000, Leap Years, 2001. Mem. Writers Guild Am., Dirs. Guild Am., Producers Guild Am. Office: Jamson Prodns Inc 9472 Rembert Ln Beverly Hills CA 90210-1720 E-mail: sandorstern@sbcglobal.net.

STERN, SUSAN TOY, human resources specialist; BA in Sociology, UCLA, 1974. Chief dep. dir. LA County Dept. Human Resources. Co-chair UCLA Fund; spkr. in field. Mem.: So. Calif. Personnel Mgmt. Assn. Human Resources (past pres.), Internat. Pub. Mgmt. Assn. Human Resources (life; pres. 2001, former mem. exec. coun., former chair Conf. rev. task force). Office: LA County Dept Human Resources 3333 Wilshire Blvd Ste 100 Los Angeles CA 90010

STERN, TODD, restaurant manager; b. 1967; Founder, mng. ptnr. Small Plates, Detroit, 2002—. Named one of 40 Under 40, Crain's Detroit Bus., 2006; recipient Best of Yr. award for Small Plates, Bon Appetit mag., 2004, Wine Enthusiast, 2004. Office: Small Plates 1521 Broadway Detroit MI 48226 Office Phone: 313-963-0497.

STERN, TODD D., government official, lawyer; b. Chgo., May 4, 1951; s. Richard and Judith (Cowen) S.; m. Jennifer Klein, Sept. 10, 1995. BA summa cum laude, Dartmouth Coll., 1973; JD cum laude, Harvard U., 1977. Bar: DC, NY. Staff atty. criminal appeals bur. Legal Aid Soc.; assoc. Paul, Weiss, Rifkind, Wharton & Garrison; gen. counsel Assoc. Mills Pollenex; v.p. Podesta Assn.; sr. counsel subcom. on tech. and the law Senate Com. on Judiciary, 1990-93; dep. asst. to Pres. and dep. staff sec. The White House, Washington, 1993-95, asst. to Pres. and staff sec., 1995-98, asst. to Pres. for spl. projects, 1998-99; counselor to sec. of Treasury, Treasury Dept., Wash., 1999; ptnr. Wilmerhale., Wash., DC. Adj. lectr. Harvard's Kennedy Sch. of Govt.; sr. counsel Senator Patrick Leahy; resident fellow German Marshall Fund of US. Contbr. articles to profl. jour. Mem. Council on Fgn. Relations, sr. fellow Ctr. for Am. Progress, Phi Beta Kappa. Office: Wilmerhale 1875 Pennsylvania Ave NW Washington DC 20006 Office Phone: 202-663-6940. Office Fax: 202-663-6363. Business E-Mail: todd.stern@wilmerhale.com.

STERN, WALTER EUGENE, neurosurgeon, educator; b. Portland, Oreg., Jan. 1, 1920; s. Walter Eugene and Ida May (McCoy) S.; m. Elizabeth Naffziger, May 24, 1946; children: Geoffrey Alexander, Howard Christian, Eugenia Louise, Walter Eugene III. AB cum laude, U. Calif., MD, 1943. Diplomate Am. Bd. Neurol. Surgery (vice chmn. 1975-80). Surg. intern, asst. resident surgery and neurol. surgery U. Calif. Hosp., 1943-46, asst. resident neurol. surgery and neuropathology, 1948; clin. clk. Nat. Hosp. Paralyzed and Epileptic, London, 1948-49; Nat. Rsch. fellow med. sci. Johns Hopkins, Balt., 1949-50; asst. resident, resident U. Calif. Svc., 1951; clin. instr. U. Calif., 1951; asst. prof. neurosurgery UCLA, 1952-56, assoc. prof., 1956-59, prof., 1959—87, prof. emeritus, 1987—, chief divsn. neurosurgery, 1952-85, chmn. dept. surgery, 1981-87; NIH spl. fellow univ. lab. physiology Oxford (Eng.) U., 1961-62. Cons. neurosurgery Wadsworth VA Hosp. Former mem., chmn. edtl. bd. Jour. Neurosurgery; contbr. articles to sci. jours., chpts. to books. Lt. to capt. M.C. AUS, 1946-48. Fellow ACS (sec.); mem. AMA, Am. Surg. Assn., Pacific Coast Surg. Assn., L.A. Surg. Soc. (pres. 1978), Am. Assn. Neurol. Surgeons (pres. 1979-80, Cushing medalist, 1992), James IV Assn. Surgeons, Western Neurosurg. Soc. (past pres.), Soc. Neurol. Surgeons (past pres., Disting. Svc. award 1999), Neurosurg. Soc. Am., Am. Neurol. Assn., Soc. Univ. Surgeons, Soc. Brit. Neurol. Surgeons (hon.), Calif. Assn. Neurol. Surgery (Disting. Svc. award 2004), Phi Beta Kappa, Sigma Xi, Alpha Omega Alpha. Epsicopalian. Home: 435 Georgina Ave Santa Monica CA 90402-1909

STERN, WALTER PHILLIPS, investment company executive; b. NYC, Sept. 26, 1928; s. Leo and Marjorie (Phillips) S.; m. Elizabeth May, Feb. 12, 1958; children: Sarah May, William May, David May. AB, Williams Coll., 1950; MBA, Harvard U., 1952. With Lazard Freres & Co., NYC, 1953-54; assoc. Burnham & Co., Inc. (predecessor firm to Drexel Burnham Lambert Group, Inc.), NYC, 1954-60, ptnr., 1960-71, sr. exec. v.p., 1972-73; mng. dir. Ea. ops. Capital Rsch. Co., 1973-95; chmn. bd. New Perspective Fund, Inc., 1973—2003, chmn. emeritus, 2003—; chmn. Capital Internat. Inc., 1973—2002, vice-chmn., 2002—; sr. ptnr. Capital Group Inc., 2002—. Chmn. Europacific Growth Fund, Inc., 1984—99; chmn. bd. dirs. Emerging Markets Growth Fund Capital Group Internat., Inc., 1987—2004, chmn., 1984—2004, chmn. emeritus, 2005—; mem. Mcpl. Securities Rulemaking Bd., 1984—87; trustee Fin. Analysts Rsch. Found., 1975—2003; chmn. bd. trustees Hudson Inst., 1983—; instr. investment mgmt. and fin. NYU, 1956—62; mem. adv. bd. South African Growth Fund, 1996—2002, Hillhouse Capital Mgmt., 2006—. Contbr. articles to profl. jours. Mem. Coun. Fgn. Rels.; chmn. fin. adv. com. Haddassah, Tel Aviv U., 1980-2007; dir. Am.-Israel Friendship League, 1996—; Rep. Jewish Coalition, 2005—; v.p., mem. exec. com. Washington Inst. Near East Policy; chmn. steering com. Freedom Trade with Israel; adv. bd., dir. Am. Committees on Fgn. Rels., 1998—; bd. visitors Monterrey Inst., 2001—; trustee The Jewish Pol. Ctr.; adv. bd. CFA Ctr. Fin. Mkt. Integrity, 2004— Mem. N.Y. Soc. Security Analysts (bd. dirs.), Fin. Analysts Fedn. (pres. 1971-72, bd. dirs.), Inst. Chartered Fin. Analysts (pres. 1976-77, bd. dirs.), Assn. Investment and Mgmt. Rsch. (bd. dirs., exec. com. 1990-92), Harvard Club, Econ. Club, Sunningdale Country Club, Calif. Club, Belle Meade County Club, Phi Beta Kappa. Jewish. Home: 450 Fort Hill Rd Scarsdale NY 10583-2413 Office: Capital Group Inc 630 5th Ave New York NY 10111-0100 also: Capital Group Inc 333 S Hope St Los Angeles CA 90071-1406 Business E-Mail: wps@capgroup.com.

STERN, WALTER WOLF, III, lawyer; b. Cin., Mar. 25, 1946; s. Walter W. Jr. and Harriet Louise Stern; (div.); 1 child, Rachael Louise. BA, Carthage Coll., 1969; JD, Marquette U., 1974. Bar: Wis. 1974, U.S. Dist. Ct. (ea. and we. dists.) Wis. 1974, U.S. Ct. Appeals (7th cir.) 1981, U.S. Supreme Ct. 1983, U.S. Dist. Ct. (no. dist.) Ill. 1999, U.S. Ct. (no. dist.) Wis. 2000. Pvt. practice, Kenosha, Wis., 1974-82, 85-91; sr. ptnr. Joling Rizzo Willems Stern & Burroughs, Kenosha, 1982-85; pvt. practice Union Grove, Wis., 1991—. Lectr. criminal law Carthage Coll., Kenosha, Wis., 1976—. Educator, Domestic Violence Project, Kenosha, 1983-94; hearing examiner Gen. Relief, Kenosha, 1990-95; candiate Cir. Judge, 2005. Fellow Am. Acad. Forensic Scis. Avocations: fishing, hunting, jogging, reading, creative writing. Home and Office: PO Box 64 Union Grove WI 53182-0064 Office Phone: 262-878-5060. Personal E-mail: walterstern@excite.com.

STERNBERG, BETTY J., school system administrator; b. NY, Jan. 30, 1950; d. Julius and Edith Jane (Meyer) Levin; m. Robert Jeffrey Sternberg, June 18, 1972 (div. Jan. 13, 1987); children: Seth, Sara. BA, Brandeis U., 1971; MA, Columbia U., 1972; PhD, Stanford U., 1978. Bur. chief Conn. Dept. Edn., Hartford, Conn., 1980-85, divsn. dir., 1985-92, assoc. commr., 1992—2003, commr., 2003—07; sch. supt. Greenwich Pub. Schools, Greenwich, Conn., 2007—. Cons. Nat. Bd. for Profl. Teaching Standards, Washington, 1992. Co-author: (textbook) Metric Multibase Mathematics, 1973, Attribute Acrobatics, 1973, People Pieces Primer, 1975; (textbook series) Math In Stride, 1987. Mem. bd. dirs. William Benton Mus. of Art U. Conn., 1989—; mem. adv. coun. Ctr. for Ednl. Excellence, 1992-93. Recipient Disting. Managerial Svc. award State of Conn., 1986. Mem. ASCD (sec. 1975-80), Conn. Assn. Suprs. of Curriculum Devel. Avocations: tennis, interior design, gardening. Office: Greenwich Pub Schools 290 Greenwich Ave Greenwich CT 06830 *

STERNBERG, PAUL, ophthalmologist, researcher; b. Chgo., Apr. 30, 1953; s. Doris Feitler and Paul Sternberg; m. Gloria May, Oct. 17, 1987; children: Matthew Gregory, Zachary Ian. BA, Harvard Coll., Cambridge, Mass, 1971—75; MD, U. Chgo., 1975—79. Diplomate Nat. Bd. Med. Examiners, 1980, cert. Am. Bd. Ophthalmology, 1985. Thomas Aaberg prof. ophthalmology Emory U. Sch. Medicine, Atlanta, 1985—; G.W. Hale prof., chmn. dept. ophthalmology Vanderbilt U. Sch. Medicine, Nashville, 2003—. Bd. sci. counselors Nat. Eye Inst., Bethesda, Md., 2003—, bd. trustees, Assn. Rsch. in Vision and Ophthalmology, Rockville, Md., 2005—. Bd. trustees Cheekwood Bot. Garden & Mus. of Art, Nashville, 2003—06. Mem.: Am. Acad. Ophthalmology (life; sec. of comm. 2000—05, bd. trustees 2005—). Office: Vanderbilt Eye Inst 1215 21st Ave S Nashville TN 37232-8808 Home Phone: 615-386-0508; Office Phone: 615-936-1453. Business E-Mail: paul.sternberg@vanderbilt.edu.

STERNBERG, ROBERT JEFFREY, dean, psychology professor, researcher; b. Newark, Dec. 8, 1949; s. Joseph Sternberg and Lillian Myriam (Politzer) Weingast; children: Seth, Sara. BA summa cum laude, Yale U., 1972; PhD in Psychology, Stanford U., 1975; D honoris causa (hon.), Complutense U., Madrid, 1994, U. Cyprus, 2000, U. Paris, 2000, U. Leuven, Belgium, 2001, Constantine the Philosopher U., Nitra, Slovakia, 2004; DSc, U. Durham, Eng., 2006, St. Petersburg U., Russia, 2006, U. Tilburg, Netherlands, 2007. Mem. faculty dept. psychology Yale U., New Haven, 1975—2005, asst. prof., 1975—80, assoc. prof., 1980—83, prof. psychology, 1983-86, dir. grad. studies, 1983—88, IBM prof. psychology and edn., 1986—, acting chmn. dept. psychology, 1992, dir. Yale Ctr. Psychology of Abilities, Competencies and Expertise, 2000—05, prof. Sch. Mgmt., 2005; dean Sch. Arts and Scis. Tufts U., Medford, Mass., 2005—, prof. psychology, 2006—; sr. scholar Ctr. for Pub. Leadership, Kennedy Sch. Govt., Harvard U., 2006—. Disting. assoc. Psychometrics Ctr., Cambridge, England, 2007—. Editor-in-chief Ency. of Human Intelligence, Psychol. Bull., 1991-96, Contemporary Psychology, 1999-2004; cons. editor Learning and Individual Differences, 1992—, Intelligence, 1977—, Devel. Rev., 1987-91, Jour. Personality and Social Psychology, 1989-91, Psychol. Rev., 1989-91; author: Intelligence, Information Processing and Analogical Reasoning, 1977, Beyond IQ, 1985, The Triarchic Mind, 1988, Metaphors of Mind, 1990, In Search of the Human Mind, 1995, 98, (with T. Lubart) Defying the Crowd, 1995, Successful Intelligence, 1997, Pathways to Psychology, 1997, Thinking Styles, 1997, Intelligence, Heredity and Environment, 1997, Love is a Story, 1998, Cupid's Arrow, 1998, Handbook of Intelligence, 2000, Psychology 101-1/2, 2002, Wisdom, Intelligence, and Creativity Synthesized, 2003. Recipient award for Excellence Mensa Edn. and Rsch. Found., 1989, Disting. Lifetime Contbn. to Psychology Conn. Psychology Assn., 1999, Disting. Scientist and Scholar award Positive Psychology Network, 2002, Anton Jurovsky award, Slovak Psychol. Soc., 2004, Interam. Psychologist award Interam. Psychol. Soc., 2005, E. Paul Torrance award, 2006; Guggenheim Found. fellow, 1985-86. Fellow AAAS, APA (bd. dirs. 2002-04, pres. 2003, past pres. divsns. 1, 10, 15, 24, trustee ins. trust 2004, McCandless Young Scientist award divsn. devel. psychology 1982, Disting. Sci. award for early career contbn. 1981, pres. 2003, Farnsworth award, Arthur W. Staats award, E.L. Thorndike award 2003, Arnheim award, 2005), Ea. Psychol. Assn. (bd. dirs., pres. 2007—), Am. Psychol. Found. (trustee 2005—), Am. Acad. Arts and Scis., Am. Psychol. Soc., Soc. Exptl. Psychologists, Internat. Assn. Cognitive Edn. and Psychology (pres.-elect 2007—); mem. Am. Ednl. Rsch. Assn. (Rsch. Rev. award 1986, Outstanding Book award 1987, Sylvia Scribner award 1996, James McKeen Cattell award 1999), Soc. Multivariate Exptl. Psychology (Cattell award 1982), Nat. Assn. Gifted Children (Disting. Scholar award 1985, E. Paul Torrance award 2006), Phi Beta Kappa, Kappa Delta Pi (Laureate chpt. 2003). Achievements include theory of successful intelligence; balance theory of wisdom; theory of mental self; investment theory of creativity; triangular theory of love; duplex theory of hate. Avocations: exercise, travel, reading, cello. Office: Tufts U Office Dean Art and Scis Ballou Hall 3d Fl Medford MA 02155 Home Phone: 617-840-7337; Office Phone: 617-627-3864. Office Fax: 617-627-3703. Business E-Mail: robert.sternberg@tufts.edu.

STERNBERG, SEYMOUR, insurance company executive; b. Bklyn., June 24, 1943; s. Max and Mollie Sternberg; m. Roslyn Jacobowitz, June 14, 1965 (div.); children: Jodi, Donna; m. Laurette Zolty, Sept. 14, 1980; 1 child, Matthew. BSEE, CCNY, 1965; MSEE in Computer Sci., Northeastern U., 1968. Mgr. Raytheon Co., Bedford, Mass., 1965-73; mgr. Data Architects, Waltham, Mass., 1973-75; dir. info. svcs. Mass. Mut. Life Ins. Co., Springfield, 1975-76, 2d v.p., 1976-77, v.p. info. svcs., 1977-81, sr. v.p. group life and health divsn., 1981-84, exec. v.p. group life and health divsn., 1984-87, sr. exec. v.p., 1987-88; sr. v.p. group ops. N.Y. Life Ins.

Co., 1989, exec. v.p., 1991, vice chmn., pres., COO, 1995-97, chmn., pres., CEO, 1997—2002, chmn., CEO, 2002—. Bd. govs. United Way Tri-State; bd. trustees Hackley School, Tarrytown, NY, NY Presbyterian Hosp., Big Bros./ Big Sisters of NYC, Northeastern U., Boston, 2004—; bd. dirs. Express Scripts Inc. Mem.: CUNY Bus. Leadership Coun., NYC Partnership and C. of C. (bd. mem.), BRT, ACLI (bd. dir. CIT group). Avocations: stamp collecting/philately, tennis. Office: NY Life Ins Co 51 Madison Ave Rm 1304 New York NY 10010 Business E-Mail: sy150@newyorklife.com.

STERNBERGER, LUDWIG AMADEUS, neurologist, educator; b. Munich, May 26, 1921; s. Hugo and Emy (Welinger) S.; m. Nancy Jeanne Hoy, Dec. 13, 1961. BA, Am. U. Beirut, 1941, MD, 1945. Fellow Sloan Kettering Meml. Cancer Ctr., NYC, 1948-50; sr. med. biochemist N.Y. State Dept. Health, Albany, 1950-54; asst. prof. medicine Northwestern U., Chgo., 1954-55; chief basic scis. div. Med. Research Labs., Edgewood Arsenal, Md., 1957-78; prof. brain research U. Rochester Med. Ctr. (N.Y.), 1978-86; prof. neurology, pathology and anatomy U. Md., Balt., 1986-92; sci. co-dir., treas. Sternberger Monoclonals, Inc., Balt., 1992—. Author: Immunocytochemistry, 1974, 3d edit, 1986; mem. editoral bd. Cell and Tissue Research, Histochemistry, Jour. Histochemistry and Cytochemistry, Jour. Neurosci. Methods, Jour. Neuroimmunology, Histochem. Jour., Electron Microscopy in Biology. Served to maj. M.C. US Army, 1955—57. Recipient Paul A. Siple prize, 1972; recipient Humboldt prize for sr. U.S. scientists, 1980, Classic Author citation Inst. Sci. Info., 1983; Senator Jacob K. Javits neurosci. investigator award, 1984; 25th most frequently cited author in sci. lit. of 1984; author of one of 17 Newcomer Superstar papers among 100 most cited of all time. Mem. Histochem. Soc. (pres. 1977-78), Am. Soc. Neurochemistry (program com. 1983-84), Am. Assn. Immunologists, Endocrine Soc., Am. Acad. Allergy, Am. Assn. Neuropathologists Lutheran. Home: 10 Burwood Ct Lutherville Timonium MD 21093-3502 Office Phone: 410-821-6719. Personal E-mail: n-l-s@att.net.

STERNE, HEDDA, artist; b. Bucharest, Romania, Aug. 4, 1910; arrived in U.S., 1941; d. Simon and Eugenie (Wexler) Lidenberg; m. Frederick Sterne (div.). Solo exhibitions including ICL Gallery, East Hampton, NY, 1980, CDS Gallery, NYC, 1982, 84, 87, 90, 95, 98, 2000, 04, 06, Queens Mus., Flushing, NY, 1985, Philippe Briet Gallery, NYC, 1993, Bibliotheque Municipale, Ville de Caen, France, 1998, Krannert Art Mus, Urbana-Champaign, Ill., 2006, U. Va. Art Mus., Charlottesville, 2007, and others; group exhibitions including Guild Hall Mus., East Hampton, 1982, Penn Plaza, NYC, 1983, CDS Gallery, 1988, Pollock-Krasner House and Study Ctr., East Hampton, 1997, Arlene Bujese Gallery, East Hampton, 1997, Lawrence Gallery, Rosemont Coll., Pa., 1997, Centro Atlantico de Arte Moderno, Las Palmas de Gran Canaria, Spain, 1999, Ulmer Mus., Ulm, Germany, 2001, Musei Civici, Veneziani, Italy, 2002, and others; permanent collections include Whitney Mus. Am. Art, NYC, Met. Mus. Art, NYC, Mus. Modern Art, NYC, Am. Acad. Arts, NY, Ford Found, NY, Rockefeller Inst., NY, Albright-Knox Art Gallery, Buffalo, Everson Mus. Art, Syracuse, Art Mus. of Chgo., and numerous others. Named to Ordre des Arts et des Lettres, Ambassador of France, NY, 1999; recipient Contemporary Am. Painting Purchase award, U. Ill., 1949, 2d prize, Art Inst Chgo. Ann., 1957, 1st prize, Art Inst. Newport Ann., 1967, Childe Hassam Purchase award, Am. Acad. Arts and Letters, 1971, Hassam and Speicher Purchase Fund award, 1984; Fulbright fellow, 1963. Mailing: CDS Gallery 76E 79st St New York NY 10021

STERNE, JOSEPH ROBERT LIVINGSTON, editor, educator; b. Phila., Apr. 25, 1928; s. Robert Livingston and Edith Eisner (Heymann) S.; m. Barbara Adele Greene, Feb. 10, 1951; children: Robert Greene, Paul Livingston, Edward Joseph, Adam Heymann, Lee Winslow Greene. BA cum laude, Lehigh U., 1948; MS, Columbia U., 1950. Reporter Salt Lake Telegram, Salt Lake City, 1948-49, Wall Street Jour., NYC, 1950-51, Dallas Morning News, 1951-53; reporter Balt. Sun, 1953-72, editorial page editor, 1972-97; sr. fellow Inst. for Policy Studies Johns Hopkins U., 1997—. Mem. Am. Soc. Newpaper Editors, Hamilton St. Club, Phi Beta Kappa. Home: PO Box 599 Sparks MD 21152-0599 Office: Johns Hopkins U Inst Policy Studies 3400 N Charles St Baltimore MD 21218-2680 Business E-Mail: jsterne@jhu.edu.

STERNER, CHRIS STEPHEN, nuclear engineer, educator; b. Reading, Pa., Nov. 19, 1943; s. Wilbur Sylvanus Sterner and Frances Corvaia; m. Karen Lee Paula Miller, Nov. 10, 1944; 1 child, Morgan Scott. AA, St. Petersburg Jr. Coll., Fla., 1985; BA, Eckerd Coll., St. Petersburg, 1989; MA, U. South Fla., Tampa, 1996. Sr. designer Gilbert/Commonwealth Assocs., Reading, 1968—80; nuc. configuration mgmt. specialist Progress Energy Corp., Crystal River, Fla., 1980—2003; adj. history prof. Edison Coll., Fla., 2004—. With USN, 1962—66. Home Phone: 941-429-2471.

STERNER, FRANK MAURICE, manufacturing executive; b. Lafayette, Ind., Nov. 26, 1935; s. Raymond E. and Madelene M. (Scipio) S.; m. Elsa Y. Rasmusson, June 29, 1958; children: Mark, Lisa. BS, Purdue U., 1958, MS, 1959, PhD, 1962. Sr. staff specialist Gen. Motors Inst., Flint, Mich., 1962-63; dir. personnel and orgnl. research Delco Electronics, Milw., 1963-66, dir. personnel devel. and research, 1966-68; partner Nourse & Sterner, Inc., Milw., 1968-69; pres., 1969-73; assoc. dean, prof. Krannert Grad. Sch. of Mgmt., Purdue U., West Lafayette, Ind., 1973-79; v.p. strategic mgmt. Johnson Controls, Inc., Milw., 1979-89; pres., chief exec. officer E.R. Wagner Mfg. Co., 1989—; pres., owner Ridgeway Devel. Inc., Milw., 1993—. Bd. dirs. Wausau Homes, Inc., E.R. Wagner Mfg. Co., Ridgeway Devel. Inc., Greenheck Fan Corp. Home: 1440 E Standish Pl Milwaukee WI 53217-1958 Office: ER Wagner Mfg Co 4611 N 32nd St Milwaukee WI 53209-6000 Office Phone: 414-449-8204. Business E-Mail: frank.sterner@erwagner.com.

STERNER, ROBERT WARNER, ecologist, science administrator; b. Elmhurst, Ill., Jan. 15, 1958; s. Paul and Helen E. (Robertson) S.; m. Joan Artley, May 31, 1984; 2 children. BS in Biology, U. Ill., Champaign, 1980; PhD in Ecology, U. Minn., Mpls., 1986. Postdoctoral rschr. Max Planck Inst. Limnology, Plön, Germany, 1986—87; asst. prof. U. Tex., Arlington, 1988—92, assoc. prof., 1992—94, U. Minn., St. Paul, 1994—99, interim dept. head, 1998—99, dept. head, 1999—2003, prof. biology dept. ecology, evolution and behavior, 1999—; dir. divsn. environ. biology NSF, 2007—. Contbr. articles to sci. jours.; co-author (with J.J. Elser): Ecological Stoichiometry: The Biology of Elements from Molecules to the Biosphere, 2002; assoc. editor: Ecology, 2005—. Activist INFACT, Mpls., 1985-86. Recipient NSF predoctoral fellowship, 1987, NSF Ecology Program award, 1988-93. Mem. AAAS, Ecol. Soc. of Am., Am. Soc. Limnology and Oceanography. Office: Divsn Environ Biology NSF 4201 Wilson Blvd Arlington VA 22230 Office Phone: 703-292-8480. Office Fax: 703-292-9064. E-mail: rsterner@nsf.edu. *

STERNHAGEN, FRANCES, actress; b. Washington, Jan. 13, 1930; Student, Vassar Coll., Perry-Mansfield Sch. Theatre; studied with Sanford Meisner, NY. Tchr. Milton Acad., Cath. U.; actress Arena Stage, Washington, DC, 1953-54. Debut Thieves Carnival, NY, 1955; plays include The Carefree Tree, The Admirable Bashville (Clarence Derwent award, Obie award), Ulysses in Night Town, Red Eye of Love, Misalliance, The Return of Herbert Bracewell, Laughing Stock, The Displaced Person, The Pinter Plays (Obie award); Broadway shows include The Skin of Our Teeth, Viva Madison Avenue, Great Day in the Morning, The Right Honorable Gentleman, The Cocktail Party, Cock-a-Doodle Dandy, Playboy of the Western World, The Sign in Sidney Brustein's Window, The Good Doctor (Tony award 1973), Equus (Drama Desk award), Angel, On Golden Pond (Drama League award), The Father, Grownups, Summer, You Can't Take It With You, Home Front, Driving Miss Daisy, Remembrance, A Perfect Ganesh, The Heiress (Tony award 1995), Long Day's Journey into Night, 1998, The Exact Center of the Universe, 1999, Morning's at Seven, 2003, The Foreigner, 2003, Echoes of the War, 2004, Seascape, 2005, Steel Magnolias, 2005; actress (films) Up The Down Staircase, 1967, Starting Over, 1979, Outland, 1981, Independence Day, 1983, Romantic Comedy, 1983, Bright Lights, Big City, 1988, See You in the Morning, 1989, Communion, 1989, Misery, 1990, Doc Hollywood, 1991, Raising Cain, 1992, Curtain Call, Land Fall, 1997, The Rising Place, 1998; (TV series) Love of Life, The Doctors, Secret Storm, Cheers, Golden Years, Under One Roof, The Road Home, E.R., Sex and the City, The Closer; (TV movies) Who Will Save Our Children?, 1978, Prototype, 1982, Resting Place, 1986, Follow Your Heart, 1990, She Woke Up, 1992, Labor of Love: The Arlette Schweitzer Story, 1993, Reunion, 1994, Tales from the Crypt, Outer Limits, Law and Order, 1990, 96, The Con, 1997, To Live Again, 1997, New York: A Documentary Film, 1999, The Laramie Project, 2001. Recipient Edith Oliver Award for Sustained Excellence, 2005.

STERNLICHT, BARRY STUART, hotel executive; b. Lake Success, NY, Nov. 27, 1960; m. Mimi Sternlicht; 3 children. BA magna cum laude, Brown U., 1982; MBA with distinction, Harvard U., 1986; PhD in bus. adminstrn. (hon.), Johnson & Wales. Pres., CEO Starwood Capital Group, LLC, Phoenix, 1991—2004; chmn., CEO Starwood Hotels and Resorts Trust, Phoenix, 1995—2004; CEO iStar Fin. Inc., 1996—97, chmn., 1996—2000, Starwood Hotels & Resorts Worldwide, Inc., White Plains, NY, 1997—2004, CEO, 1999—2004, exec. chmn., chief design officer, 2004—. Trustee Equity Residential Trust; bd. dirs. Starwood Fin. Trust, U.S. Franchise Systems and Comm.; mem. Urban Land Inst., Nat. Multi-Family Housing Coun, Young Presidents Org., World Travel & Tourism Council, Council for the U.S. and Italy. Bd. dirs. Com. to Encourage Corp. Philanthropy, Bus. Com. for the Arts, Inc., Channel 13/WNET, Nat. Leadership Advocacy Program for Juvenile Diabetes Rsch. Found. Internat., Kids in Crisis, Fairfield County Jr. Achievement, Ctr. for Christian-Jewish Understanding; bd. govs. NAREIT. Named Man of the Year, Juvenile Diabetes Rsch. Found. Internat.; recipient Preston Robert Tisch Disting. Industry Leadership award, NYU Sch. Hospitality, Tourism & Travel Admin. Office: Starwood Hotels and Resorts Worldwide 1111 Westchester Ave White Plains NY 10604-3520

STERNLICHT, BENO, research and development company executive; b. Nowy Sacz, Poland; arrived in U.S., 1949, naturalized, 1950; s. Hugo Charles and Helena (Anisfeld) Sternlicht; m. Lisa Spilberg; children: Mark David, Eric Alan, Joshua Hugh, Aaron Jonathan. BSEE, Union Coll., Schenectady, NY, 1950; MS, Columbia U., 1951, PhD, 1954, DSc (hon.), 1970. Staff engr. Thermal Power Sys., gen. engring. lab. GE, 1951-54, specialist applied mechanics, 1954-58, cons. engr., 1958-61; co-founder, 1961; since chmn. bd., tech. dir. Mech. Tech., Inc., Latham, NY; pres. Benjosh Mgmt. Corp., NY, 1983, Ameast, NYC, 1981—; co-founder Arben Internat. LLC, NYC, 1994—. Dir. Small Diesels Ltd., India, New Ea. India Ltd., Plug Power LLC; pres. Vols. Internat. Tech. Assistance, 1965—71, chmn. bd. dirs., 1971—73; chmn. com. energy tech. and space propulsion NASA, 1969—72, mem. rsch. adv. coun., 1970—72; mem. Nat. Energy Task Force, 1981; bd. chmn. Comfortex Corp., 1995—; cons. to PRC, Israel, India. Author: numerous tech. articles on energy, tech., social and ednl. fields. Mem. AIPAC, World Jewish Congress, Jewish Fedn., ORT; chmn. Lisbon Charitable Trust; advisor on energy & innovation to Pres. Carter; advisor on energy and transp. to Pres. Reagan; advisor Pres. Bush. Fellow: ASME (Machine Design award 1966); mem.: AIAA, Am. Soc. Lubrication Engrs., Nat. Acad. Engring., Navy League, Sigma Xi, Tau Beta Pi. Achievements include patents in field. Address: 123 Partridge Run Schenectady NY 12309-1321 Office Phone: 718-376-0070. Personal E-mail: Lisben26@aol.com.

STERNLICHT, SANFORD, literature educator, writer; b. NYC, Sept. 20, 1931; s. Irving Stanley and Sylvia (Hilsenroth) S.; m. Dorothy Hilkert, June 4, 1956 (dec. 1977); children: David, Daniel. BS, SUNY, Oswego, 1953; MA, Colgate U., 1955; PhD, Syracuse U., 1962. Instr. SUNY, Oswego, 1959-60, asst. prof., 1960-62, prof. and dir. grad. studies in English, 1962-72, chmn. dept. theater, 1972-84; adj. prof. English Syracuse (N.Y.) U., 1981—. Leverhulme vis. prof. English, U. York, Eng., 1965-66; Fulbright sr. specialist, vis. prof. English, U. Pecs, Hungary, 2004. Author: Gull's Way, 1961, The Blue Star Commodore, 1961, Love in Pompeii, 1967, John Webster's Imagery and the Webster Canon, 1972, John Masefield, 1977, McKinley's Bulldog, 1977 (Mil. Book Club award, Saturday Evening Post Book Club award), C.S. Forester, 1981, Padraic Colum, 1985; (with E.M. Jameson) The Black Devil of the Bayous, 1971; (with E.M. Jameson) U.S. F. Constellation: Yankee Racehorse, 1981, John Galsworthy, 1986, R.F. Delderfield, 1988, Stevie Smith, 1990, Stephen Spender, 1992, Siegfried Sassoon, 1993, All Things Herriot: James Herriot and His Peaceable Kingdom, 1995, Jean Rhys, 1997, A Reader's Guide to Modern Irish Drama, 1998, C.S. Forester and the Hornblower Saga, 1999, Chaim Potok: A Critical Companion, 2000, A Reader's Guide to Modern American Drama, 2002, A Student Companion to Elie Wiesel, 2003, A Reader's Guide to Modern British Drama, 2004, The Tenement Saga: The Lower East Side and Early Jewish American Writers, 2004, Masterpieces of Modern British and Irish Drama, 2005, Masterpieces of Jewish American Literature, 2007; editor: The Selected Short Stories of Padraic Colum, 1985, The Selected Plays of Padraic Colum, 1986, The Selected Poems of Padraic Colum, 1988, In Search of Stevie Smith, 1991, New Plays from the Abbey Theatre, 1993-1995, 96, 96-98, 99, 99-2001, 2003. Lt. (j.g.) USN, 1955-59, comdr. USNR, ret. Recipient New Poets award Writer mag., 1960, Chancellor's award SUNY, 1974; fellow Poetry Soc. Am., 1964; rsch. grantee SUNY, 1963-70; named Tchr. of Yr. Syracuse U., 1986. Mem. MLA, PEN, Shakespeare Assn. Am., Am. Conf. Irish Studies. Democrat. Jewish. Home: 128 Dorset Rd Syracuse NY 13210-3048 Office: Syracuse U Dept English Syracuse NY 13244-0001 Home Phone: 315-472-5639; Office Phone: 315-443-9480. Business E-Mail: svsternl@syr.edu.

STERNMAN, JOEL W., lawyer; b. NYC, Oct. 20, 1943; s. Abraham and Sarah (Simon) S.; children: Mark S., Cheryl A.; m. Barbara E. Shiers, March 31, 1985; children: Matthew S., Julia S. AB, Dartmouth Coll., 1965; LLB, Yale U., 1968. Bar: N.Y. 1970, U.S. Dist. Ct. (so. and ea. dists.) N.Y. 1971, U.S. Ct. Appeals (2d cir.) 1972, U.S. Supreme Ct. 1984, U.S. Ct. Appeals (6th cir.) 1985, U.S. Ct. Appeals (9th cir.) 1994, U.S. Tax Ct. 1996, U.S. Dist. Ct. (ea. dist.) Mich. 1997. Law clk. to judge U.S. Dist. Ct., New Haven, 1968-69; assoc. Rosenman Colin Freund Lewis & Cohen, NYC, 1969-77; ptnr. Rosenman & Colin LLP, NYC, 1977—2002, Katten Muchin Rosenman LLP (formerly Katten Muchin Zavis Rosenman), 2002—. Editor Yale Law Jour., New Haven, 1966-68. Mem. Phi Beta Kappa. Office: Katten Muchin Rosenman LLP 575 Madison Ave New York NY 10022-2585 Home Phone: 914-723-0947; Office Phone: 212-940-7060. E-mail: j.sternman@kattenlaw.com.

STERNS, JOEL HENRY, lawyer; b. NYC, Apr. 13, 1934; s. Barney and Yvetta S.; m. Joanne Glickman, Nov. 19, 1961; children: Rachel, Leslie, David. BS in Journalism, 1956; MPA, Princeton U., 1958; JD, NYU, 1967. Bar: N.J., D.C. Exec. asst. to commr., acting commr. N.J. Dept. Conservation and Econ. Devel., 1958-61; exec. asst. to adminstr. Bur. Security and Consular Affairs, U.S. Dept. State, 1961-62; regional programs coord. Alliance for Progress, 1962-64; exec. asst. to pres. Export-Import Bank U.S., 1964; dep. commr. N.J. Dept. Cmty. Affairs, 1967-68; counsel to gov. N.J., 1968-70; pres. firm Sterns, Herbert & Weinroth (P.A.), Trenton, NJ, 1970-88; mem. exec. com., compensation com. and mktg. com. Sterns, Herbert & Weinroth (merged with Hannoch-Weisman 1988), Roseland, NJ, 1988-91; pres. Hannoch-Weisman, Roseland, 1991-93, Sterns & Weinroth, Trenton, 1994—. Mem. lawyers adv. com. U.S. Dist. Ct. N.J., 1995—. Mem. ABA, Am. Law Inst., Am. Judicature Soc., N.J. Bar Assn. (trustee), Mercer County Bar Assn., Assn. Princeton U. Grad. Alumni (trustee 1975-77), NYU Alumni Assn. N.J. (Disting. Alumni award 1987). Home: 28 Heritage Hills Dr Washington Crossing PA 18977 Office: Sterns & Weinroth PO Box 1298 50 W State St Ste 1400 Trenton NJ 08607 Home Phone: 609-213-4898; Office Phone: 609-392-2100. E-mail: jsterns@sternslaw.com.

STERNS, WILLIAM S., III, lawyer; b. Wilkes Barre, Pa., Feb. 16, 1948; s. William S. Sterns, Jr. and Harriette B. Sterns; m. Wenke B. Thoman, May 1, 1999; children: William IV, Stefan, Olivia. BA, Colgate U., 1970; JD, N.Y. Law Sch., 1977. Bar: NY 1978, Conn. 1991. Assoc. Casey Lane & Mittendorf, NYC, 1977—80; ptnr. Jones Hirsch, 1980—96; ptnr.,corp. securities and securities group Alston & Bird LLP, 1996—. Contbr. Abington Theatre, Manhattan Theatre; patron Dorset Play House, Internat. House. Mem.: Ekwanok Country Club, The River Club, Baltusrol Golf Club. Avocations: golf, tennis, skiing, cuisine. Office: Alston & Bird LLP 90 Park Ave New York NY 10016 Office Phone: 212-210-9530. Office Fax: 212-210-9444. Business E-Mail: william.sterns@alston.com.

STERNSTEIN, ALLAN J., lawyer; b. Chgo., June 7, 1948; s. Milton and Celia (Kaganove) Sternstein; m. Miriam A. Dolgin, July 12, 1970 (div. July 1981); children: Jeffery A., Amy R.; m. Beverly A. Cook, Feb. 8, 1986 (div. 2004); 1 child, Julia S. BS, U. Ill., 1970; MS, U. Mich., 1972. Bar: Ill. 1977, US Dist. Ct. (no. dist.) Ill. 1977, US Dist. Ct. (no. dist.) Ohio 1977, US Dist. Ct. (ea. dist) Mich. 1986, US Dist. Ct. (we. dist.) Mich. 1990, US Ct. Customs and Patent Appeals 1978, US Ct. Appeals (7th cir.) 1979, US Ct. Appeals (Fed. cir.) 1982, US Dist. Ct. (ea. dist.) Wis. 2003, US Ct. Appeals (5th cir.) 2003. Patent agt. Sunbeam Corp., Oak Brook, Ill., 1972—76; ptnr. Neuman, Williams, Anderson & Olson, Chgo., 1976—84; divsn. patent counsel Abbott Labs., North Chgo., Ill., 1984—87; ptnr. Brinks Hofer Gilson & Lione, Chgo., 1987—2005, mng. ptnr., 1996—99; ptnr., head IP litigation Dykema Gossett, Chgo., 2005—. Adj. prof. law U. Ill., 1992—; lectr. Oxford U., England, 2003. Co-author: Designing an Effective Intellectual Property Compliance Program; contbr. articles to profl. jours. Legal advisor Legal Aid Soc., Chgo., 1974—76, Pub. Defender's Office, Chgo., 1974. Mem.: ABA, Licensing Execs. Soc., Am. Intellectual Property Law Assn., Patent Law Assn. Chgo. (com. chmn. 1982), Chgo. Bar Assn., Phi Eta Sigma, Sigma Gamma Tau, Sigma Tau, Tau Beta Pi. Jewish. Office: Dykema Gossett 10 S Wacker Dr Ste 2300 Chicago IL 60606 Office Phone: 312-627-2143.

STERRETT, JAMES MELVILLE, accountant, consultant; b. Chgo., Dec. 25, 1949; s. James McAnlis and Antoinette (Galligan) S.; m. Joyce Mieko Motoda, Sept. 1, 1989; 1 child, Victoria Hanako. BS in Acctg., Chaminade U., Honolulu, 1988; MBA, Chaminade U., 1991. CPA, Hawaii. Cons. Profitability Cons., Honolulu, 1985-87; pres. Sterrett Cons. Group, Honolulu, 1987-88; auditor Deloitte & Touche, Honolulu, 1988-90; acct., cons. pvt. practice, Honolulu, 1990—. Mem. Nat. Soc. Pub. Accts., Nat. Assn. Tax Practitioners, Hawaii Soc. CPA's, Delta Epsilon, Sigma. Office: 1314 S King St Ste 855 Honolulu HI 96814-1979 Office Phone: 808-591-6686.

STERRETT, SAMUEL BLACK, lawyer, former judge; b. Washington, Dec. 17, 1922; s. Henry Hatch Dent and Helen (Black) S.; m. Jeane McBride, Aug. 27, 1949; children: Samuel Black, Robin Dent, Douglas McBride. Student, St. Albans Sch., 1933-41; grad., US Mcht. Marine Acad., 1945, BS, 2004; BA, Amherst Coll., 1947; LLB, U. Va., 1950; LLM in Taxation, NYU, 1959. Bar: D.C. 1951, Va. 1950. Atty. Alvord & Alvord, Washington, 1950-56; trial atty. Office Regional Counsel, Internal Revenue Service, NYC, 1956-60; ptnr. Sullivan, Shea & Kenney, Washington, 1960-68; municipal cons. to office vice pres. U.S., 1965-68; judge U.S. Tax Ct., 1968-88, chief judge, 1985-88; ptnr. Myerson, Kuhn & Sterrett, Washington, 1988-89; of counsel Vinson & Elkins, Washington, 1990—2002; pvt. practice Washington, 2002—07, Chevy Chase, Md., 2007—. Bd. mgrs. Chevy Chase Village, 1970-74, chmn., 1972-74; 1st v.p. bd. trustees, exec. com. Washington Hosp. Ctr., 1969-79, chmn. bd. trustees, 1979-84, trustee, 1999-2007; chmn. bd. trustees Washington Healthcare Corp., 1982-87; chmn. bd. trustees Medlantic Healthcare Group, 1987-89; mem. audit com. Medstar Health, 1990-2006; trustee Prostestant Episcopal Cathedral Found., 1973-81, 99-2007, fin. com., 1998-2007, chmn., 1999-2006; governing bd. St. Albans Sch., 1977-81; trustee Louise Home, 1979-89. Wwith AUS, 1943, with U.S. Mcht. Marine, 1943-46. Fellow Am. Bar Found. (life); mem. ABA, D.C. Bar Assn., Am. Coll. Tax Counsel, Soc. of the Cincinnati, Coun. for Future, Am. Inns. of Ct., Chevy Chase Club (bd. govs. 1979-84, pres. 1984), Met. Club, Lawyers Club, Alibi Club, Alfalfa Club, Ch. of N.Y. Club, Beta Theta Pi. Episcopalian. Personal E-mail: sbsterrett@aol.com.

STERTZ, STEPHEN ALLEN, historian, educator; b. NYC, Aug. 2, 1944; s. Philip Bernard and Anne (Herman) S. BS, Columbia U., 1968; PhD, U. Mich., 1974. Rschr. Bronx County Hist. Soc., 1978—82, 1983—2003. Adj. asst. prof. history Rutgers U., Newark, 1980—82, 1986, Dowling Coll., Oakdale, NY, 1991—2000, Mercy Coll., Bronx, 1996—; vis. asst. prof. classics U. Ill., Urbana, 1982—83; adj. lectr. classics and history St. Peter's Coll., Jersey City, 2000—03, Fordham U., NYC, 2000, Montclair State U., Upper Montclair, NJ, 2002—05, Seton Hall U., South Orange, 2005—06, Met. Coll. NY, 2006—. Author: Jonathan Swift's Gulliver's Travels, 1996; editor: Concordantia in Orationem Quae Aristidis Fertur Eis Basilea, 1996; contbr articles to profl. jours. Candidate N.Y. State Legislature, 1970. Travel to Collections grantee NEH, Washington, 1984; rsch. grantee Wilbur Found., Mecosta, Mich., 1992, Soc. Farsaratul, L.I. City, N.Y., 1992, Richter Found., N.Y.C., 1996. Mem. Am. Hist. Assn., Am. Philol. Assn., Archaeol. Instn. Am. (nat. coun. 1977-78). Avocations: reading, book collecting. Office: Mercy Coll 1200 Waters Pl Bronx NY 10467 E-mail: sstertz@pipemail.mercy.com.

STERZER, FRED, research physicist; b. Vienna, Nov. 18, 1929; came to U.S., 1947, naturalized, 1952; s. Karl and Rosa (Trumer) S.; m. Betty Distel, Sept. 5, 1964 (dec.). BS in Physics, CCNY, 1951; MS in Physics, NYU, 1952, PhD in Physics, 1955. With RCA, 1954-87, RCA Labs., David Sarnoff Research Center, Princeton, NJ, 1956-87, dir. microwave tech. center, 1972-87; dir. microwave research lab. David Sarnoff Research Ctr., 1987-88; pres. MMTC, Inc., Princeton, 1988—. Herbert J. Kayser research prof., City Coll., CUNY, 1986-87. Contbr. numerous articles to profl. publs. Fellow IEEE; mem. Am. Phys. Soc., Nat. Acad. Engring., Sigma Xi, Phi Beta Kappa. Achievements include condr. research on optical components, microwave solid-state devices and circuits, med. microwave tech. Home: 4432 Province Line Rd Princeton NJ 08540-4368 Office: MMTC Inc 12 Roszel Rd Princeton NJ 08540-6234 Office Phone: 609-520-9699. Business E-Mail: sterzer@mmtc.com.

STESKAL, CHRISTOPHER JAMES, lawyer, former prosecutor; b. 1966; JD, Harvard Law Sch., 1992. Law clk. to Hon. Harry L. Hupp US Dist. Ct.; law clk. to Hon. James R. Browning US Ct. Appeals (9th Cir.); assoc. Cravath, Swaine & Moore, Howard, Rice, Nemerovski, Canady, Falk; asst. U.S. atty. (no. dist.) Calif. US Dept. Justice, 2001—07; ptnr., chair white collar practice Fenwick & West LLP, San Francisco, 2007—. Office: Fenwick & West LLP 555 California St 12th Fl San Francisco CA 94104 Office Phone: 415-875-2300. Office Fax: 415-281-1350. *

STETLER, DAVID J., lawyer; b. Washington, Sept. 6, 1949; s. C. Joseph and Norine (Delaney) S.; m. Mary Ann Ferguson, Aug. 14, 1971; children: Brian, Christopher, Jennifer. BA, Villanova U., 1971, JD, 1974. Bar: U.S. Supreme Ct. 1978, Ill. 1988, U.S. Ct. Appeals (7th cir.) 1988, U.S. Ct. Appeals (3d cir.) 1992, U.S. Dist. Ct. (ctrl. dist.) 1994, U.S. Ct. Appeals

(8th cir.) 1994. Atty. IRS, Washington, 1974-79; spl. atty. tax divsn. Dept. Justice, Washington, 1975-79; asst. atty. U.S. Atty.'s Office, Chgo., 1979-88, dep. chief spl. prosecutions div., 1985-86, chief criminal receiving and appellate divsns., 1986-88; ptnr. McDermott, Will & Emery, Chgo., 1988-98; prin. Stetler & Duffy, Ltd., Chgo., 1998—. Lectr. Atty. Gen. Trial Advocacy Inst., Washington, 1977—. Fellow Internat. Soc. Barristers, Am. Coll. Trial Lawyers; mem. ABA (chmn. midwest subcom. White Collar Crime com. 1991-93), Wong Sun Soc. San Francisco. Office: 11 S LaSalle St Ste 1200 Chicago IL 60603 Office Phone: 312-338-0202. E-mail: dstetler@stetlerandduffy.com.

STETLER, RUSSELL DEARNLEY, JR., investigator; b. Phila., Jan. 15, 1945; s. Russell Dearnley and Martha Eleanor (Schultz) S. BA with honors in Philosophy, Haverford Coll., Pa., 1966; postgrad., New Sch. Social Rsch., 1966-67. Research asst. to Bertrand Russell, 1967; lectr. Hendon Coll., London, 1968-69; pres. Archetype, Inc., Berkeley, Calif., 1971-78; pub. Westworks, Berkeley, 1977-80; pvt. investigator, 1980-90; chief investigator Calif. Appellate Project, 1990-95; dir. of investigation and mitigation N.Y. State Capital Defender Office, NYC, 1995—2005; nat. mitigation coord. Office of the Fed. Pub. Defender, Oakland, Calif., 2005—. Cons., dir. Ramparts Press, Palo Alto, 1971-80; editorial cons. Internews, Berkeley, 1973-78; faculty Caribbean Sch., Ponce, P.R., 1978-80 Author: The Battle of Bogside, 1970; co-editor: The Assassinations: Dallas and Beyond, 1976. Research grantee Atlantic Peace Found., 1969-70 Mem. Calif. Assn. Lic. Investigators, Nat. Assn. Legal Investigators, Calif. Soccer Referees Assn.-North (treas. Marin County chpt. 1982-90), Amigos de las Americas (pres. Marin chpt. 1985-88). Clubs: Mill Valley Soccer (dir. 1981), Albany-Berkeley Soccer (pres. 1977-78). Office: Office of the Fed Pub Defender 555 12th St Ste 650 Oakland CA 94607 E-mail: russell_stetler@fd.org.

STETLER-STEVENSON, WILLIAM GEORGE, pathologist; b. Trenton, NJ, Nov. 27, 1953; BS in Biochemistry cum laude, Albright Coll., 1975; PhD in Biochemistry & Molecular Biology, Northwestern U., 1983, MD, 1984. Diplomate Am. Bd. Pathology. Mem. house staff anatomic pathology McGaw Med. Ctr., 1984-87; sr. staff fellow NIH, 1987-91, med. officer, rschr., 1991—, chief extracellular matrix pathology sect., 1993—. Editl. bd. Cancer Rsch. FASEB Jour., Am. Jour. Pathology, Invasion & Metastasis; contbr. articles to profl. jours. Kemper Found. Med. scholar, 1978-79. Mem. Am. Soc. Biochemistry and Molecular Biology, Am. Soc. Investigative Pathology (Warner-Lambert/Parke-Davis award 1996). Office: Nat Cancer Inst Cell & Cancer Biology Extracellular Matrix Pathology Sect 81147 Grovemont Cir Bethesda MD 20892-4605

STETSON, CATHERINE E., lawyer; b. Albany, NY, Aug. 6, 1969; AM, Duke U., 1991; JD, U. Va. Sch. Law, 1994. Bar: Va. 1994, DC 1996. Clerk US Dist. Ct., DC, 1994—96, US Ct. of Appeals, DC Cir., 1996—97; ptnr. Hogan & Hartson LLP, Washington. Named one of Top 40 Under 40, Washingtonian, 2006, Litigation's Rising Stars, The Am. Lawyer, 2007. Mem.: Nat. Chamber Litig. Ctr., The Barristers, Edward Coke Appellate Inn of Ct., Women's Bar Assn. DC, ABA. Office: Hogan & Hartson LLP 555 13th St NW Washington DC 20004-1109 Office Phone: 202-637-5600. Office Fax: 202-637-5910. *

STETSON, JOHN BATTERSON, IV, construction executive; b. Phila., Dec. 21, 1936; s. John Batterson Stetson III and Winifred (Walton) Todd; m. Solveig Weiland, Nov. 23, 1963; children: John Batterson V, Eric Weiland, Scott Walton. BA, Yale U., 1959, MArch, 1966; postgrad., U. Pa., 1969-73. Registered architect, Pa., Mass., Fla. Staff architect Bower & Fradley, Architects, Phila., 1966-68, Young & Exley, Architects, Phila., 1968-69; project architect Day & Zimmerman Assocs., Phila., 1969-71, mgr. tech. staff, 1974-76; project mgr. Schnadelbach & Braun, Phila., 1971-74; project exec. Bldg. Scis., Inc., Balt., Kinshasa, Zaire, 1976-77; project mgr. Bldg. Scis., Inc., Balt., 1977-78; sr. cons., v.p., pres. MDC Sys. unit Day and Zimmermann, Inc., Phila., 1978-95, v.p. transp. svcs. unit, 1996-99; cons., Construction Project, 1999. Active Haverford (Pa.) Civic Assn., 1981-84. Comdr. USNR, 1959-81. Mem. Constrn. Mgmt. Assn. Am. (bd. dirs. 1986—), Am. Arbitration Assn., Constrn. Specifications Inst., Haverford Sch. Alumni Assn. Clubs: Merion Cricket (Haverford). Republican. Avocations: music, sailing. Home: 7 Druid Ln Malvern PA 19355-2825

STETSON, ROBERT FRANCIS, retired metallurgist; b. NYC, Oct. 20, 1928; s. Ralph Jerome and Margaret Mary Stetson; m. Rita Marie Jubach, Dec. 30, 1950 (dec. May 31, 1994); 1 child, Barbara A.; m. Mary Jane McKinney, June 10, 1999. Cert. in Metallurgy, Pa. State U., 1955. ICET A NSPE. Lab. technologist, insp. Babcock & Wilcox Co., Beaver Falls, Pa., 1949—58; tech. specialist materials sci. Gen. Atomics, San Diego, 1958—86, cons., 1986—98; ret., 1998; cons. NASA Marshall Space Flight Ctr., Huntsville, Ala., 2002—07. With AC US Army, 1946—47, ETO. Recipient Nat. Engring. Assocs. Achievement award, Am. Soc. Metals, 1979, James F. Lincoln Arc Welding Found. award, 1979. Fellow: Am. Soc. Metals Internat. (exec. bd. San Diego chpt. 1964—96, chmn. San Diego chpt. 1972—73). Achievements include patents for plasma orifice tip. Avocation: genealogy.

STETSON, WILLIS J., JR., (LEE STETSON), dean; BS in Bus. Adminstrn. and Econs., U. Del., 1963; MS in Psychol. Svcs., U. Pa., 1971. Tchr. Springfield HS, Pa., 1966; admissions officer U. Del., 1978; dean undergraduate admissions U. Pa., Phila., 1978—. Bd. trustees Coll. Entrance Examination Bd.; bd. dirs. Custodial Trust Co. Mem.: Nat. Assn. Coll. Admission Counseling. Office: U Pa Dean Admissions 3451 Walnut St Philadelphia PA 19104 Office Phone: 215-898-2886. *

STETTLER, STEPHEN F., performing company executive; b. Phila., May 1, 1952; s. Wallace Frederick and Catherine Sue (Brill) S. AB summa cum laude, Kenyon Coll., 1974; MFA in Directing, Cath. U. Am., 1982; MLitt in Theatre, Lincoln Coll., Oxford, Eng., 1983. Dir. dramatics Westminster Sch., Simsbury, Conn., 1975-80; acting coach Hartke Conservatory Cath. U., Washington, 1982; chair drama dept. St. Albans and Nat. Cathedral Schs., Washington, 1980-84; dir., instr. acting Nat. Theatre Inst. O'Neill Theater Ctr., Waterford, Conn., 1984-93; artistic dir. TNT/New Theatre Bklyn., 1985-90; producing dir. Weston (Vt.) Playhouse, 1988—. Lit. asst. Arena Stage Co., Washington, 1983-84; site evaluator theatres Nat. Endowment for Arts, Washington, 1990—; panelist Vt. Coun. Arts, Montpelier, Vt., NEA, Washington, D.C.; mem. capital grants com. N.Y.C. Dept. Cultural Affairs; guest instr. directing Teatret Vart, Norway. Dir.: Who's Afraid of Virginia Woolf?, Dancing at Lughnasa, Animal Fair, Rough Crossing, Nora, Donkeys' Years, Floyd Collins (Moss Hart award for best prodn. in New Eng.), Sweeney Todd, Six Degrees of Separation, A Midsummer Night's Dream (Best Play award Folger Shakespeare Libr. competition). Mem. Phi Beta Kappa. Office: Weston Playhouse 703 Main St Weston VT 05161 Business E-Mail: sstettler@westonplayhouse.org.

STETTNER, EDWARD A., political science professor; b. NYC, Feb. 18, 1940; s. Frederick Albert and Celia Carolyn S.; m. Laura Gagliardi, July 17, 1966; children: Victoria, Jeffrey, Thomas. BA, Brown U., 1962; MA, Princeton U., 1964, PhD, 1968. Lectr. polit. sci. Rutgers U., New Brunswick, N.J., 1965-66; instr. polit. sci. Wellesley (Mass.) Coll., 1966—68, asst. prof. polit. sci., 1968—74, assoc. prof., 1974—80, prof. polit. sci., 1980-95, Ralph Emerson and Alice Freeman Palmer prof. polit. sci., 1995—, assoc. dean of the coll., 1977-86, dean of the faculty, 1986—88. Author: Shaping Modern Liberalism: Herbert Croly and Progressive Thought, 1993; editor: Perspectives on Europe, 1970. Trustee Mount Ida Coll., Newton, Mass., 2000—. Mem. AAUP (mem. nat. coun. 1970-73, pres. Mass. State Conf. 1975-77), Am. Polit. Sci. Assn., New Eng. Polit. Sci. Assn., Phi Beta Kappa. Home: 67 Carriage Hill Cir Southborough MA 01772 Office: Wellesley College 106 Central St Wellesley MA 02481 Office Phone: 781-283-2198. E-mail: estettner@wellesley.edu.

STETTNER, JERALD WALTER, retired retail executive; b. Miami, Fla., Mar. 31, 1952; s. Richard A. and LeJean D. (Haberman) S.; m. Linda G. Day, Dec. 22, 1978; children: Kelly R., Jarrod M., Zachary A. BS in Behavioral Mgmt., Ga. Inst. Tech., 1974. Various mgmt. positions Eckerd Drug Co., Clearwater, Fla., 1974-87; regional v.p. Eckerd Corp., Clearwater, Fla., 1987-98, sr. v.p., 1998—2004, ret., 2004; pres., CEO Safe Harbor Properties and Investments, 2004—. Mem. Ga. Tech. Alumni Assn., Phi Delta Theta. Avocations: tennis, golf, skiing. Personal E-mail: JWStettner@aol.com.

STEUBEN, NORTON LESLIE, lawyer, educator; b. Milw., Feb. 14, 1936; s. Benjamin and Ria (Beerman) S.; m. Judith Ann Dickens, June 21, 1958; children: Sara Ann, Marc Nelson. AB, U. Mich., 1958, JD with distinction, 1961. Bar: N.Y. 1962, Colo. 1975. Assoc., then ptnr. Hodgson, Russ, Andrews, Woods & Goodyear, Buffalo, 1961-68; mem. faculty U. Colo. Law Sch., Boulder, 1968—2002, prof. law, 1974—2002, Nicholas Rosenbaum prof., 1997—2002, Nicholas Rosenbaum prof. emeritus, 2002—; of counsel Ireland, Stapleton, Pryor & Pascoe, Denver, 1980-97, 1999—2004. Lectr. Law Sch., SUNY, Buffalo, 1961-68; officer Buffalo-Niagara Indsl. Devel. Corp., 1963-68, Buffalo Opportunities Devel. Corp., 1966-68; vis prof. law U. Puget Sound. Sch. Law, 1992-93; resident tax policy advisor to the govt. of Ukraine, Treas. Dept., 1997-99. Author: Cases and Materials on Real Estate Planning, 1974, 4th edit., 2006; co-author: Problems in the Fundamentals of Federal Income Taxation, 1985, 3d edit. 1994, Problems in the Federal Income Taxation of Business Enterprises, 1985, 3d edit., 1996; co-editor: Bittker, Fundamentals of Federal Income Taxation, 1983; editor Jour. Affordable Housing & Cmty. Devel. Law, 1994-97; contbr. articles to profl. jours. Mem. Boulder Human Rights Commn., 1969-72, chmn., 1972-74; mem. Boulder Landlord-Tenant Com., 1973-74; trustee Boulder Open Space Bd., 1976-81, vice chmn., 1978-79, chmn., 1979-81; trustee Congregation Har Ha-Shem, Boulder, 1978-79, v.p., 1979-81, pres., 1982-84; mem. Boulder Housing Authority, 1982-89, vice chmn., 1984-85, chmn., 1985-88; mem. advocacy and pub. policy com. Am. Tinnitus Assn., 2002—, Cmty. Adv. Panel Roche Colo., 2004-; mem. Boulder County Aging Svcs. Found., 2005—, Boulder Housing Counselors, 2006—. Recipient S.I. Goldberg award Alpha Epsilon Pi, 1957, Disting. Svc. to Community award Buffalo Area C. of C., 1966, John W. Reed award U. Colo. Law Sch., 1970, Calhoun Cmty. Svc. award, 2005; Teaching Recognition award U. Colo.-Boulder, 1972, Teaching Excellence award, 1982; Commendation for Exceptional Assistance to Govt. of Ukraine, 1999; Presdl. Tchg. scholar U. Colo., 1989, Fulbright scholar, Ukraine, 2003-04. Mem. ABA, N.Y. State Bar Assn., Colo. Bar Assn., Boulder County Bar Assn., Am. Law Inst., AAUP, Scribes (officer, editor Scrivener 1975-76, dir. 1979-82), Barristers Soc., Order of Coif, Tau Epsilon Rho. Democrat. Home: 845 8th St Boulder CO 80302-7408 Office: 461 Wolf Law Boulder CO 80309 Home Phone: 303-447-1581; Office Phone: 303-492-7963. E-mail: norton.steuben@colorado.edu.

STEUER, RICHARD MARC, lawyer; b. Bklyn., June 19, 1948; s. Harold and Gertrude (Vengar) S.; m. Audrey P. Forchheimer, Sept. 9, 1973; children: Hilary, Jeremy. BA, Hofstra U., 1970; JD, Columbia U., 1973. Bar: NY 1974, US Dist. Ct. (ea. and so. dists.) NY 1974, US Ct. Appeals (2d cir.) 1974, US Supreme Ct. 1979, US Dist. Ct. (no. dist.) NY 1984, US Dist. Ct. (we. dist.) NY 1997, US Ct. Appeals (3d cir.) 1987, US Ct. Appeals (5th cir.) 1995, US Ct. Appeals (10th cir.) 2003, US Ct. Appeals 2004. Ptnr. Kaye Scholer LLP, NYC, 1973—2002, chair antitrust practice group, 1996—2002; ptnr. Mayer, Brown, Rowe and Maw LLP, NYC, 2002—. Adj. assoc. prof. law NYU, 1985; adj. prof. law St. John's U., 2003; lectr. in field; neutral evaluator U.S. Dist. Ct. Ea. Dist., N.Y, 1994-96. Author: A Guide to Marketing Law: Law and Business Inc., 1986; contbr. articles to profl. jours. Fellow: Am. Bar Found.; mem.: ABA (editl. bd. antitrust devel. vol. 1984—86, vice-chmn. program com. 1988—91, coun. sect. antitrust law 1993—96, chmn. publs. com. 1996—98, editl. chmn. Antitrust mag. 1998—2001, coun. sect. antitrust law 2001—04, comms. officer 2004—05, sec. 2004—05, ho. of dels. 2005—), Assn. Bar City N.Y. (chmn. antitrust and trade regulation 1995—98, antitrust and trade regulation, internat. trade, lectures and CLE coms). Office: Mayer Brown Rowe and Maw LLP 1675 Broadway New York NY 10019-5820 Office Phone: 212-506-2530. Business E-Mail: rsteuer@mayerbrownrowe.com.

STEUERT, DOUGLAS MICHAEL, engineering and construction management company executive; b. Oklahoma City, May 21, 1948; s. Douglas Anselm and Geraldine (Sparks) S.; m. Nancy Elizabeth Ridd, Aug. 22, 1970. BS in Physics, Carnegie-Mellon U., Pitts., 1971, MS in Indsl. Mgmt. Staff asst. TRW, Inc., Cleve., 1971-73, mgr. fin. rsch. and analysis, 1973-75, dir. fin. US, 1975-76, dir. fin. Europe Frankfurt, Germany, 1976-79, asst. treas. internat. Cleve., 1979-81, sr. fin. dir. automotive worldwide sector, 1981-84, contr. valve divsn., 1984-86; v.p., treas. GenCorp Inc., Ohio, 1986-87, v.p. fin. and planning Ohio, 1987-90, v.p, CFO, treas. Ohio, 1990-94, sr. v.p., CFO Ohio, 1994—99, Litton Industries, Inc., 1999—2001, Fluor Corp., Calif., 2001—. Dir. Weyerhaeuser Co., 2004—. Dir. Mental Health Assn. Summit County, 1993; mem. coun. on fin. Grad. Sch. Indsl. Adminstrn., Carnegie-Mellon U., 1994—. Mem. Fin. Execs. Inst. (nat. chpt., NE Ohio chpt.), Mfrs. Alliance for Productivity and Innovation, Conf. Bd. Coun. of CFOs, Leadership Akron, Alumni Assn. Carnegie-Mellon U. Office: Fluor Enterprises 3 Polaris Way Aliso Viejo CA 92698 Office Phone: 949-349-2000. Office Fax: 949-349-2585. *

STEVENS, ALEKSEI REUBEN, music educator, composer; b. NYC, Oct. 26, 1977; s. Mitchell Alvin and Frances Dougherty Stevens; m. Alexis Jennifer Lloyd, Aug. 6, 2005. MusB, Conn. Coll., New London, 1999; MusM, Manhattan Sch. Music, NYC, 2006. Curator, prodr., web mgr. Electronic Music Found., NYC, 2005—; freelance composer, arranger, 2005—; prof. advanced digital audio LI U., Bklyn., 2006—; music tech. faculty Hoff Barthelson Music Sch., Scarsdale, NY, 2006—; math. tutor Veritas Tutors, NYC, 2006—; piano tchr. Musika, NYC, 2006—. Composer: (Operas) Wakefield, 2006. Donor Working Families Party, NYC, 2006. Mem.: Am. Music Ctr., Electronic Music Found. (exec. bd. 2005—06). Avocations: camping, hiking, music. Home: 1617 10th Ave Brooklyn NY 11215

STEVENS, ANNE L., metal products executive, retired automotive executive; b. Reading, Pa., Dec. 1948; BS in mechanical & materials engring., Drexel U., 1980; Grad. Level Business student, Rutgers U; PhD (hon.), Ctrl. Mich. U. With Exxon Corp.; mktg. specialist plastic products divsn. Ford Motor Co., 1990—92, mgr., Quality Services Dept., 1992—95, mfr. mgr., Automotive Components Divsn., 1995, Plant mgr., Automotive Components Div. Enfield, England, 1995—97, asst. vehicle line dir., Ford Automotive Operations Dunton, England, 1997—99, dir., Manufacturing Business Office, N. Am., 1999—2000, v.p. N. Am. Assembly Ops., 2000—01, v.p. N. Am. Vehicle Ops., 2001—03, group v.p., Canada, Mexico, and S. Am., 2003—05, exec. v.p., COO, The Americas, 2005—06; chmn., CEO, pres. Carpenter Tech. Corp., Wyomissing, Pa., 2006—. Bd. dirs. Lockheed Martin Corp., 2002—, Coun. Americas; bd. trustees Drexel U.; trustee Women's Automotive Assn. Internat.; mem. advisory bd. Mexico Inst., Woodrow Wilson Internat. Ctr. for Scholars; mem. exec. advisory bd. Juran Ctr. for Leadership in Quality, U. Minn. Named one of Most Powerful Women in Bus., Fortune mag., 2005; recipient Shingo Leadership award, 2000, Circle of Distinction award, Drexel U. Coll. Engring., 2001, Eli Whitney award, Soc. Mfg. Engineers, 2003. Mem.: NAE. *

STEVENS, ART, public relations executive; b. NYC, July 17, 1935; m. Eva Sandberg, Mar. 19, 1972. BA, CCNY, 1957. Pub. relations dir. Prentice Hall, Inc., Englewood Cliffs, NJ; account exec. William L. Safire Public Relations Inc., NYC, 1966-69, v.p., 1967-68, pres., 1968-69, Lobsenz-Stevens Inc., NYC, 1970—99; instr. Fairleigh Dickinson U.; chmn. & CEO Publicis Dialog, NYC, 1999—2002; mng. ptnr. Stevens Gould Pincus, LLC, 2003—. Weekly humor commentator WINK-TV, Ft. Myers, Fla.; cons. in field. Author: The Persuasion Explosion, 1985, Sanibel Shell Shocked, 1992; weekly columnist Sanibel-Captiva (Fla.) Islander; contbr. articles to profl. jours. Bd. dirs. United Way of Putnam County, N.Y.; trustee Gotthelf Lupus Rsch. Inst. Inducted City Coll. N.Y. Comms. Alumni Hall Fame, 2001. Mem.: Public Relations Soc. Am. (sec. 2003, pres. N.Y. chpt. 2006, nat. bd., pub. rels. com., chair-elect tri-state dist., exec. com., chmn. eligibility com., counselors acad. sect.), Publicity Club N.Y. (Disting. Svc. award 1969), Gipsy Trail (pres., chmn. Carmel, N.Y.). Personal E-mail: artstevens@att.net. *Life is not an accident. The events in one's life are not accidents either. When I look back at what I have done and the lives that have been interwined with mine, it's as though it's all been scripted by a higher power.*

STEVENS, BERTON LOUIS, JR., data processing executive; b. Chgo., Apr. 4, 1951; s. Berton Louis Sr. and Mary Cover (Kochavaris) S.; m. Janet Alene Madenberg, May 20, 1990. Student, Ill. Inst. Tech., Chgo., 1969-73. Systems and applications programmer Judge & Dolph, Ltd., Elk Grove Village, Ill., 1978-91, mgr. data processing, 1991-99; bus. sys. coord. Meml. Med. Ctr., Inc., 2000-2001, lead sys. analyst, 2001—02; svc. ctr. mgr. Siemens Health Sys., 2002—04; mgr. applications Province Healthcare, Las Cruces, N.Mex., 2004—06; dir. MIS LifePoint Hosps., Las Cruces, N.Mex., 2006—. Instr. Adler Planetarium and Astron. Mus., Chgo., 1980-86; dir. Desert Moon Observatory #448. Editor and author newsletter Bert's Bull., 1987-90; editor newsletter No. Lights, 1990-98; columnist Starry Dome, 2004- Recipient Regional award North Ctrl. Region Astron. League, 1989. Mem. Nat. Assn. Sys. Programmers, Internat. Occulation Timing Assn. (sec. 1975-78), Chgo. Computer Soc., Chgo. Astron. Soc. (pres. 1977, 80, 84), Racine Astron. Soc. (pres. 1979), Astron. League (exec. sec. 1993-95, webmaster 1995-02), Desert Moon Observatory (dir.), Astron. Soc. Las Cruces (pres, 2001, 2007). Personal E-mail: bstevens@zianet.com. Business E-Mail: Berton.Stevens@lpnt.net.

STEVENS, BRAD K., men's college basketball coach; m. Tracy Stevens; 1 child, Brady. BA in Econs., DePauw U., Greencastle, Ind., 1999. Mktg. assoc. Eli Lilly and Co., Indpls.; coord. basketball ops. Butler U., Indpls., 2000—01, asst. coach, 2001—07, head coach, 2007—. Office: Butler Mens Basketball 510 W 49th St Indianapolis IN 46208 Office Phone: 317-940-9897. E-mail: bksteven@butler.edu. *

STEVENS, CHARLES THOMAS, SR., drafting technology educator; b. Atlanta, Dec. 9, 1944; s. James Thomas and Christeen Bush Stevens; m. Erendira Daphne Aparicio, June 13, 1980; children: Missy Moore, Secundina Angelic Moore, Charles Thomas Jr. AA in Applied Tech., Physics, Chattahoochee Tech. Coll., Marietta, Ga., 2002; diploma in Drafting, 2002, diploma in Drafting Aid, 2002. Cert. engring. technician, 1975, sr. engring. technician, Nat. Inst. for Certification in Engring. Technologies, 1977. HVAC designer TVA, Decatur, Ala., 1990, Oglethorpe Power Corp., Atlanta, 1992, Brown & Caldwell, Inc., Atlanta, 1997, Applied Engring. and Sci., Atlanta, 1997; drafting educator Chattahoochee Tech. Coll., Marietta, 2001—, mem. engring. adv. bd., 2001—; designer Studio Stevens, Hiram, Ga., 2002—. Mem. engring. adv. bd. Chattahoochee Tech. Coll., 2001—. Mem.: Am. Inst. Bldg. Design, Am. Soc. Cert. Engring. Technicians. Libertarian. Roman Catholic. Office: Studio Stevens 65 Lancaster Way Hiram GA 30141-5463 Home Phone: 678-773-1516; Office Phone: 678-773-1516. Business E-Mail: ctstevens@studiostevens.us.

STEVENS, CHERITA WYMAN, social sciences educator, writer; b. Erick, Okla., Jan. 12, 1938; d. Forrest Clarence and Wilma Peter Wyman; m. Paul Donald Stevens, May 30, 1958 (div. Nov. 10, 1978); children: Paul McDonald, Mark Liu. BA in Social Sci., Phillips U., 1961; MA in Sch. Law and Fin., Calif. State U., LA, 1976; cert. in ESL, U. Calif., LA. Adminstrv. credential K-12 and adult; LA, Calif. Classroom tchr. grades 7-9 South Pasadena (Calif.) Unified, 1966—74; assoc. regional pastor Disciples of Christ, Pacific Southwest, 1976—82; computer store owner Claremont (Calif.) Computer, 1982—87; tchr., prin., grant writer Cabrillo Unified Sch. Dist., Half Moon Bay, Calif., 1987—97; ESL computer lab. media instr. Chapman Edn. Ctr., Garden Grove, Calif., 1997—2007. Legis. intern Calif. State Assembly, Sacramento, 1978—80; NASD registered rep. Primerica Life/Citigroup, Orange, Calif., 2000—07; grant reviewer U.S. Dept. Edn., Washington, 2002; presenter in field; grant writer Calif. Dept. Edn./Joint Partnership Training Act, Half Moon Bay, 1996. Editor: Direction Newspaper, 1976—82; author: (software) Apartment Maintenance, 1988, Grants Tracking, 1989, Financial Management, 1991, Curriculum and Lesson Plans for the Independent Learning Lab, 1995; designer, lesson plan builder: OTAN Website, 2002—07; contributor KOCE (PBS) Schoolhouse Video Project, 2004; contbr. articles to newspapers and mag.:, author of poems. Mem. Ams. for Dem. Action, Pasadena, 1963—80; civil rights activist, 1960—69; organizer first Martin Luther King Jr. celebration in U.S. LA, 1972; active First Christian Ch., Orange, 1963—2005, Pasadena, Calif. Mem.: Assn. Calif. Sch. Adminstrs. (site rep. 1993—97, state presenter 2005, state workshop presenter, state presenter 2006, 2007). Avocations: golf, photography, genealogy. Home: 401 W La Veta Ave #220 Orange CA 92866-2649 Personal E-mail: cheri166@msn.com.

STEVENS, CONNIE, actress, singer; b. Bklyn., Aug. 8, 1938; d. Peter and Eleanore (McGinley) Ingolia; m. Maurice Elias; m. Edwin Jack Fisher (div.); children: Joely, Tricia Leigh. Pres. Forever Spring Cosmetics; founder Windfeather Foundation. Show bus. debut as vocalist with, The Three Debs, Hollywood, at age 16; appeared in: Finians Rainbow for Hollywood Repertory Co.; numerous motion pictures, including Way, Way Out, Scorchy, Eighteen and Animals, Young and Dangerous, Drag Strip Riot, Rock-a-bye Baby, Parish, Susan Slade, Palm Springs Weekend, The Grissom Gang, Never Too Late, Grease II, 1983, Back to the Beach, 1987, Bring Me the Head of Dobie Gillis, 1988, Love Is All There Is, 1996; starred in TV series Wendy and Me and TV series Hawaiian Eye, 1959-62, Head Over Heals, 1997, Titus, 2000-02, TV films for ABC-TV Movie-of-the-Week; Call Her Mom, 1972, Playmates, Mister Jericho, Cole Porter in Paris, The Sex Symbol, 1974, Starting From Scratch, 1988, James Dean: Live Fast, Die Young, 1997; guest star on TV with, Bob Hope, Red Skelton, Englebert Humperdinck, Tom Jones, Perry Como and Laugh-In; TV appearance comedy spl. Harry's Battles; headliner at Flamingo Hotel, Las Vegas, also, Hilton Internat., Sands Hotel, Desert Inn, Aladdin, MGM, Sahara, 1969-76; stage appearances include The Wizard of Oz at Carousel Theatre in So. Calif., Any Wednesday at Melodyland, Anaheim, Calif.; made Broadway debut in Star Spangled Girl, 1967; accompanied Bob Hope around world on his Christmas tour, 1969, Persian Gulf Christmas tour, 1987; dir., prodr., writer, editor, cinematographer: A Healing, 1997 (Santa Clarita Internat. Film Festival Award, 1998); created line of cosmetics called Forever Spring and opened the Garden Sanctuary day spa in Los Angeles Bd. dirs. Ctr. for Plastic and Reconstructive Surgery, South Vietnam. Recipient Lady of Humanities Award, Shriners Hospital, 1991, Humanitarian of the Year, Sons of Italy, 2001, Distinguished Civilian Service Medal, 2002.

STEVENS, DAVID ALEC, medical educator; b. NYC, June 3, 1940; m. Julie Anne Teece, Aug. 15, 1964; children: Joseph John, Emily Beth Stevens Marsh. BA, Cornell U., Ithaca, NY, 1960; MD, U. Rochester, NY, 1965. Diplomate Nat. Bd. Med. Examiners, Am. Bd. Internal Medicine and Infections Diseases; med. lic. Wis., Calif. Intern, asst. resident dept. medicine U. Wis. Hosps., Madison, 1965-67; rsch. assoc. Nat. Cancer Inst., Bethesda, Md., 1967-69; resident dept. medicine UCLA Med Ctr., 1969-70; fellow divsn. infectious diseases, dept. medicine Stanford U., Calif., 1970—72, asst. prof. divsn. infectious diseases dept. medicine, 1972—78, assoc. prof. divsn. infectious diseases, dept. medicine, 1978—85, prof., 1985—, assoc. chief divsn. infectious diseases, 1992—2003; epidemiologist Santa Clara County-Valley Med. Ctr., San Jose, Calif., 1972—, assoc. chief dept. medicine, 1972—, chief divsn. infectious diseases, 1972—. Co-dir. microbiology lab. Santa Clara Valley Med. Ctr., 1972—; prin. investigator Infectious Diseases Rsch. Lab., Calif. Inst. Med. Rsch., San Jose, 1973—, bd. regents, 1978-90, 92—, sec.-treas., 1979-81, sci. dir. coun., 1986-88, pres., 1992—, Internat. Agy. Rsch. Cancer, WHO, Lyon, France, 1976; mycology ref. lab. Pub. Health Lab. Svcs. Dept. Microbiology, U. London, 1979; dir. clin. labs. Calif. Inst. Med. Rsch., 1980—; co-dir. AIDS program Santa Clara Valley Med. Ctr., 1986-88, assoc. dir., 1988-98; lectr. fourth ann. O.J. Farness lecture, U. Ariz., Tucson, 1999; Ian Murray Meml. lectr. British Soc. Mycopathology, Canterbury, Eng., 1985; spl. lectr. fourth ann. Japanese Soc. Med. Mycopathology, Chiba, 1996, Focus on Fungal Infections 17, San Diego, 2007; keynote spkr. Focus on Fungus Infections 13, Maui, Hawaii, 2003. Author: (with others) Coccidioidomycosis, 1980; mem. editl. bd. various profl. jours.; contbr. articles to profl. jours, chpt. to books. With USPHS, 1967-69. Recipient Charles Smith Meml. award, Coccidioidomycosis Study Group, 2006. Fellow ACP, Am. Soc. Microbiology (chair mycology 1992-93, divsn. lectr. mycology ann. gen. meeting 2001), Infectious Diseases Soc. Am., Am. Acad. Microbiology; mem. AMA, AAUP, AAAS, Am. Fedn. Clin. Rsch., Am. Soc. Clin. Investigation, Fedn. Am. Scientists, Med. Mycology Soc. Ams. (Rhoda Benham medal 1999), Calif. Med. Assn., Western Assn. Physicians, Santa Clara County Med. Soc. (Outstanding Achievement in Medicine award 2003), Internat. Soc. Human and Animal Mycology (clin. mycology com. 1985-91, Lucille Georg medal 2006). Achievements include patents for antigenic preparation and diagnostic method for identification of Nocardia infections; use of synthetic molecules to stimulate leukocytes, and topical therapy with collectins; antifungal vaccines. Avocations: jazz, running, stamp collecting/philately. Home: 19070 Portos Dr Saratoga CA 95070-5169 Office: Santa Clara Valley Med Ctr 751 S Bascom Ave San Jose CA 95128-2699

STEVENS, DAVID BOYETTE, law educator; b. Augusta, Ga., Jan. 31, 1923; s. Henry Boyette and Floreid Elizabeth (Miller) S.; m. Willa King Horner, July 18, 1942; children: David Boyette, Caroline Elizabeth, Paul King. BS in Bus., U. N.C., 1949, JD, 1951; LLM, Duke U., 1956. Bar: N.C. 1951, U.S. Ct. Mil. Appeals 1965, U.S. Supreme Ct. 1967. Commd. 2d lt. U.S. Army Air Force, 1944; advanced through grades to col. USAF, 1968; asst. prof. internat. law U.S. Air Force Acad., Colorado Springs, Colo., 1959-63; judge adv., acting dir. U.S. Air Force Judiciary, Washington, 1963-70; ret., 1970; asst. prof. bus. East Carolina U., Greenville, N.C., 1970-74, prof., 1984—, dir. EEO Office, 1974-81, univ. atty., 1970—. Divsn. chmn. United Fund Svc., East Carolina U., 1972; mem. Greenville Bd. Adjustments, 1983—. Recipient Meritorious Achievement award USAF, 1970, Outstanding Svc. award East Carolina U. Law Soc., 1978. Mem. Fed. Bar Assn., N.C. Bar Assn., Pitt County Bar Assn., Nat. Assn. Coll. and Univ. Attys., Kiwanis (pres. Greenville 1976-77, lt. gov. 1979-80, Disting. Lit. Gov. ward 1981), Delta Theta Phi. Democrat. Baptist. Home: 304 Francis Asbury Ln Greenville NC 27858

STEVENS, DENNIS MAX, auditor; b. Jersey City, Sept. 3, 1944; m. Susan Gail Brown, Mar. 15, 1969; children: Julie Ayn, Daniel Ross. BBA, Rutgers U., 1966; MA in Acctg., U. Mo., 1968. CPA Mo. Staff Peat, Marwick, Mitchell and Co., St. Louis, 1968-80, ptnr., 1980-84; sr. v.p., internal auditor Southwestern States Bankcard Assn., Dallas, 1985-86, sr. v.p., CFO, 1986-89; corp. planner NCH Corp., Irving, Tex., 1989-95, dir. corp. audit, 1995—2002; dir. internal audit Alamo Group, Seguin, Tex., 2002—. Contbr. articles to profl. jours. 1st lt. US Army, 1969—70. Mem.: AICPA (mem. electronic data processing auditing stds. com. 1979—84), Inst. Mgmt. Accts., Inst. Internal Auditors, Beta Gamma Sigma, Beta Alpha Psi. Home: 23711 Legend Gln San Antonio TX 78258-4316 Office Phone: 830-372-9580. Personal E-mail: den.stevens@yahoo.com.

STEVENS, DIANA LYNN, elementary school educator; b. Waterloo, Iowa, Dec. 12, 1950; d. Marcus Henry and Clarissa Ann (Funk) Carr; m. Paul John Stevens; 1 child, Drew Spencer. BS, Mid Am. Nazarene Coll. (now Mid-Am. Nazarene U.), Olathe, Kans., 1973; M in Liberal Arts, Baker U., Baldwin, Kans., 1989. Elem. tchr. Olathe (Kans.) Sch. Dist. #233, 1975—. Artwork appeared in traveling exhibit ARC/Nat. Art Edn. Assn., 1968, Delta Kappa Gamma Bull., 2001. Olathe Sch. Dist. Action grantee, 1996-97, Summer Reading grantee Olathe Pub. Schs., 2007; recipient Excellence in Edn. award Olathe Pub. Schs. Found., 2002. Mem. NEA, Kans. Edn. Assn., Olathe Edn. Assn. (social com. Olathe chpt.), Coll. Ch. of the Nazarene, Delta Kappa Gamma (profl. affairs com. mem., chpt. membership chair 2006-, Excellence in Edn. award 2002), Beta Omega (membership chair, 2d v.p. 2006-). Avocations: portrait art, reading, walking. Home: 217 S Montclaire Dr Olathe KS 66061-3828

STEVENS, DONALD KING, retired aeronautical engineer, consultant; b. Danville, Ill., Oct. 27, 1920; s. Douglas Franklin and Ida Harriet (King) S.; m. Adele Carman de Werff, July 11, 1942; children: Charles August, Anne Louise, Alice Jeanne Stevens Kay. BS with high honors in Ceramic Engrng., U. Ill., 1942; MS in Aeros. and Guided Missiles, U. So. Calif., 1949; grad., U.S. Army Command and Gen. Staff Coll., 1957, U.S. Army War Coll., 1962. Staff mem. Ill. State Geol. Survey, 1938—40; air defense officer (434th AAA Bn) in England, Algeria. Tunisia, Italy, 1942—44; regimental staff officer 473d Infantry Regiment, Italy, 1945; commd. 2d lt. US Army, 1942; ceramic engr. Harbison-Walker Refractories Co., Pitts., 1945—46; antiaircraft and guided missiles br. The Arty. Sch. US Army, Ft. Bliss, Tex., 1949—52, commdr. 2d battalion 1st guided missile group, 1954—56, mem. weapons sys. evaluation group Office Sec. Def. Washington, 1957—61, chief J2 plans br. UN command/US Forces Korea, 1962—63, advanced through grades to col., 1963, comdr. Niagara-Buffalo def. 31st arty. brigade Lockport, NY, 1963—65, chief air def. and nuc. br. war plans divsn. Washington, 1965—67, dir. US ballistic missile def. studies DEPEX and X-66 for Sec. Def., 1965—66, chief strategic forces divsn. office dep. chief of staff mil. ops., 1967—69, chief J5 spl. weapons plans U.S. European command Germany, 1969—72, ret., 1972. Co-authored layout of McGregor Range, N.Mex, as guided missile firing range; guest lectr. U.S. Mil. Acad., 1958-59; mem. Study Group Army Air Def. Sys. for the 1970's, The AADS-70 Study in 1964 defined requirements for SAM-D, later named 'Patriot' 1964; cons. US Army Concepts Analysis Agy., Bethesda, Md., 1973-95; cons. on strategy Lulejian & Assocs., Inc., 1974-75; cons. nuc. policy and plans to Office Asst. Sec. of Def., 1975-80, 84-93; cons. Sci. Applications, Inc., 1976-78. Contbr. articles to profl. jours. Asst. camp dir. Piankeshaw Area coun. Boy Scouts Am., 1937; mem. chancel choir, elder First Christian Ch., Falls Church, Va., 1957-61, 65-69, 72-2002, elder emeritus 2004-; elder, trustee Presbyn. Ch., Niagara Falls, NY, 1963-65. Decorated D.S.M., Legion of Merit, Bronze Star, Order of St. Barbara. Mem. Am. Ceramic Soc., Assn. U.S. Army, U. Ill. Alumni Assn., U. So. Calif. Alumni Assn., Rotary, Keramos, Niagara Falls Country Club, Ill. Club (Washington), Terrapin Club, Sigma Xi, Sigma Tau, Tau Beta Pi, Phi Kappa Phi, Alpha Phi Omega. Disciples of Christ. Achievements include pioneer in tactics and deployment plans for Army surface-to-air missiles. Address: 5916 5th St N Arlington VA 22203-1010 Personal E-mail: dkstevens@starpower.net.

STEVENS, ELISABETH GOSS (MRS. ROBERT SCHLEUSSNER JR.), journalist, writer, graphic artist; b. Rome, NY, Aug. 11, 1929; d. George May and Elisabeth (Stryker) Stevens; m. Robert Schleussner, Jr., Mar. 12, 1966 (dec. 1977); 1 child, Laura Stevens BA, Wellesley Coll., 1951; MA with high honors, Columbia U., 1956. Editl. assoc. Art News Mag., 1964-65; art critic and reporter Washington Post, Washington, 1965-66; freelance art critic and reporter Balt., 1966—; contbg. art critic Wall Street Jour., NYC, 1969-72; art critic Trenton (NJ) Times, 1974-77; art and architecture critic The Balt. Sun, 1978-86; critic-at-large srqradio-.com, 2004—; art correspondent Sarasota Herald Tribune, 2005—07; contbg. writer The Senses mag., 2007. Author: Elisabeth Stevens' Guide to Baltimore's Inner Harbor, 1981, Fire and Water: Six Short Stories, 1982, Children of Dust: Portraits and Preludes, 1985, Horse and Cart: Stories from the Country, 1990, The Night Lover: Art & Poetry, 1995, In Foreign Parts, 1997, Household Words, 1999, 2d edit., 2000, Eranos, 2000, Cherry Pie & Other Stories, 2001, numerous poems; contbr. articles short stories to jours., newspapers and popular mags.; one-woman shows include Coll. Notre Dame of Md., 1997, Galerie Francoise, Lutherville, Md., 2000, Kirkland Libr., Linton, NY, 2007, exhibited in group shows at Corcoran Gallery of Art, Washington, Towson State U., Balt., Atelier A/E, NYC, Stephen Gang Gallery, Govt. Ho., Annapolis, U. Minn., Morris, Cooperstown Art Assn., NY, Armory Art Ctr., West Palm Beach, Fla., Venice Art Ctr., Fla., Ft. Meyers Alliance for the Art, Katharine Butler Gallery, Sarasota, Fla., 2004, Combined Talents: Fla. Internat., Tallahassee, 2005, Mus. Fine Arts, Tallahassee, 2005, Silvermine Guild Arts Ctr., Wilton, Conn., 2006, N.Mex. Printmakers, Santa Fe, 2006—07, Kirkland Libr., Clinton, NY, 2007, Old Print Shop, NYC. Recipient A.D. Emmart award for journalism, 1980, Critical Writing citation Balt.-Washington Newspaper Guild, 1980, fiction awards Md. Poetry Rev., 1992, 93, 94, 2d prize Lite Circle, 1994, 1st prize in fiction Lite Circle, 1995, 96, Balt. Writers Alliance Play Writing Contest award, 1994; art critics' fellow NEA, 1973-74, fellow MacDowell Colony, 1981, Va. Ctr. for Creative Arts, 1982-85, 88-90, 92, 93, 95, 97, 2000, 07, Ragdale Found., 1984, 89, Yaddo, 1991, Villa Montalvo, 1995; Work-in-Progress grantee for poetry Md. Art Coun., 1986, Creative Devel. grantee for short fiction collection Balt. Mayor's Com. on Art and Culture, 1986. Mem. Coll. Art Assn., Authors Guild, Fla. Printmakers Assn., Soc. Am. Graphic Artists, Women Contemporary Artists Sarasota. Home: Bards Castle 5353 Creekside Trail Sarasota FL 34243

STEVENS, ELIZABETH MCCARTHA, secondary school educator; m. James Gordon Stevens; children: Jay Stone, Grant Stone; m. James W. Stone II (div.). BS in Secondary Edn., Auburn U., Ala., 1977; M in Secondary Edn., U. Ala., Birmingham, 1979. Cert. sci. tchr. Ala. Tchr. biology McAdory H.S., McCalla, Ala., 1971—75, Leeds H.S., Ala., 1975—84; tchr. 7th grade sci. Pizitz Mid. Sch., Vestavia Hills, Ala., 2002—04, tchr. 8th grade sci., 2004—. Chmn. sci. dept. Pizitz Mid. Sch., Vestavia Hills, Ala., 2004—; chmn. sci. curriculum review com. Vestavia Hills City Schs., 2005—. Mem., donor Birmingham Mus. Art, Ala., 1999—. Recipient grant, Legacy, Ptnrs. in Environ. Edn., 2003. Mem.: Ala. Nat. Bd. Cert. Tchrs. Network, Pi Lambda Theta. Avocations: scuba diving, photography, golf, tennis, travel. Home: 6535 Harper's Dairy Loop Bessemer AL 35022 E-mail: bethstevens7@aol.com.

STEVENS, GARY, retired jockey; Jockey, 1991. Named winner, Breeder's Cup Turf Race, 1990, Breeder's Cup Juvenile, 1993, Breeder's Cup Distaff, 1994. Achievements include being a top money winner, 1991. Office: Jockey's Guild Inc PO Box 150 Monrovia CA 91017-0150

STEVENS, GARY LEE, state senator; b. McMinnville, Oreg., Aug. 21, 1941; m. Rita Stevens; children: Anna, Matthew, Natalie. BA, Linfield Coll., 1963; MFA, U. Oreg., 1965, PhD, 1984. Dir. Kodiak Oral History Project; gen. mgr. No. Processors Inc., 1970—75; mayor Kodiak, Kodiak Island Borough; mem. Alaska Ho. of Reps., 2000—02, Alaska Senate, 2003—04. Prof. U. Alaska, Kodiak, Alaska, 1975—2000. Pres. Kodiak Sch. Bd.; presiding officer Borough Assembly; bd. dirs. Alaska Humanities Forum, Alaska Mcpl. League, Alaska Conf. Mayors. 1st lt. US Army, 1966—69. Decorated Army Commendation medal, Nat. Def. medal. Mem.: Nat. Assn. Counties (edn. steering com.), Alaska Hist. Soc. (pres.), Rotary (gov.). Republican. Office: Rm 417 State Capitol Juneau AK 99801-1182 E-mail: senator_gary_stevens@legis.state.ak.us.

STEVENS, GEORGE RICHARD, business consultant, public information officer; b. Chgo., Sept. 6, 1932; s. George and Irene (Kaczmarek) S.; m. Jeanne E. Sowden, Aug. 2, 1957; children: Stacey, Samantha, Pamela. BS with honors, Northwestern U., 1954. CPA, Ill. With Arthur Andersen & Co., 1954-78, mng. ptnr. Brussels, 1957—71, ptnr. Chgo., 1971-78; pres. Daubert Industries, Oak Brook, Ill., 1978-80, G.R. Stevens Group, 1981—; founder, pres. Stevens Ctr. for Pub. Policy Studies, 1981—. Commr. Ill. Ednl. Facilities Authority, 1989-04. Commr. Ill. State Scholarship Commn., 1981-87; vice chmn. Ill. Ind. Higher Edn. Loan Authority, 1982-88. Home and Office: 22615 N Las Lomas Ln Sun City West AZ 85375-2022

STEVENS, GLADSTONE TAYLOR, JR., retired industrial engineer, retired educator; b. Brockton, Mass., Dec. 16, 1930; s. Gladstone Taylor and Blanche Ruth S.; m. Jane A. Crouch, July 20, 1953; children— Robert, Bartlett. BSM.E., U. Okla., 1956; MSM.E., Case Inst. Tech., 1962; PhD in Indsl. Engrng, Okla. State U., 1966. Registered profl. engr., Tex., Okla. Project engr. E.I. duPont, Orange, Tex., 1956-59; research engr. Thompson-Ramo-Wooldridge, Cleve., 1960-62; asst. prof. mech. and indsl. engrng. Lamar U., Beaumont, Tex., 1962-64; asst. prof. to asso. prof. indsl. engrng. Okla. State U., Stillwater, 1966-75; prof., chmn. dept. indsl. engrng. U. Tex., Arlington, 1975-98; ret., 1998. Author: (with J.E. Shamblin) Operations Research: A Fundamental Approach, 1974, Economic and Financial Analysis of Capital Investments, 1993; Engineering Economy, 1983. Served with AUS, 1948-52. Recipient E.L. Grant award, 1974, AMOCO Teaching award, 1979, Wellington award, 1992. Fellow Am. Inst. Indsl. Engrs.; mem. Sigma Xi, Alpha Pi Mu (nat. pres.), Tau Beta Pi, Sigma Tau, Omicron Delta Kappa. Home: 2501 Spanish Trl Apt 212 Arlington TX 76016-1410 Office: U Tex Indsl Engrng Arlington TX 76019-0001

STEVENS, GLENN H., lawyer; Grad., Johns Hopkins U.; JD, NYU. Positions in legal dept. US West Inc., 1979—92; atty. pvt. practice, 1992—94; v.p., gen. counsel, sec. Maxtor Corp., Milpitas, Calif., 1994—2001, sr. v.p., gen. counsel, sec., 2001; spl. counsel Stevens, Littman, Biddison, Tharp & Weinberg, LLC, Boulder, Colo., 2005—. Mem.: Nebr. State Bar Assn., Colo. Bar Assn. Office: Stevens, Littman, Biddison, Tharp & Weinberg, LLC 250 Arapahoe, Ste 301 Boulder CO 80302 Office Phone: 303-443-6690. Office Fax: 303-449-9349. E-mail: glenn@slb-llc.com. *

STEVENS, HELEN JEAN, music educator; b. Nevada, Iowa, July 11, 1934; d. Paul Ellison and Helen Margaret (Ives) Stevens. MusB, U. So. Calif., 1956. Cert. secondary music tchr. Calif. Tchr. San Francisco Sch. Dist., 1956-58; prin. oboist Marin Symphony Orch., San Rafael, Calif., 1956-94, Santa Rosa (Calif.) Symphony, 1956-86; tchr. Santa Venetia Mid. Sch., San Rafael, 1958-83; asst. prof. music Sonoma State Coll., Rohnert Park, Calif., 1963-76; tchr. Davidson Mid. Sch., San Rafael, 1984-89; pvt. tchr. oboe. Oboist Evenings on the Roof Series, LA, 1953—56, Debut TV Show, LA, 1954—56, Carmel (Calif.) Bach Festival, 1954—82; prin. oboist Light Opera Curren Theatre, San Francisco, 1966—67, Marin Opera Co., San Rafael, 1980—84. Leader Sonoma County 4-H Guide Dog Project Guide Dogs for Blind, Inc., 1974—87; organist, choir dir. Korean Meth. Ch., LA, 1953—56; music dir. United Meth. Ch., St. James, Mo., 2002—. Named Outstanding Tchr., Marin Edn. Found., 1986; recipient Svc. award, PTA, 1974, Golden Bell award, Marin County Office Edn., 1984, Continuing Svc. award, Calif. Congress Parents, Tchrs. and Students, Inc., 1989. Avocations: computers, animals. Home: 14713 State Rt BB Saint James MO 65559 E-mail: stevfam@fidnet.com.

STEVENS, HERBERT FRANCIS, lawyer, educator; b. Phila., Nov. 19, 1948; s. Herbert F. and Lois Marie (Kenna) S.; m. Jane Pickard, 1994; children: Sarah, Ben. SB, MIT, 1970; JD, Catholic U. Am., 1974; ML in Tax, Georgetown U, 1983. Bar: D.C., 1975; U.S. Supreme Ct., 1980. Law clk Md. Ct. of Spl. Appeals, 1974-75; with Morgan, Lewis & Bockius, Washington, 1975-78, Lane & Edson, P.C., Washington, 1979-89, Kelley Drye & Warren, Washington, 1989-93, Nixon Peabody LLP, Washington, 1993—; adj. prof. Georgetown U. Law Ctr., 1983-98. Spkr. in field. Editor: Real Estate Aspects of the 1984 Tax Law, 1984; author: Real Estate Taxation: A Practitioner's Guide, 1986, Developer's Guide to Low Income Housing Tax Credit, 4th edit., 2000. Bd. dirs. Nat. Fund for U.S. Botanic Garden, 1992—97, exec. com. Mem. ABA, D.C. Bar Assn. Presbyterian. Home: 8301 Hackamore Dr Potomac MD 20854-3877 Office: Nixon Peabody LLP 401 9th St NW Washington DC 20004-2128 Business E-Mail: hstevens@nixonpeabody.com.

STEVENS, JAMES C., chemist; Rsch. fellow performance polymers and chems. R & D Dow Chem. Co. Contbr. articles to profl. jours. Co-recipient US Nat. Inventor of Yr. award, 1994; named one of 50 R & D Stars, Industry Week Mag., 1994; recipient Inventor of Yr. award, Mich. Saginaw Valley Patent Lawyers Assn., 1992, Carothers award, Am. Chem. Soc., Del. sect., 2004, Indsl. Chemistry award, Am. Chem. Soc., 2006, Perkin medal, Soc. Chem. Industry, 2006. Achievements include patents in field. Mailing: Dow Chem Co 2301 N Brazosport Blvd Freeport TX 77541

STEVENS, JAMES HERVEY, JR., retired financial planner; b. Balt., June 22, 1944; s. James H. and Hilda (Pearce) S.; m. Patricia Carol Donohue, Aug. 27, 1967 (div. Mar. 1983); children: James III, Carol; m. Lisa Gay Landrum, Apr. 29, 1984. BA, Duke U., 1966; MS in Fin. Scis., Am. Coll., Bryn Mawr, Pa., 1981. CLU; ChFC; CFP; registered health underwriter. Supr. New Eng. Life, Overland Park, Kans., 1969-75, agt., 1969—; v.p., treas. Creative Planning, Inc., Overland Park, 1980-95; pres. Hokanson, Lehman & Stevens, Inc., Overland Park, 1982-95; founder, chmn. Wings Over Mid-Am., Inc., 1995-97, chmn. emeritus, 1997—; chmn. Air Care Alliance, 1997—; chmn. emeritus Wings Over Mid-Am., Inc., 1997—; founder, chmn. legacy fund Angel Flight Ctrl., Inc., Kansas City, Mo. Contbg. editor monthly tax topics Kansas City Bus. Jour.; contbg. editor Pvt. Pilot Mag.; contbr. articles to profl. jours. Bd. dirs. Mo. divsn. Am. Cancer Soc., Kans. and Mo., 1982-84, Ctrl. United Meth. Ch., Kansas City, Mo., 1990-92, North Cross United Meth., 1991—; bd. dirs. Apple Valley Homes Assn., Overland Park, 1990—, pres. 1992; co-founder Kansas City Friends of Gilda's. Recipient Outstanding Young Man award, 1977; named one of Top 200 Fin. Advisors, Money Mag., 1987, Boss of Yr., Kansas City LICOMA, 1983. Mem. Kansas City Life Underwriters (pres. 1980-82, Herbert A. Hedges award 1987), Kansas City CLU & ChFC Soc. (pres. 1981-83), Mo. Life Underwriters (pres. 1984-86), Am. Soc. CLU & ChFC (vice chmn., bd. dirs.). Republican. Avocations: model railroading, collecting post-war "lionel", airline transport pilot, instrument flight instr. Home: 5200 W 98th Ter Shawnee Mission KS 66207-3221 Office: Angel Fly Ctrl Inc 10 Richards Rd Kansas City MO 64113 E-mail: jstevens10@gmail.com.

STEVENS, JEREMY R., lawyer; b. Spring Valley, Minn., Sept. 5, 1974; m. Christina Stevens; 2 children. BS in Polit. Sci., Luther Coll., 1997; JD, Hamline U. Sch. Law, 2000. Bar: Minn. 2000. Ptnr. Bird, Jacobsen & Stevens, P.C., Rochester, Minn. Articles editor: Hamline Jour. Law and Pub. Policy. Named a Rising Star, Minn. Super Lawyers mag., 2006. Mem.: Am. Trial Lawyers Assn., Minn. Trial Lawyers Assn., Minn. State Bar Assn. Office: Bird Jacobsen & Stevens PC 305 Ironwood Sq 300 3rd Ave SE Rochester MN 55904 Office Phone: 507-282-1503. E-mail: jeremy@birdjacobsen.com. *

STEVENS, JOANN A., textile, political leader, author, minister; b. Snow Hill, NC, May 15, 1957; d. Moses Lee and Annie Iola Artis; m. Willard Ray Stevens, Apr. 3, 1993; children: Thyais Artis, Jorel, Shakira. Student, Wayne C.C., Goldsboro, NC, 1983; student in criminal justice, Lenoir C.C., Kinston, NC, 1984. Ordained elder Bapt. Ch., 1983; cert. substance abuse counselor N.C., 1986, Min. Inst. Shaw Divinity Sch., 1987, protective intervention Caswell Ctr., Dept. Human Resource, 1988, Safety E.I. Dupont, 1989. Founder, owner JoAnn's Christian Supply, Bibile and Bookstore, Snow Hill, NC, 1989—93; founder, counselor Spectrum's Substance Abuse, N/A, A/A Group, Snow Hill, NC, 1991—94; founder Rosenwald Ctr. Cultural Enrichment, 2001—; co-founder Power of Prayer Bible Inst. and Sem., 2002—04. Incorporator Spectrum for Living, Snow Hill, NC, 1990—93; assoc. pastor Cry Out Loud Ministries, 2006—; presenter in field. Author: The Holy Spirit, Is He a Stranger in Your House?, 1997 (1999), Could it Be I'm Chosen? (Fear, Peer Pressure, Rejection), 1999; host (TV Show) Appearances on various morning TV shows., 2002—03; singer: You Can Love Again, 1985; author: Fear, Peer Pressure Rejection- Could it be I'm Chosen. Policy coun. chair person Greene Lamp Headstart Inc., Kinston, NC; v.p. Greene County Interfaith Vols., Snow Hill, NC, 1999—2001; host Parad in Honor Local Africa. Am. Heroes, 2004; cert. grantwriter HUD; press sec. Com. To Elect Don Davis for Mayor, Snow Hill, NC, 2002; sec. Snow Hill Dem. Party, Snow Hill, NC; asst. regional chmn. Dem. Get Out to Vote Campaign, 2002; coord. ticket sales Mal Williams Gospel World Tour, Germany, 1996; bd. dirs. Legal Aide, NC, 2002—. Recipient Cert. of Achievement, Goshen Rubber Co., 1984, Cert. of Award, Snow Hill Primary Sch., 1985, Cert. of Appreciation, State of NC, Dept. of Correction & Human Resources, 1985 -1986, Award of Merit, East Carolina U. Sch. of Medicine / Project Concern Internat., 1988 - 1990, Cert. of Recognition, Self Image Bldg. Program, 1989, Letter of Appreciation, First Lady Hillary Rodham Clinton, 1998, Letter of Recognition, N.C. Gen. Assembly - Marian McLawhorn 9th Dist., 1999 -2001, Friends of Project Head Start award, 1999, cert. of Excellence, N.C. Hist. Preservation Office, 2003; Nat. Trust Diversity scholar, 2004. Mem.: N.C. Ctr. for Non Profit Gifts In Kind Internat., Nat. Trust. for Hist. Preservation, Greene County Arts & Hist. Soc. (bd. dirs. 2001—03, neighborhood affairs com., vice chmn. hist. commn. 2002—03). Achievements include initiated process of Nat. Register Nomination for Snow Hill Colored, Greene Co. Sch; partnering with Vocational Rehabilitation to open first transitional house in Greene County, NC; Established Rosenwald Center, counties first community development corporation. Avocations: travel, reading, counseling, research, history. Home: PO Box 343 Snow Hill NC 28580 Home Phone: 252-560-6221; Office Phone: 252-747-4912. Personal E-mail: rcenter@earthlink.net.

STEVENS, JOHN, professional hockey coach, retired professional hockey player; b. Campbellton, NB, Can., May 4, 1966; m. Stacy Stevens; children: John, Nolan. Defenseman Hershey Bears, 1984—90, Phila. Flyers, 1986—88, Springfield Indians, 1990—96, Hartford Whalers, 1990—94, Phila. Phantoms, 1996—99, asst. coach, 1999—2000, head coach, 2000—06; asst. coach Phila. Flyers, 2006, head coach, 2006—. Office: Phila Flyers Wachovia Ctr 3601 S Broad St Philadelphia PA 19148-5250 *

STEVENS, JOHN PAUL, United States supreme court justice; b. Chgo., Apr. 20, 1920; s. Ernest James and Elizabeth (Street) Stevens; m. Elizabeth Jane Sheeren, June 7, 1942 (div. 1979); children: John Joseph(dec.), Kathryn Stevens Jedlicka, Elizabeth Jane Stevens Sesemann, Susan Roberta Stevens Mullen; m. Maryan Mulholland Simon, Dec. 1979. AB, U. Chgo., 1941; JD magna cum laude, Northwestern U., 1947. Bar: Ill. 1949. Practiced in, Chgo.; law clk. to Justice Wiley B. Rutledge U.S. Supreme Ct., Washington, 1947—48; assoc. Poppenhusen, Johnston, Thompson & Raymond, 1949—52; assoc. counsel, sub-com. on study monopoly power, com. on judiciary U.S. Ho. of Reps., Washington, 1951—52; ptnr. Rothschild, Stevens, Barry & Myers, 1952—70; judge U.S. Ct. Appeals (7th cir.), Chgo., 1970—75; assoc. justice U.S. Supreme Ct., Washington, 1975—. Lectr. anti-trust law Northwestern U. Sch. Law, 1953—54, U. Chgo. Law Sch., 1955—58; mem. Atty. Gen.'s Nat. Com. to Study Anti-Trust Laws, 1953—55; chief counsel to commn. investgating the judgment of People v. Isaacs Ill. Supreme Ct., 1969; appellate judge seminar NYU Sch. Law, 1972. With USNR, 1942—45. Decorated Bronze Star. Mem.: Am. Law Inst., Fed. Bar Assn., Ill. Bar Assn., Am. Bar Assn., Chgo. Bar Assn. (2d v.p. 1970), Order of Coif, Phi Delta Phi, Psi Upsilon, Phi Beta Kappa. Office: US Supreme Ct One First St NE Washington DC 20543

STEVENS, JOSEPH CHARLES, psychology professor; b. Grand Rapids, Mich., Feb. 28, 1929; s. Joseph, Jr. and Anne Katheryn Stevens. AB, Calvin Coll., Grand Rapids, 1950; MA, Mich. State U., 1953; PhD, Harvard U., 1957. Instr., asst. prof. psychology Harvard U., 1957-66; fellow emeritus John B. Pierce Found. Lab., sr. rsch. scientist Yale U., 1966—. Cons. in field. Author: Laboratory Experiments in Psychology, 1965; co-editor: Sensation and Measurement, 1974; mem. editl. bds. profl. jours.; contbr. numerous articles to profl. jours. Grantee NSF; Grantee NIH, Air Force Office Sci. Rsch. Fellow AAAS, Am. Psychol. Soc., NY Acad. Scis.; mem. Acoustical Soc. Am., Optical Soc. Am., Soc. Neuroscience, Ea. Psychol. Assn., Gerontol. Soc. Am. Office: 290 Congress Ave New Haven CT 06519-1403 Business E-Mail: jstevens@jbpierce.org.

STEVENS, KENNETH ALLEN, retired defense department worker; b. Exeter, NH, June 21, 1933; s. Albert Howard and Helen Susan (Sewall) S. BA, U. N.H., 1961. With Dept. Def., 1961-88. Bd. dirs. Columbia (Md.) Dem. Club, 1988-90; mem. Howard County (Md.) Dem. Ctrl. Com., 1990-94; vol. Office Human Rights, Howard County, 1989-2001; mem. Howard County Charter Rev. Commn., 2003-04; steering com., Democracy for Howard County, 2005-. Staff sgt. USAF, 1953-57. Mem. ACLU (coord. Howard County chpt. 1988-98). Democrat. Avocations: computer games, crossword puzzles.

STEVENS, KENNETH NOBLE, electrical engineer, educator; b. Toronto, Ont., Can., Mar. 23, 1924; arrived in U.S., 1948, naturalized, 1962; s. Cyril George and Catherine (Noble) Stevens; m. Phyllis Fletcher, Jan. 19, 1957 (div. 1979); children: Rebecca, Andrea, Michael Hugh, John Noble; m. Sharon Manuel, Jan. 14, 1994; children: Kendra Wenyu Manuel, Mackenzie Yin Ying Manuel. BASc., U. Toronto, 1945, MASc., 1948; Sc.D., MIT, 1952. Instr. U. Toronto, 1946—48; faculty MIT, Cambridge, 1948—, prof. elec. engring., 1963—, Clarence J. LeBel prof., 1977—. Vis. fellow Royal INst. Tech., Stockholm, 1962—63; cons. to industry, 1952—; vis. prof. phonetics U. Coll., London, 1969—70; mem. Nat. Adv. Coun. on Neurol. and Communicative Disorders and Stroke, NIH, 1982—86. Author (with A.G. Bose): Introductory Network Theory; author: Acoustic Phonetics, 1998; contbr. articles to profl. jours. Trustee Buckingham Browne and Nichols Sch., 1974—80. Recipient Quintana award, Voice Found., 1992, medal, European Speech Comm. Assn., 1995, Nat. Medal of Sci., 1999; fellow, Guggenheim, 1962. Fellow: IEEE (James L. Flanagan Speech and Audio Processing award 2004), Am. Acad. Arts and Scis., Acoustical Soc. Am. (exec. com. 1963—66, v.p. 1971—72, pres.-elect 1975—76, pres. 1976—77, Gold medal 1995); mem.: NAE, NAS. Office: MIT 77 Massachusetts Ave Cambridge MA 02139-4307 Home: 15298 SE Oregon Tr Dr Clackamas OR 97015

STEVENS, KENNETH T., retail executive; b. 1952; Grad., DePauw U., 1974; student, U. Redlands; MBA, U. So. Calif. Former ptnr. McKinsey & Co., Inc.; former sr. v.p. and treas. Pepsico; exec. v.p. mktg. Taco Bell divsn. of Pepsico, 1993—94, pres. and COO, 1994—97; chmn. and CEO Banc One Retail Group, 1997—2000; pres. and COO inChord Comm., 2001—02; exec. v.p. and COO Bath & Body Works divsn. of Ltd. Brands, Inc., 2002—03, pres., 2003—04; CEO Express (subs. Limited Brands), 2004—06; exec. v.p., CFO Limited Brands, Inc., 2006; pres., COO,sec., treas. Tween Brands, Inc., 2007—, also bd. dir., 2007—. Bd. mem. Spartan Stores, 2002—. Office: Tween Brand Inc 8323 Walton Pkwy New Albany OH 43054-9522 *

STEVENS, LAUREN ROGERS, writer, environmentalist; b. Phila., May 3, 1938; s. Lewis Miller and Elizabeth (Morgan) Stevens; m. Beverly Decker, June 20, 1964 (div. Dec. 1987); children: Rebecca Fasciano, Jeffrey L., Jennifer Wu; m. Peggy Brooks, June 26, 2004; 1 adopted child, Tamirat Brooks-Stevens. BA, Princeton U., 1960; MA, U. Iowa, 1962. Tchr. English lang. & environ. studies Williams Coll., Williamstown, Mass., 1963-81, dean of freshmen, 1970-81; founder, pub., editor Advocate Newsweekly, Williamstown, Mass., 1981-83. Writer, freelance, 1983—. Author: The Double Axe, 1961, Skiing: Downhill and Cross Country, 1991; co-author (with Deborah Burns): Most Excellent Majesty, 1988; co-author: (with Richard W. Babcock) Old Barns in the New World: Reconstructing History, 1996; author: The Berkshire Book, 2006; columnist: Berkshire Eagle; author: Hikes and Walks in the Berkshire Hills, 2004; contbr. articles to mags. and newspapers. Founder Hoosic River Watershed Assn., Williamstown, 1986, co-pres., 1994—96, exec. dir., 1997—2002; leader Mahican-Mohawk Trail, N.Y., Vt., Mass., 1992—; co-founder Greylock A Better Chance, Williamstown, 1968; deacon First Congl. Ch., Williamstown, 1985—, moderator, 2000—03. Mem.: The Trustees of Reservations, Phi Beta Kappa. Democrat. Avocations: hiking, canoeing, cross country skiing. Home: 203 Lesure Rd Stamford VT 05352

STEVENS, LINDA K., lawyer; BA cum laude, Kalamazoo Coll., 1984; JD cum laude, U. Mich., 1987. Bar: Ill. 1987, US Dist. Ct. (no. dist. Ill.) 1987, US Dist. Ct. (ctrl. dist. Ill.), US Ct. Appeals (7th cir.) 1993, US Ct. Appeals (4th cir.). Ptnr. Schiff Hardin, Chgo. Adj. faculty Northwestern U. Sch. Law, Nat. Inst. Trial Advocacy. Contbr. articles to law jours. Mem.: ABA. Office: Schiff Hardin 6600 Sears Tower Chicago IL 60606-6473 Office Phone: 312-258-5667. Office Fax: 312-258-5600. E-mail: lstevens@schiffhardin.com. *

STEVENS, LORETTA MARIE, special education educator; b. Bethpage, NY, Nov. 26, 1955; d. Hamilton Thomas and Evelyn Barbara Pendergast; m. Louis C. Stevens, Apr. 2, 1987 (dec.); children: Erin Michelle Cook, Megan Colleen Oneill. BS, Shenandoah U., Winchester, Va., 1995; MEd, James Madison U., Harrisonburg, Va., 1997; M of Ednl. Adminstrn., Shenandoah U., Winchester, Va., 2005. Cert. elem. edn. tchr. Va., 1995, spl. edn. tchr. Va., 1997, ednl. adminstr. Va., 2005. Learning disabilities specialist Warren County Pub. Schs., Front Royal, Va., 1995—2004, ednl. diagnostician, 2004—06, supr. spl. edn., 2006—. Lead tchr. for learning disabilities Warren County Pub. Schs., Front Royal, Va., 1996—2004, spl. edn. dept. chairperson, 1997—2004; individual edn. plan coord. Warren County Pub. Schools, Front Royal, Va., 1999—; mentor new spl. educators Old Dominion U., Newport News, Va., 1997—. Pres. PTA, Manassas Park, Va., 1986—89; mem./advisor 4-H Club, Warren County, Va., 2002—04; dir. children's choir St. John the Bapt. Cath. Ch., Front Royal, Va., 1989—93, dir. adult modern music choir, 1993—98. Mem.: ASCD, Va. Coun. Spl. Edn. Adminstrs., Internat. Coun. Learning Disabilities, Therapeutic Riding Assn., Internat. Reading Assn., Learning Disabilities Assn., Coun. for Exceptional Children (Professionall Recognized Spl. Educator 200-2005). Achievements include development of Educational program to improve learning for students who are slow learners. Avocations: horseback riding, hiking. Office: Warren County Public Schs 210 N Commerce Ave Front Royal VA 22630 Home Phone: 540-636-4625; Office Phone: 540-635-2171 ext. 247.

STEVENS, LORI ANN LABEAU, school librarian, educator; b. Yakima, Wash., Dec. 31, 1959; d. Raymond L. and Irene A. LaBeau; m. Mark D. Stevens, Apr. 24, 1981; children: Elisabeth A., Jared S., Mark D., Jonathan R. BMus, Brigham Young U., 1983; MLS, Emporia State U., 1999. Pub. svcs.- media ref. libr. Orem Pub. Libr., Utah, 1991—99; media instrn. libr. Utah Valley State Coll., Orem, 1999—. Contbr. chapters to books. Chair libr. adv. commn. City of Orem, 2002. Recipient Merit award, Utah Humanities Coun., 2001, Trustees award Excellence, Utah Valley State Coll. Bd. Trustees, 2002. Mem.: ALA (assoc.; chair 2001—05), Video Round Table ALA (assoc.; program chair 2004), Music Libr. Assn., Mountain Plains Chpt. (assoc.; mem. at large 2002—03), Utah Libr. Assn. (assoc.; mem. at large 2002—05, Spl. Recognition award 2005), Music Libr. Assn. (assoc.; chair film music roundtable 2005—). Mem. Lds Ch. Avocations: singing, piano, hiking, travel, gardening. Home Phone: 801-226-2547. Home Fax: 801-863-7065. Personal E-mail: stevenlo@uvsc.edu.

STEVENS, MARK WHITNEY, art critic; b. NYC, Aug. 14, 1951; s. Whitney Stevens and Rhoda (Winton) Kraft; m. Annalyn Swan, June 12, 1977; children: Emmelyn Swan, Julia Philippa. AB, Princeton U., 1973; MA, Cambridge U., Eng., 1975. Art critic Newsweek, NYC, 1977-87, The New Republic, Washington, 1986—94, Vanity Fair, NYC, 1988—92, NY Mag., NYC, 1994—. Author: (art history) Richard Diebenkorn, 1984, (novel) Summer in the City, 1984; co-author (with Annalyn Swan), de Kooning: An American Master, 2004 (Nat. Book Critics Guild prize for biography, 2004, Pulitzer Prize for Biography, 2005); also numerous articles and essays on art. Office: NY Magazine 444 Madison Ave New York NY 10022

STEVENS, MARTIN BRIAN, publisher; b. NYC, Dec. 29, 1957; s. David Robert and Shirley Stevens. Grad. high sch. Advt. artist Unitron Pubs., NYC, 1977, Westchester Publs., Elmsford, 1978; founder, CEO The Composing Rm., NYC, 1979—83; pub. Retailers Forum, Centerport, 1981—, Swap Meet mag., 1990—; founder, CEO Forum Pub. Co., 1981—. Pub. 8 bus. directories; rep. 6 bus. book pubs.; founder Rodeo Dr. Limousine Svc., 1990—93, Mercedes-Benz Limousine Svc., 1990—93; founder, CEO Party Fun House, Inc., 2004—. Named Top Mail Order Dealer, Nat. Mail Dealers Counsel, 1978. Mem. Mail Order Bus. Bd. (pres. 1978-80), Better Bus. Bur., Nat. Assn. Self-Employed, Nat. Assn. Desktop Pub., L.I. Assn., Can. Direct Mail Assn. Avocations: weight training, reading. Office: Forum Pub Co 383 E Main St Centerport NY 11721-1538

STEVENS, MAY, artist; b. Boston, June 9, 1924; d. Ralph Stanley and Alice Margaret (Dick) S.; m. Rudolf Baranik, June 5, 1948; 1 child, Steven. BFA, Mass. Coll. Art, 1946; postgrad., Academie Julian, Paris, 1948-49, Art Students League, 1948. Mem. faculty Sch. Visual Arts, NYC, 1964-96, Skowhegan Sch. Painting and Sculpture, 1992, Vt. Studio Ctr., 1997, 2005, Santa Fe Art Inst., 2000, 2003. Lectr. Royal Coll. Art, London, 1981, U. Wis.-Racine, 1973, Coll. Art Assn., Washington, 1975; sole juror Am. Drawing Biennial, Coll. William and Mary, Williamsburg, Va., 2000; lectr. Coll. Santa Fe, 1998, Santa Fe Art Inst., 2003. One-woman shows include Terry Dintenfass Gallery, NYC, 1971, Cornell U., 1973, Douglass Coll., Rutgers U., 1974, Lerner-Heller Gallery, NYC, 1975, 76, 78, 81, Clark U., 1982, Boston U. Art Gallery, 1984, Frederick S. Wight Gallery, UCLA, 1985, U. Md., College Park, 1985, Real Art Ways, Hartford, Conn., 1988, New Mus. Contemporary Art, 1988, Orchard Gallery, Derry, No. Ireland, 1988, Kenyon Coll., Gambier, Ohio, 1988, Greenville County Art Mus., SC, 1991, Herter Gallery, U. Mass., Amherst, 1991, U. Colo., Boulder, 1993, U. N.Mex., Albuquerque, 1996, Mary Ryan Gallery, NYC, 1996-97, 99, 2001, 03, 05, 07, Mus. Fine Arts, Boston, 1999, LewAllen Contemporary, Santa Fe, 1998, Minn. Inst. Art, 2005, Nat. Mus. Women in the Arts, Washington, 2005, Springfield Art Mus., Mo., 2006; exhibited in group shows at Santa Fe Art Inst., 2002, Mus. Fine Art, Santa Fe, 2002, Guild Hall, East Hampton, NY, 2002, Hobart & William Smith Colls., 2002, We. Wash. U. Bellingham, 2002, UBS Paine Webber Art Gallery, NYC, 2002, Deutsche Bank, NYC, 2002, Bass Mus. Art, Miami Beach, Fla., 2002, Bklyn. Mus., 2003, Nat. Mus. Women in the Arts, Washington, 2003, Danese Gallery, NYC, 2003, Tamarind Inst., Albuquerque, N.Mex., 2004, Harwood Mus., Taos, N.Mex., 2004, Ctr. Contemporary Arts Warehouse, Santa Fe, N.Mex., 2004, Nat. Acad. Design, NYC, 2004, Evo Gallery, Santa Fe, 2005, Mason Gross Sch. Arts, Rutgers U., New Brunswick, NJ, 2006, others; represented in permanent collections: Met. Mus. Art, NYC, Mus. Modern Art, NYC, Moca, LA, San Francisco Mus. Art, New Mus. Contemporary Art, Whitney Mus., Bklyn. Mus., Herbert F. Johnson Mus., Cornell U., Mus. Fine Arts Boston, De Cordova Mus., Lincoln, Mass., Harwood Mus., Taos, N.Mex., Joslyn Art Mus., Omaha, Nat. Mus. Women in Arts, Washington, Minn. Inst. Art, Mpls., Springfield Mus. Art, Mo., Mcnhy Art Mus., San Antonio, Tex., McCormick Pl. Ctr. Art Coll., Chgo., Jacksonville Art Mus., Fla., Cleve. Mus. Art, Ill., U. Miami, Fla.; contbr. articles to various mags. Recipient Childe Hassam Purchase awards Nat. Inst. Arts and Letters, 1968, 69, 75, N.Y. State Coun. on Arts award, 1974, Disting. Alumna award Mass. Coll. Art, 1997, Disting. Artist award Coll. Art Assn., 2001, Edwin Palmer Meml. prize NAD, 2004; Andy Warhol Found. grantee for project space Headlands Ctr. for Arts, Sausalito, Calif., 2001; MacDowell Colony fellow, 1971, 72, 74, 75, 81, 82, 84, Bunting Inst. fellow Radcliffe Coll., 1988-89; Line Assn. grantee for artists books, 1978; grantee NEA, 1983, Guggenheim, 1986; honoree Women's Caucus for Art, 1990. Mem.: NAT, Coll. Art Assn.

STEVENS, MICHAEL N., lawyer; b. Rockville Centre, NY, Jan. 24, 1949; BA, Temple U., 1971; JD, Bklyn. Law Sch., 1974. Bar: NY 1975, US Dist. Ct. Ea. Dist. NY 1975, US Dist. Ct. So. Dist. NY 1975, US Ct. Appeals 2nd Cir. 1975. Joined Wilson, Elser, Moskowitz, Edelman & Dicker LLP, NYC, 1979, ptnr., 1983—. Mem.: NY State Med. Malpractice Def. Assn., NY State Bar Assn. Office: Wilson Elser Moskowitz Edelman & Dicker LLP 150 E 42nd St 23rd Fl New York NY 10017-5639 Office Phone: 212-490-3000 ext. 2265. Office Fax: 212-490-3038. Business E-Mail: stevensm@wemed.com.

STEVENS, PAUL SCHOTT, lawyer; b. New Orleans, Nov. 19, 1952; s. Miles Gordon and Rosemary Louise (Schott) S.; m. Joyce Lynn Pilz, Aug. 18, 1979; Paul Schott Jr., Alexander Holmes, Andrew Colby, Carl Bernard. BA magna cum laude, Yale U., 1974; JD, U. Va., 1978. Bar: D.C. 1979, U.S. Dist. Ct. D.C. 1979, U.S. Ct. Appeals (D.C. cir.) 1979, U.S. Ct. Appeals (fed. cir.) 1983, U.S. Supreme Ct. 1982. Assoc., prin. Dickstein, Shapiro & Morin, Washington, 1978-85, ptnr., 1989-93; dep. dir., gen. counsel Pres.'s Blue Ribbon Commn. on Def. Mgmt., Washington, 1985-86; legal adviser NSC, Washington, 1987, exec. sec., 1987-89; spl. asst. to Pres. for nat. security affairs The White House, Washington, 1987-89; exec. asst. to Sec. of Defense, Washington, 1989; sr. v.p., gen. counsel Investment Co. Inst., Washington, 1993-97; sr. v.p., gen. counsel Mut. Funds and Internat. Enterprise, Charles Schwab & Co., Inc., San Francisco, 1997-99; ptnr. Dechert LLP, Washington, 1999—2004; pres., CEO Investment Co. Inst., 2004—. Bd. dirs. ICI Mut. Ins. Co.; lectr. law Washington Coll. Law, Am. U., Washington, 1980-83; trustee M.G. Stevens Corp., New Orleans, 1978—; quality of markets com. NASDAQ Stock Market, Inc., 1997, investment cos. com. NASD Regulation, Inc., 1999; adv. bd. Ctr. Banking and Fin. Law, Boston U., 1996—. Author: U.S. Armed Forces and Homeland Defense: The Legal Framework, 2001. Chmn. bd. dirs. Student Conservation Assn., Charlestown, N.H., 1986-87, bd. dirs., 1985-91, 94-96, sec., gen. counsel, 1991-93; mem. fin. coun. Cath. Diocese of Arlington, 2006—; mem. Life Guard Soc. of Mt. Vernon, 2005-, mem. bd. trustees, Yale Libr. Assoc., 2006-. Recipient medal for disting. pub. svc. Dept. Def., 1989; Bates fellow Yale U., 1973, Scholar of House, 1973-74; Rotary Internat. Found. grad. fellow, 1978, U.S.-Japan Leadership fellow Japan Soc., 1989-90, assoc. fellow Saybrook Coll., Yale U., 1993—. Mem.: ABA (chmn. standing com. law and nat. security 1995—98), Fed. Bar Assn., Coun. Fgn. Rels., Federalist Soc., Internat. Bar Assn., DC Bar Assn., Soc. of Sons of the Am. Revolution, Soc. War 1812, Soc. of Mayflower Descendants, Jamestowne Soc., Cosmos Club, Elizabethan Club, Yale Club, Met. Club. Republican. Roman Catholic. Office: Investment Co Inst 1401 H St NW Washington DC 20005 Business E-Mail: paul.stevens@ici.org.

STEVENS, QUALLS E., neurosurgeon; s. Quillens E. and Patricia A. Stevens. DO, NY Coll. Osteo. Medicine, Old Westbury, 2002; MBA, NY Inst. Tech., Old Westbury, 2002. Resident in neurosurgery Bromenn Healthcare, Normal, Ill., 2002—. Vol. physician, Monrovia, Liberia, 2004. Scholar, Hattie Strong Found., 2001; Resident fellow, Depuy Spine, 2006, Synthes, 2006. Mem.: Am. Brain Tumor Assn. (assoc.), AO- N.Am. (assoc.), North Am. Spine Soc. (assoc.), Ill. State Neurosurgical Soc. (assoc.), Am. Coll. Osteo. Surgeons (assoc.). Independent. Achievements include research in cervical instrumentation. Avocations: travel, soccer.

STEVENS, RICHARD YATES, state senator; b. Raleigh, NC, Dec. 12, 1948; s. Floyd L. and Luna (Yates) Stevens; m. Jere Ann Gilmore, Sept. 13, 1980; children: Charles Andrew, Katherine Elizabeth. BA in Polit. Sci., U. N.C., 1970, JD, 1974, MPA, 1978. Bar: N.C. 1974. Asst. dean men U. NC, Chapel Hill, 1970-71, asst. residence dir., 1971-75, asst. Office Student Affairs, 1973-75; pvt. practice Chapel Hill, NC, 1974-76; adminstrv. asst. City of Durham, NC, 1975-76, budget officer, 1976-78, dir. adminstrn., 1978-79, dir. fin. and program devel., 1979-80; from asst. county mgr. to county mgr. Wake County, NC, 1980—2000; mem. NC State Senate, 2003—. Coord. N.C. State Govt. intern program, Inst. Govt., 1971; adj. prof. polit. sci. N.C. State U., 1980, 92, 94; sr. budget advisor N.C. Gov.'s Transition Team, 2000—01. Bd. visitors U. N.C., Chapel Hill, 1991—95, trustee, 1995—2003, chmn., 1997—99; chmn. bd. dirs. U. N.C. Endowment Fund, 1997—99; chmn. U. N.C. Found., 1997—99. Mem.: ASPA (Nat. Pub. Svc. award 2000), NC Mus. Natural Scis. Soc. (bd. dirs. 1987—88, treas. 1988—89, pres.-elect 1989—90, pres. 1990—91), NC City-County Mgmt. Assn. (bd. dirs. 1991—92, 2d v.p. 1997—98, 1st v.p. 1999—99, pres. 1999—2000), NC Bar, Nat. Assn. County Adminstrs. (bd. dirs. 1989—92), Internat. City-County Mgmt. Assn. (life), Yates Mill Assn. (bd. dirs. 2001—07), Cary Acad. (bd. dirs.), U. NC Gen. Alumni Assn. (dir. 1978—80, 1983—88, treas. 1988—98, chmn.-elect 1999—2000, chmn. 2000—01, Disting. Svc. medal 1994), U. NC Pub. Adminstrn. Alumni Assn. (pres. 1977—79, dir. 1982—84, Disting. Pub. Svc. award 1998), Carolina Club (vice chmn. 1993—94, chmn. 1994—98, 2002—). Home: 132 Lochwood Dr W Cary NC 27518 Office: NC Gen Assembly Rm 406 Legislative Office Bldg Raleigh NC 27601-2808 Office Phone: 919-733-5653.

STEVENS, RISË, performing arts association administrator; b. NYC; m. Walter Surovy; 1 child, Nicolas. Student, Juilliard Sch.; Hon. Degree Smith Coll., Coll. of Senecas, Russell Sage Coll., Rider Coll., U. Pa., Baylor U., Rice U., Mercy Coll., Mannes Coll Music, Hobart Coll., Cleve. Inst. Music, Va. Commonwealth U. Co-gen. mgr. Met. Opera Nat. Co., NYC, 1980-88; pres. The Mannes Coll. Music, NYC, 1975-78; mng. dir. Met. Opera Bd., NYC. Performer Prague Opera, Vienna State Opera, Royal Opera, NY Met. Opera, 1938-61, starred in films, concerts, TV, and radio. Mem. Nat. Endowment for Arts (co-chair music panel 1981-83), N.Y. State Coun. on Arts (chmn. music panel), Met. Opera Guild (bd. dirs.), Wagnerian Soc. Buenos Aires, Sigma Alpha Iota. Office: Met Opera Assn Lincoln Ctr New York NY 10023

STEVENS, ROBERT BOCKING, lawyer; b. UK, June 8, 1933; naturalized, 1971; s. John Skevington and Enid Dorothy (Bocking) S.; m. Katherine Booth, Dec. 23, 1985; 1 child, Robin; children by previous marriage: Carey, Richard. BA, Oxford U., 1955, BCL, 1956, MA, 1959, DCL, 1984; LLM, Yale U., New Haven, Conn., 1958; LLD (hon.), NY Law Sch., 1984, Villanova U., Pa., 1985, U. Pa., Phila., 1987; DLitt. (hon.), Haverford Coll., Pa., 1991. Bencher, Gray's Inn, 1999. Barrister-at-law, London, 1956; tutor in law Keble Coll. Oxford U., 1958-59; asst. prof. law Yale U., 1959-61, assoc. prof., 1961-65, prof., 1965-76; provost, prof. law and history Tulane U., 1976-78; pres. Haverford Coll., 1978-87; chancellor, prof. history U. Calif., Santa Cruz, 1987-91; counsel Covington and Burling, Washington and London, 1991—; master Pembroke Coll., Oxford, 1993-2001; mem. Essex Court Chambers, 1966—; sr. rsch. fellow U. Coll., London, 2001—06. Vis. prof. U. Tex., 1961, U. East Africa, 1962, London Sch. Econs., 1963, Stanford U., 1966, Brookings Instn., 1967-68, U. Coll. London, 1991-94, U. Hong Kong, 1998, Yale U., 1999, George Washington U., 2003, Cardozo Law Sch., 2004; cons. UN, HEW, US Dept. State; hon. fellow, Keble Coll., Oxford U., 1985, Pembroke Coll., Oxford U., 2001. Author: The Restrictive Practices Court, 1965, Lawyers and the Courts, 1967, In Search of Justice, 1968, Income Security, 1970, Welfare Medicine in America, 1974, Law and Politics, 1978, The Law School, 1983, The Independence of the Judiciary, 1993, The English Judges, 2002, 2d edit., 2005, From University to Uni, 2004, 2d edit., 2005. Chair Marshall Memorial Commn., 1994—2001, Sulgrave Manor, 2001—06; mem. Nat. Humanities Coun., 1982—86. Fellow, Russell Sage Found., 1967—68, Cromwell Found., 2005; grantee, Rockefeller Found., 1962—64, Ford Found., 1962—64, 1973—74, Nuffield Found., 1975;, NEH, 1973—74, 2005. Office: Covington and Burling 265 Strand London WC2R 1BH England Home: 19 Burgess Mead Oxford OX2 6XP England Office Phone: 44-20-7067-2213. Business E-Mail: rstevens@cov.com.

STEVENS, ROBERT DAVID, librarian, educator; b. Nashua, NH, Aug. 11, 1921; s. David Philip and Ruth (Ackley) S.; m. Helen Medora Conrad, Jan. 16, 1943; children: Ruth Wilson Robertson, Hope Conrad. AB magna cum laude, Syracuse U., 1942; BS in L.S. with honors, Columbia, 1947; MA, Am. U., 1955, PhD, 1965. Employed Libr. Congress, Washington, 1947-64, coord. pub. law, 480 programs, 1962-64; dir. Libr. East West Ctr., Honolulu, 1964-65; dean Grad. Sch. Library Studies U. Hawaii, 1966-75; chief cataloging div. Copyright Office, 1975-80, coordinator copyright collections, 1980; lectr. grad. Sch. Libr. Studies, U. Hawaii, 1981-91; chief exec. officer Molesworth Inst. West, Inc., 1984-91, chmn., 1991-96. Fulbright lectr. U. Indonesia, 1971; US del. Intergovtl. Conf. Planning Nat. Libraries Infrastructures, 1974 Author: Role of the Library of Congress in International Exchange of Government Publications, 1955, Toshokan Kyoryoku, 1970, Documents of International Organizations, 1974, Japanese and US Research Libraries at the Turning Point, 1977, Short History of the School of Library and Information Studies, 1991; contbr. articles to profl. publs. Served to lt. USNR, 1943-46. Mem. Hawaii Library Assn. (pres. 1966-67), ALA (mem. council 1967-70, mem. US, Japan adv. com. 1972-79, chmn. 1974-76, Rlms policy and rsch. com. 1977-81), Assocs. U. Hawaii Library (vice chmn. 1981-84), Japan Library Assn., Hui Dui, Phi Beta Kappa, Pi Sigma Alpha. Clubs: 15 (Honolulu). Democrat. Home: 3-3400 Kuhio Hwy Apt C208 Lihue HI 96766-1084

STEVENS, ROBERT EDWARD, engineering company executive; b. Kansas City, Mo., Oct. 30, 1957; s. Kenneth E. and Nina (France) S. BS in Chem. Engring., U. Mo. Rolla (now Mo. U. Sci. and Tech.), Rolla, 1980; MS in Engring. Mgmt., U. Mo. Rolla (now Mo. U. Sci. and Tech.), 1985. Process design engr. The Pritchard Corp., Kansas City, Mo., 1981-83;

process engr. Procter & Gamble, Cape Girardeau, Mo., 1986-87, tech. mgr., 1987-90; from project engring. mgr. to site mgr. Bechtel, 1990—99, engring. mgr. Mex., 1999-2000, project mgr., 2000-01, resident engring. mgr. Egypt, 2001, sys. engring. mgr. Hanford, 2002—. Contbr. to Properties of Gases and Liquids, 1987. Chmn. bd. dirs. Wesley Found., St. Louis, 1993-98; corp. devel. coun. U. Mo. Rolla (now Mo. U. Sci. and Tech.), chair benchmarking com., 1996-2000, chair distance learning com., 2001-03, mem. chem. engring. indsl. adv. bd., 2002—. Recipient Stan Adams Reliability award P & G Paper Div., 1990, Pres.'s award for team excellence Shell Oil Co., 1994; Nat. Merit scholar, 1976. Mem.: AIChE (life), Acad. Chem. Engrs. (bd. dirs. 2006—), Am. Soc. Engring. Mgmt., Project Mgmt. Inst., Nat. Fire Protection Assn., B-Reactor Mus. Assn., Chem. Heritage Found./Robert Boyle Soc, George C. Marshall Inst., Alpha Chi Sigma Ednl. Found. (bd. dir. 2003—), Mo. U. Sci. and Tech. Wesley Found. Alumni Assn. (pres. 1988—97, named outstanding contr. 1983, 1988), Order of the Golden Shillelagh, Tau Beta Pi, Alpha Chi Sigma (expansion com 2002—04, N.W. Dist. com. 2004—, cert. appreciation 1991, Hall of Fame Selection Adv. Bd. 2004—, Kuebler award Selection Com. 2006—). Methodist. Home and Office: 11220 W Florissant # 369 Florissant MO 63033-6741

STEVENS, ROBERT J., aerospace transportation executive; b. McKeesport, Pa. BS summa cum laude, Slippery Rock U., 1976; grad., Dept. Def. Sys. Mgmt. Coll.; M in Engring. and Mgmt., Polytechnic U. N.Y.; M in Bus., Columbia U. With Fairchild Republic Co.; gen. mgr. to v.p., CFO Loral Sys. Manufacturing Co. (acquired by Lockheed Martin), 1987—93; exec. v.p., sr. v.p., CFO, air traffic mgmt. Lockheed Martin, 1993—96; pres., air traffic mgmt. Lookheed Martin, 1996—98; pres., COO energy and environ. bus Lockheed Martin, 1998—99, v.p. strategic devel. Bethesda, Md., 1998—99, exec. v.p., CFO, 1999—2001, pres., COO, 2000—04, pres., CEO, 2004—, chmn., 2005—. Commr. Commn. Future of US Aerospace Industry, 2001—02; chmn., bd. dirs. Sandia Corp.; presiding dir., bd. dirs. Monsanto Co., 2002—; assoc. fellow Am. Inst. Aeronautics and Astronautics; mem., internat. adv. bd British-American Business Coun. Served USMC. Recipient Disting. Alumni award, Slippery Rock Univ., 2003, Exec. Yr., Nat. Mgmt. Assn., 2004; fellow Fairchild Fellowship, Am. Aeronautical Soc. Fellow: Am. Astronautical Soc.; mem.: Aerospace Industries Assn. (mem. exec. com.). *

STEVENS, ROBERT JAY, magazine editor; b. Detroit, July 25, 1945; s. Jay Benjamin and Louise Ann (Beyreuther) S.; m. Dahlia Jean Conger, Aug. 15, 1970; children— Sandra Lee, Julie Ann. Student, Huron Coll., SD, 1963-66, Wayne State U., 1968-71. Sr. staff writer Automotive News, Detroit, 1968-71; editor Excavating Contractor mag., Cummins Pub. Co., Oak Park, Mich., 1971-78, Chevrolet's Pro Jour., Sandy Corp., Southfield, Mich., 1978—79, Cars and Parts mag., Cars and Parts Corvette mag. Amos Press, Sidney, Ohio, 1979—; truck editor Automotive Design & Devel. mag., 1971-78. Lectr., speaker in field. Contbr. articles to profl. jours.; author: numerous poems. Served with AUS, 1966-68, Vietnam. Decorated Air medal, Bronze star, Commendation medal; recipient Alphomega Publs. award, 1965—, Robert F. Boger Meml. award for outstanding constrn. journalism, 1975, U.L.C.C. nat. editl. award, Am. Pub. Works Assn., 1978, Moto award for outstanding automotive journalism, Internat. Automotive Media Conf., 1997, 1998, 1999, 2000, 2001, Internal. Automotive Media Conf., 2002, Best of Divsn. award, Internat. Automotive Media Conf., 2001, Folio mag. Editl. Excellence award, 2001. Mem. Detroit Auto Writers (past dir.), Internat. Motor Press Assn., Antique Automobile Club Am. (Lifetime Achievement award 2005. Republican. Presbyterian. Home: 653 Ridgeway Dr Sidney OH 45365-3432 Office: PO Box 482 911 Vandemark Rd Sidney OH 45365 E-mail: bstevens@carsandparts.com.

STEVENS, ROBERTA A., librarian; BA, MLS, SUNY Buffalo; MA in English, SUNY Binghamton. Assoc. dir. tech. ops. Fairfax County Pub. Libr., Va., 1981—85; customer services officer, cataloging distbn. svc. Libr. of Congress, 1985—89, spl. asst. to assoc. libr. for cultural affairs, 1990—95, spl. asst. to dir. nat. services, libr. services. Bicentennial prog. mgr. Libr. of Congress, 2000; project mgr. Nat. Book Festival, 2001—. Mem.: ALA (coun. mem. 2001—, com. on legis. 2001—, mem. exec. bd. 2006—). Office: Libr of Congress 101 Independence Ave SE Washington DC 20540-1400 Office Phone: 202-707-1550. Office Fax: 202-707-0312. Business E-Mail: rste@loc.gov. *

STEVENS, ROGER TEMPLETON, writer; b. Syracuse, NY, Jan. 11, 1927; s. Raymond Alfred and Mabel Eunice Stevens; m. Mildred Lorraine Hasbrouck, June 12, 1948 (dec. Aug. 1978); children: Margaret Ann, David Keith; m. Barbara Ann Wilkinson, July 14, 1979. AB in English, Union Coll., Schenectady, NY, 1949; MA in Math., Boston U., 1959; MS in Systems Engring., Va. Inst. Tech., Blacksburg, 1975; PhD in Elec. Engring., Calif. Western U., 1978. Tech. writer Raytheon Mfg. Co., Waltham, Mass., 1950—51; engr. Lab. for Electronics, Boston, 1951—55; sr. engr. Spencer Kennedy Labs., Boston, 1955—56, Avco Mfg. Co., Boston, 1956—57, Electronics Systems, Inc., Boston, 1957—60; supr., video and display Sanders Assocs., Nashua, NH, 1960—65; mem. tech. staff The Mitre Corp., Bedford, Mass., 1965—67, 1983—92, 1970—74; sr. rsch. engr. The Dikewood Corp., Albuquerque, 1967—70, 1974—81; sect. head EG & G Inc., Albuquerque, 1981—83. Author: Operational Test and Evaluation, 1979, Graphics Programming in C, 1988, Fractal Programming with C, 1989, Fractal Programming with Turbo Pascal, 1990, Advanced Fractal Programming in C, 1990, Fractal Programming and Ray Tracing with C++, 1991; author: (with Christopher Watkins) Advanced Graphics Programming in C and C++, 1991, Advanced Graphics Programming with Turbo Pascal, 1991; author: The C Graphics Handbook, 1992, Learning C with Fractals, 1993, Quick Reference Guide to Computer Graphics Terms, 1993, Object Oriented Graphics Programming in C++, 1994, Using PCX Graphics Files, 1995, Understanding Self-Similar Fractals, 1995, The C++ Graphics Handbook, 1996, Graphics Programming with Java, 1997, Computer Graphics Dictionary, 2002, Creating Fractals, 2005. With USN, 1945—46, Pacific. Mem.: AF and AM, Shriners. Avocations: computers, photography. Home: 17 Castle Rock Rd Rio Rancho NM 87124 Personal E-mail: rogerstevens76@msn.com.

STEVENS, RON A., lawyer, advocate, surveyor; b. Indpls., Sept. 4, 1945; s. Granville Thomas and Charlotte May (Wheeler) S.; m. Judy Rohde, June 15, 1968; children: Samuel Thomas, Alison Elizabeth. BA, Okla. State U.; JD with honors, Ill. Inst. Tech., 1976. Bar: Ill. 1976. Staff atty. Legal Assistance Found. Chgo., 1976-79; staff atty., dir. housing agenda Bus. and Profl. People for Pub. Interest, Chgo., 1979-81; chief housing divsn. Office of Cook County State's Atty., Chgo., 1981-82; campaign coord. north lakefront Washington for Mayor, Chgo., 1982-83; program officer The Joyce Found., Chgo., 1983-86; pres. Citizens for a Better Environment, Chgo., 1986-89; pres., CEO United Way Santa Fe County, 1989—2003; dir. cmty. impact svcs. United Way Am., 2003—06; pres. ChangeWays LLC, 2006—. Adv. bd. state support ctr. on environ. hazards Nat. Ctr. for Policy Alternatives, Washington, 1987-89; chair Local Bd. EFSP, 1989—, Santa Fe Affordable Housing Roundtable, 1992-97; chair Exec. Leadership Coun. for Cmty. Schs, 1998—; bd. dirs. No. N.Mex. Grantmakers Assn., v.p., 1999, pres., 2000. Mem. bldg. code enforcement com. Mayor's Transition Team Housing Task Force, Chgo., 1983, steering com. Chgo. Ethics Project, 1986-88; founder, chmn. Progressive Chgo. Area Network, 1981-84; bd. dirs. Uptown Recycling Sta., Chgo., 1987-89; mem. South Ctrl. Regional Coun., United Way of Am., 1993-98. Mem. Chgo. Coun. Lawyers (chmn. housing com. 1978-81, bd. govs. 1981-83, bd. dirs. Fund for Justice, 1986-88), Chgo. Area Runners Assn. (founder, v.p. 1977-81). Home and Office: 7006 Stone Mill Pl Alexandria VA 22306-1329

STEVENS, ROSEMARY ANNE, medicine and public health historian, artist; b. Bourne, Eng. came to U.S., 1961, naturalized, 1968; d. William Edward and Mary Agnes (Tricks) Wallace; m. Robert B. Stevens, Jan. 28, 1961 (div. 1983); children: Carey, Richard; m. Jack D. Barchas, Aug. 9, 1994. BA, Oxford U., Eng., 1957; Diploma in Social Adminstrn., Manchester U., Eng., 1959; MPH, Yale U., 1963, PhD, 1968; LHD (hon.), Hahnemann U., 1988; DSc (hon.), Northeastern Ohio U. Coll. Medicine, 1995; DSc, Rutgers U., 1995. Various hosp. adminstrv. positions, Eng., 1959-61; rsch. assoc. Med. Sch. Yale U., 1962-68, asst. prof. Med. Sch., 1968-71; assoc. prof. Med. Sch., 1971-74, prof. pub. health Med. Sch., 1974-76; master Jonathan Edwards Coll., 1974-75; prof. dept. health systems mgmt. and polit. sci. Tulane U., New Orleans, 1976-78, chmn. dept. health systems mgmt., 1977-78; prof. history and sociology of sci. U. Pa., Phila., 1979—2002, chmn. dept., 1980-83, 86-91, UPS Found. prof., 1990-91, dean Sch. Arts and Scis., Thomas S. Gates prof., 1991-96, Stanley I. Sheerr prof., 1997—2001, prof. emeritus, 2002—. Prof. emeritus U. Pa., Phila., 2002-; vis. lectr. Johns Hopkins U., 1967-68; guest scholar Brookings Instn., Washington, 1967-68; acad. visitor London Sch. Econs., 1962-64, 1973-74; DeWitt Wallace disting. scholar social medicine and pub. policy, dept. psychiatry Weill Cornell Med. Coll., 2005—. Author: Medical Practice in Modern England: The Impact of Specialization and State Medicine, 1966, new edit., 2003, American Medicine and the Public Interest, 1971, rev. edit., 1998, In Sickness and in Wealth: American Hospitals in the Twentieth Century, 1989, rev. edit., 1999, (with others) Foreign Trained Physicians and American Medicine, 1972, Welfare Medicine in America, 1974, new edit., 2003, Alien-Doctors: Foreign Medical Graduates in American Hospitals, 1978, The Public-Private Health Care State, 2007; editor: (with others) History and Health Policy in the United States: Putting the Past Back In. Bd. dirs. Milbank Meml. Fund. Rockefeller Humanities fellow, 1982-83, Guggenheim fellow, 1984-85; Bellagio Study and Conf. scholar, 1984; recipient Frohlich medal Royal Soc. Medicine, London, 1986, Baxter Found. prize distinction in health svcs. rsch., 1990, James A. Hamilton Book award Am. Coll. Healthcare Execs. best book, 1990, Welch medal distinction in history of medicine Am. Assn. History Medicine, 1990, Arthur Viseltear award history pub. health Am. Pub. Health Assn., 1990, Nicholas E. Davies award Piedmont Hosp., Atlanta, 1997, Investigator award in health policy rsch. Robert Wood Johnson Found., 1998-2003, Carlson award for extraordinary contbns. to history of medicine Cornell U., Weill Med. Coll, 2000., Lifetime Achievement award Am. Assn. History Medicine, 2002. Fellow Am. Acad. Arts and Scis.; mem. AAAS (chmn. sect. history and philosophy of sci., 2002-03), Inst. Medicine of Nat. Acad. Sci., Am. Sociol. Assn., Am. Assn. for History of Medicine, Coll. Physicians Phila., Century Assn. Home: 500 E 77th St Apt 419 New York NY 10162 Office Phone: 212-746-5798. Business E-Mail: ras2023@med.cornell.edu.

STEVENS, ROY W., sales and marketing executive; b. Ottumwa, Iowa, Oct. 28, 1924; s. Manley O. and Ruth (Worrell) S.; m. Donna R. Borman, June 7, 1952 (dec. Jan. 1973); children: Katharine Anne Stevens Dillon, Thomas W., John M.; m. Beth A. Murphy, Apr. 20, 1974; children: Carrie Theresa, Elizabeth Mary. BSc, U. Iowa, 1948. With Coca-Cola Co., 1948-54, Gen. Foods Corp., 1954-67; exec. v.p. Riviana Foods, Houston, 1967-73; v.p. mktg. Hiram Walker Inc., Detroit, 1973-75, pres., 1975-80, Maidstone Wine & Spirits Inc., LA, 1980-91, Kahlua Group (Allied Domecq), 1987-91; exec. v.p. The Century Coun., Los Angeles, 1991-98. Bd. dirs., past chmn. Detroit Met. YMCA; bd. dirs. L.A. Met. YMCA. Lt. (j.g.) USN, 1943-46. Mem. Jonathan Club, Sigma Alpha Epsilon. Episcopalian. Home: 1444 S Marengo Ave Pasadena CA 91106-4228

STEVENS, ROY W., microbiologist, researcher, photographer; BS, State Univ. of N.Y., Albany, 1956, MS, 1958; PhD, Albany Med. Coll., 1965. Diplomate Am. Bd. Med. Microbiology, cert. emeritus Am. Bd. Med. Microbiology, 2002. Rsch. scientist Wadsworth Ctr., N.Y. State Dept. Health, Albany, 1967—70, assoc. rsch. scientist, 1970—73, prin. rsch. scientist, 1973—79, dir. lab. diagnostic immunology, 1979—85, dir. retrovirology and immunology lab., 1985—91; adj. prof. microbiology and immunology Albany Med. Coll., 1982—92; assoc. prof. sch. pub. health State Univ. N.Y., Albany, 1988—98; pres. Bio-med. Resource Group, Albany, 1991—2001. Trustee Bender Sci., Albany, 1986-98; chair Bender Sci. Ltd. Cmty. Found., Albany, 2002—; mem. libr. devel. com. U. at Albany, 2001—, chair 2003-06. Fellow Am. Acad. Microbiology (emeritus 2002), Assn. Med. Lab. Immunologists (pres. 1989), Am. Soc. Microbiology (chmn. clin. and diagnostic immunology divsn. 1997-98), Nat. Assn. Photoshop Profls. Home: 507 Acre Dr Schenectady NY 12303-5226

STEVENS, SCOTT, retired professional hockey player; b. Kitchener, Ont., Canada, Apr. 1, 1964; Defenseman Washington Capitals, 1982—90, St. Louis Blues, 1990—91, NJ Devils, 1991—2005, capt., 1992—2005, cons., 2005—. Played in NHL All-Star Game, 1985, 89, 91-94, 96; named to NHL All-Rookie Team, 1982-83, Sporting News All-Star Second Team, 1987-88, NHL All-Star First Team, 1987-88, 93-94, 2004, NHL All-Star Second Team, 1991-92, Sporting News All-Star First Team, 1993-94; recipient Conn Smythe Trophy, 2000; set NHL record for games played by a defensemen. Achievements include being a member of Stanley Cup Champion NJ Devils, 1995, 2000, 2003; having his number, 4, retired by NJ Devils, 2006. Office: c/o NJ Devils Nat Newark Bldg 744 Broad St 33rd Fl Newark NJ 07102

STEVENS, SHANE, novelist; s. John and Caroline (Royale) S. MA, Columbia U. Mem. numerous writers confs. including Bread Loaf, Santa Barbara Writers Conf. Author: Go Down Dead, Way Uptown in Another World, Dead City, Rat Pack, By Reason of Insanity, The Anvil Chorus; (as J.W. Rider) Jersey Tomatoes (Best Novel award), Hot Tickets; contbr. articles to pubs. including N.Y. Times, Life, Washington Post; screenwriter: By Reason of Insanity, The Me Nobody Knows. Mem. Authors Guild, Writers Guild Am.

STEVENS, SHARON COX, lawyer; b. 1948; m. Michael Callahan. BA, Washington State Univ.; JD, McGeorge Sch. Law. Bar: Oreg. 1977. Ptnr. Callahan & Stevens, Keizer, Oreg. Mem.: ABA (bd. gov. 2004—). Office: Callahan & Stevens 5845 Shoreview Lane N PO Box 20937 Keizer OR 97307-0937 also: Callahan & Stevens 156 Chemawa Rd N Salem OR 97303-5356 Office Phone: 503-240-4133.

STEVENS, SHEILA MAUREEN, retired teachers union administrator; b. Glendale, Calif., Nov. 1, 1942; d. Richard Chase and Sheila Mary (Beatty) Flynn; m. Jan Whitney Stevens, Sept. 12, 1964; children: Ian Whitney, Bevin Michelle. AA in Liberal Arts, Monterey Peninsula Coll., Calif., 1963; BA in Anthropology, Calif. State U., Long Beach, 1969; postgrad. studies in Edn., U. Guam, 1976-77. Tchr. U.S. Trust Territory of the Pacific, Koror, Palau Island, 1968-72, Kolonia, Ponape Island, 1972-76, Dept. Edn., Agana, Guam, 1976-79; newspaper editor Pacific Daily News (Gannett), Agana, 1979-83; comm. dir. Guam Fedn. of Tchrs., Agana, 1983-84, exec. dir., 1984-85, Alaska Fedn. Tchrs., Anchorage, 1985-87; labor rels. specialist N.Y. State United Tchrs., Watertown, 1987-93, regional staff dir. Potsdam, 1993—2003; ret., 2003. Mem. Gov.'s Blue Ribbon Panel on Edn., Agana, Guam, 1983-85; leadership devel. coord. Am. Fedn. Tchrs., Washington, 1983—; trainer positive negotiations program Situation Mgmt. Sys., Hanover, Mass., 1988—. Author, editor: Pacific Daily News, 1981-83 (Guam Press Club awards 1981, 82, 83); contbr. articles to mag. and jours. Mem. task force on labor policy, com. on self determination, Govt. of Guam, Agana, 1984-85, Adult Basic Edn. Planning Com., 1985; mem. labor studies adv. bd., Anchorage, Alaska, 1989, regional compact coalition N.Y. State Edn. Dept., Albany, 1994; del. NY State Labor Religion Coalition. Named Friend of Edn., Carthage (N.Y.) Tchrs. Assn., 1990. Mem. NOW, ACLU, ASCD, AAUW, Am. Fedn. Tchrs. Comm. Assn. (Best Editorial award 1984), Indsl. Rels. Rsch. Assn. Democrat. Methodist. Avocations: travel, reading, free-lance writing, cross country skiing. Personal E-mail: seawings49@hotmail.com.

STEVENS, STANLEY DAVID, historian, researcher, retired librarian, archivist; b. San Francisco, Nov. 10, 1933; s. David Franklin and Ellen Myrtle (Wixson) S.; m. Carli Ann Lewis, Sept. 3, 1960; adopted children: Alexander Lewis, Nikolas Harriman, Brooke Cayton Stevens. BA, San Jose State U., Calif., 1959. Conf. officer polit. and security com. 14th Gen. Assembly, UN, NYC, 1959; map libr. U. Calif., Santa Cruz, 1965-93, ret., 1993, coord. Hihn-Younger Archive, Univ. Libr., 1994—. Mem. Cartographic Users Adv. Coun., 1976-86, chmn., 1982-86; presenter in field; adj. prof. libr. sci. San Jose State U., 1989, 91. Author: Index to Guinn's Biographical Record of Santa Cruz, San Benito, Monterey and San Luis Obispo Counties, Catalog of aerial photos by Fairchild Aerial Surveys, Inc. now in the collections of the Dept. Geography, UCLA, 1982, Correspondence of Charles B. Younger Sr. and Charles B. Younger Jr., Santa Cruz, California Attorneys and Counsellors at Law, vols. 1-13, 1996—, indexed edit. Santa Cruz County, Calif., 1997, Index to Personal Names, Portraits & Illustrations Appearing in California City, County & Regional Histories 1867-1910, 2005; editor: Santa Cruz County History Jour., 1994-96, 98, Index to Sidewalk Companion to Santa Cruz Architecture, 3d edit., 2005; co-author: A Legal History of Santa Cruz County: an account of the local bench and bar through the end of the Twentieth Century, 2006, The Rowland Website & The Content of the Leon Rowland Collection, 2006, Index to Lime Kiln Legacies: The History of the Lime Industry in Santa Cruz County, 2007, others; prodn. editor: Index to Boulder Creek Mountain Echo, 1896-1916, 1999; contbr. articles to profl. jours. Mem. adv. com. archaeol. program Cabrillo Coll., Aptos, Calif., 1985—; bd. dirs. Santa Cruz County Hist. Soc., 1985-94, chmn. publs. com., 1985-96, mem. programs adv. coun., 1994-95; mem. Santa Cruz Orgn. for Progress and Euthenics, 1987—; bd. dirs. Friends of U. Calif.-Santa Cruz Libr., 1994-97; founding mem. Rschr. Anonymous, Santa Cruz, 1993—; mem. U. Calif.-Santa Cruz Emeriti Group, sec.-treas. 1996—; mem. collections adv. com. Santa Cruz City Mus. Natural History, 1995—; mem. hist. publs. com. Mus. Art and History, 2000—, chmn., 2006—; vol. Spl. Collections, Univ. Libr., U. Calif., Santa Cruz, 1994—. With U.S. Army, 1954-56. Recipient honors award geography and map divsn. for outstanding achievement in map librarianship Spl. Librs. Assn., 1981, cert. of commendation Santa Cruz Hist. Soc., 1986, appreciation cert. for svcs. Assn. Info. and Image Mgmt., 1989, Proclamation of Honor, Santa Cruz County Bd. Suprs., 1998, Historian of Yr. award History Forum of Santa Cruz Mus. of Art and History, 2001; grantee Librs. Assn. U. Calif., 1981-82, Rsch. grantee Office of Pres., U. Calif., 1985-86. Mem. ALA (publs. com. Map and Geography Round Table 1985-86, editl. bd. Meridian 1989-2000, honors award Map and Geography Round Table 1992), ACLU (chmn. bd. dirs. Santa Cruz County chpt. 1962-68, bd. dirs. No. Calif. br. 1973-76), Western Assn. Map Librs. (hon. life, founding pres. 1967-68, treas. 1968-89, editor Info. Bull. 1969-84, Exec. Com. award 1984, Stanley D. Stevens Hon. Map presented at 30th anniversary meeting 1997, Calif. Hist. Soc., Calif. Map Soc., Pajaro Valley Hist. Assn., Santa Cruz County Geneal. Soc., Capitola Hist. Soc., El Paso de Robles Hist. Soc. (life). Democrat. Avocations: researching local history, listening to jazz and classical music. Home: 231 13th Ave Santa Cruz CA 95062-4831 Office: U Calif Dean E McHenry Libr Santa Cruz CA 95064 Business E-Mail: sstevens@library.ucsc.edu.

STEVENS, STANLEY M., lawyer; b. Dec. 21, 1948; m. Kristin Stevens. BA, U. Mo., Columbia, 1970; JD, U. Chgo., 1973. Bar: Ga. 1973, US Dist. Ct. No. Dist. Ga. 1974, Ill. 1976, US. Dist. Ct. No. Dist. Ill. 1977, Fla. 1987, US Dist. Ct. Mid. Dist. Fla. 1987. Exec. v.p., chief legal counsel, sec. Equity Office Properties Trust, Chgo., 1996—. Office: Equity Office Properties Trust 2 N Riverside Plz Ste 2100 Chicago IL 60606 Office Phone: 312-466-3362. Business E-Mail: stan_stevens@equityoffice.com.

STEVENS, SUFJAN, musician; b. Detroit, July 1, 1975; Band mem. Marzuki, Holland, Mich.; solo career, 1999—; dir., co-founder, owner Asthmatic Kitty Records, Mich., 1999—. Musician: (albums) A Sun Came, 2000, Enjoy Your Rabbit, 2001, Greetings from Michigan: The Great Lakes State, 2003, Seven Swans, 2004, Illinois, 2005, The Avalanche, 2006, Songs for Christmas, 2006. Recipient New Pantheon award, 2006. Office: Asthmatic Kitty Records PO Box 1282 Lander WY 82520 Business E-Mail: info@asthmatickitty.com.

STEVENS, SUSAN SELTENREICH CIRILLO, special education educator; b. Rockville Centre, NY, Apr. 16, 1962; d. Richard Paul and Estelle Duboise Seltenreich; m. John Stafford Cirillo (div.); children: Adam Cirillo, Jeremy Cirillo, Nicholas Cirillo; m. Peter Stevens, Oct. 4, 2003. AS in Early Childhood Edn., SUNY, Farmingdale, 1982; BS in Edn., SUNY, Geneseo, 1986; MEd, U. North Tex., 1992. Cert. lay min. United Meth. Ch. of N.Y., local lay min. United Meth. Ch. of N.Y.; spl. edn. tchr. N.Y., tchr. nursery, kindergarten, grades 1-6 N.Y., spl. edn. tchr. K-12 Wash., tchr. ESL Wash., elem. edn. tchr. Wash., early childhood educator Wash., spl. edn. tchr. Tex., tchr. ESL Tex., elem. edn. tchr. Tex., kindergarten tchr. Tex. Spl. edn. tchr. United Cerebral Palsy of Queens, Jamaica, NY, 1987—88; elem. and ESL educator Herbert Marcus Elem. Sch., Dallas Ind. Sch. Dist., 1988—92, spl. edn. educator Hillcrest H.S., 1994—96; enrichment educator The Huntington Learning Ctr., Issaquah, Wash., 1999—2000; spl. edn. educator Beaver Lake Mid. Sch., Issaquah Sch. Dist., 2000—02; spl. edn. educator Silas Wood 6th Grade Ctr., South Huntington Union Free Sch. Dist., Huntington Sta., NY, 2000—. Author: (poetry) Mellie the Muskrat, 2004. Lay min., mem. edn. com., Sunday sch. educator, children's sermon min. Dix Hills (N.Y.) United Meth. Ch., 2002—05; Sunday sch. educator Faith United Meth. Ch., Issaquah, 2000—02, St. John's Luth. Ch., Columbia, Md., 1996—98; Sunday sch. educator, mem. worship and music coun. Preston Meadow Luth. Ch., Plano, Tex., 1988—96. Fellow ednl. grantee, South Huntington Parent Tchr. Ctr., 2004. Mem.: Coun. Exceptional Children (assoc.). Avocations: poetry, travel. Home: 3 Wexford St Huntington NY 11743 Office: Silas Wood 6th Grade Ctr 23 Harding Pl Huntington Station NY 11746 Home Phone: 631-427-0702; Office Phone: 631-425-5515. Personal E-mail: susanc001@msn.com. E-mail: sstevens@shufsd.org.

STEVENS, TED (THEODORE FULTON), senator; b. Indpls., Nov. 18, 1923; s. George A. and Gertrude (Chancellor) S.; m. Ann Mary Cherrington, Mar. 29, 1952 (dec. 1978); children: Susan B., Elizabeth H., Walter C., Theodore Fulton, Ben A.; m. Catherine Chandler, 1980; 1 child, Lily Irene. BA, U. Calif. at Los Angeles, 1947; LL.B., Harvard U., 1950. Bar: Calif., Alaska, D.C., U.S. Supreme Ct. bars. Pvt. practice, Washington, 1950-52, Fairbanks, Alaska, 1953; U.S. atty. Dist. Alaska US Dept. Justice, Fairbanks, 1953-56; legis. counsel US Dept. Interior, Washington, 1956—57, asst to sec., 1958—59, solicitor, 1960; pvt. law practice Anchorage, 1961-68; mem. Alaska Ho. of Reps., 1965-68, majority leader, speaker pro tem, 1967-68; US Senator from Alaska, 1968—; minority whip, 1977—81; majority whip, 1981—85; pres. pro tempore, 2003—07; chair appropriations com., 1997—2001, 2003—05, commerce com., 2005—; co-chair sci. com., 2005—. Served in USAF, 1943—46. Decorated Disting. Flying Cross, Air medal, Yuan Hai medal. Mem. ABA, Alaska Bar Assn., Calif. Bar Assn., D.C. Bar Assn., Am. Legion, VFW. Lodges: Rotary, Pioneers of Alaska, Igloo #4. Republican. Episcopalian. Office: US Senate 522 Hart Senate Bldg Washington DC 20510-0001

STEVENS, THELMA KAPLAN, artist, educator; b. NYC, Dec. 4, 1932; d. Nathan and Shirley (Laufer) Kaplan; m. Jay P. Stevens, Mar. 17, 1956; children: Wendy, Andrew BS, Pratt Inst., 1954; MS, Queens Coll., 1959; PhD, Fordham U., 1980. Tchr. art pub. schs., NY, 1954—88; instr. Grad. Sch. Fordham U., NYC, 1979; pres. Isis Gallery Ltd., Searingtown, NY,

1982—. Pres. Reunions to Remember, Manhasset, NY, 1996—. Co-author: Super Sculpture, 1974; contbr. numerous articles to profl. jours Mem. Internat. Soc. Edn. Thru Art (N.Y. state rep. 1989—), U.S. Soc. for Edn. Thru Art, N.Y. State Art Tchrs. Assn., Nat. Art Edn. Assn. (dir. ea. region U.S. and Can. secondary art edn. 1986-89, N.Y. State Art Educator of Yr. 1983), James Madison H.S. Alumni Assn. (pres. 1995-2004, bd. dirs.) Avocations: travel, reading, cooking, theater. Studio: Reunions to Remember 565 Plandome Rd # 130 Manhasset NY 11030 Office Phone: 516-944-2240.

STEVENS, THOMAS CHARLES, lawyer; b. Auburn, NY, Oct. 17, 1949; s. Alice (Kerlin) S.; m. Christine Eleanor Brown, June 2, 1973; children: Erin, Leigh, Timothy. BA, SUNY, Albany, 1971; JD, Duke U., 1974. Bar: Ohio 1974. Mng. ptnr. Thompson, Hine & Flory, Cleve., 1991-96; vice-chmn. KeyCorp., Cleve., 1996—, chief adminstrv. officer, 1996—. Bd. dirs. KeyCorp. Trustee Greater Cleve. Growth Assn., 1993-96, Greater Cleve. Roundtable, 1993-2003,(chmn. of bd. trustees), Playhouse Sq. Found., 1998—, Greater Cleve. (Ohio) Partnerships, 2003—; active Leadership Cleve., 1992-93, Young Audiences, 1999—, 1999 United Way Campaign; mem. Fin. Svcs. Roundtable, 1997—. Mem. ABA, Cleve. Bar Assn., Am. Soc. Corp. Secs., N.Y. Bankers Assn., Nisi Prius. Office: KeyCorp 127 Public Sq Cleveland OH 44114-1306 E-mail: thomas_stevens@keybank.com.

STEVENS, THOMAS M., real estate company executive; m. Lindy Stevens. Cert. Residential Broker, Residential Specialist, Grad. Realtor Inst. Sales assoc., 1972; prin. broker; sr. v.p. and divsn. mgr. Shannon & Luchs, 1979; founder Coldwell Banker Stevens, 1993—; sr. v.p. Mid-Atlantic NRT Inc., pres. and COO DC and Va. ops., sr. v.p. bus. devel. Mem. Wolf Trap Found. for Performing Arts, Fairfax C. of C., Cerebral Palsy Campaign of Nat. Capital Area. Named one of Real Estate's 25 Most Influential Thought Leaders, Realtor Mag., 2006. Mem.: Nat. Assn. Realtors (first v.p. 2004—05, pres.-elect 2005—06, pres. 2006—07), Va. Assn. Realtors (pres. 1989, Realtor of Yr. 1991), Northern Va. Assn. Realtors (chmn. issues mobilization com., chmn. strategic planning com., chmn. by-laws com., pres. 1985, Disting. Svc. award 1978, Realtor of Yr. 1986), Northern Va. Bldg. Industry Assn. *

STEVENS, WARREN, actor; b. Clark's Summit, Pa., Nov. 2, 1919; s. Albert Clifford and Helen Dodd (Blakeslee) S.; m. Barbara Helen Fletcher, Sept. 9, 1969; children— Adam Fletcher, Matthew Dodd; 1 son by previous marriage, Laurence Blakeslee. Student, U.S. Naval Acad., 1939-40. Appeared on: New York stage in Gallileo, 1947, Sundown Beach, 1948, Smile of the World, 1949, Detective Story, 1949; appeared in numerous motion pictures, since 1950, including, Barefoot Contessa, Forbidden Planet; appeared on: numerous television shows, including Richard Boone Rep. With USN, 1937-40; with USAAF, 1942-46. Mem. Actors Studio.

STEVENS, WILBUR HUNT, accountant; b. Spencer, Ind., June 20, 1918; s. John Vosburgh and Isabelle Jane (Strawser) S.; m. Maxine Dodge Stevens, Sept. 28, 1941; children: Linda Maxine Piffero, Deborah Anne Augello. BS, MBA, U. Calif., Berkeley, 1949. CPA, Calif.; cert. fraud examiner, fin. svcs. auditor. Staff acct. McLaren, Goode, West & Co., San Francisco, 1949-52; mng. ptnr. Wilbur H. Stevens & Co., Salinas, Calif., 1952-70; regional ptnr. Fox & Co., CPAs, Salinas, 1970-73, nat. dir. banking practice Denver, 1973-80; pres., chmn. Wilbur H. Stevens, CPA, PC, Salinas, 1980-94; chmn. Stevens, Sloan & Shah, CPAs, 1994—. Adj. prof. acctg. U. Denver, 1975-78; faculty mem. Assemblies for Bank Dirs., So. Meth. U., Dallas, 1976-81, Nat. Banking Sch., U. Va., Charlottesville, 1979-87; chmn., dir. Valley Nat. Bank, 1963-71, Pacific Ag Credit, Inc., 1997—, Pacific Valley Bank, 2002-05; dir. World Travel, Inc.; v.p., dir. Dirs. Coun. Ind. Banks, Global Uplift, Inc.; mem. bus. adv. coun. NRCC. Editor Issues in CPA Practice, 1975; contbr. articles to profl. jours. Capt. AUS, 1942-53. Decorated Bronze Star, Burma Star, UK, China Victory medal; Frank G. Drum fellow U. Calif., Berkeley, 1949. Fellow Am. Bd. Forensic Acctg.; mem. AICPA (v.p. 1971), Am. Acctg. Assn., Am. Assembly Collegiate Schs. Bus. (accreditation coun. 1975-78, 81-84), Nat. Assn. State Bds. Accountancy (pres. 1976-77, strategic initiatives com. 1997-99), Inst. Internal Auditors (fin. svcs. group), Am. Acad. Cert. Consultants and Experts, Calif. Soc. CPAs (pres. 1968-69, Disting. Svc. award 1988), Acctg. Rsch. Assn. (pres. 1973-75), Acad. Acctg. Historians, Assn. Cert. Fraud Examiners, Am. Coll. Forensic Examiners, Ctrl. Calif. Past Masters Assn. (pres. 1998), Burma Star Assn., CBI Vets. Assn., 14 AF Assn., Hump Pilots Assn., Salinas C. of C. (pres. 1960), Commonwealth Club Calif., Masons (master 1992, 97, Hiram award 1998, grand lodge com. taxation), Knight Templar (comdr. 2000), Royal Arch (high priest 1998, grand chpt. inspector 1999-2000), Cryptic Masons (illus. master 2000), Fedn. Knight Masons Am., Knight of York (Cross of Honor), Allied Masonic Degrees (sov. master 2001 York Rite Coll.), Royal Order Scotland, 32 degree Scottish Rite, Nat. Sojourners (pres. Monterey Bay chpt. 1996), Heroes of '76 (comdr. John C. Fremont chpt. 1996-97), Fed. for Collingwood Libr. and Mus., Red Cross of Constantine, Salinas High Twelve Club (pres. 1995), Philalethes Soc., QCCC, London, Rotary (dist. gov. 1983, chmn. internat. fellowship CPAs 1994-96, Paul Harris fellow 1973), Phi Beta Kappa, Beta Gamma Sigma (v.p. 1949), Beta Alpha Psi. Republican. Methodist. Home: 38 Santa Ana Dr Salinas CA 93901-4136 Office: 975 W Alisal St Ste D Salinas CA 93901-1148

STEVENS, WILLIAM DOLLARD, mechanical engineer, consultant; b. Bayonne, NJ, Aug. 4, 1918; s. William B. and Beatrice (Dollard) S.; m. Mary E. King, Oct. 12, 1940; children: Sandra A. (Mrs. Jeffrey N. Melin), Barbara E. (Mrs. Dennis Gallagher), William K. BSME, Rensselaer Poly. Inst., 1940; postgrad., Case Inst. Tech., 1958; DSc (hon.), N.J. Inst. Tech., 1986. Various engring. and mgmt. positions Babcock & Wilcox Co., NYC, 1940-62; v.p. equipment div. Foster Wheeler Corp., Livingston, NJ, 1962-73, sr. v.p., 1972-74, exec. v.p., 1974-78, chmn. bd., 1978-81, dir., 1974-86, dir. emeritus, 1986-90; bd. of dir. Am. Soc. for Macro Engring., 1992—2001. Instr. Pratt Inst., 1946-47; bd. overseers N.J. Inst. Tech., 1978-94. Contbr. articles to profl. jours.; patentee in field Chmn. fund drive ARC, Hackensack, N.J., 1956; planning commr., Hackensack, 1955-58; trustee Bergen County Mental Health Consultation Ctr., 1955-58; bd. dirs. Metals Properties Coun.; mem. coun. Rensselaer Polytech. Inst., 1983—. Lt. USNR, 1943-45. Fellow ASME; mem. Nat. Acad. Engring., Sigma Xi, Tau Beta Pi, Phi Kappa Tau, Pi Tau Sigma. Methodist. Home and Office: 3302 Pointe Gate Rd Livingston NJ 07039 E-mail: wmdstevens3@verizon.net.

STEVENS, WILLIAM GRANT (GRANT STEVENS), plastic surgeon; b. Orange, Calif., Nov. 13, 1953; s. William Raymond Stevens and Donna Lynn (Stabbert) Watson; m. Sheri Diane Eagle, Aug. 13, 1977; 1 child, Catherine Eagle. BS, U. Oreg., 1976; MD, Washington U., 1980. Lic. Calif., 1981, Idaho, 1994, diplomate Nat. Bd. Med. Examiners, 1981, Am. Bd. Plastic Surgery, 1989. Intern Harbor UCLA Med. Ctr., Torrance, 1980-81, resident, 1981-83; hand surgery fellow Washington U., St. Louis, 1983-84, resident plastic surgery, 1984-85, chief resident, 1985-86; med. dir. Marina Outpatient Surgery Ctr., LA, 1988—; med. dir. hand therapy svcs. Washington Hosp., 1988—93; chmn. surgical dept. Daniel Freeman Marina Hosp., Marina del Rey, Calif., 1989—96, assoc. med. dir. Marina Breast Ctr., 1991—92, physician advisor, Skin Care POD, 1995—98. Mem. editl. bd. Wounds: A Compendium of Clin. Rsch. & Practice, 1988, mem. editl. adv. bd. Plastic Surgery Products, 1998—2006, Cosmetic Surgery Times, 1998—2006, frequent TV appearances include Personal Story, TLC, Hard Copy, Plastic Surgery Before & After, Discovery Health, The Perfect Cut, frequently featured in The Argonaut, Glamour, LA Times Mag., Plastic Surgery News, Longevity, LA Times, LA Mag., Daily Breeze, Cosmetic Plastic Surgery Times, Cosmetic Plastic Surgery Mag., Cosmetic Surgery Mag.; contbr. articles to profl. journals. Pres. Native Sons of the Golden West, Santa Monica, 1989—; active Boys and Girls Club Marina Del Rey. Recipient Kovitz sr. prize in Surgery, 1980, cert. of tribute, City of LA, 1996, GTE Cmty. Spirit award, 1996, cert. of recognition, Calif. State Assembly, 1997, cert. of Spl. Congl. Recognition, 1997, cert. of recognition, Calif. State Senate, 1997; Louis & Dorothy Kovitz fellowship in Surg. Rsch., 1979. Fellow: Am. Soc. for Laser Medicine & Surgery, Internat. Coll. Surgeons, Am. Coll. Surgeons; mem.: AMA (Physician Recognition award), Internat. Soc. Aesthetic Plastic Surgery, Internat. Confederation for Plastic, Reconstructive and Aesthetic Surgery, LA County Med. Assn., Am. Coll. Surgeons, Southern Calif. ch., Calif. Med. Assn. (adv. panel on plastic surgery sect. asst. sec. 1991—92, adv. panel on plastic surgery sect. sec. 1992—93, adv. panel on plastic surgery chmn. 1993—94), Lipoplasty Soc. N.Am., Barnes Hosp. Plastic Surg. Soc., Plastic Surgery Ednl. Found., LA Society of Plastic Surgeons, Inc., Am. Soc. for Aesthetic Plastic Surgery, Inc., Am. Soc. Plastic Surgeons, Am. Soc. Plastic & Reconstructive Surgeons, Inc. (young plastic surgeons com. 1991—93, CPT com. 1992—93, practice devel. com. 1992—93, govt. rels. com. 1992—95), Phi Beta Kappa. Republican. Office: 4644 Lincoln Blvd Ste 552 Marina Del Rey CA 90292 Office Phone: 866-588-7507. *

STEVENS, WILLIAM KENNETH, lawyer; b. Chgo., Apr. 19, 1917; s. Ernest James and Elizabeth (Street) S.; m. Anne Hughes, Jan. 4, 1943; children: Anne Elizabeth Stevens Fishman, William Hughes Stevens, Mary Carol Stevens Williams, Martha Street Stevens Gingrich. AB cum laude, U. Calif., Berkeley, 1938; MA, U. Chgo., 1940; JD, Harvard U., 1948. Bar: Ill. 1948, Fla. 1977. With First Nat. Bank Chgo., 1948-74, asst. v.p., 1958-61, v.p., 1961-74; ptnr. McDermott, Will & Emery, Chgo., 1974-85, Myers Krause & Stevens, Naples, Fla., 1986—2001; of counsel Fowler White Boggs Banker, Naples, Fla., 2001—. Author: Illinois Estate Administration, 1968. Chmn. Ill. Inst. Continuing Legal Edn., 1971-72; pres. Hinsdale (Ill.) Pub. Libr., 1977-79. Lt. USNR, 1941-45. Recipient Disting. Svc. award Chgo. Estate Planning Coun., 1981. Fellow Am. Coll. Trust and Estate Counsel; mem. ABA, Am. Law Inst., Chgo. Bar Assn., Ill. Bar Assn., Fla. Bar Assn. (bd. cert. estate planning and probate lawyer), Internat. Acad. Estate and Trust Law. Clubs: Mid-Day, Hinsdale Golf; Chikaming Country (Lakeside, Mich.), The Club at Pelican Bay (Naples). Office: Ste 600 5811 Pelican Bay Blvd Naples FL 34108-2711 E-mail: wstevens@fowlerwhite.com.

STEVENS, WILLIAM TALBERT, financial services executive; b. Houston, Mar. 11, 1952; s. Talbert Maxton and Peggy Elizabeth (Cagle) S.; m. Christine Leslie Treml, May 24, 1975; 1 child, Anne Kathleen. BBA, Pacific Western U., 1988. Mgr. Capital Fin. Svcs., Akron, Ohio, 1975-80, Beneficial Mgmt., Columbus, Ohio, 1980-85; v.p. Mid Am. fed. Savs. and Loan, Columbus, 1985-87, Lender's Svc., Inc., Pitts., 1987-89; pres. Equity Mgmt. Svcs., Inc., Pitts., 1989-90; sr. v.p. CBC Cos., Pitts., 1990—2001, Gen. Am. Corp., Pitts., 2001—06, exec. v.p., 2006—, Fiserv Lending Solutions, 2006—. Mem. faculty, bd. govs. Nat. Inst. Consumer Credit Mgmt. Marquette U., Milw., 1988-94. Recipient Pres.'s Disting. Achievement Beneficial Mgmt., 1982, 83. Avocation: golf. Office: Gen Am Corp 700 Grant St Pittsburgh PA 15219 also: CBC Cos 520 E Main St Carnegie PA 15106-2051 Office Phone: 412-261-4791. Business E-Mail: william.stevens@fiserv.com.

STEVENS, YVETTE MARIE See KHAN, CHAKA

STEVENSON, ADLAI EWING, III, lawyer, retired senator; b. Chgo., Oct. 10, 1930; s. Adlai Ewing and Ellen (Borden) S.; m. Nancy L. Anderson, June 25, 1955; children: Adlai Ewing IV, Lucy W., Katherine R., Warwick L. Grad., Milton Acad., 1948; AB, Harvard U., 1952, LL.B., 1957. Bar: Ill. 1957, D.C. 1977. Law clk. Ill. Supreme Ct., 1957-58; assoc. Mayer, Brown & Platt, Chgo., 1958-66, ptnr., 1966-67, 81-83, of counsel, 1983-91; treas. State of Ill., 1967-70; U.S. senator from Ill., 1970-81; chmn. SC&M Internat. Ltd., Chgo., 1991-95, pres., 1995-98, chmn. bd., 1998—; co-chmn. Huamei Capital Co., Inc., 2005—. Mem. Ill. Ho. of Reps., 1965-67; Dem. candidate for gov. of Ill., 1982, 86. Capt. USMCR, 1952-54. Office: 71 S Wacker Dr 27th Fl Chicago IL 60606

STEVENSON, AMANDA (SANDY STEVENS), librettist, composer, songwriter; b. Bklyn., Oct. 24, 1943; d. Haakon and Grace Svendsen. Cert. Nat. Bur. Document Examiners. Composer, librettist, Nellie Bly, Victorine, (screenplay) The Last Assignment Mem. Actors Equity Assn., BMI, Songwriters Guild. Democrat. Avocations: chess, art history, songwriting.

STEVENSON, BEN, performing company executive; b. Portsmouth, Eng., Apr. 4, 1936; arrived in U.S., 1968; s. Benjamin John and Florence May (Gundry) S.; m. Joan Toastivine, Jan. 6, 1968. Grad., Arts Ednl. Sch., London, 1955. Artistic dir. Harkness Ballet Youth Dancers, 1968—71, Chgo. Ballet, 1974—75, Houston Ballet, 1973—2003, artistic dir. emeritus, 2003—; co-dir. Nat. Ballet, Washington, 1971—74; artistic dir. Tex. Ballet Theater, 2003—. Mem. dance panel Tex. Commn. Arts, 1977; guest tchr. Am. Ballet Theatre, Joffrey Ballet, Royal Ballet, London, Beijing Dance Acad. Dancer Theatre Arts Ballet, London, 1952-54, Sadler's Wells Theatre Ballet, 1955-56, Royal Ballet, 1956-60, London Festival Ballet, 1960-62; appearances in Wedding in Paris, 1954-55, Music Man, London, 1962-63, Half a Sixpence, also, Boys in Syracuse, London, 1964; prin. dancer, ballet master, London Festival Ballet, 1964-68; prin. ballets choreographed include Three Faces of Eve, 1965, Cast Out, 1966, Sleeping Beauty (full length), 1967, 71, 76, 78, Fervor, 1968, Three Preludes, 1968, Forbidden, 1969, Cinderella (full length), 1969, 71, 73, 74, 76, Bartok Concerto, 1970, Nutcracker (full length), 1972, 76, Symphonetta, 1972, Courant, 1973, Swan Lake (full length), 1977, L, 1978, Britten Pas de Deux, 1979, Four Last Songs, 1979, Space City, 1980, Peer Gynt (full length), 1981, Zheng Ban Qiao, 1982, The Prince of Pagodas, 1986 Recipient 1st prize London Choreographic competitions, 1965, 66, 67, modern ballet choreography Internat. Ballet Competition, Varna, Bulgaria, 1972, Gold medal for choreography Internat. Ballet Competition, 1982, Dance mag. award, 2000; named Order of Brit. Empire, 1999. Asso. mem. Royal Acad. Dancing (Adeline Genee Gold medal 1955) Office: Tex Ballet Theatre 6845 Green Oaks Rd Fort Worth TX 76116 Office Phone: 817-763-0207 817-763-0207. E-mail: bstevenson@texasballettheater.org. *

STEVENSON, BRADFORD ALLEN, management consultant; s. James Richard and Sara Jean Stevenson; m. Sarah Alaine Powers, Aug. 8, 2001; children: Paige Anne, Braden Allen. BS in Criminal Justice, So. Ill. U.; MBA, So. Ill. U., Albuquerque, 2007. Cert. program enhancement instr. TWD N.Mex, 2006. COO Exec. Intelligence Svcs., Inc, Albuquerque, 1990—2004, Trans-World Dynamics, LLC, Albuquerque, 2004—. Bus. coach TWD Ind., Albuquerque, 1991—2007. Contbr. articles to profl. jours. Staff sgt. spl. forces US Army, 1984—90. Decorated Combat Inf. badge US Army, Jungle Expert award. Home: PO Box 82066 Albuquerque NM 87198 Office: Trans-World Dynamic LLC PO Box 82512 Albuquerque NM 87198 Home Phone: 505-991-1079; Office Phone: 505-266-3614. Personal E-mail: brad@thepowerofthanks.com. Business E-Mail: brad@transworldynamics.com.

STEVENSON, BRYAN ALLEN, lawyer; b. Milton, Del., Nov. 14, 1959; s. Howard Carlton and Alice Gertrude (Golden) S. BA, Eastern Coll., St. Davids, Pa., 1981; MPP, Kennedy Sch. Govt., Cambridge, Mass., 1985; JD, Harvard U., 1985. Bar: Ga. 1985, Ala. 1987. Staff atty. So. Prisoners Def. Com., Atlanta, 1985-89; exec. dir. Ala. Capital Representation Resource Ctr., Montgomery, 1989-95; dir. Equal Justice Initiative of Ala., Montgomery, 1995—, exec. dir.; asst. prof. clin. law NY U. Sch. Law, 1998, assoc. prof. clin. law, 2002, prof. of clin. law, 2003—. Vis. prof. law NYU Sch. Law, 1997, U. Mich. Law Sch., 1995. Contbr. articles to publs. Recipient MacArthur Found. award, Thurgood Marshall medal of justice, Nat. Human Rights award Reebol Human Rights Found., 1989, ACLU Medal of Liberty, 1991, ABA Wisdom Award for Pub. Svc., 1991; Harvard Law Sch. Pub. Interest fellow, 1985. Avocations: music, piano and keyboards. Office: Equal LJustice Initiative of Alabama 122 Commerce St Montgomery AL 36104-2538 also: NY U Sch Law 245 Sullivan St 628 New York NY 10012 Office Phone: 212-998-6456. Office Fax: 212-995-4031. Business E-Mail: bstevenson@eji.org. *

STEVENSON, C. DONALD, youth organization executive, folk artist; b. Greensboro, NC, Dec. 4, 1932; s. C. Donald Sr. and Sue Holland Stevenson; m. June Lee Keefe, Feb. 22, 1955 (div. June 30, 1977); m. Judy Kaye Helms, May 16, 1978; children: Kimberly Sue, Donald Scott. Student, Appalachian State U., Boone, NC, 1951—54. Cert. mfg. tng. program GE, Lockland, Ohio, 1961. Mfg. planner rocket engine mfg. GE, Lockland, Ohio, 1955—59, quality control planner, 1959—61; dist. scout exec. Fort Steuben area coun. Boy Scouts Am., Steubenville, Ohio, 1961—65, dist. scout exec. greater Cleve. area coun., 1965—71, explorer exec. Piedmont coun. Gastonia, NC, 1971—75; vol. svc. coord. State of NC, Western Carolina Ctr., Morganton, 1975—81; self employed portrait artist, 1981—85; adaptive equipment specialist Appalachian State U., Boone, NC, 1985—93; owner Fourth Creek Folk Art Studio, Morganton, NC, 1994—. Mem. Hist. Courthouse Commn., Morganton, NC, 1980—84; burke county disaster chmn. ARC, Morganton, NC, 1988—94, nat. disaster team mem. Washington, DC, 1989—92; children's sunday sch. tchr. First Presbyn. Ch., Morganton, NC, 1978—85. Mem.: Southern Highland Craft Guild (fin. com. 2001). Democrat. Presbyterian. Avocations: painting, gardening, woodcarving, photography. Home: 308 Forest Hill Morganton NC 28655-4326 Office: Fourth Creek Folk Art Studio 308 Forest Hill Morganton NC 28655-4326 Office Phone: 828-433-6118. Personal E-mail: donstevenson@bellsouth.net.

STEVENSON, CHERYL D., science educator, researcher; PhD, Tex. A&M Univ., 1969. With Ill. State Univ., 1977—, disting. prof., phys. chemistry. Contbr. several articles to peer-reviewed jours. Recipient award for Rsch. at an Undergraduate Institution, Am. Chem. Soc., 2007. Office: 219 Science Laboratory Bldg 214 Julian Hall 4160 Dept Chemistry Illinois State University Normal IL 61790-4160 Office Phone: 309-438-7300. Business E-Mail: cdsteve@ilstu.edu. *

STEVENSON, DAVID JOHN, planetary scientist, educator; b. Wellington, New Zealand, Sept. 2, 1948; arrived in US, 1971, permanent resident; s. Ian McIvor and Gwenyth (Carroll) S. BS in Physics, Victoria U., New Zealand, 1971, MS in Physics, 1972; PhD in Theoretical Physics, Cornell U., 1976. Rsch. fellow Australian Nat. U., Canberra, Australia, 1976-78; asst. prof. UCLA, LA, 1978-80; assoc. prof. Calif. Inst. Tech., Pasadena, 1980-84, prof., 1984—, George van Osdol prof., 1995—. Chmn. divsn. geol. & planetary scis. Calif. Inst. Tech., 1989-94; mem. NASA solar system exploration subcom., 2000—. Assoc. editor ICARUS, 1990—; Contbr. 100 articles to profl. jours. Named Fulbright scholar, USA, 1971-76; in 1996, at suggestion of discoverers asteroid, (5211) Stevenson, named in his honor. Fellow Am. Geophysical Union (Whipple award 1994, Harry H. Hess medal 1998; pres. planetary scis. sect. 2000-02), Royal Soc. London, 1993, AAAS; Am. Astron. Soc. (Urey prize 1984), NAS (fgn. assoc.). Office: Calif Inst Tech 1200 E California Blvd Pasadena CA 91125-0001 Office Phone: 626-395-6534. Office Fax: 626-585-1917. E-mail: djs@gps.caltech.edu.

STEVENSON, DAVID WAYNE, municipal official; b. Commerce, Tex., Aug. 9, 1957; s. Billy Wayne Stevenson and Constance Marie-Essary Underwood; m. Tami Gail Thomas; children: James David, Ashlei Gail Jones, John Thomas, Amber Michelle. Degree in acctg., Tyler Comml. Coll., 1976. Office mgr. Fountain & Holdredge CPA, Athens, Tex., 1976—78; brakeman Union Pacific RR, Mineola, Tex., 1978—86; firefighter City of Mineola, 1986—94, city sec., 1994—. Firefighting instr. Tex. A&M, College Station; mem. homeland security adv. bd. East Tex. Coun. of Govts., Kilgore, 2003—; mem. adv. bd. Nat. Coun. Readiness and Preparedness, Washington, 2005—. Chief Mineola Vol. Fire Dept., 1997—. Named Mineola Man of Yr., Mineola C. of C., 1997, Mineola Firefighter of Yr., Mineola Fire Dept., 1990, 1994; named to Leadership Mineola, C. of C., 1997. Mem.: Tex. State Fireman's and Fire Marshal's Assn., Wood County Fire Chiefs Assn. (pres. 1998—99), Kiwanis (pres. 1997). Methodist. Avocations: hunting, golf, reading. Office: City of Mineola 300 Greenville Ave Mineola TX 75773 Office Phone: 903-569-6183. Business E-Mail: dstevenson@mineola.com.

STEVENSON, EDWARD WARD, retired otolaryngologist, surgeon; b. Chester, SC, Jan. 9, 1926; s. Thomas M. and Annie Lou (Ward) S.; m. Dorothy Giles, Sept. 2, 1947; children: Sally Anne Stevenson Yeilding, Laura Stevenson Healy, Nancy Stevenson Schonbeger (dec.), Molly Stevenson Walker. B in Medicine, Duke U., 1945; MD, U. Md., Balt., 1949. Intern Bapt. Meml. Hosp., Memphis, 1949-50; resident Med. Coll. Va. Hosp., Richmond, 1953-55; fellow Ochsner Found. Hosp., New Orleans, 1955-56; staff otolaryngologist Ochsner Clinic, 1956-57; pvt. practice Birmingham, 1957-60, 65-94, 1965—94; instr., clin. asst. prof. surgery U. Ala., 1957-94; pvt. practice Decatur, 1960-65; ret., 1994. Faculty Tulane U. Sch. Medicine, 1956-57; staff Bapt. Med. Ctr. Montclair, Birmingham, vice chmn. 2007. Contbr. articles to profl. jours. Bd. dirs. So. Mus. Flight, Birmingham, 1989—, Ala. Aviation Hall Fame, chmn., bd. dirs., 2003—, vice chmn. 2006—; pres. Birmingham Aero Club, 1996. Lt. M.C. USNR, 1949—53. Mem. AMA, ACS, Am. Laryngol., Rhinol. and Otol. Soc. (sec.- treas. so. sect. 1990-93, v.p. so. sect. 1993-94), Am. Soc. Head and Neck Surgery, Am. Acad. Otolaryn., Jefferson County Med. Soc., Ala. Otolaryn. Soc. (founder, pres. 1971), Med. Assn. State Ala., Morgan County Med. Soc. (pres. 1964-65), Tri-State Otolaryn. Assembly (co-founder), Birmngham Otolaryn. Soc. (pres. 1984), Newcomen Soc. US, Birmingham-Jefferson Hist. Soc. (pres. 2007), Birmingham Downtown Rotary Club. Methodist. Avocations: aerobatic flying, world travel. Home: 4249 Antietam Dr Birmingham AL 35213-3221 E-mail: edstevenson@bellsouth.net.

STEVENSON, FRANCES KELLOGG, retired museum program director; b. Boston; d. Charles Summers and Alice deGueldry (Stevens) S.; m. James Richard Wein, 1971 (div. 1989). BA, Wells Coll., Aurora, NY, 1967; MA, Oxford U., England, 1972; MBA, U. Pa., Phila., 1992. Publs. officer Nat. Portrait Gallery Smithsonian Instn., Washington, 1974—2001, strategic planning officer, 2001—06; ret., 2006. Bd. mem. Am. Friends of St. Hilda's Coll., Oxford U.; mem. St. John's Episcopal Ch., Georgetown. James E. Webb fellow Smithsonian Instn., 1988-89. Mem.: Sulgrave Club. Home: 2724 Ordway St NW Apt 4 Washington DC 20008-5047

STEVENSON, HOWARD HIGGINBOTHAM, business educator; b. Salt Lake City, June 27, 1941; s. Ralph Shields and Dorothy Dee (Higginbotham) S.; m. Fredericka O'Connell; children: William, Charles, Andrew. BS, Stanford U., 1963; MBA, Harvard U., 1965, DBA, 1969. Asst. prof. Harvard U., Cambridge, Mass., 1968—78, prof., 1982—, sr. assoc. dean for fin. adminstrn., 1991-94, sr. assoc. dean external rels., 2000—04, sr. assoc. provost resources and planning, 2004—05, vice provost resources and planning, 2005—06; sr. assoc. dean, dir. of pub. activities Harvard Bus. Sch., Boston, 2006—. Faculty chair, owner, pres., mgr. Program Exec. Edn., 1998—2000; chmn. publs. rev. bd. Harvard Bus. Sch. Press, 1999—2000; faculty chmn. Latin. Am. Adv. Bd., 1999—2001; v.p. Simmons Assocs., Boston, 1970—71; v.p. fin. adminstrn. Preco Corp., West Springfield, Mass., 1978—81; bd. dirs. Landmark Comms. Inc., Norfolk, Va., Camp Dresser and McKee Inc., Cambridge, The Baupost

Group, Inc., Boston, Commonwealth Capital Ptnrs., Boston, Nat. Pub. Radio, Washington. Co-author: Policy Formation and Administration, 1984, New Business Ventures and the Entrepreneur, 1985, 89, 94, 99, 6th edit., 2007, Entrepreneurial Ventures, 1992, 2d edit., 1999, Do Lunch or Be Lunch: The Power of Predictability in Creating Your Future, 1997, (with David Amis) Winning Angels: The Seven Fundamentals of Early Stage Investing, 2001, (with David Amis) Winning Angels: Mentors in a Network of Success, 2003, (with Laura Nash) Just Enough: Tools for Creating Success in Your Work and Life, 2004, (with Eileen Shapiro) Make Your Own Luck, 2005, (with Jane Wei-Skillern, James Austin, Herman Leonard) Entrepreneurship in the Social Sector, 2007. Trustee Rural Land Found., Lincoln, Mass., 1973-78, Boston Ballet, 1991-2004, Suffield Land Conservancy, Conn., 1978-82; dir. Sudbury Valley Trustees, 1991-2004, pres. bd. trustees, 1996-2000; trustee, dir. Nat. Pub. Radio Found., 1998-2003, Mass. Chpt. Nature Conservancy, dir., Nat. Pub. Radio, 2004-, trustee, Mt. Auburn Hosp., 2006-, fin. com., Care Group, Inc., 2006-. IBM Nat. Merit scholar, 1959; Ford Found. fellow, 1965. Mem. Fin. Execs. Inst., Acad. Mgmt., Harvard Club (N.Y.C.). Office: Harvard Bus Sch Rock Center 314 Soldiers Field Boston MA 02163

STEVENSON, JAMES LARAWAY, engineering company executive, electronics engineer, computer engineer, communications engineer, engineering educator; b. Detroit, Oct. 25, 1938; s. Joseph Morley and Kittie Harriet (Laraway) S.; m. Jeanie Lorraine Minkstein, Aug. 7, 1965; children: Amy Jean, Brian Morley. AAS in Electronics Engring., US Armed Forces Staff Coll., 1958; BSEE in Electronics Engring., MIT, 1960, MSEE in Electronics Engring., 1962; DSc in Electronics and Computer Engring., Buxton U., 1994. Cert. master radio and telecom. engr. Internat. Assn. Radio, Telecomm., Electromagnetics Inc.; 1st class cert. competency Associated Pub. Safety Comm. Officers, Inc.; lic. 1st Class FCC Commercial Radiotelephone, 1964. With USN Mercury Space Project, 1957-63, Office of Naval Rsch. (Naval Rsch. Lab., Naval Air Sta. and Flight Test Ctr., Patuxent River MD/Argonne Nat. Lab.), DC, 1962—63, London, 1962—63; engr. Sta. WBCM-FM, Bay City, Mich., 1964-65; chief engr. Sta. WCRM, Clare, Mich., 1965-66, Sta. WSMA, Marine City, Mich., 1966; engr. Sta. WWJ-AM-FM-TV, Detroit, 1966-79; owner, mgr. Twin Oaks Comms. Engring. now Twin Oaks Comms. Engring. P.C.), North Branch, Mich., 1972—. Charter pilot, flight and ground instr. G. B. DuPont Co., Almont Marlette Aviation Inc., 1977-82; expert legal witness, 1968—; corp. edn. dean's adv. coun. Colls. Bus. Adminstr., Sci., Engring. and Tech., Saginaw Valley State U., 1997—; curriculum adv. com. ITT Tech. Inst., Canton, Mich., 2002—; mem. Intern. Engring. Consortium, 2005-; cons. in field. Mem. editl. advisory panel: eWeek Mag., 2004; contbr. articles to profl. jours. Jury foreman, Lapeer County Circuit Ct, 1974; sr. divsn. judge Detroit Met. Sci. and Engring. Fair, 1975—, Mich. State Sci. and Engring. Fair, 2000—; spl. awards judge Intel Internat. Sci. and Engring. Fair, Detroit, 2000; search and rescue pilot, mission comdr., capt. Mich. wing CAP, 1961-81; cubmaster Boy Scouts Am., North Branch, 1983-85; hon. state chmn. bus. adv. coun. Rep. Congl. Com., 2002—. With USN, 1957—63. Recipient appreciation award CAP, 1980, North Branch Area Schs., 1985, Century award Boy Scouts Am., 1984, Chairman's award, Saginaw Valley Engrg. Coun., 1991, 2001, Intl. Scientist of Yr. award, IBC, Cambridge, 2002. Mem. AIAA, IEEE (sr., chmn. N.E. Mich. sect. 1987-88, 1995-2006, bd. dirs. 1984—), NSPE, Am. Soc. for Engring. Edn. (profl. mem.), Internat. Assn. Radio, Telecom., Electromagnetics (master mem.), Am. Inst. Physics (assoc.), Mich. Soc. Profl. Engrs. (flint chpt.), Network and Sys. Profls. Assn., Saginaw Valley Engring. Coun. (chmn. 1990-91, 2000-01, sec.-treas. 1992-95, Outstanding Leadership award 1991, 2001), Engring. Soc. Detroit (profl.), Profl. Activities Coun. Engrs. (chmn. U.S. activities bd. 1985—), Network and Systems Profls. Assn., Nat. Pilots Assn. (sr. pilot citation, Safe Pilot award 1978), Aircraft Owners and Pilots Assn., Network and Systems Profls. Assn., North Br. C. of C. (charter), Tri-County Econs. Club, Am. Legion, (vice-commander North Br. club 2001-02), Lions (sec. North Br. club 1985-90, pres. 1990-91), Radio Club Am., Tri-County Econs. Club, Sigma Alpha Epsilon (Order of Minerva honoree). Conservative. Methodist. Avocations: computers, amateur radio, flying. Office: Twin Oaks Comms Engring PC 2465 Johnson Mill Rd PO Box 340 North Branch MI 48461-0340 Office Phone: 810-688-2633. Personal E-mail: stepthe8@aol.com.

STEVENSON, JEFFREY SMITH, physiologist, educator; b. Salt Lake City, Utah, June 15, 1951; s. Wilford Stevenson. BS, Utah State U., Logan, 1975; MS, Mich. State U., East Lansing, 1977; PhD, NC State U., Raleigh, 1980. Prof. Kans. State U., Manhattan, 1980—. Recipient Agway Inc. Young Scientist award, Am. Dairy Sci. Assn., 1990, Pharmacia Animal Health Physiology award, 2002, Rsch. Award, Nat. Assn. Animal Breeders, 1998. Office: Kansas State Univ Dept Animal Scis and Industry Manhattan KS 66506-0201 Office Phone: 785-532-1243.

STEVENSON, JOANNE SABOL, nursing educator, consultant, retired dean; b. Steubenville, Ohio, June 8, 1939; d. Joseph A. and Susan (Ploskunak) Sabol; m. Robert J. Stevenson, Aug. 6, 1966; children: James J., Michael J. BS, Ohio State U., 1963, MS, 1964, PhD, 1970. Prof. Ohio State U., Columbus, 1970-95, dir. Ctr. for Nursing Rsch. Coll. Nursing, 1972-84, emeritus prof. dept. adult health and illness, 1995—, assoc. dean acad. affairs and rsch., 1998—2002, cons., 2006—; prof. emeritus Rutgers U., Newark, 2002—; prof. Mt. Carmel Coll. of Nursing, Columbus, Ohio, 2003—. Author: Issues and Crises During Middlescence (Book of Yr. 1977), 1977, (with J. Larabee) A Plan for Nurse Staffing in Hospital Emergency Services, 1978, (with T. Tripp-Reimer) Knowledge About Care and Caring: State of the Art and Future Developments, 1990, 1990 Directory of Nurse Researchers, 3d edit., 1990, (with J.J. Fitzpatrick and N. Polis) Nursing Research and Its Utilization: Proceedings of International State of the Science Congress (Book of Yr. 1994), 1994, (with H. Sommers) Alcohol Use, Misuse, Abuse and Addiction, 2005; editor Ann. Rev. of Nursing Rsch.; contbr. articles to profl. jours. Pres. bd. trustees Friendship Village Columbus. NIH predoctoral fellow; Fulbright scholar to Brazil, 1995-96; recipient Am. Jour. Nursing Book of Yr. award, 1977, 94, 95, 96, others. Fellow AAAS, Am. Acad. Nursing (chmn. knowledge devel. and utilization think tank); mem. AAUP, ANA (cabinet on rsch., coun. nurse researchers), Ohio Nurses Assn., Midwest Nursing Rsch. Soc. (pres. 1991-93), Am. Coll. Sports Medicine, Sigma Theta Tau (chmn. rsch. com.), Alpha Tau Delta, Phi Beta Delta. Office: 127 S Davis Ave Columbus OH 43222 E-mail: jstevenson@mchs.com.

STEVENSON, JOSIAH, IV, management consultant; b. Jamaica, NY, Oct. 4, 1935; s. Josiah and Ruth Lillian (Leech) S.; m. Jane Margaret Kupfer, Sept. 1, 1957; children: Josiah V., Todd Sander. AB, Dartmouth Coll., 1957; MBA, Amos Tuck Sch. Bus., 1958. Instr. U. Md.-Far East, 1959—61; account supr. Benton & Bowles, Inc., NYC, 1961—66; group product mgr., gen. mgr. Japan Chesebrough-Pond's Inc., Greenwich, Conn., 1967—77; dir. devel. Dartmouth Coll., 1977—84, Boston Symphony Orch., 1984—95; v.p. Curtis Inst. Music, Phila., 1995—2003; mng. ptnr. Dover Stevenson & Assocs., 1987—. Trustee Opera North. With USAF, 1958-61. Mem. US C. of C., Assn. Fund Raising Profls. (Mass. chpt. bd. dirs., v.p. 1993-95, Greater Phila. chpt. bd. dirs., v.p. fin. 1996-2003), Dartmouth Club, Tokyo Lawn Tennis Club, Yale-Dartmouth Club (NYC), Badminton and Tennis Club (Boston). Episcopalian. Home: 23 Spring Pond Rd PO Box 1810 Norwich VT 05055-1810 Office Phone: 802-649-1547. E-mail: jstevenson@valley.net.

STEVENSON, LAURA CAROLINE, writer, educator; b. Ann Arbor, Mich., Sept. 8, 1946; d. Charles Leslie and Louise Ellen (Destler) S.; m. Michael William O'Connell, Sept. 27, 1969 (div. July 1981); children: Katharine O'Connell, Margaret O'Connell; m. Franklin D. Reeve, Dec. 22, 1997. AB with highest honors, U. Mich., 1968; MPhil, Yale U., 1971, PhD, 1974. Lectr. history U. Calif., Santa Barbara, 1970-71; prof. humanities Bradford Coll., Haverhill, Mass., 1980-83, Marlboro (Vt.) Coll., 1986—. Author: Praise and Paradox, 1984, 2d edit., 2002, Happily After All, 1990, The Island and the Ring, 1991, All the King's Horses, 2001, A Castle in the Window, 2003. Recipient Grant-in-Aid, Am. Coun. Learned Socs., 1975; Andrew W. Mellon Faculty fellow Harvard U., 1982-83, Rsch. fellow NEH, 1996-97. Mem.: Windham County Farm Bur., Vt. Natural Resources Coun., Authors Guild, Royal Oak Found., Assn. Late-Deafened Adults, Beatrix Potter Soc., Phi Beta Kappa. Soc. Of Friends. Avocations: gardening, farming. Home: PO Box 14 Wilmington VT 05363-0014 Office: Marlboro Coll Dept Humanities Marlboro VT 05344 Home Phone: 802-464-3712; Office Phone: 802-258-9285. Business E-Mail: lsteve@marlboro.edu.

STEVENSON, NANCY NELSON, museum director; b. Annapolis, Md., Oct. 23, 1950; d. Perry Waldemar and Grace Anne Nelson; m. Roger Stevenson Jr., Nov. 18, 1972; children: Jennifer Loren, Matthew Austin. BA, Sarah Lawrence Coll., 1972. Tchr. Montgomery County (Md.) Pub. Schs., 1972—76; bd. dirs. Jr. League of Washington, 1988—89, 1990—92; trustee Nat. Mus. Women in the Arts, Washington, 1996—, sec. bd. of trustees, 1997—98, treas. bd. of trustees, 1998—2002, v.p. bd. trustees, 2002—04, pres. bd. trustees, 2004—. Co-author French immersion curriculum, 1974. Pres. Country Pl. Citizens Assn., Potomac, Md., 1983-84. Office: Nat Mus Women in the Arts 1250 New York Ave NW Washington DC 20005-3970

STEVENSON, PAUL MICHAEL, physics professor, researcher; b. Denham, Eng., Oct. 10, 1954; came to U.S., 1983; s. Jeremy and Jean Helen (Jennings) S. BA, Cambridge U., Eng., 1976; PhD, Imperial Coll., London, 1979. Rsch. assoc. U. Wis., Madison, 1979-81, 1983-84; fellow European Orgn. for Nuclear Rsch., Geneva, 1981-83; sr. rsch. assoc. Rice U., Houston, 1984-86, asst. prof. physics, 1986-89, assoc. prof., 1989-93; prof. physics, 1993—. Contbr. articles to profl. jours. Avocation: music. Business E-Mail: stevenson@physics.rice.edu.

STEVENSON, ROBERT EDWIN, microbiologist, consultant; b. Columbus, Ohio, Dec. 2, 1926; s. Arthur Edwin and Mary Lucille (Beman) S. BS, Ohio State U., 1947, MS, 1950, PhD, 1954. Cert. Am. Bd. Microbiology. Virologist USPHS, Cin., 1954-58; head cell culture sect., Tissue Bank U.S. Naval Med. Sch., Bethesda, Md., 1958-60; head cell culture and tissue material sect. Nat. Cancer Inst., Bethesda, 1960-63, chief viral carcinogenesis br., 1963-67; mgr. biolog. scis., corp. devel. dept. Union Carbide Corp., Tarrytown, NY, 1967-72; v.p., gen. mgr., Frederick (Md.) div. Litton Bionetics, 1972-80; dir. Am. Type Culture Collection, Rockville, Md., 1980-93; dir. emeritus, 1993. Dir. Large Scale Biology, Inc., Rockville, 1984-90; cons. Am. Assn. Tissue Banks, 1999—; chmn. biotech. adv. com. Dept. Commerce, Washington, 1985-93; lectr. Yale U. Coll. Med., 2006. With USN, 1944-45. Recipient Hyatt award, AATB, 2004. Fellow Inst. for Soc., Ethics & Life Scis.; mem. Tissue Culture Assn. (pres. 1988-90), World Fedn. Culture Collections, U.S. Fedn. Culture Collections (pres. 1988-90), Am. Soc. Micrbiology, Cosmos Club (Washington). Avocations: painting, cross country skiing. Home: 27 Evart's Ln Madison CT 06443-2564 Office Phone: 703-827-9582.

STEVENSON, ROBERT MURRELL, music educator; b. Melrose, N.Mex., July 3, 1916; s. Robert Emory and Ada (Ross) S. AB, U. Tex., El Paso, 1936; grad., Juilliard Grad. Sch. Music, 1938; MusM, Yale, 1939; PhD, U. Rochester, 1942; STB cum laude, Harvard U., 1943; BLitt, Oxford U., Eng.; Th.M., Princeton Theol. Sem.; DMus honoris causa, Cath. U. Am., 1991; LHD honoris causa, Ill. Wesleyan U., 1992; LittD honoris causa, Universidade Nova de Lisboa, 1993. Instr. music U. Tex., 1941-43, 46; faculty Westminster Choir Coll., Princeton, NJ, 1946-49; faculty rsch. lectr. UCLA, 1981, mem. faculty to prof. music, 1949—. Vis. asst. prof. Columbia, 1955-56; vis. prof. Ind. U., Bloomington, 1959-60, U. Chile, 1965-66, Northwestern U., Chgo., 1976, U. Granada, 1992; adj. prof. Cath. U. Am., 1991—; cons. UNESCO, 1977; Louis Charles Elson lectr. Libr. of Congress, Washington, 1969; inaugural prof. musicology Nat. U. Mex., 1996; spkr. Dumbarton Oaks Pre-Columbian Music Workshop, 1998, Internat. Colonial Music Congress, Lima, Peru, 2000; lectr. Tureck Bach Rsch. Found., Oxford U., 2000; hon. prof. Conservatorio Nacional, Peru, 2000, Real Conservatorio Superior, Madrid, 1991-2003; hon. lectr. Royal Conservatory, Madrid, 2004; keynote spkr. Morales Colloquium, Oxford U., 2004. Author: Music in Mexico, 1952, Patterns of Protestant Church Music, 1953, La musica en la catedral de Sevilla, 1954, 85, Music Before the Classic Era, 1955, Shakespeare's Religious Frontier, 1958, The Music of Peru, 1959, Juan Bermudo, 1960, Spanish Music in the Age of Columbus, 1960, Spanish Cathedral Music in the Golden Age, 1961, La musica colonial en Colombia, 1964, Protestant Church Music in America, 1966, Music in Aztec and Inca Territory, 1968, Renaissance and Baroque Musical Sources in the Americas, 1970, Music in El Paso, 1970, Philosophies of American Music History, 1970, Written Sources for Indian Music Until 1882, 1972, Christmas Music From Baroque Mexico, 1974, Foundations of New World Opera, 1973, Seventeenth Century Villancicos, 1974, Latin American Colonial Music Anthology, 1975, Vilancicos Portugueses, 1976, Josquin in the Music of Spain and Portugal, 1977, American Musical Scholarship, Parker to Thayer, 1978, Liszt at Madrid and Lisbon, 1980, Wagner's Latin American Outreach, 1983, Spanish Musical Impact Beyond the Pyrenees, 1250-1500, 1985, La Música en las catedrales españolas del Siglo de Oro, 1993; contbg. editor: Handbook Latin Am. Studies, 1976—; editor Inter-Am. Music Rev., 1978—; contbr. to New Grove Dictionary of Music and Musicians, 17 other internat. encys. Decorated Army Commendation ribbon, 1946; fellow Folger Shakespeare Library, 1950, Ford Found., 1953-54, Gulbenkian Found., 1966, 81, Guggenheim Found., 1962, NEH, 1974, Comité Conjunto Hispano-Norteamericano (Madrid), 1989; recipient Fulbright rsch. awards, 1958-59, 64, 70-71, 88-89, Carnegie Found. tchg. award, 1955-56, Gabriela Mistral award OAS, 1985, Heitor Villa Lobos Jury award OAS, 1988, OAS medal, 1986, Cert. Merit Mexican Consulate San Bernardino, Calif., 1987, Silver medal Spanish Ministry Culture, 1989, Gold medal Real Conservatorio Superior, 1994, 97, 1st Lifetime Achievement award Sonneck Soc., 1999, All-Calif. Constantine Penunzio award, 2004. Mem. Real Academia de Bellas Artes (hon.), Hispanic Soc. Am., Am. Liszt Soc. (cons. editor), Heterofonia (cons. editor), Brazilian Musicol. Soc. (hon.), Portuguese Musicol. Soc. (hon.), Argentinian Musicol. Soc. (hon.), Venezuelan Musicol. Soc. (hon.), Am. Musicol. Soc. (hon.), Orden Andrés Bello, Primera Clase, Venezuela, 1992. Avocation: playing piano. Office: UCLA Dept Music 405 Hilgard Ave Los Angeles CA 90095-9000 Business E-Mail: info@ericdilauro.com.

STEVENSON, THOMAS RAY, plastic surgeon; b. Kansas City, Mo., Jan. 22, 1946; s. John Adolph and Helen Ray (Clarke) S.; m. Judith Ann Hunter, Aug. 17, 1968; children: Anne Hunter, Andrew Thomas. BA, U. Kans., 1968, MD. Diplomate Am. Bd. Plastic and Reconstructive Surgery, Am. Bd. Surgery. Resident in gen. surgery U. Va., Charlottesville, 1972-78; resident in plastic surgery Emory U., Atlanta, 1980-82; asst. prof. surgery U. Mich., 1982-88, assoc. prof. surgery, 1988-89. Chief plastic surgery Ann Arbor VA Hosp., 1982—, U. Calif., Davis, 1989—. Served to maj. USAR, 1978-80. Fellow ACS; mem. Am. Soc. Plastic and Reconstructive Surgery, Am. Bd. Plastic Surgery, chair-elect 2006- Office: UC Davis Divsn Plastic Surg 2221 Stockton Blvd 2d Fl Sacramento CA 95817-2214

STEVENSON, WILLIAM ALEXANDER, retired justice of Supreme Court of Canada; b. Edmonton, Alta., Can., May 7, 1934; s. Alexander Lindsay and Eileen Harriet (Burns) S.; m. Patricia Ann Stevenson; children: Catherine, Kevin, Vivian, James. BA, U. Alta., Edmonton, 1956, LLB, 1957; LLD (hon.), U. Alta., 1992. Called to Alta. bar, 1958. Ptnr. Hurlburt Reynolds Stevenson & Agrios, Edmonton, 1957-68; prof. U. Alta., 1968-70; ptnr. Reynolds Stevenson & Agrios, Edmonton, 1970-75; judge Dist. Ct. Alta., Edmonton, 1975-79; justice Ct. of Queens Bench Alta., Edmonton, 1979-80, Ct. of Appeal Alta., Edmonton, 1980-90, Supreme Ct. Can., Ottawa, Ont., 1990-92. Officer Order of Can., 1997. Co-author: Civil Procedure Guide, 1995. Mem. Can. Bar Assn., Can. Inst. for Adminstrn. Justice (pres. 1983-85, hon. dir.), Nat. Jud. Inst. (hon. dir.), Legal Archives Soc. Alta (hon. dir.). Home: 7 Laurier Pl Edmonton AB Canada T5R 5P4 E-mail: wmstevenson@shaw.ca.

STEVENSON, WILLIAM HENRI, author; b. London, June 1, 1924; s. William and Alida (Deleporte) S.; m. Glenys Rowe, July 28, 1945; children: Andrew, Jacqueline, Kevin, Sally. Student, Royal Navy Coll., 1942. Fgn. corr. Toronto (Ont., Can.) Star, 1948-58; Toronto Globe & Mail, 1958-63; Ind. TV News, London, Eng., 1964-66; CBC, 1966-77; ind. writer, broadcaster, 1977—. Author: Travels In and Around Red China, 1957, Rebels in Indonesia, 1964, Chronicles of the Israeli Air Force, 1971, A Man Called Intrepid, 1976, Ninety Minutes at Entebbe, 1976, The Ghosts of Africa, 1981; producer: TV documentaries; movie screenplays include The Bushbabies, 1970. Served as aviator Royal Navy, 1942-45. Mem. Assn. Naval Aviation U.S.A., Authors Guild, Royal Overseas League (London). Mem. Progressive Conservative Party Can. Mem. Church of England. Clubs: Royal Bermuda Yacht, Royal Hong Kong Yacht. Office: care Paul Gitlin Agy 15th Fl 353 Lexington Ave Fl 15 New York NY 10016-0941 Address: 25 Roxborough E Toronto ON Canada M4W Z2G

STEVER, DONALD WINFRED, lawyer; b. Altoona, Pa., Jan. 25, 1944; s. Donald Winfred and June Lily (Bargfrede) S.; m. Betsy Jean Seaman, May 28, 1968 (div. Oct. 1975); 1 child, Heather Elene; m. Margo Leaman Taft, July 30, 1976; children: David Whittaker, James Taft. BA, Lehigh U., 1965; JD, U. Pa., 1968. Bar: Conn. 1968, N.H. 1969, D.C. 1983, N.Y. 1983, U.S. Dist. Ct. N.H. 1969, U.S. Dist. Ct. Conn. 1986, U.S. Dist. Ct. (so. dist.) N.Y. 1985, U.S. Dist. Ct. (no. and we. dists.) N.Y. 1990, U.S. Ct. Appeals (1st cir.) 1974, U.S. Ct. Appeals (10th cir.) 1980, U.S. Ct. Appeals (5th, 11th and Fed. cirs.) 1982, U.S. Ct. Appeals (2d cir.) 1990, U.S. Supreme Ct. 1972. Atty. Aetna Life & Casualty co., Hartford, Conn., 1968-69, Office of N.H. Atty. Gen., Concord, 1969-72, asst. atty. gen., chief environ. protection, 1972-77; atty. pollution control sect. U.S. Dept. Justice, Washington, 1978-79, chief pollution control sect., 1979-80, chief environ. def. sect., 1980-82; prof. Pace U. Sch. Law, White Plains, NY, 1982-87, adj. prof. environ. law, 1987-92; ptnr. Sidley and Austin, NYC, 1987-93, Dewey Ballantine, NYC, 1993—2004, Kirkpatrick and Lockhart LLP, 2004—. Bd. dirs. Environ. Law Inst., Washington, chmn., 1996-97, 99-2003; bd. dirs. Hudson Valley Writers Ctr. Inc., chair, 2007—; bd. dirs. Sleepy Hollow, N.Y., Friends of Rockefeller State Park Preserve, Inc. Author: Seabrook and The Nuclear Regulatory Commission, 1980; Law of Chemical Reation and Hazardous Waste, 1986; editor: Environmental Law & Practice, 1992; co-editor Environmental Law & Practice, 1992. Bd. dirs. Biddeford Pool (Maine) Improvement Assn., 1989-93; mem. conservation adv. com. Village of North Tarrytown, N.Y., 1989-93; trustee Village of Sleepy Hollow, 1998-2003. Mem. Biddeford Pool Yacht Club (treas. 1989-92, sec. 1992-2000, rear commodore 2000-02, vice commodore 2002-07, commodore 2007—), Sleepy Hollow Country Club, Abenakee Club, Mill Reef Club. Avocations: golf, tennis, sailboat racing, early music. Home: 157 Millard Ave Sleepy Hollow NY 10591-1412 Office: Kirkpatrick & Lockhart Creston Gates Ellis LLP 599 Lexington Ave New York NY 10022-6030 Office Phone: 212-536-4861. E-mail: don.stever@klgates.com.

STEVER, HORTON GUYFORD, aerospace scientist, educator, aerospace engineer, consultant; b. Corning, NY, Oct. 24, 1916; s. Ralph Raymond and Alma (Matt) Stever; m. Louise Risley Floyd, June 29, 1946; children: Horton Guyford, Sarah, Margarette, Roy. AB, Colgate U., 1938, ScD (hon.), 1958; PhD, Calif. Inst. Tech., 1941; LLD, U. Pitts., 1966, Lehigh U., 1967, Allegheny Coll., 1968, Ill. Inst. Tech., 1975; DSc, Northwestern U., 1966, Waynesburg Coll., 1967, U. Mo., 1975, Clark U., 1976, Bates Coll., 1977; DH, Seton Hill Coll., 1968; D.Engring., Washington and Jefferson Coll., 1969, Widener Coll., Poly. Inst. N.Y., 1972, Villanova U., 1973, U. Notre Dame, 1974; DPS, George Washington U., 1981. Staff radiation lab. MIT, Cambridge, Mass., 1941—42, asst. prof., 1946—51, assoc. prof. aero. engring., 1951—56, prof. aero. and astro., 1956—65, head depts. mech. engring., naval architecture, marine engring., 1961—65, assoc. dean engring., 1956—59, exec. officer guided missiles program, 1946—48; chief scientist USAF, 1955—56; pres. Carnegie-Mellon U., Pitts., 1965—72; dir. NSF, Washington, 1972—76; sci. adviser, chmn. Fed. Council Sci. and Tech., 1973—76; dir. Office Sci. and Tech. Policy, sci. and tech. adviser to Pres., 1976—77, sci. cons., corp. trustee, 1977—. Secretariat guided missiles com. Joint Chiefs of Staff, 1945; sci. liaison officer London Mission, OSRD, 1942—45; guided missiles tech. evaluation group Rsch. and Devel. Bd., 1946—48; sci. adv. bd. to chief of staff USAF, 1947—69, chmn., 1962—69; steering com. tech. adv panel on aeros. Dept. Def., 1956—62; chmn. spl. com. space tech. NASA, chmn. rsch. adv. com. missile and spacecraft aerodynamics, 1959—65; mem. Nat. Sci. Bd., 1970—72, ex-officio, chmn. exec. com., 1972—75; mem. Def. Sci. Bd., 1962—68; adv. panel U.S. Ho. Reps. Com. Sci. and Astronautics, 1959—72; mem. Pres.'s Commn. on Patent System, 1965—67; chmn. U.S.-USSR Joint Commn. Sci. and Tech. Cooperation, 1973—77, Fed. Council Arts and Humanities, 1972—76; Pres. com. Nat. Sci. medal, 1973—77. Author: Flight, 1965, In War and Peace: My Life in Sci and Tech, 2002; contbr. articles to profl. jours. Past trustee Colgate U., Shady Side Acad., Sarah Mellon Scaife Found., Buckingham Sch; trustee Univ. Rsch Assn., 1977—, pres., 1982—85; trustee Woods Hole Oceanographic Inst., 1980—, Sci. Svc., 1982—, Univ. Corp. for Atmospheric Rsch., 1980—83; bd. dirs. Saudi Arabia Nat. Ctr. for Sci. and Tech., 1978—81; bd. govs. U.S. Israel Binat. Sci. Found., 1972—76, chmn., 1972—73; mem. Carnegie Commn. on Sci., Tech. and Govt., 1988—93. Recipient Pres.'s Cert. of Merit, 1948, Exceptional Civilian Svc. award, USAF, 1956, Scott Gold medal, Am. Ordinance Assn., 1960, Disting. Pub. Svc. medal, award, Dept. Def., 1969, NASA, 1988, Nat. Medal of Sci., 1991. Fellow: AAAS, AIAA (hon.; pres. 1960—62), Am. Phys. Soc., Royal Soc. Arts, Am. Philos. Soc., Am. Acad. Arts and Scis., Royal Aero. Soc.; mem.: NAE (chmn. aero. and space engring. bd. 1967—69, fgn. sec. 1984—88), NAS (chmn. assembly engring. 1979—83, chmn. policy divsn. 1995—97), Royal Acad. of Engring. of Great Britain (fgn. mem.), Acad. Engring. of Japan (fgn. mem.), Cosmos Club, Phi Beta Kappa, Tau Beta Pi, Sigma Gamma Tau, Sigma Xi. Episcopalian.

STEVES, GALE C., marketing professional, writer, editor-in-chief, publishing executive; b. Mineola, NY, Dec. 20, 1942; d. William Harry and Ruth (May) Steves; m. David B. Stocker, Mar. 31, 1972 (div. Apr. 1978); m. Philip L. Perrone, Aug. 14, 1983. BS, Cornell U., 1964; MA, NYU, 1966. Editl. asst. Ladies Home Jour., NYC, 1966-69; seafood consumer specialist U.S. Dept. Commerce, NYC, 1969-73; editor food Homelife mag., NYC, 1973-74; editor food and equipment Co-Ed mag., NYC, 1974-76, Am. Home mag., NYC, 1976-78; editor kitchen design and equipment Woman's Day mag., NYC, 1979-83; editor-in-chief Woman's Day Spls., NYC, 1983-91; v.p., editor-in-chief Home Mag. Group, NYC, 1991—2001; pres. Open House Prodns., NYC, 2001—03, 2005—; v.p., editl. dir., pub. AMI Mini Mags. Group, NYC, 2003—05. Bd. dirs. Les Dames d'Escoffier, Coun. Sr. Ctrs. and Svcs. N.Y.C., Catskill Ctr. Cons. and Econ. Devel. Author: Game Cookery, 1974, The International Cook, 1980, Creative Microwave Cooking, 1981; author: (with Lee M. Elman) Country Weekend Cooking, Home Magazine's Best Little Houses, 1998; mem. editl. bd. Sr. Summary, N.Y.C., 1982—88. Co-chmn. Alder Lake Restoration Soc.; chmn. alumni adv. bd. Coll. Human Ecology, Cornell U., 1993—97, mem. univ. coun., 1996—2000, mem. pres.'s coun. Cornell

Women; mem. adv. bd. Cornell Plantations, 1998—2005; bd. mem. Catskill Ctr. Conservation and Econ. Devel. Mem.: Garden Writers Assn. Am., Am. Soc. Mag. Editors, Internat. Furnishings and Design Assn., Acad. Women Achievers YWCA N.Y.C. Address: 185 West End Ave Ste 26C New York NY 10023-5551

STEWARD, DAVID JOHN, retired anesthesiologist, educator, researcher; b. Luton, England, Feb. 2, 1934; arrived in US, 1991; s. William John and Kathleen Steward; m. Mary Louise Roberts, Mar. 18, 1988; children: Jennifer, Nigel. MB BS, U. London, 1958. Cert. Am. Bd. Anesthesiology, 1969. Resident anesthesia U. Toronto, Canada, 1964—65, resident internal medicine, 1966—67, sr. resident anesthesia, 1967—68, prof. anesthesiology, 1978—84; registrar anesthesia Southampton Gen. Hosp., England, 1965—66; chief of anesthesiology Hosp. for Sick Children, Toronto, Canada, 1972—84; chief anaesthesia BC Children's Hosp., Vancouver, Canada, 1984—91; prof. anesthesiology U. BC, Vancouver, 1984—91, hon. prof. anaesthesia, 2005—; prof. anesthesiology U. So. Calif., LA, 1991—2001; dir. anesthesiology Childrens Hosp. LA, 1991—2001. Chmn. com. on pediat. anaesthesia World Fedn. Socs. Anaesthesia, 1984—88; chmn. sci. program com. Can. Anaesthetists Soc., Toronto, 1984—85; cons. Can. China Child Health Found., Vancouver, 1986—; chmn. med. adv. com. BC Children's Hosp., Vancouver. Author: (textbook) Manual of Pediatric Anesthesia, 1979, 5th edit., 2001; editor: Anesthesia for Uncommon Pediatric Diseases, 1982, 2nd edit., 1989, Pediatrics for the Anesthesiologist, 1993; mem. editl. bd.: Can. Jour. Anaesthesia, Jour. Pediat. Anaesthesia. Flight lt. Royal Can. Air Force, 1960—65. Recipient Robert M. Smith award, Am. Acad. Pediat., 2000. Fellow: Royal Coll. Physicians Can.; mem.: Royal Coll. Surgeons Eng. and Wales, Royal Coll. Physicians Eng. and Wales, Am. Soc. Anesthesiology (life), Assn. Pediat. Anaesthetists, Acad. Anesthesiology. Avocations: sailing, photography, travel. Home: 5396 Goldfinch Way Blaine WA 98230 Home Phone: 360-371-8618. Personal E-mail: davidjsteward@telus.net.

STEWARD, DAVID L., technology company executive; b. Clinton, Mo. m. Thelma Steward; children: David, Kimberly. BS, Ctrl. Mo. State U., 1973. Various sales and mktg. positions Wagner Elec., Mo. Pacific Railroad, Fed. Express; founder, chmn. World Wide Tech., Maryland Heights, Mo., 1990—. Bd. dir. St. Louis Cmty. Coll. Found., Civic Progress of St. Louis, St. Louis Regional Chamber and Growth Assn., Mo. Tech. Corp., Webster U., BJC Health Sys., First Banks, Inc., St. Louis Sci. Ctr., United Way of Greater St. Louis Bd., Greater St. Louis Area Coun. of Boy Scouts of Am., Harris-Stowe State Coll. African-Am. Bus. Leadership Coun., RCGA, Barnes-Jewish Hosp.; chaired (with wife) United Way's 2000 African-American Leadership Giving Initiative. Named 14th Best Am. Entrepreneur, Success Mag., 1998, Minority Small Bus. Person of Yr., Small Bus. Adminstrn., 1997—98, Entrepreneur of Yr. in Tech., Ernst & Young, 1998, #1 African-Am.-Owned Bus. in US, Black Enterprise Mag., 2000; named to Small Bus. Adminstrn. Hall of Fame, 2001. Office: World Wide Technology 58 Weldon Pkwy Maryland Heights MO 63043-3237

STEWARD, JAMES, museum director, art history educator; BA, U. Va., Charlottesville; MA, NYU, NYC; PhD in art hist., Oxford U., England. Prof. hist. art U. Mich., Ann Arbor; dir. U. Mich. Mus. Art, Ann Arbor. Office: U Mich Mus Art 915 E Washington St Ste 0540 Ann Arbor MI 48109 Office Phone: 734-764-0395. E-mail: jsteward@umich.edu.

STEWARD, JAMES BRIAN, lawyer, pharmacist; b. Cleve., Mar. 25, 1946; s. Louis Fred and Helen Elaine Steward; m. Betty Kay Krans, Dec. 14, 1968; children: Christina Lynn, Brian Michael. BS in Pharmacy, Ferris State Coll., 1969; JD, U. Mich., 1973. Bar: Mich. 1973, U.S. Dist. Ct. (we. dist.) Mich. 1979, U.S. Ct. Appeals (6th cir.) 1980, U.S. Supreme Ct. 1986, cert.: elder law atty., Nat. Elder Law Found. Pharmacist Revco Pharmacies, Grand Rapids, Mich., 1969-70, Coll. Pharmacy, Ypsilanti, Mich., 1970-73; assoc. Bridges & Collins, Negaunee, Mich., 1973-80; ptnr. Steward, Peterson, Sheridan & Nancarrow, Ishpeming, Mich., 1980-94, Steward & Sheridan, Ishpeming, 1995—. Mem., chmn. Negaunee Commn. on Aging, 1974-86; mem., chmn., sec. Marquette County Commn. on Aging, 1976-82; trustee, v.p., pres. Negaunee Bd. Edn., 1984-88, 91-95; mem., chmn., adv. bd. trustee Greater Ishpeming Area Cmty. Fund, 1995—; mem. combined ad hoc com. Marquette County Commn. on Aging, 1996; bd. mem. Noquemanon Trails Network, 2000—; mem. econ. restructuring com. Ishpeming Main St. program, 2004. Mem.: Am. Soc. for Pharmacy Law, Marquette County Bar Assn. (sec.-treas., v.p., pres.), Mich. Bar Assn. (awards com. 1996—2004, chmn.), Nat. Acad. Elder Law Attys., Wawonowin Country Club, Ishpeming Ski Club, Superiorland Cross Country Ski Club, Rho Chi, Phi Delta Chi. Avocations: cross country ski racing, running, mountain bike racing, classic cars, water-skiing. Office: 205 S Main St Ishpeming MI 49849-2018

STEWARD, SHERRY ANN, information technology executive, educator; b. Ft. Campbell, Ky., Aug. 22, 1959; d. Vincent John Nappa and Mary Emma Woodward; m. J.R. Hooper, June 1977 (div. Oct. 1982); children: Amanda Renee Hooper, James Robert Hooper; m. W.H. Steward, Dec. 4, 1992. BA in English, Rollins Coll., 1996; MA in English and Tech. Writing, U. Ctrl. Fla., 1999; MS in Info. Tech., Barry U., 2001; PhD in Texts and Tech., U. Ctrl. Fla., 2004—. Sr. logistics specialist Harris Corp., Palm Bay, Fla., 1981—89; sr. documentation specialist Ea. Test Range, Malabar, Fla., 1989—93; sr. tech. writer DME Corp, Orlando, Fla., 1993—96; program mgr. Dimensions Internat., Inc., Orlando, 1996—2005, Technologist Dimensions Internat., 1996—2005; dir. applied rsch. and life cycle support DEI Svcs. Corp., Winter Park, 2005—. Contbr. articles to profl. jours. Mem.: IEEE (adcom 2000—03, 2004—05), Simulation Interoperability Stds. Orgn., Internat. Soc. Logistics, Army Aviation Assn. Am., Armed Forces Comm. Electronics Assn. (v.p. publicity 2002—03), Nat. Def. Indsl. Assn. Democrat. Roman Catholic. Achievements include 25 years in the acquisition and development of defense technologies and 10 years in flight and weapons simulations; ground-based tactical maintenance training devices; interactive technical documentation. Office: DEI Svcs Corp 7213 Sandscove Ct Winter Park FL 32792 Office Phone: 407-678-3388. E-mail: ssteward@deicorp.net.

STEWARD, WELDON CECIL, architecture educator, architect, consultant; b. Pampa, Tex., Apr. 7, 1934; s. Weldon C. and Lois (Maness) S.; m. Mary Jane Nedbalek, June 9, 1956; children: Karen A., W. Craig. Cert. in architecture and planning, Ecole des Beaux Arts, Fontainebleu, France, 1956; B.Arch., Tex. A&M U, 1957; MS in Architecture, Columbia U., 1961; LHD (hon.), Drury Coll., 1991. Registered architect, Tex., Nebr. Designer Perkins & Will, Architects, White Plains, NY, 1961-62; asst. prof. architecture Tex. A&M U., College Station, 1962-67, assoc. chmn. Sch. Architecture, 1966-69, assoc. dean, prof. Coll. Environ. Design, 1969-73; dean, prof. Coll. Architecture U. Nebr., Lincoln, 1973-2000, emeritus dean, prof. arch. and planning, 2000—; founding pres. Joslyn Castle Inst. Sustainable Cmtys., Omaha, 1996—; W. Cecil Steward dist. chair sustainable arch. U. Nebr., Lincoln, 2000—02; founding dir. Nebr. Ctr. for Sustainable Constrn., 2003; editor-in-chief Greensource Report, Atlanta, 2002—04; founding chmn. UN-Habitat North/North Network Urban Sustainability and Leadership, 2004—. Adj. prof. Sch. Arch. U. Hawaii, 1999—; ednl. cons. People's Republic of China, 1979—; project dir. Imo State U. Planning, Nigeria, 1981-88; vis. prof. Tong ji U., Shanghai, 1984; hon. prof. N.W. Inst. Architects Engrs., Xian, 1989; specialist Design USA, USSR, 1990; co-chmn. nat. coordination com. AIA Nat. Coun. Archtl. Registration Bd. Intership, Washington, 1980-81; bd. visitors Drury Coll., 1980-97, Coll. Arch. U. Miami, Fla., 1993-96, Judson Coll., 1998-2000; mem. nat. design rev. bd. GSA, Washington, 1994—; mem. founding bd. dirs. East/West Pacific Arch., U. Hawaii, 1995—; vice chmn. Design Futures Coun., Reston, Va., 1995-2000; sr. fellow Design Futures Coun., 1999. Designer, Quinnipiac Elem. Sch., New Haven, Conn., 1961 (Am Assn. Sch. Adminstrs. Exhibit 1969), J.J. Buser Residence, Bryan, Tex., 1969, Steward Urban Residence, Lincoln, Nebr., 1994. Mem. Lincoln Architects, Engrs. Selection Bd., 1979-88; mem. Nat. Com. for U.S.-China Rels., N.Y.C., 1981—, Nebr. Capitol Environ. Commn., 1989-97; bd. dirs. Downtown Lincoln Assn., 1996-2006, KZUM Pub. Radio, 1997-2001; mem. Lincoln/Lancaster County Planning Commn., 1996-2004, chmn., 2003-04; co-chmn. steering com. City of Lincoln Downtown Master Plan, 2004—; bd. dirs. Lincoln Children's Mus., 1996-2001; profl. adviser nat. design competition Wick Alumni Ctr., Lincoln, 1981; steering com. Internat. Coun. Tall Bldgs., 1992-96. Recipient T.R. Russel award for Newsletters, 2003; named Disting. Alumnus, Tex. A&M U., 1998; Grad. fellow Columbia U., 1960. Mem. AIA (pres. Brazos chpt. 1969, chmn. profl. devel. com. 1979, bd. dirs. 1979-90, dir. Cen. States 1987-90, nat. pres. 1991-92, Coll. of Fellows 1983, Tri-Nat. com. 1991-02, Nebr. Gold medal 1997, nat. AIA/ACSA Topaz award for excellence in architecture 1999, honor award for excellence in urban design 2005, charter award for excellence Congress for New Urbanism 2005); mem. Am. Planning Assn. (chair Dubai Internat. award for sustaining cmty. 2000), Nebr. Soc. Architects (bd. dirs. 1977-2000), Archtl. Found. Nebr. (bd. dirs. 1981-94, treas. 1981-94), Assn. Collegiate Schs. Architecture (bd. dirs. 1975-79), Nat. Archtl. Accrediting Bd. (bd. dirs. 1986-89, pres. 1988-89), Kazakhstan Union Architecture, Assn. Siamese Architects, Royal Inst. Canadian Architects, Fedn. Mexican Achitects, Japan Inst. Architects (hon.), Tau Sigma Delta (medal 1999), Phi Kappa Phi, Phi Beta Delta. Home: 125 N 11th St Lincoln NE 68508-3605 Office: U Nebr Coll Architecture Lincoln NE 68588 Home Phone: 402-475-1275; Office Phone: 402-472-0087. Business E-Mail: csteward1@sustainabledesign.com. E-mail: csteward1@unl.edu.

STEWART, ADAM MARK, hotel executive; b. Jan. 27, 1981; s. Gordon Stewart. B in Hospitality Mgmt., Fla. Internat. U. CEO Sandals Resorts Internat., Miami, 2006—. Spkr. in field. Recipient Paul Harris Fellow, Rotary Internat., 2006. Office: Sandals 4950 SW 72nd Ave Miami FL 33155 Office Phone: 305-284-1300. Office Fax: 305-667-8996. *

STEWART, ALEC THOMPSON, physicist, educator; b. Windthorst, Sask., Can., June 18, 1925; s. Arthur and Nelly Blye (Thompson) Stewart; m. Alta Aileen Kennedy, Aug. 4, 1960 (dec. Sept. 2000); children: A. James Kennedy, Hugh D., Duncan R.; m. Annabel C. Wenzel, Apr. 21, 2004. BSc, Dalhousie U., Halifax, NS, Can., 1946, MSc, 1949; PhD, Cambridge U., Eng., 1952; LLD, Dalhousie U., Halifax, NS, Can., 1986. Research officer Atomic Energy Can., Chalk River, Ont., Canada, 1952-57; assoc. prof. Dalhousie U., Halifax, 1957-60; assoc. prof. to prof. U. N.C., Chapel Hill, 1960-68; head physics Queen's U., Kingston, Ont., 1968-74, prof. physics, 1968-90, prof. physics emeritus, 1990—. Vis. prof. various univs., Can., Europe, Japan, China, Hong Kong; creator and chair adv. com. series of internat. positron confs. Author: 2 books; contbr. over 100 articles to profl. jours. Dir. Can. Olympic Tng. Regatta Kingston, 1976—82, Marine Mus. Great Lakes, Kingston, 1988—94. Decorated officer Order of Can.; recipient CAP medal for achievement in physics, 1992, Canada 125 medal, 1992, Queen Elizabeth II Golden Jubilee medal 2002. Fellow Am. Phys. Soc., Royal Soc. Can. (pres. Acad. Sci. 1984-87), Japan Soc. for Promotion Sci.; mem. Can. Assn. Physicists (pres., other offices 1970-74). Achievements include research in solid state physics, behavior of phonons, electrons, positrons and postronium in crystals and liquids; developed a series of conferences on positron annihilation: nuclear reactor safety, possible hazards of power frequency electric and magnetic fields, emergency measures following a nuclear accident, state of nuclear technology in Canada. Office: Queens U Dept Physics Kingston ON Canada K7L 3N6

STEWART, AMY LEE, lawyer; b. Fla. d. Marshall J. and Patricia R. Stewart; m. David William Bailin; children: Patricia C. Bailin, Hannah G. Bailin, Clara L. Bailin, Sarah F. Bailin, Emma S. Bailin. BA in Econ., Wellesley Coll., 1981; JD, NYU, 1986. Bar: Ga. 1987, Mass. 1987, Ark. 1988, cert.: (Coll. Mediators); Lex Mundi Coll. Mediators. Jud. clk. U.S. Dist. Ct., Little Rock, 1986—88; assoc. Rose Law Firm, Little Rock, 1988—92, mem., 1992—. Mem. Ark. Supreme Ct. Commn. on Model Jury Instrns.-Civil, 2005—; adj. prof. law U. Ark., Little Rock, 2001—. Mem. Leadership Program, C. of C., Little Rock. Named one of 40 Under 40, Ark. Bus., 1999, Mid-South Super Lawyer, 2006. Mem.: Ark. Bar Assn. (mem. ho. dels. 2002—05). Avocations: reading, hiking. Office: Rose Law Firm 120 East Fourth St Little Rock AR 72201 Office Phone: 501-375-9131.

STEWART, ANNETTE, judge; b. Paris, Tex., Jan. 1, 1928; d. Ray Bryan and Mary Christene (Plumer) Stewart. BA, U. Tex., Austin, 1949; MEd, U. Tex., 1952; LLB summa cum laude, So. Meth. U., 1966. Bar: Tex. 1966. Assoc. Parnass, McGuire & Handy, 1966-67; ct. reporter Ct. Domestic Rels., Dallas, 1957-66, 67-74, judge, 1975-77, 301st Dist. Ct., Dallas, 1977-83, 305th Dist. Ct., 1985-86, Ct. Appeals, Dallas, 1983-84, 86-92, sr. judge, 1993—. Fellow Tex. Bar Found.; mem. State Bar Tex., Tex. Bar Found., Dallas Bar Assn., P.E.O., Phi Beta Kappa. Democrat. Presbyterian.

STEWART, ARDEN RUTH, retired automotive executive; d. Oliver Shaw and Helen (Neitzel) Stewart; children: Mark, Todd. BA, Baldwin Wallace Coll., 1952. Trainee GM, Cleve., 1952—57; tchr. Elyria City Bd. Edn., Ohio, 1967—85; pres., CEO AAR, Inc., Cleve., 1984—2005. Pres. Elyria Schs. PTA, 1967; treas. Homeowners Assn., North Ridgeville, Ohio, 1988-89; mem. adv. com. bus. and tech. Cuyahoga CC Recipient Weatherhead 100 award Case Western Res. U., 1990, 91, 92, 93, 94, 95. Mem.: Navy League US, PGA Nat. Mem. Club. Republican. Episcopalian. Avocations: music, scuba diving, dance, piano, computers. Home: 32889 Brownstone Ln PO Box 39359 North Ridgeville OH 44039-0359 also: 37 Princewood Ln PO Box 33599 Palm Beach Gardens FL 33420-3599 Personal E-mail: arden9201@aol.com.

STEWART, ARTHUR IRVING, III, (ART STEWART), management consultant; b. Plainfield, NJ, Aug. 1, 1958; s. Arthur Irving Jr. and Audree Claire (Rollerson) S. BS in Mass Comm., Emerson Coll., 1982; Profl. Devel. cert. in Sr. Exec. Leadership, Georgetown U., 2004, postgrad., 2005—; M in Policy Mgmt., Georgetown U. Pub. Policy Inst., 2007. Intern Sta. KYW Newsradio/TV, Phila., 1977; news anchorman, reporter Sta. WLBR-WUFM-FM, Lebanon, Pa., 1984; ops. mgr. Sta. WMSP-FM, Harrisburg, Pa., 1984-86; sr. account exec. mktg. and sales promotion Sta. WFCC-FM, Chatham, Mass., 1987-88; account mgr. Vizwiz Film-Video, Inc., Brookline, Mass., 1989-90; pub. rels. account exec. The Interface Group, Needham, Mass., 1991-92; sr. account exec. pub. rels. Mullen Advt., 1992-93; pres., sr. counsel Stewart Strategies Group, LLC, Wayne, Pa., 1993—. Dir. mktg. and pub. rels. Cape and Islands Chamber Music Festival, Cape Cod, Mass., 1988; asst. organist The United Parish, Brookline, 1982-84. Producer (radio concert broadcasts) Harrisburg Symphony Orch., 1984-86, documentary on U.S. debut tour of Westminster Cathedral Choir of London, 1985, investigative report on acid rain, 1985 (Excellence in Broadcasting award), documentary on Nat. Cathedral Washington, 1986 (Excellence in Broadcasting award). Editor OUTREACH newsletter Trinity Ch., Boston, 1990-94; staff media rels. 72d genl. conv. Episcopal Ch. U.S.A., 1997. Recipient Excellence in Broadcasting award Pa. Assn. Broadcasters; named to Outstanding Young Men in Am., 1996. Mem. Am. Polit. Sci. Assn., Pub. Rels. Soc. Am., Greater Wash. Bd. Trade, Leadership, Inc., Phila., Am. Guild Organists, Edn. Com., Pub. Rels. Com., Anti Defamation League, Washington Ind. Writers, World Affairs Coun., World Future Soc. Episcopalian. Avocations: running, bicycling, travel, the arts, politics. Home Phone: 610-721-0611; Office Phone: 610-407-0182. E-mail: results@stewartgrp.com.

STEWART, BOBBY GENE, laboratory director; b. Jesse, W.Va., Apr. 18, 1940; s. Leonard Mart and Zeta Marie Stewart; m. Linda May Smith, Mar. 17, 1961; children: Barbara Lynn, Ramona Jean Stewart Pinkerman. Cert. in med. tech., Army Med. Svc. Sch., 1960; cert. blood banking specialist, 10th Med. Rsch. Lab., Landstuhl, Germany, 1961. Lic. nursing home adminstr. Mo., cert. clin. lab. scientist, bioanalytical lab. mgr. Med. and x-ray technologist Oceana (W.Va.) Med. Ctr., 1962-68; clin. mgr., med. technologist Sigourney (Iowa) Med. Clinic, 1968-69; staff med. and x-ray technologist Van Buren County Hosp., Keosauqua, Iowa, 1969; dir. lab. and x-ray svcs. Scotland County Hosp., Memphis, Mo., 1969-71; dir. lab. svcs. Keller Meml. Hosp., Fayette, Mo., 1971-95, Regional Med. Assocs., Fayette, 1995-97; med. technologist Boyce and Bynum Pathology Labs., 1998-99, Mo. Cancer Assocs., Columbia, 1999—2002. Mem. city coun. City of Fayette, 1977—85, mayor pro-tem, 1980—85, chmn. parks and recreation com., 1977—80, chmn. elec. dist. com., 1981—85. With US Army, 1959—62. Mem.: Hawaii State Soc. Am. Med. Technologists (pres. 2004—), Mo. State Soc. Am. Med. Technologists (v.p. 1973—74, pres. 1975—76, legis. chmn. 1975—90, v.p. 1989—90, 2004—, Med. Technologist of Yr. 1977, Pres.'s award 2001), Am. Med. Technologists (dist. councillor 1977—81, 1988—93, nat. bd. dirs. 1993—2002, nat. treas. 1994—96, nat. v.p. 1996—97, nat. pres. 1997—99, 2001—02, nat. sch. liaison 2002—, Disting. Achievement award 1976, Exceptional Merit award 1981, Nat. Silver Svc. award 1997, Nat. Pillar award 1998, Nat. Order Golden Microscope award 2000, Technologist of Yr. 2002, Nat. Pillar award 2006, Dusty Rhodes Life award 2007). Avocations: tennis, golf, swimming. Home: 91-1012 Wahipana St Kapolei HI 96707-2922 Personal E-mail: bgslms@hawaiiantel.net.

STEWART, BURTON GLOYDEN, JR., retired banker; b. Clayton, NC, Mar. 14, 1933; s. Burton Gloyden and Evelyn I. (Stallings) S.; m. Patricia Taylor, June 16, 1956; children: Burton Gloyden III, H. Taylor. AB, Duke U., 1955; grad., Sch. Banking of the south, 1970; exec. program, U. N.C., 1975. With Allstate Ins. Co., 1957-66, regional sales mgr. Charlotte, NC, 1964-66; with Branch Banking and Trust Co., Wilson, NC, 1966-98, sr. v.p., mgr. corp. planning and mktg. divsn., 1972-81, dir. investor rels., 1981-98, ret., 1998. Dir. Branch Corp., 1974-82; dir. N.C. Payments System, 1980-89, v.p., 1983-86, chmn. bd. 1986-89; bd. dirs., chmn. Electronic Fin. Svcs., Inc., 1988-90. Bd. dirs., treas. Wilson Arts Coun., 1969-71; bd. dirs. Wilson Heart Assn., 1968, Wilson United Way, 1974-80, 86-89, campaign chmn., 1977, pres., 1979, chmn. strategic planning com., 1986-90; mem. N.C. Gov.'s Efficiency Study Commn., 1985, N.C. Goals and Policy Bd., 1985-93; local com. Cypress Glen Retirement Cmty., 1991—, chmn., 1999-2001; fin. com., trustee United Meth. Ret. Homes, Inc., 1999—, chmn., 2002—; trustee UMRH Found., 1999—, chmn., 2002—. Lt. USNR, 1955-57. Mem. Bank Investor Rels. Assn. (bd. dirs. 1984-98, v.p. 1984-87), Wilson Country Club, Dunes Club. Methodist. Address: 1107 Salem St NW Wilson NC 27893-2139

STEWART, CARL E., federal judge; b. Shreveport, La., 1950; BA magna cum laude, Dillard U., 1971; JD, Loyola U., New Orleans, 1974. Atty. Piper & Brown, Shreveport, La., 1977—78; staff atty. La. Atty. Gen. Office, Shreveport, 1978—79; asst. US atty. Office US Atty. (we. dist.) La., Shreveport, 1979—83; prin. Stewart & Dixon, Shreveport, 1983—85; spl. asst. dist. atty., asst. prosecutor City of Shreveport, 1983—85; judge La. Dist. Ct., 1985—91, La. Ct. Appeals (2d cir.), 1991—94, US Ct. Appeals (5th cir.), 1994—. Bd. trustees Cmty. Found. Shreveport-Bossier, Shreveport, La., 1994—2004, Am. Inns. Ct. Found.; chmn. nat. search com. Boy Scouts Am. Capt. JAGC other, 1974—77, Ft. Sam Houston, Tex. Recipient Am. Silver Buffalo awrd, Boy Scouts Am., 2002. Mem.: La. State Bar Assn. (bench/bar liaison com.), La. Conf. Ct. Appeal Judges, Black Lawyers Assn. Shreveport-Bossier, Am. Inns of Ct. (Harry Booth/Henry Politz chpt. Shreveport), Nat. Bar Assn., Omega Psi Phi (Rho Omega chpt.). Office: US Ct Appeals 5th Cir 300 Fannin St Ste 2299 Shreveport LA 71101-3124 Home Phone: 318-636-4829; Office Phone: 318-676-3765. *

STEWART, CARLETON M., retired bank executive, director; b. Chgo., 1921; s. Carleton Merrill and Margaret (Lyon) S.; m. Alicia Dewar (dec.); 3 children; m. Kathryn White. Student, Stanford U., 1939-42; grad. in indsl. adminstrn., Harvard U., 1943, MBA, 1947. With Citibank, 1947-76, v.p. NYC, 1960-67, sr. v.p. in charge of Asia Pacific area, 1967-69, sr. v.p. in charge of South Asia, Middle East and Africa, 1969-73, sr. officer London, 1973-76; dir. Grindlay's Bank Ltd., London, Banque Internat. pour L'Afrique Occidentale, Paris, 1973-76; chmn. bd., chief exec. officer Am. Security Corp. and Am. Security Bank, Washington, 1976-80; chmn. bd. Internat. Bank Miami, 1983-85; dir. Travelers Asset Mgmt. Internat. Corp., NYC, 1985-87, ret., 1987—. Mayor Longboat Key, Fla., 1987-88, town commr., 1984-90, ethics com., 1990-99, chmn. 1992-94; mem. Planning Commn., Sarasota County, Fla., 1990-92. Capt. AUS, 1943-46.

STEWART, CHARLES LESLIE, lawyer; b. Fayetteville, Ark., Aug. 12, 1919; s. Charles Leslie and Ruth (Want) Stewart; m. Edalee Esther Gastrock, Aug. 30, 1941; children: William Paul, Thomas Alan, Katherine Jean, Robert Edward. AB, U. Ill., 1940; MA, La. State U., 1941; student, George Washington U. Law Sch., 1944-45; JD, U. Chgo., 1947. Bar: Ill. 1948, U.S. Supreme Ct. 1954. Economist Dept. Agr., 1941—42; adminstrv. asst. OPA, 1942-43, Bd. Econ. Warfare, 1943; exec. dir. Chgo. divsn. ACLU, 1946—47; assoc. Mayer, Brown, Rowe & Maw, Chgo., 1947-55, ptnr., 1956-67, 70-71, resident ptnr. charge European office, Paris, 1967-70; v.p., gen. counsel Hart Schaffner & Marx, Chgo., 1971-73, v.p., sec., gen. counsel, 1974-83, Hartmarx Corp., Chgo., 1983-84, v.p., sec., sr. counsel, 1984, of counsel legal dept., 1985-89; arbitrator Mandatory Arbitration Program Cir. Ct., Cook County, Ill., 1990—2005. Mem. Am. Law Inst., 1983-90. Mem. Glencoe (Ill.) Bd. Edn., 1965-66; mem. planning com. Corp. Counsel Inst., Northwestern U. Sch. Law and Ill. Inst. Continuing Legal Edn., 1978-84, vice-chmn., 1983, chmn., 1984; mem. Glencoe Union Ch. Served with Rsch. and Analysis Br., OSS, AUS, 1943-45., sec. projects com., 1944-45. Mem. ABA, Ill. State Bar Assn., Chgo. Bar Assn. (com. devel. of law 1977-91, vice chmn. 1984-85, chmn. 1985-86, corp. law com. 1981-91, corp. law depts. com. 1981-83, sr. lawyers com. 1987-92), Am. Soc. Corp. Secs. (adv. com. Chgo. regional group 1978-83, vice chmn. 1979-80, chmn. 1980-81, nat. dir. 1981-84, exec. com. 1983-84, corp. practices com. 1982-87, assoc. mem. 1986-91), Delta Phi. Avocations: genealogy, history, bridge.

STEWART, CONNIE WARD, retired academic administrator; b. Athens, Ga., Nov. 19, 1938; d. Fred Tendal and Elsie (Janes) Ward; m. D.G. Stewart, 1960 (div. 1967); 1 child, Sheri Lyn; m. Nick Vista, Apr. 16, 1982. AB in Journalism, U. Ga., Athens, 1959, MA, 1968; postgrad., George Washington U., Washington, 1979; cert. in ednl. mgmt., Harvard U., Cambridge, Mass., 1985. Cert. elem. and secondary tchr., Ga. Promotion-pub. rels. staff Sta. WSB-TV, Atlanta, 1959—61; assoc. dir. Ga. Scholarship Commn., Atlanta, 1967; faculty U. Ga. Journalism Sch., Athens, 1967—70; dir. orientation U. Ga., Athens, 1970—71; project mgr. Planned Mgmt. Corp., Tampa, Fla., 1976—77; dir. policy comm., mem., Carter-Mondale adminstrn. HEW, Washington, 1977—79; orgnl. staff U.S. Dept. Edn., Washington, 1979; v.p. Mich. State U., East Lansing, 1980—87; assoc. v.p. Emory U., Atlanta, 1987—93; ret., 1993. Dir. Cmty. Forum on Children and Families Ga. State U., 1995; mil. acad. screening com. Office U.S. Senator Donald Riegle, Lansing, Mich., 1984-86. Editor, columnist Oconee Enterprise, 1971-72. Steering com. Carter for Pres. Campaign, Fla., 1975—76; exec. com. Mich. Sesquicentennial Celebratoin, 1985—87; mem. Ga. Scholarship Commn., 1965—67, Ga. Motion Picture-TV Adv. Bd., 1972—76, Ga. Gov.'s Commn. on Edn., 1965—67, Mich. Film and TV Coun., 1984—86; exec. com. Comm. Coun., The Atlanta Project, 1992—94; vol. mentor in pub. schs. Success-by-Six program, 1993—96;

trainer vols. United Way, 1993—96, Big Bros./Bis Sisters Teach One program, 1997—99; docent Carter Presdl. Libr./Mus., 1998—; bd. councilors Carter Presdl. Ctr., 2005—; bd. dirs. Olympic Acad., 1987—88, Atlanta Olympics Organizing Com. for Olympic Games, 1991—93. Recipient Outstanding Alumna award Henry W. Grady Coll. of Journalism and Mass Communications, U. Ga., 1993, hon. alumnus award Mich. State U., 1987; disting. svc. award Ga. Edn. Advancement Coun., 1990. Mem. Coun. for Advancement and Support Edn., Nat. Assn. State Univs. and Land Grant Colls. (univ. rels. coun. 1984-87), Atlanta C. of C. (Forward Atlanta 1989), Soc. Profl. Journalists, Nat. Press Club (Washington), Pub. Rels. Soc. Am., Phi Beta Kappa (v.p. Mich. State U. chpt. 1986, pres. 1987), Phi Kappa Phi, Sigma Delta Chi, Theta Sigma Phi, Di Gamma Kappa, Zeta Tau Alpha. Democrat. Avocations: travel, reading, poetry. Home: 2848 Warrington Close Tucker GA 30084-2598

STEWART, CRAIG E., lawyer; b. Cleve., 1946; AB cum laude, Harvard U., 1968, JD, 1972. Bar: Mass. 1973, US Dist. Ct. Dist. Mass., US Ct. of Appeals (1st cir.), Mass. Supreme Jud. Ct., US Supreme Ct., US Dist. Ct. (no.dist.) Ga. Law clk. to Hon. Newell Edenfield U.S. Dist. Ct., No. Dist. Ga., 1972-73; ptnr. Palmer & Dodge, Boston, Edwards Angell Palmer & Dodge. Contbr. ABA (sect.litig.& tort trial and ins. practice sect.) past chair, Mass. Bar Assn., Boston Bar Assn., Self-Insurers and Risk Managers Com., Nat. Trial Acad., Mem. Mass. Bar Found. (past pres.), trustee Mass. CLE Inc., mem. Mass. IOLTA Com. (apptd.by supreme jud. ct.), CPR Internat. Inst. Conflict Prevention and Resolution. Office: Edwards Angell Palmer & Dodge 111 Huntington Ave Boston MA 02199-7613 Office Phone: 617-239-0164. Office Fax: 617-227-4420. Business E-Mail: cstewart@eapdlaw.com.

STEWART, CYNTHIA WILLIS, minister; b. Friendship, Guyana, Dec. 13, 1944; arrived in U.S., 1985; d. William Nathaniel and Hilloise Isola Willis; m. Ronald Eustace Stewart, June 3, 1990. BSc magna cum laude, Mich. State Univ., 1973; MA in Comm. Arts, Cornell Univ., 1980; MDiv, Hood Theol. Sem., 1983; DD, Drew Univ., 1990. Lic. local preacher 1979, admitted on trial 1981, Deacon's Orders 1982, Elder's Orders 1983; cert. Pub. Rels. Sch. of Pub. Rels., Eng., 1975. Pastor Alleyne A.M.E. Zion Ch., Guyana, South America, 1982—85; bishop's adminstrv. asst., presiding elder, advisor Guyana Conf., 1982—88, bishop's adminstrv. asst., presiding elder, 1992—96, Guyana, Barbados, Trinidad, Tobago Conf., 1996—98; assoc. min. First A.M.E. Zion Ch., Bklyn., 1986—92; pastor Westbury A.M.E. Zion Ch., NY, 1992—2000; presiding elder L.I. Dist., N.Y. Conf., 2000—01, Westchester Dist., N.Y. Conf., 2001—. Editor, design and layout artist, contbg. writer: Missionary Seer; contbr. articles pub. to non-profit jours. Bd. dirs. Harriet Tubman Home Inc.; adminstrv. bds. Theol. Sem., Christian Edn., Sch. and Coll.; pres. elder's coun. A.M.E. Zion Ch., first v.p.; chmn. bd. Christian Edn. and Admission Com.; mem. Budget Com., Holy Orders Com., N.Y. Conf.; bd. trustees N.Y. Conf., M. Ardelle Shaw Retreat Ctr. Recipient Excellence in Christian Life and Conduct, GW Griffin Meml. Preaching award, Hood Theol. Sem., Nat. Sojourner Truth Meritorious Svc. award, Nat. Assn. of Negro Bus. and Profl. Women's Club. Mem.: NAACP, Ch. Women United, World Fedn. of Meth. and Uniting Ch. Women, Ministerial Alliance, Nat. Coun. of Negro Women (life), Assn. of Christian Educators (life), A.M.E. Zion Ch. Min. and Lay Assn. (life). Home: 1129 Pembrooke St Uniondale NY 11553-1408

STEWART, D. SCOTT, engineering educator, consultant; b. Pitts., Oct. 2, 1955; s. Donald Ralph and Shirley Grace Stewart; m. Marcella Lee Vancil; 1 child, Cameron Scott. BS, SUNY, Buffalo, 1976; PhD, Cornell U., Ithaca, NY, 1981. From asst. prof. to assoc. prof. U. Ill., Urbana, 1981—2005, prof. mech. sci. and engring., 2005—. Cons. Los Alamos Nat. Lab., N.Mex., 1983—2007. Fellow, Cornell U., 1976; Nat. Acad. fellow, NRC, 2007—08. Fellow: AIAA (assoc.), Inst. Physics, Am. Phys. Soc.; mem.: Tau Beta Pi, Phi Kappa Phi. Baptist. Achievements include first to detonation shock dynamics; modern theory of detonation instability; research in advanced multi-scale computation and analysis. Home: 409 E Oakbrook Cir Urbana IL 61802 Office: U Ill Dept Mech Sci and Engring 268 Mech Eng Bld MC-244 Urbana IL 61802 Office Phone: 217-333-7947. Office Fax: 217-244-6534; Home Fax: 217-244-6534. Business E-Mail: dss@uiuc.edu.

STEWART, DANIEL CLARK, lawyer; b. Morristown, NJ, Sept. 23, 1947; BA, Brown U., 1969; JD, Duke U., 1972. Bar: Tex. 1972. Ptnr. Winstead, Sechrest & Minick, P.C., Dallas; ptnr., head Insolvency & Reorganization Sect. Vinson & Elkins LLP, Dallas. Mem. ABA, State Bar Tex. (bankruptcy and reorganization law com. 1979—, bankruptcy adv. comsn. to Tex. Bd. Legal Specialization 1981—), Dallas Bar Assn. (chmn. ethics com. 1979 and bankruptcy and coml. law sect. 1979-80). Office: Vinson & Elkins LLP Trammell Crow Ctr 2001 Ross Ave, Ste 3700 Dallas TX 75201 also: 26 Fl 666 Fifth Ave New York NY 10103 Office Phone: 214-220-7761. E-mail: dstewart@velaw.com.

STEWART, DAVID JAMES, oncologist, educator; m. Lesley Gayle Carruthers, 2002. MD, Queen's U., Kingston, Ont., 1974. Faculty assoc. and instr. U. Tex. M.D. Anderson Hosp. and Tumor Inst., Houston, 1978—79, asst. prof. and asst. internist devel. therapeutics, 1979—80; med. oncologist and clin. asst. prof. of medicine Ottawa Regional Cancer Ctr. and U. of Ottawa, Ont., Canada, 1980—84, med. oncologist and prof. of medicine, cellular and molecular medicine (pharmacology), 1988—2003, med. oncologist and assoc. prof. of medicine and pharmacology, 1984—88; chief of the divsn. of med. oncology Ottawa Civic Hosp., Canada, 1989—99; oncologist U. Tex. M.D. Anderson Cancer Ctr., Houston, 2003—, prof. medicine, 2003—, chief exptl. therapeutics dept. thoracic/head and neck med. oncology, 2003—06, dep. chair dept. thoracic/head and neck med. oncology, 2006—. Contbr. over 500 articles and abstracts to profl. jours., chapters to books. Mem.: Am. Assn. for Cancer Rsch., Am. Soc. of Clin. Oncology. Achievements include research in Of anticancer agents, mechanisms of resistance to chemotherapy and methods of overcoming resistance. Avocations: running, skiing, hiking. Office: UT MD Anderson Cancer Center 1515 Holcombe Blvd Houston TX 77030 Home Phone: 713-665-0374; Office Phone: 713-792-6363. Personal E-mail: dstewart@mdanderson.org.

STEWART, DAVID MARSHALL, librarian; b. Nashville, Aug. 1, 1916; s. David and Mary (Marshall) Stewart; m. Gladys Carroll, June 9, 1947; 1 child, James Marshall. BA, Bethel Coll., 1938; BSLS, George Peabody Coll., 1939. Circulation asst. Vanderbilt U. Library, 1938-39; county librarian Ark. Library Commn., 1939-40; Tenn. supr. WPA library service projects, 1940-42; librarian Memphis State U., 1942-46; spl. asst. to chief card div. Library of Congress, Washington, 1947; librarian CIA, Washington, 1948-60; chief librarian Nashville Pub. Library, 1960-85; Instr. Peabody Library Sch., 1966-80. Bd. dirs. Coun. Cmty. Agys., Nashville, Friends Chamber Music, Nashville, Travelers Aid, Nashville; v.p. bd. Mid.-E. Tenn. Arthritis Found. Served to lt. comdr. USNR, 1942—46. Mem.: ALA, Pub. Libr. Assn. Am. (chmn. stds. com. 1964—65, pres. 1966—67), Southeastern Libr. Assn., Tenn. Libr. Assn. (chmn. legis. com. 1961—65, v.p. 1965, pres. 1966, Honor award 1983), Alumni Assn. Bethel Coll. (dir., Disting. Alumni award 1992), Coffe House Club (Nashville), Kiwanis. Democrat. Mem. United Meth. Ch. Home: 6342 Torrington Rd Nashville TN 37205-3157

STEWART, DAVID PENTLAND, lawyer, educator; b. Milw., Dec. 24, 1943; s. James Pentland and Frederica (Stockwell) S.; children from previous marriage: Jason, Jonathan; m. Jennifer Kilmer, June 21, 1986; children: Daniel, Mary Elizabeth. AB, Princeton U., 1966; JD, MA, Yale U., 1971; LLM, N.Y.U., 1975. Bar: N.Y. 1972, U.S. Dist. Ct. (ea. and so. dists.) N.Y. 1973, U.S. Ct. Appeals (2d cir.) 1973, D.C. 1976. Assoc. Donovan, Leisure, Newton & Irvine, NYC, 1971-76; atty. adviser, office of legal adviser U.S. Dept. State, Washington, 1976-82, asst. legal adviser, 1982—. Adj. prof. law Georgetown U., Washington, 1984—, Am. U., Washington, 1985-86, Johns Hopkins U. Sch. Advanced Internat. Studies, 2000—; vis. lectr. Sch. Law U. Va., 1993-96, Nat. Law Ctr., George Washington U., 1993-99. Co-editor: (ann. vols.) Digest of United States Practice in International Law, 1989—2005; contbr. articles to profl. jours. Served to maj. USAR, 1970-87. Mem. ABA, Am. Law Inst., Am. Soc. Internat. Law., Internat. Law Assn., Internat. Bar Assn. (adv. coun. procedural aspects internat. law inst.). Office: US Dept State Office Legal Adviser Washington DC 20520-6310 Business E-Mail: stewartdp@state.gov.

STEWART, DAVID WAYNE, marketing educator, psychologist, consultant, dean; b. Baton Rouge, Oct. 23, 1951; s. Wesley A. Stewart, Jr. and Edith L. (Richhart) Moore; m. Lenora Francois, June 6, 1975; children: Sarah Elizabeth, Rachel Dawn. BA, N.E. La. U., 1972; MA, Baylor U., 1973, PhD, 1974. Rsch. psychologist HHS, La., 1974-76; rsch. mgr. Needham, Harper & Steers Advt., Chgo., 1976-78; assoc. prof. Jacksonville (Ala.) State U., 1978-80, Vanderbilt U., Nashville, 1980-86, sr. assoc. dean, 1984-86; prof. U. So. Calif., LA, 1986-90, Ernest W. Hahn prof. mktg., 1990-91, Robert Brooker rsch. prof. mktg., 1991—, chmn. dept. mktg., 1995-99, dep. dean faculty, 1999-2001, dep. dean, 2001—04, chmn. dept. mktg., 2006—; dean Anderson Sch. Mgmt. U. Calif., Riverside. Mgmt. cons., 1978—. Author, co-author: Secondary Research: Sources and Methods, Effective Television Advertising: A Study of 1000 Commericals, Consumer Behavior and the Practice of Marketing, Focus Group: Theory and Practice, Attention, Attitude, and Affect in Response to Advertising, Nonverbal Communication and Advertising, Marketing Champions; editor: Jour. of Mktg., 1999-2002, Jour. Acad. Mktg. Sci., 2006—; contbr. articles to profl. jours.; editor: Jour. of Mktg., 1999-2002; mem. editl. bd. Jour. Pub. Policy and Mktg., Jour. Mktg., Jour. Advt., Jour. Promotion Mgmt., Current Issues and Rsch. in Advt., Jour. Internat. Consumer Mktg., Jour. Managerial Issues, Jour. Promotion Mgmt., Jour. Advt. Rsch., others; past pres. policy bd. Jour. Consumer Rsch., Acad. Mgmt.; editor-in-chief Jour. Acad. Mktg. Sci. Recipient Outstanding Contbn. to Advt. Rsch. award, Am. Acad. Advt., 1998, named Disting. Mktg. Educator, Acad. Mktg. Sci., 2006. Fellow APA (coun. rep.), Am. Psychol. Soc. (charter); mem. Soc. for Consumer Psychology (past pres.), Inst. Mgmt. Scis., Decision Sci. Inst., Am. Mktg. Assn. (pres. acad. coun. 1997-98, v.p. fin. 1998-99), Assn. for Consumer Rsch., Am. Statis. Assn. (chair sect. on stats. in mktg. 1997), Acad. of Mgmt., Acad. Mktg. Sci. (bd. govs. 2004—). Republican. Baptist. Office: Office Dean Anderson Hall 122 Anderson Grad Sch Mgmt Univ Calif Riverside Riverside CA 92521 Office Phone: 213-740-5037. Business E-Mail: david.stewart@marshall.usc.edu.

STEWART, DAVID WITHERINGTON, business consultant; b. Marion, Ind., Feb. 9, 1939; s. Edgar Allen Jr. and Faye Maxine (Cummings); m. Ruth Ada Valk, Aug. 26, 1961, (div.); m. Annette Louise Witherington, Dec. 17, 1962 (dec. Aug. 1999); children: Edna (dec.), Geoffrey. BS in Physics, U. Fla., Gainesville, 1959. Sr. engr. Atlas Gen. Dynamics/Convair, Cape Canaveral, Fla., 1959—63; lead engr. Gemini-Titan Martin Canaveral, Cape Canaveral, 1963—66; lead engr. Sprint Martin-Orlando, Orlando, Fla., 1966—67; lead engr. Apollo Rockwell Internat., Kennedy Space Center, Fla., 1967—74, lead engr. avionics, 1975—78, prime system integ. engr. shuttle, 1978—79, supr. orbiter software, 1979—81, project mgr. software, 1982—84, project mgr. design, 1984—85, project mgr. adv. programs, 1985—89, mgr. adv. program, 1989—91, project mgr. adv. program and bus. devel., 1991—92, program devel. mgr. Fla. ops. space sys. divsn., 1992—96; owner, pres. L&D Consulting, Titusville, Fla., 1996—; owner, gen. mgr. Coreopsis Publs., 2004—. Author: Edie and the Gobie, 1966. Pres. North Brevard Environ. Action Com., Titusville, 1970-73; chmn. Marine Resources Coun. East Fla., 1996-97, 2000—02; pres.-elect Space Coast Devel. Commn., 1995-96; sec. Space Coast Grant Profls. Network, 1997-99; pres. Brevard Adult Literacy Vols., Inc., 2000—04; vol., treas. Brevard Humanity Ctr., Inc, 2000—. Mem. Inst. Cert. Profl. Mgrs. (cert. mgr.), Am. Cons. League (accredited profl. cons.). Republican. Unitarian Universalist. Mailing: PO Box 5869 Titusville FL 32783-5869 Personal E-mail: david@davidwstewart.com.

STEWART, DEBORAH CLAIRE, dean; b. Freeport, Ill., Sept. 14, 1951; Student, Monterey Peninsula Coll., 1969-71; BS in Zoology, U. Calif., Davis, 1973; MD, U. Calif., San Francisco, 1977. Diplomate Am. Bd. Peds. Intern Children's Hosp. L.A., 1977-78, resident in peds., 1978-79, fellow in adolescent medicine, 1979-81, attending physician emergency med. svcs., 1980-81; med. dir. comprehensive adolescent program dept. ob-gyn. Charles R. Drew Postgrad. Med. Sch., LA, 1981-83; asst. prof. dept. ob-gyn. UCLA/Charles R. Drew Postgrad. Med. Sch., 1982-83; mem. ped. staff Children's Hosp. of Orange County, Orange, Calif., 1983-86, U. Calif. Irvine Med. Ctr., Orange, 1983-99; assoc. prof. ob-gyn., assoc. prof. medicine U. Calif., Irvine, 1983-99, dir. child sexual abuse program, 1983-99, assoc. prof. clin. peds., chief divsn. gen. peds., dir. adol, 1988-95, assoc. dean for med. student and resident affairs, 1992-99; med. dir. child protection ctr. Meml. Miller Children's Hosp., Long Beach, Calif., 1995-99; assoc. dean med. edn. program U. Calif.-San Francisco, Fresno, 1999—. Project dir. South Ctrl. L.A. Sexual Trauma Program, 1983; med. cons. L.A. Commn. on Assaults Against Women, 1982-84, Calif. Children's Svcs., 1980-85, Sexual Assault Protocol Office of Criminal Justice Planning, 1984-86, Sexual Assault Protocol L.A. County, 1984-86; med. dir. Child Abuse Svcs. Team County of Orange, 1987—; physician mem. Calif. State Atty. Gen.'s Investigative Pilot Projects Rsch. and Evaluation Adv. Panel; cons. County of Orange Coroner's Office, 1994-99. Contbr. articles to profl. jours.; presenter in field; reviewer: Ped. and Adolescent Gyn., 1988—, Jour. Adolescent Health Care, 1986—, Peds., 1988—, Am. Jour. Obs. and Gyn., 1991— Mem. med. adv. bd. Planned Parenthood, 1983-94. Fellow Am. Acad. Pediatrics (pres. Dist. IX Chpt. 4, 1995-97, sec. chpt. IV, chair chpt. IV com. on child abuse 1983—); mem. N.Am. Soc. Pediatric And Adolescent Gynecology (co-chair collaborative rsch. com. 1988—), Orange County Ped. Assn. Office: U Calif San Francisco-Fresno Med Edn Program 2615 E Clinton Ave Fresno CA 93703-2223 E-mail: deborah.stewart@ucsfresno.edu.

STEWART, DEBRA WEHRLE, educational association administrator, political science professor; b. Petersburg, Va., May 22, 1943; BA in Philos. and Polit. Sci., Marquette U., 1965; MA in Govt., U. Md., 1967; PhD in Polit. Sci., U. NC, 1975. Instr. polit. sci. European divsn. U. Md., Nuremberg, Germany, 1967—69; instr. polit. sci. and pub. adminstrn. NC State U., Raleigh, 1974—75, asst. prof., 1975—78, acting dir. MPA prog., 1978, assoc. prof., 1979—83, assoc. dean Grad. Sch., 1983—86, prof., 1984—, interim vice provost, dean Grad. Sch., 1986—88, dean Grad. Sch., 1988—2000, vice provost, 1995—98, vice chancellor, dean Grad. Sch., 1998—2000; pres. Coun. Grad. Schs., Washington, 2000—. Interim chancellor U. NC, Greensboro, 1994; mem. com. on assessment of rsch. doctorate NRC, 1992-95; mem. Grad. Record Exam. Bd., 1992-96, chmn.-elect, 1994-95, chmn., 1995-96; bd. dirs. Coun. Grad. Schs., 1990—, chmn.-elect, 1992-93, chmn., 1993-94; mem. Test English as Fgn. Lang. Bd., 1992-95; councilor Oak Ridge Assoc. Univs., 1988-92, bd. dirs., 1993—, chair-elect 1997—; bd. dirs. Nat. Phys. Scis. Consortium, 1998—; mem. exec. com. Coun. So. Grad. Schs., 1989-91; trustee Triangle U. Ctr. Advanced Studies, 1989—; mem. Commn. on Peer Rev. and Accreditation, Nat. Assn. of Schs. of Pub. Affairs and Adminstrn., 1997-99. Author: The Women's Movement in Community Politics: The Role of Local Commissions on the Status of Women, 1980, (with G. David Garson) Organizational Behavior and Public Management, 1983, 3rd edit. (with Vasu and Garson), 1998; editor: Women in Local Politics, 1980; mem. editl. bd. Rev. Pub. Pres. Adminstrn., 1981-89, Annals Pub. Adminstrn., 1982-84, Women and Politics, 1980-88, Politics and Policy, 1983-86; contbr. articles to profl. jours., chpts. to books. Recipient edn. award YWCA Acad. Women, 1988 Mem. Nat. Assn. State Univs. and Land-Grant Colls. (bd. dirs. 1992-94, exec. com. coun. on rsch. policy and grad. edn. 1989-92, chmn. 1990-91), Am. Soc. for Pub. Adminstrn. (com. on status of women in pub. adminstrn. 1976-78, com. on profl. stds. and ethics 1980-89, chmn. com. on whistle blowing and dissent channels of profl. stds. and ethics com. 1985-86, Burchfield award 1976), So. Polit. Sci. Assn. (nominating com. 1978, coord. pub. adminstrn. sect. 1979), Women's Forum NC, Phi Kappa Phi, Pi Sigma Alpha, Pi Alpha Alpha. Office: Coun Grad Schs 1 Dupont Cir NW Ste 430 Washington DC 20036-1136 Office Phone: 202-223-3791. E-mail: president@cgs.nche.edu.

STEWART, DONALD GEORGE, musician, composer, music industry executive; b. Sterling, Ill., Jan. 8, 1935; s. Donald Balmer and Elinore Maud (Denison) S.; m. Susan Ann Trainer, June 13, 1963 (div. 1979); 1 child, Elizabeth Ann. MusB, Ind. U., 1960; postgrad., Manhattan Sch., 1960-62; student, Sch. of Jazz, 1958-60; studied with Roy Harris, Bernhard Heiden, Gunther Schuller. 2d clarinetist Birmingham (Ala.) Symphony, 1954-56, Fla. Symphony, Orlando, 1963; musician with numerous jazz groups including Ornette Coleman, David Baker, Sammy Davis, 1957-65; woodwind player Orch. USA, NYC, 1963-65; libr. Harkness Ballet, NYC, 1967-72; founder, clarinetist Boehm Quintette, NYC, 1968-88; music asst. N.Y. State Coun. on the Arts, NYC, 1972-75; freelance copyist NYC, 1958-88; founder, pres. Trillenium Music Co., 1986—, clarinetist, saxophonist, 1958—; pres. Opera North, Norwich, Vt., 1987-89; musician Sarasota Jazz Ensemble and Sarasota Pops, 2005—. Founder, treas. Chamber Music Am., N.Y.C., 1977-81; panelist Vt. Coun. on the Arts, 1976-78. Composer Piccolo Concerto, 1973, August Lions for Youth Orch., 1978, Song of Arion, 1985 (2d prize Am. Harp Soc.), First Blue Symphony, 1988, Book of Sliding Things, 1989, Green Mountain Christmas Card (opera), 1995, Never Seek to Tell Thy Love (voice and ensemble), 1998, Duo for Violin and Cello, 1999, Flute Quartet, 2003, Third Symphony, 2005; others; transcriber wind chamber music; composer, arranger for G. Schirmer, Boosey and Hawkes, Carl Fischer, Trillenium Music Co.; recs. for Columbia, Orion, New World, Margun and Marlboro, 1964—; participant Marlboro Festival, Vt., 1966-68, Berkshire Festival, Mass., summer 1965, 68. Vt. Coun. on the Arts fellow, 1985, Nat. Endowment for Arts grant, 1978—. Mem. ASCAP, Am. Fedn. Musicians, Am. Soc. Music Copyists (bd. dirs. 1970-87, treas. 1984-87), Am. Music Ctr., Music Pub.'s Assn. Democrat. Congregationalist. Office: Trillenium Music Co PO Box 51059 Sarasota FL 34232-0329 Office Fax: 941-377-9043. Business E-Mail: don@trillmusic.com.

STEWART, DONALD M., college president; b. Chgo., July 8, 1938; m. Isabel Carter Johnston; children: Jay Ashton, Carter Mitchell. BA, Grinnell Coll., 1959; MA, Yale U., 1962; MPA, Harvard U., 1969, postgrad., 1975. Asst. to rep. for West Africa Ford Found., 1962-64, program asst. Mid. East Africa Project, 1964-66, asst. rep. Cairo, asst. for North Africa, 1966-67; program officer Mid. East Africa Program, 1968-70; exec. asst. to pres. U. Pa., 1970-72; researcher Ford Found. Study Award, Washington, 1972-73; dir. Community Leadership Seminar Program, 1973-74, Continuing Edn., 1973-74, Higher Edn. Research, 1973-74; instr. City Planning and Pub. Policy Analysis, 1973-74; pres. Spelman Coll., 1976-87, Coll. Bd., NYC, 1987—99; sr. program officer, spl. adv. to pres. Carnegie Corp., NYC, 1999—2000; pres., CEO Chgo. Cmty. Trust, 2000—05. Bd. dirs. Bankers Life of Iowa Ins. Co., Nat. Bank of Ga., vis. prof. Harris Sch. Pub. Policy Studies, Univ. Chgo. Pres., treas. Atlanta Symphony Orch.; trustee, mem. adv. council of pres., mem. governing bd. Grinnell Coll.; mem. Council on Fgn. Relations; bd. dirs. Com. forEcon. Devel.; pres. Com. on Arts and Humanities; trustee Atlanta Botanical Gardens; mem. research com. Ind. Sector Adv. Com. Fellow Am. Acad. Arts & Scis.; mem. Nat. Acad. Pub. Adminstrn. (bd. dirs.). Office: Harris Sch Pub Policy Studies Univ Chgo 1155 East 60th St Chicago IL 60637 *

STEWART, DORIS MAE, biology professor; b. Sandsprings, Mont., Dec. 12, 1927; d. Virgil E. and Violet M. (Weaver) S.; m. Felix Loren Powell, Oct. 8, 1956; children: Leslie, Loren. BS, Coll. Puget Sound, 1948, MS, 1949; PhD, U. Wash., 1953. Instr. U. Mont., Missoula, 1954-56, asst. prof., 1956-57, U. Puget Sound, Tacoma, 1957-58; head sci. dept. Am. Kiz Lisesi, Istanbul, Turkey, 1958-62; rsch. asst. prof. U. Wash., Seattle, 1963-67, rsch. assoc. prof., 1967-68; assoc. prof. Cen. Mich. U., Mt. Pleasant, 1970-72, U. Balt., 1973-81, prof., 1981-95, prof. emeritus, 1995—. Contbr. numerous articles to profl. jours. Mem. Am. Physiol. Soc., Sigma Xi. Home: 1103 Frederick Rd Baltimore MD 21228-5032

STEWART, DOROTHY K., librarian; b. Bristol, Conn., Sept. 28, 1928; d. Robert and Anna Esther (Schwirtz) Konopask; m. David Benjamin Stewart, Sept. 27, 1952 (div. Nov. 1979); children: Douglas Neil, Diane Alison. BA in Romance Langs. and Lit. cum laude, Boston U., 1950; MSLS, Cath. U. Am., Washington, DC, 1959. Children's libr. Brookline Pub. Libr., Mass., 1953-55, Takoma Park Libr., Md., 1955-57; reference libr. US Geol. Survey, 1961; libr. Washington Internat. Sch., 1979-80, Office Sea Grant NOAA, Rockville, Md., 1980-82; info. specialist Life Ring, Inc., Silver Spring, Md., 1983-84; pub. svc. libr. Urban Inst., Washington, 1984-85; user svcs. coord. ERIC Clearinghouse on Tchg. and Tchr. Edn., Washington, 1985-97; ret., 1997. Active, past pres. PTA, Rockville, Md., 1973-78; chmn., mem. com. adv. com. Potomac Libr., 1975-85; vol. English Conversation Club, 2005-. Mem. Capital PC User Group, French lang. clubs, Phi Beta Kappa, Beta Phi Mu. Democrat. Avocations: travel, hiking, birding, computers. Personal E-mail: dkstewart24@comcast.net.

STEWART, E(DWARD) NICHOLSON, investment management executive; b. Bronxville, NY, Sept. 28, 1940; s. Edward Nicholson and Helen (Davis) S.; m. Mary Patricia Hunter, Aug. 8, 1964; children: Pamela S. Burke, Wendy S. Leary. Student, Hamilton Coll., 1959-62; BA, New Sch. Social Rsch., 1965. Dir. membership Investment Co. Inst., NYC, 1968; v.p. Lord, Abbett & Co., NYC, 1969-74; pres. Trevor Stewart Burton & Jacobsen Inc., NYC, 1974-95, CEO, 1990—2004, chmn., 1995—. Pres., bd. dirs. Robert Hampton Tapp Found., 1993—. Co-founder, editor Hackley Rev., 1963-68. Trustee Hackley Sch., 1971-87, treas., 1972-87, v.p. 1980-87; pres. Hackley Alumni Assn., Inc., 1967-69. Mem. USN League (Marine Corps com. N.Y. 1986—), Naval War Coll. Found. (life), Marine Corps Univ. Found. (assoc.), U.S. Naval Inst., Nat. Def. Indsl. Assn. (life), Union League Club (bd. govs. 1985-87, 95-97, vice-chmn. 1987, pres. 1989-90), Pendennis Club (Louisville), Sleepy Hollow Country Club (bd. govs. 1993-96, sec. 1995, 2001-2003, asst. sec. 2000, v.p. 2003-2004, pres. 2005-06), Econ. Club N.Y., The 200 Club (bd. dirs.), Delta Kappa Epsilon. Republican. Office: 405 Lexington Ave Ste 4700 New York NY 10174

STEWART, ELIZABETH ANNELLA, gynecologist, researcher; b. Atlanta, Apr. 24, 1959; married. BA molecular biology magna cum laude, Vanderbilt U., 1980; MD, Harvard U., 1985. Cert. Nat. Bd. Med. Examiners 1986, Mass. License Registration 1988, Am. Bd. Ob-Gyn. 1993, diplomate in ob-gyn. and reproductive endocrinology Am. Bd. Ob-gyn., 1995, cert. Am. Bd. Ob-Gyn., Annual Recertification 2003. Intern Obstetrics & Gynecology, Magee Women's Hosp., Pitts., 1985—86; resident Obstetrics & Gynecology, Brigham & Women's Hosp., 1986—89, fellow, Reproductive Endocrinology Boston, 1990—92; clin. dir., Ctr. Uterine Fibroids, Brigham and Women's Hosp., Boston, 1998—; asst. prof. ob-gyn and reproductive biology Harvard Med. Sch., 1995—2003, assoc. prof., 2003—; assoc. ob-gyn. Brigham and Women's Hosp., Boston, 1989—; asst. gynecologist Mass. General Hosp., Boston, 1989—90; assoc. in ob-gyn. Mass. Inst. Tech. Med. Dept., Cambridge, 1989—90; clinical dir., Ctr. for Uterine Fibroids Brigham and Women's Hosp., 1998—; assoc. gynecologist Faulkner Hosp., Boston, 2005—. Rsch. asst., Dept. of Surgery Vanderbilt U. Sch. of Medicine, 1981, summer fellow, Diabetes Ctr., 82; clinical assoc. Nat. Institutes of Health (NIH), Clinical Elective in Endocrinology and Metabolism, 1984; med. dir., Quality Assurance Com. Fertility and Endocrinology Unit, Brigham and Women's Hosp., Boston, 1993—95; assoc. dir., Lab. of Cell Biology, Dept. of Obstetrics, Gynecology and Reproductive Biology Brigham and Women's Hosp., Harvard Med. Sch., 1995—99; cons., Reproductive Sciences Program U. Mich., 2000; visiting prof. of ob-gyn. Kuwait U., Kuwait, 2000; cons. for Women's Health Care Emirates Palomar Med. Tech. Services, Abu Dhabi, United Arab Emirates, 2000; assoc. dir., Reproductive Endocrinology Fellowship Program Brigham and Women's Hosp., 2002—04; ad hoc mem. Bd. of Sci. Counselors, Review of Epidemiology Br. Nat. Inst. of Environ. Health Sciences, Nat. Institutes of Health, 2005. Recipient First Prize, Boston Fertility Soc. Prize Paper Competition, 1991, Berlex Scholar Award, 1993, First Prize, Boston Obstetrical Soc. Prize Paper Competition, 1994, Second Prize, Boston Fertility Soc. Prize Paper Competition, 1996, Partners in Excellence Award, Partners HealthCare System, 1996, Bear and Eagle Feather Mentoring Award, Four Directions Summer Rsch. Program, Harvard Med. Sch., 2000, Partners in Excellence Award, Partner's Health Care System, 2000, Residency Teaching Award in Reproductive Endocrinology, Brigham and Women's Hospital, 2004, Leadership Award for Clinical Innovation, Brigham and Women's Physician's Org., 2004. Fellow: Am. Coll. Ob-Gyn.; mem.: Soc. for Gynecologic Investigation, Soc. of Reproductive Endocrinologists, Am. Soc. for Reproductive Medicine, Mortar Bd. Hon. Soc., Phi Beta Kappa. Achievements include U.S. Patent 6440445: Methods and Compounds for Treatment of Abnormal Uterine Bleeding. Office: Brigham and Women's Hosp 75 Francis St Boston MA 02115 Office Phone: 617 732-4285. Office Fax: 617 566-7752. Business E-Mail: eastewart@partners.org. *

STEWART, ELLEN D., theater producer; Former fashion designer; founder, dir. La MaMa Exptl. Theatre Club, NYC, 1961—. Vis. prof. Inst. Drama, Republic of Korea. Prodr. innovative theatre, most recently Antigone, a part of SEVEN: Seven Greek Plays in Repertory; dir., most recently Perseus, Great Jones Rep. Co.; active in internet theatre exch. Named Officer Ordre des Arts et Lettres, Republic France; named to Theatre Hall of Fame, 1993; recipient Margo Jones award, 1969, MacArthur Genius award, Les Kurbas award disting. svc. to art and culture, Ukraine, Order of Sacred Treasure Gold Rays with Rossette, Emperor Japan, 1994, Human Rights award, Philippines. Mem.: Seoul Internat. Theatre Inst. Office: La MaMa ETC 74A E 4th St New York NY 10003-8903 Office Phone: 212-254-6468. Business E-Mail: lamama@lamama.org.

STEWART, GEOFFREY S., lawyer; b. Kansas City, Mo., Oct. 21, 1951; s. Gordon D. and Patricia S. Stewart; m. Marybeth Boyle, July 28, 1979; children: John, Elisabeth Cameron. AB, AM, Brown U., 1973; JD, Harvard U., 1976. Bar: NY, DC, US ct of appeal (1st, 4th, 6th, 9th, 11th, dc & fed. cirs.), various dists. cts., US Supreme Ct. Assoc. Davis, Polk & Wardwell, NYC, 1976-79, Washington, 1980-81; spl. counsel Dept. Justice, Washington, 1981-82, dep. asst. atty. gen., 1983; assoc. Hale & Dorr, Washington, 1985-86, ptnr., 1986, Jones Day, NYC. Assoc. counsel Iran arms sales/contra diversion Office of Ind. Counsel, Wash., 1987-90. Contbr. articles to profl. jour. Mem. ABA, DC Bar Assn. Editor Harvard Jour. on Legis. Office: Jones Day 222 E 41st St New York NY 10017 Office Phone: 212-326-3939, 212-326-7877. Office Fax: 212-755-7306. Business E-Mail: gstewart@jonesday.com.

STEWART, GILBERT WRIGHT, computer science educator; b. Washington, Oct. 1, 1940; s. Gilbert Wright and Ruth (Blount) S.; m. Mary Lynn Tharp, 1964; children: Michael, Laura; m. Astrid Schmidt-Nielsen, Apr. 29, 1978. AB, U. Tenn., 1962, PhD, 1968. Programmer Union Carbide Nuclear Co., Oak Ridge, 1959-62, 63-64, 65-68, computer div. Gen. Electric Co., Phoenix, 1964-68; asst. prof., assoc. prof. U. Tex.-Austin, 1968-72; assoc. prof. Carnegie-Mellon U., Pitts., 1972-74, U. Md., College Park, 1974-76, prof. Computer Sci. Dept.; prof. computer sci. Carnegie-Mellon U., 1976—; cons. Argonne Nat. Lab., Ill., 1974—, Nat. Bur. Standards, Gaithersburg, Md., 1979—; dir. Lab. Parallel Computation U. Md., 1983. Author: Introduction to Matrix Computations, 1974; co-author: (with Dougarra, Bunch and Moler) LINPACK Users' Guide, (with I.G. Sun) Matrix Perturbation Theory; translator: Gauss's Theoria Combinations. Woodrow Wilson fellow, 1962; NSF grantee, 1983 Mem. NAE, Soc. Indsl. and Applied Math., Am. Math. Assn., Am. Statis. Assn. Democrat. Office: U Md Dept Computer Sci College Park MD 20742-0001 Office Phone: 301-405-2681, 301-405-6707. E-mail: stewart@cs.umd.edu.

STEWART, GORDON CURRAN, retired insurance institute executive; b. Chgo., July 22, 1939; s. Henry Stewart and Evangeline (Williams) Bolton; m. Elizabeth Knorr, June 19, 1965 (div. 1968); m. Zanne Early, Dec. 20, 1995; 1 child, Katarina Guadalupe Hadley. BA, Oberlin Coll., 1960; MA, U. Chgo., 1962; student, U. Vienna, Austria, 1963; MFA, Yale U., 1967. Instr. Amherst Coll., Mass., 1967-68; dir. Bus. Comm. for Arts, NYC, 1969-71; exec. asst. Mayor of NYC, 1971-73; dir., writer NYC, LA, UK, 1973-78; dep. chief speechwriter President of US, Washington, 1978-81; instr. Bus. and Govt. Acad. forums, U.S. and fgn. countries, 1981-82; v.p. AMSE, NYC, 1982-89; exec. v.p. Ins. Info. Inst., NYC, 1989-91, pres., 1991—2006; ret. Cons. Am. Bus. Conf., Washington, 1982-89, Internat. Commn. for Ctrl. Am., Washington, 1986-88, Coun. on Competitiveness, Washington, 1987-88, Def. Sci. Bd., Washington, 1988-89; pres., CEO Mind, Inc. Writer films: The Store, 1978, Joey, 1978, Gallery, 1978; dir. (play) The Elephant Man (1st US prodn.), 1977, Jesse, 1975, Cowboy Mouth, 1976, Sleep, 1977, (films) The Blazers, 1975; condr. Beggar's Opera, 1969, West Side Story, 1970. Dir. NY Urban Coalition, NYC, 1984-88; dir. policy Samuels for Gov., NY, 1974; speechwriter numerous dem. campaigns, 1974-81; mem. fin. coun. Dem. Nat. Com., 1984-88; mem. adv. coun. Dem. Leadership Coun., 1984-90. Woodrow Wilson fellow Woodrow Wilson Found., 1961. Mem. Writers Guild Am. (west), Judson Welliver Soc. of Chief Presdl. Speechwriters (sec.-treas.), Coun. Fgn. Rels., Century Assn., Phi Beta Kappa, Yale Club. Avocations: politics, music.

STEWART, HAROLD BROWN, biochemist; b. Chatham, Ont., Can., Mar. 9, 1921; s. John Craig and Margaret Gertrude (Brown) S.; m. Audrey Pauline Blake, Oct. 14, 1950; 1 dau., Ann Margaret. MD, U. Toronto, 1944, PhD, 1950, Cambridge U., Eng., 1955. Prof. biochemistry U. Western Ont., London, 1956—; chmn. dept. biochemistry U. Western Ont., 1964-72, dean grad. studies, 1972-86, prof. emeritus, 1986—. Med. Research Council Can. vis. scientist dept. biochemistry U. Cambridge, Eng., 1971-72 Contbr. articles in biochemistry to sci. jours. Served with Royal Canadian Navy, 1945-46. Mem. Canadian, U.K. biochem. socs., Canadian Physiol. Soc., Am. Soc. Biochemistry and Molecular Biology, Coll. Physicians and Surgeons of Ont. Home: 118 Baseline Rd E London ON Canada N6C 2N8

STEWART, JAMES B., journalist, writer; b. Quincy, Ill. BA in History, DePauw U., 1973; JD, Harvard U., 1976. Assoc. Cravath, Swaine & Moore LLP, 1976—79; exec. editor Am. Lawyer mag., 1979—83; sr. spl. writer Wall St. Jour., NYC, 1983—88, "Page One" editor, 1988-92; reporter The New Yorker mag., NYC, 1993—; editor-at-large Smart Money mag. Bloomberg prof. bus. journalism Columbia U., NYC. Author: The Partners: Inside America's Most Powerful Law Firms, 1984, Wendell Phillips: Liberty's Hero, 1986, The Prosecutors: Inside the Offices of the Government's Most Powerful Lawyers, 1987, Den of Thieves, 1993, Blood Sport: The President and His Adversaries, 1996, Holy Warriors: The Abolitionists and American Slavery, 1997, Follow the Story: How to Write Successful Nonfiction, 1998, Blind Eye, 1999, Heart of a Soldier: The Story of Love, Heroism and September 11, 2002, Disney War: The Battle for the Magic Kingdom, 2005. Pulitzer prize for Explanatory Journalism, 1987,Gerald Loeb award, 1987, 1988, George Polk award, 1988, Edgar Allan Poe award Mystery Writers Am., 2000 Mem.: NY State Bar Assn. Office: The New Yorker 4 Times Square New York NY 10036 E-mail: jbs32@columbia.edu.

STEWART, JANE, psychology professor; b. Ottawa, Ont., Can., Apr. 19, 1934; d. Daniel Wallace and Jessie Stewart; m. Dalbir Bindra, Aug. 5, 1959 (dec. 1981). BA with honours, Queen's U., Kingston, Ont., 1956; PhD, U. London, 1959; DSc (hon.), Queen's U., 1992. Sr. rsch. biologist Ayerst Labs., Montreal, Que., 1959-63; part-time instr. psychology Sir George, Montreal, 1962-63; assoc. prof. psychology Williams U., Montreal, 1963-69; prof., chmn. psychology SGW Univ. (now Concordia U.), Montreal, 1969-75; prof. psychology Concordia U., Montreal, 1975—. Dir. Ctr. for Studies in Behavioral Neurobiology, Concordia U., Montreal, 1990-97. Fellow: APA, AAAS, Can. Psychol. Assn., Royal Soc. Can.; mem.: NY Acad. Sci., Soc. for Neurosci. Office: Concordia Univ 7141 Sherbrooke St W Montreal PQ Canada H4B 1R6

STEWART, JOAN HINDE, academic administrator; b. NYC, Aug. 11, 1944; d. Wade and Dorothy (Ronning) H.; m. Philip Robert Stewart, Jan. 31, 1970; children: Anna Faye, Justin. Student, Université Laval Summer Sch, Quebec, 1963, Middlebury Coll. Summer Sch., 1964-65; BA summa cum laude, St. Joseph's Coll., 1965; student, Salzburg Summer Sch., Austria, 1966; MPhil, Yale U., 1969, PhD, 1970. Tchg. assoc. French Yale U., New Haven, 1967—69, acting instr. French, 1969—70; instr. French Wellesley Coll., 1970—71, asst. prof. French, 1971—72, NC State U., Raleigh, 1973—77, assoc. prof. French, 1977—81, prof. French, 1981—99, asst. head dept. fgn. langs. and lits., 1978—82, asst. dean rsch. and grad. programs, 1983—85, acting head dept. fgn. langs. and lits., 1984—85, head dept. fgn. langs. and lit., 1985—97; prof., dean liberal arts U. SC, 1999—2003; prof. French, pres. Hamilton Coll., Clinton, NY, 2003—. Author: The Novels of Mme Riccoboni, 1976, Colette, 1983, 1996, Gynographs: French Novels by Women of the Late Eighteenth Century, 1993; editor: Mme Riccoboni's Lettres de Mistriss Fanni Butlerd, 1979; co-editor: Isabelle de Charrière's Lettres de Mistriss Henley, 1993, Marie Riccoboni's Histoire d'Ernestine, 1998. Chmn. N.C. Humanities Coun., 1988-89. Fellow Camargo Found., Cassis, France, 1979, Nat. Humanities Ctr., 1982-83, (sr.) ctr. for humanities Wesleyan U., 1990; NEH summer seminar fellowship, Princeton U., 1980; NEH fellowship Coll. Tchrs. and Ind. Scholars, 1990-91, 1994-95; fellow Ctr. d'Etude du XVIII Siecle, U. Paul Valery, Montpellier, France, 1995, Liguria Study Ctr. for the Arts and Scis., Bogliasco, Italy, 1997, Beinecke Rare Book and Manuscript Libr., Yale U., 1997; stipend younger humanists NEH, 1973; travel grantee ACLS, 1983; travel to collections grantee NEH, 1984; vis. scholar European Humanities Rsch. Ctr., Oxford U., 1995. Mem. AAUP, MLA, Am. Assn. Tchrs. French. Address: Hamilton Coll Pres Office 198 College Hill Rd Clinton NY 13323 Office Phone: 315-859-4104. E-mail: jstewart@hamilton.edu.

STEWART, JOHN HARGER, music educator; b. Cleve., Mar. 31, 1940; s. Cecil Tooker and Marian (Harger) S.; m. Julia Wallace, Aug. 14, 1977; children: Barbara, Cecily Bronwen. BA, Yale U., 1962; MA, Brown U., 1972; cert., New Eng. Conservatory, 1965. With various operas including Santa Fe Opera, N.Y.C. Opera, Met. Opera, U.S. and Europe, 1965—; lectr. Mt. Holyoke Coll., South Hadley, Mass., 1988-90; dir. vocal activities Washington U., St. Louis, 1990—, dir. Friends of Music. Office: Dept Music Washington U Campus Box 1032 One Brookings Dr Saint Louis MO 63130-4899 Home Phone: 314-533-0665; Office Phone: 314-935-5597. Business E-Mail: jstewart@wustl.edu.

STEWART, JOHN LINCOLN, former academic administrator; b. Alton, Ill., Jan. 24, 1917; s. Frederick William and Hilda (Denovan) S.; m. Joan Elsdon Guthridge, Sept. 23 1939 (div. 1964); children: Leslie Cythera Stewart Chalmers, Ann Guthridge Stewart Nutt; m. Ruth Peabody Quinn, July 11, 1964; stepchildren: Geoffrey Cornelius Quinn, Andrew Dean Quinn. AB, Denison U., 1938, ArtsD (hon.), 1964; MA, Ohio State U., 1939, PhD, 1947. From tchg. asst. to instr. Ohio Sate U., Columbus, 1939-47; instr. UCLA, 1947-49; from asst. prof. to prof. English Dartmouth Coll., Hanover, N.H., 1949-64; prof. Lit. U. Calif., San Diego, 1964-87, provost John Muir Coll., 1965-87. Author: Exposition for Science and Technical Students, 1950, The Essay, 1952, John Crowe Ransom, 1962, The Burden of Time, 1965; (with others) Horizons Circled, 1974, Ernst Krenek, 1990; contbr. articles to profl. jours. Assoc. dir. Hopkins Ctr. for Arts, 1961-64; dir. Mandeville Ctr. for Arts, 1974-76; mem. Dartmouth Community Symphony Orch., 1949-58; trustee Kinhaven Music Sch., 1960-64, Fla. West Coast Symphony, 1958, Oakland Cmty. Orch., 1997-2002; bd. dirs. Theater and Arts Found. San Diego County, 1970; pres. La Jolla (Calif.) Friends Sch. Music, 1971-73, Friends of Music, U. Calif., San Diego. Served with Aus, 1942-45. Howard Found. fellow, 1953-54, Dartmouth Coll. fellow, 1962-63. Democrat. Avocation: performer with music ensembles. Home: 2361 E 29th St Oakland CA 94606-3511

STEWART, JOHN MURRAY, bank executive; b. Summit, NJ, Apr. 2, 1943; s. Robert John Stewart and Mary Catherine Grabhorn; m. Sandra Meyers Frazier, 1966 (div. 1997); children: Jennifer Bricar Crone, Catherine Dorothy Lochead; m. Rebecca Marie Mellen, July 10, 1998. BA, U. Va., Charlottesville, 1965; MBA, NYU, 1983. Trust officer, v.p. Bankers Trust Co., NYC, 1965-82, Morgan Guaranty Trust Co., NYC, 1982-83; mgr., pres., dir. Morgan Trust Co. Fla., Palm Beach, 1983-89; pres., dir. Bankers Trust Co. Fla., 1989-93; founder, pres. pvt. capital group SunTrust Bank, Orlando, Fla., 1993-96; pres., dir. Harris Trust/Bank of Montreal, West Palm Beach, 1996—2001; contbg. writer Cannon Fin. Inst., 2004—; sr. trust advisor Wachovia Bank, 2006—. Campaign chmn. Palm Beach Cmty. Chest, 1985, 1986; exec. com. Tampa Bay and Palm Beach County Local Initiatives Support Corp.; mem. planned giving coun. U. Va., 1997—, pres. alumni club, 1990—98; vestryman Bethesda By the Sea Ch., Palm Beach, 1986—89, 1992—94, treas., 1986—87, Cathedral Ch. of St. Luke, Orlando, 1996; bd. dirs. Orlando Opera Co., 1994—96, Palm Beach Opera Co., 1996—2001. Mem. Fla. Bankers Assn. (chmn. trust bus. devel. com. 1989, planning commn., chmn. trust legis. com. 1990), NY State Bankers Assn. (mem. trust bus. devel. com. 1978-82), NY Yacht Club (NYC), St. Petersburg Yacht Club, Isla del Sol Country Club (St. Petersburg), Monmouth Boat Club (Red Bank, NJ), SAR (pres. Palm Beach chpt. 1997-98). Home: 1049 Pinellas Bayway S Tierra Verde FL 33715 Office Phone: 561-313-4444. Personal E-mail: uva1965@msn.com.

STEWART, JOHN NORMAN, scenic artist; b. San Bernadino, Calif., May 2, 1940; s. John T. and Rachel (Powell) S.; m. Judith Kay Coleman, Sept. 1959 (div. 1961); 1 child, Pamela Joy Perrini; m. Barbara Lyn Perlman, Feb. 6, 1966; 1 child, Dawn Sheryl; m. Valerie Anne DeRenzo, Dec. 9, 2001 Student, Chouinard Art Inst., 1958—60, Art Ctr., LA, 1966. Ind. artist. sculptor, scenic artist, 1958—2002; artist Cottonwood, Calif., 2002—. Muralist Hilton Hotels, Reno, 1993—94; artist Disney Studios (WED), Glendale, Calif., 1981—83; scenic artist Universal Studios, North Hollywood, Calif., 1976—81; free lance artist Self Employed, Sun Valley, Calif., 1966—76. Scenic and portrait artist (films) Smokey and the Bandit parts I and II, Blues Brothers, Extremities, Xanadu, Harvest Home, Saint Elmo's Fire, Vibes, E. T.-The Extraterrestrial, Love at First Bite, Poltergeist, Bachelor Party, One From the Heart, Ghostbusters, Space Balls, Karate Kid, Starman, Bonfire of the Vanities, 1990, Naked Gun 2 1/2, 1991, Addams Family The Movie, 1991, Public Eye, Johnnie Zombie, Addams Family 2, Deep Space Nine, Murder She Wrote, George of the Jungle, Home Alone 3, Men in Black, Notorious, (TV shows) Tonight Show, Grammy Awards Show, 1987, All in the Family, Soul Train, Wheel of Fortune, Osmonds, Battlestar Gallactica, V, Bionic Woman, Dinosaurs, Dark Shadows, (TV commls.) Krispy Krunchies, Pepsi, McDonalds, Unical, Coke, (film promotionals) Airport '77, Beau Geste, The Sting, 7% Solution, Swashbuckler, Paramount Pictures Logo; artist: (watercolor) Mechanica; paintings and sculptures represented in pvt. collections including Richard Nixon, Barry Goldwater, John Wayne, Milton Perlman, Herschel Bernardi; exhibitions include Gallery Hawaii, Copenhagen Galleri, Space Gallery, Emerson Gallery, La Jolla Fine Arts Gallery, Lakeland (Ohio) Coll.; author: Changing Patterns Computer Graphics Program for Atari-800, 1981, computer illustrations for Hilton Hotels, 20th Century Fox TV, Besure Corp.; portrait artist for Bette Davis, James Brolin, Norman Lloyd, Ben Cross, Henry Winkler, Ricardo Montelban, Marty Feldman, Elton John; murals Walt Disney, Hilton Hotel Reno (Nev.); prodr. (CD-ROMs) The Art of John N. Stewart, 1996, The Stewart Collection, 1995-96, (web site) The Art of John N. Stewart, 1996; composer: Peruvian Suite, 1997, Piano Abstract, 1998. Mem. L.A. Art Assn. Chouinard scholar Glendale (Calif.) Art Assn., 1958. Mem. Nat. Watercolor Soc., IATSE (v.p. scenic and title artists 1989-92), Order of DeMolay, Calif. Art Club. Republican. Mem. Foursquare Ch. Avocations: piano, computers, photography, enjoying nature. Home and Office: 19700 Sweet Brier Pl Cottonwood CA 96022 E-mail: j@jstewart.com.

STEWART, JOHN PATRICK, art educator, researcher; b. Ft. Leavenworth, Kans., Mar. 11, 1945; s. John Smith Stewart and Marilyn E. Miller; 1 child, Amy Lynn Gallaher. BFA in Printmaking and Sculpture, U. Colo., Boulder, 1967; MFA in Printmaking and Sculpture, U. Calif., Santa Barbara, 1969. Instr., head printmaking U. NC, Greensboro, 1969—73; prof. printmaking and painting U. Cin., 1973—. One-man shows include Prescott Coll., Ariz., 1970, Nicholls State U. Gallery, Thibodaux, La., 1971, Pyramid Gallery, Washington, 1972, 1974, 1978, East Ctrl. State U., Ada, Okla., 1973, Okla. State U., Stillwater, 1973, Galeria de las Americas, San Juan, PR, 1974, 1976, Gimpel/Weitzenhoffer Gallery, NYC, 1975, Contemporary Art Ctr., Cin., 1978, Nat. Armory, Washington, 1979, A.J. Wood Galleries, Phila., 1980, Osuna Gallery, Washington, 1981, 1982, 1986, Foire Internat. D'Art Contemporain, Paris, 1982, Carl Solway Gallery, Cin., 1985, So. Ohio Mus., Portsmouth, 1991, 2001, Closson's Art Gallery, Cin., 1999, exhibited in group shows at Cin. Art Mus., 1981, Cin. Commn. on Arts, 1981, Osuna Gallery, Washington, 1983, 1987, Louisville Art Gallery, Ky., 1984, Coll. of Mt. St. Joseph, Cin., 1984, U. Va., Blacksburg, 1984, Rosenthal Fine Arts Ltd., Chgo., 1985, 1990, Allegheny Coll., Meadville, Pa., 1986, Carl Solway Gallery, Cin., 1986, 1989, Cin. Art Acad., 1987, U. Cin., 1988, 1993, Tangeman Fine Arts Gallery, U. Cin., 1988, Miami U. Mus., Oxford, Ohio, 1989, Dayton Art Inst., Ohio, 1991, The Machine Shop Gallery, Cin., 1993, Contemporary Art Ctr., 1994, Wright State U., Dayton, 1995, The Univ. Club, Cin., 1995, Aronoff Ctr. for Arts, 1995, Riffe Ctr. for Arts, Columbus, 1996, 1998, So. Ohio Mus., Portsmouth, 1997, Dayton Visual Arts Ctr., 1998, Christ Hosp., Cin., 2000, Closson's Art Gallery, 2001, Oglebay Inst., Wheeling, W.Va., 2002, Reed Gallery, Cin., 2004, Heart Hosp. of Mercy, Fairfield, Ohio, 2005. Office: Univ Cin Sch Art Coll Design Art Architect and Planning Cincinnati OH 45221

STEWART, JOHN TODD, economist, consultant; AB, Stanford U., 1961; MA, Tufts U., 1962, MALD, 1970. With Am. Fgn. Svc., 1962-98; U.S. amb. to Republic of Moldova, 1995-98; dep. head U.S. diplomatic missions to Can., Costa Rica and Jamaica; dir. office maritime and land transport Dept. of State, Washington; dir. GATT affairs Pres.'s Spl. Rep. for Trade Negotiations; dep. dir. Inst. Internat. Econs., Washington, 1998—2002; diplomat-in-residence Am. U., 2003—04. Vis. fellow Inst. Internat. Econs., 2002—. Home and Office: PO Box 3200 Sun Valley ID 83353 Office Phone: 208-622-7343. E-mail: todd.stewart@stanfordalumni.org.

STEWART, JOHN WRAY BLACK, college dean; b. Coleraine, Northern Ireland, Jan. 16, 1936; s. John Wray and Margaret Reid (Black) S.; m. Felicity Ann Patricia Poole, Aug. 7, 1965; children: J.W. Matthew, Hannah Louise. BSc with honors, Queen's U., Belfast, Northern Ireland, 1958, BSA with honors, 1959, PhD, 1963, DSc, 1988. Registered profl. agrologist. Sci. officer chem. rsch. divsn. Ministry of Agr., Belfast, 1959-64; asst. prof. soil sci. dept. U. Sask., Saskatoon, Canada, 1966-71, assoc. prof., 1971-76, prof., 1976-81, dir. Sask. Inst. Pedology, 1981-89, dean Coll. Agr., 1989-99, prof. emeritus, 1999—, dean emeritus, 1999—, interim dir. Inter-Am. Inst. for Global Change Rsch., 2002, 2005. Tech. expert, cons. FAO/IAEA, U.N.D.P., Vienna, 1971, Vienna, 1974—75; mem. program com. Can. Global Change, 1985—98; sec.-gen. Sci. Com. on Problems of Environ., Paris, 1988—92, pres., 1992—95, editor-in-chief, 1999—2006; cons. UNESCO, Paris, 1990; trustee Internat. Inst. Tropical Agr., Nigeria, 1991—97; chair sci. adv. com. Inter-Am. Inst. for Global Change Rsch., 1994—2001. Contbr. articles to profl. publs., chapters to books. Fellow: Can. Soc. Soil Sci., Berlin Inst. Advanced Study, Am. Soc. Agronomy, Soil Sci. Soc. Am., Agrl. Inst. Can.; mem.: Internat. Soc. Soil Sci., Brit. Soc. Soil Sci. Avocations: golf, tennis. Personal E-mail: stew9250@telus.net.

STEWART, JON (JONATHAN STEWART LEIBOWITZ), comedian, actor; b. NYC, Nov. 28, 1962; m. Tracy McShane, 2000; children: Nathan Thomas, Maggie Rose. BS in Psychology, Coll. William and Mary, 1984. Actor: (TV films) Since You've Been Gone, 1998; (films) Mixed Nuts, 1994, Wishful Thinking, 1997, Half Baked, 1998, The Faculty, 1998, Playing by Heart, 1998, Big Daddy, 1999, The Office Party, 2000, Jay and Silent Bob Strike Back, 2001, Death to Smoochy, 2002, (voice) Doogal, 2006; host: (TV series) Short Attention Span Theater, 1989; You Wrote It, You Watch It, 1992; The Daily Show, 1999— (Emmy award Outstanding Variety, Music or Comedy Series, 2004); (TV special) The Daily Show with Jon Stewart: Indecision 2000 (Emmy award, 2001, George F. Peabody award, 2001); The Daily Show with Jon Stewart: Indecision 2004 (George F. Peabody award, 2005); exec. prodr., writer: (TV series) The Daily Show, 1996—; writer, host The Jon Stewart Show, 1993; writer (TV series) The Sweet Life, 1989; author: (book) Naked Pictures of Famous People, 1998; co-author (with Ben Karlin and David Javerbaum): The Daily Show With Jon Stewart Presents America (The Book): A Citizen's Guide to Democracy Inaction, 2004 (Book of the Year, Publishers Weekly, 2004, Quills award for best humor book, best audio book, 2005, Thurber Prize for American Humor, 2005). Named one of Time Mag. 100 Most Influential People, 2005; recipient George F. Peabody award, 2005. Office: The Daily Show 604R W 52nd St New York NY 10019-5013 *

STEWART, JON DOUGLAS, lawyer; b. Chicopee, Ga., Sept. 8, 1938; s. Marvin Jones and Lillian Monteen (Cozens) S.; m. Helen Helms, Feb. 22, 1964; children: Jon Douglas Jr., William Andrew. BA, Emory U., 1960, LLB, 1962. Bar: Ga. 1962, U.S. Dist. Ct. (no. dist.) Ga. 1962, U.S. Ct. Appeals (5th cir.) 1962, U.S. Dist. Ct. (mid. dist.) Ga. 1964, U.S. Supreme Ct. 1968, U.S. Dist. Ct. (so. dist.) Ga. 1976, U.S. Ct. Appeals (11th cir.) 1982. Assoc. Green, Buckley, De Rieux & Jones, Atlanta, 1962-68; ptnr. Stewart Melvin & Frost, Gainesville, Ga., 1968—. Chair Gainesville Cmty. Concert, 1973; chair adminstrv. bd. Gainesville 1st United Meth. Ch., 1979-81, tchr. Serendipity Sunday Sch.; chmn. Emory Univ. Law Alumni Assn. Fellow Am. Bar Found. (life), Ga. Bar Found. (mem., chair bd. trustees 1983-93), Ga. Lawyers Found. (life); mem. ABA (Ga. state del. ho. of dels. 1985—, bd. gov. 2002-2005), State Bar of Ga. (pres.-elect, pres., treas., bd. govs., Disting. Svc. award 1992). Avocations: acting, singing. Office: Stewart Melvin & Frost Suite 600 Hunt Tower 200 Main St NW Gainesville GA 30501-3649 Office Phone: 770-536-0101. Business E-Mail: dstewart@smf-law.com.

STEWART, JOSEPH GRIER, lawyer; b. Tuscaloosa, Ala., July 24, 1941; s. Jesse Grier and Kyle Vann (Pruett) S.; m. Linda Louise Hogue, Mar. 2, 1963; children: Joseph Grier Jr., Robert Byars, James Vann. BS, U. Ala., Tuscaloosa, 1963, LLB, 1966. Bar: Ala. 1966, U.S. Dist. Ct. (no. dist.) Ala. 1968, U.S. Dist. Ct. (middle Dist.of Ala.), 1996, U.S. Tax Court. Ptnr. Burr & Forman LLP, Birmingham, Ala., 1968—. Mem. ABA, Ala. State Bar, Birmingham Bar Assn. (chmn. com. 1989-90), Ala. Law Inst., Kiwanis, Birmingham Tip Off Club (pres. 1988-89). Methodist. Office: Burr & Forman LLP 420 20th St N Ste 3400 Birmingham AL 35203-5200 Office Phone: 205-251-3000.

STEWART, JOSEPH TURNER, JR., retired pharmaceutical executive; b. NYC, Apr. 30, 1929; s. Joseph Turner and Edna (Pride) S.; m. Carol Graham, Aug. 7, 1954; children: Lisa D., Alison D. BS with honors, U.S. Mcht. Marine Acad., 1951; MBA, Harvard U., 1954. Systems analyst Warner Lambert Co., Morris Plains, NJ, 1954-56, budget dir. internat., 1956-60, asst. div. controller consumer products group, 1960-62, div. controller group, 1962-66; dir. adminstrn. and fin. Proprietary Drug div. Warner Lamber Co., 1966; dir. Lactona Products div. Warner Lamber Co., 1967; controller Beech-Nut subs. Squibb Corp., NYC, 1968, v.p. fin., 1968-71, v.p. planning, corp. staff parent corp., 1971-79, v.p. fin. and planning parent co., 1979-82, sr. v.p. corporate affairs parent co., 1982-89; also bd. dirs.; cons. Johnson & Johnson, 1990-98. Bd. dirs. Gen. Am. Investment Corp. 1987-. Trustee Tax Found., 1985-89, US Mcht. Marine Acad. Found., 2004-; commr. N.J. State Commn. on Income and Expenditures, 1985-88; mem. adv. com. Grad. Sch. Indsl. Adminstrn., Carnegie Mellon U., 1986-91; trustee New Sch. for Social Rsch., 1990-98, U. Medicine and Dentistry of N.J. Found., 1989—; bd. dirs. Liposome Co., 1995-2000; vis. coun. Marine Biol. Lab., 1995—; bd. advisors U.S. Mcht. Marine Acad., 2002—, trustee alumni found., 2003— John Hay Whitney Opportunity fellow, 1952-54. Mem.: Harvard (N.Y.C.). Personal E-mail: kingpin497@aol.com.

STEWART, JULIA A., food service executive; m. Jon Greenawalt (div.); 2 children. BA in Communications, San Diego State U., 1977. Regional mktg. dir. Carl's Jr. Restaurant, 1978—80; regional mktg. mgr. Burger King Corp., 1980—84; mktg. dir. Spoons Grill & Bar Stuart Anderson's Black Angus/Cattle Co. Restaurants, 1985, mktg. v.p., 1986—91; western region v.p. operations Taco Bell Yum! Brands, 1991, nat. v.p. franchise, license Taco Bell, 1997—98; pres. domestic div. Applebee's Internat., Inc., 1998—2001; pres, COO Internat. House Pancakes (IHOP), 2001—, CEO, 2002—, chmn., 2006—. Bd. dirs. Avery Denison, Town Hall, LA, Women's Franchise and Distbn. Forum; mem. Elliott Inst. Leadership Coun.; bd. visitors UCLA Anderson Sch. Mgmt.; trustee Calif. Sci. Ctr. Found. Named one of Top Fifty Women in foodservice, Nation's Restaurant. Mem.: Nat. Restaurant Assn. (pres. mktg. executives group), Calif. Restaurant Assn. (exec. bd. mem.), Women's Foodservice Forum (past pres., founding mem.). Avocations: cooking, skiing. Office: IHOP 450 N Brand Blvd Glendale CA 91203-1903

STEWART, J.W., energy executive, lawyer; b. Mar. 2, 1944; BSEE, Univ. Tex., Arlington, 1966; JD, Univ. Houston, 1973. V.p. legal, sec. Hughes Tool Co.; chmn., pres., CEO BJ Services, Houston, 1990—. Office: BJ Services 5500 N W Ctrl Dr Houston TX 77092 Mailing: BJ Services PO Box 4442 Houston TX 77210-4442 *

STEWART, KENNETH L., lawyer; b. Nashville, Ark., Feb. 26, 1954; BSBA in Acctg., U. Ark., 1976; JD, Vanderbilt U., 1979. Bar: Tex. 1979. Ptnr.-in-charge, Dallas office and mem. corp. banking and bus. practice Fulbright & Jaworski, LLP, Dallas, 1979—. Editor: Vanderbilt Law Rev. Chmn. Dallas Bus. Hall of Fame, 2001, Jr. Achievement Dallas Inc., 2002—03. Mem. ABA, Dallas Bar Assn., State Bar Tex., Dallas Citizens Coun., Greater Dallas C. of C. (dir. 2005-06), Order of Coif. Office: Fulbright & Jaworski LLP 2200 Ross Ave Ste 2800 Dallas TX 75201-2784 Office Phone: 214-855-8000. Office Fax: 214-855-8200. Business E-Mail: kstewart@fulbright.com.

STEWART, KENT KALLAM, analytical biochemistry educator; b. Omaha, Sept. 5, 1934; s. George Franklin and Grace S.; m. Margaret Reiber, June 10, 1956; children: Elizabeth, Cynthia, Richard, Robert. Student, U. Chgo., 1951-53; AB, U. Calif., Berkeley, 1956; PhD, Fla. State U., 1965. Guest investigator Rockefeller U., NYC, 1965-67, research assoc., 1967-68, asst. prof., 1968-69; research chemist U.S. Dept. Agr., Beltsville, Md., 1970-75, lab. chief Nutrient Composition Lab., 1975-82; prof., head dept. food sci. and tech. Va. Poly. Inst. and State U., Blacksburg, 1982-85, prof. biochemistry, anaerobic microbiology, food sci./tech., 1985—96, prof. emeritus of biochemistry; adj. prof. dept. chemistry and biochemistry U. Tex., Austin, 1996—2004. Editor Jour. Food Composition and Analysis, 1987-97, also 3 books; contbr. articles to profl. jours., co-author book; patentee in field. Capt. USMCR, 1956-59. Fellow AAAS, Inst. Food Technologist. Home: 3900 Glengarry Dr Austin TX 78731-3812 Office Phone: 512-458-1072. E-mail: stewart.kent@gmail.com.

STEWART, LINDSAY D., lawyer, apparel executive; b. Portland, Oreg. married. BA in Econs., Willamette U., Salem, Oreg., 1969, JD, 1973. Bar: Oreg. 1973. Pvt. practice atty.; corp. counsel Ga.-Pacific Corp.; asst. corp. counsel Nike, Inc., Beaverton, Oreg., 1981—83, gen. counsel, 1983—91, v.p., gen. counsel, 1991—96, v.p. law and corp. affairs, 1996—2001, v.p., chief of staff, 2001—. Mem. Oreg. State Internat. Trade Commn. Avocations: tennis, golf, running. Office: Nike Inc 1 Bowerman Dr Beaverton OR 97005-0979 Office Phone: 503-671-6453. *

STEWART, LUCILLE MARIE, retired special education coordinator, educator; b. Pitts., Feb. 24; d. William H. and Edna (Hoffman) S. BEd, Duquesne U.; MEd, U. Pitts.; postgrad., Columbia U., U. Calif., Calif. State U. Cert. elem. and secondary tchr., spl. edn. tchr., supr., adminstr. Tchr., group leader mentally retarded Ednl. Alliance, NYC, 1950—53; tchr. Lincoln State Sch., Ill., 1953; tchr., program leader, sec. Edn. Alliance, NYC, 1954-58; tchr. mentally retarded Ramapo Ctrl. Sch. Dist., Spring Valley, NY, 1958-60, tchr. seriously emotionally disturbed, 1960-64, supr. presch. program for educationally disadvantaged, 1965-67; program dir. Pomona Camp for Retarded, NY, summers 1960-63; tchr. mentally retarded Stockton Sch., San Diego, 1964-65; tchr. mentally retarded sch. Cathedral City Sch., 1967-78; program specialist spl. edn. Palm Springs Unified Sch. Dist., Calif., 1978-95, prin. elem. summer schs., 1971-72; prin.-tchr. Summer Extended Sch. for Spl. Students, summer 1979-99. Exec. com. U. Calif. Extension, area adv. com.; spl. edn. surrogate parent Palm Springs Unified Sch. Dist. Vol. Palm Springs Unified Dist. HS Alternative Program, 2001—. Mem. NEA, AAUW, ASCD, Calif. Adminstrs. Spl. Edn., Coun. Exceptional Children (adminstrn. divsn., early childhood-learning handicap divsns.), Am. Assn. Childhood Edn., Autism Soc., Coachella Valley, Learning Disabilities Assn., Desert Theater League, Alpha Kappa Alpha, Phi Delta Kappa, Delta Kappa Gamma.

STEWART, LYNNE F., lawyer; b. Bklyn., Oct. 8, 1939; d. John and Irene Feltham. BA in Polit. Sci., Wagner Coll., 1961; M in Libr. Sci., Pratt U., 1964; JD, Rutgers U., 1975. Bar: NJ 1975, NY 1976. Mem.: Nat. Lawyers Guild. Office: The Lynne Stewart Del Com 350 Broadway Ste 700 New York NY 10013 Office Phone: 212-625-9696. *Convicted of conspiracy, providing material support to terrorists, & defrauding the US government, Feb. 10, 2005; sentenced to 28 months in prison, Oct. 16, 2006; disbarred from practicing law, April 25, 2007.* *

STEWART, MARLENE METZGER, financial planning practitioner, insurance agent; b. Portland, Oreg., Nov. 1, 1937; d. Eddie Charles and Helen M. (Grant) Metzger; m. Robert W. Stewart, Aug. 1, 1964 (dec. Jan. 1967); m. Melvin N. McBurney, Feb. 14, 1985. BA, U. Oreg., 1959; MA, U. Tex., El Paso, 1971. CLU, CFP. Exec. dir. Summer 72 Youth Com. Office of Mayor, Portland, 1972; registered rep. Mut. Life Ins. Co. N.Y., Portland, 1973-76, Prudential Life Ins. Co., Portland, 1976-77; ptnr. N.W. Fin. Planning, Portland, 1977-79; pres. Horizons Unltd. Fin. Planning, Portland, 1979-86; prin. EMR Fin. Adv. Svcs., Inc., Portland, 1986-89; registered rep. KMS Fin. Svcs., Inc., Portland, 1979—; owner Stewart Fin. Group, 1991—. Mem.-at-large nat. bd. YMCA's, 1971-73; bd. dirs. Met. YMCA, Portland, 1971-75; bd. dirs. YWCA, Portland, 1989-92, treas., 1990-92, chmn. investment com.; chmn. planned giving com. Arthritis Found., 1984-86; mem. planned giving com. Willamette Falls Hosp. Found., 2007—. Bill Bottler scholar Portland chpt. CLU and Chartered Fin. Cons., 1981. Mem. Fin. Planning Assn., Oreg. Soc. Inst. CFP's (treas. 1985-86, Internat. Assn. Fin. Planners (pres. Oreg. chpt. 1987-88), Nat. Assn. Ins. & Fin. Adv., Soc. of Fin. Svc. Profls. and Portland Chpt. (treas. Portland chpt. 1985-86), Fin. Planning Assn. (mem. nat. task force on career devel. 2002), Estate Planning Coun. Portland, Assocs. Good Samaritan (steering com., chmn. 1991-92), Rotary (past chmn. World Cmty. Svc. com. 1998-2000). Republican. Presbyterian. Avocations: swimming, travel, reading, gardening. Office: 5901 SW Macadam Ave Ste 135 Portland OR 97239 Office Phone: 503-224-2034. E-mail: stewfg@aol.com.

STEWART, MARTHA KOSTYRA, entrepreneur, lecturer, author; b. Jersey City, Aug. 3, 1941; d. Edward and Martha (Ruszkowski) Kostyra; m. Andy Stewart, July 1, 1961 (div. 1990); 1 child, Alexis Gilbert. BA European History and Archtl. History, Barnard Coll. Former model; former stockbroker NYC; former profl. caterer; mag. owner, editor-in-chief Martha Stewart Living, 1990—97; CEO Martha Stewart Living Omnimedia, 1997—2003, chief creative officer, 2003—04, chmn., 1997—2004, founding editl. dir., 2004—. Lifestyle cons. for K-Mart Corp., 1987; bd. dirs., NYSE, 2002-04. Host (TV show) Martha Stewart Living, 1993-2004, The Apprentice: Martha Stewart, 2005, (TV talk show) Martha 2005-; Author: (with Elizabeth Hawes) Entertaining, 1982, Weddings, 1987; Martha Stewart Hors d'Oeurvres: The Creation and Presentation of Fabulous Finger Food, 1984, Martha Stewart's Pies and Tarts, 1985, Martha Stewart's Quick Cook Menus: Fifty-two Meals You Can Make in Under an Hour, 1988, The Wedding Planner, 1988, Martha Stewart's Gardening: Month by Month, 1991, Martha Stewart's New Old House: Restoration, Renovation, Decoration, 1992, Martha Stewart's Christmas, 1993, Martha Stewart's Menus for Entertaining, 1994, Holidays, 1994, Good Things: The Best of Martha Stewart Living, 1997, Four Seasons of Great Menus to Make Every Day, 1997, Hors D'Oeuvres Handbook, 1999, The Best of Martha Stewart Living: Weddings, 1999, The Barefoot Contessa Cookbook: Secrets from the East Hampton Specialty Food Store for Simple Food and Party Platters You Can Make at Home, 1999, (with Ina Garten) Favorite Comfort Food, 1999, The Martha Stewart Living Cookbook, 2000, Halloween: The Best of Martha Stewart Living, 2001, Classic Crafts and Recipes Inspired by the Songs of Christmas, 2002, Martha Stewart Living 2003, Recipes, 2002, Simple Home Solutions, 2004, The Martha Rules, 2005, Martha Stewart's Baking Handbook, 2005, Martha Stewart's Homekeeping Handbook: The Essential Guide to Caring for Everything in Your Home, 2006; contbr. (magazine) Blueprint: Design Your Life, 2006-; appeared in semi-monthly cooking segment on Today Show; syndicated columnist, NY Times. Named one of World's 100 Most Influential People, Time Mag., 2005, 50 Most Powerful Women in Bus., Fortune mag., 2006. Office: 10 Saugatuck Ave Westport CT 06880-5720 also: care Susan Magrino Agy 40 W 57th St Fl 31 New York NY 10019-4001

STEWART, MELBOURNE GEORGE, JR., physicist, researcher; b. Detroit, Sept. 30, 1927; s. Melbourne George and Ottilie (Tuholke) S.; m. Charlotte L. Ford, Jan. 23, 1954; children— Jill K., John H., Kevin G. AB, U. Mich., 1949, MS, 1950, PhD, 1955. Research assoc. dept. physics AEC, Ames Lab., Iowa State U., 1955-56, asst. prof., 1956-62, assoc. prof., 1962-63; prof. Wayne State U., Detroit, 1963-94, prof. emeritus, 1994—, chmn. dept. physics, 1963-73, assoc. provost for faculty relations, 1973-86; hon. research fellow Univ. Coll., London, 1986-87,93. Editorial bd.: Wayne State U. Press, 1969-73. Served with AUS, 1946-47. Mem. Am. Phys. Soc., AAAS, Sigma Xi, Phi Beta Kappa. Office: Dept Physics Wayne State U Detroit MI 48202

STEWART, MICHAEL B., lawyer, mechanical and aerospace engineer; b. Royal Oak, Mich., Nov. 5, 1963; s. Colin M. and Jacqueline P. Stewart; children: Elizabeth and Caitlin. BSME, U. Mich, 1987, BA in English, 1987, MS in Aerospace Engring., 1988, JD, 1991. Assoc. Dykema Gossett PLLC, Bloomfield Hills, Mich., 1991-96; founding and mnging. ptnr. Rader, Fishman & Grauer PLLC, Bloomfield Hills, 1996—. Contbr. articles to profl. jours. Named 40 Under 40 Honoree Crain's Detroit Bus., 1998. Mem. ABA, Intellectual Property Law Assn., Mich. Patent Law Assn., Mich. Bar Assn., Oakland County Bar Assn. (chmn. continuing legal edn. subcom. for IP com. 1998), Optimists (bd. dirs. 1993-97), Delta Theta Phi (dean., bd. govs., Detroit alumni senate). Avocations: bicycling, woodworking. Office: Rader Fishman & Grauer PLLC 39533 Woodward Ave Ste 140 Bloomfield Hills MI 48304-5098 Business E-Mail: mbs@raderfishman.com.

STEWART, MICHAEL GLENN, otolaryngologist, educator; b. Bowling Green, Ky., Sept. 17, 1962; s. Michael Joseph and Barbara (Weisser) S. B in Engring. summa cum laude, Vanderbilt U., 1984; MD, Johns Hopkins U., 1988; MPH, U. Tex., 1996; Gen. Surgery, Baylor Coll. Medicine, 1990, Otolaryngology, 1994. Diplomate Am. Bd. Otolaryngology. Asst. prof. Baylor Coll. Medicine, Houston, 1994-99, assoc. prof., 1999—2005, dir. residency edn. dept. otolaryngology, 1996—2005, asst. dean clin. affairs, 1998-2000, gen. dir. affil. med. svc., 1999—2005, assoc. dean clin. affairs, 2000—05; prof., chmn. Dept. Otorhinolaryngology Weill Cornell Med. Coll., NYC, 2005—; otorhinolaryngologist-in-chief NY Presbyn. Hosp., 2005—. Chief otolaryngology Ben Taub Gen. Hosp., 1994-2005; chmn. med. bd. Harris County Hosp. Dist., Houston, 1999-2000; sr. examiner Am. Bd. Otolaryngology. Editor Rev. Head and Neck, 1994—; reviewer Archive Otolaryngology-Head and Neck, 1997—, Jour. Trauma, 1998—, Otolaryngology-Head and Neck Surgery, 1998—, Cancer, 2001—; assoc. editor, mem. editl. bd. Am. Jour. Rhinology, 2003—; mem. editl. bd. Archives of Otolaryngology-Head and Neck Surgery, 2005—. Recipient Outstanding Clin. Rsch. award Kelsey-Seybold Found., 1992, 93, Houston Disting. Surgeon award Assn. Perioperative Nurses, 2005. Fellow: ACS, Am. Rhinologic Soc., Am. Laryngol., Rhinol. and Otol. Soc., Am. Acad. Otolaryngology Head and Neck Surgery (Disting. Svc. award 2004); mem.: Assn. Acad. Depts. Otolaryngology (sec.-treas.), Soc. Univ. Otolaryngologists (pres.-elect). Office Phone: 646-962-4777. Business E-Mail: mgs2002@med.cornell.edu.

STEWART, MICHAEL MCFADDEN, speech professional; b. Eupora, Miss., Aug. 24, 1938; s. Judge Ernest and Billie Rivers (McFadden) S.; m. Barbara Ann Dickerson, June 2, 1962; children: Michael Jr., Mark Robert (dec. Dec. 1997). BS, La. State U., 1961. Registered corp. coach. Cons. E.K. Williams & Co., Birmingham, Ala., 1964-66, br. mgr., 1966-68, Miami, Fla., 1968-69, Marcoin, Inc., Balt., 1969-73, dist. mgr. Falls Church, Va., 1973-74; v.p. Marcoin Western Ops., Inc., Houston, 1974-77; dir., v.p. Marcoin, Inc., Atlanta, 1977-85; ptnr. Cherokee/G & S Assocs., Atlanta, 1985-88; pres. Stewart & Stewart, Inc., Dunwoody, Ga., 1988—, The Sales Power Resource Group, Inc., Atlanta, 1991-95. Cons., speaker AMA, NYC, 1989—, Duffy-Vinet Inst., Langhorne, Pa., 1987-92, The Sullivan Group, Guilford, Conn., 1990-92; guest speaker SBA, Bell South Success Symposium Series, 1990-91. Author: How to Get Started with a Small Business Computer, 1984, Quality Customer Service, 1990, Using Your Financial Statements to Boost Your Bottom Line Profits, 1990, Computerizing Your Business, 1991, The Magic of Customer Service, 1991, Bring Home the Bacon, 1992, Customer Service Excellence: How to Implement a Corporate-wide Program, 1992, Strategic Relationship Selling, 1992, Transition into Sales Management, 1992, Sales Managememt Call Reluctance Workshop, 1992, Negotiating with Style, 1992, Meeting Today's Competitive Challenges, 1992, Creative Management in Tough Economic Times, 1993, Relationship Empowered Technical Selling, 1993, Consultative Relationship Selling, 1993, Customer-Centered Sales Management Leadership, 1993, Customer Centered Selling, 1993, Being Different in a Niche Market, 1993, Moving, Shaking and Prospecting, 1993, 50/250 The Smart Way, 1993, Customer-Centered Relationship Selling, 1994, Working Sucessfully with Others, 1994, Fundamentals of Quality Customer Service, 1994, Sales Are The Life-Blood Service is the Heart Beat, 1994, Customer-Centered Value Selling, 1994, Customer-Centered Sales Management, 1994, Make the Number by Selling Value, 1995, Hiring Smart, 1995, Customer-Centered Sales Management, 1995, Live the Spirit, 1996, Sell Value, Not Price, 1996; contbg. author: Chicken Soup for the Soul at Work, 1996, Relationship Centered Value Selling, 1997, Professional Sales Skills, 1997, Sales Negotiation for Higher Profits, 1998; contbg. author: Reach for the Stars, 1998, Close More Sales!, 1999, Close More Sales With Premise, 2000, Developing A Productive Sales Orientation, 2000, Motivational Sales Management, 2000, Basic Sales Training Boot Camp, 2001, DNA of Sales Success: Hiring and Motivating Blue-Chip Sales Persons, 2002, Leading Explosive Growth-Encouraging Passionate Sales Performance, 2002, others; co-author: Embracing Change-Understanding and Managing Transitions in Life and Work, 2002, Target Your Time For Sales Success, 2005, The Dirty Dozen: 12 Killer Mistakes That Murder Sales, 2005, 24 Karat Sales Standards: Two Dozen Gold Nuggets to Help You Sell More New Business, 2005, Plan Every Call to Sell More New Business, 2006; contbr. articles to profl. jours. Fin. officer Atlanta Colts Youth Assn., 1979; vol. speaker Am. Cancer Soc., 1994—. Capt. U.S. Army, 1961-64. Recipient Silver award Carlson Learning Co., Mpls., 1990, numerous other awards. Mem. Ga. Speakers Assn. (past pres., past dir., Mem. of Yr. 1996), Nat. Spkrs. Assn. (cert. speaking profl.), Dunwoody Country Club, Dunwoody Gridiron Club (pres. 1981), Lambda Chi Alpha. Episcopalian. Avocation: golf. Home: 490 Tavern Cir Atlanta GA 30350-4455 Office Phone: 770-512-0022. Personal E-mail: mike@stewartsalesdynamics.com.

STEWART, MILTON ROY, lawyer; b. Clovis, N.Mex., Dec. 16, 1945; s. Virgil Maurice and E. Marie (Collins) S. BA, Ind. U., 1968, JD summa cum laude, 1971. Bar: Oreg. 1971, U.S. Ct. Appeals (9th cir.) 1971, U.S. Dist. Ct. (no. dist.) Oreg. 1971. Assoc. Davies, Biggs et al, Portland, Oreg., 1971-75; v.p., gen. counsel U.S. Datacorp, Portland, 1975-77; pvt. practice Portland, 1977-86; bus. devel. ptnr. Davis, Wright, Tremaine, Portland, 1987—2006; spl. counsel AIG Corp., NY, 2007—. Bd. dir. Lex Mundi assn. internat. law firms. Past chmn., mem emeritus Oreg. chpt. Nat. Multisclerosis Soc., 1994—, immediate past mem.; bd. dirs. Nat. Multiple Sclerosis Soc.; emeritus bd. visitors Ind. U. Law Sch.; active Bd. Ind. U. Found. Capt. U.S. Army, 1968-78 State Farm Found. fellow, 1970, John H. Edwards fellow Ind. U. Found., 1971. Mem. Oreg. State Bar Assn., Wash. State Bar Assn., Multnomah Athletic Club, Astoria Golf and Country Club. Office: Davis Wright Tremaine 1300 SW 5th Ave Ste 2200 Portland OR 97201-5667 Business E-Mail: miltstewart@dwt.com.

STEWART, MIZELL, III, editor; b. Ohio, 1966; m. Valerie Morgan-Stewart. BA, Bowling Green State U., Huron, Ohio, 1991. Reporter Springfield News-Sun, Ohio; reporter & editor Dayton Daily News, Ohio; local news editor Akron Beacon Jour., Ohio, 1994—2000, mng. editor, 2006, editor, 2006—; mng. editor Tallahassee Dem., Fla., 2000—03, editor & v.p., 2003—05. Office: Akron Beacon Journal PO Box 640 Akron OH 44309-0640 Office Phone: 330-996-3700. Office Fax: 330-376-9235. *

STEWART, MURRAY BAKER, retired lawyer; b. Muskogee, Okla., May 16, 1931; s. Francis and Fannie Penelope (Murray) S.; m. Roseanna Furgason; children: Melinda, Jeffrey, Cheryl. BA, U. Okla., 1953, JD, 1955; postgrad., Georgetown U., 1958-59. Bar: Okla. 1955; CLU, ChFC. Judge adv. U.S. Army, 1955-59; ptnr. Stewart & Stewart, Tulsa and Muskogee, Okla., 1955, 62-72; asst. v.p. First Nat. Bank and Trust Co. of Tulsa, 1959-62, 77-78; mem. Hutchins, Stewart, Stewart & Elmore, Tulsa, 1972-77; atty. cons. advanced underwriting Metlife Ins. Co., NYC, 1978-94; assoc. Metlife Securities, Inc., SEC Registered Investment Advisors, 1984-94; of counsel Brumley & Bishop, Tulsa, 1997-99; ret., 1999. Cons. on Am. Indian books; lectr. in field. Contbr. articles to profl. and hist. jours.; prodr. texts and videos on history, investment and bus. Fellow Life Mgmt. Inst.; mem. Okla. Bar Assn., Okla. Indian Bar Assn., Sons Confederate Vets. (judge advocate Army of Trans-Mississippi 1998-2000, Kans. divsn. 2002-05), Civil War Roundtable Tulsa, Sons Union Vets. Civil War. Office: PO Box 1000 Broken Arrow OK 74013-1000

STEWART, PAMELA WIDDUP, language educator, musician; b. Waynesburg, Pa., May 11, 1952; d. Howard Dawson Widdup and Clara Kay Blair; m. William Berns Stewart Jr., May 27, 1972; children: Sean Timothy, Christopher James, Patrick Howard. BS in Edn., Indiana U. of Pa., 1973; MS in Edn., U. Dayton, Ohio, 1979. Lic. secondary sch. counselor Pa. State Dept. Edn., 1987. Tchr. German and English Brooke HS, Wellsburg, W.Va., 1974—79; tchr. German Trinity HS, Washington, Pa., 1986—87; counselor McGuffey Mid. Sch., Claysville, Pa., 1987—2004; tchr. German McGuffey HS, 2005—. Organist Washington St. Meth. Ch., Waynesburg, 1968—72, Newlonsburg Presbyn. Ch., Murrysville, Pa., 1983—84, Claysville Presbyn. Ch., 1984—87; organist, freelance musician various churches in Washington County, Pa., 1987—95; organist Ctr. Presbyn. Ch., McMurray, Pa., 1995—96, Trinity Presbyn. Ch., McDonald, Pa., 1996, Faith United Presbyn. Ch., Washington, 1996—; charter pianist, organist Wahington Cmty. Arts Choir, 2004—06. Deacon Ch. of the Covenant, Washington, 1989—91; ad hoc or acting mem. of worship and music coms. Faith United Presbyn. Ch., Washington, 1996. Mem.: McGuffey Edn. Assn., Pa. State Edn. Assn., Am. Guild Organists. Presbyterian. Avocations: cooking, photography, travel, gardening. Home: 788 Rural Valley Rd Washington PA 15301 Office: McGuffey HS 86 McGuffey Dr Claysville PA 15323 Home Phone: 724-345-3551; Office Phone: 724-948-3328. Personal E-mail: bstewart@libcom.com. Business E-Mail: stewardp@mcguffey.k12.pa.us.

STEWART, PATRICIA CARRY, foundation administrator; b. Bklyn., May 19, 1928; d. William J. and Eleanor (Murphy) Carry; m. Charles Thorp Stewart, May 30, 1976. Student, U. Paris, 1948—49; BA, Cornell U., 1950. Fgn. corr. Irving Trust Co., NYC, 1950-51; with Janeway Rsch. Co., NYC, 1951-60, sec., treas., 1955-60; with Buckner & Co. and successor firms, NYC, 1961-73, ptnr., 1962-70, v.p., treas., 1970-71, pres., treas., 1971-73, Knight, Carry, Bliss & Co., Inc., NYC, 1971-73, G. Tsai & Co., Inc., 1973; v.p. Edna McConnell Clark Found. Inc., 1974-92. Dir. Cmty. Found. Palm Beach and Martin Counties, 1993-2001, chair, 1998, 2000; allied mem. N.Y. Stock Exch., 1962-73; past mem. nominating com. Am. Stock Exch., N.Y. Stock Exch., N.Y.C. Fin. Svcs. Corp.; dir. emeritus, past chmn. Investor Responsibility Rsch. Ctr. Trustee emerita, vice chair Cornell U.; mem. bd. life overseers Cornell Med. Coll.; mem. vis. com. Grad. Sch Bus., Harvard U., 1974-80; bd. dirs. NOW Legal Def. and Edn. Fund, 1984-92, Women in Founds./Corp. Philanthropy, 1980-86; v.p. fin. com. Women's Forum, 1982-90; vice chmn. CUNY, 1976-80; bd. dirs. United Way of Tri-State, 1977-81, Inst. for Edn. and Rsch. on Women and Work; voting mem. Blue Cross and Blue Shield Greater N.Y., 1975-82; trustee N.Y. State 4-H Found., 1970-76, Intenrt. Inst. Rural Reconstrn.,

1974-79; mem. N.Y.C. panel White House Fellows, 1976-78; mem. bus. adv. coun. The Hosp. Chaplaincy. Recipient Elizabeth Cutter Morrow award YWCA, 1977, Catalyst award Women Dirs. in Corps., 1978, Trustee medal CUNY, 1983, Acomplishment award Wings Club N.Y. 1984, Women's Funding Coalition Innovators for Women$hare award, 1986, Banking Industry Achievement award Nat. Assn. Bank Women, 1987, Cert. Disting. Accomplishments Barnard Coll., 1989; named to YWCA Acad. Women Achievers. Mem. Fin. Women's Assn. N.Y., Country Club of Fla. (bd. dirs.), Univ. Club (N.Y.C), Gullane Golf Club (Scotland), North Berwick Golf Club (Scotland), Dunbar Golf Club (Scotland), St. Andrews Club (Delray Beach, Fla.), Phi Beta Phi. Home and Office: 2613 N Ocean Blvd Delray Beach FL 33483-7367 also: Halfland Barns North Berwick EH395PW Scotland Home Phone: 561-278-5387. Personal E-mail: stewartpc@aol.com.

STEWART, PATRICK, actor; b. Mirfield, Eng., July 13, 1940; s. Alfred and Gladys (Barraclough) S.; m. Sheila Falconer, Mar. 3, 1966 (div. 1990); 2 children; m. Wendy Neuss, Aug. 25, 2000 (div. 2003). Trained, Bristol Old Vic Theatre Sch. Actor: (theatre) Treasure Island (U.K., debut), 1959, (U.S.) A Midsummer Night's Dream (Broadway debut), 1970, A Christmas Carol, 1991, 92, 94; (TV series) Star Trek: The Next Generation, 1987-94, Eleventh Hour, 2006, (narrator) High Spirits with the Ghostman, 2005, (mini series) Fall of Eagles, 1974, I, Claudius, 1977, Tinker, Sailor, Soldier, Spy, 1979, Maybury, 1981, Smiley's People, 1982, Playing Shakespeare, 1983, When the Lion Roars, 1992, (voice) 500 Nations, 1995, Mysterious Island, 2005, (TV movies) The Gathering Storm, 1974, Anthony and Cleopatra, 1974 (Olivier award best supporting actor), North and South, 1975, The Madness, 1976, Hamlet, Prince of Denmark, 1980, Little Lord Fauntleroy, 1980, John Paul II, 1984, The Devil's Disciple, 1987, Death Train, 1993, In Search of Dr. Seuss, 1994, (also co-prodr.) The Canterville Ghost, 1996, Moby Dick, 1997, Safe House, 1998, (voice) Animal Farm, 1999, (also exec. prodr.) A Christmas Carol, 1999, (also exec. prodr.) King of Texas, 2002, The Lion in Winter, 2003; host on Saturday Night Live, 1994, (films) Hennessy, 1975, Hedda, 1975, Excalibur, 1981, The Plague Dogs (voice) 1982, Dune, 1984, Uindii, 1984, Lifeforce, 1985, Code Name: Emerald, 1985, Wild Geese II, 1985, The Doctor and the Devils, 1985, Lady Jane, 1986, L.A. Story, 1991, Robin Hood: Men in Tights, 1993, Gunmen, 1994, Star Trek: Generations, 1994, The Pagemaster, 1994 (voice), Jeffrey, 1995, Let It Me Be (aka Love Dance), 1995, Star Trek: First Contact, 1996, Conspiracy Theory, 1997, Safe House, 1997, Dad Savage, 1997, Master Minds, 1997, (voice) Prince of Egypt, 1998, X-Men, 2000, (voice) Jimmy Neutron: Boy Genius, 2001, Star Trek: Nemesis, 2002, X-Men 2, 2003, (voice) Back to Gaya, 2004, Steamboy, 2004, The Game of Their Lives, 2005, (voice) Chicken Little, 2005, X-Men: The Last Stand, 2006, TMNT, 2007; assoc. prodr. Star Trek IX: Insurrection, 1998; assoc. artist with Royal Shakespeare Co., 1967—; recording: Prokofiev: Peter and the Wolf (Grammy award best spoken word album for children 1996). Office: Flying Freehold Productions 233 Wilshire Blvd Ste 600 Santa Monica CA 90401 also: William Morris Agy 151 El Camino Dr Beverly Hills CA 90212 *

STEWART, PAUL ARTHUR, pharmaceutical company executive; b. Greensburg, Ind., Sept. 28, 1955; s. John Arthur and Alberta Jeannette (Densford) S.; m. Susan Rhodes, Dec. 20, 1975; children: John Rhodes, Daniel Robbins. BS, Purdue U., 1976; MBA, Harvard U., 1987. Grad. asst. Purdue U., West Lafayette, Ind., 1977; asst. treas. Stewart Seeds Inc., Greensburg, 1997-82, sec., treas., 1982-84; cons. The Boston Cons. Group Inc., Chgo., 1986; founder, owner PASCO Group, mgmt. and computer cons., aircraft leasing, 1979-87; mgr. bus. planning agrichems. Eli Lilly & Co., Indpls., 1987-88, dist. sales mgr. agrichems., 1989-90, tech. acquisition mgr. med. devices and diagnostics divsn., 1990-92; dir. mktg. info. and bus. devel. IVAC Corp. subs. Eli Lilly & Co., 1992-94, advisor corp. fin. and investment banking, 1994-96; mgr. global bus. devel. (animal health) Eli Lilly & Co., 1996—. Author: (nonfiction) A Harvard MBA's Advice to His Sons, 2005. Mem. Greensburg-Decatur County Bd. Airport Commrs., 1980-85, pres., 1980-81, 83; mem. Decatur County Data Processing Bd., 1982-85; deacon 2d Presbyn. Ch. Indpls., 1991-92, elder, 1996-99; bd. dirs. Friends of Nat. Inst. Nursing Rsch., NIH, 1995-98, Park Tudor Sch., Indpls., 1997-2003. Mem.: Indpls. Legal Aid Soc. (bd. dirs. 2004—), Harvard Bus. Sch. Alumni Assn. (bd. dirs. 1999—2003, v.p. 2001—03), Alpha Gamma Rho. Republican. Presbyterian. Office: Eli Lilly & Co Lilly Corp Ctr Indianapolis IN 46285-0001 Office Phone: 317-277-6120. Personal E-mail: pstewart@mba1987.hbs.edu.

STEWART, RICHARD BURLESON, law educator; b. Cleve., Feb. 12, 1940; s. Richard Siegfreid and Ruth Dysert (Staten) Stewart; m. Alice Peck Fales, May 13, 1967 (div. June 1992); children: William, Paul, Elizabeth; m. Jane Laura Bloom, Sept. 20, 1992; children: Emily, Ian. AB, Yale U., 1961; MA (Rhodes scholar), Oxford U., Eng., 1963; LLB, Harvard U., 1966; D (hon.), Erasmus U., Rotterdam, 1993, U. Rome La Sapienza, 2005. Bar: DC 1968, U.S. Supreme Ct. 1971. Law clk. to Hon. Potter Stewart U.S. Supreme Ct., 1966-67; assoc. Covington & Burling, Washington, 1967-71; asst. prof. law Harvard U., 1971-75, prof., 1975-82, Byrne prof. adminstrv. law, 1982-89, assoc. dean, 1984-86; asst. atty. gen. environment and natural resources div. Dept. Justice, Washington, 1989-91; prof. law NYU Law Sch., NYC, 1992-94, Emily Kempin prof. law, 1994—2002, John Edward Sexton prof. law, 2002—, univ. prof., 2002—; of counsel Sidley & Austin, 1992—. Spl. counsel U.S. Senate Watergate Com., 1974; vis. prof. U. Calif., Berkeley Law Sch., 1979—80, U. Chgo. Law Sch., 1986—87, Georgetown U., 1991—92, Europen U. Inst., 1995; dir. Ctr. Environ. and Land Use Law, 1992—, Health Effects Inst.; mem. adv. bd. Environ. Def. Author: (book) The Reformation of American Administrative Law (in Chinese), 2002; author: (with P. Menell) Environmental Law and Policy, 1994; author: (with S. Breyer, C. Sunstein and M. Spitzer) Administrative Law and Regulation, 1979, Administrative Law and Regulation, 5th edit., 2002; author: (with E. Rehbinder) Integration Through Law: Environmental Protection Policy, 1985, Integration Through Law: Environmental Protection Policy, paper edit., 1987; author: (with R. Revesz) Markets v. Environment?, 1995; author: (with R. Revesz and P. Sands) Environment, the Economy, and Sustainable Development, 2001; author: (with J. Wiener) Reconstructing Climate Policy, 2003; editor (with R. Revesz): (book) Analyzing Superfund: Economics, Science, and Law, 1995. Fellow: Am. Acad. Arts and Scis.; mem.: ABA, Am. Law Inst. Office: NYU Law Sch 40 Washington Sq S New York NY 10012-1099 Home Phone: 212-337-0662; Office Phone: 212-998-6170. Business E-Mail: stewartr@juris.law.nyu.edu.

STEWART, RICHARD DONALD, internist, educator, writer; b. Lakeland, Fla., Dec. 26, 1926; s. LeRoy Hepburn and Zoa Irene (Hachet) S.; m. Mary Leeuw, June 14, 1952; children: R. Scot, Gregory D., Mary E. AB, U. Mich., 1951, MD, 1955, MPH, 1962; MA, U. Wis. Milw., 1979; PhD in English, U. Wis., Milw., 1997. Diplomate Am. Bd. Internal Medicine, Am. Bd. Med. Toxicology, Acad. Toxicol. Scis. Intern Saginaw (Mich.) Gen. Hosp., 1955-56; resident in internal medicine U. Mich. Med. Ctr., Ann Arbor, 1959-62; dir. med. rsch. sect. Dow Chem. Co., Midland, Mich., 1962-66; staff physician Midland Hosp., 1962-66; assoc. prof. preventive medicine Med. Coll. Wis., Milw., 1966-68, prof., chmn. dept. environ. medicine, 1968—78, prof. emergency med., 1989—91, adj. prof. dept. pharmacology and toxicology, 1978—. Cons. Children's Hosp. Wis., 1989-93, Internal Medicine St. Mary's Hosp., Racine, Wis., 1983-93; prof., dir. med. toxicology fellowship Dept. Emergency Medicine Milw. Regional Med. Ctr., 1989-91; sr. attending staff, 1967-90; staff Internal Medicine St. Luke's Hosp., Racine, 1983-93; med. dir. Poison Control Ctr. Southeastern Wis., 1989-93; corp. med. advisor S.C. Johnson & Son, Inc., Racine, 1971-78, corp. med. dir., 1978-89. Author: (med. biography) Leper Priest of Molokai, 2000. Mem. adv. med. staff Milw. Fire Dept., 1975—. Cadet USAF, 1945-46. Fellow ACP, Am. Coll. Occupl. Medicine, Am. Acad. Clin. Toxicology, Acad. Toxicological Scis.; mem. AMA, Soc. Toxicology, Wis. State Med. Soc., Racine Acad. Medicine, Rotary Internat., Phi Theta Kappa, Phi Kappa Phi, Sigma Tau Delta. Achievements include invention of medical devices including the hollow fiber artificial kidney and capillary artificial lung; being leader of team that performed first human dialyses with the Hollow Fiber Artificial Kidney, beginning Aug.4, 1967. This artificial kidney is universally used for long-term dialysis. Avocations: hiking, literature, creative writing. Home and Office: 5337 Wind Point Rd Racine WI 53402-2322 Office Phone: 262-639-6483.

STEWART, RICHARD EDWIN, insurance consulting company executive; b. Washington, Nov. 4, 1933; s. Irvin and Florence Elsie (Dezendorf) S.; m. Barbara Lewis Dickson, Oct. 29, 1993. BA, W.Va. U., 1955; BA (Rhodes scholar), Oxford U., Eng., 1957, MA, 1961; JD, Harvard, 1959. Bar: N.Y. 1960. Assoc. Royall, Koegel & Rogers, NYC, 1960-63; asst. counsel to Gov. of N.Y., 1963-64, 1st asst. counsel, 1965-66; supr. ins. N.Y. State Ins. Dept., 1967-70; sr. v.p., gen. counsel First Nat. City Bank, NYC, 1971-72; sr. v.p., dir. Chubb & Son Inc., NYC, 1973-81; sr. v.p. Chubb Corp., NYC, 1973-81, CFO, 1974-81; gov. N.Y. Ins. Exch., NYC, 1979-81; chmn. Stewart Econs., Inc., NYC, 1981-90, Chapel Hill, NC, 1990—2005, San Francisco, 2005—. Mem. adv. com. HUD, 1968-72; mem. Adminstrv. Conf. U.S., 1970-74; bd. dirs. Am. Arbitration Assn., 1970-80; mem. UN panel experts on Transnational Bank failure, 1991. Co-author: Automobile Insurance...For Whose Benefit?, 1970, Watergate: Implications for Responsible Government, 1974, Medical Malpractice, 1977, Managing Insurer Insolvency, 1988, Insurance Insolvency Guarantees, 1990, A Brief History of Underwriting Cycles, 1991, Niche Insurance Companies, 1997, Information Technology and Insurance Agent Licensing, 1998, The Loss of the Certainty Effect, 2002, Managing Insurer Insolvency, 2003; author: Reason and Regulation, 1972, Insurance and Insurance Regulation, 1980, Arbitration and Insurance without the Common Law, 2004, The Attorney General, the SEC and the Commissioners of Insurance, 2007. Trustee Coll. Ins., N.Y., 1970-78, Am. Coll. Life Underwriters, 1990-93; mem. Mayor's Com. on Taxi Regulation, 1979-82, ABA Com. to Improve Liability Ins. System, 1989; mem. panel experts on transnat. bank failure UN, 1991; mem. spl. panel U.S. Senate Com. on Presdl. Campaign Practice, 1974. Served with AUS, 1959. Mem. Nat. Acad. Pub. Adminstrn., Nat. Acad. Social Ins., Cosmos Club of Washington, Century Club of N.Y.C., Phi Beta Kappa Assn. Home and Office: One Embarcadero Ctr Ste 500 San Francisco CA 94111 Office Phone: 415-315-1771. Business E-Mail: res@stewarteconomics.com.

STEWART, RICHARD WILLIAMS, lawyer; b. Harrisburg, Pa., Aug. 21, 1948; s. Alexander H. and M. Winifred (Williams) S.; m. Mary A. Simmonds, June 7, 1975; 1 child, Anne W. AB cum laude, Franklin and Marshall Coll., 1970; JD, Duke U., 1973. Bar: Pa. 1973, U.S. Dist. Ct. (mid. dist.) Pa. 1975, U.S. Tax Ct. 1984. Assoc. Stone & Sajer, New Cumberland, Pa., 1973-77; ptnr. Stone, Sajer & Stewart, New Cumberland, 1977-87, Johnson, Duffie, Stewart & Weidner, Lemoyne, Pa., 1987—. Solicitor West Shore Sch. Dist., Lemoyne, Pa., 1977-93, No. York County Sch. Dist., Dillsburg, Pa., 1984—, Camp Hill Sch. Dist., 1986—, Fairview Twp., 1987-98; v.p. Cedar Cliff Abstract Agy., 1980-87; v.p. Secured Land Transfers, Inc., Camp Hill, Pa., 1985-2000, pres., 2000-05; pres. Lawyers Realty LLC, 2006—. Chmn. Cumberland County Rep. Com., 1981-84; mem. Rep. State Com. Pa., 1990—. Mem. ABA, Pa. Bar Assn. (house of dels. 2004-), Cumberland County Bar Assn. (pres.2004), Supreme Ct. of Pa. (disciplinary bd. 1998—, vice chmn. 2003, chmn. 2004), Ctrl. Pa. Estate Planning Coun. (bd. dirs. 1983-85), Pa. Sch. Solicitors Assn. (pres. 1995), Rotary (bd. dirs. West Shore). Presbyterian. Home: 1811 Warren St New Cumberland PA 17070-1148 Office: 301 Market St Lemoyne PA 17043-1628 Office Phone: 717-761-4540.

STEWART, RITA JOAN, academic administrator; b. Muncie, Ind., June 6, 1945; d. John Marion and Crystalee Masterson; children: Jon Lewis, Robert Forrest. BS, Ball State U., 1967, MA, 1974. Tchr. Blue River H.S., Mt. Summit, Ind., 1968-69, Sunnyside Elem. Sch., New Castle, Ind., 1967-68; copywriter, announcer Sta. WTIM, Taylorville, Ill., 1974-75; dir. Kitselman Conf. Ctr. Ball State U., Muncie, Ind., 1978-2000, dir. conf. and spl. events, 2000—. Contbr. articles to profl. jours. Precinct committeewoman Henry County Dem. Party, New Castle, Ind., 1969-70; precinct chmn. March of Dimes, New Castle, Ind., 1974-75; chmn. edn. com. West Viwe Sch. Coun., Muncie, 1987-88; sec., bd. dirs. PAL Club, Muncie, 1988-93; pres., bd. dirs. Altrusa Club Found., Muncie, 1997-98, v.p., 2001-01, pres., 2002. Mem.: AAUW (v.p. 1984—85), Ind. Conf. Dirs. Assn., Assn. Collegiate Conf. and Event Dirs. Internat. (dir. region 8 1999—2000, pres. elect 2006—07, internat. bd. dirs., pres. 2007—, Mentor Yr. award 2004), Altrusa Club of Muncie (pres. 2002—03), Kappa Delta Pi (Disting. Svc. award 1995). Methodist. Office: Ball State U Confs and Spl Events Muncie IN 47306 Home: # 1-203 4501 N Wheeling Ave Muncie IN 47304-1277 Office Phone: 765-285-1396. Office Fax: 765-285-5457. Business E-Mail: conferences@bsu.edu.

STEWART, ROBERT S., construction executive; B, MBA, U. Wash. With Weyerhaeuser Co., 1977—2000; sr. v.p. strategic planning and mktg. Centex Corp., Dallas, 2000—05, sr. v.p. strategy and corp. devel., 2005—. Bd. dirs. Tex. Bus. and Edn. Coalition. Office: Centex Corp PO Box 199000 Dallas TX 75219-9000 Office Phone: 214-981-5000. Office Fax: 214-981-6859. *

STEWART, ROD (RODERICK DAVID STEWART), singer; b. North London, Eng., Jan. 10, 1945; m. Alana Collins, Apr. 6, 1979 (div. 1984); children: Kimberly, Sean; child with Kelly Emberg: Ruby Rachel; m. Rachel Hunter, Dec. 15, 1990 (div. Nov. 2, 2006); children: Renée, Liam; m. Penny Lancaster, June 16, 2007; 1 child, Alistair Wallace Leader singer Jeff Beck Group, 1968—69, The Faces, 1969—75; solo artist, 1969—. Singer: albums (with Jeff Beck Group) Truth, 1968, Beck-Ola, 1969; (with The Faces) The First Step, 1970, Long Player, 1971, A Nod Is As Good as a Wink...To a Blind Horse, 1971, Ooh La La, 1973, Coast to Coast/Overture & Beginners, 1973, Snakes and Ladders/The Best of Faces, 1976; (solo albums) An Old Raincoat Won't Ever Let You Down, 1969, Gasoline Alley, 1970, Every Picture Tells a Story, 1971, Never a Dull Moment, 1972, Sing it Again Rod, 1973, Smiler, 1974, Atlantic Crossing, 1975, The Best of Rod Stewart, 1976, The Best of Rod Stewart Vol. II, 1976, A Night on the Town, 1976, Foot Loose & Fancy Free, 1976, Blondes Have More Fun, 1978, Greatest Hits Vol. I, 1979, Foolish Behaviour, 1980, Tonight I'm Yours, 1981, Absolutely Live, 1981, Camouflage, 1984, (with Jeff Beck) Get Workin', 1985, Out of Order, 1988, Storyteller: The Complete Anthology 1964-1990, 1990, Downtown Train, 1990, Vagabond Heart, 1991, You Wear It Well, 1992, The Mercury Anthology, 1992, Once In A Blue Moon Vintage, 1993, Ridin High, The Rod Stewart Album, Unplugged...And Seated, 1993 (Grammy nomination, Best Pop Male Vocal for "Have I Told You Lately"), Spanner in the Works, 1995, Handbags and Gladrags, 1996, When We Were the New Boys, 1998, Human, 2001, It Had to Be You...The Great American Songbook, 2002, As Time Goes By...The Great American Songbook, Vol.:II, 2003, Stardust-...The Great American Songbook, Vol.:III, 2004, Thanks for the Memory: The Great American Songbook, Vol. 4, 2005, Ain't That Loving You Baby, 2005, Gold, 2005, Still the Same...Great Rock Classics of Our Time, 2006; performer (films)Rod Stewart - The Best of Rod Stewart, Rod Stewart and The Faces - The Final Concert, 1974, Rod Stewart and Faces, 1975, Rod Stewart Live at Los Angeles Forum, 1980, Rod Stewart-Tonight He's Yours, short and long versions, 1981, The Rod Stewart Concert Video, 1984, Rod Stewart -Storyteller 1984-91, 1991, Rod Stewart - Vagabond Heart; composer (films) Night at the Roxbury, 1998, Almost Famous, 2000, About Schmidt, 2002 and several others; performer Olympic Torch Concert Live, 2004 and several others. Named Rock Star of Year Rolling Stone mag., 1971; recipient British Rock and Pop Lifetime Achievement award, 1992, named an Honorary Knight Commander of the Most Excellent Order of the British Empire by Queen Elizabeth II, 2007; inducted into the Rock & Roll Hall of Fame, 1994. Office: Warner Bros Records 3300 Warner Blvd Burbank CA 91505-4694 *

STEWART, ROGER CHARLES, consumer products executive; b. Indpls., Sept. 23, 1949; s. Charles Thomas and Mary Pearl Stewart. BS in Sci., Purdue, 1971, MS in Indsl. Admin., 1974. Staff disposable fin. analysis Procter Gamble, Cin., 1978-80, staff spl. assign analysis, 1980, assoc. dir. tissue, 1981-83, dir. soft drinks Lexington, Ky., 1983-85, dir. sys. RVI Wilton, Conn., 1986, dir. internat. treasury Cin., 1987-98, v.p. global treasury, 1998—. Lectr. Krannert Sch., Purdue U., West Lafayette, Ind., 1992—. Past pres. Cancer Family Care, 1978—; fundraiser local charities. Avocations: playing marimba, travel, biking. Home: 5415 N Fort Valley Rd Flagstaff AZ 86001-7711 E-mail: stewart.rc.@pg.com.

STEWART, RUTH ANN, public policy educator; b. Chgo., Apr. 4, 1942; d. Elmer Ashton and Ann (Mitchell) Stewart; m. David Levering Lewis; children: Allegra Stewart, Jason Lewis, Allison Lewis, Eric Lewis. Student, U. Chgo., 1960-61, Simmons Coll., 1963; BA, Wheaton Coll., Norton, Mass., 1963; MS, Columbia U., 1965; postgrad., Fisk U., 1970, Harvard U., 1976, postgrad., 1987. Mktg. mgr. Macmillan Co., NYC, 1968-70; asst. chief Schomburg Ctr. Rsch. Black Culture, NYC, 1970-80; assoc. dir. external svcs. N.Y. Pub. Libr., 1980-86; asst. Libr. Congress Nat. Programs, Washington, 1986-89; assoc. Dir. Resource Devel., Washington, 1989-95; sr. policy analyst arts, humanities & social legis. Congl. Rsch. Svc., Washington, 1989-97; rsch. prof. cultural policy Ctr. Urban Policy Rsch. Bloustein Sch. Planning and Pub. Policy, Rutgers U., New Brunswick, NJ, 1997—2003; clin. prof. Wagner Grad. Sch. Pub. Svc., NYU, NYC, 2003—. Trustee, sec. Wheaton Coll., Norton, 1980—99; mem. libr. vis. com. Harvard U., 1975—88, MIT, 1986—90. Cons. editor: Jour. Arts Mgmt. Law and Soc., 1998—, founding co-editor: book series Public Life of the Arts, 1998—. Bd. dirs. Nat. Pk. Found., Washington, 1978—84, Fund Folk Culture, Santa Fe, 1991—2003, Lab. Sch. Washington, 1992—94, Women's Fgn. Policy Group, 1999—2003, Bklyn. Bot. Garden, 2000—, Studio in Sch., 2000—, Cooper-Hewitt Nat. Design Mus., Smithsonian Instn., 2003—; mem. rsch. adv. coun. Ctr. Arts and Culture, Washington, 1997—2006; sch. com. Alvin Ailey Sch., 1998—. Fellow, NY State Coun. Arts. Mem.: Coun. Fgn. Rels., ArtTable (nat. bd. dirs. 2002—03), Friends of Edn., Mus. Modern Art. Office: NYU Wagner Sch 295 Lafayette St New York NY 10012 Office Phone: 212-998-7480.

STEWART, S. JAY, automotive executive; b. Pineville, W.Va., Sept. 18, 1938; s. Virgil Harvey and Lena Rivers (Repair) S.; m. Judith Ann Daniels, June 3, 1961; children: Julie Annette, Jennifer Amy, Steven Jay. BSChemE, U. Cin., 1961; MBA, W.Va. U., 1966. Various positions in engring., mfg., mktg. Monsanto Co., St. Louis, 1961-73; dir. mktg. Ventron Corp. subs. Thiokol, Inc., Beverly, Mass., 1973-77, gen. mgr., 1977-79; pres. Dynachem Corp. subs. Thiokol, Inc., Tustin, Calif., 1979-82; group v.p. Thiokol Corp., Newtown, Pa., 1982; group v.p. splty. chems. Morton Internat., Inc. (formerly Morton Thiokol, Inc.), Chgo., 1983-86; pres., chief oper. officer Morton Internat., Inc., Chgo., 1986-94, also bd. dirs., 1994—99, chmn. bd., CEO, 1994—99; chmn. Autoliv, Inc., Stockholm, 2001—07, lead ind. dir., 2007—. Mem. Household Internat. Inc., Autoliv, Inc.; trustee Rush Presbyn.-St. Luke's Med. Ctr., Chgo., 1987—; Trustee Mus. Scis. and Industry; mem. exec. comm., Soc. Chem. Industry. Recipient Disting. Alumnus award U. Cin., 1984. Mem. Am. Chem. Soc., Am. Inst. Chem. Engrs., Chem. Mfrs. Assn. (bd. dirs. 1984-87, 94), Comml. Devel. Assn., Chem. Mktg. Assn. (bd. dirs. 1990), Comml. Club Chgo., The Chgo. Club, Econ. Club Chgo. Republican. Methodist. Office: Autolive Inc Klarabergsciadukten 70 Sec E Box 70381 SE 10724 Stockholm Sweden *

STEWART, SHARON ROSE, mathematics professor; b. Fillmore, NY, Dec. 16, 1946; d. Eldyn Benjamin and Elizabeth Ann Simons; m. Brian William Stewart, July 24, 1971; children: Sheila, David, Anna. BA, Houghton Coll., NY, 1968; MS in Edn., SUNY, Geneseo, 1971; A in Practical Theology, Christ Nations Inst., Dallas, 1978; cert. in libr. studies, Meml. U. of Nfld., St. John's, Can., 1992. Cert. tchr. N-9, tchr. math. 7-12 NY. Math. tchr. Corinth Ctrl. Sch., NY, 1968—69, Belmont Ctrl. Sch., NY, 1969—71, Lindsay Collegiate and Vocat. Inst., Ont., Canada, 1971—72; tchr. A. Garrigus Acad. and Collegiate Inst., St. Lunaire-Griquet, Nfld., 1973—74, 1982—83; libr. technician Ctrl. Nfld. Regional Coll., Grand Falls-Windsor, 1987—92, math. prof., 1992—96, Hazard Cmty. and Tech. Coll., Ky., 1997—. Bd. dirs. Evangel Pentecostal Assembly, Grand Falls-Windsor, 1996—97; adult tchr. Victory Assembly of God, Hazard, 1997—. Mem.: Ky. Math. Assn. of 2-Yr. Colls., Gideons Internat. Ladies Aux. Avocations: reading, travel, painting. Office: Hazard Cmty and Tech Coll 1 Community College Dr Hazard KY 41701 Office Phone: 606-487-3119. E-mail: sharon.stewart@kctcs.edu.

STEWART, SHIRLEY S., retired elementary school educator; b. Adams Run, SC, Oct. 17, 1939; d. Herbert and Ella (Harris) Simmons; children: Charlette, Kieshea. BS Edn., Carlin U., Orangeburg, SC. Tchr. Minnie Huge Elem. Sch., Hollywood, SC, Farm Sch. for Farmworkers Families, Ravanal, SC, Baptist Elem. Sch., SC. Adminstr. grants USDA, Charleston, SC, 1990—. Cmty. activist Salvation Army, Charleston, SC, 1988—; vol. helper to seniors in need of help Adams Run; cmty. organizer Mt. Nebo AMF Ch., Adams Run, SC, 1963—; Missionary Mt. Nebo AME Ch. Avocations: reading, cooking, acting, model. Office: PO Box 11 5065 Hwy 174 Adams Run SC 29426

STEWART, SUE S., lawyer; b. Oct. 9, 1942; d. Fraizer McVale and Carolyn Eliabeth (Hunt) S.; m. Arthur L. Stern, III, July 31, 1965 (div.); m. children: Anne, Mark Alan; m. John A. Ciampa, Sept. 1, 1985 (div.); m. Stephen L. Raymond (dec.). BA, Wellesley Coll., 1964; postgrad., Harvard U. Law Sch., 1964-65; JD, Georgetown U., 1967. Bar: N.Y. 1968. Clk. to judges Juvenile Ct., Washington, 1967-68; mem. Nixon, Hargrave, Devans & Doyle (now Nixon Peabody LLP), Rochester, NY, 1968-74, ptnr., 1975—2001, mng. ptnr., 1998—2001, ret., 2001; sr. v.p., gen. counsel U. Rochester, 2003—. Lectr. in field; trustee Found. of Monroe County (N.Y.) Bar, 1976-78; v.p. & Gen. Counsel Univ. Rochester, NY, 2003-. Author: Charitable Giving and Solicitation. Sec., dir. United Cmty. Chest of Greater Rochester, 1973-87, 1992-; trustee, sec. Internat. Mus. Photography at George Eastman House, Rochester, 1974-97, 2000-03, Genesee Country Mus., Mumford, N.Y., 1976-2002; bd. dirs. Ctr. for Govtl. Rsch., 1990-97; trustee, chmn. United Neighborhood Ctr. of Greater Rochester Found., 1991-2003; trustee, chmn. exec. com. Nat. Ctr. Edn. and Economy, 1997-; dir. Canandaigua Nat. Bank, NY, 2000-. Mem. ABA (chmn. task force on charitable giving, exempt orgns. com. tax sect. 1981-2003), N.Y. State Bar (exec. com. tax sect. 1974-76, chmn. com. exempt orgns. 1975-76), Monroe County Bar Assn. (trustee 1974-75), BNA Portfolio, Pvt. Found. Distbns. (Athena award 2000, de Tocqueville award 2003). Office: Office of Counsel 266 Wallis Hall PO Box 270040 Rochester NY 14627-0040 Office Phone: 585-273-2167.

STEWART, SUSAN MARIE, psychologist, educator; b. Des Plaines, Ill., Dec. 16, 1969; d. James Edward and Dorothy Ann (Luszcz) Burroughs BA with honors, Ea. Ill. U., 1992; MA with honors, Roosevelt U., 1995; PhD, U. Tenn., 2001. Asst. prof. mgmt. Roosevelt U., 2000—03, Wash. State U., 2003—05, U. Puget Sound, Tacoma, 2005—. Presenter in field. Author: jour. articles, book chpts., mag. articles, conf. proc. Recipient numerous grants, scholarships, tchg., rsch. and svc. awards. Mem. APA, Acad. Mgmt., Soc. Human Resource Mgmt., Soc. Indsl./Orgnl. Psychology, Beta

Gamma Sigma, others. Roman Catholic. Avocations: theater, museums, drawing, music. Office: U Puget Sound 1500 N Warner St #1032 Tacoma WA 98416-1032 Office Phone: 253-879-3569. Office Fax: 253-879-3156.

STEWART, TIMOTHY GLEN, organist; b. Atlanta, Sept. 18, 1960; s. Glen A. Stewart and Carol Ann Hicks; m. Melodee Beth Adams, Sept. 6, 1986. BS in Chemistry, Ga. State U., Atlanta, Ga., 1982; MS in Metallurgy, Ga. Inst. of Tech., Atlanta, Ga., 1985; PhD in Ednl. Psychology, Ga. State U., Atlanta, Ga., 1992. Chemistry lab asst. DeKalb Coll., Decatur, Ga., 1978—79; organist/asst. choir dir. Tucker Christian Ch., Tucker, Ga., 1981—88; metallurgy lab instr. Ga. Tech, Atlanta, 1983—84; chemistry/math instr. DeKalb Coll., Decatur, Ga., 1986—88; organist Indian Creek Bapt. Ch., Stone Mountain, Ga., 1988—91; owner/operator Stewart Musical Svcs., Loganville, Ga., 1991—; dir. music ministries/organist Westminster Presbyn. Ch., Snellville, Ga., 1992—93; organist First Bapt. Ch., Avondale Estates, Ga., 1995—; v.p. Miller Pipe Organ Svcs., Inc., Buford, Ga., 1995—2002; organist Two Tuners Music Ministry, Loganville, 2006—. Author: The Elemental Book of Facts, 1982; musician: (recordings) Christmas Music for Everyone, 1987, Music from Roswell United Methodist Church, 2002. Mem.: Planetary Soc., Am. Guild of Organists. Achievements include development of Advanced MIDI organ voice module. Avocations: genealogy, classic television, chemistry, extra-biblical studies, astronomy. Home Phone: 770-554-6768. Personal E-mail: tgstewart@earthlink.net.

STEWART, TONY, professional race car driver; b. Rushville, Ind., May 20, 1971; NASCAR Driver Joe Gibbs Racing Team. Recipient Hoosier Auto Racing Fans 1st-Yr. Driver award, 1989, USAC Sprint Rookie of Yr. award, 1991, Indpls. Speedrome midget series Rookie of Yr. award, 1991, ESPY award, Best Driver, 2006. Achievements include recognized as International Karting Foundation Grand National champion, 1983; recognized as World Karting Association National Champion, 1987; won first USAC national midget victory, Hut Hundred, Terre Haute, Ind., 1993; finished 5th in points, finished 2d Copper World Classic, Phoenix; won NASCAR Busch Series Grand National division debut, 1999; won Penzoil 400, 1999; won Checker Auto Parts/Dura-Lube 500, 1999; won Exide NASCAR 4000, 1999; won Winston Cup, 2002; won Brickyard 500, 2005; won Nextel Cup Championship, 2005; won his first Daytona 300, 2006; won his first USAC victory, Indpls., 1991; won Nextel Cup Series DIRECTV 500, Pepsi 400, Banquet 400, Bass Pro Shops 500, & Dickies 500, 2006; won Nextel Cup Series Budweiser Shootout & Gatorade Duel 150, 2007; won Nextel Cup USG Sheetrock 400, Chicagoland Speedway, 2007, Allstate 400, 2007. Office: c/o Joe Gibbs Racing 13415 Reese Blvd W Huntersville NC 28078-7933 *

STEWART, VERLINDSEY LAQUETTA, accounting educator; b. Birmingham, Ala., Dec. 27, 1965; d. Nathan Jr. and Shirley Ruth Brown; m. Kelvin Lorenzo Stewart I, June 22, 1991 (div. Feb. 1999); 1 child, Kelvin Lorenzo II. BS in Acctg., Ala. A&M U., Normal, 1988, MS in Bus. Edn., 1995, AA Cert. in Bus. Edn., 1997; EdD in Higher Edn. Leadership, Nova Southeastern U., Ft. Lauderdale, Fla., 2004. Cert. tchr. bus. 7-12 Ala. Jr. acct. Childress Acctg., Huntsville, Ala., 1990-93; acctg. clk. Appeal Beauty Salon, Huntsville, 1988-94; receptionist Coop. Ext., Normal, Ala., 1992-94; grad. asst. Ala. A&M U., Normal, 1995; student tchr. J.O. Johnson H.S., Huntsville, Ala., 1995; acctg. instr. J.F. Drake State Tech., Huntsville, 1996—. Cons. Jr. Achievement, Huntsville, 1995—96. Post-reviewer: (book) College Accounting 9th, 1999 (Honorarium 1999). Vol. Habitat for Humanity, Huntsville, 1995-97; vol. asst. leader Girl Scouts North Ala., Huntsville, 1995-96. Recipient Adminstrv. Acad. award Rust Coll., 1999, Emerging Leaders Sch. award Ala. Edn. Assn., 1994, Ala. Master Tchr. Seminar, 2001. Mem. Nat. Bus. Edn., Ea. Star Mitzpah Ctr., Phi Beta Lambda (adviser 1998—), Delta Sigma Theta. Democrat. Baptist. Avocations: aerobics, weightlifting, reading, jazz. Office: JF Drake State Tech Coll 3421 Meridian St N Huntsville AL 35811-1544 Personal E-mail: vbdst28@aol.com.

STEWART, WILLIAM JAMES, cardiologist; b. Cleve., Aug. 17, 1951; s. James B. and Virginia Stewart; m. Denise Elizabeth Balk, Dec. 30, 1972; children: Emily, Travis. AB in Biology cum laude, Harvard U., 1973; MD, U. Cin., 1977. Diplomate Am. Bd. Internal Medicine with subspecialty in cardiovascular disease; lic. physician, Ohio. Intern/resident U. Mich. Affiliated Hosps., Ann Arbor, 1977-80; clin. fellow dept. cardiology Boston U. Hosp., 1980-82; clin./rsch. fellow Cardiac Ultrasound Lab. Mass. Gen. Hosp./Harvard Med. Sch., Boston, 1982-84; staff physician Cleve. Clinic, 1984—, dir. Echo Lab, 1992—. Clin. assoc. in medicine Boston U., 1980-82; rsch. fellow in medicine Harvard Med. Sch., 1982-84; asst. prof. medicine Ohio State U., Cleve. Clinic Health Scis. Campus, 1992-94, assoc. prof., 1995—. Contbr. numerous articles and abstracts to profl. jours., chpts. to books; reviewer Circulation, Jour. Am. Coll. Cardiology, Jour. Am. Soc. Echocardiography, Echocardiography, Am. Heart Jour., Am. Jour. Cardiology, Brit. Heart Jour., Annals of Thoracic Surgery, Jour. Thoracic and Cardiovascular Surgery, Am. Jour. Cardiac Imaging; editl. bd. Echocardiography, 1992-96, Jour. Am. Soc. Echocardiography, 1991—. Christian youth leader. Fellow Am. Coll. Cardiology (Ohio chpt. adv. expert team in echocardiography 1995—), chmn. task force tng. in echocardiography 1994, mem. echocardiography com. 1991-96); mem. Am. Heart Assn. (mem. edn. com. N.E. Ohio chpt. 1985-88), Am. Soc. Echocardiography (chmn. com. on echocardiography in emergency medicine 1997, chmn. sci. sessions 1996, abstract chmn. sci. sessions 1994, mem. physicians' edn. and tng. com. 1993—, abstract vice chmn. 1993, bd. dirs. 1989-92), Internat. Soc. Ultrasound in Cardiac Surgery (pres. 1994—), Greater Cleve. Soc. Echocardiography (founder, bd. dirs. 1985—). Episcopalian. Avocations: jogging, sailing, skiing, music. Office: Cleveland Clinic Found Dept Cardiology F-15 9500 Euclid Ave Dept Cleveland OH 44195-0002 *

STEWART SIMPSON, DONNAMAY ANGELA, interior designer; b. Mandeville, Jamaica, W.I., Dec. 31, 1965; d. Ermine Stewart and Mary Ester Stewart Bromfield; m. Everton Seymour Simpson (div.); 1 child, Dimitre Andre Simpson. Student, Miami Dade C.C., 1986. Sec. Jamaica Transformer Co., 1986—87; secretarial clk. Pat Thompson Constrn. Co., Jamaica, 1987—89; ops. mgr. Blaise Trust, Mandeville, Jamaica, 1989, Nat. Car Rental, Mandeville, Jamaica, 1989—90; sec., accounts clk. Simpsons Wholesale Co., Elizabeth, Jamaica, 1990—91; ops. mgr. Simpson Supermarket, Elizabeth, Jamaica, 1991—94, Wesley Plz., Mandeville, Jamaica, 1995—97; owner Angelique Enterprises, Miramar, Fla., 1997—; fgn. exch. teller Ft. Lauderdale Internat. Airport, 1999—2001. Songwriter: Hill Top Records, 2006, Amercord. Interior decorator, stage performer Perfect Praise Sch. Dance, Fla., 2002; conf. spkr. Women's Empowerment Conf. Believers and Achievers Internat., 1998. Mem.: Reagan Ranch Found., Paralyzed Vets. Am., USO, U.S. Navy Meml., Internat. Poetry Soc. Avocations: dance, writing, design, motivational speaking. Home: 1980 SW 103d Terr Miramar FL 33025 Office: Angelique Enterprises 1980 SW 103d Terr Miramar FL 33025 Office Phone: 954-295-8694. E-mail: Dimitre01@aol.com.

STEYER, THOMAS FAHR, investment company executive; BA in Economics and Polit. Sci., summa cum laude, Yale U.; MBA, Stanford U., 1983. Assoc. risk arbitrage dept. Goldman, Sachs & Co.; with mergers and acquisitions dept. Morgan Stanley & Co.; founder, sr. mng. mem. Farallon Capital Mgmt. LLC, 1986—; mng. dir. Hellman & Friedman LLC, 1986—. Bd. dirs CapitalSource, Chevy Chase, Md. Office: Hellman & Friedman LLC One Maritime Plz 12th Fl San Francisco CA 94111 also: Farallon Capital Mgmt Ste 2100 One Maritime Plaza San Francisco CA 94111 *

STIBBE, AUSTIN JULE, retired accountant; b. St. Paul, Mar. 29, 1930; s. Austin Julius and Agnes Dorothea (Delaney) S.; m. Mary Elizabeth King, May 29, 1952; children: Anne Marie, Craig Jule, David King, Karen Lee. BSB in Acctg., U. Minn., 1952. CPA, Minn., Wis. Tax acct. Ernst & Ernst, Mpls., 1955-60; corp. tax mgr. EcoLab, Inc., St. Paul, 1960-65; audit mgr. Coopers & Lybrand, Mpls., 1965-74; v.p. Wilkerson, Guthmann & Johnson, Ltd., St. Paul, 1974-93, of counsel, 1993—2006; ret., 2006. Exec. officer Twin Cities Squadron, U.S. Naval Sea Cadet Corps, Mpls., 1974-80; bd. dirs., treas., mem. Twin Cities coun. Navy League, 1970—, pres., 1979-81, treas., 1975-79, 81-91; mem. adv. coun. to dept. acctg. U. Minn., Mpls., 1983-86; bd. dirs., chmn. audit com. St. Paul Area Coun. Chs., 1985-87; mem. adv. bd. Headwaters Soc., 1987-88; mem. fin. reporting com. United Way St. Paul Area, 1981-93, mem. audit com., 1991-93; dist. commr. staff Indianhead coun. Boy Scouts Am., 1962-65. Lt. USN, 1952-55. Mem. Minn. Soc. CPAs (life), U.S. Naval Inst. (life), Belle Taine Lake Assn. (dir. 1995-2001, treas. 1996-2001), Hubbard County COLA Print Com., 1995-98, Friends of Heritage, 1996—, Hubbard County Works of Improvement (steering com. 2001), VFW (life), Am. Legion. Presbyterian. Avocations: music, boating, history. Home: PO Box 41 Nevis MN 56467-0041 E-mail: austib30@msn.com.

STIBBE, CRAIG JULE, engineer; b. St. Paul, Apr. 2, 1956; s. Austin Jule and Mary Elizabeth Stibbe; m. Jane Marie Denery, May 9, 1981; children: Matthew Jule, Kevin Lowell, Aileen Marie. Cert. Chief A Stationary Engr., Minn., 1986, Class D Water Operator, Minn., 2004. Engr. Mid-America Dairymen, Inc., Farmington, Minn., 1981—84, Am. Hoist and Derrick, St. Paul, 1984—85, Jacob Schmidt Brewing Co., 1985—88, NW Airlines, 1989—2005, Packaging Corp. Am., Mpls., 2006—, Rock-Tenn. Co., St. Paul, 2007—. Boiler technician third class USN, 1976—80. Mem.: Mensa. Home: 20060 Akin Rd Farmington MN 55024 Office: Rock-Tenn Co 2250 Wabash Ave Saint Paul MN 55114 Personal E-mail: cjstibbe@charter.net.

STIBER, JULIE ANNE, social worker; b. Binghamton, NY, May 1, 1962; d. Max Linwood and Ruth Mary S. BA, Albertus Magnus, New Haven, Conn., 1984; MSW, So. Conn. State U., New Haven, Conn., 1991. LCSW Conn., 1993, DCSW Conn., 1996. Asst. dir. Coord. Coun. Children in Crisis, New Haven, 1996—99; clin. coord. social work Priority Care, New Haven, Bridgeport and Norwalk, Conn., 1999—2000; dir. social work svcs. New Eng. Home Care, Conn., 2000—; clin. cons. Dept. Children & Families, State of Conn. Mem.: Nat. Assn. Social Workers (children's com. 2001—, diplomate in clin. social work 1996). Democrat. Episcopalian. Avocations: running, painting, drawing, jewelry, cooking. Office: State of Conn Dept Children & Families 1 Long Wharf New Haven CT 06511

STICE, DWAYNE LEE, broadcasting company executive; b. Paducah, Ky., Aug. 10, 1956; s. Freeman D. and Dorris Olive (Lee) S. AA, Paducah Community Coll., 1976; BS, Murray State U., 1977; MS, Southern Ill. U., 1983. Lic. funeral dir., Ky. Dir. Johnson-Lambert Funeral Home, Calvert City, Ky., 1974-81; gen. mgr. Paducah Area Transit System, 1980-92; pres. Sta. WCCK-FM, Stice Comm., Inc., Calvert City, 1990—2001; human resources, programming WPSD-TV, Paducah, Ky., 2001—. Adj. bus. instr. Paducah Community Coll., 1979-91, Lindsey Wilson Coll., Columbia, Ky., 1991; adj. reporter CBS Radio Network, 1997-2000; cons. in field. Contbr. articles to profl. jours. Mem. Calvert Area Devel. Assn.; transp. com. Purchase Area Devel. Dist.; organist St. Matthew by the Lake Luth. Ch., 1986—, Calvert City United Meth. Ch., 2004—. Outstanding grantee Ky. Transp. Cabinet, 1985, 86. Mem. Ky. Pub. Transit Assn. (pres. 1988-91), Ky. Broadcasters Assn. (bd. dirs. 1997-2000), Marshall C. of C. (bd. dirs., vice chmn. govt. affairs 1998), Paducah C.C. Alumni Assn. (pres. 1983), Hon. Order Ky. Cols., Travelers Protective Assn. (pres. Paducah chpt. 1989-90), Lions, Masons (master Calvert City 1984), Shriners, Order Ea. Star, Phi Kappa Phi, Phi Theta Kappa. Methodist. Avocations: travel, baseball, antique clocks, automobiles. Office: WPSD-TV 100 TV Ln Paducah KY 42003 E-mail: ky4202956@yahoo.com.

STICH, ROBERTA LYNN, not-for-profit fundraiser, social worker; b. NYC, May 23, 1948; d. Melvin Harold Stich and Shirley Pearl Kaplan-Stich. Student, U. Rochester, 1965—67; BA, Bklyn. Coll., 1970; MSW, Hunter Coll., 1972; postgrad., Stanford Law Sch., 1980—85. Lic. master social worker N.Y. Legal asst. Howard Deutsch Atty. at Law, NYC, 1977—80, Donald Lindover Atty. at Law, NYC, 1982; rsch. asst. sociology dept. Stanford (Calif.) U., 1986—87; rsch. asst. Merit Co., Jerusalem, 1989—91; fundraiser Nat. Symphony Orch. Assn., Washington, 1991—95, Nat. Rep. Senatorial Com., Washington, 1995—97, Nat. Capital Teleservices, LLC, Washington, 1997—. Telephone solicitor Nat. Children's Ctr. Value Village Project Inc., Beltsville, Md., 1992—. Mem. Smithsonian Instn., Washington, 1996—, Phillips Collection, 2005, U.S. Holocaust Mus., Washington, 2000—, Rep. Nat. Com., 2002—. Mem.: Nat. Trust Historic Preservation, Stanford Alumni Assn. (life). Republican. Jewish. Avocations: surfing the Internet, cassettes and videos, casino gambling, travel, fashion. Home: Apt 208 1255 New Hampshire Ave NW Washington DC 20036 Office: CAPTEL 300 5th St NE Washington DC 20002 Office Phone: 202-547-4614. E-mail: robersti@aol.com.

STICH, STEPHEN PETER, philosophy educator; b. NYC, May 9, 1943; s. Samuel Joseph and Sylvia Lucille (Siegel) S.; m. Judith Ann Gagnon, Dec. 20, 1971; children: Jonathan Andrew, Rebecca Elizabeth. BA summa cum laude with distinction, U. Pa., 1964; PhD, Princeton U., 1968. Teaching asst. Princton U., 1965; asst. prof. U. Mich., 1968-73, assoc. prof., 1973-78, dir. grad. studies in philosophy, 1973-74, assoc. chmn. dept. philosophy, 1975-76; assoc. prof. U. Md., 1978-81, prof., 1981-86, dir. grad. studies in philosophy, 1982-83; prof. U. Calif., San Diego, 1986-89, dir. cognitive sci. program, 1988-89; prof. philosophy and cognitive sci. Rutgers U., New Brunswick, 1989—, acting chair dept. philosophy, 1992-93, dir. rsch. group on evolution and higher cognition, 1997—, bd. govs. prof., 1998—. Prof. Linguistic inst., Linguistic Soc. Am., summer 1982; dir. Summer Seminar for Coll. Tchrs. NEH, 1983, 89; vis. sr. lectr. U. Sydney, 1984-85; vis. fellow Australian Nat. U., 1992; Jemison prof. humanities U. Ala., Birmingham, 1993; adj. prof. CUNY Grad. Ctr., 1994-97; Erskine fellow Canterbury U., Christchurch, New Zealand, 1996; cons. Pres. Commn. for Nat. Priorities in the Eighties, Pres. Commn. on Ethics in Medicine and Biomed. and Behavioral Rsch.; mem. selection com. Mellon Fellowships in the Humanities, 1983-84; mem. Fulbright Selection Com., 1981-83, chair, 1983; vis. fellow Australian Nat. U., Rsch. Sch. Social Scis., 1992; hon. prof. philosophy U. Sheffield, 2005-. Author: From Folk Psychology to Cognitive Science, 1983, The Fragmentation of Reason, 1990, Deconstructing the Mind, 1996, Mindreading, 2003; editor: Innate Ideas, 1975; (with others) The Recombinant DNA Debate, 1979, Philosophy and Connectionist Theory, 1991, Mental Representation, 1994; editor Evolution and Cognition Series; mem. editl. bd. Linguistics and Philosophy, 1984—, Mind and Language, 1985—, Cognitive Sci., 1990—, Minds and Machines, 1991—, Pragmatics and Cognition, 1991—, Philosophical Studies, 1992—, Philosophy of Sci., 1992—, Cognition, 1993—, Neural Network Modeling and Connectionism; mem. editl. adv. bd. Studies in Cognitive Sys.; contbr. articles to profl. jours., chpts. to books. Woodrow Wilson Nat. Fellowship Found. fellow, 1964-65, Woodrow Wilson dissertation fellow, 1967, Danforth grad. fellow, 1964-67, H.H. Ford fellow Princeton U., 1967, Coun. Philos. Studies Summer Inst. fellow, 1971, Am. Coun. Learned Socs. fellow, 1978-79, Rutgers U. competitive fellow, sch. liberal arts fellow U. Otago, Dunedin, New Zealand, 2001; recipient fellowships NEH, 1974, 83-84, 96, Ctr. for Advanced Study in Behavioral Scis., Stanford, Calif., 1983; Fulbright sr. rsch. scholar, Bristol (U.K.) U., 1978-79; grantee U.S.-Israel Ednl. Found., 1979, NRC and U.S. Nat. Com. for Internat. Union of History and Philosophy of Sci., Hannover, West Germany, 1979, NSF, 1981-82. Mem. Am. Philos. Assn., Soc. for Philosophy and Psychology (pres. 1982-83, exec. com. 1980-82, 83-84, chair program com. 1979-80), Philosophy of Sci. Assn., Brit. Soc. for Philosophy of Sci., Fulbright Alumni Assn. Office: Rutgers U Philosophy Dept Davison Hall Douglass Campus New Brunswick NJ 08901-2882 Office Phone: 732-932-9861 x131. E-mail: stich@ruccs.rutgers.edu.

STICK, MICHAEL ALAN, lawyer; b. Elizabeth City, NC, June 2, 1954; s. David and Phyllis (Stapells) S.; m. Debra Joan Braselton, May 22, 1993. BA, Davidson Coll., NC, 1976; JD, U. NC, 1981. Bar: Ill. 1981, US Dist. Ct. (no. dist.) Ill. 1982, US Ct. Appeals (7th cir.) 1983, US Ct. Appeals (8th cir.) 1986. Assoc. Jenner & Block, Chgo., 1981-84, Butler, Rubin, Newcomer, Saltarelli & Boyd, Chgo., 1984-87; ptnr. Butler, Rubin, Saltarelli & Boyd, Chgo., 1988—. Staff mem. Law Rev. U. NC, 1979—80. Mem. ABA, Chgo. Bar Assn. Avocation: travel. Office: Butler Rubin Saltarelli & Boyd 70 W Madison St Ste 1800 Chicago IL 60602 Office Phone: 312-444-9660.

STICK, THOMAS HOWARD FITCHETT, architect, construction litigation consultant; b. Balt., Feb. 28, 1938; s. Gordon M. F. and Anne Howard (Fitchett) S.; m. Rosalie Wade Reynolds, 1959 (div. 1982); children: H. Edward M., Alexander W., David F.; m. Joyce Yeargin Carr, 1982 (div. 1989); m. Alyce C. Cushing, 1989. BA in Psychology, Yale U., 1960; postgrad., Md. Inst., 1962, U. Pa. Grad. Sch. Arch., 1964. Registered arch., Pa., Md., Del., N.J., Va., Maine, N.Y., D.C., Mass., N.H., N.C., Vt., Tenn., Okla., Colo., Ind., Ga., Ill., Mich., Ky., Kans., Ohio, Peoples Republic of China; cert. recommendation Nat. Coun. Archtl. Registration Bds. Arch. Vincent G. Kling & Ptnrs., Phila., 1964-74, B.J. Hoffman & Assocs., Berwyn, Pa., 1974; ptnr. Grim & Stick, Ardmore, Pa., 1975-77; prin. Stick Assocs., Gladwyne, Pa., 1977-80; corp. arch. Gino's Inc., King of Prussia, Pa., 1980-81; mgr. constrn. adminstrn. Ballinger Co., Phila., 1981-83; sr. constrn. claims cons. MDC Sys. Corp., Phila., 1984-85; chief arch. Day & Zimmermann Inc., Phila., 1985—, discipline mgr., 1987—, corp. arch., 1995—; dir. Day & Zimmermann Internat. Corp., Phila., 2000—. V.p. F-S Found., 1986, also bd. dirs. One-man show in photography Ea. Camera Gallery, 1972. Named Arch. of Best Food Plant of Yr., Food Engring. Mag., 1992. Mem. AIA, Pa. Soc. Archs., Bldg. Ofcls. and Code Adminstrs. Internat., Internat. Conf. Bldg. Ofcls., So. Bldg. Code Congress Internat., Constrn. Specifications Inst., Nat. Fire Protection Assn., Soc. War of 1812 (sec. 1977-82), Soc. of Cincinnati, Soc. Colonial Wars, SR, Descs. of Lords of the Md. Manors, Mil. Order of Loyal Legion of U.S., Huguenot Soc., Am. Clan Gregor Soc., St. Andrew's Soc. of Balt., St. George's Soc. of Balt., Merion Cricket Club (Haverford, Pa.), Yale Club, Sovereign Mil. of Temple of Jerusalem (comdr.), Sovereign Order of St. John of Jerusalem (Knight of Justice), Knights Malta, Zeta Psi. Home: 1501 Monticello Dr Gladwyne PA 19035-1206 Office: Day & Zimmermann Internat 240 Continental Dr Newark DE 19713-4328

STICKEL, FREDERICK A., publishing executive; b. Weehawken, NJ, Nov. 18, 1921; s. Fred and Eva (Madigan) S.; m. Margaret A. Dunne, Dec. 4, 1943; children: Fred A., Patrick F., Daisy E., Geoffrey M., James E., Bridget A. Student, Georgetown U., 1939-42; BS, St. Peter's Coll., 1943. Advt. salesperson Jersey Observer daily, Hoboken, NJ, 1945-51; retail advt. salesperson Jersey Jour., Jersey City, 1951-55, advt. dir., 1955-66, publisher, 1966-67; gen. mgr. Oregonian Pub. Co., Portland, Oreg., 1967-72, pres., 1972-86, publisher, 1975—. Bd. regents U. Portland; adv. bd. Portland State U., St. Vincent's Hosp.; bd. dirs. Portland Rose Festival Assn., United Way Oreg.; chmn. Portland Citizens Crime Commn. Capt. USMC, 1942-45. Mem. Assn. for Portland Progress (dir.), Portland C. of C. (dir.), Oreg. Newspaper Pubs. Assn. (past pres.), Pacific N.W. Newspaper Assn. (past pres.), Newspaper Assn. Am., University Club, Multnomah Athletic Waverley Country Club, Arlington Club, Rotary. Office: Oregonian Pub Co 1320 SW Broadway Portland OR 97201-3499 Office Phone: 503-221-8140. Office Fax: 503-294-4175. *

STICKLE, DAVID WALTER, microbiologist; b. Boston, Apr. 18, 1933; s. Harold Edwards and Lucille Margaret (Magee) S.; m. Mary Elizabeth DeLong, July 29, 1972. BS in Chemistry, Biology, Tufts U., 1955; MS in Pharmacy and Health, Northeastern U., Boston, 1968; MPH, U. N.C., 1969, DrPH, 1971. Bacteriologist Mass. Dept. Pub. Health, Boston, 1959-63, supr. immunology unit, 1963-68; UNC/CDC lab. dir.'s program Ctrs. for Disease Control, Atlanta, 1968-71; chief, clin. lab. improvement program Divsn. Med. Labs./Minn. Dept. Health, Mpls., 1971-82, acting dir., 1977-78, asst. dir., 1978-88. Ex-officio mem. Minn. Soc. Clin. Pathologists Exec. Com., Mpls., 1977-78; mem. Proficiency Testing Com., Minn. Acad. Family Physicians, Mpls., 1977-83; adj. asst. prof. U. Minn., Mpls., 1977-88; assoc. prof. emeritus, U. Minn., 1988—. Editor: Med. Lab. Forum periodical, 1973-88. Proctor Nat. Registry of Microbiology, Mpls. Examinations for Minn., 1987-92; instr. Edina Community Edn. Programs, Minn., 1992. With U.S. Army, 1955-57. Lab. tng. grantee Ctr. for Disease Control, HEW, Atlanta, 1977-78, 1978-80, 1979-81. Mem. Am. Soc. Microbiology, Phi Sigma, Sigma Xi. Achievements include serologic tests for systemic candidiasis which were in use for many years by the Ctrs. for Disease Control, U.S. Dept. of Health and Human Svcs.

STICKLER, GUNNAR BRYNOLF, pediatrician; b. Peterskirchen, Germany, June 13, 1925; came to U.S., 1951, naturalized, 1958; s. Fritz and Astrid (Wennerberg) S.; m. Duci M. Kronenbitter, Aug. 30, 1956; children: Katarina Anna, George David. MD, U. Munich, Germany, 1949; PhD, U. Minn., Mpls., 1957. Diplomate Am. Bd. Pediatrics, ofcl. examiner and mem., 1965-95. Resident in clin. pathology Krankenhaus III Orden, Munich, 1950; resident in pathology U. Munich, 1950-51; intern Mountainside Hosp., Montclair, NJ, 1951-52; fellow in pediatrics Mayo Grad. Sch., Rochester, Minn., 1953-56; sr. cancer research scientist Roswell Park Meml. Inst., Buffalo, 1956-57; asst. to staff Mayo Clinic, Rochester, 1957-58, cons. in pediatrics, 1959-69, head sect. pediatrics, 1969-74; prof. pediatrics, chmn. dept. pediatrics Mayo Clinic and Mayo Med. Sch., 1974-80. Mem. test com. III Nat. Bd. Med. Examiners, 1973-75; vis. prof. at various univs and instns., including U. Dusseldorf (Germany) and U. Munich, 1971, Pahlavi U., Iran, 1975, Olga Hosp., Stuttgart, Germany, 1978, Martin Luther King Hosp., Los Angeles, 1979, U. Man., 1981; mem. emeritus staff Mayo Clinic, 1989. Mem. editl. bd. Clin. Pediatrics, 1968-76, 79-97, European Jour. Pediatrics, 1976-84, Pediatrics, 1983-89; contbr. more than 290 articles to med. publs. Active parent support groups in field of cyclic vomiting syndrome; life pres. Stickler Syndrome support group, 1997—. Recipient Humanitarian award Chgo. region chpt. Nat. Found. Ileitis and Colitis, 1978, award for excellence of subject matter and presentation So. Minn. Med. Assn., 1978 Mem. Am. Acad. Pediatrics (Disting. Svc. award Minn. chpt. 1999), Soc. Pediatric Rsch., Am. Pediatric Soc., Nat. Coun. Reliable Health Info., Midwest Soc. Pediatric Rsch. (coun. 1967-69, pres. 1970-71, Founders award 1996), N.W. Pediatric Soc. (pres. 1973-74) Achievements include description of hereditary progressive arthropthalmopathy in 1965, now called Stickler syndrome; and the treatment otitis media, hypophosphatemic rickets, renal disease; research in areas of parents' fears and the need of routine physical examinations in adolescents, and the excesses of alternative medicine. Office: Mayo Clinic Emeritus Ctr Rochester MN 55905

STICKLER, RICHARD E., federal agency administrator; b. W.Va., 1944; BS, Fairmount State U., 1968. Cert. mine safety profl. Internat. Soc. Mine Safety. With Bethenergy Mines, Bethlehem, Pa., 1996—97, various positions including coal miner, capt. mine rescue team, shift foreman, supt., mine mgr.; with Performance Coal Co., Charleston, W.Va.; dir. Pa. Bur. Deep Mine Safety, 1997—2003; asst. sec. labor for mine safety, Mine Safety & Health Adminstrn. US Dept. Labor, 2006—. Office: US Dept Labor 1100 Wilson Blvd Arlington VA 22209-3939 *

STICKNEY, JESSICA, former state legislator; b. Duluth, Minn., May 16, 1929; d. Ralph Emerson and Claudia Alice (Cox) Page; m. Edwin Levi Stickney, June 17, 1951; children: Claudia, Laura, Jeffrey. BA, Macalester Coll., St. Paul, Minn., 1951; PhD (hon), Rocky Mtn. Coll., Billings, Mont., 1986. Rep. State of Mont., 1989-92. Mem. Gov.'s Commn. on Post-Sec. Edn., Mont., 1973-75. Mem. Sch. Bd. Trustees, Miles City, Mont., 1968-74; mem., chmn. zoning bd., Miles City, 1975-89; mem. Govt. Study Commn., Miles City, 1974-76, United Ch. Christ Bd. Homeland Ministries, 1975-81; chmn., conf. moderator United Ch. Christ Bd. Mont.-Northern Wyo. Conf., 1980-82; chmn. Town Meeting on the Arts, Mont., 1980; mem., chmn. Miles Community Coll. Bd., 1975-89, chmn. 1978-80. Recipient Disting. Citizen's award, Macalester Coll., 2006. Mem. Mont. Arts Coun. (chmn. 1982-85), Western States Arts Found. (vice chmn. 1984), Nat. Assembly State Arts Agys. (bd. dirs. 1982-88), AAUW (pres. 1964-66). Democrat. Avocations: writing, sewing, painting, reading.

STICKNEY, JOHN, editor; BA, Williams Coll., 1968. With People mag., 1982, Money mag., 1983—88; mktg. comm. mgr. NY Times Syndication Sales Corp., 1997—2002, sr. editor, 2002—. Freelance writer; author: 2 books.

STICKNEY, NANCY CARVER, state legislator; b. Bethel, Maine, July 20, 1936; d. Irving L. and Ruth W. (Homsted) Carver; m. Wallace E. Stickney, 1957; children: Peter, Christopher J., Daniel C., Adam K. BS, U. NH, 1960. Mem. NH Ho. of Reps. (dist. 26), Concord, Maine, 1997—2000. Methodist. Home: PO Box 177 North Salem NH 03073-0177 Office: NH State Legis State House Concord NH 03301

STICKNEY, ROBERT ROY, fisheries educator; b. Mpls., July 2, 1941; s. Roy E. and Helen Doris (Nelson) S.; m. LuVerne C. (Whiteley), Dec. 29, 1961; children: Robert Roy, Marolan Margaret. BS, U. Nebr., 1967; MA, U. Mo., 1968; PhD, Fla. State U., 1971. cert. fisheries scientist. Rsch. assoc. Skidaway Inst. Oceanography, Savannah, Ga., 1971—73, asst. prof., 1973—75, Tex. A and M U., Coll. Sta., 1975—78, assoc. prof., 1978—83, prof., 1983—84; prof. zoology, dir. Fisheries Rsch. Lab., So. Ill. U., Carbondale, 1984—85; dir. Sch. of Fisheries U. Wash., Seattle, 1985—91, prof., 1985—96; dir. Sea Grant Coll. program Tex. A&M U., Coll. Sta., 1996—. Author: Principles of Warmwater Aquaculture, 1979, Estuarine Ecology of the Southeastern U.S. and Gulf of Mex., 1984; editor: Culture of Non Salmonid Freshwater Fishes, 1986, 1992, Flagship: A History of Fisheries at the U. of Washington, 1989; co-editor: Fisheries: Harvesting Life from Water, 1989, Culture of Salmonid Fishes, 1992, Fisheries: Harvesting Life from Water, 1995, Principles of Aquaculture, 1994, Fish Culture in the United States: A Hist. Survey, 1996, Responsible Marine Aquaculture, 2002, Aquaculture: An Introductory Text, 2005; editor: revs. in Fisheries Sci., Ency. of Aqua-culture, World Aquaculture mag.; contbr. articles to profl. jours. Served in USAF, 1959-63. Mem.: Sea Grant Assn. (pres. 2003—04). Home Phone: 979-279-3094; Office Phone: 979-845-3854. Personal E-mail: rrstickney@aol.com. E-mail: stickney@tamu.edu.

STIEBER, TAMAR, journalist; b. Bklyn., Sept. 15, 1955; d. Alfred and Florence (Spector) Stieber. Student, Rockland C.C., 1972—75, West Chester CC, NY, 1973—74; BA in Film cum laude, U. Calif., Berkeley, 1985, postgrad. in comparative lit., 1985—86; grad. Police Res. Acad. cum laude, Napa Valley Coll., 1988. Office mgr., confidential sec. AP, San Francisco, 1981—83; stringer Daily Californian, Berkeley, Calif., 1983—84; film rsch. tchg. asst. U. Calif., Berkeley, 1984—86; libr. and rsch. asst. Pacific Film Archive, Berkeley, 1984—86; intern San Francisco Examiner, 1984; reporter Sonoma (Calif.) Index-Tribune, 1987—88, Vallejo (Calif.) Times-Herald, 1988—89, Albuquerque Jour., 1989—94, freelancer, 1994—. Recipient Pulitzer Prize for specialized reporting, 1990, 1st pl. pub. svc. divsn., N.Mex. Press Assn., 1990, Pub. Svc. award, Albuquerque Press Club, 1990, 1st pl. newswriting, N.Mex. Press Assn., 1991, Hon. Mention, AP Mng. Editors, 1994. Mem.: AAUW, Phi Beta Kappa. Home: PO Box 9835 Santa Fe NM 87504-9835 E-mail: tstieber@isp.com.

STIEF, LOUIS JOHN, chemist; b. Pottsville, Pa., July 26, 1933; s. Louis Norman and Dorothy Elizabeth (Bassler) S.; m. Kathleen J. Talbot, Nov. 30, 1963 (div. 1980); children: Andrew, Lorraine. BA, La Salle Coll., 1955; PhD, Catholic U. Am., 1960. Nat. Acad. Scis.-NRC postdoctoral rsch. assoc. Nat. Bur. Standards, Washington, 1960-61; NATO postdoctoral fellow, ind. researcher chemistry dept. Sheffield (Eng.) U., 1961-63; sr. scientist, sr. chemist Melpar, Inc., Falls Church, Va., 1963-68; NAS-NRC sr. postdoctoral rsch. assoc. NASA/Goddard Space Flight Ctr., Greenbelt, Md., 1968-69, astrophysicist, 1969-76, head br. astrochemistry, 1976-90, sr. scientist, 1990—2004, emeritus scientist, 2004—. Research: numerous publs., especially in Jour. Chem. Physics and Jour. Phys. Chemistry. Recipient Alumni Achievement award Cath. U. Am., 1985; NASA fellow Queen Mary Coll., U. London, 1981-82 Fellow: Washington Acad. Sci.; mem.: Am. Astron. Soc. (divsn. planetary sci.), Royal Soc. Chemistry, Am. Chem. Soc. (Hillebrand prize Chem. Soc. Washington 2002), Sigma Xi.

STIEFEL, ETHAN, dancer, performing company executive; b. Tyrone, Pa. s. Alan and Mima Stiefel. Studies with Mikhail Baryshnikov, Sch. Classical Ballet, 1987; student, Fordham U., 1995—. From mem. to prin. dancer NY City Ballet, 1989-95, prin. dancer, 1995-96, Am. Ballet Theatre, NYC, 1997—; artistic dir. Stiefel and Stars, 2002—, Stiefel and Students, 2004—, Ballet Pacifica, 2004—06; prin. dancer, artistic assoc. Kings of the Dance, 2006—. With Zurich Ballet, 1992-93; guest artist N.Y.C. Ballet, 1998-99, Atlanta Ballet, 1999, Royal Ballet, 1999—. Dancer prin. roles include Le Corsaire, Romeo & Juliet, Giselle, Les Patineurs, Onegin, Swan Lake, Theme and Variations, Raymonda, Don Quixote, A Midsummer Night's Dream, La Bayadere, The Dream, The Four Temperaments, Apollo, Stars and Stripes, Harlequinade, Tarantella, Tchaikovsky Pas de Deux, Chaconne, Prodigal Son, La Fille Mal Gardee, The Nutcracker, Robbins' ballets Dances at a Gathering, West Side Story Suite, The Goldberg Variations, The Cage, Quiet City, Martins' ballets Fearful Symmetries, Ash, Tchaikovsky Pas de Quatre, The Sleeping Beauty, King of the Dance, Tharp Ballets Known by Heart, Push Comes to Shove, In The Upper Room, others; appeared in PBS TV prodn. Le Corsaire, 1999, Born to be Wild, 2002, The Dream, 2004; artistic dir. Steifel & Stars, 2001—, artistic dir Performance Project, 2004; guest artist Teatro Colon, 1999, Hamburg Ballet, 2000, Kirov Ballet, 2001, 04, Verona, Italy, 2003, Washington Opera, 2003, Budapest Opera, 2003, others; starring role: (film) Center Stage, 2000. Recipient Silver medal Prix de Lausanne, 1989, Statue award Princess Grace Found., 1999; emerging dance artist grantee Princess Grace Found. U.S.A., 1991-92 Office: care Peter S Diggins Assoc 133 W 71st St Ste 8-B New York NY 10023 Office Phone: 212-874-4534. Personal E-mail: festspiel@aol.com.

STIEFEL, LINDA SHIELDS, lawyer; b. Syracuse, NY, Nov. 14, 1948; d. Harold F. and Ellen (Brown) Shields; m. John L. Stiefel, Sept. 20, 1969; 1 child, John L. BS, Tusculum Coll., 1988; JD, Akron Sch. Law, 1991. Bar: Ohio 1992, D.C. 1993, N.Y. 1998, U.S. Dist. Ct. (no. dist.) Ohio 1993, U.S. Supreme Ct. 1997. Judicial law clk. Stark County Common Pleas, Canton, Ohio, 1991-94; pvt. practice Louisville, Ohio, 1992-97, Cape Vincent, NY, 1998—. Trustee, mem. exec. com. Am. Handweaving Mus., 1997-2001. Mem. ABA, NOW, N.Y. State Bar Assn., Jefferson County Bar Assn. Methodist.

STIEGEL, MICHAEL ALLEN, lawyer; b. Greenfield, Mass., Sept. 15, 1946; s. Sid James and Ida Eleanor (Solomon) S.; m. Marsha Palmer, Sept. 10, 1983. BA, U. Ariz., Tucson, 1968; JD cum laude, Loyola U., Chgo., 1971. Bar: Ill. 1971, US Dist. Ct. Ill. 1971, US Ct. Appeals (7th cir.) 1971, US Ct. Appeals (1st cir.) 1975, US Ct. Appeals (6th cir.) 1991, US Supreme Ct. 1975, Wis. 1985, Fla. 1987. Law clk. to fed. judge William Lynch U.S. Dist. Ct. Ill., Chgo., 1971—72; mng. ptnr. Arnstein & Lehr, Chgo., 1985—98; ptnr. Michael Best and Friedrich, 1998—, co-chair trial dept., 1998—2003, elected mgmt. com., 2003—. Adj. prof. law Northwestern U.; faculty Nat. Inst. Trial Advocacy, La. State U. Trial Advocacy Program, 1995-2000. Contbr. articles to profl. jours. Mem. fin. com. Lynn Martin for Senate, Ill., 1989-90. Mem. ABA (pres., sects. on litig. and bus. law, vice chmn. trial evidence com. litig. sect. 1990-91, co-chmn. trial evidence com. 1991-95, lawyers conf. stds.andards for admissibility of technologically sophisticated evidence comm., co-chair nat. CLE programs 1995-97, coun. 1997-2000, mem. exec. com. 2000—, budget officer 2000-02, revenue officer, 2002-06, litig. sect. advisor, uniform laws commn., litig. sect. liaison, drafting com. on Model Punitive Damages Act, appointee to Nat. Conf. Attys. & CPA, 2005, atty.-client privilege task force liaison), Ill. Bar Assn., Fla. Bar Assn., Wis. Bar Assn., Chgo. Bar Assn. (chair large firm com. 2002-04), Econ. Club Chgo. (membership com.). Avocations: sports, reading, horse racing syndications. Office: Michael Best Friedrich 70 W Madison St Ste 3500 Chicago IL 60602-4224 Office Phone: 312-836-5073. Business E-Mail: mastiegel@michaelbest.com.

STIEHM, E. RICHARD, pediatrician, educator; b. Milw., Jan. 22, 1933; s. Reuben Harold and Marie Dueno S.; m. Judith Hicks, July 12, 1958; children: Jamie Elizabeth, Carrie Eleanor, Meredith Ellen. BS, U. Wis., 1954, MD, 1957. Diplomate Am. Bd. Pediat., Am. Bd. Allergy and Clin. Immunology (bd. dirs. 1977-83), Am. Bd. Diagnostic Lab. Immunology. Intern Phila. Gen. Hosp., 1957-58; fellow in physiol. chemistry U. Wis., 1959-61, asst. prof. pediat., 1965—68, assoc. prof., 1968—69; med. officer USNR, Johnsville, Pa., 1961-63; resident in pediat. Babies Hosp., NYC, 1963-65; rsch. fellow in pediat. immunology U. Calif., San Francisco, 1965-68; assoc. prof. UCLA, 1969—72, chief divsn. immunology, allergy and rheumatology, 1969—2003, prof., 1972—, assoc. dir. Ctr. for Interdisciplinary Rsch. in Immunologic Diseases, 1981-82, co-dir. Cystic Fibrosis Ctr., 1988—95, vice chair acad. affairs dept. pediat., 1989—99; vis. scientist metabolism br. Nat. Cancer Inst., Bethesda, Md., 1982-88. Vis. prof. Yale U., Mayo Clinic, U. Cin., Great Ormond St. Hosp., U.K., U. Wis.; bd. sci. dirs. Immune Deficiency Found., 1981—, Eczema Found., 1988—, Pediat. AIDS Found., 1989-99; task force on pediatric allergy NIH, 1977; mem. gen. clin. rsch. ctr. study sect. NIH, 1978-82, 84-88; adv. com. Hartford Fellowship, 1984-88; co-dir. LA Pediatric AIDS Consortium, 1988—. Editor: Immunologic Disorders in Infants and Children, 1972, 80, 89, 96, 2004; Am. editor: Pediatric Rsch., 1984-89; assoc. editor: Pediat. Update, 2003-; mem. editl. bd. Pediat., 1972-78, Pediat. in Rev., 1978-81, Jour. Allergy and Clin. Immunology, 1976-80, Jour. Clin. Immunology, 1985-89, Jour. Asthma Pediatric Allergy and Immunology, 1987-91, Am. Jour. Diseases of Children, 1987-97, Contemporary Pediat., 1991-96, Am. Jour. Clin. Nutrition, 1992-97; contbr. articles to profl. jours. Commr. HHS Commn. on Childhood Vaccines, 1988-90; mem. clin. rsch. adv. com. Nat. Found. March of Dimes, 1992-97, 2004-09. Recipient Career Devel. award Nat. Inst. Allergy and Infectious Diseases, 1967-69, E. Mead Johnson award for Pediat. Rsch., 1974, Alumni Citation award U. Wis. Med. Sch., 1988, Lifetime Achievement award Immune Deficiency Found., 1995, Med. Sci. award UCLA Med. Alumni, 1999, Disting. Alumni award Babies and Children's Hosp. Alumni Assn., N.Y., 1999, Abbott award Am. Soc. Microbiology, 2007; Markle scholar, 1967-72. Fellow AAAS; mem. Am. Assn. Immunologists, Western Soc. Pediat. Rsch. (coun. 1977-80, pres. 1983, Ross Rsch. award 1971), Soc. Pediat. Rsch., Am. Pediat. Soc., Am. Acad. Allergy, Asthma and Clin. Immunology, Am. Acad. Pediat. (infectious diseases com. 1971-77), Am. Soc. Clin. Investigation, Clin. Immunology Soc., Phi Beta Kappa, Alpha Omega Alpha. Office: UCLA Dept Peds Divsn Immunology 10833 Le Conte Ave Los Angeles CA 90095-3075 Office Phone: 310-825-6481. Business E-Mail: estiehm@mednet.ucla.edu.

STIEHM, JUDITH HICKS, political scientist; b. Madison, Wis., Oct. 9, 1935; d. Stratton Elson and Eleanor Spencer (Kilbourn) Hicks; m. E. Richard Stiehm, July 12, 1958; children: Jamie Elizabeth, Carrie Eleanor, Meredith Ellen. Student, Oberlin Coll., 1953; BA in E. Asian Studies, U. Wis., 1957; MA in Am. History, Temple U., 1961; PhD in Polit. Theory, Columbia U., 1969. Dir. resident hons. program U. So. Calif., LA, 1970-73, asst. prof., 1970-74, assoc. prof., 1974-83, dir. program for study of women and men in soc., 1975-81, prof. polit. sci., 1983, vice provost, 1984-87; provost Fla. Internat. U., Miami, 1987-91, prof. polit. sci., 1987—. Vis. prof. U. Wis., 1994, U.S. Army Peacekeeping Inst., U.S. Army War Coll., 1995-96, U.S. Army Strategic Studies Inst., U.S. Army War Coll., 1996, U. So. Calif., 2002-; lectr. U. Wis., Madison, 1966-69, UCLA, 1969-70; vis. lectr. San Francisco State U., 1965-66; affiliate NAS Project, 1981-82; cons. UN Div. for the Advancement of Women, Calif. Elected Women, Dept. HEW, AAUW, LWV L.A., UN Lessons Learned Unit, Dept. Peacekeeping Ops. Author: Nonviolent Power: Active and Passive Resistance in America, 1972, Bring Me Men and Women..., 1981, Arms and the Enlisted Woman, 1989, The U.S. Army War College: Military Education in a Democracy, 2002, Champions for Peace: Women Winners of the Nobel Peace Prize, 2006; editor: The Frontiers of Knowledge, 1976, Women and Men's Wars, 1983, Women's Views of the Political World of Men, 1984, It's Our Military, Too!, 1996; mem. editorial bd. Western Polit. Quar., 1972-75, Signs, 1981-84, Women and Politics, 1986-88, 2000-. Mem. Calif. Postsecondary Edn. Commn., 1978, Calif. Adv. Coun. on Vocat. Edn., 1978-82, Def. Adv. Com. on Women in Svcs., 1979-82; bd. dirs. So. Calif. and Miami chpts. ACLU. Named Woman of Yr., Santa Monica YWCA, 1981; recipient Outstanding Civilian Svc. medal U.S. Army, 1996, U. Wis. Disting Alumni award, 2006. Mem. Am. Polit. Sci. Assn. (exec. coun. 1989, sec. 2000), Western Polit. Sci. Assn. (pres. 1986), Women's Caucus Polit. Sci. (pres. 1996-97), Nat. Council for Research on Women (exec. council 1982), Council on Fgn. Relations, Phi Beta Kappa, Phi Kappa Phi (Victoria Schuck Book award 1990). Avocations: tennis, skiing, stained glass. Home: 434 24th St Santa Monica CA 90402-3102 Personal E-mail: stiehmj@fiu.edu.

STIER, MARY P., publishing executive; b. Memphis, Nov. 9, 1956; m. Jeff Stier; 2 children. BA in comm., broadcasting, U. Iowa, 1978; DHL (hon.), Grand View Coll., Des Moines. With Gannett Co., 1982—2007, v.p. Ctrl. Region Newspaper Divsn., 1990—93, pres. Midwest Newspaper Group, 1993—2000, sr. group pres. Midwest Newspaper Group, 2000—07; retail advt. mgr. Iowa City Press-Citizen, 1982—84, advt. dir., 1984—87, pres., pub., 1987—91, Rockford (Ill.) Register Star, 1991—2000, The Des Moines Register, 2000—07; founder, CEO Brilliance Group, Des Moines, 2007—. Bd. trustees Drake U. Named one of Top 30, Nat. Orgn. Female Execs., Most Powerful Women in Bus., Fortune mag., 2002; recipient Athena award, Council of 100, Star of Hope award, Juvenile Diabetes Rsch. Found., Iowa ch., 2006. Mem.: The Greater Des Moines Partnership, Am. Press Inst., Iowa Newspaper Assn., Newspaper Assn. Am., Phi Beta Kappa. Office: Des Moines Register PO Box 957 Des Moines IA 50304-0957 Office Phone: 515-284-8041. E-mail: mpstier@dmreg.com, mary@thebrilliancegroup.net. *

STIERS, DAVID OGDEN, actor, conductor; b. Peoria, Ill., Oct. 31, 1942; s. Kenneth Truman and Margaret Elizabeth (Ogden) S. Diploma drama div., Juilliard Sch., 1973. Actor, Actors Workshop, 1962, Calif. Shakespeare Festival, 1963-68, mem., The Committee, 1968-70, San Francisco (revue)/Broadway season City Center Acting Co., N.Y.C., 1974; Broadway appearances include Ulysses in Nighttown, 1974, The Magic Show, 1974-75; other stage appearances include King Lear, 1981; regular on TV series MASH 1977-83, Two Guys, a Girl, and a Pizza Place, 1998, Love & Money, 1999, Teacher's Pet (voice), 2000-02, The Dead Zone, 2002-, Lilo & Stitch: The Series (voice), 2003-; other TV appearances include Mary Tyler Moore Show, 1976, 77, Rhoda, 1977, Matlock, 1987, 88, 89, Alf, 1988, Wings, 1990, Dr. Quinn, Medicine Woman, 1997, Ally McBeal, 1998, The Practice, 1999, Bull, 2000, Arli$$, 2002, Touched by an Angel, 2003, Frasier, 2003; TV film appearances include Charlie's Angels, 1976, A Circle of Children, 1977, A Love Affair: The Eleanor and Lou Gehrig Story, 1978, Sergeant Matlovich Vs. the US Air Force, 1978, Breaking Up Is Hard To Do, 1979, Damien: The Leper Priest, 1980, The Day the Bubble Burst, 1982, Anatomy of an Illness, 1984, The First Olympics-Athens 1896, 1984, The Bad Seed, 1985, North and South, 1985, North and South Book II, 1986, Mrs. Delafield Wants to Marry, 1986, Perry Mason: Case of the Notorious Nun, 1986, Perry Mason: Case of the Shooting Star, 1986, The Kissing Place, 1990, How to Murder a Millionaire, 1990, American Eyes, 1991, The Last of His Tribe, 1992, Taking Liberty, 1993, Past Tense, 1994, To Face Her Past, 1996, Justice League of America, 1997, Murder, She Wrote: The Last Free Man, 2001, Black River, 2001, Cable Beach, 2004; film appearances include: Drive, He Said, 1972, Oh God!, 1977, The Cheap Detective, 1978, Magic, 1978, The Man With One Red Shoe, 1985, Creator, 1985, Better Off Dead, 1985, The Accidental Tourist, 1988, Another Woman, 1988, Doc Hollywood, 1991, Beauty and the Beast (voice), 1991, Iron Will, 1994, The Toolshed, 1994, Bad Company, 1995, Pocahontas (voice), 1995, Steal Big, Steal Little, 1995, Mighty Aphradite, 1995, Everyone Says I Love You, 1996, The Hunchback of Notre Dame (voice), 1996, Meet Wally Sparks, 1997, Jungle 2 Jungle, 1997, Beauty and the Beast: The Enchanted Christmas (voice), 1997, Justice League of America, 1997, Belle's Magical World (voice), 1997, Reagan, 1998, Krippendorf's Tribe, 1998, Pocahontas: Journey to a New World (voice), 1998, MacArthur, 1999, Love & Money, 1999, The Stand-In, 1999, Tomcats, 2001, Atlantis: The Lost Empire (voice), 2001, The Majestic, 2001, The Assistant, 2001, Lilo & Stitch (voice), 2002, Stitch! The Movie (voice), 2003, Teacher's Pet (voice), 2004, Hoodwinked (voice), 2005; artistic assoc. The Acting Co., N.Y.C.; prin. guest condr. Yaquina Orch., 1989; now resident condr. Yaquina Chamber Orch.; guest condr. 70 orchs. including San Diego Symphony, Dallas Symphony Orch., Utah Symphony Orch., Chgo. Symphony Orch., Va. Symphony Orch., N.C. Symphony Philharm., Ft. Wayne Philharm., Calif. Symphony Orch., also orchs. in Honolulu, Portland, Maine, Grand Rapids, Mich., Peoria, Ill. Mem. NARAS, Conductors Guild, Am. Symphony Orch. League, Internat. Horn Soc., Magic Castle, Players Club.

STIFEL, FREDERICK BENTON, minister, biochemist, nutritionist; b. St. Louis, Jan. 30, 1940; s. Carl Gottfried and Alma J. (Clark) Stifel; m. Gail Joane Stewart, Aug. 10, 1963; children: Tim, Faith, Seth, Elizabeth. BS, Iowa State U., 1962, PhD, 1967; MDiv., Melodyland Sch. Theol., Anaheim, Calif., 1979. Ordained to ministry Evang. Presbyn. Ch., 1981. Lab. supr., research chemist U.S. Army Med. Research and Nutrition Lab., Denver, 1968-74, Letterman Army Inst. Research, San Francisco, 1974-76; intern pastor Melodyland Christian Ctr., Anaheim, 1979-80; assoc. pastor Faith Presbyn. Ch., Aurora, Colo., 1980—, moderator bd. deacons, 1997—; pastor Outreach and Missions, 1999—. Chmn. care candidates com. Presbytery of West, Denver, 1985—88, Denver, 1991—94, Denver, 2003—; v.p. Love Inc. Metro Denver, 1987—90; regional coord. Nat. Assn. Single Adult Leaders, 1987—90, coord. Denver area, 1990—95; mem. Denver Seminary Commn., 1995—, mem. world outreach com., 1998—99; regional coord. Colo. Pregnancy Ctrs., Inc., 1992—94, Rocky Mountain Prayer Network, 1994—96, Christian Family Svcs., 1990—; bd. dirs. St. James Bible Coll., Kiev, Ukraine, 1997—, faculty; bd. dirs. Profl. Publs.; faculty Life of Jesus Bible Coll., Yellow Water, Ukraine; bd. dirs. Internat. Project Adv. Bd., Heart for the World, Inc. Contbr. articles to profl. jours. Young Life leader Hinkley HS, Aurora, 1968—74; vice chmn. Young Life com. Marin County, Calif., 1974—76; mem. parent adv. coun. IMPACT drug intervention team Rangeview HS, Aurora, 1985—89, mem. accountability com., 1989—96; mem. Friends of Arts, 1992—96; del. Iowa and Colo. State Rep. Conv., Denver, 1984, Colorado Springs, 2002. Capt. Med. Svc. Corps US Army, 1967—70. Recipient Sci. Achievement award, U.S. Army Sci. Conf., 1968, 1970, Parents of the yr. award, Rangeview HS, 1992—93; Ralston Purina Rsch. fellow, 1962—63, Borden Agrl. scholar, 1962. Mem.: Am. Sci. Affiliation, Am. Soc. Clin. Nutrition, Am. Soc. Nutritional Scis., Evang. Theol. Soc., Sigma Xi, Kappa Sigma, Gamma Sigma Delta, Alpha Zeta, Phi Kappa Phi, Phi Eta Sigma. Avocations: reading, hiking, swimming, poetry, gardening. Home: 3492 S Blackhawk Way Aurora CO 80014-3909 Office: Faith Presbyn Ch 11373 E Alameda Ave Aurora CO 80012-1023 Office Phone: 303-364-7271. Business E-Mail: fstifel@faithpc.org.

STIFELMAN, MARC LEE, toxicologist, risk management consultant; s. Alan Stifelman and Phyllis Nebret; m. Loretta Amy Vosk, Nov. 7, 1992. BS, Rutgers U., New Brunswick, NJ, 1989; MS, U. Wash., Seattle, 1998. Corps officer Nat. Oceanic and Atmospheric Adminstrn., Seattle, 1992—94; environ. cons. Seattle, 1995—96; rsch. asst. U. Wash., Seattle, 1996—98; toxicologist US EPA, Seattle, 1998—. Surveyor NOAA, 1992—94. Lt. j.g. NOAA Corps, 1992—95. Mem.: Soc. Toxicology (risk assessment and ethical, legal, and social issues com. 1998—). Achievements include human health risk assessment for Coeur d'Alene Basin. Office: US EPA 1200 Sixth Ave Mail Stop OEA-095 Seattle WA 98101 Office Phone: 206-553-6979. Business E-Mail: stifelman.marc@epa.gov.

STIFF, ROBERT MARTIN, newspaper editor; b. Detroit, Aug. 25, 1931; s. Martin L. and Gladys (Mathews) S.; m. Cindy Rose, Aug. 30, 1980; children: David Alan, Amy Anne, Kirsten Marie. BA in Radio and Journalism, Ohio State U., 1953. All-Am. sports editor Ohio State U., Daily Lantern, 1952—53; reporter, bur. chief, city editor Painesville Telegraph, Ohio, 1953-61; deskman, asst. city editor, sports editor, city editor, day editor, state editor, asst. mng. editor St. Petersburg Times, Fla., 1961-67; editor St. Petersburg Evening Ind., 1967-84; dir. St. Petersburg Times Pub. Co., 1969-84; exec. editor, v.p. Tallahassee Democrat, 1985-91; pres. Bob Stiff & Assocs., Tallahassee, 1991-95; exec. editor JMT Assocs., 1991—92, 1994—95; mng. editor About Fla., 1991-94; editor Lexington (NC) Dispatch, 1995—2006. Mem. Pulitzer Prize Jury, 1982-83; dir. devel. and pub. rels. Fla. Taxwatch Inc., 1992-94; bd. dirs. NC AP News Coun., 1995-2001, v.p., 1997-99, pres., 1999-2000; pres. Empty Stocking Fund, 1995-2006. Bd. dirs. NC AP News Coun., 1995—2001, v.p., 1997—99, pres., 1999—2000; bd. dirs. Cancer Svcs. Davidson County, 1996—2004, NC Open Govt. Coalition, 2004—06, U. NC, Chapel Hill, Sch. Journalism Found., 2004—06; pres. Capital Press Assn., 1998—2001; bd. dirs. NC Daily Newspaper Assn., 1995—2006, v.p., 1998—99, pres., 1999—2000. Mem.: Nat. Coun. Editl. Writers, NC Press Assn. (bd. dirs. 1999—2000, 2002—05), AP Mng. Editors Assn., Fla. Bar Found. (bd. 1990—92), Fla. Soc. Newspaper Editors (pres. 1975—76, dir. 1971—84, 1990—93), Am. Soc. Newspaper Editors Found. (bd. dirs., treas. 1986—90), Am. Soc. Newspaper Editors (dir. 1981—87), AP Assn. Fla. (pres. 1970—71), Lexington Kiwanis (bd. dirs. 1996—2000, 2003—06), Sigma Delta Chi (pres. West Coast chpt. 1970—71).

STIFFLER, JACK JUSTIN, electrical engineer; b. Mitchellville, Iowa, May 22, 1934; s. John Justin and Helen Irene (Roorda) S.; m. Ardis Ann Ackerman, Aug. 21, 1955; 1 child, Julia Alise; m. Sally Voris Burns, Apr. 20, 1989. AB magna cum laude in Physics, Harvard U., Cambridge, Mass., 1956; MSEE, Calif. Inst. Tech., Pasadena, 1957, PhD, 1962; postgrad., U. Paris, 1957-58. Engr. Hughes Aircraft Corp., Culver City, Calif., 1956-57; mem. tech. staff Jet Propulsion Lab., Pasadena, Calif., 1959-67; cons. scientist Raytheon Corp., Sudbury, Mass., 1967-81; co-founder, exec. v.p. Sequoia Systems, Inc., Marlborough, Mass., 1981—97; co-founder, CTO Reliable Tech., Inc., 1998—; cons., 1997—. Lectr. Calif. Inst. Tech., U. So. Calif., UCLA, Northeastern U. Author: Theory of Synchronous Communications, 1971; contbr. chpts. to books, articles to profl. jours. Fellow: IEEE; mem.: Woods Hole Oceanographic Inst. (hon.), Sigma Xi, Phi Beta Kappa. Office Phone: 508-353-5611. Personal E-mail: stiffler@capecod.net.

STIFFLER, STUART ALDEN, retired library director; b. St. Louis, Jan. 16, 1934; s. James Henry Stiffler and Marcella Eugenia Alden; m. Muriel Watkins (dissolved); children: Douglas, Christine. BA, Hiram Coll., 1955; MA, We. Res. U., 1956, MLS, 1957; postgrad., Ind. U., 1966; cert. in exec. mgmt., Miami U., 1976. Ref. asst. Enoch Pratt Free Libr., Balt., 1958—59; asst. to assoc. libr. Hiram (Ohio) Coll., 1960—67; dir. Shafer Libr., Findlay (Ohio) Coll., 1968—73; dir. libr. Behrend Coll., Pa. State U., Erie, 1974—77; dir. Cole Libr, Cornell Coll., Mt. Vernon, Iowa, 1978—83; dir. libr. Ky. Wesleyan Coll., Owensboro, Ky., 1983—85, Daymar Coll., Owensboro, 1986—97. Faculty Hiram Coll., 1965, honors program faculty, 1965—67; chair nominating com. Ohio Coll. Libr. Ctr., 1970, exec. com., 70; pres. Erie Area Libr. Consortium, Erie, Pa., 1974. Reviewer: Iowa History; contbr. articles to profl. jours. Mem. Friends of the Libr., Hiram Coll., 1990, Friends of Libr., Juniata Coll., Huntington, Pa., 2003—; sponsor Children Internat., Kansas City, 1995—; exec. com. Boy Scout Am., Mt. Vernon, 1974—76; sponsor Big Brothers Big Sisters, Owensboro, 1994—96. Recipient Genealogist's Documentation award, Alden Kindred, Inc., 2002; scholar, We. Res. U., 1956. Mem.: ALA. Democrat. Unitarians. Avocations: numismatics, genealogy, history. Home: PO Box 522 401 4th St Huntingdon PA 16652-1423 Personal E-mail: stustiff@verizon.net.

STIFF-ROBERTS, ADRIENNE D., electrical engineer, educator; d. Lee Vernon and Renee Flood Stiff; m. Francis L. Roberts, Jr., Aug. 11, 2001. BS in Physics, Spelman Coll., Atlanta, Ga., 1999; BSEE, Ga. Inst. Tech., Atlanta, Ga., 1999; MSEE, U. Mich., Ann Arbor, Mich., 2001, PhD in Applied Physics, 2004. Asst. prof. Dept. Elec. and Computer Engring. Duke U., Durham, NC, 2004—. Contbr. articles to profl. jours. Recipient Elec. and Computer Engring. Outstanding Sr. Scholar award, Ga. Inst. Tech., 1999, Excellence in Tech. Comm. commendation, 2005; fellow, David and Lucille Packard Found., 1999—2004, AT&T Labs., 1999—2004; grantee, NSF, 2006; scholar, NASA, 1994—99. Mem.: IEEE, Materials Rsch. Soc., Golden Key Honor Soc., Sigma Pi Sigma, Phi Beta Kappa. Office: Duke University Dept of ECE Box 90291 Durham NC 27708-0291 Office Phone: 919-660-5560. Office Fax: 919-660-5293. Business E-Mail: adrienne.stiffroberts@duke.edu.

STIFTEN, EDWARD J., corporate financial executive; Corp. contr. Gen. Dynamics Corp.; exec. v.p., chief adminstrv. officer Clark Refining & Mktg., Inc.; v.p., CFO BJC HealthCare, 1998—2004; sr. v.p., CFO Express Scripts, Inc., Md. Heights, Mo., 2004—. Office: Express Scripts Inc 13900 Riverport Dr Maryland Heights MO 63043 Office Phone: 314-702-7667. Office Fax: 314-702-7037. *

STIGLER, STEPHEN MACK, statistician, educator; b. Mpls., Aug. 10, 1941; s. George Joseph and Margaret (Mack) S.; m. Virginia Lee, June 27,1964; children: Andrew, Geoffrey, Margaret, Elizabeth. BA, Carleton Coll., 1963, DSc (hon.), 2005; PhD, U. Calif., Berkeley, 1967. Asst. prof. U. Wis., Madison, 1967-71, assoc. prof., 1971-75, prof., 1975-79, U. Chgo., 1979—, chmn. dept., 1986—92, 2005—, Ernest DeWitt Burton Disting. Svc. prof., 1992—. Trustee Ctr. Advanced Study in the Behavioral Scis., Stanford, Calif., 1986-92, 93-2006, chmn., 1995-99, 2002-06. Author: The History of Statistics, 1986, Statistics on the Table, 1999; contbr. articles to jours. in field. Recipient Rsch. award Humboldt Found., 2005; Guggenheim Found. fellow, 1976-77; Ctr. for Advanced Study in Behavioral Scis. fellow, 1978-79. Fellow: AAAS, Royal Statis. Soc. (Fisher lectr. 1986), Am. Statis. Assn. (editor Jour. 1979—82), Inst. Math. Stats. (Neyman lectr. 1988, pres. 1993—94, LeCam lectr. 2006), Am. Acad. Arts and Scis. (mem. coun. 1995—99); mem.: Am. Philos. Soc., Brit. Soc. for History Sci., History of Sci. Soc., Bernoulli Soc., Statis. Soc. Can., Internat. Statis. Inst. (mem. coun. 1999—2001, pres. 2003—05), Quadrangle Club, Phi Beta Kappa, Sigma Xi. Office: U Chgo Dept Statistics 5734 S University Ave Chicago IL 60637-1514 Office Phone: 773-702-8328. Business E-Mail: stigler@galton.uchicago.edu.

STIGLIANO, JOSE MARIA, information technology executive, computer scientist; b. Buenos Aires, Dec. 9, 1953; s. Jose and Yvonne Suzanne (Engel) S.; m. Daniela Saida Farinelli, Dec. 14, 1988; children: Veronica Maria, Carolina Maria, Jose Nicolas. Cert. in electronics, L.A. Huergo Tech. Coll., 1973; cert. systems analysis, U. Del Salvador, 1975; BSBA, Am. U., 1990; MS in Mgmt., Boston U., 1992; PhD in Mgmt., Clayton U., 1993; BS in Mgmt. Info. Systems, U. of State of N.Y., 1996; MSc in Computer Sci., Boston U., 1997. Programmer Ministry of Justice, Buenos Aires, 1973-76; analyst, programmer CTC Svc. Bur., Buenos Aires, 1976-77; systems analyst Aurora S.A., Buenos Aires, 1977-78; computer systems officer Internat. Fund Agrl. Devel. UN, Rome, 1981-88; info. tech.coord. Internat. Fund Agrl. Devel. of U.N., Rome, 1988—2005, dir. info. tech. divsn., 2006—. Lectr. U. Del Salvador, Buenos Aires, 1975-77; cons. in field. Contbg. author: Encyclopedia of Information Systems, 2002; inventor in field. Recipient IFAD Merit award, 1988, IFAD Svc. award, 1990. Mem. IEEE, IEEE Computer Soc., IEEE Comms. Soc., Engring. Mgmt. Soc., Software Engring. Tech. Coun., Soc. Internat. Devel. (life), Assn. Computing Machinery, Boston U. Gen. Alumni Assn., Argentine Soc. for Informatics and Ops. Rsch. Avocations: music, bass guitar. Office: Internat Fund Agrl Devel 107 Via Del Serafico 00142 Rome Italy Personal E-mail: j.stigliano@computer.org. Business E-Mail: j.stigliano@ifad.org.

STIGLITZ, JOSEPH EUGENE, economics professor, former federal official; b. Gary, Ind., Feb. 9, 1943; s. Nathaniel David and Charlotte (Fishman) Stiglitz; m. Anya Schiffrin, Oct. 29, 2004; children from previous marriage: Siobhan, Michael, Edward, Julia. BA, Amherst Coll., Mass, 1964; DHL, Amherst Coll., 1974; PhD in Econs., MIT, 1966; MA (hon.), Yale U., 1970; D in Econs. (hon.), U. Leuven, 1994. Asst. prof. econs. MIT, 1966—67; asst. prof. Cowles Found., Yale U., New Haven, 1967—68, assoc. prof., 1968—70, prof. econs., 1970—74; vis. fellow St. Catherine's Coll., Oxford, England, 1973—74; Joan Kenney professorship Stanford U., 1974—76, prof. econs. & senior fellow, Hoover Inst., 1988—2001; Oskar Morgenstern dist. fellow Inst. Advanced Studies Math., Princeton, NJ, 1978—79; Drummond prof. polit. economy Oxford U., England, 1976—79; prof. econs. Princeton U., 1979—88; mem., Coun. Econ. Advisors Exec. Office of the Pres., Washington, 1993—97, chmn., 1995—97; sr. v.p., chief economist World Bank, Washington, 1995—2000; sr. fellow Brookings Inst., Washington, 2000; Stern visiting prof. Columbia U., 2000; prof. economics & fin. Columbia U. Grad. Sch. of Bus., Dept. of Econ. and Sch. of Internat. and Public Affairs, 2001—; prof. exec. MBA programs Columbia U.; chmn. Columbia U. Com. Global Thought; chair Brooks World Poverty Inst., U. Manchester, England, 2005. Tapp rsch. fellow Gonville and Caius Coll., Cambridge, England, 1966—70; vis. prof. dept. econs. U. Canterbury, Christchurch, New Zealand, 1967; sr. rsch. fellow social sci. divsn. Inst. for Devel. Studies U. Coll. Nairobi, 1969—71; cons. World Bank, State of Alaska, Seneca Indian Nation, Bell Comm. Rsch. Editor: Jour. Econ. Perspectives, 1986—93; Am. editor: Rev. of Econ. Studies, 1968—76, assoc. editor: Am. Econ. Rev., 1968—76, Energy Econs., Managerial and Decision Econs., mem. editl. bd.: World Bank Econ. Rev.; author: Whither Socialism?, 1996, Frontiers of Development Economics: The Future in Perspective, 2000, New Ideas About Old Age Security: Toward Sustainable Pension Systems in the 21st Century, 2001, Globalization and Its Discontents, 2002, The Rebel Within: Joseph Stiglitz and the World Bank, 2002, The Roaring Nineties, 2003; co-author (with C.E. Walsh): Principles of Macroeconomics, 2002, Economics, 2002; co-author: (with R. K. Sah) Peasants Versus City-Dwellers: Taxation and the Burden of Economic Development, 2002; co-author: (with B. Greenwald) Towards a New Paradigm in Monetary Economics, 2003; co-author: (with Andrew Charlton) Fair Trade For All: How Trade Can Promote Development (Initiative for Policy Dialogue Series), 2006. Recipient John Bates Clark award, Am. Econ. Assn., 1979, Internat. prize, Accademia Lincei, 1988, Union des Assurances de Paris prize, 1989, The Nobel Prize in Economic Sciences, 2001, Rechtenwald Prize, Germany, 1998; fellow, Guggenheim, 1969—70; scholar guest, The Brookings Inst., Washington. Fellow: Inst. for Policy Rsch. (sr. 1991—93), Brit. Acad. (corr.); mem.: NAS (fellow, 1988), Econometric Soc., Am. Acad. Arts and Scis.(fellow, 1983), Am. Econ. Assn. (exec. com. 1982—84, v.p. 1985). Office: Columbia U Uris Hall Rm 814 3022 Broadway New York NY 10027 E-mail: jes322@columbia.edu. *

STIGWOOD, ROBERT COLIN, film producer, television producer, radio producer, theater producer; b. Adelaide, Australia, Apr. 16, 1934; came to Eng., 1956; s. Gordon and Gwendolyn (Burrows) S. Student, Sacred Heart Coll., Adelaide. Worked as copywriter for advt. agy., Adelaide; opened talent agy. London, 1962; liquidated firm, 1965; became bus. mgr. for group Graham Bond Orgn.; became co-mng. dir. NEMS Enterprises, 1967; prin. Robert Stigwood Orgn., 1967; formed RSO Records, 1973; dir. Polygram, 1976; co-founder (with Rupert Murdoch) R&R Films, 1979. Founder Music for UNICEF. 1st ind. record producer in Eng. with release of single Johnny Remember Me; producer: films, including Jesus Christ Superstar, 1973, Tommy, 1975, Survive, 1976, Saturday Night Fever, 1977, Grease I, 1978, Grease II, 1982, Moment By Moment, 1978, Sergeant Pepper's Lonely Hearts Club Band, The Fan, 1981, Times Square, 1980, Gallipoli, 1980, Staying Alive, 1983, Evita, 1996; stage musicals in Eng. and U.S., including, Hair, Oh! Calcutta, The Dirtiest Show in Town, Sweeney Todd, Pippin, Jesus Christ Superstar, Evita, Grease, Saturday Night Fever; TV producer in Eng. and U.S.; co-prodns. include The Entertainer (dramatic spl.); All in the Family (series), The Prime of Miss Jean Brodie (dramatic series). Recipient Tony award for best musical (Evita); named Internat. Producer of Yr. ABC Interstate Theatres, Inc., 1976. Mem. Royal Bermuda Yacht Club. Clubs: Royal Bermuda Yacht. Avocations: yachting, tennis. Office: Barton Manor East Cowes Isle of Wight England

STILES, GARY LESTER, cardiologist, molecular pharmacologist, educator; b. NYC, May 22, 1949; s. Robert L. and Vivian M. (Cano) S.; m. Alexis H. Stiles; children: Heather B., Wendy A. BS in Chemistry, St. Lawrence U., 1971; MD, Vanderbilt U., 1975. Diplomate Am. Bd. Internal Medicine, sub.-bd. Cardiovascular Medicine. Resident in internal medicine Vanderbilt U., Nashville, 1975-78; from fellow in cardiology to prof. Duke U., Durham, NC, 1978—90, prof. medicine, 1990—; CMO, v.p. Duke Health Sys., 1999—2004; exec. v.p. Wyeth Pharms., Collegeville, Pa., 2004—, chief med. officer, 2004—. Mem. sci. adv. coun. Alta. Heritage Found., Edmonton, Can., 1990-2006; mem. pharmacology study sect. NIH, Bethesda, Md., 1988-91. Mem. editl. bd. Jour. Biol. Chemistry, 1990-95, Molecular Pharmacology, 1991-99. Recipient Katz prize Am. Heart Assn., 1983, award Am. Fedn. Clin. Rsch., 1989; grantee Am. Heart Assn., 1987-90; named one of America's Top Cardiologistst, Consumers' Research Coun. Am. Fellow Am. Coll. Cardiology (award 1993); mem. Internat. Churchill Soc., Assn. Am. Physicians, Am. Soc. Clin. Investigation. Republican. Achievements include patent in field. Office: Wyeth Pharms 500 Arcola Rd Collegeville PA 19426 Office Phone: 484-865-8700. Business E-Mail: stilesg@wyeth.com. *

STILES, JULIA, actress; b. NYC, Mar. 28, 1981; d. John O'Hara and Judith Stiles. B in English, Columbia U., 2005. Actor: (TV films) Before Women Had Wings, 1997, The '60s, 1999; (films) I Love You, I Love You Not, 1996, The Devil's Own, 1997, Wicked, 1998, Wide Awake, 1998, 10 Things I Hate About You, 1999, Down to You, 2000, Hamlet, 2000, State and Main, 2000, Save the Last Dance, 2001 (Teens Choice Drama award, 2001), The Business of Strangers, 2001, O, 2001, The Bourne Identity, 2002, A Guy Thing, 2003, Carolina, 2003, Mona Lisa Smile, 2003, The Prince & Me, 2004, The Bourne Supremacy, 2004, Edmond, 2005, A Little Trip to Heaven, 2005, The Omen, 2006, The Bourne Ultimatum, 2007; TV guest appearances include Ghostwriter, 1992, Promised Land, 1996, Chicago Hope, 1994; actor: (plays) Fran's Bed, 2005. Volunteer Habitat for Humanity, Costa Rica, Amnesty Internat. Named one of 25 Hottest Stars under 25, Teen People mag., 2002; voted one of, People Mag.'s 50 Most Beautiful People, 2001. Democrat. Office: Clare Ryu c/o United Talent Agy 9560 Wilshire Blvd Beverly Hills CA 90212 *

STILES, OWEN RODGER, social studies educator; b. NYC, July 31, 1945; s. Owen Russell Stiles and Madalyn Geneva Reinbolt; m. Martha M. Stiles, Dec. 30, 1974; children: Darienne Rnee, Andrea Lynn, Merinda Marie, Corrinne Marie. AA, Grossmont Coll., El Cajon, Calif., 1972; BBA, Nat. U., San Diego, 1985; MA, Azusa Pacific U., Calif., 1992. Commd. ensign USN, 1963, ret., 1983; tchr. Roosevelt Jr. HS, San Diego, 1989—93, Gompers Secondary Sch., San Diego, 1993—95, Laytonville HS, Calif., 1995—97, Gridley HS, Calif., 1998—. Willard fellow, Econ Ed Found., 1991. Mem.: Sons of Union Vets. of Civil War, Sons of Am. Revolution, Kiwanis (pres. Gridley chpt. 1989—). Home: 284 Hazel St Gridley CA 95948

STILES, THOMAS BEVERIDGE, II, retired investment company executive; b. Easton, Pa., Oct. 4, 1940; s. Ezra Martin and Vivien (de Fay) S.; m. Elaine Ann Patyk, July 2, 1966 (div. Oct. 1980); children— Thomas Beveridge III, Jonathan Ezra; m. Barbara Toll Alexander, Mar. 7, 1981. BA, Yale U., 1963; MBA, Harvard U., 1968. V.p. Laird, Inc., NYC, 1968-73; sr. v.p., dir. Smith Barney Harris Upham and Co., Inc., NYC, 1973-82; exec. v.p., dir. E.F. Hutton & Co. Inc., NYC, 1982-87; chmn., CEO Shearson Lehman Advisors Asset Mgmt. Co., NYC, 1988-90, 99—, Bernstein Macaulay, NYC, 1988-90; CEO, chmn. Greenwich Street Advisors, NYC, 1990-97; mng. dir. Smith, Barney, Inc., NYC, 1993-99, retired, 1999—. Bd. dirs., pres. Cedar Lawn Cemetery, Paterson, N.J., 1973—. Bd. dirs. Sanford C. BErnstein Fund, 2003—. 1st lt. M.I., U.S. Army, 1963-66. Fellow Fin. Analysts Fedn.; mem. N.Y. Soc. Security Analysts, El Niguel Country Club (Calif.). Republican. Presbyterian. Avocations: political science, tennis, swimming. E-mail: tom.stiles@cox.net.

STILES, VIRGINIA FORD, data processing executive, poet; b. Memphis, June 3, 1961; d. Margaret Berry and John Edward Ford, adopted d. Mattie Virginia Martin; m. Allen Wesley Stiles, Aug. 9, 2003; children: Lakeisha Lashun Williams, Teresita Louise Cornelius. Lic. Tax Preparer, H&R Block Tax Sch., 1992. Data entry clk. H&R Block, LA, 1992—93; ms mgmt. specialist USN, Norfolk, Va., 1996. Tax examiner IRS, Memphis, 1987—88. Singer (author): (anthology) Memphis Miracle (Editor's Choice award, 2000); author: I Think (Best Poet, 2002). Recipient Veterans Integrity, Patriotism Recognition, Am. Legions, 2000, Pub. greeting cards, anthology, and CD, Internat. Libr. of Poetry, 2001. Mem.: Phi Theta Kappi Honor Soc. (hon.). Personal E-mail: virginiallen@aol.com.

STILL, CHARLES NEAL, retired neurologist, medical educator, consultant; b. Richmond, Va., Apr. 15, 1929; s. Charles Wright and Ruth (Kemp) S.; m. Dorothy Lee Varn, Dec. 27, 1958; children: Charles Herbert, Carl Nelson, Sara Alice. BS in Chemistry, Clemson U., 1949; MS in Biochemistry, Purdue U., 1951; MD, Med. U. SC, 1959; MA in Religion, Luth. Theol. So. Sem., Columbia, SC, 2007. Diplomate Am. Bd. Psychiatry and Neurology. Instr. chemistry Clemson (S.C.) U., 1951-52; rotating intern U. Chgo. Clinics, 1959-60; neurology fellow Sch. Medicine Johns Hopkins U., Balt., 1960-63; resident in neurology Johns Hopkins-Balt. City Hosp., 1960-63; NIH rsch. fellow Harvard U.-McLean Hosp., Belmont, Mass., 1963-65; chief neurology svcs. William S. Hall. Psychiat. Inst., Columbia, S.C., 1965-81, assoc. dir. gen. psychiatry and neurology, 1989-92; dir. C. M. Tucker Human Resources Ctr., Columbia, 1981-88; clin. prof. neuropsychiatry USC Sch. Medicine, Columbia, S.C., 1981-88, prof. neuropsychiatry, 1989—2004, clin. prof. neuropsychiatry and behavioral sci. Sch. Medicine, 2004; ret., 2004. Instr. chemistry U.S. Mil. Acad., West Point, N.Y., 1953-55; assoc. clin. prof. neurology Med. U. S.C., Charleston, 1973-92; assoc. prof. neuropsychiatry U. S.C. Sch. Medicine, Columbia, 1976-78, prof. neuropsychiatry, 1978-81. Author: (with others) Handbook of Clinical Neurology, 1976, Neurologic Clinics, 1984, Movement Disorders, 1986; editor The Recorder Columbia Med. Soc., 1991-2003, editor emeritus, 2003—; mem. editl. bd. Jour. S.C. Med. Assn., 1980-2006, Jour. Applied Gerontology, 1983-88; contbr. articles to profl. jours. Chmn. grants rev. bd. S.C. Dept. Mental Health, Columbia, 1973-78; mem. exec. bd. Alzheimer's Assn. Columbia, 1985-93, pres. Mid-State chpt. Alzheimer's Assn., 1991-92; med. dir. Alzheimer's Disease Registry, Columbia, 1989-92, Alzheimer's Daycare Ctr., Columbia, 1989-92; mem. Gov.'s Adv. Coun. to Alzheimer's Disease and Related Disorders Resource Coordination Ctr., 1995-99. 1st lt. U.S. Army, 1952-55. Fellow: Am. Geriatrics Soc. (emeritus), Am. Acad. Neurology (emeritus), Gerontol. Soc. Am. (emeritus), Am. Inst. Chemists (life); mem.: AMA (life), Am. Chem. Soc. (emeritus). Baptist. Avocations: writing, photography. Home: 2 Culpepper Cir Columbia SC 29209-2234 Personal E-mail: cndstill@aol.com.

STILL, HOMER IBSON, information technology executive; b. Tulsa, Oct. 3, 1945; children: Walter D., Sarisa D., Joshua H., Homer Isaac, Quillie Mae Elisabeth. Student in Bus. Mgmt. and Programming, Tulsa Jr. Coll.; AA in Liberal Arts and Sci., Okla. Mil. Acad., Claremore, 1965; BS in Indsl. and Managerial Psychology, Okla. State U., Stillwater, 1969, BA in History, 1969. Cert. project mgmt. specialist, instr., cons. IBM Southwestern Region, planning and estimating specialist, instr., cons. IBM Southwestern Region. Sr. EDP systems engr., computer security mgr. Am. Airlines, Inc., 1974—82; sr. cons. Trans World Airlines, 1982—87; adv. system engr., account mgr., bus. analyst, program/project mgmt. cons., worldwide bus. cons., sr. ptnr. IBM, 1987—93; chief operating and info. officer, exec. v.p. Genesis Industries, Inc., 1994—95; computer and operations cons., 1995—98; sr. mgr., program mgr. Sabre Inc., 1998—2001; security screener Dept. Homeland Security, 2002—03; sr. program and project mgr. Capital One Auto Fin., 2003—04; flow team mem., mem. exec. mentoring program Target Corp., 2005—06; master program mgr. Capitol One Finance, 2005—06. Active reserve US Army, 1967—70, infantry officer, capt., brevet col., dep. commdg. officer Presidio of San Francisco US Army, 1970—73, Vietnam, active reserve US Army, 1974—79, 95th Infantry Divsn., Tulsa. Recipient SAR medal for outstanding cadet, Okla. Mil. Acad., 1965. Mem.: MENSA, Phi Theta Kappa. Conservative. Baptist. Avocations: fishing, hunting, reading, travel. Personal E-mail: homerstill@hotmail.com.

STILLER, BEN, actor, television producer; b. NYC, Nov. 30, 1965; s. Jerry Stiller and Anne Meara. m. Christine Taylor, May 13, 2000, children: Ella Olivia, Quinlin Dempsey. Student, UCLA. Actor: (theatre) The House of Blue Leaves, 1985, This Is How It Goes, 2005; (films) Hot Pursuit, 1987, Empire of the Sun, 1987, Fresh Horses, 1988, Next of Kin, 1988, That's Adequate, 1989, Elvis Stories, 1989, Stella, 1990, Highway to Hell, 1992, Reality Bites, 1994, Heavyweights, 1995, Happy Gilmore, 1996, Flirting With Disaster, 1996, Zero Effect, 1998, There's Something About Mary, 1998, Your Friends and Neighbors, 1998, Permanent Midnight, 1998, Nobody Knows Anything, 1998, The Suburbans, 1999, McClintock's Peach, 1999, Black and White, 1999, Mystery Men, 1999, The Independent, 2000, Keeping the Faith, 2000, Meet the Parents, 2000, The Royal Tannenbaums, 2001, Orange County, 2002, Duplex, 2003, Nobody Knows Anything, 2003, Along Came Polly, 2004, Envy, 2004, Meet the Fockers, 2004, Madagascar (voice), 2005, Danny Roane: First Time Director, 2006, School for Scoundrels, 2006, Night at the Museum, 2006; actor, dir. (films) Reality Bites, 1994, The Cable Guy, 1996, Zoolander, 2001; actor, prodr. (films) Dodgeball: A True Underdog Story, 2004; actor, exec. prodr. (films) Starksy & Hutch, 2004, Tenacious D: The Pick of Destiny, 2006; prodr.: Blades of Glory, 2007; TV appearances include Kate McShane, 1975, Kate & Allie, 1986, Miami Vice, 1987, The Ben Stiller Show (also writer, dir.)(Emmy award for writing), 1992-93, Frasier, 1993, Duckman, 1995, Friends, 1997, Saturday Night Live, 1998, 2000, Freaks and Geeks, 2000, The Simpsons (voice), 2002, Undeclared, 2002, The King of Queens, 2002, Curb Your Enthusiasm, 2004, King of the Hill (voice), 2004, Arrested Development, 2004, 05; co-editor (with Marla Hamburg Kennedy) Looking at Los Angeles. Named Man of Yr., Hasty Pudding Theatricals, Harvard U., 2007; named one of 50 Most Powerful People in Hollywood, Premiere mag., 2005, 100 Most Powerful Celebrities, Forbes.com, 2007. *

STILLER, JENNIFER A., lawyer; b. Washington, May 4, 1948; d. Ralph Sophian and Joy (Dancis) Stiller. AB in Econs. and History, U. Mich., 1970; JD, NYU, 1973. Bar: Pa. 1973, U.S. Dist. Ct. (mid. dist.) Pa. 1977, U.S. Supreme Ct. 1978, U.S. Dist. Ct. (ea. dist.) Pa. 1983, U.S. Ct. Appeals (3rd cir.) 1983, U.S. Ct. Appeals (D.C. cir.), 1996. Dep. atty. gen. Pa. Dept. Justice, Harrisburg, 1973-75, Pa. Dept. Health, Harrisburg, 1975-78; sr. staff atty. Am. Hosp. Assn., Chgo., 1978-80, mgr., dept. fed. law, 1980-81; gen. counsel Ill. Health Fin. Authority, 1981-82; sr. assoc. Berriman & Schwartz, King of Prussia, Pa., 1983-85, Wolf, Block, Schorr & Solis-Cohen, Phila., 1985-88, Montgomery, McCracken, Walker & Rhoads, LLP, Phila., 1988-90; ptnr. Montgomery, McCracken, Walker & Rhoads, Phila., 1990-2000, chair health law group, 1991-2000; sr. counsel Tenet Healthcare Corp., Phila., 2000-2001; pvt. practice Haverford, Pa., 2001—. Contbr. articles to profl. jours. Fellow Am. Health Lawyers Assn. (bd. dirs. 1997-2003, exec. com. 2002-03); mem. ABA (gov. com. Health Law Forum 1994-95), Pa. Soc. Healthcare Attys. (pres. 1995). Avocations: gardening, bicycling, hiking, music. Office: Law Office Jennifer A Stiller 625 Haydock Ln Haverford PA 19041-1207 Home Phone: 610-649-9817; Office Phone: 610-642-3366. Business E-Mail: stiller@healthregs.com.

STILLER, JERRY, actor; b. NYC, June 8, 1927; s. William and Bella S.; m. Anne Meara, Sept. 14, 1953; children: Amy, Benjamin. BS in Speech and Drama, Syracuse U., 1950. Actor with nat. co. of Peter Pan, 1951, also at Henry St. Playhouse, 1941, Cherry Lane Theatre, N.Y.C., 1947, Billy Barnes Showboat, Chgo., 1950, Erie (Pa.) Playhouse, 1951, 52, Memphis Arena Theatre, 1952, Phoenix Theatre, 1954, 55, 56, Shakespeare Festival Theatre, Stratford, Conn., 1955, Compass Players, 1959, mem. Shakespeare Co. in Central Park, N.Y.C., 1957, 71, Two Gentlemen, 1971, Much Ado, 1988; Broadway appearances include The Golden Apple, 1954, The Ritz, 1975, Unexpected Guests, 1977, Hurlyburly, 1985, Three Men on a Horse, 1993, What's Wrong With This Picture?, 1994, The Three Sisters, 1997; film appearances include The Taking of Pelham 1-2-3, 1974, Airport '75, 1975, The Ritz, 1976, Those Lips, Those Eyes, 1979, Nadine, 1986, That's Adequate, 1986, Hairspray, 1986, Shoeshine (Acad. award nomination, short subject 1989), A Pair of Jokers, 1990, The Pickle, 1992, Stag, 1996, Camp Stories, 1996, The Deli, 1997, Die Story Von Monty Spinnerratz, 1997, The Fish in the Bathtub, 1998, The Independent, 2001, On the Line, 2001, Serving Sara, 2002, Zoolander, 2003, Hairspray, 2007, The Heartbreak Kid, 2007; Off-Broadway appearances include Boubouroche, 1971, Passione, 1980, Prairie du Chien, 1985, After-Play, 1995-96; mem. comedy team, Anne Meara, 1961—, Ed Sullivan Show 36 appearances; night club appearances include Compass Players, St. Louis, 1957, Happy Medium, Chgo., 1960, also Village Gate, Village Vanguard, Blue Angel, Bon Soir and, Phase Two, N.Y.C., Mr. Kelly's, Chgo., Hungry I, San Francisco, The Establishment, London, The Sands, Flamingo, Las Vegas, Harrah's, Reno and Lake Tahoe, Trump Plaza, QE II; co-star: daily

TV series Take Five with Stiller and Meara, 1977-78; actor TV series Joe and Sons, 1975, Tattinger's, 1987, The Detective, The Sunset Gang, PBS, 1991, Seize the Day, 1990, The Hollow Boy, American Playhouse, 1991, Seinfeld, 1993-98, Subway Stories, King of Queens, 1998-2007; commercials: Blue Nun, United Van Lines, Amalgamated Bank, Vermeer Liquor, Nike, AT&T, Glad Bags, Total Cereal; AOL, Video (co-host with Anne Meara): So You Want to be an Actor?; animation: Teachers Pet "Pretty Boy", 2000-02, Lion King III, 2003, Lion King 1Y2, 2004; author: Married to Laughter (Grammy nomination for audio), 2000. Recipient Disting. Alumnus award Syracuse U., 1973, Voice of Imagery award, 1975, Arents Pioneer Medal, 1979, 1st Biffy award Balt. Internat. Film Festival, Entertainment Father of Yr. award, 1977, Syracuse Walk of Stars, 1994, Syracuse U. award for Achievement in the Arts, Am. Comedy award for role in Seinfeld, 1998, Fourth Ann. Alan King award in Jewish humor (with Anne Meara), Am. Comedy award Seinfeld, 1998, Productive Aging award Jewish Coun. Aging, 2004, Thalia award (with Anne Meara) Humbert Coll., Toronto, 2004; nominated Emmy award for role in Seinfeld, 1997, Ellis Island Medal of Honor, 2000; received joint star with wife on the Hollywood Walk of Fame, 2007.

STILLER, SHALE DAVID, lawyer, educator; b. Rochester, NY, Feb. 23, 1935; s. Maurice Aaron and Dorothy (Salitan) S.; m. Ellen M. Heller; children: Lewis B., Michael J., Kenneth R.; stepchildren: William Heller, Lawrence Heller. BA, Hamilton Coll., 1954; LLB, Yale U., 1957; MLA, Johns Hopkins U., 1977. Bar: Md. 1957. Ptnr. corp. and securities, tax, trusts and estates practices DLA Piper, Balt., 1992—. Lectr. U. Md. Law Sch., 1963—. Contbr. articles to profl. jours. Trustee Johns Hopkins U., Assn. Jewish Charities, Peabody Inst.; trustee, vice chmn. Johns Hopkins Hosp. and Sch. Medicine; pres. The Harry and Jeanette Weinberg Found., Leonard & Helen Stulman Found., Charles Crane Family Found.; bd. mem. Bright Star Found., Shelter Found., Hittman Family Found.; mem. adv. bd. Tax Mgmt., 1972-93; chmn. Jud. Nominating Commn., Balt., 1979-83; officer, bd. dirs. Park Sch., 1973-79, pres., 1982-86; pres. Jewish Family Agy., 1972-74. Mem. ABA, Am. Law Inst., Am. Coll. Tax Counsel, Am. Coll. Trust and Estate Counsel, Order of Coif. Democrat. Jewish. Office Phone: 410-654-6835. Office Fax: 410-654-4900. Business E-Mail: sstiller@theweinbergfoundation.org.

STILLER, STEPHEN JOSEPH, mathematics educator; b. El Paso, Nov. 9, 1977; s. Lawrence Joseph and Kathy Ellen Stiller. B in Math. Edn., SUNY, Geneseo, 2000; MPhil, SUNY, Buffalo, 2004. Cert. Secondary Math. Edn. NY, 2000, Cognitive Coach Ctr. for Cognitive Coaching, 2005. Tutor access opportunity program SUNY, Geneseo, 1997—99, tutor, 1998—2000; camp counselor Camp Cory the YMCA, Penn Yan, NY, 1999; math tchr. New Hanover Pub. Schs., Wilmington, NC, 2000—01, Wake County Pub. Schs., Raleigh, 2001—02; math. tchr. Buffalo Pub. Schs., 2002—, staff devel. specialist, 2003—. Head math 9 dept. Buffalo Pub. Schs., 2002—, facilitator for tchr. edn., 2003—, coach for math tchrs., head algebra dept., 2004—, health promotion com. leader, nutritional svcs. com. mem., 2006—. Distbr. bags food, water, and bibles, several U.S. cities, 2001—06. Mem.: NEA, Nat. Coun. Suprs. Math., Nat. Coun. Tchrs. Math. Home Phone: 716-541-4238; Office Phone: 716-816-4238.

STILLINGS, DENNIS OTTO, research association administrator, consultant; b. Valley City, ND, Oct. 30, 1942; s. Harlow Cecil and Ruth Alice (Wolff) S. BA, U. Minn., 1965. Tchr. Henry (S.D.) Pub. Schs., 1965-66, Darby (Mont.) Pub. Schs., 1966-68; tech. rsch. libr., then mgr. hist. dept. Medtronic, Inc., Mpls., 1968-79; instr. humanities U. Minn., Mpls., 1970-72; founding dir., then curator Bakken Libr., Mpls., 1976-80; ind. antiquarian hist. cons. Mpls., 1979-81; sole proprietor Archaeus Project, Kamuela, Hawaii, 1981—2006; exec. dir. Five Mountain Med. Cmty., 1996-97, also bd. dirs., 1996—2006; ret., 2006. Cons. Ctr. for Sci. Anomalies Rsch., Ann Arbor, Mich., 1993—97; bd. mem. Kohala Ctr., 2001—06; bd. dirs. Dan Carlson Enterprises, Mpls., Barnes County Hist. Soc. Columnist Med. Progress Through Technology, 1974-76; columnist Med. Instrumentation, 1973-76, guest editor, 1975; editor: Cyberphysiology: The Science of Self-Regulation, 1988, Cyberbiological Studies of the Imaginal Component in the UFO Contact Experience, 1989, The Theology of Electricity: On the Encounter and Explanation of Theology and Science in the 17th and 18th Centuries, 1990, Project 2010: On the Current Crisis in Health and Its Implications of the Hospital for the Future, 1992; founding editor: (jours.) Artifex, 1981-93, Archaeus, 1982-84, Healing Island. Fellow Am. Inst. Stress; mem. Soc. Sci. Exploration. Avocations: jungian psychology, golf, fishing, travel. Home and Office: 724 4th Ave NW Valley City ND 58072 Personal E-mail: stillings@gmail.com.

STILLINGS, IRENE ELLA GRACE CORDINER, retired foundation executive; b. Boston, Aug. 17, 1918; d. Matthew Wilson and Susan F. (Mason) Cordiner; m. Gordon A. Stillings, May 13, 1945; children: David Gordon, Susan Irene. Student, Radcliffe Coll., 1936-39; diploma, Burdett Coll., 1941. Sec., bookkeeper Boston Refrigerator Co., 1941-42; sec., tchr. Burdett Coll., 1942-44; sec., bookkeeper Gertrude Rittenburg, Boston, 1944-46. Town chmn. Heart Fund, Woodland, Maine, 1953-61; Brownie leader Girl Scouts U.S., 1954-58; pres. Woodland Woman's Club 1961-63; sec. PTA, 1961-62; chmn. Baileyville Superintending Sch. Com., 1962-64; chmn. women's activities Nat. Found., East Washington County, 1959-61; pres. Hosp. Aid, 1961-63; chmn. Newcomers Coll. group YWCA, 1965-66, chmn. theatre group, 1968-70, pres. Suburbanites, 1970-71; Stamford (Conn.) chmn. Expt. in Internat. Living, 1965-68; bd. dirs. YWCA of Stamford, 1969-78, chmn. antique show, 1960-77, chmn. devotion, 1970-92, ann. Antique Show benefit, 1970-77; pres. New Suburbanites, Stamford, 1994-95, ret. 1996. Mem. Mass. Hort. Soc., St. Luke's Guild (treas. 1954-63), Radcliffe Club, Stamford Woman's Club (treas. 1975-79, program com., co-chmn. Am. home dept. 1974, 75, pres. 1981-83, bd. dirs. 1981—, 2d v.p. fin. 1979-81, 83-85, 87-89, chmn. bldg. investment 1979-81, parliamentarian 1990—, pres., newcomers/suburbanites, 1994-95), Theta Alpha Chi. Episcopalian. Home: 277 W Hill Rd Stamford CT 06902-1708

STILLMAN, BRUCE, molecular biologist; b. Melbourne, Australia, Oct. 16, 1953; came to U.S., 1979; s. Graham and Jessie (England) S.; m. Grace Begley, Mar. 21, 1981; children: Keith, Jessica. BSc with honors, U. Sydney, 1975; PhD, Australian Nat. U., 1979. Staff investigator Cold Spring Harbor Lab., NY, 1981-83, sr. staff investigator, 1984-85, sr. scientist, 1985-90, asst. dir., 1990-93, dir. cancer ctr., 1992—, dir., 1994—2003, pres., CEO, 2003—. Contbr. scientific papers to profl. publs. Apptd. to Order of Australia, 1999; Rita Allen Found. scholar, 1981-85; Cancer Rsch. fellow Damon Runyon-Walter Winchell, 1979-80, Alfred P. Sloane, Jr., GM Cancer Rsch. Found., 2004. Fellow Royal Soc. London; mem. AAAS, Am. Soc. Microbiology, Am. Soc. Biochem. and Molecular Biology, Am. Assn. Cancer Rsch., NAS. Office: Cold Spring Harbor Lab PO Box 100 Cold Spring Harbor NY 11724-0100

STILLMAN, CHARLES ALLEN, lawyer; b. Bklyn., Sept. 8, 1937; s. Max and Anne (Parness) S.; m. Marilyn Norma Radezky, Aug. 30, 1959; children: Nina, Robert, Jay. BA, NYU, 1958, JD, 1962. Bar: NY 1962. Law clk. to Hon. Irving R. Kaufman, US Ct. Appeals (2d cir.), 1959-62; asst. US atty. So. Dist. NY, 1962-66; assoc. Phillips, Nizer, Benjamin, Krim & Ballon, 1966-68; assoc. Louis Bender, Esquire, 1968-69; ptnr. Botein Hays Sklar & Herzberg, NYC, 1969-72; practice, NYC, 1972-77; ptnr. Stillman & Friedman, NYC, 1977—; adj. assoc. prof. trial advocacy Fordham U., 1978-85; hearing officer for environ. protection hearings NY Conv. Ctr.; mem. spl. investigation Roosevelt Island Tramway Accident, 1981-82. Chmn. lawyers div. Am. Friends of Hebrew U.; mem. Lawyers Com. on the Criminal Justice Act, 1977-86, ABA, Fed. Bar, NYC Bar Assn., NY County Lawyers Assn., NY State Bar Assn., NY Coun. Def. Lawyers (dir., 1987-92); coun. mem. Am. Coll. Trial Lawyers, Internat. Acad. Trial Lawyers; trustee, NYC Sch. Constrn. Authority, 2000-03. Recipient: Torch of Learning award, Am. Friends of Hebrew U., lawyers divsn., 1984, Norman S. Ostrow award NY Coun. Def. Lawyers, 1992, Human Rels. award Anti-Defamation League, 1993, Louis Dembitz Brandeis Medal for Disting. Legal Svc., Brandeis U., 1997, Milton S. Gould award for Outstanding Advocacy, Office of Appellate Defender, 1999, Robert M. Morgenthau award Police Athletic League, 2003. Office: Stillman & Friedman PC 425 Park Ave New York NY 10022 E-mail: cstillman@stillmanfriedman.com.

STILLMAN, CORY, professional hockey player; b. Peterborough, Ont., Can., Dec. 20, 1973; m. Mara Stillman; children: Riley, Madison, Chase. Left wing Calgary Flames, 1995—2001, St. Louis Blues, 2001—03, Tampa Bay Lightning, 2003—04, Carolina Hurricanes, 2005—. Achievements include being a member of Stanley Cup Champion Tampa Bay Lightning, 2004, Carolina Hurricanes, 2006. Office: Carolina Hurricanes RBC Ctr 1400 Edwards Mill Rd Raleigh NC 27607

STILLMAN, ELINOR HADLEY, retired lawyer; b. Kansas City, Mo., Oct. 12, 1938; d. Hugh Gordon and Freda (Brooks) Hadley; m. Richard C. Stillman, June 25, 1965 (div. Apr. 1975). BA, U. Kans., 1960; MA, Yale U., 1961; JD, George Washington U., 1972. Bar: D.C. 1973, U.S. Ct. Appeals (10th cir.) 1975, U.S. Ct. Appeals (9th cir.) 1976, U.S. Ct. Appeals (2d cir.) 1976, U.S. Ct. Appeals (5th cir.) 1983, U.S. Ct. Appeals (4th cir.) 1985, U.S. Supreme Ct. 1976. Lectr. in English CUNY, 1963-65; asst. editor Stanford (Calif.) U. Press., 1967-69; law clk. to judge U.S. Dist. Ct. D.C., Washington, 1972-73; appellate atty. NLRB, Washington, 1973-78; asst. to solicitor gen. U.S. Dept. Justice, Washington, 1978-82; supr. appellate atty. NLRB, Washington, 1982-86, chief counsel to mem. bd., 1986-88, 94-00, chief counsel to chmn. bd., 1988-94; ret., 2000. Mem.: D.C. Bar Assn., Order of Coif, Phi Beta Kappa. Democrat.

STILLMAN, GREGORY N., lawyer; b. Portsmouth, Va., Apr. 29, 1948; BA, U. Richmond, 1970; JD, Washington & Lee U., 1974. Bar: Va. 1974. Mng. ptnr., litig, intellectual property, antitrust Hunton & Williams LLP, Norfolk, Va., and mem. exec. com. Contbr. The Va. Lawyer, 1980-86. Burls scholar. Fellow Am. Coll. Trial Lawyers (Va. State chmn., 1998-2000); mem. Va. Bar Assn., Fed. Bar Assn., Richmond Bar Assn., Va. Assn. Def. Attys., Norfolk-Portsmouth Bar Assn., Phi Delta Phi. Office: Hunton & Williams PO Box 3889 Crestar Bank Bldg 500 E Main St Ste 1000 Norfolk VA 23510-2204 Office Phone: 757-640-5314. Business E-Mail: gstillman@hunton.com.

STILLMAN, JEANNE BETSOCK, public health administrator, consultant; b. Bethlehem, Pa., Dec. 15, 1942; d. Paul Thomas and Juliana Habera Betsock; m. David George Stillman, 1965; children: J. Alexander, Gregory D., Juliana E. C. BA, Am. U., 1964; MSPH, U. N.C., 1971; postgrad., Columbia U. Sch. Pub. Health, 1979-81. Assoc. dir. Quaker Svc./AFSC, Lome, Togo, 1969-70; from instr. to lectr. health adminstrn. Sch. Pub. Health U. N.C., Chapel Hill, 1971-74, rsch. assoc. Population Ctr., 1971-74; staff assoc., Tunisia project mgr. The Population Coun., NYC, 1982-83; dir. N.Y. office Inst. for Devel. Tng., NYC, 1989-93; Nigeria project mgr. The Africa-Am. Inst., NYC, 1993-96; prin. Strategies for Devel., Inc., Hastings-on-Hudson, NY, 1998—. Dep. dir. devel. The Children's Village, Dobbs Ferry, 2002; mem. adv. com. UN Population Fund, NYC, 1998; cons. in field. Assoc. editor, contbr. International Encyclopedia of Population, 2 vols., 1982; editor: (tng. manuals) Training Course in Women's Health, 2nd edit., 11 vols., 1993; editor, writer: UNHCR Manual for Health Services in Afghan Refugee Camps, 1985; project dir.: (video) Population and People of Faith, 1991 (NY Internat. Film Festival Bronze medal 1992). Ch. coord. Habitat for Humanity, Hastings-on-Hudson, 1997—2000; vol. Internat. Microcredit Summit Meeting of Couns., NYC, 1998; bd. sec. Greater Westchester Youth Orch. Assn., Valhalla, NY, 1997-99; parent fund vol. Phillips Exeter Acad., 1998-; mem. Ch. Vestry, 2001-04; vol. Bus. Coun. of Westchester, 2002—; vol. emergency preparedness ARC, 2002-04; mem. adv. bd. youth symphony UN, 2006—; sec. Pub.-Pvt. Alliance Found., 2006—. Mem. APHA, Assn. Devel. Officers (bd. dirs. 2003-06), UN Assn. USA (Westchester chpt., exec. dir. 2006-, bd. dirs., sec. 2002—, Mid-Atlantic rep., mem. coun. of chpts. and divsns. steering com. 2005—, bd. dirs. So. N.Y. divsn. 2005—, v.p. 2006—), Am. Freedom Assn. (hon. bd. dirs. 2003—). Democrat. Episcopalian. Avocations: reading, theater, music. Office: Strategies for Development Inc 166 Edgars Ln Hastings On Hudson NY 10706-1108 Office Phone: 914-478-3450. Office Fax: 914-478-7859. Business E-Mail: jbs@stratdev.com.

STILLMAN, MARGARET (PEGGY STILLMAN), library director; m. Peter R. Stillman; children: Lindsay H. and Walker H. Forehand. BA in Edn., U. Richmond, 1973; MA in Edn., Va. Commonwealth U., 1974; MLS, U. Md., 1977. Children's libr. to dir. Chesapeake Pub. Libr. Sys., Va., 1975-85, dir., 1985—; acting asst. city mgr. City of Chesapeake, 1999—2002. Chmn. bd. Libr. Va., chmn. bldg. com. Chmn. State Adult Literacy Initiative, 1989-95; mem. Govs. Rural Econ. Devel. Task Force, 1990-92, U. Va. Continuing Edn. Ctr. Coun., 1990-94; bd. dirs. United Way Hampton Rds., 1995—, Vol. Hampton Rds., 1996-98, Va. Stage Co., 1979-85 (v.p. 1981-82), Colonial Girl Scouts, 1993-95, Cultural Alliance, 1985-91, Tidewater Red Cross, 1980-83. Recipient Outstanding Young Career Woman of Va. award, 1978; named Outstanding Profl. Woman, 1993, Woman of Yr., Hampton Roads C. of C., Women's Divsn., 2003, First Citizen of Chesapeake, Chesapeake Rotary Club, 2005; named one of Strong, Smart, and Bold Women of SW Hampton Roads, 2000. Mem. Pub. Libr. Assn. (bd. dirs. 1997-98, chmn. leadership devel. com. 1997, mem. pres.'s 2000 com.), Libr. Va. Found. (bd. dirs. 1996—), WHRO Found. (bd. dirs. 1997—), ALA (mem. awards com., mem. advancement for literacy award com., mem. adult lifelong learning com.). Office: Chesapeake Pub Libr Sys 298 Cedar Rd Chesapeake VA 23322-5598 E-mail: stillman@chesapeake.lib.va.us.

STILLMAN, MICHAEL ALLEN, dermatologist; b. NYC, Apr. 12, 1943; s. Aaron and Anne (Turansky) S.; m. Susan Fuchs, July 8, 1973; children: Julie, Jeremy. BA, Clark U., 1963; MD, SUNY, 1967. Diplomate Am. Acad. Dermatology. Med. intern Maimonides Hosp., Bklyn., 1967—68; dermatology resident NYU Med. Ctr. and Bellevue Hosp., NYC, 1970—73; pvt. practice Mt. Kisco, NY, 1973—. Cons. dermatology U.S. Mil. Acad., West Point, N.Y., 1973-75 Contbr. essays and articles to profl. jours. and newspapers Bd. trustees South Salem (NY) Libr., 1990-98; boys varsity tennis coach John Jay H.S., Katonah, NY, 1996. Capt. USAF, 1968-70, Vietnam Decorated Combat Inf. badge Fellow Am. Soc. Dermatol. Surgeons, Am. Acad. Dermatology; mem. N.Y. State Med. Soc., Noah Worcester Dermatology Soc Avocations: tennis, jogging, writing. Home: 33 Mead St Waccabuc NY 10597-1107 Office: Mt Kisco Med Group 111 Bedford Rd Katonah NY 10536 Office Phone: 914-232-3135.

STILLMAN, NINA GIDDEN, lawyer; b. NYC, Apr. 3, 1948; d. Melvin and Joyce Audrey (Gidden) S. AB with distinction, Smith Coll., 1970; JD cum laude, Northwestern U., 1973. Bar: Ill. 1973, U.S. Dist. Ct. (no. dist.) Ill. 1973, U.S. Dist. Ct. (ea. dist.) Wis. 1979, U.S. Dist. Ct. (no. dist. trial bar) Ill. 1983, U.S. Ct. Appeals (7th cir.) 1974, U.S. Supreme Ct. 1981, U.S. Dist. Ct. (ctrl. dist.) Ill. 1994, U.S. Dist. Ct. (ea. dist.) Tex., 1996, U.S. Dist. Ct. (Colo.), 1999, U.S. Dist. Ct. (ND) 2002. Assoc. Vedder, Price, Kaufman & Kammholz, Chgo., 1973-79, ptnr., 1980—2004, Morgan, Lewis and Bockius, LLP, Chgo., 2004—. Adv. bd. occupational health and safety tng. program U. Mich., Ann Arbor, 1980-83; adj. faculty Inst. Human Resources and Indsl. Rels., Loyola U., Chgo., 1983-86, bd. advisors, 1986—. Author: (with others) Women, Work, and Health: Challenge to Corporate Policy, 1979, Occupational Health Law: A Guide for Industry, 1981, Employment Discrimination, 1981, Personnel Management: Labor Relations, 1981, Occupational Safety and Health Law, 1988; contbg. author: Occupational Medicine: State of the Art Reviews, 1996; contbr. articles to profl. jours. Legal advisor, v.p. Planned Parenthood Assn. Chgo., 1979—81; sec. jr. governing bd. Chgo. Symphony Orch., 1983; trustee Merit Sch. Music, 2000—, vice chmn. bd. trustees, 2001—. Recipient Svc. award Northwestern U., 1994. Mem.: ABA (occupl. safety and health law com. 1978—), Human Resources Mgmt. Assn. Chgo. (bd. dirs. 1986—88, officer), Am. Inns of Ct. (v.p. Wigmore chpt. 1988—89), Chgo. Bar Assn. (chmn. labor and employment law com. 1986—87), Northwestern U. Sch. Law Alumni Assn. (pres. 1991—92), Univ. Club Chgo. (bd. dirs. 1988—2001, sec. 1999—2000, v.p. 2000—01), The Chgo. Com., Econ. Club Chgo., Lawyers Club, Smith Coll. Club Chgo. (pres. 1972). Avocations: travel, reading, the arts, collecting art. Office: Morgan Lewis and Bockius LLP 77 W Wacker Dr Ste 600 Chicago IL 60601 Office Phone: 312-324-1150. Business E-Mail: nstillman@morganlewis.com.

STILLMAN-MYERS, JOYCE L., artist, educator, writer, illustrator, consultant; b. NYC, Jan. 19, 1943; d. Murray W. and Evelyn (Berger) Stillman. BA, NYU, 1964; student, Art Students League, 1965, Pratt Inst., 1972; MFA, L.I. U., 1975; postgrad., Calif. Inst. Integral Studies, 1994—. Tchr. N.Y.C. Pub. Schs., 1964-71; artist, 1974-76, Louis K. Meisel Gallery, NYC, 1975-84, Tolarno Gallery, Melbourne, Australia, 1976—, Allan Stone Gallery, NYC, 1990—; founder CoCreative Inst. Art, Fingerlakes Region, NY. Assoc. prof. Towson U., Md., 1981; vis. assoc. prof. Towson State U., 1982; tchr. Tompkins Cortland C.C., 1988; lectr. Cornell U., 1990; founder Ithaca Women Artists Salon, Artistic Applications Decorative Arts Ctr.; prof. art studies Tompkins County C.C., 1986; pvt. art instr., Odessa, NY, 1986—. One-woman shows include Ctrl. Hall Gallery, Port Washington, 1975, Tolarno Gallery, Melbourne, 1976, Louis K. Meisel Gallery, N.Y.C., 1977, 1980—82, Heckscher Mus., Huntington, N.Y., 1980, Holtzman Gallery, Towson (Md.) State U., 1982, Roslyn Oxley Gallery, Sydney, 1976, 1982, Tomasulo Gallery, Union Coll., N.J., 1983, Stages Keuka Coll., Keuka Park, N.Y., 1985, New Visions, Ithaca, N.Y., 1989, Her-Chambliss, Hot Springs, Ark., 1990, Artist on the Lake, Hector, N.Y., 1992, Arnot Mus., Elmira, N.Y., Mus. Modern Art Christmas Card Collection, 1994, Arnot Mus., Elmira, N.Y., 2002, over 75 group shows, designer, Mus. Modern Art Christmas Card Collection, 1978—81, 1994, Time-Life Poster, 1978, Doing Dionysos, Arts of the So. Trees, 2000—02. Mem. Literacy Vols. Am. Recipient Flower Painting award, Artist's Mag., 1986, Distinctive Merit award, Art Dir.'s Club 58th Ann., 1979; grantee Pub. Svc., N.Y. State Creative Artist's, 1979. Mem.: AAUW, Nat. Assn. Women Artists.

STILLS, STEPHEN, musician, vocalist, composer; b. Dallas, Jan. 3, 1945; m. Kristen Stills; 2 children. Vocalist, guitarist Buffalo Springfield band, 1966-68, Crosby, Stills & Nash, 1968-69, 77, 82, Crosby, Stills, Nash, & Young, 1969-71, solo career, 1971—. Albums include Stephen Stills, 1970, Stephen Stills II, 1971, Stephen Stills, 1975, Illegal Stills, 1976, Thoroughfare Gap, 1978, Right by You, 1984, (with Buffalo Springfield) Buffalo Springfield, 1967, (with Buffalo Springfield) Buffalo Springfield Again, 1967, Last Time Around, 1969, (with Crosby, Stills, Nash, & Young) Deja Vu, 1970, Four Way Street, 1972, (with Crosby, Stills, Nash, Young) So Far, 1974, American Dream, 1989, (with Crosby, Stills, Nash) Crosby, stills and Nash, 1969, Crosby, Stills and Nash, 1977, Daylight Again, Live It Up, Replay (best of), After The Storm, 1994, (with Manassas) Manassasm 1972, Down The Roadm 1973; singles include (solo) Love the One You're With, 1971, Super Session, (with Buffalo Springfield) For What It's Worth, 1967, (with Crosby, Stills, Nash, & Young) Woodstock, Ohio, Teach Your Children, 1970, Stills Alone, 1991. Inducted into Rock and Roll Hall of Fame, 1997. Office: Vision Records 13385 W Dixie Hwy North Miami FL 33161-4134

STILLWAGON, GARY BOULDIN, radiation oncologist; b. Memphis, Dec. 30, 1951; s. Jack Wright and Ida Jean (Bouldin) S.; m. Leta Fern Miller, Jan. 20, 1979. BS in Physics, Ga. Inst. Tech., 1974, MS in Nuclear Engring., 1975, PhD, 1978; MD, U. Tenn., 1983. Diplomate Nat. Bd. Med. Examiners, Am. Bd. Radiology in Radiation Oncology; cert. FLEX, 1983. Med. physicist Meth. Hosp., Memphis, 1974; rsch. asst. Ga. Inst. Tech., Atlanta, 1975-78; radiation safety officer, physicist VA Med. Ctr., Memphis, 1978-80, cons. radiation safety, 1980-83; fellow in radiation oncology Johns Hopkins U. and Hosp., Balt., 1983-87; asst. prof. oncology and radiology Johns Hopkins U. Sch. Medicine, Balt., 1987—. Vis. rschr. radiobiology lab. U. Utah, 1978; com. mem., site visitor, radiation therapy oncology group, coop. group Nat. Cancer Inst., 1989—; cons. in field. Contbr. articles to profl. jours. Active Boy Scouts Am., Bapt. Ch. Sunday Sch. Dept. of Energy fellow, 1976-78, Clin. fellow Am. Cancer Soc., 1986-87. Fellow Am. Coll. Radiology; mem. AAAS, AMA, Health Physics Soc., Am. Assn. Physicists in Medicine, Am. Nuclear Soc., Am. Soc. Therapeutic Radiology and Oncology, Am. Soc. Clin. Oncology, Sigma Xi. Republican. Home: 655 River Chase Rdg NW Atlanta GA 30328-3568 Office: 1000 Johnson Ferry Rd Atlanta GA 30342

STILLWELL, R. NEWCOMB, lawyer; b. Oct. 2, 1956; AB magna cum laude, Princeton Univ., 1979; JD cum laude, Harvard Univ., 1984. Bar: Mass. 1984. Assoc. Ropes & Gray, Boston, 1984—93, ptnr. corp. dept., 1993—, co-leader private equity practice group. Lectr. Harvard Law Sch. Former bd. dir. Hotchkiss Sch.; chmn. Volunteers of Am. of Mass. Office: Ropes & Gray 1 International Pl Boston MA 02110-2624 Office Phone: 617-951-7316. Office Fax: 617-951-7050. Business E-Mail: newcomb.stillwell@ropesgray.com.

STILLWELL, WALTER BROOKS, III, lawyer; b. July 30, 1946; s. Walter Brooks Jr. and Selpha T. (Everson) S.; m. Carolyn E. Laws, Dec. 20, 1992; children: Walter, Haviland. BA cum laude, Wake Forest U., 1968; JD, U. Ga., 1971. Bar: Ga. 1971, U.S. Dist. Ct. (so. dist.) Ga. 1971, U.S. Ct. Appeals (D.C. cir.) 1976, U.S. Ct. Appeals (11th cir.) 1981, U.S. Dist. Ct. (no. dist. 1996) Ga., U.S. Supreme Ct., 1977. Assoc. Hunter, Maclean, Exley & Dunn, P.C., Savannah, Ga., 1971-74, ptnr., 1974—; dir. First Nat. Bank, 2002—. Trustee Savannah Tech. Coll. Found., 2002-; adv. dir. Century South Bank of Coastal Region, N.A., 1993-2001; v.p. and dir. W.E.T., Inc., 1991-96; adv. coun. Savannah (Ga.) Econ. Devel. Authority, 2004—. Alderman City of Savannah, 1974-92, mayor-pro-tem, 1990-92; chmn. Chatham County Bd. Elections, 1999-2002. Mem. State Bar of Ga. (real property sect., exec. com. 1986-93, chmn. 1992), Am. Coll. Real Estate Lawyers, Savannah Bar Assn. (pres. 1999-2000). Office: Hunter Maclean Exley & Dunn PC 200 E Saint Julian St Savannah GA 31401-2700

STIMAC, JOHN ANTHONY, small business owner, poet, cartoonist, inventor; b. Kansas City, Kans., Nov. 12, 1946; s. Max George and Lola Mae Stimac; m. Sherry Lynn Stimac, Apr. 30, 1965 (dec. Sept. 24, 2005); children: Mary Ann, John Anthony, Christopher John. Union painter Local 43, Leavenworth, Kans., 1973—79; owner Heritage Painting Co., Kansas City, Kans., 1979—85, J-Duncan's Painting Co., Kingsville, Mo., 1985—2001, John Stimac Painting Co., Kingsville, 2001—. Cartoons, Highlights for Children, 1983; contbr. poems to books and jours. With US Army, 1963—65. Recipient Editors Choice awards, Internat. Libr. of Poetry, 2001—02. Mem.: Soc. of Poets (Lifetime Mem. award 2005). Achievements include invention of inventive systems minor images. Avocations: guitar, instrumental music. Home and Office: 13 NW 1621 Rd Kingsville MO 64061 Office Phone: 816-682-5075.

STIMMEL, BARRY, cardiologist, educator, internist, dean; b. Bklyn., Oct. 8, 1939; s. Abraham and Mabel (Bovit) S.; m. Barbara Barovick, June 6, 1970; children: Alexander, Matthew. BS, Bklyn. Coll., 1960; MD,

SUNY, Bklyn., 1964. Diplomate: Nat. Bd. Med. Examiners, Am. Bd. Internal Medicine. Resident Mt. Sinai Hosp., NYC, 1964-65, 67-69; asst. dean admissions and student affairs Mt. Sinai Sch. Medicine, CUNY, 1970-71, assoc. dean, 1971-81, asst. prof. medicine, 1972-75, assoc. prof., 1975-83, prof. medicine and med. edn., 1984—, assoc. dean acad. affairs, 1975-81, assoc. attending physician, 1975-83, acting chmn. dept. med. edn., 1979-94, dean admissions, acad. affairs and student affairs, 1981-94, dean grad. med. edn., 1994—, attending physician, 1984—, Katherine and Clifford Goldsmith prof. medicine (cardiology), 1998—. Mem. com. planning, priorities and evaluation N.Y. Met. Regional Med. Program, 1971-73; adv. com. Nat. Ctr. Urban Problems CUNY, 1970-71; adv. com. methadone maintenance Office of Drug Abuse Svcs. State N.Y., 1976-79; sci. adv. bd. Nat. Coun. Drug Abuse, 1978-84, N.Y. State Bd. Profl. Med. Conduct, 1983-97; bd. dirs. Am. Soc. Addiction Medicine, N.Y. State Coun. on Grad. Med. Edn., Greater N.Y. Hosp. Assn. Task Force on Health Manpower. Author: Heroin Dependency: Medical Social and Economic Aspects, 1975, Cardiovascular Effects Mood Altering Drugs, 1979, Pain, Analgesia, Addiction, 1984, Ambulatory Care, 1983, The Facts about Drug Use, 1993, Drugs Abuse and Social Policy in America: The War That Must Be Won, 1996, Pain and Its Relief Without Addiction, 1997, Alcoholism, Drug Addiction and the Road to Recovery: Life on the Edge, 2002; editor Advances in Alcohol and Substance Abuse, 1980-91, Jour. Addictive Diseases, 1991—; assoc. editor Am. Jour. Drug and Alcohol Abuse, 1979-85; contbr. chpts. to books, articles to profl. jours. With M.C. USNR, 1965—67. Mem. AAUP, Am. Assn. Physicians Assts. (adv. bd. 1972-73), Am. Assn. Higher Edn., Soc. Study of Addiction to Alcohol and Other Drugs, Assn. Med. Edn. and Rsch. Substance Abuse, Inst. Study of Drug Addiction, Am., N.Y. heart assns., Am., N.Y. State socs. internal medicine, Soc. Internal Medicine County of N.Y. (dir.), Am. Coll. Cardiology, Greater N.Y. Coalition on Drug Abuse, NYS Coun. on Grad. Medical Edn., N.Y. Acad. Medicine, Nat. Coun. Alcoholism, Rsch. Soc. on Alcoholism, Am. Ednl. Research Assn., Am. Fedn. Clin. Rsch., Am. Soc. Addiction Medicine. Office: Mt Sinai Sch Med 5 E 98th St Fl 3 New York NY 10029-6501 Office Phone: 212-241-6694. E-mail: barry.stimmel@mssm.edu.

STIMPERT, MICHAEL ALAN, retired agricultural products company executive; b. Madisonville, La., Aug. 21, 1944; s. Warren Eugene and Louisa (Beale) S.; m. Kim Kathleen Agee, Apr. 17, 1970 (div. 1985); 1 child, Kelly Kathleen; m. Helen Marie Evans, June 27, 1987; children: Katherine Helen, Michael Adam. Student, Washburn U., 1962-64, U. Copenhagen, 1964; BA, Western Res. U., 1967; MBA, Harvard U., 1974. Asst. to group v.p. Gold Kist Inc., Atlanta, 1974, mgr. internat. div., 1975-80, dir. spl. markets and staff services, 1980-81, group v.p., 1982-86; v.p. ops. and govt. affairs Golden Peanut Co., Atlanta, 1986-89, exec. v.p., 1989-95; sr. v.p. Gold Kist Inc., Atlanta, 1996—2007. Chmn. bd. dirs. Sunpower, Inc., Athens, Ohio, Fundatropicos, Turrialba, Costa Rica; immediate past chmn. Global Health Action, Atlanta. Bd. dirs. Global Health Action, Tropics Found., Atlanta. Lt. (j.g.) USN, 1967-72, Vietnam. Mem. Assn. for Corp. Growth, Japan-Am. Soc. Ga., Harvard Bus. Sch. Club Atlanta, Cherokee Town and Country Club. Democrat. Roman Catholic.

STIMPSON, CATHARINE ROSALIND, literature educator, writer; b. Bellingham, Wash., June 4, 1936; d. Edward Keown and Catharine (Watts) Stimpson. AB, Bryn Mawr Coll., 1958; BA, MA, Cambridge U., Eng., 1960; PhD, Columbia U., 1967. Mem. faculty Barnard Coll., NYC, 1963—80; prof. English, dean of grad. sch., vice provost grad. edn. Rutgers U., New Brunswick, NJ, 1980—92, univ. prof., 1991—; chmn. bd. scholars Ms. Mag., NYC, 1981—92; dir. fellows program MacArthur Found., 1994—97; univ. prof., dean Grad. Sch. Arts and Sci. NYU, NYC, 1998—. Author: Class Notes, 1979, Where the Meanings Are, 1988; editor: Signs: Jour. Women in Culture and Soc., 1974—81, Women in Culture and Society book series, 1981; contbr. Change Mag., 1992—93. Chmn. N.Y. Coun. Humanites, 1984—87, Nat. Coun. Rsch. on Women, 1984—89; trustee Bates Coll., 1990—2007; pres. Assn. Grad. Schs., 2000—01; bd. dir. Stephens Coll., Columbia, Mo., 1982—85, Legal Def. and Edn. Fund, 1991—96. Fellow, Woodrow Wilson Found., 1958, Nat. Humanities Inst., 1975—76; Fulbright fellow, 1958—60, Rockefeller Humanities fellow, 1983—84. Mem.: PBS (bd. dirs. 1994—2000), NOW, PEN, MLA (exec. coun., chmn. acad. freedom com., 1st v.p., pres. 1990). Democrat. Home: 29 Washington Sq W Apt 15C New York NY 10011-9199 Office: NYU 6 Washington Sq N New York NY 10003-6668 Office Phone: 212-998-8040. Business E-Mail: catharine.stimpson@nyu.edu.

STINE, JEFFREY KIM, environmental historian, curator; b. San Diego, Feb. 25, 1953; s. Howard Henry and Dorothy (Graham) S.; m. Marcel Chotkowski LaFollette, July 28, 1986. BA, U. Calif., Santa Barbara, 1975, PhD, 1984. Cons. House Com. on Sci. and Tech., Washington, 1984—85, US Army Corps of Engrs., Washington, 1985—89; curator of engring. and environ. history Smithsonian Inst., Washington, 1989—, chair, divsn. medicine and sci., 2005—. Cons. Carnegie Commn. on Sci., Tech. and Govt., Washington, 1990, Libr. of Congress, 1995; commr. U.S., Can., Mex. Trilateral Com. on Environ. Edn., 1992-95. Editor: (series) Technology and the Environment, 1993-2001, (book reviews) Tech. and Culture, 1987-94; author: (Congl. report) A History of Science Policy in the United States, 1940-85, 1986; co-editor: Technology and Choice, 1991; author: Mixing the Waters: Environment, Politics, and the Building of the Tennessee-Tombigbee Waterway, 1993, Twenty Years of Science in the Public Interest, 1994; co-editor: Going Underground: Tunneling Past, Present, and Future, 1998. Pres. Am. Soc. for Environ. History, 1999—2001; trustee Pub. Works Hist. Soc., 1990—97, 1999—2001, pres., 2002—03. Recipient Congl. fellow Am. Hist. Assn., 1984, Weyerhaeuser award Forest History Soc., 1984, James Madison prize Soc. for History in the Fed. Govt., 1992, Wesley Johnson prize Nat. Coun. Pub. History, 1993, Abel Wolman award Pub. Works Hist. Soc., 1994, Charles Thompson prize Soc. for History in the Fed. Govt., 1999. Mem. Am. Hist. Assn., Soc. for History of Tech., Am. Soc. for Environ. History, Forest History Soc., Pub. Works Hist. Soc., Nat. Coun. on Pub. History. Democrat. Office: Nat Mus Am History Smithsonian Instn MRC 627 PO Box 37012 Washington DC 20013-7012 Business E-Mail: stine@si.edu.

STINE, JOHN ANDREW, communications engineer, researcher; b. Miami, Fla., Oct. 4, 1959; s. Carl William and Mary Biggers Stine; m. Martha Jane Byrd, Apr. 13, 1985; children: Andrew Joseph, Harry James, Brian Edward, Mary Elizabeth, Bridget Anne, Christopher William. BS in Gen. Engring., U.S. Mil. Acad., West Point, NY, 1981; MSEE, U. Tex., Austin, 1990, MS in Mfg. Sys., 1990, PhD in Elec. Engring., 2001. Registered profl. engr., Va., 1992. Commd. 2d lt. U.S. Army, 1981, advanced through grades to maj., 1981, ret., 2007. platoon leader A Co. 10th engr. bn. 3rd inf. div. Schweinfurt, Germany, 1982—83, exec. officer A Co. 10th engr. bn. 3rd inf. div., 1983—85, brigade engr. 2d brigade, 2d armored div. Ft. Hood, Tex., 1985—86, comdr. C Co. 17th engring. bn. 2d armored div., 1986—87, asst. divsn. engr. 2d armored div., 1987—88, operation rsch. sys. analyst test and experimentation command, 1993—96; constrn. mgr. Def. Spl. Weapons Agy. (now Def. Threat Reduction Agy.), Kirtland AFB, N.Mex., 1997—2001; asst. prof. elec. engring. U.S. Mil. Acad., West Point, NY, 1990—93; comm. engr. MITRE Corp., McLean, Va., 2001—04, prin. investigator in advanced tactical networking, 2004—. Contbr. articles to profl. jours. Decorated Army Commendation medal 3rd inf. divsn. U.S. Mil. Acad., Army Meritorious Svc. medal 2d armored divsn., Army Commendation medal, Army Meritorious Svc. Medal, Army Commendation medal U.S. Army Test and Experimentation Command, Army Meritorious Svc. medal, Def. Meritorious Svc. medal Def. Threat Reduction Agy.; recipient Best Dept. Rsch. award, U.S. Mil. Acad., 1993. Mem.: IEEE Comm. Soc. (sr. Best Paper award Dynamics Spectrum Access Networks Conf. 2007). Roman Catholic. Achievements include patents pending for wireless networking protocols. Office: MITRE Corp 7515 Colshire Dr Mc Lean VA 22102 Home Phone: 703-257-6478; Office Phone: 703-983-6281. Office Fax: 703-983-1370. Personal E-mail: stine@ieee.org. Business E-Mail: jstine@mitre.org.

STINE, KATIE KRATZ, state legislator; b. Dec. 6, 1956; BS, U. Cin.; JD, No. Ky. U. Atty.; mem. Ky. Ho. of Reps., Frankfort, 1995-98; senate pres. pro-tempore Ky. Senate, Frankfort, 1999—, mem. judiciary com. on com. rules. Active Jr. League Cin., Episcopal Ch. Women, No. Ky. Right to Life; former vice chair Ft. Thomas Bd. Adjustments. Mem. DAR, Ky. Bar Assn., Ft. Thomas Garden Club. Republican. Office: Ky Senate 24th Dist 702 Capitol Ave Rm 204 Frankfort KY 40601-3448 Home: 21 Fairway Dr Southgate KY 41071-3023

STINE, RICK D., editor; B in Journalism, English and Mathematics, U. of Richmond. Joined Dow Jones & Co., 1983, reporter Dow Jones Capital Markets Report, writer Dow Jones cable television dept.; news editor Dow Jones News Svc., 1989—95, asst. mng. editor, 1995—97, deputy mng. editor, 1997—99, mng. editor Jersey City, 1999—. Office: Dow Jones News Svc Harborside Fin Ctr 800 Plaza Two Jersey City NJ 07311-1199

STINE, ROBERT HOWARD, retired pediatrician, allergist; b. Nov. 1, 1929; s. Harry Raymond and Mabel Eva (Newhard) S.; m. Lois Elaine Kihlgren, Oct. 22, 1960; children: Robert E., Karen E. Burnham, Jonathan N. BS in Biology, Moravian Coll., 1952. Diplomate in pediatrics and in pediatric allergy Am. Bd. Pediatrics, Am. Bd. Allergy and Immunology. Intern St. Luke's Hosp., Bethlehem, Pa., 1960-61, resident in surgery, 1961-62; physician Jefferson Med. Coll., Phila., 1956-60; resident in pediatrics U. N.Y., Syracuse, 1962-64; resident in allergy Robert A. Cooke Inst. Allergy Roosevelt Hosp., NYC, 1964-65; clin. instr. pediatrics U. Ill., Chgo., 1965-71; mem. courtesy staff Proctor Community Hosp., Peoria, Ill., 1966-77, mem. active staff, 1977—, chmn. dept. medicine, 1988—89; pres. elect. med. staff, 1990-91; pres. med. staff, 1991-92; mem. teaching staff St. Francis Hosp., Peoria, 1969—2002; clin. instr. pediatrics Rush-Presbyn. St. Luke's Hosp., Chgo., 1971—2002; ret. Vol. Heartland Cmty. Health Clinic, Peoria, Ill., 2002—04. Lt. (j.g.) USN, 1953—56. Fellow Am. Acad. Pediatrics (emeritus), Am. Acad. Allergy Asthma and Immunology, Am. Coll. Allergy and Asthma, Am. Assn. Cert. Allergists Am. Coll. Chest Physicians (emeritus); mem. Ill. Soc. Allergy and Clin. Immunology, Peoria Med. Soc. (pres.-elect 1993, pres. 1994), Christian Med. and Dental Soc. Home: 105 Hollands Grove Ln Washington IL 61571-9623

STINEHART, ROGER RAY, lawyer; b. Toledo, Jan. 27, 1945; s. Forrest William and Nettie May (Twyman) S.; m. Martha Jean Goodnight, Sept. 19, 1970; children: Amanda Jean, Brian Scott. BS, Bowling Green State U., Ohio, 1968; JD, Ohio State U., 1972. Bar: Ohio 1972. Fin. analyst Gen. Electric, Detroit, 1968-69; assoc. Gingher & Christensen, Columbus, Ohio, 1972-76, ptnr., 1976-80; sr. v.p., gen. counsel, sec. G.D. Ritzy's, Inc., Columbus, 1983-85; ptnr. Jones, Day, Reavis & Pogue, Columbus, 1980—83, 1985—2000, Jones Day, Columbus, Ohio, 2000—. Adj. prof. law Capital U., Columbus, 1976-79; mem. adv. com. Ohio securities divsn. Dept. Commerce, Columbus, 1979—; fellow Columbus Bar Found., 1992—; adv. bd. The Entrepreneurship Inst., 1992-95. Contbr. Ohio State U. Coll. Law Jour., 1970-72. Gen. counsel, trustee Internat. Assn. Rsch. on Leukemia and Related Diseases, 1975-2000; v.p., trustee Hospice of Columbus, 1978-80; trustee Cen. Ohio chpt. Leukemia Soc. of Am., Columbus, 1983-93, v.p., 1985-87; trustee Ohio Cancer Rsch. Assocs., Columbus, 1983—, v.p., 1990—; dir. Rotary Internat., Columbus Chapter, 2004-, v.p., 2005-; chmn. Social Com., 2001-03, Internat. Com., 2003-04, Adopt-a-School Com., 2003-04, group study exchange com., team leader, Dist. 6690, 2004-05, dist. chmn., 2005-06. With USMCR, 1963-68. Mem. ABA (bus. law com., franchise law com.), Ohio State Bar Assn. (corp. law com., franchise law com.), Columbus Bar Assn. (securities law com., chmn. 1981-83, bus. law com., franchise law com.), Sigma Tau Delta, Beta Gamma Sigma. Home: 2155 Waltham Rd Columbus OH 43221-4149 Office: Jones Day 325 J McConnell Blvd Columbus OH 43215-5017

STINEHART, WILLIAM, JR., retired lawyer; b. LA, Dec. 15, 1943; s. William Sr. and Martha T. S.; m. Patricia Kidney, June 22, 1968; children: Jacqueline Elaine, William III. BA with distinction, Stanford U., 1966; LLB, UCLA, 1969. Bar: Calif. 1970, US Dist. Ct. (cen. dist.) Calif. 1970. Assoc. Gibson, Dunn & Crutcher LLP, LA, 1969-76, ptnr. tax dept., 1977—; ret., 2005. Bd. dir. Tribune Co. Trustee Harvard Westlake Sch., N. Hollywood, 1983-89, SW Mus., 1986-89. Mem. LA County Bar Assn., Order of Coif, LA Country Club, Beach Club of Santa Monica, Calif., LA Tennis Club. Republican. Episcopalian. Office: Gibson Dunn & Crutcher LLP 2029 Century Pk E Los Angeles CA 90067-3026 Office Phone: 310-552-8557. Office Fax: 310-552-7027. Business E-Mail: wstinehart@gbsondunn.com. *

STINES, FRED, JR., publisher; b. Newton, Iowa, Mar. 16, 1925; s. Fred and Nella (Haun) S.; m. Dorothy G. McClanahan, Sept. 5, 1953 (dec.); children: Steven, Scott, Ann; m. Mary K. Devin, Sept. 12, 1989. B.C.S., U. Iowa, 1949. With Meredith Corp., Des Moines, 1949-90, sales promotion and mdse. mgr., 1955-63, advt. dir., 1963-66, pub., 1966-73, pub. dir. mag. div., 1973-76, v.p., gen. mgr. books and newspapers, 1976-83, sr. v.p., 1983-87, pres. book pub., 1986-90, corp. v.p. spl. projects, 1988-90; pres., prin. Concepts in Mktg., 1990—. Cert. instr. Dale Carnegie courses, 1958-63. Bd. dirs. Des Moines Ballet Assn., North Am. Outdoor Group, Mpls., 1992-95; bd. dirs., v.p. Jr. Achievement of Ctrl. Iowa. Served with AUS, 1946-49. Named Farm Marketing Man of Year, 1972 Mem. Future Farmers Am. Found. (nat. chmn. 1971), Rotary Internat., Des Moines Golf and Country Club, Phi Gamma Delta (sect. chief 1983, nat. bd. dirs. 1985-89), Alpha Kappa Psi, Alpha Delta Sigma. Clubs: Des Moines Golf and Country (dir., pres. 1981, pres. Ednl. Found.). Home: Concepts in Mktg 680 58th Pl West Des Moines IA 50266-6007

STINES, JOE, library director, educator; MLS, U. Tenn., Knoxville; postgraduate student in Pub. Rels., U. Tenn. Coll. Comm. Rsch. assoc. U. Tenn. Energy and Environ. Resource Ctr.; head libr. Joint Rsch. Ctr. Libr.; with Hillsborough County, Fla., 1985; dir. librs. Tampa-Hillsborough County Pub. Libr. Sys., Fla., 1991—. Adj. faculty mem. U. South Fla. Sch. Libr. and Info. Sci. Contbr. articles to profl. publs. Recipient Outstanding Cmty. Communicator award, Tampa Ednl. Cable Consortium, 1998. Mem.: ALA, Fla. Libr. Assn. (vice chmn. legis. com.), Pub. Libr. Assn., Tampa Bay Libr. Consortium (pres. 1999). Office: John F Germany Pub Libr 900 N Ashley Dr Tampa FL 33602-3788 Office Phone: 813-273-3660. Office Fax: 813-273-3707. E-mail: stinesj@hillsboroughcounty.org.

STING, (GORDON MATTHEW SUMNER), musician, songwriter, actor; b. Newcastle Upon Tyne, Eng., Oct. 2, 1951; s. Ernest Matthew and Audrey (Cowell) Sumner; m. Frances Eleanor Tomelty, May 1, 1976 (div. Mar. 1984); children: Joseph, Fuschia Katherine; m. Trudie Styler, Aug. 22, 1992; children: Brigette, Michael, Jake, Eliot, Paulina, Giacomo Luke. Grad., Warwick U., Coventry, Eng.; doctorate (hon.), Northumbria U., 1992; degree (hon.), Berklee Coll. Music, Boston, 1994. Schoolmaster, Newcastle Upon Tyne, Eng., 1975-77; songwriter, singer, bass player with rock group The Police, 1977-86; mng. dir. Kaliedescope Cameras, London, from 1982; singer, songwriter, 1986—. Albums (with The Police) Outlandos D'Amour, 1978, Reggatta De Blanc, 1979, Zenyatta Mondatta, 1980, Ghost in the Machine, 1981, Synchronicity, 1983, singles Every Breath You Take, 1986; appearance: (Broadway plays) Three Penny Opera, 1989; solo (albums) The Dream of the Blue Turtles, 1985, Bring On The Night, 1986, Nothing Like the Sun, 1987, The Soul Cages, 1991, Ten Summoner's Tales, 1993 (Grammy award, Best Long Form Music Video, 1994), Demolition Man, soundtrack, 1993, Mercury Falling, 1996, Brand New Day, 1999, Sacred Love, 2003 (Grammy award, Best Pop Collaboration With Vocals for song "Whenever I Say Your Name" with Mary J. Blige, 2003), appeared (films) Quadrophenia, 1979, The Secret Policeman's Other Ball, 1981, Brimstone and Treacle, 1982, Dune, The Bride, Plenty, 1985, Julia and Julia, 1987, Stormy Monday, 1988, Resident Alien, 1990, The Grotesque, 1995, Lock, Stock and Two Smoking Barrels, 1998, voice artist (TV series) Captain Planet and the Planeteers, 1990—92, rec. soundtracks (films) Brimstone and Treacle, Party, Party, The Secret Policeman's Other Ball, 1982, The Emperor's New Groove, 2000. Named to Rock and Roll Hall of Fame (The Police), 2003; recipient 15 Grammy awards with The Police and as solo artist, 13 BMI awards, 4 Brit awards, Downbeat mag. Readers' Poll Pop/Rock Musician of Yr. award, 1989, Downbeat mag. Readers' Poll Pop/Rock group award, 1989, Internat. Rock award for Video Legend, 1991, Star on the Hollywood Walk of Fame, 2000, Golden Globe award Kate and Leopold, 2001. Mem.: Rainforest Found. (co-founder), Amnesty Internat., Performing Rights Soc. also: Firstars 3520 Hayden Ave Culver City CA 90232-2413 also: A & M Records Inc 70 Universal City Plz Universal City CA 91608-1011 Office: KSM 826 Broadway Fl 4 New York NY 10003-4826 *

STINGEL, RUDOLF, artist; b. Merano, Italy, 1957; One-man shows include pittura austriae - Positionen aus Osterreich I/III, Galerie Elisabeth & Klaus Thoman, Innsbruck, 2000, Monochrome/Monochrome?, Florence Lynch Gallery, NYC, 2001, Stanze, Museo d'arte moderna e contemporanea, 2001, Collector's Choice, Neue Galerie Graz am Landesmuseum Joanneum, 2002, Penetration, Friedrich Petzel Gallery, NYC, 2002, Marianne Boesky Gallery, NYC, 2002, ReProdukton - Gruppenausstellung, Galerie Bernhard Knaus, Mannheim, 2002, International Landscape, Galerie Rodolphe Janssen, Brussels, 2002, Dreams and Conflicts: The Dictatorship of the Viewer, La Biennale di Venezia, Venice, 2003, Walk Ways, U. South Fla. Contemporary Art Mus., 2003, Invite - Silver Convention, Galerie Giti Nourbakhsch, Berlin, 2003, Ruina - Aesthetic of Destruction, Galeria Helga de Alvear, Madrid, 2004, Miradas y conceptos en la Coleccion Helga de Alvear, 2005, Home Depot, Museum fur Moderne Kunst, Frankfurt, 2004, Art Underfoot - Carpeting the Walker Entry, Walker Art Ctr., Mpls., 2004, Sadie Coles HQ, London, 2004, None of the Above, SI Swiss Inst., NYC, 2004, Singular Forms (Sometimes Repeated): Art from 1951 to the Present, Solomon R Museum, NY, 2004, Power, Corruption and Lies, Roth Horowitz, NYC, 2004, Museum fur Kunst, Frankfurt, 2004, Galleria Massimo de Carlo, Milan, 2004, EURAC tower, Bolzano, Italy, 2005, MART, Roverto, Italy, 2005, Hayward Gallery, London, 2005, Universal Experience: Art, Life, and the Tourist's Eye, Mus. Contemporary Art, 2005, The Red Thread, Howard House Contemporary, Seattle, 2005, exhibited in group shows at Examining Pictures, Mus. Contemporary Art Chgo., 1999, GOOD TIMING, Georg Kargl Fine Arts, Vienna, 2005, Whitney Biennial: Day for Night, Whitney Mus. Am. Art, NYC, 2006.

STINNETT, HESTER, art school administrator, educator; BFA, Hartford Art Sch.; MFA, Tyler Sch. Art, Phila. Lectr. U. of Arts, Phila., 1982-85, Bryn Mawr (Pa.) Coll., 1985-86; asst. prof. Tyler Sch. Art Temple U., Phila., 1986—; assoc. dean Tyler Sch. Art, Phila., 1992—. Vis. artist Pa. Acad. Fine Arts, Phila., 1984-85. Author: Water-Base Screenprinting, 1988; exhibited in group show Dolan/Maxwell Gallery, 1988; prodr. Electrical Matter, 1989-92; dir. Contemporary Viewpoints, 1987-89. Office: Tyler Sch Arts Temple U 7725 Penrose Ave Elkins Park PA 19027 Office Fax: 215-782-2799. Business E-Mail: hester.stinnett@temple.edu.

STINNETT, MARK ALLAN, lawyer; b. Jackson, Miss., Sept. 15, 1955; s. Allan J. and Joan (Mouser) S.; m. Carol Fowler, Sept. 5, 1992; children: Michelle, Michael. BA in Polit. Sci. with honors, Tex. Tech U., 1977; JD with honors, U. Tex., 1980. Bar: Tex. 1980, US Dist. Ct. (no. and ea. dists.) Tex. 1981, US Ct. Appeals (5th cir.) 1993, US Supreme Ct. 2006. Founding ptnr., mng. ptnr. Stinnett Thiebaud & Remington L.L.P., Dallas, 2000—; shareholder Cowles & Thompson, Dallas, 1986—2000. Mem. Philmont Ranch com. Boy Scouts Am., chmn. program task force. Fellow Tex. Bar Found., Dallas (Tex.) Bar Found.; mem. ABA, Am. Bd. Trial Advocates, Am. Inns of Ct., Am. Coll. Legal Medicine, Am. Health Lawyers Assn., State Bar of Tex., Dallas Bar Assn., Tex. Assn. Def. Counsel, Dallas Assn. Def. Counsel, Def. Rsch. Inst., Inns Ct. (barrister Dallas chpt. 1988-91), Tex. Ctr. Legal Ethics and Professionalism, Nat. Eagle Scout Assn., Philmont Staff Assn. (pres. 1994-98, editor High Country mag. 1998—). Avocations: backpacking, hiking, military history, writing. Home: 3801 Sonoran Dr Colorado Springs CO 80922 Office: Stinnett Thiebaud & Remington LLP 1445 Ross Ave Ste 2500 Dallas TX 75202-2702 Office Phone: 214-954-2200. Business E-Mail: mstinnett@strlaw.net.

STINNETT, TERRANCE LLOYD, lawyer; b. Oakland, Calif., July 22, 1940; s. Lloyd Monroe and Gertrude (Hyman) S. BS, Stanford U., 1962; JD magna cum laude, U. Santa Clara, 1969. Bar: Calif. 1970, U.S. Dist. Ct. (no. dist.) Calif. 1970, U.S. Dist. Ct. (ea. ctrl. and so. dists) Calif. 1975, U.S. Ct. Appeals (9th cir.) 1970, U.S. Supreme Ct. 1975. Law clk. to judge Calif. Ct. Appeals, San Francisco, 1969-70; assoc. Hyman, Rhodes & Aylward, Fremont, Calif., 1970-71, Glicksberg, Kushner & Goldberg, San Francisco, 1972-77; mem. Goldberg, Stinnett Meyers & Davis, San Francisco, 1977—2006; gen. counsel Fremont Bank, 2007—. Bd. dirs. Fremont Bancorp, Fremont Bank, vice-chmn. bd., 1998-2000. Mem. ABA, Calif. State Bar Assn., Bar Assn. San Francisco (chmn. bench bar liaison com. for U.S. Bankruptcy Ct., No. Dist. of Calif. 1997). Republican. Roman Catholic. Home: 131 Alamo Hills Ct Alamo CA 94507-2243 Office: Fremont Bank 39150 Fremont Blvd Fremont CA 94538 Office Phone: 510-505-5335. Business E-Mail: terrance.stinnett@fremontbank.com.

STINSMUEHLEN-AMEND, SUSAN, artist; b. Balt., Nov. 5, 1948; d. William I. and Geraldine S. (Dodds) Hamilton; m. Richard E. Amend, Nov. 27, 1987; children: Jason Stinsmuehlen, Wyatt Amend. Student, Hood Coll., U. Tex. Designer, owner Renaissance Glass Co., Austin, 1973-87; artist, glass, paint and mixed media dba Impresa, Inc., L.A. and Ojai, Calif., 1987—. Mem. Art in Pub. Places Panel, Austin, 1986-87; cons. Nat. Endowment for the Arts, Washington, 1986, 87, Cmty. Redevel. Agy., L.A., 1990-92; artist trustee Am. Craft Coun., 1988-92; lectr., lead artist Hollywood Blvd. Streetscape Team, Hollywood, Calif., 1991-94; lead artist Canoga Park, Calif., Pedestrianscape and Madrid Theater Project, City of L.A., 1996-2000; mem. Arts Commn., Ojai, Calif., 2000—; mem. Hollywood Art and Design Adv. Panel, 1994-2003; lead artist Canoga Pk., Calif., 1996-2000; guest lectr., artist Puchuck Glass Sch., 1980-92, 94-95, 97, 2005, R.I. Sch. Design, 1980, 2006, Mass. Coll. Art, 1980, Dallas Mus. Art, 1981, Japanese Glass Conf., 1985, Calif. Coll. Arts, Oakland, 1985, 89, Australian Glass Conf., 1987, Penland Sch. Craft, N.C., 1996; artist-in-residence Pilchuck Glass Sch., Wash., 2006, Internat. Ctr. for Contemporary Art, Mus. Glass, Tacoma, 2006; interviewer archive project Focus on the Masters, Ventura, Calif.; educator in field. One-woman shows include Mattingly Baker Gallery, Dallas, 1984, Kurland Summers Gallery, L.A., 1985, 88, 90, 92, Traver Sutton Gallery, Seattle, 1986, Habatat Galleries, Detroit, 1991, The Nest Gallery, Ojai, Calif., 1997, The Glass Gallery, Bethesda, Md., 2000, Carnegie Mus. Art, Oxnard, Calif., 2004, Sandy Carson Gallery, Denver, 2005, D&A Fine Arts, L.A., 2005, 07, Coll. the Sequoias Art Gallery, Visalia, Calif., 2006; exhibited in group shows at Whatcom Mus., Bellingham, Wash., 1992, 94, Finegood Art Gallery, West Hills, Calif., 1993-94, Miller Gallery, N.Y.C., 1994, The Wignall Mus., Chaffey Coll., Rancho Cucamonga, Calif., 1995, Traver Gallery, Seattle, 1995, Smithsonian Inst. Travelling Exhbn., 1999, Muckenthaler Cultural

Arts Ctr., Calif., 1999, Loveland (Colo.) Mus. Gallery, 1998, 99, Fresno Art Mus., 1998, SOFA Chgo., 1998, Santa Cruz Mus. Art and History, 1999, Smithsonian Inst., 1998-2000, L.A. County Mus. Art, 1999, Orange County Mus. Art, 1999, L.A. Mcpl. Art Gallery, 2003, Reynolds Gallery, Richmond, Va., 2003, Nathan Larramendy Gallery, 2004, Ojai Valley Mus., 2003-05, San Francisco Mus. Craft & Design, 2005, L.A. Mcpl.Art Gallery, 2005, Beatrice Wood Ctr. Arts, 2005-07, William Traver Gallery, Seattle, 2006, 07, Robert V. Fullerton Art Mus., San Bernandino, 2007—, others, Palos Verdes Art Ctr., Calif.; represented in permanent collection Am. Airlines, Dallas, Renwick Gallery Nat. Mus. Art, Washington, The Jewish Mus., N.Y.C., The Corning (N.Y.) Mus. Glass, Detroit Inst. Arts, Leigh Yawkey Woodson Mus., Wausau, Wis., Oakland (Calif.) Mus., Wagga Wagga City Art Gallery, NSW, Australia, Nishida Mus., Toyoma, Japan, Pilchuck Glass Ctr., Stanwood, Wash., Mus. Art & Design, N.Y.C., L.A. (Calif.) County Mus. Art, Radisson Hotel, Austin, AT&T, Dallas, AT&T, N.Y.C., Marshall Fields Corp. Collection, Chgo., City of L.A., Mus. Am. Art/Smithsonian Instn., Carnegie Art Mus., Mus. Glass, Theoma, Wash., Ojas Valley Cmty. Hosp., others plus numerous pvt. collections. Nat. Endowment for the Arts grantee, Washington, 1982, 88; Hauberg fellowship Pilchuck Glass Sch., 2001. Mem. Glass Art Soc. (hon. life; bd. dirs. 1982-86, pres. 1984-86), Mus. Contemporary Art (L.A.), L.A. County Mus. Avocations: gardening, swimming, walking, hiking, golf. E-mail: impresa@pobox.com.

STINSON, ALAN LYNN, insurance company executive; b. 1945; BA, U. Tex., 1968. CPA. Ptnr. Deloitte & Touche LLP, 1980—94; exec. v.p., CFO Alamo Title Holding Co., 1994—98; exec. v.p. fin. ops. Fidelity Nat. Fin., Inc., Jacksonville, Fla., 1998—99, exec. v.p., CFO, 1999—2006, exec. v.p., CFO, COO, 2006, exec. v.p., COO, 2006—07, CEO, 2007—. Mem.: Am. Inst. CPAs. Office: Fidelity Nat Fin Inc 601 Riverside Ave Jacksonville FL 32204-2950 *

STINSON, KENNETH E., construction and mining company executive; b. Chgo., May 24, 1946; BS in Civil Engring., U. Notre Dame; MS in Civil Engring., Stanford U. Pres. Kiewit Constrn. Grp. Inc., Omaha, 1992—96, chmn., 1993—96; pres. Peter Kiewit Sons' Inc., Omaha, 1997—2000, chmn., 1997—, CEO, 1998—2004. Bd. dirs. ConAgra Foods, Inc., Omaha, 1996—, Valmont Industries, Inc., Omaha, 1996—. Recipient Outstanding Projects and Leaders awards, ASCE, 2003, Star of Courage award, Nebr. Med. Ctr., 2005. Mem.: NAE. Office: Kiewit Corp 3555 Farnam St Omaha NE 68131 Office Phone: 402-342-2052. Office Fax: 402-271-2939. *

STINSON, MARION DENNIS, lawyer, land use planner, judge; b. Alton, Ill., Aug. 19, 1953; s. George Washington and Clara Alevia (Keene) S.; m. Shirley Joan Cartwright, Feb. 13, 1971; children: Casey René (dec.), Marion David. AA magna cum laude, Rogers State Coll., Claremore, Okla., 1992; BA summa cum laude, Northeastern State U., Tahlequah, Okla., 1997; JD, Oklahoma City U., 2002. Leadman Stresscon Inc., Tulsa, 1971-74; crane operator Gardner-Denver, Pryor, Okla., 1974-79; laborer Lone Star Industries, Pryor, 1979-88; owner, mgr. sml. bus. Pryor, 1988-90; concrete finisher United Bridge Constrn., Joplin, Mo., 1990-91; sec. Grand Gateway Econ. Devel. Assn., Vinita, Okla., 1991-93; coord. cmty. devel. Grand Gateway Econd. Devel. Assn., Vinita, Okla., 1993-94, dir. cmty. devel., 1994-95, dir. cmty./econ. devel. Big Cabin, Okla., 1995—2003, dep. exec. dir., 1999—2003. Bd. trustees Town of Salina, 1990-91; com. chmn. MESTA, Pryor, 1995-98; citizen's adv. com. chmn. Mayes County Commrs., Pryor, 1997-98; mem. oversight com. Multiple Local Govts., Delaware/Adair County, Okla., 1995-99; mem. Salina (Okla.) Bd. Edn., 1995-98, v.p., 1996-97, pres., 1997-98; precinct chmn. Dem. Party, Salina, 1996; chmn. bd. N.E. Okla. Little League, Salina, 1994-96; bd. dirs. Pryor Sr. Citizens, Inc., 1996, Cmty. Devel. Soc., 1995-2003; com. mem. Okla. Dept. Commerce, 1994-96, bd. govs., O.D. Mayor Found., 2003—. Recipient Acad. Achievement award Northeastern State U., 1997, scholarship Okla. Scholar Leadership Enchancement Program, 1996, Cert. of Achievement, Okla. Mcpl. League, 1995, 96, 97, 98. Mem. Okla. Floodplain Mgmt. Assn. (cert. floodplain mgr., sec. com. 1996-98), Am. Planners Assn., Salina Area C. of C. (bd. dirs. 1996), Phi Theta Kappa, Alpha Chi. Democrat. Baptist. Avocations: boating, golf, movies, football. Office: Stinson Law Firm PO Box 922 Pryor OK 74362 Office Phone: 918-825-3399. Personal E-mail: stinsonlawfirm@sbcglobal.net.

STINSON, MARY FLORENCE, retired nursing educator; b. Wheeling, W.Va., Feb. 11, 1931; d. Rolland Francis and Mary Angela (Voellinger) Kellogg; m. Charles Walter Stinson, Feb. 12, 1955; children: Kenneth Charles, Karen Marie Wiberg, Kathryn Anne Kartye. BSN, Coll. Mt. St. Joseph, 1953, postgrad., 1983; MEd, Xavier U., Cin., 1967; postgrad., U. Cin., 1981. Staff nurse contagious disease ward Cin. Gen. Hosp., 1953-54, asst. head nurse med. and polio wards, 1955, acting head nurse, clin. instr., 1955-56; instr. St. Francis Hosp. Sch. Practical Nursing, Cin., 1956-57, Good Samaritan Hosp. Sch. Nursing, Cin., 1957—66; instr. refresher courses for nurses Cin. Bd. Edn. and Ohio State Nurses Assn. Dist. 8, 1967—70; coord. sch. health office Coll. Mt. St. Joseph, Ohio, 1969-72, instr. dept. nursing, 1974-79, asst. prof., 1979-89; RN assessor pre-admission screening sys. providing options & resources today Coun. on Aging Southwestern Ohio, 1989-90, quality assurance coord. pre-admission screen sys. providing options & resources today program, 1990-93, quality assurance supr. pre-admission screen sys. providing options & resources today and elderly svcs. programs, 1993-94; quality assurance mgr. Coun. Aging Southwestern Ohio, 1995-2000; ret., 2000. Staff nurse St. Francis/St. George Hosp., Cin., 1988-89; vol. ombudsman Pro Srs. of S.W. Ohio, 2005—. Charter mem. Adoptive Parents Assn. St. Joseph Infant and Maternity Home, 1966—70; women's com. for performing arts series Coll. Mt. St. Joseph; chmn. by-law com. Coll. Mt. St. Joseph Nursing Honor Soc., 1996—98; active St. Antoninus Rosary Altar and Sch. Soc., 1973—84, St. Antoninus Athletic Club, com. chmn., 1969—70; bd. dirs. Coll. Mt. St. Joseph Alumni Assn., 1982—84, sec., 1968—69, v.p., 1969—70, pres., 1970—71, chmn. revision of constn., 1976—77; homecoming chmn. Coll. Mt. St. Joseph, 1970, co-chmn., 1977, co-chair com. to celebrate 75 years of nursing edn., 2001—02; mem. com. to plan 50th ann. of graduation Coll. Mt. St. Joseph Alumni Assn., 2003. Mem. River Squares Club (v.p. 1967), Sigma Theta Tau (charter Omicron Omicron chpt. 1998—), St. Antonious Adult Social Group (pres. 2005-). Democrat. Roman Catholic. Home: 5549 Cleander Dr Cincinnati OH 45238-4266 Personal E-mail: flostinson@current.net.

STINSON, STANLEY THOMAS, project manager; b. Dothan, Ala., Dec. 17, 1961; s. Leonis and Betty Lois (Harrison) S.; m. Sharin B. Clark, Aug. 25, 1984; children: Sarah Ashley, Amy Rebecca, Rachel Elizabeth, Thomas Clark. AS in Computer Sci., Enterprise State Jr. Coll., 1982; BSBA cum laude, Troy State U., 1984; MBA, Samford U., 1989. Fin. sys. engr. NCR Corp., Birmingham, Ala., 1984-87; sr. sys. specialist Systematics Inc., Birmingham, 1987-88, sys. engr., 1988-90, sr. sys. engr., 1990; cons. devel. analyst Systematics, Inc., Little Rock, 1990-92; sr. sys. engr. Systematics Fin. Svcs., Atlanta, 1992-93; sr. applications programmer/analyst Capital City Bank, Tallahassee, 1993-96; sys. cons. Consultec, Inc., Tallahassee, 1996-98; ind. contractor, 1998—2002; founder, pres. DP Answers Inc., 1999—2001; sr. sys. analyst Deutsche Fin. Svcs., St. Louis, 2002; sr. staff E-Trade Consumer Fin. Corp., 2003—05; lead analyst IT applications GE Money, 2005—. Baptist. Avocations: golf, personal computer. Home and Office: 5998 Peachtree Dr Hillsboro MO 63050 Personal E-mail: banking_dp@earthlink.net.

STIPE, MICHAEL, musician, film producer; b. Decatur, Ga., Jan. 4, 1960; Student, U. Ga. Singer R.E.M., 1980—; owner C-OO. Albums (with R.E.M.) Chronic Town, 1982, Murmur, 1983 (Rolling Stone Critics Poll Best Album of Yr., 1983), Reckoning, 1984, Fables of the Revolution, 1985, Life's Rich Pageant, 1986, Dead Letter Office, 1987, Document, 1987, Eponymous, 1988, Green, 1989, Out of Time, 1991 (Grammy award, Best Alternative Music Performance, 1992), Automatic for the People, 1992 (4 Grammy nominations, 1992), Monster, 1994, Songs That Are Live (4 song CD), 1995, New Adventures in Hi-Fi, 1996, Up, 1998, Reveal, 2001, In Time: The Best of R.E.M., 2003, guest artist for following groups 10,000 Maniacs, 1987, Indigo Girls, 1989, soundtrack Man on the Moon, 1999; prodr.: (films) Being John Malkovich, 1999, Saved!, 2004, (TV films) Olive, the Other Reindeer, 1999, Stranger Inside, 2001; exec. prodr.: (films) Velvet Goldmine, 1998, Spring Forward, 1999, Our Song, 2000, Thirteen Conversations About One Thing, 2001, Everyday People, 2004, Johnny Berlin, 2005; albums (with R.E.M.) Around the Sun, 2004, songs (with R.E.M.) Orange Crush (MTV Video Music award, Best Post Modern Video, 1989), Losing My Religion (6 MTV Video Music awards, 1991, Best Group Pop Vocal Performance, Best Short Form Music Video, Grammy Awards, 1992), Everybody Hurts (4 MTV Video Music awards, 1994). Named Rolling Stone Critics Poll Best New Group, 1983, Rolling Stone Group Artist of Yr., 1992, Rolling Stone Male Vocalist of Yr., 1992; named one of Top Newsmakers of Yr., Out mag., 1998; named to Rock & Roll Hall of Fame, with R.E.M., 2007; recipient Top Modern Rock Artist award, Top World Album award, Billboard Music Awards, 1991, Best Internat. Group award, Brit Awards, 1992, 1993, 1995, Video Vanguard award, MTV Video Music Awards, 1995. Address: REM PO Box 8032 Athens GA 30603-8032 *

STIPE, ROBERT EDWIN, retired design educator; b. Easton, Pa., July 18, 1928; s. J. Norwood and Ethel M. Stipe; m. Josephine Davis Weedon, 1952; children: Daniel W., Frederick Norwood. AB in Econ., Duke U., 1950, LLB, 1953; MRP, U. N.C., 1959. Urban planning cons. City and Town Planning Assocs., Chapel Hill, NC, 1956-57; asst. dir., prof. pub. law and govt. U. N.C. Inst. Govt., Chapel Hill, NC, 1957-74; sr. Fulbright rsch. fellow London U., 1968-69; dir. Divsn. Archives and History N.C. Dept. Cultural Resources, Raleigh, NC, 1974-75; vis. prof. U. N.C., Chapel Hill, 1975-77; prof. design N.C. State U., Raleigh, 1976-89, emeritus prof. design, part time prof. design, 1989—2000. Lectr. Inst. Advanced Studies, Bratislava, Slovak Republic, 1992-96; bd. trustees US com. Internat. Coun. on Monuments and Sites, Preservation Action, Nat. Coun. on Preservation Edn., Hist. Preservation Fund NC, Alliance for Preservation Hist. Landscapes, Old Salem Inc., Stagville Ctr. for Preservation Tech.; emeritus trustee Nat. Trust for Hist. Preservation; bd. adv. Nat. Alliance Preservation Commn. Author, editor articles and publs. in fields of historic preservation, landscape conservation, design, urban planning and planning law; contbr. chapters to books. Mem. Chapel Hill Design Review Bd.; trustee Chapel Hill Preservation Soc.; founder, trustee Chapel Hill HIstorical Soc. Fellow U.S. Com. Internat. Coun. on Monuments and Sites, 1986; recipient Disting. Svc. award Ruth Coltrane Cannon award, N.C. Soc. for Preservation of Antiquities, 1973, Sec. of Interior's Disting. Conservation Svc. award, 1978, Spl. award outstanding contbns. to landscape architecture Am. Soc. Landscape Archiects, N.C. chpt., 1985, Louise DuPont Crowninshield award for Superlative Lifetime Achievement in Historic Preservation, Nat. Trust for Historic Preservation, 1988, Dist. Svc. and Profl. Leadership award Nat. Coun. for Preservation Edn., 1989, Charles S. Murphy award, Duke U. Law Sch. Alumni Assn., 2003, Antoinette Downing Book award Soc. Archtl. Historians, 2005. Mem. Cosmos Club (Washington), Sigma Pi Kappa (First Disting. mem. 1994), Sigma Lambda Alpha (disting. mem. 1996), Phi Delta Phi. Home: 100 Pine Ln Chapel Hill NC 27514-4331 Personal E-mail: bobstipe@mindspring.com.

STIPETIC, WERNER See HERZOG, WERNER

STIREWALT, JOHN NEWMAN, coal company executive; b. Springfield, Ill., July 14, 1931; s. Newman Claude and Genevieve (Henton) S.; m. Joan Marie McCarthy, Dec. 26, 1957; children: Genevieve, Janice, James, Christopher. AB, U. Miami, 1953; grad. execs. program, Carnegie Mellun U., 1978. Salesman Kaiser Aluminum, Indpls., 1957-63; dist. sales mgr. Consol. Coal, Detroit, 1963-67, Cleve., 1967-73, gen. sales mgr. Detroit, 1973-76, asst. v.p., 1976-79; v.p. mktg. Youghiogheny and Ohio Coal Co., St. Clairsville, 1979-81; v.p. mktg. Crown Coal and Coke Co. Pitts., 1981-85, Arch Mineral, 1985-90; sr. v.p. Crown Coal & Coke Co., 1990—. Exec. reservist U.S. Dept. Interior emergency solid fuels adminstrn., 1971, U.S. Energy Dept., 1991-97. Chmn. coun. Cub Scouts, Highland, Mich., 1976; mem. Mich. Energy Task Force, 1966; pres. bd. trustees Wheeling Country Day Sch., 1980-84; trustee Wheeling Symphony; bd. dirs. Teen Challenge for New Life Inc. Served with U.S. Army, 1954-56. Mem.: Vinyard Christian Fellowship, Ft. Henry Club, Symposiarchs, Wheeling Country Club, Sigma Chi. Home: 130 Spring Hill Ln Wheeling WV 26003-7746 Office: Crown Coal and Coke Co Pittsburgh PA 15220 Home Phone: 304-336-7888; Office Phone: 412-920-1908.

STIRITZ, MARETTE MCCAULEY, English language educator, consultant; b. Center Point, Ark., Dec. 9, 1931; d. Edrie Delos and Lucyle Virginia (Dautrieve) McCauley; m. Charles Wayne Jackson, July 1, 1950 (dec. June 1986); children: Charles, Retta, Shelia; m. John David Stiritz, Dec. 3, 1992. BSE, Ark. State U., 1962; MA, U. Ark., 1965, PhA, 1986. Tchr. elem. Plum Bayou (Ark.) Pub. Schs., 1950-52; tchr. Laura Connor H.S., Augusta, Ark., 1955-59, Swifton (Ark.) Elem. Sch., 1959-60, Swifton H.S., 1962-63; prof. English So. Ark. U., Magnolia, 1965-78, U. Cen. Ark., Conway, 1978—96; cons., 1996—. Cons. high schs., Conway, Morrilton, Vilonia, 1983—, Ark. Dept. Edn., Little Rock, 1982, 84; lectr. U. Chile, Santiago, 1989, Moscow Pedagogical U., 1991, 92, Academica Inst. Chileno-Norteamericano, Santiago, 1994; speaker 8th Bi-ann. Conf. Profs. Fgn. Langs., Chile, 1992, 9th Conf., Chile, 1994. Author: A Grammar for All Seasons, 1996, Using Language Effectively, 1996; editor: What the American Children Like to Read, 1995; contbr. articles to profl. jours.; book reviewer Ark. Elem. Coun., 1980—. Del. Faulkner County Dems., Conway, 1984; exec. sec., founder Columbia Tchrs. Eng., Magnolia, 1974-78. Mem. Ark. Coun. Tchrs. English (pres. 1979-80, bd. dirs. 1989-93), Ark. Philol. Assn., Nat. Coun. Tchrs. English, Ark. Coll. Tchrs. English (pres. 1992-93), Conway Rotary Internat. Breakfast Club (charter), Conway Shakespeare Club (v.p. 2005-06, pres. 2006—), Alpha Chi (region II v.p. 1992-93. Democrat. Methodist. Home: 3414 Rhondas Ct Conway AR 72032-9168 Office Phone: 501-329-5048. Personal E-mail: JorMStiritz@conwaycorp.net.

STIRITZ, WILLIAM P., food products executive; b. Jasper, Ark., July 1, 1934; s. Paul and Dorothy (Bradley) Stiritz; m. Susan Ekberg, Dec. 4, 1972; children: Bradley, Charlotte, Rebecca, Nicholas. BS, Northwestern U., 1959; MA, St. Louis U., 1968. Mem. mktg. mgmt. staff Pillsbury Co., Mpls., 1959—62; staff Gardner Advt. Co., St. Louis, 1963; with Ralston Purina Co., St. Louis, 1963—97, pres., CEO, chmn., 1981—97; chmn., CEO Agribrands Internat., St. Louis, 1997—2001; chmn. Ralcorp Holdings, St. Louis, Energizer Inc. Bd. dirs. Am. Freightways, Angelica Corp., Ball Corp., Boatmen's Bancshares, Inc., Gen. Am. Life Ins. Co., May Dept. Stores, S.C. Johnson & Son, Reins. Group Am., Vail Resorts; bd. dirs., chmn. Ralston Purina, Ralcorp.; chmn. Westgate Equity Group, LLC; bd. dirs. Fedennted Dept. Stores. Served USN, 1954—57. Business E-Mail: william.stiritz@purina.nestle.com.

STIRLING, JAMES PAULMAN, investment banker; b. Chgo., Mar. 30, 1941; s. Louis James and Beverly L. (Paulman) S.; m. Ellen Adair Foster, June 6, 1970; children— Elizabeth Ginevra, Diana Leslie, Alexandra Curtiss. AB, Princeton U., 1963; MBA, Stanford U., 1965. CFA. Vice pres. corp. fin. Kidder, Peabody & Co. (now UBS), NYC and Chgo., 1965-71, 84-86, sr. v.p. corp. fin., 1987—; asst. to sec. U.S. Dept. Commerce, Washington, 1976-77. Chmn. bd. Northwestern Meml. Mgmt. Corp., Chgo., 1989—; trustee Northwestern Meml. Hosp., Chgo., 1985—. Pres. jr. bd. Chgo. Symphony, 1968—70; mem. exec. coun. Chgo. Metropolis 2020; trustee Chgo. Symphony, 1970—75, Tchrs. Acad. for Math. Sci., 1991—95. Mem. CFA Soc. Chgo. (bd. dirs.), CFA Leadership Coun. (chmn.), Bond Club Chgo., Nat. Econ. Hon. Soc., Chicago Club, Racquet Club (Chgo.), Onwentsia Club (Lake Forest, Ill.). Office: UBS Tower One N Wacker Dr Ste 2500 Chicago IL 60606-4302

STITES, SUSAN KAY, writer, human resources specialist, consultant; b. Colorado Springs, Colo., Sept. 20, 1952; d. William Wallace and Betty Jane (Kosley) Stites; m. Gerald Frederick Simon, Aug. 14, 1988. BA, Wichita State U., 1974; MA, Northwestern U., 1979. Human resources mgr. Montgomery Ward, Chgo., 1979-83; mgr. tng. Lands' End, Dodgeville, Wis., 1983-87; dir. human resources Ctrl. Life Assurance, Madison, Wis., 1988-90; owner Mgmt. Allegories, Madison, 1987—. Author: Delegating for Results, 1992, Business Communications, 1992, Managing with a Quality Focus, 1994, Training Orientation for the Small Business, 1994, Powerful Performance Management, 1994, Safety Management Techniques, 1995, Teaching First Aid and CPR, 1995, Alive at 25, 1995, Strategic Thinking and Planning, 1995, Teaching Alice at 25, 1996, Fundamentals of Industrial Hygiene, 1996, Recruiting, Developing and Retaining Volunteers, 1996, Creating a Credit Union University: An Administrator's Guide, 1997, 2d. edit., 2001, Creating a Corporate University, 1997, Strategic Thinking for the Automotive Industry, 1997, Managing Sales and Service, 1997, Sales and Service Management in Credit Unions, 1997, Provide Training Without Straining Your Budget, 1997, Car America Sales Training Manual, 1998, Introduction to Community Organizing, 1998, Car America Leader's Guide, 1998, Effective Loan Interviewing, 1999, Driven to Extremes, 2000, Safety Inspections, 2001, Job Safety Analysis, 2001, Incident Investigations, 2001, Ergonomics for the Small Business, 2003, Creating a Safety Culture: Strategies for Small Business, 2004, Preventing Slips, Trips and Falls, 2006, How May I Help You? Service with a Smile and a Story, 2006, Prevention Strategies for Construction's Focus Four Hazards, 2007, Prescription For The Flu, 2007, Protecting Your Workers From A Flu Pandemic, 2007. Vol. tutor Japanese students in English, Evanston, Ill., 1977—80; reader to the blind Chgo. Coun. for Blind, 1974—76. Named Outstanding Woman of the Yr., Wichita State U., 1974. Mem.: ASTD (v.p. membership 1986, chpt. pres. 1988, Region V awards chair 1992). Nat. Storytelling Network, Mendota Yacht Club (treas. 1990—94), Rotary (vol. fundraiser). Avocations: sailing, windsurfing, gardening, cooking, travel. Office: Mgmt Allegories 3788 Highridge Rd Madison WI 53718-6206

STITH, LAURA DENVIR, state supreme court justice; b. St. Louis, Oct. 30, 1953; m. Donald George Scott; children: Lisa, Rebecca, Cynthia. BA magna cum laude, Tufts U., 1975; JD magna cum laude, Georgetown U., 1978. Law clk. to Hon. Robert E. Seiler, Mo. Supreme Ct., 1978—79; assoc. Shook, Hardy & Bacon, Kansas City, Mo., 1979—84, ptnr., 1984—94; judge. Mo. Ct. Appeals (we. dist.), 1994—2001; judge Mo. Supreme Ct., 2001—. Speaker Mo. New Judges Sch. Author: articles on appellate practice, products liability and civil procedure. Tutor, mentor Operation Breakthrough, St. Vincent's Sch.; founding dir., mem. Lawyers Encouraging Academic Performance. Mem.: Assn. Women Lawyers of Greater Kansas City (speaker, past pres.), Mo. Bar Assn., Kansas City Metropolitan Bar Assn. Office: Supreme Ct Mo PO Box 150 Jefferson City MO 65102

STITH-CABRANES, KATE, law educator; b. St. Louis, Mar. 16, 1951; d. Richard Taylor and Ann Carter (See) Stith; m. Jeffrey Leonard Pressman, Dec. 23, 1970 (dec. Mar. 1977); m. José Alberto Cabranes, Sept. 15, 1984; children: Alejo, Benjamin José; stepchildren: Jennifer, Amy. BA, Dartmouth Coll., 1973; MPP, J.F.K. Sch. of Govt., 1977; JD, Harvard U., 1977. Bar: D.C. 1979. Law clk. to Judge Carl McGowan US Ct. of Appeals, Washington, 1977-78; law clk. to Justice Byron White US Supreme Ct., Washington, 1978-79; staff economist Coun. of Econ. Advisers, Washington, 1979-80; spl. asst. Dept. of Justice, Washington, 1980-81, asst. U.S. atty. NYC, 1981-84; assoc. prof. Yale Law Sch., New Haven, 1985-90, prof. of law, 1990—97, Lafayette S. Foster prof. law, 1998—, dep. dean, 1999—2001, 2003—04; mem. adv com. Fed. Rules of Criminal Procedure, 1995—2001. Mem. Permanent Commn. on the Status of Women, State of Conn., Hartford, 1990-96. Author: (with José A. Cabranes) Fear of Judging: Sentencing Guidelines in the Federal Courts, 1998 (Cert. of Merit ABA); contbr. articles on criminal law and constl. law to profl. jours. Trustee Dartmouth Coll., Hanover, N.H., 1989-2000, Women's Campaign Sch., 1994—, Fed. Bar Found., 1998-2004. Mem. Am. Law Inst., Coun. Fgn. Rels., Conn. Bar Found. (bd. dirs. 1987—, chair 1999-2002). Office: Yale Law Sch PO Box 208215 New Haven CT 06520-8215 E-mail: kate.stith@yale.edu.

STITLE, STEPHEN A., bank executive; B in Econs. and Polit. Sci., Ind. U., JD cum laude. Bar: US Supreme Ct., US Dist. Ct. (so. dist. Ind.), Ind., Washington. Corp. v.p., bd. dirs., mem. mgmt. and policy coms. Eli Lilly and Co.; chmn. Ind. bank Nat. City Corp., 1995, chmn., pres., CEO Nat. City Bank Ind., corp. exec. v.p., pres. Ind. Banking, 1999—. Bd. dirs. Ctrl. Ind. Corp. Partnership, Ctr. Leadership Devel., Indpls. C. of C., US Auto Club, Sagamore Inst. Policy Rsch., Ind. C. of C. Bd. dirs. Ind. U. Found., Heart Ctr. Ind., YMCA, Greater Indpls. Progress Com., Pacers Basketball Corp. Found., Simon Youth Found. Office: Nat City Corp 101 W Washington St Indianapolis IN 46255 Office Phone: 317-267-7900. *

STITLEY, JAMES WALTER, JR., food manufacturing executive; b. York, Pa., May 23, 1944; s. James Walter and Geraldine Salome (Horn) S.; m. Tresa Rose Adkins, 1996. BS in Chemistry, Millersville U., 1970. Med. technician York Hosp., 1962-66; rsch. biochemist Carter-Wallace, Inc., Cranbury, N.J., 1970-75; mgr. Ward Labs. divsn. Ward Foods, East Orange, N.J., 1975-77; mgr. tech. svcs. Pepperidge Farms, Inc., Norwalk, Conn., 1977-86; dir. tech. devel. Am. Inst. Baking, Manhattan, Kans., 1986-88; dir. baking and cereal sci. rsch. and biscuit product devel. internat. Campbell Soup Co., Camden, N.J., 1988-90; nat. dir. rsch. and tech. Domino's Pizza, Inc., 1990-91, divsn. v.p. consumer and product rsch., 1992—; pres., CEO TechnoVation Network, Inc., 1992—; dir. new product innovation Weider Nutrition Internat., Salt Lake City, 1999—. Cons. biochemistry and toxicology. Contbr. articles to profl.jours. Asst. scoutmaster Boy Scouts Am. Mem. AAAS, Am. Chem. Soc., Am. Mgmt. Assn., Am. Assn. Cereal Chemists, Am. Inst. Baking (ednl. adv. com. 1978—), Instrument Soc. Am. (assoc. dir.-food industry liaison), Am. Astron. Rsch. Group, York Astron. Soc. (v.p. 1960). Achievements include patents in field. Office: Schiff Nutrition Internat 2002 S 5070 W Salt Lake City UT 84104 Home: 5519 Philadelphian Ct West Jordan UT 84088-6232 E-mail: sitf2000@yahoo.com.

STITT, DAVID TILLMAN, judge; b. St. Louis, Apr. 9, 1943; s. David Leander and Jane Wilkinson (Dupuy) S.; m. Elizabeth Celia Santino, Apr. 30, 1981; children: Rachel Elizabeth Botkin, Samuel Thornton. AB, Davidson Coll., 1964; JD, U. Tex., 1969. Assoc. Galland, Kharasch, Calkins & Brown, Washington, 1969-71; asst. corp. counsel D.C., Washington, 1971-73, asst. U.S. atty., 1973-74; asst. county atty. Fairfax County, Va., 1975-80, county atty., 1980-91; ptnr. Venable, Baetjer & Howard, McLean, Va., 1991-95; judge Cir. Ct. Fairfax County, Va., 1995—. Lt. U.S. Army, 1964-66, Vietnam. Mem. Va. State Bar Coun. (exec. com. 1991-93), Local Govt. Attys. of Va. (pres. 1983-84, Disting. Svc. award 1991), Conf. of Local Bar Assn. (chmn. 1990-91), Fairfax Bar Assn. (pres. 1986-87). Presbyterian. Home: 6503 Smoot Dr Mc Lean VA 22101-4003 Office: Fairfax County Circuit Ct 4110 Chain Bridge Rd Fairfax VA 22030-4009 Office Phone: 703-246-2221.

STITT, DOROTHY JEWETT, journalist; b. Houston, Sept. 4, 1914; d. Harry Berkey and Gladys (Norfleet) Jewett; m. James Wilson Stitt, Feb. 14, 1939; children: James Harry (dec. 1999), Thomas Paul. AB, Rice U., 1937; MS, Columbia U., 1938. Reporter Houston Post, 1936-38, asst. city editor, 1938; editor of publs. Jewett Family of Am., 1971-94, editor emeritus, 1994—. Spl. asst. to pub. Jewett Genealogy Vols. III and IV, 1995-97; Jewett family Dir.-for-Life, 1995—; gen. chair Jewett Family Reunion, 1996; exec. com. Jewett 2000 Millennium Reunion. Author, editor: The 100th Anniversary Yearbook and History of the George Taylor Chapter, DAR, 1895-1995, 1994, Easton Red Cross Fiftieth Anniversary Booklet and History—Fifty Years of Service, 1967. Adv. bd. Easton Salvation Army, pub. chmn., 1956—, chmn. bd. dirs., 1964, bd. treas., 1981; bd. dirs., pub. chmn. Easton chpt. ARC, 1952-67, vol. Lehigh Valley chpt., 1995-96, 98; founding chmn., pres. Easton JC Wives, 1950-53; fin. com. Little Stone House Mus. Assn., 1974-76, 80, organizing bd. dirs. sec. and pub. chmn., 1974-91; bd. dirs. Easton United Comty. Chest/United Way, 1957-60, publicity chmn. for United Way 1st campaign, 1960; active Easton Civil Def. Comms., 1956-60; charter mem. bd. Montgomery County Pa. Girl Scouts USA, 1946-48, publicity chmn., initiator and editor county newsletter; den mother cub scouts Easton Boy Scouts Am., 1948-55; capt. renovation campaign area YWCA, 1956; mem. March Sch., Easton PTA, 1948-57, sec., 1952-54, v.p., 1954-56, bylaws chmn., 1953, Easton H.S., 1954-61, membership chmn., 1955-57, 59-60; bd. dirs. Easton Young Woman's Christian Assn., 1965-68, publicity chmn. Y-Teen com., 1953-68; sponsoring dir. Easton area H.S. Students weekly TV 30-minute news program, 1955-56; class agent 60th reunion Pulitzer Grad. Sch. Journalism Class of 1938 Columbia U., 1998 Recipient citation, United Way of Easton, 1960, cited for outstanding svcs., Easton chpt. ARC, 1967, cert. for outstanding svc. and support, 1997, Molly Pitcher Gold medal, SAR, 1980, plaques, Salvation Army, 1982, 1991, 2005, Vol. Svc. cert., 2005, plaques, Jewett Family of Am., 1993, citation for outstanding svc. in restoration and pub. of Little Stone Ho. Mus., Hist. and Geneal. Soc. Northampton County, 1993, cert. of recognition, State Senate of Pa., 2005. Mem. AAUW (treas. Easton br. 1950-52, newsletter initiator and editor 1951-60, rep. of br. to UN N.Y.C. conf. 1961-68, internat. rels. chair 1960-68; Pa. achievement award 2000), UDC (Jefferson Davis chpt./Houston), DAR (George Taylor chpt. regent 1974-80, 89-95, vice regent 1980-83, historian 1971-74, 95—, pub. chair 1969—, Pa. state chair vol. svcs. 1995-98, DAR chmn. Kressler Meml. Garden, Easton, 1999—), DAR, PEO (chpt. AF Houston), Easton Tavern House Soc., World Affairs Coun. Phila., Woman's Club of Easton (pres. 1961-64, bd. dirs. 1957—, pub. chair 1952-68, 70-82, 92-96, parliamentarian 1984-92, 2000—, spl. fin. chair 1969-78, legis. chair 1982-84, internat. affairs chair 1996-2000, history update chair 1997—, Outstanding Woman of Yr. 1992, Gold Medal of Honor 1992), Pa. Northeastern Dist. Regents Club (pres. 1980-83, treas. 1997—2003), Northampton Country Club (Niners' Golf chair 1957-91), Women's Golf Assn. (constn. and bylaws chair, publicity chmn. 1957-92, parliamentarian 1960-92), Libr. of Congress Assn. (founding nat. mem., charter assoc.). Republican. Episcopalian. Avocations: history, antiques, golf, swimming. Home: 110 Upper Shawnee Ave Easton PA 18042-1356

STITT, FRANK, food service executive; b. Cullman, Ala. m. Pardis Stitt. Attended, Tufts U., Boston, U. Calif. Berkeley. Cook Chez Panisse; chef, owner Highlands Bar & Grill, Birmingham, Ala., 1982—, Chez FonFon, Bottega, Bottega Café. Mem. bd. dirs. Chef's Collaborative, Southern Foodways Alliance; state wide chair Share Out Strength; food chair Magic Moments Wine Auction, An Event in Three Acts; mem. Leadership Birmingham, 1993. Author: Frank Stitt's Southern Table: Recipes and Gracious Traditions from Highlands Bar and Grill; cons. editor Saveur mag., 1994. Named a Rising Star of Am. Cuisine, James Beard Found.; named Best Chef: Southeast, 2001; named one of Top 25 Hot New Am. Chefs, Food and Wine Mag., 25 Shining Stars, Ind. Restaurant mag.; recipient 2006 Jack Daniel Lifetime Achievement award, Southern Foodways Alliance Hall of Fame. Office: Highlands Bar & Grill 2011 11th Ave Birmingham AL 35201 Office Phone: 205-939-1400. *

STITT, MARI LEIPPER, poet; b. Salem, Ohio, May 1, 1923; d. Robert and Myrtle (Cost) Leipper; m. Rodney Dean Stitt, Apr. 22, 1944; children: Dana Lovelace, Rodney D. Jr. BA in Music, San Diego State U., 1946; MA in Human Rels., Calif. Western U., 1966. Dir. religious edn. Ctrl. Congl. Ch., 1941-50; tchr. sociology San Diego Evening Coll., 1966-84; writer poetry, 1984—. Green Party. Episcopalian. Home: The Academy Village 7761 S Vivaldi Ct Tucson AZ 85747-9632 Personal E-mail: marilstitt@cox.net. *Did we miss the point? Somehow the stories of the Garden of Eden, Cain and Abel, and the Tower of Babel seemed so simple—take only what you need, care for your brother, stay with your own kind. After all our pious ponderings, why don't we get it?.*

STITT, THOMAS PAUL, SR., lawyer; b. Sellersville, Pa., Oct. 2, 1943; s. James Wilson and Dorothy (Jewett) Stitt; m. Suzanne Ruth Reifsnyder, June 19, 1970 (div. Sept. 1982); children: Alicia Ann, Rebecca Jean; m. Melinda May Millheim, Aug. 20, 1983 (div. June 2000); children: Thomas Paul, Victoria Elizabeth, Andrew James; m. Donna L. Pum, Feb. 14, 2001. AB, Duke U., 1965; JD, So. Meth. U., 1968. Bar: Tex. 1968, Pa. 1969, U.S. Dist. Ct. (ea. dist.) Pa. 1971, U.S. Supreme Ct. 1986. Assoc. Coffin and DeRaymond, Easton, Pa., 1971-73; jr. ptnr. Coffin, DeRaymond, Shipman & Stitt, Easton, 1973-75; sr. ptnr. Coffin, DeRaymond, Shipman, Stitt, Lewis & Walters, Easton, 1975-87, Stitt and Cordts, Easton, 1987-94; pvt. practice Easton, 1994-2000, 2002—; ptnr. Stitt & Narlesky, 2001—02. Sr. ptnr. Star Enterprises Partnerships, Lehigh Valley, Pa., 1986-2000; solicitor Borough of Stockertown, Pa., 1974-84, Easton Suburban Water Authority, 1987-2006; bd. dirs. Keystone Food Products, Inc., Easton; v.p. Jewett Family of Am., 1985-94, 96-99 Solicitor Lehigh Valley chpt. ARC, 1988-90, bd. dirs., 1990-96, chmn. 1994-96; trustee, elder First Presbyn. Ch., Easton, 1973-79, 80-86; pres. State Theater, Inc., Easton, 1988-91; bd. dirs. Easton Pub. Libr., 1973-78, pres., 1978. 1st lt. U.S. Army, 1969-71. Mem. ABA (Silver Key award 1968), Northampton Country Club (bd. dirs. 1987-96), AAA Northampton County (v.p., bd. dirs. 1973—, chmn. bd. dirs. 2004—), Masons, Shriners, Rotary. Republican. Avocations: reading, golf, tennis, swimming, travel. Office: 576 Nazareth Pike Nazareth PA 18064

STITZIEL, JUDD, foreign affairs officer; s. William Franklin and Mariel Reeves Stitziel. BA magna cum laude, Yale U., New Haven, Conn., 1992; MA, Johns Hopkins U., Balt., 1996, PhD, 2001. Reporter FDC Reports, Inc., Chevy Chase, Md., 1993—94; vis. asst. prof. Wesleyan U., Middletown, Conn., 2001, Cornell U., Ithaca, NY, 2002; ind. hist. cons. Washington, 2002—03; mgr. rsch. and info. Odell, Simms & Associates, Falls Church, Va., 2003—05; compliance specialist US Dept. State, Washington, 2005—. Cons. History Associates, Inc., Rockville, Md., 1999—2003. Author: Fashioning Socialism: Clothing, Politics and Consumer Culture in East Germany, 2005. Recipient John Snell Meml. prize, So. Hist. Assn., 1995; Berlin Program fellow, Social Sci. Rsch. Coun., 1997—98, rsch. fellow, Humboldt U., Berlin, 1997, Bielefeld U., Germany, 1996. Mem.: Phi Beta Kappa.

STOB, MARTIN, retired physiology educator; b. Chgo., Feb. 20, 1926; s. Cornelius and Theodora (Sluis) S BS, Purdue U., 1949, MS, 1951, PhD, 1953. Mem. faculty Purdue U., Lafayette, Ind., 1953—, assoc. prof. animal scis., 1958-63, prof., 1963-92; ret., 1992. Contbr. articles to profl. jours. Patentee prodn. of fermentation estrogen Served with USN, 1944-46; ETO, PTO Name Best Tchr. Sch. Agr., 1970, Best Counselor Sch. Agr., 1977, Best Counselor Purdue U., 1977 Fellow AAAS Episcopalian. Home: 6218 W Rd 75 N West Lafayette IN 47906

STOBAUGH, ROBERT BLAIR, oil industry executive; b. McGehee, Ark., Oct. 15, 1927; s. Robert B. and Helen (Parris) S.; m. Beverly Ann Parker, Oct. 18, 1947 (dec. 1990); children: Blair, Susan, William (dec.), Clay; m. June Gray Milton, Dec. 7, 1991. BS in Chem. Engring., La. State U., 1947; DBA, Harvard Bus. Sch., 1968. Refinery engr. Exxon Corp., Baton Rouge and Venezuela, 1947-52; engring. mgr. Caltex Oil Co., NY, Bahrain, London, 1952-59; mgr. econ. evaluation Monsanto Co., Houston, 1959-65; lectr. Harvard Bus. Sch., Boston, 1967-70, assoc. prof., 1970-71, prof., 1972-83, Charles E. Wilson prof., 1984-96, Charles E. Wilson prof. emeritus, 1996—, chmn. doctoral programs, 1984-89, dir. energy project, 1972-83, chmn. tech. and ops. mgmt. area, 1981-83. Bd. dirs. 11 cos.; adj. prof. mgmt. Rice U., 2002-06. Co-author: Money in the Multinational Enterprise, 1973, Energy Future (best-seller list N.Y. Times and Time mag.), 1979, How To Build an Effective Small-Company Board, 1996; author: Nine Investments Abroad and Their Impact at Home, 1976, Innovation and Competition, 1988; co-editor: Technology Crossing Borders, 1984; contbr. articles to profl. jours. Mem. bd. advisors Inst. Estudios Superiores de la Empresa, Barcelona, Spain, 1973-80; co-chmn. The Dumbarton Oaks Symposium on Energy Efficiency, Washington, 1979; bd. dirs. Alliance to Save Energy, Washington, 1979-94; expert testimony Congress; adv. cabinet-level depts. White House and UN; trustee French Libr. and Cultural Ctr., Boston, 1995-2004, Houston Firefighters' Relief and Retirement Fund, 2006—. Named to Hall of Distinction, La. State U., 1987. Fellow Acad. Internat. Bus. (pres. 1979-80), Coun. on Fgn. Rels., Am. Econ. Assn., Nat. Assn. Corp. Dirs. (bd. dirs. 1996-2005, vice-chmn. blue rimmon commn.), Harvard Club (NY), Forest Club (Houston) Episcopalian. Office: Harvard Bus Sch Soldiers Field Rd Boston MA 02163-1317 E-mail: rstobaugh@hbs.edu.

STOBB, MARY JEAN, retired association administrator; b. Winnipeg, Man., Can., Oct. 16, 1934; came to U.S., 1955; d. Rudolph Edwin and Milla Elida (Corneliussen) Rasmussen; m. Gordon Wesley Stobb, June 14, 1958; children: Barbara Jean, David Gordon, William Eric. BS in Home Econs., U. Man., 1955. Cert. home economist. County home agt. U. Minn. at Stearns County, St. Cloud, 1955-58, U. Minn. at Mille Lacs County, Milaca, 1962-67; pvt. practice home economist Little Falls, Minn., 1967-71; interviewer Mid-Continent Surveys, Inc., Mpls., 1971-78, Rsch. Triangle Inst., Inc., Research Triangle Park, NC, 1976-78; dir. nutrition Region V Elderly Nutrition Program, Little Falls, Minn., 1978-80; dist. dir. Minn. unit Green Thumb, Inc., Wadena, Minn., 1980—89, mgr. field ops., 1989—95; field ops. coord. Green Thumb, Inc. (now Experience Works, Inc.), Minn., 1995—2003, ret., 2003. Key leader Riverwood Ramblers 4-H Club, Little Falls, 1968—70, 1971—79; county clothing leader Morrison County, Little Falls, 1974—75; chair adv. com. North Ctrl. Minn. Coun. on Aging, 2003—05, Ctrl. Minn. Coun. Aging, 2006—; commr. Little Falls Housing and Devel. Authority, 2005—; mem. adv. bd. Morrison County Interfaith Hospitality Network, 2004—06; pres. United Ch. Women's Assn., Little Falls, 1977—79; lay leader First United Ch., 2003—05, outreach chair, 1976—78, fin. chair, 1987—93, chair mission and ministry com., 1996—2002, mem. mission and ministry com., 2006—. Named 4-H Leader of Yr. Morrison County 4-H Leaders, 1974. Mem.: Minn. Home Econs. Assn. (dist. pres. 1969—71, chmn. home economists in homemaking 1972—73, by-laws chair 1977—78, del. 1981, 1982, dist. pres. 1986—87), Am. Assn. Family and Consumer Scientists (dist. pres. 1986—87), Internat. Fedn. Home Economists, Morrison County Interfaith Hospitality Network (host coord. 2005—), Mid-Sota Home Economists in Homemaking Club (Little Falls) (pres.). Methodist. Avocations: singing, gardening, walking. Home: 17861 Riverwood Dr Little Falls MN 56345 E-mail: maryjeans@charter.net.

STOBER, WILLIAM JOHN, II, economics professor; b. Boston, Mar. 24, 1933; s. Ralph William and Marjorie Cairncross (Duthie) S.; m. Jeannine Lynn Defries, Sept. 10, 1955. B.Sc., Washington and Lee U., 1955; MA, Duke U., 1957, PhD, 1965. Instr., then asst. prof. econs. N.C. State U., Raleigh, 1959-65; asst. prof., then asso. prof. La. State U., 1965-69, acting head dept. econs., 1968-69; mem. faculty U. Ky., 1969—, prof. econs., 1974-97, chmn. dept., 1979-86, 90-95, dir. grad. studies, 1979-86, prof. emeritus, 1997—. Mem. Beta Gamma Sigma. Democrat. Home: 516 Mundys Lndg Versailles KY 40383-9468

STOBERSKI, MICHAEL EDWARD, lawyer; b. Troy, NY, Oct. 18, 1966; s. John S. and Winifred A. S.; m. Holly S. Sedarat, Oct. 21, 1994. BA, U. San Diego, 1988, JD, 1991. Bar: Calif. 1991, Nev. 1992, U.S. Dist. Ct. (so. dist.) Calif. 1991, Nev. 1992, U.S. Ct. Appeals (9th cir.) 1992. Shareholder Olson, Cannon, Gormley & Desruisseaux, Las Vegas, Nev., 1991—. Counsel Clark County Pro Bono Project, Las Vegas, 1992-96, named Rookie of Yr. 1992-93. Mem. ABA, Def. Rsch. Inst., Clark County Bar Assn. Avocations: golf, skiing, scuba diving. Office: Olson Cannon Et Al 9950 W Cheyenne Ave Las Vegas NV 89129

STOBO, JOHN DAVID, academic administrator, physician; b. Somerville, Mass., Sept. 1, 1941; BA, Dartmouth Coll., 1963; MD, SUNY, Buffalo, 1968. Intern Osler Med. Services, Johns Hopkins, Balt., 1968-69, asst. med. resident, 1969-70, chief med. resident, 1972-73; research assoc. NIH, Bethesda, 1970-72; asst. prof. Mayo Clinic and Research Found., Rochester, Minn., 1973-76; assoc. prof. Moffitt Hosp., San Francisco, 1976-82, prof., head section rheumatology, clin. immunology, 1982-85; William Osler prof. medicine, chmn. dept. medicine John Hopkins Hosp. and Univ., Balt., 1985-94, vice dean clin. sci., assoc. v.p. medicine, 1994—97; v.p. Johns Hopkins Health System, Balt., 1994—97; chmn., CEO Johns Hopkins Healthcare LLC, Balt.; pres. U. Tex. Med. Br., Galveston, 1997—. Mem. transp. and immunobiology adv. com. NIAID, 1976—81; vice chmn. rsch. com. Arthritis Found., 1982—84, chmn. rsch. com., 1984—86, sr. investigator, 1974—77; mem. bd. sci. counselors Nat. Cancer Inst., 1982—; mem. sci. adv. bd. exec. com. Lupus Rsch. Inst.; mem. rsch. adv. bd. DuPont Co., 1987—94. Mem. editl. bd.: Jour. Immunology, 1981—86, Jour. Lab. and Clin. Investigation, 1977—82, Arthritis and Rheumatism, 1980—85, Jour. Reticuloendothelial Soc., 1982—84, Jour. Clin. Investigation, 1981—86, Jour. Clin. Immunology, 1982—87, Jour. Molecular and Cellular Immunology, 1984—86, Rheumatology Internat., 1984—86, Jour. Immunology, 1875—1987; contbr. numerous articles to profl. jours. Recipient Merck award, 1967, Maimonides Med. Soc. award, 1968. Fellow: ACP, Am. Clin. and Climatol. Assn.; mem.: AAAS, Assn. Profs. Medicine (sec.-treas. 1991—92, pres. 1994—95), Am. Soc. Clin. Investigation, Am. Fedn. Clin. Rsch., Assn. Am. Physicians, Am. Assn. Immunologists, Am. Rheumatism Assn. (sec., treas., 1st v.p. 1985—89), Am. Coll. Rheumatology (pres. 1989—90), Inst. Medicine, Md. Soc. Internal Medicine, Interurban Clin. Club, Balt. City Med. Soc., Alpha Omega Alpha. Office: U Texas Med Br Pres Office 301 University Blvd Galveston TX 77555-5302

STOCK, ANN, federal official; m. Stuart C. Stock; 1 child. Grad., Purdue U. Dep. press sec. to V.p. Walter F. Mondale, 1980, 84; regional dir. pub. rels. Bloomingdales Dept. Stores, 1982—86, ops. v.p., 1986—89, v.p. pub. rels., 1989—93; dep. asst. to Pres. and Social Sec. The White House, Washington, 1993-97; v.p. institutional affairs The Kennedy Ctr., Washington, 1997—. Asst. sec. Kennedy Ctr. Bd. Trustees; bd. dirs. Young Concert Artists, Cultural Alliance Greater Washington, United Artists. Mem. Capital Children's Mus. (co-founder), The Women's Forum, N.Y. Fashion Group (former program chmn.), Washington Woman Roundtable (founder), "Race for the Cure" (co-founder). Office: Institutional Affairs The Kennedy Ctr Washington DC 20566-0001 Office Phone: 202-416-8703.

STOCK, DAVID EARL, mechanical engineering educator; b. Balt., Feb. 2, 1939; s. Walter E. and Minnie H. (Bauer) S.; m. Mary R. Wilford, Aug. 4, 1962; children: Joseph W., Katherine W. BS, Pa. State U., 1961; MS, U. Conn., 1965; PhD, Oreg. State U., 1972. Test engr. Pratt & Whitney Aircraft, East Hartford, Conn., 1961-65; vol. Peace Corps, Ghana, 1965-68; prof. Wash. State U., Pullman, 1972—. Contbr. articles to profl. jours. Fellow ASME (chair multiphase flow com. 1988-90, Freeman scholar 1994, chair exec. com. fluid engring. divsn., 2000-01). Office: Wash State U Sch Mech Materials Engr PO Box 642920 Pullman WA 99164-2920 Home Phone: 509-332-5637; Office Phone: 509-335-3223. Business E-Mail: stock@wsu.edu.

STOCK, JAMES H., economics professor; b. Munich, Dec. 24, 1955; arrived in U.S., 1956; s. James H. and Barbara F. Stock; m. Anne E. Doyle; children: Christopher, Corey. BS, Yale U., 1978; MA, U. Calif., Berkeley, 1982, PhD, 1983. Asst. to assoc. prof. Harvard U., Cambridge, Mass., 1983—90, prof. polit. econ., 1991—2002, prof. econ., 2002—, U. Calif., Berkeley, 1990—91. Adv. panel Bus. Cycle Indicators, 1982—; cons. European Ctrl. Bank, 2000—; acad. adv. Fed. Res. Bank, Boston. Chair bd. editors: Rev. Econ. and Stats., 1992—2002; author: Introduction to Econometrics, 2003; contbr. articles to profl. joours. Grantee, Nat. Bur. Econ. Rsch., 1987—91, NSF, 2004; Sloan Rsch. fellow, 1988—90. Fellow: Am. Acad. Arts & Sciences; mem.: NSF (econ. panel mem.), Econometric Soc. Office: Harvard Univ M4 Littauer Ctr Cambridge MA 02138

STOCK, STEPHEN MICHAEL, broadcast journalist; b. Colorado Springs, May 16, 1961; s. Ray Kesecker and Juanita Madeline (Keller) Stock; m. Lynn Victoria Peithman, July 20, 1985; 1 child, Michael Stephen Ray. BA, U.N.C., 1983. From engring. tech. to gen. assignment reporter WDBJ-TV, Roanoke, Va., 1983-86; from investigative reporter to weekend anchor, producer WECT-TV, Wilmington, N.C., 1986-87; bur. chief Anderson, S.C. WYFF-TV, Greenville, S.C., 1987-91; investigative reporter-bur. chief Ocala, Fla. WESH-TV, Orlando, 1991—2005, chief investigative reporter, 2005—; standby SE corr. NBC NewsChannel, 1995—. Guest lecr. Marion County Sheriff's Office, Ocala, 1993—98, U. Fla. Press Club, Gainesville, 1993; participant Media Studies Initial Advanced Power Reporting Seminar The Poynter Inst., 1998, participant Getting Wired Seminar, 2001. Adv. bd. mem. Jack Eckerd Youth Camp E-Kel-Etu, Silver Springs, Fla., 1996—; founder Ocala/Marion County Town Mtg. on Violence, 1996; adv. bd. mem. Fla. Environthon, Ocala/Silver Springs, 1993; v.p., bd. dirs. Ocala Habitat for Humanity, 1996—99; elder First Presbyn. Ch., Ocala, 1996—99, Fort King Presbyn. Ch., Ocala, 2005—. Named TV Journalist of Yr., RTNDA of Carolinas, 1989; recipient TV Agrl. News Coverage award, S.C. Agr. Co., 1989, Fla. Media award, Fla. Emergency Mgmt. Assn., 1997, 5 Emmy awards, Alfred I. DuPont Columbia U. Silver Baton, 2004, George Foster Peabody award, 2004, Sigma Delta Chi award, 2003, 1st Pl. Individual Achievement award, AP, 2004, Best in Show-TV award, Fla. AP, 2005, Best Investigative Report award, 2005; Ethics fellow, Poynter Inst. Media Studies, 2004. Mem.: Ctrl. Fla. Press Club (Best Gen. News 1994, Merit Recognition for Spot News 1995, Best Spot News award 1996, Best Investigative Report award 1996, Merit Gen. News award 1996), Investigative Reporters and Editors Assn., Soc. Profl. Journalists (Finalist Non-deadline News 1999, 1st pl. TV Investigations Market 1-100 Green Eyeshade award 2000, Fla. Sunshine State award for best investigative reporting 2000, Sunshine State award Best Investigative 2006, RTNDA Communicator award of distinction, Green Eyeshade award 2006). Avocation: Avocations: wine collecting, photography, sports, gardening, carpentry. Office Phone: 352-208-2605. Personal E-mail: stocknews@earthlink.net.

STOCK, STUART CHASE, lawyer; b. St. Louis, July 19, 1946; s. Sheldon Harry and Muriel Cecil (Lovejoy) Stock; m. Judith Ann Stewart, July 18, 1970; 1 child, Frederick Chase. BS in Engring., with highest distinction, Purdue U., 1968; JD magna cum laude, Harvard U., 1971. Bar: Mo. 1971, Ind. 1973, DC 1974. Law clk. to Chief Judge Henry J. Friendly U.S. Ct. Appeals 2d cir., New York, 1971-72; law clk. to Justice Thurgood Marshall U.S. Supreme Ct., Washington, 1972-73; assoc. Covington & Burling, Washington, 1974-78, ptnr., 1978—, chmn. of firm, exec. com., chmn. mgmt. com. Lectr. law U. Va., Charlottesville, 1987—90. Mem.: Am. Law Inst. Office: Covington & Burling PO Box 7566 1201 Pennsylvania Ave NW Washington DC 20044 Business E-Mail: sstock@cov.com.

STOCKAR, HELENA MARIE MAGDALENA, artist; b. Bratislava, Czechoslovakia, Mar. 22, 1933; came to the U.S., 1968; d. Arnost J. and Helen R. (Strakova) Kubasek; m. Ivo J. Stockar, Oct. 31, 1959; children: David, Laura Bates. Diploma, Graficka Skola, Prague, 1952, Music Conservatory, 1954. Piano tchr. Music Sch., Prague, 1954-68; company pianist State Ballet/Breacrest Sch., R.I., 1968-74; piano tchr. Music Tchr. Assn., R.I., 1968-86. One-woman shows include Warwick Mus., RI, 1986, Brown U., Providence, 1987, Westerly Art Gallery, RI, 1987, Westerly Art Gallery/Morin-Miller, 1988—89, Galerie Horizon, Paris, 1989, Barnes & Noble, Warwick, 1999—2000, Bohemian Gallery, NYC, 1999, Hoxie Gallery, Westerly, 2000, Happy White Gallery, Barrington, RI, 2000, CC RI, Lincoln, 2000, 2004, Pittenween Art Festival, Scotland, 2001, 2004, Pawtucket Congl. Ch., 2002, Bell St. Chapel, Providence, 2002, Courthouse Ctr. Arts, West Kingston, R.I., 2003, McGrath Courthouse, Wakefield, RI, 2005, Courthouse Ctr. Arts, West Kingston, R.I., 2007, Gallery Z, Providence, 2007, two-person shows, RI State Com. Nat. Mus. Women in the Arts, Triboro Studio, 1995, Bush Gallery, Bryce Studio, Providence, 2001, Monserat Gallery, Soho, 2002, Courthouse Ctr. for the Arts, West Kingston, R.I., 2002, De Blois Gallery, Newport, 2002, Stonington Vineyards Gallery, Conn., 2002, Teichman Gallery, Cape Cod, Mass., 2003, Gallery Z, Providence, 2003—04, exhibited in group shows at World Congress Czechoslovak Soc. Art and Sci., Washington, 1988, Prague, 1992, Morin-Miller Internat., N.Y.C., 1989, Ariel Gallery, Soho, N.Y.C., 1989, Art Expo N.Y.C., 1989, New Eng. Internat. Art Expo, 1993, R.I. State Com. Nat. Mus. Women Arts, 1995, Providence Art Club, 1996—97, Sarah Doyle Galery, Brown U., Providence, 1997, Visions, Newport, 2001—02, Gallery Z, Providence, 2003—05, 2006, 2007, Krause Gallery, 2003, 2005, 2007, Breslin Fine Arts, Inc., Warwick, RI, 2003—05, Warwick Mus., 2003, Charmed Gallery, East Greenwich, RI, 2004—05, BFA Boston Internat. Fine Art Show, 2005, BFA Art Expo, N.Y.C., N.Y., 2005, BFA Contemporary Art Fair, Edinburgh, 2005, BFA Art Ireland, Dublin, 2005, Real Art Ways, Hartford, Conn., 2006, 2007, Ct. House Ctr. for the Arts, West Kingston, RI, 2006, De Blois Gallery, Newport, RI, 2005, 2007, front cover, Medicine & Health, RI, 2007, Represented in permanent collections; featured on TV shows. Participant Art in Public Places: Convention Ctr., Providence, 1994. Recipient Second prize Nat. Competition of Children's Book Illustration, Prague, 1965. Mem.: Czechoslovak Soc. Art and Sci. Avocations: travel, gardening. Personal E-mail: istockar@aol.com.

STOCKARD, JAMES ALFRED, lawyer; b. Lake Dallas, Tex., Aug. 4, 1935; s. Clifford Raymond and Thelma Gladys (Gotcher) S.; m. Mary Sue Hogan, Aug. 17, 1956; children— Bruce Anthony, James Alfred, Paul Andrew. BA with honors, N. Tex. State U., Denton, 1956; LLB magna cum laude, So. Methodist U., 1959. Bar: Tex. 1959. Pvt. practice, Dallas, 1959-62; with Employers Casualty Co., Dallas, 1962-65; v.p. Southland Life Ins. Co., Dallas, 1965-77, sr. v.p., gen. counsel, dir., 1977-87; exec. v.p., gen. counsel, sec. Southland Fin. Corp., Dallas, 1978-87; dir. Tex. Life, Accident, Health and Hosp. Svc. Ins. Guaranty Assn., 1978-84, chmn. bd., 1980-84; ptnr. Butler & Binion, Dallas, 1987-2000; pvt. practice Dallas, 2000—; counsel Employers Gen. Ins. Group, Inc., 1994—2006. Bd. dirs. Ins. Systems Am., Atlanta; pres., bd. dirs. Dallas County Mcpl. Utility Dist. 1, Irving, Tex.; gen. counsel, bd. dirs. Lone Star Life Ins. Co., 1988-99. Contbr. legal jours. Mem. exec. com., precinct chmn. Dallas

County Dem. Com., 1971. Mem.: ABA, Tex. Bar Assn., Dallas Bar Assn., Assn. Life Ins. Counsel. Methodist. Home: 3607 Asbury St Dallas TX 75205-1848 Office: 7501 Inwood Rd Dallas TX 75209-4019 Personal E-mail: jastockard@sbcglobal.net.

STOCKARD, SUSAN ANTONIA WILLIAMS See CHANNING, STOCKARD

STOCKBAUER, ROGER LEWIS, retired physicist, researcher; b. Victoria, Tex., Feb. 3, 1944; s. Fred Ferdinand and Elizabeth (Nitschman) S.; m. Catherine Pauline Jones, June 10, 1972; children: Robbin Renee, Kathryn Elizabeth, Marc Daniel. BA, Rice U., 1966; MS, U. Chgo., 1968, PhD, 1973. Rsch. assoc. U. Chgo., 1972-73; rsch. physicist Nat. Inst. Stds. and Tech., Gaithersburg, Md., 1973-89; prof. physics La. State U., Baton Rouge, 1989—2005; ret., 2004. Editor: High Tc Superconducting Thin Films, 1990; contbr. articles to profl. jours. Recipient Silver medal US Dept. Commerce, 1983; NRC fellow, 1973-75. Fellow Am. Phys. Soc., Am. Vacuum Soc.; mem. AAAS, AAUP, Materials Rsch. Soc., Sigma Xi. Personal E-mail: rlstockbauer@mac.com.

STOCKBURGER, JEAN DAWSON, lawyer; b. Scottsboro, Ala., Feb. 4, 1936; d. Joseph Mathis Scott and Mary Frances (Alley) Dawson; m. John Calvin Stockburger, Mar. 23, 1963; children: John Scott, Mary Staci, Christopher Sean. Student, Gulf Park Coll., 1954-55; BA, Auburn U., 1958; M in Social Work, Tulane U., 1962; JD, U. Ark., Little Rock, 1979. Bar: Ark. 1979, U.S. Dist. Ct. (ea. dist.) Ark. 1980. Assoc. Mitchell, Williams, Selig, Gates & Woodyard and predecessor, Little Rock, 1979-85, ptnr., 1985-94, of counsel, 1994—. Bd. dirs., sec. Cen. Ark. Estate Coun., Little Rock, 1984—85, 2d v.p., 1985—86, pres., 1987—88. Assoc. editor: U. Ark. Law Rev., 1978—79. Bd. dirs. Little Rock Cmty. Mental Health Ctr., 1994—, v.p., 1996—99, pres., 1999—2001; bd. dirs. Sr. Citizens Activities Today, Little Rock, 1983—88, treas., 1986—88; bd. dirs. Vol. Orgn. for Ctrl. Ark. Legal Svcs., 1986—91, sec., 1987—88, chmn., 1989—91, H.I.R.E. Inc., 1994—2001. Mem. ABA, Ark. Bar Assn. (chmn. probate and trust law sect. 1986-88), Pulaski County Bar Assn. (bd. dirs. 1994-97), Ark. Bar Found., Am. Coll. Trust and Estate Counsel. Democrat. Methodist. Office: Mitchell Williams Selig Gates & Woodyard 425 W Capitol Ave Ste 1800 Little Rock AR 72201-3525 Home Phone: 501-661-0791; Office Phone: 501-688-8818. Business E-Mail: jstockburger@mwsgw.com.

STOCKEBRAND, LARRY DEAN, physical education educator, director; b. Iola, Kans., Dec. 25, 1956; s. Gerald D. Stockebrand and Carolyn Ann Orr; m. Janet Kay Brilke, Dec. 31, 1983; children: Eric, Steven, Paul. AA, Ft. Scott C.C., Kans., 1976; BSE, Emporia State U., Kans., 1979. Cert. phys. edn. tchr. Kans. K-8 phys. edn. tchr. Yates Ctr. Elem. Sch., Yates Center, Kans., 1980—, coord. jump rope for heart, 1980—. Jr. h.s. track coach Yates Ctr., 1980—2007; jr. h.s. football vol. coach Yates Ctr. Jr. H.S., 1980—86; basketball coach Yates Ctr. H.S., 1980—87. Mem.: NRA, NEA, Kans. Assn. Health, Phys. Edn., Recreation and Dance, Kans. Edn. Assn., Kans. Rifle Assn. Avocations: fishing, gardening, walking, hunting, fitness. Home: 1207 Nighthawk Rd Yates Center KS 66783 Office: Yates Center Elementary School Box 160 Yates Center KS 66783 Office Phone: 620-625-8870. Business E-Mail: lstockebrand@usd366.net.

STOCKER, ARTHUR FREDERICK, classics educator; b. Bethlehem, Pa., Jan. 24, 1914; s. Harry Emilius and Alice (Stratton) S.; m. Marian West, July 16, 1968. AB summa cum laude, Williams Coll., 1934; A.M., Harvard U., 1935, PhD, 1939. Instr. Greek Bates Coll., 1941—42; asst. prof. classics U. Va., 1946—52, assoc. prof. Va., 1952—60, prof. Va., 1960—84, prof. emeritus Va., 1984—, chmn. dept. Va., 1955-63, 68-78, assoc. dean Grad. Sch. Arts and Scis. Va., 1962—66; vis. asst. prof. classics U. Chgo., summer 1951. Editor: (with others) Servianorum in Vergilii Carmina Commentariorum Editio Harvardiana, Vol. II, 1946, Vol. III, 1965; assoc. editor: Classical Outlook. Served with USAAF, 1942-46; col. (ret.); with USAAFR, then USAFR. Sheldon Traveling fellow, Harvard U., 1940—41. Mem. Va. Classical Assn. (pres. 1949-52), Mid. West and South Classical Assn. (pres. So. sect. 1960-62, pres. 1970-71), Nat. Huguenot Soc. (pres. gen. 1989-91), Am. Philol. Assn., Mediaeval Acad. Am., Poetry Soc. Va. (pres. 1966-69), Soc. Colonial Wars in the State of Va., Sons of the Revolution, S.A.R. (chpt. pres. 1972, 91), Huguenot Soc. Va. (pres. 1981-83), Raven Soc. (Raven award 1977), Phi Beta Kappa, Omicron Delta Kappa. Republican. Presbyterian (elder). Clubs: Masons, Red-Land (Charlottesville, Va.), Colonnade (Charlottesville, Va.), Farmington Country (Charlottesville, Va.), Commonwealth (Richmond, Va.), Williams (N.Y.C.), Army and Navy (Washington). Home: 250 Pantops Mountain Rd Charlottesville VA 22911-8682

STOCKER, CHRISTINE MARIE, language educator; b. Detroit, Oct. 14, 1946; d. Norman Robert and Verna Mary. BA in English, U. Windsor, Ont., Can., 1968; MA in Comparative Lit., U. Mich., Ann Arbor, 1969; cert. in Paralegal, Oakland C.C., 1993. Designer Inst. Continuing Legal Edn., Ann Arbor, Mich., 1968—70; mgr. Donaldson Lufkin and Jenerette, NYC, 1980—82; cons. Warner Comms., NYC, 1982—83; assoc. prof. Madonna U., Livonia, Mich., 1986; pvt. practice tutor lang. Farmington Hills, Mich., 1994—. Tchr. ESL Lang. Ctr. Internat., Southfield, Mich., 1996—2000; assoc. prof. Oakland C.C., Farmington Hills, Mich., 2000, tutor, 2004—05; assoc. prof. St. Mary's Coll., Orchard Lake, Mich., 2002. Editor, writer: Human Life Internat.; prodr.: Radio programs, 1986—88; promotions, editor St. Gabriel Media, 1987—94; contbr. articles to profl. jours. Mem.: Human Life Internat. (vol.), Mystical Rose Soc. (founder 1988—, contbr. articles to newsletter), Mensa. Business E-Mail: specialinterestgroup@yahoo.com.

STOCKER, JOYCE ARLENE, retired secondary school educator; b. West Wyoming, Pa., May 13, 1931; d. Donald Arthur and Elizabeth Mae (Gardner) Saunders; m. Robert Earl Stocker, Nov. 26, 1953; children: Desiree Lee Stocker Stackhouse, Rebecca Lois Stocker Genelow, Joyce Elizabeth Stocker Scrobola. Grad. cum laude, Coll. Misericordia, Dallas, 1953; Master's equivalency diploma, Pa. Dept. Edn., 1991. Cert. tchr., Pa. Tchr. music and lang. arts West Pittston (Pa.) Sch. Dist., 1953-60; tchr. music and choral Wyoming Area Sch. Dist., Exeter, Pa., 1970-78, tchr. English composition, 1978-93, chmn. lang. arts dept., 1982-90, dir. nat. history day activities, 1982-93. State cons. Nat. History Day, 1996—. Organist, choir dir. United Meth. Ch., Wyo., 1958—; dir. W. Wyo. Centennial Choir, 1998; mem. adminstrv. bd. West Wyo., 2000—; mem. worship com. United Meth. Ch. and Interch. Coun., Wyo. and West Wyo., chmn. worship com., dir. music, organist, mem. nominating com.; judge history day, Wyo., 1986—; chmn. centennial Wyo., 1988, organizer, dir. choirs various venues. Recipient Tchr. of Yr. award DAR, 1992-93, Wilkes U., 1990, citation Pa. Senator Musto, Pa. Rep. Mundy, Pres. Clinton, 1999, Medallion award Coll. Misericordia, 2003; named Outstanding Educator, Times Leader, 1993; honoree Wyo. United Meth. Ch. Choir, 1999. Mem. NEA, Pa. Edn. Assn., Wyo. Edn. Assn., N.E. Pa. Writing Coun., Nat. Coun. Tchrs. English, Women Educators Internat., Orgn. Am. History, Pa. Music Educators Assn., Music Educators Nat. Coun., Nat. Coun. Social Studies, Pa. Assn. Sch. Retirees (mem. vol. of yr. com., mem. exec. bd., mem. bd. region III, named Vol. of Yr. 1998), Pa. Sch. Employees Retirement Sys. (social svcs. com.), Pa. Retired Pub. Sch. Employees Assn. (Luzerne-Wyoming counties chpt.), Pa. Coun. Social Studies, Wyo. Monument Commemorative Assn., Delta Kappa Gamma (recording sec. 1991—, accompanist Pa. state chorus, 1999—, 2000—, pres. Alpha Rho chpt. 2002-04, chmn. nominating com., parliamentarian 2004-06), Phi Mu Gamma. Methodist. Avocations: reading, writing, sewing, hunting, fishing. Office: Wyoming Area Sch Dist 20 Memorial St Exeter PA 18643-2659

STOCKERT, AMY L., chemistry professor; b. Muskegon, Mich., May 18, 1977; d. Donald E. and Peggy R. Nielson; m. Dennis A. Stockert, June 12, 1999. PhD, Ohio State U., Columbus, 2004. Postdoctoral rschr. Ohio State U., 2004—05; vis. asst. prof. biology Ohio No. U., Ada, 2005—06, asst. prof. biochemistry, 2006—. Facutly advisor Cir. K, Ada, 2006—07; girl scout trainer, vol. Girl Scouts Am., Ada, 2006—07. Recipient Fall Symposium Seminar Presentation award, Ohio State Biochemistry Program, 2003. Mem.: Am. Soc. Biochemistry and Molecular Biology, Ohio Acad. Sci., Sigma Xi Sci. Rsch. Soc., Am. Assn. Coll. Pharmacy, Am. Chem. Soc., Kiwanis. Achievements include research in the mechanistic understanding of xanthine oxidase. Home: 621 Clint Dr Ada OH 45810 Business E-Mail: a-stockert@onu.edu.

STOCKHOLM, CHARLES M., diversified financial services company executive; BA, Stanford Univ.; grad. degree, Am. Grad. Sch. Internat. Mgmt. Sr. officer Citibank; chmn. Citibank Internat.; sr. exec. vice-pres. Crocker Nat. Bank; mng. dir. Trust Co. West; chmn. bd. dir. Matson Navigation Co., Inc., Alexander & Baldwin, Inc. Trustee Am. Graduate Sch. Internat. Mgmt., Asian Art Mus. San Francisco.

STOCKMAN, DAVID ALAN, investment banker, former congressman; b. Ft. Hood, Tex., Nov. 10, 1946; s. Allen and Carol (Bartz) S. BA in Am. History cum laude, Mich. State U., East Lansing, 1968; postgrad., Harvard U. Div. Sch., 1968—70. Spl. asst. to Rep. John Anderson US Congress, 1970-72; exec. dir. Rep. Conf., Ho. of Reps., 1972-75; mem. US Congress from 4th Dist. Mich., 1977—81; chmn. Rep. Econ. Policy Task Force, 1977-81; dir., Office Mgmt. & Budget Exec. Office of the Pres., Washington, 1981-85; mng. dir. Salomon Bros., NYC, 1985-88; sr. mng. dir. The Blackstone Group, NYC, 1988-99; founder Heartland Indsl. Ptnrs., 1999—; CEO Collins & Aikman, Southfield, Mich., 2003—05. Mem. Nat. Commn. on Air Quality, 1978. Author: The Triumph of Politics: Why the Reagan Revolution Failed, 1986. Fellow, Inst. Politics, 1974. Mem. Coun. on Fgn. Rels. Office: Heartland Indsl Ptnrs 55 Railroad Ave Greenwich CT 06830 Home Phone: 203-661-0007; Office Phone: 203-861-2622. Business E-Mail: david.stockman@heartlandpartners.com.

STOCKMAN, JAMES ANTHONY, III, pediatrician; b. Phila., 1943; MD, Jefferson Med. Coll., 1969. Diplomate Am. Bd. Pediat. Intern Childrens Hosp. Pa., 1969—70, resident in pediat., 1970—72; fellow in pediatric hematology/oncology SUNY, Syracuse, 1972—74; now clin. prof. Duke U.; also with U. N.C., Chapel Hill; pres. Am. Bd. Pediat., Chapel Hill. Office: Office of the Pres Am Bd Pediatrics 111 Silver Cedar Ct Chapel Hill NC 27514-1512 Office Phone: 919-929-0461.

STOCKMAN, JENNIFER BLEI, political organization administrator; b. Phila., Dec. 5, 1954; d. William Harry and Florence (Sussberg) Blei; m. David. A. Stockman, Nov. 10, 1983; children: Rachel, Victoria. BS, U. Md., 1976; MBA in Fin., George Washington U., 1983. Systems engr. IBM Corp., Washington, 1976-78, mktg. rep., 1978-81, staff mktg. mgr., 1981-83; dir. tech. trade Sears World Trade, Washington, 1983-84, v.p. tech. investment, 1984-85; founder Stockman & Associates Inc., Greenwich, Conn., 1985, past pres., CEO. Co-chair Rep. Majority for Choice (formerly Rep. Pro-Choice Coalition); bd. mem. WISH List. Pres. Solomon R. Guggenheim Mus., NYC, 2003—; phography com. MOMA; co-chair Bruce Mus. Council; nat. adv. bd. Aspen Art Mus. Named Republican Woman of Year award, Conn. Women's Forum; recipient Heart of Greenwich, YMCA. Republican. Avocations: tennis, swimming, children. Office: Republican Majority For Choice 1660 L St NW Ste 609 Washington DC 20036-5676 Home: 1850 Henry Cowgill Rd Camden Wyoming DE 19934 Business E-Mail: jbstockman@aol.com.

STOCKMEYER, NORMAN OTTO, law educator, consultant; b. Detroit, May 24, 1938; s. Norman O. and Lillian R. (Hitchman) S.; m. Marcia E. Rudman, Oct. 1, 1966; children: Claire, Kathleen, Mary Frances. AB, Obelin Coll., 1960; JD, U. Mich., 1963. Bar: MIch. 1963, U.S. Ct. Appeals (6th cir.) 1964, U.S. Supreme Ct. 1974. Legis. grad. fellow Mich. State U., 1963; legal counsel Senate Judiciary Com., Mich. Legislature, 1964; law clk. Mich. Ct. Appeals, 1965, commr., 1966-68, rsch. dir., 1969-76; assoc. prof. law Thomas M. Cooley Law Sch., 1977-78, prof., 1978—. Vis. prof. Mercer U. Sch. Law, 1986, Calif. Western Sch. Law, 1993; lectr. Mich. Judicial Inst., 1995. Editor Mich. Law of Damages, 1989; contbr. numerous articles to state and nat. legal jours. Named one of 88 Greats, Lansing State Jour., 1988. Fellow Am. Bar Found. (life); mem. ABA (chmn. Mich. membership 1972-73, ho. of dels. 1988-92, editl. bd. Compleat Lawyer 1990-99), Nat. Conf. Bar Founds. (trustee 1985-90, sec. 1988-89), Mich. State Bar Found. (pres. 1982-85, trustee 1971-92), State Bar Mich. (chmn. Young Lawyers sect. 1971-72, rep. assembly 1972-79, bd. commrs. 1985-93), Ingham County Bar Assn. (bd. dirs. 1981-85), Mich. Assn. Professions (bd. dirs. 1981-84, Profl. of Yr. 1988), Thomas M. Cooley Legal Authors Soc. (pres. 1982-83), Scribes (bd. dirs. 1994—, pres. 2005—), Delta Theta Phi (dean Christiancy Senate 1962, Outstanding Prof. 1984). Address: PO Box 13038 Lansing MI 48901-3038 Home Phone: 517-339-2246; Office Phone: 517-371-5140 x 2727. Business E-Mail: stockmen@cooley.edu.

STOCKNER, LINDA ANN, elementary school educator; b. Ft. Knox, Ky., May 23, 1956; d. Armand M. and Lois J. King; m. Terry J. Stockner, July 22, 1978; children: Christopher, Kelly. BS in Edn., Bowling Green State U., 1978, MEd, 1985. 7th and 8th grade English tchr. Woodmore Schs., Woodville, Ohio, 1978—79; 5th grade tchr. Eastwood Local, Pemberville, Ohio, 1979—85, 4th grade tchr., 1985—89, 3d grade tchr., 1989—. Career edn. bldg. rep. Pemberville Elem., Ohio, 1984—. Sunday sch. supt. 1st Bapt. Ch. Greater Toledo, Holland, Ohio, 2000—05, Sunday sch. tchr., 2004—. Recipient Career Edn. Planning Team of Yr., Ohio Dept. Career Edn., 1994. Mem.: Ea. Star (Palestine chpt.). Republican. Bapt. Avocations: going to the beach, reading, teaching Sunday school. Home: 1055 Louisiana Ave Perrysburg OH 43551 Personal E-mail: las1055@hotmail.com.

STOCKS, RUNDELL KINGSLEY, management, construction, education and general consultant; b. Kokstad, South Africa, Feb. 14, 1925; s. Gerald Restall and Edith Hannah (Duffy) S.; m. Janet Alma Parish, Mar. 23, 1949 (dec. 1964); 1 child, Virginia Anne Stocks Garde. Grad., Kingswood Coll., Grahamstown, South Africa, 1942. Chmn., mng. dir. Stocks Constrn., Port Alfred, South Africa, 1946-57; tech. clk. Vecor Ltd., Vanderbijlpark, South Africa, 1957-60; gen. mgr. F.A. Poole Group, Pretoria, South Africa, 1960-64; dir. gen. mgr. Stocks Group, Pretoria, South Africa, 1964-75; Pretoria dir. Eastern Province Bldg Soc., 1970-86; chmn. non exec. Habitech Group, Pretoria, 1975-85; chmn. Gem Valley Estates (Pty) Ltd., 1969—; external examiner U. Pretoria, 1970—2000. Mem. bldg. rsch. adv. com. Coun. for Sci. and Indsl. Rsch., 1972-88, nat. exec. com. Bldg. Industries Fedn. South Africa, exec. com. Master Builders Assn. of Pretoria, mgmt. com. Nat. Devel. Fund for Bldg. Industry, mem. South African affiliate Internat. Com. on Tall Bldgs. With South African Navy, 1943-46. Fellow Chartered Inst. Mgmt., Chartered Inst. Bldg. (hon., pres. 1977-78); mem. South African Inst. Mgmt. (hon. life), South African Inst. Pers. Mgmt. Christian Scientist. Home: Gem Valley Farm Pretoria Transvaal South Africa Office: 442 Clark St Waterkloof Pretoria Transvaal 0181 South Africa Home Phone: 012-808-5701, 046-624-1677.

STOCKS, WILLIAM L., federal judge; Bar: N.C. Chief bankruptcy judge for mid. dist. N.C. U.S. Bankruptcy Ct., Greensboro, 1993—. Office: US Bankruptcy Ct 101 S Edgeworth St Greensboro NC 27401-2219 Office Phone: 336-358-4080.

STOCKSTILL, DAVID H., musician, research historian, lecturer; b. New Orleans, La., July 24, 1937; s. David H. and Doris (Fleming) Stockstill. BS, U. South Miss., Hattiesburg, 1964, MEd, 1972. Tchr. Hancock County Schs., Bay St. Louis, Miss., 1964—91; pipe organist Bay St. Presbyn. Ch., Hattiesburg, 1994—. Textbook selection com. Miss. Pub. Schs., 1985—91, accreditation com., 1985—91. Rschr., composer, pub. (various monographs);, performer concerts in various churches, synagogues, universities and theaters. Bd.dirs. Picayune Main St. Inc., Miss., 1995—2006; chmn. hist. com., 1995—2005; former officer Am. Guild Organists; elder Presbyn. Ch. Am. Named Citizen of Yr., Picayune C. of C., 2004. Mem.: Am. Harp Soc. (past pres. La. Chpt.), Picayune Main St., Inc., Organ Hist. Soc., Railroad Hist. Soc. Republican. Presbyn. Avocations: reading, photography, architecture. Home: 605 S Curran Ave Picayune MS 39466 Office: Bay St Presbyn Ch 204 Short Bay St Hattiesburg MS 39402 Office Phone: 601-299-0735. Personal E-mail: dhstill@bellsouth.net.

STOCKTON, DAVID A., lawyer; BA, Emory U., 1978; JD with honors, U. NC, Chapel Hill, 1982. Bar: Ga. 1982. Ptnr. Corp. Group Kilpatrick Stockton LLP, Atlanta. Mem.: ABA (mem. Fed. Regulation of Securities sub-com.), Atlanta Bar Assn., State Bar of Ga. (chmn. Bus. Law Sect.), Order of the Coif. Office: Kilpatrick Stockton LLP Ste 2800 1100 Peachtree St Atlanta GA 30309 Office Phone: 404-815-6500. Office Fax: 404-541-3402. E-mail: DStockton@KilpatrickStockton.com.

STOCKTON, JOHN HOUSTON, retired professional basketball player; b. Spokane, Wash., Mar. 26, 1962; m. Nada Stepovich, Aug. 16, 1986; 1 child, John Houston. Grad., Gonzaga U., 1984. With Utah Jazz, Salt Lake City, 1984—2003. Mem. U.S. Olympic Basketball Team, 1992. Named All-Star Co-Most Valuable Player, NBA, 1993; named one of 50 Greatest Players in NBA History, 1996; named to All-Star team, NBA, 1989—94, All-NBA 1st team, 1994. Achievements include being NBA Assists leader, 1987-92; sharing single-game playoff record for most assists, 24, 1988; leading NBA in most assists per game, 1988-93; leading NBA with highest steals per game avg., 1989, 92; being NBA Steals leader, 1989, 92; being holder of NBA single season rec. most assists, 1991.

STOCKTON, RICHARD LEE, lawyer; b. Bremen, Fed. Republic of Germany, Aug. 8, 1949; s. A.L. Waldo and Ursula (Siemon) S.; children: Tracy, Andrea, Brantley, Laura. BA, Princeton U., 1971; JD, U. Fla., 1979. Bar: Fla. 1979. Assoc. Holland & Knight, Lakeland, Fla., 1980-88, ptnr. Lakeland and Orlando, 1988—; commd 2d lt. USAF, 1971, advanced through grades to capt., resigned, 1980. Author: (chpts. in treatise) Estate and Personal Finance Planning, 1986. Mem. Fla. Bar Assn. (co-chmn. cert. com., mem. exec. coun., real property probate and trust law sect.), Cen. Fla. Estate Planning Coun., Planned Giving Adv. Coun. Cen. Fla. Avocations: tennis, volleyball, bridge. Office: Holland & Knight 200 S Orange Ave Ste 2600 Orlando FL 32801-3453

STOCKTON, SUSAN, food products executive; Attended, U. Dayton, Mus. Sch., Peter Kump New York Sch. of Cooking. Owner landscape and floral design store, graphic design firm, Boston, catering co.; chef, food stylist Food Network, 1993, exec. chef, v.p. Culinary Prodn.; founding mem. Food Network Kitchens. Avocation: cooking. Office: Home of Food Network 75 9th Ave New York NY 10011

STOCKWELL, JOHN, screenwriter, director, actor; b. Galveston, Tex., Mar. 25, 1961; s. John Stockwell and Ellen (Richards) Samuels. BA, Harvard U., 1982. Actor: (films) So Fine, 1981, Losin' It, 1983, Eddie and the Cruisers, 1983, My Science Project, 1985, City Limits, 1985, Top Gun, 1986, Born to Ride, 1991, Aurora: Operation Intercept, 1995, I Shot a Man in Vegas, 1995, The Nurse, 1997, Stag, 1997, Legal Deceit, 1997, (TV films) Quarterback Princess, 1983, Billionaire Boys Club, 1987, The Eyes of the Panther, 1990, Hart to Hart: Crimes of the Hart, 1994, (TV miniseries) North and South, 1985; exec. prodr.: (TV series) Rocky Point, 2005; dir.: (films) Crazy/Beautiful, 2001, Into the Blue, 2005; writer, dir.: (films) Under Cover, 1987, Blue Crush, 2002; actor, writer, dir.: (TV films) Cheaters, 2000, (films) Dangerously Close, 1986; actor, dir., prodr.: (films) Touristas, 2006. Mem. Writers Guild Am., Dirs. Guild Am., Screen Actors Guild. *

STOCKWELL, LINDA M., principal; b. Mpls., Oct. 8, 1948; d. Irving Gordon and Neomie Lillian Reishus; m. David Lewis Stockwell, Dec. 20, 1969 (div.); children: Joel David, Jaime Lynn O'Brien. BA in Elem. Edn., Augsburg Coll., 1970; MS in Curriculum and Supervision, No. Ill. U., 1985. Cert. elem. sch. tchr. 1-6, elem. sch. prin. Minn. Dept. Edn. Elem. sch. tchr. Bloomington Pub. Schs., Minn., 1970—72, Menominee Cath. Ctrl. Schs., Menominee, Mich., 1974—76, Valley View Pub. Schs., Romeoville, Ill., 1981—85, curriculum coord., 1985—88, assoc. prin., 1988—92; elem. sch. prin. Rochester Pub. Schs., Minn., 1992—. Com. mem. Gloria Dei Luth. Ch., Rochester, Minn., 1998—2005. Recipient Ofcl. Core Knowledge Sch., Core Knowledge Found., 2000-2005. Mem.: Rochester Elem. Sch. Prins. Assn. (pres., v.p., sec.), Nat. Assn. Elem. Sch. Prins., ASCD. Home: 605 29th St NW Rochester MN 55901 Office: Washington Elem School 1200 11th Ave NW Rochester MN 55901 Home Phone: 507-281-9874. Business E-Mail: listockwell@rochester.k12.mn.us.

STOCKWELL, ROBERT PAUL, linguist, educator; b. Oklahoma City, June 12, 1925; s. Benjamin P. and Anna (Cunningham) S.; m. Lucy Louisa Floyd, Aug. 29, 1946; 1 child, Paul Witten; m. Donka Minkova, Jan. 13, 2005. BA, U. Va., 1946, MA, 1949, PhD, 1952. Instr. English, Oklahoma City U., 1946-48; mem. linguistics staff Sch. Langs., Fgn. Service Inst., State Dept., 1952-56; mem. faculty UCLA, 1956-94, prof. English, 1962-66, prof. linguistics, 1966—94, chmn. dept., 1966-73, 80-84, prof. emeritus, 1994—. Mem. com. lang. programs Am. Coun. Learned Socs., 1965-69 Author: (with J.D. Bowen) Patterns of Spanish Pronunciation, 1960, Sounds of English and Spanish, 1965, (with J. D. Bowen, J.W. Martin) The Grammatical Structures of English and Spanish, 1965, The Major Syntactic Structures of English, 1973, (with P.M. Schachter, B.H. Partee) Foundations of Syntactic Theory, 1977, Workbook in Syntactic Theory and Analysis, 1977, (with Donka Minkova) English Words: History and Structure, 2001; also numerous articles.; editor: (with R.S.K. Macaulay) Linguistic Change and Generative Theory, 1972, (with Donka Minkova) Studies in the History of the English Language: A Millennial Perspective, 2003; assoc. editor: Lang., 1973-79, Festschrift: Rhetorica, Phonologica, Syntactica: A Festchrift for Robert P. Stockwell, 1988. Served with USNR, 1943-45. Am. Coun. Learned Socs. fellow, 1963-64. Mem. Linguistic Soc. Am. (exec. com. 1965-68), Philol. Assn. Great Britain. Home: 1929 Manning Ave #301 Los Angeles CA 90025 Office: UCLA Linguistics Dept Los Angeles CA 90095 Business E-Mail: stockwel@ucla.edu.

STOCKWELL, WILLIAM F., not-for-profit fundraiser, consultant; b. Belmont, Mass., Oct. 1, 1948; s. Fred F. and Marjorie (Werner) Stockwell; m. Sara Gray Stockwell, June 16, 1973; children: Quentin F., Carl W. BA, Rutgers U., 1971; MEd, Boston U., 1975. Dir. devel. Eaglebrook Sch., Deerfield, Mass., 1980-83, Hyde Sch., Bath, Maine, 1983-84, Western Regional Coun. on Alcoholism, Lewiston, Maine, 1992-94; dealer Target/1 Fundraiser, Auburn, Maine, 1985-95, 2006, Campagne Assn., Manchester, NH, 1999—2006; cons. William F. Stockwell Fundraising and Nonprofit Mgmt. Cons., Waterford, Maine, 1984—. Dir. numerous workshops, presentations, retreats and studies including Arthur Griffin Ctr. for Photographic Art, Winchester, Mass., 1997, Shaw House, Bangor, Maine, 1998, Bear Mountain Learning Cmty., South Waterford, Maine, 1998, Cary Med. Ctr., Caribou, Maine, 1998, Deertrees Found., Ltd., Harrison, Maine, 1998, Calais Regional Hosp., 1998, Bridgton (Maine) Pub. Libr., 1998, Watershed Ctr. for Ceramic Arts, Nobleboro, Maine, 1999, Lincoln Home, Newcastle, Maine, 1999, Carriage and Driving Ctr., Skyline Farm, North Yarmouth, Maine, 1999, USM-Sr. Coll., Portland, Maine, 1999, Maine Bar Found., Augusta, 2000, Hyde Sch., Bath, Me., 2001, Eagle Hill Sch., Hardwick, 2001, among others. Trustee Western Maine Health, Norway, Maine, 1990—2005; dir., pres. Oxford Hills Assn. Devel. Corp., Norway, 1985-94; corporator Norway Savs. Bank, 1986—, Maine Health, 1999—; mem. annual fund steering com., parent vol. Eagle Hill Sch., 1999—2004. Mem. Maine Hosp. Assn. (healthcare governance coun. 1991—2004), Kiwanis (dir. Norway-Paris chpt. 1986-88). Republican. Avocations: semi-precious gems, gardening. Home: PO Box 84 264 Passaconaway Rd Waterford ME 04088-0084 Office: PO Box 84 Waterford ME 04088 E-mail: fndrsr@fndrsr.com.

STODDARD, ALEXANDRA, interior designer, educator, writer; b. Weston, Mass., Nov. 8, 1941; d. Robert Powell and Barbara Rutledge (Green) Johns; m. Brandon Stoddard (div.); children: Alexandra Brandon, Brooke Goodwin; m. Peter Megargee Brown, May 18, 1974. Diploma in design, N.Y. Sch. Interior Design, 1961. Designer McMillen, Inc., NYC, 1963-77; pres., CEO Alexandra Stoddard Inc., NYC, 1977—. Founder, pres. Design & Art Soc., Ltd., N.Y., 1987—. Author: Style for Living: How to Make Where You Live You, A Child's Place: How to Create a Living Environment for Your Child From Birth through Adolescence, Reflections on Beauty: Lectures and Notes on Interior Design, The Postcard as Art: Bring the Museum Home (Cert. of Merit award 1986), Living a Beautiful Life: 500 Ways to Add Elegance, Order, Beauty and Joy To Every Day of Your Life, 1997, Alexandra Stoddard's Living Beautifully Together, Alexandra Stoddard's Book of Color, Gift of a Letter, Daring to be Yourself, 1990, Creating a Beautiful Home, 1992, Grace Notes, Making Choices, Alexandra Stoddard's Tea Celebrations, The Art of the Possible, Mothers: A Celebration, Gracious Living in a New World, The Decoration of Houses, Open Your Eyes - 1000 Simple Ways to Bring Beauty into Your Home and Life Each Day, Feeling at Home - Defining Who You are and How You Want to Live, 1999, Choosing Happiness: Keys to a Joyful Life, 2002, Things I Want My Daughters to Know--A Small Book About the Big Issues in Life, 2004, Time Alive: Celebrate Your Life Every Day, 2005; contbg. editor Country Antiques and Collectibles, Decorating with Americana; back page columnist Design Times--The Art of Interiors; columnist McCall's mag.; contbr. articles to profl mags. and jours. Founding mem., chmn. spiritual direction com. Ch. of Heavenly Rest, 1975-77; former mem. bd. regents Cathedral St. John the Divine; dame Am. Soc. of Order of St. John Hosp. of Jerusalem. Recipient Burlington prize, 1975, award for design Greenwich Arts Coun., 1985, Interior Design award Brandeis U., 1986, cert. of spl. merit Graphic Art Inst., Designer of Yr. award Kips Bay Boys and Girls Club, 1997, Disting. Womans' award Northwood U., 1999, Lit. Lion, 100th Anniversary prize 2000 Stonington (Conn.) Libr. Mem. English Speaking Union, New Eng. Soc. Republican. Episcopalian. Home: 1125 Park Ave New York NY 10128-1243 Office: Rev John Rathbone House 87 Water St Stonington CT 06378-1432 also: 1125 Park Ave Ste 6A New York NY 10128-1243 Office Phone: 212-289-5509.

STODDARD, ALLAN LEE, writer, musician; b. Perry, Okla., Sept. 1, 1944; s. Leland Luellan and Lena Ethel Stoddard; m. Katherin Ann Gilpen, Apr. 28, 1974; m. Diana Elizabeth Doyle, Apr. 21, 1973 (div. Sept. 1973). Musician The Intruders, Okla., 1959—67; lead guitar The Greenmen, 1965; band leader The Shirelles, 1967—71; prin., owner Cherokee Heart Pub. Co., Shawnee, Okla., 1967—. Musician The Drifters, 1966—67, The Olympics, 1966—67; band leader Mickey Hargitay, 1966—67, 1970, Wolfman Jack, 1966—67; prodr. for Mel Fender and Ashley Fender. Author: Single Pick, 1973 (featured Billboard mag., 1973), Lady You've Been On My Mind, 1973 (featured Billboard mag., 1973), Oklahoma Trade Tokens & Baggage Checks, 2003, Oklahoma Territory and Indian Territory Collectibles, 2003; appearances on (TV program) Danny's Day, Okla. City Channel 4, 1978, featured with Roy Clark, Dub Taylor, and Johnny Gimble (Roy Clark jam) Enid Quail Hunt, 1979; music video writer: Hit and Run Lover, 1990; contbr. articles to profl. jours. including Nat. Treasure Pubs. Vol. Alan Lee Christmas benefit party mentally handicapped children Enid State Sch., 1972; vol. Oklahoma Cystic Fibrosis Found., 2003; musician benefit fundraiser REST Homeless Shelter, Oklahoma City, 2000; mem. Nat. D-Day Mus., New Orleans, 2006; bd. dirs. Washington Irving Mus., Stillwater, Okla., 2000—. With Nat. Guard, 1961—67. Mem.: Philbrook Art Mus., Western Heritage Assn. Republican. Baptist. Avocations: metal detecting, treasure hunting, writing songs, collecting rare indian painting. Home: 1615 East Main Shawnee OK 74801 Office Phone: 405-878-0355.

STODDARD, PATRICK CLARE, retired military systems consultant, computer engineer; b. June 13, 1941; s. Frank Eudaly and Mary Clarann (Burns) Stoddard; m. Anneliese Barg, Sept. 18, 1963; children: Patrick Frank, Conni Maryann. Student, Cleve. Inst. Electronics, 1967—68, U. Md., 1961—63. Enlisted USAF, 1959, radar technician, 1959—67, re-signed, 1967; asst. engr. Univac divsn. Sperry Rand, Minn., 1967—68, field engr. Minn., 1968; sys. engr. Hydrospace Challenger Rsch., Inc., Md., 1968—73; sr. engr. Control Data Corp., Arlington, Va., 1973—74, prin. engr. computer scis., 1974—78, mil. sys. cons., 1978—2002; ret., 2002. Contbr. numerous studies in support of mil. sys. devel. Recipient Bill Norris Shark Club award, Control Data Corp., 1978. Roman Catholic. Achievements include patents for electronic oil slick control. Home: 55 Mohegan Rd Groton CT 06340-5537 Personal E-mail: local538@mindspring.com.

STODDARD, PETER HAWKINS, education educator, consultant; b. Biloxi, Miss., June 10, 1949; s. Richard Williams Stoddard and Winifred Gertrude Hawkins; 1 child, Matthew Richard. BA, Hiram Coll, 1967—71; MSW, San Francisco State U., 1979—81; PhD, Case Western Res. U., 1981—83. Reporter Charlotte Observer, NC, 1971—73; transp. mgr. Jesica/Gunne Sax, Ltd., San Francisco, 1973—74; news editor Alameda Times Star, Calif., 1975—77; social worker San Francisco Welfare Dept., 1977—79; aid to the mayor City of San Francisco, 1979—81; prof. of social work Moorhead State U., Moorhead, Minn., 1983—84, U. of Tenn. Grad. Social Work Sch., Knoxville, 1984—88, Austin Peay State U., Clarksville, Tenn., 1988—. Dir. Ctr. for Social Rsch./ Coun. of Cmty. Services, Nashville, 1986—89; founder and exec. dir. Montgomery County Coun. of Cmty. Services, Clarksville, 1993—94; founder and dir. APSU Cmty. Outreach Partnership Ctr., Clarksville, 1992—96, Vol. Ctr. of Clarksville, Tenn., 1995—96; co-founder Family Guidance Ctr., Clarksville. Author: (book) An Atlas of Montgomery County, Tennessee; contbr. articles to profl. jours. Bd. mem. Nat. Assn. of Planning Councils, Dallas; governor's task force on social svc. block grants State of Tenn., 1996—97; task force mem. Governor's Task Force on Manpower Needs in Mental Health, Nashville, 1987—89, SF Mayor's Task Force on Housing Needs, San Francisco, 1980—81; sec. and bd. mem. Red River Improvement Corp., Clarksville, Tenn.; pres. Cmty. Services Orgn., Clarksville, Tenn., 1993—96, AAUP Austin Peay State U. Chpt., Clarksville, Tenn., 2000—03. Fellow NIMH fellowship, NIMH, 1981—82; grantee Austin Peay State U. Tower grant, Austin Peay State U., 1989. Mem.: Austin Peay State U. Faculty Senate (senator 1998—2002), Coun. on Social Work Edn. Accreditation Com. (licentiate; u. accreditation team insp. 1998—2003), AAUP (life; chpt. pres. 2000—03). Democrat-Npl. Unitarian Universalist. Office: Austin Peay State Univversity College St Clarksville TN 37040 Personal E-mail: stoddardp@apsu.edu.

STODDARD, PHILIP HENDRICK, foreign affairs analyst, consultant, writer; b. Iowa City, Apr. 30, 1929; s. George Dinsmore and Margaret (Trautwein) S.; m. Carol Cannon, Jan. 19, 1952 (div. 1959); children: Michele, Christopher, Eric; m. Doris Joyce Mills, Dec. 26, 1960; children: Leah, Evan. BA, U. Ill., 1950; MA, Princeton U., 1955, PhD, 1963. Asst. prof. SUNY New Paltz, 1958-60; analyst, 1963-80; with U.S. Dept. State, Washington, dep. asst. sec., 1980-83; exec. dir. Middle East Inst., Washington, 1983-87; cons. Nat. Intelligence Coun., Washington, 1988-90, dir., analytic group, 1990-94; ret., 1994; mem., dir. Ctrl. Intelligence's Sr. Rev. Panel, 1996-97. Author: Teskilat-i Mahsusa, 1993; editor: Change and the Muslim World, 1981; editor, co-translator: The Turkish Battle at Khaybar, 1997 (in English and Turkish); contbr. articles to profl. jours. State Dept. fellow Coun. Fgn. Rels., 1979-80. Sgt. USMC, 1951-53. Named Disting. Fed. Exec., U.S. Govt.; recipient Nat. Intelligence Disting. Svc. medal. Mem. Middle East Inst., Middle East Studies Assn., Turkish Studies Assn., Am. Fgn. Svc. Assn., Phi Beta Kappa, Sigma Chi. Home: 6000 Springfield Dr Bethesda MD 20816-1232

STODDARD, ROBERT H., geography educator; b. Auburn, Nebr., Aug. 29, 1928; s. Hugh P. and Nainie L. (Robertson) S.; m. Sally E. Salisbury, Dec. 10, 1955; children: Martha, Andrew R., Hugh A. BA, Nebr. Wesleyan, Lincoln, 1950; MA, U. Nebr., 1960; PhD, U. Iowa, 1966. Instr. Nebr. Wesleyan, 1961-63, asst. prof., 1963-67, U. Nebr., Lincoln, 1967-71, assoc. prof., 1971-81, prof., 1981—2001. Vis. prof. Tribhuvan U., Kathmandu, Nepal, 1975-76, U. Colombo, Sri Lanka, 1986; inst. instr. Okla. State U., Stillwater, 1966; TV instr. Nebr. Ednl. TV Higher Edn., Lincoln, 1969; instr. Career Opportunity Program, Lincoln, 1973; dir. Geog. Edn. of Nebr., Lincoln, 1989-95. Author: Field Techniques, 1982; 1st author: Human Geography, 1986, 2d edit., 1989; editor and contbr.: Sacred Places, 1997, Mem. subcom. Lincoln-Lancaster Planning Com., 1974-78. Recipient Robert Stoddard award for Svc., GORABS. Mem. Assn. Am. Geographers, Nat. Coun. for Geog. Edn. (Disting. Tchg. Achievement award 1992). Democrat. Unitarian Universalist. Office: U Nebr Geog Program Lincoln NE 68588-0368

STODDARD, ROGER ELIOT, scholar; b. Boston, Dec. 2, 1935; s. Merton Edgar and Helen (Bonney) S.; m. Helen Louise Heckel, May 24, 1958; children: Alison Louise, Christopher Paine AB, Brown U., 1957. Asst. curator Harris Coll. Am. Poetry and Plays, Brown U., Providence, 1961-63, curator, 1963-65; asst. to librarian Harvard U. Houghton Library, Cambridge, Mass., 1958-61, asst. librarian, 1965-69, assoc. librarian, 1969-85, sr. curator, 1995—2004; curator rare books Harvard Coll. Library, Cambridge, Mass., 1985—2004; lectr. English Harvard U., Cambridge, Mass., 1984-86, sr. lectr., 1986—2004, assoc., 2004—. Faculty mem. Columbia U. Rare Book Sch., N.Y.C., 1984-85; sec. Friends of Harvard Coll. Libr., Cambridge, Mass., 1983-98. Author: Catalogue of Books & Pamphlets Unrecorded in Wegelin's Early American Poetry, 1969, The Houghton Library 1942-82, 1982, Poet & Printer in Colonial & Federal America, 1983, The Parkman Dexter Howe Library, part 1: Early New England Books, 1983, Marks in Books, Illustrated and Explained, 1985 (N.E. Book Show award, 1986, Am. Libr. Assn. award, 1987), Put a Resolute Hart to a Steep Hill: William Gowans Antiquary and Bookseller, 1990; editor: A Glance at Private Libraries, 1991, Edmond Jabès in Bibliography, 1998, 2001, John Laurent, Maine Painter: An Annotated Register of Paintings, Prints and Drawings, 2000, Julien Offray de La Mettrie, 1709-1751: A Bibliographical Inventory, 2001, A Library-Keeper's Business: Essays, 2002, Abundant Bibliophiles: Hubbard Winslow Bryant on the Private Libraries of Portland 1863-1864, 2004, Andrée Chedid, A Bibliography, 2006, Jacques-Charles Brunet, Le Grand Bibliographe, 2007; contbr. articles to profl. jours. Mem. Records and Archives Com., Concord, Mass., 1985-87; bd. dirs. Louisa May Alcott Meml. Assn., Concord, 1983—2004. Huntington Library fellow, San Marino, Calif., 1978, 2005; W.F. Milton fellow Harvard U. Med. Sch., Boston, 1978-80; D.W. Bryant fellow Harvard U., 1992. Mem. Bibliog. Soc. Am. (coun. mem. 1982-88), Bibliography of Am. Lit. (supervisory com. chmn. 1982-91, pres. 1996-2000), Am. Antiquarian Soc. (coun. mem. 1989-93), Assn. Internat. de Bibliophilie, Baxter Soc. Portland, Colonial Soc. Mass. (corr. sec. 1993-97), Bibliog. Soc. London (hon. sec. for Am. 1992—), Bibliog. Soc. Va., Grolier Club (N.Y.C.), Harvard Club (N.Y.C.), Club of Odd Vols. Boston (exec. com. 1985-87), Soc. of Printers Boston, Phi Beta Kappa. Home: 9 Birchwood Ln Lincoln MA 01773-4907 Office: Harvard Univ Barker Ctr 12 Quincy St Cambridge MA 02138-6502

STODDARD, STEPHEN DAVIDSON, ceramics engineer, retired state senator; b. Everett, Wash., Feb. 8, 1925; s. Albert and Mary Louise (Billings) S.; m. Joann Elizabeth Burt, June 18, 1949 (dec. Oct. 1993); children: Dorcas Ann, Stephanie Kay; m. Barbara L. Seitz, Feb. 18, 1995. Student, Tacoma Coll., Wash., 1944, Conn. Coll., New London, 1946; BS, U. Ill., Urbana, 1950. Asst. prodn. supr., asst. ceramic engr. Coors Porcelain Co., Golden, Colo., 1950-52; ceramics-powder metallurgy sect. leader Los Alamos (N.Mex.) Sci. Lab., U. Calif., 1952-82; pres., treas. Materials Tech. Assocs., Inc., 1978-94; cons. Ceramic Age Mag., 1958-60; Cons. Nuclear Applications for Ceramic Materials, 1958-60; Jury commr. Los Alamos County, 1969; justice of peace, 1956-62; mem. Los Alamos Sch. Adv. Council, 1966; mcpl. judge Los Alamos, 1976—77; chmn. Los Alamos Ordinance Rev. Com., 1958; Mem. Republican County and State Central Com., 1955—; county commr. Los Alamos, N.Mex., 1966-68; mem. Los Alamos County Planning Commn., 1962-63, N.Mex. Senate, 1980-92. Bd. dir. Los Alamos Econ. Devel. Corp., 1982-99, U. N.Mex. Los Alamos Found.; mem. Los Alamos Pub. Sch. Found., 2006-, vice chmn., 2007-. Patentee in field. Bd. dirs. Los Amigos de Valles Caldera, 2006—; vice chmn. Amigos de Valles Coldera, 2006—; vestryman Episcop. Ch., 1999—2002; bd. dirs. Sangre de Cristo coun. Girl Scouts U.S.A., 1965—71; N.Mex. chpt. Nature Conservancy, 1988—97, v.p., 1993—94, disting. trustee, 2001; bd. dirs. Southwestern Assn. on Indian Affairs, Inc., 1987—91, chmn., 2000—02; chmn. bd. dirs. Los Alamos Vis. Nurses, 1995—2004; chmn. Gov.'s Commn. in Nat. and Cmty. Svc., 2001, Los Alamos County 50th Anniversary Com., 1998—99; trustee, vice chmn. Valles Caldera Nat. Preserve, 2000—02; chmn. Los Alamos Vis. Nurses, 2000—, Los Alamos 50th Anniversary Com., 1998—99; mem. Los Alamos Edn. Group, 1995—. With AUS, 1943—46. Decorated Bronze Star, Purple Heart, Combat Infantry Badge; recipient disting. alumni award U. Ill. Coll. Engring., 1986, Leopold Conservation award N.Mex. Nature Conservancy, 1988, Cmty. Svc. award. Fellow Am. Inst. Chemists, Am. Ceramic Soc. (treas. 1972-74, pres. 1976-77, disting. life 1984); mem. Nat. Inst. Ceramic Engrs. (PACE award 1965, Greaves Walker award 1984), Am. Soc. Metals, N.Mex. Soc. Profl. Engrs. (Ingeniero Veterano de Neuvo Mejico award 1992), Los Alamos C. of C. (citizen of yr. award 1992, Living Treasure of Los Alamos 2000), Masons, Shriners (pres. 1994-95), Elks (dist. dep. grand exalted ruler 1968-69), Los Alamos Golf Assn. (dir. 1964-66), Am. Legion (nat. legis. coun. 1992-94), Kiwanis (pres. 1964, lt. gov. 1968-69), Sigma Xi, Alpha Tau Omega. Episcopalian. Home: 4557 Trinity Dr Los Alamos NM 87544-1862 E-mail: sbstoddard@msn.com.

STODDART, J(AMES) FRASER, chemistry professor; b. Edinburgh, May 24, 1942; widowed; 2 children. BSc, Edinburgh U., Scotland, 1964; PhD, Edinburgh U., 1966, DSc, 1980; DSc (hon.), Birmingham U., 2005, U. Twente, 2006. Postgrad. student U. Edinburgh, Scotland, 1964-66; NRC postdoctoral fellow Queen's U., Kingston, Ont., Canada, 1967-70; Imperial Chem. Industries rsch. fellow U. Sheffield, England, 1970, lectr. in Chemistry, 1970—82, reader in Chemistry, 1982—91; sci. rsch. coun. sr. vis. fellow UCLA, 1978; rschr. ICI Corp. Lab., Runcorn, England, 1978-81; prof. Org. Chem. Birmingham U., England, 1990-97, hon. prof. chemistry, 1997—2002, chair organic chemistry, 1990, head Sch. Chem., 1993-97; Saul Winstein chair, organic chemistry UCLA, 1997—2003, Fred Kavil Chair Nanosystems Sciences, 2003—; acting co-dir. Calif. NanoSystems Inst., 2002—03, bd. dir., 2000, dir., 2003—. Vis. prof. Tex. A&M U., 1980, Messina U., Italy, 1985-87, Ecole Nationale Supérieure de Chemie de Mulhouse, 1987; invited lectr. in supramolecular and macromolecular sci.; hon. prof. East China U. Sci. and Tech. in Shanghai, 2005; Carnegie Centenary vis. professorship, U. Scotland, 2005; mem. scientific adv. bd. Ctr. for Nanoscale Sci. and Tech., Rice U. Mem. editl. adv. bd. Crystal Growth and Design, Journal Organic Chemistry, Organic Letters; mem. internat. adv. bd. Collection of Czechoslovak Chem. Communications, Angewandte Chemie; mem. editl. bd. Chemistry- A European Jour., Synthesis, Journal of Inclusion Phenomena, Bioorganic Chemistry Reviews, Organic Letters; editor Royal Society of Chemistry Series of Monographs on Supramolecular Chemistry; contbr. a significant number of articles to profl. jours. Recipient Hope prize 1964, RSC Perkin Divsn. Career award 1980, 81, 82, Internat. Izatt-Christensen award in macrocyclic chemistry, 1993, Chaire Bruylants award, U. Louvaine-La-Neuve, Belgium, 1994, Adolf Steinhofer Found. award, 1995, Nagoya Gold Medal award in organic chemistry, 2004, Mack Meml. award, Ohio State U., 2006. Fusion award, U. Nev., 2006, King Faisal Internat. prize Sci. King Faisal Found.; Leverhulme rsch. fellow, 1988-89, Humboldt Fellowship, 1998; named Alumnus of Yr., U. Endinburgh, 2005, Knight Bachelor, 2006. Fellow Royal Soc., Royal Soc. Chem., German Acad. Natural Scis., AAAS, Sci. Divsn. Royal Netherlands Acad. Arts and Sciences; mem. Chem. Soc.(Carbohydrate Chemistry award, 1978), Am. Chem. Soc. (Arthur C. Cope Scholar award, 1999, PSME Divsn. Arthur K. Doolittle award, 2005). Achievements include being co-creator of the world's densest memory circuit in 2007. Office: UCLA Dept Chem & Biochem 607 Charles E Young Dr East Los Angeles CA 90095-1569 Office Phone: 310-206-7078. Office Fax: 310-206-1843. Business E-Mail: stoddart@chem.ucla.edu.

STODDART, MERVIN, religious studies educator, pastor; b. Saint James, Jamaica, Mar. 7, 1957; s. Raphael George Stoddart and Merdiena Cynthia Brown; m. Aneita Jenkins, Apr. 21, 2003; children: Mervin, Mario Keith, Lorian Elise. Grad. in Edn. with distinction, Coll. of Arts, Sci. & Tech., Kingston, Jamaica, 1985; BA, Martin U., Indpls., 1997, MA, 1998. Cert. min. Gravel Ground Bapt. Ch., Jamaica, 1980; tchr. Assn. Christian Schs. Internat., 2004. Tchr. Ministry Edn., Montego Bay, St. James, Jamaica, 1975—85, Belair Sch., Manchester, Jamaica, 1985—86; instr. Bapt. Bible Coll. Indpls., 1990—99; founding headmaster Oaks Acad., Indpls., 1999; headmaster Antioch Christian Acad., Indianapolis, 1999—2000; tchr. Ctrl. Fla. Christian Acad., Ocoee, 2000—03, Found. Acad., Winter Garden, Fla., 2003—. Asst. pastor Jamaica Bapt. Union, St. James, Jamaica, 1978—85; pastor Gravel Ground Bapt. Ch., Clarendon, Jamaica, 1980—81; freelance reporter Jamaica Gleaner, St. James, 1980—86; pastor Greater N.E. Bapt. Ch., Indpls., 1995—97; founding headmaster Christian Acad., Indpls., 1996—97; career counselor Martin U., Indpls., 1998—99; freelance writer Jamaica Observer, Kingston, Jamaica, 2000—. Cmty. svc. African Cultural Renaissance Movement, Kingston, 1982—85; trained cub master Boys Scouts Am., Indpls., 1989—95; evangelist Bapt. Ch., Jamaica, 1972—; youth camp counselor Jamaica Bapt. Union, Trelawny, Jamaica, 1976—80; vol. Christ's Agents, Montego Bay, St. James, 1976—80; choir dir., pianist Providence Bapt. Ch., St. James, 1974—80; dir. counseling Billy Graham Evangelistic Crusade, Montego Bay, St. James, 1981—81; mem. sch. coun. T. C. Sch. #98, Indpls., 1996—98. Lance cpl. Jamaica Combined Cadets Force, 1969—75, St. James. Mem.: Assn. Christian Scs. Internat. (licentiate; tchr. accreditation com. 1995—), Jamaica Tchrs. Assn. Housing Trust (life; founding mem. 1979). Independent. Avocations: chess, travel, soccer, cricket, swimming. Home: 1057 Vizcaya Lakes Rd Ocoee FL 34761 Office: Found Acad 125 E Plant St Winter Garden FL 34787 Home Phone: 407-462-5048; Office Phone: 407-656-3677. Personal E-mail: inmerv@hotmail.com. Business E-Mail: mstoddart@foundationacademy.net.

STODOLA, MARK ALLEN, mayor, former prosecutor; b. Mpls., May 18, 1949; s. Robert Allen and Elizabeth (Abeler) S.; 1 child, Allison. BA in Journalism and Polit. Sci., U. Iowa, 1971; JD, U. Ark., 1974. Bar: Ark. 1974, U.S. Dist Ct. (we. and ea. dists.) Ark. 1975, U.S. Ct. Appeals (8th cir.). Assoc. Givens & Buzbee, Little Rock, 1974-75; dep. pub. defender Pulaski County, Little Rock, 1975-76; pub. defender North Little Rock City, Ark., 1976-85; ptnr. Stodola & Smith, North Little Rock, 1976-85; city atty. City of Little Rock, Ark., 1985—90, prosecuting atty., 1990—96, mayor, 2007—. Instr. criminal justice U. Ark, Little Rock, 1976-85. Mem. exec. com. Dem State Com., Little rock, 1976—; mem. exec. com. Dem. Nat. Com., Washington, 1981-83; nat. pres. Young Dems. Am., Washington, 1981-83. Served to 1st lt. USAFR, 1969-74. Mem. ABA, Ark. Bar Assn., Pulaski Bar Assn. (Lawyer's award, 1981), Nat. Inst. Mcpl. Law Officers, Am. Trial Lawyers Assn. Lodges: Rotary. Avocations: rugby, hist. preservation. Office: City Hall 500 W Makham Ste 203 Little Rock AR 72201 *

STODT, F. CHLOE, piano educator; d. Leo Francis and Mary Ellen Stodt. BA in Music Edn. and Piano, St. Ambrose U., Davenport, Iowa, 1974; MMus in Piano Performance, U. Colo., 1976; MA in Theology and Liturgical Studies, U. Notre Dame, 1978; DMA in Piano Performance and Pedagogy, U. Iowa, 2003. Dir. music and liturgy St. Joseph's Parish, Stratford, Ontario, Canada, 1978—80, St. Patrick's Parish, Kansas City, Mo., 1980—84; asst. prof, then assoc. prof. music Black Hawk Coll., Moline, Ill., 1986—88; dir. cmty. music, instr. piano Augustana Coll., Rock Island, 1988—93; dir. music ministries South Pk. Presbyn. Ch., Rock Island, 1993—2005; instr. piano West Music Conservatory, Moline, Ill., 2005—. Recipient Music award, State Iowa, 1970—71; Italian Lang. scholar, U. Iowa, 1992, Piano Accompanying scholar, U. Colo., 1975, Presdl. scholar, St. Ambrose U., 1970—74. Mem.: Coll. Music Soc., Nat. Guild Piano Teachers, Am. Guild Organists (exec. bd. mem., sub-dean, newsletter editor 1984—2005), Pi Kappa Lambda. Independent. Avocations: swimming, bicycling, wildflowers, morel mushrooms. Office: 2201 7th Ave Moline IL 61265 Home Phone: 563-326-3713.

STOEBUCK, WILLIAM BREES, law educator; b. Wichita, Mar. 18, 1929; s. William Douglas and Donice Beth (Brees) S.; m. Mary Virginia Fields, Dec. 24, 1951; children: Elizabeth, Catherine, Caroline. BA, Wichita State U., 1951; MA, Ind. U., 1953; JD, U. Wash., 1959; SJD, Harvard U., 1973. Bar: Wash. 1959, US Supreme Ct. 1967. Pvt. practice, Seattle, 1959—64; asst. prof. law U. Denver, 1964—67; assoc. prof. U. Wash., Seattle, 1967—70, prof., 1970—95, Judson Falknor prof., 1995—99, prof. emeritus, 1999—; of counsel Karr, Tuttle, Campbell, Seattle, 1988—. Vis. prof. Hastings Coll. Law, 1987, Wash. & Lee U., 1979—80; guest lectr. U. Tubingen, 1996; spkr., cons. in field. Author: Washington Real Estate: Property Law, 1995, 2d edit., 2004, Washington Real Estate: Transactions, 1995, 2d edit., 2004, Basic Property Law, 1989, Law of Property, 1984, 3d edit., 2000, Nontrespassory Takings, 1977, Contemporary Property, 1996, 2d edit., 2002; contbr. articles to profl. jours. Bd. dirs. Cascade Symphony Orch., 1978-83, Forest Park Libr., 1975-80; ch. elder, congregational pres. 1st lt. USAF, 1951—56. Mem. Pacific Real Estate Inst., Am. Coll. Real Estate Lawyers, Wash. State Bar Assn., Assn. Am. Law Schs., Order of Coif, Seattle Yacht Club. Republican. Presbyterian. Avocations: baroque music, boating, history. Home: 3515 NE 158th Pl Lk Forest Park WA 98155-6649 Office: Sch Law Univ Washington William H Gates Hall Seattle WA 98195-3020 Office Phone: 206-543-4917. Business E-Mail: stoebuck@u.washington.edu.

STOECKER, DAVID THOMAS, retired banker; b. St. Louis, June 8, 1939; s. John Garth and Marie (Zahler) S.; m. Ann E. Conrad, Aug. 18, 1962; children— Lisa Ann, Susan Jane. BS, Ind. U., 1963. Sr. v.p. comml. loans Mercantile Trust Co. N.Am., St. Louis, 1965-80; pres. Gravois-Merc. Bank, St. Louis, 1980-87; pres., chief exec. officer Bank of South County, St. Louis, 1987-95; chmn. bd., CEO Ctrl. West End Bank, St. Louis, 1996—2006; ret., 2006. Served to 1st lt. AUS, 1963—65. Mem.: Robert Morris Assocs. (pres. St. Louis 1980), Sunset Country Club. Methodist. Office: 415 Debaliviere Saint Louis MO 63112

STOELTJE, BEVERLY JUNE, liberal studies educator; b. Rotan, Tex., Apr. 1, 1940; d. Roger Caswell and Laura Inez (Kennedy) Smith; children: Gretchen, Rachael; m. Richard Bauman, Nov. 26, 1977; children: Mark, Andrew. BA, U. Tex., 1961, MA, 1975, PhD, 1979. Asst. prof. English U. Tex., Austin, 1983-86; assoc. prof. anthropology, folklore/ethnomusicology Ind. U., Bloomington, 1986—, mem. Am. studies faculty, 1986—, mem. African studies faculty, 1989—. Cons. S.W. Ednl. Devel. Lab., Austin, 1976, Tex. Women's History Project, San Antonio, 1981; dir. Folk Arts Survey Tex., Austin, 1977, 78; dir. USIA linkage performance Ind. U. and U. Ghana, 1989-93; assoc. dir. Ind. Ctr. Global Change World Peace, 1994-95. Author: Children's Handclaps, 1979; editor: (with C.B. Cohen and R. Wilk) Beauty Queens on the Global Stage, 1996; editor (essay collection) Feminist Revision in Folklore Studies, 1988, Women, Language, and Law in Africa, 2002; contbr. articles to profl. jours. and chpts. in books. Fulbright rsch. fellow Ghana, 1989-90; grantee Tex. Commn. for Humanities, 1980; Weatherhead scholar Sch. Am. Rsch., 1997-98. Mem. African Studies Assn., Am. Folklore Soc. (exec. bd. 1981-84), Am. Anthropol. Assn., Law and Soc. Office: Dept Anthropology Student Bldg Ind U Bloomington IN 47405 Office Phone: 812-855-8014. Business E-Mail: stoeltje@indiana.edu.

STOERI, WILLIAM R., lawyer; b. 1955; BA in History and Phil. summa cum laude, Kalamazoo Coll., 1978; student, U. Erlangen, Nurenberg, Germany, 1978—79; JD, Yale U., 1982. Bar: Minn. 1982. Law clerk, Hon. Diana E. Murphy US Dist. Ct., Minn. Dist., 1982—84; assoc. Dorsey & Whitney LLP, Mpls., 1984—89, ptnr., trial dept., 1990—, and co-chair, profl. malpractice group. Mem.: Phi Beta Kappa. Office: Dorsey & Whitney LLP Ste 1500 50 S Sixth St Minneapolis MN 55402-1498 Office Phone: 612-343-7942. Office Fax: 612-340-8800. Business E-Mail: stoeri.bill@dorsey.com.

STOESEN, ALEXANDER RUDOLPH, retired history educator; b. Austin, Texas, Apr. 9, 1932; s. Andrew Robert William and Laura Tomine (Thompson) S.; m. Carol Annette Cronk, Aug. 22, 1959 (dec. Feb. 1999); children: Robert Andrew, William Darden, Carolyn Anne. BA, The Citadel, 1954; MA, U. Rochester, 1958; PhD, U. N.C., 1965. Tchr. Washington Sq. Reading Ctr., NYC, 1958-59; asst. prof. history Newberry Coll., SC, 1964-66; from asst. to prof. history Guilford Coll., Greensboro, NC, 1966-99, chmn. dept. history, 1972-77, 82-84, 90-91; Lilly fellow Duke U., Durham, NC, 1976-77. Mem., past chair NC Hwy. Hist. Marker Adv. Commn., Raleigh, 1986-91, 94-98, 2001—; v.p. So. Assn. Pre-Law Advisers, 1989-91, pres., 1991-93; mem. Pre-Law Advisers Nat. Coun., 1991-93, cons., 1993—. Author: Guilford College: On the Strength of 150 Years, 1987, Guilford County Since 1890, Part II of History of Guilford County, 1981, Guilford County: A Brief History, 1993; author: (with others) The North Carolina Experience, 1984, Encyclopedia of Southern History, 1979; contbg. author: Encyclopedia of North Carolina, 2006; contbr. articles to profl. jours. and reviews to newspapers. Mem. Greensboro Sit-Ins Twentieth Anniversary Com., 1979-80, 30th Anniversary Com., 1989-90, 40th Ann. Com., 1999-2000; chmn. bd. trustees Unitarian Ch. of Greensboro, 1979-81; trustee Greensboro Hist. Mus., 1997-99; vol. Habitat for Humanity, various countries, 2001—; vol. Quaker workteam in Ramallah, Palestine, 1999, 2001. 1st lt. US Army, 1955-57, capt. USAR, 1969. Recipient Congl. Leadership award Thomas Jefferson dist. Unitarian-Universalist Assn., Excellence in Tchg. Award, Guilford Coll., 1995, Appreciation award Guilford County Bd. of Pub. Health, 2000, Christopher Crittenden award State NC, 1990, 2000; grantee NEH, 1975, 82. Mem. Am. Hist. Assn., Hist. Soc. NC (coun. 1988-90, sec. 1990-96, v.p. 1997-98, pres. 1998-99, Hugh T. Lefler undergrad. history award com. 1983, chmn. 1984), N.C. Lit. and Hist. Assn. (Mayflower Cup book prize com. 1987, 91), So. Hist. Assn., Orgn. Am. Historians (chmn. membership com., 1991-96), Assn. of Citadel Men (life). Democrat. Avocations: bicycling, bicentennial memorabilia collector, gardening, bird watching, whitewater rafting. Personal E-mail: astoesen54@bellsouth.net.

STOESSINGER, JOHN GEORGE, political science professor; b. Vienna, Oct. 14, 1927; arrived in US, 1947; s. Oscar and Irene Stoessinger; m. Carolyn Stoessinger, 1966 (div. 1985); children: Richard Victor (dec.), Anna. BA, Grinnell Coll., 1950, LLB (hon.), 1970; MA, Harvard U., 1952, PhD, 1954; LLB (hon.), Am. Coll. in Switzerland, Leysin, 1981; LHD (hon.), Drury U., 2007. Prof. polit. scis. CUNY, NYC, 1957-83; dir. polit. affairs divsn. UN, NYC, 1967-74; disting. prof. internat. affairs Trinity U., San Antonio, 1983-2000; disting. prof. global diplomacy U. San Diego, 2000—. Teaching fellow Harvard U., Cambridge, Mass., 1952-54; asst. prof. polit. sci. Wellesley (Mass.) Coll., 1954-56; vis. prof. internat. affairs Columbia U., N.Y.C., 1963-67, Princeton (N.J.) U., 1978. Author: The Might of Nations, 1962, 10th edit., 2000 (Bancroft prize 1963), Nations at Dawn, 1979, 6th edit., 1996, Henry Kissinger, 1979, Why Nations Go To War, 1983, 10th edit., 2007. Active UNA-USA, NY, 1960—. Mem. Coun. on Fgn. Rels. (book rev. editor Fgn. Affairs 1968-78). Jewish. Avocation: classical music. Office: U San Diego 5998 Alcala Park San Diego CA 92110 Home: 601 Neptune Ave Encinitas CA 92024 Office Phone: 760-632-8682. Personal E-mail: johngstoessinger@cox.net.

STOFFEL, PAUL T., investment company executive; m. Gayle Stoffel. MBA, Harvard Bus. Sch. Various positions to bd. dirs. Centex Corp.; chmn. Triple S Capital Corp., Paul Stoffel Investments. Bd. dirs. Holly Corpn., Dallas, 2001—. Co-founder Gayle and Paul Stoffel Found.; bd. mem. Dallas Symphony Orch., Southwestern Med. Found., Zale Lipshy Hosp., St. Paul U. Hosp.; bd. dirs. Dallas Symphony Assn., Dallas Symphony Found. Named one of Top 200 Collectors, ARTnews mag., 2005—06. Mailing: 5949 Sherry Ln Ste 1465 Dallas TX 75225

STOFFEL, ROBERT E., delivery service executive; B bus. mgmt., Univ. Ill. Joined UPS, Atlanta, Guam, 1975, ops. mgr., indsl. engring. mgr., v.p. quality, v.p. transp. process mgr., sr. v.p., COO logistics group, 2000—02, pres. supply chain solutions, 2002—03, sr. v.p. supply chain group. mem. mgmt. com., 2004—. Office: UPS 55 Glendale Pky Atlanta GA 30328 *

STOFFERSON, TERRY LEE, financial analyst; b. Omaha, Apr. 22, 1957; s. Dale Leslie and Alma Rose (Flores) S. BSBA, U. Nebr., Omaha, 1980; MBA, DBA, Calif. Coast U., Santa Ana, 1998. Auditor Alexander Grant & Co., CPA's, Omaha, 1979-81; budget mgr. Archbishop Bergan Mercy Hosp., Omaha, 1981-86; controller Lafayette (La.) Gen. Med. Ctr., 1986-87; chief fin. officer Opelousas (La.) Gen. Hosp., 1987-89; assoc. adminstr. fin. County of Fresno Valley (Calif.) Med. Ctr., 1989-94; v.p. fin. Trinity Med. Ctr., Minot, N.D., 1994-96; exec. v.p. St. Catherine Hosp., Garden City, Kans., 1996-2001; sr. v.p. Provena St. Joseph Hosp., Elgin, Ill., 2001—02; v.p. adminstrn. La Rabida Children's Hosp., Chgo., 2003—05; CFO Twelve Oaks Med. Ctr., Houston, 2006—. Cons. in field. Mem. Healthcare Fin. Mgrs. Assn. (advanced), Nat. Assn. Accts. (contr.'s coun. 1988, 89), Am. Hosp. Assn., Am. Coll. Healthcare Execs Lodges: Optimist (pres. 1988). Republican. Presbyterian. Avocations: fishing, electronics, photography. Office Phone: 404-501-5768, 713-964-8780. E-mail: drterrbear@aol.com.

STOFFLE, CARLA JOY, university library dean; b. Pueblo, Colo., June 19, 1943; d. Samuel Bernard and Virginia Irene (Berry) Hayden; m. Richard William Stoffle, June 12, 1964; children: Brent William, Kami Ann. AA, So. Colo. State Coll., Pueblo, 1963; BA, U. Colo., 1965; MLS, U. Ky., 1969; postgrad., U. Wis., 1980. Head govt. publ. dept. John G. Crabbe Library, Eastern Ky. U., Richmond, 1969-72; from head pub. svcs. to asst. chancellor edn. svcs. U. Wis. Parkside Libr., Kenosha, 1972—85; dep. dir. U. Mich. Libr., Ann Arbor, 1986—91; prof. libr. sci. U. Ariz., Tucson, 1991—, dean librs. and Ctr. for Creative Photography, 1991—, acting dir. Sch. Info. Resources and Libr. Sci., 1999—2001. Adv. bd. Bowker Librs., NY, 1985—90; bd. dirs. Trejo Foster Found., 2000—; state adv. com. Ariz. State Dept. of Libr. Archives and Pub. Records, 2000—; adv. com. U. Mich. Sch. Libr. Sci., 1986—92, OCLC Rsch. Librs., 1995—2000. Co-author: Administration of Government Documents Collection, 1974, Materials and Method for History Research, 1979, Materials and Methods for Political Science Research, 1979; mem. editl. bd. The Collection Bldg., 1978—95, The Bottom Line, 1989—95, Internet and Higher Edn., 1998—99, The Univ. Ariz. Press, 1992—. Vol. Peace Corps, Barbados, West Indies, 1965—67; mem. bd. Pima County Pub. Libr., 2004—; mem. bd. libr. examiners Ariz. State Libr. Named Outstanding Alumnus, Coll. Libr. and Info. Sci., U. Ky., 1989; recipient Pres.'s award, Ariz. Ednl. Media Assn., 1993, YWCA Tucson Outstanding Woman of 1992: A Woman on the Move award, 1992, Ariz. Libr. of Yr. award, 2000, Dir.'s award for Outstanding Svc., Sch. Info. Resources Libr. Sci., 2006. Mem.: ALA (councilor 1983—93, exec. bd. dirs. 1985—93, treas. 1988—93, endowment trustee 1988—93, endowment campaign com. 1989—93, pres. adv. com. 1993—96, legis. com. 1994—96, nominations com. 1997, Lippincott award com. 1997, spectrum scholarship com. 1998—2002, endowment trustee 2001—, chair com. accreditation 2002—04, libr. and outreach svcs. adv. com. 1997-99, chair 1997-98, Miriam Dudley Bibliographic Instrn. Libr. of Yr. award 1991, Acad. Rsch. Libr. of Yr. 1992, Edith Futas Catalyst for Change award 2002, Equality award 2003, Loleta Fyan award Jury 2003—04), Greater Western Libr. Alliance (incoming chair 2006—), Ctr. Rsch. Librs. (budget and fin. com. 1994—2001, exec. com., bd. dirs. 1998—, treas. 1999—2000, vice chair, bd. dirs. 2001—03, chair, bd. dirs. 2003), Ariz. State Libr. Assn., Assn. Coll. Rsch. Librs. (bd. dirs. 1978—84, mem. exec. com. 1981—84, pres. 1982—83, planning com. 1993—95, chair nat. conf. planning com. 1995—97), Assn. Rsch. Librs. (com. stats. and measurement 1994—2003, bd. dirs. 1997—2001, mem. steering com. Scholarly Pub. and Acad. Resource Coalition 1998—2001, mem. govt. documents digitization project work group 2004—, bd. dirs. info. policies com. 2004—). Office: U Arizona Main Libr 1510 E University Blvd Tucson AZ 85721-0055 Office Phone: 520-621-2101. E-mail: stofflec@u.library.arizona.edu. *

STOHLER, CHRISTIAN S., dean, dental educator; DMD, U. Bern, Switzerland, 1972, DrMedDent, 1975. Cert. in oral surgery U. Bern, 1976, in prosthodontics U. Bern, 1979. Vis. asst. prof. U. Mich., 1979—81; assoc. prof. prosthodontics U. Bern, 1981—83; vis. assoc. prof. U. Mich. Sch. Dentistry, 1983—84, assoc. prof., 1984—90, prof., 1990—95; rsch. scientist Ctr. for Human Growth and Devel., U. Mich., 1991—98; dir. rsch. U. Mich. Sch. Dentistry, 1994—97; chair dept. biologic and material sci. U. Mich., 1995—2003, William R. Mann prof., 1997—2002, Robert and Natalie Roberts prof., 2002—03; dean Balt. Coll. Dental Surgery, U. Md., 2003—. Mem. bd. scientific counselors Nat. Inst. Dental and Craniofacial Rsch., 2000—; past pres. IADR/AADR Neuroscience Group, Assn. of U. TMD/Orofacial Pain Groups. Assoc. editor: Journal of Orofacial Pain. Office: U Maryland Baltimore Coll Dental Surgery 666 W Baltimore St Baltimore MD 21201 Business E-Mail: cstohler@dental.umaryland.edu.

STOHR, DONALD J., federal judge; b. Sedalia, Mo., Mar. 9, 1934; s. Julius Leo and Margaret Elizabeth (McGaw) Stohr; m. Mary Ann Kuhlman, July 31, 1957; 5 children. BS, St. Louis U., 1956, JD, 1958. Bar: Mo. 1958, U.S. Dist. Ct. (ea. dist.) Mo. 1958, U.S. Ct. Appeals (8th cir.) 1966, U.S. Supreme Ct. 1969. Assoc. Hocker Goodwin & MacGreevy, St. Louis, 1958-63, 66-69; asst. counselor St. Louis County, 1963-65, counselor, 1965-66; U.S. atty. Ea. Dist. Mo., St. Louis, 1973-76; ptnr. Thompson & Mitchell, St. Louis, 1969-73, 76-92; judge U.S. Dist. Ct. (ea. dist.) Mo., St. Louis, 1992—. Mem. ABA, Mo. Bar Assn., Am. Judicature Soc., St. Louis Met. Bar Assn. Office: 111 S 10th St Rm 16 182 Saint Louis MO 63102

STOIA, VIOREL G., life underwriter; b. Aberdeen, SD, Feb. 13, 1924; s. John and Seana (Biliboca) S.; m. Donna Marie Maurseth Stoia, Sept. 10, 1949; children: Marsha Jo, Nancy Kay, Gregory Allen, Thomas John, James Vincent. BBA, U. Minn., 1949; D in Pub. Svc. (hon.), No. State U., 2002. CLU, ChFC, Am. Coll. Sr. agt. Northwestern Mut. Life, Milw., 1950—95; with Stoia Kusler and Assoc., Aberdeen, SD, 1995—. Co-founder, chmn. bd. Student Loan Fin. Corp., 1978—2003; mng. ptnr. Aberdeen Real Estate Ptnrs., 1979—92; co-founder, mng. ptnr. Tel Serv, 1983—97; co-founder Northwest Regional Health and Fitness Ctr., 1999—. Co-founder, pres. Northeastern Mental Health Ctr., 1957-59, North Plains Hospice, 1980-84; sec. Edn. Asst. Corp., 1978-97; bd. dirs. SD Crippled Children's Hosp., Avera Health Sys., 1996-2003; trustee Aberdeen YMCA, 1969-73, St. Luke's Hosp., 1969-96; co-founder, trustee Northern State U. Found., 1972-99; co-founder Great Plains Edn. Found., 1999—, Aberdeen Downtown Assn., 1999, Blackstone Devel. Corp., 2000, N.E. Regional Health and Fitness Ctr., 1999—. USN, C.P.O., 1942-46. Named Outstanding Civic Leader of Am., 1967; recipient Jefferson award Nat. Inst. of Pub. Svc., Sioux Falls, 1980, George award Aberdeen C. of C., 1979, 94, Gov.'s award for excellence in econ. devel., 2000, Disting. Trustee award SD Assn. Healthcare Orgns., 2002. Mem. Aberdeen Devel. Corp. (pres. 1972-87), Aberdeen Jr. C. of C. (pres. 1956), S.D. Soc. CLU's (co-founder, pres. 1958-59), Nat. Assn. Life Underwriters, Aberdeen Dist. Life Underwriters (pres. 1953-54), S.D. Assn. Life Underwriters (pres. 1959-60), Million Dollar Round Table (life), Moccasin Creek Country Club (v.p. 1969-75). Republican. Roman Catholic. Avocations: jogging, hunting, reading. Home: 1022 N Main St Aberdeen SD 57401-2426 Office: Stoia Kusler & Assoc PO Box 98 304 1/2 S Main St Aberdeen SD 57401-4146 Office Phone: 605-225-3382. Personal E-mail: stoia@nvc.net.

STOIBER, CARLTON RAY, nuclear law consultant, freelance/self-employed cartoonist; b. Vallejo, Calif., July 5, 1942; s. Raymond F. and Grace Stoiber; m. Susanne Alexander, Sept. 10, 1966. BA summa cum laude, U. Colo., 1964, JD, 1969; LLM, U. London, 1975; diploma cum laude, Hague Acad. Internat. Law, 1975. Bar: Colo. 1969, DC 1970, US Supreme Ct. 1973. Atty. US Dept. Justice, Washington, 1969-71, dir. Office of Indian Rights, 1972-74; asst. gen. counsel US NRC, Washington, 1975-80, US Arms Control and Disarmament Agy., Washington, 1980-81; dir. Office Nuclear Export Control US Dept. State, Washington, 1981-85, dir. Office Nuclear Non-Proliferation Policy, 1988-91, dir. Office Nuclear Tech. and Safeguards, 1991-93; counselor US Mission to UN Agys., Vienna, 1985-88; dir. Internat. Programs USNRC, 1993-99; cons. Sci. Applications Internat. Corp., 1999—; cartoonist Issues in Sci. & Tech., 2000—. Rhodes scholar, 1964, Norlin award for disting. achievement U. Colo., 1994. Mem. Reform Club, Am. Soc. Internat. Law, Am. Assn. Editl. Cartoonists, Phi Beta Kappa. Avocations: mountain climbing, birding. Personal E-mail: crstoiber@earthlink.net.

STOIBER, SUSANNE A., health science organization administrator; BA, MPA, U. Colo.; MS, London Sch. Econs. Principal analyst for health care fin. programs Congressional Budget Office; adminstr. of clinical research Nat. Inst. of Health; dir. divsn. soc. and econ. studies NRC US Dept. HHS, 1990-94, various sr. positions, 1994—98; exec. officer Inst. Medicine, 1998—. Contbr. articles to profl. jours. Recipient NIH Directors Award, 1985, Presidential Rank Award for lifetime achievement in Senior Exec. Service. Office: Inst Medicine 500 5th St NW Washington DC 20418-0007 Fax: 908-771-8618.

STOICHEFF, BORIS PETER, physicist, researcher; b. Bitol, Macedonia, June 1, 1924; s. Peter and Vasilka (Tonna) S.; m. Lillian Joan Ambridge, May 15, 1954; 1 child, Richard Peter. BSc, U. Toronto, 1947, MA, 1948, PhD, 1950, DSc (hon.), 1994, U. Skopje, Macedonia, 1981, York U., 1982, U. Windsor, 1989; DSc (hon.), U. Western Ontario, 2007. McKee-Gilchrist postdoctoral fellow U. Toronto, Ont., Canada, 1950-51; postdoctoral fellow NRC Can., Canada, 1951-53, sr. rsch. officer, 1954-64; vis. scientist MIT, 1963-64; prof. physics U. Toronto, Canada, 1964-89, univ prof., 1977-89, univ. prof. emeritus, 1989—, chmn. engring. sci., 1972-77, H.L. Welsh lectr., 1984; sr. fellow Massey Coll., 1979—; exec. dir. Laser and Lightwave Rsch. Ctr., Ont., Canada, 1988-91. Mem. NRC Can., 1977-83; govt. appointee to coun. Assn. Profl. Engr. Ont., 1985-91; vis. sci. Stanford U., 1978; Walter E. Kaskan lectr. SUNY, Binghamton, 1980; Elizabeth Laird Meml. lectr. U. Western Ont., 1985; UK/Can. Rutherford lectr., 1989; v.p. Internat. Union Pure and Applied Physics, 1994-96. Author: Gerhard Herzberg: An Illustrious Life in Science, 2002; contbr. articles to profl. jours. Decorated officer Order of Can., 1982; I.W. Killam scholar, 1977-79; Geoffrey Frew fellow Australian Acad. Sci., 1980. Fellow Royal Soc. Can. (co-fgn. sec. 1995-2000, Henry Marshall Tory medal 1989), Royal Soc. London, Am. Phys. Soc., Optical Soc. Am. (pres. 1976, William F. Meggers award 1981, Frederic Ives medal 1983, Disting. Svc. award 2002), Indian Acad. Sci. (hon.), Macedonian Acad. Sci. and Arts (hon.), Am. Acad. Arts and Sci. (fgn. hon.); mem. Can. Assn. Physicists (pres. 1984, Gold medal 1974). Achievements include development of techniques for high resolution Raman spectroscopy of gases and determination of geometrical structures many molecules; use of lasers in spectroscopic investigations including Brillouin and Raman scattering and two photon absorption; observation of stimulated Raman absorption and stimulated Brillouin scattering resulting in generation of intense hypersonic waves in solids; use of Brillouin spectra to measure elastic constants of rare gas crystals; generation of tunable coherent VUV radiation for use in atomic and molecular spectroscopy. Home: 66 Collier St Apt 6B Toronto ON Canada M4W 1L9 Office: U Toronto Dept Physics Toronto ON Canada M5S 1A7 Office Phone: 416-978-2948. Business E-Mail: bps@physics.utoronto.ca.

STOJKOVIC, DUSAN, lawyer; b. Zemun, Yugoslavia, Apr. 26, 1976; s. Sava and Dragica (Filip) Stojkovic. BA, Bernard M. Baruch Coll., 1997; JD, Harvard Law Sch., 2000. Bar: NY 2001. Assoc. LeBoeuf, Lamb, Greene & MacRae, L.L.P., NYC, 2000—05, Simmons & Simmons, London, 2005—. Mem. Sierra Club, NYC, 1995—2004. Belle Zeller scholar, CUNY, 1996. Avocations: travel, writing on-line film reviews, rock concerts. Office: Simmons & Simmons CityPoint One Ropemaker St London EC2Y 9SS England Office Phone: 011-44-20-7825-4234. Office Fax: 011-44-20-7628-2070. Business E-Mail: dusan.stojkovic@simmons-simmons.com.

STOKER, DAVID ALLEN, plastic surgeon; b. Miami, Fla., July 6, 1969; BA/BS in Biology and Polit. Sci. (grad. with honors), Stanford U., 1991; MD, U. Calif. Sch. Medicine, San Francisco, 1995. Diplomate Am. Bd. Plastic Surgery, lic. Calif. and NY. Intern, plastic surgery NYU Med. Ctr., 1995—96, resident, general surgery, 1996—99, resident, plastic surgery, Inst. Reconstructive Plastic Surgery, 1999—2000, chief resident, plastic surgery, Inst. Reconstructive Plastic Surgery, 2000—01; med. staff St. Johns Health Ctr., Santa Monica, Calif., 2001—, UCLA Med. Ctr., Calif., 2001—, Centinela Hosp. Med. Ctr., 2001—, Marina Outpatient Surgery Ctr., 2001—, Daniel Freeman Marina Hosp., 2001—; plastic surgeon in private practice Marina Plastic Surgery Associates, Marina Del Ray, Calif., 2001—; clin. asst. prof. surgery Keck Sch. Medicine, U. So. Calif., 2006—. Teaches course: Liposuction: Comprehensive and Integrated Am. Soc. Plastic Surgeons, 2006, Am. Soc. for Aesthetic Plastic Surgery, 2007; rsch. experience at various institutions, 1985—2006; presenter in field. Contbr. articles to profl. jours.; author: (textbook) Chpt. on Liposuction and Body Contouring; plastic surgery expert Dr. Phil, featured on Learning Channel and Discovery Health Channel. Named one of Top Plastic Surgeons in the nation with spl. mention about experience in liposuction, tummy tucks and breast surgery, NY Times, NY Times Style Mag., 2005; recipient 1st Place, Plastic Surgery Educational Found., 1993, British Journal Surgery award, 1999, Howard Hughes Med. Inst. Major Grant for Undergrad. Rsch., 1991. Fellow: Am. Coll. Surgeons; mem.: Am. Soc. for Anesthetic Plastic Surgery, Am. Soc. Plastic Surgeons, Alpha Omega. Achievements include being nationally recognized for research in power-assisted liposuctionand anatomy of the facial nerve as it relates to facelifts; pioneering research with power-assisted liposuction, the safest and most effective lipoplasty method available, contributed to a major advance in the field of body contouring. Office: 4644 Lincoln Blvd Ste 552 Marina Del Rey CA 90292 *

STOKES, ANNE DOROTHY, retired educational association administrator; b. Elyria, Ohio, Nov. 29, 1928; d. Edgar Pier and Dorothy Anne (Day) Gates; m. Kenneth Irving Stokes, June 30, 1951 (dec.); children: Alan, Randall, Bradley, Harlan. BA, Oberlin Coll., Ohio, 1950; MEd, U. Fla., 1970, EdS, 1974, EdD, 1977. Cert. K-12 tchr., Minn.; cert. parent educator. Kdg. tchr. Elyria Pub. Schs., 1950-51, Hamden (Conn.) Pub. Schs., 1951-53; owner, tchr. Lads N Lassies Kdg., Glen Ellyn, Ill., 1961-65; trainer, cons. Head Start, Bradford and Putnam Cty., Fla., 1968-69; instr. U. Fla., Gainesville, 1968-72, curriculum developer, 1972-73; edn. dir. Palmer King Day Care, Gainesville, 1971-72; interim prof. U. Minn., Mpls., 1977-78, Concordia Coll., St. Paul, 1986; coord. early childhood family edn. St. Louis Park (Minn.) Schs., 1979-96, ret., 1996. Sec. evaluation com. Minn. State Family Edn. Resources of Minn., Dept. Edn., 1986-99; cons., spkr. schs. and chs.; bd. dirs. Bell Nursery Sch. Project, Gainesville, 1970-73; mem. ethics com. Minn. Coun. of Family Rels., 1991-99. Author: The Thinking Parent, 1993, Career Education Manual for Teachers and Supervisors, 1976; contbr. articles to profl. jours. Informal lobbyist Early Childhood Family Edn., Minn. State Capitol; spkr., workshop leader Adult Faith Resources, 1996-2000; ind. cons. parent edn., 2000—. Career Growth fellowship Bush Found. U. Minn., 1983; fellowship U. Fla., 1969. Mem. ASCD, Assn. for Childhood Edn. Internat., Minn. Coun. on Family Rels., Nat. Assn. for Edn. of Young Children, Phi Kappa Phi, Pi Lambda Theta. Mem. United Ch. of Christ. Avocations: writing, travel, painting. Home: 787 Plymouth Rd Claremont CA 91711-4249

STOKES, ARCH, lawyer, writer; b. Atlanta, Sept. 2, 1946; s. Mack B. and Rose Stokes; m. Maggie Mead; children: Jennifer Jean, Austin Christopher, Susannah Rose, Travis, Emmarose. BA, Emory U., 1967, JD, 1970. Bar: Ga. 1970, US Dist. Ct. (no. dist.) Ga. 1970, US Ct. Appeals (5th cir.) Ga. 1970, US Ct. Mil. Appeals 1971, US Ct. Appeals (9th cir.) Ga. 1980, (2d cir.) Ga. 1990, US Supreme Ct. 1981, US Dist. Ct. (no. dist.) Calif. 1981, US Ct. Appeals (11th cir.) Calif. 1982, US Ct. Appeals (7th cir.) Calif. 1986, US Ct. Appeals (1st cir.) Calif. 1992, US Ct. Appeals (8th cir.) Calif. 1991, US Dist. Ct. (no. dist.) NY 1991, US Dist. Ct. (ea. dist.) Mich. 1986. Ptnr. Stokes Lazarus & Carmichael, Atlanta, 1972-92, Stokes & Murphy, Atlanta, 1992—, San Diego, Pitts., 1992—, Las Vegas, Ithaca, NY, 2001—. Author: The Wage & Hour Handbook, 1978, rev. edit., 2000, The Equal Employment Opportunity Handbook, 1979, The Collective Bargaining Handbook, 1981. Founding mem. adv. bd. William F. Harrah Hotel Coll., U. Nev., Las Vegas, also vis. spkr.; vis. spkr. Cornell U., Johnson and Wales U., U. Houston, Ga. State U. Recipient Hal Holbrook award Internat. Platform Assn., 1990. Mem. ABA, ATLA, Union Internat. des Avocats, Internat. Soc. Hospitality Cons., Confrérie de la Chaîne des Rotisseurs, Am. Hotel and Lodging. Office: Shea Stokes ALC 3593 Hemphill St College Park GA 30337-0468 Office Phone: 404-766-0076. Business E-Mail: astokes@sheastokes.com.

STOKES, B. R., transportation executive, consultant; b. Anadarko, Okla., Feb. 20, 1924; s. Robert Allan and Ethel Nan (James) S.; m. Joan Pringle, Oct. 22, 1950; children: Timothy, Leigh, Lindsey, Celia. Student, U. Okla., 1941-44; BA, U. Calif., Berkeley, 1947. Reporter, writer Oakland (Calif.) Tribune, 1946-58; dir. info. San Francisco Bay Area Rapid Transit Dist., 1958-61, asst. gen. mgr., 1961-63, gen. mgr., 1963-74; exec. v.p. Am. Public Transit Assn., Washington, 1974-80; sr. v.p. internat. ATE Mgmt. and Service Co., Inc., 1980-95. Dir. gen. Saudi Arabian Public Transport

Co., 1980-81 Served with USNR, 1942-46. Recipient Salzberg medal Syracuse U., 1975; inductee Am. Pub. Transit Assn. Transit Hall of Fame, 1996; Reid Found. fellow, 1954. Office: 1911 Fort Myer Dr Arlington VA 22209-1603

STOKES, JAMES CHRISTOPHER, lawyer; b. Orange, NJ, Mar. 19, 1944; s. James Christopher and Margaret Mary (Groome) S.; m. Eileen Marie Brosnan, Sept. 7, 1968; children: Erin Margaret, Michael Colin, Courtney Dorothy. AB, Holy Cross Coll., 1966; JD, Boston Coll., 1975. Bar: Hawaii 1975, U.S. Ct. Appeals (1st and 9th cirs.) 1976, Mass. 1977, U.S. Ct. Internat. Trade 1988. Officer USMC, 1966-72; assoc. Carlsmith, Carlsmith, Wichman & Case, Honolulu, 1975-76, Bingham, Dana & Gould (now Bingham McCutchen LLP), Boston, 1976-82, ptnr. London, 1980-84, Boston, 1982—. Contbr. articles to profl. jours. Active personnel bd. Town of Wellesley, Mass., 1984-89, chmn. bd., 1988-89, town moderator, 1992-97; trustee U.S.S. Constitution Mus., 2004, chmn., 2007. Capt. USMC, 1966-72, Vietnam. Mem. Hawaii Bar Assn., Mass. Bar Assn., Internat. Bar Assn., Boston Bar Assn., Harvard Club (Boston), Wellesley Club. Roman Catholic. Office: Bingham McCutchen LLP 150 Federal St Boston MA 02110-1713 Office Phone: 617-951-8222. Business E-Mail: james.stokes@bingham.com.

STOKES, JAMES SEWELL, environmental services administrator, not-for-profit developer; b. Englewood, NJ, Jan. 24, 1944; s. James Sewell III and Doris Mackey (Smith) S.; m. Esther Moger, Aug. 19, 1967; children: Jessica Neale, Elizabeth Sewell BA, Davidson Coll., NC, 1966; LLB, Yale U., 1969. Bar: Ga. 1969. Asst. to gen. counsel Office Gen. Counsel of the Army, Washington, 1969-72; assoc. Alston, Miller & Gaines, Atlanta, 1972-77; ptnr. Alston & Bird (previously Alston, Miller & Gaines), Atlanta, 1977—2005, chmn. environ. group, 1987—96, chmn. bus. devel. com., 1996—2005; mem. ptnr.'s com. Alston & Bird, Atlanta, 1995-98; chmn. mgmt. com., Atlanta, 1998; pres. Ga. Conservancy, Atlanta, 2005—. Mem. Gov.'s Environ. Adv. Coun., 1991-2004, chmn., 1997-99; chmn. Gov.'s Conf. on Pollution Prevention and the Environment, 1997; spkr. in field Contbr. articles to profl. jours. Mem. Metro Atlanta Chamber Clean Water Initiative, 2000, Ga. Future Forestry Commn., 2005, Atlanta Regional Commn. Environ. & Land Use Com., 2005—; exec. com. Livable Cmtys. Coalition, 2005—; chmn. Metro Atlanta Chamber Water Com., 2002; mem. Trust for Public Land Ga. Bd., 1986-91; co-chmn. Spotlight on Ga. Artists V, 1986; mem. City of Atlanta Zoning Rev. Bd., 1978-85, chmn., 1984-85; bd. dirs. Brookwood Hills Civic Assn., 1975-77, pres., 1977; bd. dirs. Nexus Contemporary Arts Ctr., Atlanta, 1987-92, vice chmn. capital campaign, 1989, chmn. nominating com., 1988, chmn. fundraising com., 1987-88; bd. dirs. Butler St. YMCA N.W. br., 1973-75, Dynamo Swim Club, 1988-91, Arts Festival Atlanta, 1994-98; trustee Inst. Continuing Legal Edn., Athens, 1980-81, Trinity Sch., Atlanta, 1988, 1997-2003, Charles Loridans Found., 1994-2005; mem. session Trinity Presbyn. Ch., 1986-89, 1997-2000, clk. of session, 1988-89, chmn. cmty. concerns com., 1987-88, chmn. pers. com., 1989-90, 1999-2005, chmn. assoc. pastor search com., 1991-92, 2004-05; bd. dirs. Park Pride, 1992, Ga. C. of C., 1998-2005, Hambidge Ctr., 2000-2003, chmn. environ. com., 1987-92, environ. legal counsel, 1981-87; mem. spl. program Leadership Atlanta, 1979-80, Leadership Ga., 1985, Inst. Ga. Environ. Leadership, 2004. Capt. U.S. Army, 1969-72 Decorated D.S.M.; recipient Spl. award Atlanta chpt. AIA, 1988, Mayor Andrew Young, 1985; named one of 96 Most Influential Atlantans, Atlanta Bus. Chronicle, 2005, One of 100 Most Influential Georgians, Ga. Trend Mag., 2006. Mem. ABA (natural resources sect.), State Bar Ga. (chmn. environ. law sect. 1979-82), Atlanta Bar Assn., City of Atlanta Hist. Preservation (policy steeering com. 1989), Atlanta C. of C. (water resources task force 1982-87, solid waste task force 1989, air quality task force 1993-97, environ. affairs com. 1998—2005), Ga. Indsl. Developers Assn. (hazardous waste com. 1983-84), Phi Beta Kappa, Omicron Delta Kappa. Avocations: swimming, bird watching, community activities, travel. Office: Ga Conservancy Ste 200 817 W Peachtree St Atlanta GA 30308 Office Phone: 404-876-2900 ext. 200. Office Fax: 404-872-9229. Business E-Mail: jstokes@gaconservancy.org.

STOKES, KATHLEEN SARAH, dermatologist, educator; b. Springfield, Mass., Oct. 18, 1954; d. John Francis and Margaret Cecelia (MacDonnell) Stokes; m. William Walter Greaves; children: Ian R., Spencer W., Malcolm W. BS, U. Utah, 1978, MS, 1980; MD, Med. Coll. Wis., 1987. Diplomate Am. Bd. Dermatology. Intern in internal medicine Med. Coll. Wis., Milw., 1987-88, resident in dermatology, 1988-90, chief resident, 1990-91, asst. clin. prof. dermatology, 1991—; pvt. practice, Milw., 1991—. Contbr. articles to med. jours., including Critical Care Medicine, Jour. Pediatric Dermatology. Named A Top Physician, Milw. mag., 1996, 2000, 04 Fellow Am. Acad. Dermatology, Milw. Acad. Medicine; mem. AMA, Wis. Dermatol. Soc. (sec.-treas. 2003-04, pres. 2005-06), Women's Dermatologic Soc., Tempo, Alpha Omega Alpha. Office: Affiliated Dermatologists 2300 N Mayfair Rd Milwaukee WI 53226-1505

STOKES, LOUIS, lawyer, former congressman; b. Cleve., Feb. 23, 1925; s. Charles and Louise (Stone) S.; m. Jeanette Francis, Aug. 21, 1960; children: Shelley, Louis C., Angela, Lorene. Student, Case We. Res. U., 1946—48; JD, Cleve. Marshall Law Sch., 1953; 26 hon. doctorate degrees, 1953—2001. Bar: Ohio 1953. Mem. 91st-105th Congresses from 11th (formerly 21st) Ohio dist., Washington, 1969—99; sr. counsel Squire, Sanders and Dempsey, Washington, 1999—. Former chmn. appropriations subcom. on VA, HUD and Ind. Agys.; Disting. vis. prof. Mandel Sch. Applied Social Scis. Case We. Res. U., 1999—. Served with AUS, 1943-46. Decorated Congl. DSM; recipient numerous awards for civic activities including Disting. Svc. award Cleve. br. NAACP; Certificate of Appreciation U.S. Commn. on Civil Rights. Mem. ABA, ACLU, Cuyahoga County Bar Assn., Cleve. Bar Assn., Urban League, Am. Legion, Masons, Kappa Alpha Psi. Democrat. Office: Squire Sanders & Dempsey Key Tower Bldg Cleveland OH 44114 Office Phone: 202-626-6697. Business E-Mail: lstokes@ssd.com.

STOKES, MACK BOYD (MARION BOYD STOKES), bishop; b. Wonsan, Korea, Dec. 21, 1911; arrived in U.S., 1929; s. Marion Boyd and Florence Pauline (Davis) Stokes; m. Ada Rose Yow, June 19, 1942; children: Marion Boyd III, Arch Yow, Elsie Pauline. Student, Seoul Fgn. High Sch., Korea; AB, Asbury Coll., 1932; BD, Duke, 1935; postgrad., Boston U. Sch. Theol., 1935-37, Harvard, 1936-37; PhD, Boston U., 1940; LLD, Lambuth U., Jackson, Tenn., 1963; DD, Millsaps Coll., 1974. Resident fellow systematic theology Boston U., 1936-38, Bowne fellow in philosophy, 1938-39; ordained to ministry Meth. Ch., deacon, 1938, elder, 1940; vis. prof. philosophy and religion Ill. Wesleyan U., 1940-41; prof. Christian doctrine Candler Sch. Theology, Emory U., 1941-56, asso. dean, Parker prof. systematic theology, 1956-72, chmn. exec. com. div. of religion of grad. sch., 1956-72; acting dean Candler Sch. Theology, Emory U. (Candler Sch.), 1968-69; bishop-in-residence Peachtree Rd. United Meth. Ch. Atlanta, 1988—. Faculty mem. Inst. Theol. Studies Oxford U., 1958; del. Meth. Ecumenical Conf., 1947, 52, 61, 71, Holston, Gen. confs., S.E. Jurisdictional Conf., 1956, 60, 64, 68, 72; chmn. com. ministry Gen. Conf. Meth. Ch., 1960; nat. com. Nature Unity We Seek, 1956—; mem. gen. com. ecumenical affairs theol. study com. United Meth. Ch., 1968—72, com. on Cath.-Meth. rels., 1969—, bishop, 1972—. Author: (book) Major Methodist Beliefs, 1956, Major Methodist Beliefs, rev. 15th edit., 1990, The Evangelism of Jesus, 1960, The Epic of Revelation, 1961, Our Methodist Heritage, 1963, Crencas Fundamentals Dos Methodistas, 1964, Study Guide on the Teachings of Jesus, 1970, The Bible and Modern Doubt, 1970, Major United Methodist Beliefs, 1971, Major United Methodist Beliefs, Korean transl., 1977, Major United Methodist Beliefs, rev. with added study guide, 1998, The Holy Spirit and Christian Experience, 1975, The Holy Spirit and Christian Experience, Korean transl., 1985, Twelve Dialogues on John's Gospel, 1975, Jesus, The Master-Evangel, 1978, Can God See the Inside of an Apple?, 1979, Questions Asked by United Methodists, Philippine transl., 1980, The Bible in the Wesleyan Heritage, 1981, Respuestas A Preguntas Que Hacen Los Metodistas Unidos, 1983, The Holy Spirit in the Wesleyan Heritage, 1985, The Holy Spirit in the Wesleyan Heritage, Spanish transl., 1992, The Holy Spirit in the Wesleyan Heritage, Korean transl., 1992, Scriptural Holiness of the United Methodist Christian, 1988, Talking with God: A Guide of Prayer, 1989, Theology for Preaching, 1994, Questions and Answers about Life and Faith, 2000, Person-to-Parson, 2007. Trustee Emory U., Millsaps Coll., Rust Coll., Wood Jr. Coll. Methodist. Home: PO Box 497 Waynesville NC 28786 *Faith in God and basic trust in people. Knowing the direction in which to go, and moving with divine assistance toward it with persistence, resourcefulness, imagination and patience.*

STOKES, PATRICK T., brewery company executive; b. Washington, Aug. 11, 1942; m. Anna-Kristina Stokes. BS, Boston Coll., 1964; MBA, Columbia U., 1966. Fin. analyst Shell Oil Co., 1966-67; v.p. materials acquisitions Anheuser-Busch Cos., Inc., St. Louis, 1979-81, v.p., group exec., 1981—86; COO Campbell Taggart Inc. (subs. Anheuser-Busch Cos. Inc.), Dallas, 1986-90, CEO, 1990—2002; sr. exec. v.p. Anheuser-Busch Cos., Inc., St. Louis, 2000—02, pres., CEO, 2002—06, chmn., 2006—, Anheuser-Busch Internat., Inc, 1999—. Bd. dirs. Anheuser-Busch Cos. Inc., 2000—. Served to 1st lt. U.S. Army, 1967-69. Recipient Award of Excellence in Commerce, Boston Coll. Alumni Assn., 1991. Office: Anheuser-Busch Companies Inc 1 Busch Place Saint Louis MO 63118-1852 *

STOKES, PAUL MASON, lawyer; b. Miami Beach, Fla., July 16, 1946; s. Walter Johnson and Juanita (Hemperley) S.; m. Carol Crocker, Sept. 12, 1970; children: Macon Lanford, Walter Ashley, Mary Juanita. BA, Duke U., 1968; JD, U. Chgo., 1971. Bar: Fla. 1971. Law clerk to hon. Milton Pollack U.S. Dist. Ct. (so. dist.) N.Y., NYC, 1971—72; assoc. Smathers and Thompson, Miami, Fla., 1972—77, ptnr., 1977—88, Kelley Drye & Warren L.L.P., Miami, 1988—99, Stokes McMillan Maracini & Autunez P.A., Miami, 1999—. Adj. prof. law U. Miami, Coral Gables, Fla., 1987-94, 2005-; pub. defender City of Miami Springs, Fla., 1974, City of Hialeah, Fla., 1974-75. Mem. Code Enforcement Bd. Miami Springs, 1990-92; regent Trinity Internat. U., Deerfield, Ill., 1989-98; mem. Permanent Jud. Commn., Presbytery of Tropical Fla., 1997-00; bd. dirs. Greater Miami Youth for Christ; com. on ministry, Presbytery of Tropical Fla., 2007-. Fellow Am. Coll. Trust and Estate Coun.; mem. Dade County Bar Assn. (probate and guardianship ct. com. 1988—, bd. dirs. 1989-92, 94-2000, 2004—05), Fla. Bar (cert. wills, trusts and estates), Am. Radio Relay League, Phi Beta Kappa, Order of Coif. Democrat. Presbyterian. Avocation: amateur radio. Office: Stokes McMillan Marcini & Antunez PA One SE 3d Ave Ste 1750 Miami FL 33131 Home Phone: 305-887-0643; Office Phone: 305-379-4008. Business E-Mail: pstokes@smpalaw.com.

STOKES, RICHARD FRANCIS, lawyer; b. Teaneck, NJ, Jan. 7, 1946; s. Edwin Matthew and Norma S. (Bonn) S.; m. Sally Scott, Mar. 28, 1970; children: Sarah S., Richard Hunter. BA, Colgate U., 1967; JD, Duke U., 1970. Bar: Del. 1970, US Dist. Ct. Del. 1970., Del. Superior Ct. 1999. Law clk. Superior Ct., Wilmington, Del., 1970, ptnr. Tunnell & Raysor, Georgetown, Del., 1978—96, with Del. Ct. Common Pleas, 1996-99; counsel Beebe Hosp., Lewes, Del., 1983—95. Elder Rehoboth Beach Presbyn. Ch., Del., 1983—; chmn. Sussex County Dem. Exec. Com. 1986-88; mem. Abraham Lincoln Bicentennial Commn. Capt. USAF, 1971-75. Mem. Terry Carey Am. Inn Ct. (pres. 2006—), Rotary (sec. 1983). Home: 137 E Side Dr Rehoboth Beach DE 19971-1311 Home Phone: 302-226-7861; Office Phone: 302-856-5264. Business E-Mail: richard.stokes@state.de.us.

STOKES, WILLIAM JAMES, musician; b. June 24, 1940; MusB, Eastman Sch. Music, Rochester, NY, 1962; AB in Music, St. Andrews Presbyn. Coll., Laurinburg, NC, 1964; M Sacred Music, Union Theol. Sem., NYC, 1967. Dir. music, organist 2d Presbyn. Ch., Richmond, Va., 1967—84, Cathedral of All Souls, Asheville, NC, 1984—2000; interim dir. music Congl. Ch., New Canaan, Conn., 2002—04, St. Luke's Episcopal Ch., Forest Hills, NY, 2006—. Fellow Washington Nat. Cathedral, Washington, 1976—77. Mem.: Am. Guild Organists (assoc.; past dean Richmond chpt., Choirmaster cert.). Home: 408 W 34th St Apt 1B New York NY 10001 Personal E-mail: williamjnyc@aol.com.

STOKEY, NANCY L., economist, educator; BA in Economics, U. Pa., 1972; PhD in Economics, Harvard U., 1978. Asst. prof. Kellogg Grad. Sch. Mgmt., Northwestern U., 1978—82, assoc. prof., 1982—83, prof., 1983—87, dept. chmn., 1987—89, Harold L. Stuart prof. managerial economics, 1988—90; vis. lectr. Harvard U., 1982; vis. prof. economics U. Minn., 1983, U. Chgo., 1983—84, prof. ecnomics, 1990—96, Frederick Henry Prince prof. economics, 1997—. Vis. scholar rsch. dept. Fed. Reserve Bank, Mpls., 2000—01. Author (with Robert E. Lucas, Jr. and Edward C. Prescott): Recursive Methods in Economic Dynamics, 1989. Fellow: Am. Econ. Assn. (v.p. 1996—97, nominating com. 1998, exec. com. 2000—02), Am. Acad. Arts and Scis., Econometric Soc. (coun. mem. 1996—98, 1999—2001); mem.: NAS. Home Phone: 773-477-9640; Office Phone: 773-702-0915. Office Fax: 773-702-8490. Business E-Mail: n-stikey@uchicago.edu.

STOKKE, DIANE REES, lawyer; b. Kansas City, Mo., Jan. 29, 1951; d. William James and Marybeth (Smith) Rees; m. Larry Ernst Stokke, June 9, 1973; children: Michelle, Megan, Carly. AB magna cum laude, Gonzaga U., 1972; JD with high honors, U. Wash., 1976. Bar: Wash. 1976, U.S. Dist. Ct. (ea. dist.) Wash. 1976, U.S. Dist. Ct. (we. dist.) Wash. 1976, U.S. Ct. Appeals (9th cir.) 1980. Assoc. Preston, Thorgrimson, Ellis & Holman, Seattle, 1976-83; ptnr. Kirkpatrick & Lockhart Preston Gates Ellis LLP (formerly known as Preston, Gates & Ellis LLP), Seattle, 1983—. Atty. Seattle Ctr. Found., 1977-83. Trustee Seattle Infant Devel. Ctr., 1984—86, Fremont Pub. Assn., 1994—2001, 2003—05. Gonzaga U. scholar, 1968. Mem. ABA, Wash. State Bar Assn. (spl. dist. counsel 1985-88), Seattle-King County Bar Assn., Wash. Women Lawyers, Order of Coif, Wash. Women Real Estate Lawyers, Am. Coll. of Mortgage Attys., Comml. Real Estate Women. Roman Catholic. Office: Kirkpatrick Lockhart Preston Gates Ellis LLP 925 Fourth Ave Ste 2900 Seattle WA 98104-1158 Office Phone: 206-623-7580. Business E-Mail: diane.stokke@klgates.com.

STOKLOSA, GREGORY A., publishing executive; BS, U. Mich.; MA in Mgmt., Northwestern U. Various fin. positions Kraft Gen. Foods, Inc.; from asst. treas. global corp. fin. to exec. v.p., CFO RR Donnelley & Sons, Chgo., 1993—2000, exec. v.p., 2000—05, CFO, 2000—05; v.p., CFO Hollinger Internat. Inc., Chgo., 2005—. Office: Hollinger International Inc 350 N Orleans St Chicago IL 60654 Office Phone: 312-321-2299. Office Fax: 312-321-0629.

STOKOE, KENNETH H., II, civil engineer, educator; BSCE, U. Mich., 1966, MSCE, 1967, PhD, 1972. Instr. Univ. Mich., 1971; asst. prof. Univ. Mass., 1972—73, Univ. Tex., Austin, 1973—78, assoc. prof., 1978—83, prof. civil engring., 1983—85, Brunswick Abernathy Regents prof., 1985—97, Cockrell Family Regents Chair, 1997—99, Jennie C. and Milton T. Graves chair in engring., 2000—. Contbr. articles to prof. jours. Mem.: Nat. Acad. Engring., Am. Soc. Civil Engineers, Am. Soc. Nondestructive Testing, Am. Soc. Testing & Materials, Earthquake Engring. Rsch. Inst., Internat. Soc. Soil Mech. & Geotechnical Engring., Seismological Soc. Am., Soc. Exploration Geophysicists, Transp. Rsch. Bd., Soc. Profl. Engineers. Office: U Tex at Austin Dept Archl and Environ Engring 1 Univeristy Sta C1792 Austin TX 78712-0280

STOLARIK, M. MARK, history professor; b. St. Martin, Slovak Republic, Apr. 22, 1943; s. Imrich and Margita (Vavro) S.; m. Anne Helene Ivanco, June 15, 1968; children: Roman Andrej, Matthew Mark. BA, U. Ottawa, 1965, MA, 1967; PhD, U. Minn., 1974. Ast. prof. history Cleve. State U., 1972-76; hist. rschr. Nat. Mus. of Man, Ottawa, Ont., Canada, 1977-78; pres. Balch Inst. for Ethnic Studies, Phila., 1979-91; prof. history, chair dept. Slovak history and culture U. Ottawa, 1992—. Cons. Harvard Ency. Ethnic Groups, Cambridge, Mass., 1976-80; advisor State Hist. Records Bd., Harrisburg, Pa., 1982-91; cons. Ency. Canada's Peoples, 1991—99. Author: film documentary Vianoce-Slovak Christmas, 1978 (2d prize 1979), Slovaks in Bethlehem, Pa., 1985, The Slovak Experience, 1870-1918, 1989. Mem. Pa. adv. com. to U.S. Commn. on Civil Rights, 1985-91. Lehigh U. fellow, 1976. Mem. 1st Cath. Slovak Union, Nat. Slovak Soc., Can. Slovak League (pres. 1994-99). Roman Catholic. Home Phone: 613-825-6015; Office Phone: 613-562-5800 x1286. Business E-Mail: stolarik@uottawa.ca.

STOLBERG, MARY MARGARET, historian; b. Denver, Colo., Sept. 8, 1956; d. David Fox and Anne Stewart (Brand) S.; m. Lynn Doyle, Jan. 18, 1986 (div. 2000). BA, U. Chgo., 1977; MA, U. Va., 1986, PhD, 1991. Reporter S.W. Times Record, Fort Smith, Ark., 1977-78, The Pitts. Press, 1978-84; lectr., asst. prof. Appalachian State U., Boone, N.C., 1990-93; ind. scholar Boone, N.C., 1993—. Author: Fighting Organized Crime, 1995, (Little Brown award 1995), Bridging the River of Hatred, 1998, Looking Beyond Race, 2000; also articles in Sat. Eve. Post, Jour. of Policy History. Democrat. Episcopalian. Home: PO Box 90 Vilas NC 28692-0090 Agent: David Hendin Lit Enterprises PO Box 990 Nyack NY 10960-0990

STOLBERG, SHERYL GAY, journalist; b. NYC, Nov. 18, 1961; d. Irving and Marcia Dawn (Papier) S. BA, U. Va., 1983. Reporter Providence Jour. Bulletin, 1983-87, L.A. Times, 1987-97; sci. & med. corr. NY Times, Washington, 1997—2002, congl. corr., 2002—06, White House corr., 2006—. Recipient Unity award Lincoln U., 1987. Office: NY Times Wash Bur 7th Fl 1627 I St NW Washington DC 20006-4007

STOLL, ANDREW LAWRENCE, psychopharmacologist; b. Newark, May 14, 1959; BA, Boston U., 1981; MD, N.J. Med. Sch. Resident in psychiatry McLean Hosp., Belmont, Mass., 1987-91, dir., psychopharmacology rsch. lab.; neurosci. fellow Harvard Med. Sch., Boston, 1991-93, Ethel Dupont-Warren fellow, 1991-92, asst. prof. psychiatry, 1994—; former dir. psychopharmacology Brigham and Women's Hosp., Boston. Spkr. in field. Author: The Omega-3 Connection: The Groundbreaking Anti-depression Diet and Brain Program, 2001; contbr. articles to peer-reviewed publications. Recipient Tchr. Yr. award, Harvard Longwood Psychiatry Residency Tng. Program, Klerman award, National Alliance for Research on Schizophrenia and Depression, 1999. Achievements include being the first to report the use of omega-3 fatty acids as an effective mood stabilizer and anti-depressant in a controlled study of bipolar patients. Home: 171 Grant St Lexington MA 02420-2119 Office: McLean Hosp Psychopharmacology Rsch Lab 115 Mill St Belmont MA 02478 Office Phone: 617-855-2459. Office Fax: 617-855-3619. Business E-Mail: alstoll@mclean.harvard.edu. *

STOLL, HOWARD LESTER, JR., dermatologist; b. Buffalo, June 13, 1928; s. Howard L. and Margaret (Kahler) S.; m. Jacklyn Fay Straight, June, 1948; children— Shelley, Margaret, Amy, Howard III AB, Harvard U., 1948; MD, U. Pa., 1952. Diplomate Am. Bd. Dermatology. Intern E.J. Meyer Hosp., Buffalo, 1952, resident in dermatology, 1953-55; sr. cancer research surgeon Roswell Park Meml. Inst., Buffalo, 1958-59, assoc. cancer research dermatologist, 1959-67, chief, sect. dermatology, 1984-92; mem. courtesy staff Mercy Hosp., Buffalo, 1958-70; asst. in dermatology E.J. Meyer Meml. Hosp., Buffalo, 1962-72. Clin. assoc. prof. dermatology Sch. Medicine, SUNY-Buffalo, 1976-91, clin. prof., 1991—. Served to capt. U.S. Army, 1955-57 Mem. Am. Acad. Dermatology, Soc. Investigative Dermatology, Buffalo-Rochester Dermatologic Soc. Office: Roswell Park Meml Inst Elm & Carlto Sts 666 Elm St Buffalo NY 14263-0002 Home Phone: 716-649-1761; Office Phone: 716-845-3378.

STOLL, JOHN ROBERT, lawyer, educator; b. Phila., Nov. 29, 1950; s. Wilhelm Friedrich and Marilyn Jane (Kremser) S.; m. Christine Larson, June 24, 1972; children: Andrew Michael, Michael Robert, Meredith Kirstin, Alison Courtney. BA magna cum laude, Haverford Coll., 1972; JD, Columbia U., 1975. Bar: Ind. 1975, U.S. Dist. Ct. (no. and so. dists.) Ind. 1975, U.S. Ct. Appeals (7th cir.) 1978, U.S. Dist. Ct. (no. dist.) Ill. 1980, (so. dist.) N.Y. 1993, Ill. 1981, N.Y. 1989. Atty. Barnes & Thornburg, South Bend, Ind., 1975-80, Mayer, Brown & Platt, Chgo. and N.Y.C., 1980—. Adj. prof. law Northwestern U., Chgo., 1985—94, DePaul U., Chgo., 1987; lectr. in bus. St. Mary's Coll., Notre Dame, Ind., 1977-78. Contbr. articles to profl. jours. Fellow Am. Coll. Bankruptcy; mem. ABA, Ind. State Bar Assn., Am. Bankruptcy Inst., Phi Beta Kappa. Office: Mayer Brown & Platt 71 S Wacker Dr Chicago IL 60606-4637

STOLL, NEAL RICHARD, lawyer; b. Phila., Nov. 7, 1948; s. Mervin Stoll and Goldie Louise (Serody) Stoll Wilf; m. Linda G. Seligman, May 25, 1972; children: Meredith Anne, Alexis Blythe. BA in History with distinction, Pa. State U., 1970; JD, Fordham U., 1973. Bar: N.Y. 1974, U.S. Dist. Ct. (ea. dist.) N.Y. 1974, U.S. Ct. Appeals (2d cir.) 1974, U.S. Ct. Appeals (11th cir.) 1982, U.S. Dist. Ct. (ea. dist.) Mich. 1983, U.S. Dist. Ct. (so. dist.) N.Y. 1974, U.S. Supreme Ct. 1986. Assoc. Skadden, Arps, Slate, Meagher & Flom, LLP, NYC, 1973-81, mem., 1981—. Lectr. Practicing Law-Inst., N.Y.C. Author: (with others) Aquisitions Under the Hart Scott Rodino Antitrust Improvements Act, 1980; contbr. articles to profl. pubs. Mem. Assn. Bar City of N.Y. (mem. trade regulation com. 1983-85), ABA, N.Y. State Bar Assn. Democrat. Office: Skadden Arps Slate Four Times Sq New York NY 10036-6522 Office Phone: 212-735-3660. Business E-Mail: nstoll@skadden.com.

STOLL, RICHARD GILES, lawyer; b. Phila., Oct. 2, 1946; s. Richard Giles and Mary Margaret (Zeigler) S.; m. Susan Jane Nicewonger, June 15, 1968; children: Richard Giles III, Christian Hayes. BA magna cum laude, Westminster Coll., 1968; JD, Georgetown U., 1971. Bar: DC 1971, US Dist. Ct. DC 1971, US Ct. Appeals DC 1971, US Ct. Appeals (4th cir.) 1977. Assoc. Arent, Fox, Kintner, Plotkin & Kahn, Washington, 1971-73; atty. Office of Gen. Counsel EPA, Washington, 1973-77, asst. gen. counsel, 1977-81; dep. gen. counsel Chem. Mfrs. Assn., Washington, 1981-84; ptnr. Freedman, Levy, Kroll & Simonds, Washington, 1984-2001, Foley & Lardner, Washington, 2001—. Instr. environ. law and policy U. Va., Charlottesville, 1981-90. Co-author: Handbook on Environmental Law, 1987, 88, 89, 91, Practical Guide to Environment Law, 1987; contbr. articles to profl. jours.; moderator, panelist legal ednl. TV broadcasts and tapes ABA and Am. Law Inst. Elder Georgetown Presbyn. Ch.; bd. dirs., mem. exec. com. Georgetown Ministry Ctr., 2004-06, pres. 2006—; bd. dirs. Westminster Ingleside Found., Washington, 2004—. Capt., USAR, 1968-76. Recipient Alumni Achievement award Westminster Coll., 1998. Mem. ABA (sect. environment, energy and resources, chmn. water quality com. 1980-82, hazardous waste com. 1983-85, coun. mem. 1985-88, sect. chmn. 1990-91, sect. adminstrv. law co-chmn. rulemaking com. 2004-06, chmn. sponsorship com. 2004-07, mem. coun. 2005—), Washington Golf and Country Club, Cosmos Club. Avocations: piano, golf, music composition. Office: Foley & Lardner 3000 K St NW Washington DC 20007 Business E-Mail: rstoll@foley.com.

STOLL, WILHELM, mathematics professor; b. Freiburg, Germany, Dec. 22, 1923; arrived in U.S., 1960; s. Heinrich and Doris (Eberle) S.; m. Marilyn Jane Kremser, June 11, 1955; children: Robert, Dieter, Elisabeth, Rebecca. PhD in Math, U. Tübingen, Fed. Republic Germany, 1953, habilitation, 1954. Asst. U. Tübingen, 1953-59, dozent, 1954-60, ausserplanmässiger prof., 1960; vis. lectr. U. Pa., 1954-55; temp. mem. Inst. Advanced Study, Princeton, 1957-59; prof. math. U. Notre Dame, 1960-88, Vincent J. Duncan and Annamarie Micus Duncan prof. math., 1988-94, prof. emeritus, 1994—, chmn. dept., 1966-68, co-dir. Ctr. for Applied Math., 1992. Vis. prof. Stanford U., 1968-69, Tulane U., 1973, U. Sci. and Tech., Hefei, Anhui, People's Republic of China, summer, 1986; adviser Clark Sch., South Bend, Ind., 1963-68; Japan Soc. Promotion Sci. fellow, vis. prof. Kyoto U., summer 1983. Publs. in field. Fellow: AAAS. Achievements include research in complex analysis several variables. Home: 2601 Covington Commons Dr #44-46 Fort Wayne IN 46804-7333

STOLL, WILLIAM FREDERICK, JR., lawyer; b. Youngstown, Ohio, June 28, 1948; s. William Frederick and Elizabeth Jayne (Walsh) Stoll; m. Patricia Ann Musial, 1969 (div.); children: Eric Walsh, Todd William. BS in Fgn. Service, Georgetown U., 1969; JD, Case Western Res. U., 1973. Bar: Ohio 1973, U.S. Dist. Ct. (no. dist.) Ohio 1974. Assoc. Roth & Stephens, Youngstown, Ohio, 1973—75; atty. Westinghouse Electric Corp., Pitts., 1975—77, counsel, 1977—78, chief counsel, 1978—82, asst. gen. counsel, 1982—84, assoc. gen. counsel, 1982—93, v.p., dep. gen. counsel, 1993—96; chief legal officer, exec. v.p. Borden, Inc., 1996—2003, Lennox Internat., 2004—. Mem. bd. dirs. AEP Industries, Inc. Mem. bd. of governors Georgetown U. Alumni Assn. Mem.: ABA. Office: Lennox Internat 2140 Lake Park Blvd Richardson TX 75080 Office Phone: 972-497-5000. *

STOLLAR, BERNARD DAVID, biochemist, educator; b. Saskatoon, Sask., Aug. 11, 1936; came to US, 1960. s. Percy and Rose (Direnfeld) S.; m. Carol A. Singer, Oct. 7, 1956; children: Lawrence, Michael, Suzanne. BA, U. Sask., Saskatoon, 1958, MD, 1959. Intern U. Sask. Hosp., 1959-60; postdoctoral fellow Brandeis U., Waltham, Mass., 1960-62; asst. prof. dept. pharmacology Tufts U. Schs. Medicine and Dental Medicine, Boston, 1964-67, asst. prof. dept. biochemistry, 1967-68, assoc. prof. biochemistry/pharmacology, 1968-74, prof., 1974—2005, prof. emeritus, 2005—, acting chmn. dept. biochemistry and pharmacology, 1984-86, chmn. dept. biochemistry, 1986-2001; interim dean Sackler Sch. Grad. Biomed Sci., Tufts U., 2002—04. Vis. prof. internat. course in immunology and immunochemistry Mexico City, 1971; sr. fellow Weizmann Inst. Sci., Rehovot, Israel, 1971-72; vis. prof. chemistry Wellesley Coll., Mass., 1976, U. Tromsö, Norway, 1981; Dozor vis. prof. Ben-Gurion U. Sch. Medicine, Beer Sheva, Israel, 1986; cons. USAF Office Sci. Rsch., 1966-69, Seragen, Inc., 1983-88, Cetus, 1982-85, Gene-Trak, 1986-89, Alkermes, Inc., 1989-94, Catalytic Antibodies, Inc., 1993-98; 3d ann. alumni lectr. U. Sask. Coll. Medicine, 1989; mem. allergy/transplantation rsch. com. NIH/NIAID, 1990-94; mem. sci. vis. com. Okla. Med. Rsch. Found., 1996-98; mem. panel Israel Cancer Rsch. Found., 1996-2000. Contbr. over 200 articles to profl. jours., chpts. to books; exec. editl. bd. Analytical Biochemistry, 1988—; editl. bd. Jour. Immunology, 1981-85, Molecular Immunology, 1980-95, Arthritis and Rheumatism, 1986-89, Jour. Immunological Methods, 1988—. Mem. adult edn. com. Temple Reyim, Newton, Mass., v.p., 2001-04, 1st v.p. 2004-05, pres. 2005-07. Capt. USAF, 1962—64. Recipient (with Carol Stollar) 2d Century award Jewish Theol. Sem. and Temple Reyim, 1997; rsch. grantee NSF, NIH, 1964-2005; sr. fellow Weizmann Inst. Sci., 1971-72. Mem. Am. Assn. Immunologists. Office: Tufts Univ Sch Medicine Dept Biochemistry 136 Harrison Ave Boston MA 02111-1800 Home Phone: 617-965-0226; Office Phone: 617-636-2948. Business E-Mail: david.stollar@tufts.edu.

STOLLE, RUSSELL ROBERT, chemicals executive; b. Houston; BA, Valparaiso U., Ind., 1984; JD with honors, U. Tex., 1987. Bar: Tex. 1987, US Patent and Trademark Office 1988. Intern Tex. Supreme Ct., Austin, Tex., 1987; assoc. Baker & Botts, Houston, 1987-89; patent atty. Texaco Inc., Austin, 1990-94; chief patent and licensing counsel Huntsman Corp., Austin, 1994—2000, v.p., chief tech. counsel, 2000—02, v.p., dep. gen. counsel, 2002—06, sr. v.p. global pub. affairs and comm., 2006—. Mem. Am. Intellectual Property Law Assn., Licensing Execs. Soc., Austin Intellectual Property Law Assn. Office: Huntsman Corp 10003 Woodloch Forest Dr The Woodlands TX 77380 Office Phone: 281-719-6000. *

STOLLER, CLAUDE, architect; b. NYC, Dec. 2, 1921; s. Max and Esther (Zisblatt) S.; m. Anna Maria Oldenburg, June 5, 1946 (div. Oct. 1972); children: Jacob, Dorothea, Elizabeth; m. Rosemary Raymond Lax, Sept. 22, 1978. Student, Black Mountain Coll., NC, 1942; M.Arch., Harvard U., 1949. Architect Architects Collaborative, Cambridge, Mass., after 1949, Shepley, Bulfinch, Richardson & Abbot, Boston, 1951; co-founder, partner firm Marquis & Stoller, San Francisco, 1956; pvt. practice architecture NYC and San Francisco, 1974-78; founder, partner Stoller/Partners, Berkeley, Calif., 1978, Stoller, Knoerr Archs., 1988-95. Mem. faculty Washington U., St. Louis, 1955-56; mem. faculty U. Calif., Berkeley, 1957-91, prof. architecture, 1968-92, acting chmn. dept., 1965-66, chair grad. studies, 1984-91, prof. emeritus, 1991—; mem. Berkeley Campus Design Rev. Bd., 1985-91, chmn., 1992-93; commr. Calif. Bd. Archtl. Examiners, 1980-90, mem. exam. com., 1985-88; mem. diocesan commn. arch. Episcopal Diocese Calif., 1961-98; vis. arch. Nat. Design Inst., Ahmedabad, India, 1963; planning commr. City of Mill Valley, 1961-66, Marin County Planning Commn., 1966-67; mem. pub. adv. panel archtl. svcs. GSA, 1969-71; citizens urban design adv. com. City of Oakland, Calif., 1968; vis. com. nat. archtl. accrediting bd. U. Minn. and U. Wis., Milw., 1971; coun. Harvard Grad. Sch. Design Assn., 1976-77; mem. design rev. com. The Sea Ranch, Calif., 1990-2002. Prin. works include St. Francis Sq. Coop. Apts., San Francisco, 1961, Pub. Housing for Elderly, San Francisco, 1974, Learning Resources Bldg, U. Calif., Santa Barbara, 1975, Menorah Park Housing for Elderly, San Francisco, 1979, San Jose State U. Student Housing Project, 1984, Delta Airlines Terminal, San Francisco Internat. Airport, 1988. Served with AUS, 1943-46. Recipient numerous awards including AIA Honor awards, 1963, 64, AIA Bay Region Honor award, 1974, Concrete Reinforced Steel Inst. award, 1976, AIA award, 1976, CADA Site I Solar Housing award Sacramento, Calif., 1980, State of Calif. Affordable Housing award, 1981, PG&E Suntherm award, 1981, San Francisco Housing Authority award, 1983, Orchid award City of Oakland, 1989, Citation for achievement and svc. U. Calif., Berkeley, 1991, Design award Berkeley Design Advocates. Fellow AIA. Home: 2816 Derby St Berkeley CA 94705-1325 Business E-Mail: stoller@berkeley.edu.

STOLLER, JOHN R., lawyer; b. NYC, Oct. 16, 1948; BA, Valparaiso U., 1970, JD, 1973. Bar: Minn. 1973, Colo. 1978, Mich. 1993. Editor-in-chief Calparaiso U. Law Rev., 1972—73; law clk. to Justice Walter F. Rogscheske Minn., 1973—74; assoc. HArstad & Rainbow, 1974—78; spl. asst. atty. gen. Minn. Dept. Transp., 1974—78; atty. The Mountain States Telephone and Telegraph Co., 1978—83; v.p., gen. counsel, sec. Beta West Properties, Inc., 1984—90; gen. counsel, sec. Pulte Homes, Inc., Bloomfield Hills, Mich., 1990—2005, sr. v.p., 1999—2005. Mem.: ABA, Am. Soc. Corp. Secs., Am. Corp. Counsel Assn., State Bar Mich., Denver Bar Assn., Colo. Bar Assn., Minn. Bar Assn. *

STOLLERMAN, GENE HOWARD, internist, educator; b. NYC, Dec. 6, 1920; s. Maurice William and Sarah Dorothy (Mezz) S.; m. Corynne Miller, Jan. 21, 1945 (dec. Mar. 1997); children: Lee Denise Stollerman Meyburg, Anne Barbara Stollerman DiZio, John Eliot; m. Vita Mark, Nov. 9, 1997. AB summa cum laude, Dartmouth Coll., 1941; MD, Columbia U., 1944. Diplomate Am. Bd. Internal Medicine. Clin. tng. Mt. Sinai Hosp., NYC, 1944-46, chief med. resident, 1948; Dazian research fellow microbiology NYU Med. Sch., 1949-50, mem. dept. medicine, 1951-55; med. dir. Irvington House for Cardiac Children, 1951-55; prin. investigator Sackett Found. Research in Rheumatic Diseases, 1955-64; asst. prof. medicine Northwestern U., 1955-57, assoc. prof., 1957-61, prof. medicine, 1961-65; prof., chmn. dept. medicine U. Tenn., 1965-81, Goodman prof., 1977-81; physician-in-chief City of Memphis Hosps., 1965-81; prof. medicine Boston U. Sch. Medicine, 1981-95, prof. pub. health, 1991-95, prof. medicine and pub. health emeritus, 1996—. Chief sect. gen. internal medicine Univ. Hosp., Boston U. Med. Ctr., 1983-86; Disting. physician VA Med. Ctr., Bedford, Mass., 1986-89; assoc. chief of staff Geriatrics and Extended Care, 1989-92; clin. dir. Bedford div. Geriatric Rsch., Ednl. and Clin. Ctr., 1989-92; dir. VA Health Svcs. Rsch. Field, 1990-93; chmn. research career program com. NIAMD-NIH, 1967-70; mem. commn. streptococcal and staphylococcal diseases U.S. Armed Forces Epidemiol. Bd., 1956-74; adv. bd. immunization practices Center for Disease Control, 1968-71; expert adv. panel cardiovascular disease WHO, 1966—; mem. Am. Bd. Internal Medicine, 1967-73, chmn. cert. exam. com., 1969-73, mem. exec. com., 1971-73; chmn. Panel on Bacterial Vaccines, FDA, 1973-80; mem. nat. adv. council Nat. Inst. Allergy and Infectious Diseases, NIH, 1978-82; mem. Dept. Health & Human Services nat. vaccine adv. com. Editor-in-chief Advances in Internal Medicine, 1968-93, Jour. Am. Geriatric Soc., 1984-88; co-editor Hosp. Practice, 1990—, editor, 1998—; contbr. chpts. to Braunwald's Textbook of Cardiology, Harrison's Textbook of Medicine, Cecil & Loeb Textbook of Medicine, others; contbr. articles to profl. jours. Served as capt. M.C., AUS, 1946-48. Recipient Bicentennial award in internal medicine Columbia U., 1967, Disting. Alumnus award Mt. Sinai Hosp., 1989, Thewlis award Am. Geriatric Soc., 1990, Mentor award Infectious Disease Soc. Am., 2004. Master ACP (bd. regents 1978, v.p. 1984, Bruce medal for preventive medicine 1985), Am. Coll. Rheumatology; mem. Am. Heart Assn. (mem. exec. com., pres. coun. on rheumatic fever and congenital disease 1965-67), Am. Fedn. Clin. Rsch., Am. Rheumatism Assn., Am. Soc. Clin. Investigation, Cen. Soc. Clin. Rsch. (v.p. 1973-74, pres. 1974-75), Assn. Profs. Medicine (pres. 1975-76), Am. Assn. Immunologists, Assn. Am. Physicians, Infectious Disease Soc. Am. (coun. 1968-70), Phi Beta Kappa, Alpha Omega Alpha. Personal E-mail: gstollerman@valley.net.

STOLLEY, ALEXANDER, advertising executive; b. Coethen Anhalt, Germany, May 12, 1922; arrived in US, 1923, naturalized, 1929; s. Mihail and Tatiana (Rainich) Stolarevsky; m. Patricia Martin, June 26, 1944 (dec. Aug. 1970); children: Christopher, Peter, Laura Stolley Smith, Annabel Stolley Hetzer, Megan Stolley Berry; m. Bette Scott Vogt, June 15, 1973. ME, U. Cin., 1948. With Cin. Milacron, Inc., 1941-50, dir. employee relations, 1948-50; with Northlich, Stolley, Inc., Cin., 1950-89, exec. v.p., 1959-67, pres., 1967-84; chmn. Northlich, Stolley, LaWarre, Inc. (formerly Northlich, Stolley, Inc.), Cin., 1984-89. Mem. exec. com. Cincinnatus Assn., 1968-73, sec., 1970-71, v.p., 1971-72, pres., 1972-73; mem. Cin. Council on World Affairs, 1969—; chmn. Contemporary Arts Center, Cin., 1966-67; mem. exec. com. Cin. Conv. and Visitors Bur., 1975, chmn. long range planning com., 1983; trustee Cin. Symphony Orch., 1969-75. Served to 1st lt. AUS, 1943-46. Mem. Bus., Profl. Advt. Assn., Greater Cin. C. of C. (exec. com. 1982-83) Clubs: Cin. Country, Literary, Gasparilla Beach, Lemon Bay Golf, Boca Bay Pass. Home: 7333 Scotland Way Apt 2312 Sarasota FL 33921 Home Phone: 941-923-1428. Personal E-mail: astolley@sover.net.

STOLLEY, PAUL DAVID, medical educator, researcher; b. Pawling, NY, June 17, 1937; s. Herman and Rosalie (Chertock) Stolley; m. Jo Ann Goldenberg, June 13, 1959; children: Jonathan, Dorie, Anna. BA, Lafayette Coll., 1957; MD, Cornell U., 1962; MPH, Johns Hopkins U., 1968; MA (hon.), U. Pa., 1976. Diplomate Am. Coll. Preventive Medicine, Am. Coll. Epidemiology. Intern U. Wis. Med. Ctr., 1962—63, resident in medicine, 1963—64; med. officer USPHS, Washington, 1964—67; asst. prof. Johns Hopkins Sch. Pub. Health, Balt., 1968—71, assoc. prof., 1971—76; Herbert C. Rorer prof. medicine U. Pa. Sch. Medicine, Phila., 1976—91; prof. dept. epidemiology U. Md. Sch. Medicine, Balt., 1991—2002; staff epidemiologist Public Citizen Health Rsch. Group, 2002—04. Co-author: Foundations of Epidemiology, 3d edit., 1995, Epidemiology: Investigating Disease, 1995 (Am. Med. Writers Assn. award, 1996); contbg. author: Case-Control Studies, 1982, mem. editl. bd.: New Eng. Jour. Medicine, 1989—93, Millbank Quar., Health and Soc., 1986—, assoc. editor: Clin. Pharmacology and Therapeutics, 1987—93; contbr. articles to med. jours. Charter mem. Physicians for Social Responsibility, 1961—. Lt. comdr. USPHS, 1964—67. Fellow: ACP; mem.: Johns Hopkins Soc. Scholars, Internat. Epidemiol. Assn. (treas. 1982—84), Am. Epidemiol. Soc. (pres. 1994—), Soc. Epidemiol. Rsch. (pres. 1982—84), Inst. Medicine of NAS, Am. Coll. Epidemiology (pres. 1987—89). Office Phone: 410-706-3610. Personal E-mail: pstolley@aol.com.

STOLLEY, RICHARD BROCKWAY, journalist; b. Peoria, Ill., Oct. 3, 1928; s. George Brockway and Stella (Sherman) S.; m. Anne Elizabeth Shawber, Oct. 2, 1954 (div. 1981); children: Lisa Anne, Susan Hope, Melinda Ruth, Martha Brockway; m. Lise Jane Hilboldt, 1997. BS in Journalism, Northwestern U., 1952, MS, 1953; LLD, Villa Maria Coll., 1976, Hartwick Coll., 2005. Sports editor Pekin (Ill.) Daily Times, 1944-46; reporter Chgo. Sun-Times, 1953; mem. staff weekly Life mag., 1953-73, bur. chief Los Angeles, 1961-64, Washington, 1964-68, sr. editor Europe, 1968-70, asst. mng. editor NYC, 1971-73; mng. editor monthly Life mag., NYC, 1982-86; founding mng. editor People mag., NYC, 1974-82, Picture Week mag., NYC, 1985-86; dir. spl. projects Time Inc., NYC, 1987-89; editl. dir. Time Inc. Time Warner Inc., NYC, 1989-93, sr. editl. adviser, 1993—. Author: Sinatra: An Intimate Portrait of a Very Good Year, 2002; introd. to Leigh A. Wiener, Marilyn: A Hollywood Farewell: The Death and Funeral of Marilyn Monroe, 1990, Forward To Life: The Platinum Anniversary Collection, 2006; editor People Celebrates People: The Best of 20 Unforgettable Years, 1994, rev. edit., 1996, Life: Our Century in Pictures, 1999, Life: Century of Change, America in Pictures, 1900-2000, 2000, LIFE: World War 2, 2001; exec. prodr. (TV) Extra, 1995-96; editl. cons. Our American Century series Time-Life Books, 1998-99. Bd. govs. Nat. Parkinson Found., Miami, Fla., Lensic Performing Arts Ctr., Santa Fe, N.Mex., 2005—. With USN, 1946-48. Recipient Alumni merit award Northwestern U., 1977, Alumni medal Northwestern U., 1994, Henry Johnson Fisher award for lifetime achievement in mag. pub., 1997, Mag. Profl. of Yr. award Assn. for Edn. in Journalism and Mass Comm., 2002; inducted into Am. Soc. Magazine Editors' Hall of Fame, 1996, Hall of Achievement Medill Sch. Journalism Northwestern U., 1997. Mem. Am. Soc. Mag. Editors (pres. 1982-84), Nat. Press Club, Overseas Press Club (pres. 2004-06), Century Assn., Sigma Delta Chi. Home: 1243 Canyon Rd Santa Fe NM 87501

STOLOV, WALTER CHARLES, medicine physiatrist, educator; b. NYC, Jan. 6, 1928; s. Arthur and Rose F. (Gordon) S.; m. Anita Carvel Noodelman, Aug. 9, 1953; children: Nancy, Amy, Lynne. BS in Physics, CCNY, 1948; MA in Physics, U. Minn., 1951, MD, 1956. Diplomate Am. Bd. Phys. Med. and Rehab., Am. Bd. Electrodiagnostic Medicine. Physicist U.S. Naval Gun Factory, Nat. Bur. Stds., Washington, 1948-49; teaching and rsch. asst. U. Minn., Mpls., 1950-54; from instr. to assoc. prof. U. Wash., Seattle, 1960-70, prof., 1970-99, prof. emeritus, 1999—, also chmn., 1987-99, prof. emeritus, 1999—. Editl. bd. Archives Phys. Medicine and Rehab., 1967-78, Muscle and Nerve, 1983-89, 92-95; cons. Social Security Adminstrn., Seattle, 1975—; sec. Am. Bd. Electrodiagnostic Medicine, 1995—. Co-editor: Handbook of Severe Disability, 1981; contbr. articles to profl. jours. Surgeon USPHS, 1956-57. Recipient Townsend Harris medal CCNY, 1990. Fellow: AAAS, Am. Heart Assn.; mem.: Am. Spinal Cord Injry Assn., Am. Assn. Electrodiagnostic Medicine (pres. 1987—88, Lifetime Achievement award 2001), Assn. Acad. Physiatrists, Am. Congress Rehab. Medicine (Essay award 1959), Am. Acad. Phys. Medicine and Rehab. (Disting. Clinician award 1987). Avocations: dance, singing. Office: U Wash Box 356490 1959 NE Pacific St Seattle WA 98195-0001 Office Phone: 206-543-7065.

STOLPER, PINCHAS ARYEH, religious organization executive, rabbi; b. Bklyn., Oct. 22, 1931; s. David Bernard and Nettie (Rosch) S.; m. Elaine Liebman, Nov. 22, 1955; children: Akiva Psachia, Michal Hadassah Cohen, Malka Tova Kaweblum. BA, Bklyn. Coll., 1952; MA, New Sch. for Social Rsch., 1971. Rabbinical ordination Chaim Berlin-Gur Aryeh Rabbinical Acad., 1956; dir. L.I. Zionist Youth Commn., 1956-57; adminstrv. dean, adviser to English-speaking students Ponevez Yeshiva, Bnai Brak, Israel, 1957-59; also prin., instr. English and Talmud Nahalim Bnai Akiva H.S., 1959-77; nat. dir. youth div. Union Orthodox Jewish Congregations Am., Nat. Conf. Synagogue Youth, NYC, 1959-76, founder NCSY, Torah Fund, Ben Zakai Honor Soc., 1959-76; editor Jewish Youth Monthly, 1967—; exec. v.p. Union Orthodox Jewish Congregations Am., 1976-94, sr. exec., 1994—. Adj. prof. Jewish studies Touro Coll., N.Y., 1975—; mem. publs., Israel, campus commns., staff mem. responsible for edn., Talmud Torah, day sch. commns. Union Orthodox Jewish Congregations Am., 1965—; del. White House Conf. on Children and Youth, 1961; cons. N. Am. Jewish Youth Conf., 1967—. Author: Tested Teen Age Activities, 1961, rev. edit., 1964, Day of Delight, 1961, Tefilah, Text and Source Book, 1963, Revelation What Happened on Sinai, 1966, Prayer, The Proven Path, 1967, The Road to Responsible Jewish Adulthood, 1967, Jewish Alternatives in Love, Dating and Marriage, 1985, The Sacred Trust, Love, Dating and Marriage, The Jewish View, 1996, Beyond Belief, Revelation for the Modern Jew, 1996, Living Beyond Time: The Mystery and Meaning of the Jewish Festivals, 2003, Purim in a New Light: Mystery, Grandeur and Depth, 2003, Chanukah in a New Light, 2005, Hidden Lights: Chanukah and the Jewish/Greek Conflict, 2005; contbr. numerous articles, plays, and revs. to Jewish publs.; columnist The Jewish Press, 1994. Nat. dir. Nat. Conf. Synagogue Youth, 1995-98; bd. dirs. Chaim Berlin Torah Schs.-Mesivta Rabbi Chaim Berlin-Rabbinical Acad., 1965—; pres. David Dov Found. Recipient Alumi Amudim award Mesivta Rabbi Chaim Berlin-Gur Aryeh Inst., 1967, award Assn. Orthodox Jewish Tchrs., 1975, citation Rabbinical Coun. Am., 1984, Jabotinsky medal, 1990, Alumnus of Yr. award Flatbush Yeshiva, 1989, Joseph K. Miller Achdut Yisrael award Shaalvim Yeshiva, 1993. Mem. Rabbinical Coun. Am. Jewish. Home: 603 Twin Oaks Dr Lakewood NJ 08701-7147 Office: Union Orthodox Jewish Cong of Am 11 Broadway New York NY 10004-1303 E-mail: PinchasStolper@aol.com.

STOLPIN, WILLIAM ROGER, printmaker; b. Flint, Mich., June 25, 1942; s. William and Dorothy Florence (Mitchell) S.; m. Kathleen Diane Poyner, Aug. 14, 1970; children: Krishna Ann, James Mitchell. BME, Kettering U., 1965; AA, Charles Stewart Mott C.C., Flint, 1978; postgrad., Ea. Mich. U., 1992. Jr. reliability engr. GM Corp., Flint, 1968—76, sr. reliability engr., 1976—80, supr. quality control, 1980—83, mgr. product assurance, 1983—89, asst. staff engr. Warren, Mich., 1990—93; printmaker, print pub. Flint, 1969—80; printmaker, print pub., co-founder DAS Print Co., Holly, Mich., 1980—; art faculty Flint Inst. Arts, Mich., 2006—. Resident artist Robert T. Longway Planetarium, Flint, 1975—. Printmaker: (lithograph) ...And the Santa Maria, 1969 (Smithsonian permanent collection 1973), (serigraph) One Giant Leap For Mankind, 1970 (Smithsonian permanent collection 1973), numerous pub. serigraphs, lithographs, intaglio prints and woodcuts, 1969—. Grant reviewer Greater Flint Arts Coun., 1989-90, 2000-02, v.p., 1973-74, programming and planning, 1988, mktg. and pub. rels., 1999-2007, bd. dirs., 1999-2007; pres. Buckham Fine Arts Project, Flint, 1993-94, bd. dirs., 1993-2000; bd. dirs. Whaley Hist. House, Flint, 1997-2000; adv. com. U. Mich. Flint Art Gallery, 1997-2000, Shiawassee Arts Coun., 1999-2000, Alma Coll., 1999-2001; accessions and collections com. Flint Inst. Arts, 2000—, art sch. com., 2007; grant reviewer Oakland County Office Arts, Culture and Film, 2002—. Recipient 1st in Graphics award Internat. Platform Assn., 1969, Koegler Meml. award Left Bank Gallery, 1991, 1st in Overall Attitude, Mich. Renaissance Festival, 1998, 99, 1st prize all media award Left Bank Gallery, 1998, Purchase prize Saginaw Art Mus., 1994, 98, hon. mention Ann Arbor Art Ctr., 2003, 04, 1st prize Flint (Mich.) Art Fair, 2004, Third prize 2006; Fed. Design and Art in Transp. grantee, 2002. Mem. AAAS, AIAA, Internat. Assn. for Astron. Arts, Am. Soc. for Quality, Nat. Stereoscopic Assn., Soc. Automotive Engrs., Soc. Am. Graphic Artists, Flint Artist's Market, Detroit Artist's Market, Assn. Sci. Fiction and Fantasy Artists, Mich. Assn. Printmakers, Am. Print Alliance, Am. Color Print Soc., Mid Am. Print Coun., Internat. Ctr. for the Print, Wood Engravers Network, Mich. Guild Artists and Artisans. Avocations: directing community theater, participant in michigan renaissance festival, stereoscopic imaging. Studio: DAS Print Co 12201 Gage Rd Holly MI 48442-8339 Personal E-mail: bill@stolpinart.com.

STOLTE, LARRY GENE, marketing executive, retired computer and publishing company executive; b. Cedar Rapids, Iowa, Sept. 17, 1945; s. Ed August and Emma Wilhelmina (Tank) S.; m. Rebecca Jane Tappmeyer, June, 1970; children: Scott Edward, Ryan Gene. BBA with highest distinction, U. Iowa, 1971; MBA, Trinity U., 2000. CPA Ill., Mo., Minn., Mich., Wis., personal fin. specialist, Ill., Mo., Minn., Mich., Wis., cert. profl. cons. to mgmt., Nat. Bur. Profl. Mgmt. Cons. Tax and auditing acct. McGladrey Pullen & Co., Cedar Rapids, 1971—73; v.p., gen. mgr. TLS Co. (subs. CCH Computax Inc.), Cedar Rapids, 1973—92; re-engring. cons. CCH, Inc., Riverwoods, Ill., 1992—94; nat. dir. mktg. McGladrey & Pullen, Cedar Rapids, 1994—97; sr. v.p., mng. dir. Web Site Dynamics & Stolte Enterprises, Cedar Rapids, 1997—2000; ptnr. NY Life Ins. Co. & NY Life Securities, Inc., Cedar Rapids, 2001—03; personal fin. advisor Thrivent Fin., 2004—. Sgt. USMC, 1964-67. Mem. AICPA, Nat. Assn. Computerized Tax Processors (pres.), Am. Mgmt. Assn., Am. Mktg. Assn., Inst. Mgmt. Accts. (cert.), Nat. Bur. Profl. Mgmt. Cons. (cert.), Sales and Mktg. Execs. Internat. (cert. mktg. exec., cert. sales exec.), Inst. Cert. Mgmt. Cons. (cert.). Methodist. Address: 3000-A Towne House Dr NE PO Box 0489 Cedar Rapids IA 52406-0489 Office Phone: 319-393-5885 ext 161. Personal E-mail: larrystolte@hotmail.com.

STOLTZMAN, RICHARD LESLIE, clarinetist; b. Omaha, July 12, 1942; s. Leslie Harvey and Dorothy Marilyn (Spohn) S.; m. Lucy Jean Chapman, June 6, 1976; children: Peter John, Margaret Anne. MusB summa cum laude, Ohio State U., 1964; MusM magna cum laude, Yale U., 1967; postgrad., Columbia U. Tchrs. Coll., 1967-70. Mem. faculty Calif. Inst. Arts, 1970-75, New Eng. Conservatory, 1996. Western regional dir. Young Audiences, Inc., 1972-74, mem. nat. bd. Appeared in concerts throughout U.S., Europe, Japan, Hong Kong, Australia, 1976—; rec. artist, 1974—; debut LaScala, Milan, 1981, Carnegie Hall, N.Y.C., 1982; appeared in world premiere of Einar Englund concerto Helsinki Festival, 1991, Toru Takemitsu concerto (Fantasma/Cantos) Wales BBC, 1991, U.S. premiere of Lukas Foss concerto L.A. Philharm. Orch., 1991, Copland concert, 1993 (Emmy award for best performing arts video 1993), world premiere of Leonard Bernstein sonata for clarinet and orch. Pacific Music Festival, Sapporo, Japan, 1994, world premiere of Steven Hartke concerto PBS, Tenn., 2001, world premiere of William Thomas McKinley concerto 9 Shades of Lament, Boston Civic Orch., 2001, of Einojuhani Rautavaara Concerto, Nat. Symphony, Carnegie Hall, 2002. Recipient Horatio Parker award Yale U., 1966, Avery Fisher prize, 1977, Martha Baird Rockefeller award, 1973, Grammy award, 1983, 95, Avery Fisher artist award, 1986, Disting. Alumnus award Ohio State U., 1990, Sanford medal Yale U., 2005. Home: 6 Lincolnshire Way Winchester MA 01890-3048 Office: 201 W

54th St Apt 4C New York NY 10019-5521 Office Phone: 212-581-5197. E-mail: stohome@comcast.net. *Be mindful of the breath. It gives life to the sound which sends music to the soul.*

STOLZ, ALAN JAY, youth camp executive; b. NYC, May 7, 1931; s. Irving H. and Pearl (Maltz) S.; m. Sandra Stolz (div.); m. Gail C. Stolz; children: Maryann Stolz Levanti, Gary M. AB, Wabash Coll., 1953; LHD (hon.), London Inst., 1973. Cert. lifetime camp dir. Colo. Outdoor Inst., state instr. emergency med. svc. Pres. Camp Cody, Inc., Freedom, NH; ptnr., prin. 72d St Assocs. Real Estate Corp., NYC. Cons., profl. witness U.S. Senate and Ho. Reps., White House, Washington; cons. youth camp health various govtl. agys., Washington; guest spkr. Am. Free Enterprise program, Moscow and St. Petersburg, Russia, 1993; spkr. Internat. Youth Conf., Toronto, Ont., Can., 1994, Orlando, 1995, Washington, 2002; pres. Alanor, Inc., Fla., 1994—; apptd. consumer affairs specialist NH Atty. Gen. Office, Dept. of Justice, Fraud and Anti-Trust Bur. Author: National Camp Directors Guide, 1990; contbr. articles to profl. jours. Founding mem. USAF Mus. in Britain; primary instr. EMS, Westport, Conn., v.p., 1996—, bd. dirs.; vol. staff lectr. Maritime Aquarium, Norwalk, Conn., 2000—; instr. trainer ARC, 1999, Conn. and NH; advisor explorer adv. coun. Boy Scouts Am.; justice of peace State of NH, quorum mem.; bd. govs. Judaica Mus., Riverdale, NY, 1994—; vol. dist. coord. NH marine patrol Aux. State Dept. Safety, 1991—; mem. Am. Friends Brit. Mus., 1998—. Sgt. U.S. Army, 1955-57. Recipient honor award Emergency Med. Svcs., 1989, 97, 99, Environ. Youth Honors award White House-EPA, 1994, Citation for 60 yrs. svc. to Boy Scouts Am., Conn. State Legislature, 1994, Gov.'s Exec. Coun., NH, 1995, Cold War Recognition cert. U.S. Dept. Def., 1999, numerous awards Boy Scouts Am., honored for safety patrol svc., 1996, White House Med. Corps Secret Svc. citation for svcs. on presdl. visit, 1999, Congressional Record Congratulations citation for a quarter century EMS vol. leadership, 1999, Congratulations citation from Conn. Gov., State Legislature and Town Mayor, 1999, ARC Unsung Heroes award, 2000, 03, Vol. of Yr. award Emergency Med. Svcs., 2000, 10 Yrs. Nat. Educator award 2005, 20 Yrs. Nat. Registered Svc. award, 2005, Fairfield County Hero award Bridgeport Hosp., 2005; named Conn. Vol. of Yr., Carosel Mag., 1990, Conn. Man of Yr., Spotlight Mag., 1991, Disting. Svc. award EMS, Conn. State, 2001, 1st Pl. Nat. Gold award, EMS Vols., 2001, Nat. Disting. Svc. Lifetime Achievemnt award Assn. Ind. Camps Divsn., Colo. Internat. Camping Conf., 2003. Mem. Am. Camp Assn. (life, nat. legis. chmn. 1970-86, nat. bd. dirs. 1972-84, nat. v.p. 1984-86), NH Camp Dirs. Assn. (pres. 1974-76, state sec./hon. bd. mem. 1976—, Nat. Lifetime Disting. Svc. award 2003), Nat. Assn. Emergency Med. Svcs. Educators, Am. Legion, US Army Alumni, Kiwanis, Rotary, Gold's Dragoons. Republican. Jewish. Avocations: archaeology, photography, aviation, history, medical research. Office: 5 Lockwood Cir Westport CT 06880-1640 Home: 46 Gailan Rd Freedom NH 03836 Personal E-mail: g.c.stolz@aol.com.

STOLZ, BENJAMIN ARMOND, foreign language educator; b. Lansing, Mich., Mar. 28, 1934; s. Armond John and Mabel May (Smith) S.; m. Mona Eleanor Seelig, June 16, 1962; children: Elizabeth Mona, John Benjamin. AB, U. Mich., Ann Arbor, 1955; certificat, U. Libre de Bruxelles, Belgium, 1956; A.M., Harvard U., 1957, PhD, 1965. Mem. faculty U. Mich., 1964-2001, prof. Slavic langs. and lits., 1972-2001, chmn. dept., 1971-85, 89-91; prof. emeritus, 2001—. Cons. in field. Editor: Papers in Slavic Philology, 1977, Studies in Macedonian Language, Literature, and Culture, 1995; co-editor: Oral Literature and the Formula, 1976, Cross Currents, 1982-85, Language and Literary Theory, 1984, Mich. Slavic Publs., 1990—; co-editor, translator: (Konstantin Mihailovic): Memoirs of a Janissary, 1975; contbr. articles to profl. pubs. Served to lt. (j.g.) USNR, 1957-60. Recipient Orion E. Scott award humanities U. Mich., 1954, Fulbright scholar, 1955-56; Fgn. Area fellow Yugoslavia, 1963-64; Fulbright-Hays rsch. fellow Eng. and Yugoslavia, 1970-71; grantee Am. Coun. Learned Socs., 1968-70, 73, Internat. Rsch. and Exchs. Bd., 1985, 87, Woodrow Wilson Ctr., 1992. Mem. Am. Assn. Advancement Slavic Studies, Am. Assn. Tchrs. Slavic and East European Langs., Phi Beta Kappa, Phi Kappa Phi, Delta Upsilon. Home: 3423 Riverbend Dr Ann Arbor MI 48105

STOLZ, THEODORA, psychologist; b. Athens, Greece, Jan. 13, 1958; d. Bernhard and Evelyn Stolz; children: Lynette, Constantine. BA in Psychology, Marymount Manhattan Coll., 1981; PhD, Hofstra U., 1991. Lic. psychologist N.Y., 1991, N.J., 1994. Pvt. practice, Staten Island and Bklyn., 1991—; assoc. psychologist, program mgr. Staten Island Devel. Disabilities Svcs, 1989—, bd. dirs., 1989—; contractual mil. psychologist Homeland Security, NJ, 2005—. Author: Cognitive Factors in Pathological Gambling, 1991., Hofstra U. fellow, 1989. Mem.: APA, Deborah Orgn. Avocations: dollhouse building, bicycling, needlepoint, music, meditation. Office: 68 Guyon Ave Staten Island NY 10306-2019

STOLZBERG, MARK ELLIOTT, psychologist; b. NYC, Apr. 30, 1944; s. Seymour and Ruth (Petesky) S.; m. Marilyn Goldberg, Mar. 18, 1972; children: Susan Beth, David Jonathan, Daniel Jason. BA, Hofstra U., Hempstead, NY, 1966, PhD, 1986; MA in Exptl. Psychology, C.W. Post Coll., Greenvale, NY, 1970; postgrad. in clin. psychology, SUNY, Albany, 1973. Diplomate in clin. psychology Am. Bd. Profl. Psychology. Intern in clin. psychology Maimonides Hosp., Bklyn., 1972-73; pres. Stolzberg Rsch., LLC, Stony Brook, NY, 1976—. Adj. lectr. Bklyn. Coll., 1973; faculty Coll. Optometry, SUNY, 1985-86; cons. clin. psychologist to numerous nursing homes, 1994—. Contbr. articles to profl. jours. Co-pres. North Shore SEPTA, 1999-2001. Grad. fellow C.W. Post Coll., 1968-70, SUNY, Albany, 1970-72, N.Y. State War Svc. scholar; recipient Disting. Achievement award for Rsch., N.Y. State Optometric Assn., 1983. Mem. Ind. Practitioners of Geropsychology (founder, past pres.), N.Y. State Psychol. Assn. (pres. divsn. on aging 2004), Aircraft Owners and Pilots Assn., Nat. Aeronautics Assn. Achievements include setting two U.S. transcontinental speed records for piston-engine aircraft. Home and Office: 3 Seabrook Ct Stony Brook NY 11790-3305 Personal E-mail: markst1@verizon.net.

STOMFAY-STITZ, ALINE MARIA, education educator; b. Newark; d. Adolph and Irene (Badowska) Wegrocki; m. Emery Stomfay-Stitz (dec.); children: Peter, John, Robert. BA, Barnard Coll., NYC; MA, Case We. Res. U., Cleve.; EdD, No. Ill. U., DeKalb, 1984. Asst. prof. Coll. St Scholastica, Duluth, Minn., 1984—85, St. Leo Coll., Fla., 1985—87, Nicholls State U., Thibodaux, La., 1989—91; assoc. prof. edn. Christopher Newport U., Newport News, Va., 1991—96. Vis. prof., assoc. prof. edn. U. No. Fla., Jacksonville, 1996-2003; assoc. editor Joun. Early Childhood Tchr. Edn. Author: Peace Education in America 1828-1990, 1993; author (book chpt.): Toward Education That is Multicultural, 1992, Multicultural Education for the 21st Century, 1993; contbr. articles to profl. jours. Mem.: Internat. Peace Rsch. Assn., Nat. Assn. for Early Childhood Tchr. Educators, Am. Ednl. Rsch. Assn. (SIG exec. coun.). Business E-Mail: astomfay@unf.edu.

STONE, ALAN, container company executive; b. Chgo., Feb. 5, 1928; s. Norman H. and Ida (Finkelstein) S.; m. Joanie B. Stone; children: Christie-Ann Stone Weiss, Joshua. BSE, U. Pa., Phila., 1951; cert. in Advanced Mgmt., U. Chgo., 1960. Trainee, salesman Stone Container Corp., Chgo., 1951-53, dir. mktg. service, 1954-64, gen. mgr., regional mgr., 1964-72, sr. v.p. adminstrn., gen. mgr. energy div., 1972—, also dir., sr. v.p. purchasing and transp.; pres. North La. and Gulf R.R./Ctrl. La. and Gulf R.R., 1985-92, Atlanta St. Andrews and Bay Line R.R., 1992-94, Abbeville-Grimes R.R., 1992-94, Apache R.R., 1992-94. Bd. dirs., exec. com. Stone Container Corp., 1960—; cons. Chgo. Mfg.; pres. No. La. Gulf Railroad, 1985, Ctrl. La. Gulf Railroad, 1985. Pres. Jewish Vocat. Svc., Chgo., 1975-77, bd. dirs., 2005—; v.p. Sinai Temple, Chgo., 1977-84; bd. dirs. Jewish Fedn. Chgo., 2005; vice-chmn. Roycemore Sch., Evanston, Ill., 1982-87; pres. Emergency Fund for Needy People, 1993-2007, chmn., 2003—; trustee Brewster Acad., Wolfeboro, N.H.; vol. exec. for overseas needs Citizen's Democracy Corps; vol. cons. Exec. Svc. Corps., 1992—, project mgr., 1997, bd. dirs., 2002—; bd. dirs. Gastrointestinal Rsch. Found., Intermodal Transp. Inst., U. Denver, 1997—; cancer adv. bd. Northwestern U. Mem. Standard Club, Tavern Club, Bryn Mawr Country Club, Tamarisk Country Club, Long Boat Key Club, Execs. Club Chgo., Beta Alpha Psi, Phi Eta Sigma, Zeta Beta Tau. Avocations: golf, sports, reading, travel, cultural activities. Office: Stone Container Corp 645 N Michigan Ave Ste 800 Chicago IL 60611-3775 Home Phone: 312-649-5727; Office Phone: 312-981-5016. Personal E-mail: alanstone3@aol.com.

STONE, ALAN JAY, retired academic administrator; b. Ft. Dodge, Iowa, Oct. 15, 1942; s. Hubert H. and Bernice A. (Tilton) S.; m. Jonieta J. Smith; 1 child, Kirsten K. Stone Morlock. BA, Morningside Coll., Sioux City, Iowa, 1964, HD, 2001; MA, U. Iowa, Iowa City, 1966; MTh, U. Chgo., 1968, DMin, 1970; PhD (hon.), Kyonggi U., Korea, 1985; LLD, Stillman Coll., Tuscaloosa, Ala., 1991, Sogong U., Korea, 1992, Alma Coll., Mich., 2001. Admissions counselor Morningside Coll., Sioux City, Iowa, 1964-66; dir. admissions, asso. prof. history George Williams Coll., Downers Grove, Ill., 1969-73; v.p. coll. relations Hood Coll., Frederick, Md., 1973-75; v.p. devel. and fin. affairs W.Va. Wesleyan Coll., Buckhannon, 1975-77; dir. devel. U. Maine, 1977-78; pres. Aurora U., Ill., 1978-88, Alma Coll., 1988-2000; pres., CEO Alzheimer's Assn., Chgo., 2001—02; ret., 2002; lectr. for cruises. Home: 28897 N 94th Pl Scottsdale AZ 85262 Personal E-mail: thestones3@cox.net.

STONE, ALAN JOHN, manufacturing company executive, real estate company executive; b. Dansville, NY, Sept. 9, 1940; s. Guthrie Boyd and Doris Irene (Wolfanger) S.; m. Sandra Barber, Aug. 22, 1964; children: Teri, Timothy, Michael. BSME, Rochester Inst. Tech., 1963; MBA, U. Pitts., 1964. Engrng. aide Xerox Corp., Webster, N.Y., 1960-63; gen. mgr. mech. component divsn. Stone Conveyor Co., Inc., Honeoye, N.Y., 1964-67, v.p. sales, 1968; co-founder, CEO Stone Constrn. Equipment Inc., Honeoye, 1969-86, also cons., bd. dirs., 1969—; founder, pres. Canandaigua Apts. Inc., NY, 1967—83; pres. Wildtrak, Inc., 1983—; founder, gen. ptnr. Stone Properties, 1986—2002; mng. mem. Stone Family Properties, LLC, 2002—. Dir., co-founder Baker Rental Svc., Inc., 1973-75; met. adv. bd. Chase Lincoln Bank, 1981-84; co-founder, dir. Royal Lines Ltd., 1989-91; v.p. Naples Biol. Rsch. Sta. Inc., 1996-98; bd. dirs. Canandaigua Nat. Bank & Trust Co., 1986-, chmn. 1994-2004; co-founder, ptnr. Storage Assocs., 1996-2001; mem., City Mini Storage, LLC, 2001—, mng. mem., 2001-04. Patentee in field. Mem. Town of Richmond (N.Y.) Planning Bd., 1970-75, chmn., 1970-71; mem. Honeoye Ctrl. Sch. Bd. Edn., 1971-76, pres., 1974-75; com. chmn. pack 10 Boy Scouts Am., 1975-78; mem. Ontario County Overall Econ. Devel. Com., 1976-81; bd. dirs. F.F. Thompson Hosp., 1987-91; chmn. fin. com. United Meth. Ch., Allens Hill, 1995—2001; trustee Honeoye Pub. Libr., 1998-2003. Mem. Honeoye C. of C., Constrn. Industry Mfrs. Assn. (exec. mem. new bus. challenges coun. 1980-83), Honeoye Valley Assn. (dir. 1991-95, treas. 1993-95), Griswold and Cast Iron Collectors Assn. (treas. 1994-96, chmn. fin. com. 1996-2002), Honeoye Area Hist. Soc. (bicentennial com. 1989), Grand Slam Club, Safari Club Internat., Found. N.Am. Wild Sheep. Methodist.

STONE, ANDREW GROVER, lawyer; b. LA, Oct. 2, 1942; s. Frank B. and Meryl (Pickering) S.; 1 child, John Blair; m. Susan Anselmo, Feb. 14, 2003. BA, Yale U., 1965; JD, U. Mich., 1969. Bar: D.C. 1970, U.S. Dist. Ct. D.C. 1970, U.S. Ct. Appeals (D.C. cir.) 1972, Mass. 1981. Assoc. Rogers & Wells, Washington, 1969-71; atty. Bur. Competition, FTC, Washington, 1971-80; antitrust counsel Digital Equipment Corp., Maynard, Mass., 1980-83, mgr. N.E. law group, 1983-86, mgr. headquarters sales law group, 1986-88; asst. general counsel U.S. (acting), 1987, 88; corp counsel Washington, 1988-90; corp. counsel, pub. sect. mktg. Thinking Machines Corp., Cambridge, Mass., 1990-91, corp. counsel, 1992-95; pvt. practice on-site legal svcs. Marblehead, Mass., 1995—2006; v.p., gen. counsel Hologic Inc., Bedford, Mass., 2006—. Corp. mem. Tenacre Country Day Sch., Wellesley, Mass., 1981-88. Mem. ABA (bus. law sect.), Mass. Bar Assn. (internat. law steering com. 1993-94), Boston Bar Assn. (membership com. 1998-2000, chair corp. counsel com. 1995-98, chair gen. counsel forum 1995—), Am. Arbitration Assn. (comml. arbitrator), New Eng. Corp. Counsel Assn.

STONE, ANN ELIZABETH, marketing agency executive, consultant, entrepreneur, volunteer; b. Bridgeport, Conn., Aug. 9, 1952; d. Jack Reginald and Edith Pauline (Christiansen) Wesche; m. Roger J. Stone, June 15, 1974 (div. Dec. 1990). BA in History and Comm., George Washington U., 1974; postgrad., Wharton Sch. Bus., Washington, 1975—76. Mktg. mgr. Human Events, Washington, 1974—76; v.p. polit. div. The Viguerie Co., Falls Church, Va., 1976—82; chmn. Capstone Lists, Alexandria, Va., 1983—, Unique Graphics, Alexandria, 1985—; vice chmn. George Washington Nat. Bank, Alexandria, 1988—; ptnr. Weintraub-Stone Direct, Inc., Woodland Hills, Calif., 1991—; pres. The Stone Group Inc. (formerly Ann E.W. Stone & Assocs.), Alexandria, 1982—. Bd. dirs. Action Products; spkr. in field. Co-host (TV show) The Alexandria Forum, TV appearances Larry King Live, Lehrer News Hour, Good Morning Am., Politically Incorrect, others; contbr. articles to profl. jours. Pres.'s exec. global adv. bd. European/Am. Women's Coun., 2003; internat. chair Empowered Women Internat. and Women Immigrant Network; arbiter Va. Bar Assn.; trustee apptd. by gov. Va. Hist. Preservation Found.; fin. dir. Alexandria Rep. Party, 1989—92; chmn. D.C. Young Reps., Washington, 1975—77; Republican candidate for mayor Alexandria, 1991; chmn., foundr Reps. for Choice, Alexandria, 1989—; bd. dirs. Campaigns and Elections Mag., Washington, 1987—, Am. Heart Assn., 1990—, chmn., 1993—94; bd. dirs. Nat. Womens History Mus., The Washington Ctr., Response mag., Influence mag. Named one of Women Who Changed Politics in Am., Campaigns and Elections mag., 1992. Mem. Direct Mktg. Assn. Washington (bd. dirs. 1974—), Renaissance Women (bd. dirs. 1985—), Alexandria C. of C. (bd. dirs. 1982), Alexandria Soc. for Preservation of Black Heritage, Animal Welfare League, Lions Club, Alexandria Seaport Fedn. (past bd. dirs.), Direct Mktg. Club (Washington). Lutheran. Avocations: reading, travel, historical renovation, rock collecting, music. Office: 205 S Whiting St 250 Alexandria VA 22304 Office Phone: 703-329-1982, 703-370-8282. Personal E-mail: tsgrp@aol.com.

STONE, BRUCE, lawyer; Grad. with high honors, U. Fla.; grad. with highest honors, Fla. State U. Shareholder Goldman, Felcoski & Stone, Coral Gables, Fla. Adj. prof. U. Miami Sch. Law. Named one of 45 Best Trusts and Estates Attys. in US, Town and Country, 1998, Top 100 Attys., Worth mag., 2005—06; recipient Friend of the Trust Industry award, Fla. Bankers Assn., 2001. Fellow: Am. Coll. Trust and Estate Counsel (bd. regents); mem.: Phi Beta Kappa. Office: Goldman Felcoski & Stone PA 95 Merrick Way Ste 440 Coral Gables FL 33134 Office Phone: 305-446-2800. Office Fax: 305-446-2819. E-mail: brucestone@gfsestatelaw.com. *

STONE, CURTIS, celebrity chef; b. 1976; Chef Savory Hotel, Melborne, Australia, The Grill Room, Café Royal, London; sous chef Mirabelle; head chef Quo Vadis, London, Restaurant 301. Host Dinner in a Box, UK Food, 2002, Surfing the Menu, ABC Australia, 2003, 2005, My Restaurant Rules, Network 7, Australia, 2004, Take Home Chef, TLC, 2006—, guest appearances Taste Today, Taste Network, Great Food Live, UK Food, Saturday Kitchen, BBC2, This Morning; author: Surfing the Menu, 2004, 2005; columnist Delicious Mag., Australia. Avocations: surfing, skiing.

STONE, DAVID PHILIP, lawyer; b. NYC, Sept. 11, 1944; s. Robert and Laura Stone; m. Arlene R. Stone, June 11, 1966; children: Aaron J., Rachel E. AB, Columbia U., 1967; JD, Harvard U., 1970. Bar: NY 1971. Assoc. Cahill, Gordon & Reindel, NYC, 1970-74, Baer & McGoldrick, NYC, 1974-76, Weil, Gotshal & Manges, L.L.P., NYC, 1976-79, ptnr., 1979—2005. Office: Weil Gotshal & Manges LLP 767 5th Ave New York NY 10153-0119 Business E-Mail: david.stone@weil.com.

STONE, DONALD DIAMOND, investment and sales executive; b. Chgo., June 25, 1924; s. Frank J. and Mary N. (Miller) Diamondstone; m. Catherine Mauro, Dec. 20, 1970; 1 child, Jeffrey. Student, U. Ill., 1942-43; BS, DePaul U., 1949. Pres. Poster Bros., Inc., Chgo., 1950-71, Revere Leather Goods, Inc., Chgo., 1953-71; owner Don Stone Enterprises, Chgo., 1954—; v.p. Horton & Hubbard Mfg. Co. Inc. div. Brown Group, Nashua, N.H., 1969-71, Neevel Mfg. Co., Kansas City, Mo., 1969-71. Mem. adv. bd. San Diego Opera; founder Don Diego Meml. Scholarship Fund; mem. bd. overseers U. Calif., San Diego, chancellor's assoc.; mem. exec. bd. Chgo. Area council Boy Scouts of Am. Served with U.S. Army, 1943-46. Clubs: Bryn Mawr Country (Lincolnwood, Ill.) (dir.), Carlton, La Jolla Beach and Tennis, La Jolla Country, Del Mar Thoroughbred. Home: 1001 Genter St Apt 5C La Jolla CA 92037

STONE, DONALD RAYMOND, lawyer; b. Madison, Wis., Mar. 6, 1938; s. Donald Meredith and June Dorothy (Graffenberger) S.; m. Dorothy Tetzlaff, June 23, 1962; children: Randall, Brian. BS in Physics, U. Wis., 1960, JD, 1963. Bar: Minn. 1963, D.C. 1987, U.S. Supreme Ct. 1987. Patent atty. Honeywell, Inc., Mpls., 1963-66; patent atty. firm Burd, MacEachron, Braddock, Bartz & Schwartz, Mpls., 1966-68; with Medtronic, Inc., Mpls., 1968-87, v.p., then sr. v.p. product assurance and regulation, 1973-77, sr. v.p., sec., gen. counsel, 1977-80, sr. v.p., 1980-85, v.p., 1985-87; ptnr., mem. Burditt, Bowles & Radzius, Chartered, Washington, 1987-90; ptnr. McKenna & Cuneo, L.L.P., Washington, 1990-2001, Kirkpatrick & Lockhart LLP, Washington, 2001—03, of counsel, 2003; ret., 2003. Condr. seminars, 1974—. Contbr. articles to profl. jours. Bd. dirs., 1st v.p. East Side Neighborhood Services, Inc., Mpls., 1976-80; bd. dirs. Guthrie Theater Found., 1979-85; mem. allocations com. United Way Mpls., 1979-86, chmn. allocations com., 1985, bd. dirs. 1985-86; mem. Citizens League of Twin Cities, 1965-86. Mem. ABA, D.C. Bar Assn., Fed. Bar Assn., Hennepin County Bar Assn., Am. Soc. Quality, Am. Intellectual Property Law Assn., Advanced Med. Tech. Assn. (past chmn. legal and regulatory sect., std. sect., 1975-87), Nat. Elec. Mfrs. Assn. (past chmn. med. electronics sect., 1970-76), Minn. State Bar Assn., Minn. Intellectual Property Law Assn. (past sec.), Minn. Corp. Counsel Assn., Order of Coif, Phi Delta Phi, Kappa Sigma. Episcopalian.

STONE, EDMUND CRISPEN, III, banker; b. Charleston, W.Va., Nov. 29, 1942; s. Edmund C. and Sallie Ragland (Thornhill); S.; m. Annette Margarethe Isaksen, Nov. 26, 1965 (div.); 1 child, Kristine Margarethe; m. Barbara J. Sarff, June 15, 2000. BS, U.S. Mil. Acad., 1964; MBA, U. Va., 1972. V.p. Wachovia Bank, Winston-Salem, N.C., 1972-81; exec. v.p. First Am. Corp., Nashville, from 1981; vice chmn. First Am. Nat. Bank Nashville, 1988; exec. v.p. Regions Fin. Corp. (formerly First Ala. Bancshares, Inc.), Birmingham, 1988—2005; ret. Contbg. author: The International Banking Handbook, 1983. Mem. export policy task force U.S. C. of C., 1980-81. With inf. U.S. Army, 1964-70, Vietnam, Iran. Decorated Bronze Star (Valor) with oak leaf cluster, Vietnamese Cross of Gallantry, others; hon. mem. Imperial Iranian Spl. Forces, 1968. Mem. Assn. of Grads. U.S. Mil. Acad. (trustee 1992-93, 98-2001, 2001—). Republican. Avocations: golf, sailing, hunting, fishing. Home Phone: 205-870-7097. E-mail: cris.stone@regions.com.

STONE, EDWARD C., physicist, researcher; b. Knoxville, Iowa, Jan. 23, 1936; s. Edward Carroll and Ferne Elizabeth (Baber) Stone; m. Alice Trabue Wickliffe, Aug. 4, 1962; children: Susan, Janet. AA, Burlington Jr. Coll., 1956; MS, U. Chgo., 1959, PhD, 1964, DSc (hon.), 1992, Washington U., St. Louis, 1992, Harvard U., 1992, U. So. Calif., 1998. From rsch. fellow in physics to prof. Calif. Inst. Tech., Pasadena, Calif., 1964—94, Voyager project scientist, 1972—, chmn. divsn. physics, math. and astron., 1983—88, v.p., 1988—2001, dir. jet propulsion lab., 1991—2001, David Morrisroe prof. physics, 1994—, mem. Draper Lab., 2001, vice provost for spl. projects, 2004—. Cons. Office of Space Sci., NASA, 1969—85, adv. com. outer planets, 1972—73; high energy astrophysics mgmt. oper. working group NASA, 1976—84, cosmic ray program working group, 1980—82, outer planets working group, 1981—82, solar sys. exploration com., 1981—82, U. rels. study group, 1983; exec. com. Com. on Space Rsch. Interdisciplinary Sci. Commn., 1982—86; com. on space astronomy and astrophysics Space Sci. Bd., 1979—82, steering group study on maj. directions for space sci., 1984—85; mem. Space Sci. Bd., NRC, 1982—85; commn. on phys. sci., math. and resources NRC, 1986—89; adv. com. vis. sr. scientist program NASA/Jet Propulsion Labs., 1986—90; com. on space policy NAS/NAE, 1988—89; chmn., chief sci. advisor The Astronomers, KCET, 1989—91; chmn. adv. panel NAS/WQED TV program "Sail on, Voyager!", 1989—90; v.p. COSPAR Bur., 2001—. Mem. editl. bd. Space Sci. Instrumentation, 1975—81, Space Sci. Rev., 1982—85, Astrophysics and Space Sci., 1982—, Sci. mag. Bd. dir. W.M. Keck Found., 1994—. Named an asteroid Edward C. Stone in his honor, 1996; named to Hall of Fame, Aviation Week and Space Tech., 1997, Hall of Honor, Burlington Comm., 1999; recipient medal for exceptional sci. achievement, NASA, 1980, Am. Edn. award, 1981, DSM, 1981, 1998, 2001, Dryden award, 1983, Disting. Pub. Svc. medal, 1985, Outstanding Leadership medal, 1986, 1995, Achievement award, Soc. for Tech. Comm., 1984, Space Achievement award, AIAA, 1986, Oppenheimer Mem. Lecture Aviation Week and Space Tech. Aerospace Laureate, 1989, Sci. Man of Yr. award, ARCS Found., 1991, Nat. Medal of Sci., 1991, Golden Plate award, Am. Acad. Achievement, 1992, COSPAR award, 1992, LeRoy Randle Grumman medal, 1992, Disting. Pub. Svc. award, Aviation/Space Writers Assn., 1993, Internat. von Karman Wings award, 1996, Space Flight Award, Am. Astron. Soc., 1997, Alumni award, S.E. C.C., Burlington, Iowa, 1997, CEO of Yr. award, ARC, 1998, Allan D. Emil Meml. award, Internat. Astronautical Fedn., 1999, Carl Sagan award, Am. Astronautical Soc. and Planetary Soc., 1999, Prof. Achievement award, Alumni, U. Chgo., 2002, Nat. Award for Op., Assn. for Unmanned Sys., Nat. Medal of Sci., Pres. Bush; fellow Sloan Found., 1971—73. Fellow: AAAS (award 1993), AIAA (assoc.; Calif. coun. sci. and tech. 1996—2001, Space Sci. award 1984, von Karman lectureship in astronautics 1999), Internat. Astron. Union, Am. Geophys. Union, Am. Phys. Soc. (exec. com. 1974—76, chmn. cosmic physics divsn. 1979—80); mem.: NAS, Sci. Edit. Bd., Comm. of Phys. Sci., Math., and Applications, NRC, Am. Philos. Soc., Calif. Assn. Rsch. in Astronomy (bd. dirs., vice-chmn. 1986—88, vice-chmn. 1986—2003, bd. dirs., vice-chmn. 1991—94, chmn. bd. dirs. 1994—97, bd. dirs., vice-chmn. 1997—2000, chmn. bd. dirs. 2000—03), Royal Aero. Soc., Nat. Space Club (bd. govs., Sci. award 1990), Astron. Soc. Pacific, Am. Philos. Soc. (Magellanic award 1992), Am. Astron. Soc. (divsn. planetary sci. com. 1981—84, Space Flight award 1997), Internat. Acad. Astronautics (trustee 1989—2001, v.p. 2001—). Office: Calif Inst Tech Space Radiation Lab M/C 220-47 Pasadena CA 91125 Office Phone: 626-395-8321. Business E-Mail: ecs@srl.caltech.edu.

STONE, EDWARD HARRIS, II, landscape architect; b. Lanesboro, Pa., Aug. 28, 1933; s. Frank Addison and Beth Lee (Brennan) S.; m. Diane Gertrude Berg, June 11, 1955; children: Randel Harris, Deborah Dee. BS, SUNY, 1955. Landscape architect Harmon, O'Donnell & Henninger, Denver, 1955-56, U.S. Forest Service, Colo., 1958-61; regional landscape architect Alaska, 1961-64; regional landscape architect, Colo., 1964—65; chief landscape architect U.S. Forest Service, U.S. Dept. Agr., Washington, 1966-79, asst. dir. for recreation, 1979-85; ret., 1985; with C-3 Co., Bowie,

Md., 1986—. Founder Edward H. Stone, Clockmaker, Bowie, Md., 1989—. Exhibitions include The White House, Washington, Md. Hist. Soc. With US Army, 1956—58. Recipient Arthur S. Flemming award for outstanding fed. govt. service U.S. Jr. C. of C., 1969 Fellow Am. Soc. Landscape Architects (pres. 1975-76); mem. Sigma Lambda Alpha (hon.) Home and Office: 13200 Forest Dr Bowie MD 20715-4390

STONE, EDWARD HERMAN, lawyer; b. July 20, 1939; s. Sidney and Ruth Stone; m. Penni G. Gray (dec. 1990); children: Andrew, Matthew; m. Elaine Ornitz, Dec. 22, 1995. BS in Acctg., U. Ill., 1961; JD, John Marshall Law Sch., 1967. Bar: Ill. 1967, Calif. 1970, cert.: Calif. (specialist probate, estate planning, and trust law). With IRS, 1963—71; assoc. Eilers, Baranger, Myers & Smith, 1971—72; pvt. practice Newport Beach, Calif., 1972—88, Santa Ana, Calif., 1988—89; mem. Davis, Samuelson, Goldberg & Blakely (formerly Cohen, Stokke & Davis), Santa Ana, 1984—88; ptnr. Edward H. Stone A Law Corp., Irvine, Calif., 1990—. Instr. income and estate taxes Western States U. Sch. Law, 1971—72; temporary judge Orange County Superior Ct.; mediator tax cases in appeals IRS ADR, 2000—; moderator, spkr. in field Continuing Edn. Bar Calif., 1999—. Contbr. articles to profl. jours. Pres. Jewish Family Svcs. Orange County, 1975; v.p., bd. dirs. Jewish Fedn. Orange County, 1985—88; bd. dirs. Heritage Points Orange County, 1992—95, Eastbluff Homeowners Cmty. Assn., Newport Beach, 1980—82, pres., 1981—82. Mem.: Orange County Bar Assn. (vice-chmn. estate planning probate and trust law sect. 1976—77, chmn. sect. 1977—78, instr. Probate Clinic 1980, chairperson ADR com. 1996, spkr. in substantive law, dir. 1977—82, past chmn. profl. edn. coun., chmn.del. real property and probate sect, chmn. del. real property and probate sect. state bar conv. 1992—), Phi Alpha Delta (pres. alumni chpt. 1975—76). Office Phone: 949-833-7708.

STONE, EDWARD LUKE, investor, realtor; b. Englewood, NJ, Jan. 18, 1937; s. James and Anna (Druskin) S.; m. Cassandra Reeve, Mar. 15, 1969. BA, Yale U., 1958; postgrad., Cambridge U., Eng., 1959; MBA, Harvard U., 1966. Dir. fin. planning Yale U., New Haven, 1966-69; pres. HDC, Inc., Boston, 1969-77; ptnr. Dane, Falb, Stone, Boston, 1977-81; exec. dir. White House Preservation Fund, Washington, 1981-90; trustee Newport Art Mus., 1991-94; chmn. Stone and Cranwell, Newport, R.I., 1995-99; pres. Hogan and Stone, Newport, 1996-99; broker Benchmark Assocs., Middletown, RI, 1999—2001; chmn. Edward L. Stone Realty llc, Newport, 2002—. Cons. Booz Allen Hamilton, Bethesda, Md., 1987-88. Trustee Nat. Mus. of Women in the Arts, Washington, 1988-90, Tudor Pl. Found., Washington, 1988-95, The Washington Home, 1988-95, Touro Synagogue Friends, 1996—; chmn., pres. Royal Arts Found., 2006—; gov. Newport Health Care Corp., 1997—; co-chmn. The Isaac Bell House, 1995—. Mem. Newport Reading Rm., Spouting Rock Beach Assn., Somerset Club, Elizabethan Club, Phi Beta Kappa. Avocation: early 19th century American decorative arts. Office Phone: 401-849-9262. Personal E-mail: estone3137@aol.com.

STONE, ELAINE MURRAY, writer, composer, television producer; b. NYC, Jan. 22, 1922; d. H. and Catherine Fairbanks Murray-Jacoby; m. F. Courtney Stone, May 30, 1944; children: Catherine Gustavson, Pamela Webb, Victoria Mattson. Student, Juilliard Sch., 1939—41; BA, N.Y. Coll. Music, 1943; licentiate in organ, Trinity Coll. Music, London, 1947; student, U. Miami, 1952, Fla. Inst. Tech., 1963; PhD (hon.), World U., 1985, Oxford U., Eng., 1998. Organist, choir dir. St. Ignatius Episc. Ch., 1940-44; accompanist Strawbridge Ballet on Tour, NYC, 1944; organist All Saints Episc. Ch., Ft. Lauderdale, 1951-54, St. John's Episc. Ch., Melbourne, Fla., 1956-59, First Christian Ch., Melbourne, 1962-63, United Ch. Christ, Melbourne, 1963-65, piano studio, Melbourne, 1955-70; editor-in-chief Cass Inc., 1970-71; dir. continuity radio Sta. WTAI, AM-FM, Melbourne, 1971-74; mem. sales staff Engle Realty Inc., Indialantic, Fla., 1975-78; v.p. pub. relations Consol. Cybertronics Inc., Cocoa Beach, Fla., 1969-70; writer, producer Countdown News, Sta. KXTX-TV, Dallas, 1978-80; assoc. producer Focus News, Dallas, 1980. Host producer TV show, Focus on History, 1982-94, Episc. Digest, 1984-90; judge Writer's Contest sponsored Brevard Cmty. Coll., 1987; v.p. Judges Fla. Space Coast Writer's Conf., 1985—, chmn., 1987. Author: The Taming of the Tongue, 1954, Love One Another, 1957, Menéndez de Avilés, 1968, Bedtime Bible Stories, Travel Fun, Sleepytime Tales, Improve Your Spelling for Better Grades, Improve Your Business Spelling, Tranquility Tapes, 1970, The Melbourne Bi-Centennial Book, 1976, Uganda: Fire and Blood, 1977, Tekla and the Lion, 1981 (1st pl. Nat. League Am. Pen Women), Brevard County: From Cape of the Canes to Space Coast, 1988, Kizito, Boy Saint of Uganda, 1989 (2d pl. Nat. League Am. Pen Women 1990), Christopher Columbus: His World, His Faith., His Adventures, 1991 (1st pl. Nat. League Am. Pen Women 1992), Elizabeth Bayley Seton: An American Saint, 1993 (3d pl. Nat. League Am. Pen Women 1994), Dimples The Dolphin, 1994 (1st pl. Fla. Space Coast Writer's Guild, 1994), Brevard at The Edge of Sea and Space, 1995, The Widow's Might, 1996 (1st pl. Space Coast Writer's Contest), Carter G. Woodson Father of Black History, 1997 (1st pl. Am. Heritage Contest Nat. Soc. Daus. of Am. Revolution 1997), Maximilian Kolbe: Saint of Auschwitz, 1997 (Cath. Bestseller list 1997), Albert's Jungle Piano, 1997 (1st pl. Nat. League Am. Pen Women 1997, 2d pl., Nat. League of Am. Pen Women, 1999), Mother Teresa: A Life of Love, 1999, The Taming of the Tongue, 1999, C.S. Lewis: Creator of Narnia, 2001 (3d place Nat. League Am. Pen Women 2001), Mary and the Apparitions of Guadalupe, Lourdes and Fatima, 2003, A Saint and His Lion The Story of Tekla of Ethiopia, 2003, A New Life (1st place Fla. Assn. Univ. Women 2003), Saints of the Americas, 2004, Dorothy Day: Champion of the Poor, 2004, Courtney's Seawall (2d pl. award); composer: Christopher Columbus Suite, 1992 (1st pl. Pen Women Music Awards 1992, 2d pl. 1993), Florida Suite for cello and piano, 1993, Two Crowns of St. Maximilian, 1998 (1st pl. in music Nat. League Am. Pen Women 1997), Pastorale, 2000 (1st pl. Nat. League Am. Pen Women, Washington, 2000), Anima Christi, 2000 (hon. mention Nat. League Am. Pen Women, Washington, 2000); contbr. articles to mags., newspapers including N.Y. Herald Tribune, Living Church, Christian Life, Episcopal Life; space corr. Religious News Service, Kennedy Space Ctr., 1962-78. Exec. bd. Women's Assn., Brevard Symphony, 1967—; heritage com. Melbourne Bicentennial Commn.; mem. Evangelism Commn. Episc. Diocese Cen. Fla., 1985-94; v.p. churchwomen group Holy Trinity Episcopal Ch., Melbourne, 1988-89, Stephen minister, 1988—, pres. churchwomen group, 1989—; bd. dirs. Fla. Space Coast Council Internat. Visitors, Fla. Space Coast Philharm., 1989—, Aid for the Arts, 1994; appointee Hist. Preservation Com., Melbourne, Fla., 2003. Recipient 1st place for piano Ashley Hall, 1935-39, S.C. State Music Contest, 1939, 1st place for piano composition Colonial Suite, Constitution Hall, Washington 1987, 88, 89, 3d place for vocal composition, 1989, honorable mention for article, 1989, 2nd place for piano composition, 1989, award lit. contest Fla. AAUW, 1989, 1st place award Fla. State PEN Women, 1990, 1st Place award Nat. Black History Essay Contest, 1990, 2d place Nat. League Am. Pen Women, 1999, 2d place for music composition, 1999, named Woman of Achievement, 1999, Disting. Author of Yr. plaque Fla. Space Coast Writers Guild, 1992, 96, Woman of Achievement plaque AAUW, 1997, Martha Ingram award Excellence in Arts, Ashley Hall, Charleston, 2004; honoree Nat. Polish Alliance, 3d place award for essay "Remembering C.S. Lewis" Mount Dora Festival of Music and Literature, 2001. Mem. ASCAP, Nat. League Am. PEN Women (1st place awards Tex. 1979, 1st place award for duet, Washington, 2000, pres. Dallas br. 1978-80, organizing pres. Cape Canaveral br. 1969, pres. 1988-90, 96—), Women in Comms., DAR (Fla. state chmn. music 1962-63), Colonial Dames Am. (organizing pres. Melbourne chpt. 1994), Nat. Soc. DAR (organizing regent Rufus Fairbanks chpt. 1981-85, vice regent 1987—, historian 1989—, Fla. state chmn. Am. Heritage), Children Am. Revolution (past N.Y. state chaplain), Am. Guild Organists (organizing warden Ft. Lauderdale), Space Pioneers, Fla. Press, Aid for the Arts, Space Coast Writers Guild (past v.p.).

STONE, ELIZABETH CECILIA, anthropology educator; b. Oxford, Eng., Feb. 4, 1949; d. Lawrence and Jeanne Cecilia (Fawtier) S.; m. Paul Edmund Zimansky, Nov. 5, 1976. BA, U. Pa., 1971; MA, Harvard U., 1973; PhD, U. Chgo., 1979. Lectr. anthropology SUNY, Stony Brook, 1977-78, asst. prof., 1978-85, assoc. prof., 1985-95, prof., 1995—2002. Participated archaeol. in Eng., Iran, Iraq, Afghanistan; dir. archaeol. projects Ain Dara, Syria, Tell Abu Duwari, Iraq, Ayanis Survey, Turkey. Author: Nippur Neighborhoods, 1987; co-author: (monograph) Old Babylonian Contracts from Nippur 1, 1976, Adoption in Old Babylonian Nippur and the Archive of Mannum-meshu-lissur, 1991, The Iron Age Settlement at Ain Dara, Syria, 1999, The Anatomy of a Masopotamian City: Survey and Soundings of Mashkan-Shapin, 2004; editor: Settlement and Society: Essays Dedicated to Robert McCormack; co-editor: The Cradle of Civilization Recent Archaeology in Iraq-Biblical Archaeologist, 1992, Velles Paraules: Ancient Near Eastern Studies in Honor of Miguel Civil on the Occasion of His 65th Birthday, 1991; mem. editl. bd. Bull. Am. Schs. Oriental Rsch., 1993-95, 99—; contbr. articles to profl. jours. Assoc. trustee Am. Schs. of Oriental Rsch., 1983-90. Recipient P.E. MacAllister Field Archaeology award Am. Sch. Oriental Rsch., 2002, SUNY Rsch. Recognition award, 2003, Am. Schs. of Oriental Rsch. Spl. Recognition award, 2004; named Woman of the Yr. in Sci., Three Village Cmty., 2004; Fulbright fellow, 1986-87; rsch. grantee Nat. Geog. Soc., 1983, 84, 88, 90, 97-99, 2002, 2003-06, Am. Schs. of Oriental Rsch., 1987, 88, NSF, 1989-95, 2000—06, NEH, 1989-93, 2005-06, Andrew Mellon Found., 2003, USAID, 2003-04, State Dept., 2005-06, 07, World Monument Fund, 2005-06. Office: SUNY Dept Anthropology Stony Brook NY 11794-0001 Home Phone: 631-751-3824; Office Phone: 631-632-7627. Business E-Mail: estone@notes.cc.sunysb.edu.

STONE, F. L. PETER, lawyer; b. Wilmington, Del., Feb. 24, 1935; s. Linton and Lorinda (Hamlin) S.; m. Therese Louise Hannon, Apr. 7, 1969; 1 child, Lisa Judith. AB, Dartmouth Coll, 1957; LLB, Harvard U., 1960. Bar: Del. Supreme Ct. 1960, U.S. Ct. Appeals (3d cir.) 1964, U.S. Supreme Ct. 1965, U.S. Ct. Appeals (fed. cir.) 1983. Assoc. Connolly, Bove & Lodge, Wilmington, 1960-64; dep. atty. gen. State of Del., Wilmington, 1965-66; atty. Del. Gen. Assembly, Dover, 1967-68; counsel Gov. Del., Dover, 1969; U.S. atty. Dist. of Del., Wilmington, 1969-72; ptnr. Connolly, Bove, Lodge, & Hutz, Wilmington, 1972-97; counsel Trzuskowski, Kipp, Kelleher & Pearce, Wilmington, 1997—98, 2001—02; dep. atty. gen., counsel to ins. dept. State of Del., 1998-2001; dep. commr. Del. Ins. Dept., 2002—05. Mem. Del. Agy. to Reduce Crime, 1969-72, Del. Organized Crime Commn., 1970-72, State Drug Abuse Coun., 1990-93, State Judicial Nominating Commn., 1991-93, State Coun. Corrections, 1992-99; co-founder, adj. prof. criminal justice progra, West Chester (Pa.) U., 1975-79; chmn. Gov.'s Harness Racing Investigation Com., 1977, Del. Jai Alai Commn., 1977-78, Del. Govs. Corrections Task Force, 1986-88. Contbr. articles to profl. jours. Chmn. UN Day, Del., 1989; mem. Del. Gov.'s Task Force on Prison Security, 1994—95; trustee Leukemia Soc. Am., NYC, 1972—74, Marywood Coll., Scranton, Pa., 1974—79, Ursuline Acad., Wilmington, 1974—80; bd. dirs. Boys and Girls Club Del., 1997—, Seamen's Ctr., Port of Wilmington, 2001—; Rep. candidate for atty. gen. Del., 1990; mem. Rep. exec. com. Wilmington region, 1991—2000; chmn. re-election campaign Del. Ins. Commr., 1996. Mem. Port of Wilmington Maritime Soc. (bd. dirs., chair 1998-2000), Wilmington Country Club, Rehoboth Beach Country Club, Lincoln Club Del. (pres. 1994), Wilmington Rotary (bd. dirs. 1995-97), Nat. Assn. Former U.S. Attys. (bd. dirs. 1995-98). Roman Catholic. Avocations: hiking, tennis, golf, music, mountain climbing. Office: 7234 Lancaster Pike Ste 300D Hockessin DE 19707 Home Phone: 610-388-0902. *My major accomplishment has been establishing and maintaining a close relationship with my family, first and foremost, regardless of what activities and accomplishments were pursued in my professional, political and community life.*

STONE, FLORENCE SMITH, film presenter and film festival producer, consultant; b. Balt., June 15, 1938; d. Howard Chandler and Mary (Burnam) Smith; m. Roger David Stone; 1 child, Leslie Burnam. BA, Vassar Coll., 1960; cert. Inst. Arts Adminstrn., Harvard U., 1978. Asst. to v.p. for pub. rels. Transam. Corp., San Francisco, 1962—64; newsletter editor U.S. Embassy, Rio de Janeiro, 1964—66; coord. cmty. rels. Am. Mus. Natural History, NYC, 1970—79, coord. spl. progrm, 1977—84; dir. Washington Office Earthwatch, 1985—90; ind. cons. to mus. and ednl. orgns. Washington, 1990—; artistic dir., founder Environ. Film Festival, Washington, 1993—. Co-chmn. Margaret Mead Film Festival, 1977-84, Trustee The Textile Mus., Washington, 1994—, Laura Boulton Found., N.Y.C., 1980-99, Mus. of the Hudson Highlands, Cornwall-on-Hudson, N.Y., 1974-96; mem. adv. com. Margaret Mead Film Festival, N.Y.C., 1992—; active Trees for Georgetown Com., Washington, 1996—. Mem.: Textile Soc., Women in Film and Video, Ind. Film and Video Assn., Internat. Documentary Assn., Am. Assn. Mus., Cosmos Club, Cosmopolitan Club, Georgetown Garden Club. Democrat. Avocations: textiles, films, trees, performing arts, outdoor activities. Office: Environ Film Festival 1228 1/2 31st St NW Washington DC 20007-3402 Office Phone: 202-342-2564. Business E-Mail: flostonc@igc.org.

STONE, FRED MICHAEL, lawyer; b. Bklyn., Jan. 20, 1943; s. Nathan and Rose (Silverman) Stone; m. Bonnie B. Dobkin, Aug. 14, 1965; children: Jonathan, Jennifer. AB cum laude, Bklyn. Coll., 1964; JD, Harvard U., 1967; LLM, NYU, 1971. Bar: N.Y. 1968. Assoc. Cadwalader, Wickersham & Taft, NYC, 1967-69; asst. gen. counsel Standard & Poor's/Intercapital, Inc., NYC, 1969-71; v.p., gen. counsel Neuwirth Funds, 1971-73, Mocatta Metals Corp., NYC, 1973-76; sr. v.p., gen. counsel Am. Stock Exch., Inc., NYC, 1976-86; exec. v.p., gen. counsel Jamie Securities Co., Caronan Ptnrs., NYC, 1986-88; sr. v.p., gen. counsel, sec. M.D. Sass Assocs., Inc., NYC, 1989-2000; chmn. exec. com. Amex Commodities Exch., 1980-81; dir. Am. Gold Coin Exch., Inc., 1981-85; exec. v.p., dir. Revere Copper and Brass, Inc., 1986-88; dir. Ea. Electric Motor Co., Inc., 1987-88; mng. dir. Chase & M.D. Sass Ptnrs., 1998-2000; sr. mng. dir., exec. counsel Millennium Ptnrs., L.P., NYC, 2000—. Ofcl. advisor drafting com. to Revise Uniform Securities Act Nat. Conf. Uniform State Law Commrs., 1981—85; sec., treas. steering com. Taxaple Mcpl. Bondholders Protective Com., 1990—95; lectr. in field. Mem. Manalapan (N.J.) Twp. Zoning Bd. Adjustment, 1975—86, 2000—03, chmn., 2001—02; mem. N.J. regional adv. com. Anti-Defamation League of B'nai B'rith, 1991—; vice chmn. Manalapan Dem. Com., 1988—96; Dem. candidate Manalapan Twp. Com., 1989, 1993. Mem.: ABA (subcom. pvt. investment entities 1994—), Nat. Futures Assn. (mem. nominating com. 1986—88), Nat. Assn. Securities Dealers (arbitrator 1986—), Assn. Bar City of N.Y. (mem. chorus), Harvard U. Law Sch. Assn. Democrat. Jewish. Home: 15 Kingsley Dr Manalapan NJ 07726-3134 Personal E-mail: fstone@mlp.com.

STONE, GEOFFREY RICHARD, lawyer, educator; b. Nov. 20, 1946; s. Robert R. and Shirley (Weliky) S.; m. Nancy Spector, Oct. 8, 1977; children: Julie, Mollie. BS, U. Pa., 1968; JD, U. Chgo., 1971. Bar: N.Y. 1972. Law clk. to Hon. J.S. Kelly Wright U.S. Ct. Appeals (D.C. cir.), 1971-72; law clk. to Hon. William J. Brennan, Jr. U.S. Supreme Ct., 1972-73; asst. prof. U. Chgo., 1973-77, assoc. prof., 1977-79, prof., 1979-84, Harry Kalven Jr. disting. svc. prof., 1984—, dean Law Sch., 1987-93, provost, 1994—2002, Harry Kalven, Jr. Disting. Svc. Prof. Law, 2003—. Author: Constitutional Law, 1986, 5th edit., 2005, The Bill of Rights in the Modern State, 1992, The First Amendment, 1999, Eternally Vigilent: Free Speech in the Modern Era, 2001, Perilous Times: Free Speech in Wartime, 2004 (25th Annual Robert F. Kennedy Book award, 2005); editor The Supreme Ct. Rev., 1991—; contbr. articles to profl. jours. Recipient Robert F. Kennedy Book award, Los Angeles Times Book prize for Best Book of Yr. in History. Fellow AAAS; mem. Chgo. Coun. Lawyers (bd. govs. 1976-77), Am. Law Inst. Assn. Am. Law Schs. (exec. com. 1990-93), Order of Coif. Office: U Chgo 1111 E 60th St Chicago IL 60637-5418 Business E-Mail: gstone@uchicago.edu.

STONE, GREGORY PAUL, lawyer; b. Ventura, Calif., July 21, 1952; BS in Chem. Engring., MS in Chem. Engring., Calif. Inst. Tech., 1974; JD, Yale U., 1977. Bar: Calif. 1977. Law clk. to Hon. William Matthew Byrne, Jr. US Dist. Ct. (ctrl. dist. Calif.), 1977—78; ptnr. Munger, Tolles & Olson LLP, LA, 1978—. Bd. dirs. Constl. Rights Found., Pasadena Playhouse, Huntington-USC Inst. on Calif. and the West. Named one of Top 10 Trial Lawyers in Am., Nat. Law Jour., 2006; recipient Jack E. Froelich Meml. award, Donald S. Clark award, John F. Casky Prize for trial advocacy. Mem.: ABA, State Bar Calif., LA County Bar Assn. Office: Munger Tolles & Olson LLP 355 S Grand Ave 35th Fl Los Angeles CA 90071-1560 Office Phone: 213-683-9255. Office Fax: 213-683-5155. E-mail: Gregory.Stone@mto.com. *

STONE, HAROLD B., artist, educator; b. Ft. Worth, Sept. 26, 1951; s. Harold Ben and Joy Walker Stone; m. Ann Nelson, Mar. 6, 1976; 1 child, Stephen Thomas. BS, Tex. A&M U., 1972; MA, MFA, U. Tulsa, Okla., 1981. Instr. drawing and design Dunwoody Coll. of Tech., Mpls., 1988—2005; dir. Mpls. Drawing Workshop, 1996—. Fine art instr. Tulsa Jr. Coll., 1981—84; instr. art and art history Century C.C., Mahtomedi, Minn., 1988—95. Author: Exploring Life Drawing, 2006. Office: Mpls Drawing Workshop 250 3rd Ave N # 328 Minneapolis MN 55403 Home Phone: 612-267-3550; Office Phone: 612-267-3550.

STONE, HAZEL ANNE DECKER, artist; b. Salt Lake City, Oct. 30, 1934; d. Carl Marcellus and Hazel Sheets (Van Cott) Decker; m. William Samuel Stone, July 20, 1956; children: Cynthia Anne Stone Barkanic, Lisa Marie. BS, RN, U. Utah, 1956; postgrad. in arts and humanities, Ariz. State U., 1979-81; studied with various artists, Ariz., N.Mex., 1985—. Nurse out-patient dept. Salt Lake County Hosp., 1956-57; instr. med.-surg. nursing U. Utah Coll. Nursing, 1957-59; watercolor fine artist. Art exhbn. juror in field, 1998—; workshop instr. in field. One-woman shows include Sun Cities Mus. Art, Sun City, Ariz., 1997, Downtown Deli, Phoenix, 1999, Galerie van Friend, Scottsdale, Ariz., 2003—04, two person exhbns., Church of the Beatitudes, Phoenix, 1994—95, 2003, Gallery Nineteen, 1996, three person exhbns., Grady Gammage Meml. Auditorium, Ariz. State U., 2002, Casa Grande Art Mus., 2002, exhibitions include Ariz. Artists Guild, 1986, 1988—90, 1992—97, 2005, Tucson Mus. of Art, 1988, Ariz. Watercolor Assn., 1989 (Merchant award), 1991, 1993—95 (Award of Merit, 1998), 1997—2000, 2001—05 (Award of Merit, 2005), Vistas, 1989, 1991, 1993, Sun Cities Art Mus., Ariz., 1994, Contemporary Watercolorists of Ariz., 1994—2006 (award of Excellence, 1997, Merit award, 1998, Merchant award, 2001, Award of Excellence, 2004, Merchant award, 2006, 2003, award of Excellence, 2000), Foothills Art Ctr., Golden, Colo., 1994, Bareiss Gallery, Taos, N.Mex., 1995, 13th Ann. Women's Nat. Juried Art Exhbn., Fayetteville, Ark., 1995, Q Artists, 1995—96, 1998, 2000—02, Stables Gallery, Taos, 1996, Wenatchee Valley Coll., Wash., 1997, 1999—2000, Van Vechten-Lineberry Taos Art Mus., 1997, Chandler Ctr. for Arts, Ariz., 1997, 2000, 2005, Farmington Mus. at Gateway Pk., N.Mex., 1999, West Valley Art Mus., Surprise, Ariz., 1999, Sangre de Cristo Arts Ctr., Pueblo, Colo., 1999, Tubac Ctr. of the Arts, Ariz., 1999, 2003, Watercolors Gallery, Pitts., 1999—2000, Woodmere Art Gallery, Phila., 1999—2000, Crary Art Gallery, Warren, Pa., 2000 (Hon. Mention award, 2000), Colo. Springs Fine Arts Ctr., 2001, Bellevue Art Mus., Wash. 2001, Hiestand Art Gallery, U. Miami, Oxford, Ohio, 2001, Showcase Gallery, San Diego, 2001 (Merchant award, 2001), 2005, Acad. of Art Gallery, Calif., 2002, Minnetrista Cultural Ctr., Muncie, Ind., 2002 (Hon. Mention award, 2002), Noyes Mus. of Art, Oceanville, NJ, 2002, Albuquerque Art Mus., 2002, City of Brea Gallery, Calif., 2002, Fine Arts Ctr., Colo. Springs, 2003, Art Ctr., Western Colo. Ctr. for Arts, Grand Junction, 2003, Beverly Arts Ctr., Chgo., 2003 (Merit award, 2003), Mill Atelier Gallery, Santa Fe, 2003, Cynon Valley Mus., Aberdare, Wales, 2004 (ISEA USA Wales medallion, 2003, 2004), John Stobart's Three Rivers Gallery, Pitts., 2003, AIS, Seattle, 2004, Plains Art Mus., Fargo, ND, 2004, Springfield Art Mus., Mo., 2004, Lee County Alliance of Arts, Ft. Myers, Fla., 2004 (Medallion, 2004), Wichita Art Mus., Kans., 2004, 2005, So. Alleghenies Mus. Art, Loretto, Pa., 2005, Showcase Gallery, San Diego, 2005, Shemer Art Ctr. and Mus., 2005, Mountain Shadow Gallery, Tucson, 2005, Internat. Soc. Expl. Artists, Cardiff, Wales, 2005, Kirsten Gallery, Seattle, 2005, So. Alleghenies Mus. Art, Loretto, Pa., 2005, Berman Mus. Art, Ursinus Coll., Collegeville, PA, 2005—06, The Continental Ctr., 2006, Kaewyn Gallery, Bothell, Wash., 2006, Sweetwater Ctr. Arts, Sewickley, 2006, Hist. Nicolai Fechin House, Taos Art Mus., 2006, galleries, Vision Gallery, Chandler, Ariz., 1997— (2d Place award, Chandler Ostrich Festival Fine Arts Print Contest, 1998), The Park Gallery, Litchfield Park, Ariz., 2003—04, Mountain Shadow Galley, Tucson, 2005—, mag., The Artist's Mag.; contbr. Docent Phoenix Art Mus., 1979-80, master docent, 1989-96; mem. Ariz. Women's Caucus Art, 1988-91. Finalist Ann. Art Competition in Exptl. Art, The Artist's Mag., 1996. Mem.: Red River Watercolor Soc., Transparent Watercolor Soc. Am., Waterworks (exhbn. chair 2003—), Q Artists, Contemporary Watercolorists Ariz. (gen. chmn. 2002—04, exhbn. chmn. 2002—04, signature), Ariz. Watercolor Assn. (assoc. 1985—88, juried 1988—, bd. mem. 1994—2001, Coatimundi Honor Soc. 1995, Nat. Watercolor Exhbn. co-chair 1999, Royal Scorpion 2000, Nat. Watercolor Exhbn. chair 2000, signature), Ariz. Artists Guild (juried 1986—), Watercolor West (juried), Watercolor Art Soc. - Houston, Taos Nat. Soc. Watercolorists (signature), Phila. Water Color Soc. (signature), Pa. Watercolor Soc. (signature), N.W. Watercolor Soc. (signature), Mo. Watercolor Soc., Internat. Soc. Exptl. Artists (signature), Calif. Watercolor Assn., San Diego Watercolor Soc. (assoc.), Nat. Watercolor Soc. (assoc.), La. Watercolor Soc. (assoc.), Am. Watercolor Soc. (assoc.). Home: 3621 E Pasadena Ave Phoenix AZ 85018-1511 Office Phone: 602-956-3783. Personal E-mail: hazelstone@earthlink.net.

STONE, JACQUELYN ELOIS, lawyer; b. Williamsburg, Va., Jan. 7, 1958; d. William Thomas and Sara Elizabeth (Cumber) Stone. BA in Am. Govt., U.Va., 1980; JD, Harvard U., 1985. Bar: Va. 1985. Legis. asst. US Ho. of Reps., Washington, 1980-82; assoc. McGuire, Woods, Battle & Boothe, LLP (now McGuireWoods LLP), Richmond, Va., 1985—94, ptnr., 1994—, mem. bd. partners, firmwide hiring ptnr. & recruiting com. chair, mem. diversity com. Bd. mem. Arts Coun. of Richmond, past pres.; bd. mem. Jr. Achievement of Ctrl. Richmond, Richmond Eye & Ear Hosp., Venture Richmond, asst. sec.; exec. com. mem. Va. Performing Arts Found.; mem. local adv. com. Local Initiatives Support Corp.; bd. mem. Va. Commn. for the Arts. Recipient Outstanding Woman Award, YWCA, 2000, Women of Achievement award, Met. Richmond Women's Bar Assn., 2005, Themis award, DuPont Women's Lawyer Network, 2005. Mem.: ABA (mem. bus. law sect. 1985—), Am. Immigration Lawyers Assn., Old Dominion Bar Assn. (mem. exec. com. 1990—92), Va. Bar Assn. (exec. com. young lawyers sect. 1988—90, chmn. membership com. 1988—90), Va. State Bar. Baptist. Avocation: travel. Office: McGuireWoods LLP One James Ctr 901 E Cary St Richmond VA 23219-4030 Office Phone: 804-775-1046. Office Fax: 804-698-2183. Business E-Mail: jstone@mcguirewoods.com.

STONE, JAMES HOWARD, management consultant; b. Chgo., Mar. 4, 1939; s. Jerome H. and Evelyn Gertrude (Teitelbaum) S.; divorced; children: Margaret Elisa, Emily Anne, Phoebe Jane. AB cum laude, Harvard U., 1960; MBA, Harvard Bus. Sch., 1962. Cert. mgmt. cons.,

1977. From staff analyst to exec. com. Stone Container Corp., Chgo., 1962—83, former exec. and audit coms., 1983—96; founder, owner, CEO, pres. Stone Mgmt. Corp., Chgo., 1969—; dir. privately-owned beverage mfr. Sheridan Beverage Co., Chgo., 1989—96; dir. privately-owned distributor and fabricator metals and metal products Fullerton Metals Co., Northbrook, Ill., 1993—98; pres. JEMP, Inc., Chgo., 2002—. Mem. strategic alliance Boston Cons. Group, 1990—; trustee, sec., exec. com. Roosevelt U., Chgo., 1983—, exec. com. edn. alliance, 1994—; co-chmn. commn. fgn. and domestic affairs Northwestern U., Evanston, Ill., 1981-85, bus. plan judge Kellogg Grad. Sch. Mgmt., 1994—; mem. vis. com. libr., lectr. U. Chgo., 1980—, The Chgo. Com., 1986—, Mid-Am. Com., Chgo., 1993-98; bd. overseers, lectr. IIT Stuart Sch. Bus., 1993—; bd. dirs. Cinema Chgo./Chgo. Film, Festival, Pilgrim Chamber Players, pres.; past pres., regional dir. Chgo. chpt. Inst. Mgmt. Cons.; past dir. Chgo. Roundtable Coun. Logistics Mgmt.; past pres., dir. Harvard Bus. Harvard Bus. Sch. Club Chgo. Contbr. articles in various trade jours. Mem. Chgo. Coun. Fgn. Rels., 1967, bd. dirs., 1974-78; bd. dirs., mem. exec. com. NCCJ, Chgo., 1985, presiding co-chmn., 1990-97; trustee Hadley Sch. Blind, Winnetka, Ill., 1985-96, chmn. planning com., 1989-96, Hadley life trustee, 1996—; vice chmn. fin. com. North Shore Congregation Israel, 1995-98; bd. dirs. Suzuki-Orff Sch., 1997-03; pres. Pilgrim Chamber Players, 2002—; former presiding co-chair Chgo. region Nat. Conf. Christians and Jews; sec., trustee, mem. exec. com. Roosevelt U.; mem. Chgo. Alliance Com.; life trustee Hadley Sch. for the Blind; vis. com. libr., patron U. Chgo.; with Northwestern U. Asher Sch. Psychiatry, Med. Sch.; bd. overseers Ill. Inst. Tech. Stuart Sch. Bus.; pres.'s cir., former dir. Chgo. Coun. Fgn. Rels.; advisor DCFS; mem. JVS Duman Loan Com.; dir. Blue Gargoyle, Little City Found.; past vice chmn. fin. com. North Shore Congregation Israel. Recipient Spirit of Life award, 2003. Mem. Coun. Logistics Mgmt. (dir. Roundtable-Chgo. 1990-94, lectr. Northwestern U. Ill. Inst. Tech.), The Exec. Club Chgo., Econs. Club Chgo., Harvard Club Chgo. (dir. 1995—), Harvard Bus. Sch. Club Chgo. (dir. 1992—, pres. 1997-99), Traffic Club Chgo., Std. Club, Northmoor Country Club, Mid-Day Club, The Casino Club, MidAm. Club, Arts Club, Juvenile Protective Assn. (trustee 1999—, dir.), The East Bank Club, Little City Found. Avocations: reading, golf, travel, writing. Office Phone: 312-236-0800. Business E-Mail: stonem@stonemgnt.com.

STONE, JAMES MERRILL, lawyer; b. Columbus, Ohio, Mar. 7, 1952; s. Irving Joseph and Dessie (Flauhaus) S. m. Winifred Ann Storkan, Apr. 11, 1981; children: Jennifer Elizabeth, Jeffrey Joseph. BA, Ohio State U., 1976; JD summa cum laude, Cleve. State U., 1986. Bar: Ohio 1986, U.S. Dist. Ct. Ohio 1986, U.S. Ct. Appeals (6th cir.) 1986. Tech. dir. Karamu House, Cleve., 1974-77; pres., gen. mgr. Merrill Stone Assocs., Inc., Cleve., 1977-83; ptnr. McDonald, Hopkins, Burke and Haber Co. LPA, Cleve., 1986—2006; ptnr., resident mgr. Jackson Lewis LLP, 2006—. Contbr. articles to profl. publs. Awards com. chairperson U.S. Inst. Theatre Tech., Cleve., 1984-89; bd. dirs. Cleve. Pops Orch., 2004-; Deacon Solon Cmty. Ch., Ohio. Frew scholar Cleve. State U., 1986. Mem. ABA, Cleve. Bar Assn., Soc. Human Resource Mgmt., Delta Theta Phi (Jaeger award 1984), City Club (Cleve.), Union Club. Republican. Home: 32638 Haver Hill Dr Solon OH 44139-1913 Office: Jackson Lewis LLP 29225 Chagrin Blvd Ste 275 Cleveland OH 44122 Home Phone: 440-349-0974; Office Phone: 216-591-0404 ext. 1418. Business E-Mail: james.stone@jacksonlewis.com.

STONE, JAMES ROBERT, surgeon; b. Greeley, Colo., Jan. 8, 1948; s. Anthony Joseph and Dolores Concetta (Pietrafeso) S.; children: Jeffrey, Marisa; m. Monica Syr-Tucker, Nov. 2005. BA, U. Colo., 1970; MD, U. Guadalajara, Mex., 1976; MBA, Madison U., 2002. Diplomate Am. Bd. Surgery, Am. Bd. Surg. Critical Care, Am. Bd. Forensic Medicine. Intern Md. Gen. Hosp., Balt., 1978-79; resident in surgery St. Joseph Hosp., Denver, 1979-83; pvt. practice Grand Junction, Colo., 1983-87; staff surgeon, dir. critical care Va. Med. Ctr., Grand Junction, 1987-88; dir. trauma surgery and critical care, chief surgery St. Francis Hosp., Colorado Springs, Colo., 1988-91; pvt. practice Kodiak, Alaska, 1991-92; with Summit Surg. Assocs., 1992-96; asst. dir. trauma Tristate Trauma System, Erie, Pa., 1996-99; med. dir. LifeStar Aeromed, Erie, Pa., 1997-99; dir. trauma, sr. assoc. physician, med. dir. emergency svcs. ISJ Mayo Health, 1999—2001; clin. prof. surgery U. Minn. Med. Sch., Mpls., 1999—2001, dir. trauma/EMS med. dir., sr. assoc.; gen., thoracic and vascular surgery Caylor-Nickel Clinic, Bluffton, Ind., 2001—02, Emergency Medicine of Ind., Ft. Wayne, Ind., 2002—04; CEO Guymon Surg. Cons., Okla., 2004—. Asst. clin. prof. surgery U. Colo. Health Sci. Ctr., Denver, 1984-96; pres. Stone Aire Cons., Grand Junction, 1988—; owner, operator Jjnka Ranch and Stuno Ranch, Flourissant, Colo.; spl. advisor CAP, wing med. officer, 1992-96; advisor med. com. unit, 1990-92; advisor Colo. Ground Team Search and Rescue, 1994-96; cons. Am. Med. Forensic Specialists, Berkeley, Ca., 2002-; Guymon surigical cons., 2004—. Contbr. articles to profl. jours.; inventor in field. Bd. dirs. Mesa County Cancer Soc., 1988-89, Colo. Trauma Inst., 1988-91; chmn. Guymon Pioneer Days Rodeo. Colo. Speaks out on Health grantee, 1988; recipient Bronze medal of Valor Civil Air Patrol; named one of Am.'s Top Surgeons, 2007. Fellow Denver Acad. Surgery, Southwestern Surg. Congress, Am. Coll. Chest Physicians, Am. Coll. Surgeons (trauma com. Colo. chpt.), Am. Coll. Critical Care; mem. Am. Coll. Physician Execs., Soc. Critical Care (task force 1988—), Assn. Air Med. Physicians. Roman Catholic. Avocations: horse breeding, hunting, fishing. Home Phone: 580-333-6544; Office Phone: 580-338-6666. Business E-Mail: jrstone@ptsi.net.

STONE, JED, lawyer; b. Chgo., Sept. 30, 1949; s. William P. and Bernice (Birenhotz) S.; children— Meghan Elizabeth, Allison Leigh, Benjamin William. B.A. with honors, Lake Forest Coll., 1971; J.D. Chgo. U. 1975. Bar: Ill. 1976, Wis. 1984, U.S. Dist. Ct. (no. dist.) Ill. 1976, U.S. Ct. Appeals (7th cir.) 1983, U.S. Ct. Appeals (5th cir.) 1985, U.S. Ct. Appeals (11th cir.) 1986, U.S. Supreme Ct. 1984, U.S. Dist. Ct. (cen. dist.) Ill. 1988. Cert. Criminal Trial Adv.; diplomate Nat. Bd. Trial Advocacy, 1984. Staff atty. Lawyer's Com. Civil Rights Under Law and Land of Lincoln Legal Aid, Cairo, Ill., 1975; sr. staff atty. Prairie State Legal Services, Waukegan, Ill., 1975-77; ptnr. The Law Offices of Jed Stone, Ltd., Chgo.; lectr. Ill. Inst. Continuing Legal Edn., Ill. State Bar Assn. Law Edn. Series; mem. faculty Nat. Criminal Def. Coll., Macon, Ga., 1994, 95; vis. lectr. Russian Acad. of Law & Sci., St. Petersburg, Russia, 1995. Author: (with others) Defending Illinois Criminal Cases, 1988; author: Illinois Criminal Defence Motions, 1993. Mem. Ill. Coalition Against the Death Penalty (pres. 1995); pres., bd. dirs. Prairie State Legal Svcs., Inc., 1982-84; bd. dirs., Lake County Urban League, Waukegan, 1981—; bd. mem. alumni bd. gov's. Lake Forest College, Ill., 1981-87, treas., pres. 1994-95, bd. dirs. Ill. Attys. for Criminal Justice. Mem. NAACP (life), Urban League (life), Nat. Assn. Criminal Def. Lawyers (various coms.), Ill. Attys. Criminal Justice (bd. dirs. 1986—), Lake County Bar Assn. (chmn. criminal law sect. 1983-86). N.Y. State Defender Assn. (faculty defender inst.). Democrat. Jewish. Office: Stone & Associates LLC 415 Washington St Ste 107 Waukegan IL 60085 E-mail: jstone@jedstone.com. *

STONE, JEREMY JUDAH, professional society administrator; b. NYC, Nov. 23, 1935; s. I.F. and Esther (Roisman) S.; m. Betty Jane Yannet, June 16, 1957. BS magna cum laude, Swarthmore Coll., 1957, LL.D. (hon.), 1985; PhD, Stanford U., 1960. Research mathematician Stanford Research Inst., 1960-62; mem. profl. staff Hudson Inst., Croton-on-Hudson, 1962-64; research asso., arms control and disarmament Harvard Ctr. Internat. Affairs, 1964-66; asst. prof. math., lectr. polit. sci. Pomona Coll., Claremont, Calif., 1966-68; pres. Fedn. Am. Scientists, Washington, 1970-2000, Catalytic Diplomacy, 1999—. Author: Containing the Arms Race; Some Concrete Proposals, 1966, Strategic Persuasion, 1967, "Every Man Should Try." Adventures of a Public Interest Activist, 1999. Recipient award for pub. svc. Forum on Physics and Soc., Am. Phys. Soc., 1979, Fedn. of Am. Scientists Pub. Svc. award, 1994; Social Sci. Rsch. Coun. fellow in econs. Stanford U., 1968-69, Coun. Fgn. Rels. internat. affairs fellow, 1969-70. Mem. Coun. Fgn. Rels., Internat. Inst. Strategic Studies, Phi Beta Kappa. Home and Office: 5615 Warwick Pl Bethesda MD 20815-5503 E-mail: Jstone@catalyticdiplomacy.org.

STONE, JOSHUA JAMES, military officer; b. Jacksonville, NC, Sept. 25, 1975; s. James Kenneth and Patricia Ann Stone; m. Stacey Ann Mayberry (div.); m. Maeyoung Crosby, Feb. 13, 2004; children: Gregory, Hannah, Tyler, Dyasia, Samari. AA, Centra Tex. Coll., Ga., 2004. Cannon crew mem. US Army, Schofield Barracks, Hawaii, 1996—2000, chem. specialist Ft. Stewart, Ga., 2000—07, electronic warfare officer, 2007—. With US Army, 1996—. Mem.: Chem. Corp. Cath. Avocations: hunting, classic cars, sports. Home: 407 Lancaster Hinesville GA 31313 Office: 1-30th In Ft Steward Fort Stewart GA 31314 Business E-Mail: joshua.j.stone@us.army.mil.

STONE, JOSS (JOSCELYN EVE STOKER), singer; b. Dover, Eng., Apr. 11, 1987; d. Richard and Wendy Stoker. Winning contestant Jr. Star for a Night, BBC TV talent show, 2002; former back-up singer for Britney Spears. Spokeswoman The Gap, 2005. Singer: (albums) The Soul Sessions, 2003, Mind Body & Soul, 2004 (Capital Award, London's favourite UK album, 2005), Introducing Joss Stone, 2007, (songs) Family Affair (Grammy award for Best Group Vocal R&B Performance, 2007); actor: (films) Eragon, 2006. Recipient Brit Award best British female solo artist, 2005, Brit Award best British urban act, 2005, Grammy Nomination best new artist, 2005, Grammy Nomination best female pop vocal performance, 2005, Grammy Nomination best pop vocal performance, 2005. *

STONE, KARIN L., bank executive; B, Gustavus Adolphus Coll., St. Peter, Minn.; MBA, U. Minn., Mpls. Various positions in mut. fund bus. and mktg. systems area Fin. Advisors subs. to chief of staff to chmn. and CEO Am. Express, head strategic and oper. devel. Am. Express Fin. Direct; with Ford Motor Credit Co., Walker Digital, Nat. City Corp., Cleve., 2001—, sr. v.p. corp. mktg. Founding mem., mem. adv. bd. NE Ohio Exec. Mktg. Forum. Bd. trustees Cleve. Inst. Music, Gustavus Adolphus, Cmty. Partnership for Arts and Culture; mem. steering com. Coll. 360. Office: Nat City Corp Nat City Ctr 1900 E Ninth St Cleveland OH 44114-3484 Office Phone: 216-222-2000. *

STONE, LARRY DEAN, consumer products company executive; b. North Wilkesboro, NC, July 18, 1951; s. Clyde D. and Irene (Mamess) Stone; m. Diane Adams, Aug. 23, 1969; children: Larry Jr., Chris. Student in bus., Wilkes Community Coll., Wilkesboro, NC, 1971. With mailroom and printshop Lowe's Cos., Inc., North Wilkesboro, 1969-70, area gen. mgr., 1986-89; office trainee Lowe's of Hickory, NC, 1970-71; office and credit mgr. Lowe's of Raleigh, NC, 1971-75, sales mgr. NC, 1975-78; store mgr. Lowe's of Cary, NC, 1978-83, Lowe's of North Wilkesboro, 1983-86; v.p. store merchandising Lowe's Cos., North Wilkesboro, 1989-92, v.p. merchandising, 1992-95, sr. v.p. sales opers., 1995-96, exec. v.p. store opers., 1996, sr. exec. v.p. store opers., 2003—05, sr. exec. v.p. merchandising and mktg., 2005—06, pres., COO, 2006—. Bd. dir. North Wilkesboro Mchts. Assn., 1985, North Wilkesboro Homebuilders Assn., 1985. With US Army, 1970—76. Mem.: Rotary (treas. North Wilkesboro chpt. 1982-84), Elks. Republican. Baptist. Avocations: golf, swimming. Office: Lowe's Cos Inc PO Box 1111 North Wilkesboro NC 28656 *

STONE, LAWRENCE MAURICE, lawyer, educator; b. Malden, Mass., Mar. 25, 1931; s. Abraham Jacob and Pauline (Bernstein) S.; m. Anna Jane Clark, June 15, 1963; children: Abraham Dean, Ethan Goldthwaite, Katharine Elisheva. AB magna cum laude, Harvard U., 1953, JD magna cum laude, 1956. Bar: Mass. 1956, Calif. 1958. Rsch. asst. Am. Law Inst., Cambridge, Mass., 1956-57; assoc. Irell and Manella, LA, 1957-61, ptnr., 1963, 79-96, of counsel, 1997—; internat. tax coordinator U.S. Treasury Dept., Washington, 1961-62, tax. legis. counsel, 1964-66; prof. law U. Calif., Berkeley, 1966-78. Vis. prof. law Yale U., New Haven, 1969, Hebrew U. Jerusalem, 1973-74, U. So. Calif., L.A., 1984; mem. adv. group to commr. IRS, Washington, 1973-74; mem. President's Adv. Commn. on Tax Ct. Appointments, Washington, 1976-80; tax advisory bd. Little Brown Co., 1994-96. Author: (with Doernberg) Federal Income Taxation of Corporations and Partnerships, (with Klein, Bankman and Bittker) Federal Income Taxation; bd. editors Harvard Law Rev., 1955-56. Fellow Am. Coll. Tax Counsel; mem. ABA, Am. Law Inst., Internat. Fiscal Inst., Am. Arbitration Assn., L.A. County Bar Assn. (recipient Dana Latham award 1995), Phi Beta Kappa. Office: Irell & Manella 1800 Avenue Of The Stars Los Angeles CA 90067-4276

STONE, LAWRENCE MYNATT, publishing executive; b. Balt., June 24, 1945; s. David G. and Clara Ruth (Coxey) S.; m. Lois V. Smith, June 10, 1967; children: Bradley Michael, Geoffrey David. BA, U. Iowa, 1968. Prof. Northeastern Bible Coll., Essex Fells, NJ, 1968-69; missionary Africa Evangelical Fellowship, Ndola, Zambia, 1969-71; asst. to production mgr. Am. Bible Soc., NYC, 1971-72; book club mgr. Iversen-Norman Assocs., NYC, 1972-75; editl. v.p. Thomas Nelson Pubs., Nashville, 1976-85; pres. Rutledge Hill Press, Nashville, 1985-99, pub., 1999—2004, pub. emeritus, 2005—. Book and libr. adv. com. U.S. Info. Agency, Washington, 1984-88; editor in field; ghost writer. Office: Rutledge Hill Press PO Box 141000 Nashville TN 37214-1000 Home Phone: 615-292-7322. Personal E-mail: larryrhp@aol.com. Business E-Mail: lstone@thomasnelson.com.

STONE, LINDA, former computer company executive, consultant, speaker, writer; Grad., Evergreen State Coll.; M. in Edn., Cognitive Psychology, and Librarianship, U. of Washington. Primary sch. teacher; sch. librarian Seattle; systems analyst, market devel. mgr., software evangelist and asst. for special projects for CEO John Sculley Apple Computer, 1986—93; joined as dir. special projects under Nathan Myhrvold Microsoft Corp., 1993, co-founder, dir. Virtual Worlds Group / Social Computing Group, v.p. corp. and industry initiatives, 2000—02; cons., 2002—. Adj. faculty NYU Tisch Sch. Arts, 1998—99; speaker, expert online social life and virtual communities. Contbr. NY Times, Newsweek, Wired, The Economist, The Boston Globe and hundreds of blogs. Nat. bd. World Wildlife Fund, Philanthropic Collaborative for Integrative Medicine; advisory bd. Rochester Inst. Tech. Lab Social Computing; advisor hidden brain drain task force Center for Work-Life Policy. Named Outstanding Regional Volunteer of the Year, F.I.R.S.T. 2002; named one of 100 leaders of the digital revolution, Upside mag., 1996. Achievements include coined the term continuous partial attention to describe the way people work and live with information and communication overload.

STONE, MARVIN JULES, hematologist, oncologist, educator; b. Columbus, Ohio, Aug. 3, 1937; s. Roy J. and Lillian (Bedwinek) S.; m. Jill Feinstein, June 29, 1958; children: Nancy Lillian, Robert Howard. Student, Ohio State U., 1955-58; SM in Pathology, U. Chgo., 1962, MD with honors, 1963. Diplomate Am. Bd. Internal Medicine, (Hematology, Med. Oncology). Intern ward med. svc. Barnes Hosp., St. Louis, 1963-64, asst. resident, 1964-65; clin. assoc. arthritis and rheumatism br. Nat. Inst. Arthritis and Metabolic Diseases, NIH, Bethesda, Md., 1965-68; resident in medicine, ACP scholar Parkland Meml. Hosp., Dallas, 1968-69; fellow in hematology-oncology, dept. internal medicine U. Tex. Southwestern Med. Sch., Dallas, 1969-70, instr. dept. internal medicine, 1970-71, asst. prof., 1971-73, assoc. prof., 1974-76, clin. prof., 1976—, chmn. bioethics com., 1979-81; mem. faculty and steering com. immunology grad. program, Grad. Sch. Biomed. Scis., U. Tex. Health Sci. Ctr., Dallas, 1975, adj. mem., 1976—. Dir. Charles A. Sammons Cancer Ctr., chief oncology, dir. immunology, co-dir. divsn. hematology-oncology, attending physician Baylor U. Med. Ctr., Dallas, 1976—; v.p. med. staff Parkland Meml. Hosp., Dallas, 1982. Contbr. chpts. to books, articles to profl. jours. Chmn. com. patient-aid Greater Dallas/Ft. Worth chpt. Leukemia Soc. Am., 1971-76, chmn. med. adv. com., 1978-80, bd. dirs., 1971-80; mem. v.p. Dallas unit Am. Cancer Soc., 1977-78, pres., 1978—; mem. adv. bd. Baylor U. Med. Ctr. Found., Marvin J. Stone Libr., Baylor Inst. Immunology Rsch., 1999. With USPHS, 1965-68. Recipient Wings of Eagles award, Baylor Health Care Sys., 2001, Disting. Svc. award, U. Chgo., 2002, Lifetime Achievement award, Internat. Soc. Study of Waldenstrom's Macroglobulinemia, 2004. Master ACP (gov. No. Tex. 1993-97, laureate Tex. chpt. 2000); fellow Royal Soc. Medicine (London); mem. AMA, Am. Assn. Immunologists, Am. Soc. Hematology, Internat. Soc. Hematology, Coun. Thrombosis, Am. Heart Assn. (established investigator 1970-75), Am. Soc. Clin. Oncology (edn. com. 2002-05, career devel. com. 2002-05), Am. Osler Soc. (bd. govs. 1997-2000, 2005—, v.p. 2001-03, pres. 2003-04), Am. Assn. for Cancer Rsch., So. Soc. Clin. Investigation, Tex. Med. Assn., Dallas County Med. Soc., Clin. Immunology Soc., Phi Beta Kappa, Sigma Xi, Alpha Omega Alpha. Office: Baylor U Med Ctr Charles A Sammons Cancer Ctr 3500 Gaston Ave Dallas TX 75246-2096 Business E-Mail: marvins@baylorhealth.edu.

STONE, MARY ANN, literature and language educator; b. Freelandville, Ind., Jan. 30, 1934; d. Ralph D. and Leona Green; m. Paul R. Stone, Dec. 27, 1953; children: Sunny, Karen, Kerry, Kevin. BS, Ind. State U., 1964, MS, 1983. Lang. arts tchr. Ganada HS, Ganada, Ariz., 1983—2002. Pres. Ganada Edn. Assn., Ganada, Ariz., chmn. lang. arts; faculty coun. Ganada HS. Chmn. bd. dirs. Ganada Presbyn. Avocations: reading, gardening, needlecrafts. Home: 586 Bay N Ct Franklin IN 46131 E-mail: magreenstone@earthlink.net.

STONE, MERRILL BRENT, lawyer; b. Jersey City, Aug. 16, 1951; s. Leonard and Claire (Orlean) S.; m. Geri Ellen Satkin, Nov. 24, 1976; children: Jacqueline Blair, Erica Lauren. AB summa cum laude, Rutgers U., 1973; JD, Columbia U., 1976. Bar: N.J. 1976, N.Y. 1977, Fla. 1981, U.S. Dist. Ct. N.J. 1976, U.S. Dist. Ct. (so. dist.) N.Y. 1977, U.S. Dist. Ct. (so. dist.) Fla. 1983. Assoc. Kelley Drye & Warren, NYC, 1976-84, resident Miami, 1983-85, ptnr. NYC, 1985—, mng. ptnr., 1992—2003. Editor: (comments section) Columbia Human Rights Law Rev., N.Y.C., 1975-76. Trustee Greater Miami C. of C., 1984-85. Named Harlan Fiske Stone Scholar, Columbia Law Sch., N.Y.C., 1975-76. Mem. ABA (bus. bankruptcy com. sect. on bus. law, banking law com.), Am. Soc. Corp. Secs., Fla. Bar Assn., Club 101, Phi Beta Kappa, Pi Sigma Alpha. Office: Kelley Drye & Warren LLP 101 Park Ave New York NY 10178-0002 Business E-Mail: mstone@kelleydrye.com.

STONE, MICHAEL HOWARD, psychiatry educator; b. Syracuse, NY, Oct. 27, 1933; s. Moses Howard and Corinne (Gittleman) S.; m. Clarice Joan Kestenbaum, (div. 1979); children: David, John; m. Beth Janine Eichstaedt. BA, Cornell U., 1954, MD, 1958. Diplomate Am. Bd. Psychiatry and Neurology. Residency in psychiatry Columbia Coll. of Physicians & Surgeons, NYC, 1963-66; asst. prof. psychiatry Columbia Coll. Physicians and Surgeons, NYC, 1973-77; assoc. prof. Cornell Med. Coll., NYC, 1977-80; prof. psychiatry U. Conn., Farmington, 1980-84; clin. dir. U. Conn. Dept. Psychiatry, Farmington, 1980-84; prof. clin. psychiatry Mt. Sinai Sch. Medicine, NYC, 1984-85, Cornell Med. Coll., NYC, 1985-88, Columbia Coll. Physicians and Surgeons, NYC, 1988—; dir. research Middletown (N.Y.) Psychiat. Ctr. Visiting prof. psychiatry Albert Einstein Med. Ctr., N.Y.C., 1987—; lectr. in field, 1987-; prof. clin. psychiatry Columbia Coll. Physicians and Surgeons. Author: The Borderline Syndromes, 1980, The Fate of Borderline Patients, 1990; editor: Borderline Disorders, 1981, Treating Schizophrenic Patients, 1983, Essential Papers on Borderline, 1985, Personality Disorders: Treatable and Untreatable, 2006; host (TV show) Most Evil, 2006-07; contbr. over 200 articles to profl. jours. Recipient Hematology Fellowship NIH, 1961-63. Fellow Am. Psychiat. Assn.; mem. Am. Pschopathol. Assn., Am. Coll. Psychiatrists. Republican. Jewish. Avocations: piano, collecting rare books, languages. Home and Office: 225 Central Park W New York NY 10024-6027 Home Phone: 212-799-1449; Office Phone: 212-758-2000. Personal E-mail: mhstonemd@yahoo.com.

STONE, OLIVER, film director, producer, scriptwriter; b. NYC, Sept. 15, 1946; s. Louis and Jacqueline (Goddet) S.; m. Najwa Sarkis May 22, 1971 (div. 1977); m. Elizabeth Stone June 6, 1981 (div. 1993); 2 children. Student, Yale U., 1965; BFA, NYU Film Sch., 1971. Tchr., Cholon, Vietnam, 1965-66; wiper U.S. Mcht. Marine, 1966; taxi driver NYC, 1971. Screenwriter: Midnight Express, 1978 (Acad. award for screenplay, Writers Guild Am. for screenplay), Evita, 1996; screenwriter, dir.: Seizure, 1974 The Hand, 1981, (with John Milius) Conan, the Barbarian, 1982 (writer), Scarface, 1983, (writer with Michael Cimino) Year of the Dragon, 1985, (writer with David Lee Henry) 8 Million Ways to Die, 1986; dir., writer (with Richard Boyle) Salvador, 1986, Platoon, 1986 (Acad. award for best dir., Dirs. Guild award, British Acad. award),(documenatary) Looking for Fidel, 2004; co-writer, dir.: Wall Street, 1987, Talk Radio, 1988, The Doors, 1991, Any Given Sunday, 1999; screenwriter, prodr., dir.: Born on the Fourth of July, 1989 (Acad. award for best dir. 1990), Heaven & Earth, 1993, Comandante, 2003, Looking for Fidel, 2004, Alexander, 2004, World Trade Center (Hollywood Dir. of the Yr. Hollywood Awards, 2006), 2006; co-writer, prodr., dir.: JFK, 1991, Natural Born Killers, 1994, Nixon, 1995 (Acad. award nominee for best screenplay with Stephen J. Rivele and Christopher Wilkinson 1996); prodr.: Love, Death, 1972, Sugar Cookies, 1973, Reversal of Fortune, 1991, South Central, 1992, Zebrahead, 1992, The Joy Luck Club, 1993, The New Age, 1994, The People vs. Larry Flynt, 1996, Savior, 1998, The Corruptor, 1999, (TV mini-series) Wild Palms, 1993; exec. prodr. The Iron Mze, 1991, Freeway, 1996, Killer: A Journal of Murder, 1996, Indictment: The McMartin Trial, 1995 (Emmy award), Cold Around the Heart, 1997, The Last Days of Kennedy and King, 1998, The Day Reagan was Shot, 2003; dir. only (short film) Last Year in Viet Nam, 1971, Mad Man of Martinique, 1979, U-Turn, 1992, Persona Non Grata, 2003; film appearances include The Battle of Lover's Return, 1971, The Hand, 1981, Platoon, 1986, Wall Street, 1987, Born on the Fourth of July, 1989, The Doors, 1991, Nixon (voice only), 1995, Any Given Sunday, 1999. Served with U.S. Army, 1967-68. Decorated Purple Heart with oak leaf cluster, Bronze Star; Lifetime Achievement award, Stockholm Internat. Film Festival, 2004. Mem. Writers Guild Am., Dirs. Guild Am., Acad. Motion Picture Arts and Scis.

STONE, PATRICIA A., special education services professional, consultant; d. Henry and Rita Belair; m. James Henry Stone, Oct. 27, 1984; children: Cassandra L., Allison M., Brian J. BS, Fitchburg State Coll., Mass., 1984; MEd, Lesley Coll., Cambridge, Mass., 1989; cert. in advanced grad. study in ednl. leadership, Rivier Coll., Nashua, NH, 2006. Cert. elem. edn. N.H., Mass., spl. edn. N.H., Mass., assessment specialist N.H., spl. edn. adminstrn. N.H. Tchr. spl. edn. Sch. Adminstrv. Unit 28 Windham Sch. Dist., NH, 1985—99, Sch. Adminstrv. Unit 57 Salem Sch. Dist., 1999—2001, assessment specialist, 2001—04, asst. dir. student svcs., 2004—06, dir. student svcs., 2006—. Chmn. bd. Windham Coop. Kindergarten, NH, 1996—97; adj. instr. U. N.H., Durham, 2004—; exec. bd. United Way Success by 6, Salem, 2004—. Mem.: ASCD, NH Assn. Spl. Edn. Adminstrs., NH Assn. Sch. Psychologists, Assn. Specialization Intellectual Functioning, Alpha Delta Kappa. Avocations: reading, crafts. Home: 11 Brookdale Rd Salem NH 03079-1902 Office: SAU 57 Salem Sch Dist 38 Geremonty Dr Salem NH 03079

STONE, RICHARD ALAN, medical educator; b. Combridge, Mass., Nov. 21, 1945; s. Jack David and Abigail Stone. BA, Brown U., Providence, 1964; attended, Columbia U., NY, 1966; MD, Tufts U., Boston, 1970. Cert. Nat. Bd. Med. Examiners, 1971, diplomate Am. Bd. Internal Medicine, 1973, Am. Bd. Nephrology, 1976, lic. Calif., 1975. Intern medicine Montefiore Hosp., Bronx, 1970—71, asst. resident medicine, 1971—72; fellow nephrology Duke U. Med. Ctr. Dept Biochemistry, Durham, NC, 1972—74; asst. prof. medicine U. Calif. Sch. Medicine, La Jolla, 1974—78, assoc. prof. medicine, 1978—79; dir. Vets. Adminstrn. Hosp. Hemodialysis Unit, San Diego, 1974—79; chmn. nephrology section. Eisenhower Med. Ctr., Rancho Mirage, Calif., 1979—, chmn. dept. medicine, 1982—84, sr. attending physician, 1985—; ASH specialist clin. hypertension, 1999—. Contbr. articles various profl. jours. Mem.: Riverside County Heart Assn., Internat. Soc. Nephrology, Am. Soc. Artificial Internal Organs, Southern Calif. Kidney Found., Nat. Kidney Found., Am. Assn. Advancement Scis., Am. Heart Assn., Am. Fed. Clin. Rsch., Am. Soc. Nephrology. Office: Eisenhower Medical Ctr 39000 Bob Hope Dr Ste 316 Rancho Mirage CA 92270-3221

STONE, RICHARD JAMES, lawyer; b. Apr. 30, 1945; s. Milton M. and Ruth Jean (Manaster) S.; m. Lee Lawrence, Sept. 1, 1979; children: Robert Allyn, Katherine Jenney, Grant Lawrence. BA in Econs., U. Chgo., 1967; JD, UCLA, 1970. Bar: Calif. 1971, Oreg. 1994, D.C., 2000, Wash. State, 2004. Assoc. O'Melveny & Myers, LA, 1971-77; dep. asst. gen. counsel US Dept. Def., Washington, 1978-79; asst. to sec. US Dept. Energy, Washington, 1979-80; counsel Sidley & Austin, LA, 1981, ptnr., 1982-88; ptnr., head litig. dept. Milbank, Tweed, Hadley & McCloy, LA, 1988-94; mng. ptnr. Zelle & Larson, LLP, LA, 1994-97; counsel Ball Janik LLP, Portland, Oreg., 1998—2006, ptnr., 2007—. Gen. counsel and staff dir. Study of L.A. Civil Disturbance for Bd. Police Commrs., 1992; adj. prof. law Lewis and Clark Northwestern Sch. Law, 1998-99; lawyer rep. 9th Cir. Jud. Conf., 1998-99; mem. legal ethics com. Oreg. State Bar, 2002-03, com. on spl. rules, 2002-03. Editor-in-chief: UCLA Law Rev., 1970. Mem. Pub. Sector Task Force, Calif., State Senate Select Com. on Long Range Policy Planning, 1985-86, U.S. del. Micronesian Polit. Status Negotiations, 1978-79; with U.S. Mil. Acad. at West Point, Oreg. Field Force, 2003—; mem. adv. panel Coun. Energy Resource Tribes, 1981-85; mem. vestry St. Aidan's Episcopal Ch., 1990-93, 97-98, sr. warden, 1998; dir. Legal Aid Found. L.A., 1991-99, officer, 1994-98, pres., 1997-98; dir. Portland City United Soccer Club, 1999-2000; classic coach, 2002-04. Recipient Amos Alonzo Stagg medal and Howell Murray Alumni medal U. Chgo., 1967; honoree Nat. Conf. Black Mayors, 1980; recipient spl. citation for outstanding performance Sec. Dept. Energy, 1981. Fellow Am. Bar Found.; mem. ABA, Fed. Bar Assn., Calif. Bar Assn., Oreg. Bar Assn., Wash. Bar Assn., L.A. County Bar Assn. (trustee 1986-88), D.C. Bar Assn., Assn. Bus. Trial Lawyers, Multnomah County Bar Assn., Phi Gamma Delta. Home: 3675 NW Gordon St Portland OR 97210-1285 Office: Ball Janik LLP 101 SW Main St 11th Fl Portland OR 97204-3228 Office Phone: 503-228-2525. Business E-Mail: rstone@bjllp.com.

STONE, ROBERT G., JR., water transportation executive; BA, Harvard U., 1947. Chmn. & pres. States Marine Lines; chmn. Kirby Corp., 1983—95, chmn. emeritus & dir., 1995—. Bd. dir. Chubb Corp., Core Industries Inc., Corning Inc., NovaCare Inc., Pittston Co., Russell Reynolds Assoc., Tandem Computers Inc., Tejas Gas Corp.; mem. bd. adv. Arcadia Partners; lead investor Industrial Capital Group, Intersouth Partners, Morgan Holland Venture Partners, Mayfield Fund. Fellow Harvard Corp., 1975—95, sr. fellow, 1995—2002. With US Army, 1943—45. Fellow: Am. Acad. Arts & Sci.; mem.: N.Y. Yacht Club (commodore), Augusta Nat. Golf Club. Achievements include world record in 2000 meter heavyweight crew, captain, 1947. Office: Kirby Corporation Suite 1000 55 Waugh Dr PO Box 1745 Houston TX 77251-1745

STONE, ROGER DAVID, environmentalist; b. NYC, Aug. 4, 1934; s. Patrick William and Kathleen Mary Stone; married; 1 child. BA in English, Yale U., 1955. Asst. to pub. Time Mag., 1959-61, corr., news bur. chief San Francisco, Rio, Paris, 1961-68; asst. to pres. Time Inc., NYC, 1968-70; v.p. internat. dept. Chase Manhattan Bank, NYC, 1970-74; pres. Ctr. for Inter-Am. Rels., NYC, 1975-82; v.p. World Wildlife Fund, 1982-86, sr. fellow, 1986-90; vis. fellow, cons. on environ. issues Coun. on Fgn. Rels., 1990-92; vice chmn. ECO Inc., Washington, 1992-96; pres. Sustainable Devel. Inst., Washington, 1993—. Vis. lectr. Yale Ctr. Internat. and Area Studies, 1994-95; mem. external adv. bd. Yale Inst. Biospheric Studies. Author: Dreams of Amazonia, 1985, The Voyage of the Sanderling, 1990, Wildlands and Human Needs, 1991, The Nature of Development: Reports from the Rural Tropics on the Quest for Sustainable Economic Growth, 1992, Fair Tide: Sailing Toward Long Island's Future, 1996, Tropical Forests and the Human Spirit = Journeys to the Brink of Hope, 2001; guest editor: Am. Prospect, 2007—; contbr. chpts. to books; contbr. articles to Time, Life, Life en Espanol, Fgn. Affairs, N.Y. Times, Internat. Herald Tribune, Christian Sci. Monitor, Harvard Bus. Rev., USA Today Mag., Cruising World, Conservation Found. Letter, others. Bd. dirs. Astrolabe, Inc., Cintas Found.; v.p. Armand G. Erpf Fund, Sotterley Found.; sec. St. Mary's River Watershed Assn.; former bd. dirs. U. Andes Found.; former bd. dirs. and exec. com. World Wildlife Fund-U.S., Ctr. for Inter-Am. Rels., Ams. Found., Accion Internat., Arts Internat., others. Lt. (j.g.) USN, 1956-59. Mem.: Century Assn. Democrat. Episcopalian. Avocation: sailing. Home: 1527 30th St Nw # B-32 Washington DC 20007 Office Phone: 202-338-1017. Fax: 202-337-9639. E-mail: susdev@igc.org.

STONE, SAMUEL BECKNER, lawyer; b. Martinsville, Va., Feb. 4, 1934; s. Paul Raymond and Mildred (Beckner) S.; m. Shirley Ann Gregory, June 18, 1955; children: Paul Gregory, Daniel Taylor. BSEE, Va. Polytech. Inst. & State U., 1955; JD, George Wash. U., 1960. Bar: Md. 1960, Calif. 1963, Patent and Trademark Office. Patent examiner, 1955-58; patent adv. Naval Ordinance Lab., Silver Spring, Md., 1958-59; assoc. Thomas & Crickenberger, Washington, 1959-61, Beckman Instruments Inc., Fullerton, Calif., 1961-65, Lyon & Lyon, LA, 1965-72, ptnr., 1972—2002, mng. ptnr. Irvine, Calif., 1982-2000. Judge Disneyland Com. Svc. Awards, Anaheim, 1987. Mem. Orange County Bar Assn. (bd. dirs. 1988-91, travel seminar chair 1986-92), Orange County Patent Law Assn. (pres. 1987, bd. exec. com. 1987-90), Calif. Bar Assn. (intellectual property sect. bd. 1987-90), Am. Arbitration Assn. (intellectual property panel neutral arbitrators 1997-2000), Am. Electronics Assn. (lawyers com. 1988-99, co-chair 1996-97), Orange County Venture Group (dir. 1985-99, pres. 1996-97), Rams Booster Club (dir. 1984-90), Pacific Club (mem. legal adv. com., chair 1989-92, bd. dirs. 1999-2002). Republican. Avocations: tennis, waterskiing, music. Home: 1612 Antigua Way Newport Beach CA 92660-4344 Office: Orrick Herrington & Sutcliffe LLP 4 Park Plz Ste 1600 Irvine CA 92614 Office Phone: 949-567-6700. Business E-Mail: sstone@orrick.com.

STONE, SHARON, actress; b. Meadville, Pa., Mar. 10, 1958; d. Joe and Dorothy S; m. George Englund Jr. (div.); m. Michael Greenburg, Aug. 18, 1984 (div. Jan. 20, 1987); m. Phil Bronstein, Feb. 14, 1998 (div. Jan. 29, 2004); 3 adopted sons, Roan Joseph, Laird Vonne, Quinn. Diploma in Creative Writing and Fine Arts, Edinboro State U. Model Eileen Ford Modeling Agy.; owner Chaos prodn. co. Actress (films) Stardust Memories, 1980, Deadly Blessing, 1981, Irreconcilable Differences, 1984, King Solomon's Mines, 1985, Allan Quatermain and the Lost City of Gold, 1986, Cold Steel, 1987, Police Academy 4: Citizens on Patrol, 1987, Action Jackson, 1988, Above the Law, 1988, Beyond the Stars, 1989 (Personal Choice award), Total Recall, 1990, Year of the Gun, 1991, Diary of a Hitman, 1991, He Said/She Said, 1991, Scissors, 1991, Basic Instinct, 1991, Where Sleeping Dogs Lie, 1992, Last Action Hero, 1993, Sliver, 1993, Intersection, 1994, The Specialist, 1994, (also co-prodr.) The Quick and the Dead, 1995 (also co-prodr.), Casino, 1995 (Golden Globe award for best actress in film 1996, Acad. award nominee for best actress 1996), Diabolique, 1996, Last Dance, 1996, Sphere, 1998, The Mighty, 1998 (Golden Global nominee), Antz, 1998 (voice), Gloria, 1999, The Muse, 1999, Simpatico, 1999, Beautiful Joe, 2000, Picking Up the Pieces, 2000, Cold Creek Manor, 2003, Cold Creek Manor, 2003, Catwoman, 2004, Jiminy Glick in La La Wood, 2004, A Different Loyalty, 2004, Broken Flowers, 2005, Alpha Dog, 2006, Basic Instinct 2, 2006, Bobby, 2006; TV appearances include Not Just Another Affair, 1982, Bay City Blues, 1983, Calendar Girl Murders, 1984, The Vegas Strip Wars, 1984, War and Remembrance, 1988, Tears in the Rain, 1988, (guest) The Larry Sanders Show, 1994, Big Guns Talk: The Story of the Western (tv spl.), 1997; narrator: Harlow: The Blond Bombshell, 1993, If These Walls Could Talk 2, 2000, Harold and the Purple Crayon, 2001, Cold Creek Manor, 2003. Office: Care Guy McElwaine PO Box 7304 North Hollywood CA 91603-7304 *

STONE, SHELLEY CLYDE, III, art educator, archaeologist; b. Washington, May 15, 1952; s. Shelley Clyde Stone Jr. and Charlene Fairchild Stone; m. Fleur Delis Dahilig, June 12, 1998; children: Rachel Jade, Lourdes Grace. BA, Ind. U., Bloomington, 1974; PhD, Princeton U., NJ, 1981. Prof. art history Calif. State U., Bakersfield, 1998—, chair liberal studies, 2002—. Recipient Rome prize, Am. Acad., Rome, 1981; John Williams White fellow, Arthur Parsons fellow, Am. Sch. Classical Study, Athens, 1977-79. Mem.: Archaeol. Inst. Am., Coll. Art Assn. Office: Calif State Univ Liberal Studies 9001 Stockdale Hwy Bakersfield CA 93311-1022 Home Phone: 661-873-9035; Office Phone: 661-654-6029. Office Fax: 661-654-6100. Business E-Mail: sstone@csub.edu.

STONE, STUART LEE MORRISON, librarian, language educator; b. St. Louis, June 4, 1949; s. Norwood Lee Stone and Antoinette Aubouchon Engle. BS in Edn., The U. Mo., 1971; M of Libr. and Info. Sci., The Cath. U. Am., 1979, post-MLS, 1980—82. Cert. secondary edn. U. Mo., 1971, English as a fgn. lang. tchr. The Cambridge Sch., Ltd., London, 1982. Quadri-lingual rsch. asst. The Inter-Am. Def. Coll. / OAS, Washington, 1972—75; tchr. French, Spanish, & history The Wash. Ethical Soc. H.S., 1975—77; sr. staff asst. The U.S. Ho. Subcom. Postal Pers. and Modernization, 1980—82; tchr. English and Am. history The Am. Lang. Inst., Lisbon, Portugal, 1982—86; asst. libr. IMF, Washington, 1986—87; sr. cataloger, Portuguese-French-Spanish-Gaelic Libr. Congress, 1987—2002, recommending officer Scots-Gaelic, 1997—, sr. acquisitions specialist Europe and L.Am., 2000—, founder, coord. Scots Gaelic Lang. Table, 2004—. Instr. beginning and intermediate Scots-Gaelic Am. Gaelic Soc., Alexandria, Va., 1999—; mem. planning com. US Nat. Mod, 2006—. Translator (seminar instr. / U. Sao Paulo): (international library online networking) Training Manual / MARC Name Authorities; author: (ednl. discussion kit) Inauguration: An American Beginning (Presdl. Inaugural Com. award, 1981). Ward rep. bldgs. and grounds com. Fairlington Villages, Arlington, Va., 2003—06. With US Army, 1972—75. Decorated Joint Svc. Commendation medal Sec. Def. Pentagon. Fellow: Soc. Antiquaries Scotland; mem.: Libr. Congress (profl. assoc.), Am. Gaelic Soc. (newsletter editor asst. 1997—2000, Gaelic instr. 1997—), Am. Legion. Home: 3079 S Buchanan St C-2 Arlington VA 22206 Business E-Mail: ssto@loc.gov.

STONE, SUSAN A., lawyer; b. 1961; BA summa cum laude, Yale U., 1983; JD cum laude, Harvard U., 1987. Bar: Calif. 1987, U.S. Dist. Ct. (no. dist.) Calif. 1987, U.S. Ct. Appeals (9th cir.) 1987, U.S. Dist. Ct. (ctrl. dist.) Calif. 1988, Ill. 1990, U.S. Dist. Ct. (no. dist.) Ill. 1990, U.S. Ct. Appeals (7th cir.) 1990. Asst. U.S. atty. U.S. Dept. Justice, LA; law clk. to Judge William J. Orrick, U.S. Dist. Ct. for No. Dist. Calif.; ptnr. Sidley & Austin (until 2001 merger), Chgo.; ptnr. litig. Sidley Austin Brown & Wood, Chgo., 2001—, and co-chair practice devel. com. Former adj. prof. trial practice DePaul U. Coll. Law, Chgo. Named one of Top Young Litigators Under 40, Ill. Legal Times, One of 40 Attorneys Under 40, Chgo. Lawyer. Mem. ABA, Ill. Bar Assn., Calif. State Bar, Phi Beta Kappa. Office: Sidley Austin Brown & Wood LLP Bank One Plz 10 S Dearborn St Chicago IL 60603 Office Phone: 312-853-2177. Fax: 312-853-7036. E-mail: sstone@sidley.com.

STONE, TODD M., military officer; b. Plattsburgh, NY, May 20, 1982; s. Theodore T and Shelly R Stone; m. Lori A Bernardo, June 2, 2007. Diploma, Franklin Acad. High Sch., Malone, 2000. Cannon crewman USMC, Camp Pendleton, Calif., 2001—04, gunner Quantico, 2004—07, sect. chief, 2007—. Sgt. USMC, 2004—07, Quantico, VA. Decorated Combat Action Ribbon USMC, Presdl. Unit Citation. R-Consevative. Catholic. Achievements include combat veteran. Avocation: travel. Home: 209 Badore Rd Malone NY 12953 Home Phone: 518-483-5891.

STONE, VAN COURTRIGHT, not-for-profit developer; b. Deland, Fla., June 22, 1946; s. Wilfred Arthur and Catherine Louise Stone; m. Nancy M. Stone, July 19, 1969 (div. 1989); 1 child, Edana A. Stone Neundorf; m. Lisa L. Stone, Dec. 22, 1990; children: Melisa A., Wesley Alan. BA, Wichita State U., 1968; JD, Washburn U., 1974. Exec. v.p., officer S.W. State Bank, Topeka, Kans., 1974-81; pres. Nat. Bank of Andover, Kans., 1985-87; corp. atty. various corps., 1987-91; COO Gerber Bus. Devel. Corp., Petaluma, Calif., 1991-94; exec. dir. Lions of Ill. Found., Sycamore, 1995—. Bd. dirs. Ill. Sch. for the Visually Impaired, Jacksonville, Ill. Eye Fund, Chgo., mng. dir. Lions of Ill. Endowment Fund, 1995—; pres., N.Am. Conf. of Lions Founds., 2000—. Author: (newsletter) Lions Share, 1995—; contbr. articles to profl. jours. Capt. U.S. Army, 1968-71. Decorated 3 Bronze Stars; recipient Presl. medal of honor Ill. Coll. of Optimetry, 1999, Meritorious Svc. award Deicke Ctr., 1999; Lions of Ill. Found. fellow laureate, 2002. Mem. VFW (life), No. Aurora Lions Club, Lions Club Internat. (Melvin Jones fellow), Andover C. of C. (pres. 1986), Phi Sigma Rho, Tau Kappa Alpha, Phi Alpha Delta. Republican. Methodist. Avocations: golf, running, bridge, writing, bowling. Office: Lions Ill Found 2814 Dekalb Ave Sycamore IL 60178-3117 Home Phone: 630-262-8304; Office Phone: 815-756-5633 227.

STONE, VICTOR J., retired law educator; b. Chgo., Mar. 11, 1921; s. Maurice Albert and Ida (Baskin) Stone; m. Susan Abby Cane, July 14, 1951; children: Mary Jessica, Jennifer Abby, Andrew Hugh William. AB, Oberlin Coll., 1942; JD, Columbia U., 1948; LLD, Oberlin Coll., 1983. Bar: N.Y. 1949, Ill. 1950. Assoc. Columbia U., NYC, 1948-49, Sonnenschein, Chgo., 1949-53; rsch. assoc. U. Chgo., 1953-55; from asst. prof. to prof. law U. Ill., Champaign, 1955—91, prof. law emeritus, 1991—, assoc. v.p. acad. affairs, 1975-78. Mem. jud. adv. coun. State of Ill., 1959—61; mem. com. jury instns. Ill. Supreme Ct., 1963—79, reporter, 1973—79; mem. Ill. State Appellate Defender Commn., 1973—83, vice-chmn., 1973—77, 1979—83; bd. dirs. Champaign County Ct.-Apptd. Spl. Adv. Program, 1995—99, pres., 1998—99. Co-editor: Illinois Pattern Jury Instructions, 1965, 1971, 1977, Civil Liberties and Civil Rights, 1977. Trustee Oberlin Coll., 1982—97, AAUP Found., 1983—90. Lt. USNR, 1942—46. Ford Found. fellow, 1962—63. Fellow: Ill. Bar Found. (charter 1986—); mem.: ACLU (bd. dirs. Ill. divsn. 1986—96, exec. com. 1991—96, Roger Baldwin award for lifetime achievement 2002), CASA (bd. dirs. 1994—98, pres. 1998—99), AAUP (pres. chpt. 1964—65, pres. Ill. conf. 1968—70, gen. counsel 1978—80, pres. 1982—84, mem. coun. 1982—90), ABA, Chgo. Bar Assn., Am. Bar Found. (life), Ill. Bar Assn. (chmn. individual rights and responsibilities 1971—72, mem. coun. civil practice and procedure 1978—82, Elmer Gertz award in civil liberties and civil rights 2003), State Univs. Annuitants Assn. (pres. 1994—95, mem. state exec. com. 1995—97). Office: U Ill Coll Law 504 E Pennsylvania Ave Champaign IL 61820-6909 Business E-Mail: v-stone@uiuc.edu.

STONE, VOYE LYNNE, women's health nurse practitioner; b. Grandfield, Okla., Apr. 17, 1941; d. Clint Voy and Mattie Evelyn (Averyt) Wynn; m. Don Dale Stone, Dec. 19, 1964; children: Melinda Anne Stone Phelps, Tari Elisabeth Stone Newhouse. Student, Bapt. Hosp. Sch. Nursing, Oklahoma City, 1965; diploma in nursing, U. Okla., Oklahoma City, 1965; BS, St. Joseph's Coll., North Windham, Maine, 1985; grad. women health care nursing program, U. Tex., Dallas, 1990; MS, U. Okla., 1996. Cert. women's health nurse; cert. legal nurse cons. Dietary cons. Frederick Meml. Hosp., 1967; pub. health nurse Dept. Health, State of Okla., Frederick, 1985; insvc. educator Frederick Meml. Hosp.; women's health nurse practitioner Dept. Health, State of Okla., Oklahoma City, 1990. Vol., unit pres. Am. Cancer Soc.; vol. ARC; pres. adv. coun. 4-H Club; pres. local PTA. Named one of Outstanding Young Women of Am., 1970. Mem. AWHONN, Am. Acad. Nurse Practitioners, ANA, Okla. State Nurses Assn., Okla. Pub. Health Assn., Okla. Mental Health Assn., PEO, Beta Sigma Phi (various offices, Girl of Yr. 1976, 77, 78), Sigma Theta Tau, Phi Kappa Phi, First United Methodist Ch. Home: 21918 CR EW 184 Frederick OK 73542-9727

STONE, WILLIAM EDWARD, academic administrator, consultant; b. Peoria, Ill., Aug. 13, 1945; s. Dean Proctor and Katherine (Jamison) S.; m. Deborah Ann Duncan; children: Jennifer, Allison, Molly. AB, Stanford U., 1967, MBA, 1969. Asst. dean Stanford U., 1969—71, asst. to pres., 1971—77; exec. dir. Stanford Alumni Assn., 1977—90, pres., CEO, 1990—98; pres., dir. Stanford Alumni Assn. divsn. Stanford U., 1998—2001, Stanford Sierra Programs LLC, South Lake Tahoe, Calif., 1998—2001, Alpine Chalet, Inc., Alpine Meadows, Calif., 1987—2001; pres.-emeritus Stanford Alumni Assn. Stanford U., 2001—, cons. in ednl. advancement, 2001—; prin. eAdvancement Consortium, 2001—. Dir. Coun. Alumni Assn. Execs., 1989-93, v.p., 1990-91, pres., 1991-92; trustee Coun. for Advancement and Support of Edn., 1988-91; bd. dirs. Univ. ProNet, Inc., chmn., 1990-92, sec. 1996-00. Bd. dirs. North County YMCA, 1975-76; bd. dirs., chmn. nominating com. faculty club Stanford U., 1979-81; trustee Watkins Discretionary Fund, 1979-82; mem. cmty. adv. bd. Resource Ctr. Women; dir. Stanford Hist. Soc., 2002—, v.p., 2003-06, pres., 2006—. Recipient K.M. Cuthbertson award Stanford U., 1987, Tribute award Coun. for Advancement and Support of Edn., 1991, Steuben Apple award, 2002, Stanford Assocs. award of merit, 2005. Mem.: Stanford Assocs., Stanford Faculty Club. Home: 1061 Cathcart Way Stanford CA 94305-1048 Office Phone: 650-494-6959. Business E-Mail: stone@eadvancement.org.

STONEBRAKER, MICHAEL R., electrical engineering, computer science educator; BS, Princeton U., 1965; MS, U. Mich., 1966, PhD, 1971. Asst. prof. U. Calif., Berkeley, 1971-76, assoc. prof., 1976-81, prof., 1981-99; ret., 1999; founder, CTO StreamBase Sys., Inc., Lexington, Mass., 2003—. Vis. engr. Nat. Bur. Stds., 1972; founder, cons., mem. bd. dirs. Relational Tech., Inc., 1980—, v.p. engring., 1984; vis. prof. Pontifico Univ. Catholique, Rio de Janeiro, 1976, U. Calif., Santa Cruz, 1977-78, U. Grenoble, France, 1984-85; founder, CTO INGRES Corp. (now INGRES Products Divsn. of ASK Computer Sys.), Illustra Info. Sys., Inc.; spkr. in field. Contbr. articles to profl. jours. Named one of 8 innovators driving the Silicon Valley wealth explosion, Forbes mag., 1998, Top 25 Chief Tech. Officers, InfoWorld mag., 2006; recipient ACM Sys. Software award, 1992, John von Neumann medal, IEEE, 2005. Mem. ACM (past chmn. spl. interest group on mgmt. of data, SIGMOD Innovations award 1992; NAE, 1998-. Office: Streambase Systems Inc 181 Spring St Lexington MA 02421 Office Phone: 781-761-0800.

STONECIPHER, DAVID A., insurance company executive; b. 1941; m. Nancy Berend; 4 children. Degree, Vanderbilt U., 1962; M Agrl. Sci., Ga. State U., 1967. With Life Ins. Co. Ga., Altanta, 1967-92, sr. v.p., actuary Atlanta, 1978—84, exec. v.p., 1984—89, pres., COO, 1989—91, CEO, 1991—92, Southland Life Ins. Co, Altanta, 1991—92; CEO elect Jefferson-Pilot Corp., Greensboro, NC, 1992; pres., CEO Jefferson Pilot Corp., Greensboro, NC, 1993—2004, Jefferson-Pilot Life Ins. Co., 1993—2004; chmn. Jefferson-Pilot Corp., Greensboro, NC, 1998—2004, non-exec. chmn., 2005—06. Bd. dir. Bassett Furniture Industries, Inc., McKenney's Corp., Internat. Home Furnishings Ctr., Inc., Fin. Services Roundtable, Lincoln Nat. Corp., Phila., 2006—. Bd. dirs. McCallie Sch. Served US Army, 1962—64. Fellow, Soc. of Actuaries, 1970. Mem.: Am. Acad. Actuaries, Soc. Actuaries, Am. Coun. Life Insureres (past chmn.). Office: Lincoln Nat Corp Ctr Sq W Tower Ste 3900 1500 Market St Philadelphia PA 19102-2112

STONEHILL, ERIC, lawyer; b. Rochester, NY, Feb. 27, 1950; BA with distinction, Northwestern U., 1970; JD, Cornell U., 1973, MBA, 1981, cert. hosp. and health svc. adminstrn., 1981. Bar: N.Y. 1974, D.C. 1981, U.S. Dist. Ct. (we. dist.) N.Y. 1974, U.S. Dist. Ct. (no. dist.) N.Y. 1976. Assoc. Harris Beach PLLC, Rochester, 1973—81, ptnr., 1982—. Adj. instr. Rochester Inst. Tech., 1990-92. Contbr. articles to profl. jours. Bd. dirs. Rochester Eye and Human Parts Bank, 1983-91, 92-2001, pres., 1987-90. Mem. Am. Health Lawyers Assn., N.Y. State Bar Assn. (mem. health law sect.), D.C. Bar Assn., Monroe County Bar Assn., Sloan Alumni Assn., Phi Beta Kappa. Office: Harris Beach PLLC 99 Garnsey Rd Pittsford NY 14534 Office Phone: 585-419-8641.

STONEHILL, LLOYD HERSCHEL, gas industry executive, mechanical engineer; b. South Bend, Ind., May 20, 1927; s. Charles Myers and Bertha M. (Reed) S.; m. Jean Carole Herzer, Dec. 30, 1961; children: Mark, Bill, John, Rob. BSME, Purdue U., 1949. Registered profl. engr., La. Chief engr. Rothschild Boiler & Tank Works, Shreveport, La., 1949-54; chmn. bd. dirs. Frankfort (Ind.) Bottle Gas, Inc., 1956—. Patentee in field. Founding pres. Clinton County Hosp. Authority, Frankfort, 1974; membership chmn. Clinton County Hosp. Found., Frankfort, 1982-83, 89. With U.S. Army, 1954-56. Recipient Heroism award Elks Lodge, Frankfort, 1959. Mem. Nat. Propane Gas Assn. (mktg. awards 1986, 87), Am. Legion, Purdue Alumni Assn. (Clinton County Chpt. mem. pres.' coun.), Hudson Inst., Rotary (sec. 1963-65, Paul Harris fellow), Lambda Chi Alpha (sec. 1946-47). Republican. Mem. Christian Ch. Avocations: collecting old violins, sailing, reading. Home: 1258 Forest Dr Frankfort IN 46041-3230 Office: Frankfort Bottle Gas Inc 1555 McKinley Ave Frankfort IN 46041-1805

STONEMAN, MARK L., lawyer; b. Cleve., Jan. 11, 1971; s. Dean L. and Diana G. Stoneman; m. Jill L. Stoneman, June 24, 2000; children: William J., Nathaniel D. BS in Bus. Adminstrn., U. Mo., Columbia, 1993, JD, 1996; master degree in Accountancy, U. Mo., St. Louis, 2002. Lic.: Mo. 1996, Ill. 1997. Assoc. Armstrong Teasdale LLP, St. Louis, 1996—2004, ptnr., 2004—. Contbr. chapters to books. Tchg. vol. Jr. Achievement, St. Louis, 2004; bd. mem. Metro Theater Co., St. Louis, 2001—04. Recipient Order of the Coif, U. Mo., 1996, Fred L. Howard award for Excellence in Appellate Advocacy, 1996, Pacioli award, 2002; scholar Lynn and Peggy Ewing Scholar, U. Mo. Law Sch. Found., 1994-95, Curator's Scholar, U. Mo., 1994-95, Mary Fiser Meml. Scholar, 1994-95, Law Rev. Fellows Scholar, 1995-96. Mem.: Phi Kappa Phi, Mo. Law Rev. Office: Armstrong Teasdale LLP One Metropolitan Sq Ste 2600 Saint Louis MO 63102 Home Phone: 314-909-1968; Office Phone: 314-621-5070. Office Fax: 314-621-5065. Business E-Mail: mstoneman@armstrongteasdale.com.

STONER, GARY DAVID, cancer researcher; b. Bozeman, Mont., Oct. 25, 1942; married; 2 children. BS, Mont. State U., 1964; MS, U. Mich., 1968, PhD in Microbiol., 1970. Asst. rsch. scientist U. Calif., San Diego, 1970-72, assoc. rsch. scientist, 1972-75; cancer expert Nat. Cancer Inst., 1976-79; assoc. prof. pathology Med. Coll. Ohio, 1979-83; prof. pathology, 1983-92; prof. internal medicine and pathology Ohio State U., Columbus,

1992, assoc. dir. Ctr. for Molecular and Environ. Health, 1993—2003, assoc. dir. basic rsch. Comp Cancer Ctr, 1994—, prof., chmn. divsn. environ. health scis. Sch. Pub. Health, 1995—2003; prof. internal medicine, dir. program Ohio State U. Comprehensive Cancer Ctr., Columbus. Cons. Nat. Heart Lung & Blood Inst., 1974—, EPA, 1979—, Nat. Cancer Inst., 1979—, Nat. Toxicol. Program, 1981—; mem. study sect. NIH, 1980-92, 2003—, Am. Cancer Soc., Ohio, 1982—, Am. Cancer Soc., Nat., 1995-2002. Grantee Nat. Cancer Inst., EPA, U.S. Army R & D Command. Fellow AAAS; mem. Soc. Toxicology, Am. Assn. Cancer Rsch., Am. Assn. Pathologists, Internat. Soc. Cancer Chemoprevention. Achievements include research in carcinogenesis in human and animal model respiratory and esophageal tissues, carcinogenic metabolism, mutagenesis, in vitro transformation of epithelial cells and chemoprevention. Office: Ohio State U Divsn Hematology/Oncology Dept Internal 1148 CHRI 300 W 10th Ave Columbus OH 43210-1240 Home Phone: 614-888-2133; Office Phone: 614-293-3268. Business E-Mail: stoner.21@osu.edu.

STONER, JAMES LLOYD, retired foundation administrator, clergyman; b. Point Marion, Pa., Apr. 23, 1920; s. Martin Clark and Bess (Hare) S.; m. Janice Faller Evans, Aug. 28, 1943; children: Thomas Clark, James Douglas and Geoffrey Lloyd (twins). BS, Bethany Coll., 1941, DD (hon.), 1958; BD, MA, Yale U., 1944. Ordained to ministry Christian Ch., 1943; minister in Hamden, Conn., 1942-44; assoc. exec. sec. U. Tex., YMCA, 1944-45; dir. Student Christian Fellowship, Bowling Green State U., 1945-47, Univ. Christian Mission, Fed. Council Ch. and Nat. Council Chs., 1947-56; minister North Christian Ch., Columbus, Ind., 1956-66; asst. gen. sec. for exec. operations Nat. Council Chs., 1966-72; sr. minister Central Christian Ch., Austin, Tex., 1972-80; dep. exec. dir. Found. for Christian Living, Pawling, N.Y., 1980-83, exec. dir., 1983-87. Chmn. com. recommendations Internat. Conv. Christian Chs., 1962-65; bd. mgrs. United Christian Missionary Soc., 1956-63; mem. adv. bd. Am. Bible Soc., 1966-72; life mem. coun. Christian Unity, Christian Ch.; a founder, 1st pres. LINK Award, Ridgewood, N.J., 1966-72; mem. Austin Conf. Chs., pres., 1973-75; rep. Tex. Conf. Chs., 1976-80; mem. goals com. Austin Tomorrow; mem. adv. bd. 1st Comml. Bank of Lakeway, Austin, Tex., 1990-95. Author: Down-to-Earth Meditations That Give You a Lift, 2000; contbr. articles to profl. publs. A founder, bd. dirs. Fellowship Christian Athletes, Kansas City, Mo., 1956-68; trustee Tougaloo (Miss.) Coll., 1968-74; trustee emeritus Lakeway Ch.; v.p., mem. exec. com. Ecumenical Ctr. Continuing Edn., Yale, 1966-72; mem. exec. com. Boy Scouts Am., Austin, 1980, Dutchess County council, 1981-82; bd. mgrs. New Milford Hosp., 1983-88; bd. dirs. Holiday Hills YMCA, 1983-87; com. mem. Town of Pawling 200th Anniversary, 1985-88, Lakeway Ecumenical Ch.; cofounder Holy Week Palm Observance, Lakeway,Tex. Mem. Pawling C. of C. (exec. com. 1984-87), Fellowship of Christian Athletes (nat. adv. bd. 1994—), Masons (32 degree), Pawling Rotary Club (pres. 1983-84, dist. gov.-elect 1991-92, dist. gov. 1992-93, Paul Harris fellow), Shriners, Austin Rotary Club (spl. lifetime mem.), Lake Travis/Lakeway Rotary Club (hon.), Alpha Psi Omega, Beta Theta Pi. Home: Summit 1034 Liberty Pk Dr 323 Austin TX 78746 *Fill every day with rainbow colors, and punctuate life with a positive outlook... Even the Cross of Christ is a positive sign.*

STONER, JOHN RICHARD, federal agency administrator; b. Ypsilanti, Mich., May 11, 1958; s. Richard P. and Marjorie G. Stoner; m. Diane Leslie Snow. BA in Govt., Lawrence U., 1981, B in Music Edn., 1981; MS in Mgmt., U. Md., 2004, MBA, 2005. Staff asst. Senator Robert Kasten Jr., Washington, 1981-82; staff asst. Wis. Office Fed.-State Rels., Washington, 1982-83; intergovtl. rels. officer U.S. Dept. Transp., Washington, 1983-86, congl. rels. officer, 1989-91; dir. Office of Program and Policy Support, Rsch. and Spl. Programs Adminstrn., Dept. Transp., Washington, 1991-93; exec. dir. Republican Nat. Lawyers Assn., 1993-97; rep. Primerica Fin. Svcs., 1993-97, mortgage banker, 1998—; state govt. rels. mgr. Am. Trucking Assn., Inc., Alexandria, Va., 1986-88; researcher George Bush for Pres. Com., 1988; staff asst. Office of Pres.-Elect, Washington, 1988-89; state dir. The Century Coun., Washington, 2000—03. Admissions contact Washington area Lawrence U., 1986-87; softball team mgr. Montgomery County Recreation League. Recipient Eagle Scout award Boy Scouts Am., 1972; Mortar Bd. scholar, 1980; Senate Rep. Policy Com. Legis. fellow, 1993-96. Republican. Mem. Ch. of Christ, Scientist. Avocations: water-skiing, organ. Home: 10409 Brunswick Ave Silver Spring MD 20902-4845 Office: The Century Coun 1310 G St NW Washington DC 20005-3000

STONESIFER, PATTY (PATRICIA Q. STONESIFER), foundation administrator; b. Indpls., 1956; m. Michael Kinsley; 2 children from previous marriage. BA, Ind. U., 1982. Editor-in-chief Que Corp., Indpls.; sr. mgr. Microsoft Press, 1988-89; gen. mgr. Microsoft Can., 1989-90; gen. mgr., then v.p. product support svcs. consumer divsn. Microsoft Corp., Redmond, Wash., 1990-93, sr. v.p. consumer divsn., 1993—96; chairwoman, pres. Gates Learning Found., 1997—99; co-chair, pres., CEO Bill & Melinda Gates Found., Seattle, 2000—. Mem. US delegation to UN Gen. Assembly Spl. Session on AIDS; mem., bd. dirs. Viacom Inc., 2000—, The Seattle Found., Amazon.com. Mem. bd. regents Smithsonian Inst. Named one of 25 Most Influential People in Am., Time mag., 1996. Fellow: Am. Acad. Arts & Sci. (founding bd. mem.). Office: Bill & Melinda Gates Found PO Box 23350 Seattle WA 98102

STONESTREET, JEANNINE LEE, edcuator; b. Silver Spring, Md., Nov. 22, 1970; d. Randy Vernon and Frances Kathleen Merritt; m. Bruce Wayne Stonestreet, June 5, 1993; children: Brandon Patrick, Justin Wayne, Nicole Alexandra. Grad. in Elem. Edn., U. Md., College Park, 1993; grad. in Guidance Counseling, Johns Hopkins U., Balt., 2001. Cert. tchr. Md., 1993. Elem. sch. tchr. Fields Rd. Elem. Sch., Gaithersburg, Md., 1993—99; tchr. mentor Frederick County Pub. Schs., Frederick, Md., 2000—03; adj. instr. Frederick CC, 2003—05; instr. Hagerstown CC, Md., 2005—. Bd. mem. Tchr. Acad., Hagerstown, 2005. Office: Hagerstown CC 11400 Robinwood Dr Hagerstown MD 21742 Home Phone: 301-293-1818; Office Phone: 301-790-2800 258. Business E-Mail: stonestreetj@hagerstowncc.edu.

STONG, ROGER ALAN, lawyer; b. Chgo., May 2, 1962; s. Robert Evert and Therese (Countess Raczynski) Stong; m. Phyllis Ann Hoffman, Apr. 9, 1994; 1 child, Heather Nicole Ross. BA, U. Va., 1983; JD, Ind. U., 1985; MBA, U. Okla., 1986. Bar: Okla. 1986, U.S. Dist. Ct. (we. dist. Okla.) 1991. Assoc. Crowe & Dunlevy, Oklahoma City, 1986—93, dir., shareholder, 1993—. Fellow: Okla. Bar Found.; mem.: ABA, Oklahoma County Bar Assn., Okla. Bar Assn. (chair Bus. and Corp. Law sect. 2002—03), Okla. C. of C., Okla. Lawyers for Children (asst. sec. 1998—), Okla. State C. of C. (bd. dirs. 2006—, dir. 2006—), U. Va. Alumni Assn., U. Okla. Alumni Assn., Ind. U. Alumni Assn., Okla. Hist. Soc. Republican. Roman Cath. Home: 2205 NW 56th St Oklahoma City OK 73112 Office: Crowe & Dunlevy 20 N Broadway Oklahoma City OK 73102 Office Phone: 405-235-7700. Office Fax: 405-272-5255. Business E-Mail: stongr@crowedunlevy.com.

ST-ONGE, DENIS ALDERIC, geologist, research scientist, educator; b. Ste-Agathe, Man., Can., May 11, 1929; s. Adolphe and Jeanne M (Ritchot) St-Onge; m. Jeanne Marie Behaegel, Jan. 7, 1955; children: Marc R, Nicole J M. BA, Coll. St-Boniface, 1951; Lic. Sci., U. Louvain, Belgium, 1957, DSc, 1962; DSc (hon.), U. Man., 1990. Research scientist Geol. Survey, Ottawa, Ont., Canada, 1958-68, sect. head, 1982-85; chief sub. div. Quaternary Geology, 1985-87, dir. terrain scis. div., 1987-91, sci. advisor Polar Continental Shelf Project, 1991-97; prof. geography U. Ottawa, 1968-82, chmn. geography, 1974-77, vice dean grad. studies, 1977-80, prof. emeritus, 1998—, bd. govs., 2000—; scientist emeritus Geol. Survey Can., 1997—. Chmn. bd. dirs. Fluxnet Can., 2002—07, Cases, 2003—07. Author: (book) Geomorphologie Ellef-Ringnes Island, 1965, Quaternary Geology, Inman River Region, N.W.T. Canada, 1995; contbr. articles to profl jours. Pres Ont Francophone PTA, 1967—69. Decorated Officer Order of Can; recipient medal, Queen Elizabeth II, 1979, Commemorative medal, Govt. of Can., 1992, Medal of Honor, Univ Liege, Belgium, 1980, medal, A Cailleux, 1991, Can 125, 1992, Royal Scottish Geog, Soc, 1994, Golden Jubilee medal, Queen Elizabeth II, 2002. Fellow: Explorers Club (internat. fellow 2005), Arctic Inst. N.Am., Geol. Assn. Can. (pres. 1984—85, J. W. Ambrose medal 2001), Royal Can. Geog. Soc. (bd. dirs. 1980—2001, pres. 1992—98, chmn. Partnership Group Sci. Engrs. 1999—2001, Camsell medal 2005, 75th Ann. medallion 2005); mem.: Can. Geosci. Coun. (pres. 1996—97), Assn. Quebecoise pour l'etude du Quaternaire (hon.), Can. Quaternary Assn., Internat. Union Quaternary Rsch. (hon.), Can. Assn. Geographers (pres. 1979—80, Award Svc. to Profession 2000). Avocations: swimming, skiing, photography. Office: Geolog Survey of Canada 601 Booth St Ottawa ON Canada K1A OE8 Home: 1188 Agincourt Rd Ottawa ON Canada K2C 2H9 Home Phone: 613-225-4267; Office Phone: 613-947-1652. Business E-Mail: dstonge@nrcan.gc.ca.

STONNINGTON, HENRY HERBERT, physician, association administrator, educator; b. Vienna, Feb. 12, 1927; arrived in U.S., 1969; m. Constance Mary Leigh Hammersly. MB, BS, Melbourne U., Victoria, Australia, 1950; MS, U. Minn., 1972. Diplomate Am. Bd. Phys. Medicine and Rehab., 1973. Pvt. practice, Sydney, N.S.W., Australia, 1955-65; clin. tchr. U. N.S.W., Sydney, 1965-69; resident in Phys. Medicine and Rehab. Mayo Clinic, Rochester, Minn., 1969-72, mem. staff, 1972-83; assoc. prof. Mayo Med. Sch., Rochester, 1975-83; chmn. dept rehab. medicine Med. Coll. Va., Va. Commonwealth U., Richmond, 1983-88, prof. rehab. medicine, 1983-89, dir. rsch. tng. ctr., 1988-89; v.p. med. svcs. Sheltering Arms Hosp., Richmond, 1985-92; prof. and chmn. dept. phys. medicine and rehab. U. Mo., Columbia, 1992-94; med. dir. Meml. Rehab. Ctr., Savannah, Ga., 1994-97; clin. prof. rehab. medicine Emory U., Atlanta, 1997—2000; clin. prof. medicine sect. phys. medicine and rehab. La. State U., 2001—. Med. dir. rehab. svcs. Meml. Hosp., Gulfport, Miss., 1998—; clin. prof. phys. med. and rehab. La. State U. Med. Sch., 2001—. Editor: Brain Injury, 1987—2001, Pediatric Rehabilitation, 1997—2000; contbr. articles to profl. jours. Recipient award Rsch. Tng. Ctr. Model Sys., Nat. Inst. Disability and Rehab. Rsch., Washington, 1987, 88, Disting. Clinician award Am. Acad. Phys. Medicine and Rehab., 2002. Fellow Australian Coll. Rehab. Medicine, Australasian Faculty Rehab. Medicine, Royal Coll. Physicians Edinburgh (Scotland), Am. Acad. Phys. Medicine and Rehab. (named Disting. Physician 2002), Am. Coun. Rehab. Medicine, Am. Assn. Acad. Physiatrists; mem. Internat. Brain Injury Assn. (v.p. for sci. affairs 1998-2002, bd. govs., Founder's award 2004). Personal E-mail: hencon2731@bellsouth.net.

STOOKESBERRY, DENISE, music educator, musician; d. Sylvester and Gladys Sauer; m. David Stookesberry, Nov. 18, 1989; children: John H. Kilper, Katherine M. MusM in Voice Performance, Washington U., St. Louis, 1994. Cert. K-12 music tchr. Mo. Pvt. practice voice tchr., St. Louis, 1990—; choral dir. Duchesne HS, St. Charles, Mo., 1984—89, St. Charles HS, 2000—04, John Burroughs Sch., St. Louis, 2005—; voice tchr. Washington U., 1994—2000. Soloist, choir dir. Temple Israel, St. Louis, 1995—; singer St. Louis Symphony Orch. Singer: Union Ave. Opera, 1978, 1979, Opera Theater St. Louis, 1996, Ohio Light Opera, 1997, (Madame Butterfly) Pensacola Opera, 1998, (recital) 20th Century Works, 2000. Founder Opera Unltd. Recipient Friends of Music award, Wash. U., 1993; scholar, St. Louis U., 1975—79; Music Tech. grantee, St. Charles Sch. Dist., 2003. Mem.: Am. Choral Dirs. Assn. (assoc.), Music Educators Nat. Conf. (assoc.), Nat. Assn. Tchrs. Singing (assoc.; treas. 1997—2000). Avocation: hiking. Home: 12551 Merrick Dr Saint Louis MO 63146 Office: John Burroughs Sch 755 S Price Rd Saint Louis MO 63124 Office Phone: 314-993-4045 254. Business E-Mail: dstook@jburroughs.org.

STOOKEY, NOEL PAUL, folksinger, composer; b. Balt., Dec. 30, 1937; s. George William and Dorothea (St. Aubrey) S.; m. Mary Elizabeth Bannard, Sept. 4, 1963; children: Elizabeth Drake, Katherine Darby, Anna St. Aubrey. Student, Mich. State U., 1955-58; HHD (hon.), Husson Coll., 1978. Prodn. mgr. Cormac Chem. Corp., N.Y.C., 1959-60; artist in residence Northfield Mount Hermon Sch., 1999. Released album of songs Birds of Paradise, 1954; sang professionally, master ceremonies events, Mich. State U., 1955-58; profl. singer, Greenwich Village, N.Y.C., 1960-61; mem. folksinging group, Peter, Paul and Mary, 1961—; solo rec. artist for Warner Bros., 1971-74; producer folk albums for Scepter Records, Verve/Folkway Records; founder, Neworld Media, rec. studio Neworld Records, 1977-81; rec. artist: Paul And, 1971, One Night Stand, 1972, Real to Reel, 1976, Something New and Fresh, 1978, Band and Bodyworks, 1979, Wait'll You Hear This, 1982, There is Love, 1985, State of the Heart, 1985, In Love Beyond Our Lives, 1990; host Maine Pub. TV broadcasting series "E-Maine", 1997. Mem. AFTRA, Screen Actors Guild, ASCAP, Delta Upsilon. Clubs: St. Botolph's (Boston). Personal E-mail: stook@celestat.com. Business E-Mail: neworld@celestat.com.

STOOPLER, ERIC T., dentist, dental educator; b. NYC, Nov. 15, 1973; s. Stanley and Francine Stoopler; m. Melanie Sass, Sept. 5, 2004. BA, Binghamton U., Vestal, NY, 1994; DMD, U. Pa., Phila., 1999. Diplomate Am. Bd. Oral Medicine, 2004, Am. Bd. Spl. Care Dentistry, 2006. Asst. prof. oral medicine U. Pa., Sch. Dental Medicine, Phila., 2002—. Author: Burket's Oral Medicine, 11th edit.; contbr. articles to profl. jours. Grantee, Multiple Myeloma Rsch. Found., 2005. Mem.: Spl. Care Dentistry Assn., Am. Acad. Oral Medicine. Achievements include research in oral amyloid in multiple myeloma. Office: Univy Pa 240 S 40th St Philadelphia PA 19104 Office Phone: 215-746-0112. Business E-Mail: ets@pobox.upenn.edu.

STOOPLER, MARK BENJAMIN, physician; b. NYC, Sept. 29, 1950; s. Alex and Blanche Sylvia (Kappel) S.; m. Lynn Sara Fruchter, Jan. 10, 1982; children: David Andrew, Emily Rachel, Jesse Bryan. BS, Tulane U., 1971; MD, Cornell U., 1975. Diplomate Am. Bd. Internal Medicine, Am. Bd. Oncology. Intern and resident in internal medicine North Shore U. Hosp., Manhasset, N.Y., 1975-78, Meml. Sloan-Kettering Cancer Ctr., NYC, 1975-78, asst. chief resident in medicine, 1978, fellow in med. oncology, 1978-80; asst. attending physician Presbyn. Hosp., NYC, 1980-93, assoc. attending physician, 1993—; asst. clin. prof. medicine Columbia U. Coll. of Physicians and Surgeons, NYC, 1980-93; assoc. clin. prof. medicine, 1993—. Contbr. articles to profl. jours. Tulane U. scholar, 1970-71; named one of Am.'s Top Drs. Castle Connolly Guide, 2003-07, Best Drs. NY Mag., 2006, 07. Fellow ACP; mem. Am. Soc. of Clin. Oncology, Am. Fedn. for Clin. Research, Internat. Assn. for the Study of Lung Cancer, Phi Beta Kappa. Office: Columbia-Presbyn Med Ctr 161 Fort Washington Ave New York NY 10032-3713 Office Phone: 212-305-8230.

STOOPS, BOB, college football coach; b. Youngstown, Ohio, Sept. 9, 1960; BS, Univ. Iowa, 1983. Grad. asst. coach Univ. Iowa, 1983—84, vol. coach, 1985—87; asst. coach Kent State, 1988; defensive backs coach Kans. State, 1989—90, co-defensive coord., 1991—95; def. coord., asst. head coach Univ. Fla., 1996—98; head football coach Univ. Okla., 1998—. Named Bear Bryant Nat. Coach of Yr., 2000, Coach of Yr., AP, 2000, Eddie Robinson/FWAA Coach of Yr., 2000, Woody Hayes Nat. Coach of Yr., 2000, 2003, Nat. Coach Yr., Am. Heart Assn., 2000, Football News, 2000, Walter Camp awards, 2000, 2003, Big 12 Coach Yr., 2000, 2003, Dallas Morning News, 2004, 2006, Region IV Coach of Yr., AFCA, 2003, Bobby Dodd Nat. Coach of Yr., 2003; recipient Paul "Bear" Bryant award, Nat. Sportscasters & Sportswriters Assn., 2000, George Munger award, Maxwell Football Club, 2000. Achievements include coaching U. Okla. to 2000 BCS Nat. Championship. Office: OU Football 180 W Brooks St Norman OK 73019

STOOPS, DANIEL J., lawyer; b. Wichita, Kans., May 27, 1934; s. Elmer F. and Margaret J. (Pickrell) S.; m. Kathryn Ann Piepmeier, Aug. 28, 1954; children: Sharon, Janet. BA, Washburn U., Kans., 1956, JD, 1958. Bar: Kans. 1958, Ariz. 1959, US Dist. Ct. Kans. 1958, US Dist. Ct. Ariz. 1960, US Ct. Appeals (9th cir.) 1975, US Supreme Ct. 1971. Assoc. Wilson, Compton, & Wilson, Flagstaff, Ariz., 1959-64; ptnr. Wilson, Compton & Stoops, Flagstaff, Ariz., 1964-67, Mangum, Wall & Stoops, Flagstaff, 1967-77, Mangum, Wall, Stoops & Warden, Flagstaff, 1977—2005, of counsel, 2005—. Editor Washburn Law Rev., 1958. Pres. Flagstaff Festival of the Arts, 1988-89, Flagstaff Sch. Bd., 1961-73, Ariz. Sch. Bd. Assn., 1971 Fellow Ariz. Bar Found., Am. Bar Found., Am. Coll. Trial Lawyers (state chmn. 1984-85), Internat. Soc. Barristers; mem. Ariz. Bar Assn. (pres. 1980-81), Masons. Republican. Methodist. Avocations: golf, political and historical reading and research. Office: Mangum Wall Stoops & Warden 100 N Elden St Flagstaff AZ 86001-5295 Home Phone: 928-774-2833; Office Phone: 928-779-6951. Business E-Mail: dstoops@mwswlaw.com.

STOPNIK, SCOTT H., lawyer; BBA, U. Miami, 1992; JD, NY Law Sch., 1995. Bar: NY 1996, US Dist. Ct. Ea. Dist. NY, US Dist. Ct. So. Dist. NY. Ptnr. Wilson, Elser, Moskowitz, Edelman & Dicker LLP, NYC. Mem.: Assn. of the Bar of the City of NY. Office: Wilson Elser Moskowitz Edelman & Dicker LLP 150 E 42nd St 23rd Fl New York NY 10017-5639 Office Phone: 212-490-3000 ext. 2747. Office Fax: 212-490-3038. Business E-Mail: stopniks@wemed.com.

STOPPARD, TOM (TOMAS STRAUSSLER), playwright; b. Zlin, Czechoslovakia, July 3, 1937; arrived in Eng., 1946; s. Eugene and Martha Stoppard Straussler, Kenneth Stoppard (Stepfather); m. Jose Ingle, 1965 (div., 1972), 2 sons; m. Miriam Moore-Robinson, 1972 (div. 1992), 2 sons MLitt (hon.), U. Bristol, Eng., 1979, Brunel U., 1979, U. Sussex, 1980. Journalist Western Daily Press, Bristol, Eng., 1954-58, Evening World, Bristol, 1958-60; free-lance reporter, 1960-63. Bd. dir. Royal Nat. Theatre, London, 1989—. Author: (plays) The Gamblers, 1965, Rosencrantz and Guildenstern Are Dead, 1966 (Plays and Players Best Play award 1967, Best Play Tony award 1968), Enter a Free Man, 1968, The Real Inspector Hound, 1968, Albert's Bridge, 1969 (Prix Italia 1968), If You're Glad I'll Be Frank, 1969, After Magritte, 1970, Dogg's Our Pet, 1971, Jumpers, 1972 (Evening Standard Best Play award 1972, Plays and Players Best Play award 1972), Travesties, 1974 (Evening Standard Best Play award 1974, Best Play Tony award 1976), Dirty Linen and New-Found-Land, 1976, Every Good Boy Deserves Favor, 1974, Night and Day, 1978 (Evening Standard Best Play award 1978), Dogg's Hamlet, Cahoot's Macbeth, 1979, The Real Thing, 1982 (Evening Standard Best Play award 1982, Best Play Tony award 1984, Best Fgn. Play Tony award 1984), Hapgood, 1988, Artist Descending a Staircase, 1988, Arcadia, 1993 (Evening Standard Best Play award 1993, Oliver award 1994), Indian Ink, 1995, Invention of Love, 1997 (Evening Standard Best Play award 1997), The Coast of Utopia (trilogy), 2002 (Drama Desk award outstanding play 2007, Tony award best play, 2007), Rock 'n' Roll, 2006 (Evening Standard Best Play award, 2006); (play adaptations) Tango by Slawomir Mrozek, 1966, The House of Bernarda Alba by Federico Garcia Lorca, 1973, Undiscovered Country (based on Das Weite Land by Arthur Schnitzler), 1979, On the Razzle (based on Einen Jux will er sich machen by Johann Nestroy), 1981, Rough Crossing (based on The Play's the Thing by Ferenc Molnar), 1984, Dalliance (based on Liebelei by Arthur Schnitzler), 1986, Henry IV (Pirandello), 2003, Heroes (trans. Gérald Sibleyras), 2005; (radio plays) The Dissolution of Dominic Boot, 1964, M is for Moon Among Other Things, 1964, If You're Glad I'll Be Frank, 1966, Albert's Bridge, 1967, Where Are They Now?, 1970, Artist Descending A Staircase, 1972, The Dog It Was That Died, 1982, In the Native State, 1991; (radio serial episodes) The Dales, 1964, A Student's Diary, 1965; (screenplays) The Romantic Englishwoman, 1975, Despair, 1978, The Human Factor, 1980, (with Terry Gilliam and Charles McKeown) Brazil, 1985 (Best Screenplay Acad. award nominee 1985, Best Screenplay L.A. Critics Circle award 1985), Empire of the Sun, 1987, The Russia House, 1990; (author, dir.) Rosencrantz and Guildenstern Are Dead, 1990 (Grand prize Venice Film Festival 1990), Billy Bathgate, 1991, (with Marc Norman) Shakespeare in Love, 1998 (Golden Globe award and Oscar best screenplay), Enigma, 2001; (teleplays) A Walk on the Water, 1963, A Separate Peace, 1966, Teeth, 1967, Another Moon Called Earth, 1967, Neutral Ground, 1968, The Engagement (based on his radio play The Dissolution of Dominic Boot), 1970, One Pair of Eyes, 1972, (with Clive Exton) Boundaries, 1975, Three Men in a Boat, 1975, Professional Foul, 1977, Squaring the Circle: Poland 1980-81, 1985; (translator) Largo Desolato by Vaclav Havel, 1987; (novel) Lord Malquist and Mr. Moon, 1966; contbr. short stories to Introduction 2, 1964. In 1977, a visit to Russia raised concerns for human rights issues; concerns are manifested in work and involvement with orgns. such as Amnesty Internat., Com. Against Psychiatric Abuse, and Index on Censorship. Decorated knight comdr. Order Brit. Empire, Order of Merit; Ford Found. grantee, 1964; recipient John Whiting award Arts Coun. Great Britain, 1967, Evening Standard Most Promising Playwright Drama award, 1972, Shakespeare prize Hamburg, Germany, 1979. Fellow: Royal Soc. Literature. Office: Peters Fraser Dunlop Drury Ho 34-43 Russell St London WC2B 5HA England

STOPPELMAN, JEREMY, Internet company executive, entrepreneur; b. Arlington, Va., 1978; BS in computer engring., U. Ill., 1999; student, Harvard Bus. Sch., 2003—04. With @Home Networks, X.com, Confinity; v.p. engring. PayPal, 2002—03; co-founder & CEO Yelp Inc., San Francisco, 2004—. Office: Yelp Inc 650 Mission St #2 San Francisco CA 94105 E-mail: info@yelp.com. *

STORANDT, MARTHA, psychologist; b. Little Rock, June 2, 1938; d. Farris and Floy (Montgomery) Mobbs; m. Duane Storandt, Dec. 15, 1962; 1 child, Eric AB, Washington U., St. Louis, 1960, PhD, 1966. Lic. psychologist, Mo. Staff psychologist VA, Jefferson Barracks, Mo., 1967-68; asst. prof. to prof. Washington U., St. Louis, 1968—. Mem. nat. adv. council on aging Nat. Inst. on Aging, 1984-87; editor-in-chief Jour. Gerontology, 1981-86 Author: Counseling and Therapy with Older Adults, 1983; co-author: Memory, Related Functions and Age, 1974; co-editor: The Clinical Psychology of Aging, 1978, The Adult Years: Continuity and Change, 1989, Neuropsychological Assessment of Dementia and Depression in Older Adults: A Clinician's Guide, 1994. Recipient Disting. Service award Mo. Assn. Homes for the Aging, 1984. Fellow APA (pres. divsn. 20 1979-80, council rep. 1983-84, 86-88, Disting. Sci. Contbn. award divsn. adult devel. and aging 1988, Master Mentor award divsn. adult devel. and aging 2000, Disting. Contbns. to Clin. Geropsychology divsn. clin. psychology 2002), Gerontol. Soc. Am. Office: Washington U Dept Psychology Saint Louis MO 63130

STORANDT, PETER, educational consultant; AB, Cornell U.; PhD in English, U. Mass., Amherst. Asst. to dean U. Calif., Davis; asst. dean admissions Harvard U., Tufts U.; dir. admissions Yale U. Sch. Mgmt., NY Law Sch.; now ptnr. Ivy Success Inc., Garden City, NY. Exec. bd. mem. Nat. Network Law Sch. Officers, 1987—90; founder New England Assn. of Grad. Admissions Profls. Office: IvySuccess 1225 Franklin Ave Ste 325 Garden City NY 11530 *

STORCH, ARTHUR, theater director; s. Sam and Bessie (Goldner) S.; children: Max Darrow, Alexander English, Bess Martin. BA, New Sch.

Social Research, 1949. Actor in Broadway prodns. End as a Man, 1953, Time Limit, 1955, Girls of Summer, 1956, Look Homeward, Angel, 1957, Night Circus, 1958, The Long Dream, 1960, The Best Man, 1961; motion pictures The Strange One, 1956, Girls of the Night, 1959, The Exorcist, 1974; dir. off-Broadway Two by Saroyan, 1961, Three by Three, 1962, Talking to You (London debut), 1962, The Typists and the Tiger, 1963, The Owl and the Pussycat, 1964, The Impossible Years, 1965, The Local Stigmatic, 1970, Under the Weather, 1965, Golden Rainbow, 1967, The Chinese and Dr. Fish, 1969, Promenade All, 1970, 42 Seconds from Broadway, 1973, Tribute, 1978, Twice Around the Park, 1982, Clarence, 1986; Of Mice and Men, 1988; dir. nat. tour The King and I, 1989; dir. Syracuse Stage Waiting for Lefty, Noon, Of Mice and Men, 1974, 75, La Ronde, The Butterfingers Angel. Mornings at Seven, Dynamo, 1975-76, A Quality of Mercy, The Seagull, 1976-77, 1976-77, Love Letters on Blue Paper, End of the Beginning, 1977-78, Loved, 1978, Naked, 1979, The Comedy of Errors, 1980, The Impromptu of Outremont, 1982, The Double Bass, 1984, Arms and the Man, Handy Dandy, Cyrano de Bergerac, Romeo and Juliet, 1986, Of Mice and Men, NYC, 1987, Fugue, 1988, Seven By Beckett, 1988, Look Homeward Angel, Wait Unitl Dark, Dangerous Corner, 1990, A Walk in the Woods, 1989, Finding Donis Ann, 1990, Androcles and the Lion, 1991; Lend Me a Tenor, 1992; Awake and Sing, 1993; dir., actor Love Letters, 1992. Founder, producing artistic dir. Syracuse Stage; chmn. drama dept. Syracuse U., 1974-92, Arthur Storch Theatre, 1992; artistic dir. Berkshire Theatre Festival, Stockbridge, Mass., 1995-98. Home: 400 W 43d St Apt 13A New York NY 10036

STORCH, DAVID, manufacturing executive; Degree, Ithaca Coll., NY, 1975. Pres. AAR Aircraft Turbine Ctr.; pres., COO AAR Corp., Wood Dale, Ill., 1989—, CEO, 1996—. Bd. dirs. AAR Corp., Whittman-Hart Inc., Prentice Women's Hosp. Bd. trustees Ithaca (N.Y.) Coll., 2000—. Mem.: Young Pres. Org. Internat., Econ. Club Chgo. Office: AAR Corp 1100 North Wood Dale Rd Wood Dale IL 60191

STORCH, GERALD L. (JERRY STORCH), retail executive; BA cum laude, Harvard U., 1978, MBA with hons., 1981, JD magna cum laude, 1982. Ptnr. McKinsey & Co., Boston, 1982—93; sr. v.p. strategic planning Dayton Hudson Corp., Mpls., 1993—98; pres. fin. services & new bus. Target Corp., Mpls., 1999—2001, vice chmn., 2001—05; chmn., CEO Toys R Us, Inc., Wayne, NJ, 2006—. Office: Toys R Us Inc 1 Geoffrey Way Wayne NJ 07470 *

STORER, MARYRUTH, law librarian; b. Portland, Oreg., 1953; d. Joseph and Carol Storer; m. David Bailey, 1981; children: Sarah, Allison. BA in History, Portland State U., 1974; JD, U. Oreg., 1977; M in Law Librarianship, U. Wash., 1978. Bar: Oreg. 1978. Assoc. law libr. U. Tenn., Knoxville, 1978-79; law libr. O'Melveny & Myers, LA, 1979-88; dir. Orange County Pub. Law Libr., Santa Ana, Calif., 1988—. Mem. Am. Assn. Law Librs. (exec. bd. 1999-2002), So. Calif. Assn. Law Librs. (pres. 1986-87), Coun. Calif. County Law Librs. (sec./treas. 1990-94, pres. 1994-96), Arroyo Sero Libr. Network (chair 2000-03). Democrat. Episcopalian. Office: Orange County Public Law Library 515 N Flower St Santa Ana CA 92703-2304 Office Phone: 714-834-3002.

STOREY, BRIT ALLAN, historian; b. Boulder, Colo., Dec. 10, 1941; s. Harold Albert and Gladys Roberta (Althouse) S.; m. Carol DeArman, Dec. 19, 1970; 1 child, Christine Roberta. AB, Adams State Coll., Alamosa, Colo., 1963; MA, U. Ky., 1965, PhD, 1968. Instr. history Auburn (Ala.) U., 1967-68, asst. prof., 1968-70; dep. state historian State Hist. Soc. Colo., Denver, 1970-71, acting state historian, 1971-72, rsch. historian, 1972-74; hist. preservation specialist Adv. Coun. on Hist. Preservation, Lakewood, Colo., 1974-88; sr. historian Bur. Reclamation, Lakewood, 1988—. Contbr. articles to profl. publs. Mem. Fed. Preservation Forum (pres. 1990-91), Nat. Coun. Pub. History (sec. 1987, pres.-elect 1990-91, pres. 1991-92), Orgn. Am. Historians (com. 1983-86, chmn. 1985-86), Victorian Soc. Am. (bd. dirs. 1977-79), Western History Assn. (chmn. com. 1982-86), Colo.-Wyo. Assn. Mus. (sec. 1974-76, pres. 1976-77), Cosmos Club (Washington). Avocation: birding. Home: 7264 W Otero Ave Littleton CO 80128-5639 Office: Bur Reclamation Denver Fed Ctr D 5300 Bldg 67 Denver CO 80225-0007

STOREY, CHARLES PORTER, lawyer; b. Austin, Tex., Dec. 4, 1922; s. Robert Gerald and Frances Hazel (Porter) S.; m. Helen Hanks Stephens, Oct. 14, 1950; children: Charles Porter, Harry Stephens, Frederick Schatz. BA, U. Tex., 1947, LLB, 1948; LLM, So. Methodist U., 1952. Bar: Tex. 1948. Pvt. practice law, Dallas, 1948—; sr. counsel Carrington Coleman Sloman & Blumenthal, LLP. Pres. Dallas Day Nursery Assn., 1958, Greater Dallas Coun. Chs., 1970-71; chmn. Internat. Com. YMCA, 1969-71; nat. bd. dirs. U.S. YMCA, 1964-75; pres. Children's Devel. Ctr., Dallas, 1959; trustee Baylor Coll. Dentistry, 1981-90, Hillcrest Found., 1994—; trustee emeritus Southwestern Legal Found., chmn. 1980-90. 1st lt., pilot USAAF, 1943-45, ETO. Decorated Air medal. Master emeritus Dallas Inn of Ct. (pres. 1991-93); fellow Am. Coll. Trial Lawyers, Am. Bar Found., Tex. Bar Found.; mem. ABA, Tex. Bar Assn. (bd. dir. 1976-79), Dallas Bar Assn. (pres. 1975), Philos. Soc. Tex., Dallas Country Club, Phi Delta Phi, Phi Delta Theta. Home: 5855 Farquhar Ln Dallas TX 75209 Office: 901 Main St Ste 5500 Dallas TX 75202 Office Phone: 214-855-3052. Fax: 214-758-3753. E-mail: cstorey@ccsb.com.

STOREY, FRANCIS HAROLD, business consultant, retired bank executive; b. Calgary, Alberta, Can., June 20, 1933; s. Bertwyn Morrell and Hilda Josephine (Masters) S.; m. Willomae Saiter, Apr. 25, 1954; children: Daryl, Elizabeth, Brian, Shelley. Student, Gonzaga U., 1953, Pacific Coast Bankers Sch., 1974-76. Designated Certified Profl. Cons. Bank trainee Wash. Trust Bank, Spokane, 1950-56; owner Storey & Storey, Spokane, 1956-64; agt. Bankers Life Nebr., Spokane, 1964-67; sr. v.p. Old Nat. Bank, Spokane, 1967-87, U.S. Bank of Wash., Spokane, 1987-90; pvt. practice cons. Spokane, 1990—. Bd. dirs. Output Tech. Corp. Bd. dirs. Spokane Bus. Incubator, 1985-96, United Way of Spokane, 1987-95; bd. dirs., treas., fin. chair, gen. conv. dep. Episc. Diocese Spokane Dep., 1969-2001; trustee Spokane Symphony Soc., 1986-93, Spokane Area Econ. Devel. Coun., 1982-89; mem. adv. bd. Intercollegiate Ctr. Nursing Edn., 1990-96, chair, 1996; bd. dirs. Coalition for Women on Streets, treas., fin. chmn., 1999-2001. Mem.: Inland N.W. Soc. Consulting Profls., Acad. Profl. Consultants and Advisors, Spokane Club, Spokane Rotary (bd. dirs. Spkane Rotary Club 21 2003—05, trustee Spokane Rotary Found. 2004—, v.p. 2005). Episcopalian. Avocations: golf, reading, travel. Home: 214 E 13th Ave Spokane WA 99202-1115 E-mail: fhstorey@comcast.net.

STOREY, JAMES MOORFIELD, lawyer; b. Boston, Apr. 12, 1931; s. Charles Moorfield and Susan Jameson (Sweetser) S.; m. Adair Miller, Aug. 28, 1954 (div. 1973); children: Barbara Sessums Storey McGrath, Mary Sweetser Storey Meley, Susan Adair Storey Frank, Eliza Allison Tebo Storey Anderson, Alice Leovy Storey Wille; m. Isabelle Helene Boeschenstein, May 17, 1973. AB, Harvard U., 1953, LL.B., 1956. Bar: Mass. 1956. Atty. SEC, Washington, 1956-57, legal asst. to chmn., 1957-59; assoc. Gaston, Snow, Motley & Holt, Boston, 1959-62; ptnr. Gaston, Snow, Motley & Holt (name changed to Gaston Snow & Ely Bartlett), Boston, 1962-87, Dechert Price & Rhoads, Boston, 1987-94, ret., 1994, profl. trustee, corp. dir., 1994—. Trustee Mt. Auburn Cemetery, Cambridge, Mass., 1980-. Co-author: Mutual Fund Law Handbook, 1998, The Uneasy Chaperone, 2000. Mem. ABA, Boston Bar Assn., Tavern Club Boston (pres. 1985-87), Century Assn. of N.Y. Unitarian Universalist. Home: 89A Mt Vernon St Boston MA 02108-1330 Office: 5 Boylston Pl Boston MA 02116 Office Phone: 617-728-0429. Personal E-mail: jandistorey@worldnet.att.net.

STOREY, KENNETH BRUCE, biology professor; b. Taber, Alta., Can., Oct. 23, 1949; s. Arthur George and Madeleine Una (Mawhinney) S.; m. Janet Margaret Collicutt, June 6, 1975; children: Jennifer, Kathryn. BSc with honors, U. Calgary, Alta., 1971; PhD, U. B.C., Vancouver, Can., 1974. Asst. prof. Duke U., Durham, NC, 1975-79; assoc. prof. Carleton U., Ottawa, Ont., Canada, 1979-85, prof., 1985—, Can. Rsch. chair, 2001—. Chair. Can. rsch. molecular physiology, Canada; adj. prof. in botany and zoology Stellenbosch U., South Africa; lectr. in field. Editor Cell and Molecular Responses to Stress, Functional Metabolism; mem. editl. bd. Jour. Comparative Physiology, 1995—, Jour. Thermal Biology, 2007-; contbr. over 510 articles to profl. jours. Recipient E.W.R. Steacie award Nat. Sci. and Engring. Rsch. Coun. Can., 1984-86, Killam Sr. Rsch. fellow, 1993-95. Fellow AAAS, Royal Soc. Can.; mem. Can. Biochem. Soc. (Ayerst award 1989), Can. Soc. Zoology, Soc. Cryobiology. Avocations: movies, music, renaissance art. Office: Carleton U Dept Biology 1125 Colonel By Drive Ottawa ON Canada K1S 5B6 Office Phone: 613-520-3678. Business E-Mail: kenneth_storey@carleton.ca.

STOREY, MITCHEL D., sports medicine physician; MD, Phila. Coll. Osteopathic Medicine, Pa. Cert. Family Practice, Sports Medicine. Intern Cmty. Gen. Osteopathic Hosp., Harrisburg, Pa.; fellow, sports medicine, The Sports Medicine Clinic Northwest Hosp. and Med. Ctr., Seattle, physician, The Sports Medicine Clinic. Team physician Seattle Mariners, 1984—, Blanchet HS, Seattle Pacific U. Athletics; med. dir. Seafair Hydroplane Races. Avocations: golf, fishing, hunting, swimming. Office: The Sports Medicine Clinic 10330 Meridian Ave N Ste 300 Seattle WA 98133 Office Phone: 206-368-6100. *

STOREY, NORMAN C., lawyer; b. Miami, Fla., Oct. 11, 1943; BA cum laude, Loyola-Marymount U., LA, 1965; JD, U. Ariz., 1968. Bar: Ariz. 1968. Law clk. to Hon. James A. Walsh U.S. Dist. Ct. Ariz.; ptnr. Squire, Sanders & Dempsey, L.L.P., Phoenix. Fin. coun. Diocese Phoenix Cath. Ch.; mem. mens art coun. Phoenix Art Mus. Mem.: State Bar Ariz. Office: 40 N Central Ave Ste 2700 Phoenix AZ 85004-4498 Business E-Mail: nstorey@ssd.com.

STOREY, RICHARD D., academic administrator, biology professor; m. Martha Storey; children: Beth, Justin. BS, Univ. N.Mex.; MS, PhD, Univ. Okla. Asst. prof., assoc. prof. Colo. Coll., Colo. Springs., 1978—92, prof., biology dept. Colo. Springs, 1992—99, dean of faculty, 1999—2004, acting pres., 2000; chancellor Univ. Mont. Western, Dillon, 2004—. Office: Univ of Montana Western Office of the Chancellor 710 S Atlantic Dillon MT 59725 *

STOREY, ROBERT DAVIS, retired lawyer; b. Tuskegee, Ala., Mar. 28, 1936; s. Dewitt Herald and Katie Pearl (Johnson) Storey; m. Juanita Kendrick Cohen, May 9, 1959; children: Charles Kendrick, Christopher Robert Ransom, Rebecca Kate. AB, Harvard U., 1958; JD, Case Western Res. U., 1964; LHD, Tri-State U., 2000. Bar: Ohio 1964. Atty. East Ohio Gas Co., Cleve., 1964-66; asst. dir. Legal Aid Soc., Cleve., 1966-67; assoc. Burke, Haber & Berick, Cleve., 1967-70, ptnr., 1971-93, Thompson, Hine & Flory, L.L.P., Cleve., 1994—2004; ret., 2004. Bd. dirs. Verizon Comm., Inc., NYC. Trustee Kresge Found., Phillips Exeter Acad., 1968—83, Cleve. State U., 1971—80, chmn., 1979—80; bd. overseers Harvard U., 1978—84. Capt. USMC, 1958—61. Named Chief Marshal, 25th Reunion, Harvard Class of 1958, 1983; recipient Charles Flint Kellogg award, Assn. Episcopal Colls., 1984. Mem.: Soc. Benchers, Union Club. Episcopalian. Home: 1803 Asturias St Saint Augustine FL 32080-4074

STOREY, SUSAN, investment banker; b. Dublin; 1 child. Student, U. Coll. Dublin, York U., Toronto, Can. Fgn. exch. trader CIBC Wood Gundy, 1982—87, v.p., 1987—88, with bank derivatives group London, 1988—90, derivatives mgr. Toronto, 1990—96, head global derivatives trading, 1996—98, mng. dir., head global trading Debt Capital Markets, 1998—. Former chair Can. Com. for Professionalism; past pres. Forex Can.; voting mem. Fed. Res. Bank, N.Y. Fgn. Exch. Com.; ex-officio mem. Can. Fgn. Exch. Com. Bank Can. Chair CIBC Wood Gundy Children's Miracle Found.; vice chair Children's Aid Found.; bd. mem. Ireland Fund. Named one of 25 Most Powerful Women in Banking, U.S. Banker, 2003. Office: BCE Place 161 Bay St PO Box 500 Toronto ON Canada M5J 2S8

STORIE, ERIC DUANE, science administrator; b. Lenoir, NC, May 20, 1954; s. Clarence Lee and Daisy Puett Storie; m. Jean Ward Bumbarger; children: Kathryn Elizabeth, Erin Christine. MS in Biology, U. NC, Charlotte, 1983. Dir. environ. tech. Roanoke-Chowan C.C., Ahoskie, NC, 1992—2003; dir. biotech. Coll. of The Albemarle, Elizabeth City, NC, 2003—. Mem. com. on anti-bioterrorism curricula NC Dept. of C.C.s, Raleigh, 2002—03. Mem. Union Concerned Scientists, 2003; advisor Green Party, Midland, NC, 2004. Mem.: Am. Inst. Biol. Scis., Human Anatomy and Physiology Soc. Avocations: hiking, bicycling. Office: Coll of The Albemarle 1208 N Road St Elizabeth City NC 27909 Home Phone: 252-357-1532; Office Phone: 252-335-0821 ext 2202. Office Fax: 252-335-2011. E-mail: estorie@albemarle.edu.

STORIN, MATTHEW VICTOR, academic administrator, educator, retired editor; b. Springfield, Mass., Dec. 24, 1942; s. Harry Francis and Blanche Marie S.; m. Keiko Takita, Aug. 1, 1975; 1 child, Kenyatta; children by previous marriage: Karen, Aimee, Sean. BA, U. Notre Dame, 1964. Reporter Springfield Daily News, 1964-65, Griffin-Larrabee News Bur., Washington, 1965-69; Washington corr., city editor, Asian corr., nat. editor, asst. mng. editor, dep. mng. editor, mng. editor Boston Globe, 1969-85; dep. mng. editor U.S. News & World Report, Washington, 1985-86; editor, sr. v.p. Chgo. Sun-Times, 1986-87; editor The Maine Times, Topsham, 1988-89; mng. editor N.Y. Daily News, 1989-91, exec. editor, 1991-92, Boston Globe, 1992-93, editor, 1993—2001; assoc. v.p., prof. Am. studies U. Notre Dame, 2002—. Recipient Disting. Polit. Reporting award Am. Assn. Polit. Sci., 1969, Yankee Quill award New Eng. Chpt. Sigma Delta Chi, 1997. Home: 1741 W North Shore Dr South Bend IN 46617 Office Phone: 574-631-0477. E-mail: mstorin@nd.edu.

STORING, PAUL EDWARD, retired foreign service officer; b. Ames, Iowa, Oct. 24, 1929; s. James Alvin and Edith Nora (Ryg) S.; children: Mimi Storing Harlan, Felice Storing Kite. Student, U Oslo, Norway, 1950-51; BA, Allegheny Coll., 1952; MA with honors, Colgate U., 1956; postgrad., U. Wis., Madison, 1955-59. Fgn. service officer Dept. State, Washington, Mex. and Scandinavia, 1960-80; spl. asst. U.S. Sect. Internat. Boundary and Water Commn. U.S. And Mex., Washington, 1980-99; ret. Contbr. articles to profl. jours. Served to cpl. U.S. Army, 1953-55 Fellow U. Wis., 1957-58; Fulbright fellow U. Oslo, 1959-60 Mem. Am. Fgn. Svc. Assn., Fulbright Assn., Phi Beta Kappa, Delta Tau Delta (pres. Alpha chpt. 1949-50). Baptist. Avocations: music, photography, travel. Home: 9006 Opera Alley Manassas VA 20110 E-mail: storingpe@netscape.net.

STORK, DONALD ARTHUR, advertising executive; b. Walsh, Ill., June 17, 1939; s. Arthur William and Katherine Frances (Young) S.; m. Joanna Gentry, June 9, 1962; 1 child, Brian Wesley. BS, So. Ill. U., 1961; postgrad., St. Louis U., 1968—69. With Naegele Outdoor Advt., Mpls. and St. Louis, 1961—63; acct. exec. Richard C. Lynch Advg., 1963—64; media exec. Gardner Advt. Co., 1964—69; v.p. mktg. Advanswers Media/Programming, 1975—79; pres. Advanswers divsn. Wells/BDDP, NYC, 1979—98; pres. Advanswers unit Omnicom, St. Louis, 1998—2002, pres. PHD unit, 2002—04; ret., 2004. Bd. dirs. Trailblazers, Inc.; corp. devel. St. Louis Art Mus., 1999—2005. Capt. Mo. Air N.G., 1961—67. Recipient Journalism Alumnus of Yr. award So. Ill. U., Alumni Achievement award. Mem. St. Louis Advtsg. Club, Mensa, Mo. Athletic Club, St. Clair Country Club (bd. dirs. 2001), Alpha Delta Sigma (Aid to Advtg. Edn. award). Home: 27 Symonds Dr Belleville IL 62223-1905 Office: Media Mgmt Inc 14755 N Outer Forty Dr Chesterfield MO 63017 Office Phone: 314-910-0373. Personal E-mail: dastork@sbcglobal.net.

STORK, GILBERT, chemistry professor; b. Brussels, Dec. 31, 1921; s. Jacques and Simone (Weil) Stork; m. Winifred Stewart, June 9, 1944 (dec. May 1992); children: Diana, Linda, Janet, Philip. BS, U. Fla., 1942; PhD, U. Wis., 1945; DSc (hon.), Lawrence Coll., 1961, U. Paris, 1979, U. Rochester, 1982, Emory U., 1988, Columbia U., 1993, U. Wis., 1997. Sr. rsch. chemist Lakeside Labs., 1945—46; instr. chemistry Harvard U., 1946—48, asst. prof., 1948—53; assoc. prof. Columbia U., NYC, 1953—55, prof., 1955—67, Eugene Higgins prof., 1967—92, prof. emeritus, 1992—, chmn. dept., 1973—76. Lectr. and cons. in field; chmn. Gordon Steroid Conf., 1958—59. Recipient Baekeland medal, 1961, Harrison Howe award, 1962, Edward Curtis Franklin Meml. award, Stanford, 1966, Gold medal, Synthetic Chems. Mfrs. Assn., 1971, Nebr. award, 1973, Roussel prize in steroid chemistry, 1978, Edgar Fahs Smith award, 1982, Nat. Medal of Sci., 1982, Linus Pauling award, 1983, Tetrahedron prize, 1985, Remsen award, 1986, Cliff S. Hamilton award, 1986, Mony Ferst award, Sigma Xi, 1987, George Kenner award, 1992, Robert Robinson award, 1992, Chem. Pioneer award, Am. Inst. Chemists, 1992, Welch Found. award in chemistry, 1993, Allan R. Day award, 1994, Wolf prize in chemistry, Wolf Found., Israel, 1996, Phila. Chemists Club award, 1998, Barton Gold medal, U.K., 2002, Ryoji Noyori award, Soc. Synthetic Organic Chemistry Japan, 2003, Eminent Scientists award, Japanese Soc. for the Promotion Sci., 2005; fellow, Guggenheim, 1959. Fellow: NAS (award in chem. sci. 1982), Am. Philos. Soc., Am. Acad. Arts and Scis., Royal Soc., French Acad. Scis., Royal Soc. Chemistry (Barton Gold medal 2002); mem.: Am. Chem. Soc. (chmn. organic chemistry divsn. 1967, award in pure chemistry 1957, award for creative work in synthetic organic chemistry 1967, Nichols medal 1980, Arthur C. Cope award 1980, Willard Gibbs medal 1982, Roger Adams award in organic chemistry 1991, Herbert C. Brown award in organic chemistry 2005), Chem. Soc. Japan (hon.), Pharm. Soc. Japan (hon.), Chemists Club (hon.). Home: 188 Chestnut St Englewood Cliffs NJ 07632-1908 Office: Columbia U Dept Chemistry Chandler Hall New York NY 10027 Home Phone: 201-871-4032; Office Phone: 212-854-2178. Business E-Mail: gjs8@columbia.edu.

STORK, VERA LEE, retired elementary school educator; b. Galveston, Tex., Dec. 21, 1942; d. Leslie Don and Ethel F. (Wakefield) Ward; m. Jack E. Stork; children: James Ward, Melissa Gayle. BS in Edn., Southwest Tex. State U., 1965; MEd, Sam Houston State U., 1974. Counselor's cert. U. Houston Clear Lake. Tchr. Port Isable (Tex.) Sch. Dist., 1965-67, Galveston Sch. Dist., 1974—; counselor Rosenberg Elem. Sch., Galveston, Tex., Boliver Elem. Sch., Galveston, 1995—2000; ret., 2000. Life mem. Tex. State PTA; first v.p. Rosenberg Sch. PTA, Galveston; active Galveston Hist. Soc., 1986-87, Galveston Hospice Group, 1986-87; mem. Leon County Rep. Women, 2000—; chmn. Neighbors Helping Neighbors, Hilltop Lakes, 2004-06; Hilltop Lakes Beautification Com., 2000—; mem. Hilltop Lakes Aux. Scholarship Com., 2005—, chairperson, 2006; pres. Hilltop Lakes Chapel Aux., 2007. Mem. AAUW (treas. 1978-79), LWV, Am. Field Service (pres. 1982-84), Assn. Tex. Profl. Women (bldg. rep.), Delta Kappa Gamma (project com., ceremonies com. Omicron chpt. 1975—). Beta Sigma Phi (Beta Kappa Mu chpt., 2002—, pres., 2003-04), Red Hat Soc. (La Chapequx chpt., 2004—). Episcopalian. Home: PO Box 1158 Normangee TX 77871-1158

STORM, HUNTER ALEXANDRA (EUGENIA LYNN MORRIS), information security engineer; b. Charleston, W.Va., Mar. 4, 1968; d. Eugene Paul, Jr. and Nora Jean (Harless) Morris. AA with honors, Scottsdale CC, Ariz., 1996; BA, Ariz. State U., Tempe, 1999. Microsoft office user specialist master Microsoft, 2000, cert. Win2K Profl. Microsoft, 2001, profl. Win2K server Microsoft, 2002, Network+ Profl. CompTIA, 2001, ArcSight security analyst ArcSight, 2006. Entrepreneur, entertainer Morgan Le Fey Entertainment and Promotions, 1986—99; sys. adminstr., tech. support analyst KAET-TV Eight, Tempe, Ariz., 1998—99; sr. field engr., project mgr. Wells Fargo/MicroAge, 1999—2001; tech. lead Am. Express/Alliance Cons., Phoenix, 2001—03; lead engr., project mgr. Charles Schwab, Phoenix, 2003—04; sys. arch. Wells Fargo/Datatek, Chandler, Ariz., 2005—06; dir. info. security Go Daddy Software, Scottsdale, Ariz., 2002; info. security engr. Wells Fargo, Chandler, Ariz., 2006—. Entrepreneur, cons. H.A.S. IT Cons., Phoenix, 1996—2005; spkr. in field. Singer: Asphalt Playground; asst. editor Much Ado About Mensa; contbr. articles to popular mags.; host, writer (TV series) Backstage Pass. Named Wells Fargo Enterprise Assoc. of the Month, MicroAge, 2000; recipient Cert. of Achievement, Ariz. State U. West Student Comm. Conf., 1998, Legends of Svc. award, MicroAge, 2000, 1st pl., Long Beach Half Marathon, 2000, Cactus Speed Classic Half Marathon, Tucson 5000, 2000, Chandler Run for the Gold 5K, 2000, Phoenix Coyotes/Runner's Den 10K, 2000. Mem.: Mensa, Predator Inline Speed Club, Phi Theta Kappa. Democrat. Achievements include research in system migration processes and documentation; design of systems and process improvements. Avocations: inline speed skating, kickboxing, bodybuilding, motorcycling, reading. Home Phone: 480-343-7383. Personal E-mail: hunterstorm@hotmail.com.

STORM, J. RENI, nurse, consultant; d. Edmund Francis and M. Helen (Saltzmann) Corrado; m. John A. Storm, Feb. 14, 1970 (div. Sept. 1990); 1 child, Kierston L Storm-Dubois. AAS in Nursing cum laude, Dutchess C.C., Poughkeepsie, NY, 1978; BS in Health Care Cmty., SUNY, New Paltz, 1987; workshop, Scottsdale Sch. for Artists, 2001; MA in Legal and Ethical Studies, U. Balt., 2003. RN NY. Clin. nurse III St. Vincent Hosp., Santa Fe, 1992—. Cmty. edn., mental health players NY State Psychiat. Ctr., Poughkeepsie, 1984—86; pvt. practice consulting legal nurse, Santa Fe, 2003—06; surveyor Accreditation Assn. for Ambulatory Health Care, Inc., 2006. Contbg. editor: (novel) Seas Raging, White Horse Flying; contbg. costume designer The Jungle Book, N.Mex. Ballet, creator (coloring book); exhibitions include 1st Nat. Bank Santa Fe, Limner Gallery, NYC, Santa Fe Soc. Artists, Kiva Gallery; actor: (debut) Inherit the Wind, Agatha Christie's Spider Web (Critical acclaim reviews, 1990); polit. cartoon strip, Udo. Mem. Santa Fe Coun. on Internat. Rels., N.Mex., 2002—03; mem., educator Cmty. Mental Health Players, Poughkeepsie, NY, 1984—86; tutor for cmty. immigrants Literacy Vols., Santa Fe, 2001—02; mem. founding group Santa Fe Living Wage Network, 2003—; rehab. group leader for stroke patients Santa Fe Care Nursing Home, 1999—2000; pres., bd. dirs. Mid Hudson Kennel Club, 1986—88; sponsor World Vision, Rhinebeck, NY, 1989—99; nursing, health care advisor KSK Buddhist Ctr., Santa Fe, 2001—03; AKC judges edn. coord. Mastiff Club Am., Rhinebeck, NY, 1986—88; pres. Dutchess County SPCA, Poughkeepsie, NY, 1986—88; v.p. Santa Fe Soc. Artists, 1997—98. Recipient Cmty. Svc. award for Devel. Contbn., Dutchess County SPCA Bd. Dirs., 1988; scholar, Union Plus, 2002. Mem.: Legal Nurse Consultants (Puget Sound chpt.), Am. Assn. Legal Nurse Cons. Achievements include development of long range plan for community project/Dutchess County SPCA. Avocations: world travel and cultures, cartooning, painting, writing, public speaking. Personal E-mail: renistorm@yahoo.com.

STÖRMER, HORST LUDWIG, physicist; b. Frankfurt-Main, Fed. Republic Germany, Apr. 6, 1949; arrived in U.S., 1977; s. Karl-Ludwig and Marie (Ihrig) S.; m. Dominique A. Parchet, 1982. Studied Physics, JW Goethe Univ.; PhD, U. Stuttgart, 1977. From tech. staff to dir. phys. rsch. lab. AT&T Bell Labs., Murray Hill, NJ, 1977—97; prof. physics and applied physics Columbia U., NYC, 1998—. Adj. physics dir. Lucent Tech., 1997—. Decorated Officier de la Legion d'Honneur France, Grosses Verdienstkreuz Mit Stern Germany; recipient Otto Klung prize, 1985,

Benjamin Franklin medal in physics, 1998, Nobel prize in Physics, 1998, N.Y.C. Mayor's award for excellence in sci. and tech., 2000; fellow Bell Labs., 1983. Fellow: NAS, Am. Acad. Arts and Scis., Am. Phys. Soc. (Buckley prize 1984). Office: Columbia U Dept Physics 538 W 120th St New York NY 10027-6601 also: Lucent Technologies 700 Mountain Ave New Providence NJ 07974-1208

STORMER, JOHN ANTHONY, retired minister, writer, publisher; b. Altoona, Pa., Feb. 9, 1928; s. Regis Walter and Mary Ann (Forr) S.; m. Elizabeth Ruth Lewis, July 2, 1951; 1 child, Holly. BS in Journalism, San Jose State U., Calif., 1954; DLitt (hon.), Manahath Sch. Theology, Hollidaysburg, Pa., 1965; LittD (hon.), Shelton Coll., 1976. Ordained to ministry Bapt. Ch., 1968. Pastor Heritage Bapt. Ch., Florissant, Mo., 1968-86; supt. Faith Christian Acad., Florissant, 1968—99; owner Liberty Bell Press, Florissant, 1963—. Bd. dirs. Internat. Coun. Christian Chs., 1965-87; dir. I Chronicles 12:32 Ministry, Florissant, 1985—; leader bible studies for legislators, Jefferson City, Mo., 1977—. Author: None Dare Call It Treason, 1964, The Death of a Nation, 1968, Growing of God's Way, 1984, NDCIT—25 Years Later, 1990, None Dare Call It Education, 1999, Betrayed by the Bench, 2005. Mem. rep. state com., state chmn. Mo. Young Reps., 1962-64, state del. Rep. Nat. Conv., San Francisco, 1964; tchr. legis. bible studies Mo. State Capital, Jefferson City, Mo., 1977—. With USAF, 1950-53. Mem. Am. Legion, Rotary Internat. Office: PO Box 32 Florissant MO 63033 Office Phone: 314-838-1477. *Through the resurrected life of the Lord Jesus Christ, individuals who have received Him have everything they need to be and do all that God the Father calls them to.*

STORMES, JOHN MAX, systems analyst; b. Manila, Oct. 7, 1927; s. Max Clifford and Janet (Heldring) S.; m. Takako Sanae, July 29, 1955; children: Janet Kazuko, Alan Osamu. BS, San Diego State U., 1950; BA, U. So. Calif., 1957, MA, 1967. Cert. secondary and community coll. tchr., sr. profl. human resources. Editing supr. Lockheed Propulsion Co., Redlands, Calif., 1957-61; proposals supr. Rockwell Internat., Downey, Calif., 1961-62; publs. dir. Arthur D. Little, Inc., Santa Monica, Calif., 1962-63; publs. coord. Rockwell Internat., Downey, 1963-68; project dir. Gen. Behavioral Systems, Inc., Torrance, Calif., 1969-73; tng. and comm. cons. Media Rsch. Assocs., Santa Cruz, Calif., 1973—; instrl. design supr. So. Calif. Gas Co., LA, 1985-2001; adj. assoc. prof. Alliant U., Alhambra, Calif., 2001—02. Lectr. Calif. State U., Northridge, 1991-2003; tng. cons. Nat. Ednl. Media, Chatsworth, Calif., 1966-81, comm. cons. Opinion Rsch. Calif., Long Beach, 1974-. Co-author: TV Communications Systems For Business and Industry, 1970; contbg. author: ASTD's In Action series of casebooks, 1996-99. Curriculum adv. bd. communications dept. Calif. State U., Fullerton, 1964-78. Sgt. U.S. Army, 1953-55, Japan. Mem. Soc. Tech. Communication (sr. mem., 2nd v.p. Orange County chpt. 1962-63), Internat. Soc. Performance and Instruction (v.p. L.A. chpt. 1989, pres. 1990). Democrat. Episcopalian. Avocations: photography, sailing. Home and Office: 136 Alamo Ave Santa Cruz CA 95060 Home Phone: 831-427-1558. Personal E-mail: jmstormes@comcast.net.

STORMONT, RICHARD MANSFIELD, hotel executive; b. Chgo., Apr. 4, 1936; s. Daniel Lytle and E. Mildred (Milligan) S.; m. Virginia Louellen Walters, Nov. 21, 1959; children: Stacy Lee Freeman, Richard Mansfield, John Frederick. BS, Cornell U., 1958. Cert. hosp. adminstrn.; cert. hosps. industry profl. Food cost analyst, sales rep. Edgewater Beach Hotel, Chgo., 1957-58; asst. sales mgr. Marriott Hotels, Inc., Washington, 1962-64, dir. sales Atlanta, 1964-68, resident mgr., 1969-71; gen. mgr. Marriott Hotel, Dallas, 1971-73, Phila., 1973-74, Atlanta, 1974-79; pres. Hardin Mgmt. Co., 1979-80; v.p. Marriott Franchise div. Marriott Corp., Washington, 1980-83, v.p. ops. Courtyard by Marriott, 1981-83; pres. The Stormont Cos. Inc., 1984—2004; chmn. Stormont Trice Corp., 1993-2000, Stormont Noble Devel. LLC, 2004—06; pres. The Stormont Cos., LLC, 2004—. Pres. Atlanta Conv. and Visitors Burs., 1975-76, vice chmn. bd., 1976-77, chmn., 1998-99, chmn. bd. exec. com., 1998-2000; trustee Young Harris Coll.; bd. dirs. Better Bus. Bur.; exec. com. Ctrl. Atlanta Progress, 1979-80; exec. coun. Boy Scouts Am.; bd. dirs., chmn. tourism divsn. Ga. Dept. Industry, Trade and Tourism, 1999-2001; chmn. bd. trustees Lenbrook Square Found., Inc., 2007—; chmn. bd. dirs. Atlanta St. Patricks Day Found., 2005-06. Paul Harris fellow Rotary Internat., 2006-07; recipient Disting. Salesman of Yr. award Marriott, 1967, Obi T. Brewer award for Decade of Outstanding Svc., 1979, Atlanta Hospitality Hall of Fame award, 2006. Mem. Sales and Mktg. Execs. (exec. v.p. 1969-70, pres. Atlanta 1970-71), Am. Hotel-Motel Assn. (exec. com., bd. dirs. 1993-95, Most Valuable Vol. Ga. 1999), Ga. Hospitality and Travel Assn. (founder 1975, bd. dir., pres. 1989-90, chmn. bd. 1991-92, Hotelier of Yr. award 1977, Hall of Fame 2001), Ga. Bus. and Industry Assn. (bd. dirs.), Atlanta Hotel Assn. (pres. 1976), So. Innkeepers Assn., Atlanta C. of C. (v.p. 1978-79), Gwinnett C. of C. (bd. dirs.), Cornell Soc. Hotelmen (pres. Ga. chpt. 1976, regional v.p. 1989-91), Cornell U. Hotel Soc. (SE Hotelier of Yr.), Rotary (Atlanta, bd. dirs. 1999-2007, pres. 2007—). Home and Office: 2980 Nancy Creek Rd NW Atlanta GA 30327-2000 Office Phone: 404-355-4038. E-mail: dstormont@bellsouth.net.

STORMS, CLIFFORD BEEKMAN, lawyer; b. Mount Vernon, NY, July 18, 1932; s. Harold Beekman and Gene (Pertak) S.; m. Barbara H. Grave, 1955 (div. 1975); m. Valeria N. Parker, July 12, 1975; children: Catherine Storms Fischer, Clifford Beekman. BA magna cum laude, Amherst Coll., 1954; LLB, Yale U., 1957. Bar: N.Y. 1957. Assoc. Breed, Abbott & Morgan, NYC, 1957—64; with CPC Internat., Inc., Englewood Cliffs, NJ, 1964—97, v.p. legal affairs, 1973—75, v.p., gen. counsel, 1975—88, sr. v.p., gen. counsel, 1988—97, atty. alternate dispute resolution, corp. dir., 1997—; bd. dirs. Corn Products Internat. Inc., 1997—2005; pvt. practice Greenwich, Conn., 1997—. Bd. dirs. Atlantic Legal Found., Indian Harbor Yacht Club; mem. Conn. Alternate Dispute Resolution panel Ctr. Pub. Resources. Trustee emeritus Food and Drug Law Inst. Mem. ABA (com. of corp. gen. counsel), Am. Arbitration Assn. (panel arbitrators large complex case program), Assn. Gen. Counsel (pres. 1992-94), Assn. Bar City NY (sec., com. on corp. law depts. 1979-81), Phi Beta Kappa. Home: 19 Burying Hill Rd Greenwich CT 06831-2604 Office: Ste 100 Two Sound View Dr Greenwich CT 06830 Office Phone: 203-622-4995. Personal E-mail: cbstorms@aol.com.

STORNES, MARK, professional sports team executive; married; children: Matt, Ryan, Scott, Meghan. BBA in Acctg., Cleve. State U., 1983. Sr. auditor Grant Thornton, 1983—87; positions up to exec. v.p., COO TransAmerica Mailings, Inc., 1987—96; sr. v.p. fin. and adminstrn., CFO Cleve. Cavaliers/Quicken Loans Arena, 1996—2001, exec. v.p., COO, 2001—02, CEO, 2003—. Exec. dir. Cavaliers Charities, 1999; treas. Downtown Cleve. Alliance; trustee Berea Ednl. Fund Found. Mem.: Bluecoats, Inc. Office: Cleve Cavaliers One Center Ct Cleveland OH 44115-4001 *

STORR, ROBERT, curator, art educator, painter; b. Portland, Maine, Dec. 28, 1949; s. Richard J. and Virginia V. Storr; m. Rosamund Helen Morley, Sept. 1, 1979; children: Katharine, Susannah. BA, Swarthmore Coll., 1972; postgrad., Sch. Art Inst. of Chgo., 1975-78; MFA, Skowhegan Sch. Painting and Sculp, Maine, 1978. Assoc. dean N.Y. Studio Sch., NYC, 1987-88; asst. prof. Tyler Sch. Art, Phila., 1989; Avery prof. Bard Coll., Annandale On Hudson, NY, 1990-91; sr. curator painting and sculpture Mus. Modern Art, NYC, 1991—2002; Rosalie Solow prof. of modern art NYU Inst. of Fine Arts, NYC, 2002—06; dean Sch. Art Yale Univ., New Haven, 2006—. Vis. artist Cooper Union, N.Y.C., 1988-89; vis. artist, critic R.I. Sch. Design, Providence, 1988; lectr. art mus., univs. and art schs. in U.S. and abroad; coordinating curator at Moma, 1995. Author: Philip Guston, 1986; co-author: Chuck Close, 1987, (with Lars Hitue) Susan Rothenberg 15 Years a Survey, 1990, (with Kirk Varnedoe) From Bauhaus to Pop: Masterworks Given By Phillip Johnson, 1996; also exhbn. catalogues; contbg. editor Art in Am.; mem. editorial bd. Art Jour.; contbr. articles to profl. jours.; exhibitions include Inst. Contemporary Art Phila., 1991, Moma, 1991, 93, 94, 95, 96. Penny McCall Found. grantee, 1988, Peter Norton Family Found. grantee, 1990. Mem. Internat. Assn. Art Critics.

STORRER, SCOTT A., insurance company executive; B, DePauw U., Greencastle, Ind.; MBA, Boston U. Various mgmt. positions Liberty Mut. Group, 1993—2001; sr. v.p. disability mgmt. & customer svc. CIGNA Corp., 2001—02, sr. v.p. healthcare svc. ops., 2002—05, sr. v.p. info. tech., 2004—05, exec. v.p. svc. ops. & info. tech., 2005—. Office: CIGNA Corp 900 Cottage Grove Rd Bloomfield CT 06002 Office Phone: 860-726-6000. *

STORRER, WILLIAM ALLIN, theater educator, consultant; b. Highland Park, Mich., Mar. 22, 1936; s. Fredrick Ray and Margaret Ann (Pitts) S.; m. Carol A. Tuthill, Nov. 6, 1964 (div. June 1969); 1 child, Kirsten; m. Patricia Alice Whalley, Dec. 30, 1976. Student, Albion Coll., 1954-56; AB in Engring. Scis., Harvard U., 1959; MFA in Theatre Arts, Boston U., 1962; PhD in Comparative Arts, Ohio U., 1968. Electronics engr. Raytheon Co., Wayland, Mass., 1958-60; tech. dir. small stage Boston Arts Festival, 1961, 62; dir. dramatics Melrose HS, Mass., 1962—63; dir. playhouse and repertory theatre, instr. drama-speech Hofstra U., 1963-66, instr. opera, 1965; asst. prof. theatre, dir. univ. theatre, U. Toledo, 1968-69; assoc. prof. theatre and film, dir. Southampton Coll., LI U., 1969—73; asst. prof. cinema studies and still photography Ithaca Coll., NY, 1973—76; assoc. prof. media arts U. SC, Columbia, 1976—82; pres. MINDaLIVE Creative Mind Enhancement, Newark, 1980—. Assoc. prof. theater and speech World Campus Afloat, Chapman Coll., 1972; edn. media specialist Newark Bd. Edn., 1990-94, Linden Bd. Edn., 1994-95, Harrison Bd. Edn., 1995-96, Rosa Parks Fine and Performing Arts HS, Paterson, NJ, 1996-2004, dir. Storrer/Storre/Storer Family Inst., adj. prof. U. Tex., 2004-. Author: The Architecture of Frank Lloyd Wright, A Complete Catalog, 1974, 4th edit. 2007, The Frank Lloyd Wright Companion, 1993, 2d edit., 2006; contbr. articles to popular mags. and profl. jours. Grantee Graham Found. for Advanced Studies in Fine Arts, 1987, 94. Home: Frankfort MI 49635-1121 Office: PO Box 1121 Frankfort MI 49635 Office Phone: 231-352-9343.

STORRS, ELEANOR EMERETT, science administrator, consultant; b. Cheshire, Conn., May 3, 1926; d. Benjamin Porter and Alta Hyde (Moss) S.; m. Harry Phineas Burchfield, Jr., Nov. 29, 1963; children: Sarah Storrs, Benjamin Hyde. BS with distinction in Botany, U. Conn., 1948; MS in Biology, NYU, 1958; PhD in Chemistry, U. Tex., 1967. Asst. biochemist Boyce Thompson Inst. for Plant Rsch., Yonkers, NY, 1948-62; rsch. scientist Clayton Found. Biochem. Inst., U. Tex., Austin, 1962-65; biochemist Pesticides Rsch. Lab., USPHS, Perrine, Fla., 1965-67; dir. dept. biochemistry Gulf South Rsch. Inst., New Iberia, La., 1967-77; adj. prof. chemistry U. Southwestern La., Lafayette, 1974-77; rsch. prof. biology Fla. Inst. Tech., Melbourne, 1977-94, cons. on leprosy-armadillo programs, 1975-94, mem. Faculty Senate, 1979-84, prof. emeritus, 1994—. Cons. in rehab. and prevention deformities leprosy Pan Am. Health Orgn., WHO, Venezuela, Argentina, Brazil, Mex., 1972-90; dep. v.p. Coll. Hansenology in Endemic Countries, 1980-85 Author: (with H.P. Burchfield) Biochemical Applications of Gas Chromatography, 1962, (with Burchfield, D.E. Johnson) Guide to the Analysis of Pesticide Residues, 2 vols, 1965; also articles, book chpts. Grantee NIH, 1968-88, CDC, 1969-73, WHO, 1973-93, Leprosy Program, 1978-93, German Leprosy Relief Assn., 1973-78, Nat. Coun. Episc. Ch., 1975-77, Brit. Leprosy Relief Assn., 1981-88; recipient plaque La. Health Dept., 1972, Disting. Alumni award U. Conn., 1975, Gold award Am. Coll. Pathologists and Am. Soc. Clin. Pathologists, 1974, Gerard B. Lambert award for spl. recognition, 1975. Fellow AAAS; mem. AAUW, Internat. Leprosy Assn., Am. Recorder Soc., Early Music Assn., Sigma Xi. Episcopalian (vestryman). Clubs: Appalachian (Boston); Green Mountain (Bear Mountain, N.Y.). Achievements include pioneering devel. leprosy in exptl. animal (armadillo) reproduction. Home: 72 Riverview Ter Melbourne FL 32903-4640 *Children display interests early in their lives, and in my life, this early interest - in animals, and the beauty of nature - is one which I have never lost, but one which seems to become more important now with the passing of years. Parents can help mold a child, but should mold the child in the child's interests as my parents did, not in a mold designed by them.*

STORRS, GLENN WILLIAM, museum administrator, paleontologist; b. Poughkeepsie, N.Y., Jan. 12, 1957; s. Emory Parker and Elizabeth Archard Storrs; m. Robin Anne Talerico, Mar. 5, 1964; children: William Emory, Oliva Evangeline, Ian Robert. BS, Syracuse U., N.Y., 1979; MA, U. of Tex., Austin, 1981; MPhil, PhD, Yale U., New Haven, Conn., 1986. Mus. Leadership Inst. Getty Found., Calif. Sr. mus. asst. Peabody Mus. of Natural History, New Haven, 1986—91; sr. rsch. fellow U. of Bristol, England, 1991—96; Withrow Farny curator of vertebrate paleontology Cin. Mus. Ctr., 1995—, dir. of sci. rsch., 2001—04, asst. v.p., 2004—. Adj. prof. geology U. Cin., 1995—. Contbr. articles to profl. jours. Recipient Investigation of a unique Mississipian tetrapod locality and its paleofauna grant, NSF, 2003—06, Spaceflight Edn. Opportunities (NSEO) Live In-Flight Edn. Downlink grant, NASA, 2005. Mem.: Yellowstone - Bighorn Rsch. Assn., Am. Assn. Mus., Soc. of Vertebrate Paleontology, Beta Theta Pi. Achievements include research in anatomy, systematics and evolution of fossil reptiles. Office: Cin Mus Ctr 1301 Western Ave Cincinnati OH 45203

STORY, JOAN H., lawyer; b. Parsons, Kans., Feb. 7, 1944; AB, Occidental Coll., 1965; MA, UCLA, 1968; JD, U. Calif., Davis, 1977. Bar: Calif. 1977. Ptnr., mem. exec. com. Sheppard, Mullin, Richter & Hampton LLP, San Francisco. Co-chair Calif. adv. bd. Trust for Pub. Land. Volume editor U. Calif. at Davis Law Rev., 1976-77. Mem. alumni bd. govs. Occidental Coll., 1982-85. Mem.: Practicing Law Inst. (real estate law adv. com.), Am. Coll. Real Estate Lawyers, Bar Assn. San Francisco, State Bar Calif. (mem. real property law sect.), U. Calif. Davis Law Sch. Alumni Assn. (bd. dirs.), Lambda Alpha. Office: Sheppard, Mullin, Richter & Hampton LLP 17 Fl Four Embarcadero Ctr San Francisco CA 94111 Office Phone: 415-774-3211. Office Fax: 415-434-3947. E-mail: jstory@sheppardmullin.com.

STORY, JULIE ANN, language educator; b. Muncy, Pa., Aug. 6, 1959; d. Phillip Mason Story and Mary Lee Peters. BA in English, Lock Haven U., 1982; MA in English, Ind. U. Pa., 1984. Assoc. dir. undergraduate writing ctr., lectr. English Pa. State U., U. Pk., 1987—2003; English instr. Juniata Coll., Huntingdon, Pa., 1987—89; dir. writing ctr., writing specialist Lock Haven U., Pa., 1998, 2003—. Internship coord. writing ctr. Pa. State U., University Park; cons. in field; faculty advisor Dangling Modifier. Mem. Pa. State Commn. for Women, University Park. Grantee, Ctr. Excellence Learning and Tchg., 2001. Mem.: Nat. Coun. Tchrs. English, Conf. Coll. Composition Comm., Ctrl. Pa. Writing Ctrs. Assn. (bd. dirs.), Nat. Conf. Peer Tutoring in Writing (adv. bd.), Mid-Atlantic Writing Ctrs. Assn. (bd. dirs.), Internat. Writing Ctrs. Assn., Phi Kappa Phi, Sigma Tau Delta. Democrat. Avocations: gardening, walking, photography, reading, movies. Home: 33 Julia Dr Lock Haven PA 17745 Office: Lock Haven Univ Pa 19 Russell Hall Lock Haven PA 17745 Office Phone: 570-484-3847. Business E-Mail: jstory@lhup.edu.

STORY, RICHARD DAVID, publishing executive; b. Okla. s. Richard Truman S.; m. Jennifer Willoughby Crandall, Sept. 25, 1988. Sr. editor NY Mag.; editl. dept. USA Today, Travel + Leisure, Reader's Digest, Esquire Mag.; sr. editor InStyle Mag.; features editor Vogue Mag.; editor-in-chief Departures Mag., 2000—. Named to Okla. Journalism Hall of Fame, 1989. Mem.: Am. Soc. Mag. Editors (bd. dir. 2007—, Nat. Mag. award for Single-Topic Issue, Departures Mag. 2007). Office: Departures 16th Fl 1120 Ave Of Americas New York NY 10036 Office Phone: 212-382-5689. Office Fax: 212-827-6463. *

STORY, SUSAN N., utilities executive; b. 1960; B in Indsl. Engring., Auburn U., Ala.; MBA, U. Ala., Birmingham. Nuc. power plant engr. Southern Co., 1982, dir. human resources, v.p. real estate and corp. svcs., v.p. supply chain mgmt., exec. v.p. engring. and constrn. svcs. Southern Co. Generation and Energy Mktg., pres., CEO Gulf Power, 2003—. Mem. exec. coun. Fla. Coun. of 100; bd. trustees Fla. Chamber Found., US Naval Aviation Mus. Found.; chmn. Enterprise Fla. Tech. Innovation and Entrepreneurship Coun.; chair Auburn Alumni Engring. Coun.; vice chair bd. dirs. Enterprise Fla., Inc., 2005—07; bd. dirs. Fla. Coun. of 100, Fla. C. of C., Gt. NW Econ. Devel. Coun., Fla., Pensacola Area C. of C., Assn. Edison Illuminating Cos., Edison Electric Inst. CEO Com., Southeastern Electric Exch. CEO Com., Fla. Electric Reliability Coordinating Coun.; bd. mem. Ala. Engring. Hall of Fame. Named Fla. Econ. Devel. Vol. of Yr., So. Econ. Devel. Coun., 2005, Bus. Leader of Yr., Pensacola Area C. of C., 2007; named one of Top 10 Women in Bus., Birmingham Bus. Jour., 2002; recipient Presdl. Achievement award, Sacred Heart Hosp., 2004, Women Breaking the Corp. Glass Ceiling award, Women's Bus. Ctr., 2004, Woman of Distinction award, Girl Scouts, Outstanding Engring. Alumnus award, Auburn U. Coll. Engring., Leaders and Legends award for Environ. Leadership, 2006, Ethics in Bus. award, U. West Fla. and Combined Rotary Clubs of Pensacola region, 2006, Internat. Women's Day award, World Trade Ctr. Miami, 2007. Office: Gulf Power Co One Energy Pl Pensacola FL 32520 *

STORY, TIMOTHY KEVIN (TIM STORY), film director; b. LA, Mar. 13, 1970; married; 1 child. Grad., U. So. Calif. Dir.: (films) One of Us Tripped, 1997, Barbershop, 2002, Taxi, 2004, Fantastic Four, 2005; dir., co-editor, writer (films) The Firing Squad, 1999, writer Urban Menace, 1999; prodr., dir.: (TV series) Standoff, 2006; The 12th Man, 2006.

STORY, TYLER JAMES, psychologist, educator; b. Sacramento, Dec. 21, 1975; s. Michael K. and Garlinn H. Story; m. Lisa Barcelo Story, Aug. 11, 2001. BA cum laude, Cornell U., Ithaca, NY, 1998; MA in Psychology, UCLA, 2002; PhD in Psychology, U. Calif., LA, 2005. Lic. Psychologist NC Bd. Psychology, 2006. Post-doctoral fellow in neuropsychology Duke U. Med. Ctr., Durham, 2005—07, asst. prof., 2007—. Treas. Traction Inc., Durham, 2005—06. Fellowship, UCLA, 2000—01. Mem.: APA, Nat. Acad. Neuropsychology (assoc.), Am. Acad. Clin. Neuropsychology (assoc.). Avocations: running, hiking, mountain biking, travel. Office: Duke U Med Ctr 932 Morreene Rd Box 3333 Durham NC 27710 Office Phone: 919-684-2116. Business E-Mail: tyler.story@duke.edu.

STOSS, FREDERICK WARREN, librarian, educator; b. Gloversville, NY, Aug. 12, 1950; s. Dayton Robert and Katherine Gretchen (Ruzicka) Stoss; m. Dorothy Katherine Holderle, Aug. 24, 1974; 1 child, Kaeti Elizabeth. BA in Biology, Hartwick Coll., 1972; MS in Zoology, SUNY, Brockport, 1974; MLS, Syracuse U., 1982. Tech. rsch. assoc. U. Rochester Med. Ctr., NY, 1974—78; rsch. assoc. Syracuse Rsch. Corp., 1978—82; libr. dir. Ctr. for Environ. Info., Rochester, 1982—90; rsch. assoc. U. Tenn., Knoxville, 1990—96; scis. libr. U. Buffalo, 1996—. Lab. instr. U. Rochester, 1975—78; adj. lectr. Syracuse U., 1983—85; vis. lectr. U. Buffalo, 1997—2002; mem. editl. adv. bd. Environment Abstracts, 1988—, Electronic Green Jour., 1990—, Counterpoise, 1999—2005. Assoc. editor: Information Resources in Toxicology, 2001. Pres. Seth Green chpt. Trout Unlimited, Rochester, 1989—90; mem. spkrs. bur. Susquahanna River Basin Commn., 2005—; mem. panel on environment Rochester Dem. and Chronicle Readers, 2005—. Mem.: ALA (chair task force on the environment 1995—99, coord. social responsibilities round table 1999—2002, team trainer Librs. Build Sustainable Cmtys. Team 1999—2002, co-chair task force on the environment 2002—, OLOS adv. com. 2003—06, STS/ACRL cont. edn. subcom. co-chair 2005—07, publ. com. 2005—, com. on legis. subcom. fed. librs. 2006—), N.Am. Assn. Environ. Edn. (non-formal environ. edn. guidelines trainer), N.Y. State Outdoor Edn. Assn., Spl. Librs. Assn. (chair environ. info. divsn. 1988, pres. So. Appalachian chpt. 1994—95, Outstanding Divsn. Mem. award, Environ. Resource Mgmt. divsn., Environment and Resource Mgmt. Divsn. 1994), Nat. Sci. Tchrs. Assn., N.Y. Libr. Assn., SUNY Libr. Assn., Sierra Club (chair environ. edn. com. 2001—06), Sigma Xi (Outstanding Grad. Rsch. award 1974). Democrat. Lutheran. Avocations: fly fishing, nature photography. Office: Univ Buffalo Sci Eng Libr 228-B Capen Hall Buffalo NY 14260 Office Phone: 716-645-2947 ext. 224. Business E-Mail: fstoss@buffalo.edu.

STOSSEL, JOHN, news analyst; BA in Psychology, Princeton U., 1969. Prodr., reporter Sta. KGW-TV, Portland, Oreg.; consumer editor WCBS-TV, NYC, Good Morning Am.; consumer corr. 20/20, 1981—, ABC news corr. Weekly consumer reporter ABC Radio Info. Network, Author: Shopping Smart: The Only Consumer Guide You'll Ever Need, 1980, Give Me a Break, 2004, Myths, Lies and Downright Stupidity: Get Out the Shovel--Why Everything You Know Is Wrong, 2006. Recipient 19 Emmy awards, 5 awards for Excellence in Consumer Reporting Nat. Press Club, award Nat. Environment Devel. Assn., award Retirement Rshc. Found., George Polk award Outstanding Local Radio and Television Reporting. Office: 20/20 147 Columbus Ave Fl 8 New York NY 10023-5900

STOSSEL, SCOTT HANFORD, editor, writer; b. Boston, Aug. 7, 1969; s. Thomas Peter and Anne (Hanford) Stossel; m. Susanna Joy Pueschel, July 1, 2000. BA, Harvard Coll., 1991. Spl. projects editor Atlantic Monthly, Boston, 1992-93, staff editor, 1993-96, editl. dir. new media, 1994-96; assoc. editor The Am. Prospect, Cambridge, Mass., 1996-97, exec. editor, 1997—2002; sr. editor The Atlantic Monthly, Boston, 2002, mng. editor Washington, 2006—. Contbr. columns in newspapers; contbr. The New Yorker, The New Republic; author: (biography) Sarge: The Life and Times of Sargent Shriver, 2004. Mem. Harvard Club Boston, Belmont Hill Club. Episcopalian. Avocations: tennis, squash, soccer, basketball. Office: The Atlantic Monthly The Watergate 600 New Hampshire Ave NW Washington DC 20037

STOSSEL, THOMAS PETER, medical educator, researcher, director; b. Chgo., Sept. 10, 1941; m. Kerry Maguire, 1997. AB, Princeton U., NJ, 1963; MD, Harvard U., Cambridge, Mass., 1967; MD (hon.), U. Linkoping, Sweden, 1989, U. Geneva, 2004. Diplomate Am. Bd. Internal Medicine. Ho. staff medicine Mass. Gen. Hosp., Boston, 1967-69, chief hematology-oncology, 1976-90; staff assoc. NIH, Bethesda, Md., 1967-71; fellow to sr. assoc. Med. Ctr. Children's Hosp., Boston, 1971-76; prof. medicine Harvard Med. Sch., Boston, 1982—; chief divsn. exptl. medicine Brigham Women's Hosp., Boston, 1991—, co-dir. hematology divsn., 1998—2006, dir. translational medicine div., 2006—. Sci. bd. Biogen Corp., 1987—2002, Dyax Corp., 1996—2002; clin. rsch. prof. Am. Cancer Soc., 1987—; bd. dirs. Zymequest, Inc., Critical Biologics Corp. Author (with B. Babior): (book) 2d edit., 1984, Hematology, A Pathophysiological Approach, 1994; editor (with R. Handin and S Lux): Blood, Principles & Practice of Hematology, 1995, 2d edit., 2003; contbr. articles to profl. jours. Bd. dirs. Am. Coun. Sci. and Health, 2006—. Lt. comdr. USPHS, 1969—71. Mem.: NAS, Am. Acad. Arts and Scis., Assn. Am. Physicians, Am. Soc. Cell Biology, Am. Soc. Hematology (pres. 1997, Damashek prize 1983, Thomas prize 1993), Am. Soc. Clin. Investigation (pres. 1987), Am. Fedn. Clin. Rsch., Inst. Medicine. Achievements include patents in field. Office: Brigham & Womens Hosp Karp 625 1 Blackfan Cir Boston MA 02115 Home Phone: 617-489-1299; Office Phone: 617-355-9001. Business E-Mail: tstossel@partners.org.

STOTLAR, DOUGLAS W., transportation executive; b. Newbury, Ohio; BS, Ohio State Univ. Freight ops. supr. through regional mgr. Con-Way Transp. Svcs., Ann Arbor, Mich., 1985—96, v.p., gen mgr. Con-Way NOW, 1996—99, exec. v.p. ops., 1999—2002, exec. v.p., COO, 2002—04, pres., CEO, 2004—05, Con-Way Inc. (formerly CNF Inc.), San Mateo, Calif., 2005—. V.p., mem. exec. com. Am. Trucking Assn.; bd. dir. Am. Transp. Rsch. Inst. Office: Con-Way Inc 2855 Campus Dr Ste 300 San Mateo CA 94403-2512 *

STOTLER, ALICEMARIE HUBER, federal judge; b. Alhambra, Calif., May 29, 1942; d. James R. and Loretta M. Huber; m. James Allen Stotler, Sept. 11, 1971. BA, U. So. Calif., 1964, JD, 1967. Bar: Calif. 1967, U.S. Dist. Ct. (no. dist.) Calif. 1967, U.S. Dist. Ct. (ctrl. dist.) Calif. 1973, U.S. Supreme Ct. 1976; cert. criminal law specialist. Dep. Orange County Dist. Attys. Office, 1967-73; mem. Stotler & Stotler, Santa Ana, Calif., 1973-76, 83-84; judge Orange County Mcpl. Ct., 1976-78, Orange County Superior Ct., 1978-83, U.S. Dist. Ct. (ctrl. dist.) Calif., LA, 1984—. Assoc. dean Calif. Trial Judges Coll., 1982; lectr., panelist, numerous orgns.; standing com. on rules of practice and procedure U.S. Jud. Conf., 1991-98, chair, 1993-98; chair 9th cir. Pub. Info. and Cmty. Outreach, 2000-04; mem. exec. com. 9th Cir. Jud. Conf., 1989-93, Fed. State Jud. Coun., 1989-98, jury com., 1990-92, planning com. for Nat. Conf. on Fed.-State Jud. Relationships, Orlando, 1991-92, planning com. for We. Regional Conf. on State-Fed. Jud. Relationships, Stevens, Wash., 1992-93; chair dist. ct. symposium and jury utilization Ctrl. Dist. Calif., 1985, chair atty. liaison, 1989-90, chair U.S. Constn. Bicentennial com., 1986-91, chair magistrate judge com., 1992-93; mem. State Adv. Group on Juvenile Justice and Delinquency Prevention, 1983-84, Bd. Legal Specializations Criminal Law Adv. Commn., 1983-84, victim/witness adv. com. Office Criminal Justice Planning, 1980-83, U. So. Calif. Bd. Councilors, 1993-2001; active team in tng. Leukemia Soc. Am., 1993, 95, 97, 2000; legion lex bd. dirs. U. So. Calif. Sch. Law Support Group, 1981-83. Winner Hale Moot Ct. Competition, State of Calif., 1967; named Judge of Yr., Orange County Trial Lawyers Assn., 1978, Most Outstanding Judge Orange County Bus. Litig. Sect., 1990. Mem. ABA (jud. adminstrn. divsn. and litig. sect. 1984—, nat. conf. fed. trial judges com. on legis. affairs 1990-91), Am. Law Inst., Am. Judicature Soc., Fed. Judges Assn. (bd. dirs. 1989-92), Nat. Assn. Women Judges, U.S. Supreme Ct. Hist. Soc., Ninth Cir. Dist. Judges Assn., Calif. Supreme Ct. Hist. Soc., Orange County Bar Assn. (mem. numerous coms., Franklin G. West award 1984), Calif. Judges Assn. (mem. com. on jud. coll. 1978-80, com. on civil law and procedure 1980-82, Dean's coll. curriculum commn. 1981), Calif. Judges Found. Office: Ronald Reagan Fed Bldg & Courthouse 411 W 4th St Santa Ana CA 92701-4500

STOTLER, EDITH ANN, retired grain company executive; b. Champaign, Ill., Oct. 11, 1946; d. Kenneth Wagner and Mary (Odebrecht) S. Student, Mary Baldwin Coll., 1964-66; AB, U. Ill., 1968. Asst. v.p. Harris Trust and Savs. Bank, Chgo., 1969-83; mgr. Can. Imperial Bank of Commerce, Chgo., 1983, sr. mgr., 1983-85, asst. gen. mgr. group head, 1985-88, v.p., dir. utilities, 1988-90; ptnr. Stotler Grain Co., Champaign, Ill., 1990—2002; pres. Homer Grain Co., Champaign, 1990-2000; pres., bd. dirs. S&I Grain Co., 1990-2000, SEMCO Energy Inc., 1987—2004. Bd. dirs., audit com., fin. com. SEMCO Energy Inc.; compensation com. Strategic Capital Bancorp, Inc., 2002—03. Past pres. liberal arts and scis. constituent bd., mem. pres.'s coun. U. Ill.; trustee, mem. fin. com. Countryside Sch., 1997—2000; mem. dean's bus. coun. U. Ill. Bus. Coll., 2007, exec. com. dean's bus. coun., 1998—2005; bd. dirs. Champaign County YMCA, 2000—03; bd. dirs., treas. bd., chair investment and fin. coms. Champaign Pub. Libr. Found.; past mem. investment com., bd. trustees 4th Presbyn. Ch.; bd. dirs. Spurlock Mus., Urbana. Mem.: U. Ill. Found., Art Club (past pres., v.p.), Krannert Art Mus. Coun., Champaign Country Club (chair house com.), U. Ill. Found., Book Club. Avocations: needlepoint, reading, tennis, golf, cooking. Home: 1010 W Clark Champaign IL 61821

STOTSKY, ADAM, communications executive; b. 1969; BA, Western Va. U., 1991. Sr. account mgr. Fallon McElligott, Mpls., NYC; v.p., Mktg. Travel Channel; sr. v.p. J. Walter Thompson Worldwide's Entertainment Practice; v.p., Brand Mktg. Sci Fi Channel, 2002—. Named one of 40 Executives Under 40, Multichannel News, 2006. Office: Sci Fi Channel 30 Rockefeller Plz New York NY 10112 Office Phone: 212-413-5000. Office Fax: 212-413-6509.

STOTT, BRIAN, software company executive, consultant; b. Eccles, Eng., Aug. 5, 1941; came to U.S., 1983; s. Harold and Mary (Stephens) S.; m. Patricia Ann Farrar, Dec. 3, 1983. BSc, Manchester U., 1962, MSc, 1963, PhD, 1971. Asst. prof. Mid. East Tech. U., Ankara, Turkey, 1965—68; lectr. Inst. Sci. and Tech., U. Manchester, England, 1968—74; assoc. prof. U. Waterloo, Ont., Canada, 1974—76; cons. Electric Energy Rsch. Ctr. Brazil, Rio de Janeiro, 1976—83; prof. Ariz. State U., Tempe, 1983—84; chmn. Power Computer Applications Corp., Mesa, Ariz., 1984—2000; pres. Stott Inc. Cons. in field. Contbr. numerous articles to rsch. publs. Fellow IEEE (Millennium medal); mem. NAE. Home and Office: 10222E Southwind Lane #1004 Scottsdale AZ 85262 Business E-Mail: brianstott@ieee.org.

STOTT, DON S., precious metals products executive; b. Washington, Feb. 17, 1934; s. Marion McClelland Stott and Mabelle Louise (Maidem) Vanice; m. Dorothy Greene, June 21, 1962 (div.); children: David Michael, Melissa Ann; m. Bonnie Jean Peltomen, Dec. 4, 2002. Owner DS Theatres, DC and Phila., 1956—67, Bijou Iced Creme Parlours, Phila., 1967—71; hotel owner Wyman, Alma House and Grand Imperial Hotels, Silverton, Colo., 1971—94; pres. Colo. Gold, Montrose, 1977—. Author: Where the Mountains Meet the Sky, Three Feet to Silverton, Trails Among the Columbines, Consequences, numerous newspaper columns. Past pres. Montrose Hist. Soc., Valley Symphony, Kiwanis Club, Early Words Toastmasters, Am. Theatre Organ Soc., Silverton C. of C.; bd. dirs. Ariz. Opera. Republican. Avocations: trains, antiques, architecture. E-mail: gold@gwe.net.

STOTT, GRADY BERNELL, lawyer; b. Bailey, NC, Sept. 19, 1921; s. William Willard and Zettie Harriett (Bissette) S.; m. Mays Beal, May 9, 1952; children: Sue J., Caroline Beal. AB, Duke U., 1947, JD, 1952. Bar: N.C. 1952. Dist. atty. 27th Jud. Dist., Gastonia, NC, 1957-62; partner firm Stott, Hollowell, Palmer & Windham, Gastonia, 1960—. Served with USMC, 1943-48. Fellow Am. Bar Found., Am. Coll. Trial Lawyers; mem. N.C. State Bar (pres. 1978-79), Am. Bar Assn. (del. 1980), N.C. Bar Assn., Assn. Ins. Attys. Clubs: Masons. Democrat. Methodist. Office: 401 E Franklin Blvd Gastonia NC 28054-7152 Office Phone: 704-864-3425. Personal E-mail: gbs@shpw.com.

STOTT, PETER WALTER, investment company executive; b. Spokane, Wash., May 26, 1944; s. Walter Joseph and Rellalee (Gray) S.; m. Julie L. Neupert, Oct. 12, 1996; 1 child, Preston. Student, Portland State U., 1962-63, 65-68, U. Americas, Mexico City, 1964-65. Founder, bd. chmn. emeritus Market Transport Ltd., Portland, Oreg., 1969—2006; pres. Columbia Investments, Ltd., Portland, 2005—; vice chmn., prin. ScanlanKemperBard Cos., Portland, 2005—. Pres., CEO, prin. Crown Pacific, 1988-2004; bd. dir. Con-Way Inc. Mem. pres.'s adv. bd. athletics Portland State U., mem. cabinet Building Our Future campaign; trustee Portland Art Mus.; founding bd. dir. Crater Lake Nat. Park Trust; bd. dir. Portland State U. Found. With USAR, 1966-72. Mem. Nat. Football Found. and Hall of Fame, Oreg. Sports Hall of Fame (lifetime), Stop Oreg. Litter and Vandalism (founders' circle), Arlington Club, Mazamas Club, Multnomah Athletic Club, Racquet Club, Univ. Club, Waverly Country Club, Valley Club. Republican. Roman Catholic. Office: Columbia Investments Ltd Ste 2600 1211 SW Fifth Ave Portland OR 97204 Business E-Mail: pstott@skbcos.com.

STOTT, THOMAS EDWARD, JR., retired engineering executive; b. Beverly, Mass., May 14, 1923; s. Thomas Edward and Mildred (Ayers) S.; m. Mary Elizabeth Authelet, Feb. 26, 1944; children: Pamela, Randi, Wendy, Thomas E., Diana. BS, Tufts U., 1945. Design engr. Bethlehem Steel, Quincy, Mass., 1956-59, project engr., 1959-64, sr. engr. basic ship design, 1960-63, project coordinator, 1963-64; pres. Stal-Laval, Inc., Elmsford, N.Y., 1964-84, Thomas Stott & Co., Cummaquid, Mass., 1984-88; ret., 1988. Bd. dirs. Friends of Prisoners, Inc., 1990-05; deacon West Parish Barnstable, Mass., 1994-96, 2002-04, moderator, 1996-99. With USNR, 1944-46. Decorated (4) WWII medals with 5 combat stars, Combat ribbon. Fellow ASME (chmn. marine com., chmn. gas turbine div. exec. com., chmn. nat. nominating com., exec. sec. gas turbine div., Centennial medal 1980, R. Tom Sawyer award 1981, Dedicated Svc. award 1989), Soc. Naval Architects and Marine Engrs. Republican. Home: 51 Kates Path Yarmouth Port MA 02675-1448 Personal E-mail: tstott7668@aol.com.

STOTTER, HARRY SHELTON, banker, lawyer; b. NYC, Aug. 28, 1928; s. Jack and Adele Stotter; m. Marilyn H. Knight, Nov. 7, 1954; children: Jeffrey Craig, Cheryl dee. Student, L.I. U., 1948-49; JD, St. John's U., 1952; postgrad., NYU Law Sch., 1956-57. Bar: N.Y. 1952, N.J. 1974, U.S. Supreme Ct. 1983. Pvt. practice in, NYC, 1952-53, 54-56; atty. U.S. Dept. Def., 1953; with trust div. Bank of N.Y., 1956-63; exec. v.p., sr. mgmt. com. Summit Bank (now Bank of Am.), NJ, 1963-84; exec. v.p. Chase Manhattan Bank, NYC, 1984-94; dir., vice chmn. Chase Manhattan Trust Co. Fla., Palm Beach, Fla., 1984-87; pvt. trust and estates law practice NJ, 1974-2000; former mem. probate com. N.J. Supreme Ct. Jud. Conf. Mem. N.Y.C. and Bergen County estate planning couns.; former pres. Bergen County coun. Girl Scouts Am.; bd. dirs., pres., chief exec. officer Bergen County United Way; treas. 2d Century Fund, Hackensack Hosp.; bd. dirs. Holy Name Hosp., Teaneck, N.J. With USN, World War II; brig. gen. Army N.G. Mem. ABA (co-chmn. nat. conf. lawyers and corp. trustees 1991-93), Am. Bankers Assn. (chmn. trust counsel com. 1991-93), N.Y. Bar Assn., N.J. Bar Assn., N.Y. County Lawyers Assn., Bergen County Bar Assn. (former trustee, former chmn. probate and estate planning com.), Fed. Bar Assn., NY Mil. Assn. US, Nat. Guard Assn.

STOTTER, LAWRENCE HENRY, lawyer; b. Cleve., Sept. 24, 1929; s. Oscar and Bertha (Lieb) S.; m. Ruth Rapoport, June 30, 1957; children: Daniel, Jennifer, Steven. BBA, Ohio State U., 1956, LLB, 1958, JD, 1967. Bar: Calif. 1960, U.S. Supreme Ct. 1973, U.S. Tax Ct. 1976. Pvt. practice, San Francisco, 1963—; ptnr. Stotter and Coats, San Francisco, 1981-97; sole practitioner, 1997—; mem. faculty Nat. Judicial Coll.; mem. Calif. Family Law Adv. Commn., 1979-80. Editor in chief: Am. Bar Family Advocate mag, 1977-82; TV appearances on Phil Donahue Show, Good Morning America. Pres. Tamalpais Conservation Club, Marin County, Calif.; U.S. State Dept. del. Hague Conf. Pvt. Internat. Law, 1979-80; legal adv. White House Conf. on Families, 1980—. Served with AUS, 1950-53. Mem. ABA (past chmn. family law sect.), Am. Acad. Matrimonial Lawyers (past nat. v.p.), Calif. State Bar (past chmn. family law sect.), San Francisco Bar Assn. (past chmn. family law sect.), Calif. Trial Lawyers Assn. (past chmn. family law sect.) Home and Office: 2244 Vistazo St E Belvedere Tiburon CA 94920-1970 Home Phone: 415-435-3568; Office Phone: 415-435-3568. Personal E-mail: lhstotter@aol.com.

STOTTLEMYER, DAVID LEE, federal official; b. Waynesboro, Pa., June 1, 1935; s. Omar Samuel and Miriam (Noll) S.; m. Jane Ann Hembree, Aug. 26, 1961; children: Todd Andrew, Kristen Elizabeth, Kathryn Ann. AB, Miami U., Oxford, Ohio, 1959; M. Pub. and Internat. Affairs (NDEA fellow), U. Pitts., 1964, also postgrad. Program and budget analyst Exec. Office of Pres., Office of Mgmt. and Budget, Washington, 1964-69; sr. mgmt. officer UN, NYC, 1969-70; adviser internat. orgn. affairs US Mission to UN, NYC, 1971-72, counsellor internat. orgn. affairs, 1973-75, counsellor UN resources mgmt., 1976-77; also mem. U.S. del. 26th-31st gen. assemblies, mem. UN Com. on Contbns., 1971; mem. UN Adv. Com. on Adminstrv. and Budgetary Questions, 1973-77; dir. policy mgmt. staff Bur. Internat. Orgn. Affairs, US Dept. State, Washington, 1977-80, exec. asst. to asst. sec. of state for internat. orgn. affairs, 1980; mem. staff Office of Vice-Pres., Washington, 1981-83; dir. adminstrv. mgmt. service UN, NYC, 1984-85; exec. asst., dir. Office of Under-Sec.-Gen. for Adminstrn. and Mgmt., UN, NYC, 1986-87; pvt. practice as cons., 1987-90; dir. industry rels. NASA, Washington, 1990-91, dir. office nat. svc., 1992-93; retired, 1993; cons. pvt. practice, 1993—. Served with AUS, 1953-56. Recipient Superior Honor award State Dept., 1975 Mem. Am. Fgn. Svc. Assn. Home and Office: 12363 Grantley Ct Lake Ridge VA 22192 Office Phone: 703-967-0216. E-mail: davestot@comcast.net.

STOTTLEMYER, TODD A., business association executive; BA, Coll. William and Mary; JD cum laude, Georgetown U., 1991. Corp. v.p. BDM Internat. Inc.; exec. v.p., CFO, chief adminstrv. officer BTG Inc.; mng. dir. McGuireWoods Capital Group; pres. McGuireWoods Cons.; CEO Apogen Technologies; pres., CEO Nat. Fedn. Ind. Bus., Washington, 2006—. Mem. Profl. Svcs. Coun.; vice chmn. bd. dirs. No. Va. Tech. Coun. Bd. dirs. Fairfax County C. of C., Am. Red Cross of Nat. Capital Region, INOVA Health System Foundation. Mem.: Phi Beta Kappa. Home: Nat Fedn Ind Bus 1201 F St NW Ste 200 Washington DC 20004

STOTTS, TERRY L., former professional basketball coach; b. Cedar Falls, Iowa, Nov. 25, 1957; s. Frank and Jayne (Phelps) Stotts; m. Jan S. Stotts. BS in zoology, U. Okla., 1983, MBA, 1988. Profl. basketball player Montana Golden Nuggets, CBA, Spain, France; head coach Albany Patoons, 1990—91; asst. Fort Wayne Fury, 1991—92; advance scout Seattle SuperSonics, 1992—93, asst. coach, 1994, Milw. Bucks, 1998—2002, head coach, 2005—07; asst. coach Atlanta Hawks, 2002, head coach, 2002—04. Head coach Western Conf. NBA All-Star Game, 1994, 96, 98. *

STOTZKY, GUENTHER, microbiologist, educator; b. Leipzig, Germany, May 24, 1931; arrived in US, 1939; s. Moritz Stotzky and Erna (Angres) Kester; m. Kayla Baker, Mar. 17, 1958; children: Jay, Martha, Deborah. BS, Calif. Poly. State U., 1952; MS, Ohio State U., 1954, PhD, 1956. Spl. sci. employee Argonne Nat. Lab. USAEC, Lemont, Ill., 1955; rsch. assoc. dept. botany U. Mich., Ann Arbor, 1956-58; head soil microbiology Ctrl. Rsch. Labs. United Fruit Co., Norwood, Mass., 1958-63; chmn., microbiologist Kitchawan Rsch. Labs. Bklyn. Botanic Garden, Ossining, NY, 1963-68; assoc. prof. dept. biology NYU, 1967-70, prof. dept. biology, 1970—, chmn. dept. biology, 1970-77. Editor: Soil Biochemistry, 1990-2000; series editor Marcel Dekker, Inc., 1986-92; contbr. over 290 articles to profl. jours., chpts. to books. With USCG, 1957. Recipient Selman A. Waksman Hon. Lecture award Theobald Smith Soc., 1989, Honored Alumnus of Yr. award Calif. Poly. State U., 1992, fellowship Japanese Soc. for Promotion of Sci., 1996; named Disting. Vis. Scientist, U.S. EPA, 1986-89. Fellow AAAS, Am. Soc. Agronomy, Soil Sci. Soc. Am.; mem. Am. Acad. Microbiology, Am. Soc. Microbiology (Fisher Co. award for applied and environ. microbiology 1990, Excellence in Tchg. award N.Y.C. br. 1994). Jewish. Avocations: gardening, reading, music. Office: NYU Dept Biology 1009 Silver Ctr New York NY 10003 Home Phone: 212-533-3269; Office Phone: 212-998-8268. Business E-Mail: gs5@nyu.edu.

STOUCK, JERRY, lawyer; b. Washington, Mar. 24, 1955; s. Alex and Eileen Marion (Tepper) S.; m. Mindy A. Buren, Feb. 18, 1984; children: Danielle, David, Rachel. BA magna cum laude, Wesleyan U., 1977; JD, NYU, 1980. Bar: U.S. Dist. Ct. D.C. 1981, U.S. Ct. Fed. Claims 1981, D.C. Ct. Appeals, 1981, Md. Ct. Appeals 1983, U.S. Ct. Appeals (4th cir.) 1983, U.S. Dist. Ct. Md. 1985, U.S. Ct. Appeals (fed. cir.) 1992, U.S. Supreme Ct. 1993, U.S. Ct. Appeals (D.C. cir.) 1997. Law clk. to Hon. Pettine U.S. Dist. Ct. R.I., 1980-81; assoc. McKenna, Conner & Cuneo, Washington, 1981-83, Shulman, Rogers, Gandel, Rockville, Md., 1984-87, Spriggs & Hollingsworth, Washington, 1983-84, 87-89, ptnr., 1989—2005; shareholder Greenberg Traurig, LLP, Washington, 2005—. Mem. Phi Beta Kappa. Office: Greenberg Traurig LLP 800 Connecticut Ave NW Washington DC 20006 Office Phone: 202-331-3173. Business E-Mail: stouckj@gtlaw.com.

STOUDEMIRE, AMARE CARSARES, professional basketball player; b. Lake Wales, Fla., Nov. 16, 1982; Player Phoenix Suns, 2002—. Mem. US Olympic Basketball Team, Athens, Greece, 2004. Named NBA Rookie of Yr., 2003, MVP, Rookie Challenge, 2004; named to NBA All-Rookie Team, 2003, Western Conf. All-Star Team, NBA, 2007, All-NBA First Team, 2007. Achievements include being the only high school student selected in the 2002 NBA Draft. Office: c/o Phoenix Suns 201 E Jefferson St Phoenix AZ 85004 *

STOUDT, RALPH JOSEPH, JR., language educator; b. Reading, Pa., Sept. 23, 1928; s. Ralph Joseph Stoudt Sr. and Anna Thompson; m. Barbara Ann Holmes, Aug. 31, 1957; children: Dorothy Anna, Charlotte Lyzabeth. BA, Albright Coll., Reading, 1950; postgrad., Princeton Theol. Sem., NJ, 1950—51; MA, U. Va., Charlottesville, 1959; PhD, U. Mich., Ann Arbor, 1964. Dist. scout exec. Bucks County coun. Boy Scouts Am., Doylestown, Pa., 1951—55, Blue Ridge coun. Boy Scouts Am., Roakoke, Va., 1955—58; asst. prof. Vanderbilt U., Nashville, 1964—66; asst. prof., then assoc. prof. U. Va., 1966—95, assoc. prof. emeritus, 1995—. Mem.: Va. Speech and Hearing Assn., Am. Lang. Hearing Assn. Presbyterian. Avocations: photography, genealogy, travel.

STOUGHTON, W. VICKERY, healthcare executive; b. Peoria, Ill., Mar. 1, 1946; s. Warner Vickery and Mary Olive (McNamara) S.; m. Anne Stoughton; children: Zachary Benjamin, Samantha. BS, St. Louis U., 1968; MBA, U. Chgo., 1973. Asst. dir. Boston Hosp. for Women, 1973-74, Peter Bent Brigham Hosp., Boston, 1975-77, dir., 1978-80; pres. The Toronto Hosp., Ont., Can.; asst. prof. U. Toronto, 1982-90, assoc. prof., 1991; vice chancellor health affairs, chief exec. officer Duke U. Hosp., Durham, N.C., 1991-92; pres. Smithkline Beecham Clin. Labs., Collegeville, Pa., 1992-95, Smithkline Beecham Diagnostic Systems, King of Prussia, Pa., 1996; chmn., CEO Careside, Culver City, Calif., 1996—; dir. Biomira, 1988—. Bd. dirs. Sun Life Assurance Co. Bd. dirs. Toronto Symphony, 1983-86, Toronto United Way, 1988-91. Served to capt. AUS, 1969-72. Fellow Am. Coll. Hosp. Adminstrs. Home: 8820 Lookout Mountain Ave Los Angeles CA 90046-1820

STOUT, ALASTAIR, music director, composer; b. Derby, England, England, Aug. 1, 1975; s. Edward and Lindsay Stout. MusB, Royal Coll. Music, London, 1997; MusM, Guildhall Sch. Music and Drama, London, 1998; PhD, U. London, 2002. Asst. organist Wesley's Chapel, London, 1993—2001; organist, dir. music Coraopolis United Meth. Ch., Pa., 2001—. Composer Shetland Choral Soc., Lerwick, Scotland, 2003. Composer: (contemporary classical music) String Quartet No. 1 (Young Composer of Wales award, 1999), (contemporary classical piano work) Pour Les Notes Repetees (William Mathias Composition award, 2005), (contemporary classical operatic work) Releasing the Sky. Mem. Am. Guild Organists, Pitts., 2002. Home: 1439 1/2 Ridge Ave Coraopolis PA 15108 Office: Coraopolis United Meth Ch 1205 Ridge Ave Coraopolis PA 15108 Home Phone: 412-269-3431; Office Phone: 412-264-3727. Office Fax: 412-264-4787. Personal E-mail: stout@icubed.com.

STOUT, LEON JAMES, archivist, librarian; b. Long Branch, NJ, Oct. 10, 1947; s. Leon E. Stout and Verna May Porter; m. Dolores Anne Altmyer, Aug. 22, 1969; children: David James, Christine Anne Smith. BA, Pa. State U., 1969, MA, 1972; MLS, U. of Pitts., 1974. Archivist Pa. State U. Librs., University Park, 1974—2002, head, pub. svcs. and outreach spl. collections, 2002—. Cons. in field. Author: (reference book) Pennsylvania State University in International Dictionary of Library Histories; contbr. articles to profl. jours. Mem. U.S. Nat. Hist. Pubs. and Records Commn., Washington, 2002—, Pa. State Hist. Records Adv. Bd., Harrisburg, 1989—; apptd. rep. State Coll. Borough Hist. Resources Commn., State College, Pa., 1992—. Recipient Award for Outstanding Contbns. to Librs., Pa. State U. Librs., 1991, Fellows' Posner prize for Outstanding Articles in the Am. Archivist, Soc. of Am. Archivists, 1995; fellow Andrew K. Mellon Rsch. fellow in archives, Bentley Hist. Libr., U. of Mich., 1987; grantee Archival Rsch. grantee, U.S. Nat. Hist. Pubs. and Records Commn., 1991—93, Archives and Records Mgmt. grantee, Pa. Hist. and Mus. Commn., 1985—86. Fellow: Soc. of Am. Archivists (pres. 2001—02); mem.: Midwestern Archives Conf., Mid-Atlantic Regional Archives Conf. (chair 1989—91). Roman Catholic. Avocations: travel, golf, genealogy, photography. Office: Pennsylvania State University 104 Paterno Library University Park PA 16802 Home Phone: 814-238-4855; Office Phone: 814-863-3381. E-mail: lys2@psu.edu.

STOUT, LYNN ANDREA, law educator; b. Albany, NY, Sept. 14, 1957; d. Warren White and Sally (Cowan) Stout. BA, Princeton U., 1979, MPA, 1982; JD, Yale U., 1982. Law clk. to the Hon. Gerhard A. Gesell US Dist. Ct. D.C., Washington, 1982-83; assoc. Williams & Connolly, Washington, 1983-86; prof. George Washington U., Washington, 1986-90; prof. Law Ctr. Georgetown U., Washington, 1990—2001, dir. Georgetown-Sloan Project on Bus. Insts.; prof. law UCLA, 2001—, Paul Hastings prof. corp. & securities law, 2006—; prin. investigator UCLA-Sloan Found. Rsch. Program on Bus. Orgns.; prof. (corp. and Securities Law) UCLA, Wash. Vis. prof. Harvard Law Sch., NYU Law Sch., George Washington U. Nat. Law Ctr.; guest scholar Brookings Inst., Washington. Contbr. articles to law jours. Bd. trustee Eaton Vance family of mutual funds. Vis. scholar Nat. Merit scholar, 1975. Mem.: Am. Assn. of Law Sch. (past chair Sect. on Law and Econ. and Sect. Bus. Assns.), Am. Law and Econs. Assn. (bd. dirs.), Phi Beta Kappa. Office: UCLA Sch Law Box 951476 Los Angeles CA 90095-1476 Office Phone: 310-206-8402, 310-825-4841. Office Fax: 310-825-6023. E-mail: stout@law.ucla.edu. *

STOUT, MARY WEBB, dean; b. Richmond, Va., Dec. 24, 1947; d. Frank Edmond Webb and Edith Diuguid (Harris) Webb Steger; m. Teddy Alvin Stout, July 8, 1972. BA, Mary Washington Coll., 1970; MEd, U. Va., Charlottesville, 1972; Edn. Specialist, Coll. William and Mary, 1991, EdD, 1995; cert. in Multimedia Devel., George Mason U., 2003; cert. in Orgnl. Transformation, Nat. Def. U., 2007. Cert. in Multimedia Devel. George Mason U., 2003, in Orgnl. Transformation Nat. Def. U., 2007, water safety instr. Red Cross, CPR Red Cross. Tchr. Harrisonburg City Sch., Va., 1970-71, Buckingham County Sch., Va., 1972-73; guidance counselor So. European Task Force US Army, Vicenza, Italy, 1973-78, edn. specialist Quartermaster Sch. Ft. Lee, Va., 1978-80, edn. specialist Tng. Support Ctr. Ft. Eustis, Va., 1980-82; edn. specialist Hdqs. Tng., Doctrine Command, Ft. Monroe, Va., 1982-83; edn. svc. specialist Combined Arms Ctr., Ft. Leavenworth, Kans., 1983-88; instrnl. systems specialist Hdqs. TRADOC, Ft. Monroe, 1988-98; supervisory edn. svc. specialist Hdqs. US Army Pers. Command, Alexandria, Va., 1998-2000; edn. program specialist OSD Office of Chancellor Edn. and Profl. Devel., Arlington, Va., 2000—03; online faculty U. Phoenix, 2002—; edn. program specialist OSD Civilian Pers. Mgmt. Svcs., Arlington, 2003—05; acad. dean, dep. dir. U.S. Marine

Corps War Coll., Quantico, Va., 2005—. Mem. devel. bd. Sch. Edn. Coll. William and Mary, 2002—. Legis. affairs rep. Running Man Homeowners Assn., Yorktown, Va., 1996—98; treas. Massanetta Springs Alumni Assn., Harrisonburg, Va., 1988—2002, membership chmn., 1998—2002, pres., 2002—04, reunion com., 2004—07; mem. Living Waters campaign devel. bd. Massanetta Springs Renovation, 2007—; bd. dirs. Living Waters, 2007—. Recipient Alumni award, Massanetta Springs Alumni Assn., 1996. Mem.: ASTD, Assn. Ednl. Comm. and Tech., Assn. Study Higher Edn., U. Mary Washington Alumni Assn., Coll. William and Mary Alumni Assn., U. Va. Alumni Assn., Kappa Delta Pi. Presbyterian. Avocation: running. Home: 6006 River Dr Mason Neck VA 22079-4127 Office: Marine War Coll Marine Corps Univ 2076 South St Quantico VA 22134 Personal E-mail: mstout8895@aol.com.

STOUT, MAYE ALMA, retired secondary school educator; b. Reliance, SD, Mar. 3, 1920; d. Jesse Wilbur and Susie Maude (Fletcher) Moulton; m. Dennis William Stout, Jan. 6, 1943; children: Perry Wilbur, David Jay. BA, Dakota Wesleyan U., Mitchell, SD, 1969. Tchr. Rural Lyman County Sch., Iona/Oacoma, SD, 1939—42, Vivian Pub. Sch., SD, 1942, Rural Lyman County Sch., Reliance, Tenn., 1944-45, Reliance Cons. Dist., 1945-46, 49-51, Ft. Pierre Ind. Sch. Dist., SD, 1954—67, Kadoka Ind. Sch., SD, 1967—82; ret. Asst. editor: Jackson/Washabaugh County History 2, 1989; contbr. articles to books and publs. Vol. bingo Kadoka Care Ctr., 1982-2005, vol. Veterans and Meml. Day svcs., 1987-2004; pres. Kadoka Cmty. Betterment Assn., 1987; vol. Meals for Elderly; Sunday sch. tchr. asst.; tchr. 55 Alive, 1991-93; pres. Pierre/Ft. Pierre ACEI; tchr. Sunday sch. 5th grade 1st United Meth. Ch., 1953-67; deliverer meals to the elderly Mem. Am. Legion Aux. (dist. pres. 1985-89, chmn. com. Dept. Fgn. Rels. 1990-91, dept. chmn. constitution and by-laws com. 1992-93). Republican. Methodist. Avocations: reading, crocheting, travel. Address: PO Box 231 Kadoka SD 57543-0231 E-mail: mastout@gwtc.net.

STOUT, SHARON SPARKES, elementary school educator, counselor; d. Thomas and Frances Sparkes; m. Marvin Stout (div.); children: Franchesca Stout Jorgensen, Megan Stout Farias. BS in Edn., Ga. So. U., 1971, MEd, 1973; Cert. Advanced Grad. Studies, Fitchburg State Coll., 1983. Lic. mental health counselor Mass., marriage and family therapist Mass.; ednl. psychologist Mass., rehab. therapist Mass., cert. prin., reading tchr., elem. tchr., spl. edn. tchr., sch. psychometrist Ga. Spl. edn. tchr. Bulloch County Schs., Statesboro, Ga., 1971—73; learning disability specialist Screven County Schs., Sylvania, Ga., 1973—75; spl. edn. tchr. Harwich (Mass.) Pub. Schs., 1975—77, Eastham (Mass.) Elem. Sch., 1977—78; elem. sch. tchr. Chatham (Mass.) Pub. Schools, 1978—86, counselor, 1986—, devel., coord. caring for each student and bully prevention program, 2001—. Founder, dir. Cape Cod Learning Ctr., Harwich, 1980—87. Edn. chmn. Jr. Women's Club, Harwich, 1975—77; co-president Harwich Parent, Tchr. and Friends Orgn., Harwich, 1977—78; v.p. Cape Cod chpt. Mass. Assn. for Children with Learning Disabilities. Grantee, Dept. of Justice, 2001—03, Mass. Dept. Edn., 2003—06. Office: Chatham Pub Schs 147 Depot Rd Chatham MA 02633 Home Phone: 508-240-1572; Office Phone: 508-945-5135. Personal E-mail: capecod2000@comcast.net. Business E-Mail: sstout@chatham.k12.ma.us.

STOUTE, STEVE, advertising executive, former recording industry executive; b. NYC, June 26, 1970; 1 child. Attended, Syracuse U. Road mgr., 1992; A&R dir. RCA Records; ptnr. Track Masters Entertainment; pres. black music Sony Music, sr. v.p. A&R; pres. black music Universal Music Group, exec. v.p. Interscope, Geffen and A&M; co-founder PASS, 1999; ptnr. Arnell Group; founder, chmn., chief creative officer Translation Consultation & Brand Imaging, NYC, 2004—; owner Carol's Daughter, Zino Plainum. Exec. prodr.: (albums) It Was Written, 1996, Ill Na Na, 1996, I Can Love You, 1997, Share My World, 1997, Allure, 1997, Soundtrack to the Streets, 1998, I Can See Clearly Now, 1999, Love, Vol 4, 2000, Best of Nas, 2002, God's Son, 2002, I Can/Heaven, 2003; exec. prodr.: (single) Hate Me Now/If I Ruled the World, 1999; co-prodr.: (soundtrack) Def Jam's How to Be a Player, 1997, The Grinch, 2000, Ali, 2001; prodr.: Phenomenon, 1997. Bd. dirs. Diddy Runs the City, 2003. Recipient Power Broker of Yr., VIBE Awards, 2004, Humanitarian award, NY Police Dept/NY Fire Dept., 2004. Office: Translation Consultation & Brand Imaging 145 W 45th St New York NY 10036-4008 Office Phone: 212-299-5310. *

STOVAL, LINDA, political coach, consultant; b. Kans. m. Toby Stoval. Chairperson Wyo. Dem. Party, 2001—03; polit. leadership coach, 2005—. Mgr. Trauner for Congress, 2006; mem. campaign staff to local presdl. activist; ogranizer; campaign cons.; owner Gravilas Coaching & Consulting. Former chair Make-A-Wish, Wyo.; former vice chair Habitat for Humanity, Wyo.; former chair Serve Wyo. (Americorps).

STOVALL, CARLA JO, former state attorney general; b. Hardner, Kans., Mar. 18, 1957; d. Carl E. and Juanita Joe (Ford) Stovall. BA, Pittsburg State U., Kans., 1979; JD, U. Kans., 1982, MPA, 1993. Bar: Kans. 1982, U.S. Dist. Ct. Kans. 1982. Pvt. practice, Pitts., 1982—85; atty. Crawford County, Pitts., 1984—88; gov. Kans. Parole Bd., Topeka, 1988—94; atty. gen. State of Kans., Topeka, 1995—2002. Lectr. law Pittsburg State U., 1982—84. Mem. bd. govs. U. Kans. Sch. Law; Nat. Ctr. Missing and Exploited Children; Am. Legacy Found.; Nat. Crime Prevention Coun.; Coun. State Govts.; mem. bd. govs. Kans. Children's Cabinet; pres. NAAG, 2001—02, chmn. exec. com. midwest region, sexually violent predator com., 1995—96; Bd. dirs., sec. Pittsburg Family YMCA, 1983—88. Named Outstanding Atty. Gen., Nat. Assn. Attys. Gen., 2001, Topeka Fraternal Order of Police's Amb. to Law Enforcement; recipient Champion award, Campaign Tobacco Free Kids, 2002, Adam Walsh Children's Fund Rainbow award, Nat. Ctr. Missing and Exploited Children, 2001, Kelley-Wyman award, Nat. Assn. Attys. Gen., 2001, Person of the Yr., Kans. Peace Officer Assn.'s Law Enforcement, Morton Baud Allied Profl. award, Nat. Orgn. Victim Assistance, Father Ken Czillinger award, Nat. Parents Murdered Children, Disting. Svc. to Kans. Children award, Kans. Children's Svc. League, Woman of Achievement award, Miss Kans. Pageant. Mem.: NAAG (pres. 2001—02), AAUW (bd. dirs. 1983—87), ABA, Bus. and Profl. Women Assn. (Young Careerist award 1984), Nat. Coll. Dist. Attys., Kans. County and Dist. Attys. Assn., Crawford County Bar Assn. (sec. 1984—85, v.p. 1985—86, pres. 1986—87), Kans. Bar Assn., Kans. Assn. Commerce and Industry (Leadership Kans. award 1983), Pittsburg Area C. of C. (bd. dirs. 1983—85, Leadership Pitts. award 1984), Pittsburg State U. Alumni Assn. (bd. dirs. 1983—88). Republican. Methodist. Avocations: travel, photography, tennis. Home: 138 S Blue Bells Ct Garden Plain KS 67050-9225

STOVALL, FRANCES MIDDAGH, journalist, preservationist; b. Lawrenceville, Ill., Dec. 7, 1921; d. John Judy and Rebecca (Fowler) Middagh; m. Jack N. Stovall, Aug. 16, 1941 (dec. 2004; children: Richard Middagh Stovall, Frances Tshudy, John Fowler Stovall, Susan Calvert G. Carter. Student, McMurry Coll., 1938-41. Woman's Page editor Odessa (Tex.) News Times, 1937-40; reporter Abilene (Tex.) Reporter News, 1938-41. Author: Clear Springs and Limestone Ledges, A History of San Marcos and Hays County, 1986; editor: San Marcos Bicentennial Cookbook, 1976, Cottage Kitchen Cookbook, 1983, Cottage Kitchen, Second Helping, 1986, Twenty Years In Cottage Kitchen, 1996, Historical Markers in Hays County, 2005-06; columnist San Marcos Daily Record, 1986-2007. Founder Heritage Assn. San Marcos, 1975, bd. dirs., 1975-2006, hon. life mem., 1989—; chmn. City of San Marcos Bicentennial Commn., 1972-76, Hays County Hist. Commn., 1987-2006; initiator Main St. in San Marcos, 1989; founder Preservation Assocs., Inc., 1986, Friends of Hays County Hist. Commn., 1990-2007. Named Woman of Yr. Beta Sigma Phi, San Marcos, 1976, 96, Vol. of Yr., Rotary Club San Marcos, 1995; recipient Tex. award for hist. preservation Tex. Hist. Commn., Austin, 1990, John Ben Shepperd Leadership award Tex. Hist. Commn., Austin, 1991, Lifetime Achievement award Tex. Hist. Commn., Austin, 1993; Preservation award named in her honor, 1999, The Frances Stovall Collection within the San Marcos City libr. dedicated in her honor, 2001. Mem. DAR, Nat. Trust for Hist. Preservation, Tex. Hist. Found., Tex. State Hist. Assn., Spring Lake Garden Club, Magna Charta Dames. Avocation: history. Home: 20 Timbercrest St San Marcos TX 78666-3018

STOVALL, JERRY COLEMAN, insurance company executive; b. Houston, July 31, 1936; s. Clifford Coleman and Maxine (Lands) S.; m. Elsie Hostetter, June 20, 1959; 1 child, Brent Allen. BBA, U. Houston, 1968. Adminstr. home office Am. Gen. Life, Houston, 1955-63, agt., agy. mgr., 1963-66, agy. mgr., regional dir. agys., regional v.p., 1969-74; sr. brokerage cons. Conn. Gen. Life, Houston, 1966-69; sr. v.p., dir. mktg. Capitol Life Inst. Co., Denver, 1974-78; v.p., dir. mktg. Integon Life Ins. Corp., Winston-Salem, N.C., 1978-81; pres. Life of Mid-Am. Ins. Co., Topeka, 1981-85, Victory Life Ins. Co., Topeka, 1981-85, chmn., pres., chief exec. officer, 1981-87; pres., retired chief exec officer Integon Life Ins. Co., Winston-Salem, N.C., 1987-91; pres. Lamar Life Ins. Co., 1992-95, ret., 1995; pres., CEO Am. Pub. Holding Inc., 1996-2000, ret., 2000. Bd. dirs., vice-chmn., Ga. Internat. Life; vice-chmn. Mktg. One Inc. Bd. dirs. Jr. Achievement Miss., Inc.; bd. trustees Miss. Bapt. Found. With U.S. Army, 1955-57. Mem. Nat. Assn. Life Cos., Nat. Assn. Life Underwriters, Am. Soc. CLUs (Gold Key soc.), Am. Coun. Life Ins., Exec. Round Table (chmn. 1995), The Country Club of Jackson. Home: 1406 Mossycup Ln Livingston TX 77351-3074

STOVALL, LOU, printmaker; b. Athens, Ga., Jan. 1, 1937; Attended, RI Sch. Design; BFA, Howard U. Founder & dir. Workshop Inc., 1968—. Ind. Day invitation, White House (at Nancy Reagan's request), 1982, Am. Beauty Rose print, DC Area Host Com. Dem. Nat. Conv. (at Mayor Marion Barry's request), 1988, Breathing Hope print, Howard U. pres. inauguration, exhibitions include Art Lou Stovall, Strathmore Hall, 2004, Art Silkscreen Printmaking, Howard U. Gallery, 2001. Named Washingtonian Yr., 1979; recipient Bd. Dir.'s Award, Source Theatre Co., Washington DC, 1988, Mayor's Art Award Excellence Artistic Design, Washington DC, 1985; Workshop Grants, Nat. Endowment Arts, 1972, 1973, 1974, Individual Artist Fellowship Grant, 1972, Stern Family Grant Fund, 1968—74. Mem.: DC Commn. Arts & Humanities. Office: Workshop Inc 3145 Newark St NW Washington DC 20008 Office Phone: 202-966-4202. Office Fax: 202-362-0116. E-mail: lou@loustovall.com.

STOVER, CARL FREDERICK, foundation executive; b. Pasadena, Calif., Sept. 29, 1930; s. Carl Joseph and Margarete (Müller) S.; m. Catherine Swanson, Sept. 3, 1954; children: Matthew Joseph, Mary Margaret Stover Marker, Claire Ellen Stover Herrell; m. Jacqueline Kast, Sept. 7, 1973. BA magna cum laude, Stanford U., 1951, MA, 1954. Instr. polit. sci. Stanford U., 1953-55; fiscal mgmt. officer Office Sec. Dept. Agr., 1955-57; assoc. dir. conf. program pub. affairs Brookings Instn., 1957-59, sr. staff govtl. studies, 1960; fellow Center Study Democratic Instns., Santa Barbara, Calif., 1960-62; asst. to chmn. bd. editors Ency. Brit., 1960-62; sr. polit. scientist Stanford Research Inst., 1962-64; dir. pub. affairs fellowship program Stanford U., 1962-64; pres. Nat. Inst. Pub. Affairs, Washington, 1964-70, Nat. Com. U.S.-China Relations, 1971-72; pres., dir. Federalism Seventy-Six, Washington, 1972-74; dir. cultural resources devel. Nat. Endowment Arts, 1974-78; pres., dir. Cultural Resources, Inc., Washington, 1978-85; bd. dirs. H.E.A.R. Found., 1976-86, treas., 1976-80, pres., 1980-86. Bd. dirs. Ctr. for World Lit., pres., 1987-90, chmn., 1990-92; pvt. profl. cons., 1970—; scholar-in-residence Nat. Acad. Pub. Adminstrn., 1980-82; cons. in field. Author: The Government of Science, 1962, The Technological Order, 1963; Founding editor: Jour. Law and Edn., 1971-73; pub. Delos mag., 1987-92. Treas. Nat. Com. U.S.-China Rels., 1966-71, 82-87, 89-94, bd. dirs., 1966-74, 79-98, dir. emeritus, 1998—; bd. dirs. Coord. Coun. Lit. Mags., 1966-68, H.E.A.R. Found., 1976-86, treas., 1976-80; trustee Inst. of Nations, 1972-76, Nat. Inst. Pub. Affairs, 1967-71, Kinesis Ltd., 1972-78; vol. Nat. Exec. Svc. Corps, 1984-89; mem. Fellowship of Reconciliation Fellow AAAS, Phi Beta Kappa (hon. lectr. 1972-87); mem. Am. Soc. Pub. Adminstrn., Fedn. Am. Scientists, Soc. Internat. Devel., Jordan Soc. (dir. 1982-84), Nat. Acad. Pub. Adminstrn. (hon.), Internat. Soc. Panetics (pres. 1991-95, chmn. 1995-98, chmn. emeritus 1999—, bd. govs. 1991—, founding mem. 1991—). Democrat. Presbyterian. Home and Office: 4109 Metzerott Rd College Park MD 20740-2082 Home Phone: 301-935-5263. E-mail: carlfstover@aol.com.

STOVER, ELLEN L., health scientist, psychologist; b. Bklyn., Nov. 21, 1950; d. Ralph and Charlotte (Tulchin) Simon; m. Alan B. Stover, June 3, 1973; children: Elena Randall Simon, Randall Alan Simon, Samantha Anne Simon. BA with honors, U. Wis., 1972; PhD, Catholic U., 1978. Cons. NIMH, Rockville, Md., 1972-74, exec. sec. drug abuse rsch. review com., 1974-76, spl. asst. to assoc. dir. extramural programs Rockville, Md., 1976-77, chief, small grants program, 1977-79, asst., acting & chief rsch. resources br., 1980-85, dep. dir., div. basic scis., 1985-88, dir. office AIDS, 1988-97, dir. divsn. mental disorders, behavioral rsch. and AIDS, 1997—; dir. Ctr. Mental Health Rsch. on AIDS. Dir. divsn. AIDS, health, behavior NIMH. Recipient Superior Svc. award USPHS, 1987, 92, 93, Dir.'s award NIH, 1996, Presdl. Rank award, 2001. Mem. APA, Am. Psychol. Soc. Avocations: gardening, dance. Office: NIMH 6001 Executive Blvd Rm 6217 Bethesda MD 20892-0001 Office Phone: 301-443-9700. Business E-Mail: estover@nih.gov.

STOVER, JILL S., school librarian, writer; BA in Hist., Ohio State U., 2001; MS in Libr. Sci., U. NC, 2004; student in Mktg., Va. Commonwealth U., Richmond, 2005—. Undergraduate svcs. libr. James Branch Cabell Libr. Va. Commonwealth U. Contbr. articles to profl. publs. Mem.: ALA, Reference and User Svcs. Assn., Assn. Coll. and Rsch. Librs., Phi Beta Kappa. Office: Va Commonwealth U Librs 901 Park Ave PO Box 842033 Richmond VA 23284-2033 Office Phone: 804-828-8964. E-mail: jsstover@vcu.edu.

STOVER, MILES RONALD, management consultant; b. Glendale, Calif., Dec. 23, 1948; s. Robert Miles and Alberta Mae (Walker) S.; m. Cynthia McNeil, Jan. 25, 1975; children: Christopher, Matthew. BS, U. So. Calif., 1974; MBA, Pepperdine U., 1979; PhD, Kennedy Western U., 2005. Cert. fraud examiner; cert. turnaround profl.; cert. profl. cons.; cert. mgmt. cons.; cert. confidentiality officer; cert. insolvency advisor. V.p., gen. mgr., CFO Johnson Controls Inc., LA, 1974-82; gen. mgr. MG Products Inc., San Diego, 1982-84; exec. v.p., gen. mgr. ICU Med. Inc., Mission Viejo, 1984-86; v.p., COO B.P. John Inc., Santa Ana, Calif., 1986-88; gen. mgr. MG Products Inc., San Diego, 1988-90; pres. Lucks Co., Kent, Wash., 1991-96, also bd. dirs.; prin. Crossroads LLC, 1998—2002; pres. Turnaround, Inc., 1996—98, 2002—. Cons. Turnaround Mgmt. Assn., Tacoma, 1990. With USN, 1967-71. Decorated Gallantry Cross USN; recipient award for Productivity US Senate, 1978, Congl. medal of Distinction Nat. Rep. Congl. Com.; named Businessman of Yr. Wash., 2006. Mem. Inst. Mgmt. Cons., Turnaround Mgmt. Assn., Am. Bankruptcy Inst., Nat. Assn. Corp. Dirs., Assn. Cert. Fraud Examiners, Assn. Insolvency and Restructuring Advisors, Inst. Mgmt. Accts., Mensa. Republican. Methodist. Home: 3415 A St NW Gig Harbor WA 98335-7843 Home Phone: 253-851-7687; Office Phone: 253-857-6730. Business E-Mail: mstover@turnaround-inc.com.

STOVER, RICHARD L., investor; b. Uniontown, Pa., Oct. 11, 1942; s. Louis John and Sarah Virginia Stover; m. Dorothea Gerber Stover, June 19, 1965; children: Kristin Stover Matheny, Douglas Richard. BSBA, The Pa. State U., 1965. Sr. v.p. Mellon Fin. Corp., Pitts., 1969—89; exec. v.p. Bank of New Eng. Corp., Boston, 1989—91; exec. v.p. and chief credit officer Equimark Corp., Pittsburgh, Pa., 1991—93; mng. dir. GE Capital Corp., Stamford, Conn., 1993—94; founder and prin. Stover & Assocs., Wexford, Pa., 1994—96; founder and mng. dir. ARC Capital, Pittsburgh, Pa., 1995—96; pres. First Western Bancorp, Inc., New Castle, Pa., 1996—99; mng. prin. Birchmere Capital, Wexford, Pa., 2000—. Dir. SAFAS Corp., Clifton, NJ, 1995—, Bliley Technologies, Inc., Erie, Pa., 1999—, Ductmate Industries, Inc., Charleroi, Pa., 2004—. Bd. dirs. Inst. for Transfusion Medicine, Pitts., 1978; chmn. bd. suprs. Marshall Twp., Wexford, Pa., 1995—2001; vice chmn. WQED Multimedia, Pitts., 2002. Lt. USN, 1965—69. Mem.: Bonita Bay Club, Treeesdales Golf and Country Club, The Duquesne Club. Avocations: golf, travel, exercise, history. Office: Birchmere Capital 5000 Stonewood Dr Ste 220 Wexford PA 15090 Home Phone: 724-625-3191; Office Phone: 724-940-2300. Office Fax: 724-940-2383. Business E-Mail: rstover@birchmere.net.

STOWE, ALEXIS MARIANI, accountant, consultant; b. Binghamton, NY, May 3, 1950; d. Albert Joseph and Gilda Ann (DiNardo) Mariani; m. Dennis James Stowe, June 3, 1972 (dec. Nov. 1988); children: Cort Andrew, Derek Anthony, Jilda Ann. Student, Le Moyne Coll., 1968-70; BS in Acctg., SUNY, Buffalo, 1972; MS in Acctg., SUNY, Albany, 1974; MS in Taxation, Southeastern U., 1980. CPA, N.Y., Va.; cert. fraud examiner; cert. govt. fin. mgr., cert. info. sys. auditor; cert. info. technology profl., cert. massage therapist. In-charge acct. Ernst & Young, CPA's, Buffalo, 1973-74; sr. corp. acct. Moog, Inc., East Aurora, N.Y., 1974-76; auditor U.S. Gen. Acctg. Office, Washington, 1976-78, 79-80; tax law specialist IRS, Washington, 1978-79; pvt. practice CPA Woodbridge, Va., 1980-87; v.p., contr. M.T. Hall, Ltd., Woodbridge, 1987-91; audit mgr. U.S. Dept. Health and Human Svcs., Washington, 1991-93; oversight mgr. Resolution Trust Corp., Washington, 1993-94; v.p., prin. Gardiner, Kamya, CPA's, Washington, 1994-97; v.p., ptnr. Leon Snead & Co., PC, Rockville, Md., 1998—2002; v.p., prin. Gardiner, Kamya, CPAs, Washington, 2002—05; dir. profl. svcs. Mgmt. Concepts., Washington, 2005; dir. Washington fed. practice Price Waterhouse Coopers, Washington, 2005—. Trustee pension plan M.T. Hall, Ltd., Woodbridge, 1987—90; team leader CFO task force Pres.'s Coun. on Integrity and Efficiency, Washington, 1991—93; instr. Inspector Gen. Auditor Tng. Inst., Ft. Belvoir, Va., 1992—2000; mem. task force on grants Govtl. Acctg. Stds. Bd., Norwalk, Conn., 1992—96; mem. faculty Assn. Cert. Fraud Examiners, 1995—. Contbr. articles to profl. jours. N.Y. Regents scholar, 1968-72. Mem.: AICPA, Nat. Assn. Massage and Bodywork, Inst. Internal Auditors, Info. Sys. Audit Control Assn., Assn. Cert. Fraud Examiners, Assn. Govt. Accts. (vice chair publs. 1994—98, Author's award 1991), Va. Soc. CPAs, Cath. Daus. of Am., Beta Gamma Sigma, Chi Omega. Roman Catholic. Office: 1800 Tysons Blvd Mc Lean VA 22102 Home: 908 N Wayne St Apt 301 Arlington VA 22201 Office Phone: 703-918-1049. Business E-Mail: alexis.m.stowe@us.pwc.com.

STOWE, CHARLES ROBINSON BEECHER, management consultant, educator, lawyer; b. Seattle, July 18, 1949; s. David and Edith Beecher (Andrade) Stowe; m. Laura Everett, Mar. 9, 1985. BA, Vanderbilt U., Nashville, 1971; MBA, U. Tex., Dallas, 1975; JD, U. Houston, 1982; PhD, U. Warsaw, Poland, 1998. Bar: Tex. 1982, US Dist. Ct. (so. dist.), Tex. 1984, US Tax Ct. 1984. Acct. exec. Engleman Co., Dallas, 1974-75; dir. Productive Capital Assoc., 1975-81; instr. Richland Coll., Dallas, 1976; acct. Arthur Andersen and Co., 1976-78; pres. Stowe and Co., 1978—; prof. dept. gen. bus., fin. Coll. Bus. Adminstrn., Sam Houston State U., 1982—, dir. office internat. programs, 1997-2001. Bd. dir. Office Internat. Programs Sam Houston State U., Tex., adminstrv. intern asst. to pres., 1985; bd. dirs. Entrepreneurship Inst., dir., 2006—; cons. in field. Editor: Houston Journal International Law, 1981—82; co-editor: Knowledge Cafe for Intellect Product and Intellectual Entrepreneurship, 2001, Knowledge Cafe for Intellectual Entrepreneurship, Intellectual Product, Intellectual Capital, 2001; author: Bankruptcy I Micro-Mash Inc., 1989, 3d edit., 2005, The Implications of Foreign Financial Institutions on Poland's Emerging Entrepreneurial Economy, 1999; co-author: CPA; contbr. articles to profl. jour. Team chief, US Mil. liaison, Rep., 1994; founder Young Am.'s Found., 1969—; trustee Stowe-Day Found., 1979—80; vol., faculty State Bar Tex., Profl. Devel. Program, 1988—; vol., mediator Dispute Resolution Ctr., Montgomery County; mediator so. dist. US Dist. Ct., Tex., 1993; pub. affairs officer George C. Marshall European Ctr. Security Studies, 1997; vestry St. Stephen's Episcopal Ch., Huntsville, Tex., 2002—05. Capt. Res. USNR, 1971—74. Decorated Navy Achievement medal, Gold Star Navy, US, Def. Meritorious Svc. medal (oak leaf cluster), Navy Meritorious Svc. award, Legion of Merit; recipient Freedoms Found. award; fellow Summer fellow Tex. Coordinating Bd., 1988, Prince-Babson Fellow Entrepreneurship Symposium, 1991. Mem.: Res. Officers Assn., Naval Res. Assn., Tex. Assn. Realtors, Pub. Rels. Soc. Am., Assn. Computer Educators Tex. (bd. dirs. 2000—03, editor 2002—05), Tex. State Bar Coll. (bd. dirs. 2001—05), Walker County Bar Assn. (pres. 1987—88), State Bar Tex. (vol. faculty profl. devel. program 1988—90, vice chmn. profl. efficiency and econ. rsch. com. 1993, chmn. law office mgmt. com. 1993—94), Am. Arbitration Assn., ABA, US Navy League, Dallas Vanderbilt Club (pres. 1977—78). Office: PO Box 537 Huntsville TX 77342-0537

STOWELL, CHRISTOPHER R., performing company executive, choreographer, retired dancer; b. NYC, June 8, 1966; s. Kent and Francia (Russell) S. Student, Pacific N.W. Ballet Sch., 1979-84, Sch. Am. Ballet, 1984-85. Entered corps de ballet San Francisco Ballet, 1986, promoted to soloist, 1987, prin., 1990—2001; freelance choreographer for ballet and opera cos., 2001—; ballet master Balanchine Trust, 2001—; artistic dir. Oreg. Ballet Theater. Guest artist Ballet Met, Ohio, Pacific N.W. Ballet, Seattle, and with Jean Charles Gil, Marseilles, France, Asami Maki Ballet, Tokyo. Created leading roles in Handel-A Celebration, Con Brio, The Sleeping Beauty, New Sleep, Connotations, Pulcinella, Meistens Mozart; other roles include Calcium Light Night, Rubies, The Sons of Horus, The Four Temperaments, Hearts, Tarantella, Flower Festival, La Fille Mal Garde, Haffner Symphony, Forgotten Land, The End, Agon, In the Middle Somewhat Elevated, Le Quattro Stagioni, Swan Lake, Job, Company B, Tchaikousky Pas de Deux, Maelstrom, Mercutio in Romeo and Juliet, The Dance House, Stars and Stripes, Ballo Della Regina, Drink to me Only With Thine Eyes, Pacific; performed in Reykjavik Arts Festival, Iceland, 1990, San Francisco Ballet at the Paris Opera Garnier, 1994, Bolshoi Theatre, Moscow, 1998; artistic dir. Oreg. Ballet Theatre, Portland, 2003—. Avocations: cooking, reading, camping. Office: Oreg Ballet Theatre 818 SE 6th Ave Portland OR 97214 *

STOWELL, KENT, retired ballet director; b. Rexburg, Idaho, Aug. 8, 1939; s. Harold Bowman and Maxine (Hudson) S.; m. Francia Marie Russell, Nov. 19, 1965; children: Christopher, Darren, Ethan. Lead dancer San Francisco Ballet, 1957—62, NYC Ballet, 1962—68; ballet dir., ballet master Frankfurt (Fed. Republic Germany) Opera Ballet, 1973—77; artistic dir. Pacific NW Ballet, Seattle, 1977—2005. Prof. dance Ind. U., Bloomington, 1969-70; bd. dirs. Sch. of Am. Ballet, Dance/USA, Washington, 1986—; bd. dirs. Sch. Am. Ballet, NYC, 1981—; mem. Goodwill Games Arts Com., Seattle, 1987—; chmn. dance panel NEA, 1981-85. Grantee NEA, 1980, 85; fellow NEA, 1979. Choreographer: Silver Lining, Cinderella, Carmina Burana, Coppelia, Time & Ebb, Faurè Requiem, Hail to the Conquering Hero, Firebird, Over the Waves, Nutcracker, The Tragedy of Romeo and Juliet, Delicate Balance, Swan Lake, Time and Ebb, Through Interior Worlds, Quaternary, Orpheus. Recipient Arts Service award King County Arts Commn., 1985, Outstanding Contbn. to Pacific NW Ballet State of Wash., 1987, Best Dance Co. award The Weekly Newspaper, Seattle, 1987, Gov. Arts award, 1988, Dance Mag. award, 1996, Lifetime Achievement award U. Utah, 2004,

Lifetime Achievement in Arts award ArtsFund, 2004, award Seattle (Wash.) Ctr., 2004, Entrepreneur of Yr. award Ernst and Young, 2004, Mayor's Art award, 2004. Office: Pacific NW Ballet 301 Mercer St Seattle WA 98109-4600

STOWELL, ROBERT EUGENE, pathologist, retired educator; b. Cashmere, Wash., Dec. 25, 1914; s. Eugene Francis and Mary (Wilson) S.; m. Eva Mae (Chambers), Dec. 1, 1945; children: Susan Jane, Robert Eugene Jr. Attended, Whitman Coll., 1932-33; BA, Stanford Univ., 1936, MD, 1941; PhD, Washington Univ., 1944. Fellow in cytology Wash. U. Sch. Medicine, St. Louis, 1940-42; rsch. fellow Barnard Free Skin and Cancer Hosp., St. Louis, 1940-42, rsch. assoc., 1942-48; asst. resident in pathology Barnes, McMillan, St. Louis Children's Hosps., St. Louis, 1942-43, resident in pathology, 1943-44, asst. pathologist, 1944-48; instr. in pathology Washington U. Sch. Medicine, St. Louis, 1943-45, asst. prof., assoc. prof., 1948; advanced med. fellow Inst. for Cell Rsch., Stockholm, 1946-47; chmn. dept. oncology U. Kans. Med. Ctr., Kans. City, Kans., 1948-51, prof. pathology and oncology, dir. cancer rsch., 1948-59, chmn., 1951-59; sci. dir. Armed Forces Inst. Pathology, Washington, 1959-67; chmn. dept. pathology Sch. of Medicine U. Calif., Davis, 1967-69, asst. dean Sch. Medicine, 1967-72, prof. pathology Sch. Medicine, 1967-82, prof. emeritus, 1982—; dir. div. pathology Sacramento Med. Ctr., 1967-69. Vis. prof. U. Md. Sch. Medicine, Balt., 1960-67; acting dir. Nat. Ctr. for Primate Biology, U. Calif., Davis, 1968-69, dir., 1969-71; cons. U.S. Atomic Energy commn., Los Alamos, N.Mex., 1949-54; NIH, 1949-74; Cancer Control Div. USPHS, 1949-59, others; mem. adv. med. bd. Leonard Wood Meml. found., Washington, 1965-67, numerous univs.; prin. investigator, chmn. Expert Panel on Authentication Review of Selected Materials Submitted to the FDA Relative to Application of Searle Lab. to Market Aspartame, 1977-78; Assessment of the Practical Risk to Human Health from Nitrilotriacetic Acid in Household Laundry Products, 1984-85. Contbr. 121 articles, 34 abstracts to jour. in field; editor 35 biomed. books, monographs and conf. reports, 1941-88; mem. editorial bd. Cancer Rsch., 1949-59, Lab. Investigation, 1952-71, editor, 1967-71. Recipient Meritorious Svc. Award, Dept. Army, 1963; Exceptional Civilian Svc. Award, Dept. Army, 1965; Disting. Svc. Award U. Calif., 1988, Robert E. Stowell ann. Med. Student Award Outstanding Excellence in Pathology, 1981—; Robert E. Stowell ann. lectureship established U. Calif. Sch. Medicine, 1991 and Am. Registry of Pathology, Washington, 1991; endowed Robert E. Stowell professorship, 2002-. Mem. AMA; Am. Registry of Pathology (bd. dir. 1976-83, exec. com. 1976-82, v.p. 1976-78, pres. 1978-79, Disting. Svc. Award 1995), Am. Assn. Cancer Rsch., Am. Assn. Pathologists (Gold-headed Cane Award 1990), Am. Assn. Pathologists and Bacteriologists (councilor 1965-72, v.p. 1969-70, pres. 1970-71); Am. Soc. Clin. Pathologists; Am. Soc. Exptl. Pathology (councilor 1962-66, v.p. 1963-64, pres. 1964-65); Calif. Med. Soc.; Calif. Soc. Pathologists; Binford-Dammin Soc. Infectious Disease Pathologists; Coll. Am. Pathologists; Histochem. Soc.; Internat. Acad. Pathology (councilor 1954-61, pres.-elect 1958-59, pres. 1995-60); Disting. Svc. Award 1970; Diamond Jubilee Award 1981; Stowell-Orbison Award established 1982—); Soc. Cryobiology (bd. gov. 1968-71); Soc. Exptl. Biology and Medicine; U.S. and Can. Acad. Patholog;, Yolo County Med. Soc.; Assn. Mil. Surgeons U.S. (sustaining membership award 1965), Univ. Associated for Rsch. and Edn. in Path. (bd. dir. 1975-90, sec.-treas. 1978-82, hon. dir. 1990-2002); Sigma Xi; Alpha Omega Alpha. Home: 44752 N El Macero Dr El Macero CA 95618-1090

STOWERS, CARLTON EUGENE, writer; b. Brownwood, Tex., Apr. 14, 1942; s. Ira Milton and Fay Eloise (Stephenson) S.; m. Patricia Ann Folks, Mar. 2, 1981; children: Anson, Ashley. Student, U. Tex., Austin, 1961-63. Sportswriter Abilene (Tex.) Reporter News, 1963-64; sports editor Roswell (N.Mex.) Daily Record, 1964-65; sportswriter Lubbock (Tex.) Avalanche Jour., 1965-67; sports editor Amarillo (Tex.) Globe News, 1967-72; reporter, columnist Dallas Morning News, 1972-81; freelance writer Cedar Hill, Tex., 1981—. Editor Dallas Cowboys Weekly, 1985-89. Author: The Randy Matson Story, 1971, Spirit, 1973; author: (with E.B. Hughes) Doc, 1976; author: (with Trent Jones) Where the Rainbows Wait, 1978; author: (with Wilbur Evans) Champions, 1978; author: The Overcomers, 1978; author: (with Roy Rogers and Dale Evans) Happy Trails, 1979; author: pub. softcover as Terlingua Teacher, 1982, 2005, The Unsinkable Titanic Thompson, 1982, softcover, 1988, Journey to Triumph, 1988, Partners in Blue: The 100-Year History of the Dallas Police Department, 1983; author: (with Billy Olson) Reaching Higher, 1984; author: The Dallas Cowboys: The First 25 Years, 1984, The Cowboy Chronicles, 1984; author: (ghosted for Pam Lontos) Don't Tell Me It's Impossible Until I've Already Done It, 1988; author: Careless Whispers, 1986 (Edgar Allan Poe award Mystery Writers Am., Oppie award S.W. Booksellers Assn.), The Cotton Bowl: The First 50 Years, 1986; author: (with William C. Dear) Please...Don't Kill Me: The True Story of the Milo Murder, 1989 (Literary Guild selection); author: (with Larry Wansley) The FBI Undercover: The True Story of Special Agent 'Mandrake', 1989; author: Innocence Lost, 1990, A Hero Named George, 1991, Hard Lessons, 1994, Open Secrets, 1994, Sins of the Son, 1995; author: (with Marcus Allen) Marcus, 1997; author: To the Last Breath, 1998 (Edgar Allan Poe award Mystery Writers Am.); author: (with Rev. Carroll Pickett) Within These Walls, 2002 (Violet Crown award, 2002, PEN S.W. Book award finalist, 2005); author: Scream at the Sky, 2003, Death in a Texas Desert, 2003, Where Dreams Die Hard, 2005, Oh, Brother How They Played the Game, 2007. Recipient numerous journalism awards. Home: 1015 Randy Rd Cedar Hill TX 75104-3035 Office Phone: 972-291-4831. E-mail: cstowers1@tx.rr.com.

STOWERS, JAMES EVANS, JR., investment company executive; b. Kansas City, Mo., Jan. 10, 1924; s. James Evans Sr. and Laura (Smith) S.; m. Virginia Ann Glasscock, Feb. 4, 1954; children: Pamela, Kathleen, James Evans III, Linda. AB, U. Mo., 1946, BS in Medicine, 1947. Chmn. bd. Am. Century Investment Mgmt. Inc., Am. Century Cos., Inc.; Am. Century Group of Mutual Funds, Kansas City, 1958—. Author: Why Waste Your Money on Life Insurance, 1967, Principles of Financial Consulting, 1971, Yes, You Can...Achieve Financial Independence, 1992; co-author: (with Jack Jonathan) The Best is Yet to Be: A Story of Innovation, Generosity & Success, 2007 Co-founder, chmn. Stowers Inst. for Med. Rsch., Kansas City, 1995—. Capt. USAAF, 1943-45; with USAFR, 1945-57. Mem. Kansas City C. of C., Sigma Chi Republican. Office: Am Century Svcs 4500 Main St Kansas City MO 64111-1816 *

STOWERS, LELA M., retired academic administrator; b. Tahlequah, Okla., Mar. 21, 1935; d. Thomas Jefferson and Leona May (Simpson) Heaton; m. Gerald D. Stowers, Nov. 8, 1952; children: Allan, Kevin, Kathryn LeAnn Stowers Miller. BS, Northeastern State U., Tahlequah, 1984. Credit check clk. Pub. Fin., El Cajon, Calif., 1958—59; acct. dept. motor vehicles Hatch Chevrolet, El Cajon, 1959—63; acct. Success Motor Co., Tahlequah, 1964—65; asst. admissions registrar, counselor Northeastern State U., Tahlequah, 1965—85, asst. to grad. dean, 1985—94; ret., 1994. Co-chmn. Relay for Life, Am. Cancer Soc., 2006—; chmn. long range planning com., Sunday sch. tchr., vice chmn. bldg. com., trustee Meth. Ch. Recipient Disting. Svc. award, Okla. Assn. Collegiate Registrars and Admissions Officers, 1994. Mem.: AAUW (v.p. 1993—2003, pres., spkr. local, state and regional meetings, Outstanding Longterm Mem. 1998—99), Cherokee County Ret. Tchrs., Nature and Garden Club Tahlequah. Democrat. Avocations: travel, sightseeing, crafts, musicals. Home: 18097 S Prairie Ave Tahlequah OK 74464

STOWERS, MARK DAVID, chemicals executive; b. Houston, Feb. 9, 1957; s. Charles Henry Stowers, Jr. and Eleanor Ann (Schutz) Fowler; m. Sarah Kent Upham, Sept. 2, 1984; children: Rosemary Diane, Samuel Huntington, Elizabeth Ann. BS in Biology, Appalachian State U., Boone, NC, 1977; MS in Microbiology, N.C. State U., 1980, PhD in Microbiology, 1982. Postdoctoral assoc. Cornell U., Ithaca, NY, 1982-83; sr. project leader NPI, Inc., Salt Lake City, 1983-86; head, biol. scis. rsch. Eastman Kodak Co., Rochester, NY, 1986-89; bus. dir. Monsanto Co., St. Louis, 1989-95, v.p. ops. Naples, Fla., 1995—96; v.p. mktg. Seminic Inc., Oxnard, Calif., 1996—98; v.p. bus. devel. Seminis Inc., Oxnard, Calif., 1998—2000; pres., CEO MBI Internat., Lansing, Mich., 2000—06, Draths Corp.; v.p. R&D Broin Cos., 2006—. Bd. dirs. BioPlastics Inc., Natura, Inc., MBI Internat. Bd. dirs. Pierce Coll. Found., 2000—01. Rsch. grantee NSF, 1984, AID, 1985, Dept. Energy, 2001-06, EPA, 2001-03, 02-03, USDA, 2002-06, US Dept. Energy, 2002-03, US Dept. Agr., 2002-03; named Disting. Alumnus, Coll. Agr. and Life Scis. NC State U., 2003. Mem. AAAS, Am. Soc. for Microbiology, Soc. for Indsl. Microbiology, Assn. Univ. Tech. Mgrs., Inst. Food Technologists. Conservative. Methodist. Achievements include patents for use of a protease in the extraction of Chlamydial, Gonococcal and Herpes Antigens. Avocations: golf, cross country skiing, basketball, fly fishing. Home: 412 E 21st St Sioux Falls SD 57105-1927 Office: Poet Rsch 4615 N Lewis Ave Sioux Falls SD 57104 Office Phone: 605-965-6438. Personal E-mail: mdstowers@yahoo.com.

STOWMAN, DAVID L., lawyer; b. Rothsay, Minn., 1943; m. Judy Stowman; 4 children. BA, Moorehead State Univ.; JD, Univ. N.D. Co-founder NW Minn. Legal Services. Capt. USMC, 1965—69, Vietnam (1968-69). Named one of Minn. Top 25 Lawyers, Law & Politics mag., 2001. Mem.: ABA, Minn. State Bar Assn. (pres.-elect 2003, pres. 2004). Avocations: running, water-skiing. Office: Stowman Law Office PO Box 845 Detroit Lakes MN 56502-0845 also: Stowman Law Office 1100 W Lake Dr Detroit Lakes MN 56501 Office Phone: 218-847-5644.

STOYTCHEVA, LILIA STEFANOVA, concert pianist, educator; b. Sofia, Bulgaria, July 13, 1962; arrived in US, 1995; d. Stefan Sotirov Stoytchev and Liliana Georgieva Sarafova. Studied with Liuba Entcheva, Bulgarian State Conservatory, M in Piano summa cum laude, 1987; M of Music summa cum laude, Winthrop U., Rock Hill, SC, 1997; MusD in Piano Performance, U. Iowa, Iowa City, 2005. Instr. piano Bulgarian State Conservatory, Sofia, 1988—92; asst. prof. piano Sofia's U. "Kliment Ohridski", 1988—90; prof. piano State Conservatory, Czech Republic, 1992—95; asst. prof. Ctrl. State U., Wilberforce, Ohio, 2003—06; assoc. prof. piano North Greenville U., Tigerville, SC, 2006—. Composer: 1300 Anniversary Bulgaria, 1981; musician (solo pianist): Symphony Orch. of the Bulgarian State Conservatory, 1987, Symphony Orch. of Biel/Bienne, 1992, The Jihoceske Chamber Orch. of South Bohemia, 1992, Acad. Symphony Orch., U. Iowa, 2002; musician: (pianist) Harper Hall, 2001, 2002, Clapp Hall, 2001, 2002, Rudolf Steiner House and St. Cyprianus Ch. Eng., 2001, Hancher Auditorium, 2002, Concert Hall at the Conservatory of Stravanger, 2002, Salle Munch at Ecole Normal de Musique, 2002, Schuster Ctr. for Performing Arts, 2004, Steinway Gala Concert, Hamlin Recital Hall, North Greenville U., 2006, Gunter Theater at Peace Ctr., 2007. Recipient award, Nat. Composition Competition, Bulgaria, 1981, Internat. Piano Competition, Italy, 1988, John Simms award, 1998, 1999, 2001, award, Maia Quartet Competition, 2001; fellow Internat. Piano Master Classes with Norma Fisher, London, UK, 2001, Internat. Piano Master Classes with Nelson Delle-Vigne, John Perry, Phillippe Entremont and Einar Nokleberg, Paris, 2002; grantee, George Soros Found. Open Soc., Sofia, 1992; scholar Internat. Piano Master Classes with Rudolf Buchbinder and Victor Merzhanov, Switzerland, 1992, 1993, Walter Hautzig Piano Master Classes, S.C., 1995, 1996, Internat. Piano Workshop, Stavanger, Norway, 2002. Mem.: Studio of the Young Musician, Coll. Music Soc., Phi Kappa Phi. Avocations: travel, fine arts, languages. Personal E-mail: lstoytch@hotmail.com.

STRAATSMA, BRADLEY RALPH, ophthalmologist, educator; b. Grand Rapids, Mich., Dec. 29, 1927; s. Clarence Ralph and Lucretia Marie (Nicholson) S.; m. Ruth Campbell, June 16, 1951; children: Cary Ewing, Derek, Greer. Student, U. Mich., 1947; MD cum laude, Yale U., New Haven, Conn., 1951; DSc (hon.), Columbia U., NYC, 1984; JD cum laude, U. West LA, 2002. Diplomate Am. Bd. Ophthalmology (vice chmn. 1979, chmn. 1980). Intern New Haven Hosp., Yale U., 1951-52; resident in ophthalmology Columbia U., NYC, 1955-58; spl. clin. trainee Nat. Inst. Neurol. Diseases and Blindness, Bethesda, Md., 1958-59; assoc. prof. surgery/ophthalmology UCLA Sch. Medicine, 1959-63, chief div. ophthalmology, dept. surgery, 1959-68, prof. surgery/ophthalmology, 1963-68, prof. ophthalmology, 1968—2001, dir. Jules Stein Eye Inst., 1964-94, chmn. dept. ophthalmology, 1968-94, prof. emeritus, 2001—; ophthalmologist-in-chief UCLA Med. Ctr., 1968-94. Lectr. numerous univs. and profl. socs. 1971—; cons. to surgeon gen. USPHS, mem. Vision Research Tng. Com., Nat. Inst. Neurol. Diseases and Blindness, NIH, 1959-63, mem. neurol. and sensory disease program project com., 1964-68; chmn. Vision Rsch. Program Planning Com., Nat. Adv. Eye Coun., Nat. Eye Inst., NIH, 1973-75, 75-77, 85-89; mem. med. adv. bd. Internat. Eye Found., 1970-79; mem. adv. com. on basic clin. rsch. Nat. Soc. to Prevent Blindness, 1971-87; mem. med. adv. com. Fight for Sight, 1960-83; bd. dirs. So. Calif. Soc. to Prevent Blindness, 1967-77, Ophthalmic Pub. Co., 1975-93, v.p. 1990-93, Pan-Am. Ophthalmol. Found., 1985-95; chmn. sci. adv. bd. Ctr. for Partially Sighted, 1984-87; mem. nat. adv. panel Found. for Eye Rsch., Inc., 1984-94; mem. cons. com. Palestra Oftalmologica Panamericana, 1976-81; coord. com. Nat. Eye Health Edn. Program, 1989; mem. sci. adv. bd. Rsch. to Prevent Blindness, Inc., 1993—2003. Editor-in-chief Am. Jour. Ophthalmology, 1993-2002; mem. editorial bd. UCLA Forum in Med. Scis., 1974-82, Am. Jour. Ophthalmology, 1974-91, Am. Intra-Ocular Implant Soc. Jour., 1978-79, EYE-SAT Satellite-Relayed Profl. Edn. in Ophthalmology, 1982-86; mng. editor von Graefe's Archive for Clin. and Exptl. Ophthalmology, 1976-88; contbr. over 500 articles to med. jours. Trustee John Thomas Dye Sch., LA, 1967-72. Lt. USNR, 1952-54. Recipient William Warren Hoppin award NY Acad. Medicine, 1956, Univ. Service award UCLA Alumni Assn., 1982, Miguel Aleman Found. medal, 1992, Benjamin Boyd Humanitarian award Pan Am. Assn. Ophthalmology, 1991, Lucian Howe medal, Am. Ophthalmological Soc., 1992, Internat. Gold Medal award 3rd Singapore Nat. Eye Ctr. Internat. Meeting and 11th Internat. Meeting on Cataract, Implant, Microsurgery and Refractive Keratoplasty, 1998, award of merit in retinal rsch. Retina Rsch. Found., 2002, Jose Rizal gold medal Asia-Pacific Acad. Ophthalmology, 2003, Gold medal Barraquer Inst., 2005, Fellow Royal Australian and New Zealand Coll. Ophthalmologists (hon.); mem. Academia Ophthalmologica Internationales (pres. 1998-2002), Am. Acad. Ophthalmology (bd. councillors 1981, Life Achievement award 1999), Found. of Am. Acad. Ophthalmology (trustee 1989, chmn. bd. trustees 1989-92), Am. Acad. Ophthalmology and Otolaryngology (pres. 1977), Am. Soc. Cataract and Refractive Surgery, AMA (asst. sec. ophthalmology sect. 1962-63, sec. 1963-66, chmn. 1966-67, coun. 1970-74), Am. Ophthalmol. Soc. (coun. 1985-90, v.p. 1992, pres. 1993), Assn. Rsch. in Vision and Ophthalmology (Mildred Weisenfeld award 1991), Assn. U. Profs. of Ophthalmology (trustee 1969-75, pres.-elect 1973-74, pres. 1974-75), Assn. VA Ophthalmologists, Calif. Med. Assn. (mem. ophthalmology adv. panel 1972-94, chmn. 1974-79, sci. bd. 1973-79, ho. of dels. 1974, 77, 79), Chilean Soc. Ophthalmology (hon.), Columbian Soc. Ophthalmology (hon.), Glaucoma Soc. Internat. Congress of Ophthalmology (hon.), Heed Ophthalmic Found. (chmn., bd. dirs. 1990-98), Hellenic Ophthalmol. Soc. (hon.), Internat. Coun. Ophthalmology (bd. dirs. 1993-, Internat. Duke-Elder medal 2006), LA County Med. Assn., LA Soc. Ophthalmology, Pan-Am. Assn. Ophthalmology (coun. 1972—, pres. elect 1985-87, pres. 1987-89, Harry S. Gradle Tchg. award 2007), Peruvian Soc. Ophthalmology (hon.), Retina Soc., Barraquer Inst. Ophthalmology (pres. 1996-05), Academia Ophthalmol. Internat. (pres. 1998-02), Internat. Coun. Ophthalmology (pres. found. 2002-, Jules Francois medal 2002, Philip M. Corboy award 2005, Internat. Duke-Elder medal 2006, Prince Abdul Aziz Ahmed Al-Saud Prevention of Blindness award, 2007), The Jules Gonin Club. Republican. Presbyterian. Avocations: music, scuba diving. Home: 3031 Elvido Dr Los Angeles CA 90049-1107 Office: UCLA 100 Stein Plz Los Angeles CA 90095-7065 Business E-Mail: straatsma@jsei.ucla.edu.

STRACHER, DOROTHY ALTMAN, education educator, consultant; b. NYC, May 11, 1934; d. Joseph and Gussie (Newman) Altman; m. Alfred Stracher, July 4, 1954; children: Cameron Altman, Adam Reed, Erica Terri. BA, Bklyn. Coll., 1955; MA, Columbia U., NYC, 1957; postgrad., U. Copenhagen, 1958-59; acad. vis., Oxford U., Eng., 1973-74; PhD, Hofstra U., Hempstead, NY, 1979. Cert. English and social sci. tchr. NY. Coord. secondary reading Ctrl. Moriches Sch. Dist., NY, 1974-78; coord. reading East Williston Sch. Dist., NY, 1978-79; specialist reading and writing SUNY, Old Westbury, 1979-81; adj. prof. dept. reading Hofstra U., Hempstead, NY, 1979-82; asst. prof. edn. LI U., Bklyn., 1982-83, Coll. New Rochelle, 1983-85; sr. learning diagnostic specialist child devel. div. LI Jewish Hosp., Bklyn., 1985-86; prof. Dowling Coll., Oakdale, NY, 1986—, acad. chair Sch. Edn., 1991-93, coord. elem. edn. dept., 2000-01, acad. chair Sch. Edn., 2001—05. Cons. Johnson & Johnson, Inc., Princeton, NJ, 1982—, Sanford Sch. Dist., Fla., 1983, Lawrence Sch. Dist., NY, 1984, Sch. Dist. 7, NYC, 1984—; vis. prof. U. East London, 1994. Author (with others): First the Fundamentals, 1980, What Do You Call a Well-Behaved Martian?, A Manual for Thinkers' Parents, 1981, Integrating Assessment, 1982; editor: Differentiated Curricula, 1986, A Literature Based Integrated Curriculum: Grades Pre-K, 1989, Successful Strategies for Learning Disabled College Students: Reading, Writing and Reasoning, 1991, 3d edit., 2005; co-author: Commitment to Excellence, 2002; contbr. articles to profl. jours. Bd. dirs. Roslyn (N.Y.) Sch. Dist., 1975—84, v.p., 1980—82, pres., 1982—84; mem. adv. bd. Children's Sch. Sci., Wood Hole, Mass., 1976—82. Recipient Academic Excellence award, Dowling Coll., 2005, 2006. Mem.: NOW, LWV (bd. dirs. 1961—70), Nat. Assn. Gifted Edn., Internat. Reading Assn., Orton Soc., Coun. Exceptional Children, Kappa Delta Pi. Avocations: reading, writing, travel. Home: 47 The Oaks Roslyn NY 11576-1704 Office Phone: 631-244-3306. Business E-Mail: strached@dowling.edu.

STRACK, HAROLD ARTHUR, retired electronics executive, military officer, financial consultant, musician, writer; b. San Francisco, Mar. 29, 1923; s. Harold Arthur and Catheryn Jenny (Johnsen) S.; m. Margaret Madeline Decker, July 31, 1945; children: Carolyn, Curtis, Tamara (dec.). Student, San Francisco Coll., 1941, Sacramento Coll., 1947, Sacramento State Coll., 1948, U. Md., 1962, Indsl. Coll. Armed Forces, 1963. Commd. 2d lt. USAAF, 1943; advanced through grades to brig. gen. USAF, 1970; comdr. 1st Radar Bomb Scoring Group Carswell AFB, Ft. Worth, 1956-59; vice comdr. 90th Strategic Missile Wing SAC Warren AFB, Cheyenne, Wyo., 1964; chief, strategic nuclear br., spl. studies group Joint Chiefs of Staff, 1965-67, dep. asst. to chmn. JCS for strategic arms negotiations, 1968; comdr. 90th Strategic Missile Wing SAC Warren AFB, Cheyenne, 1969-71; chief Studies, Analysis and Gaming Agy. Joint Chiefs Staff, Washington, 1972-74, ret., 1974; v.p., mgr. MX Peacekeeper Program v.p. strategic planning Northrop Electronics Divsn., Hawthorne, Calif., 1974-88; ret., 1988. 1st clarinetist, Cheyenne Symphony Orch., 1969-71. Mem. Cheyenne Frontier Days Com., 1970-71. Decorated D.S.M., Legion of Merit, D.F.C., Air medal, Purple Heart, Presdl. citation, Army, Air Force and Joint Svc. Commendation medals. Mem. Inst. Nav., Am. Def. Preparedness Assn., Air Force Assn., Aerospace Edn. Found., Am. Fedn. Musicians, Orde Pour le Merite, Cheyenne Frontier Days "Heels". Home: 707 James Ln Incline Village NV 89451-9612 *The precepts which have guided me recognize the dignity of the individual and human rights. I believe that living by the Golden Rule contributes to the quality of life by making us better and more useful citizens while favorably influencing others. Integrity, ideals, and high standards reinforce one's own character. While taking pride in accomplishment, show gratitude for opportunity and humility for success. Lead by example and always do your best. Service to humanity and country is the highest calling, and the satisfaction of a job well done, approbation, respect and true friendship are one's greatest rewards.*

STRACK, STEPHEN NAYLOR, psychologist; b. Rome, NY, Nov. 13, 1955; s. Ralph and Grace (Naylor) S.; m. Leni Ferrero. BA, U. Calif., Berkeley, 1978; PhD, U. Miami, Fla., 1983. Psychologist L.A. County Dept. Mental Health, 1984-85; staff psychologist VA Outpatient Clinic, LA, 1985—, dir. tng., 1992-97. Clin. assoc. U. So. Calif., L.A., 1986-95; adj. prof. Calif. Sch. Profl. Psychology, L.A., 1989—; clin. prof. Fuller Grad. Sch. Psychology, Pasadena, Calif., 1986—. Author (test): Personality Adjective Check List, 1987; co-author: Differentiating Normal and Abnormal Personality, 1994, 2d edit., 2006, Death and the Quest for Meaning, 1997, Essentials of Million Inventories Assessment, 1999, 2d edit., 2002, Handbook of Personology and Psychopathology, Pioneers of Personality Science, 2005, Millon Coll. Counseling Inventory, 2006; cons. editor Jour. Personality Disorders, 1992—, Omega, 1997—, Jour. Personality Assessment, 1999—, Assessment, 2007. U.S. Dept. VA grantee, 1986-93, 96-2000. Fellow APA, Soc. for Personality Assessment; mem. Internat. Soc. for the Study of Personality Disorders, Calif. Psychol. Assn., Soc. for Interpersonal Theory and Rsch., Soc. for Rsch. in Psychopathology, Western Psychol. Assn. Office: VA Outpatient Clinic 351 E Temple St Los Angeles CA 90012-3328 Home Phone: 626-799-1481. Personal E-mail: snstrack@aol.com.

STRADER, JAMES DAVID, lawyer; b. Pitts., June 30, 1940; s. James Lowell and Tyra Fredrika (Bjorn) S.; m. Ann Wallace, Feb. 8, 1964; children: James Jacob, Robert Benjamin. BA, Mich. State U., 1962; JD, U. Pitts., 1965. Bar: Pa. 1966, US Dist. Ct. (we. dist.) Pa. 1966, US Dist. Ct. (ea. dist.) Pa. 1973, US Dist. Ct. (mid. dist.) Pa. 1985, US Ct. Appeals (4th and 5th cirs.) 1977, US Ct. Appeals (3d and 11th cirs.) 1981, US Supreme Ct. 1982, W.Va. 1996. Assoc. Peacock, Keller & Yohe, Washington, 1967-68; atty. US Steel Corp., Pitts., 1968-77, gen. atty. worker's compensation, 1977-84; assoc. Caroselli, Spagnolli & Beachler, Pitts., 1984-87; ptnr. Dickie, McCamey & Chilcote, Pitts., 1987—. Bd. trustees Mt. Lebanon Pub. Libr., 2002—, pres., 2004—05; del. Dem. Mid-Yr. Conv., 1974; mem. Dem. Nat. Platform Com., 1976; commr. Mt. Lebanon, Pa., 1974—78. Capt. US Army, 1965—67. Mem. ABA (sr. vice-chmn. worker's compensation com. 1978-94), Pa. Bar Assn. (chmn. worker's compensation law sect. 1994-95), Pa. Bar Inst. (bd. dirs. 2001-),State Bar W.Va., Allegheny County Bar Assn., Valley Brook Country Club. Democrat. Presbyterian. Office: Dickie McCamey & Chilcote 2 PPG Pl Ste 400 Pittsburgh PA 15222-5491 Home Phone: 412-343-2368; Office Phone: 412-392-5419. Business E-Mail: jstrader@dmclaw.com.

STRADER, TIMOTHY RICHARDS, lawyer; b. Portland, Oreg., Jan. 17, 1956; s. Charles J. and Carol Jane (Dwyer) S.; m. Lisa M.K. Bartholomew, May 21, 1988; children: Kelly Meehan, Erin Dwyer. BBA in Mgmt., U. Notre Dame, 1978; JD, Willamette U., Salem, Oreg., 1981; LLM in Taxation, U. Fla., Gainesville, 1982. Bar: Oreg. 1981, Wash. 2004. Assoc. McEwen, Hanna, Gisvold & Rankin, Portland, 1982-85, Bullivant, Houser, Bailey, Hanna, Portland, 1985-87, Hanna, Urbigkeit, Jensen, et al., Portland, 1987-88, Hanna, Murphy, Jensen, Holloway, Portland, 1988-89; mem. Hanna Strader, P.C., Portland, 1989—. Mem. editorial bd. State Bar Estate Planning Newsletter, 1987—. Mem. alumni bd. Jesuit H.S., Portland, 1982-94, trustee, 1993-99; bd. dirs. Valley Cath. Sch., Beaverton, 1989-95; mem. Estate Planning Coun., Portland, 1990—, bd. dirs., 2000—, v.p., 2005, pres., 2006. Mem. ABA, Multnomah Bar Assn., Multnomah Athletic Club, Waverley Country Club. Office: Hanna Strader PC 1300 SW 6th Ave Ste 300 Portland OR 97201-3461 Office Phone: 503-273-2700. E-mail: tstrader@hannastrader.com.

STRADLEY, WILLIAM JACKSON, lawyer; b. Houston, Oct. 27, 1939; s. Samuel and Mary Stradley; m. Emmalee H. Stradley, Apr. 16, 1960; children: Lisa D., William M. BS, U. Houston, 1964, JD, 1967. Bar: Tex. 1967, U.S. Dist. Ct. (so. dist.) Tex. 1967, U.S. Ct. Appeals (5th cir.) 1967, U.S. Supreme Ct. 1970, cert.: (civil trial law), Tex. Bd. Legal Specialization (personal injury trial law). Of counsel Mithoff Law Firm; mem. faculty trial advocacy course Law Sch. U. Houston, 1982. Pres. Police Adv. Com., 1981—84, sec., 1980—81; bd. dirs. Houston Coun. Human Rels., 1982—84; mem. adminstrv. bd. St. Luke's United Meth. Ch.; co-chair fed. judiciary appts. com. State Bar Tex., 1991, mem. cont. legal edn. com., 1991, adminstrn. justice com., spl. com. professionalism. Named Texas Super Lawyers, 2005; named one of, 2003, 2004; recipient Pub. Svc. award, Houston Police Dept., 1984, Texas Super Lawyers, 2006. Mem.: Assn. Trial Lawyers Am., Tex. Trial Lawyers Assn. (dir. emeritus, chmn. ethics com., by-laws com.), Houston Bar Assn. (chmn. tort and compensation sect. 1980—81, chmn. cont. legal edn. com., com. on professionalism), Houston Trial Lawyers Assn. (bd. dirs. 1980—82, v.p. 1983—84, pres. 1985—86), Am. Bd. Trial Advocates (pres., treas. 1980—82, v.p. Houston 1983—84), Houston Bar Found. (charter), The Houstonians Club, Houston Club. Home: 64 E Broad Oaks Dr Houston TX 77056-1226 Office: 3450 One Allen Ctr Houston TX 77002 Office Phone: 713-654-1122.

STRAFER, G. RICHARD, lawyer; b. Evanston, Ill., Jan. 19, 1951; BA, U. Wis.-Madison, 1976; JD, Northeastern U., 1980; LLM, Georgetown U., 1983. Bar: DC, U.S. Dist. Ct., DC, U.S. Ct. Appeals, DC Cir. 1980, Fla. 1984. Appellate law fellow Appellate Litig. Clin. Prog. Georgetown U. Law Ctr., 1981—83; pvt. practice G. Richard Strafer, PA. Contbr. articles to law jours. Mem.: ABA, Fla. Assn. Criminal Defense Lawyers, Nat. Assn. Criminal Defense Lawyers. Office: 2400 S Dixie Highway Ste 200 Miami FL 33133 Office Phone: 305-857-9090. Office Fax: 305-854-2103.

STRAHAN, MICHAEL ANTHONY, professional football player; b. Houston, Nov. 21, 1971; s. Gene and Louise Strahan; m. Wanda Hutchins, 1992 (div. 1996); children: Tanita, Michael Jr.; m. Jean Strahan, July 18, 1999 (div. July 20, 2006); children: Isabella, Sophia. Grad, Tex. State U., 1992. Defensive end N.Y. Giants, 1993—. Co-author (with Jay Glazer): Inside the Helmet: Life as a Sunday Afternoon Warrior, 2007. Co-chair Meet the Giants Fundraisers. Named First Team All-American, 1992, NFL Defensive Player of the Yr., 2001, NFL All-Pro, AP, 2003; named to NFL Pro-Bowl, 1997—99, 2001—03, 2005. Achievements include set NFL single season sack record (22.5), 2001. Office: Giants Stadium East Rutherford NJ 07073

STRAHILEVITZ, MEIR, inventor, researcher, psychiatry educator; b. Beirut, July 13, 1935; s. Jacob and Chana Strahilevitz; m. Aharona Nattiv, 1958; children: Michal, Lior. MD, Hadassah Hebrew U. Med. Sch., Jerusalem, Israel, 1963. Diplomate Am. Bd. Psychiatry and Neurology, Royal Coll. Physicians and Surgeons Can. Asst. prof. Washington U. Med. Sch., St. Louis, 1971-74; assoc. prof. So. Ill. U., Springfield, 1974-77, U. Chgo., 1977, U. Tex. Med. Br., Galveston, 1978-81; chmn. dept. psychiatry Kaplan Hosp., Rehovot, Israel, 1987-88; clin. assoc. prof. U. Wash., Seattle, 1981-88; prof. U. Tex. Med. Sch., Houston, 1988-92. Contbr. articles to profl. jours. Fellow Am. Psychiat. Assn., Royal Coll. Physicians and Surgeons Can. Achievements include discovery of protective effects of nitric oxide on psychiatric patients; invention of the use of antibodies to receptors and their fragments as drugs of immunoadsorption treatment of hyperlipidemia, cancer, autoimmune disease, atherosclerosis and coronary artery disease; patents for immunological and affinity adsorption methods; specific adsorption devices with automatic regeneration of adsorbent utilized in automated fluid purification and analytical and preparatory applications; treatment methods for psychoactive drug dependence; immunological methods for treating psychoactive drug intoxication; methods of improved targeting of drugs and visualization ligands, particularly in the treatment and diagnosis of cancer; immunoassay methods for psychoactive drugs; devices for removing species from the blood circulatory system. Office: PO Box 25008 Seattle WA 98165-1908 Personal E-mail: mstrahilevitz@pol.net.

STRAHLE, RON E., elementary school educator, social studies educator; b. Vincennes, Ind., Jan. 22, 1957; m. Gail F. Gervais, Aug. 5, 1964; children: Nicholas J., Alexander M. AS in Gen. Edn., Vincennes U., Ind., 1977; BS in Elem. Edn., Ind. U., Bloomington, 1980; M in Elem. Edn., Ball State U., Muncie, Ind., 1985, endorsement in Gifted Edn., 1986. Cert. tchr. Ind., 1981, lic. sch. adminstrn. Ind. U., 1995. Gifted/talented tchr. Monroe Ctrl. Sch. Corp., Parker City, Ind., 1983—91; tchr. social studies grade 6 Brownsburg Cmty. Sch. Corp., 1991—. Mem.: KC. Home: 412 Dover Rd Brownsburg IN 46112 Office: Brownsburg Cmty Sch Corp 1250 E Airport Rd Brownsburg IN 46112 Home Phone: 317-858-1036; Office Phone: 317-858-1036. Personal E-mail: rang412@aol.com. Business E-Mail: rstrahle@brownsburg.k12.in.us.

STRAHLER, ALAN H., geography educator, researcher, writer; b. NYC, Apr. 27, 1943; s. Arthur Newell and Margaret Elizabeth S.; m. Kristi Margaret Schrader, Feb. 4, 1967; 1 child, Amy Leona. BA, Johns Hopkins U., 1964, PhD, 1969; Doctorat scientarum (hon.), Cath. U. Louvain, 2000. Asst. prof. U. Va., Charlottesville, 1969—74; asst. prof., assoc. prof. U. Calif., Santa Barbara, 1974—82; prof. Hunter Coll., NYC, 1982—88, Boston U., 1988—. Mem. Moderate-Resolution Imaging Spectometer Sci. Team, NASA, 1989, NASA Deep Space Climate Obs. Sci. Team, 2000. Author, co-author phys. geography textbooks including 9 major titles in 17 edits.; contbr. numerous articles to profl. publ. Recipient numerous grants NSF and NASA, 1978—, Outstanding Contbr. to Remote Sensing medal Assn. Am. Geographers, 1993. Fellow: AAAS. Achievements include development of body of rsch. on remote sensing of forests and vegetation emphasizing math. models of forest structure and viewing of forests by imaging instruments on space-borne platforms; prodn. of global maps of land cover and surface reflectance using satellite data. Office: Boston U Dept of Geography 675 Commonwealth Ave Boston MA 02215-1406

STRAHLMAN, RICHARD SCOTT, pediatrician; s. Richard and Carol Ann Strahlman; m. Teresa Flores, May 11, 1996; children: John Wesley, Stephanie Leigh, Matthew Scott, Michael Allen. MD, Johns Hopkins U., Balt., 1978. Diplomate Am. Bd. Pediats. Instr. in pediats. Johns Hopkins U. Sch. of Medicine, Balt., 1985—; chief of pediats. Patuxent Med. Group, Columbia, Md., 1997—2004; pediatrician Columbia Med. Practice, Md., 2004—. Cons. in field, Columbia, 1995—. Author: (chpts. in med. textbooks) Primary Pediatric Care. Named Top Doc, Balt. Mag., 2002. Fellow: Am. Acad. Pediats. Office: Columbia Med Practice 5500 Knoll N Dr Columbia MD 21045 Home Phone: 301-865-5161; Office Phone: 410-964-6300. Office Fax: 410-964-6227.

STRAHM, MARY ELLEN, music educator; d. Edward Carey and Mary Margaret McBride; m. Shaun Robert Strahm, Feb. 16, 1976. MusB in Pipe Organ, Ohio U., Athens, 1971; MA in Music Edn., Ohio State U., Columbus, 1978. Elem. vocal music specialist Licking Valley Sch. Dist., Newark, Ohio, 1972—2003, St. Nicholas Sch., Zanesville, Ohio, 2003—06, Bishop Fenwick Sch., Zanesville, 2006—. Dir. of music St. John's Luth. Ch., Evang. Luth. Ch. Am., Zanesville, 2000—. Vol. Eastside Food Pantry, Newark, 1988—98; bd. dirs. Friends and Alumni of Sch. of Music, Ohio U., Athens, 1990—99. Mem.: Friends and Alumni of Sch. of Music of Ohio U. (v.p. 1995—97, bd. dirs. 1990—99), Am. Guild Organists, Ohio Music Edn. Assn. (25-Yr. award 1998), Music Educators Nat. Conf. (assoc.). Democrat. Lutheran. Avocations: walking, reading, photography. Home: 5512 Licking Valley Rd NE Nashport OH 43830 Office: Bishop Fenwick Sch 1030 E Main St Zanesville OH 43701 Home Phone: 740-763-2794; Office Phone: 740-453-2637.

STRAHM, SAMUEL EDWARD, retired veterinarian; b. Fairview, Kans., Feb. 9, 1936; s. Silas Tobias and Martha Mary (Beyer) S.; m. Barbara Jean Wenger, June 1; children: Gregory Lee, Bryan Scott, Andrea Marie Enloe. BS, DVM, Kansas State U., 1959. Owner Osage Animal Clinic Inc., Pawhuska, Okla., 1959—2007, pres., 1985—2007; ret., 2007. Bd. dirs. 1st Nat. Bank, Pawhuska, Okla.; bd. cons. Profl. Exam Svc., 1990-2000; adv. bd. USDA Users, 1991-95; adv. com. Pew Nat. Health Profession Vet. Medicine, 1991; state adv. coun. Okla. Coop. Extension Svcs., 2000—, chmn.-elect, 2000-01, chmn., 2001-07. Bd. dirs. Okla. Sch. Bd. Assn., 1977-98, 2d v.p., 1993, 1st v.p., 1994, pres., 1996; active Okla. All-State Sch. Bd., 1993, Pawhuska Sch. Bd., 1974-98, 2001-06, pres., 2003-06; active Pawhuska Planning Commn., 1965-70, Okla. State U. Centennial Commn., Stillwater, 1986-91; bd. dirs. Nat. Sch. Bd. Assn., 1996-99, exec. com., 1997-99, western reg. chmn., 1996. Recipient Disting. Alumni award Coll. Vet. Medicine Kans. State U., 1994, Fairview HS, 2004, Outstanding Svc. award Nat. Sch. Bds. Assn., 1997, Disting. Svc. award Nat. Bd. Exam. Com., 2000, Friend of Yr. award Okla. Coop. Extension, 2002. Mem.: Acad. Vet. Consultants, AVMA (pres. 1989—90, coun. govt. affair 1992—98, coun. edn. 2003—06, AVMA award 1986), Am. Vet. Med. Found. (chmn. 1995—98, treas. 2004—), Am. Assn. Theriogenealogy, Am. Assn. Bovine Practitioners (Practitioner of Yr. award 2002), Am. Assn. Vet. State Bds., Am. Assn. Vet. Specialty Bd. (rep. coun. on edn.), Am. Assn. Food Hygiene Vets. (bd. dirs. 2000—06), Nat. Bd. Vet. Med. Examiners (Disting. Svc. award 2000), Okla. Vet. Med. Assn. (all offices 1959—, Veterinarian of Yr. 1990, Disting. Svc. award 1998), Kans. Vet. Med. Assn., Okla. Bd. Vet. Med. Examiners (pres.), Pawhuska C. of C. (pres. 1968), Toastmasters Club, Pawhuska Jaycees (all offices 1959—69). Republican. Baptist. Avocations: gardening, fishing, flying. Home: PO Box 1256 Pawhuska OK 74056-1256 Office: Osage Animal Clinic Inc PO Box 1209 Pawhuska OK 74056-1209

STRAIGHT, ELSIE HOSKING, retired librarian, sculptor; b. Moresby, Cumberland, Eng., 1914; arrived in U.S., 1923, naturalized, 1926; d. Thomas E. and Anne (Molyneaux) Hosking; 1 child, Elaine W. Sanders. AA, Art Inst. Pitts., 1940, NY Sch. Applied Design, 1941; BA, Roger Williams Coll., 1969; MLS, U. RI, 1974. Libr. St. Raphael Acad., Pawtucket, RI, 1960—68, Elmhurst Acad., Portsmouth, RI, 1968—74; libr. dir. Ringling Sch. Art and Design, Sarasota, Fla., 1974—81; ret.; cons. U. South Fla., Sarasota, 1981—. Manatee Art League, Bradenton, Fla., 1980—82, 1983, 1984, Plaza Art Show, Sarasota, 1983, Longboat Key Art Ctr., 1984, Represented in permanent collections Mus. of the Circus, Ringling Mus. Art; author: (novels) Between the Dark and the Daylight, 2001, Land of the Dead, 2002; contbr. articles to publs. Mem.: Manatee Writers Guild, Fla. West Coast Writers, Ringling Sch. Art Libr. Assn., Artcenter Manatee, Art Librarian's Soc. (dir. 1980). Avocation: writing. Home: 435 Edwards Dr Sarasota FL 34243-2038

STRAIGHT, RICHARD COLEMAN, photobiologist, natural philosopher; b. Rivesville, W.Va., Sept. 8, 1937; BA, U. Utah, 1961, PhD in Molecular Biology, 1967. Asst. dir. radiation biology summer inst. U. Utah, 1961-63; supervisory chemist med. svc. VA Hosp., 1965—; dir. VA Venom Rsch. Lab., 1975—; adminstrv. officer rsch. svc. VA Ctr., 1980—; dir. Dixon laser inst. U. Utah, Salt Lake City, 1985-90; pres. Western Inst. for Biomed. Rsch., Salt Lake City, 1990—2003. Dir. Utah Ctr. for Photo Medicine, Salt Lake City, 1993-; assoc. chief of staff for rsch. VA Salt Lake City Health Care Sys., 1997-2003; chmn. bd. dirs. VAMCU FEd. Credit Union, 1980-; cons. to NIH, NSF, Dept. Def., 1985-. Assoc. editor Lasers in Surgery and Medicine, 1990-95, Jour. Biomed. Optics, 1998—. Mem. AAAS, Am. Chem. Soc., Am. Soc. Photobiology, Biophysics Soc., Am. Soc. for Laser Medicine and Surgery, Utah Life Sci. Industries Assn. (charter). Achievements include research in photodynamic action on biomonomers and biopolymers, tumor immunology, effect of antigens on mammary adenocarcinoma of C3H mice, biochemical changes in aging, venom toxicology, mechanism of action of photoactive drugs, optical imaging and spectroscopy. Office: Protherics-Utah Univ Utah PO Box 58603 Salt Lake City UT 84158 Office Phone: 801-913-4799. E-mail: rcsrcsrcs3@aol.com.

STRAIN, EDWARD RICHARD, psychologist; b. Indpls., Apr. 12, 1925; s. Edward Richard and Ernestine (Kidd) S.; children: Chadwick Edward, Sarah Abigail, Zachary Richard. AB, Butler U., 1948; PhD, Duke U., 1952. Clin. psychologist Ohio State Med. Ctr., Columbus, 1952-53, Ind. U. Med. Ctr., Indpls., 1953-56; pvt. practice cons. psychology, Indpls., 1956—. Lectr. dept. psychology Butler U., Indpls., 1958-68; pres. Marion County (Ind.) Mental Health Assn., 1967-69. Mem. 500 Festival Assocs., Indpls., 1961—; pres. Perry Twp. (Ind.) Rep. Club, 1968-69; founder Downtown Sr. Citizens Ctr., 1961; vestryman Episcopal Ch., 1975-77, 86-88, sr. warden, 1976-77. Recipient Disting. Tech. Alumni award Arsenal Tech. H.S., 1993, Hansen H. Anderson Cmty. Svc. Merit medal Arsenal Tech. H.S., 1994. Mem. Masons, Rotary, Indpls. Club, Skyline Club. Office Phone: 317-372-2062. Personal E-mail: erstrain@comcast.net.

STRAIN, JAMES ARTHUR, lawyer; b. Alexandria, La., Oct. 11, 1944; s. William Joseph and Louise (Moore) S.; m. Cheryl Sue Williamson, Aug. 19, 1967; children: William Joseph, Gordon Richard, Elizabeth Parks. BS in Econs., Ind. U., 1966, JD, 1969. Bar: Ind. 1969, U.S. Dist. Ct. (so. dist.) Ind. 1969, U.S. Ct. Appeals (7th cir.) 1972, U.S. Supreme Ct. 1975, U.S. Ct. Appeals (5th cir.) 1978. Instr. Law Sch. Ind. U., Indpls., 1969-70; law clk. to Hon. John S. Hastings 7th Cir. Ct. Appeals, Chgo., 1970-71; assoc. Cahill, Gordon & Reindel, NYC, 1971-72; law clk. to Hon. William H. Rehnquist U.S. Supreme Ct., Washington, 1972-73; assoc. Barnes, Hickam, Pantzer & Boyd, Indpls., 1973-75; ptnr. Barnes, Hickam, Pantzer & Boyd (name changed to Barnes & Thornburg), 1976-96, Sommer Barnard, PC, Indpls., 1996—. Adj. asst. prof. law Ind. U. Sch. Law, 1986-92. Mem., bd. dirs. The Penrod Soc., Indpls., 1976—, Indpls. Symphonic Choir, 1988-91, Festival Music Soc., Indpls., 1990-96. Mem. 7th Cir. Bar Assn. (meetings chmn. Ind. chpt. 1979-88, portraits 1988-89, bd. govs. 1989—, 1st v.p. 1995, pres. 1996). Avocations: photography, music. Office: Sommer Barnard PC Ste 3500 One Indiana Sq Indianapolis IN 46204 Home Phone: 317-686-1928; Office Phone: 317-713-3500. Business E-Mail: strain@sommerbarnard.com.

STRAIN, JAMES ELLSWORTH, pediatrician, educator, retired medical association administrator; b. Lincoln, Nebr., Apr. 23, 1923; s. Elmer Ellsworth and Tessa Elizabeth (Stevens) Strain; m. Ruby Lee Shepard; children: James A., John D., Janet M. Strain McKinney, Jeffrey Lee Phillips-Strain. AB, Phillips U., Enid, Okla., 1945; MD, U. Colo., Denver, 1947. Diplomate Am. Bd. Pediat. (examiner 1984-89, mem. 1989-93, emeritus mem. 1993—). Intern Mpls. Gen. Hosp., 1947—48; resident in pediat. Denver Children's Hosp., 1948—50, pres. med. staff, 1964, dir. genetic unit, 1982—86; pvt. practice specializing in pediat. Denver, 1950—86; exec. dir. Am. Acad. Pediat., Elk Grove Village, Ill., 1986—93, ret., 1993. Pres. med. bd. Colo. Gen. Hosp., 1969—70; clin. prof. pediat. U. Colo. Med. Ctr., 1969—86, 1993—, U. Chgo., 1987—93; mem. Colo. Med. Adv. Coun. for Title 19, 1968—75, chmn., 1968—71; mem. Task Force on Iowa Health Care Sds. Project, 1984—85; presenter numerous profl. confs. Editl. bd. Pediat. in Rev., reviewer Jour. Pediat.; contbr. articles to profl. publs. Mem. Colo. Commn. on Children and Youth, 1971—75; trustee Phillips U., 1974—. Capt. US Army, 1953—55. Recipient Disting. Alumnus award, Phillips U., 1974, Florence Sabin award, U. Colo., 1984, Excellence in Pub. Svc. award, U.S. Surgeon Gen., 1988, Abraham Jacobi award, AMA and Am. Acad. Pediat., 1994, James E. Strain Child Advocacy award established in his name, Denver Children's Hosp., 1983. Fellow: Am. Acad. Pediat. (Clifford Grulee award 1985); mem.: AMA, APHA, Inst. Medicine NAS, Ambulatory Pediatric Assn., Can. Pediatric Soc., Denver Med. Soc., Colo. Med. Soc., Alpha Omega Alpha. Republican. Mem. Christian Ch. (Disciples Of Christ). Avocations: fishing, sports, reading. Personal E-mail: jstrain121@aol.com.

STRAIT, GEORGE, musician; b. Poteet, Tex., May 18, 1952; m. Norma Strait; 1 child, George Bubba Jr. Degree in Agr., S.W. Tex. State U. Singer Care Err Cooolsey, Tenn., 1983—. Albums include Blue Clear Sky (Country Music Assn. Album of Yr. 1996), Strait Out of the Box (boxed set), Easy Come, Easy Go, Right or Wrong, Strait from the Heart, Strait Country, Does Ft. Worth Ever Cross Your Mind, 1985 (Country Music Assn. Album of Yr. 1985), Pure Country, 1986, No. 7, Something Special, 1986, Ocean Front Property, 1987, If You Aint Lovin' (You Aint Livin'), 1988, Beyond the Blue Neon, 1989, Livin' It Up, 1990, Ten Strait Hits, 1991, Chill of An Early Fall, 1991, Greatest Hits Volume I, II, Lead On, 1994, Strait Out of the Box, 1995, Blue Clear Sky, 1996 (Country Music Assn. Album of Yr. 1996), Carrying Your Love With Me, 1997 (Country Music Assn. Album of Yr. 1997), One Step at a Time, 1998 (Country Music assn. Album of Yr. 1998), Always Never the Same, 1999, Merry Christmas Wherever You Are, 1999, Latest Greatest Straitest Hits, 2000, George Strait, 2000, The Road Less Traveled, 2001, 20th Century Masters, 2002, Honkytonkville, 2003, 50 Number Ones, 2004, Somewhere Down in Texas, 2005, It Just Comes Natural, 2006, (Single Record of Yr. & Song of Yr. awards for Give It Away, Acad. Country Music, 2007), Live at Texas Stadium, 2007, other platinum albums; #1 country hits include Fool Hearted Memory, 1982, Amarillo By Morning, 1983, You Look So Good in Love, 1984, The Chair, 1986, Baby Blue, 1989, Beyond the Blue Moon, 1989, Baby's Gotten Good At Goodbye, 1989, Love Without End, Amen, 1990, I've Come to Expect It From You, 1990, Chill of An Early Fall, 1991, If I Know Me, 1991, The Big One, 1995, Good News Bad News (Due with Lee Ann Womack), 2005 (Country Music Assn. Musical Event of Yr. 2005); (movie) Pure Country, 1992. Served with U.S. Army, until 1975. Recipient Entertainer of Yr. award Country Music Assn., 1989, 90, Entertainer of Yr. award Acad. Country Music, 1990; named Male Vocalist of Yr. Country Music Assn., 1985, 86, 96, Male Vocalist of Yr. Acad. Country Music, 1984, 85, 89, SRO Touring Artist of Yr., 1990, Top Country Vocalist Am. Music Awards, 1991, Entertainer of Yr. 1990, Country Music Assn., Tex Ritter Award for Pure Country, 1993, Voice of the Yr. ASCAP, 1995, Male Vocalist of Yr. 1997, Country Music Assn. Avocations: golf, skiing, fishing, hunting, Steer-roping.

STRAIT, VIOLA EDWINA WASHINGTON, librarian; b. El Paso, Tex., Aug. 29, 1925; d. Leroy Wentworth and Viola Edwina (Wright) Washington; m. Freeman Adams, Mar. 6, 1943; 1 child, Norma Jean (Mrs. Louis Lee James); m. Clifford Moody, Jan. 8, 1950; 1 child, Viola Edwina III (Mrs. Paul M. Cunningham); m. Amos O. Strait, Dec. 9, 1972. Bus. cert., Tillotson Coll., 1946, BA, 1948; MS in Libr. Sci., U. So. Calif., 1954. Substitute tchr. El Paso Pub. Schs., 1948; sec., bookkeeper U.S.O.-YWCA, El Paso, 1948-50; libr. asst. Spl. Svcs. Libr., Ft. Bliss, Tex., 1950-53, libr., 1954-71; equal employment opportunity officer Ft. Bliss, 1971-72; dep. equal employment opportunity officer Long Beach (Calif.) Naval Shipyard, 1972-85; with Temp. Job Mart, Torrance, Calif., 1986-87; substitute tchr. Ysleta Ind. Sch. Dist., 1988-89; profl. libr. Eastwood Hts. Elem. Sch., 1989-90; sec. Shiloh Bapt. Ch., El Paso, 1991-92; br. mgr. El Paso Pub. Libr., 1992-96, retired, 1996. Host, prodr. (gospel music video with Viola Washington Strait), Time Warner TV, Cable Channel 15, 2003—04. Sec. Sunday sch. Bapt. Ch., 1956-66, 92-96, min. music, 1958-72, supr. young adult choir, 1966-72, pres. sr. choir, 1969-71; disc jockey Sta. KELP, El Paso, 1970-72; host radio show Sta. KTEP, U. Tex., El Paso, 1994-2004; hon. chmn. for ann. observance of Nat. Libr. Week, City of El Paso, 1970. Mem. ALA, Border Region Libr. Assn. (chmn. scholarship com. 1970), NAACP (sec. 1996), Alpha Kappa Alpha. Democrat. Baptist. Avocations: piano, reading. Personal E-mail: vstrait@aol.com.

STRAIT, WILLIAM ROBERT, computer technician; b. Troy, NY, July 22, 1943; s. Ralph Ernest Strait and Ruth Edna Copping; m. Sandra Vada Sanborn, Aug. 10, 1994; children: Stefan Michael, Sean Eric. BS, Union Coll., 1965; MS, Northeastern U., Boston, 1967; PhD, Rensselaer Poly. Inst., 1975. Instr. Union Coll., Schenectady, NY, 1967—80; dir. MIS, OMRDD, Albany, NY, 1980—84; asst. dir. MIS, Nathan Kline Rsch. Inst., Orangeburg, NY, 1984—89; pres. Computer Solutions Ctr., Suffern, NY, 1989—90; v.p. Merritech, Tampa, Fla., 1990—91, SOS Techs., Tampa, 1991—92; sr. cons. Automation Rsch. Systems, Tampa, 1992—95; asst. dir. IT, U. South Fla., Tampa, 1995—2001; chief info. officer Ctr. Fla. C.C., Ocala, 2001—. Bd. dirs. Fla. Assn. Ednl. Data Systems, Speede Com. (AACRAO), Washington. Founder, chair bd. Com. for Better Govt., Schenectady, NY, 1976—79; instr. Red Cross, Tampa, Fla., 1990—95. Mem.: Rotary (Tampa chpt. bd. dirs. 1993—97, Paul Harris fellow 1997), Sigma Xi. Avocations: jogging, bicycling, woodworking, stained glass. Home: 9643 SW 74th Ave Ocala FL 34476 Office: Ctrl Fla CC 3001 SW College Rd Ocala FL 34478

STRAJA, SORIN RADU, chemical engineer, mathematician, computer programmer; b. Bucharest, Romania; s. Radu and Sonica Straja; m. Mihaela Cirstea, Mar. 26, 1982. MS, Poly. Inst., Bucharest, 1979, PhD, 1987. Chem. engr. Plastics Processing, Bucharest, 1979—81; rsch. and devel. cons. Chem. and Biochem. Energetics Inst., Bucharest, 1982—89; cons., vol. USDA, Washington, 1991—92; chemist U. Md., Balt., 1992—93; dir. occupl. health and safety dept. Temple U., Phila., 1993—95, asst. prof. stats., 1994—2001; v.p. Inst. Regulatory Sci., Columbia, Md., 1996—. Cons. Montgomery Investment Tech., Radnor, 1995—. *Over twenty-five years experience working with the industry, academia, and government agencies in the United States and Europe. Proven expertise in mathematical modeling and software development applied in chemical and biochemical engineering, risk analysis, financial engineering, environmental and health sciences. Author of three books and over fifty scientific papers published in internationally recognized and refereed journals. Editor of Environment International and contributing editor of Technology (formerly Jour. of the Franklin Institute). Received the "Nicolae Teclu" prize of the Romanian Academy of Sciences, a certificate of appreciation for teaching from Temple University and a certificate of appreciation from the United States Department of Agriculture for significant volunteer contributions* Editor: Environmental International, 1993-99; contbg. editor: Technology, 1996—; contbr. numerous articles to profl. jours. Recipient Nicolae Teclu award Romanian Acad. Scis., 1983, Cert. Appreciation, USDA, 1992, Cert. Appreciation for Tchg., Temple U., 1999. Mem. AIChE, ACS. Avocations: history, geography. Home and Office: Inst Regulatory Sci 5406 Hildebrand ct Columbia MD 21044-1918 Office Phone: 410-997-6396.

STRAKA, ANGELINE C., broadcast executive; BS, MLS, U. Pitts.; JD cum laude, Duquesne U., Pitts. Spl. asst. US atty. US Atty.'s Office; with US Vets. Adminstrn., H.J. Heinz Co., Westinghouse Electric Corp.; v.p., dep. gen. counsel, sec. CBS Corp., 1992—2000, sr. v.p., dep. gen. counsel, sec., 2006—; sr. v.p. gen. counsel, sec. Infinity Broadcasting Corp., 2000—01; with law dept. Viacom, 2001—05, v.p., assoc. gen. counsel, co-head corp. transactions & securities practice group, asst. sec. Mem.: Pa. Bar Assn., NY Bar Assn. Office: CBS Corp 51 W 52nd St New York NY 10019-6188 Office Phone: 212-975-4321. *

STRAKA, LASZLO RICHARD, retired publishing consultant; b. Budapest, Hungary, June 22, 1934; came to U.S., 1950, naturalized, 1956; s. Richard J. and Elisabeth (Roeck) S.; m. Eva K. von Viczian, Jan. 20, 1962 (div. May 1981); children: Eva M., Monika E., Viktoria K. BA cum laude,

NYU, 1959. Acct. Greatrex Ltd., NYC, 1952-53; pres. Maxwell Macmillan Internat. Pub. Group, NYC, 1991-92; with Pergamon Press, Inc., Elmsford, NY, 1954-90, v.p., 1964-68, exec. v.p., treas., 1968-74, pres., 1974-75, 80-88, chmn. bd., 1975-77, 88-90, vice chmn. bd., 1977-80, 88-89, also dir.; vice chmn. bd. Pergamon Books Ltd., Oxford, England, 1986-88; group v.p. Macmillan Inc., NYC, 1989-91; pub. cons. Alta Loma, Calif., 1992—2005; ret., 2005. Treas. Brit. Book Centre, Inc., N.Y.C., 1956-67; pres. Pergamon Holding Corp., 1981-86; chmn. bd. Microforms Internat., Inc., 1971-87. D. dirs., sec. Szechenyi Istvan Soc., N.Y.C., 1967-80, 89-93. Mem. Phi Beta Kappa. Home: 6405 Caledon Pl Alta Loma CA 91737 Home Phone: 909-912-4140. Personal E-mail: nagyapul@yahoo.com.

STRAMPEL, WILLIAM DERKEY, dean, medical educator; b. Saugatuck, Mich., Feb. 8, 1948; married; 3 children. BA, Hope Coll., 1970; DO, Chgo. Coll. Osteopathic Medicine, 1976. Intern Madigan Army Med. Ctr., Fort Lewis, Wash., 1976—77, resident in medicine, 1977—79; fellow in pulmonary disease Fitzsimons Army Med. Ctr., Aurora, 1980—82; staff internal medicine svc. and dir. intensive care 121 Evacuation Hosp., Seoul; pulmonary staff and dir. intensive care Fitzsimons Army Med. Ctr., Aurora, Colo.; divsn. surgeon First Infantry Divsn. Irwin Army Cmty. Hosp., Fort Riley, Kans., dep. comdr., dir. med. edn., Evans Army Cmty. Hosp., Fort Carson, Colo.; chief Quality Assurance Divsn., Dept. of Army, Office Surgeon Gen., 1991—94; dir. med. edn. Brooke Army Med. Ctr., 1994—96; comdr. Brooke Army Med. Ctr. and Great Plains Med. Command, 1996—97; dir. quality mgmt. Office Sec. Def.; chief med. officer Tricare Mgmt. Activity; spl. asst. for ops. and readiness to U.S. surgeon gen.; leader Mich. State U. Health Team; sr. assoc. dean Mich. State U., Coll. Osteo. Medicine, 1999—2002, prof. internal medicine, 2001—, acting dean, 2001—02, dean, 2002—. Served to col. US Army. Office: A314 E Free Hall East Lansing MI 48824-1316

STRANC, CATHLEEN L., music educator; d. George H. and Nancy L. Stranc. MusB in Bus. in Bus., So. Ill. U., 1982, MusB in edn., 1984; MusM in edn., VanderCook Coll. Music, Chgo., 1995. Cert. edn. Ill., 1984. Choral and instrumental music educator Jersey Cmty. Sch. Dist., Jerseyville, Ill., 1985—95; instrumental music educator Edwardsville (Ill.) Sch. Dist., 1995—. Guest condr. Madison County Band Festival, 2006. Named Employee of the Month, Edwardsville Sch. Dist., 1998, 2000, 2004, 2005, 2006, 2007; recipient Outstanding Mid. Sch. Activity Sponsor award, 2005. Mem.: NEA, Madison County Band Dirs. Assn. (sec. 2002—), Ill. Grade Sch. Music Assn. (sec./treas. dist. 5 2005—), Ill. Edn. Assn. (region 45 elections com. chair 2000—), Edwardsville Edn. Assn. (sec. 1998—, Local Leadership award 2005), Ill. Music Educator Assn. (dist. 6 profl. devel. chair 2000—06), Women's Internat. Band Dirs. Assn. (life), Nat. Band Assn. (life), Phi Kappa Phi (life). Office: Edwardsville Community SchoolDistrict #7 #1 District Dr Edwardsville IL 62025 Home: 5 Jennifer Dr Glen Carbon IL 62034 Home Phone: 618-346-6711; Office Phone: 618-655-6800. Personal E-mail: cstranc@sbcglobal.net.

STRAND, CURT ROBERT, hotel executive; b. Vienna, Nov. 13, 1920; naturalized Am. citizen, 1943; m. Fleur Lillian Emanuel, June 14, 1946. BS, Cornell U., 1943. Supt. service Plaza, NYC, 1947-49; asst. to v.p. Hilton Hotels Corp., 1949-53; v.p. Hilton Internat. Co., NYC, 1953-64, exec. v.p., 1964-67, pres., chief exec. officer, 1967-86, chmn., 1986-87. Sr. v.p., dir. Trans World Air Lines, Inc.; lectr. Cornell U. Sch. Hotel Adminstrn., Ecole Superieure de Scis. Econs., Paris, NYU, Houston U.; sr. cons. Am. Express; mem. adv. panel com. Am. Hotel and Motel Assn.; dir. Sherry Netherland Corp.; mem. exec. com. Bd. Exec. Svc. Corps, Aspen. Mem. coun. Cornell U.; adv. bd. Aspen Found.; bd. govs. Snowmass Resort Assn., also pres.; fellow Aspen Inst. With Mil. Intelligence US Army, 1943—46. Mem. Cornell Soc. Hotelmen (Hotelier of Yr. 1986), Aspen Exec. Svc. Corps (mem. bd., v.p.), Snowmass Club. Home: PO Box 6359 Snowmass Village CO 81615

STRAND, FRED P., mathematics educator; b. ND; m. Donalee Strand. BS in Edn., Mayville State Univ., 1980. Math. tchr. Hatton (ND) H.S. Vol. St. John Luth. Ch. Named ND Tchr. of Yr., 2006. Luth. Office: Hatton High Sch 503 Fourth St Hatton ND 58240 Business E-Mail: fred.strand@sendit.nodak.edu. *

STRAND, MARGARET N., lawyer; b. White Plains, NY, Apr. 27, 1946; BA, U. Rochester, 1968; MA, U. RI, 1971; JD, Coll. William and Mary, 1976. Bar: Va. 1976, DC 1977, US Supreme Ct. Chief, environ. def. sect. environ. and natural resources divsn. U.S. Dept. Justice, Washington, 1984—91; ptnr. Venable LLP, Washington. Lectr. George Washington U., 1993—2002; chair environ. law com. Transp. Rsch. Bd., Nat. Acad. Scis.; bd. dirs. Environ. Law Inst.; mem. editl. bd. Environ. Law Reporter, Nat. Wetlands News. Author: Wetlands Deskbook, 1997; contbr. chapters to books, articles to profl. jours. Mem.: ABA. Office: Venable LLP 575 7th St NW Washington DC 20004 Office Phone: 202-344-4699. Office Fax: 202-344-8300. Business E-Mail: mnstrand@venable.com.

STRAND, MARK, poet; b. Summerside, PEI, Can., Apr. 11, 1934; came to U.S., 1938. s. Robert Joseph and Sonia (Apter) S.; m. Antonia Ratensky, Sept. 14, 1961 (div. June 1973); 1 dau., Jessica; m. Julia Rumsey Garretson, Mar. 15, 1976; 1 son, Thomas Summerfield. BA, Antioch Coll., 1957; BFA, Yale, 1959; MA, U. Iowa, 1962. Instr. English U. Iowa, 1962-65; asst. prof. Mt. Holyoke Coll., 1967; assoc. prof. Bklyn. Coll., 1971-72; Bain-Swiggett lectr. Princeton, 1973; Hurst prof. poetry Brandeis U., 1974-75; prof. U. Utah, 1981-93; U.S. poet laureate Library of Congress, Washington, 1990-91; prof. Johns Hopkins U., 1994—97; Andrew MacLeish disting. svc. prof. U. Chgo., 1997—. Fulbright lectr. U. Brazil, Rio de Janeiro, 1965-66; adj. assoc. prof. Columbia U., 1969-72; vis. prof. U. Wash., 1968, 70, U. Va., 1977, Wesleyan U., 1979, Harvard U., 1980; vis. lectr. Yale, 1969-70, U. Va., 1976, Calif. State U., Fresno, 1977, U. Calif., Irvine, 1979. Author: Sleeping with One Eye Open, 1964, Reasons for Moving, 1968, Darker, 1970, The Story of Our Lives, 1973 (Edgar Allan Poe award Acad. Am. Poets 1974), The Sargeantville Notebook, 1974, The Monument, 1978, Elegy for My Father, 1978, The Late Hour, 1978, Selected Poems, 1980, The Planet of Lost Things, 1982, The Night Book, 1983, Mr. and Mrs. Baby and Other Stories, 1985, Rembrandt Takes a Walk, 1986, William Bailey, 1987, The Continuous Life, 1990, Dark Harbor, 1993, Hopper, 1994, Blizzard of One, 2000 (Pulitzer Prize), Man and Camel, 2006; Editor: The Contemporary American Poets, 1968, New Poetry of Mexico, 1970, 18 Poems from Quechua, 1971, The Owl's Insomnia, 1973, The Best American Poetry 1991, The Golden Ecco Anthology, 1994; co-author: 89 Clouds, 1999; co-editor: Another Republic: Seventeen European and South American Writers, 1976, The Art of the Real, 1983, Traveling in the Family, 1987; translator: Souvenir of the Ancient World, 1976. Recipient award Am. Acad. and Inst. Arts and Letters, 1975, Utah Gov.'s award in arts, 1992, Bobbitt Nat. prize for poetry, 1992, Bollingen prize for poetry Yale Univ. Libr., 1993; Fulbright scholar in Italy, 1960-61; Ingram Merrill Found. grantee, 1966; Nat. Endowment for Arts grantee, 1967-68, 78-79, 86-87; Rockefeller Found. grantee, 1968-69; Guggenheim fellow, 1975-76; Acad. Am. Poets fellow, 1979; MacArthur Found. fellow, 1987; Pulitzer Prize in Poetry, Blizzard of One, 1999, Wallace Stevens prize, 2004. Fellow Acad. Am. Poets; mem. Am. Acad. and Inst. Arts and Letters. E-mail: ms3091@columbia.edu.

STRAND, MELVIN LEROY, English educator; b. Waseca, Minn., Mar. 15, 1936; s. Carl Morris and Dorothy Mae Robran S. BS, Minn. State U., Mankato, 1961, MS in Edn., 1968; MS, Bemidji State U., Minn., 1972; EdD, U. S.D., 1976. Tchr. English Rockford (Ill.) Secondary Schs., 1960-61, Rochester (Minn.) Secondary Schs., 1961-63, Richfield (Minn.) Secondary Schs., 1963-82; asst. prof. English King Saud U., Abha, Saudi Arabia, 1982-92; prof. English Saudi Arabian Am. Oil Co., Dhahran, Saudi Arabia, 1994, Royal Saudi Navy, Dhahran, 1995-96, Ctrl. Tex. Coll., Killeene, 1996—. Author: The Basic Sentence, 1989, Sentence to Paragraph, 1990; subject of nat. Saudi Arabian telecast Guest of Kingdom, 1991; contbr. articles to jours. in field. Vol., instr. AARP 55-Alive; active Minnesotans for Responsible Recreation, Nat. Arbor Day Found., Bemidji State U., WASECA County DFL, Am. Refugee Com., Internat. Planned Parenthood Com.; com. mem. Dem. Congrl. Campaign; active Grace Luth. Ch. With USAF, 1955—59. Recipient, USAF Missile Badge, 1958. Mem. NEA, AARP, Minn. Edn. Assn., Nat. Coun. Tchrs. English, Edn. Minn., AmVets, Vets for Common Sense, MSU Found., Minn. Young DFL, Minn. Sr. Fed., N.H. Arbor Day, WASECA Arts Council, Alliance for Ret. Am., Sojourners, Am. Fedn. Tchrs., Ret. Educators Assn. Minn., Edn. Minn., Stroke Assn., Disabled Am. Vets, Mankato Alumni Assn., Sierra Club, World Wildlife Fund, Nature Conservancy, Nat. Parks Conservation Assn., Childreach Plan Internat., Interfaith Alliance, Friends Waseca Pub. Libr., Waseca Area Found., Nat. Geographic Soc., Wellstone Action, Pi Delta Epsilon. Dfl. Lutheran. Avocations: world travel, reading, writing, environmental concerns. Home: 13342 382nd Ave Waseca MN 56093-4200 Personal E-mail: MLS2@myclearwave.net.

STRAND, ROGER GORDON, federal judge; b. Peekskill, NY, Apr. 28, 1934; s. Ernest Gordon Strand and Lisabeth Laurine (Phin) Steinmetz; m. Joan Williams, Nov. 25, 1961. AB, Hamilton Coll., 1955; LLB, Cornell U., 1961; grad., Nat. Coll. State Trial Judges, 1968. Bar: Ariz. 1961, U.S. Dist. Ct. Ariz. 1961, U.S. Supreme Ct. 1980. Assoc. Fennemore, Craig, Allen & McClennen, Phoenix, 1961-67; judge Ariz. Superior Ct., Phoenix, 1967-85, U.S. Dist. Ct. Ariz., Phoenix, 1985—2001, now sr. judge. Assoc. presiding judge Ariz. Superior Ct., 1971-85; lectr. Nat. Jud. Coll., Reno, 1978-87; mem. jud. conf. U.S. com. on info. tech., 1996-2002; mem. 9th Cir. Jud. Coun. Past pres. cen. Ariz. chpt. Arthritis Found. Lt. USN, 1955-61. Mem. ABA, Ariz. Bar Assn., Maricopa County Bar Assn., Nat. Conf. Fed. Trial Judges, Phi Delta Phi, Aircraft Owners and Pilots Assn. Lodges: Rotary. Avocations: computer applications, golf, fishing. Home: 5825 N 3rd Ave Phoenix AZ 85013-1537 Office: Sandra Day O'Connor US Courthouse SPC 57 401 W Washington Phoenix AZ 85003-2156 Office Phone: 602-322-7550. Business E-Mail: roger_strand@azd.uscourts.gov.

STRANDBERG, MALCOM WOODROW PERSHING, physicist; b. Box Elder, Mont., Mar. 9, 1919; s. Malcom and Ingeborg (Riestad) S.; m. Harriet Elisabeth Bennett, Aug. 2, 1947 (dec.); children— Josiah R.W., Susan Abby, Elisabeth G., Malcom B. S.B., Harvard Coll., 1941; PhD, M.I.T., 1948. Research asso. M.I.T., Cambridge, 1941-48, asst. prof. physics, 1948-53, asso. prof., 1953-60, prof., 1960-88, prof. emeritus, 1988—. Author: Microwave Spectroscopy, 1954; patentee in field. Fellow Am. Phys. Soc., Am. Acad. Arts and Scis., IEEE, AAAS; mem. Am. Assn. Physics Tchrs. Episcopalian. Home: 82 Larchwood Dr Cambridge MA 02138-4639 Office: Mass Inst Tech 36-597 Cambridge MA 02139 Office Phone: 617-253-2563. Business E-Mail: mwpstr@mit.edu.

STRANDJORD, M. JEANNINE, telecommunications industry executive; B in Acctg. and Bus. Adminstrn., U. Kans. CPA. V.p. fin. Macy's Midwest; with Kans. city Power & Light Co., Ernst and Whinney; v.p. fin. and distrbn. AmeriSource, Inc. (subs. Sprint), 1985—90, controller, 1986—90, sr. v.p., treas., 1990—98, sr. v.p. fin. global markets group, 1998—2003; sr. v.p. fin. svcs. Sprint Corp., 2003, sr. v.p., chief integration officer, 2003—. Bd. dirs. Am. Century Mutual Funds, DST Sys., Inc., Euronet Worldwide. Trustee Rockhurst U. Office: 6200 Spring Pkwy Overland Park KS 66251

STRANG, GILBERT, mathematics professor; SB, MIT, 1955; BA, MA, Oxford U., 1957, PhD, UCLA, 1959. C.L.E. Moore instr. MIT, 1959—61, asst. prof., math., 1962—64, assoc. prof., math., 1964—70, prof. math., 1970—; NATO postdoctoral fellow Oxford U., 1961—62. Chmn. MIT Com. on Pure Math., 1975—79; mem. NSF Adv. Panel on Math., 1977—80, chmn., 1979—80; hon. prof. Xian Jiaotong Univ., China, 1980; mem. US Nat. Com. on Math., 2001—04, chair, 2003—04, Joint Policy Bd. for Math., 1999; mem. Abel Prize Com., Oslo, 2003—05; invited lectr. in field. Jour. editor for several peer-reviewed jours.; contbr. articles to profl. jours.; co-author (with George Fix): An Analysis of the Finite Element Method, 1973; co-author: (with Truong Nguyen) Wavelets and Filter Banks, 1996; co-author: (with Kai Borre) Linear Algebra, Geodesy, and GPS, 1997; author: Linear Algebra and Its Applications, 1976, 1980, 1988, 2005, Calculus, 1991, Introduction to Linear Algebra, 1993, 1998, 2003. Recipient von Neumann medal, US Assn. for Computational Mechanics, Su Buchin prize, Internat. Congress of Indsl. and Applied Math.; William Barton Rogers Scholar, MIT, 1952—55, Rhodes Scholar, Balliol Coll., Oxford U., 1955—57, NSF Fellow, UCLA, 1957—59, Alfred P. Sloan Fellow, 1966—67, Fairchild Scholar, Calif. Inst. Tech., 1980—81, hon. fellow, Balliol Coll., Oxford, 1999. Fellow: Am. Acad. Arts and Sciences; mem.: Math. Assn. Am. (mem. sci. policy com. 1992—95, Chauvenet prize 1977, Deborah and Franklin Tepper Haimo awards for Disting. Coll. or Univ. Tchg. of Math. 2007, Northeastern Sect. Tchg. award 2006), Irish Math. Soc. (hon.), Soc. for Indsl. and Applied Math. (coun. 1977—82, and Am. Math. Soc. Com. on Applied Mathematics 1990—92, v.p. edn. 1991—96, pres. 1999—2000, chair, Com. on Sci. Policy 2001—02, award for disting. svc. to profession 2003). Office: Dept Math MIT Room 2-240 Cambridge MA 02139 Office Phone: 617-253-4383. Office Fax: 617-253-4358. Business E-Mail: gs@math.mit.edu.

STRANG, NATHAN THOMAS, military officer; b. Niskayuna, NY, July 9, 1978; s. Thomas Strang, Sr. and Teresa Gallo; m. Katherine Foster, July 27, 2002; 1 child, William. BA in Govt. and Internat. Studies, Manhattan Coll., Riverdale, NY, 2000. Commd. ens. USN, advanced through grades to lt.; naval flight officer Sea Control Squadron 24, Jacksonville, Fla., 2003—06, Patrol Squadron 4, Kaneohe, Hawaii, 2006—. Decorated Navy Commendation medal, Air Medal, Navy/Marine Corps Achievement,edal. Mem.: Tailhook Assn., US Naval Inst. Office: Patrol Squadron 4 MCB Hawaii Kaneohe HI 96744 Home Phone: 904-535-4306. Personal E-mail: jaspernavy@hotmail.com. Business E-Mail: nathan.strang@navy.mil.

STRANG, RUTH HANCOCK, pediatrician, educator, cardiologist, priest; b. Bridgeport, Conn., Mar. 11, 1923; d. Robert H.W. and Ruth (Hancock) Strang. BA, Wellesley Coll., 1944, postgrad., 1944—45; MD, N.Y. Med. Coll., 1949; MDiv, Seabury We. Theol. Sem., 1993. Diplomate Am. Bd. Pediat.; ordained deacon Episc. Ch., 1993, priest Episc. Ch., 1994. Intern Flower and Fifth Ave. Hosp., NYC, 1949—50, resident in pediat., 1950—52; mem. faculty N.Y. Med. Coll., NYC, 1952—57; fellow cardiology Babies Hosp., NYC, 1956—57, Harriet Lane Cardiac Clinic, Johns Hopkins Hosp., Balt., 1957—59, Children's Hosp., Boston, 1959—62; mem. faculty U. Mich. Hosp., Ann Arbor, 1962—89, prof. pediat., 1970—89, prof. emeritus, 1989—; priest-in-charge St. Johns Episcopal Ch., Howell, Mich., 1994—. Dir. pediat. Wayne County Gen. Hosp., Westland, Mich, 1965-85; mem. staff U. Mich. Hosps., 1962-89; mem. med. adv. com. Wayne County chpt. Nat. Cystic Fibrosis Rsch. Found., 1966-80, chmn. med. adv. com. nat. found., Detroit, 1971-78; cons. cardiology Plymouth (Mich.) State Home and Tng. Sch., 1970-81; diocesan coun. Diocese Mich., 2003-05, mem. com. on nominations and elections Diocesan Conv., 2003, chmn. com., 2004. Author: Clinical Aspects of Operable Heart Disease, 1968; contbr. numerous articles to profl. jours. Mem. citizen's adv. coun. Juvenile Ct., Ann Arbor, 1968—76; mem. med. adv. bd. Ann Arbor Continuing Edn. Dept., 1968—77; v.p. Am. Heart Assn. Mich., 1989, pres., 1991; bd. dirs. Livingston Cmty. Hospice, 1995—99; bd. mgrs. Emrich Episcopal Retreat Ctr., 1998—; mem. Diocesan Com. for World Relief, Detroit, 1970—72; trustee Episcopal Med. Chaplaincy, Ann Arbor, 1971—96; mem. bishop's com. St. Aidan's Episc. Ch., 1966—69, sec., 1966—68, vestry, 1973—76, 1978—80, 1984—86, 1990—91, sr. warden, 1975—76, 1978, 1986, 1990; del. Episc. Diocesan Conv., 1980, 1991; mem. Congl. Life Circle Episcopal Diocese Mich., 1995—2001, mem. loans and grants com., 1995—99, mem. com. on reference ann. diocesan conv., 1995-98, chmn., 1996; mem. Diocese Mich. Clergy Family Project, 1996—98; co-dean Huron Valley area coun. Diocese Mich., 1998—2000; bd. trustees Ecumenical Theol. Sem., 1996—, chair acad. affairs com., 2000—; mem. Congl. Devel. Commn., 2001—03; bd. dirs. Livingston County Cath. Social Svcs., 2004—. Recipient Alumnae Life Achievement award, Baldwin Sch., 2005. Mem. AMA, Am. Acad, Pediat., Am. Coll. Cardiology, Mich. Med. Soc., Washtenaw County Med. Soc., N.Y. Acad. Medicine, Am. Heart Assn., Women's Rsch. Club (membership sec. 1966-67), Ambulatory Pediat. Assn., Am. Assn. Child Care in Hosps., Am. Assn. Med. Colls., Assn. Faculties of Pediat. Nurse Assn./Practitioners Programs (pres. 1978-81, exec. com. 1981-84), Episc. Clergy Assn. Mich., Northside Assn. Ministries (pres. 1975, 76, 79-80), Soc. Companions of Holy Cross. Home: 4500 E Huron River Dr Ann Arbor MI 48105-9335 E-mail: stjohns@saintjohnsepiscopalhowell.org.

STRANG, WILLIAM GILBERT, mathematician, educator; b. Chgo., Nov. 27, 1934; s. William Dollin and Mary Catherine (Finlay) S.; m. Jillian Mary Shannon, July 26, 1958; children— David, John, Robert. SB, MIT, 1955; BA (Rhodes scholar), Oxford U., Eng., 1957; PhD (NSF fellow), UCLA, 1959. Asst. prof. mathematics MIT, 1959-63, assoc. prof., 1963-66, prof., 1966—. Pres. Wellesley-Cambridge Press; hon. prof. Xian Jiaotong U., People's Republic of China, 1980. Author: An Analysis of the Finite Element Method, 1973, Linear Algebra and Its Applications, 1976, Introduction to Applied Mathematics, 1986, Calculus, 1990, Introduction to Linear Algebra, 1993, Wavelets and Filter Banks, 1996, Linear Algebra, Geodesy, and GPS, 1997. Recipient Chauvenet prize Math. Assn. Am., 1977; Sloan fellow, 1966-67, Hon. fellow Balliol Coll., Oxford, 1999; Fairchild scholar, 1981. Mem. Soc. Indsl. and Applied Math. (pres. 1999-2000). Home: 7 Southgate Rd Wellesley MA 02482-6606 Office: MIT Math Dept Rm 2-240 Cambridge MA 02139 Office Phone: 617-253-4383. Business E-Mail: gs@math.mit.edu.

STRANGE, CURTIS NORTHROP, professional golfer; b. Norfolk, Va., Jan. 30, 1955; s. Thomas Wright Strange Jr. and Nancy (Ball) Neal; m. Sarah Jones; children: Thomas Wright III, David Clark. Student, Wake Forest U., 1974—76. Profl. golfer, 1976—; mem. PGA Tour, Champions Tour, 2005—; lead golf analyst ABC. Mem. US Team Ryder Cup, 1983, 85, 87, 89, 95. Named to Collegiate Golf Hall of Fame, 1987, Wake Forest Hall of Fame, 1988, World Golf Hall of Fame, 2007; named PGA Player of Yr., 1988; recipient Golf Writers Player of Yr. award, 1985, 87, 88. Achievements include winning the Southeastern Amateur, 1973, NCAA, 1974, Western Amateur, 1974, Walker Cup, 1974, Ea. Amateur, 1975, 76, North and South Amateur, 1975, 76, Va. State Amateur, 1976, World Amateur Cup, 1975; winner, PGA Tour events including the Pensacola Open, 1979, Michelob-Houston Open, 1980, Mfrs. Hanover Westchester Classic, 1980, Sammy Davis Jr.-Greater Hartford Open, 1983, LaJet Golf Classic, 1984; winner, Honda Classic, 1985, Panasonic Las Vegas Invitational, 1985, Canadian Open, 1985, 87, Houston Open, 1986, Fed. Express St. Jude Classic, 1987, NEC World Series of Golf, 1987; winner, Ind. Ins. Agt. Open, 1988, Meml. Tournament, 1988, US Open, 1988, 89, Nabisco Championships, 1988; led the PGA money list, 1985, 87, 88. Avocations: hunting, fishing. Mailing: Champions Tour 112 PGA TOUR Blvd Ponte Vedra Beach FL 32082 *

STRANGE, DONALD ERNEST, healthcare company executive; b. Ann Arbor, Mich., Aug. 13, 1944; s. Carl Britton and Donna Ernestine (Tenney) Strange; m. Lyn Marie Purdy, Aug. 3, 1968 (div. Mar. 2001); children: Laurel Lyn, Chadwick Donald. BA, Mich. State U., 1966, MBA, 1968. Asst. dir. Holland (Mich.) City Hosp., 1968-72, assoc. dir., 1972-74; exec. dir. Bascom Palmer Eye Inst./Anne Bates Leach Eye Hosp., U. Miami, Fla., 1974-77; v.p. strategic planning and rsch. Hosp. Corp. Am., Nashville, 1977-80, group v.p. Boston, 1980-82, regional v.p., 1982-87; chmn., chief exec. officer HCA Healthcare Can., Toronto, 1985-87; exec. v.p. Avon Products, Inc., NYC, 1987-89; chmn. Sigecom, Ltd., Greenwich, Conn., 1989-94, U.S. HomeCare Corp., 1990-91; exec. v.p., COO, dir. EPIC Healthcare Group, Dallas, 1991-93; chmn, CEO TransCare Corp., Dallas, 1993-95; chmn., CEO First New Eng. Dental Ctrs., Inc., Boston, 1996-98; pres., CEO Behavorial Healthcare Ptnrs., Inc., Quincy, Mass., 2000; sr. v.p. Bon Secours Health Sys. Inc., Mariottsville, Md., 2001—06, COO, 2006—. Dir. Altoona (Pa.) Regional Health Sys., 2004—, Bon Secours Cottage Health Sys., Grosse Pointe, Mich., 2002—07. Trustee Boston Ballet, 1998—2001, chmn. bd. overseers, 1999—2001. Mem. Harvard Club (Boston), Nat. Arts Club (N.Y.). Episcopalian. Office: Bon Secours Health Sys Inc 1505 Marriottsville Rd Marriottsville MD 21104-1399 Office Phone: 410-442-5511. Business E-Mail: don_strange@bshsi.com.

STRANGE, HENRY HAZEN, judge; b. Oleary, PEI, Can., July 26, 1939; s. Henry Hazen and Marion Yvonne (Copp) S.; m. Heather Susan Carson, July 30, 1966; children: Elizabeth Marion, Jennifer Jody. BBA, U. N.B., Fredericton, 1961, BA, 1963, B in Civil Laws, 1964. Pvt. practice barrister, solicitor, N.B., 1964-66; spl. asst. to dir. of pub. rels. Centennial Commn., Ottawa, Ont., Canada, 1966-67; crown prosecutor Dept. Justice, Fredericton, N.B., 1967-71, dir. pub. prosecutions N.B., 1971-81; judge Provincial Ct., N.B., 1981—, chief judge N.B., 1987-97. Chmn. Can. Coun. Chief Judges, 1995. Apptd. as Queen's Counsel, N.B., 1977. Avocations: salmon fishing, sports. Home: 664 Woodstock Rd Fredericton NB Canada E3B 5N7 Office: Provincial Ct PO Box 6000 Fredericton NB Canada E3B 5H1 Home Phone: 506-459-4523; Office Phone: 506-459-4523. Personal E-mail: hazen.strange@gnb.ca.

STRANGFELD, JOHN R., JR., diversified financial services company executive; Various mgmt. pos. Prudential Fin., 1977—89, chmn., PRICOA Capital Group Europe London, 1989—95, sr. mng. dir., Pvt. Asset Mgmt. Group, 1995—96, exec. in charge of Global Asset Mgmt. Group, 1996—2000, chmn., CEO Prudential Securities, 2000—01, CEO, Prudential Investment Mgmt. of Prudential Ins., 2001—02, exec. v.p., 2001—02, vice chmn. investments div., 2002—. Mem. bd. Wachovia Financial Svcs., LLC. Office: Prudential Financial Inc 751 Broad St Newark NJ 07102-3777 *

STRANTZ, NANCY JEAN, law educator, consultant; b. Calgary, Alta., Can., 1958; 1 child. LLB, U. Alta., 1981; JD, South Tex. Coll. Law, Houston, 1990; BA in Social Scis., U. N.D., Grand Forks, 1997. Bar: Alta. 1982. Articling lawyer Carma Developers Ltd., Calgary, 1981-82; barrister and solicitor Stewart & Stewart, Calgary, 1982-83; rsch. asst., author Can. Inst. Resources Law, U. Calgary, 1984-85; corp. counsel Chevron Can. Resources, 1985-90, Gulf Can. Resources, 1991-94, 98; asst. prof. U. N.D. Sch. Law, Grand Forks, 1994-97; contracts adminstr. Longview Fibre Co., 2007—. Land and legal cons. N.J. Strantz Cons., Calgary, 1991-94, 1998, 2007; adj. faculty U. Calgary, Mt. Royal Coll., So. Alta Inst. Tech., Calgary, 1991-94. Co-author: A Reference Guide to Hardrock Mining in Canada; contbr. articles to profl. jours. Trustee Rocky Mountain Mineral Law Found., 1994-97. Pvt. Can. Dept. Nat. Def., Naval Res., 1975. Recipient award and grants. Mem. Law Soc. Alta. Avocation: swimming.

STRASBAUGH, WAYNE RALPH, lawyer; b. Lancaster, Pa., July 20, 1948; s. Wayne Veily and Jane Irene (Marzolf) S.; m. Carol Lynne Taylor, June 8, 1974; children: Susan, Wayne T., Elizabeth. AB summa cum laude, Bowdoin Coll., 1970; AM in History, Harvard U., 1971, PhD in History, 1976, JD cum laude, 1979. Bar: Ohio 1979, Pa. 1983, U.S. Tax Ct. 1980, U.S. Ct. Fed. Claims 1980, U.S. Ct. Appeals (fed. cir.) 1982, U.S. Dist. Ct. (no. dist.) Ohio 1979, U.S. Dist. Ct. (ea. dist.) Pa. 1983. Assoc. Jones Day

Reavis & Pogue, Cleve., 1979-82, Morgan Lewis & Bockius, Phila., 1982-84, Ballard Spahr Andrews & Ingersoll, LLP, Phila., 1984-88, ptnr., 1988—, chmn. tax group, 2001—. Mem. ABA (tax sect., chmn. com. 1992-94, 2007—), Am. Coll. Tax Counsel (regent 2003—), Phila. Bar Assn. (tax sect., chmn. fed. tax com. 1992, coun. mem. 1995, sec.-treas. 1996, vice-chmn. 1997-98, chmn. 1999-2000). Episcopalian. Office: Ballard Spahr Andrews & Ingersoll LLP 1735 Market St Ste 5100 Philadelphia PA 19103-7599

STRASBURGER, VICTOR C., pediatrician; b. Balt., Oct. 7, 1949; s. Arthur Charles and Marjorie (Cohen) S.; m. Alison Reeve, Aug. 18, 1984; children: Max, Katya. BA summa cum laude, Yale U., 1971; MD, Harvard U., 1975. Intern Children's Hosp.- U. Wash., Seattle, 1975-76, residency, 1976-77, Boston Children's Hosp., 1977-78; dir. adolescent medicine Bridgeport (Conn.) Hosp., 1979-86; vis. lectr. St. Mary's Hosp. Med. Sch., London, 1986-87; chief div. adolescent medicine sch. medicine U. N.Mex., Albuquerque, 1987—, prof. pediats., 1997—. Cons. Nat. PTA, Washington and Chgo., 1978-86. Author: Rounding Third and Heading Home, 1974, Adolescent Medicine: A Practical Guide, 1991, 2d edit., 1998, Getting Your Kids to Say No in the '90's When You Said Yes in the '60's, 1993, (with B. Wilson) Children, Adolescents, and the Media, 2002, (with R. Brown, P. Braverman, C. Holland, P. Rogers and S. Coupey) Care of the Adolescent: A Handbook for Primary Care, 2006; editor: Basic Adolescent Gynecology, 1990; editor-in-chief Adolescent Medicine: State of the Art Revs., 1989—. Recipient Adele Hofmann award, 2000. Fellow Am. Acad. Pediatrics (Holyroyd-Sherry award 2000), Soc. for Adolescent Medicine; mem. Phi Beta Kappa. Office: U NM Sch Medicine Dept Pediatrics MSC10 5590 1 Univ New Mexico Albuquerque NM 87131-0001 Home Phone: 505-856-7943; Office Phone: 505-272-0338. E-mail: vstrasburger@salud.unm.edu.

STRASFOGEL, IAN, stage director, playwright; b. NYC, Apr. 5, 1940; s. Ignace and Alma (Lubin) S.; m. Judith Hirsch Norell, Feb. 15, 1973; children: Daniella Elizabeth, Gabrielle Sandra. BA, Harvard U., 1961. Adminstrv. asst. N.Y.C. Opera Co., 1962-64, stage dir., 1964—; tchr. music Julliard Sch. Music, NYC, 1965-66, Augusta (Ga.) Coll., 1967-68; founder, previous artistic dir. Augusta Opera Co., from 1967; chmn. dept. opera New Eng. Conservatory, Boston, 1968-72; prof. opera U. Mich., Ann Arbor, 1980; freelance opera dir., playwright Rosenstone & Wander Agency, NYC, 1982—. Stage dir. Balt. Civic Opera, Kansas City Lyric Theatre, Netherlands Opera Co., 1973—, N.Y.C. Opera, San Francisco Opera, Stuttgart Opera, Alte Oper Frankfurt, Edinburgh Festival, Aix-en-Provence Festival, Aspen Music Festival; dir. music theatre project Tanglewood Festival, Lenox, Mass., 1971-73; gen. dir. Opera Soc. Washington, 1972-75; artistic cons. Phila. Lyric Opera, 1973; dir. New Opera Theatre, Bklyn. Acad. Music, 1976-79. Author: Il Musico (music by Larry Grossman), 1990-91 The Caregiver (play), 1999, Jewish Ensemble Theatre, Detroit; editor: Ba-Ta-Clan, 1970. Served with AUS, 1966-68. Henry Russell Shaw travelling fellow, 1961-62; Ford Found. internship in performing arts, 1962-64; grantee: Internat. Inst. Edn., 1965, Berrillon Kerr Found., 1997 (for The Caregiver). Mem. Phi Beta Kappa. Home: 915 W End Ave New York NY 10025-3535

STRASSELS, SCOTT A., pharmacist, researcher; m. Ann Strassels, 1994; 1 child, Noah B. BS, U. Ariz., Tucson, 1988, PharmD, 1989; PhD, U. Wash., Seattle, 2005. Bd. cert. pharmacotherapy specialist 1996. Clin. rsch. pharmacist New Eng. Med. Ctr., Boston, 1997—2000; asst. prof. U. Tex., Austin, 2005—. Office: Univ Tex 2409 University Ave PHR 3208E Austin TX 78712 Office Phone: 512-471-5657. Business E-Mail: scotts1@mail.utexas.edu.

STRASSER, GABOR, management consultant; b. Budapest, Hungary, May 22, 1929; s. Rezso and Theresa (Seiler) S.; m. Linda Casselman Pemble, Aug. 16, 1958 (div. 1976); children: Claire Margaret, Andrew John; m. Joka Verhoeff, Feb. 2, 1978; children: Steven Verhoeff, Tessa Christina. BCE, City Coll. N.Y., 1954; MS, U. Buffalo, 1959; PMD, Harvard, 1968; MDiv, Va. Theol. Sem., 1992. Research engr. Bell Aircraft Co., Buffalo, 1956-61; project leader Boeing Airplane Co., Seattle, 1961-62; dept. head Mitre Corp., Bedford, Mass., Washington, 1962-68; v.p. Urban Inst., Washington, 1968-69; tech. asst. to pres.'s sci. adviser White House, 1969-71, exec. sec. pres.'s sci. and tech. policy panel, 1970-71; dir. planning Battelle Meml. Inst., Columbus, Ohio, 1971-73; pres. Strasser Assocs., Inc., Washington, 1973-92. Author, editor: Science and Technology Policies-Yesterday, Today, Tomorrow, 1973; Contbr. articles to profl. jours. and theol. lit. Served to 1st lt., C.E. USAR. Recipient 1st nat. award Gravity Research Found., 1952

STRASSER, KURT ALBERT, law educator, researcher, author, dean; b. Oak Ridge, Tenn., July 20, 1947; s. George Albert and Doris Maupin (Adams) S.; m. Jane Wyatt, Aug. 23, 1969; 1 child, Julia Wyatt. BA, Vanderbilt U., 1969, JD, 1972; LLM, Columbia U., 1979, JSD, 1986. Bar: Tenn. 1972, U.S. Dist. Ct. (mid. dist.) Tenn. 1972, Conn. 1986. Rsch. asst. Inst. Govt, U. NC, Chapel Hill, NC, 1971; assoc. Neal & Harwell, Nashville, 1972-74; asst. prof. Mercer U. Law Sch., Macon, Ga., 1974—77, assoc. prof., 1977—80, prof., 1980—81, U. Conn. Law Sch., Hartford, 1981—98, assoc. dean acad. affairs, 1996—99, Phillip I. Blumberg Prof. Law, 1999—, interim dean, 2006—. Vis. prof. Exeter U., Exeter, England, 1984, 1991, Free U. of Berlin, 2003; dir. Conn. Environ. Entrepreneurial Ctr., Hartford, 1994—. Co-author: Regulating Utilities with Management Incentives, 1989, Law of Corporate Groups—Specific Statutory Law, 1992, Law of Corporate Groups—State Statutory Law, 1995, Law of Corporate Groups-Enterprise Liability, 1998. Mem. ABA, Environ. Law Inst. Democrat. Avocation: sailing. Home: 93 State St Wethersfield CT 06109-1851 Office: University Connecticut Law School 65 Elizabeth St Hartford CT 06105-2290 Business E-Mail: KStrasse@law.uconn.edu.

STRASSER, RICHARD JOSEPH, JR., federal agency administrator; b. NYC, July 15, 1947; s. Richard Joseph Sr. and Lillian Mary (Murray) Strasser; m. Christine Therese Avery, Oct. 18, 1969; children: Richard, Mary Patricia, Therese, Clare, Moira, Christine. BA in Govt., Seton Hall U., 1969; M. in Pub. Admistrn., Am. U., 1983. Mgmt. intern US Postal Svc., Washington, 1969-71, acting postmaster Walnut Creek, Calif., 1972, mgr. mktg. Washington, 1973-80, dir. office of policy, 1981-86, asst. postmaster gen. planning, 1987-90, sr. asst. postmaster gen. mktg. and customer svc., exec. v.p., CFO, 2000—. Mem. Corp. Planning 100, N.Y.C., 1986—, Conf. Bd. Coun. on Svcs. Mktg., 1991—. Soccer coach, Arlington, 1982-85, 88—. Roman Catholic. Office: US Postal Svc 475 Lenfant Plz SW Rm 5021 Washington DC 20260-0004

STRASSFIELD, CHRISTINA MOSSAIDES, curator; d. Paul and Melika Mossaides; m. Paul Joseph Strassfield, July 9, 1983; children: Zoe Paula, Joseph Daniel, Peter Mossaides. BA with honors in Art History and Anthropology, CUNY, 1980; M, CUNY, Flushing, 1984. Mus. curator Guild Hall Mus., East Hampton, NY, 1987—. Bd. mem. LI Mus. Assn., NY, 2000—02, Long Ho. Art Com., East Hampton, NY, 2000—06; mem. Arttable, NYC, 2006. Home: P O Box 1429 Water Mill NY 11976-1429 Office: Guild Hall Museum 158 Main St East Hampton NY 11937 Office Phone: 631-324-0806. Office Fax: 631-324-2722. Personal E-mail: strassfield@optonline.net. Business E-Mail: museum@guildhall.org.

STRASSLER, MARC A., lawyer; b. 1948; m. Meryl Strassler. BA, Bklyn. Coll., CUNY; JD, George Washington U. Bar: 1973. Joined Pathmark Stores Inc., Carteret, NJ, 1974, v.p., gen. counsel, sec., sr. v.p., gen. counsel, sec., 1998—. Office: Pathmark Stores Inc 200 Milik St Carteret NJ 07008 Office Phone: 732-499-3000. *

STRASSNER, HOWARD TAFT, JR., obstetrician, educator; b. Tulsa, Okla., Dec. 2, 1948; BA in Biochemistry, U. Chgo., 1970, MD, 1974. Diplomate Am. Bd. Ob-gyn. Intern Columbia Presbyn. Med. Ctr., NYC, 1974, resident ob-gyn., 1974—78; fellow maternal fetal medicine L.A. County-U. So. Calif. Med. Ctr., 1978—80; physician, dir. sect. maternal fetal medicine Rush U. Med. Ctr., Chgo., 1980—, co-dir. Rush Perinatal Ctr. John M. Simpson prof., chmn. Rush U. Med. Ctr., Chgo. Office: Rush Med Ctr 1653 W Congress Pkwy Chicago IL 60612 Office Phone: 312-942-6678. Business E-Mail: howard.t.strassner@rush.edu.

STRATAS, BYRON ARISTOTLE, ophthalmologist; b. Williamsburg, Va., Dec. 18, 1958; s. Nicholas and Rene Stratas; m. Caroline Barden Stratas; children: Ashleyanne Rene, Grace, Hughes Byron. BA in Psychology (hon.), U. NC, Chapel Hill, 1981; MD, East Carolina U., Greenville, 1986. Lic. Chiron Keratorefractive Surgery NC, 1992, Summit Tech. Excimer Laser Rush Presbyn. Med. Ctr., Ill., 1995, C-LASIK and Mini-Fellowship Med. Coll. Va., 1997, Visx Johns Hopkins U., 1997, Custom Vue NC, 2001, Crystalens NC, 2004, Intralase NC, 2004, Restor Lens NC, 2005. Ophthalmologist Eye Assocs. Wilmington, NC, 1990—. Ophthalmologist Youth With A Mission, Mercy Ship Anastasis, Port Antonio, Jamaica, 1989, Guinea, West Africa, 1992; opthalmologist Hosp. St. Croix, Leogane, Haiti, 1995, 1996, 1997, ophthalmologist, 1998, 1999, Med. Ministries Internat., Costa Rica, 2002, Lighthouse for Christ Eye Ctr., Mombasa, Kenya, 2004. Fellow: ACS, Am. Acad. Ophthalmology and Refractive Surgery Interest Group (corr.); mem.: AMA (corr.), Christian Ophthalmology Soc. (corr.), Christian Med. Soc. (corr.), New Hanover/Pender Count Med. Soc. (corr.), NC Med. Soc. (corr.), Internat. Soc. Refractive Surgery (corr.), Am. Soc. Cataract and Refractive Surgery (corr.), Am. Acad. Ophthalmology (corr.). Avocations: golf, water sports, fishing, hunting. Office: Eye Assocs Wilmington 1729 New Hanover Med Park Dr Wilmington NC 28403 Home Phone: 910-763-4608; Office Phone: 910-763-3601. Office Fax: 910-763-4608.

STRATAS, TERESA (ANASTASIA STRATAKI), soprano; b. Toronto, Ont., Can., May 26, 1938; Studied with Irene Jessner, 1956-59; grad., U. Toronto, 1959; LLD (hon.), McMaster U., 1986, U. Toronto, 1994; degree (hon.), Juilliard Sch. Music, 1995, Eastman Sch. Music, 1998, U. Rochester, 1998. Winner Met. Opera auditions, 1959; major roles in opera houses throughout world include: Mimi in La Bohème; Tatiana in Eugene Onegin; Susanna in The Marriage of Figaro; Nedda in Pagliacci; Marenka in The Bartered Bride; Three Heroines in Il Trittico; Violetta in La Traviata; title role in Rusalka; Jennie in Mahagonny; created title role in completed version of Lulu (Alban Berg), Paris Grand Opera, 1979; film appearances Kaiser von Atlantis, Seven Deadly Sins; Zefirelli's La Traviata, Salome, Lulu, Paganini, Zarewitsch, Eugene Oregin; Broadway debut in Rags, 1986; creator the role of Marie Antoinette Ghosts of Versailles world premiere Met. Opera, 1992; sang both female leading roles Il Tabarro, Pagliacci double bill opening Met. Opera, 1994, numerous recs. including Richard Strauss' Salomé, Songs of Kurt Weill. Decorated Order of Can.; recipient 3 Grammy awards, Emmy award, Drama Desk award, 1986, 3 Grammy nominations, Tony nomination, 1986, Tiffany award, 1994, Highest Paedeia award, 1996, Gemini award, 1997; named Performer of Yr., Can. Music Council, 1979. Home: 6150 Blackjack Ct N Punta Gorda FL 33982-9606

STRATHAIRN, DAVID, actor; b. San Francisco, Calif., Jan. 26, 1949; m. Logan Goodman; 2 children. Attended, Williams Coll., Ringling Bros. Clown Coll. Numerous stage appearances including: I'm Not Rappaport, Salonika, A Lie of the Mind, The Birthday Party, Danton's Death, Mountain Language, L'Atelier, A Moon for the Misbegotten, Temptation; Actor (films) Return of the Secaucus Seven, 1980, Lovesick, 1983, Silkwood, 1983, The Brother From Another Planet, 1984, Iceman, 1984, Enormous Changes at the Last Minute, 1985, When Nature Calls, 1985, At Close Range, 1986, Matewan, 1987, Eight Men Out, 1988, Stars and Bars, 1988, Dominick and Eugene, 1988, Call Me, 1988, The Feud, 1989, Memphis Belle, 1990, City of Hope, 1991, Big Girls Don't Cry...They Get Even, 1992, Bob Roberts, 1992, Shadows and Fog, 1992, A League of Their Own, 1992, Sneakers, 1992, Passion Fish, 1992, April One, 1993, Lost in Yonkers, 1993, The Firm, 1993, A Dangerous Woman, 1993, The River Wild, 1994, Dolores Claiborne, 1995, Losing Isaiah, 1995, Home for the Holidays, 1995, Mother Night, 1996, Beyond the Call, 1996, Song of Hiawatha, 1997, The Climb, 1997, Bad Manners, 1997, L.A. Confidential, 1997, With Friends Like These..., 1998, Simon Birch, 1998, Meschugge, 1998, A Small Miracle, 1998, A Midsummer Night's Dream, 1999, A Map of the World, 1999, Limbo, 1999, Harrison's Flowers, 2000, A Good Baby, 2000, The Victim, 2001, Ball in the House, 2001, Speakeasy, 2002, Blue Car, 2002, The Root, 2003, Twisted, 2004, Heavens Fall, 2005, Missing in America, 2005, Good Night, and Good Luck (Coppa Volpi award for Best Actor, Venice Film Festival), 2005, The Notorious Bettie Page, 2005, Steel Toes, 2006, The Shovel, 2006, Heavens Fall, 2006, We Are Marshall, 2006, Matters of Life and Death, 2007, Fracture, 2007, The Bourne Ultimatum, 2007; (TV films) Broken Vows, 1985, The Feud, 1989, Wiseguy, 1990, Heat Wave, 1990, Judgment, 1990, Without Warning: The James Brady Story, 1991, Lethal Innocence, 1991, O Pioneers!, 1992, The American Clock, 1993, Beyond the Call, 1996, In the Gloaming, 1997, Evidence of Blood, 1998, Freedom Song, 2000, The Miracle Worker, 2000, Lathe of Heaven, 2002, Master Spy: The Robert Hanssen Story, 2002, Paradise, 2004; (TV series) Another World, 1987, The Days and Nights of Molly Dodd, 1988-90, Big Apple, 2001; (TV appearances) Miami Vice, 1985, Spense: For Hire, 1987, The Equalizer, 1988, Day One, 1989, Wiseguy, 1990, Big Apple, 2001, The Sopranos, 2004 *

STRATHE, MARLENE I., academic administrator; BS, Iowa State U., MS in Counseling Psychology, PhD in Ednl. Rsch. and Measurement; EdS in Ednl. Psychology, U. No. Iowa, 1973. Faculty mem., assoc. dean Coll. Edn., asst. v.p. academic affairs U. No. Iowa; provost U. ND, 1993—98; provost, v.p. academic affairs U. No. Colo., 1998—2003; provost, sr. v.p. Okla. State U., Stillwater, 2003—, interim sys. CEO, pres., 2007—. Exec. com. mem. Higher Learning Commn. Bd. Trustees. Contbr. articles to profl. jours. Recipient Fulbright Award, 1995, Virgil Lagomarcino Award for Excellence in Edn., Iowa State U. Office: Okla State U 107 Whitehurst Stillwater OK 74078 Office Phone: 405-744-6384. E-mail: marlene.strathe@okstate.edu. *

STRATIGOS, WILLIAM NARGE, computer company executive; b. Huntington, NY, Mar. 14, 1946; s. Narge G. and Portia R. (Kleros) Stratigos; m. Deborah Feller, Jan. 4, 1981; children: Stephanie, Elena. BA in Biology cum laude, NYU, 1972, DDS, 1977. Lic. dentist N.Y. Mgr. div. Med. Ctr. NYU, NYC, 1966-74; mng. ptnr., dentist Stratigos et al, NYC, 1978-88; pres. Sigma Imaging Sys. Inc., NYC, 1988-95; also bd. dirs. Sigma Imaging Sys., Inc., NYC; v.p. Wang Software, N.Y., Inc., NYC, 1995-97, Eastman Software, Inc., NYC, 1997; v.p., bd. dirs. R2K, Inc., NYC, 1997—; pres. Comfidex Corp., NYC, 1998—. Bd. dirs. Animal Med. Ctr. Author: (book) Hot Spot, 1993. Fellow: NYU Acad. Oral Rehab.; mem.: First Dist. Dental Soc., Dental Soc. State of N.Y., Assn. Image & Info. Mgmt. Internat. (bd. dirs., treas. exec. com., chmn. accreditation com.), Omicron Kappa Upsilon. Greek Orthodox. Achievements include patents in field. Avocations: writing, chess, bowling. Office: R2K Inc 83 Maiden Ln New York NY 10038 Personal E-mail: wstratigos@aol.com.

STRATMAN, DEBORAH, filmmaker, film and video educator; Attended, U. Ill., 1985—86; BFA, Sch. of the Art Inst. of Chgo., 1986—90; MFA, Calif. Inst. of the Arts, 1992—95. Asst. instr. Cmty. Film Workshop, Chgo., 1988; contact printer Allied Film & Video, Chgo., 1989; tech. programmer, visiting artists; program Sch. Art Inst. Chgo., Chgo., 1989—90; staff audio visual dept. Mich. & Adams, 1990—91; projectionist, The Film Ctr. Art Inst. Chgo., 1990—92; co-op & tech. dir. Chgo. Filmmakers, 1991—92; 35 mm projectionist Cal Arts, Valencia, Calif., 1992—95; dir./prodr. Ind. Film/Video Prodn. Pythagoras Productions, 1995—2002; visiting instr. -live action film/video Calif. Inst. Arts, Valencia, 2002; adj. asst. prof.-dept. film, video & new media Sch. Art Inst., Chgo., 1998—2003; adj. asst. prof.-art & architecture dept. U. Ill., Chgo., 2003—. Prodr.: (films) My Alchemy, 1990, Upon a Time, 1991, A Letter, 1992, Possibilities, Dilemmas, 1992, the train from l.a. to l.a., 1992, In Flight: Day No. 2,128, 1993, Palimpsest, 1993, Waking, 1994, Iolanthe, 1995, On the Various Nature of Things, 1995 (Ann Arbor Film Festival, 1996), From Hetty to Nancy, 1997 (Athens Internat. Film/Video Festival: best experimental, 1998), The BLVD, 1999 (Athens Internat. Film/Video Festival: best documentary, 2000), Untied, 2001, In Order Not to Be Here, 2002 (THAW Film/Video Festival: best of festival, 2002, Chgo. Underground Film Festival: best experimental, 2002, Film Festival: Gecko Award, 2002, Media City Film Festival: hon. mention, 2003, Ann Arbor Film Festival: best experimental & best narrative integrity, 2003), Meet Adiljan, 2003. Bd. dirs. Experimental Film Coalition, 1989—92, Chgo. Filmmakers, 2000—01. John Simon Guggenheim Meml. Found., 2003, prodn./post-prodn. grant, Danish Film Inst. Workshop, 1995—96, Fulbright Grant, Iceland, 1995—96, Baltic-Nordic Fund, Denmark, 1996, finalist stipend, Studio Film & Tape, Roy W. Dean Film Grant, 1998, Chinese Adventure Capital Grant, Durfee Found., 2000, Pub. Art Grant, Gunk Found., 2000, Cmty. Arts Assistance Grants, 1999, 2000, 2001, Wendover Residency, Ctr. Land Use Interpretation, 2001, audio post prodn. residency, Experimental Sound Studio, 2001, Ill. Arts Coun. Spl. Assistance Grant, 1995, 1997, 2002, post prodn. residency, Wexner Ctr. Arts, 1998, 1999, 2001, 2002, Cal Arts Deans Coun. Grant, 2002, Artist's Fellowship-Media Arts, Ill. Arts Coun., 2000, 2002, Guggenheim Fellowship, 2003. Office: U Ill Chgo Sch Art & Design 106 JH MCC 036 929 W Harrison Chicago IL 60607-7038 Office Phone: 312-899-5105. E-mail: dstrat1@uic.edu.

STRATMAN, JOSEPH LEE, oil and gas industry executive, consultant, retired chemical engineer; b. Louisville, Oct. 15, 1924; s. Dominic Herman and Mary Ann (Wolf) S.; m. Elizabeth Jewell Doyle, July 1, 1950; children: Joseph Lee, Mary Elizabeth, Sharon Ann, Judith Ann. BChemE, U. Louisville, 1947. Registered profl. engr., Tex. Chem. engr. Pan Am. Refining Corp., Texas City, Tex., 1947-55, operating supr., 1955-61; mgr. Texas City Refining, Inc., Texas City, Tex., 1961-69, v.p., 1969-80, sr. v.p., 1980-88; pvt. practice, 1988-2001. Bd. dirs., exec. com., treas., chmn. Galveston County ARC, 1966-73; bd. dirs., exec. com., chmn. Texas City Jr. Achievement, 1966-73; treas. Texas City Refining Good Govt. Fund., 1983-88. With USNR, 1945-46. Mem. AIChE. Roman Catholic.

STRATMANN, GAYLE G., lawyer, consumer products company executive; b. Columbia, Mo., Sept. 13, 1956; BS, MEd, U. Mo., 1979; JD cum laude, U. Mo. Sch. of Law, 1987. Bar: Mo. 1987, Ill. 1988. Atty. Greensfelder, Hemker & Gale, St. Louis, Eveready Battery Co., Inc. (div. of Energizer Holdings), 1990—96, asst. gen. counsel, 1996—2002, v.p. legal ops., 2002—03; sr. v.p., gen. counsel Energizer Holdings, 2003—. Author: Church Employment and the First Amendment, 1986; contbr. articles to numerous profl. jours. Mem.: ABA, Mo. Bar Assn., St. Louis Bar Assn. Office: Energizer Holdings 533 Maryville University Dr Saint Louis MO 63141

STRATON, JOHN CHARLES, JR., investment banker; b. Warwick, NY, Apr. 18, 1932; s. John Charles and Helen (Sanford) S.; m. Sally M. Strawhand (div. Mar. 1970); children: John Charles III, Sara; m. Marion S. Holder, Feb. 18, 1974 (div. Mar. 1997); 1 child, Ashley Holder Straton; m. Donna S. DeCoursey, June 24, 1998. BA, U. Va., 1954. With Jas. H. Oliphant and Co., NYC, 1956—, gen. ptnr., 1962—, 1st v.p., 1972-75; v.p. Spencer Trask & Co., Inc., NYC, 1975-77, Hornblower, Weeks, Noyes & Trask, NYC, 1977-78, Loeb Rhoades, Hornblower & Co., 1978-79, Shearson Loeb Rhoades, 1979-81; v.p., fin. cons. Shearson Lehman Bros., NYC, 1981-93; sr. v.p. Smith Barney, NYC, 1993—, Saloman Smith Barney, NYC, 1997—, Smith Barney, NYC, 2004—. Assessor Village of Tuxedo Park, N.Y., 1963-70. Vestryman St. Mary's, Tuxedo, N.Y. Served to maj. AUS, 1954-56; ret. Mem. U. Va. Alumni Assn. N.Y. (pres., treas. 1973-90), Mil. Order Fgn. Wars (comdr. 1981-86, treas. 1986—), Pilgrims of U.S., Am. Legion, Tuxedo Park Club, Sigma Phi Epsilon. Home: 2 Ledge Rd Tuxedo Park NY 10987 Office: 450 Lexington Ave New York NY 10017

STRATT, RICHARD MARK, chemistry researcher, educator; b. Phila., Feb. 21, 1954; s. Stanford Lloyd and Florence Clair (Sussman) S. SB in Chemistry, MIT, 1975; PhD, U. Calif., Berkeley, 1979. Postdoctoral rsch. assoc. U. Ill., Champaign, 1979-80; NSF postdoctoral rsch. assoc., 1980; asst. prof. chemistry Brown U., Providence, 1981-85, assoc. prof., 1986-88, prof., 1988—, dept. chair, 1996—99, Harrison S. Kravis prof., 1999—2000, Newport Rogers prof. chemistry, 2004—, prof. physics, 2006—. Mem. editl. bd. Jour. Chem. Physics, 2002-04, Molecular Physics, 2003—; mem. adv. bd. Jour. Phys. Chemistry, 1999—; contbr. articles to profl. jours. Alfred P. Sloan fellow, 1985-89; Fulbright scholar Oxford U., 1991-92. Fellow Am. Phys. Soc.; mem. Am. Chem. Soc. (chmn.-elect theoretical chem. subdivsn. 1997-98, chair 1998-99, program chair phys. chem. divsn. 2000-01, chair 2001-02), Sigma Xi, Phi Lambda Upsilon. Office: Brown U Dept Chemistry Providence RI 02912-0001 Office Phone: 401-863-3418. Business E-Mail: Richard_Stratt@brown.edu.

STRATTON, EVELYN LUNDBERG, state supreme court justice; b. Bangkok, Feb. 25, 1953; came to US, 1971 (parents Am. citizens); d. Elmer John and Corrine Sylvia (Henricksen) Sahlberg; children: Luke Andrew, Tyler John; m. Jack A. Lundberg. Student, LeTourneau Coll., Longview, Tex., 1971-74; AA, U. Fla., 1973; BA, U. Akron, 1976; JD, Ohio State U., 1978. Bar: Ohio 1979, U.S. Dist. Ct. (so. dist.) Ohio 1979, U.S. Ct. Appeals (6th cir.) 1983. Assoc. Hamilton, Kramer, Myers & Cheek, Columbus, 1979-85; ptnr. Wesp, Osterkamp & Stratton, 1985-88; judge Franklin County Ct. Common Pleas, 1989-96; justice Ohio Supreme Ct., 1996—. Vis. prof. Nat. Jud. Coll., 1997—; spkr. legal seminars. Contbr. articles to profl. jours. Trustee Ohio affiliate Nat. Soc. to Prevent Blindness, 1989—, bd. dirs., trustee Columbus Coun. World Affairs, 1990-99, chmn. bd. dirs., 1999—; bd. dirs., trustee Dave Thomas Adoption Found., 1996—, ArCh-Safe Found., 1997—; mem. women's bd. Zephyrus League Cen. Ohio Lung Assn., 1989—; mem. Alliance Women Cmty. Corrections, 1993—. Recipient Gold Key award LeTourneau Coll., Gainesville, Fla., 1974, Svc. commendation Ohio Ho. of Reps., 1984, Scholar of Life award St. Joseph's Orphanage, 1998. Mem. ABA, ATLA, Columbus Bar Assn. (bd. govs. 1984-88, 90—, lectr.), Ohio Bar Assn. (jud. adminstrv. and legal reform com., coun. dels. 1992-96, Ohio Cmty. Corrections Orgn. (trustee 1995—), Columbus Bar Found. (trustee 1986-91, officer, sec. 1986-87, v.p. 1987-88), Am. Inns of Ct., Women Lawyers Franklin County, Phi Alpha Delta (pres. 1982-83). Office: Ohio Supreme Ct 65 S Front St Columbus OH 43215 *

STRATTON, JOHN ALFRED, electrical engineer, educator; b. Rochester, NY, Sept. 12, 1941; s. Burton Elbridge and Alice Adele (Howie) Stratton; m. Lois Averett; children: Thomas C., Linda S. Palmer, Ann-Marie Giannosa. AAS, Rochester Inst. Technology, 1962, BS, 1964; MSEE, Rensselaer Poly. Inst., Troy, NY, 1966. Profl. engr. Sys. planning engr. NY State Elec. & Gas, Binghamton, 1966—69; asst. prof. Alfred State Coll., NY, 1969—71; from prof. elec. engring. tech. to chair dept., assoc. dean Rochester Inst. Tech., 1971—99, chair mfg. & mech. engring. technology, pckg. sci., 1999—2003, prof. elec./mech. engring., 2003—. Cons. in field. Past pres. Classis of Rochester Reformed Ch. in Am. Mem. IEEE, Inst. Power Engring. Soc., Am. Soc. Engring. Edn. (chair zone 1). Avocation: riding trains. Home: 43 Queensway Rd Rochester NY 14623-

4627 Office: Rochester Inst Technology 78 Lomb Memorial Dr Rochester NY 14623-5604 Home Phone: 585-334-7315; Office Phone: 716-475-2017. Business E-Mail: jasite@rit.edu.

STRATTON, JOHN G., telecommunications industry executive; V.p. merchandising Jersey Camera; dir. retail sales & ops., v.p. mktg., pres. Phila. region Bell Atlantic Mobile, 1993—2000; pres. NW area Verizon Wireless, 2000—01, v.p., chief mktg. officer, 2001—07; exec. v.p., chief mktg. officer Verizon Communications, NYC, 2007—. Office: Verizon Comm 1095 Ave of the Americas New York NY 10036 *

STRATTON, MARGARET ANNE, minister; b. Concordia, Kans., Oct. 10, 1948; d. Charles Edward and Marie Teresa Kier; m. Mick Stratton, June 9, 1973; children: James, Grace. BS Home Econs., Kans. State U., 1973; M Theology, Caribbean Comty. Ministerial Acad., Orlando, Fla., 1994; MDiv, So. Meth. U., 2000. Ordained elder United Meth. Ch., 2003. Pastor United Meth. Diamond Hill Parish and Mission, Ft. Worth, 2000—06, Robinson Dr. United Meth. Ch., Waco, Tex., 2006—. Chmn. Task Force on Hunger, Ctrl. Tex. Conf.; mem. Hispanic com.; mem. Confessing Movement United Meth. Ch.; clergy leadership initiative Tex. Meth. Found.; bd. dirs. Johnson Hill Children's Program, Eutaw, Ala., 1993—95. Recipient grants in field. Mem.: Christian Friendds of Israel Am., Confession Movement, Battalion of Deborah, Lifewatch, Nat. Assn. United Meth. Evangelists. Avocation: wood sculpting and carving. Office: 2801 Robinson Dr Waco TX 76706 Home: 5001 Stadium Dr Fort Worth TX 76133 Home Phone: 817-923-8777; Office Phone: 254-662-3155. Business E-Mail: margaretstratton@sbcglobal.net.

STRATTON, MARIANN, retired military nursing executive; b. Houston, Apr. 6, 1945; d. Max Millard and Beatrice Agnes (Roemer) S.; m. Lawrence Mallory Stickney, nov. 15, 1977 (dec.). BSN, BA in English, Sacred Heart Dominican Coll., 1966; MA in Mgmt., Webster Coll., 1977; MSN, U. Va., 1981. Cert. adult nurse practitioner. Ensign USN, 1966, advanced through grades to rear adm., 1991; patient care coord. Naval Regional Med. Ctr., Charleston, SC, 1981-83; nurse corps plans officer Naval Med. Command, Washington, 1983-86; dir. nursing svcs. U.S. Naval Hosp., Naples, Italy, 1986-89, Naval Hosp., San Diego, 1989-91; chief pers. mgmt. Bur. Medicine & Surgery, Washington, 1991-94; dir. USN Nurse Corps, Washington, 1991-94; ret. USN, 1994. Decorated Disting. Svc. medal, Meritorious Svc. medal with two stars, Naval Achievement medal, Navy Commendation medal. Mem. Interagy. Inst. Fed. Health Care Execs., Am. Volksporting Assn., Tex. Wanders, D'Vine Women, Garden Vols. of South Tex., U. Va. Raven Soc., Fiber Artists San Antonio.

STRATTON, ROBERT, retired electronics executive; b. Vienna, Aug. 14, 1928; came to U.S., 1959, naturalized, 1966; s. Kenneth Kurt and Eugenie (Schwatzer) S.; m. Elfriede Karlberger, Jan. 11, 1980; children: David Alexander, Valerie Pam. B.Sc. in Physics, Manchester U., 1949, PhD in Theoretical Physics, 1952. Rsch. physicist Met. Vickers Elec. Co., Manchester, Eng., 1952-59; with Tex. Instruments, Inc., Dallas, 1959-94, dir. physics rsch. lab., 1963-71, assoc. dir. cen. rsch. labs., 1971-72, dir. semiconductor R & D, 1972-75, dir. cen. rsch. labs., 1975-77, asst. v.p., dir. cen. rsch. labs., 1977-82, v.p. corp. staff, dir. cen. rsch. labs., 1982-94; dir. Indsl. Outreach Elec. Materials Sci. Tech. Ctr., dir. Engring. and Tech. Inst., U. Tex., Austin, 1994-96. Contbr. articles to profl. jours. Bd. dirs. Indsl. Rsch. Inst., 1985-88, Coun. on Superconductivity for Am. Competitiveness, 1987-90; adv. bd. dirs. Tex. Ctr. for Superconductivity, 1989-2000. Fellow IEEE, Inst. Physics (U.K.), Am. Phys. Soc.; mem. NAE. Personal E-mail: rstratton@tx.rr.com.

STRATTON, WALTER LOVE, lawyer; b. Greenwich, Conn., Sept. 21, 1926; s. John McKee and June (Love) Stratton; m. DeAnna Weinheimer, Oct. 1, 1994; children from previous marriage: John, Michael, Peter(dec.), Lucinda. Student, Williams Coll., 1943; AB, Yale U., 1948; LLB, Harvard U., 1951. Bar: N.Y. 1952. Assoc. Casey, Lane & Mittendorf, NYC, 1951-53, Donovan, Leisure, Newton & Irvine, NYC, 1956-63, ptnr., 1963-84, Gibson, Dunn & Crutcher, 1984-93, Andrews Kurth, NYC, 1993-95; of counsel Andrews Kurth, NYC, 1996—2006. Asst. U.S. atty. U.S. Dist. Ct. (so. dist.) N.Y., NYC, 1953—56; lectr. Practising Law Inst. With USNR, 1945—46. Fellow: Am. Coll. Trial Lawyers; mem.: ABA, N.Y. State Bar Assn., Fed. Bar Coun., Greenwich Riding and Trails Assn., Colo. Arlberg Club, Indian Harbor Yacht Club. Office Phone: 203-869-8294. Personal E-mail: wstratton@msn.com.

STRATTON-CROOKE, THOMAS EDWARD, financial consultant; b. NYC, June 28, 1933; s. Harold and Jeanne (Stifft); children: Karen, John Ryland; m. Suzanne Williams, Oct. 21, 1989 Student, Hunter Coll., 1951-52; BS in Marine Engring. and Transp., U.S. Maritime Acad., 1952-56; student, Washington U., St. Louis, 1961; MBA in Internat. Mktg., Banking and Fin., NYU, 1967. Commd. ensign USN, 1956, advanced through grades to lt., 1957; with Goodyear Internat. Corp., Akron, Ohio, 1960-63, Esso Internat., NYC, 1963—67; dir. market info. and devel. Hotel Corp. Am., Boston, 1967—71; with Continental Grain Co., NYC, 1971—75; dir. charter contracts Conoco, Stamford, Conn., 1975—77; cons. A. T. Kearney, Cleve., 1977—79; investment banker E. F. Hutton, Cleve., 1979—82, AG Edwards and Sons, Inc., Cleve., 1982—89; sr. fin. advisor, registered investment advisor, asst. v.p., sr. fin. cons. Merrill Lynch, Cleve., 1989—. Chmn. Indsl. Devel. Resch. Coun., Atlanta, 1970, Indsl. Devel. Resch. Coun., Snow Mass, Colo., 1971; lectr. bus. U. R.I., Kingston, 1968-70, tchr. Bus. Coll. Internat., 1986-89 Contbr. articles to profl. jours. Mem. Findley Lake (N.Y.) Hist. Soc.; mem. Nat. Task Force Reps. for Pres. Reagan, Cleve., 1982— Officer (ret.) USN. Mem. Naval Res. Officers Assn., Naval Res. Assn., Great Lakes Hist. Soc., Soc. Naval Architects/Engrs., Findley Lake N.Y. Area C. of C., Navy League, Civil War Roundtable, NYU Alumni Assn., U.S. Coast Guard Club (Cleve.), Univ. Club, Circumnavigators Club (life), Internat. Shipmasters Assn., Propeller Club, Army Club, Navy Club, French Creek Hist. Soc., Town Club (Jamestown, N.Y.), Masons (32d degree), Naval Masonic Lodge, Shriners, Cleve. City Club, Kings Point Alumni Assn., Civil War Round Table, U.S. Mcht. Marine Acad., English Speaking Union (chpt. bd. dirs.), York & Scottish Rites Avocations: sailing, skiing, birdwatching, gardening, sports car and motorcycle enthusiast. Office: Merrill Lynch One Cleveland Ctr 1375 E 9th St Cleveland OH 44114-1798 Office Phone: 216-363-6717, 877-375-6717. Office Fax: 216-539-0941. Personal E-mail: tommyes@aol.com. Business E-Mail: thomas_stratton-crooke@ml.com.

STRAUB, CHESTER JOHN, federal judge; b. Bklyn., May 12, 1937; s. Chester and Ann (Majewski) Straub; m. Patricia Morrissey; children: Chester, Michael, Christopher, Robert. AB, St. Peter's Coll., 1958; JD, U. Va., 1961. Bar: N.Y. 1962, U.S. Dist. Ct. (so. and ea. dists.) N.Y. 1963, U.S. Ct. Appeals (2d cir.) 1967, U.S. Supreme Ct. 1978. Assoc. Willkie Farr & Gallagher, NYC, 1963—71, ptnr., 1971—98; mem. N.Y. State Assembly, 1967—72, N.Y. State Senate, 1973—75, Dem. Nat. Com., 1976—80; judge U.S. Ct. Appeals (2d cir.), 1998—. Past mediator U.S. Dist. Ct. (so. dist.) N.Y.; neutral evaluator U.S. Dist. Ct. (ea. dist.) N.Y.; chmn. jud. screening com. State of N.Y., 1988—94, first dept. jud. screening com., 1983—94, Senator Moynihan's jud. selection com., 1976—98. With US Army, 1961—63. Mem.: ABA, Assn. of Bar of City of N.Y.C., N.Y. State Bar Assn. Office: US Ct Appeals 2530 US Courthouse 500 Pearl St New York NY 10007 *

STRAUB, GREGORY S., priest; b. Irvington, NJ; Degree, Dickinson Coll., 1970; MDiv, Phila. Div. Sch., 1973; DMin, Drew U., 1990. Ordained deacon, 1973, priest, 1974; deacon intern St. Thomas Ch., Lancaster, Pa., priest asst. to rector, interim rector; rector Emmanuel Ch., Chestertown, Md., 1976—2005; exec. officer Gen. Conv., NYC, 2005—. Dep. Gen. Conv. triennial meeting, 1985, 97, 2000, 03, asst. sec. for voting, 03. Mem.: Nat. Episcopal Historians and Archivists Orgn., Episcopal Ch. Hist. Soc. Episcopalian. Office: DFMS Gen Conv Office 815 2nd Ave 4th Fl New York NY 10017

STRAUB, PETER FRANCIS, novelist; b. Milw., Mar. 2, 1943; s. Gordon Anthony and Elvena (Nilsestuen) S.; m. Susan Bitker, Aug. 27, 1966; children: Benjamin Bitker, Emma Sydney Valli. BA, U. Wis., 1965; MA, Columbia U., NYC, 1966. English tchr. Univ. Sch., Milw., 1966-68. Bd. dirs. U. Wis. Author: Marriages, 1973, Julia, 1975, If You Could See Me Now, 1977, Ghost Story, 1979, Shadowland, 1980, Floating Dragon, 1983, Leeson Park and Belsize Square, 1984, Wild Animals, 1984, Blue Rose, 1985, Koko, 1988, Mystery, 1989, Houses Without Doors, 1990, Mrs. God, 1991, The Throat, 1993, The Hellfire Club, 1996, Mr. X, 1999, Pork Pie Hat, 1999, Magic Terror, 2000, Lost Boy Lost Girl, 2003, In the Night Room, 2004, Sides, 2007, 5 Stories, 2007; (with Stephen King) The Talisman, 1984, Black House, 2001; editor: Peter Straub's Ghosts, 1995, Conjunctions #39, 2002, Library of America H.P. Lovecraft Tales, 2005. Bd. dir. Fence, Conjunctions, Am. Poetry Rev., Poets & Writers. Recipient Brit. Fantasy award, August Derleth award, 1983, World Fantasy awards World Fantasy Conv., 1989, 93, World Horror Assn. awards, 1993, 98, 99, 2000, 03, 04, Grand Master award World Horror Conv., 1997, award Internat. Horror Guild, 1999, 2003; sponsor Peter Straub Disting. Lectureship on Popular Culture, U. Wis. Mem. PEN, Horror Writers Assn. (life; Achievement award, 2006), Century Assn. Avocations: jazz, opera, classical music. Personal E-mail: pstraub@nyc.rr.com.

STRAUB, PETER THORNTON, lawyer; b. St. Louis, Mar. 27, 1939; s. Ralph H. and Mary Louise (Thornton) S.; m. Wendy B. Cubbage, Dec. 29, 1964; children: Karl Thornton, Philip Hamilton, Ellen Elizabeth. AB, Washington and Lee U., 1961, LLB, 1964. Bar: Mo. 1964, Va. 1964, US Dist. Ct. (ea. dist.) Mo. 1967, US Circuit Ct. Appeals (8th cir.) 1969, US Supreme Ct. 1970. US Circuit Ct. Appeals (DC cir.) 1971, Ct. Mil. Appeals 1970, US Tax Ct. 1971, US Bankruptcy Ct. 1991. Assoc. Evans & Dixon, St. Louis, 1966-68; asst. pub. defender St. Louis County, St. Louis, 1968-69; asst. US Atty. St. Louis, 1969-71; trial atty. internal security div. Dept. Justice, Washington, 1971-72, atty.-adviser office of dep. atty. gen., 1972-73, dir. office criminal justice, spl. asst. to atty. gen., 1974; minority counsel com. on judiciary US Ho. of Reps., Washington, 1973-74; gen. counsel SSS, Washington, 1974-76; pvt. practice Law Offices of Peter T. Straub, Alexandria, Va., 1976—. Pres., gov. bd. Alexandria Cmty. Mental Health Ctr., 1982—95; mem. No. Va. Estate Planning Coun., 1981—; pres.'s coun. Trinity Coll., Washington, 1980—87; adv. bd. Am. Heart Assn., Alexandria, 1991—92, Salvation Army, Alexandria, 1991—, v.p., 1994—96, chmn., 1997—99, Alexandria Cmty. Shelter Adv. Bd., 1995—97; Va. escheat atty. City of Alexandria, 1994—2002; dist. chmn. Boy Scouts Am., 1998—2001, risk mgmt. com. Nat. Capital Area coun., 2006—; adv. bd. Hospice No. Va., 2000—; mem. Econ. Opportunity Commn. City of Alexandria, 2006—; bd. dirs. Friends of the Washington and Old Dominion Trail, 2002—, Parc East Condominium, 1990—, sec., 1992—2006; bd. dirs. Sigma Nu Ednl. Found., Inc., 2000—; charter mem. bd. dirs. Alexandria Country Day Sch., 1983—90. With US Army, 1964—66, capt. USAR, 1966—72. Recipient certificate of award Dept. Justice, 1970, certificate of appreciation Law Enforcement Assistance Adminstrn. Dept. Justice, 1974, Silver Beaver award Boy Scouts Am., Washington, 1987, Collins award Alexandria Coun. Persons with Disabilities, 1993, Cmty. Svc. award Am. Indian Alliance, 1995. Mem.: FBA, ABA, Nat. Acad. Elder Law Attys., Va. Trial Lawyers Assn., Alexandria Bar Assn., Mo. Bar Assn., Bar Assn. Met. St. Louis, Va. State Bar Assn., Optimists (bd. dirs., pres. Alexandria chpt. 1984, lt. gov. Nat. Capitol Va. Dist. 1987—89, treas. 1999—2001), Nat. Eagle Scout Assn., Sigma Nu. Republican. Congregationalist. Avocations: scouting, reading, bicycling. Office: 1225 Martha Custis Dr # 103 Alexandria VA 22302-2040 Office Phone: 703-820-3600. Office Fax: 703-820-8602. Business E-Mail: pstraub@straublawoffices.com.

STRAUB, TERRENCE D., metal products executive; BBA, Ind. U., Bloomington; M in Internat. Pub. Policy, Johns Hopkins Sch. Advanced Internat. Study. Spl. asst. congl. affairs to Pres. Jimmy Carter White House, Washington, 1977—81; mgr. govtl. affairs US Steel, Washington, 1981, dir. govtl. affairs, gen. mgr. govtl. affairs Steel & Diversified Businesses, gen. mgr. govtl. affairs Energy, v.p. govtl. affairs USX Corp., 1991, mem. corp. policy com., 1996, sr. v.p. pub. policy & govtl. affairs, 2003—, mem. corp. mgmt. com., 2004. Mem. Industry Sector Adv. Com.; chmn. Coun. US Prodrs. Am. Iron and Steel Inst.; chmn. oper. com. Steel Alliance; lectr. Am. U., George Washington U., Conn. Coll., Harvard U. Inst. Politics at Kennedy Sch. Govt. Mem. adv. com. Export-Import Bank; vice chmn. Ctr. Nat. Policy; mem. adv. bd. Manna Inc., Washington; mem. Fed. City Coun., Washington Econ. Club. Office: US Steel 600 Grant St Pittsburgh PA 15219-2800 Office Phone: 412-433-1121. *

STRAUCH, BERISH, plastic surgeon, hand and cosmetic surgeon; b. NYC, Sept. 19, 1933; m. Rena (Feuerstein), June 12, 1955; children: Robert, Laurie. BS, Columbia U., 1955, MD, 1959. Diplomate Am. Bd. Surgery, Am. Bd. Plastic Surgery, qualification in hand surgery. Intern Bellevue Hosp., NYC, 1959—60; resident gen. surgery Montefiore Med. Ctr., Bronx, NY, 1960—63; hand surgery fellow Roosvelt Hosp., NYC, 1961; resident plastic surgery Stanford U., Palo Alto, Calif., 1966—67, chief resident, 1967—68; asst. prof. plastic surgery Albert Einstein Coll. Medicine, Bronx, NY, 1970—76, assoc. prof., 1976—81; chief plastic surgery svc. Montefiore Med. Ctr. and Albert Einstein Coll. Medicine, Bronx, NY, 1978—87; prof. plastic surgery Albert Einstein Coll. Medicine and Montefiore Med. Ctr., Bronx, NY, 1981—; acting chmn. dept. Montefiore Med. Ctr. and Albert Einstein Coll. Medicine, Bronx, NY, 1987—89, chmn., 1989—. Instr. Stanford U., 1967-68; vis. plastic surgeon Sing Sing Prison, N.Y., 1968-75. Co-author: (with others) Atlas of Microvascular Surgery: Anatomy and Operative Approaches, 1993 (Best Healt Sci. Book, Doody's Rating Svc. 1993); co-editor: Textbook on Microsurgery, 1976, (with others) Grabb's Encyclopedia of Flaps, 3 vols., 1990, (Outstanding Publ. in Clin. Medicine, Assn. Am. Pub. 1990), 2d edit. 1997; contbr. articles to profl. journals. and 20 chpts. to sci. books; assoc. editor Plastic and Reconstructive Surgery, 1982-88; founder, editor-in-chief Jour. Reconstructive Microsurgery, 1984—. Capt. Med. Corp. U.S. Army, 1964-66, Mem. AAAS, ACS, Am. Soc. for Reconstructive Microsurgery (founder, past sec., treas., pres., chmn. Founder's Lectr. 1988), Am. Assn. Plastic Surgeons, Internat. Soc. Reconstructive Microsurgery (chmn. founding coun. 1983-84, pres. 1984-85). Med. Soc. State of N.Y., Am. Trauma Soc. (founding mem.), N.Y. Acad. Sci., Am. Soc. for Peripheral Nerve Surgery (pres. 1993-94), and others. Office: Montefiore Med Pk 1625 Poplar St Ste 200 Bronx NY 10461-2653 Business E-Mail: bstrauch@montefiore.org.

STRAUCH, EDWARD HUGO, writer, retired literature and language professor; b. Chgo., June 18, 1925; s. Moritz Franz and Ida (Pfeffer) Strauch; m. Patricia A. D'Andrea (div.); 1 child, Jason Edward; m. Arlene M. Russie, 1954 (div. 1959); children: Julia, Lydia. Diplôme Supérieur, Sorbonne U., Paris, 1950; BA in English and French, Calif. State U., LA, 1958, MA in English and Edn., 1961; PhD in Comparative Lit., Ind. U., Bloomington, 1969. Cert. instr. Calif. Dir. humanities program Nasson Coll., Caen, France, 1966—70; assoc. prof. English U. Guam, Mangilao, 1971—75; vis. prof. English Pahlavi U., Shiraz, Iran, 1975—76; writer multimedia English Free U., Teheran, 1976—77; prof. English Mohammed V U., Rabat, Morocco, 1977—78; head English dept. U. Maiduguri, Nigeria, 1979—86; assoc. prof. English U. Guam, Mangilao, 1987—95; ret., 1995. Author: How Nature Taught Man to Know, Imagine and Reason, 1995, Beyond Literary Theory: Literature as a Search for the Meaning of Human Destiny, 2001, The Creative Conscience as Human Destiny, 2004; contbr. articles to profl. jours. Ensign USN, 1943—46. Mem.: MLA. Avocations: art, writing, music. Home: U Guam PO Box 5256 Mangilao GU 96923

STRAUCH, JOHN L., lawyer; b. Pitts., Apr. 16, 1939; s. Paul L. and Delilah M. (Madison) S.; m. Gail Lorraine Kohn, Dec. 5, 1991; children: Paul L., John M., Lisa E. BA summa cum laude, U. Pitts., 1960; JD magna cum laude, NYU Sch. Law, 1963. Law clk. to Judge Sterry Waterman US Ct. Appeals (2d cir.), St. Johnsbury, Vt., 1963-64; assoc. Jones, Day, Reavis & Pogue, Cleve., 1964-70, ptnr., litig. group, 1970—, chair, litig. group, 1993—2004. Mem. Statutory Com. on Selecting Bankruptcy Judges, Cleve., 1985-88; mem. lawyers com. Nat. Ctr. for State Cts. Editor-in-chief: NYU Law Rev., 1962-63; contbr. chpt. to book. Pres., trustee Cleve. Task Force on Violent Crimes, 1985-88; trustee Legal Aid Soc., Cleve., 1978, Cleve. Greater Growth Assn., 1985-86, Citizens Mental Health Assembly, 1989-90, lawyers com. Nat. Ctr. for State Cts., 1989—. Fellow Am. Coll. Trial Lawyers (life); mem. ABA, Ohio Bar Assn., Cleve. Bar Assn. (trustee 1980-83, pres. 1985-86), Fed. Bar Assn. (trustee Cleve. chpt. 1978-79, v.p. Cleve. chpt. 1979-80), Sixth Fed. Jud. Conf. (life), Ohio Eighth Jud. Conf. (life), Order of Coif, Inns of Ct., Oakmont Country Club, The Country Club, Kiawah Island Club, Phi Beta Kappa. Office: Jones Day North Point 901 Lakeside Ave Cleveland OH 44114-1190

STRAUCH, KATINA PARTHEMOS, college librarian, publishing executive; m. Bruce Strauch; children: Raymond, Ileana. MLS, U. NC-Chapel Hill. Head libr., collection dept. Coll. Charleston (SC) Librs.; founder & dir. Charleston Conf., 1980—; founder & editor Against the Grain, 1989—. Chair bd. Charleston Report, 1996—, Charleston Advisor, 1999—; bd. dirs. Inst. Mus. & Libr. Svc., 2004—. Author: Legal & Ethical Issues in Acquisitions, 1990. Recipient Disting. Alumnus award, U. NC-Chapel Hill Sch. Libr. & Info. Sci., 1992, SC Outstanding Libr. award, 1996. Mem.: ALA, Reference & User Svcs. Assn. (Louis Shores-Greenwood Pub. Group award 2007), Assn. Libr. Collections & Technical Svcs. (Leadership in Libr. Acquisitions award 1997). Office: Coll Charleston Librs 66 George St Charleston SC 29424 also: Charleston Info Group LLC MSC 98 The Citadel Charleston SC 29409 Office Phone: 843-953-5530. Office Fax: 843-953-8019. E-mail: strauchk@cofc.edu, kstrauch@comcast.net.

STRAUCHEN, JAMES ARTHUR, medical educator, pathologist; b. NYC, July 11, 1948; s. Murray and Helen Strauchen; m. Vivienne Sari Gold, May 27, 1972; children: Jennifer Mia, Katherine Sinead. BA magna cum laude, Columbia Coll., NYC, 1968; MD with honors, NY U., NYC, 1972. Diplomate Am. Bd. Pathology, 1978, cert. hematology Am. Bd. Pathology, 1981, diplomate Am. Bd. Internal Medicine, 1975, cert. med. oncology Am. Bd. Internal Medicine, 1977, hematology Am. Bd. Internal Medicine, 1978. Asst. prof. pathology Stanford U., Sch. Medicine, Palo Alto, Calif., 1978—81; assoc. prof. pathology U. Rochester, Sch. Medicine, NY, 1982—83; prof. pathology and neoplastic diseases Mt. Sinai Sch. Medicine, NYC, 1983—, vice chair dept. pathology, 2005—. Pres. NY Cancer Soc., NYC, 2006—07. Lt. comdr. USPHS, 1974—78. Mem.: Soc. for Study of Blood, NY Path. Soc., Arkadi M. Rywlin Pathology Club, Assn. Dirs. Anatomic and Surg. Pathology, Am. Soc. Hematology (assoc.), Phi Beta Kappa, Alpha Omega Alpha (pres. 1971—72). Office: Mt Sinai Sch Medicine 1 Gustave Levy Pl New York NY 10029 Office Phone: 212-241-9142. Office Fax: 212-289-2899. Business E-Mail: james.strauchen@mssm.edu.

STRAUGHAN, WILLIAM THOMAS, structural engineering consultant, educator; b. Shreveport, La., Aug. 2, 1936; s. William Eugene and Sara Chloetilde (Harrell) S.; m. Rubie Ann Barnes, Aug. 20, 1957; children: Donna Ann, Sara Arlene, Eugene Thomas. BS, MIT, 1959; MS, U. Tex., 1986; PhD, Tex. Tech. U., 1990. Registered profl. engr., Fla., Ill., Iowa., La., Tex., Wash. Project engr. Gen. Dynamics Corp., Chgo., 1959—60; chief project, design engr. Gen. Foods Corp., Kankakee, Ill., 1960—64; mgr. plant engring. Std. Brands Inc., Clinton, Iowa, 1964—66; regional mgr. Air Products & Chems., Inc., Creighton, Pa., 1966—68; gen. mgr. Skyline Corp., Harrisburg, NC, 1968—70; cons. Charlotte, NC, 1970—72; dir. engring. and Fla. ops. Zimmer Homes Corp., Pompano Beach, 1972—73; v.p. engring. and mfg. Nobility Homes, Inc., Ocala, Fla., 1973—78, Moduline Internat., Inc., Lacey, Wash., 1978—85; rsch. engr. U. Tex., Austin, 1985—86; lectr., rschr. Tex. Tech. U., Lubbock, 1987—90; assoc. prof. U. New Orleans, 1990—92; asst. prof. dept. civil engring. La. Tech. U., Ruston, 1992—98. Tchr. 30 different courses, 1987—; adj. prof. Coll. Engring., La. Tech. U., 2001-05, vis. prof., 2005-; cons. in field, Dubach, La., 1992—; condr. workshops in field; apptd. spokesman Mfrd. Housing Industry before U.S. Congress. Contbr. articles to numerous profl. jours. Vol. engring. svcs. Lubbock Fire Safety House, 1990; judge sci. fair Ben Franklin H.S., New Orleans, 1990. Recipient T.L. James Svc. award La. Tech. U., 1994; grantee Urban Waste Mgmt. and Rsch. Ctr., New Orleans, 1991, Shell Devel. Co., 1993, La. Edn. Quality Support Fund, Insituform Techs., Inc., Trenchless Tech. Ctr., PABCO, Inc., InLiner USA, Inc., 1995, others; numerous grants in field. Mem. ASME (life), ASCE (Student chpt. Tchr. of Yr. award 1995, 98), Nat. Coun. Structural Engrs. Assns., Structural Engrs. Assn. La., Phi Kappa Phi, Sigma Xi, Chi Epsilon. Avocations: flying, skiing, motorcycling, camping, reading. Home: 199 Sellers Rd Dubach LA 71235-3218 Personal E-mail: drtomstraughan@msn.com.

STRAUS, DAVID A., architectural firm executive; b. Medford, Oreg., 1943; m. Sherry Straus; 2 children. BArch, U. Oreg., 1967. Registered architect, Oreg. Founding ptnr. Skelton, Straus & Seibert, Medford, 1989—. Mem Oreg Transp Comn, Rogue Valley Area Comn Transp. Past pres Medford Arts Comn, Arts Coun Southern Oreg; coach Rogue Valley Soccer Asn; leader Boy Scouts Am; bd dirs, past pres Schneider Mus Art SOSC; bd dirs Medford YMCA, Rogue Valley Art Asn. Lt USNR, Vietnam. Mem.: AIA (pres. so. Oreg. chpt.), Archit Found Oreg (past bd. dirs.), Medford/Jackson County CofC (past bd. dirs., Mem of the Yr 2000), Univ Oreg Alumni Asn, Oreg Club Southern Oreg (past pres.), Univ Club Medford (past pres.), Rotary. Office: Skelton Straus & Seibert Arch 26 Hawthorne St Medford OR 97504-7114 Office Phone: 541-779-4363. Business E-Mail: dstraus@sssarchitects.com.

STRAUS, KATHLEEN NAGLER, academic administrator, educator; b. NYC, Dec. 3, 1923; d. Maurice and Mildred (Kohn) Nagler; m. Everet M. Straus, May 29, 1948 (dec. Nov. 1967); children: Peter R., Barbara L. BA in Econs., Hunter Coll., 1944; postgrad., Columbia U., 1944—45, Am. U., 1946—47, Wayne State U., 1976—78. Various positions, 1944—50, 1966; dep. dir. Model Neighborhood Agy., City of Detroit, 1968—70; dir. social svcs. Southeastern Mich. Coun. Govts., Detroit, 1970—74; staff coord. Edn. Task Force, Detroit, 1974—75; exec. dir. People and Responsible Orgns. for Detroit, 1975—76; staff dir. edn. com. Mich. Senate, Lansing, 1976—79; assoc. exec. dir. Mich. Assn. Sch. Bds., Lansing, 1979—86; dir. cmty. rels. and devel. Ctr. for Creative Studies, Detroit, 1986—87, pres., 1987—91; mem. Mich. Bd. Edn., 1992—, pres., 2003. Mem. Mich. Bd. for Pub. Jr. and C.C.s, Lansing, 1980-92, v.p., 1989, pres., 1991; cons. Met. Columbus (Ohio) Schs. Com., 1975-76; mem. steering com. Mich. Edn. Seminars, 1979-86; mem. Adv. Com. on Higher Edn. Needs in S.W. Mich., 1971-72, Ad Hoc Com. on Equal Access to Higher Edn., 1970-71, Citizens Action Com. on Sch. Fin. Contbr. articles to profl. jours. Active numerous civic orgns.; vice chmn. downtown br. Met. Detroit YWCA, 1970-74; bd. dirs. Citizens for Better Care, Inc., 1973-78; mem. edn. com. New Detroit, Inc., 1972—; trustee Detroit Sci. Ctr., Inc., 1975—; founder, pres. Mich. Tax Info. Coun., 1982—; v.p. bd. dirs. Univ. Cultural Ctr. Assn., 1986-91;

trustee Comprehensive Health Planning Coun. Southeastern Mich., 1977-78; mem. Wayne County Art and History Commn., 1988; co-chmn. Nat. Arts Program, 1987-88; bd. dirs. North Ctrl. Regional Edn. Libr.; bd. dirs. North Ctrl. Regional Edn. Lab.; bd. mem. Midwest Regional Edn. Lab. Recipient Amity citation, Detroit, 1966, Disting. Cmty. Svc. award Am. Jewish Com., 1988, Common Coun., Detroit, 1976, resolution Mich. Ho. of Reps., 1986, Mich. Senate, 1988, Educator of Yr. Wayne State U., 1999, Disting. Warrior award Detroit Urban League, 2000; named to Mich. Edn. Hall of Fame, 1997; inducted into Mich. Women's Hall of Fame, 2000, Lifetime Achievement award Anti Defamation League, 2004, Multi Cultural Edn. award Nat. Conf. Cmty. and Justice, 2004, Lifetime Achievement award Communities in Schs. Mem.: LWV (pres. Detroit 1961—63), Alpha Chi Alpha. Democrat. Avocations: travel, theater, concerts. Home: 7431 Deep Run 210 Bloomfield Hills MI 48301 Office: State Bd Edn PO Box 30008 Lansing MI 48909-7508 Office Phone: 517-373-3900. Business E-Mail: strausk@michigan.gov.

STRAUS, LEON STEPHAN, physicist; b. Takoma Park, Md., May 29, 1943; s. Sidney and Ruth Straus; m. Cheryl Sarran Straus, Apr. 4, 1970; children: Jonathan, Jennifer. BS in Physics, Antioch Coll., Yellow Springs, Ohio, 1965; M Physics, Georgetown U., 1970, PhD in Physics, 1971. Mem. rsch. staff Ctr. Naval Analyses, Alexandria, Va., 1973-75, field rep. CTF 69 Naples, Italy, 1975-77, project mgr. Alexandria, 1977-79, field rep. CTF 69 and CTF 66/67 Naples, Italy, 1979-82, assoc. dep. dir. Alexandria, 1982-85, field rep. CTF 72 Kamiseya, Japan, 1985-87, program mgr. Alexandria, 1987-90, field rep. COMSIXTHFLT Gaeta, Italy, 1990-92, project mgr. Alexandria, 1992-95, tech. dir. spl. projects, 1995-97, dep. dir. info. ops. warfare team, 1997-2000; pvt. contractor, 2001—. Asst. AEC, Germantown, Md., 1968-71. Contbr. articles to profl. jours. Vol. Jewish lay leader USN, Naples, 1975-77, 79-82. Recipient Fellowship Georgetown U., Washington, 1965-68. Mem. Acoustical Soc. Am., Navy Submarine League. Jewish. Achievements include planning, evaluating and documenting tests/exercises and conducting studies associated with U.S. Navy and joint strategy, tactics, force planning, communication and technology. Office Phone: 954-298-2513. Personal E-mail: strausconsult@aol.com.

STRAUS, MARC JOSHUA, internist, poet; b. NYC, 1943; married; 2 children. AB, Franklin and Marshall Coll., 1964; MD, SUNY, Bklyn., 1968. Straight med. intern Kings County Hosp., Bklyn., 1968-69; staff assoc. Nat. Cancer Inst., NIH, Bethesda, Md., 1969-71; sr. cancer rsch. internist, head Cell Kinetics Lab. Barnes Hosp., St. Louis, 1972—74, resident in medicine, 1971-72, fellow in hematology, 1974; chief sect. med. oncology Univ. Hosp., Boston, 1974-78; assoc. prof. medicine Boston U. Sch. Medicine, 1974-78; prof. medicine NY Med. Coll., Valhalla, 1978—, chief divsn. neoplastic diseases, 1978-82; pvt. practice, White Plains, NY, 1982—. Rsch. pathologist Mallory Inst. Pathology, Boston, 1974-78; chief oncology Westchester County Med. Ctr., 1978-82; staff physician St. Agnes Hosp., White Plains, St. Joseph's Hosp., Yonkers, Hudson Valley Hosp., Peekskill, NY, Putnam Hosp., Carmel, NY; co-founder (with Livia Straus) Hudson Valley Center for Contemporary Art, Peekskill, NY, 2002-. Recipient Robert Penn Warren award lectr. Yale U. Med. Sch., 1998; Yaddo fellow in poetry, 1993. Fellow ACP, Am. Coll. Physician Execs.; mem. Am. Assn. for Cancer Rsch., Am. Soc. Clin. Oncology. Office: 707 Westchester Ave Ste 110 White Plains NY 10604-3155 also: Hudson Valley Ctr for Contemporary Art 1701 Main St PO Box 209 Peekskill NY 10566 Office Phone: 914-788-7166. Business E-Mail: mstraus@mdx-med.com, info@hvcca.com.

STRAUS, OSCAR S., II, foundation executive; b. NYC, Nov. 6, 1914; s. Roger Williams and Gladys (Guggenheim) S.; m. Marion Miller Straus, 1941 (div. 1982); 1 child, Oscar S. III.; m. Joan Sutton, 1982. AB, Princeton U., 1936; postgrad., U. Dijon, summer 1936, Sch. Bus. Adminstrn. Harvard U., 1938. Pvt. sec. Internat. Labor Office, Geneva, 1937-38; U.S. fgn. svc. officer, 1940-42; divisional asst. Dept. State, 1942-43, 44-45; treas., dir., v.p., chmn. fin. com. Am. Smelting & Refining Co., 1945-59; ptnr. Guggenheim Bros., 1959-83; pres., dir. Guggenheim Exploration Co., Inc., 1963-73; gen. ptnr. Straus Minerals, 1973-88; chmn., bd. dirs. Daniel and Florence Guggenheim Found., NYC. Chmn., bd. dirs. Fred L. Lavanburg Found. Trustee emeritus Am. Mus. Natural History, Mystic Seaport, Conn.; hon. chmn. Rensselaerville (N.Y.) Inst.; trustee Congregation Emanu-El. Mem.: Coun. Fgn. Rels., Knickerbocker Club, Doubles Club, Megantic Fish and Game Club, Cruising Club Am. Jewish. Home: 40 S Howells Point Rd Bellport NY 11713 Office: 950 3rd Ave New York NY 10022

STRAUS, ROBERT, behavioral sciences educator; b. New Haven, Jan. 9, 1923; s. Samuel Hirsh and Alma (Fleischner) Straus; m. Ruth Elisabeth Dawson, Sept. 8, 1945; children: Robert James, Carol Martin, Margaret Dawson, John William. BA, Yale U., 1943, MA, 1945, PhD, 1947. Asst. prof. Yale U., 1948—51, rsch. assoc. applied physiology, 1951—53; acting dir. Conn. Child Study and Treatment Home, New Haven, 1952—53; assoc. prof. preventive medicine SUNY Upstate Med. Ctr., 1953—56; prof. med. sociology U. Ky., Lexington, 1956—59, prof. dept. behavioral sci. Coll. Medicine, also chmn. dept., 1959—87; dir. for sci. devel. Med. Rsch. Inst. San Francisco, 1991—93. Vis. fellow Yale U., 1968—69; vis. prof. U. Calif., Berkeley, 1978, 86; sec. Com. Med. Sociology, 1955—57; chmn. Coop. Com. Study Alcoholism, 1961—63, Nat. Adv. Com. on Alcoholism, 1966—69; mem. Nat. Adv. Coun. on Alcohol Abuse and Alcoholism, 1984—87; trustee Med. Rsch. Inst. San Francisco, 1988—93; mem. Calif. Pacific Med. Ctr. Rsch. Coun., 1993. Author: Medical Care for Seamen, 1950; author: (with S.D. Bacon) Drinking in College, 1953; author: Alcohol and Society, 1973, Escape From Custody, 1974, A Medical School is Born, 1996; co-editor: Medicine and Society, 1963; mem. editl. bd.: Jour. Studies on Alcohol, 1950—2000. Pres. Bluegrass R.R. Mus., 1980. Mem.: Inst. Medicine NAS, Acad. Behavioral Medicine Rsch., Am. Pub. Health Assn. (lifetime achievement award sect. on alcohol, tobacco and other drugs 1993), Assn. Behavioral Scis. and Med. Edn. (pres. 1974), Am. Sociol. Assn. (chmn. med. sociology sect. 1967—68, Leo G. Reeder award Disting. Contbn. to Med. Sociology 1998), Sigma Xi, Phi Beta Kappa. Home: 656 Raintree Rd Lexington KY 40502-2874 Personal E-mail: randrstraus@insightbb.com. Business E-Mail: rstraus@uky.edu.

STRAUSBAUGH, CARL ALAN, plant pathologist; s. Carl Dennis and Mary Katie Strausbaugh; m. Cynthia Strausbaugh, June 0, 1989; 1 child, Ben Lee. PhD, Wash. State U., Pullman, 1988. Rsch. plant pathologist USDA-ARS, Kimberly, Idaho, 2004—. Office: USDA-ARS 3793 North 3600 East Kimberly ID 83341 Home Phone: 208-734-1574; Office Phone: 208-423-6594. Office Fax: 208-423-6555. Business E-Mail: carls@nwisrl.ars.usda.gov.

STRAUSBERG, ROBERT L., federal agency administrator; Head, sequencing tech. br. Nat. Ctr. for Human Genome Rsch., NIH, 1994—96; dir., office of cancer genomics Nat. Cancer Inst., NIH, 1999—; v.p., rsch. The Inst. for Genomic Rsch., 2003—04; v.p. human genomic medicine J. Craig Venter Institute, Rockville, Md., 2004—. Office: J Craig Venter Institute 9704 Medical Ctr Dr Rockville MD 20850

STRAUSER, DAVID ROSS, healthcare educator, director; b. Sept. 4, 1968; m. Mary Ellen Chryst, Apr. 7, 1990; children: Matthew, David, John. MS, U. Wis., 1990, PhD, 1995. Asst. prof. U. Memphis, 1995-2001, dir. rehab. studies, 1998-2000, assoc. prof., 2001—05, U. Ill., Champaign, 2005—06, assoc. dir. Disability Rsch. Inst., 2006—. Dir. cmty. based job readiness program U. Memphis, 1997—2001; dir. Ctr. Rehab. and Employment Rsch., 2000—05; owner Vocat. Consulting Svcs.; presenter in field; commr. Commn. Rehab. Counselors Cert., 2001—06, rsch. cons.; commr. Commn. Disability Mgmt. Specialists, 2007—. Contbr. articles to nat. and internat. jours.; mem. editl. rev. bd.: leading jours. in field; co-editor: Jour. of Rehabilitation. Recipient New Faculty Rsch. award Nat. Coun. on Rehab. Edn., Rsch. award Am. Counseling Rehab. Assn., 2002, 03, Dean's Excellence award for rsch. and scholarship, 2004, Rehab. Svcs. Adminstrn. Commn. award, 2004. Mem. APA, Am. Rehab. Counseling Assn. (com. on rsch. and knowledge, Rsch. award 2002). Roman Catholic. Office: U Ill Dept Cmty Health 116 Huff Hall 1206 S 4th St Champaign IL 61820 Home Phone: 217-355-8714; Office Phone: 217-244-3936. Personal E-mail: drstrauser@insight.bb.com. Business E-Mail: strauser@uiuc.edu.

STRAUSER, ROBERT WAYNE, lawyer; b. Little Rock, Aug. 28, 1943; s. Christopher Columbus and Opal (Orr) S.; m. Atha Maxine Tubbs, June 26, 1971 (div. 1991); children: Robert Benjamin, Ann Kathleen; m. Terri D. Seales, Oct. 17, 1998. BA, Davidson Coll., NC, 1965; postgrad., Vanderbilt U., Nashville, 1965-66; LLB, U. Tex., Austin, 1968. Bar: Tex. 1968, U.S. Ct. Mil. Appeals 1971. Staff atty. Tex. Legis. Coun., Austin, 1969-71; counsel Jud. Com., Tex. Ho. of Reps., Austin, 1971-73; chief counsel Jud. Com., Tex. Constl. Conv., Austin, 1974; exec. v.p. and legis. counsel Tex. Assn. Taxpayers, Austin, 1974-85; assoc. Baker Botts, LLP, Austin, 1985-87, ptnr., 1988—. Assoc. editor Tex. Internat. Law Jour., 1968. Mem. Tex. Ho. Speakers Econ. Devel. Com., Austin, 1986-87; assoc. dir. McDonald Obs. Bd. Visitors, 1988—; bd. dirs. Tex. Assn. Bus. and C. of C., 2000-2002; mem. Dean's Roundtable, U. Tex. Law Sch.; bd. dirs. Austin Symphony Orch. Soc., 1985—, v.p., 1993-94, nominating com., 1998-2002. Capt. USNR, ret. Named Rising Star of Tex., Tex. Bus. Mag., 1983. Fellow Tex. Bar Found.; mem. State Bar of Tex. (tax sect.), Austin Bar Assn., Austin Bar Found., Headliners Club (Austin). Office: Baker & Botts 1600 San Jacinto Blvd Austin TX 78701 Office Phone: 512-322-2535. Business E-Mail: robert.strauser@bakerbotts.com.

STRAUSER, SUSAN PARKYN, performing arts educator, singer; d. Harold Mann and Helen Ruth (Knapp) Parkyn; m. George John Strauser; 1 child, Andrew. BS in Music Edn., West Chester U., Pa., 1964; MEd in Music, West Chester U., 1967; postgrad., Ind. U., 1976—80. Profl. singer, 1959—; prof. voice William Paterson U., Wayne, NJ, 1974—75; artistic dir. Vocal Arts Studio, Wallkill, NY, 1985—; voice seminar dir. Delaware Valley Opera, Narrowsburg, NY, 1985—86; prof. voice SUNY, Orange/Middletown, 1990—2004, voice program dir. Ulster/Stone Ridge, 2000—. Seminar presenter in field; artistic dir. Empire Artists of N.Y., Wallkill, 1992—; appeared with N.J. Symphony Orch., Hudson Valley Philharmonic Orch., West Chester Symphony, Ind. U. Philharm. and Opera Theatre; guest artist West Islip Symphony Orch. of L.I.; performances with opera and musical theatre cos. as well as in concert, oratorio and recital presentations include numerous leading roles; numerous appearances for cable TV Lunch N Listen series, Heroines-Women of the Musical Stage. Contbr. articles to profl. jours. Bd. dirs. Delaware Valley Opera, 1986. Recipient U.S. Congl. Citation in the Benjamin Gilman Congress, 1995, Theodore Presser Found. award, Westchester U., 1962, N.J. Opera Festival winner, Nat. Arion award. Avocation: genealogy. Home and Office: PO Box 412 37 DuBois St Wallkill NY 12589 Office Phone: 845-895-3959. Personal E-mail: parkyn@frontiernet.net.

STRAUSS, ALBRECHT BENNO, retired language educator, editor; b. Berlin, May 17, 1921; came to U.S., 1940; s. Bruno and Bertha (Badt) S.; m. Nancy Grace Barron, July 30, 1978; 1 child, Rebecca Ilse; stepchildren: Carolyn, Kathryn BA, Oberlin Coll., 1942; MA, Tulane U., 1948; PhD, Harvard U., 1956. Instr. English Brandeis U., 1951-52; teaching fellow gen. edn. Harvard U., 1952-55; instr. English Yale U., 1955-59; asst. prof. English U. Okla., Norman, 1959-60, U. N.C., Chapel Hill, 1960-64, assoc. prof., 1964-70, prof., 1970-91, prof. emeritus, 1991—; lectr. Duke Inst. for Learning in Retirement, 1993—2005. Editor Studies in Philology, 1974-80; sec. editorial com. Yale Edit. of Works of Samuel Johnson, 1975—; mem. editorial com. Ga. Edit. Works of Tobias Smollett, 1973-95; contbr. articles to lit. publs. Served with U.S. Army, 1942-46 Recipient Tanner Teaching award U. N.C., 1966; Fulbright fellow, Germany, 1983-84 Mem. MLA, South Atlantic MLA, Am. Soc. Eighteenth-Century Studies (pres. Southeastern group 1980-81), Johnsonians. Republican. Jewish. Home: 396 Lakeshore Ln Chapel Hill NC 27514-1728 Personal E-mail: strausshaus@mindspring.com.

STRAUSS, CAROLYN, broadcast executive; b. NYC, July 13, 1963; BA, Harvard U., 1985. Temp Documentaries Dept. HBO, 1986, asst. original programming, 1986—89, mgr. original programming, 1989—90, dir. original programming, 1990—94, v.p. original programming, 1994—99, sr. v.p. original programming, 1999—2002, exec. v.p. original programming, 2002—04, pres. entertainment, 2004—. Named one of 100 Most Powerful Women in Entertainment, Hollywood Reporter, 2006. Mailing: HBO Entertainment 1100 Avenue of Americas New York NY 10036 *

STRAUSS, CINDI, curator; b. Suffern, NY, Feb. 19, 1969; m. Chris Ballou. BA, Hamilton Coll., Clinton, NY, 1987—91; MA in History of Decorative Arts, Cooper-Hewitt/Parsons Sch. Design, NYC, 1992—95. Asst. curator decorative arts and rienzi Mus. Fine Arts, Houston, 1997—2001, assoc. curator decorative arts and rienzi, 2001—03, curator modern and contemporary decorative arts and design, 2003—. Adv. coun. Houston Ctr. Contemporary Craft, 2000—. Author: (exhibition catalogue) Crafting a Collection, Ornament as Art: Avant-Garde Jewelry from the Helen Williams Drutt Collection; contbr. collection catalogue. Grantee Lisa Taylor Rsch. fellowship, Cooper-Hewitt Mus., 1993—94, fellowship, Am. Friends Attingham, 1996. Mem.: Rice Design Alliance (bd. mem. 2003—06), Hamilton Coll. Art Adv. Bd., Am. Ceramics Cir. Office: Mus Fine Arts Houston PO Box 6826 Houston TX 77265-6826 Office Fax: 713-639-7399.

STRAUSS, DEBORAH, foundation administrator; AB, MA, U. Chgo. Cert. Fund Raising Exec. Dir. devel. pub. rels. Chgo. Child Care Soc.; exec. dir. IT Resource Ctr., Chgo., 1985—. Mem. mgmt. team Nat. Strategy for Nonprofit Tech.; chair Tech. Resource Consortium; bd. mem. Alliance for Nonprofit Mgmt., Donors Forum of Chgo.; mem. Mayor's Coun. of Tech. Advisors, co-chair Bridging the Digital Divide Com. Mem.: Assn. of Fundraising Profls. (mem. Chgo. Chap. Bd., Benjamin Franklin Award 1993). Office: IT Resource Ctr Ste 1005 29 E Madison St Chicago IL 60602-4529 Office Phone: 312-372-4872. Office Fax: 312-372-7962. E-mail: dstrauss@itresourcecenter.org.

STRAUSS, DIANE CAROL WHEELER, librarian, educator, writer; b. Milw., Feb. 14, 1943; d. Charles Clifton and Olga (Bondeli) Wheeler; m. Robert P. Strauss, Nov. 26, 1969 (div. 1973). BS, U. Wis., Milw., 1966, MS in Libr. Sci., 1967. Young adult libr. Enoch Pratt Free Libr., Balt., 1967-68; materials analyst U. Wis., Madison, 1968-69; legis. libr. Dept. Labor Libr., Washington, 1970-72; social scis. libr. U. NC, Chapel Hill, 1973—75, head bus. adminstrn./social scis. reference dept., 1975—92, assoc. univ. libr. svcs., 1992—2006, interim head collections, 2005—06, assoc. univ. libr. collections and svcs., 2006—. Author: Handbook of Business Information, 1988; also articles. Mem. ALA (Gale Rsch. award 1990), Spl. Librs. Assn. (pres. NC chpt. 1980-81), NC Online Users Group (pres. 1978), Beta Phi Mu (pres. Epsilon chpt. 1991-93). Office: U NC Davis Libr CB #3900 Chapel Hill NC 27514-8890 Home Phone: 919-286-7895; Office Phone: 919-962-1301. Business E-Mail: dstrauss@email.unc.edu.

STRAUSS, GWEN B., writer, editor; b. Deschapelles, Haiti, May 19, 1963; d. Julian Max Strauss and Katie Cowles Nichols; m. Jody Gerard Jenkins, June 22, 1996; children: Noah Jenkins, Sophie Jenkins, Eliza Jenkins. BA in Poetry, Hampshire Coll., 1986; MA in Edn., Wheelock Coll., 1987. Tchg. asst. Park Sch., Boston, 1986—87; freelance writer France, 1990—2003; editl. asst. Frank Books, Paris, 1992; editor Design Press, Savannah, Ga., 2002—04; dir. French campus Savannah Coll. of Art and Design, Lacoste, France, 2005—. Editl. cons. So. Poetry Rev., Savannah, 2003. Author: (poetry book) Trail of Stones, 1989, (children's book) Night Shimmy, 1991; contbr. short stories and poetry to various lit. jours. Finalist Nat. Poetry Series, 1995, Allen Ginsburg Poetry prize, 2003; recipient hon. mention, Atlanta Rev., 2001. Mem.: Authors Guild, Amnesty Internat., Planned Parenthood. Democrat. Avocations: gardening, sailing. Office: SCAD Rue Basse 84480 Lacoste France Personal E-mail: gbs0885@aol.com. Business E-Mail: gstrauss@scad.edu.

STRAUSS, HARLEE SUE, environmentalist, consultant; b. New Brunswick, NJ, June 19, 1950; d. Robert Lemuel and Helene (Marcus) S. BA, Smith Coll., 1972; PhD, U. Wis., 1979. Postdoctoral fellow dept. biology MIT, Cambridge, 1979-81; congrl. sci. fellow U.S. House of Reps., Washington, 1981-83; spl. asst. Am. Chem. Soc., Washington, 1983-84; spl. cons. Environ. Corp., Washington, 1984-85; rsch. assoc. Ctr. for Tech., Policy and Indsl. Devel. MIT, Cambridge, 1985-86, rsch. affiliate, 1986-92; sr. assoc. Gradient Corp., Cambridge, 1986-88; pres. H. Strauss Assocs., Inc., Natick, Mass., 1988—. Exec. dir. Silent Spring Inst., Inc., 1994-95; adj. assoc. prof. Sch. Pub. Health, Boston U., 1990-94; lectr. Sch. Medicine, Tufts U., Boston, 1988-95; mem. steering com. Boston Risk Assessment Group, 1986-95. Co-editor, author Risk Assessment in Genetic Engineering, 1991; author: Biotechnology Regulations, 1986, book chpts. in field. Active Instl. Biosafety Com., Army Rsch. Lab., Natick, 1989—94, Army Sci. Bd., 1994—2001. Mem. AAAS, Am. Chem. Soc., Assn. for Women in Sci. (chmn. com. New England chpt. 1986-88, co-chmn. legis. com. 1985-93), Biophys. Soc. (chmn. com. 1983-84, Congl. Sci. fellow 1981-83), Soc. for Risk Analysis (pres. New England chpt. 1991-92, pres.-elect 1995-2000). Jewish. Avocations: travel, hiking. Office: H Strauss Assocs Inc 21 Bay State Rd Natick MA 01760-2942 Office Phone: 508-651-8784. Personal E-mail: hstrauss@aol.com. Business E-Mail: h.strauss@rcn.com.

STRAUSS, HERBERT LEOPOLD, chemistry professor; b. Aachen, Germany, Mar. 26, 1936; came to U.S., 1940, naturalized, 1946; s. Charles and Joan (Goldschmidt) S.; m. Carolyn North Cooper, Apr. 24, 1960; children: Michael Abram, Rebecca Anne, Ethan Edward. AB, Columbia U., 1957, MA, 1958, PhD, 1960; postgrad, Oxford U., 1960-61. Mem. faculty U. Calif., Berkeley, 1961—, prof. chemistry, 1973—2003, prof. grad. divsn., 2003—, vice chmn. dept. chemistry, 1975-81, 92-95, asst. dean. Coll. Chemistry, 1986-92, assoc. dean, 1995—. Vis. prof. Indian Inst. Tech., Kanpur, 1968-69, Fudan U., Shanghai, 1982, U. Tokyo, 1982, U. Paris du Nord, 1987; mem. IUPAC Commn. I.1, 1990-2005. Author: Quantum Mechanics, 1968; assoc. editor Ann. Rev. Phys. Chemistry, 1976-85, editor, 1985-2000. Recipient Bomen-Michaelson award Coblentz Soc., 1994, Ellis Lippincott award Optical Soc. Am., 1994, The Berkeley Citation, 2003; Alfred P. Sloan fellow, 1966-70. Fellow Am. Phys. Soc., AAAS; mem. Am. Chem. Soc., Sigma Xi, Phi Beta Kappa, Phi Lambda Upsilon. Achievements include research in elucidation of vibrational spectra associated with large amplitude molecular motion in gases, liquids and solids. Home: 2447 Prince St Berkeley CA 94705-2021 Office: U Calif Dept Chemistry Berkeley CA 94720-1420 Home Phone: 510-848-3522; Office Phone: 510-642-7114. Business E-Mail: hls@berkeley.edu.

STRAUSS, JEROME FRANK, III, reproductive endocrinologist, educator; b. Chgo., May 2, 1947; s. Jerome Frank (Jr.) and Josephine (Newberger) Strauss; m. Catherine Blumlein, June 20, 1970; children: Jordan L., Elizabeth J. BA, Brown U., 1969; MD, U. Pa., 1974, PhD, 1975. Asst. prof. U. Pa. Sch. Medicine, Phila., 1976—83, assoc. prof., 1983—85, prof., 1985—, assoc. chair, 1987—, assoc. dean, 1990—98; Luigi Mastroianni jr. prof. and founding dir. Ctr. Rsch. on Women's Health and Reproduction, Phila., 1990—94; prof. Inst. Medicine NAS, 1994—; dean, exec. v.p. med. affairs, prof. ob-gyn. Va. Commonwealth U. Sch. Medicine, Richmon, 2005—. Biochem. endocrinology study sect. NIH, 1983—87, Nat. Adv. Child Health and Human Devel. Coun., 2002—06; chmn. population rsch. com. NICHHD, 1989—92; chair Reproductive Scientist of the Ams. Network, 1995—; dir. Ctr. Excellence in Women's Health, 1996—2002; co-chair Indo-U.S. Joint Working Group on Reproductive Sci. and Contraceptive Tech., 1999—; bd. dirs. Burroughs Wellcome Fund, 2003—; trustee Berlex Found., 2005—; Cheung Kong lectr., prof. Heilongjiang U. Chinese Medicine, 2006—. Editor: Lipoprotein and Cholesterol Metabolism in Sterodogenic Tissues, 1985, Current Topics in Membrane Research, 1987, Uterine and Embryonic Factors in Early Pregnancy, 1991, New Achievements in Research of Ovarian Function, 1995, Cell Death in Reproductive Physiology, 1997, Molecular Biology in Reproductive Medicine, 1999, Ovarian Function Research: Present and Future, 1999, Reproductive Medicine Molecular, Cellular and Genetic Fundamentals, 2002, New Frontiers in Contraceptive Research, 2004, Yen and Jaffe's Reproductive Endocrinology, 2004, Peterm Birth, 2007, Steroids jour., 1993—; assoc. editor Ency. of Reproduction, 1998—, assoc. editor, mem. editl. bd. Jour. Lipid Rsch., 1982—90, corr. editor Jour. Steroid Biochem. and Molecular Biology, 1990—99, mem. editl. bd. Endocrinology, 1986—90, 1997—2000, Biology of Reprodn., 1986—90, 1999—2003, Jour. of Women's Health, 1991—, Jour. Soc. Gynecologic Investigation, 1993—, Placenta, 1995—98, Trends in Endocrinology and Metabolism, 1999—, Reference en Gynecologie Obstetrique, 1999—, Seminars in Reproductive Endocrinology, 2000—, Jour. Endocrinology, 2000—06, Human Reproduction Update, 2001—05, Science, 2004—, assoc. editor Molecular Human Reproduction, 2007—. Recipient Transatlantic medal, Brit. Endocrine Soc., 1998, Disting. Grad. award, U. Pa., 2005, NAS Inst. Medicine, 2005. Fellow: Internat. Acad. Human Reproduction; mem.: Perinatal Rsch. Soc., Am. Soc. for Reproductive Medicine, Soc. for Study of Reproduction (bd. dirs. 1989—91, Rsch. award 1992), Endocrine Soc., Soc. Gynecologic Investigation (pres. 2003, Pres.'s Achievement award 1990, Disting. Scientist award 2006). Home: 2808 Monument Ave Unit 3 Richmond VA 23221 Office: Va Commonwealth U Dean's Office Sch Medicine 1101 E Marshall St Rm 1-070 Richmond VA 23298 Business E-Mail: jfstrauss@vcu.edu.

STRAUSS, JOHN STEINERT, dermatologist, educator; b. New Haven, July 15, 1926; s. Maurice Jacob and Carolyn Mina (Ullman) Strauss; m. Susan Thalheimer, Aug. 19, 1950; children: Joan Sue, Mary Lynn. BS, Yale U., 1946, MD, 1950. Intern U. Chgo., 1950-51; resident dermatology U. Pa., Phila., 1951-52, 54-55, fellow dermatology, 1955-57, instr., 1956-57; mem. faculty Boston U. Med. Sch., 1958-78, prof., 1966-78; head dept. dermatology U. Iowa, Iowa City, 1978-98, prof. dermatology, 1978-00, prof. emeritus, 2000—. Mem. editl. bd.: Archives of Dermatology, 1970—79, Jour. Am. Acad. Dermatology, 1979—89, Jour. Investigative Dermatology, 1977—82; contbr. articles to profl. jours. With USNR, 1952—54. Fellow James H. Brown Jr., 1947—48, USPHS, 1955—57; grantee. Fellow: Am. Acad. Dermatology (pres.); mem.: Internat. Com. Dermatology (pres. 1992—97), Internat. League Dermatol. Socs. (pres. 1992—97), 18th World Congress Dermatology (pres.), Am. Bd. Med. Spltys. (exec. com. 2001—04), Coun. Med. Splty. Socs. (pres.), Am. Fedn. Clin. Rsch., Ctrl. Soc. Clin. Rsch., Assn. Am. Physicians, Am. Dermatol. Assn. (sec., pres.), Am. Bd. Dermatology (bd. dirs., pres., assoc. exec. dir., exec. cons.), Dermatology Found. (pres.), Soc. Investigative Dermatology (sec.-treas., pres.). Achievements include research in sebaceous glands and pathogenesis of acne. Office: U Iowa Hosp & Clinics Dept Dermatology 200 Hawkins Dr # BT2045-1 Iowa City IA 52242-1009 Office Phone: 319-356-7546.

STRAUSS, JON CALVERT, retired academic administrator; b. Chgo., Jan. 17, 1940; s. Charles E. and Alice C. (Woods) S.; m. Joan Helen Bailey, Sept. 19, 1959 (div. 1985); children: Susan, Stephanie; m. Jean Anne

Sacconaghi, June 14, 1985; children: Kristoffer, Jonathon. BSEE, U. Wis., 1959; MS in Physics, U. Pitts., 1962; PhD in E.E., Carnegie Inst. Tech., 1965; LLD (hon.), U. Mass., 1996. Assoc. prof. computer sci., elec. engring. Carnegie Mellon U., Pitts., 1966-70; dir. computer ctr., prof. computer sci. Tech. U. Norway, Trondheim, Norway, 1970; vis. assoc. prof. elec. engring. U. Mich., Ann Arbor, 1971; assoc. prof. computer sci. Washington U., St. Louis, 1971-74, dir. computing facilities, 1971-73; dir. computing activities U. Pa., Phila., 1974-76, faculty master Stouffer Coll. House, 1978-80, prof. computer, info. scis., prof. decision sci. Wharton Sch., 1974-81, exec. dir. Univ. Budget, 1975-78, v.p. for budget, fin., 1978-81; prof. elec. engring. U. So. Calif., Los Angeles, 1981-85, sr. v.p. adminstrn., 1981-85; pres. Worcester Poly. Inst., Mass., 1985-94; v.p., chief fin. officer Howard Hughes Med. Inst., Chevy Chase, Md., 1994-97; pres. Harvey Mudd Coll., Claremont, Calif., 1997—2006. Cons. Electronics Assocs., Inc., 1965, IBM Corp., 1960-64, Westinghouse Elec. Corp., 1959-60; bd. dirs. Transamerica Income Fund, Variable Ins. Fund, United Educators Ins., mem. NSF Nat. Sci. Bd., 2004-. Contbr. articles on computer systems and university mgmt. to profl. jours.; co-holder patent. Bd. dirs. Presbyn.-U. Pa. Med. Ctr., Phila., 1980-81, U. So. Calif. Kenneth Norris Jr. Cancer Hosp., L.A., 1981-85, Med. Ctr. of Ctrl. Mass., 1986-94, Worcester Acad., 1986-91, Mass. Biotech. Rsch. Inst., 1985-94. Mem. New. Eng. Assn. Schs. and Colls., Inc., Commn. on Instns. of Higher Edn., Nat. Collegiate Athletic Assn. (pres.'s commn. 1990-94). Avocations: hiking, running, swimming. Office: Harvey Mudd Coll Kingston Hall Rm 201 301 E 12th St Claremont CA 91711-5980 Office Fax: 909-321-8360. Business E-Mail: jon_strauss@hmc.edu.

STRAUSS, JUDY PERKINS, psychologist, educator; b. Fairfield, Iowa, Feb. 8, 1948; d. Charles R Perkins and Elizabeth J Ovrom; children: Abby A Bradecich, Jackie R, Elly B. PhD, U. Iowa, 1993. Asst. prof. Augustana Coll., Rock Island, Ill., 1993—2000, Calif. State U., Long Beach, 2000—. Contbr. articles articles to various psychology jours. Champion for diversity certification tchg. program Calif. State U., Long Beach, Calif., 2004—05. Recipient Outstanding Tchg. Asst. award, U. Iowa, 1990-1991, 4 rsch. awards, Calif. State U., Long Beach. Mem.: Profl. Human Resources Assn., Soc. Human Resource Mgr., Am. Psychol. Soc., Soc. Indsl. Orgnl. Psychologists, Acad. Mgmt. Home Phone: 562-597-8725.

STRAUSS, MARK, editor; b. Nov. 8, 1966; married. BA, Macalaster Coll.; MS, Columbia Sch. Jour., NYC; MA in Middle East Studies and Internat. Economics, Johns Hopkins U. Paul H. Nitze Sch. Advanced Internat. Studies. Former rsch. asst. Brookings Inst. Foreign Policy Studies Prog.; formerly with SAIS Review, Discover Mag., Spy Mag.; sr. editor, web manager Foreign Policy Mag., 1997—2005; editor The Bulletin of Atomic Sciences, 2005—. TV and Radio Apperances CNN, Fox News, NPR, BBC; contbr. articles to Slate, Chronicle of Higher Education, Washington Post, New Republic, Spectator, Brown Journal of World Affairs, and Washington Monthly. Recipient General Excellence award under 100,00 circulation, Nat. Mag. Awards, Am. Soc. Mag. Editors, 2007. Office: Bulletin Atomic Sciences 6042 South Kimbark Ave Chicago IL 60637 Office Phone: 773-834-1800. Business E-Mail: mstrauss@thebulletin.org. *

STRAUSS, MICHAEL, mortgage company executive; BA in Bus. Adminstrn., Washington U., St. Louis. V.p., dir. Empire State Mortgage Bankers Assn.; founder Am. Home Mortgage Holdings, 1987, chmn., pres., CEO. Office: Am Home Mortgage Holdings 538 Broadhollow Rd Melville NY 11747 Office Phone: 866-805-7600. *

STRAUSS, PAUL, shadow senator; b. NYC; m. Kathy Strauss; children: Abigail, Samantha. BA, Am. U.; JD, Wash. Coll. Law. Atty. Law Offices of Paul Strauss & Assocs., PC, 1993—, various locally elected govt. positions including at-large mem. of Dem. State Com. and chmn. of Dem. Party Statehood Com. Washington; chmn. to commr. Advisory Neighborhood Commn., 1986—96; DC shadow senator to US Congress Washington, 1997—. Legis. asst. council's com. on consumer and regulatory affairs, Washington; union organizer Hotel and Restaurant Employee's Local 25. Pres. NW Youth Alliance, Inc.; atty. mem., panel chmn. Bd. Real Property Assessment and Appeals, Washington. Mem.: Internat. Assn. Assessment Officers, African-Am. Coalition (hon. chmn.). Democrat. Office: John A Wilson Bldg 1350 Pennsylvania Ave, NW Washington DC 20004 Office Phone: 202-727-7890. Office Fax: 202-727-9672. E-mail: paulstrauss@aol.com. *

STRAUSS, PETER L(ESTER), law educator; b. NYC, Feb. 26, 1940; s. Simon D. and Elaine Ruth (Mandle) S.; m. Joanna Burnstine, Oct. 1, 1964; children: Benjamin, Bethany. AB magna cum laude, Harvard U., 1961; LLB magna cum laude, Yale U., 1964. Bar: DC 1965, US Supreme Ct. 1968. Law clk. US Ct. Appeals DC Cir., 1964-65, US Supreme Ct., 1965-66; lectr. Halle Selassie U. Sch. Law, Addis Ababa, Ethiopia, 1966-68; asst. to solicitor gen. Dept. Justice, Washington, 1968-71; assoc. prof. law Columbia U., 1971-74, prof., 1974—, Betts prof., 1985—, vice-dean, 1996, 2001—02. Gen. counsel Nuclear Regulatory Commn., 1975-77, Adminstrv. Conf. U.S., 1984-95; Byrne vis. prof. Sch. Law Harvard U., Cambridge, Mass., 1994; bd. dirs. Ctr. for Computer Assisted Legal Instrn., 2002—. Mem. adv. bd. Lexis Electronic Author's Press, 1995-99; editor: SSRN Administrative Law Abstracts, 1997-2006; author: (with Abba Paulos translator) Fetha Negast: The Law of the Kings, 1968; (with others) Administrative Law Cases and Comments, 2003; Administrative Justice in the United States, 2002; Legal Methods: Understanding and Using Cases and Statutes, 2005; Administrative Law Stories, 2005; Legislation: Understanding and Using Statutes, 2006; contbr. articles to profl. jours. Recipient John Marshall prize Dept. Justice, 1970, Disting. Svc. award Nuclear Regulatory Commn., 1977. Mem. ABA (chair sect. administrv. law and regulatory practice 1992-93, Disting. Scholarship award 1988), Am. Law Inst. Office: Columbia U Law Sch 435 W 116th St New York NY 10027-7201 Home Phone: 914-478-3221; Office Phone: 212-854-2370. Business E-Mail: strauss@law.columbia.edu.

STRAUSS, ROBERT PHILIP, economics professor; b. Cleve., May 11, 1944; s. Harry and Carrie S.; m. Celeste G. Meade, Jan. 11, 1980; children: Sarah Elizabeth, David Anthony, Elena Nicole. AB in Econs., U. Mich., 1966; MA, U. Wis., 1968, PhD in Econs., 1970. Fellow Inst. Research on Poverty, 1968-69; asst. prof. econs. U. N.C., Chapel Hill, 1969-73, assoc. prof., 1973-79; econ. policy fellow Brookings Instn., Washington, 1971-72; economist U.S. Congress Joint Com. Taxation, 1975-78; prof. econs. and pub. policy Carnegie-Mellon U., Pitts., 1979—, assoc. dean Sch. Urban and Pub. Affairs, 1981-83, dir. Ctr. for Pub. Fin. Mgmt., 1984-91; dir. research Pa. Tax Commn., 1979-81. Vis. prof. econs. and pub. policy U. Rochester, 1992-94. Mem. Pa. Local Tax Reform Commn., 1987; sec. faculty Carnegie-Mellon U., 1991-92. Recipient Exceptional Service award U.S. Treasury, 1972, Disting. Service award Pitts. Tax Execs. Inst., 1987, Georgescu Roegen award, 1998, Steven B. Gold award, Assn. Pub. Policy and Mgmt. Nat. Tax Assn. and Fedn. Tax Adminstrs., 2005; named to Alumni Hall of Fame, Cleveland Heights H.S., 2004; grantee NSF, U.S. Dept. Labor, U.S. Treasury, HUD, Social Security Adminstrn.; William C. Lincoln fellow, 2005-06. Mem. Am. Econ. Assn., Econometric Soc., Nat. Tax Assn., Pub. Choice Soc., Assn. for Pub. Policy and Mgmt., Am. Soc. for Pub. Adminstrn., Nat. Tax Assn. (bd. dirs. 1995-98). Clubs: Cosmos. Home: 2307 Country Pl Export PA 15632-9059 Office: 5000 Forbes Ave Pittsburgh PA 15213-3890 Office Phone: 412-268-4798. E-mail: rpstrauss@att.net.

STRAUSS, SIMON WOLF, chemist, materials scientist; b. Bedzin, Keltz, Poland, Apr. 15, 1920; arrived in U.S., 1929; s. Israel Calvin and Anna (Hops) S.; m. Mary Jo Boehm, Dec. 27, 1957; children: Jack Calvin, Ruth Ann. BS in Chemistry, Poly. Inst. Bklyn., 1944, MS in Chemistry, 1947, PhD in Chemistry, 1950. Rsch. chemist Nat. Bur. Stds., Washington, 1951-55; from phys. chemist to head chem. metallurgy sect. Naval Rsch. Lab., Washington, 1955-63; sr. staff scientist Air Force Systems Command, Washington, 1963-80; ind. tech. cons. Washington, 1980—. Mem. bd. civil svc. examiners for sci. and tech. pers. U.S. Naval Dist. of Washington, 1959-63; mem. air force panel expert tech. reviewers patents for secrecy considerations Office Air Force Judge Adv. Gen., Washington, 1965-80; co-chair com. on career planning and appraisal of sci. and engrs. Air Force Sys. Command, Washington, 1966-67; air force mem. in-house com. mgmt. rev. tech. info. program, Dept. Def., 1967; chair rsch. steering com. Air Force Dir. of Sci. Tech., Washington, 1976-80; mem., chair editl. adv. com. Washington Acad. Jour., 1983-87, chair com. on scholarly activities, 1984-88. Author: Advanced Composites: An Historical Perspective, Retiring Presidential Lecture, 1987; prin. compiler 75 Years of Scientific Thought, 1987; mem. bd. reviewers Jour. Chem. Engring. Data, 1965-66; contbr. articles to profl. jours. Judge Internat. Sci. Engring. Fair, 1970, 72, 73; nat. evaluator space shuttle student involvement program NSTA, NASA, Washington, 1984, 85. With U.S. Army, 1944-45. Recipient Air Force Exceptional Civilian Svc. medal, 1980, first Disting. Career in Sci. award Wash. Acad. Scis., 1988, Disting. Svc. award, 1990. Fellow AAAS, Wash. Acad. Scis. (first Disting. Scholar-in-Residence 1984-89, pres.-elect 1985-86, pres. 1986-87, life mem. fund trustee 1988—), Am. Inst. Chemists; mem. Math. Assn. Am., Air Force Assn., Cosmos Club, Air Force Materials Lab. (hon. life), Sigma Pi Sigma, Phi Lambda Upsilon, Sigma Xi. Achievements include 3 patents for electrodeposition of Cadmium on high strength steel; research and development of advanced composites technology; the development of equations for the estimation of surface tensions, viscosities and densities of liquid metals as a function of temperature. Home: 4506 Cedell Pl Temple Hills MD 20748-3805 *Living a life not just for oneself contributes not only to the elevation of humankind, but also to the ennoblement and enrichment of one's own life.*

STRAUSS, STANLEY ROBERT, lawyer; b. NYC, June 3, 1915; s. Maurice M. and Blanche Anna (Danciger) S.; m. Margaret Inglis Forbes, Mar. 13, 1944 (div. 1950); m. Helen Anne Cummings, Dec. 31, 1975 (dec. 1980). BA cum laude, Williams Coll., 1936; LLB, Columbia U., 1940. Bar: N.Y. 1941, D.C. 1964, U.S. Ct. Appeals (1st cir.) 1977, U.S. Ct. Appeals (3d cir.) 1986, U.S. Ct. Appeals (4th cir.) 1974, U.S. Ct. Appeals (5th cir.) 1970, U.S. Ct. Appeals (6th cir.) 1977, U.S. Ct. Appeals (8th cirs.) 1975, U.S. Supreme Ct. 1965. Assoc. Howard Henig, NYC, 1940-41; atty. NLRB, Washington, 1946-52, supervising atty., 1953-59, chief counsel, 1959-63; assoc. Vedder, Price, Kaufman & Kammholz, Washington, 1963-65, ptnr., 1965-90; of counsel Ogletree, Deakins, Nash, Smoak & Stewart, Washington, 1990—. Co-author: Practice and Procedure Before the National Labor Relations Board, 3d edit., 1980, 4th edit., 1987, 5th edit., 1996. Officer US Army, 1941—45, PTO. Decorated Bronze Star; Horn scholar, Columbia U. Law Sch., 1937—40. Mem. ABA, Fed. Bar Assn., D.C. Bar Assn., Kenwood Country Club. Avocations: golf, tennis. Home: 4956 Sentinel Dr Bethesda MD 20816-3594 Office: Ogletree Deakins Nash 2400 N St NW Fl 5 Washington DC 20037-1154 Home Phone: 301-229-2382; Office Phone: 202-887-0855. E-mail: stanleystrauss@odense.com.

STRAUSS, ULRICH PAUL, chemist, educator; b. Frankfurt, Germany, Jan. 10, 1920; s. Richard and Marianne (Seligmann) S.; m. Esther Lipetz, June 20, 1943 (dec. Sept. 1949); children— Dorothy, David; m. Elaine Greenbaum, Nov. 23, 1950; children— Elizabeth, Evelyn. AB, Columbia U., 1941; PhD, Cornell U., 1944. Sterling fellow Yale U., 1946-48; faculty Rutgers U., New Brunswick, NJ, 1948—, prof. phys. chemistry, 1960-90, prof. emeritus, 1990—; also dir. Sch. Chemistry, 1965-71, chmn. dept. chemistry, 1974-80. Prof. emeritus Rutgers U., 1990—. Mem. editorial bd. Macromolecules, 1990-93; contbr. articles to profl. jours. Recipient Sci. achievement award Johnson Wax Co., 1986; NSF sr. fellow Nat. Center Sci. Research, Strasbourg, France, 1961-62; Guggenheim fellow U. Oxford, Eng., 1971-72 Fellow N.Y. Acad. Scis.; mem. Am. Chem. Soc. (chmn. phys. chemistry group N.J. sect. 1956, councillor 1961-72, honored by 1-day symposium at nat. meeting N.Y.C. 1986, Excellence in Edn. award N.J. sect. 1994). Home: 227 Lawrence Ave Highland Park NJ 08904-1837 Office: Rutgers U Dept Chemistry New Brunswick NJ 08903 Business E-Mail: strauss@rci.rutgers.edu.

STRAUSSLER, TOMAS See STOPPARD, TOM

STRAUTINS, VILNIS, music educator, retired performing company executive; b. Lubana, Madona, Latvia, Dec. 28, 1939; s. Fricis Strautins and Emma (Bundzis) Strautina; m. Dzidra Markevica, Dec. 31, 1964; children: Ineta, Peteris. MA, Latvian Music, Riga, 1965. Prin. flutist Latvian Nat. Symphony Orch., Riga, 1961-89, mng. dir., 1989-97; prof. flute Latvian Music Acad., Riga, 1971—. Mem.: Latvian Correspondence Chess Fedn. (pres. 2001—). Lutheran. Avocation: correspondence chess. Office: Latvian Music Acad Kr Barona 1 LV-1050 Riga Latvia E-mail: vstrautins@apollo.lv.

STRAVALLE-SCHMIDT, ANN ROBERTA, lawyer; b. NYC, Jan. 2, 1957; Grad. cum laude, Phillips Exeter Acad., 1975; student, Occidental Coll., 1975-78, Oxford Coll., Eng., 1976-77; BS cum laude, Boston Coll., 1980; JD, Boston U., 1987; MBA, Rensselaer Poly. Inst., 2002. Bar: Conn. 1987, U.S. Dist. Ct. Conn. 1988, U.S. Supreme Ct. 1993. Consulting staff Arthur Andersen, Boston, 1980-82; supr. CID ops. Aetna Life & Casualty, Hartford, Conn., 1982-84; summer intern US Atty.'s Office, Boston, 1985; jud. clk. Hon. Judge Thayer III NH Supreme Ct., 1987-88; trial lawyer Day, Berry & Howard, Hartford, Conn., 1988-91; sr. lawyer comml. litig. and appellate practice Berman & Sable, Hartford, Conn., 1991-96; dir. maj. case unit Travelers Property and Casualty Corp., Hartford, Conn., 1996-98; sr. atty. Robinson & Cole, Hartford, Conn., 1998-2000; dir. legal svcs., gen. counsel Conn. Resources Recovery Authority, Hartford, Conn., 2000—04; gen. counsel, in-house mgr., legal, IP, warranty and reliability Jacobs Vehicle Sys. (subs. Danaher Corp.), Bloomfield, Conn., 2005—. Brief judge Nat. Appellate Advocacy Competition, 1996; online faculty U. Phoenix, 2002—, moot court judge, U. Conn., 1992, 2004. Mem. editl. bd. Conn. Bar Jour., 1990-99; contbr. articles to profl. jours. Mem. Hebron Dem. Town Com., Hebron Bd. Fin., 1995-99, Hebron Sch. Bldg. Com., 1997-99; justice of peace, 1997-99; apptd. mem. Hebron Bldg. Com., 1997-99; bd. dirs. Lawyers Without Borders, 2004; mem. adv. bd. Discovery Ctr., 2004—; mgr. Lawyers at Risk and Neutral Observer Program. Hennessey scholar Boston U. Sch. Law, 1987. Mem. ABA, Conn. Bar Assn. (founder, chair appellate practice com. litigation sect. 1994-96, mem. exec. com. litigation sect., pro bono exec. com, 2004, chair pro bono initiative, corp. counsel sect. 2004). Home: 54 Monte Alto Rd Santa Fe NM 87508 Office: Jacobs Vehicle Sys Subsidiary Danagher Corp 22 E Dudley Tour Rd Bloomfield CT 06002 Home Phone: 505-466-1877. Personal E-mail: astravalle@comcast.net.

STRAVINSKA, SARAH, dance educator; b. Pitts., Nov. 12, 1940; d. Robert Edwin Williams and Alice Elizabeth Markey Hildeboldt; m. George Lawrence Denton, May 10, 1959 (div. 1973); children: Kathryn, Michael, Laura, David. BFA in Dance, Fla. State U., 1977, MFA in Dance, 1979; Cert. in Ballet, Vaganova Inst., Leningrad, Russia, 1990; Cert., Raoul Gelabert Kinesiology Ins, NYC, 1980. Dancer Ballet Russe, NYC, 1957-58; dance choreographer Dutchess County Ballet, Beacon, NY, 1960-65; instr. Brevard C.C., Cocoa, Fla., 1969-73; chair dept. dance Randolph/Macon Woman's Coll., Lynchburg, Va., 1979-84; asst. prof. dance U. So. Miss., Hattiesburg, 1984-86; prof. and coord. dance U. La., Lafayette, 1986—. Dir. State of La. Danse Project, Lafayette, 1991-94. Choreographer: Mama! Stop the Bombs, 1989, The Yellow Wallpaper, 1990, Spring Night, 1998, Serrano!, 2002, Feather, Stone and Light, 2003, The Littlest Angel, 2005; reconstructor of classical ballets: Les Sylphides, 1991, Giselle, 1992, Swan Lake, 1993, Raymonda, Pas de Quatre, 1994. Dir. concerns for children La Danse with Acadiana Arts Coun., Lafayette, 1987-93; mem. Arts in Edn. Program, Lafayette, 1987—, coord. The Othello Project, 2003-04. Grantee Mellon Found., 1982. Mem. Am. Coll. Dance Festival Assn. (bd. dirs., festival coord. 1989-91), Dance History Scholars, CORPS de Ballet Internat. (founder), Phi Kappa Phi. Episcopalian. Avocations: writing, music, reading, biking. Office: Univ of La PO Box 43690 Lafayette LA 70504-3690 Personal E-mail: dancepro@macfriends.net.

STRAWDERMAN, WILLIAM E., statistics educator; b. Westerly, RI, Apr. 25, 1941; s. Robert Lee and Alida Browning (Dow) S.; m. Susan Linda Grube; July 20, 1985; children: Robert Lee, William Edward, Heather Lynne. BS, U. R.I., 1963; MS, Cornell U., 1965, Rutgers U., 1967, PhD, 1969. Mem. tech. staff Bell Tel. Labs., Holmdel, NJ, 1965-67; vis. asst. prof. Stanford (Calif.) U., 1969-70; instr. Rutgers U., New Brunswick, NJ, 1967-69, prof. stats., 1970—. Contbr. more than 140 articles to profl. jours. Fellow: Inst. Math. Stats., Am. Statis. Assn. Office: Rutgers U Statistics Dept Hill Ctr-Busch Campus New Brunswick NJ 08903 Home Phone: 908-874-4357; Office Phone: 732-445-2697. Business E-Mail: straw@stat.rutgers.edu.

STRAWHECKER, KENNETH EDWARD, research scientist; b. West Chester, Pa., Dec. 22, 1971; s. Edward Russell and Barbara Lynne Strawhecker; m. Trisha Ann Koch, May 22, 2004; 1 child, Caleb Kenneth. BSChemE, Drexel U., Phila., 1997; MS in Materials Sci. and Engring., Pa. State U., University Park, 1999, PhD in Materials Sci. and Engring., 2001. Applications scientist Veeco Instruments, Chadds Ford, Pa., 2005—. Office: Veeco Metrology 223 Wilmington-West Chester Pike St 114 Chadds Ford PA 19317 Office Phone: 610-361-9550 106.

STRAWHECKER, PAUL JOSEPH, fundraising consultant; b. Oct. 31, 1947; s. John Leslie and Leone Francis (Kalamaja) Strawhecker; m. Margaret Ellen Baumann, Aug. 31, 1974; children: Risa Nicole, Ryan John. Student, St. Joseph's Sem., 1963-67, Blessed John Neumann Coll., 1968-68; BA, Creighton U., 1970, postgrad. Law Sch., 1971-73; MPA, U. Nebr., 1980. Advanced cert. fundraising exec. Assn. Fundraising Profls. Rsch. specialist mayor's office City of Omaha, 1970, spl. asst. to mayor, 1971, mgr. spl. programs, 1972-73; dir. spl. resources Father Flanagan's Boys Home, Boys Town, Nebr., 1974-81; v.p. for devel. Luth. Hosps. and Homes Soc. Am., Fargo, N.D., 1982-86; asst. administr. Sacred Heart Gen. Hosp., Eugene, Oreg., 1986-87; v.p. Northwood U., Midland, Mich., 1987-94; pres. Paul J. Strawhecker, Inc., Omaha, 1995—. Adj. prof. U. Nebr., Omaha, 1995—; treas. Credit Union, 1975; clk., treas., liaison officer Village of Boys Town, 1974-81; writer Am. Soc. Planning Ofcls.; past owner The Wooden Spoon Ltd., Omaha.; exec. com. Assn. Philanthropic Counsel. Author: Fund Raising, 1997, Capital Campaigns, 1998, Resource Development, 1999. Chmn. Met. Area Planning Agy. Coun. Ofcls. Goals Com. for Human Svcs., 1976; mem. Omaha/Douglas County Criminal Justice Commn., 1977-80; mem. adv. com. Douglas County Office on ChildrenYouth, Midland County Cmty. Corrections, 1991-92; bd. dirs. "Say Yes" to Youth, 1990-92; chmn. urban affairs com. Met. Area Planning Agy. Mem. Assn. Fundraising Profls. (cert., pres. ND area chpt., bd. dirs. 1994-95, pres. Mich. chpt. bd. dirs. 1987-90, pres. Nebr. chpt. bd. dirs. 1997-99, vice chair nat. bd. 1991, nat. found. bd. 2000—, bd. mem. chair 2007—, U.S.A. Found.), Nat. Assn. Hosp. Devel. (spkr. 1983), Internat. City Mgmt. Assn. (spkr. 1971), Multi Hosp. Devel. Assn. (pres. 1986), Leadership Midland (alumni and steering com. 1990-92), Phi Kappa Psi. Roman Catholic. Home: 3424 N 129th Cir Omaha NE 68164-4240 Office: Paul J Strawhecker Inc 4913 Dodge St Omaha NE 68132-2917 Home Phone: 402-493-8049; Office Phone: 402-556-5785. Business E-Mail: paul@pjstraw.com.

STRAWN, MELVIN NICHOLAS, artist, educator; b. Boise, Aug. 5, 1929; s. Milton Rozell and Irma Belle Strawn; m. Bernice Iva Strawn, June 14, 1951; children: Clare Lynn, Daniel Paul, Stanley Milton, Benjamin Joseph, Angela Mary, Thomas Melvin. BFA, Calif. Coll. Arts and Crafts, 1955, MFA, 1956. Art instr. Midwestern U., Wichita Falls, Tex., 1956—57, Mich. State U., East Lansing, 1957—59; asst./assoc. prof. Antioch Coll., Yellow Springs, Ohio, 1959—69; prof., dir. Sch. Art U. Denver, 1969—85; prof., chair art dept. Western Mich. U., Kalamazoo, 1985—88; prof. emeritus U. Denver, 1985—. Juror Colo. Watercolor Soc., Denver. Major retrospective exhbn., Denver Ctrl. Libr., 2006. Pvt. US Army, 1951—53. Avocations: fly fishing, photography, cross country skiing, hiking. Home: 8905 Hwy 285 Salida CO 81201 Office Phone: 719-539-2637. Personal E-mail: mels@chaffee.net.

STRAWSER, JERRY R., dean; BBA in Acctg., Tex. A&M U., 1983, MS in Acctg., 1984, PhD in Acctg., 1985. CPA Tex., 1985. Asst. prof. La. State U., 1985—90, Arthur Andersen & Co. rsch. fellow, 1989—90; assoc. prof. Conn. Bauer Coll. Bus., U. Houston, 1990—97, assoc. dean academic and rsch. programs, 1995—99, prof. and Arthur Anderson & Co. alumni prof. acctg. and taxation, 1997—2001, interim dean, 1999—2001; dean Mays Bus. Sch., Tex. A&M U., 2001—, Devel. Coun. chair bus., 2001—, Leland/Weinke chair acctg., 2001—. Mem. editl. bd. Issues in Acctg. Edn., 1998—. Co-author: (books) Auditing Theory and Practice, 1985—2001, Managerial Accounting, 1990—2000, Auditing & Assurance Services, 2004. Recipient Outstanding Tchg. award, Alpha Kappa Psi, 1985, George W. Fair award for tchg. excellence, 1986, Melcher award for rsch. excellence, 1992, 1995, Master Tchg. award, NationsBank, 1994, Disting. Faculty award, Exec. MBA Alumni Assn., 2000; Arthur Andersen rsch. fellowship, 1989, Melcher tchg. fellow, 1991, Melcher svc. fellow, 1993. Mem.: Am. Assn. Acctg., Assn. to Advance Collegiate Schools of Bus. Office: Tex A&M U Mays Bus Sch 4113 TAMU 3003 Wehner College Station TX 77843-4113 Office Phone: 979-845-4711. Office Fax: 979-845-6639. Business E-Mail: jstrawser@tamu.edu. *

STRAYER, BARRY LEE, retired judge; b. Moose Jaw, Sask., Can., Aug. 13, 1932; s. Carl John and Nina Naomi Strayer; m. Eleanor Lorraine Staton, July 2, 1955; children: Alison Lee, Jonathan Mark, Colin James. BA, U. Sask., Can., 1953, LLB, 1955; BCL, Oxford U., Eng., 1957; SJD, Harvard U., 1966. Bar: Sask., 1959. Crown solicitor Gov. Sask., Regina, 1959-62; prof. law U. Sask., 1962-68; dir. constitutional rev. Gov. Can., Ottawa, 1968-72, dir. constitutional law, 1972-74, asst. dep. minister justice, 1974-83; judge trial divsn. Fed. Ct. Can., Ottawa, 1983-94; jud. mem. Competition Tribunal Can., Ottawa, 1986-93; judge Fed. Ct. Appeal of Can., 1994—2004; chief justice Ct. Martial Appeal Ct. of Can., 1994—2004. Sessional lectr. U. Ottawa, 1973-78; constitutional advisor Rep. Seychelles, 1979; adviser Hongkong Govt. Bill of Rights, 1989. Author: Judicial Review of Legislation, 1968, Canadian Constitution and the Courts, 1983, 3d edit., 1988; contbr. articles to profl. jours. Mem.: Larrimac Golf Club, Rideau Club. Home: 504 Queen Elizabeth Dr Ottawa ON Canada K1S 3N4

STRAZZELLA, JAMES ANTHONY, lawyer, educator; b. Hanover, Pa., May 18, 1939; s. A.F. and T.A. Strazzella. AB, Villanova U., 1961; JD, U. Pa., 1964. Bar: Pa. 1964, DC, 1965, US Dist. Ct. (ea. and mid. dist.) Pa. 1969, US Ct. Appeals (3rd cir.) 1964, US Ct. Appeals (D.C. cir.) 1965, US Ct. Appeals (4th cir.) 1983, US Supreme Ct. 1969, US Dist. Ct. DC. Law clk. to Hon. Samuel Roberts Pa. Supreme Ct., 1964-65; asst. U.S. atty. D.C., 1965-69; vice dean, asst. prof. law U. Pa., Phila., 1969-73; faculty Temple U., Phila., 1973—; James G. Schmidt chair in law, 1989—; acting dean, 1987-89. Chief counsel Kent State investigation Pres.'s Commn. Campus Unrest, 1970; chmn. Atty. Gen.'s Task Force on Family Violence,

Pa., 1985-89; mem., chmn. justice ops. Mayor's Criminal Justice Coordinating Commn., Phila., 1983-85; Pa. Joint Coun. Criminal Justice, 1979-82; mem. Com. to Study Pa.'s Unified Jud. Sys., 1980-82; Jud. Coun. Pa., 1972-82; chmn. criminal procedural rules com. Pa. Supreme Ct., 1972-85; mem. task force on prison overcrowding, 1983-85, rsch. adv. com., 1988, Pa. Commn. on Crime and Delinquency; chmn. U.S. Magistrate Judge Merit Selection Com., 1991, mem., 1989, 90, 91; co-chair Mayor's Transition Task Force on Pub. Safety, Phila., 1992; designate D.C. Com. on Adminstrn. of Justice Under Emergency Conditions, 1968; del. D.C. Jud. Conf., 1985, 95. Contbr. articles to profl. jours. and books. Adv. coun. Wagner Free Inst. Sci., 2005—; mem. adv. bd. dirs., past pres. A Better Chance in Lower Merion; dir. Hist. Fire Mus., Phila., 1978—, 1st v.p., 2002—07; bd. dirs. Coun. Legal Edn. Opportunity Bd., 1997—, Lower Merion Hist. Soc., 1998—2000, Neighborhood Civic Assn., Bala-Cynwyd, Pa., 1984—87; bd. trustees Bala Cynwyd Pub. Libr., 1999—2005; pres. Smith Meml. Playground & Playhouse in Fairmount Pk., 2003—. Recipient award for disting. tchg. Linback Found., 1983, Advancement of Justice award Pa. Atty. Gen., 1989, Disting. Pub. Svc. award Assn. State and County Detectives, 1989, Spl. Merit award Pa. Assn. Police Chiefs, 1989, significant contbn. to legal scholarship and edn. Beccaria award Phila. Bar Assn. and Nat. IAB Assn., 1995. Fellow: Am. Bar Found.; mem.: St. Thomas More Soc. (pres. 1985—86, St. Thomas More award 1996, past dir. Phila. area), Phila. Bar Assn. (criminal justice sect., appellate cts. com.), Pa. Bar Assn. (commn. profl. stds. 1981—84, chmn. criminal law sect. 1986—88, Merit award 1987), FBA (Phila. crim. law com. adv. bd. 1988—93, chmn. nat. criminal law com. 1991—92), Am. Law Inst., ABA (faculty appellate judges seminars 1975—2003, various coms., acad. advisor appellate judges edn. com. 1993—2003, reporter task force on federalization criminal law 1998—99), Order of the Coif (past mem. exec. bd. U. Pa.). Roman Catholic. Office: Temple U Law Sch 1719 N Broad St Philadelphia PA 19122-6002

STREAMAS, JOHN, ethnic and American studies professor; s. Edward Streamas and Hideko Kato; m. Valerie Boydo, Oct. 31, 1996. AB, Miami U., Oxford, Ohio, 1977; MA, Syracuse U., NY, 1981; PhD, Bowling Green State U., Ohio, 2001. Grad. tchg. asst. Syracuse U., NY, 1979—80, Miami U., Oxford, Ohio, 1981—85, rsch. asst., 1978—83; instr. Franklin U., 1985—94; grad. asst. Bowling Green State U., Bowling Green, 1996—98; asst. prof. Wash. State U., Pullman, 2001—. Proofreader Ross Lab., Columbus, Ohio, 1987—2001; tchr. langs. Berlitz Sch. Langs., Ft. Thomas, Ky., 1981. Author short stories, poems. Mem.: Am. Studies Assn. (minority scholars com. 2005—), Western Lit. Assn., Japanese Am. Nat. Mus., Nat. Japanese Am. Hist. Soc., Multi-Ethnic Lit. US, Assn. Asian Am. Studies, Internat. Soc. Study Time, Am. Studies Assn. (Wise Susman prize 2000), MLA, AAUP. Office: Wash State U PO Box 644010 Wilson Hall 112A Pullman WA 99164-4010 Home Phone: 509-334-5303; Office Phone: 509-335-4791. Business E-Mail: streamas@wsu.edu.

STREAR, JOSEPH D., public relations executive; b. NYC, Nov. 5, 1933; s. Morris and Betty (Birenbaum) S. BA, CCNY, 1955. Pres. AC&R Pub. Relations, Inc., NYC, 1972-82; mng. ptnr. Kanan, Corbin, Schupak & Aronow, Inc., NYC, 1982-84; pres. Strear, David & Mitchell, Inc., NYC, 1984-91; prin. Joseph Strear Pub. Rels., NYC, 1992—. 1st lt. U.S. Army, 1955-57. Mem. Pub. Rels. Soc. Am. Avocation: sports. Office: 408 W 57th St New York NY 10019-3053

STREATOR, EDWARD, retired diplomat, management consultant; b. NYC, Dec. 12, 1930; s. Edward James and Ella (Stout) S.; m. Priscilla Craig Kenney, Feb. 16, 1957; children: Edward James, III, Elinor Craig Garcia-Garcia, Abigail Merrill Squance. AB, Princeton U., 1952. Commd. fgn. service officer Dept. State, 1956; assigned ICA, 1956-58; 3d sec. embassy Addis Ababa, Ethiopia, 1958-60; 2d sec. embassy Lome Togo, 1960-62; intelligence research specialist Office Research and Analysis for Africe, Dept. State, Washington, 1962-63, staff asst. to sec. state, 1964-66, chief polit.-mil. affairs unit, 1966-67; dep. dir. polit.-mil. affairs, 1967-68; dep. dir. polit. affairs U.S. Mission to NATO, 1968-69; dep. dir. Office NATO and Atlantic Polit.-Mil. Affairs, Dept. State, 1969-73; dir. office, 1973-75; dep. U.S. permanent rep. to NATO, dep. chief U.S. Mission to NATO, 1975-77; minister, dep. chief of mission Am. embassy, London, 1975-84; ambassador, U.S. rep. OECD Paris, 1984-87. Bd. dirs. South Bank, 1991-99; chmn. New Atlantic Initiative, 1996-2000. US dels. NATO and OECD Ministerial Meetings, 1964, 66, 69-75, 85-87; mem. 10th SEATO Coun. Min. Meeting, 1965; 2d spl. Inter-Am. Conf., 1965, Conf. Security and Coop., Europe, 1973; mem. Coun., Royal United Svcs. Inst., 1987-92, vice patron, 1991—; exec. com. The Pilgrims, UK, 1988-90, Internat. Inst. Strategic Studies, 1988-99; coun. mem. Royal United Svcs. Inst. Def. Studies, 1988-1992; gov. Ditchley Found., 1988-, English Speaking Union, 1988-94; pres. Am. C. of C., UK, 1988-94; chmn. European Coun. Am. C. of C., 1992-94; bd. dirs. Brit-Am. Arts Assn., 1987-99; dir. Brit. Mus. Natural History Internat. Found.; devel. com. Nat. Gallery, UK, 1991-95; adv. bd. Inst. US Studies-U. London, 1993-99; mem. founding coun. Oxford Inst. Am. Studies, 1989-2001; adv. com. Fulbright Commn., 1995-2001; pres., trustee Northcoate Parkinson Fund, 2004-07, Train Found., 2007-. Recipient Presdl. Meritorious Svc. award, 1986, Wilbur Carr award Dept. of State, 1987, Benjamin Franklin medal Royal Soc. Arts, 1992. Mem. Knickerbocker Club NY, Pilgrims NY, Met. Club Washington, Beefsteak Club, Garrick Club, White's Club London, Mill Reef Club Antigua, Century Assn. NY. Episcopalian. Mailing: 535 Park Ave New York NY 10065 Office Phone: 212-486-6688. Personal E-mail: estreator@nyc.rr.com.

STREB, PAUL GERARD, arbitrator; b. Balt., Dec. 8, 1945; s. Edwin and Marie (W.) S.; m. Mary Ament, Nov. 16, 1973. AB in Philosophy, Mount St. Mary's Coll., 1967; JD, U. Balt., 1973. Bar: Md. 1973, U.S. Ct. Appeals (Fed. cir.) 1986. Adminstrv. judge U.S. Civil Svc. Commn. and U.S. Merit Systems Protection Bd., Washington, 1973-83; atty. U.S. Merit Systems Protection Bd., Washington, 1983-90, dep. dir. regional ops., 1990-91; adminstrv. law judge U.S. Dept. HUD, Washington, 1991-94; chief adminstrv. law judge U.S. Merit Systems Protection Bd., Washington, 1994-2001; bd. dirs. fgn. svc. grievance bd. U.S. Dept. State, Washington, 2001—03. Sec. Fed. Administrative Law Judges Conf., 1993-94; arbitrator Fed. Mediation and Conciliation Svc, 2002-. Vol. atty. for Homeless Persons Representation Project, Balt., 1990-91. Lt. U.S. Army, 1967-70, Vietnam. Decorated Purple Heart, U.S. Army; recipient Chmn.'s Legal Excellence award Merit Systems Protection Bd., 1987. Avocations: running, swimming, biking, travel, the arts.

STRECK, FREDERICK LOUIS, III, lawyer; b. St. Louis, Nov. 6, 1960; s. Frederick Louis Jr. and Joan Kathrine (Faerber) S.; m. Michelle Renee Harding; children: Frederick IV, Robert Harding, Joseph Walter, Samuel Franklin. BBA, Tex. Christian U., Ft. Worth, 1983; JD, St. Mary's U., 1986. Bar: Tex. 1986, US Dist. Ct. (no. dist.) Tex. 1987, US Ct. Appeals (5th cir.) 1987; bd. cert. in personal injury trial law, civil trial advocacy; diplomate Am. Bd. of Trial Advocacy. Atty. Kugle, Stewart, Dent & Frederick, Ft. Worth, 1986-89, The Dent Law Firm, 1990—. State del. Dem. Party, Tex., 1988. Named Tex. Super Lawyer, Tex. Monthly Mag., 2003—. Fellow Tex. State Bar Coll.; mem. ABA, ATLA, Am. Coll. Barristers (sr. counsel), Tex. Trial Lawyers Assn., Million Dollar Adv. Forum, Am. Coll. Barristers (sr. counsel). Democrat. Roman Catholic. Avocations: wine collecting, golf, fishing, scuba diving. Office: The Dent Law Firm 1120 Penn St Fort Worth TX 76102-3417 Office Phone: 817-332-3117. Office Fax: 817-332-5809. Personal E-mail: fstreck3@yahoo.com.

STRECKER, DAVID EUGENE, lawyer; b. Carthage, Mo., Nov. 29, 1950; s. Eugene Albert and Erma Freida (Wood) S.; m. Katherine Ann Pugh; children: Charles David, Carrie Christina. BA, Westminster Coll., 1972; JD, Cornell U., 1975, M in Indsl. Labor Rels., 1976. Bar: NY 1976, Okla. 1981, US Dist. Ct. (no. dist.) NY 1976, US Dist. Ct. (ea. dist.) Okla. 1984, US Dist. Ct. (we. dist.) Okla. 2000, US Dist. Ct. (we. and ea. dists.) Ark. 2000, US Ct. Appeals (no. dist.) Okla. 1981, US Ct. Appeals (10th cir.) 1982, US Ct. Appeals (6th cir.) 1990, US Supreme Ct. 1991, US Dist. Ct. (ea. dist.) Tex. 2006. Assoc. Conner & Winters, Tulsa, 1980-85, ptnr., 1985-91, Shipley, Inhofe & Strecker, Tulsa, 1991-95, Strecker & Assocs. P.C., Tulsa, 1995—. Instr. paralegal program Tulsa Jr. Coll., 1985—, mem. adv. com., 1986-91; mem. Cornell Secondary Schs. Com., Tulsa, 1985—; instr. labor rels. Okla. State U., 1995—; master Am. Inns of Ct. Bd. dirs., v.p. Tulsa Sr. Svcs., 1988-91; mem. pers. com. Philbrook Art Mus. Capt. JAGC, U.S. Army, 1976-80. Mem. ABA, Okla. Bar Assn. (chmn. labor sect. 1990-91), Tulsa County Bar Assn. (continuing legal edn. com. 1981—), Soc. for Human Resource Mgmt., Tulsa Area Human Resources Assn. (gen. counsel 1989-2000, v.p. 1994-98, bd. dirs. family and children's svcs. 2000—04), Kappa Alpha. Democrat. Episcopalian. Avocations: jogging, golf. Home: 5112 E 107th St Tulsa OK 74137-7238 Office: Midcontinent Tower 401 S Boston Ste 2150 Tulsa OK 74103-4009 Home Phone: 918-298-4652; Office Phone: 918-582-1716. E-mail: destreck@juno.com, david.strecker@streckerlaborlaw.com.

STRECKER, JUDY ELLEN, music educator; d. Robert Joseph and Tressie Eulala Gibson; m. Jerome John Strecker, Dec. 28, 1990. MusB, Incarnate Word U., 1965; MA, Eastman Sch. Music, 1971; D of Musical Arts, U. Colo., 1979. Chair music dept. Incarnate Word Coll., San Antonio, 1971—76; dir. music St. Alphonsus Ch., Greenwell Springs, La., 1985—87; chair music dept. St. Mary of Plains Coll., Dodge City, Kans., 1987—90, Frank Phillips Coll., Borger, Tex., 1992—. V.p. faculty assoc. Frank Phillips Coll., 1996—98; adjudicator Nat. Guild Piano Tchrs., 1990—; organist 1st Meth. Ch., Pampa, 1992—94. Musician: (albums) Afternoon of Jazz, 1998, Recorder Music. Regional dir. Tex. Jr. Colls. Choral Festival, San Antonio, 1997—98; organist various chs., Borger, 1992—. Recipient NISOD Excellence award, U. Tex., Austin, 1998; fellow, Eastman Sch. Music, Rochester, N.Y., 1976—79. Mem.: Am. Coll. Musicians (piano judge 1990—), Tex. Assn. Music Schs., Tex. Music Educators Assn. Home: Box 835 Fritch TX 79036 Office: Frank Phillips Coll 1301 W Roosevelt Borger TX 79008 Personal E-mail: judystrecker@aol.com.

STREEB, GORDON LEE, diplomat, economist; b. Windsor, Colo., Dec. 24, 1935; s. Gerhard O. and Amelia (Martin) S.; m. Alice Junette Thomas, Aug. 11, 1962; children: Kurt, Kent, Kerry-Lynn. BSBA, BSChemE, U. Colo., 1959; PhD in Econs., U. Minn., 1978. Fgn. service officer U.S. Dept. State, Berlin, 1963-65; vice consul Am. Consulate, Guadalajara, Mex., 1965-67; instr. econs. U. Minn., 1968; examiner Bd. Examiners, 1972-73; internat. economist for trade policy Bur. Econ. and Bus. Affairs, Washington, 1973-77; econ. counselor U.S. mission European Office of the UN and other internat. orgns., Geneva, 1977-80; exec. asst. to undersec. of state on econ. affairs Washington, 1980-81; dep. asst. sec. state for econ. and social affairs Bur. Internat. Orgn. Affairs, Washington, 1981-84; dep. chief mission Am. Embassy, New Delhi, 1984-88; sr. inspector Dept. State, Washington, 1988-90; amb. to Zambia Am. Embassy, Lusaka, 1990-93; diplomat-in-residence The Carter Ctr., Atlanta, 1994-95, assoc. exec. dir. peace program, 1995—2004; vis. prof. Emory U., Atlanta, 2004—. Bd. dirs. Coun. on Fgn. Rels.; mem. adv. bd. Engrs. Without Borders-USA. Home: 2680 Churchwell Ln Tucker GA 30084-2402 Business E-Mail: gstreeb@emory.edu.

STREEM, JAMES KENNETH, musician, educator; b. Cleve., Jan. 15, 1934; s. Irving Earl and Geraldine W. Streem; m. Prudence Vitale, July 4, 1968 (dec. June 29, 2000). BS, Juilliard, 1956, MS, 1959. Mem. piano faculty Cleve. Music Sch. Settlement, 1960—68; prof. piano Fla. State U., Tallahassee, 1968—2003; concert debut Carnegie Hall, NYC, 1966. Lectr. in field. Composer: (film score) Double Stop, 1967; author: 125 Pianists on the Legend of Vladimir Horowitz, 1996; performer: Steinway concert series, Kosciusko Found., Alice Tully Hall, numerous recitals throughout U.S.; soloist: with symphony orch. Trustee Temple Israel, Tallahassee, 1975—82, 1987—93. With US Army, 1958—63. Home: 2604 Stonegate Dr Tallahassee FL 32308 E-mail: jks1115@earthlink.com.

STREEP, MERYL (MARY LOUISE STREEP), actress; b. Summit, NJ, June 22, 1949; d. Harry, Jr. and Mary W. Streep; m. Donald J. Grummer, Sept. 15, 1978; children: Henry, Mary Willa, Grace, Louisa. BA, Vassar Coll., 1971; MFA, Yale U., 1975, DFA (hon.), 1983, Dartmouth Coll., 1981. Co-founder Mothers & Others for a Livable Planet. Appeared with: Green Mountain Guild; actress: (Broadway plays) Trelawny of the Wells, 1975; (plays) 27 Wagons Full of Cotton (Theatre World award); A Memory of Two Mondays; Henry V; Secret Service; The Taming of the Shrew; Measure for Measure; The Cherry Orchard; Happy End; Wonderland; Taken in Marriage; Alice in Concert (Obie award, 1981); Mother Courage, 2006; (films) Julia, 1977; The Deer Hunter, 1978 (Best Supporting Actress award nat. Soc. film Critics, Acad. award nomination, 1978); Manhattan, 1979; The Seduction of Joe Tynan, 1979; Kramer vs. Kramer, 1979 (N.Y. Film Critics' award, Los Angeles Film Critics' award, both for best actress, Golden Globe award, Acad. award for best supporting actress, 1980); The French Lieutenant's Woman, 1981 (Los Angeles Film Critics award for best actress, Brit. Acad. award, Golden Globe award for best actress, Acad. award nomination, 1982); Sophie's Choice, 1982 (Acad. award for best actress, Los Angeles Film Critics award for best actress, Golden Globe award for best actress, 1983); Still of the Night, 1982; Silkwood, 1983 (Acad. award nomination); Falling in Love, 1984; Plenty, 1985; Out of Africa, 1985 (Los Angeles Film Critics award for best actress, Golden Globe award, 1985); Heartburn, 1986; Ironweed, 1987 (Acad. award nomination); A Cry in the Dark, 1988 (named Best Actress N.Y. Film Critics' Circle, Best Actress Cannes Film Festival, 1989, Acad. award nomination); She-Devil, 1989; Postcards From the Edge, 1990; Defending Your Life, 1991; Death Becomes Her, 1992; The House of Spirits, 1993; The River Wild, 1994; The Bridges of Madison County, 1995 (Acad. award nominee for best actress, 1996); Before and After, 1996; Marvin's Room, 1996; Dancing at Lugnasa, 1998; One True Thing, 1998; Music of the Heart, 1999 (Acad. award nominee for best actress); The Hours, 2002; Adaptation, 2002 (Southeastern Film Critics Assn. award for best supporting actress, 2002, Chgo. Film Critics Assn. award for best supporting actress, 2003, Golden Globe for best supporting actress, 2003); The Manchurian Candidate, 2004; Lemony Snicket's A Series of Unfortunate Events, 2004; Prime, 2005; A Prairie Home Companion, 2006 (Best Supporting Actress, Nat. Soc. Film Critics, 2007); Dark Matter, 2007; The Devil Wears Prada, 2006 (Best Supporting Actress, Nat. Soc. Film Critics, 2007, Best Performance by an Actress in a Motion Picture-Musical or Comedy, Golden Globe awards, Hollywood Fgn. Press Assn., 2007); Evening, 2007; (voice only) Rabbit Ears: The Tale of Peter Rabbit, 1987; Rabbit Ears: The Tale of Jeremy Fisher, 1987; The Tailor of Gloucester, 1988; Rabbit Ears: The Fisherman and His Wife, 1989; Chrysanthemum, 1999; Artificial Intelligence: AI, 2001; The Ant Bully, 2006; actress: (TV films) Secret Service, 1977; The Deadliest Season, 1977; Uncommon Women and Others, 1979; Alice at the Palace, 1982; actress, exec. prodr. First Do No Harm, 1997; narrator The Velveteen Rabbit, 1984 (Emmy award Best Children's Rec.); A Vanishing Wilderness, 1990; actress: (TV miniseries) Holocaust, 1978 (Emmy award for Outstanding Lead Actress in a Mini-series, 1978); Angels in America, 2003 (Screen Actors Guild Award for best actress, Golden Globe for best actress, Emmy award Outstanding Lead Actress in a Mini-series or a movie, 2004). Named Officer, French Ordre des Arts et des Lettres, 2000; named one of 100 Most Influential People, Time Mag., 2006; recipient Mademoiselle award, 1976, Woman of Yr. award, B'nai Brith, 1979, Hasty Pudding Soc., Harvard U., 1980, Best Supporting Actress award, Nat. Bd. of Rev., 1979, Best Actress award, 1982, Star of Yr. award, Nat. Assn. Theater Owners, 1983, People's Choice award, 1983, 85, 86, 87, 1990, Women in Film Crystal award, 1998, Gotham award for Lifetime Achievement, 1999, Bette Davis Lifetime Achievement award, 1999, Lifetime Achievement award, Am. Film Inst., 2004, most nominated actor ever for an Academy Award. Office: Creative Artists Agy 9830 Wilshire Blvd Beverly Hills CA 90212-1825

STREET, ERICA CATHERINE, lawyer; b. Lansing, Mich., July 5, 1958; d. Cassius English and Helen Joanna (Hoesman) S.; 1 child, Chelsea Nicole Pratte. BA, Hillsdale Coll., 1979; JD, U. Mich., 1981. Bar: Minn. 1982, U.S. Dist. Ct. Minn. 1982, U.S. Ct. Appeals (8th cir.) 1983. Assoc. Best & Flanagan, Mpls., 1981-85; sr. counsel Fingerhut Corp., Minnetonka, Minn., 1985-89, Target Stores, Mpls., 1989-97, asst. gen. counsel, 1997-99; pres. Dayton Hudson Brands Inc., Mpls., 1999-2000, Target Brands, Inc., Mpls., 2000—04, E. Street Assocs., PLLC, Deephaven, 2004—07; assoc. gen. counsel Fingerhut Direct Mktg., Inc., 2007—. Office Phone: 952-656-3933. Business E-Mail: erica.street@fingerhut.com.

STREET, HUSTON, professional baseball player; b. Austin, Tex., Aug. 2, 1983; s. James, Janie. Attended, Tex. Univ., 2002—03. Relief pitcher Oakland Athletics, 2004—. Named Ctrl. Tex. Coll. Pitcher Yr, 2003, USA Baseball Athlete Yr., 2003; recipient Rookie of the Yr., Major League Baseball Am. League, 2005. Achievements include first-team NCAA All-American, 2003; two-time first-tem All-Big 12, 2002-2003. Office: Oakland Athletics 7000 Colliseum Way Oakland CA 94621 Personal E-mail: jrstreet4@aol.com.

STREET, JOHN CHARLES, linguistics educator; b. Chgo., Apr. 3, 1930; s. Charles Larrabee and Mary Louise (Rouse) S.; m. Eve Elizabeth Baker, June 4, 1975. BA, Yale, 1951, MA, 1952, PhD, 1955. Asst. prof. English Mich. State U., 1957-59; asst. prof. linguistics and Mongolian langs. Columbia, 1959-62; vis. asst. prof. linguistics U. Wash., 1962-63; assoc. prof. linguistics U. Wis., Madison, 1963-65, prof. linguistics, 1965-92, prof. emeritus Madison, 1992—. Author: The Language of the Secret History of the Mongols, 1957, Khalkha Structure, 1963, The Journal of Oliver Rouse, 1983, An Ellis Family of Devon and Newfoundland, 1994, A Genealogy of the Rouses of Devon, 2002. Research asso. Am. Council Learned Socs., 1959-62. Served with AUS, 1955-57.

STREET, JOHN F., mayor; b. Norristown, Pa., Oct. 15, 1943; m. Naomi Street; children: Sharif, Rasida, Lateef, Akeem. BA in English, Oakwood Coll., 1966; JD, Temple U., 1975. Pvt. law practice, 1975—80; city councilman City of Phila., 1979-98, coun. pres., 1992-98, past chmn. licenses and inspections, appropriations coms., chmn. Whole, Rules & Fiscal Stability, Intergovt. coop. com., 1992—; mem. Phila. Gas Commn., 1984-89, chmn., 1992—; mayor City of Phila., 2000—. Named one of 100 Most Influential Black Americans, Ebony mag., 2006. Avocations: running, bicycling. Office: City Hall Rm 215 Philadelphia PA 19107 *

STREET, PAUL SHIPLEY, lawyer; b. Klamath Falls, Oreg., Mar. 4, 1948; s. Leon Rex and Mary Rebecca (Shipley) S.; children: Adam, Blake. BA, Coll. Idaho, 1970; JD, U. Wash., 1973. Bar: Idaho 1973, U.S. Dist. Ct. Idaho 1973, Idaho Supreme Ct. 1973. Law clerk Idaho Supreme Ct., Boise, 1973-74; pres., mng. ptnr. Moffatt, Thomas, Barrett, Rock & Fields, Boise, 1974—99; sr. v.p., gen. counsel, corp. sec. Bldg. Materials Holding Co., San Francisco, 1999—, chief adminstrv. officer, 2001—. Sec. BMC West Corp., Boise. Co-author: Idaho Law Review, 1991, Digest of Environmental Law of Real Property, 1991. Pres. Coll. Idaho Alumni Assn., Caldwell, 1986, Am. Diabetes Assn., 1984—; formerly bd. dirs. First United Meth. Ch., Boise; chairperson United Way of Ada County, Boise, 1982-83. Mem. ABA (sec. mem. patent, trademark and copyright law; litigation, econs. law practice), Am. Soc. Med. Assn. Counsel, Am. Soc. Law and Medicine, Am. Arbitration Assn., Idaho State Bar (chmn. corp. and securities law sect. 1992-93), Boise Bar Assn., Boise Ins. Adjusters Assn., Real Estate Lawyers Assn., Boise Area C. of C. (vice chmn. 1991—). Avocation: bird hunting. Office: Bldg Materials Holding Corp Four Embarcadero Ctr Ste 3200 San Francisco CA 94111 Office Phone: 415-627-9100. Office Fax: 415-627-9119. *

STREET, PICABO, Olympic athlete; b. Triumph, Idaho, Apr. 3, 1971; Downhill skier U.S. Ski Team, 1994—. Autobiography Picabo: Nothing to Hide. Named World Cup Downhill Women's Champion, 1995, 1996; recipient Silver medal Women's Downhill Alpine Skiing, Olympic Games, Lillehammer, 1994, Bronze and Gold medals, World Championships, 1996, Gold medals (3) Women's Super Giant Slalom Alpine Skiing, Nagano, Japan, 1998, medal, Winter Olympics. Office Phone: 208-578-9880.

STREET, ROBERT LYNNWOOD, civil, mechanical and environmental engineer; b. Honolulu, Dec. 18, 1934; s. Evelyn Mansel and Dorothy Heather (Brook) S.; m. Norma Jeanette Ensminger, Feb. 6, 1959; children: Brian Clarke (dec.), Deborah Lynne, Kimberley Anne. Student, USN ROTC Program, 1952-57; MS, Stanford U., 1957, PhD (NSF grad. fellow 1960-62), 1963. Mem. faculty Sch. Engring. Stanford U., 1962—2005, prof. civil engring., assoc. chmn. dept. Sch. Engring., 1970-72, chmn. dept. Sch. Engring., 1972-80, 94-95, prof. fluid mechanics and applied math. Sch. Engring., 1972—2004, founding dir. environ. fluid mechanics lab. Sch. Engring., 1985-91, assoc. dean rsch. Sch. Engring., 1971-83, vice provost acad. computing and info. sys., 1983-85, vice provost, dean rsch. and acad. info. sys., 1985-87, v.p. for info. resources, 1987-90, acting provost, 1987, v.p. librs. and info. resources, 1990-92, vice provost, dean of librs. and info. resources, 1992—94, William Alden and Martha Campbell prof. Sch. Engring., 1997—2004, prof. emeritus fluid mechanics, applied math, 2005, design cons. Engring. Libr., 2007. Vis. prof. U. Liverpool, Eng., 1970-71, Ctr. for Water Rsch., U. Western Australia, 1985; vis. prof. mech. engring. James Cook U., Australia, 1995; trustee Univ. Corp. Atmospheric Rsch., 1983-94, chmn. sci. programs evaluation com., 1981, treas. corp., 1985, vice chmn. bd., 1986, chmn. bd., 1987-91; bd. dirs., sec.-treas. UCAR Found., 1987-91; bd. govs. Rsch. Libr. Group, 1990-91; chmn. Com. Preservation Rsch. Libr. Materials, Assn. Rsch. Librs., 1993; mem. higher edn. adv. bds. computer corps., 1983-94; mem. basic energy sci. adv. com. U.S. Dept. Energy, 1993-96; bd. dirs. Stanford U. Bookstore, Inc., 1993-98; cons. Design of Libr., Sch. Engring., Stanford U., 2007. With C.E.C., USN, 1957-60. Sr. postdoc. fellow Nat. Ctr. Atmospheric Rsch., 1978-79, faculty fellow, 2007; sr. Queen's fellow in marine sci., Australia, 1985; fellow N.E. Asia-U.S. Forum on Internat. Policy at Stanford U., 1985-89; named to Beverly Hills H.S. Hall of Fame, 2005. Fellow: AAAS; mem.: NAE (Sect. 4 peer com. 2006—), ASME (R.T. Knapp award 1986), ASCE (chmn. publs. com. hydraulics divsn. 1978—80, Walter Huber prize 1972, Hilgard Hydraulic Engring. prize 2002, Rouse Hydraulic Engring. award 2005), Am. Meteorol. Soc., Oceanographic Soc., Am. Geophys. Union, Sigma Xi, Phi Beta Kappa, Tau Beta Pi. Office: Stanford U Environ Fluid Mechs Lab Dept Civil/Environ Engring Stanford CA 94305-4020 Home Phone: 650-493-7598; Office Phone: 650-723-4969. Business E-Mail: street@stanford.edu.

STREET, SHARON, philosophy educator; BA in Philosophy, Amherst Coll., 1995; PhD in Philosophy, Harvard U., 2002. Asst. prof. philosophy NYU, 2002—. Spkr. in field. Author: A Darwinian Dilemma for Realist Theories of Value, 2006. Mailing: NYU Silver Ctr Rm 503 100 Washington Sq E New York NY 10003 Office Phone: 212-998-8324. Office Fax: 212-995-4179. Business E-Mail: sharon.street@nyu.edu.

STREET, TERRY M., artist, educator; b. Bklyn., Dec. 11, 1929; d. William George Nappenbach and Marie Virginia Caron; m. Norman Street, Oct. 11, 1962 (dec. Sept. 1979); children: Lesa, David. Student, Chinourd Art Sch., 1948, Art Students League, 1950—53, Am. Art Sch., 1953—54, NYU Inst. Fine Art, 1953—54, Nat. Acad. Design, 1953—58, Vrijy Acad., 1956. Cert. tchr. Calif. Instr. Traphagen Sch. Design, NY, 1959, Conejo Valley Adult Sch., Thousand Oaks, Calif., 1980—93; art dir. Dwight Sch. for Girls, NJ, 1960—62, Carden Conejo Sch., Calif., 1965—93; exhibit specialist Smithsonian, Wash., 1962—63; founder, dir. Burke Sch. Art, Va., 1968—70; art cons. for occupl. therapists Pediatric Rehabilitation, Poland, Slovakia, Hungary, 1988—90; founder, dir. Hawthorne Studio, Portland, Oreg., 1993—. Instr. St. Francis Svcs., Portland, 2000—. Exhibitions include Knickerbocker Art Guild, 1955, Allied Artists Nat. Acad. Design, NY, 1956, Smithsonian Art Inst., Wash., DC, 1964, Gallery 33, Portland, Oreg., 1997—98, Hawthorne Studio; illustrator: Problem Solving in Occupational Therapy; numerous pvt. collections. Cons. park and recreation Children's Art Festival, Calif.; charter mem. Nat. Women's Mus.; coun. mem. St. Francis Ch., Portland. Fogg Mus. of Haravard U. scholar, 1954, Louis Comfort Tiffany fellow, 1956. Mem.: Allied Artists, Oriental Art Soc., Oreg. Soc. Artists, Keizer Art Assn., Watercolor Soc. Oreg., Nat. Watercolor Soc. (assoc.), Northwest Watercolor Soc. (assoc.), Art Students League (life). Home and Office: Hawthorne Studio 3511 SE Francis St Portland OR 97202 E-mail: tstreetart@msn.com.

STREET, TISON, music educator; b. Boston, May 20, 1943; s. Jabez Curry and Leila Street. BA, Harvard Coll., Cambridge, Mass., 1965; MA, Harvard U., Cambridge, Mass., 1971. Instr. chamber music Harvard U., 1978—79, assoc. prof. music, 1979—83; tchg. assoc. music Boston U., 1995—2002. Vis. lectr. U. Calif., Berkeley, 1971—72, City Coll., NYC, 1987; violinist, concertmaster Harvard Chamber Orch., Cambridge, 1991—96; violinist Boston Ballet Orch., 1968—2006, Boston Pops Esplanade Orch., 1988—97. Composer: String Quartet, 1972, Bright Sambas, 1992, Colonial Scenes, 2004. Recipient Rome prize, Am. Acad. Rome, 1973—74, award, Am. Acad. Arts & Letters, NYC, 1973; fellow, Guggenheim Found., NYC, 1981. Democrat. Buddhist. Avocations: hiking, swimming. Home: 69 Appleton St #4 Boston MA 02116

STREET, WILLIAM MAY, retired beverage company executive; b. Louisville, 1938; Grad., Princeton U., 1960; MBA, Harvard U., 1963. V.p. Brown-Forman Corp., Louisville, 1969, dir., mem. exec. com., 1971, sr. v.p., 1977, vice chmn., 1983, pres., 2000; pres., COO Brown-Forman Beverage Co. Divsn., Louisville, 1986-94; pres., CEO Brown-Forman Beverages Worldwide Divsn., 1994—; pres. Brown-Forman Corp., 2001—03; ret., 2003. Dir. Papa John's Internat. Chmn. Ky. Horse Racing Authority. Office: Brown-Forman Beverages Worldwide 850 Dixie Hwy Louisville KY 40210-1038 Home Phone: 502-897-7320.

STREETEN, BARBARA WIARD, ophthalmologist, medical educator; b. Candia, NH, Mar. 3, 1925; d. Robert Campbell Wiard and Gertrude Sarah Matheson; m. David Henry Palmer Streeten, Aug. 2, 1952; children: Robert Duncan, Elizabeth Anne, John Palmer. AB magna cum laude, Tufts U., 1945, MD cum laude, 1950. Diplomate Am. Bd. Ophthalmology. Jr. resident in gen. pathology Mallory Inst., Boston City Hosp., 1951-52; fellow in ophthalmic pathology Mass. Eye and Ear Infirmary, Boston, 1952-53; resident in ophthalmology Wayne County Gen. Hosp., Eloise, Mich., 1953-56; from jr. to sr. clin. instr. ophthalmology U. Mich. Med. Sch., Ann Arbor, 1956-60; from asst. prof. to prof. ophthalmology SUNY Health Sci. Ctr. (now called SUNY Upstate Med. U.), Syracuse, 1964—, dir. eye pathology lab., 1966—; from asst. prof. to prof. pathology SUNY Health Sci. Ctr., Syracuse, 1968—. Contbr. more than 120 articles to profl. jours., chapters to books. Mem. vision study sect. Nat. Eye Inst., NIH, Bethesda, Md., 1977-80, mem. bd. sci. counselors, 1982-86; mem. editl. bd., mem. editl. adv. com. Ophthalmology jour., 1982-94; gen. editor Investigative Ophthalmology and Visual Sci., 1979-82, mem. editl. bd., 1987-92. Grantee Nat. Eye Inst., NIH, 1975—2002. Mem. Am. Assn. Ophthalmic Pathologists (charter, past pres., bd. dirs., Zimmerman medal 1997), Am. Acad. Ophthalmology (honor award 1990), Verhoeff Ophthalmic Pathology Soc. (past pres.), Assn. for Rsch. in Vision and Ophthalmology (past sect. chmn.), Internat. Soc. Ophthalmic Pathology (co-v.p. N.Am. 1990-92), Phi Beta Kappa, Alpha Omega Alpha. Episcopalian. Achievements include establishment of elastic system nature of the suspensory ligament of the ocular lens; ultrastructural and immunopathologic contributions to diseases of the ocular connective tissue matrix, particularly those related to cataract and glaucoma. Home: 334 Berkeley Dr Syracuse NY 13210-3000 Office: SUNY Upstate Med Univ WH Rm 2107 766 Irving Ave Syracuse NY 13210-1602

STREETER, OSCAR EDWARD, JR., radiation oncologist; b. Roanoke, Va., May 20, 1955; s. Oscar Edward Sr. and Betty (Richardson) S.; m. Paulette Y. Saddler; 1 child, Rebecca. BS in Biology, USC; MD, Howard U., 1982. Diplomate Am. Bd. Med. Examiners. Intern U. Calif., Irvine, 1983-85; resident Howard U. Med. Ctr., Washington, 1986-89; resident tng. program dir. dept. radiation oncology U. So. Calif. Sch. Medicine, LA, 1990-94, asst. prof. radiation oncology, 1990-95, asst. prof. clin. radiation oncology, 1995-97, assoc. prof. clin. radiation oncology, 1997—; dept. radiation oncology chief physician LAC, U. So. Calif. Med. Ctr., 1992-94, U. So. Calif. Norris Cancer Ctr., 1994—. Chair cancer com. U. So. Calif. Sch. Medicine, LA, 1997, med. exec., 1995—, acad. tech. adv. com., 1997; mem. leadership coun. U. So. Calif. Cancer Ctr., 1995—. Contbr. articles to profl. jours. Chmn. NBLIC/Western Region, LA, 1995—; adv. bd. Wellness Com. Foothills, Pasadena, Calif., 1995—; bd. dirs. Real Men Cook Found., LA, 1993—, Women of Color Breast Cancer Survivors Project, L.A., 1995—; mem. Real Men Cook Found., 1994; mem. Maxine Waters-35th Dist. Com. Svc., Mem. of Congress; mem. health svcs. Office of Willie Brown Jr. Spkr. of Assembly 13 Dist. Grantee U. So. Calif., 1993, 93-96, U. Calif., 1993-95, Biotech. Comms., LA, 1995; named one of Top 100 Black Physicians in Am., Black Enterprise Mag., 2001; named to America's Top Doctors, 2001-06, Best Doctors in Am., 2003-06. Office: USC/Norris Comprehensive Cancer Ctr 1441 Eastlake Ave Los Angeles CA 90089-0112 Business E-Mail: ostreeter@aol.com. *

STREETER, ROBERT DAVENPORT, electrical engineer, consultant; b. Springfield, Mass., Sept. 17, 1941; s. William Allen Streeter and Muriel Ethel Davenport; m. Carole Janet Riley, Mar. 21, 1970 (dec. Nov. 2004); children: John Riley, Susan Streeter Billian; m. Donna Jean Preston Smith, Feb. 18, 2006. B in Elec. Engring., Ohio State U., 1964; MSEE, Purdue U., 1968. Registered profl. engr., Ind. Engr. WBNS Radio-TV, Columbus, Ohio, 1961—64, Ohio State U. Rsch. Found., Columbus, 1962—64, The Magnavox Co., Fort Wayne, Ind., 1965—82; pres. A M Stereo, Inc., Fort Wayne, 1982—; engring. fellow Raytheon, Fort Wayne, 1985—. Contbr. articles to profl. jours. Mem.: IEEE, Eta Kappa Nu (life). Achievements include invention of AM stereo, microelectromechanical systems. Avocations: private pilot, amateur radio, bicycling. Home: 6111 Eagle Creek Dr Fort Wayne IN 46814-3213 Office: Raytheon 1010 Production Rd Fort Wayne IN 46808 Personal E-mail: r.streeter@ieee.org.

STREETER, STEPHANIE ANNE, former printing company executive; b. Boston, Sept. 19, 1957; d. Andrew Geoffrey Galef and Suzanne Jane (Cohen) Sidy; m. Edward Stanley Streeter, Feb. 22, 1980. BA in Polit. Sci., Stanford U., 1979. Mgr. market analysis Xerox Small Bus. System, Sunnyvale, Calif., 1980-81; regional sales mgr. Xerox Office Products Divsn., Sunnyvale, Calif., 1981-83; product mgr. Decision Data Computer Corp., Horsham, Pa., 1983-85; sr. product mgr. Avery Dennison Corp., Covina, Calif., 1985-88, bus. mgr. indexes, 1988-89, bus. mgr. computer supplies, 1989-90, dir. mktg., computer products, 1990-91, v.p. gen. mgr. label divsn. Diamond Bar, Calif., 1991-93, v.p., gen. mgr., Avery Dennison Brands, 1993—96, worldwide group v.p., 1996—2000; COO idealab!, Pasadena, Calif., 2000; pres., COO Banta Corp., Menasha, Wis., 2001—02, pres., CEO, 2002—04, chmn., pres., CEO, 2004—07. Bd. dirs. Banta Corp., 2001—07, Kohl's Corp., 2007—. Bd. dirs. Wis. Mfrs. and Commerce. Fellow Internat. Women's Forum. Democrat. Avocations: bicycling, skiing. *

STREETMAN, BEN GARLAND, electrical engineering educator; b. Cooper, Tex., June 24, 1939; s. Richard E. and Bennie (Morrow) S.; m. Lenora Ann Music, Sept. 9, 1961; children: Paul, Scott. BS, U. Tex., 1961, MS, 1963, PhD, 1966. Fellow Oak Ridge Nat. Lab., 1964-66; asst. prof. elec. engring. U. Ill., 1966-70, assoc. prof., 1970-74, prof., 1974-82; rsch. prof. Coordinated Sci. Lab., 1970-82; prof. elec. engring. U. Tex., Austin, 1982—, dir. Microelectronics Rsch. Ctr., 1984—96, Dula D. Cockrell Centennial chair engring., 1989—, dean Coll. Engring., 1996—. Bd. dir. Nat. Instruments. Author: Solid State Electronic Devices 6th edit., 2005. Recipient Frederick Emmons Terman award Am. Soc. Engring. Edn., 1981, AT&T Found. award, 1987; named Disting. Alumnus, U. Tex. at Austin, 1998, Aldert Vander Ziel award, 2005. Fellow IEEE (life, Edn. medal 1989), Electrochem. Soc.; mem. NAE, Am. Acad. Arts and Scis., Tau Beta Pi, Eta Kappa Nu, Sigma Xi. Office: U Tex at Austin Dean of Engring 1 University Sta C2100 Austin TX 78712-0284

STREETMAN, JOHN WILLIAM, III, museum director; b. Marion, NC, Jan. 19, 1941; s. John William, Jr. and Emily Elaine (Carver) S.; children: Katherine Drake, Leah Farrior, Burgin Eaves. BA in English and Theatre History, Western Carolina U., 1963; cert. in Shakespeare studies, Lincoln Coll., Oxford (Eng.) U., 1963. Founding dir. Jewett Creative Arts Ctr., Berwick Acad., South Berwick, Maine, 1964-70; exec. dir. Polk Mus. Art, Lakeland, Fla., 1970-75; dir. Mus. Arts and Sci., Evansville, Ind., 1975—; chmn. mus. adv. panel Ind. Arts Commn., 1977-78. Mem. Am. Assn. Museums, Assn. Ind. Museums (bd. dirs.) Episcopalian. Office: Evansville Mus Arts History and Sci 411 SE Riverside Dr Evansville IN 47713-1037

STREISAND, BARBRA JOAN, singer, actress, film director; b. Bklyn., Apr. 24, 1942; d. Emanuel and Diana (Rosen) S.; m. Elliott Gould, Mar. 1963 (div.); 1 son, Jason Emanuel; m. James Brolin, July 1, 1998. Grad. high sch., Bklyn.; student, Yeshiva of Bklyn.; Doctorate of Arts and Humanities (hon.), Brandeis U., 1995. NY theatre debut Another Evening with Harry Stoones, 1961; appeared in Broadway musicals I Can Get It for You Wholesale, 1962, Funny Girl, 1964-65; motion pictures include Funny Girl, 1968, Hello Dolly, 1969, On a Clear Day You Can See Forever, 1970, The Owl and the Pussy Cat, 1970, What's Up Doc?, 1972, Up the Sandbox, 1972, The Way We Were, 1973, For Pete's Sake, 1974, Funny Lady, 1975, The Main Event, 1979, All Night Long, 1981, Nuts, 1987, Meet the Fockers, 2004; actor, prodr. (films): A Star is Born, 1976; prodr., dir., actor (films) Yentl, 1983, The Prince of Tides, 1991, The Mirror Has Two Faces, 1996 (ASCAP Award for score, 1996; exec. prodr.: (TV movies) Serving in Silence: The Margarethe Cammermeyer Story, 1995; (TV spls.) My Name is Barbra, 1965 (5 Emmy awards), Color Me Barbra, 1966, Barbra Streisand: The Concert, 1995 (Cable ACE award for best performance and for best direction, Two Emmy awards), Barbra Streisand: Timeless, 2001 (Emmy award); rec. artist on Columbia Records; (albums) People, 1965, My Name is Barbra, 1965, Color Me Barbra, 1966, Barbra Streisand: A Happening in Central Park, 1968, Barbra Streisand: One Voice, Stoney End, 1971, Barbra Joan Streisand, 1972, The Way We Were, 1974, A Star is Born, 1976, Superman, 1977, The Stars Salute Israel at 30, 1978, Wet, 1979, (with Barry Gibb) Guilty, 1980, Emotion, 1984, The Broadway Album, 1986, Til I Loved You, 1989; other albums include: A Collection: Greatest Hits, 1989, Just for the Record, 1991, Back to Broadway, 1993, Concert at the Forum, 1993, The Concert Recorded Live at Madison Square Garden, 1994, The Concert Highlights, 1995, Higher Ground, 1997, A Love Like Ours, 1999, Christmas Memories, 2001, The Essential Barbara Streisand, 2002, The Movie Album, 2003, Guilty Pleasures, 2005, Guilty Too, 2005, Nur das Beste, 2006, Live in Concert 2006, 2007. Recipient: Emmy award, CBS-TV spl. (My Name Is Barbra), 1964, Acad. award as best actress (Funny Girl), 1968, Golden Globe award (Funny Girl), 1969, co-recipient Acad. award for best song (Evergreen), 1976, Georgie award AGVA 1977, Grammy awards for best female pop vocalist, 1963, 64, 65, 77, 86, for best song writer (with Paul Williams), 1977, 2 Grammy nominations for Back to Broadway, 1994; Nat. Acad. of Recording Arts & Sciences Lifetime Achievement Award, 1994, Cecil B. Demille Lifetime Achievement Award, 2000, Life Achievement award, Am. Film Inst., 2001, Liberty & Justice Award, Rainbow/PUSH Coalition, 2001, Humanitarian award, Human Rights Campaign, 2004; Inducted into French Legion Of Honor, 2007 Office: Barbra Streisand c/o Martin Erlichman Assoc Inc 5670 Wilshire Blvd Ste 2400 Los Angeles CA 90036 also: Nigro Karlin Segal 10100 Santa Monica Blvd Ste 1300 Los Angeles CA 90067

STREISAND, ROBERT L., thoracic surgeon; s. Max and Florence Streisand; m. Gail Hollick Streisand; children: Adam, Eve, Rachael, Danielle. BS, Trinity Coll., West Hartford, Conn.; MD, SUNY, Bklyn., 1966. Chief thoracic surgery White Plains Hosp., NY, 1985—2000, St. Johns Hosp., Yonkers, NY, 2000—; sr. attending thoracic surgeon Laurence Hosp., Bronxville, NY, 2000—. Med. cons. Med. Mut. Liability Ins. Co., NYC, 1995—. Lt. col. USAF, 1973—75. Fellow: Soc. Thoracic Surgeons, Am. Coll. Surgeons. Avocations: skiing, scuba diving. Office: 10 Chester Ave White Plains NY 10601

STREIT, MICHAEL J., state supreme court justice; b. Sheldon, Iowa, Apr. 14, 1950; married; 1 child. BA, U. Iowa, 1972; grad., U. San Diego Sch. Law, 1975. Cert.: (U.S. Ct. Appeals) 1996. Atty. priv. practice, 1975—83; asst. atty. Lucas County, 1975—79, atty., 1979—83; judge Iowa Dist. Ct., Fifth Judicial Dist., 1983—96, Iowa Ct. of Appeals, 1996—2001; justice Iowa Supreme Ct., 2001—. Mem. Iowa Supreme Ct. Education Advisory Com., Iowa Supreme Ct. Judicial Technology Com., Judges Assn. Education Com. Mem.: Iowa State Bar Assn., Blackstone Inn of Ct., Iowa Jud. Inst. Office: Iowa Supreme Ct Jud Branch Bldg 1111 E Ct Ave Des Moines IA 50319 *

STREITWIESER, ANDREW, JR., retired chemistry professor; b. Buffalo, June 23, 1927; s. Andrew and Sophie Streitwieser; m. Mary Ann Good, Aug. 19, 1950 (dec. May 1965); children: David Roy, Susan Ann; m. Suzanne Cope Beier, July 29, 1967 (dec. Apr. 2006); m. Joyce Hessel, May 2007. AB, Columbia U., 1949, MA, 1950, PhD, 1952; postgrad. (AEC fellow), MIT, 1951-52. Faculty U. Calif., Berkeley, 1952-92, prof. chemistry, 1963-92, prof. emeritus, 1993—. Cons. to industry, 1957—. Author: Molecular Orbital Theory for Organic Chemists, 1961, Solvolytic Displacement Reactions, 1962, (with J.I. Brauman) Supplemental Tables of Molecular Orbital Calculations, 1965, (with C.A. Coulson) Dictionary of Pi Electron Calculations, 1965, (with P.H. Owens) Orbital and Electron Density Diagrams, 1973, (with C.H. Heathcock and E.M. Kosower) Introduction to Organic Chemistry, 4th edit., 1992, A Lifetime of Synergy with Theory and Experiment, 1996; also numerous articles; co-editor: Progress in Physical Organic Chemistry, 11 vols., 1963-74. Recipient Humboldt Found. Sr. Scientist award, 1976, Humboldt medal, 1979, Berkeley citation, 1993. Fellow AAAS; mem. NAS, Am. Chem. Soc. (Calif. sect. award 1964, award in Petroleum Chemistry 1967, Norris award in phys. organic chemistry 1982, Cope scholar award 1989), Am. Acad. Arts and Scis., Bavarian Acad. Scis. (corr.), Phi Beta Kappa, Sigma Xi. Achievements include research in organic reaction mechanisms; application molecular orbital theory to organic chemistry; chemical structures on carbon acidities; f-element organometallic chemistry. Office: U Calif Dept Chemistry Berkeley CA 94720-1460 Home Phone: 510-841-6877; Office Phone: 510-642-2204. Business E-Mail: astreit@berkeley.edu.

STREKOWSKI, LUCJAN, chemistry professor; came to U.S., 1981; s. Antoni and Janina S.; m. Alewtina Smirnova, Oct. 14, 1967; children: Rafal, Anna. BS in Polymer Chemistry with distinction, Mendeleev Inst. Chemistry, Moscow, 1967; PhD in Organic Chemistry, Polish Acad. Scis., 1972; DSc in Chemistry, Adam Mickiewicz U., Poznan, Poland, 1976. Instr. organic chemistry Adam Mickiewicz U., Poznan, 1971-72, asst. prof. dept. chemistry, 1972-78, assoc. prof. dept. chemistry, 1978-81; rsch. assoc. dept. chemistry U. Fla., Gainesville, 1981-84; asst. prof. dept. chemistry Ga. State U., Atlanta, 1984-89, assoc. prof. dept. chemistry, 1989-96, prof. dept. chem., 1996—. Vis. prof. U. Fla., Gainesville, 1979-80, 81, Australian Nat. U., 1980, U. Kans., Lawrence, 1972-73. Editor: Pyridine-Metal Complexes, Vol. 14, Part 6, 1985; N.Am. editor Heterocyclic Comms.; mem. editl. bd. Arkivoc; contbr. more than 250 articles to profl. jours.; patentee in field. Recipient award, Polish Ministry Sci., 1997, Polish Chem. Soc., 1973, Polish Acad. Scis., 1972, Ga. State U., 1993; grantee Am. Chem. Soc.-Petroleum Rsch. Fund, 1985—2006, Solvay Pharms., 1992—93, Nat. Diagnostics, 1991—93, NIAID/NIMH, 1988—89, Rohm and Hass Co., 1988, Am. Cancer Soc., 1987—89, Rsch. Corp., 1985—94, Milheim Found. Cancer Rsch., 1985—86, DuPont Co., 1996—2000, Small Bus. Innovation Rsch. Program, 2000—02, FBI, 2002—, Coley Pharms., 2003—04, Ga. Rsch. Alliance, 2004—05. Mem. Am. Chem. Soc., Internat. Soc. Heterocyclic Chemistry, Internat. Acad. Scis. of Nature and Soc. (mem. presidium). Avocation: classical music. Office: Ga State Univ Dept Chemistry Atlanta GA 30303 Office Phone: 404-651-0999. Business E-Mail: lucjan@gsu.edu.

STRELTZER, JON, psychiatry professor; b. Denver, Sept. 22, 1944; s. John Ellis and Sarah Ann Streltzer; m. Sheila Ledesma, Aug. 7, 1993; children: Robin Leilani Bodin, Audrey Luana, James Ormand. BA in Philosophy, Yale U., New Haven, Con., 1966; MD, U. Colo., Denver, 1970. Lic. psychiatrist Am. Bd. Psychiatry & Neurology, 1976, addiction psychiatry Am. Bd. Psychiatry & Neurology, 1993, pain mgmt. Am. Bd. Psychiatry & Neurology, 2000. Asst. prof. psychiatry U. Hawaii, Honolulu, 1974—80, assoc. prof. psychiatry, 1980—84, residency tng. dir., dept. psychiatry Med. Sch., 1982—96, prof. psychiatry, 1984—. Chair 17th World Congress on Psychosomatic Medicine, Waikoloa, Hawaii, 2003; sec. Internat. Coll. Psychosomatic Medicine, 2003—. Editor: (medical books) Culture and Psychopathology, 1997, Culture and Psychotherapy, 2001, Clinical Competence in Cultural Psychiatry, 2004; author: (medical textbook) Handbook of Consultation-Liaison Psychiatry, 2007. Bd. dirs. Drug Addiction Svcs. Hawaii, Honolulu, 2005—. Fellow: Internat. Coll. Psychosomatic Medicine (sec. 2003—07), Am. Psychiat. Assn. (life Eldridge award 1985); mem.: Am. Acad. Addiction Psychiatry (chair task force cronic pain 2001—03), Am. Bd. Anesthesiology, Soc. Study Culture and Psychiatry, World Assn. Cultural Soc. (treas. 2005—, 2005—), Acad. Psychosomatic Medicine, Am. Psychosomatic Soc. D-Liberal. Avocations: squash, golf. Office: Univ Hawaii Dept Psychiatry 1356 Lusitana St Honolulu HI 96813 Office Fax: 808-586-2940; Home Fax: 808-586-2940. Business E-Mail: streltzerj@dop.hawaii.edu.

STREMSTERFER, JOHN GARY, foundation administrator, consultant; b. Springfield, Ill., Aug. 4, 1974; s. Gary Wilbur and Marianne Stremsterfer; m. Trina Ann Madonia, July 5, 2003; 1 child, Ileana. AA, Springfield Coll. Ill., 1994; BA, Ill. Coll., Jacksonville, 1996. Dunn fellow, legislative liaison Ill. Gov.'s Office, Springfield, 1996—98; dir. instl. advancement Ursuline Acad., Springfield, 1998—2001; dir. maj. gift devel. U. Ill. Found., Springfield, 2001—03; exec. dir. Sangamon County Cmty. Found., Springfield, 2003—. Cons. Shea Consulting Svcs., Dallas, 2000—. Bd. dirs. Ursuline Acad., Springfield, 2001—04, Donors Forum Ill., Chgo., 2007; chairperson Leadership Springfield, 2003—07, Springfield Works, 2004—07. Am. Marshall Meml. fellow, German Marshall Fund, 2006. Mem.: Alliance Ill. Cmty. Founds. (chair legis. com. 2005—06), Assn. Fundraising Profl., Coun. Founds., Sangmo Club. Office: Sangamon County Cmty Found 1 W Old State Capitol Plz Ste 816 Springfield IL 62704 Home Phone: 217-546-4658; Office Phone: 217-789-4431. Office Fax: 217-789-4635. Business E-Mail: stremsterfer@sccf.us.

STRENG, WILLIAM PAUL, lawyer, educator; b. Sterling, Ill., Oct. 17, 1937; s. William D. and Helen Marie (Conklen) S.; children: Sarah, John. BA, Wartburg Coll., 1959; JD, Northwestern U., 1962. Bar: Iowa 1962, Ill. 1962, Ohio 1964, Tex. 1975. Law clk. to U.S. circuit judge Lester L. Cecil, Cin., 1963-64; assoc. firm Taft, Stettinius & Hollister, Cin., 1964-70; atty.-advisor Office Sec. Tax Policy, Office Tax Legis. Counsel, Dept. Treasury, Washington, 1970-71; dep. gen. counsel Export-Import Bank U.S., Washington, 1971-73; prof. law Sch. Law, So. Methodist U., Dallas, 1973-80; vis. prof. Coll. Law Ohio State U., Columbus, 1977; ptnr. firm Bracewell & Patterson, Houston, 1980-85; Vinson & Elkins prof. of law U. Houston Law Ctr, 1985—. Vis. prof. Rice U., NYU Law Sch., 1990, U. Tex. Sch. Law, 2002, Yokohama (Japan) Nat. U., 2005; disting. vis. prof. U. Hong Kong Law Faculty, 1992; Fulbright prof. U. Stockholm Law Faculty, 1993; vis. fellow law faculty Victoria U., Wellington, New Zealand, 1996; vis. law lectr. U. Leiden, Netherlands, 1997, 98, 2000, 07; cons. Bracewell & Patterson (now Bracewell & Giuliani), 1985—; lectr. various confs. Am. Law Inst., World Trade Inst., Practicing Law Inst., Internat. Fiscal Assn., ABA, Tex. State Bar. Author: International Business Transactions-Tax and Legal Handbook, 1978, Estate Planning, 1991, 2006, International Business Planning: Law and Taxation, 6 vols., 1982, 3d edit., 2007, Tax Planning for Retirement, 2001, revised edit., 2007, Doing Business in China, 1990, 1996, Federal Income Taxation of Corporations and Shareholders--Forms, 1995—2007, Choice of Entity, 1994, 1999, Choic of Entity, 2007, U.S. International Estate Planning, 1996, revised, 2006. Served with USMC, 1962. Lutheran. Home: 1903 Dunstan Rd Houston TX 77005-1619 Office: U Houston Law Ctr Houston TX 77204-6060 Home Phone: 713-529-4802; Office Phone: 713-743-2148. Business E-Mail: wstreng@uh.edu.

STRENIO, ANDREW JOHN, JR., lawyer; b. Erie, Pa., Apr. 3, 1952; s. Andrew and Mary Coletta (Rodgers) S.; m. Judith Lee Ferington, Aug. 31, 1974; children: Elizabeth Ann, Andrew John III, Stephen Peter. AB, Princeton U., 1974; JD cum laude, M in Pub. Policy, Harvard U., 1978; MPP, Harvard U, 1976. Bar: DC 1980, US Supreme Ct., 1986. Research assoc. Huron Inst., Cambridge, Mass., 1978-79; assoc. Wald, Harkrader & Ross, Washington, 1980; staff economist, atty. Pres.' Council of Econ. Advisers, Washington, 1980-81; asst. dir. regulatory evaluation, Bur. Consumer Protection FTC, Washington, 1982-84; commr. ICC, Washington, 1984-85, FTC, Wash., 1986—91; ptnr. Sidley, Wash., DC. Author: The Testing Trap, 1981; contbr. articles to mags. Mem. ABA, DC Bar Assn. Democrat. Roman Catholic. Avocation: sports. Office: Sidley 1501 K St NW Washington DC 20005 Office Phone: 202-736-8614. Office Fax: 202-736-8711.

STRETCH, JOHN JOSEPH, social worker, educator, management consultant; b. St. Louis, Feb. 24, 1935; s. John Joseph and Theresa Carmelita (Fleming) S.; children: Paul, Leonmarie, Sylvan, Adrienne, Sharonalice; m. Barbara Ann Stewart, Mar. 16, 1985; children: Margaret, Thomas. AB, Maryknoll Coll., Glen Ellyn, Ill., 1957; MSW, Washington U., St. Louis, 1961; PhD, Tulane U., 1967; MBA, St. Louis U., 1980. LCSW 1985. Instr. Tulane U., 1962—68, asst. prof., 1968; assoc. prof. social work St. Louis U., 1968—71, prof., 1972—, asst. dean Sch. Social Service, 1976-87, dir. doctoral studies, 1976-94, dir. MSW. program, 1985-86, bd. dirs., exec. com. Ctr. for Social Justice, 1987—, instnl. rev. bd. Sch. Social Svc., 1987—92; dir. rsch. Social Welfare Planning Coun. Met. New Orleans, 1962—69. Cons. to United Way Met. St. Louis, Cath. Charities of Archdiocese of St. Louis, Cath. Svcs. for Children and Youth, Full Achievement, Mo. Province of S.J., Cath. Commn. on Housing, Cath. Family Svcs., Youth Emergency Svcs., Mo. State Dept. Social Svcs., U.

Mo. Extension Svc., St. Joseph's Home for Boys, Marian Hall Ctr. for Adolescent Girls, Boys Town-Girls Town of Mo., A World of Difference, Anti Defamation League of B'nai Brith, Prog. Youth Ctr., Foster Care Coalition of Greater St. Louis, Rankin-Jordan Children's Rehab. Hosp., 1999-2000, Ill. St. Claire County Sch. Sys.'s Old Man River Project, 2002—05, Prison Performing ARts, 2005-06, Family Resource Ctr., 2004—; expert witness on homeless U.S. House Select Com. on Families, Children and Youth, 1987; resource spl. task force on homeless Office of Sec. U.S. Dept. HUD, 1989; survey design cons. U.S. Office of The Insp. Gen., 1990; methodology expert on homelessness U.S. Census Bur., 1989; expert homeless policy GAO hearings, 1992; chair Mo. Assn. for Social Welfare Low Income Housing, 1982—; chmn. St. Louis Low Income Housing Preservation Com., 1985; mem. Comprehensive Housing Affordabiltiy Strategies (CHAS) Mo. Statewide Planning Group, Mo. Housing Devel. CHAS citizen's com., State of Mo. Affordable House Task Force, Mo. Housing Devel. Corp., 1998-2002, Mo. Inst. Psychiatry, 1995, University City Sch. Dist., 1990; mgmt. cons. People's Issues Task Force Agrl. div. Monsanto Chem. Inc., 1992, regional office NCCJ, 1990-92; vis. prof. Nat. Cath. U. Am. Sch. Social Svcs., 1991, 92, U. Bristol, Eng., 1992, U. Calif. Sch. Pub. Health, Berkeley, 1990; cons. Mo. Speaker of the Ho. statewide legis. task force, 1990-92, Russian Am. Summer U., 2000; statewide grant project reviewer emergency shelter grant program Mo. Dept. Social Svcs., 1989—, chair, 2000—; homeless svcs. grant reviewer City of St. Louis, 1996-97; book award judge Alpha Sigma Nu. Mem editl. bd. Social Work, 1968-74, Health Progress, 1988—01, Social Work Administration, 2003—; manuscript referee Jour. Social Svc. Rsch., 1977-99; mgmt. and evaluation content referee Wadsworth Press, Human Svcs. Press, Thompson Press, Allyn and Bacon Press, Sage Press, Haworth Press; editor, contbr. chpts. to books, articles to profl. jours. Mem. Mo. Assn. Social Welfare, 1980—, Salvation Army Family Haven, 1987, 2000—; mem. leadership coun. Success by Six, 1990—2004; organizer Mo. State Nat. Coalition for the Homeless, 1989; mem. DuBourg Soc. St. Louis U., 1989; evaluation cons. Prison Performing Arts, 2005—06; bd. dirs. Beyond Housing, Inc., 1985—, pres., 1993—95; bd. dirs. Housing Comes First, 1995—99, Adequate Housing for Missourians, 2002—, Neighborhood Housing Svc., 2004—05, Nat. Coalition for Homeless, 2004—05; mem. adv. bd. Salvation Army Family Haven, 1988—; bd. dirs., mem. exec. com. Cmty. Asset Mgmt. Co.; chmn. venture grant com. United Way of Greater St. Louis, 1988—91, vice chmn. day care allocation com., 1985—95, mem. process and rev. com., 1991—93, mem. inter-orgnl. priorities com., 1991—93; appointee instnl. representation nat. Jesuits social concern group St. Louis U., 1993—2004, mem. exec. and support tng. group, 1987—92, mem. instnl. rev. bd., 1979—2004. NIMH Career Leadership Devel. fellow, 1965-67, Fed. Ednl. grantee Ill. Sch. Sys., 2002; recipient Scholar of Yr. award Sch. Social Svc., St. Louis U., 1987; named Vol. of Yr. Ecumenical Housing Prodn. Corp., 1990; Presdl. scholar Sch. Social Svc., 1992, Fulbright Sr. scholar, 2004—. Mem.: ACLU (charter compensation benefits com. St. Louis faculty senate 2004—05), AAUP (St. Louis U. chpt. exec. com. 1990—2002, pres. 1994—2002), U.S. Census Bur. (subcom. health stats. for minorities and spl. populations of U.S. 1988—2004), Nat. Consumers Union (com. on vital and health stats.), Coun. on Social Work Edn., Mo. Assn. for Social Welfare (bd. dirs., evaluation cons. family resourse ctr. 2005—, Outstanding State-Wide Mem. of Yr. 1987, nominee Elaine Aber Humanitarian award 2005), Nat. Assn. Social Workers, Acad. Cert. Social Workers (charter mem.), Amnesty Internat., Common Cause. Democrat. Roman Catholic. Home: 9100 Litzsinger Rd Saint Louis MO 63144-2214 Office: 3550 Lindell Blvd Saint Louis MO 63103-1021 Office Phone: 314-977-2715. Business E-Mail: stretchj@slu.edu. *My entire professional life has been in the field of social work. My personal and professional values are derived from a dual commitment to empower the uniqueness of individuals and to enhance the development of caring communities. These goals have organized and directed my professional practice, teaching and writing. I believe that the profession of social work has a unique and singular mission in society. That mission is to advocate for and consciously bring about the social development of all people.*

STREVEY, TRACY ELMER, JR., army officer, surgeon, health facility administrator; b. Shorewood, Wis., Apr. 24, 1933; s. Tracy Elmer and Margaret (Rees) S.; m. Victoria Crowley (div.); children: Virginia Ann, Tracy Elmer III, Andrew Victor; m. Elizabeth Sommers; children: Stephanie Jean, James Sommers. Student, Pomona Coll., 1951-54; MD, U. So. Calif., 1958; student, Armed Forces Staff Coll., 1970-71, U.S. Army War Coll., 1977-78. Diplomate Am. Bd. Surgery, Am. Bd. Thoracic Surgery. Intern Los Angeles County Gen. Hosp., 1958-59; commd. officer U.S. Army, 1959, advanced through grades to maj. gen., 1983; resident in gen. surgery Letterman Gen. Hosp., San Francisco, 1962-66; resident in thoracic and cardiovascular surgery Walter Reed Gen. Hosp., Washington, 1968-70; comdg. officer 757 Med. Detachment OA, Ludwigsburg, Germany, 1959-61; ward officer orthopaedic svc. 75th Sta. Hosp., Stuttgart, Fed. Republic Germany, 1961-62; chief profl. svc., chief surgery 85th Evacuation Hosp., Qui Nhon, Vietnam, 1967; comdg. officer 3d Surg. Hosp., Dong Tam, Vietnam, 1967-68; asst. chief thoracic and cardiovascular surgery service Fitzsimons Army Med Ctr., Denver, 1971-73, chief thoracic and cardiovascular surgery service, 1973-75; asst. dir. med. activities and dir. Profl. Edn. Gorgas Hosp., Panama Canal Zone, 1975-77; chief dept. surgery Walter Reed Army Med. Ctr., Washington, 1978-81; comdr. Brooke Army Med. Ctr., Ft. Sam Houston, Tex., 1981-83, Tripler Army Med. Ctr., Hawaii, 1983-86, U.S. Army Health Svcs. Command, San Antonio, 1986-88; ret. U.S. Army, 1988; CEO Nassau County Med. Ctr., 1988-93; pres., CEO N.Y. Hosp Med. Ctr. Queens, NYC, 1993-94; v.p. N.Y. Hosp. Care Network, NYC, 1994-95; v.p. for med. affairs Sisters of Mercy Health Sys., St. Louis, 1995-99; prin. Strevey Cons. Assocs., LLC, 1999—2003. Asst. clin. prof. surgery U. Colo. Med. Ctr., Denver, 1973-75; prof. surgery Uniformed Services U. Health Scis., Bethesda, 1978-2003, vice chmn. dept. surgery, 1978-81 Contbr. articles to profl. jours. Mem. reg. bd. Am. Heart Assn. Decorated D.S.M., Legion of Merit with 2 oak leaf clusters, Meritorious Service medal with 2 oak leaf clusters, Purple Heart, Army Commendation Medal for Valor, Vietnam Cross of Gallantry with Palm; recipient Outstanding Service award U. So. Calif. Med. Alumni Assn., 1983 Fellow ACS, Am. Coll. Chest Physicians, Am. Coll. Cardiology, Am. Coll. Physician Execs. (disting.); mem. Assn. Mil. Surgeons U.S., Soc. Thoracic Surgeons, Western Thoracic Surg. Assn., Am. Assn. Thoracic Surgery, Masons. Avocations: ham radio, scuba diving, golf, computers. Home and Office: 1509 Woodgate Dr Saint Louis MO 63131-4724 Personal E-mail: tstrevey@aol.com.

STREVIG, JANICE LEE, music educator; b. Balt., Oct. 19, 1957; BS, Towson U., Towson, Maryland, 1975—79; postgrad., U. Iowa, 1980—90, Temple U., 1980—90, Bucknell U., 1980—90, Towson U., 1980—90, Peabody Conservatory, 1980—90. Tchr. Balt. County Pub. Schools, Baltimore, Md., 1980—. Freelance pit musician, Md., 1980—; performer Sentimental Journey Big Band, Balt., 1980—; pvt. clarinet tchr., Balt., 1979—95. Girls fastpitch softball coach Lansdowne (Md.) H.S. Jayvee, 1989—97; soloist Catonsville (Md.) United Meth. Ch., 1998—, dir. vocal ensemble, 2000—. Mem.: Md. Music Educators Assn. (chm. exhibits 1987—, bd. dirs. 1987—), Music Educators Nat. Conf. (25 Yr. Svc. award 2004), Kappa Delta Pi (v.p. 1978—79). United Methodist. Avocations: playing women's baseball, crossword puzzles, reading. Home Phone: 410-265-6222; Office Phone: 410-887-0854. Personal E-mail: jbrahms@comcast.net.

STRIANESE, MICHAEL T., communications systems company executive; b. Mar. 13, 1956; Grad., St. John's U. CPA. With Ernst & Young; dir. spl. projects Loral Skynet, 1991—96; v.p. & contr., C31 & systems integration ctr. Lockheed Martin Corp., 1996—97; v.p. fin., contr. L-3 Comm. Holdings Inc., NYC, 1997—2000, sr. v.p. fin., 2000—05, sr. v.p., CFO, 2005—06, interim CEO, 2006, pres., CEO, 2006—. Bd. dirs. L-3 Communications, Inc., 2006—. Avocations: boating, skiing. Office: L-3 Comm Holdings Inc 600 Third Ave New York NY 10016 Office Phone: 212-697-1111. Office Fax: 212-867-5249. *

STRICHERZ, VINCENT C., journalist; b. Sioux Falls, SD, Nov. 11, 1952; s. Leo P. and Agnes Susan Fox Stricherz; m. Regina J. Hills, Feb. 25, 1984. BA in Polit. Sci. and Mass Comm., U. SD, Vermillion, 1977. News dir. KORN Radio, Mitchell, SD, 1978—79; city editor Daily Rep., Mitchell, 1979—81; reporter UPI, Lincoln, Nebr., 1981—82, bur. mgr., reporter Omaha, 1982—83; mng. editor Daily Sentry-News, Slidell, La., 1984; reporter, asst. city editor Indpls. Star, 1985—87; reporter, editor Seattle Times, 1988—90; freelance writer Seattle, 1991; city editor, reporter Jour.-Am./King County Jour., Bellevue, Wash., 1992—98; sci. writer media rels. U. Wash., Seattle, 1998—. Steering com. mem. Regional Pub. Info. Network, Seattle, 2001—. Constrn. vol., pub. rels. vol. Habitat Humanity Seattle/South King County, Seattle, 2000—. Recipient 1st Place award, Soc. Profl. Journalists, 1994, Bronze medal, Coun. Advancement & Support Edn., 2002, 2005, Silver medal, 2006. Mem.: Nat. Assn. Sci. Writers. Independent. Roman Catholic. Avocations: history, music. Office: Univ Wash Box 351207 Seattle WA 98195-1207 Business E-Mail: vinces@u.washington.edu.

STRICK, GERALD JAY, lawyer; b. N.Y.C., Oct. 19, 1934; s. Abraham and Esta (Schlaff) S.; children: Susan D., Daniel F. BA, Hobart Coll., 1955; JD, U. Mich., 1962; cert. Nat. Coll. State Trial Judges, 1971; cert. in correctional adminstrn. U. So. Calif., 1975. Bar: Ariz. 1963, U.S. Dist. Ct. Ariz. 1963, U.S. Ct. Appeals (9th cir) 1969, U.S. Ct. Appeals (fed. cir.) 1993. Assoc. Kramer, Roche, Burch & Streich, Phoenix, 1963-66; ptnr. Harrison, Strick, Myers & Singer, Phoenix, 1966-71; judge Superior Ct. Ariz., Phoenix, 1971-83; ptnr. Treon, Strick, Lucia & Aguirre, P.A., Phoenix, 1983—; mem. Ariz. Commn. on Jud. Conduct, 1993-2000; mem. faculty Nat. Inst. Trial Advocacy, 1977—, Ariz. Coll. Trial Advocacy, 1986—; adj. prof. Coll. Law Ariz. State U., 1995, vis. prof., 1994; master bencher Sandra Day O'Connor Inn of Ct.; cons. NAS, 1979-82. Majority counsel Ariz. Ho. Reps., 1969. E-mail: gerald.strick@tsla.com.

STRICK, JEREMY, curator; BA in History of Art with highest honors, U. Calif., Santa Cruz, 1977; postgrad., Harvard U. Asst. curator 20th Century art Nat. Gallery Art, Washington, 1986-89, assoc. curator 20th Century art, 1989-93, acting dept. dept. 20th Century art, 1992-93, curator Nat. Sculpture Garden project, 1989-93; curator modern art St. Louis Art Mus., 1993-96; Frances and Thomas Dittmer curator 20th Century painting and sculpture Art Inst. Chgo., 1996-99; dir. Mus. Contemporary Art, LA, 1999—. Curator N.Y. Interpreted: Joseph Stella and Alfred Stieglitz, Nat. Gallery Art, 1987, Milton Avery, 1990, Mark Rothko: The Spirit Myth, 1990-95, asst. curator A Century of Modern Sculpture: The Patsy and Raymond Nasher Collection, 1987, co-curator Twentieth-Century Art: Selections for the Tenth Anniversary of the East Building, 1987; curator Brice Marden: A Painting, Drawings, Prints, St. Louis Art Mus., 1993, Currents 58: Susan Crile—The Fires of War, 1994, Louise Bourgeois: The Personages 1946-1954, 1995, Currents 60: Jerald Ieans, 1994, Masterworks from Stuttgar: The Romantic Age in German Art, 1995, Currents 66: Michael Byron, 1996, Currents 67: Leonardo Drew, 1996; curator The Sublime Is Now: The Early Work of Barnett Newman, Walker Art Ctr., Mpls., Pace Gallery, N.Y.C., 1994; curator In the Light of Italy: Corot and Early Open-Air Painting, Nat. Gallery Art, Bklyn. Mus., St. Louis Art Mus., 1996; lectr., symposia participant and organizer, 1980—; juror Showhegan awards, 1995. Contbg. author: Works by Antoine-Louis Barye in the Collection of the Fogg Art Museum, Vol. IV, 1982; contbr. articles to exhbn. catalogs, newspapers, mags., ency. Instnl. fellow Samuel H. Kress Found., Paris, 1983-85, fellow Mrs. Giles Whiting Found., 1985-86. Office: Mus Contemporary Art Dept 20th Century Painting 250 S Grand Ave Los Angeles CA 90012-3021 Home: 261 N Bundy Dr Los Angeles CA 90049-2825 E-mail: jstrick@moca.org.

STRICKER, STEVE, professional golfer; b. Edgerton, Wis., Feb. 23, 1967; m. Nicki Stricker; 1 child, Bobbi Maria. Student, U. Ill. Profl. golfer, 1990—. Mem. US team Alfred Dunhill Cup, 1996, Presidents Cup, 1996, 2007. Named winner, Victoria Open, Can., 1990, Can. PGA, 1993, Kemper Open, 1996, Motorola Western Open, 1996, World Golf Championships - Accenture Match Play Championship, 2001, The Barclays, 2007, PGA TOUR Comeback Player of Yr., 2006. Office: PGA Tour 112 PGA Tour Blvd Ponte Vedra Beach FL 32082 *

STRICKHOLM, JEAN, musician, music company executive, retired elementary school educator; b. Madison, Wis., Oct. 27, 1933; d. Hulsey and Eloise May (Boeker) Cason; m. Harry Jean Cason Strickholm, June 30, 1956; children: Karen, Sally Tayeb, Douglas, Glenn. Student, Red Fox Music Camp, Marlboro, Mass., 1952—54; BS, U. Rochester, Rochester, NY, 1955; MS, Queens Coll., Flushing, NY, 1959. Cert. tchr. N.Y. Dept. Edn., 1955, elem. edn. K-12 N.J. Dept. Edn., 1969, tchr. social studies K-12 N.J. Dept. Edn., 1973. Tchr. Gt. Neck Pub. Schs., Gt. Neck, NY, 1955—58, Tenafly Pub. Schs., NJ, 1969—70, Englewood Pub. Schs., NJ, 1970—98, ret., 1998. Co-dir., mgr., fund raiser, performer All Seasons Chamber Players, Demarest, NJ, 1981—. Chmn. Bergen County Equal Opportunities Study Com., Hackensack, NJ, 1969—70; active Civil Rights Movement Bergen County, 1961—70. Recipient award, Bergen County Fair Housing Coun., 1961—70. Mem.: Chamber Music Am. (assoc.). Democrat. Avocations: swimming, gardening, reading. Home Phone: 201-768-1331; Office Phone: 201-768-1331.

STRICKLAND, ANTHONY, state representative; b. Fort Ord, Calif., Feb. 17, 1970; m. Audra Strickland. Student, Cochise C.C., Ariz.; BA in Polit. Sci., Whittier Coll. Calif. Mem. Calif. Assembly, 1998—. Mem. adv. bd. Food Share; founding pres. So. Calif. Taxpayers' Alliance; hon. bd. dirs. Doris Tate Crime Victims' Bur.; bd. dirs.Go N Strong Basketball Camp; hon. bd. dirs. Moorpark Boys & Girls Club; bd. dirs. Ventura County United Way. Republican. Office: PO Box 942849 Rm 4098 Sacramento CA 94249 Address: 2659 Townsgate Rd Westlake Village CA 91361

STRICKLAND, ARVARH EUNICE, history professor; b. Hattiesburg, Miss., July 6, 1930; s. Eunice and Clotiel (Marshall) S.; m. Willie Pearl Elmore, June 17, 1951; children: Duane Arvarh, Bruce Elmore. BA, Tougaloo Coll., 1951; MA, U. Ill., 1953, PhD, 1962; LHD (hon.), Tougaloo Coll., 2007. Tchr. Hattiesburg Schs., 1951-52; instr. Tuskegee Inst., 1955-56; prin. supr. Madison County Schs., Canton, Miss., 1956-59; asst. prof. history Chgo. State U., 1962-65, assoc. prof. history, 1965-68, prof., 1968-69, U. Mo., Columbia, 1969-96, prof. emeritus, 1996—, chmn. dept. history, 1980-83, interim dir. black studies program, 1994-96, sr. faculty assoc., Office of V.P. acad. affairs, 1987-88, assoc. v.p. acad. affairs, 1989-91. Author: History of the Chicago Urban League, 1966, reprint, 2001, (with Reich and Biller) Building the United States, 1971, (with Reich) The Black American Experience to 1877, 1974, The Black American Experience since 1877, 1974; editor: Working with Carter G. Woodson, (with Lorenzo J. Greene) The Father of Black History: A Diary, 1928-1930, 1989, Selling Black History for Carter G. Woodson: A Diary, 1930-33, 1996, (with Robert E. Weems) The African American Experience: A Historiographical and Bibliographical Guide, 2000. Commr. Planning and Zoning, Columbia, Mo., 1977-80, Boone County Home Rule Charter, 1982, Mo. Peace Officers Standards and Tng. Commn., 1988-89; co-chmn. Mayors Com. to Commemorate Contbns. of Black Columbians, Columbia, 1981; mem. exec. subcom. Mayor's Ad Hoc Election '82 Com., 1982; bd. dirs. Harry S. Truman Library Inst., 1987-96, U. of Mo.-Columbia Health Sys., 2003—. Recipient Disting. Svc. award Ill. Hist. Soc., 1957, Byler Disting. Prof. award U. Mo., 1994, St. Louis Am.'s Educator of Yr. award, 1994, Disting. Faculty award U. Mo.-Columbia Alumni Assn., 1995, Tougaloo Coll. Alumni Hall of Fame, 1995, Alumni Achievement U. Ill. Coll. Liberal Arts and Scis., 1997, Disting. Svc. award State Hist. Soc. Mo., 1997. Mem. Orgn. Am. Historians, Am. Hist. Assn., Assn. Study Afro-Am. Life and History (Carter Godwin Woodson Scholars medallion 1999), So. Hist. Assn., State Hist. Soc. Mo. (Disting. Svc. award 1997), Boone County Hist. Soc. (bd. dirs. 1998-2002, 2d v.p. 1999, 1st v.p. 2000-02), Kiwanis, Alpha Phi Alpha, Phi Alpha Theta (internat. v.p. 1991-93, pres. 1994-95, chair adv. bd. 1996-97, Disting. Svc. award 1997, Columbia Values Diversity award, 2005). Democrat. Methodist. Home: 4100 Defoe Dr Columbia MO 65203-0252 Office: U Mo Dept History 101 Read Hall Columbia MO 65211-7500 E-mail: stricklanda@missouri.edu.

STRICKLAND, BONNIE RUTH, psychologist, educator; b. Louisville, Nov. 24, 1936; d. Roy E. and Billie P. (Whitfield) S. BS, Ala. Coll., 1958; MS, Ohio State U., 1960, PhD (USPHS fellow), 1962. Diplomate: clin. psychology Am. Bd. Examiners in Profl. Psychology. From asst. to asso. prof. psychology Emory U., Atlanta, 1962—73, dean of women, 1964—67; prof. psychology U. Mass., Amherst, 1973—2003, prof. emeritus, 2003—, chmn. dept. psychology, 1976—77, 1978—82, assoc. to chancellor, 1983—84. Mem. adv. coun. NIMH, 1984-87; Sigma Xi nat. lectr., 1991-93. Adv. editor numerous psychology jours., acad. pub. houses; contbg. author texts personality theory.; contbr. of numerous articles on social personality and clin. psychology to profl. jours.; contbg. author of two citation classics. Recipient Outstanding Faculty award Emory U., 1968-69; Chancellor's medal disting. service U. Mass., 1983. Fellow APA (pres. divsn. clin. psychology 1983, pres. divsn. gen. psychology 2005, chmn. bd. profl. affairs 1980-83, chmn. policy and planning bd. 1983-85, pres. 1987, bd. dirs. 1986-87, Outstanding Leadership award 1992, Disting. Contbns. and Psychology in the Pub. Interest award 1999, Presdl. Citation 2001), Am. Psychol. Soc. (founder 1988, bd. dirs. 1989-93), New Eng. Psychol. Assn. (Disting. Contbns. award 2002), Am. Assn. Applied and Preventive Psychology (founder 1990, bd. dirs. 1990-94, pres. 1992-94), Acad. Clin. Psychology (chmn. 1982-83). Home: 558 Federal St Belchertown MA 01007-9754 Office: U Mass Dept Psychology Amherst MA 01003-7710

STRICKLAND, DELPHENE COVERSTON, judge; b. Ponca City, Okla. d. Harry Ethelbert and Mary Louise (Reed) Coverston; m. Thomas Whitney Strickland, Aug. 31, 1946; children: Mary Herrington, Thomas Whitney. BA, John B. Stetson U., 1944; JD, U. Fla., 1945; postgrad., Fla. State U., 1965-70, Nat. Jud. Coll., Reno, 1979-80. Bar: Fla. 1945, US Dist. Ct. (so. dist.) Fla. 1946, US Dist. Ct. (no. dist.) Fla. 1966, US Dist. Ct. (no. dist.) Tex. 1979, US Dist. Ct. Hawaii 1980, US Supreme Ct. 1980, US Ct. Appeals (11th cir.) 1983. Assoc. Rogers & Morris, Ft. Lauderdale, Fla., 1945-46, Clayton, Arnow, Johnson & Duncan, Gainesville, Fla., 1946-51; pvt. practice Delphene Strickland Law Offices, Gainesville, 1951-59; legal rsch. asst. Fla. Supreme Ct., Tallahassee, 1960-68, exec. asst., 1968-70, mem. legis. ref. com., 1970—72; gen. counsel Fla. Dept. Transp., 1972; adminstrv. law judge Tallahassee; ret., 1972—82; part time gen. practice DC Strickland, 2002—. Adj. prof. U. Fla., Gainesville, Fla. State U., Tallahassee; Fla. del. to 1983 11th Cir. Jud. Conf.; mem. Fla. Bd. Bar Examiners, 1970-, sr. mem. 1980-; sr. mem. Fla. Traffic Ct., 1970—; mem. efficiency com. Fla. Supreme Ct., 1984—; organizer, charter mem. Leon Safety Coun. Contbr. articles to law jours. Sunday sch. tchr. St. Paul United Meth. Ch., Tallahassee, 1970-2002. Fellow ABA Judicial Div. Nat. Conf. Adminstrv. Law Judges; mem. ABA (chmn. nat. conf. adminstrv. law judges 1983-84, exec. coun. 1985—), Fla. Govt. Bar Assn. (past pres., Earnie Webb award 1988), Fla. Assn. Women Lawyers (past pres.), Tallahassee Women Lawyers Assn. (past pres., founder,), Nat. Assn. Women Lawyers (Fla. del., charter mem.), Nat. Assn. Women Judges (charter mem.), Am. Arbitration Assn., AAUW (past pres. Gainesville), Supreme Ct. Hist. Soc., Fla. Supreme Ct. Hist. Soc. (organizer, charter, trustee), Fla. Govt. Bar Assn. (organizer, charter, past pres.), Tallahassee Bar Assn., North Fla. Legal Svcs., DAR (state del. Tallahassee, 99th nat. congress Washington 1989—), Nat. Soc. Daughters of the Am. Revolution, Nat. Soc. US Daughters 1812, United Daughters of the Confederacy, The Nat. Soc. Colonial Dames XVII Century, Capital City Country Club, Am. Camellia Soc., Tallahassee Camellia Soc., Am. Rose Soc., Tallahassee Rose Soc., Thomasville Camellia Soc, Thomasville Rose Soc., Apalachee Audubon Soc., Saint Andrew Soc. (organizer, charter mem.), Appalachian Trail Conservancy, Continental Divide Trail Alliance, Inc., Zonta, Phi Alpha Delta. Home: 2802 Sterling Dr Tallahassee FL 32312-3030 Personal E-mail: delphinesjd@net.com.

STRICKLAND, DONALD BENNETT, lawyer; b. Feb. 25, 1931; BA, Duke U., Durham, NC, 1953, JD, 1956; MA, U. Md., College Park, 1970. Bar: NC. Commd. 2d lt. USAF, 1956, advanced through grades to col., with Judge Advocate Corps. Washington, ret., 1985; asst. dist. atty. 8th Jud. Dist., Goldsboro, NC, 1985—93; ptnr. Bland, Hechin, Smith & Strickland, Goldsboro, 1993—. Decorated Legion of Merit with one oak leaf cluster USAF. Mem.: Mil. Officers Assn. (pres. Goldsboro chpt. 1993—94). Office: 306 E Mulberry St Goldsboro NC 27534

STRICKLAND, DOROTHY, education educator; BS, Newark State Coll.; MA, PhD, NYU. Elem. sch. tchr. N.J. pub. sch. sys., reading cons., learning disabilities specialist; prof. edn. Rutgers U., New Brunswick, NJ, 1985—, Samuel DeWitt Proctor Prof. Edn., 2002—. Active in numerous state and nat. adv. bds. Author: Language Literacy and the Child, Process Reading and Writing: A Literature Based Approach, The Administration and Supervision of Reading Programs, Educating Black Children: America's Challenge, Family Storybook Reading, Listen Children: An Anthology of Black Literature, Families: An Anthology of Poetry for Young Children, Teaching Phonics Today, 1998, Beginning Reading and Writing, 2000, Supporting Struggling Readers and Writers, 2002, Preparing Our Teachers, 2002, Language Arts: Learning and Teaching, 2003, Learning About Print in Preschool Settings, 2004. Inducted into the Reading Hall of Fame, pres., 1997-98. Mem. Nat. Coun. Tchrs. English (Rewey Belle Inglis award for Outstanding Woman in English Education Annual Conv., rsch. award, Outstanding Educator in Lang. Arts award 1998), Internat. Reading Assn. (past pres., Outstanding Tchr. Educator of reading award). Home: 131 Coccio Dr West Orange NJ 07052-4121 Office: Rutgers U Dept Edn Grad Sch Edn New Brunswick NJ 08903

STRICKLAND, FRANK B., lawyer; b. Washington, July 12, 1936; BA, Vanderbilt U., 1958; LLB, Emory U., 1966. Bar: Ga. 1966, US Dist. Ct., no. mid. & so. dists. Ga., US Ct. Appeals, 11th circuit, US Supreme Ct. Ptnr. Wilson Strickland & Benson, Atlanta, 1971—2000, Holland & Knight, Atlanta, 2000—01, Strickland Brockington Lewis, Atlanta, 2001—. Mem. State Ethics Commn., Ga., 1987—90, pres. Ga., 1989—90; mem. Jud. Nominating Commn., Ga., 2003—; trustee Atlanta Metro Grp.; mem. Fulton County Bd. Registration & Elections; trustee Inst. Continuing Edn., Ga.; gen. counsel Rep Party, Ga., 1993—95; chmn. bd. Legal Svcs. Corp., 2003—; dir. Atlanta Legal Aid Soc. & Fed. Def. prog., 1984—88. Comdr. (ret.) USCGR. Mem.: Rep. Nat. Lawyers Assn. (bd. gov., chmn. Ga. chptr. 2002—), Federalist Soc. (chmn. Atlanta lawyers chptr. 1996—), Nat. Assn. Coll. & Univ. Attys., Lawyers Club Atlanta, State Bar Ga. (bd. gov. 1985—), Atlanta Bar Assn. (pres. 1985—86), ABA (ho. del. 1985—87), Atlanta Vanderbilt Alumni Assn. (past pres.). Republican. Office: Strickland Brockington Lewis LLP Midtown Proscenium 1170 Peachtree St NE Ste 2000 Atlanta GA 30309-7673 Office Phone: 678-347-2211. E-mail: fbs@sbllaw.net. *

STRICKLAND, HUGH ALFRED, lawyer; b. Rockford, Ill., May 3, 1931; s. Hugh and Marie (Elmer) S.; m. Donna E. McDonald, Aug. 11, 1956; children: Amy Alice, Karen Ann. AB, Knox Coll., 1953; JD, Chgo. Kent Coll. Law, 1959. Bar: Ill. 1960. Partner firm McDonald, Strickland & Clough, Carrollton, Ill., 1961—; asst. atty. gen. Ill., 1960-67; spl. asst. gen. Ill., 1967-69; pres. McDonald Title Co. Mem. Greene County Welfare Svcs. Com., 1963—, Ill. Heart Assn., 1961-65; trustee Thomas H. Boyd Meml. Hosp., 1972-95; pres. Long Lake Assn. Vilas County, Inc., 2002—. With AUS, 1953-55. Recipient award for meritorious service Am. Heart Assn., 1964 Fellow Ill. Bar Found. (charter); mem. ABA, Ill. Bar Assn., Greene County Bar Assn. (past pres.), Southwestern Bar Assn. (past pres.), Ill. Def. Counsel, Am. Judicature Soc., Def. Rsch. Inst., Elks Club, Westlake Country Club (v.p. 1968-70, dir.), Big Sand Lake Country Club, Phi Delta Theta, Phi Delta Phi. Methodist. Home: 827 7th St Carrollton IL 62016-1421 Office: 524 N Main St PO Box 71 Carrollton IL 62016-1027 Office Phone: 217-942-3115. Personal E-mail: mcdslawyers@aol.com. Business E-Mail: has3@irtc.net.

STRICKLAND, JULIA B., lawyer; b. San Francisco, Aug. 21, 1954; Student, Dartmouth Coll.; BA with honors, Univ. Calif., San Diego, 1975; JD, UCLA, 1978. Bar: Calif. 1978. Summer intern Stroock & Stroock & Lavan LLP, LA, 1977, ptnr., chair, fin. svcs. litig. practice, mem., operating exec. com, 1996—. Chair, consumer fin. svcs. litig. program Practising Law Inst., 1997—. Bd. of editors Banking Law Jour., editorial bd. Wall St. Lawyer, frequent lectr., writer in field. Named a Super Lawyer, LA Mag.; named one of Top 50 Women Litigators, LA Daily Jour., 2004. Mem.: Mortgage Bankers Assn., Assn. Bus. Trial Lawyers (bd. dir.). Office: Stroock & Stroock & Lavan LLP 2029 Century Pk E Los Angeles CA 90067-3086 Office Phone: 310-556-5806. Office Fax: 310-556-5959. Business E-Mail: jstrickland@strook.com.

STRICKLAND, MARSHALL HAYWARD, bishop; b. Rome, Ga., Oct. 8, 1933; s. Albert A. Strickland and Elzie Greer Strickland Morton; 1 child, Marshall H. II. BA, Livingstone Coll., 1951; PhD, St. Mary's Theol. Sem., Balt.; MDiv, Hood Theol. Sem., 1955, DD (hon.), Allen U. Pastor Patten Meml. AME Zion Ch., Chattanooga, David Stan AME Zion Ch., Lancaster, SC, Hood Meml. AME Zion Ch., Bristol, Tenn., Big Zion AME Ch., Mobile, Ala., Pa. Ave. AME Zion Ch., Balt.; bishop Mid Atlantic I dist. AMEZ Ch., Balt., sec.; bishop AMEZ, Balt., 1992—. Bd. bishops AME Zion Ch., chmn. commn. judiciary, chmn. Am. Bible Soc., 1st vice chair brotherhood pension svc., 1st vice chair Christian edn., 2d vice chair bicentennial commn., trustee Livingstone Coll.; past mem. Ala. Consultation Ch. Union; guest pastor Gen. Conf. AME Ch., St. Paul Cathedral, others; spkr. in field; guest on various radio and TV stas. Author: William E. Fine: Kennedy-The Dreamer, Church and State: Not Separate, Our Heritage is Our Religion, The Black Church: Black America's Salvation, The Black Church: Solving Black America's Crisis, Health Care: Preaching Prevention from the Pulpit, Rebuilding Our Cities in Partnership with the Black Church: A Master Plan; contbr. articles to profl. jours. Former chmn. bd. dirs. Mobile Community Action Authority; past mem. Commn. Organic Union; founder Zion Outreach Ctr., Balt. Recipient Humanitarian award, Zion Outreach Svcs. Associated Black Charities, Econ. Devel. award, HUB, Flood Relief Support award, Jamaican Assn. Md. Mem.: NAACP (past pres. Bristol chpt., Recognition awards Bristol and Balt. chpts.). Office: 2000 Cedar Circle Dr Baltimore MD 21228-3743

STRICKLAND, ROBERT LOUIS, retired retail executive; b. Florence, SC, Mar. 3, 1931; s. Franz M. and Hazel (Eaddy) S.; m. Elizabeth Ann Miller, Feb. 2, 1952; children: Cynthia Anne, Robert Edson. AB, U. N.C., 1952; MBA with distinction, Harvard U., 1957. Bd. dirs. Lowe's Cos., Inc., North Wilkesboro, NC, 1961—2000, sr. v.p., 1970—76, exec. v.p., 1976—78, chmn. bd., 1979—98, chmn. exec. com., 1988—98, mem. office of pres., 1970—78, chmn. emeritus, 1999; founder Sterling Advt., Ltd., 1966. V.p., mem. adminstrv. com. Lowe's Profit-Sharing Trust, 1961-87, chmn. ops. com., 1972-78; mgmt. com. Lowe's ESOP Plan, 1978-97; bd. dirs. Lowe's Cos., Wilkesboro, NC, T.Rowe Price Assocs., Balt., 1991-2001, Hannaford Bros. Co., Portland, Maine, Krispy Kreme Corp., Winston-Salem, NC, Wholesale Club, Indpls., Summit Comms., Atlanta; vice chair, bd. dirs. Revelstroke Co., Calgary, Can.; panelist investor rels. field, 1972-99; spkr., panelist employee stock ownership, 1978-2000; spkr. on investor rels., London, Edinburgh, Glasgow, Paris, Zurich, Frankfurt, Milan, Vienna, Singapore, Tokyo. Author: Lowe's Cybernetwork, 1969, Lowe's Living Legend, 1970, Ten Years of Growth, 1971, The Growth Continues, 1972, 73, 74, Lowe's Scoreboard, 1978; contbr. articles to profl. jours. Mem. NC Ho. of Reps., 1962-64, Rep. Senatorial Inner Circle, 1980-95; exec. com. NC Rep. Com., 1963-73; trustee U. NC, Chapel Hill, 1987-95, chmn. bd., 1991-93; dir., dep. chmn. Fed. Res. Bank of Richmond, 1996-98; com. on bus. laws and the economy NC, 1994-97; dir. US Coun. Better Bus. Burs., 1981-85; bd. dirs., v.p. Nat. Home Improvement Coun., 1972-76; bd. dirs. NC Sch. Arts Found., 1975-79, NC Bd. Natural and Econ. Resources, 1975-76; bd. dirs., govt. affairs com. Home Ctr. Inst., co-chmn. Home Ctr. to Israel Del., 1984; trustee, sec. bd. Wilkes CC, 1964-73; chmn., pres. bd. dirs. Do-It-Yourself Rsch. Inst., 1981-89; pres. Hardware Home Improvement Coun. City of Hope Nat. Med. Ctr., LA, 1987-89. With USN, 1952-55, lt. Res. 1955-62. Named Wilkes County NC Young Man of Yr., Wilkes Jr. C. of C., 1962; recipient Bronze Oscar of Industry award Fin. World, 1969-74, 76-79, Silver Oscar of Industry award, 1970, 72-74, 76-79, Gold Oscar of Industry award as best of all industry, 1972, 87, Excellence award in corp. reporting Fin. Analysts Fedn., 1970, 72, 74, 81-82, cert. of Distinction Brand Names Found., 1970, Retailer of Yr. award, 1971, 73, Disting. Mcht. award, 1972, Spirit of Life award City of Hope, 1983, Free Enterprise Legend award Students Free Enterprise, 1994; named to Home Ctr. Hall of Fame, 1985. Mem. Nat. Assn. Over-Counter Cos. (bd. advisers 1973-77), Newcomen Soc., Employee Stock Ownership Assn. (pres. 1983-85, chmn. 1985-87), James Madison Club, Federalist Soc., Forsyth Country Club, Piedmont City Club, Roaring Gap Club (NC), Ponte Vedra Inn and Club (Fla.), Harvard Club (NY), Scabbard and Blade, Phi Beta Kappa, Pi Kappa Alpha. Home: 226 N Stratford Rd Winston Salem NC 27104-3132 also: 721 5th Ave Apt GH New York NY 10022 Office: 2000 W 1st St Winston Salem NC 27104-4225 Home: 67 Ponte Vedra Blvd Ponte Vedra Beach FL 32082 Personal E-mail: lowchair@aol.com.

STRICKLAND, SHAWN, communications executive; b. 1973; BA, Harvard U.; MBA, Columbia U. Position with Corp. Devel. Prog. Bell Atlantic; exec. dir., FTTP Video Product. Mgmt. Verizon Comm., v.p., FiOS TV Product Mgmt. Named one of 40 Executives Under 40, Multichannel News, 2006. Office: Verizon Communications Inc 140 W St New York NY 10036

STRICKLAND, SYLVIA RAYE, social worker; b. Grand Prarie, Tex., Feb. 21, 1945; d. Nathaniel and Flora Evelyn Strickland; m. Julian B. Angel, Oct. 6, 1973 (div. Apr. 1983); 1 child, Sarah Renee Angel. BSW, U. So. Colo., Pueblo, 1986; MSW, N.Mex. Highlands U., Las Vegas, N.Mex., 1987. Lic. psychotherapist 1998, cert. grief recovery specialist Grief Recovery Inst., 2005. Social worker Highland Park Nursing Home, Pueblo, 1988; social worker III El Paso County Social Svcs., Colorado Springs, Colo., 1988—89; resident svcs. coord. Villa Santa Maria, Colorado Springs, Colo., 1990—91, ballot initative circulator, 1992; social worker Medalion Health Ctr., Colorado Springs, 1993—99, coord. activities personal care unit, 1993—96, resident family rep., 1999—. Vol. Hospice of Comforter, 1994—96; active St. Paul's Cath. Ch.; sec. Social Work Action Team, U. So. Colo., 1984—85. Mem.: Colo. Soc. Clin. Social Work (chmn. program 1999—), Assn. Rsch. and Enlightenment, SOS Investment Club. Avocations: choir, water colors, attending concerts, quilting. Home: PO Box 38123 Colorado Springs CO 80937-8123

STRICKLAND, TED, governor, former congressman; b. Lucasville, Ohio, Aug. 4, 1941; s. Orville and Carrie Strickland; m. Frances Smith. BA in Hist., Asbury Coll., Wilmore, Ky., 1963; MDiv, Asbury Theol. Seminary, Wilmore, Ky., 1967; PhD in Counseling Psych., U. Ky., Lexington, 1980. Min.; dir. social svcs. Ky. Meth. Home; consulting psychologist So. Ohio Correctional Facility, 1985—92, 1994—96; asst. prof. psych. Shawnee State U., Portsmouth, Ohio, 1988—92, 1994—96; mem. US Congress from 6th Ohio dist., 1993—95, 1997—2007, mem. energy & commerce com., vets. affairs com., ranking minority mem. oversight and investigations subcommittee; gov. State of Ohio, Columbus, 2007—. Dem. nominee for Gov., Ohio, 2006. Co-recipient Outstanding Psychologist award, Nat. Alliance Mentally Ill, 2004. Mem.: Ohio Psychol. Assn., APA. Democrat. Methodist. Office: Office Gov Vern Riffe Ctr 77 S High St 30th Fl Columbus OH 43215-6117 *

STRICKLAND, THOMAS L., lawyer; b. Houston, May 16, 1952; BA with honors, La. State Univ., 1974; JD with honors, Univ. Texas, Austin, 1977. Bar: Tex. 1977, Colo. 1979. Law clk. Judge Carl. O. Bue, Jr., US Dist. Ct. So. Dist. Tex., 1977—79; dir. policy & rsch. Office of Colo. Gov., 1982—84; ptnr. Brownstein Hyatt & Farber, Denver, 1984—99; U.S. Atty. Colo. Dist., 1999—2001; ptnr. Hogan & Hartson LLP, Denver, 2003—07; exec. v.p., chief legal officer UnitedHealth Group, Mpls., 2007—. Legal counsel Denver Metro C. of C.; commr. Colo. Transp. Commn., 1985—89, chmn., 1987—88, Metro. Transp. Develop. Commn., Colo., 1989—90. Dem. nominee U.S. Senate from Colo., 1996, 2002; founding bd. mem. Great Outdoors Colo.; bd. mem. Children's Hosp., Denver, Denver Pub. Schools Found. Mem.: ABA, Colo. Bar Assn., State Bar Tex., Denver Bar Assn., Omicron Delta Kappa. Democrat. Mailing: UnitedHealth Group PO Box 1459 Minneapolis MN 55440-1459 *

STRICKLAND, WILLIAM JESSE, lawyer; b. Newport News, Va., Mar. 21, 1942; BSBA, U. Richmond, 1964, JD, 1969. Bar: Va. 1969, US Dist. Ct. Ea. Dist. Va., US Dist. Ct. We. Dist. Va., US Ct. Appeals 4th Cir., US Ct. Claims, US Tax Ct. Mem McGuire Woods LLP, Richmond, Va., 1969—, firm mng. ptnr., 1996—. Bd. dirs. Cableform Inc., Zion Crossroads, Va., Eimeldingen Corp., Indpls, World Affairs Coun., Greater Richmond. Mem. exec. com. Va. Found. for Rsch. & Econ. Edn., Inc., bd. dirs. U. Richmond Law Sch. Found.; mem. coun. Va. Inst. Marine Sci.; founder Marine Corps Heritage Found.; bd. dirs. World Affairs Coun. Greater Richmond. Capt. USMC, 1964—67. Mem. ABA (com. on tax exempt fin.), Va. Bar Assn., Richmond Bar Assn., Nat. Assn. Bond Lawyers, Va. Govt. Fin. Officers Assn., Va. Local Govt. Attorneys Assn., Va. Bond Club. Office: McGuire Woods LLP One James Ctr 901 E Cary St Richmond VA 23219-4030 Office Phone: 804-775-4350. Office Fax: 804-698-2185. Business E-Mail: wstrickland@mcguirewoods.com.

STRICKLER, IVAN K., dairy farmer; b. Carlyle, Kans., Oct. 23, 1921; s. Elmer E. and Edna Louise (James) S.; m. Madge Lee Marshall, Aug. 7, 1949; children— Steven Mark, Thomas Scott, Douglas Lee. BS, Kans. State U., 1947. Owner, mgr. dairy farm, Iola, Kans., 1947—; tchr. farm tng. to vets. World War II, 1947-54; judge 1st and 2d Nat. Holstein Show, Brazil, 1969-70, Internat. Holstein Show, Buenos Aires, 1972, Nat. Holstein Show, Ecuador, 1978, 10th Nat. Holstein Show, Brazil, 1980, Holstein Show, Australia, Mex. and Argentina, 1981, Lang Lang, 1984, Adelaide (Australia) Royal Show, 1987; pres Mid-America Dairymen, Inc., Springfield, Mo., 1981—. Appointed chmn. Nat. Dairy Bd., 1985-90; dairy leader 4-H Club, 1962-75; dir. Iola State Bank; rep. U.S. Internat. Dairy Symposium, 1994, Belo Horinzote, Brazil. Author: Wholly Cow We Did It, 1996 (Centennia Honor roll 1997). Trustee Allen County Community Jr. Coll.; mem. agr. edn. and rsch. com. Kans. State U. (recipient Medallion-highest honor, 2000), U.S. Agrl. Trade and Devel. Mission, Algeria and Tunisia, 1989. With USN, 1942-46, PTO. Recipient Silver award Holstein Friesian Assn. Brazil, 1969, Top Dairy Farm Efficiency award Ford Found., 1971, Master Farmer award Kans. State U. and Kans. Assn. Commerce and Industry, 1972, Gold award Holstein Friesian Assn. Argentina, 1972, Richard Lynng award Nat. Dairy Bd., 1990, award of merit Gamma Sigma Delta, 1987, Alumni medallion Kans. State U., 1999; named Man of Yr. World Dairy Exposition, 1978; portrait in Dairy Hall of Fame Kans. State U., 1974; Guest of Hon. Nat. Dairy Shrine, 1985; selected First Dairy Leader of Yr., 1996; inductee Kans. Co-op Hall of Fame, 1999. Mem. Mid Am. Dairymen (sec. corporate bd. 1971-81, pres. 1981-95), Holstein Friesian Assn. Am. (nat. dir. 1964-72), Dairy Shrine (nat. dir. 1971-81), United Dairy Industry Assn. (dir. 1971-79), Nat. Holstein Assn. Am. (pres. 1979-80), Alpha Gamma Rho (highest honor 1989, Hall of Fame 1998). Mem. Christian Ch. (elder, bd. dirs.). Club: Nat. Dairy Shrine (pres. 1978). Home: PO Box 365 Iola KS 66749-0365 Office: Mid America Dairymen Inc 1641 N Dakota Rd Iola KS 66749

STRICKLER, JEFFREY HAROLD, pediatrician; b. Mpls., Oct. 14, 1943; s. Jacob Harold and Helen Cecelia (Mitchell) S.; m. Karen Anne Stewart, June l8, 1966; children: Hans Stewart, Liesl Ann. BA, Carleton Coll., 1965; MD, U. Minn., 1969. Diplomate Am. Bd. Pediatrics. Resident in pediatrics Stanford U., Calif., 1969-73; pvt. practice Helena, Mont., 1975—2005; chief staff Shodair Children's Hosp., Helena, 1984-86; consulting ptnr. Strickler Enterprises, 2006—. Dir. maternal-child health Lewis and Clark County, Helena, 1978-88; chief of staff St. Peters Hosp., Helena, 1994-96; bd.chmn. Helena Health Alliance, 1996-99; founding mem., bd. dirs. Caring Found. Mont., 1992-2005. Mem. Mont. Gov.'s Task Force on Child Abuse, 1978-79; mem. steering com. Region VIII Child Abuse Prevention, Denver, 1979-82; bd. dirs. Helena Dist. 1 Sch. Bd., l982-88, vice chmn., 1985-87. Maj. M.C., USAF, 1973-75. Fellow: Am. Acad. Pediatrics (vice chmn. Mont. chpt. 1981—84, chmn. 1984—87, mem. nat. nominating com. 1987—90, chmn. 1989—90, coun. on govt. affairs 1990—96, future of pediatric edn. II 1996—2000, Wyeth award 1987); mem.: Am. Bd. Pediatrics (PMCP-G practice performance com. 2001—), Rotary (youth exch. chmn. dist. 539 1984—88, pres. Helena 1988—89, polio plus chair dist. 5390 1996—, asst. gov. dist. 5390 2002—04, dist. gov. elect 2005—06, gov. 2006—07). Avocations: skiing, hiking. Home: PO Box 161815 2125 Yellowtail Rd Big Sky MT 59716-1815 Office Phone: 406-431-4331. Personal E-mail: j.strickler@3rivers.net.

STRICKLER, MATTHEW M., lawyer; b. Bryn Mawr, Pa., June 27, 1940; s. Charles S and Mary Webster (Cornman) S.; m. Margaret Renshaw, Sept. 3, 1966; children: Matthew David, Andrew Kellogg, Timothy Webster, Edward Charles. AB, Haverford Coll., 1962; JD, Harvard U., 1965. Bar: Pa. 1965, U.S. Supreme Ct. 1975. Assoc. Ballard, Spahr, Andrews & Ingersoll, Phila., 1965-74, ptnr., 1974—2002, sr. counsel, 2003—; dir. legal affairs Sch. Medicine Temple U., Phila., 2003—. Adj. prof. Temple U. Sch. Law, Phila., 1993—. Editor: Representing Health Care Facilities, 1981. Bd. dirs. Phila. chpt. Girl Scouts Am., 1978-96, v.p., 1984-90, 94-96; bd. dirs. Kardon Inst. Arts, 2000—, treas., 2003-05, chmn., 2005—. Mem. ABA, Pa. Bar Assn., Phila Bar Assn., Am. Acad. Healthcare Attys., Am. Health Lawyers Assn., Nat. Assn. Coll. and Univ. Attys., Union League Phila., Pocono Lake Preserve, Meridian Bridge Club. Office: Temple U Sch Medicine 3420 N Broad St Rm 107 Philadelphia PA 19140 Office Phone: 215-707-6766. Business E-Mail: mstrick@temple.edu.

STRICKLER, SCOTT MICHAEL, lawyer; b. Miami Beach, Fla., May 24, 1961; s. Lawrence Jerome and Barbara Susan (Fogelman) S.; m. Joy Ann Kohler, June 24, 1995; 1 child, Megan Halle. BS in Journalism, U. Md., 1981, JD with honors, 1985. Bar: Md. 1985, DC 1987, US Dist. Ct. (dist. Md.) 1988, US Supreme Ct. 2005. Jud. law clk. 5th Jud. Cir. Md., Annapolis, 1985-86; assoc. Stephen E. Moss, P.A., Bethesda, Md., 1986-89; ptnr., v.p. Moss, Strickler & Weaver, P.A., Bethesda, 1990-94, Moss & Strickler, P.A., Bethesda, 1994; ptnr. Strickler, Sachitano & Hatfield, P.A. (formerly Moss Strickler & Sachitano, P.A.), Bethesda, 1995—. Coach, dir. Bowie Boys and Girls Club, Md., 1976-81; dir. Bowie Basketball Sch., Inc., 1978-82; basketball coach Peninsula Athletic League, Annapolis, 1985-86, Olney Boys and Girls Club, Md., 1987, I-270 Sports Club, Gaithersburg, Md., 1991, Sports Challenge Internat., Palm Harbor, Fla., 1993. Named one of Top 100 Attys., Worth mag., 2006. Mem. ABA (family law sect.), Md. State Bar Assn. (family law sect.), Montgomery County Bar Assn. (chair family law sect. 1998-99), Inst. Sports Attys., Kappa Tau Alpha. Avocations: basketball coach, participatory athletics, memorabilia collection. Office: Strickler Sachitano & Hatfield PA 4550 Montgomery Ave Ste 900N Bethesda MD 20814-3304 Office Phone: 301-657-8805. Office Fax: 301-657-8815. E-mail: sstrickler@modernfamilylaw.com. *

STRICKON, HARVEY ALAN, lawyer; b. Bklyn., Nov. 9, 1947; s. Milton and Norma (Goodhartz) S.; m. Linda Carol Meltzer, July 2, 1972; children: Joshua Andrew, Meredith Cindy, Erica Stacey. BBA, CCNY, 1968; JD, NYU, 1971. Bar: NY 1972, US Dist. Ct. (so. and ea. dists.) NY 1973, US Ct. Appeals (2d cir.) 1973, US Supreme Ct. 1975, US Dist. Ct. (no. dist.) NY 1980, US Dist. Ct. (we. dist.) NY 1981, US Dist. Ct. Ariz. 1991, US Dist. Ct. Conn., 1996, US Tax Ct. 2006. Law clk. U.S. Dist. Ct. (ea. dist.) N.Y., Bklyn., 1971-73; assoc. Moses & Singer, NYC, 1973-80; from assoc. to ptnr. Kaye, Scholer, Fierman, Hays & Handler, NYC, 1980-91; from ptnr. to counsel Paul, Hastings, Janofsky & Walker LLP, NYC, 1991—. Mem. complaint mediation panel, departmental disciplinary com. appellate div., 1st dept. Supreme Ct. State N.Y.; mem. mediation panel U.S. Dist. Ct. (ea. dist.) N.Y.; mem. mediation register U.S. Bankruptcy Ct. (so. and ea. dists.) N.Y. Co-author: Enforcing Judgments and Collecting Debts in New York, 1996. Mem. Nassau County Rep. Com., Great Neck, N.Y., 1982—; chmn. bd. dirs. Flushing Community Vol. Ambulance Corps. Inc., N.Y., 1981-86, vice chmn., 1987-92. Mem. ABA, N.Y. State Bar Assn., Assn. Bar City N.Y. (chmn. com. on profl. discipline and complaint mediation panel com. on profl. discipline), Am. Judicature Soc., Assn. Comml. Fin. Attys., N.Y. Law Inst., Bankruptcy Lawyers Bar Assn., (bd. govs. 1987-89, corr. sec. 1989—), Am. Bankruptcy Inst. Republican. Jewish. Home: 11 West Brook Rd Great Neck NY 11024-1219 Office: Paul Hastings Janofsky & Walker LLP 75 E 55th St New York NY 10022-3205 Office Phone: 212-318-6380. E-mail: harveystrickon@paulhastings.com, hastrick@optonline.net.

STRIDER, MARJORIE VIRGINIA, artist, educator; b. Guthrie, Okla. d. Clifford R. and Marjorie E. (Schley) S. BFA, Kansas City Art Inst., 1962. Faculty Sch. Visual Arts, NYC, 1970-2001; artist-in-residence City U. Grad. Ctr. Mall, NYC, 1976, Fabric Workshop, Phila., 1978, Grassi Palace, Venice, Italy, 1978. One-woman shows include Pace Gallery, N.Y.C., 1963-64, Nancy Hoffman Gallery, N.Y.C., 1973-74, Weather Spoon Mus., U.N.C., Chapel Hill, 1974, City U. Grad. Center Mall, 1976, Clocktower, N.Y.C., 1976, Sculpture Center, N.Y.C., 1983, Steinbaum Gallery, N.Y.C., 1983, 84, Andre Zarre Gallery, 1993, 95, Outdoor Installation, N.Y.C., 1997, Selby Gallery, Ringling Sch. of Art, Sarasota, Fla., 1998, Neuberger Mus., Purchase, N.Y., 1999; exhibited in group shows at Sculpture Center, N.Y.C., 1981, Drawing Biennale, Lisbon, Portugal, 1981, Newark Mus., 1984, William Rockhill Nelson Mus., Kansas City, 1985, Danforth Mus., Framingham, Mass., 1987, Delahoyd Gallery, N.Y.C., 1992; represented in permanent collections Guggenheim Mus., N.Y.C., U. Colo., Boulder, Albright-Knox Mus., Buffalo, Des Moines Art Center, Storm King (N.Y.) Art Center, Larry Aldrich Mus., Ridgefield, Conn., City U. Grad. Center, N.Y.C., Hirschhorn Mus. and Sculpture Garden, Washington, Santa Fe (N. Mex.) Mus. of Art, also pvt. collections. Grantee Nat. Endowment for Arts, 1973, 80, Longview Found., 1974, Pollock-Krasner Found., 1990, Florsheim Art Fund, 1998, 2000; Va. Ctr. for Creative Arts fellow, 1974, 92, Millay Colony for Arts fellow, 1992, Yaddo Colony, 1996-97 Home Phone: 845-246-1301; Office Phone: 845-246-1301. Business E-Mail: m_strider@hvc.rr.com.

STRIDIRON, IVER ALLISON, former attorney general; b. St. Thomas, VI, May 29, 1945; m. Priscilla Blyden; 4 children. BA Lincoln U., 1969; JD, Howard U. Sch. of Law, 1974. Atty. U.S. Nuclear Regulatory Commn., U.S. Commn. on Civil Rights, Washington, 1974—77; pvt. practice St. Thomas, V.I., 1977—99; mem. V.I. Legis., 1981—83, 1985—89, pres., 1987—88; atty. gen. V.I., 1999—2004. Democrat.

STRIEBY, B. LORRAINE, artist; b. Morgantown, W.Va., Dec. 5, 1938; d. Charles Willis Ayer and Margaret Ann Ferko; m. Michael Strieby (dec.); children: Vicki Parzyk, Lisa Magistro, Lori Constantine, Ann; m. Stanley Veerin Gunn, Nov. 22, 2003. BA in Bus. Edn., Calif. State U., Northridge, 1976, secondary tchg. credential, 1977. Tchr. L.A. Unified Sch. Dist., 1978—81. Pres. Women Painters West, LA, 1995—97. Exhibitions include Art Concepts Gallery, Tacoma, 1997, Black Sheep Gallery, Hardwarden Castle, Wales, 1999, Westminster Gallery, London, 1999, S.E. La. U. Gallery, Hammond, 2000, Segreto Gallery, Santa Fe, 2002, Barlow Gallery, New Orleans, 2004, Mus. Making Music, Carlsbad, Calif., 2004, Williamson Art Gallery and Mus., Liverpool, Eng., 2004, Sotto South Gallery, Savannah, Ga., 2004—06, Barrie Holt Gallery, New Orleans, 2006, Charlevoix Street Gallery, Albuquerque, 2006, Adobe Ranch Gallery, Chatsworth, Calif. Various positions Rep. Women West Valley, LA, 1990—99. Recipient Golden Products award, Nat. Acrylic Painters Assn. Home: PO Box 4928 Chatsworth CA 91311 Office Phone: 818-261-3968. E-mail: adobeart818@earthlink.net.

STRIEFSKY, LINDA A(NN), lawyer; b. Carbondale, Pa., Apr. 27, 1952; d. Leo James and Antoinette Marie (Carachilo) S.; m. James Richard Carlson, Nov. 3, 1984; children: David Carlson, Paul Carlson, Daniel Carlson. BA summa cum laude, Marywood Coll., 1974; JD, Georgetown U., Washington, DC, 1977. Bar: Ohio 1977. Assoc. Thompson Hine LLP (formerly Thompson, Hine & Flory), Cleve., 1977-85, ptnr., 1985—. Loaned exec. United Way N.E. Ohio, Cleve., 1978; trustee ideastream, Mus. Theater Edn. Programming. Mem. ABA (real estate fin. com. 1980-87, vice chmn. leader liability com. 1993-97, mem. non-traditional real estate fin. com. 1987—, chair securitization and spl. financing techniques com. 2006—), Am. Bar Found., Am. Coll. Real Estate Lawyers (bd. govs. 1994-98, 06—, treas. 1999), Internat. Coun. Shopping Ctrs., Nat. Assn. Office and Indsl. Parks, Urban Land Inst. (chmn. Cleve. dist. coun. 1996-2000), Cleve. Real Estate Women (mem. adv. bd. 2007-), Ohio Bar Assn. (bd. govs. real property sect. 1985-97), Greater Cleve. Bar Assn. (chmn. bar applicants com. 1983-84, exec. coun. young lawyers sect. 1982-85, chmn. 1984-85, mem. exec. coun. real property sect. 1980-84, Merit Svc. award 1983, 85), Pi Gamma Mu. Democrat. Roman Catholic. Home: 2222 Delamere Dr Cleveland OH 44106-3204 Office: Thompson Hine LLP 3900 Key Ctr 127 Public Square Cleveland OH 44114-1216 Office Phone: 216-566-5733. Business E-Mail: linda.striefsky@thompsonhine.com.

STRIER, KAREN BARBARA, anthropologist, educator; b. Summit, NJ, May 22, 1959; d. Murray Paul and Arlene Strier. BA, Swarthmore Coll., 1980; MA, Harvard U., 1981, PhD, 1986. Lectr. anthropology Harvard U., Cambridge, Mass., 1986—87; asst. prof. Beloit Coll., Wis., 1987—89, U. Wis., Madison, 1989—92, assoc. prof., 1992—95, prof., 1995—, dept. chair, 1994—96. Panel mem. U.S. Dept. Edn., Washington, 1989—92. Author: (book) Faces in the Forest, 1999, Primate Behavioral Ecology, 2d edit., 2003; co-author: Planning, Purposing, and Presenting Science Effectively; mem. editl. bd.: Internat. Jour. Primatology, 1990—, Primates, 1991—, Yearbook of Phys. Anthropology. Recipient Presdl. Young Investigator award, NSF, 1989—94. Fellow: AAAS, Am. Anthropol. Assn.; mem.: NAS, Animal Behavior Soc., Internat. Primatological Soc., Am.

Assn. Phys. Anthropologists. Office: U Wis Dept Anthropology 5403 Social Sci Bldg 1180 Observatory Dr Madison WI 53706-1320 Office Phone: 608-262-0302. E-mail: kbstrier@wisc.edu.

STRIGL, DENNIS F., telecommunications industry executive; b. Apr. 13, 1946; BBA, Canisius Coll.; MBA, Dickinson U. With NY Tel. Co., 1968, AT&T; pres. Ameritech Mobile Commn., 1984—89; v.p. product mgmt. network svcs. Bell Atlantic, 1989—91; pres., CEO Bell Atlantic Mobile and Bell Atlantic Global Wireless, 1991—97, Bell Atlantic Global Wireless, 1997—2000, Verizon Wireless Joint Venture, 2000—07; exec. v.p. Verizon Comm., Inc., Bedminster, NJ, 2000—07, pres., COO, 2007—. Mem. bd. dirs. Verizon Wireless, Anadigics Inc., PNC Fin. Services Grp., PNC Bank. Chmn. bd. trustees Canisius Coll. Named to Pinnacle Soc. for disting. alumni, Fairleigh Dickinson U.; recipient Cellular Industry Achievement award. Mem.: Cellular Telecom. & Internet Assn. (chmn. bd. dirs. 1996—97). Office: Verizon Wireless 180 Washington Valley Rd Bedminster NJ 07921 *

STRIKER, CECIL LEOPOLD, archaeologist, educator; b. Cin., July 15, 1932; s. Cecil and Delia (Workum) S.; m. Ute Stephan, Apr. 27, 1968. BA, Oberlin Coll., 1956; MA, NYU, 1960, PhD, 1968; MA (hon.), U. Pa., 1972. From instr. to asst. prof. Vassar Coll., 1962-68; assoc. prof. U. Pa., Phila., 1968-78, prof. history art, 1978—2006, chmn. dept. history of art, 1980-87, prof. emeritus, 2006—; field archaeologist Dumbarton Oaks Center for Byzantine Studies, 1966-80, fellow, 1972-73. Adj. prof. Sabanci U., 1999—; dir. survey and excavation, Myrelaion, Istanbul, 1965-66; co-dir. Kalenderhane Archaeol. Project, Istanbul, 1966-78, Aegean Dendrochronology Project, 1977-88; gen. archaeol. cons. Istanbul Metro and Bosphorus Tunnel Project, 1985-87; dir. Archtl. Dendrochronology Project, 1988—; cons. Integrated Study of Hagia Sophia Structure, 1991-95. Mem. editorial bd. Architectura: Zeitschrift für Geschichte der Architektur, 1986—. Adv. bd. Ctr. for Advanced Study in the Visual Arts, 1986-88, Samuel H. Kress Found. Art History Fellowship Program, 1986-87. With U.S. Army, 1954-57. Fulbright grant in Germany, 1960-62, NEH grant, 1985-86; art historian in residence Am. Acad. in Rome, 1973. Mem. Archaeol. Inst. Am., Coll. Art Assn., Am. Rsch. Inst. in Turkey (fellow 1965-66, pres. 1978-84, hon. dir. 2002), Coun. Am. Overseas Rsch. Ctr. (chmn. 1980-84), Soc. Archtl. Historians, Turkish Studies Assn., U.S. Nat. Com. for Byzantine Studies, Koldewey Gesellschaft, German Archaeol. Inst. (corr.). Office Phone: 215-573-9702. Business E-Mail: cstriker@sas.upenn.edu.

STRIKWERDA, CARL JAMES, dean; b. Grand Rapids, Mich., Aug. 23, 1952; s. Alfred Charles Strikwerda and Bernice Bonwens; m. Gail Margaret Bossenga, June 7, 1975; children: Laurna Margaret Bossenga, Timothy James Strikwerda. BA, Calvin Coll., Grand Rapids, 1976; MA, U. Chgo., 1976; PhD, U. Mich., Ann Arbor, 1983. Asst. prof. U. Kans., Lawrence, 1989—92, assoc. prof., 1992—98, assoc. dean liberal arts and scis., 1998—2004; dean faculty arts and scis. Coll. William and Mary, Williamsburg, Va., 2004—. Hist. cons. Liberty Meml. Mus., Kansas City, Mo., 2001—05. Author: A House Divided, 1997; editor: Politics of Immigrant Workers, 1993, Consumers Against Capitalism?, 1998. Rsch. fellow, German Marshall Fund, Washington, 1995—96, Kemper fellow, U. Kans., 2001. Mem.: Coun. Colls. Arts and Scis. (sec.-treas. 2006—). Lutheran. Home: 115 Hempstead Rd Williamsburg VA 23188 Office: Coll William and Mary PO Box 8795 Williamsburg VA 23187

STRIMBU, VICTOR, JR., lawyer; b. New Phila., Ohio, Nov. 25, 1932; s. Victor and Veda (Stancu) S.; m. Kathryn May Schrote, Apr. 9, 1955 (dec. 1995); children: Victor Paul, Michael, Julie, Sue; m. Marjorie Bichsel, Oct. 23, 1999. BA, Heidelberg Coll., 1954; postgrad., Western Res. U., 1956-57; JD, COlumbia U., 1960. Bar: Ohio 1960, U.S. Supreme Ct. 1972. With Baker & Hostetler LLP, Cleve., 1960—, ptnr., 1970—. Bd. dirs. North Coast Health Ministry; mem. Bay Village (Ohio) Bd. Edn., 1976-84, pres., 1978-82; mem. Bay Village Planning Commn., 1967-69; life mem. Ohio PTA; mem. Greater Cleve. Growth Assn.; trustee New Cleve. Campaign, 1987-94—, North Coast Health Ministry, 1989-2001, Heidelberg Coll., 1996—; mem. indsl. rels. adv. com. Cleve. State U., 1979—, chmn., 1982,1999, vice chmn., 1998. With AUS, 1955-56. Mem. ABA, Ohio Bar Assn., Greater Cleve. Bar Assn., Ohio Newspaper Assn. (minority affairs com. 1987-90), Ct. of Nisi Prius Club. Republican. Presbyterian. Office: Baker & Hostetler LLP 3200 National City Ctr 1900 E 9th St Ste 3200 Cleveland OH 44114-3485 Office Phone: 216-621-0200.

STRINER, HERBERT EDWARD, economics professor; b. Jersey City, Aug. 16, 1922; s. Harry and Pearl (Strynar) S.; m. Erma Steinert, Dec. 9, 1943 (div. 1970); children: Richard Alan, Deborah Jane; m. Iona V. Meredith. AB, Rutgers U., 1947, MA, 1948; PhD (Maxwell fellow 1949-50), Syracuse U., 1951. Asst. prof. Syracuse U., 1951; economist Interior Dept., 1951-54; program dir. NSF, 1954-55, Nat. Planning Assn., 1955-57; sr. analyst Operations Research Office, Johns Hopkins, 1957-59; program dir. Brookings Inst., 1959-61, Stanford Research Inst., 1961-62; program devel. dir. Upjohn Inst., Washington, 1962-69; dean Coll. Continuing Edn. Am. U., Washington, 1969-72, dean Coll. Bus., 1974-81, prof. econs. and mgmt., 1981-89; cons. Los Alamos Nat. Lab., 1990-91; chief planning and policy NIH, 1972-73; pres. U. Research Corp., 1973-74; assoc. faculty mem. Johns Hopkins U., 1997. Chmn. bd. dirs. NetTalon Corp. Inc., 2002—04. Author: Toward a Fundamental Program for the Training, Employment and Economic Equality of the American Indian, 1968, Continuing Education as a National Capital Investment, 1972, Regaining The Lead: Policies for Economic Growth, 1984; co-author: Local Impact of Foreign Trade, 1960, Civil Rights, Employment and the Social Status of American Negros, 1966; Contbr. profl. jours. Mem. rev. panel Pres.'s Cabinet Com. Juv. Delinquency, 1961-63, D.C. Youth Employment Com., 1963, Pres.'s Task Force Am. Indians, 1967, White House Conf. Aging, 1971; bd. dirs. Opportunities Industrialization Ctr., NAACP, Washington. Officer inf. U.S. Army, 1943-46. Decorated Breast Order of Yun Hui with Ribbon, World War II Govt. China. Home: 3158 Gracefield Rd # 416 Silver Spring MD 20904

STRINGER, C. VIVIAN, women's college basketball coach; b. Edenborn, Pa., 1948; m. William D. Stringer (dec.); children: David, Janine, Justin. Grad., Slippery Rock State Coll. Head coach Cheyney State Coll., 1971—83, U. Iowa, 1983—95, Rutgers U., 1995—. Head coach US Select Team tour China, 1980, World U. Games, Kobe, Japan, 1985, World Championship Zone Qualification Tournament, Sao Paulo, Brazil, 1989, US Pan-Am. Games, Havana, Cuba, 1991. Finalist Naismith Nat. Coach of Yr. award, 2000, 2001, 2003; named to Women's Basketball Hall of Fame, 2001; recipient Phila. Sportswriters' Coach of Yr., 1980, 1981, NCAA Wade Trophy Women's Nat. Coach of Yr., 1982, Converse Women's Nat. Coach of Yr., 1988, Naismith award, Converse, Sports Illus., USA Today, LA Times and Black Coaches Assn. Women's Coach of Yr., 1993. Mem. Amateur Basketball Assn. US (bd. dirs.). Achievements include 1st person (male or female) to lead 3 different schools to the NCAA final four; recorded 750th career win, 2006. *

STRINGER, GRETCHEN ENGSTROM, consulting volunteer administrator; b. Pitts., Feb. 25, 1925; d. Birger and Gertrude Anne (Schuchman) Engstrom; m. Loren F. Stringer, Oct. 3, 1953 (dec. Sept. 1992); children: Lizbeth, Pamela, William E., Frederick E. BA, Oberlin Coll., 1946; Cert. in Teaching, U. Pitts., 1951, SUNY, Buffalo, 1964, M, 1996. Cert. vol. adminstr. Owner, founder, pres. Vol. Cons., Clarence, NY, 1979—; owner, founder, officer Non Profit Mgmt. Ctr., Buffalo, 1995-2000. Founding pres., bd. dirs. Ctrl. Referral Svc. Author: The Board Manual Workbook, 1980, rev., 2004, The Instructors Guide, 1982, A Magical Formula, 1980; co-author: Non Profit Management Education, 1998; contbr. articles to profl. jours. Exec. dir. Vol. Action Ctr., United Way Buffalo and Erie County, 1978-81; founding vice chair Erie County Commn. on Status of Women, 1989-2000; pres. Girl Scout Coun. of Buffalo and Erie County, chair, gen. mgr. cadette encampment; bd. dirs. Clarence Ctrl. Sch. Dist., 1976-86; chair, gen. mgr. Buffalo and Erie County Bicentennial Parade, 1976, Erie County Ski Swap; bd. dirs. Longview Protestant Home for Children Bd., Millard Fillmore Jr. Bd., Prevention is Primary, N.Y. Bd. State Foster Care Youth Ind. Project, others; Cmty. Hero Torch Bearer Summer Olympics, 1996; del. White House Conf. on Small Bus., 1995; vol. steering com. Martin House Restoration Corp., 1988—. Recipient Pinny Wilson Vol. award Buffalo and Erie County, 1981, Continuing Svc. award Mass. Mutual, 1987, Girl Scouts Thanks Badge, 1983, Susan Reid Greene Russell award Jr. League of Buffalo, 1994, Assoc. of Yr. award Am. Bus. Women, 1997, Women Bus. Advocate of Yr. Small Bus. Adminstrn., 1998, Prime Time award Coord. Care, 1999, Woman of Achievement award AAUW, Buffalo chpt., 2001, Woman of Achievement award Every Woman Opportunity Ctr., 2004. Mem. Nat. Assn. Women Bus. Owners (bd. pres. Buffalo chpt. 1998-2000), N.Y. Assn. Vol. Ctrs. (founding exec. bd.), Vol. Adminstrs. Western N.Y. (founding pres. 1980), Buffalo Ambassadors of C. of C. (bd. dirs.), Women's Pavilion Pan Am. Centennial 2001 (founder, pres. bd. dirs. 1999-2001), Jr. League Buffalo, Inc. (sustainer v.p. 1998-2000), Assn. Vol. Adminstrn. (chair, gen. mgr. nat. conf. 1986, nat. trainer, re-cert. chair, subcom. vol. adminstrn. higher edn.). Office: Vol Cons 9015 Cliffside Dr Clarence NY 14031-1460 Office Phone: 716-633-8264. E-mail: gestringer@adelphia.net.

STRINGER, SIR HOWARD, entertainment company executive; b. Cardiff, Wales, Feb. 19, 1942; arrived in U.S., 1965, naturalized, 1985; s. Harry and Marjorie Mary (Pook) Stringer; m. Jennifer Kinmond Patterson, July 29, 1978; children: David Ridley, Harriet Kinmond. BA, MA in Modern History, Oxford U., Eng., 1964; PhD (hon.), London Arts Inst., 2003, U. Glamorgan, 2005, Am. Film Inst., 2007. Prodr., dir. CBS News, NYC, 1973—76, pres., 1986—88, exec. v.p., 1984—86; exec. prodr. CBS Reports, 1976—81, CBS Evening News with Dan Rather, 1981—84; pres. CBS Broadcast Group, 1988—95; chmn., CEO Tele-TV, 1995—97; pres. Sony Corp. Am., 1997—98, chmn., CEO, 1998—, Sony Corp., 2005—, bd. mem., 2005—; corp. head Sony Corp. Entertainment Bus. Group; bd. mem. Sony BMG Music Entertainment, Sony Ericsson. Chmn. bd. trustees Am. Film Inst.; bd. mem. Am. Theatre Wing, NY Presbyn. Hosp., Am. Friends of the British Mus., Corp. Leadership Com. Lincoln Ctr. for the Performing Arts; bd. trustee Paley Ctr. Media (formerly Mus. TV and Radio); trustee Teach for Am.; bd. mem. Carnegie Hall. Sgt. US Army, 1965—67, Vietnam. Decorated US Army Commendation medal for meritorious achievement for svc. in Vietnam; named a Living Legend of NY, 2005; named Knight Bachelor, Queen Elizabeth, 1999, hon. fellow Merton Coll., Oxford, 2000, hon. fellow Welsh Coll. Music and Drama, 2001; named one of World's 100 Most Influential People, Time Mag., 2005; named to Broadcasting and Cable Hall of Fame, 1996, Royal TV Soc. Welsh Hall of Fame, Wales, 1999; recipient Columbia Dupont award, Columbia Journalism Sch., 1979, 1981, Overseas Press Club awards, 1974, 1979, 1982, IRTS Found. award, 1994, honored Uncommon Vision Media Industry, Museum Moving Image, 1994, First Amendment Leadership award, Radio and TV News Dirs. Found., 1996, Steven J. Ross Humanitarian award, UJA-Federation NY, 1999, highest award, Ctr. for Communications, 2000, award, Literary Partners, Pub. Svc. award, Phoenix House, 2002, award, NY Hall of Sci., Dinner Champions honoree, Nat. Multiple Sclerosis Soc., 2002, medal of Honor, St. George Soc., 2004, Disting. Svc. award honoree, Big Brothers Big Sisters NYC, 2005, Teach Am. Annual award, 2001, Disting. Leadership award, Internat. Emmy Founders, 2002, honored, Alliance Lupus Rsch., 2007, Visionary award, Paley Ctr. Media (formerly Mus. Radio and TV), 2007. Mem.: Coun. on Fgn. Rels. Presbyterian. Office: Sony Corp of Am 550 Madison Ave New York NY 10022-3211 also: Sony Corp 1-7-1 Konan Minato ku Tokyo 108-0075 Japan

STRINGER, JOHN, retired materials scientist; b. Liverpool, Eng., July 14, 1934; came to U.S., 1977, naturalized, 1996; s. Gerald Hitchen and Isobel (Taylor) S.; m. Audrey Lancaster, Feb. 4, 1957; children: Helen Caroline, Rebecca Elizabeth. BS in Engring., U. Liverpool, 1955, PhD, 1958, D in Engring., 1974. Chartered engr., U.K. Lectr. Univ. Liverpool, England, 1957-63, prof. materials sci., 1966-77; fellow Battelle Columbus (Ohio) Labs., 1963-66; sr. project mgr. Electric Power Rsch. Inst., Palo Alto, Calif., 1977-81, sr. program mgr., 1981-87, dir. tech. support, 1987-91, dir. applied rsch., 1991-95, tech. exec. Applied Sci. and Tech., 1995-96, exec. tech. fellow, 1997—2004; ret. Chmn. Sci. and Tech. Edn., Merseyside, Liverpool, 1971-74; pres. Corrosion and Protection Assn., London, 1972; mem. Nat. Material Adv. Bd., 1992-95, basic energy scis. adv. com., U.S. Dept. Energy, 1992-98, chmn., 1996-98. Mem. editl. bd.: Oxidation of Metals Jour., 1971—; author: An Introduction to the Electron Theory of Solids, 1967; editor: (book) High Temperature Corrosion of Advanced Materials, 1989, Chlorine in Coal, 1991, Applied Chaos, 1992; contbr. over 350 articles to profl. jours. Recipient U.R. Evans award Inst. Corrosion, U.K., 1993, Campbell Meml. Lectr. of ASM Internat., 1995. Fellow AAAS, NACE Internat. (Willis Rodney Whitney award 2004), AIME, Inst. Energy, Royal Soc. Arts, Instn. Corrosion (hon.), ASM Internat. Office Phone: 650-365-2471. Personal E-mail: jstringer@izambard.com, johnstringer@comcast.net.

STRINGER, L. E. (DEAN), retired lawyer; b. Sayre, Okla., June 22, 1936; s. Rex Herman and Bessie (Morris) S.; m. Carol Ann Woodson, Aug. 31, 1963; children: Craig Woodson, Laura DeAnn. BA, Okla. State U., 1958; LLB, Harvard U., 1961. Bar: Okla. 1961, US Ct. Appeals (10th cir.) 1962, US Dist. Ct. (we. dist.) 1963, US Supreme Ct. 1972. Assoc. Crowe, Boxley, et al (now Crowe & Dunlevy), Oklahoma City, 1961—68, mem., dir., 1968—2000, chmn. bd., 1999—2000. Pres. Crowe & Dunlevy, P.C., 1979-81, chmn. litigation dept., 1987-2000, ret. 2000; bd. dirs. Okla. Inst. for Child Advocacy, 2003-, v.p., 2004, pres.-elect, 2005, pres. 2006. Pres. Okla. State U. Alumni Assn., 1972-73; bd. regents Okla. State U. and A&M Colls., Stillwater, 1986-94, vice-chmn., 1989-90, chmn., 1990-91; chmn. Okla. State U. Found., Stillwater, 1982-85; pres. Friends of the Libr., Okla. State U., 2000—; bd. dirs. Okla. Heritage Assn., 1995-2000; pres. adv. com. Okla. State U./OKC, 1998—, chmn., 2000—; mem. regents edn. adv. com. Okla. State Regents for Higher Edn., 1995-2001; trustee Youth Svcs. Oklahoma County, Inc., 2001—, vice chmn. 2002-04, chmn. 2004-07. Maj. Okla. N.G., 1961-71. Recipient Disting. Alumnus award Okla. State U., 1979, Neil E. Bogan Professionalism award, Okla. Bar Assn., 2005; inducted Hall of Fame Okla. State U. Alumni Assn, 1998. Fellow Am. Bar Found. (adv. rsch. com. 1996-2000); mem. Okla. Bar Assn. Democrat. Methodist. Home: 325 NW 17th St Oklahoma City OK 73103-3424

STRINGER, SCOTT M., city manager, former state legislator; b. NYC, Apr. 29, 1960; BA, John Jay Coll. Mem. NY State Assembly, Dist. 67, Albany, NY, 1992—2005, mem. Edn., Higher Edn., Housing, and Judiciary coms.; borough pres. Manhattan, NY, 2006—. Dist. coord. NY State Assemblyman Jerrold Nadler. Mem.: NAACP, Nat. Women's Polit. Caucus, West Side Crime Prevention Program, NYC Americans for Dem. Action, Manhattan New Dem. Coalition. Office: Office Manhattan Borough Pres 1 Centre St 19th Fl New York NY 10007

STRINGER, WILLIAM JEREMY, university official; b. Oakland, Calif., Nov. 8, 1944; s. William Duane and Mildred May (Andrus) S.; m. Susan Lee Hildebrand; children: Shannon Lee, Kelly Erin, Courtney Elizabeth. BA in English, So. Meth. U., Dallas, 1966; MA in English, U. Wis., Madison, 1968, PhD in Ednl. Adminstrn., 1973. Dir. men's housing Southwestern U., Georgetown, Tex., 1968-69; asst. dir. housing U. Wis., Madison, 1969-73; dir. residential life, assoc. dean student life, adj. prof. Pacific Luth., Tacoma, 1973-78; dir. residential life U. So. Calif., 1978-79, asst. v.p., 1979-84, asst. prof. higher and post-secondary edn., 1980-84; v.p. student life Seattle U., 1984-89, v.p. student devel., 1989-92, assoc. provost, 1989-95, assoc. prof. edn., 1990—, chair ednl. leadership, 1994—97, chair strategic planning, 1997—2000, chair profl. studies, 2001—. Author: How to Survive as a Single Student, 1972, The Role of the Assistant in Higher Education, 1973. Bd. dirs. NW Area Luth. Social Svcs. of Wash. and Idaho, pres.-elect, 1989, pres., 1990-91; bd. dirs. Seattle Coalition Ednl. Equity; chair parents' coun. Pacific Luth. U., 2006-. Recipient John Hubbard Leadership award, 1984; Danforth Found. grantee, 1976-77. Mem. AAUP, Nat. Assn. Student Pers. Adminstrs. (bd. dirs. region V 1985-97, mem. editl. bd. Jour. 1995-2001, Disting. Svc. to Profession award 2000, faculty fellow 2002-, chair 2005-), Am. Coll. Pers. Assn., Phi Eta Sigma, Sigma Tau Delta, Phi Alpha Theta, Lambda Chi Alpha Lutheran. Home: 4553 169th Ave SE Bellevue WA 98006-6505 Office: Seattle U Dept Edn Seattle WA 98122 E-mail: stringer@seattleu.edu.

STRINGFELLOW, GERALD B., engineering educator; b. Salt Lake City, Apr. 26, 1942; s. Paul Bennion and Jean (Barton) S.; m. Barbara Farr, June 9, 1962; children: Anne, Heather, Michael. BS, U. Utah, 1964; PhD, Stanford U., 1968. Staff scientist Hewlett Packard Labs., Palo Alto, Calif., 1967-70, group mgr., 1970-80; disting. prof. elec. engring., materials sci. U. Utah, Salt Lake City, 1980—, chmn., 1994-98, adj. prof. physics, 1988—, dean Coll. Engring., 1998—2003. Cons. Tex. Instruments, Dallas, 1995-97, AT&T-Bell Labs., Holmdel, N.J., 1986-90, Brit. Telecom., London, 1989-92; editor-in-chief Phase Diagrams for Ceramics, Vol. IX. Author: Organometallic Vapor Phase Epitaxy, 1989, 2d edit., 1999; editor: Metal Organic Vapor Phase Epitaxy, 1986, 2004, American Crystal Growth, 1987, Alloy Semiconductor Physics and Electronics, 1989, Phase Equilibria Diagrams-Semiconductors and Chalcogenides, 1991, High Brightness LEDs, 1997; prin. editor Jour. Crystal Growth, 1998-2003; letters editor Jour. Electronic Materials, 1992-99; contbr. over 360 articles to profl. jours. Recipient U.S. Sr. Scientist award Alexander von Humboldt Soc., Bonn, Germany, 1979, Gov.'s Sci. Tech. medal State of Utah, 1997, John Bardeen award TMS, 2003; guest fellow Royal Soc., London, 1990. Fellow IEEE, Japan Soc. Promotion of Sci.; mem. Am. Phys. Soc., Electronic Materials Com. (pres. 1985-87), Nat. Acad. Engring. Achievements include pioneering development of organometallic vapor phase epitaxy, development of theories of thermodynamic properties of alloy semiconductors; discovery of phenomenon of compositional latching in alloy semiconductor layers grown by epitaxial techniques. Office: U Utah Dept ECE 3280 MEB Salt Lake City UT 84112-1109 Business E-Mail: stringfellow@coe.utah.edu.

STRINGFIELD, SHERRY, actress; b. Colorado Springs, Colo., June 24, 1967; m. Larry Joseph, 1998; 1 child. BFA, SUNY, Purchase, 1989. Theater appearances include Goose and Tom Tom, Hurly Burly, Devil's Disciple, A Dream Play, Hotel Baltimore, The Kitchen, Tom Jones; appeared in (TV series) Guiding Light, 1989-92, NYPD Blue, 1993, ER, 1994-96, 2001- (Emmy nominee Outstanding Lead Actress in a Drama Series, 1995), Going Home, 2000; (films) Burnzy's Last Call, 1995, 54, 1998, Borderline, 1998, Autumn in New York, 2000, Viva Las Nowhere, 2001; (TV movies) Border Line, 1999, Going Home, 2000; (TV appearances) Touched by an Angel, 1999, Third Watch, 2002.

STRINGHAM, LUTHER WINTERS, retired economist, retired health facility administrator; b. Colorado Springs, Colo., Dec. 14, 1915; s. Luther Wilson and Fern (Van Duyn) S.; m. Margret Ann Pringle, Dec. 1, 1942 (dec. May 1998); 1 child, Susan Jean; m. Kathryn Cochran Baehr, June 19, 1999. BA summa cum laude, U. Colo., 1938, MA in Econs, 1939; Rockefeller fellow pub. adminstrn., U. Minn., 1939-40, Nat. Inst. Pub. Affairs, 1940-41. Economist Dept. Commerce, also OPA, 1941-43; intelligence officer Def. Dept., 1946-55; program analysis officer Office of the Sec. HEW, 1956-63, chmn. sec.'s com. mental retardation, 1961-63; exec. dir. Nat. Assn. for Retarded Children, 1963-68; intergovtl. relations officer HEW, 1968-77; planning dir. Central Va. Health Systems Agy., 1977-83. Dir. TV series Healthy Virginians, 1981-83. Mem. Pres.'s Com. Employment Handicapped, 1963-68; pres. Music for People, Inc., 1971-74; lectr. CUNY, 1971-76; mem. nat. coun. Boy Scouts Am., 1963-83; co-founder Older Virginians for Action, 1983-84; bd. dirs. Capital Area Agy. Aging, 1984-87; Midlothian Dist. rep. Keep Chesterfield Clean Corp. Capt. AUS, 1943-46; lt. col. USAFR, 1946-56. Mem. Greater Richmond C. of C. (mem. quality coun. 1993-94), Va. Hist. Soc., Phi Beta Kappa, Pi Gamma Mu, Delta Sigma Rho. Home: 2500 Durhamshire Pl Cheltenham Midlothian VA 23113 E-mail: lstringham2005@comcast.net.

STRINGHAM, PETER E., advertising executive; b. Winnipeg, Man., Can., Apr. 24, 1949; s. Elwood and Gabriel (Wellington) S.; m. Alberta McLeod, June 19, 1950; children: Thomas, John Peter, Wells. Sr. v.p. Gordon Hill Advt., Toronto, Ont., Canada, 1974—80; pres. Stringham & Grant Tandy Inc., Winnipeg, Canada, 1980—; pres., chief exec. BBDO Canada; chmn., CEO N.Am. Young & Rubicam; group gen. mgr. N.Am. HSBC Holdings plc, London, 2001—07; CEO Young & Rubicam Brands, NYC, 2007—. Office: Young & Rubicam Brands 285 Madison Ave New York NY 10017 *

STRINGHAM, PHYLLIS JOAN, retired music educator; b. Grand Rapids, Mich., Jan. 30, 1931; d. Wilhelmina Johanna and Harry Newton Stringham. MusB, Calvin Coll., Grand Rapids, Mich., 1952; MusM, U. Mich., Ann Arbor, Mich., 1955. Organist Chatham (Va.) Hall Girls Sch., 1955—59; prof. of music Carroll Coll., Waukesha, Wis., 1959—2001. Owner and mgr. Phylllis Stringham Concert Mgmt., Waukesha, Wis., 1964—. Musician concert organist. Mem.: Am. Guild of Organists. Avocation: reading. Home: 1101 Belmont Dr Waukesha WI 53186 Office: Phyllis Stringham concert Mgt 1101 Belmont Dr Waukesha WI 53186 Home Phone: 262-542-7197; Office Phone: 262-542-7197. Business E-Mail: pstringh@sbcglobal.net.

STRIPLING, BETTY KEITH, artist, retired medical/surgical nurse; b. Stephenville, Tex., Aug. 22, 1930; d. Fred Lancaster and Myrtle Ethel (Patton) Keith; m. Warren Lee Stripling, Mar. 22, 1952 (div. 1961); children: Keith, Kelley, David(dec.). Student, John Tarleton Agrl. Coll., 1948-50, Tarleton State U., 1980-85. Clk.-typist Kimbell-Food Products Co., Ft. Worth, 1950-52; LVN Stephenville Hosp. and Clinic, 1963, LVN floor duty, 1963-64, LVN surgery, 1964-66, Ft. Worth Osteo. Hosp., 1966-68; LVN, charge nurse Sunset Nursing Home, Stephenville, 1968-80, LVN, DON, 1973-78; LVN, charge nurse Cmty. Nursing Home, Stephenville, 1980-86, 89-94, pvt. duty nurse, 1986-89, cmty. nursing home LVN, 1998-99; freelance painter, 1999—2002. Democrat. Home: 3219 Kenilworth Dr Arlington TX 76001-5207 Personal E-mail: bjstrip@ont.com.

STRITCH, ELAINE, singer, actress; b. Detroit, Feb. 2, 1925; d. George Joseph and Mildred (Jobe) S.; m. John M. Bay, Feb. 2, 1973 (dec. 1973). Student drama workshop, New Sch. for Social Research; studies in singing with Burt Knapp, Drama Workshop, from 1948. Appeared in Broadway prodns. Loco, 1946, Three Indelicate Ladies, 1947, Yes M'Lord, 1949, Pal Joey, 1962, On Your Toes, Bus Stop, 1955, Sail Away, 1961, Who's Afraid of Virginia Woolf?, 1962, 65, Wonderful Town, 1967, Private Lives, 1968, Company, 1970, also London prodn., 1972, At Home at the Carlyle, 2005, 2006; appeared in Follies in Concert, NYC, 1982; (films) The Scarlet Hour, 1956, Three Violent People, 1956, A Farewell to Arms, 1957, The Perfect Furlough, 1958, Who Killed Teddy Bear?, 1965, Pigeons, 1971, The Spiral Staircase, 1975, Providence, 1977, September, 1988, Cocoon II: The Return, 1988, Cadillac Man, 1990, Out to Sea, 1997, Screwed, 2000, Small Time Crooks, 2000; numerous television appearances, including (series) My Sister Eileen, 1960-61, The Trials of O'Brien, 1965-66, (British) Two's

Company, 1975-76, The Ellen Burstyn Show, 1987, Stranded, 1986; (TV movie) Chance of a Lifetime, 1991; (TV miniseries) An Inconvenient Woman, 1991, Elaine Stritch: At Liberty, 2002 (Emmy award Outstanding Individual Performance in a Variety or Music Program, 2004, Drama Desk award, outstanding solo performance, Drama Desk award, outstanding book of a musical, Tony award for best solo musical performance HBO 1991); author: Am I Blue?: Living With Diabetes and, Dammit, Having Fun, 1984. Recipient Nightlife award, outstanding cabaret female vocalist in a major engagement, 2006.

STRITTMATTER, PETER ALBERT, astronomer, educator; b. London, Eng., Sept. 12, 1939; came to U.S., 1970. s. Albert and Rosa S.; m. Janet Hubbard Parkhurst, Mar. 18, 1967; children— Catherine D., Robert P. BA, Cambridge U., Eng., 1961, MA, 1963, PhD, 1967. Staff scientist Inst. for Astronomy, Cambridge, Eng., 1967-70; staff scientist dept. physics U. Calif.-San Diego, La Jolla, 1970-71; assoc. prof. dept. astronomy U. Ariz., Tucson, 1971-74, prof. dept. astronomy, 1974—, Regent's prof., 1994—. Dir. Steward Observatory, Tucson, 1975—; mem. staff Max Planck Inst. Radio-astronomy, Bonn, W. Germany, 1981— Contbr. articles to profl. jours. Recipient Sr. award Humboldt Found., 1979-80, Karl Schwarzschild medal, 1998. Fellow Royal Astron. Soc.; mem. Am. Astron. Soc., Astronomische Gesellschaft. Office: U Ariz Steward Obs Tucson AZ 85721-0001

STROBAUGH, TERENCE PHILIP, JR., molecular biologist, microbiologist; b. Altoona, Pa., Dec. 19, 1958; s. Terence Philip Strobaugh, Sr. and Lois Ann Strobaugh. BA in Psychology, Pa. State U., University Park, 1988, BS in Life Sci., 1992. Molecular biologist, microbiologist USDA, Agrl. Rsch. Svc., Ea. Regional Rsch. Ctr., Wyndmoor, Pa., 1994—. Presenter in field. Contbr. articles to profl. jours. Mentor Mentornet, San Jose, Calif., 2000—06; parish rep. Malvern Laymen's Retreat League, Pa., 1985—2006. Recipient Cert. of Merit for Outstanding Performance rating, USDA, 1997, Silver medal for Achievement in Recognition of Outstanding Pub. Svc., Fed. Exec. Bd. Excellence in Govt. Awards Program, 1999. Mem.: Nittany Lion Club, Suburban Cyclists Unlimited (ride coord. 2001—02, Most Improved Male Cyclist 2001), Internat. Soc. for Philos. Enquiry (assoc.). Roman Catholic. Avocations: bicycling, photography, genealogy, chess. Home: 1272 Quakertown Ave Pennsburg PA 18073 Office: USAD-ARS-ERRC 600 E Mermaid Ln Wyndmoor PA 19038 Home Phone: 215-541-4001; Office Phone: 215-233-6455. Office Fax: 215-233-6581; Home Fax: 215-541-4001. Personal E-mail: terence.strobaugh1989@psualum.com. Business E-Mail: terence.strobaugh@ars.usda.gov.

STROBEL, MARTIN JACK, lawyer, manufacturing and distribution company executive; b. NYC, July 4, 1940; s. Nathan and Clara (Sorgen) S.; m. Hadassah Orenstein, Aug. 15, 1965; children: Gil Michael, Karen Rachel. BA, Columbia U., 1962; JD, Cleve. Marshall Law Sch., 1966; completed advanced bus. mgmt. program, Harvard U., 1977. Bar: Ohio bar 1966. Counsel def. contract adminstrn. services region Def. Supply Agy., Cleve., 1966-68; with Dana Corp., Toledo, 1968—, gen. counsel, 1970—, dir. govt. relations, 1970-71, asst. sec., 1971—, v.p., 1976—, sec., 1982—. Mem. ABA, Fed. Bar Assn., Machinery and Allied Products Inst., Ohio Bar Assn., Toledo Bar Assn. Office: Dana Corp 4500 Dorr St Toledo OH 43615

STROBEL, PAMELA B., energy executive; b. Chgo., Sept. 9, 1952; BS highest honors, U. Ill., 1974, JD cum laude, 1977. Bar: Ill. 1977, U.S. Dist. (ctrl. and no. dists.) Ill. 1977, U.S. Ct. Appeals (7th cir.) 1981, U.S. Claims Ct. 1983, U.S. Ct. Appeals (fed. cir.) 1985. Ptnr. Sidley & Austin, Chgo., 1988-93; exec. v.p., gen. counsel Commonwealth Edison Co., Chgo., 1993—2000; exec. v.p. Exelon Corp., Chgo., 2000—, exec. v.p., chief adminstrv. officer, 2003—; pres. Exelon Energy Delivery Co., Chgo., 2000—, vice-chair, 2000—01, CEO, vice-chair, 2001—02, chmn., CEO, 2002—03. Mem. Kappa Tau Alpha (staff 1975-77). Office: Exelon Corp PO Box 805398 Chicago IL 60680-5398

STROBEL, RUSS M., gas industry executive, lawyer; b. NYC, May 2, 1952; BA, Northwestern U., 1974; JD magna cum laude, U. Ill., 1977. Bar: Ill. 1977. Ptnr. Jenner & Block, Chgo., Friedman & Koven; sr. v.p., gen. counsel, & sec. Nicor Inc., Naperville, Ill., 2000—02; pres. Nicor Gas, Naperville, Ill., 2002—, CEO, 2003—, chmn., 2005—; exec. v.p. Nicor Inc., Naperville, Ill., 2002, pres., 2002—05, chmn., pres., CEO, 2005—. Dir., mem. exec. com. Am. Gas Assn. Bd. dir. USO Ill.; mem. adv. com. Gene Siskel Film Ctr., Art Inst. Chgo. Mem.: Econ. Club Chgo., Comml. Club Chgo. (mem. civic com.), Order of the Coif. Office: Nicor Inc 1844 Ferry Rd Naperville IL 60563-9600 *

STROBER, MYRA HOFFENBERG, education educator, consultant; b. NYC, Mar. 28, 1941; d. Julius William Hoffenberg and Regina Scharer; m. Samuel Strober, June 23, 1963 (div. Dec. 1983); children: Jason M., Elizabeth A.; m. Jay M. Jackman, Oct. 21, 1990. BS in Indsl. Rels., Cornell U., 1962; MA in Econs., Tufts U., 1965; PhD in Econs., MIT, 1969. Lectr., asst. prof. dept. econs. U. Md., College Park, 1967-70; lectr. U. Calif., Berkeley, 1970-72; asst. prof. grad. sch. bus. Stanford (Calif.) U., 1972-86, assoc. prof. sch. edn., 1979-90, prof. edn., 1990—, assoc. dean acad. affairs, 1993-95, interim dean, 1994; program officer in higher edn. Atlantic Philanthropic Svcs., Ithaca, N.Y., 1998-2000. Organizer Stanford Bus. Conf. Women Mgmt., 1974; founding dir. ctr. rsch. women Stanford U., 1974-76, 79-84, dir. edn. policy inst., 1984-86, dean alumni coll., 1992, mem. policy and planning bd., 1992-93, chair program edn. adminstrn. and policy analysis, 1991-93, chair provost's com. recruitment and retention women faculty, 1992-93, chair faculty senate com. on coms., 1992-93; mem. adv. bd. State of Calif. Office Econ. Policy Planning and Rsch., 1978-80; mem. Coll. Bd. Com. Develop Advanced Placement Exam. Econs., 1987-88; faculty advisor Rutgers Women's Leadership Program, 1991-93. Author: (with others) Industrial Relations, 1972, 1990, Sex, Discrimination and the Division of Labor, 1975, Changing Roles of Men and Women, 1976, Women in the Labor Market, 1979, Educational Policy and Management: Sex Differentials, 1981, Women in the Workplace, 1982, Sex Segregation in the Workplace: Trends, Explanations, Remedies, 1984, The New Palgrave: A Dictionary of Economic Theory and Doctrine, 1987, Computer Chips and Paper Clips: Technology and Women's Employment, Vol. II, 1987, Gender in the Workplace, 1987, Challenge to Human Capital Theory: Implications for the HR Manager, American Economic Review, 1995, Rethinking Economics Through a Feminist Lens, Feminist Economics, 1995, Making and Correcting Errors in Economic Analyses: An Examination of Videotapes, (with Agnes M.K. Chan) the Road Winds Uphill All the Way: Gender, Work, and Family in the U.S. and Japan, 1999, (with Jay M. Jackman) Fear of Feedback, 2003, Children As a Public Good, 2004, Can Harvard Ever Play a Positive Role for Women in Higher Education?, 2005; editor (with Francine E. Gordon) Bringing Women Into Management, 1975, (with others) Women and Poverty, 1986, Industrial Relations, 1990, Challenges to Human Capitol Theory: Implications for HR Managers, 1995, (with Sanford M. Dornbusch) Feminism, Children and the New Families, 1988, Rethinking Economics Through a Feminist Lens, 1995, (with Agnes M.K. Chan) The Road Winds Uphill All The Way: Gender, Work and Family in the U.S. and Japan, 1999, (with Jay M. Jackman) Fear of Feedback, 2003, Application of Mainstream Economics Constructs to Education: A Feminist Analysis, 2003, Children as a Public Good, 2004, Feminist Economics: Implications for Education, 2005, Can Harvard Ever Play a Positive Role for Women in Higher Education, 2005; Habits of the Mind: Challenges for Multidisciplinarity, 2006; Faculty Salaries and Maximization of Prestige, 2007, (with Tatiana Melguizo); mem. bd. editors Signs: Jour. Women Culture and Soc., 1975-89, assoc. editor, 1980-85; mem. bd. editors Sage Ann. Rev. Women and Work, 1984—; mem. editorial adv. bd. U.S.-Japan Women's Jour., 1991—; assoc. editor Jour. Econ. Edn., 1991—; contbr. chpt. to book, articles to profl. jours. Mem. rsch. adv. task force YWCA, 1989—; chair exec. bd. Stanford Hillel, 1990-92; bd. dirs. Resource Ctr. Women, Palo Alto, Calif., 1983-84; pres. bd. dirs. Kaider Found., Mountain View, Calif., 1990-96; bd. trustees Mills Coll., 2004—. Fellow Stanford U., 1975-77, Schiff House Resident fellow, 85-87. Mem.: NOW (bd. dirs. legal def. and edn. fund 1993—98), Ctr. Gender Equality (bd. dirs. 2000—), Internat. Assn. Feminist Econs. (assoc. editor Feminist Econs. 1994—, pres. 1997), Indsl. Rels. Rsch. Assn., Am. Ednl. Rsch. Assn., Am. Econ. Assn. (mem. com. status of women in profession 1972—75). Office: Stanford U School Edn Stanford CA 94305 Office Phone: 650-723-0387. Business E-Mail: myra.strober@stanford.edu.

STROBER, SAMUEL, immunologist, educator; b. NYC, May 8, 1940; s. Julius and Lee (Lander) S.; m. Linda Carol Higgins, July 6, 1991; children: William, Jesse; children from a previous marriage: Jason, Elizabeth. AB in Liberal Arts, Columbia U., 1961; MD magna cum laude, Harvard U., 1966. Intern Mass. Gen. Hosp., Boston, 1966-67; resident in internal medicine Stanford U. Hosp., Calif., 1970-71; rsch. fellow Peter Bent Brigham Hosp., Boston, 1962-63, 65-66, Oxford U., England, 1963-64; rsch. assoc. Lab. Cell Biology Nat. Cancer Inst. NIH, Bethesda, Md., 1967-70; instr. medicine Stanford U., 1971-72, asst. prof., 1972-78, assoc. prof. medicine, 1978-82, prof. medicine, 1982—, Diane Goldstone Meml. lectr., 1978-97, John Putnam Merrill Meml. lectr., chief div. immunology & rheumatology, 1978-97. Investigator Howard Hughes Med. Inst., Miami, Fla., 1976-81; chmn., bd. dirs. La Jolla Inst. for Allergy and Immunology; founder Dendreon, Inc. Assoc. editor: Jour. Immunology, 1981-84, Transplantation, 1981-85, 99—, Internat. Jour. Immunotherapy, 1985—, Transplant Immunology, 1992—, Biol. Bone Marrow Transplantation, 1999—; contbr. articles to profl. jours. Served with USPHS, 1967-70. Recipient Leon Reznick Meml. Rsch. prize, Harvard U., 1966. Mem. Am. Assn. Immunology, Am. Soc. Clin. Investigation, Am. Coll. Rheumatology, Transplantation Soc. (councilor 1986-89), Am. Soc. Tranplantation Physicians, Western Soc. Medicine, Am. Assn. Physicians, Clin. Immunology Soc. (pres. 1996), Alpha Omega. Office: Stanford U Sch Medicine 300 Pasteur Dr Palo Alto CA 94304-2203

STROCK, JAMES MARTIN, communications executive, writer, entrepreneur; b. Austin, Tex., Aug. 19, 1956; s. James Martin Strock Sr. and Augusta (Tenney) Cumby. AB, Harvard U., 1977, JD, 1981; postgrad, New Coll. Oxford U., 1981—82. Bar: Colo. 1983. Tchg. asst. Harvard U., 1980—81; spl. cons. to majority leader U.S. Senate, Washington, 1982—83; spl. asst. to adminstr. EPA, Washington, 1983—85, asst. adminstr. for enforcement, 1989—91; spl. counsel U.S. Senate Com. on Environment and Pub. Works, Washington, 1985—86; assoc. Davis, Graham & Stubbs, Denver, 1986—88; acting dir., gen. counsel U.S. Office Pers. Mgmt., Washington, 1988—89; sec. for environ. protection State of Calif., Sacramento, 1991—97; prin. James Strock & Co., Scottsdale, Ariz., 1997—; sr. fellow, exec. edn. R.H. Smith Sch. bus. U. Md., 2003—. Adj. prof. U. So. Calif., 1996-97; mem. Intergovtl. Policy Adv. Com., rep. U.S. Trade, 1991-97; mem. Calif. State Pers. Bd., 1998; guest prof. U. Konstanz, 1998; bd. dir. Raoul Wallenberg com. of the U.S.; mem. Calif. State Personnel Bd., 1997-99; spkr. in field Author: Reagan on Leadership, 1998, Theodore Roosevelt on Leadership, 2001; contbr. articles to profl. jours. Capt. JAGC USAR, 1987—96. Recipient Ross Essay award ABA, 1985, Environ. Leadership award Calif. Environ. Bus. Coun., 1994, Fed. Republic Germany Friendship award, 1996; Environ. Soc. India fellow, 1997, commendation Calif. Dist. Attys. Assn., 1997 Mem. Coun. Fgn. Rels., Authors' Guild, Phi Beta Kappa. Republican. Office: Ste B-111-601 15029 N Thompson Peak Pky Scottsdale AZ 85260 Business E-Mail: jms@jamesstrock.com.

STROCK, ROBERT S., retired education educator; b. Sewickley, Pa., Oct. 19, 1921; s. Paul Blazier and Jessie Serene Strock. BS, Geneva Coll., 1947; EdM, Shippensburg U., 1964; postgrad., Colo. State U., 1965, U. Tenn., 1966, U. Miami, 1968, Ind. U., 1969. Cert. tchr. Dept. Pub. Instrn., Pa., Nat. Coun. Bus. Schs. Acctg. tchr. Duffs Iron City Coll., Pitts., 1947—50; stock control clk. H.H. Robertson Co., Inc., Ambridge, Pa., 1950—57; tchr. Baden (Pa.)-Economy Sch. Dist., 1957—67; asst. prof. Slippery Rock (Pa.) U., 1967—72; assoc. prof. Indiana U. Pa., 1972—99, prof. emeritus, 2002—. Dir. homecoming parades Indiana U. Pa., 1974—98, Geneva Coll., 2000, 05, 06. Mem. Indiana Boro Coun., 1991—94, Bd. Elections, Beaver, Pa., 2002—. Staff sgt. USAF, 1943—45. Recipient Outstanding Prof. award, Student Pa. State Edn. Assn., 1992, Patriotic Achievement award, Mil. Order of the World Wars Chpt. 200, 1993, Pres. medal of distinction, Indiana U. Pa., 1998, Disting. Svc. award, Alumni Assn. Geneva Coll., 2007. Mem.: 27th Air Transp. Group WWII, Friends of Nat. Parks Gettysburg, Nat. Trust Hist. Preservation, Beaver County Geneal. Soc., Beaver Heritage Soc. (trustee), CWPT History Channel Club (life), Am. Legion, Alpha Phi Omega, Delta Pi Epsilon (treas. chpt. 1973—76), Theta Xi. Republican. Methodist. Avocations: genealogy, travel, collecting miniature bottles, collecting postcards. Home: 222 Fourth St Beaver PA 15009

STROCK, WILLIAM C., lawyer; b. Cleve., Sept. 22, 1942; s. Harry Kenneth and Mabel T. (Moseley) S.; m. Anne B. Turner, June 26, 1965; children: William Matthew, Anne Elizabeth. BA, So. Meth. U., 1964, JD, 1967. Bar: Tex. 1967, admitted to practice: US Supreme Ct., US Ct. Appeals (5th Cir.), US Ct. Appeals (8th Cir.), US Ct. Appeals (11th Cir.), US Dist. Ct. (No. Dist.) Tex., US Dist. Ct. (So. Dist.) Tex., US Dist. Ct. (Ea. Dist.) Tex., US Dist. Ct. (We. Dist.) Tex., US Dist. Ct. (Dist. Colo.), Supreme Ct. Tex. Labor rels. atty. Gen. Dynamics Co., Ft. Worth, 1967-70; ptnr. Seay, Gwinn, Crawford, Mebus & Blakeney, Dallas, 1970-82; ptnr., labor and employment law Haynes & Boone LLP, Dallas, 1982—. Mem. adj. faculty So. Meth. U., 1983—90, mem. adj. faculty employment law & labor law, 1990. Contbg. editor Developing Law Law, 2nd edit., 1983; editor: Employment Law Handbook, 1989; assoc. editor Jour. of Air Law and Commerce, 1966—67. Named a Tex. Super Lawyer, Tex. Monthly Mag., 2003, 2004; named one of Best Lawyers in Dallas, D Magazine, 2001, 2003. Fellow: Coll. of Labor & Employment Lawyers; mem.: Labor Law Tex. Bd. of Legal Specialization (adv. com.), Tex. Assn. Bus. (chmn. employment law subcom. 1988), Tex. Bar Found., ABA (labor and employment law sect.). Republican. Presbyterian. Office: Haynes and Boone LLP 901 Main St Ste 3100 Dallas TX 75202-3789 Office Phone: 214-651-5623. Office Fax: 214-200-0655. Business E-Mail: bill.strock@haynesboone.com.

STRODE, JOSEPH ARLIN, lawyer; b. DeWitt, Ark., Mar. 5, 1946; s. Thomas Joseph and Nora (Richardson) S.; m. Carolyn Taylor, Feb. 9, 1969; children: Tanya Briana, William Joseph. BSEE with honors, U. Ark., 1969; JD, So. Meth. U., 1972. Bar: Ark. 1972. Design engr. Tex. Instruments Inc., Dallas, 1969-70; patent agent Tex. Instruments, Dallas, 1970—72; assoc. Bridges, Young, Matthews, Drake, Pine Bluff, Ark., 1972-74, ptnr., 1975—. Chmn. Pine Bluff Airport Commn., 1993; bd. dirs. United Way Jefferson County, Pine Bluff, 1975-77, campaign chmn., 1983, pres., 1986, exec. com., 1983-87; bd. dirs. Leadership Pine Bluff, 1983-85. Mem. Ark. Bar Assn., Jefferson County Bar Assn. (pres. 1995), Pine Bluff C. of C. (dir. 1981, 84, 94, 97), Ark. Wildlife Fed. (dir. 1979-81), Jefferson County Wildlife Assn. (dir. 1973-80, pres. 1974-76), Kiwanis (lt. gov. Mo.-Ark. divsn. 1983-84, chmn. lt. govs. 1983-84), Order of Coif, Tau Beta Pi, Eta Kappa Nu. Home: 7600 Jay Lynn Ln Pine Bluff AR 71603-9387 Office: 315 E 8th Ave Pine Bluff AR 71601-5005 Office Phone: 870-534-5532. Business E-Mail: joestrode@bridgesplc.com.

STROEVE, PIETER, chemical engineering researcher, educator; b. Velp, Gelderland, Netherlands, Sept. 15, 1945; arrived in US, 1959; s. Antonie and Frederika Wilhelmina Stroeve; m. Diane Barrett; children: Dale, Maryke, Yoly, Jodie. Student, Contra Costa Coll., 1962-65; BSChemE, U. Calif., Berkeley, 1967; MSChemE, MIT, 1969, ScD, 1973. Sr. scientist Weizmann Inst. Sci., Rehovot, Israel, 1973—74; asst. prof. U. Nijmegen, The Netherlands, 1974-77; postdoctoral rschr. Weizmann Inst. Sci., 1977; from asst. to assoc. prof. SUNY, Buffalo, 1977-81; assoc. prof. U. Calif., Davis, 1981-83, prof. dept. chem. engring. and material sci., 1983—. Cons. Los Alamos (N.Mex.) Nat. Lab., 1983—86, Ames Nat. Lab., 1995—97, Procter and Gamble Co., 2003; vis. prof. Max-Planck Inst., Mainz, Germany, 1996; Frontis prof. nanotech. Wageningen U., Netherlands, 2003—04; co-dir. NSF Ctr. on Polymer Interfaces and Macromolecular Assemblies; co-founder ATA Co., Nanotech. Co. Solar Cells, Q1NanoSys. Author, editor (books): Integrated Circuits, 1985, Biomedical Engineering, 1983; editor: Transport with Chemical Reaction, 1981, Molecular Engineering of Ultrathin Polymeric Films, 1987, Macromolecular Assemblies in Polymeric Systems, 1992; author: (book) Polymer-Layered Silicate and Silica Nanocomposites, 2005; contbr. over 190 articles to profl. jours. Recipient Tchg. award, U. Calif., Davis, 1984, 1990, 1991, 1995, 2006, 2d Pl. award Big Bang bus. plan competition, 2005; grantee NSF, 1985, 1987—89, 1994—2002; P.J. Flory fellow, IBM Almaden Rsch. Ctr., 1988—89. Mem. Am. Inst. Chem. Engrs., Am. Chem. Soc. Office: U Calif Davis Dept Chem Engring and Material Sci Davis CA 95616 Office Phone: 530-752-0400, 530-752-8778. Business E-Mail: pstroeve@ucdavis.edu.

STROGATZ, STEVEN H., mathematics professor; AB, Princeton U., 1980; BA, Cambridge U., 1982, MA, 1986; PhD, Harvard U., 1986. Marshall scholar Cambridge U., 1980—82; postdoctoral fellow Harvard U., 1986—89; taught in dept. math. MIT, 1989—94; with theoretical and applied math. dept. Cornell U., NY, 1994—, prof., theoretical and applied mechanics NY, dir., Ctr. for Applied Math. NY. Spkr. in field. Contbr. articles to profl. jours.; author: Nonlinear Dynamics and Chaos: With Applications to Physics, Biology, Chemistry, and Engineering, 1994, Sync: The Emerging Science of Spontaneous Order, 2003. Recipient Presdl. Young Investigator awatd, NSF. Mem.: Soc. Math. Biology, Soc. for Indsl. and Applied Math. (Joint Policy Bd. for Math. Communications award 2007). Seminal research on human sleep and circadian rhythms, scroll waves, coupled oscillators, synchronous fireflies, Josephson junctions, and small-world networks has been featured in publications such as, Nature, Science, Scientific American, NY Times, US News and World Report, New Yorker, Discover, American Scientist, Science News, Newsweek, Die Zeit, and London's Daily Telegraph, and broadcast programs such as, BBC Radio, National Public Radio, CBS News, and numerous other mass media outlets. Office: Cornell U Theoretical and Applied Mechanics 223 Kimball Hall Ithaca NY 14853-1503 Office Phone: 607-255-5999. Business E-Mail: shs7@cornell.edu. *

STROH, RAYMOND EUGENE, retired personnel executive; b. Bloomington, Ill., Aug. 13, 1942; s. Harry William and Felcie Cleo (Weaver) S.; m. Peggy Jane Whitacre, June 12, 1966 (dec. Jan. 2002); children: Rebecca Jane, David Ray. BA, So. Ill. U., 1966, U. Ill., 1977. Pers. technician Ill. Dept. Mental Health, Springfield, Ill., 1966-67; pers. officer Andrew McFarland Mental Health Ctr., Springfield, 1967-68, Manteno (Ill.) State Hosp., 1968-69; chief pers. officer Ill. Dept. Law Enforcement, Springfield, 1969-75, Ill. Dept. Revenue, Springfield, 1975-81, Ill. Dept. Mental Health, Springfield, 1981-82; pers. exec. Ill. Dept. Cen. Mgmt. Svcs., Springfield, 1982-2001; ret. State govt. chmn. U.S. Savs. Bond Campaign, Springfield, 1978-82. Bd. dirs. Consumer Credit Counseling Svc., Springfield, 1988-94, sec., 1994; coun. exec. bd. Boy Scouts Am., Springfield, 1987—, v.p., 1987-99, dist. commr., 1979-86, unit commr., 1970-79; bd. dirs. Ill. State Employees Credit Union, 1984-85. Recipient Patriotic Svc. awards U.S. Treasury Dept., 1979-82, Silver Beaver award Boy Scouts Am., 1987, Dist. award of merit, 1981, Area Pres. awards, 1985, 86, Scouters Key award, 1976, Order of the Arrow Vigil Honor, 1998. Mem. NRA, U. Ill. Alumni Assn., So. Ill. U. Alumni Assn., Exptl. Aircraft Assn., Aircraft Owners and Pilots Assn., Cessna Owner Orgn., Nat. Geog. Soc., Cornell U. Lab. of Ornithology, Ill. Audubon Soc., Abraham Lincoln Gun Club, Union County (Tenn.) Hist. Soc., Wabash R.R. Hist. Soc., Am. Rose Soc., Theta Delta Chi. Republican. Lutheran. Avocations: aviation, fishing, model railroading, gardening, birding. Home: 2111 Warwick Dr Springfield IL 62704-4147

STROHECKER, LEON HARRY, JR., orthodontist; b. Schuylkill Haven, Pa., Aug. 14, 1932; s. Leon Harry and Anna (Fabian) S.; m. Juanita Mary Puyoou, Apr. 13, 1957; children: Sandra Lee Strohecker Beckett, Leon Harry III. Student, U. Pa., 1950-53, DDS, 1957, orthodontic cert., 1960. Bd. cert. Am. Bd. Orthodontics. Pres., pvt. practice, Lansdale, Pa., 1961—; dir. Face Head & Neck Pain and Trauma Ctr., Lansdale, 1987-99. Bd. dirs. Artman Home Retirement Ctr., Ambler; treas., bd. dirs. Valley Ctr. Mental Health Clinic, Lansdale, 1984—2002; guest lectr. in field. Pres. Lansdale Rotary Club, 1967-68; coun. mem. Trinity Luth. Ch., Lansdale, 1977-85, chmn. fin. com., 1980-85. Lt. (j.g.) USN, 1957-59. Named Internat. Health Profl. of Yr., Internat. Biographical Ctr., 2003; recipient Spoke award, Jr. C. of C., 1963, Spark Plug award, 1963, Widsom award of Honor, Best Orthodontist vote, 2 Lansdale area newspapers, One Thousand Great Ams. award, Internat. Biographical Ctr., 2001, 2002. Mem. ADA, Internat. Acad. Head, Neck and Facial Pain, Internat. Coll. Cranio-Mandibular Orthopedics, Am. Acad. Pain Mgmt. (diplomate), Am. Assn. for Functional Orthodontics, Am. Profl. Practice Assn., Am. Soc. Dentistry for Children, Am. Acad. Oral Medicine, Am. Assn. Orthodontists, Am. Assn. Stomatologists, Am. Acad. Oral Medicine, Middle Atlantic Orthodontic Soc., Pa. Orthod ontic Soc., Phila. Orthodontic Soc., Pa. Dental Assn., Second Dist. Dental Assn., Montgomery-Bucks Dental Soc., Alpha Omega, Omicron Kappa Epsilon. Avocations: tennis, travel, bridge, water sports. Home: 1512 Cedar Hill Rd Ambler PA 19002-1406 Office: 456 E Hancock St Lansdale PA 19446-3803 Home Phone: 215-643-1818; Office Phone: 215-855-7717. Personal E-mail: lstrohecker@hotmail.com.

STROHM, BRUCE C., lawyer, real estate company executive; b. 1955; BS, U. Ill.; JD, Northwestern U. Ptnr. Rosenberg & Liebentritt, PC, Chgo.; exec. v.p., gen. counsel, sec. Equity Residential, Chgo., 1995—. Office: Equity Residential 2 N Riverside Plaza Chicago IL 60606 Office Phone: 312-474-1300. *

STROHMEYER, JOHN, writer, retired editor; b. Cascade, Wis., June 26, 1924; s. Louis A. and Anna Rose (Saladunas) S.; m. Nancy Jordan, Aug. 20, 1949 (dec. 2000); children: Mark, John, Sarah; m. Sylvia Ciernick Broady, Oct. 25, 2003. Student, Moravian Coll., 1941—43; AB, Muhlenberg Coll., 1947; MA in Journalism, Columbia U., 1948; LHD (hon.), Lehigh U., 1983. With Nazareth Item, Pa., 1940—41; night reporter Bethlehem Globe-Times, Pa., 1941—43, 1945—47; investigative reporter Providence Jour.-Bull., 1949—56; editor Bethlehem Globe-Times, 1956—64, v.p., 1961—84, dir., 1963—84. African-Am. journalism tchr. in Nairobi, Freetown, 1964; Atwood prof. journalism U. Alaska, Anchorage, 1987-88, writer-in-residence, 1989—; Clendinen Prof., U. S. Fla., 2001. Author: Crisis in Bethlehem: Big Steel's Struggle to Survive, 1986, Extreme Conditions: Big Oil and The Transformation of Alaska, 1993, Historic Anchorage, 2001. Lt. (j.g.) USNR, 1943-45. Pulitzer Traveling fellow, 1948; Nieman fellow, 1952-53; recipient Comenius award Moravian Coll., 1971; Pulitzer prize for editl. writing, 1972; Alicia Patterson Found. fellow, 1984, 85. Mem. Am. Soc. Newspaper Editors, Pa. Soc. Newspaper Editors (pres. 1964-66), Anchorage Racquet Club. Home (Summer): 6633 Lunar Dr Anchorage AK 99504-4550 Home (Winter): 11975 W Edgeview Ct Crystal River FL 34429 E-mail: jstroh@gci.net.

STROJNIK, TADEJ, neurosurgeon, researcher; b. Ljubljana, Slovenia, July 11, 1963; s. Franc and Marija (Petrič) S.; m. Irena Šurca, June 6, 1987; children: Tom, Maša. MD, U. Ljubljana, 1989, MSc, 1994, PhD, 1998.

Physician Health Ctr., Ptuj, Slovenia, 1989-90; resident in neurosurgery Univ. Clinic Neurosurgery, Ljubljana, 1995—96, Tchg. Hosp., Maribor, Slovenia, 1990-95, neurosurgeon, 1996—; asst. prof. U. Ljubljana, 2002—. Aitken Clin. Rsch. fellow, 1998-99. Mem. Med. Chamber Slovenia, Slovene Med. Soc., Slovenian Neurosurg. Soc. (sec. 1997-2001), European Assn. Neurosurgeons, Ctrl. European Neurosurg. Soc. (bd. dirs.). Roman Catholic. Avocations: photography, fishing, reading. Office: Tchg Hosp Dept Neurosurgery Ljubljanska 5 2000 Maribor Slovenia Office Phone: 386 2 3211511. Business E-Mail: tadejistrojnik@sb-mb.si.

STROKE, HINKO HENRY, physicist, researcher; b. Zagreb, Croatia, June 16, 1927; came to U.S., 1943, naturalized, 1949; s. Elias and Edith (Mechner) S.; m. Norma Bilchick, Jan. 14, 1956; children: Ilana Lucy, Marija Tamar. BEE, N.J. Inst. Tech., 1949; MS, MIT, 1952, PhD, 1955. From rsch. asst. to rsch. assoc. Princeton (N.J.) U., 1954-57; rsch. staff lab. electronics, lectr. dept. physics MIT, 1957-63; assoc. prof. physics NYU, NYC, 1963-68, prof., 1968—. Dept. chmn. NYU, 1988-91; prof. associé, U. Paris, 1969-70, Ecole Normale Supérieure, 1976; vis. scientist Max Planck Inst. für Quantenoptik, Garching, U. Munich, 1977-78, 81-82, 93; cons. Atomic Instrument Co., MIT Sci. Translation Svc., Tech. Rsch. Group, Cambridge Air Force Rsch. Ctr., Am. Optical Corp., ITT Fed. Labs., NASA, others; mem. com. on line spectra of elements NAS-NRC, 1976-82; sci. assoc. CERN, Geneva, 1983—. Contbg. author: Nuclear Physics, 1963, Atomic Physics, 1969, Hyperfine Interactions in Excited Nuclei, 1971, Francis Bitter: Selected Papers, 1969, Atomic Physics 3, 1973, Nuclear Moments and Nuclear Structure, 1973, A Perspective of Physics, Vol. 1, 1977, Atomic Physics 8, 1983, Lasers in Atomic, Molecular, and Nuclear Physics, 1989—, Symposium on Probing Luminous and Dark Matter, 2000; editor: Comments on Atomic, Molecular and Optical Physics, The Physical Review-The First Hundred Years, Benjamin Bederson: Works, Comments and Legacies, Advances in Atomic, Molecular and Optical Physics, Vol. 51. Mem. Chorus Pro Musica, 1951—54, 1957—63, Münchener Bach-Chor, Munich, 1977—82, 1992; Choeur pro Arte Lausanne, 1983—; mem. Collegiate Chorale, NY, 1964—94, Dessoff Choirs, 1994—, Westchester Oratorio Soc., 2001—. Recipient Sr. U.S. Scientist award Alexander von Humboldt Found., 1977; NATO sr. fellow in sci., 1975 Fellow AAAS, Am. Phys. Soc. (publs. oversight com. 1991-93), Optical Soc. Am.; mem. IEEE (life), European Phys. Soc., Soc. Française de Physique, Sigma Xi, Tau Beta Pi, Omicron Delta Kappa. Office: NYU Dept Physics 4 Washington Pl New York NY 10003-6621 Office Phone: 212-998-7679. Business E-Mail: henry.stroke@nyu.edu.

STROLLA, CORY C., lawyer; b. Omaha, Nebr., Jan. 1, 1973; s. Carmine and Susan Strolla. JD, Stetson Coll. Law, Gulfport, Fla., 1997. Bar: US Fed. Ct. (no., mid. so. dists.), Fla. 1997, cert.: Fla. Internat. U. US Transp. Intoxilyzer; intoxilyzer tech. operator. Asst. state atty. State Atty. Office, West Palm Beach, Fla., 1998—2000; assoc. Meldon and Barbarette PA, Gainesville, Fla., 2000—01; pvt. practice West Palm Beach, 2001—. Adj. prof. Palm Beach CC; judge youth ct. Palm Beach County, 1998—; trial team coach U. Fla., Gainesville, 2000; mem. law adv. coun. Stetson Coll. Law, Gulfport, 2006—, mem. alumni adv. bd.; lectr. in field. Contbr. articles to profl. jours. Past pres. Bus. Network Internat., West Palm Beach, Fla. Mem.: Fla. Bar Assn. (criminal law divsn.), Fla. Assn. Criminal Def. Lawyers, Nat. Assn. Criminal Def. Lawyers. Office: 2247 Palm Beach Lakes Blvd Ste 107 West Palm Beach FL 33409 Office Phone: 561-802-8987.

STROM, BRIAN LESLIE, internist, educator; b. NYC, Dec. 8, 1949; s. Martin and Edith (Singer) S.; m. Elaine Marilyn Moskowitz, June 4, 1978; children: Shayna Lee, Jordan Blair. BS, Yale U., 1971; MD, Johns Hopkins U., 1975; MPH, U. Calif., Berkeley, 1980. Diplomate Am. Bd. Internal Medicine, Am. Bd. Epidemiology. Intern in medicine U. Calif., San Francisco, 1975-76, resident in medicine, 1976-78, research fellow in clinical pharmacology, 1978-80; from asst. prof. to assoc. prof. medicine and pharmacology U. Pa., Phila., 1980-93, prof. medicine, 1993—, prof. biostatistics & epidemiology, 1995—. Adj. asst. prof. clin. pharmacy Phila. Coll. of Pharmacy and Sci., 1981-90, adj. assoc. prof., 1990-93, adj. prof., 1993—; mem. U. Pa. Cancer Ctr., 1981—; attending staff Hosp. U. Pa., 1980—, co-dir Clin. Epidemiology Unit, 1980-91, dir., 1991-2001; dir. Clin. Pharmacology Cons. Svc., 1981-82; dir. Ctr. for Clin. Epidemiology and Biostats., 1993—, chair dept. biostats. and epidemiology, 1995—; lectr. in field; George S. prod. pub. health and preventive medicine, 2002—; cons. CDC, 1981, Coun. for Internat. Orgn. of Med. Scis., Geneva, Switzerland, 1981-83, Office of Tech. Assessment, Congress of U.S., 1980-81, Aging Rev. Com., Nat. Inst. Aging, 1982, Ministry of Pub. Health, State of Kuwait, 1982, Royal Tropical Inst., Amsterdam, 1983, others. Editl. cons. Johns Hopkins U. Press, J.B. Lippincott; referee Annals of Internal Medicine, Archives of Internal Medicine, Clin. Pharmacology and Therapeutics, Digestive Diseases and Sci., Internat. Jour. Cardiology, Internat. Jour. Epidemiology, Jour. AMA, Jour. Gen. Internal Medicine, Med. Care, Primary Care Tech., Sci.; editor Pharmaepidemiology and Drug Safety; mem. editl. bd. 7 jours.; contbr. numerous articles to profl. jours. Nat. Acad. Scis. grantee, Rockefeller Found. grantee, NIH grantee, many others. Fellow ACP, Am. Coll. Epidemiology, Am. Epidemiology Soc.; mem. Am. Fedn. Med. Rsch., Am. Pub. Health Assn., Am. Soc. Clin. Pharmacology and Therapeutics, Am. Soc. Clin. Investigation, Am. Assn. Physicians, Internat. Soc. Pharmacoepidemiology, Internat. Epideliol. Assn., Soc. for Epidemiologic Rsch., Soc. Gen. Internal Medicine, Inst. Medicine, Inst. Medicine. Democrat. Jewish. Avocations: hiking, bicycling, camping, skiing. Home: 332 Hidden River Rd Narberth PA 19072-1111 Office Phone: 215-898-2368. Business E-Mail: bstrom@cceb.med.upenn.edu.

STROM, KRISTINA CHASE, writer, consultant; b. Schenectady, NY, Dec. 28, 1948; d. Raymond Olaf and Lois Moulton Strom; children: Kia Strom Kuresman, Kamala Strom Kuresman, Kimberly Strom Kuresman, Kara Strom Kuresman. PhD, Universal Life Sem. Lic. in ins. Ohio; ordained clergy Ohio, Minn. Asst. buyer, buyer Hess's Dept. Store, Allentown, Pa., 1968—69; educator Xavier U., New Orleans, 1970; columnist Denver Free Press, 1972; co-founder, owner New World Ctr. Bookshop and Foodshop, 1973—74; tchr. Beth Adam Religious Sch., Cin., 1981—88, art dir., 1987—89, prin., 1988—89; editor Beth Adam Newsletter, Cin., 1982—86; designer Del Favero Enterprises, Cin., 1984—90; store mgr. B. Dalton Books, Cin., 1990—91; systems operator TriStateOnline Greater Cin. Consortium Colls. and Univs., 1999, adminstr., 1999; pvt. practice Glendale, Ohio, 1968—; freelance artist, 1970—; design and bus. cons., 1985—. Columnist, staff writer Silent Messages, Cin., 1996—99; moderator Wells List, 1995—; owner, mgr. CelestialPerspectives.com, Cin., 1999—. Exhibitions include Mich. State U., 2003—04, Represented in permanent collections Millennium Challenge; author: Denim and Lace, An historical mystery of first love, timeless love, numerous poems; co-editor, contbr. From Eulogy to Joy, A Heartfelt Anthology, Feathered Star, 2003, Monkey Wrench New Quilts from an Old Favorite, 2004, Seven Sisters New Quilts from an Old Favorite, 2005, Goose River Anthology, 2007; contbr. articles to profl. jours. Pres. Kindervelt #17 Cin. Children's Hosp. Aux., 1983—85. Mem.: Smithsonian Nat. Mus. Am. Indian, Nat. Ctr. for Preservation of Medicinal Herbs, The Nature Conservancy, Nat. Audubon Soc., Am. Quilter's Soc., Sierra Club; Twilight Club Ctr. Evolutionary Ethics. Avocations: gardening, genealogy, book collecting, anthropology, archaeology. Home: 171 West Sharon Road Glendale OH 45246-4334 Personal E-mail: kristinastrom@celestialperspectives.com.

STROM, LYLE ELMER, judge; b. Omaha, Nebr., Jan. 6, 1925; s. Elmer T. and Eda (Hanisch) Strom; m. Regina Ann Kelly, July 31, 1950 (dec.); children: Mary Bess, Susan Frances(dec.), Amy Claire, Cassie A., David Kelly, Margaret Mary, Bryan Thomas. Student, U. Nebr., 1946-47; AB, Creighton U., 1950, JD cum laude, 1953. Bar: Nebr. 1953. Assoc. Fitzgerald, Brown, Leahy, Strom, Schorr & Barmettler and predecessor firm, Omaha, 1953-60, ptnr., 1960-63, gen. trial ptnr., 1963-85; judge U.S. Dist. Ct. Nebr., Omaha, 1985-87, chief judge, 1987-94, sr. judge, 1995—. Adj. prof. law Creighton U., 1959-95, clinical prof., 1996—; mem. com. pattern jury instrns. and practice and proc. Nebr. Supreme Ct., 1965-91; spl. legal counsel Omaha Charter Rev. Commn., 1973; chair gender fairness task force U.S. Ct. Appeals (8th cir.), 1993-97. Exec. com. Covered Wagon Coun. Boy Scouts Am., 1953—57, bd. trustees, exec. com. Mid-Am. Coun., 1988—; chmn. bd. trustees Marian H.S., 1969—71; mem. pres. coun. Creighton U., 1990—95. With U.S. Maritime Svc., 1943—46. Fellow Am. Coll. Trial Lawyers, Internat. Acad. Trial Lawyers; mem. Nebr. Bar Assn. (ho. of dels. 1978-81, exec. coun. 1981-87, pres. 1989-90), Nebr. Bar Found. (bd. trustees 1998—), Omaha Bar Assn. (pres. 1980-81), Am. Judicature Soc., Midwestern Assn. Amateur Athletic Union (pres. 1976-78), Rotary (pres. 1993-94), Alpha Sigma Nu (pres. alumni chpt. 1970-71). Republican. Roman Catholic. Office: US Dist Ct Roman Hruska Courthouse 111 S 18th Plz Ste 3190 Omaha NE 68102 Office Phone: 402-661-7320.

STROM, MILTON GARY, lawyer; b. Rochester, NY, Dec. 5, 1942; s. Harold and Dolly (Isaacson) S.; m. Barbara A. Simon, Jan. 18, 1975; children: Carolyn, Michael, Jonathan. BS in Econ., U. Pa., 1964; JD, Cornell U., 1967. Bar: N.Y. 1968, U.S. Dist. Ct. (W. dist.) N.Y. 1968, U.S. Ct. Claims 1969, U.S. Ct. Mil. Appeals 1969, U.S. Ct. Appeals (D.C. cir.) 1970, U.S. Supreme Ct. 1972, U.S. Dist. Ct. (so. dist.) N.Y. 1975. Atty. SEC, Washington, 1968-71; assoc. Skadden, Arps, Slate, Meagher & Flom, NYC, 1971-76, ptnr., 1977—2004, of counsel, 2004—. Served with USCGR, 1967-73. Mem. ABA, N.Y. State Bar Assn. (corp. law sect.), Assn. of Bar of City of N.Y., Internat. Bar Assn., Beach Point Club. Republican. Jewish. Avocations: tennis, skiing, golf. Office: Skadden Arps Slate Meagher & Flom 4 Times Sq Fl 42 New York NY 10036-6522 Office Phone: 212-735-2300. Business E-Mail: mstrom@skadden.com.

STROM, PARIS SCOTT, education educator; s. Robert D. Strom. BFA, Ariz. State U., 1991, MA, 1994, PhD in Ednl. Psychology, 1997. Cert. secondary tchr. Ariz., instr. CC Ariz. Ariz. State Bd. Dirs. Faculty Ariz. State U., Tempe, 1998—99, rsch. assoc. Office Parent Devel. Internat., 1990—2001, asst. dir., 2002—; tchr. Scottsdale Pub. Schs., 1997—99, Peoria Pub. Schs., Ariz., 1999—2001; assoc. prof. Coll. Edn. Auburn U., Ala., 2001—. Co-author: Teaching Through Play, Adolescent Guidance in Japan; contbr. articles to profl. jours. Recipient Gerald & Emily Leischuck Outstanding Tchg. award, Auburn U., 2005; grantee, Motorola, 2000—02, Nat. Adv. Coun., Auburn U., 2002—04. Mem.: Am. Assn. Behavioral and Social Scis., Am. Ednl. Rsch. Assn. Office: Auburn U 4036 Haley Ctr EFLT Auburn University AL 36849-5221 Office Phone: 334-844-3077. Business E-Mail: stromps@auburn.edu.

STROM, SUSAN G., special education educator; d. Maurice and Celia Kornblit; m. Douglas S. Strom, June 18, 2000. BS, Temple U., Phila., 1975; MEd, Wilkes U., Wilkes-Barre, Pa., 1997—2000. Diplomate cert. addictions counselor Pa. Cert. Bd., cert. alcohol and drug abuse Calif.; lic. addictions counselor Alvernia Coll., 1993. Therapist Progressions, Reading, Pa., 1996—98; spl. edn. tchr. Reading HS, 1998—2000, Antelope Valley HS, Lancaster, Calif., 2000—. Organizer AIDS Walk, Lancaster, 2002—06. Recipient Outstanding Young Women of Am. award, 1986. Office: Antelope Valley HS 44900 N Division St Lancaster CA 93535 Business E-Mail: sstrom@avhsd.org.

STROMAN, SUSAN, choreographer, theater director; b. Wilmington, Del., Oct. 17, 1954; d. Charles and Frances Stroman; m. Mike Ockrent, 1996 (dec. Dec. 2, 1999); stepchildren: Ben, Natasha. Grad., U. Del. Choreographer Flora Roberts Inc. Dancer Chgo., 1977—78, Whoopee!, 1979, Richard III, 1980, Peter Pan, 1983, choreographer (off-Broadway) Broadway Babylon, 1984, Sayonara, 1987, Flora, the Red Menace, 1987, Shenandoah, 1988, Slasher, 1988, Rhythm Ranch, 1989, The Roar of the Greaspaint-The Smell of the Crowd, 1990, Gypsy, 1991, And the World Goes 'Round, 1991 (Outer Critics' Cir. award for choreography, 1991), A Christmas Carol, 1994, (Broadway plays) Crazy for You, 1992 (Tony award for best choreography, 1992, Drama Desk award for choreography, 1992, Outer Critics' Cir. award, 1992, Laurence Olivier award for choreography, 1993), Picnic, 1994, Show Boat, 1994 (Tony award for best choreography, 1995, Astaire award Theatre Devel. Fund, 1995), Big, 1996 (Tony nomination for best choreography, 1996), Oklahoma, 2002 (Laurence Olivier Award for choreography, 2002, Tony nomination for best choreography, 2002), (Operas) Don Giovanni, 1989, A Little Night Music, 1990, 100 in the Shade, 1992, (spl.) Liza Minnelli: Stepping Out at Radio City Music Hall, 1991 (Emmy nomination for choreography, 1993), (films) The Producers, 2005; choreographer, conceiver (Broadway plays) Steel Pier, 1997 (Tony nomination for best choreography, 1997), dir., choreographer The Music Man, 2000 (Tony nomination for best choreography, 2000, Tony nomination for best dir., 2000), The Producers, 2001 (Tony award for best choreography, 2001, Tony award for best dir., 2001, Drama Desk Award for best dir. musical, 2001, Touring Broadway award, best direction, League Am. Theatres and Producers, 2005), The Frogs, 2004, dir., choreographer, conceiver Contact, 2000 (Tony award for best choreography, 2000, Lucille Lortel Award for outstanding direction, 2000, Tony nomination for best dir., 2000), Thou Shalt Not, 2001, Double Feature, 2004, co-conceiver Trading Places, Equity Libr. Theatre Informals, 1983, dir., co-conceiver (off-Broadway) Living Color, 1986, co-conceiver, choreographer (TV spl.) Sondheim-A Celebration at Carnegie Hall, 1992, asst. dir., asst. choreographer (Broadway plays) Musical Chairs, 1980; dir.(TV spl.): An Evening With the Boston Pops-A Tribute to Leonard Bernstein, 1989. Recipient Disting. Achievement in Musical Theatre Award, Drama League, 2001, Elan award, 2005. Address: Flora Roberts Agy Penhouse A 157 W 57th St New York NY 10019-2210

STROMBERG, CLIFFORD DOUGLAS, lawyer; b. NYC, June 1, 1949; s. George M. and Greta (Netzow) Stromberg; m. Ava S. Feiner, June 25, 1972; children: Kimberly, Eric. BA summa cum laude, Yale U., 1971; JD, Harvard U., 1974. Bar: NY 1975, DC 1975, US Dist. Ct. (so. and ea. dists.) NY 1975, US Ct. Appeals (DC cir.) 1975, US Ct. Appeals (2nd cir.) 1975, US Supreme Ct. 1980. Law clk. to judge U.S. Dist. Ct. (ea. dist.) N.Y., 1974-75; assoc. Arnold & Porter, Washington, 1975-78, 80-83; dep. exec. sec. HHS, Washington, 1978-80; cons. FTC, Washington, 1980; ptnr. Dorsey & Whitney, Washington, 1983-84, Hogan & Hartson, Washington, 1984—. Adj. asst. prof. emergency medicine George Washington U. Sch. Medicine, 1991-97. Co-author: Mental Health and Law: A System in Transition, 1975, Alternatives to the Hospital: Ambulatory Surgery Centers and Emergicenters, 1984, Entrepreneurial Health Care: How to Structure Successful New Ventures, 1985, The Psychologist's Legal Handbook, 1988, Access to Hospital Information: Problems and Strategies: 4 Frontiers of Health Services Management 3-33, 1987, Healthcare Provider Networks: Antitrust Issues and Practical Considerations in Devels. in Antitrust Law, 1990, Healthcare Credentialing: Implications for Academic Medical Centers, 1991; mem. editl. bd. Harvard Law Rev., 1972-73; editor in chief Healthspan: The Report of Health Business and Law, 1984-87; cons. editor: Managed Care Law Strategist, 1999-2002; contbr. articles to profl. jours. Bd. dirs. Nat. Children's Eye Care Found., Washington, 1985-87. Teaching fellow in govt. Harvard U., 1973-74. Fellow Am. Bar Found.; mem. ABA (chair working group health care reform 1993-96, state membership chmn. 1984, bd. dirs. forum com. health law 1987-90, adv. com. govt. affairs 1993-98, governing bd., individual rights and responsibilities sect., exec. coun., 1980-90, sec. 1984-87, chair-elect 1987-88, chair 1988-89, legal aid and indigent defendants com. 1982-87), Am. Health Lawyers Assn., Nat. Assn. Coll. and Univ. Attys., Phi Beta Kappa. Office: Hogan & Hartson 555 13th St NW Washington DC 20004-1161 Office Phone: 202-637-5699. Business E-Mail: cdstromberg@hhlaw.com.

STROMBERG, GREGORY, printing ink company executive; b. Milw., Feb. 10, 1948; s. Clifford Norman and Margaret Betty (Hoover) S.; m. Gail Elizabeth Steinbach, Aug. 22, 1970; children: Christopher, Brian, Ellen. BS, Marquette U., Milw., 1970; MBA, Jones Internat. U., 2006. Office contact salesman Continental Can Co., Milw., 1970-78; sales rep. Sun Chem. Co., Milw., 1978-82; v.p., gen. mgr. Acme Printing Ink Co., Milw., 1982—; exec. v.p. Can. ops. Acme Printing Ink Can. Ltd., 1985—, pres., 1990—, v.p. sales/mktg. metal divsn., 2000—. Bd. dirs. Can. Ops. Acme Inks of Can.; pres. Toobee Internat., Inc., Milw., 1981—; v.p., dir. mktg. and internat. sales INX Internat. Ink Co., 1991—. Author: Toobee Air Force Flight Training Manual, 1983. Advisor Milw. Jr. Achievement, 1974; sponsor Muscular Dystrophy, 1983; asst. mem. com. toys for Tots, Children's Hosp., Milw., 1983; active United Meth. Men. Mem. Internat. Metal Decorators Assn., Am. Mgmt. Assn. Internat., Am. Soc. Quality Control, Nat. Metal Decorators Assn., Nat. Assn. Printers and Lithographers, Nat. Assn. Printing Equipment and Suppliers, Exec. Agenda of Wis Home: N69w23448 Donna Dr Sussex WI 53089-3245 E-mail: mitze@execpc.com.

STROMBERG, PATRICIA ROBERTS, retired school librarian; b. Cin., Apr. 23, 1932; d. Richard Bickmore and Ruth Hessler Roberts; children: Mark Alan Stromberg, Ruth Ann Stromberg Batson. BS in Edn., U. Cin., Ohio, 1954; postgrad., Our Lady of the Lake Coll., San Antonio, 1973-75; MA in Edn., U. Colo., Denver, 1979. Tchr. Cin. Pub. Schs., 1954-56, 1970-71, Mt. Healthy (Ohio) Pub. Schs., 1972-73; library media specialist Jefferson County Pub. Schs., Golden, Colo., 1976—97; ret. Mem. basic list com., Jefferson County Schs., 1976-77, Pleasant View Sch., 76-90, Peiffer Sch., 1990-97; computer cons. JEFFCO Schs., 1983-88; co-chair gifted and telented com. Pleasant View Sch., Golden, Colo., 1987-90; pres. JEFFCO Ednl. Media Specialists, 1990-92. Ruling elder on session Green Mt. Presbyn. Ch., 1982-84, 88-91, 2001-03, 06—, chair worship and fellowship/evangelism coms., 1988, 89, 2003-05, ch. mission com., 2006—; mem. social justice and peacemaking commn. Presbytery of Denver, 1989-92; mem. ministry evaluation Cmty. Green Mt. Presbyn. Ch., 1992; vol. Hospice of St John, 1995-. Title IV-C Drama grantee Pleasant View Sch., 1981-84, Jeff Found. Venture grantee, 1985, CCIRA Star grantee, 1996. Mem. AAUW, Nat. Assn. Advancement and Perpetuation of Storytelling, Jefferson County Internat. Reading Assn. (sec. 1978-79, area membership rep. 1991-95), Jefferson County Ret. Sch. Employees Assn., Colo. Coun. (chair Books for Kids com. 1998—) Internat. Reading Assn. (workshop presenter), Jefferson County Spellbinders Assn., Phi Delta Kappa. Republican. Avocations: internat. study children's lit., travel, storytelling, gardening, photography. Home and Office: 12834 W Iliff Ave Lakewood CO 80228-4334 Office Phone: 303-988-3563. Personal E-mail: pstrawberry32@aol.com.

STROMBERG, ROSS ERNEST, lawyer; b. Arcata, Calif., May 5, 1940; s. Noah Anders and Anne Laura (Noyes) S.; m. Toni Nicholas, Dec. 16, 1961; m. Margaret Telonicher, Oct. 3, 1965; children: Kristin, Matthew, Gretchen, Erik. BS, Humboldt State U., 1962; JD, U. Calif., Berkeley, 1965. Bar: Calif. 1966, U.S. Dist. Ct. (no. dist.) Calif. 1966, U.S. Ct. Appeals (9th cir.) 1966. Assoc. Hanson Bridgett, San Francisco, 1965-70, ptnr., 1970-85, Epstein Becker Stromberg & Green, San Francisco, 1985-90, Jones Day, San Francisco, 1990—. Past chmn. Jones Day's Healthcare Specialized Industry Practice; pres. Stromberg Vineyards, Healdsburg, Calif., 2002—. Author: Economic Joint Venturing, 1985, Acquisition and Enhancement of Physician Practices, 1988. Pres. Am. Acad. Hosp. Attys. of Am. Host. Assn., Chgo., 1978; bd. dirs. Sutter Med. Ctr., Santa Rosa, 2001—, chair, 2003—; pres. East Bay AHEC, Oakland, Calif., 1984—87; bd. dirs. Am. Cancer Soc., Oakland, 1984—95, Wildflowers Inst., San Francisco, 1984—; chair Pediat. Dental Initiative of the North Coast, Healdsburg, Calif., 2004. Mem.: Am. Health Lawyers Assn. Democrat. Office: Jones Day 26th Fl 555 Calif St San Francisco CA 94104 Office Phone: 415-875-5724. Business E-Mail: restromberg@jonesday.com.

STROMBOM, DAVID GLEN, designer; b. Pullman, Wash., Apr. 18, 1951; s. Donald A. and Dona S.; m. Cathy J. (Powers), June 17, 1972; 1 child, Paul Davis. Student, Whitman Coll., 1968—70; BS in Architecture, Wash. State U., 1973; MArch, Harvard U., 1977. Registered arch., Wash. Vol. U.S. Peace Corps, Marrakech, Morocco, 1973-75; designer Seattle, 1978-82; prin. The Strombom Architects, Seattle, 1982-91; dir. David Roberts Bowman, Ltd., 1991—; assoc. Internat. Devel. Bus. Cons., Washington, 1996—, Islamabad, Pakistan, 1996, Port au Prince, Haiti, 1997-99, Bali, Indonesia, 1999, Chiang Mai, Thailand, 1999, Venice, Italy, 2002. Fulbright scholar Ahmedabad, India, 1977-78; vis. prof. Ahmedabad Sch. Architecture; designer Ctr. Devel. Studies and Activities, Pune, India. Office Phone: 206-283-1023. E-mail: davidstrombom@comcast.net.

STROME, STEPHEN, distribution company executive; b. Lynn, Mass., June 20, 1945; s. David and Rose (Cantor) S.; m. Phyllis Ruth Fields, Jan. 14, 1967; children: Michael, Rochelle. BA, Hillsdale Coll., Mich., 1967; MBA, Wayne State U., 1968. Trainee KMart Corp., Detroit, 1968-69, mgr. work measurement Troy, Mich., 1970-73; mgr. tng., edn. Fruehauf Corp., Detroit, 1974-76, regional mgr. labor relations, 1976-78; dir. ops. Handleman Co., Clawson, Mich., 1978-80, account exec., 1980-82, v.p. computer software div. Troy, 1983-85, pres. computer software/video div., 1986-87, exec. v.p., 1987-89, exec. v.p., chief oper. officer, 1990, pres., CEO, 1991-2001, chmn., CEO, 2001—. Home: 4597 Kiftsgate Bnd Bloomfield Hills MI 48302-2331 Office: Handleman Co 500 Kirts Blvd Troy MI 48084-4142

STROMINGER, JACK LEONARD, biochemist; b. NYC, Aug. 7, 1925; AB, Harvard U., 1944; MD, Yale U., 1948; DSc (hon.), Trinity Coll., Dublin, 1975, Washington U., 1988. From asst. prof. to prof. pharmacology sch. med. Washington U., St. Louis, 1955-61, prof. pharmacology and microbiology, 1961-64; prof. pharmacology and chem. microbiology med. sch. U. Wis., Madison, 1964-68; prof. biochemistry Harvard U., 1968-83, chmn. dept. biochemistry and molecular biology, 1970-73, Higgins prof. biochemistry, 1983—; head tumor virol. divsn. Dana-Farber Cancer Inst., Boston, 1977—. Recipient John J. Abel award, 1960, Paul-Lewis Lab award, 1962, Rose Payne award Am. Soc. Histocompat. & Immunogen., 1986, Hoechst-Roussel award, 1990, Pasteur medal, 1990, Albert Lasker Award for Basic Med. Rsch., 1995; named Passano Found. laureate, 1993. Mem. NAS (mem. inst. medicine, Microbiology award 1968, Selman Waxman award 1968), AAAS, Am. Soc. Biol. Chemists, Am. Soc. Pharmacology & Exptl. Therapeutics, Am. Assn. Immunologists, Am. Soc. Microbiologists, Am. Chem. Soc., Am. Acad. Arts & Sci., European Molecular Biol. Orgn., Sigma Xi. Address: Harvard U Dept Molecular & Cell Bio 7 Divinity Ave Cambridge MA 02138-2019 Office: Dana Farber Cancer Inst Dept Biochem 44 Binney St Boston MA 02115-6084 Office Phone: 617-495-2733, 617-632-3083. E-mail: jlstrom@fas.harvard.edu.

STRONACH, BELINDA, former retail executive; b. Newmarket, Ont., Can., May 2, 1966; d. Frank Stronach; m. Donald Walker, 1990 (div. 1995); children: Nikki, Frank; m. Johann Olov Koss, 2000 (div. 2003). Student, York U., Toronto; JD (hon.), McMaster U. With Magna Internat. Inc., Aurora, Ont., Canada, 1985—2004, CEO, 2001—04, pres., 2002—04. Mem., bd. dirs. Magna Internat. Inc., 1988—2004, U.S. Chamber of Commerce; mem., Dean's Coun. J.F.K. Sch. Govt., Harvard U.; mem., Dean's Advisory Coun. Joseph L. Rotman Sch. Mgmt., U. Toronto; ran for leadership of Can. Conservative Party, 2004; mem. Parliament for

Newmarket-Aurora, Ont.; internat. trade critic Official Opposition, Canada; mem. standing com. on fgn. affairs and internat. trade Ho. Commons; founding mem. Can. Automotive Partnership Coun.; mem. Ont. Task Force on Productivity, Competitiveness and Econ. Progess; dir. Yves Landy Found. Named Most Powerful Businesswoman in Can., Nat. Post, 2001, Global Leader of Tomorrow, World Econ. Forum, 2001, #2 World's Most Powerful Women in Bus., Fortune mag., 2002; named one of World's 100 Most Influential People, Time Mag., 2004.

STRONACH, CAREY ELLIOTT, physicist, researcher; b. Boston, Aug. 8, 1940; s. Ralph Howard and Frances Burns (Maynard) S.; m. Joan Alice Louise Venner, Aug. 20, 1966; children: John Maynard, Howard Stanley. BS, U. Richmond, Va., 1961; MS, U. Va., Charlottesville, 1963; PhD, Coll. William and Mary, Williamsburg, Va., 1976. Instr. physics Va. State U., Petersburg, 1965-66, asst. prof., 1966—76, assoc. prof., 1976—80, prof., 1980—2006, prof. emeritus, 2006—. Dir. Muon Spin Rotation Rsch. Program, 1977-2006, Superconducting Materials Rsch. Program, 1988-97, Nanostructured Materials Rsch. Program, 1997-2001, Galactic Cosmic Radiation Rsch. Program, 1993-97, U.S.-France Joint Muon Spin Rotation Rsch. Program, 1985-91, Magnetic Materials Lab. Devel. Program, 1999-2001; radiation safety officer; mem. Solid State Physics Rsch. Inst., 1983-87; founding dir. Ctr. Interactive Micromagnetics, 2001-06; vis. assoc. prof. U. Alta, 1978-79; guest scientist Brookhaven Nat. Lab.; organizing com. Internat. Symposium on the Electronic Structure and Properties of Hydrogen in Metals, 1982, Internat. Symposium on the Physics and Chemistry of Small Clusters, 1986, From Clusters to Crystals, 1991, Sci. and Tech. Atomically Engineered Materials, 1995, Internat. Symposium on Cluster and Nanostructure Interfaces, 1999, Internat. Symposium Clusters and Nano-Assemblies: From Physical to Life Sciences, 2003; sci. adv. com. European Workshop Spectroscopy of Subatomic Species in Non-Metallic Solids, 1985, govs. com. on Superconducting Supercollider, 1987; TV physics lectr., 1991-94; adv. com. Internat. Conf. Muon Spin Rotation, 1996-2005, chmn., 1999-2002; assoc. Va. Inst. Pub. Policy, 2004-; cons. Marco Polo Project AAAS, 2002—; leadership coun. So. Poverty Law Ctr. Contbr. articles to profl. jours.; playwright; editor of sci. textbooks. Internat. adv. com. on acad. freedom Bar Ilan U., Israel, 2005—; pres. Petersburg area chpt. Va. Coun. Human Rels., 1965—67; active Petersburg Commn. Cmty. Rels. Affairs, 1974—77; long-range transp. adv. com. City of Petersburg, 1994—98; steering com. Gilmore for Gov., 1997; active Dramatists Guild; sec. adv. coun. bds. and commns. Commonwealth Coun., 1998—2002; active Richmond Playwrights Forum, 1999—, Virginians for Warner, 2001; reviewer of rsch. proposals Nat. Sci. Found.; corr. sec. Petersburg Dem. Com., 1974—77, active, 1972—85, vice chmn., 1981—85. Fellow duPont Corp., 1961-63, NSF, 1971-72, NASA, 1976; recipient Patrick Henry award Va. Gov. James C. Gilmore III, 2001. Mem.: AAUP (chpt. pres. 1968—70), AAAS, Nat. Ctr. for Sci. Edn., Richmond Realists and Naturalists Assn., Air Force Assn., Internat. Soc. on Muon Spectroscopy (founding mem.), WWII Meml. Soc. (charter), NY Acad. Scis., Planetary Soc., High Speed Rail/Maglev Assn. (govt. rels. com. 1992—97, Maglev task force 1994—97), Va. Assn. Scholars (bd. govs. 1999—, pres. 2004—), Southeastern Univs. Rsch. Assn. (site sel. com. 1980—81, materials sci. com. 1983—86, trustee 1983—98, sci. and tech. com. 1986—88, rules com. 1988—92, edn. com. 1992—94, new projects com. 1994—95, Jefferson Lab. com. 1995—98), Va. Acad. Sci. (sec. astronomy, math. and physics sect 1983—84, chmn. 1984—85), Nat. Assn. Scholars, Am. Assn. Physics Tchrs., Am. Phys. Soc., Met. Opera Guild, Americans United Separation Ch. and State, The Churchill Ctr., Bertrand Russell Soc., Scholars for Peace in Mid. East, Tri-univ. Meson Facility Users Group, Richmond Area Free Thinkers, Coun. Secular Humanism (assoc.), Pi Mu Epsilon, Sigma Pi Sigma, Sigma Xi (chpt. sec. 1977—78, chpt. pres. 1980—84, 1987—88), Phi Beta Kappa. Achievements include co-devel. of low-energy muon beam line at the AGS of Brookhaven Nat. Lab.; rsch. in pion-nucleus interactions, heavy-ion reactions, muon spin rotation studies of high-temperature superconductors and related materials, fullerenes, heavy-fermion materials, ferromagnetic metals, metal hydrides, fatigue in metals and other materials; participation in the establishment of the Southeastern Universities Research Association and the Thomas Jefferson Nat. Accelerator Facility; discovery of formation of muonium and muonated radicals in Buckminsterfullerene; discovery of simultaneous high-temp. superconductivity and magnetic ordering in strontium yttrium ruthenate. Home: 2241 Buckner St Petersburg VA 23805-2207 Office Phone: 804-732-8993. Personal E-mail: cestronach@comcast.net.

STRONE, MICHAEL JONATHAN, real estate consultant, lawyer, art consultant; b. NYC, Feb. 26, 1953; s. Bernard William and Judith Semel (Sogg) S.; m. Andrea Nan Acker, Jan. 27, 1979; children: Noah Gregory, Joshua Samuel. BA cum laude, Colby Coll., Waterville, Maine, 1974; JD, Fordham Law Sch., Bronx, NY, 1978. Bar: NJ 1978, NY 1979, Conn. 1988, US Ct. Appeals (2d and 3d cirs.) 1979, US Dist. Ct. (so. and ea. dists.) NY 1979, US Dist. Ct. NJ 1979. Assoc. Ratheim Hoffman et al, NYC, 1978-80, Botein Hays et al, NYC, 1980-84; v.p., assoc. gen. counsel, asst. sec. GE Investment Corp., Stamford, Conn., 1984-2000; v.p., gen. counsel real estate GE Asset Mgmt. Inc., 2000—02, sr. cons., 2002—; CEO Oracle Investment Advisors, LLC, 2002—, Oracle Fin., LLC, 2004—; pres. Kokoro Japanese Art Advisors, 2007—. Cons. First Am. Title Ins. Co., 2002—05, Title Assoc., 2004—06; bd. dirs. Internat. Netsuke Soc., 2005—, Holm & Drath, 2005—, spl. counsel, 2005—07; prin. Kokoro Japanese Art Advisors, 2007—. Columnist: Jour. Internat. Netsuke Soc., 2002—, mem. editl. bd.:, 2005—; contbr. articles to profl. jours. in field. Bd. dirs. NY chpt. Juvenile Diabetes Found., NYC, 1981-89, vice chmn., 1981-88; mem. fin. com. Juvenile Diabetes Found. Internat., 1981-86; asst. prin. bassist Westchester Symphony Orch., Scarsdale, NY, 1982-2000, pres., 1982-87, chmn. bd., 1982-90, exec. mng. dir., 1990-93; vice chmn. ann. dinner NCCJ, 1987; bd. dirs. Parkinson's Disease Found., 1989-96, chmn. merger com., 1991-96; bd. dirs. Parkinson's Action Network, 1994-98; founding mem., trustee Congregation Sulam Yaakov, 2005-07; trustee Jewish Cmty. Ctr. of Harrison, 1996-2003, mem. ritual com., 1996-2004, chmn., 2000-03, chmn. alt. svcs. com., lay cantor, 1997-2005; founding mem., lay cantor Congregation Sulam Yaakov, 2005—; chmn. county United Way Campaign, 1999, bd. dirs., gen. coun. Harrison Little League, 2001—, coach, 1989-2005; bd. dirs., v.p., gen. counsel Mariners Hockey, Inc., 2003-04, v.p. adminstrn., 2004-05, exec. mng. dir., 2005-07; mem. zoning bd. appeals, Village of Harrison, 2003—; mem. bd. dirs. NY Gilbert & Sullivan Players, 2006-, mem. exec. com., 2006—; chmn. strategic task force, 2006-07, chmn. bd., 2007—; coach Babe Ruth League, 2006—, WBA, 2006—, Sr. Little League, 2006—, Sr. Little League, 2007—. Recipient Gerald I. Phillippe Dist. Cmty. Svc. award, Juvenile Diabetes Found., 1994, Lifetime Achievement award, Juvenile Diabetes Rsch. Found. Internat., 2003. Mem. ABA (chmn. pension plan investments 1989-91, chmn. asset mgmt. 1992-94, 95-97, significant legis. coms. 1985-92, chmn. subcom. on joint ventures 1988-90), Am. Coll. Real Estate Lawyers (com. professionalism 1994—, vice chmn. 1999-2000), Nat. Assn. Real Estate Investment Mgrs. (sr. legal officers adv. com. 1993-2003, ann. forum chair 1997), Colby Coll. Alumni Coun. (nominating com. 1994-97), Fordham Law Alumni Assn., Internat. Netsuke Soc. (bd. dirs. 2005—, v.p. 2007—). Republican. Jewish. Avocations: political memorabilia, antiquarian books, coaching. Home: 10 Genesee Trail Harrison NY 10528-1802 Office: PO Box 6 Harrison NY 10528-0006 Office Phone: 914-899-9000. Personal E-mail: michael@strone.com. Business E-Mail: mstrone@oracleinvest.com.

STRONG, ANNSLEY CHAPMAN, interior designer, volunteer; b. Paterson, NJ, July 18, 1947; d. Donald John and Margaret Brawley Chapman; m. George Gordon Strong, Jr., Nov. 30, 1974; children: George Gordon III, Courtney Chapman Strong Thomas, Meredith Annsley, Alexis Palmer. BA, Wheaton Coll., Norton, Mass., 1969. Cert. N.Y. Sch. Design, 1969. Interior Designers Guild, 1975. Pres. Strong Studio Designs, La Canada, Calif., 1984—. Treas., commr. AYSO Region 13, Pasadena, Calif., 1993—97; mem. Bishop Stevens Found. Bd., Pasadena, Calif., 1994—; co-founder La Canada Sports Coalition, 1996; chmn. bd. Hathaway Sycamores, Pasadena, Calif., 2008—; past chair Verdugo Hills Hosp. Found., 2008—; bd. vice chair Verdugo Hills Hosp., Glendale, 2007—. Recipient 20th Century award, Pasadena YMCA, 1990, Bill Carroll Lifetime Achievement award, Am. Youth Soccer Orgn., 2000. Republican. Avocations: painting, piano, bridge, skiing, golf. Office Phone: 818-957-0086.

STRONG, BRENDA, actress; b. Brightwood, Oreg., Mar. 25, 1960; BA, Ariz. State U. Actor(guest appearances): (TV series) St. Elsewhere, 1985, MacGyver, 1986, Cheers, 1986, Dallas, 1987, Hotel, 1987, Star Trek: The Next Generation, 1988, Matlock, 1989, Father Dowling Mysteries, 1990, Anything But Love, 1991, Twin Peaks, 1991, Blosson, 1991, 1992, Murphy Brown, 1991, 1996, Scorch, 1992, Sibs, 1992, Herman's Head, 1992, 1993, Picket Fences, 1993, The John Larroquette Show, 1996, Party of Five, 1996, 3rd Rock from the Sun, 1996, Seinfeld, 1996, 1997, Any Day Now, 1999, Sports Night, 1999, 2000, Get Real, 2000, Michael Richards Show, 2000, Ally McBeal, 2001, CSI: Crime Scene Investigation, 2001, Gilmore Girls, 2001, Dawson's Creek, 2001, 7th Heaven, 2001, 2002, The Court, 2002, Malcolm in the Middle, 2002, Nip/Tuck, 2003, Everwood, 2002, 2003, 2004, 2005, Desperate Housewives, 2004— (Screen Actors Guild Award for outstanding performance by an ensemble in a comedy series, 2005, 2006),: (TV films) Kenny Rogers as the Gambler, Part III: The Legend Continues, 1987, Spaceballs, 1987, People Like Us, 1990, Island City, 1994, Going to the Mat, 2004; (films) Malice, 1993, My Life, 1993, The Craft, 1996, Get a Job, 1998, Black Dog, 1998, Undercurrent, 1999, The Deep End of the Ocean, 1999, Terror Tract, 2000, Teddy Bears' Picnic, 2002, Red Dragon, 2002, Missing Brendan, 2003, The Work and the Glory, 2004, The Work and the Glory: American Zion, 2005. Bd. dirs. Montana Shakespeare Co., Helena. Office: Desperate Housewives Touchtone Television 100 Universal City Plaza Bldg 2128 Ste G Universal City CA 91608

STRONG, GARY EUGENE, university librarian; b. Moscow, Idaho, June 26, 1944; s. Authur Dwight and Cleora Anna (Nirk) S.; m. Carolyn Jean Roetker, Mar. 14, 1970; children: Christopher Eric, Jennifer Rebecca. BS in Edn., U. Idaho, 1966; AMLS, U. Mich., 1967. Adminstrv. and reference asst. U. Idaho, 1963-66; extension libr. Latah County Free Libr., Moscow, 1966; head libr. Markeley Residence Libr. U. Mich., 1966-67; libr. dir. Lake Oswego Pub. Libr., Oreg., 1967-73, Everett Public Libr., Wash., 1973-76; assoc. dir. services Wash. State Libr., Olympia, 1976-79, dep. state libr., 1979-80; state librarian Calif. State Libr., Sacramento, 1980-94; dir. Queens Borough Pub. Libr., Jamaica, NY, 1994—2003; dir. emeritus Calif. State Library Found., 1994—2003; univ. libr. UCLA, 2003—. Adj. prof. Queens Coll. Grad. Sch. of Libr. and Info. Scis., 2000-03; chief exec. Calif. Libr. Svcs. Bd., 1980-94; founder, bd. dirs. Calif. State Libr. Found., 1982-94, Calif. Literary Campaign, 1984-94, Calif. Rsch. Bur., 1992; bd. dirs. No. Regional Libr. Bd., 1983-94, Queens Libr. Found., 1994-2003; mem. adv. bd. Ctr. for the Book in Libr. of Congress, 1983-86; mem. nat. adv. com. Libr. of Congress, 1987-89; chmn. adv. bd. Calif. Libr. Constrn. and Renovation Bond Act Bd., 1989-94; vis. lectr. Marylhurst Coll., Oreg., 1968, Oreg. Divsn. Continuing Edn., 1972, San Jose State U. Sch. Libr. Svc., 1990; mem. N.Y. State Adv. Coun. Librs., 1996-97; mem. chancellor's task force ednl. tech. and librs. CUNY, 1996-97; convenor Archons of the Colophon, 1997-98; regents adv. coun. librs. N.Y. State, 1999-2003; mem. various coms., UCLA; lectr. and cons. in field. Host, producer: cable TV Signatures Program, 1974-76, nationwide videoconfs. on illiteracy, censorship, 1985; author: On Reading-in the Year of the Reader, 1987, U.S. Patriot's Act: Protecting Patron's Rights, 2002; editor Calif. State Library Found. Bull., 1982-94 (H.W. Wilson Periodical award 1988), Western Americana in the Calif. State Library, 1986, On Reading-In the Year of the Reader, 1987, Chinatown Photographer: Louis J. Stellman, 1989, Local History Genealogical Resources, 1990, Literate America Emerging, 1991; curator Queens Libr. Gallery, 1998; contbr. articles to profl. jours.; editor, designer and pub. of various books. Bd. dirs., v.p. Pacific N.W. Bibliog. Ctr., 1977-80; bd. dirs. Thurston Mason County Mental Health Ctr., 1977-80, pres., 1979-80; bd. dirs. Coop. Library Agy. for Sys. and Svcs., 1980-94, vice chmn., 1981-84; bd. dirs. Sr. Svcs. Snohomish County, 1973-76, HISPANEX (Calif. Spanish lang. database), 1983-86; bd. govs. Snohomish County Hist. Assn., 1974-76; mem. psychiat. task force St. Peters Hosp., Olympia, 1979-80; co-founder Calif. Ctr. for the Book, bd. dirs., 1987-94; mem. adv. bd. Calif. State PTA, 1981-86, Gov.'s Tech. Conf., 1993-94; mem. adv. com. Sch. Libr. Sci., UCLA, 1991-94, Sch. Libr. and Info. Studies, U. Calif., Berkeley, 1991-94, Libr. Sch. Queens Coll., 1996-2003, libr. sch. St. John's U., 1996-98; mem. Oreg. Coun. Pub. Broadcasting, 1969-73, Calif. Adult Edn. Steering Com., 1988-94, N.Y. State Adv. Coun. on Librs., 1996-97; chmn. collaborative coun. Calif. State Literacy Resource Ctr., 1993-94; bd. dirs. Queens coun. Boy Scouts Am., 1994-2003; v.p. 100 Yr. Assn. N.Y., 1996-2003; mem. Chancellor's Task Force on Ednl. Tech. and Librs., CUNY, 1996-97; participant N.Y. Pub. Libr. Conf. of World Libr. Leaders, 1996; trustee Flushing Cemetery Assn., 1998-2003; mem. com. on intellectual property rights and the engring. info. infrastructure Nat. Rsch. Coun., 1998-2000; chair organizing com. China-U.S. Libr. Conf., 2001, 05; mem. info. tech. planning bd. UCLA, 2003—, mem. privacy and data protection adv. bd., 2004—, mem. accreditation steering com. Western Assn. Schs. and Colls., 2005—06; mem. libr. adv. com., Calif. Rare Book Sch., 2003—; mem. adv. com. Libr. Sch., San Jose State U., 2006—. Oreg. Libr. scholar, 1966; recipient Disting. Alumnus award U. Mich., 1984, Disting. Svc. award, Calif. Literacy Inc., 1985, Spl. Achievement award, Literacy Action, 1988, Assn. Specialized and Coop. Libr. Agys. Exceptional Achievement award 1992, Gov.'s award of Achievement, Govt. Tech. Conf., 1994, Advancement of Literacy award, Pub. Libr. Assn., 1994, John Cotton Dana award, Libr. Adminstrn. and Mgmt. Assn., 1994, Charlie Robinson award, Pub. Libr. Assn., 2002; named Libr. of Yr., Calif. Assn. Libr. Trustees and Commrs., 1994, Disting. Svc. award, Chinese Am. Libr. Assn., 1996, 21st Century Libr. award, Syracuse U., 2002, Knowledge Trust Honors award for edn., 2006; named Bus. Person of Yr., Queens C. of C., 2002. Mem.: ALA (legis. com. 1980—82, commn. on freedom and equality of access to info. 1983—86, legis. com. 1995—97, chair intellectual property subcom. 1995—98, chmn. conf. librs. Beijing 1996, rep. Internat. Fedn. of Libr. Assn. nat. organizing com. 1996—2001, intellectual property com. 1998—2001, chair China U.S. planning com. for chair U.S. libr. coop. conf. 2001, Fedn. of Libr. Assn. UN rep. 2001—03, chair China U.S. planning com. for chair U.S. libr. coop. conf. 2003, IFLA governing bd. 2004—07, Humphrey award for Internat. Librarianship 2003), Rsch. Librs. Group (chmn. programs coun. 2006—), Oakshire Computer Libr. Ctr. (program coun. chair rsch. librs. group 2006—), The Digital Dilemma, Assn. of Coll. and Rsch. Libraries, Assn. Specialized and Coop. Libr. Agys., Western Coun. State Librs. (pres. 1989—91), Chief Officers of State Libr. Agys. (pres. 1984—86), Calif. Libr. Assn. (govt. rels.com. 1980—94), Pacific N.W. Libr. Assn. (hon. life mem., pres. 1978—79), Oreg. Libr. Assn. (hon. life mem., pres. 1970—71), Assn. of Rsch. Librs. (mem. task force on rsch. tchg. and learning 2005—, mem. task force spl. collections 2007—), Libr. Adminstrn. and Mgmt. Assn. (bd. dis. 1980—88, pres. 1984—85), Am. Printing History Assn., Metro (bd. dirs. 1994—2003, treas. 1996—99, 1st v.p. 1999—2001), Queens County C. of C. (bd. dirs. 1996—2003, named Bus. Person of Yr. 2002), Jamaica Devel. Corp., Everett Area C. of C. (bd. dirs. 1974—76), Zamorano Club, The Typophiles, Guild of Book Workers, Grolier Club, The Book Collectors Club of L.A., Roxburghe Club, Sacramento Book Collectors Club, Book Club of Calif. Office: UCLA Libr Box 951575 Los Angeles CA 90095-1575 Office Phone: 310-825-1201. Business E-Mail: gstrong@library.ucla.edu.

STRONG, GEORGE GORDON, JR., lawyer, management consultant; b. Toledo, Apr. 19, 1947; s. George Gordon and Jean Boyd (McDougall) S.; m. Annsley Palmer Chapman, Nov. 30, 1974; children: George III, Courtney, Meredith, Alexis. BA, Yale U., 1969; MBA, Harvard U., 1971; JD, U. San Diego, 1974. Bar: Calif. 1974, U.S. Dist. Ct. (cen. dist.) Calif. 1974; CPA, Calif., Hawaii, cert. mgmt. cons. Contr. Vitredent Corp., Beverly Hills, Calif., 1974-76; sr. mgr. Price Waterhouse, LA, 1976-82, ptnr., 1987—2001, mng. ptnr. west region dispute analysis and corp. recovery, 1993—99, mem. policy bd., bd. dirs., 1995-98, mem. combination bd., 1997-98; bd. ptnrs., prin. Pricewaterhouse Coopers LLP, LA, 1998-2001, mem. global oversight bd., 1998—2001; exec. v.p., COO Internat. Customs Service, Long Beach, Calif., 1982-84; CFO Uniform Software Systems, Santa Monica, Calif., 1984-85; exec. v.p., COO Cipherlink Corp., 1986; pres. Woodleigh Lane, Inc., Flintridge, Calif., 1985-87; mng. dir., gen. counsel sec. and bd. mem. Cornerstone Rsch., 2002—. Chmn. bd. dirs. LA SPCA; treas. Andover Abbot Alumni Assn. Southern Calif.; chmn. bd. trustees Harvard Bus. Sch. Assn. So. Calif. Scholarship Fund. Mem. ABA, AICPA, Calif. State Bar, Calif. Soc. CPAs, Andover Abbott Alumni So. Calif. (bd. dirs., treas.), Inst. Mgmt. Cons., Harvard Bus. Sch. Alumni Assn. (bd. dirs. 1996-99), Harvard Bus. Sch. Assn. So. Calif. (bd. dirs., trustees scholarship fund 1992—, pres. 1988-89, dir. 1996-99, 2001-03, 06—), Harvard Club NY, Harvard Club Boston, Yale Club NY, Lincoln Club, Calif. Club, Olympic Club, Jonathan Club, Annandale Golf Club, Coral Beach and Tennis Club, Mid Ocean Golf Club, Royal Bermuda Yacht Club, Valley Hunt Club, Tuckers Point Golf Club (Bermuda), Park Meadows Country Club. Republican. Presbyterian. Avocations: golf, tennis, bridge. Home: 5455 Castle Knoll Rd La Canada Flintridge CA 91011-1319 Office: Cornerstone Research 633 W Fifth St 31st Fl Los Angeles CA 90071-3509 Office Phone: 213-553-2600. Personal E-mail: gstrong@cornerstone.com.

STRONG, GEORGE HOTHAM, private investor, consultant; b. Johnstown, Pa., July 15, 1926; s. George Hite and Mary Elizabeth (Hotham) S.; m. Mary Louise Lyon, Sept. 19, 1953; children: Cynthia Strong Hibbard, Dexter, Sarah Strong Bornstein. AB magna cum laude, Allegheny Coll, 1949; MBA, Harvard U., 1951. V.p. Smith Barney & Co., NYC & Boston, 1951-67, Norlin Corp., NYC, 1967-73, Am. Medicorp, Bala-Cynwyd, Pa., 1974-78; cons. A.D. Little, Cambridge, Mass., 1973-74; sr. v.p., dir. Universal Health Svcs., King of Prussia, Pa., 1978-84; pvt. practice investor NYC, 1985—. Served on 16 pub. and pvt. corp. bds. Served to sgt. US Army, 1944—46, Italy. Mem. Harvard Club (NYC), Union League Club (Phila.), Seabright (NJ) Lawn Tennis Club, Seabright Beach Club, Rumson (NJ) Country Club, Phi Beta Kappa. Republican. Episcopalian. Home: 946 Navesink River Rd Rumson NJ 07760-2330

STRONG, JOHN DAVID, insurance company executive; b. Cortland, NY, Apr. 12, 1936; s. Harold A. and Helen H. Strong; m. Carolyn Dimmick, Oct. 26, 1957; children: John David, Suzanne. BS, Syracuse U., 1957; postgrad., Columbia U., 1980. With Kemper Group, 1957-90, Kemper Corp., 1990-96, Empire sales divsn. mgr., 1972-74, CEO, 1988-93, chmn. bd., 1989-93; vice chmn. Millikin Assocs., 1993-96, chmn., 1996; exec. v.p., dir. Facilitators, Inc., 1995-98. Mem. adv. coun. Sch. Bus., Millikin U., 1975-79, 84—; bd. dirs. United Way of Decatur and Macon County, Ill., 1976-83, campaign chmn., 1978-79, pres. bd. dirs., 1979-81; pres. United Way of Ill., 1981-83; bd. dirs. DMH Commn. Svcs. Corp., 1985-97, chmn., 1988-90; bd. dirs. Decatur-Macon County Econ. Devel. Found., 1983-88, DMH Health Systems, 1987-94, Richland C.C. Found., 1987-90, Symphony Orch. Guild of Decatur, 1992-96, DMH Found., 1988-97; bd. dirs. Ill. Ednl. Devel. Found., 1983-90, pres., 1986-87; bd. dirs. Decatur Meml. Hosp., 1985-94, vice chmn., 1988, chmn., 1990-92; bd. dirs. Ctrl. Ill. Health Assocs., Inc., 1994, vice chmn., 1994-96; mem. steering com. Decatur Advantage, 1981-93, pres., 1988-93. Capt. USAR, 1958-69. Mem. Metro Decatur C. of C. (bd. dirs. 1977-80, chmn. 1983-84), Decatur Club (bd. dirs. 19080-83, pres. 1983), Country Club of Decatur (bd. dirs. 1993-99, pres. bd. 1995-97), Union League Club Chgo., Bull Valley Golf Club, Anvil Club, Union League Club of Chgo., Bull Valley Golf Club, Alpha Kappa Psi. Personal E-mail: jack@strongs.net.

STRONG, JOHN OLIVER, plastic surgeon, educator; b. Montclair, NJ, Feb. 1, 1930; s. George Joseph and Olivia (LeBrun) S.; m. Helen Louise Vrooman, July 19, 1958 (dec. Mar. 1973); m. Deborah Sperberg, May 20, 1978; children: John Jr., Jean LeB., Andrew D. BS, Yale U., 1952; MD, U. Pa., 1957. Cert. vol. paleontologist Calif. Practice medicine specializing in plastic and reconstructive surgery, Santa Ana, Calif., 1964-97; asst. clin. prof. plastic and reconstructive surgery U. Calif., Irvine, 1970—. Chief of staff Western Med. Ctr., Santa Ana, 1996-97, interim chmn. bd., 1996-97, bd. dirs.; bd. dirs. United Western Med. Ctrs., Healthcare Found. Orange County, chmn.; vol. Anza Borrego Desert State Pk., steering com., 1998-2003. Vol. Anza -Borrego Desert State Pk. Fellow ACS; mem. Calif. Med. Assn. (chmn. sci. adv. panel 1983-89), Calif. Soc. Plastic Surgeons (pres. 1991-92). Republican. Office: PO Box 94 Borrego Springs CA 92004-0094 Address: 511 Seaward Rd Corona Del Mar CA 92625-2600 Personal E-mail: jostrong1@sbcglobal.net, jhnos@netscape.net.

STRONG, JOHN SCOTT, finance educator; b. Phila., Aug. 28, 1956; s. John S. and Thelma J. (Willard) S. BS, Washington & Lee U., 1978; M of Pub. Policy, Harvard U., 1981, PhD in Bus. Econs., 1986. Rsch. fellow Harvard U., Cambridge, Mass., 1983-85, 89-90, 93, vis. asst. prof. econs., 1989-90; prof. fin. Coll. William and Mary, Williamsburg, Va., 1985—. Cons. on econs. and fin. Republic of Indonesia, 1987-99, MITI, Japan, 1988-89, European Bank for Reconstruction and Devel., 1993-95, Govt. of Bolivia, 1994, Govt. of Russia, 1996, Govts. of Brazil, Argentina and Uruguay, 1997, Govt. of Peru, 1998, World Bank, 1997—, Inter-Am. Devel. Bank, 2002—, U.S. Dept. Transp., 1999-02. Author: Why Airplanes Crash: Aviation Safety in a Changing World, 1992, Moving to Market: Restructuring Transport in the Former Soviet Union, 1996; co-author 2 books on airline deregulation; contbr. articles to profl. jours. Fulbright scholar, 1978-79; grad. fellow NSF, 1979-82. Business E-Mail: john.strong@business.wm.edu.

STRONG, JOHN WILLIAM, lawyer, educator; b. Iowa City, Aug. 18, 1935; s. Frank Ransom and Gertrude Elizabeth (Way) S.; m. Margaret Waite Cleary, June 16, 1962; children— Frank Ransom, Benjamin Waite. BA, Yale U., 1957; JD, U. Ill., 1962; postgrad, U. N.C., 1966-67. Bar: Ill. 1963, Oreg. 1976. Assoc. firm LeForgee, Samuels, Miller, Schroeder & Jackson, Decatur, Ill., 1963-64; asst. prof. law U. Kans., 1964-66; assoc. prof. Duke U., 1966-69; prof. U. Oreg., 1969-75; legal counsel Oreg. Task Force on Med. Malpractice, 1976; prof. U. Nebr., 1977-84, dean, 1977-82, vice chancellor for acad. affairs, 1981-84; Rosenstiel Disting. prof. law U. Ariz., 1984-98, prof. emeritus, 1998—. Nat. sec.-treas. Order of the Coif, 1992-98; cons. Nat. Judicial Coll. Author: (with others) Handbook on Evidence, 5th edit., 1999. Served with U.S. Army, 1957-59. Mem. Ill. Bar Assn., Oreg. Bar Assn., ABA, Am. Law Inst., Phi Delta Phi. Independent. Congregationalist. Office: U Ariz Coll Law Tucson AZ 85721-0001 Home: PO Box 8063 Black Butte Ranch OR 97759 Business E-Mail: strong@law.arizona.edu.

STRONG, JUDITH ANN, chemist, educator; b. June 19, 1941; d. Philip Furnald and Hilda Bernice (Hulbert) S. BS cum laude, SUNY, Albany, 1963; MA, Brandeis U., 1966, PhD, 1970. Asst. prof. chemistry Moorhead State U., Minn., 1969—73, assoc. prof., 1973—81, prof., 1981—, chmn. chemistry dept., 1984—86, dean social and natural scis., 1986—97, assoc. v.p. acad. affairs, 1997—. Recipient Gov.'s Acts of Kindness Vol. award, 1997; fellow, NSF, 1965—67. Mem.: Minn. Acad. Sci., Assn. Women in Sci., Am. Chem. Soc., Soroptimist Internat. (gov. North Ctrl. region

2002—04, program coun. 2004—), Sigma Xi. Home: 1209 12th St S Moorhead MN 56560-3707 Office: Minn State U Moorhead Academic Affairs Moorhead MN 56563-0001 Office Phone: 218-477-2075. Business E-Mail: strong@mnstate.edu.

STRONG, KARIN HJORT, artist, educator; b. NYC, Jan. 30, 1956; d. Corrin Peter and Mette Hjort (Matthiesen) S. BA, Boston U., 1981; AA, Pratt U., 1985. Art tutor Hampshire Coll., Amherst, Mass., 1977; co-founder, mgr., tchr. Poland Springs (Maine) Cmty. Program, 1977-79; tchr. Southampton Cultural Ctr., 1989-96; tchg. asst. master workshop on art L.I. Univ., Southampton, NY, 1990. Bd. mem. Catharine Lorillard Wolfe Art Club, Inc., N.Y.C., 1989-96; painting judge Pen and Brush Club, Inc., N.Y.C., 1995; art show judge J.L.C. Art Ctr., Inc., Stony Brook, N.Y., 1995. Artist represented by Gallery East, Images Gallery, Lizan Tops Gallery, others. Vol. coord. Appalachian Mountain Club, Boston, 1981; monkey trainer to aid quadreplegics Boston U., 1981; spkr., event M.C. CLWAC, Nat. Arts Club, N.Y.C., 1992-95; spkr., lectr. Jimmy Ernst Artist Alliance, East Hampton, N.Y., 1993, Southampton Artists, 1994. Mem. Soc. Animal Artists, Southampton Artists (bd. mem., exhbn. chair, publicity com. 1988-90), Catharine Lorillard Wolfe Art Club, Inc. (pres. 1992-95). Avocations: music, playing guitar, flute and dulcimer, sports, writing.

STRONG, MARCELLA LEE, music specialist, educator; b. East Liverpool, Ohio, Oct. 16, 1954; d. Carl and Ruth I. (White) Hinkle; m. David Lee Strong, Feb 19, 1977. BA magna cum laude, U. Toledo, 1976; MA in Early Childhood Edn., Kent State U., 1982. Cert. music, elem. tchr., Ohio. Music instr. Cardinal Local Schs., Parkman and Huntsburg, Ohio, 1977—. Choir dir. G.V. Nazarene Ch., Orwell, Ohio 1981-83; organist, mem. bd. deacons and stewardship com., sr. choir, jr. choir and ch. band dir. Huntsburg Congl. Ch., 1985—; mem., officer Orwell Farm Bur.; band dir. Kent State U. Coll. for Kids, 1995—. Mem. Cardinal Edn. Assn. (negotiator 1982, 84, 87, 90, 93, 96, 99, 2002, sec. 1983-84, treas. 1984-85, pres. 1985-86, 89-91, 1997-2002), Ohio Music Educators Assn., Kappa Delta Pi, Mu Phi Epsilon, Delta Kappa Gamma. Democrat. Avocations: spectator sports, travel, reading, chess, member international trivia team. Home: PO Box 370 78 Chaffee Dr Orwell OH 44076-0370 E-mail: dlsmls@yahoo.com.

STRONG, SUSAN CLANCEY, writer, communications executive, editor; b. Cin., Nov. 10, 1939; d. William Power and Elizabeth (Browne) Clancey; m. Oliver Swigert, 1957 (div. 1972); children: Silvia, David Mack; m. Richard Devon Strong, 1977. BA, Northwestern U., 1965; MA, U. Calif., Berkeley, 1972, PhD, 1979. Tchr. Helen Bush Parkside Sch., Seattle, 1965-66, Taipei (Taiwan) Lang. Inst., 1967-68; acting instr. U. Calif., Berkeley, 1972-78, teaching fellow, 1979, lectr., 1979-84, St. Mary's Coll., Moraga, Calif., 1982-85; pvt. practice Orinda, Calif., 1985-90, 97—; sr. rsch. assoc. Ctr. for Econ. Conversion, 1990-96. Mem. Contra Costa County Conflict Resolution Panels, Calif., 1987-90; affiliate Support Ctr./CTD, San Francisco, 1987-90; del. UN Conf. on Econ. Conversion, Moscow, 1990; co-founder "The Who's Counting?" Project, 1996; founder The Metaphor Project, 1997. Author: The GDP Myth: How It Harms Our Quality of Life, and What Communities are Doing About It, 1995; editor Deficit Delirium, 1993, Shaping A New Conversion Agenda, 1995; author poetry; columnist, book reviewer, film reviewer. Mem. Bay Area Global Tomorrow Com., 1986; co-founder Peace Economy Working Group, 1988; co-founder Peace Economy Campaign, 1988; mem. Peace Action Nat. Strategy Com., 1989-95, co-chair strategy com., 1992-93; conf. co-chmn. Nat. Sane/Freeze Congress, 1989-90, rep. nat. bd. advisors Nat. Peace Action, Washington, 1989-95; mem. bd. advisors Peace and Environ. Project, San Francisco, 1986-88; chmn. No. Calif. Sane Freeze, San Francisco, 1985-89; co-convenor The Natural Step Open Space Com. Conf., San Francisco, 1997. Mem. Phi Beta Kappa. Democrat. Episcopalian. Avocations: music, gardening. Mailing: PO Box 892 Orinda CA 94563-2124 Office Phone: 925-254-7198. Office Fax: 925-254-3304. Business E-Mail: sstrong@metaphorproject.org.

STRONG, VIRGINIA WILKERSON, freelance writer, former special education educator; b. Vernal, Utah, Mar. 19, 1935; d. Arbun C. and Mildred (Wyman) Wilkerson; m. David Smith, Oct. 6, 1950 (div. Jan. 1960); children: Anna Smith Blyton, Dorothy Smith Wolf, Wendell Lee Smith, Ava Smith Eatman, Karen Smith Ritter; m. Lawrence D. Strong, June 1961 (div. May 1973); children: Lawrence D. Jr., Jeffrey A. BA, U. Miss., 1970, MEd, 1972; PhD, Ohio U., 1985; cert. film, TV, and digital entertainment media, UCLA, 2006. Cert. elem. edn. tchr., spl. edn. K-12 tchr., ednl. adminstrn., 1991; cert screenwriter, UCLA, 1995. Rsch. asst. U. Miss., University, 1968-70, Utah State U., Logan, 1974-78; tchr. spl. edn. various schs., nr. Oxford, Miss., 1969-74; instr. spl. edn., project coord., rsch. asst. Ohio U., Athens, 1978-82; supr. spl. edn. Meigs County Bd. Edn., Pomeroy, Ohio, 1982-84; tchr. spl. edn., dept. chmn. L.A. Unified Sch. Dist., 1986-93, co-faciliator alcohol drug abuse, 1990-93; freelance writer, owner, mgr. Fenix Devel., Henderson, Calif., 1990—. Early childhood adv. Utah Bd. Edn., Salt Lake City, 1976, evaluator edn. programs, Salt Lake City and Logan, 1976-77; curriclum developer Meigs County, 1982-84; dir. gifted edn. workshop Ohio U., 1980; acting dir. edn., cons. North Miss. Retardation Ctr., Oxford, 1993-94; creative cons. student film Patience UCLA, 2005. Author: The Role of the Special Education Supervisor, 1985, (screenplays) To See the Elephant, Dark Encounters; contbr. articles to newspapers. Elector Dem. Party, Logan, 1976; religious instr. LDS Ch., various locations, 1953-97. U.S. Dept. Edn. grantee Utah State U., 1976. Mem. ASCD, Kappa Delta Pi, Phi Delta Kappa. Avocations: genealogy, gemology, photography, history buff, travel.

STRONG, WENDI ELLEN, insurance company executive; BA in Psychology, U. North Tex., Denton, MA in Journalism. With Halt & Assocs., Dallas, Hill & Knowlton; dir. pub. rels. and advt. Rosewood Hotels and Resorts; dir. corp. comm. Kimberly-Clark Corp.; v.p. strategic comm. Assocs. First Capital Corp.; with USAA (United Svcs. Automobile Assn.), 2000—, v.p. corp. comm., sr. v.p. comm. programs, 2001, exec. v.p. corp. comm. Office: USAA 9800 Fredericksburg Rd San Antonio TX 78288 Office Phone: 210-498-8222. E-mail: wendi.strong@usaa.com. *

STRONG-CUEVAS, ELIZABETH, sculptor; b. St. Germain en Laye, France, Jan. 22, 1929; Am. citizen; d. George and Margaret (Strong) de Cuevas; 1 child, Deborah Carmichael. BA, Vassar Coll., Poughkeepsie, NY, 1952. Instr. Arts Students' League, NYC; student John Hovannes. One-woman shows include Lee Ault Gallery, NYC, 1977-78, Tower Gallery, Southampton, NY, 1980, Iolas-Jackson Gallery, NYC, 1983, 85, Guild Hall Mus., East Hampton, NY, 1985, Benton Gallery, Southampton, NY, 1987, Kerr Gallery, NYC, 1988, Grounds for Sculpture, Hamilton, NJ, 1999, Island Weiss Gallery, NYC, 2004-05, 07, Vassar Coll., Poughkeepsie, NY, 2006, Island Weiss Gallery, NYC, 2007; group shows include Guild Hall, East Hampton, 1980, 84, 98, Art Students League of NY, 1982, Bruce Mus., Greenwich, Conn., 1984, 85, Tower Gallery, NYC, 1984, Kouros Gallery, Ridgefield, Conn., 1985, Andre Zarre Gallery, NYC, 1985, Susan Blanchard Gallery, NYC, 1986, Ruth Vered Gallery, East Hampton, 1986-88, Benton Gallery, Southampton, 1987, 1990, Benson Gallery, Bridgehampton, NY, 1989, 99, Koln Art Fair, Germany, 1989, 1991, Feingarten Galleries, NYC, 1990, Marisa del Re Biennale III, 1993, IV, 1994, Parrish Mus., Southampton, 1994, Grounds for Sculpture, Hamilton, NJ, 1994-96, Shidoni, Tessuque, N.Mex., 1995-98, Barnard-Biderman Fine Art, Southampton, 1997, The Tolman Collection, Singapore, 1997-98, Earl McGrath Gallery, 1998, Bulgari, NY, 2000, Grounds for Sculpture, Hamilton, 2000, 02, Russian Am. Cultural Ctr., 2001, Clark Fine Art, Southampton, 2001, 2003, The Ross Sch., East Hampton, 2003, Island Weiss Gallery, NYU, 2004-06, Kouros Gallery, NYC, 2003, UBS Bank Gallery, 2005, Ann Norton Sculpture Gardens, West Palm Beach, Fla., 2006; represented in pvt. collections at Bruce Mus., Greenwich, Conn., Grounds for Sculpture, Hamilton, NJ Guild Hall Mus., Heckscher Mus., Huntington, NY, East Hampton Garden, East Hampton, 1982, Park Ave. Ter., NY, 1997. Recipient First prize, Guild Hall, NY, 1985. Mem. Vassar Club (NY). Avocation: yoga. Personal E-mail: strongworks@sc-sculpture.com.

STRONGIN, JONATHAN DAVID, physician; b. Kingston, NY, June 19, 1951; s. Jack and Thelma (Kaufman) S.; m. Ellen Wells Seely, June 11, 1983; children: Jessica, Matthew. BA, Columbia Coll., 1973; PhD, MD, Columbia U., 1982. Diplomate Am. Bd. Internal Medicine, Am. Bd. Pulmonary Disease, Am. Bd. Critical Care Medicine. Intern, resident Cambridge (Mass.) Hosp., 1982-84; med. resident Beth Israel Hosp., Boston, 1984-85; pulmonary fellow Mass. Gen. Hosp., Boston, 1985-97; physician Pulmonary Assocs. of Greater Boston, 1994—96. Pres. med. staff Whidden Meml. Hosp., Everett, Mass., 1995-97; trustee Melrose Wakefield Health Care Corp., 1996-98; med. dir. respiratory care, pres. med. staff Cambridge Health Alliance. Fulbright scholar, 1976-77. Fellow Am. Coll. Physicians, Am. Coll. Chest Physicians. Avocation: running.

STRONG-TIDMAN, VIRGINIA ADELE, marketing professional; b. July 26, 1947; d. Alan Ballentine and Virginia Leona (Harris) Strong; m. John Fletcher Tidman, Sept. 23, 1978. BS, Albright Coll., Reading, Pa., 1969; postgrad., U. Pitts., 1970-73, U. Louisville, 1975-76. Exec. trainee Pomeroy's divsn. Allied Stores, Reading, 1969-70; mktg. rsch. analyst Heinz U.S.A., Pitts., 1970-74; new products mktg. mgr. Ky. Fried Chicken, Louisville, 1974-76; dir. Pitts. office M/A/R/C, 1976-79; assoc. rsch. dir. Henderson Advt., Inc., Greenville, SC, 1979-81; sr. v.p., dir. rsch. Bozell, Jacobs, Kenyon & Eckhardt, Inc., Dallas, 1981-86, sr. v.p., dir. rsch. and strategic planning Atlanta, 1986-88; sr. v.p., dir. mktg. svcs. Bozell, Inc., Atlanta, 1988-91; sr. v.p., mng. ptnr. Henderson Adv., Inc., 1991-95; prin. Ender-Ptnr., Inc., 1995-96; v.p. mktg. Booth Rsch. Svcs., Inc., 1996-98; COO Moore & Symons, Inc., 1998—. Cons. mktg. rsch. Greenville Zool. Soc., 1981; adj. prof. So. Meth. U., 1984-85. Mem. Am. Mktg. Assn. (Effie award N.Y. chpt. 1982). Republican. Episcopalian. Home: 146 Northshores Dr Seneca SC 29672

STROOCK, DANIEL WYLER, mathematician, educator; b. NYC, Mar. 20, 1940; s. Alan Maxwell and Katherine (Wyler) S.; m. Lucy Barber, Nov. 21, 1962; children: Benjamin, Abraham. AB, Harvard Coll., 1962; PhD, Rockefeller U., 1966. Vis. mem. Courant Inst., N.Y. U., 1966-69, asst. prof., 1969-72; asso. prof. math. U. Colo., Boulder, 1972-75, prof., 1975-84, chmn. dept. math, 1979-81; Simons prof. math. MIT, 1984—. Adj. prof. U. Colo., Beijing Normal U. Author: (with S.R.S. Vanadhan) Multidimensional Diffusion Processes, 1979, (with J.D. Deutschel) Large Deviations, 1989, Probability Theory, An Analytic View, 1993, An Introduction to the Analysis of Paths on a Rieman Manfold, 1999, Markov Processes from K. Ito's Perspective, 2003; editor Math. Zeitschrift, 1992-2000, Ill. Jour. Math., 1975-80, Transactions of Am. Math. Soc., 1974-80, Annals of Probability, 1988-93, Advances in Math., 1995—, Jour. Functional Analysis, 1994—; contbr. articles on probability theory to profl. jours. Guggenheim fellow, 1978-79 Mem. Am. Acad. Arts and Scis., Nat. Acad. Scis., Polish Acad. Arts & Scis. (fgn. mem.). Democrat. Jewish. Home: 55 Frost St Cambridge MA 02140-2247 Office: MIT Dept Math Cambridge MA 02139

STROOCK, MARK EDWIN, II, public relations company executive; b. NYC, Nov. 6, 1922; s. Irving Sylvan and Blanche (Loeb) S.; m. Hanna Marks Eiseman, June 24, 1945 (dec. May 2003); children— Mark E., Carolyn E. BA, Bard Coll., 1947. Reporter The New York Journal of Commerce, 1947-50; writer Barrons, NYC, 1950-51; mng. editor Fairchild Publ., NYC, 1952-53; bus. editor World Mag., NYC, 1953-54; contbg. editor Time Mag., NYC, 1954-56; with Young & Rubicam Inc., NYC, 1956-87, sr. v.p., dir. corp. rels., cons., 1987—. Bd. trustee N.Y. Urban League, 1971-78, Alvin Ailey Dance Theatre, N.Y.C., 1977-84, Friends of the Theatre Mus. City N.Y., 1977-85, Arts Horizons, N.Y.C., 1998—; vice-chmn. Covenant House, N.Y.C., 1978-90; exec. com., mktg. and communications com., assoc. nat. commr. Anti-Defamation League, 1992—. With U.S. Army, 1943-46. Democrat. Jewish. Home: 50 Park Ave Apt 11B New York NY 10016-3075 Office: Young & Rubicam Inc 285 Madison Ave New York NY 10017-6486

STROOCK, THOMAS FRANK, oil and gas company executive; b. NYC, Oct. 10, 1925; s. Samuel and Dorothy (Frank) S.; m. Marta Freyre de Andrade, June 19, 1949; children: Margaret, Sandra, Elizabeth, Anne. BA in Econs., Yale U., 1948; LLB (hon.), U. Wyo., 1995; PhD (hon.), Universidad del Valle, Guatemala, 2001. Landman Stanolind Oil & Gas Co., Tulsa, 1948-52; pres. Stroock Leasing Corp., Casper, Wyo., 1952-89, Alpha Exploration, Inc., 1980-89; ptnr. Stroock, Rogers & Dymond, Casper, 1960-82; dir. First Wyo. Bank, Casper, 1967-89; mem. Wyo. Senate, 1969-89, chmn. appropriations com., 1983-89, co-chmn. joint appropriations com., 1983-89, mem. mgmt. and audit com., pres., 1988-89; mem. steering com. Edn. Commn. of States; amb. to Guatemala Govt. of U.S., 1989-93; pres. Alpha Devel. Corp., 1992—; prof. pub. diplomacy U. Wyo., Laramie, 1993—2002, chmn. internat. adv. bd., 2001—. Dir. Wyo. Med. Ctr., 1996-2004. Rep. precinct committeeman, 1960-68; pres. Natrona County Sch. Bd., 1966, 69; pres. Wyo. State Sch. Bds. Assn., 1965-66; chmn. Casper Cmty. Recreation, 1955-60; chmn. Natrona County United Fund, 1963-64, Wyo. State Rep. Com., 1975-78, exec. com. 1954-60; del. Rep. Nat. Conv., 1956-76, 92; regional coord. campaign George Bush for pres., 1979-80, 87-88; chmn. Western States Rep. Chmn. Assn., 1977-78; chmn. Wyo. Higher Edn. Commn., 1969-71, Wyo. Health Access Task Force, 2003-04; mem. Nat. Petroleum Coun., 1972-77; chmn. trustees Sierra Madre Found. for Geol. Rsch., New Haven; chmn. Wyo. Nat. Gas Pipline Authority, 1987-88; bd. dirs. Ucross Found., Denver; mem. Nat. Pub. Lands Adv. Coun., 1981-85; trustee Nature Conservancy, 1993-2005; chmn. Wyo. Health Reform Commn., 1993-95, Universidad del Valle Found., Guatemala City, 1995-2000, trustee, 2000-2005. Sgt. USMC, 1943-46. Mem. Rocky Mountain Oil and Gas Assn., Petroleum Assn. Wyo., Kiwanis, Casper Country Club, Casper Petroleum Club, Yale Club N.Y. Republican. Unitarian Universalist. Home and Office: PO Box 2875 Casper WY 82602-2875 Office Phone: 307-234-8925.

STROPKI, JOHN M., JR., electric power industry executive; BS indsl. engring., Purdue Univ.; MBA, Ind. Univ. Sales trainee Lincoln Electric Holdings, 1972, dist. mgr., nat. sales mgr., 1992—94, exec. vice-pres., 1996, dir., 1998—, COO, 2003—04, CEO, 2003—04, chmn., pres., CEO, 2004—. Mem. Am. Lung Assn.; Juvenile Diabetes Research Found.; mem. bd. Greater Cleveland Growth Assn., Great Lakes Sci. Ctr. Mem.: Nat. Electrical Manufacturers Assn. (mem. bd. gov.), Gas & Welding Distbr. Assn., Manufacturers Alliance/MAPI (pres. coun.), Am. Welding Soc. (hon.). Office: Lincoln Electric Holdings 22801 St Clair Ave Cleveland OH 44117 Office Phone: 216-481-8100. Office Fax: 216-486-1751. *

STROSCIO, MICHAEL ANTHONY, physicist, researcher; b. Winston-Salem, NC, June 1, 1949; s. Anthony and Norma Lee (Sidbury) S.; m. Mitra Dutta; children: Elizabeth de Clare, Charles Marshall Sidbury, Gautam Dutta. BS, U. N.C., 1970; MPhil in Physics, Yale U., 1972, PhD in Physics, 1974. Physicist Los Alamos Sci. Lab., N.Mex., 1975-78; sr. staff mem. Johns Hopkins U. Applied Physics Lab., Laurel, Md., 1978-80; prof. mgr. for electromagnetic research Air Force Office of Sci. Research, Washington, 1980-83; spl. asst. to research dir. Office of Under Sec. Def., Washington, 1982-83; policy analyst White House Office of Sci. and Tech. Policy, Washington, 1983-85; prof. dir. for microelectrons, prin. scientist U.S. Army Research Office, Research Triangle Park, NC, 1985—2001; adj. prof. depts. physics and elec. and computer engring. N.C. State U., Raleigh, 1985—; Richard and Loan Hill prof. depts. bioengring., elec. and computer engring., physics U. Ill., Chgo., 2001—, dir. grad. studies, 2002—04. Adj. prof. depts. elec. engring. and physics Duke U., Durham, 1986-2005, dept. physics U. Ill., Chgo., 2002—; vis. prof. dept. elec. engring. U. Va., Charlottesville, 1990-95, U. Md., College Park, 1996-97; mem. congrl. coun. Duke U. Chapel, 1989-91; lectr. UCLA, 1987, U. Mich., 1988; cons. U.S. Dept. Energy, Washington, 1985-90; vice-chmn. White House Panel on Sci. Comm., Washington, 1983-84; chmn. Dept. Def. Rsch. Instrumentation Com., Washington, 1982; assoc. mem. Adv. Group on Electron Devices, 1985-91, liaison Nat. Laser Users Facility, Rochester, N.Y., 1984; liaison Panel on Sci. Comm. and Nat. Security, NAS, 1982, Panel on Materials for High-Density Electron Packaging, 1987-90; U.S. Army liaison to JASON, 1991-2001; mem. U.S. Govt. coord. com. on Semicondr. Rsch. Corp., 1992-2001; reviewer Irish Sci. Found. Author: Positronium: A Review of the Theory, 1975, Onslow Families, 1977, Quantum Heterostructures: Microelectronics and Optoelectronics, 1999, Phonons in Nanostructures, 2001, Biological Nanostructures and Applications of Nanostructures in Biology, 2004; editor: Quantum-Based Electronic Devices and Systems, 1998, Advanced Semiconductor Lasers and Applications to Optoelectronics, 2000, Advanced Semiconductor Heterostructures, 2003; reviewer: Army Rsch. Office, US Dept. Energy, NSF, Office of Naval Rsch., Dept. Commerce and the Natural Scis., Engring. Rsch. Coun. Can., 1981—, Irish Sci. Found., 2003, referee jours., —; contbr. articles to profl. jours. Capt. USAF, 1974-75. Grantee Los Alamos Sci. Lab., 1977, Air Force Office Sci. Rsch., 2002—, Army Rsch. Office, 2003—, Def. Advanced Rsch. Projects Agy., 2002—, Dept. Homeland Security, Def. Threat Reduction Agy., NSF, SRC, 2004-06. Fellow AAAS, APS, IEEE (exec. com. for plasma sci. 1983—, Harry Diamond Meml. award 1998), Yale Sci. and Engring. Assn. (exec. bd. dirs. 1983—), Army Rsch. Lab.; mem. Nat. Geneal. Soc., Phi Beta Kappa. Achievements include patents in field. Home: 2045 Central Ave Wilmette IL 60091-2383 Office: U Ill Dept Elec and Computer Engring MC154 851 S Morgan St Chicago IL 60607 Home Phone: 847-920-1479; Office Phone: 312-413-5968. Business E-Mail: stroscio@uic.edu, m.stroscio@gte.net.

STROSS, CYNTHIA, lawyer; b. Seattle, May 7, 1967; BA magna cum laude, Kenyon Coll., 1999; JD cum laude, Cornell Univ., 1994. Bar: Wash. 1994. Assoc. atty., litig., alternative dispute resolution Savitt & Bruce, LLP, Seattle. Contbr. articles to numerous profl. jours. Named Wash. Rising Star, SuperLawyer Mag., 2006. Mem.: ABA, Wash. Bar Assn. Office: Savitt & Bruce LLP Puget Sound Plz Ste 1410 1325 Fourth Ave Seattle WA 98101

STROSS, JEOFFREY KNIGHT, internist, educator; b. Detroit, May 2, 1941; s. Julius Knight and Molly Ellen S.; m. Ellen Nora Schwartz; children: Wendy, Jonathan. BS in Pharmacy, U. Mich., 1962, MD, 1967. Diplomate Am. Bd. Internal Medicine. Intern Univ. Mich. Hosp., Ann Arbor, 1967-68, resident in internal medicine, 1971-73; instr. internal medicine U. Mich., Ann Arbor, 1973-74, asst. prof., 1974-79, assoc. prof., 1979-87, prof., 1987—. Contbr. numerous articles to med. jours. Served to maj. USAF, 1969-71. Nat. Heart, Lung and Blood Inst. grantee, 1975—. Fellow ACP; mem. Soc. for Gen. Internal Medicine (regional chmn. 1984-86). Jewish. Home: 824 Asa Gray Dr Ann Arbor MI 48105-2853 Office: U Mich Med Sch 3119 Taubman Ann Arbor MI 48109-0376 E-mail: jstross@umich.edu.

STROSS, RANDALL E., business history professor, columnist; BA, Macalester Coll.; PhD in History, Stanford Univ. Prof. bus. history San Jose State Univ. Digital Domain columnist New York Times; columnist U.S. News & World Report; vis. scholar History Dept. & Prog. in History and Philosophy of Sci. and Tech., Stanford Univ. Author: eBoys: The First Inside Account of Venture Capitalists At Work, Steve Jobs and the NeXT Big Thing, The Microsoft Way, Technology & Society in Twentieth-Century America; contbr. articles to Wall Street Journal, The New Republic, Fortune. Rsch. fellowship, Nat. Endowment for the Humanities. Mailing: New York Times 229 W 43d St New York NY 10036 Office Phone: 212-556-7395.

STROSSEN, NADINE, legal association administrator, educator; b. Jersey City, Aug. 18, 1950; d. Woodrow John and Sylvia (Simicich) S.; m. Eli Michael Noam, Apr. 25, 1980. AB, Harvard U., 1972, JD magna cum laude, 1975; LHD (hon.), U. Vt., 1992; LHD, U. RI, 1992; JD (hon.), San Joaquin Coll. Law, 1996; LHD (hon.), Rocky Mountain Coll., 1996, Mass. Sch. Law, 2000. Jud. clk. Minn. Supreme Ct., St. Paul, 1975-76; assoc. Lindquist & Vennum, Mpls., 1976-78, Sullivan & Cromwell, NYC, 1978-83; prof. clin. law, supervising atty. Civil Rights Clinic NYU Sch. Law, 1984-88; prof. law NY Law Sch., NYC, 1988—; adj. prof. Columbia U., 1990—; pres. ACLU, NYC, 1991—. Editor Harvard Law Rev., 1975; contbr. chpts. to books, articles to profl. jours.; author: In Defense of Pornography: Free Speech and the Fight for Women's Rights, 1995. Mem. Coun. Fgn. Rels., 1994—. Recipient Outstanding Young Person award Jaycees Internat., 1986; named one of Ten Outstanding Young Ams., US Jaycees, 1986; adj. fellow Yale U. Calhoun Coll., 1997-. Mem. ACLU, Nat. Coalition Against Censorship (bd. dirs. 1988—), Human Rights Watch (exec. com. 1989-91), Harvard Club (NYC). Avocations: travel, skiing, singing. Office: NY Law Sch 57 Worth St New York NY 10013-2960 also: ACLU 125 Broad St 18th Fl New York NY 10004 E-mail: nstrossen@aclu.org. *

STROTE, JOEL RICHARD, lawyer; b. NYC, Apr. 19, 1939; s. Jack and Fortuna (Benezra) S.; children: Jared, Noah, Sebastian; m. Elisa Ballestas, Dec. 14, 1991. BA, U. Mich., 1960; JD, Northwestern U., 1963. Bar: N.Y. 1964, D.C. 1965, Calif. 1967, U.S. Dist. Ct. (cen. dist.) Calif. 1967, U.S. Supreme Ct. 1971, Nev., 2003. Assoc. Damman, Blank, Hirsh & Heming, NYC, 1964-65, ICC, Washington, 1965-66, Capitol Records, Hollywood, Calif., 1966-67; ptnr. Strote & Whitehouse, Beverly Hills, Calif., 1967-89; of counsel Selvin, Weiner & Ruben, Beverly Hills, Calif., 1989-94; ptnr. with Cohen, Strote & Young, 1992-94; sole practice law, 1994—. Judge pro tem L.A. County Mcpl. Ct., 1973—; probation monitor Calif. State Bar Ct., L.A., 1985—; pres. Liberace Found., Las Vegas, Nev., 1987-2005; bd. chmn. Tuesday's Child, L.A., 1989-91. Mem. Thousand Oaks Arts Commn., 1997-99. Cpl. USMC, 1963-64. Mem. Calif. State Bar Assn., L.A. County Bar Assn., L.A. Copyright Soc., Beverly Hills Bar Assn., Assn. Internat. Entertainment Lawyers, Internat. Fedn. of Festival Orgns. Democrat. Jewish. Avocations: swimming, bicycling, hiking, opera, travel. Office: 200 N Westlake Blvd Ste 204 Westlake Village CA 91392 Home Phone: 805-494-1324; Office Phone: 818-707-1923. Personal E-mail: joelstrote@verizon.net.

STROTHER, ALLEN, biochemical pharmacologist, researcher; b. Nolan County, Tex., Feb. 20, 1928; s. Henry Allen and Minnie Etta (Taylor) S.; m. Julia Ann Gutch, Feb. 7, 1957; children: Wesley Allen, Lori Ann. BS, Tex. Tech U., 1955; MS, U. Calif., 1957; PhD, Tex. A&M U., 1963. Rsch. asst. Tex. A&M, Coll. Sta., 1959-63; rsch. biochemist FDA, Washington, 1963-65; asst. prof. pharmacology Loma Linda (Calif.) U., 1965-70, assoc. prof., 1970-75, prof., 1975-95, retired, vol. faculty, 1995—, prof. emeritus Physiology and Pharmacology, 1997—. Cons. WHO, Geneva, 1982-86. Contbr. numerous articles to profl. jours.; chpt. to WHO Bull. Pilot CAP/USAF Search and Rescue San Bernardino, Calif., 1967-95; pilot examiner CAP Air Force Aux., Norton AFB, 1970-86. Named Investigator of Yr. Walter E. McPherson Soc., Loma Linda U., 1984, Basic Sci. Fellow of Yr., 1986, Outstanding Faculty Rschr. of Yr. award, 1997. Mem. Am. Soc. Pharmacology and Exptl. Therapeutics, Am. Chem. Soc., Xzenobiotic Soc. Avocations: flying, golf. Home: 74448 Nevada Cir E Palm Desert CA 92260-2269 Office: Loma Linda U Sch Medicine Dept Physiology and Pharmacology Loma Linda CA 92354

STROTHER, JAMES M., lawyer; b. 1951; BA, JD, Univ. Minn. Pvt. practice, Mpls.; asst. gen. counsel Norwest Corp. (now Wells Fargo Home Mortgage), 1986—98; gen. counsel Wells Fargo Home Mortgage, 1998—2001; dep. gen. counsel Wells Fargo & Co., San Francisco, 2001—03, exec. v.p., gen. counsel, 2004—. Office: Wells Fargo & Co 633 Folsom St San Francisco CA 94107 *

STROTHER, PATRICK JOSEPH, public relations executive; b. St. Louis, Dec. 14, 1953; s. Arch Oscar Strother and Mary Margaret Boyle; m. Patricia Henning; children: Sara Ann, Ryan Joseph. BS with distinction, U. Minn., 1978; MBA, U. St. Thomas, St. Paul, 1982. V.p. investor rels. First Bank System, Mpls., 1983-90; pres. Cevette and Co. Advt. and Pub. Rels., Mpls., 1990-92; founder, pres. Strother Comms. Group Pub. Rels., Mpls., 1992—. Adj. prof. Coll. St. Thomas, St. Paul, 1984-86, Coll. St. Catherine, St. Paul, 1986-92, vis. assoc. prof., U. Minn. Sch. Journalism, 1999. Bd. dirs. Trade Acceptance Group, Ltd.; bd., Human Devel. and Edn., Coll. Univ. Minn. Mem. Pub. Rels. Soc. Am., Counselors Acad., Nat. Investor Rels. Inst., Minn. Guitar Soc. Avocations: 6 and 12 string guitars, studio recording, weightlifting, reading, bicycling, fine art collector. E-mail: pats@scgpr.com.

STROTHMAN, JAMES EDWARD, editor-in-chief; b. Pitts., Mar. 27, 1939; s. Edward Charles and Harriet Hope (Jones) S.; m. Eleanor Shawfield Jacobs, Sept. 9, 1961; children— Joseph, Jill, Stuart. BA in Journalism, Pa. State U., University Park, 1961. Asst. city editor, city hall reporter Williamsport Grit, Pa., 1961-64; with Miami Herald, Fla., 1964-67; aerospace writer AP, Cape Kennedy, Fla., 1967-69; reporter Los Angeles bur. Electronic News, 1969-71, sr. editor computer news sect., 1971-73, mng. editor, 1973; sr. info. rep. corp. hdqrs., then program adminstr. data processing divsn. hdqrs. IBM Corp., 1973-77, mgr. ea. area comm. data processing divsn., 1977-79, field comm. mgr. data processing divsn., 1979-81, mgr. comm. rsch. divsn., 1981; free-lance writer and cons. Strothman Assocs., 1981-82; editor-in-chief MIS Week, NYC, 1982-88; free-lance writer, cons., 1988-89; editor-in-chief Computer Pictures, Chappaqua, NY, 1989-94; news editor InTech Mag. and ISA On Line Instrument Soc. Am. (ISA), Research Triangle Park, NC, 1994-2000. Online editor, eCommerce Bus. Mag., 2000-01; assoc. editor InTech Mag., 2001-02; freelance writer, mktg. comm. cons., 2003—. Episcopalian.

STROTHMAN, WENDY JO, literary agent; b. Pitts., July 29, 1950; d. Walter Richard and Mary Ann Strothman; children: Andrew Richard, Margaret Ann; m. John P. Bishop, Aug. 27, 2005. Student, U. Chgo., 1979-80; AB, Brown U., 1972. Copywriter, mktg. U. Chgo. Press, 1973-76, editor, 1977-80, gen. editor, 1980-83, asst. dir., 1983; dir. Beacon Press, Boston, 1983-95; v.p., pub. adult, trade and reference Houghton-Mifflin, Boston, 1995-96, exec. v.p. trade and reference divsn., 1996—2002, lit. agent, 2003—. Trustee Brown U., 1990-96, Deerfield Acad., 2003—. Edtl. adv. bd. Scholarly Pub., 1993-94; bd. editors Brown Alumni Monthly, 1983-89; chmn., 1986-89. Bd. dirs. Editorial Project for Edn., trustee, 1987-91, treas., 1988-90. Fellow Brown U., 1997—. Mem. Renaissance Soc. (bd. dirs. 1980-83), Assn. Am. Pubs. (Freedom to Read com.), Pubs. Lunch Club (N.Y.C.), PEN New Eng. (adv. bd.), Examiner Club, NacRe Reins. Corp. (bd. dirs.). Office: The Strothman Agy LLC One Faneuil Hall Marketplace Third Fl Boston MA 02109

STROTMAN, LINDA ANN, language educator; b. Cin., Mar. 12, 1950; d. Cyril Joseph and Marjorie Ann Bastian; m. Thomas F. Strotman, July 25, 1973; children: Michael, David, Anthony. AB, Thomas More Coll., Ft. Mitchell, Ky., 1972; MEd in Spanish, Xavier U., Cin., 1978. Spanish tchr. Marian HS, Cin., 1972—76, Covington Cath. HS, Ky., 1984—92, St. Ursula Acad., Cin., 1993—. Mem.: Am. Assn. Tchrs. of Spanish and Portuguese. Business E-Mail: lstrotman@saintursula.org.

STROUCKEN, ALBERT P. L., consumer products company executive, former chemical company executive; b. July 9, 1947; Exec. v.p. industrial chemicals divsn. Bayer Corp., 1992—97; gen. mgr. inorganic chemicals divsn. Bayer AG, 1997—98; pres., CEO H.B. Fuller Co., St. Paul, 1998—2006, chmn., 1999—2006; chmn., CEO Owens-Illinois, Inc., Toledo, 2006—. Bd. dir. Baxter Internat., Owens Illinois. Bd. dir. Twin Cities United Way; chmn. Minn. Bus. for Early Learning. Office: Owens-Illinois Inc One SeaGate Toledo OH 43666

STROUD, JAMES STANLEY, retired lawyer; b. Wimbledon, ND, Jan. 26, 1915; s. Herbert Montgomery and Amanda Getchell (Longfellow) S.; m. Marjorie Marsh Hovey, Sept. 11, 1940; children: Jay Stanley, Steven Hovey. AB, Jamestown Coll., 1936; JD, U. Chgo., 1939. Bar: Ill. 1939, U.S. Supreme Ct. 1945, D.C. 1972. Counsel Ill. Mcpl. Code Commn., Chgo., 1939-40; bill drafter Ill. Legis. Ref. Bur., Springfield, 1941; from assoc. to ptnr. Mayer, Brown Row & Maw LLP, Chgo., 1941-71, ptnr.-in-charge Washington, 1972-80, ret., 1982. Bd. dirs. Chgo. Community Renewal Found., 1962-70; mem. adminstrv. bd. Nat. United Meth. Ch., Washington, 1982-84; coord. Extended Family Program, 1981-82. Capt. AUS, 1943-46. Home: Cottage 304 3300 Darby Rd Haverford PA 19041-1063

STROUD, JOHN FRED, JR., judge; b. Hope, Ark., Oct. 3, 1931; s. John Fred and Clarine (Steel) S.; m. Marietta Kimball, June 1, 1958; children: John Fred III, Ann Kimball, Tracy Steel. Student, Hendrix Coll., Conway, Ark., 1949-51; BA, U. Ark., 1959, LLB, 1960. Bar: Ark. 1959, Tex. 1988, US Supreme Ct. 1963, cert.: Ark. (mediator). Ptnr. Stroud & McClerkin, 1959-62; city atty. City of Texarkana, Ark., 1961; legis. asst. to US Senator John L. McClellan, 1962-63; ptnr. Smith, Stroud, McClerkin, Dunn & Nutter, 1963-79, 81-95; assoc. justice Ark. Supreme Ct., Little Rock, 1980; judge Ark. Ct. Appeals, Little Rock, 1996—2001, chief judge, 2001—04. Chmn. Texarkana Airport Authority, 1966-67, Texarkana United Way Campaign, 1988; pres. Caddo area coun. Boy Scouts Am., 1971-73; former trustee Ark. Nature Conservancy; former bd. dirs. Ark. Cmty. Found.; mem. adv. bd. Donald W. Reynolds Inst. On Aging; former pres. Red River Valley Assn.; former commr. Red River Compact Commn.; past vice chmn. Ark. Water Code Study Commn.; chmn. bd., chmn. coun. ministries Meth. Ch. Lt. col. USAF, 1951-56, Res. ret. Recipient award of exceptional accomplishment Ark. State C. of C., 1972, 86, Silver Beaver and Disting. Eagle awards Boy Scouts Am., Joint Presdl. award of excellence Ark. Bar Assn. and Ark. Bar Found., 2007; named Outstanding Young Man of Texarkana, 1966, One of Five Outstanding Young Men of Ark., 1967, Outstanding Alumnus of U. Ark. Law Sch., 1980. Fellow Am. Bar Found.; mem. ABA, Ark. Bar Assn. (chmn. exec. coun. 1979-80, pres. 1987-88, C.E. Ransick award of excellence 1990-91, Presdl. award of excellence and Charles L. Carpenter Meml. award 1997-98, Golden Gavel award 2006), Four States Area Estate Planning Coun. (past chmn.), State Bar Tex., Miller County Bar Assn. (past pres.), Texarkana Bar Assn. (pres. 1982-83), Ark. Bar Found. (chmn. 1974-75, chmn. trust com. 2003-06), Am. Coll. Trust and Estate Counsel (chmn. Ark. chpt. 1986-91), S.W. Ark. Bar Assn., N.E. Tex. Bar Assn., Assn. Atty.-Mediators, Texarkana C. of C. (pres. 1969, C.E. Palmer award 1979), U. Ark. Law Alumni Soc. (bd. dirs.), Texarkana Country Club (pres. 1990-92), Rotary (pres. Texarkana 1965-66) Avocations: tennis, golf, hunting, fishing. Office: 405 Walnut Texarkana AR 71854 Office Phone: 870-772-0718. Personal E-mail: jstroudadr@yahoo.com.

STROUD, PATRICIA TYSON, writer; b. Phila., Dec. 22, 1932; d. George Peterson and Jane (Chapman) Huber; m. Noel J. Tyson, Sept. 8, 1956 (dec. July 1982); children: John Tyson II, Peter H. Tyson, Lisa Tyson Ennis; m. Morris Wistar Stroud III, Mar. 11, 1989 (dec. Apr. 1990); m. Alexander McCurdy III, Nov. 16, 1991. AB, Smith Coll., Northampton, Mass., 1955. Writer, pub. rels. releases First Pa. Bank, Phila., 1968-69; editor, Frontiers Acad. Natural Scis., Phila., 1979-82; writer pvt. practice, Phila., 1982—. Author: Thomas Say: New World Naturalist, 1992, The Emperor of Nature: Charles Lucien Bonaparte and His World, 2000, The Man Who Had Been King: The American Exile of Napoleon's Brother Joseph, 2005; contbr. articles to profl. jours. Pres. bd. dirs. Ga. Farm Found., 1990—; bd. dirs. Hist. Bartram's Garden, 1992—98, U. Pa. Press, 1999—2003. Avocations: reading, gardening, piano. Personal E-mail: patriciatysonstroud@verizon.net.

STROUD, ROBERT EDWARD, lawyer; b. Chester, SC, July 24, 1934; s. Coy Franklin and Leila (Caldwell) S.; m. Katherine C. Stroud, Apr. 8, 1961; children: Robert Gordon, Margaret Lathan. AB, Washington and Lee U., 1956, LLB, 1958. Bar: Va. 1959, U.S. Ct. Appeals (4th cir.) 1967, U.S. Tax Ct. 1959. Assoc. McGuire Woods, LLP, Charlottesville, Va., 1959-64; ptnr. McGuire Woods, LLP, Charlottesville, Va., 1964—2002, exec. com., 1978-89. Lectr. math. Washington and Lee U., 1957-59; lectr. bus. tax Grad. Bus. Sch., U. Va., Charlottesville, 1969-87, lectr. corp. taxation law sch., 1985-91; lectr. to legal edn. insts., lectr. in corp. law Washington and Lee Law Sch., Lexington Va., 1984. Co-author: Buying, Selling and Merging Businesses, 1975; editor-in-chief Washington and Lee Law Rev., 1959; editor: Advising Small Business Clients, Vol. 1, 1978, 4th edit., 1994, Vol. 2, 1980, 3d edit., 1990; contbr. articles to profl. jours. Pres. Charlottesville Housing Found., 1968-73; mem. mgmt. coun. Montreat Conf. Ct., NC, 1974-77; trustee Presbyn. Found., 1972-73, Union Theol. Sem., Va., 1983-91; bd. dirs. Presbyn. Outlook Found., 1968-02, pres., 1985-88; mem. governing coun. Presbyn. Synod of the Virginias, 1973-78, moderator of coun., 1977-78, moderator of Synod, 1977-78; trustee, v.p. Va. Tax Found., 1984-95; adv. bd. Westminster Orgn. Concert Series, 1989-93; bd. dirs. Shannon Found. for Excellence in Pub. Edn., Charlottesville, 1996—; adv. bd. Ashlawn-Highland Summer Festival, 1989-03, pres., 1994-00; bd. dirs. Ash Lawn Opera Festival Found., 2003-05, gov. coun. Presbyn. Presbytery of the James, 1993-96, moderator of coun., 1995-96; moderator of presbytery, 1997; dir. Nat. Soc. Arts and Letters, Va. and NC chpt., 2005-, treas., 2006-. Capt. inf. US Army, 1958, with res. 1958-70. Fellow Am. Bar Found., Va. Law Found.; mem. ABA, Am. Judicature Soc., Nat. Soc. Arts and Letters, Va. State Bar, Va. Bar Assn., Washington and Lee Law Sch. Assn. (governing coun. 1974-80, pres. 1979-80), Order of the Coif (hon.), Phi Delta Sigma, Omicron Delta Kappa, Phi Delta Phi. Democrat. Home: 345 Terrell Ct Charlottesville VA 22901-2171 Office: McGuire Woods LLP PO Box 1288 Charlottesville VA 22902-1288 E-mail: rstroud@mcguirewoods.com.

STROUD, ROBERT MICHAEL, biophysicist, educator, biotechnologist; b. Stockport, Eng., May 24, 1942; BA in Natural Sci., Cambridge U., Eng., 1964, MA in Natural Sci., 1968; MS in Crystallography, London U., 1965, PhD, 1968. Asst. prof. chemistry Calif. Inst. Tech., Pasadena, 1971-75, assoc. prof., 1975-77; prof. biochemistry, biophysics U. Calif., San Francisco, 1977—. Cons. NIH, 1976—, DeWitt Stetten lectr., 1984—. Editor Ann. Rev. Biophysics and Biomolecular Structure; mem. editorial bd. Protein Engring., Jour. Structural Biology; contbr. articles to profl. jours. Research grantee NIH, 1971—, NSF, 1971—. Fellow Royal Soc. Medicine, Am. Acad. Arts and Scis.; mem. NAS (elected mem.), UK Biophys. Soc., Am. Biophys. Soc. (pres. coun.), Fedn. Exptl. Biologists. Avocation: windsurfing. Business E-Mail: stroud@msg.ucsf.edu.

STROUP, DARRYL RAY, systems engineer; b. Denver, Colo., Aug. 5, 1953; s. Norman Glen and Darlene Edna (Porath) Stroup; m. Mary Meta Vensel, Dec. 9, 1972; children: Jared Norman, Caryn Meta Hill, Elizabeth Marie. BSEE cum laude, U. Utah, 1977; MSEE, Air Force Inst. Tech., Dayton, Ohio, 1981. Sys. flight test engr., USN Test Pilot Sch., Md., 1984; Program Management Def. Sys. Mgmt. Coll., Va., 1991. Chief FB 111 AMP avionics test engr. USAF, McClellan AFB, Calif., 1985—86, chief B-2 offensive avionics test engr. Edwards AFB, Calif., 1986—89; chief advanced sys. br. Asst. Sec. of Air Force (Acquisition), Pentagon, DC, 1989—90; lead F-15 program element Fighter Divsn., Asst. Sec. of Air Force (Acquisition), Pentagon, 1990—92; mgr. avionics, nav., and precision targeting sys. Adroit Sys. Inc, Alexandria, Va., 1992—96; CNS ATM lead sys. integration engr. USN, Patuxent River, Md., 2003—07, EW sys. team lead, 2007—. Contbr. articles to jours. Rsch. asst. Program in Occupl. Therapy Wash. Sch. of Medicine, St Louis, Mo., 1998—99; rsch. design engr. Ctrl. Inst. for the Deaf, St Louis, Mo., 2000; vol. Luth. Family Assn. and Luth. Hour Ministries, St Louis, 1999—2003. Maj. USAF, 1972—92. Decorated Meritorious Svc. medal USAF, Air Force Commendation medal. Mem.: Swedish Colonial Soc. Lutheran - Missouri Synod. Office: USN NAWCAD Bldg 2805 Patuxent River MD 20670 Home Phone: 301-866-9220. Office Fax: 301-757-6459. Business E-Mail: darryl.stroup@navy.mil.

STROUP, KALA MAYS, former education commissioner, educational alliance administrator; BA in Speech and Drama, U. Kans., 1959, MS in Psychology, 1964, PhD in Speech Comm. and Human Rels., 1974; EdD (hon.), Mo. Western State Coll., 1996; LHD (hon.), Harris-Stowe State Coll., 2000. V.p. acad. affairs Emporia (Kans.) State U., 1978-83; pres. Murray State U., Ky., 1983-90, S.E. Mo. State U., Cape Girardeau, 1990-95, Am. Humanics, Kansas City, Mo., 2002—; commr. higher edn., mem. gov.'s cabinet State of Mo., Jefferson City, 1995—2002. Pres. Mo. Coun. on Pub. Higher Edn.; mem. pres.'s commn. NCAA; cons. Edn. Commn. of States Task Force on State Policy and Ind. Higher Edn.; adv. bd. NSF Directorate for Sci. Edn. Evaluation; adv. com. Dept. Health, Edn. and Welfare, chair edn. com.; citizen's adv. coun. on state of Women U. S. Dept. Labor, 1974-76. Mem. nat. exec. bd. Boy Scouts Am., nat. exploring com., former chair profl. devel. com., mem. profl. devel. com., exploring com., Young Am. awards com., 1986-87, north ctrl. region strategic planning com., bd. trustees, nat. mus. chair; mem. Gov.'s Coun. on Workforce Quality, State of Mo.; bd. dirs. Midwestern Higher Edn. Commn.; chair ACE Leadership Commn.; mem. bd. visitors Air U.; v.p. Missourians for Higher Edn.; bd. dirs. St. Francis Med. Ctr. Found., 1990-95, Cape Girardeau C. of C., 1990-95, U. Kans. Alumni Assn.; pres. Forum on Excellence, Carnegie Found.; adv. bd. World Trade Ctr., St. Louis, Svc. Mems. Opty. Colls., 1997—; mem. Mo. Higher Edn. Loan Authority, 1995—, depts. econ. devel. & agrl. Mo. Global Partnership, 1995—, Mo. Tng. & Employment Coun., 1995-2002, Concordia U. Sys. Advancement Cabinet, State Higher Edn. Exec. Officers, 1995—, mem. com. workforce edn. and tng., 1996; bd. govs. Heartland's Alliance Minority Participation, 1995-2002; chair, mem. workforce devel. com. NPEC coun. U.S. Office of Edn., 1997—; bd. dirs. Midwestern Higher Edn. Com. Distributed Learning Workshop, 1998-2002, Dept. Natural Resources Minority Scholarship Adv. Bd.; chair Show Me Results sub-cabinet Educated Missourians; mem. Pub. Policy Initiative Stakeholder Com., 1999—; mem. Coun. Higher Edn. transfer and pub. interest com.; mem. access/diversity com. State Higher Edn. Exec. Officers; trustee, mem. adv. coun. Assn. Governing Bds. of Univs. and Colls. Ctr. for Pub. Edn., 2000—. ACE fellow; recipient Alumni Honor Citation award U. Kans., Award Distinction Profl. Black Men's Club, S.E. Mo., 1990, Dist. Svc. to Edn. award Harris-Stowe State Coll., 1996; named to U. Kans. Womans Hall of Fame, Ohio Valley Conf. Hall of Fame, 1997. Mem. Am. Assn. State Colls. and Univs. (past bd. dirs., mem. Pres.'s Commn. on Tchr. Edn., Task Force on Labor Force Issues and Implications for the Curriculum), Mortar Board, Phi Beta Kappa, Omicron Delta Kappa, Phi Kappa Phi, Rotary (found. Ednl. awards com.). Office Phone: 816-561-6415.

STROUP, RICHARD L., lawyer; b. Shelby, Ohio, May 17, 1948; BSME, Ohio Northern U., 1970; JD, U. Va., 1976. Bar: Va. 1976, DC 1977, lic.: US Ct. Appeals (Fed. Cir.) 1982, registered: US Patent & Trademark Office. Law clk. to Hon. Francis C. Brown Trial Divsn., US Ct. of Claims, 1976—77; patent examiner US Patent & Trademark Office; ptnr. Finnegan, Henderson, Farabow, Garrett & Dunner LLP, Washington, leader, Litig. Sect., mem. mgmt. com. Mem.: Internat. Trademark Assn., Am. Intellectual Property Law Assn., ABA, Va. Bar Assn., Bar Assn. DC, DC Bar Assn., Phi Kappa Phi, Tau Beta Pi. Office: Finnegan Henderson Farabow Garrett & Dunner LLP 901 New York Ave NW Washington DC 20001-3315 Office Phone: 202-408-4000. Office Fax: 202-408-4400. Business E-Mail: richard.stroup@finnegan.com.

STROUP, RICHARD LYNDELL, economist, educator, writer; b. Sunnyside, Wash., Jan. 3, 1943; s. Edgar Ivan and Inez Louise (Kellett) S.; m. Sandra Lee Price, Sept. 13, 1962 (div. Sept. 1981); children— Michael, Craig; m. Jane Bartlett Steidemann Shaw, Jan. 1, 1985; 1 child, David. Student, MIT, 1961-62; BA, MA, U. Wash., 1966, PhD in Econs., 1970. Asst. prof. econs. Mont. State U., Bozeman, 1969-74, assoc. prof. econs., 1974-78; dir. Office Policy Analysis, Dept. Interior, 1982-84; prof. econs. Mont. State U., 1978—2006, dept. head, 2003—06; pres. Polit. Economy Rsch. Inst., Raleigh, NC, 2007—. Sr. fellow Property and Environ. Rsch. Ctr., Bozeman, 1980-. Author: Eco-nomics, 2003; co-author: Natural Resources, 1983, Economics: Private and Public Choice, 11th edit., 2005, Basic Economics, 1993, What Everyone Should Know About Economics and Prosperity, 1993, Common Sense Economics, 2005; editor: Cutting Green Tape, 2000; also articles, 1972—; mem. editorial bd. Regulation, 1993—. Adj. scholar Cato Inst., 1993—. Mem. Am. Econ. Assn., Western Econ. Assn., So. Econ. Assn., Mont Pelerin Soc., Phila. Soc., Assn. Pvt. Enterprise Edn. (Hayeck Endowed chair econs. 2005). Episcopalian. Office: NCSU Econ 4102 Nelson Hall 2801 Founders Dr Raleigh NC 27695 Business E-Mail: rstroup@ncsu.edu,

STROUPE, ASHLEY W., engineer; BS in Physics, Harvey Mudd Coll., 1990; MS in Elec. and Computer Engring., George Mason U., 1998; MS in Robotics, Carnegie Mellon U., 2001, PhD in Robotics, 2003. Staff engr., Jet Propulsion Lab. NASA, 2003—. Mem., Lunar Ice Discovery Intiative Robotics Inst., Carnegie Mellon U., 1998—99, mem. mobile autonomous robot software project, 2000—03, mem., Minnow Project, 2000—03; robotic construction crew project tech. lead NASA, 2003—05, mem. Mars Exploration Rover flight project, 2003, mem. Mars Exploration Rovers Engring. Team, Jet Propulsion Lab, 2004—, single command approach and instrument placement, 2004—, wide area prospecting Jet Propulsion Lab. software lead, 2005—. Contbr. multiple conf. papers, book chpts. and jour. articles in robotics. Office: NASA-Jet Propulsion Lab M/S 82-105 4800 Oak Grove Dr Pasadena CA 91109 Office Phone: 818-393-7111. Office Fax: 818-393-3254. Business E-Mail: Ashley.W.Stroupe@jpl.nasa.gov.

STROUSE, JEAN, writer; b. LA, Sept. 10, 1945; d. Carl David and Louise (Friedberg) S. BA, Radcliffe Coll., 1967. Editl. asst. N.Y. Rev. of Books, 1967-69; freelance writer NYC, 1969-72; editor Pantheon Books, NYC, 1972-75; freelance writer NYC, 1975-79, 1983—2003; book critic Newsweek Mag., NYC, 1979-83; dir. Cullman Ctr. for Scholars and Writers N.Y. Pub. Libr., NYC, 2003—. Selection com. J.S. Guggenheim Found., N.Y.C., 1995-97, trustee, 1987-94, 2001—04, fellow, 1977, 86; exec. coun. Authors Guild; Ferris prof. journalism Princeton U., 1998; John J. Rhodes chair in Am. instns. and pub. policy Barrett Honors Coll., Ariz. State U., 2003. Author: Alice James, A Biography, 1980, Morgan American Financier, 1999; editor: Women & Analysis: Dialogues on Psychoanalytic Views of Femininity, 1974. Recipient Bancroft prize, Columbia U., 1981; fellow, NEH, 1976, 1992, John D. and Catherine T. MacArthur Found., 2002—06. Fellow, Am. Acad. Arts & Sci.; mem. Soc. Am. Historians (pres. 2001-02), Am Philos Soc, The Century Assn., Phi Beta Kappa (vis. scholar 1996-97).

STROUSS, CARLETON O., lawyer; BA, Bucknell Univ., 1974; JD, Pa. State Univ., 1977. Bar: Pa. 1977. Atty. Pa. Dept. Transp., 1980—85; chief counsel Pa. Turnpike Commn., 1985—87; adminstrv. ptnr. & mem. mgmt. com. Kirkpatrick & Lockhart Nicholson Graham LLP, Harrisburg, Pa. Trustee emeritus Wilson Coll.; mem. Transp. Rsch. Bd. Com. Contract Law. Master: James S. Bowman Am. Inn of Ct.; mem.: ABA (Forum on Constrn. Industry), Pa. Bar Assn. (chmn. Civil Litigation sect. 1991—93, chmn. Constrn. Litigation Com. 1986—90). Office: Kirkpatrick & Lockhart Nicholson Graham LLP Payne Shoemaker Bldg 240 N Third St Harrisburg PA 17101-1507 Office Phone: 717-231-4503. Office Fax: 717-231-4501. Business E-Mail: cstrouss@klng.com.

STROUSTRUP, BJARNE, computer science and engineering professor; b. Aarhus, Denmark, 1950; m. Marian Stroustrup; children: Annemarie, Nicholas. Grad., U. Aarhus, 1975; PhD in Computer Sci., Cambridge U., 1979. Joined Computer Sci. Rsch. Ctr., Bell Telephone Labs., Murray Hill, NJ, 1979; mem. AT&T Bell Labs. Rsch., head Large-Scale Programming Rsch. Dept., mem. Info. and Sys. Software Rsch. Lab.; Coll. Engring. chair prof. computer sci. Tex. A&M U., College Station, Tex., 2002—. Author: The C++ Programming Language, 1985, 1991, 1997, 2000; contbr. articles to profl. jours. Named one of Am.'s twelve top young scientists, Fortune Mag., 1990; recipient ACM Grace Murray Hopper award, 1993. Fellow: IEEE (Computer Entrepreneur Award 2004), Computer Hall of Fame; mem.: NAE, Tex. Acad. of Medicine, Engring. and Sci., Sigma Xi (William Procter Prize for Scientific Achievement 2005). Achievements include designer and original implementer of C++ programming language. Avocations: hiking, running, music, travel. Office: Tex A&M U Dept Computer Sci TAMU 3112 College Station TX 77843-3112 also: AT&T Rsch 180 Park Ave Florham Park NJ 07932-0971 E-mail: bs@cs.tamu.edu.

STROUTH, BARON HOWARD STEVEN, geologist, mining engineer; b. Frankfurt, Germany, Sept. 28, 1919; arrived in U.S., 1941; s. Baron Karl Siegfried and Ida (Morck) von Strauss; m. Penelope Ann Creamer-Osteen, Nov. 3, 1951. BSc, U. Sorbonne, 1939; PhD in Engring., Bretton Woods U., 1965; PhD in Engring. (hon.), Rochedale U., Can., 1970. Asst. mgr. Drexel Bros. Ltd., NYC, 1941—43; pres. Std. Mining, NYC, 1951-58, Stanleigh Uranium Mine, Toronto, Can., 1954-61; mng. dir. Norsul Oil and Mining Quito, Ecuador, 1961-71; dir., officer Mining and Oil Cos., various locations; founder, operator Stanleigh Uranium and Norsul Oil. Sr. trustee Weinguetter Baron K. S. von Strauss, Erben Trust, Vaduz, 1954—. Translator: author Rilke The Cornet, 1960, A Window to the Morrow, 1963, A Sonata for Frankfurt, 1967, Cities of the Break of Dawn, 1988, Beauty is Forever, 1996. Maj. USAR, 1943-69, ret. Recipient Conspicuous Svc. Cross, Gov. Dewey, 1947, French, Czech, Cambodian decorations. Fellow Explorers Club; mem. Can. Inst. Mining Engrs. (life), Am. Inst. Mining Engrs. (sr.; Legion of Honor), St. James Club (London), Ontario Club Toronto. Achievements include patents for mining and oil processes. Avocations: collector, antique books, pre-colombian art, antique maps.

STROYD, ARTHUR HEISTER, JR., lawyer; b. Pitts., Sept. 5, 1945; 1 child, Elizabeth. AB, Kenyon Coll., 1967; JD, U. Pitts., 1972. Bar: Pa. 1972, U.S. Dist. Ct. (we. dist.) Pa. 1972, U.S. Ct. Appeals (3d cir.) 1972. Law clk. to judge U.S. Ct. Appeals (3d cir.), Phila., 1972—75; with Reed, Smith, LLP, Pitts., 1975—2006, mng. ptnr., Allegheny Region, 1997—2001; ptnr. Del Sole Cavanaugh Stroyd, LLC, Pitts., 2007—. Mem. Nat. Adv. Coun. on Child Nutrition, U.S. Dept. Agriculture, 1984-85. Mem. Mt. Lebanon Zoning Hearing Bd., 1978-81; pres. bd. dirs. Mt. Lebanon Sch. dist., 1981-87; solicitor Allegheny County Rep. Com., 1988-95; pres. bd. dirs. Ctr. for Theatre Arts, Pitts., 1984-93; grad. Leadership Pitts., 1991-92; chair bd. dirs. Mt. Lebanon Hosp. Authority, 1993-01; bd. dirs. Neighborhood Legal Svcs. Assn., 1989-91, U. Pitts. Cancer Inst., 1993—, Leadership Pitts. Inc., 2006—, Material Handling Industry Found., 2006—; mem. alumni coun. Kenyon Coll., 1996-00; bd. dirs. Edn. Policy and Issues Ctr., 2000-03. Lt. USNR, 1969-71. Fellow Am. Coll. Trial Lawyers; mem. ABA, Pa. Bar Assn. (commn. for justice initiatives in Pa. 2004—), Allegheny County Bar Assn. (past pres., bd. govs., past chair civil litig. sect., past chmn. judiciary com.), Acad. Trial Lawyers (pres., bd. govs.), mem. Pa. Supreme Ct. Civil Procedural Rules Com., Duquesne Club, Pitts. Golf Club, Hist. Soc. We. Pa. (bd. dirs. 2000—). Episcopalian. Avocations: skiing, motorcycling, golf. Office: Del Sole Cavanaugh Stroyd LLC Ste 300 200 1st Ave Pittsburgh PA 15222 Office Phone: 412-261-2393. Business E-Mail: astroyd@dscslaw.com.

STRUBBE, THOMAS R., insurance industry executive; b. Ft. Wayne, Ind., Mar. 30, 1940; s. Rudolph C. and Maverne E. (Wagoner) S.; children: Tracy Lynn, Patrick Thomas, Christina Lee. BS, Ind. U., 1962; JD, Tulane U., 1965. Bar: Ind. 1965, Ill. 1969. Atty. Lincoln Nat. Life Ins. Co., Ft. Wayne, Ind., 1965-66, asst. counsel, 1967-68; with Washington Nat. Corp., Evanston, Ill., 1968-90, counsel, 1968-73, gen. counsel, 1973-79, corp. sec., 1970-84, v.p., 1975-79, sr. v.p., 1979-83, exec. v.p., 1983-84, pres., 1984-90, also bd. dirs., mem. exec. com.; pres., CEO Osborn Labs. Inc., Olathe, Kans., 1990-98, Guarantee Res. Life Ins. Co., Chgo., 1998-99, also bd. dirs., ret., 2000. V.p., bd. dirs., exec. com. Chgo. chpt. Epilepsy Found. Am., 1975—79; trustee Glencoe Union Ch., Ill., 1984—87; Stephen leader Trinity Luth. Ch., Kans., 2003—; bd. dirs. Assn. Retarded Citizens Ill., 1985—89, Northlight Theater, 1984—89. Lt. USNR, 1965—71. Lincoln Found. grantee, 1964. Mem. ABA, Assn. Life Ins. Counsel, Nat. Investor Rels. Inst., Am. Soc. Corp. Secs., Home Office Life Underwriters Assn., Ind. Bar Assn., Ill. Bar Assn., Skokie Country Club (Ill.), Shadow Glen Golf Club (Kans.), Hallbrook Country Club (Kans.), Hideaway Beach Club (Fla.), Rotary, VFW, Lambda Chi Alpha, Delta Sigma Pi. Home (Summer): 9210 Oak Valley Dr De Soto KS 66018-7994 Home (Winter): 6000 Royal Marco Way Unit 350 Marco Island FL 34145 Personal E-mail: tomstrubbe@yahoo.com.

STRUBEL, ELLA DOYLE, advertising executive, public relations executive; b. Chgo., Mar. 14, 1940; d. George Floyd and Myrtle (McKnight) D.; m. Richard Craig G'sell, Apr. 26, 1969 (div. 1973); m. Richard Perry Strubel, Oct. 23, 1976; stepchildren: Douglas Arthur, Craig Tollerton. BA magna cum laude, U. Memphis, 1962; MA, U. Ill., 1963. Staff asst. Corinthian Broadcasting Co., NYC, 1963-65; dir. advt. and pub. rels. WANE-TV, Ft. Wayne, Ind., 1965-66; asst. dir. advt. WBBM-TV, Chgo., 1966-67, mgr. sales promotion, 1967-69, dir. advt. sales promotion and info. svcs., 1969-70; dir. pub. rels. Waltham Watch Co., Chgo., 1973-74; mgr. advt. promotion and pub. rels. WMAQ-TV, Chgo., 1974-76; v.p. corp. rels. Kraft, Inc., Glenview, Ill., 1985-87; sr. v.p. corp. affairs Leo Burnett Co., Inc., Chgo., 1987-92, exec. v.p., 1992-98; mng. dir. EllaQuent Designs, 2002—. Pres. women's bd. Rehab. Inst. Chgo., 1982—84; chair Chgo. Network, 1994—95, Rehab. Inst. Chgo., 1998—2001; vice chair Chgo. Pub. Libr. Found.; bd. dirs. Rehab. Inst. Chgo. Named Outstanding Woman in Comms. in Chgo., YWCA, 1995, one of 100 Most Influential Women in Chgo., Crain's Chgo. Bus., 1996, Who's Who in Chgo. Bus., 2002. Mem. Casino Club, Econ. Club. Democrat. Presbyterian. Office: #1254 55 W Goethe St Chicago IL 60610-7406 Office Phone: 312-255-0235. Business E-Mail: estrubel@aol.com.

STRUBEL, RICHARD PERRY, Internet company executive; b. Evanston, Ill., Aug. 10, 1939; s. Arthur Raymond and Martha (Smith) S.; m. Linda Jane Freeman, Aug. 25, 1961 (div. 1974); children: Douglas Arthur, Craig Tollerton; m. Ella Doyle G'sell, Oct. 23, 1976. BA, Williams Coll., 1962; MBA, Harvard U., 1964. Assoc. Fry Cons., Chgo., 1964-66, mng. prin., 1966-68; with N.W. Industries, Inc., Chgo., 1968-83, v.p. corp. devel., 1969-73, group v.p., 1973-79, exec. v.p., 1979-83, pres., 1983; chmn. bd., pres. Buckingham Corp., NYC, 1972-73; pres., chief exec. officer Microdot Inc., Chgo., 1983-94; mng. dir. Tandem Ptnrs. Inc., Chgo., 1990-99; with UNext Inc., Deerfield, Ill., 1999, pres., COO, 1999—2004, vice chmn., dir., 2004—. Trustee Mut. Funds of The No. Trust Co., Chgo., and various mutual funds of Goldman Sachs Asset Mgmt., N.Y.C.; bd. dirs. Gildan Activewear, Inc., Montreal, Que., Can. Trustee U. Chgo.; mem. visiting com. Divinity Sch., U. Chgo.; mem. adv. bd. Martin Marty Ctr. Mem. Casino Club, Chicago Club, Comml. Club, Racquet Club of Chicago, Commonwealth Club, Econ. Club. Presbyterian. Office: UNext Inc Ste 455 111 N Canal St Chicago IL 60606

STRUBLE, JAMES CURTIS, ambassador; b. Visalia, Calif., Oct. 29, 1953; s. Arthur James and Ezella Ruby (Meek) S.; m. Susan Mary Briggs, Dec. 9, 1976; children: Peter James, Dale. BA in Slavic Lang. & Lit., U. Calif., Berkeley, 1975, BA in History, 1975. Vice consul Am. Consulate Gen., Monterrey, Mex., 1977-79; consul Am. Embassy USSR, Moscow, 1981-83; first sec. Am. Embassy Spain, Madrid, 1983-86; consul gen. Am. Embassy Honduras, Tegucigalpa, 1986-88; program assoc. Hoover Institution, Stanford, Calif., 1988—89; gen. consul Am. Embassy Thailand, Bangkok, 1994—96; dep. chief of mission Am. Embassy Ecuador, Quito, 1996—99; dir., office of Brazilian and So. cone affairs U.S. Dept. State, Washington, 1999—2001, dep. asst. sec., bureau of western hemisphere affairs, 2001—02, prin. dep. asst. sec., 2002, acting asst. sec., 2002—03, U.S. amb. to Peru Lima, 2003—. Mem.: Am. Fgn. Svc. Assn. Avocations: coin collecting/numismatics, history. Office: Am Embassy APO Lima AA 34031-5000 Peru

STRUCK, NORMA JOHANSEN, artist; b. West Englewood, NJ, Feb. 17, 1929; d. Hans Christian and Amanda (Solberg) Johansen; m. H. Walter Struck, Aug. 21, 1955; children: Steven, Laurie. Student, N.Y. Phoenix Sch. Design, 1946-50, Art Students' League, NYC, 1976-77. Staff artist Norcross, Inc., NYC, 1950-60, free-lance artist, 1967-75; artist portraits, prints Scafa-Tornabene, Nyack, NY, 1976—; artist portraits, paintings U.S.N., U.S. Coast Guard, Washington, 1976—. Com. bd. mem. Navy Art Coop. Liaison, N.Y.C., 1976-80, Coast Guard Art Program, N.Y.C., 1980—, Navy Hist. Mus., Washington. One-woman shows include Valley Cottage Gallery, NY, Bergen Co. Playhouse, Oradell, NJ, NY Yacht Club, 2003, Nabisco Co., Fairlawn, NJ, 1987; exhibited in group shows Navy Hist. Mus., Washington, 1976, Navy Combat Art Gallery, Washington, World Trade Ctr., 1979, USCG, New Eng. Air Mus., Windsor Locks, Conn., 1984, Fed. Hall, NYC, 1986, 93-97, Salmagundi Club, NYC, Officers Club, Governor's Island, Hudson Valley Show, White Plains, NY, Intrepid Mus., NYC, Alexander Hamilton U.S. Custom House, Newington-Cropsey Mus., NY, Bergen County Mus. Art & Sci., NJ; represented in permanent collections U.S. Pentagon, Washington, Henie-Onstad Mus., Oslo, World Figure Skating Hall of Fame and Mus., Colorado Springs, Alexander Hamilton Custom House, NYC, Nat. ARts Club, NYC. Recipient Louis E. Seley award, Navy Art Program, 1979; Grumbacher award, Catherine Lorillard Wolfe, Nat. Arts Club, N.Y.C., 1978; George Gray award Coast Guard Art Program, Governors Island, N.Y., 1983, 89. Fellow Am. Artists Profl. League (pres.'s award 1979); mem. Portrait Soc. Am., Art Students League (life), Hudson Valley Assn. (bd. dirs. 1985-88, M. Dole award 1980), Soc. Illustrators, Salmagundi Club, Portrait Soc. Am., Inc., Mus. of Women in the Arts (charter). Avocations: antiques, gourmet cooking. Home: 910 Midland Rd Oradell NJ 07649-1904 E-mail: njstruck99@cs.com.

STRUELENS, MICHEL MAURICE JOSEPH GEORGES, political science professor, consultant; b. Brussels, Mar. 10, 1928; m. Godelieve De Wilde, Aug. 2, 1949; children: Alain, Patricia, Brigitte, Bernard, Jean Paul (dec.). BA, Coll. St. Pierre, Brussels, 1944; MA, Antwerp U., Belgium, 1949; PhD, Am. U., Washington, 1968. Insp. econ. affairs Congo Govt., Leopoldville, 1950-54, chief insp. econ. affairs, 1954-55, dep. commr. transp., 1955-57; dir. Info. and Public Relations Office for Congo, Brussels, 1957-58, Congo Tourism Pavillion, Internat. World's Fair, Brussels, 1958-59; dir. gen. Belgian Congo and Ruanda Urundi Tourist Office, Congo, 1959; chmn. African Commn. Internat. Union Ofcl. Travel Orgns., Geneva, 1959-60; ofcl. Katanga rep. in U.S., NYC, 1960-63; dir. gen. Internat. Inst. for African Affairs in Can., 1963-64; spl. asst. to prime minister Democratic Republic Congo, fgn. affairs minister, adviser to Congo UN del., adviser Congo embassy Washington, NYC, 1964-66; dir. Eurafrica, Consultants on Fgn. Affairs, Washington, 1966—; prof. polit. sci., French, internat. bus. Am. U., 1968-93; prof. emeritus, 1993; dir. Ctr. Rsch and Documentation on European Community Am. U., 1971—, chmn. faculty rels. com., 1986-87, chmn. grad. studies com., SIS, 1989-90; dir. E.C. Inst. in Europe, 1978-93, U. Antwerp Exchange Program, 1979-83. Dir. EPSCI/ESSEC (France) Exchange Program, 1980-84, chmn. internat. bus. dept., 1980-84; dir. exchange program Bus. Sch. of Poly., U. Madrid, 1981-84; investment adviser, 1977—; adminstr. French Parish,, 1974-75, Ctr. Studies on Internat. Relations, 1987-96, Econs. and Bus., La Rochelle, France, 1987-96; exec. v.p. Eglise St. Louis Corp., French-Speaking Union, Washington, 1974-75; mgr. by agreement with European Communities, European Documentation Ctr. (CERDEC), accessing by satellite EC Data Banks, 1985— and providing through WCL Libr. of Am. U., On Line Pub. Access Cataloging, 1991—. Author: (with Inforcongo) Congo Belge et Ruanda-Urundi, 1958; monograph Le Canada à l'Heure de l'Afrique, 1964; The United Nations in the Congo - or ONUC and International Politics, 1976. Recipient Internat. Union Ofcl. Travel Orgns. Poster award Brussels, 1958, Etoile de Service en Argent King of Belgium, 1956; chevalier de l'Ordre Royal du Lion, 1957; Faculty award for outstanding contbn. to acad. program devel. Coll. Bus. Adminstrn., Am. U., 1979; Faculty award for outstanding teaching, 1980, 82, 84; Faculty award for outstanding service to Am. U., 1981 Mem. Golden Key, Phi Sigma Alpha. Clubs: Cosmos (Washington); Bukavu Royal Sports (founder 1950, pres. 1951-54, hon. pres. 1957) (Congo). Lodges: Rotary. Home: 1374 Woodside Dr Mc Lean VA 22102-1536 Office: Am U 4400 Mass Ave NW Washington DC 20016-8071 *"Ad Augusta per Angusta". Using Latin, French writer Victor Hugo said it all! Nothing comes easy and "success," a very personal perception indeed, requires a great deal of luck, perseverance and hard work. True success, though, is directly related to the pursuit of happiness, which in turn is a state of mind. If and when I reach eternity, I'll then be able to tell how successful I was during my passage on earth.*

STRUIF, L. JAMES, lawyer; b. Alton, Ill., Sept. 18, 1931; s. Leo John and Clara Lillie (Bauer) S.; m. Shirley Ann Spatz, Mar. 24, 1965; children: Scott B., Jamie Lynn Pehowski, Susan Marie Bazzell, Jeffrey James. BS, Northwestern U., 1953; JD, U. Ill., Champaign, 1960. Bar: Ill. 1960, U.S. Dist. Ct. (so. dist.) Ill. 1960. Gen. counsel So. Ill. U., 1960-64; pvt. practice Struif Law Offices, Alton, Ill., 1964—. Lectr. So. Ill. U., Edwardsville, 1960-65. Author: Guide to Law for Laymen, Field Guide to 150 Prairie Plants of S.W. Ill. Scoutmaster Boy Scouts Am., Alton, 1966-69; active civil rights worker, Miss., 1964; trustee The James and Aune Nelson Found. With USN, submarines 1953-57, Pacific. Recipient Chmns. award Madison County Urban League, Blazing Star award The Nature Inst. Democrat. Mem. United Ch. of Christ. Avocations: nature, gardening, science, piano, mathematics. Office: The Struif Law Offices 2900 Adams Pkwy Alton IL 62002-4857 Office Phone: 618-463-0700. Business E-Mail: struiflaw@piasa.net.

STRUKOFF, RUDOLF STEPHEN, retired music educator; b. Rostov, Don, Russia, July 18, 1935; came to U.S., 1951; s. Stephen and Olga (Flemming) S.; m. Donna Lee Hill, May 31, 1959; children: Rudolf Stephen, Jr., Robbin Stanley, Regan Stuart. B Music Edn., Andrews U., 1960; studied with Roger Wagner and Robert Shaw, 1960—63; MusM, Mich. State U., 1964, PhD in Music, 1970. Instr. music Mich. State U., East Lansing, 1963-65; asst. prof. Ind. State U., Terre Haute, 1966-69; assoc. prof. Andrews U., Berrien Springs, Mich., 1969-76; prof. music Gov's. State U., Univ. Park, Ill., 1977-97. Chorus master Ill. Philharm. Chorus, Park Forest, Ill., 1982-84; music dir. Univ. Cmty. Chorale, Univ. Park, Ill., 1978-96, Chamber Orch., Univ. Park, 1978-96. Composer: The Greatest of These, 1970, Childhood Sketches, 1973; singer (opera) Attila by Verdi, 1979; condr. Christmas Oratorio by Saint-Saens, 1986, Stabat Mater by Rossini, 1988, German Requiem by Brahms, 1989, Requiem by Mozart, 1990, Mass in C by Beethoven, 1991, Mass in E Flat by Schubert, 1992, Requiem in C Minor by Cherubini, 1993, Cathedral Series, Joliet, Ill., Mass in B Flat by Haydn, St. Liborius, Steger, Ill., 1994, Symphony #2 (Hymn of Praise), Temple Anshe Sholom, 1994, Olympia Fields, Ill., Requiem by Mozart, St. Liborius, Steger, Ill., 1995, Messiah by Handel, Ctr. for Performing Arts, University Park, Ill., 1995, Concert Overture and Requiem by Cherubini, 1996; rec. artist (CD) How Great Thou Art, 2003, My Native Land, 2003. Lectr. Lyric Opera, Chgo., 1979-89, Libr. Lectr. Series, Park Forest, 1982, Career Days, Chgo., 1982-97, Symposium on Soviet Russia, Univ. Park, 1985, Ill. Philharmonic Workshop Series, 1991-96. Mem. ASCAP, Chgo. Singing Tchrs. Guild (pres. 1984-86, 91-93, bd. dirs. 1986-96), Am. Choral Dirs. Assn., Nat. Assn. Tchrs. Singing, Nat. Assn. Schs. Music, Pi Kappa Lambda. Avocations: antiques, golf, reading.

STRULL, GENE, technology consultant, retired manufacturing executive; b. Chgo., May 15, 1929; s. Albert and Helen (Wolf) S.; m. Joyce Landsbaum, July 6, 1952; children— David Jay, Brian Lee. BSEE, Purdue U., 1951; MS, Northwestern U., 1952, PhD in Elec. Engring, 1954. With Westinghouse Electric Corp., Pitts., later Balt., 1954-93, supervisory engr., adv. engr., mgr. solid state tech.-aerospace, 1958-68, mgr. sci. and tech. systems devel. div., mgr. advanced tech. labs., 1968-78, dep. gen. mgr. systems devel. div., 1979-81, gen. mgr. advanced tech. div., 1981-93, exec. dir. tech., 1987-93. Cons. Army Sci. Bd., 1979-83, NRC-NAS, 1980-82, Def. Sci. Bd., 1981-83, NSF, 1992—; cons. NASA, 1967-87, com. chmn., 1976-78; adv. com. panel USNR, 1989. Contbg. author: Integrated Electronic Systems, 1970, Integrated Circuit Technology, 1967; contbr. articles to profl. jours.; patentee in field. Gene Strull Tech. Ctr. at Westinghouse Electric Corp. Advanced Tech. Labs. named in his honor, Balt., 1993; named Outstanding Elec. Engr. award Purdue U., 1994. Fellow IEEE (life, Govt. Industry Svc. award 1987, Frederik Philips award 1991); mem. Md. Acad. Scis. (chmn. 1978-80). Home: One Gristmill Ct # 606 Baltimore MD 21208

STRUM, BRIAN J., real estate company officer; b. Bklyn., Nov. 27, 1939; s. Max J. and Beatrix (Galitzky) S.; m. Mickey Weiss, Nov. 19, 1966; children: Ira, Howard, Beth. BA, Bklyn. Coll., 1960; LLB, NYU, 1963. Bar: N.Y. 1964, N.J. 1969; CLU; counselor of real estate. Atty. Gilbert, Segall and Young, NYC, 1963-65; assoc. res. atty. Prudential Ins. Co. Am., NYC, 1965-67, various positions, law dept., 1967-75, v.p. real estate investments, 1975-86; chmn. Prudential Property Co., Newark, 1986—94; CEO Prudential Realty Group, Newark, 1992-94; Silverstein chair of real estate devel. NYU, 1995-98. Pres., trustee Prudential Realty Trust, 1985-94; mem. adv. bd. Chgo. Title & Trust Co., N.Y.C., 1982-96. Editor: Financing Real Estate in the Inflationary Eighties, 1981; contbr. articles to profl. jours. With USAR, 1963-69. Recipient Disting. Cmty. Svc. award Brandeis U., 1983, Urban Leadership award NYU, 1990, Good Scout award N.Y.C. coun. Boy Scouts Am., 1991, Nat. Achievement awrd D.A.R.E. Am., 1993. Fellow Anglo Am. Real Property Inst. (charter); mem. ABA (chmn. real property, probate and trust law sects. 1984-85), N.Y. State Bar Assn. (chmn. real property sect. 1975-76), Urban Land Inst. (coun. mem.), Am. Coll. Real Estate Lawyers (charter), Am. Soc. Real Estate Counselors. Home: 435 Pine Ln Haworth NJ 07641-1308 Office Phone: 201-384-1400. Personal E-mail: mstrum77@aol.com.

STRUM, JAY GERSON, lawyer; b. NYC, July 6, 1938; s. John and Dorothy (Chaikind) S.; m. Patricia Ann Burtis, Jan. 25, 1969; children: Daniel, Jennifer. BA in polit. sci. magna cum laude, CCNY, 1959; LLB, Harvard U., 1962. Bar: N.Y. 1963, U.S. Dist. Ct. (so. and ea. dists.) N.Y. 1963, U.S. Ct. Appeals (2d cir.) 1965, U.S. Supreme Ct. 1979. Ptnr. SEC, NYC, 1963-65, Coon, Dubow, Kleinberg & Strum, 1965-67; assoc. Kaye, Scholer, Fierman, Hays & Handler, 1967-70; ptnr. Kaye, Scholer LLP, 1971—2007. Mem. ABA, Assn. of Bar of City of N.Y., Harvard Club (N.Y.C.), Phi Beta Kappa. Clubs: Harvard (N.Y.C.). Office: Kaye Scholer Fierman Hays & Handler LLP 425 Park Ave New York NY 10022-3506

STRUNJO, JACOB ANTHONY, elementary school educator; b. Germany, Mar. 6, 1951; arrived in US, 1957; s. Ivan and Katherine Strunjo; m. Nancy Strunjo; children: Kara, Kyle, Kate, Kirstin, Gerrit. Student, Greenfield CC, 1970—71, North Adams State Coll., Mass., 1971—73, U. Mass., 1975—76, Westfield State Coll., 2004—05. 3d grade tchr. Orange Elem. Schs., Mass. Home: 21 Shingle Brook Rd Orange MA 01364 Office: Orange Elem Schs 3 Dester St Ext Orange MA 01364

STRUNK, ROBERT CHARLES, physician; b. Evanston, Ill., May 29, 1942; s. Norman Wesley and Marion Mildred (Ree) S.; m. Juanita; children: Christopher Robert, Alix Elizabeth. BA in Chemistry, Northwestern U., 1964, MS in Biochemistry, 1968, MD, 1968. Lic. MD, Ariz., Colo., Mass., Mo. Resident in pediatrics Cin. Children's Hosp., 1968-70; pediatrician Newport (R.I.) Naval Hosp., 1970-72; rsch. fellow in pediatrics Harvard Med. Sch., Boston, 1972-74; asst. prof. pediatrics U. Ariz. Health Sci. Ctr., Tucson, 1974-78; dir. clin. svcs. Nat. Jewish Ctr. for Immunology and Respiratory Med., Denver, 1978-87; sabbatical leave Boston Children's Hosp., 1984-85; dir. divsn. allergy and pulmonary medicine Children's Hosp., St. Louis, 1987-98; pediatrician Barnes and Allied Hosp., St. Louis, 1987—; prof. pediatrics Washington U. Sch. Medicine, St. Louis, 1987—, Strominger prof., 2002—. Recipient Allergic Disease Acad. award Nat. Inst. Allergy and Infectious Disease of NIH. Mem. Am. Acad. Allergy and Immunology, Am. Thoracic Soc. Office: Washington U Sch Med Dept Pediatrics 1 Childrens Pl Saint Louis MO 63110-1002

STRUNZ, KAI, research scientist, educator; arrived in US, 2002; MS, Saarland U., Saarbruecken, Germany, 1996, PhD summa cum laude, 2001. Rsch. asst. Brunel U., London, 1995—97; engr. R&D Electricite de France, Paris, 1997—2002; asst. prof. U. Wash., Seattle, 2002—. Mem. editl. bd. IEEE Transactions on Power Electronics, 2006—, IET Renewable Power Generation, 2007—. Mem. editl. bd.: IET Renewable Power Generation, 2007—. Sgt. German Armed Forces, 1986—88. Recipient Best Master Degree in Saarland award, German Soc. Elec. and Electronic Engrs., 1996, Dr. Eduard Martin prize, Saarland U., 2002, Outstanding Tchg. award, Dept. Elec. Engring., U. of Wash., 2004; grantee CAREER award, NSF, 2003. Mem.: IEEE (mem. editl. bd. Transactions on Power Electronics 2006—), Internat. Assn. Hydrogen Energy. Achievements include research in multiscale modeling and simulation of electric networks; Stochastic modeling and simulation of electric networks; optimization of electric network design and operation. Office: Univ Washington Box 352500 Seattle WA 98195 Business E-Mail: strunz@u.washington.edu.

STRUTHERS, MARGO S., lawyer; BA, Carleton Coll., 1972; JD cum laude, U. Minn., 1976. Atty., shareholder Moss & Barnett, P.A. and predecessor firms, Mpls., 1976-93; ptnr. Oppenheimer Wolff & Donnelly, LLP, Mpls., 1993—. Mem. Am. Health Lawyers Assn., Minn. State Bar Assn. (bus. law sect., former chair nonprofit com., former chair and former mem. governing coun. health law sect.). Office: Oppenheimer Wolff & Donnelly LLP Plaza VII 45 S 7th St Ste 3300 Minneapolis MN 55402-1614 Office Phone: 612-607-7427, 612-607-7000. Business E-Mail: mstruthers@oppenheimer.com.

STRUTIN, KENNARD REGAN, lawyer, educator, librarian; b. Bklyn., Dec. 1, 1961; s. Fred and Estelle (Brodzansky) S. BA summa cum laude, St. John's U., Jamaica, NY, 1981; JD, Temple U. Sch. Law, Phila., 1984; MLS, St. John's U., 1994. Bar: N.Y. 1986, U.S. Dist. Ct. (ea. and so. dists.) N.Y. 1990, U.S. Dist. Ct. (no. and we. dists.) N.Y. 1991, U.S. Ct. Appeals (2d cir.) 1990, U.S. Ct. Appeals (fed. cir.) 1991, U.S. Tax Ct. 1991, U.S. Ct. Mil. Appeals 1991, U.S. Supreme Ct. 1990. Atty. pvt. practice, West Hempstead, N.Y., 1986; trial atty. Nassau County Legal Aid Soc., Hempstead, N.Y., 1987-88, Orange County Legal Aid Soc., Goshen, N.Y., 1988-90; atty. pvt. practice, West Hempstead, N.Y., 1990-91; staff atty. N.Y. State Defenders Assn., Albany, N.Y., 1991-93; adj. asst. prof. St. John's U., Jamaica, N.Y., 1993-96; small claims tax assessment hearing officer Supreme Ct., Nassau, Suffolk, N.Y., 1993-96; law libr. Syracuse U. Coll. Law, 1996-98; legal info. cons., 1998—2004; dir. legal info. svcs. N.Y. State Defenders Assn., Albany, 2004—. Spkr. lawyer in classroom Nassau County Bar Assn., Mineola, N.Y., 1987-94, pre-release program Correctional Facilities, Lower Hudson Valley, N.Y., 1989-94, CLE programs, 1999-. Author: ALI-ABA's Checklist Manual on Representing Criminal Defendants, 1998, Insider's Guide: Criminal Justice Resources on the Web, 2002; co-author: (computer-assisted, interactive instrnl. program) Legal Research Methodology, 1997; columnist NY Law Jour., 2005-; contbr. articles to profl. jours. Recipient Orange County Exec. Recognition award, 1990, 93, 2nd place winner libr. divsn. Donald Trautman Ctr. for Computer-Assisted Legal Instrn. Lesson Writing Competition, 1996-97. Mem. Beta Phi Mu.

STRUVE, GUY MILLER, lawyer; b. Wilmington, Del., Jan. 5, 1943; s. William Scott and Elizabeth Bliss (Miller) S.; m. Marcia Mayo Hill, Sept. 20, 1986; children: Andrew Hardenbrook, Catherine Tolstoy, Frank Leroy Hill, Guy Miller, Beverly Marcia Wise Hill (dec.), Elena Wise Struve-Hill. AB summa cum laude, Yale U., 1963; LLB magna cum laude, Harvard U., 1966. Bar: NY 1967, DC 1986, US Dist. Ct. (so. dist.) NY 1970, US Dist. Ct. (ea. dist.) NY 1973, US Dist. Ct. (no. dist.) Calif. 1979, US Dist. Ct. DC 1987, US Dist. Ct. (we. dist.) NY 1991, US Dist. Ct. (no. dist.) NY 2000, US Ct. Appeals (2d cir.) 1969, US Ct. Appeals (DC cir.) 1973, US Ct. Appeals (8th cir.) 1976, US Ct. Appeals (9th cir.) 1979, US Supreme Ct. 1971. Law clk. Hon. J. Edward Lumbard, Chief Judge United States Ct. Appeals for 2d Circuit, 1966-67; assoc. Davis Polk & Wardwell, NYC, 1967-72, ptnr., 1973—, Ind. Counsel's Office, 1987-94. Mem. ABA, NY State Bar Assn., Assn. Bar City NY (chmn. com. antitrust and trade regulation, 1983-86, chmn. com. fed. cts. 1998-2001), Am. Law Inst, Civil War Preservation Trust (trustee), Juvenile Diabetes Rsch. Found. (lay rev. com.). Office: Davis Polk & Wardwell 450 Lexington Ave Fl 30 New York NY 10017-3982 Office Phone: 212-450-4192. Business E-Mail: struve@dpw.com.

STRYER, LUBERT, biochemist, educator; b. Tientsin, China, Mar. 2, 1938; BS with honors, U. Chgo., 1957; MD magna cum laude, Harvard U., 1961; DS (hon.), U. Chgo., 1992. Helen Hay Whitney fellow Harvard U., also Med. Research Council Lab., 1961-63; from asst. prof. to assoc. prof. biochemistry Stanford U., 1963-69; prof. molecular biophysics and biochemistry Yale U., 1969-76; Winzer prof. neurobiology Stanford U. Sch. Medicine, 1976—2004, chmn. dept. structural biology, 1976-79, prof. emeritus, 2004—; chmn. sci. adv. bd. Affymetrix, Inc., 1993—; founder, chmn., chief sci. officer Senomyx, Inc., La Jolla, Calif., 1999-2001, chmn. sci. adv. bd., 2001—. Cons. NIH, NRC; pres., sci. dir. Affymax Rsch. Inst., Palo Alto, Calif., 1989-90; mem. sci. adv. bd. Jane Coffin Childs Fund, 1982-90, Rsch. to Prevent Blindness, 1984-93, Pew Scholars Profs. in Biomed. Scis.; chmn. sci. adv. bd. Perlegen Sciences, Inc. Mem. editorial bd.: Jour. Molecular Biology, 1968-72, Jour. Cell Biology, 1981-84; assoc. editor: Annual Revs. Biophysics and Bioengineering, 1970-76. Trustee Helen Hay Whitney Found., 1997—2001, McKnight Endowment for the Neuroscis., 1999—2007. Named 2006 Nat. Medal Sci. Laureate, NSF, 2007; recipient Alcon award in vision Alcon Rsch. Inst., 1992, Disting. Inventors award, Intellectual Property Owners' Assn., 1994, Molecular Bioanalytics award German Soc. Biochemistry and Molecular Biology, 2002, Frank Westheimer prize Harvard U., 2006, Carl Branden award Protein Soc., 2007. Fellow AAAS (Newcomb Cleveland prize 1992), Am.

Acad. Arts and Scis.; mem. NAS, Am. Chem. Soc.(award in biol. chemistry Eli Lilly & Co., 1970), Am. Soc. Biol. Chemists, Biophys. Soc., Am. Philos. Soc., Phi Beta Kappa. Office: Stanford Sch Medicine Fairchild Ctr D221 Stanford CA 94305-5125

STRYKER, DAVID MICHAEL, lawyer; b. Bloomington, Ind., Nov. 5, 1958; m. Josie Bizzari; children: Joshua, Joseph, Hannah, Samuel. BA in English lit., Ind. U., 1980, JD magna cum laude, 1983. Bar: Ill. 1984, NY 1990. Clk. to Hon. Robert H. Bork US Ct. Appeals, DC Cir., 1984; ptnr. Kirkland & Ellis, 1984—94; sr. litig. counsel Siemens Corp., NYC, 1994—98, assoc. gen. counsel, 1998—2004, corp. compliance officer; sr. v.p., gen. counsel BASF Corp., Florham Park, NJ, 2004—. Exec. editor Ind. Law Jour., 1982—83. Mem.: Order of Coif. Avocations: running, camping, fishing. Office: BASF Corp 100 Campus Dr Florham Park NJ 07932 Office Phone: 973-245-6000.

STRYKER, JAMES WILLIAM, retired automotive executive, former military officer; b. Grand Rapids, Mich., Apr. 20, 1940; s. John Alvin and Marian (Anderson) S.; m. Eleanor Marie Finger, Sept. 26, 1964; children: James William II, Marian Marie Jenkins, Kathryn Alison Greenbauer. BS, U.S. Mil. Acad., 1963; student, Def. Lang. Inst., 1968—69; MA, U. Mich., 1972; postgrad., U.S. Army Command and Gen. Staff Coll., 1978. Commd. 2d lt. U.S. Army, 1963, battery exec. officer 6th/20th field arty. Ft. Carson, Colo., 1964-65, advisor Joint US Mil. Assistance Group Vietnam, 1965—66, battery comdr. 4th/3d field arty. Ft. Hood, Tex., 1967-68, advisor Joint US Mil. Assistance Group Thailand, 1969—70; S-3 ops. officer 1st/7th F.A., Ft. Riley, Kans., 1972-73; asst. prof. history U.S. Mil. Acad., West Point, NY, 1973-77; chief nuc. ops. Ctrl. Army Group NATO, Heidelberg, Germany, 1978-81; dir., project mgr. tank-automotive command U.S. Army, Warren, Mich., 1981-86, ret., 1986; program mgr. military vehicles operation GMC Truck, Pontiac, Mich., 1987-95; cross brand portfolio mgr. Pontiac-GMC Divsn. GM Corp., Detroit, 1996-98, asst. brand mgr. product full size and mid size vans, 1999-2001, asst. brand mgr. product alternative fuels and mobility, 2001—02, product mgr. alternative fuels and mobility, 2002—04; ret., 2004. Author: (with others) Encyclopedia of Southern History, 1977; co-author: Early American Wars, 1978. Torch bearer Olympic Winter Games, Salt Lake City, 2002. Decorated Legion of Merit, Bronze Star medal, Def. Meritorious Svc. medal, Meritorious Svc. medal with oakleaf cluster, Army Commendation medal with oakleaf cluster, U.S. Army/Vietnamese Cross of Gallantry with palm and gold star; Olympic torchbearer Winter Olympics, 2002. Mem.: NRA (endowment), Nat. Def. Indsl. Assn. (dir. Detroit chpt. 1991—97, 2d v.p. 1995, 1st v.p. 1995—96, pres. 1996—97, adv. 1997—2000), Trout Unltd., Ruffed Grouse Soc. (banquet com. Detroit 1998—2003), Assn. U.S. Army (dir. Detroit chpt. 1990—95), Ducks Unltd., Pheasants Forever, Nodrog Setter Club Mich., Gordon Setter Club Am. Avocations: hunting, skeet shooting, trout fishing, field training english and gordon setters. Home: 168 First St Romeo MI 48065-5000

STRYKER, JOAN COPELAND, retired obstetrician, retired gynecologist, educator; b. Swayzee, Ind., Apr. 17, 1918; d. Kenneth Bayard and Elsie Weser Copeland; m. Walter Stryker (dec.); children: Sara Gill, Peter, David; m. Dawson James Lewis. BS, U. Ill., Urbana, 1939; MD, U. Ill., Chgo., 1943. Resident U. Mich., Ann Arbor, 1943—46, fellow, 1946—47; asst. prof. Wayne State U., Detroit, 1965—85, prof., 1985—2001, prof. emeritus, 2001—. Chief menopausal clinic Hutzel Hosp., Detroit, 1992—2001. Chief investigator (book) Addicted Neonatals. Med. dir. Planned Parenthood, Detroit, 1965—70, treas., 1970; staff mem. WHO, 1958—61. Named Tchr. of Yr., Wayne State U. Sch. Medicine, 1990; recipient Disting. Svc. award, 1988, Pathfinders award in medicine, 1991. Mem.: ACOG (pres., Cmty. Svc. award, Gynecologist of Yr. 1994), Am. Menopausal Soc., Alpha Omega Alpha, Sigma Xi. Avocations: sailing, skiing. Home: 9784 Hawthorne Glen Dr Grosse Ile MI 48138

STRYKER, STEVEN CHARLES, lawyer; b. Omaha, Oct. 26, 1944; s. James M. and Jean G. (Grannis) S.; m. Gina; children: Ryan, Kevin, Gerrit, Courtney. BS, U. Iowa, 1967, JD with distinction, 1969; postgrad. studies, Northwestern U. Grad. Sch. Bus, 1969-70, DePaul U., 1971. Bar: Iowa 1969, Tex. 1986; CPA Ill., Iowa. Sr. tax acct. Arthur Young & Co., Chgo., 1969-72; fed. tax mgr. Massey Ferguson, Des Moines, 1972-74; fed., state tax mgr. FMC Corp., Chgo., 1974-78; gen. tax atty. Shell Oil Co., Houston, 1978-81, asst. gen. tax counsel, 1981-83, gen. mgr., 1983-86, v.p., gen. tax counsel, 1986—2000; pvt. practice Houston, 2000—. Mem. ABA, AICPA, Tex. Bar Assn., Tax Execs. Inst. Home and Office: 2117 Del Monte Houston TX 77019

STUART, ALICE MELISSA, lawyer; b. NYC, Apr. 7, 1957; d. John Marberger and Marjorie Louise (Browne) S. BA, Ohio State U., 1977; JD, U. Chgo., 1980; LLM, NYU, 1982. Bar: NY 1981, Ohio 1982, Fla. 1994, US Dist. Ct. (so. dist.) Ohio, 1983, US Dist. Ct. (so. and ea. dists.) NY 1985. Assoc. Schwartz, Shapiro, Kelm & Warren, Columbus, Ohio, 1982-84, Paul, Weiss, Rifkind, Wharton & Garrison, NYC, 1984-85, Kassel, Neuwirth & Geiger, NYC, 1985-86, Phillips, Nizer, Benjamin, Krim & Ballon, NYC, 1987—92; pvt. practice NYC, 1992—98; atty. LeBoeuf, Lamb, Greene & MacRae, NYC, 1998—. Adj. prof. So. Coll., Orlando, Fla., 1997-98. Surrogate Speakers' Bur. Reagan-Bush Campaign, NYC, 1984; mem. Lawyers for Bush-Quayle Campaign, NYC, 1988. Mem. ABA, NY State Bar Assn., Women's Nat. Rep. Club (bd. dirs. 2004—), Winston Churchill Meml. Libr. Soc., Jr. League, Soc. Mayflower Descs. (bd. dirs. NY chpt. 2002-07, counselor NY chpt. 2002-07), Jamestowne Soc. (life), New Eng. Soc. (bd. dirs. 2007-), Women's Nat. Rep. Club (bd. dirs. 2004—), Phi Beta Kappa, Phi Kappa Phi, Alpha Lambda Delta. Republican. Office: LeBoeuf Lamb Greene & MacRae 125 W 55th St New York NY 10019-5369 Home Phone: 516-759-6987; Office Phone: 212-424-8669. Business E-Mail: astuart@llgm.com.

STUART, CAROLE, publishing executive; b. NYC, Feb. 22, 1941; d. Frank and Sally (Stern) Rose; m. Lyle Stuart, Feb. 4, 1982; 1 child, Jennifer Susan Livingston. Student, Bklyn. Coll. Pub. Lyle Stuart, Inc., Secaucus, NJ; assoc. pub. Carol Pub. Group, NYC; pub. Barricade Books, Inc., NYC. Author: Why Was I Adopted?, To Turn You On, 39 Sex Fantasies for Women; author: (with Claire Ciliotta) Why Am I Going to the Hospital?; author: I'll Never Be Fat Again, How To Lose 5 Pounds Fast, The Thank You Book. Mem.: Authors Guild, Women's Media Group, Wine and Food Soc. N.Y. Home: 1530 Palisade Ave Apt 6L Fort Lee NJ 07024-5402 Office: Barricade Books Ste 308A 185 Bridge Plz N Fort Lee NJ 02024

STUART, CHARLES EDWARD, electrical engineer, oceanographer; b. Durham, NC, Feb. 9, 1942; s. Charles Edward and Wilma Kelly Stuart; m. Margaret Ann Robinson, Jan. 9, 1982; children: Marjorie Kelly, Heather Alison BSEE, Duke U., 1963. Engr. Westinghouse Electric Corp., Balt., 1963—65; sr. engr. Booz Allen Hamilton, Chevy Chase, Md., 1966—68; rsch. dir. B-K Dynamics Inc., Huntsville, Ala., 1969—78; oceanographer Office of Naval Rsch., Arlington, Va., 1979—84; dir. Maritime Sys. Office Advanced Rsch. Projects Agy., Arlington, 1985—98; with def. programs US Dept. Energy, Washington, 1998—99; pres. Competitive Enterprise Solutions, LLC, Arlington, 2000—. Contbr. articles to profl. jours. Recipient Am. Def. Preparedness Assn. Bushnell award career contbns. undersea warfare, 1996 Mem. IEEE (sr., ad. com. 1991-93), Assn. Unmanned Vehicle Systems (trustee 1989-93) Methodist. Achievements include rsch. in antisubmarine warfare, cybersecurity and unmanned undersea vehicle technology. Office: Competitive Enterprise Solutions LLC PO Box 567 Slidell LA 70458 Business E-Mail: cstuart@cesllc.com.

STUART, CYNTHIA MORGAN, retired academic administrator; b. Harrisburg, Pa, June 29, 1949; d. Paul William and Bernice Leona (Boyer) M.; m. David Edward Stuart, June 14, 1971. Student, Elizabethtown Coll., Pa., 1967-69; BA, U. N.Mex., 1971, MPA, 1982, ABD in Ednl. Leadership, 2003. Admissions counselor U. N.Mex., Albuquerque, 1974-77, asst. dir. admissions, 1977-80, assoc. dir. admissions, 1980-83, dir. admissions, 1983—2005, Univ. articulation officer, 1989—2005, dir. student outreach svc., 1991-95, enrollment mgmt. team mem., 1998—2005; ret., 2005. Mem. N.Mex. Coordinating Coun. Secondary Sch. and Coll., 1983-92; chair Coun. for Common Concerns, Albuquerque, 1987-95; mem. N.Mex. Articulation Com., Santa Fe, 1983-95; mem. adv. bd. Albuquerque Tech. Vocat. Inst., 1991—. Compiler, editor Statewide Statistical Profile Report, N.Mex. HS, 1983-90; cover photographer Prehistoric New Mexico, 2d edit., 1994, Glimpses of the Ancient Southwest, 1995. Coord. United Way, Albuquerque, 1980-81; elected del. N.Mex. Dem. Conv., 1982; mem. issues and advocacy com. Albuquerque Bus. Edn. Compact, 1991-93; mem. Am. Indian Edn. Initiative, Albuquerque, 1992—; Coll. Bd. del., 1991—. Recipient sys. devel. grant Commn. on Higher Edn., Santa Fe, 1995. Mem. Am. Assn. Collegiate Registrars and Admissions Officers (reporting officer of transfer credit N.Mex. 1979—), Rocky Mountain Assn. Collegiate Registrars and Admissions Officers (v.p. 1979-81, pres. 1983-84), N.Mex. Assn. Collegiate Registrars and Admissions Officers (sec.-treas. 1978-82, pres. 1991-92, Outstanding Svc. award 1990), N.Mex. Am. Coll. Testing Coun. (chair 1996-97, state rep. 1997—2005, trustee Am. Coll. Testing 1999-2002, del. to Coll. Bd. 1991—2005). Democrat. Avocations: photography, travel, drawing, music. Home: 423 Tulane Dr SE Albuquerque NM 87106-1417 E-mail: cstuart@unm.edu.

STUART, DABNEY, poet, language educator; b. Richmond, Va., Nov. 4, 1937; s. Walker Dabney Jr. and Martha (vonSchilling) S.; m. Sandra Westcott, Jan. 20, 1983; children: Martha, Nathan vonSchilling, Darren Wynne AB, Davidson Coll., 1960; AM, Harvard U., 1962. Instr. Coll. William and Mary, Williamsburg, Va., 1961-65; prof. English Washington and Lee U., Lexington, Va., 1965—2002, S. Blount Mason Jr. prof. English, 1991—2002. Vis. prof. Middlebury (Vt.) Coll., 1968-69, Ohio U., Athens, 1975, U. Va., Charlottesville, 1981-83. Author: The Diving Bell, 1966, A Particular Place, 1969, The Other Hand, 1974, Friends of Yours, Friends of Mine, 1974, Round and Round, 1976, Nabokov: The Dimensions of Parody, 1978, Rockbridge Poems, 1981, Common Ground, 1982, Don't Look Back, 1987, Narcissus Dreaming, 1990, Sweet Lucy Wine, 1992, Light Years: New and Selected Poems, 1994, Second Sight: Poems for Paintings by Carroll Cloar, 1996, Long Gone, 1996, The Way to Cobbs Creek, 1997, Settlers, 1999, Strains of the Old Man, 1999, No Visible Means of Support, 2001, The Man Who Loves Cezanne, 2003, Family Preserve, 2005. Recipient Dylan Thomas prize Poetry Soc. Am., 1965, Gov.'s award State of Va., 1979, Libr. Va. Poetry award, 2006; NEA lit. fellow, 1975, 82, Guggenheim fellow, 1987-88, Individual Artist fellow Va. Commn. for Arts, 1995, resident fellow Rockefeller Study and Conf. Ctr., Bellagio, Italy, 2000. Avocations: food, travel, painting. Home: 30 Edmondson Ave Lexington VA 24450-1904

STUART, FRANK ADELL, county official; b. Tahoka, Tex., Dec. 18, 1928; s. John Franklin and Mary Elizabeth (Reed) S.; m. Mary Louise Wheat Crelia, Feb. 2, 1962; children: Rita, Donna, Franklin, Burce, Susan, Mary, Chris. BBA, Tex. Tech U., 1979. Asst. cashier Am. State Bank, Lubbock, Tex., 1949-52, Citizen Nat. Bank, Lubbock, 1953-59; acct. in pvt. practice Lubbock, 1960-63; asst. mgr. Gibson Discount Ctr., Lubbock, 1964-77; tax. assessor and collector Lubbock County, Lubbock, 1979-94, ret., 1994. Served to col. Tex. State Guard, 1988-98. Mem. Tax Assessor-Collectors Assn. Tex., Lubbock C. of C., Masons, YorkRite, Scottish Rite, Shriners, Yellow House Lodge, Daylight Lodge. Baptist. Home: 2704 57th St Lubbock TX 79413-5605 E-mail: stuart2704@aol.com.

STUART, GERARD WILLIAM, JR., investment company executive, alderman, city official; b. Yuba City, Calif., July 28, 1939; s. Gerard William and Geneva Bernice (Stuke) S.; m. Lenore Frances Lorona, 1981. Student, Yuba Jr. Coll., 1957-59, Chico State Coll., 1959-60; AB, U. Calif., Davis, 1962; MLS, U. Calif., Berkeley, 1963. Rare book libr. Cornell U., 1964-68; bibliographer scholarly collections Huntington Libr., San Marino, Calif., 1968-73, head acquisitions libr., 1973-75; sec.-treas., dir. Ravenstree Corp., 1969-80, pres, chmn. bd., 1980—, William Penn Ltd., 1981—. Councilman City of Yuma, 1992-96, deputy mayor, 1995; bd. dirs Ariz. Humanities Coun., 1993-99, Yuma Libr. Found., 1997, chmn., 1997-98, 99-2001, 05—. Lilly fellow Ind. U., 1964-63. Mem. Bibliog. Soc. Am., Rolls-Royce Owners Club, Grolier Club (N.Y.C.), Zamorano Club (L.A.), Phi Beta Kappa, Alpha Gamma Sigma, Phi Kappa Phi.

STUART, GLEN R(AYMOND), lawyer; b. Kimpese, Congo, Mar. 4, 1959; came to U.S., 1960; s. Charles H. and Jeannette B. (Spinney) S.; m. Susan K. Sharpless, May 26, 1984; children: Jennifer Jacqueline, David Charles, Andrew William. BA, Franklin and Marshall Coll., 1981; JD, U. Va., 1984. Bar: Pa. 1984, U.S. Dist. Ct. (ea. dist.) Pa. 1984, U.S. Dist. Ct. (mid. dist.) Pa. 1986, U.S. Ct. Appeals (3rd cir.) 1988, U.S. Supreme Ct. 1997. Hiring ptnr. Morgan, Lewis & Bockius, LLP, Phila., 1984—. Mem. ABA, Pa. Bar Assn., Phila. Bar Assn., Order of Coif. Democrat. Baptist. Avocations: soccer, golf, softball, tennis. Home: 21 Harvey Ln Malvern PA 19355-2907 Office: Morgan Lewis & Bockius LLP 1701 Market St Philadelphia PA 19103-2903 Office Fax: 215-963-5001. Business E-Mail: gstuart@morganlewis.com.

STUART, GREG, marketing professional, writer; BA, U. Wash., Seattle, 1983. Media planner William Esty Advt., Inc., 1984—85; media supr. Jordan McGrath Case & Taylor, 1985—90; v.p., assoc. media planning dir. Levine Huntley Vick & Beaver, 1990—91; dir. comms. strategies Wells, Rich, Green BDDP, 1992—93; sr. v.p., gen. mgr. Interactive Mktg. Divsn. Wunderman Cato Johnson Agency, Young & Rubicam, NYC, 1993—96; exec. v.p. Interactive Imaginations, 1996; founder, prin. Greg Stuart Consulting, 1996—99; v.p. bus. devel. Flycast Comms., San Francisco, 1999—2000; CEO, pres. DeltaClick, Inc., San Francisco, 2000—01; pres., CEO Interactive Advt. Bur., NYC, 2001—06. Entrepreneur-in-residence, venture ptnr. iMinds Ventures, San Francisco; bd. dirs. Rapt Inc., Allyes; spkr. in field. Co-author: What Sticks: Why Most Advertising Fails and How to Guarantee Yours Succeeds, 2006. Office: 3 Kellis Way PO Box 337 Bridgehampton NY 11932 Office Phone: 212-380-4704. Office Fax: 978-477-5822. E-mail: greg@gregstuart.com. *

STUART, HAROLD CUTLIFF, lawyer, business executive; b. Okla. City, July 4, 1912; s. Royal Cutliff and Alice (Bramlitt) S.; m. Joan Skelly, June 6, 1938 (dec. 1994); children: Randi Stuart Wightman, Jon Rolf; m. Frances Langford, Nov. 18, 1994. JD, U. Va., 1936. Bar: Okla. 1936, DC 1952. Ptnr. Stuart, Biolchini, Turner & Givray, Tulsa; judge Common Pleas Ct., 1941-42; asst. sec. USAF, 1949-51; chmn. bd. 1st Stuart Corp., radio, oil, real estate and investments, Tulsa; dir. Lowrance Electronics, Inc., Tulsa. Spl. cons. to sec. Air Force, 1961-63; mem. Okla. Hwy. Commn., 1959-63; bd. dirs. Great Empire Broadcasting Inc., Wichita, Kans. Trustee emeritus Lovelace Found., Albuquerque; trustee N.Am. Wildlife Fedn; mem. Nat. Eagle Scout Coun. Boy Scouts Am., Disting. Eagle Scout; past pres. Air Force Acad. Found., chmn. bd. Served from 1st lt. to col. USAAF, 1942-46, ETO. Decorated Bronze Star and 6 battle stars; comdr. Order of St. Olav; King Haakon 7th Victory medal; medal of Liberation (Norway); Croix de Guerre (Luxembourg); named to Okla. Aviation and Space Hall of Fame, Okla. Hall of Fame. Mem. ABA, Okla. Bar Assn., DC Bar Assn., Air Force Assn. (dir., nat. pres., chmn. bd. 1951-52), Tulsa C. of C., Tulsa Headliner, Falcon Found. (vice chmn.), Ducks Unltd. (trustee), Southern Hills Country Club, The Boston Club (Tulsa), Burning Tree Club (Washington), Willoughby Golf Club, The Amb. Club (Stuart, Fla.), Delta Kappa Epsilon. Democrat. also: Ste 600 2431 E 61st St Tulsa OK 74136-1235 E-mail: stuar28@adelphia.net.

STUART, HENRY LEE, retired rail transportation executive; b. San Francisco, Aug. 4, 1921; s. Henry Lee Stuart and Lucile Edna McClelland; m. Carollyne Banner, June 26, 1987; m. Jacquline Frederica Molthan, Aug. 29, 1946 (dec. Nov. 12, 1985); children: Henry M., Lee, Shelly. BS, U. Calif., Berkeley, 1948. V.p., dir. Interstate RR Co., Andover, Va., 1956—63; asst. gen. mgr. So. Rlwy. Sys., Charlotte, 1963, supr., 1964, dir. svc. control, 1965—66; gen. mgr. Metro Atlanta Rapid Transit Authority, 1966—72; dir. transp. studies URS Covedale and Colpitts, NYC, 1973—76; v.p., dir. Wyer Dick & Co., Livingston, NJ, 1977—85. Dir. 1st Nat. Bank Appalachia, Va., 1961—63. Photographer (exhibitions) Morris Graves Mus. Art, Eureka, Calif., 2000. V.p. Lonesome Pine Coun. BSA, Pikeville, Ky., 1959—63; pres. Sr. Citizens Found., Eureka, 2004—06. 1st lt. Air Corps US Army, 1942—46. Named Transp. Man Yr., Nat. Def. Transp. Assn., 1971. Avocation: photography. Home: 1090 Murray Rd #9 Mckinleyville CA 95519

STUART, JACQUELYN L., state supreme court justice; b. Atmore, Ala., Sept. 23, 1955; m. George Stuart; children: Tucker, Shepard, Kelly. BA in Sociology and Edn., Auburn U., 1977; JD, U. Ala., 1980. Asst. atty. gen. State of Ala.; exec. asst. to commr. and spl. asst. atty. gen. Ala. Dept. Corrections; asst. dist. atty. Baldwin County; dist. judge, 1989—97; judge Ala. Cir. Ct., 1997—2001; justice Ala. Supreme Ct., 2001—. Faculty advisor Nat. Judicial Coll., Reno; former pres. Ala. Council of Juvenile & Family Ct. Judges; pres. Blue Ridge Inst. for Juvenile & Family Ct. Judges, 2002. Former pres. Heritage Junior Women's Club, Bay Minette Kiwanis Club, Jubilee Woman's Club; bd. mem. Ala. Federation of Women's Clubs. Republican. Office: Ala Supreme Ct 300 Dexter Ave Rm 3-215 Montgomery AL 36104-3741 Office Phone: 334-229-0626. Business E-Mail: lstuart@appellate.state.al.us.

STUART, JEFFREY L., mathematics professor, consultant; m. Susan Stuart. BA in Math. & Physics, Pomona Coll., Claremont, Calif., 1980; MS in Math., PhD in Math., U. Wis., Madison, 1986. Vis. asst. prof. math. No. Ill. U., DeKalb, 1986—87; prof. math. U. So. Miss., Hattiesburg, 1987—2001, Pacific Luth. U., Tacoma, 2001—. Recipient K.T. Tang Faculty Excellence in Rsch. award, Pacific Luth. U., 2004—05, Faculty Excellence in Tchg. award, U. So. Missisippi, 2000, Disting. Tchg. award, Miss.-La. Sect. Math. Assn. Am., 2000. Mem.: Soc. Indsl. and Applied Math., Math. Assn. Am., Am. Statis. Assn. (v.p. Miss. chpt. 2000—01), Internat. Linear Algebra Soc. (sec.-treas. 2000—), Phi Beta Kappa. Office: Math Dept Pacific Lutheran Univ Tacoma WA 98447 Office Phone: 253-535-7403. Business E-Mail: jeffrey.stuart@plu.edu.

STUART, JILL, apparel designer; m. Ron Curtis, 1986; children: Morgan, Chloe, Sophie. Student, RI Sch. of Design. Sold jewelry and handbag designs Bloomingdales, NYC; founded accessory line Jill Stuart, NYC, founded women's wear line, 1993—, launched intimate apparel, eyewear, denim and footwear lines, 2000—. Office: Jill Stuart Offices 550 7th Ave New York NY 10018 Office Phone: 212-921-2600.

STUART, JODI MARIE, language educator; b. Staples, Minn., Nov. 4, 1980; d. Floyd Edgar and Esther Frost; m. Lucas A. Stuart, July 7, 2001. BA in English, U. Alaska, Anchorage, 2003. Substitute tchr. Kenai Peninsula Borough Sch., Soldotna, Alaska, 2004—06; project GRAD/ACCESS Kenai Peninsula Coll., Soldotna, 2006—, adj. faculty preparatory English. Mem.: Nat. Coun. Tchrs. English. Office: Kenai PeninsulaColl 34820 Coll Dr Soldotna AK 99669

STUART, JOSEPH MARTIN, art museum administrator; b. Seminole, Okla., Nov. 9, 1932; s. Arch William and Lillian (Lindsey) S.; BFA in Art, U. N.Mex., 1959, MA in Art, 1962; m. Signe Margaret Nelson, June 18, 1960; 1 dau., Lise Nelson Stuart. Dir., Roswell (N.Mex.) Museum and Art Center, 1960-62; curator U. Oreg. Mus. Art, 1962-63; dir. Boise (Idaho) Gallery Art, 1964-68, Salt Lake (City) Art Ctr., 1968-71, S.D. Art Mus., Brookings, 1971-93; prof. art S.D. State U., 1971-93; represented in permanent collections: Civic Fine Arts Ctr., Sioux Falls, S.D., Coll. Idaho, Eureka Coll., Salt Lake Art Ctr., Sioux City (Iowa) Art Ctr., U. N.Mex. Art Mus., West Tex. State U. With USN, 1951-55. Mem. Phi Kappa Phi. Unitarian. Author: Index of South Dakota Artists, 1974; Art of South Dakota, 1974, Harvey Dunn: Son of the Middle border, 1984, Art for a New Century, 1989; The Legacy of South Dakota Art, 1990; author numerous exhbn. catalogs. Office Phone: 505-466-6625.

STUART, MARIE JEAN, physician, hematologist, researcher; b. Bangalore, India, Sept. 11, 1943; came to U.S., 1967; d. Norman and Dorothy (Dias) S. BS, MB, Madras U., India. Asst. prof. pediatrics SUNY Health Sci. Ctr., Syracuse, 1972-76, assoc. prof., 1976-81, prof. pediatrics, 1981-87; prof. chief hematology and oncology div. St. Christophers Hosp. for Children and Temple U., Phila., 1987-97; prof. thrombosis rsch. Temple U., 1987-97; dir. NIH Comprehensive Sickle Cell Ctr. Thomas Jefferson U., Phila., 1998—. Mem. nat. child health com. Nat. Inst. Child Health and Human Devel., Bethesda, Md., 1982-86; mem. nat. heart, lung and blood rsch. tng. com., NIH, Bethesda, 1993-2000; mem. NIH Sickle Cell Disease Adv. Coun., 2000-04; mem. NIH Erythrocyte and Leucocyte Biology Study Sect., 2003—. Mem. editl. bd. Biology of the Neonate, 2000—; contbr. chpts. to books, articles to profl. jours. Docent Phila. Mus. Art, 2005. Recipient Rsch. award Temple U., 1997. Mem. Am. Fedn. Clin. Research. Am. Pediatric Soc., Soc. for Pediatric Research. Avocations: music, art. Home: 227 S 6th St Apt 1 NW Philadelphia PA 19106 Office Phone: 215-955-9820. Business E-Mail: marie.stuart@jefferson.edu.

STUART, NANCY GIOVINAZZO, secondary school educator; b. LA, Aug. 8, 1931; d. Joseph and Carmelita Mary (Frontino) Giovinazzo; m. Jay William Stuart, Jr., July 28, 1951; children: Tani Lynn Stuart Robertson, Joel Vanni; 1 foster child, Hilary Davis. AA, UCLA, 1952, BS, 1954, MS, 1967. Tchr. Washington High Sch., L.A. Unified Sch. Dist., 1954-60, tchr. Gardena High Sch., 1960-63, tchr. Carson High Sch., 1963-91, chair dept. health, master tchr., 1970—91, retired, 1991, preferred substitute tchr., 1992—; mentor Calif. Acad. Math. and Sci. at Calif. State U., Dominguez Hills, 1993—2000. Drill team-pep units sponsor, 1968-81; founder Bird Seed Baby Parenting Experience, Carson H.S., 1970-91, sponsor peer counseling tng. program, 1984-91; workshop leader in field. Author: Death and Dying: A Teaching Guide and Workbook for Health Education, 1989, For Phsical Edn. and Dance, 1956, Adaptive Physical Edn., 1958, For Health Edn. CPR, 1976, 1980. Tchr. rep. L.A. Unified Sch. Dist. on City of L.A. Drug Commn., 1968-69. Grantee State of Calif., 1985. Mem. Calif. Assn. for Health, Phys. Edn., Recreation and Dance (Health Edn. Tchr. of Yr. 1988), AAUW, Calif. Ret. Tchrs. Assn., Delta Kappa Gamma, Alpha Delta Kappa. Home: 17502 Valmeyer Ave Gardena CA 90248-3356 Office: Carson High Sch 22328 Main St Carson CA 90745-4599 Home Phone: 310-323-0121. Personal E-mail: ngs54@earthlink.net.

STUART, NANCY RUBIN (NANCY ZIMMAN STETSON), journalist, writer, television producer; b. Boston, Nov. 25, 1944; d. Stuart Wendell and Ethel (Rabinovitz) Zimman; m. William W. Stetson, Apr. 28, 2001; children: Elisabeth, Jessica. BA, Tufts U., 1966; MA in Teaching, Brown U., 1967; PhD (hon.), Mt. Vernon Coll., 1995. Playwright, dir. Equity Library Theatre, Roundabout, Joseph Jefferson and St. Clement's theaters, N.Y.C., 1971-74; freelance reporter Westchester-Gannett newspapers and mags., 1975-77, N.Y. Times, NYC, 1977—. Faculty affiliate Bush Ctr. in

Child Devel., Yale U., New Haven, 1981-86; mem. Westchester County Women's Adv. Bd., chair, 1988; bd. dirs. Women Writing Women's Lives Seminar; mem. faculty SUNY, Purchase, 1994-95, Fordham U., N.Y.C., 1996-99. Author: The New Suburban Women, Beyond Myth and Motherhood, 1982, The Mother Mirror: How a Generation of Women is Changing Motherhood in America, 1984, Isabella of Castile: The First Renaissance Queen, 1991, American Empress: The Life and Times of Marjorie Merriweather Post, 1995, Club Dance: The Show, The Steps, The Spirit of Country, 1998, The Reluctant Spiritualist: The Life at Maggie Fox, 2005; writer, assoc. prodr: TV series America's Castles for A&E Network, 1996—99 (Telly award, 1999, Telly award (3), 2001, Writing Communicator award, 1999), The Gold Coast for The Grand Tour A & E TV, 1997, writer prodr., prodr.: TV series Restore America, 1999; writer prodr., prodr. (TV series) Restore America, 2001 (3 Telly awards); writer/assoc. prodr.: TV series Eccentrics, 1999 (Crystal award, Telly award), The N.Y. Times, 1977—; writer Baltimore Sun, American History Magazine; contbg. editor: Parents mag., 1987—91,: McCalls, Savvy, Travel & Leisure, Ladies Home Jour., 1980—92; theater critic: Stamford Advocate, 1994—96; co-prodr.:. Recipient Washington Irving award Westchester Libr. Assn., 1993, Telly award finalist, 2001; Am. Antiquarian Soc. fellow, 2005; Time, Inc.-Bread Loaf Writers' Colony scholar, 1979. Fellow MacDowell Colony; mem. Author's Guild, Am. Soc. Journalists and Authors (Author of Yr. award 1992, Outstanding Nonfiction book award, 2005, hon. mention oustanding book award, gen. nonfiction 2006), PEN, Nat. Arts Club. Avocations: skiing, sailing, ballet, classical music, dance. Personal E-mail: thewriteway@aol.com.

STUART, PAMELA BRUCE, lawyer; b. NYC, Feb. 13, 1949; d. J. Raymond and Marion Grace (Cotins) S. AB with distinction, Mt. Holyoke Coll., 1970; JD cum laude, U. Mich., 1973. Bar: N.Y. 1974, D.C. 1975, U.S. Dist. Ct. D.C. 1979, U.S. Ct. Appeals (D.C. cir.) 1980, U.S. Supreme Ct. 1980, U.S. Dist. Ct. Md. 1989, Md. 1992, Va. 1993, U.S. Ct. Appeals (4th cir.) 1993, Fla. 1994, U.S. Dist. Ct. (ea. dist.) Va. 1994, U.S. Dist. Ct. (no. dist.) N.Y. 1996, U.S. Dist. Ct. (so. dist.) Fla. 1998, U.S. Dist. Ct. (so. dist.) N.Y. 1999, U.S. Dist. Ct. (ea. dist.) N.Y. 1999, U.S. Dist. Ct. (mid. dist.) Fla. 2001. Trial atty., deputy asst. dir. Bur. of Consumer Protection, FTC, Washington, 1973-79; asst. U.S. atty. U.S. Atty's Office, Washington, 1979-85; sr. trial atty. Office of Internat. Affairs, U.S. Dept. Justice, Washington, 1985-87; atty. Ross, Dixon & Masback, Washington, 1987-89; mem. Lobel, Novins, Lamont & Flug, Washington, 1989-92; pvt. practice, Washington, 1992—. Instr. Nat. Inst. for Trial Advocacy, Atty. Gen.'s Advocacy Inst., Legal Edn. Inst., Fed. Practice Inst.; mem. Jud. Conf. D.C., 1985-88, 1991-2004; mem. Jud. Conf., D.C. Cir., 1996, 98, 2000; assoc. mem. Consular Corps Washington; legal analyst CNN, MSNBC, Fox News, other TV networks. Author: The Federal Trade Commission, 1991; contbr. articles to profl. jours. Bd. dirs. Anacostia Econ. Devel. Corp., 1993—, Anacostia Holding Co., Inc. Mem. ATLA, ABA (internat. criminal law com., chmn., 1993-96, chmn. fed. crime rules subcom. white collar crime com. sect. criminal justice 1997-99), Bar Assn. D.C. (bd. dirs. 1995-2001, 03—, sec. 2003-04, treas. 2005-06), Asst. U.S. Attys. Assn. D.C. (exec. coun. 1993-99, pres. 1998-99), Women's Bar Assn. D.C., Fla. Bar (exec. coun. real property probate and trust law sect. 1999—), Alumnae Assn. Mt. Holyoke Coll. (bd. dirs. 1986-89, 92-95, mem. art adv. bd. Art Mus. 2005—, Alumnae medal of honor 1990), Edward Bennett Williams Inn of Ct. (master of bench), Fed. City Club (bd. govs. 1992—, pres. 2005-06), Cosmos Club. Avocations: writing, interior design, investments, piano, art. Home: 5115 Yuma St NW Washington DC 20016-4336 Office: The J Raymond Stuart Bldg 1750 N Street NW Washington DC 20036 Office Phone: 202-835-2200. Personal E-mail: pamstuart@aol.com.

STUART, ROBERT, container manufacturing executive; b. Oak Park, Ill., Aug. 3, 1921; s. Robert S. and Marie (Vavra) Solinsky; m. Lillian C. Kondelik, Dec. 5, 1962 (dec. May 1978); m. Lila Winterhoff Peters, May 21, 1982. BS, U. Ill., Chgo., 1943, LLD, 1982. Sec.-treas., gen. mgr. Warren Metal Decorating Co., 1947-49; asst. to gen. mgr. Cans, Inc., 1950-52; asst. to v.p., then v.p. Nat. Can Corp., Chgo., 1953-59, exec. v.p., 1959-63, pres., 1963-69, chief exec., 1966-69, chmn. bd., CEO, 1969-73, chmn. bd., 1973-83, chmn. fin. com., 1983, mem. corp. devel. com., until 1986, chmn. emeritus, 1986—. Past pres., bd. dirs. Corp. Responsibility Group of Greater Chgo. Past pres., bd. dirs. Chgo. Crime Commn.; past dir. Nat. Crime Prevention Coun.; founding chmn. Nat. Minority Supplier Devel. Coun., 1972-73, Lloyd Morey Scholarship Fund: Freedoms Found. at Valley Forge, past trustee; past mem. adv. bd. Salvation Army, Broader Urban Involvement and Leadership Devel.; chmn. emeritus World Federalist Assn.; past bd. dirs., past moderator Millard Congl. Ch.; past pres. Ctrl. Ch. Chgo.; chmn. emeritus Assn. to Unite the Democracies. Capt. AUS, 1943-46. Mem.: Rotary (past pres. Chgo. club, past dist. gov.), Little Ship Club (London), Yacht Club, Chgo. Club, Masons (32d degree, Red Cross of Constantine), Alpha Kappa Lambda (past nat. pres.). Lutheran. Home and Office: 233 SW 43d Ter Cape Coral FL 33914

STUART, ROBERT KENNETH, internist, hematologist, oncologist, educator; b. Baton Rouge, July 6, 1948; s. Walter Bynum and Rita Bess (Kleinpeter) S.; m. Gail Elaine Wiscarz, June 12, 1971 (div. Dec. 1988); children: R. Morgan, Elaine C.; m. F. Charlene Gates, Nov. 2, 1991. BS, Georgetown U., 1970; MD, Johns Hopkins U., Balt., 1974. Diplomate Am. Bd. Internal Medicine. Resident in medicine Johns Hopkins Hosp., Balt., 1974-76, oncology fellow Oncology Ctr., 1976-78; rsch. fellow Sloan-Kettering Inst., NYC, 1978-79; asst. prof. Johns Hopkins U., Balt., 1979-84, assoc. prof., 1984-85; prof. medicine Med. U. S.C., Charleston, 1985—; assoc. dir. Hollings Cancer Ctr., Charleston, 1993-97; chmn. dept. oncology King Faisal Specialist Hosp and Rsch. Ctr., Riyadh, Saudi Arabia, 1997-2001; prof. medicine Med.U. S.C., Charleston, 2001—. Bd. dirs. Aplastic Anemia Found., Balt., 1982-93, med. adv. bd., 1993-98; mem. nat. team Tour of Hope, 2004. Democrat. Roman Catholic. Office: Medical Univ of South Carolina 171 Ashley Ave Charleston SC 29425-0100 E-mail: stuartrk@musc.edu.

STUART, SPENCER RAYMOND, management consultant; b. Balt., Sept. 25, 1922; s. William Moore Stuart and Helen Lenore Raymond; m. Eugenia Presler Birdsall, Sept. 24, 1949; children: Spencer Raymond Stuart Jr., Cooper B., Eugenia Anne. BS, Haverford Coll., 1947. Mgr. mktg. and advt. Martin Senour Paint Co., Chgo., 1947—52; cons. Booz Allen and Hamilton, Chgo., 1952—55; prin. Heidrick and Struggles, Chgo., 1955; founder, CEO Spencer Stuart, Exec. Search Consultants, Chgo., 1956—74, founder, chmn. NYC, 1974—, Dean Witter Coun. of Mgmt. Advisors, NYC, 1990—92; mgmt. cons., corp. dir. Palm City, Fla., 1974—2001. Dir., chmn. compensation and mgmt. succession com., chmn. corp. governance com. Enhance Fin. Svcs. Group, NYC, 1986—2001; dir., chmn. audit com., mem. compensation stock option and mgmt. succession com. UST, Inc., Greenwich, Conn., 1977—97; dir., mem. audit and compensation com. U.S. Timberlands Co., L.P., NYC, 1997; dir., mem. exec. com., chmn. compensation and mgmt. succession com. Western Airlines, LA, 1984—87; dir., chmn. compensation and corp. strategy coms. Allegheny Internat., Pitts., 1984—89; panelist Am. Mgmt. Assn., Presidents Assn., NYC, 1960—72; exec. compensation Blue Ribbon com. Nat. Assn. Corp. Dirs., Washington, 1974—97; past dir. Assn. Exec. Recruiting Consultants, NYC; dir. Mass. Co./Keystone Custodian Funds, Boston, 1982—97. Contbr. articles to newspapers and profl. jours. Reception com. Econ. Club, Chgo., 1956—65; chmn. exploring divsn. Boy Scouts Am., Stamford, Conn., 1974—86, founder, chmn. corp. adv. bd. Fairfield County, Conn., 1975—86; trustee, pres. Silvermine Guild of Artists, New Canaan, Conn., 1972—79; trustee Green Mountain Coll., Poultney, Vt., 1980—84; chmn. fundraising dinner com., athlete of decade program Am. Cancer Soc., NYC, 1977—82; panelist Aspen (Colo.) Inst. Humanistic Studies, 1948—58; mem. Conf. Christians and Jews, Conn., 1960—68. 1st lt. AUS, 1943—46, ETO. Decorated Bronze Star, Purple Heart; recipient Wm. H. Splurgen III award for disting. svc., Nat. Exploring Coun., Boy Scouts Am., 1978, Profl. Leadership award, Newcomen Soc. Am., 1981, Heidrick award, Assn. Exec. Search Consultants, 1995. Mem.: Hassayampa Golf Club, The Sky Club, Eldorado Country Club, Univ. Club N.Y.C. Avocations: golf, exercise, writing, computers, art.

STUART, WALTER BYNUM, III, retired banker; b. Baton Rouge, Oct. 5, 1922; s. Walter Bynum and Rosa (Gauthreaux) S.; m. Rita Kleinpeter, May 20, 1944; children— Walter Bynum IV, Robert, Douglas, Ronald, Scott. BS, La. State U., 1943. Adminstrv. mgr. Kaiser Aluminum & Chem. Corp., 1946-63; v.p. First Nat. Bank Commerce, New Orleans, 1963-65, sr. v.p., 1965, exec. v.p., 1965-73; vice chmn. bd., dir. 1st Nat. Bank Commerce, New Orleans, 1973-78; exec. v.p. 1st Commerce Corp., New Orleans, 1972-73, pres., 1973-75, vice-chmn. bd., 1975-78, dir., 1973-78; pres. Am. Bank & Trust Co., Lafayette, La., 1978-86, cons., ret., 1986. Assoc. dir., mem. faculty Sch. Banking La. State U., 1973-75, dir., 1975-78; mem. Faculty Assemblies for Bank Dirs. Campaign group chmn. industry com., mem. United Fund for Greater New Orleans Area, 1974; mem. research com. Pub. Affairs Research Council La., 1973-76, v.p., trustee, 1973-76; bd. dirs. Bur. Govtl. Research, 1973-77, Council Better La., 1975—; pres. New Orleans Indsl. Devel. Bd., 1973-75. Served to lt. (j.g.) USNR, 1943-46. Mem. C. of C. of Greater New Orleans Area (v.p. 1973-75, bd. dirs.), Am. Bankers Assn., La. Bankers Assn. (pres. 1977), Am. Mgmt. Assn., Kappa Alpha, Delta Sigma Pi, Beta Gamma Sigma. Democrat. Roman Catholic. Home: 10100 Hillview Dr Apt 2109 Pensacola FL 32514-5481 *Recognizing that life is the experiencing of reality, and that reality is simply a continuing series of problems, I long ago decided that I would treat a problem as an opportunity. Every incident of difficulty has always invited my intense interest as a challenge, and my thoughts have been immediately marshalled for positive effort. My life has been most rewarding because I believe that "a problem is an opportunity!".*

STUART, WALTER BYNUM, IV, lawyer; b. Grosse Tete, La., Nov. 23, 1946; s. Walter Bynum III and Rita (Kleinpeter) S.; m. Lettice Lee Binnings, May 18, 1968; children: Courtney Lyon, Walter Burke V. Student, Fordham U., 1964—65; BA, Tulane U., 1968, JD, 1973. Bar: La. 1973, N.Y 1980, U.S. Dist. Ct. (ea. and we. dists.) La. 1974, U.S. Tax Ct. 1974, U.S. Supreme Ct. 1981, U.S. Dist. Ct. (so. dist.) Colo. 1987, U.S. Dist. Ct. (so. dist.) Tex. 1989. Ptnr. Stone, Pigman, Walther, Wittman and Hutchinson, New Orleans, 1973—78, Singer Hutner Levine Seeman and Stuart, New Orleans, 1978—81, Gordon, Arata, McCollam and Stuart, New Orleans, 1981—88, Vinson & Elkins LLP, Houston, 1988—, adminstrv. ptnr. NYC, 2003—. Instr. Tulane U. Law Sch., 1978-82; mem. faculty Banking Sch. of the South; bd. dirs. Inst. Politics; mem. adv. bd. City Atty.'s Office, New Orleans, 1978-79. Bd. dirs., gen. counsel Houston Grand Opera, 1992-2003. Named one of Best Lawyers in Am., N.Y. Super Lawyers, NY. Area's Best Lawyers, N.Y. Mag., Best Lawyers, Corp. Counsel Mag., Tex. Super Lawyers, Houston's Top 100, Tex. Monthly Mag. Mem. ABA, La. Bar Assn., Tex. Assn. Bank Counsel (pres. 1994-95), La. Bankers Assn. (chmn. bank counsel com.). Office: Vinson & Elkins 666 Fifth Ave 26th Fl New York NY 10103-0040 also: First City Tower 1001 Fannin St, Ste 2300 Houston TX 77002-6760 Office Phone: 212-237-0020, 212-237-0007. E-mail: wstuart@velaw.com.

STUART, WILLIAM CORWIN, judge; b. Knoxville, Iowa, Apr. 28, 1920; s. George Corwin and Edith (Abram) S.; m. Mary Elgin Cleaver, Oct. 20, 1946; children: William Corwin II, Robert Cullen, Melanie Rae, Valerie Jo. BA, State U. Iowa, 1941, JD, 1942. Bar: Iowa 1942. Pvt. practice, Chariton, 1946-62; city atty., 1947-49; mem. Iowa Senate from, Lucas-Wayne Counties, 1951-61; justice Supreme Ct. Iowa, 1962-71; judge U.S. Dist. Ct., So. Dist. of Iowa, Des Moines, 1971-86, sr. judge, 1986—. With USNR, 1943-45. Recipient Outstanding Svc. award Iowa Acad. Trial lawyer, 1987, Iowa Trial Lawyers Assn., 1988, Spl. award Iowa State Bar Assn., 1987, Disting. Alumni, U. Iowa Coll. Law, 1987. Mem. ABA, Iowa Bar Assn., Am. Legion, All For Iowa, Order of Coif, Omicron Delta Kappa, Phi Kappa Psi, Phi Delta Phi. Clubs: Mason (Shriner). Presbyterian. Home: PO Box 130 Chariton IA 50049-0130

STUBBART, DAVID JAMES, elementary school educator; b. Framingham, Mass., Sept. 26, 1977; s. John Crawford and Fern Elizabeth Stubbart; m. Laura Michelle Opdenbrouw, July 20, 2006. BS in Edn., Framingham State Coll., Mass., 1999, EdM, 2003. Cert. elem. edn. grades 1-6 Mass., 2000, reading tchr. grades K-12 Mass., 2004. Educator grade 1 Town of Natick, Mass., 1999—99; educator-grade 1 Town of Westborough, Westborough, Mass., 2000—03; educator-grade 3 Town of Southborough, Mass., 2003—. Unit leader YMCA, Hopkinton, Mass., 1999—2000. Coord. Boy Scouts Am., Ashland, Mass., 1995—95. Mem.: Alpha Upsilon Alpha (assoc.). Office: Town of Southborough 28 Cordaville Rd Southborough MA 01772 Personal E-mail: davidstubbart@yahoo.com.

STUBBE, RAY WILLIAM, minister, writer; b. Milw., Aug. 15, 1938; s. Clarence Arnold and Ruby Otillie (Mueller) Stubbe. *Grandfather, Julius F. Mueller, emigrated in 1889 from Germany at age 4. Though he lost both his parents, and was schooled only through 8th grade, he eventually worked his way up to become a superintendent in a cast iron foundry. In later years, his innovative techniques drew inquiries from numerous foreign foundry men throughout the world and, upon retirement, he traveled to Sao Paulo, Brazil where he successfully modernized a foundry. His boundless energy and value on education was the reason that he flew bi-planes in the 1920's, built a reflecting telescope in the 1930's, sang in a civic male chorus, and travelled by car in the 1930's to every state including Canada and Mexico.* BA, St. Olaf Coll., 1962; MDiv, Northwestern Luth. Theol. Sem., 1965; postgrad., U. Chgo., 1967. Ordained to ministry Evang. Luth. Ch. Am., 1965. Mission devel. bd. Am. missions Luth Ch. in Am., Oak Creek, Wis., 1965-66; organizer, pastor All Saints Luth Ch., Oak Creek, 1966-67; enlisted USN, 1955; commd. ensign USNR, 1963, advanced through grades to lt., comdr. chaplain corps, 1971; augmented to USN, 1971; chaplain, 1967-85; ret. USN, 1985. Interviews on national televised programs. Author: Inside Force Recon, 1989, Khe Sanh Chaplain, 1970, Paddles, Parachutes, Patrols, 1979, Aarugha, 1989, Valley of Decision, 1991, The Final Formation, 1995, Khe Sanh and the Mongol Prince, 2002, Battalion of Kings, 2005, B5-T8 in 48 QXD: The Secret Official History of the North Vietnamese Army of the Siege at Khe Sanh, Vietnam, Spring, 1968, 2006, numerous poems; editor: Khe Sanh Veteran/Red Clay, 1996—98; contbr. articles to profl. jours. Founder, pres. emeritus Khe Sanh Vets., Inc., 1988—; spkr. numerous vet. assemblies; chaplain Wis. Vietnam Vets., Milw., 1984—, 3d Marine Divsn. Assn., 1988. Decorated Bronze Star with combat V; recipient Legion of Honor award, Chapel Four Chaplains. Mem.: DAV (life), VFW (life), Mil. Chaplains Assn. of USA (life), Wis. Acad. Scis., Arts and Letters (life), Spl. Ops. Assn. (life), 3d Marine Divsn. Assn. (life), Spl. Forces Assn. (life), Force Reconnaissance Assn. (life), Soc. Bibl. Lit., Vietnam Vets. Am. (life), Marine Corps Hist. Found. (life), Wis. Vietnam Vets. (life), Mil. Officers Assn. Am. (life), Mil. Chaplains Assn. (life), Pi Kappa Delta. Lutheran. Home: 8766 Parkview Ct Wauwatosa WI 53226-2729 *The most powerful Words of God have always been communicated to me by the occasional people encountered in life's pathways. These are the quiet ones whose very being reflect possibilities of being the image of God we all are; living Words of God who make us know we are free, forgiven, loved, blessed with value and future; heroes, who at great risk and pain to themselves, transform negatives into positives; great, good people who empty themselves into servants and incarnate love into all human conditions. When the vision they offer becomes life's task of who to become, all of life becomes a gift of everdeepening wells which nourish everything living with the deep underground stream, which is God.*

STUBBERUD, ALLEN ROGER, electrical engineering educator; b. Glendive, Mont., Aug. 14, 1934; s. Oscar Adolph and Alice Marie (LeBlanc) S.; m. May B. Tragus, Nov. 19, 1961; children: Peter A., Stephen C. BS in Elec. Engring, U. Idaho, 1956; MS in Engring, UCLA, 1958, PhD, 1962. From asst. prof. to assoc. prof. engring. UCLA, 1962-69; prof., then prof. emeritus, elec. engring. U. Calif., Irvine, 1969—, assoc. dean engring., 1972-78, dean engring., 1978-83, chair elec. and computer engring., 1993-98, interim dean engring., 1994-96; chief scientist U.S. Air Force, 1983-85. Dir. Elec. Communications and Systems Engring. divsn. NSF, 1987-88. Author: Analysis and Synthesis of Linear Time Variable Systems, 1964, (with others) Feedback and Control Systems, 2d edit., 1990, (with others) Digital Control System Design, 2d edit., 1994; contbr. articles to profl. jours. Recipient Exceptional Civilian Svc. medal USAF, 1985, 90, Meritorious Civilian Svc. medal, 1996. Fellow IEEE (Centennial medal 1984, Millennium medal 2000), AIAA, AAAS, NYAS; mem. INFORMS, Sigma Xi, Sigma Tau, Tau Beta Pi, Eta Kappa Nu. Office: Univ Calif Elec Engring Dept zotcode 2625 Irvine CA 92697-2625 E-mail: arstubbe@uci.edu.

STUBBLEFIELD, JOHN K., JR., food products executive; m. Sharon Stubblefield; 2 children. BBA in Acctg., U. Houston, 1970. V.p. adminstrn. Langazorta Internat., 1976-84; controller Sysco Corp., Houston, 1984-86, v.p. fin. Denver, 1986-92, v.p., controller, sr. v.p. Houston, 1993—99, CFO, 1994—, sr. v.p. fin. & admin., 1999—2003, exec. v.p. fin. and adminstrn., CFO, 2003—, also bd. dirs., 2003. Office: Sysco Corp 1390 Enclave Pkwy Houston TX 77077-2099 *

STUBBS, DONALD CLARK, retired secondary school educator; b. Providence, Mar. 6, 1935; s. Edward J. and Margaret Eleanor (Clark) S.; m. Lorraine Alice Thivierge, Apr. 3, 1969 (dec. Jan. 1986); 1 child, Derek C.; m. Sarah E. Andrews, Apr. 23, 1999. AB, Cath. U. Am., Washington, 1959, MS, 1966; postgrad., St. John's U., NYC, 1960. Tchr. Bishop Loughlin Meml. High Sch., Bklyn., 1959-61, Bishop Bradley High Sch., Manchester, NH, 1961-66; tchr., sci. dept. chair LaSalle Mil. Acad., Oakdale, NY, 1966-69, Ponaganset Regional High Sch., Glocester, RI, 1969-2000; ret., 2000. Home: 35 Shove St Woonsocket RI 02895-5741 E-mail: naddad@aol.com.

STUBBS, GERALD, biochemist, educator; b. Hobart, Australia, May 9, 1947; came to the US, 1976; m. Rebecca Lynn Harris; children: Andrew, Tamsin, Anneliese, Rachel. BSc, Australian Nat. U., 1968; DPhil, U. Oxford, 1972. Sci. asst. Max Planck Inst., Heidelberg, Germany, 1973-76; rsch. assoc. Brandeis U., Waltham, Mass., 1976-83; asst. prof. Vanderbilt U., Nashville, 1983-87, assoc. prof., 1987-90, prof., 1990—. Contbr. articles to profl. jour. Achievements include determination of molecular structure of tobacco mosaic virus. Office Phone: 615-322-2018. Business E-Mail: gerald.stubbs@vanderbilt.edu.

STUBBS, KENDON LEE, retired librarian; b. Washington, Apr. 6, 1938; s. Donald Harrison and Rosalee Adelia (Brown) S.; m. Patricia Townsend, June 3, 1961; children: Christopher, Peter, Timothy. BA, St. John's Coll., Annapolis, Md., 1960; MA, U. Va., 1964; MS, Columbia U., 1965. Sr. asst. in manuscripts U. Va. Libr., Charlottesville, 1965, reference libr., 1966-76, acting acquisitions libr., 1967-68, assoc. univ. libr., 1976-87, assoc. univ. libr. for pub. svcs., 1987-92, acting univ. libr., 1993, assoc. univ. libr., 1994-98, dep. univ. libr., 1998—2003, ret., 2003. Cons. US Dept. Edn., Washington, 1982—84. Author: Quantitative Criteria for Academic Research Libraries, 1984; editor: Cumulated Assn. Research Libraries Statistics, 1981, Rsch. Libr. Statistics, 1990, ARL Statistics, 1992-95, Japanese Text Initiative on World Wide Web, 1995—; contbr. articles on library stats., rsch. to profl. publs., Internet. Mem. Assn. of Rsch. Librs. (mem. stats. com., vis. program officer 1995-97), Bibliog. Soc. U. Va. (pres. 1975-78, v.p. 1978-99).

STUBBS, LU, sculptor, educator; b. NYC, Aug. 16, 1925; d. Thomas Benedetti and Clara Benvenuto; m. Harold L. Stubbs, Nov. 16, 1945; children: Susan Lee, Mahi Swan. Grad. highest honors, Sch. Boston Mus. Fine Arts, 1963, grad., 1964. Art cert. L'Accademia di Belle Arti, Perugia, Italy, 1971. Tchg. grad. asst. Mus. Sch., Boston, 1963—64, Boston Ctr. Edn., 1964—76, Milton Acad., Mass., 1967—68, Boston U., 1976—77. Bronze sculpture, Three Women, Bookline Mass., 1975, Deborah Sampson Revolutionary War Heroine, Sharon, Mass., 1989, Foxtale Family, Children's Libr., Foxboro, Mass., 2000, Pregnant Woman II, Cooley Dickinson Hosp., Nothampton, 2001, Mary Lyon, Holyoke Coll, South Hadley, Mass., 2006. Vol. Svc. Net., Northampton, Mass., 2000—; mem. Arts Coun., Northampton, Mass., 2005—07. Grantee, Nat. Endowment Arts and Humanites, 1977, Browne Fund, Boston, 1987. Fellow: Nat. Sculpture Soc.; mem.: New England Sculptor's Assn., Sharon Creative Arts Assn. Avocations: gardening, creative writing.

STUBBS, WILL, JR., pharmaceutical company manager; b. Birmingham, Ala., Feb. 26, 1955; s. Will, Sr. and Elizabeth S.; 1 child, Will III. BS in Mgmt. and Econs. cum laude, Fisk U., 1977. Sys. engr. Procter & Gamble, Jackson, Tenn., 1977-78, prodn. team mgr., 1978-80; large parenterals labeling/packaging supr. Abbott Labs., Rocky Mount, N.C., 1980-81, large parenterals terminal sterile filling supr., 1981-85, aseptic sterilization supr., 1985-88, small parenterals terminal sterile fill supr., 1988-90, aseptic filling supr., 1990-93, sr. prodn. supr., 1993-95, pharm. prodn. mgr., 1995-2001, terminal sterile filling prodn. mgr., 2001—02, small volume parenterals labeling/packaging prodn. mgr., 2002—04, pharm. prodn. mgr., 2004; labeling and packaging prodn. mgr. Hospira Inc., Rocky Mount, 2004—. Contbr. poetry to Fisk Herald. Mem. econ. growth task force Rocky Mount City Coun., 1992-94; bd. dirs. Nash Edgecombe Econ. Devel. Inc., Rocky Mount, 1994-99, vice chmn. bd. dirs., 1998, chmn., 1999; mem. Adult Basic Edn. Bd., 1980-84; pres. Rocky Mount Pan Hellenic Coun., 1991-93. Named to Outstanding Young Men of Am., Jayucees, 1983, 5th Dist. Scholar of the Yr., Omega Psi Phi, 1977; recipient internship Mobil Oil Corp. Mem. Omega Psi Phi (Vice-Basileus grad. chap. 1989-91). Democrat. Baptist. Avocations: community service, travel, music, swimming, jogging. Home: 1028 Niblick Dr Rocky Mount NC 27804-9655 Office: 4285 N Wesleyan Blvd Rocky Mount NC 27804-8612 Office Phone: 252-977-5961. Business E-Mail: will.stubbsjr@hospira.com.

STUBER, CHARLES WILLIAM, retired genetics educator, researcher, director; b. St. Michael, Nebr., Sept. 19, 1931; s. Harvey John and Minnie Augusta (Wilks) S.; m. Marilyn Martha Cook, May 28, 1953; 1 child, Charles William Jr. BS, U. Nebr., 1952, MS, 1961; PhD, N.C. State U., 1965. Vet., agrl. instr. Broken Bow HS, 1956-59; rsch. asst. U. Nebr., Lincoln, 1959-61; rsch. geneticist Agrl. Rsch. Svc., USDA, Raleigh, NC, 1962-75, supervisory rsrch. geneticist, rsch. leader, 1975-98, collaborator, 1998—; prof. genetics & crop sci. NC State U., Raleigh, 1975-98, prof. emeritus, 1998—, dir. Ctr. Plant Breeding and Applied Plant Genomics, 2006—. Assoc. editor Crop Sci. Jour., 1979-82, tech. editor, 1984-86, editor, 1987-89; contbr. over 200 articles to profl. jour., chpt. to books. Chmn. coun. on ministries and numerous offices Highland United Meth Ch., Raleigh. Lt. USN, 1952-56. Named Outstanding Sci. of Yr., USDA-ARS, 1989; recipient Genetics and Plant Breeding award Nat. Coun. Comml. Plant Breeders, 1995, Award of Merit, U. Nebr. Alumni Assn., 1997; inductee USDA-Agrl. Rsch. Svc. Sci. Hall of Fame, 1999; Vol. 45 of MAYDICA dedicated to Charles W. Stuber, 2000. Fellow: Crop Sci. Soc. Am. (editor-in-chief 1987—91, pres. 1992—93, Crop Sci. Rsch. award 1995, DeKalb Genetics Crop Sci. Disting. Career award 1999), Fellow Am. Soc. Agronomy (pres. 2002); mem.: Am. Genetic Assn. (sec. 1984—86), Genetics Soc. Am., Phi Kappa Phi, Sigma Xi. Avocations: windsurfing, water-skiing. Home: 1800 Manuel St Raleigh NC 27612-5510 Office: NC State U NC Agril Res Svc 4124 Williams Hall Raleigh NC 27695-7620 Office Phone: 919-515-5834. Office Fax: 919-515-7959. Personal E-mail: cstuber2@aol.com.

STUBER, SCOTT, film company executive; Past mktg. dept. Universal Pictures; exec. Donner/Schuler-Donner Prodns.; v.p. prodn. Universal Pictures, Universal City, Calif., 1997—2000, exec. v.p. prodn., 2000—01, co-pres. prodn., 2001—03, vice chmn., worldwide prodn., 2003—05, prodr., 2006—. Actor: (films) Free Willy 2: The Advanture Home, 1995, Assassins, 1995; assoc. prodr.: Volcano, 1997; prodr.: The Break-Up, 2006, You, Me and Dupree, 2006; exec. prodr.: (films) Accepted, 2006, Dead Silence, 2007. Office: Universal Pictures 100 Universal City Plaza Universal City CA 91608 *

STÜBGEN, JOERG-PATRICK, neurologist; b. Tripoli, Libya, Sept. 7, 1959; s. Fritz Hans Georg and Marie-Louise Hildegard Stübgen; m. Dana Annenberg; 1 child, Charlotte. MD, U. Pretoria, South Africa, 1983. Diplomate Am. Bd. Psychiatry and Neurology. Intern Grey's Hosp., Pietermaritzburg, South Africa; neurology resident U. Pretoria, South Africa, 1984—89, neuromuscular fellow, asst. prof. dept. neurology, 1990—91, assoc. prof., 1991—92; asst. prof. Cornell U., NYC, 1995—99, assoc. prof. dept. neurology, 2000—. Contbr. over 30 articles to profl. jours., chapters to books. Named one of Best Doctors in Am., 2003—04, America's Top Physicians, Consumer's Rsch. Coun. Am., 2005, Top Doctors N.Y. Metro Area, Castle Connelly Med. Ltd., 2006. Fellow: South Africa Coll. Medicine, Am. Bd. Electrodiagnostic Medicine, Royal Coll. Physicians and Surgeons Can., Am. Assn. Electro-Diagnostic Medicine, Coll. Physicians South Africa; mem.: AMA, Med. Soc. State N.Y., N.Y. Med. Soc., Am. Acad. Neurology. Lutheran. Avocations: road running, travel. Office: Cornell Univ Med College 525 E 68th St New York NY 10021 Home Phone: 212-288-5047; Office Phone: 212-746-2334. Business E-Mail: pstuebge@med.cornell.edu.

STUCKI, MARGARET ELIZABETH, art gallery director, writer, painter; b. West New York, NJ, Jan. 9, 1928; d. William Eugene and Elise (Hohl) Stucki. BA in Philosophy, Barnard Coll., 1949; MA in Fine Art, Columbia U., 1959; postgrad., Art Students League N.Y.C., 1949-51; ABD, NYU, 1961; PhD, Freedom U., Orlando, Fla., 1975. Prof. art Hartwick (N.Y.) Coll., 1962-72; dir. Stucki-Linstead Art Gallery and Mus., Pocatello, Idaho, 1994—. Founded A.D. 2000+ Christian Greeting Cards, 1999. One-woman shows include Wichita Art Assn., Kans., 1967, Swiss Ctr., N.Y.C., 1975, Capitol Bldg., Augusta, Maine, 1978, U.S. Senate, Washington, 1987, Idaho TV 8, 1998, Idaho State U. Women's Art Show, 2000, exhibitions include Treasure Valley Juried Exhbn., Boise State U., 1998, prin. works include oil painting The Crucifixion, Temple Bapt. Ch., Tallahassee, portraits; author: The Revolutionary Mission of Modern Art or Crud and Other Essays on Art, 1973, War on Light: The Destruction of the Image of God in Man Through Modern Art, 1975, Eco-Elegia: Elegies in Ecology, 1981, Gullible's Travels: An Educational Tax Exempt Trip Around the World in a Hot Air Balloon, 1987, October: A Thoreaunal, 2002, Margaret Stucki: A Pictorial Autobiography of the Swiss-American Artist (1928—), 2004, Croak: USSR-USA Top Secret Weather Control Tesla-Tech, 2005. Pub. spkr. Rorschach Soc. Projective Techniques, London, 1968, 3d Internat. Congress Social Psychiatry, Zagreb, Yugoslavia, 1970, Women for Constl. Gov., Washington, 1975, nat. convs., Boston, 1977, West Palm Beach, Fla., 1988, Rotary Club, Farmington, Maine, 1979. Recipient 4 awards for photography, 1951, 1961, 1997, 1999, Poetry prize, Swiss Civic Cultural Soc., 1983; grantee, Rsch. Coun., Finger Lakes, N.Y., 1967. Office: Stucki-Linstead Mus & Art Gallery 1050 E Center St Pocatello ID 83201-5201 Office Phone: 208-234-0478.

STUCKY, SCOTT WALLACE, federal judge, lawyer; b. Hutchinson, Kans., Jan. 11, 1948; s. Joe Edward and Emma Clara (Graber) S.; m. Jean Elsie Seibert, Aug. 18, 1973; children: Mary-Clare, Joseph. BA summa cum laude, Wichita State U., 1970; JD, Harvard U., 1973; MA, Trinity U., 1980; LLM with high honors, George Washington U., 1983; postgrad., Nat. War Coll., 1993. Bar: Kans. 1973, U.S. Dist. Ct. Kans. 1973, U.S. Ct. Appeals (10th cir.) 1973, U.S. Ct. Mil. Appeals 1974, U.S. Supreme Ct. 1976, D.C. 1979, U.S. Ct. Appeals (D.C. cir.) 1979. Assoc. Ginsburg, Feldman & Bress, Washington, 1978-82; chief docketing and svc. br. Nuclear Regulatory Commn., Washington, 1982-83; legis. counsel USAF, Washington, 1983-96; gen. counsel US Senate Armed Services Com., 1996—2001, prin. minority counsel, 2001—03, gen. counsel, 2003—06; judge US Ct. Appeals for the Armed Forces, Washington, 2006—. Lectr. bus. law Maria Regina Coll., Syracuse, N.Y., 1977; congrl. fellow Office Senator John Warner, 1986; res. judge adv. USAF Res., Washington, 1982-2003; col. Appellate Mil. Judge, USAF Ct. Criminal Appeals, 1991-95, 97-98, 2001-03; sr. reservist USAF Judiciary, 1995-97, Air Res. Pers. Ctr., 1998-99, Air Force Legal Svcs. Agy., 1999-2001. Contbr. articles to profl. jours. Capt. USAF, 1973-78. Decorated Legion of Merit, Air Force Meritorious Svc. medal with two oak leaf clusters. Mem. Fed. Bar Assn., Judge Advs. Assn. (bd. dirs. 1984-88), Res. Officers Assn., Wichita State U. Alumni Assn. (pres. chpt. 1981-86, nat. bd. dirs. 1986-92), Adoption Svc. Info. Agy. (bd. dirs. 1998-2002, 04-07), Army and Navy Club (Washington), Mil. Order of Loyal Legion US (state comdr. and recorder 1984-92, nat. treas. 1987-89, nat. vice comdr. 1989-93, nat. comdr.-in-chief 1993-95), Sons of Union Vets Civil War (chpt. vice-comdr 1986-88), Phi Delta Phi, Phi Alpha Theta, Phi Kappa Phi, Omicron Delta Kappa (bd. dirs. 2006—), Sigma Phi Epsilon. Republican. Episcopalian. Office: US Ct Appeals for the Armed Forces 450 E St NW Washington DC 20442

STUCKY, STEVEN (EDWARD), composer, conductor; b. Hutchinson, Kans., Nov. 7, 1949; s. Victor Eugene and Louise Doris (Trautwein) Stucky; m. Melissa Jane Whitehead, Aug. 22, 1970; children: Maura Catharine, Matthew Steven. MusB, Baylor U., 1971; MFA, Cornell U., 1973, DMA, 1978. Vis. asst. prof. Lawrence U., Appleton, Wis., 1978-80; prof. Cornell U., Ithaca, NY, 1980—, chmn. dept. music, 1992-97; vis. prof. Eastman Sch. of Music, 2001—02; Ernest Bloch vis. prof. U. Calif., Berkeley, 2003. Composer-in-residence L.A. Philharm. Orch., 1988—, Am. Acad. Rome, 2006. Author: Lutoslawski and His Music, 1981 (Deems Taylor award ASCAP 1982); composer: Sappho Fragments, 1982, Voyages, 1984, Boston Fancies, 1985, Dreamwaltzes, 1986, Concerto for orch., 1987, Son et Lumière, 1988, Angelus, 1990, Impromptus, 1991, Four Poems of A.R. Ammons, 1992, Ancora, 1994, Double Flute Cto., 1994, Fanfares and Arias, 1994, Pinturas de Tamayo, 1995, Music for Saxophones and Strings, 1996, Cradle Songs, 1997, Concerto Mediterraneo, 1998, Ad Parnassum, 1998, American Muse, 1999, Nell'ombra, nella luce, 2000, Etudes, 2000, Partita-Pastorale, after J.S.B., 2000, Concerto for Percussion and Wind Orchestra, 2001, Skylarks, 2001, Colburn Variations, 2002, Whispers, 2002, Album Leaves, 2002, Spirit Voices, 2003, Jeu de timbres, 2003, Second Concerto for Orchestra, 2003 (Pulitzer Prize for music, 2005), To Whom I Said Farewell, 2003, Sonate en forme de préludes, 2004, Piano Quartet, 2005, Three New Motets, 2005, Radical Light, 2007; received commn. from Nat. Endowment for Arts, 1982, Koussevitzky Found., 1991, Meet the Composer, 1995, 2004. Bd. advisors Barlow Endowment, 1993-97; bd. dirs. MacDowell Colony, 1993-95, Koussevitzky Found., 2006—, Am. Acad. in Rome, 2006-. Fellow Guggenheim Found., Nat. Endowment for the Arts, Bogliasco Found., Goddard Lieberson fellow Am. Acad. Arts and Letters. Fellow: Am. Acad. Arts and Scis.; mem.: AAAL. Office: care Philip Wilder 21C Media Group 162 56th St Ste 506 New York NY 10019 Office Phone: 212-245-2110 ext. 205. Personal E-mail: stevenstucky@mac.com.

STUDDARD, (CHRISTOPHER) RUBEN, singer; b. Birmingham, Ala., July 14, 1978; s. Kevin Studdard Sr. and Emily Studdard. Graduated, Ala. A&M U., 2000. Singer, jazz and soul band Just a Few Cats; singer, gospel group God's Gift. Backup singer: American Idol: The Search for a Superstar, 2002; singer, 2003 (named American Idol, 2003), (single) Flying Without Wings, 2003, (albums) Soulful, 2003, I Need an Angel, 2004, The Return, 2006; singer: (with various artists) American Idol Season 2: All Time, 2003; cameo Scooby Doo 2: Monsters Unleashed, 2004; nominee commentator: I Wanna Thank My Mama: The BET Awards 2004 Nomination Special; performer: American Idol Tour, 9th Annual Walk of Fame Honoring Aretha Franklin, 2003, Fromage, 2003, American Idol Christmas, 2003, 3rd Annual BET Awards, 2003, Good Morning America, 2004; guest appearances Oprah Winfrey Show, 2003, 2004, Making the Video, Ruben Studdard: Flying Without Wings, 2003, American Juniors, 2003, Sharon Osbourne Show, 2003, Late Show with David Letterman, 2004, The Ellen DeGeneres Show, 2004, Mad TV, 2004, One on One, 2004, Jimmy Kimmel Live, 2004. Nominee Grammy award for best male vocal R&B performance. He was nicknamed the 'Velvet Teddy Bear' by the legendary soulful diva Gladys Knight. During the competition he acknowledged his home town of Birmingham, Alabama by wearing a t-shirt adorned with the city area code "205." The state declared March 11 'Ruben Studdard Day'. Office: J Records 745 5th Ave New York NY 10151 Office Phone: 646-840-5600.

STUDEBAKER, JOHN MILTON, utilities engineer, consultant, educator; b. Springfield, Ohio, Mar. 31, 1935; s. Frank Milton and Monaruth (Beatty) S.; m. Virginia Ann Van Pelt, Mar. 12, 1960; 1 child, Jacqueline Ann Allcorn. BS in Law, LaSalle U., Chgo., 1969; MS and PhD in Indsl. Engring., Columbia Pacific U., San Rafael, Calif., 1984. Cert. plant engr. Am. Inst. Plant Engrs., profl. cons. Acad. Profl. Cons. & Advisors. Indsl engr. Internat. Harvest Co., 1957-60, supr. indsl. engring., 1960-66, gen. supr. body assembly, 1967-68, mgr. indsl. engring., 1968-70; mgr. manufacturing engring. Lamb Electric Co., 1970—76, Cascade Corp., 1976—88; engring. mgr. Bundy Tubing Corp., Winchester and Cynthia, Ky., 1988—98; chmn. The Studebaker Group, Inc., Alexandria, Va., 1998—; pres. Studebaker Energy Cons., LLC, 1998—. Instr. numerous univs. including Boston U., Clemson U., Cornell U., Harvard U., Duquesne U., U. Ala., U. Ill., U. Wis., Ga. State U., James Madison U., Tex. Tech. U., U. Calif., Calif. State U., Columbia U., Fairleigh Dickinson U., San Francisco State U.; instr. Am. Mgmt. Assn., Rochester Inst. Tech., Ctr. for Profl. Advancement. Author: Slashing Utility Costs Handbook, Natural Gas Purchasing Handbook, Electricity Retail Wheeling Handbook, Electricity Purchasing Handbook, Utility Negotiation Handbook, ESCO Handbook. Mem. NSPE, Am. Inst. Facility Engrs. (cert.), Assn. Energy Engrs. (instr.). Republican. Home and Office: PO Box 708 Winchester KY 40392-0708 Office Phone: 859-744-1018. Business E-Mail: jstudebaker@studebakerenergy.net.

STUDEMAN, BILL (WILLIAM OLIVER STUDEMAN), aerospace transportation executive, former federal agency administrator, retired naval officer; b. Brownsville, Tex., Jan. 16, 1940; s. Oliver Jennings and Gail (McDavitt) S.; m. Gloria Diane Jeans, Sept. 12, 1964; children: Kimberly, Michael, Kate. BA, U. of S. Sewanee, 1962; student, Def. Intelligence Sch., 1966-67; M in Internat. Affairs, George Washington U., 1973; postgrad., Naval War Coll., 1973, Nat. War Coll., 1981; DSc in Strategic Intelligence (hon.), Def. Intelligence Coll., 1987. Commd. ensign USN, 1963, advanced through grades to admiral, 1992; ret., 1995; analyst Naval Intelligence Support Ctr., Washington, 1974-75; exec. asst. Office Naval Intelligence, Washington, 1975-76; officer in charge FOSIC Norfolk, CINLANTFLT, Norfolk, Va., 1976-78; asst. chief of staff COMSIXTHFLEET, Gaeta, Italy, 1978-80; exec. asst. Office of VCNO, Washington, 1981-82; comdg. officer Navy Operational Intel Command, Washington, 1982-84; dir. long range planning USN, Washington, 1984-85; dir. Naval Intelligence, Washington, 1985-88, Nat. Security Agy., MD, 1988-92; dep. dir. CIA, Washington, 1991-95; sr. v.p., dep. gen. mgr. for intelligence & info. superiority, Northrop Grumann Mission Systems Northrop Grumman Corp. (formerly TRW), Reston, Va., 1996—. Mem. Commn. on Intelligence Capabilities of the US Regarding Weapons of Mass Destruction, 2004. Decorated Legion of Merit with two gold stars, Naval and Intelligence D.S.M.; recipient President's Nat. Security medal. Mem. Armed Forces Comm. and Electronics Assn., Nat. Mil. Intelligence Assn., Naval Intelligence Profls., Assn. Former Intelligence Officers. Episcopalian. Avocations: sailing, rebuilding cars.

STUDER, LOUIS, priest, religious organization administrator; b. Algona, Iowa, Oct. 24, 1949; s. Paul Otto and Marcella Bertha (West) Studer. BA in Sociology, Lewis U., 1971; MDiv in Theology, Weston Coll. Sch. Theology, 1975; MS in Edn. Adminstrn. and Supervision, So. Ill. U., 1979; PhD in Philosophy of Edn., St. Louis U., 1984. Ordained priest Roman Cath. Ch., 1976. Assoc. pastor St. Patrick's Parish, McCook, Nebr., 1976—77; prin. St. Henry's Seminary, Belleville, Ill., 1977—84; dir. campus ministry U. Minn., Duluth, Minn., 1984—86; dir. Pre-Novitiate Program, Omaha, 1986—89, St. Louis, 1989—91; vocation dir. Oblate House Theology, Chgo., 1991—96; sabbatical program Jerusalem, Israel, Cambridge, Mass., 1996—97; dir. Shrine of Our Lady of the Snows & Missionary Assn. of Mary Immaculate, Belleville, 1997—. Provincial coun. mem. Oblates of Mary Immaculate, St. Paul, 1990—99. Author: (book) The High School Seminary in U.S. Today, 1984. Bd. dirs. Bethany Place, Belleville, 1998—. Home: 442 S De Mazenod Dr Belleville IL 62223 Office: Nat Shrine of Our Lady of the Snows 442 S DeMazenod Dr Belleville IL 62223

STUDER, WILLIAM ALLEN, security consultant, retired military officer; b. Chgo., July 27, 1939; s. William Gotlieb and Annette Elizabeth (Bruzek) S.; m. Donna Barnes Bray, Dec. 26, 1961; children: Scott, Shannon. BS in Indsl. Mgmt., Ga. Tech., 1962; MS in Guidance and Counseling, Troy State U., 1975, MS in Mgmt., 1978; graduate, Air War Coll., Maxwell AFB, Ala., 1981, Air Command and Staff Coll., 1975. Commd. 2d lt. USAF, 1961, advanced through grades to maj. gen., 1989; legis. liaison U.S. Senate, Washington, 1981-83; dir. fighter ops./tng. USAF Hdqrs. Europe, Ramstein AB, Fed. Republic Germany, 1983-84; vice comdr. 10th Tactical Reconnaissance Wing RAF USAF, Alconbury, Eng., 1984-85, comdr. 10th Tactical Reconnaissance Wing RAF, 1985-86, cmdr. 81st Tactical Fighter Wing RAF Bentwaters, Eng., 1986-87, comdr. 316th Air Div/Kaiserslautern Ramstein AB, Fed. Republic Germany, 1987-88, vice comdr. 12th Air Force/U.S. So. Command Bergstrom AFB, Tex., 1988-90, comdr. 13th Air Force Clark AFB, The Philippines, 1990-91; dir. ops. CENTCOM/J-3, MacDill AFB, Fla., 1992-94; ret. USAF, 1994; dir. pub. safety dept. Hillsborough County, Tampa, Fla., 1994—2005, emergency preparedness cons., 2005—; pres. Studer & Assoc., Tampa. Decorated D.S.M., Legion of Merit with oak leaf cluster, DFC with three oak leaf clusters, Bronze Star, Air medal with 35 oak leaf clusters; Legion of Honor, Bronze Cross medal (The Philippines). Mem. Daedalians, Quiet Birdmen, Rotary. Avocations: golf, reading, hiking. Home: 5309 Bayshore Blvd Tampa FL 33611 Office: Studer & Assoc Tampa FL 33611 Office Phone: 813-758-5106. Personal E-mail: studerdm@verizon.net.

STUDER, WILLIAM JOSEPH, library director; b. Whiting, Ind., Oct. 1, 1936; s. Victor E. and Sarah G. (Hammersley) S.; m. Rosemary Lippie, Aug. 31, 1957 (dec.); children: Joshua E., Rachel Marie. BA, Ind. U., 1958, MA, 1960, PhD (Univ. fellow), 1968. Grad. asst. divsn. libr. sci. Ind. U., 1959-60, reference asst., 1960-61; spl. intern Libr. of Congress, 1961-62, reference libr., sr. bibliographer, 1962-65; dir. regional campus librs. Ind. U., Bloomington, 1968-73, assoc. dean univ. librs., 1973-77; dir. librs. Ohio State U., Columbus, 1977-2000, prof. emeritus libr. sci., 2000—, coord. univ. oral history program, 2001—. Mem. Libr. Svcs. and Constrn. Act Adv. Com. of Ind., 1971-76; mem. Adv. Coun. on Fed. Libr. Programs in Ohio, 1977-85, chmn., 1980-81; adv. coun. Libr. Svcs. and Tech. Act, 1997-99; mem. ARL Office Mgmt. Studies Adv. Com., 1977-81, ARL Task Force on Nat. Libr. Network Devel., 1978-83, bd. dirs., 1981-84, chmn., 1981-83, com. on preservation, 1985-88, vice-chmn., 1989-90, chmn., 1991-92, task force on scholarly comm., 1983-87, com. stats. and measurement, 1993-99, chmn., 1997-98; network adv. com. Libr. Congress, 1981-88; libr. study com. Ohio Bd. Regents, 1986-87; mem. steering com. Ohio Libr. and Info. Network (OhioLINK), 1987-90; vice-chmn. Ctr. Rsch. Librs., 1993-94, chmn., 1994-95, sec., chmn. membership com., 1990-93; adv. coun. OhioLink Libr., 1992-2000, chmn., 1991-92, policy adv. coun., governing bd., 1991-92. Contbr. articles to profl. jours. Trustee Online Computer Libr. Ctr. Inc., 1977-78; del. Online Computer Libr. Ctr. Users Coun., 1983-91; rsch. librs. adv. com. Online Computer Libr. Ctr., 1989-95, vice-chmn., chmn.-elect, 1993-94, chmn., 1994-95; bd. dirs. Ohio Network of Librs. Ohionet, 1977-87, chmn., 1980-82, 86-87, treas., 1983-86; mem. Columbia U. Sch. Libr. Svc. Conservation Programs, vis. com., 1987-90; nat. adv. coun. to commn. on preservation and access, 1989-92; treas. Monroe County (Ind.) Mental Health Assn., 1968-76; budget rev. com. United Way, 1975-77; bd. dirs. Mental Health Assn. Recipient citation for participation MARC Insts., 1968-69, Disting. Alumni award Ind. U., 1978, OhioLINK Founders award, 2002. Mem. ALA, Ohio Libr. Assn. (bd. dirs. 1980-83), Assn. Coll. and Rsch. Librs. (bd. dirs. 1977-81, com. on activities model for 1990, 1981-82, chmn. libr. sch. curriculum task force 1988-89), Ohio State U. Retirees Assn. (pres.-elect 2004-05, pres., 2005-06), Acad. Libr. Assn. Ohio, Torch Club (pres. 1993-94), Phi Kappa Phi (pub. rels. officer 1982-83, sec. 1983-85), Phi Eta Sigma, Alpha Epsilon Delta., Beta Phi Mu. Home: 724 Olde Settler Pl Columbus OH 43214-2924 Office: Ohio State U William Oxley Thompson Meml Libr 1858 Neil Ave Columbus OH 43210-1286 Office Phone: 614-688-0204. Business E-Mail: studer.2@osu.edu.

STUDIN, JAN, publishing executive; From acct. mgr. to v.p. Woman's Day, 1982—95, v.p., advt. dir., 1995—96; v.p., pub. Woman's Day Hachette Filipacchi Mags., Inc., NYC, 1996—2002; v.p., pub. Parents Mag., 2002—06, Better Homes & Gardens Mag., 2006—. Office: Better Homes & Gardens 125 Park Ave New York NY 10017 Office Phone: 212-557-6600. *

STUDNESS, CHARLES MICHAEL, economist; b. Mpls., Nov. 2, 1935; s. Leo C. and Alma (Mehus) S.; m. Harriet Leah Katz, Oct. 27, 1968; children: Erica, Lisa, Roy. BA, U. Minn., 1957, MA, 1958; PhD in Econs., Columbia U., 1963. Lectr. CCNY, 1961-64, U. Minn., Mpls., 1964-65; economist Fed. Res. Bank N.Y., NYC, 1965-67, N.Y. Stock Exchange, NYC, 1967-68, Eastern Airlines, NYC, 1968-70, Baker Weeks, NYC, 1970-76, E.F. Hutton, NYC, 1976-79; pres. Studness Rsch., Manhasset, NY, 1979—; lectr. Baruch Coll., NYC, 1968-74. Contbg. editor Public Utilities Fortnightly, 1990—. Columnist, Pub. Utilities Fortnightly, 1979—. Personal E-mail: studness@optonline.net.

STUDWELL, WILLIAM EMMETT, librarian, writer; b. Stamford, Conn., Mar. 18, 1936; s. Alfred Theodore and Mary Alice (Baker) S.; m. Ann Marie Stroia, Aug. 28, 1965 (dec. 2003); 1 child, Laura Ann. BA, U. Conn., 1958, MA, 1959; MLS, Cath. U. Am., 1967. Tech. abstracter Libr. Congress, Washington, 1963-66, asst. editor decimal classification office, 1966-68; head libr. Kirtland C.C., Roscommon, Mich., 1968-70; head/prin. cataloger No. Ill. U., DeKalb, 1970-2000; freelance writer, editor, 2001—. Mem. US Adv. Com. to Chemistry Sects., Universal Decimal Classification, 1968-72; chmn. adv. group Libr. Rsch. Ctr., Urbana, Ill., 1982-84. Author: Chaikovskii, Delibes, Stravinskii, 1977, Christmas Carols, 1985, Adolphe Adam and Leo Delibes, 1987, Ballet Plot Index, 1987 (named one of Outstanding Academic Books, Choice Mag., 1989), Cataloging Books, 1989, Library of Congress Subject Headings, 1990, Opera Plot Index, 1990, Christmas Card Songbook, 1991, Subject Access to Films and Videos, 1992, Popular Song Reader, 1994, Christmas Carol Reader, 1995, National and Religious Song Reader, 1996, Americana Song Reader, 1997, Minor Ballet Composers, 1997, State Songs of the United States, 1997 (academic best seller), Publishing Glad Tidings, 1998, College Fight Songs, 1998, Barbershops, Bullets, and Ballads, 1999, Circus Songs, 1999, The End of the Year, 1999, The Classic Rock and Roll Reader, 1999, They Also Wrote, 2000, The Big Band Reader, 2000, The Clandestine Classical Music Reader, 2000, Forward! Forward! Is the Word, 2000, College Fight Songs II, 2001, Lest We Forget, 2001, A Fable, A Fantasy, and a Farewell, 2002, The French Violin School, 2002, Suzannah's Redemption, or The Devil Gets His Due, 2003, The Man Who Invented God and Other Fantastic Tales, 2004, Ten Terrible Tales, 2005, College Fight Songs III, 2005, The Christmas Carol in the New Millennium, 2006, An Easy Guide to Christmas Carols, 2006, Seven Deadly Singles, 2007; asst. editor Western Assn. of Map Librs. Info. Bull., 1989—94; editor: Music Reference Svcs. Quar., 1991—99, Resources in Music History Book Series, 1999—, The Millennia Collection, 2000—; contbg. editor Technicalities, 1996—2004; contbr. articles to profl. jours. US expert on Christmas Carols; internat. recognized expert on Am. Coll. fight songs; internat. leader to devel. standardization code for libr. congress subject headings; leading internat. proponent multinat., multicultural and multilingual subject access sys. Named most productive author among librs. in US, Coll. and Rsch. Librs. Mag., 1983-87, 93-97, Outstanding Alumnus, Sch. Libr. and Info. Sci., Cath. U. Am., 2002. Mem. Ill. Assn. Coll. and Rsch. Librs. (exec. bd. 1980-85, newsletter editor 1980-85, lifetime achievement award 1992), Ill. Libr. Assn., Librs. for Social Responsibility (editor newsletter 1986-87, bd. dirs. 1986-94). Home: 3332 S Forrester St Bloomington IN 47401-7115

STUDZINSKI, JOHN JOSEPH PAUL, investment banking executive; b. Mass., Mar. 19, 1956; arrived in Eng., 1984; s. Alfred and Jennie S. AB, Bowdoin Coll., 1978; MBA, U. Chgo., 1980. Investment banker Morgan Stanley & Co. Ltd., NYC, 1980; head, corp. fin. Morgan Stanley Internat. Inc., London, 1989—92, head, mergers & acquisitions European bus., 1992—97, head, investment banking Europe, 1997—2001, dep. chmn, 2001—03; co-chief exec., corp. investment banking, and markets (CIBM) HSBC Holdings, 2003—06; sr. mng. dir. The Blackstone Group, 2006—, mem. exec. com., 2006—. Chmn. Bus. Action on Homelessness, London, 1999—; founder Passage Day Centre, London, 2000—; trustee Tate Gallery, 1998—; life trustee Sir John Soane Mus., 1999—; trustee Human Rights Watch, NYC, 1999—, Bowdoin Coll. Named to Knight of the Order of St. Gregory, Pope John Paul II, 2001; recipient Prince of Wales Ambassador's award, 2000, dist. alumnus, U. Chgo., 2002. Avocations: performing arts, hiking, outdoor survival. Office: The Blackstone Group 40 Berkeley Sq London W1J 5AL England *

STUEBING, EDWARD WILLIS, research scientist; b. Cin., Sept. 9, 1942; s. Edward Norman and Ruth Marcella (Glass) S.; m. Mary Ann Brown (div. 1980); children: Barbara Jean, Jennifer Jane. BS with high honors, U. Cin., 1965; PhD, Johns Hopkins U., Balt., 1970. Rsch. scientist U.S. Army Frankford Arsenal, Phila., 1971—77, U.S. Army, Edgewood R&D Ctr., Aberdeen Proving Ground, Md., 1977—; joint svcs. bus. area mgr. CB Def. Supporting Sci. and Tech., 1994—2003, chief scientist for physical scis., 1999—2001, team leader aerosol sci., 1992—. Adj. prof. Drexel U., Phila., 1973-1976; invited lectr. nat. and internat. scientific meetings. Contbr. articles to profl. jours. Dir. Civic Assn., Kingsville, Md., 1989-92; pres. Gunpowder Valley Conservancy, Md., 1990-94, treas., 1995—; elder Presbyn. Ch., Franklinville, Md., 1993—. Capt. U.S. Army, 1970-71. Recipient Army R&D Achievement award, 1974, 85, medal for Meritorious Civilian Svc., 1984, The Outstanding Fed. Profl. of 1984 award Fed. Exec. Bd., 1984, William H. Walker award, 1989. Mem. Am. Assn. for Aerosol Rsch. (chmn. nat. meeting 1983, dir. 1998—2001), Am. Chem. Soc., Am. Phys. Soc., Phi Beta Kappa, Sigma Xi. Avocations:

trombone, sailing. Home: PO Box 233 Gunpowder MD 21010-0233 Office: Attn AMSRD ECB RT TA Bldg E5951 5183 Blackhawk Rd Aberdeen Proving Ground MD 21010-5424 Office Phone: 410-436-3089.

STUEBNER, ERWIN AUGUST, JR., internist; b. Phila., Oct. 9, 1944; s. Erwin August and Frances Badge (Quinn) S.; m. Jane Sigrid Christensen, Sept. 21, 1968; children: Eric Jay, Andrew Todd, Scott August. AB, Dartmouth Coll., 1966; MD, Northwestern U., Chgo., 1970. Diplomate Am. Bd. Internal Medicine. Intern, resident U. Mich., Ann Arbor, 1970-74; physician Williamstown Med. Assocs., Mass., 1976—; chmn. dept. medicine North Adams Regional Hosp., Mass., 1991—2003, 2005—07. Corporator North Adams Regional Hosp., 1992-; bd. dirs. Med. Profl. Mut. Ins. Co., Boston, 1995-. Fundraising chmn. Campaign for New Athletic Field, Williamstown, Mass., 1995-96. Maj. U.S. Army, 1974-76; trustee No. Berkshire Health Sys., 2002—. Mem. ACP, Am. Heart Assn. (exec. com. 1978-94), Mass. Med. Soc. (trustee 1988-94, 2000—06, alt. trustee 1994-2000, 06—), Berkshire Dist. Med. Soc. (pres. 1984-86, exec. com. 1982-). Avocations: hiking, tennis, travel, classical music. Office: Williamstown Med Assn 197 Adams Rd Williamstown MA 01267-2930

STUEHRENBERG, PAUL FREDERICK, librarian; b. Breckenridge, Minn., Mar. 14, 1947; s. Henry Ernest Frederick and Marian Violet (Sandberg) S.; m. Suzanne Elaine Draper, June 14, 1969 (div. Apr. 1982); m. Carole Lee DeVore, Aug. 1, 1983. BA, Concordia Sr. Coll., 1968; MDiv, Concordia Sem., 1972; STM, Christ Sem., 1974; MA, U. Minn., 1978, PhD, 1988. Asst. libr. U. Minn., Mpls., 1974-82; monographs libr. Yale Divinity Libr., New Haven, 1982-91, div. libr., 1991—; adj. assoc. prof. in theol. lit. Yale Divinity Sch., New Haven, 1993—. Asst. pastor Christ Meml. Luth. Ch., Plymouth, Minn., 1974-82; adj. pastor Bethesda Luth. Ch., New Haven, 1984—; sec. Luth. Student Found., Mpls., 1978-81. Contbr. articles to profl. jours. Sec. North Haven (Conn.) Libr. Bd., 1989-2003. Mem. Am. Theol. Libr. Assn. (pres. 2004-05), Soc. Bibl. Lit., Am. Acad. Religion, North Haven Meml. Libr. Assn. Home: 280 Bayard Ave North Haven CT 06473-4307 Office: Yale U Div Sch Libr 409 Prospect St New Haven CT 06511-2167 E-mail: paul.stuehrenberg@yale.edu.

STUFANO, THOMAS JOSEPH, criminologist, author, inventor; b. Newport, RI, July 23, 1955; s. Thomas and Zoe Anne (Halsey) S.; 1 child, Christine Anne; m. Rene Ellen Goldfarb, Nov. 10, 1994. BSc in Criminal Justice, Pacific Western U., 1988; disting. grad., U.S. Air U., 2000; postgrad., Eurotech. Rsch. U., 1997; MBA in Mil. Scis., Touro U., 2001. Legis. rschr. R.I. Ho. of Reps., Providence, R.I., 1978-79; sub com. investigator U.S. Ho. of Reps., Washington, 1979-81; law enforcement staff rschr. State of Fla., 1981-88; exec. dir. Diversified Technologies and System Inc., 1989—; CEO U.S. Dept. Homeland Security, 2002—; chief of police Smithville, Tenn., 2006—. Cons. crime commn. State of Fla., 1986-87, U.S. Govt., Washington, 1990-92, State of R.I., 1979-80; mem. Pres.' Commn. on Aviation Security and Terrorism. Author: Human Element in Business, 1992, Combating Terrorism, 1994, Investigators Pretext Investigation Manual, 1998, BEA Training Manual, 1998; Applied Impact Theory patentee, 1999; contbr. articles to profl. jours. Mem. Rep. Senatorial Inner Circle, Washington, 1992—; instr. ARC, Fla., 1994—; mem. adv. bd. Nat. Civil Def., Washington, 1988—; mem. Presdl. Round Table. Recipient Presdl. Commendation Pres. of U.S., 1988, 91, 94, Commendation U.S. Ho. of Reps. and Senate, 1982, 91, 94, commendation Prime Minister Lady Margaret Thatcher, 1991, Citation R.I. Ho. of Reps., 1980, Gov. of Mass., 1980, Tenn., Fla., Ky., 1990, Commendation U.S. Dept. of State, 1992, Min. Intelligence Security, Eng., 1996, Meritorious Achievement award for global antiterrorism, 1997, 20th Century Achievement award ABI, 1998, Millennium Hall of Fame award, 1998, 500 Leaders of Influence award IBI, 1998. Mem. Air Force Assn., Internat. Narcotic Enforcement Officers Assn., Internat. Assn. Chiefs Police, Res. Officers Assn., World Assn. of Investigators, Internat. Assn. Counter Terrorism and Security Profls., Tenn. Assn. Chiefs Police, USAF/SARCAP (instr. search/rescue command pilot), Aircraft Owners and Pilots Assn., Profl. Assn. of Diving Instrs. (instr., Platnuim Diving award 1989), Am. Shorin Kempo Karate Assn. (5th degree blackbelt), Order of Ky. Cols. Roman Catholic. Avocations: scuba diving, airplane pilot, parachuting, bicycling, Karate.

STUFFT, WILLIAM DAVID, music educator; b. Somerset, Pa., Oct. 26, 1947; s. William Denton Stufft, Freda Mildred (Daniels) Stufft; m. June Carol Gestine, June 12, 1971; 1 child, Carolyn Joy. BS in Music Edn., Indiana U. Pa., 1969, MEd, 1978; postgrad., Alliance Theol. Sem., 1978, U. Pitts., 1979—80. Tchr. band Meyersdale Sch. Dist., Meyersdale, Pa., 1969—78; min. music Tallmadge Alliance Ch., Tallmadge, Ohio, 1978—82; pastor Oakhill Alliance Ch., Warrendlae, Pa., 1982—85; prof. music Toccoa Falls Coll., Toccoa Falls, Ga., 1985—. Musical dir. Toccoa Symphony Orch., Toccoa, Ga., 2001—, trumpet and aux. percussion, 1989—2001; dir. concert band Toccoa Falls Coll., Toccoa Falls, 1985—. Author: Preparing to Take the Praxis # in Music; contbr. articles to profl. jours. Spec 4 US Army, 1970—72. Mem.: Ga. Music Educators Assn., Pa. Music Educators Assn. (pres., pres.-elect 1970—77), Music Educators Nat. Conf. Avocations: woodworking, writing, playing trumpet, composing music. Home: 927 Skyline Dr Toccoa GA 30577 Office: Toccoa Falls College Falls Rd Toccoa Falls GA 30598

STUHAN, RICHARD GEORGE, lawyer; b. Braddock, Pa., July 1, 1951; s. George and Pauline Madeline (Pavlocik) S.; m. Mary Ann Cipriano, Aug. 23, 1975; children: Brendan George, Sara Katherine, Brian Christopher, Caitlin Emily. BA summa cum laude, Duquesne U., 1973; JD, U. Va., 1976. Bar: Va. 1976, D.C. 1977, U.S. Ct. Appeals (D.C. cir.) 1977, U.S. Ct. Appeals (4th cir.) 1977, U.S. Claims Ct. 1979, U.S. Supreme Ct. 1980, U.S. Ct. Appeals (3d cir.) 1981, U.S. Ct. Appeals (11th cir.) 1982, U.S. Dist. Ct. (no. dist.) Ohio 1985, Ohio 1986. Assoc. Arnold & Porter, Washington, 1976-84; of counsel Jones Day, Cleve., 1984-86, ptnr., 1987—. Pres. Womankind Maternal and Prenatal Care; chmn. devel. com. Doan Brook Watershed Partnership. Mem. Va. Law Review, 1974-76. Recipient Gold Medal for Gen. Excellence, Duquesne U., 1973; named Ohio Super Lawyer, Law and Politics Media, Inc. Mem. Cleve. Bar Assn. (chmn. jury svc. com.), Internat. Assn. Def. Counsel, Order of Coif. Democrat. Roman Catholic. Avocations: tennis, swimming, basketball, home repair. Home: 2865 Falmouth Rd Shaker Heights OH 44122-2838 Office: Jones Day 901 Lakeside Ave Cleveland OH 44114-1190 Home Phone: 216-561-3595; Office Phone: 216-586-7148. Business E-Mail: rgstuhan@jonesday.com.

STUHLDREHER, DAVID BROSNAN, urologist; b. Indpls., Feb. 11, 1961; s. William Daniel and Eleanor Sue Stuhldreher; m. Pratima V. Stuhldreher, Nov. 24, 1990; children: Jason, Rachel. BS in Biology, Ind. U., Bloomington, 1983; MD, Ind. U., Indpls., 1987. Diplomate Am. Bd. Urology. Urologist Urology of Ind., Indpls., 1993—. Named one of Top Urologists in Indpls., 2001; recipient, 2003. Mem.: Am. Urol. Assn., Highland Club, Sigma Chi. Republican. Roman Catholic. Avocations: reading, travel, golf, tennis. Home: 3228 Henback Way Indianapolis IN 46220 Office: Urology of Ind 1270 N Post Indianapolis IN 46219

STUHLINGER, ERNST, physicist; b. Niederrimbach, Germany, Dec. 19, 1913; came to U.S., 1946, naturalized, 1955. s. Ernst and Pauline (Werner) S.; m. Irmgard Lotze, Aug. 1, 1950; children: Susanne, Tilman, Hans Christoph. PhD, U. Tuebingen, Germany, 1936; PhD (hon.), Tech. U., Berlin. Asst. prof. Technische Hochschule, Berlin, Germany, 1936-41; guidance and control equipment rocket Devel. Center, Peenemuende, Germany, 1943-45; with Guided Missile Devel. Office, Ft. Bliss, Tex., 1946-50; physicist Ordnance Missile Labs., Huntsville, Ala., 1950-56, Army Ballistic Missile Agy., 1956-60; dir. Space Scis. Lab., George C. Marshall Space Flight Center, NASA, Huntsville, Ala., 1960-68; assoc. dir. for sci. George C. Marshall Space Flight Center, NASA, 1968-76; sr. research scientist, adj. prof. U. Ala. at Huntsville, 1976-84; sr. research assoc. Teledyne Brown Engring. Corp., Huntsville, 1984-88; cons. aerospace cos. Vis. scientist Tech. U. Munich, W. Germany, 1978, Max Planck Inst. Nuclear Physics, Heidelberg, 1983-85; cons. Teledyne-Brown Engring., 1984-90. Author: Ion Propulsion for Space Flight, 1964; co-author: Skylab, A Guidebook, 1973, Project Viking, 1976, Aufbruch in Den Weltraum, 1992, Wernher von Braun, Crusader for Space, 1994. Served with German Army, 1941-43, Russian Campaign. Recipient Humboldt prize Tech. U. Munich, 1978, Rainer Bauer award Ala.-Germany Partnership, 2002; induction Ala. Aviation Hall of Fame, 2001. Fellow Am. Astronautical Soc., mem. Von Braun Astron. Soc. (dir.), German Roentgengesellschaft (hon.), German Physikalische Assn., Hermann Oberth Assn. (hon.), Internat. Foerderkreis for Raumfahrt (hon. pres. 2004—). Rsch. cosmic rays, nuclear physics, electric space propulsion, manned missions to Mars. Home: 3106 Rowe Dr SE Huntsville AL 35801-6151

STUHR, ELAINE RUTH, state legislator; b. Polk County, Nebr., June 19, 1936; m. Boyd E. Stuhr, 1956; children: Cynthia (Stuhr) Zluticky, Teresa (Stuhr) Robbins, Boyd E., Jr. BS, U. Nebr. Tchr. jr. and sr. vocat. h.s. Nebr. schs.; senator Nebr. Unicameral, Lincoln, 1994—; chmn. Nebr. retirement sys. com.; vice chair natural resources com.; commr. edn. com. of states; farmer Bradshaw, Nebr. Former asst. instr. U. Nebr., Lincoln; participant farmer to farmer assignment to Russia with Winrock, Internat., 1993, to Lithuania with Vol. Overseas Coop. Asistance, 1993; former pres. Agrl. Womens Leadership Network; former mem. bd. dirs. Feed Grains Coun., Nebr. Corn Bd. Past pres., bd. dirs. Found. for Agrl. Edn. and Devel.; former mem. exec. com. and bd. dirs. Agrl. Coun. Am.; nat. pres. Women Involved in Farm Econs., state pres.; mem. adv. com. Nebr. Extension Sv.; bd. dirs. Heartland Ctr. for Leadership Devel.; past chmn. Nebr. Agrl. Leadership Coun. Republican. Office Phone: 402-471-2756. E-mail: estuhr@unicam.state.ne.us.

STUKEL, JAMES JOSEPH, academic administrator, mechanical engineer, educator; b. Joliet, Ill., Mar. 30, 1937; s. Philip and Julia (Mattivi) S.; m. Mary Joan Helpling, Nov. 27, 1958; children: Catherine, James, David, Paul. BS in Mech. Engring, Purdue U., 1959; MS, U. Ill., Urbana-Champaign, 1963, PhD, 1968. Research engr. W.Va. Pulp and Paper Co., Covington, Va., 1959-61; mem. faculty U. Ill., Urbana-Champaign, 1968—, prof. mech. engring., 1975—, dir. Office Coal Research and Utilization, 1974-76, dir. Office Energy Research, 1976-81, dir. pub. policy program Coll. Engring., 1981-84, assoc. dean Coll. Engring. and dir. Expt. Sta., 1984-85; dean Grad. Coll., vice chancellor for research U. Ill. at Chgo., 1985-86, exec. vice chancellor, vice chancellor academic affairs, 1986-91, interim chancellor, 1990-91, chancellor, 1991-95, pres., 1995—. V.p. Chgo. Tech. Park Corp., 1985-88. pres., 1990-91; exec. sec. midwest Consortium Air Pollution, 1972-73, chmn. bd. dirs., 1973-75; mem. adv. bd. regional studies program Argonne (Ill.) Nat. Lab., 1975-76; adv. com. Energy Resources Commn., 1976; chmn. panel on dispersed electric generating techs. Office Tech. Assessment, U.S. Congress, 1980-81; chmn. rev. adv. bd. tech. rev. dist. heating and combined heat and power systems Internat. Energy Agy, OECD, Paris, 1982-83; cons. in field. Contbr. articles to profl. jours. Pres. parish council Holy Cross Roman Cath. Ch., Urbana, 1967-68. Mem. ASCE (State-of-the-Art of Civil Engring. award 1975), ASME, AAAS, Sigma Xi, Phi Kappa Phi, Pi Tau Sigma. Home: 2650 N Lakeview Ave Apt 1610 Chicago IL 60614-1819 Office: 364 Henry Adm Bldg M/C 346 Urbana IL 61801

STUKENBERG, MICHAEL WESLEY, lawyer; b. Freeport, Ill., Feb. 22, 1951; s. Wesley W. and Nancy Jack (Baker) S.; m. Amanda Reed Eggert, July 21, 1973; children: Sarah Reed, William Robinson. BA, Princeton U., 1973; JD, Vanderbilt U., 1976. Bar: Tex. 1977, U.S. Tax Ct. 1977, U.S. Dist. Ct. (so. dist.) Tex. 1982. Assoc. firm Branscomb P.C., Corpus Christi, Tex., 1976-81, shareholder, 1981—. Gov. Art Mus. South Tex., Corpus Christi, 1990-96; dir., pres. Corpus Christi Estate Planning Coun., 1989-98; trustee, chair bd. trustees YMCA Corpus Christi, 1997-. Fellow Am. Coll. Trust and Estate Counsel; mem. ABA, Tex. Bar Assn. (tax sect.), Tex. Acad. of Probate and Trust Lawyers, Coll. of State Bar of Tex., Corpus Christi Yacht Club. Episcopalian. Home: 3502 Aransas St Corpus Christi TX 78411-1302 Office Phone: 361-888-9261. E-mail: mstukenberg@branscombpc.com.

STULBERG, SAMUEL DAVID, surgeon, physician; b. Lansing, Mich., Jan. 14, 1943; s. Julius and Esther (Leiberman) Stulberg; m. Jann Dragovich, Aug. 17, 1996; children: Lisa Michele, Debra Beth, Mark Jeffrey. BA cum laude, Harvard Coll., Cambridge, Mass., 1961—65; MD, U. Mich. Med. Sch., Ann Arbor, 1965—69; D Honoris Causa (hon.), U. Mediterrean, Marseilles, France, 1997. Orthop. surg. resident Harvard U., Cambridge, Mass., 1970—75; founder and dir., joint reconstruction and implant svc. Northwestern Meml. Hosp., Chgo., 1986—; prof., clin. orthop. surgery Northwestern U., Feinberg Sch. Medicine, Chgo., 1994—. Author: (book) Arthritis of the Hip & Knee; contbr. chapters to books, articles to profl. jours. Bd. dirs. Rehab. Inst. Chgo., 1996—2005; bd. mem. ACLU, Chgo., 1986—2005. Recipient Elven J. Berkheiser Prize, Inst. Medicine Chgo., M.E. Muller award, Helsinki, 2005; fellow, Orthopaedic Rsch. and Edn. Found. Fellow: Am. Acad. Orthop. Surgeons (life); mem.: Internat. Soc. for Computer Assisted Orthop. Surgery (pres. 2003—04), Internat. Soc. for Tech. in Arthroplasty, Internat. Soc. Arthroscopy, Knee Surgery and Orthop. Sports Medicine, Knee Soc. N.Am., Hip Soc. N.Am., Am. Assn. Hip and Knee Surgeons, Am. Orthop. Assn. Liberal. Jewish. Achievements include being a leader in the development of the field of computer-assisted orthopedic surgery; being a leader in the development of concepts, techniques and instruments for minimally invasive orthopedic surgery; design of multiple joint replacement systems, including: The Columbus Computer Assisted Knee System, The Continuum Knee System, The MicroLoc Knee System; patents for a computer-assisted surgical system; methods and instruments for performing radial impaction grafting for revision total hip surgery; invention of surgical systems for carrying out robotic and computer assisted surgery. Avocations: travel, running, photography, boating. Office: Northwestern Orthop Inst 680 N Lake Shore Dr #1028 Chicago IL 60611 Home Phone: 312-828-0737; Office Phone: 312-664-6848. Office Fax: 312-475-5624. E-mail: jointsurg@northwestern.edu.

STULC, JAROSLAV PETER, surgeon, educator; b. Teplitz, Czechoslovakia, Sept. 14, 1947; came to U.S., 1948; s. Jaroslav Pavel and Emilie Vanca Stulc; m. Diana Susan Minassian, Dec. 27, 189; children: Alexan Christopher, Evan Thomas. BA, Cornell Coll., Mt. Vernon, Iowa, 1969; MD, U. Iowa, 1973; student, U.S. Naval War Coll., Newport, RI, 1997-98. Diplomate Am. Bd. Surgery. Intern SUNY, Syracuse, 1973-75; resident in surgery Georgetown U., Washington, 1975-80, instr. surgery, 1979-80; instr. surgery, fellow transplant surgery Loyola U., Chgo., 1980-83; fellow surg. oncology Roswell Park Cancer Inst., Buffalo, 1983-85, attending surgeon, 1985-90; asst. prof. surgery SUNY, Buffalo, 1988-91; chief surgery VA Hosp., Buffalo, 1990-91; attending surgeon Trover Clinic Found., Madisonville, Ky., 1991—. Clin. faculty U. Louisville, 1991—; co-dir. Mahr Cancer Ctr., Madisonville, 1992—. Editor Ky. Med. Jour., Physician Focus; contbr. articles and abstracts to publs. Vis. lectr. outreach program Am. Cancer Soc., bd. dirs. Ky. chpt., 1993—. Capt. USNR. Fellow Naval War Coll., R.I., 1997, 98. Fellow ACS (cert. advanced trauma life support), Internat. Coll. Surgeons; mem. AMA, AAAS, Am. Soc. Gastrointestinal Endoscopy, Am. Soc. Abdominal Surgeons, Am. Soc. Clin. Oncology, Soc. Am. Gastrointestinal Surgeons, Nat. Surg. Adjuvant Breast and Bowel Protocl, Ea. Coop. Oncology Group, Iowa Jr. Acad. Sci., Chgo. Assn. Immunologists, Roswell Park Surg. Soc., Buffalo Surg. Soc., Acad. Surg. Rsch., Assn. Acad. Surgery, Adrian Kantrowitz Surg. Rsch. Soc., VFW, Tri Beta. Presbyterian. Office: Trover Clinic Found 435 N Kentucky Ave Madisonville KY 42431-1768 Home: 202 Day Break Dr Hanson KY 42413 Home Phone: 270-828-1680; Office Phone: 270-825-4204. E-mail: gent1969@hotmail.com.

STULL, DONALD DAVID, anthropologist, educator; b. Sebree, Ky., June 25, 1946; s. Emerson Bosse and Marjorie Dunville Stull; m. Laura Kriegstrom Poracsky, Mar. 25, 1947; m. Paula Jean Jensen (div.); children: Todd Weldon, Erin Kirsten McAnulty. BA, U. Ky., Lexington, 1968; MA, U. Colo., Boulder, 1970, PhD, 1973; MPH, U. Calif., Berkeley, 1975. Assoc. dir. nat. clearinghouse on child neglect and abuse, children's divsn. Am. Humane Assn., Denver, 1973—74; prof. anthropology U. Kans., Lawrence, 1975—, chair, dept., 1994—2001. Author: (book) Slaughterhouse Blues: The Meat and Poultry Industry in North America, Doing Team Ethnography: Warnings and Advice, Kiikaapoa: The Kansas Kickapoo; editor: Any Way You Cut It: Meat Processing and Small-Town America, Collaborative Research and Social Change: Applied Anthropology in Action, Culture and Agriculture Jour., Human Organization Jour.; prodr.: (ethnographic films) Neshnabek: The People; Return to Sovereignty: Self-Determination and the Kansas Kickapoo; Another Wind Is Moving: The Off-Reservation Indian Boarding School; contbr. articles to profl. jours. Recipient Louise Byrd Grad. Educator award, U. Kans., 1998, Hon. Citizen, Garden City, Kans., 2001, Irvin Youngberg award for Rsch. Achievement in Applied Sci., Kans. Endowment Assn., 2002, Wally and Marie Steeples Faculty award for Outstanding Svc. to People of Kans., U. Kans., 2004. Fellow: High Plains Soc. Applied Anthropology (Omer C. Stewart Meml. Award 1995), Am. Anthrop. Assn., Soc. Applied Anthropology (pres. 2005—07); mem.: Nat. Assn. Practice of Anthropology, Phi Kappa Phi. Achievements include being one of the first to conduct modern social science research on the consequences of the meat and poultry industry for workers and communities in the United States. Avocation: novice trick roper. Office: Univ Kans 1415 Jayhawk Blvd 622 Fraser Hall Lawrence KS 66045 Home Phone: 785-842-8055; Office Phone: 785-864-2641. Office Fax: 785-864-5224. E-mail: stull@ku.edu.

STULL, DONALD LEROY, architect; b. Springfield, Ohio, May 16, 1937; s. Robert Stull and Ruth Branson; m. Patricia Ann Ryder, Dec. 29, 1959 (div. Dec. 1985); children: Cydney Lynn, Robert Branson, Gia Virginia. BArch, Ohio State U., 1961; MArch, Harvard U., 1962. Registered arch. Calif., Conn., Fla., Ky., Maine, Md., Mass., Mo., N.H., N.J., N.Y., Pa., R.I., Tenn., Va., D.C., Wash. Pres. Stull Assocs., Inc., Boston, 1966-83, Stull and Lee, Inc., Boston, 1983—. Mem. Loeb fellowship com. Harvard Grad. Sch. Design, Cambridge, 1969-80; mem. adv. bd. Boston Archtl. Ctr., 1972-80, Mus. Nat. Ctr. of Afro-Am. Artists, Boston, 1978—, Ohio State U. Sch. Architecture, 1980—; design prof. Harvard Grad. Sch. Design, 1974-81; mem. vis. design studio, Rice U., Houston, spring 1993; mem. vis. com. Yale Sch. Art and Architecture, New Haven, 1972-76, William Henry Bishop chair Yale Sch. Architecture, 1975; mem. nat. presdl. design award jury Nat. Endowment for Arts, 1984, 88; bd. overseers The Inst. of Contemporary Art, Boston, 1996-98. Trustee Shaw U., 1973-75, Boston Found. for Architecture, 1992—; mem. design adv. panel, Balt., 1976-80; chmn. Mass Art Commn., Boston, 1978-80; commr. Boston Art Commn., 1980-92; mem. Design Adv. Group, Cambridge, 1980-90, 94—; commr. Boston Civic Design Commn., 1987—; adv. com. Suffolk Sch. Bus. Mgmt., 1989-95; bd. dirs Hist. Boston, 1990-98, Mus. of Afro-Am. History, Boston, 1979—; trustee Mass. Coll. Art, 1995-2000, 03-. Recipient Presdl. Design award Nat. Endowment for Arts, 1988; named one of Outstanding Young Men of Boston, 1969, Outstanding Young Men in Am., 1970, Centennial Yr. Outstanding Alumnus Ohio State U., 1970. Fellow AIA (nat. design com. 1972-84); mem. Boston Soc. Archs. (bd. dirs. 1969, 1999-2001, AIA Regional Design award 1975, 80-89, Honor award 1997), Nat. Coun. Archtl. Registration Bds., Mass. Soc. Archs. (bd. trustees 1995). Office: Stull and Lee Inc 38 Chauncy St Ste 1100 Boston MA 02111-2301 Office Phone: 617-426-0406. E-mail: dstull@stullandlee.com.

STULL, EVALYN MARIE, artist; b. Hays, Kans., June 7, 1949; d. Harold Kenneth Gossett and Helen Marie Loreg; m. Dennis Eugene Kincaid, Dec. 4, 1967 (div. 1968); children: Pamela Sue Kincaid, Mark Allen Kincaid; m. Kenneth Eugene Stull, Dec. 4, 1973 (dec. July 27, 2006); children: Daniel Eugene, Carl Andrew. A in Gen. Studies, Morgan CC, Ft. Morgan, Colo., 1994. Owner Stull's Kinder Day Care, Fort Morgan, Colo., 1994, Paintings by Evalyn Stull, Chase, Kans., 2001—07; with Sunflower Diversified, Greatbend, Kans., 1998—99. Bd. dirs. Rice County Arts Coun., Sterling Coll., Kans., 2003—06. Exhibitions include Kans. State Fair, Hutchinson, 1996—98. Home and Office: 201 Cedar/PO Box 134 Chase KS 67524

STULL, FRANK WALTER, elementary school educator; b. Easton, Pa., June 4, 1935; s. George Washington and Minnie Elizabeth S.; m. Darlene Joy Hunsicker, Aug. 2, 1958; children: James, Ronald, Wendy. BS, East Stroudsburg State Coll., 1956; MEd, Lehigh U., 1966. Cert. tchr., N.J. Tchr. Korea Heung-Up Bank, Seoul, Korea, 1957-58, Howell Twp. Elem. Sch., Freehold, NJ, 1958-59, Holland Twp. Elem. Sch., Milford, NJ, 1959-91. Bd. dirs., sec., treas., mgr. Hunterdon County Sch. Employees Fed. Credit Union, Phillipsburg, N.J., 1969-87, mem. adv. com., 1995; merit badge counselor Boy Scouts Am., 1970-84, cubmaster, 1971-72; treas., mem. Hist. Preservation Commn. Holland Twp., 1993—; bd. govs. Riegel Ridge Cmty. Ctr., 1997-2000; trustee, scholarship coord. C&E Found., 1997—. Recipient Meritorious Svc. award N.J. Credit Union League, 1988, Tchr. Recognition award State N.J. Gov., 1987, Disting. Achievement award for rsch. and preservation of history of Holland Twp. and surrounding areas; named Outstanding Elem. Tchr. Am., 1972; Experienced Tchr. in Geography fellow Pa. State U., 1967. Mem. NEA, Holland Twp. Edn. Assn., Hunterdon County Edn. Assn., N.J. Edn. Assn., Phi Delta Kappa (chartered mem. Zeta Gamma chpt.). Avocations: photography, travel. Home and Office: 16 Beaver Lane Easton PA 18045-1917

STULTING, ANDRIES ANDRIESSEN, ophthalmologist; b. Cape Town, South Africa, Aug. 29, 1948; s. Andries Andriessen and Magdalena (Van Huyssteen) Stulting; m. Lemainé Fouché, Dec. 15, 1973; children: Lizette, Liesl. MB ChB, U. Pretoria, 1973, MMed in Ophthalmology, 1981. Intern S.A. Def. Force, Pretoria, 1974; sr. houseman H.F. Verwoerd and Kalafong Hosps., Pretoria, 1975-76, med. officer, 1976, sr. med. officer, 1976-77, sr. med. officer, registrar dept. ophthalmology, 1977-81, sr. specialist, 1982; head dept. ophthalmology U. of the Free State, 1982—. V.p. Colls. of Medicine of South Africa, 1998—2007. Chmn. Bloemfontein Children's choir, 1992-97; chmn. Free State Govern Sch. Bodies, 1993-97; vice chmn. South African Schs. Governing Bodies, 1993-97; chmn. Ctrl. H.S., 1992-97. Recipient Bloemfonteiner of Yr., Publicity Com. of Bloemfontein, 1996. Fellow ACS, Am. Acad. of Ophthalmology; mem. Ophthalmol. Soc. of South Africa (pres. 1989-91, 97-99), Health Professions Coun. of South Africa, South African Med. Assn. (past vice chmn., past pres. free state br.). Dutch Reformed Ch. Avocations: reading, writing, light classical music, sport photography. Home: 50 Gascony Crescent Bloemfontein 9301 South Africa Office: Dept Ophthalmology PO Box 339 Bloemfontein South Africa Home Phone: 0027514362163; Office Phone: 0027514052151. Personal E-mail: aaseyedoc@lantic.net. Business E-Mail: stultinga@fshealth.gov.za.

STULTS, WALTER BLACK, management consultant, trade association administrator; b. Hightstown, NJ, Oct. 25, 1921; s. C. Stanley and Nettie M. (Black) S.; m. Ann D. Haynes, June 28, 1947 (dec. 2002); children: Andrew Haynes, Thomas Stanley; m. Jean Morris Curtin, 2003. BA, Williams Coll., 1943; MA (Woodrow Wilson fellow), Princeton U., 1949. Teaching asst. Princeton (N.J.) U., 1946-49; legis. asst. to U.S. Senator

Robert Hendrickson, Washington, 1949-50; staff dir. U.S. Senate Small Bus. Com., Washington, 1950-61; pres. Nat. Assn. Small Bus. Investment Cos., Washington, 1961-86; prin. W.B. Stults, Cons., Chapel Hill, NC, 1979-99. Dir. Pardee & Curtin Lumber Co., Pardee Resources Co., Phila.; chmn. Coun. Small and Ind. Bus. Assns., 1976-81. Pres. Carol Woods Residents Assn.; dir. Carol Woods Retirement Comty., 1995-97, 2001-06. With USAAF, 1943-46. Mem. Am. Soc. Assn. Execs., The Exchequer Club, Masons. Congregationalist.

STULTZ, JACK C., career military officer; m. Lauralyn Brown; 4 children. BA, Davidson Coll., 1974; grad., Command Gen. Staff Coll., Army War Coll. Advanced through grades to Lt. Gen. U.S. Army, 1974—, platoon leader, exec. officer, comdr. Co. B. 20th engr. battalion, 1974—79; various positions including brigade asst. ops. officer, battalion personnel officer, comdr., divisn. asst. ops. officer, 108th divsn. U.S. Army Reserve, 1979—87; with 32d Transp. Group, 1987—91, group exec. officer, 1991—95, comdr., 1998—99, 257th Transp. Battalion, Gainsville, Fla., 1995—98; dep. comdg. gen. 143rd Transp. Command (TRANSCOM), 1999—2002, comdr. Orlando, 2002—04; dir. movements, distbn., transp. combined forces land land component command, Kuwait, 2003—04; dep. comdg. gen. U.S. Army Reserve Command, 2005—06; chief U.S. Army Reserve, 2006—; comdg. gen. U.S. Army Reserve Command, 2006—; ops. mgr. Proctor and Gamble, Orlando, Fla. Decorated Def. Superior Svc. Medal, Legion of Merit, Bronze Star with oak leaf cluster, Meritorious Svc. Medal with three oak leaf clusters, Army Commendation Medal with four oak leaf clusters, Army Achievement Medal. Office: US Army Reserve 1401 Deshler St SW Fort Mcpherson GA 30330-2000

STULTZ, NEWELL MAYNARD, retired political science professor; b. Boston, June 13, 1933; s. Irving Washburn and Marjorie May (MacEachern) S.; m. Elizabeth Petronella Olckers, Apr. 6, 1958; children: Elliot Andries, Amy Elizabeth. AB, Dartmouth Coll., 1955; MA, Boston U., 1960, PhD, 1965; MA hon., Brown U., 1968. Fulbright exchange scholar U. Pretoria, South Africa, 1955-56; asst. prof. polit. sci. Northwestern U., Evanston, Ill., 1964-65; asst. prof. to prof. polit. sci. Brown U., Providence, 1965—2003, assoc. grad. dean, 1970-74, assoc. dean of faculty, 1993-98, assoc. provost, 1998-2000; ret., 2003. Vis. fellow Yale U.-South African Research Program, 1977; vis. prof. U. South Africa, Pretoria, 1980; James Gathings lectr. Bucknell U., Lewisburg, Pa., 1980 Author: Afrikaner Politics in South Africa, 1974, Who Goes to Parliament?, 1975, Transkei's Half Loaf, 1979, (bibliography) South Africa, 1989, 2d edit., 1993; co-author: South Africa's Transkei, 1967; co-editor: Governing in Black Africa, 1970, 2d edit., 1986 V.p. World Affairs Council R.I., 1983. Served as lt. (j.g.) USN, 1956-59. Fulbright fellow, 1955-56; NDEA grantee, 1959-62; Ford Found. fellow, 1962-64; Rockefeller Found. fellow, 1976-77 Unitarian Universalist. Home: 371 New Meadow Rd Barrington RI 02806-3729 Office: Brown U Dept Polit Sci PO Box 1844 Providence RI 02912-1844 Office Phone: 401-863-1567. Business E-Mail: newell_stultz@brown.edu.

STUMBO, GREGORY D., state attorney general; b. Huntington, W.Va., Aug. 14, 1951; s. Harold James and Pluma Jean (Martin) Stumbo; m. Mary Karen Henderson, Aug. 18, 1973; children: Brooks, Elizabeth Morgan, Kassidy Ream. B in Gen. Sci., U. Ky., Lexington, 1973; JD, U. Louisville, 1975. Asst. county atty. Floyd County, Prestonsburg, Ky., 1976-78; trial commr. to dist. ct. Adminstrv. Office of Cts., State Ky., Prestonsburg, 1978-79; mem. Ky. Ho. Reps., Frankfort, 1980—2003, majority fl. leader, 1985—2003; atty. gen. State of Ky., 2003—. Bd. dirs. First Guaranty Nat. Bank, Martin, Ky. Mem. Gov.'s Task Force on Coal Transp., Frankfort, 1983, Ky. Lottery Commn., Frankfort, 1988, Ky. Task Force on Edn. Reform, 1989—. Recipient Disting. Svc. award Ky. Cir. Judges Assn., 1980, Cert. of Appreciation, Western Ky. U., Bowling Green, 1982, Disting. Alumni award, U. Louisville, 1985. Mem. ABA, Ky. Bar Assn. Democrat. Baptist. Avocations: hunting, fishing, golf. Address: 108 Ridgewood Dr Prestonsburg KY 41653 Office: Office of Atty Gen State Capitol Rm 116 700 Capitol Ave Frankfort KY 40601 Office Phone: 502-696-5300. *

STUMER, MARK BRADLEY, lawyer, consultant, restaurateur; b. NYC, May 31, 1969; s. Nathan and Roberta Adele (Klau) S. LLB, SUNY, Albany, 1991; JD, N.Y. Law Sch., 1995. Bar: N.Y. 1995, U.S. Dist. Ct. (ea. and so. dists.) N.Y., 1995. Pres. Marker Entertainment, Inc., 1992—95, Mark B. Stumer & Assoc., P.C., NYC, 1995—; owner Tja! Restaurant, NYC, 1999—; pres. Soho Consulting Group, NYC, 1996—, Stumer Watson PC. Gen. counsel Tribeca Ventures, Inc., Abaya, Inc., Lima's Taste, Inc., KC Enterprises, Inc., Bella Inca, Bubbys, Inc., Pinch, Inc., Sage, Inc., Merchant Ivory Prod., Inc., Aldem Internat., Inc., Cense Apparel, Inc., Lighting Workshop, Inc., Tapas Food and Wine, Inc., Sapa, Inc., others; pres. Stumer Watson, P.C.; bd. dirs. Global Logistics, Inc., Global Logistics Acquisition Corp., First Arlington, Inc., IBN Cons., Inc., Arlington Consulting Svcs., Inc.; lectr. in field. Contbr. articles to profl. jours. including Nat. Restaurant Assn., Restaurant Law, The Legal Monitor, and The Restaurateur; pub. Restaurant Law newsletter, Restaurant and Bar Law newsletter, Entertainment Law & Fin., Bus. Lawyer, Civil Rights Jour. Mem. ABA, N.Y. State Bar Assn. (former chmn. copyright sect. student divsn. 1993-94, civil rights com.), Nat. Assn. Trial Lawyers, Nat. Employment Lawyers Assn. (N.Y. chpt.), Young Entreprenuers Orgn., Nat. Restaurant Assn., N.Y. State Restaurant Assn., N.Y. County Lawyers Assn., Assn. Trial Lawyers Am., N.Y. Prestige Lawyers Assn., Porsche Club Am., Porsche Club N.Y. Office: Mark B Stumer & Assocs PC 200 Park Ave S New York NY 10003-1008 Office Phone: 212-633-2225. E-mail: mstumer@newyorklawfirm.org.

STUMP, DAVID JAMES, philosopher, educator; b. Santa Monica, Calif., Mar. 21, 1955; s. John and Sarah Stump. BA, U. Calif., Berkeley, 1977; MA, Northwestern U., Ill., 1984, PhD, 1988. Prof., philosophy U. San Francisco, 1992—. Editor: Disunity of Science. Postdoctoral fellowship, NSF, 1989-1990. Mem.: The Internat. Soc. History of Philosophy of Sci. (steering com. 2003—06). Office: U San Francisco 2130 Fulton St San Francisco CA 94118 Office Phone: 415-422-6153.

STUMP, EARL SPENCER, psychologist; b. Parkersburg, W.Va., Dec. 12, 1943; s. Amos Earl Stump and Harriet Gertrude (White) Stiff; m. Ann Chadwick, Sept. 30, 1967 (div. 1985); 1 child, Andrea Renee; m. Joan Irene Croft, Sept. 28, 1985; m. Suzan Woodhead, Mar. 19, 2005. BA, Ohio State U., 1966; MS in Corrections, Xavier U., 1971; PhD, Ohio U., 2000. Lic. psychologist, Ohio, profl. clin. counselor; cert. rehab. counselor. Psychiat. aide Harding Hosp., Worthington, Ohio, 1965-67; psychology trainee Athens (Ohio) State Hosp., 1966-67; psychologist Ohio Dept. Rehab. and Correction, Columbus, 1967-97; supr. psychology and clin. dir. Chillicothe (Ohio) Correctional Inst., 1977-97. Pvt. practice psychology Columbus Mental Health Clinic, Columbus, 1976-77; instr. psychology Hocking Tech. Coll., Chillicothe, 1973-78; adj. prof. Ohio U., Athens, 2002; psychologist Scioto Point Valley Mental Health Ctr., Chillicothe. Mem.: APA, Ohio Psychol. Assn. Home: 15 N May Ave Athens OH 45701-1817 Personal E-mail: estump@columbus.rr.com.

STUMP, JOHN SUTTON, retired lawyer; b. Clarksburg, W.Va., Aug. 7, 1929; s. John Sutton and Helen (Mannix) S.; m. Elaine Claire Scammahorn, Sept. 14, 1968; children— John Sutton IV, James Felix. Student, Washington and Lee U., 1946-47, LL.B., 1957; BS in Commerce, U. N.C., 1951. Bar: W.Va. 1957, Va. 1957, D.C. 1983. Assoc. Jackson, Kelly, Holt & O'Farrell, Charleston, W.Va., 1957-58, Boothe, Dudley, Koontz & Boothe, Alexandria, Va., 1958-61, Boothe, Dudley, Koontz & Blankingship, Fairfax and Alexandria, Va., 1962-63; ptnr. Boothe, Dudley, Koontz, Blankingship & Stump, Fairfax and Alexandria, 1963-71, Boothe, Prichard & Dudley, 1971-87, McGuire, Woods, Battle & Boothe LLP, 1987-99. Served to lt. comdr. USNR, 1951-54, 61-62. Fellow Am. Coll. Trial Lawyers; mem. Am. Law Inst. Home: 8329 Weller Ave Mc Lean VA 22102-1717 Office: 1750 Tysons Blvd Mc Lean VA 22102-4208

STUMP, PATRICK MARTIN, musician; b. Glenview, Ill., Apr. 27, 1984; Lead singer, guitarist Fall Out Boy, 2001—. Musician: (albums) Fall Out Boy's Evening Out With Your Girlfriend, 2002, Take This to Your Grave, 2003, From Under the Cork Tree, 2005, Infinity on High, 2007, (songs) Sugar, We're Going Down, 2003 (MTV2 award, MTV Video Music Awards, 2005), Dance, Dance, 2005 (Choice Music Single award, Choice Rock Track award, Teen Choice Awards, 2006, Viewer's Choice award, MTV Video Music Awards, 2006); actor: (films) Bedussey, 2005. Recipient Choice Music Rock Group award, Teen Choice Awards, 2006. Office: Fall Out Boy Inc Box 219 1187 Wilmette Ave Wilmette IL 60091

STUMP, RICHARD CARL, environmental services administrator, consultant; b. Reading, Pa., Aug. 14, 1952; s. Richard Carl Stump; m. Brenda Lee Roughton, Jan. 11, 1974; children: Richard, Nathan, Jonathan Grad. high sch., Muhlenberg, Pa. Cert. radon testing specialist. Pres. Suburban Water Testing Labs., Temple, Pa., 1978—, Suburban Property Inspections, Inc., Temple, Pa., 1996—. Cons. in field. Mem. Am. Water Works Assn., Pa. Assn. Accreditation Environ. Labs., Am. Chem. Soc., Aircraft Owners and Pilots Assn. Avocations: amateur radio, aviation, private pilot. Office: Suburban Water Testing Labs 4600 Kutztown Rd Temple PA 19560-1548

STUMPE, WARREN ROBERT, county official, retired engineering executive; b. Bronx, NY, July 15, 1925; s. William A. and Emma J. (Mann) S.; children: Jeffrey, Kathy, William. BS, U.S. Mil. Acad., 1945; MS, Cornell U., 1949; MS in Indsl. Engring, N.Y. U., 1965; grad., Command and Gen. Staff Coll., 1972, Army War Coll., 1976; PhD (hon.), Milw. Sch. Engring., 1982. Registered profl. engr., N.Y., Fla., Wis. Commd. 2d lt., C.E. U.S. Army, 1945, advanced through grades to capt., 1954; with (65th Engr. Bn.), 1945-48; asst. prof. mechanics U.S. Mil. Acad., 1951-54; resigned, 1954; from capt. to col. Res., 1958-79; dep. gen. mgr., gen. engring. div. AMF, Stamford, Conn., 1954-63; exec. v.p. Dortech, Inc., Stamford, 1963-69; dir. systems mgmt. group Mathews Conveyor div. REX, Darien, Conn., 1969-71; dir. research and devel. Rexnord, Inc., Milw., 1971-73, v.p. corp. research and tech., from 1973, v.p. bus. devel. sector, 1981-83, v.p., chief tech. officer, 1983-86; pres. Rexnord Techs., Milw., 1986-87; v.p. Radian Corp., Milw., 1987—90; civilian aide to sec. army for State of Wis., 1981-85; alderman City of Mequon, 1994—97, pres. coun., 1996—97, county supr., 1998—. Mem. adv. bd. technology transfer program U. Wis.-Whitewater. Contbr. articles to profl. jours. Founder, pres. No. Little League, Stamford, 1965-69; pres. Turn of River Jr. High Sh. PTA, 1967-68; vice chmn. for Wis. Dept. Def., Nat. Com. Employer Support Guard and Res.; bd. regents Milw. Sch. Engring.; mem. liaison coun. Coll. Engring., U. Wis., also mem. indsl. adv. coun.; mem. adv. coun. Marquette U.; mem. Wis. Gov.'s Task Force on Energy, Coun. Great Lakes Govs.' Regional Econ. Devel. Commn., 1987-88; bd. dirs. MRA-Inst. Mgmt., Inc. Mem. Am. Water Pollution Control Fedn., Indsl. Rsch. Inst. (pres., dir.), Wis. Assn. Rsch. Mgrs. (founder), West Point Soc. Wis., Tau Beta Pi, Phi Kappa Phi. Clubs: Wis., Ozaukee Country. Personal E-mail: warrenstumpe@aol.com.

STUMPF, DAVID ALLEN, pediatric neurologist; b. LA, May 8, 1945; s. Herman A. and Dorothy F. (Davis) S.; children: Jennifer F., Kaitrin E.; m. Elizabeth Dusenbery, Feb. 2, 1989; children: Todd Coleman, Shilo Walker. BA, Lewis and Clark Coll., 1966; MD cum laude, U. Colo., 1972, PhD, 1972. Diplomate Am. Bd. Pediat., Am. Bd. Psychiatry and Neurology, lic. MD State of Ill. Pediatric intern Strong Meml. Hosp., Rochester, NY, 1972-73, resident, 1973-74; resident in neurology Harvard Med. Sch., Boston, 1974-77; dir. pediatric neurology U. Colo. Health Sci. Ctr., Denver, 1977-85; chief neurology Children's Meml. Hosp., Chgo., 1985-89; chmn. neurology, Benjamin and Virginia T. Boshes prof. Northwestern U., 1989-98, prof. neurology and pediatrics, 1999—2001; pres. and CEO Oyxis, LLC, 1999—2001; med. dir. United Healthcare, Chgo., 2005—. Mem. sci. adv. com. Muscular Dystrophy Assn., 1981-87; bd. dirs. Northwestern Meml. Corp., Chgo. Mem. editl. bd. Neurology, 1982-87; contbr. articles to sci. jours. Recipient Lewis and Clark Coll. Disting. Alumni award, 1991; NIH grantee, 1979-84; Muscular Dystrophy Assn. grantee, 1977-89; March of Dimes grantee, 1983-85. Fellow Am. Acad. Neurology (treas. 2005-07); mem. Child Neurology Soc. (counsellor 1982-84, pres. 1985-87), Am. Neurol. Assn., Am. Pediatric Soc., Soc. Pediatric Rsch., Internat. Child Neurology Assn. (sec. 2002-04). Presbyterian. Home: 540 Judson Ave Evanston IL 60202-3084 Office Phone: 312-424-6905. E-mail: david@stumpf.org.

STUMPF, HEINRICH JOSEF, psychometrician, research consultant; b. Cologne, Germany, Dec. 10, 1951; came to U.S., 1991; s. Friedrich Hubert and Johanna Luise (Bauer) Stumpf; m. Doris Elisabeth Hoffmann, May 10, 1990. Diploma in Psychology, U. Bonn, Germany, 1975, PhD, 1978. Sci. employee German Nat. Scholarship Found., Bonn, Germany, 1978-91; sr. rsch. assoc. Ctr. for Talented Youth, Johns Hopkins U., Balt., 1991-95; rsch. cons. Ctr. for Talented Youth Johns Hopkins U., Balt., 1996—. Contbr. to German Encyclopedia of Psychology. Mem. German Psychol. Assn., Assn. for Psychol. Sci., N.Y. Acad. Scis. Achievements include: sr. author of the Cube Perspective Test of Spatial Ability, 1983, the German Personality Research Form, 1985 and the Spatial Test Battery of the Ctr. for Talented Youth; contbr. to German Ency. Psychology; contbr. about 50 scientific publications. Personal E-mail: stumpfhj@aol.com.

STUMPF, JOHN G., bank executive; b. Pierz, Minn., 1953; BS in Acctg., St. Cloud State U., 1976; MBA in Fin., U. Minn. V.p. loan adminstrn. Norwest Nat. Bank, 1982—83, sr. v.p., chief credit officer, 1982—89; chmn., CEO Norwest Bank Ariz., 1989—91; regional pres. Greater Colo./Ariz Norwest Bank, Colo., 1991—94, head Tex., 1994—98; head southwestern banking group Wells Fargo & Co., San Francisco, 1998—2000, exec. v.p. we. banking group, 2000—02, group exec. v.p. cmty. banking, 2002—05, pres., COO, 2005—07, pres., CEO, 2007—. Bd. chmn. Visa U.S.A.; bd. dir. Visa Internat., The Clearing House. Bd. dir. San Francisco Zool. Soc., Bay Area chpt. Jr. Achievement, San Francisco Com. on Jobs; trustee San Francisco Mus. Modern Art. Mem.: Fin. Services Roundtable, Calif Bus. Roundtable. Office: Wells Fargo & Co 420 Montgomery St San Francisco CA 94163 *

STUMPF, WALTER ERICH, cell biology and pharmacology professor, researcher; b. Oelsnitz, Sachsen, Germany, Jan. 10, 1927; arrived in U.S., 1963; m. Ursula Emily Schwinge, May 20, 1961; children: Andrea, Martin, Carolin, Silva. MD summa cum laude, Humboldt U., Berlin, 1952; PhD in Pharmacology, U. Chgo., 1967; D of Human Biology (hon.), U. Ulm, Germany, 1987. Resident in neurology and psychiatry Humboldt U., Berlin, 1954-57, U. Marburg, Germany, 1957-61, resident in radiobiology, 1961-62; rsch. assoc. U. Chgo., 1963-67, asst. prof., 1967-70; assoc. prof. U. N.C., Chapel Hill, 1970-73, prof., 1973-95, mem. labs. for reproductive biology and neurobiology program, mem. Cancer Rsch. Ctr., Carolina Population Ctr., mem. curriculum in toxicology. Vis. psychiatrist Maudsley Hosp., London, 1959; vis. prof. Max-Planck Inst. for Cell Biology, Wilhelmshaven, Germany, 1975, U. Ulm, 1981, U. Sao Paulo, Brazil, 2000-02; rsch. advisor Chugai Pharm. Co., Ltd., Tokyo, 1992-95; lectr. U. São Paulo, 1997, 2000, Ain Shams U., Cairo, 1998; cons. Harris Mfg. Co., North Billerica, Mass., Rsch. Triangle Inst., Chemistry and Life Scis. Divsn., Rsch. Triangle Park, N.C., Merck Sharp and Dome, Westpoint, Pa., Glaxo Wellcome, Rsch. Triangle Park; exec. com. NRC, Inst. of Lab. Animal Resources, NAS, 1979-81, coun. Inst. of Lab. Animal Res., 1978-81, com. Soc. for Exptl. Biology and Medicine, 1987-92, founder Internat. Inst. Drug Distbn. Cytopharmacology and Cytoxicology, Chapel Hill, 1995—. Editor: Autoradiography of Diffusible Substances, 1969, Anatomical Neuroendocrinology, 1975, Autoradiography and Correlative Imaging, 1995; author: Drug Localization in Tissues and Cells, 2003; mem. editl. bd. Neuroendocrinology Letters, 1979-87, Exptl. Aging Rsch., 1975-85, Jour. Histochemistry and Cytochemistry, 1982-90, Cell and Tissue Rsch., 1982-88, Molecular and Cellular Neurosci., 1989-94, Biomed. Rsch., 1991-94, Histochemistry, 1992-96; contbr. articles to profl. jours. Recipient Humboldt Found. award, 1989. Mem. AAAS, Am. Assn. Anatomists, N.Y. Acad. Scis., Soc. for Exptl. Biology and Medicine, Soc. for Neurosci., Endocrine Soc., Internat. Brain Rsch. Orgn., Am. Soc. Zoologists, Histochem. Soc. (coun. 1977-81), Histochem. Gesellschaft (Feulgen lectureship 1982), Internat. Soc. Study Xenobiotics (charter), Internat. Inst. Drug Distbn. Cytopharmacology and Cytotoxicology (founder). Home: U NC Sch Medicine 2612 Damascus Church Rd Chapel Hill NC 27516-8043 Office: Internat Inst Drug Distribution Cytopharmacology & Cytotoxicology Chapel Hill NC 27516 Business E-Mail: stumpfwe@email.unc.edu.

STUMPFF, ROBERT THOMAS, retired academic administrator; b. Lewistown, Pa., June 25, 1945; s. Harry Clarence and Marjorie Louise (Bossinger) Stumpff; m. Sylvia Simmons, Apr. 22, 1972; children: Robert Dale, Cherie Lynn Stumpff Zimmer. BS, U. Md., 1968; cert., U. Ky., 1978. Asst. dir. athletics U. Md., College Park, 1968-69, asst. dir. Md. student union, 1969-72, assoc. dir. Md. student union, 1973-80, acting dir. Md. student union, 1974-75, bus. mgr. athletics, 1980-81, asst. athletic dir., 1982-88, asst. dir. gen. svcs., facilities mgmt., 1988—2005; dir. pub. works City of College Park, 2005—. Cons. U.S. Naval Acad. Athletic Assn., Annapolis, Md., 1984. Author, editor: Maryland Wrestling, 1964—65, 1968—69, asst. editor: Maryland Basketball, 1964—65, 1968—69, Maryland Football Guide, 1965—69. Asst. min. St. Paul's Luth. Ch., Fulton, Md., 1996—; mem. ch. coun. Abiding Savior Luth. Ch., Columbia, Md., 1986—87; mem. Luth. campus ministry bd. U. Md., 1995—2006. Mem.: Nat. Recycling Coalition, Md. Recylcers Coalition (bd. dirs. 1997—, chair 2003—), Md.-Del. Solid Waste Assn., Nat. Solid Wastes Mgmt. Assn., Solid Waste Assn. N.Am. (bd. dirs. Mid-Atlantic chpt. 1992—94, cert. mcpl. solid waste mgr.), Am. Pub. Works Assn., U. Md. M Club Found. (life; bd. dirs. 1970—, past pres.), U. Md. Alumni Assn. (life), U. Md. Terrapin Club, Omicron Delta Kappa (Sigma chpt. faculty sec.-treas. 1972—76, faculty adviser 1976—91, faculty coord. 1991—2005). Avocations: reading, sightseeing. Home: 8206 Bubbling Spring Laurel MD 20723-1079 Home Phone: 301-725-1533; Office Phone: 301-474-4194 ext. 220. Business E-Mail: rstumpff@collegeparkmd.gov.

STUNKARD, ALBERT JAMES, psychiatrist, educator; b. NYC, Feb. 7, 1922; s. Horace Wesley and Frances (Klank) Stunkard. BS, Yale U., 1943; MD, Columbia U., 1945; MD (hon.), U. Edinburgh, 1992, La. State U., 2006. Intern in medicine Mass. Gen. Hosp., Boston, 1945—46; resident physician psychiatry Johns Hopkins Hosp., 1948—51, rsch. fellow psychiatry, 1951—52; 1rsch. fellow medicine Columbia U. Svc., Goldwater Meml. Hosp., NYC, 1952—53; Commonwealth rsch. fellow, then asst. prof. medicine Cornell U. Med. Coll., 1953—57; mem. faculty U. Pa., 1957—73, 1976—, prof. psychiatry, 1962—73, 1976—, Kenneth Appel prof. psychiatry, 1968—73, chmn. dept., 1962—73; prof. psychiatry Med. Sch., Stanford U., 1973—76. Contbr. 450 articles on psychol., physiol., sociol., therapeutic and genetic aspects of obesity to profl. jours. Capt. M.C. AUS, 1946—48. Recipient Disting. Svc. award, Am. Psychiat. Assn., 1994, Goldberger award, AMA, 1990, Willendorf award, Internat. Assn. Study of Obesity, 1998, Sarnat award mental health, NAS Inst. Medicine, 2004, Disting. Achievement medal medicine, Columbia U. Coll. Physicians and Surgeons, 2005; fellow, Ctr. Advanced Study in Behavioral Scis., 1971—72. Mem.: Soc. Behavioral Medicine (past pres.), Assn. Rsch. Nervous and Mental Diseases (past pres.), Am. Psychosomatic Soc. (past pres.), Acad. Behavioral Medicine Rsch. (past pres.), Am. Assn. Chmn. Depts. Psychiatry (past pres.), Inst. Medicine of NAS. Achievements include contributions to the behavioral, pharmacological, community and surgical treatment of obesity and to understanding of sociological, physiological, psychological and genetic aspects of the disorder; contributions also to nosology and treatment of the eating disorders. Office: U Pa Sch Medicine Dept Psychiatry 3535 Market St 3rd Flr Philadelphia PA 19104-2641 Business E-Mail: stunkard@mail.med.upenn.edu.

STUNTEBECK, CLINTON A., lawyer; b. Hibbing, Minn., May 25, 1938; s. Robert F. and S. Mary Stuntebeck; m. Mary Joan Carmody; children: Robin, M. Alison, Susan, John, William. BA in Psychology, U. Minn., 1960; LLB, U. Maine, 1968. Bar: Pa. 1969, U.S. Dist. Ct. (ea. dist.) Pa. 1969. Ptnr. emeritus, chmn. corp. fin. and securities, mem. exec. com. Schnader, Harrison, Segal & Lewis, Phila. Bd. dirs. HMG Courtland Properties, Cimento Tupi Shipping, Markel Corp., Greater Phila. First Partnership for Econ. Devel.; lectr. corp. and securities law. Contbr. articles to profl. jours. Pres. Radnor (Pa.) Twp. Bd. Commn., 1981—83, 1992—2001; founder, bd. dirs. Radnor Enhancement Cmty. Trust; bd. visitors U. Maine Sch. Law; trustee Cabrini Coll.; bd. dirs. Am. Heart Assn., Ctr. for Responsible Leadership and Governance, Villanova U. Capt. USAF, 1960—68. Mem. ABA, Am. Law Inst., Pa. Bar Assn., Phila. Bar Assn., Securities Industry Assn. (law and compliance com.), Nat. Assn. Corp. Dirs., U. Maine Law Alumni Assn. (pres. 1974-76), Federalist Soc., AF Assn., Mil. Order Fgn. Wars US, Union League Phila., Phila. Country Club, Sunday Breakfast Club, Corinthian Yacht Club. Avocations: sailing, skiing, golf. Office: Schnader Harrison Segal 1600 Market St Ste 3600 Philadelphia PA 19103-7287 Office Phone: 215-751-2034. E-mail: cstuntebeck@schnader.com.

STUNTZ, JEAN ALLISON, history professor; b. Orange, Tex., Apr. 8, 1957; d. Homer Clyde and Billie Williams Stuntz. JD, Baylor Law Sch., 1980; PhD, U. No. Tex., 2000. History prof. West Tex. A&M U., Canyon, Tex., 2001—. Author: (historical monograph) Hers, His, and Theirs: Community Property Law in Spain and Early Texas. Office: West Texas A&M Univ 2402 N 3rd Canyon TX 79016 Home Phone: 806-655-0680. Business E-Mail: jstuntz@mail.wtamu.edu.

STUNTZ, LINDA GILLESPIE, government official, lawyer; b. Bellefontaine, Ohio, Sept. 11, 1954; d. J. Bradshaw Gillespie and Freda Taylor; m. Reid P.F. Stuntz, May 23, 1981; children: Joseph Gillespie, Grace Reid. AB, Wittenberg U., 1976; JD, Harvard U., 1979. Bar: D.C. 1979, U.S. Dist. Ct. D.C. 1980, U.S. Temp. Emergency Ct. Appeals 1980, U.S. Ct. Appeals (D.C. cir.) 1980, U.S. Supreme Ct. 1983. Assoc. Jones, Day, Reavis & Pogue, Washington, 1979-81, 87-89; assoc. minority counsel Energy and Commerce Com., U.S. Ho. of Reps., Washington, 1981-86, minority counsel, staff dir., 1986-87; dep. under sec. for policy, planning and analysis U.S. Dept. Energy, Washington, 1989-92, acting asst. sec. for fossil energy, 1991, acting asst. sec. for domestic and internat. energy policy, 1992, dep. sec. energy, 1992—; ptnr. Van Ness Feldman, 1993—95, Stuntz, Davis & Staffier, P.C., 1995; dir. Raytheon Co., Waltman, Mass., 2004. Bd. dir. Schlumberger Ltd. Mem. Fed. Energy Bar Assn. Republican. Office: Raytheon Co 870 Winter St Waltham MA 02451-1449 Office Phone: 781-522-3000.

STUNZ, JOHN HENRY, JR., retired physician, consultant; b. Freeland, Pa., May 20, 1921; s. John Henry and Anna Amelia (Gross) Stunz; m. Geraldine Kutz, July 2, 1944 (dec. Oct. 10, 2003); children: Beverly A. Stunz Boyd, Geri Stunz Konstantin. BA, U. Pa., 1943, MD, 1946. Diplomate Am. Bd. Occupl. Medicine. Intern U.S. Naval Hosp., Saint Albans, NY, 1946-47; pvt. practice Freeland, 1949-50; plant physician Harrison Radiator div. Gen. Motors Corp., Lockport, NY, 1950-52, med. dir., 1952-78, Cadillac Motor Car div. Gen. Motors Corp., Detroit, 1978-86; occupational medicine cons. Preferred Med. Assocs., Southfield,

Mich., 1987-98, ret., 1998. Pres. Niagara County (N.Y.) Bd. Health, 1966; acting commr. health Niagara County, 1972-73. Lt. (j.g.) M.C., USNR, 1946-49. Fellow Am. Coll. Occupl. and Environ. Medicine; mem. Mich. State Med. Soc., Oakland County Med. Soc. (environ. health com. 1988), Mich. Occupl. and Environ. Med. Assn. (bd. dirs. 1985-88), Detroit Occupl. Physicians Assn. Republican. Presbyterian. Avocations: stamp collecting/philately, boating, golf. Home: 735 Ardmoor Dr Bloomfield Hills MI 48301-2417

STUPAK, BART T., congressman, lawyer; b. Milw., Feb. 29, 1952; m. Laurie Ann Olsen; children: Ken, Bart Jr. (dec.). AA in Criminal Justice, Northwestern Mich. C.C., Traverse City, 1972; BS in Criminal Justice, Saginaw Valley State Coll., 1977; JD, Thomas M. Cooley Law Sch., 1981. Patrolman Escanaba City Police Dept., 1972-73; state trooper Mich. Dept. State Police, 1973-84; instr. State Police Tng. Acad., 1980-82; atty., 1981-84, Hansley, Neiman, Peterson, Beauchamp, Stupak, Bergman P.C., 1984-85; ptnr. Stupak, Bergman, Stupak P.C., 1985-88; mem. Mich. Ho. of Reps., 1989-90; prin. Bart T. Stupak P.C., 1991—; mem. US Congress from 1st Mich. dist., 1993—. Mem. commerce subcom., ranking dem. on oversights and investigation, telecom. and Internet, environment and hazardous materials, commerce trade, consumer protection. Nat. committeeman Boy Scouts Am., coach Menominee Youth Baseball Assn., Little League; active Wildlife Unltd., Menominee Woods and Streams Assn., Menominee County Hist. Soc.; adv. com. Bay Pines Juv. Detection Ctr.; bd. dir. Cmty. Action Agy. Recipient Fed. Legislator of Yr. award, Mich. Credit Union League, Great Lakes legis. of Yr. award, Great Lakes Maritime Task Force, 2003. Mem. Nat. Rifle Assn., Sons of the Am. Legion, Knights of Columbus, Elks Club, State Employees Retirees Assn., fin. com. Holy Spirit Catholic Ch. Democrat. Roman Catholic. Office: US Congress 2352 Rayburn House Office Bldg Washington DC 20515-2201 also: Iron County Courthouse Ste 3 2 S Sixth St Crystal Falls MI 49920-1438 Office Phone: 202-225-4735, 906-875-3751. Office Fax: 202-225-4744, 906-875-3889. E-mail: stupak@mail.house.gov. *

STUPPARD-BYARS, DORIS J., minister; b. El Dorado, Ark., Feb. 19, 1941; d. Jimmy D. and Mozella Massey; m. Mark Byars, July 31, 2004; m. Emanuel Stuppard, Aug. 1, 1986 (div. Sept. 1, 1995); m. Van J. Whaley, Mar. 1962 (div. June 1983); children: Stephanie A. Whaley-Jones, Ralph S. Whaley, Tiffany L. Whaley-LeConte. BA in Family Life Ed & Ministry, Spring Arbor U., Spring Arbor, Mich., 1997; BS in Psycology, Detroit Inst. of Tech., Detroit, Mich., 1978. Ma Dept. of Pub. Health, Mich., 1994; cert. Tchg. Fla. State Bd. of Edn., Fla., 1985, Child Care Adminstrn. Dade County C.C., Fla., 1987. Girl scouts leader Girl Scouts Of Am., Detroit, 1966—68; exec. dir. & founder Multi-Racial Family Study & Del. Ctr., Ypsilanti, Mich., 1979—; pres. of cloverlawn block club Cloverlawn Block Club, Detroit, 1970—71; leader Adult Deliverance Study, Detroit, 1976—78; alternative sch. tchr. Ace Sch., Detroit, 1976—78; outreach min. Old Path Temple COGIC, Detroit, 1977—83; pres. of chalmers block club Chalmers Block Club, Detroit, 1978—79; evangelist (min.) Trinity Deliverance Ch., Detroit, 1979—; asst. pastor Outer Dr. United Meth. Ch., Detroit, 1995—97; leader Children's Refuge Ho. (MRFDC), Brightmoor Cmty., Mich., 1993—95. Cons. Noble Mid. Sch., Detroit, 2000—01; youth group counselor Go Lightly Elem. & Jr. High, Detroit, 1998—99; learning for life instr. Boy Scouts Of Am., Detroit, 1997—97. Author: (religous novel) The Unction it Takes to Function, (religous instruction) Hey Churchmember! Put Your Money Where Your Mouth Is!; singer (soprano): (concert) 2nd Annual Women's Conf. of Institutional Bapt. Ch. 100 Woman Concert; speaker 2nd Annual Women's Conf. of Inst. Bapt. Ch. Candidate for city coun. Detroit City Coun., Detroit, 2001—01; candidate state rep. State of Mich., Detroit, 2002—02; candidate charter commr. City of Detroit, Detroit, 1980—80. Recipient Cert. of Appreciation, Wayne County Sherrif Dept.: Exec. Dir. Robert Ficano, 2003, Cert. of Appreciation for Children's Feeding Program, City Of Detroit, 1979. Master: Word Of Deliverance (assoc.; evangelist 2004—05); mem.: Hartford Meml. Bapt. Ch. (min. 1993—2000), Leadership To Go (corr.; exec. dir. 2004—05). Independent. Achievements include Outstanding Young Woman of the Yr. DIT: 1977; Outstanding Young Woman of Am.: 1978. Avocation: traveling evangelist. Home: 1870 Meadow Woods Blvd Ypsilanti MI 48197-4570 Home Phone: 734-483-9016; Office Phone: 734-483-0557. Personal E-mail: messengerd7@aol.com.

STURCKOW, FREDERICK W. (RICK), astronaut; b. La Mesa, Calif., Aug. 11, 1961; s. Karl H. and Janette R. Sturckow; m. Michele A. Street. BS in Mech. Engring., Calif. Poly. State U., 1984. Commd. 2d lt. USMC, 1984, advanced through grades to lt. col.; with MCAS, Beaufort, SC, Sheik Isa Air Base, Bahrain, 1990; mission comdr. Operation Desert Storm; F/A-18 E/F project pilot Naval Air Warfare Ctr.-Aircraft Divsn., Patuxent River, Md., 1993; astronaut NASA, Houston, 1994—, with Vehicle Systems and Ops. Br., also served as dep. shuttle ops. br., astronaut office, lead for Kennedy Space Ctr. Ops. support, chief astronaut office, Capcom Br. Pilot STS-88 Endeavor Mission (first Internat. Space Station assembly mission), 1998, STS-105 Discovery Mission, 2001; crew comdr. STS-117 Atlantis Mission, 2007. Decorated Single Mission Air medal with combat "V", 4 Strike/Flight Air medals, Def. Superior Svc. medal, Navy and Marine Corps Commendation medal, Navy and Marine Corps Achievement medal, NASA Space Flight medals (2). Mem.: Soc. Exptl. Test Pilots, Marine Corps Assn. Achievements include logged 4,000 flight hours in over 50 different aircraft; logged 568 hours in space; pilot STS-88 Endeavour (1998) and STS-105 Discovery (2001). Avocations: flying, physical training. Office: Astronaut Office/CB NASA Johnson Space Ctr Houston TX 77058 *

STURDIVANT, JAMES M., lawyer; b. Tulsa, Sept. 14, 1937; s. Ben S. and Elizabeth (Carlock) S.; m. Carol A. Baker, 1961 (div. Feb. 1975); children: Anne Carol, Catherine Abby; m. Barbara Dunn, Feb. 4, 1978; children: David Andrew, John Michael. BBA, U. Okla., 1959, JD, 1964. Bar: Okla. 1964, U.S. Tax Ct. 1964, U.S. Ct. Claims 1964, U.S. Dist. Ct., no. we. & so. dist. Okla. 1964, U.S. Ct. Appeals, 10th circuit 1971, U.S. Supreme Ct. 1975. Lawyer Gable & Gotwals, Inc., Tulsa, 1964—. Trustee River Parks Authority, Tulsa County, Okla., 1989-97; Okla. Jud. Nomin. Commn. 1981-87, chmn. 1985-87; Ctr. Am. & Internat. Law, trustee 1997-, rsch fellow 2000-; bd. dir. Tulsa Area United Way 2003- (exec. comm. 2003-, Alexis de Tocqueville Soc. chmn. 2004); bd. visitors Univ. Okla. Coll. Arts & Sci. 1997-, Coll. Law 2002-. Officer infantry USMC, 1959—61. Mem. ABA (house del. 1992-04, bd. gov. 2004-); Am. Coll. Trial Lawyers (fellow, state chmn. 2000-02), Okla. Bar Assn. (v.p., bd. gov. 1976, chmn. profl. responsibility commn. 1978, chmn. adminstrn. justice comm.1994-97, mem. tort reform task force, 2004), Okla. Bar Found. (trustee 1988—); Tulsa County Bar Assn.(Dist. Svc. award, 1992, Outstanding Young Lawyer, 1968). Life Fellow, Am. Bar Found; Okla. Bar Found; Am. Inns of Ct. (founding master, Hudson-Hall-Wheaton chptr.). Republican. Methodist. Office: Gable & Gotwals 1100 ONEOK Plz 100 W 5th St Tulsa OK 74103-4217 Home Phone: 918-747-1234; Office Phone: 918-595-4800. Business E-Mail: jsturdivant@gablelaw.com. *

STURGES, KEITH, information technology executive; MBA, U. Warwick, United Kingdom. V.p. advanced svcs. divsn. Oracle Corp.; CEO homecare divsn. Misys Healthcare, chief mktg. officer, 2004—05; pres. SirsiDynix Internat., 2007—. Office: SirsiDynix 101 Washington St SE Huntsville AL 35801

STURGES, SHERRY LYNN, recording industry executive; b. Long Beach, Calif., Dec. 11, 1946; d. Howard George and Alice Myrtle Fairbairn; m. Jeffery Alan Sturges, Dec. 30, 1969; children: Allisun Malinda, Jay. Grad. high sch., Las Vegas, Nev. V.p. Soultime, Inc., Las Vegas, 1968-69, Universe, Inc., Las Vegas, 1971-76; co-developer, owner Fun Trax Music Video and Audio Recording Studios, Westwood, Calif., 1986—. Creative cons. John Debella Show, 1990, M.T.V., L.A., 1990, KCET-TV, L.A., 1990,KTLA-TV, L.A., 1991. Co-writer song The Sharing of Love for TV series Murder, She Wrote, 1996, feature film The Ride, 1997; song writer (film) The Ride, 1997. Officer PTA, Woodland Hills, Calif., 1977-86, pres., 1984-86; vol. Connie Stevens Charity Orgn., Beverly Hills, Calif., 1980-84; vol. Crossroads Sch. for Arts and Sci., Westwood Meth. presch., West L.A. Bapt. Sch., Northridge United Meth. Ch., St. Vincent's Parents Coun., St. Joseph the Worker Sch., Chatsworth H.S., Sepulveda Nursery Sch., Nat. Neurofibromatosis Found., Life Steps Found., Westwood Village Assn., San Joaquin Valley Actors Repertory Co., 1997—. Recipient Outstanding Contribution award L.A. Unified Sch. Dist., Oxnard Unified Sch. Dist., 1998, 99. Mem. Am. Soc. Composers, Authors and Pubs. Republican. Avocations: collecting dolls, plates and figurines. Home: 29468 Sequoia Rd Santa Clarita CA 91387-6246

STURGULEWSKI, ARLISS, state legislator, director; b. Blaine, Wash., Sept. 27, 1927; BA, U. Wash., Seattle; LLD (hon.), U. Alaska, Anchorage, 1993. Mem. Assembly Municipality of Anchorage; interim exec. dir. Alaska Sci. and Tech. Found., 1995. Vice chmn. New Capital Site Planning Commn., mem. Capital Site Selection Com.; chmn. Greater Anchorage Area Planning and Zoning Commn.; mem. Alaska State Senate, 1978-93; Rep. nominee Office Gov. Alaska, 1986, 90. Home: 2957 Sheldon Jackson St Anchorage AK 99508-4469 Office: 3201 C St Ste 405 Anchorage AK 99503-3967 Business E-Mail: a.sturgulewski@swallingcpas.com.

STURKEN, CRAIG C., retail executive; Sr. v.p. Big Star Food Stores, 1989—90; chmn. Can. ops. Spartan Stores Inc., 1990—93, group v.p. Mich. ops., then pres. A&P Mich., 1993—97, chmn., CEO midwest region, 1997—2000, pres., CEO atlantic region, 2000—03, chmn., pres., CEO, 2003—. Office: Spartan Stores 850 76th St SW Grand Rapids MI 49518 *

STURLEY, MICHAEL F., law educator; b. Syracuse, NY, Feb. 14, 1955; s. Richard Avern and Helen Elizabeth (Fisher) S.; m. Michele Y. Deitch, July 2, 1989; children: Jennifer Diane, Elizabeth Claire. BA, Yale U., 1977, JD, 1981; BA in Jurisprudence, Oxford U., 1980, MA, 1985. Bar: N.Y. 1984, U.S. Dist. Ct. (so. and ea. dists.) N.Y. 1984, U.S. Supreme Ct. 1987, U.S. Ct. Appeals (11th circuit) 2001, U.S. Ct. Appeals (2nd circuit) 2004. Law clk. to Judge Amalya L. Kearse, U.S. Ct. Appeals for 2d Cir., NYC, 1981-82; law clk. to Justice Lewis F. Powell, Jr. U.S. Supreme Ct., Washington, 1982-83; assoc. Sullivan & Cromwell, NYC, 1983-84; asst. prof. law U. Tex. Law Sch., Austin, 1984-88, prof., 1988—. Vis. prof. Queen Mary and Westfield Coll., U. London, 1990, advisor Restatement (3d) of Property (servitudes), 1989-2000. Author: (with David W. Robertson and Steven F. Friedell) Admiralty and Maritime Law in the United States, 2001; compiler, editor: The Legislative History of the Carriage of Goods by Sea Act and the Travaux Préparatoires of The Hague Rules, 3 vols., 1990; mem. editl. bd. Jour. Maritime Law and Commerce, 1989—, book rev. editor, 1993—; contbg. author: Benedict on Admiralty, 1990—; contbr. articles to legal jours. Mem. Am. Law Inst., Maritime Law Assn. (proctor), Comité Maritime Internat. (titulary) Office: U Tex Sch Law 727 E Dean Keeton St Austin TX 78705-3224 Office Phone: 512-232-1350.

STURM, WILLIAM CHARLES, lawyer; b. Milw., Aug. 4, 1941; s. Charles William and Helen Ann (Niesen) S.; m. Kay F. Sturm, June 10, 1967; children: Patricia, Elizabeth, Katherine, William, Susan. BS in Bus. Adminstrn., Marquette U., 1963; JD, 1966. Bar: Wis. 1966, U.S. Dist. Ct. (ea. dist.) Wis. 1966, U.S. Supreme Ct. 1980. Sole practice, Milw., 1966—77; ptnr. Rausch, Hamell, Ehrle & Sturm, S.C., Milw., 1977—81, Rausch, Hamell, Ehrle, Sturm & Blom, Milw., 1981-83, Rausch, Hamell, Ehrle & Sturm, 1983-95, Rausch, Hamell, Sturm & Israel S.C., 1995-98, Rausch, Sturm, Israel & Hornik, S.C., 1999—. Asst. prof. Marquette U., 1982-91; lectr. U. Wis., Milw., 1991-97, sr. lectr. 1997-2002. Contbr. articles to profl. jours. Mem. adv. bd. Pallotine Order, 1985—; bd. dirs. Pius XI H.S., 2002-2004. Recipient Editors award Wis. Med. Credit Assn., 1980, Recipient Outstanding Alumni Pius XI H.S., 2002. Mem. ABA, Wis. Bar Assn., Comml. Law League Am. (exec. coun. midwestern dist. 1981-83, 86-88, chmn. state membership com. 1981-88, nat. nominating coun. 1984-86, 1988-89, 2004-05, sec., 2d v.p. midwestern dist. 1989-90, 1st v.p. midwestern dist. 1990-91, chmn. 1991-92, nat. bd. govs. 1997-2000, pres. elect 2000-01, pres. 2001-02), Acad. Legal Studies in Bus., Midwest Bus. Law Assn. (sec. 1988-89, v.p. 1989-90, pres. 1990-91), Healthcare Fin. Mgmt. Assn., Beta Alpha Psi (faculty v.p. Psi chpt. 1985-88, Eta Theta chpt. 1992-99), Midwest Bus. and Health Assn. (v.p. procs. 1987-88, v.p. program 1988-89, pres. 1989-90), Westmoor Country Club (Milw.); Kiwanis (pres. 1979, lt. gov. div. 5, 1980). Office: 2448 South 102nd St Milwaukee WI 53227 Office Phone: 414-328-1400. E-mail: wsturm@wiscollect.com.

STURMAN, DEBORAH MUSCHA, lawyer, columnist; d. Herman Getzie and Gladys Freiman Sturman; 1 child, Rachel Zipporah. Prix D'Excellence, Royal Brussels Conservatory of Music, Belgium, 1992; JD, UCLA, 1995. Bar: Calif. 1995, D.C. 2000, NY 2001. Of counsel Milberg Weiss Bershad Hynes & Lerach LLP, NYC, 1995—2001, Milberg, Weiss, Bershad, & Schulman, 2001—06, Law Office of Deborah Sturman, 2006—. Legal columnist Manager Mag., Hamburg, Germany, 2003—. Musician (French horn soloist): Telemann Concerti Mozart Chamber Music for winds, 1982; musician: (French horn sect. leader) Royal Philharmonic Belgium; musician: West German Broadcasting Orch.; dir.(prodr.): (radio and TV) Singing and Swinging in the Cloister Tavern, 1984, The Woodwind Quintet in Old and New Clothes, 1985; columnist: Mgr. Mag.; contbr. numerous columns. Mem. Calif. Holocaust Era Ins. Oversight Com., Sacramento, 2000—. Mem.: Calif. Holocaust Era Ins. Oversight Com., Hadassah (life). Democrat. Jewish. Avocations: music, writing. Office: Sturman LLC 112 Madison Ave New York NY 10016 Home Phone: 212-367-7017; Office Phone: 212-784-6263. Business E-Mail: sturman@sturman.ch.

STURNER, LYNDA, performing company executive; b. Buffalo, July 1, 1941; d. Samuel and Rachel Louise Sturner; m. Jerome S. Traum, Sept. 23, 2001 (dec.); children: Daniel Matthew Traum, Edward Hart Traum stepchildren: David A. Traum, Norman Traum. BFA, Boston U., 1963. Instr. Boston U., 1983. Actor: (Broadway plays) Oliver, 1964—66, Bingo the Musical, 2007; prodr.: Triangle Prodns., 1981—87; co-prodr.: The Juniper Tree, 1982; artistic dir.: Playwrights Forum Inc., 1982—88; Provincetown Repertory Theatre, 2004—05; playwright: Woman's Project Lab., 1989—97; contbg. author: TheaterMania.com, 1999—2007; author: (plays) Look What You Made Me Do, 2000 (Audience Choice award, 2001), Art Brute, 2001, The Death of Huey Newton; co-author Sextet, 2001. Bd. dir. Castle Hill Truro Ctr. for the Arts, 1980—99, Music Theatre Group, NYC, v.p., 1981—2001; bd. dir. Provincetown Theatre Co., 1999—2003; co-pres. League of Profl. Theatre Women, NYC. Mem.: League of Profl. Theatre Women, Screen Actors Guild, Actors Equity Assn. Democrat. Jewish. Personal E-mail: lynda_sturner@yahoo.com.

STURR, JAMES WILLIAM, JR., bandleader, recording industry executive, clarinetist, saxophonist, small business owner; b. Springfield, Mass., Sept. 25, 1952; s. James William Sr. and Margaret Lillian (Gallagher) S. AA, Valley Forge Mil. Acad., 1964; BA, U. Scranton, 1966. Pres., bus. owner Starr Record Co., 1969—; pres. United Polka Artists; owner Jimmy Sturr Travel Agy. Composer: Men Don't Leave; album I'm Sturr Crazy (Album of Yr.); song A Little Bit of Poland (Song of Yr.); albums include Live at Gilly's, 1991, When It's Polka Time at Your House, 1991, A Jimmy Sturr Christmas, 1992, Sturr It Up, 1992, Polka Christmas, 1993, Polka Saturday Night, 1994, Polka Your Troubles Away, 1994, Attitude in Polkas, 1994, I Love to Polka, 1995, Saturday Night Polka, 1995, Polka! All Night Long, 1996, Living On Polka Time, 1997, Polka Favorites, 1997, Pure Polka, 1997, Dance With Me, 1998, Life's A Polka, 1998, Polkapalooza, 1999, Jimmy Sturr Polka, 2000, Touched By a Polka, 2000, Gone Polka, 2001, Top of the World, 2002, Let's Polka 'Round, 2003, Rock 'N Polka, 2004, Shake, Rattle and Polka!, 2005, Polka in Paradise, 2006 (Best Polka Album, Grammy Awards, 2007) and others; has featured a number of high profile guest on albums such as, Willie Nelson, Jo-El Sonnier, Flaco Jimenez, Bill Anderson, Oak Ridge Boys, Brenda Lee, Arlo Guthrie, Mel Tillis, Rhonda Vincent, Béta Fleck and Boots Randolph; appeared at the Grand Old Opry, Carnegie Hall, NY, Lincoln Ctr., NYC, Avery Fisher Hall, NYC, Palace of Culture, Warsaw, Poland, The Nashville Network, Mohegan Sun Casino, Uncasville, Conn., Tropicana and Taj Mahal, Atlantic City, NJ, Patowatomi Casino, Milwaukee, Wis., Soaring Eagle, Mt. Pleasant, Mich., The President's Casino, Biloxi, Miss., Mountaineer Race Track and Gaming Resort, Chester, West Va., Stardust Hotel and Casino, Las Vegas; host, nationally syndicated TV show; guest appearances on CNN, ABC, NBC, FOX News, and Saturday Night Live, (TV commercials) Budweiser, Pontiac, Mrs. T's Pierogies (Nat. spokesperson for Mrs. T's Pierogies); owner of music publishing co.; owner, host syndicated radio show, Polka Session, 1964-. Anchorman Cerebral Palsy telethons, Am. Cancer Soc. telethons, active numerous others. Recipient 16 Grammy awards (including Best Polka Album), 5 Gold Album awards, (with orchestra) Commendation of Excellence, Broadcast Music Inc. (the only one ever awarded in the polka field); named #1 Polka Band in the country, Man of Yr., Valley Forge Military Acad.; inducted into Polka Hall of Fame. Mem. Elks. Achievements include receiving more consecutive Grammy nominations then anyone in history of musical awards; honored with a Star of Fame in the walkway of Main Street in small hometown of Florida, NY. Also on display signs at each entrance of the small town, Hometown of Polka King Jimmy Sturr.

STURROCK, PETER ANDREW, space science and astrophysics educator; b. South Stifford, Essex, Eng., Mar. 20, 1924; came to U.S., 1955; s. Albert Edward and Mabel Minnie Sturrock; m. Marilyn Fern Stenson, June 29, 1963; children: Deirdre, Colin; 1 child from previous marriage, Myra. BA, Cambridge U., Eng., 1945, MA, 1948, PhD, 1951. Scientist Telecomms. Rsch. Establishment, Malvern, England, 1943-46, Nat. Bur. Standards, Washington, 1949-50, Ecole Normale Superieure, Paris, 1950-51, Atomic Energy Rsch. Establishment, Harwell, 1951-53; fellow St. John's Coll., Cambridge U., 1952-55; rsch. assoc. Stanford (Calif.) U., 1955-61, prof. dept. applied physics, 1961-98, dir. Inst. for Plasma Rsch., 1964—74, 1980—83; dep. dir. Ctr. for Space Sci. and Astrophysics, 1983-92, dir., 1992-98. Author: Static and Dynamic Electron Optics, 1955, Plasma Physics, 1993, The UFO Enigma, 1999; editor: Plasma Astrophysics, 1967, Solar Flares, 1980, Physics of the Sun, vols. I, II, III, 1986. Recipient Gravity prize Gravity Found., 1967, Hale prize Am. Astron. Soc., 1986, Henryk Arctowski medal NAS, 1990, Space Sci. award AIAA, 1992; European Ctr. for Nuclear Rsch. fellow, 1957-58. Fellow AAAS, Royal Astron. Soc., Am. Phys. Soc.; mem. Internat. Astron. Union, Internat. Acad. Astronautics, Soc. Sci. Exploration (pres. 1982-2001, Dinsdsale prize 2006). Office: Stanford U Dept Physics Varian Bldg Rm 302 Stanford CA 94305

STURTEVANT, BRERETON, retired lawyer, federal official; b. Washington, Nov. 24, 1921; d. Charles Lyon and Grace (Brereton) S. BA, Wellesley Coll., 1942; JD, Temple U., 1949; postgrad., U. Del., 1969-71. Bar: D.C. 1949, Del. 1950. Research chemist E.I. duPont DeNemours & Co., 1942-50; law clk. Del. Supreme Ct., 1950; gen. practice law Wilmington, Del., 1950-57; partner Connolly, Bove & Lodge, Wilmington, 1957-71; Examiner-in-Chief U.S. Patent and Trademark Office Bd. Appeals, Washington, 1971-88. Adj. prof. law Georgetown U., 1974-79. Trustee Holton-Arms Sch., Bethesda, Md., 1977-96, chmn. or mem. all coms., trustee emerita, 1997—. Mem. ABA, Exec. Women in Govt. (charter mem., chmn. 1978-79) Clubs: Wellesley College, Washington-Wellesley (pres. 1982-84). Episcopalian. Achievements include first woman law clerk for the Delaware Supreme Court; first woman US Patent Office examiner-in-chief. Home: 1227 Morningside Ln Alexandria VA 22308-1042

STURTEVANT, PETER MANN, JR., television news executive; b. Northampton, Mass., Feb. 27, 1943; s. Peter Mann and Katharine Bryan (Hobson) S.; m. Anne Elizabeth Fitzpatrick, July 12, 1969 (div. Dec. 1984); 1 child, Amanda Hadden; m. Toni E. Siegel, Apr. 14, 1985; 1 child, Gillian Lee. BA in Polit. Sci., Wilmington Coll., 1965; MA in Journalism, U. Iowa, 1967. Assoc. prodr. CBS News, Washington, 1967-71, bur. chief Viet Nam Saigon, 1971-73, nat. news editor NYC, 1974-80, asst. v.p. spl. events, 1981-83, producer 60 Minutes, 1984-85; exec. bus. news editor CNN, NYC, 1985-86; prodr. Today's Bus. Buena Vista TV, NYC, 1987; dir. news coverage CNBC, Fort Lee, NJ, 1988-90, v.p., mng. editor Ft. Lee, NJ, 1991-94; sr. v.p. Internat. Bus. News NBC, 1994-98; disaster relief, instr. Am. Red Cross, 1999—. Trustee Wilmington Coll., 2000—. Named Disting. Alumnus, Wilmington Coll., 1975, 97; named to Journalism Hall of Fame, U. Iowa Grad. Sch. Journalism, 1988; named to Wilmington Coll. Sports Hall of Fame, 1997. Mem. Nat. Acad. Cable Programming (nominated ACE award 1992, 93, 94), Soc. Profl. Journalists, Deadline Club N.Y., The Asia Soc., Overseas Press Club (bd. dirs.). Episcopalian. Avocations: racquet sports, landscaping, travel, stamp collecting/philately, parenting. Home: 90 Riverside Dr # 8D New York NY 10024-5306

STURTZ, DONALD LEE, surgeon, educator, military officer; b. Coshocton, Ohio, Apr. 18, 1933; s. Walter Raymond and Helene Josephine (Kubic) S.; m. Alice Marie McGuire, June 11, 1955; children: Jimalee, Janel. BS, US Naval Acad., Annapolis, Md., 1955; MD, U. Pa., Phila., 1965; diploma med. care catastrophe, Soc. Apothecaries London, 1996. Diplomate Am. Bd. Surgery. Surg. resident USN, Phila., 1965-70, ship's surgeon, 1970-71; staff surgeon Bethesda Naval Hosp., USN, 1971-80; chief of surgery San Diego Naval Hosp., USN, 1980-84; exec. officer Oakland Naval Hosp., USN, Calif., 1984-85; prof. clin. surgery USN, Bethesda, Md., 1985-87, commd. Naval Med. Command, 1987-88, Atlantic fleet surgeon, Supreme Allied Command surgeon Norfolk, Va., 1989-91; prof. surgery USUHS, Bethesda, Md., 1991—. Contbr. articles to profl. jours. Mem. nat. adv. cabinet Guideposts, 1980—. Recipient B.D. Larrey award for Surgical Excellence, Surgical Dept. USUHS, Bethesda, 1988, Exceptional Svc. medal, Uniformed Svcs. U., 1998. Fellow ACS (gov. 1985-88); mem. Am. Assn. for Surgery of Trauma, Assn. Mil. Surgeons, USN Inst. Republican. Presbyterian. Avocations: travel, gardening, antiques, music, reading. Office: USUHS Dept Surgery 4301 Jones Bridge Rd Bethesda MD 20814-4799 Office Phone: 301-295-9825. Personal E-mail: sturtz@aol.com.

STUTTS, JAMES F., lawyer, energy executive; b. Dec. 1944; BA in English, U. Va., 1967; MBA, U. Pa., 1970; JD, U. Richmond, 1977. Bar: Va. 1977, Pa. 1992. V.p. corp. fin. Wheat, First Securities; ptnr. McSweeney, Stutts & Burtch, Richmond, Va.; assoc. McGuire, Woods, Battle & Boothe, LLP, Richmond, Va., 1985—87, ptnr., 1987—97; v.p., gen. counsel Dominion Resources Inc., Richmond, Va., 1997—2007, sr. v.p., gen counsel, 2007—. Office: Dominion PO Box 26532 Richmond VA 23261-6532 *

STUTTS, WILLIAM FLOYD, JR., lawyer, educator; b. El Dorado, Ark., Nov. 8, 1952; s. William Floyd and Marilyn Martin Stutts; m. Susan P. Campbell, May 16, 1992. BA, U. Tex., 1973; JD, U. Va., 1976. Bar: Tex. 1976, U.S. Dist. Ct. (we. dist.) Tex. 1992. Law clk. U.S. Ct. Appeals (5th cir.), Austin, 1976-77; assoc. Baker & Botts, Houston, 1978-85; ptnr. Baker Botts, Austin, 1987—, Clark, Thomas, Winters, Austin, 1985-87. Adj. prof. U. Tex. Law Sch., Austin, 1997—; instr., cons. Internat. Law Inst.,

Washington, 1998, 2001. Bd. dirs. Ballet Austin, 1988-96, Austin Oita Sister City Com., 1990—, Travis County Bar Assn., 1995-96, Capital Area Coun. Boy Scouts Am., Austin, 1996—. Fellow Am. Coll. Investment Counsel, Tex. Bar Found. (life); mem. ABA, Am. Bankruptcy Inst., Comml. Law League of Am. Lutheran. Home: 1405 Hardouin Ave Austin TX 78703 Office: Baker Botts 98 San Jacinto Blvd # 1500 Austin TX 78701 E-mail: william.stutts@bakerbotts.com.

STUTZ, CATHLEEN KINSELLA, education educator; m. Guy Stutz. BA in English, U. Pa., 1983, MS in Ed., 1983; EdD, Boston U., 1995. Asst. prof. edn. Assumption Coll., Worcester, Mass., 1995—, chair dept. edn., 2003—. Recipient US Prof. of Yr. award, Carnegie Found. for Advancement of Tchg. and Coun. for Advancement and Support of Edn., 2006. Office: Dept Edn Assumption Coll 500 Salisbury St Worcester MA 01609 Office Phone: 508-767-7553. *

STUTZ, PEARL HEWLETT, retired photojournalist; b. Rochester, NY, Apr. 28, 1927; d. Herbert Henry Hewlett and Carolyn Amanda Brockmann; m. Peter Swan Stutz, May 23, 1953 (dec. July 1988); children: Eric Edward, Carolyn Edith Stutz Kourofsky. BA in Journalism, Ohio State U., 1949; MLS, SUNY, Geneseo, 1971. Cert. profl. libr. and media specialist, N.Y. Reporter Pampa (Tex.) Daily News, 1949, Great Falls (Mont.) Tribune, 1950; staff photographer Democrat and Chronicle, Rochester, 1950-56; libr. dir. Irondequoit Pub. Libr., Rochester, 1976-91; ret., 1991. Libr. cons. Cancer Action, Inc., Rochester, 1992-01. Named Disting. Communicator, Women in Comms., 1996. Achievements include first woman press photographer for large-city newspaper.

STUTZMAN, DONNA J., minister; b. Lemoyne, Ohio, Apr. 29, 1936; d. David O. Kaser and Opal M. Stockwell; m. Darrell A. Stutzman, June 7, 1958 (dec. Sept. 1993); children: Denzel, Devon, Dawn, Dara, Desmond. BS in Child and Family Cmty. Svc., Bowling Green State U., Ohio, 1987; MA in Christian Psychology, Cornerstone U., Lake Charles, La., 1992. Ordained minister Nat. Conservative Christian Ch., 1999; lic. social worker Ohio. Pvt. piano tchr., Wauseon, Ohio, 1958—; case mgr. Fulton County Maumee Valley Guidance Ctr., Defiance, Ohio, 1987—89; assoc. pastor First Ch. of God, Wauseon, 1989—91; mental health profl. Fulton County Health Ctr., Wauseon, 1991—99; social worker, music coord. Fulton Manor Nursing Home, Wauseon, 1998—; hospice chaplain Cmty. Health Profls., Archbold, Ohio, 1999—; pastor Hope Christian Fellowship, Wauseon, 1991—; in-patient hospice chaplain Defiance, Ohio, 2007—. Spirituality group facilitator Fulton County Health Ctr. Psychiat. Unit, 2003—. Vol. coord. Habitat for Humanity, 2003. Mem.: AAUW, Am. Acad. Bereavement, Am. Assn. Christian Counselors, Nat. Christian Counselors Assn., Phi Upsilon Omicron. Avocations: reading, music. Home: 701 Burr Rd Unit 5 Wauseon OH 43567 E-mail: djstutzman@aol.com.

STUTZMAN, THOMAS CHASE, SR., lawyer; b. Portland, Oreg., Aug. 1, 1950; s. Leon H. and Mary L. (Chase) S.; m. Wendy Jeanne Craig, June 5, 1976; children: Sarah Anne, Thomas Chase Jr. BA with high honors, U. Calif. Santa Barbara, 1972; JD cum laude, Santa Clara U., 1975. Bar: Calif. 1976; cert. family law specialist. Pvt. practice, San Jose, Calif., 1976—79; pres., sec., CFO Thomas Chase Stutzman, PC, San Jose, 1979—. Instr. San Jose State U., 1977—78. Bd. dirs. Santa Cruz Campfire, 1978-80, Happy Hollow Park, 1978-80, 83-86, Pacific Neighbors, pres., 1991-92. Mem. Calif. Bar Assn., Santa Clara County Bar Assn. (chmn. environ. law com. 1976-78, exec. com. family law), Assn. Cert. Family Law Specialists, San Jose Jaycees (Dir. of Yr. 1976-77), Lions (dir. 1979-81, 2d v.p. 1982-83, 1st v.p. 1983-84, pres. 1984-85), Scottish Rite, Masons, Phi Beta Kappa. Congregationalist. Office: 1625 The Alameda Ste 626 San Jose CA 95126-2207 Home Phone: 408-997-7454; Office Phone: 408-294-4600. Business E-Mail: stutzman@tomstutzman.com.

STWALLEY, WILLIAM CALVIN, physics and chemistry professor; BS, Calif. Inst. Tech., 1964; PhD, Harvard U., 1968. Asst. prof. U. Iowa, Iowa City, 1968-72, assoc. prof., 1972-75, prof. dept. chemistry, 1975-93, prof. dept. physics and astronomy, 1977-93, dir. Iowa Laser Facility, 1979-93, dir. Ctr. for Laser Sci. and Engring., 1987-89, George Glockler prof. physical scis., 1988-93; program dir. NSF, Washington, 1975-76 (leave of absence); prof. and head dept. physics, prof. chemistry U. Conn., Storrs, 1993—, bd. trustees disting., prof., 2002—. Program chmn. Internat. Laser Sci. Conf., 1985, co-chmn., 1986, chmn., 1987; lectr. Chinese Acad. Scis., 1986. Editor books in field; contbr. numerous articles to profl. publs. Recipient Conn. medal of sci., 2005—; Japan Soc. for Promotion of Sci. fellow, 1982; Sloan fellow, 1970-72; numerous grants in field, 1970—. Fellow AAAS, Am. Phys. Soc. (sec.-treas. divsn. chem. physics 1984-90, vice chair/chair Topical Group on Laser Sci. 1989-92, vice chair/chair divsn. atomic, molecular and optical physics 2005-), Optical Soc. Am. (William F. Meggers award 1998), Conn. Acad. Sci. and Engring., Conn. Acad. Arts and Scis.; mem. Am. Chem. Soc. Office: U Conn Unit 3046 Dept Physics Storrs Mansfield CT 06269-3046 Office Phone: 860-486-4924. Business E-Mail: w.stwalley@uconn.edu.

STYCOS, MARIA NOWAKOWSKA, adult education educator; b. Lwow, Poland, June 4, 1937; arrived in U.S., 1964; d. Marian Zygmunt Nowakowski and Julia Demska Nowakowska; m. Joseph Mayone Stycos; 1 child, Marek. BA, King's Coll. U. London, London, 1958; MA, Cornell U., 1967, PhD, 1977. Part time asst. prof. Ithaca Coll., NY, 1975—81; dir. Handwerker Art Gallery, Ithaca, NY, 1981—82; asst. prof. State U. of N.Y., Cortland, NY, 1982—86; sr. lectr. Cornell U., Ithaca, NY, 1986—. Cons. Cornell U. project in Costa Rica, Costa Rica, 1986; faculty adv. com. Johnson Mus. Art, Cornell U. Co-author (with E. Sanchez-Blake): Voces Hispanas Siglo XXI Entrevistas con autores en DVD, 2005; contbr. chapters to books, articles to profl. jours. including Asociacion Internat. de Letras y Cultura Femenina Hispanica, Revista/Rev, Interamericana P.R., Dictionary of the Lit. of the Iberian Peninsula, others. Planning bd. mem. Village of Lansing, NY, 2002—. Mem.: MLA, Congreso Internat. Sobre Lit. Centroamericana. Avocations: music, art, gardening, travel, poetry. Office: Romance Studies Cornell Univ Ithaca NY 14853 Business E-Mail: mns2@cornell.edu.

STYER, DENISE MARIE, psychologist; d. Kenneth James and Mary Ellen Styer; 1 child, James Kenneth Marketti. BA, U. Wis., Milw., 1990; MA, Alfred Adler Inst. Minn., 1995; PsyD, Adler Sch. Profl. Psychology, 2001. Lic. Profl. Counselor Ill., 2001. Therapist, intake coord. SAFE Alternatives, Naperville, Ill., 2000—01; clin. coord. Self Injury Recovery Svcs. Alexian Bros. Behavioral Hosp., Hoffman Estates, Ill., 2001—. Mem.: APA (prevention rschr. adv. bd. 2005). Home Phone: 708-638-8235; Office Phone: 708-638-8235. Personal E-mail: drdenisestyer@comcast.net.

STYER, JANE M., computer scientist, consultant; b. Bethlehem, Pa., Apr. 14, 1957; d. LeRoy V. and Pauline M. (Diehl) S. Assoc in Gen. Edn., NCACC, 1977, Assoc in Applied Sci., 1979; BS in Computer Sci., St. Francis de Sales Coll., 1985, cert. profl. legal sec., 1986. PC technician A+ cert. 1997. Legal sec., asst. Lower Saucon Police Dept.; asst. to treas., bookkeeper Lehigh Valley Motor Club, Allentown, Pa.; title ins. agt., real estate and probate paralegal, office mgr. various attys., Lehigh & Delaware Valleys, Pa., 1976—92; owner, mgr. Abstractors' Svcs., Bingen, Pa., 1982—; quality control theory checker, tax preparer H & R Block, 1992—2002. Mem. exec. com., comptr. Northampton County Drop In Ctr., 2002—04. Mem. NAFE, Nat. Assn. Legal Secs. (Continuing Legal Edn. Recognition award 1988), Lehigh-Northampton Counties (chmn. continuing legal edn. com. 1984-88, seminar chmn. 1985-88), Pa. Assn. Notaries, Single Sq. Dancers U.S.A. (nat. sec. 1986-87), Bachelors and Bachelorettes, Internat. (sec. Mid-Atlantic region 1980-84). Avocations: camping, square and round dancing, horseback riding. Office: Abstractors' Svcs 3228 Bingen Rd Bethlehem PA 18015-5707

STYER, JOANNE LOUISE, retired dietician; b. Melin, Oreg., Nov. 23, 1931; d. Raymond Louis Hosford and Gladys Lorraine Loomis; m. Lawrence Henry Styer, Aug. 20, 1955. BS in Foods and Nutrition and Instnl. Mgmt., U. Wis., Stout, 1954; postgrad., George Washington U., U. Md., U.S. Internat. U. Lic. reg. dietitian. Intern St. Mary's Hosp., Rochester, Minn., 1955; chief therapeutic dietitian Glen Dale Hosp., Washington, 1956; chief dietitian George Washington U. Med. Ctr., Washington, 1956—68; asst. dir. food svc. Montgomery County (Md.) Pub. Schs., 1968—69, dir. food svc., 1969—92; dietetic cons. Carriage Hill Nursing Home; ret. Cons. N.Y.C. Homeless Food Svc., Montgomery County Pub. Schs., USDA Commodity Processing, N.Y.C. Prison Food Svc. Evaluation; mem. adv. bd. D.C. Dairy Coun.; mem. industry adv. bd. Nat. Frozen Food Assn. Mem. editl. review panel Sch. Food Svc. Rsch. Review. Past chmn. nutrition com. D.C. Heart Assn.; nutrition com. Am. Heart Assn.; food chmn. Montgomery County Disaster Com.; nutrition com. Montgomery County Heart Assn.; expert task force USDA, Am. Cancer Soc. Named Disting. Alumni, U. Wis., Stout, 1989. Mem.: Md. Sch. Bus. Ofcls. (sect. chmn. food svc.), Md. Sch. Food Svc. Assn. (past pres.), D.C. Dietetic Assn. (past pres.), Md. Dietetic Assn., Am. Dietetic Assn. (chmn. dietetic practice group for sch. food svc.). Home: 11342 Kings Valley Dr Damascus MD 20872 Personal E-mail: lcapthook1@aol.com.

STYMIEST, BARBARA, stock exchange executive; MBA, Richard Ivey Sch. Bus. Audit ptnr., Fin. Svcs. Group Ernst & Young, 1978—87; exec. v.p., CFO Nesbitt Burns Corp., Ltd., Canada, 1992—99; chair, bd. govs. Toronto Stock Exch. (now TSX Group Inc.), 1997—99, CEO, 1999—, also. bd. dirs.; COO Royal Bank Can. Mem. ICAO Task Force, 1996; gov. Can. Investor Protection Fund, 1996; chair Joint Industry Coord. Com., 1995—97; alt. gov. Can. Securities Inst., 1995, gov., 1997—; mem. task force on std. setting CICA, 1996—98. Mem. ofcl. Bd. Forest Hills United Ch., 1984; bd. mem. Rehab. Inst. Toronto, 1996, Hincks Dellcrest Children's Ctr., 1990—97, chair, bd. dirs., 1993—96. Named one of 50 Most Powerful Women, Fortune Mag., 2005; grantee Inst. Charted Accts. Ont. Fellow: Inst. Chartered Accts. Ont. Office: Royal Bank Canada 200 Bay St M5J 2J5 Toronto ON Canada

STYNE, DENNIS MICHAEL, physician, educator; b. Chgo., July 31, 1947; s. Irving and Bernice S.; m. Donna Petre, Sept. 5, 1971; children: Rachel, Jonathan, Juliana, Aaron. BS, Northwestern U., 1969, MD, 1971. Diplomate Am. Bd. Pediat. Intern in pediatrics U. Calif., San Diego, 1971-72, resident in pediatrics, 1972-73, Yale U., New Haven, 1973-74; fellow in pediatric endocrinology U. Calif., San Francisco, 1974-77, asst. prof. pediatrics, 1977-83, assoc. prof. Davis, 1983-90, prof., 1990—, chair pediatrics, 1989-97; prof., sect. chief and Rumsey chair of pediatric endocrinology U. Calif. Davis Med. Ctr., Sacramento, 1997—. Author numerous book chpts., contbr. articles to profl. jours. Mem. Endocrine Soc., Soc. Pediat. Rsch., Am. Pediat. Soc., Am. Acad. Pediat., Lawson Wilkins Soc. for Pediat. Endocrinology, Western Assn. of Physicians. Avocations: sailing, music. Office: UC Davis Med Ctr Dept Pediat 2516 Stockton Blvd Fl 3 Sacramento CA 95817-2208

STYNES, STANLEY KENNETH, retired chemical engineer, educator; b. Detroit, Jan. 18, 1932; s. Stanley Kenneth and Bessie Myrtle (Casey) S.; m. Marcia Ann Meyers, Aug. 27, 1955; children: Peter Casey, Pamela Kay, Suzanne Elizabeth. BS, Wayne State U., 1955, MS, 1958; PhD, Purdue U., 1963. Lab. asst. U. Chgo., 1951; instr. Purdue U., 1960-63, asst. prof. chem. engring. Wayne State U., Detroit, 1963-64, assoc. prof., 1964-71, prof., 1971-92, dean engring., 1972-85, prof. emeritus, 1992—. Dir. Energy Conversion Devices, Inc., Rochester Hills, Mich., 1978—2005, MacMedia, Holland, Mich.; cons. Schwayder Chem. Metallurgy Co., 1965, chemistry dept. Wayne State U., 1965—66, Claude B. Schneible Co., Holly, Mich., 1968. Contbr. engring. articles to profl. jours. Mem. coun. on environ. strategy S.E. Mich. Coun. Govts., 1976—81; sec.-treas. Mich. Ednl. Rsch. Info. Triad; trustee Sci. Ctr. Met. Detroit, 1980—92; mem. ops. com. MACTV, 2000; sec. Friends of Herrick Dist. Libr., 2003; bd. dirs. Program for Minorities in S.E. Mich., Sci. and Engring. Fair of Met. Detroit, pres., 1983; bd. dirs. Midwest Program for Minorities in Engring., Friends of Herrick Dist. Libr.; treas. bd. dirs. Mac Media, 2002—; bd. dirs. Hope Acad. Sr. Profls., 2004. Ford Found. fellow, 1959-63; DuPont fellow, 1962-63; Wayne State U. faculty research fellow, 1964-65 Fellow: AIChE (past chmn. Detroit sect.), Mich. Soc. Profl. Engrs. (pres. 1987—88), Engring. Soc. Detroit (past bd. dirs.); mem.: Adult Learning Inst. (bd. dirs. 1994—99), Engring. Sci. Devel. Found. (pres. 1992—94), Am. Chem. Soc., Hope Acad. Sr. Profls. (bd. dirs. 2004—), Phi Lambda Upsilon, Omicron Delta Kappa, Tau Beta Pi, Sigma Xi. Presbyterian. Home: 145 Columbia #609 Holland MI 49423-2980 Personal E-mail: stanley.stynes@sbcglobal.net.

STYRON, ROSE, human rights activist, poet, journalist; b. Balt., Apr. 4, 1928; d. Benjamin Bernei and Selma (Kann) Burgunder; m. William Styron, May 4, 1953; children: Susanna, Polly, Thomas, Alexandra. BA, Wellesley Coll., 1950; MA, Johns Hopkins U., 1952; LHD (hon.), Briarcliff Coll., 1976, SUNY, Purchase, 1991, Trinity Coll., 2000. Bd. dirs. Amnesty Internat., USA, NYC, 1973-83, chair nat. adv. coun., 1984-94. Author: (poems) From Summer to Summer, 1965, Thieves' Afternoon, 1973, By Vineyard Light, 1995; co-author, translator: Modern Russian Poetry, 1972; contbr. editorials, profiles, articles, book revs. and poetry to maj. newspapers and mags. Chair, judge Robert F. Kennedy Meml. Human Rights Award, 1983—; mem. adv. bd. Reebok Found. for Human Rights, 1987—; mem. exec. bd. Human Rights Watch, N.Y.C., 1975-94; bd. dirs. Acad. of Am. Poets, 1995—, Equality Now, 1993—; chmn. adv. coun. Roxbury (Conn.) Libr., 1990-92; bd. dirs. N.Y. Found. for Arts, N.Y.C., 1986-94, Lawyers Com. for Human Rights, N.Y.C., 1981—, Rainforest Found., 1989-95, Assn. to Benefit Children, 1993—, Folger Shakespeare Libr., 1994-00; bd. overseers NYU Faculty of Arts and Scis., 1994—. Mem. P.E.N. (chair freedom-to-write com. 1983-89, bd. dirs. 1983-93), Coun. Fgn. Rels., Vineyard Haven Yacht Club. Democrat. Home: 12 Rucum Rd Roxbury CT 06783-1906

STYSLINGER, LEE JOSEPH, JR., manufacturing executive; b. Birmingham, Ala., June 28, 1933; s. Lee Joseph and Margaret Mary (McFarl) S.; m. Catherine Patricia Smith, Apr. 30, 1960; children: Lee Joseph III, Jon Cecil, Mark Joseph. Student, U. Ala., 1952. Pres., chief exec. officer Altec, Inc. and predecessors, truck equipment mfrs., Birmingham, 1956-89, chief exec. officer, chmn. bd., 1989-92, chmn., 1992—. Bd. dirs. Jemison Investment Co., Birmingham, Ala., Electronic Healthcare Systems. Mem. Country Club Birmingham, Mountain Brook Club, Shoal Creek Club, Willow Point Golf and Country Club, Jupiter Island Club (Hobe Sound, Fla.), Seminole Golf Club (Juno Beach, Fla.), Lyford Cay Country Club (Bahamas), Rotary, NY Yacht Club (N.Y.C.). Roman Catholic. Home: 3260 E Briarcliff Rd Birmingham AL 35223-1305 Office: 210 Inverness Center Dr Birmingham AL 35242-4834

SU, CHING-HUA, materials scientist; b. Taipei, Taiwan, Oct. 10, 1954; s. Draw-Ming Su and Kuo-In Ho; m. Yuk Yin Ma Su, May 19, 1995; children: Jeanne, Wynne, Charmain, Grace. BS in Materials Science, National Tsing-Hua U., Taiwan, 1976; PhD in Materials Science, Marquette U., Milw., 1985. Rsch. asst. Marquette U., 1979-84; sr. scientist U. Space Rsch. Assn., Huintsville, Ala., 1985-93, dir., 1993-94; rsch. scientist NASA/Marshall Space Flight Ctr., Huintsville, Ala., 1994—. Cons. in field. Author: (books) Semiconductor & Semimetals, 1983, Current Research Topics in C. Growth, 1995. Avocations: travel, bridge, basketball. Office: EM30 NASA Marshall Space Flight Ctr Huntsville AL 35812 Business E-Mail: ching.h.su@nasa.gov.

SU, FEI, electrical engineer, researcher; s. Xiaomin and Miaoyu (Yu) Su; m. Min Zhang. PhD, Duke U., Durham, NC, 2006. Rsch. asst. Duke U., Durham, 2001—06; sr. engr. Intel Corp., Folsom, Calif., 2006—. Reviewer in field. Co-author: Digital Microfluidic Biochip: Synthesis, Testing and Reconfiguration Techniques, 2006; contbr. articles to profl. jours. Recipient Outstanding Dissertation award, European Design Automation Assn., 2006; grantee, ACM/SIGDA, 2005; Travel grant, IEEE Computer Soc., Design and Tech. Com., 2004. Mem.: IEEE (test coun. test tech., Best Paper award 2007). Achievements include research in design-for-test, testing and computer-aided design (CAD) for SoC and mixed microsystems.

SU, HUA, medical educator; d. Zuyou Su and Rongzhen Cao; m. Jianqin Ye, Mar. 2, 1957; 1 child, Julia Ye. MD, Nanjing Med. U., China, 1982. Cert. ednl. commn. for fgn. med. grads. Ednl. Commn. US, 1997. Asst. prof. Xian Med. U., 1986—87, lectr., 1987—89, assoc. prof., 1994—; postgrad. rschr. U. Calif., San Francisco, 1992—96, asst. rsch. physician, 1996—2003, asst. prof., 2003—. Contbr. articles to profl. jours. Recipient Distinctive Rsch. Paper award, Conf. Electron Microscopy in North-West China, 1987, Xian Br. Chinese Med. Assn., 1988; grantee, Nat. Family Planning Assn. China, 1986, Xian Med. U., 1986; Cheng scholar, Chinese Adminstrn. Health, 1989. Mem.: Am. Heart Assn. (Scientist Devel. grantee 2005), Am. Soc. Gene Therapy. Office: Univ California San Francisco 513 Parnassus Ave HSW 901B San Francisco CA 94143-0793 Office Fax: 415-476-2956. Business E-Mail: hua.su@ucsf.edu.

SU, KENDALL LING-CHIAO, engineering educator; b. Fujian, China, July 10, 1926; came to U.S., 1948; s. Ru-chen and Sui-hsiong (Wang) S.; m. Jennifer Gee-tsone Chang, Sept. 10, 1960; children: Adrienne, Jonathan. BEE, Xiamen U., Peoples Republic China, 1947; MEE, Ga. Inst. Tech, 1949; PhD, Ga. Inst. Tech., 1954. Jr. engr. Taiwan Power Co., Taipei, Republic China, 1947-48; asst. prof. Ga. Inst. Tech., Atlanta, 1954-59, assoc. prof., 1959-65, prof., 1965-70, Regents prof., 1970-94, Regents' prof. emeritus, 1994—. Mem. tech. staff Bell Labs., Murray Hill, N.J., 1957. Author: Active Network Synthesis, 1965, Time-Domain Synthesis of Linear Networks, 1969, Fundamentals of Circuits, Electronics, and Signal Analysis, 1978, Handbook of Tables for Elliptic-Function Filters, 1990, Fundamentals of Circuit Analysis, 1993, Analog Filters, 1996. Fellow IEEE (life); mem. Sigma Xi (pres. Ga. Inst. Tech. chpt. 1968-69, 72-73, Faculty Rsch. award 1957), Phi Kappa Phi, Eta Kappa Nu. Methodist. Business E-Mail: ksu@ece.gatech.edu.

SU, SUNYU, physicist; b. Jinjiang, Fujian, China, Apr. 8, 1955; s. Guangjun Su and Linfeng Wang; m. Rong Luo, Dec. 29, 1986; children: Charles, Robin. MSc, U. of NB, 1986; PhD, U. of Toronto, 1991. Postdoctal fellow U. of Toronto, 1991—93; rsch. assoc. NRC Can., Winnipeg, 1993—96; MRI scientist Toshiba Am. MRI, Inc., South San Francisco, 1996—2000; mgr., open MRI coils USA Instruments, Inc., Aurora, Ohio, 2000—03; open segment program mgr. GE Med. Sys.-USA Instruments, Inc., 2003—06; program mgr. GE Healthcare Coils, Aurora, Ohio, 2006—. Cons. Toshiba Am. MRI, Inc., South San Francisco, 2000—02. Reviewer: Internat. Soc. Magnetic Resonance in Medicine Ann. Meeting Procs. Abstracts; contbr. articles to profl. jours. Recipient CEO award, GE Healthcare Coils., 2006, Mgmt. award, GE Healthcare Coils, 2006. Mem.: Internat. Soc. of Magnetic Resonance in Medicine. Achievements include development of solenoidal array concept for magnetic resonance imaging, patents for sandwiched solenoidal array coil; flexible, region-selectable inherently de-coupled sandwiched solenoidal array coil; uneven counter-rotational coil; double counter-rotational coil; quadreture detection coil for interventional MRI; open structure breast coil and support arrangement for interventional MRI; patents pending in field. Office: GE Healthcare Coils 1515 Danner Dr Aurora OH 44202 Office Phone: 330-995-8586. Business E-Mail: sunyu.su@med.ge.com.

SUAREZ, LUIS EDGARDO, civil engineering educator; b. Jujuy, Argentina, May 14, 1957; came to U.S., 1983; s. Luciano and Maria Mercedes (Colche) S.; m. Rosana Martinez-Cruzado, Dec. 30, 1994. MS in Engring. Mechanics, Va. Poly Inst., 1984, PhD in Engring. Mechanics, 1986. Jr. engr. Atomic Energy Commn. Argentina, Cordoba, 1981; instr. part-time dept. of structures U. Cordoba, 1981-82, asst. prof. grad. programs, 1987-89; rsch. asst. engring. sci. and mechanics Va. Poly. Inst., Blacksburg, 1983-86, asst. prof. engr. sci. and mechanics dept., 1986-87; asst. prof. gen. engring. dept. U. P.R., Mayaguez, 1989-91, assoc. prof. gen. engring. dept., 1991-96, prof. civil engring., 1996—. Proposal reviewer U.S. Army Rsch. Office, Mayaguez, 1991, NSF, Washington, 1994-95; paper reviewer Jour. Vibration and Acoustics, Jour. Engring. for Industry, Jour. Engring. Structures, Jour. Engring. Mechanics, Jour. Vibration and Control, AIAA Jour., Jour. of Sound and Vibration, Jour. Nonlinear Dynamics; panelist to select scholarships Battelle, Raleigh, 1991-92; chmn. 5th Pan Am. Congress of Applied Math., 1997, tech. chmn. South Eastern Conf. Theoretical and Applied Mechanics Congress, 2001, 06. Co-author: Multinational Seismic Design Codes, Handbook, 1992, A Visual Introduction to SAP 2000, 2002; mem. editl. bds. Jour. Engineering Structures, Vibration and Control Mechanics; co-editor Jour. Revista Internacional de Desastres Naturales, Accidentes e Infraestructura Civil; contbr. articles to profl. jours. Cunningham fellow Va. Poly. Inst., 1986, Disting. prof., dept. gen. engring., 1994, Disting. prof. civil engring., 1996, 99, 2005; grantee U.S. Army Rsch. Office, 1990, Nat. Ctr. for Earthquake Engring. Rsch., 1992-96, Langley Rsch. Ctr. NASA, 1999, FEMA, 2001-03, U.S. Army Corps. Engrs., 2003-05, U.S. Geol. Survey, 2003-04. Mem. ASCE, ASME, AIAA, Internat. Conf. Bldgs. Offcls., Soc. Exptl. Mechanics, Earthquake Engring. Rsch. Inst., The Vibration Inst., Am. Soc. Engring. Edn., Am. Acad. Mechanics, Sigma Xi (Rsch. award Va. Tech. chpt. 1987). Roman Catholic. Achievements include development of methods for seismic analysis of mechanical equipment that are used in industry, several methods for dynamic analysis of large structural systems. Office: Univ Puerto Rico Civil Engring Dept PO Box 9041 Mayaguez PR 00681-9041 Home Phone: 787-832-5217; Office Phone: 787-832-4040 ext. 3669. E-mail: lsuarez@uprm.edu.

SUAREZ, SALLY ANN TEVIS, health facility administrator, nurse, consultant; b. Jersey City, Jan. 23, 1944; d. Paul John and Gertrude Marie (Clancey) Tevis; 1 child, Maria E. Diploma, St. Mary Hosp. Sch. Nursing, 1965; BA in Health Edn. and Nursing, Jersey City State Coll., 1966, MA in Health Sci., 1977. Staff nurse St. Mary Hosp., Hoboken, N.J., 1965, Bayonne (N.J.) Hosp., 1966, Jersey City Med. Ctr., 1965-66; adminstr. Hoboken Med. Arts Family Health Ctr., 1969-75; adj. faculty Jersey City State Coll., 1976-77; adminstrv. supr. St. Mary Hosp., Hoboken, 1977-80; dir. North Hudson Commn. Action Corp. Clinic, West New York, N.J., 1979-88; nursing clin. dir. St. Mary Hosp., Hoboken, 1988-89; corp. dir. nursing Francisan Health System N.J., 1989-92; dir. maternal child health svcs. St. James Hosp., Newark, 1992-93, dir. Family Care Ctr., Cathedral Healthcare Sys., 1993-97, dir. nursing, 1992—97; ind. cons., 1995—2003; v.p. Med. Resource Network, 1997—2003; med. case mgr. MCR, 2000—03, Corvel Corp., 2003—04; coord. family health ctr. North Hudson Cmty. Action Corp., 2004—06; coord. case mgmt. U. Medicine and Dentistry N.J. Univ. Hosp., 2006—. Instr. nursing St. Mary Hosp. Sch. Nursing; cons. Creative Concepts in Counseling, Rutherford, N.J., 1979-82, Com. for Cytogenetics, Newark, 1986-88; cons. in health svcs., 1996—; v.p. Med. Resource Network, 1998-2003; case mgr. workers' compensation, critical care MCR, 2000-2003; case mgr. workers' compensation CorVel Corp., 2003-2004; health ctr. coord. North Hudson Cmty. Action Corp. Health Ctr., 2004-2006; case mgr. and coord UMDNJ, 2006—. Active Hudson County ARC, 1984-88, United Way, 1984-94; mem. Hudson County Perinatal Consortium Bd., 1987-92, Gateway Consortium, 1993-96; mem. adv. bd. Health Start, 1995-97, N.J. Assn. Women Bus. Owners, 1996-98; bd. dirs. Passaic Head Start; mem. adv. bd. Harrison Care Inst., 2005—. Mem. U.S. Assn. Women Bus. Owners, Am. Cancer Soc., N.J. Family Planning Forum (exec. com. 1980-86), Family Planning Assn. N.J. (exec. com. 1986-88). Democrat. Roman Catholic. Avocation: alternative healing. Home: 113 Wilson Ave Rutherford NJ 07070-2726 Office Phone: 973-972-4655. Personal E-mail: nursesrch@aol.com.

SUAREZ-OROZCO, CAROLA ELISABETH, psychology professor; b. Switzerland, Mar. 16, 1957; arrived in U.S., 1962; d. Rene Guy Jacqnat-Francillan and Carola Marietta Peters; m. Marcelo Mario Suarez-Orozco, Jan. 15, 1977; 1 child, Lucas. BA in Devel. Studies, U. Calif., Berkeley, 1978; MA in Clin. Psychology, John F. Kennedy U., 1980; PhD in Clin. Psychology, Calif. Sch. Profl. Psychology, 1993. Vis. scholar Harvard U., Grad. Sch. Edn., 1994—95, lectr., 1997—2002, mng. dir. immigrant projects, 1997—2002; exec. dir. David Rockefeller Ctr. for Latin Am. Studies Harvard U., 2002—03; sr. rsch. assoc. Harvard U., Grad. Sch. Edn., 2003—04; assoc. prof. N.Y. U., Steinhardt, 2004—05, prof., 2005—, chair applied psychology, 2005—. Author (M. Suarez-Orozco): Transformations: Immigration, Family Life & Achievement Motivation Among Latino Adolescents, 1995 (Best Book award Soc. Rsch. on Adolescents, 1996); co-author (M. Suarez-Orozco and D. Qin-Hillard): Interdisciplinary Perspectives on the New Immigration, 6 vols., 2001; author (M. Suarez-Orozco): Children of Immigration, 2001; author: (I. Todorova) Understanding the Social World of Immigrant Youth, 2003; author: (M. Suarez-Orozco and D. Qin-Hillard) Immigration: An Interdisciplinary Reader, 2005; contbr. chapters to books, to profl. jours. Mem.: Am. Psychol. Assn., Soc. Rsch. Adolescence, Am. Ednl. Rschrs. Assn. Achievements include research in intersection of cultural and psychological factors in adaptation of immigrant and ethnic minority youth and families. Avocations: reading, gardening, travel. Office: NY Univ Applied Psychology 239 Greene St 4th Flr New York NY 10003

SUBAK-SHARPE, GERALD EMIL, electrical engineer, educator; b. Vienna, June 15, 1925; came to U.S., 1959, naturalized, 1967; s. Robert and Nelly (Brull) S.; m. Genell Jackson, Nov. 23, 1963; children: David, Sarah and Hope (twins). BS with 1st class honors, Univ. Coll., London, 1951; PhD, U. London, 1965; ScD, Columbia U., 1969. Rsch. engr. Brit. Telecommunications Rsch., Taplow, England, 1951-58; mem. tech. staff Bell Labs., Murray Hill, NJ, 1959-64, cons., 1977-78; assoc. prof. elec. engring. Manhattan Coll., Bronx, NY, 1966-68; prof. elec. engring. CCNY, NYC, 1968—; v.p. G.S. Sharpe Communications Inc., 1981—. Author: (with A.B. Glaser) Integrated Circuit Engineering, 1978; contbr. articles on network structure and semicondr. theory to profl. jours. Served as lt. Royal Warwickshire Regt., 1944-47. Recipient Prof. of Yr. award Eta Kappa Nu/CCNY, 1985-86. Fellow Instn. Elec. Engrs. (London); mem. IEEE (sr.), N.Y. Acad. Scis., Nat. Trust for Historic Preservation Home: 606 W 116th St Apt 71 New York NY 10027-7024 Office: CCNY Dept Elec Engring Convent Ave New York NY 10027 also: Knollcroft East Chatham NY 12060

SUBBARAO, KALANIDHI, economist; b. Kakinada, Andhra Pradesh, India, June 30, 1940; s. Sanjeeva Rao and Sharadabai K.; m. Sundari Bhanu, May 1969; children: Sanjeev, Sharada. BA in Econs., Andhra U., 1963; MA in Econs., U. Delhi, 1965, PhD in Econs., 1973. Lectr. in econs. U. Delhi, 1965-75, read/assoc. prof. dept. commerce, 1975-77; Ford Vis. Rsch. fellow U. Calif., Berkeley, 1981-83; prof. econs. Inst. Econ. Growth U. Delhi, 1977-88; cons. World Bank Resident Mission, Delhi, 1988, World Bank, Washington, 1988-90, economist to sr. economist, 1990-94, prin. economist program team leader, 1994-95, prin. economist thematic group leader, 1996-99, lead economist, 1999—2002; cons., 2002—. Rev. jours. in field. Editl. bd.: Indian Jour. of Agrl. Econs.; author several books, including: Poverty Reduction and the World Bank: Progress in Fiscal 1996 and 1997, 1997, Safety Net Programs and Poverty Reduction: Lessons from Cross-Country Experience, 1997, Enhancing Women's Contribution to Economic Development, 1994, Agricultural Price Policy and Income Distribution in India, 1986, Improving Nutrician in India, 1989, Letting Girls Learn, 1991, India's Public Distribution System: A National and International Perspective, 1997. Doctoral fellow Indian Coun. Social Sci. Rsch., Delhi, 1972-73; Ford vis. rsch. fellow Ford Found., Berkeley, 1981-83. Mem. Indian Soc. Agrl. Econs. (life), Indian Econometric Soc. (life). Avocations: photography, cricket. Office: World Bank 1818 H St NW Washington DC 20433-0001 E-mail: ksubbarao@worldbank.org.

SUBBIONDO, JOSEPH L., academic administrator; V.p. academic affairs U. Pacific, Stockton, Calif.; dean Santa Clara U. Coll. Arts & Sciences, St. Mary's Coll. Calif. Sch. Liberal Arts, Moraga; pres. Calif. Inst. Integral Studies, San Francisco, 1999—. Author: Borrowed Time, 1972; co-author: Fifty Years of Innovations in Undergraduate Education: Change & Stasis in the Pursuit of Quality, 1999; editor: John Wilkins & 17th-Century British Linguistics, 1992; contbr. articles. Office: Calif Inst Integral Studies Office of the Pres 1453 Mission St San Francisco CA 94103 Office Phone: 415-575-6105. Office Fax: 415-575-1268. E-mail: jsubbiondo@ciis.edu. *

SUBER, ROBIN HALL, former medical and surgical nurse; b. Bethlehem, Pa., Mar. 14, 1952; d. Arthur Albert and Sarah Virginia (Smith) Hall; m. David A. Suber, July 28, 1979; 1 child, Benjamin A. BSN, Ohio State U., 1974. RN, Ariz., Ohio. Formerly staff nurse Desert Samaritan Hosp., Mesa, Ariz. Lt. USN, 1974-80. Mem. ANA, Sigma Theta Tau.

SUBIAUL, FRANCYS, anthropologist, psychologist, educator; b. Santa Clara, Cuba, June 2, 1976; s. Francisco Subiaul and Alfonso Ana Alfonso. PhD, Columbia U., NYC, 2004. Cert. psychologist Mich., 2007. Post doctoral fellow U. La., Lafayette, 2004—06; asst. prof. George Washington U., Washington, 2007—. Contbr. articles to profl. jours. Grantee, James S. McDonnell Found., 2005—. Office: The George Washington Univ 1922 F Street NW 406E Washington DC 20052 Home Phone: 337-322-9595; Office Phone: 202-994-7208. Office Fax: 202-994-2589; Home Fax: 202-994-2589. Business E-Mail: subiaul@gwu.edu.

SUBLER, EDWARD PIERRE, advertising executive; b. Shelby, Ohio, Mar. 24, 1927; s. Leo John and Dorotha (Armstrong) S.; m. Alice Ellen Carpenter, Sept. 8, 1956; children: Leo, Scott, Dorotha. BA, Denison U., Granville, Ohio, 1950; grad. advanced mgmt. course, Emory U., Atlanta. Mgr. product advt. Westinghouse Electric Co., Mansfield, Ohio, 1950—65; mgr. advt. and sales promotion Bell & Howell Co., Chgo., 1965-69; v.p. mdsg. Westinghouse Consumer Products Co., 1969-76; sr. v.p. Ketchum Advt., Pitts., 1976-92, ret., 1992; v.p. Pacific Garden Co., Millheim, Pa., 1998—2005, pres., bd. dir. Trustee BCB Anglers, Baie Jeanne Assn., Tanglewood Assn. Served with USN, 1945-46. Mem. Am. Mktg. Assn., Am. Assn. Advt. Agencies (regional chmn.), Catawba Island Club, Bus./Profl. Adv. Assn. (Pitts. Advt. Exec. of Yr. 1988), US Power Squadron, Baie Jeanne Assn. (bd. dir.). Home: 2465 Circleville Rd Unit 122 State College PA 16803-3390 Personal E-mail: esubler@yahoo.com.

SUBLETT, ROGER H., academic administrator; b. Ark. m. Cynthia Sublett; 3 children. BS, MA, U. Ark.; PhD in Am. History, Tulane U. Assoc. v.p. academic affairs U. Evansville, Ind., dean Coll. of Grad. and Continuing Studies Ind., dir. spl. programs Coll. of Alternative Programs Ind.; dir. Kellogg Nat. Fellowship/Leadership Program W. K. Kellogg Found., 1991—2001, program dir. Higher Edn. and Leadership, 1991—2001; faculty mem. Union Inst. & Univ., Cin., 2001—, interim v.p. for nat. undergraduate programs, provost, COO, acting pres., pres., 2003—. Co-author: Leading from the Heart. Bd. trustees Ctr. for Ethical Leadership, Seattle, OmniMed, Boston. Named Leadership Scholar, James MacGregor Burns Acad. of Leadership, U. Md.; recipient Spirit of Leadership Award, Kellogg Fellows Leadership Alliance, 2005. Fellow: James MacGregor Burns Acad. Leadership; mem.: Coalition for Adult Edn. Orgns. (pres. 1989—90), Assn. for Continuing Higher Edn. (life; v.p. 1984—89, Outstanding Svc. Award), Ctr. for Ethical Leadership (sr. scholar). Office: Union Inst & Univ Office of the President 440 E McMillan St Cincinnati OH 45206-1925 *

SUBOLESKI, STANLEY C., federal agency administrator, mining engineer; BS, Pa. State U., 1963, PhD in Mining Engring., 1978; MS, Va. Tech. U., 1968. Mining engr. North American Coal Corp., 1963—65; gen. supt. Underground Mines, Ctrl. Div. Consolidation Coal Co., 1969—74; v.p. Mining Div. Continental Ill. Nat. Bank, 1977—81; v.p. mining devel, treas. A.T. Massey Coal Co., 1981—88, v.p. ops. strategy, pres. United Coal Co., v.p. Norfolk Southern Ops., 1993—97; cons. mining engr., 2000—01; exec. v.p., interim COO Massey Energy Co., 2001—03; commr. Fed. Mine Safety and Health Review Commn., Washington, 2003—. Instr. Va. Tech. U., 1963—65, prof., head Dept. Mining Engring., 1998—2000; instr. Pa. State U., 1974—77, Centennial professor mining engring., chmn. Mining Engring. Sect., 1988—93. Mem.: NAE, Soc. Mining, Metallurgy and Exploration (mem. exec. com. Coal and Energy Div.). Office: Fed Mine Safety and Health Review Commn 601 New Jersey Ave NW, Ste 9500 Washington DC 20001 Office Phone: 202-434-9921.

SUBOTNICK, ALI, curator, writer; Receptionist Artforum; with editl. office Art News; host radio program WPS1.org; co-founder The Wrong Gallery, NYC. Vis. critic sch. of arts Columbia U.; spkr. in field. Curator MFA Thesis Exhibition, Columbia U. Sch. of Arts, 2004, 4th Berlin Biennial, 2006; editor: Parkett mag.; co-editor: Charley mag.; contbr. articles to profl. jours.

SUBRAMANIAM, SHIVAN SIVASWAMY, insurance company executive; b. Madras, India, Feb. 15, 1949; came to U.S., 1970; s. Kodaganullor Sivaswamy and Seethalakshmi S. B.E. in Mech. Engring. with honors, Birla Inst. Tech., Pilani. India, 1970; MS in Ops. Research, Poly. Inst. Bklyn., 1972; S.M. in Mgmt., MIT, 1978. Indsl. engr. Midland Container Corp., Ridgewood, N.J., 1971-74; mgmt. sci. analyst Allendale Ins. Co., Johnston, RI, 1974-76, sr. mgmt. sci. analyst, 1976-77, sr. fin. staff officer, 1978-80, v.p., treas., 1980-83, sr. v.p. fin., chief fin. officer, 1983-91, exec. v.p., 1991-92, pres., 1992-93, pres., CEO, 1993-95, chmn., pres., CEO, 1995—99; pres., CEO FM Global, Johnston, RI, 1999—2002, chmn., pres., CEO, 2002—. Mem. Fin. Execs. Inst. (membership chmn. 1982-84, Providence chpt. pres. 1985-86), Nat. Assn. Corp. Treas. Office: FM Global 1301 Atwood Ave Johnston RI 02919 *

SUBRAMANIAN, GUHAN, law educator; b. 1970; BA in Econs., Harvard U., 1992, JD, MBA, Harvard U., 1998. Bar: NY 1999. Assoc. McKinsey & Co., 1998—99; lectr. Harvard Bus. Sch., 1999—2001; Joseph Flom asst. prof. law and bus. Harvard Law Sch., Cambridge, Mass., 2002—04, Joseph Flom prof. law and bus., 2004—. Office: Harvard Law Sch 1563 Massachusetts Ave Cambridge MA 02138 Office Phone: 617-495-9784. Office Fax: 617-496-5156. Business E-Mail: subraman@law.harvard.edu.

SUBRAMANIAN, TIRUNELVELI SATYANANDAM, physicist; s. Tirunelveli Mahadevan and Subbalakshmi Satyanandam; m. Uma Balam, Mar. 18, 1976; 1 child, Raja Satyam Iyer. MS, U. Madras, Madurai, 1965, U. Detroit, 1972; PhD, U. Calif., Davis, 1979. Dir. radiation protection Bhabha Atomic Rsch. Ctr., Bombay, Maharashtra, 1965—70; rsch. assoc. Lawrence Berkeley Lab., Calif., 1979—81; dir. med. physics Hollywood Meml. Hosp., Fla., 1983—87; cons. med. physicist NorthBay Cancer Ctr., Fairfield, Calif., 1987—. Bd. mem. Shiva Murugan Temple, Concord, Calif., 1993—97. Mem.: Am. Assn. Physicists Medicine, Am. Coll. Radiology. Conservative. Hindu. Achievements include research in neutron, heavy ion physics for cancer treatment. Avocations: gardening, tennis, travel. Home Phone: 925-932-8346; Office Phone: 707-429-7905.

SUCATO, DANIEL J., orthopaedic surgeon; s. Justin and Ilde Sucato; m. Lisa Sucato; children: Daniel, Emma, Matthew. BA magna cum laude, Canisius Coll., Buffalo, 1987; MD, U. Buffalo, 1991, MS in Biophysics, 1997. Orthopaedic resident U. Buffalo, 1991—97, basic sci. rsch. fellow, 1992—93; pediatric orthopaedic surgery fellow Tex. Scottish Rite Hosp., Dallas, 1997—98, assoc. prof. orthopaedic surgery, U. Tex. at Southwestern Med. Ctr., Dallas, 1998—. Active staff mem. Children's Med. Ctr. Dallas. Contbr. articles to profl. jours., including Jour. Bone and Joint Surgery; cons. reviewer Spine, Jour. of Spinal Cord Medicine, Jour. of Bone and Joint Surgery, mem. editl. bd. Spine Universe. Active smem. Recipient Dr. William Beaumont award, AMA, 2005; Hip Preserving fellowship, Bern, Switzerland, 1998, SRS Internat. Traveling Fellow, 2003. Mem.: N.Am. Spine Soc., Tex. Med. Assn., Pediatric Orthopaedic Soc. N.Am., Am. Acad. Orthopaedic Surgeons, Scoliosis Rsch. Soc. (travelling fellow 2003). Office: Texas Scottish Rite Hosp 2222 Welborn St Dallas TX 75219 Office Phone: 214-559-7557. Office Fax: 214-559-7570. Business E-Mail: dan.sucato@tsrh.org.

SUCH, DOMINGO P., III, lawyer; BA cum laude, Washington U., St. Louis, MBA; JD cum laude, Loyola U. Chgo. Sch. Law. Ptnr. McDermott, Will & Emery LLP, Chgo. Mem. profl. adv. com. Chgo. Cmty. Trust, Loyola U. Med. Ctr.; mem. Body of Knowledge com. of bd. dirs. Family Firm Inst., mem. faculty; lectr. Loyola U. Chgo. Sch. Law and Grad. Sch. Bus. Contbr. articles to profl. publs. Named one of Top 100 Attys., Worth mag., 2006. Mem.: Chgo. Estate Planning Coun., Asian Am. Bar Assn., ABA, Chgo. Bar Assn. (chair, former legis. liaison Trust Law Com., past chmn. probate practive com.). Office: McDermott Will & Emery LLP 227 W Monroe St Chicago IL 60606-5096 Office Phone: 312-984-7683. Office Fax: 312-984-7700. E-mail: dsuch@mwe.com.

SUCHANEK, WOJCIECH LUKASZ, materials scientist, researcher; b. Oswiecim, Poland, 1969; arrived in US, 1999, permanent resident, 2004; s. Franciszek and Lucyna Suchanek; m. Figen Suchanek, 1996; 1 child, Melissa Ann. BS, U. Mining and Metallurgy, Cracow, Poland, 1991, MS, 1992; DSc, Tokyo Inst. Tech., 1996. Rsch. assoc. Tokyo Inst. Tech., Materials and Structures Lab., 1996—98; postdoctoral fellow U. Pierre Marie Curie, Lab. Chimie Matière Condensée, Paris, 1998—99; rsch. assoc. dept. ceramic and materials engring. Rutgers U., Piscataway, NJ, 1999—2001; rsch. scientist Sawyer Tech. Materials LLC (formerly Sawyer Rsch. Products), Eastlake, Ohio, 2001—04, sr. rsch. scientist, 2004—. Contbr. chapters to books, review papers and articles to profl. jours. Recipient Young Rschr. award, IUMRS Internat. Conf., 1997; fellow, Centre Internat. Etiudants Stagiaires, 1998—99; scholar, Ministry Edn., Sci. and Culture of Japan (Monbusho), 1993—96; Rsch. grantee, Rsch. Inst. Solvothermal Tech, Japan, 1998—2001. Achievements include patents in field; patents pending in field. Avocations: travel, photography, classical music, movies, sports. Office: Sawyer Tech Materials LLC 35400 Lakeland Blvd Eastlake OH 44095 Office Fax: 440-951-1480. Personal E-mail: w_suchanek@yahoo.com. Business E-Mail: wls@sawyerllc.com.

SUCHOMEL, MARK, publishing executive; With Contemporary Books, Chgo.; sales mgr. Chgo. Rev. Press (acquired by IPG), Chgo., 1986—87; with Independent Pub. Group, Chgo., 1987—, v.p. sales, mktg., pres., 1998—. Exec. coun. The Quills. Named One of 11 for the Millennium-those who will help shape publ. in 21st century, Publishers Weekly. Office: IPG 814 N Franklin St Chicago IL 60610 Office Phone: 312-337-0747. Office Fax: 312-337-0747.

SUCHY, ALBERT FRANCIS, marine architect; b. Phila., Pa., Aug. 16, 1952; s. Albert Francis Suchy and Jeannette Elise (Brinker) Sucny; m. Mary Jayne Ruggeri, Sept. 2, 1979; children: Kathryn Anne, Daniel Albert, Elizabeth Mary. BS, USCG Acad., New London, Conn., 1974; MS in Naval Arch. and Marine Engring., MIT, Cambridge, Mass., 1980, degree in oceans engring., 1980, MS in Mgmt., 1994. Lic. profl. naval arch. and marine engr. Wash. Commd. ensign USCG, 1974, advanced through grades to capt., ret., 2000; strategic planner Intel Corp., Hudson, Mass., 2000—03; ship ops. mgr. Woods Hole Oceanographic Inst., Mass., 2003—. Mem.: Soc. Naval Archs. and Marine Engrs. Democrat. Roman Catholic. Home: 85 Haystack Rd Reading MA 01867 Office: Woods Hole Oceanographic Inst Mail Stop # 27 Woods Hole MA 02543 Office Phone: 508-289-2624. Business E-Mail: asuchy@whoi.edu.

SUCKEWER, SZYMON, physics professor; arrived in US, 1975; MS in Physics, Moscow U., 1962; PhD in Physics, Warsaw U., 1966, DSc in Physics, 1971. With Plasma Physics Lab. Princeton U., NJ, 1975—87, prof. mech. and aerospace engring., 1987—. Contbr. articles to sci. jours. Recipient W.E. Lamb medal, 2005. Fellow: Optical Soc. Am., Am. Phys. Soc. (Arthur L. Schawlow prize in Laser Sci. 2007). Achievements include patents in field. Office: Mech and Aerospace Engring Princeton U Engring Quad Princeton NJ 08544 Office Phone: 609-258-4738. Office Fax: 609-258-1139. E-mail: suckewer@princeton.edu. *

SUDAN, RAVINDRA NATH, electrical engineer, physicist, educator; b. Chineni, Kashmir, India, June 8, 1931; came to U.S., 1958, naturalized, 1971; s. Brahm Nath and Shanti Devi (Mehta) S.; m. Dipali Ray, July 3, 1959; children: Rajani, Ranjeet. BA with first class honors, U. Punjab, 1948; diploma, Indian Inst. Sci., 1952, Imperial Coll., London, 1953; PhD, U. London, 1955. Engr., Brit. Thomson-Houston Co., Rugby, Eng, 1955-57; Engr. Imperial Chem. Industries, Calcutta, India, 1957-58; research assoc. Cornell U., Ithaca, N.Y., 1958-59, asst. prof. elec. engring., 1959-63, assoc. prof., 1963-68, prof., 1968-75, IBM prof. engring., 1975—2001, IBM prof. engring. emeritus, 2001—, dir. Lab. Plasma Studies, 1975-85, dep. dir. Cornell Theory Ctr., 1985-87, prof., 1987—. Cons. Lawrence Livermore Lab., Los Alamos Sci. Lab., Sci. Applications Inc., Physics Internat. Co.; vis. research asso. Stanford U., summer 1963; cons. U.K. Atomic Energy Authority, Culham Lab., summer 1965; vis. scientist Internat. Center Theoretical Physics, Trieste, Italy, 1965-66, summers 1970, 73, Plasma Physics Lab. Princeton U., 1966-67, spring 1989, Inst. for Advanced Study, Princeton, N.J., spring 1975; head theoretical plasma physics group U.S. Naval Research Lab., 1970-71, sci. adviser to dir., 1974-75; chmn. Ann. Conf. on Theoretical Aspects of Controlled Fusion, 1975, 2d Internat. Conf. on High Power Electron and Ion Beam Research and Tech., 1977 Mem. editl. bd. Physics of Fluids, 1973-76, Comments on Plasma Physics, 1973, Nuclear Fusion, 1976-84, Physics Reports, 1990—; co-editor Handbook of Plasma Physics; contbr. over 220 articles to sci. jours. Recipient Gold medal Acad. Scis. of the Czech Republic, 1993. Fellow IEEE, AAAS, Am. Phys. Soc. (Maxwell prize 1989), Nat. Rsch. Coun. (chmn. Plasma Sci. com. 1993—). Achievements include patents (with S. Humphries, Jr) intense ion beam generator.

SUDARSKY, JERRY M., industrialist; b. Russia, June 12, 1918; s. Selig and Sara (Ars) S.; m. Mildred Axelrod, Aug. 31, 1947; children: Deborah, Donna (dec.). Student, U. Iowa, 1936—39; BS in Chem. Engring., Poly. U. Bklyn., 1942; DSc (hon.), Poly. U. NY, 1976; PhD Hebrew U. Jerusalem (hon.), 2002. Founder, CEO Bioferm Corp., Wasco, Calif., 1946-66; cons. to Govt. of Israel, 1966—72; founder, chmn. Israel Chems., Ltd., Tel Aviv, 1967-72; chmn. I.C. Internat. Cons., Tel Aviv, 1971-73; vice chmn., bd. dirs. Daylin, Inc., LA, 1972-76; pres., chmn. J.M.S. Assocs., LA, 1976—; vice chmn. bd. dirs. Jacobs Engring. Group Inc., Pasadena, Calif., 1982-94; chmn., CEO Health Sci. Prop. Holding Corp., 1994-97; chmn. Alexandria Real Estate Equities, Pasadena, 1997—2007, chmn. emeritus, 2007—. Mem. sci. adv. bd. Calif. Tech. Ventures, Pasadena, 2000—. Patentee in field of indsl. microbiology. Bd. govs. Hebrew U., Jerusalem; trustee Polytechnic U. NY, 1976—; bd. dirs. Mgmt. Edn. Assn., UCLA, 1990-99. Served with USNR, 1943-46. Mem. AAAS, Am. Chem. Soc., Brentwood Country Club, Sigma Xi. E-mail: jmsudarsky@sbcglobal.net.

SUDBRINK, JANE MARIE, sales and marketing executive; b. Sandusky, Ohio, Jan. 14, 1942; niece of Arthur and Lydia Sudbrink. BS, Bowling Green State U., 1964; postgrad., Kinderspital-Zurich, Switzerland, 1965. Field rep. Random House and Alfred A. Knopf Inc., Mpls., 1969-72, Ann Arbor, Mich., 1973, regional mgr. Midwest and Can., 1974-79, Can. rep., mgr., 1980-81; psychology and ednl. psychology adminstrv. editor Charles E. Merrill Pub. Co. div. Bell & Howell Corp., Columbus, Ohio, 1982-84; sales and mktg. mgr. trade products Wilson Learning Corp., Eden Prairie, Minn., 1984-85; fin. cons. Merrill Lynch Pierce Fenner & Smith, Edina, Minn., 1986-88; sr. editor Gorsuch Scarisbrick Pubs., Scottsdale, Ariz., 1988-89; regional mgr. Worth Publs., Inc. - von Holtzbrinck Pub. Grp., NYC, 1988-97; mktg. assoc. Harcourt Brace Coll. Pubs., Northbrook, Ill., 1997-98, cons. Mid-Atlantic Redion, Midwest, Manitoba, Can., 1998—; mktg. assoc. W.W. Norton & Co., Northbrook, Ill., 1998—. Lutheran. Home and Office: 3801 Mission Hills Rd Northbrook IL 60062-5729 Business E-Mail: jsudbrink@wwnorton.com.

SUDBURY, DAVID MARSHALL, lawyer; b. Blytheville, Ark., Oct. 31, 1945; s. John Graham and Avis Wheatley (Miller) S.; m. Holly Jane Ritger, Dec. 27, 1967; children: Erin Elizabeth, Gregory Marshall. BA, So. Meth. U., 1967, JD, 1970. Bar: Tex. 1970, Okla. 1971, US Dist. Ct. (we. dist. Okla.) 1971, US Dist. Ct. (so. dist. Tex.) 1974, US Dist. Ct. (no. dist. Tex.) 1976, US Ct. Appeals (5th cir.) 1979, US Supreme Ct. 1981. Asst. sec., atty. Wilson & Co. Inc., Oklahoma City, 1970-74; ptnr. Nelson and Harding, Houston, 1974-76; v.p., gen. counsel, sec. Comml. Metals Co., Dallas, 1976—. Bd. dirs. Dallas Repertory Theatre, 1982-85; bd. dirs. The 500 Inc., Dallas, 1978-82, pres., 1980-81. Mem. ABA, Tex. Bar Assn., Dallas Bar Assn. (bd. dirs. corp. counsel sect. 1987-93, chmn. 1992-93), Houston Bar Assn., Okla. Bar Assn., Am. Soc. Corp. Secs. (dir. 1984-86, pres., officer Dallas regional group 1978-81). Office: Comml Metals Co 6565 N MacArthur Blvd #800 Irving TX 75039-2461 Office Phone: 214-689-4300. *

SUDDABY, GLENN T., prosecutor, lawyer; b. 1956; BA, SUNY, 1980; JD, Syracuse U., 1985. Bar: NY 1986, Mass. 1986, Fed. Dist Ct. 1986. Asst. dist. atty. Onondaga County Dist. Atty.'s Office, 1986—89; assoc. Menter, Rudin & Trivelpiece, Syracuse, NY, 1989—92; chief asst. dist. atty. Onondaga County Dist. Atty.'s Office, 1992; 1st chief asst. dist. atty. Onandaga County Dist. Atty.'s Office, 1998—2002; US atty. (no. dist.) NY US Dept. Justice, 2002—. Office: PO Box 7198 100 S Clinton St Syracuse NY 13261 Office Phone: 315-448-0672.

SUDERS, JOAN MARY, elementary school educator; b. Phila., Apr. 20, 1948; d. John Joseph and Stephany Rita Povilaitis; m. Daniel Charles Suders, Aug. 2, 1975; children: Daniel John, Stephany Rebecca. BS, Gwynedd-Mercy Coll., 1970; MEd, Shippensburg U., 1973. Cert. reading specialist Pa., 1998, reading recovery specialist Shippensburg U. Tchr. Cumberland Valley Sch. Dist., Mechanicsburg, Pa., 1970—. Tchr. religious edn. St. Katharine Drexel Ch., Mechanicsburg, 1994—2006; min. of eucharist St Katherine Drexel Parish, Mechanicsburg, 1996—. Mem.: Beta Sigma Phi (officer Laureate Epsilon chpt.). Office Phone: 717-766-0217. Personal E-mail: jdsuders@verizon.net. Business E-Mail: jsuders@cvschools.org.

SUDHAKAR, NORI, materials scientist, researcher; s. Siva Prasad Venkata and Parameswari Nori. PhD in Physics, Indian Inst. Tech., Kanpur, 2004. Rschr. low temperature lab. physics dept. Indian Inst. Tech., Kanpur, 1990—2005; postdoctoral rsch. assoc. materials sci. and engring. NC State U., Raleigh, 2006—. Contbr. articles to profl. jours. Mem.: Metals, Minerals and Materials Soc. Achievements include research in synthesis of novel transitiona metal oxides, nanomagnetic materials, study of electrotransport and magnetic properies of exotic materials showing giant magnetoresitance at low temperatures. Home: Apt # 205 2516 Avent Ferry Rd Raleigh NC 27606 Office: NC State U Materials Sci and Engring Raleigh NC 27695-7907 Home Phone: 919-833-2537; Office Phone: 919-515-7219. Office Fax: 919-515-7724. Personal E-mail: norisud@gmail.com. E-mail: nsudhak@ncsu.edu.

SUDHIVORASETH, NIPHON, pediatrician, immunologist, allergist; b. Bangkok, 1940; MD, Chulalongkorn Hosp. U., Bangkok, 1966. Diplomate Am. Bd. Pediatrics, Am. Bd. Allergy and Immunology. Intern Ch. Home Hosp., Balt., 1967-68; resident in pediatrics St. Lukes Hosp., NYC, 1968-69, Beth Israel Hosp., NYC, 1969-70; fellow in allergy Metro Hosp., N.Y. Med. Coll., NYC, 1970-72; staff Marshall Meml. Hosp., Tex., 1978—; pvt. practice. Mem. AMA, Am. Acad. Allergy, Asthma, and Immunology, Am. Acad. Pediats., Am. Coll. Allergy and Immunology. Office: PO Box 2087 705 S Grove St Marshall TX 75670-5220

SUDHOF, THOMAS CHRISTIAN, molecular genetics educator; b. Göttingen, Germany, Dec. 22, 1955; Degree in medicine, RWTH, Aachen, Germany, 1977; MD, Georgia Augusta U., Göttingen, Germany, 1982. Postdoctoral fellow Max-Planck-Inst. Biophysikallsche Chemie, Göttingen, 1982-83; postdoctoral fellow dept. molecular genetics U. Tex. Southwestern Med. Ctr., Dallas, 1983-85, asst. prof. dept. molecular genetics, 1987-89; asst. investigator U. Tex. Southwestern Med. Ctr., Howard Hughes Med. Inst., Dallas, 1986-89, assoc. prof. dept. molecular genetics, 1989-91, prof. dept. molecular genetics, 1991—, Gill disting. chair neurosci. rsch., 1995—, dir. center for neurosci., 1998—. Loyd B. Sands disting. chair in neurosci.; mem. molecular, cellular and devel. neurobiology rev. com. NIMH, 1995—. Mem. editl. bd. Jour. Biol. Chemistry and of Neuron; contbr. numerous articles to profl. publs. Recipient W. Alden Spencer award Columbia U., 1993, Wilhelm Feldberg award, 1994, Molecular Biology award NAS, 1997, MetLife award for Alzheimers Rsch. MetLife Found., 2004, Freedom to Discover Achievement award for Neuro-Science, Bristol-Myers Squibb, 2004. Office: UT Southwestern Med Ctr 5323 Harry Hines Blvd Dallas TX 75390-9111

SUDMEYER, ALICE JEAN, art gallery owner; b. Goldbeach, Oreg., Feb. 17, 1946; d. Harold Leo Enz Sr. and Zoa Jane (Mercer) Enz; m. Larry Gene Orrell, Jan. 11, 1970 (div. July 1974); children: Aaron Jay, Zoa Jean Easterling; m. Larry Everett Sudmeyer, Apr. 28, 1978. A Fine Arts and Letters, Mt. Hood C.C., 1977. Adminstr. dir. Art's OK!, San Diego, 1987—93; with Margaret Harwell Art Mus., Poplar Bluff, Mo., 1999—; owner, operator, artist Alice Jean Sudmeyer Artworks Gallery and Studio, Fredericktown, 2000—. With USAR, 1970—2006, ret. USAR, 2006. Decorated Liberation of Kuwait medal, Army Commendation medal, Southwest Asia medal. Mem.: DAV (life), VFW (life), Am. Legion (life). Avocations: gardening, yoga, music. Home and Office: 715 South Wood Ave Fredericktown MO 63645 Personal E-mail: jean4me@charter.net.

SUE, ALAN KWAI KEONG, dentist; b. Honolulu, Apr. 26, 1946; s. Henry Tin Yee and Chiyoko (Ohata) S.; m. Ginger Kazue Fukushima, Mar. 19, 1972; 1 child, Dawn Marie. BS in Chemistry with honors, U. Hawaii, 1968; BS, DDS, U. Calif., San Francisco, 1972. Film editor, photographer Sta. KHVH-TV ABC, Honolulu, 1964-71; staff dentist Strong-Carter Dental Clinic, Honolulu, 1972-73; dentist Waianae Dental Clinic, Honolulu, 1972-73; pvt. practice Pearl City, Hawaii, 1973—; chief exec. officer Dental Image Specialists, Pearl City, 1975—; dental dir. Hawaii Dental Health Plan, Honolulu, 1987—; dental cons. Calif. Dental Health Plan, Tustin, 1987—, Pacific Group Med. Assn., The Queen's Health Care Plan, Honolulu, 1993—. Dental cons. Pacific Group Med. Assn., 1994—; cons. Hawaii Mgmt. Alliance Assn., 1996—; bd. dirs. Kula Bay Tropical Clothing Co., Hawaiian Ind. Dental Alliance; mem. exec. bd. St. Francis Hosp., Honolulu, 1976-78, chief dept. dentistry, 1976-78; mem. expert med. panel Am. Internat. Claim Svc., 1995—. Mem. adv. bd. Health Svcs. for Sr. Citizens, 1976—; mem. West Honolulu Sub-Area Health Planning Coun., 1981-84; mem. dental task force Hawaii Statewide Health Coordinating Coun., 1980, mem. plan devel. com., 1981-84; vol. oral cancer screening program Am. Cancer Soc.; v.p. Pearl City Shopping Ctr. Merchants Assn., 1975-84, 92-93, pres., 1994—. Regents' scholar U. Calif., San Francisco, 1968-72. Fellow Pierre Fauchard Acad., Acad. Gen. Dentistry; mem. ADA, Acad. Implants and Transplants, Am. Acad. Implant Dentistry, Hawaii Dental Assn. (trustee 1978-80), Honolulu County Dental Soc. (pres. 1982), Am. Acad. and Bd. Head, Facial, Neck Pain and TMJ Orthopedics, Intertel, Internat. Platform Assn., Mensa, Porsche Club, Pantera Owners Club, Mercedes Benz Club. Democrat. Avocations: cars, tennis, photography, gardening. Office: Dental Image Specialists 850 Kam Hwy Ste 116 Pearl City HI 96782-2691 Office Phone: 808-455-4191. E-mail: oraldr928@tennis.com.

SUE, MICHAEL ALVIN, allergist; b. LA, Apr. 15, 1956; MD, U. Chgo., 1980. Diplomate Am. Bd. Internal Medicine, Am. Bd. Allergy and Immunology. Intern, resident and fellow West Los Angeles VA Med. Ctr., LA, 1980-86; allergist Kaiser Permanent, Panorama City, Calif., 1986—. Fellow Am. Coll. Allergy, Asthma, and Immunology; mem. Am. Acad. Allergy, Asthma, and Immunology. Office: Kaiser Permanente 13652 Cantara St Panorama City CA 91402-5497

SUEDFELD, PETER, psychologist, educator; b. Budapest, Hungary, Aug. 30, 1935; emigrated to US, 1948, naturalized, 1952; s. Leslie John and Jolan (Eichenbaum) Field; m. Gabrielle Debra Guterman, June 11, 1961 (div. 1980); children: Michael Thomas, Joanne Ruth, David Lee; m. Phyllis Jean Johnson, Oct. 19, 1991. Student, U. Philippines, 1956-57; BA, Queens Coll., 1960; MA, Princeton U., 1962, PhD, 1963. Rsch. assoc. Princeton U.; lectr. Trenton State Coll., 1963-64; vis. asst. prof. psychology U. Ill., 1964-65; asst. prof. psychology Univ. Coll. Rutgers U., 1965-67, assoc. prof., 1967-71, prof., 1971-72, chmn. dept., 1967-72; prof. psychology U. B.C., Vancouver, 1972-2001, head dept., 1972-84, dean faculty grad. studies, 1984-90, disting. scholar-in-residence, P. Wall Inst. Adv. Studies, 2000, dean and prof. emeritus, 2001—. Chmn. Can. Antarctic Rsch. Program, 1994—98; Disting. vis. scholar Ohio State U., 2000—03; affiliated prof. U. Haifa, 2005—; cons., lectr. in field. Author: Restricted Environmental Stimulation: Research and Clinical Applications, 1980; editor: Attitude Change: The Competing Views, 1971, Personality Theory and Information Processing, 1971, The Behavioral Basis of Design, 1976, Psychology and Torture, 1990, Restricted Environmental Stimulation: Theoretical and Empirical Developments in Flotation REST, 1990, Psychology and Social Policy, 1991, Light from the Ashes, 2001, Understanding the Bush Doctrine, 2007; editor Jour. Applied Social Psychology, 1975-82; assoc. editor Environment and Behavior, 1992—; contbr. articles to profl. jours. Served with US Army, 1955-58. Recipient Antarctica svc. medal, NSF, US Navy, 1994, Zachor award, Parliament of Can., 2000; grantee, NIMH, 1970—72, Can. Coun., 1973—2006, Nat. Rsch. Coun. Can., 1973—90, NIH, 1980—84, Can. Space Agy., 2003—. Fellow Royal Soc. Can., Can. Psychol. Assn. (pres. 1998-99, Donald O. Hebb award 2001), APA, Am. Psychol. Soc., Acad. Behavioral Medicine Resch., Soc. Behavioral Medicine, NY Acad. Sci., Royal Can. Geog. Soc.(hon.); mem. Internat. Soc. Polit. Psychol. (v.p. 1999-2001, Harold D. Lasswell award 2001, Roberta Sigel award 2005), Internat. Acad. Astronautics (corr.), Soc. Exptl. Social Psychology, Phi Beta Kappa, Sigma Xi. Office: U BC Dept Psychology Vancouver BC Canada V6T 1Z4 Home Phone: 604-687-8886; Office Phone: 604-822-5713. Business E-Mail: psuedfeld@psych.ubc.ca.

SUEHRSTEDT, WENDY P., bank executive; V.p. comml. loan rev. TD Banknorth, 1990, sr. v.p. comml. credit policy and adminstrn., 1991—94, sr. v.p. retail and small bus. banking, 1994—97, exec. v.p. and chief retail banking officer, 1997—2006, sr. exec. v.p., 2006—, pres. & CEO Mid-Atlantic divsn., 2006—. Former chair Maine Group Robert Morris Associates; chair cmty. investment divsn. United Way Greater Portland, bd. dirs., Maine Devel. Found. Named one of 25 Most Powerful Women in Banking, US Banker, 2006. Avocations: travel, cooking. Office: TD Banknorth 2 Portland Sq Portland ME 04112 *

SUEN, CHING YEE, computer scientist, educator, researcher; b. Chung Shan, Kwang Tung, China, Oct. 14, 1942; s. Stephen and Sin (Kan) S; m. Sheung Ling Chan, May 12, 1970; children: Karwa, Karnon. BSc in Engring., U. Hong Kong, 1966, MSc in Engring., 1968; MASc., U. B.C., 1970, PhD, 1972. Asst. prof. computer sci. Concordia U., Montreal, Can., 1972-76, assoc. prof., 1976-79, prof., 1979—, chmn., 1980-84, dir. Centre for Pattern Recognition and Machine Intelligence, 1988—, assoc. dean faculty engring. and computer sci., 1993-97, disting. chair artificial intelligence and pattern recognition, 2001—. Vis. scientist Rsch. Lab. of Electronics, MIT, Cambridge, 1975, 76, 78-79; invited prof. Ecole Polytechnique Fédérale de Lausanne, Switzerland, 1979, Institut de Recherche d'Informatique et d'Automatique, Rocquencourt, France, 1976, 78, 79, founder, Vision Interface, 1986; founder, co-chmn. Internat. Conf. on Document Analysis and Recognition, St.-Malo, France, 1991, Tsukuba Sci. City, Japan, 1993, chmn., Montreal, Can., 1995; founder, chmn. Internat. Workshop on Frontiers in Handwriting Recognition (hon. chair, 2002), gen. chair Internat. Conf. on Pattern Recognition, Quebec City, Canada, 2002; organizer numerous confs. Author: Computational Analysis of Mandarin, 1979, Computational Studies of the Most Frequent Chinese Words and Sounds, 1986, (with Z.C. Li, T.D. Bui, Y.Y. Tang) Computer Transformation of Digital Images and Patterns, 1989; editor: (with R. De Mori) Computer Analysis and Perception Vol. 1, Visual Signals, 1982, Computer Analysis and Perception Vol. 2, Auditory Signals, 1982, (with R. De Mori) New Systems and Architectures for Automatic Speech Recognition and Synthesis, 1985, (with R. Plamondon and M.L. Simner) Computer Recognition and Human Production of Handwriting, 1989, Frontiers in Handwriting Recognition, 1990, Operating Expert System Applications in Canada, 1992, (with P.S.P. Wang) Thinning Methodologies for Pattern Recognition, 1994; assoc. editor: Signal Processing, 1979—2006, Pattern Recognition Letters, 1982—, Pattern Recognition, 1983—2005, dep. editor, 2005-06, editor-in-chief, 2007-; assoc. editor: IEEE Transactions on Pattern Analysis and Machine Intelligence, 1986-89, Internat. Jour. Pattern Recognition and Artificial Intelligence, 1986—, Pattern Analysis and Applications, 1998—, Internat. Jour. on Document Analysis and Applications, 1998—2006; founder, editor-in-chief: Computer Processing of Chinese and Oriental Langs., 1982-93; adviser: IEEE Transactions on Pattern Analysis and Machine Intelligence, 1989-92; author more than 300 publs.; patentee in field. Recipient award Fedn. Chinese Can. Profls., 1988; Rsch. fellow Concordia U., 1998; Swire scholar U. Hong Kong, 1967, ITAC/NSERC award Info. Tech. Assn. Can. and Natural Scis. and Engring. Rsch. Coun. Can., 1992, Internat. Assn. Pattern Recognition and Internat. Conf. Document Analysis and Recognition award, 2005. Fellow IEEE (advisor Computer Soc.), Royal Soc. Can., Internat. Assn. for Pattern Recognition; mem. (life) Chinese Lang. Computer Soc. (v.p. 1987-90, pres. 1990-93, award 1988), Can. Image Processing and Pattern Recognition Soc. (pres. 1984-90, award 1997). Office: Concordia Univ Dept Computer Sci 1455 Maisonneuve W Ste VE-3-189 Montreal PQ Canada H3G 1M8 Office Phone: 514-848-2424 x3006.

SUER, MARVIN DAVID, architectural consultant; b. Phila., Apr. 4, 1923; m. Gertrude Litvin, 1947; children: Marsha Suer Clark, Sharon, Deborah Suer Berman. BArch, U. Pa., 1950. Registered architect, Pa. Ptnr. Suer & Livingston, 1961-62, Suer, Livingston & Demas, 1962-69; dir. tech. prodn. Eshbach, Pullinger, Stevens & Bruder, Phila., 1969-74; assoc. Ballinger, Phila., 1974-79, Bartley Long Mirenda, Phila., 1979-85, S.T. Hudson Internat., Phila., 1986-95; archtl. cons., 1996—. Archtl. works include State Hosp. for Crippled Children addition, 1964, Huey Elem. Sch., Phila., 1964, Dist. No. 4 Health Ctr., Phila., 1967, Stephen Smith Towers, 1969, Foxchase Br. Libr., 1969. Chmn. bd. trustees Phila. Found. for Architecture, 1980-81. With C.E., AUS, 1943-46. Fellow AIA (pres. Phila. chpt. 1968, 125th Yr. citation 1982); mem. Tau Sigma Delta. Home: 305 Overlook Ave Willow Grove PA 19090-2806

SUES, HANS-DIETER, paleontologist, zoologist, educator; b. Rheydt, Germany, Jan. 13, 1956; came to U.S., 1977; s. Guenther and Lieselotte (Dehmel) S.; m. Elizabeth Bailey, May 12, 1990. Candidate in Geology, Johannes Gutenberg U., Mainz, Germany, 1975; MS, U. Alberta, Can., 1977; AM, Harvard U., 1978, PhD, 1984. Postdoctoral fellow McGill U., Montreal, Can., 1984-85, Nat. Mus. Natural History, Washington, 1986-90; geologist Dept. Paleobiology Nat. Mus. Natural History, Smithsonian Inst., 1990—92, assoc. dir. rsch. and collections Washington, 2004—; adj. assoc. rsch. scientist Lamont-Doherty Earth Observatory, Columbia U., 1989—98, adj. sr. rsch. scientist, 1998—; asst. prof. zoology U. Toronto, 1992—94, assoc. prof. zoology, 1994—97, fellow Trinity Coll., 1996—2002, prof. zoology, 1997—2002; assoc. cur. Dept Vertebrate Palaeontology Royal Ontario Mus., Toronto, 1992—96, cur.-in-charge Dept. Vertebrate Palaeontology, 1994—96, sr. cur. Dept. Palaeobiology, 1996—2002, v.p. collections and rsch., 1992—2002; cur. Sect. Vertebrate Paleontology Carnegie Mus. Natural History, Pittsburgh, 2002—04, assoc. dir. sci. and collections, 2002—04. Editor: Evolution of Herbivory in Terrestrial Vertebrates, 2000; co-editor: Terrestrial Ecosystems through time, 1992, In the Shadow of the Dinosaurs, 1994; contbr. chpts. to books, articles to nature, sci. and tech. jours. Recipient Postdoctoral award Govt. Can., 1984, Postdoctoral fellowship Smithsonian Instn., 1985, Connaught Jr. Faculty award Connaught Found., 1992. Fellow Linnean Soc. London, AAAS, Royal Soc. Can.; mem. Soc. Systematic Biologists, Soc. Vertebrate Paleontology (v.p., pres.), Nat. Geograpic Soc. (rsch. and exploration com.), Am. Assn. of Mus. (peer reviewer, accreditation com.), Internat. Coun. Mus., Natural Sci. Collections Alliance (bd. dirs.), Palaeontological Assn., Paleontological Soc., Soc. Preservation Natural History Collections, Soc. Study Mammalian Evolution, Willi Hennig Soc. Home: 776 Manning Ave Toronto ON Canada M6G 2W6 Office: Royal Ontario Mus 100 Queen's Park Toronto ON Canada M5S 2C6 E-mail: hdsues@rom.on.ca. *

SUESS, FRED, plastic surgeon; MD, Downstate Med. Sch., NY. Cert. Am. Bd. Plastic Surgery, 1982. Intern St. Luke's Hosp., NYC; surg. resident Highland Gen. Hosp., Oakland, Calif.; resident in plastic surgery U. Calif. Med. Ctr., San Francisco; pvt. practice San Francisco, 1979—; mem. staff Calif. Pacific Med. Ctr., St. Francis Hosp. Mem.: San Francisco Med. Soc., Lipoplasty Soc. N.Am., Calif. Soc. Plastic Surgeons, Am. Soc. Aesthetic Plastic Surgery, Am. Soc. Plastic & Reconstructive Surgeons. Office: Aesthetic Enhancement Clinic Ste 500 1700 California St San Francisco CA 94109 Office Phone: 415-567-1791. Office Fax: 415-567-4906. E-mail: info@aestheticenhancement.net. *

SUESS, JAMES FRANCIS, retired clinical psychologist; b. Evanston, Ill., Aug. 8, 1950; s. James Francis and Rae Love (Miller) S.; m. Linda Grace Powell, July 31, 1976; 1 child, Misty Lynne. BS, U. So. Miss., 1974, MS, 1978, PhD, 1982. Lic. psychologist, NY, Ala.; diplomate Am. Bd. Profl. Psychology, Am. Bd. Med. Psychotherapists, Profl. Assn. Custody Evaluators, Am. Coll. Forensic Examiners, Am. Bd. Forensic Medicine. Assoc. psychologist State of Miss., Ellisville, 1978-80; clin. psychologist SUNY Med. Sch./Erie County Med. Ctr., Buffalo, 1982-84, supervising clin. psychologist, 1984-87, assoc. dir., 1987—2005; prof. dept. psychology Clinic South Ala., 2001—05; prof. emeritus SUNY, 2005—. Dir. practica SUNY Med. Sch., 1982-90, faculty counsel, 1988—; cons. Buffalo Dept. Social Svcs., 1985—; mem. spkrs. bur. Erie Alliance for Mentally Ill, 1986—; vis. prof. U. Guadalajara Sch. Medicine, 1985—; clin. dir. Stickney Adolescent Ctr. Mobile MHC, 1993-97; clin. dir. Physicians' Psychiat. Clinic, 1997—; CEO Stillwood Clin. Group, 1998—; adj. prof. dept. psychology U. South Ala., 2000—; clin. dir. Adm. Mc Collough Inst. of Rejuvenology. Author: Annotated Bibliography of Sex Roles, 1972, Personality Disorder and Self Psychology, 1991, (textbook) Enduring My Journey Throug Life: The Borderline Personality Disorders, 2005; contbr. chpts. to books, numerous articles to refereed jours. including Perceptual and Motor Skills, Jour. Clin. and Consulting Psychology, Am. Annals of Deaf, Assessment of Children. Mem. small bus. adv. coun. Nat. Congl. Com., 2005—. With USAR, 1969-76. Fellow Am. Orthopsychiat. Assn. (life, diplomate), Soc. Personality Assessment; mem. APA, Am. Bd. Forensic Exam (life), Ala. Lic. Psychol. (pres.), Mobile Assn. Psychol. (pres.). Home: 507 Evergreen Rd Mobile AL 36608-3845 Office: The Stillwood Clin Grp 717 Executive Park Dr Ste B Mobile AL 36606-2843 Office Fax: 251-342-8599. Personal E-mail: drjfsuess@comcast.net.

SUESS, JAMES FRANCIS, retired psychiatry educator; b. Rock Island, Ill., Nov. 27, 1919; s. Joseph John and Elizabeth Ida (Dalton) S.; m. Rae Love Miller, Mar. 24, 1946; children: Rae Anne, James Francis, John Randall. B Med. Sci., Northwestern U., 1950, MD, 1952; postgrad., Coll. Physicians and Surgeons, Columbia U. and N.Y. Psychiat. Inst., 1958. Diplomate Am. Bd. Psychiatry and Neurology (examiner various times). Intern USPHS Hosp., New Orleans, 1952-53; resident in psychiatry Warren (Pa.) State Hosp., 1953-56, clin. dir., 1956-62; asst. prof. psychiatry U. Miss. Med. Sch., Jackson, 1962-65, assoc. prof., 1965-69, prof., 1969-82; prof. emeritus, 1982—; chmn. dept., 1967-69, 73-75; asst. dean, 1978-82. Assoc. chief staff for edn. VA Med. Ctr., Jackson, 1978-82; vis. prof. Inst. Psychiatry, London, 1977, 83; ref. editl. bd. Am. Jour. Psychiatry, Washington; invited cons. to 5 Soviet republics, USSR, 1979; invited cons. in psychiatry, China, 1979. Contbr. articles to med. jours., including Am. Jour. Psychiatry, Jour. Med. Edn., chpts. to books. Capt. U.S. Army, 1941-45. Fellow Am. Psychiat. Assn., So. Psychiat. Assn. (edn. com. 1973-77), Miss. Psychiat. Assn. (pres. 1968-69); mem. Am. Assn. Dirs. Psychiat. Tng. (a founder, exec. bd. 1969-71). Avocations: piano, organ, golf, duplicate bridge. Home: 1415 Radcliffe St Jackson MS 39211-4824 E-mail: jamespsychman@cs.com.

SUEYOSHI, AMY HARUKO, social sciences educator; b. Daly City, Calif., Feb. 4, 1971; d. Ernest and Miyako Ihara Sueyoshi. BA, Barnard Coll., NYC, 1993; PhD, UCLA, 2002. Asst. prof. San Francisco State U., 2002—, dir. ethnic studies program, 2007. Cons. Asian Americans for Equality, NYC, 1995—96. Editor: O-musubi, 2002—05; contbr. articles to profl. jours. Cmty. devel. ext. agt. U.S. Peace Corps, Mindif, Extreme North, Cameroon, 2002—05; translator Queer and Women's Resources Ctr., Osaka, Japan, 2005, Kansai Queer Film Festival, Osaka, 2005; fundraiser Asian Pacific Islander Queer Women and Transgender Coalition, San Francisco, 2006—07. Fellow, Japan Found., 2003; Project 88 fellow, UCLA, 1996—2000, JSPS Rsch. fellow, Social Sci. Rsch. Coun., 2005, Mayers fellow, Huntington Libr., 2006—07. Fellow: Inst. Am. Cultures; mem.: Nat. Assn. Ethnic Studies. Achievements include research in Queer Asian American history. Office: San Francisco State Univ ETHS 1600 Holloway San Francisco CA 94132 Home Phone: 415-664-7697; Office Phone: 415-405-0774. Business E-Mail: sueyoshi@sfsu.edu.

SUFIAN, SANDY M., education educator; d. David P. and Beverly Sufian; m. Elias Murciano, Jan. 7, 2006. PhD, NYU, NYC, 1999; MPH, Oreg. Health Scis. U., 2001. Asst. prof. U. Ill., Chgo., 2002—. Chair Global Network Rschrs. HIV/AIDS Mid. East, Chgo., 2003—. Author: (book) Healing the Land and the Nation; editor: Reapproaching Borders. Fellow, Littauer Found., 2006—, NEH. Mem.: Disability History Assn. Office: U Ill 808 S Wood St 9th Fl DME Chicago IL 60612 Home Phone: 773-728-2881. Office Fax: 312-413-2048. Business E-Mail: sufians@uic.edu.

SUFLAS, STEVEN WILLIAM, lawyer; b. Camden, NJ, Oct. 7, 1951; s. William V. and Dorothy (Stafre) S.; m. Rochelle B. Volin, Apr. 15, 1978; children: Allison, Rebecca, Whitney. BA, Davidson Coll., 1973; JD with honors, U. N.C., 1976. Bar: N.J. 1976, Pa. 1978, U.S. Dist. Ct. N.J., U.S. Ct. Appeals (3d cir.). Field atty. NLRB, Phila., 1976-80; assoc. Archer & Greiner P.C., Haddonfield, NJ, 1980-86, ptnr., 1986—2002, Ballard, Spahr, Andrews & Ingersoll LLP, Voorhees, NJ, 2002—. Fellow Coll. of Labor and Employment Lawyers; mem. ABA, Pa. Bar Assn., Phila. Bar Assn., NJ Bar Assn. (exec. com. labor and employment law sect. 1985—, chmn. 1999-2001), Order of Coif, Omicron Delta Kappa. Office: Ballard Spahr Andrews & Ingersoll Plaza 1000 Ste 500 Main St Voorhees NJ 08043-4636 Office Phone: 856-761-3466. Business E-Mail: suflas@ballardspahr.com.

SUGAHARA, BYRON MASAHIKO, transportation executive; b. Jan. 22, 1940; s. Kay and Yone (Kuwahara) Sugahara; m. Nancy Shaw Hall, June 5, 1977; children: Christopher, Abigail, Alexandra. BA, Harvard Coll., 1962. From v.p. to pres. Gt. Am. Lines, Roseland, NJ, 1985—. Bd. dirs. Peck Sch., Morristown, NJ, 1993—95. 1st lt. US Army, 1963—65. Mem.: Am. Bur. Shipping, Tokyo Club, Henryville Conservation Club. Avocations: fly fishing, golf. Office: Great American Lines 5 Becker Farm Rd Ste 4 Roseland NJ 07068-1779 Home: 533 Indian Harbor Rd Vero Beach FL 32963

SUGAR, JOSEPH ROBERT, music educator, conductor, musician; b. Worcester, Mass., Dec. 14, 1928; s. Elias George and Emily Angeline (David) Sugar; m. Clara Anne Steele, Dec. 26, 1955; children: Thomas Elias, Robert Albert. AA, Bergen Jr. Coll., Teaneck, NJ, 1948; BA, LI U., 1950; MA, Columbia U., 1955; profl. diploma, 1956. Brass instr. LI U., NY, 1949, prof., advisor to music chmn. for courses music edn. C. W. Post Coll. Greenvale, NY, 1990—, dir. music edn., 1990-2001; asst. bands. Ind. U., Bloomington, Ind., 1950; dir. Instrumental Music, Matawan, NJ, 1954-56; band dir. Upsala Coll., East Orange, NJ, 1956-57; band. dir., instr. music Bethpage Elem. Sch., NY, 1957-66; instr. baton twirling Bethpage HS, 1957-67; band. dir. Hewlett-Woodmere Jr. HS, NY, 1966-78; asst. band dir., instr. baton twirling Hewlett HS, 1967-69, band dir., 1983-84, dir. jazz ensemble, 1983-89; band dir. Dowling Coll., Oakdale, NY, 1977-79; dist. dir. music Hewlett-Woodmere Pub. Schs., 1978-89. Summer band sch. co-dir., Manasquan, NJ, 1955—64; creative music cultural workshop, Bethpage, 1959—62; dir. NY Jazz Ensemble, Hempstead, 1976, Kismet Shrine Temple Band, 1997—; clinician numerous music festivals, 1970—; choral dir., instrumentalist Air Force Band of Rockies, 504th Air Force Band, Colorado Springs. Performer: Indpls. Symphony Orch., 1950, Joe Sugar and the Big Band, 1980—; musician (numerous entertainers including): Vic Damone, Diahann Carroll, Al Martino, Jerry Vale, Georgia Gibbs, Toni Arden, Johnny Ray, Eddie Fisher, Cab Calloway, Marilyn Michaels, Frankie Lane, Henny Youngman, Anna Maria Alberghetti, Patti Page, Bobby Rydell, Buddy Greco, Billy Eckstine, Julius La Rosa, The Four Aces, Don Cornell, Connie Francis; musician: (with Audio-Fidelity) (albums) 20th Century Fox, Paramount, MGM, 1958—61; author: Where

Are We Headed in Music Education?, 1960, Twirling Tips in 3 Volumes, 1963, Presidents March, 1982; composer, condr.: albums Ten Nights in a Harem, 1963. Mem. Boy Scouts Am.; youth choir dir. Levittown Presbyn. Ch., NY, 1966. With USAF, 1950—52. Named Man of the Yr., Wantagh C. of C., 1979; named to Tchr. Hall of Fame, Hewlett-Woodmere Pub. Schs., 1990; recipient Merit award, Music Belongs, 1972, 1st Pl. award, E. Nat. Music Festival, 1977, Apprecation of Outstanding Leadership award, Black Music Caucus, 1982, cert. of Merit award, NY State Senate, 1982, citation, Town of Hempstead, 1982, Oustanding Ret. Band Dirs. award, NY State Band Dirs. Assn., 2007, Disting. Svc. award, Hewlett-Woodmere Pub. Schs., 1989; grantee, Ford Found., 1962. Mem.: DAV (life), NY State Coun. Music Adminstrs. (Disting. Svc. award 1990), Internat. Trumpet Guild, Nat. Assn. Jazz Educators, Nassau Music Educators Assn. (pres. 1970, mem. adv. bd. 1980—, Pres. award 1970, Svc. award 1973, 1987), NY State Sch. Music Assn. (pres. 1980—82, Disting. Svc. award 1989), NY State Adminstrs. Music Edn. (pres. 1987—), Music Educators Nat. Conf. (life; pres. ea. divsn. 1985—87), Wantagh Friends Libr., Jones Beach Power Squadron (sr.), Wantagh Spiked Shoe (past pres., award 1979), Am. Legion (past cmdr., award 1978), Kiwanis (past pres., award 1979), Wantagh Dads and Booster (past pres.), Masons, Tri M, Kappa Kappa Psi, Phi Delta Kappa, Phi Mu Alpha (life). Republican. Home: 1594 Milburn Ct Wantagh NY 11793-3330 Office: LI U CW Post Coll Music Dept 720 Northern Blvd Greenvale NY 11548-1319 Business E-Mail: jsugar@liu.edu.

SUGAR, RONALD D., aerospace transportation company executive; b. Toronto, July 1948; m. Valerie Sugar; 2 children. BSEE summa cum laude, UCLA, 1968, MS, 1969, PhD, 1971. Dir. advanced R & D programs TRW Inc., Cleve., 1981-83, chief engr., dep. program mgr. Milstar Satellite payload program, 1983-87, v.p., gen. mgr. space comms. divsn., 1987-92, v.p. strategic bus. devel. space and def. sector, 1992-94, exec. v.p., CFO, 1994-96, exec. v.p., gen. mgr. automotive electronics group, 1996-98, exec. v.p. spl. projects, 1998-99, pres., COO space and info. sys. sector, 1999-2000; pres., COO Litton Industries, Inc., Woodland Hills, Calif., 2000—01, Northrop Grumman Corp., LA, 2001—03, pres., CEO, chmn., 2003—06, chmn., CEO, 2006—. Mem. Nat. Security Telecom. Adv. Com.; bd. dirs. Chevron Corp., 2005—. Nat. trustee Boys & Girls Clubs of Am.; dir. LA Philharmonic Assn.; trustee U. So. Calif. Recipient Engring. Alumnus of the Yr., UCLA, 1996, Daniel Epstein Engring. Mgmt. award, U. So. Calif., 2003, Found. award, USMC, 2003. Fellow: Royal Aeronautical Soc., Am. Inst. of Aeronautics and Astronautics; mem.: NAE, Aerospace Industries Assn. (vice chmn.), Assn. of US Army. Office: Northrop Grumman Corp 1840 Century Park E Los Angeles CA 90067-2199 *

SUGARBAKER, PAUL H., oncologist, surgeon; b. Balt., Md., Nov. 28, 1941; MA in Immunology, Harvard U. Grad. Sch. Arts & Scis., 1983; MD, Cornell U., 1967; PhD (hon.), U. Liege, Belgium, 1999. Cert. Surgery. Intern, surgery Peter Bent Brigham Hosp., Boston, 1967—68, resident, 1968—73; fellow Mass. Gen. Hosp., Boston, 1973—76; sr. investigator, surgery branch & head, colorectal cancer sect. Nat. Cancer Inst., Bethesda, Md., 1976—86; dir., surgical oncology Emory U. Sch. Medicine, Atlanta, 1986—89; dir. surgical oncology Washington Cancer Inst., Washington Hosp. Ctr., Washington, 1989, dir., peritoneal surface malignancy program; private practice Sugarbaker Oncology Assocs., Washington. Mem. med. adv. bd. Find Cancer Experts; delivered Burchenal Lecture Meml. Sloan-Kettering Cancer Ctr. Numerous editl. bds. that include Journal of Hepato Pancreatico Biliary Surgery, European Journal of Surgical Oncology and the International Journal of Surgical Sciences; contbr. articles to profl. jours., chapters to books. Recipient E.T. Krementz award for best rsch. develop., Ulm, Germany. Mem.: ACS, Internat. Soc. Regional Cancer Therapy (founding mem.), Am. Assn. Cancer Rsch., Assn. Academic Surgery. Achievements include being an internationally recognized oncologic surgeon with expertise in gastrointestinal cancers, liver tumors, mesothelioma and soft tissue sarcomas. Office: Sugarbaker Oncology Assocs Washington Hosp Ctr 106 Irving St NW Ste 3900 Washington DC 20010 Office Phone: 202-877-3908. Office Fax: 202-877-8602. *

SUGARMAN, ALAN WILLIAM, educational consultant; b. Boston, Sept. 26, 1924; s. Henry and Dorothy (Adams) S.; m. Alice Mulhall, 1974; children: Michael, Susan, Ellen, William, Jane, James. BS, Boston U., 1948; MA, Columbia U., 1949, EdD, 1967; postgrad., SUNY, Albany, 1954-56. Entrance examiner Boston U., 1947-48; tchr. Public Schs. Hudson, NY, 1950-54, prin. jr. high sch., 1954-56, prin. sr. high sch., 1956-61; prin. Spring Valley (N.Y.) Sr. High Sch., 1961-67; dir. secondary edn. Ramapo Central Sch. Dist. No. 2, Spring Valley, 1967-69, asst. supt. instrn., 1969-73; prin. Ramapo Sr. High Sch., Spring Valley, 1969; supt. schs. Connetquot Central Sch. Dist. Islip, Bohemia, NY, 1973-80, Ft. Lee (N.J.) Sch. Dist., 1980—2000; nat. spkr., cons., 2000—. Adj. prof. NY U., NYC, U. PR, Rio Piedras, Hofstra U., 1967—; prof. Fordham U., NYC, 1969. Athletic dir. East River Day Camp, N.Y.C., summer 1949; group worker St. John's Guild, summer 1950; asst. dir. Tenn. Work Camp, Unitarian Service Com., summer 1951; dir. spl. activities Hudson Youth Bur., Hudson, N.Y., summer 1952; exec. dir. Jewish Community Center, Hudson, 1953-56; chmn. vis. coms. Middle States Commn. Colls. and Secondary Schs., 1958-76; chmn. county leadership tng. com., mem. Rockland County exec. council Boy Scouts Am., 1956; bd. dirs. Bergen County Red Cross; corr. sec. Rockland County Negro Scholarship Fund, Inc.; pres. Spring Valley Youth Activities Com., 1956-58; bd. dirs., past campaign co-chmn. Greater Hudson Community Chest; bd. dirs., 2d v.p. Hudson Youth Recreation Center, 1958-61; bd. dirs. Rockland County br. Am. Cancer Soc., 1958-61, Columbia Meml. Hosp., 1959-61; chmn. Town of Islip Health Usage Com., 1973; bd. dirs. Am. Heart Assn. N.J. affiliate, 1993—. Served with AUS, 1944-46, ETO. Recipient Disting. Svc. award Hudson Jr. C. of C., 1960, Ft. Lee Citizen of Yr. award VFW, Bergen County Citizen of Yr. award VFW, 1989, N.J. State Elks Alcohol and Drug Prevention award, 1989, St. Michael's award, 1992, PBA Silver Life Card award, 1993, EIA award Greek Orthodox Archdiocese, 1993; named Adminstr. of Yr., Fordham U., 1990, B'nai Brith Man of Yr., 1995. Mem. Nat. Honor Soc. Secondary Schs. (hon.), Nat. PTA (hon. life), Am. Assn. Sch. Adminstrs., Assn. Supervision and Curriculum Devel., Nat. Sch. Public Relations Assn., Assn. Sch. Bus. Ofcls., Nat. Soc. Study Edn., DAV, VFW, Jewish War Vets., Rotary (bd. dirs.), Phi Delta Kappa (Adminstr. of Yr. award 1990), Kappa Delta Pi, Pi Gamma Mu. Office: 400 Fairview Ave Fort Lee NJ 07024 Home: 494 Country Club Dr Egg Harbor City NJ 08215-5132 Personal E-mail: amwsintac@msn.com.

SUGARMAN, GEORGE, artist; b. NYC, May 11, 1912; s. Herman and Rachel S. BA, CCNY, 1935. Adj. prof. art Hue Hunter Coll., 1961-68, also Yale U., Princeton U. One-man shows Widdifield Gallery, N.Y.C., 1958, Radich Gallery, N.Y.C., 1961, 64, 65, 66, Phila. Art Alliance, 1965, Dayton's Gallery 12, Mpls., 1966, Galerie Schmela, Dusseldorf, Germany, 1967, Galerie Ziegler, Zurich, Switzerland, 1967, 70, Kaiser Wilhelm Mus., Krefeld, Germany, 1969, Staditsches Mus., Leverkusen, 1969, Kunsthalle, Basel, Switzerland, 1970, Haus Am Waldsee Mus., Berlin, 1970, Stedelijk Mus., Amsterdam, 1970, Gallery 118, Mpls., 1971, Zabriskie Gallery, N.Y.C., 1974, Dag Hammarskjold Plaza Sculpture Garden, N.Y.C., 1974, Robet Miller Gallery, N.Y.C., 1977, 78, Galerie Liatowitsch, Basel, 1979, Rudolf Zwirner Gallery, Cologne, W. Ger., 1981, Joslyn Art Mus (retrospective), Omaha, 1981-82, Fuller-Goldeen Gallery, San Francisco, 1984, Robert Miller Gallery, N.Y.C., 1985, Whitney Mus. Am. Art, N.Y.C., 1985, Contemporary Sculpture Ctr., Tokyo, 1993; group shows include, São Paulo (Brazil) Biennale, 1963, Whitney Mus. Am. Art, 1966, Los Angeles County Mus. Art, 1967, Internat. Pavilion, Biennale, Venice, Italy, 1968, Mus. Modern Art, N.Y.C., 1969, Whitney Mus., 1976, Washburn Gallery, NYC, 2006; represented in permanent collections, Walker Art Center, Mpls., Kunstmuseum, Zurich, Mus. Modern Art, Whitney Mus. Am. Art, Art Inst. Chgo., Met. Mus., N.Y.C.; sculpture commns., World Trade Center, Brussels, Albert M. Greenfield Sch., Phila., Empire State Mall, Albany, N.Y., Fed. Ct. Bldg., Balt., Akron (Ohio) Public Library, Lincoln Nat. Life Found., Ft. Wayne, Ind., Internat. Airport, Miami, Fla., Detroit Gen. Hosp., Wills Eye Hosp., Phila., Summer-Best Sta., Buffalo, Southland Life Bldg., Dallas, Columbia Plaza, Cin., Allegheny Landing, Pitts., Joslyn Sculpture Garden, Omaha, Bellevue Park, Wichita Falls, Tex., VA Hosp., Martinsburg, W.Va., Columbia Plaza, Cin., Storm King Art Ctr., Mountainville, N.Y., Mercantile Bank, San Antonio, GTE, Irving, Tex., NCNB Pla., Tampa, Fla., Koll Ctr. Irvine, North Irvine, Calif., The Pavillions at Buckland Hills, Manchester, Conn., Crystal Tower, Kobe, Japan, Mitsui Marine Co., Chiba, Japan, Cultural Ctr., Miyazaki, Kyushu, Japan, Suderman Sq., Jakarta, Indonesia. With USN, 1941—45. Recipient 2d prize Pitts. Internat., 1961-62; Am. Acad. and Inst. Arts and Letters award; Longview Found. grantee, 1961, 62, 63; Ford Found. grantee, 1965; Nat. Found. Arts grantee, 1966, special award Sculpture Triennale Osaka, Japan, 1992. Home: 230 Park Ave Rm 545 New York NY 10169-0599

SUGARMAN, IRWIN J., lawyer; b. Dayton, Ohio, June 17, 1943; s. Nathan and Esther (Goldstein) S.; 1 child, Alexander David Sugarman. BA, Rutgers U., New Brunswick, NJ, 1965; JD, Rutgers U., Newark, 1968. Bar: N.Y. 1968. Law clk. to Judge Edmund Palmieri U.S. Dist. Ct. for So. Dist. N.Y., NYC, 1968-69; assoc. Debevoise Plimpton Lyons & Gates, NYC, 1969-79; ptnr. Schulte Roth & Zabel, NYC, 1979—. Bd. dirs. Santa Fe Opera, 1989-94. Office: Schulte Roth & Zabel 919 3rd Ave Fl 23 New York NY 10022-4774 E-mail: irwin.sugarman@srz.com.

SUGARMAN, MICHAEL, physician, rheumatologist; b. Galveston, Tex., May 26, 1945; s. Harold and Amelia Sugarman; m. Hilda Roberta Krug, Aug. 26, 1967; children: Jason, Steven. BS, U. Calif., Berkeley, 1966; MD, U. Calif., San Francisco, 1970. Diplomate Am. Coll. Physicians, Am. Coll. Rheumatology. Rheumatologist Fullerton (Calif.) Internal Medicine Ctr., Fullerton, Calif., 1976-94. Pres. St. Jude Heritage Med. Group, 1996—. Bd. trustees St. Jude Hosp. Fellow Am. Coll. Rheumatology, Orange County Rheumatism Soc.; mem. AMA, Orange County Med. Assn. Office: St Jude Heritage Med Group 433 W Bastanchury Rd Fullerton CA 92835-3404 Home Phone: 714-525-4422; Office Phone: 714-446-7819.

SUGARMAN, MYRON GEORGE, lawyer; b. San Francisco, Nov. 7, 1942; s. Irving Carden and Jane Hortense (Weingarten) S.; m. Cheryl Ann Struble, June 8, 1968 (div. 1993); children: Andrew, Amy, Adam; m. Cynthia Wilson Woods, Apr. 16, 1994. BS, U. Calif., Berkeley, 1964, JD, 1967. Bar: Calif. 1967, US Tax Ct. 1994. Assoc. Cooley Godward Kronish LLP, San Francisco, 1972-77, ptnr., 1977—. Served to capt. US Army, 1968-71. Fellow Am. Coll. Trust and Estate Counsel, Am. Coll. Tax Counsel, Am. Bar Found.; mem. U. Calif. Alumni Assn. (bd. dirs. 1985-88), U. Calf. Berkeley Found. (bd. trustees), San Francisco Tax Club (pres. 1990), San Francisco Grid Club, Order of Coif, Phi Beta Kappa, Beta Gamma Sigma. Avocations: skiing, tennis. Office: Cooley Godward Kronish LLP 101 California St 5th Fl San Francisco CA 94111-5800 Office Phone: 415-693-2040. Office Fax: 415-693-2222. Business E-Mail: msugarman@cooley.com.

SUGARMAN, PAUL RONALD, lawyer, educator, academic administrator; b. Boston, Dec. 14, 1931; m. Susan J. Sugarman; children: Amy J., Ellen L. AA, Boston U., 1951, JD cum laude (Law Week award 1954, asso. editor law rev. 1952-54), 1954; LLD (hon.), Suffolk U., 1989. Bar: Mass. 1954, U.S. Supreme Ct. 1965. Ptnr. Sugarman & Sugarman, Boston, 1967-90, 94—; prof. law, dean Suffolk U. Law Sch., Boston, 1990-94. Mem. Atty. Gen. Mass. Hwy. Law Study Commn., 1965, Mass. Gov.'s Select Com. on Jud. Needs, 1976; bd. bar overseers Supreme Jud. Ct., 1984-88, chmn., 1985-88; advocate Am. Bd. Trial Advocates; spl. master, commr. Boston Mcpl. Ct. Report Supreme Jud. Ct. of Mass., 1990. Trustee Mass. Bar Found., 1980-81; bd. visitors Boston U. Sch. Law, 2005—. Served as officer AUS, 1955-58. Recipient Courageous Adv. award, Mass. Acad. Trial Attys., 1984, William O. Douglas First Amendment Freedom award, Anti-Defamation League, 1986, Silver Shingle award for svc. to legal profession Boston U. Sch. Law, 1989, Jurisprudence award Am. Orgn. for Rehab. through Tng. Fedn., 1991, Civil Justice award Am. Bd. trial Adv., 1993, Lifetime Achievement award, Mass. Acad. Trial Attys., 2007. Fellow: Internat. Soc. Barristers, Mass. Bar Found., Am. Coll. Trial Lawyers, Am. Bar Found.; mem.: ATLA (gov. 1966—68, pres. Mass. chpt. 1968—70), ABA, Boston U. Sch. Law Alumni Assn. (pres. 1979—80), Boston Bar Assn., Mass. Bar Assn. (pres. 1976—77, chmn. com. on recall of ret. judges 1982—86, chmn. Jud. Adminstrn. Sect. Coun., chmn. 2000—01, Task Force on Jud. Conduct Commn., Gold Medal award 1991). Office: Sugarman and Sugarman PC One Beacon St Boston MA 02108 Business E-Mail: psugarman@sugarman.com.

SUGARMAN, PAUL WILLIAM, lawyer; b. Cambridge, Mass., July 31, 1947; s. Louis Edward and Natalie (Waldman) S.; m. Susan Lee Richard, July 16, 1978; children: Sarah, Emily, Hannah. BA magna cum laude (hon.), Harvard U., 1969; JD, Yale U., 1975. Bar: Calif. 1976, US Dist. Ct. (no. dist.) Calif. 1976, US Ct. Appeals (9th cir.) 1976. Law clk. to judge U.S. Dist. Ct. (no. dist.) Calif., San Francisco, 1975-76; assoc. Heller, Ehrman, White & McAuliffe, San Francisco, 1976-81, ptnr., 1982; shareholder Heller, Ehrman LLP, San Francisco. Spkr. in field. Contbr. articles to profl. jour. Vol. U.S. Peace Corps, Ethiopia, 1969-72. Mem. ABA (litig., tort & ins. practice sect.), Calif. Bar Assn., San Francisco Bar Assn., Phi Beta Kappa. Home: 1200 Sunnyhills Rd Oakland CA 94610-1818 Office: Heller Ehrman LLP 333 Bush St San Francisco CA 94104-2806 Office Phone: 415-772-6000, 415-772-6217. Office Fax: 415-772-6268. Business E-Mail: paul.sugarman@hellerehrman.com.

SUGARS, JANEAL M., opera singer, vocal educator; b. Wichita falls, Tex., Jan. 11, 1954; d. Thomas R. and Jane Sugars. B, U. Houston, 1977; M in music, U. Tex., Austin, 1978, postgrad.; profl. diploma, Juillard Sch. Music, 1982. Head voice dept. Houston Music Inst. Tchg. asst. U. Tex., 2007—. Office: Houston Music Inst 14511 Memorial Dr Houston TX 77079 Office Phone: 281-556-1644.

SUGERMAN, ABRAHAM ARTHUR, psychiatrist, educator; b. Dublin, Jan. 20, 1929; came to U.S., 1958, naturalized, 1963; s. Hyman and Anne (Goldstone) S.; m. Ruth Nerissa Alexander, June 5, 1960; children: Jeremy, Michael, Adam, Rebecca. BA, Trinity Coll., 1950, MB, BChir, BA in Obstetrics, 1952; DSc, SUNY Bklyn., 1962. Diplomate Am. Bd. Psychiatry and Neurology. House officer Meath Hosp., Dublin, 1952—53, St. Nicholas Hosp., London, 1953—54; sr. house physician Brook Gen. Hosp., London, 1954; registrar in psychiatry Kingsway Hosp. Derby and Kings Coll. Med. Sch., Newcastle, England, 1955—58; clin. psychiatrist Trenton Psychiat. Hosp., NJ, 1958—59; rsch. fellow Downstate Med. Ctr., Bklyn., 1959—61; chief investigative psychiatry sect. N.J. Bur. Rsch., Princeton, 1961—73; cons. psychiatry, 1964—80; cons. rsch., assoc. psychiatrist Carrier Clinic, Belle Mead, NJ, 1968—72, 1978—90, dir. outpatient svcs., 1972—74, 1977—78, med. dir., 1974—77; dir. rsch. Carrier Found., Belle Mead, 1972—79; med. dir. addiction recovery svcs. Cmty. Mental Health Ctr. U. Medicine and Dentistry of N.J., Piscataway, 1990—93; cons. psychiatry Med. Ctr., Princeton, 1972—2001, assoc. in psychiatry, 2001—03, attending, 2003—, sr. attending, 2005—; clin. assoc. prof. psychiatry Rutgers Med. Sch. (now Robert Wood Johnson Med. Sch.), New Brunswick, NJ, 1972—78, clin. prof., 1978—. Vis. prof. Rutgers Ctr. for Alcohol Studies, 1977-83, Hahnemann Med. Coll., Phila., 1978-93; contbg. faculty Grad. Sch. Applied and Profl. Psychology, Rutgers U., 1974-78. Editor: (with Ralph E. Tarter) Alcoholism: Interdisciplinary Approaches to an Enduring Problem, 1976, Expanding Dimensions of Consciousness, 1978; contbr. articles to profl. jours. Bd. dirs. N.J. Mental Health R & D Fund, Princeton, 1968-74; v.p. Jewish Family Svc., Trenton, 1972-78; 1st v.p. Trenton Hebrew Acad., 1972-75. Fellow Am. Psychiat. Assn. (disting. life), Am. Coll. Neuropsychopharmacology, Am. Coll. Clin. Pharmacology, Am. Coll. Psychiatrists, Royal Coll. Psychiatrists; mem. AMA, Soc. Biol. Psychiatry, Assn. Rsch. Nervous and Mental Diseases. Office: 256 Bunn Dr Princeton NJ 08540-2859 Home Phone: 609-883-5368; Office Phone: 609-924-6711.

SUGG, JEANNE D., library director; m. John Sugg; 1 child, James; 1 child, Jeff. BA, Trevecca Nazarene U., Nashville; MLS, Vanderbilt U. Peabody Coll. Libr. coord. Arabian-Am. Oil Co., Saudi Arabia, 1981—89; dir. pub. svcs. Tenn. State Libr. & Archives, Nashville, 1989, state libr. & archivist, 2005—. Mem.: Tenn. Libr. Assn., Chief Officers State Libr. Agencies. Office: Tenn State Libr & Archives 403 7th Ave N Nashville TN 37243 Office Phone: 615-741-7996. Office Fax: 615-532-9293. Business E-Mail: jeanne.sugg@state.tn.us. *

SUGG, ROBERT PERKINS, retired judge; b. Eupora, Miss., Feb. 21, 1916; s. Amos Watson and Virgie Christian (Cooper) S.; m. Elizabeth Lorraine Carroll, June 23, 1940; children: Robert Perkins, Charles William, John David. Student, Wood Jr. Coll., 1933—34, Miss. State U., 1935—37, Jackson Sch. Law, 1939—40. Bar: Miss. Practice law, 1940; chancery judge, 1951—71; assoc. justice Miss. Supreme Ct., 1971—83; county pros. atty. Webster County, Miss., 1949—50; spl. chancery judge Hinds, Scott and Jasper counties, Miss., 1989; sr. judge, 1990—2000. Mem. adv. coun. Nat. Ctr. for State Cts., 1973-79. Bd. govs. Miss. Jud. Coll., 1973-80; literacy missions assoc. Home Mission Bd. of So. Bapt. Conv., 1983—; tchr. internat. class First Bapt, Ch., Jackson, Miss., 1980-2004, tchr. adult Bible class, 1973-2002, mem. fin. com. 1995-98, vision com. 1996-97, legal com. 1998-2001, missions com., 1997-2001. Named Outstanding Citizen, Eupora Jr. C. of C., 1970, Alumnus of Year, Wood Jr. Coll., 1973; recipient Svc. to Humanity award Miss. Coll., 1976, Literacy Missions Svc. award Home Mission Bd. of So. Bapt. Conv., 1995. Mem. Miss. State Bar, CAP (Miss. Wing, squadron comdr. 1974-76), Am. Legion (post comdr. 1950) Democrat. Baptist (chmn. bd. deacons 1964). Home: 1067 Meadow Heights Dr Jackson MS 39206-6021 Personal E-mail: judgesugg@jam.rr.com.

SUGGS, KENNETH, lawyer; b. Greenville, SC, Sept. 24, 1946; BA Economics, Clemson Univ., 1964; JD cum laude, Univ. of S.C. Bar: S.C. Bar 1975, Fourth Cir. Ct. of Appeals, Eleventh Cir. Ct. of Appeals, U.S. Supreme Ct. Found., ptnr. Suggs & Kelly, P.C., Janet, Jenner, & Suggs. Pres. S.C. Trial Lawyers Assoc, 1981; bd. gov. Assoc. of Am. Trial Lawyers (ATLA); founding fellow So. Trial Lawyers Assoc.; pres. Richmond County Bar Assoc., 1999; bd. gov. Assoc. of Am. Trial Lawyers (ATLA), 1989—2000, parliamentarian, 2000—01, treas., 2001—02, sec., 2002—03, v.p., 2003—04, pres. elect, 2004—. Communications technician USN, 1968—72. Recipient S.C. Trial Lawyers Assoc. Pres. Award, 1988, S.C. Trial Lawyers Public Citizen Award, 2002; fellow Am. Coll. of Trial Lawyers, Clemson Univ. Alumni, 2000. Office: Janet, Jenner & Suggs Woodholme Center 1829 Reisterstown Rd Suite 320 Baltimore MD 21208

SUGGS, MICHAEL EDWARD, lawyer; b. Conway, SC, Nov. 9, 1962; s. Edward and Rebecca S. BSBA, U. S.C., 1985, JD, 1992. Bar: S.C. 1992, U.S. Dist. Ct., S.C., 1995. Asst. pub. defender Def. Corp. Horry County, Conway, SC, 1993—. Troop 847 com. Boy Scouts Am., Loris, S.C., 1985—; coun. City of Loris, 1994—, mayor pro-tem, 1998-2000, 06—. Recipient Eagle Scout award Boy Scouts Am., 1976. Mem. S.C. Assn. Criminal Def. Lawyers, Horry County Bar Assn., Loris C. of C. Methodist. Home: 4932 Circle Dr Loris SC 29569-3146 Office: Def Corp Horry County PO Box 1666 203 Laurel St Conway SC 29526

SUGIHARA, KENZI, publishing executive; b. Kearny, NJ, Oct. 4, 1940; s. Kyuichi and Shinobuko (Yamaguchi) S.; m. Roslyn Forbes, Dec. 1966; children: Kenichi, Takeo, Akira, Fumio; m. Nancy Elizabeth Kirsh, June 8, 1981; 1 child, Toshiro. BA, NYU, 1963. Supr. McGraw Hill, Inc., NYC, 1965-67; assoc. dir. coll. product dept. Harcourt Brace Jovanovich Inc., NYC, 1978-82, dir. electronic pub., 1982-83; v.p., pub. Bantam Electronic Pub. div., pub. Bantam Reference Books, Bantam Profl. Books, Bantam Doubleday Dell, NYC, 1983-93; v.p., pub. Random House Reference & Electronic Pub. (Random House Inc.), NYC, 1993-95; pres. Sugihara and Rose, NYC, 1995—; pres., pub. ToExcel divsn. Kaleidoscope Software Corp., NYC, 1998—2001; pub. Iuniverse; CEO, pres. SelectBooks, Inc., NYC, 2001—. Democrat. Presbyterian. Home: 585 West End Ave Apt 15D New York NY 10024-1715 Office: SelectBooks Inc One Union Sq West Ste 909 New York NY 10003 Office Phone: 212-206-1997. Business E-Mail: kenzi@selectbooks.com.

SUGIKI, SHIGEMI, ophthalmologist, educator; b. Wailuku, Hawaii, May 12, 1936; s. Sentaro and Kameno (Matoba) Sugiki; m. Bernice T. Murakami, Dec. 29, 1958; children: Kevin S., Boyd R. AB, Washington U., St. Louis, 1957, MD, 1961. Intern St. Luke's Hosp., St. Louis, 1961-62; resident in ophthalmology Washington U., 1962-65; chmn. dept. ophthalmology Straub Clinic, Honolulu, 1965-70, Queens Med. Ctr., Honolulu, 1970-73, 80-83, 88-90, 93-2000; clin. prof. ophthalmology Sch. Medicine U. Hawaii, 1997. Maj. M.C., AUS, 1968-70. Decorated Hawaiian N.G. Commendation medal, 1968. Fellow ACS; mem. AMA, Hawaii Med. Assn., Honolulu County Med. Soc., Am. Acad. Ophthalmology, Contact Lens Assn. Ophthalmologists, Pacific Coast Oto-Ophthal. Soc., Pan-Pacific Surg. Assn., Am. Soc. Cataract and Refractive Surgery, Am. Glaucoma Soc., Internat. Assn. Ocular Surgeons, Am. Soc. Contemporary Ophthalmology, Washington U. Eye Alumni Assn., Hawaii Ophthal. Soc., Rsch. To Prevent Blindness. Home: 2398 Aina Lani Pl Honolulu HI 96822-2024 Office: 1380 Lusitana St Ste 714 Honolulu HI 96813-2443 Office Phone: 808-528-5333. Personal E-mail: vision2damax@yahoo.com.

SUGINTAS, NORA MARIA, healthcare executive; b. Evergreen Park, Ill., Mar. 12, 1956; d. George and Mary (Navickas) S. BS in Biol. Scis. with highest distinction, U. Ill., Chgo., 1978; DVM, U. Ill., 1982. Lic. veterinarian Ill. Profl. hosp. specialist Abbott Labs., Detroit, 1983—87; anesthesia and critical care patient monitoring equipment acct. exec. Shiley, Inc., Detroit, 1987—91; anesthesia and critical care monitoring equipment sales exec. and cons. Ohmeda, Detroit, 1991—94; regional mgr. Criticare Systems, Detroit, 1994—95, nat. acct. dir., 1995—96; dir. corp. accounts Isolyser Health Care, 1996—98; cons. healthcare industry, 1998—2000; v.p. HealthCare Partnerships Healthgrades, Inc., Detroit, 2001—. Journalist The Lithuanian World-Wide Daily Newspaper, 1975; author: The Production of S-Adenosylmethionine by Saccharomyces cerevisiae and Candida utilis. Troop leader Girl Scouts Lithuanian, Chgo., 1972-77, camp dir., 1977; mem. Mirage Mid. Eastern Dance Ensemble. Recipient Louis Pasteur award for Acad. Excellence in the Biol. Scis. and Ind. Rsch. U. Ill., 1978. Mem. Internat. Platform Assn., Chelsea Park Assn. (bd. dirs., treas.), Mich. Orchid Soc., Econ. Club Detroit, Kirk Garden Guild, Phi Beta Kappa. Republican. Avocations: hiking, nature preservation, photography, dance, international politics.

SUGIYAMA, AKIKO, artist; b. Noheji, Japan; arrived in US, 1974; BA, Joshibi Daigaku, Tokyo, Japan, 1974. Tchr. Deland Mus. Art, Fla., 1982—85. Deland Mus. Art, Fla., 1984 (best in show), fine craft shows including, Phila. Mus. Art, Smithsonian Craft Show, Am. Craft Exposition, exhibitions include Polk Mus. Art, Lakeland, Fla., 1990, Gulf Coast Art Ctr., Belleair, Fla., 1997, Gaye Wilson Gallery, Southampton, NY, 2001, Gallery Camino Real, Boca Raton, Fla., 2005, Represented in permanent collections Daytona Beach Internat. Airport, Fla., Laventhol and Howarth, Tampa, Fla., Van Wezel Performing Arts Hall, Sarasota, Fla. Fellow, Fla., 1990—91, 2002—03. Mem.: Am. Craft Coun. (Achievement award 2004, 2005). Achievements include development of own unique paper construct techniques. Avocations: cello, gardening, cooking. Home: 5 Bay Hill Dr Ormond Beach FL 32174 Home Phone: 386-672-2319.

SUGIYAMA, KAZUNORI, music producer; b. Tokyo, Aug. 18, 1950; came to U.S., 1976; s. Hiroshi and Michiko (Maeda) S.; m. Emi Fukui, Aug. 11, 1981. BS, Waseda U., 1974, postgrad., 1974-75; MA, Boston U., 1977. Jr. adminstrv. officer Japanese Mission to UN, NYC, 1978-88; rep. N.Y. Toshiba EMI Records, Jazz Div., Tokyo, 1990-93; rep. U.S., exec. producer DIW/Avant Records, Tokyo, 1991—; exec. producer Tzadik Records, NYC, 1995—; mem. adv. bd. The New Grove Dictionary of Jazz, 1997—2004. Corr. Jazz Life, Tokyo, 1980-88; columnist OCS News, N.Y.C., 1982-90; columnist Asahi Newspaper, 1998-99. Rec. engr. (album) Bud and Bird/Gil Evans, 1988 (Grammy); prodr. V/Ralph Peterson, 1990 (Jazz Album of Yr.); co-prodr. The Nurturer/Geri Allen, 1991 (2d pl. Jazz Album of Yr.), Big Band & Quartet/David Murray, 1992 (Best Prodn. Jazz Album of Yr.), Picasso/David Murray, 1993 (3d pl. Jazz Album of Yr.); translator Autobiography of Miles Davis, 1989. Mem. NARAS, USTA. Avocations: tennis, travel. Office: 93 Mercer St Apt 3W New York NY 10012-4452 E-mail: info@tzadik.com.

SUGIYAMA, TORU TOM, automotive executive; b. Hiratsuka, Japan, Aug. 15, 1956; s. Tadatsugu and Hatsue Sugiyama. MBA, Calif. State U., 1994, MS in Acctg., 1997; MS in Engring., Oakland U., 1997, PhD in Engring., 2003. CPA Ill., 2005. Mgr. Denny's Japan Co., Ltd., Tokyo, 1979—80; indsl. engr. NHK Spring Co., Ltd., Yokohama, Japan, 1980—82; acct. mgr. NHk Spring Co., Ltd., Yokohama, Japan, 1983—89; mgr. NHK Internat. Corp., Southfield, Mich., 1992—96, corp. sec., treas., 1996—2001, pres., CEO Wixom, Mich., 2001—03, also bd. dirs.; treas. Gen. Seating Can., 2001—05; bd. dirs. Gen. Seating Am., 2001—03. Lectr. Oakland U., Rochester, Mich., 1998—. Avocations: golf, tennis, swimming. Office: NHK Internat Corp 50706 Varsity Ct Wixom MI 48393

SUGLIA, JOSEPH VINCENT, writer, educator; s. Theresa Joyce and Robert Louis Suglia. BA, Binghamton U., 1994; PhD, Northwestern U., 2002. Lectr. English DePaul U., Chgo., 2000—, Roosevelt U., Chgo., 2002—, St. Augustine Coll., Chgo., 2004—, Columbia Coll., Chgo., 2005—, DeVry U., Chgo., 2006—. Author: (novels) Years of Rage, 2005, Watch Out, 2006, (literary criticism) Hölderlin and Blanchot on Self-Sacrifice, 2004. Home Phone: 773-404-1158. Personal E-mail: josephsuglia@yahoo.com.

SUGRUE, THOMAS J., history professor, social sciences educator; b. Detroit, July 24, 1962; s. Thomas J. and Sharon R. Sugrue; m. Dana L. Barron, May 30, 1993; children: Anna Linn Barron, John Michael Barron. BA in History summa cum laude, Columbia U., 1984; BA in History with honors, Cambridge Univ., 1986; AM in History, Harvard U., 1987; MA in History, Cambridge U., 1989; PhD in History, Harvard U., 1992. Lectr. history U. Pa., Phila., 1991—92, asst. prof. history, 1992—97, assoc. prof. history, 1997—98, assoc. prof. history and sociology, 1998—2000, Bicentennial Class of 1940 prof. history and sociology, 2000—04, Kahn prof. history and sociology, 2004—. Rsch. fellow Brookings Instn., Washington, 1990—91; vis. assoc. prof. NYU, NYC, 1998; trustee and vice chair of bd. Hist. Soc. Pa., Phila., 2000—; dir. Urban History Assn., Cin., 2000—02; vis. prof. Ecole des Hautes Etudes en Sciences Sociales, Paris, 2002. Author: The Origins of the Urban Crisis (Bancroft Prize in History 1998, Taft Prize in Labor History 1997, President's Book Award SSHA, 1996, Urban History Assn. Best Book Award 1997); editor: (book series) Politics and Culture in Modern America; editor, author (collection of essays) W.E.B. DuBois, Race, and the City. Founding mem. Scholars, Artists, and Writers for Social Justice, NYC, 1996—98; vice chair and commr. Phila. Hist. Commn., Phila., 2001—; bd. chair Bread and Roses Cmty. Fund, 2004—. Recipient Phi Beta Kappa, Columbia U., 1983, Sidney Hillman Found. award. for Nat. Teach-In with the Labor Movement., 1997, Disting. Lectr., Orgn. of Am. Historians, 2002—, John Simon Guggenheim fellowship, 2005; fellow, Alphonse Fletcher Sr. Found., 2005; grantee program in non-profits, univs., cmtys., schs., Kellogg Found. through U. Pa.Ctr. Cmty. Partnerships, 1998—2001, grant for Conf. (co-PI), Nat. Endowment Humanities, 1994-96; scholar, Harry S. Truman Found., 1982-84, 1986-88, Josephine De Kármán Found. fellow, 1989-90, Com. for Rsch. on the Urban Underclass, Dissertation grant and fellow, Social Sci. Rsch. Coun., 1990-91, Am. Coun. of Learned Societies fellow, ACLS, 1995-96. Mem.: Inst. for Advanced Study, Social Sci. History Assn. (program com. chair 1997—98), Am. Studies Assn., Am. Sociol. Assn., Urban History Assn. (bd. mem., prize com. mem., program com. mem. 2000—04), Orgn. of Am. Historians (program com. 2001—03). Avocations: architecture, travel, gardening. Home: 129 Carpenter Ln Philadelphia PA 19119 Office: U Pa 208 College Hall Philadelphia PA 19104 Home Phone: 215-848-8448; Office Phone: 215-898-0293. Business E-Mail: tsugrue@sas.upenn.edu.

SUH, BYUNGSE, medical educator; b. Ansung, Korea, Mar. 6, 1941; came to U.S., 1964; s. Sang Keun and Chong Sang (Lee) S.; m. Youngjoo Lee, Dec. 21, 1974; children: Jason, Jessica, Janice. BS, Chungang U., Seoul, Korea, 1962; MA, U. Kans., 1967, PhD, 1969; MD, U. Miami, 1973. Diplomate Am. Bd. Internal Medicine; diplomate Am. Bd. Infectious Diseases. Asst. prof. medicine Temple U. Sch. Medicine, Phila., 1978-83, assoc. prof. medicine, 1983-90, prof. medicine, 1990—. Contbr. articles to profl. jours. Fellow Infectious Diseases Soc. Am., Am. Coll. Physicians, Coll. Physicians Phila., Am. Coll. Clin. Pharmacology; mem. Am. Soc. Microbiology, Alpha Omega Alpha. Office: Temple U Sch Medicine Sect Infectious Diseases Broad and Ontario Sts Philadelphia PA 19140 Office Phone: 215-707-3807. Business E-Mail: bingsuh@temple.edu.

SUH, DAE-SOOK, political science professor; b. Hoeryong, Korea, Nov. 22, 1931; came to U.S., 1952; s. Chang-Hee and Chong-Hee (Paek) S.; m. Yun-Ok Park, Oct. 29, 1960; children: Maurice, Kevin. BA, Tex. Christian U., 1956; MA, Ind. U., 1958; PhD, Columbia U., 1964. Asst. prof. U. Houston, 1965-67, assoc. prof., 1968-71; prof. polit. sci., dir. Ctr. for Korean Studies, U. Hawaii, Honolulu, 1972-95, Korea Found. prof. policy studies, 1994-99; George L. Paik prof. Yonsei U., 1999; prof. polit. sci. U. Hawaii, Manoa, Hawaii, 1972—. Vis. prof. polit. sci. UCLA, 2005. Author: The Korean Communist Movement, 1967, Documents of Korean Communism, 1970, Korean Communism, 1980, Kim Il Sung, 1988, Kim Il Sung and Kim Jong Il, 1996. Mem. Conv. Ctr. Authority, Honolulu, 1989-94. Grantee Social Sci. Rsch. Coun.-Am. Coun. Learned Socs., 1963, East-/West Ctr., Columbia U., 1971, The Woodraw Wilson Internat. Ctr. for Scholars, 1985, Fulbright, 1988. Mem. Am. Polit. Sci. Assn. (life), Assn. for Asian Studies. Avocations: tennis, golf. Office: U Hawaii Manoa Dept Political Sci 2424 Maile Way Honolulu HI 96822-2223 Home: 5150 Via EL Molino Thousand Oaks CA 91320-6996 Personal E-mail: daesook@roadrunner.com.

SUH, JUNG SOOK KY, personnel consultant; d. Keum Joon and Jung Ja Suh. BA, Calif. State U., Fullerton, 1996; MS in Orgnl. Psychology, Alliant Internat. U., Alhambra, Calif., 2001, PhD, 2005; postgrad., Oxford U., Eng., 2000. V.p. Packy B., Inc., Bellflower, Calif., 1995—2001; cons. Optimal Mgmt. Consulting, Long Beach, Calif., 2001—. Adj. faculty Long Beach City Coll., 2002—, Mt. San Antonio Coll., Walnut, 2005—. Mem.: NEA, Calif. Tchrs. Assn.

SUH, MARY, editor; Nat. editor Ms; editor Newsday; op-ed editor NY Times, Week in Review editor. Contbr. Minerva: Quar. Report on Women & the Military. Office: NY Times 229 W 43rd St New York NY 10036 Office Phone: 212-556-1748. Office Fax: 212-556-3738.

SUH, WONSUK WARREN, radiation oncologist; s. Chai-Pill and Myung-Hi Suh; m. Jeewon Park, Nov. 22, 2000; children: Ryan Joonwon, Sidney Chaewon. BA, Cornell U., 1991; MD, U. Chgo., 1996; MPH, Harvard U., 1996. Diplomate internal medicine and radiation oncology. Resident internal medicine Mayo Clinic, Rochester, Minn., 1996—99; from radiation oncology resident to chief resident U. Mich., Ann Arbor, 2000—04; faculty radiation oncologist Dana-Farber/Brigham & Women's Cancer Ctr., Boston, 2004—. Contbr. articles to profl. jours. Named Eminent Scientist Yr. in Radiation Oncology, Internat. Rsch. Prom Coun., 2006—07; recipient H. Hughes award, 1990. Mem.: Am. Coll. Radiology (mem. appropriateness criteria expert panel, rectal and anal cancers 2006—), Am. Soc. Therapeutic Radiation and Oncology (health svcs. outcome rsch. leadership com. 2004—, adj. prostate radiation panel chair 2007—), Am. Soc. Clin. Oncology (mem. new tech. com., PET evaluation 2002—, Merit award 2003). Office: Dana Farber/Brigham Women's Cancer Ctr Dept Radiation Oncology 75 Francis St ASB1-L2 Boston MA 02115 Office Phone: 617-732-7936.

SUHLER, JOHN STUART, investor; b. Des Moines, May 10, 1943; s. Lester F. and Irene (Holmberg) S.; m. Charlotte Kay Thompson, Dec. 30, 1966; children: Ashley Thompson, Courtney Ruth, Brooke Thompson. BS, U. Kans., 1965. Co-owner Dalton (Mass.)-Hinsdale News, 1965-66; promotion writer Look mag., Des Moines, 1965-66; cons. Benson, Stagg & Assos., NYC, 1966-68; salesman Metromail div. Metromedia, NYC, 1968-69; circulation dir. Psychology Today, CRM div. Boise Cascade, Del Mar, Calif., 1969-70, assoc. pub., 1970-71, pub., 1971-73; v.p., pub. Psychology Today Pub. Group, 1973-74, Ziff Davis Pub. Co.; pres. CBS Publs., Consumer Pub. div. CBS Inc., NYC, 1974-79, CBS/Pub. Group, v.p. CBS Inc., 1979-81, Veronis, Suhler and Assocs. Inc. (now Veronis Suhler Stevenson), 1981—; gen. ptnr. VS&A Communications Ptnrs., L.P., 1987—. Pub. Univ. Daily Kansan, 1964-65; bd. dirs. Access Intelligence. Trustee William Allen White Found. Mem. Mag. Pubs. Assn. (former dir.), Nat. Assn. Broadcasters, Assn. Bus. Pubs., Direct Mktg. Assn., Assn. Am. Pubs. (former dir.), Info. Industry Assn., Wee Burn Club, Edgartown (Mass.) Yacht Club, Vineyard (Mass.) Golf Club, Long Boat Key (Fla.) Club, Sigma Chi. Office: Veronis Suhler Stevenson 350 Park Ave New York NY 10022

SUHR, PAUL AUGUSTINE, lawyer; b. Sonwunri, Chonbuk, Korea, Jan. 20, 1940; arrived in US, 1966; s. Chong-ju and Oksuk (Pang) So; m. Angeline M. Kang Suhr; 1 child, Christopher. BA, Campbell Coll., Buies Creek, NC, 1968; MA, U. N.C., Greensboro, 1970; MS, U. N.C., Chapel Hill, 1975; JD, N.C. Cen. U., 1988. Bar: NC 1989, US Dist. Ct. (ea. and mid. dist.) NC 1989, US Ct. Appeals DC 1990, US Ct. Appeals (4th cir.) 1992. Bibliographer NC Divsn. of State Libr., Raleigh, 1975-78; dir. Pender County Pub. Libr., Burgaw, NC, 1978-80; libr. Tob. Lit. Svc., NC State U., Raleigh, 1980-85; pvt. practice law Law Offices of Paul A. Suhr, PLLC, Raleigh and Fayetteville, NC, 1989—. Author short stories and novelettes various lit. mags., jours. and revs. Mem. Human Resources and Human Rels. Adv. Commn., City of Raleigh, 1990-95, chmn., 1994-95. NC Humanities Com. grantee, 1979-80; recipient Presdl. award President of Korea, 1992. Mem. ABA, ATLA, Am. Immigration Lawyers Assn., NC Bar Assn., NC Trial Lawyers Assn., Wake County Bar Assn. (bd. dirs. 1996-97, 2003—), DC Bar Assn. Democrat. Roman Catholic. Avocations: gardening, fishing, writing. Office: 1110 Navaho Dr Ste 502 Raleigh NC 27609-7322 Office Phone: 919-876-4707. Personal E-mail: paulsuhr@aol.com.

SUHRHEINRICH, RICHARD FRED, federal judge; b. Lincoln City, Ind., 1936; BS, Wayne State U., 1960; JD cum laude, Detroit Coll. Law, 1963; LLM (hon.), U. Va., 1990, Detroit Coll. Law, 1992. Bar: Mich. Law clerk Stringari, Fritz & Fiott, 1963; assoc. Moll, Desenberg, Purdy, Glover & Bayer, 1963—67; asst. prosecutor Macomb County, 1967; ptnr. Rogensues, Richard & Suhrheinrich, 1967; assoc. Moll, Desenberg, Purdy, Glover & Bayer, 1967—68; ptnr. Kitch, Suhrheinrich, Saurbier & Drutchas, 1968—84; assoc. prof. of law Detroit Coll. of law, 1975—85; judge US Dist. Ct. (ea. dist.) Mich., Detroit, 1984—90, US Ct. Appeals (6th cir.), Lansing, 1990—2001, sr. judge, 2001—. Law prof. Thomas M Cooley Law Sch., 2003—; mem. State of Mich. Atty. Discipline Bd., Atty. Grievance Commn. Bd. trustees Brighton Hosp. Mem.: Ingham County Bar Assn., State Bar Mich., Mich. State Univ.-Detroit (bd. trustees 1985—2003, pres. 1999—2001). Office: US Ct Appeals 6th Cir USPO & Fed Bldg 315 W Allegan St Rm 241 Lansing MI 48933-1514 *

SUHRSTEDT, BARBARA LYNN, concert pianist, voice educator; b. Massillon, Ohio, Dec. 6, 1945; d. Donald Charles and Elizabeth Ann Fetrow; m. Gerhardt John Suhrstedt, Oct. 25, 1969 (dec. Dec. 29, 2005). MusB, Oberlin Conservatory of Music, 1967; MusM, Boston U., 1970. Instr. piano South Shore Conservatory of Music, Hingham, Mass., 1971—84; pvt. piano studio Newton, Watertown and Somerville, Mass., 1975—90; concert pianist, 1980—2005; soprano Ch. of the Adent, Boston, 1980—90; pvt. voice studio Newton, Watertown and Somerville, 1982—. Artist, clinician state convs. Music Tchrs. Nat. Assn., 1989—2002; mem. internat. jury 3d Igor Stravinsky Competition for Young Pianists Stravinsky Sch. Music and Art, Lomonosov, Russia, 2002; participant St. Petersburg (Russia) Arts Festival, 2002. Musician: (CDs) A Four-Hand Feast, 1989, Dances for Duettists, 1998, Elegie, 2007, (concerts) Peterhof's Grand Palace, Rimsky-Korsakov Conservatory, 1998—2001. Bd. dirs. FLAME Russian sister-city orgn., Framingham, Mass., 1999—. Mem.: Nat. Assn. Tchrs. of Singing. Episcopalian. Avocation: reading. Home: 112 Central St # 4 Somerville MA 02143-1200 Personal E-mail: bsuhrstedt@aol.com.

SUI, ANNA, fashion designer; b. Dearborn Heights, Mich., 1955; d. Paul and Grace S. Grad., Parsons Sch. Design. Founder, designer Anna Sui, 1988—. Opened outlet SoHo dist., 1992, NYC, Anna Sui Boutiques, Osaka, Tokyo, 1997; designer Sui Anna Sui, 1995-, Anna Sui cosmetic line, fragrance line, 1999, skincare line, 2000. First runway show, 1991. Recipient Perry Ellis award new fashion talent Coun. Fashion Designers Am., 1992. Achievements include launching an Anna Sui Boho Barbie with Mattel, 2006. *

SUI, HAICHANG, electrical engineer, researcher; arrived in US, 2001; BS, Shanghai Jiao Tong U., 2001; MS, U. Calif. San Diego, La Jolla, 2004—, PhD, 2007. Engring. intern Ericsson Wireless Comm. Inc., San Diego, 2002, Motorola Inc., Arlington Heights, Ill., 2006; rschr. U. Calif. San Diego, La Jolla, 2002—07; comm. sys. engr. Tex. Instruments Inc., San Diego, 2007—. Contbr. scientific papers to confs., articles to profl. jours. Cal-(IT)2 fellow, U. Calif., San Diego, 2001. Mem.: IEEE.

SUINN, RICHARD MICHAEL, psychologist; b. Honolulu, May 8, 1933; s. Maurice and Edith (Wong) S.; m. Grace D. Toy, July 26, 1958; children: Susan, Randall, Staci, Bradley. Student, U. Hawaii, 1951-53; BA summa cum laude, Ohio State U., 1955; MA in Clin. Psychology, Stanford U., 1957, PhD in Clin. Psychology, 1959; Doctorate (hon.), Calif. Sch. Profl. Psychology, 1999. Lic. psychologist, Colo.; diplomate Am. Bd. Profl. Psychology. Counselor Stanford U., Calif., 1958-59, rsch. assoc. Med. Sch., 1964-66; asst. prof. psychology Whitman Coll., Walla Walla, Wash., 1959-64; assoc. prof. U. Hawaii, Honolulu, 1966-68; prof. Colo. State U., Ft. Collins, 1968-99, head dept. psychology, 1972-93, emeritus prof., 2000—. Cons. in field; psychologist US Ski Teams, 1976, Olympic Games, US Women's Track and Field, 1980 Olympic Games, US Ski Jumping Team, 1988, US Shooting Team, 1994; mem. sports psychology adv. com. US Olympic Com., 1983-89; reviewer NIMH, 1977-80, 94-98. Author: The Predictive Validity of Projective Measures, 1969, Fundamentals of Behavior Pathology, 1970, The Innovative Psychological Therapies, 1975, The Innovative Medical-Psychiatric Therapies, 1976, Psychology in Sport: Methods and Applications, 1980, Fundamentals of Abnormal Psychology, 1984, 88, Seven Steps to Peak Performance, 1986, Anxiety Management Training, 1990; editorial bd.: Jour. Cons. and Clin. Psychology, 1973-86, Jour. Counseling Psychology, 1974-91, Behavior Therapy, 1977-80, Behavior Modification, 1977-78, Jour. Behavioral Medicine, 1978-83, Behavior Counseling Quar., 1979-83, Jour. Sports Psychology, 1980-91, Clin. Psychology: Science and Practice, 1994-97, Professional Psychology, 1994-97; author: tests Math. Anxiety Rating Scale, Suinn Test Anxiety Behavior Scale, Suinn-Lew Asian Self-identity Acculturation Scale. Mem. City Coun., Ft. Collins, 1975-79, mayor, 1978-79; mem. Gov.'s Mental Health Adv. Coun., 1983, Colo. Bd. Psychologist Examiners, 1983-86. Recipient cert. merit US Ski Team, 1976, APA Career Contbn. to Edn. award, 1995, Lifetime Contbn. to Ethnic Minority Issues award, 2004, Raymond D. Fowler award, 2005; NIMH grantee, 1963-64; Office Edn. grantee, 1970-71. Fellow APA (chmn. bd. ethnic minority affairs 1982-83, chmn. edn. and tng. bd. 1986-87, policy and planning bd. 1987-89, publs. bd. 1993-97, bd. dirs. 1990-93, pres.-elect 1998, pres. 1999, chmn. membership com. 2005, chmn. presdl. task force on enhancing diversity, 2005), Behavior Therapy and Rsch. Soc. (charter); mem. Am. Psychol. Found. (trustee 2000-04), Assn. for Advancement Psychology (trustee 1983-86), Assn. for Advancement Behavior Therapy (sec.-treas. 1986-89, pres. 1992-93), Asian Am. Psychol. Assn. (bd. dirs. 1983-88), Am. Bd. Behavior Therapy (bd. dirs. 1987-2000), Phi Beta Kappa, Sigma Xi. Home: 808 Cheyenne Dr Fort Collins CO 80525-1560 Office: Colo State U Dept Psychology Fort Collins CO 80523-0001 Office Phone: 970-491-1351. Business E-Mail: suinn@lamar.colostate.edu.

SUISSA, DAVID, advertising executive; Exec. creative dir., chmn. bd. Suissa Miller Advt. (merged with Dailey & Assoc.), LA; co-vice chmn. Dailey & Assoc., LA, 2004. Publ.: OLAM Mag.

SUIT, HERMAN DAY, radiation oncologist, medical educator; b. Houston, Feb. 8, 1929; BA, U. Houston, 1948; MD, Baylor U., 1952; PhD, Oxford U., Eng., 1956. Cert. Radiation Oncology (England), 1956, Radiation Oncology, 1957. Intern Jefferson David Hosp., Houston, 1952-53, resident in radiation oncology, 1953-54; postdoctoral tng., radiation oncology Oxford United Hosp., England, 1957, Nat. Cancer Inst., 1959; house surgeon registrar Churchill Hosp., Oxford, 1954, rsch. asst. radiobiol. lab., 1954-56, registrar in radiotherapy, 1956-57; sr. asst. surgeon radiation br. Nat. Cancer Inst., 1957-59; asst. radiotherapist U. Tex. M.D. Anderson Hosp. and Tumor Inst., Houston, 1959-63, assoc. radiotherapist, 1963-68, radiotherapist, 1968-71, chief sect. exptl. radiotherapy, 1962-70; Andres Soriano Disting. prof. radiation oncology Harvard Med. Sch., 1970—; head dept. radiation oncology Mass. Gen. Hosp., Boston, 1970—2000, radiologist, oncologist. Mem. staff NASA Manned Spacecraft Ctr., 1969-71; annual oration in radiation oncology, Radiological Soc. of N.Am., 1997. Named a Disting. Alumnus, U. Houston, 2005; named Disting. Alumni Assn. award, Baylor College of Medicine, 1978, Janeway Lectr., Am. Radium Soc., 1987; recipient Charles F. Kettering prize, GM Cancer Rsch. Found., 1997, Gray medal, Internat. Comm. on Radiation Units and Measurments, Inc., 2001. Mem. AAAS (subcom. radiation biology), AMA, Am. Coll. Radiology, Am. Soc. Therapeutic Radiology and Oncology (pres. 1980-81, recipient Gold medal, 1990), Am. Assn. Cancer Rsch. Office: Mass Gen Hosp Cancer Ctr Dept Radiation Therapy 55 Fruit St Boston MA 02114 Office Phone: 617-724-1155. Office Fax: 617-726-1805.

SUITOR, DORCAS P., elementary school educator; b. Albany, Vt., Aug. 5, 1944; d. Abner Joseph and Eulalee Dorothy Poutry; m. David Douglas Suitor, Dec. 24, 1966; children: Daphne Joan Morris, Dorothea Joy Alter. BS in Edn., Johnson State Coll., 1966. Cert. tchr. Vt. Tchr. 2d grade C.P. Smith Sch., Burlington, Vt., 1966—67, Swanton Elem. Sch., 1967—71; tchr. title I Sheldon Elem. Sch., 1973—75, St. Anne's Elem. Sch., Swanton, 1974—75; tchr. 1st grade Swanton Elem. Sch., 1975—94, tchr. k-1, 1994—99, tchr. 1st grade, 1999—. Mem. adv. bd. Project Scope, Swanton, 2002—06; mem. local stds. bd. Franklin Northwest Dist., 1999—; mem. tech. task force Swanton Elem. Sch., 1999—2006, grade 1 math leader, 2005—; presenter in field. Mentor new tchr. FNW Supervisory Union, Swanton, 2003—; supr. student tchrs. U. Vt. and Johnson State Coll. Swanton Elem. Sch., 2001—04; trustee Meml. United Meth. Ch., Swanton, 2005—, Swanton Town Libr., 2005—. Recipient Outstanding Vt. Tchr. award, 2006. Mem.: ASCD, Nat. Coun. Tchrs. Math., Franklin Northwest NEA (30 Yrs. Svc. to Children award 1999), Vt. Coun. Reading. Democrat. United Methodist. Avocations: reading, cooking, making educational games, gardening. Home: 17 Dunning St Swanton VT 05488 Office: Swanton Elem Sch 113 Grand Ave Swanton VT 05488 Personal E-mail: davdor1@aol.com.

SUITS, BERNARD HERBERT, philosophy educator; b. Detroit, Nov. 25, 1925; s. Herbert Arthur and Helen Dorothy (Carlin) S.; m. Nancy Ruth Berr, July 3, 1952; children— Mark, Constance; m. Cheryl Ann Ballantyne, June 14, 1996. BA, U. Chgo., 1944, MA, 1950; PhD, U. Ill., 1958. Investigator venereal disease USPHS, 1950-51; personnel officer Detroit Civil Service Commn., 1952-54; instr. philosophy U. Ill., Urbana, 1958-59; asst. prof. Purdue U., 1959-66; asso. prof. U. Waterloo, Ont., 1966-72, prof. philosophy, chmn. dept., 1971-74, asso. dean arts for grad. affairs, 1981-84. Vis. prof. U. Lethbridge, Alta., Can., 1980, U. Bristol, Eng., 1980, disting. prof. emeritus U. Waterloo, 1995. Author: The Grasshopper: Games, Life, and Utopia, 1978, paper, 1990, 2d edit., 2005; contbr. to profl. jours. and books; featured guest on seven-week TV Ontario series The Academy of Moral Philosophy, 1982. Served with USNR, 1944-46. Recipient Disting. Tchg. award U. Waterloo, 1983. Mem.: Philosphic Soc. Study of Sport (pres. 1973). Office: U Waterloo Dept Philosophy Waterloo ON Canada E-mail: bernard.suits@sympatico.ca.

SUJANSKY, EVA BORSKA, pediatrician, geneticist, educator; b. Bratislava, Slovak Republic, Feb. 14, 1936; d. Stefan and Terezia (Kaiserova) Borsky; m. Eduard Sujansky, Apr. 2, 1960 (dec. Sept. 1979); children: Paul, Walter. MD, Comenius U., Bratislava, Czechoslovakia, 1959. Diplomate Am. Bd. Pediats., Am. Bd. Med. Genetics. Resident in pediats. U. Iowa, Iowa City, 1969-71; fellow in human genetics Mt. Sinai Sch. Medicine, NYC, 1971-73; clin. geneticist Beth Israel Hosp., NYC, 1973-74; dir. clin. genetics Sch. Medicine, U. Colo., Denver, 1974-90, assoc. prof. pediats., 1981—, assoc. prof. biochemistry, biophysics and genetics, 1981—98; co-dir. divsn. genetic svcs. The Children's Hosp., U. Colo., Denver, 1990—2000. Contbr. articles to profl. jours. Fellow Am. Acad. Pediats., Am. Soc. Human Genetics, Am. Coll. Med. Genetics (founding fellow). Avocations: fine arts, reading, travel. Office: U Colo Med Ctr/TCH 1056 E 19th Ave Denver CO 80218-1007 Office Phone: 303-861-6395. Business E-Mail: sujansky.eva@tchden.org.

SUKAPDJO, WILMA IRENE, language educator; b. Indpls., Nov. 8, 1936; d. Wilson Homer and Della Irene Warren; m. Humam Sukapdjo, Apr. 12, 1960; children: Tina, Stephen, Amye. AB, Butler U., Indpls., 1958, MS, 1967; post grad., Trinity Coll. of the Bible and Sem., Newburgh, Ind. Tchr. French U. Wis., Madison, Gadjah Mada U., Jakarta, Indonesia, Plainfield H.S., Ind., Columbus Jr. H.S., Ben Davis H.S., Indpls.; tchr. langs. Iupui Continuing Edn., Wilhum Acad., Carmel, Oasis, Indpls. Vol. guide Eiteljorg Indian Mus., 1999—2006. Recipient Di Vinci Diamond award, Cambridge, England, 2006. Mem.: Colonial Williamsburg Found., Indpls.

Mus. Art, Japan Am. Soc. Ind., Tomodachi Japan-Am. Club (pres.), Omicron Psi, Phi Kappa Phi. Republican. Presbyterian. Avocation: travel. Office: Wilhum Acad Foreign Lang 622 S Range Line Rd Ste Q Carmel IN 46032-2152 Office Phone: 317-843-2874.

SUKKARIYAH, BESHR, soil scientist; b. Baalbeck, Lebanon, Jan. 8, 1973; s. Fadel Sukkariyah and Soleima Succarieh. BS in Agr. with distinction, Am. U. Beirut, 1995, Diploma of Ingenieur Agricole, 1995, MS in Soil Sci., 1998; PhD in Soil Chemistry, Va. Poly. Inst. & State U., Blacksburg, 2003. Rsch. & tchg. asst. Va. Poly. Inst. & State U., 2000—03, tchg. faculty, 2004—05, postdoctoral rsch. assoc., 2005—. Contbr. articles to profl. jours. Lt. Lebanese Army, 1999—2000. Mem.: Water Environment Fedn., Bd. Engrs. Lebanon, Soil Sci. Soc. Am. Avocations: hiking, camping, soccer, bicycling. Home: 119 Hearthstone Dr Apt E Blacksburg VA 24060 Office: 351B Smyth Hall Blacksburg VA 24061 Business E-Mail: bsukkari@vt.edu.

SUKO, LONNY RAY, judge; b. Spokane, Wash., Oct. 12, 1943; s. Ray R. and Leila B. (Snyder) Suko; m. Marcia A. Michaelson, Aug. 26, 1967; children: Jolynn R., David M. BA, Wash. State U., 1965; JD, U. Idaho, 1968. Bar: Wash. 1968, U.S. Dist. Ct. (ea. dist.), Wash. 1969, U.S. Dist. Ct. (we. dist.), Wash. 1978, U.S. Ct. Appeals (9th cir.) 1978. Law clk. U.S. Dist. Ct. Ea. Dist., Wash., 1968—69; assoc. Lyon, Beaulaurier & Aaron, Yakima, Wash., 1969—72; ptnr. Lyon, Beaulaurier, Weigand, Suko & Gustafson, Yakima, Wash., 1972—91; ptnr., shareholder Lyon, Weigand, Suko & Gustafson, Yakima, Wash., 1991—95; U.S. magistrate judge Yakima, Wash., 1971—91, 1995—2003; judge U.S. Dist. Ct., 2003—. Mem.: Phi Kappa Phi, Phi Beta Kappa. Office: PO Box 2726 Yakima WA 98907-2726

SUKONECK, IRA DAVID, lawyer; b. Newark, Jan. 20, 1947; s. Edward and Mae (Rosenkrantz) S.; m. Vicki Sherman, Oct. 29, 1972; children: Marc, Randi. BS in Pharmacy, Northeastern U., 1969; JD, Suffolk U., 1972. Bar: Mass. 1972, N.J. 1973, U.S. Dist. Ct. N.J. 1973, U.S. Supreme Ct. 1978; cert. workers compensation law atty. Assoc. ptnr. Braff, Harris & Sukoneck, Livingston, N.J., 1973—. Mem. ABA, N.J. Bar Assn., Assn. Trial Lawyers Am., Am. Inns of Ct., N.J. Workers Compensation Def. Assn. Office: Braff Harris Sukoneck 570 W Mount Pleasant Ave PO Box 657 Livingston NJ 07039-0657 E-mail: isukoneck@bhs-law.com.

SUL, YI CHUL, neurologist; b. Seoul, May 5, 1947; arrived in US, 1976; s. Tae Woon Sul and Jung Sook Suh; m. Kyu Won, Nov. 21, 1976; children: Caroline, Douglas, Joseph. MD, Yonsei U., Seoul, 1972. Diplomate Am. Bd. Psychiatry and Neurology, Am. Bd. Neurophysiology. Clin. instr. Vanderbilt U., Nashville, 1981-82; v.p. Lakeside Neurology, PC, Grosse Pointe Woods, Mich., 1985—; asst. clin. prof. Mich. State U., Lansing, 1995—. Adj. clin. asst. prof. U. Osteo. Medicine and Health Sci., 1998—99; clin. asst. prof. Coll. Osteo. Medicine U. Health Sci., 2000—; chief neurology sect. St. John N.E. Cmty. Hosp., Detroit, 2002—03; mem. neurosci. adv. group St. John Health Sys., 2004—06. Pres. Lakside Neurology, 2005—; sec. Christian Assn. Med. Mission, Detroit, 1991—95, pres., 1999—2001; med. mission Thailand, 1994, China, 1997; chairperson adminstrv. bd. Korean United Meth. Ch., Detroit, 1997—98, chairperson bd. trustees, 2001. Capt. Republic of Korea Army, 1972—75. Grantee, Muscular Dystrophy Assn., 1981—82. Fellow: Am. Assn. Electrodiagnostic Medicine; mem.: AMA, Mich. State Med. Soc., Am. Clin. Neurophysiology Soc., Am. Acad. Neurology. Home: 20720 Green Ct Grosse Pointe Woods MI 48236-1459 Office: Lakeside Neurology PC 20867 Mack Ave Ste 6 Grosse Pointe Woods MI 48236-1356 Home Phone: 313-884-2774; Office Phone: 313-882-2922. Personal E-mail: yisul21@comcast.net.

SULDS, JONATHAN L., lawyer; b. NYC, Feb. 6, 1950; s. Irvin D. adn Vivienne (Sheinberg) S.; m. Katharine Cooper, June 24, 1978; children: Amy, Benjamin, Michael. BA, MA, Colgate U., 1971; JD, Harvard U., 1974. Ptnr., co-chmn. mgmt. com. Gibson Dunn and Crutcher, NYC, 1984—98; now ptnr., labor and employment practice group Akin Gump Strauss Hauer & Feld LLP, NYC, 1998—. Lectr. Cornell U. Sch. Indsl. and Labor Rels., Ithaca, NY, 1985—. Author: New York Employment Law, 1998, New York Employment Discrimination Handbook, 2001; contbr. numerous articles profl. journals. Office: Akin Gump Strauss Hauer & Feld LLP 590 Madison Ave New York NY 10022-2524 Office Phone: 212-872-1042. Office Fax: 212-872-1002. Business E-Mail: jsulds@akingump.com.

SULEMAN, AMER, internist, cardiologist; b. Lahore, Punjab, Pakistan, Mar. 21, 1967; s. Sheikh Mohammad and Nusrat Suleman; m. Mahvash Amer, May 31, 1999. BA, BS, Punjab U., Lahore, 1986; MBBS, King Edward Med. Coll., Lahore, 1990. Diplomate Am. Bd. Internal Medicine. House officer internal medicine and cardiology Mayo Hosp., Lahore, 1991; clin. instr. dept. pathology SUNY, Buffalo, 1991-92, clin. instr. dept. medicine, 1992-95; fellow dept. cardiology Alton Ochsner Med. Ctr., New Orleans, 1995-97; staff cons. internal medicine and cardiology Denton (Tex.) Regional Med. Ctr., 1997—. CME editor: Internet Text Book of Medicine; mem. editl. adv. bd.: Internat. Jour. Family Practice; contbr. articles to profl. jours. Founding mem. Muscular Dystrophy Welfare Assn., Pakistan, 1986-87, Art and Cultural Orgn. Pakistan, 1985; incharge youth wing Internat. Red Cross, Punjab, 1986; vol. physician AlShifa Clinic, Bedford, Tex., 1999—. Recipient Sci. Poster Recognition awards So. Med. Assn., 1999; Merit scholar Govt. Pakistan, 1982; Rsch. grantee KOS Pharm., 2000. Fellow Royal Soc. Medicine, Am. Inst. Stress; mem. ACP, Am. Soc. Hypertension. Avocations: poetry, literature, community service, playing chess. Home: 3529 San Patricio Dr Plano TX 75025-4427 Fax: (940) 381-2613. E-mail: asuleman@pol.net.

SULG, MADIS, manufacturing executive, entrepreneur; b. Tallinn, Estonia, May 25, 1943; came to U.S., 1950; s. Hand Eduard and Erika (Turk) S.; m. Mary Diane Detellis, Dec. 30, 1967; children: Danielle Marie, Michaella Erika. SB in Engring. Mgmt., MIT, 1965, SM in Mgmt., 1967. Cons. Barss, Reitzel & Assocs., Cambridge, Mass., 1970—71; mgr. planning and research Converse Rubber Co., Wilmington, Mass., 1971—75; dir. bus. planning and devel. AMF, Inc., Stamford, Conn., 1975—79; sr. v.p. planning and devel. Bandag, Inc., Muscatine, Iowa, 1978—88; pres. Prime Investments, 1988—, Muscatine Natural Resources Corp., 1981—88; chmn., CEO Sieg Auto Parts, Davenport, Iowa, 1989—93; COO Hammer's Plastic Recycling, Iowa Falls, Iowa, 1994, PURethane, Inc., West Branch, Iowa, 1994—98; COO, Bytec, Inc., Clinton Township, Mich., 1999—2001; prin. M&D Mgmt. Assocs., 1989—; mng. mem. Maddi's Gallery, LLC, 2001—, Maddi's Southern Bistro, LLC, 2007—. With U.S. Army, 1968-70. Presbyterian. Avocations: bridge, jogging, swimming. Home: 11238 Home Place Lane Charlotte NC 28227 Office Phone: 704-907-1289. Personal E-mail: madissulg@aol.com.

SULKIN, HOWARD ALLEN, academic administrator; b. Detroit, Aug. 19, 1941; s. Lewis and Vivian P. (Mandel) S.; m. Constance Annette Adler, Aug. 4, 1963; children— Seth R., Randall K. PhB, Wayne State U., 1963; MBA, U. Chgo., 1965, PhD, 1969; LHD (hon.), De Paul U., 1990. Dir. program rsch., indsl. rels. ctr. U. Chgo., 1964-72; dean Sch. for New Learning, De Paul U., Chgo., 1972-77; v.p. De Paul U., Chgo., 1977-84; pres. Spertus Inst. Jewish Studies, Chgo., 1984—. St. Paul's vis. prof. Rikkyo U., Tokyo, 1970—; cons., evaluator North Ctrl. Assn., Chgo., 1975—. Contbr. articles to profl. jours. Sec.-treas. Grant Park Cultural and Ednl. Cmty., Chgo., 1984—; bd. dirs. Chgo. Sinai Congregation, 1972—, pres., 1980-83; bd. dirs. Grant Park Conservancy, Legacy Charter Sch., Parliament of World's Religions, 1989—, chmn., 1989-; mem. exec. com. Loop Alliance. Mem.: Tavern, The Standard. Office: Spertus Inst of Jewish Studies 618 S Michigan Ave Chicago IL 60605-1901

SULLEBARGER, JOHN THOMPSON, internist, educator, cardiologist; b. Plainfield, NJ, May 2, 1957; s. Franklyn Jackson and Joanne Abbott (Aspinall) S.; m. Lorrie Jeanne Miller, June 14, 1980; children: Jeffrey Franklyn, Melissa Jeanne. Student, U. Mainz, 1977; AB, Dartmouth Coll., 1979; MD, Johns Hopkins U., 1983. Intern U. Rochester, NY, 1983-84, resident in medicine, 1984-86, fellow in cardiology, 1986-89, from sr. instr. to asst. prof., 1989-92; asst. prof. U. South Fla., Tampa, 1992-96, assoc. prof., 1997-99; dir. CCU Tampa Gen. Hosp., 1997—; clin. assoc. prof. U. South Fla., Tampa, 2004—. Dir. Cardiac Catheterization Lab. James Haley VA Hosp., Tampa, 1992—99; dir. interventional cardiology U. South Fla., 1994—99; attending physician Strong Meml. Hosp., Rochester, 1989—92; pres. Fla. Cardiovascular Inst., 2004—. Author: (with others) book chapters; contrb. articles to profl. jours. Chmn. Bd. Christian Svc., 1st Bapt. Ch., Rochester, 1991-92. Fellow ACP, 1992, Am. Coll. of Cardiology, 1991, Counc. on Clin. Cardiology of Am. Heart Assn., 1991, N.Y. Cardiological Soc., 1992. Fellow ACP, Soc. Cardiac Angiography and Interventions, Am. Coll. Cardiology, N.Y. Cardiol. Soc.; mem. Am. Heart Assn. (fellow coun. on clin. cardiology), Tampa Internat. Heart Found. (founder 2004-). Avocation: music. Office: 509 S Armenia Ste 200 Tampa FL 33609 Office Phone: 813-353-1515.

SULLENBERGER, ARA BROOCKS, mathematics professor; b. Amarillo, Tex., Jan. 3, 1933; d. Carl Clarence and Ara Frances (Broocks) Cox; m. Hal Joseph Sullenberger, Nov. 2, 1952; children: Hal Joseph Jr., Ara Broocks Sullenberger Switzer. Student, Randolph-Macon Woman's Coll., 1951—52, So. Meth. U., 1952, U. Tex., Arlington, 1953, Amarillo Coll., 1953—54; BA in Math., Tex. Tech. U., 1955, MA, 1958; postgrad., Tex. Christian U., 1963—67, U. N. Tex., 1969—80, Tarrant County Coll., 1972—73. Cert. tchr., Tex. Math. tchr. Tom S. Lubbock H.S., Tex., 1955—56; instr. math. Tex. Tech U., Lubbock, 1956—63; tchg. fellow math. Tex. Christian U., Ft. Worth, 1963—64; chmn. dept. math. Ft. Worth Country Day Sch., 1964—67; instr. math. Tarrant County Coll.-South, Ft. Worth, 1967—70, asst. prof. math., 1970—74, assoc. prof. math., 1974—95; prof. emeritus, 1995—; ret., 1995. Adj. prof. math. Tex. Christian U., 1996; cons. Project Change, Ft. Worth, 1967-68; math. scis. advisor Coll. Bd., Princeton, N.J., 1979-83; math. book reviewer Prentice-Hall, McGraw Hill, D.C. Heath, Prindle, Weber & Schmidt, MacMillan, Harcourt, Brace Jovanovich, West, Worth, Saunders, Wadsworth. Contbr. articles to profl. jours.; author book supplement to Intermediate Algebra, 1990. Active Jr. League, Ft. Worth, 1954—73, sustaining mem., 1973—; editor newsletter Crestwood Assn., Ft. Worth, 1984, 1986, 1991, membership sec., 1985, 1990—91, 1995, 1999, pres., 1988—89, 1998—99, crime patrol capt., 1993, 2000—01, v.p., 1993, treas., 1987, 1996, 2003, sec., 1997—98, crime patrol sec., 1999, crime patrol sec.-treas., 2001—05, fin. com. chair, 2004—05, 2006—. Recipient award for excellence in teaching Gen. Dynamics, 1968. Mem. Math. Assn. Am. (life), Nat. Coun. Tchrs. Math. (life), Am. Math. Assn. Two-Yr. Colls. (life), Tex. Math. Assn. Two-Yr. Colls. (charter, v.p. 1997-99), Tex. Jr. Coll. Tchrs. Assn., Ft. Worth League Neighborhood Assn. (v.p. 1999-2000, del. 2004-05), Pi Beta Phi. Republican. Episcopalian. Avocation: reading. Home: 600 Eastwood Ave Fort Worth TX 76107-1020 Personal E-mail: halnara@sbcglobal.net.

SULLENDER, JOY SHARON, retired elementary school educator; b. Bloomington, Ind., Apr. 9, 1932; d. Fred Laymond and Edith (Parrish) Medaris. BS, Ind. U., 1959, MS, 1965; postgrad., Ind. U./Purdue U., Indpls., 1991. Cert. tchr. elem. edn. 1-8. Tchr. Monroe Sch., Salem, Ind., 1952-55, Pekin (Ind.) Sch., 1955-61, Highland Park (Ill.) Sch., 1961-62, George Julian Sch. #57, Indpls., 1962—2000; ret., 2000. Mem. prin.'s adv. coun. Indpls. Pub. Schs., 1985-95, supts. adv. coun., 1982-90; state mentor student tchrs., 1969—. Author col.: Let's Be Informed, 1993-95. Class sponsor Best Friends, Indpls., 1990—; vol. Toys for Foster Children, Indpls., 1991—; workshop presenter Alpha Epsilon State, Anderson, South Bend, 1994, 95. NSF grantee, 1971. Mem. PTA (tchr. rep. 1993-95), Ind. Sch. Women's Club (v.p. 1989-91, pres. 1992-94), Woman's Dept. Club (v.p. 2002—, corr. sec. 2007-), Delta Kappa Gamma (pres. 1978-80, state com. 1989—, state corr. sec. 1997-99). Home: 1310 N Bazil Ave Indianapolis IN 46219-4244

SULLINS, KEN, mathematics, science and computer science educator; BA in Math., Oakland U., Rochester, Mich., 1970; MAT in Math., Oakland U., 1975. Tchr. 8th grade math. East Hills Jr. High, Bloomfield Hills, Mich., 1972; tchr. 7th grade math. and sci. Imlay City (Mich.) Jr. High, 1972—73; tchr. math. Croswell (Mich.)-Lexington HS, 1973—76; tchr. Carsonville (Mich.)-Port Sanilac Jr.-Sr. HS, 1976—81; tchr. pre-calculus St. Clair C.C., Port Huron, Mich., 1977—81; tchr. Chelsea (Mich.) HS, 1981—99; tchr. math. Ripley (Tenn.) HS, 1998—99; press operator JAC Products, Saline, Mich., 2000; text layout technician Sheridan Books, Inc., Ann Arbor, Mich., 2000—01; instr. Mansfield (Pa.) U., 2001—; adj. instr. math., sci., computer tech. Empire State Coll., Corning, NY, 2004—. Presenter in field. Contbr. articles to profl. jours. Mailing: 146 Barber Hollow Rd Tioga PA 16946 Office Phone: 607-962-1421. Business E-Mail: kenneth.sullins@esc.edu.

SULLIVAN, ALFRED DEWITT, academic administrator; b. New Orleans, Feb. 2, 1942; s. Dewitt Walter and Natalie (Alford) Sullivan; m. Marilyn Janie Hewitt, Sept. 1, 1962 (div. May 1989); children: Alan, Sean; m. Dorothy Madeleine Hess, Apr. 1993. BS, La. State U., 1964, MS, 1966; PhD, U. Ga., 1969. Asst. prof. Va. Poly. Inst. and State U., Blacksburg, 1969—73; assoc. prof., then prof. Miss. State U., Starkville, 1973—88; dir. Sch. Forest Resources Pa. State U., University Park, 1988—93; dean coll. natural resources U. Minn., St. Paul, 1993—2002, vice provost academic programs & facilities Mpls., 2002—06, spl. asst. to pres., 2006—. Assoc. Danforth Found., 1981. Contbr. articles to profl. jours. Fellow, Am. Coun. Edn., 1987—88, NDEA fellow, U. Ga., 1966—69. Mem.: Soc. Am. Foresters. Office: U Minn 234 MorH 0262 100 Church St SE Minneapolis MN 55455 Office Phone: 612-626-3838. E-mail: sulli031@umn.edu.

SULLIVAN, ALISON ELIZABETH, pediatrician, child psychiatrist; b. Bronx, NY, May 17, 1976; d. Shirley Anne and Colm Sullivan. BA, Coll. of the Holy Cross, Mass., 1998; MD, Columbia U., NYC, 2002. Resident in pediat., adult psychiatry and child psychiatry Mt. Sinai Hosp., NYC, 2002—. Home: 215 East 95th St Apt 7G New York NY 10128 Home Phone: 914-213-5936. Personal E-mail: alison.sullivan@mssm.edu.

SULLIVAN, ANDREW M., online journalist, editor, news blogger; b. Aug. 1963; BA, Magdalen Coll., Oxford; MPA, Harvard John F. Kennedy Sch. Govt., 1986, PhD, 1990. Editl. writer intern The Daily Telegraph, London, Centre For Policy Studies; intern The New Republic, 1986, assoc. editor, dep. editor, 1990, acting editor, 1991, editor, 1991—96, currently sr. editor; taught moral and polit. theory in govt. dept. Harvard John F. Kennedy Sch. Govt., 1987; freelancer Wall Street Journal, Washington Post, Daily Telegraph, Esquire and NY Mag., Telegraph, 1990; started monthly column Esquire, 1990; columnist Time Mag., 2000—07; blogger, editor andrewsullivan.com, 2000—; blog writer time.blogs.com/daily-dish, 2006—07; sr. editor and blogger Atlantic Monthly (TheAtlantic.com), 2007—. Testified before Congress on the Defense of Marriage Act in 1996; spkr. in field at many universities and colleges. Author: (essay) The Politics of Homosexuality, 1993, What's So Bad About Hate, 1999, Virtually Normal: An Argument About Homosexuality, 1995, Love Undetectable: Notes on Friendship, Sex, and Survival, 1998, The Conservative Soul: How We Lost It, How to Get It Back (Hardcover), 2006, (reader) Same-Sex Marriage: Pro and Con, (cover stories) When Plagues End, NY Times, 1996, The Scolds, NY Times, 1998, Why Are Men So Different (provoked a cover story in Time and documentary on the Discovery Channel), 2000; contbg. writer, columnist NY Time Mag., regular contbr. NY Times Book Review, weekly columnist Sunday Times of London, contbg. columnist The Advocate, LA, Calif., contbg. editor NY Sun, regular guest Real Time with Bill Maher, Chris Matthews Show, guest appearances Nightline, Face the Nation, Meet the Press, Crossfire, Hardball, The O'Reilly Factor, Larry King Show, Reliable Sources, Hannity and Colmes, and many others. Named Editor of Yr., Adweek Mag., 1996; Harkness Fellowship, Harvard John F. Kennedy Sch. Govt., 1984. Office: The New Republic 1331 H St NW Ste 700 Washington DC 20005 Address: Sunday Times of London One Pennington St London E9 81ST England also: The Advocate 6922 Hollywood Blvd Ste 1000 Los Angeles CA 90028 also: NY Sun 105 Chambers St New York NY 10007 Office: Atlantic Monthly Group The Watergate 600 NH Ave NW Washington DC 20037 Office Phone: 202-508-4444, 800-788-7197, 323-871-1225, 212-406-2000, 212-522-1212. Office Fax: 202-628-9383, 323-467-6805, 212-522-0003. E-mail: andrewmsullivan@aol.com, andrew@andrewsullivan.com. *

SULLIVAN, AUSTIN PADRAIC, JR., retired diversified food company executive; b. Washington, June 26, 1940; s. Austin P. and Janet Lay (Patterson) Sullivan; m. Judith Ann Raab, June 1, 1968 (dec. Oct. 1995); children: Austin P. III, Amanda, Alexander; m. Marie Elise de Golian, Aug. 1, 1997; stepchildren: Lauren Gibbons, Georgia Gibbons, Samuel Gibbons. BA cum laude, Princeton U., 1964. Spl. asst. to dep. dir. N.J. Office Econ. Opportunity, Trenton, NJ, 1956—66; prof. staff mem. Com. on Edn. and Labor, U.S. Ho. of Rep., Washington, 1967—71, legis. dir., 1971—76; dir. govt. relations Gen. Mills, Inc., Mpls., 1976—78, v.p., corp. dir. govt. rels., 1978—79, v.p. pub. affairs, 1979—93, v.p. corp. comm. and pub. affairs, 1993—94, sr. v.p. corp. rels., 1994—2005; ret., 2005. Lectr. fed. labor market policies Harvard U., Mass., 1972—76, Boston U., 1972—76. Mem. Nat. Commn. on Employment and Tng., 1979—81, U.S. Sec. Agr. Adv. Com. on Agrl. Biotech., 2000—03; chmn. Governor's Coun. on Employment and Tng., 1976—82; bd. dir., exec. com. Urban Coalition Mpls., 1978—80, Guthrie Theatre, Mpls., 1978—84, Minn. Citizens for the Arts, 1980—83; co chmn. Governor's Commn. on Dislocated Workers, Minn., 1988—89; chmn. Pub. Affairs Coun., 1993—94; bd. dir. Minn. C. of C., 1993—99; trustee Minn. Pub. Radio, 1999—; bd. advisors Dem. Leadership Coun., 1986—. Served in USMC, 1957—59. Recipient Eleanor Roosevelt Fellow in Interracial Rels., 1964—65. Mem.: Grocery Mfr. Assn. (govt. affairs coun. 1991—2004, chmn. biotech. task force 1999—2004), Coun. of Pub. Affairs Exec. (chmn. 1989—90), Medica (bd. dir. 2001—), Greater Mpls. C. of C. (exec. com. 1980—86, 1990—93, bd. dir. 1986—), Mpls. Club (bd. governor's 2001—). Home: 17830 County Rd 6 Minneapolis MN 55447-2905 Office: Ste 252 700 Twelve Oaks Center Dr Wayzata MN 55391

SULLIVAN, BARRY, lawyer; b. Newburyport, Mass., Jan. 11, 1949; s. George Arnold and Dorothy Bennett (Furbush) S.; m. Winnifred Mary Fallers, June 14, 1975; children: George Arnold, Lloyd Ashton. AB cum laude, Middlebury Coll., 1970; JD, U. Chgo., 1974. Bar: Mass. 1975, Ill. 1975, Va. 1995, US Dist. Ct. (no. dist.) Ill. 1976, US Ct. Appeals (7th cir.) 1976, US Ct. Appeals (10th cir.) 1977, US Supreme Ct. 1978, US Ct. Appeals (11th cir.) 1986, US Ct. Appeals (5th and 9th cirs.) 1987, US Ct. Appeals (fed. cir.) 1993, US Ct. Appeals (DC cir.) 1994, US Ct. Appeals (4th cir.) 1997, US Ct. Appeals (2d and 3d cirs.) 2002, US Ct. Appeals (6th and 8th cirs.) 2004, US Dist. Ct. (ctrl. dist.) Ill. 2006. Law clk. to judge John Minor Wisdom U.S. Ct. Appeals (5th cir.), New Orleans, 1974-75; assoc. Jenner & Block, Chgo., 1975-80; asst. to solicitor gen. of U.S. U.S. Dept. of Justice, Washington, 1980-81; ptnr. Jenner & Block, Chgo., 1981-94, 2001—; prof. law Washington and Lee U., Lexington, Va., 1994-2001, dean, 1994-99, v.p., 1998-99; Fulbright prof. U. Warsaw, Poland, 2000—01; lectr. in law U. Chgo., 2001—02; spl. asst. state's atty. Cook County, Ill., 2002—03. Vis. fellow Queen Mary and Westfield Coll., U. London, 2001; spl. asst. atty. gen. State of Ill., 1989—90; lectr. in law Loyola U., Chgo., 1978—79; adj. prof. law Northwestern U., Chgo., 1990—92, 1993—94, vis. prof., 1992—93; vis. prof. Ctr. for Am. law studies U. Warsaw, 2002—03, 2005; sr. lectr. Irving B. Harris Grad. Sch. Pub. Policy, U. Chgo., 2005—; Jessica Swift Meml. lectr. constl. law Middlebury Coll., 1991; Rufus Monroe and Sophie Payne lectr. U. Mo., Columbia, 2003; Charles L. Ihlenfeld lectr. pub. policy and ethics W.Va. U., 2005. Assoc. editor U. Chgo. Law Rev., 1973-74; mem. editl. bd. Dublin U. Law Jour., 2004-; contbr. articles to profl. jours. Mem. nat. adv. bd. Ctr. for Religion, The Professions, and The Pub., U. Mo., Columbia, 2003—; trustee Cath. Theol. Union at Chgo., 1993—2003, trustee emeritus, 2003—; mem. vis. com. Irving B. Harris Grad. Sch. Public Policy Studies U. Chgo., 2001—, U. Chgo. Divinity Sch., 1987—2001; mem. adv. panel Fulbright Sr. Specialist Program, 2001—04; mem. adv. bd. Internat. Human Rights Inst. DePaul U., 2003—; trustee U. Chgo. Court Theatre, 2003—05; mem. bd. visitors So. Ill. U. Sch. Law, 2006—; mem. adv. bd. Project DV-Leap, George Washington U. Law. Sch., 2006—; mem. Cmty. Renewal Soc. Chgo., 2006—. Yeats Soc. scholar, 1968, Woodrow Wilson fellow, Woodrow Wilson Found., 1970, Nat. Honor scholar, Univ. Chgo., 1970—74. Fellow Am. Bar Found., Phi Beta Kappa; mem. ABA (chmn. coord. com. on AIDS 1988—94, standing com. on amicus curiae briefs 1990—97, coun. sect. individual rights and responsibilities 1993—98, sect. legal edn. com. on law sch. adminstrn. 1994—98, chair sect. legal edn. com. on professionalism 1999—2000, co-chair sect. individual rights/responsibilities com. amicus briefs 2002—04, sect. legal edn. stds. rev. com. 2002—05, co-chair sect. individual rights/responsibilities com. bill rights 2002—, standing com. amicus curiae briefs 2004—), Lawyers Club Chgo., Supreme Ct. Hist Soc. (Ill. membership chair 2002—03), Ill. State Bar Assn., Appellate Lawyers Assn., Am. Law Inst., Bar Assn. 7th Fed. Cir. (vice chmn. advminstrv. justice com. 1985—86), Va. State Bar (chair sec. on edn. of lawyers 1998—99) Democrat. Roman Catholic. Home: 5555 S Everett Apt A1-2 Chicago IL 60637 Office: Jenner & Block LLP 330 N Wabash Ave Chicago IL 60611 Office Phone: 312-923-2652. Business E-Mail: bsullivan@jenner.com.

SULLIVAN, BERNARD JAMES, accountant; b. Chgo., June 25, 1927; s. Bernard Hugh and Therese Sarah (Condon) S.; m. Joan Lois Costello, June 9, 1951; children: Therese Lynn Scanlan, Bernard J., Geralyn M. Snyder. BSc, Loyola U., Chgo., 1950. CPA, Ill. Staff Bansley and Kiener, Chgo., 1950-66, ptnr., 1966-82, mng. ptnr., 1982—. Bd. dirs. Associated Acctg. Firms, Internat.; exec. com. Moore Stephens and Co., U.S.A., 1984—, Arbitrator Nat. Assn. Security Dealers. Served with USN, 1945-46. Mem. Am. Inst. CPA's, Ill. Soc. CPA's, Govt. Fin. Officer Assn., Internat. Found. Employee Benefit Plans, Delta Sigma Pi. Clubs: Beverly Country (Chgo.), Metropolitan (Chgo.). Lodges: Elks, K.C. Avocations: golf, sports, travel. Home: 9636 S Kolmar Ave Oak Lawn IL 60453-3214 Office: Bansley & Kiener 8745 W Higgins Rd Ste 200 Chicago IL 60631-2704 Home Phone: 708-423-1990; Office Phone: 312-263-2700. Business E-Mail: bsullivan@bk-cpa.com.

SULLIVAN, BRENDAN V., JR., lawyer; b. Providence, Mar. 11, 1942; AB, Georgetown U., 1964, JD, 1967. Bar: RI 1967, DC 1970, US Dist. Ct. DC 1970, US Ct. Appeals (DC cir.) 1970, US Supreme Ct. 1972, US Dist. Ct. Md. 1974, US Ct. Appeals (3d cir.) 1979, US Ct. Appeals (4th cir.) 1981, US Ct. Appeals (6th cir.) 1991, US Ct. Appeals (9th cir.) 1996, US Ct. Fed. Claims 1998, US Ct. Appeals (fed. cir.) 2003, US Ct. Appeals (2d cir.) 2007. Mem. Williams & Connolly LLP, Washington. Lectr. Practicing Law Inst., 1981—, Md. Inst. for Continuing Profl. Edn. of Lawyers, Inc., 1979—, D.C. Criminal Practice Inst., 1975-81. Author: Grand Jury Proceedings, 1981, Techniques for Dealing with Pending Criminal Charges or Criminal Investigations, 1983, White Collar Criminal Practice Grand Jury, 1985. Capt. US Army, 1968—69. Named one of 75 Best Lawyers In Washington, Washingtonian mag., 2002, 100 Most Influential Lawyers, Nat. Law Jour., 2006. Fellow Am. Coll. Trial Lawyers; mem. ABA, R.I. Bar Assn., D.C. Bar. Office: Williams & Connolly 725 12th St NW Washington DC 20005-5901 Office Phone: 202-434-5800.

SULLIVAN, CHARLES, dean, educator, author; b. Boston, May 27, 1933; s. Charles Thomas and Marion Veronica (Donahue) S.; divorced; children: Charles Fulford, John Driscoll, Catherine Page. BA in English, Swarthmore Coll., 1955; MA, NYU, 1968, PhD in Social Psychology, 1973; MPA, Pa. State U., 1978. Predoctoral fellow NYU, 1964-68; postdoctoral fellow Ednl. Testing Svc., Princeton, NJ, 1973-74; asst. prof. psychology Ursinus Coll., Collegeville, Pa., 1973-78; mgmt. cons., 1978-86; adj. prof. Pa. State U., Radnor, Pa., 1978-80; prof., head dept. pub. adminstrn., dir. student svcs. Southeastern U., Washington, 1986-89; asst. dean Grad. Sch. Arts and Scis. Georgetown U., Washington, 1989-92, assoc. dean Grad. Sch. Arts and Scis., 1992-97, professorial lectr., dept. psychology, 1994-95; exec. dir. Doylestown Found., Doylestown, Pa., 1958-73; assoc. dean, prof. Coll. Profl. Studies U. San Francisco, 1997-98. Adj. prof. social and behavioral scis. U. Md., 1984-96; lectr., spkr. on lit. and art Cooper-Hewitt Mus., N.Y.C., Nat. Soc. Arts and Letters, Washington, Martin Luther King Jr. Libr., Washington, Met. Mus. Art, N.Y.C., Smithsonian Instn., Washington, Children's Book Fair, N.Y.C., Nat. Mus. Women in Arts, Lombardi Cancer Rsch. Ctr., Georgetown U., Arts Club of Washington, Phillips Collection, Corcoran Gallery of Art, U. San Francisco Multicultural Lit. Program, Nat. Mus. Am. History, New Coll. of Calif., others. Author: Alphabet Animals, 1991, The Lover in Winter, 1991, Numbers at Play, 1992, Circus, 1992, Cowboys, 1993, A Woman of A Certain Age, 1994, Out of Love, 1996, American Folk, 1998, In a Certain Place, 1999, The Lovers' Companion, 2002; editor: America in Poetry, 1988, 2d edit., 1992, 3d edit., 1996, Imaginary Gardens, 1989, Ireland in Poetry, 1990, Children of Promise, 1991, 2d edit., 2001, Loving, 1992, American Beauties, 1993, Here Is My Kingdom, 1994, Fathers and Children, 1995, Imaginary Animals, 1996, Dancing in the Wind, 2002; contbr. poems in various periodicals. Trustee Folger Poetry Bd., 1988-92; Nat. Soc. Arts and Letters, 1992-94, 2002-04, Am. Acad. Liberal Edn., 1995—, San Francisco Art Inst., 2000-05, Pacific Ctr. for Photog. Arts, 2003—05; pres. Am. Found. Arts, 1995—; collectors com. Nat. Gallery Art, Washington, 1998-2006; mem. Dir.'s Cir., San Francisco Mus. Modern Art, 1998-2006. Recipient Best Books for Young Adults award, Young Adult Libr. Svcs. Assn., 1992, 1998, Best Books for Teens award, N.Y. Pub. Libr., 1992, 1993. Mem.: The Family Club, Cosmos Club. Personal E-mail: artsfound@earthlink.net.

SULLIVAN, CHARLES, JR., retired lawyer; b. Beaumont, Tex., Oct. 20, 1943; BS, Lamar U., 1967; JD, U. Houston, 1973. Bar: Tex. 1973. Mem. Fulbright & Jaworski L.L.P., Houston, retired ptnr. Mem. ABA, State Bar Tex., Houston Bar Assn. Office: Fulbright & Jaworski LLP 1301 Mckinney St Ste 5100 Houston TX 77010-3031 E-mail: csullivan@fulbright.com.

SULLIVAN, CHRISTOPHER DAVID, real estate broker, real estate attorney; b. NYC, Oct. 6, 1966; m. Anne Marie Houlihan, Sept. 3, 1966. JD, U. of the Pacific, 1997. Bar: Nev. 2002, Utah 1998. Mng. ptnr. Sullivan/Brown The Law Firm, Las Vegas, Nev., 2004—; broker, owner Chris Sullivan Realty, Las Vegas, 2005—. Mem. Urban Land Inst., Las Vegas, 2004—. Bd. dirs. Project Sunshine, Las Vegas, 2003—06. Mem.: Clark County Bar Assn., State Bar of Utah (assoc.), State Bar of Nev. (assoc.). Office: Sullivan-Brown 332 S Jones Blvd Las Vegas NV 89107 Home Phone: 702-855-0233; Office Phone: 702-471-0112, 702-547-0115. Office Fax: 702-567-0116. E-mail: thisisyourleader@yahoo.com.

SULLIVAN, CONNIE CASTLEBERRY, artist; b. Cin., Jan. 8, 1934; d. John Porter and Constance (Alf) Castleberry; m. John J. Sullivan, June 6, 1959; children: Deirdre Kelly, Margaret Graham. BA, Manhattanville Coll., 1957. Spl. lectr. Cin. Contemporary Art Ctr., 1984, Toledo Friends of Photography, 1991, U. Ky. Art Mus., 1993, Dennison U. Sch. Art, 1993, El Instituto de Estudios Norte Americanos, Barcelona, 1994, Ctr. for Photography, Bombay, India, 1997, Miami U. Art Mus., Oxford, Ohio, 1998, Alice and Harris K. Weston Gallery, Aronoff Ctr. for the Arts, Cin., 2000, Columbus Mus. Art, Ohio, 2001, Mus. Fine Arts St. Petersburg, Fla., 2002. One-woman shows include Contemporary Art Ctr. Cleve., 1982, Cin. Contemporary Arts Ctr., 1983, Fogg Art Mus., Cambridge, Mass., 1983, 90, Neikrug Gallery, N.Y.C., 1984, Camden Arts Ctr., London, 1987, Evanston Art Ctr., Chgo., 1987, Silver Image Gallery Ohio State U., Columbus, 1988, Jean-Pierre Lambert Galerie, Paris, 1988, 96, David Winton Bell Gallery, Brown U., Providence, 1989, Toni Burckhead Gallery, Cin., 1989, Rochester Inst. Tech., 1991, Fotomus. im Münchner Stadtmus., Munich, 1992, U. Ky. Art Mus., Lexington, 1993, Internat. Photography Hall, Kirkpatrick Mus. complex, Oklahoma City, 1993, Institut d'Estudios Fotografics de Catalunya, Barcelona, Spain, 1994, Cheekwood Art Mus., Nashville, 1994, Museo Damy di Fotografia Contemporanea, Brescia, Italy, 1995, Photography Gallery U. Notre Dame, Ind., 1995, Louisville Visual Art Assoc., Watertower, Louisville, KY, 1995, Jean-Pierre Lambert Galarie, 1996, Museo Damy, Milan, 1997, Ctr. for Photography, Bombay, India, 1997, Miami U. Art Mus., Oxford, Ohio, 1998, Aronoff Ctr. for the Arts, Cin., 2000, Vine St. Studios, Houston, 2000, Columbus Mus. Art, 2001, Visual Studies Worshop Gall. Rochester, NY, 2000, NuNatte Duo Centre Photography, OP Photo Gall., Hong Kong, 2000, FotoFest, 2000; exhibited in numerous group shows including Robert Klein Gallery, Boston, 1981, Cin. Art Mus., 1981, 84, 85, 93, Witkin Gallery, N.Y.C., 1984, Milw. Art Mus., 1986, Dayton (Ohio) Art Inst., 1987, J.B. Speed Art Mus., Louisville, 1988, Trisolini Gallery Ohio U., 1989, Ohio U., Athens, l989, Centre Nat. Photographie, Paris, 1989, Cleve. Ctr. for Contemporary Art, 1991, Tampa Mus. Art, 1991, 93, Images Gallery, 1991, Dayton Art Inst./Mus. Contemporary Art Wright State U., Dayton, 1992, Bowling Green State U. Sch Art, 1992, Carnegie Arts Ctr., Covington, Ky., 1993, POLK Mus. Art, Lakeland, Fla., 1993, Tampa (Fla.) Mus. Art, 1993, Adams Landing Fine Art Ctr., Cin., 1995, Cheekwood Mus. Art, Nashville, 1995, Photo Forum Gallery, 1995, 96, Jean-Pierre Galerie, 1996, Soros Ctr. Contemporary Art, Kiev, Ukraine, 1996, Dom Khudozhnikiv, Kharkiv, Ukraine, 1996, Wolf Photographic Galleries, Cin., 1996, Columbus Mus. Art, 1996, Mus. fine Arts, St. Petersburg, Fla., 1997, Louisville Visual Art Assn., Water Tower, 1997, Mus. Damy di Fotografia Contemporanea, Brescia, Italy, 1998, Kharkiv Mcpl. Art Gallery, Kharkiv, Ukraine, 1999, Jean-Pierre Lambert Gallery, Paris, 1999, Huntington (W.Va.) Mus. Art, 2000, Centre Socio-Cultural Galerie Pierre Tal Coat, Hunnebont, France, 2000; represented in numerous permanent collections Tampa Mus. of Art, Münchner Stadt Mus., Munich, Germany, Museo Damy, Brescia, Italy, Ctr. Creative Photography, Tucson, Detroit Inst. Arts, Biblioteque National, Paris, Internat. Photography Hall of Fame and Mus., Kirkpatrick Ctr. Mus. Complex, Okla. City, Nelson Gallery-Atkins Mus., Kansas City, Ctr. for Photography, Bombay, Milw. Art Mus., Mus. Photography Arts, San Diego, Musee Nat. D'Art Modern, Cin. Art Mus., High Mus., Atlanta, Mus. Fine Arts, St. Petersburg, Fla., Centre Georges Pompidou, Paris, Denver Art Mus., Boston Mus. Fine Arts, Stanford U. Mus. Art, Palo Alto, Indpls. Art Mus., New Orleans Mus. Art, Fogg Mus., Cambridge, Mass., numerous others; also pvt. collections; author: Petroglyphs of the Heart, Photographs by Connie Sullivan, 1983; work represented in numerous publs. Trustee Images Ctr. for Fine Photography, Cin., 1986-94. Named Hyde Park Living Person of Yr., 1996; recipient Juried Show, Toledo Friends Photography, 1986, Best of show, 1988, Images Gallery, 1986, Pres.'s Coun. for Arts award, Manhattanville Coll., 1991, Treasure of the Month award, Mus. Fine Arts St. Petersburg, Fla., 1995; fellow Arts Midwest fellow, NEA, 1989—90; grantee Aid to Individual Artists grantee, Summerfair, 1987, travel grantee, Ohio Arts Coun., 1995, 1997, 2000, Artist Projects, 1999, 2000. Mem. McDowell Soc. Avocations: travel, reading, gardening, music. Home: 1950 Mount Vernon Dr Fort Wright KY 41011 Fax: 513-871-6931.

SULLIVAN, DANIEL F., academic administrator, sociologist, educator; b. Jan. 19, 1944; m. Ann H. Sullivan; 3 children. BS in Math., St. Lawrence U., 1965; PhD in Sociology, Columbia U., 1971. Ctrl. office supr. N.Y. Tel. Co., Syracuse, 1966—67; rsch. assoc. Barnard Coll., 1969—73, instr. sociology, 1970—71; asst. prof. sociology, sr. rsch. assoc. Cornell U., 1974—76; asst. prof. sociology Carleton Coll., 1971—79, assoc. prof. sociology, 1979—86, dean acad. devel. and planning, 1979—81, v.p. for planning and devel., 1981—86, sec. of the coll., 1981—86; pres. Allegheny Coll., Meadville, Pa., 1986—96, prof. sociology, 1986—96; pres. St. Lawrence U., Canton, NY, 1996—, prof. sociology, 1996—. Mem. adv. com. NSF Divsn. Undergrad. Edn., 1991—; chair bd. trustees St. Lawrence Aquarium and Ecol. Ctr., 1998—; bd. dirs. N.Y. Commn. for Ind. Colls. and Univs., mem. exec. com., 2003; trustee Commn. on Ind. Colls. and Univs., 2002—. Co-author: Research on Human Subjects: Problems and Processes of Social Control in Bio-Medical Experimentation, 1973, Applying Market Research in College Admissions, 1983, What Works: Building Natural Science Communities, 1991. Mem.: Western Pa. Hist. Soc. (trustee 1994—), Am. Assn. Colls. and Univs. (bd. dirs. 2003—). Office: St Lawrence Univ 23 Romoda Dr Canton NY 13617 Office Phone: 315-229-5892. Business E-Mail: dsullivan@stlawu.edu. *

SULLIVAN, DANIEL J., artistic director; b. Wray, Colo., June 11, 1940; s. John Martin and Mary Catherine (Hutton) Sullivan; children: Megan, John, Rachel M. BA, San Francisco State U. Actor Actor's Workshop, San Francisco, 1963—65; actor, dir. Lincoln Ctr. Repertory Theatre, NYC, 1965—73; resident dir. Seattle Repertory Theatre, 1979—81, artistic dir., 1981—97. Actor: (plays) Tiger at the Gates, 1968, Camino Real, 1970, The Good Woman of Setzuan, 1970, The Playboy of the Western World, 1971, Enemies, 1972, The Merchant of Venice, 1973, A Streetcar Named Desire, 1973; asst. dir. (plays) Hair, 1968; dir.: (plays) I'm Not Rappaport, 1985, 2002, The Heidi Chronicles, 1989, Conversations With My Father, 1992, The Sisters Rosensweig, 1993, An American Daughter, 1997, A Moon for the Misbegotten, 2000, Proof, 2000 (Tony award best direction), Major Barbara, 2001, Morning's at Seven, 2002, Short Talks on the Universe, 2002, A Retreat from Moscow, 2003, Sight Unseen, 2004, Brooklyn Boy, 2005, Julius Caesar, 2005, After the Night and the Music, 2005, Rabbit Hole, 2006, Stuff Happens, 2006 (OBIE award Village Voice, 2006, Lucille Lortel award outstanding dir., 2007). Recipient Drama Desk award, NY Theatre Critics award, 1972, MR. Abbott award lifetime achievement in Am. theatre, Stage Directors and Choreographers Found., 2007. Mem.: Nat. Endowments for Arts. Democrat. Office: Seattle Rep Theatre PO Box 900923 Seattle WA 98109-9723 *

SULLIVAN, DANIEL JOSEPH, theater critic; b. Worcester, Mass., Oct. 22, 1935; s. John Daniel and Irene Ann (Flagg) S.; m. Helen Faith Scheid, 1965; children: Margaret Ann, Benjamin, Kathleen. AB, Holy Cross Coll., 1957; postgrad., U. Minn., 1957-59, U. So. Calif., 1964-65, Stanford U., 1978-79. Reporter Worcester Telegram, Mass., 1957, Red Wing Republican Eagle, Minn., 1959, St. Paul Pioneer Press, 1959-61; music and theater critic Mpls. Tribune, 1961—64; comedy writer Dudley Riggs' Brave New Workshop, 1961-64; music, theater reviewer NY Times, 1965—68; theater critic L.A. Times, 1969-90. Dramaturg Eugene O'Neill Theatre Ctr., Waterford, Conn., 1972-73, 93-98; instr. O'Neill Nat. Critics Inst., Waterford, 1977-92, assoc. dir., 1993-98, dir., 1999—; adj. prof. U. Minn., Mpls., 1990—; juror theater panel Nat. Endowment for Arts, 1983; juror Pulitzer Prize for Drama, 1985, 89, 92; pres. LA Drama Critics Circle, 1970-71, Ctr. for Arts Criticism, St. Paul, 1992-95. Mem. Am. Theater Critics Assn. (founding). Office Phone: 612-522-9053. Personal E-mail: sulli008@yahoo.com.

SULLIVAN, DANIEL S., federal agency administrator; married; 3 children. B in Economics magna cum laude, Harvard U.; JD, MS in Fgn. Svc. cum laude, Georgetown U. Law clk. to Hon. Andrew Kleinfeld US Ct. Appeals (9th cir.); law clk. to Chief Justice Warren Matthews Alaska Supreme Ct.; atty. Perkins Coie, LLP; dir., acting sr. dir. Internat. Econ. Directorate The White House, Washington; asst. sec. for econ. and bus. affairs US Dept. State, Washington, 2006—. With USMC, strategic advisor, spl. asst. to comdr. U.S. Ctrl. Command (CENTCOM) USMC, 2005—06. Decorated Def. Meritorious Svc. Medal; named one of 10 Outstanding Young Americans, U.S. Jr. C. of C.; recipient Outstanding Svc. award, Nat. Security Coun. Office: US Dept State Bur Econ and Bus Affairs 2201 C St NW Washington DC 20520

SULLIVAN, DENNIS C., lawyer; b. San Francisco, 1946; AB, U. Calif., Berkeley, 1968, JD, 1972. Bar: Calif. 1972. Counsel Pacific Gas & Elec., 1972—76; assoc. Wilson Sonsini Goodrich & Rosati, 1976—78; founding ptnr. Mosher Pooley & Sullivan, 1978—88; ptnr. Graham & James, Palo Alto, Calif., 1988—93, Gray Cary Ware & Freidenrich, 1993—2004; ptnr., co-chmn. Capital Markets practice group DLA Piper Rudnick Gray Cary, Ea. Palo Alto, Calif., 2005—. Office: DLA Piper Rudnick Gray Cary 2000 University Ave Palo Alto CA 94303 Office Phone: 650-833-2243. Office Fax: 650-833-2001. Business E-Mail: dennis.sullivan@dlapiper.com.

SULLIVAN, DENNIS JAMES, JR., retired hospitality and music executive; b. Jersey City, Feb. 23, 1932; s. Dennis James and Mary Theresa (Coyle) S.; m. Constance Rosemary Shields, Jan. 31, 1953; children: Denise Sullivan Morrison, Mary Agnes Sullivan Wilderotter, Colleen Sullivan Bastkowski, Andrea Sullivan Doelling. AB, St. Peters Coll., 1953; postgrad., U. Md., 1955; MBA, U. Pa., 1973. Various line and staff positions N.J. Bell, 1955-61, N.Y. Telephone Co., 1961-64, 67-68, AT&T, NYC, 1964—67, 1968—72, dir. mktg., 1972-74, asst. v.p., 1974-76; v.p. mktg. Ohio Bell Telephone Co., Cleve., 1976-78; v.p. consumer info. services AT&T-Am. Bell, Parsippany, N.J., 1978-83; exec. v.p. Cin. Bell Telephone Co., 1983-84, pres., 1984-87, also bd. dirs.; exec. v.p., chief fin. officer Cin. Bell Inc., 1987-93; exec. counselor Dan Pinger Pub. Rels., 1993-2000; pres., CEO Gaylord Entertainment, Nashville, 2000—02. Bd. dirs. Fifth Third Bancorp & Bank, Anthem Ins. Co., The Future Now, Intefrated Techs. Inc., Kalthoff Internat. Author: Videotex, IEE Nat. Conf., 1981. Bd. dirs. Boy Scouts, Cin. Bd. Edn., 1993-97; gen. chmn. United Way, 1990—. Lt. (j.g.) USN, 1953-55, ret. comdr. USNR, 1976. Mem. Fin. Exec. Inst., Commonwealth Club, Cin. Country Club, Queen City Club, Legatus. Roman Catholic. E-mail: dennisj37@marcocable.com.

SULLIVAN, DENNIS P., mathematics professor; b. Port Huron, Mich., 1941; PhD, Princeton U., 1965; doctorate (hon.), Ecole Normale Superieure de Lyon, France, 2002. Albert Einstein chair in Sci., grad. ctr. CUNY; disting. prof. math. SUNY, Stony Brook. Invited spkr. Internat. Congress of Math., 1970, 86. Recipient Elie Cartan prize, French Acad. Sciences, 1981, King Faisal Internat. prize of Sci., 1994, Nat. Medal Science in Math., 2004. Mem.: Am. Math. Soc. (Veblen prize 1971, Leroy P. Steele prize for Lifetime Achievement 2006), NAS. Office: Graduate Ctr CUNY 365 Fifth Ave New York NY 10016-4309

SULLIVAN, DIANE P., lawyer; b. Elizabeth, NJ; BA cum laude, Fairfield U., 1984; JD, U. Pa., 1987. Bar: NJ 1987, U.S. Dist. Ct. (NJ Dist.) 1987, U.S. Dist. Ct. (So. and ea. dist. NY) 2003. Ptnr. mass torts and product liability group Dechert LLP, Princeton, NJ, 2001—. Bd. trustees Trial Attys. NJ, 2000—04; mem. policy com. Dechert LLP; lectr. in field. Named one of Top 40 Litigators Under 40, Nat. Law Jour., 2002, The Nation's Top Litigators, 2007, Top 10 Lawyers in the Country, Lawyers Weekly USA, 2005. Mem.: ABA, Internat. Assn. Def. Counsel (mem. trial acad. faculty 2002), Def. Rsch. Inst., NJ State Bar Assn. Office: Dechert LLP Princeton Pike Corp Ctr PO Box 5218 Princeton NJ 08543-5218 Office Phone: 609-620-3232. Office Fax: 609-620-3259. E-mail: diane.sullivan@dechert.com. *

SULLIVAN, DOROTHY RONA, state official; b. Jan. 7, 1941; d. Lewis Robert and Dorothy (Hopkins) Sullivan. BA, Boston U., 1963; MEd, State Coll. Boston, 1966; CAGS, Boston U., 1972; postgrad., Northeastern U., 1970—71, Boston Coll., 1974—78, U. Mass., 1980. Rsch. asst. Boston Lying-In Hosp., 1963—64; employment counselor Mass. Divsn. Employment Security, Boston, 1964—66, sr. employment counselor, 1966—67, prin. employment counselor, 1967—70, employment office mgr., 1970—75, supr., 1975—78, chief rsch. dept., 1978—88, dir. def. employment analysis, 1985—87; chief rsch. dept. Mass. Divsn. Employment and Tng., 1989—98, 1998—2002. Supr. cmty. counselor interns and rehab. adminstrn. interns Northeastern U. Grad. Sch. Edn., 1968—74; supr. pub. adminstrn. interns Suffolk U., 1976; supr. econ. interns Boston U., 1979, Regis Coll., 1984, U. Mass.-Boston, 1998; presenter in field. Author: Boston Employment Service Guide, 1969, Careers and Training in the Allied Health Field, 1989, Higher Skills, Higher Wages and Higher Achievement, 1997, Career Families and Career Paths, 1997, Massachusetts Cities and Towns, 1978—82, Outplacement Program, 1993, Presentation and Performance Portfolio, 1998; editor: Mass. Trends, 1978—82; mem. editl. bd. Memos to the Gov., Mgmt. Advice from the Commonwealth's Experts in Pub. Adminstrn., 2003; contbr. articles to profl. jours.; exhibitions include Brookline Arts Ctr., Brookline Pub. Libr., Chatham Creative Arts Ctr. Recorder Gov.'s Conf. on Rehab., 1970; mem. Gov.'s Commn. Employment of Handicapped, 1972—78, Pres.'s Com. Employment of Handicapped, 1975—78; exec. bd. Greater Boston coun. Camp Fire Girls, 1971—73; R.S.V.P. adv. bd. Boston Commn. Affairs of the Elderly, 1977—78; mem. adv. com. equal employment opportunity practices Dept. Pers. Adminstrn., 1984—85; mem. adv. group Mass. Occupl. Info. Coordinating Com., 1991—98; mem. adv. bd. Mass. Ctr. Civic Edn., 2001—; bd. dirs. Doric Dames, Mass. State Ho., 2004—; 2nd v.p. Doric Docents, 2006; bd. dirs. Ethas (Boston Sr. Svcs. Agy.), 2004—. Recipient Recognition award, Nat. Occupl. Info. Coordinating Com., 1994, Exceptional Achievement award, U.S. Sec. Labor, 2003, Pres. Vol. Svc. award, 2004. Mem.: ASPA, AACD, ACA (recorder), Am. Bus. Women's Assn. (del. nat. conv. 1980, 1983, pres. Boston chpt. 1982, Woman of Yr,. Boston chpt. 1983), Am. Econ. Assn., Am. Acad. Polit. and Social Sci., Am. Fedn. State, County and Mcpl. Employees (exec. bd. local 164 1972—73, 1974—76), Nat. Rehab. Assn. (Mass. sec. 1971—72, exec. bd. 1972—74, v.p. 1974—75, pres. 1976—77), Nat. Career Devel. Assn., Am. Personnel Guidance Assn. (nat. recorder conf. 1968), Am. Soc. Pub. Adminstrn. (life; region I-II liaison, sect. women in pub. adminstrn. 1988—90, Mass. chpt. coun., officer, treas. 1997, sec. 1998, v.p. 1998—, pres.-elect 1999, pres. 2000, nat. coun. campaign for internat. rels.), Charitable Irish Soc., Rockport Art Assn. (patron), Boston Ctr. for Internat. Visitors, Chatham Swim Club. Home: 33 Morey Rd Roslindale MA 02131-1037 also: Eldredge Sq Chatham MA 02633

SULLIVAN, DWIGHT H., military lawyer; b. 1961; m. Lynne I. Sullivan. BA, U. Md.; grad., U. Va. Sch. Las, 1986. Atty. USMC, 1987—97; mng. atty. ACLU Md., Balt., 1997—2003; appellate def. counsel Navy-Marine Corps Divsn., 2003—04; atty. advisor Ct. of Appeals for the Armed Forces, 2004—05; chief def. counsel US Dept. Def. Office Mil. Commns., 2005—. Col. USMCR, 2005—. Office: Office Mil Commns The Pentagon Washington DC 20301

SULLIVAN, E. THOMAS, law educator; b. Amboy, Ill., Dec. 4, 1948; s. Edward McDonald and Mary Lorraine (Murphy) S.; m. Susan A. Sullivan, Oct. 2, 1971. BA, Drake U., 1970; JD, Ind. U., Indpls., 1973. Bar: Ind. 1973, Fla. 1974, D.C. 1975, Mo. 1980. Law clk. to Judge Joe Eaton, U.S. Dist. Ct. for So. Dist. Fla., Miami, 1973-75; trial atty. U.S. Dept. Justice, Washington, 1975-77; sr. assoc. Donovan, Leisure, Newton & Irvine, Washington, 1977-79; prof. law U. Mo., Columbia, 1979-84; assoc. dean, prof. Washington U., St. Louis, 1984-89; dean U. Ariz. Coll. Law, Tucson, 1989-95; William S. Pattee prof. law, dean U. Minn. Law Sch., Mpls., 1995—2002, Irving Younger prof. law, 2002—, sr. vice-pres., provost, 2004—. Fellow Am. Bar Found., mem. Am. Law Inst., Am. Econ. Assn. Office: U Minn Law Sch Walter F Mondale Hall Office 381 229 19th Ave S Minneapolis MN 55455 Home: 182 Bank St Se Minneapolis MN 55414-1042

SULLIVAN, EDWARD DELANO, lawyer, investor; s. Joseph Daniel and Eugenia Rose Sullivan; m. Elizabeth Wilhelmina Frank, June 26, 1954; children: Elizabeth Sullivan Rolfe, Kathleen Sullivan Fleming, Maureen Sullivan Fengler, Caroline Sullivan Piper, Alice Sullivan Tucker, April Sullivan Fitzgerald, Virginia Elaine. BS in Bus. Adminstrn., U. Conn., Storrs, 1954; JD, U. Okla. Coll. Law, Norman, 1958; grad. Judge Advocate Course Res., U. Va., Charlottesville, 1965; grad. Nat. Sec. Seminar, Indsl. Coll. of Armed Forces, 1974; grad. Sr. Staff Judge Advocate course, Air U., 1976; grad., U.S. Air Force War Coll., 1978. Bar: Okla. 1958, Conn. 1960, U.S. Supreme Ct. 1967, Fla. 1979; cert. in mgmt. devel. Fla. Atlantic U., 1977, pub. purchasing officer Nat. Inst. Govtl. Purchasing, lic. comml. pilot with seaplane rating FAA. Pvt. practice, Bridgeport, Conn., 1960—, Fort Lauderdale, Fla., 1979—. Dir. Nat. Inst. Govtl. Purchasing, 1965—68. Col. JAG USAF, 1954—84. Decorated Commendation medal with Oak Leaf Cluster USAF, Humanitarian medal, Meritorious Svc. medal, Legion of Merit medal; named Hon. Lt. Col. Aide-de-Camp, Ala. State Militia, 1976, Hon. Mayor, City of San Antonio, 1996; recipient Committment to Corporate Spirit plaque, Warren Robins AFB, GA, 1984, Boston Bar Assn. award, 1971. Mem.: SAR (chpt. pres. 1990—91, Fla. state pres. 1998—99, nat. trustee 1999—2000, pres. coun. of state pres.'s 1999—2000), ABA (sr.), Ga. Govtl. Purchasing Assn. (hon.), Freedon Found. (life), Air Force Assn., Pilgrim John Howland Soc., Delano Kindred (com. mem.), Gen. Soc. of Mayflower Descendants (asst. gen. 1996—99, dep. gov. gen. 1999—2002, counsellor gen. 2003—05, gov. gen 2005—), Res. Officers Assn. U.S. (life), Nat. Gavel Soc. (life), Mil. Officers Assn. Am. (life), Mayflower Soc. State of Fla. (gov. John Alden Colony (Ft. Lauderdale chpt.) 1988—90, state dep. gov. 1990—93, state gov. 1993—96, Fla. counsellor 2003—05), Hugenot Soc. Fla. (pres. (Louis Du Bois chpt.)), Alden Kindred, Phi Alpha Delta. Address: 2837 NE 27th St Fort Lauderdale FL 33306-1912

SULLIVAN, EDWARD JOSEPH, lawyer; b. Bklyn., Apr. 24, 1945; s. Edward Joseph and Bridget (Duffy) S.; m. Patte Hancock, Aug. 7, 1982; children: Amy Brase, Molly Elsasser, Mary Christine. BA, St. John's U., 1966; JD, Willamette U., 1969; MA, cert. Urban Studies, Portland State U., 1973; LLM, Univ. Coll., London, 1978; diploma in law, Univ. Coll., Oxford, 1984; MA, U. Durham, 1999. Bar: Oreg. 1969, D.C. 1978, Wash. 2001, U.S. Dist. Ct. Oreg. 1970, U.S. Ct. Appeals (9th cir.) 1970, U.S. Supreme Ct. 1972. Counsel Washington County, Hillsboro, Oreg., 1969-75; legal counsel Gov. of Oreg., Salem, 1975-77; ptnr. O'Donnell, Sullivan & Ramis, Portland, Oreg., 1978-84, Sullivan, Josselson, Roberts, Johnson & Kloos, Portland, Salem and Eugene, Oreg., 1984-86, Mitchell, Lang & Smith, Portland, 1986-90, Preston Gates & Ellis, Portland, 1990—2003; owner Garvey Schubert Barer, Portland, Oreg., 2003—. Bd. dirs., pres. Oreg. Law Inst. Contbr. numerous articles to profl. jours. Chmn. Capitol Planning Commn., Salem, 1975-77, 78-81. Mem. ABA (local govt. sect., com. on planning and zoning, adminstrv. law sect.) Oreg. State Bar Assn., D.C. Bar Assn., Wash. State Bar Assn., Am. Judicature Soc., Am. Polit. Sci. Assn. Democrat. Roman Catholic. Office: Garvey Schubert Barer 121 SW Morrison Ste 1100 Portland OR 97204-3141 Office Phone: 503-228-3939. Business E-Mail: esullivan@gsblaw.com.

SULLIVAN, EDWARD LAWRENCE, lawyer; b. Boston, May 8, 1955; s. Edward L. and Dorothy L. (Gregory) S.; m. Susan M. Griffin, Dec. 2, 1983; children: Erica A., Brittany M. BA in Polit. Sci., St. Anselm Coll., 1977; JD, St. Louis U., 1980. Bar: Mo. 1980, Mass. 1981, Ill. 1981, D.C. 1986. Atty., Ill. divsn. Peabody Coal Co., Fairview Heights, 1980-85; legis. counsel Peabody Holding Co., Washington, 1985-88; dir., legal and pub. affairs, western divsn. Peabody Coal Co., Flagstaff, Ariz., 1988-90; sr. counsel Peabody Holding Co., St. Louis, 1990-94; gen. counsel Powder

River Coal Co., Gillette, Wyo., 1994-95; gen. counsel, western region Peabody Holding Co., St. Louis, 1995—2000; sr. counsel Peabody Energy Corp. (formerly known as Peabody Holding Co.), St. Louis, 2000—. Industry rep. royalty policy com. U.S. Dept. Interior, Washington, 1995—. Mem. Bar Assn. Met. St. Louis. Office: Peabody Energy Corp 701 Market St Ste 700 Saint Louis MO 63101-1895 Office Phone: 314-342-3400.

SULLIVAN, EMMET G., judge; b. Washington, June 4, 1947; s. Emmet A. and Eileen G. Sullivan; m. Nan Sullivan; children, Emmet, Erik. BA in Polit. Sci., Howard U., 1968, JD, 1971. Law clk. to Hon. James A. Washington, Jr. Superior Ct. D.C.; from assoc. to ptnr. Houston and Gardner, 1973-80; ptnr. Houston, Sullivan & Gardner, 1980-84; judge Superior Ct. D.C., 1984-92, U.S. Dist. Ct., D.C., 1992—94, U.S. Ct. Appeals, D.C. cir., 1994—. Commr. D.C. Judicial Nominating Commn. Mem. bd. dir. & exec. com. Council for Ct. Excellence, Washington; mem. Com. on Criminal Law & chmn. legis. subcommittee Judicial Conf. U.S.; mem. bd. dir. Frederick Abramson Memorial Found., DC. Reginald Heber Smith fellow; recipient Thurgood Marshall Award of Excellence. Office: US Courthouse Rm 2327 333 Constitution Ave NW Washington DC 20001-2822

SULLIVAN, EUGENE JOHN JOSEPH, manufacturing executive, director; b. NYC, Nov. 28, 1920; s. Cornelius and Margaret (Smith) S.; m. Gloria Roesch, Aug. 25, 1943; children: Eugene John Joseph, Edward J., Robert C., Elizabeth Ann Hansler. BS, St. John's U., 1942, D in Commerce, 1973; MBA, NYU, 1948. With chem. divsn. Borden, Inc., NYC, 1946—, beginning as salesman, successively asst. sales, 1957-58, exec. v.p., 1958-64; pres. Borden Chem. Co. divsn. Borden, Inc.; v.p. Borden, Inc., 1964-67, exec. v.p., 1967-73, pres., COO, 1973-79, chmn., pres., CEO, 1979-86; prof. St. John's U., 1987—2003. Bd. dirs. W.R. Grace & Co.; chmn. bd. dirs. Hamilton Fund; trustee Atlantic Mut. Ins. Co. Trustee, vice chmn., past sec. St. John's U., chmn. bd. dirs., 1999—; trustee N.Y. Med. Coll., Cath. Health Assn., Cath. Charities U.S.A., 1999—; chmn. Commn. on Cath. Health Care. Served as lt. USNR, 1942-46; lt. Res. Mem. Coun. Fgn. Rels., Knights of Malta, Knights of Holy Sepulchre, Knights of St. Gregory, Univ. Club, Plandome Country Club. Personal E-mail: gene5978@aol.com.

SULLIVAN, EUGENE RAYMOND, federal judge; b. St. Louis, Aug. 2, 1941; s. Raymond Vincent and Rosemary (Kiely) S.; m. Lis Urup Johansen, June 18, 1966; children— Kim, Eugene II. BS, U.S. Mil. Acad., 1964; JD, Georgetown U., 1971; HDL (hon.), New Eng. Sch. Law, 2001. Bar: Mo. 1972, D.C. 1972. Law clk. to Hon. M.C. Matthes US Ct. Appeals (8th Cir.), St. Louis, 1971—72; assoc. Patton Boggs & Blow LLP, Washington, 1972—74; asst. spl. counsel to Pres. The White House, Washington, 1974; trial counsel US Dept. Justice, Washington, 1974—82; dep. gen. counsel Dept. Air Force, US Dept. Def., Washington, 1982—84; gen. counsel USAF, Washington, 1982—86; gov. of Wake Island, 1984—86; judge US Ct. Appeals AF, Washington, 1986—90, 1995—2002, chief judge, 1990—95, sr. judge, 2002—; co-founder, prin. Gavel Consulting Group, 2003—. Mem. Fed. Commn. To Study Honor Code at West Point, 1989-90. Author: (book) The Majority Rules, 2005. Trustee U.S. Mil. Acad., 1989—; bd. Duke Law, Ethics, and Nat. Security Ctr., 2001-. Airborne ranger US Army, 1964—69, Vietnam, ranger instr. Decorated Bronze Star, Air medal, airborne badge, ranger badge, others; Castle award, West Point Soc., 2001, Medal of Justice, Romania, Medal of Defense, 1st Class, Hungary, Defense Minister Citation, ROC; installed as Disting. Mem. Army Ranger Training Brigade, 2006. Republican. Roman Catholic. Avocation: writing. Business E-Mail: esullivan@gavelconsultinggroup.com, judgesullivan@west-point.org.

SULLIVAN, FRANK, JR., state supreme court justice; b. Mar. 21, 1950; s. Frank E. and Colette (Cleary) S.; m. Cheryl Gibson, June 14, 1972; children: Denis M., Douglas S., Thomas R. AB cum laude, Dartmouth Coll., 1972; JD magna cum laude, Ind. U., 1982; LLM, U. Va., 2001. Bar: Ind. 1982. Mem. staff Office of U.S. Rep. John Brademas, 1974-79, dir. staff, 1975-78; with Barnes & Thornburg, Indpls., 1982-89; budget dir. State of Ind., 1989-92; exec. asst. Office of Gov. Evan Bayh, 1993; assoc. justice Ind. Supreme Ct., 1993—. Chair Ind. Supreme Ct. Judicial Technology & Automation Com. Mem. ABA (vice chair appellate judges conf.), Ind. State Bar Assn., Indpls. Bar Assn. Home: 5854 Lawton Loop West Dr Indianapolis IN 46216-2009 Office: Ind Supreme Ct State House Rm 321 Indianapolis IN 46204-2728 Home Phone: 317-549-3926; Office Phone: 317-232-2548.

SULLIVAN, FRANK C., manufacturing executive; BA, U. N.C., 1983. Various comml. lending corp. fin. 1st Union Nat. Bank and Harris Bank, 1983-87; regional sales mgr. AGR Co. RPM Group, Inc., 1987-89, dir. corp. devel., 1989-91, v.p., 1991-93, CFO, 1993-98, exec. v.p., 1998-99, pres., 1999—2002, pres., CEO, 2002—. Bd. dir. Timken Co. Bd. mem. Greater Cleveland Chpt., Am. Red Cross, Cleveland Rock & Roll Hall of Fame & Mus. Morehead scholar, 1983. Mem.: Cuyahoga County Bluecoats. Office: RPM International PO Box 777 2628 Pearl Rd Medina OH 44256 Office Phone: 330-273-5090. *

SULLIVAN, G. CRAIG, household products executive; b. 1940; BS, Boston Coll., 1964. With Procter & Gamble Co., 1964-69, Am. Express Co., 1969-70; regional sales mgr. Clorox Co., Oakland, Calif., 1971-76, v.p. mktg., 1976-78, mgr. food svc. sales devel., mgr. bus. devel., 1978-79, gen. mgr. food svc. products divsn., 1979-81, v.p. food svc. products divsn., 1981, v.p. household products, 1981-89, group v.p. household products, 1989-92, chmn. bd., pres., CEO, 1992-99, chmn. bd., CEO, 1999—2003; ret., 2003.

SULLIVAN, GEORGE EDWARD, writer; b. Lowell, Mass., Aug. 11, 1927; s. Timothy Joseph and Cecilia Mary (Shea) S.; m. Muriel Agnes Moran, May 24, 1952; 1 son, Timothy. BS, Fordham U., Bronx, NY, 1952. Pub. relations mgr. Popular Library, NYC, 1952-55; pub. relations dir. AMF, NYC, 1955-63. Adj. prof. Fordham U. Author: Mathew Brady, His Life and Photographs, 1994 (named a Notable Children's Trade Book in Field of Social Studies, Nat. Coun. Social Studies and Children's Book Coun., Teenage Book of Yr. NY Pub. Libr., Recommended Children's Book for Reading and Sharing, 1994, Recommended as a Book of Gt. Interest, Gt. Books for Boys, 1998), Slave Ship, The Story of the Henrietta Marie, 1994 (named Best Book of 1994 Selection, Parents Mag., Best Children's Book of Yr. Selection, Children's Book Com., Bank St. Coll. Edn.), The Day Women Got the Vote, 1994, Pitchers: Twenty Seven of Baseball's Greatest, 1994(named Teenage Book of Yr., NY Pub. Libr., A Recommended Book for Reluctant Young Adult Reader, ALA), Black Artists in Photography, 1995, Women War Spies, 1996, Alamo, 1996, Black Artists as Photographers, 1840-1940, 1996(named Teenage Book of Yr., NY Pub. Libr., A Best Children's Book of Yr. Selection, Children's Book Com., Bank St. Coll. Edn.), Glovemen: Twenty-Seven of Baseball's Greatest, 1996 (named a Teenage Book of Yr., NY Pub. Libr., A Recommended Book for Reluctant Young Adult Reader, ALA), Not Guilty: Six Times When Justice Failed, 1996, To the Bottom of the Sea, 1998, Burnin' Rubber: Behind the Scenes in Stock Car Racing, 1998, One Hundred Years in Photographs, 1999, Picturing Lincoln: Famous Photographs that Popularized the President, 1999(Selected as a Notable Social Studies Trade Book, Children's Book Coun., named a Best Children's Book of Yr. Selection, Children's Book Com., Bank St. Coll. Edn.), Portraits of War, Civil War Photographers and Their Work, 2000, One Hundred Years in Photographs, 2000, The Civil War at Sea, 2001 (Selected as a Notable Social Studies Trade Book, Children's Book Coun., named a Teenage Book of Yr., NY Pub. Libr.), In Their Own Words: Lewis & Clark, 2001, In Their Own Words: Harriet Tubman, 2001, In Their Own Words: Helen Keller, 2001 (named a Best Children's Book of Yr. Selection, Children's Book Com., Bank St. Coll. Edn.), Power Football, 2001, In Their Own Words: The Wright Brothers, 2002 (Selected by US Agy. for Internat. Devel. to Promote Reading in North Africa, reprinted in Arabic), In Their Own Words: Abraham Lincoln, 2002 (Named a Best Children's Book of Yr. Selection, Children's Book Com., Bank St. Coll. Edn.), Mr. President: A Book of U.S. Presidents, 2004, The Civil War Photographs of Mathew Brady, 2004, Journalists at Risk: Reporting America's Wars, 2005, Built to Last, 2005, Berenice Abbott, Photographer: An Independent Vision, 2006, Helen Keller: Her Life in Pictures, 2007. Served with USN, 1945-48. Mem. PEN, Authors Guild, Soc. Children's Book Writers & Illustrators. Roman Catholic. Office Phone: 212-689-9745. Personal E-mail: gjsbooks@rcn.com.

SULLIVAN, GEORGE MURRAY, transportation executive, consultant, retired mayor; b. Portland, Oreg., Mar. 31, 1922; s. Harvey Patrick and Viola (Murray) S.; m. Margaret Eagan, Dec. 30, 1947; children: Timothy M., Harvey P. (dec. July 1996), Daniel A., Kevin Shane, Colleen Marie, George Murray, Michael J., Shannon Margaret, Casey Eagan. D.P.A. (hon.), U. Alaska, 1981. Line driver Alaska Freight Lines, Inc., Valdez-Fairbanks, 1942-44; US dep. marshal Alaska Dist., Nenana, 1946-52; mgr. Alaska Freight Lines, 1952-56; Alaska gen. mgr. Consol. Freightways Corp. of Del., Anchorage, 1956-67; mayor of Anchorage, 1967-82; exec. mgr. Alaska Bus. Council, 1968; sr. cons. to pres. Western Air Lines Inc., 1982-87; former legis. liaison for Gov. of Alaska; now cons. Past mem. Nat. Adv. Com. on Oceans and Atmosphere, Joint Fed.-State Land Use Planning Commn.; past chmn. 4-state region 10 adv. com. OEO; mem. Fairbanks City Council, 1955-59, Anchorage City Council, 1965-67, Greater Anchorage Borough Assembly, 1965-67, Alaska Ho. of Reps., 1964-65. Trustee U. Alaska Found.; chmn. Anchorage Conv. and Visitors Bur.; bd. dirs. Western council Boy Scouts Am., 1958-59. Served with U.S. Army, 1944-46. Mem. Nat. Def. Transp. Assn. (life mem., pres. 1962-63), Nat. League Cities (dir.), Pioneers of Alaska, Alaska Mcpl. League (past pres.), Anchorage C. of C. (exec. com. 1963-65, treas. 1965-66, dir.), Alaska Carriers Assn. (exec. com.), Alaska Transp. Conf. (chmn.), U.S. Conf. Mayors (exec. com.), VFW (comdr. Alaska 1952) Clubs: Elks. Home and Office: George M Sullivan Co 1345 W 12th Ave Anchorage AK 99501-4252 Office Phone: 907-272-2918. *America is truly the land of opportunity, and I feel that the success with which God has blessed my life attests to this fact. I have been blessed four times. Not only was I born in America, but I have lived my life in Alaska. My other two blessings are my wonderful and supportive wife and our eight healthy children.*

SULLIVAN, GLENN D., music educator; b. Ridgewood, NJ, Mar. 1, 1975; s. Gerald W. and Beverly Sullivan. MusB Music Mgmt., William Paterson U., 1998. Music instr. Partesi Music Svcs., Inc., South Plainfield, NJ, 1993—. Pvt. music instr., Wayne, NJ, 1991—. Asst. dir. N.J. Diocesan Honors Band, 1998—; asst. music dir. Pentecostal Lighthouse Ch., Paterson, NJ, 1990—98, Midvale Gospel Ch., Wanaque, NJ, 2000—02, 2004—. Mem.: Music Educators Nat. Conf. Avocations: computers, music. Home: 31 Emerson Pl Wayne NJ 07470 E-mail: gds3175@optonline.net.

SULLIVAN, GORDON R., military association executive, retired military officer; b. Boston, Sept. 25, 1937; s. Russsell Edgar and Penuel Edith (Gordon) S.; m. Miriam Gay Loftus, June 20, 1965; children: John, Mark, Elizabeth. BA in History, Norwich U., 1959, D Mil. Sci. (hon.), 1991; MA in Polit. Sci., U. N.H., 1974. Commd. 2d lt. U.S. Army, 1959, advanced through grades to gen., 1990, ret., 1995; student Armor Officer Basic Course U.S. Army Armor Sch., Ft. Knox, Ky., 1959-60; platoon leader Co. B, 1st Medium Tank Bn., 66th Armor, 2d Armored Div., Ft. Hood, Tex., 1960; student Armor Communication Class U.S. Army Armor Sch., Ft. Knox, 1960; communications officer 1st Medium Tank Bn., 66th Armor, 2d Armored Div., Ft. Hood, 1960-61; comdr. Co. A, 1st Medium tank Bn., 66th Armor,. 2d Armored Div., Ft. Hood, 1961; bn. communications officer 3d Medium Tank Bn. (Patton), 40th Armor, U.S. Army Pacific, Republic of Korea, 1961-62; platoon leader Co. A 3d Medium Tank Bn., 40th Armor, U.S. Army Pacific, Korea, 1962; asst. civil guard/self def. corps advisor 21st Inf. Div., Mil. Assistance Adv. Group, Vietnam, 1962-63; adminstrv. officer, later exec. asst. Office of Asst. Chief of Staff, J2 Div., Mil. Assistance Command, Vietnam, 1963-64; student Armor Officer Advanced Course U.S. Army Armor Sch., Ft. Knox, 1964-65; S-4 (Logistics) 3d Bn., 32d Armor, 3d Armored Div., U.S. Army Europe, 1965-66; comdr. Co.A, 3d Bn., 32d Armor, 3d Armored Div., U.S. Army Europe, 1966; assignment officer, later staff officer Combat Arms Sect., Mil. Pers. Div., Office of Dep. Chief of Staff for Pers., U.S. Army Europe, 1966-68; student U.S. Army Command Gen. Staff Coll., Ft. Leavenworth, Kans., 1968-69; pers. svcs. officer Plans and Ops. Div., G-1, Hdqrs., I Field Force, Vietnam, 1969-70; pers. mgmt. officer Pers. Actions Sect., Armor Br., Office of Pers. Ops., Washington, 1970-73; student Internat. Rels. U. N.H., Durham, 1973-74; comdr. 4th Bn., 73d Armor, 1st Inf. Div. (Forward), U.S. Army Europe, 1975-76; chief of staff 1st Inf. Div. (Forward), U.S. Army Europe, 1976-77; student U.S. Army War Coll., Carlisle Barracks, Pa., 1977-78; asst. chief of staff G-3 (Ops.)/Dir. Plans and Tng., 1st Inf. Div. and Fort Riley, Kans., 1978-79, G-3 (Ops.), VII Corps, U.S. Army Europe, 1980-81; comdr. 1st Brigade, 3d Armored Div., U.S. Army Europe, 1981-83; chief of staff 3d Armored Div., U.S. Army Europe, 1983; asst. comdt. U.S. Army Armor Sch., Ft. Knox, 1983-85; dep. chief of staff for support Cen. Army Group, Europe, 1985-87; dep. comdt. U.S. Army Command and Gen. Staff Coll., Ft. Leavenworth, 1987-88; comdg. gen. 1st Inf. Div. (Mechanized), Ft. Riley, 1988-89; dep. chief of staff for ops. and plans US Army, Washington, 1989-90, vice chief of staff, 1990-91, chief of staff, 1991-95; pres. Coleman Federal, 1995—97; pres., COO Assn of the US Army, Arlington, Va., 1998—. Bd. dirs Newell Rubbermaid, 1999-, Electronic Warfare Associates, Inc., Inst. Def. Analysis Co-author (with Michael V. Harper) Hope Is Not a Method, 1996; editor: Portrait of an Army, 1991. Chmn. bd. trustees, Norwich U., chmn. emeritus Marshall Legacy Inst. Decorated D.S.M., Def. Superior Svc. medal, Legion of Merit, Bronze Star, Purple Heart, Meritorius Svc. medal with oak leaf cluster, Joint Svc. Commendation medal, Army Commendation medal with oak leaf cluster, Army Achievement medal, Combat Infantryman badge. Mem. Assn. of U.S. Army, Armor Assn. Office: Assn of the US Army 2425 Wilson Blvd Arlington VA 22201

SULLIVAN, GREGORY PAUL, secondary school educator; b. Buffalo, June 13, 1957; s. Jerome Patrick and Gloria Mae (Struble) S.; m. Sarah Davis Houston, May 17, 1986; children: Patrick Benjamin, Ryan Christopher. BS in Indsl. Edn., State U. Coll., Oswego, NY, 1979; MA in Indsl. Edn., Ball State U., 1983. postgrad. collegiate profl. teaching cert. Grad. asst. mfg. lab. Ball State U., Muncie, Ind., 1982-83; tchr. tech. edn. John Rolfe Mid. Sch., Richmond, Va., 1979-86, Horton Mid. Sch., Pittsboro, N.C., 1986-88, Dunbar Mid. Sch., Lynchburg, Va., 1988-93; supr. career-tech. programs Lynchburg City Schs., 1993—. Coord./judge regional and nat. mfg. contest Tech. Edn. and Collegiate Assn., 1988—; coord. Eisenhower Grant, 1991-92. Asst. dir. Camp Minnehaha, Minnehaha Springs, W.Va., 1979-88. Named Va. Tchr. of Yr., Va. Dept. Edn., 1993. Mem. Soc. Mfg. Engrs. (internat. edn. com. career guidance 1984, 91), Internat. Tech. Edn. Assn. (mem. editl. rev. bd. The Tech. Tchr., delphi com. critical issues and concerns tech. edn. 1992), Coun. Tech. Tchr. Edn. (student svcs. com. 1991), Va. Tech. Edn. Assn. (v.p. 1997, 98), Va. Coun. Tech. Edn. Suprs. (pres. 1997), Phi Delta Kappa, Epsilon Pi Tau, Kappa Delta Pi. Avocations: intramural sports, golf, tennis, running. Office: Lynchburg City Schools PO Box 2497 Lynchburg VA 24505-2497 Home: 1512 Sanglоe Pl Lynchburg VA 24502

SULLIVAN, JAMES EDWARD, poet; b. Cohasset, Mass., July 11, 1928; s. James J. Jr. and E. Louise (Hyland) S.; m. Frances Elizabeth Lynch, Aug. 11, 1963 (dec. Oct. 1976); children: Julia Marietta, John Franklin Joseph. AB, Boston Coll., 1948, MA, 1950. Dir. Woods Meml. Libr., Barre, Mass., 1967-94; ptnr. Crisis and Climax, 1989—. Lectr. in history, Boston Coll., 1962-63. Author: American Town: Barre, Mass., 1774-1974, 1974, In Order of Appearance: 400 Poems, 1988, numerous poems, plays; weekly contbr. original poetry Barre (Mass.) Gazette, 1981—. Selectman, Town of Barre, 1986-92, bd. chmn., 1988-92. Sgt. U.S. Army, 1950-52. Mem.: Am. Legion (past comdr. Barre Post 2). Democrat. Roman Catholic. Home: PO Box 451 Barre MA 01005-0451

SULLIVAN, JAMES F., physicist, researcher; b. Cin., Mar. 7, 1943; s. James E. and Alma L. (Lienesch) S.; m. Sylvia J. Kasselmann, Aug. 16, 1969; 1 child, Robert L. BS, Xavier U., Cin., 1965, MS, 1969. Instr. physics Brebeuf Prep. Sch., Indpls., 1965-67, OMI Coll. Applied Sci., U. Cin., 1968-71, asst. prof. physics, 1971-77, assoc. prof. physics, 1977-88, prof. physics, 1988—; dept. head math., physics, computing tech. U. Cin. OMI Coll. of Applied Sci., 2002—. Summer faculty rschr. Solar Energy Rsch. Inst., Golden, Colo., 1980; mem. high sch. evaluation team N. Ctrl. Assn., Cin., 1983-85; vis. prof. Arcada Polytechnic Inst., Finland, 2001; rep. U. Cin. Grad. Ceremony, Delta Acad. Mansoura, Egypt, 2004. Author: Technical Physics, 1988; Co-author: Laboratory Manual for General Physics, 1973, 83, 90, 92, Physics for Technology Laboratory Manual, 1995, 97. Organizer of events St. Xavier H.S. Alumni, Cin., 1983—; vol. examiner Am. Radio Relay League for U.S. Fed. Comm. Commn., Newington, Conn., 1984—; judge physics category Ohio State Sci. Fair, Delaware, Ohio, 1986—; chief negotiator faculty and librs. U. Cin., 1995. Received John B. Hart award (disting. svc. to Southern Ohio sect. of Am. Assn. of Physics Tchrs.), 2001; named Faculty Mem. of Yr., Gamma Alpha chpt. Tau Alpha Phi, 1983. Fellow Ohio Acad. Sci.; mem. AAUP (v.p. U. Cin. chpt. 1994-96, bd. dirs. 2004—), Am. Assn. Physics Tchrs. (founder, past pres., assoc. sec. So. Ohio sect. 1993—, com. on instrnl. media 1994-98, chief organizer and presenter Fundamentals of Radio workshop Toronto 1985, Columbus, Ohio 1986, Bozeman, Mont. 1987, Orono, Maine 1992, Boise, Idaho 1993, South Bend, Ind. 1994, College Park, Md. 1996, Denver, 1997, com. on metric measurements, 2000-03), Ohio Valley Amateur Radio Assn. (pres. 1997—), Am. Soc. Engring. Edn. Achievements include supervising successful attempt of OMI Coll. Applied Sci. contact of shuttle Challenger during STS-51F mission, 1985. Office: Univ Cin 2220 Victory Pkwy Cincinnati OH 45206-2822

SULLIVAN, JAMES GERALD, small business owner; b. Bad Axe, Mich., Sept. 13, 1935; s. John Thomas and Frances Eugena (O'Henley) Sullivan; m. Florence Marie Tack, Sept. 12, 1959; children: Kevin Michael, Kathleen Marie. Student, U. Detroit, 1957—58, Highland Park Coll., 1959—60. Owner Jerry's Barber Shop, Kinde, Bad Axe, Mich., 1963-66, 79—; purchasing agt. Thumb Elec. Coop., Ubly, Mich., 1966-79, Walbro Corp., Cass City, Mich., 1979-80; sales rep. Thumb Blanket, Bad Axe, Mich., 1980-81, Sta. WLEW, Bad Axe, 1981-82; regional mgr. Pri Am. Fin. Svcs., Bad Axe, 1985—; treas. Colfax Twp., Bad Axe, 1979-90; rural letter carrier U.S. Postal Svc., Bad Axe, 1982-98, ret., 1998. Loss clk., Toplis & Harding Wagner & Gliddon, Detroit, 1959-61; inventory control clk., Carrick Products Co., Royal Oak, Mich., 1957-59. Pres. Huron County Twp. Assn., Mich., 1988—90; leader Boy Scouts Am., Bad Axe, 1975—77; lector Ushers Club, Sacred Heart Ch., Eucharistic min. With US Army, 1954—56. Mem. Huron County Rural Letter Carriers Assn. (pres. 1988-2003), Armed Forces Vets. Club of the Nat. Rural Letter Carriers Assn. (Mich. divsn., state sec. 1999—), Am. Legion, 4-H Club (pres. 1948-50), Lions (pres. 1979-80, 2006-07), Cmty. Club (pres. 1976-77), KC (mem. coun. #1546), Tip of the Thumb Dance Club (pres. 2005). Republican. Roman Catholic. Avocations: gardening, golf, swimming, fishing. Home: 122 W Richardson Rd Bad Axe MI 48413-9108

SULLIVAN, JAMES KIRK, management consultant; b. Greenwood, SC, Aug. 25, 1935; s. Daniel Jones and Addie (Brown) S.; m. Elizabeth Miller, June 18, 1960; children: Hal N., Kim J. BS in Chemistry, Clemson U., 1957, MS, 1964, PhD, 1966; postgrad. program for sr. execs., MIT, 1975; DSc (hon.), U. Idaho, 1990. Prodn. supr. FMC Corp., South Charleston, W.Va., 1957-62, tech. supt. Pocatello, Idaho, 1966-69, mktg. mgr. NYC, 1969-70; v.p. govtl. and environ. affairs Boise (Idaho) Cascade Corp., 1970-98; exec. com., chmn. trust and investment com., dist. bd. dirs. Key Bank of Idaho, 1983—2006; sr. ptnr. Veritas Advisors, LLP, 1999—2006; state chmn. Idaho State Republican Com., 2004—. Bd. dirs., chmn. audit com. Key Trust Co. of the West, 1980—83; mem. Accreditation Bd. Engring. and Tech., Inc., 1994—99; bd. dirs. Pub. Employees Retirement Sys. of Idaho. Contbr. articles to profl. jours.; patentee in field. Mem. Coll. of Forest and Recreation Resources com. Clemson U., mem. Golden Tiger Soc.; mem. Idaho Found. Pvt. Enterprise and Econ. Edn., Idaho Rsch. Found., Inc., Idaho Task Force on Higher Edn., Len B. Jordan Pub. Affairs Symposium; trustee Idaho Children's Emergency Fund, 1984—90, Bishop Kelly HS, 1987—89; chmn. adv. bd. U. Idaho Coll. Engring., 1966—70, 1980—87, centennial campaign, 1987—89, rsch. found., 1980—82; chmn. adv. bd. Am. Forest and Paper Assn., Govtl. Affairs Com., Environ. Com., Options Adv. Group, Idaho State Rep. Com.; pres Ore-Ida coun. Boy Scouts Am., St. Al's Found.; trustee St. Al's Med. Ctr.; bd. dirs. Idaho Found. for Excellence in Higher Edn., Exptl. Program to Stimulate Competitive Rsch. NSF, NW Nazarene Coll., 1988—90, Boise Philharm., 1996—99, Boise Master Chorale, 1995—98. Recipient Presdl. Citation U. Idaho, 1990, Disting. Eagle award Boy Scouts Am., 2005, Good Shepard award Presbyn. Ch., 2005, Outstanding Citizen award SARMC, 2007. Mem. AIChE, Am. Chem. Soc., Bus. Week Found. (chmn. Bus. Week 1980), Am. Forest and Paper Assn. (environ. and health coun., product and tech. com., solid waste task force), Bus. Roundtable (environ. com.), Idaho Assn. Commerce and Industry (past chmn. bd. dirs.), C. of C. of U.S. (pub. affairs com.). Republican. Home: 5206 Sorrento Cir Boise ID 83704-2347 Personal E-mail: j.kirksullivan@att.net.

SULLIVAN, JAMES LEO, organization executive; b. Somerville, Mass., Dec. 11, 1925; s. James Christopher and Anna Agnes (Kilmartin) S.; m. Anne Dorothy Hevner, Jan. 20, 1951; children: Maura, Mark, Lianne, Christopher. BS in History and Govt. cum laude, Boston Coll., 1950, MEd in Adminstrn. and Fin., 1958; DCS (hon.), Suffolk U., 1990. Asst. town mgr., Arlington, Mass., 1957-62; town mgr. Watertown, Conn., 1962-65; chief adminstrv. officer Town of Milton, Mass., 1965-68; city mgr. Cambridge, Mass., 1968-70, 74-81, Lowell, Mass., 1970-74; sr. rsch. asst. MIT, Cambridge, 1970-71; pres. Greater Boston C. of C., 1981-91, H.M.S. Mktg., Boston, 1991—. Chmn. Mass. Gov.'s Local Govt. Adv. Com., 1978; del. to Orgn. Econ. and Coop. Devel., Paris, 1979; chmn. New Eng.-Can. Bus. Coun., 1983; pres. Careers for Later Years, 1983; bd. dirs. Input-Output Computer Svcs., Imugen Inc., Mass. Bus. Devel. Corp., New Eng. Cert. Devel. Corp. Trustee Emerson Coll., 1984-88, mem. fin. and investment com., 1985-88; bd. dirs. Bunker Hill C.C. Coll. Found., 1988—; mem. Adv. Com. on Reorgn. of Mass. Ct. Sys., 1991—, chmn. budget subcom. 1991—; bd. overseers Univ. Hosp. Boston. With USN, 1943-46. Mem. Mass. League of Cities and Towns (pres. 1978), Mass. Mayors Assn., Internat. City Mgmt. Assn., Nat. League Cities, Am. C. of C. Execs. (bd. dirs. 1988—), World Trade Club (bd. govs. 1986—). E-mail: jls1225@aol.com.

SULLIVAN, JEREMY R., psychologist, educator; b. Austin, Tex., Dec. 5, 1975; s. Arthur G. Sullivan and Vikki K. Schorlemmer, Rodney N. Schorlemmer (Stepfather); m. Amanda M. Hendley, Aug. 16, 2003. BS, Sam Houston State U., Huntsville, Tex., 1994—98; PhD, Tex. A&M U., College Station, 1998—2003. Cert. sch. psychologist NASP, 2004, lic. specialist in sch. psychology Tex. State Bd. Examiners Psychologists, 2004, psychologist Tex. State Bd. Examiners Psychologists, 2005. Grad. rsch. asst. Tex. A&M U., 1999—2002; psychology internship Cypress-

Fairbanks Ind. Sch. Dist., Houston, 2002—03; sch. psychologist, 2003—05; asst. prof. U. Tex., San Antonio, 2005—. Contbr. chapters to books, articles to profl. jours. Mem.: NASP, APA, Tex. Assn. Sch. Psychologists.

SULLIVAN, JEROME H., educational association administrator; MPA, U. Maine. With U. Maine, 1966, Kent State U., Iowa State U.; dir. fin. aid and student employment U. Colo., Boulder; exec. dir. Am. Assn. Collegiate Registrars and Admissions Officers, Washington, 1998—. Office: Am Assn Collegiate Registrars and Admissions Officers One Dupont Cir NW Ste 520 Washington DC 20036 Office Phone: 202-293-9161. E-mail: sullivanj@aacrao.org. *

SULLIVAN, JIM, artist; b. Providence, Apr. 1, 1939; s. James Henry, Jr. and Frances Winifred (Welch) S.; m. Marie-Louise Paulson. BFA, R.I. Sch. Design, 1961; postgrad., Stanford U., 1962-63. Prof. art Bard Coll., Annandale-on-Hudson, NY, 1966—95, prof. emeritus, 1995—. One-man shows Paley and Lowe Gallery, N.Y.C., 1971, 73, Henri Gallery, Washington, 1974, Fischback Gallery, N.Y.C., 1974, Willard Gallery, N.Y.C., 1978, Nancy Hoffman Gallery, N.Y.C., 1980, 82, 84, 86, 88, 2004, Foker Skulima Gallery, Berlin, Germany, Anne Jaffe Gallery Bay Harbor Islands, Fla. 1990; exhibited in group shows including, Whitney Mus., Mus. Modern Art, Columbus Gallery Fine Arts, Worcester Art Mus., Corcoran Gallery Art, Washington; pub. collections including Met. Mus., Whitney Mus., Albany State Mus., Wadsworth Atheneum, Philip Morris Inc., Owens Corning Coll., Amerada Hess, Carie Secrist Gallery, 2006. Juror Fulbright Fellowship Program, 1996, 1999; bd. dirs. Schoharie Land Trust. Recipient Hinda and Richard Rosenthal award, Am. Acad. Arts and Letters, 1973; grantee Stanford U., 1962—63, R.I. Sch. Design European Honors program, Rome, 1960—61, Nat. Endowment for Arts, 1982; Fulbright fellow, 1961—62, Guggenheim fellow, 1972—73. Address: Box 219 Rum Hill Rd Jefferson NY 12093 also: 59 Wooster St New York NY 10012

SULLIVAN, JOHN, news correspondent; Corr. Trenton Bur. NY Times. Office: NY Times Trenton Bur PO Box 021 Trenton NJ 08625-0021 also: NJ State House 125 W State St Trenton NJ 08625-0021 Office Phone: 609-292-5173 ext. 3. E-mail: jsullivan@nytimes.com.

SULLIVAN, JOHN A., congressman; b. Tulsa, Okla., Jan. 1, 1965; s. Daniel and Mag Sullivan; m. Judith Marie Beck; children: Tommy, Meredith, Sydney, Daniel. BBA, Northeastern State U., Tahlequah, Okla., 1992. Real estate broker; mem. Okla. State Ho. Reps., 1995—2002, US Congress from 1st Okla. dist., 2002—, mem. energy and commerce com., co-chair Congl. Fatherhood Caucus, vice chair Congl. Native Am. Caucus. Republican. Office: US House Reps 114 Cannon House Office Bldg Washington DC 20515-3601 Office Phone: 202-225-2211. Office Fax: 202-225-9187. *

SULLIVAN, JOHN CORNELIUS, JR., lawyer; b. Erie, Pa., Oct. 23, 1927; s. John Cornelius and Catherine J. S.; m. Helen E. Kennedy, Feb. 3, 1951; children: John III, Timi Ann, Michael, Elizabeth. BA in Econs., Allegheny Coll., 1953; LLB, Dickinson Sch. Law, 1959. Bar: Pa. 1960, U.S. Supreme Ct. 1976. Sales rep. IBM Corp., 1953-56; mem. firm Nissley, Clecker & Fearen, Harrisburg, Pa., 1959-63, Nauman, Smith, Shissler & Hall, Harrisburg, 1964—97, of counsel, 1997—. Asst. city solicitor City of Harrisburg, 1964-68, city solicitor, 1968-70; gen. counsel Harrisburg Redevel. Authority, 1964-68, Harrisburg Mcpl. Authority, 1964-87; solicitor Silver-Spring Twp., 1970-81; dir. accounts and fin. City of Harrisburg, 1963; mem. Pa. House of Reps., 1963-64. Assoc. editor Dickinson Law Rev., 1958-59; editor Dauphin County Reporter, 1961-63. Chmn. bd. dirs. Harrisburg Pub. Library, 1965-73; bd. dirs., sec. Harrisburg Hosp.; bd. dirs. Harrisburg Hosp. Found., 1975-89. Mem. Pa. Bar Assn., Dauphin County Bar Assn. (past. dir.), The Pa. Soc. (N.Y.C.), Phi Gamma Delta. Home: 107 Sample Bridge Rd Mechanicsburg PA 17050-1940 Office: 200 N 3rd St Fl D18 Harrisburg PA 17101-1518

SULLIVAN, JOHN DAVID, business association executive; b. Bisbee, Ariz., Jan. 13, 1948; s. Lloyd John and Marjorie Jane (Kingsbury) S.; m. Patricia Mary Mathis, 1999. BA, U. Pitts., 1969, MA, 1972, PhD, 1983. Rschr. Inst. for Econ. Rsch., LA, 1974-75; mem. rsch. staff Pres. Ford Com., Washington, 1976; dir. bus. edn. U.S. C. of C., Washington, 1977-82; asst. dir. The Democracy Program, Washington, 1982-83; program coord. Ctr. for Internat. Pvt. Enterprise, Washington, 1984-89; dir. Washington office Internat. Ctr. for Econ. Growth, 1989-91; exec. dir. Ctr. for Internat. Pvt. Enterprise, Washington, 1991—. Trustee Internat. Devel. Conf., Washington, 1988—. Contbr. articles to jours. in field; mem. editl. bd. Econ. Reform Today, 1991—. Speechwriter, vol. Reagan-Bush campaign, Washington, 1980, 84. Mem. Internat. Studies Assn. Republican. Roman Catholic. Avocations: photography, cooking. Office: Ctr for Internat Pvt Enterprise 1615 H St NW Washington DC 20062-0001

SULLIVAN, JOHN DOMINIC, theater producer, writer; b. La Crosse, Wis., Oct. 6, 1963; s. Arthur John and Eleanor Elizabeth (Skemp) Sullivan. BFA, U. Wis., Superior, 1986. Asst. dir. Duluth Playhouse, Minn., 1985; freelance arts cons. La Crosse, Wis., 1993—; play prodr. Great River Steamboat Co., La Crosse, Wis., 1996—97; stage mgr. La Crosse Cmty. Theatre, Wis., 1997; mng. dir. Fairbanks Shakespeare Theatre, Alaska, 1997. Author: (plays) Murder on the Mississippi, 1996, The Cabaret Killer, 1997. Democrat. Roman Catholic. Personal E-mail: johndom6@yahoo.com.

SULLIVAN, JOHN E., III, lawyer; b. Boston, Nov. 11, 1958; BA magna cum laude in Hist. and Econs., Boston Coll., 1980; JD, U. Tex. Sch. Law, 1984. Bar: Mass. 1985, Ill. 1985, Ohio 1986, US Dist. Ct. (no. dist. Ohio) 1987, US Dist. Ct. (no. dist. Tex.) 1987, US Ct. Appeals (5th cir.) 1988, US Ct. Appeals (6th cir.) 1991, US Supreme Ct. 1995, US Tax Ct. 1997. Founding mem. Sullivan & Sullivan, Ltd. Contbr. articles to profl. jours. Named one of Top 100 Attys., Worth mag., 2005. Mem.: Ohio State Bar Assn., Cleve. Estate Planning Coun., Internat. Tax Planning Assn. Office: Sullivan & Sullivan Ltd Ste 350 25201 Chagrin Blvd Beachwood OH 44122 Office Phone: 216-896-0001. Office Fax: 216-896-0002. E-mail: jesullivan3@sullivanandsullivan.com. *

SULLIVAN, JOHN F., III, lawyer; BBA with highest honors, U. Okla., 1984; JD with honors, U. Houston, 1987. Bar: Tex. 1987, US Dist. Ct. (so., ea., no., and we. dists.) Tex., US Ct. Appeals (5th cir.), bar: US Supreme Ct. Joined Fulbright & Jaworski LLP, Houston, 1987—, ptnr. and chair, hiring com. Assoc. editor Houston Law Rev. Trustee Oncology Svcs. Found. Fellow: Tex. Bar Found., Houston Bar Found.; mem.: ABA, Tex. Assn. Civil Trial and Appellate Specialists, State Bar of Tex., Houston Bar Assn., Tex. Assn. Def. Counsel, Order of Coif, Beta Gamma Sigma. Office: Fulbright & Jaworski LLP Ste 5100 1301 McKinney Houston TX 77010-3095 Office Phone: 713-651-5637. Office Fax: 713-651-5246. Business E-Mail: jsullivan@fulbright.com.

SULLIVAN, JOHN J., lawyer; b. Boston; m. Grace Rodriguez; 3 children. BA in History and Polit. Sci., Brown U., 1981; JD, Columbia U., 1985. Law clk. to Justice David H. Souter U.S. Supreme Ct.; counselor to asst. atty. gen. office of legal counsel U.S. Dept. Justice; ptnr. Mayer, Brown, Rowe & Maw, LLP, 1993—2004; legal counsel, dep. gen. counsel US Dept. Def., Washington, 2004—05; gen. counsel US Dept. Commerce, Washington, 2005—. Office: US Dept Commerce Herbert Clark Hoover Bldg 14th St and Constitution Ave NW Rm 5870 Washington DC 20230 Office Phone: 202-482-4772. Office Fax: 202-482-0042. *

SULLIVAN, JOHN L., political science professor; BA summa cum laude, Univ. Minn., 1967; PhD, Univ. NC, 1970; Postdoctoral Rsch. Fellow, Yale Univ., 1970—71. Faculty, dept. statistcs, polit. sci. Iowa State Univ., 1971—72; faculty, polit. sci. Ind. Univ., 1972—75; faculty, dept. polit. sci. Univ. Minn., 1975—, prof., 1983—99, regents' prof., 1999—, Arleen C. Carlson chair in Am. politics, 2001—04. Vis. prof. Victoria Univ. of Wellington, New Zealand, 1984; adj. assoc. prof., Hubert H. Humphrey Inst. Pub. Affairs Univ. Minn., 1975—83, co-dir. Ctr. for Study of Polit. Psychology, 1995—2004; Benedict disting. vis. prof. Carleton Coll., 1991, 98, 2000, 01. Co-editor (founder): Political Methodology, 1972—85; co-editor: Quantitative Applications to the Social Sciences, 1979—86, American Journal of Political Science, 1985—88, Political Psychology, 1997—2004; editl. bd. American Political Science Review, 1996—2001. Recipient Harold Lasswell award for Disting. Scientific Contributions, Internat. Soc. Polit. Psychology, 2002. Fellow: Am. Acad. Arts & Scis. Office: Coll Liberal Arts Twin Cities Campus Univ Minn 101 Pleasant St SE Minneapolis MN 55455 Office Phone: 612-624-4305. Business E-Mail: jsull@umn.edu. *

SULLIVAN, JOHN W., lawyer; b. NYC, Oct. 30, 1947; BA, SUNY, Stony Brook, 1968; JD, NYU, 1973. Bar: NY 1974, US Dist. Ct. No., So., Ea. & We. Districts NY. Ptnr. Wilson, Elser, Moskowitz, Edelman & Dicker LLP, NYC. Mem.: ABA, NY County Lawyer's Assn., Assn. of the Bar of the City of NY, NY State Bar Assn. Office: Wilson Elser Moskowitz Edelman & Dicker LLP 150 E 42nd St 23rd Fl New York NY 10017-5639 Office Phone: 212-490-3000 ext. 2454. Office Fax: 212-490-3038. Business E-Mail: sullivanj@wemed.com.

SULLIVAN, JOSEPH PETER, risk and insurance management consultant; b. Boston, Sept. 8, 1939; s. Joseph Francis and Mary Anna S.; m. Rachael Anne Cullen, Dec. 22, 1974; children: Philip, Sandra, Susan, Frederick. B Gen. Studies, U. Nebr., 1968; MA, U. No. Colo., 1973, Cen. Mich. U., 1976. Sr. acct. exec. Arkwright Ins., Greenwich, Conn., 1977-83; v.p. Frenkel & Co., NYC, 1983-84; sr. account exec. Republic Hogg Robinson, NYC, 1984-85; v.p. Alexander & Alexander, NYC, 1985-92, Hugh Wood Inc., NYC, 1992-93, Crawford-THG, NYC, 1993-98; sr. v.p. Frontline Ins. Mgrs., Tampa, Fla., 1998—. Assoc. Miller-Heiman Internat., 1986-92; instr. Dale Carnegie and Assocs., 1980-87; ajd. prof. ins. The Coll. of Ins., N.Y.C., 1991-98. Mem. membership com. Met. Rep. Club; bd. advisors The Salvation Army. With US Army, 1956—77, with ETO, Korea and Vietnam. Decorated Bronze Star. Mem. Assn. Former Intelligence Officers (life), Ret. Officers Assn. (bd. dirs. Knickerbocker chpt.), Soc. CPCU's, Am. Soc. CLU's, Nat. Assn. Health Underwriters, Profl. Liability Underwriting Soc., N.Y. Soc. Security Analysts, Soc. Competitive Intelligence Profls., Toastmasters, N.Y. Athletic Club, Rotary, Masons, Shriners. Republican. Roman Catholic. Avocations: american history, photography, collecting old photographic prints and antique photographic equipment. Home and Office: 15920 Dawson Ridge Dr Tampa FL 33647-1324 Office Phone: 813-903-8073. Personal E-mail: sully15920@earthlink.net.

SULLIVAN, KATHLEEN, elementary school educator; b. Vt. Grad., Pa. State Univ. Tchr. Quaker Sch., Phila., Ripton Sch., 1991—92, Warren (Vt.) Sch., 1992—. Leader Vt. Math. Network, 1994—. Named Vt. Tchr. of Yr., 2007. Office: Warren Elem Sch 293 School Rd Warren VT 05674 Home Phone: 802-496-5867; Office Phone: 802-496-2487. Business E-Mail: katie@warrenschool.org.

SULLIVAN, KATHLEEN MARIE, lawyer, educator, former dean; b. 1955; BA, Cornell U., 1976; Oxford U., Eng., 1978; JD, Harvard U., 1981. Bar: NY 1982, US Supreme Ct. 1985, Mass. 1988, Calif. 2006. Law clk. Hon. James L. Oakes U.S. Ct. Appeals (2d cir.), 1981-82; pvt. practice, 1982-84; asst. prof. Harvard U., Cambridge, Mass., 1984-89, prof., 1989-93, Stanford U. Law Sch., Calif., 1993—, Robert E. Paradise fellow, 1995-96, Stanley Morrison prof., 1996—, dean, Richard E. Lang prof. law, 1999—2004; of counsel Quinn Emanuel Urquhart Oliver & Hedges LLP, Redwood Shores, Calif., 2005—. Vis. prov. U. So. Calif. Law Ctr., 1991, Stanford U., 1992; lectr., commentator on constnl. law. Co-editor: (with Gerald Gunther) Constitutional Law, 15th edit., 2004. Named one of 100 Most Influential Lawyers Nat. Law Jour., 2000, 2006, The 50 Most Influential Women Lawyers in Am., 2007, 100 Most Influential Lawyers in Calif., Daily Jour.; recipient Albert M. Sacks-Paul A. Freund award for Teaching Excellence, Harvard, 1992, John Bingham Hurlbut award for excellence in tchg. Stanford U., 1996. Fellow Am. Acad. Arts and Scis, Am. Philosophical Soc.; bd. trustees, The Century Found. Office: Quinn Emanuel Urquhart Oliver & Hedges LLP 555 Twin Dolphin Dr Ste 560 Redwood City CA 94065 also: Stanford U Law Sch Crown Quadrangle 559 Nathan Abbott Way Stanford CA 94305-8610 Office Phone: 650-801-5000. Business E-Mail: sullivan@law.stanford.edu. *

SULLIVAN, KATHRYN D., geologist, former astronaut, former science association executive; b. Paterson, NJ, Oct. 3, 1951; d. Donald P. and Barbara K. Sullivan (dec.). BS in Earth Scis., U. Calif., Santa Cruz, 1973; PhD in Geology, Dalhousie U., Halifax, NS, Can., 1978; Dr. (hon.), Halhousie, Halifax, NS, Can., 1985, SUNY, Utica, 1990, Stevens Inst., 1992, Ohio Dominican U., 1998, Kent State U., 2002; Doctorate (hon.), St. Bonaventure U., 2005. Astronaut NASA, 1979—93, mission specialist flight STS-41G, 1984, mission specialist flight STS-31, 1990, payload comdr. flight STS-45, 1992; chief scientist NOAA, Washington, 1993—96; pres., CEO Ctr. Sci. and Industry, Columbus, Ohio, 1996—2005, sci. advisor. Adj. prof. Rice U., Houston, 1985-92, geology, Ohio State U., Columbus, Ohio; mem. Nat. Commn. on Space, 1985-86; mem. exec. panel Chief of Naval Ops., 1988-96; chair, Ohio Aerospace and Defense Adv. Coun., 2003; mem. Nat. Sci. Bd., 2005—; served on Pews Oceans Commn.; advisor, Nat. Geographic, Smithsonian Inst., Pub. TV; bd. dirs. Am. Electric Power. Oceanography officer, Capt. USNR; private pilot. Recipient Space Flight medal NASA, 1984, 90, 92, Exceptional Svc. medal, 1988, 91, Nat. Air and Space Mus. trophy Smithsonian Instn., 1985, Outstanding Leadership medal, 1992, AAS Space Flight Achievement award, 1991, AAS Prather Eva award, 1992, Lone Sailor award, US Navy Meml. Found., 1997, Juliette award for Nat. Women of Distinction, Girl Scouts U.S.A., 2002, Aviation Week & Space Tech. Aerospace Legend award, 2005; named one of Ten Outstanding Young People of the World award, Jaycees Internat., 1987, Ten Outstanding Young Americans award, US Jaycees, 1987; inductee Ohio Veteran's Hall of Fame, 2001, Ohio Women's Hall of Fame, 2002, Astronaut Hall of Fame, 2004. Fellow AAAS; mem. AIAA (Haley Space Flight award, 1991, Legends Aerospace Laureate 2005), Geol. Soc. Am., Am. Geophys. Union, Soc. Women Geographers, Nat. Sci. Bd. (Public Svc. award, 2003), Explorers Club, Woods Hole Oceanographic Institution, Assn. Space Explorers. First Am. woman to walk in space.

SULLIVAN, KENNETH WAYNE, engineer; b. NYC, Apr. 15, 1957; s. William A. and Helen J. Sullivan; m. Christina A. Eastwood, Sept. 10, 1983 (div. Apr. 1997); children: Daniel, Sarah. AAS, SUNY, Farmingdale, 1978, BS, 2003. Draftsman, jr. designer Cosentini Assoc., NYC, 1981—84; sr. designer Syska & Hennessy Engrs., NYC, 1984—88; project engr. Sikorski Engring. Assn., Jericho, NY, 1990—93, Lehr Assocs., NYC, 1993—99, Sear Brown, Melville, NY, 1999—2003; project mgr. Estee Lauder Co., 2003—05; project engr. AKF Engrs., NYC, 2005—. Recipient award, Am. Sch. and U. Archtl. Portfolio, 2000. Mem.: ASHRAE, Project Mgmt. Inst., Nat. Trust Hist. Preservation, Delta Mu Delta. Roman Catholic. Avocations: reading, history, music, running. Home: 21 Ferney St Hicksville NY 11801-5147 Office: AKF Engrs 1501 Broadway New York NY 10036 Personal E-mail: sullk11801@yahoo.com.

SULLIVAN, KEVIN B., former lieutenant governor, state legislator; b. Hartford, Conn., Aug. 20, 1949; s. John (dec.) and Gwendolyn Price (Bancroft) S.; m. Carolyn Thornberry, 1985. AB, Trinity Coll., 1971; JD, U. Conn., 1982. Polit. cons. in pvt. practice, West Hartford, Conn., 1973-74; adminstrv. clk. edn. com. Conn. Ho. of Reps., Hartford, 1974-76; legis. asst. State Commr. Edn., 1976-81; atty. Byrn Slater Sandler Shulman & Rouse, Hartford, 1981—; councilman Town of West Hartford, 1981-86, mayor, 1983-85, dep. mayor, 1985-86; mem. from Dist. 5 Conn. Senate, Hartford, 1986—2004, Pro Tempore, 1997—2004; lt. gov. State of Conn., 2004—07. Chmn. edn. com., mem. internship and transp. coms., dep. minority leader Conn. State Senate. Mem. ABA, Hartford Bar Assn., Greater Hartford Jaycees (Man of Yr. 1983), Pi Gamma Mu. Founded State Capitol Vietnam Veterens Meml. Democrat.

SULLIVAN, KEVIN F., federal official; b. Chgo., 1958; m. Jo Anne Y. Sullivan; 4 children. BSM, Purdue U., 1980; MS in Mass Comm., Iona Coll., 2004. Mem. pub. rels. dept. Dallas Mavericks, NBA, 1982—2000; v.p. sports comm. NBC, 2000—04; sr. v.p. corp. comm. and media rels. NBC Universal, 2004—05; asst. sec. for comm. & outreach US Dept. Edn., Washington, 2005—06; asst. to Pres. for comm. The White House, Washington, 2006—. Office: The White House 1600 Pennsylvania Ave Washington DC 20500 Office Phone: 202-401-0768.

SULLIVAN, KEVIN PATRICK, lawyer; b. Waterbury, Conn., June 9, 1953; s. John Holian Sullivan and Frances (McGrath) Coon; m. Peggy Hardy, June 13, 1975 (div. Jan. 1985); m. Jarnine Welker, Feb. 15, 1985; children: S. Craig Lemmon, Michael Scott Lemmon, Lindsay Michelle Lemmon. BS in Polit. Sci., BS in Police Sci. cum laude, Weber State Coll., 1979; JD, Pepperdine U., 1982. Bar: Utah 1982, U.S. Dist. Ct. Utah 1982, U.S. Ct. Appeals (10th cir.) 1986, U.S. Supreme Ct. 1986. Assoc. Farr, Kaufman & Hamilton, Ogden, Utah, 1982-87; ptnr. Farr, Kaufman, Hamilton, Sulivan, Gorman & Perkins, Ogden, 1987-91, Farr, Kaufman, Sullivan, Gorman & Perkins, Ogden, 1991—. Judge pro tem Utah 2d Cir. Ct.; city prosecutor of South Ogden, 1990-92. Mem. Eccles Community Art Ctr., Victim's Rights Com. of 2d Jud. Dist. Mem. ABA (criminal justice sect., litigation sect., justice and edn. fund lawyers' coun.), ACLU, ATLA, Utah Bar Assn. (criminal law, young lawyer, litigation sects., unauthorized practice law com.), Utah Trial Lawyers Assn., Utah Assn. Criminal Def. Lawyers, Weber County Bar Assn. (criminal law sect., pres.-elect 1993, pres. 1994), Weber County Pub. Defenders Assn. (assoc. dir. 1987), Weber State Coll. Alumni Assn., Amicus Pepperdine, Elks, Kiwanis, Phi Kappa Phi. Mem. Lds Ch. Avocations: skiing, golf, tennis, fishing. Home: 2731 E 6425 S Ogden UT 84403-5461 Office Phone: 801-394-5526. E-mail: KevinSullivan@qwest.net.

SULLIVAN, LAURA PATRICIA, lawyer, insurance company executive; b. Des Moines, Oct. 16, 1947; d. William and Patricia S. BA, Cornell Coll., Iowa, 1971; JD, Drake U., 1972. Bar: Iowa 1972. Various positions Ins. Dept. Iowa, Des Moines, 1972-75; various legal positions State Farm Mut. Auto Ins. Co., Bloomington, Ill., 1975-81, sec. and counsel, 1981-88, v.p., counsel and sec., 1988—; v.p., sec., dir. State Farm Cos. Found., 1985—; sec. State Farm Lloyd's, Inc., 1987—; v.p., counsel and sec. State Farm Fire and Casualty Co., 1988—, State Farm Gen. Ins. Co., 1988—, also bd. dirs.; v.p. counsel, sec., dir. State Farm Life and Accident Assurance Co.; v.p. counsel, sec. State Farm Annuity and Life Assurance Co., State Farm Life Ins. Co.; dir. State Farm Indemnity Co., Bloomington, Ill., 1995—; sec., dir. State Farm Fla. Ins. Co., 1998—. Bd. dirs. Ins. Inst. for Hwy. Safety, Nat. Conf. Ins. Guaranty Funds, chmn., 1995-97. Trustee John M. Scott Indsl. Sch. Trust, Bloomington, 1983-86, Cornell Coll., 1999—; bd. dirs. Scott Co., 1983-86, Bloomington-Normal Symphony, 1980-85, YWCA of McLean County, 1993-95; chmn. Ins. Inst. for Hwy. Safety, 1987-88. Mem. ABA, Iowa State Bar Assn., Am. Corp. Counsel Assn., Am. Soc. Corp. Secs. Office: State Farm Mut Automobile Ins Co 1 State Farm Plz Bloomington IL 61710-0001

SULLIVAN, LAWRENCE MATTHEW, lawyer; b. Wilmington, Del., Sept. 5, 1937; BA Philosophy, Kings's Coll., 1959; LLB, Cath. U. Am., 1964. Bar: US Supreme Ct./Del. 1965, US Dist. Ct./Del. 1966. Pvt. practice, 1965; asst. county atty. New Castle County, 1966—67, register of wills, 1966—70; pub. defender State of Del., 1970; instr. bus. and real estate law Wilmington Coll., 1969—78, Del Tech. and Cmty. Coll., 1978—80, Del. State Coll., 1980—82, Brandywine Coll.; vice chmn. and mem. various com., Criminal Justice Coun., Del. Co-author: Del. Fundamentals of Real Estate, 1980. Named Del. Outstanding Young Rep. of Yr., Del., 1965, Wilmington's Young Man of Yr., Wilmington Del., 1966, one of Outstanding Young Men of Am., 1968; recipient Reginald Heber Smith award, Nat. Legal Aid and Defender Assn., 2006. Mem.: ABA (Charles H. Dorsey, Jr. award 2006), New Castle County Officials Assn. (pres. 1968—70), Del Trial Lawyers Assn., Del. Bar Assn., Trial Lawyers Am., Am. Arbitration Assn., Sentencing Accountability Commn., Gov. Crime Reduction Task Force, Del. Agy. to Reduce Crime, Del Supreme Ct. Commn. on Del. Ct. 2000, Del Supreme Ct. Planning and Long Range Ct. Planning Com., Phi Alpha Delta. Office: Lawrence M Sullivan Pub Defender Del 1010 Concord Ave # 201 Wilmington DE 19802-3367

SULLIVAN, MARCIA WAITE, lawyer; b. Chgo, Nov. 30, 1950; d. Robert Macke and Jacqueline (Northrop) S.; m. Steven Donald Jansen, Dec. 20, 1975; children: Eric Spurlock, Laura Macke, Brian Northrop. BA, DePauw U., 1972; JD, Ind. U., 1975. Assoc. Arnstein, Gluck, Weitzenfeld & Minow, Chgo., 1975-76; ptnr. Greenberger and Kaufmann, Chgo., 1976-86, Katten Muchin Rosenman LLP, Chgo., 1986—. Adj. prof. Kent Coll. Law, Ill. Inst. Tech., Chgo., 1991—94; pres. Chgo. Real Estate Exec. Women, 2000—01. Mem. editl. adv. bd.: Real Estate Chgo., 2001—02. Mem. NNCREW Found. Grant Making Com, 2003—04. Mem.: ABA, Chgo. Bar Assn. Avocations: bicycling, cross country skiing, gardening, camping. Office: Katten Muchin Rosenman LLP 525 W Monroe St Chicago IL 60661-3693 Home Phone: 847-256-2496; Office Phone: 312-902-5535. Business E-Mail: marcia.sullivan@kattenlaw.com.

SULLIVAN, MARGARET M., editor-in-chief; d. John and Elaine (Saab) Sullivan; m. Charles "Bud" Anzalone; children: Alex, Grace. BA in English, Georgetown U., 1979; MS with distinction, Medill Sch. Journalism, Northwestern U., 1980. Clk. Washington bur. Gannett News Svc., 1977—80; Buffalo-area stringer N.Y. Times, 1984—89; reporter, news-feature reporter, columnist Buffalo News, 1980—87, asst. city editor, 1987—89, asst. mng. editor, 1989—98, mng. editor, 1998—99, editor, 1999—. Instr. journalism SUNY, Buffalo, 1991—93. Named One of Buffalo's Outstanding Young Bus. Leaders, Bus. 1st newspaper, 1992; named to Medill Sch. Journalism Hall of Achievement, 2003; recipient Award for Internat. Understanding, Rotary Found., 1987, Young Leadership award, YMCA, 1987. Mem.: Kappa Tau Alpha. Office: Buffalo News 1 News Plaza PO Box 100 Buffalo NY 14240 Office Phone: 716-849-4444.

SULLIVAN, MARK J., federal agency administrator; b. Arlington, Mass. m. Laurie Bell; 3 children. BA, St. Anselm Coll. Spl. agent office inspector gen. HUD, 1978—83; spl. agent U.S. Secret Svc., U.S. Dept. Homeland Security, Detroit, 1983—90, spl. agent fraud divsn. Washington, 1990—91, spl. agent presdl. protection divsn., 1991—96, asst. spl. agent in charge office protective ops., 1996—97, resident agent in charge Columbus, Ohio, 1997—98, spl. agent in charge conterfeit divsn., 1998—99, asst. spl. agent in charge presdl. protective divsn., 1999—2000, dep. asst. dir. office protective ops. fed. sr. exec. svc., 2000—02, dep. spl. agent in charge vice presdl. protective divsn., 2002—03, dep. asst. dir. office human resources and training, asst. dir. office protective ops., 2003—06, dep. dir., 2006, dir., 2006—. Recipient Disting. Presdl. Rank award, 2005. Office: US Secret Svc Personnel Divisn 245 Murray Dr Bldg 410 Washington DC 20223

SULLIVAN, MARTIN EDWARD, museum director; b. Troy, NY, Feb. 9, 1944; s. John Francis and Helen Edna (Lynch) S.; m. Katherine Mary Hostetter, May 9, 1981; children: Abigail, Bethany. BA in History, Siena Coll., 1965; MA in History, U. Notre Dame, 1970, PhD in History, 1974. Exec. dir. Ind. Commn. for Humanities, Indpls., 1972-75; dir. pub. programs NEH, Washington, 1976-81; pres. Inst. on Man and Sci., Rensselaerville, N.Y., 1981-83; dir. N.Y. State Mus., State Edn. Dept., Albany, N.Y., 1983-90, The Heard Mus., Phoenix, 1990-99, Historic St. Mary City, Md., 1999; adj. prof. history St. Mary's Coll. Md. Trustee Am. Indian Ritual Object Repatriation Found., N.Y.C., 1992-98; chmn. U.S. Govt. Cultural Property Adv. Com., 1995-2003. Author: Museums, Adults and the Humanities, 1981, Inventing the Southwest: The Fred Harvey Company and Native American Art, 1996; contbr. articles to profl. jours. Trustee Am. Fedn. Arts, 1994-98; mem. Native Am. Repatriation Act Adv. Com., 1992-2005. With U.S. Army, 1966-68. Mem. Am. Assn. Mus. (v.p. 1990-93, mem. accreditation commn. 1997—; named to Centennial Honor Roll, 2006). Democrat. Home: PO Box 428 Saint Marys City MD 20686-0428 Office: PO Box 39 Saint Marys City MD 20686-0039 Office Phone: 240-895-4960. E-mail: mesullivan@smcm.edu.

SULLIVAN, MARTIN J., insurance company executive; With fin. dept. Am. Internat. Underwriters Ltd., 1971—83, property mgr., 1983—88, London office mgr., regional mktg. mgr. for U.K. and Ireland, 1988—89, asst. mng. dir., 1989—91, CEO, 1991—93, pres., UK/Ireland div., 1993—95, pres., 1997—98; sr. v.p. Am. Internat. Group, Inc., 1995—98, exec. v.p. NYC, 1998—2002, co-COO, 2002—05, vice chmn., 2002—05, pres., CEO, 2005—. Office: Am Internat Group Inc 70 Pine St New York NY 10270 *

SULLIVAN, MARY ANN, artist; b. Columbus, Ohio, June 17, 1952; d. Thomas Joseph and Mary Jane (neeHouck) Sullivan; 1 child, Benjamin James. BFA in Illustration, Columbus Coll. Art and Design, 1974. Designer, illustrator Gibson Greeting Cards, Cin., 1974—78; freelance comml. artist Artwear, Albuquerque, 1984—90; exhibiting fine artist Fine Arts Ctr. En Taos, Taos, N.Mex., 1984—86, Spangler Cummings Gallery, Columbus, 1984—88, El Taller Gallery, Taos, N.Mex., 1984—94, Roberta Kuhn Gallery, Columbus, 1988—92, various galleries, 1992—. Songs of the Earth, 1976, one-woman shows include El Taller Gallery, N. Mex., 1988, 1990, Wilmington Coll., 2001, exhibited in group shows at Ohio State Fair, 1974—2001, Spangler Cummings Gallery, Ohio, Roberta Kuhn Gallery, Grand Ctrl. Galleries, N.Y.C., 1985, Society of Illustrators, NYC, others. Mem.: Ohio Art League. Avocations: books, interior decorating.

SULLIVAN, MARY ANNE, lawyer, government agency administrator; BA in Philosophy summa cum laude, Fordham U., 1973; JD, Yale U., 1976. Law clk. to Hon. Walter K. Stapleton U.S. Dist. Ct., Wilmington, Del., 1976-77; assoc. Hogan & Hartson, Washington, 1977-84, ptnr., 1985-94; dep. gen. counsel Environ. and Civilian and Def. Nuclear Programs, U.S. Dept. Energy, Washington, 1994-98; gen. counsel U.S. Dept. Energy, Washington, 1998—. Instr. Lawyers Com. for Civil Rights; spkr. in field. Contbr. articles to profl. jours. Active Dem. Party, 1982—; sr. domestic issues advisr Geraldine Ferraro in Mondale Campaign; with debate prep. team Senator Bentsen in Dukakis Campaign; counsel to Clinton Campaign and Clinton/Gore Transition Team, 1992. Office: US Dept Energy Gen Counsel Rm 6A-245 1000 Independence Ave SW Washington DC 20585-0001 Fax: 202-586-1499.

SULLIVAN, MARY E., retired secondary educator, past state legislator; b. June 29, 1932; m. Charles M. Sullivan; children: Charles M. Jr., Ethel M., Mary E., Kathleen M., Mark C., Ursula M. AB, Regis Coll., 1954; MA, Boston Coll., 1955. Asst. prof. stats. Bentley Coll., Waltham, Mass., 1966-72; asst. prof., registrar Husson Coll., 1973-79; mem. staff Maine Dept. Manpower Affairs Rsch., 1980-81; math. tchr. John Bapst Meml. H.S., 1981-97; also mem. Maine Ho. of Reps., 1992-94. City councilor City of Bangor, Maine, 1985—, mayor, 1988-89. Mem. Maine Munic Assn. (past pres.). Democrat. Home: 143 Bright St Waltham MA 02453-6584

SULLIVAN, MARY ROSE, retired English language educator; b. Boston, May 13, 1931; d. John Joseph and Elinor Mary (Crotty) Sullivan BA, Emmanuel Coll., Boston, 1952; MA, Cath. U. Am., 1957; PhD, Boston U., 1964. Tchr. Woburn Pub. Schs., Mass., 1957-60; faculty Emmanuel Coll., Boston, 1960-66; prof. English U. Colo., Denver, 1966-96; ret., 1996. Book reviewing staff San Diego Mag., 1980—90. Author: Browning's Voices in the Ring and the Book, 1969; co-editor: (3 vols.) letters of E.B. Browning to M.R. Mitford, 1836-54, 1983, Women of Letters: Selected Letters of E.B. Browning to M.R. Mitford, 1987, Crime Classics, 1990, Elizabeth Barrett Browning: Selected Poetry and Prose, 1993; editl. bd. English Lang. Notes, 1970-96. Served to capt. USNR, 1952—83. Am. Coun. Learned Socs. fellow, 1973. Mem. MLA, Boston Browning Soc., Mystery Writers of Am.

SULLIVAN, MICHAEL, writer, retired mathematics professor; b. Chgo., Jan. 8, 1942; s. Michael and Catherine Sullivan; m. Mary Rita Doody (dec.); children: Kathleen, Michael III, Dan, Colleen. BS, DePaul U., Chgo., 1962; MS, Ill. Inst. Tech., Chgo., 1963, PhD, 1967. Prof. math. Chgo. State U., 1965—97; prof. emeritus, 1997—. Dir. Scott-Jones Inc., Half Moon Bay, Calif., 1987—2006; cons. Authors Coalition of Am., 2001—. Author: Calculus and Analytic Geometry, 3d edit., 1990, Mathematics for Business, 8th edit., 2005, Basic Calculus, 8th edit., 2005, Finite Mathematics, 9th edit., 2005, Algebra with Review, 7th edit., 2005, Trigonometry, Right Angle EGLL, 4th edit., 2006, Precalculus EGU, 4th edit., 2006, Algebra and Trigonometry EGU, 4th edit., 2006, College Algebra EGU, 4th edit., 2006, Precalculus, Right Triangle, Concepts, 2007, Precalculus, Unit Circle, Concepts, 2007, College Algebra, Concepts, 2007. Chmn. Oak Lawn Youth Commn., Ill., 1979—85; pres. St. German Sch. Bd., Oak Lawn, 1985—88, St. German Holy Name Soc., Oak Lawn, 1984. Mem.: Text and Acad. Authors Assn. (pres. 2001—04). Avocations: tennis, chess, gardening, travel. Home: 9529 S Tripp Ave Oak Lawn IL 60453

SULLIVAN, MICHAEL EVAN, investment company executive; b. Phila., Dec. 30, 1940; s. Albert and Ruth (Liebert) S. BS, N.Mex. State U., 1966, MA, 1967; BS, U. Tex., 1969; MBA, U. Houston, 1974; MS, U. So. Calif., 1976, MPA, 1977; BS in Acctg., U. La Verne, Calif., 1981; PhD in Adminstrn., U. So. Calif., 1983. Sr. adminstrv. and tech. analyst Houston Lighting & Power Co., 1969—74; electronics engr. US Govt., Point Mugu, Calif., 1974—77; mem. tech. staff Hughes Aircraft Co., El Segundo, Calif., 1977—78; staff program adminstr. Ventura divsn. Northrop Corp., Newbury Park, Calif., 1978—79; divsn. head engring. Navastrogru, Point Mugu, 1978—82; br. head, divsn. head spl. programs head operational sys. Pacific Missile Test Ctr., Calif., 1983—90, head tech. devel. office, head capability devel., 1993—98; regional coord. far west, exec. com., exec. bd. Fed. Lab. Consortium, 1999—. CNO, dir. rsch., devel. and acquisition The Pentagon, Washington, 1987-88, dir. rsch. devel. test and evaluation and tech., 1990-93; pres., chmn. bd. Diversified Mgmt. Sys., Inc., Camarillo, Calif., 1978—. Author: The Management of Research, Development, Test and Evaluation Organizations; Organization Behavior Characteristics of Supervisors-Public versus Private Sectors; Self-Actualization in RDT & E Organizations: Self-Actualization in a Health Care Agency; others. V.p., bd. dirs. Ventura County Master Chorale and Opera Assn.; bd. dirs. So. Calif. Assn. of Pub. Adminstrn. (also mem. fin. com., programs com., student aid com., exec. bd., exec. com. fed. lab. consortium). Served with U.S. Army, 1958-62. Ednl. Rsch. Info. Clearing House fellow, 1965-67, Ednl. Rsch. Tng. Program fellow N.Mex. State U., 1967. Mem. IEEE, Am. Math. Soc., Math. Assn. Am., Am. Statis. Assn., IEEE Engring. Mgmt. Soc., Am. Soc. Pub. Adminstrn., So. Calif. Assn. Pub. Adminstrn. (bd. dirs., various coms.), Assn. Fedn. Tech. Transfer Execs., Fed. Mgrs. Assn., Am. Assn. Individual Investors, Mcpl. Mgmt. Assts. So. Calif., Acad. Polit. Sci., Internat. Soc. for the Sys. Scis., Assn. MBA Execs., Tech. Transfer Soc., Internat. Fedn. for Sys. Rsch., Phi Kappa Phi, Pi Gama Mu. Home: PO Box 273 Port Hueneme CA 93044-0273 Office: PO Box 447 Camarillo CA 93011-0447 Office Phone: 805-985-3792. Personal E-mail: mikedmsinc@aol.com.

SULLIVAN, MICHAEL J., prosecutor; b. Oct. 3, 1954; m. Terry Sullivan, 1975; children: Joseph, Kelly, Allyson, James. BA, Boston Coll., 1979; JD, Suffolk U., 1983. Assoc. Bolles and Pritchard, 1983—90; ptnr. McGovern and Sullivan, 1990—95; mem. Mass. Ho. Reps. (Dist. 7), 1991—95; dist. atty. Plymouth County, Mass., 1995—2001; US atty. Dist. Mass. US Dept. Justice, Boston, 2001—; acting dir. Bur. Alcohol, Tobacco, Firearms & Explosives, US Dept. Justice, 2006—. Office: US Attys Office John Joseph Moakley Courthouse 1 Courthouse Way Boston MA 02210 also: Bur Alcohol Tobacco Firearms & Explosives 650 Massachusetts Ave NW Rm 8000 Washington DC 20226 *

SULLIVAN, MICHAEL J., labor union administrator; b. Indpls., 1945; Sheet metal worker Brad Snodgrass Sheet Metal Inc., R.M. Cotton Inc., Nyland Sheet Metal Inc.; bus. rep. Sheet Metal Workers' Internat. Assn., 1973, 1976, bus. mgr. and fin. sec./treas., Local 20, 1979—94, gen. exec. coun., 1983—94, gen. sec./treas., 1994—99, pres., 1999—. Pres. Ind. Bldg. and Constrn. Trades Coun.; v.p. State AFL-CIO; mem. Ind. Workers Compensation Commn.; chmn. Labor Inst. Tng.; pres. Sheet Metal Workers' Internat. Assn.'s Mich.-Ind. Coun.; bd. dir. Nat. Coordinating Com. for Multiemployer Plan, ULLICO, Washington, Am. Cmty. Partnerships. Mem. Hoosier Alliance Against Drugs. Office: Sheet Metal Workers' Internat Assn 1750 New York Ave NW Washington DC 20006 *

SULLIVAN, MICHAEL JOHN, lawyer, former ambassador; b. Omaha, Sept. 22, 1939; s. Joseph Byrne and Margaret (Hamilton) S.; m. Jane Metzler, Sept. 2, 1961; children: Michelle, Patrick, Theresa. BS in Petroleum Engring., U. Wyo., 1961, JD, 1964. Bar: Wyo. 1964, U.S. Ct. Appeals (10th cir.) 1968, U.S. Supreme Ct. 1980. Assoc. Brown, Drew, Apostolos, Barton & Massey, Casper, Wyo., 1964-67; ptnr. Brown, Drew, Apostolos, Massey & Sullivan, Casper, Wyo., 1967-86, 95-98; gov. State of Wyo., Cheyenne, 1987-95; amb. to Ireland Dublin, 1998-2001; spl. counsel Rothgerber, Johnson & Lyons, LLP, Casper, Wyo., 2001—. Trustee St. Joseph's Children's Home, Torrington, Wyo., 1986-87; bd. dirs. Natrona County Meml. Hosp., Casper, 1976-86. Mem. ABA, ATLA, Wyo. Bar Assn., Wyo. Trial Lawyers Assn., Rotary (pres. Casper club). Democrat. Roman Catholic. Avocations: fly fishing, golf, tennis, jogging. Office: Casper Bus Ctr 123 W 1st St Ste 200 Casper WY 82601 Home: 1124 S Durbin St Casper WY 82601-4328 E-mail: msullivan@rothgerber.com.

SULLIVAN, MICHELLE CORNEJO, lawyer; b. St. Louis, June 29, 1958; m. Dennis Keith Sullivan, May 18, 1985. BS, U. Calif., Berkeley, 1980; JD, U. Santa Clara, 1983. Bar: Calif., 1984; US Dist. Ct. (no. dist.) Calif., 1984, (so. dist.) Calif., 1985; cert. family law specialist. Legal dept. Four-Phase Computers, Cupertino, Calif., 1984; asst. dist. atty. San Benito County, Hollister, Calif., 1984-85; assoc. Walters & Ward, Rancho Bernardo, Calif., 1986-87, Law Offices of Rebecca Prater, Carlsbad, Calif., 1987-88; pvt. practice Escondido & San Diego, Calif., 1988—. Pres. Women in Networking, San Diego, 1987; western horse show judge Calif. State Horseman's Assn., 1985; adv. com. San Diego Regional Conf. on Women, trustee, 1993-95. Law Faculty scholar U. Santa Clara, 1982-83. Mem.: ABA, Lawyers Club (v.p. North County chpt. 1988—89), San Diego Trial Lawyers Assn. (family law sect.), Bar Assn. No. San Diego County (chair family law sect. 1996—98, chair, cert. family law specialist 2004, bd. dirs. 2005—07, treas. 2007), San Diego County Bar Assn. (cert. specialist), State Bar Assn., Rancho Bernardo C. of C. (amb. 1986—87), Escondido Rotary Main Club. Avocations: western horseback riding, golf, sailing, scuba diving. Office: 16516 Bernardo Center Dr Ste 220 San Diego CA 92128-2518 Office Phone: 858-451-9390. Business E-Mail: msullivan@fullspectrumlaw.com.

SULLIVAN, MORTIMER ALLEN, JR., lawyer; b. Buffalo, Sept. 19, 1930; s. Mortimer Allen Sr. and Gertrude (Hinkley) S.; m. Maryanne Calella, Nov. 20, 1965; children: Mark Allen, Michael John. BA, U. Buffalo, 1954. Bar: N.Y. 1964, U.S. Dist. Ct. (we. dist.) N.Y. 1966, U.S. Dist. Ct. (no. dist.) N.Y. 1967, U.S. Supreme Ct. 1970. Counsel liability claims Interstate Motor Freight System, Grand Rapids, Mich., 1964-82. V.p. J.P.M. Sullivan, Inc., Elmira, N.Y., 1959-67; govt. appeal agt. U.S. Selective Service System, 1967-71; dep. sci. staff Erie County (N.Y.) Sheriff's Office, 1971—, lt., 1986—. Inventor (with others) in field; creator, dir. video depiction JudiVision, 1969; composer High Flight, 1983. Chmn. com. on Constn. and Canons Episcopal Diocese of Western N.Y., 1975-96; bd. dirs. Erie County Law Enforcement Found., Inc., 1987—; bd. dirs. Orchard Park (N.Y.) Symphony Orch., 1975-97, v.p., 1977-79, 91-94. With USAF, 1954-57; spl. agt. Air Force Office of Spl. Investigations, 1972-87, col. res. ret. Decorated Legion of Merit. Mem. Erie County Bar Assn. (chmn. law and tech. com., 1970-81), Transp. Lawyers Assn., Kappa Alpha Soc., Wanakah (N.Y.) Country Club. Republican. Avocation: aviation. Home: 19 Knob Hill Rd Orchard Park NY 14127-3917 Office: PO Box 1003 Orchard Park NY 14127-8003 Home Phone: 716-662-3270; Office Phone: 716-667-7800. Personal E-mail: masulaw@aol.com.

SULLIVAN, NEIL MAXWELL, oil and gas company executive; b. May 25, 1942; s. Thomas James and Jane Mason (Ginn) S.; m. Holly Abolt; children: Margaret Blair, Mason Pedrick. BS, Dickinson Coll., 1970; MS, Tulane U., 1994; postgrad., U. S.C., 1992. Exploration geologist Bass Enterprises, Midland, Tex., 1976—77; dist. geologist Am. Trading and Prodn. Co., Midland, 1977—78; divsn. geologist Anadarko Prodn. Co., Midland, 1978—79, chief geologist, 1979—80, v.p. exploration, regional mgr. Houston, 1980—82; mgr. exploration ops. Valero Producing Co., San Antonio, 1982—85, v.p. exploration New Orleans, 1985—87; pres. Bluebonnet Petroleum Co., New Orleans, Eastover, 1987—97; v.p. exploration Forcenergy, Inc., Houston, 1997—98; pres. GAPCO Energy, Houston, 1998—; COO Tex. Keystone, Inc., Pitts., 2002—05; v.p. exploration and prodn. Gulf Keystone Petroleum, Ltd., 2002—05. Mem. Dept. adv. bd. Interior Outer Continental Shelf Com., 1985-87 Editor: Petroleum Exploration in Thrust Belts and Their Adjacent Forelands, 1976, Ancient Carbonate Reservoirs and Their Modern Analogs, 1977, Guadalupian Delaware Mountain Group of West Texas and Southeast New Mexico, 1979, Deep Water Sands in the Gulf Coast Region, 1988, Offshore Louisiana Geology: An Onshore Exploration Model, 1988, Risk: Evaluation and Management, 1989, Volga-Ural Basin Analysis, 1993, Northern Marginal Zone of the Pricaspian Basin, 1996. Bd. dirs. Permian Basin Grad. Ctr., Midland, 1979; com. chmn. Mus. of S.W., Midland, 1978. Served with USAF, 1964-68. Mem. Geol. Soc. Am., Am. Assn. Petroleum Geologists (cert. petroleum geologist), Houston Geol. Soc., New Orleans Geol. Soc. (chmn. continuing edn. com. 1987-89), South Tex. Geol. Soc. (chmn. nominating com. 1985), Soc. Econ. Paleontologists and Mineralogists (pres. Permian Basin sect. 1979), Elks. Home: 3894 Ash Dr Allison Park PA 15101-3103 Office Phone: 412-222-9600. Business E-Mail: neil.sullivan@gapcoenergy.com. E-mail: nsullivan525@yahoo.com.

SULLIVAN, NEIL SAMUEL, physicist, researcher, educator, former dean; b. Wanganui, Wellington, New Zealand, Jan. 18, 1942; came to U.S., 1983; s. Reynold Richard and Edna Mary (Alger) S.; m. Robyn Annette Dawson, Aug. 28, 1965; children: Raoul Samuel, Robert Alexander and David Charles (twins). BSc with 1st class honors, U. Otago, New Zealand, 1964, MSc in Physics, 1965; PhD in Physics, Harvard U., 1972. Postdoctoral rsch. Centre d'Etudes Nucleaires, Saclay, France, 1972-74, rsch. physicist, 1974-82; prof. physics U. Fla., Gainesville, 1982—, chair physics dept., 1989—, co-founder Microkelvin Rsch. Lab.; assoc. dean rsch. Coll. Liberal Arts and Scis., U. Fla., 1999—2001, dean, 2001—07. Co-prin. investigator U.S. Nat. High Magnetic Field Lab., Tallahassee, 1990-. Contbr. numerous articles on quantum solids and nuc. magnetism to profl. jours. Recipient prix Saintour, Coll. de France, Paris, 1978, prix LaCaze, Acad. des Scis., Paris, 1982; Fulbright exch. grantee, 1965; Frank Knox Meml. fellow Harvard U., Cambridge, Mass., 1965-67. Fellow Am. Phys. Soc.; mem. AAAS, Am. Assn. Physics Tchrs., Inst. Physics, Soc. Francaise de Physique, European Phys. Soc., Groupement Ampere. Achievements include investigation of fundamental properties of solid hydrogen and solid helium at very low temperatures; studies of molecular motions using nuclear magnetic resonance; orientational disorder in molecular crystals, cryogenic detectors for dark matter particles and other cosmological relics of big bang theory; discovery of quadrupole glass phase of solid hydrogen, anomalous nuclear spin-lattice relaxation of solid 3He at interfaces; development of NMR techniques to study molecular dynamics at very low temperatures, quantum diffusion in solid hydrogen; design of ultra-sensitive low-noise cryogenic UHF detectors; subspecialities include condensed matter physics, low temperature physics, high magnetic fields. Office Phone: 352-392-0780. E-mail: sullivan@phys.ufl.edu. *

SULLIVAN, NICHOLAS G., science educator; b. Phila., Dec. 20, 1927; s. Edward James and Florence (Delaney) S. BS, Cath. U. Am., 1950; MSc, U. Pitts., 1954; PhD, U. Notre Dame, 1961. Asst. prof. U. Notre Dame (Ind.), 1961-63; asst. prof., assoc. prof., prof. La Salle Coll., Phila., 1963-78, asst. to pres., 1972-74; prof. sci. Manhattan Coll., Riverdale, NY, 1979—. Vis. prof. U. Alaska, Anchorage, 196l, U. NSW, Sydney, Australia, 1963; chmn. U.S. Deep Caving Team. Author: Speleology, the Study of Caves, 1962; contbr. over 200 articles on speleology to profl. jours. Trustee Gwynedd (Pa.) Mercy Coll., 1963-75, Nat. Speleological Found., Washington, 1978-84, Charles Lindbergh Found., 1989—. Fellow Nat. Speleological Soc. (hon. life, trustee 1955-79, pres. 1957-63), Royal Geog. Soc., AAAS, N.Y. Acad. Scis., Explorers Club (pres. 1989-92, trustee 1968—, Explorer's medal Phila. chpt. 1978, Sweeney medal 1979); mem. Sydney Speleological Soc. (hon. life), South African Speleological Soc. (hon. life), Rittenhouse Club, Bankstown Sports Club (Sydney). Avocation: speleology.

SULLIVAN, OWEN, employment services executive; Grad., Marquette U., Milw. Various sales, sales mgmt. and product mgmt. positions IBM; pres. Fin. Svcs. Group Metavante, pres. Enterprise Solutions Group; owner Sullivan Advisors, LLC; exec. v.p., CEO Jefferson Wells subs. Manpower, Inc., 2003—, CEO Right Mgmt. subs., 2004—. Bd. dirs. Ministry HealthCare, Circuit Check Inc. Bd. dirs. Children's Hosp. and Health Sys., Inc. Office: Right Mgmt 200 S Executive Dr Ste 140 Brookfield WI 53005 Office Phone: 262-957-3612. *

SULLIVAN, PATRICIA A., academic administrator; b. Staten Island, NY; m. Charles Sullivan. AB cum laude, St. John's U., 1961; MS in Biology, NYU, 1964, PhD in Biology, 1967. Tchg. fellow, NIH pre-doctoral fellow NYU; post-doctoral fellow in cell biology Upstate Med. Ctr., Syracuse, NY; vis. fellow Cornell U., 1976; tchr. Wells Coll., NY; dir. biology honors program Tex. Woman's U., 1979-81; dean Salem Coll., Winston-Salem, 1981-87; v.p. acad. affairs Tex. Woman's U., 1987-94, interim pres., 1993-94; chancellor U. N.C., Greensboro, 1995—. Pres. Assn. Tex. Colls. and Univs. Acad. Affairs Officers, Assn. So. Colls. for Women, N.C. Assn. Chief Acad. Officers; active numerous coms. Tex. Higher Edn. Coordinating Bd.; lectr. in field. Contbr. articles to profl. jours. Office: U NC at Greensboro Office of Chancellor PO Box 26170 Greensboro NC 27402-6170

SULLIVAN, PATRICIA EILEEN, physical therapist, educator; b. Wilmington, Del., Mar. 5, 1946; 1 child, Kathryn. BS, Northeastern U., 1968; MS, Northwestern U., 1975; PhD, Boston U., 1989; D in Phys. Therapy, Mass. Gen. Hosp. Inst. Health Profs., Boston, 2005. Phys. therapist Mass. Gen. Hosp., Boston, 1968-69, 72-74, Kaiser Permanent, San Francisco, 1969-72; assoc. phys. therapy program Northwestern U. Med. Sch., Chgo., 1974—87; asst. prof. Boston U., 1975-88; assoc. prof., coord. internat. scholars program, dir. Internat. Ctr., Inst. Health Profls., Mass. Gen. Hosp., 1990—. Lectr. dept. orthopedics Harvard Med. Sch.; adj. prof. Curtin U., Perth, Australia; vis. faculty Mahidol U., Bangkok; chmn. Marblehead Disabilities Commn.; cons. in field. Co-author: (textbooks) Integrated Approach to Therapeutic Exercise, 1982, Clinical Procedures in Therapeutic Exercise, 1986, Clinical Decision Making in Therapeutic Exercise, 1994, Clinical Procedures, 2nd edit., 1995. Mem. Am. Phys. Therapy Assn. (v.p. Mass. chpt. 1990-92, sec. 1973-74, chief del. 1980-86), Republic of China Phys. Therapy Assn. Avocations: sailing, cross country skiing. Office: Inst Health Profls 36 First Ave Boston MA 02129-4724 Office Phone: 617-724-2261. Business E-Mail: PSullivan8@mghihp.edu.

SULLIVAN, PATRICIA W. (TERRY SULLIVAN), real estate trainer; b. Hempstead, NY, July 25, 1936; d. Gilbert Hudson and Vera (Morgan) Wehmann; m. Richard J. Sullivan, June 8, 1957 (div. Apr. 1982); children: Katherine, Gillian Stewart, Adam W. BS, Skidmore Coll., 1958; MS, Syracuse U., 1965. Mgr. Purtell & Wigdale, Inc., Cedarburg, Wis., Merrill Lynch Real Estate, Cedarburg; office mgr. Coldwell Banker Real Estate, Cedarburg; sales mgr. Coldwell Banker Residential Brokerage, Mequon, WI; owner, trainer, cons. Terry Sullivan Tng. and Seminars, Belgium, Wis., 1991—; sales mgr. Coldwell Banker, Mequon, Wis. Contbr. articles to profl. jours. Named Wis. Cert. Real Estate Brokerage Mgr. of Yr., 1990. Mem.: Wis. Cert. Residential Brokers (cert., pres. 1988), Wis. Cert. Residential Specialists (cert., pres. 1982, Cert. Residential Specialist of Yr. 1983), Wis. Realtors Assn. (v.p. 1982—83, bd. dirs. 1983—86, GRI 1975, Instr. of Yr. 1988, Disting. Svc. award 1992), Realtors Nat. Mktg. Inst. (dir. RS coun. 1983—86, CRS 1978, CRB 1981), Oazukee Bd. Realtors (pres. 1979, bd. dirs. 1977—79, Realtor of Yr. 1979), Women's Coun. Realtors (pres. Milw. chpt. 1982, bd. dirs. 1983—90, PMN 2005, WCR of Yr. 1983), Nat. Women's Coun. Realtors (pres. 1990), Nat. Assn. Realtors (bd. dirs. 1989—90, Omega Tau Rho award 1983, Outstanding Educator of Yr. award for medium states 1989). Address: Terry Sullivan Tng & Seminars 5342 Sandy Beach Ln Belgium WI 53004-9731 E-mail: rlterry@hotmail.com.

SULLIVAN, PATRICK JAMES, lawyer; b. Orange, Calif., Sept. 17, 1943; s. Leo Charles Sullivan and Virginia (Wohosky) Souza; m. Pamela Pressler, Aug. 17, 1974; children: Shannon, Erin. BA, U. So. Calif., 1965; JD, Loyola U., Los Angeles, 1974. Bar: (Calif.) 1974, (U.S. Ct. Appeals (9th cir.)) 1978, (U.S. Supreme Ct) 1979, U.S. Ct. Appeals (3d cir.) 1983, U.S. Tax Ct. 1986, U.S. Ct. Appeals (2d and 8th cirs.) 1989. Trial atty. U.S. Dept. Justice, Washington, 1974—75; ptnr. Sullivan, Jones & Archer, San Diego and San Francisco, 1975—83, Hewitt, Sullivan & Marshall, San Diego, 1983—87, King & Ballow, 1987—90, The Sullivan Law Firm, San Diego, 1990—. Arbitrator San Diego Superior Ct., 1979—83; lectr. U. Calif. Securities Regulations Inst., 1985; chmn. Am. Law Inst. Anti-Trust Conf., 1988, 91; mem. faculty Hastings Ctr. for Trial and Appellate Advocacy, 1989—92, Calif. Continuing Edn. of Bar, 1989—. Served to 1st lt. US Army, Vietnam. Decorated Bronze Star. Fellow: Am. Bar Found.

(life); mem.: ABA (litigation and anti-trust sects., ho. dels.), Am. Bd. of Trial Advocates, Nat. Inst. Trial Adv. (faculty 1986—), Am. Judiciary Soc., Am. Law Inst., Am. Inn Ct. (master 1992—2002), Rotary (Newhall, Calif.). Republican. Roman Catholic. Home: 335 Whitewood Pl Encinitas CA 92024-3137 Office: 810 Mission Ave Ste 300 Oceanside CA 92054

SULLIVAN, PEGGY, librarian, consultant; b. Kansas City, Mo., Aug. 12, 1929; d. Michael C. and Ella (O'Donnell) Sullivan. AB, Clarke Coll., 1950; MS in Libr. Sci., Cath. U. Am., 1953; PhD, U. Chgo., 1972. Children's pub. libr., Mo., Md., Va., 1952-61; sch. libr. specialist Montgomery County (Md.) Pub. Schs., 1961-63; dir. Knapp Sch. Librs. Project, 1963—68, Jr. Coll. Libr. Info. Ctr., 1968-69; asst. prof. U. Pitts., 1971-73; dir. Office for Libr. Pers. Resources, ALA, Chgo., 1973-74; dean of students, assoc. prof. Grad. Libr. Sch., U. Chgo., 1974-77; asst. commr. for ext. svcs. Chgo. Pub. Libr., 1977-81; dean Coll. Profl. Studies, No. Ill. U., DeKalb, 1981-90; dir. univ. librs. No. Ill. U., 1990-92; exec. dir. ALA, 1992-94; assoc. Tuft & Assocs., 1995-98; dean Grad. Sch. Libr. and Info. Sci. Rosary Coll., 1995-97. Instr. grad. libr. edn. programs, 1958-73, UNESCO cons. on sch. librs., Australia, 1970; trustee Clarke Coll., 1969-72; sr. ptnr. Able Cons., 1987-92; cons. in field. Author: The O'Donnells, 1956, Many Names for Eileen, 1969, Problems in School Media Management, 1971, Carl H. Milam and the American Library Association, 1976, Opportunities in Library and Information Science, 1977; co-author: Public Libraries: Smart Practices in Personnel, 1982; editor: Realization: The Final Report of the Knapp School Libraries Project, 1968. Mem.: ALA, Ill. Libr. Assn., Cath. Libr. Assn., Caxton Club, Chgo. Lit. Club. Roman Catholic. Home and Office: 2800 N Lake Shore Dr Apt 816 Chicago IL 60657-6266 Office Phone: 773-549-5361. Business E-Mail: pslibcon@alumni.uchicago.edu. *Opportunities to use my abilities in a variety of public services have enriched my life, as I hope the results have enriched and empowered others.*

SULLIVAN, ROBERT EDWARD, lawyer; b. San Francisco, May 18, 1936; s. Edward C. S. and Mary Jane (Sullivan); m. Maureen Lois Miles, June 14, 1958 (dec. 1972); children: Teresa Ann, Andrew Edward, Edward Braddock; m. Lynn Bryant, Aug. 28, 2002. BS, U. San Francisco, 1958; LLB, U. Calif-Berkeley, 1961. Bar: Calif. 1962. Assoc. Pillsbury, Madison & Sutro, San Francisco, 1963-70, ptnr., 1971—2000, Pillsbury Winthrop LLP, San Francisco, 2001—05, Pillsbury Winthrop Shaw Pittman LLP, San Francisco, 2005—. Lectr. bus. law Calif. Continuing Edn. Bar and Practicing Law Inst.; v.p., treas., dir. MPC Ins., Ltd., 1986-93. Contbr. articles to profl. jours. Bd. dirs., exec. com. mem., sec. San Francisco Opera Assn., 1993—. 1st lt. U.S. Army, 1961-63. Mem. ABA, State Bar Calif. (com. corps. 1979-82, chmn. 1981-82, mem. exec. com. bus. law sect. 1982-85, vice chmn. 1983-84, chmn. 1984-85, advisor 1985-86, mem. partnership com. 1990-92, chmn. ltd. liability co. drafting com. 1992-93), San Francisco Bar Assn., Bankers Club San Francisco (bd. dirs., sec.). Democrat. Roman Catholic. Office: Pillsbury Winthrop Shaw Pittman LLP 50 Fremont St San Francisco CA 94105-2228

SULLIVAN, ROBERT EMMET, JR., lawyer; b. Detroit, Oct. 2, 1955; s. Robert Emmett Sr. and Gloria Marie (Lamb) S. BA in Polit. Sci. and Sociology, Wayne State U., Detroit, 1977; M in Urban Planning, U. Mich., 1979; JD, U. Detroit, 1983; postgrad., Oxford U., Eng., 1981. Bar: Mich. 1984, US Dist. Ct. (we. dist.) Mich. 1984, US Dist. Ct. (ea. dist.) Mich. 1984, US Ct. Appeals (6th cir.) 1984, US Ct. Appeal (D.C. cir.) 1984, US Tax Ct. 1984, DC 1985, US Supreme Ct. 1987. Planning commr. City of Detroit, 1982-85; shareholder Sullivan, Ward, Asher & Patton, PC, Detroit, 1984—2007; mem., bd. dirs. Internat. Inst. Metro. Detroit. Contbr. articles to profl. jours. Active St. Scholastica Parish Ch., North Rosedale Park Civic Assn., Detroit Hist. Soc. Moffitt scholar, 1982, 83. Mem. AIA, Detroit Bar Assn., Am. Planning Assn., Am. Inst. Cert. Planners. Roman Catholic. Home: 7464 Wilshire West Bloomfield MI 48322-2875 Personal E-mail: resulliv@umich.edu.

SULLIVAN, ROBERT EMMETT, pediatric dentist, educator; b. Sioux City, Iowa, May 28, 1932; s. Joseph A. and Daisy B. (Stanieforth) S.; m. Mary Ann Haerer, Sept. 22, 1961. BA, Morningside Coll., 1954; DDS, U. Nebr., 1961, MSD, 1963. Diplomate Am. Bd. Pediat. Dentistry. Prof., chair pediat. dentistry U. Nebr. Coll. Dentistry, Lincoln, 1963—; prof. pediats. U. Nebr. Coll. Medicine, Omaha, 1969—. Contbr. articles to profl. jours. With U.S. Army. Fellow Am. Acad. Pediat. Dentistry, Am. Coll. Dentists, Internat. Coll. Dentistry; mem. ADA, VFW, Am. Soc. Dentistry for Children, N.E. Nebr. Dental Assn., Lincoln Dist. Dental Assn. Democrat. Avocation: music. Home: 2530 Ridge Rd Lincoln NE 68512-2418

SULLIVAN, ROBERT JOHN, lawyer; b. Butte, Mont., Feb. 22, 1954; s. James David and Margorie (Ostoj) S.; m. Mary R. White, Feb. 18, 1984; children: Brian Robert, Patrick Leland. BA, U. Mont., 1976, JD, 1980; attended, Nat. Inst. Trial Advocacy, 1985. Bar: Mont. 1980, U.S. Dist. Ct. Mont. 1980, U.S. Ct. Appeals (9th cir.) 1980. Dep. county atty. Missoula (Mont.) County Atty.'s Office, 1980-85; assoc. Boone Karlberg P.C., Missoula, 1985—87, ptnr., 1987—. Mem. ABA, Western Mont. Bar Assn. (treas. 1989, v.p. 1990, pres. 1990-91), Mont. State Bar Assn. (trustee, mem. character and fitness com., 1991-, chmn. 2001-02, pres.-elect 2002-03, pres. 2003-04, past pres. 2004-05). Avocations: biking, skiing, outdoors. Office: Boone Karlberg PC 201 W Main St Ste 300 PO Box 9199 Missoula MT 59807-9199

SULLIVAN, ROBERT S., college dean; BA in Math., Boston Coll., 1966; PhD in Ops. Mgmt., Pa. State U., 1968; MBA in Prodn. Mgmt., Cornell U., 2003. Various U. Tex., Austin, 1968—91; dean graduate sch. Indsl. Adminstrn. Carnegie Mellon U., Pitts., 1991-95; dir. IC2 inst. U. Tex., Austin, 1995-97; dean Kenan-Flagler U. N.C., Chapel Hill, 1998—2003; dean Rady Sch. Mgmt. U. Calif., San Diego, 2003—. Peace Corps. vol. Addis Ababa U., 1968-70. Office: U Calif Rady Sch Mgmt 9500 Gilman Dr La Jolla CA 92093-0093 Office Phone: 858-822-0830. Business E-Mail: rss@ucsd.edu.

SULLIVAN, SHAUN STUART, lawyer; b. Albany, NY, Dec. 25, 1940; s. Charles Patrick and Dorothy Beatrice (Stuart) S.; m. Bonnie Sullivan; children: Sara Stuart, Jennifer Landon. AB with honors, Fairfield U., 1962; LLB, Fordham U., 1966. Bar: N.Y., Conn., U.S. Dist. Ct. (so. dist.) N.Y., U.S. Dist. Ct. Conn., U.S. Ct. Appeals (2d cir.), U.S. Supreme Ct. Assoc. Cahill, Gordon, NYC, 1966-69, Wiggin & Dana, New Haven, 1969—. Fellow Am. Coll. Trial Lawyers (chair ADR comm., chair state of Conn. 1997-99, Best Lawyers 1987-2005), Internat. Acad. Trial Lawyers (chmn. state of Conn. 2004—); mem. Internat. Bar Assn. (chair litig. sect. bus. law 1999-2001), Am. Bar Found., Conn. Bar Found. Home: 40 Cliff St New Haven CT 06511-1344 Office Phone: 203-498-4400. Business E-Mail: ssullivan@wiggin.com.

SULLIVAN, STEPHEN GENE, psychiatrist, pharmacologist, health facility administrator; b. Manchester, NH, Feb. 27, 1947; BS, Georgetown U., 1970; MS, NYU, 1976, PhD, 1977, MD, 1984. Assoc. research scientist NYU Sch. Med., 1978-81, rsch. asst. prof. pharmacology, 1981-82, adj. asst. prof. pharmacology, 1984-91; intern Beth Israel Med. Ctr., NYC, 1984, resident in psychiatry, 1984-88, physician-in-charge Clin. Psychopharmacology Lab., 1988-90; sci. dir. The Corp. for Clin. Psychopharmacology Research, NYC, 1988-99; pvt. practice NYC, 1986—. Instr. psychiatry Mt. Sinai Sch. Med. CUNY, 1986-88, asst. clin. prof. psychiatry, 1988-90. Author, adminstr.: (Web site) speciesaccounts.org, 2001—; contbr. numerous articles to profl. jours., author ten book chpts., 1976—. Med. scientist tng. program fellow NIH, 1970-76, 82-83, postdoctoral fellow, 1976-77. Mem. AAAS, AMA, Am. Psychiat. Assn., N.Y. Acad. Scis. Avocation: composing music. Office: 533 E 13th St New York NY 10009-3508 Office Phone: 212-979-9145.

SULLIVAN, STEVEN R., lawyer; b. St. Louis, Aug. 1960; BBA summa cum laude, U. Mo., St. Louis, 1981; JD with distinction, U. Mo., Kans. City, 1994. CPA 1982. Atty. Arthur Andersen & Co., Kohn, Shands, Elbert, Gianoulakis & Giljum, 1985—87, Union Electric Co. (now Ameren EU), 1987—95; assoc. gen. counsel Anheuser-Busch Co., 1995—98; v.p. regulatory policy, gen. counsel, sec. Ameren EU, 1998—2003; sr. v.p. govtl./regulatory policy, gen. counsel, sec. Ameren Corp., St. Louis, 2003—. Mem.: Mo. Bar Assn., Bar Assn. Met. St. Louis, Mo. Soc. CPA., Am. Soc. Corp. Sec., Edison Electric Inst. Office: Ameren Corp 1 Ameren Plz 1901 Chouteau Ave Saint Louis MO 63103 Office Phone: 314-621-3222. Office Fax: 314-554-3801. *

SULLIVAN, STUART FRANCIS, anesthesiologist, educator; b. Buffalo, July 15, 1928; s. Charles S. and Kathryn (Duggan) S.; m. Dorothy Elizabeth Faytol, Apr. 18, 1959; children: John, Irene, Paul, Kathryn. BS, Canisius Coll., 1950; MD, SUNY, Syracuse, 1955. Diplomate Am. Bd. Anesthesiology. Intern Ohio State U. Hosp., Columbus, 1955—56; resident Columbia Presbyn. Med. Ctr., 1958—60; fellow Columbia-Bellevue Hosp. Ctr., NYC, 1960—61; instr. anesthesiology Columbia U. Coll. Physicians and Surgeons, NYC, 1961—62, assoc., 1962—64, asst. prof., 1964—69, assoc. prof., 1969—73; prof. dept. anesthesiology UCLA, 1973—91, vice chair anesthesiology, 1974—77, exec. vice chair, 1977—90, acting chmn., 1983—84, 1987—88, 1990—91, prof. emeritus, 1991—. Capt. M.C., USAR, 1956-58. Fellow NIH, 1960-61; recipient research career devel. award NIH, 1966-69. Mem. Assn. Univ. Anesthetists, Am. Physiol. Soc., Am. Soc. Anesthesiologists. Home: 101 Foxtail Dr Santa Monica CA 90402-2047 Office: UCLA Sch Medicine Dept Anesthesiology Los Angeles CA 90095-0001

SULLIVAN, TERESA ANN, law and sociology educator, academic administrator; d. Gordon Hager and Mary Elizabeth (Finnegan) S.; m. H. Douglas Laycock, June 14, 1971; children: Joseph Peter, John Patrick. BA, Mich. State U., 1970; MA, U. Chgo., 1972, PhD, 1975. Asst. prof. sociology U. Tex., Austin, 1975-76, assoc. prof. sociology, 1981-87, dir. women's studies, 1985-87, prof. sociology, 1987—, prof. law, 1988—, assoc. dean grad. sch., 1989-90, 1992-95, chair dept. sociology, 1990-92, vice provost, 1994-95, v.p., grad. dean, 1995—2002; asst. prof. sociology U. Chgo., 1977-81; exec. vice-chancellor acad. affairs U. Tex. Sys., 2002—06; provost, exec. v.p. academic affairs U. Mich., Ann Arbor, 2006—. Pres. Southwestern Sociol. Assn., 1988-89; mem. faculty adv. bd. Hogg Found. Mental Health, 1989-92; mem. sociology panel NSF, 1983-85. Author: Marginal Workers Marginal Jobs, 1978; co-author: As We Forgive Our Debtors, 1989 (Silver Gavel 1990), Social Organization of Work, 1990, 4th edit., 2007; co-author: The Fragile Middle Class, 2000; contbr. articles and chpts. to profl. jours. Bd. dirs. Calvert Found., Chgo., 1978, CARA, Inc., Washington, 1985; mem. U.S. Census Bur. Adv. Com., 1989-95, chmn., 1991-92; mem. sociology panel NSF, 1983-85; trustee St. Michael's Acad., 1996-2001. Leadership Tex. 1994. Fellow AAAS (liaison to Population Assn. Am. 1989-91, chair sect. K 1996), Sociol. Rsch. Assn., Am. Sociol. Assn. (sec. 1995—, editor Rose Monograph Series 1988-92), Philos. Soc. Tex., Soc. Study of Social Problems (chair fin. com. 1986-87), Population Assn. Am. (bd. dirs. 1989-91, chair fin. com. 1990-91), Assn. Grad. Schs. (pres. 2001-2002). Roman Catholic. Avocation: reading. Office: 503 Thompson St Ann Arbor MI 48109-1340 Home: 2197 Gray Fox Ct Ann Arbor MI 48103 Office Phone: 734-764-9292. Business E-Mail: tsull@umich.edu.

SULLIVAN, THOMAS CHRISTOPHER, coatings company executive; b. Cleve., July 8, 1937; s. Frank Charles and Margaret Mary (Wilhelmy) S.; m. Sandra Simmons, Mar. 12, 1960; children: Frank, Sean, Tommy, Danny, Kathleen, Julie. BS, Miami U., Oxford, Ohio, 1959. Div. sales mgr. Republic Powdered Metals, Cleve., 1961-65, exec. v.p., 1965-70; chmn. bd., CEO RPM, Internat., Medina, Ohio, 1971—2002, chmn. bd., 2003—. Bd. dirs. Cleve. Clinic Found., Kaydon Corp., Ann Arbor, Mich. Trustee emeritus Culver (Ind.) Ednl. Found.; former trustee Cleve. Tomorrow; bd. advisors Urban Cmty. Sch., Cleve., Malachi House, Cleve.; trustee City Year Cleve.; trustee Cath. Diocese of Cleve. Found. Lt. (j.g.) USNR, 1959-60. Mem.: Nat. Assn. Securities Dealers (bd. govs. 1986—88, long-range strategic planning com.), Nat. Paint and Coatings Assn. (past chmn. bd., CEO, mem. exec. com.). Roman Catholic. Office: RPM Internat 2628 Pearl Rd Medina OH 44256-7623 Business E-Mail: tsullivan@rpminc.com.

SULLIVAN, THOMAS JAMES, retired manufacturing company executive; b. Franklin, NH, Mar. 26, 1923; s. James J. and Helen (Mullin) S.; m. Anne Clark, Aug. 31, 1963. AB, Holy Cross Coll., 1947; JD, Harvard U., 1949. With Gen. Dynamics Corp., 1949-61, asst. div. mgr., 1959-61; sr. assoc. Harbridge House, Cambridge, Mass., 1961-63; with Hydraulic Research & Mfg. Co., Valencia, Calif., 1963-71, v.p., 1964-68, exec. v.p., 1968-69, pres., 1969-71; v.p. Textron, Inc., Providence, 1971-73; pres. Walker/Parkersburg (W. Va.) Co., 1973-81, Sprague Meter, Bridgeport, Conn., 1981-84, Dimetrics Inc., Diamond Springs, Calif., 1984-86. Served with USAAF, 1943-46. Fellow Nat. Contract Mgmt. Assn. Home: 2186 Augusta Ct San Luis Obispo CA 93401-4500 E-mail: tsullivan0323@aol.com.

SULLIVAN, THOMAS PATRICK, lawyer; b. Evanston, Ill., Mar. 23, 1930; s. Clarence M. and Pauline (DeHaye) Sullivan; m. Anne Landau; children from previous marriage: Margaret Mary, Timothy Joseph, Elizabeth Ann. Student, Loras Coll., 1947—49; LLB cum laude, Loyola U., Chgo., 1952; LLD (hon.), U. Notre Dame, 2006. Bar: Ill. 1952, Calif. 1982, N.Mex 1997. Assoc. Jenner & Block, Chgo., 1954—62, ptnr., 1963—77, 1981—; U.S. atty. No. Dist. Ill., Chgo., 1977—81. Co-chair Ill. Gov.'s Commn. Capital Punishment, 2000—02; chair Capital Punishment Reform Study Com., 2005—. Contbr. articles to profl. jours. With US Army, 1952—54. Decorated Bronze Star; named laureate, Acad. Ill. Lawyers, Person of Yr., Chgo. Lawyer Mag., 2004; recipient medal of excellence, Loyola U. Law Sch., 1965, Damen award, 2004, award, Ill. Pub. Defender Assn., 1972, Justice John Paul Stevens award, 2000, Ctr. on Wrongful Convictions award, Northwestern U., 2003, Albert E. Jenner, Jr. Pro Bono award, 2003, Lifetime Achievement award, Legal Assistance Found. Chgo., 2005. Fellow: Am. Coll. Trial Lawyers; mem.: ABA (John Minor Wisdom Pub. Svc. and Professionalism award 2003), Chgo. Coun. Lawyers, Am. Judicature Soc. (Justice award 2004), Am. Law Inst., Fed. Bar Assn., Chgo. Bar Assn., Fed. 7th Cir. Bar Assn., Ill. Bar Assn. Office: Jenner & Block 330 N Wabash Ave Ste 4100 Chicago IL 60611-5697 Office Phone: 312-923-2928. Business E-Mail: tsullivan@jenner.com.

SULLIVAN, THOMAS PATRICK, academic administrator; b. Detroit, July 8, 1947; s. Walter James and Helen Rose (Polosky) S.; m. Barbara Jean Fournier, Aug. 9, 1968; children: Colleen, Brendan. BA in English, U. Dayton, 1969; M. Edn. and Adminstrn., Kent State U., 1971; postgrad., U. Mich., 1988. Tchr. Resurection Elem. Sch., Dayton, Ohio, 1968-69; adminstr. residence hall Kent (Ohio) State U., 1969-71; program mgr. residence hall Ea. Mich. U., Ypsilanti, 1971-73, adminstrv. assoc., 1973-76, dir. housing, 1976-83; assoc. provost Wayne County Community Coll., Belleville, Mich., 1983-84, dir. budget and mgmt. devel. Detroit, 1984-85, sr. v.p. acad. affairs, acting provost, 1985-86, acting exec. dean Belleville, 1986-88, dir. budget and mgmt. devel. Detroit, 1988-89; pres. Cleary Univ., Ypsilanti, 1989—. Part-time instr. English and math. Schoolcraft Coll., Livonia, Mich., 1980-90. Home: 9835 Whisperwood Ln Brighton MI 48116-8859 Office: Cleary Univ 3601 Plymouth Rd Ann Arbor MI 48105-2659

SULLIVAN, TIMOTHY, lawyer; b. Detroit, May 16, 1948; s. Paul Gilmary and Virginia (Rosier) S.; m. Marsha Rosenberg Sullivan, June 19, 1971; children: Eileen A., Hugh V. BA Journalism, U. Mich., 1970; JD, Georgetown U., 1975. Bar: Va. 1975, D.C. 1976. Contract negotiator CIA, Washington, 1973-75; assoc. Fried, Frank, Harris, Shriver & Kampelman, Washington, 1975-78; ptnr. Capell, Howard, Knabe & Cobbs P.A., Washington, 1978-83, Dykema Gossett, Washington, 1983-95, Adduci, Mastriani & Schaumberg, LLP, 1995—2001. Lectr. in field. Narrator (audio cassette) How to Negotiate Government Contracts, 1986. Citizen mem. Alexandria Commn. Persons with Disabilities, Va., 1992-99, vice-chmn. 1997-98, 98-99. Sgt. U.S. Army, 1970-73. Mem. ABA, Nat. Contract Mgmt. Assn., U. Club Washington (bd. govs. 2003-2004, sec. 2003-05, v.p. 2005-06, pres. 2006-07), Congl. Country Club (v.p. 1998-99, bd. govs. 1995-2000, pres. 1999-2000). Roman Catholic. Avocations: reading, sports. Office: Thompson Coburn LLP 1909 K St NW 6th Fl Washington DC 20006-1167

SULLIVAN, TIMOTHY E., bank executive; B, U. Ill.; MBA, U. Calif., Berkeley. Various tech. and ops. mgmt. positions including chief info. officer First Interstate Bank, Ariz.; chief info. officer Kaiser Found. Health Plan; exec. v.p., group tech. exec. Wells Fargo, San Francisco; corp. exec. v.p., chief info. officer SunTrust Banks, Inc., Atlanta, 2003—. Office: SunTrust Banks Inc PO Box 4418 Atlanta GA 30302-4418 Office Phone: 404-588-7711. Office Fax: 505-827-6173. *

SULLIVAN, TIMOTHY JACKSON, museum and retired academic administrator, educator; b. Ravenna, Ohio, Apr. 15, 1944; s. Ernest Tulio and Margaret Elizabeth (Caris) Sullivan; m. Anne Doubet Klare, Jan. 21, 1973. AB, Coll. William and Mary, Williamsburg, Va., 1966; JD, Harvard U., Cambridge, Mass., 1969; LLD (hon.), U. Aberdeen, Scotland, 1993, Old Dominion U., Norfolk, Va., 2005, Centre Coll., Danville, Ky., 2007. Asst. prof. law Coll. William and Mary, Williamsburg, Va., 1972—75, assoc. prof., 1975—78, prof., 1978—85, Bryan prof. law, dean, 1985—92, pres., 1992—2005, pres. emeritus, 2005—; exec. asst. for policy to Gov. Charles S. Robb State of Va., Richmond, Va., 1982—85; atty. Freeman, Drapers' Co., London, 1992; pres., CEO The Mariners Mus., Newport News, Va., 2006—. Vis. prof. law U. Va., Charlottesville, 1981; exec. dir. Gov.'s Commn. on Va.'s Future, Richmond, 1982—84; vice-chmn. Gov.'s Commn. on Fed. Spending, Richmond, 1986; mem. Gov.'s Fellows Selection Com., 1985—90, Gov.'s Commn. on Sexual Assault and Substance Abuse on the Coll. Campus (chmn. enforcement subcom.), 1991—92; counsel Commn. on Future of Va.'s Jud. Sys., 1987—89; chair VA Rhodes Scholarship Commn., 1998—2003; mem. Livery Drapers Co., 2003; chair appeals panel Internat. Commn. Holocaust Era Ins. Claims, 2002—06. Mem. Va. State Bd. Edn., Richmond, 1987—92; chair Gov.'s Task Force on Intercollegiate Athletics, 1992—93; pres. The Mariner's Mus., Newport News, Va., 2006—. Decorated Bronze Star; named Outstanding Virginian, Va. 4-H Found., 1999. Fellow: Va. Bar Fedn., Am. Bar Fedn.; mem.: ABA, Va. Bar Assn., Va. State Bar, Am. Arbitration Assn. (bd. dirs. 2000—03), Cosmos Club, Univ. Club (Washington), Bull and Bear Club, Omicron Delta Kappa, Phi Beta Kappa. Democrat. Avocations: wine, swimming, reading, golf. Office: Coll William and Mary Office of Pres Emeritus PO Box 8795 Williamsburg VA 23187-8795 also: The Mariners Museum 100 Museum Dr Newport News VA 23606 Home Phone: 757-220-0423; Office Phone: 757-591-7707. Business E-Mail: tjsull@wm.edu, tsullivan@marinersmuseum.org.

SULLIVAN, TIMOTHY PATRICK, telecommunications company executive; b. Springfield, Ill., Mar. 4, 1942; s. Jeremiah Joseph and Genevieve Anastasia (Stapleton) S.; m. Kathleen Veronica Logue, May 4, 1974; children: Timothy Patrick Jr., Michael Sean, Shannon Kathleen, Jennifer Hillary, Thomas Brendan. BSEE, U. Notre Dame, 1964; postgrad., Syracuse U., 1966-67. Tech. mgr. IBM Corp., Poughkeepsie, NY, 1964—68, Hursley, England, 1968—69, middle mgr. Poughkeepsie, San Jose, 1969—77, sr. mgr. Research Triangle Park, NC, 1977—81, corp. cons. Armonk, NY, 1981—83, product mgr. Research Triange Park, NC, 1983—85; v.p., officer No. Telecom, Richardson, Tex., 1985—92; pres., CEO Connectware, Inc., 1993—97; CEO Com World, Inc., 1997—98; pres. Optical Networking, SBU, Lucent Techs., Richardson, Tex., 1998—2000; pres. optical networking group Lucent Techs., Holmdel, NJ, 2001—03; pres., CEO Cebatech Inc., Eatontown, 2004—07; chief tech. officer Internap, 2007—. Bd. dirs., chmn. Corp. for Open Systems, McLean, Va., 1992; bd. dirs. AXONLINK; mem. adv. bd. Monmouth U., Corrigent Sys., Reactive Nanotech., Arcana Networks, Carrius Techs.; mem. exec. adv. coun. Nat. Comms. Forum, Chgo., 1989-90; chmn. bd. Osinet Corp., 1991. Inventor storage subsystems in field, 1969-71; author: Captain, 1974; contbr. articles to profl. jours. Adv. bd. Dallas Mus. of Art, 1988-92; mem. North Tex. Commn., Dallas, 1988-91. Republican. Roman Catholic. Avocations: creative writing, chess, golf. Home: 170 Red Hill Rd Middletown NJ 07748 Office Phone: 908-601-2244. Personal E-mail: tpskvs@ix.netcom.com. Business E-Mail: sullivan@cebatech.com.

SULLIVAN, TRUDY F., apparel executive; m. Michael Sullivan; children: Catherine, Anne. BA, Manhattanville Coll.; grad. studies, Simmons Coll. Buyer Jordan Marsh; mgmt. positions with The Avenue, Decelle, T. Deane, Filene's; pres. J. Crew Group, Inc., 1997—2001; group pres. Liz Claiborne casual & Liz Claiborne woman Liz Claiborne, Inc., NYC, 2001—02, exec. v.p., 2002—06, pres., 2006—07; pres., CEO The Talbots, Inc., Hingham, Mass., 2007—. Office: The Talbots 1 Talbots Dr Hingham MA 02043 *

SULLIVAN, WILLIAM BEAUMONT, lawyer; b. Kansas City, Mo., May 12, 1945; s. Raymond Sidney and Georgia Belle (Sykes) S.; m. Donna Ray Daniel, Nov. 25, 1966; 1 child, Georgia Marie. BA magna cum laude in Economics, U. Va., 1967; JD cum laude, Harvard U., 1970. Bar: DC 1970, NC, 1990, US Ct. Appeals DC, 3rd, 4th, 6th, and 11th Circuits, various dist. and bankruptcy courts. Assoc. Arent, Fox, Kintner, Plotkin & Kahn, Washington, 1970-77, ptnr., 1978-90, head bankruptcy dept., 1982-90; mem. Womble, Carlyle, Sandridge & Rice PLLC, Winston-Salem, NC, 1990—, bankruptcy and creditors' rights practice group leader. Fellow Am. Bar Found., Am. Coll. Bankruptcy; mem. ABA, NC Bar Assn., Am. Bankruptcy Inst., Am. Arbitration Assn., Harvard U. Law Sch. Assn., Walker Chandler Inn of Ct. Avocations: word puzzles, music, golf. Office: Womble Carlyle Sandridge & Rice PLLC PO Box 84 Winston Salem NC 27102 Office Phone: 336-721-3506. Office Fax: 336-733-8365. Business E-Mail: wsullivan@wcsr.com.

SULLIVAN, WILLIAM FRANCIS, lawyer; b. San Francisco, May 6, 1952; s. Francis Michael and Jane Frances (Walsh) S.; children: Matthew, Meghan, Kathleen; m. Kait Sullivan. AB, U. Calif., Berkeley, 1974; JD, UCLA, 1977. Bar: Calif. 1977, U.S. Dist. Ct. (no. dist.) Calif. 1977, U.S. Ct. Appeals (9th cir.) 1977, U.S. Dist. Ct. (ea. dist.) Calif. 1978, U.S. Ct. Appeals (D.C. cir.) 1979, U.S. Ct. Appeals (fed. cir.) 1985, U.S. Dist. Ct. (so. dist.) Calif. 1986, U.S. Dist. Ct. (cen. dist.) Calif. 1990, U.S. Supreme Ct. 1986. Assoc. Chickering & Gregory, San Francisco and Washington, 1977-81, Brobeck, Phleger & Harrison, San Diego and San Francisco, 1981-84, ptnr., 1984—2002, mng. ptnr. San Diego, 1992-96, 2001—03, securities litig. group leader, 2002—03, firmwide mng. ptnr., 1996-98; ptnr. Paul Hastings Janofsky & Walker LLP, San Diego and LA, 2003—, chair nat. securities litig. practice group, mem. litig. steering com., 2003—. Named Calif. Lawyer of Yr. in Securities, Chambers USA, 2006; named an

Best Lawyers in Am. Mem. ABA, Assn. Bus. Trial Lawyers (bd. govs. San Diego chpt. 1993-95), Calif. Bar Assn. (litig. sect.), San Francisco Bar Assn., San Diego Bar Assn., Barristers Club San Francisco (bd. dirs. 1984-86, pres. 1985), Calif. Young Lawyers Assn. (bd. dirs. 1986-89, sec. 1987-99, 1st v.p. 1988-89), Am. Arbitration Assn. Democrat. Roman Catholic. Home: 1089 Prospect Blvd Pasadena CA 91103 Home Phone: 626-584-1909; Office Phone: 213-683-6000. Business E-Mail: williamsullivan@paulhastings.com.

SULLIVAN, WILLIAM J., state supreme court justice; b. Waterbury, Conn., Mar. 12, 1939; Student, St. Thomas Sem., 1958-59; BA in Polit. Sci., Providence Coll., 1962; B in Civil Law, Coll. William and Mary, 1965, JD, 1970. Priv. practice, Waterbury, 1967—78; civil service commr. State of Conn., 1974—75; corp. counsel City of Waterbury, 1976—78; judge Conn. Superior Ct., 1978-97, Conn. Appellate Ct., 1997-99; assoc. justice Conn. Supreme Ct., 1999-2001, chief justice, 2001—06, sr. justice, 2006—. Captain US Army, 1965—66. Decorated 2 Bronze Stars for meritorious svc. US Army, Air Medal. Office: Conn Supreme Ct Supreme Ct Bldg 231 Capitol Ave Hartford CT 06106-1548 Office Phone: 860-757-2116.

SULLIVAN, WILLIAM JOHN, osteopath; b. Pitts., Kans., Nov. 5, 1963; s. William Leroy and Joan Elizabeth (Prete) S; div.; 1 child, Lauren Marie. BS in Biology, Pittsburg State U., 1986; DO, U. Health Scis., Kansas City, Mo., 1990. Diplomate Nat. Bd. Osteo. Med. Examiners, Am. Bd. Internal Medicine, Am. Assn. Med. Rev. Officers. Intern Riverside Hosp., Wichita, Kans., 1990-91; resident Deaconess Hosp., St. Louis, 1991-94; pvt. practice Med. Cons. of Pitts., LLC, Kans., 1994—; active staff Mt. Carmel Med. Ctr., 1994—, med. dir. occupl. health, med. dir. employee health, 1995—2002, med. dir. cardiomyopathy clinic, 1997—, chief medicine, 1998—, chief-of-staff-elect, 1999—, pres. med. staff, 2001—. Mem. adv. bd. dirs. Cmty. Nat. Bank, Pittsburg; med. staff sec. Mt. Carmel Med. Ctr., Pittsburg, 1999; clin. instr. Pittsburg State U. Sch. Nursing; participating physician Pittsburg Free Clinic; clin. adv. Pittsburg State U. Pre-Med Club; mem. health occupations adv. bd. Unified Sch. Dist. #250; physician Congl. Health Ministries; consulting physician Cmty. Health Clinic S.E. Kans., 2006—. Mem. exec. bd. dirs. Pitts. Family YMCA, pres.-elect, 2003, pres., 2004—, chief internal medicine, 1995—; bd. dirs. Pitts. State U. Alumni Assn., nat. 2d v.p., 2003-04. Lt. col. Kans. Army N.G., 1988—. Fellow ACP; mem. VFW, Kans. Med. Soc., Am. Assn. Med. Rev. Officers, N.G. Assn. U.S., KC, Crawford County Med. Soc. (pres. 2000), Am. Legion, Sigma Chi (life loyal Sig program). Republican. Roman Catholic. Avocations: music, golf, stamp collecting/philately. Office: Med Consultants Pitts LLC 1015 Mt Carmel Pl Pittsburg KS 66762 Home: 1502 Woodland Terr Pittsburg KS 66762 Office Phone: 620-231-8849. Personal E-mail: wsullivan21@cox.net.

SULLIVAN, WILLIAM LITSEY, lawyer; b. Harrodsburg, Ky., Nov. 1, 1921; s. Charles Blount and Anne Litsey Sullivan; m. Elizabeth Dorsey Sullivan, Apr. 21, 1951; children: John Charles, William L. Jr. BA, Centre Coll. Ky., Danville, 1943; LLB, U. Ky., Lexington, 1948; degree in Humanities (hon.), Henderson C.C., Ky., 2004. Founder and ptnr. Dorsey and Sullivan, Henderson, Ky., 1956—95; ptnr. Sullivan and Sullivan, 1995—99; of counsel Stoll Keenan Ogden PLLC, 1999—. Mem. Ky. State Senate, Frankfort, Ky., 1953—58, 1966—82; commr. aeronautics State of Ky., Frankfort, Ky., 1959—60; acting judge Ky. Supreme Ct., 1978; chmn. Ky. State Lottery, Louisville, 1988—89; mem. Ky. Racing Commn., 1990—94. Chmn. Coll. Found., Inc., Henderson, Ky., 1980—. 1st lt. USAAF, 1943—45. Named winner, Internat. Formula One Air Race, France, 1976, Outstanding Alumnus, Centre Coll., 1976, Disting. Citizen, City of Henderson, Ky., 2004; named to Ky. Aviation Hall of Fame, Ky. Aviation Mus., 2004. Mem.: ABA, Ky. Bar Assn. Democrat. Presbyterian. Avocations: hunting, fishing, golf, flying. Office: Stoll Keenan Ogden PLLC 201 C N Main Henderson KY 42420 Office Phone: 270-831-1900.

SULLIVAN, WILLIAM P., electronics executive; b. Yakima, Wash., 1949; BS, U. Calif.-Davis. With Hewlett-Packard Co., 1976—99, various positions, 1976—95, gen. mgr. Optical Comm. Divsn., 1995—97, gen. mgr. Comm. Semiconductor Solutions Divsn., 1997—98, gen. mgr., v.p. Components Group (now Semiconductor Products Group), 1998—99; senior v.p., gen. mgr. SPG Agilent Technologies Inc. (spin-off from HP Co.), 1999—2002; exec. v.p., COO Agilent Technologies Inc., 2002—05, pres., CEO, 2005—. Bd. dir. Children's Discovery Mus., San Jose, Calif., Lumileds, URS Corp., 2006—. Office: Agilent Technologies Inc 395 Page Mill Rd Palo Alto CA 94306 *

SULLIVAN STEMBERG, MAUREEN, interior designer; b. Brookline, Mass., July 8, 1951; d. Loretta McDermott and Herbert Michael Sullivan; m. Thomas George Stemberg, Mar. 11, 1975 (div. Sept. 0, 1989). AA in polit. sci., Newton Jr. Coll., 1969—71; degree in art history, Boston Coll., 1972—73; Fine Arts Program, Mus. of Fine Arts Sch., 1973—75; Architecture and Design, Boston Ctr. of Architecture, 1982—85. ASID, MA, 1987. CEO, interior designer Interiors of Wellesley, Inc., Wellesley, Mass., 1977—80; CEO, head designer Maureen Sullivan Stemberg Interiors, Boston-Palm Beach, 1980—98; design and fashion editor Palm Beach Illus., Palm Beach, Fla., 1990—95; CEO BabySuites.Com, Boston, 2003—04; chief creative officer Connoisseur Pub., Inc., Boston, 2004—. Chmn. and co-chairman, ann. flower show Mass. Hort. Soc., Boston, 1990—94. Designer Mahaney Baseball Club House, U. Maine (Top 5 Design winner for Baseball Complex Devel., 1994), Various Hotel Interiors (Top 20 Hotel Designers for Holiday Inns Inc., 1991), Trump Plaza, other Club Colette, Palm Beach, Fla.; contbr. articles to mag. Fund raiser Barcelona Summer Olympics, Mass., Spain, 1990—92, Am. Cup, Boston, 1993—95; trustee Boston Opera Co., 1977—81. Mem.: United Way of Mass. Bay, Nat. Trust for Hist. Preservation, Dana Farber Cancer Inst. Pediat. (hon.; dir. 1996—97), Nat. Musuem of Women in the Arts (hon.; coun. mem. 1991—93), Am. Soc. of Interior Designers (assoc.). Home: 118 Huntington Ave Ste 1403 Boston MA 02116 Home Phone: 617-266-5664; Office Phone: 617-266-5664. E-mail: maureen@connoiseurpublishing.com, intdesignmss@aol.com.

SULLIVAN-SZUTS, BETTY ANNE, academic administrator, educator; b. Phila., Dec. 23, 1939; d. Rowland Thomas and Elizabeth Catherine Moriarty; m. Robert Lloyd Sullivan, Sept. 21, 1957 (div.); children: Lisa Anne Sullivan, Brent Rowland Sullivan, Jamie Alexandra Sullivan; m. Ivan Ramon Szuts, May 6, 1995. BS in Home Econs. Edn., Douglass Coll., Balt., 1975; EdM in Supervision and Adminstrn., Rutgers U., New Brunswick, N.J., 1978, EdD in Adult and Continuing Ednl. Adminstrn., 1989. Cert. sch. adminstr. NJ, prin./supr. NJ, tchr. home econs. NJ. Tchr. home econs. Freehold Regional HS Dist., NJ, 1975—80; state supr. home econs. edn. NJ State Dept. Edn., Trenton, 1980—81; dir. and tchr. in-svc. Rutgers U., New Brunswick, NJ, 1981—89; vice prin. Monmouth County Vo-Tech H.S. Dist., Middletown, NJ, 1990—91; dir. Suffolk County Respite Care Program, Patchogue, NY, 1991—94; dir. gerontology program and instr. aging courses Union County Coll., Cranford, NJ, 1994—96; supr. student tchrs. Georgian Ct. Coll., Lakewood, NJ, 1994—96; vis. prof. dept. sociology Wheaton Coll., Norton, Mass., 1996—97; dir. model Tex. safe home program N.W. Assistance Ministries, Houston, 2000—02; grant coord. N. Harris Coll., 2002—03; seminar leader Spirited Elder and Assocs. Adj. prof. profl. studies grad. program LI U., Southampton, NY, 1991—94; rschr. Aging Tex. Well Coalition, 2002—; seminar leader Spirited Elder and Assocs., 2004—; presenter in field. Author: Spiritual Elders: Women of Worth in the Third Millennium, 1999. Chair edn. Harris County Area Agy. Aging, tng. com.; chair adv. bd. Acad. Lifelong Learning, North Harris Coll.; mem. Acts 16:5 task force Presbytery New Covenant, Houston; ruling elder Northwoods Presbyn. Ch., 2006—. Recipient Cmty. Svc. award, North Harris Coll., 2003; grantee The Aging Tex. Well Grant, 2002—03. Mem.: Phi Delta Kappa, Kappa Delta Pi, Omicron Nu. Avocations: tennis, ballroom dancing, writing, playing the organ. Home and Office: Spirited Elder and Assocs 14311 Champions Dr Houston TX 77069 Office Phone: 281-895-0321. Personal E-mail: bettyanne.ivan@sbcglobal.net.

SULLOWAY, FRANK JONES, social sciences educator, historian; b. Concord, NH, Feb. 2, 1947; s. Alvah Woodbury and Alison (Green) Sulloway; 1 child, Ryan. AB summa cum laude, Harvard U., Cambridge, Mass., 1969, AM in History Sci., 1971, PhD in History Sci., 1978. Jr. fellow Harvard U. Soc. Fellows, 1974-77; mem. Sch. Social Sci. Inst. Advanced Study, Princeton, NJ, 1977-78; rsch. fellow Miller Inst. Basic Rsch. Sci. U. Calif., Berkeley, 1978-80, vis. Miller rsch. prof., 1999—2000, vis. prof., 2000—; rsch. fellow MIT, Cambridge, 1980-81, vis. scholar, 1989-98; postdoctoral fellow Harvard U., Cambridge, 1981-82, vis. scholar, 1984-89; rsch. fellow U. Coll., London, 1982-84; Vernon prof. biography Dartmouth Coll., Hanover, NH, 1986. Author: (book) Freud, Biologist of the Mind, 1979 (Pfizer award History Sci. Soc., 1980), Born to Rebel, 1996; contbr. articles to profl. jours. Recipient Randi award, Skeptics Soc., 1997, Golden Plate award, Am. Acad. Achievement, 1997; fellow, NEH, 1980—81, NSF, 1981—82, John Simon Guggenheim Meml. Found., 1982—83, MacArthur Found., 1984—89, Dibner Inst., MIT, 1993—94, Ctr. Advanced Study Behavioral Scis., Stanford, Calif., 1998—99. Fellow: AAAS (mem. electorate nominating com. sect. L 1988—91, 1994—97), Assn. Psychol. Sci., Linnean Soc. London; mem.: History Sci. Soc. (mem. fin. com. 1987—92, mem. com. devel. 1988—92), Human Behavior and Evolution Soc., Am. Psychol. Soc. Home: 1709 Shattuck Ave Apt 205 Berkeley CA 94709-1753 Office: U Calif Dept Psychology IPSR 4125 Tolman Hall Berkeley CA 94720-1603 Home Phone: 510-540-9336; Office Phone: 510-642-7139. Business E-Mail: sulloway@berkeley.edu.

SULLY, IRA BENNETT, lawyer; b. Columbus, Ohio, June 3, 1947; s. Bernie and Helen Mildred (Koen) S.; m. Nancy Lee Pryor, Oct. 2, 1983. BA cum laude, Ohio State U., 1969, JD summa cum laude, 1974. Bar: Ohio 1974, U.S. Dist. Ct. (so. dist.) Ohio 1974. Assoc. Schottenstein, Garel, Swedlow & Zox, Columbus, 1974-78; atty. Borden, Inc., Columbus, 1978-80; sole practice Columbus, 1980—. Instr. Real Estate Law Columbus Tech. Inst., 1983-88; title ins. agt. Sycamore Title Agy., Columbus, 1983—. Bd. dirs. Rsch. Franklin County Celeste for Gov., Columbus, 1978; asst. treas. Pamela Conrad for City Coun., Columbus, 1979; treas. Leland for State Rep., Columbus, 1982, 84, Leland for City Atty., Columbus, 1985; active Ohio Dem. Bldg. Com., 1995-98; commentator Sta. WOSU, Columbus, 1980; trustee Ohio State U. Undergrad. Student Govt. Alumni Soc., 1997—, pres., 2000—. Mem. ABA, Ohio Bar Assn., Columbus Bar Assn., Agonis Club (Columbus). Democrat. Jewish. Avocations: running, coin collecting/numismatics. Home: 200 Reinhard Ave Columbus OH 43206-2616 Office: 844 S Front St Columbus OH 43206-2543 Office Phone: 614-443-3930.

SULTAN, ALTOON, artist; b. Bklyn., Sept. 29, 1948; BFA, Bklyn. Coll., 1969, MFA in Painting, 1971; student, Skowhegan Art Sch., Maine, 1970. Vis. critic Univ. Pa., Phila., 1985—88; resident faculty Skowhegan Sch. Painting & Sculpture, Maine, 1988; asst. prof. San Jose State Univ., Calif., 1991—94; vis. prof. Dartmouth Coll., NH, 1998—2001; founder Mount Ara Designs, Groton, Vt. Author: The Luminous Brush: Painting with Egg Tempera, 1999; one-woman shows include First St. Gallery, NYC, 1971, 1973, 1975, Univ. SD, Vermillion, 1975, Marlborough Gallery, NYC, 1977, 1979, 1982, 1984, 1985, 1988, 1990, 1993, 1995, 1998, Marlborough Fine Art Graphics, London, 1987, Galleria Marieschi, Monza, Italy, 1999, Tibor de Nagy Gallery, NYC, 2001, exhibited in group shows at Suffolk Mus., Stony Brook, NY, 1971, Allan Frumkin Gallery, NYC, 1975, Davis & Long Gallery, 1977, Thorpe Intermedia Gallery, Sparkill, NY, 1980, Downtown Br., Whitney Mus., NYC, 1982, Mus. Fine Arts, Boston, 1982, One Penn Plaza, NYC, 1985, Veranneman Found., Belgium, 1986, David Adamson Gallery, Washington, 1988, Flint Inst. of Arts, Mich., 1991, Am. Acad. and Inst. of Arts & Letters, NYC, 1992, Sleeth Gallery, W. Va. Wesleyan Coll., 1996, numerous others. Recipient Prix Duc de Valverde d'Ayala Valva, Fondation Monaco, 1999, Acad. award in art for egg tempera painting, Am. Acad. Arts and Letters, 1999; grantee Nat. Endowment for Arts, 1983, 1989. Mem.: NAD (academician 1995—). Studio: PO Box 2 Groton VT 05046 Office: Tibor de Nagy Gallery 724 Fifth Ave New York NY 10019

SULTAN, MARK R., plastic surgeon; b. NJ; BS, Brandeis U.; MD, Columbia U. Coll. Physicians and Surgeons, 1982. Diplomate rgery, Am. Bd. Plastic Surgery. Resident in gen. surgery Columbia-Presbyn. Med. Ctr., NYC, 1983—87, resident in plastic surgery, 1987—88, 1989—90; fellow in head and neck surgery/microvascular reconstrn. Emory U. Affiliated Hosps., Atlanta, 1988—89; attending physician dept. plastic surgery St. Luke's Roosevelt, N.Y. Eye and Ear Infirmary, NYC, 1990—; chief divsn. plastic and reconstructive surgery Beth Israel Hosp., NYC; pvt. practice plastic surgery NYC. Assoc. prof. clin. surgery Columbia U. Coll. Physicians and Surgeons, NYC. Named one of NY's Top Doctors, NY mag.; recipient Allen O. Whipple award for Outstanding Performance in Surgery. Mem.: Soc. Reconstructive Microsurgery, NY Head and Neck Soc., Northeast Regional Soc. Plastic and Reconstructive Surgeons, Am. Soc. Reconstructive Microsurgery, Am. Soc. Plastic and Reconstructive Surgeons, Am. Soc. Aesthetic Plastic Surgery, Alpha Omega Alpha Soc., Phi Beta Kappa. Office: 1100 Park Ave New York NY 10128 Business E-Mail: samson@slrsurgery.org. *

SULTAN, TERRIE FRANCES, curator; b. Asheville, NC, Oct. 28, 1952; d. Norman and Phyllis Ellen (Galumbeck) Sultan; m. Christopher French, June, 1988. BFA, Syracuse U., 1973; MA, John F. Kennedy U., 1985. Exhbn. dir. Source Gallery, San Francisco, 1982-83; adj. curator Oakland (Calif.) Mus., 1984-85; dir. pub. affairs and pub. programs New Mus. Contemporary Art, NYC, 1986-88; curator contemporary art Corcoran Gallery of Art, Washington, 1988—. Author: Representation and Text in the Work of Robert Morris, 1990, Redefining The Terms of Engagement: The Art of Louise Bourgeois, 1994, Neik Kemps: Behind the Facade of Analytical Order (a Series of Propositions), 1995, Painting Outside Painting, 1995, Petah Coyne: black/white/black, 1996, Ida Applebroog: Nothing Personal Paintings 1987-1997, 1998; also exhbn. catalogues. Mem. Am. Assn. Museums, Coll. Art Assn., ArTable. Democrat. Office: The Corcoran Gallery Art 17th St New York Ave NW Washington DC 20006

SULTANIK, JEFFREY TED, lawyer; b. NYC, July 26, 1954; s. Solomon and Anna (Tiger) S.; m. Judith Ann Chyman, Nov. 14, 1981; children: Evan A., Sara A. BA cum laude, U. Pa., Phila., 1976; JD, Hofstra U., 1979. Bar: Pa. 1979, Fla. 1980, U.S. Dist. Ct. (ea. dist.) Pa., U.S. Ct. Appeals (3d cir.). Ptnr. Fox Rothschild, LLP, Lansdale, Pa., 1979-81; solicitor Upper Merion Sch. Dist., 1995—. Solicitor Boyertown Area Sch. Dist., Pa., 1981—, North Montco Vocat.-Tech. Sch., Lansdale, 1981—, Souderton Area Sch. Dist., Pa., 1989—, Montgomery County Intermediate Unit, 1993—, Wallingford-Swarthmore Sch. Dist., 1999—, Interboro Sch. Dist., 2002, Whitehall-Coplay Sch. Dist., 2003, Colonial Sch. Dist., 1998—, Kennett Consol. Sch. Dist., 1999—; spl. counsel Owen J. Roberts Sch. Dist., 2000—, West Chester Area Sch. Dist., 2002, Hatboro-Horsham Sch. Dist., 2003, Avon Grove Sch. Dist., 2005—, Capital Area Intermediate Unit, 2005—, Parkland Sch. Dist., 2006—, Springfield Township Sch. Dist., 2006—, Upper Dublin Sch. Dist., 2006—; trustee, bd. sec. Germantown Acad., Ft. Washington, Pa., 1991—; chair edn. law group Fox Rothschild, LLP, Lansdale, Pa.; presenter in field. Columnist Your School and the Law, 1992-2003. Mem. Nat. Sch. Bds. Assn., 2001. Mem. Nat. Assn. Sch. and Coll. Attys., Nat. Sch. Bds. Assn., Pa. Sch. Bds. Assn., Inc., Pa. Assn. Sch. Bus. Ofcls. (cert. of appreciation 1991), Pa. Bar Assn. (labor and edn. sects.), Pa. Sch. Solicitors Assn. (region II dir., sec.), Pa. Assn. Sch. Personnel Admins. (Friend of PASPA award, 2005), Montgomery County Bar Assn. (mcpl. law com. 1983—), Lehigh U. Law Forums, Assn. Del. Valley Ind. Schs. Republican. Jewish. Avocations: automobiles, travel. Home: 3229 Barley Ln Lansdale PA 19446-5114 Office: Fox Rothschild LLP 1250 S Broad St Lansdale PA 19446-0431 Home Phone: 610-584-0193; Office Phone: 215-661-9407. Business E-Mail: jsultanik@foxrothschild.com.

SULTZBAUGH, JOHN STEPHAN, historian, educator; b. Harrisburg, Pa., July 25, 1950; s. John Leroy Sultzbaugh and Kathryn Mikhailovna Sass; m. Gayle Rene Reitenbach, May 3, 1980; children: Elisabeth Yvonne, Andrew John. B.Humanities summa cum laude, Pa. State U.-Harrisburg, 1972, MA, 1975; PhD, Greenwich U., Norfolk Island, Australia, 1999. Cert. tchr. Pa. Hydrologist USGS, Harrisburg, Pa., 1973—74; hydrologic technologist Susquehana River Basin Commn., Mechanicsburg, Pa., 1974—75; tchr. history, govt. Upper Dauphin Area Sch. Dist., Lykens, Pa., 1975—. Adj. journalist and photographer Upper Dauphin Sentinel, Millersburg, Pa., 1978—88, Daily News, Lebanon, Pa., 1981—83, Sunday Pa., Lebanon, 1982, Pa. Mag., Harrisburg, 1990; mem. Nat. Jr. Honor Soc. Bd./Upper Dauphin Area Sch. Dist., 2002—03; coord. student assistance program Upper Dauphin Sch. Dist., 1991—98; cons. reader Pa. History Textbook Commn., Harrisburg, 2003. Contbr. poetry in jours. Recipient Editors award, Poetry.com, 2004. Mem.: Nat. Edn. Assn., Am. Soc. Authors, Composers and Pubs., Intersoc. Color Coun., Mensa. Democrat. Eastern Orthodox. Achievements include patents for variable pitch fluid impeller; research in blending colored music for instructional and theraupeutic applications; entry in Guniness Book of World Records. Avocations: aquatics, classical music, photography, philosophy. Home: 261 Romberger Rd Elizabethville PA 17023 Office: Upper Dauphin Area Sch Dist 2668 State Rt 209 Lykens PA 17048 Office Phone: 717-580-6719.

SULYK, STEPHEN, retired archbishop; b. Balnycia, Western Ukraine, Oct. 2, 1924; s. Michael and Mary (Denys) Sulyk. Student, Ukrainian Cath. Sem. of Holy Spirit, Fed. Republic Germany, 1945—48, St. Josaphat's Sem., 1948—52; Licentia in Sacred Theology, Cath. U. Am., 1952. Ordained priest Ukrainian Cath. Ch., 1952. Assoc. pastor, Omaha, 1952; assoc. pastor Bklyn., 1953, Minersville, Pa., 1954, Youngstown, Ohio, 1955; pastor Ch. Sts. Peter and Paul, Phoenixville, Pa., 1955, St. Michael's Ch., Frackville, Pa., 1957—61, Assumption of Blessed Virgin Mary Ch., Perth Amboy, NJ, 1962—81; sec. Archeparchy Chancery, 1956—57; adminstr. St. Nicholas, Phila., 1961; archbishop Met. of Ukraine-Rite Catholics of Archeparchy, Phila., 1981—2000; ret., 2000. Vice-chmn. Priests Senate, 1977—78, chmn.; pres. Ascension Manor, Inc.; archbishop Ukranian Rite Caths. Archeparchy Phila., Met. Ukranian-Rite Caths. U.S.A.; chmn. ad-hoc inter-rite com. Nat. Cath. Conf. Bishops/U.S. Cath. Conf., 1991. Mem.: Presidium of Synod of Ukranian Cath. Bishops (treas.), Coll. Bishops of Roman Cath. Ch., Providence Assn. Am. (Supreme Protector). Office: Archdiocese of Phila 827 N Franklin St Philadelphia PA 19123-2004

SULYOK, PAUL DAVID, music educator, composer; b. St. Johnsbury, Vt., July 14, 1958; s. Kalman Laszlo and Catherine Hagerman Sulyok. MusB in Music Edn., Westminster Choir Coll., 1981. Cert. Music Comprehensive 2100 N.J., 1981. Dir. activities Childrens' Fresh Air Home, North Wildwood, NJ, 1976—86; vocal, choral, drama tchr. East Windsor (N.J.) Schs., 1983—91, Upper Freehold Schools, Allentown, NJ, 1991—; childrens' theater dir. Green Apple Theater, Hightstown, NJ, 1993; music dir. On With The Show Bravo Cable Network, NYC, 2001. Guild mem., entertainer Boheme Opera N.J., Trenton, 1993; musical dir., accompanist Off Broad St. Theater, Hopewell, 1995. Composer (and author): (musical play) Audition, 1993; composer: (author) (musical plays) Luigi's, 1995; composer: (and author) many children's musicals. Hospice vol. Hyacinth Orgn., New Brunswick, 1988—91; sch. bd. mem. Ewing Presbyn. Nursery Sch., 1998—2000; mem. choir, pianist Ewing Presbyn. Ch., 1995. Mem.: NEA, Ctrl. N.J. Orff-Schulwerk Assn., Music Educators Nat. Conf., Boheme Opera N.J. Guild (adv. bd./fundraising 1993). Democrat. Presbyterian. Avocations: piano, composing, travel, theater. Home: 27 Chippin Ct Robbinsville NJ 08691 Office: Upper Freehold Regional Schools 27 High St Allentown NJ 08501 Personal E-mail: sulyokpaul@aol.com.

SULZBERGER, ARTHUR OCHS, newspaper executive; b. NYC, Feb. 5, 1926; s. Arthur Hays and Iphigene (Ochs) Sulzberger; m. Barbara Grant, July 2, 1948 (div. 1956); children: Arthur Ochs, Karen Alden; m. Carol Fox, Dec. 19, 1956 (dec. Aug. 1995); 1 adopted child, Cathy 1 child, Cynthia Fox; m. Allison Stacey Cowles, Mar. 9, 1996. BA, Columbia, 1951; LL.D., Dartmouth, 1964, Bard Coll., 1967; L.H.D., Montclair State Coll., 1972, Tufts U.; LLD (hon.), U. Scranton; L.H.D., Columbia U., 1992. With N.Y. Times, NYC, 1951—, asst. treas., 1958—63, pres., 1963—79, pub., 1963—92, chmn., CEO, 1963—97, chmn. emeritus, 1997—, also bd. dirs. Dir. Times Printing Co., Chattanooga. Trustee emeritus Columbia U.; trustee Met. Mus. Art, chmn. bd. trustees, 1987—. Capt. USMCR, WWII, Korea. Mem.: SAR, Met. Club (Washington), Explorers Club, Overseas Press Club. Office: NY Times Co 229 W 43rd St New York NY 10036-3959

SULZBERGER, ARTHUR OCHS, JR., newspaper publisher; b. Mt. Kisco, NY, Sept. 22, 1951; s. Arthur Ochs Sulzberger and Barbara Winslow Grant; m. Gail Gregg, May 24, 1975; children: Arthur Gregg, Ann Alden. BA, Tufts U., 1974; grad. Prog. for Mgmt. Dev., Harvard U. Bus. Sch., 1985. Reporter The Raleigh (N.C.) Times, 1974—76; corr. AP, London, 1976—78; Washington corr. NY Times, 1978—81, city hall reporter, 1981, asst. metro editor, 1981—82, group mgr. advt. dept., 1983—84, sr. analyst corp. planning, 1985, prodn. coordinator, 1985—87, asst. pub., 1987—88, dep. pub., 1988—92, pub., 1992—; chmn. NY Times Co., 1997—. Chmn. NY Outward Bound Ctr., 2002—. Office: The NY Times 229 W 43rd St New York NY 10036-3959 *

SUMANT, ANIRUDHA, materials scientist, researcher; arrived in US, 1998; children: Alkesh, Suchir. PhD, U. Pune, India, 1998. Postdoctoral fellow Argonne Nat. Lab., Ill., 1998—2001, materials scientist, 2006—; scientist Light Matrix Techs., Inc., 2001—02, MER Corp., Tucson, 2001—02; staff scientist U. Wis., Madison, 2002—06. Mem.: Am. Vacuum Soc. (chmn. group 2007—). Achievements include patents pending in field. Office: Argonne Nat Lab 9700 S Cass Ave Argonne IL 60439 Office Phone: 630-252-4854. Business E-Mail: sumant@anl.gov.

SUMANTH, DAVID JONNAKOTY, industrial engineer, educator; b. Machilipatnam, India, Jan. 28, 1946; arrived in U.S., 1972; s. John Devraj and Nancy (David) Jonnakoty; m. Chaya J. Victor, June 26, 1974; children: John J., Paul J. BE, Osmania U., India, 1967, ME, 1969; MS in Indsl. Engring., Ill. Inst. Tech., 1974, PhD in Indsl. Engring., 1979. Tchg./rsch. asst. Ill. Inst. Tech., Chgo., 1973-78, instr., 1979; asst. prof. indsl. engring. U. Miami, Coral Gables, Fla., 1979-83, founding dir. productivity research group, 1979—, dir. grad. studies, 1980-83, assoc. prof. indsl. engring., 1983-88, Coll. Engring. coordinator MBA/MSIE, 1984-93, prof. indsl. engring., 1987—. Chmn. confs. Author: Productivity Engineering and Management, 1984, internat. student edit., 1985, Spanish edit., 1990, Indian edit., 1990, coll. custom series edit., 1994, also instrs. manual, (script) Total Productivity Management, 1985; editor: Productivity Management Frontiers-I, 1987, II, 1989, Productivity and Quality Management Frontiers III, 1991, IV, 1993, V, 1995, VI, 1997, VII, 1998, X, 2004; author: Total Productivity Management, 1998. Recipient over 65 honors, awards and recognitions including YMCA Edn. Gold medal, 1969, Freedoms Found., 1987;, Alexander Orr award of Tchg. Excellence, U. Miami, 2000; fellow U. Miami Eaton Honors Coll., 1986, fellow World Acad. Productivity Sci., 1989; gov.'s appointee as sr. judge Fla. Sterling award, 1992-93, judge, 1993-98. Mem. Am. Inst. Indsl. Engrs. (sr. mem., pres. Miami chpt. 1982-83, bd. dirs. 1983-84, nat. asst. dir. productivity mgmt. 1984—, chairperson rsch. com. 1987, Outstanding Indsl. Engr. of Yr. Miami chpt. 1983, 84); Productivity Ctr. (trustee 1985-89), Internat. Soc. for Productivity and Quality Rsch. (founder 1993, founding pres. 1993-95, chmn. 1995-97, pres. 2004—, Distinguished Prof. Univ. Francise Marroguin, 2006). Republican. Baptist. Avocations: reading, writing, people. Office: U Miami Productivity Rsch Group Coral Gables FL 33124 Office Phone: 305-284-2366. Business E-Mail: dsumanth@miami.edu.

SUMERS, ANNE RICKS, ophthalmologist, museum director; b. Beverly, Mass., May 8, 1957; d. David Frank and Anne Russell (Russell) Ricks; m. Elliott H. Sumers, May 31, 1983; children: Ben, Ted. BA in English Lit. with honors, U. Mich., 1979; MD, U. Cin., 1983. Diplomate Am. Bd. Ophthalmology. Intern Mt. Auburn Hosp., Cambridge, Mass., 1984; resident in ophthalmology NYU/Bellevue Hosp., 1984-87; ptnr. Ridgewood Ophthalmology, PC, NJ, 1990—; dir. NJ Childrens Mus., Paramus, NJ, 1992—; co-owner Saddle River Market, NJ, 1995—2002. Team ophthalmologist NY Giants Football Team, 1994—, NJ Nets, 1999-2002; state coord. NJ Turn Off Your TV Week, 1994-96; Democratic candidate for US Congress (NJ-5), 2002; spkr. in field. Author: The Offical M.D. Handbook, 1983, Be A Better Mother—Today!, 1999; writer, host Channel 11/WPIX Wonder Zone, 1993; Democratic candidate for US Congress (NJ-S) 2002; interviewed on Good Morning Am., Am.'s Talking, CBS This Morning, NJN Discover NJ, Comcast Cablevision, Cablevision, Fox Channel 5 Good Day NY, 1992—, NBC Nightly News, various radio shows; contbr. articles to popular mags. Named one of 10 NJ Women of Yr., NJ Woman Mag., 1993; profiled in AMA News, Med. Econs., The NY Times, Star Ledger, Argus and other newspapers and mags. Fellow Am. Acad. Ophthalmology (media spokesperson, media info. com.); mem. AMA, Assn. Youth Museums, NJ Acad. Ophtholmology (bd. gov. 1997), Alpha Omega Alpha. Office: Ridgewood Ophthalmology PC 1200 E Ridgewood Ave Ridgewood NJ 07450-3937

SUMIDA, GREGORY ZIO, artist, photographer, musician, astronomer; b. LA; One-man shows include Palm Springs Desert Mus., 1973, Desert S.W. Art Gallery, 1974, Pioneer Mus. and Haggin Art Gallery, 1975, Potlatch Art Gallery, 1976, Maxwell Galleries, San Francisco, 1977, Smith Gallery, N.Y.C., Troy's Gallery, Ariz., 1984, 1986, 1986, Zantman Galleries, Palm Desert, Calif., 1990, Legacy Gallery, 1991, 2002, exhibited in group shows, Scottsdale, 2000, Artist Focus Show Legacy Gallery, 2000—01, Eitejorg Mus., 2002, Visions of the West, 2003—07, Legacy of Am. West, 2003, 2005, Weatherburn Gallery, 2003, Mountain Oyster's Club Art Show, 2003—07, Contemporary Western Art Show, 2003—05, Sylvan Gallery's Miniature Show, 2003, 2005—07, Trees Pl. Small Works Holiday Exhbn., 2003—07, Big Horn Galleries Summer Roundup, 2004—07, Tex. Art Gallery Auction, 2004—06, Phippen Mus. Miniature Masterpieces Art Show, 2005, 2006, 2007, Settlers West Show, 2005—06, Nat. Exhibits Found. Mus. Show, Lubbock, Tex., 2005, Trees Pl. Gallery, 2006—07, numerous others; contbr. artwork to mags. and jours. including Cowboys and Indian Mag., Jour. Pharm. Med., Art Talk, and Southwest Art. Mem.: Oil Painters Am., Soc. Am. Impressionism. Office: PO Box 9210 Stockton CA 95208-1210 Office Phone: 209-464-3532. Personal E-mail: ziogregory@hotmail.com.

SUMIDA, KEVIN P.H., lawyer; b. Honolulu, Feb. 14, 1954; s. William H. and Dorothy A. Sumida. BA in Philosphy, Case Western Res. U., 1976; JD, U. Pa., 1979. Bar: Hawaii 1979, U.S. Ct. Appeals (9th cir.) 1981. Assoc. Fong & Miho, Honolulu, 1979-81; law clk. to hon. judge Harold M. Fong U.S. Dist. Ct., Honolulu, 1981-82; assoc. Matsui & Chung, Honolulu, 1982-89; ptnr. Matsui Chung Sumida & Tsuchiyama, Honolulu, 1989—2005, Sumida & Tsuchiyama, Honolulu, 2006—. Bd. dirs., officer Farrington Alumni and Community Found., Honolulu, 1980—; commr. Nat. Conf. Commrs. Uniform State Laws, 2005-. Mem. ABA (litigation sect., tort and ins. practice sect.), Hawaii Bar Assn. Avocation: music. Office: Sumida & Tsuchiyama 735 Bishop St Ste 411 Honolulu HI 96813 Office Phone: 808-356-2600. Business E-Mail: ksumida@sthawaii.com.

SUMIYOSHI, TOMIKI, psychiatrist, researcher; b. Tokyo, Dec. 18, 1964; s. Hiroshi and Fusako (Naganuma) S.; m. Sawako Suemasa, Apr. 4, 1993. MB, MD, Kanazawa U., Japan, 1989, PhD, 1993. Med. diplomate. Resident Fukui Prefectural Psychiat. Hosp., Japan, 1990; ward administr., dir. neurochemistry rsch. Kanazawa U. Hosp., Japan, 1991—93; rsch. assoc. dept. psychiatry Case Western Res. U., Cleve., 1993-95; asst. prof. dept. psychiatry, dir. psychopharmacology rsch. Saitama Med. Sch., Japan, 1995—96; asst. prof. dept. neuropsychiatry, dir. neurochemistry rsch. Toyama Med. and Pharm. U., Japan, 1996—2000; assoc. prof. dept. neuropsychiatry U. Toyama Sch. Medicine, 2000—; apptd. psychiatrist Health and Welfare Ministry Japan, 1996—. Vis. prof. dept. psychiatry Vanderbilt U., Nashville, 2000—02; rsch. bd. adv. Am. Biog. Inst., Inc., 2005—; opinion leaders panel Time, 2007—; cons. in field. Author: Clinical Perspective of the New Antipsychotic Drugs, 2001, Relapse in Schizophrenia, 2002; contbr. articles to profl. jours. Rep. athlete The Nat. Athletic Meeting, Hachinohe, Japan, 1993; mem. TIME Opinion Leader's Panel, 2007-. Recipient Psychiat Rsch. award, Saburo Matsubara Meml. Fund, Kanazawa, Japan, 1993, Young Investigator award, Nat. Alliance for Rsch. on Schizophrenia and Depression, Chgo., 1995, NY, 2001, Meml. Travel award, Am. Coll. Neuropsychopharmacology, 2001; fellow Rsch. fellow, Min. Edn. and Sci., Japan, 2000—02; scholar, Rotary, 1994—95. Mem. Soc. Neurosci., NY Acad. Scis., World Fedn. Socs. Biol. Psychiatry, Coll. Internat. Neuropsychopharmacologicum, Schizophrenia Internat. Rsch. Soc., Japanese Soc. Psychiatry and Neurology, Japanese Soc. Biol. Psychiatry (prize 1996), Japanese Soc. Neuropsychopharmacology, Japanese Soc. Clin. Neuropsychopharmacology, Japanese Soc. for Brain Scis., Japanese Soc. Clin. Neurophysiology, Japan Soc. Psychiat. Diagnosis, Japanese Soc. Prevention in Psychiat. Disorders, Japanese Soc. Schizophrenia Rsch. Avocations: foreign languages, classical music, figure skating, foreign travel. Home: 144-14-B2 Nishiaraya Toyama 939-8251 Japan Office Phone: +81-76-434-7323. Business E-Mail: sumiyo@med.u-toyama.ac.jp.

SUMLIN, MARGARET (MARGIE) BROWN, special education educator; b. Ann Arbor, Mich., Nov. 2, 1950; d. Willis Radcliff and Eulalie (Draughon) Brown. BS, U. Ala., 1972; MA, U. South Ala., 1976. Cert. spl. edn. tchr., Ala. Spl. edn. tchr. Morningside Elem. Sch., Tuscaloosa, Ala., 1972-73; spl. edn. tchr., community coord. A.P. Brewer Developmental Ctr., Mobile, Ala., 1973-75; spl. edn. tchr. Crichton Elem. Sch., Mobile, 1975-77, Scarborough Mid. Sch., Mobile, 1977-82, Cornerstone Group Home, Mobile, 1982; spl. edn. tchr., edn. coord. Brookwood Recovery Ctr., Mobile, 1984-90, Wilmer Hall Children's Home, Mobile, 1991, art therapy tchr., 1991—92; spl. edn. coord., tchr. The Murray Sch. at Wilmer Hall, Mobile, 1992—2002, prin., spl. edn. coord., 2003—. Ednl. cons. Parkside Recovery Ctr., Mobile, 1989-90; art therapy coord. Wilmer Hall Children's Home, 1991—; founder, organizer Friends of Wilmer Hall, 1992—. Author: (program model) Classroom Structure for Emotionally Disturbed Students, 1984. Bd. dirs. Women of Ch., St. Paul Ch., Mobile, 1991—, Mobile Pub. Libr., 1992—; vol. fundraiser Am. Cancer Soc., 1992; vol. tutor Project Hope Group Home, 1974, Rotary Rehab. Ctr., 1976; vol. coord. Vol. Mobile, 1982, Mobile County Sch. System, 1984; bd. dirs. Cornerstone Group Home (pres. 1985-86); vol. Mobile Pre-Sch. for the Deaf, 1979, Rotary Rehab. Ctr. In-Patient Svcs., 1977. Named a Point of Light by Pres. George Bush, 1991. Mem. Jr. League of Mobile (vol. fundraiser 1990-91), Nat. Soc. of Colonial Dames of Am. Episcopalian. Avocations: reading, hand sewing, beach activities. Office: Wilmer Hall Childrens Home 3811 Old Shell Rd Mobile AL 36608 Business E-Mail: msumlin@wilmerhall.org.

SUMME, GREGORY LOUIS, health products executive; b. Ft. Mitchell, Ky., Nov. 25, 1956; s. James Augustine and Mary Elizabeth (McQueen) S.; m. Susan Louise Stevie, Aug. 1, 1981; children: Heather, Erin. BSEE, U. Ky., 1978; MS, U. Cin., 1980; MBA with distinction, U. Pa., 1983. Design engr. Mostek Corp., Dallas, 1980-81; mktg. specialist Gen. Electric Plastics Europe, The Netherlands, 1982; ptnr. McKinsey & Co. Inc., Atlanta and Hong Kong, 1983—92; gen, mgr., comml. motors GE, 1992—93; pres. automotive products group, aerospace engines, gen. aviation avionics Allied Signal Inc., 1993—98; pres., COO PerkinElmer, Inc., Wellesley, Mass., 1998—99, chmn., pres., CEO, 1999—. Contbr. articles to profl. jours. Alex Proudfoot fellow Wharton Sch., U. Pa., 1981-83; named to Univ. Ky. Coll. Engring. Hall of Distinction. Mem. IEEE, Eta Kappa Nu. Roman Catholic. Avocations: running, squash, golf. Office: PerkinElmer Inc 45 William St Wellesley MA 02481

SUMMER, DONNA (LA DONNA ADRIAN GAINES), singer, songwriter, actress; b. Boston, Dec. 31, 1948; d. Andrew and Mary Gaines; m. Helmut Sommer (div.); 1 child, Mimi; m. Bruce Sudano; children: Brooklyn, Amanda. Has sold over 20 million records. Singer, 1967—; actress: (German stage prodn.) Hair, 1967-75, (Vienna Folk Opera prodns.) Porgy and Bess, (German prodns.) The Me Nobody Knows, (cable TV spl.) Donna Summer Special, 1980; recorded albums including The Wanderer, Star Collection, Love To Love You Baby, Love Trilogy, Four Seasons of Love, I Remember Yesterday, The Deep, Shut Out, Once Upon A Time, Bad Girls, On The Radio, Walk Away, She Works Hard For The Money, Cats Without Claws, All Systems Go, 1988, Another Place and Time, 1989, Mistaken Identity, 1991, Endless Summer, 1994, Christmas Spirit, 1994, I'm a Rainbow, 1996, Live & More Encore, 1999; subject My Life VH1 Concert, 1999; recorded theme song for Hunchback of Notre Dame, Disney; forerunner of disco style. Named Best Rhythm and Blues Female Vocalist, Nat. Acad. Rec. Arts and Scis., 1978, Best Female Rock Vocalist, 1979, Favorite Female Pop Vocalist, Am. Music Awards, 1979, Favorite Female Vocalist of Soul Music, 1979, Soul Artist of Yr., Rolling Stone mag., 1979; recipient Best Favorite Pop Single award, 1979, Best-selling Black Music Album for Female Artist award Nat. Assn. Record Merchandizers, 1979, Ampex Golden Reel award for album On the Radio, 1979, Best-selling Album for Female Artist, 1980, Ampex Golden Reel award for single On the Radio, 1980, Ampex Golden Reel award for album Bad Girls, Best of Las Vegas Jimmy award for best rock performance, 1980, Grammy award for best inspirational performance, 1984. Office: 2401 Main St Santa Monica CA 90405-3515

SUMMER, EMILY EUGENIA, artist, art educator; d. Charles Edgar and Emily Eugenia Summer. BS, Miss. U. for Women, 1945; LHD (hon.), MIss. U. for Women, 2005; MA, Columbia U., 1948. Supr. art Clarksdale (Miss.) City Schs., 1948—49; adj. prof. art Miss. U. for Women, Columbus, 1949—58, assoc. prof. art, 1958—78, prof. art, 1978—80, asst. dean Sch. Arts and Scis., 1980—82, head divsn. fine and performing arts, 1982—85, prof. emerita art, 1985—. One-woman shows include Ricks Meml. CArnegie Libr., Yazoo City, Miss., 1962, First Nat. Bank, Jackson, Miss., 1974, Mcpl. Libr., Amory, Miss., 1975, Miss. State U., Starkville, 1978, Rosenzweig Arts Ctr., Columbus, 2001, Fine Arts Gallery, Miss. U. for Women, 02, exhibitions include Hunter Gallery, 1963, Birmingham Mus. Art, 1968, Nat. Arts Club, 1980, numerous others, exhibited in group shows at Itawamba Jr. Coll. Gallery, Fulton, Miss., 1986, Hinds C.C. Gallery, Raymond, Miss., 1987, Shelton State C.C. Gallery, Tuscalosa, Ala., 1988, Miss. U. for Women, 1970—86, Miss. Mus. Art, Jackson, 2002, 2007, Miss. Gov.'s Mansion, 2001, Walter Anderson Mus. Art, Ocean Springs, Miss., 2007, Represented in permanent collections Miss. Mus. Art, Miss. U. for Women, also numerous pvt. and corp. collections. Bd. govs. artist registry Brooks Meml. Art Mus., Memphis, 1971—72; Miss. rep. bd. dirs. Southeastern Coll. Art Assn., 1964—71; rschr., trainer Nat. Mus. Am. Art, Washington, 1992—93; mem. Columbus/Lowndes County United Way, 1997—. Recipient Alumni Achievement award, Miss. U. for Women, 1986, Honored Artist, Nat. Mus. Women Artists, 2001, Lowndes County Alumni Svc. award, Plymouth Bluff Ctr., Columbus, 2003, Medal of Excellence, Miss. U. for Women, 2003, numerous others; Eugenia Summer Art Gallery named in her honor, Miss. U. for Women, 2002, Danforth assoc., 1977—83, rsch. grantee, Miss. U. for Women, 1976, 1978, 1979. Mem.: Miss. Mus. Art Rembrandt Soc., Nat. Audubon Soc., Lauren Rogers Mus. Art, Nat. Mus. Women in Arts (honored artist 2002), Coll. Art Assn. Am. (life), Nature Conservancy, John Muir Soc., Sierra Club, Garden Clubs Miss. (life), Kappa Pi, Phi Kappa Phi. Democrat. Roman Catholic. Home: 915 5th Ave S Columbus MS 39701

SUMMERFIELD, GALE, director, educator; children: Tai Hsiao, Thomas Hsiao. PhD, U. Mich., 1987. Assoc. prof. Monterey (Calif.) Inst. Internat. Studies, 1987—98, U. Ill., Champaign, Ill., 1998—, dir. WGGP, 1998—. Author: Women and Gender Equity in Development Theory and Practice, Women's Rights to House and Land: China, Laos, Vietnam; contbr. articles to profl. jours. Bd. dirs. Nat. Coun. Rsch. on Women, NYC, 2004—05; trustee Assn. Social Econs., 2002—05. Office: University of Illinois at Urbana 910 South Fifth St Champaign IL 61820 Office Phone: 217-333-1977. Office Fax: 217-333-6270. Business E-Mail: summrfld@uiuc.edu.

SUMMERFIELD, JOHN ROBERT, textile curator; b. St. Paul, Feb. 21, 1917; s. Isaac and Irene (Longini) S.; m. Anne Benson, July 14, 1945. SB in Mech. Engring., MIT, 1938; MBA, U. Calif., Berkeley, 1947, PhD in Econs., 1954. Asst. prof. Sloan Sch. Mgmt., MIT, 1952-54; br. chief CIA, Washington, 1954-56; project leader The Rand Corp., Santa Monica, Calif., 1956—62; corp. economist Douglas Aircraft Co., Santa Monica, Calif., 1962—66; v.p. econ. planning Western Airlines, LA, 1966-70; staff v.p. econ. planning Pan Am. Airways, NYC, 1970-71; pres. Summerfield Assocs., Pacific Palisades, Calif., 1972-92; vis. curator Fowler Mus. Cultural History, UCLA, 1993—. Co-curator exhbns. of antique Minangkabau ceremonial textiles from West Sumatra, Textile Mus., Washington, 1990-91, Santa Barbara (Calif.) Mus. Art, 1991, Bellevue (Wash.) Art Mus., 1992, Utah Mus. Fine Art, 1992, Fowler Mus. of Cultural History, UCLA, 1999, Iris and B. Gerald Cantor Gallery, Coll. Holy Cross, 2003, 05, 07. Served to lt. USNR, 1942-45. E-mail: summrfld@arts.ucla.edu.

SUMMERFORD, BEN LONG, retired artist, educator; b. Montgomery, Ala., Feb. 3, 1924; s. Ben Long and Ollie Jo (Gilchrist) S.; m. Christene Morris, Jan. 30, 1951 (dec.); children: Jeffrey (dec.), Rebecca, James. Student, Birmingham-Southern Coll., 1942-43; BA, Am. U., 1948, MA, 1954; student, Ecole des Beaux Arts., Paris., 1949-50. Staff art dept. Am. U., 1950-88, chmn. dept., 1957-66, 70-86, prof., 1960-88; prof. emeritus, 1988—; artist in residence Dartmouth Coll., 1993. One-man shows include, Balt. Mus. Art, Goucher Coll., Franz Bader Gallery, Washington, Jefferson Place Gallery, Washington, Phillips Collection, Washington, Washington County Mus. Fine Arts, Hagerstown, Md.; represented in permanent collection, Watkins Gallery, Phillips Gallery Art, Corcoran Gallery Art, all Washington, 50 yr RetoSelective exhibitions Wah. County Mus. of Fine Arts, Md, 2004, numerous group shows of paintings. Served to ensign USNR, 1943-46. Fulbright fellow, France, 1949-50; J. Paul Getty scholar, Phillips Collection, 1990-91. Home: 15 Chatfield Dr Shepherdstown WV 25443

SUMMERHILL, RONALD RAYMOND, psychotherapist, psychologist; s. Walter Edward Summerhill and Vernon Joenell Goldsmith; m. Wanda Jean Owens, Dec. 31, 1979 (div. Jan. 24, 1994); children: Valorie Lenee Summerhill Mullins, Ronald Raymond II. BA in Bus. Mgmt., St. Mary's Coll. of Calif., Moraga, Calif., 1985; MS in Adminstrn., Ctrl. Mich. U., Mt. Pleasant, Mich., 1992; M in Human Rels., U. Okla., Norman, Okla., 1993; D of Psychology, Argosy U., Phoenix, 2004. Lic. Master Social Worker Iowa, 1996; cert. Sch. Psychologist Ariz., 2001, Nat. Counselor NBCC, 1996, lic. Profl. Counselor Nebr., 1996, Mental Health Practitioner Nebr., 1996. Capt., navigator USAF, Omaha, 1986—92; social worker Nebr. HHS, Omaha, 1994—96; exec. dir. Tiller Therapeutic Svcs., Inc., Bellevue, Nebr., 1996—99; psychologist assoc. Ariz. Dept. of Juvenile Corrections, Phoenix, 1999—2000; clin. supr. ValueOptions, Phoenix, 2000—00; psychology assoc. Ariz. Dept. of Health, Phoenix, 2000—01; sch. psychologist Cave Creek Unified Sch. Dist., Cave Creek, Ariz., 2001—03, Scottsdale Unified Sch. Dist., Scottsdale, Ariz., 2004—. Internship neuropsychology Kingsbrook Jewish Med. Ctr., Bklyn., 2003—04. Capt. USAF, 1986—92, Omaha, Nebr. Decorated Achievement Medal USAF, Accommodation Medal. Mem.: APA, ACA, NASP. R-Consevative. Protestant. Avocations: travel, musician, outdoorsman. Office: Scottsdale Unified Sch Dist #48 6720 E Continental Scottsdale AZ 85257-3226 Home Phone: 623-434-4293; Office Phone: 480-484-5828. Office Fax: 480-484-5801. Business E-Mail: rsummerhill@susd.org.

SUMMERS, ANITA ARROW, finance educator; b. NYC, Sept. 9, 1925; d. Harry I. and Lillian (Greenberg) Arrow; m. Robert Summers, Mar. 29, 1953; children: Lawrence H., Richard F., John S. BA, Hunter Coll., 1945, DHL (hon.), 1995; MA, U. Chgo., 1947. Sr. econ. analyst Standard Oil Co. N.J., NYC, 1947-54; asst. in econs. Yale U., New Haven, 1956-59; lectr. dept. econs. Swarthmore (Pa.) Coll., 1965-71; sr. economist Fed. Res. Bank Phila., 1971-75, research officer, 1975-79; adj. prof. pub. policy U. Pa., Phila., 1979-82, prof. pub. policy and mgmt., 1982—, dept. chair, 1983-88, univ. ombudsman, 2001—03, co-dir Wharton Urban Decentralization Project, 1987-97, dir. rsch. Wharton Real Estate Ctr., 2003—, sr. scholar Nat. Ctr. on the Edn. Quality of the Workforce, 1991—95. Expert witness schs. fin. Md., Mass., Va., 1980-85, Md., Va., 1996, Calif., 2003, bd. dirs. William Penn Found., Phila., 1993-98; chair bd. dirs. Mathematica Policy Rsch., Inc., Princeton, N.J., 1993—. Author: Economic Report on the Philadelphia Metropolitan Area, 1985, Economic Development within the Philadelphia Metropolitan Area, 1986, Local Fiscal Issues in the Philadelphia Metropolitan Area, 1987; editor: Urban Change in the United States and Western Europe, 1992, 99; contbr. articles to profl. jours. Chair econ. subcom. Pa. Three Mile Island Commn., Harrisburg, 1979; pres. Lower Merion (Pa.) LWV, 1963-65; mem. Mayor's Econ. Roundtable, Phila., 1984-88; mem. rsch. policy coun., 1992-94, Com. for Econ. Devel. Rockefeller Found. resident scholar, Bellagio, Italy, 1986. Mem. Am. Econ. Assn., Assn. for Pub. Policy and Mgmt. (policy coun. 1986), Phi Beta Kappa. Avocations: needlepoint, cooking. Office: U Pa Wharton Sch Dept Pub Policy and Mgmt Philadelphia PA 19104 Office Phone: 215-898-4076. Business E-Mail: summers@wharton.upenn.edu.

SUMMERS, CAROL, artist; b. Kingston, NY, Dec. 26, 1925; s. Ivan Franklin and Theresa (Jones) S.; m. Elaine Smithers, Oct. 2, 1954 (div. Aug. 1967); 1 son, Kyle; m. Joan Ward Toth, May 6, 1974 (dec.1998). BA, Bard Coll., 1951, DFA (hon.), 1974. Tchr. Hunter Coll., Sch. Visual Arts, Haystack Mountain Sch. Crafts, Bklyn. Mus. Art Sch., Pratt Graphic Art Ctr., Chelterham Twp. Art Ctr., Valley Stream Community Art Ctr., U. Pa., Columbia Coll., U. Calif., Santa Cruz, San Francisco Art Inst., U. Utah, Logan, Art Study Abroad, Paris, Casa de Espiritus Alegres Marfil, Mex., USIS workshop tour, India, 1974, 79; folk art and textiles tour leader to Rajasthan, India, 1995-2007. Represented in permanent collections at, Mus. Modern Art, Bklyn. Mus., N.Y. Pub. Libr., Libr. of Congress, Nat. Gallery, Victoria and Albert Mus., London, Bibliotheque Nationale, Paris, Kunstmuseum, Basil, Lugano (Switzerland) Art Mus. Grenchen (Switzerland) Art Mus., Malmo (Sweden) Mus., Los Angeles County Mus., Phila. Mus., Balt. Mus., Seattle Mus., Boston Mus., Art Inst. Chgo., Am. embassies in Russia, Can., India, Thailand, Fed. Republic Germany and Eng.; traveling exhibit, Mus. Modern Art, 1964-66; retrospective exhbn. Brooklyn Mus., 1977, Nassau County Mus. Art, 1990, Belles Artes, San Miquel de Allende, Mex., 1992, Miami U. Art Mus., Oxford, Ohio, 1995, Egon Schiele Centrum Česky Krumlov, Czech Republic, 1997-98; 50-yr. retrospective at Mus. Art and History, Santa Cruz, 1999, Woodstock (N.Y.) Artists Assn., 1999, Museo del Peublo de Guarajuato, Mex., 2007; author: A Treasury of Indian Folk Textiles, 2002, Another Treasury of Indian Folk Textiles, 2006. Served with USMCR, 1944-48, PTO. Named Artist of Yr., Santa Cruz County Arts Commn., 2001; recipient Outstanding Printmaker award, Mid Am. Print Coun., 2004; fellow, Louis Comfort Tiffany Found., 1955, 1960, John Simon Guggenheim Found., 1959, Fulbright, Italy, 1961; study grantee, Italian govt., 1954—55, rsch. grantee, Coun. Internat. Exch. Scholars, India, 1993—94. Mem. NAD (academician, 1994-), Calif. Soc. Printmakers. Office Phone: 831-423-0181. Personal E-mail: carol@casaspirit.com.

SUMMERS, CATHLEEN, film producer; b. Chgo. d. Paul and Elizabeth Summers; m. Patrick Crowley. BA, U. So. Calif., 1973. Film editor, comml. producer, dir.'s asst. Roman Polanski, Rome, 1972; story editor Albert S. Ruddy Prodns. Paramount Pictures, LA, 1973-74; exec. asst. Columbia Pictures, Burbank, Calif., 1974, story editor, 1974-76; devel. exec., v.p., producer Martin Ransohoff Prodns. Columbia Pictures, 1976; sr. v.p. Tri-Star Pictures, Century City, Calif., 1984-87; motion picture producer Cathleen Summers Prodns., LA, 1989—; ptnr. ESN, Film Prodn. Resource Co.; cons., ptnr. Estudio Network. Motion picture producer, ptnr. Summers-Kouf Prodns., Burbank, 1986-87; motion picture producer Cathleen Summers Prodns., L.A., 1987, Summers-Quaid Prodns., Century City, Culver City, Calif., 1988—. Producer: (motion picture) Stakeout, 1987, DOA, 1991, Vital Signs, 1990, Mystery Date, 1991, Dogfight, 1991, The Sandlot, 1993, Stakeout II, 1993; exec. prodr. Derivations, Who New/The Real Deal, 2003. Co-founder Diane Thomas Scholarship, UCLA, 1988—; bd. dirs. L.A. chpt. Nat. Parkinsons Found.; founding bd. dirs. U.S. Comedy Arts Festival, Aspen, Colo. Mem. Am. Film Inst. (pres. 3d Decade Coun. 1995, 96, 97). Personal E-mail: july4bu@charter.net.

SUMMERS, CLYDE WILSON, law educator; b. Grass Range, Mont., Nov. 21, 1918; s. Carl Douglas and Anna Lois (Yontz) S.; m. Evelyn Marie Wahlgren, Aug. 30, 1947; children: Mark, Erica, Craig, Lisa. BS, U. Ill., 1939, JD, 1942, LLD, 1998; LLM, Columbia U., 1946, JSD, 1952; LL.D., U. Leuven, Belgium, 1967, U. Stockholm, 1978, U. Ill., 1998. Bar: N.Y. 1951. Mem. law faculty U. Toledo, 1942-49, U. Buffalo, 1949-56; prof. law Yale U., New Haven, Conn., 1956-66, Garver prof. law, 1966-75; Jefferson B. Fordham prof. law U. Pa., 1975-90, prof. emeritus, 1990—. Hearing examiner Conn. Commn. on Civil Rights, 1963-71 Co-author: Labor Cases and Material, 1968, 1982, Rights of Union Members, 1979, Legal Protection for the Individual Employee, 1989, 1996, 2002; co-editor: Labor Relations and the Law, 1953, Employment Relations and the Law, 1959, Comparative Labor Law Jour., 1984—97. Chmn. Gov.'s Com. on Improper Union Mgmt. Practices N.Y. State, 1957-58; chmn. Conn. Adv. Council on Unemployment Ins. and Employment Service, 1960-72; mem. Conn. Labor Relations Bd., 1966-70, Conn. Bd. Mediation and Arbitration, 1964-72. Guggenheim fellow, 1955-56; Ford fellow, 1963-64; German-Marshall fellow, 1977-78; NEH fellow, 1977-78, Fullbright fellow, 1984-85. Mem. Nat. Acad. Arbitrators, Internat. Soc. Labor Law and Social Legislation (pres.). Congregationalist. Office: U Pa Sch Law 3400 Chestnut St Philadelphia PA 19104-6204 Home: 608 W Phil Ellena St Apt 1a Philadelphia PA 19119-3525 Office Phone: 215-898-6867. Business E-Mail: csummers@law.upenn.edu.

SUMMERS, DAVID PATRICK, chemist, astrobiologist; s. Ernest and Virginia Joy Summers. BS signum laudis, SUNY, Albany, 1975; PhD, MIT, Cambridge, Mass., 1984. Electrochemist SRI Internat., Menlo Park, Calif., 1984—89; Nat. Rsch. Coun. sr. fellow NASA Ames Rsch. Ctr., Mountain View, Calif., 1990—92; prin. investigator SETI Inst., Mountain View, 1993—. Recipient Undergrad. Award in Analytical Chemistry, Am. Chem. Soc., 1978. Mem.: Sigma Xi, Phi Beta Kappa. Achievements include patents in field; invention of. Office: SETI Inst NASA Ames Rsch Ctr Mail Stop 239-4 Mountain View CA 94035-1000 Home Phone: 650-326-6274; Office Phone: 650-604-6206. Office Fax: 650-604-1088. E-mail: dsummers@mail.arc.nasa.gov.

SUMMERS, DAVID STEWART, neurologist, consultant; b. Canton, Ohio, Feb. 16, 1932; s. William Edward and Stewart (Jordan) Summers; m. Ada Ernestine Cumber, Nov. 30, 1957; children: David Stewart II, Timothy C. BS, Va. State U., Petersburg, 1954; MD, U. Va., Charlottesville, 1959. Diplomate Am. Acad. Pain Mgmt. Resident in neurology SUNY, Syracuse, 1960—63; asst. prof. neurology U. Rochester, NY, 1968—72; asst. prof. U. Utah Coll. Medicine, Salt Lake City, 1972—76; staff neurologist St. Vincent Health Ctr., Erie, Pa., 1976—91, Meadville Med. Ctr., Pa., 1991—93; neurologist Warren State Hosp., Pa., 1993—2000; investor, 2000—. Cons. Reflex Sympathetic Dystrophy Assn., Erie, 1988—97; mem. adv. coun. HHS, Washington, 1974—77. Contbg. author The Black Humanist Experience, 2003; contbr. articles to profl. jours. Supporter City Mission, Erie, 1991—, Planetary Soc., 2005—, Am. United Separation Ch. and State, NOW, ACLU, Am. Humanist Assn., People for the Am. Way, Ctr. Reproductive Law and Policy, Planned Parenthood, The Freedom from Religion Found., others; advisor to gov. Coun. Black Affairs, Salt Lake City, 1975; mem. Human Rights Campaign, Population Connection. Capt. M.C. USAR, 1964—67, Landstuhl, Germany. Grantee, Nat. Med. Fellowships, 1956—59; A. A. Rockefeller scholar, Williamsburg, Va., 1951—54. Mem.: AAAS, NAACP, African Sci. Fellows, Nat. Ctr. for Sci. Edn., The Planetary Soc., Nat. Soc. Scabbard & Blade, NY Acad. Scis., Menninger Soc., Am. Epilepsy Soc., Nat. Med. Assn., Am. Acad. Neurology, U. Va. Alumni Assn., Am. Legion (life). Democrat. Avocations: reading, hiking, walking.

SUMMERS, EDWIN C., lawyer, electronics executive; b. 1946; BA, Harvard U.; JD, U. Southern Calif. Bar: 1975. V.p., gen. counsel, asst. sec. Harman Internat. Industries, Wash., DC, 1998—. Mem. Inst. For Corp. Counsel, U. of Southern Calif. Contbr. articles to numerous profl. jours. Office: Harman Internat 1101 Pennsylvania Ave NW Washington DC 20004

SUMMERS, GERALD HOWARD (JERRY), lawyer; b. Chattanooga, May 28, 1941; s. Homer Howard and Millie (Dean) S. BA in Bus. Adminstrn. with honors, Auburn U., U. of South, 1963; LLB, U. Tenn., 1966. Bar: Tenn. 1966, U.S. Ct. Appeals (6th cir.) 1970, U.S. Supreme Ct. 1972. Asst. dist. atty. City of Chattanooga, 1966-69; sole practice, Chattanooga; ptnr. Summers & Wyatt; mem. Tenn. Law Revision Commn. 1976; city judge City of Soddy-Daisy (Tenn.), 1976-83; mem. Tenn. Supreme Ct. Com. on Jud. Planning, 1976, Commn. on Advt., 1978; mem. bd. advisors paralegal program Cleveland State Community Coll., 1975-76; mem. faculty polit. sci. U. Tenn., 1982; mem. Law Enforcment Commn. Hamilton County; bd. dirs. Project First Offender; mem. br. adv. bd. United Bank Chattanooga; mem. Speedy Trial Planning Commn. for Eastern Dist. Tenn. 1977-78; mem. Commn. on Criminal Rules, Tenn. Supreme Ct., 1982-83; lectr. in field. Named Young Man of Yr., Chattanooga Jaycees, 1973, 76-77, Outstanding Young Man Am., U.S. Jaycees, 1974; U. Tenn. univ. scholar, 1963-64. Fellow Tenn. Bar Found., Am. Bd. Trial Advocates (founding mem., pres. Tenn. chpt. 1986-87), Internat. Soc. Barristers, Am. Bd. Criminal Lawyers; mem. ABA, NACDL (gov. 1975-76), Tenn. Bar Assn. (chmn. criminal justice sect. 1976), Assn. Trial Lawyers Am. (chmn. young lawyers sect. 1975, bd. govs. 1985-87), Tenn. Trial Lawyers Assn. (v.p. 1972-73, pres. 1977-78), Tenn. Assn. Criminal Def. Lawyers (pres. 1975-76), Chattanooga Bar Assn. (mem. bd. govs. 1978, sec. 1981, pres.-elect 1982, pres. 1983-84), Chattanooga Trial Lawyers Assn. (pres. 1972-73), Central High Alumni Assn. (pres. 1971-73), Phi Gamma Delta (v.p. chpt. 1962-63). Club: Civitan (Chattanooga). Author: Law Office Management Manual, 1974. Office: Summers & Wyatt PC The James Bldg 735 Broad St, Ste 800 Chattanooga TN 37402-2913 Office Phone: 423-266-2385. Office Fax: 423-266-5211. E-mail: jsummers@summersandwyatt.com. *

SUMMERS, LARRY (LAWRENCE HENRY), investment company executive, political science professor, former academic administrator, former secretary of the treasury; b. New Haven, Nov. 30, 1954; s. Robert Summers and Anita A. (Summers); m. Victoria Joanne Perry, 1984 (div.); children: Pam, Ruth, Harry; m. Elisa New, Dec. 11, 2005. BS, MIT, 1975; PhD, Harvard U., 1982. Mem. faculty MIT, 1979-82; domestic policy economist, Coun. Econ. Advisors The White House, 1982-83; v.p. devel. economics, chief economist World Bank, 1991-93; prof. economics Harvard U., Cambridge, Mass., 1983-93, Nathaniel Ropes prof. polit. economy, 1987—91, pres., 2001—06, Charles W. Eliot U. prof., 2006—; under sec. for internat. affairs US Dept. Treasury, Washington, 1993-95, dep. sec., 1995-99, sec., 1999-2001; Arthur Okun Disting. Fellow in Econ., Globalization, and Governance Brookings Instn., Washington, 2001; mng. dir. D.E. Shaw & Co. LP, NYC, 2006—. Author Understanding Unemployment, 1990; co-author Reform in Eastern Europe, 1991; editor series Tax Policy and the Economy; contbr. numerous articles to profl. jours. Recipient Alan Waterman Award NSF, 1987, John Bates Clark Medal, 1993, Disting. Achievement Award Boys' & Girls' Club Greater Washington, 2000, Disting. Svc. Award Golden Slipper Club & Charities 2000, Econ. Patriot Award Concord Coalition, 2000, Stephen P. Guggan Award Inst. Internat. Edn., 2000; named one of 100 Most Influential People of 2005, Time mag. Fellow NAS, Econometric Soc., Am. Acad. Arts and Scis., Brookhaven Sci. Assocs. (bd. dirs.), Nat. Acad. Sci. Office: DE Shaw & Co LP Tower 45 39th Fl 120 W 45th St New York NY 10036 also: Kennedy Sch Govt Littauer 244 79 John F Kennedy St Cambridge MA 02138 *

SUMMERS, LORRAINE DEY SCHAEFFER, retired librarian; b. Phila., Dec. 14, 1946; d. Joseph William and Hilda Lorraine (Ritchey) Dey; m. F. William Summers, Jan. 28, 1984. BA, Fla. State U., 1968, MS, 1969. Ext. dir. Santa Fe Regional Libr., Gainesville, 1969-71; pub. libr. cons. State Libr. of Fla., Tallahassee, 1971-78, asst. state libr., 1978-84; dir. adminstrv. svcs. Nat. Assn. for Campus Activities, Columbia, SC, 1984-85; asst. state libr. State Libr. of Fla., Tallahassee, 1985—2001, ret., 2001—. Bd. dirs., sec. Southeastern Libr. Network, Inc.; cons. in field. Contbr. articles to profl. jours. Del. Pres.'s Com. on Mental Retardation Regional Forum, Atlanta, 1975; del. Fla. Gov.'s Conf. on Libr. and Info. Svcs., 1978, 90. Mem. ALA (orgn. com. 1979-83, coun. 1982-84, 93-97, resolutions com. 1983-85, mem. legislation com. 1993-95, nominating com. 1996, awards com. 1998-99, Spectrum awards jury 1999-2000), Assn. Specialized and Coop. Libr. Agys. (dir. 1976-82, chmn. planning and orgn. com. 1976-80, chmn. nominating com. 1980-81, chmn. by laws com. 1985-86, exec. bd. state libr. agy. sect. 1983-86, pres. 1987-88, chmn. stds. rev. com. 1990-92), Southeastern Libr. Assn. (exec. bd. 1976-80, v.p., pres.-elect 1994-96, pres. 1996-98, past pres. 1998-2000, nominating com. 2000-02), Fla. Libr. Assn. (sec. 1978-79, dir. 1976-80, nominating com. 1995-96), Zonta (dir. 1992-95, sec. 1999-2001). Democrat. Methodist. Personal E-mail: lorsummers@worldnet.att.net.

SUMMERS, MARC, TV host, TV personality; b. Indpls., 1951; m. Alice Summers; 2 children. Comedian, LA; magician, comedian Magic Castle; studio page CBS, LA; guest announcer Joker's Wild, 1973. Nat. spokesperson Obsessive Compulsive Found. Performer (audience warm-ups): (TV series) Soap, Alice, Star Search; host, programming cons., prodr. (TV series) Double Dare, Nickelodeon, 1986—94, host What Would You Do?, host, creator, exec. prodr. Pick Your Brain, host Home Show, ABC, Our Home, Lifetime, Biggers and Summers, Great Day Am., PAX-TV, Unwrapped, Food Network, Trivia Unwrapped, appearances on The Next Food Network Star, Oprah, The Today Show, Dateline, The Howard Stern Show, The Tonight Show, Politically Incorrect, featured in People mag., USA Today; author: Everything In It's Place, 1999.

SUMMERS, PAUL G., lawyer, former state attorney general; b. Somerville, Tenn., Mar. 28, 1950; 1 child, Isaac. BS, Miss. State U.; JD, U. Tenn. Dist. atty. gen. 25th Jud. Dist., Somerville, Tenn., 1982—90; judge Tenn. Ct. Criminal Appeals, Nashville, 1990—99; atty. gen. State of Tenn., Nashville, 1999—2006; ptnr. Waller, Lansden, Dortch & Davis LLP, Nashville, 2006—. Adj. prof. law U. Memphis; former adj. faculty Cumberland U.; pres. elect Tenn. Dist. Atty.'s Gen. Conf.; mem. Ct. Criminal Appeals, 1990—99; lectr. in field. Former mem. Tenn. Sentencing Commn.; col. Tenn. Army N.G. With USAF. Decorated Legion of Merit, Meritorious Svc. medal with Oak Leaf Cluster. Mem.: Tenn. Dist. Attys. Gen. Conf. (pres.), Tenn. Bar Assn. (former gov.). Democrat. Avocations: racquetball, rollerblading, Karate (black belt), martial arts. Office: Waller Lansden Dortch & Davis LLP Ste 2700 511 Union St Nashville TN 37219 E-mail: paul.summers@wallerlaw.com. *

SUMMERS, ROBERT, economics professor; b. Gary, Ind., June 20, 1922; s. Frank and Ella (Lipton) Samuelson; m. Anita Arrow, Mar. 29, 1953; children: Lawrence Henry, Richard Fredric, John Steven. BS, U. Chgo., 1943; PhD, Stanford, 1956; postgrad. (Social Sci. Research Council fellow), King's Coll., U. Cambridge, Eng., 1951-52. Instr. Stanford, 1949-50; mem. faculty Yale, 1952-59, asst. prof., 1956-59; staff mem. Cowles Found., 1955-59; economist RAND Corp., Santa Monica, Calif., 1959-60, cons., 1960-80. Mem. faculty U. Pa. Wharton Sch., 1959—, prof., 1967—, chmn. grad. group in econs., 1967-70, 73-76 Author: (with Lawrence R. Klein) The Wharton Index of Capacity Utilization, 1966, (with others) Strategies for Research and Development, 1967, (with others) A System of International Comparisons of Gross Product and Purchasing Power, 1975, (with others) International Comparisons of Real Product and Purchasing Power, 1978, (with others) World Product and Income, 1982; contbr. articles to profl. jours. Served with AUS, 1944-46. Ford Found. faculty rsch. fellow London Sch. Econs., 1966-67; NSF grantee 1957-59, 63-66, 80-82, 86-90, 92-94, 95-97, 97-2000, 00—03; resident scholar Rockefeller Found. Study Ctr., 1986. Fellow: AAAS, Am. Econ. Soc. (disting.), Econometric Soc. Home: 1400 Waverly Rd V-11 Gladwyne PA 19035-1271 Office: U Pa Dept Econ Philadelphia PA 19104-6297 Office Phone: 215-898-7717, 215-898-7624. Business E-Mail: rsummers@econ.upenn.edu.

SUMMERS, ROBERT SAMUEL, lawyer, author, educator; b. Halfway, Oreg., Sept. 19, 1933; s. Orson William and Estella Bell (Robertson) S.; m. Dorothy Millicent Kopp, June 14, 1955; children: Brent, William, Thomas, Elizabeth, Robert. BS in Polit. Sci., U. Oreg., 1955; postgrad. (Fulbright scholar), U. Southampton, Eng., 1955-56; LLB, Harvard U., 1959; postgrad. rsch., Oxford U., 1964-65, 74-75, 81-82, 88-89; LLD (hon.), U. Helsinki, Finland, 1990, U. Göttingen, Germany, 1994. Bar: Oreg. 1959, NY 1974. Asso. King, Miller, Anderson, Nash and Yerke, Portland, Oreg., 1959-60; asst. prof. law U. Oreg., 1960-63, asso. prof., 1964-68; vis. asso. prof. law Stanford U., 1963-64; prof. U. Oreg., 1968-69, Cornell U., 1969-76, McRoberts rsch. prof. law, 1976—. Summer vis. prof. Ind. U., 1969, U. Mich., 1974, U. Warwick, Eng., 1975, Australia Nat. U., U. Sydney, Australia, 1977; vis. Fulbright prof. U. Vienna, Austria, 1985; Goodhart vis. prof. Cambridge U., Eng., 1991-92; H. Hurst Eminent vis. scholar U. Fla., 1995; rsch. fellow Merton Coll., oxford U., 1981-82, Exeter Coll., Oxford U., 1988-89; cons. Cornell Law Project in publ. schs., N.Y., 1969-74, Law in Am. Soc. project Chgo. Bd. Edn., 1968-69; instr. Nat. Acad. Jud. Edn., 1976—; mem. faculty Salzburg Seminar in Am. Studies, 1990; ofcl. advisor Drafting commn. on New Civil Code for Russian Fedn., 1994-96. Author: Law, Its Nature, Functions and Limits, 1986, Form and Function in a Legal System - A General Study, 2005; (with Hubbard and Campbell) Justice and Order Through Law, 1973; (with Bozzone and Campbell) The American Legal System, 1973; (with Speidel and White) Teaching Materials on Commercial Transactions, 1987, Collective Bargaining and Public Benefit Conferral-A Jurisprudential Critique, 1976, The Uniform Commercial Code, 1988, 4th edit., 1995; (with White) Het Pramatisch Instrumentalisme, 1981, Instrumentalism and American Legal Theory, 1982, Lon L. Fuller-Life and Work, 1984; (with Atiyah) Form and Substance in Anglo-American Law, 1987; (with Hillman) Contract and Related Obligation, 1987; (with MacCormick and others) Interpreting Statutes-A Comparative Study, 1991, Nature of Law and Legal Reasoning, 1993; contbr. book revs. and articles to profl. jours.; editor: Essays in Legal Philosophy, vol. 1, 1968, vol. 2, 1971. Social Sci. Research Council fellow, 1964-65 Mem. Am. Law Inst., Assn. Am. Law Schs. (chmn. sect. jurisprudence 1972-73), Am. Soc. Polit. and Legal Philosophy (v.p. 1976-78), Internat. Acad. Comp. Law, Internat. Assn. of Legal and Social Philosophy Am. Soc. (pres. 1989-91), Austrian Acad. of Scis., Phi Beta Kappa. Republican. Congregationalist. Office: Cornell U Sch Law Myron Taylor Hall Ithaca NY 14853

SUMMERS, SUZANNE FRANCES HEMENWAY, elementary school educator; b. Battle Creek, Mich., June 23, 1950; d. Robert Walter and Irene (Hodges) Hemenway; m. Jacob George Summers, June 23, 1973; children: Braxton, Jennifer, Dondra. BS in Home Econs., E. Carolina U., 1972; MEd, Campbell U., 1997. Lic. elem. tchr., N.C.; cert. tchr. Nat. Bd. Profl. Tchg. Standards, Va., 2005. Substitute tchr. Wake County Pub. Schs., Raleigh, N.C., 1973-74; presch. tchr. Greenwood Forest Bapt. Kindergarten, Cary, N.C., 1978-80; substitute tchr. Wake County Pub. Schs., Raleigh, 1980-96, tchr. elem., 1996—; tchr. Cary Elem. Sch. 2d team chair Cary Elem. Sch., rep. sch. improvement 2d and 3d grades; chmn. 2d grade sci. steering com. Wake County Pub. Schs., mem. sci. leadership com. Mem. NEA, N.C. Assn. Educators, Kappa Delta Pi, Phi Kappa Phi, Phi Upsilon Omicron. Republican. Baptist. Avocations: cooking, decorating homes. Home: 239 E Cornwall Rd Cary NC 27511-3907 Office Phone: 919-460-3455. Business E-Mail: ssummers@wcpss.net.

SUMMERS, WILLIAM B., JR., brokerage house executive; b. 1950; With McDonald & Co. Investments Inc., Cleve., 1971—; pres., CEO and chmn. McDonald & Co. Securities, Cleve., 1983—; chmn. McDonald Investments Inc., Cleve., 1995—; exec. v.p. KeyCorp, 1998—2000; chmn. Key Capital Partners, 1998—2000. Office: McDonald Investment Inc 800 Superior Ave E Cleveland OH 44114-2601

SUMMERS, WILLIAM COFIELD, science educator; b. Janesville, Wis., Apr. 17, 1939; s. Crosby Hungerford and Rebecca Delores (Cofield) S.; m. Wilma Jean Poos, July 24, 1965; 1 child, Emily Alexandra. BS, U. Wis., 1961, MS, 1963, Phd, MD, 1967; MA, Yale U., 1977. Post-doctoral fellow MIT, Cambridge, Mass., 1967-68; asst. prof. Yale U., New Haven, 1968-70, assoc. prof., 1970-77, prof., 1977—. Cons. NIH, Bethesda, Md., 1976—. Editor Nucleic Acids Research Jour., 1977-79, Gene jour., 1984-91; contbr. articles to profl. jours. Cons. Anna Fuller Fund, New Haven, 1973-88, Searle Scholars Program, Chgo., 1980-84; trustee Leukemia Soc. Am., N.Y.C., 1981-85, Yale-China Assn., New Haven, 1982-88, 94-98. Mem. Am. Soc. for Microbiology, History Sci. Soc., Am. Assn. History of Medicine. Office: Yale U Box 208114 New Haven CT 06520-8114 E-mail: william.summers@yale.edu.

SUMMERS, WILLIAM KOOPMANS, psychiatrist, internist, researcher; b. Jefferson City, Mo., Apr. 14, 1944; s. Joseph S. and Amy Lydia (Koopmans) Summers; m. Angela Forbes McGonigle, Oct. 2, 1972 (div. Apr. 1985). Student, Westminster Coll., Fulton, Mo., 1962-64; BS, U. Mo., 1966; MD, Washington U., St. Louis, 1971. Internal medicine intern Barnes Hosp-Washington U., St. Louis, 1971—72; resident in internal medicine Jewish Hosp., St. Louis, 1972—73; resident in psychiatry Washington U. Sch. Medicine, St. Louis, 1973—76; asst. prof. U. Pitts., 1976—78, U. So. Calif., LA, 1978—82; asst. clin. prof. rsch. UCLA, 1982—88; rschr. Arcadia, Calif., 1988—92, Albuquerque, 1992—; pres., CEO Alzheimers Corp., Albuquerque, 1999—. Mem.: ACP, AMA, Am. Fedn. Clin. Rsch., Soc. Neurosci., N.Y. Acad. Scis., Am. Psychiat. Assn. Episcopalian. Achievements include holder of 8 patents in neuropharmacology and neuroceuticals. Avocation: gardening. Office: Alzheimers Corp 6000 Uptown NE Ste 308 Albuquerque NM 87110

SUMMERS, WILLIAM LAWRENCE, lawyer; b. Ravenna, Ohio, Mar. 6, 1942; s. Samuel Long and Harriet Cordellia (Jones) S.; m. Barbara A. Herbert; children: Melinda Ann, Shannon Lea, Heather Colleen, Kelly Lynn, Michael Patrick, Kevin James. BA in Polit. Sci. and Sociology, Kent State U., 1965; postgrad., U. Miami, 1966; JD, Cleve. State U., 1969. Bar: Ohio 1969, Ky. 1988, U.S. Dist. Ct. (no. dist.) Okla. 1971, U.S. Ct. Appeals (6th cir.) 1973, U.S. Ct. Appeals (3d and 5th cirs.) 1979,, U.S. Ct. Appeals (8th and 5th cirs.) 1981, U.S. Ct. Appeals (7th cir.) 1982, U.S. Ct. Appeals (9th and 10th cirs.) 1983, U.S. Ct. Appeals (11th cir.), 1984, U.S. Supreme Ct., 1973, U.S. Tax Ct. 1973, U.S. Dist. Ct. (so. dist.) Ala. 1984, U.S. Dist. Ct. (so. dist.) Ohio 1985, U.S. Dist. Ct. (ea. and we. dists.) Ky. 1988. Ptnr. Summers & Vargas Co. LPA, Cleve. and Lexington, Ky., 1969—. Cons. on death penalty State Pub. Defender, Santa Fe, 1980-83; lectr. in field. Named one of Ten Outstanding Young Men of Cleve., Cleve. Jaycees, 1972, Five Outstanding Young Men of Ohio, Ohio Jaycees, 1972. Fellow Am. Acad. Trial Lawyers (Roscoe Pound award 1971); mem. ABA (criminal justice sect.), Ohio State Bar Assn. (ho. of dels. 1973-75, 2002-2004), Cuyahoga County Bar Assn. (trustee 1972-76, treas. 1976-79, pres. 1982-83, other coms.), Cuyahoga County Bar Assn., Cuyahoga County Criminal Ct. Bar Assn. (pres. 1977-79), Fed. Bar Assn., Portage County Bar Assn., Ohio Assn. Criminal Def. Lawyers (bd. dirs. 1988—), Ky. Assn. Criminal Def. Lawyer (bd. dirs. 1987-2000), Bar Assn. Greater Cleve., Nat. Assn. Criminal Def. Lawyers (trustee 1977-88, chmn. various coms. Pres.'s award 1981, 1986, 90, Robert C. Heeney award 1982), Am. Judicature Soc., Thoroughbred Club Am., Delta Theta Phi, Canterbury Golf Club, Elks. Roman Catholic. Avocation: thoroughbred horse breeding. Home: 17549 Merry Oaks Trl Chagrin Falls OH 44023-5643 Office: 55 Public Square Ste 2000 Cleveland OH 44113 Office Phone: 216-591-0727. Personal E-mail: wlslawyer@aol.com.

SUMMERS-POWELL, ALAN, lawyer; BA, Yale Coll., 1985; JD, U. Pa., 1988. Bar: N.Y. 1989, N.J. 1989, U.S. Dist. Ct. (fed. dist.) N.J. 1989, D.C. 1990, Fla. 1993, U.S. Dist. Ct. (mid. dist.) Fla. 1996, U.S. Ct. Appeals (11th cir.) 1996, U.S. Tax Ct. 1997, U.S. Dist. Ct. (so. dist.) Fla. 2001, U.S. Supreme Ct. 2005. Pvt. practice, Palm Harbor, Fla. Chmn. David Leasing and Devel., Inc. Office: PO Box 6043 Palm Harbor FL 34684-0643

SUMMERTREE, KATONAH **See WINDSOR, PATRICIA**

SUMMERVILLE, RICHARD M., mathematician, academic administrator; b. Shippenville, Pa., May 20, 1939; BS in Math., Clarion State Coll., Pa., 1959; AM in Math., Washington U., St. Louis, 1965; PhD in Math., Syracuse U., 1969. Provost Christopher Newport U. Office: Christopher Newport U Office of the Provost 1 University Pl Newport News VA 23606-2998 E-mail: rsummer@cnu.edu.

SUMMITT, PATRICIA HEAD, women's college basketball coach; b. Henrietta, Tenn., June 14, 1952; d. Richard and Hazel Head; m. R.B. Summitt; 1 child, Ross Tyler. BS in Phys. Edn., U. Tenn., Martin, 1974; MS in Phys. Edn., U. Tenn., Knoxville, 1975. Head coach U. Tenn., Knoxville, 1974—. Head coach 1st US Jr. Nat. team, 1977 (2 gold medals in internat. play), US Nat. team William R. Jones Cup Games, 1979, World Championships, 1979, Pan Am. Games, 1979 (2 gold medals, 1 silver medal); asst. coach US Women's Olympic Basketball team, 1980-84, head coach, 1984 (gold medal); assoc. athletics dir., U. Tenn.; past v.p. USA BASKETBALL; past Olympic rep. adv. com. to USA BASKETBALL; bd. trustees Basketball Hall of Fame; bd. dirs. Women's Basketball Hall of Fame. Active Big Bros./Big Sisters; active spokesperson United Way, Race for the Cure, Juvenile Diabetes; hon. chair Tenn. Easter Seal Soc., 1985, 87, 88, 89; Tenn. chair Am. Heart Assn., 1994. Named Women's Basketball Coaches Assn./Converse Coach of Yr., 1983—95, Naismith Coach of Yr., 1987, 1989, 1994, 1997, Naismith Coach of Century, 2000; named one of Women of Yr., Women in Sports and Events, 1999; named to Women's Sports Found. Hall of Fame, 1990, Nat. Assn. Sport and Phys. Edn., 1996, Women's Basketball Hall of Fame, 1999, Basketball Hall of Fame, 2000; recipient Silver medal, US World U. Games, 1973, Gold medal, Pan Am. Games, 1975, Silver medal, Olympic Games, 1976, Wooden award, 1997, ARETE Award for Courage in Sports, 1999. Mem. Chi Omega. Achievements include leading the Lady Vols to the NCAA Championship, 1987, 89, 91, 96, 97, 98, 2007; led the Lady Vols to the Southeastern Conf. Championship, 1980, 85, 90, 93, 94, 95, 98, 99, 2000, 01, 02, 03, 04; became the all-time winningest coach in NCAA basketball history, March 21, 2005; first female coach ever to win 300 games, 2006. Office: U Tenn 207 Thompson-Boling Ctr and Arena 1600 Phillip Fulmer Way Knoxville TN 37996-4610 Office Phone: 865-974-0600. *

SUMNER, DANIEL ALAN, economist, educator; b. Fairfield, Calif., Dec. 5, 1950; BS in Agrl. Mgmt., Calif. State Poly. U., 1971; MA in Econs., Mich. State U., 1973, U. Chgo., 1977, PhD, 1978. Post-doctoral fellow, labor and population group, econ. dept., Rand Corp., Santa Monica, Calif., 1977-78; asst. prof. N.C. State U., Raleigh, 1978-83, assoc. prof., 1983-87, prof., 1987-92; resident fellow Resources for the Future, Washington, 1986-87; sr. economist Pres.'s Council of Econ. Advisers, 1987-88; dep. asst. sec. for econs. USDA, 1990-91, asst. sec. for econs., 1992-93; Frank H. Buck Jr. prof. dept. agrl. econs. U. Calif., Davis, 1993—. Dir. U. Calif. Agrl. Issues Ctr., 1997—; chair Internat. Agrl. Trade Rsch. Consortium, 1997-99; mem. USDA Agrl. Policy Adv. Com. for Trade, 2001-03. Author and editor books and monographs; contbr. chpts. to books, articles in profl. jours. Named Alumnus of Yr., Calif. State Poly. U., 1991; recipient Quality of Rsch. Contbn. award Am. Agrl. Econ. Assn., 1996, Policy Contbrn., 1995, fellow, 1999; Fulbright Sr. Spl. Scholar Australia, 2002. Mem. Am. Agrl. Econs. Assn., Internat. Assn. Agrl. Economists. Office: U Calif Davis Dept Agrl Econ Davis CA 95616 Office Phone: 530-752-1668. Business E-Mail: dasumner@ucdavis.edu.

SUMNER, DAVID GEORGE, trade association administrator; b. Norwich, Conn., Apr. 22, 1949; s. Raymond W. and Ruth M. (Crooks) Sumner; m. Linda Ann Churma, June 27, 1980; 1 child, Deryn Anne. BA in Polit. Sci., Mich. State U., 1970; MBA, U. Conn., 1979. Corr. Travelers Ins. Co., Hartford, Conn., 1971-72; asst. sec. Am. Radio Relay League, Newington, Conn., 1972-76, asst. gen. mgr., 1976-82, gen. mgr., 1982-85, exec. v.p., 1985—. Mem. spectrum panning and policy adv. com. US Dept. Commerce, 1994—2001; bd. dirs. Windham Regional Planning Agy., Willimantic, Conn., 1991—98; mem. Coventry Zoning Bd. Appeals, 1997—, chmn., 1999—; mem. Coventry Dem. Town Com., Conn., 1995—. Recipient Calcutta Key, Radio Soc. Gt. Britain, 1989; Radio Club Am. fellow, 1991. Mem.: Newington C. of C. (bd. dirs. 1988—90), Internat. Amateur Radio Union (sec. 1982—89, 1999—, Region I award 1989). Democrat. Congregationalist. Avocation: amateur radio. Office: Am Radio Relay League 225 Main St Newington CT 06111-1400

SUMNER, FLOYD G., retired music educator; b. New Albany, Ind., Mar. 23, 1938; s. Louis Benjamin and Flora Wheeler Sumner; m. Rochelle Deeb Sumner, Jan. 22, 1961; children: Kevin George, Christopher George. B in Medicine, U. Louisville, Ky., 1959, MA, 1963; PhD, Rutgers U., NJ, 1973. Asst. prof. Rutgers U., New Brunswick, 1973—79, assoc. prof., 1979—96, prof., 1996—2002, prof. emeritus, 2002. Assoc. dean U. Coll. Rutgers U., 1990; music dept. chair Rutgers U., 1998. Editor: Canzoni Diversi, 1994, Fantasie overo Canzoni, 1995; author: The Music Handbook, 1996. Cultural arts adv. com., Piscataway, 1980—85. Mem.: Am. Musicological Soc. Avocations: trains, trollies, covered bridges, lighthouses. Home: 55 Dunbar Ave. Piscataway NJ 08854 Personal E-mail: f.sumner@att.net.

SUMNER, GORDON, JR., retired military officer; b. Albuquerque, July 23, 1924; s. Gordon and Esstella (Berry) S.; m. Frances Fernandes, May, 1991; children: Ward T., Holly Rose. AS, N.Mex. Mil. Inst., Roswell, 1943; BA, La. State U., 1955; MA, U. Md., 1963. Commd. 2d. lt. US Army, 1944, advanced through grades to lt. gen., 1975, ret., 1978; founder, chmn. Cypress Internat., 1978-96; chmn. La Mancha Co., Inc., 1981-89, Sumner Assoc. Cons. US Depts. State and Def; amabassador at large for Latin Am.; spl. advisor US Dept. State; nat. security advisor Pres.' Bi-Partisan Commn. Ctrl. Am.; cons. Los Alamos Nat. Lab. Contbr. articles to profl. jours. Decorated D.S.M., Silver Star, Legion of Merit with three oak leaf clusters, D.F.C., Air medal with 13 oak leaf clusters, Bronze Star, Army Commendation medal with oak leaf cluster, Purple Heart. Mem. Phi Kappa Phi, Pi Sigma Alpha. Office: La Mancha Co 100 Cienega St Ste D Santa Fe NM 87501-2003 Office Phone: 505-984-8041.

SUMNER, GORDON MATTHEW See STING

SUMNER, STEPHEN C., academic administrator; m. Pamela Sumner. Prof. U. Tulsa, dir. div. fine & performing arts, 1994—2001; provost New World Sch. Art, Miami, 2001—03; pres. Rocky Mountain Coll. Art & Design, Colo. Office: Office of President Rocky Mountain Coll Art & Design 1600 Pierce St Denver CO 80214 Office Phone: 303-753-6046. E-mail: ssumner@rmcad.edu.

SUMNERS, SARAH ELIZABETH, grant manager, history professor; b. Oxford, Miss., May 16, 1980; d. William and Caraly Sumners. MEd, Miss. U. for Women, Columbus, 2004. AA lic. secondary edn. Miss., 2004. History prof. Miss. Sch. for Math and Sci., Columbus, 2003—06; grant mgr. Miss. U. for WomenCtr. for Creative Learning, Columbus, 2004—. Nominee Tchr. of Yr., Disney Found., 2005—06; named Staff Mem. of Month, Miss. U. for Women, 2005; Math. and Sci. Partnership grantee, Miss. Dept. Edn., 2004—05, 2005—06, 2006—07. Mem.: NSTA, Nat. Mid. Sch. Assn., Nat. Coun. Tchrs. Math. Liberal. Office: MUW Center for Creative Learning 1100 College St MUW-1635 Columbus MS 39701 Office Phone: 662-241-6088.

SUMWALT, ROBERT LLEWELLYN, III, federal agency administrator, pilot; b. Columbia, SC, June 30, 1956; s. Robert Llewellyn Jr. and Joyce (Mills) S.; m. Anne Macdonald, Dec. 22, 1978; 1 child, Kaylyn Mackenzie. BS, U. S.C., 1979. Flight engr., first officer Piedmont Airlines, Winston-Salem, N.C., 1981-83, chief flight engr., 1983, capt., airline instr. Charlotte, NC, 1984-89; capt. U.S. Airways, Charlotte, 1989—2005; mgr. aviation SCANA Corp., 2005—06; mem. Nat. Transp. Safety Bd. (NTSB), Washington, 2006—, vice chmn., 2006—. Chmn. Richland County Airport Commn., Columbia, S.C., 1987-89; pres. Aviatrends, Inc., Columbia, 1992—; aviation safety rsch. cons. NASA Aviation Safety Reporting Sys.; mem., Air Line Pilots Assn. Accident Investigation Bd., 2002-04, US Airways Flight Ops. Quality Assurance, 2002-04; instr. Aviation Safety & Security Program, U. So. Calif., 2003- Author: Terminal Checklist, 1991; editl. adv. bd. Profl. Pilot Mag., Alexandria, Va., 1986—; contbr. articles to profl. jours. Recipient Laura Taber Barbour award, Flight Safety Found., 2003, Air Safety award, Air Line Pilots Assn., 2004. Mem. Airline Pilots Assn. (chmn. human hactors and ergonomics com.). Presbyterian. Achievements include research on aviation safety and aircraft accident investigation. Office: Nat Transp Safety Bd (NTSB) 490 L Enfant Plz SW Washington DC 20594

SUN, CHENGHUA, composer, music educator; b. Shao Xing, Zejiang, China, Sept. 17, 1942; arrived in U.S., 1991; s. Zhiliang Sun and Fuzhen Cai; m. Ai-Yue Ding, Jan. 17, 1968; children: Tian, Sun. Bachelors Degree in Violin Performance, Conservatory of Music, Shanghai, 1966. Group leader composition Song and Dance Theatre, Hunan, China, 1974—84; dir. song and dance group Opera & Dance Theatre, Jiangsu, China, 1986—91; founding dir. Chinese Youth Orch., Dallas, 1995—99; dir. Chinese Lucky-Star Choir, Dallas, 1995—. Advisor Little Red Flower Arts Group, Nanjing, China, 1987, Greatland Choral Soc., Dallas, 1995—2000, 2005; soloist Chinese Erhu Philharm. Symphony Orch., Irving, Tex., 1996, Voice of Change Inc., Dallas, 1998; soloist Dallas Chamber Orch., 2004—05. Composer: (songs) Album of Best Songs of China Since 1949, 1980 (1st prize), violin concerto. Named Life-time Art Dir., Opera and Dance Theatre, Jiangsu, 1991; recipient Grand prize for dance music, Nat. Edn. Dept., Beijing, 1989. Mem.: Am. String Tchr.'s Assn., Chinese Muiscians Assn., Music Tchrs. Nat. Assn., Assn. Chinese Profls. (advisor 2000), Dallas Chinese Artist Assn. (dir. 1999—2003), Chinese Music Soc. Dallas (founding dir. 1994—, prodr. first Dallas Chinese Music Festival 2004). Avocations: sports, games. Personal E-mail: sunding@juno.com. E-mail: sunding421217@yahoo.com.

SUN, DONGLIAN, meteorologist; d. Detian Sun and XianZhi Shiao; m. XiaoBiao Fan, May 1, 1990; 1 child, Jean Fan. BS in Synoptic Dynamics, Nanjing Inst. Meteorology, China, 1986; MS in Numerical Model and Simulation, Chinese Acad. Meteorol. Scis., Beijing, 1989, U. Md., College Park, 1998, PhD in Satellite Remote Sensing, 2003. Sr. scientist Raytheon ITSS Inc, Lanham, Md., 1998—2000; sr. software engr. Titan/AverStar, Vienna, Va., 2000—01; rsch. scientist, severe weather ctr. lead George Mason U., Fairfax, Va., 2001—. Achievements include development of new algorithms for improving atmospheric water vapor, surface temperature and emissivity retrieval from current and future satellite measurements; the study of coastal upwelling, hurricanes, and earthquakes by combining numerical model simulations with satellite remote sensing. Home: 21700 Seneca Ayr Dr Boyds MD 22030 Office: George Mason Univ Rsch Bldg 1 Room #252 MS:5C3 4400 University Dr Fairfax VA 22030 Home Phone: 703-993-4736; Office Phone: 703-993-4736. Office Fax: 703-943-1980; Home Fax: 703-993-1980. Personal E-mail: dsun@gmu.edu. Business E-Mail: sun@atmos.umd.edu.

SUN, HUI, industrial engineer, operations research analyst; b. Luoyang, Henan, China, May 21, 1973; arrived in US, 2001; s. Yubao Sun and Jun Xu. BEng, Hefei U. Tech., China, 1993; PhD, U. Tenn., Knoxville, 2005. Cert. SAS Inst. Inc., NC, 2006. Rsch. asst. U. Tenn., 2001—05; design engr. Millennium Transit Svcs., LLC., Roswell, N.Mex., 2006—. Indsl. engr. Inst. Project Planning and Rsch. Ministry Machinery Industry, Zhengzhou, Henan, China, 1993—2001. Contbr. articles to profl. jours. Mem.: Inst. Ops. Rsch. and Mgmt. Scis., Inst. Indsl. Engrs. Achievements include research in improving the performance of manufacturing systems and supply chain using advanced optimization techniques. Home: 1901 S Sunset Ave Apt 810 Roswell NM 88203 Home Phone: 505-910-2682. Personal E-mail: hui.sun@utalum.org.

SUN, HUN H., retired electrical and biomedical engineering educator; b. Shanghai, Mar. 27, 1925; s. Yu F.and Tuk F. Sun; m. Nancy Liu, Jan. 30, 1951; 1 child, Elizabeth A. BSEE, Chiao-Tung U., Shanghai, 1946; MSEE, U. Wash., 1950; PhD, Cornell U., 1955. Asst. prof. elect. engring. Drexel U., Phila., 1953-56, assoc. prof., 1956-59, prof., 1959—65, dir. Biomed. Engring. and Scis. Inst., 1964-74, chmn. elec. engring. dept., 1973-78, E.O. Lange prof., 1978-95, prof. emeritus, 1995—; NIH spl. fellow MIT, Cambridge, Mass., 1963-64. Cons. Wright-Patterson AFB, Dayton, Ohio, 1963-65; mem. study com. NIH, Bethesda, Md., 1981-85; mem. adv. com. NSF, Washington, 1985-88; adj. prof. Temple U. Dept. Physiology, 1971-91. Author: Synthesis of R. C. Networks, 1967; editor in chief Annals of Biomed. Engring., 1984-94; mem. editl. bd. Automatica (London), 1974-90, Critical Rev. in Bioengring, 1978-81; cons. editor Elec. Engring. Monograph Series, 1964-67; contbr. chpts. to books, articles to profl. jours. Mem. Com. on Art and Sci. Franklin Inst., 1969-82. Recipient 1st Rsch. Achievement award Drexel U., 1973. Fellow IEEE (editor in chief Trans. Biomed. Engring. 1972-78); mem. Biomed. Engring. Soc. (founding), Sigma Xi (life). Home: 939 Hedgerow Ct Blue Bell PA 19422-2408 Office Phone: 215-895-2240.

SUN, JUNPING, computer science professor; BE in Computer Sci., SE U., Nanjing, China, 1982; MS, Wayne State U., Detroit, 1987; PhD, Wayne State U., 1992. Asst. and assoc. prof. Nova Southeastern U., Ft. Lauderdale, Fla., 1992—2002, prof., 2002—. Assoc. editor Jour. Engring. Letter, Hong Kong, 2005—, Internat. Jour. Computers and Their Applications, Cary, NC, 2005—. Mem.: IEEE (sr.), Assn. Computing Machinery (assoc.), Upsilon Pi Epsilon. Office: Nova Southeastern U 3301 College Ave Fort Lauderdale FL 33314 Office Phone: 954-262-2082. Office Fax: 954-262-3915.

SUN, LI, statistician; b. Changchun, Jilin, China, Aug. 5, 1957; s. Enhou Sun and Chongxin Li; m. Nancy Xiaoning Ha, Feb. 21, 1982; children: Rosy, George. BSc, U. Jilin, Changchun, Jilin, China, 1982; MSc, Acad. Sci. China, 1984; PhD, U. Toronto, 1992. Rsch. fellow U. B.C. Cancer Agy., Vancouver, 1992—2000; sr. statis. engr. Ericsson Inc, Berkeley, Calif., 2001—02; sr. statistician Edmunds.com Inc., Santa Monica, Calif., 2002—. Contbr. articles to profl. jours., chapters to books. Fellow, Natural Sci. and Engring. Rsch. Coun. Can., 1992—94; Connaught scholar, U. Toronto, 1989—92. Mem.: Am. Stats. Assn. Office: Edmunds Inc 1620 26th St Ste 400 Santa Monica CA 90404 Office Phone: 310-309-4982. Personal E-mail: liandning_sun@yahoo.com. E-mail: lsun@edmunds.com.

SUN, NILAJA, playwright, actress; b. NYC; BA, Franklin and Marshall Coll., Pa. HIV educator. Creator and performer (one-woman shows) La Nubia Latina, Black and Blue (Aaron Davis Hall's Fund for New Work, 2000), Insufficient Fare, Babylon, No Child... (Lucille Lortel award outstanding solo show, 2007, John Gassner Playwriting award, Outer Critics Cir. Awards, 2007, Outer Critics Cir. award outstanding solo performance, 2007, OBIE award performance, 2007, Theatre World award, 2007), actress (plays) Santos and Santos, On the Hills of Black America, Antigone-In-Progress, Pieces of the Throne, Time and the Conways, Due To the Tragic Events of..., The Cook, 2003. Recipient Princess Grace award. *

SUN, NORA CHI-JUN, pathologist; b. Shanghai, June 16, 1937; came to U.S., 1966; d. K.F. and S.W. Sun; m. David T. Sung; children: Thomas C.K. Lee, Anthony D. Sung. MD, Shanghai 2d Med. Coll., 1960; MS in Pathology, U. Minn., 1973. Demonstrator U. Hong Kong, 1964-66; rsch. biologist A.H. Robins Co., Richmond, Va., 1966-67; resident Med. Coll. Va., 1967—68; clin. teaching asst. Boston U. Sch. Medicine, 1968-70; resident Mallaory Inst. Pathology, 1968—70; fellow Mayo Clinic and Grad. Sch., 1970—73; asst. prof. pathology U. So. Calif., LA, 1973-76; staff pathologist John Wesley Hosp., LA, 1973-76; asst. prof. UCLA Sch. Medicine, LA, 1976-82; staff pathologist, head hematopathology Harbor-UCLA Med. Ctr., Torrance, Calif., 1976—2002; assoc. prof. UCLA Sch. Medicine, LA, 1982-88, prof. pathology, 1988—2002, prof. emeritus, 2002—. Recipient Women Achievement award Delta Kappa Gamma, Rochester, Minn., 1972, Disting. Svc. award Am. Soc. Clin. Pathologists, 1996. Mem. Internat. Assn. Chinese Pathologists (pres.-elect 1991-93, pres. 1993-95), Harbor-UCLA Med. Ctr. Faculty Soc. (pres.-elect 1990-91, pres. 1991-92). Office: Harbor UCLA Med Ctr 1000 W Carson St Torrance CA 90502-2004

SUN, QIANG, botanist; s. Meixin Sun and Xianglan You; m. Wen Ding. PhD, Tohoku U., Sendai, Japan, 2001. Asst. prof. Xiamen U., Fujian, China, 1992—97; rsch. scientist Inst. Phys. and Chem. Rsch., Sendai, Miyagi, Japan, 2001—04; postdoctoral rschr. U. Calif. Davis, 2004—. Mem.: Bot. Soc. Am., Gamma Sigma Delta. Office: Univ Calif Davis One Shields Ave Davis CA 95616 Home Phone: 530-758-1827; Office Phone: 530-752-3971. Business E-Mail: qiasun@ucdavis.edu.

SUN, RENSHENG, electrical engineer, educator; s. Shouzhi Sun and Jingrong Xu; m. Wei Zhang, July 19, 2001. BSEE, Tsinghua U., Beijing, 1999; MSEE, Villanova U., Pa., 2002; PhD, Mich. State U., East Lansing, 2005. Vis. asst. prof. Dept. Elec. and Computer Engring. Mich. State U., 2005; sr. application engr. EM Software & Sys. Inc., Hampton, Va., 2006—. Mem.: IEEE, Phi Beta Delta, Tau Beta Pi, Eta Kappa Nu. Avocations: travel, music, jogging. Office: EM Software & Sys Inc 144 Research Dr Hampton VA 23666

SUN, ROBERT ZU JEI, manufacturing company executive, inventor, educator; b. Shanghai, July 5, 1948; s. David C.H. and Evelyn (Lee) S.; m. Nan Jennifer Ronis, Sept. 20, 1986; children: Matthew Nyland, Michael Elias. BS in Elec. Engring., U. Pa., 1970. Sr. project engr. Drexelbrook Engring. Co., Horsham, Pa., 1970—78; pres., chmn. bd. Suntex Internat., Inc., Easton, 1981—. Inventor 24 Math Game, Mhing Card Game; author First In Math. online program; 5 patents in field. Pres. Coalition of Religious and Civic Orgns., Easton, 1979-81; mem. transition team Pa. Gov.-elect Tom Ridge, 1994; apptd. by Gov. Ridge to Pa. State Bd. Edn., 1995, Team Pa. Amb. Coun., 1999; mem. fin. comm. Moravian Acad., 2001, trustee, 2004, chair audit com., 2006; planning commr. City of Easton, 2005; mem. Eisenhower Commn., 2006. Recipient 2 Excellence awards for Mhing pkg. Nat. Paperbox and Pkg. Assn., 1984-85. Office: 3311 Fox Hill Rd Easton PA 18045 Office Phone: 610-253-5255. E-mail: bob@24game.com.

SUN, RUIDONG, petroleum engineer; s. Wenke Sun and Zhaoqing Zeng; m. Yuhong Liu; 1 child, Connie. BS, China U. Petroleum, Dongying, 1992; MS, China U. Petroleum, Beijing, 1995, U. Chgo., 2002. Asst. prof. China U. Petroleum, 1995—99; sr. reservoir engr. Schlumberger, Houston, 2002—. Mem.: Soc. Petroleum Engrs.

SUN, WEI, electrical engineer; b. Jilin, China, Sept. 15, 1969; arrived in US, 1997; m. Xueqin Wu, July 15, 1997; 1 child, Olivia Qing. BEE, Xidian U., China, 1992; MS, Chinese Acad. Telecom. Tech., 1995; PhD, Stevens Inst. Tech., 2001. Mem. tech. staff Bell Labs Lucent Technologies, Holmdel, NJ, 2001—02; post-doctoral rsch. fellow Villanova U., Pa., 2002—04; asst. prof. Temple U., Phila., 2004—05; sr. comm. engr. Magnolia Broadband Inc., Bedminster, NJ, 2005—. Author: Signal Processing for Mobile Communications Handbook, 2004; contbr. scientific papers to profl. jours. Mem.: IEEE, Eta Kappa Nu. Home: 104 Bluebird Dr Hillsborough NJ 08844 Home Phone: 908-874-7176. Personal E-mail: wsun@ieee.org.

SUN, YILIN, language educator; arrived in US, 1994, permanent resident; d. Jieqing Sun and Jing Mei Wu; m. Jian Zou, Aug. 24, 1980; children: Lydia Zou, David Zou. BA, Ctrl. China Normal U., Wuhan, China, 1982; MEd, U. Toronto, Can., 1989, PhD (hon.), 1992. Tchr. faculty edn. York U., Toronto, Canada, 1992—94; prof. Seattle Ctrl. C.C., 1994—, dir. faculty devel., 2000—02. Curriculum writer, rschr. Ont. Province English Lang. Instrn. for Newcomers Curriculum Guidelines Employment and Immigration Can./TESL Ont., 1993; adj. prof. Seattle Pacific U., 2004—06, Seattle U., 2006—; program lead Seattle Ctrl. C.C., 2006—. Illustrator: The Illustrated Otolaryngological Operation, 1977; contbr. chapters to books. Mem. adv. com. the yr. China City Seattle, Seattle Art Mus, Asian Art Mus., 2000—01; mem. title II grant adv. com. US Dept. Edn., Washington, 1999—99. Named Outstanding Student Orgn. Advisor, Seattle Ctrl. C.C., 1997; recipient Exceptional Faculty award, Seattle C.C. Dist., 2002, Innovation of Yr. award, League Innovation in C.C., 2002, Svc. citation, Wash. State Faculty and Staff of Color in Higher Edn. Ann. Conf. Planning Com., 2005, 2006; grantee, Office of Adult Literacy, State Bd. Cmty. and Tech. Colls., 1995, 2005, 2006; scholar, Fulbright Hayes Found., 1998, 2005. Mem.: TESOL (chmn. conf. 2006—07, chmn. affiliate leadership coun. 2005—07), Wash. Assn. Edn. Spkrs. Other Langs. (pres. 2002—03), Am. Assn. Applied Linguistics (corr.; mem. 1990—95), Am. Fedn. Tchrs. (assoc.; mem. exec. bd. 2005—07, chmn. profl. issues Wash. chpt. 2004—07, Svc. citation 2002, 2004), Global Edn. Design Team (co-chmn. 2004—06). Office: Seattle Central CC 1701 Broadway Seattle WA 98122 Home Phone: 425-687-8513; Office Phone: 206-587-5411. Office Fax: 206-344-4384. Business E-Mail: yilsun@sccd.ctc.edu.

SUN, YING-HSUAN, research scientist; b. Taipei, Taiwan, May 22, 1964; s. Tien-Shou Chou and Mei-Shieh Sun; m. Chiu-Yueh Hung, Nov. 21, 1964; children: Katherine Hung, Isabella Hung. BS, Nat. Taiwan U., 1987; MS, N.C. State U., 1994, PhD, 2001. Rsch. scientist Bio-Informatics Group, Inc., Cary, NC, 2001—03; rsch. assoc. N.C. State U., Raleigh, 2003—06. Contbr. articles to profl. jours. Biotechnology fellow, N.C. State U., 1998. Mem.: AAAS, Taiwanese Am. Assn. (pres. N.C. chpt. 2003—04), Am. Soc. Plant Biologists, N.Y. Acad. Sci. Achievements include patents pending for micro RNA in trees. Office: Forest Biotech Group NCSU 2500 Partners II 840 Main Campus Dr Raleigh NC 27695 Home Phone: 919-859-3586; Office Phone: 919-513-0015. E-mail: yhsun@unity.ncsu.edu.

SUN, YUEFENG, research scientist, educator; b. Liangshan, Shandong, China, Apr. 5, 1962; s. Xueqian Sun and Shuyuan She; m. Lilai Yan; 1 child, Yusha Yan Sun. BS, Petroleum U. China, Donying, Shandong, 1981; MS, Columbia U., NYC, 1988, PhD, 1994. Geophysicist China Nat. Petroleum Corp., Urumqi, Xinjiang, 1982—87; grad. tchg. fellow Columbia U., NYC, 1988—94; postdoctoral fellow Lamont Doherty Earth Obs., Columbia U., Palisades, 1995—97, Doherty rsch. scientist, 1998—2005; assoc. prof. The Petroleum Inst., Abu Dhabi, 2005—06, Tex. A&M U., College Station, 2007—. Mem.: Am. Assn. Petroleum Geologists, Soc. Exploration Geophysicists (assoc.), Am. Geophys. Union (assoc.). Achievements include invention of work on relating permeability to wave velocity implemented and referred to as the Sun model by Shell Oil Co., which improves world hydrocarbon reserves and production; research in theory invention; patents for method of estimation of gas hydrates; systems and methods of detecting living organisms in rocks. Home: 49 Bluefield Ave Harrington Park NJ 07640 Office: TAMU 3115 College Station TX 77843 Home Phone: 201-768-4652; Office Phone: 971-2-5085334, 979-845-0635. Office Fax: 971 2 5085200. Personal E-mail: yfsun3@yahoo.com. Business E-Mail: ysun@pi.ac.ae, sun@geo.tamu.edu.

SUN, ZUO, aerospace engineer, researcher; b. Shenyang, Liaoning, China, July 3, 1970; arrived in U.S., 1996; s. Dianfu Sun and Shuxiang Liu; m. Xinxin Zhou. PhD in Theoretical and Applied Mechanics, Northwestern U., 2001; MS, BS, Tsinghua U. Sr. mech. engr. Corning (N.Y.) Inc., 2001—02; rsch. scientist Va. Tech, Blacksburg, 2002—03; mech. engr. GE Global Rsch. Ctr., Schenectady, NY, 2003—06; sr. aerospace engr. Boeing Co., 2006—. Cons. Hewlett-Packard Corp., Portland, Oreg., 2001—02, State Nuc. Safety Bur. in China, Beijing, 1993—95. Contbr. articles to profl. jours. Recipient First Class award, Tsinghua U., Beijing, 1989; Grad. fellow, 1994, Grad. scholar, Northwestern U., 1997—2003. Mem.: ASME, AIAA (corr.), Sigma Xi (hon.). Achievements include development of new models to predict long term behavior and life of composite materials; tools to characterize micro/nano scale systems; physics-based modeling of commercial aircraft engines; design of Micro-electro-mechanical Systems; investigation of adhesion science. Home: 2307 NE 4th St # B303 Renton WA 98056 Office Phone: 206-662-2258. Personal E-mail: zuosun@yahoo.com.

SUNAMI, JOHN SOICHI, designer; b. NYC, June 10, 1949; s. Soichi and Suyeko (Matsushima) S.; m. Marialyce Norman, Apr. 21, 1973; children: Christopher Andrew-Soichi, Jennifer Kiyoko. BA, CCNY, 1969. Cert. Gemological Inst. Am. Vol. Peace Corps, Jamaica, W.I., 1969-71; jeweler NYC and Columbus, Ohio, 1971-82; dir. mktg. Knight's Inn/Cardinal Industries, Columbus, 1982; founder, exec. designer Nimbus, Columbus, 1983—. Designer/sculptor pub. artwork IntroCenter, 1990; designer logo identities for various cos.; exhibited paintings and sculpture; author poems and essays. Bd. dirs. William H. Thomas Gallery, Columbus, 1992-93, Ctrl. Cmty. House, Columbus, 2007; v.p., bd. dirs. South Side Settlement House, Columbus, 1982-93; mem. cultural diversity outreach com. United Way of Franklin County, 1993-01. Recipient 1st prize Macworld Gallery/Macworld Mag., 1985. Mem.: Ctrl. Ohio Machine Knitters. Avocations: music, travel. Home: 408 Fairwood Ave Columbus OH 43205-2244 Office: Nimbus 413 Fairwood Ave Columbus OH 43205-2202 Office Phone: 614-253-0453. Office Fax: 614-253-0257. Personal E-mail: design@nimbus-art.com.

SUND, RICK (RICHARD W. SUND), former professional sports team executive; b. Elgin, Ill., 1951; s. Bob Sund; m. Lea E. Sund; children: Hali, Patrick. Student, Northwestern U.; M in Athletic Adminstrn., Ohio U., 1974. With Milw. Bucks, 1974—78; player pers. dir. to v.p. ops. Dallas Mavericks, 1979—93; player pers. cons. Seattle SuperSonics, 1994—95, gen. mgr., 2001—07, cons., 2007—; v.p. player pers. to exec. v.p. basketball ops. Detroit Pistons, 1995—2001. Named to Ill. HS Basketball Coaches' Hall of Fame. Avocation: golf. *

SUNDARAM, CHANDRU P., urologist; arrived in US, 1992; MS, Madras Med. Coll., India, 1985; MS in Gen. Surgery, Bangalore U., India, 1988; FRCS, Royal Coll. Surgeons, England, 1989. Diplomate Am. Bd. Urology, lic. Ind., Mo. Urology residency U. Minn., Mpls., 1997; asst. prof. surgery Washington U., St. Louis, 1998—2002; assoc. prof. urology Ind. U., 2002—, dir. minimally invasive urologic surgery, 2002—; endourology fellowship Harvard Med. Sch., Boston, 1998. Dir. fellowship in minimally invasive urology Ind. U., 2002—. Contbr. articles various profl. jours., chapters to books. Recipient Resident Tchg. award, Washington U., 2002. Mem.: Endourological Soc., Soc. Laparoendoscopic Surgeons (Best Urology Video award 2005), Am. Urological Assn. Office: Ind U Sch Medicine 535 N Barnhill Dr Indianapolis IN 46202 Business E-Mail: sundaramc@netscape.net.

SUNDARAM, SHANKAR M., surgeon; b. Apr. 25, 1969; BA, Washington U., St. Louis, 1989; MD, U. Tex., Galveston, 1994. Pvt. practice Victoria Ctr. Trade Union Studies, Tex., 2004—06, North Tex. Cardiothoracic and Vascular Surgery, McKinney, 2006—. Fellow: ACS. Office: North Tex Cardiothoracic and Vascular Surgery 4510 Medical Center Dr Ste 112 Mc Kinney TX 75069-3639

SUNDBERG, MARSHALL DAVID, biology professor; b. Apr. 18, 1949; m. Sara Jane Brooks, Aug. 1, 1977; children: Marshall Isaac, Adam, Emma. BA in Biology, Carleton Coll., 1971; MA in Botany, U. Minn., 1973, PhD in Botany, 1978. Lab. technician Carleton Coll., Minn., 1973-74; teaching asst. U. Minn., Mpls., 1974-76, rsch. asst., 1976-77; adj. asst. prof. Biology U. Wis., Eau Claire, 1978-85, mem. faculty summer sci. inst., 1982-85; instr. La. State U., Baton Rouge, 1985-88, asst. prof. Biology, 1988-91, coord. dept. Biology, 1988-93, assoc. prof. Biology, 1991-97; prof., chair dept. biol. scis. Emporia State U., 1997—. Author: General Botany Laboratory Workbook, 5th revision, 1984, General Botany 1001 Laboratory Manual, 1986, General Botany 1002 Laboratory Manual, 1987, Biology 1002 Correspondence Study Guide, 1987, Boty 1202: General Botany Laboratory Manual, 1988, Biol 1208: Biology for Science Majors Laboratory Manual, 1988, 2d edit., 1989, Instructor's Manual for J. Mauseth, Introductory Botany, 1991; contbr. articles to profl. jours. Brand fellow U. Minn., 1976-77, Faculty Grants scholar U. Wis., 1984-85. Fellow Linnaean Soc. London; mem. NSTA, AAAS, Am. Inst. Biol. Scis. (coun. mem. at large 1992-95, edn. com. 1994-95, 98-2002), Nat. Sci. Tchrs. Assn., Assn. Biology Lab. Edn., Bot. Soc. Am. (chmn. tchg. sect. 1985-86, workshop com. tchg. sect. 1983-84, slide exch./lab. exch. tchg. sect. 1980-89, edn. com. 1991, 92, editor Plant Sci. Bull. 2000—, Charles H. Bessey award 1992, Centennial award 2006), Internat. Soc. Plant Morphologists, Nat. Assn. Biology Tchrs. (Outstanding 4-Yr. Coll. Tchr. award 1997, 2003), Soc. Econ. Botany, The Nature Conservancy, Sigma Xi (chpt. sec. 1982-84, 93-95, 2000-02, v.p. 1984-85, 96-97, pres. 1996, 99, 2005). Home: 1912 Briarcliff Ln Emporia KS 66801-5404 Office: Emporia State U Dept Biol Scis 1200 Commercial St Emporia KS 66801-5087

SUNDBERG, RICHARD, architectural firm executive; b. Seattle, Oct. 10, 1942; BArch, U. Wash., 1966. Registered arch., Wash., Mont., Idaho, Wyo.; cert. Nat. Coun. Archtl. Registration Bd. Arch. Ibsen Nelsen & Assocs., 1967-74; assoc. Olson/Walker Assocs., Seattle, 1975-76, ptnr., 1976-85; prin. Olson/Sundberg Archs., Seattle, 1985—2000, Olson Sundberg Kundig Allen Archs., Seattle, 2000—. Guest juror U. Wash. Sch. Architecture; mem. hist. bldg. code tech. adv. group State of Wash. Prin. works include Overlake Park Presbyn. Ch. (Seattle chpt. Merit award AIA 1989), Evergreen State Coll. (Seattle chpt. Merit award AIA, 1993, Pacific N.W. Regional Honor award, 1993, Architecture and Energy Honor award AIA, 1993), Wash. State Hist. Soc. Mus., Hill Climb Ct. (Honor award AIA, 1983), Zoo Store-Woodland Park Zool. Gardens, 98 Union/South Arcade (Honor award AIA, 1985), Pike & Virginia Bldg. (Honor award AIA, 1979), Seattle Art Mus. Downtown, Seattle's Best Coffee-various locations, Seattle Univ. Chapel, Frye Art Mus., Antioch U., Seattle U. Sch. Law (Masonry Inst. Wash. Citation award 2001, AIA Seattle Merit award 2001), Habitat for Humanity - Roxbury Estates (Builder's Choice award 2005), Maury Island Residence (NW Design awards 2006). Fellow AIA; mem. Nat. Trust Hist. Preservation. Office: Olson Sundberg Kundig Allen Archs 159 S Jackson St Ste 600 Seattle WA 98104 Office Phone: 206-624-5670. Office Fax: 206-624-3730. *

SUNDBERG, RICHARD JAY, chemistry professor; b. Sioux Rapids, Iowa, Jan. 6, 1938; BS, U. Iowa, 1959; PhD, U. Minn., 1962. Faculty dept. chemistry U. Va., Charlottesville, 1964-74, prof., 1974—. Author (with F. A. Carey) Advanced Organic Chemistry, 4th edit., 2000. Served to 1st lt. U.S. Army, 1962-64 Mem. Am. Chem. Soc. Lutheran. Office: U Va Dept Chemistry Box 400319 Charlottesville VA 22904-4319 Office Phone: 434-924-3233.

SUNDBERG, RUTH DOROTHY, hematologist, educator; b. Chgo., July 29, 1915; d. Carl William and Ruth (Chalbeck) S.; m. Robert H. Reiff, Dec. 24, 1941 (div. 1945). Student, U. Chgo., 1932-34; BS, U. Minn., 1937, MA, 1939, PhD, 1943, MD, 1953. Diplomate: Am. Bd. Pathology. Instr., asst. prof. anatomy U. Minn., 1939-53, assoc. prof., 1953-60, prof., 1960-63, prof. of lab. medicine and anatomy, 1963-73, prof. lab. medicine, pathology and anatomy, 1973-84, emeritus prof., 1984—; hematologist, dir. Hematology Labs., 1945-74, hematologist, co. dir., 1974-84. Editorial bd.: Soc. Exptl. Biology and Medicine, until 1975; mem. editorial bd.: Blood, 1960-67; assoc. editor, 1967-69. Recipient Lucretia Wilder award for research in anatomy, 1939 Mem.: Sigma Xi. Home (Summer): 322 Bishopsbridge Dr Cincinnati OH 45255-3947 Home (Winter): 12558 Shanandoah Ct Marco Island FL 34145-5023

SUNDBORG, STEPHEN V., academic administrator; s. George and Mary Sundborg. PhD, Pontifical Gregorian Univ., Rome, 1982. Ordained Jesuit, 1974. Tchr. religion and Latin Gonzaga Prep. Sch., Spokane, Wash., Jesuit High, Portland, Oreg.; tchr. theology Seattle U.; rector Seattle U. Jewish Cmty., 1986-90; provincial Oreg. Province, 1990-97; pres. Seattle U., 1997—. Office: Admin Bldg 109 900 Broadway Seattle WA 98122-4340 *

SUNDE, DOUGLAS, plastic surgeon; b. Evanston, Ill., May 18, 1960; s. Edward Albert and Marilyn S.; m. Linda Neff, 1989; children: Samuel, Joseph. AB, Stanford U., 1982; MD, U. Calif., San Francisco, 1986. Diplomate Am. Bd. Plastic Surgery. Resident in plastic surgery Stanford (Calif.) U., 1986-92, clin. instr., 1992; fellow in aesthetic surgery Manhattan Eye Ear and Throat Hosp., NYC, 1990; fellow in hand, microsurgery Davies Med. Ctr., San Francisco, 1993; pvt. practice Monterey, Calif., 1994—. Clin. asst. prof. Stanford Med. Ctr., 1998—. Contbr. articles to profl. jours. Named Nat. Merit scholar 1977. Fellow ACS; mem. Am. Bd. Plastic Surgery, Am. Soc. Plastic Reconstructive Surgery, Calif. Soc. Plastic Surgery, Alpha Omega Alpha. Office Phone: 831-372-0200.

SUNDEL, MARTIN, management consultant, psychologist, educator; b. Bronx, NY, Sept. 22, 1940; s. Louis and Pauline (Brotman) S.; m. Sandra Stone, Aug. 22, 1971; children: Adam Daniel, Jenny Rebecca, Ariel Pauline. BA cum laude, St. Mary's U., 1961; MSW., Our Lady of the Lake Univ., 1963; MA, PhD, U. Mich., 1968. Social group work supr. Valley Cities Jewish Cmty. Ctr., Van Nuys, Calif., 1963-65; asst. prof. U. Mich. Sch. Social Work, Ann Arbor, 1968-71; dir. rsch. and evaluation River Region Mental Health-Mental Retardation Bd., Louisville, 1972-77; assoc. clin. prof. dept. psychiatry and behavioral sci. Kent. Sch. Social Work, U. Louisville, 1974—77; sr. research assoc. The Urban Inst., Washington, 1977-80; pvt. practice psychology Dallas, 1980-95; Dulak Disting. prof. U. Tex., Arlington, 1980-89, prof., 1980-95, Fla. Internat. U., Miami, Fla., 1995-2000; faculty assoc. S.E. Fla. Ctr. on Aging, 1996-2000; pres. Sundel Cons. Group, 2000—. Mental health cons. UN High Commn. for Refugees in Cyprus, 1993-95; profl. adv. coun. Dallas Geriatric Rsch. Inst., 1980-89; long-range planning com. Dallas Jewish Coalition for the Homeless, 1986-95; coordinating com. Arlington Human Svcs. Project, 1981-90, Mayor's Forum on Human Svc. Needs Assessment, Ft. Worth, 1983-86; vis. prof. U. So. Calif. Sch. Social Work, spring 1985; sr. consortium rsch. fellow, Dept. Def., 1996-99; adj. prof. Kent. Sch. Social Work, U. Louisville, 1974-77. Author: (with Sandra Stone Sundel) Behavior Change in the Human Services, 1975, 5th edit., 2005; Be Assertive, 1980; co-author: Women at Midlife, 2002; co-editor: Assessing Health and Human Service Needs, 1983, Individual Change Through Small Groups, 2d edit., 1985, Midlife Myths, 1989; mem. editl. bds. and cons. to profl. jours. Named Nat. Table Tennis Champion, U1600 Round Robin Age Group of 40 Yrs. and Older, 2005; fellow, Harvard U. Lab. Cmty. Psychiatry, Boston, 1971—72. Fellow Prescribing Psychologists Register (diplomate), Internat. Coun. Prescribing Psychology (diplomate in psychopharmacology); mem. Behavior Therapy and Rsch. Soc. (charter clin. fellow). Home: 3804 Barbados Ave Hollywood FL 33026-4659 E-mail: sundelm@bellsouth.net.

SUNDERMAN, DUANE NEUMAN, chemist, research and development company executive; b. Wadsworth, Ohio, July 14, 1928; s. Richard Benjamin and Carolyn (Neuman) S.; m. Joan Catherine Hoffman, Jan. 31, 1953; children: David, Christine, Richard. BA, U. Mich., 1949, MS, 1954, PhD in Chemistry, 1956. Researcher Battelle Meml. Inst., Columbus, Ohio, 1956-59, mgr., 1959-69, assoc. dir., 1969-79, dir. internat. programs, 1979-84; sr. v.p. Midwest Rsch. Inst., Kansas City, Mo., 1984-90, exec. v.p., 1990-94, Golden, Colo., 1990-94. Dir. Nat. Renewable Energy Lab., Golden, Colo., 1990-94, dir. emeritus, 1994—. Contbr. numerous articles to profl. jours. Bd. dirs. Mid-Ohio chpt. ARC, 1982-83, U. Kansas City, 1985-90, Mo. Corp. for Sci. and Tech., Jefferson City, 1986-90, Colo. Energy Sci. Ctr., 2000-04. With USNR, 1949—59. Mem. Am. Chem. Soc. Presbyterian. Avocation: paleontology.

SUNDERMEYER, MICHAEL S., lawyer; b. Kansas City, Mo., Feb. 8, 1951; s. Edgar W. and Ruth (Shobe) S.; m. Susan Talarico; children: Kim Marie, Mark Shobe. BA, U. Kans., 1973; JD, U. Va., 1976. Bar: D.C., Md., Va., U.S. Dist. Ct. D.C., U.S. Dist. Ct. Md., U.S. Dist. Ct. (ea. dist.) Va., U.S. Dist. Ct. (no. dist.) Okla., U.S. Ct. Appeals (D.C. cir.), U.S. Ct. Appeals (2d, 3d, 4th, 5th, 6th, 9th and 11th cirs.). Law clk. to Hon. John Minor Wisdom U.S. Ct. Appeals (5th cir.), New Orleans, 1976-77; law clk. to Hon. Harry A. Blackmun U.S. Supreme Ct., Washington, 1977-78; assoc. Williams & Connolly, Washington, 1978-84, ptnr., 1985—. Editor-in-chief Va. Law Rev., 1975-76. Mem. ABA. Office: Williams & Connolly LLP 725 12th St NW Washington DC 20005-5901 Office Phone: 202-434-5000. E-mail: msundermeyer@wc.com.

SUNDGREN, DONALD E., construction executive; BS, La. State U. V.p. exec. dir. Dillingham Constrn,. Holdings, Inc., Pleasanton, Calif., 1996-97; pres., CEO Dillingham Construction Corp., Pleasanton, Calif., 1997—. Office: Dillingham Construction Holdings PO Box 1268 Placerville CA 95667-1268

SUNDHEIM, NANCY STRAUS, lawyer, computer company executive; b. Phila., June 25, 1951; B in Hist., U. Pa., 1973; JD, Harvard U., 1978. With Arnold & Porter, Washington, Ropes & Gray, Boston, Dechert, Price & Rhoads, Phila.; chief acquisitions counsel Unisys Corp., Blue Bell, Pa., 1987, dep. counsel, head corp. law group, 1990, corp. v.p., corp. sec., 1999, mem. exec. com., 1999—, sr. v.p., sec., gen. counsel, 2001—. Office: Unisys Corp Unisys Way Blue Bell PA 19424 Office Phone: 215-986-4011. Office Fax: 215-986-2312. *

SUNDICK, SHERRY SMALL, author, journalist, poet; b. Washington, July 17, 1946; d. Charles Haskell and Ruth (Behrend) Small; B.A., Am. U., 1970; m. Gary Norman Sundick, Aug. 3, 1969; children— Amy Beth, Suzanne Faye. Columnist, Today Newspapers, Rockville, Md., 1973-75; journalist The Jour. Newspapers, Chevy Chase, Md., 1975—, The Potomac Almanac, 1976-80. Recipient N.Am. Mentor Mag. Ann. Mentor Poetry award, 1973. Mem. Nat. League Am. Pen Women, Writers Center, World Poetry Soc. Jewish. Author: Celebration, 1977; (with Ruth Small) Potpourri, 1978; contbr. articles to various mags. and jours. including Md. Mag., No. Va. Mag. Design, Maine Life, Feelings, Smile, The Pen Women, Haiku Headlines, others. Address: 11809 Hunting Ridge Ct Potomac MD 20854-2152

SUNDIN, MATS JOHAN, professional hockey player; b. Sollentuna, Sweden, Feb. 13, 1971; Selected 1st round NHL entry draft Que. Nordiques, 1989, right wing, 1990—94, Toronto Maple Leafs, 1994—, capt., 1997—. Played in Europe NHL Lockout, 1994—95; mem. Swedish League All-Star Team, 1990—91, 1991—92; player NHL All-Star Game, 1996—2004. Achievements include being a member of gold medal winning Swedish Hockey Team, Torino Olympics, Italy, 2006. Office: Toronto Maple Leafs Air Canada Ctr 40 Bay St Ste 300 Toronto ON Canada M5J 2X2

SUNDLOF, STEPHEN FREDERICK, veterinary administrator; b. Peoria, Ill., May 4, 1951; m. Sandra Linden Sundlof; children: Christofer Linden, Thomas Michael. BS in Zoology/Chemistry with honors, So. Ill. Univ., Carbondale, Ill., 1973; MS in Veterinary Toxicology, U. Ill., Coll. Veterinary Med. Sciences, Urbana, Ill., 1976, BS in Veterinary Medicine with honors, 1977, DVM in Veterinary Medicine with honors, 1980, PhD in Veterinary Toxicology, 1980. Diplomate Am. Bd. Vet. Toxicology. Rsch. asst., dept. physiology and pharmacology U. Ill., Coll. Vet. Medicine, Urbana, Ill., 1973—76, rsch. asst., dept. veterinary biosciences, 1976—80; asst. prof., dept. preventative medicine Coll. Vet. Medicine, U. Fla., Gainesville, Fla., 1980—86, prof., dept. physiological sciences, 1995, assoc. prof., dept. physiological sciences, 1986—95; dir. Ctr. for Vet. Medicine FDA, Washington, 1994—. Chmn., drug abuse com., Fla. Vet. Med. Assn., 1982-85; divsn. leader, divsn. toxicology and pathophysiology, dept. preventative medicine, 1982-83; animal drug coordinator, So. Region IR-4 Project, 1982-94; vice-chair, Ineragency Coordinating Com. for Animal Production Food Safety, 1995-; rep., Fla. Prescription Abuse Data Synthesis Com, Coll. Vet. Medicine and Fla. Vet. Med. Assn., 1984-86; courtesy prof., dept. physiological sciences, Coll. Vet. Medicine, U. Fla., Gainesville, Fla., 1996; mem. US Pub. Health Svc. spl. oversight com. to review allegations of mismanagement and abuse of authority by the US FDA, Ctr. for Vet. Medicine, 1986-87; Am. Vet. Med. Assn. delegate to the WHO/FAO Codes Alimentarius Com. on Residues of Vet. Drugs in Foods, 1986-94; Inst. Food Technologists delegate to the Food Safety Workshop, 1989; mem., vet. medicine adv. com., US FDA, 1991-94, chmn. 1993-94; chmn., WHO/FAO Codes Alimentarius Com. on Residue of Vet. Drugs in Foods, 1994-; temporary advisor, WHO/FAO Joint Expert Com. on Food Additives, 1995-; mem. steering com. on Internat. Cooperation on Harmization of Tech. Requirements for Registration of Vet. Medicinal Products, Office of Internat. Epizootics, 1995-; mem. external adv. bd., Inst. Food Sci. and Engring, Tex. A7M U., 1996-97; mem., USDA Food Safety and Inspection Svc., Food Rsch. Working Group, 1996-97; US Delegate to the Codex Alimentarius Internat. Ad Hoc Task Force on Animal Feeding, 1999-2004; mem., WHO/FAO, Office of Internat. Epizootics expert consultation on non-human antimicrobial usage and antimicrobial resistence, 2004; US delegation to Japan to discuss trade implications following finding of BSE-positive cow in US, 2004-; presenter in field. Editoral reviewer, Journal Veterinary Pharmacology and Therapeutics, 1988-; contbr. articles to profl. jours. Named Hon. Diplomate, Am. Vet. Epidemiology Soc., 1996, Disting. Practitioner in the Nat. Acad. Practice in Vet. Medicine, Nat. Acad. Practices, 1997; recipient Presidential Exec. Rank award Meritorious Exec. Rank, 1999. Mem. Am. Acad. Vet. Pharmacology and Therapeutics (pres.-elect 1993-95, pres. 1995-97), Am. Acad. Vet. and Comparative Toxicologists, Am. Vet. Med. Assn. (President's award, 1997), Am. Bd. Veterinary Toxicology. Office: FDA Ctr Vet Medicine HFV-1 Office Dir 7500 Standish Pl Rockville MD 20855-2764 Fax: 301-827-4401. *

SUNDLUN, BRUCE, former governor; b. Providence, Jan. 19, 1920; s. Walter I. and Jan Z. (Colitz) Sundlun; m. Susan Garvin Dittelman, Jan. 1, 2000; children: Tracy, Stuart, Peter, Kara; stepchildren: Heather Conover, Max Dittelman. BA, Williams Coll., 1942; LLB, Harvard U., 1949; grad., Air Command and Staff Sch., 1948; DSBA (hon.), Bryant Coll., 1980; DBA (hon.), Roger Williams Coll., 1980; LLD (hon.), Johnson and Wales U., 1993, Williams Coll., 1993, U. RI, 1998; DHL (hon.), New Eng. Inst. Tech., 2005. Bar: RI and DC 1949. Asst. U.S. atty., Washington, 1949-51; spl. asst. to U.S. atty. gen., Washington, 1951-54; ptnr. Amram, Hahn & Sundlun, Sundlun, Tirana & Scher, Washington, 1958—76; v.p., gen. counsel, dir. Outlet Co., Providence, 1960-76, Outlet Comms. Inc.; pres., CEO Outlet Co., Providence, 1976-84, chmn. bd., CEO, 1984-88. Pres. Exec. Jet Aviation, Inc., Columbus, Ohio, 1970—76; apptd. by Pres. Kennedy incorporator, bd. dirs. Comm. Satellite Corp., 1962—92; bd. dirs. Worthington Industries, Nat. Bank of Washington, Miriam Hosp. Mem. adv. group Nat. Aviation Goals, 1961; chmn. Inaugural Medal Com., Washington, 1961, 65; vice chmn. Inaugural Parade Com., 1961; appointed by Pres. Carter, bd. visitors USAF Acad., 1978-80; mem. RI Capital Center Commn., 1980, RI Legis. Pay Commn., 1980; vice chmn. Providence Rev. Com., 1981, chmn., 1982-85; mem. Providence Sch. Bd., 1985-90; mem. Providence Housing Authority, 1987, chmn. 1987-90; elected del. Dem. Nat. Conv. 1964, 68, 80, 88, 92, RI Constl. Conv., 1985; Dem. candidate for gov. RI, 1986, 88, 90, 92; gov. RI, 1990-92, 1992-95; mem. exec. com. Dem. Gov. Assn., 1990-94; vice chmn. CONEG, 1992-94, chmn., 1994, chmn., vice chmn. Com. on Economy Nat. Gov. Assn., 1992-94, chmn. NE Gov. Assn., 1994; pres. Washington Internat. Horse Show, 1970-75, trustee, 1975-90; pres. Providence Performing Arts Ctr., 1978-90; bd. dirs. Touro Synagogue, Newport, RI, 1979—, Miriam Hosp., 1985-90; bd. dirs. Temple Beth El, Providence, 1979-84, v.p., 1984-88, pres., 1988-91; bd. dirs. Trinity Repertory Theater, 1980-90, chmn., 1984-90; trustee RI Philharm. Orch., 1981-90; trustee Providence Preservation Soc., 1981-90, v.p., 1987-90; trustee Newport Art Mus., 1985, pres., 1987-91; founding chmn., pres. Providence Found., 1985-86; pres. RI C. of C. Fedn., 1981-84, bd. dirs., 1977-81; pres. Greater Providence C. of C., 1978-81, bd. dirs. 1976-85; bd. dirs. New Eng. Coun., 1978, vice chmn., 1980-81, chmn., 1981-83; trustee Bryant Coll., 1989-98; gov.-in-residence U. RI, 1995—; dir. Providence Facilities Mgmt. Corp., 1998—; appointed by Pres. Clinton dir. Nat. Security Edn. Bd., 2000-05; dir. Sargent Rehab. Ctr., 1995—, Ft. Adams Found., 2000—. Lt. USAAF, 1941-45; Capt. USAFR, ret., 1980. Decorated D.F.C., Air medal with oak leaf cluster, Purple Heart; chevalier Legion d'Honneur (France); Prime Minister's medal (Israel). Mem.: Aurora Assn., Spouting Rock Beach Assn., Dunes Club, Hope Club, Clambake Club, Delta Upsilon. Democrat. Office: U RI Carlotti Bldg 175 Lower College Rd Kingston RI 02881 Home: 280 Seaside Dr Jamestown RI 02835-3031 Office Phone: 401-874-4000. Business E-Mail: sundlun@uri.edu.

SUNDQUIST, DAVID HALL, voice educator; b. July 21, 1941; MusB in Voice, Roosevelt U., 1981. Instr. ESL, German and French Berlitz Sch. Langs., Hinsdale, Ill., 1981—84; asst. prof. music and voice U. N. Tex., 1989—94, assoc. prof. music and voice with tenure, 1995—. Singer (soloist): Orchestra New Spain, 1990, Orch. New Spain, 1990, Las Vegas Symphony, 1990, U. N. Tex. Symphony Orch., 1996, U. N. Tex. Jazz Repertory Ensemble, 1996, performer concerts. Adjudicator regional auditions Metro. Opera Assn., St. Louis, 1995; adjudicator NOA Opera Competition, 1996; adjudicator preliminary auditions Marguerite McCammon Voice Competition, Ft. Worth Opera Guild, 2003; traffic appeals ct. judge, adv. com., coord. dept. recitals, mem. voice search com. PAC, 1996; chair divsn. vocal studies Voice Search Com., Traffic Appeals Ct. Com., 2005. Grant, Nat. Opera Inst., 1972—73. Mem.: Am. Guild Musical Artists, Nat. Assn. Tchrs. Singing (tenor panel regional conf. 1996, adjudicator regional conf. 2004), Pi Kappa Lambda, Phi Mu Alpha Sinfonia. Office Phone: 940-565-3759.

SUNDQUIST, DON, retired governor, retired congressman, sales executive; b. Moline, Ill., Mar. 15, 1936; s. Kenneth M. and Louise (Rohren) S.; m. Martha Swanson, Oct. 3, 1959; children: Tania, Andrea, Donald Kenneth. BA, Augustana Coll., 1957. Div. mgr. Josten's, Inc., 1961-72; exec. v.p. Graphic Sales of Am., Memphis, 1972, pres., 1973-82; mem. 98th-103rd Congresses from 7th Tenn. dist., Washington, 1983-94; gov. State of Tenn., Nashville, 1995—2003. Vice chmn. bd. Bank of Germantown, Tenn. Past mem. White House Commn. Presdl. Scholars; past chmn. Jobs for High Sch. Grads. of Memphis; chmn. Congl. Steering Com. George Bush for Pres., 1988, 92; nat. campaign mgr. Howard Baker for Pres., 1979; dir. com. ops., alt. del. Republican Nat. Conv., 1980; chmn. Shelby County Rep. Party, 1975-77; alt. del. Rep. Nat. Conv., 1976; exec. com. Rep. Nat. Com., 1971-73; nat. chmn. Young Rep. Nat. Fedn., 1971-73; sec. Bedford County Election Commn., 1968-70; chmn. Tenn. Young Rep. Fedn., 1969-70; dir. Mid-South Coliseum, Am. Council Young Polit. Leaders, 1972-74, U.S. Youth Council, 1972-75; bd. govs. Charles Edison Meml. Youth Fund; nat. adv. bd. Distributive Edn. Clubs Am.; mem. U.S. del. study tour, People's Republic of China, 1978, study tour, USSR, 1975. Served with USN, 1957-59. Mem. Kiwanis. Republican. Lutheran. Mailing: PO Box 28 Townsend TN 37882

SUNDQUIST, JAMES LLOYD, retired political scientist; b. West Point, Utah, Oct. 16, 1915; s. Frank Victor and Freda (Carlson) S.; m. Beth Ritchie, Dec. 25, 1937 (dec. 1982); children: Erik L., Mark L., James K.; m. Geraldine Coote, Dec. 3, 1983. Student, Weber Coll., 1932-34, HHD (hon.), 1990; student, Northwestern U., 1934-35; BS, U. Utah, 1939; MS in Pub. Adminstrn, Syracuse U., 1941; DDS (hon.), Carthage Coll., 1987. Reporter Salt Lake Tribune, 1935-39; adminstrv. analyst U.S. Bur. Budget, 1941-47, 49-51; reports and statistics officer Office Def. Moblzn., 1951-53; dir. mgmt. control European Command, U.S. Army, Berlin, 1947-49; asst. to chmn. Democratic Nat. Com., 1953-54; asst. sec. to gov. NY, 1955-56; asst. to U.S. Senator Clark, 1957-62; dep. under sec. agr., 1963-65; sr. fellow Brookings Instn., 1965-85, emeritus, 1985—, dir. govtl. studies, 1976-78; adj. prof. Smith Coll., 1975-78. Sec. platform com. Dem. Nat. Conv., 1960, 68 Author: Politics and Policy: The Eisenhower, Kennedy and Johnson Years, 1968, Making Federalism Work, 1969 (Louis Brownlow award for best pub. adminstrn. book), Dynamics of the Party System, 1973, 2d edit., 1983, Dispersing Population: What America Can Learn form Europe, 1975, The Decline and Resurgence of Congress, 1981 (Hardeman prize for best book on Congress), Constitutional Reform and Effective Government, 1986, 2d edit., 1992, Deseret Boy: Memories of a Utah Childhood, 2003; editor: Internat. Rev. Adminstrv. Scis., 1980—89, Beyond Gridlock?, 1993, Back to Gridlock?, 1995. Mem. Gov.'s Commn. on Va.'s Future, 1983-84 Recipient Exceptional Civilian Svc. award War Dept., 1945, Lifetime Achievement award Maxwell Sch. (Syracuse U.) Alumni Assn., 1994; sr. Rsch. fellow U. Glasgow, Scotland, 1972-73. Mem. Nat. Acad. Pub. Adminstrn., Am. Soc. Pub. Adminstrn., Am. Polit. Sci. Assn. (treas. 1980, Charles E. Merriam award 1985, Eldersveld award 1994), Am. Acad. Arts and Scis. Home: 900 N Taylor St Unit 2117 Arlington VA 22203 Office Phone: 703-294-4226. E-mail: jlsundquist@aol.com.

SUNDQUIST, M. ALEXANDRA (ALIX SUNDQUIST), diplomat, consultant; arrived in US, 1962; m. Erik Lindon Sundquist, Mar. 1, 1975; 1 child, Karin Alexandra. BA in Govt. cum laude, Smith Coll.; MA in Econ., N.Y. U. Entered fgn. svc. U.S. Dept. State, 1979; with Chase Manhattan Bank, NYC, Chemical Bank, NYC, 1970—75; comml. attache U.S. Embassy, Jeddah, Saudi Arabia, 1980—82, 1st sec. (energy attache) Paris, 1982—86, consul gen. Bordeaux, 1991—94, counselor econ. affairs Rabat, Morocco, 1995—98; economist Bur. Econ. and Bus. Affairs Dept. State, Washington, 1986—90, chief spl. trade activities divsn., 1998—99; ret., 1999; ind. fgn. affairs advisor, 1999—. Cons. U.S. Dept. State, Washington, 2000; chargé d'Affaires, Valletta, Malta; trade policy advisor Bill Bradley Pres. Campaign. Mem.: Am. Fgn. Svc. Assn., U.S. Assn. Energy Econ., Middle East Inst., Diplomatic and Consular Officers, Retired, Inc. (gov., trustee DACOR Bacon Ho. Found.). Address: 3016 N Florida St Arlington VA 22207-1808 Personal E-mail: masundq@aol.com.

SUNDSTROM, AILEEN LOIS, speech educator; b. Detroit, Mar. 2, 1925; d. Raymond and Gertrude B. (Meyer) Richard; m. Arthur E. Sundstrom, July 10, 1954. BA, Wayne State U., 1946, MA, 1947, PhD, 1964, postgrad., 1977. Tchr. speech, radio Highland Park (Mich.) High, 1947-48; English tchr. Denby High, 1948-49, Barbour Jr. High, 1949-50, Jefferson Jr. High, 1950-52, Denby High, 1952-53, Northwestern High, 1953-56, Cass Tech. High, 1957-65; asst. prof. Mercy Coll., Detroit, 1965-67; instr. performing arts dept. Henry Ford C.C., Dearborn, Mich., 1967—. Dept. spokesperson Henry Ford C.C., 1980-82, chair, 1982-88; speaker in field; text book reviewer; dir., evaluator Interpretative Reading Festival Workshops; chair various coms. Henry Ford C.C.; participant NEH, summer 1994; spl. lectr. performance communication, Oakland U., 1999-2005; forensic evaluator I.E. events, 2000-05; sponsor performance sect. Meeting of Minds, 2003, 04, 05. Contbr. articles to profl. jours. Recipient Ford Found. scholarship, 1961-62. Mem. Assn. Speech Communication, Am. Forensic Assn., Am. Assn. Univ. Women Ednl. Found., Academically Gifted and Talented, Excellence in Interpretative Reading, Mich. Assn. of Speech Communication (pres. 1985-86, presenter, chair confs. 1967—, Disting. Svc. award for festivals 1992, 93), Mich. Intercollegiate Speech League (bd. dirs. Oral Interpretation Festival/Workshops 1977—, pres. 1993-94), Speech Comm. Assn. (presenter, chair conf. programs 1967-2002), Ctrl. States Speech Assn. (presenter, chair conf. programs 1978-2001, participant NEH summer seminar 1994), Mich. High Sch. Forensic Assn., Beta Sigma Phi, Alpha Beta Pi.

SUNDSTROM, HAROLD WALTER, public relations executive; b. Chgo., Jan. 26, 1929; s. Elmer A. and Rosalind Lillian (Busse) S.; m. Mary Olin, Oct. 1, 1955; children: Geoffrey Lee, Lori Lynn, Deborah Barron. AA, Wright Jr. Coll., 1949; BA, Mich. State U., 1952, MA, 1954. Fgn. svc. info. officer USIA, Tokyo, Jakarta, Seoul, 1955-61; sr. pub. rels. assoc. Eli Lilly and Co., Indpls., 1962-66; v.p., dir. pub. rels. Eisenhower People to People Program, Kansas City, Mo., and Copenhagen, 1966-68; govt. and pub. affairs rep. North Ctrl. States Automobile Mfrs. Assn., Kansas City, 1968-69; speechwriter, pub. rels. cons. Commdr.-in-Chief U.S. Pacific Forces, Aiea, 1969-75; pres. No. Ariz. Comm., Inc., Flagstaff, 1975-79; asst. sec., dir. pub. affairs U.S. Internat. Trade Commn., Washington, 1977-87; v.p. pub. affairs and publs. Export-Import Bank U.S., Washington, 1987-89; pres. Halamar, Inc., Manassas, Va. and Easley, SC, 1983—, Silver Springs, Fla., 1983-98. Mem. Pres.'s Consumer Affairs Couns., 1977-89; freelance writer and poet. Author: The American West, 1956, Indonesia: Its People and Politics, 1957, Garuda, Introducing Indonesia, 1962, Faces of Asia: Korea, 1965, The Northern Arizona Scene, 1976, American Collie Champions, Vol. I, 1979, Vol. II, 1980, Vol. III, 1987, Collies - A Complete Pet Owners Manual, 1994, 2d edit., 2005; editor, pub. Hawaiian Dog Rev., The Alaska Cir., The Arizona Cir., Internat. Lhasa Apso Rev., Sandwich Isles Dog Gazette, 1972-76, Collie Cues, 1983-86, Travel Writer, Honolulu Sun Press, 1972-76. Active Civil War Preservation Trust, Colonial Williamsburg, Hist. Mount Vernon, Va. With U.S. Army, 1947-48, 52-53. Recipient People to People Disting. Svc. award, 1967, George Washington Honor medal Freedom Found., 1968, Silver Beaver award Boy Scouts Am., 1975. Fellow Japan Soc. N.Y., Pub. Rels. Soc. Am. (past pres. Hawaii chpt., Silver Anvil award 1973); mem. Dog Writers Assn. Am. (pres. 1984-92, Disting. Svc. award 1993), Dog Writers Ednl. Trust (vice chmn., chmn. 1999-2005), Collie Club Am. (pres. 1984-86), Collie Club Am. Found. (life, pres. 1990-92), Am. Kennel Club (del. 1986—), Pi Sigma Alpha, Phi Kappa Sigma. Republican. Avocations: pure-bred dog breeding and showing, travel, photography, conservation, preservation of historic properties. Home and Office: 1 Wadsworth Ct Greer SC 29651

SUNDSTROM, JOHNATHAN, chef; b. LA, 1967; m. JM Enos. A, New Eng. Culinary Inst., Montpelier, Vt., 1987. Chef Ritz-Carlton Laguna Niguel, Club XIX, Lodge at Pebble Beach, Stein Erickson Lodge, Carmelita; with raison d'etre, Campagne, Café Sport; cook Dahlia Lounge, sous chef, chef; exec. chef Earth & Ocean, 2002; owner, exec. chef Lark, Seattle, 2003—. Featured on Best Of, TV Food Network, Food Nation, Chefs a-field, PBS. Named Best New Chef, Food & Wine Mag., 2001, Best Chef: Northwest, James Beard Found., 2007. Avocations: gardening, Aikido. Office: Lark 926 12th Ave Seattle WA 98122 Office Phone: 206-323-5275. Business E-Mail: info@LarkSeattle.com. *

SUNEJA, VINCE H., lawyer; b. Chandigarh, Punjab, India, Oct. 8, 1974; s. Sudarshan K. and Inder Jeet Suneja. BS, Kent State U., Ohio, 1997; JD, Ohio No. U., Ada, 2001; LLM Global Health in Global Health, Georgetown U., Washington, 2007. Assoc. DKW Law Group, Pitts., 2001—03; regulatory counsel Mylan Pharm. Inc., Morgantown, W.Va., 2003—06; dir. internat. affairs Mylan Lab. Inc., Washington, 2006—. Abritrator Neibhorhood Legal Svcs., Pitts., 2002—06. Mem.: Diabetes Assn. (orgn. com. 2002—04), South Asian Bar Assn. (assoc.). R-Liberal. Hindu. Avocations: travel, tennis, exercise, theater. Home: 4850 Eisenhower Ave Unit 106 Alexandria VA 22304 Office: Mylan Lab Inc 601 Pennsylvania Ave NW Washington DC 20004 Home Phone: 412-352-0164; Office Phone: 202-220-3007. Office Fax: 202-220-3047.

SUNG, GYUNG TAK, urologist, department chairman; b. Daegu, Republic of Korea, Aug. 15, 1958; s. Ui Joon Sung and Won Ok Rho; m. Sung Jong Kyung, Feb. 7, 1989; children: Seh-Rin, Catherine, Christine. Degree, State U. NJ, 1981, Busan Coll. Medicine, Republic of Korea, 1987, Busan Nat. Grad. Sch., 1990. Resident neurology Pusan Nat. U. Hosp., Busan, 1988—92; asst. prof. Coll. Medicine Dong-N U., Busan, 1995—98, chmn. dept. urology Coll. Medicine, 2002—; rsch. fellow dept. urology Cleve. Clinic Found., 1999, co-dir. laparoscopic rsch., 1999—2001, mem. staff Urol. Inst., 2001—02. Cons. in field. Co-editor: Robotic Surgery In Urology, 2003; co-author: Laparoscopic Prestatertomy, 2003, Retropa-Floneoscope Adrenarectomy: Lateral Approach, 2003. Recipient Video award, World Congress Endourology and Shockwave, 2001. Mem.: The Korean Urol. Assn., World Endourology and Shockwave Soc. (Academic Paper 2d prize 2002), Am. Urol. Assn. (Best Video 1st prize 1999, Best Video hon. mention 2001, Best Video 2d prize 2002). Avocations: jazz, golf. Home: 8678 Scenicview Dr Broadview Heights OH 44147 Office: Dept Urology Dong A Univ Hosp 3Ga1 Dongdaesin dong Seo gu Busan Republic of Korea 602 715 Office Phone: 82 51-240-5446. Personal E-mail: sunggt@daunet.donga.ac.kr.

SUNG, HOU-MEI, curator, researcher; b. Shenyang, China; d. Yu-fan Sung and You-lan Huang; children: Mineh Ishida, Koto Ishida. BA, Nat. Taiwan U., Taipei, 1968, MA, 1974; PhD, Case Western Res. U., Cleve., 1984. Editor Nat. Palace Mus., Taipei, 1968—71, adminstrv. sec. dir., 1968—70, asst. curator, 1970—74, 1970—74; expert rep. nat. palace mus. World Expn., Osaka, Japan, 1970; lectr. John Carroll U., Cleve., 1987, The Colo. Coll., Colorado Springs, 1988; adj. asst. prof. Case Western Res. U., Cleve., 1989—90, 1989—90; adj. prof. Cleve. State U., 1998—2001; rsch. assoc. Cleve. Mus. Art, 1999—2002, 1999—2002; curator Asian art Cin. Art Mus., 2002—. Bd. mem. The Midwest Art History Soc., Cleve., 1991—95; program dir. Chinese arts and cultural celebration program Cleve. State U., 1999—2001; exec. officer Chinese Am. Faculty and Staff Assn. Cleve. State U., 2000—02; bd. mem. Cleve. Chinese Women's Assn., 2000—02, Asian Art Soc., Cin., 2002—. Dir.: (gallery reinstallation) Asian Art Gallery Reinstallation Project (NEH Planning Grant, 2004); author: (book) The Unknown World of the Ming Court Painters: The Ming Painting Academy. Grantee Rsch. Grant, Ctr. for Chinese Studies, Taiwan, 1996; Fellowship, Fulbright Scholary Exch., 2000. Office: The Cin Art Mus 953 Eden Park Dr Cincinnati OH 45202 Office Phone: 513-639-2330. Business E-Mail: hou-mei.sung@cincyart.org.

SUNG, KYU-TAIK, social worker, educator, gerontologist, researcher; b. South Kyungsang, Republic of Korea, Sept. 9, 1930; arrived in U.S., 1967; s. Jang Hwan Sung and Kyu Soon Nam; children: Choon-ho, Jin-ho, Yoon-ho, Vera. BA, Seoul Nat. U., 1956, MA, 1961; MSW, U. Mich., 1972, PhD, 1974. Prof. U. Wis. Sch. Social Work, Madison, 1975—78; prof. dept. social work Yonsei U., Seoul, Republic of Korea, 1978—96; prof. Mich. State U. Sch. Social Work, East Lansing, Mich., 1996—98; Frances Wu endowed chair prof. U. So. Calif. Sch. Social Work, 1999—2004; vis. prof. U. Mich. Sch. Social Work, Ann Arbor, 2004—. Dir., founder Ctr. for Social Welfare Rsch. Yonsei U., 1982—96; exec. dir., founder Elder Respect, Inc., 2002—; sr. rschr. Korean Inst. Gerontology; presenter/spkr. in field. Author: Social Welfare Administration, 1993, Filial Piety in Modern Times: A New Look at Intergenerational Relationship, 1995, Filial Piety in Modern Times: Changing Expressions in Modern Times, 1996, Filial Piety in Modern Times: Timely Adaptation and Practicing Patterns, 2000, Filial Piety in Modern Times: Care and Respect for the Elderly, 2005, Care and Respect for the Elderly: Filial Piety in Modern Times in East Asia, 2005; contbr. articles to profl. jours. With US Army, 1950—53. Mem.: Korean Acad. Social Welfare (past pres.), Korean Gerontol. Soc. (past pres.). Democrat. Achievements include identified components of filial piety (East Asian value of care and respect for the elderly) based on empirical data and introduced them in US profl. jours. Avocations: collecting Buddhist paintings, visiting museums. Home: 1812 Longshore Dr Ann Arbor MI 48105 Office: Univ Mich Sch Social Work 1080 S University Ann Arbor MI 48109-1106 Office Phone: 734-936-8645.

SUNGAILA, MARY-CHRISTINE (M.C. SUNGAILA), lawyer; BA in Polit. sci., Stanford U., 1988; JD, UCLA, 1991. Bar: Calif., Ctrl. Dist. Calif., U.S. Ct. Appeals (9th cir.) 1991, U.S. Supreme Ct. 1995. Extern The Honorable Dorothy W. Nelson, U.S. Ct. Appeals (9th cir.), 1990; law clk. The Honorable Alicemarie H. Stotler, U.S. Dist. Ct., Ctrl. Dist. Calif., 1991—92, The Honorable Ferdinand F. Fernandez, U.S. Ct. Appeals (9th cir.), 1993—94; litigation assoc. Irell & Manella LLP, Newport Beach, Calif., 1994—97; assoc. Horvitz & Levy LLP, Encino, Calif., 1997—2002, ptnr., 2003—. Spkr., panelist, lectr. various legal speaking engagements. Founding editor: The Newsletter of the Woman Advocate Com. of the ABA, 1996—97; contbg. editor: Jurist: Books-on-Law, 2000—01; contbr. articles to profl. jours. Mem. Gender Equity Com. Orange County Bar Assn., 1996—2000; bd. dirs. Opera Pacific, 1996—2006; bd. govs. Women Lawyers Assn. L.A., 2000—. Office: Horvitz & Levy 15760 Ventura Blvd 18th Fl Encino CA 91436 Office Phone: 818-995-0800. Office Fax: 818-995-3157. Business E-Mail: msungaila@horvitzlevy.com.

SUNI, ELLEN Y., dean, law educator; BA magna cum laude, CCNY; JD magna cum laude, Boston U. Law clerk to Chief Justice Mass. Supreme Judicial Ct., dep. legal asst. to Justices; dir. legal writing prog. Boston U. Sch. Law, asst. dean, lectr.; faculty mem. U. Mo.-Kansas City Sch. Law, 1980—, interim assoc. dean, interim dean, prof. law, 2004—, Marvin Lewis Rich Faculty Scholar. Fed. prosecutor U.S. Atty. Office, 1987—88; mem. Eighth Cir. Criminal Jury Instrns. Sub-com.; bd. mem. Pub. Interest Litigation Clinic, Police Law Inst. Contbr. articles to law jours. Legal dir. Kansas City Youth Ct.; pres. Midwestern Innocence Project. Recipient Legal Leader of Yr. Award, 2004. Office: U Mo-Kansas City Sch Law 5100 Rockhill Rd Kansas City MO 64110 Office Phone: 816-235-2372. E-mail: sunie@umkc.edu.

SUNIA, AITOFELE TOESE F., lieutenant governor; b. Mar. 26, 1943; JD, U. San Francisco. Various gov. positions including asst. atty. gen., temp. dist. ct. judge Ter. of Am. Samoa, territorial treas., 1997—2003, lt. gov., 2003—. Democrat. Office: Office Lt Governor Territory American Samoa Pago Pago AS 96799 Office Phone: 684-633-4116. Office Fax: 684-633-2269.

SUNLEY, EMIL MCKEE, economist, consultant; b. Morgantown, W.Va., July 30, 1942; s. Emil McKee and Nelle Berniece (Traer) S.; m. Judith Evelyn Steere, Dec. 23, 1966; children: Rachel Anne, Gillian Traer, Neil Steere. BA, Amherst Coll., 1964; MA, U. Mich., 1965, PhD, 1968. Economist office tax analysis Dept. Treasury, Washington, 1968-73, assoc. dir. office tax analysis, 1973-75, dep. asst. sec. for tax policy, 1977-81; sr. fellow Brookings Instn., Washington, 1975-77; dir. tax analysis Deloitte & Touche, Washington, 1981-92; asst. dir. fiscal affairs dept. Internat. Monetary Fund, 1992—2006; pvt. practice Bethesda, Md., 1992—. Cons. in field. Mem. editl. bd. Nat. Tax Jour., 1992-95. Mem. Commn. on RR Retirement Reform, 1987-90. Mem. Am. Econ. Assn., Nat. Tax Assn. (pres. 1995-96), Tax Analysts (bd. dirs. 1982-93). Episcopalian. Personal E-mail: esunley@verizon.net.

SUNSHINE, STEVEN C., lawyer; b. Buffalo, Feb. 20, 1959; s. Gary Alan and Inez B. (Goldman) S.; m. Fay E. Wheeler, Sept. 1, 1984; children: Benjamin W., Daniel W. AB, Brown U., 1981; JD magna cum laude, Boston Coll., 1984. Bar: N.Y., D.C. Attty. Shearman & Sterling, NYC, 1984-93; dep. asst. atty. gen. in charge of merger enforcement U.S. Dept. Justice, Washington, 1993-95; ptnr. Shearman & Sterling, Washington, 1995—2005; ptnr. antitrust practice Cadwalader, Wickersham & Taft LLP, 2005—07; ptnr. Skadden, Arps, Slate, Meagher & Flom LLP, Washington, 2007—. Contbr. articles to profl. jours.; editor Boston Coll. Law Rev., 1983-84; named among Top 10 Lawyers Under 40, Nat. Law Jour., 1996. Mem. ABA (vice chmn. Clayton Act com. antitrust sect. 1994-96), Order of Coif. Office: Skadden 1440 New York Ave NW Washington DC 20005 Office Phone: 202-371-7860. Business E-Mail: steve.sunshine@skadden.com.

SUNSHINE, STEVEN H., lawyer; AB, UCLA, 1973, JD, 1976. Bar: Calif. 1976. Ptnr., mem. exec. com. Bryan Cave LLP, Irvine, Calif. Office: Bryan Cave LLP 2020 Main St, Ste 600 Irvine CA 92614 Office Phone: 949-223-7200. E-mail: shsunshine@bryancave.com.

SUNSTEIN, BRUCE DAVID, lawyer; b. Phila., May 27, 1944; s. David E. and Phylis (Eisenberg) S.; 1 child, Aaron E. BS, MIT, 1965; MA, Ind. U., 1969; JD, U. Calif., Berkeley, 1973. Bar: Calif. 1973, U.S. Dist. Ct. (no. dist.) Calif. 1973, U.S. Ct. Appeals (9th cir.) 1973, U.S. Patent and Trademark Office 1974, Mass. 1977, U.S. Tax Ct. 1977, U.S. Supreme Ct. 1977, U.S. Ct. Appeals (1st cir.) 1978, U.S. Ct. Appeals (fed. cir.) 1982. Assoc. Cooper, White & Cooper, San Francisco, 1973-77; ptnr. Bromberg & Sunstein LLP, predecessor firms, Boston, 1977—. Contbr. articles to profl. jours.; author: Investor Relations Meets Intellectual Property, 2003. Named one of top Boston lawyers, Boston Mag., 2002. Mem.: Boston Patent Law Assn., Boston Bar Assn., Mass. Bar Assn., Licensing Execs. Soc., Am. Intellectual Property Lawyers Assn., IEEE, ABA. Office: Bromberg & Sunstein LLP 125 Summer St Ste 1100 Boston MA 02110-1618 Office Phone: 617-443-9292. Office Fax: 617-443-0004. Business E-Mail: bsunstein@bromsun.com.

SUNTRA, CHARLES RATAPOL, surgeon, educator; b. Detroit, Dec. 4, 1968; s. Sathien and Malee Suntra. BA summa cum laude, St. Louis U., 1991, MD cum laude, 1995. Diplomate Am. Bd. Otolaryngology, bd. eligible Am. Bd. Facial Plastic and Reconstructive Surgery. Intern gen. surgery Boston U. Sch. Medicine/Boston Med. Ctr., 1995—96; resident otolaryngology-head and neck surgery Boston U. Sch. Medicine, 1996—2000; chief resident Boston Med. Ctr./Boston U., 1999—2000; fellow facial plastic and reconstructive surgery Park Ctrl. Inst./Forest Park Hosp., St. Louis, 2000—01; med. staff Forest Pk. Hosp., St. Louis, 2000—01, Sutter Gould Med. Found., Modesto, Calif., 2001—, Doctors Med. Ctr., Modesto, 2001; asst. clin. prof. Sch. Medicine U. Calif., Davis. Presenter in field. Contbr. articles to profl. jours. Fellow: ACS, Am. Bd. Otolaryngology; mem.: Thai Physicians Assn. Am., Am. Rhinologic Soc., Am. Acad. Facial Plastic and Reconstructive Surgery, Am. Acad. Otolaryngology-Head and Neck Surgery, Phi Eta Sigma, Alpha Epsilon Delta, Beta Beta Beta, Alpha Sigma Nu, Phi Beta Kappa, Alpha Omega Alpha. Office: Gould Med Group 600 Coffee Rd Modesto CA 95355 Office Phone: 209-550-4770. Business E-Mail: suntrac@sutterhealth.org. E-mail: csuntra@email.com.

SUNUNU, JOHN EDWARD, senator; b. Boston, Sept. 10, 1964; s. John H. Sununu; m. Kitty (Halloran) Sununu; 3 children BS in Mech. Engring., Mass. Inst. Tech., 1986, MS in Mech. Engring., 1987; MBA with honors, Harvard Grad. Sch. Bus., 1991. Design engr. Remec, Inc., 1987-90; mgr., ops. specialist Pittiglio, Rabin, Todd & McGrath, 1990-92; chief fin. officer, dir. ops. Teletrol Sys. Inc., Manchester, NH, 1992—96; cons. JHS Assocs., Ltd.; mem. US Congress from 1st NH dist., 1997—2003; US senator from NH, 2003—. Com. banking, housing and urban reform US Senate, com. commerce, sci., and transp., com. fgn. relations, joint econ. com. Active NH C. of C., NH Bus. and Industry Assn., NH High Tech Coun. Recipient Friend of the Taxpayer award, Americans for Tax Reform, Guardian of Small Bus. award, Nat. Fedn. Independent Bus., Spirit Enterprise award, US C. of C. Mem.: NH Bus. and Industry Assn. Republican. Roman Catholic. Office: US Senate 111 Russell Senate Bldg Washington DC 20510 also: District Office Ste 3 1589 Elm St Manchester NH 03101 Office Phone: 202-224-2841, 603-647-7500. Office Fax: 202-228-4131, 603-647-9352. *

SUNWARD, JUSTIN HUGO, artist; b. Chgo., Feb. 20, 1939; s. Arthur Peter and Dorothy Irene Johnsen. Student, Sch. of Art Inst. of Chgo., 1951-52; diploma with honors, Frances Harrington Profl. Sch. Interior Decoration, Chgo., 1958. Represented in permanent collections Mus. Modern Art, N.Y.C., Met. Mus. Art, Whitney Mus. Am. Art, Mus. Contemporary Modern Art, Uuskila, Finland, others; contbr. art revs. to publs. Recipient numerous nat. art competition awards. Mem. Chgo. Art Critics Assn. (founding mem.). Avocations: cooking, gardening, history, architecture, travel. Office Phone: 717-232-3645.

SUPANICH, BARBARA ANN, physician; b. Detroit, Sept. 24, 1952; d. Donald George and Mildred Mary (Stanovich) Supanich. BS in Chemistry, Mercy Coll. Detroit, 1974; MD, Mich. State U., 1980. Diplomate Am. Bd. Family Practice, Am. Bd. Hospice and Palliative Medicine, 2006, lic. physician Mich., Fla., Md.; joined Sisters of Mercy, 1973. Resident in family practice Creighton U. Affiliated Hosps., Omaha, 1980—83; pvt. practice Eaton Rapids, Mich., 1983—86, Houghton Lake, Mich., 1986—92; fellow in clin. ethics Ctr. Ethics Mich. State U., East Lansing, 1992—93, asst. prof. family practice, 1993—97, assoc. prof., 1998, assoc. chair clin. svcs., dept. family practice, 1995—99, assoc. residency dir. family practice residency Munson, 1999—2005; fellow palliative medicine and hospice care Mayo Clinic, Jacksonville, Fla., 2005; med. dir. palliative medicine, sr. svcs. Holy Cross Hosp., Silver Spring, Md., 2006—. Cons. Mich. Dept. Cmty. Health, Lansing, 1996—99. Contbr. chapters to books, articles to profl. jours. Fellow: Am. Acad. Family Physicians (bd. dirs., regional dir. 2000—04, 2d v.p. 2004—05); mem.: Am. Med. Women's Assn., Mich. Acad. Family Physicians. Roman Catholic. Avocations: swimming, bicycling, mystery and science fiction novels. Home: 4013 Postgate Ter Apt 201 Silver Spring MD 20906 Office: Holy Cross Hosp 1500 Forest Glen Rd Silver Spring MD 20910 Home Phone: 301-828-0748; Office Phone: 301-754-7910. Personal E-mail: barbsupanich@comcast.net.

SUPANICK, BEVERLY JANE, language educator; b. McKeesport, Pa., July 2, 1959; d. Jacob Jr. and Patty Jane Supanick. BS, Janiata Coll., Huntington, Pa., 1982; MS, Calif. State U., Bakersfield, 1990. Cert. tchr. advanced profl. Md., racquetball pro-internat., Spanish tchr. mentor 2004. Tchr. Spanish, coach Omega HS, Bakersfield, Calif., 1984—86; substitute tchr. Bakersfield City Schs., 1986—89, bilingual educator, 1989—97; racquetball profl. Sport and Health Clubs, Bethesda, Md., 1997—; elem. Spanish specialist Prince George's County Pub. Schs., Upper Marlboro, 1999—2004, Spanish immersion educator Hyattsville, 2004—. Personal trainer Merritt Athletic Club, Annapolis, Md., 1997—98; curriculum devel. Prince George's County Pub. Schs., Upper Marlboro, 2001—02, tchr. trainer Spanish, 2002, 03; mem. adv. panel Penn divsn. Head NV, 1999—; sponsored by Ashaway Shoes, 2006. Vol. Brethren soup kitchen Good Shepherd Shelter, Bakersfield, 1983. Named #7 ranked player US, US Racquetball Assn., 1991, #3 ranked player Md., 2001, 2003, #1 ranked player Del., 2002, #13 world ranked player, Women's Profl. Racquetball Assn., 1999, recipient medals (6), nat. racquetball competitions, 1991—97; fellow, Calif. State U., 1988. Avocations: music, bicycling, jogging, weightlifting. Home: 1800 Metzerott Rd Apt 207 Hyattsville MD 20783-5104 Office: Cesar Chavez Elem Sch 6609 Riggs Rd Hyattsville MD 20782 Office Phone: 301-853-5694.

SUPANVANIJ, JANIKAN, finance educator; b. Bangkok, Aug. 6, 1971; arrived in U.S., 1993; d. Vitaya and Sopha Supanvanij. BBA, Thammasat U., Bangkok, 1993; MFN in Fin., St. Louis U., 1995, MBA in Fin. and Econs., 1997, PhD in Fin., 2003. Cert. tchg. skills. Internat. banking facility fgn. exch. dealer The Thai Mil. Bank, Ltd., Bangkok, 1993; instr. St. Louis U., 1997—2003; asst. prof. St. Cloud State U., Minn., 2003—06, assoc. prof., 2006—. Contbr. articles to profl. jours. Finalist Tchg. Excellence award, Acad. Fin., 2007; recipient Rsch. Collaboration award, St. Cloud State U., 2000—05, Disting. Rsch. award, 2000—05, Tchg. Excellence award, 2004—05, Best Paper award, Assn. Global Bus., 2004, 2005. Mem.: St. Louis U. Grad. Student Assn. (webmaster 1997—2002, GSA rsch. symposium program co-chair 2001—02, pres. 2002—03), Beta Gamma Sigma, Alpha Epsilon Lambda. Office: St Cloud State U 720 4th Ave S Saint Cloud MN 56301

SUPERNEAU, DUANE WILLIAM, geneticist, physician; b. Ogden, Utah, Dec. 31, 1950; s. Richard Edwin and Mary Ellen Superneau; children: Adam, Ashley, Allison. BA, Carroll Coll., 1973; MD, U. Wash., 1977. Diplomate Am. Bd. Pediat., Am. Bd. Med. Genetics. Asst. prof. dept. med. genetics U. So. Ala., Mobile, 1982-87, assoc. prof. dept. med. genetics, 1987-91; chief sect. med. genetics Ochsner Clinic, New Orleans, 1991—2005; dir. Genetic Svcs. La., Baton Rouge, 2005—. Clin. asst. prof. La. State U., New Orleans, 1992—. Bd. dirs. The ARC Greater New Orleans, 1991—, pres. 1994-96; bd. dirs. ARC of La., 1994—, pres., 1999-2001; bd. dirs. Jefferson Parish Human Svcs. Authority, Jefferson Parish, La., 1992-99. Roman Catholic. Office: Genetic Svcs of La 5339 O'Donovan Dr Baton Rouge LA 70808 Office Phone: 225-231-5381. Business E-Mail: duane.superneau@womans.org.

SUPINO, PHYLLIS GAIL, medical researcher, educator; m. Rene Patrick Supino, June 7, 1980; children: Lisa Michelle, Christopher Davies. BS in Biol. Scis., CCNY, 1964; EdD in Sci. Edn., Rutgers U., New Brunswick, NJ, 1976. Instr. psychology, rsch. assoc. in cognitive psychology Princeton U., 1975—77; dir. rsch. and evaluation The Ednl. Improvement Ctr. divsn. NJ. State Dept. Edn., West Orange, 1977—79; adj. instr. environ. and cmty. medicine, adj. instr. family medicine Robert Wood Johnson Med. Sch./U. Medicine and Dentistry NJ, Piscataway, 1979—90; asst. prof. pub. health in medicine, dir. data mgmt. Cornell U. Med. Coll., NYC, 1990—95; rsch. assoc. prof. emergency medicine, rsch. assoc. prof. med. edn., dir. rsch. in emergency medicine Mt. Sinai Sch. Medicine, NYC, 1996—99; assoc. rsch. prof. pub. health in medicine, dir. data mgmt., epidemiology and ednl. programs Weill Cornell Med. Coll., NYC, 1999—. Mem. editl. bd.: Cardiology, reviewer: Med. Edn.; contbr. chapters to books, articles to profl. jours. Vol. Morocco VI US Peace Corps, Washington. Recipient Phi Delta Kappa award, Rutgers U., 1976, The Howard Gilman award, The Howard Gilman Found., 1995, Best Mentor of the Yr. award, Mt. Sinai Sch. Medicine, 1998, Best Nat. Sci. Abstract award, Am. Soc. Nuc. Cardiology and Internat. Affiliates, 2001; grantee Pilot Rsch. award, Weill Med. Coll. of Cornell U. Fellow: NY Acad. Medicine; mem.: Heart Valve Soc. Am., Am. Soc. Nuc. Cardiology, Am. Heart Assn., Am. Statis. Assn., Cardiology (editl. bd. Cardiology), Am. Fedn. for Med. Rsch., Kappa Delta Pi (life). Achievements include development of first comprehensive approved course on clinical research methodology for physicians at Weill Medical College and Mount Sinai School of Medicine; Research mentor to more than 50 residents, fellows and junior faculty in medicine. Avocations: theater, vocal music.

SUPLEE, DENNIS RAYMOND, lawyer; b. Phila., Jan. 20, 1943; s. Raymond C. and Miriam C. (Morris) S.; m. Patricia H. Hickey; children:

David A., Christopher D., Richard C. BS, St. Joseph's U., 1964; LLB, U. Pa., 1967. Bar: Pa. 1967. Assoc. Schnader, Harrison, Segal & Lewis, Phila., 1967-74, ptnr. litig. practice, 1975—, mem. exec. com., 1986-89, 91-92, chmn. exec. com., 1992—98. Mem. Sec. Navy's Adv. Bd. on Edn. and Tng., Washington, 1985-86. Author: (with others) The Deposition Handbook, 4th edit., 2002, Expert Witness: Law and Practice, 1993; contbr. articles to profl. jours. Mem. adv. com. Dorland Global Health Communications, 2003-; trustee St. Joseph's U., Phila., 2004-; mem. bd. gov. Mercy Fitzgerald Hosp., 2005-. Equal Justice award, Cmty. Legal Svcs., 2003. Fellow Am. Coll. Trial Lawyers (Pa. state chmn. 1998-2000, regent for NJ & Del. 2001-), Internat. Acad. Trial Lawyers (dir. 2000-); mem. Pa. Bar Assn. (ho. of dels. 1988-89), Phila. Assn. Def. Counsel (pres. 1994-95), U. Pa. Law Sch. Am. Inn of Ct. (master); Union League. Democrat. Roman Catholic. Avocations: tennis, badminton. Office: Schnader Harrison Segal & Lewis Ste 3600 1600 Market St Philadelphia PA 19103-7286 Home: 40 S Roberts Rd Bryn Mawr PA 19010-2622 Office Phone: 215-751-2068. Office Fax: 215-751-2205. Business E-Mail: dsuplee@schnader.com.

SUPPES, CHRISTINE JOHNSON, publishing executive; b. LA, Mar. 3, 1953; d. Robert and Jane Johnson; m. Patrick Suppes; children: Alexandra Christine, Michael Patrick. Copygirl/editl. asst. San Francisco Examiner, 1972—73; pres. Gravure At Home, Stanford, Calif., 1997—2001; pub., editor-in-chief www.Fashionlines.com, Stanford, Calif., 1999—2007; chief designer Jewels by Christine, 2002—. Advt. cons. Clarum Corp., Palo Alto, Calif., 1997—, Gravure Corp., Dallas, 1997—2000; chief designer www.jewelsbyChristine.com, Stanford, Calif., 2003—; Am. rep. Of Silk, of Gold and Silver Assn., France. Author: Amanda Prescott, 1984, Clinic, 1985; contbr. revs. to San Francisco Chronicle, articles to SF Moda. Organizer, Teacher's Fund Bing School, Stanford, 1995—; mem. Peninsula chpt. NARAL, Palo Alto, 1997—2000; supporter ARC, Palo Alto, 2001. Recipient Angel of Fashion com. award, N.Y.C., 1999—. Mem.: Fine Art Mus. San Francisco, Couture Circle, French Heritage Soc. No. Calif., Fashion Group Internat., Camera Nazionale della Moda Italiana, Federation Francaise de la Couture. Office: Fashionlines 678 Mirada Ave Stanford CA 94305 Business E-Mail: suppes@fashionlines.com.

SUPPES, PATRICK, statistician, philosopher, psychologist, educator; b. Tulsa, Mar. 17, 1922; s. George Biddle and Ann (Costello) Suppes; m. Joan Farmer, Apr. 16, 1946 (div. 1970); children: Patricia, Deborah, John Biddle; m. Joan Sieber, Mar. 29, 1970 (div. 1973); m. Christine Johnson, May 26, 1979; children: Alexandra Christine, Michael Patrick. BS, U. Chgo., 1943; PhD (Wendell T. Bush fellow), Columbia U., 1950; LLD, U. Nijmegen, Netherlands, 1979; Dr. honoris causa (hon.), U. Rene Descartes, Paris, 1982, U. Regensburg, Germany, 1999, U. Bologna, Italy, 1999. Instr., Stanford U., 1950—52, asst. prof., 1952—55, assoc. prof., 1955—59, prof. philosophy, statistics, psychology and edn., 1959—92, prof. emeritus. Founder, CEO Computer Curriculum Corp., 1967—90. Author: Introduction to Logic, 1957, Axiomatic Set Theory, 1960, Sets and Numbers, books 1-6, 1966, Studies in the Methodology and Foundations of Science, 1969, A Probabilistic Theory of Causality, 1970, Logique du Probable, 1981, Probabilistic Metaphysics, 1984, Estudios de Filosofia y Metodologí de la Ciencia, 1988, Language for Humans and Robots, 1991, Models and Methods in the Philosophy of Science, 1993, Representation and Invariance of Scientific Structures, 2002; author: (with Davidson and Siegel) Decision Making, 1957; author: (with Richard C. Atkinson) Markov Learning Models for Multiperson Interactions, 1960; author: (with Shirley Hill) First Course in Mathematical Logic, 1964; author: (with Edward J. Crothers) Experiments on Second-Language Learning, 1967; author: (with Max Jerman and Dow Brian) Computer-assisted Instruction, 1965—66, Stanford Arithmetic Program, 1968; author: (with D. Krantz, R.D. Luce and A. Tversky) Foundations of Measurement, Vol. 1, 1971, Vol. 2, 1989, Vol. 3, 1990; author: (with M. Morningstar) Computer-Assisted Instruction at Stanford, 1966-68, 1972; author: (with B. Searle and J. Friend) The Radio Mathematics Project: Nicaragua, 1974-75, 1976; author: (with Colleen Crangle) Language and Learning for Robots, 1994; author: (with Mario Zanotti) Foundations of Probability with Applications, 1996. Served to capt. USAAF, 1942-46. Recipient Nicholas Murray Butler Silver medal, Columbia U., 1965, Disting. Sci. Contbr. award, APA, 1972, Tchrs. Coll. medal for disting. svc., 1978, Nat. medal Sci., NSF, 1990, Henry Chauncey award for disting. svc., Ednl. Testing Svc., 2003, Lakatos Book Award prize, London Sch. Econs., 2003, Lauener Prize in Philosophy, Lauener Found., 2004; fellow, Ctr. for Advanced Study Behavioral Scis., 1955—56, NSF, 1957—58. Fellow: APA, AAAS, Assn. Computing Machinery, Am. Acad. Arts and Scis.; mem.: NAS, Chilean Acad. Scis., European Acad. Scis. and Arts, Norwegian Acad. Sci. and Letters (fgn.), Russian Acad. Edn. (fgn.), Am. Ednl. Rsch. Assn. (pres. 1973—74), Internat. Union History and Philosophy of Sci. (pres. divsn. logic, methodology and philosophy of sci. 1975—79), Finnish Acad. Sci. and Letters, Internat. Inst. Philosophy, Croatian Acad. Scis. (corr.), Brazilian Acad. Philosophy (corr.), Nat. Acad. Edn. (pres. 1973—77), Acad. Internat. de Philosophie des Scis. (titular), Am. Math. Soc., Assn. Symbolic Logic, Am. Philos. Soc., Am. Philos. Assn., Math. Assn. Am., Sigma Xi. Home Phone: 650-321-6594; Office Phone: 650-725-6030. E-mail: psuppes@stanford.edu.

SUPUT, RAY RADOSLAV, librarian; b. Columbus, Ohio, May 13, 1922; s. Elias and Darinka (Balac) S.; m. Mary Grace Hansen, May 23, 1953 (dec. Nov. 1980); children: David Ray, Dorothy Mary; m. Milana Peradov, July 12, 1986. BA, Ohio State U., 1950; MSL.S., Case Western Res. U., 1951, PhD, 1972; MA, U. Chgo., 1955. Librarian Northwestern U., Evanston, Ill., 1951-52; reference and circulation librarian Law Library, U. Chgo., 1952-54, cataloger, 1954-57; asso. librarian Garrett-Evang. Theol. Sem., Evanston, 1957-58, head librarian, 1958-64; asst. dir. libraries and adj. lectr. dept. Slavic and E. European langs. Sch. Library Sci. Case Western Res. U., Cleve., 1964-67, acting dir. libraries, 1967-68; adj. instr. Case Western Res. U. (Sch. Library Sci.), 1965-69; librarian Case Western Res. U. (Freiberger Library), 1968-69; dir. univ. library, head dept. and prof. library sci. Ball State U., Muncie, Ind., 1969-78, univ. librarian, head dept. and prof. library service, 1978-81, prof. library service, also adj. prof. library sci., 1981-82, chmn. dept. library and info. sci., prof. library sci., 1982-87, prof. library sci., info. sci. emeritus, 1987—. Contbr. articles to profl. jours. Nat. Endowment for Humanities and Council on Library Resources Inc. grantee. Mem.: ALA, Serb Nat. Fedn., African Violet Soc. Am., Am. Theol. Libr. Assn. (life). Eastern Orthodox. E-mail: suputi@sbcglobal.net.

SURABIAN, CAROL ANNE, language educator, consultant; b. Fresno, Calif., Aug. 1, 1948; d. Harvey Graham and Jeannette Agnes Corbett; m. Ronald Dave Surabian; children: Jennifer Carol, Shelley Rebecca Vizcarra, David Christopher. BA, Calif. State U., Fresno, 1971; M, Fresno Pacific U., 2001. Tchr. Washington Intermediate Sch., Dinuba, Calif., 1984—. Organist Sts. Sahag-Mesrob Armenian Ch., Reedley, Calif., 1982—2006. Mem.: Calif. Assn. Tchrs. English (pres. Tulare County coun. 1997—2006). Avocations: reading, needlecrafts, travel. Home: 589 E Sycamore Reedley CA 93654 Office: Washington Intermediate Sch 1150 N Hayes Dinuba CA 93618 Home Phone: 559-638-1086; Office Phone: 559-595-7252. Personal E-mail: csurab132@yahoo.com. Business E-Mail: csurabia@dinuba.k12.ca.us.

SURACI, CHARLES XAVIER, JR., retired federal agency administrator, air transportation executive, consultant; b. Washington, Feb. 10, 1933; s. Charles Xavier and June Celcia (Hunter) Suraci; m. Florence Patricia De Mino, May 23, 1970. Cadet, Widener U., 1951—55; grad., Nat. Acad. Broadcasting Sch., Washington, 1959; student, Columbia Union Coll., 1962-63, 72, Catholic U., 1969; grad. extension course, CAP Staff Coll., 1974; BA, Calif. Christian Coll., 1977, HHD (hon.), 1977; grad., USAF Inspectors Gen. Sch., Eglin AFB, Fla., 1982; also grad. numerous other govt. schs. and courses. Served with USAF, 1953-57; enlisted CAP, 1957, commd. 1st lt., 1961; advanced through ranks to Col. CAP USAF Aux, 1974; co-founder Wheaton-Silver Spring Cadet Squadron; comdr. Nat. Capital Wing, 1973-76; dep. chief of staff cadet activities Middle East region, 1977-79, dir. cadet tng., 1979-82, insp. gen., 1982—. With Henry Diamond Lab. U.S. Army, Adelphi, Md., 1963—, materials publs. asst. Harry Diamond Lab., 1963—68, later asst. to motor transp. officer, now supply specialist, logistics sect.; bd. dirs. Centro Tepeyac Crisis Pregnancy Ctr., Silver Springs, Md. Mem. youth com. YMCA, Silver Spring, 1962—69, mem. bd. mgmt., 1967—; bd. dirs. Am. Youth Com.; mem. Commn. on Children and Youth Bd., Montgomery County, Md., Montgomery County Juvenile Ct. Com., 1978—86; co-chmn. Right to Life com. KC-Rosensteel Coun.; bd. dirs. Pregnancy Aid Ctr., College Park, Md.; choir mem. Blessed Sacrament Cath. Ch., Washington. Nominee Pres.'s Vol. Action award, Pres. of U.S., 1988, 1991; named Air Man of Month, USAF, 1956, Grand Marshall Meml. Day Parade, Rockville, Md., 1971, Man of Yr. State of Md., Air Force Assn., 1993; recipient Leader and Svc. award, YMCA Silver Spring, 1968, 1969, CAP Meritorious Svc. award, Dept. Def., 1969, 1977, Cert. of Commendation, Pres. Richard Nixon, 1970, CAP Exceptional Svc. award, Congressman Lester Wolff of N.Y., 1972, award, Montgomery County C. of C., 1973, Commendation, Gov. of Tenn., 1975, Letter of Commendation, Washington Mayor Walter Washington, 1977, Outstanding Patriotic Civilian Svc. award, Dept. Def., 1977, Md. Vol. Cmty. honor award, Montgomery County, 1981, Vol. Activist award, 1984, George Washington honor medal, Valley Forge Freedom Found., 1995, Patrick Henry medal for Patriotic Achievement, Mil. Order of World Wars, 1995, Honor, Md. Ho. Dels., 1974, D.C. Govt., 1977, numerous AF and CAP ribbons and medals, Dept. of Army Spl. Act or Svc. award, Dept. of Army Superior Performance award, 1987, Cmty. Svc. award, Wheaton-Kensington News, Bethesda Chevy Chase Current, Montgomery County Press Assn., 1990, Outstanding Support Aviation Career Day Tuskegee Airmen and Commdg. Gen. of D.C., Air Nat. Guard, 1992, Spl. award for tng. over 1000 youth cadets in CAP in 31 yrs., State of Md., 1986, Plaque Name Displayed at U.S. Army-Harry Diamond Lab., Pro-Life award, KC-Rosensteel Coun., 1992, 1999—2002, Frank G. Brewer Meml. Aerospace award-CAP Mid. East Region HQ, 1984, 1991, 1992, CAP-USAF Aux. Meritorious Svc. award, Mid. East Region HQ, 1993, Cert. Appreciation Aerospace Edn. of Md., Air Force Assn., 1993—95, Exceptional Svc. award, USAF Aux., 1994—95, Sr. Officer of Yr. Mid East Region, USAF Aux.-CAP, 1998, Colonel Robinson Lifetime Leadership award, Nat. Capital Wing, 2001, Leadership award, Cen. East Region Air Force Assn., 2001, numerous others, 50th Yr. award, Blessed Sacrament Ch., 2007. Mem.: Md. Pvt. Industry Coun. (bd. dirs. Opportunity Skyway program), Md. Press. Assn. Montgomery County, Nat. Officers Assn., Mil. Order of World Wars (jr. vice comdr. Bethesda chpt. 1996—, Outstanding staff officer of the yr. 2005), Tuskegee Airmen Inc., Fed. Ret. Employees Assn., Army Aviation Assn., Navy League, Nat. Aerospace Assn., Air Force Assn. (v.p. aerospace edn. Thomas W. Anthony chpt. 1996—, pres. Thomas W. Anthony chpt. 1998—, bd. dirs., nat. liaison officer to Civil Air Patrol-Aux. USAF 2004, Medal of Merit 1990, Exceptional Svc. award 1991, Disting. Svc. as Inspector Gen. 1991, Exceptional Svc. award 1994, Commd. Officer of Yr. 1995, Spl. Cert. Appreciation 1996, Mem. Distinction award Thomas W. Anthony chpt. 2000—02, Cen. East Region Chpt. Pres. of Yr. for State of Md. 2002, named Outstanding Mem. 2004, Outstanding Pres. of the Thomas W. Anthony chpt. 2004, Thomas W. Anthony Chptr. pres. of the Yr. 2005, Pres. of Yr. Thomas Anthony chpt. 2006), Alumni Assn. Widener U., Andrews AFB Officers Club, KC (chmn. Pro-Life Father Rosensteel coun., Outstanding Leadership Pro-Life activities 1990—91, Outstanding Svc. award 1993—94, Honored Guest of Yr. 1996—97, Outstanding Cmty. award 2003, 2004, Achievement award of the Yr. 2005), Chester Lodge. Democrat. Achievements include 2 plaques in his name displayed at Columbia Union Coll., Takoma Park, Md., Widener U. (formerly Pa. Mil. Coll.), Chester. Home: Rock Creek Hills 9817 La Duke Dr Kensington MD 20895-3156 Office: USAF Aux CAP Mid East Region Hdqrs Office of Insp Gen 9817 La Duke Dr Kensington MD 20895-3156 Office Phone: 301-585-0081.

SURACI, PATRICK JOSEPH, clinical psychologist; b. Rochester, NY, May 31, 1936; s. Frank and Josephine Rosalie (Marino) S. PhD in Psychology, New. Sch. for Social Rsch., NYC, 1981. Cert. clin. psychologist, N.Y. Intern in clin. psychology Morrisania Neighborhood Family Care Ctr., Montefiore Hosp., NYC, 1979-80; staff psychologist N.Y. Police Dept., 1981-83; pvt. practice NYC, 1982—. Adj. lectr. N.Y. Inst. Tech., N.Y.C., 1975-78, John Jay Coll. Criminal Justice, CUNY, 1973-81; adj. asst. prof. dept. psychology Baruch Coll., CUNY, 1983-92; vol. Manhattan Ctr. for Living, 1994-96, Police Orgn. Providing Peer Assistance, 2001—. Author: Male Sexual Armor. Erotic Fantasies and Sexual Realities of the Cop on the Beat and the Man in the Street, 1992. Mem. The Nat. Arts Club. With U.S. Army, 1959-62. Mem. N.Y. State Psychol. Assn. (task force on AIDS), Actors Equity. Office: 8 Gramercy Park S New York NY 10003-1718 Office Phone: 212-473-5966. Personal E-mail: DrSuraci@aol.com.

SURANYI, JOHN B., broadcast executive; With United Cable, United Artists Cable, EchoStar Comm. Corp., Cheetah Advanced Techs.; sr. v.p. Am. Telecasting, Inc.; sr. v.p. supply chain mgmt. DIRECTV Group, 2004, exec. v.p. customer satisfaction, pres. Sales and Svcs., 2005—. Office: DIRECTV Group 2230 E Imperial Hwy El Segundo CA 90245 Office Phone: 310-964-5000. E-mail: jbsuranyi@directv.com. *

SURAVAJJALA, MAMATHA, information technology manager; Mgr. volume planning sys., Info. Tech. Mgmt. DaimlerChrysler, Auburn Hills, Mich. Recipient Women of Color Tech. award, 2005. Office: Chrysler Group 1000 Chrysler Dr Auburn Hills MI 48326-2766

SURAWICZ, BORYS, physician, educator; b. Moscow, Feb. 11, 1917; came to U.S., 1951, naturalized, 1956; s. Josef and Mathilda (Soloweczyk) S.; m. Frida G. Van Klaveren, July 19, 1946; children: Christina M., Nina M., Tanya S., Serge J. MD, Stefan Batory U., Wilno, Poland, 1939. Mem. staffs hosps., Germany, Norway, 1945-49; staff De Goesbriand Meml. Hosp., Burlington, Vt., 1951-53, Phila. Gen. Hosp., 1953-55; instr. cardiology U. Pa., Phila., 1954-55; instr. U. Vt., Burlington, 1955-57, asst. prof. clin. and expt. medicine, 1957-62; chief div. cardiology U. Ky. Coll. Medicine, Lexington, 1962-81, assoc. prof. medicine, 1962-66, prof., 1966-81; prof. medicine Ind. U. Sch. Medicine, Indpls., 1981—. Cons. VA Hosp., Indpls. Editor: (with E.D. Pellegrino) Sudden Cardiac Death, 1964, (with C. Fisch) Digitalis, 1969; (with E. Prystowsky, C.P. Reddy) Tachycardias, 1985, Electrophysiologic Basis of ECG and Cardiac Arrhythmics, 1995, Chou's Electrocardiography in Clinical Practice, 2001; mem. editl. bds. profl. jours. Mem. AMA, ACP, Am. Heart Assn., Assn. Univ. Cardiologists (pres. 1978), Am. Coll. Cardiology (master; pres. 1979), Am. Physiol. Soc., Sigma Xi. Office Phone: 317-338-6227. Personal E-mail: bsurawic@yahoo.com.

SURBER, DAVID FRANCIS, public relations executive, consultant, television producer, journalist; b. Covington, Ky. s. Elbert and Dorothy Kathryn (Mills) Surber. BA in Physics, Thomas More Coll., Covington, Ky., 1960; LLD (hon.), London Inst. Applied Rsch., 1973. Owner P.R. Co., pub. affairs counseling, Covington, 1960—. Judge Brit. Airways Tourism Tomorrow awards, London, 2000—. Spl. corr.: Am. newspapers to Vatican II, 1965; prodr.: (TV series) Make Peace with Nature, Sta. WKRC-TV, 1973—, Strip Mining: Two Views, 1972, Energy: Where Will It Come From, How Much Will It Cost, 1975, Atomic Power for Ohio, 1976, A Conversation with the Vice President, 1976, The Bad Water, 1977, The Trans-Alaska Pipeline: A Closeup Report, 1977, Acid Rain: A World View, 1986—89, Energy Independence in the U.K., 1992, Unhappy Prospects: Acid Rain & Global Climate Change, 1995, The Kyoto Summit: Was It Global and Will It Work, 1997—98. Apptd. by Sec. of Energy to Nat. Coal Coun., 1992, 1994, 1996, 1998, 2000, 2002, 2004, 2006, chmn. comm. com., 1999—; mem. Bd. Zoning Appeals, Covington, 1964—84, chmn., 1971—84, Covington Environ. Commn., 1971—72, Commn. Strip Mining, 1967—68; pub. interest adv. com. Ohio River Valley Water Sanitation Commn., 1976—82; water quality adv. com. Ohio-Ky.-Ind. Regional Coun. Govts., 1975—82; environ. adv. coun. City of Cin., 1981—84; rehab. com. Cmty. Chest Greater Cin., 1972—78, mem. agy. admissions com., 1972—78, mem. priorities com., 1972—78; pres. bd. dirs. Cathedral Found., 1968—70; trustee Montessori Learning Ctr., 1973—75, Bklyn. Spanish Youth Choir; founding mem. Mayor's Task Force on the Environment, Cin., 1972—73; mem. Ky. Nature Preserves Commn., 1976—79; Dem. candidate for U.S. Ho. Reps., 1972. Recipient Cmty. Svc. award, Thomas More Coll., 1975. Mem.: ACLU, AFTRA, Nat. Inst. Urban Wildlife (bd. dirs. 1987—96), Tri-State Air Com. (chmn. 1973—74), Mousquetaires d'Armagnac, Izaak Walton League (pres. Ky. 1973—98, bd. dirs. Ky., nat. bd. dirs.). Office: PO Box 15555 Covington KY 41015-0555 Office Phone: 859-491-5000. Business E-Mail: surber@surber.com.

SURDAM, ROBERT MCCLELLAN, retired banker; b. Albany, NY, Oct. 28, 1917; s. Burke and LeMoyne (McClellan) S.; m. Mary Caroline Buhl, July 8, 1946; children— Peter Buhl, Robert McClellan, Mary Caroline. BA cum laude, Williams Coll., 1939. With Nat. Bank Detroit, 1947-88, exec. v.p., 1964-66, pres., 1966-72, chmn. bd., 1972-82, also bd. dirs., 1966-88. Served to lt. comdr. USNR, 1941-46. Recipient, Navy and Marine Corps. medal. Mem. Detroit Club, Country Club of Detroit, Yondotega Club, Jupiter Island Club (Hobe Sound, Fla.), Jupiter Hills Club (Tequesta, Fla.), Little Traverse Yacht Club (Harbor Springs, Mich.), Rolling Rock Club (Ligonier, Pa.), Hobe Sound Yacht Club, Little Harbor Club (Harbor Springs, Mich.). Home: 396 Provencal Rd Grosse Pointe Farms MI 48236-2959

SURESH, SUBRA, materials engineer, educator; B in Tech., Indian Inst. Tech., 1977; MS, Iowa State U., 1979; ScD, MIT, 1981. Asst. prof. engring. Brown U., 1983; R. P. Simmons Endowed Professorship MIT, 1993, head Dept. Materials Sci. and Engring., 2000—, Ford Prof. of Engring., 2002—. Clark B. Millikan Endowed Chair for visiting professorship Calif. Inst. Tech., Pasadena, 1999—2000. Author: Fatigue of Materials, 2nd ed., 1998; co-author (with A. Mortenson): Fundamentals of Functionally Graded Materials, Institute of Materials, 1998; co-author: (with L.B. Freund) Thin Film Materials: Stress, Surface Evolution and Failure, 2003; contbr. articles to profl. jours. Named one of The Most "Highly Cited Researchers" in the World in the broad area of Materials Science, Inst. for Scientific Info., 2002; recipient Outstanding Scientific Accomplishment award, U.S. Dept. of Energy, 1982, Robert Lansing Hardy Gold medal, The Metallurgical Society of AIME, 1983, Champion H. Matthewson Gold medal, 1985, Presidential Young Investigator award, NSF, 1985—90, Ford Found. Rsch. award, 1985—87, Allied Signal Found. Rsch. award, 1989, Allied Signal Found. Merit award, 1990, Disting. Alumnus award, Indian Inst. of Technol., 1997. Fellow: TMS (Disting. Scientist/Engineer award 2001), ASME, ASM Internat., Am. Acad. Arts and Sciences, Am. Ceramic Society (Ross Coffin Purdy award 1992); mem.: US Nat. Acad. Engring., NAE, Materials Rsch. Society of India (hon.). Achievements include patents in field. Office: MIT Room 8-303 77 Massachusetts Ave Cambridge MA 02139

SURFACE, JAMES LOUIS, SR., trust officer, lawyer; b. Roanoke, Va., May 20, 1941; s. Thomas James and Elizabeth (Abbott) S.; m. Judith Marcia Woodford, Aug. 11, 1962; children: Susanna Elizabeth, James Louis Jr. BA cum laude, Washington & Lee U., 1963, JD cum laude, 1965. Bar: W.Va. Assoc. Spilman, Thomas, Battle & Klostermeyer, Charleston, W.Va., 1965-71; trust officer Kanawha Valley Bank, N.A., Charleston, 1971-77; v.p., trust counsel Liberty Nat. Bank & Trust Co., Louisville, 1977-84; v.p., trust officer United Va. Bank, Richmond, 1984-85; v.p., sr. trust officer First Citizens Nat. Bank, Dyersburg, Tenn., 1985-93; sr. v.p., sr. trust officer SunTrust Bank East Tenn., Johnson City, 1993—2003; retired, 2003. Mem. adminstrv. bd. First United Meth. Ch., Dyersburg, 1988-90, pres., bd. dirs. Cmty. Concert Assn., Dyersburg, 1988-93; treas., bd. dirs. Louisville-Jefferson County Youth Orch., Louisville, 1980-84; pres., bd. dirs. W.Va. Opera Theater, Inc., Charleston, 1972-77; elder First Presbyn. Ch., Johnson City, 1998-2000; bd. dirs. Tipton-Haynes Hist. Site, 2001-06. Mem. ABA (chmn. subcom. on duties and responsibilities of successor trustee real property, probate and trust sect., Charleston 1974-75), W.Va. Bar Assn., Tenn. Bankers Assn. (treas. trust divsn. Nashville chpt. 1988-89, sec. 1989-90, v.p. 1990-91, pres. 1991-92), W.Va. Bankers Assn. (chmn. trust divsn. Charleston chpt. 1974-75), Rotary (bd. dirs. Dyersburg chpt. 1987-88), East Tenn. State U. Friends of Music (bd. dirs. 1994-99, 2000—). Democrat. Avocations: tennis, racquetball, photography, reading.

SURKIN, ELLIOT MARK, lawyer; b. Phila., Apr. 22, 1942; s. Hersh M. and Minnie (Shore) S.; m. Carol E. Foley, May 26, 1973; 1 child, Jennifer Dykema. AB, Princeton U., 1964; LLB, Harvard U., 1967. Bar: Mass. 1967. Assoc. Hill & Barlow, P.C., Boston, 1967-73, mem., 1973—2003, chmn. mgmt. com., 1988-92, chmn. real estate dept., 1996-2001; mng. ptnr. Boston DLA Piper, 2003—. Lectr. law Harvard U., 1975-96, MIT, Ctr. for Real Estate, 1996—. Chmn. bd. Boston Ctr. Arts, 1972-81, dir., mem. exec. com., 1981-83; trustee, mem. exec. com. Citi Performing Arts Ctr. (formerly Wang Ctr. for Performing Arts), Boston, 1980-2007, mem. fin. com., 1995-2005, vice chmn. bd., 1997-2005, dir. 2007—; mem. New Eng. com. Legal Def. Fund NAACP, 1976-93; chmn. bd. Trustees of Reservations, 1997-2003, bd. dir., 2003-06, chmn. Chappaquiddick local com. 1986-97, trustee 1985—, mem. standing com. 1994-2003, mem. exec. com. 1996-2003; dir. Sheriff's Meadow Found., 1994-97. Mem. ABA, Am. Law Inst., Am. Coll. Real Estate Lawyers, Mass. Bar Assn., Boston Bar Assn., St. Botolph Club, Harvard Club of Boston, Edgartown Yacht Club, Country Club of Brookline, Mass., Kiawah Island Club. Office: DLA Piper 33 Arch St 26th Fl Boston MA 02110-1447 Office Phone: 617-406-6030. Office Fax: 617-406-6130. Business E-Mail: elliot.surkin@dlapiper.com.

SURKO, STEPHEN WILLIAM, systems engineer; s. Alexander Surko and Elise Catherine Foulkes; m. Elizabeth Barry Thompson, Dec. 23, 1989; children: Katherine Helen, James Frederick Surko Thompson, Samuel Meredith Surko Thompson. BS in Ocean Engring. with distinction, U.S. Naval Acad., Annapolis, Md., 1982; MS in Mech. Engring., MIT, Cambridge, Mass., 1988, MS in Marine Engring. and Naval Architecture, 1988. Registered profl. engr., NY, 1990. Commd. ens. USN, 1982, advanced through grades to comdr., ret., 2004; sys. engr. ITS-Noesis, Arlington, Va., 2004—. Contbr. papers, articles to prof. publs. Scoutmaster Boy Scouts Am., Newport, RI, 1982—83; commr. DC Stoddert Soccer League, Washington, 2004—06. Decorated Meritorious Svc. Medal with 3 Gold Stars USN; Trident scholar. Mem.: Am. Soc. Naval Engrs. (assoc.; chmn. day tech. program com.), U.S. Naval Inst. (life), Phi Kappa Phi (assoc.), Sigma Xi (assoc.), Tau Beta Pi (life). Office: ITS-Noesis 4100 N Fairfax Dr Ste 800 Arlington VA 22203-1663 Office Phone: 703-741-0300.

SURLES, CAROL D., academic administrator; b. Pensacola, Fla., Oct. 7, 1946; d. Elza Allen and Versy Lee Smith; divorced; children: Lisa Surles, Philip Surles. BA, Fisk U., 1968; MA, Chapman Coll., 1971; PhD, U. Mich., 1978. Personnel rep. U. Mich., Ann Arbor, 1973-78, vice-chancellor-adminstrn. Flint, 1987-89; exec. asst. to pres., assoc. v.p. for human resources U. Ctrl. Fla., Orlando, 1978-87; v.p. acad. affairs Jackson State U., Miss., 1989-92; v.p. adminstrn. and bus. Calif. State U., Hayward, 1992-94; pres. Tex. Woman's U., Denton, 1994-99, Ea. Ill. U., Charleston, 1999—. Trustee Pub. Broadcasting Ch. 24, Orlando, 1985-87; bd. dirs. First State Bank, Denton, Tex., Tex.-N.Mex. Power Co., TNP-Enterprise.

Recipient Outstanding Scholar's award Delta Tau Kappa, 1983. Mem. AAUW, Am. Assn. Colls. and Univs., Golden Key Honor Soc., Mortar Bd. Soc., Dallas Citizens' Coun., Dallas Women's Found., Coun. of Pres. (Austin, Tex.), Phi Kappa Phi, Alpha Kappa Alpha. Methodist. Avocation: piano. Office: Ea Ill U 600 Lincoln Ave Charleston IL 61920-3011

SURLES, HAROLD BRADY, history professor; b. Fredericksburg, Va., May 21, 1938; m. Carolyn Ann Collins; children: Frances Catherine Rimer-Surles, John Collins. BA, Baylor U., Waco, Tex., 1960, MA, 1964; D, U. NC, Chapel Hill, 1974. Assoc. prof. history SW Va. C.C., Richlands, Va., 1974—. Gov. Appalachian dist. Civitan Internat., Birmingham, Ala., 1988—89; mem., vice chair VA Spl. Olympics, Richmond, Va., 1985—91; bd. dirs. Va. Found. for the Humanities, 1996—2002. Grantee, Fulbright Program, 1998—99, US Dept. State, 2000—04. Mem.: Phi Theta Kappa (coord. Va. region 1979—2007, bd. dirs. 1988—94, named Disting. Regional Coord. 1992, Mosal scholar 1994). Home: 219 Glenrochie Dr Abingdon VA 24211 Office: SW Va Cmty Coll U S Hwy 19 South Richlands VA 24641 Home Phone: 276-628-9096; Office Phone: 276-964-7210. Office Fax: 276-964-7720. Personal E-mail: brady_surles@hotmail.com. Business E-Mail: brady.surles@sw.edu.

SURLES, RICHARD HURLBUT, JR., retired law librarian; b. Norfolk, Va., Mar. 28, 1943; s. Richard H. and Elda Florine (Belvin) S.; m. Judith Louise Coffin, May 29, 1964; children— Stephanie Anne, Richard H. BA, Tex. A&M U., 1963; JD, U.Houston, 1967; M.L.L., U.Wash., 1969. Bar: Colo. 1971. Asst. to law librarian U. Houston, 1966-68; asst. to law librarian King county Law Library, Seattle, 1968-69; dir. of law library, prof. law U. Denver, 1969-71, U. Tenn., Knoxville, 1971-76, U. Oreg., Eugene, 1976-81, U. Ill., Champaign, 1981—98; ret., 1998. Author: Legal Periodical Management Data, 1977 Mem. Am. Assn. Law Libraries Republican. Personal E-mail: Beretta@KTC.com.

SURMA, JOHN P., JR., metal products executive; b. Pitts., 1954; BS in Acctg., Pa. State U., 1976. CPA. Acct. Price Waterhouse, 1976—81, mgr., 1981—85, sr. mgr., 1985—87, ptnr., 1987—97; sr. v.p. fin. and acctg. Marathon Oil Co., 1997—98; pres. Speedway SuperAmerica LLC, 1998—2000; sr. v.p. supply and transp. Marathon Ashland Petroleum LLC, 2000, pres., 2001; asst to chmn. USX Corp., 2001; vice chmn., CFO US Steel Corp., 2002—03, pres., COO, 2003—04, pres., CEO, 2004—06, chmn., CEO, 2006—. Exec. staff asst. to vice chmn. Fed Res. Bd. Pres. Exec. Exch. Program, 1983; bd. dirs. Mellon Fin. Corp., 2004—, Calgon Carbon Corp., 2000—, NAM; dir. & mem. exec. com. Internat. Iron & Steel Inst.; mem. Pa. Bus. Roundtable. Dir., mem. exec. com. Allegheny Conf. Cmty. Devel.; mem. bd. visitors U. Pitts. Katz Grad. Sch. Bus., Pa. State U. Smeal Coll. Bus. Mem.: AICPA, Pitts. Celebrity Hockey Team. Office: US Steel Corp 600 Grant St Pittsburgh PA 15219-2800 Office Phone: 412-433-1121. *

SURMAN, OWEN STANLEY, psychiatrist; b. Boston, Apr. 21, 1943; s. Aaron Harry and Edith Anne (Silver) S.; m. Lezlie Anne Humber, July 19, 1969 (dec. Nov. 5, 1994); children: Craig Bruce Hackett, Kathleen Bridget Lezlie; m. Amy Johnson, Oct. 1, 2000. BSc with honors, McGill U., 1964, MD, CM, 1968. Diplomate Am. Bd. Psychiatry and Neurology. Intern Balt. City Hosp., 1968—69; clin. fellow in medicine Johns Hopkins U., Balt., 1968—69; resident in psychiatry Mass. Gen. Hosp., Boston, 1969—72; clin. fellow in psychiatry Harvard Med. Sch., Boston, 1969—72; clin. asst. in psychiatry Mass. Gen. Hosp., Boston, 1975—76, asst. in psychiatry, 1977—80, asst. psychiatrist, 1980—86, assoc. psychiatrist, 1986—89, psychiatrist, 1990—; instr. psychiatry Harvard U. Med. Sch., Boston, 1975—80, asst. prof., 1980—90, assoc. prof., 1990—. Psychiat. cons. Boston Ctr. Heart Transplant, 1988-94; mem. ethics com. Mass. Ctr. Organ Transplantation, 1988—; mem. subcom. Human Studies, Mass. Gen. Hosp., 1982—, acting chmn., 1996-97, co-vice-chmn., 1999-2001, cons. transplant unit, 1975—, vice-chmn. xenotransplant adv. com., 1997-98, living related partial liver donor oversight com., 2000—; mem. Inst. for Study of Smoking Behavior and Policy, John F. Kennedy Sch. Govt., 1982-89; vis. prof. Tokyo U., 2001; mem. N.Y. State Com. on Quality Improvement in Living Liver Donation, 2002—. Contbr. articles and letters to profl. jours., chpts. to books, After Eden: A Love Story, 2005. Bd. dirs. Unitarian-Universalist Area Ch., Sherborn, Mass., 1983-86, 93-96; advancement officer troop 1 Boy Scouts Am., Sherborn, 1983-91. Lt. comdr. M.C., USNR, 1972-75. Grantee Milton Fund, 1969-70, Upjohn Corp., 1982-84, Burroughs Wellcome Co., 1984-85, Eli Lily Corp., 1989, 90-92. Fellow Am. Psychiat. Assn. (Disting.), Am. Acad. Psychosomatic Medicine (ethics com., awards com. 1994-97); mem. AAAS, Mass. Med. Soc., N.Y. Acad. Scis., Mass. ACLU, Libr. of Boston Athenaeum, Ford Hall Forum, New Eng. Poetry Club, Boston Authors Club. Avocation: creative writing. Office: Mass Gen Hosp Wang ACC 815 15 Parkman St Boston MA 02114 Office Phone: 617-724-0846. Business E-Mail: osurman@partners.org. E-mail: ossurman@yahoo.com.

SURO-BREDIE, CARMEN CECILIA, federal official; b. Washington, Aug. 19, 1947; d. Guillermo Antonio and Piedad (Castillo) Suro; m. Joseph W.B. Bredie, Oct. 26, 1974; children: Nicholas Alexander, Christopher Anthony. BA, Manhattanville Coll., 1969; MA, Johns Hopkins U., 1972; MBA, Harvard U., 1981. Dep. asst. U.S. Trade Rep. for Investment and the Uruguay Round, Washington, 1989-92, asst. for environment and intellectual property, 1992-93, asst. for L.Am., Africa and the Caribbean, 1993-95; sr. policy advisor Bur. Interam. Affairs Dept. State, Washington, 1995-96; sr. policy advisor and exec. sec. U.S. Trade Rep., Washington, 1996-00, asst. U.S. trade rep. for policy coord., 2000—. Contbr. articles to profl. publs. Coach No. Ireland Women's Coalition. Named one of Elite Women, Hispanic Bus. mag., 2005; recipient Nat. Cuban Am. Women's Assn. award, 1992. Roman Catholic. Avocations: antiques, gourmet cooking. Office: Exec Office of the Pres US Trade Rep 600 17th St NW Washington DC 20850 Office Phone: 202-395-9541. Business E-Mail: csuro-bredie@ustr.eop.gov.

SUROVELL, EDWARD DAVID, real estate company executive; b. Washington, Mar. 20, 1940; s. Samuel and Florence Deborah (Starfield) S.; m. Barbara Ann Bartelmes, Apr. 26, 1958 (div. Jan. 1974); children: David Alexander, Claire Katherine; m. Natalie A. Sallade, June 3, 1999. BA, Columbia U., 1962; postgrad., U. Mich., 1968-71. Lic. real estate broker, Mich. Copy editor Harcourt, Brace & World, Inc., NYC, 1963-65; editor Princeton (N.J.) U. Press, 1965-67, Scott, Foresman Co., Glenview, Ill., 1967-68, U. Mich., Ann Arbor, 1968-72; real estate agt. Fletcher & Klein, Inc., Ann Arbor, 1973-75; sales mgr. Charles Reinhart Co., Ann Arbor, 1975-82; pres. Edward Surovell Realtors, Ann Arbor, 1982—. Dir. United Bank and Trust, Washtenaw, 2001—. Mem. Ann Arbor City Planning Commn., 1988-91, 95-98, Downtown Devel. Authority, Ann Arbor, 1991-95; trustee Ann Arbor Dist. Libr., 1996—, pres., 2004—06; trustee Libr. Mich. Found., 2005-; bd. dirs. Mich. Shakespeare Festival, 1999—, Jackson Symphony Orch., 2000—, Chamber Music Am., 2004—; mem. Mich. Bd. Profl. Cmty. Planners, 1988-92. Mem. Nat. Assn. Realtors, Hist. Soc. Mich. (trustee 1992—), Ann Arbor Area Bd. Realtors (pres. 1985, Realtor of Yr. 1990), Univ. Mus. Soc. (bd. dirs. 1992-98, trustee Mich. Ctr. for the Book 1998-2002), Mich. Hist. Commn. (bd. mem. 2005—, pres. 2007—), Mich. Hist. Found. (bd. dirs. 2007—). Avocations: book collecting, arts philanthropy. Home: 1000 Forest Rd Ann Arbor MI 48105-1047 Office: Edward Surovell Realtors 1884 W Stadium Blvd Ann Arbor MI 48103-4504 Business E-Mail: esurovell@surovell.com.

SUROWIEC, ANDREW JULIUS, biophysicist, researcher; b. Lwów, Poland, Apr. 13, 1940; arrived in US, 1986; s. Jan Jakub and Maria (Knobloch) S.; m. Irene Regina Baranowski, Apr. 27, 1977; 1 child, Caroline Maria. Engr., Tech. U., Gliwice, Poland, 1962, MS, 1964; PhD, Silesian U., Katowice, Poland, 1972. Cert. elec. engring. Asst. prof. Silesien Sch. Medicine, Katowice, 1964-82; postdoctoral fellow Ctr. d'Etude L'Energie Nucleaire, Mol, Belgium, 1973-74; disting. vis. scientist U. Ottawa, Ont., Canada, 1983-87; asst. prof. Bowman U. Sch. Medicine, Winston-Salem, NC, 1987-88, U. So. Calif., LA, 1988-93; sr. physicist Centennial Med. Ctr., Nashville, 1993—. Peer reviewer: Cancer, Internat. Jour. Am. Cancer Soc., 1993; contbr. articles to Physics in Medicine and Biology, Bioelectromagnetics, IEEE Transactions Biomed., Internat. Jour. Hyperthermia, Biopolymers, Jour. Chem. Soc. Faraday Transactions. Grantee Nat. Sci. and Engring. Rsch. Coun., 1985. Fellow Radiation Rsch. Soc.; mem. Internat. Clin. Hyperthermia Soc., N.Y. Acad. Scis. Achievements include patent for recording system for rotating viscometer; finding of simulated materials for electromagnetic studies and cancer treatment; findings of dielectric spectroscopy of normal and cancer tissues; finding of dielectric and hydrodynamic properties of DNA. Home: 8209 Londonberry Rd Nashville TN 37221-4640 Office: Centennial Med Ctr Radiation Therapy 2300 Patterson St Nashville TN 37203-1528 Home Phone: 615-673-0205; Office Phone: 615-342-4850. Personal E-mail: andsur@aol.com.

SURPLUS, ROBERT WILBUR, retired music educator; b. Scranton, Pa., Sept. 1, 1923; s. Willard K. and Olive T. (Wrightson) S.; m. Jean Craig, June 25, 1976; children: Amy, Melanie. BS, Susquehanna U., Selinsgrove, Pa., 1945; MA, Columbia U., NYC, 1947, EdD, 1968. Music tchr., Mineola, NY, 1945-46, Butler, NJ, 1946-47; music supr. Red Lion, Pa., 1947-56; assoc. prof. Shippensburg State U., Pa., 1956-58; music tchr. Fox Lane Sch., Bedford, NY, 1958-59; instr. Columbia U., NYC, 1959-61; asst. prof. U. Minn., Mpls., 1961-65; prof. music Ea. Ky. U., Richmond, 1965-94; ret., 1994. Rsch. chmn., So. Divsn., Music Educators Nat. Conf., 1974-80, rsch. coun. mem., 1974-80; cons. Nat. Assn. Jr. Colls., 1973-75. Author: Follow the Leader, 1962, The Alphabet of Music, 1963, The Beat of the Drum, 1963, The Story of Musical Organizations, 1963; editor: A Guidebook for State Music Education Associations, 1985, Beyond the Classroom: Informing Others, 1987; contbr. articles to profl. jours. Mem.: Ky. Alliance for Arts Edn. (pres. 1974—82, adv. bd.), Ky. Music Educators Assn. (bd. dirs., pres. 1971—73, Disting. Svc. award 1983, Citation for Svc. 2004), Music Educators Nat. Conf. (pres. so. divsn. 1982—84).

SURPRISE, JUANEE, chiropractor, nutrition consultant; b. Gary, Ind., Apr. 28, 1944; d. Glenn Mark and Willia Ross (Vasser) Surprise; m. Peter E. Coakley, Feb. 12, 1966 (div. Jan. 1976); children: Thaddeus, Mariah, Darius; m. Robert T.Howell, Feb. 24, 1984. RN, Phila. Gen. Hosp. Sch. Nursing, 1965; D of Chiropractic summa cum laude, Life Chiropractic Coll., Marietta, Ga., 1981. Diplomate Nat. Bd. Chiropractic Examiners, Am. Acad. Pain Mgmt., Am. Acad. Integrated Medicine, Internat. Acad. Clin. Nutrition; bd. cert. naturopathic med. doctor; cert. clin. nutritionist, acupuncturist, Thompson technique, Nimmo receptor tonus technique. Staff nurse Children's Hosp., Balt., 1966-67; charge nurse Melrose-Wakefield Hosp., Mass., 1967-68; hosp. adminstr. Animal Hosp. of Wakefield, Mass., 1967-79; chiropractor Chiropractic Clinic of Greenville, NC, 1982-84, Family Med.-Chiropractic Clinic, Denton, Tex., 1984—; dean Sch. Nutrition Quantum-Veritis Internat. Univ. Sys., 2003—; dir. Ctr. Clin. Sci., Parker Coll. Chiropractic, Dallas, 1996-97, dir. diplomate and certification programs, 1997-2000. Mem. postgrad. faculty Northwestern U. Health Scis. Mem., chmn. Cmty. Planning Commn., North Reading, Mass., 1976-79; chmn. bldg. com. Immaculate Conception Ch., Denton, 1987-90, parish coun., 1990-92; v.p. Property Owners Assn., 2000-02. Fellow Am. Acad. Integrated Medicine; mem. Am. Assn. Pain Mgmt., Am. Chiropractic Assn., Am. Chiropractic Bd. on Nutrition (past pres.), Tex. Chiropractic Assn. (past chair), Pi Tau Delta. Republican. Roman Catholic. Avocation: health education. Office: Family Med and Chiropractic Clinic 1100 Dallas Dr Denton TX 76205-5121 Office Phone: 940-566-0000. Personal E-mail: doctormomdc@hotmail.com. Business E-Mail: info@familymedandchiro.com.

SURRIDGE, STEPHEN ZEHRING, lawyer, writer; b. NYC, Dec. 12, 1940; s. Robert George and Florence Elizabeth (Zehring) S.; m. Helen Frances McKenna, Mar. 15, 1969; children: Christopher S., Jonathan R., Matthew W., Martha H. BA magna cum laude, Yale U., 1962; MBA (with distinction), JD, U. Mich., 1969. Bar: Wis. 1969, Mich. 1969. Assoc. Quarles & Brady, Milw., 1969-76, ptnr., 1977-89; freelance writer, tchr., 1990—. Author: (monograph) Seven Thunders of Revelation, 1985, Revelation Revisited, 1995, Fatima's 'Third Secret' is Future Warning, 2004. 1st lt. US Army, 1963—65. Mem. Phi Beta Kappa. Mem. Christian Ch. Home: 4480 N Ardmore Ave Milwaukee WI 53211-1418

SURRY, MELINDA OWEN, reading coach; d. Marvin Edward and Joyce Carole Owen; m. Daniel Wayne Surry. BS, Jacksonville State U., Ala., 1988; Ednl. Specialist, U. Ala., Tuscaloosa, 1996, MA, 1993. Nat. bd. cert. tchr. Nat. Bd. for Profl. Tchg. Stds., 2005, cert. adminstr. U. Ala., Tuscaloosa, 2000. Elem. sch. tchr. W. E. Striplin Elem., Gadsden, Ala., 1988—2001; asst. prin. Eichold-Mertz Elem., Mobile, Ala., 2001—03; coach Ala. Reading Initiative McDavid-Jones Elem., Citronelle, Ala., 2003—. Master coach Ala. Reading Initiative Ala. State Dept. Edn., Foley, 2006. Vol. Habitat for Humanity, Gadsden, Ala., 1999—2000; vol. Food for the Bereaved St. Dominic Cath. Ch., Mobile, 2002—06. Named Tchr. of Yr., Striplin Elem., 1991—92; grantee, Ala. Power, 1997—98. Mem.: ASCD, Ala. Network Nat. Bd. Cert. Tchrs., Nat. Coun. Tchrs. English, Internat. Reading Assn., Kappa Delta Pi, Pi Lambda Theta, Kappa Delta Epsilon. Roman Catholic. Avocations: travel, sporting events, concerts, gardening. Office: McDavid-Jones Elementary 16520 Highway 45 Citronelle AL 36522 Home Phone: 251-602-6827; Office Phone: 251-221-1510.

SURWIT, RICHARD SAMUEL, psychology professor; b. Bklyn., Oct. 7, 1946; s. David and Ethel S.; m. Sandra E. Cummings, May 23, 1982; children: Daniel Alan, Sarah Jeanne. AB, Earlham Coll., 1968; PhD, McGill U., Montreal, Que., Can., 1972; postgrad., Harvard U., Boston. Postdoctoral fellow Harvard Med. Sch., 1972-74, instr., 1974-76, asst. prof., 1976-77; assoc. prof. psychiatry Duke U. Med. Ctr., Durham, NC, 1977-83, prof., 1980, 83—, vice chmn., 1993—; chief divsn. med. psychology Duke U., 1997, prof. psychology, 1991—; chmn. bd. dir. ZyCare Inc. (formerly Healthware Corp.), Chapel Hill, 1983—. Author: Fear: Learning to Cope, 1978, Behavioral Approaches to Cardiovascular Diseases, 1982, The Mind-Body Diabetes Revolution, 2004. Recipient rsch. devel. award NIMH, 1980, rsch. scientist award NIMH, 1993. Fellow APA, Soc. Behavioral Medicine (pres. 1994), Acad. Behavioral Medicine Rsch. Achievements include co-discovery in 1997, of UCP2, a novel gene related and diabetes and immunity; co-developer of the Diacare diabetes disease management system, Coag-Care anticoagulation management system. Home: 3804 Sweeten Creek Rd Chapel Hill NC 27514-9706 Office: Duke U Med Ctr PO Box 3842 Durham NC 27702-3842 Business E-Mail: richard.surwit@duke.edu.

SURYANARAYANAN, RAJ GOPALAN, pharmacist, researcher, consultant, educator; b. Cuddalore, Tamil Nadu, India, Apr. 19, 1955; came to U.S., 1985; s. Natesan and Pushpa (Subramanian) Rajagopalan; m. Shanti Venkateswaran, Nov. 24, 1985; children: Priya Mallika Sury, Meera Sindu Sury. B in Pharmacy, Banaras Hindu U., Varanasi, India, 1976, M in Pharmacy, 1978; MS, U. BC, Vancouver, Can., 1981, PhD, 1985. Mgmt. trainee Indian Drugs and Pharms. Ltd., Rishikesh, India, 1978; supr. Roche Products, Bombay, 1979; tchg. asst. U. B.C., Vancouver, Can., 1979, 82-83; asst. prof. pharmaceutics U. Minn., Mpls., 1985-92, assoc. prof., 1992-99, prof., 1999—, dir. grad. studies, 1994-98, William and Mildred Peters endowed chair, 2006—. Cons. numerous pharm. cos. in U.S., 1987—. Contbr. articles to profl. jours.; patentee quantitative analysis of intact tablets. Recipient numerous grants for rsch., U.S., 1985—. Mem. Am. Assn. Pharm. Scientists, Am. Assn. Colls. Pharmacy. Hindu. Avocation: sports. Office: U Minn Coll Pharmacy 308 Harvard St SE Minneapolis MN 55455-0353 Home: 2025 Autumn Pl Saint Paul MN 55113-5417 E-mail: surya001@umn.edu.

SUSAC, JOHN OBREN, neurologist, consultant; b. Powhatan Point, Ohio, Feb. 27, 1940; s. John William and Eunice Marie Susac, Glenn Howard Morris (Stepfather); m. Lois Ann Green, Sept. 5, 1959; children: Holly Beth Tabernilla, Heather Megan, John Arthur, Jeremy Lawton. MD, Ohio State, Columbus, 1965. Lic. Ohio, 1965. Neurologist Neurology, Neurosurgery, Winter Haven, Fla., 1978—. Assoc. prof. Uniformed Svcs. Health Scis., Washington, 1973—78; cons. neuroophthalmologist U.S. Dept. Army, Lt col. US Army, 1965—70. Fellow: Am. Acad. Neurology. Achievements include discovery of Susac's syndrome. Avocations: travel, hiking. Home: 300 W Lake Otis Dr SE Winter Haven FL 33880 Office: Neurology Neurosurgery 50 2d St Winter Haven FL 33880 Home Phone: 863-299-8975; Office Phone: 863-293-2107. Office Fax: 863-294-9314; Home Fax: 863-294-9314. Business E-Mail: jsusac@neurohaven.com.

SUSCHITZKY, PETER, cinematographer; Cinematographer The Skouras Agy., 1987—. Cinematographer: (films) It Happened Here, 1962, Privilege, 1967, A Midsummer Night's Dream, 1968, Charlie Bubbles, 1968, Leo the Last, 1970, Melody/Swalk, 1971, The Pied Piper, 1972, Henry VIII and His Six Wives, 1972, That'll Be the Day, 1974, All Creatures Great and Small, 1975, Lisztomania, 1975, The Rocky Horror Picture Show, 1976, Valentino, 1977, The Empire Strikes Back, 1980, Krull, 1983, Falling in Love, 1984, Dead Ringers, 1988, Where the Heart Is, 1990, Naked Lunch, 1992, The Public Eye, 1992, The Vanishing, 1993, M. Butterfly, 1993, Immortal Beloved, 1994, Crash, 1996, Mars Attacks!, 1996, eXistenZ, 1998, The Man in the Iron Mask, 1998, The Empire Strikes Back - Spl. Edition, 1999, Star Wars Trilogy- Spl. Edition, 1999, The Red Planet, 1999, Spider, 2005, A History of Violence, 2005, Shopgirl, 2005, le concile de pierre, 2005. Office: The Skouras Agency 1149 3rd St #3 Santa Monica CA 90403

SUSCOVICH, DAVID J., neuropsychologist, marriage and family therapist; b. Mt. Pleasant, Pa., Sept. 20, 1952; s. Joseph Anthony and Helen G. Suscovich; m. Edith P. Suscovich, May 23, 1980 (div. Sept. 15, 2001); children: Joseph Alfred, John David, Mark Andrew. BS/BA in Psychology and Sociology, U. Pitts., 1973, postgrad., 1974; MA in Marriage and Family Therapy, U. Conn., 1977; PsyD in Clin. Psychology, Antioch New Eng., 1997. Cert. marriage family therapist Conn., diplomate Am. Coll. Forensic Examiners, Nat. Bd. Addiction Examiners; lic. marriage and family therapist Am. Assn. Marriage and Family Therapists, Conn. Psychiat. clinician psychiatry dept. Waterby (Conn.) Hosp., 1974—80; pvt. practice individual and marriage and family therapy Naugatuck, Conn., 1987—. Clin. cons. Waterby Youth Svcs., Inc., 1988—, Salvation Army Youth Shelter, Waterby, 1995—, Conn. Dept. children and Famlites, 2001—03; clin. neuropsychology examiner Conn. Resource Group, LLC, Waterby, 1988—, Conn. Edn. Svcs., Middletown, 2001—; mental health cons. Danby (Conn.) Head Start, Conn., 1994—97; adj. faculty So. Conn. State U., New Haven, 1992—, Yale U. Sch. Medicine, New Haven, 2002—; full adj. prof., adj. Ctrl. Conn. State U., New Britain, Conn., 1994—; presenter in field; co-facilitater G.R.A.S.P. parent advocacy and support group. Weeblos Cub Scout leader Boy Scouts Am. Pack 110, Naugatuck, 1989—98; troop com. mem. Boy Scouts Am. Troop 109, Naugatuck, 1997—. Mem.: Electroencephalography and Clin. Neurosci. Soc., Conn. Assn. Marriage and Family Therapy (chair state election com. 2002—), Phi Kappa Phi. Democrat. Roman Catholic. Achievements include research in negative neurophysiological effects of stress on children and teens delaying development of executive brain functions, neurofeed back training for brain disorders. Avocations: camping, canoeing, fishing, woodworking, music. Home: 23 May St Naugatuck CT 06770 Office: 16 Orchard St Naugatuck CT 06770 Office Phone: 203-729-2565. Personal E-mail: dr_suscovich@msn.com.

SUSKIND, RONALD STEVEN, journalist, writer; b. Kingston, NY, Nov. 20, 1959; s. Walter Burton and Shirley Lila (Berman) Suskind; m. Cornelia Kennedy, May 4, 1986; children: Walter Kennedy, Harry Owen. BA in Govt. and Fgn. Affairs, U. Va., 1981; MS in Journalism, Columbia U., 1983. No. Va. field coord. Charles Robb for Gov., Alexandria, Va., 1981; campaign mgr. John Downey for U.S. Senate, New Haven, 1982; news asst., interim reporter The New York Times, 1983—85; city/state reporter The St. Petersburg Times, Fla., 1985—86; sr. editor Boston Bus. Mag., 1987—88, editor, 1988—90; staff reporter The Wall St. Jour., Boston, 1990—93, sr. nat. affairs writer Washington, 1993—2000, project reporter; contr. NY Times Mag., Esquire Mag. Instr. advanced journalism Harvard U., Cambridge, Mass., 1987—93; commentator Sta. WBUR, Boston, 1989—93. Author: (non-fiction) A Hope in the Unseen: An American Odyssey from the Inner City to the Ivy League, 1998, The Price of Loyalty: George W. Bush, the White House, and the Education of Paul O'Neill, 2004 (Investigative Reporter's and Editor's Book of Yr. award, 2004), The One Percent Doctrine: Deep Inside America's Pursuit of Its Enemies Since 9/11, 2006. Recipient Pulitzer Prize for feature writing, 1995, Benjamin Fine award, Nat. Assn. Secondary Sch. Prins., 1995, Nat. Writing award, Ball State U., 1995, Bus. Book of Yr. award, Forbes Mag., 2004. Office: c/o The Harry Walker Agency Inc 21st Fl 355 Lexington Ave New York NY 10017 Business E-Mail: ronsuskind@ronsuskind.com.

SUSKO, CAROL LYNNE, lawyer, accountant, educator; b. Washington, Dec. 5, 1955; d. Frank and Helen Louise (Davis) S. BS in Econs. and Acctg., George Mason U., 1979; JD, Cath. U., 1982; LLM in Taxation, Georgetown U., 1992. Bar: Pa. 1989, D.C. 1990; CPA, Va., Md. Tax acct. Reznick Fedder & Silverman, P.C., Bethesda, Md., 1984-85; sr. tax acct. Pannell Kerr Forster, Alexandria, Va., 1985; tax specialist Coopers & Lybrand, Washington, 1985-87; supervisory tax sr. Frank & Co., McLean, Va., 1987-88; mem. editl. staff Tax Notes Mag., Arlington, Va., 1989-90; adj. faculty Am. U., Washington, 1989—; tax atty. Marriott Corp., Washington, 1993-94; sr. tax mgr. Host Marriott Inc., Washington, 1994-99, KPMG LLP, McLean, Va., 1999—. Mem. ABA, AICPAs, Va. Soc. CPAs, D.C. Soc. CPAs, D.C. Bar Assn. Office: IRS 11166 Fairfax Blvd Ste 500 Fairfax VA 22030 Personal E-mail: l8636@aol.com. Business E-Mail: carol.l.susko@irs.gov.

SUSLICK, KENNETH SANDERS, chemistry professor; b. Chgo., Sept. 16, 1952; s. Alvin and Edith Suslick. BS with honors, Calif. Inst. Tech., 1974; PhD, Stanford U., 1978. Rsch. and tchg. asst. Stanford (Calif.) U., 1974-78; chemist Lawrence Livermore (Calif.) Lab., 1974-75; asst. prof. U. Ill., Urbana, 1978-84, assoc. prof., 1984-88, prof. chemistry, 1988—; prof. Beckman Inst. for Advanced Sci. and Tech., Urbana, 1989-92; prof. materials sci. and engring. U. Ill., Urbana, 1993—, William H. and Janet Lycan prof. chemistry, 1997—2004, Marvin T. Schmidt prof. chemistry, 2004—; founder ChemSensing, Inc., 2001—. Vis. fellow Balliol Coll., Inorganic Chemistry Lab., Oxford (Eng.) U., 1986; cons. in field. Editor: High Energy Processes in Organometallic Chemistry, 1987, Ultrasound: Its Chemical, Physical and Biological Effects, 1988, Comprehensive Supramolecular Chemistry, vol. 5, 1996; co-editor: Sonochemistry and Sonoluminescence, 1999; editl. bd. Ultrasonics, 1992-96, Ultrasonic Sonochemistry, 1996—, Accounts of Chemical Research, 2005—, Jour. Am. Chem. Soc., 2006-; patentee isotope separation by photochromatography, sonochemistry, protein microspheres, drug delivery, blood substitutes, sensors, smell-seeing, artificial olfaction; contbr. articles to profl. jours. Recipient Rsch. Career Devel. award NIH, 1985-90, NSF Spl. Creativity award 1992-94, Material Rsch. Soc. medal, 1994, R.S.C. Sir George Stokes medal 2007; fellow DuPont Found., 1979-80, Sloan Found.,

1985-87; A.C.S. Sr. Cope scholar, 2004. Fellow AAAS, Am. Acoustical Soc. Royal Soc. Arts, Mfrs. and Commerce (Silver medal 1974); mem. Am. Chem. Soc. (chmn. sect. 1987-89, Nobel Laureate Signature award 1994, Sr. Cope Scholar award 2004). Avocations: sculpting, music. Office: U Ill Dept Chemistry 600 S Mathews Ave Urbana IL 61801-3602 Business E-Mail: ksuslick@uiuc.edu.

SUSMAN, MILLARD, geneticist, educator; b. St. Louis, Sept. 1, 1934; s. Albert and Patsy Ruth S.; m. Barbara Beth Fretwell, Aug. 18, 1957; children: Michael K., David L. AB, Washington U., St. Louis, 1956; PhD, Calif. Inst. Tech., 1962. With microbial genetics research unit Hammersmith Hosp., London, 1961-62; asst. prof. genetics U. Wis., Madison, 1962-66, assoc. prof., 1966-72, prof., 1972—2002, prof. emeritus, 2002—, chmn. lab. genetics, 1971-75, 77-86, assoc. dean med. sch., 1986-95, acting dean Sch. Allied Health Professions, 1988-90, vice dean med. sch., 1994-95, spl. advisor to the dean med. sch., 1995; dir. Ctr. for Biology Edn., Madison, 1996—2002. Phage course instr., Cold Spring Harbor, N.Y., 1965; v.p. scis., Wis. Acad. Scis., Arts and Letters, 2000—. Co-author: Life on Earth, 2d edit., 1978, Human Chromosomes: Structure, Behavior, Effects, 3d edit., 1992; contbr. articles to sci. jours. Mem Genetics Soc. Am., AAAS, Sigma Xi, Phi Beta Kappa, Phi Eta Sigma, Omicron Delta Kapp. Home: 2707 Colgate Rd Madison WI 53705-2234 Office: 2432 Genetics/Biotech Ctr Bldg Madison WI 53706 Office Phone: 608-263-5075. Business E-Mail: msusman@wisc.edu.

SUSMAN, MORTON LEE, lawyer; b. Aug. 6, 1934; m. Nina Meyers, May 1, 1958; 1 child, Mark Lee. BBA, So. Meth. U., 1956, JD, 1958. Bar: Tex. 1958, U.S. Dist. Ct. (so. dist.) Tex. 1961, U.S. Ct. Appeals (5th cir.) 1961, U.S. Supreme Ct. 1961, U.S. Ct. Appeals (11th cir.) 1981, DC 1988, U.S. Ct. Appeals (DC cir.) 1988, N.Y. 1990, Colo. 1996. Asst. U.S. atty., Houston, 1961-64; 1st asst. U.S. atty., 1965-66; U.S. atty., 1966-69; ptnr. Weil, Gotshal & Manges and predecessor firm Susman & Kessler, Houston, 1969-97; ret., 1998. Lt. USNR, 1958—61. Fellow: Am. Coll. Trial Lawyers, Tex. Bar Found.; mem.: FBA (dir., Younger Fed. Lawyer award 1968), ABA, Tex. Bar Assn. Democrat. Personal E-mail: mort99@msn.com.

SUSMAN, STEPHEN DAILY, lawyer; b. Houston, Jan. 20, 1941; m. Ellen Spencer, 1999; children: Stacy Kuhn, Harry. BA magna cum laude, Yale U., 1962; JD with highest honors, U. Tex., 1965. Bar: Tex. 1965, US Supreme Ct. 1970, DC 1999, NY 2000, Colo. 2002. Law clk. to Hon. John R. Brown US Ct. Appeals (5th cir.), New Orleans, 1965-66; law clk. to Justice Hugo L. Black US Supreme Ct., Washington, 1966-67; ptnr. Fulbright & Jaworski LLP, Houston, 1966-75; spl. counsel to atty. gen. Mandell & Wright, P.C., Houston, 1975-80; founding ptnr. Susman Godfrey LLP, Houston, 1980—. Vis. prof. law U. Tex., Austin, 1975; chmn. adv. com. on discovery Tex. Supreme Ct. Contbr. articles to profl. jours. Mem. Nat. Coun. of Human Rights First; mem. bd. visitors Anderson U. Cancer Found.; mem. devel. bd. U. Tex. Health Sci. Ctr.; mem. Yale Art Gallery, Yale Devel. Found. Recipient ADL Jurisprudence award, 1995, Disting. Counselor award, State Bar Tex., 2005; named one of Nation's Top 10 Trial Litigators, Nat. Law Jour., 2006, Best Lawyers in Am. Mem. ABA (antitrust sect., mem. coun. litig. sect., chmn. task force on fast track litig.), Houston Bar Assn., Dallas Bar Assn., DC Bar Assn., NY Bar Assn., Colo. Bar, State Bar Tex., Am. Law Inst., Assn. Trial Lawyers Am., Am. Bar Trial Advs., Houston Bar Assn., Southwestern Legal Found. Rsch. Fellows, Yale Club (Houston, NYC), Houston Trial Lawyers Assn. (dir.), Tex. Assn. Civil Trial and Appellate Specialists (former pres., dir.), Order of the Coif, Friars, Phi Delta Phi. Avocations: skiing, hiking. Office: Susman Godfrey LLP Ste 5100 1000 Louisiana St Houston TX 77002-5096 Home Phone: 713-522-1856; Office Phone: 713-653-7801. Office Fax: 713-654-6670. Business E-Mail: ssusman@susmangodfrey.com.

SUSSBERG, MILTON JOEL, marketing professional; b. New Rochelle, NY, Oct. 5, 1949; s. Darwin Ralph and Carol G Sussberg; m. Linda Aland, June 27, 1971; children: Matthew H, Jordan A. BBA with distinction, U. Wis., Madison, 1971; MBA, Columbia U., 1973. Car. mktg. & sales Pearl-Wick Corp., Long Island City, N.Y., 1973-76; v.p. M. Ware Assocs., NYC, 1976-79, Meteor/SKelly, Inc., Stamford, Conn., 1979-84; pres. Robot-Coupe Internat., Norwalk, Conn., 1984-86; CEO, founder Sussberg & Co., Inc., White Plains, N.Y., 1986—; owner Savannah (Ga.) Sand Gnats Baseball Club, 1991—2005. Adj. prof. mktg. Fordham U., Bronx, NY, 1996—99. Mem.: Trump Nat. Golf Club, Phi Kappa Phi. Avocations: golf, skiing. Office: Sussberg & Co Inc Ste 308W 701 Westchester Ave White Plains NY 10604

SUSSE, SANDRA SLONE, lawyer; b. Medford, Mass., June 1, 1943; d. James Robert and Georgie Coffin (Bradshaw) Slone; m. Peter Susse, May 10, 1969 (div. May 1993); 1 child, Toby. BA, U. Mass., 1981; JD, Vt. Law Sch., 1986. Bar: Mass. 1986, U.S. Dist. Ct. Mass. 1988, U.S. Ct. Appeals (1st cir.) 1995. Staff atty. Western Mass. Legal Svcs., Springfield, 1986—. Mem. ABA, Hampden County Bar Assn. Avocations: hiking, german literature, films, skating. Address: Western Mass Legal Serv 127 State St Fl 4 Springfield MA 01103-1905 Office Phone: 413-781-7826 ext. 124. Business E-Mail: ssusse@wmls.org.

SUSSER, MERVYN WILFRED, epidemiologist, educator; b. Johannesburg, Sept. 26, 1921; came to U.S., 1965; s. Solomon and Ida Rose (Son) S.; m. Zena Athene Stein, Mar. 28, 1949; children: Ida, Ezra, Ruth. MB, BChir, U. Witwatersrand, Union of South Africa, 1950; diploma pub. health, London Conjoint Bd., 1960; DMS (hon.), U. Witwatersrand, 1993. Med. officer, then supt. Alexandra Health Centre and Univ. Clinic, Johannesburg, 1952-55; successively lectr., sr. lectr., reader, head dept. social and preventive medicine Manchester (Eng.) U., 1957-65; also med. officer div. mental health Salford, Eng.; prof., chmn. div. epidemiology Sch. Pub. Health, Columbia U., NYC, 1966-78, Gertrude H. Sergievsky prof. epidemiology, dir. Sergievsky Ctr., 1977-91; Sergievsky prof. emeritus, spl. lectr., 1992—. Hon. prof. Nat. Sch. Pub. Health, Madrid; cons. WHO, 1962, 66-72, 79, 90, NIH, NAS. Author: (with W. Watson) Sociology in Medicine, 1962, 2d edit., 1971, (with W. Watson and K. Hopper), 3d edit., 1985, Community Psychiatry: Epidemiologic and Social Themes, 1968, Causal Thinking in the Health Sciences: Concepts and Strategies of Epidemiology, 1973, (with others) Famine and Human Development: Studies of the Dutch Hungerwinter 1944-45, 1975, (with D. Rush and Z. Stein) Diet in Pregnancy: A Randomized Controlled Trial of Nutritional Supplements, 1980, Epidemiology, Health and Society: Selected Essays, 1987, (with Jennie Kline and Zena Stein) Conception to Birth: Epidemiology of Prenatal Development, 1989; editor Am. Jour. Pub. Health, 1992-98; festschrift in his honor. Pres. Com. Health in So. Africa, 1984-94. With South African Defence Force, 1940-45. Named Gaylord Anderson lectr., U. Minn. Sch. Pub. Health, 2007; recipient Disting. Svc. award, Coll. Physicians and Surgeons, Columbia U., 1994, Jubilee medal, U. Witwatersrand, South Africa, Abraham Lilienfeld award, 1999; Belding scholar, Assn. Aid Crippled Children, 1965—66, Guggenheim fellow, 1972. Fellow: APHA (Rema Lapouse lectr. 2005, John Snow award 1994, Maternal and Child Health Epidemiology Lifetime Achievement award 2005), N.Y. Acad. Medicine, Am. Epidemiol. Soc., Royal Coll. Physicians (Edinburgh), Faculty of Pub. Health Medicine of Royal Coll. Physicians U.K. (hon.), Am. Coll. Epidemiology (hon.); mem.: Physicians for Human Rights, Inst. Medicine (sr.), Soc. Pediat. Epidemiol. Rsch., Soc. Social Medicine U.K. (hon.), Soc. Epidemiol. Rsch., World Psychiat. Assn., Internat. Epidemiol. Assn. Home: 100 Pinecrest Dr Hastings On Hudson NY 10706-3702 Office: Sergievsky Ctr and Columbia U Sch Pub Health 630 W 168th St New York NY 10032-3795 Office Phone: 212-305-9081. Business E-Mail: mws2@columbia.edu.

SUSSER, SAM L., oil industry executive, consumer products company executive; married; 3 children. BBA in Fin., U. Tex., Austin. With corp. fin. divsn. and mergers and acquisitions group Salomon Bros. Inc., NYC and Dallas, 1985—87; founder Susser Holdings Corp. (formerly Southguard Corp.), 1988, CEO. Mem. adv. coun. Tex. A&M U. Coll. Bus., Corpus Christi; trustee Driscoll Found.; dir. Tex. State Aquarium, USS Lexington Mus. Office: Susser Holdings Corp 4433 Baldwin Blvd Corpus Christi TX 78408 Office Phone: 361-884-2463. Office Fax: 361-884-2494.

SUSSKIND, LAWRENCE ELLIOTT, urban planner, educator, mediator; b. NYC, Jan. 12, 1947; s. David J. and Marjorie H. (Friedman) S.; m. Miriam Mason, June 8, 1968 (div. Dec. 1982); m. Leslie Webster Tuttle, Dec. 12, 1982; children: Noah Gates, Lily Webster. AB in Sociology, Columbia U., 1968; M.C.P., MIT, 1970, PhD in Urban Planning, 1973. Asst. prof. urban and environ. planning MIT, Cambridge, 1971-74, assoc. prof., 1974-82, prof., 1982-95, Ford prof., 1995—, head dept., 1978-82, dir. MIT-Harvard Pub. Disputes Program, 1980—; exec. dir. program on negotiation Harvard Law Sch., 1984-87, visiting prof. law, 2001—. Founder Consensus Bldg. Inst., 1993— Author: Paternalism, Conflict and Co-Production, 1983, Proposition 1 1/2: Its Impact on Massachusetts, 1983, Resolving Environmental Regulatory Disputes, 1983, Breaking the Impasse, 1987, Environmental Diplomacy, 1994, Reinventing Congress for the 21st Century, 1995, Dealing With an Angry Public, 1996, Consensus Building Handbook, 1999, Negotiating on Behalf of Others, 1999, Negotiating Environmental Agreements, 1999, Better Environmental Policy Studies, 2001, Transboundary Environmental Negotiation, 2002, Breaking Robert's Rules, 2006; sr. editor, founder Environ. Impact Assessment Rev., 1980-96; mem. editl. bd. Negotiation Jour., 1984—. Recipient Disting. Planning Educator award, Assn. Collegiate Sch. Planning, 2005, Global Environment award, Internat. Assn. Impact Assessment, 2007. Mem. Am. Inst. Cert. Planners, Assn. for Conflict Resolution. Jewish. Office: MIT 9-332 Cambridge MA 02139 Office Phone: 617-492-1414. Business E-Mail: susskind@mit.edu.

SUSSKIND, LEONARD, physicist, educator; BS, CCNY, 1962; PhD, Cornell U., 1965. NSF postdoc. fellow Cornell U., Ithaca, NY, 1965-66; from asst. to prof. Physics Belfer Grad. Sch. Sci. Yeshiva U., NYC, 1966-79; Felix Bloch prof. Physics Stanford U., Stanford, Calif., 1979—. Visiting prof. Physics U. Tel Aviv 1971-72. Co-author (with James Lindesay): An Introduction To Black Holes, Information And The String Theory Revolution: The Holographic Universe, 2004; author: The Cosmic Landscape: String Theory and the Illusion of Intelligent Design, 2005. Recipient Pregel award 1975, J.J. Sakurai prize 1997; Loeb lectr. Harvard U. 1976. Mem. AAAS, Nat. Acad. Sci. Achievements include being credited as the father of String Theory; co-inventor, Holographic Principle. Office: Dept Physics Varian Bldg Rm 108 Stanford Univ Stanford CA 94305-4060

SUSSKIND, TERESA GABRIEL, publishing executive; came to U.S., 1945; d. Aaron and Betty (Fox) Gabriel; m. Charles Susskind, May 1, 1945; children: Pamela Pettler, Peter Gabriel, Amanda. Student, U. London, 1938-40. Profl. libr. Calif. Inst. Tech., Pasadena, 1946-48, Yale U., New Haven, 1948-51, Stanford (Calif.) U., 1951-52, SRI Internat., Menlo Park, Calif., 1953; founder, pres. San Francisco Press, Inc., 1959—. Active in cultural affairs; bd. govs. San Francisco Symphony, 1986-89. With Women's Royal Naval Svc., 1943—45. Mem. Town and Gown Club (Berkeley, Calif.; pres. 1984-85). Office: 660 Spruce St Berkeley CA 94707-1730

SUSSMAN, ALEXANDER RALPH, lawyer; b. Bronx, NY, Sept. 24, 1946; s. Herman R. and Claire (Blumenson) S.; m. Edna Rubin, Mar. 24, 1973; children: Jason, Carl, Matthew, Eric. AB cum laude, Princeton U., 1968; JD, Yale U., 1972. Bar: N.Y. 1973, U.S. Dist. Ct. (so. and ea. dists) N.Y. 1974, U.S. Ct. Appeals (1st, 2d, 3d, 5th, 6th, 8th, 10th, and 11th cirs.) 1983, U.S. Supreme Ct. Law clk. to Hon. Constance Baker Motley U.S. Dist. Ct., NYC, 1972-73; assoc. Cravath, Swaine & Moore, NYC, 1974-76, Fried, Frank, Harris, Shriver & Jacobson, NYC, 1977-79, ptnr., 1979—. Author: (with A. Fleischer, Jr.) Responses to Takeover Bids, 2004, Takeover Defense, 2 vols., 2004; editor Yale Law Jour., 1971-72. Bd. dirs. N.Y. Lawyers for Pub. Interest, 1983—; bd. dirs., mem. exec. com. Legal Aid Soc., 1987-93. Fulbright scholar U. Bordeaux, 1969. Mem. ABA, Am. Law Inst., N.Y. State Bar Assn., Assn. of Bar of City of N.Y. (fed. cts. com. 1984-87, jud. com. 1987-90, chmn. legal assistance com. 1988-91, Marden lectr. com. 1991-94, chmn. mergers and acquisitions com. 1995-99). Home: 20 Oak Ln Scarsdale NY 10583-1627 Office: Fried Frank Harris Shriver & Jacobson 1 New York Plz Fl 25 New York NY 10004-1980 E-mail: Alex.Sussman@ffhsj.com.

SUSSMAN, ANDREW LOUIS, research scientist; b. Dec. 14, 1968; BA in Latin Am. Studies and Anthropology, Am. U., Washington, 1991; MCRP, U. N.Mex, Albuquerque, 2002, PhD, 2003. Rsch. scientist U. N.Mex, Albuquerque, 2002—. Office Phone: 505-272-4077.

SUSSMAN, ARTHUR H., artist, painter; b. Bklyn., Mar. 30, 1927; Art & film editor Sta. KOAT-TV, Albuquerque; TV film critic; courtroom sketch artist; indsl. art cons.; owner Arthur Sussman Gallery, Albuquerque. Prin. works include Ethicon, Joe G. Maloof Corp., stained glass window, Monte Vista Christian Ch., painting, Congregation, Albuquerque, stained glass window, Las Padillos Cmty. Ctr., N.Mex, 1998, portrait Gov. Richardson, 2004, one-man shows include U. N.Mex, 1967, 1977, 1997, Nat. Acad. Design, NY, 1969, N.Mex Mus. Fine Arts Biennials, 1972, N.Mex Mus. Fine Art, 1974, 2002—03, Gallery 16, 1986, U. Judaism, LA, 1988, Albuquerque Mus. Fine Arts, 1991—93, Nat. Christian Art Exhbn., Farmington, N.Mex, 1999, Represented in permanent collections Albuquerque Mus. Fine Arts, Jewish Mus., NYC, N. Mex. Mus. Fine Art, Santa Fe, Okla. Art Ctr., Sunport, N.Mex., Bern County Ct. House, Albuquerque, Albuquerque Mus. Fine Arts. Office: PO Box 13493 Albuquerque NM 87192

SUSSMAN, BARRY, writer, demographer, editor; b. NYC, July 10, 1934; s. Samuel and Esther (Rosen) S.; m. Peggy Earhart, Jan. 20, 1962; children: Seena, Shari. BA, Bklyn. Coll., 1956. Reporter Herald Courier, Bristol, Va., 1960-62, mng. editor, 1962-65; editor Washington Post, 1965-69, city editor, 1970-73, spl. Watergate editor, 1972-74, pollster, pub. opinion analyst, 1975-87; co-founder, co-dir. Washington Post-ABC News poll, 1981-87; columnist Washington Post Nat. Weekly, 1983-87; mng. editor nat. affairs UPI, Washington, 1987; ind. pub. opinion analyst and pollster, 1988—. Adv. bd. Innovation news media cons. group, 1994—; editor Watchdog Project of the Nieman Found. for Journalism at Harvard U., 2003—. Author: The Great Coverup: Nixon and the Scandal of Watergate, 1974, What Americans Really Think, 1988, (with Lowell P. Weicker, Jr.) Maverick, 1995; editor: (with J.A. Giner) Innovations in Newspapers: The 1999 Global Report, 1999, The 2000 Global Report, 2000, The 2001 Global Report, 2001, 02, 03, 04. Recipient Drew Pearson award for Nat. Reporting, 1972, 1st Prize award Washington Newspaper Guild, 1973, Editor of Yr. award Washington Newspaper Guild, 1973. Mem. Am. Assn. for Pub. Opinion Rsch. (exec. coun. 1985-87), Am. Soc. Newspaper Editors. Jewish. Avocation: chess. Personal E-mail: bsussman@his.com. Business E-Mail: bsussman@niemanwatchdog.org.

SUSSMAN, DEBORAH EVELYN, interior designer, small business owner; b. NYC, May 26, 1931; d. Irving and Ruth (Golomb) S.; m. Paul Prejza, June 28, 1972. Student, Bard Coll., 1948-50, DHL (hon.), 1998; student, Inst. Design, Chgo., 1950-53, Black Mountain Coll., 1950, Hochschule für Gestaltung Ulm, Germany, 1957-58. Art dir. Office of Charles and Ray Eames, Venice, Calif., 1953-57, 61-67; graphic designer Galeries Lafayette, Paris, 1959-60; prin. Deborah Sussman and Co., Santa Monica, Calif., 1968-80; founder, pres. Sussman-Prejza and Co., Inc., Santa Monica, Calif., 1980-90, Culver City, Calif., 1990—. Spkr., lectr. UCLA Sch. Arch., Archtl. League N.Y.C., Smithsonian Inst., Stanford Conf. on Design, Am. Inst. Graphic Arts Nat. Conf. at MIT, Design Mgmt. Inst. Conf., Mass.; spl. guest Internat. Design Conf., Aspen, Colo.; Fulbright lectr., India, 1976; spkr. NEA Adv. Coun., 1985, Internat. Coun. Shopping Ctrs., 1986, USIA Design in Am. seminar, Budapest, Hungary, 1988. One-woman shows include Visual Arts Mus. Sch. Visual Arts, N.Y.C., 1995; participant exhbn., Moscow, 1989, Walker Art Ctr., Mpls., 1989; mem. editl. adv. bd. Arts and Arch. Mag., 1981-85, Calif. Mag., Arch. Calif. Fulbright grantee Hochschule für Gestaltung Ulm, 1957-58; recipient award AIA Nat. Inst. Honors, 1985, 88, Am. Inst. Graphic Arts, Calif. Coun. AIA, Comms. Arts Soc., LA County Bd. Suprs., Vesta award Women's Bldg. LA, Golden Arrow award Soc. Environ. Graphic Designers, 2006. Fellow Soc. Environ. Graphic Design; mem. AIA (hon., Medal for XXIII Olympiad 2004), Am. Inst. Graphic Arts (bd. dirs. 1982-85, founder LA chpt., chmn. 1983-84, Legacy medal 2004), Am. Ctr. Design (hon.), LA Art Dirs. Club (bd. dirs., award), Alliance Graphique Internat., Archs., Designers, and Planners Social Responsibility, Calif. Women in Environ. Design (adv. d.), Trusteeship (affiliate Internat. Women's Forum, chmn.'s cir. Town Hall). Democrat. Jewish. Avocation: photography. Office: Sussman/Prejza & Co Inc 3525 Eastham Dr Culver City CA 90232 E-mail: dsussman@sussmanprejza.com.

SUSSMAN, GERALD, publishing company executive; b. Balt., Feb. 21, 1934; s. Hyman Jacob and Sylvia (Applebaum) S.; m. Arla Ilene Ellison, Aug. 25, 1963; children: Daniel Leonard, Andrew Louis. BA, U. Md., 1956. Co-founder, prin. Investors Service of Md., Balt., 1956-60; coll. traveller Oxford U. Press, Inc., NYC, 1961-62, coll. sales mgr., 1962-69, gen. advt. mgr., 1970-73, v.p., dir. mktg., 1974-79, sr. v.p., dir. mktg., 1979-83, sr. v.p., dir. adminstrn. and planning, 1983—97; project mgr. Guide to the Sandia Mountains. V.p. Friends of Sandia Mountains. Mem. Assn. Am. Pubs. (chmn. mktg. com.), Assn. Am. Univ. Presses (chmn. mktg. com. 1980-81), Pubs. Advt. Club, Phi Alpha Theta. Home: 10424 City Lights Dr NE Albuquerque NM 87111-7536 Office: Oxford U Press Inc 198 Madison Ave Fl 9 New York NY 10016-4341 Personal E-mail: agsuss@comcast.net.

SUSSMAN, HOWARD SIVIN, lawyer; b. NYC, Feb. 12, 1938; s. Joseph and Dora (Sivin) S. AB cum laude, Princeton U., 1958; LLB, Columbia U., 1962. Bar: N.Y. 1964, U.S. Dist. Ct. (so. and ea. dists.) N.Y. 1967, U.S. Ct. Appeals (2d cir.) 1967, U.S. Tax Ct. 1969, U.S. Dist. Ct. (no. dist.) N.Y. 1970, U.S. Supreme Ct. 1970, U.S. Ct. Appeals (5th cir.) 1982. Assoc. Chadbourne, Parke, Whiteside & Wolff, NYC, 1963-71; asst. US atty. So. Dist. NY, 1971-77; assoc. prof. law U. Houston, 1977-82; of counsel Wood, Lucksinger & Epstein, Houston, 1982-83; pvt. practice NYC, 1983-94; ptnr. Sussman, Sollis, Ebin, Tweedy & Wood, LLP, NYC, 1995—2006; sr. counsel Sussman, Sollis, Tweedy & Wood, LLP, 2006—07; of counsel Wrobel & Schatz, LLP, NYC, 2007—. Instr. continuing legal edn. U. Houston, Nat. Inst. for Trial Advocacy; 1985-89, Stockholm, 2003-. Editor Columbia U. Law Rev., 1960-62; contbr. articles to profl. jours. Harlan Fiske Stone scholar, 1959-61, Edvard Cassels Stiftelse vis. scholar, Stockholm, 1962-63; travelling fellow Parker Sch. Fgn. and Comparative Law Columbia U., 1962-63. Mem. Assn. Bar City N.Y. (com. adminstrv. law 1974-76, profl. conf. 1979, com. fed. legis. 1984-87, com. criminal law 1987-90, com. lectr. and continuing edn. 1990-93, com. fgn. and comparative law 1993-96, arbitration com. 2002-2003), Fed. Bar Coun., Swedish Am. C. of C. (dir. N.Y. chpt. 1996—). Clubs: Princeton N.Y. Office Phone: 212-688-7373. Business E-Mail: ssetwsussman@msn.com.

SUSSMAN, JANET I., social sciences educator; b. NYC, Sept. 24, 1952; d. Joseph I. and Selma H. Sussman. BA, Douglas Coll., 1974. Pub. Harcourt Brace, NYC, 1974—76, Van Nostrand Reinhold, NYC, 1975—77, Sky & Telescope Mag., Cambridge, Mass., 1977—80, Wholistic Edn. & Svcs., Inc., Charlotte, NC, 1984—90, No. Star Dimensions, Charlotte, 1986—; pub., cons. Time Portal Pubs., Fairfield, Iowa, 1993—. Author: Timeshift: The Experience of Dimensional Change, 1996, The Reality of Time, 2005; musician: (CD) Bridges, 2002, Subtle Bodies, 2007. E-mail: timeport@lisco.com.

SUSSMAN, JEFFREY BRUCE, public relations and marketing executive; b. NYC, Mar. 15, 1943; m. Suzy Hirschland-Prudden, 1964 (div. 1981); 1 child, Robert; m. Barbara Ramsay, 1984. BA in English, NYU, 1969. Pres. Suzy Prudden Studios, NYC, 1975—81; v.p. Zachary and Front, NYC, 1981—88; pres. Jeffrey Sussman, Inc., NYC, 1988—, Sweet Silver Prodns., 2005—. Instr. mktg. New Sch. U., NYC. Author: Creative Fitness for Baby and Child, 1972, Suzy Prudden's Family Fitness Book, 1975, Fit for Life, 1977, See How They Run, 1978, Suzy Prudden's Spot Reducing Program, 1979, Suzy Prudden's Pregnancy and Back-To-Shape Exercise Program, 1980, I Can Exercise Anywhere, 1981, How to Sleep Without Drugs, 1986, Power Promoting: How to Market Your Business to the Top!, 1997; book rev. editor The Manhattan Tribune, 1969-75; contbr. book revs. to N.Y. Times Book Rev., 1974; bi-monthly columnist Weight Watchers Mag., 1977-79; monthly columnist Fortune Small Business, 2000—; contbr. articles to profl. jours. including Bottom Line Bus., Independent Bus., Small Bus. Report, N.Y. Real Estate Jour., East Hampton Star, M World mag. Press sec. NYC Coun.-Henry Stern, 1981; pvt. sec. to Nobel prize winning author Isaac Bashevis Singer. Avocations: photography, writing, music, painting, drawing. Home and Office: 249 E 48th St New York NY 10017-1526 Office Phone: 212-421-4475. Personal E-mail: marketingpro@aol.com.

SUSSMAN, JOSEPH, engineering educator, researcher; BCE, City Coll. NY; MSCE, U. NH; PhD, MIT. Dir. ctr. transp. & logistics MIT, Cambridge, Mass., 1986—91, JR East prof. civil & environ. engrng. & engrng. systems. Author: (book) Introduction to Transportation Systems, 2000, Perspectives on Intelligent Transportation Systems, 2005. Recipient Effective Teaching award, MIT Dept. Civil & Environ. Engrng., 1997, Tech. Leadership award, Move Mass. 2000, 1998, Disting. Contbn. award, Coun. Univ. Transp. Ctrs., 2003. Mem.: ASCE, Intelligent Transp. Systems Mass. (bd. dirs. 1996—2001, ann. Joseph M. Sussman Leadership award instituted 2002), Intelligent Transp. Systems Am. (bd. dirs. 1995—2001), Transp. Rsch. Bd. (exec. com. mem. 1991—98, exec. com. chmn. 1994, Roy W. Crum award for Disting. Rsch. 2002), Transp. Rsch. Forum, Am. Soc. Engrng. Edn., Boston Soc. Civil Engrs. (life). Achievements include development of new methodology for regional strategic transportation planning, ReS/SITE (Regional Strategies for the Sustainable Intermodal Transportation Enterprise); Complex, Large-Scale, Integrated, Open Systems (CLIOS) process; worked extensively on intelligent transportation systems in the U.S., Bangkok, Western Europe and Japan. Office: Mass Inst Tech Bldg 1-163 77 Massachusetts Ave Cambridge MA 02139-4307 Office Phone: 317-253-4430. Business E-Mail: sussman@mit.edu.

SUSSMAN, LAUREEN GLICKLIN, retired elementary school educator; b. NYC, Mar. 21, 1953; d. Harry and Ruth (Goldstein) G.; m. Alan Neil Sussman, May 30, 1977; children: David Efrem, Adam Jacob, Daniel Joshua. BA, Bklyn. Coll., 1974; MS, MSc, Hofstra U., 1998. Cert. tchr. nursery-6, spl. edn. tchr. all grades. Sec. McCann-Erickson, Inc., NYC, 1974-75; adminstrv. asst., tour operator EasTours divsn. Fgn. Tours, NYC, 1975-78; adminstrv. asst. Alan N. Sussman, CPA, Woodmere, NY, 1978-96; kindergarten tchr. Hebrew Acad. Long Beach (N.Y.), 1996-97; jr. HS tchr. Torah Acad. Girls, Far Rockaway, NY, 1997—2007; ret., 2007. Participant Instrumental Enrichment/IRI Skylight, N.Y., 1995, 98, Dynamic Assessment project Touro Coll., N.Y.C., 1996; CSE parent rep., adv.

Lawrence (N.Y.) Pub. Schs., 1992-97; trainer Life Tech., Cedarhurst, N.Y., 2004—05. Contbr. articles to profl. jours. Mem. Spl. Edn. PTA Lawrence Schs., 1986-2003, Sisterhood Congregation Bais Tefilah, 1990-2003; mem. Sisterhood East Meadow Jewish Ctr., chair social action, Israel affairs, 1979-81; mem. adv. bd. Kulanu of the South Shore of Nassau County, 2000—; mem. Sisterhood Kehillah Aish Kodesh, Emunah of Am. Mem.: AMIT Women (Masada chpt.), OTSAR (founder Nassau County chpt. 1987—, nat. bd. dirs., pres. Nassau chpt. 1987—2002). Democrat. Avocations: Israeli and simcha dancing, walking, reading, needlepoint. Office: Torah Acad Girls 444 Beach 6 St Far Rockaway NY 11691 Personal E-mail: lauglick@aol.com.

SUSSMAN, LEONARD RICHARD, foundation executive; b. NYC, Nov. 26, 1920; s. Jacob and Carrie (Marks) S.; m. Frances Rukeyser, May 9, 1942 (div. 1958); m. Marianne Rita Gutmann, May 28, 1958; children: Lynne, David William, Mark Jacob. AB, NYU, 1940; MS in Journalism, Columbia U., 1941. Copy editor N.Y. Morning Telegraph, news editor radio sta. WQXR, 1941; cable editor San Juan (P.R.) World Jour., also corr. Business Week mag., 1941-42; editor fgn. broadcast intelligence svc. FCC, 1942; press sec. to Gov. of P.R., 1942-43; dir. info. in N.Y. for Govt. of P.R., 1946-49; regional dir., then nat. exec. dir. Am. Coun. Judaism, 1949-66; cons. pub. affairs cons. Nationwide Ins. Cos. (and indsl. subs.), 1955-57; mem. editorial com. Coun. Liberal Chs., 1956-59; exec. dir. Freedom House, 1967-88, 96, sr. scholar in internat. communications, 1988—; evaluator Fulbright Program Bd. Fgn. Scholarships, 1990-92; exec. dir. Willkie Meml., 1970-88. Adj. prof. journalsim and mass comm. NYU, N.Y.C., 1990-99; adj. prof. Sch. for Internat. and Pub. Affairs, Columbia U., 2000-01; organizer, dir. Freedom House/Books USA, 1968-85; editor Freedom at Issue, bimonthly, 1970-81; mem. U.S. Dels. to Conf. World Communicaiton Yr./83, 1982-83; organizer acad. confs.; participant Internat. Conf. on Press Freedom, Venice, Italy, 1976, 77, Cairo, 1978, Talloires, 1981, 83, San Jose, Costa Rica, Johannesburg, and Santiago Chile, 1987, others; panel competition in space Congl. Office Tech. Assessment, 1982-83. Author: American Press-Under Siege?, 1973, Mass News Media and The Third World Challenge, 1977, Glossary for International Communications: Warning of a Bloodless Dialect, 1983, Spanish version, 1987, Power, The Press and the Technology of Freedom: The Coming of Age of ISDN, 1990, The Culture of Freedom: The Small World of Fulbright Scholars, 1992, Good News Bad News, 1994, Can A Free Press Be Responsible? To Whom?, 1995, The Press: Pressed and Oppressed, 1995, The Journalist as Pariah: Press Freedom, 1996, The Global Airscape, 1996, Democracy, Yes; Press Freedom, Maybe, 1997, Press Law Epidemic: Press Freedom, 1997, Global Warning: Press Controls Fuel the Asian Debacle, 1998, The News of the Century, 1999, Censor Dot Gov: The Internet and Press Freedom, 2000, Press Freedom in Our Genes, A Human Need, 2001, How Free? The Web and the Press, 2001, Democracy's Advocate: The Story of Freedom House, 2002, The Press at War: Marksman and Target, 2002, repub. in Freedom and Responsibility Yearbook, 2001-2002, A Global Survey of Media Independence, 2003, A Passion for Freedom: My Encounters with Extraordinary People, 2004, Historic Aspects of Freedom of the Press and New World Information and Communication in the Encyclopedia of International Media and Communications, 2003, The Unesco Withdrawral Syndrome: Shoot The UN in Americans for UNESCO, 2005, Footnotes to Freedom: 8 Decades of Striving, 2007; editor: Three Years at the East-West Divide, 1983, Today's American: How Free?, 1986; contbr. chpts. to books, articles to profl. jours. and newspapers; project dir.: Big Story-How the American Press and Television Reported and Interpreted the Crisis of Tet-1968 in Vietnam and Washington, 1977; editor: textbook series, also quar. mag. Issues, 1953-66; mem. editl. bd. Polit. Comm. and Persuasion. Trustee Internat. Coun. on Future of Univ., 1973-84; bd. dirs. World Press Freedom Com., 1977—; chmn. Friends of Survey Mag. Charitable Trust, London, 1978-92; mem. U.S. Nat. Commn. for UNESCO, 1979-85, vice chmn., 1983-85; mem. U.S. dels. to internat. conf. on space, African Aid, UNESCO, London Info. Forum; mem. Internat. Freedom of Expression Exch., 1995-2003, mem. coun., 1997-99. 2001-2002. Decorated Legion of Merit; recipient Ann. First Amendment award N.Y. br. Soc. Profl. Journalists, 1988. Mem. Internat. Inst. Comm., Internat. Press Inst., Internat. Assn. Mass Comm. Rsch., Century Club. Home: 215 E 73d St New York NY 10021-3653 Office: 120 Wall St Fl 26 New York NY 10005-3904 Business E-Mail: sussman@freedomhouse.org.

SUSSMAN, MARK RICHARD, lawyer; b. Bklyn., Feb. 4, 1952; s. Vincent E. and Rhoda (Urowsky) S.; m. Lisa Rosner, June 8, 1975; children: Corey, Randi, Samuel. BS in Civil Engring., Tufts U., 1974; JD, U. Pa., 1977. Bar: Pa. 1977, D.C. 1980, Conn. 1981. Trial atty. land and natural resources div. U.S. Dept. Justice, Washington, 1977-81; assoc. Murtha, Cullina, Richter & Pinney, Hartford, Conn., 1981-86, ptnr., 1987—; chmn. environ. dept. Murtha Cullina LLP, Hartford, Conn., 1990—. Gov.'s blue ribbon panel to evaluate environtl. permit programs, 1996. Chmn. conservation commn. Windsor, Conn., 1984-2000; mem. Conn. Hazardous Waste Mgmt. Service Recycling Task Force, 1986, Legis. Task Force on Environ. Permitting, 1992, Conn. State Implementation Plan Revision Adv. Com., 1984—. Mem. ABA (natural resources sect.), Conn. Bar Assn. (chmn. conservation and environ. quality sect. 1984-87, faculty continuing legal edn.), Conn. Bus. and Industry Assn. (steering com. environ. policies coun. 1990-93, 98—) Tau Beta Pi. Home: 62 Timothy Ter Windsor CT 06095-1652 Office: Murtha Cullina LLP City Pl 185 Asylum St Ste 29 Hartford CT 06103-3469 Home Phone: 860-688-1994; Office Phone: 203-240-6034. E-mail: msussman@murthalaw.com. *Notable cases include: Mumford Cove Assn. v. Town of Groton, 786 F. 2d 530, 640 F. Supp 392, 647 F. Supp. 671, 1986, represented homeowners assn. in Clean Water Act citizens's suit to force municipality to relocate sewer discharge pipe; City of Shelton v. Commr. of Environ. Protection, 193 Conn. 506, 1984, represented the Conn. Resources Recovery Authority in obtaining and defending permits for a solid waste landfill, Conn. Coastal Fishermen's Assn. v. Remington Arms Co., Inc., 989 F 2d 1302 (2d cir. 1993), represented defendant in Clean Water Act & RCRA citizens suit which found, in part, that lead shot may be considered a hazardous waste subject to remediation under RCRA statutory definition of hazardous waste.*

SUSSMAN, MONICA HILTON, lawyer; b. NYC, Apr. 2, 1952; BA cum laude, Syracuse U., 1973; JD, Hofstra U., 1977. Bar: Va. 1977, DC 1978. Legis. coun. NY State Gov's. Office, Washington, 1977-79; spl. asst. to under sec. US Dept. HUD, Washington, 1979-80, br. chief office State Agy. and Bond Fin. programs, 1980-82, office gen. counsel, 1982-83, also bd. dirs., 1988-95, v.p., 1989-93, treas. Nat. Housing Conf., 1990-93, pres. Nat. Housing Conf., 1997—2000, also programs and regulations dep. gen. counsel; ptnr. McDermott, Will & Emery, Washington, Peabody & Brown, Washington, 1996-99, Nixon Peadoby LLP, Washington, 1999—. Mem.: ABA, Mortgage Bankers Assn., Nat Leased Housing Assn., Va. State Bar, DC Bar Assn. Office: Nixon Peabody LLP 401 9th St NW Ste 900 Washington DC 20004 Office Fax: 202-585-8080. E-mail: msussman@nixonpeabody.com.

SUSSMAN, RICHARD, music educator, composer; b. Phila., Pa., Feb. 28, 1946; s. Rudolph and Helen Sussman; m. Barbara Rice, Apr. 3, 1993. BA, Empire State Coll., 1982—84; MM, Manhattan Sch. of Music, 1984—85. Faculty Manhattan Sch. of Music, New York, NY, 1987—; musician Donna Summer Band, 1993—96; pianist Blood, Sweat, & Tears, 1984—86, Lionel Hampton Band, 1977—78. Composer: (orchestral jazz) Dialogue for Jazz Band and Orchestra, Suite for Jazz Band and Orchestra #2, Suite for Jazz Band and Orchestra #1; musician (musician/composer): (jazz recording) Free Fall, Tributaries; composer: (jazz big band arrangement) Fletcher. Mem.: BMI, NATAS, NARAS, Am. Fedn. of Musicians. Home: 215 Elm Street Nyack NY 10960 Office: Union Street Music 215 Elm Street Nyack NY 10960 Home Phone: 845-358-9060; Office Phone: 845-358-9060. Fax: 845 358-9060. E-mail: rsussman@dti.net.

SUSSNA, EDWARD, economist, educator; b. Phila., Nov. 26, 1926; s. Louis and Manya (Prytzycka) Sussna; m. Sylvia Fishman, Mar. 8, 1953; children: Audrey Francine, Ellen Sondra. BA, Bklyn. Coll., 1950; MA, U. Ill., 1952, PhD, 1954. Instr. U. Ill., 1952-54; asst. prof. Lehigh U., 1956-57; prof. bus. adminstrn. and econs. U. Pitts., 1957—; dir. ctr. for exec. edn. Grad. Sch. Bus. U. Pitts., 1983-89; dir. mgmt. program for execs. Center for Econ. Edn., Grad. Sch. Bus., acad. dir. study program in Hong Kong and Peoples Republic China, spring 1989, 95; inaugural prof. MBA program Bratislava Sch. Econs., Slovakia, 1996. Vis. Fulbright prof. U. Tehran, Iran, adviser, 1972—73; cons. Bur. Budget, HEW, Dept. Transp., UN Indsl. Devel. Orgn., Bell Tel. Co., Alcoa, Westinghouse Corp., NSF, Pitts. Nat. Bank, Japanese Regional Bankers Assn., others; vis. prof. UCLA, 1970, Ecole Superieure des Scis. Economiques et Commerciales, Paris, 1976—77, U. E. Asia, Hong Kong, Macau, 1986; vis. scholar Internat. Inst. Mgmt., Berlin, 1982. Contbr. articles to profl. jours. With U.S. Mcht. Marine, 1944—47, with US Army, 1954—56. Ford Found. Fellowship Vis. prof., Harvard, 1960—61, Ford Found. Fellowship Guest scholar, Brookings Instn., 1962—63. Mem.: Strategic Mgmt. Inst., Am. Fin. Assn., Am. Econ. Assn., Omicron Delta, Beta Gamma Sigma. Home: 1538 S Negley Ave Pittsburgh PA 15217-1420 Personal E-mail: sussna@katz.pitt.edu.

SUSTANA, MARK, lawyer, construction executive; Grad., U. NC. Positions up to chief legal officer, corp. sec. GenTek, Inc., 1998—2005; sec., gen. counsel Lennar Corp., Miami, Fla., 2005—. Office: Lennar Corp 700 NW 107th Ave Ste 400 Miami FL 33172 Office Phone: 305-559-4000. Office Fax: 305-228-8383. E-mail: mark.sustana@lennar.com. *

SUSTAR, T. DAVID, religious organization administrator; Pres. East Coast Bible Coll., Ch. of God, Charlotte, NC, 1996-99; evangelism and home missions dir. Western N.C. Ch. of God, Charlotte, 1999—2002; sr. pastor Easley Ch. God, Easley, SC, 2004—. Pentecostal. Home: 100 Muirfield Dr Easley SC 29642-2414 Office: PO Box 443 Easley SC 29641 Office Phone: 864-859-1631. Personal E-mail: tdsustar@bellsouth.net.

SUTARDJA, SEHAT, information technology executive; b. China; m. Weili Dai; 2 children. BSEE, U. Calif., Berkeley, MS in Elec. Engring. and Computer Sci., PhD in Elec. Engring. and Computer Sci., U. Calif., Berkeley. Mgr., prin. project engr. 8X8, Inc., 1989—95; co-founder Marvell Semiconductor Inc., chmn., pres., CEO, 1995—. Named one of 400 Richest Ams., Forbes mag., 2006. Office: Marvell Semiconductor Inc 5488 Marvell Ln Santa Clara CA 95054

SUTCLIFFE, RICK (RICHARD LEE SUTCLIFFE), professional baseball player; b. Independence, Mo., June 21, 1956; m. Robin Ross. Profl. baseball player Los Angeles Dodgers, 1976-81, Cleve. Indians, 1982-84, Chgo. Cubs, 1984—91, Balt. Orioles, 1992—93, St. Louis Cardinals, 1994; sportscaster, and baseball analyst ESPN, 2000—. Mem. Am. League All-Star Team, 1983, Nat. League All-Star Team, 1989; recipient Cy Young award Nat. League, 1984. Office: ESPN ESPN Plz 935 Middle St Bristol CT 06010

SUTER, ROBERT EDUARD, emergency physician, educator; b. Decatur, Ill., Aug. 29, 1961; s. Robert Koester and Erika Ilse Suter; children: Robert E. Jr., Joseph E., Jennifer E. B, Washington U., 1982; M in Healthcare Adminstrn., Des Moines U., 1980, D of Osteopathy, 1989. Diplomate Am. Bd. Emergency Medicine. Chmn. emergency svcs. Eisenhower Army Med. Ctr., Ft. Stewart, Ga., 1993—95, Providence Hosp. and Med. Ctrs., Detroit, 1995—97; regional med. dir. Questcare Med. Svcs., Dallas, 1997—2001; chmn. emergency dept. Spring Br. Med. Ctr., Houston, 2001. Pres. Tex. Emergency Physicians; prof. Med. Coll. Ga., U. Tex. S.W. Bd. dirs. alumni assn. Des Moines U. Col. US Army, 1978—. Recipient Founders award, Continuing Edn. Coord. Bd. for EMS, 2004, Wackerle Founders award, Emergency Medicine Residents Assn., 1998, Alumnus of the Yr., Des Moines U., 2005. Fellow: Am. Coll. Osteopathic Emergency Physicians, Am. Coll. Emergency Physicians (pres. bd. dirs. 2001—); mem.: Energy Medicine Found. (chair 2006), Internat. Fedn. Emergency Medicine (pres. 2006), Soc. for Academic Emergency Medicine. Cath. Mailing: P O Box 670785 Dallas TX 75367 Home: 5926 St Marks Cir Dallas TX 75230

SUTERA, SALVATORE PHILIP, mechanical engineer, educator; b. Balt., Jan. 12, 1933; s. Philip and Ann (D'Amico) S.; m. Celia Ann Fielden, June 21, 1958; children: Marie-Anne, Annette Nicole, Michelle Cecile. BS in Mech. Engring, Johns Hopkins, 1954; postgrad., U. Paris, 1955-56; MS, Calif. Inst. Tech., 1955; PhD, Cal. Inst. Tech., 1960; MA (hon.), Brown U., 1965. Asst. prof. mech. engring. Brown U., Providence, 1960-65, asso. prof., 1965-68, exec. officer div. engring., 1966-68; prof. dept. mech. engring. Washington U., St. Louis, 1968-97, chmn. dept., 1968-82, 86-97, Spencer T. Olin prof. engring. and applied sci., 1997—2003, prof. biomed. engring., 1997—2003, sr. prof., 2003—07. Vis. prof. U. Paris VI, 1973. Assoc. editor: Jour. Biomech. Engring., 1993-97; mem. editorial bd. Circulation Rsch., 1975-82. Pres. St. Louis-Lyon Sister Cities, Inc., 2000—. Fulbright fellow Paris, 1955; recipient Nat. Marconi Sci. award UNICO, 1999. Fellow ASME, Am. Inst. of Med and Biol. Engring. (founding); mem. Biomed. Engring. Soc. (bd. dirs. 1997-2000), Internat. Soc. Biorheology, N.Am. Soc. Biorheology (pres.-elect 1986-89, pres. 1989-90), Am. Soc. Artificial Internal Organs, Am. Soc. Engring. Edn., AAAS (Lindbergh award St. Louis sect. 1988), AIAA, European Acad. Sci., Tau Beta Pi, Pi Tau Sigma. Republican. Roman Catholic. Achievements include research in fluid mechanics, heat transfer, blood flow, rheology of suspensions. Home: 830 S Meramec Ave Saint Louis MO 63105-2539 Business E-Mail: sps@wustl.edu.

SUTHERLAND, ALAN ROY, business educator; b. NYC, Jan. 15, 1944; s. Arthur Abbott and Margaret Louise S. BFA, Pratt Inst., Bklyn., 1964; MPA, NYU, 1969, PhD, 1984. Personnel dir. Manhattan Psychiat. Ctr., NYC, 1966-72; dep. dir. Rockland Children's Psychiat. Ctr., Orangeburg, NY, 1972-74, L.I. Devel. Ctr., Melville, NY, 1974-78, dir., 1978-80; program dir. Vols. Am., NYC, 1983-86; sr. staff officer Nat. Acad. Scis., Washington, 1986-88; dep. dir. U.S. Interagy. Coun. on Homeless, Washington, 1988-89; exec. dir. Travelers Aid Internat., Washington, 1989-91, AIDS Ctr. of Queens County, Rego Park, NY, 1992-96; chair dept. mgmt. studies Southeastern U., Washington, 1998-99. Prof. U. Md., College Park, 1998—. Editor: Homlessness, Health and Human Service Needs. Recipient citation N.Y.C. Coun., 1986, Stanley J. Drazak Excellence in Tchg. award U. Md., 2004. Mem. ASPA, World Futurist Soc. Lutheran. Avocation: weightlifting. Home: 1301 Delaware Ave SW #N-806 Washington DC 20024 Office: Univ of Maryland 3501 University Blvd E Adelphi MD 20783-7998

SUTHERLAND, ALLAN C., engineering executive; BS in Accountancy, U. Ill., Urbana-Champaign, 1985; MS in Taxation, DePaul U., Chgo. Sr. mgr. tax dept. Ernst & Young; mgr. fed. tax Ill. Tool Works Inc. (ITW), Glenview, Ill., 1993, dir. worldwide tax planning, v.p. leasing and investments, 1996—98, sr. v.p. leasing and investments, 1998—. Mem. commerce coun. U. Ill. Coll. Bus. and Adminstrn.; mem. fin. adv. coun. DePaul U. Mem.: AICPA, Ill. CPA Soc., Execs.' Club Chgo. Office: Ill Tool Works 3600 W Lake Ave Glenview IL 60026-1215 Office Phone: 847-724-7500. Office Fax: 847-657-4572. *

SUTHERLAND, BETSY MIDDLETON, biologist; m. John C. Sutherland, Aug. 28, 1965. BS, Emory U., 1964, MS, 1965; PhD, U. Tenn., 1967. Postdoctoral fellow Walter Reed Army Med. Ctr., Washington, 1967—69, U. Calif., Berkeley, 1969—72, asst. prof. Irvine, 1972—75, assoc. prof., 1975—77; sr. scientist Brookhaven Nat. Lab., Upton, NY, 1977—, head biology dept., radiobiology support group. Named to Alumni Hall of Fame, U. Tenn., Knoxville; recipient Outstanding Svc. to Sci. award, Suffolk County, NY, E. O. Lawrence award, U.S. Dept. Energy, 1985, Rsch. Career Devel. award, NIH; grad. fellow, Emory U., 1964—65, Oak Ridge Associated Universities, 1965—67. Achievements include patents in field. Office: Brookhaven Nat Lab Bldg 463 Biology 50 Bell Ave Upton NY 11973-5000 Office Phone: 631-344-3380.

SUTHERLAND, DONALD, actor; b. St. John, NB, Can., July 17, 1935; m. Lois Hardwick, 1959 (div. 1966); m. Shirley Douglas, 1966. (div. 1970); children: Kiefer, Rachel; m. Francine Racette, 1972; children: Roeg, Rossif, Angus. Grad., U. Toronto, 1958. Actor: London Acad. Music and Dramatic Art, Perth Repertory Theatre, Scotland, also Nottingham, Chesterfield, Bronley, Sheffield, (plays) The Spoon River Anthology, The Male Animal, The Tempest, August for People (London debut), On a Clear Day You Can See Canterbury, The Shewing Up a Blanco Posnet, Enigma Variations, 2000, Ten Unknowns, 2001 (films) The World Ten Times Over, 1963, The Castle of the Living Dead, 1964, Dr. Terror's House of Horrors, 1965, Fanatic, 1965, The Bedford Incident, 1965, Promise Her Anything, 1966, The Dirty Dozen, 1967, Billion Dollar Brain, 1967, Oedipus the King, 1967, Sebastian, 1968, Interlude, 1968, Joanna, 1968, The Split, 1968, Start the Revolution Without Me, 1970, The Act of the Heart, 1970, M*A*S*H, 1970, Kelly's Heroes, 1970, Alex in Wonderland, 1970, Little Murders, 1971, Klute, 1971, Johnny Got His Gun, 1971, Lady Ice, 1973, Steelyard Blues, 1973, Don't Look Now, 1973, Alien Thunder, 1974, S*P*Y*S, 1974, The Day of the Locust, 1975, End of the Game, 1975, Fellini's Casanova, 1976, 1900, 1976, The Eagle Has Landed, 1976, The Kentucky Fried Chicken Movie, 1977, The Disappearance, 1977, Blood Relatives, 1978, Animal House, 1978, Invasion of the Body Snatchers, 1978, The Great Train Robbery, 1979, Murder by Decree, 1979, Bear Island, 1979, A Man, A Woman and a Bank, 1979, North China Commune (voice), 1980, Nothing Personal, 1980, Ordinary People, 1980, Eye of the Needle, 1981, Gas, 1981, The Disappearance, Blood Relative, Threshold, 1981, Max Dugan Returns, 1983, Crackers, 1984, Heaven Help Us, 1985, Revolution, 1985, The Wolf at the Door, 1986, The Trouble with Spies, 1987, The Rosary Murders, 1987, Apprentice to Murder, 1988, Lock Up, 1989, Lost Angels, 1989, A Dry White Season, 1989, Bethune: The Making of a Hero, 1990, Buster's Bedroom, 1991, Backdraft, 1991, JFK, 1991, Eminent Domain, 1991, Cerro Torre: Schrei aus Stein, 1991, Buffy the Vampire Slayer, 1992, The Setting Sun, 1992, Shadow of the Wolf, 1992, The Railway Station Man, 1992, Younger and Younger, 1993, Six Degrees of Separation, 1993, The Shadow Catcher (voice), 1993, Red Hot, 1993, Benefit of the Doubt, 1993, Punch, 1994, The Puppet Masters, 1994, Disclosure, 1994, Outbreak, 1995, Bethune: The Making of a Hero, 1990, FTA, A Time to Kill, 1996, Hollow Point, 1996, The Shadow Conspiracy, 1997, The Assignment, 1997, Fallen, 1997, Without Limits, 1998, Free Money, 1998, Toscano, 1999, CSS Hunley, 1999, Virus, 1999, Instinct, 1999, Panic, 2000, Space Cowboys, 2000, The Art of War, 2000, Threads of Hope (voice), 2000, Final Fantasy: The Spirit Within(voice), 2001, Da wan, 2001, Five Moons Plaza, 2003, The Italian Job, 2003, Baltic Storm, 2003, Cold Mountain, 2003, Aurora Borealis, 2005, Fierce People, 2005, Pride & Prejudice, 2005, Lord of War, 2005, An American Haunting, 2005, Land of the Blind, 2006, Ask the Dust, 2006, Beerfest, 2006, Sleepwalkers, 2007, Reign Over Me, 2007; (TV films) Terry-Thomas, 1963, Marching to the Sea, Hamlet at Elsinore, 1964, The Death of Bessie Smith, 1965, The American Civil War, 1965, The Sunshine Patriot, 1968, Bethune, 1977, The Saint, The Avengers, Gideon's Way, The Champions, The Winter of Our Discontent, 1984, Ordeal By Innocence, 1984, Quicksand: No Escape, 1992, The Lifeforce Experiment, 1994, Oldest Living Confederate Widow Tells All, 1994, Citizen X, 1995 (Emmy award), Natural Enemy, 1997, Behind the Mask, 1999, The Hunley, 1999, The Big Heist, 2001, Uprising, 2001, Path to War, 2002, Salem's Lot, 2004, Frankenstein, 2004; (TV mini series) A Farewell to Arms, 1966; (TV series) Commander in Chief, 2005-06; guest appearance Suspense, 1963, Gideon's Way, 1965, The Saint, 1965, 1966, Man in a Suitcase, 1967, 1968, The Name of the Game, 1969, (voice) The Simpsons, 1996 and others; narrator The Poky Little Puppy's First Christmas, 1992; exec. prodr. Steelyard Blues, 1973. Decorated officier dans l'Ordre des Artes et des Lettres (France); officer Order of Can. Office: c/o Creative Artists Agy Katherine Olin 9830 Wilshire Blvd Beverly Hills CA 90212-1804 *

SUTHERLAND, DONALD SINCLAIR, music educator, musician; b. Kearny, NJ, May 27, 1939; s. Sinclair Ross Watt and Helen Angus Sutherland; m. Phyllis May Brynjulson, June 7, 1968; children: David Alan, Kaaren Sutherland Lally. MusB, Syracuse U., NY, 1961, MusM, 1963. Faculty Sch. of Music Syracuse (N.Y.) U., 1963—71; coord. Organ Dept. Peabody Conservatory Johns Hopkins U., Balt., 1975—. Adj. faculty Hamilton Coll., Clinton, NY, 1970—71. Musician: Nat. Symphony Orch., Balt. (Md.) Symphony, City London (Eng.) Symphonia, Athenee Theatre, Queen Elizabeth Hall, Notre Dame, Stephandsdom, Westminster Abbey. Fund raiser Bethesda (Md.) Cares, 1984—99; dir. music ministries Bradley Hills Presbyn. Ch., Bethesda, Md., 1969—71; organist, choir master First Universalist Ch., Syracuse, 1962—71. Recipient Disting. Alumni award, Syracuse U., 1988, Excellance in Tchg. award, Johns Hopkins U., 1997, Recognition and Appreciation award, The County Exec. of Montgomery County, Md., 1999. Mem.: Am. Guild Organists (sec. 2002—, dean Syracuse (N.Y.) chpt. 1968—70, dean D.C. chpt. 1978—80), Pi Kappa Lambda. Home: 721 Tobacco Run Drive Bel Air MD 21015-1331 Office: Peabody Institute of the Johns Hopkins U 1 East Mount Vernon Place Baltimore MD 21202 Home Phone: 410-734-4273; Office Phone: 410-659=8100 x.1359.

SUTHERLAND, DONALD WOOD, retired cardiologist; b. Kansas City, Mo., July 29, 1932; s. Donald Redeker and Mary Frances (Wood) S.; m. Margaret Sutherland, Sept. 11, 1954 (div. 1994); children: Kathleen Sutherland, Ellen Baltus, Richard, Ann, Julia McMurchie; m. Roslyn Ruggiero Elms, Mar. 31, 1995. BA, Amherst Coll., 1953; MD, Harvard U., 1957. Intern, resident Mass. Gen. Hosp., Boston, 1957-60; fellow in cardiology U. Oreg., Portland, 1961-63; pvt. practice Portland, 1963—2006; ret. Assoc. clin. prof. medicine Oreg. Health Sci. U., Portland, 1967—; chief of staff St. Vincent Hosp. and Med. Ctr., Portland, 1971-72. Contbr. articles to profl. jours. Fellow Am. Heart Assn., Am. Coll. Cardiology (pres. Oreg. chpt. 1972); mem. Multnomah Athletic Club, North Pacific Soc. Internal Medicine (pres. 1985), Pacific Interurban Clin. Club (pres. 2000). Avocations: flying, scuba diving. Home: 4405 SW Council Crest Dr Portland OR 97239 Personal E-mail: dwscardio@comcast.net.

SUTHERLAND, IVAN E., computer scientist; b. Hastings, Nebr., May 16, 1938; children: Juliet, Dean. BSEE, Carnegie Inst. Tech., 1959; MSEE, Calif. Inst. Tech., 1960; PhD in Elec. Engring., MIT, 1963; MA (hon.), Harvard U., 1966. Elec. engr., 1st lt. Nat. Security Agy., 1963; dir. office info. processing techniques Advance Rsch. Projects Agy., 1964-66; prof. elec. engring. Harvard U., 1966-68, U. Utah, Salt Lake City, 1968—73; co-founder Evans & Sutherland, 1968; rschr. Rand Corp., 1975; chmn. dept. computer sci. Calif. Inst. Tech., 1976—80; established, v.p., Tech. dir. Sutherland, Sproull, and Assocs., 1980; fellow, v.p. Sun Microsystems Lab., Menlo Park, Calif., 1990—. Honored guest spkr., elec. engring. computer sci. dept. U. Calif. Berkeley, 2006; spkr. in field. Contbr. articles to profl. publs. Recipient Smithsonian Price Waterhouse Info. Tech. Leadership award for Lifetime Achievement, Fellow award, Computer

History Mus., 2005; co-recipient, R&D 100 award, 2004. Fellow Assn. Computing Machinery (A.M. Turing award 1988); mem. NAE (First Zworkin award 1972), NAS, IEEE (John von Neumann medal 1998). Achievements include pioneer in computer graphics; inventor of computer program, known as Sketchpad, and head-mounted three-dimensional display, an integral part of many virtual reality systems; several patents in field. Office: Sun Microsystems Lab 16 Network Cir umpk16-161 Menlo Park CA 94025

SUTHERLAND, J.J., journalist; b. Bourne, Mass., June 10, 1969; s. Jeffrey Victor and Arline (Conan) S.; m. Lisa Kaarina Koopman, Feb. 13, 1993 (div. Mar. 1994), m. Verónica María Ruiz Contreras, Oct. 2002. Student, Carnegie Mellon U., 1988-89, Harvard U., 1989-94. Asst. prodr. WBUR, Boston, 1991-92, assoc. prodr., 1992-94; prodr., dir. The Connection, Boston, 1994; prodr. On the Media, NYC; with NPR, 2000—. Prodr. (radio show) The Campaign Connection, 1996. Recipient 2 Peabody awards, Alfred I duPont-Columbia U. award for Coverage of Iraq, 2007. Mem. Dark Tree. Avocations: reading, writing, chess. Office: NPR 635 Massachusetts Ave NW Washington DC 20001 *

SUTHERLAND, KIEFER, actor; b. London, Eng., Dec. 21, 1966; s. Donald and Shirley Douglas S.; m. Camelia Kath, Sept. 12, 1987 (div.1990); 1 child, Sarah Jude; m. Kelly Winn, June 29, 1996 (div.) Appearances include (theater) debut in Throne of Straw, 1977, (films) Max Dugan Returns, 1983, The Bay Boy, 1984 (Genie award nominee 1984), At Close Range, 1986, Crazy Moon, 1986, Stand By Me, 1986, The Lost Boys, 1987, The Killing Time, 1987, Promised Land, 1987, 1969, 1988, Bright Lights, Big City, 1988, Young Guns, 1988, Renegades, 1989, Chicago Joe and the Showgirl, 1990, Flashback, 1990, Flatliners, 1990, The Nutcracker Prince (voice), 1990, Young Guns II, 1990, Article 99, 1991, Twin Peaks: Fire Walk With Me, 1992, A Few Good Men, 1992, The Vanishing, 1993, The Three Musketeers, 1993, The Cowboy Way, 1994, Eye for an Eye, 1995, A Time to Kill, 1996, The Last Days of Frankie the Fly, 1996, Freeway, 1996, Truth or Consequences N.M, 1997, Dark City, 1997, Sweetheart of the Song Tra Bong, 1998, Ground Control, 1998, (voice) Dinosaur, 1998, The Breakup, 1998, Dark City, 1998, Woman Wanted, 1999, The Red Dove, 1999, Hearts and Bones, 1999, Beat, 2000, Picking Up the Pieces, 2000, Ring of Fire, 2000, The Royal Way, 2000, The Right Temptation, 2000, To End All Wars, 2001, Paradise Found, 2001, Desert Saints, 2002, Dead Heat, 2002, Behind the Red Door, 2002, Phone Booth, 2002, Taking Lives, 2004, Jiminy Glick in La La Wood, 2004, (voice) The Wild, 2006, The Sentinel, 2006; (TV movies) Trapped in Silence, 1986, Brotherhood of Justice, 1986, Last Light, 1993; (TV series) 24, 2001-(Best Performance by Actor in TV Series Drama Golden Globe award 2002, Best Performance by Actor in a Drama Series Golden Satellite award 2002, nominee Outstanding Lead Actor in Drama Series Emmy award 2002, Screen Actors Guild Award for best actor in a drama series, 2004, Screen Actors Guild Award for Outstanding Performance by a Male Actor in a Drama Series, 2006, Emmy Award for Outstanding Lead Actor in a Drama Series, 2006). Office: William Morris Agency attn: Steve Dontanville 151 El Camino Dr Beverly Hills CA 90212 *

SUTHERLAND, L(EWIS) FREDERICK, food products executive; b. Charleston, W.Va., Jan. 1, 1952; s. Lewis Frederick and Dorothy Louise (Droddy) S.; m. Barbara Hall Hoover, Aug. 24, 1974; children— Matthew, Mark BS, Duke U.; MBA, U. Pitts. V.p. Chase Mahattan Bank, NYC; asst. treas. Aramark Corp., Phila., 1980-83, treas., 1983-85, v.p., treas., 1985-87, v.p. corp. fin. and devel., 1987-91, sr. v.p., 1991-93, exec. v.p. and pres. Uniform Svcs. sector, 1993-96, exec. v.p., CFO, 1997—. Trustee WHYY, Phila.; bd. dirs. Consol. Edison. Trustee People's Light and Theatre Co. Named Treas. of Yr., Cash Flow mag., 1987. Office: Aramark Corp 1101 Market St Ste 45 Philadelphia PA 19107 *

SUTHERLAND, MARION IDA, music educator; b. Merrill, Wisc. d. Edwin August and Erna Martha Hackbarth; m. Robert D. Sutherland, Sept. 22, 1962. B in Music Edn., St. Louis Inst. of Music, 1954; M in Music, Eastman, 1956. Cert. music educator 1974. Music tchr. St. Louis Inst. Music, Clayton, Mo., 1956—58; acting vocal music dir. Carleton Coll., Northfield, Minn., 1959—60; choral music dir. Concordia Coll., River Forest, Ill., 1960—61, Chippewa Falls Mid. Sch., Wis., 1975—81; music educator St. Therese Sch., Schofield, Wis., 1981—85, St. Paul's Sch., Bloomer, Wis., 1988—93; piano and voice educator Wausau Conservatory Music, Wis., 1982—2003; ret., 2003. Mem. libr. bd. St. Louis Inst. Music, Clayton, 1956—58; cert. music adj. Wis. Music Festivals, 1982—2000, master music adj., 2000—. Author: (booklet) Life of P. Tschaikovsky, 1963. Full Yr. scholarship, Eastman, 1955—56. Mem.: Nat. Assn. of Tchrs. of Singing, Kiwanis Club (pianist 1948—50), Rotary Club (pianist 1945—50, Internat. Found. fellowship for European study 1958—59), Sigma Alpha Iota (life). Lutheran. Avocations: reading, walking, swimming, needlecrafts. Home: N3822 Hanke Rd Bryant WI 54418 Home Phone: 715-627-7945.

SUTHERLAND, PAGE HAMILTON, retired government relations executive; b. Petersburg, Va., Sept. 29, 1932; s. Alban Jackson Jr. and Virginia Brown Sutherland; m. Barbara Lee Norris, June 8, 1956; children: Barbara Sutherland Gaylor, Elizabeth Sutherland Kennon. Degree in history, U. Va., Charlottesville, 1956. Mgmt. trainee GE Supply Corp., Richmond, Va., 1958—59; prodn. control specialist Reynolds Metals Co., Richmond, 1959—62; indsl. engrng. profl. Larus & Brother Co., Richmond, 1962—67; exec. v.p. Tobacco Tax Coun., Richmond, 1967—82; regional dir. Tobacco Inst., Richmond, 1982—92; legis./govt. affairs cons. Philip Morris USA, Richmond, 1992—97. Cons. in field. Mem. Rotunda Soc., Lawn Soc., U. Va., Charlottesville, Jamestown/Yorktown Found., Williamsburg, Va., Colonial Williamsburg Found., Va. Mus. Fine Arts, 1985—; bd. dirs. Trinity Episcopal Sch., Richmond, 1977—85, chmn. bd. dirs., 1978—82; bd. dirs. Nat. Tobacco Festival, Richmond, 1974—84, chmn. bd. dirs., 1979; bd. dirs. Tobacco/Textile Mus., Danville, Va., 1976—78, Richmond on the James, 1982—88, chmn. bd. dirs., 1986—88; bd. dirs. Historic Richmond Found., 1988—98, Va. Athletics Found., U. Va., Charlottesville, 1995—98, Richmond Gentry, 1997—2007, pres., 2003—04. Served with US Army, 1956—58. Mem.: Va. Hist. Soc. Presbyterian. Avocations: college athletics, beach activities, gardening. Home: 9 E Square Ln Richmond VA 23238 Home Fax: 804-784-0390. E-mail: bns426@msn.com.

SUTHERLAND, ROBERT D., orthopedist, surgeon; b. Sewickley, Pa., Oct. 19, 1955; Grad. summa cum laude, Wash. and Jefferson Coll.; MD, Temple U., 1981. Cert. Am. Bd. Orthopaedic Surgery. Intern gen. surgery Abington Meml. Hosp., 1981—82; resident orthop. surgery Temple U. Hosp., Phila., 1982—86, Shriner's Hosp. Crippled Children; orthopedist Orthop. Assocs. Reading; staff mem. Reading Hosp. and Med. Ctr. Named one of Top 250 Golfer Doctors in Am., Golf Digest, 2006. Office: Orthop Assocs Reading 301 S Seventh Ave Ste 3220 West Reading PA 19611 also: 4885 DeMoss Rd, Ste 102 Reading PA 19606 Office Phone: 610-376-6387. Office Fax: 610-376-6387. *

SUTHERLAND, VANNA RAE, psychiatrist; BS in Biology, Tulane U., New Orleans, 1992, MD, 1996. Resident in psychiatry U. Calif., San Francisco, 1996—2000; adult psychiatrist City and County of San Francisco, 2000—03; adult psychiatrist student health ctr. Hastings Coll. Law, San Francisco, 2000—06; pvt. practice San Francisco, 2000—05, San Mateo, Calif., 2005—. Mem.: No. Calif. Psychiat. Soc., Am. Psychiat. Assn. Office: 205 E Third Ave Ste 207 San Mateo CA 94401 Office Phone: 650-375-8077.

SUTHERLAND, WILLIAM OWEN SHEPPARD, retired language educator, consultant; b. Wilmington, NC, Jan. 19, 1921; s. William Owen Sheppard and Mary Owen (Green) S.; m. Madeline Ethel Cooley, Sept. 12, 1947; children: Madeline, William, John, Thomas. AB in English with honors, U. N.C., 1942, MA, 1947, PhD, 1950. Instr. English. U. N.C., Chapel Hill, 1950-51, Northwestern U., Evanston, Ill., 1951-54; asst. prof. U. Tex., Austin, 1954-58, assoc. prof., 1958-65, prof., 1965-98, Robert A.-Thomas H. Law Centennial prof. humanities emeritus, 1998—, chmn. dept., 1983-90, faculty humanist rep. Deans of Humanities of S.W. Conf., 1980; cons. Ednl. Testing Svc. and Coll. Bd., Princeton, NJ, 1965-72, NEH, Washington, 1978—; prof. emeritus U. Tex., 1998; ret., 1998. Author: Art of the Satirist, 1965; co-editor: The Reader, 1960, Six Contemporary Novels, 1961, An Index to 18th Century Periodicals, 1800, 1956. Served to capt. C.E. U.S. Army, 1942-45. Recipient Scarborough Excellence in Tchg. award U. Tex. Austin, 1959, Liberal Arts Pro Bene Meritis award, 1996, Pres. Assocs. Tchg. award, 1982; NEH grantee, 1978-79. Mem. MLA, South Central MLA (exec. com. 1967-69), AAUP (state v.p. 1970-71), Nat. Council Tchrs. English (dir. 1974-78) Democrat. Episcopalian. Home: 3610 Highland View Dr Austin TX 78731-4033 Office: U Tex Dept English Austin TX 78712 Business E-Mail: woss@mail.utexas.edu.

SUTHERLIN, MICHAEL W., paper company executive; BSIE/BBA, Tex. Tech. Univ.; MBA, Univ. Tex., Austin. Mgmt. positions through pres. & COO Varco Internat. Inc., 1976—2003; pres., COO Joy Global Inc., Milw., 2003—06, pres., CEO, 2007—. Office: Joy Global Inc 100 E Wisconsin Ave Milwaukee WI 53202 *

SUTHERLY, CURTIS KENT, civilian military employee, journalist, writer; b. Lebawn, Pa., July 12, 1950; s. Curtis and Mildred Mary Sutherly. Grad. in Jet Aircraft Maintenance, Sheppard AFB, Witchita Falls, Tex., 1969. Lic. pvt. investigator Knoxville, Tenn., 1974. Freelance journalist, Fredericksburg, Pa., 1975—77; newspaper reporter and outdoor columnist Lebanon Daily News, Pa., 1977—85; newspaper reporter Reading Eagle News Co., Pa., 1985—86; med. records clerk VA Med. Ctr., Lebanon, 1986—87; retirement clerk US Army Mil. Personnel Office, Carlisle Barracks, Pa., 1987—88; flight sec. USAF 315th Recruiting Squadron, Mechanicsburg, Pa., 1988—. Spkr. in field. Author: (books) Strange Encounters, 1996, UFO Mysteries: A Reporter Seeks The Truth, 2001. Vol. counselor Lebanon County Jr. Conservation Sch., Lickdale, Pa., 1981—82; vol. stream restoration work and blue bird tag and release programs Ft. Indian Town Gap, Pa., 1983—84. Sgt. USAF, 1968—72. Recipient Exemplary Civilian Svc., Dept. Air Force, New Cumberland, Pa., 1994, Civilian Yr., USAF, 360th Recruiting Group, Boston, 1995, USAF 318th Recruiting Squadron, New Cumberland, 2000. Mem.: Am. Legion. Avocations: fencing, history, reading, wood furniture restoration. Home: 231 S 6th St Steelton PA 17113 Office: USAF Recruiting Office 5205 Simpson-Ferry Rd Mechanicsburg PA 17050

SUTHERS, JOHN WILLIAM, state attorney general; b. Denver, Oct. 18, 1951; s. William Dupont and Marguerite A. (Ryan) S.; m. Janet Gill, May 21, 1976; children: Alison, Catherine. BA in Govt. magna cum laude, U. Notre Dame, 1974; JD, U. Colo., 1977. Bar: Colo. 1977, U.S. Dist. Ct. Colo. 1977, U.S. Ct. Appeals (10th cir.) 1979, U.S. Supreme Ct. 2003. Dep. dist. atty. 4th jud. dist. State of Colo., Colorado Springs, 1977-79, chief dep. dist. atty. 4th jud. dist., 1979-81, dist. atty. 4th jud. dist., 1989—97; assoc. Sparks, Dix, Enoch, Colorado Springs, 1981-82; ptnr. Sparks, Dix, Enoch, Suthers & Winslow, Colorado Springs, 1982-89; sr. counsel Sparks, Dix, Colorado Springs, 1997—99; exec. dir. Colo. Dept. Corrections, 1999—2001; US atty. dist. Colo. US Dept. Justice, 2001—05; atty. gen State of Colo., Denver, 2005—. Mem. adv. bd. Sec. of State, Denver, 1983—89; Colo. commr. Uniform State Laws, 1993—97. Author: Fraud and Deceit, 1982, How to Liquidate a Lemon, 1983. Pres., chmn. bd. dirs. Cmty. Corrections of Pikes Peak Region, Inc., 1984—87; bd. dirs. Crimestoppers, Inc., Colorado Springs, 1985—88; mem. exec. com. Colo. Dist. Atty.'s Coun., 1992—97, pres., 1994—95, treas., 1993; El Paso County Rep. Ctrl. com. Colorado Springs, 1985—2001; Colo. State Rep. Ctrl. com., 1989—2001. Zimmerman Found. scholar, 1970-74. Mem. Colo. Bar Assn. (com. chmn.), El Paso County Bar Assn. (pres. 1990-91), Notre Dame Colorado Springs (pres. 1983-84). Republican. Roman Catholic. Avocations: baseball cards, golf. Office: Colo Dept Law 1525 Sherman St 5th Fl Denver CO 80203 Office Phone: 303-866-3557. Business E-Mail: john.suthers@state.co.us.

SUTIN, ALAN N., lawyer; b. New Haven, Apr. 29, 1958; BA, Emory Univ., Atlanta, 1979; JD, Univ. Ga., 1984. Bar: Ga. 1984, NY 1985, US Ct. Appeals (DC cir.), US Dist. Ct. (so., ea. districts) NY. Shareholder, chair nat. tech. media, telecom. practice Greenberg Traurig LLP, NYC. Articles editor Ga. Journ. Internat. and Comparative Law; contbr. articles to profl. journals. Mem.: ABA, State Bar of Ga., NY State Bar Assn., Assn. Bar of NYC, Computer Law Assn. Office: Greenberg Traurig LLP MetLife Bldg 200 Park Ave New York NY 10166 Office Phone: 212-801-9286. Office Fax: 212-801-6400. Business E-Mail: sutina@gtlaw.com.

SUTIN, NORMAN, retired chemist, researcher; b. Ceres, Sept. 16, 1928; arrived in US, 1956, naturalized; s. Louis and Clara (Goldberg) S.; m. Bonita Sakowski, June 29, 1958; children: Lewis Anthony, Cara Ruth. B.Sc., U. Cape Town, S. Africa, 1948, M.Sc., 1950; PhD, Cambridge U., Eng., 1953. Research fellow Durham U. (Eng.), 1954-55; research assoc. Brookhaven Nat. Lab., Upton, NY, 1956-57, assoc. chemist, 1958-61, chemist, 1961-66, sr. chemist, 1966—2001, dept. chmn., 1988-95; ret., 2001; affiliate Rockefeller U., NYC, 1958-62; vis. fellow Weizmann Inst., Rehovoth, Israel, 1965; vis. prof. SUNY-Stony Brook, 1968, Columbia U., NYC, 1968-69, Tel Aviv U., Israel, 1973-74, U. Calif.-Irvine, 1977, U. Tex. Austin, 1979; disting. prof. Rutgers U., 1999—2001. Editor: Comments on Inorganic Chemistry Jour., 1980-87; mem. editorial bd. Jour. Am. Chem. Soc., 1985-89, Inorganic Chem., 1986-89, Jour. Phys. Chem., 1987-92; contbr. articles to profl. jours. Mem. NAS, Am. Acad. Arts and Scis., Am. Chem. Soc. (recipient award for disting. svc. in advancement of inorganic chemistry 1983).

SUTMAN, FRANCIS XAVIER, retired academic administrator, chemist, writer; b. Newark, Dec. 20, 1927; s. Joseph L. and Ella (Joyce) S.; m. Mabel Ranagan, Apr. 1, 1956; children: Frank J., Catherine J., Elizabeth A. AB, Montclair State U., 1949, MA, 1952; EdD, Columbia U., 1956. Tchr. pub. secondary schs., NJ, 1949-55; instr. chemistry Upsala Coll., 1953-55; asst. prof. Wm. Paterson Coll., 1955-57; chmn., assoc. prof. natural scis. Inter-Am. U. P.R., 1957-58; prof. gen. edn., chmn. SUNY, Buffalo, 1958-62; prof. sci. edn., chmn. dept. secondary edn., dir. Merit Bilingual Ctr. Temple U., Phila., 1962—82; dean edn. Fairleigh Dickinson U., 1982—89; vis. scientist Nat. Sci. Found., 1989—93; sr. scholar U. Miami, 1995—2000, Morgan State U., 1999—2002, Temple U., Phila, 1998—2004; sr. scholar, tchg. intern supr. Richard Stockton Coll., NJ, 2004—. Tech. rsch. staff Exxon Engring. & Rsch. Lab., Linden, N.J., 1955; vis. lectr. Rutgers U.; cons. India AID Project; vis. prof., scientist Hebrew U., Israel; exec. dir. curriculum devel. coun., Rowan U., N.J., 1993-2003; del. OAS Coun. Sci. Edn. and Culture, 1971; co-dir. Environ. Edn. Conf. Environ. Protection Svc., Jerusalem, 1975; cons. fed., state, local sch. dists.; dir. sci. tech. project Huazhong U., China, 1980-87; co-dir. chem. edn. conf. Tianjin Normal U., 1984. Author: Concepts in Chemistry, 1962, 2d edit., 1968, What Kind of Environment Will Our Children Have?, 1971, Chemistry in Today's Environment (U.S. and Israel), 1977, Educating Personnel for Bilingual Settings: Today and Beyond, 1979, Learning English Through Science, 1986, Improving Learning in Science and Basic Skills Among Diverse Student Populations, 1995, We Need a Better Understanding of Inquiry in Instruction, Harvard Edn. Letter, 2000, The Science Quest: Using Inquiry/Discovery to Enhance Student Learning, 2007. Active Haddonfield (N.J.) Bd. Edn., 1976-79; v.p. alumni bd. Montclair State U., 1982-89; mem. chem. and tech. bd. Burlington County Coll., 1994—. Recipient Air Force Assn. award, 1968, N.J. Gov.'s Albert Einstein Edn. award, 1987, award Hispanic Congress of Pa., 1980, Alumni Citation Montclair State U., 1988. Fellow AAAS; mem. NSTA, Am. Chem. Soc., Am. Assn. Colls. Tchr. Edn. (chief instnl. rep. 1968-87), Nat. Assn. Rsch. Sci. Tchg. (pres.), N.J. Gov.'s Acad., Coun. Sci. Soc. Presidents, Sigma Xi, Phi Delta Kappa (pres. chpt. 2000-02). Home: 311 W Royal Ave Linwood NJ 08221-1458 Office Phone: 609-927-1260. Personal E-mail: fmsutman@msn.com. *Professional success comes when one accepts the paradoxes of human activity and accepts conflict, criticism and praise, and gives of one's self for a worthy cause.*

SUTNICK, ALTON IVAN, internist, educator, researcher, consultant, dean; b. Trenton, NJ, July 6, 1928; s. Michael and Rose (Horwitz) S.; m. Mona Reidenberg, Aug. 17, 1958; children: Amy Sutnick Plotch, Gary Benjamin Sutnick. AB, U. Pa., 1950, MD, 1954; student in Biomed. Math., Drexel U., 1961—62; student in Biometrics, Temple U., 1969—70. Diplomate Am. Bd. Internal Medicine. Rotating intern Hosp. U. Pa., 1954—55, resident in anesthesiology, 1955—56, resident in medicine, 1956, USPHS postdoctoral research fellow, 1956—57; asst. instr. anesthesiology, then asst. instr. medicine U. Pa. Sch. Medicine, 1955—57; resident in medicine Wishard Meml. Hosp., Indpls., 1957—58, chief resident in medicine, 1960—61; resident instr. medicine Ind. U. Sch. Medicine, Indpls., 1957—58; USPHS postdoctoral research fellow Temple U. Hosp., 1961—63; instr., then assoc. in medicine Temple U. Sch. Medicine, 1962—65; mem. faculty U. Pa. Sch. Medicine, 1965—75, assoc. prof. medicine, 1971—75; clin. asst. physician Pa. Hosp., 1966—71; research physician, then assoc. dir. Inst. Cancer Research (now Fox Chase Cancer Ctr.), Phila., 1965—75; vis. prof. medicine Med. Coll. Pa., Phila., 1971—74; prof. medicine Drexel U. Coll. Medicine (formerly Med. Coll. Pa.), 1975—; dean Med. Coll. Pa., 1975—89, sr. v.p., 1976—89; v.p. Ednl. Commn. Fgn. Med. Grads, 1989—95; dir. internat. med. edn. Carelift Internat., 1997—2005. Dir. clin. devel. Am. Oncologic Hosp., Phila., 1973-75; attending physician Phila. VA Hosp., 1967-89, Allegheny U. Hosps., 1971-95; cons. in field; mem. U.S. nat. com. Internat. Union Against Cancer, 1969-72; mem. Nat. Conf. Cancer Prevention and Detection, 1973, Nat. Cancer Control Planning Conf., 1973; vice chmn. Gov. Pa. Task Force Cancer Control, 1974-76, chmn. com. cancer detection, 1974-76; mem. health rsch. adv. bd. Commonwealth of Pa., 1976-78; mem. diagnostic rsch. adv. group Nat. Cancer Inst., 1974-78; chmn. coord. com., comprehensive cancer ctr. program Fox Chase Cancer Ctr., U. Pa. Cancer Ctr., 1975; cons. WHO, Govt. of India, 1979, Govt. of Indonesia, 1980, entire S.E. Asia region, 1981, U. Zimbabwe, 1989, Minister of Health of Poland, 1992, Israel Sci. Coun., 1992, U. Autonoma de Guadalajara, Mex., 1993, Generalitat de Catalunya, Spain, 1993, Ministry of Health Russian Fedn., 1993, Inst. de Pos-Graduacae Medica Carlos Chagas, Brazil, 1993, Fondazione Smith Kline, Italy, 1995, Assn. Med. Schs. Europe, 1995-99, U. Jordan, 1995, U.S.-China Ednl. Inst., 1996, Georgian Postgrad. Med. Found., 1996, Instituto Universitario de Ciencias Biomedicas, Argentina, 1996, faculty of medicine U. Saarland, Germany, 1996, Ctr. for Med. Edn., Ben Gurion U., Israel, 1996-, Hungarian Nat. Health Ins. Fund, 1996, Carelift Internat., 1997, Intercoll., Cyprus, 1997, Open Soc. Inst., 1997-99, Aieti Med. Sch., Republic of Georgia, 1997-2001, Tartu U., Estonia, 1998-99, WHO European Office, 1998, Vilnius U. and Kaunas Med. U., Lithuania, 1998-99, U. Zagreb, Croatia, 1998-99, Larnaca Hosp., Cyprus, 1998, Netherlands and Russian med. schs., Temple U., Govt. of Republic of Georgia, others; faculty of medicine Moldova State Med. and Pharm. U., 1997-, vis. prof., 2002, prof. assoc., 2003-; rep. for internat. med. and health scis. edn. MCP Hahnemann U. of the Health Scis., 1996-99; adv. com. Open Soc. Inst. Muskie Fellowship Program, 1997, working group on implementation of presdl. policy on internat. edn., 2000, selection comm. Internat. Consortium for the Advancement of Med. Edn., 2001-05; mem. adv. com. internat. health program Temple U., 2005—. Author numerous articles in field.; asst. editor: Annals Internal Medicine, 1972-75; mem. editl. bd. other med. jours. Bd. dirs. Israel Cancer Rsch. Fund, 1975—95, Am. Assocs. for Democracy in Georgia, 2000—; nat. bd. dirs. Am. Assocs. Ben Gurion U., 1991—; bd. Internat. Med. Scholar Program, 1988—89, Sight Savers Internat., 1988—91; adv. commn. Internat. Participation Phila. '76, 1973—76; bd. dirs. Phila. Coun. Internat. Visitors, 1972—77; nat. bd. dirs. Phila. divsn. Am. Assocs. Ben Gurion U., 1986—, assoc. chair, 1993—95, 2000—. Capt. M.C. US Army, 1958—60. Recipient Torch of Learning award Am. Friends of Hebrew U., 1981, medal Ben Gurion U. of Negev, Israel, 1985, medal U. Cath. de Lille, France, 1987, medal U. Belgrade, Yugoslavia, 1988, Founder's award and medal Med. Coll. Pa., 1989, St. Thomas Aquinas award Santo Tomas U. Med. Alumni Assn., The Philippines, 1989, medal Kiev Med. Inst., Ukraine, 1991, Benjamin Albagli medal Inst. de Pos-Graduacao Medica Carlos Chagas, Brazil, 1993, shield Coll. Physicians and Surgeons, Pakistan, 1993, medal Ukrainian State Med. U., 1994, medal Universidad de Cantabria, Spain, 1999, medal Hadassah-Hebrew U. Dental Sch., 1999, Negev award Am. Assocs., Ben Gurion U., 2000. Fellow ACP (internat. adv. network), Coll. Physicians Phila. (censor 1977-86, councillor 1977-86); mem. AMA (Arnold and Marie Schwartz award in medicine, 1976, Dr. William Beaumont award), AAAS, Am. Fedn. Clin. Rsch. (pres. Temple U. chpt. 1964-65), Am. Assn. Cancer Rsch., Am. Soc. Clin. Oncology, Am. Dermatoglyphics Assn., Assn. Am. Cancer Insts., Assn. Am. Med. Colls., Northeast Consortium on Med. Edn. (treas. 1983-89, chmn. 1986-87), Coun. of Deans of Pvt. Free-Standing Med. Schs. (co-founder, nat. chmn. 1983-85), Pa. Coun. Deans (chmn. 1987-89), Am. Cancer Soc. (vice chmn. service com. Phila. div. 1974-76, bd. dirs. 1974-80, chmn. awards com. 1976), Am. Lung Assn., Am. Heart Assn., NAFSA-Assn. Internat. Educators, Pan Am. Med. Assn., Phila. Coop. Cancer Assn., N.Y. Acad. Scis., Pa. Heart Assn., Heart Assn. Southeastern Pa., Pa. Med. Soc., Phila. County Med. Soc. (chmn. com. internat. med. affairs 1964-72, Strittmatter award 2006), Pa. Lung Assn., Phila. Assn. for Clin. Trials (bd. dirs. 1980-81), Health Systems Agy. Southeastern Pa. (gov. bd., exec. com. 1983-87, sec. 1985-87), Am. Assn. Ben Gurion U. (bd. dirs. 1986—), Soc. des Medecins Militaires Français, Assn. Med. Edn. in Europe, Soc. Española de Educacion Medica, Internat. Med. Sch. Affiliates Consortium (co-founder, vice chmn. 1985-87), Phi Beta Kappa, Sigma Xi, Alpha Omega Alpha (councillor 1963-65). Achievements include discovery of association of hepatitis B surface antigen with hepatitis; performed 1st studies of pulmonary surfactant in adult human lung disease; developed cancer screening system based on risk status; pioneer in describing non-A non-B hepatitis C, pioneer in showing relationship of body iron stores to cancer susceptibility and life expectancy; organized first symposium on problems of foreign medical graduates; coined word "ergasteric" for lab.-contracted disease; responsible for advances in assessment of clinical competence; demonstrated validity of clinical competence assessment using standardized patients; demonstrated reliability of clinical competence assessment across six different languages and cultures. Personal E-mail: alton@sutnick.com.

SUTPHIN, BRIAN, information technology executive; Grad. in Econs., U. Wis., Madison; law degree, Stanford U., Calif. Pvt. practice atty.; various sr. mgmt. positions in mktg., bus. devel. and engring. Sun Microsystems, Inc., Santa Clara, Calif., v.p. bus. devel., exec. v.p. corp. devel. & alliances, mem. exec. mgmt. group. Office: Sun Microsystems Inc 4150 Network Cir Santa Clara CA 95054 Office Phone: 650-960-1300. *

SUTPHIN, WILLIAM TAYLOR, lawyer; s. William Halstead and Catharine (Bonner) S.; m. Alissa L. Kramer, June 21, 1958. AB in History, Princeton U., 1957; LLB, U. Pa., 1960. Bar: N.J. 1960; U.S. Ct. Appeals (3d cir.) 1964, U.S. Supreme Ct. 1965. Assoc. Stryker, Tams & Dill, Newark, 1960-67, ptnr., 1967-73; sole practice Princeton, N.J., 1973—. Co-adj. faculty mem. Rutgers U. Govt. Svcs. Tng. Program, 1973-2003;

assoc. counsel N.J. Planning Ofcls., 1975-2003. Mem. Princeton Twp. Planning Bd., 1967—72, Regional Planning Bd. Princeton, 1970—74; atty. Green Brook (N.J.) Twp. Planning Bd., 1972—2001, Millstone (N.J.) Twp. Bd. Adjustment, 1978—98, Delaware Twp. (N.J.) Bd. Adjustment, 1982—2003, Princeton Borough Bd. Adjustment, 1983—; committeeman Twp. Princeton, 1973—75, police commr., 1974—75; treas. Youth Employment Svc. Princeton, 1981—84. Mem.: N.J. Inst. Local Govt. Attys., Princeton Bar Assn. (pres. 1981—82), N.J. Bar Assn. (chmn. ins. com. 1979—81). Home: 501 Jefferson Rd Princeton NJ 08540-3418 Office: Law Offices of William T Sutphin 34 Chambers St Princeton NJ 08542-3700 Office Phone: 609-924-9525. E-mail: william.t.sutphin@verizon.net.

SUTRO, EDMUND J., secondary school educator, consultant; b. LA, Aug. 4, 1946; s. Paul and Ethelwyn (Ziegler) S. AA, L.A. Valley Coll., Van Nuys, 1966; AB, U. So. Calif., LA, 1969, MSc, 1971; PhD, Stanford U., 1979. Cert. tchr. Calif. Tchr. Pasadena (Calif.) H.S., 1969-92, Arcadia (Calif.) H.S., 1992—. Commr. Calif. Comnn. on Tchg. Credentials, Sacramento, 1992-95; mem. adv. bd. Occidental Coll., L.A., 1990—, L.A. Times, 1971-72; reviewer Dept. Edn., Washington; guest lectr. U. So. Calif., Calif. State Coll., L.A., Calif. Inst. Tech., Stanford U.; spkr. Pasadena Star News; acad. cons., L.A.; manuscript reviewer Social Edn. Contbr. articles to profl. jours. Co-chair Calif. chpt. Bush-Quayle '92, 1992; trustee Flintridge Prep. Sch., La Canada, Calif., 1992—, Pilgrim Sch., L.A., 1990—; bd. dirs. L.A. Bach. Festival, Pasadena Chamber Orch.; prodn. chair, bd. dirs., mem. adv. bd. Hollywood Bowl Easter Sunrise Svc.; vol. Head Start, Bell Gardens/Montebello; vol. fundraiser Sta. KCET Channel 28, L.A.; charter mem. Greater L.A. Zoo Assn. Mem. ASCD, Ednl. Excellence Network, Nat. Coun. for the Social Studies, Calif. Coun. for the Social Studies, Phi Delta Kappa, Tau Kappa Epsilon (pres., past pledge trainer). Republican.

SUTTELL, PAUL ALLYN, state supreme court justice; b. Providence, Jan. 10, 1949; s. Allyn Kingsley and Pauline Louise (Stickney) S.; m. Mary Wood Cissel, May 24, 1980; children: William Theodore Stickney, Grace Wood. BA, Northwestern U., 1971; JD, Suffolk U., 1976. Assoc. Beals & DiFiore, Providence, 1977-90; legal counsel RI Home Minority Leader, 1979-82; mem. RI Ho. of Reps., Providence, 1983—90; assoc. justice RI Family Ct., Providence, 1990—2003; justice RI Supreme Ct., 2003—. Mem. Little Compton (R.I.) Rep. Town Commn., 1981-90; del. R.I. Rep. State Com., 1981-90, Rep. Nat. Conv., 1988; bd. dirs. Friends of Sakonnet Lighthouse; bd. dirs. Little Compton Hist. Soc., chmn., 1999—; mem. bd. deacons Little Compton Congregational Ch., 1995-99, chair, 1997-99. Mem. Sakonnet Preservation Assn., R.I. Agrl. Lands Preservation Com. Office: RI Supreme Ct Frank Licht Judicial Complex 250 Benefit St Providence RI 02903 E-mail: psuttell@counts.state.ri.us. *

SUTTER, BRENT COLIN, professional hockey coach, retired professional hockey player; b. Viking, Alta., Can., June 10, 1962; m. Connie Sutter; children: Merrick, Brandon, Brooke. Center NY Islanders, 1981—91, capt., 1987—92; center Chgo. Blackhawks, 1991—98; owner, pres. Red Deer Rebels (Western Hockey League), 1999—, gov., gen. mgr., head coach, 1999—2007; head coach NJ Devils, 2007—. Head coach Can. Nat. Jr. Team, 2005—07. Named to NHL All-Star Game, 1985. Achievements include being a member of Stanley Cup Champion NY Islanders, 1982, 1983. Office: c/o NJ Devils 33 Fl 744 Broad St Newark NJ 07102 also: Red Deer Rebels 4847C - 19th St Red Deer AB T4R 2N7 Canada E-mail: bsutter@reddeerrebels.com. *

SUTTER, BRUCE (HOWARD SUTTER), retired professional baseball player; b. Lancaster, Pa., Jan. 8, 1953; m. Jaymie Sutter; children: Joshua, Chad, Ben. Baseball player Chgo. Cubs, 1976-80; baseball player St. Louis Cardinals, 1981-85, Atlanta Braves, 1985—88. Mem. Nat. League All-Star Team, 1978-81, 84. Recipient Cy Young award Nat. League, 1979; named Nat. League Fireman of Year Sporting News, 1979, 81, 82, 84; inducted to MLB Hall of Fame, 2006. Office: c/o Baseball Hall of Fame 25 Main St Cooperstown NY 13326

SUTTER, DARRYL JOHN, professional sports team executive, former professional hockey coach; b. Viking, Alta., Can., Aug. 19, 1958; m. Wanda Sutter; children: Brett, Christopher, Jessie. Player Chgo. Blackhawks, 1980-86, asst. coach, 1987-88, assoc. coach, 1991-92, head coach, 1992-95, cons., 1995-97; head coach San Jose Sharks, 1997—2002, Calgary Flames, 2002—06, gen. mgr., 2003—. Named to Alberta Sports Hall of Fame, 2000; recipient Dudley Red Garrett Meml. Trophy, 1980, Commrs. Trophy, 1990. Office: Calgary Flames PO Box 1540 Stn M Calgary AB Canada T2P 3B9

SUTTER, ELEANOR BLY, retired diplomat; b. NYC, Oct. 21, 1945; d. Samuel M. and Sylvia Gertrude Bly; children: Deborah Nelson, Willis. BA, Swarthmore Coll., 1966; MA, Am. U., 1978; diploma in strategic studies, U.S. Army War Coll., 1997. Instr. English Thammasat U., Bangkok and Udornthani Tchr. Tng. Coll., 1967-71, Lomonosov State U., Moscow, 1973-74; rschr. Kennan Inst. for Advanced Russian Studies, 1977-79; fgn. svc. officer Office Soviet Internal Affairs Dept. of State, 1979-80, fgn. svc. officer Office of Strategic Nuc. Policy, 1986-88, fgn. svc. officer Office of Soviet Union Affairs, 1988-90, office dir. Washington, 1997-99, sr. inspector Office Inspector Gen., 1999-2001, dir. Office of Proliferation Threat Reduction, 2001—02; fgn. svc. officer U.S. Embassy, Kinshasa, 1980-82, London, 1982-85, Moscow, 1990-92, charge d'affaires ad interim Bratislava, 1993, dep. prin. officer, 1993-95, dep. chief of mission, 1995-96. Exec. dir., exec. sec., advisor U.S. Del. to Nuclear and Space Talks, Geneva, 1987-91; teaching fellow Russian lit. The Am. U., 1976-77; escort interpreter and translator Dept. of State, 1976. Co-author: Final Report of the Kennan Institute's Soviet Research Institutes Project, 1981. Founder Camp Wocsom, Moscow, 1974. Mem. Am. Fgn. Svc. Assn. Avocations: music, folk dance. Office: care of Fgn Svc Lounge Dept State Washington DC 20520

SUTTER, JANE ELIZABETH, conservationist, science educator; b. St. Louis, Nov. 27, 1939; d. Richard A. and Elizabeth Henby Sutter. AB in Sociology and English, Vassar Coll., 1961; MA in Health Facilities Mgmt., Webster Coll., St. Louis, 1979. Healthcare analyst, Chgo. and St. Louis, 1966-83; asst. dir. radio, TV and motion picture dept. AMA, Chgo., 1966-67; staff coord., rsch. assoc. Chgo. water quality study and environ. health study Inst. of Medicine of Chgo., 1967-69; dir. environ. health planning Comprehensive Health Planning, Inc., Chgo., 1969-73; planning assoc., spl. asst. to med. dir. Sutter Clinic, Inc., St. Louis, 1975-84; vol. activist, educator; founder, dir. for conservation and gardening for birds Wild Birds for the 21st Century (a non-profit ednl. svc.), 1994—; ednl. writer www.wildbirds.org. Author: City Approved Medical Emergency Plan of Operation O'Hare International and Midway Airports, 1971. Chmn. Opera Theatre of St. Louis Newsletter, Recitative, Vol. 1, No. 1, 1980, Vol. 1, No. 2, 1980; co-founder, com. mem. 1st Internat. Alewife Festival of Chgo., Chgo. Yacht Club, summer 1968; appointee Gov.'s Com. for Pure Air and Water, Chgo., 1968; spl. advocate N.Am. Migratory Birds particularly hummingbirds. Mem. Ladue Chapel (life), Mo. Bot. Garden St. Louis, Artists' Guild (mem. artists' sect. 1992-95, portraitist), Mo. Bird Conservation Initiative, Neotropical Bird Club (UK), Vassar Club St. Louis, Bradenton C. of C. Avocations: gardening, writing, travel, fishing, music. Home: Wild Birds for the 21st Century 7376 Pershing Blvd Saint Louis MO 63130-4206 Personal E-mail: jesutteri@sbcglobal.net.

SUTTER, JOSEPH F., aeronautical engineer, consultant, retired air transportation executive; b. Seattle, Mar. 21, 1921; m. Nancy Ann French, June 14, 1943. BA, U. Wash., 1943; Doctorate, Nova Gorica Poly. Inst., 2004. Various engrng. positions Boeing Comml. Airplane Co., Seattle, 1946—65, dir. engrng. for Boeing 747, 1965—71, v.p., gen. mgr. 747 div., 1971—74, v.p. program ops., 1974—76, v.p. ops. and product devel., 1976—81, exec. v.p., 1981—86, cons., 1986—87, 1987—. Chmn. aerospace safety adv. panel NASA, 1986; mem. Challenger Accident Commn., 1986. Served to lt. j.g. USN, 1943—45. Named Joseph F. Sutter professorship established in his honor, U. Wash., Boeing Co., 1992; named to, Interant. Air Cargo Assn. Hall of Fame, Gallery of Legends, Pacific Asian Travel Assn., 2005; recipient Master Design award, Product Engrng. mag., 1965, Franklin W. Kolk Air Transp. Progress award, Soc. Aero. Aerospace Coun., 1980, Elmer A. Sperry award, 1980, Nuts & Bolts award, Transport Assn., 1983, Nat. Medal Tech., U.S. Pres. Reagan, 1985, Sir Kingsford Smith award, Royal Aero. Soc. in Sydney, 1980, Wright Bros. Meml. Trophy, 1986, Alumnus Summa Laude Dignatus award, U. Wash., 2001. Fellow: AIAA (Daniel Guggenheim award 1990), Royal Aero Soc. (hon.); mem.: Internat. Fedn. Airworthiness (pres. 1989), Slovenian Acad. Engrg. (hon.). Office: Boeing Co PO Box 3707 Seattle WA 98124-2207

SUTTER, LAURENCE BRENER, lawyer; b. NYC, Feb. 5, 1944; s. Meyer and Beatrice Sutter; m. Betty A. Satterwhite, June 9, 1979. AB, Columbia Coll., 1965; JD, N.Y.U., 1976. Bar: N.Y. 1977, U.S. Dist. Ct. (so. and ea. dists.) N.Y. 1977. Assoc. Shea & Gould, NYC, 1976-80, Meyer, Suozzi, English & Klein P.C., Mineola, NY, 1980-82; assoc. counsel publs. Gen. Media Comm., Inc., NYC, 1982-96, sr. v.p., gen. counsel, sec., 1997—2004; sr. counsel Penthouse Media Group Inc., 2004—. With N.Y. Army N.G., 1966-72. Mem. Assn. of Bar of City of N.Y. (mem. com. on civil rights 1986-89, mem. com. on comm. and media law 1989-92, mem. com. on copyright and lit. property 1994-97), First Amendment Lawyers Assn., Nat. Arts Club, Orient (N.Y.) Yacht Club (dir. 1997-2000, sec. 2000-2001). Democrat. Jewish. Avocations: music, sailing. Office Phone: 212-702-6105.

SUTTER, WILLIAM PAUL, lawyer; b. Chgo., Jan. 15, 1924; s. Harry Blair and Elsie (Paul) S.; m. Helen Yvonne Stebbins, Nov. 13, 1954; children: William Paul, Helen Blair Sutter. AB, Yale U., 1947; JD, U. Mich., 1950. Bar: Ill. 1950, Fla. 1977, U.S. Supreme Ct. 1981. Assoc. Hopkins & Sutter (and predecessors), Chgo., 1950-57, ptnr., 1957-89, of counsel, 1989—2001. Mem. Ill. Supreme Ct. Atty. Registration Commn., 1975-81 Contbr. articles on estate planning and taxation to profl. jours. Chmn. Winnetka Caucus Com., 1966-67; pres., trustee Lucille P. Markey Charitable Trust, 1983-98; precinct capt. New Trier Twp. (Ill.) Rep. party, 1960-68; asst. area chmn. New Trier Rep. Orgn., 1968-72; trustee Gads Hill Center, pres., 1962-70, chmn., 1971-80; trustee Northwestern Meml. Hosp., 1983-98, life trustee, 1998—; bd. dirs. Chgo. Hort. Soc., 1982-2005, life dir., 2005—; mem. dean's coun. Sch. Medicine, Yale U., 1991-97; bd. visitors Waisman Ctr., U. Wis., 1996-2002; corr. sec. Yale U. Class of 1945, 1990—. Served to 1st lt. AUS, 1943-46 Fellow Am. Bar Found., Am. Coll. Trust and Estate Counsel (bd. regents 1977-83, exec. com. 1981-83); mem. ABA (ho. dels. 1972-81, chmn. com. on income estates and trusts, taxation sect. 1973-75), Ill. Bar Assn. (bd. govs. 1964-75, pres. 1973-74), Chgo. Bar Assn. (chmn. probate practice com. 1963-64), Am. Law Inst., Internat. Acad. Estate and Trust Law, Am. Judicature Soc., Ill. LAWPAC (pres. 1977-83), Order of Coif, Phi Beta Kappa, Phi Delta Phi, Chi Psi, Mid-Day Club, Indian Hill Club, Gulf Stream Golf Club, Country Club Fla., Ocean Club (Fla.) (bd. govs. 1993-99, sec. 1993-97, pres. 1997-99), Lawyers Club Chgo. Episcopalian. Home: 2 Par Club Cir Village Of Golf FL 33436 Personal E-mail: WPSutter@aol.com.

SUTTERBY, LARRY QUENTIN, internist; b. North Kansas City, Mo., Sept. 11, 1950; s. John Albert and Wilma Elizabeth (Henry) Sutterby; m. Luciana Risos Magpuri, July 5, 1980; children: Leah Lourdes, Liza Bernadette. BA in Chemistry, William Jewell Coll., 1972; MD, U. Mo., Kans. City, 1976. Resident in internal medicine Mt. Sinai Hosp., Chgo., 1976-79; physician Mojave Desert Health Svc., Barstow, Calif., 1979-86; pvt. practice Barstow, 1986-2001; med. cons. State of Calif., LA, 2001—. Med dir Mojave Valley Hospice, 1983—2001, VNA Hospice, Barstow, 1994—2001, Optioncare Home Health Servs, 1995—2001. Recipient Loving Care Award, Vis Nurse Asn Inland Counties, 1988. Democrat. Roman Catholic. Avocation: astronomy. Office: 311 S Spring St Ste 900 Los Angeles CA 90013

SUTTIE, JOHN WESTON, biochemist; b. La Crosse, Wis., Aug. 25, 1934; married; 2 children. BS, U. Wis., 1957, MS, 1958, PhD, 1960. Fellow biochemist Nat. Inst. Med. Rsch, England, 1960-61; asst. prof. to assoc. prof. biochemistry U. Wis., Madison, 1961-69, prof., 1969—2001, chair nutrition sci., 1988-97, Katherine Berns Van Donk Steenbock prof. nutrition, 2000, prof. emeritus, 2002—. Mem. Bd. on Agriculture & Natural Resources, 1996—2001, Food and Nutrition Bd., 2004—07. Assoc. editor Jour Nutrition, 1991-97; editor Jour. Nutrition, 1997-2003; asst. editor Ann. Rev. Nutrition, 2005—. Recipient Disting. Achievement in Nutrition Rsch., Bristol-Myers Squibb/Mead Johnson, 2002. Fellow Am. Heart Assn. Coun. Nutrition, Physical Activity and Metabolism, Am. Soc. for Nutrition (Osborne and Mendel award 1980, Mead Johns award 1974, Conrad Elvehjem award, 2004); mem. NAS, Am. Soc. Expl. Biology and Medicine, Am. Soc. Biochemistry and Molecular Biology, Internat. Soc. Thrombosis and Hemostasis (Hemostasis Career award 1989). Business E-Mail: suttie@biochem.wisc.edu.

SUTTLE, STEPHEN HUNGATE, lawyer; b. Uvalde, Tex., Mar. 17, 1940; s. Dorwin Wallace and Ann Elizabeth Suttle; m. Rosemary Williams Davison, Aug. 3, 1963; children: Michael Barrett, David Paull, John Stewart. BA, Washington and Lee U., 1962; LLB, U. Tex., 1965. Bar: Tex. 1965, U.S. Dist. Ct. (no. and we. dists.) Tex. 1965, U.S. Ct. Appeals (5th cir.) 1967, U.S. Supreme Ct. 1970. Law clk. to Hon. Leo Brewster U.S. Dist. Ct., Ft. Worth, 1965-67; ptnr. McMahon, Surovik, Suttle, P.C., Abilene, Tex., 1970—. Pres. Abilene Boys Clubs, Inc., 1975—76; bd. dirs. Abilene Cmty. Theater, 1979—80, Abilene Fine Arts Mus., 1977—78. Fellow: Tex. Bar Found., Am. Bd. Trial Advocates (pres. Tex. 2003), Am. Coll. Trial Lawyers; mem.: ABA, Tex. Bar Assn. (dir. 1999—2002), Abilene Bar Assn. (pres. 1987—88), Am. Judicature Soc. (bd. dirs. 1981—84), Tex. Young Lawyers Assn. (chmn. bd. dirs. 1976), Def. Rsch. Inst., Tex. Assn. Def. Counsel, Assn. Def. Trial Attys., State Bar Tex. (dir. 1999—2002), Abilene Country Club. Episcopalian. Home: 1405 Woodland Trl Abilene TX 79605-4705 Office: McMahon Surovik Suttle PC PO Box 3679 Abilene TX 79604-3679 E-mail: ssuttle@mcmahonlawtx.com.

SUTTON, BETTY, congresswoman, lawyer; b. Barberton, Ohio, July 31, 1963; m. Doug Sutton; 2 children. BA in Polit. Sci., Kent State U., 1985; JD, U. Akron, 1990. Coun.-at-large Barberton City Coun., 1990-91; v.p. Summit County Coun., 1991-92; mem. Ohio Ho. Reps. from dist. 47, 1993—2000; atty. Faulkner, Muskovitz & Phillips LLP, 2001—06; mem. US Congress from 13th Ohio dist., 2007—, mem. rules com., budget com., 2007—. Vice chmn. Judiciary & Criminal Justice Com., mem. Civil & Comml. Law, Ways & Means, Ins. Pub. Utilities & Elec. Twp. Com. Recipient Outstanding Performance in Const. Law Fed. Bar Assn., 1989, Am. Jurisprudence award, 1989. Mem. ABA, Akron Child Guidance Adv. Coun., Assn. Trial Lawyers Am., Ohio Acad. Trial Lawyers, Summit County Trial Lawyers, Fed. Dem. Women. Democrat. Office: 1721 Longworth House Office Bldg Washington DC 20515 also: 1655 W Market St Rm 435 Akron OH 44313 Office Phone: 330-865-8450. Office Fax: 330-865-8470. *

SUTTON, BEVERLY JEWELL, psychiatrist; b. Rockford, Mich., May 27, 1932; d. Beryl Dewey and Cora Belle (Potes) Jewell; m. Harry Eldon Sutton, July 7, 1962; children: Susan, Caroline. MD, U. Mich., 1957. Diplomate Am. Bd. Pediat., Am. Bd. Psychiatry and Neurology. Rotating intern St. Joseph Mercy Hosp., Ann Arbor, Mich., 1958; resident in child psychiatry Hawthorne Ctr., Northville, Mich., 1958-62; resident in pediat. U. Hosp./U. Mich. Med. Ctr., Ann Arbor, 1959-61; resident in psychiatry Austin (Tex.) State Hosp., 1962-64, dir. children's svc., 1964-89, dir. psychiat. residency program, 1989—, dir. tng. and rsch., 1993-98. Cons. in field. Contbr. articles to profl. jours. Active numerous civic orgns. Recipient Outstanding Achievement award, YWCA, 1989, Jackson Day award, Tex. Soc. Child and Adolescent Psychiatry, 1989, Showcase award, Tex. Dept. Mental Health/Mental Retardation, 1990. Fellow Am. Acad. Child and Adolescent Psychiatry (life), Am. Psychiat. Soc., Am. Pediatric Assn.; mem. Tex. Soc. Child and Adolescent Psychiatry (pres. 1979-80), Tex. Soc. Psychiat. Physicians (Disting. Svc. award 1990), AMA, Tex. Med. Soc., Am. Genetics Soc. Office: Seton Shoal Creek Hosp 3501 Mills Ave Austin TX 78731 Business E-Mail: bsutton@seton.org.

SUTTON, CECILIA (CECE SUTTON), bank executive; b. Charlotte, NC; B in Psychology, U. SC; MBA, Winthrop U. Branch manager First Union Corp., Raleigh and Cary, NC, consumer credit sales mgr. Charlotte, NC, 1984—86, consumer banking mgr. Greenville, SC, 1986—89, consumer bank training dir. Charlotte, NC, 1988—89, area exec. Rock Hill, SC, 1989—92, head SC Gen. Banking Group Greenville, SC, 1992—93, area exec. Rock Hill, SC, 1993—95, consumer banking exec. SC, exec. v.p. SC, 2001; exec. v.p., head retail Wachovia Corp. (merged with First Union Corp), Charlotte, 2001—. Chmn. Consumers Bankers Assn., 2006—. Office: Wachovia Corp 301 S Coll St Charlotte NC 28288-0018

SUTTON, DOLORES, actress, writer; b. NYC; BA in Philosophy, NYU. Appeared in broadway plays including Man With the Golden Arm, 1956, Career, 1958, Machinal, 1960, Rhinoceros, Liliom, She Stoops to Conquer, Hedda Gabler, Anna Karenina, Eccentricities of a Nightingale, Brecht on Brecht, Young Gifted and Black, Luv, The Friends, The Web and the Rock, The Seagull, Saturday, Sunday, Monday, The Little Foxes, What's Wrong With This Picture, The Cocktail Hour, My Fair Lady (Broadway revival), 1994, My Fair Lady (nat. tour), 1993-94; films include The Trouble With Angels, Where Angels Go, Trouble Follows, Crossing Delancey, Crimes and Misdeameanors, Tales of the Darkside; TV appearances include Studio One, Hallmark Hall of Fame Prodn. AH, Wilderness, Theatre Guild of the Air: Danger, Suspense, Gunsmoke, Valiant Lady, General Hospital, From These Roots, As the World Turns, Edge of Night, F. Scott Fitzgerald in Hollywood, Patty Hearst Story, All in the Family, Bob Newhart Show, All My Children, others, (TV writer) Lady Somebody, 1999, The Secret Storm, Loving; playwright: Down at the Old Bull and Bush, The Web and the Rock; Born Yesterday, 1995, A Perfect Ganesh, 1995, Detail of a Larger Work, 1995, The Front Page, 1996, The Exact Center of the Universe, 1997, A Drop in the Bucket, 1997, Spring Storm (newly discovered Tennessee Williams play), 1997, Signs and Wonders, 1998, It Gives Me Great Pleasure, 2001, Company Comin', 2006, and others; prodns. Free Ascent, 2001, Burial Society, 2001, The Find, 2002, (narrator) What If?, LA Opera, 2007. Mem. Actors Studio, League of Profl. Theatre Women (bd. dirs.), Ensemble Studio Theatre (bd. dirs.). Personal E-mail: suttonplace@webtv.net.

SUTTON, FRANCIS XAVIER, social services administrator, consultant; b. Oneida, Pa., July 7, 1917; s. Frank James and Rose Marie (Burns) S.; m. Ruth Jacqueline Young, Aug. 24, 1948 (dec. July 2002); children: Peter, Sean, Philip, Elizabeth. BS, Temple U., 1938; MA, Princeton U., 1940, Harvard U., 1941, PhD, 1950; DLitt (hon.), Aga Khan U., Karachi, 2003. Jr. fellow, Soc. Fellows Harvard U., Cambridge, Mass., 1946-49, asst. prof., lectr., 1949-54; program officer, overseas rep. Ford Found., NYC, 1954-67, dep. v.p., acting v.p., 1968-83; cons. Ford Found. and Harvard U., 1983-85; acting pres. Social Sci. Rsch. Coun., NYC, 1985-86, also bd. dirs., chmn., 1985-92; cons. Rockefeller Found., U.S. Agy. for Internat. Devel. and World Bank, NYC and Washington, 1987-92; acting dir. Rockefeller Study and Conf. Ctr., Bellagio, Italy, 1990-92; cons. Aga Khan U., 1992—. Author: The American Business Creed, 1956; editor: A World to Make/Development in Perspective, 1989; contbr. articles to profl. jours. and chpts. to books. Pres. Am. Found. for Intellectual Coop. with Europe, N.Y.C., 1987-93; mem. bd. fgn. scholarships Dept. State, Washington, 1961-63; bd. dirs. Nat. Ctr. on Adult Literacy, U. Pa., Phila., 1990-97; mem. adv. bd. Ctr. on Philanthropy, City Univ., N.Y.C., 1988—. Capt. U.S. Army Air Corps, 1941-45. Fellow AAAS; mem. Council on Fgn. Relations, Assn. for Asian Studies (Disting. Service award 1984). Clubs: Century Assn. (N.Y.C.). Democrat. Avocation: piano playing. Home: 80 Bellair Dr Dobbs Ferry NY 10522-3504 E-mail: fxsutton@aol.com.

SUTTON, GREGORY PAUL, obstetrician, gynecologist; b. Tokyo, Dec. 12, 1948; (parents Am. citizens); s. Vernon S. And Vonna Lou (Streeter) S.; m. Judith Craigie Holt, June 26, 1977; children: Anne Craigie, James Streeter. BS in Chemistry with honors, Ind. U., 1970; MD, U. Mich., 1976. Diplomate Am. Bd. of Ob/Gyn. Prof. gynecol. oncology Ind. U. Sch. Medicine, Indpls., 1986-97; Mary Fendrich Hulman prof. Gynecologic Oncology Ind. U. Sch. Med., Indpls., 1997-2000; mem. staff St. Vincent Hosp. and Health Svcs., 2000—01. Cancer Clin. fellow Am. Cancer Soc., Phila., 1981-83; recipient Career Devel. award Am. Cancer Soc., 1986-89. Fellow: Am. Coll. Obstetrics and Gynecology (chair Ind. sect. 2000—03); mem.: ACS (com. on cancer, Ind. state liaison), Hoosier Oncology Group, Soc. of Gynecologic Oncologists, Bayard Carter Soc., Ind. State Med. Soc., Marion County Med. Soc., Gynecologic Oncology Group (cert. Spl. Competence in Gynecologic Oncology 1985). Avocations: swimming, bicycling, woodworking, sailing, crossword puzzles. Office: 8301 Harcourt Rd Ste 202 Indianapolis IN 46260-1453 E-mail: gsutton@stvincent.org.

SUTTON, HARRY ELDON, geneticist, educator; b. Cameron, Tex., Mar. 5, 1927; s. Grant Edwin and Myrtle Dovie (Fowler) S.; m. Beverly Earlene Jewell, July 7, 1962; children: Susan Elaine, Caroline Virginia. BS in Chemistry, U. Tex., Austin, 1948, MA, 1949; PhD in Biochemistry, U. Tex., 1953. Biologist U. Mich., 1952-56, instr., 1956-57, asst. prof. human genetics, 1957-60; assoc. prof. zoology U. Tex., Austin, 1960-64, prof., 1964-99, chmn. dept. zoology, 1970-73, asso. dean Grad. Sch., 1967-70, 73-75, v.p. for research, 1975-79, Ashbel Smith prof. emeritus molecular genetics and microbiology, 2000—. Mem. adv. council Nat. Inst. Environ. Health Scis., 1968-72, council sci. advs., 1972-76; mem. various coms. Nat. Acad. Scis.-NRC; cons. in field; bd. dirs. Associated Univs. for Research in Astronomy, 1975-79, Argonne Univs. Assn., 1975-79, Univ. Corp. for Atmospheric Research, 1975-79, Associated Western Univs., 1978-79 Author: Genes, Enzymes, and Inherited Disease, 1961, An Introduction to Human Genetics, 1988, Genetics: A Human Concern, 1985; editor: First Macy Conference on Genetics, 1960, Mutagenic Effects of Environmental Contaminants, 1972, Am. Jour. Human Genetics, 1964-69. Trustee S.W. Tex. Corp. Public Broadcasting, 1977-80, sec., 1979-80; bd. dirs. Ballet Austin, 1978-84, 98-2004; mem. Austin Arts Commn., 1991-95. Served with U.S. Army, 1945-46. Mem. AAAS, Am. Soc. Human Genetics (dir. 1961-69, pres. 1979), Genetics Soc. Am., Am. Soc. Biochem. and Molecular Biology, Am. Chem. Soc., Tex. Genetics Soc. (pres. 1979), Am. Genetic Assn., Headliners Club (Austin), Town and Gown Club. Achievements include research and publications in human genetics. Home: 1103 Gaston Ave Austin TX 78703-2507 Office: Univ Tex Sect Molecular Genetics & Microbiology Austin TX 78712 Business E-Mail: eldon.sutton@mail.utexas.edu.

SUTTON, JEFFREY PAUL, physician, scientist; b. NYC, July 6, 1958; MD, U. Toronto, Ontario, Can., 1982, MSc in med. sci., 1985, PhD in physics, 1988. Intern U. Toronto, 1982-83, fellow in med. sci., 1983-84; fellow Can. Psychiat. Research Found., 1984-85; research fellow Med. Research Coun. of Can., 1985-88; clin. fellow in psychiatry Harvard Med. Sch., Boston, 1988-91; vis. scientist in brain and cognitive scis. MIT,

Cambridge, 1988-95, rsch. affiliate in brain and cognitive scis., 1995—; instr. psychiatry Harvard Med. Sch., Boston, 1991-93, asst. prof., 1993—; dir. neural sys. group Mass. Gen. Hosp., 1995—2001; dir. Nat. Space Biomed. Rsch. Inst., 2001—. Recipient NIH Rsch. Career Scientist award, 1994—. Mem. AMA, Am. Phys. Soc., Am. Psychiat. Assn., Soc. for Neurosci. Office: Nat Space Biomed Rsch Inst One Baylor Plaza NA-425 Houston TX 77030

SUTTON, JEFFREY S., federal judge; b. Dhahran, Saudi Arabia, 1960; BA, Williams Coll., 1983; LLB, Ohio State Univ., 1990. Clk. Second Circuit Ct. for Judge Thomas Meskill, 1990—91, Supreme Ct. for Justice Scalia and ret. Justice Powell, 1991—92; assoc. Jones, Day, Reavis & Pogue, Columbus, Ohio, 1992—95; adj. law prof. Ohio State Univ., Ohio, 1994—; Solicitor Ohio State, Ohio, 1995—98; ptnr. Jones, Day, Reavis & Pogue, Columbus, Ohio, 1998—2003; judge US Ct. Appeals, (6th cir.), Cin., 2003—. Office: Office Clerk US Ct Appeals 6th Cir 532 Potter Stewart US Cthse 100 E 5th St Cincinnati OH 45202-3988 *

SUTTON, JOHN F., JR., lawyer, educator, dean; b. Alpine, Tex., Jan. 26, 1918; s. John F. and Pauline Irene (Elam) S.; m. Nancy Ewing, June 1, 1940; children: Joan Sutton Parr, John Ewing. JD, U. Tex., 1941. Bar: Tex. 1941, U.S. Dist. Ct. (we. dist.) Tex. 1947, U.S. Ct. Appeals (5th cir.) 1951, U.S. Supreme Ct. 1960. Assoc. Brooks, Napier, Brown & Matthews, San Antonio, 1941; spl. agt. FBI, Washington, 1942—45; assoc. Matthews, Nowlin, Macfarlane & Barrett, San Antonio, 1945—48; ptnr. Kerr, Gayer & Sutton, San Angelo, Tex., 1948—50, Sutton, Steib & Barr, San Angelo, 1951—57; prof. U. Tex.-Austin, 1957—65, William Stamps Farish prof., 1965—84, A.W. Walker centennial chair, 1984—88, emeritus, 1988—, dean Sch. Law, 1979—84. Editor: (with Wellborn) Materials on Evidence, 8th edit., 1996, (with Dzienkowski) Cases and Materials on Professional Responsibility of Lawyers, 1989, (with Schuwerk) Guideline to the Texas Disciplinary Rules of Professional Conduct, 1990, (with Dzienkowski) Cases and Materials on Professional Conduct, 2d edit., 2002; contbr. articles to profl. jours. Served to 1st lt. JAGC USAR, 1948—53. Fellow Am. Bar Found. (life), Tex. Bar Found. (life); mem. ABA (com. on ethics 1970-76), State Bar Tex. (com. on rules of profl. conduct, com. adminstrn. rules of evidence), Philos. Soc. Tex., Order of Coif, U. Tex. Club, Phi Delta Phi, North Austin Rotary (pres. 1969). Presbyterian. Home: 3830 Sunset Dr San Angelo TX 76904-5956 Office: U Tex Sch Law 727 E Dean Keeton St Austin TX 78705-3224 Business E-Mail: jsutton@mail.law.utexas.edu.

SUTTON, JOHN PAUL, lawyer; b. Youngstown, Ohio, July 24, 1934; m. Jane Williamson, Aug. 20, 1958; children: Julia, Susan, Elizabeth. BA, U. Va., 1956; JD, George Washington U., 1963. Bar: Calif. 1965. Patent examiner U.S. Patent Office, Washington, 1956, 59-62; law clk. U.S. Ct. Customs and Patent Appeals, Washington, 1962-64; assoc. Flehr, Hohbach, Test, Albritton & Herbert, San Francisco, 1964-68; ptnr. Limbach, Limbach & Sutton, San Francisco, 1969-91; spl. counsel Heller, Ehrman, White & McAuliffe, San Francisco, 1992-95; of counsel Medlin & Carroll, San Francisco, 1995, Bryan, Hinshaw & Barnet, San Francisco, 1996-99; sole practice San Francisco, 2000—. Adj. instr. Practicing Law Inst., 1968-69; continuing edn. program Calif. State Bar, 1972, 75, U. Calif. Law Sch., Berkeley, 1975, 84. Contbr. articles to legal jours. Served with USNR, 1956-59. Mem.: Am. Chem. Soc., Fedn. Internat. des Conseils en Propriete Indsl. (pres. U.S. sect. 2003—06), State Bar Calif. (exec. com. patent sect. 1975—77), San Francisco Patent Law Assn. (pres. 1976), Calif. Patent Law Assn. (pres. 1975). Democrat. Episcopalian. Home and Office: 2421 Pierce St San Francisco CA 94115-1131 Home Phone: 415-922-6426; Office Phone: 415-929-7408. Personal E-mail: JohnPSutton@earthlink.net.

SUTTON, JOHNNY KEANE, prosecutor, lawyer; b. June 1960; B in Internat. Bus., U. Tex., 1983, JD, 1987. Criminal trial prosecutor Harris County Dist. Atty. Office; asst. dist. atty. Harris County Dist. Atty.'s Office, 1987—95; criminal justice policy dir. to Gov. State of Tex., 1995—2000; assoc. dep. atty. gen. US Dept. Justice, Washington, 2001; policy coord. Bush-Cheney Transition Team, US Dept. Justice; US atty. (we. dist.) Tex. US Dept. Justice, 2001—. Avocation: baseball (played for the Longhorns, starting lef-fielder on 1983 Nat. Championship team). Office: US Attys Office 601 NW Loop 410 Ste 600 San Antonio TX 78216 *

SUTTON, JULIA, musicologist, dance historian; b. Toronto, July 20, 1928; d. Samuel L. and Anne R. (Rubin) Sumberg. AB summa cum laude, Cornell U., 1949; MA, Colo. Coll., 1952; PhD, U. Rochester, 1962. Instr. music history New Sch. for Social Rsch., 1962-63; instr. music Queens Coll., CUNY, 1963-66; instr. music history and musicology New Eng. Conservatory Music, 1967—90, instr. and prof. musicology, 1967—90, chmn. dept. music history and musicology, 1971-90, chmn. faculty senate, 1971-73, prof. emerita, 1992. Vis. asst. prof. George Peabody Coll. for Tchrs., 1966-67; instr. NYU, summers 1963, 64; pvt. tchr. piano, 1949-65; lectr., rsch. dir. in musicology, music as related to the dance; presenter numerous workshops and summer insts. on Renaissance dance. Dance dir. N.Y. Pro Musica prodn. An Entertainment for Elizabeth, Caramoor, N.Y., Saratoga, N.Y., U. Ariz., Stanford U., UCLA, 1969, ann. nationwide tours, 1970-1973; dance dir. Descent of Rhythm and Harmony, Colorado Springs, Colo., 1970, Renaissance Revisited, Phila., 1972, An Evening of Renaissance Music and Dance, York U., Toronto, 1974; author: Jean Baptiste Besard's Novus Partus 1617, 1962; editor: Thoinot Arbeau: Orchesography 1588, 1967; translator, editor: Fabritio Caroso: Nobiltà di dame 1600, 1986, reprinted 1995; producer, co-dir. (tng. video) Il Ballarino, 1991; contbr. numerous articles to profl. jours. and Internat. Ency. of Dance, The New Grove Dictionary of Music and Musicians 1st and 2d edit., Die Musik in Geschichte und Gegenwart, 1st edit. Mem. Am. Musicological Soc., Soc. of Dance History Scholars, Phi Beta Kappa. Office Phone: 617-244-2482. E-mail: jsutton@lasell.edu.

SUTTON, KAREN E., museum director; b. New Brunswick, NJ, Aug. 26, 1952; d. Alfred Michael and Carmen (Collado) Sutton; children: Sloane, Brooke, Devon, Megan, Christopher. BA, Hofstra U., 1974; postgrad., NYU, 1987—89. Asst. to dir. Mus. Am. Folk Art, NYC, 1975-76, acting dir., 1976-77, bd. dirs., exec. com. officer, 1980-88, gallery dir., 1989-92, dir. ops., 1992-94, dep. dir. planning and adminstrn., 1994-95; v.p. Sotheby's, NYC, 1995-96, sr. v.p. adminstrn., 1996-2001, sr. v.p. worldwide mktg., 2001—. Bd. dirs. Family Dynamics, N.Y.C., 1976-80. Mem.: NY Women in Real Estate, Cosmopolitan Club (younger members chmn.). Democrat. Episcopalian. Office: Sotheby's 1334 York Ave New York NY 10021-4806 Home: 132 E 72 St New York NY 10021 Home Phone: 212-535-5935; Office Phone: 212-606-7410. E-mail: karen.sutton@sothebys.com.

SUTTON, KIM ROCHELL, education educator; b. Goldsboro, NC, Nov. 5, 1962; d. James D. and Minnie L. Staton; m. Michael W. Sutton, July 11, 1997; children: Christopher M. Maxwell, Sarah A. Maxwell, Ryan M. BS, Mo. State U., Springfield, 1999; MEd, William Woods U., Fulton, Mo., 2005. Cert. human devel. & child care Mo. Dept. Elem. & Secondary Edn., 2006. Child & family devel. instr. SW Mo. State U., 2000—02; early childhood instr. Ozarks Tech. Cmty. Coll., Springfield, 2003—; online early childhood instr. Mo. State U., West Plains, 2006—07; online edn. instr. Kendall Coll., Chgo., 2006—. Early childhood cons. Early Childhood Consulting, Springfield, 2000—. Team leader Mo. Ctr. Accreditation, Springfield, 2003—07. Mem.: Mo. Assn. Edn. Young Children (assoc.; bd. mem. 2006—), Air Force Sergeants Assn. (life), Golden Key. Achievements include design of online child and family development courses; development of continuing education child development associate program. Office: Ozarks Tech Cmty Coll 1001 E Chestnut Expressway Springfield MO 65802 Business E-Mail: suttonk@otc.edu.

SUTTON, LEE, biology professor; s. Leonard F. and Jerri Sutton; m. Brooks Sykes, May 31, 2003; 1 child, Charlie. PhD, NC State U., Raleigh, 2002. Lic. 100 ton capt. USCG, 1997. Biology prof. East Carolina U., Greenville, NC, 2002—. Participant Jeanie B Tall Ships, Pepsi Am.'s Sail, 2006; sailing capt., instr. Outer Banks Sail and Kayak. Home Phone: 804-519-0174.

SUTTON, LYNN SORENSEN, librarian; b. Detroit, July 31, 1953; d. Leonard Arthur Edward and Dorothy Ann (Steele) Sorensen. AB, U. Mich., 1975, MLS, 1976. Dir. Med. Libr. South Chgo. Cmty. Hosp., 1976-77; corp. dirs. librs. Detroit-Macomb Hosp. Corp., Detroit, 1977-86; dir. librs. Harper Hosp., Detroit, 1987-88; dir. Sci. and Engring. Libr. Wayne State U., Detroit, 1989-95, dir. undergrad. libr., 1996—2004; dir. Z. Smith Reynolds Libr. Wake Forest U., Winston-Salem, NC, 2004—. Cons. Catherine McAuley Health Sys., Ann Arbor, Mich., 1993. Contbr. articles to profl. jours. Mem. ALA, Assn. Coll. and Rsch. Librs. (budget and fin. com. 1995—), Mich. Health Scis. Librs. Assn. (pres. 1987-88), Met. Detroit Med. Libr. Group (pres. 1983-84), Phi Beta Kappa, Beta Phi Mu. Office: Z Smith Reynolds Libr Wake Forest U Box 7777 Reynolda Station Winston Salem NC 27109 Office Phone: 336-758-5090. Business E-Mail: suttonls@wfu.edu. *

SUTTON, NEAL S., lawyer; b. Grand Forks, ND, Sept. 9, 1945; BA, U. Houston, 1969, JD, 1972. Bar: Tex. 1972, US Ct. Appeals (5th cir.) 1972. Atty. pvt. practice; gen. counsel, sec. Cameron Iron Works (acquired by Cooper Industries Inc. in 1989), Houston, 1977—89; assoc. gen. counsel Cooper Industries Inc., Houston, 1989—91; v.p., sec., gen. counsel Smith Internat. Inc., Houston, 1991—92, v.p. adminstrn., gen. counsel, sec., 1992—94, sr. v.p. adminstrn., gen. counsel, sec., 1994—2006, sr. v.p. law, 2006—. Adj. assoc. prof. adminstrv. sci. Rice U. Jones Grad. Sch. Adminstrn., 1989—93; gulf coast dist. dir. Petroleum Equipment Suppliers Assn. Bd. dirs. Harris County Edn. Found., 1997—. Mem.: Am. Corp. Counsel Assn. (dir. Houston chpt. 1984—87, pres. Houston chpt. 1985—86, mem. nat. bd. dirs. 1988—96), State Bar Tex., Houston Bar Assn. (dir. corp. counsel sect. 1991—93), ABA. Office: Smith Internat Inc PO Box 60068 Houston TX 77205-0068 *

SUTTON, PHILIP D. (PHILIP DIETRICH SUTTON), psychologist, educator; b. June 20, 1952; s. Clifton C. and Ida-Lois (Dietrich) S.; m. Kathleen E. Duffy, June 17, 1973; children: Heather, Shivonne. BA, So. Ill. U., 1974; MA, U. Chgo., 1975; PhD, U. Utah, 1979. Lic. psychologist, Colo. Psychologist VA Hosp., Salt Lake City, 1975-76; psychology intern Salt Lake Cmty. Mental Health Ctr., 1976-78; counselor, instr. Counseling Ctr. U. Utah, 1976-78; counselor, acting dir. spl. svcs. program Met. State Coll., Denver, 1978-80; staff psychologist Kaiser-Permanente Health Plan, 1980—83; pvt. practice Boulder, 1983—. Adj. prof. U. Colo., 1979-83; cons. spl. program for disacvantaged students in higher edn. HEW, 1980. Mem. APA, Biofeedback Soc., Am. Soc. Behavioral Medicine. Office: Box 1781 Nederland CO 80466 Personal E-mail: pdsphd@aol.com.

SUTTON, RONNIE NEAL, state legislator, lawyer; b. Pembroke, NC, June 17, 1941; s. Willie French and Vergie Mae (Oxendine) S.; m. Genny Chavis, June 19, 1967; children: Ronette, Fonda Lynn. BA, U. West Fla., 1970; MS, Naval War Coll., 1977; MA, Ctrl. Mich. U., 1979; JD, U. N.C., 1985. Commd. ensign USN, 1958, advanced through grades to comdr., ret., 1982; atty. Sutton Law Office, Pembroke, 1985-97; rep. N.C. Ho. of Reps., Raleigh, 1993—. Bd. dirs. Lumber River Legal Svcs., Pembroke, N.C. Cancer Inst., Lumberton. Chmn. Robeson County Dem. Party, Lumberton, 1991-92. Mem. Pembroke Kiwanis Club (pres. 1991-92, Kiwanian of Yr. 1992). Democrat. Home: 2940 Philadelphus Rd Pembroke NC 28372-8308 Office: NC Ho of Reps Jones St Raleigh NC 27601 Home Phone: 910-843-2353; Office Phone: 910-521-4797. E-mail: rons@ncleg.net.

SUTTON, SAMUEL J., lawyer, educator, engineer; b. Chgo., July 21, 1941; s. Samuel J. and Elaine (Blossom) S.; m. Anne V. Sutton, Aug. 28, 1965; children: Paige, Jean, Leah, Jepson. BA in History and Philosophy, U. Ariz., 1964, BSEE, 1967; JD, George Washington U., 1969. Bar: Ariz. 1969, D.C. 1970, U.S. Ct. Appeals (fed. cir.) 1983. Patent atty. Gen. Electric Co., Washington, Phoenix, 1967-70; ptnr. Cahill, Sutton & Thomas, Phoenix, 1970-95, of counsel, 1995—. Prof. law Ariz. State U., Tempe, 1975-2004; expert witness Fed. Dist. Cts., 1983—; trial cons. to numerous lawyers, 1972—; arbitrator Am. Arbitration Assn., Phoenix, 1971—. Author: Patent Preparation, 1976, Intellectual Property, 1978, Art Law, 1988, Law, Science and Technology, 1991, Licensing Intangible Property, 1994, Commercial Torts, 1995, Patent Litigation, 1996, 120-hr. multimedia series on intellectual property, 1999—; pub. sculptures installed at Tanner Sq., Phoenix, Tucson Art Inst., Mobil Corp., Mesa, Ariz., Cox Devel. Co., Tempe, Ariz., Downtown Phoenix, Desert Bot. Garden, Phoenix, Gateway Ctr., Sedona Sculpture Garden, Construct Gallery, Phoenix. Chmn. air pollution hearing bd. City of Phoenix, Maracopa County, 1970-85. Recipient Patent prize Patent Resources Group, 1979, Publ. award IEEE, 1967, Genematus award U. Ariz., 1964, Disting. Achievement award Ariz. State U., 1980, Construct Sculpture prize, 1989. Avocation: large scale steel sculpture. Office: PO Box 32694 Phoenix AZ 85064-2694 E-mail: sam.sutton@cox.net.

SUTTON-CREECH, DONNA LYNN, gifted and talented educator; b. Arcadia, La., Dec. 14, 1963; d. Jerry Lamar and Betty Muse Sutton; m. Stephen Orel Creech, July 9, 2005. BA, La. Tech. U., 1984, MA, 1985, EdD in curriculum and instruction, 2002. Compensatory edn. tchr. Bienville Parish Sch. Sys., Arcadia, La., 1985—90; parttime computer instr. Northwest La. Tech. Coll., Minden, La., 2002—04; gifted program tchr. Bienville Parish, Sch. Sys., Arcadia, 1990—. Computer workshop presenter Bienville Parish La. Libr., Arcadia, La., 2003. Publr. genealogy column, Bienville Democrat. Participant Tech Rome 1987, La. Tech. U. Named Tchr. of Yr., Ringgold Elem. Sch., 1995; recipient Daughters of Am. Revolution Outstanding Jr. Mem. award, Dorcheat-Bistineau, 1997; La. Heritage Edn. grant, La. Divsn. Archaeology and Hist., 2003. Mem.: DAR (Dorcheat-Bistineau chpt. officer, vice regent, historian, chpt. chair, Dorcheat-Bistineau chpt. scholarship com., Good Citizens award), Phi Delta Kappa, Krewe of Gemini, Colonial Dames Seventeenth Century (state jr. mem. chair 2001—04, Martha Randolph chpt. v.p. 2002—04, state pages chair), Nat. Soc. Magna Carta Dames and Barons, USA Order of Crown of Charlemagne. Republican. Baptist. Avocations: genealogy, reading, travel, painting.

SUUBERG, ERIC MICHAEL, chemical engineering educator; b. NYC, Nov. 23, 1951; s. Michael and Aino (Berg) S.; m. Ina Inara Vatvars, Apr. 26, 1987; 1 child, Alessandra Anna. BSChemE, MSChemE, MIT, 1974, BS in Bus. Mgmt., 1974, MS in Bus. Mgmt., 1976, ScD in Chem. Engring., 1978. Asst. prof. chem. engring. Carnegie-Mellon U., Pitts., 1977-81; asst. prof. engring. Brown U., Providence, 1981-84, assoc. prof. engring., 1984-90, prof. engring., 1990—, rep. exec. com. fluids, thermal and chem. processes group, 1991—97, assoc. dean faculty, 2003—05; co-dir. Brown, Superfund Basic Rsch. Program, 2005—. Vis. scientist Centre National de la Recherche Scientifique, Mulhouse, France, 1988; invited lectr. Ministry Edn., Monbusho, Japan, 1991, 93, 2003; vis. prof. Tallinn Tech. U., 2001. Mem. internat. editl. bd. Fuel, 1988—, mem. editl. adv. bd. Energy and Fuels, 1990—93, 1998—2000, Americas editor Fuel, 2000—, contbr. over 100 articles to profl. jours. Elected mem. Estonian Am. Nat. Coun., N.Y.C., 1984-99, v.p. 1996-99, bd. dirs. 2002—. Vice Chancellor's Rsch. Best Practice fellow U. Newcastle, Australia, 1995; Fulbright scholar, 2000-01. Mem. AIChE, Combustion Inst., Am. Chem. Soc. (chmn. divsn. fuel chemistry 1991, bd. dirs.-at-large 1995-97, trustee 2002—, H.H. Storch award in fuel chemistry Am. Chem. Soc. 1999). Office: Brown Univ Divsn Engring Box D Providence RI 02912 E-mail: eric_suuberg@brown.edu.

SUVARI, MENA, actress; b. Newport, RI, Feb. 9, 1979; d. Ando and Candance Suvari; m. Robert Brinkmann, Mar. 4, 2000. Actor: (TV films) Atomic Train, 1999; (TV series) Six Feet Under, 2004—; (films) Nowhere, 1997, Snide and Prejudice, 1997, Kiss the Girls, 1997, Slums of Beverly Hills, 1998, The Rage: Carrie 2, 1999, American Pie, 1999, American Beauty, 1999, American Virgin, 2000, Loser, 2000, Sugar & Spice, 2001, American Pie 2, 2001, The Musketeer, 2001, Sonny, 2002, Spun, 2002, Trauma, 2004, Beauty Shop, 2005, Domino, 2005, Rumor Has It..., 2005, The Dog Problem, 2006, Factory Girl, 2006, Brooklyn Rules, 2007, Stuck, 2007. Office: c/o Gersh Agy 232 N Canon Dr Beverly Hills CA 90210

SUWYN, MARK A., paper company executive; b. Denver, Aug. 8, 1942; BS in Chemistry, Hope Coll., Holland, Mich., 1964; PhD in Inorganic Chemistry, Wash. State U., Pullman, 1967. R & D to gen. mgmt. positions DuPont Co., 1967-91, sr. v.p. imaging and med. products, 1989-92; exec. v.p. distbn., dir. Internat. Paper, Purchase, NY, 1992-95; chmn., CEO La.-Pacific Corp., Portland, Oreg., 1996—2004, NewPage Corp., 2006—. Bd. dirs. NewPage Holding, Maple Timber Acquisition. Office: NewPage Corp Delaware Courthouse Plaza NE Dayton OH 45463 Office Phone: 877-855-7243. *

SUYCOTT, MARK LELAND, program manager, retired military officer; b. Riverside, Calif., Oct. 3, 1956; s. Morgan L. Suycott and Dixie L. (Drury) Bobbitt; m. Lisa Lyn Brammer, Oct. 1, 1983. BSCE, U. Mo., 1979; MS in Aero. Engring., Naval Postgrad. Sch., Monterey, Calif., 1987; test flight officer, U.S. Naval Test Pilot Sch., Patuxent River, Md., 1987; student, Def. Sys. Mgmt. Coll., Ft. Belvoir, Va., 1994. Commd. ensign USN, 1979, advanced through grades to comdr., 1995; aviation armament divsn. officer Fighter Squadron 33, Virginia Beach, Va., 1981-84; flight test project officer Pacific Missile Test Ctr., Point Mugu, Calif., 1987-89; air ops. officer Comdr. U.S. 7th Fleet, Yokosuka/Manama, Japan/Bahrain, 1989-91; ops./maintenance officer Fighter Squadron 11, San Diego, 1992-93; dep. asst. program mgr. Naval Air Sys. Command, Arlington, Va., 1994-97; prof. Def. System Mgmt. Coll., Fort Belvoir, Va., 1997-99; sr. sys. engr. SAIC Space and Def. Group, San Diego, 2000-01, prin. sys. engr. and program mgr., 2001—03, sr. project mgr., program mgr., 2004—. Asst. dist. commr. Boy Scouts Am.; chaplain Al Bahr Shrine, 2006. Decorated Def. Meritorious Svc. medal, Meritorious Svc. medal (2), Navy Commendation medal (2), Navy Achievement medal; named Outstanding Grad., U.S. Naval Test Pilot Sch.; recipient Woodbadge award, Boy Scouts Am., Disting. Commr. award, Commr.'s Key award, Dist. award of Merit. Mem.: VFW, AIAA (sr.), Inst. Navigation, Tailhook Assn., Nat. Eagle Scout Assn. (life), Masons (life), Naval Aviation Found., Rancho Bernardo Shrine Club (pres. 2007—), Scottish Rite (32d degree), Shriners (life; club pres. 2007), Am. Legion, Chi Epsilon, Tau Beta Pi, Omicron Delta Kappa, Alpha Phi Omega (life). Avocations: bicycling, sailing, skiing. Address: SAIC 10260 Campus Point Dr MS c2 San Diego CA 92121-1522

SUYDAM, JOHN J., lawyer; b. NYC, 1960; BA, SUNY, Albany, 1982; JD, NYU, 1985. Bar: NY 1986. Chmn. O'Sullivan, LLP, NY; head O'Melveny & Myers, LLP, NY, mem. policy com., co-chair merger and acquisitions/private equity practice group, 2002—06; chief legal officer, v.p. Apollo Investment Corp., NYC, 2006—. Mem.: ABA. Office: Apollo Investment Corp 9 W 57th St New York NY 10019 *

SUYENAGA, ELSIE SAKAE, retired elementary school educator; b. Honolulu, Dec. 19; d. Shigeharu Shimizu-Jinbo and Misao Jinbo; m. James Saburo Suyenaga; 1 child, Matthew Masao. BA, Pasadena Coll., 1963; postgrad., U. Hawaii, 1963—81. Sec. Nuuanu Bapt. Ch., 1954—62; tchr. Ewa Beach (Hawaii) Elem. Sch., 1964—89. Exch. tchr. Laurel Elem. Sch. LA Sch. Dist., 1968—69; advisor student coun. Laurel Elem. Sch. Sec. Palisades Cmty. Assn., 1977; treas. Neighborhood Bd., Pearl City, 1982; legis. chmn., treas. Pearl City Cmty. Assn., 1984—85; treas. local chpt. PTA; active polit. campaigns. Recipient Student Coun. Advisor award, Ewa Beach Elem. Sch., 1978, Dist. award, PTA, 1976, Merit Cert., Pearl City Cmty. Assn., 1977, Recognition award, Ewa Beach Kiwanis, 1986; Fed. grant, 1963. Mem.: DAV, Am. Mus. Natural History, Hawaii Edn. Assn. (bd. trustees 1986—), Leeward Tchrs. Assn. (treas., polit. sect. chmn. 1986), Hawaii State Tchrs. Assn. (dir. 1981—83, sec. fin. com. 1981, vice-chmn. 1982, Merit Cert. 1969), Alpha Delta Kappa (treas. Lambda chpt. 1980—81). Democrat. Baptist. Home: 6354 San Diego Ave Riverside CA 92506 E-mail: suyenaga@charter.net.

SUZIEDELIS, VYTAUTAS A., retired engineering corporation executive; b. Kaunas, Lithuania, June 22, 1930; s. Simas and Antanina S. BS, Northeastern U., 1954; MS, NYU, 1955. With Stone & Webster Engring. Corp., Boston, 1956-90, chief power engr., 1972-74, v.p., 1974-76, sr. v.p., 1976-79, exec. v.p., 1979-87, dir., 1975-87, cons., 1987-90; pres. Vasair Corp., Brockton, Mass., 1977-91; ret., 1991. Mem. ASME, Aircraft Owners and Pilots Assn., Pi Tau Sigma (hon.). Republican. Roman Catholic. Home: 6849 Grenadier Blvd Ph 5 Naples FL 34108-7223 Personal E-mail: vasuziedelis@cs.com.

SUZUKI, AKIRA, physics professor; b. Tokyo, Apr. 14, 1949; s. Masatsugu and Takako (Tanbo) S.; m. Keiko Sawamura, Sept. 13, 1992. BSc, Sci. U. Tokyo, 1973; PhD, U. Reading, Eng., 1982. Rsch. assoc. Purdue U., West Lafayette, Ind., 1982-85; chief scientist Canon Inc. Rsch. Ctr., Atsugi, Japan, 1986-93; assoc. prof. Sci. U. Tokyo, 1993-98, prof. physics, 1998—, chmn., 2002—; prof. Inst. Pure and Applied Physics Tokyo U. Sci., 1998—. Contbr. articles to profl. jours. Mem. IEEE, Am. Phys. Soc., NY Acad. Scis. Avocations: tennis, golf, music. Office: Sci U Tokyo Ctr Solid State Physics 1-3 Kagurazaka Tokyo 162 Japan

SUZUKI, BOB H., retired academic administrator; b. Jan. 1936; MS mech. engring., Univ. Calif. Berkeley. Formerly v.p. acad. affairs Calif. State Univ., Northridge; pres. Calif. State Poly. Univ., Pomona, 1991—2003; ret., 2003. Recipient Human Rights award Leadership Asian and Pacific Island Affairs, NEA, 1976. Home: 3012 W Ross Ave Alhambra CA 91803

SUZUKI, HIDETARO, violinist; b. Tokyo, June 1, 1937; arrived in U.S., 1956; s. Hidezo and Humi (Sakai) S.; m. Zeyda Ruga, May 16, 1962; children: Kenneth Hideo, Nantel Hiroshi, Elina Humi. Diploma, Toho Sch. Music, Tokyo, 1956, Curtis Inst. Music, 1963. Prof. violin Conservatory Province Que., Canada, 1963-79, Laval U., Quebec, Canada, 1971-77, Butler U., Indpls., 1979—. Concertmaster Que. Symphony Orch., 1963-78, Indpls. Symphony Orch., 1978-2005; performed as concert violinist Can., U.S., Ea. and Western Europe, Cuba, Japan, S.E. Asia, India, USSR 1951-; guest condr. orchs. in numerous concerts, broadcasts, 1968—; mem. jury Mont. Internat. Competition, 1979, Internat. Violin Competition, 1979, Internat. Violin Competition of Indpls., 1982, 86, 90, 94; artistic dir. Suzuki and Friends chamber music series, 1980—; rec. artist (CDs, violin and piano) Dialogue, Dialogue II, Pas de deux.

SUZUKI, HOWARD KAZURO, retired anatomist, educator; b. Ketchikan, Alaska, Apr. 3, 1927; s. Goerge K. and Tsuya S.; m. Tetsuko Fujita, Sept. 12, 1952; children: Georganne, Joan, James, Stanley. BS, Marquette U., 1949, MS, 1951; PhD, Tulane U., 1955. Instr. anatomy Yale U. Sch. Medicine, 1955-58; asst. prof. anatomy U. Ark. Med. Center, Little Rock, 1958-62, asso. prof., 1962-67, prof., 1967-70; prof. anatomy, asso. dean health related professions U. Fla., Gainesville, 1970-71; prof. anatomy U. Fla. (Coll. Medicine), 1970-71; dean U. Fla. (Coll. Health Related Professions), 1971-79; prof. anatomy U. Fla. (Coll. Medicine and Health Related Professions), 1979-90, ret., 1990. Cons. NIH, VA, NASA; vis. research prof. U. Utah Sch. Medicine, 1962 Contbr. articles to profl. jours.

Bd. dirs. Civitan Regional Blood Bank, 1977—; regional v.p. Fla. Retarded Citizens Assn., 1974-76; mem. Fla. Adv. Council on Vocat. Edn., 1978-86, chmn., 1981; active United Way. Fellow AAAS; mem. Soc. Exptl. Biol. Medicine, Am Assn. Anatomists, Am. Soc. Allied Health Professions, Am. Soc. Marine Artists, Sigma Xi. Episcopalian. Home: 4331 NW 20th Pl Gainesville FL 32605-3436 E-mail: hksuzuki@aol.com.

SUZUKI, ICHIRO, professional baseball player; b. Kasugai, Japan, Oct. 22, 1973; m. Yumiko Suzuki. Player Orix Blue Waves, Japan, 1992—2001; right fielder Seattle Mariners, 2001—. Named Pacific League MVP, 1994—96, Am. League Rookie of Yr., 2001, Am. League MVP, 2001, All-Star Game MVP, 2007; named to Am. League All-Star Team, 2001—07, All-Tourney Team, World Baseball Classic, 2006; recipient Matsutaro Shoriki prize, 1994—95, 8 Gold Glove awards, Nippon Profl. Baseball League, 7 Best Nine Team titles, Japan, Silver Slugger award, 2001, Am. League Gold Glove award, 2001—06. Achievements include being the second player in history to win rookie and MVP award in the same season; being second player in MLB history to lead league in batting average and stolen bases in a season, 2001; being first player in MLB history to have over 200 hits in each of his first four years; holding MLB record for singles in a season (225), 2004; holding MLB record for hits in a single season (262), 2004; leading Am. League in Batting Avg. (.350), 2001, and (.372), 2004; helping his national team Japan win the first ever World Baseball Classic 2006; became third fastest to reach 1,500 hits on July 29, 2007 against the Oakland Athletics. Office: Seattle Mariners PO Box 4100 Seattle WA 98104 *

SUZUKI, JON BYRON, medical educator, periodontist, microbiologist; s. George K. and Ruby Suzuki. BA in Biology, Ill. Wesleyan U., 1968; PhD in Microbiology magna cum laude, Ill. Inst. Tech., 1971; DDS magna cum laude, Loyola U., 1978. Lic. lab. dir. Hawaii Dept. Health. Med. technologist Ill. Masonic Hosp. and Med. Ctr., Chgo., 1966—67; instr. lab. in histology and parasitology Ill. Wesleyan U., Bloomington, 1967—68; med. technologist Augustana Hosp., Chgo., 1968—69; rsch. assoc., instr. microbiology Ill. Inst. Tech., Chgo., 1968—71; clin. rsch. assoc. U. Chgo. Hosps., 1970—71; clin. microbiologist St. Luke's Hosp., Columbia Coll., Physicians and Surgeons, NYC, 1971—73; assoc. med. dir. Paramed Tng. and Registry, Vancouver, BC, Canada, 1973—74; dir. clin. labs. Registry of Hawaii, 1973—74; chmn. clin. labs. edn. Kapiolany C.C., U. Hawaii, Honolulu, 1974; lectr. periodontics, oral pathology Loyola U. Med. Ctr., Maywood, Ill., 1974—90; lectr. stomatology Northwestern U. Dental Sch., Chgo., 1982—90; NIH rsch. fellow depts. pathology and periodontics Ctr. for Rsch. in Oral Biology, U. Wash., Seattle, 1978—80; prof. dept. periodontics and microbiology U. Md. Coll. Dental Surgery, Balt., 1980—90; attending faculty divsn. dentistry and oral and maxillofacial surgery Johns Hopkins Med. Inst., Balt., 1985—96; practice specializing in periodontics Balt. and Pitts.; prof., dean Sch. Dental Medicine U. Pitts., 1989—2000, prof., dir. periodontics residency program, 2002—04. Cons. Dentsply Internat., York, Pa., U.S. Army, Walter Reed Med. Ctr., Washington, U.S. Army, Ft. Gordon, Ga., USN, Nat. Naval Med. Command, Bethesda, The NutraSweet Col, Chgo., FDA, Rockville, Md., 1995—, Phillips Oral Health Care, Snoqualmie, Wash.; oral biology/medicine study sect. NIH, Bethesda, 1985-90; nat. adv. dental rsch. coun. NIH/NIDCR, Bethesda, 1994-98; vis. scientist Moscow State U., USSR, 1972, NASA, Houston, 1976-92; lectr. Internat. Congress allergology, Tokyo, 1973. Author: Clinical Laboratory Methods for the Medical Assistant, 1974; mem. editl. bd. Jour. Clinical Dentistry, Jour. Practical Hygiene, Jour. Acad. Gen. Dentistry; contbr. articles on rsch. in microbiology, immunology and dentistry to profl. jours. Instr. water safety ARC, Honolulu, 1973—90. Recipient Pres.'s medallion Loyola U., Chgo., 1977; named Alumnus of Yr., Ill. Wesleyan U., 1977, Loyola U., Chgo., 1997. Fellow Acad. Dentistry Internat., Am. Coll. Dentists, Internat. Coll. Dentists, Am. Coll. Stomatognathic Surgeons; mem. ADA (chair coun. sci. affairs 1998), AAUP, Am. Acad. Periodontology (diplomate), Am. Dental Edn. Assn., Am. Inst. Biol. Scis., Internat. Soc. Biophysics, Internat. Soc. Endocrinologists, Ill. Acad. Sci., Am. Internat. Assn. Dental Rsch. (pres. Md. chpt.), Am. Coll. Microbiology (diplomate, examiner), Am. Soc. Clin. Pathology (specialist microbiology), N.Y. Acad. Scis., Sigma Xi, Omicron Kappa Upsilon (past nat. pres., exec. sec. 1989—, treas. 2006—), Beta Beta Beta. Office: Temple Univ Dentistry Office of the Dean 3223 N Broad St Philadelphia PA 19140 E-mail: jsuzuki@temple.edu.

SUZUKI, KUNIHIKO, biomedical educator, researcher; b. Tokyo, Feb. 5, 1932; arrived in U.S., 1960; s. Nobuo and Teiko (Suzuki) Suzuki; m. Kinuko Ikeda, Dec. 20, 1960; 1 child, Jun. BA in History and Philosophy of Sci., Tokyo U., 1955, MD, 1959; MA (hon.), U. Pa., 1971. Diplomate Nat. Bd. Med. Licensure Japan. Rotating intern USAF Hosp. Tachikawa, Tokyo, 1959-60; asst. resident in neurology Bronx (N.Y.) Mcpl. Hosp. Ctr.-Albert Einstein Coll. Medicine, 1960-61, resident in neurology, 1961-62, clin. fellow in neurology, 1962-64; instr. in neurology Albert Einstein Coll. Medicine, Bronx, 1964, asst. prof., 1965-68; assoc. prof. U. Pa. Sch. Medicine, Phila., 1969-71, prof. neurology and pediatrics, 1971-72; prof. neurology Albert Einstein Coll. Medicine, 1972-86, prof. neurosci., 1974-86; prof. neurology and psychiatry, faculty curriculum in neurobiology U. N.C. Sch. Medicine, Chapel Hill, 1986—2002, prof. emeritus neurology and psychiatry, 2002—; dir. UNC Neurosci. Ctr., Chapel Hill, 1986-99, dir. emeritus, 1999—; prof. Future Sci. and Tech. Joint Rsch. Ctr. Tokai U., Japan, 2003—, dir. Inst. Glycotechnology, 2003—. Staff dept. neuropsychiatry Tokyo U. Faculty Medicine, 1960, U. Pa. Inst. Neurol. Scis., 1969—72; attending physician Bronx Mcpl. Hosp. Ctr., 1976—86, Hosp. Albert Einstein Coll. Medicine, 1977—86; vis. prof. fellowship Japan Soc. for Promotion Sci., 1980, Yamada Sci. Found., 1981; mem. neurology B study sect. NIH, 1971—75, guest scientist, 1984—85, program com. mental retardation and devel. disabilities, 1989—92; mem. basic neurosci. task force Nat. Inst. Neurol. and Communicative Disorders and Stroke, 1978, adv. panel directions and opportunities for future rsch., 83; bd. sci. counselors NIH, 1980—84; mem. adv. com. on fellowships Nat. Multiple Sclerosis Soc., 1974—77; jury St. Vincent Internat. award for Med. Sci., 1979; mem. adv. com. Eunice Kennedy Shriver Ctr., Waltham, Mass., 1974—84; mem. U.S. Nat. Com. for Internat. Brain Rsch. Orgn., 1985—89. Editor: Ganglioside Structure and Function, 1984; editor: (chief) Jour. Neurochemistry, 1977—82; dep. chief editor Jour. Neurochemistry, 1975—77, mem. editl. bd. Jour. Neuropathology and Exptl. Neurology, 1981—83, Neurosci., 1975—, Molecular Chem. Neuropathology, 1983—, Neurochem. Rsch., 1985—89, Metabolic Brain Disease, 1985—87, Molecular Brain Rsch., 1985—, Jour. Molecular Neurosci., 1987—, Devel. Neurosci., 1987—, Jour. Neurosci. Rsch., 1993—97; contbr. Mem. Nat. Adv. Commn. on Multiple Sclerosis, 1973—74; mem. med. adv. bd. United Leukodystrophy Found., 1982—86, 1997—, Nat. Tay-Sachs and Allied Diseases Assn., 1971—2001, Canavan Found., 1992—. Recipient A. Weil award, Am. Assn. Neuropathologists, 1970, Saul R. Korey Lectureship, 1993, M. Moore award, 1975, Jacob K. Javits Neurosci. Investigator award, NIH, 1985, 1992, Humboldt Sr. Rsch. award, Humboldt Found., 1990, Eminent Scientist award, Inst. Phys. Chem. Rsch., Japan, 1995, Japan Acad. prize, 2002. Mem.: AAAS, Japan Soc. Inherited Metabolic Disease (hon.), Am. Soc. Human Genetics, Internat. Brain Rsch. Orgn., Japanese Neurochem. Soc., Japanese Med. Soc. Am. (Disting. Scientist award 1985), Am. Acad. Neurology, Am. Soc. Biochemistry and Molecular Biology, Soc. for Neurosci., Internat. Soc. for Neurochemistry (coun. 1987—89, treas. 1989—93, pres. 1993—95), Am. Soc. for Neurochemistry (pres. 1985—87, coun. 1973—77, 1987—91, Basic Neurochemistry Lectureship 1995), Inst. Medicine NAS. Avocations: piano, photography, birdwatching, skiing. E-mail: kuni.suzuki@attglobal.net.

SUZUKI, NOBUTAKA, chemistry professor; b. Nishio, Aichi, Japan, Nov. 8, 1942; s. Kihachiro and Masayo (Miwa) S.; m. Fumiko Sato, Mar. 21, 1971; children: Mina, Kumi. B of Chemistry, Nagoya U., Japan, 1966, D of Chemistry, 1972. Asst. prof. dept. chemistry Mie U., Tsu, Japan, 1971-88, assoc. prof., 1988; sr. rschr. Biophoton project JRDC, Sendai, Japan, 1988-90; assoc. prof. Shimonoseki (Japan) Nat. U. Fisheries, 1990-92, prof., 1993—2002, Hiroshima U., Japan, 2002—06, dean dept. biol. functional chemistry, 2004—05; chief Internat. Tech. Exch. Soc. Rsch. Inst., Nagoya, Japan, 2006—. Postdoctoral staff Johns Hopkins U., Balt., 1977-79; vis. prof. Asian Sch. Internat. Tech. Exch. Soc. Rsch. Inst., Brunswick, Ohio, 2000—. Author: Natural Products Chemistry, 1975, 2d rev. edit., 1983, Bioluminescence and Chemiluminescence, Current Status, 1991, Oxygen Radicals, 1992, Chemistry of Functional Dyes, Vol. 2, 1993, Bioluminescence and Chemiluminescence, Status Report, 1993, Bioluminescence and Chemiluminescence: Fundamentals and Applied Aspects, 1994, Maillard Reactions in Chemicals, Food, and Health, 1994, Food Factors: Chemistry and Cancer Prevention, 1997, Bioluminescence and Chemiluminescence, Molecular Reporting and Photons, 1997, Food Factors for Cancer Prevention, 1997, The Maillard Reaction in Foods and Medicine, 1998, Recent Research Developments in Agricultural and Biological Chemistry, Vol. 2, 1998, Advances in Shrimp Biotechnology, 1998, Dictionary of Biochemistry, 3d edit., 1998, Bioluminescence and Chemiluminescence: Perspectives for the 21st Century, 1999, Recent Development of Food Factors for the Aging Prevention, 1999, Agricultural and Biological Chemistry, Vol. 3, 1999, Future in Fisheries Science, 1999, Food Sciences, 2001, Bioluminescence and Chemiluminescence, 2000, 01, Bioluminescence and Chemiluminescence, Progress and Current Applications, 2002, Research Advances in Food Science, 2002, Trends in Comparative Biochemistry and Physiology, 2002, Near Infrared Spectroscopy, 2002, Trends in Comparative Biochemistry & Physiology, Vol.9, 2002; editor: The Roles of Oxygen in Chemistry and Biochemistry, 1988, (book/tape) Scientific English in Fisheries, 1992, English for Science and Technological Experiments, 1994, English for Pharmacy and Medical Science, 1995, English for International Conference, 1995, Oxidative Degradation and Antioxidative Activities of Food Constituents, 2002, Life-style Related Diseases and Food Functions, 2003, Amazing Power of Marine Foods, 2003, Biological Sciences in Foods, 2004, Current Topics in Food Science & Technology, 2005; mem. editl. bd. ITE Letters on Batteries, New Techs. and Medicine, 2000—, award com. chmn., 2000—. Recipient Rsch. award Internat. Battery Material Assn., 1997, Spl. award Internat. Tech. Exch. Soc.-Internat. Battery Material Assn., 1998, Kozawa award, 2003, Yeager-Kozawa award, 2004; grantee Naito Meml. Found., 1977, Tokai Sci. Rsch. Found., 1986, Agrl. Biol. Chemistry Japan, 1990, Kiei-Kai Sci. Rsch. Found., 1991-96, Skylark Rsch. Found., 1992, The Sci. and Tech. Agy., Japan, 1994-96, Internat. Tech. Exch. K-Found., 1996-97, Internat. Battery Material Assn., 1998—, Nakatani Electronic Measuring Tech. Assn. Japan, 1998-99, Daikin Rsch. Inst., Japan, 2002-03; grant-in-aid Sci. and Tech. Agy. of Japan, 1998—, Rsch. Devel. Corp. Japan, 1998, Small Bus. Promotion Corp., Japan, 2000, grantee Daikin Rsch. Inst., Japan, 2000-2004, Taki Chem. Co., 2004—, Catalysts of Chems. Ind. Co., 2005-2006, Nishimura Co. Japan, 2005—, Yokota Md., 2005—. Mem. Am. Soc. for Photobiology, Agrl. Biol. Soc. Japan, Chem. Soc. Japan, Internat. Tech. Exch. Soc. (award 1995, bd. dirs. 1995—, v.p. 2000—, grantee 1998—). Business E-Mail: suzukin@hiroshima-u.ac.jp.

SUZUKI, TSUNEO, molecular immunologist; b. Nagoya, Aichi, Japan, Nov. 23, 1931; s. Morichika and Toshiko (Kita) S.; widowed; children: Riichiro, Aijiro, Yozo. BS, U. Tokyo, 1953, MD, 1957; PhD, U. Hokkaido, 1967. Asst. prof. U. Kans. Med. Ctr., Kansas City, 1970-79, assoc. prof., 1979-83, prof., 1983—2003, prof. emeritus, 2003—, interim chair, 1994-98. Mem. NIH Study Sect., Washington, 1983-87. Contbr. articles to profl. jours. Fellow U. Wis., 1963-66, 69-70, U. Lausanne, Switzerland, 1966-67, U Toronto, 1967-69; recipient Travel award Fulbright Found., 1962, Sr. Investigator award U. Kans. Med. Ctr., 1990. Mem. Am. Assn. Immunologists, Am. Soc. Biological Chemists (Travel award 1988). Home: 3620 W 73rd St Prairie Village KS 66208-2903 Office: U Kans Med Ctr/Dept Microbiology 3901 Rainbow Blvd Rm 3001 Orr Major Kansas City KS 66160-0001 E-mail: tsuzuki@kumc.edu.

SVAHN, JOHN ALFRED, federal agency administrator; b. New London, Conn., May 13, 1943; s. Albert Russell and Esther Marilu (Caffero) S.; m. Jill Weber, July 12, 1977; children: Kirsten Marie, John Alfred III. BA in Polit. Sci, U. Wash., 1966; postgrad., U. Pacific, 1970-73, Georgetown U., 1973-74. Spl. asst. to dir. Calif. Dept. Public Works, 1968-70; chief dep. dir. Calif. Dept. Social Welfare, 1971-73, dir., 1973; acting commr. Community Services Adminstrn., HEW, Washington, 1973-74; commr. Assistance Payments Adminstrn., 1973-76; dep. adminstr. Social and Rehab. Service, 1974-75; adminstr. Social and Rehab. Svcs., 1975-76; mgr. Haskins and Sells, 1976-79; pres. John A. Svahn, Inc., Annapolis, Md., 1979-81; U.S. commr. social security Balt., 1981-83; undersec. HHS, Washington, 1983-84; assst. to Pres. for policy devel. Washington, 1984-86; chmn. Maximus Inc., Washington, 1988-94; U.S. commr. Commn. for Study of Alternatives for Panama Canal, 1987-92; exec. v.p. The Wexler Group, Washington, 1995—; chmn. Captial Assocs., Inc., 1994—; bd. dirs. Logisticare, Inc., 2000—, EpicEdge, Inc., 2001—. Mem. Nat. Devel. Disability Adv. Council, 1975-76, Pres.'s Transition Team, 1980-81, Calif. Health Care Commn., 1972, pub. affairs com. United Way Am., 1987—; chmn. Govs. Commn. on Corrections Health Care, Md., 1990—; assoc. mem. Calif. Republican State Cen. Com., 1970-72; bd. dirs. Nat. Aquarium, Balt.; bd. dirs. Health Care Svcs. NAS Inst. Medicine, 1987-92; bd. dirs. Logisticare, Inc., 2001-; bd. dirs. Epic Edge, Inc., 2001-04; mem. Gov.'s Privatization Coun., 1992—. Served to lt. USAF, 1966-68. Named Outstanding Young Man in HEW, 1974; recipient Sec.'s citation, 1975, Adminstr.'s spl. citation, 1975 Mem. Annapolis Yacht Club, Sailing Club of the Chesapeake, Kent Island Yacht Club, Phi Delta Phi, Zeta Psi. Republican. Office: 4790 Caughlin Pkwy 317 Reno NV 89509 Personal E-mail: jacksvahn@aol.com.

SVALYA, PHILLIP GORDON, lawyer; b. Ferndale, Mich., June 28, 1943; s. John Michael and Ann Marie Svalya; children: Daniel Gordon, Karina Renee. BS, U.S. Naval Acad., Annapolis, Md., 1966; JD, U. Santa Clara, Calif., 1973. Bar: Calif. 1974, U.S. Dist. Ct. (no. dist.) Calif. 1974. Pvt. practice, Sunnyvale, Mountain View, Calif., 1974-81, Cupertino, Calif., 1981—. Officer, bd. dir. Albanian Health Fund, Phillis Found. Lt. USN, 1966-70, capt. USN SEAL ret., 1970-91. Mem. Calif. Bar Assn., Santa Clara County Bar Assn., Santa Clara County Trial Lawyers Assn., Sunnyvale/Cupertino Bar Assn., Underwater Demolition Team-SEAL Assn., Million Dollar Advocates Forum. Republican. Avocations: hiking, gardening. Office: Phillip G Svalya Inc 10455 Torre Ave Cupertino CA 95014-3203 Office Phone: 408-252-5211.

SVEINSSON, LINDA RODGERS, engineering company executive; b. Tuscaloosa, Ala., July 1, 1938; d. Eric and Sarah Ella (Haughton) Rodgers; m. Hjalmar Sveinsson, May 29, 1971; children: Martha M. Moreno, Stephen R.M. Moreno, III. BA in Math., Birmingham-So. Coll., 1960; MS in Indsl. Engring., U. Ala., 1972. Sys. analyst U. Ala. Med. Ctr., Birmingham, 1967-69; sys. mgr. Internat. Data Sys., New Orleans, 1969-70; computer scientist Computer Scis. Corp., Silver Spring, Md., 1973-76; computer sys. specialist Sys. Devel. Corp., McLean, Va., 1976-78; mem. tech. staff Bell Labs., Holmdel, NJ, 1978—80, tech. supr. Columbus, Ohio, 1980—85; mgr. bus. devel. No. Telecom., Inc., Research Triangle Park, N.C., 1985-88; dept. mgr. network ops. and mgmt. systems GTE Fed. Systems, Ctr., 1988-94; cons. Bell Atlantic, 1994-95, AT&T Solutions, 1996-97, Mitretek Sys., 1998—. Mem. IEEE, Phi Beta Kappa, Alpha Pi Mu. Republican. Methodist. Home: 8911 Old Courthouse Rd Vienna VA 22182-2107 Office: 3150 Fairview Park Dr S Falls Church VA 22042 Business E-Mail: linda.sveinsson@mitretek.org.

SVENDSBYE, LLOYD AUGUST, academic administrator, theologian, educator; b. Hamlet, ND, May 26, 1930; s. Anders A. and Gudrun J. (Birkelo) S.; m. Annelotte Frieda Erika Moertelmeyer, Dec. 20, 1958. BA, Concordia Coll., Moorhead, Minn., 1951, DD (hon.), 1983; BTh, Luther Theol.Sem., 1954; postgrad, U. Erlangen, Germany, 1954-55, Columbia U., 1959-60; ThD, Union Theol. Sem., 1966; LLD (hon.), Gettysburg Coll., 1977; LHD (hon.), Kilian C.C., 1992. Ordained to ministry, 1955; asst. pastor Our Saviours Luth. Ch., Mpls., 1955-56; adminstrv. asst. to dir. 3d Assembly Luth. World Fedn., 1956-57; asst. prof. religion Concordia Coll., 1957-59; asst. pastor Trinity Luth. Ch., Bklyn., 1959-61; chmn. dept. religion Concordia Coll., 1962-66; editor in chief Augsburg Publ. House, Mpls., 1966-71; v.p., dean St. Olaf Coll., 1971-74; pres., prof. ch. history Luther Theol. Sem., St. Paul, 1974-82; pres. Northwestern Luth. Theol. Sem., 1976-82; pres., prof. ch. history Luther Northwestern Theol. Sem., 1982—87; pres. Augustana Coll., Sioux Falls, SD, 1987-92; ret., 1992. V.p. Am. Luth. Ch., 1981-87; Mem. Am. Luth. Ch.-Luth. Ch. Am. coop. com., 1974-78; Luth. World Fedn. Com. on Info. Services, 1971-76; mem. Com. on Luth. Unity, 1978-82, Commn. To Form a New Luth. Ch., 1982-86; mem. ch. coun. Normandale Luth. Ch., 2003—, pres., 2005-07; mem. steering com. Tuesday Open House Mindekirken, 2004—; bd. dirs. Norway House, 2005—. Chmn. senate dist. 49A, Dem. Farm Labor Com., 1970-71; bd. dirs. Luth. Brotherhood, 1970-95, Luth. Gen. and Health Care Sys., Park Ridge, Ill., 1981-87; trustee Luth. Deaconess Hosp., Mpls., 1970-71, Fairview-Southdale Hosp., 1975-87, Fairview Cmty. Hosps., 1979-87. Recipient Alumni Achievement award Concordia Coll., 1974 Mem. Phi Beta Kappa. Home: 2500 Quentin Ct Minneapolis MN 55416-1900 Home Phone: 952-927-0987. E-mail: annelloy@aol.com.

SVENDSEN, ALF, artist, educator; b. Bklyn., Mar. 24, 1930; s. Alf and Anna Thordina (Fjeldberg) S. BFA cum laude, Syracuse U., 1955; MFA summa cum laude, U. Notre Dame, 1965. Asst. sculptor Ivan Mestrovic, Notre Dame, Ind., 1955-56; sculptor Hall of African Man Am. Mus. Natural History, NYC, 1966-68; tchr. art Mt. Anthony H.S., Bennington, Vt., 1969-71; prof. Delaware County C.C., Media, Pa., 1971-89. Exhibited work at New Sch. Social Rsch., N.Y.C., 1958, N.Y. Six Gallery, 1962, Berkshire (Mass.) Mus., 1970, Gallery 14 Sculptors, N.Y.C., 1974, Darmouth (N.H.) Coll., 1978, Deshong Mus., Chester, Pa., 1981, Art Sutton, Que., 1998, Mary Bryan Gallery, Jeffersonville, Vt., 1999. With USN, 1948-52. Home: 465 Daigle Dr Enosburg Falls VT 05450-5088 E-mail: alfsvenden@earthlink.net.

SVENGALIS, KENDALL FRAYNE, law librarian, educator, publishing executive, writer; b. Gary, Ind., May 16, 1947; s. Frank Anthony and Alvida Linnea (Matheus) S.; children: Hillary Linnea, Andrew Kendall; m. Ellen Christine Haffling, June 16, 2001. BA, Purdue U., 1970, MA, 1973; MLS, U. R.I., 1975. Reference librarian Roger Williams Coll., Bristol, RI, 1975, Providence (R.I.) Coll., 1975-77; asst. law librarian R.I. State Law Library, Providence, 1976-82, state law librarian, 1982—2002. Adj. prof. libr. and info. studies U. R.I., 1987—; pres. RI Law Press, 1996—. Author: The Legal Information Buyer's Guide and Reference Manual, 1996 (Best Legal Reference Book of 1996), 11th edit., 2007, Gary, Indiana: A Centennial Celebration, 2006; editor: The Criv Sheet, 1988—94; contbr. articles to profl. jours. Chmn. jud. branch United Way Com. R.I., 1980; pres. Verdandi Male Chorus, 2000—. Recipient AALL Joseph L. Andrews Bibliographical awd. Mem. Am. Assn Law Librs. (state, ct. and county libr. spl. interest sect., Connie E. Bolden Significant Publ. award 1993, 99, bd. dirs. 1986-88, 96-99), Law Librs. New Eng. (treas. 1983-85, v.p. 1985-86, pres. 1986-87), Com. on Rels. with Info. Vendors (editor 1988-94), New Eng. Law Libr. Consortium (v.p. 1990-92, pres. 1992-94), Jussi Bjorling Soc. (v.p.), R.I. Swedish Heritage Assn. (v.p.) Republican. Lutheran. Home: 204 Wyassup Rd North Stonington CT 06359 Office Phone: 860-535-0362. Personal E-mail: ksven@comcast.net, rilawpress@comcast.net.

SVENSON, CHARLES OSCAR, investment banker; b. Worcester, Mass., June 28, 1939; s. Sven Oscar and Edahjane (Castner) S.; m. Sara Ellen Simpson, Nov. 15, 1968; children: Alicia Lindall, Tait Oscar. AB, Hamilton Coll., 1961; LL.B., Harvard U., 1964; LL.M., Bklyn. Law Sch., 1965. Bar: N.Y. 1965, U.S. Dist. Ct. (so. dist.) N.Y. 1965, U.S. Ct. Appeals (2d. cir.) 1965. Atty. Dewey, Ballantine, Bushby, Palmer & Wood, NYC, 1964-68; v.p. Goldman Sachs & Co., NYC, 1968-75; sr. v.p. Donaldson, Lufkin & Jenrette, NYC, 1975-89, mng. dir., 1989-2000; sr. mng. dir. Brock Capital Group LLC, NYC, 2002—. Trustee Kirkland Coll., Clinton, N.Y., 1976-78; trustee Hamilton Coll., Clinton, 1979-83, 90—. Mem. ABA, N.Y. State Bar Assn., Assn. of Bar of City of N.Y. Clubs: Tuxedo (Tuxedo Park, N.Y.); Harvard (N.Y.C.). Home: 1185 Park Ave New York NY 10128-1308 Office: Brock Capital Group LLC 295 Madison Ave 46th FL New York NY 10017 Office Phone: 212-209-3000. Business E-Mail: csvenson@brockcapital.com.

SVENSSON, LARS GEORG, cardiovascular and thoracic surgeon; came to U.S., 1986; s. Karl-Georg and Marianne S.; m. Marion Frances Robinson, June 14, 1986. MB, BCh, U. Witwatersrand, Johannesburg, South Africa, 1978, MSc (Med.), 1983, PhD, 1986. Diplomate Gen., Vascular and Cardiothoracic Surgery. Resident in surgery Johannesburg Hosp., 1981-86; fellow cardiovascular surgery Cleve. Clinic Found., 1986-87, Baylor Coll. of Medicine, Houston, 1987-89, resident cardiothoracic surgery, 1989-91; attending surgeon Meth. Hosp., VA Med. Ctr., Houston, 1991-92, Lahey Clinic, Burlington, Mass., 1993—2001, dir. Aortic Surgery Ctr. and Marfan Syndrome Clinic, 1993—2001; dir. Cleve. Clinic Found., 2001—, dir. Aorta Ctr. and Marfan Syndrome Clinic, 2001—. Spkr. in field. Contbr. numerous articles to profl. jours. including Jour. Vascular Surgery, Chest, Ann. Thoracic Surgery, Jour. Thoracic, Cardiovascular Surgery and Anesthesia.; mem. editorial bd. Annals of Thoracic Surgery, Annals of Cardiovasc. and Thoracic Surgery. Recipient Good Fellowship award Treverton Coll., 1970, Cert. of Merit South African Sugar Assn., 1972, Robert Niven award 1974-76, DeBakey Heart Fund Rsch. award 1988, 89, 90, 91, V.A. Rag Rsch. Fund award 1992; Dana Fund Rsch. fellowship, 1994, David Lurie Rsch. fellowship 1985; Davis and Geck Surg. Rsch. scholarship, 1985. Fellow Am. Coll. Surgeons, Royal Coll. Surgeons, Coll. Surgeons and Physicians of South Africa, Royal Coll. Surgeons in Can. in Vascular and Cardiothoracic Surgery, Am. Coll. Cardiology; mem. AMA, Soc. Thoracic Surgeons. Achievements include animal research to find methods of intraoperatively locating the spinal cord blood supply and methods to prevent paraplegia after aortic surgery; investigation of methods to protect the brain, spinal cord and kidneys; study of hydrogren injection to localize spinal cord supply in humans, study of intrathecal papaveine in patients undergoing aortic surgery, minimizing use of homologous blood for major aortic surgery, particularly of the ascending and aortic arch; novel operations for ascending and aortic arch surgery; first reported replacement of the entire aorta from the heart to the aortic bifurcation during a single operation; pioneered a technique for doing minimal access "keyhole" heart surgery; (with E. Stanley Crawford) wrote the first definitive textbook on the aorta entitled Cardiovascular and Vascular Disease of the Aorta; devel. an approach for minimal access to the heart for heart operations. Office Phone: 216-445-4813. Business E-Mail: svenssl@ccf.org.

SVENSSON, ROBERT CHARLES WILHELM, physicist, researcher; b. Göteborg, Sweden, Sept. 11, 1947; s. Carl-Eric George and Lilly Maria S. BS in Physics, Göteborgs U., 1983, MS in Physics, 1991, PhD in Environ. Scis. with specialization in Phys. Chemistry, 1994. Lectr. Merchant Marine Acad., Göteborg, 1983—; physicist Applied Scis., Inc., Cedarville, Ohio, 1991-92; electronic design engr. Göteborg, 1982—; instr. Merchant Marine Acad., Göteborg, 1982-93; asst. prof. Chalmers U. Tech., Göteborg, 1994-96, assoc. prof., 1996—. Organizer Conf. TEC '93, Chalmers U. of Tech., 1993; guest speaker workshop, U. Eindhoven, Holland, 1993; cons. physicist Applied Scis., Cedarville, 1991-92, Space Exploration Assoc., 1993; specialist Thermionic Energy Conversion Conf.; presenter MIT, 1999; invited TEC specialist US Nat. Rsch. Coun. 2000; invited spkr., Russia, 2003; vis. rsch. prof. W.Va. U., Morgantown, 2004-06. Contbr. articles to profl. jours; patentee in field. Mem. ASME, Soc. Automotive Engrs. Lutheran. Avocations: artistic photography, electronics design, power sports. Home: Dörravägen 1 Landvetter S-43893 Sweden Office: Chalmers U Tech S-40272 Göteborg Sweden Personal E-mail: drlomo@yahoo.com. Business E-Mail: term@chalmers.se, rcsvensson@mail.wvu.edu.

SVENSSON, SVEN EILIF, civil engineer, consultant; b. Copenhagen, Dec. 15, 1945; s. Palle and Agnes Svensson; m. Dorte Merete Ahlbom, Aug. 10, 1968; children: Trine, Rikke, Jakob. MSc, Tech. U. Denmark, 1970, PhD, 1973; postgrad., Univ. Coll., London. Civil engring. Rambøl & Hannemann, Copenhagen, 1974-85, dir., 1985-90, ES Cons. Ltd., Copenhagen, 1990—. Cons. Great Belt Link Brige, Copenhagen, 1990—, Oresund Link Bridge, Copenhagen, 1993—; vis. prof. U. Coll., London, 1997—. Contbr. articles to profl. jours. Mem. ASCE, Nat. Acad. of Tech. Scis. Denmark. Avocations: music, tennis. Home: Bistrupvej 92B Birkeroed 3460 Denmark Office: ES-Consult DTU Scion Dr Neergaards Vej 15 DK 2970 Horsholm Denmark E-mail: eilif@es-consult.dk.

SVETLOVA, MARINA, ballerina, retired choreographer; b. Paris, May 3, 1922; arrived in U.S., 1940; d. Max and Tamara (Andreieff) Hartman. Studied with Vera Trefilova, Paris, 1930-36, studied with L. Egorova and M. Kschessinska, 1936-39; studied with A. Vilzak, NYC, 1940-57; D (hon.), Fedn. Francaise de Danse, 1988. Ballet dir. So. Vt. Art Ctr., 1959-64; dir. Svetlova Dance Ctr., Dorset, Vt., 1965-95; prof. ballet dept. Ind. U., Bloomington, 1969-92, prof. emeritus, 1992—, chmn. dept., 1969-78. Choreographer Dallas Civic Opera, 1964—67, (ballets) Ft. Worth Opera, 1967—83, San Antonio Opera, 1983, Seattle Opera, Houston Opera, Kansas City Performing Arts Found., The Fairy Queen, 1966, L'Histoire du Soidat, 1968, ballerina Ballet Russe de Monte Carlo, 1939—41, guest ballerina Ballet Theatre, 1942, London's Festival Ballet, Teatro dell Opera, Rome, Nat. Opera Stockholm, Suomi Opera, Helsinki, Finland, Het Nederland Ballet, Holland, Cork Irish Ballet, Paris Opera Comique, London Palladium, Teatro Colon, Buenos Aires, others, prima ballerina Met. Opera, 1943—50, N.Y.C. Opera, 1950—52; performer: (ballets) Graduation Ball; contbr. articles to profl. jours. Mem.: Nat. Soc. Arts and Letters (nat. dance chmn.), Conf. Ballet in Higher Edn., Am. Guild Mus. Artists (bd. dirs.). Office: 2100 E Maxwell Ln Bloomington IN 47401-6119 Office Phone: 812-330-0567.

SVIOKLA, JOHN JULIUS, technology consultant; b. Brockton, Mass., July 3, 1957; s. Sylvester Charles and Katherine Bravendar (McCaig) S.; m. Eileen Marie Harvey, Aug. 12, 1987; children: John, Michael, Patrick. BA, Harvard U., 1979, MBA, 1983, D of Bus. Adminstrn., 1986. Banker Mark Twain Bank Inc., St. Louis, 1986; asst. prof. to assoc. prof. Harvard Bus. Sch., Boston, 1986—98; v.p. DiamondCluster Internat., Chgo., 1998—2001, vice chmn., 2000—. Dir. Cosmo, Inc., Braintree, Mass., Ctr. Expert Systems, Cambridge, Mass. Dir. Found. Faces of Children-At-Children's Hosp., Boston, 1987. Recipient Detur prize Harvard U., 1979; IBM fellow Harvard, 1982. Mem. Am. Assn. Artificial Intelligence, Inst. Mgmt. Sci. Clubs: Harvard Faculty (Cambridge); Harvard (Boston). Avocations: drawing, bicycling, yoga. Office: Diamond Mgmt & Tech Cons 875 North Michigan Ave Ste 3000 Chicago IL 60611

SVOBODA, JANICE JUNE, nurse; d. Alfred A. and Jessie (Boor) Hinke; m. Glenn R. Svoboda, July 20, 1957; children: Melora, Kevin, Craig. Diploma, Luther Hosp., Eau Claire, Wis., 1954; student, U. Wis., Madison, 1955—57; BS in Health Edn. cum laude, U. Wis., Milw., 1980; student, Alverno Coll., Milw., 1991-92. Cert. U. Wis., 1955. Pub. health nurse Ozaukee County, Wis., 1979, 86; asst. instr. nursing Milw. Area Tech. Coll., 1979-83; instr. seminar Cardinal Stritch Coll., Milw., 1985-87; nutritional counselor Nutri-Sys., Grafton, Wis., 1987-90. Instr. seminar Milw. Area Tech. Coll., 1983, 90, coping with stress course, 1985-86, assertiveness training course, 1985, health seminars Alverno Coll., Milw., 1991-95, designed and implemented alternative health and healing seminar, Alverno Coll., 1994-97; pvt. practice holistic nurse cons., nutrition and herbal therapy, 1997—; lectr. pub. on nutrition and anti aging. Mem. Am. Holistic Nurses Assn. (cert. and recert.), Ctr. for Sci. in the Pub. Interest.

SVOBODA, JOANNE DZITKO, artist, educator; b. Dec. 24, 1948; d. John Richard and Joanna Frances (Rygiel) Dzitko; m. Peter W. Svoboda, Sept. 3, 1972; children: Kimberly Anne, Lauren Anne. Student, Parsons Sch. Design, 1966, Kean Coll., 1970; BA, Jersey City State Coll., 1970, MA, 1975; postgrad., Tchrs. Coll., Columbia U., 1972, Chubb Inst., 1983-84. Art tchr., Jersey City, 1966-70, Henry Snyder H.S., Jersey City, 1970-80; tng. specialist Johnson & Johnson Baby Products, Skillman, N.J., 1984-89; cons., 1989—; pres. Mgmt. Strategies Internat., 1991—. Computer instr. Raritan Valley C.C., 1999—. Exhibited Courtney Gallery, Jersey City State Coll., 1970, 74, Long Valley, 1979-80; contbr. articles in field to various publs. Trustee Jersey City Mus. Assn., 1973-79, chmn. fine arts dept., 1972-79; mem. curriculum revision com. Jersey City Bd. Edn., 1976; mem. Washington Twp. Shade Tree Commn., 1979-81, chmn., 1981; mem. Washington Twp. Hist. Heritage Commn., 1981-85; active encouraging establishment of hist. zone Long Valley, landmarks, Jersey City and Washington Twp. Grantee N.J. State Dept. Edn., 1973; recipient awards N.J. Fedn. Jr. Woman's Clubs: black and white photography, 1979, crafts, 1979, 1st pl. color photography, 1980, free form, 1981. Mem. Am. H.S. Assn. (asst. exec. dir. 1997-99, 2000-), Inst. Raritan Valley CC. (2000-). Office: PO Box 1216 Marshalls Creek PA 18335 Office Phone: 570-223-9600. E-mail: joan@joansvoboda.com.

SVOBODA, PATRICIA HELEN, art historian; b. Washington, Dec. 22, 1950; d. Ladislav Maurice and Marie Martina (Vojta) S. BFA in Graphic Design, U. Wash., Seattle, 1974, BA in Art History, 1974, MA in Art History, 1980. Graphic artist freelance, Seattle, Washington, 1971—86; art history rschr. for exhbns. Collaboration of Seattle Art Mus. & U. Wash., Seattle, 1977—78; graphic artist U. Rsch. Tech. Edn. Ctr., Rockville, Md., 1984; graphic artist, adminstrv. asst. US Dept. Commerce Office Publs. Svc., Washington, 1984—88; lectr. art history Phillips Collection, Washington, 1987—; coord. rsch. Smithsonian Instn. Nat. Portrait Gallery, Washington, 1988—; lectr. art history Georgetown U., Washington, 1989—97. Rep. Art Svcs. Internat., Alexandria, Va., 1990-92; contbr. Inst. for Classical Studies, Prague, Czech Republic, 1993-94, Inst. for the Classical Tradition, Boston U., 1995, Mus. of Decorative Arts, Prague, Czech Republic, 1996. Author: Zoe Dusanne, 1980; interviewer for Northwest Traditions, 1978; prin. work includes Seattle YMCA mural Olympic Race, 1982; contbr. articles to profl. jours. Keyworker Combined Fed. Campaign, Washington, 1985-88; participant Internat. Partnerships among Mus. Programs Am. Assn. Mus., 2003-05. Recipient Nat. Pks. Svc. Purchase Prize award Soc. Illustrators, 1974, Cert. of Performance award Smithsonian Instn., 1989-2006. Mem. Am. Assn. Mus., Internat. Coun. Mus., Coll. Art Assn., Czechoslovak Soc. Arts & Scis., Internat. Soc. for Classical Tradition, U. Wash. Alumni Assn. Avocations: literature, history, langs., music, photography. Office: Smithsonian Instn Nat Portrait Gallery Victor Bldg-Ste 4100 PO Box 37012 Washington DC 20013-7012 Business E-Mail: svobodap@si.edu.

SWACKER, FRANK WARREN, lawyer; b. NYC, May 18, 1922; m. Irene Maloney Michael; children: Carolyn, Frances, Michele, Ruth. BA, Union Coll., Schnectady, 1947; JD, U. Va., 1949; LLM in Internat. Law, NYU, 1961. Bar: Va. 1948, NY 1950, Ohio 1962, Wis. 1969, DC 1977, Fla. 1991, US Ct. Internat. Trade 1978, US Supreme Ct. 1952. Pvt. practice, NYC, 1949—54, 1964—68, Washington, 1977—84, Clearwater, Fla., 1984—89, St. Petersburg, Fla., 1994—; atty. Caltex Petroleum Corp., NYC, 1955—60, Marathon Oil Co., Ohio, 1961—63; counsel Shearman & Sterling, NYC, 1964—67; internat. counsel Allis-Chalmers Corp., Milw., 1968—78; sr. mem. Swacker & Assocs., P.C., Springfield, Va., 1980—84, chmn., pres. firm, sr. mem. Largo, Fla., 1989—93; vice chmn. Lasergate Sys., Inc., 1995—99. Spl. asst. dep. atty. gen. State of NY, 1950; govtl. adviser US, P.I., Algeria; lectr. Ohio No. U., 1962, NY World Trade Inst., 1976; adj. prof. Stetson U. Coll. Law, St. Petersburg, Fla., 1996-2000, LLM internat. adv. coun., 1997—. Author: Business International Guide for Going Global, 1999, Boardroom Conspiracies: A Courtroom Drama, 2005, Who Murdered Mom: A Legal Drama, 2007; co-author: World Trade Without Barriers: World Trade Organization and Dispute Resolution, vol. 2, 1996; co-editor, contbr.: Bus. and Legal Aspects of Latin Am. Trade and Investment, 1977, Reference Manual on Doing Business with Latin America, 1979; contbr. articles to profl. jours. Mem. internat. bus. adv. bd. U. So. Fla., 1993-94. Lt. (j.g.) USN, 1943-46, WWII. Mem. ABA (lectr. 1978, internat. comml. arbitration com. 1991—), Nat. Law Inst., Am. Arbitration Assn. (roster of neutrals, 1960-2005), Nat. Arbitration Forum (arbitration panel), World Intellectual Property Orgn. (arbitration panel), CPR Internat. Inst. for Conflict Prevention and Resolution (internat. and Fla. arbitration panels 2005—), Authors Guild. Office Phone: 727-394-0265. Personal E-mail: frankswacker@aol.com.

SWAD, STEPHEN M., mortgage company executive; b. Aug. 10, 1961; married; 2 children. BBA, U. Mich. CPA. Deputy chief acct. US Securities Exchange Commn., 1995; ptnr. KPMG LLP, 1998; v.p., deputy controller Time Warner, 1998, v.p. financial planning and analysis, exec. v.p. finance & admin. Turner Entertainment Group, 2002—03; exec. v.p., CFO AOL, 2003—07; appointed CFO Fannie Mae, 2007—. Office: Fannie Mae 3900 Wisconsin Ave NW Washington DC 20016-2892 *

SWADENER, JOHN GREGORY, research scientist; s. Nina and John Richard Swadener; m. Kay Swadener, June 23, 1984; 1 child, Michael John. PhD, U. Tex., 1998. Rsch. asst. prof. U. Tenn., Knoxville, Tenn., 1998—2001; tech. staff mem. Los Alamos Nat. Lab., Los Alamos, N.Mex., 2001—. Adj. faculty mem. U. Memphis, 2002—05. Fellow Texas Space Grant Consortium, NASA, Ripperger Engineering Mechanics. Mem.: Materials Rsch. Soc. D-Liberal. Protestant. Avocations: hiking, travel. Office: Los Alamos Nat Lab PO Box 1663 Los Alamos NM 87545 Home Phone: 505-661-2376; Office Phone: 505-667-9952. Business E-Mail: swadener@lanl.gov.

SWAFFAR, GLENDA JEAN, director; d. Glen Edward and Imagean Perkins; m. J.D. Swaffar, Aug. 27, 1992; children: Leeann Glynette Pratt, Mark Tillman Pratt. BA, U. Mo., Columbia, 1969; MS summa cum laude, U. Mo.-Kans. City, 1988, Edn. Specialist, 1990. Cert. tchr./media specialist Mo. Dept. Elem. and Secondary Edn., 1983. Media specialist Hickman Mills HS, Kans. City, 1985—99, instrnl. facilitator, A+ coord., 1999—. Adv. com. Tchr. Edn. U. Mo., Kans. City; elector for bishop Episcopal Ch., Kans. City, 1984—85. Mem.: Mo. Assn. Sch. Librs. (assoc.), Am. Assn. Sch. Librs. (assoc.), ASCD (assoc.), Internat. Reading Assn. (assoc.), Phi Kappa Phi. Achievements include successfully writing grant to secure funding and then led staff of 100 teachers through a three-year improvement process to prepare our school for designation by the state as an A+ high school. Avocations: reading, travel, swimming, scrapbooks, fabric arts. Office: Hickman Mills HS 9010 Old Santa Fe Rd Kansas City MO 64138 Office Phone: 816-316-7259. Office Fax: 816-316-7248. Business E-Mail: glendas@hickmanmills.org.

SWAFFORD, JEANNE, education educator; d. Doris Wardrep Swafford; m. Vance Durrington, July 11, 1992; 1 child, Isaac David Swafford Durrington. BS, Mid. Tenn. State U., Murfreesboro, 1974, MEd, 1977, ednl. specialist, 1985; PhD, U. Ga., Athens, 1989. Tchr. Sumner County Sch. Dist., Gallatin, Tenn., 1974—75, Cannon County Sch. Dist., Woodbury, Tenn., 1975—77, Morgan Local Sch. Dist., McConnelsville, Ohio, 1977—80; coord. devel. studies Iowa Wesleyan Coll., Mt. Pleasant, 1981—83; assoc. prof. Tex. Tech U., Lubbock, 1989—2001; coord. reading svc. U. Tenn., Chattanooga, 1983—86; assoc. prof. Miss. State U., Starkville, 2001—. Cons. Ednl. Broadcasting Corp. Channel Thirteen, N.Y.C., 2006—. Author: (book) Content Area Literacy Instruction for the Elementary Grades; contbr. articles to profl. jours. Recipient Honor for Outstanding Tchrs., Martha Holden Jennings Found., 1988; Del Jones Meml. scholar, U. Ga., Coll. Edn., 1988—89. Mem.: Miss. Reading Assn., Nat. Coun. Tchrs. of English, Internat. Reading Assn., Nat. Reading Conf. (publ. com. 1999—2003, program area co-chair 2004—06). Office: Miss State Univ PO 9705 Mississippi State MS 39762 Home Phone: 662-320-4873; Office Phone: 662-325-1151.

SWAGEL, PHILLIP L., federal agency administrator; married; 3 children. AB magna cum laude, Princeton U.; PhD, Harvard U. Economist Fed. Reserve Bd., 1992—94, Internat. Monetary Fund, 1996—2002; sr. economist Coun. Econ. Advisors, Exec. Office of the Pres., 2000—01, chief of staff, 2002—05; resident scholar Am. Enterprise Inst., 2005—06; asst. sec. for econ. policy US Dept. Treasury, Washington, 2006—. Vis. asst. prof. Northwestern U., 1994—96. Office: US Dept Treasury 1500 Pennsylvania Ave Washington DC 20220 *

SWAGER, CLEO MARIE, secondary school educator; b. Columbus, Ind., Feb. 21, 1951; d. Louis Cleo and Mable Marie Swager. BS in Edn., St. Francis Coll., Ft. Wayne, Ind., 1974, MS in Edn., 1982. Tchr. Paulding (Ohio) Exempted Village Sch., 1975—2005. Camp dir. Girl Scouts Limberlost, 1976—78, 1980—82, Luth. Outdoor Ministries, Indpls., 2006. Life mem., leader Girl Scouts US; reading camp dir. Luth. Outdoor Ministries; minister Lutheran Ch. ELCA; Stephen minister ELCA Lutheran Ch.; Christian edn. chmn. Faith Lutheran Ch., 1975—2006, VBS dir., 1975, 1978, 1981, 1984, 1987, 1990, 1993, 1996, 1999, 2001, 2003. Nominee Ohio Tchr. of Yr.; named Logan Legend, Girl Scouts US, Limberlost Coun. Mem.: Beta Sigma Phi.

SWAGER, TIMOTHY MANNING, chemistry educator; b. Sheridan, Mont., July 1, 1961; married; two children. BS in Chemistry with highest honors, Mont. State U., 1983; PhD in Chemistry, Calif. Inst. Tech., 1988. Postdoctoral fellow MIT, Cambridge, Mass., 1988-90; asst. prof. chemistry U. Pa., 1990-96, prof. chemistry, 1996, MIT, Cambridge, 1996—, John D. MacArthur prof., 2005—, chemistry dept. head, 2005—. Cons. EPA, 1993-95, Hannoch Weisman, Counselors at Law, 1996-97, Wolf, Greenfield & Sacks P.C., 1999—; mem Internat. Adv. Com. for Metallomesognes, 1994—; co-organizer Materials Chemistry Workshops, 1995-97; assoc. dir., Inst. for Soldier Nanotechnologies; mem. sci. adv. bd. E-ink, Cambridge, 1999—, Polaroid Corp., 1999—, Nomadics, Inc., Stillwater, Okla., 1999—; lectr. and presenter in field. Mem. editl. adv. bd. Chemistry of Materials, 1997—, Accounts Chem. Rsch., 1998—, Jour. Polymer Sci., 1999—, Jour. Am. Chem. Soc., 2000; contbr. numerous articles to profl. jours. Recipient Merck Index Undergrad. Chemistry award, 1983, DuPont Young Faculty award, 1993-96, Phila. Sect. award Am. Chem. Soc., 1996, Union Carbide Innovation Recognition award, 1997, 98, Homeland Security award, Christopher Columbus Fellowship Found., 2003, 2005, Lemelson-MIT prize, 2007; named Young Investigator NSF, 1992-97, Young Investigator, Office Naval Rsch., 1992-95; Camille Dreyfus Tchr. scholar, 1995-97, Arthur C. Cope scholar Am. Chem. Soc., 2000; IBM grad. fellow, 1984-87, Advanced Techs. Grad. fellow Aerojet Gen., GM, TRW, 1988, Alfred P. Sloan rsch. fellow, 1994-96. Mem. Internat. Liquid Crystal Soc.; fellow Am. Acad. Arts & Sciences Achievements include patents for Ring-Opening Polymerization of 3,4-Dimethylene Cyclobutene Derivatives, Synthesis of Polyacetylene from High Energy Polymer Formed by Ring-Opening Metathesis Polymerization, Calixarene-Based Transition Metal Complexes and Photonic Devices Comprising the Same, Derivatized Polythiophenes and Devices Comprising Same, Electroluminescence in Light Emitting Polymers Featuring Deaggregated Polymers, Conducting Polymer Hybrid Materials and Sensors, Stable Chemically Sensitive Fluorescent Polymer Films; research on polymer science, liquid crystals, synthetic conductors, chemical sensors, molecular recognition, molecular electronics; worked with colleagues to develop explosive-sniffing technology. Office: MIT Room 18-597 77 Massachusetts Ave Cambridge MA 02139-4307 Office Phone: 617-253-4423. Office Fax: 617-253-7929. E-mail: tswager@mit.edu. *

SWAGGERTY, CHRISTINA L., microbiologist, researcher; BS in Microbiology, Tex. A&M U., College Station, 1993, PhD in Vet. Microbiology, 2001. Rsch. microbiologist USDA, College Station, 2001—. Mem. small grp. involvement Grace Bible Ch., College Station, 1989—2007. Recipient Vis. Scientist award, Houghton Trust, 2006; grantee Travel grant, 2004, US Poultry & Egg Assn., 2006—07. Mem.: Soc. Leukocyte Biology, Soc. Microbiology. R-Conservative. Office: USDA 2881 F&B Rd College Station TX 77845 Office Phone: 979-260-9397. Office Fax: 979-260-9332. Business E-Mail: swaggerty@ffsru.usda.gov.

SWAILES, WILLIAM E., counseling administrator; b. Balt., July 28, 1945; m. Heidi Robin Raudleht, May 19, 1968. Stockbroker Foster & Marshall, Bellevue, Wash., 1978—81; investment mgr. Advanced Personal Finances, Medina, Wash., 1982—; chmn. EWR, Inc., Bellevue, 2002—. Author: (book) Money in your Life, 1986. Chgo. area chmn. Ill. Coll. Rep. Fedn., 1968—69; hon. chmn. for Wash. state NRCC Bus. Adv. Coun., 2004; founder, min. Leyden Tolerants Ch., 1973—. With US Army, 1964—67, Germany and Vietnam. Recipient Ronald Reagan Rep. Gold medal, Nat. Rep. Congl. Com., 2004, Wash. State Businessman of Yr., 2005, Congl. medal of distinction, 2006; Monmouth Honor scholar, Monmouth Coll., 1963. Mem.: Am. Assn. Retired Persons (past pres. Bellevue chpt.).

SWAIM, C. HALL, lawyer; b. Delta, Colo., Dec. 31, 1939; s. H. Albert and Janet S.; m. Patricia Fahey, Oct. 9, 1976. Grad. geophys. engr., Colo. Sch. Mines, 1961; JD, NYU, 1964. Asst. counsel Tex. Instruments Inc., Dallas, 1964-71; assoc. Hale and Dorr LLP, Boston, 1971-74, ptnr., 1974—. Served to capt. U.S. Army, 1965-67, Vietnam. Mem. ABA, Mass. Bar Assn., Boston Bar Assn., Comml. Law League Am. Office: Wilmer Hale 60 State St Boston MA 02109-1816 Office Phone: 617-526-6716. Personal E-mail: hall.swaim@wilmerhale.com.

SWAIM, MARK WENDELL, physician, molecular biologist, gastroenterologist, photographer; b. Winston-Salem, NC, Dec. 4, 1960; s. Donnie Lee and Bernice Earline (Brown) S. BA summa cum laude, U. N.C., 1983; MD, Duke U., 1990, PhD with honors, 1990. Diplomate Am. Bd. Internal Medicine, Am. Bd. Gastroenterology and Hepatology. Resident dept. medicine Duke U. Med. Ctr., Durham, NC, 1990-93, fellow gastroenterology, 1993-97, clin. med. instr., 1994-2000, fellow in advanced hepatology and endoscopy, 1997-98, attending physician, 1998-2000, Durham VA Med. Ctr., 1998-2000; asst. prof. medicine Gastrointestinal Ctr., U. Tex.-M.D. Anderson Cancer Ctr., Houston, 2000—02; dir., prin. investigator, med. dir. Regional Rsch. Inst., Jackson, Tenn., 2002—; founder Southeastern Liver Inst., Jackson, 2002—. Assoc. dept. medicine Duke U., 1998-2000; instr. clin. medicine Duke U. Sch. Medicine, 1994-2000, mem. admissions com.; instr. U. Tenn. Sch. Medicine, 2004—; asst. prof. medicine Gastrointestinal Ctr., U. Tex. M.D. Anderson Cancer Ctr., Houston; vis. med. resident Nat. Taiwan U., Taipei, 1991, 92; vis. physician Saratov (Russia) Med. U., 1995; faculty senator U. Tex. M.D. Anderson Cancer Ctr., 2000-02; book rev. panelist The Pharos of Alpha Omega Alpha; cons. physician Al-Jazeira Hosp., Abu Dhabi, United Arab Emirates; mem. med. adv. bd. Axium Pharms., Inc.; cons. Intermune Pharms. Contbr. articles to profl. jours., Ency. Brit. Great Ideas Today, 1996; photography pub. in Am. Photo. Recipient Brody award for history of medicine, 1998, Davison award for tchg. excellence, 2000; NIH Med. Sci. Tng. Program fellow, 1983-90, numerous acad. scholarships and grants. Fellow: ACP (winner assocs. competition 1994); mem.: Internat. Liver Cancer Assn., European Assn. for Study of Liver, Houston Acad. Medicine, Tex. Med. Assn., Am. Liver Found. (bd. dirs. Tex. chpt.), Engel Soc., Am. Coll. Forensic Examiners, Reticuloendothelial Soc., Am. Assn. for Study Liver Diseases, Am. Soc. for Gastrointestinal Endoscopy, Am. Coll. Gastroenterology, Sigma Pi Sigma, Phi Lambda Upsilon, Sigma Xi, Phi Beta Kappa, Alpha Omega Alpha (pres. Duke chpt. 1989). Avocations: photography, chamber music, writing, travel. Home: 61 Valley Oak Loop Jackson TN 38305 Office: 45 Physicians Dr Jackson TN 38305 Office Phone: 731-664-2200. Personal E-mail: markswaim@msn.com.

SWAIM, MICHAEL E., lawyer, former mayor; BA, UCLA, 1967, MA, 1968, JD, 1971. Lawyer Simon, McKinsey & Miller, 1971-78; pvt. practice, 1978—; mayor City of Salem, Oreg., 1997—2003. Office: Law Office 270 Cottage St NE Salem OR 97301 E-mail: mswaim@open.org.

SWAIMAN, KENNETH FRED, pediatric neurologist, educator; b. St. Paul, Nov. 19, 1931; s. Lester J. and Shirley (Ryan) S.; m. Phyllis Kammerman Sher, Oct. 1985; children: Lisa, Jerrold, Barbara, Dana. BA magna cum laude, U. Minn., 1952, BS, 1953, MD, 1955; postgrad., 1956-58. Diplomate Am. Bd. Psychiatry and Neurology, Am. Bd. Pediatrics, Am. Bd. Psychiatry and Neurology with Spl. Competence in Child Neurology. Intern Mpls. Gen. Hosp., 1955-56; resident in pediatrics, fellow in pediatrics to chief resident U. Minn. Hosp., 1956-58, spl. fellow in pediatric neurology, 1960-63, dir. pediatric neurology tng. program, 1968-94, various to interim head dept. neurology, 1994-96; chief pediatrics U.S. Army Hosp., Ft. McPherson, Ga., 1958-60; asst. prof. pediatrics, neurology U. Minn. Med. Sch., Mpls., 1963-66, prof., dir. pediatric neurology, 1969-96, mem. internship adv. coun. exec. faculty, 1966-70, interim head dept. neurology, 1994-96; postgrad. fellow pediatric neurology Nat. Inst. Neurologic Diseases and Blindness, 1960-63, assoc. prof., 1966-69. Cons. pediatric neurology Hennepin County Gen. Hosp., 1963—, Mpls., St. Paul-Ramsey Hosp., St. Paul Children's Hosp., Mpls. Children's Hosp.; vis. prof. numerous univs. including Loyola U., 1982, U. N.Mex., 1982, U. Ind. Med. Sch., 1983, U. Kyushu, Shiga, Nagoya, Tokyo, 1985, Driscoll Children's Hosp., Corpus Christi, Tex., 1986, Inst. Nacional de Pediatria, Mexico City, 1986, U. de Concepion, Chile, 1989, Beijing U. Med. Sch., 1989, Xian Med. U., China, 1989, Children's Hosp. of Mich., Detroit, 1990, Hong Kong Child Neurology Soc., 1995, Tartu, Estonia, 1997, Krem, Austria, 1997, Santiago, Chile, 1997, Kaunas, Lithuania, 1998, ICNA Ednl. Seminar, Tartu, 1998, Montevideo, Uruguay, 1999, others; lectr. in field; guest worker NIH, NICHD, Bethesda, Md., 1978-79, 79-81. Author: (with Francis S. Wright) Neuromuscular Diseases in Infancy and Childhood, 1969, Pediatric Neuromuscular Diseases, 1979, (with Stephen Ashwal) Pediatric Neurology Case Studies, 1978, 2d edit., 1984, Pediatric Neurology: Principles and Practice, 1989, 4th edit., 2006; editor: (with John A. Anderson) Phenylketonuria and Allied Metabolic Diseases, 1966, (with Francis S. Wright) Practice Pediatric Neurology, 1975, 2d edit., 1982, Pediatric Neurology: Principles and Practice, 4th edit., 2006; mem. editl. bd. Annals of Neurology, 1977-83, Neurology Update, 1977-82, Pediatric Update, 1977-85, Brain and Devel. (Jour. Japanese Soc. Child Neurology), 1980—, Neuropediatrics (Stuttgart), 1982-92; editor-in-chief: Pediatric Neurology, 1984—; contbr. articles to sci. jours. Chmn.

Minn. Gov.'s Bd. for Handicapped, Exceptional and Gifted Children, 1972-76; mem. human devel. study sect. NIH, 1976-79, guest worker, 1978-81. Served to capt. M.C. U.S. Army, 1958-60. Fellow Am. Acad. Pediatrics, Am. Acad. Neurology (rep. to nat. coun. Nat. Soc. Med. Rsch., A.B. Baker Neurol. Edn. Lifetime Achievement award 2005); mem. Soc. Pediatric Rsch., Ctrl. Soc. Clin. Rsch., Ctrl. Soc. Neurol. Rsch., Internat. Soc. Neurochemistry, Am. Neurol. Assn., Minn. Neurol. Soc., AAAS, Midwest Pediatric Soc., Am. Soc. Neurochemistry, Child Neurology Soc. (1st pres. 1972-73, Hower award 1981, Founder's award 1996, chmn. internat. affairs com., 1991-96, mem. long range planning com. 1991-97, chmn. fin. com. 1995—), Internat. Assn. Child Neurologists (exec. com. 1975-79, chmn. global edn. com. 1996-99), Profs. of Child Neurology (1st pres. 1978-80, mem. nominating com. 1986-92), Japanese Child Neurology Soc. (Segawa award 1986, mem. nominating com. 1986-92, chair internat. affairs com. 1991—, mem. long range planning com. 1991-98), Soc. de Psiquiatria y Neurologia de la Infancia y Adolescencia, Internat. Child Neurology Assn. (chair internat. edn. com. 1996-99), Lithuanian Child Neurology Soc. (hon., pres. 2000—), Child Neurology Found. (pres. 2000-03), Phi Beta Kappa, Sigma Xi. Office: U Minn Med Sch Dept Pediatric Neurology 1821 University Ave W Saint Paul MN 55104-2801 also: UMHC Box 486 420 Delaware St SE Minneapolis MN 55455-0374 E-mail: pncomm@uswet.net, cnfc@childneurologyfoundation.org.

SWAIN, CLIFFORD H., lawyer; b. Phila., 1941; married. BA, Yale Univ., 1963; LLB, Univ. Pa., 1968. Bar: Pa. 1968. With Drinker Biddle & Reath LLP, 1993—, ptnr., real estate practice group, former adminstrv. chair, former mng. ptnr. Office: Drinker Biddle & Reath LLP One Logan Sq 18th & Cherry Sts Philadelphia PA 19103-6996 Office Phone: 215-988-2796. Office Fax: 215-988-2757. Business E-Mail: clifford.swain@dbr.com.

SWAIN, DAVID O., manufacturing executive; b. Lizton, Ind., July 30, 1942; B of Aeronautical Engring., Purdue U., D (hon.), Rose-Hulman Inst. Tech. Engr. Gemini project McDonnell Douglas, 1954—72, engr. tactical missile programs,. tomahawk and harpoon/standoff land attack missile, 1972—87; v.p., gen. mgr. strategic bus. devel. McDonnell Douglas Astronautics Co., 1987—91; sr. v.p., c-17 program mgr. McDonnell Douglas Aerospace, 1981—94; v.p., gen. mgr. advances sys. and tech. Phantom Works McDonnell Douglas, 1994—97; v.p. engring. The Boeing Co., 1997—99; pres. Boeing Phamtom Works, 1999—2001; exec. v.p. The Boeing Co., 2002—, chief operating officer integrated defense systems, 2003—. Chmn. NASA Aerospace Tech. Adv. Com. Bd. dirs. Nat. Action Coun. Minorities in Engring., Chgo.'s Mus. Sci. and Industry. Recipient Disting. Engring. ALumnus award, Purdue U., 1993, Outstanding Aerospace Engr. award, 1999, Indsl. Rsch. Inst. medal, 2006. Fellow: AIAA, Royal Aeronautical Soc.; mem.: Soc. Automotive Engrs. Office: The Boeing Co PO Box 516 Saint Louis MO 63166

SWAIN, DONALD CHRISTIE, retired academic administrator, historian, educator; b. Des Moines, Oct. 14, 1931; s. G. Christie and Irene L. (Alsop) S.; m. Lavinia Kathryn Lesh, Mar. 5, 1955; children: Alan Christie, Cynthia Catherine. BA, U. Dubuque, 1953; MA in History, U. Calif., Berkeley, 1958, PhD, 1961; D (hon.), U. Louisville, 1995, Bellarmine Coll., 1995. Asst. rsch. historian U. Calif., Berkeley, 1961-63, mem. faculty Davis, 1963-81, prof. history, 1970-81, acad. asst. to chancellor, 1967-68, asst. vice chancellor acad. affairs, 1971, vice chancellor acad. affairs, 1972-75; acad. v.p. U. Calif. System, Berkeley, 1975-81; pres. U. Louisville, 1981-95, pres. emeritus, 1995—, prof. history, 1981-95; ret., 1995. Author: Federal Conservation Policy, 1921-33, 1963, Wilderness Defender: Horace M. Albright and Conservation, 1970; co-editor: The Politics of American Science 1939 to the Present, 1965. Recipient William B. Hellestine award Wis. State Hist. Soc., 1967, Disting. Tchg. award U. Calif., Davis, 1972, Wilson Wyatt award U. Louisville Alumni Assn., 1995; named Louisvillian of Yr., 1995. Democrat. Presbyterian. Office: U Louisville Alumni Ctr Louisville KY 40292-0001 Personal E-mail: dcsandlls@aol.com.

SWAIN, JUDITH LEA, cardiologist, educator; b. Long Beach, Calif., Sept. 24, 1948; m. Edward W. Holmes. BS in Chemistry with deptl. honors, UCLA, 1970; MD, U. Calif., San Diego, 1974. Diplomate Am. Bd. Internal Medicine, cardiovasc. disease; lic. physician Calif., Pa., N.C. Intern in medicine Duke U. Med. Ctr., 1974-75, resident in medicine, 1975-76, fellow in cardiology, 1976-80, assoc. in medicine, 1979-81, from asst. prof. medicine to assoc. prof. medicine, 1981-91, asst. prof. physiology, 1981-88, assoc. prof. microbiology & immunology, 1988-91, Herbert C. Rorer prof. med. scis., prof. genetics, 1991-92, mem. molecular biology grad. group, 1991-92, chief cardiovasc. divsn., 1991-92; chair dept. medicine Stanford (Calif.) U., 1996—; dir. Coll. Integrated Life Scis. U. Calif., San Diego, 2004—. Vis. asst. prof. dept. genetics Harvard Med. Sch., Boston, 1985-86; mem. search com. for dir. Ctr. for Aging, Duke U. Med. Ctr., 1991—, mem. exec. com. deptl. awards selection, 1992—, chmn. combined degree dir. search com., 1993, mem. clin. rsch. ctr. adv. com., 1993-94, mem. grad. student admissions com., 1993, mem. search com. for chief cardiovasc. surgery, 1992, dept. medicine intern selection com., 1992—; mem. instnl. rev. com. Pa. Muscle Inst., 1993; cardiology adv. com. Nat. Heart, Lung, & Blood Inst., 1989-93; dir. USA-Russia Cardiovasc. Rsch. Program, 1992—; mem. NIH Task Force on Heart Failure, 1992-93, dirs. standing com. on clin. rsch. NIH, 1995—; cons. Netherlands Rsch. Initiative in Molecular Cardiology, 1993; external adv. com. Ctr. for Prevention of Cardiovasc. Disease, Harvard Sch. Pub. Health, 1993—; adv. coun. NHLBI, 1995—, Friends of NHLBI com., 1996—, lectr. in field. Exec. editor: Trends in Cardiovascular Medicine, 1990-93; mem. editl. bd. Circulation Rsch., 1991—, Circulation, 1991—, Jour. Clin. Investigation, 1992—; cons. editor: Circulation, 1993—; contbr. articles to med. jours. Mem. exec. com. Coun. on Basic Sci., Am. Heart Assn., 1986-93, chmn. Katz Prize Award Com., 1989-92, rsch. rev. com., 1990-93, fellowship rsch. com., 1992—, program com., 1992—, mem. Levine Young Investigator Awards Com., Coun. on Clin. Cardiology, 1994—, mem. Basic Sci. Coun.; bd. dirs. Southeastern Pa. Heart Assn., 1992—. Recipient Bristol-Myers Squibb Cardiovasc. Achievement award, 1992, also numerous rsch. grants. Fellow Am. Coll. Cardiology (internat. edn. com. 1994—, chair cardiovasc. rsch. com. 1996—), Coll. Physicians of Phila.; mem. Assn. Univ. Cardiologists, Assn. Am. Physicians, Assn. Prof. of Cardiology, Am. Soc. Cell Biology, Am. Fedn. Clin. Rsch., Am. Soc. Clin. Investigation (pres.-elect 1994—, councilor 1991—), Internat. Soc. Heart Rsch. (councilor 1988—), Interurban Clin. Club, Clin. and Climitol. Soc., John Morgan Soc. Office: U Calif Sch Medicine 410 Pepper Canyon Hall 9500 Gilman Dr La Jolla CA 92093-0602 Office Phone: 858-534-7658. E-mail: jlswain@ucsd.edu.

SWAIN, LAURA TAYLOR, federal judge; b. Bklyn., 1958; d. Justus E. and Madeline V. (Allgood) Taylor; m. Andrew J. Swain, 1991. AB, Harvard U., 1979, JD, 1982. Bar: Mass. 1982, N.Y. 1983, U.S. Dist. Ct. (so. and ea. dists.) N.Y. 1983. Law clk to chief judge U.S. Dist. Ct. (so. dist.) N.Y., 1982-83; assoc. Debevoise & Plimpton, NYC, 1983-95, counsel, 1995-96; U.S. bankruptcy judge U.S. Bankruptcy Ct., Bklyn., 1996-2000; judge U.S. Dist. Ct. (So. Dist.), NY, 2000—. Mem. N.Y. State Bd. Law Examiners, Albany, 1986-96; mem. multistate bar exam. com. Nat. Conf. Bar Examiners, 1987-99, mem. testing, R&D devel. com., 1990-94, mem. long range planning com., 1994-96; cons. N.Y. Profl. Edn. Project, 1995-96; adv. com. for fules of banruptcy procedures Judicial Conf. U.S., 2002-. Co-contbr. articles on employee benefits, employee stock ownership plans, acctg. and bankruptcy to profl. publs.; contbg. author: New York Insurance Law, 1991. Trustee Diocese of N.Y. (Episcopal), 1991-92; mem. Dessoff Choirs, N.Y.C., 1984-92; bd. dirs. Episcopal Charities, Inc., 1996-2003, Coalition Consumer Bankruptcy Debtor Edn., 1998—. Mem. ABA, Assn. of Bar of City of N.Y., Met. Black Bar Assn., N.Y. State Bar Assn., Nat. Conf. Bankruptcy Judges, Nat. Assn. Women Judges, Fed. Judges Assn. (bd. dirs. 2005-). Episcopalian. Avocation: music. Office: US Courthouse 40 Centre St Rm 1205 New York NY 10007

SWAIN, MARY ANN PRICE, university official; b. Chardon, Ohio, Apr. 20, 1941; d. A. David and Mary A. Price; m. Donald B. Swain, June 27, 1964; children: Judy, Brenda. BA in Psychology, DePauw U., 1963; MA in Psychology, U. Mich., 1964, PhD in Psychology, 1969. Dir. Sch. Nursing Doctoral Program U. Mich., Ann Arbor, 1975—76, chmn. dept. nursing rsch., 1977—82, assoc. v.p. acad. affairs, 1983—93, interim co-dir. pers., 1986—88, interim dir. affirmative action, 1988—89, interim v.p. student svcs., 1990—92; provost and v.p. acad. affairs SUNY, Binghamton, 1993—. Evaluation site visotor U. Balt. Sch. Law, 1996—97, Tes. Wesleyan U., 1998—99, U. Va. Sch. Nursing, Charlottesville, 1994—95; chmn. coun. acad. affairs Nat. Assn. State Univs. and Land Grant Colls., 1998—99. Co-author (with H. Erickson and E. Tomlim): Modeling and Role-modeling: A Theory and Paradigm for Nursing, 1983. Chmn. campaign United Way Broome COunty, Binghamton, 1998—99; pres. bd. dirs. Vis. Nurses Assn. Huron Valley, Ann Arbor, 1989—92. Fellow Woodrow Wilson fellow, 1963. Mem.: Am. Psychol. Soc., Am. Assn. Higher Edn., Am. Soc. Quality Control, Sigma Theta Tau, Phi Beta Kappa, Golden Key Hon. Soc. Office: SUNY at Binghamton Provost Office PO Box 6000 Binghamton NY 13902-6000 Office Phone: 607-777-2141. E-mail: mswain@binghamton.edu.

SWAIN, MARY MADGALENE DICKERSON, pediatrics nurse; b. Talladega, Ala., May 4, 1954; d. Quincy Jackson and Dorothy Arizona Dickerson; m. Michael Swain, May 3, 1986; children: Cassaundrian Averitte, Victor Dickerson, Tumika Shears. AAS, Gadsden State C.C., 1996; LPN, N.F. Nunnelley Tech. Coll., 1985. Lic. clin. skills observer Ala.; cert. minister of health Ala., 2005. LPN, acting unit mgr., unit coord. Northport Health Svcs., Lineville, Ala., 1987—95; case mgr. Dixie Nursing Svc., Batesville, Miss., 1995—97; DON Ball Healthcare Svc., Roanoke, Ala., 1997—2000; RN postpartum Coosa Valley Bapt. Med. ctr., Sylacauga, Ala., 2000—02; dir. parish nurse svcs. Christ Deliverance Christian Ctr., Talladega, 2001—. RN supr. Talladega Healthcare Ctr., 2002—03; staff parish nurse Sylacauga Alliance for Family Enhancement, 2002—. Author: He Has Always Been There, 2003. Avocations: writing, reading, learning. Home: 709 Glenwood Rd Talladega AL 35160-2954 Office: A Remnant's Place 121 N Court Sq Talladega AL 35160

SWAIN, ROBERT, artist; b. Austin, Tex., Dec. 7, 1940; s. Robert O. and Beth (Brower) S.; m. Annette Carol Leibel, Oct. 4, 1969. BA, Am.U., 1964, Prof. fine arts Hunter Coll.; vis. artist to various schs., univs., including Bklyn. Mus. Art Sch., 1975, 77, 78; dept. architecture Harvard U. Grad. Sch. Design, 1977 One-man shows, Thenan Gallery, N.Y.C., 1965, Fischbach Gallery, N.Y.C., 1968-69, Everson Art Museum, N.Y.C., 1974, Susan Galdwell Gallery, N.Y.C., 1974, 75, 78, Tex. Gallery, Houston, 1975, Columbus (Ohio) Gallery Fine Arts, 1976, Nina Freundenhein Gallery, Buffalo, 1978, group shows include, Mus. Modern Art, N.Y.C., 1968, Grand Palais, Paris, 1968, Kunsthaus, Zurich, Switzerland, 1969, Tate Gallery, London, 1969, Corcoran Gallery Art, Washington, 1969, Whitney Mus. Am. Art, N.Y.C., 1971, Albright-Knox Gallery, Buffalo, 1971, Mus. Modern Art Internat. Circulating Exhbn.-Latin Am., 1974-75; represented in permanent collections, Corcoran Gallery Art, Walker Art Center, Mpls., Va. Mus. Fine Arts, Richmond, Everson Art Mus., Columbus Gallery Fine Arts, Detroit Inst. Art, Albright-Knox Mus., works include archtl. installations, Am. Republic Ins. Co., Des Moines, 1969, N.K. Winston Corp., N.Y.C., 1969, Schering Labs., Bloomfield, N.J., 1970, Skidmore, Owings and Merrill, N.Y.C., 1970, Kahn & Mallis Assos., N.Y.C., 1972, Harris Bank, Chgo., 1977, Powell/Kleinschmidt Chgo., 1977, Travenol Labs., Deerfield, Ill., 1977, Skidmore, Owings and Merrill, Chgo., 1977. John Simon Guggenheim Meml. Found. fellow, 1969; Nat Endowment for Arts grantee, 1976 Home and Office: 57 Leonard St Fl 4 New York NY 10013-2919

SWAIN, SCOTT D., finance educator, researcher; s. Reginald Vance and Barbara Mason Swain; m. Jennifer R. Alexander, June 7, 2002; 1 child, Elliott Mason. BS Physics, Francis Marion U., Florence, SC, 1989; BSEE, Clemson U., SC, 1991; MBA, U. SC., Columbia, 1996, PhD in Bus. Adminstrn., 2002. Ocean rescue City of Myrtle Beach, SC, 1986—88; instr. U. SC, Columbia, 1998—2002; prof. mktg. Boston U., 2002—. Owner MRKT-PHD listserv, Boston, 1997—. Spl. program coord. DSS, Florence, SC, 1988—89. Lt. jg USN, 1990—94. Recipient Outstanding Sr. Elec. Engring., Clemson U., 1991; grantee, Boston U., 2003—06; Francis M. Hipp MBA fellow, U. SC, 1994—96, William Douglas Dargan Merit scholar, Francis Marion U., 1986—88, Patriot scholar. Mem.: IEEE, APA, Soc. Consumer Psychology, Assn. Consumer Rsch., Am. Mktg. Assn. (bd. dirs. doctoral spl. interest group 2006—, sec. doctoral spl. interest group 2000—02), Soc. Mktg. Advances, Acad. Mktg. Sci., Mktg. Sci. Inst., Beta Gamma Sigma, Chi Delta Chi, Eta Kappa Nu, Phi Kappa Phi. Avocations: guitar, surfing, rock collecting, golf, reading. Home: 18 Devens Rd Swampscott MA 01907 Office: Boston University - School of Management 595 Commonwealth Avenue Boston MA 02215 Home Phone: 617-353-5978; Office Phone: 617-353-5978.

SWAIN, SUSAN MARIE, communications executive; b. Phila., Dec. 23, 1954; d. Samuel B. Swain and Marie Paget. BA in Comms. magna cum laude, U. Scranton, Pa., 1976, Doctorate (hon.), 2000. Reporter Sta. WDAU-TV, Scranton, 1975-76; pub. rels. staff Up With People, Inc., Tucson, 1976—78; supr. Raytheon Service Co., Cambridge, Mass., 1978-80; research assoc. Nat. Counsel Assocs., Washington, 1980-82; producer C-SPAN Cable Network, Washington, 1982-83, dir. pub. relations, 1983-87, v.p. corp. communications, mem. exec. mgmt. com., 1987-89, sr. v.p., 1989—95, exec. v.p., co-chief oper. officer, 1995—; also creator & host "American Writers", C-SPAN. Officer The Nat. Cable Satellite Corp.; bd. mem. C-SPAN Ednl. Found.; bd. mem., dir. Talbot's Inc. Moderator (TV program) C-SPAN Viewer Call-In, 1982—; editl. mgr. Booknotes, 1997, Booknotes: Life Stories, 1999, Booknotes: Stories from History, 2001, Booknotes: On American Character, 2004. Trustee U. Scranton, 1992—2000. Recipient Alumni award U. Scranton, 1976, Disting. Achievement award, 1991. Mem. Cable Telecom. Adminstrn. and Mktg., Mus. TV and Radio, Cable TV Pub. Affairs Assn. (bd. dirs. 1986-90, sec. 1988-89), Washington Cable Club, Alpha Sigma Nu. Roman Catholic. Avocations: sailing, biking. Office: C-SPAN 400 N Capitol St NW Ste 650 Washington DC 20001-1550 E-mail: sswain@c-span.org.

SWAINSON, JOHN A., software company executive; b. Canada; 3 children. BS in Engring., U. British Columbia. Joined as systems engr. IBM, Vancouver, Canada, 1978, various mgmt. positions in mktg. and services and mfg. and devel., mgr. market devel. and support, IBM Canada Software Solutions Lab. Toronto, Canada, 1991—93, dir. application devel. mktg., software solutions div., 1993—94, v.p., application devel. solutions and dir., IBM Canada Software Solutions Lab. Toronto, Canada, 1994, gen. mgr. applications and integration middleware, 1997—2004, v.p. sales software div., 2004; pres. Computer Associates Internat. Inc., Islandia, NY, 2004—05, CEO-elect, 2004—05; pres., CEO Computer Associates Internat. Inc. (now named CA, Inc.), Islandia, NY, 2005—, also bd. dir. Mem. IBM Worldwide Mgmt. Coun., IBM Strategy Team, IBM Sr. Leadership Team; bd. gov. IBM Acad. Technology. Office: Computer Assocs Internat Inc (CA Inc) One Computer Assocs Plz Islandia NY 11749 *

SWAISGOOD, HAROLD EVERETT, biochemist, educator; b. Ashland, Ohio, Jan. 19, 1936; s. Ray Weaver and Jennie (Morr) S.; m. Janet Cromwell, Sept. 15, 1956; children: Mark Harold, Ronald Ray. BS, Ohio State U., 1958; PhD in Chemistry (NIH fellow), Mich. State U., 1963. Rsch. asst. Mich. State U., 1958-63; rsch. assoc. NIH, 1963—64; asst. prof. food sci. and biochemistry N.C. State U., 1964-67, assoc. prof., 1967-72, prof., 1972-84, William Neal Reynolds prof., 1984—2001, prof. emeritus William Neal Reynolds, 2001—, Alumni Disting. Grad. Rsch. prof., 1997. Vis. prof. U. Lund, Sweden, 1974, chmn. biotech. program, 1986-92; bd. mem. Coun. Agrl. Sci. and Tech., 2004—. Editor for Ams., Comments on Agr. and Food Chemistry; assoc. editor Jour. Food Biochemistry, 1983-2000; mem. editl. bd. Jour. Dairy Sci, 1975-85, Jour. Food Sci. 1978-83; regional editor Nahrung-Food, 1995-2002; contbr. articles, chpts. to profl. publs. USPHS fellow, 1963-64. Fellow Am. Chem. Soc. (agriculture food chem. divsn., award advancement of application of agrl. and food chemistry sponsored by IFF 1994), Am. Dairy Sci. Assn. (pres. 1999-2000, dairy rsch. found. award, 1985, Borden award 1987); mem. AAAS, Am. Inst. Nutrition, Am. Soc. Biochemists and Molecular Biologists, Inst. Food Technologists, Coun. Agrl. Sci. and Tech. (bd. dir.), Sigma Xi, Phi Kappa Phi, Gamma Sigma Delta. Democrat. Methodist. Achievements include research in protein structure, interactions, and functionality; characteristics and applications of immobilized enzymes; patents in field. Office: NC State U Dept Food Sci Raleigh NC 27695-7624 Business E-Mail: harold_swaisgood@ncsu.edu.

SWALIN, RICHARD ARTHUR, scientist, company executive; b. Mpls., Mar. 18, 1929; s. Arthur and Mae (Hurley) S.; m. Helen Marguerite Van Wagenen, June 28, 1952; children: Karen, Kent, Kristin. BS with distinction, U. Minn., 1951, PhD, 1954. Rsch. assoc. GE, 1954-56; mem. faculty U. Minn., Mpls., 1956-77, prof., head Sch. Mineral and Metall Engring., 1962-68, assoc. dean Inst. Tech., 1968-71, dean Inst. Tech., 1971-77; acting dir. Space Sci. Center, 1965; v.p. tech. Eltra Corp., NYC, 1977-80; v.p. R & D Allied-Signal Corp., Morristown, NJ, 1980-84; dean Coll. Engring. and Mines U. Ariz., Tucson, 1984-87, prof., 1984-94; pres. Ariz. Tech. Devel. Corp., Tucson, 1987; prof. emeritus U. Ariz., Tucson, 1995—. Guest scientist Max Planck Inst. für Phys. Chemie, Göttingen, Fed. Republic Germany, 1963, Lawrence Radiation Lab., Livermore, Calif., 1967; cons. to govt. and industry; bd. dirs. emeritus Medtronic Corp., BMC Industries; corp. adv. bd. AMP Inc., 1990-93. Author: Thermodynamics of Solids, 2d edit, 1972; Contbr. articles to profl. jours. Dir. div. indsl. coop. U. Ariz. Found., 1985-86; trustee Midwest Research Inst., 1975-78, Sci. Mus. Minn., 1973-77, Nat. Tech. U., 1983-90. Recipient Disting. Teaching award Inst. Tech., U. Minn., 1967, Leadership award U. Minn. Alumni, 1993; NATO sr. fellow in sci., 1971. Mem. Sigma Xi, Tau Beta Pi, Phi Delta Theta, Gamma Alpha. Home: Splendido 518 13500 Rancho Vistoso Blvd Oro Valley AZ 85755 Personal E-mail: rswalin@gmail.com.

SWALLOW, KATHLEEN CLINEDINST, chemistry professor; b. Balt., Jan. 21, 1948; d. Clinton Richard and Virginia Catherine (Martin) Clinedinst; m. Stephen Thaxter Swallow, June 20, 1970; children: Lindsey Ellen, Clinton Peloubet. BS, U. Richmond, 1970; PhD, MIT, 1978; Dr. Honoris Causa, U. West, Timisoara, Romania, 2006. Asst. prof. Wellesley Coll., Mass., 1977—82, 1989—90; pres. Interstate Labs., Newburyport, Mass., 1980—82; mgr. Analytical Labs MODAR, Inc., Natick, Mass., 1982—85; sr. assoc. Gradient Corp., Cambridge, Mass., 1986—89; from assoc. prof. to prof. Merrimack Coll., North Andover, Mass., 1990—97, prof., 1997—, dean sci. and engring. dept., 1998—2003. Chair dept. chemistry Merrimack Coll., North Andover, 1995—97, 2005—; vis. scientist, prof. MIT, 1996—; Fulbright sr. specialist in environ. sci., 2004—; cons. MODAR, Inc., 1985—92. Contbg. author: Ground Water Quality and Analysis at Hazardous Waste Sites, 1992; patentee supercritical water oxidation. Moderator, Town of West Newbury, 1985—; chmn. governing bd. First Religious Soc. of Newburyport, 1984, 2002. Disting. Alumna Westhampton Coll. Class of 1970, Richmond, Va., 1995 Mem. Am. Chem. Soc. (chmn. Norris com. northea. sect. 1996), Sigma Xi, Gamma Sigma Epsilon, Phi Beta Kappa Unitarian Universalist. Home: 131 River Rd West Newbury MA 01985-1103 Office: Merrimack Coll 315 Turnpike St North Andover MA 01845-5806 Business E-Mail: kathleen.swallow@merrimack.edu.

SWALM, THOMAS STERLING, retired military officer, aviations systems consultant; b. San Diego, Sept. 28, 1931; s. Calvin D. and Margaret A. (Rynning) S.; m. Charlene La Vern Garner, June 26, 1954; children: Edward Steven, Lori Ann. BS, U. Oreg., Eugene, 1954; MS in Pub. Adminstrn., George Washington U., Washington, 1964; grad., Air Command and Staff Coll., Montgomery, Ala., 1964; MA, Nat. War Coll., Washington, 1974. Commd. USAF, 1954, advanced through grades to maj. gen., 1982, instr. fighter-interceptor weapons sch. Tyndall AFB, Fla., 1956, pilot 434th Fighter-Day Squadron George AFB, Calif., 1957-58, engring. test pilot and flight examiner 50th Tactical Fighter Wing, 10th Tactical Fighter Squadron Toul-Rosieres AFB, France, and Hahn AFB, Fed. Republic Germany, 1958-61, hdqrs. 12th Waco, Tex., 1961-64, instr. pilot, flight examiner 4453d Combat Crew Tng. Wing Davis-Monthan AFB, Ariz., 1965-66, flight comdr. 12th Tactical Fighter Wing Cam Ranh Bay AFB, Republic Vietnam, 1966-67; comdr. air-to-air flight, instr. and chief R&D/OT&E sect. Fighter Weapons Sch., Nellis AFB, Nev., 1967-70; comdr., leader Thunderbirds USAF, 1970-73, chief fighter attack directorate Kirtland AFB, N.Mex., 1974-75, dep. dir. test and evaluation, 1975-76, from vice comdr. to comdr. 8th Tactical Fighter Wing Kunsan AFB, Republic of Korea, 1976-78, comdr. 3d Tactical Fighter Wing Clark AFB, Philippines, 1978-79, comdr. 57th Fighter Weapons Wing, comdt. fighter weapons sch. Nellis AFB, Nev., 1979-80, comdr. 833d air div. Holloman AFB, N.Mex., 1980-81, comdr. tactical air warfare ctr. Eglin AFB, Fla., 1981-86, ret., 1986; pres. T. Swalm and Assocs., Ft. Walton Beach, Fla., 1986-91; v.p. Melbourne Systems Div. Grumman Corp., 1991-95; pres. T. Swalm and Assocs., Melbourne, Fla., 1995—. V.p. Applications Group Internat., Inc., Atlanta, 1986—89; bd. dirs. Nat. Correlation Working Group. Mem. editorial bd. Jour. Electronic Def., 1983-86; contbr. articles to profl. jours. Hon. chmn. Heart Assn., Las Vegas, Nev., 1972; exec. dir. Boy Scouts Am., Las Vegas and Alamagordo, N.Mex., 1970-81; chmn. AFA Scholarship Found., 1989-91; active Fla. Govs. Coun. for TQM, 1992-94; bd. dirs. Jr. Achievement, Ctrl. Fla., 1992-94; mem. USAF scientific adv. bd., 1994-98. Decorated D.S.M., Legion of Merit with two oak leaf clusters, DFC, Air medal with 14 oak leaf clusters, Vietnam Service medal with three service stars, Republic Vietnam Campaign medal; recipient R.V. Jones Trophy Electronic Security Command, 1984, Exceptional Civilian Svc. award USAF, 1999. Mem. Air Force Assn. (exec. advisor, Jerome Waterman award 1985, Jimmy Doolittle fellow 1986), Thunderbirds Pilots Assn., Old Mission Beach Athletic Club (founder), Assn. Old Crows (editl. bd. R.V. Jones trophy 1984), Order of Daedalians (flight capt.), Melbourne C of C. (trustee 1993-95), Sigma Nu. Republican. Presbyterian. Avocations: golf, tennis, sailing.

SWAMIKANNU, XAVIER, environmental engineer, state official; b. Penang, Malaysia, Aug. 1, 1958; s. Swamikannu Savarimuthu and Rosary Swamikannu; m. Laveeza Bhatti, Apr. 21, 1959; 1 child, Romin Swamikannu Savri. PhD in Environ. Sci. & Engring., U. Calif., LA, 1994. Environ. engr. Calif. EPA - Water Quality Control Bd., LA, 1989—99, chief, coastal storm water program, 1999—2003, spl. asst., storm water pollution control, 2003—04, chief storm water permitting, 2005—. Tech. adv. on storm water pollution USEPA Office of Water, Washington, 1989—; expert panelist Nat. Water Rsch. Inst., Pomona, Calif., 1997—97; mem. com. NAS/NRC, 2006—. Lector St. Anastasia Cath. Ch., LA, 1999—2004. Named Disting. scholar, U. Calif., 1993. Mem.: ASCE, Water Environment Fedn., Internat. Water Assn., Am. Water Works Assn. Roman Catholic. Achievements include development of water quality design stds. for Calif; So. Calif. storm water monitoring; Santa Monica Bay restoration policy; storm water pollution control. Avocation: travel. Home: 7732 Stewart Ave Los Angeles CA 90045 Office: Calif EPA - Water Quality

Control Bd 320 W 4th St Los Angeles CA 90013 Home Phone: 310-338-0644; Office Phone: 213-620-2094. Office Fax: 213-576-6625; Home Fax: 310-242-9222. Business E-Mail: xswamikannu@waterboards.ca.gov.

SWAN, ALAN CHARLES, law educator; b. Kalimpong, West Bengal, India, Dec. 29, 1933; came to U.S., 1945; s. Charles Lundeen and Kathleen Vivian (Doucette) S.; m. Mary Joe Smith, Aug. 28, 1954; children—Kathleen Jeanette, Amalie Christine, Alan Charles. B.A., Albion Coll., 1954; J.D., U. Chgo., 1957. Bar: N.Y. 1958. Assoc. Milbank, Tweed, Hadley & McCloy, N.Y.C., 1957-61; asst. gen. counsel AID, Washington, 1961-66; asst. v.p. U. Chgo., professorial lectr. Grad. Sch. Bus., 1966-72; prof. law U. Miami, Coral Gables, Fla., 1972—; mem. Nat. Lawyers Com. for Soviet Jewry, 1971-80. Author: The Regulation of International Business and Economic Relations, 2d edit., 2001; contbr. articles to profl. jours. Trustee Plymouth Congregational Ch., Miami, 1998-2001; mem. Miami Com. on Fgn. Relations, 1976—, sec. of state adv. com. on pvt. internat. law, 1995—. Mem. Am. Law Inst, ABA, Am. Soc. Internat. Law, Internat. Law Assn., Fla. Bar Assn. Democrat. Home: 14901 SW 82nd Ave Miami FL 33158-1906 Office: U Miami Sch Law Coral Gables FL 33124 Office Phone: 305-284-2411. E-mail: aswan@law.miami.edu.

SWAN, ANNALYN, writer; b. Biloxi, Miss. d. Ethelynn Swan; m. Mark Whitney Stevens, June 12, 1977; children: Emmelyn Swan, Julia Philippa. Former writer Time mag.; former music critic & sr. arts editor Newsweek; has also written for The New Republic, The Atlantic Monthly, NY Times Mag. Co-author (with Mark Stevens): de Koonig: An American Master, 2004 (Nat. Book Critics Circle Award for biography/autobiography, 2005, Pulitzer Prize for biography, 2005).

SWAN, BARBARA J., lawyer, utilities executive; BA in History, Macalester Coll., St. Paul, 1973; JD, William Mitchell Coll. of Law, St. Paul, 1979. Atty. Axley Brynelson Law Firm, 1981—87; assoc. gen. counsel Wis. Power and Light (subs. Alliant Energy), 1987—93, gen. counsel, 1993—94, v.p., gen. counsel, 1994—98, pres., 2004—; exec. v.p., gen. counsel Alliant Energy, 1998—. Mem. Edison Electric Inst. Gen. Counsel Com. Bd. mem. Nat. Assn. Mfrs., 2001—07; pres. Alliant Energy Found., 2004—; bd. mem. Forward Wisconsin, Madison Symphony Orch., 2004—, Greater Madison C. of C., 2005—, Am. Players Theater, 2007—. Office: Alliant Energy PO Box 77007 4902 N Biltmore Ln Madison WI 53707-1007

SWAN, GEORGE STEVEN, law educator; b. St. Louis; s. Raymond Albert and Lorene Catherine (Kennedy) Swan. BA, Ohio State U., 1970; JD, U. Notre Dame, 1974; LLM, U. Toronto, 1976, SJD, 1983. Bar: Ohio 1974, U.S. Dist. Ct. (so. dist.) Ohio 1975, U.S. Supreme Ct. 1987, U.S. Ct. Appeals (6th and 11th cirs.) 1993, U.S. Ct. Appeals (10th cir.) 1994, DC 1997, Ga. 1997, Fla. 1997, U.S. Dist. Ct. (no. dist.) Ga. 1997, Minn. 1998, La. 1999, Mass. 1999; CLU, ChFC, CFP. Asst. atty. gen. State of Ohio, Columbus, 1974-75; jud. clk. Supreme Ct. Ohio, Columbus, 1976-78; asst. prof. Del. Law Sch., Wilmington, 1980-83, assoc. prof., 1983-84; prof. law St. Thomas U. Law Sch., Miami, Fla., 1984-88; jud. clk. U.S. Ct. Appeals (7th cir.), Chgo., 1988-89; assoc. prof. N.C. Agrl. & Tech. State U., Greensboro, 1989—. Vis. prof. John Marshall Law Sch., Atlanta, 1996—97, Atlanta, 2000—01. Contbr. articles to profl. jours. Mem.: Am. Polit. Sci. Assn., Fin. Planning Assn., Soc. Fin. Svc. Profls., La. State Bar Assn., Nebr. State Bar Assn., Mass. Bar Assn., Fla. Bar, State Bar Ga., DC Bar, Ohio State Bar Assn., Phi Kappa Phi. Office: Merrick Hall 1601 E Market St Greensboro NC 27411 Office Phone: 336-334-7656 ext 7022. Business E-Mail: swan@ncat.edu.

SWAN, MARA E., employment services executive; BBA, U. Buffalo; M in Indsl. Rels., U. Minn. Human resources mgr. Miller Brewing Co.; chief people officer global ops. Molson Coors Brewing Co.; sr. v.p. global human resources Manpower, Inc., Milw., 2005—. Office: Manpower Inc 5301 N Ironwood Rd Milwaukee WI 53217 Office Phone: 414-961-1000. *

SWAN, MICHAEL K., lawyer; b. Kilgore, Tex. BBA, Tex. A&M, 1964; LLB, Univ. Tex., 1967. Bar: Tex. 1967, US Supreme Ct. 1971, US Dist. Ct. (so., no., we., ea. districts) Tex., cert.: Civil Trial Law, Tex. Bd. Legal Specialization. Assoc. Reynolds White Allen & Cook, 1971—75, mng. ptnr., 1981—88; ptnr., gen. litig. Andrews & Kurth, 1988—92; now ptnr.-in-charge Houston, head litig. practice and mem. mgmt. com. Akin Gump Strauss Hauer & Feld LLP, Houston, 1992—. Mem. JAGC US Army, 1967—71. Fellow: Houston Bar Found., Tex. Bar Found.; mem.: ABA, Am. Bd. Trial Advocates, State Bar of Tex. (dir. 1982—85), Houston Bar Assn., Phi Alpha Delta. Office: Akin Gump Strauss Hauer & Feld LLP 44th fl 1111 Louisiana St Houston TX 77002-5200 Office Phone: 713-220-5862. Office Fax: 713-236-0822. Business E-Mail: mswan@akingump.com.

SWAN, PEER ALDEN, public utility executive; b. Beverly, Mass., 1944; s. E.M. and Stella Swan; m. Nancy Carol Mosier, Jan. 24, 1969; children: Michael, Ashley. AA, Orange Coast Coll., Costa Mesa, Calif., 1966; BA, Calif. State U., Fullerton, 1973. Fin. analyst Brunswich, Costa Mesa, 1974-76; asst. treas. Pacific Sci. Co., Newport Beach, Calif., 1977-84, treas., 1984-98. Dir. SC Bancorp, Downey, Calif., 1992-97, Met. Water Dist. of So. Calif., 1999-2002. Dir. Irvine (Calif.) Ranch Water Dist., 1979—, Orange County Sanitation Dist., Fountain Valley, Calif., 1985—2001, So. Calif. Water Com., Irvine, 1984—92, Nat. Water Rsch. Inst., Fountain Valley, 1991—2001. Capt. US Army, 1966—71, Vietnam. Avocations: sailing, hiking. Home: 7 Terraza Dr Newport Coast CA 92657-1510 Business E-Mail: pswan@ix.netcom.com.

SWAN, PHILIP GEORGE, librarian, educator, director, artist; b. Camp Springs, Md., Feb. 7, 1969; s. Philip George and Diana Morse Swan; m. Jennifer Marguerite Hubert, Sept. 27, 2001. BA, U. Mich., 1991; MA, Coll. William and Mary, 1994; MS in Info., U. Mich., 1996. Libra, asst. mgr. Queensborough Pub. Libr., Jamaica, NY, 1997—99; head libr., assoc. prof. Hunter Coll., NYC, 2000—. Chesebrough Pond's Nat. Arts Competition, 1987, juried exhibition, The Haven (Second Pl. Nationally, 1987), Dansforth Gallery, 2000, Longbeach Island Found. Arts, 2002; author: (peer reviewed article) Collection Building (Emerald Publishing's 2003 Highly Commended Award, 2002); contbr. articles to profl. jours. Scholar, Coll. William and Mary and Colonial Williamsburg Found., 1993—94. Mem.: ALA, Libr. Assn. CUNY (co-chair 2002—04, co-chair electronic info. svcs. com. 2002—04), Assn. Coll. and Rsch. Libr. (coll. libr. sect. comm. com. 2001—04). Office: Hunter Coll 129 E 79th St 2nd Flr New York NY 10075

SWAN, ROBERT, explorer, adventurer, foundation administrator; b. Durham, Eng., 1956; BA in Ancient History, Durham U., 1976—79; LittD, Robert Gordon U., 1993. Mem., In Footsteps of Scott, Antarctic Expedition planning and fund Raising, 1979—84; mem. British Antarctic Survey, 1980—81; founder Robert Swan Found., 1993—; v.p. Countryside Mgmt. Assn., 1995. Vis. prof., sch. environ. Leeds Metropolitan U., 1992; keynote spkr. Earth Summit, Rio de Janeiro, 1992; planner and fund raiser One Step Beyond, South Pole Challenge Expedition, 1994—96; invited spkr. UN Goodwill Ambassador with Special Responsibility for Youth, 1989; spl. envoy to dir. gen. UNESCO, 1994. Named one of the Top Ten Presenter on Leadership and Teamwork, Time Mag.; recipient Polar medal, Her Majesty Queen Elizabeth II, 1987, Order British Empire, 1996, Smithsonian award for Info. Tech. in Edn. and Academia, 1998, European Union Ambassador for the Environment, 2003, UN Environ. Program Global 500 award, 1989. Mem.: Amstel Club (hon.). Achievements include first person to walk to both the South (Jan. 11, 1986)(arrived with Roger Mear and Gareth Wood) and North (May 14, 1989) Poles (reaches with 8 from 7 nations); In 1988-89, walk to the North Pole encompassed Icewalk, an international student expedition which included 22 participants from 15 nations; In 1996-97 organized One Step Beyond, The South Pole Challenge, which included 35 young explorers from 25 nations together at Antarctica; Mission Antarctica, the beginning of a five year challenge dedicated to the preservation of Antarctic Wilderness; In Jan., 2002, Mission Antarctica removes 1,000 tons of garbage from the Russian Antarctic station Bellingshausen; In August, 2002, participated in the World Summit on Sustainable Development in Johannesburg. Accompanied by 45 young people from 30 nations, including sponsoring companies; Antarctic yacht 2041 travels 12,000 kilometers overland to report back to World Leaders 10 years after addressing them during the first Earth Summit in Rio de Janiero; Inspire Antarctic Expeditions (IAE) 1 in 2003, led first corporate expedition to Antarctica (42 people from 18 nations); IAE 2 in 2004, brings 44 people from 15 nations in search of sitre for the future E-Base. The yacht 2041 participates in the Sydney to Hobart Race, placing 24th and 4th in the yacht's class; IAE 3 in 2005, a team of young people and corporate personnel from around the world work to refurbish the accommodation unit for the E-base (52 people from 21 nations); IAE 4 in 2006 with focus on teamwork and education, led a team of teachers, students and corporate personnel to Antarctica; IAE 5 in 2007 led corporate leaders, entrepreneurs in the field of renewable energy, journalists, teachers and deserving student to the Antarctic, Leadership on the Edge expedition; On the IAE 5 expedition hopes to launch the world's first online eduction center (E-Base) on King George Island, Antarctica, to offer children a real-time glance at life on the ice. Office: Robert Swan Found UK c/o Lucinda Swan Stable Cottage Camphill Bedale North Yorks DL82LS England Address: Mission Antarctica Found USA Inc 561 Keystone Ave PMB #640 Reno NV 89503 Office Phone: 44 1845 567783, 702-292-1378. E-mail: rswan@2041.com. *

SWAN, ROBERT H., Internet company executive; BS in Mgmt., SUNY, Buffalo; MBA, SUNY, Binghamton. Fin. positions Gen. Electric, 1985—99; CFO GE Transportation Systems, 1994—97; v.p. fin. GE Med. Systems, 1997—98; v.p. fin., CFO GE Lighting, 1998—99, Webvan Group, 1999—2001, COO, 2000—01, CEO, 2001; CFO, exec. v.p. TRW Inc., 2001—02; exec. v.p., CFO EDS, Plano, Tex., 2003—06; sr. v.p. fin., CFO eBay Inc., San Jose, Calif., 2006—. Office: eBay Inc 2145 Hamilton Ave San Jose CA 95125 Office Phone: 972-604-6000. Office Fax: 972-605-6033. *

SWAN, SUSAN LINDA, history professor; b. Everett, Wash., May 31, 1943; d. Joseph William Franckevitch and Doris Aline (Doolittle) Berry; m. Victor LaMarr Swan, June 19, 1965 (div. Apr. 1994); 1 child, Kerrigan Aline. BA in History, U. Wash., 1965, BA in English, 1965; MA in History, Western Wash. U., 1969; PhD in History, Wash. State U., 1976. Employment interviewer Wash. State Employment Security, Tacoma, 1971-72; asst. prof. history Wash. State U., Pullman, 1977-82, student affairs officer III, 1984-94, assoc. prof. gen. edn. program, 1994—; rsch. assoc. Nat. Coord. Spl. Hist. Projects, Mex., 1991-92. Student affairs com. Wash. State U., chair acad. advising and reinstatement subcom., mus. adv. subcom.; chpt. advisor Alpha Phi Omega, 1995—99; advisor Sikh Student Assn., 2002—04. Co-author: Breve Historia de las Sequias en Mexico, 1995; adaptation editor: Study Guide for the Heritage of World Civilizations, vol. I, 2001, vol. II, 2002; contbg. editor: Reading About the World, I, II, 3d edit., 1999; contbr. articles to profl. jours Vol. Pullman Meml. Hosp. Aux., 1983—92; group leader Sacajawea coun. Camp Fire, Pullman, 1984—90. Recipient Faculty award, Wash. State U. Multicultural Student Svcs., 2002. Mem.: AAAS, Assn. Faculty Women (treas. 1998—99), Am. Mus. Women in the Arts, N.Y. Acad. Scis., Seattle Art Mus., Phi Kappa Phi, Phi Alpha Theta (pres. 1974—75). Avocations: watercolors, gardening. Home: PO Box 1284 Pullman WA 99163-1284 Office: Wash State Univ Dept History Pullman WA 99164-4030

SWAN, WILLIAM, actor; b. Buffalo, Feb. 6, 1932; s. Earl B. and Irene (Hall) S. Student, Geller Workshop, LA. Appeared in films including Lady in a Cage, Hotel, The Parallax View, Winter of Frozen Deams, 2007; over 200 TV guest appearances include Streets of San Francisco, Quincy, Perry Mason, Felony Squad, Twilight Zone, Have Gun Will Travel, Cannon, Barnaby Jones; appeared in off-Broadway plays including Anne of a Thousand Days, Night Fishing in Beverly Hills, The Locked-In Syndrome; appeared in regional theatre prodns. of A Delicate Balance, The Rehearsal, The Cocktail Hour, California Suite, The Middle Ages, Stained Glass, What the Butler Saw, The Price, Golf with Alan Shepard, Moby-Dick-Rehearsed, Medea and Electra, The Miracle Worker, All the Way Home, The Night of the Iguana, 2006, and others; actor: (TV) Walter Hines on All My Children, 1982-2000, Dr Ralph Jennings on The Young and the Restless, Rex Whitmore on As The World Turns. Trustee Berkshire Theatre Festival, Stockbridge, Mass., 1984-2001. Sgt. U.S. Army, 1948-49, ETO. Mem. Acad. TV, Arts and Scis., The Players, The Yale Club. Democrat. Avocation: tennis. Home: 141 E 55th St Apt 12B New York NY 10022-4034 Office: Barberry Close Monterey MA 01245

SWANER, LYNN E, education educator; d. Norris S and Susan L Gaynor; m. Damon K Swaner, Aug. 10, 1996; 1 child, Ashley E. EdD, Columbia U., 2003. Nat. cert. counselor. Asst. prof. C.W. Post Campus of L.I. U., Brookville, NY, 2005—. Cross-site evaluator, mem. planning bd. Bringing Theory to Practice Project, Am. Assn. Colls. and Univs., Washington, 2004—. Sec. South Yaphank Cmty. Assn., Yaphank, NY, 2004—05. Recipient Binghamton U. award for the Humanities, 1996. Mem.: Phi Beta Kappa. Achievements include commissioned literature review on mental health, engaged learning, and civic development published by Am. Assn. Colls. and Univs. Office: CW Post Campus of LI U Dept of Counseling 720 Northern Blvd Brookville NY 11548 Home Phone: 631-205-5410; Office Phone: 516-299-2815.

SWANEY, THOMAS ROBBINS, venture capitalist; b. L.A., Apr. 28, 1952; s. George Robbins and Marian (Smoliga) S.; m. Ines Veronique Szilard, Aug. 31, 1974; children: Elizabeth Marian, Peter Thomas. BA in Econs. and Math., U. Calif., Berkeley, 1974; postgrad., U. Minn., 1974-75. Treasury analyst Fed. Home Loan Bank, San Francisco, 1976-78; fin. analyst Bank of Am., San Francisco, 1978-81; fin. cons. Chase Manhattan Bank, San Francisco, 1981-83, Am. Express, San Francisco, 1984-86; v.p. Bear Stearns, San Francisco, 1986-89; pres. Harwood Capital Inc., Walnut Creek, Calif., 1989—. Bd. dirs. West Oakland Devel. Assn., Calif., Am. Petroleum Inst., Sacramento. Bd. dirs. Kisha Soc., San Francisco, 1991-93; elder St. John's Presbyn. Ch. Berkeley. Mem. Sacramento Petroleum Assn., Calif. Ind. Petroleum Assn., World Affairs Coun. No. Calif., No. Calif. Geol. Soc., No. Calif. Cogeneration Assn., World Forum Silicon Valley, Indo Am. C. of C., U. Calif. Alumni Assn. (bd. dirs.), U. Calif. Berkeley Entrepreneurs Forum, Commonwealth Club, Ind. Petroleum Assn. Am. Avocations: tennis, numismatics. Office: Harwood Capital Inc 1255 Treat Blvd #300 Walnut Creek CA 94597 Office Phone: 510-658-6398.

SWANGO, COLLEEN JILL, science educator; b. Izmir, Turkey, Sept. 8, 1956; d. Charles Irvan Swango and Altamae Silva. BS in Edn., Ind. U., 1978; MS in Edn., Ind. U.-Purdue, 1984. Lic. tchr. Ind. Tchr. Share's Inc., Shelbyville, Ind., 1978—85, supervising tchr., 1979—85; sci. tchr. Brownsburg (Ind.) Jr. High, 1986—, chair sci. dept., 1993—. Co-prodr.: Help! I'm Teaching Middle School Science, 2003. Mem.: Nat. Sci. Tchrs. Assn., Hoosier Assn. Sci. Tchrs., Brownsburg Classroom Tchrs. Assn. (past pres., rep.). Independent. Methodist. Avocations: music, reading, theater, travel. Home: 104 Sterling Dr Pittsboro IN 46167

SWANK, HILARY, actress; b. Lincoln, Nebr., July 30, 1974; d. Stephen and Judy Swank; m. Chad Lowe, Sept. 28, 1997 (separated 2006). Attended, Santa Monica Coll. Actor: Buffy the Vampire Slayer, 1992, The Next Karate Kid, 1994, Sometimes They Come Back...Again, 1996, Kounterfeit, 1996, The Way We Are, 1997, Heartwood, 1998, Boys Don't Cry, 1999 (Golden Globe for Best Actress, 2000, Academy award for Best Actress, 2000), Affair of the Necklace, 2000, The Gift, 2000, The Affair of the Necklace, 2001, Insomnia, 2002, The Core, 2003, Million Dollar Baby, 2004 (best actress, Boston Film Critics award, 2004, Golden Globe award for best actress, 2005, Screen Actors Guild award, for outstanding performance by female actor in leading role, 2005, Acad. award for Best Actress, 2005), The Black Dahlia, 2006, The Reaping, 2007; (TV films) Cries Unheard: The Donna Yaklich Story, 1994, Terror in the Family, 1996, Dying to Belong, 1997, The Sleepwalker Killing, 1997, Iron Jawed Angels, 2004; (TV series) Evening Shade, 1991-92, Camp Wilder, 1992, Beverly Hills, 90210, 1997-98, Leaving L.A., 1997; actor, exec. prodr. (films) 11:14, 2003, Freedom Writers, 2007; (TV appearances) Growing Pains, 1985, Harry and the Hendersons, 1991. Named one of Time Mag. 100 Most Influential People, 2005; recipient Little Screen/Big Star award, TV Land, 2006, Emery award, Hetrick-Martin Inst., 2006, star on the Hollywood Walk of Fame, 2007. Avocations: sky diving, river rafting, skiing, swimming. *

SWANKER-GIBSON, JAHNN HANSEN, mental health nurse; b. Amsterdam, NY, Apr. 21, 1949; d. John Nichols and Andrienne M. (Hansen) Swanker; m. David Michael Gibson, Aug. 31, 1970; 1 child, Rebecca Lynne Gibson. BA in Psychology, Plattsburgh State, NYC, 1971; AAS in Nursing, Adirondack Cmty. Coll., Glens Falls, NY, 1987. RN N.Y. Med. social worker Cohoes Meml. Hosp., NY, 1973; asst. residence mgr. Alternatives in Mankind, Saratoga Springs, 1980—83; RN Saratoga Hosp., 1987—89, Wesley Nursing Home, 1990—92, Fulton County, Johnstown, 1992—93, Lexington Ctr., Gloversville, 1993—98; RN psychiat. dept. St. Mary's Hosp., Amsterdam, 1999—, RN unit QI, 2001—. Author: Susan's Sailing Adventures, 2001; editor: (newsletter) Armchair Yachtsman, 1974—76; contbr. articles to perodicals. Chmn. svc. and rehab. Am. Cancer Soc., Saratoga Springs, NY, 1981—82; mem. Victorian Ball com. Johnstown Libr., 1997—98; pres. Johnstown Hist. Soc., 1998, coord. tea and fashion show, 1995—97; soup kitchen vol. Saratoga Springs, NY, 1990—92; treas. Ch. Women's Assn., Saratoga Springs, 1986. Mem.: Eclectic Soc. Study Club, Clio Study Club, Mayfield Yacht Club (long range planning com. 1973, sec. 1974—86, historian 1993—, Daniel C. Shepard award 1965, Ladies' Cup 1980, 1982, 1983, 1986, Bill Chatterton award 1996), Students' Study Club. Republican. Presbyn. Avocations: sailing, reading, history, writing, church choir. Home: 302 Melcher St Johnstown NY 12095

SWANKIN, DAVID ARNOLD, lawyer, consumer products company executive; b. Boston, Jan. 18, 1934; s. Max and Anne (Rotefsky) S.; m. Jeanne Phyllis Herrick; 1 dau., Sheryl. AB, Brandeis U., 1954; MS, U. Wis., 1957; JD, George Washington U., 1962. Mgmt. intern U.S. Dept. Labor, Washington, 1957-60, spl. asst. to asst. sec. labor, 1961-63, dep. asst. sec. labor, 1967; dir. Bur. Labor Standards, 1967-68; exec. sec. Pres.'s Consumer Adv. Council, Washington, 1964; exec. dir. Pres's Com. on Consumer Interests, Washington, 1965-66; Washington rep. Consumer's Union, 1969-71; exec. dir. Consumer Interests Found., 1971-73; sr. partner Swankin & Turner, 1973—. Pres. Citizen Advocacy Ctr. 1994—; cons. U.S. Dept. Labor; pres. Citizen Advocacy Ctr., 1994—. Mem. president's coun. Brandeis U., 1968-69; mem. PEW Health Profls. Commn., 1997-98. Served with AUS., 1954-56. Recipient Jump award U.S. Govt., 1969 Office: 1400 16th St NW Washington DC 20036-2217 Home: 102 Gresham Pl Falls Church VA 22046 Business E-Mail: davidswankin@cacenter.org.

SWANN, BRIAN, writer, humanities educator; b. Wallsend, Northumberland, Eng., Aug. 13, 1940; came to U.S., 1963, naturalized, 1980; s. Stanley Frank and Lilyan Mary (Booth) S.; m. Roberta Metz. BA, Cambridge U., Eng., 1962, MA, 1965; PhD, Princeton U., 1970. Instr. Princeton U., 1964-65, lectr., 1968-70, asst. prof., 1970-72; instr. Rutgers U., 1965-66; asst. prof. humanities Cooper Union for Advancement Sci. and Art, NYC, 1972-75, assoc. prof., 1975-80, prof., 1980—, acting dean, 1990-91. Dir. Bennington Writing Workshops, 1988-91. Author: The Middle of the Journey, 1982, A Basket Full of White Eggs, 1988, Song of The Sky: Versions of Native American Song-Poems, 1993, The House With No Door, 1998, Wearing the Morning Star: Native American Song-Poems, 1996, Autumn Road, 2005, Snow House, 2005, other books, translations; editor: Smoothing The Ground: Essays of Native American Oral Literature, 1983; (with Arnold Krupat) Recovering the Word, 1987, I Tell You Now: Autobiographical Essays by Native American Writers, 1987, Coming to Light: Contemporary Translations of the Native American Literatures, 1992, (with Krupat) Here First: Autobiographical Essays by Contemporary Native American Writers, 2000, Voices from Four Directions: Contemporary Translations of the Native Literatures of North America, 2003; editor The Smithsonian Series of Essays on Native American Literatures, 1990-98, Algonquian Spirit: Contemporary Translations of the Algonquian Literatures of North America, 2005. NEA fellow, 1981; Creative Arts in Pub. Service grantee, 1982. Office: Cooper Union Adv Sci & Art Faculty Humanities & Social Sci Cooper Sq New York NY 10003

SWANN, CHARENA RAI, psychotherapist, social worker; b. Chamersburg, Pa., June 18, 1962; d. Nathaniel McNabb and Brenda Keepler; m. Lynn Swann, June 23, 1991; children: Shafer, Braxton. BA Social Work, Calif. U. Pa., Calif., Pa., 1984; MA Social Work, U. Pitts., 1985, PhD, 2002. Psychiatric soc. worker Western Psychiatric Inst. & Clinic, Pitts., 1984—; psychotherapist Sewickley Valley Hosp., Pitts., 1995—. Adv. bd. Summerbridge Pitts., 1999—2002; bd. mem. Children's Mus., 1998—. Fundraiser, mentor Girls Hope Pitts., 1998—2002. Mem.: Am. Psychol. Soc., Link, Jack and Jill of Am. Baptist. Avocations: reading, exercise.

SWANN, LYNN CURTIS, sportscaster, former professional football player; b. Alcoa, Tenn., Mar. 7, 1952; s. Willie and Mildred (McGarity) Swann; m. Charena Swann; 2 children. BA, U. So. Calif., 1974. Wide receiver Pitts. Steelers, 1974-83; commentator ABC Sports, 1976—; founder, pres. Swann, Inc. Bd. dirs. H.J. Heinz Co., Wyndham Internat. Inc.; chairman President's Coun. Phys. Fitness and Sports, 2002. Entertainment and media apppearances as dancer with Twyla Tharp and Peter Martines Omnibus TV Spl., 1980, guest star Night of 100 Stars I, 1982, 100 Stars II, 1985; host and narrator Britten's Young Person's Guide to Orchestra, Wheeling Symphony Orch., 1982; host of 13 part art edn. spl. Arts Alive, PBS, 1984; major character in episodes Paper Chase, 1984, Hotel, 1984, Love American Style, 1985; other appearances on various TV shows including 20/20, Good Morning America, Merv Griffin, Hollywood Squares, others; intermittent host daily talk show Pittsburgh 2Day, 1985 Spokesman for Big Bros./Big Sisters Assn.; trustee Pitts. Ballet Theatre, creator youth scholarship program; bd. dirs. Scott Newman Juvenile Drug and Alcohol Prevention Found.; bd. dirs. U. So. Calif. Sch. Journalism Alumni Assn. Named All Pro, 1976 77, 78, Most Valuable Player in Super Bowl X, 1976, Pitts. Multiple Sclerosis Athlete of Yr., 1980, NFL Man of Yr., 1981; holder 4 Super Bowl records, 2d in 2 categories; mem. Pitts. Steelers All-Time Team, 50th Anniv.; named to NFL Hall of Fame Team of Decade/1970's, AP, UPI, Kodak All Am. Teams, Pop Warner Hall of Fame; recipient Image award NAACP, 1979, Ebonics Soc. award, Outstanding Alumni award U. So. Calif., 1984, Oleg Cassini Competitors Fashion award, 1985. Mem. Screen Actors Guild, AFTRA. Office: Swann Inc 506 Hegner Way #2 Sewickley PA 15143-1552

SWANN, NAT HENDERSON, JR., physician; b. Danville, Va, Nov. 2, 1927; s. Nat Henderson, Sr. and Mary Stokes S.; m. Sarah Hayes, Aug. 7, 1952; children: Nat H. III, Wayland Hayes. AB in Chemistry, U. N.C., Chapel HIll, 1950, MD, 1954. Fellow Royal Soc. Medicine/London. Resident in internal medicine Med. Coll., Va., 1954-56, Boston VA Hosp., 1956-57, Cleve. VA (Crile) Hosp., 1957-58; specialist internal medicine Chattanooga, 1958—. Med. dir. Chattem, Inc., Chattanooga, 1960—; cons. rheumatic heart clin. Children's Hosp., Chattanooga, 1959-63; chief of staff Downtown Gen. Hosp., Chattanooga, 1986-90. Contbr. articles to profl. jours. Dir. Physician's Giving, United Way, Chattanooga, 1980; mem. Chattanooga Met. Coun., 1961; bd. spkr. Air Pollution Control Bd., Chattanooga, 1962; bd. dirs. The Salvation Army. With U.S. Army Med. Corps, 1946-47. Recipient Disting. Achievement award Am. Heart Assn. Fellow: ACP, Internat. Coll. Angiology, Royal Soc. Medicine, Am. Coll. Angiology, Am. Coll. Chest Physicians (assoc.); mem.: AMA, Am. Coll. Cardiology, Athenians Club (Chattanooga), Torch Club (Chattanooga), Mountain City Club (bd. dir.), Rotary (bd. dir.). Avocations: short story and novel writer, golf, tennis. Home: 412 Brady Point Rd Signal Mountain TN 37377-2206 E-mail: natswann@mindspring.com.

SWANN, RICHARD ROCKWELL, lawyer, banker; b. Orlando, Fla., May 7, 1940; s. Pervie P. and Maesther (Mears) Swann; m. Doris Orr (dec. Oct. 1983); children: Dorothy Orr, Christian Mears, Campbell Thornal, Doris Reed. AB, Duke U., 1961, JD, 1963. Bar: Fla. 1963. Mem. Swann & Haddock, Orlando, 1963—90, Swann & Hadley, 1990—. Chmn. bd. First Fidelity Savs. & Loan, Orlando, Am. Pioneer Savs. Bank, Orlando, Am. Pioneer, Inc., Orlando; dir. Overseas Pvt. Investment Corp., Washington, 1977—82; bd. govs. Overseas Investment Reins, 1978—82. Mem.: ABA, Fla. Bar Assn., Orange County Bar Assn. Democrat. Office: 1031 W Morse Blvd Ste 350 Winter Park FL 32789 Office Phone: 497-647-2777. Business E-Mail: rswann@swannhadley.com.

SWANSBURG, RUSSELL CHESTER, retired nursing educator, writer, consultant; b. Cambridge, Mass., Aug. 6, 1928; s. William W. and Mary A. (Pierce) S.; m. Laurel Clark, Sept. 1951; children: Philip Wayne, Michael Gary, Richard Jeffrey. Diploma, N.S. Hosp. Sch. Nursing, 1950; BSN, Western Res. U., Cleve, 1952; MA in Nursing Edn., Columbia U., NYC, 1961; PhD, U. Miss., University, 1998. CNAA. Asst. adminstr. U. South Ala. Med. Ctr., Mobile, 1980—85; prof. U. South Ala., Mobile, 1981—86, v.p., 1984—86; prof. Auburn U., Montgomery, 1986—88, Med. Coll. Ga., Augusta, 1989—90; vis. prof. La. State U. Sch. Nursing, New Orleans, 1990—92; instr. U. of Incarnate Word, San Antonio, 1993—2003; ret., 2006. Mil. cons. USAF Surgeon Gen., 1972; sr. med. svc. cons., 1973-76; nurse cons. VA Med. Ctr., Tuskegee, Ala., 1987-88; mem. editl. adv. bd. Nursing Adminstrn. Manual, 1980, 86, 90. Author: Team Nursing: A Programmed Learning Experience, 1968, Inservice Education, 1968, The Measurement of Vital Signs, 1970, The Team Plan, 1971, Management of Patient Care Services, 1976, Strategic Career Planning and Development, 1984, The Nurse Manager's Guide to Financial Management, 1988, Management and Leadership for Nurse Managers, 1990 (Book of Yr. Selection, Am. Jour. Nursing 1990), 3d edit., 2002 (Book of Yr. Selection, Am. Jour. Nursing 2002), 4th edit., 2006, Introductory Management and Leadership for Clinical Nurses, 1993, 2d edit., 1999 (Book of the Yr. Selection, Am. Jour. Nursing 1999), Staff Development: A Component of Human Resource Development, 1994, Budgeting and Financial Management for Nurse Managers, 1997, (audiovisual course) Nurses & Patients: An Introduction to Nursing Management, 1980; contbr. articles to profl. publs Bd. dir. Air Force Village Found., Alzheimer's Care and Rsch. Found. Col. USAF, 1956-76. Decorated Air Medal with oak leaf clusters, Legion of Merit, Air Force commendation medal with oak leaf cluster, Meritorious Svc. medal with oak leaf cluster, Vietnam Svc. medal, Am. Expeditionary medal, Republic of Vietnam Svc. medal; recipient award for outstanding work in hosp. adminstrn. Ala. State Nurses' Assn., 1985, Outstanding Nursing Svc. Adminstrn. award, 1981, Outstanding Nurse Rschr. 1984, Disting. Svc. award Air Force Village Found., 1999, Disting. Alumnus award Frances Payne Bolton Sch. Nursing Case Western Res. U., 2006, Vol. Achievement award Air Force Village Tex. Assn. Homes and Svcs. for Aging, 2007. Fellow AONE, Ala. Orgn. Nurse Execs. (past state pres.); mem. Coun. Grad. Edn. Adminstrn. in Nursing (sec.), Ala. Acad. Sci., Tex. Assn. Homes and Svcs. For Aging (Vol. Achievement award, 2007), Sigma Xi, Phi Kappa Phi, Sigma Theta Tau. Home and Office: 4917 Ravenswood Dr Apt 350 San Antonio TX 78227-4356 Office Phone: 210-673-9475. Personal E-mail: swansburg@sbcglobal.net.

SWANSEN, SAMUEL THEODORE, lawyer; b. Milw., June 6, 1937; s. Theodore Lawrence and Clarinda Dingwall (Crittenden) S.; m. Donna Rae Elizabeth Maloney, June 27, 1959; children: Jessica Swansen Bonelli, Theodor Arthur, Christopher Currie. AB, Dartmouth Coll., 1959; JD, U. Wis., 1962. Bar: Wis. 1962, Pa. 1964, U.S. Supreme Ct. 1969, accredited estate planner: Nat. Assn. Estate Planners & Couns. 1995. Law clk. to presiding justice Wis. Supreme Ct., Madison, 1962-63; assoc. Dechert, Price & Rhoads, Phila., 1963-68, 70-73, ptnr., 1973-93; asst. dist. atty. City of Phila. Dist. Atty.'s Office, 1968-70, chief frauds div., 1969; pvt. practice Phila., 1963—93, Blue Bell, Pa., 1994—. Adj. prof. law Temple U., Phila., 1970-80; lectr. Pa. Bar Inst., Nat. Bus. Inst., Ctr. Profl. Edn., 1985—. Editor, author U. Wis. Law Rev., 1960-62. Corp. mem. Anna T. Jeanes Found., Fox Chase, Phila, 1985—93, Associated Svcs. for the Blind, Phila, 1974—91, Bach Festival of Phila., 1989—, pres., 1993—97, 2003—06; founding dir. Global Bach Cmty., 2000—, pres., 2001—, 2003—06; violinist North Penn Symphony Orch., 1973—, trombonist, 1973—; mem. Nat. Network of Estate Planning Attys., 1993—, Nat. Acad. Elder Law Attys., 1993—, Wealth Counsel, 2005—; bd. dirs. Friends Rehab. Program, Inc., Phila., 1966—73, 1985—94, Franklin Found., Phila., 1969—; v.p., sec., bd. dirs. Foulkeways at Gwynedd, 1979—97, pres., 1986—97; chmn. bd. dirs. Friends Life Care at Home, Inc., 1990—, bd. dirs., 1990—, Friends Retirement Concepts, Inc., Gwynedd, sec. bd. dirs., 1985—96; hon. bd. dirs. Friends Neighborhood Guild; pres. Greater Phila. Fedn. Settlements, 1970—72; dir., sec. Energy Islands Internat., Inc., 1963—; pres. emeritus Foulkeways at Gwynedd, 1997; mem. Gwynedd Monthly Meeting of Friends, 1974—. Fellow Esperti Peterson Inst. Wealth Strategies Planning, 1996—. Mem. ABA, Pa. Bar Assn., Phila. Bar Assn., Montgomery County Bar Assn., Dartmouth Club Phila., Delta Upsilon, Phi Delta Phi. Republican. Mem. Soc. Of Friends. Home: 221 Morris Rd Ambler PA 19002-5202 Office: 660 Sentry Pky Ste 200 Blue Bell PA 19422-2317 Office Phone: 610-834-9810. Personal E-mail: sam@samswansen.com.

SWANSON, ALFRED BERTIL, orthopaedic and hand surgeon, educator; b. Kenosha, Wis, Apr. 16, 1923; s. O.P. and Esther (Person) S.; children: Karin Louise, Miles Raymond; m. Genevieve de Groot, MD, Dec. 27, 1969; 1 son, Eric Alfred. BS, U. Ill., 1944, MD, 1947. Diplomate: Am. Bd. Orthop. Surgery. Intern St. Luke's Hosp., Chgo., 1947; spl. tng. orthop. surgery Ill. Crippled Children's Hosp. Sch., Chgo., 1948, St. Luke's Hosp., 1949, Northwestern U. Med. Sch., 1950, Ind. U. Med. Ctr., 1951; practice medicine specializing in orthopaedic/hand surgery Grand Rapids, Mich., 1954—2001; chief hand surgery fellowship, orthopaedic research dir. Blodgett Meml. Hosp.-Spectrum Health East, 1962—; dir. emeritus Grand Rapids Orthopaedic Surgery Residency Tng. Program. Chief of staff Mary Free Bed Children's Hosp. and Orthop. Ctr., Juvenile Amputee Clin., 1963-65, 67-68, 73-78; prof. surgery Mich. State U., Lansing; chmn. Grand Rapids Internat. Symposium on Implant Arthroplasty, 1970-92; nat. and internat. lectr. in field. Author: Implant Resection Arthroplasty in the Hand and Extremities, 1973; Contbr. numerous sci. articles and exhibits in field; producer teaching films. Served with USNR, 1944-45; served to capt. M.C. AUS, 1952-54. Decorated medal of Honor So. Vietnam, 1967; recipient Profl. Medicine award Mich. Internat. Council, 1977; recipient Resolution of Tribute State of Mich., 1986, Order of Merit Orthop. Rsch. Soc., 1982, 89, 91, Disting. Svc. in Health Care award Hosp. Council West Mich., 1984, Nat. Vol. Svc. Citation Arthritis Found., 1984, U. Ill. Alumni Achievement award, 1985, Orthop. Overseas Spl. award for personal svc. and recruitment of orthop. and hand surgery vols. for So. Vietnam and Peru, Disting. Svc. award Arthritis Found., 1990, Cert. of Appreciation, Lifetime Sci. Achievement Award, Nat. Arthritis Found., 2003; Op. Desert Storm, US Dept. VA, 1991; named prof. h.c. Orthop. Alumni of Shriners Hosp. Crippled Children Mexico City; named to Grand Rapids Hall of Fame, 2001. Fellow ACS; mem. Am. Med. Writers Assn., AMA (Disting. Svc. award 1966, 69, Sci. Achievement award 1996), Am. Acad. Orthop. Surgeons (Kappa Delta award 1982), Pan Am. Med. Assn., Pan Pacific Surg. Assn., Assn. Mil. Surgeons, Am. Acad. Cerebral Palsy, Brit. Club Surgery of Hand, Italian Soc. Surgery of Hand, Brazilian, Colombian, South African, Japanese, Argentinian, So. Am., Caribbean Hand soc., Internat. Fedn. Soc. Surgery Hand (sec.-gen. 1978-83, pres. 1983-89, hist. 1989—, Pioneer in Hand Surgery award 1995), Groupe d'Etude de la Main, Am. Assn. Hand Surgeons, Am. Soc. Surgery Hand (pres. 1979-80), Am., Clin., Mich., Lamplighter's orthop. soc., Am. Orthop. Assn., Am. Orthop. Foot Soc., Am. Soc. Plastic and Reconstructive Surgeons, Peruvian Soc. Plastic and Reconstructive Surgeons, Mich. Med. Soc. (Disting. Service award 1966, Nat. Pres. award 1979, 84, Cmty. Svc. award 1993), Assn. Orthop. Chmn., European Rheumatoid Arthritis Surg. Soc., Norwegian Soc. Rheumatoid Surgery, Ga. Orthop. Soc., Fla. Orthop. Soc., Ark. Orthopaedic Soc., Orthop. Letters Club, Brazilian, Latin Am., Chilean, Columbian, Internat., Argentinian, Peruvian, Belgian, Turkish soc. Orthop. Surgery and Traumatology, Internat. Soc. Rehab. Disabled, Rheumatoid Arthritis Surg. Soc., Soc. Am. Inventors, Soc. Biomaterials, Internat. coll. Surgeons, Internat. Soc. Orthop. and Traumatology Rsch., Internat. Soc. Prosthetics and Orthotics Alternative Methods Internat. Stability (founder, chmn. 1983—), Internat. Trees Corps (founder, chmn. 1983—), Airplane Owners and Pilots Assn., World Affairs Coun. Western Mich. (chmn. numerous coms.), Cascade Hills Country Club (Grand Rapids), Rotary Internat. (Paul Harris award), many others. Congregationalist. Achievements include inventing implants for replacement arthritic joints. Office: Spectrum Health Blodgett Campus 1840 Wealthy St SE MC-504 Grand Rapids MI 49506-2969

SWANSON, CHARLES WALTER, lawyer; b. Bluefield, W.Va., Mar. 6, 1954; s. Don B. and Ann (Hughes) S.; m. Linda Susan Doak, Aug. 12, 1978 (div.); m. Pamela Lynn Reeves, Dec. 10, 1988. BA, Pfeiffer Coll., 1976; JD, U. Tenn., 1979. Bar: Tenn. 1979, U.S. Dist. Ct. (ea. dist.) Tenn. 1979, U.S. Ct. Appeals (6th cir.) 1983. Spl. judge juvenile ct. Knoxville (Tenn.) County, 1979-81; asst. city atty. City of Knoxville, 1981-84; assoc. Pryor, Flynn, Priest & Harber, Knoxville, 1984—94; ptnr. Sheppeard Swanson Mynett & McMillan, PLC, Knoxville, 1994—. Atty. city council Knoxville, 1985—. Contbg. author: 6th Circuit Federal Practice Guide, 1996. Mem. ABA, Tenn. Bar Assn.(bd. dirs., pres. young lawyer's conf. 1985-90, chmn. litigation sect. 1993-1994, mem. ho. of delegates, 1991-98, bd. govs., 1999-, pres.-elect 2003-04, pres. 2004-), Knoxville Bar Assn. (pres. 2002), Tenn. Trial Lawyers Assn., Knoxville Barristers (exec. com., pres. 1989), Nat. Inst. Mcpl. Law Officers, Delta Sigma, Phi Delta Phi. Democrat. Methodist. Avocations: softball, tennis, golf, hiking. Office: Sheppeard Swanson Mynett & McMillan, PLC PO Box 2149 Knoxville TN 37901-2149 Office Phone: 423-546-3653. Office Fax: 865-637-7300. E-mail: cswanson@shepswan.com.

SWANSON, DANIEL G., lawyer, economist; s. David E. (Stepfather) and Nancy N. Kuizenga; m. Anita Borrego; 1 child, Christopher. AB, U. Calif., Berkeley, 1979; AM, Harvard U., Cambridge, Mass., 1985, JD, 1984, PhD, 1985. Bar: Calif. 1984. Ptnr. Gibson, Dunn & Crutcher LLP, LA, 1985—. Office: Gibson Dunn & Crutcher LLP 333 S Grand Ave Los Angeles CA 90071 Office Phone: 213-229-7430. Office Fax: 213-229-6430. Business E-Mail: dswanson@gibsondunn.com.

SWANSON, DAVID C., publishing executive; Account exec. R.H. Donnelley, 1985, exec. v.p. sales, 1995—97, exec. v.p., gen. mgr. proprietary ops., 1997—98, exec. v.p. corp. strategy, 1998—99, pres. Donnelley Directory Svcs., 1999—2000, pres., COO, 2000—02, bd. dirs., 2001—, CEO, 2002—, chmn., 2002—06. Bd. dirs. Yellow Pages Assn., 2003—, v.p. bd. dirs. Office: RH Donnelley 1001 Winstead Dr Cary NC 27513 Office Phone: 919-297-1600. *

SWANSON, DAVID P., lawyer; b. 1955; BA, St. Cloud State U., 1978; JD, Vanderbilt U., 1981. Bar: Ill. 1981, Minn. 1983. Ptnr., co-chair, project devel., fin. group Dorsey & Whitney LLP, Mpls., and chair, agribus., coop. law. Dir. North Country Devel. Fund, Ralph K. Morris Found. Recipient Honored Cooperator award, Nat. Coop. Bus. Assn. Mem.: Nat. Soc. of Accountants for Cooperatives, Nat. Coop. Bus. Assn. Office: Dorsey & Whitney LLP Ste 1500 50 S Sixth St Minneapolis MN 55402-1498 Office Phone: 612-343-8275. Office Fax: 612-340-7800. Business E-Mail: swanson.dave@dorsey.com.

SWANSON, DON RICHARD, university dean; b. LA, Oct. 10, 1924; s. Harry Windfield and Grace Clara (Sandstrom) S.; m. Patricia Elizabeth Klick, Aug. 22, 1976; children— Douglas Alan, Richard Brian, Judith Ann. BS, Calif. Inst. Tech., 1945; MA, Rice U., 1947; PhD, U. Calif., Berkeley, 1952. Physicist U. Calif. Radiation Lab., Berkeley, 1947-52, Hughes Research and devel. Labs., Culver City, Calif., 1952-55; research scientist TRW, Inc., Canoga Park, Calif., 1955-63; prof. Grad. Library Sch., U. Chgo., 1963-92, dean, 1963-72, 77-79, 86-90, prof. bio-sci. coll. divsn. and divsn. humanities, 1992-96, prof. emeritus, 1996—. Mem. Sci. Info. Council, NSF, 1960-65; mem. toxicology info. panel Pres.'s Sci. Advisory Com., 1964-66; mem. library vis. com. Mass. Inst. Tech., 1966-71; mem. com. on sci. and tech. communication Nat. Acad. Scis., 1966-69 Editor: The Intellectual Founds. of Library Education, 1965, The Role of Libraries in the Growth of Knowledge, 1980; co-editor: Operations Research: Implications for Libraries, 1972, Management Education: Implications for Libraries and Library Schools, 1974; mem. editorial bd.: Library Quarterly, 1963-93; contbr.: chpt. to Ency. Brit, 1968—; sci. articles to profl. jours. Trustee Nat. Opinion Research Center, 1964-73; Research fellow Chgo. Inst. for Psychoanalysis, 1972-76. Served with USNR, 1943-46. Recipient Award of Merit Am. Soc. for Info. Sci. and Tech., 2000. Mem.: Am. Soc. for Info. Sci. Home: 5468 S Ingleside Ave Chicago IL 60615-5062 Office: U Chgo Divsn Humanities 1010 E 59th St Chicago IL 60637-1512 Business E-Mail: d-swanson@uchicago.edu.

SWANSON, DONALD ALAN, geologist; b. Tacoma, July 25, 1938; s. Leonard Walter and Edith Christine (Bowers) S.; m. Barbara Joan White, May 25, 1974. BS in Geology, Wash. State U., 1960; PhD in Geology, Johns Hopkins U., 1964. Geologist U.S. Geol. Survey, Menlo Park, Calif., 1965—68, 1971—80, Hawaii National Park, 1968—71, sr. geologist Cascades Volcano Obs. Vancouver, Wash., 1980—90, rsch. scientist-in-charge, 1986—89, sr. geologist Seattle, 1990—96; assoc. dir. Volcano Systems Ctr. U. Wash., 1993—96; scientist-in-charge Hawaiian Volcano Obs., 1997—2004. Affiliate prof. U. Wash., 1992—; adj. prof. U. Hawaii, 2002--; cons. U.S. Dept. Energy, Richland, Wash., 1979-83; volcanologist New Zealand Geol. Survey, Taupo, 1984; advisor Colombian Volcano Obs., Manizales, 1986. Assoc. editor Jour. Volcanology and Geothermal Rsch., 1976—, Jour. Geophys. Rsch., 1992-94; editor Bull. of Volcanology, 1985-90, exec. editor, 1995-99; contbr. numerous articles to profl. jours. Recipient Superior Svc. award U.S. Geol. Survey, 1980, Meritorious Svc. award U.S. Dept. Interior, 1985, Disting. Svc. award, U.S. Dept. Interior, 2005; postdoctoral fellow NATO, 1964-65. Fellow Geol. Soc. Am., Am. Geophys. Union, AAAS; mem. Sigma Xi. Avocation: hiking. Home: 417 Linaka St Hilo HI 96720-5927 Office: US Geol Survey Hawaiian Volcano Obs PO Box 51 Hawaii National Park HI 96718-0051 Office Phone: 808-967-8863. Business E-Mail: donswan@usgs.gov.

SWANSON, DONALD FREDERICK, retired food company executive; b. Mpls., Aug. 6, 1927; s. Clayton A. and Irma (Baiocchi) S.; m. Virginia Clare Hannah, Dec. 17, 1948; children— Donald Frederick, Cynthia Hannah, Janet Clare Webster. BA, U. Minn., 1948. With Gen. Mills, Inc., 1949-85, div. v.p., dir. marketing flour, dessert and baking mixes, 1964-65, v.p., gen. mgr. grocery products div., 1965-68, v.p., corporate adminstrn. officer consumer foods group, fashion div., transp. and purchasing depts., advt. and marketing services, 1969, exec. v.p. craft, game and toy group, fashion group, direct marketing group, travel group, dir., 1968-76, sr. exec. v.p. consumer non-foods, 1976-85, chief financial officer, 1977-79, sr. exec. v.p. restaurants and consumer non-foods, 1980-81, vice chmn. restaurants and consumer non-foods, 1981-85. Ret. chmn. bd. Soo Line Corp. Served with AUS, 1946-47. Mem. Mpls. Club, Wayzata Country Club, Royal Poinciana Golf Club, Phi Kappa Psi. Home: 2171 Gulf Shore Blvd N Apt 504 Naples FL 34102-4685

SWANSON, JACQUELINE V., academic administrator, educator, women's health nurse practitioner; b. Houston, Feb. 12, 1944; d. Ivan Jack and Edith Wilson; m. James Swanson, Aug. 21, 1965; children: Jim, Charlotte, Robert, Guy, Danny. BS, Tex. Woman's U., 1967, MS, 1974; PhD, U. North Tex., Denton, 1989. Cert. clin. nurse specialist, in maternal-newborn health, women's health nurse practitioner Planned Parenthood of Rocky Mountains, sexual assault nurse examiner. Various clin. nursing positions, Tex. and Kans., Tex., 1967-73; supr. obstet. and nursery Harris County Hosp. Dist., Houston, 1970-73; instr. Prairie View (Tex.) A&M U., 1973-75; asst. prof. Tex. Woman's U., Denton, 1975-85; labor and delivery nurse Tarrant County Hosp. Dist., Ft. Worth, 1987-89; assoc. prof., chmn. dept. nursing Ft. Hays State U., Hays, Kans., 1989-94; dir. BS nursing program Lamar U., Beaumont, Tex., 1994-95; prof., dean Coll. Nursing, Mont. State U. No., Havre, 1995—98, prof. nursing, 1998-2000; assoc. prof. nursing Tarleton State U., 2000—03, women's health nurse practioner Student Health Clinic, 2003—04; clin. instr. Tex. Christian U., 2005; dean Sch. Nursing Bacone Coll., 2005—. Contbr. articles to profl. jours.; presenter U.S. and internat. Mem. Denton Area War on Drugs. Mem. AAUP, ANA, Nat. Assn. Nurse Practioners Women's Health, Assn. Women's Health, Obstetric and Neonatal Nurses, Kans. State Nurses Assn., Tex. Nurses Assn., Tex. Nurse Practioner's Assn., Mont. Nurses Assn., Internat. Coun. on Women's Health Issues, Internat. Soc. for Univ. Nurses, Sigma Theta Tau. Home: 416 N 16th Muskogee OK 74401

SWANSON, JEAN LAURIE, music educator; b. Rice Lake, Wis., Jan. 18, 1958; d. Orville Melvin Johnson and Arlene May Steinmeyer; m. Gary Raymond Swanson, Dec. 22, 1979; children: Benjamin, Eliza, Jacob. MusB, U. Wis., Superior, 1981, M Profl. Devel., 1990. K-12 music tchr. Solon Springs Sch. Dist., Wis., 1981—2005, jr. and sr. HS vocal music tchr., 2006—. Choir dir. Our Saviors Luth. Ch., Solon Springs, 2003—; soprano Duluth Superior Symphony Chorus, Minn., 2005—. Author: (manual) K-6 Music Curriculum Guide, 1991. Mem.: Am. Fedn. Tchrs. (03 2005). Home: 12060 S Holly Lucius Rd Solon Springs WI 54873 Office: Solon Springs Sch Dist 8993 E Baldwin Ave Solon Springs WI 54873

SWANSON, LORI A., state attorney general, lawyer; b. Dec. 16, 1966; m. Gary Swanson. BA in Journalism and Polit. Sci. with distinction, U. Wis., Madison, 1989; JD magna cum laude, William Mitchell Coll. Law, St. Paul, 1995. Atty. Hatch, Eiden & Pihlstrom, Mpls., 1995—99; dep. atty. gen. State of Minn., St. Paul, 1999—2002, solicitor gen., 2003—06, atty. gen., 2007—. Chair consumer adv. coun. Fed. Res. Bd. Govs., Washington, 2004—. Democrat. Office: Office of Atty Gen 1400 Bremer Tower 445 Minnesota St Saint Paul MN 55101 Office Phone: 651-296-3353. *

SWANSON, LYNNETTE SUE, special olympics coordinator, special education educator; d. Carl Robert and Betty Jane Krambier; m. David John Swanson, June 2, 1984. BS cum laude, Brenau U., Gainesville, Ga., 2004. Cert. spl. edn. Ga., 2005. Spl. edn. paraprofl. Gwinnett County Pub. Schs., Lawrenceville, Ga., 1994—2000, coord. spl. olympics, 2000—; asst. coach athletics Spl. Olympics World Games, Shanghai, 2007. Coach Ga. women's volleyball team Spl. Olympics USA, Dublin, 2003. Mem.: Nat. Rlwy. Hist. Soc., Kappa Delta Pi, Phi Theta Kappa. Avocations: volunteer coaching, travel, crafts. Home: 4875 Five Forks Trickum Rd Lilburn GA 30047 Office: Gwinnett County Spl Olympics 950 McElvaney Ln Lawrenceville GA 30044 Home Phone: 770-925-3703; Office Phone: 678-985-3592. Personal E-mail: DL_SWANSON@BELLSOUTH.NET. E-mail: lynnette_swanson@gwinnett.k12.ga.us.

SWANSON, PEGGY EUBANKS, finance educator; b. Ivanhoe, Tex., Dec. 29, 1936; d. Leslie Samuel and Mary Lee (Reid) Eubanks; m. B. Marc Sommers, Nov. 10, 1993. BBA, U. North Tex., 1957, M. Bus. Edn., 1965; MA in Econs., So. Meth. U., 1967, PhD in Econs., 1978. Instr. El Centro Coll., Dallas, 1967-69, 71-78, bus. div. chmn., 1969-71; asst. prof. econs. U. Tex., Arlington, 1978-79, asst. prof. fin.; 1979-84, assoc. prof., 1984-86, chmn. dept. fin. and real estate, 1986-88, prof. fin., 1987—, interim dean Coll. Bus. Adminstrn., 1999—2000, John and Judy Goolsby disting. prof., 2004—. Expert witness various law firms, primarily Tex. and Calif., 1978—; cons. Internat. Edn. Program, 1992-99; curriculum cons. U. Monterrey, Mexico, 1995, New Saudi Arabia U., 1999. Contbr. articles to acad. profl. jours. Vol. Am. Cancer Soc., Dallas, Arlington, 1981—, Meals on Wheels, Arlington, 1989—; mem. adv. bd. Ryan/Reilly Ctr. for Urban Land Utilization, Arlington, 1986-88. Mem. Fin. Exec. Inst. (chmn. acad. rels. 1987-88), Internat. Bus. Steering Com. (chmn. 1989-91), Am. Fin. Assn., Am. Econ. Assn., Fin. Mgmt. Assn. (hon. faculty mem. Nat. Honor Soc. 1985-86, program com. 1998-99), Southwestern Fin. Assn. (program com. 1987-88, 96), Midwest Fin. Assn. (program com. 1997-98, 98-99), Acad. of Internat. Bus. (program com. 1992-95), Acad. Disting. Tchrs., Phi Beta Delta (membership com. 1987-89). Republican. Episcopalian. Avocations: tennis, gardening. Home: 4921 Bridgewater Dr Arlington TX 76017-2729 Office: U Tex at Arlington PO Box 19449 Arlington TX 76019-0001 Office Phone: 817-272-3841. Business E-Mail: swanson@uta.edu.

SWANSON, RICHARD EVERETT, physics professor, dean; b. Biloxi, Miss., Dec. 15, 1948; s. Dustin Herbert and Dorothy Mae Swanson; m. Leigh Ross Ross, June 5, 1970; children: Serena Bree, Shane Richard, Kyle Ross. B, USAF Acad., Colorado Springs, Colo., 1970; M, Ohio State U., Columbus, 1971; PhD, U. N.Mex., Los Alamos, 1981. Commd. 2d lt. USAF, 1966, advanced through grades to lt. col.; weapons devel. Air Force Armament Lab., Eglin AFB, Fla., 1971—73; explosives rsch. Los Alamos Nat. Lab., 1973—75; physics instr. U.S. Mil. Acad., West Point, NY, 1976—77; laser rsch. Air Force Weapons Lab., Albuquerque, 1977—79; guest scientist Los Alamos Nat. Lab., 1979—81; physics prof. USAF Acad., Colorado Springs, 1981—88. C.c. rep. N.C. Transfer Adv. Com., Raleigh, NC, 2003—. Co-author (videodisc) Skylab Physics, Physics of Flight. Sec. United Way of Moore County, Pinehurst, NC, 2000—04; bd. dirs. Sandhills Food Bank, Southern Pines, NC, 2004—06. Decorated Joint Meritorious Svc. medal U.S. European Command; grantee, N.C. C.C. Sys., 1993—95. Mem.: Am. Assn. Physics Tchrs. (assoc.), Phi Kappa Phi, Pi Mu Epsilon. Mem. Lds Ch. Avocations: handball, horseback riding. Home: PO Box 2258 Southern Pines NC 28388 Office: Sandhills Cmty Coll 3395 Airport Rd Pinehurst NC 28374 Home Phone: 910-246-9823; Office Phone: 910-695-3715. Business E-Mail: swansonr@sandhills.edu.

SWANSON, RICHARD WILLIAM, retired statistician; b. July 26, 1934; s. Richard and Erma Marie (Herman) Swanson; m. Laura Yoko Arai, Dec. 30, 1970. BS, Iowa State U., Ames, 1958, MS, 1964. Ops. analyst Stanford Rsch. Inst., Monterey, Calif., 1958—62; statistician ARINC Rsch. Corp., Washington, 1964—65; sr. scientist Booz-Allen Applied Rsch., Vietnam, 1965—67, LA, 1967—68; sr. ops. analyst Control Data Corp., Honolulu, 1968—70; mgmt. cons. Honolulu, 1970—73; exec. v.p. SEQUEL Corp., Honolulu, 1973—75; bus. cons. Hawaii Dept. Planning and Econ. Devel., Honlulu, 1975—77; tax rsch. and planning officer Dept. Taxation, 1977—82; ops. rsch. analyst U.S. Govt., 1982—89, shipyard statistician, 1989—97; ret., 1997. Mem.: Hawaiian Acad. Sci., Sigma Xi. Home: 583 Kamoku St Apt 3505 Honolulu HI 96826-5241 Personal E-mail: hnlrichardswanson@msn.com.

SWANSON, ROBERT LAWRENCE, oceanographer, academic program administrator; b. Balt., Oct. 11, 1938; s. Lawrence Wilbur and Hazel Ruth Swanson; m. Dana Lamont, Sept. 12, 1963; children: Lawrence Daniel, Michael Nathan BSCE, Lehigh U., 1960; MS Oceanography, Oreg. State U., 1965, PhD Oceanography, 1971. Cert. hydrographer. Commd. ensign U.S. Coast and Geodetic Survey (now NOAA), 1960, advanced through grades to capt., 1978; ops. officer U.S. Pathfinder, 1965; comdg. officer U.S. Mariner, 1966; chief oceanog. divsn. Nat. Ocean Survey, NOAA, Rockville, Md., 1969—72; mgr. Marine Ecosys. Analysis, N.Y. Bight project, Stony Brook, 1973—78; dir. Office Marine Pollution Assessment NOAA, Rockville, 1978—83, rsch. assoc. Sea Grant Stony Brook, 1983—84; comdg. officer U.S. Rschr., Miami, Fla., 1984—86; chief internat. activities group NOAA, Rockville, 1986, exec. dir. Office Oceanic and Atmospheric Rsch., 1986—87; dir. Waste Reduction and Mgmt. Inst. SUNY, Stony Brook, 1987—, assoc. dean Sch. Marine and Atmospheric Scis., 2003—. Adj. prof. Marine Scis. Rsch. Ctr., SUNY, Stony Brook, 1976—; mem. Suffolk County Coun. Environ. Quality, 1988—, vice chair, 1996—2006, chair, 2006—; mem. N.Y. State Oversight Com. Brookhaven Nat. Lab., 1996—2006; mem. Coastal Mgmt. Commn. Villages Head-of-the-Harbor and Nissequogue, 1994—2002; chmn. Coastal Mgmt. Commn. Villages Head Harbor and Nissequogue, 1995—97, 1999—2001; trustee Three Village Hist. Soc., 1994—2002; co-chair L.I. Environ. Econ. Roundtable, 1995—2000; adv. bd. Evan L. Lit Meml. Fund, 1998—; trustee Village of Head of the Harbor, 2002—, deputy mayor, 2006—; cons. in field. Co-author, co-editor: Oxygen Depletion and Associated Benthic Mortalities in N.Y. Bight, 1979; co-editor: Floatable Wastes and the Region's Beaches; mem. editl. bd. N.Y. Bight Monograph Series, 1973-81, Chemistry and Ecology, 1995-2003; co-author Images of America, Stony Brook, 2003; co-pub. Waste Mgmt. Rsch. Report, 1988-95; mem. adv. bd. L.I. Hist. Jour., 1995-2003, mem. editl. bd., 2004- Recipient Karo award Am. Soc. Mil. Engrs., 1972; Silver medal Dept. Commerce, 1973; Program and Adminstrn. Mgmt. award NOAA, 1975, Unit citation, 1981; sr. exec. fellow John F. Kennedy Sch. Govt., Harvard U., 1983, Spl. Achievement award, 1987, NOAA Corps. Commendations, 1987; named Man of Yr. for environment Three Village Times, 1998 Mem. N.Y. Acad. Scis., ASCE (chmn. hydrography and oceanography com. 1972-74), AAAS, Am. Geophys. Union, Marine Tech. Soc. (chmn. marine pollution com. 1982-92), Cosmos Club, Sigma Xi (pres. SUNY Stony Brook chpt. 1998—) Presbyterian. Home: 46 Harbor Hill Rd Saint James NY 11780-1217 Office: SUNY Waste Reduction And Mgmt Ins Stony Brook NY 11794-5000 Office Phone: 631-632-8704. Business E-mail: lswanson@notes.cc.sunysb.edu.

SWANSON, ROBERT LEE, lawyer; b. Fond du Lac, Wis., July 15, 1942; s. Walfred S. and Edna F. (Kamp) S.; m. Mary Ruth Francis, Aug. 19, 1967; children: Leigh Alexandra, Mitchell Pearson. BS, U. Wis., 1964; JD, Valparaiso U., 1970; LLM, Boston U., 1979. Bar: Wis. 1970, U.S. Dist. Ct. (ea. dist.) Wis. 1970, U.S. Dist. Ct. (we. dist.) Wis. 1974, U.S. Dist. Ct. (we. dist.) Okla. 2002, U.S. Tax Ct. 1981, U.S. Dist. Ct. (cen.) Ill. 1988, Okla. 1999, U.S. Ct. Appeals (7th cir.) 1999. Atty. Kasdorf, Dahl, Lewis & Swietlik, Milw., 1970-73; atty., ptnr. Wartman, Wartman & Swanson, Ashland, Wis., 1973-80; city atty. City of Ashland, Wis., 1976-80; atty., ptnr. DeMark, Kolbe & Brodek, Racine, Wis., 1980-95; ptnr. Hartig, Bjelajac, Swanson & Koenen, Racine, 1995-99, Okla. Indigent Def. Sys., Lincoln County, 2000—02; pvt. practice Robert Lee Swanson Law Office, 2000—. Lectr. civil rights and discrimination laws, 1980—; lectr.bus. law Cardinal Strich U., 1996—99; lectr. bus. law U. Wis.-Parkside, 1997—99; adj. prof. civil procedure Northeastern State U., Broken Arrow, Okla., 2005—; participating atty. Alliance Def. Fund, 2000—; legal columnist Burlington Std. Press, 1991—95, Wis. Restaurant Assn. Mag., 1986. Bd. dirs. North Ctrl. Regional Airport, Chandler, 2003—; chmn. Ashland County Rep. Party, 1976—79; v.p., bd. dirs. Meml. Med. Ctr., Ashland, 1975—80; bd. trustees Kendrick Mcpl. Authority, Okla., 2001—; vice comdr. USCG Aux. Bayfield (Wis.) Flotilla, 1975—81; vol. atty. ACLU Wis., 1975—90. 1st lt. US Army, 1964—66. Named one of Outstanding Young Men of Am., Jaycees, 1978; recipient Disting. Achievement in Art and Sci. of Advocacy award Internat. Acad. Trial Lawyers, 1970. Mem. Okla. Criminal Def. Lawyers Assn., Racine County Bar Assn. (bd. dirs. 1986-89), Wis. Acad. Trial Lawyers, Def. Rsch. Inst., Am. Hockey Assn. U.S. (coach, referee 1983-90), Am. Legion, Okla. Limousin Assn. (parliamentarian, treas. 2004, bd. dirs. 2005-). Avocations: softball, volleyball, hockey. Home: RR 1 Box 478 Stroud OK 74079-9723 Office: 109 1/2 W 9th St Chandler OK 74834 Office Phone: 405-258-4850. Personal E-mail: rswanson.atty@sbcglobal.net.

SWANSON, ROY ARTHUR, classicist, educator; b. St. Paul, Apr. 7, 1925; s. Roy Benjamin and Gertrude (Larson) S.; m. Vivian May Vitous, Mar. 30, 1946; children: Lynn Marie (Mrs. Gerald A. Snider), Robin Lillian, Robert Roy (dec.), Dyack Tyler, Dana Miriam (Mrs. Jon Butts). BA, U. Minn., 1948, BS, 1949, MA, 1951; PhD, U. Ill., 1954. Prin. Maplewood Elementary Sch., St. Paul, 1949-51; instr. U. Ill., 1952-53, Ind. U., 1954-57; asst. prof. U. Minn., Mpls., 1957-61, assoc. prof., 1961-64, acting chmn. classics, 1963-64, prof. classics, chmn. comparative lit., 1964-65; prof. English Macalester Coll., St. Paul, 1965-67, coord. humanities program, 1966-67; prof. comparative lit. and classics U. Wis.-Milw., 1967—, prof. English, 1990-96, prof. emeritus, 2003—, chmn. classics dept., 1967-70, 86-89, chmn. comparative lit., 1970-73, 76-83, coord. Scandinavian studies program, 1982-96. Cons. St. Paul Tchrs. Sr. High Sch. English, 1964 Author: Odi et Amo: The Complete Poetry of Catullus, 1959, Heart of Reason: Introductory Essays in Modern-World Humanities, 1963, Pindar's Odes, 1974, Greek and Latin Word Elements, 1981, The Love Songs of the Carmina Burana, 1987, Pär Lagerkvist: Five Early Works, 1989; editor Minn. Rev., 1963-67; Classical Jour., 1966-72; contbr. articles to profl. jours. With AUS, 1944-46. Decorated Bronze Star; recipient Disting. Teaching award U. Minn., 1962, Disting. Teaching award U. Wis.-Milw., 1974, 91, 99, Festschrift, 2005. Home: 11618 N Bobolink Ln Mequon WI 53092-2804 Office: U Wis French/Italian/Comp Lit PO Box 413 Milwaukee WI 53201-0413 Business E-Mail: rexcy@uwm.edu.

SWANSON, ROY JOEL, lawyer; b. Houston, Feb. 21, 1945; s. Roy J. and Daisy Lee (Peper) S.; m. Lynn Northway, Apr. 5, 1986; children: Emily Rebecca, Nell Cameron. BSChemE, U. Tex., 1967; MBA, JD, Harvard U., 1972. Bar: Tex. 1972. Assoc. Baker & Botts, Houston, 1972-80, ptnr., exec. com., sr. v.p., 1980; pvt. practice Houston. Office: 3000 One Shell Plz Houston TX 77002 Office Phone: 713-229-1330.

SWANSON, STEPHEN OLNEY, minister, retired English educator; b. Mpls., Aug. 31, 1932; s. Carl R. and Dorothy Olney Swanson; m. Judith Seleen Swanson, June 10, 1956; children: Scott, Shelley, Noel, Kim, Brian. BA, St. Olaf Coll., 1954; grad. in theology, Luther Theol. Sem., St. Paul, 1958, BD, 1960; MA, U. Oreg., 1964, ArtsD, 1970. Ordained to ministry Evang. Luth. Ch. Am., 1958. Instr. theology Augustana Coll., Sioux Falls, SD, 1957; instr. writing U. Oreg., Eugene, 1964—66; asst. prof. English and writing Tex. Luth. Coll., Seguin, 1966—70; assoc. prof. English and writing Camrose (Alta.) Univ. Coll., 1970—73; prof. writing St. Olaf Coll., Northfield, Minn., 1976—99. Parish pastor Luth. congregations, Minn., 1958-61, Oreg., 1962-65, Sask., 1973-74; interim pastor 40 congregations, Minn., Iowa, Wis., Alta., Sask., 1956—; dir. creative writing Tex. Luth. Coll., 1966-70, Camrose Univ. Coll., 1970-73; coach wrestling, football, volleyball, hockey, Tex., Can., Minn.; co-owner Nine-Ten Press, Northfield, 1997—; adj. prof. Waldorf Coll., Forest City, Iowa, 2004-07; v.p., Friends of Third World Found., Kenyon, Minn., 2007-. Author 26 books for adults, teens and children, including Is There Life After High Sch., 1991, The Earthkeeper Mystery Series, 4 vols., 1994, Moving Out on Your Own, 1995, The First Fall: Ytterboe Hall, 1946, 1997; playwright 6 plays; contbr. articles to jours.; columnist Now and Then, 1998-99; metal sculpture exhbns. include Luth. Brotherhood Corp. Gallery, Mpls., 1992, 94, 98, Waldorf Coll., Forest City, Iowa, 1999, Luther Coll., Decorah, Iowa, 2002, Art Ctr. of St. Peter, Minn., 2003, Thrivent Fin. Corp. Gallery, Mpls., 2003, St. Olaf Coll., Northfield, Minn., 2003, Am. Swedish Inst., Mpls., Minn., 2004, Edge Gallery, Big Fork, Minn., 2005. Recipient award Minn. Arts Bd., 1987, Blandin Found., Grand Rapids, Minn., 1988-89; fellow NDEA, Washington, 1968-69. Mem.: Blue Key (hon.), Am. Swedish Inst. Avocations: metal sculpture, fishing, Volvo repair. Home: 910 St Olaf Ave Northfield MN 55057

SWANSON, STEVEN R., astronaut; b. Syracuse, NY, Dec. 3, 1960; s. Stanley and June Swanson; m. Mary Drake Young; 3 children. BS in Engring. Physics, U. Colo., 1983; MAS in Computer Sys., Fla. Atlantic U., 1986; PhD in Computer Sci., Tex. A&M U., 1998. Software engr. GTE, Phoenix; sys. engr. aircraft ops. divsn. NASA, Johnson Space Ctr., Houston, 1987—89, flight simulation engr. for shuttle tng. aircraft, 1989—98, astronaut, mission specialist candidate, 1998—. Crew mem., spacewalker STS-117 Atlantis Mission, 2007. Recipient NASA Exceptional Achievement medal, Johnson Space Ctr. Cert. Accomodation, Flight Simulation Engring. award. Mem.: Phi Kappa Phi. Avocations: mountain biking, basketball, skiing, weightlifting, running, woodworking. Office: Astronaut Office/CB NASA Johnson Space Ctr Houston TX 77058 *

SWANSON, VICTORIA CLARE HELDMAN, lawyer; b. Aug. 28, 1949; d. Paul F. and Anne F. (Thomas) Schmitz; m. Louis M. Heldman, Sept. 21, 1971 (div. 1973); m. John Askins, Feb. 28, 1975 (div. 1977); m. Thomas C. Swanson, Feb. 13, 1988 (div. 2004). BA in journalism with distinction, Ohio State U., 1972; JD, U. Detroit, 1975. Bar: Mich. 1975, Colo. 1984, U.S. Dist. Ct. (ea. and we. dists.) Mich. 1975, U.S. Ct. Appeals (6th cir.) 1977, U.S. Ct. Appeals (3d cir.) 1980, U.S. Supreme Ct. 1983, U.S. Ct. Appeals (10th cir.) 1984, U.S. Ct. Appeals (5th cir.) 1989, cert.: NBTA (civil trial advocate) 1994. Assoc. Lopatin, Miller, Bindes & Freedman, Detroit, 1973—76; ptnr. Schaden, Swanson & Lampert, Detroit, 1977—90, Sears, Anderson & Swanson, P.C., Colorado Springs, Colo., 1991—96, Sears & Swanson, Colorado Springs, 1997—. Adj. prof. U. Detroit Sch. Law, 1982. Author (chpt.): (non-fiction) Anatomy of a Personal Injury Lawsuit, 1992; author, editor: handbook Colorado Auto Litigators Handbook, 1995, Colorado Courtroom Handbook, 1998, author, editor: 2nd edit., 2006, Colorado Evidence Handbook, 2005; co-author (with Richard F. Schaden): (non-fiction) Product Design Liability, 1982; co-author: (with others) Women Trial Lawyers: How They Succeed in Practice and in the Courtroom, 1986. Mem.: Mich. Trial Lawyers Assn., Colo. Trial Lawyers Assn. (past pres., Kripke Lifetime Achievement award 2005), Assn. Trial Lawyers Am., Colo. Bar Assn., Mich. Bar Assn. Home Phone: 719-481-4210; Office Phone: 719-471-1984. Business E-Mail: victoria@searsandswanson.com.

SWANSON, WALLACE MARTIN, lawyer; b. Fergus Falls, Minn., Aug. 22, 1941; s. Marvin Walter and Mary Louise (Lindsey) S.; children: Kristen Lindsey, Eric Munger. BA with honors, U. Minn., 1962; LL.B. with honors, So. Methodist U., 1965. Bar: Tex. 1965. Assoc. Coke & Coke, Dallas, 1965-70; ptnr. firm Johnson & Swanson, Dallas, 1970-88; prin. Wallace M. Swanson, P.C., Ennis, Tex., 1988—; chmn., CEO Ace Cash Express Inc., Irving, Tex., 1987-88, State St. Capital Corp., 1990—. Served with USNR, 1960-65. Mem. Tex. Bar Found., State Bar Tex. (securities com. 1972-86, chmn. 1978-80, coun. bus. law sect. 1980-86), Crescent Club. Methodist. Address: 6234 FM 879 Ennis TX 75119 Home Phone: 214-522-4400; Office Phone: 214-520-7000. Personal E-mail: wallaceswanson@yahoo.com.

SWANSON, WILLIAM FREDIN, III, manufacturing executive; b. Pitts., Mar. 6, 1960; s. William Fredin Jr. and Marjorie Beatrice (Davis) S.; m. Jane Anne Crosby, June 30, 1990; children: Elisabeth Anne, William Fredin IV. BSME, U. Va., 1982; M in Mgmt., Northwestern U., 1985. Asst. to v.p. mfg. Bridgestone/Firestone, Inc., Akron, Ohio, 1985-87, project mgr. Decatur, Ill., 1987-89, operating mgr., 1989-92; plant mgr. Am. Roller Co., Walkerton, Ind., 1992-95, mfg. mgr. Union Grove, Wis., 1995—2002; pres. Diamond Holding Corp., Marietta, Ga., 2002—07; CEO Signs and More, Inc., Cartersville, Ga., 2007—. Mem. alumni admissions orgn. Kellogg Grad. Sch. Mgmt., Northwestern U., Evanston, Ill., 1986-97, CEO roundtable Cobb County, 2002—; chmn. long range planning com. Antioch (Ill.) United Meth. Ch., 1997-98, adminstrv. coun., 2000-02, lay leader, 2001-02; coach youth soccer YMCA, 2003-2004, t-ball, 2004, basketball, 2004-2005. Mem.: Kiwanis. Avocations: golf, spectator sports, reading. Home: 1701 Kenbrook Ct Acworth GA 30101 Office: Signs and More Inc 481 E Main St Cartersville GA 30121 Personal E-mail: wfswansoniii@bellsouth.net. Business E-Mail: bills@signsmoreinc.com.

SWANSON, WILLIAM HENRY, defense equipment manufacturing company executive; b. Bakersfield, Calif., Feb. 9, 1949; s. William H. and Rosemary O. (Pavicich) Swanson; m. Cheryl K. Allen, Dec. 21, 1968. BSIE, Calif. Poly. State U., 1972; MBA, Golden Gate U., 1977; JD (hon.), Pepperdine U., 2002. Assoc. engr. Raytheon Co., 1972—74, project engr., 1974—75, mfg. program mgr., 1975—77, test engring. mgr., 1977—80, mgr. mfg. group, 1980—81; mfg. mgr. Equipment div. Waltham, Mass., 1981—83; plant mgr., Missile Systems div. Andover, Mass., 1984—90; asst. gen. mgr., Missile Systems div., 1989—90; sr. v.p., gen. mgr., Missile Systems div., 1990—95; exec. v.p. Raytheon Co., 1995—2002; gen. mgr. Electronic Systems div., 1995—97; chmn., CEO Raytheon Systems Co., 1997—99; pres., Electronic Systems div., 1999—2002; pres. Raytheon Co., 2002—03, pres., CEO, 2003—04, chmn., CEO, 2004—. Mem. President's Nat. Security Telecommunications Adv. Com. Exec. com. Bus.-Higher Edn. Forum; mem. Sec. Air Force Adv. Bd.; bd. adv. CIA Officers Meml. Found.; bd. dir. Medal Honor Found., Rose Fitzgerald Kennedy Greenway Conservancy; mem. Calif. Poly. State U. President's Cabinet, Pepperdine U. Bd. Regents. Named Outstanding Indsl. Engring. Grad., Calif. Poly. State U., 1972, Outstanding Indsl. Engring. Alumni, 1981; recipient Captains Industry Award, Inst. Indsl. Engr., Semper Fidelis Award, USMC Scholarship Found., 2002, Laurel Award, Aviation Week & Space Tech., 2003. Fellow: Royal Aero. Soc. (UK), Am. Inst. Aeronautics & Astronautics, Tau Beta Pi; mem.: Aerospace Industries Assn., Nat. Def. Indsl. Assn., Air Force Assn., Navy League (Rear Adm. John J. Bergen Leadership Medal for Industry), Assn. US Army, Blue Key, Alpha Pi Mu. Republican. Roman Catholic. Office: Raytheon Co 870 Winter St Waltham MA 02451 *

SWANSON, ZONA LUCIEL, retired elementary school educator; b. Orr, ND, Nov. 14, 1923; d. Fred L. and Hilda Dora (Rose) Neumann; m. Lyle R. Swanson, June 23, 1943; children: Barbara Jean Swanson Serr, Daniel Raymond. AA, Mayville State Tchrs., ND, 1941—43; BA, Mayvill State Tchrs., ND, 1959; MEd, U. N.D., Grand Forks, 1966. Elem. tchr., rural schools, Larimore, ND, 1950—52; tchr., grades 1-8, small town sch. Kempton, 1954—59; tchr., grades 5-8, small town sch. Arvilla, 1952—54; tchr., grades 5 & 7, AFB Grand Forks, 1959—69; tchr., grade 6 Viking Grade Sch., Grand Forks, 1969—89; retired, 1989. Sec. Grand Forks Edn. Assn., 1960—61; pres. N.D. Classroom Tchr.'s Assn., Bismarck. Active Girl Scouts, U.S., Civil Air Patrol, Farmer's Union, Larimore United Luth. Ch. Mem.: VFW, NEA (life), N.D. Edn. Assn. (life), Am. Legion. Democrat. Lutheran. Avocations: stamp collecting/philately, reading, doll collecting, teddy bear collecting. Home: 2429 W Fallcreek Ct Grand Forks ND 58201 Personal E-mail: zswanson@webtv.net.

SWANSTROM, LEE LERAY, surgeon; b. Douglas, Wyo., Apr. 3, 1957; married. Grad., U. Colo., U. Paris, France; MD, Creighton U., 1983. Cert. Am. Bd. Surgery. Resident, gen. surgery Emanuel Hosp., Portland, Oreg., 1983—88; fellow, surgical endoscopy U. Western Ont., Canada; clin. prof. Oreg. Health Scis. Univ., Portland, Oreg.; dir., Gastrointestinal and Minimally Invasive Surgery Clinic (GMIS) Oreg. Clinic, Portland, Oreg., program dir., minimally invasive surgery; chmn., sect. gen. and vascular surgery Legacy Emanuel and Good Samaritan Hosp. Mem. Natural Orifice Surgery Consortium for Assessment and Rsch.; dir. Legacy Minimally Invasive Surgery Program. Co-editor-in-chief Surgical Innovation; contbr. articles to prof. jours. Named one of Portland Monthly Top Docs, 2006—07; recipient Golden Scalpel award for Excellence in Tchg., Maricopa Med. Ctr., Phoenix, Ariz., 2005—06. Fellow: Am. Coll. Surgeons; mem.: Soc. for Surgery of the Alimentary Tract (mem. exec. com.), Soc. Am. Gastrointestinal and Endoscopic Surgeons (past pres.). With a team of surgeons, performed the first transgastric endoscopic cholecystectomy, NOTES (Natural Orifice Translumenal Endoscopic Surgery-removing the gall bladder without making incisions on the surface of the skin, also less pain, less risk of infection and reduced recovery time) in the US in 2007. Office: Oreg Clinic GMIS Good Samaritan Med Bldg 1040 NW 22nd Ste 560 Portland OR 97210 Address: 2055 Exchange St Ste 270 Astoria OR 97103 Office Phone: 503-325-9597. Office Fax: 503-281-0561, 503-281-0575. *

SWANSTROM, THOMAS EVAN, economist; b. Green Bay, Wis., May 17, 1939; s. Alfred Enoch and Elizabeth Nan (Thomas) S.; m. Nancy Anne Roche; children: Amy, Scott. Student, U. Notre Dame, 1957-59; BA, U. Wis., 1962, MA, 1963; postgrad., Am. U., 1963-66. Economist, U.S. Bur. Labor Statistics, Washington, 1963-66. Dir. rsch/ Population Ref. Bur., Washington, 1966-68; economist Sears, Roebuck & Co., Chgo., 1968-70, market analyst, 1970-72, mgr. catalog rsch., 1972-75, asst. mgr. econ. rsch., 1974-80, chief economist, 1980-90; pres. Consumer Econs., Chgo., 1991—; mem. bus. rsch. adv. coun. Bur. Labor Stats. Contbr. articles to industry publs. Mem. Conf. Bus. Economists, The Caxton Club. Home Phone: 312-315-7829. Personal E-mail: tevanswan@aol.com.

SWANTON, SUSAN IRENE, retired library director; b. Rochester, NY, Nov. 29, 1941; d. Walter Frederick and Irene Wray S.; m. Wayne Holman, Apr. 12, 1969 (div. June 1973); 1 child, Michael; ptnr. James Donald Lathrop; children: Kathryn, Kristin. AB, Harvard U., 1963; MLS, Columbia U., 1965. Libr. dir. Warsaw (N.Y.) Pub. Libr., 1963-64, Gates Pub. Libr., Rochester, NY, 1965—2003; ret., 2003. Pres. Drug and Alcohol Coun., Rochester, 1985-91, mem. adv. coun., 1992-94; bd. dirs., co-chair info. svcs. Rochester Freenet, 1995—; sec. Gates Hist. Preservation Commn., 2000-03, Friends of Rochester Pub. Libr., 2004—; chmn. Gates Dem. Com., 2004—; v.p., sec. Friends of Gates Pub. Libr., 2004—; newsletter editor Empire (N.Y.) Friends Roundtable, 2004—. Mem. Gates Hist. Soc. (bd. dirs., pres. 1998—2002, v.p. 2002—03), Gates-Chili C. of C. (pres. 1982, sec. 1990-94, 2004—, bd. dirs. 2003, Citizen Yr. 1994), Harvard Club of Rochester (mem. adv. bd.). Home: 284 Gatewood Ave Rochester NY 14624-1622 E-mail: sswanton@ggw.org.

SWANTON, VIRGINIA LEE, writer, publisher; b. Oak Park, Ill., Feb. 6, 1933; d. Milton Wesley and Eleanor Louise (Linnell) Swanton. BA, Lake Forest Coll., Ill., 1954; MA in English Lit., Northwestern U., 1955; cert. in acctg., Coll. of Lake County, Ill., 1984. Editorial asst. Publs. Office, Northwestern U., Evanston, Ill., 1955-58; reporter Lake Forester, Lake Forest, 1959; editor Scott, Foresman & Co., Glenview, Ill., 1959-84; copy editor, travel coord. McDougal Littell/Houghton Mifflin, Evanston, 1985-94; sr. bookseller B. Dalton Bookseller, Lake Forest, Ill., 1985—2004; author, pub. poetry books, reference works Gold Star Publ. Svcs., Lake Forest, 1994—. Contbr. articles to profl. jours. Former sec. bd. dirs., newsletter editor Career Resource Ctr., Inc., Lake Forest; current events discussion vol. Lake Forest/Lake Bluff Sr. Ctr.; mem. bd. deacons First Presbyn. Ch. Lake Forest. Mem.: Lake Forest/Lake Bluff Hist. Soc. (vol.), Chgo. Women in Pub. Presbyterian. Avocation: gardening. Office: Gold Star Publ Svcs PO Box 125 Lake Forest IL 60045-1333

SWANY, DOUGLAS MARTIN, education educator; s. Douglas Martin Swany and JoAnn Hope Burke; m. Lynn Burgin, Mar. 28, 1969; children: Victoria Kaytlin, Cole Martin, Noah Burgin. PhD, U. Calif., Santa Barbara, 2003. Asst. prof. U. Del., Newark, 2003—. Office: Univ Delaware Dept Computer and Info Science Newark DE 19713 Home Phone: 302-737-9377; Office Phone: 302-831-2324.

SWARD, ANDREA JEANNE, information and computer scientist, musician; b. Hackensack, NJ, June 25, 1951; d. George Frederick and Carol Jeanne (Snoad) Lankow; m. Jeffrey Edwin Sward, June 7, 1975. Student, U. Minn., Duluth, 1969-72; BA in Psychology, Calif. State U., Fullerton, 1973, MS in Info. Sci., 1974, MS in Edn., 1976; cert. Bus. Intelligence and Data Warehousing, U. Calif. Irvine, 2003. Librarian, prof. Calif. State U., Fullerton, 1972—97; violist Anaheim Cultural Arts Ctr. Orch., Calif., 1978-80, Anaheim Civic Light Opera, 1978-80, Calif. European Tour Orch., Fullerton, 1978-79, Fullerton Cmty. Orch., Fullerton, 1978—86; computer programmer, analyst Hughes Aircraft, Fullerton, 1980-81, Smith-Kline/Beckman, Fullerton, 1981-83, ConAgra/Hunt-Wesson, Irvine, 1983—2004; librarian Downey City Library, Calif., 1985, Orange Pub. Library, Calif., 1985—90, Huntington Beach Library, Calif., 1985—; sys. analyst New Century Mortgage, Irvine, Calif., 2004—07; IT analyst Lehman Brothers, Irvine, Calif., 2007; sys. data analyst Kelley Blue Book, 2007—. Adj. faculty CC Dist., Calif., 1993—2002. Editor: Vis À Vis: An Interdisciplinary Journal, 1972—74; contbr. articles to profl. jours. Mem., contbr. Newport Harbor Art Mus., Newport Beach, Calif., 1975—, Los Angeles County Mus. of Art, 1975—, ACLU, 1976—, Cousteau Soc., 1978—, Audubon Soc., 1985—, Amigos de Bolsa Chica, 1985—, Spl. Olympics, 1987—; wildlife rehabilitator Wetlands and Wildlife Care Ctr., Orange County, 1999—. Fridley (Minn.) Edn. Assn. scholar, 1969, Spl. Edn. Assn. scholar, 1972; Edwin Carr fellow, 1976; Ptnrs. in Excellence grantee, 1979. Mem. ALA, Assn. for Computing Machinery, Calif. Library Assn., Calif. Reading Assn., Reading Educators Guild, Penguini Poets and Philosophers Guild of Placentia (co-founder). Democrat. Avocations: sports, reading, dance, theater, art. Home: PO Box 7019 Huntington Beach CA 92615-7019 Office Phone: 949-260-7427. E-mail: ajsward@yahoo.com.

SWARENS, CORK (C.C. SWARENS), medical association administrator; Pub. rels. dir. Mo. State Med. Assn., Jefferson City, 1972—77, asst. exec. sec., chief lobbyist, 1977—95, exec. v.p., 1995—. Recipient Med. Exec. Achievement award, AMA, 2005. Mem.: Mo. Soc. Govtl. Cons., Mo. Soc. Assn. Execs., Am. Assn. Med. Soc. Execs., Ducks Unlimited. Office: Missouri State Med Assn 113 Madison St PO Box 1028 Jefferson City MO 65102 Office Phone: 573-636-5151. Office Fax: 573-636-8552. Business E-Mail: cswarens@msma.org. *

SWARLIS, LINDA, library and information scientist; d. Clarence Leroy and Helen Louise Jacobs; children: Amber, Andrew. BS in Edn., Clarion U., Pa., 1979; MLS, U. Pitts., Pa., 1984. Libr. dir. Winchester Thurston Sch., Pittsburgh, Pa., 1984—88, Sewickley Acad., Sewickley, Pa., 1988—95; head libr. Lincoln H.S., Gahanna, Ohio, 1995—97; dir. of info. services and libr. Columbus Sch. for Girls, Columbus, Ohio, 1997—. Pres. Pitts. Area Ind. Schools Assn., Pa., 1989—95. Recipient Outstanding Svc. award, Gahanna Kiwanis Club for Key Club Leadership, 1995—97; Distance Ind. scholarship, U. North Tex., 2004—. Office: Columbus Sch for Girls 56 S Columbia Ave Columbus OH 43209 Home Phone: 614-844-6093; Office Phone: 614-252-0781 129. Office Fax: 614-252-0571. E-mail: lswarlis@columbusschoolforgirls.org.

SWAROOP, ANAND, medical educator; MSc in Biochemistry, G.B. Pant U., Pant Nagar, India, 1997; PhD in Biochemistry, Indian Inst. Sci., Bangalore, India, 1982. Post-doctoral assoc., dept. molecular biophysics & biochemistry Yale U., New Haven, 1982—86; assoc. rsch. scientist, dept. human genetics Yale U. Sch. Med., New Haven, 1986—87, Nat. Rsch. Svc. Award post-doctoral fellow, dept. human genetics, 1987—88, assoc. rsch. scientist, dept. human genetics, 1988—90; asst. prof., dept. ophthalmology U. Mich., Ann Arbor, Mich., 1990—96, asst. prof., dept. human genetics, 1990—98, faculty mem., grad. program in cellular & molecular biology, 1991—, assoc. prof., dept. ophthalmology & visual sciences, 1996—2000, faculty mem., neuroscience grad. program, 1996—, assoc. prof., dept. human genetics, 1998—2002, prof., dept. ophthalmology and visual sciences, 2000—, prof., dept. human genetics, 2002—; coord., dir., Ctr. for Retinal and Macular Degeneration U. Mich. Med. Sch. W.K. Kellogg Eye Ctr., Ann Arbor, Mich., 2001—, dir., Sensory Gene Microarray Node, Harold F. Falls Collegiate prof. ophthalmology & visual sciences, 2003—. Scientist, Lab. of Genetics Salk Inst., La Jolla, Calif., 2000. Contbr. articles to profl. jours.; reviewer of several jours., mem. editl. bd. Molecular Vision, 1995—, Investigative Ophthalmology & Visual Science, 2002—. Mem.: Soc. for Neuroscience, Assn. for Rsch. in Vision and Ophthalmology, Am. Soc. Human Genetics, AAAS. Office: U Mich Kellogg Eye Ctr 1000 Wall St Ann Arbor MI 48105 Office Phone: 734-763-3731. Office Fax: 734-647-0228. Business E-Mail: swaroop@umich.edu. *

SWARTOUT, HANK B., oil and gas industry executive; b. Apr. 6, 1951; m. Carol Swartout; 4 children. Student in Petroleum Engring. Technol., Southern Alberta Inst.of Technol., 1972; BS with honours in Petroleum Engring., U. Wyo., 1976. Prodn. engr. Amerada Hess, ND, 1977; v.p. construction Nabors Drilling, 1978; rig design and construction Dreco; mgr. Bawden Western Oceanic Offshore; pres. Cypress Drilling (acquired Precision Drilling), 1985; chmn., pres., CEO Precision Drilling Corp., Calgary, AB, Canada, 1987—. Recipient Disting. Alumnus, Southern Alberta Inst. of Technol., 1999, Pinnacle award, Fraser Milner Casgrain LLP, 2003. Office: Precision Drilling Corp 4200 150-6th Ave SW T2P 3Y7 Calgary AB Canada

SWARTOUT, WILLIAM R., mathematician, educator, director; s. Charles W. and June Swartout; m. Janet P. Swartout; children: Robin, David. BS in Math. Scis. with distinction, Stanford U., Palo Alto, Calif., 1974; MS in Elec. Engring. & Computer Sci., MIT, Cambridge, Mass., 1977, PhD in Computer Sci., 1981. Dir., intelligent sys. divsn. U. So. Calif. Info. Scis. Inst., Marina del Rey, 1989—99; dir. of tech. U. So. Calif. Inst. for Creative Technologies, Marina del Rey, 1999—. Rsch. assoc. prof. computer sci. U. So. Calif., 1985—2006, rsch. prof. computer sci., 2006—. Mem. Air Force Sci. Adv. Bd., Washington, 2003—, Bd. Army Sci. and Tech., Washington, 2004—, Joint Forces Command Transformation Adv. Group, 2004. Fellow: Am. Assn. Artificial Intelligence (mem. bd. councilors 1989—92); mem.: Assn. Computing Machinery (chair Spl. Interest Group on Artificial Intelligence 1985—87). Presbyterian. Achievements include pioneering research in automatic program explanation, and development of virtual humans. Avocations: photography, bicycling. Office: Univ So Calif Inst Creative Technologies 13274 Fiji Way Marina Del Rey CA 90292 Home Phone: 310-457-4592; Office Phone: 310-574-5705.

SWARTZ, ANNE, art historian; d. Muriel Fonda, Maryanne Swartz (Stepmother); 1 child. PhD, Case Western Res. U. Prof. Savannah Coll. Art and Design, Ga., 1994—. Guest curator Pattern and Decoration: An Ideal Vision in Am. Art Hudson River Mus. Contbr. articles to profl. jours. Recognition awards chair Women's Caucus for the Arts. Fulbright scholar, Japan, 2002—03. Mem.: Coll. Art Assn., Feminist Art Project. Office: Savannah Coll Art and Design PO Box 3146 Savannah GA 31402-3146 Home Phone: 908-204-0482.

SWARTZ, B. K., JR., (BENJAMIN KINSELL SWARTZ JR.), archaeologist, educator; b. LA, June 23, 1931; s. Benjamin Kinsell and Maxine Marietta (Pearce) S.; m. Cyrilla Casillas, Oct. 23, 1966; children: Benjamin Kinsell III, Frank Casillas. AA summa cum laude, L.A. City Coll., 1952; BA, UCLA, 1954, MA, 1958; PhD, U. Ariz., Tucson, 1964. Curator Klamath County Mus., Oreg., 1959-61, rsch. assoc., 1961-62; asst. prof. anthropology Ball State U., Muncie, Ind., 1964-68, assoc. prof., 1968-72, prof., 1972-2001, prof. emeritus, 2001—. Vis. sr. lectr. U. Ghana, 1970-71; exch. prof. U. Yaounde, Cameroon, 1984-85; field rschr. N.Am. and West Africa; mem. exec. bd., pres. Am. Com. to Advance the Study of Petroglyphs and Pictographs and its rep. to Internat. Fedn. Rock Art Orgns.; mem. overseas ed. bd. Rock Art Rsch.; mem. adv. bd. Am. Com. for Preservation of Archaeol. Collections. Contbr. revs. and articles to profl. jours.; author books, monographs in field, including: West African Culture Dynamics, 1980, Indiana's Prehistoric Past, 1981, Rock Art and Posterity, 1991, Procs. of 1st Internat. South African Rock Art Assn. Conf., 1991. Klamath County chmn. Oreg. Statehood Centennial, 1959. With USN, 1954-56. Fellow AAAS, Ind. Acad. Sci.; mem. Current Anthropology (assoc.), Soc. Am. Archaeology, Internat. Com. Rock Art, Sigma Xi, Lambda Alpha (nat. coun., exec. sec.). Home: 805 W Charles St Muncie IN 47305-2235 Personal E-mail: 01bkswartz@bsu.edu.

SWARTZ, DONALD PERCY, physician; b. Preston, Ont., Can., Sept. 12, 1921; s. Simon Wingham and Lydia Ethel Swartz; m. Norma Mae Woolner, June 24, 1944 (dec. May 1980); children: Ian Donald, Rhonda Swartz Peterson; m. Isabelle Liz Dales, Apr. 21, 1984. BA, U. Western Ont., 1951, MD cum laude, 1951, MSc cum laude, 1953. Intern Victoria Hosp., London, Ont., 1951-52; asst. resident Westminster Hosp., London, 1953-54; resident Johns Hopkins U., Balt., 1954-58; asst. prof. ob-gyn. U. Western Ont., London, 1958-62; prof. Columbia U., NYC, 1962-72; dir. ob-gyn. Harlem Hosp.; prof. dept. ob-gyn. Albany (N.Y.) Med. Coll., 1972-99, prof. emeritus, 2000—, chmn., 1972-79, chief sect. gen. gynecology, 1982-88, head. div. gen. gynecology, 1988—99, acting chmn., 1992, hon. attending, 2006—. Vis. prof. dept. Ob-Gyn. U. Rochester, N.Y., 1981 Assoc. editor: Advances in Planned Parenthood. Vice pres., pres. Assn. Planned Parenthood Physicians, 1972-74. Served with RCAF, 1942-45. NRC Can. fellow, 1952-53; Am. Cancer Soc. fellow, 1956-57; Markle scholar, 1958-63 Fellow ACOG, Royal Coll. Surgeons Can., Am. Gynecologic Soc., Am. Gyn-Ob Soc., Am. Fertility Soc., Royal Soc. Health, Soc. Gynecologic Surgeons. Home: 24 Devon Rd Delmar NY 12054-3534 Office: Albany Med Coll 47 New Scotland Ave Albany NY 12208-3412 E-mail: swartzd@mail.amc.edu. *It has been a privilege and a challenge to participate in the forefront of the revolutionary changes in the health care of women during the past five decades. Acceptance, initiation and implementation of positive change have been guidelines for gratifying action.*

SWARTZ, EUGENE ROBERT, JR., music educator, minister; b. Cleve., Mar. 19, 1957; s. Eugene Robert and Sarah Jane Swartz; m. Vicki Ann Masters, July 31, 1959; children: Sarah Frances Bourque, Amanda Leah Dickens. AAS in Engring. Tech., Dabney Lancaster C.C., Clifton Forge, Va., 1977; BS in Music Edn., U. Tenn., Knoxville, 1987, MS in Music Edn., 1989. Cert. music edn. Md. State Dept. Edn., 2005. Worship pastor Friendship Bapt. Ch., Sykesville, Md., 1999—2003; dept. chair, dir. choral activities Owings Mills H.S., 2003—. Music dir. Wash. Bible Coll., Lanham, Md., 1994—97. Bd. mem. Adult Literacy Bd., New Roads, La., 1990—92. Hamilton Conducting scholar, U. Tenn., 1986—87. Mem.: Md. Music Educators Assn. (state choral festival dir. 1998—99), Nat. Educators Assn., Am. Choral Dirs. Assn., Music Educators Nat. Conf. Conservative. Baptist. Avocation: car and truck shows. Home: 665 Tanglewood Dr Eldersburg MD 21784 Office: Owings Mills High Sch 124 Toll Gate Rd Owings Mills MD 21117 Home Phone: 410-552-6609; Office Phone: 410-887-1700. Personal E-mail: jeeps4jesus@aol.com. E-mail: eswartz@bcps.org.

SWARTZ, JAMES EDWARD, chemistry professor, educator, dean; b. Washington, June 12, 1951; s. Donald M. and Geneva R. (Henderson) S.; m. Louanne L. Curtis, June 6, 1980 (dec. 1986); m. Cynthea Mosier, Apr. 1, 1988. BS in Chemistry, Stanislaus State Coll., Turlock, Calif., 1973; PhD in Chemistry, U. Calif., Santa Cruz, 1978. Instr. U. Calif., Santa Cruz, 1978; rsch. fellow Calif. Inst. Tech., Pasadena, 1978-80; asst. prof. Grinnell (Iowa) Coll., 1980-86, assoc. prof. chemistry, 1986-93, prof., 1993—, v.p. acad. affairs, dean, 1998—. Vis. prof. U. Minn., Mpls., 1986—87; mem. adv. coun. Iowa Energy Ctr., chair, 2006—; cons.-evaluator Commn. Higher Edn., N. Cent. Assn., 1995—; bd. dirs. Am. Conf. Acad. Deans, 2000—03; mem. exec. com. Associated Colls. of the Midwest, 2003—06. Contbr. articles to profl. jours. Grantee Petroleum Rsch. Fund, 1981-83, Rsch. Corp., 1981-83, 84-86, 86-88, NSF, 1982-84, 90-93, 91-94. Mem. AAAS, Am. Chem. Soc., Iowa Acad. Scis., Am. Wind Energy Assn. Home: 1233 Summer St Grinnell IA 50112-1547 Office: Grinnell Coll Office of Dean Grinnell IA 50112-1690 Home Phone: 641-236-5204; Office Phone: 641-269-3100. Business E-Mail: swartz@grinnell.edu.

SWARTZ, JAMES R., chemical engineer, educator; B in Chem. Engring., S.D. Sch. Mines and Tech.; DSci, MIT, 1978. Rsch. scientist Eli Lilly & Co., Indpls., Genentech, Inc., San Francisco, 1981—2003, dir. dept. fermentation rsch. and process devel.; prof. chem. engring. Stanford U., Palo Alto, Calif., 2003—. Mem. NAE, Am. Chem. Soc. Office: Dept Chem Engring Stanford U Keck 185 381 North South Mall Stanford CA 94305-5025 E-mail: swartz@chemeng.stanford.edu.

SWARTZ, JEFFREY B., apparel executive; MBA, Amos Tuck Sch. Dartmouth Coll. Exec. vice-pres. Timberland Co., 1990—91, COO, 1991—98, pres., CEO, 1998—. Office: Timberland 200 Domain Dr Stratham NH 03885

SWARTZ, JON DAVID, psychologist, educator; b. Houston, Dec. 28, 1934; s. Orville Elmo and Nina June (Baker) S.; m. Carol Joseph Hampton, Oct. 20, 1966; children: Eric Jason McFarland, Sally Katherine Baker, Edward Joseph Bryson. BA, U. Tex., Austin, 1956, MA, 1961, PhD, 1969, postgrad., 1973-74. Rsch. and tng. asst. dept. psychology U. Tex., 1956-62, asst. prof. dept. edni. psychology, 1969-72; assoc. prof. psychology, chmn. U. Tex.-Permian Basin, 1974-78, chmn. anthropology and sociology, 1975-78, field dir., 1962-65; asst. dir. Austin Longitudinal Rsch. project, 1965-69, co-dir., 1969-74; research scientist Hogg Found. for Mental Health, 1972-74; prof. edn. and psychology Southwestern U., Georgetown, Tex., 1978-90, vis. prof. psychology, 1991, dir. testing and guidance, 1978-81, holder Brown vis. chair, 1978-82, assoc. dean for librs. and learning resources, 1981-90; coord., adminstrv. head Killeen office Cen. Counties Ctr. for MHMR Svcs., Temple, Tex., 1990-91; chief psychol. svcs. Temple, Tex., 1991-99; pvt. practice Tex., 2000—. Lectr. Nat. U., Mexico, 1962, U. Ctrl. Tex., 1994, Temple Coll., 1994. Author: (with W.H. Holtzman) Inkblot Perception and Personality, 1961, (with C.C. Cleland) Mental Retardation: Approaches to Institutional Change, 1969, Administrative Issues in Institutions for the Mentally Retarded, 1972, Exceptionalities Through the Lifespan: An Introduction, 1982, Multihandicapped Mentally Retarded, 1973, (with W.H. Holtzman, R. Diaz-Guerrero) Personality Development in Two Cultures, 1975; editor: (with C.C. Cleland, L.W. Talkington) Profoundly Mentally Retarded, 1976, (with R.K. Eyman, C.C. Cleland) Research with the Profoundly Retarded, 1978, Holtzman Inkblot Technique: An Annotated Bibliography (supplement), 1988, (with R.C. Reinehr, W.H. Holtzman) Holtzman Inkblot Technique: An Annotated Bibliography 1956-1982, 1983, (with R.C. Reinehr) Handbook of Old-Time Radio, 1993, Holtzman Inkblot Technique: Research Guide and Bibliography, 1999, Southwestern University Bibliographic Series, 1986-1990, Historical Dictionary of Old-Time Radio, 2007; contbr.: Handbook of Texas, 1996; editl. assoc. Current Anthropology, 1971-77; assoc. editor: Am. Corrective Therapy Jour., 1971-81, Exceptional Children, 1982-84; mem. editl. bd. Tex. Psychologist, 1979-83, Phi Kappa Phi Jour./Nat. Forum, 1976-80; editl. cons. Mental Retardation, 1972-77; rev. editor Jour. Biol. Psychology, 1972-80, Revista Interamericana de Psicologia, 1983-89; reviewer Sci. Books, Films, 1978—; cons. editor Jour. Personality Assessment, 1981-90; spl. features editor: Scientifiction: The First Fandom Report, 2002—; rev. editor The National Fantasy Fan, 2003—; frequent contbr. Paperback Parade, 2004—; contbr. over 500 articles to profl. jours. Mem. Mayor's Drug Abuse Panel, Odessa, Tex., 1975-78; chmn. adv. bd. Human Potentials Ctr., Permian Basin Cmty. Ctrs. for Mental Health and Mental Retardation, Odessa and Midland, Tex., 1975-78; bd. govs. Mood-Heritage Mus., 1984-90. US Office Edn. fellow, 1964-66, U. Tex. fellow, 1973-74; recipient Franklin Gilliam prize Humanities Rsch. Ctr. U. Tex., 1965, Spencer Rsch. award Nat. Acad. Edn., 1972, Faculty Fellowship award Southwestern U., 1981. Fellow AAAS, Am. Psychol. Soc., Soc. Personality Assessment (life); mem. Western Rsch. Conf. on Mental Retardation, Am. Acad. Mental Retardation, Southwestern Psychol. Assn., Bell County Psychol. Assn., Sigma Xi, Psi Chi, Mu Alpha Nu, Delta Tau Kappa, Phi Kappa Phi, Phi Delta Kappa, Nat. Fantasy Fan Fedn. (Franson award 2005), First Fandom. Personal E-mail: jon_swartz@hotmail.com. *All my life I have had teachers, in school and out, who challenged me to do more than I thought I was capable of doing. Any success I have achieved, I owe to them and their efforts in my behalf.*

SWARTZ, MELODY A., biomedical engineer, educator; BSChemE, Johns Hopkins U., Balt., 1991; PhD in Chem. Engring., MIT, Cambridge, 1998. Environ. engr. Pohnpei and Yap State EPA, Federated States of Micronesia, Faeroe Islands, 1991—92; lectr. dept. chem. engring. Tufts U., Mass., 1998; postdoctoral rsch. fellow cellular biomechanics MIT Dept. Mech. Engring. and Harvard Med. Sch. Brigham and Women's Hosp., Pulmonary Divsn., 1998—99; Donald and June Brewer asst. prof. depts. biomedical engring. and chem. engring. Northwestern U., Ill., 1999—2003; asst. prof. Inst. Bioengineering Fed. Inst. Tech., Lausanne, Switzerland, 2003—. Adj. asst. prof. biomedical engring. Northwestern U. Contbr. articles to sci. jours. Named one of Brilliant 10, Popular Sci. mag., 2006. Mem.: Microcirculatory Soc., Internat. Soc. Lymphology, Biomedical Engring. Soc., AIChE. Office: Swiss Fed Inst Tech Inst Bioengineering LMBM Station 15 1015 Lausanne Switzerland E-mail: melody.swartz@epfl.ch. *

SWARTZ, MELVIN JAY, lawyer, writer; b. Boston, July 21, 1930; s. Jack M. and Rose (Rosenberg) S.; children: Julianne, Jonathan Samuel. BA, Syracuse U., 1953; LLB, Boston U., 1957. Bar: N.Y. 1959, Ariz. 1961. Assoc. Alfred S. Julian, NYC, 1957-59; ptnr. Finks & Swartz, Youngtown, Sun City, Phoenix, 1961-70, Swartz & Jeckel, P.C., Sun City, Youngtown, Scottsdale, Ariz., 1971-82. Author: Don't Die Broke, A Guide to Secure Retirement, 1974, rev. edit., 2000, (book and cassettes) Keep What You Own, 1989, rev. edit., 2000, Retire Without Fear, 1995, Harry You Bastard, (Don't You Dare Leave Me Broke) 2007; columnist News-Sun, Sun City, 1979-83; author column Swartz on Aging. Bd. dirs. Valley of the Sun Sch. for Retarded Children, 1975-79. Mem. ABA, Ariz. Bar Assn., N.Y. Bar Assn., Maricopa County Bar Assn., Scottsdale Bar Assn., Ctrl. Ariz. Estate Planning Coun., Masons (Phoenix). Jewish. Office: 3416 N 44th St Unit 22 Phoenix AZ 85018-6044 Office Phone: 602-954-6381. Business E-Mail: melvinjayswartz@yahoo.com.

SWARTZ, MICHAEL D., statistical geneticist; b. Boston, Jan. 24, 1974; s. Robert J. and Adele M. Swartz. BA, BS, Trinity U., San Antonio, 1997; MA, Rice U., Houston, 2002, PhD, 2004. Instr. dept. epidemiology M.D. Anderson Cancer Ctr., U. Tex., Houston, 1999—2004, post-doctoral fellow, 2004—; rsch. asst. prof. stats. dept. Tex. A&M U., College Station, 2004—06. Contbr. articles to profl. jours. Vol. Kairos Found., Houston, 1989. Recipient Chairman's award for svc. to dept. stats., Rice U. Dept. Chair, 2002; fellow Tng. fellowship in cancer prevention, Nat. Cancer Inst., M.D. Anderson Cancer Ctr., 2006—, Nat. Cancer Inst. & Dept. Stats., Tex. A&M U., 2004—06; Keck fellowship in computational biology, Keck Ctr., Rice U., 1998—2000, Tng. fellowship in cancer prevention, Nat. Cancer Inst., M.D. Anderson Cancer Ctr., 2000—04. Mem.: Am. Stats. Assn., Internat. Genetic Epidemiology Soc., Phi Beta Kappa. Achievements include development of a new method for gene mapping. Avocation: swing dancing. Office: U Tex MD Anderson Cancer Ctr Dept Epidemiology Unit PO Box 301439 Houston TX 77230 Business E-Mail: mdswartz@mdanderson.org.

SWARTZ, MICHAEL FREDERICK, physician assistant; b. Nyskauna, NY, Sept. 2, 1979; s. Kurt and Julie Swartz. BS, D'Youville Coll., Buffalo NY, 2001. Physician's asst. SUNY Upstate Med. U., Syracuse, 2001—. Contbr. articles to profl. jours. Recipient Du Couet Musarra scholar, D'Youville Coll., 2001, Good Citizenship award, Am. Legion, 1996. Mem.: Lambda Sigma (life; treas. 1998—98). Democrat-Npl. Episcopalian. Achievements include research in Prevention of muscle damage during a heart attack. Office: SUNY Upstate Medical University 750 E Adams St Syracuse NY 13210 Home Phone: 315-469-1970; Office Phone: 315-464-6255.

SWARTZ, MORTON NORMAN, medical educator; b. Boston, Nov. 11, 1923; s. Jacob H. and Janet (Heller) Swartz; m. Cesia Rosenberg, Sept. 18, 1956; children: Mark David, Caroline Joan. BA, Harvard Coll., 1945; MD, Harvard U., 1947; MD (hon.), U. Geneva, Switzerland, 1988. Diplomate Am. Bd. Internal Medicine. Med. intern and resident Mass. Gen. Hosp., Boston, 1947—50, chief resident in medicine, 1953—54, chief infectious disease unit, 1956—90, chief James Jackson Firm, med. svcs., 1990—; USPHS postdoctoral rsch. fellow Johns Hopkins U., McCollum-Pratt Inst. Enzymology, Balt., 1954—56; assoc. prof. medicine Harvard Med. Sch., Boston, 1967—73, prof., 1973—. Vis. assoc. prof. biochemistry Stanford Med. Sch., Palo Alto, Calif., 1969—70; chmn. Nat. Inst. Child Health and Devel., 1995—97, bd. sci. counselors. Co-author: Osteomyelitis, 1971; editor: Current Clinical Topics in Infectious Diseases, 1980—2002; assoc. editor: New Eng. Jour. Medicine, 1981—2002; contbr. articles to profl. jours. 1st lt. US Army, 1950—52. Mem.: ACP (Disting. Tchr. award 1989), Inst. Medicine, Infectious Diseases Soc. Am. (Bristol award 1984, Feldman award 1989, Soc. Citation award 2003), Assn. Am. Physicians, Am. Soc. for Clin. Investigation, Am. Soc. Biochemistry and Molecular Biology. Jewish. Avocations: biology, birdwatching, cosmology. Home: 54 Shaw Rd Chestnut Hill MA 02467-3122 Office: Mass Gen Hosp Dept Medicine Bulfinch Bldg #127 Boston MA 02114-2696 Home Phone: 617-469-0068. Business E-Mail: mswartz@partners.org.

SWARTZ, RENEE BECKER, library advocate, civic volunteer; b. Newark, Feb. 25, 1935; d. Sidney David and Adeline (Kleinberg) Becker; m. Harry Mason Swartz, Mar. 8, 1931; children: Stephen, Addi-Lyn, Sidney. Student, Rutgers U., 1950-52, Bryn Mawr Coll., 1952-53; BA, Barnard Coll.-Columbia U., 1955. Planning com. N.J. White Ho. Conf. on Librs. and Info. Sci., 1975-79, del. selection com., mem. programs com., 1978-79; chair del. White Ho. Conf., 1979; re-elected permanent N.J. rep. Nat. Commn. Follow-up Activities White Ho. Conf., 1991, chairperson nat. awards com., 1984-86, chair fundraising com., 1989-90; chmn. N.J. Del. White Ho. Conf. of Librs. and Info. Svcs., 1991—. Pres. Friends of Monmouth County Libr. Assn., 1964-68; founding mem. N.J. Citizens for Better Librs., 1982; chair bldg. com. Dorothy L. Spiwak Meml. Libr., Rumson, N.J., 1971-73, trustee, 1971—; active N.J. Libr. Devel. Com., 1973-84; chair, bd. trustees Grad. Sch. of Comm., Info. and Libr. Studies, Rutgers U., 1980—, chair, 1983—; gov. appointee N.J. State Libr. Adv. Coun., 1975, chair, 1986—, Monmouth County Libr. Commn., 1965—, chair, 1976—; past trustee Barnard Coll., pres. Alumnae Assn., 1981-84, trustee, 1981-85; founder NJ Ctr. for the Book, 2001—, chair, state coord.; presdl. appointee Nat. Inst. Mus. and Libr. Svcs. Bd., 2004— Recipient Hanna G. Solomon award, Greater Red Bank sect. Nat. Coun. Jewish Women, 1979, Pres. medal, Barnard Coll.-Columbia U., 1984, Columbia U. medal, 1985, Woman of Achievement award, Monmouth County Adv. Com., 1991; named Nat. Trustee of Yr., ALA, 1991. Mem. Nat. Citizens Com. for Pub. Libraries (steering com. 1980-84), Am. Library Trustee Assn. (pres. com. 1983, nat. intellectual freedom com. 1984—), N.J. Library Assn. (centennial com. 1986-89, chairperson N.J. Ednl. Inst. com. 1987-88, N.J. Trustee of Yr. 1980, 99), N.J. Library Trustee Assn. (exec. com. 1976-81, regional rep. 1983-86), Assn. N.J. Library Commrs. (pres. 1973-75), Capitol Hill Club, Lotus Club N.Y., Ocean Club NJ, Cosmos Club Avocations: tennis, sailing, walking. Office Phone: 732-431-7235. Business E-Mail: rswartz@co.monmouth.nj.us. *

SWARTZBAUGH, MARC L., lawyer; b. Urbana, Ohio, Jan. 3, 1937; s. Merrill L. and Lillian K. (Hill) S.; m. Marjory Anne Emhardt, Aug. 16, 1958 (deceased May 20, 2000); children: Marc Charles, Kathleen Marie, Laura Kay. BA magna cum laude, Wittenberg Coll., 1958; LLB magna cum laude, U. Pa., 1961. Bar: Ohio 1961, U.S. Dist. Ct. (no. dist.) Ohio 1962, U.S. Claims Ct. 1991, U.S. Ct. Appeals (6th cir.) 1970, U.S. Ct. Appeals (3d cir.) 1985, U.S. Ct. Appeals (Fed. cir.) 1995, U.S. Supreme Ct. 1973. Law clk. to judge U.S. Ct. Appeals (3d cir.), Phila., 1961-62; assoc. Jones, Day, Reavis & Pogue, Cleve., 1962-69, ptnr., 1970-98; ret., 1998; cons., 1998—. Note editor U. Pa. Law Rev., 1960-61; co-author: Ohio Legal Ethics, 2001, Ohio Legal Ethics Law under the New Rules, 2006; contr. articles to profl. jours. Co-chmn. Suburban Citizens for Open Housing, Shaker Heights, Ohio, 1966; v.p. Lomond Assn., Shaker Heights, 1965-68; trustee The Dance Ctr., Cleve., 1980-83; amb. People to People Internat., 1986; chmn. legal divsn. Cleve. campaign United Negro Coll. Fund, 1989-96; tutor Cleve. Reads, 2003; endower of keyboard instruments chair, Cleve. Orch., 2004. Mem. ABA (litigation sect., sr. lawyers divsn.), Fed. Bar Assn., Ohio Bar Assn., Cleve. Bar Assn., Rowfant Club, Order of Coif, Beta Theta Pi. Democrat. Avocations: poetry, painting, music, photography, book collecting. Office: Jones Day N Point 901 Lakeside Ave E Cleveland OH 44114-1190

SWARTZLANDER, EARL EUGENE, JR., engineering educator, former electronics company executive; b. San Antonio, Feb. 1, 1945; s. Earl Eugene and Jane (Nicholas) S.; m. Joan Vickery, June 9, 1968. BSEE, Purdue U., 1967; MSEE, U. Colo., 1969; PhD, U. So. Calif., 1972. Registered profl. engr., Calif., Colo., Tex. Devel. engr. Ball Bros. Rsch. Corp., Boulder, Colo., 1967-69; Hughes fellow, mem. tech. staff Hughes Aircraft Co., Culver City, Calif., 1969-73; mem. rsch. staff Tech. Svc. Co., Santa Monica, Calif., 1973-74; chief engr. Geophys. Systems Corp., Pasadena, Calif., 1974-75, staff engr. to sr. staff engr., 1975-79, project mgr., 1979-84, lab. mgr., 1985-87; dir. ind. R&D TRW Inc., Redondo Beach, Calif., 1987-90; Schlumberger Centennial prof. engring. dept. elec. and computer engring. U. Tex., Austin, 1990—2006, prof., 2006—. Gen. chmn. Internat. Conf. Wafer Scale Integration, 1989, Internat. Conf.

Application Specific Array Processors, 1990, 94, 11th Internat. Symposium on Computer Arithmetic, 1992, 31st Ann. Asilomar Conf. on Signals, Sys., and Computers, 1997, others; chmn. 3d Internat. Conf. Parallel and Distributed Sys., Taiwan, 1993, 12th Internat. Conf. on Application-Specific Systems, Architectures and Processors, 2000; mem. tech. adv. bd. ECIT, Queen's U., Belfast, 2005—, Arithmatica. Author: VLSI Signal Processing Systems, 1986; editor: Computer Design Development, 1976, Systolic Signal Processing Systems, 1987, Wafer Scale Integration, 1989, Computer Arithmetic Vol. 1 and 2, 1990, Application Specific Processors, 1996; editor-in-chief Jour. of VLSI Signal Processing, 1989-95, IEEE Transactions on Computers, 1991-94, IEEE Transactions on Signal Processing, 1995; editor: IEEE Transactions on Computers, 1982-86, IEEE Transactions on Parallel and Distributed Systems, 1989-90; hardware area editor ACM Computing Revs., 1985—; assoc. editor: IEEE Jour. Solid-State Circuits, 1984-88; contbr. more than 300 articles to profl. jours. and tech. conf. procs. Bd. dirs. Casiano Estates Homeowners Assn., Bel Air, Calif., 1976-80, pres., 1978-80; bd. dirs. Benedict Hills Estates Homeowners Assn., Beverly Hills, Calif., 1984-2006, pres., 1990-95. Recipient Disting. Engring. Alumnus award Purdue U., 1989, U. Colo., 1997, Outstanding Elec. Engr. award Purdue U., 1992, knight Imperial Russian Order St. John of Jerusalem (Knights of Malta), 1993. Fellow: IEEE (hist. com. 1996—2004, fellows com. 2000—03, 3d Millennium medal 2000); mem.: Assn. for Computing Machinery, IEEE Solid-State Cirs. Coun. (bd. govs. 1986—91, sec. 1992—93, treas. 1994—97), IEEE Signal Proc. Soc. (bd. govs. 1992—94), IEEE Computer Soc. (bd. govs. 1987—91, Golden Core award 1996), Omicron Delta Kappa, Sigma Tau, Eta Kappa Nu. Office: U Tex Austin Dept Elec Computer Engring Austin TX 78712 Home Phone: 310-271-4213; Office Phone: 310-702-5756.

SWARZ, JEFFREY ROBERT, investment banker, biotechnologist, neuroscientist; b. Nov. 9, 1949; s. Irvin Brad and Blanche S. (Marcus) S.; m. Kathy Helen Kafer, June 20, 1976. BS with honors, U. Calif., Irvine, 1971; PhD, U. Rochester, 1976. Postdoctoral fellow in neurovirology Johns Hopkins U. Sch. Medicine, Balt., 1976-79; staff fellow infectious diseases NIH, Bethesda, Md., 1979-80; dir. biotech. group Teknekron Rsch. Inc., McLean, Va., 1980-81; pres. AgroBiotics, Inc., Balt., 1981-82; from sr. scientist to dir. mktg. and sales Pall Corp., Glen Cove, N.Y., 1982-85, dir. mktg. and sales, 1985-86; biotech./healthcare analyst Goldman Sachs & Co., Glen Cove, N.Y., 1986-92; dir. CS First Boston, NYC, 1992-99; ptnr. Partner-Eagle Ptnrs., NYC, 1999—; prodr. Shadow Prodns.; mng. dir. Life Sci. Group, Greenwich, Conn., 2001—07; mng. dir. healthcare investment banking Friedman Billings Ramsey, NYC, 2007—. Cons. U.S. Senate Subcom. on Sci., Tech. and Space, 1979-80; prodr. Shadow Prodns., 1998—. Author: (with others) Genetic Engineering: Issues and Trends, 1982; contbr. articles to profl. jours. Recipient Rsch. award Bank of Am., 1970-71, Nat. Rsch. Svc. award 1976-79; NIH fellow 1975-76. Mem.: N.Y. Acad. Sci., N.Y. Athletic Club, U. Club. Democrat. Jewish. Office: Friedman Billings Ramsey 299 Park Ave New York NY Office Phone: 212-381-9285. Business E-Mail: jswarz@fbr.com.

SWATOS, WILLIAM HENRY, JR., priest, sociologist; b. Paterson, NJ, Sept. 25, 1946; s. William H. Sr. and Lucille (MacNab) S.; children (by previous marriage): Giles S., Eric B.; m. Joanne Longstreet, Oct. 29, 2002. AB, Transylvania U., 1966; MDiv summa cum laude, Episc. Theol. Sem., Lexington, Ky., 1969; MA, U. Ky., 1969, PhD, 1973. Ordained to ministry Episcopal Ch., 1969. Mem. sociology faculty King Coll., Bristol, Tenn., 1973-80; vicar St. Mark's Episc. Ch., Silvis, Ill., 1980-94; mem. sociology faculty No. Ill. U., 1984-88; chair dept. edn. Diocese of Quincy, 1988-90, 93-96. Mem. faculty Black Hawk and Scott C.C., Moline, Ill., Bettendorf, Iowa, 1988-96; adj. prof. Augustana Coll., Rock Island, Ill., 2005—; priest-in-charge Christ Ch. Limestone Twp., Ill., 2006—. Editor: Time, Place and Circumstance, 1990, Religious Politics in Global and Comparative Perspective, 1989, Religious Sociology, 1987; editor Sociol. Analysis/Sociology of Religion, 1989-94; editor-in-chief Encyclopedia of Religion and Society, 1998; mng. editor Interdisciplinary Jour. Rsch. on Religion, 2004—; contbr. articles to profl. jours. Recipient Templeton prize in humility theology, 1996; full grantee World Soc. Found., Zurich, Switzerland, 1987, grantee NEH, 1974, 79, 85, 89, rsch. grantee Soc. for the Sci. Study of Religion, 1984-85, 91-92; Inst. Studies Religion sr. fellow Baylor U, 2004—; named Disting. Alumnus Dept. of Sociology, U. Ky., Lexington, 1990. Fellow Soc. Sci. Study of Religion (program chair 2004); mem. Assn. for the Sociology of Religion (editor 1989-94, book rev. editor 1986-88, exec. coun. 1984-86, exec. officer 1996—, gen. editor Religion and the Social Order Series 2004—), Religious Rsch. Assn. (sec. 1990-91, bd. dirs. 1986-89, exec. officer 1994—). Home and Office: 618 SW 2nd Ave Galva IL 61434-1912 E-mail: bill4329@hotmail.com.

SWATT, STEPHEN BENTON, communications executive, consultant; b. LA, June 26, 1944; s. Maurice I. and Lucille E. (Sternberger) S.; m. Susan Ruth Edelstein, Sept. 7, 1968; 1 child, Jeffrey Michael. BSBA, U. Calif., 1966, M in Journalism, 1967. Writer San Francisco Examiner, 1967; reporter United Press Internat., LA, 1968-69; producer news Sta. KCRA-TV, Sacramento, 1969-70, reporter news, 1970-79, chief polit. and capitol corres., 1979-92; mng. ptnr. NCG Porter Novelli, Sacramento, 1992—2003, sr. counselor, 2003—. Adj. prof., guest lectr. Calif. State U., Sacramento. Contbr. articles to profl. jours. With USCG, 1966. Recipient No. Calif. Emmy NATAS, 1976-77, Pub. Svc. award Calif. State Bar, 1977, Exceptional Achievement Coun. advancement and Support of Edn., 1976, Nat. Health Journalism award Am. Chiropractic Assn., 1978. Mem. Soc. Profl. Journalists (8 awards), Capitol Corres. Assn., U. Calif. Alumni Assn., Sacramento Press Club. Avocations: hiking, jogging, fishing. Office: Porter Novelli 1215 K St # 2100 Sacramento CA 95814 Office Phone: 916-443-3354. Business E-Mail: steve.swatt@porternovelli.com.

SWAYZE, CHARLES J., JR., lawyer; b. Greenwood, Miss., May 14, 1944; BBA, Univ. Miss., 1966, JD, 1969; LLM, George Washington Univ., 1973. Bar: Miss. 1969, US Ct. Mil. Appeals 1969, US Supreme Ct. 1973. Prosecuting atty. City of Greenwood, Miss., 1974—75, Leflore County, 1976—2000; mem. Whittington, Brock & Swayze PA, Greenwood, Miss. Pres. So. Conf. of Bar Pres. Capt. JAGC US Army, 1969—73. Fellow: Miss. Bar Found., Am. Bar Found.; mem.: ABA, Miss. Bar Assn. (pres. 2004), Phi Delta Phi. Office: Whittington Brock & Swayze PA 308 Fulton St PO Box 941 Greenwood MS 38930 *

SWAYZE, PATRICK, actor, dancer; b. Houston, Aug. 18, 1952; s. Patsy Swayze. Student, Harkness Sch., Joffrey Ballet Sch. Dancer (Broadway) Goodtime Charley, Grease; film appearances include (debut) Skatetown, U.S.A., 1979, The Outsiders, 1983, Uncommon Valor, 1983, Red Dawn, 1984, Grandview U.S.A., 1984, Youngblood, 1986, Dirty Dancing, 1987, Steel Dawn, 1987, Tiger Warsaw, 1988, Road House, 1989, Next of Kin, 1989, Ghost, 1989, Point Break, 1991, City of Joy, 1992, Father Hood, 1993, Tall Tale, 1994, To Wong Foo, Thanks for Everything, Julie Newmar, 1995, Three Wishes, 1995, Letters From a Killer, 1997, Vanished, 1998, Black Dog, 1998, Letters from a Killer, 1998, Without a Word, 1999, The Winddrinker, 2000, Wakin' Up In Reno, 2000, Forever Lulu, 2000, Green Dragon, 2001, Donnie Darko, 2001, Waking Up in Reno, 2002, One Last Dance, 2003, 11:14, 2003, Dirty Dancing: Havana Nights, 2004; (tv series) Hollywood Squares, 1998; (TV movies) King Solomon's Mines, 2004; (off-Broadway) Guys and Dolls, 2006. Recipient Golden Apple award. Office: William Morris 151 S El Camino Dr Beverly Hills CA 90212-2775

SWAZEY, JUDITH POUND, academic administrator, science educator; b. Bronxville, NY, Apr. 21, 1939; d. Robert Earl and Louise Titus (Hanson) Pound; m. Peter Woodman Swazey, Nov. 28, 1964; children: Elizabeth, Peter. AB, Wellesley Coll., 1961; PhD, Harvard U., 1966. Rsch. assoc. Harvard U., 1966-71, lectr., 1969-71, rsch. fellow, 1971-72; cons. com. brain scis. NRC, 1971-73; staff scientist neuroscis. rsch. program MIT, Cambridge, 1973-74; assoc. prof. dept. socio-med. scis. and cmty. medicine Boston U., 1974-77, prof., 1977-80, adj. prof. Schs. Medicine and Pub. Health, 1980—; exec. dir. Medicine in the Pub. Interest, Inc., Boston and Washington, 1979-82, 89-93; pres. Coll. of the Atlantic, Bar Harbor, Maine, 1982-84, Acadia Inst., Bar Harbor, 1984-2001, founding pres., sr. scholar, 2001—. Mem. Army Sci. Bd., 1987-92. Author: Reflexes and Motor Integration, the Development of Sherrington's Integrative Action Concept, 1969, (with others) Human Aspects of Biomedical Innovation, 1971, (with R.C. Fox) The Courage to Fail, a Social View of Organ Transplants and Hemodialysis, 1975, rev. edit., 1978, 02 (hon. mention Am. Med. Writers Assn., C. Wright Mills award Am. Sociol. Assn.), Chlorpromazine in Psychiatry, a Study of Therapeutic Innovation, 1974, (with K. Reeds) Today's Medicine, Tomorrow's Science, Essays on Paths of Discovery in the Biomedical Sciences, 1978; editor: (with C. Wong) Dilemmas of Dying, Policies and Procedures for Decisions Not to Treat, 1981, (with F. Worden and G. Adelman) The Neurosciences: Paths of Discovery, 1975, (with R.C. Fox) Spare Parts, Organ Replacement in American Society, 1992, Japanese transl., 1999, (with C. Messikomer and A. Glicksman) Society and Medicine. Essays in Honor of Renée Fox, 2002; assoc. editor IRB: A Jour. of Human Subjects Rsch., 1979-00; mem. editl. bd. Sci. and Engring. Ethics, 1994—; contbr. articles to profl. jours. Mem. Maine Dept. Human Svcs. Bioethics Adv. Com. (chair 1991-94); mem. Commn. on Rsch. Integrity, 1994-95; bd. dirs. Maine Bioethics Network, 1994-99. Wellesley Coll. scholar, 1961; Wellesley Coll. Alumnae fellow Harvard U., 1966, NIH predoctoral fellow, 1966, Radcliffe Coll. grad. fellow, 1966. Fellow AAAS (sci. freedom and responsibility com. 1986-89, nominations com. 2003-2004), Inst. Medicine of NAS (mem. health scis. policy bd. 1986-89), Grad. Record Exam. (bd. dirs. 1987-91), Phi Beta Kappa, Sigma Xi (mem. ethics com. 2004-). Office: PO Box 243 Bar Harbor ME 04609-0243 Business E-Mail: jswazey@verizon.net.

SWEARER, WILLIAM BROOKS, lawyer; b. Hays, Kans. Grad., Princeton U., 1951; law degree, U. Kans., 1955. Bar: Kans. 1955. Pvt. practice, Hutchinson, Kans., 1955—; ptnr., now counsel Martindell, Swearer & Shaffer, LLP, Hutchinson, 1955—. Mem. Kans. Bd. Discipline for Attys., 1979-92, chmn., 1987-92; mem. Kans. Commn. on Jud. Qualifications, 2003-. With U.S. Army, 1952-53, Korea. Mem. ABA (ho. of dels. 1995-2000), Am. Bar Found. (state chair 1998-2002), Kans. Bar Assn. (pres. 1992-93, various offices, mem. coms.), Kans. Assn. Sch. Attys. (pres. 1989-90), Reno County Bar Assn. Office: PO Box 1907 Hutchinson KS 67504-1907 Office Phone: 620-662-3331. Business E-Mail: wbs@martindell-law.com.

SWEAT, KEN GUNTER, educator, consultant; s. Wallace Cameron and Renate Laurie Sweat. MS, Ariz. State U., Glendale, 1995. Lectr. Ariz. State U., 2000—. Home: 312 E Butler Dr Phoenix AZ 85020 Office: Ariz State U 4701 W Thunderbird Rd Glendale AZ 85306-4908 Home Phone: 602-674-0679; Office Phone: 602-543-6938. Office Fax: 602-543-6073. E-mail: kengsweat@asu.edu.

SWEATMAN, KELLY, information technology executive; Student, Loyola Coll., Balt., 1983; BA in Bus. Mgmt., Washington Coll., Chestertown, Md., 1985; MBA, U. Md., College Park, 1987. Asst. to contbr. Balt. Window Factory, 1983—85; ops. rsch. analyst MIE MSS (Shock Trauma), Balt., 1986—87; officer MNC Info. Svcs., Balt., 1987—96; v.p. MBNA Tech., Newark, Del., 1996—. Recipient MBNA Hallmark award, MBNA Tech., 1998. Mem.: AAUW, Balt. Choral Arts Soc.

SWEATON, CHERYL ANNE, bank customer service specialist; b. New Milford, Conn., Oct. 26, 1957; d. Hugh Edward Brown and Charlotte Anne Miller Brown McCoy, Lawrence Wayne McCoy (Stepfather); life ptnr. Jeffrey Alan Patterson; children: Lyn K. John, Alyssa Lee Zuckerman Cain, Ashley Megan Zuckerman. Assoc. Sci., Va. Coll., Salem, 1997. Acctg. mgr., purchasing dir. Shenandoah Robe Co., Roanoke, Va., 1999—2002; inventory control Cloverdale Co., Roanoke, 2002—03; recovery specialist Wachovia Bank NA, Roanoke, 2005—, customer info. verification, 2007—. Vol. Habitat for Humanity, Roanoke, 2006—07. Mem.: Nat. Trust Hist. Preservation (assoc.), Colonial Williamsburg Found. (assoc.). Libertarian. Nazarene. Avocations: weight training, painting, poetry, needlecraft, music. Home: 816 Mountain Ave SE Roanoke VA 24013 Office: Wachovia Bank NA Plantation Road and Lila Drive Roanoke VA 24019 Home Phone: 540-345-6104; Office Phone: 866-211-6980.

SWECKER, CHRIS (CHRISTOPHE E. SWECKER), protective services official, former federal agency administrator; b. El Ferrol, Spain, July 14, 1956; married; 3 children. BS, Appalachian State U., 1978; JD, Wake Forest U., 1981. Bar: Va., NC, U.S. Ct. Appeals (4th cir.), U.S. Supreme Ct. Asst. dist. atty. (1st dist.) State of NC, 1981—82; various positions FBI, 1981—87, supr., acting asst. spl. agent in charge Miami, 1987—94, asst. spl. agent in charge Houston, 1994—98, insp., 1998—99, spl. agent in charge Charlotte, NC, 1999—2004, asst. dir. Criminal Investigative Divsn. Washington, 2004—06, acting exec. asst. dir. for law enforcement services, 2006; head corp. security Bank of Am. Corp., Charlotte, NC, 2006—. Office: Bank of Am Corp 100 N Tryon St Bank of Am Corp Ctr Charlotte NC 28255

SWEE, DAVID ETHAN, physician; b. NYC, Sept. 3, 1947; s. Eugene and Joan (Shalit) S.; m. Karen Virginia Hermanson, Dec. 30, 1971; children: Kendra Olivia, Julia Elizabeth. BA, Grinnell Coll., 1969; MD, Dalhousie U., 1975. Diplomate Am. Bd. Family Practice. Dir. premed. programs dept. family medicine U. Medicine and Dentistry NJ-Robert Wood Johnson Med. Sch., Piscataway, NJ, 1977-85, dir. fellowship program, 1985-87, med. dir. family practice ctr., vice chair dept. New Brunswick, 1987-91, prof., chmn. dept. family medicine, 1991—2005, acting sr. assoc. dean. edn., 2005—06, assoc. dean. edn., 2006—. Chief dept. family medicine Robert Wood Johnson U. Hosp., New Brunswick, 1991-05; site surveyor, liaison com. on med. edn. Coun. on Med. Edn., Chgo., 2006—. Editor, main author: Teaching Family Medicine in Medical School: A Companion to Predoctoral Education in Family Medicine, 1991. Grantee Prudential Ins. Co., 1987-89, US Dept. HHS, 1984-87, 91-04, 93-96, 96-99, 99-02, 02-05; Bishop fellow Am. Coun. Edn., 2002-03. Fellow Am. Acad. Family Physicians; mem. Soc. Tchrs. Family Medicine (bd. dirs. 1985-89, group on predocotoral edn. 1984—, group on faculty devel. 1985—). Avocations: music (piano), writing. Home: 259 Lawrence Ave Highland Park NJ 08904-1837 Office: 675 Hoes Ln Rm R102 Piscataway NJ 08854 Home Phone: 732-249-7822. Business E-Mail: swee@umdnj.edu.

SWEED, PHYLLIS, publishing executive; b. NYC, Dec. 6, 1931; d. Paul and Frances (Spitzer) S.; m. Leonard Bogdanoff (dec. Oct. 1975); children: Patricia Romano (dec. June 1994), James Alan. BA, NYU, 1950. Asst. buyer Nat. Bellas Hess, NYC, 1950; assoc. editor Fox-Shulman Pub., NYC, 1951-57; significant products and components editor Product Engring. mag. McGraw-Hill Pub., NYC, 1957—61; mng. editor Haire Pub., NYC, 1962-66; editor Gifts & Decorative Accessories Mag., 1966-78; sr. v.p. Geyer-McAllister Pub., NYC, 1978-98, editor-in-chief, co-pub., 1978—98; dir. editl. devel. Gifts & Decorative Accessories, NYC, 1998-99; prin. P.S. Comms. & Mktg., 1999—; editor-in-chief, pub. Gift Executive, 1999—. Bd. dirs. Frances Hook Scholarship Fund, 1989-96. Recipient Editl. Excellence award Indsl. Mktg., 1964, Nat. Assn. Ltd. Edit. Dealers award, 1993, 96, MagWeek Excellence award, 1992, Dallas Mktg. Ctr. award, 1969, 80, 82. Mem. Nat. Assn. Ltd. Edit. Dealers (assoc.), Internat. Furnishings and Design Assn. Avocations: gardening, collecting antique Belleek. Office: 505 LaGuardia Pl Ste 17D New York NY 10012-2004 Personal E-mail: psweed505@aol.com.

SWEEM, BILLY DON, bishop, religious organization administrator; b. Bartlesville, Okla., Aug. 7, 1942; s. Verl D. and Viola J. (Benner) Sweem; m. Roberta Marie Hawthorn, Dec. 26, 1990; children: Mark A., Kevin L., Chad D. Dipl., Internat. Bible Inst. & Sem., Portsmount, Fla.; ThD magna cum laude, Bethel Full Gospel Sem., Okla. Ordained to ministry Gospel Mins. and Chs. Internat., 1991, Ind. Assemblies Fellowship, 1991. Evangelist Lighthouse Temple, Colorado Springs, 1977—80, Tulsa, 1980—85; youth pastor Echoes of Faith, Las Vegas, Nev., 1985-89; exec. dir. Billy Sweem Gospel Ministries, Tulsa, 1990—. Evangelist United Meth. Coop. Ministries, Tulsa, 1990—. Missionary India, Pakistan and Philippines. Special interest in church planting and mission works with orphans and troubled teens world-wide. Home: Internat Independent Assemblies Inc St Luke Ind Assemblies Ministries PO Box 2171 Bartlesville OK 74005-2171 Home Phone: 918-338-2423; Office Phone: 918-337-4754. Personal E-mail: bishopbdsweem@sbcglobal.net.

SWEENEY, ANNE M., cable television company executive; b. Nov. 4, 1957; m. Philip Miller; children: Rosemary, Christopher. BA, Coll. of New Rochelle, NYC, 1979; EdM, Harvard U., 1980. With Nickelodeon/Nick at Nite, 1981-93, sr. v.p. program enterprises; chmn., CEO Fx Networks, NYC, 1993-96; exec. v.p. Disney/ABC Cable Networks, pres. Disney Channel Walt Disney Co., 1996—98, pres. Disney/ABC Cable Networks, Disney Channel, 1998—2000, pres. ABC Cable Networks Group, Disney Channel Worldwide, 2000—04, co-chair Media Networks divsn., pres. Disney/ ABC TV, 2004—. Bd. dirs. Mus. Radio & TV; hon. chair Cable Positive. Bd. trustees Coll. of New Rochelle, Harvard U. Ptnrs. Coun.; hon. chair Cable Positive; bd. dirs. Walter Kaitz Found, Spl. Olympics Internat. Named one of 50 Most Powerful Women in Bus., Fortune mag., World's 100 Most Powerful Women, Forbes mag., 100 Most Powerful Women in Entertainment, Hollywood Reporter, 2004, 2005, 2006, 100 Most Powerful Women, Forbes mag., 2005—06, 50 Women to Watch, Wall St. Journal, 2005, Wall St. Jour., 2006, 50 Most Powerful Women in Bus., Fortune mag., 2006, Next 20 Female CEOs, Pink Mag. & Forté Found., 2006; named to Hall of Achievement, Am. Advt. Fedn., 1996; recipient Lucy award, Women in Film, 2002, Chair Award, Caucus for TV Prodrs., Writers, and Dirs., 2003, President's award, Cable TV Pub. Affairs Assn., 2004. Mem. Nat. Acad. Cable Programming (bd. dirs.), Women in Cable NY (founding mem.), Women in Cable (Exec. of Yr. 1994, Woman of Yr. 1997, Advocate Leader award So. Calif. Chpt. 1998). Office: The Walt Disney Co 500 S Buena Vista St Burbank CA 91521 *

SWEENEY, CLAYTON ANTHONY, lawyer, business executive; b. Pitts., Oct. 20, 1931; s. Denis Regis and Grace Frances (Roche) S.; m. Sally Dimond, Oct. 4, 1958; children: Sharon, Lorrie, Maureen, Clayton Anthony, Tara, Megan. BS, Duquesne U., 1957, LLB, 1962. Bar: Pa. 1962, U.S. Supreme Ct. 1968. Supr. transp. claims H.J. Heinz Co., Pitts., 1955-57; mgr. market research Murray Corp. Am., Pitts., 1957-62; ptnr. Buchanan, Ingersoll, Rodewald, Kyle and Buerger, Pitts., 1962-78; sr. v.p. Allegheny Ludlum Industries, Inc., Pitts., 1978-81; exec. v.p., chief adminstrv. officer Allegheny Internat., Inc., Pitts., 1981-84, vice chmn., 1984-85; ptnr., mng. dir. Dickie, McCamey & Chilcote, Pitts., 1986-98, also bd. dirs.; pres. Sweeney Metz Fox McGrann & Schermer, 1998-2000; with Schnader Harrison Segal & Lewis, LLP, Pitts., 2000—. Bd. dirs. Wilkinson Sword Group Ltd., U.K., Landmark Savs. and Loan Assn., Liquid Air N.Am., Halbouty Energy Co., Koppers Holding Corp., Koppers Industries, Inc., Schaefer Mfg., Inc., Schaefer Marine, Inc., Schaefer Equipment, Inc.; adj. prof. Duquesne U. Sch. Law; lectr. Pa. Bar Inst.; mem. procedural rules com. Supreme Ct. Pa. Named Disting. Alumnus Sch. Law Duquesne U., 1997. Bd. dirs. Met. Pitts. Pub. Broadcasting, Inc., Diocesan Sch. Bd., Roman Cath. Diocese Pitts., Toner Inst., Christian Assocs. of Southwestern Pa., Wesley Inst., Inc., Jr. Achievement S.W. Pa., YMCA Western Pa.; chmn. Seton Hill Coll.; mem. St. Thomas More Sch. Bd., Bethel Park, Pa.; chmn. St. Francis Med. Ctr., St. Francis Health System; chmn. bd. DePaul Inst. With U.S. Army, 1953-55. Named one of 100 Most Disting. Living Alumni, Duquesne U. Century Club, 1978. Mem. Acad. Trial Lawyers Allegheny County, ABA, Pa. Bar Assn., St. Thomas More Soc. Home: 232 Thornberry Cir Pittsburgh PA 15234-1025 Office: Schnader Harrison Segal & Lewis LLP Ste 2700 Fifth Ave Pl 120 Fifth Ave Pittsburgh PA 15222-3010 Office Phone: 412-577-5225. Business E-Mail: csweeney@schnader.com.

SWEENEY, DAVID BRIAN, lawyer; b. Seattle, June 23, 1941; s. Hubert Lee and Ann Louise (Harmon) S.; m. Janice Kay Goins, June 18, 1983; children: Stuart, Jennifer, Ann, Katharine. BA Magna cum laude, Yale U., 1963; LLB, Harvard U., 1967. Bar: Wash. 1968, U.S. Dist. Ct. (we. dist.) Wash. 1968, U.S. Ct. Appeals (9th cir.) 1968. Assoc. Roberts, Shefelman, Lawrence, Gay and Moch, Seattle, 1968-75; ptnr. Roberts, Shefelman, Lawrence, Gay & Moch (then Robert & Shefelman, then Foster, Pepper & Shefelman), 1976—2002; of counsel Smith & Zuccarini, P.S., Bellevue, Wash., 2002—. Mem. Seattle-King County Bar Assn., Wash. State Bar Assn., ABA, Estate Planning Coun. Seattle, College Club, Harbor Club. Home: 17506 SE 46th St Bellevue WA 98006-6527 Office: Smith & Zuccarini PS 2155 112th Ave NE Bellevue WA 98004 Home Phone: 425-641-8323; Office Phone: 425-990-1586. Business E-Mail: d.sweeney@smithzuccarini.com.

SWEENEY, DAWN M., trade association administrator; BA in Govt., Colby Coll., 1981; MBA, George Washington. Multiple leadership positions Nat. Rural Electric Coop. Assn., Internat. Dairy Foods Assn.; pres., CEO AARP Services, Inc., 2002—; grp. exec. officer for Membership AARP, 1999—2002; pres., CEO-elect The Nat. Restaurant Assn., 2007—. Mem. bd. dirs. Save the Children, 2007—, AARP Fin., Focalyst; chmn. Save the Children's Washington Leadership Coun. Named a Woman Worth Watching, Profiles in Diversity Jour., 2006, Women Who Means Business, Washington Bus. Jour., 2006. Office: Nat Restaurant Assn 1200 17th St NW Washington DC 20036 Office Phone: 202-331-5900. Office Fax: 202-331-2429. E-mail: info@dineout.org. *

SWEENEY, DEIDRE ANN, lawyer; b. Hackensack, NJ, Mar. 17, 1953; AB cum laude, Mt. Holyoke Coll., 1975; JD, Fordham U., 1978. Assoc. Curtis, Mallet-Prevost, Colt & Mosle, NYC, 1978—84, Eaton & Van Winkle, NYC, 1984—86; ptnr. Jacobs, Persinger & Parker, NYC, 1986—2002; of counsel McCanliss and Early, LLP, NYC, 2002—. Hi-five scholarship com. CUNY, 2000—07. Mem. Assn. of Bar of City of N.Y.

SWEENEY, DON PATRICK, music coordinator, conductor, writer; b. NYC, Jan. 8, 1952; s. John James and Eileen Bernadett (Gillen) S.; m. Catherine Mary Burkhimer, Sept. 19, 1981; 1 child, John William. Grad. high sch., Fresh Meadows, NY. Music coord. Carson/Tonight Prodn., Burbank, Calif., 1976-92; music supr. Jay Leno Tonight Show, 1992-95; ind. prodr. TV spls. and commls., 1995—; bandleader SRO Orchestra, Canoga Park, Calif., 1980—. Featured drummer Earl Rose Trio, concerts thoughout Can., U.S.; with symphonies Corpus Christi, Tex., Asheville, N.C., Pacific Symphony, Calif. Personal E-mail: sroband@earthlink.com.

SWEENEY, GERALD BINGHAM, lawyer; b. Waterbury, Conn., July 4, 1946; s. James W. and Aletha E. (Bingham) S.; m. Carolyn S. Chin, Sept. 18, 1976; 1 child, Patricia M. Chin-Sweeney. BS in Engring., Rensselaer Poly. Inst., 1968; JD, Columbia U., 1971. Bar: NY 1972, NJ 1976, Calif. 1986, Ill. 1998. With Owen and Turchin, NYC, 1971—74; atty. Avon Products, Inc., NYC, 1974-76; sr. counsel Revlon, Inc., NYC, 1976-81, regulatory counsel, 1981-83, v.p. divsn. counsel, 1983-87; v.p. gen. counsel Barnes-Hind, Inc., Sunnyvale, Calif., 1987-88, Coburn Optical Industries, Inc., Tulsa, 1987-88; prin. Sweeney & Assocs., Parsippany, NJ, 1988-92; mng. mem. Sweeney Lev, Montclair, NJ, 1992—; dir., pres. C.S. Properties, Inc. (real estate), 1995—; dir. Addition Tech., Inc. (med. devices),

2001—; dir., voting mem. Tech. Dirs., LLC (angel investing), 1998—; gen. counsel Wesley Jessen Visioncare Inc., 1998—2000, Large Scale Biology Corp., 2005. Trustee Llewellyn Pk. Preservation Found., 2007—. Exec. v.p. NJ Common Cause, Trenton, 1983; trustee Hosp. Ctr., Orange, NJ, 1986-95. Mem. ABA, NY Bar Assn., NJ Bar Assn., Calif. Bar Assn., Ill. Bar Assn., Crane Bldg. Assn., Inc. (dir., pres., treas. 2004—). Home: 24 Oak Bend Llewellyn Pk West Orange NJ 07052 Home Phone: 973-736-2250; Office Phone: 973-509-1800.

SWEENEY, JACK, publishing executive; b. Jersey City; m. Ellie Sweeney; children: Jake, Jessica. BA in English, King's Coll., Wilkes-Barre, Pa. With adv. dept. Washington Post, 1968—74; adv. dir. Trenton Times, 1974—78, Boston Herald, 1978—80, Houston Chronicle, 1980—83, dir. sales and mktg., 1983—86, v.p. sales and mktg., 1986—91, v.p., gen. mgr., 1991, assoc. pub., 1998—2000, pres., 1998—, pub., 2000—. Exec. com., bd. trustees United Way Tex. Gulf Coast; exec. com., bd. dirs. Greater Houston Partnership; chmn. Be A Super Host Com. Super Bowl 2004, Houston. Mem.: Tex. Daily Newspaper Assn. (Pat Taggart Meml. Award 2000), Newspaper Assn. Am. Office: Houston Chronicle 801 Texas Ave Houston TX 77002 *

SWEENEY, JAMES LEE, engineering educator; b. Waterbury, Conn., Mar. 22, 1944; s. James Wallace and Aletha B. S.; m. Susan L. Van Every, Aug. 21, 1971; children: Erin, Ryan, Regan, Wesley. BSEE, MIT, 1966; PhD in Engring.-Econ. Sys., Stanford U., 1971. With Stanford U., 1967—, prof. engring.-econ. sys., 1971—, chmn. dept. engring.-econ. sys., 1991—, prof. and chmn. dept. ops. rsch., engring.-econ. sys., 1996—99, prof. mgmt. sci. and engring., 2000—; sr. fellow Hoover Inst., 2001—; dir. office energy sys., modeling and forecasting U.S. Fed. Energy Adminstrn., Washington, 1974-76. Dir. Energy Modeling Forum, 1978-85, chmn. Inst. Energy Studies, 1981-84, cons. faculty Sch. of Law, 1980-82, mem. steering com. Ctr. Econ. policy Rsch., 1982—, dir., 1984-86; sr. fellow Ctr. for Econ. Policy Rsch., 1997—; dir. Precourt Inst. Energy Efficiency; cons. Cornerstone Rsch., NRC, Exxon Mobil. Author: The California Electricity Crisis, 2001; co-author: Macroeconomics Impacts of Energy Shocks, 1987, Fuels to Drive Our Future, 1990; editor: Handbook of Natural Resources and Energy Economics, 1985, 93; contbr. numerous publs., in field to profl. jours. Bd. pres. Stanford Campus Residential Leaseholders, 1998—. Recipient Disting. Svc. award Fed. Energy Adminstrn., 1975. Mem. Am. Econ. Assn., Internat. Assn. Energy Econs. (Past v.p. for publs.), Rotary (past pres.), Menlo Circus Club, Eta Kappa Nu, Tau Beta Pi. Home: 445 El Escarpado Stanford CA 94305-8430 Office: Stanford U Dept Mgmt Sci and Engring Terman Engring Ctr Rm 459 380 Panama Way Stanford CA 94305-4023 Business E-Mail: jim.sweeney@stanford.edu.

SWEENEY, JOHN E., former congressman; b. Troy, NY, Aug. 9, 1955; m. Gayle Ford; 3 children. AA in Liberal Arts, Hudson Valley CC, 1978; BA in Polit. Sci. and Criminal Justice, Russell Sage Coll., 1981; JD, Western New Eng. Sch. Law, 1991. Bar: NY 1991. Dir. Rensselaer County Stop-DWI prog., Troy; ptnr. Cholakis, Sweeney and Wollowitz, Troy, 1991—95; exec. dir., chief counsel NY State Rep. Party, 1992—94; commr. labor State of NY, Albany, 1995-97, dep. chief of staff to Gov. George Pataki, 1997—98; mem. US Congress from 20th NY dist., 1999—2007, mem. Rep. steering com., mem. appropriations com., vice chmn. transp., treasury and housing and urban devel. appropriations subcommittee. Recipient President's award, Mental Health Assn. NY State, Inc., 2002, Friend of Farm Bur. award, NY Farm Bur., 2004, Guardian award, Partnership for Drug-Free Am., 2004. Republican. Roman Catholic.

SWEENEY, JOHN JOSEPH, labor union administrator; b. Bronx, NY, May 5, 1934; m. Maureen Sweeney; children: John, Patricia. Degree in Econs., Iona Coll. Rsch. asst. Internat. Ladies' Garment Workers; v.p., chair exec. coun. com. on health care Am. Fedn. Labor and Indsl. Orgns.; contract dir., NYC Local 32B Svc. Employees Internat. Union, 1960, pres., 1980; v.p. AFL-CIO, 1980—95, pres., 1995—. Author: America Needs A Raise: Fighting for Economic Security and Social Justice, 1996; co-author: Solutions for the New Work Force, 1989; co-editor: Family & Work: Bridging the Gap, 1987. Mem.: Democratic Socialists of Am. Office: Am Fedn Labor & Indsl Orgns 815 16th St NW Washington DC 20006-4104 *

SWEENEY, JOSEPH J., lawyer, manufacturing executive; AB, Harvard Coll., 1970; JD, Boston U., 1973. Sr. atty. Data Gen. Corp.; v.p., gen. counsel MIPS Computer Systems, Inc.; v.p. adminstrn. MIPS Technologies, Inc.; with Applied Materials Inc., Santa Clara, Calif., 1993—, group v.p. legal affairs & intellectual property, corp. sec., 2002—05, sr. v.p., gen. counsel, corp. sec., 2005—. Office: Applied Materials 3050 Bowers Ave PO Box 58039 Santa Clara CA 95054-3299 *

SWEENEY, LEO JOSEPH, university administrator; b. Jan. 7, 1927; BA, U. Mo., Kansas City, 1951. Dir. admissions and registrar U. Mo., Kansas City, 1957-89, asst. vice chancellor, 1989-92, cons., 1992—. Home: 9727 Aberdeen Dr Shawnee Mission KS 66206-2148 Office Phone: 816-236-1017. Business E-Mail: sweeneyl@umkc.edu.

SWEENEY, MARGARET MARY, federal judge; b. 1955; BA in History, Coll. Notre Dame, Md., 1977; JD, U. Del. Law Sch., 1981. Bar: Supreme Ct. Pa., DC Ct. Appeals. Master Del. Family Ct., 1981—83; atty. Fedorko, Gilbert, & Lanctot, 1983—85; law clk. to Hon. Loren A. Smith US Ct. Fed. Claims, 1985—87; trial atty. gen. litig. sect., environ. and nat. resources divsn. US Dept. Justice, 1987—99, atty. adv. office intelligence policy and rev.; spl. master US Ct. Fed. Claims, 2003—05, judge, 2005—. Mem.: US Ct. Fed. Claims Bar Assn. (mem. bd. 1990—, pres. 1999). Office: US Ct Fed Claims 717 Madison Pl NW Washington DC 20005 Office Phone: 202-219-9657. *

SWEENEY, NEAL JAMES, lawyer; b. Paterson, NJ, Nov. 1, 1957; s. Bernard Thomas and Mary Agnes (Keneally) S.; m. Mary Elizabeth Finocchiaro, Oct. 27, 1984; children: Daniel Fulton, Clare Kenneally, Moira Ann. BA in History and Polit Sci., Rutgers U., 1979; JD, George Washington U., 1982. Bar: Ga. 1982, US Dist. Ct. (no. dist.) Ga. 1982, US Dist. Ct. (no. dist.) Tex. 1982, US Claims Ct. 1984, US Ct. Appeals (5th cir.) 1987. Assoc. Smith, Currie & Hancock, Atlanta, 1982-87, ptnr., 1988-98; ptnr. Construction and Pub. Contracts Practice Kilpatrick Stockton LLP, Atlanta, 1998—. Co-author: Construction Business Handbook, 1985, Holding Subcontractors to Their Bids, 1986, Subcontractor Default, 1987, The New AIA Design and Construction Documents, 1988, Proving and Pricing Claims, 1995, Fifty State Construction Lien and Bond Law, 2000, Who Pays For Defective Design?, 1997, Design-Build Contracting Claims, 1999, Design-Build Contracting Handbook, 2001; editor: Construction Subcontracting, 1991, Common Sense Construction Law, 1997, Aspen Construction Law Update, 1992—; notes editor G.W.U.J. Internat. Law and Econs., 1981-82. Mem. ABA (pub. contract law sect., forum com. on constrn. industry), Atlanta Bar Assn. (bd. mem. construct law sect.), Am. Arbitration Assn. (panel of arbitrators), Water Environment Fedn. (editl. adv. bd. 1994-97), Design Build Inst. of Am. (pres. SE chpt. 2006-). Roman Catholic. Home: 120 Forrest Lake Dr NW Atlanta GA 30327 Office: Kilpatrick Stockton LLP 1100 Peachtree St NE Ste 2800 Atlanta GA 30309-4530 Office Phone: 404-815-6616. Office Fax: 404-541-3408. Business E-Mail: nsweeney@kilstock.com.

SWEENEY, PAUL W., JR., lawyer; BA cum laude, U. So. Calif., 1972; JD, Columbia U., 1975. Bar: D.C. 1975, Calif. 1984. White House Fellow Chief of Staff Asst. to Pres. for Intergovernmental Affairs, Washington, 1979—81; adminstrv. ptnr. & mem. mgmt. com Kirkpatrick & Lockhart Nicholson Graham LLP, LA. Contbr. articles to profl. jours. Bd. dir. Prevent Child Abuse Am., Hollywood Wilshire YMCA, Public Counsel. Mem.: Am. Law Inst. Office: Kirkpatrick & Lockhart Nicholson Graham LLP 7th Fl 10100 Santa Monica Blvd Los Angeles CA 90067-4003 Office Phone: 310-552-5055. Office Fax: 310-552-5001. Business E-Mail: psweeney@klng.com.

SWEENEY, RICHARD JAMES, finance professor; b. San Diego, Jan. 13, 1944; s. John Joseph and Catherine Scott (Spahr) S.; m. Joan Long, June 19, 1965; children: Robin Scott, Erin Michaela. BA, UCLA, 1965; PhD, Princeton U., 1972. Acting asst. prof. econs. UCLA, 1968-71; asst. prof. Tex. A&M U., College Station, 1971-73; dep. dir. office of internat. monetary research U.S. Dept. Treasury, Washington, 1973-77; Charles M. Stone prof. econs. and fin. Claremont (Calif.) McKenna Coll., 1977-89, chmn. dept. econs., 1987-89; Bolton Sullivan & Thomas A. Dean chair internat. fin. Georgetown U., Washington, 1989—. Vis. assoc. prof. econs. U. Va., Charlottesville, 1975; vis. prof. bus. adminstrn. Dartmouth Coll., Hanover, N.H., 1979; vis. prof. fin. Gothenburg (Sweden) Sch. Econs., 1991—. Author: A Macro Theory with Micro Foundations, 1974, Principles of Microeconomics, Macroeconomics, 1980, Wealth Effects and Monetary Theory, 1988, Profit-Making Speculation in Foreign Exchange Markets, 1992; author, editor: Capital Control in Emerging Market Economies, 1997, Exchange-Rate Policies for Emerging Market Economies, 1999; contbr. articles to profl. jours. Fellow Woodrow Wilson Found., 1965, NSF, 1966-68. Mem. Western Econ. Assn. (editor Econ. Inquiry jour. 1984-96), Am. Econ. Assn., Am. Fin. Assn., Western Fin. Assn., Phi Beta Kappa. Independent. Avocations: writing, weightlifting, walking, aerobics. Office: McDonough Sch Bus Georgetown U Washington DC 20057-0001 Home Phone: 703-684-5957; Office Phone: 202-687-3742. Business E-Mail: sweeneyr@georgetown.edu.

SWEENEY, ROBERT DAVID, retired communications engineer; b. Nashville, Aug. 28, 1921; s. John Henry and A. Letty (Bateman) Sweeney; m. Mildred Kathleen Rose, July 14, 1941 (dec. Aug. 1973); children: Robert, Mary, Barbara; m. Marie Ruby Simmons, Dec. 14, 1974; children: Rick, Alan, Robbie. Comm. Engr., Capitol Radio Engring. Inst., Washington, 1942; Elec. Engr., U.S. Mil. Acad., West Point, NY, 1950. Commd. U.S. Army, 1951, advanced through grades to col., 1969; comm. and electronic instr. Norwich U., Norfield, Vt., 1948-50; asst. instr. U.S. Army Mil. Acad., West Point, 1950-51; bn. comdr., asst. divsn. signal officer 1st Armored Divsn., Ft. Hood, Tex., 1951-52; commdg. officer 59th Signal Support Co., 1952-53; radio engr. Japan Signal Bn., 1953-56; signal officer 61st Anti Aircraft Artillery Groups, Milw., 1956-60; officer in charge Down Island Comm. Systems, U.S. Comm. Detachment, Taiwan, 1960-61; comm.-electronics officer 28th N.Am. Air Defense Command, Hamilton AFB, Calif., 1961-64; chief Pacific field office U.S. Army Strategic Comm. Command, Okinawa, 1964-67; post signal officer The Infantry Ctr., Ft. Benning, Ga., 1967-68; dep. dir. Comm. Systems Engring. Mgmt. Agy., 1st Signal Brigade, Vietnam, 1968-69; dept. dir. comm.-electronics dept. U.S. Army Infantry Sch., Ft. Benning, 1969-73; congl. aide-dist. rep. Congressman 3rd Dist. Ga., Washington, 1974-83; ret. Counselor Boy Scouts Am., Ft. Riley, Kans., 1950—. Decorated Legion of Merit with oak leaf cross, Bronze Star with 3 oak leaf crosses, Air Medal, Purple Heart. Mem.: Armed Forces Comm.-Elec. Assn. (charter pres. 1968, Merit award), Assn. Elec. Engrs., Odd Fellows, Fraternal Order Eagles. Democrat. Baptist. Avocations: amateur radio, chess, football, baseball, tennis. Home: 4828 Allegheny Dr Columbus GA 31907-1734 Personal E-mail: sweeneyrd@hotmail.com.

SWEENEY, SARINA MARIE, psychologist, consultant; b. Chester, Pa., Nov. 20, 1978; d. William T. and Catherine M. Sweeney. BS, St. Joseph's U., Phila., 1997—2001; MA in Counseling Psychology, Immaculata U., 2004. Cert. sch. psychologist Pa. 2004. Therapeutic support staff Pvt., West Chester, Pa., 1999—2003; behavior specialist cons. Chester County Intermediate Unit, Downingtown, Pa., sch. psychologist, 2004—. Mem.: APA, Nat. Assn. Sch. Psychologists, Chi Sigma Iota. Office: Chester County Intermediate Unit 455 East Boot Rd Downingtown PA 19335 Office Phone: 484-237-5035.

SWEENEY, SHAWNA ELIZABETH, political science professor, researcher; b. New Bedford, Mass., Aug. 9, 1967; d. John Brennan and Elizabeth Theresa Sweeney. BA magna cum laude, U. Mass., Dartmouth, 1992; MA, SUNY, Binghamton, 1997, PhD, 2006. Sr. rsch. assoc. Ctr. Policy Analysis, U. Mass. Dartmouth, 1998—; asst. prof. policy studies dept. U. Mass., Dartmouth, 2005—. Guest editl. asst. spl. issue Spill Sci. and Tech. Bull., 2001—02; human rights cons. World Bank, 2003—06; rsch. asst. SUNY Human Rights Data Set funded by NSF and World Bank, Binghamton, NY, 2006—06; ofcl. coord. ann. policy studies lecture series U. Mass., Dartmouth; inaugural affiliate econ. rights working group Human Rights Inst. U. Conn. Grantee, NSF, 2003—06; scholar, SUNY Binghamton, 1993—98. Mem.: Internat. Studies Assn., So. Polit. Sci. Assn., Am. Polit. Sci. Assn. Avocations: travel, animal welfare, photography, kayaking, hiking. Office: U Mass Dartmouth 285 Old Westport Rd Dartmouth MA 02719 Home Phone: 508-993-8335; Office Phone: 508-999-8254. Business E-Mail: ssweeney@umassd.edu.

SWEENEY, THOMAS JOSEPH, JR., lawyer; b. NYC, Oct. 29, 1923; s. Thomas Joseph and Johanna M. (Flynn) S.; m. Robin Virginia Thwaites, May 30, 1947; children: Thomas Joseph, III, Deidre Ann. BA, N.Y. U., 1947; JD, Columbia U., 1949. Bar: N.Y. 1949. Assoc. in law Columbia U. Law Sch., 1949-50; assoc. Cravath, Swaine & Moore, NYC, 1950-62; with Morgan Guaranty Trust Co. N.Y., 1962-89, v.p., 1965-76, sr. v.p., sr. trust officer, 1976-89, chmn. instl. trust and investment com., 1989-99; ptnr. Decker, Hubbard, Welden & Sweeney, NYC. Bd. dirs. W.R. Kenan Fund. Trustee Pinkerton Found., Jean and Louis Dreyfus Found. 2d lt. USAAF, 1943-45. Mem. N.Y. State Bar Assn. Democrat. Roman Catholic. Home: 525 Teaneck Rd Ridgefield Park NJ 07660-1100 Office: Decker Hubbard Welden & Sweeney 420 Lexington Ave New York NY 10170

SWEENEY, TIM, computer game developer, programmer; Founder, CEO, chief architect Epic Games (founder originally under name Potamac Computer Games, formally called Epic MegaGames, Inc.), 1991—. Credited to game ZZT, 1991, Onesimus: A Quest for Freedom, 1992, Kiloblaster, 1992, Jill of the Jungle: Jill Saves the Prince, 1992, Jill of the Jungle: Jill Goes Underground, 1992, Jill of the Jungle, 1992, Brix, 1992, Zone 66, 1993, Xargon, 1993, Solar Winds: The Escape, 1993, Traffic Department 2192, 1994, Jazz Jackrabbit, 1994, Unreal Engine, 1995—98, Tyrian, 1995, Extreme Pinball, 1995, Tyrian 2000, 1999, The Wheel of Time, 1999, Unreal Tournament, 1999, Deus Ex, 2000, Deus Ex (Game of Year Edit.), 2001, Unreal Tournament 2003, 2002, Unreal Championship, 2002, Tactical Ops: Assault on Terro, 2002, Unreal II: The Awakening, 2003, Devastation, 2003, Unreal Tournament 2004, 2004, Thief: Deadly Shadows, 2004, Shadow Ops: Red Mercury, 2004, Star Wars: Republic Commando, 2005, Grand Theft Auto: Liberty City Stores, 2005, Brothers in Arms: Road to Hill 30, 2005, Gears of War (Limited Collector's Edit.), 2006. Co-recipient Rave Award-Games, WIRED Mag., 2007. Avocation: exotic sports cars. Office: Epic Games Inc 620 Crossroads Blvd Cary NC 27518-6965 *

SWEENY, PETER MICHAEL, lawyer; b. Boston, Aug. 17, 1947; s. John Sweeny and Marguerite Veronica (Caulfield) Shine; m. Sousan Fakhry Omana, Dec. 18, 1981; children: Kaitlin Anne, Lauren Elizabeth, Hannah Sousan, Mora Katherine. B.A., Georgetown U., 1971; J.D., Seton Hall U., 1974. Bar: Va. 1976, U.S. Dist. Ct. (ea. dist.) Va. 1977, U.S. Ct. Appeals (4th cir.) 1977, D.C. 1978, U.S. Dist. Ct. D.C. 1978, U.S. Ct. Appeals (D.C. cir.) 1978, U.S. Supreme Ct. 1979. Staff atty. Occupational Safety and Health Rev. Commn., Washington, 1974-76; assoc. Ashcraft & Gerel, Alexandria Va. and Washington, D.C., 1977-84, ptnr., 1985-86; ptnr. Thacher, Swiger, Sweeny & Day, Fairfax, Va., 1986-89; pvt. practice, 1989-. Mem. ABA, Va. State Bar, Loudoun County Bar Assn., Assn. Trial Lawyers Am., Ct. Practice Inst. (diplomate). Democrat. Mem. Ch. of Jesus Christ of Latter-day Saints. Home: 36552 Innisbrook Cir Purcellville VA 20132-9010 Office Phone: 571-258-0900. Personal E-mail: pmsweeny@mac.com.

SWEET, DENNIS C., III, lawyer; b. Jackson, Miss., 1955; married; 3 children. BS, Tougaloo Coll., 1977; JD, George Washington U. Nat. Law Ctr., 1980. Bar: DC 1981, Ala. 1984, US Supreme Ct. 1985, Miss. 1986. Former staff atty. Pub. Defender's Office, Washington, So. Poverty Law Ctr., Montgomery, Ala., 1984—86; del. Fifth Circuit Judicial Conf., 1987; mem. Miss. Ho. Rep., 1992—96; ptnr. Sweet & Freese, PLLC, Jackson, Miss., 2003—. Tchg. mem. Intro. Trial Advocacy, Harvard Law Sch., 1983—96. Named one of Am. Top Black Lawyers, Black Enterprise Mag., 2003. Mem.: Assn. Trial Lawyers Assn., Miss. Trial Lawyers Assn., DC Bar, Ala. State Bar, Miss. Bar (mem. bd. commrs. 1990—93), Hinds County Bar Assn., Magnolia County Bar Assn. Avocations: auto racing, fishing, horseback riding, basketball. Office: Sweet & Freese PLLC 200 S Lamar St Ste 410 N Tower Jackson MS 39207: PO Box 1178 Jackson MS 39215 Office Phone: 601-965-8700.

SWEET, HARVEY, set and lighting designer; b. Detroit, Oct. 27, 1943; s. Sam and Rose Sweet; m. Susan Perrett, Mar. 16, 1964 (div. Mar. 1975); children: Deborah Anne, Rebecca Lynn, Jason Aaron; m. Patricia Ravn, Sept. 9, 1978 (div. July 1987); m. Peggy Lynn Krueger, May 12, 2007; 1 stepchild, Caitlin M. Dugan. BS, Ea. Mich. U., 1965; MS, U. Wis., 1967, PhD, 1974. Instr. U. ND, Grand Forks, 1967-69; asst. prof. Boise State Coll., Idaho, 1972-73; instr. U. Wis., Madison, 1973-74; prof. of theater arts U. No. Iowa, Cedar Falls, 1974-89; dir. lighting Landmark Entertainment Group, LA and Tokyo, 1989-91; cons. Advanced Tech., Tokyo, 1991; tech. writer Walt Disney Imagineering, Glendale, Calif., 1992; project mgr., sr. designer, sr. estimator, tech. writer Tru Roll, Inc., Glendale, Calif., 1993-99; project mgr. estimator tech. sales LVH Entertainment Sys., Oxnard, Calif., 1999—2002, mgr. theatrical rigging divsn., 2002—03, v.p. rigging systems, 2003—04, v.p. installation sys. and sales, 2004—05; v.p. sales LA Propoint, 2005—. Owner, operator Sweet Studios Theatrical Equipment, Cedar Falls, 1981-89; dir. theater tech. and design U. No. Iowa, 1974-87; mem. tech. stds. working group Entertainment Svcs and Tech. Assn., 2002-2004, mem. rigging cert. working group, 2002-2004, mem. fire safety curtain stds. task group, 2003—, chair, 2004-, E1.22 Fire Safety Curtain Stds., chair E1.6-1Powered Rigging Stds. Task Group, 2005-. Author: Graphics for the Performing Arts, 1982, Handbook of Scenery, Properties and Lighting I and II, 1988, 2nd edit., 1995, The Complete Book of Drawing for the Theatre, 1995; scenic designer Summer Spl. Repretory Theatre, 1988, Timberlake Playhouse, 1988-89; lighting designer, scenic designer, tech. dir. various coll. theatrical prodns., 1964-89; themed lighting designer Sanrio Puroland, Tokyo, 1989, exec. dir. lighting, 1990. Mem. US Inst. for Theatre Tech. (vice commr. 1979-81, commr. 1981-87, mem. graphic stds. bd. 1979-86, edn. commn. 1983-88, mem. publs. com. 1986-89, bd. dirs. 1989). Avocations: travel, cooking. Office: LA Propoint 9051 Sunland Blvd Sun Valley CA 91352 Office Phone: 818-767-6800, 818-767-6800.

SWEET, JAMES M., lawyer; b. Mpls., Apr. 23, 1945; BA, Wheaton Coll., 1967; JD, Coll. William & Mary, 1973. Bar: Pa. 1973. Joined Drinker Biddle & Reath LLP, Phila., 1973, chmn., litig. dept., 1997—2000, chmn., CEO, mgmt. com., 2000—05, ptnr., insurance, pharm., medical device litig. practice areas. Founder, chmn. bd. Cornerstone Christian Acad. Officer USN. Fellow: Salzburg Seminar, Austria. Office: Drinker Biddle & Reath One Logan Sq 18th & Cherry Sts Philadelphia PA 19103-6996 Office Phone: 215-988-2936. Office Fax: 215-988-2757. Business E-Mail: james.sweet@dbr.com.

SWEET, LOWELL ELWIN, lawyer, writer; b. Flint, Mich., Aug. 10, 1931; s. Leslie E. and Donna Mabel (Latta) S.; m. Mary Ellen Ebben, Aug. 29, 1953; children: Lawrence Edward, Diane Marie, Sara Anne. BA in Psychology, Wayne State U., 1953; LLB, U. Wis., 1955. Bar: Wis. 1955, U.S. Dist. Ct. (ea. dist.) Wis. 1955, U.S. Dist. Ct. (no. dist.) Ill. 1958. Ptnr. Morrissy, Morrissy, Sweet & Race and successor firms, Elkhorn, Wis., 1957—70; ptnr., pres. Law Office Lowell E. Sweet SC, Elkhorn, 1970—2001, Sweet & Maier, S.C., Elkhorn, 2002—03, Sweet, Maier and Cox, S.C., Elkhorn, 2003—04, Sweet & Maier, S.C., Elkhorn, 2004—. Instr. gen. practice sect. U. Wis. Law Sch., 1978, 79, 86, 90; lectr. real estate law Wis. Bar, Gateway Tech., Carthage Coll. Inst., 1974—. Author: Phased Condominiums for Matthew Bender, 1992; co-editor: Condominium Law Handbook, 1981, 93; co-editor: Supplement to the Wisconsin Condominium Handbook, 2004; contbg. editor: Wisconsin Methods of Practice-Condo Section, 2004; mem. editl. bd. Workbook for Wis. Estate Planners, 1990. Mem. Walworth County Rep. com.; sect. Wis. Jt. Survey Commn. on Debt Mgmt. With CIC, U.S. Army, 1955-57. Named Outstanding Young Man of Am., Elkhorn Jaycees, 1966; recipient citation for svc. in drafting Wis. Condominium Law, Wis. Legislature, 1978. Fellow ABA, Wis. Law Found.; mem. Wis. Bar Assn. (gov. 1972-75, 91-93, 99-01), Walworth County Bar Assn., Am. Judicature Soc., The Best Lawyers in Am., Am. Coll. Real Estate Lawyers, Kiwanis, Lions, Moose, KC. Home: 3530 Westshire Cir Delavan WI 53115 Office: Sweet & Maier SC PO Box 318 114 N Church St Elkhorn WI 53121-0318 Home Phone: 262-728-2176; Office Phone: 262-723-5480. Business E-Mail: lsweet@wisclaw.com.

SWEET, VICTORIA, medical educator, physician; BS in Math., Stanford U., 1971; MD, U. Calif., Irvine, 1977; PhD, U. Calif., San Francisco, 2003. Assoc. clin. prof. U. Calif., San Francisco, 1970—. Attending physician Laguna Honda Hosp., San Francisco, 1990—, San Francisco Gen. Hosp., San Francisco, 2005—. Author: Rooted in the Earth, Rooted in the Sky, 2006. Mem.: Am. Assn. History of Medicine. Office: Univ Calif 1947 Alameda De Las Pulgas Redwood City CA 94061-3211

SWEETENHAM, JOHN W., medical educator; b. Billericay, England, Mar. 19, 1956; s. George H. and Joyce Sweetenham; m. Caroline A. Herriott; children: Matthew J., Michael G. BSc, MBBS, U. London, England, 1980; DM, U. Southampton, England, 1990. Sr. lectr. U. Southampton, England, 1990—2000; prof. medicine U. Colo., Denver, 2000—04, U. Ariz., Tucson, 2004—05, Cleve. Clinic Found., 2005—. Contbr. articles to profl. jours. Fellow: Royal Coll. Physicians London. Achievements include research in clinical cancer research. Office: Cleveland Clinic Found 9500 Euclid Ave Cleveland OH 44195 Home Phone: 440-542-0268; Office Phone: 216-445-6707. Office Fax: 216 44 9464. Business E-Mail: sweetej@ccf.org.

SWEETENHAM, PAUL, retail executive; With Allders Internat., 1984; area mgr. Burton Group; retail ops. dir. Champion Sports; head retail ops. T.K. Maxx TJX Cos., Inc., 1993—94, planning and distbn. dir. T.K. Maxx, 1994—95, divisional mdse. mgr. T.K. Maxx, 1995—97, sr. mdse. mgr. T.K. Maxx, 1997, asst. v.p. T.K. Maxx, gen. mdse. mgr., v.p. T.K. Maxx, 1998—99, sr. v.p., gen. mdse. mgr. T.K. Maxx, 1999—2000, pres. T.K. Maxx, 2001—06, pres. T.K. Maxx Europe, 2006—07, sr. exec. v.p., group pres. Europe, 2007—. Office: TJX Cos Inc 770 Cochituate Rd Framingham MA 01701 Office Phone: 508-390-1000. Office Fax: 508-390-2091. *

SWEETLAND, LORAINE FERN, librarian, educator; b. Morristown Corners, Vt., Aug. 13, 1933; d. William Eric and Sibyl Bedina (Bailey) Bloomfield; m. Ronald David Sweetland, July 1, 1950 (dec.); children:

Kathy L. (dec.), Dale J. Bettis. BS in Elem. Edn., Columbia Union Coll., Takoma Pk., Md., 1968; MS in LS, Syracuse U., NY, 1973. Tchr. 1st and 2d grade Beltsville Seventh-day Adventist Sch., Md., 1960-67; asst. libr., cataloger Vt. Tech. Coll., Randolph Ctr., 1968-69; middle sch. libr. Barre City Schs., Vt., 1970-74; tchg. prin. Cen. Vt. Seventh-day Adventist Sch., Barre, 1974-76, Brooklawn Seventh-day Adventist Sch., Bridgeport, Conn., 1976-81; med. libr. Washington Adventist Hosp., Takoma Park, Md., 1981-85; dir. libr. svcs. Seventh-day Adventists World Hdqs., Silver Spring, Md., 1985-95. Med. libr. cons., Balt., 1983-95; pres. Oasis, 1993-94; tchr. Home Study Internat., Silver Spring, Md., 1995-98, IPS-Info. Problem Solvers, Crossville, Tenn., 1998-99. Editor South East Packards Newsletter, 2005—; book reviewer Libr. Jour., 1990-98. Trustee Randolph Pub. Library, Vt., 1970-71; sec. Nat. Area Hosp. Coun., Washington, 1985; treas. Plateau Food Buying Club, 1999-04; founder, club coord. Adventist Food Buying Club, Crossville, 2006-; sch. bd. chair Inez Wrenn Seventh-day Adventist Sch., Crossville, 1999-06. Mem. Laurel Rotary Club (bull. editor 1990-94). Republican. Avocations: gardening, computers.

SWEETMAN, KIMBERLY BURKE, librarian, consultant; b. Framingham, Mass., May 17, 1970; m. Peter Sweetman, May 14, 2003. BA in Film Studies, U. Mass., Amherst, 1992; MA, Emory U., Atlanta, 1994; MLS, Cath. U. Am., Washington, DC, 1995. Head Interlibrary Loan NYU Librs., NYC, 1998—2001, head Access Svcs. dept., 2001—. Cons. in field. Co-author: Access Services in ARL Libraries (SPEC Kit), 2005; author: Managing Student Assistants: A How to Do it Manual for Librarians, 2006. Mem.: ALA, Assn. Coll. and Rsch. Librs. (mem. rsch. com. 2004—07). Office: Bobst Library 70 Washington Square South New York NY 10012 Home Phone: 212-995-8718; Office Phone: 212-998-2532.

SWEETNAM, JAMES E., manufacturing executive; BS in Applied Sci. and Engring., US Mil. Acad., West Point, NY; MBA, Harvard U. Various engring. positions Air Products and Chems.; various mgmt. positions Can. Liquid Air; exec. dir. Drivetrains Cummins Engine Co., 1988—89, group mng. dir. Holset Engring. Co. Ltd. subs., v.p., 1993—97; pres. Cummins Electronics, 1989—93; v.p., gen. mgr. Heavy-Duty Transmission Divsn. of Truck bus. Eaton Corp., Cleve., 1997, ops. v.p. Heavy-Duty Transmission Clutch and Aftermarket Ops. for Truck bus., 2000—01, sr. v.p., pres. Truck Group, 2001—. Bd. trustees ideastream, Cleve. Office: Eaton Corp Eaton Ctr 1111 Superior Ave Cleveland OH 44114-2584 Office Phone: 216-523-5000. *

SWEETSER, SUSAN W., lawyer, advocate, retired state legislator; b. Dec. 13, 1958; d. Robert Joseph and Lucretia Rose (Donnelly) Williams. BA in Polit. Sci./Environ. Adminstrn. with high honors, Johnson State Coll., Vt., 1982; JD magna cum laude, Vt. Law Sch., 1985; MBA, U. Pa., 2002. Bar: N.Y. 1986, Vt. 1986, U.S. Dist. Ct. Vt. 1989; CLU, ChFC, CFP. Confidential law clk. Appellate div. N.Y. Supreme Ct., Albany, 1985-86; assoc. Gravel & Shea, Burlington, Vt., 1986-90; atty. Nat. Life Ins. Co., Montpelier, Vt., 1990—2002; mem. Vt. State Senate, 1992-96; 2nd v.p. women's markets MassMutual Fin. Group, Springfield, Mass. Victims rights adv. Essex Junction, Vt., 1980—; adj. prof. bus. law St. Michael's Coll., Winooski, Vt., 1991—, Johnson State Coll., 1995-97; justice of peace Town of Essex, 1991-95; chair judiciary com., 1994-96; mem. Health and Welfare Com.; former mem. Appropriations Com.; mem. Housing and Conservation Trust Fund Study Com., Civil Rights Study Com., Adoption Law Reform Study Com. Author articles on victims rights. Trustee Vt. State Colls., Waterbury, 1979-81, Univ. Health Ctr., 1992-94, bd. dirs.; mem. ethics com. Fanny Allen Hosp., Winooski, Vt., 1989-92; v.p. Lyric Theatre, Burlington, 1989-95; mem. Vt. Rep. State Com., Montpelier, chmn. Rep. State Conv., 1988, 92, 96; founder, pres. Survivors of Crime, Inc. Recipient Achievement award Vt. Law Enforcement Coordinating Com., 1990, Vt. Ctr. for Prevention and Treatment of Sexual Abuse and The Safer Soc. Program, 1991, Nat. recognition for victims rights work The Giraffe Project, 1991, award Nat. Found. for Improvement of Justice, 1993; named 754th Point of Light by former Pres. George Bush, 1992, Am. Heroine Ladies Home Jour., 1991, Legislator of Yr. Nat. Rep. Legislators Assn., 1995, Working Mother Mag. Working Mother of Yr., 1998. Fellow AAUW, Life Mgmt. Inst.; mem. Vt. Bar Assn., N.Y. State Bar Assn., Internat. Assn. Fin. Planners (chmn. legis. affairs Greater Vt. chpt. 1988-91). Roman Catholic. Avocations: skiing, flower gardening, running, camping, horseback riding. Office: 15 Cindy Ln Essex Junction VT 05452-3307

SWEEZY, JOHN WILLIAM, political party official; b. Indpls., Nov. 14, 1932; s. William Charles and Zuma Frances (McNew) S.; BS in Mech. Engring., Purdue U., 1956; MBA, Ind. U., 1958; student Butler U., 1953-54, U. Ga., 1954-55, Ind. Cen. Coll., 1959; m. Carole Suzanne Harman, July 14, 1956; children: John William, Bradley E. Design, test engr. Allison div. GM, Indpls., 1953-57; power sales engr. Indpls. Power & Light Co., 1958-69; dir. pub. works City of Indpls., 1970-72; chmn. Marion County Rep. Cen. Com., 1972—; bd. dirs. Lorco Engring., Indpls., Indpls. Industrial Products, Acme Screw & Mfg., Inc., Telnet, Inc., Landmarks Ltd., Innovative Investment Co. Bd. dirs. Indpls. Humane Soc.; chmn. 11th Dist. Rep. Com., 1970, 73—; chmn. Nat. Assn. Urban Rep. County Chmn.; alt. del. Rep. Nat. Conv., 1968, del., 1972, 76, 80, 84, 88, 92, 96, del., mem. credentials com., 1984, 88; mem. credentials com., 1980, spkr. presenter, 1996; mem. Rep. Nat. Com., 1984—, exec. com., 1984—; mem. Warren Schs. Citizens Screening Com., 1958-72; bd. dirs. Warren Devel. Com. With AUS, 1953-55. Mem. AMA, Mensa, Sigma Iota Epsilon. Home: 2089 S German Church Rd Indianapolis IN 46239-9620

SWENDIMAN, ALAN ROBERT, lawyer; b. Arlington, Va., Apr. 5, 1947; s. Robert Charles and Jessie (Birse) S.; m. Kathleen Shea, Oct. 8, 1977; children: Shelley Christine, Robert Alan. AB in Polit. Sci., U. N.C., 1969; JD, Georgetown U., 1973. Bar: Md. 1973, D.C. 1974, U.S. Dist. Ct. D.C. 1974, U.S. Dist. Ct. Md. 1974, U.S. Ct. Appeals (D.C. cir.) 1974, U.S. Ct. Appeals (4th cir.) 1974, U.S. Supreme Ct. 1980. Law clk. to chief judge US Dist. Ct. Md., 1973-74; ptnr. Jackson & Campbell, Washington, 1974—92, 1993—2005, mng. ptnr., 1989-90; gen. counsel Fed. Labor Rels. Authority, Washington, 1992-93, Gen. Services Adminstrn., Washington, 2005—06; dir. adminstrn. office Exec. Office of Pres., 2006—. Edn. appeal bd. US Dept. Edn., 1982—90; gen. counsel Legal Svcs. Corp., Washington, 1983—84; adj. prof. George Mason Law Sch., 1988—91; mem. White House Presdl. Personnel, 1989. Gen. counsel Nat. Capital Cmty. Found.; past chmn. bd. Columbia Lighthouse for the Blind; bd. dirs. Jr. Achievement, Leadership Greater Washington, Providence Hosp. Found.; trustee Goodwill of Greater Washington. Mem. DC Bar Assn., Md. Bar Assn., Montgomery County Bar Assn., Jud. Conf. DC Cir., Greater Washington Bd. Trade, U. NC Alumni Assn., Barristers Club, Counsellors Club, DC, Rotary, Phi Beta Kappa, Phi Eta Sigma. Office: Office Adminstrn 1650 Pennsylvania Ave NW Ste 532 Washington DC 20503

SWENSEN, CLIFFORD HENRIK, JR., psychologist, educator; b. Welch, W.Va., Nov. 25, 1926; s. Clifford Henrik and Cora Edith (Clovis) S.; m. Doris Ann Gaines, June 6, 1948; children: Betsy, Susan, Lisa, Timothy, Barbara BS, U. Pitts., 1949, MS, 1950, PhD, 1952. Diplomate Am. Bd. Profl. Psychology. Instr. U. Pitts., 1951-52; clin. psychologist VA, 1952-54; from asst. prof. to assoc. prof. U. Tenn., Knoxville, 1954-62; assoc. prof. psychology Purdue U., West Lafayette, Ind., 1962-65, prof., 1965—, dir. clin. tng., 1975-85; vice chair U. Senate, 1994-95. Vis. prof. U. Fla., 1968-69, U. Bergen, Norway, 1976-77, 83-84; cons. VA, 1981 White House Conf. on Aging, others; Am. Psychol. Assn.-NSF Disting. Sci. lectr., 1968-69; Fulbright-Hays lectr., Norway, 1976-77 Author: An Approach to Case Conceptualization, 1968; Introduction to Interpersonal Relations, 1973; contbr. chpts. to books, articles to profl. jours. Mem. Ind. Gov.'s Task Force Alzheimer's Disease and Related Senile Dementia, 1998—. Served with USN, 1944-46 Recipient Gordon A. Barrows Meml. award for disting. contributions to psychology, 1990; named to Hall of Fame, Brentwood Pa. H.S., 2001. Fellow APA (pres divsn. cons. psychology 1976-77, Presdl. citation 1999, Cert. achievement 2000), Assn. for Psychol. Sci., Soc. Personality Assessment, Am. Assn. Applied and Preventive Psychology, Acad. Clin. Psychology; mem. Midwestern Psychol. Assn., Southeastern Psychol. Assn., Ind. Psychol. Assn., Gerontol. Soc., Sigma Xi, Psi Chi. Republican. Mem. Ch. of Christ Home: 1700 Lindberg Rd 229 West Lafayette IN 47906 Office: Purdue U Dept Psychol Scis West Lafayette IN 47907 Office Phone: 765-494-6977. E-mail: cswensen@psych.purdue.edu.

SWENSEN, DAVID FREDERICK, investment advisor; b. River Falls, Wis., Jan. 26, 1954; s. Richard David and Grace Marie (Hartman) Swensen; m. Susan Candler Foster, June 26, 1982 (div.); 3 children. BA, BS, U. Wis., 1975; MA, Yale U., 1976, M in Philosophy, 1978, PhD, 1980. Assoc. Salomon Bros., NYC, 1979-82; sr. v.p. Shearson Lehman, NYC, 1982-85; chief investment officer Yale U., New Haven, 1985—, adj. prof. investment strategy, lectr. econs., 1985—. Bd. dirs. Endowment Advisors, Inc., Endowment Realty Investors Inc.; trustee Carnegie Inst. of Wash., 1991—; bd. mem., treas. Hopkins Sch. Com. of Trustees Inc., 1998—; mem. Yale New Haven Hosp. Investment Com., 2000—; com. mem. Courtauld Inst. Art Investment Com., 2002—; trustee Brookings Inst., 2004. Author: Pioneering Portfolio Management: An Unconventional Approach to Institutional Investment, 2000, Unconventional Success: A Fundamental Approach to Personal Investment, 2005. Fellow: Berkeley Coll.; mem.: Tchrs. Insurance and Annuity Assn. (trustee 2003—), Am. Fin. Assn., Am. Econ. Assn., Elizabethan Club (trustee 1991). Avocations: squash, tennis, skiing, bicycling. E-mail: swen@invsmtp.invest.yale.edu.

SWENSON, ADA PEREZ, artist; m. Roy Swenson, Oct. 30, 1994; children: Miguel Weissman, Wendy Robin Weissman. Student, Stony Brook U., 1965—66, Indian River C.C., 2002—05, Art Student League, 1951—54; studied with, Richard Cardoff, 1965—68, John Seerey Lester, 2004. Coord. Indian River County Main Libr. Art Exhibit, Indian River, 2004—. Art coord. Cultural Coun. Indian River, 2007; artist-in-residence Everglade Nat. Park, 2005—07. One-woman shows include Bahia Redonda Resort and Marina, Venezuela, 1999, Port de Plaisance, St. Maarten, Netherlands, 1999, Harbor Village, Bonaire, Netherlands, 1999, Vero Beach Main Libr., Fla., 2002—06, Count Down Studio, N.Y.C., 2000—06, 2006, Everglades Nat. Park Mus., Homestead, Fla., 2005, exhibitions include Vero Beach Mus., Vero Beach Main Libr., 2001—04, 2005, 2006, Meghan Candler Gallery, Vero Beach, 2004, 2005, 2006, Arte Direct Galley, Naples, Fla., 2004—06, Everglades Nat. Park Visitors Ctr. Mus., 2005—06, Represented in permanent collections U. Fla. Rsch. Ctr., Ft. Pierce, S.C. State Park, Dillon, Littman Jewelers, Bonaire, Count Down Studio, Everglades Nat. Park; art coord. for cultural coun. Indian River Main Libr., Vero Beach, 2006. Jr. League Indian River. Recipient Scholastic Art award, Pratt U., 1948, awards, AE Backus Mus., Ft. Pierce, 2002, Ctr. for the Arts, Vero Beach, 2002, Everglades Nat. Park, 2004. Mem.: Vero Beach Art Club, Nat. Acad. Profl. Plein Air Painters, Am. Impressionist Soc., Plein Air Painters of East Coast, Fla. Watercolor Soc. Home: 256 Marina Dr Fort Pierce FL 34949 Office Phone: 772-595-3158. Personal E-mail: apswenson@comcast.net.

SWENSON, CONSTANCE RAE, lawyer; d. Albin Linus Peterson and Lillian; m. Keith Howard Swenson, June 20, 1970; children: Jeffrey, Melissa, Stacy, Justin. BA in Zoology, Rockford Coll., Ill., 1968; BA in French with honors, Portland State U., 1996; diploma in Law Studies, East China Sch. Law and Politics, Shanghai, 1988; diploma in Spanish, El Centro Idiomas y Estudios, Mex., 1993; cert. in Environ. and Natural Resources Law, Northwestern Sch. Law, Portland, 1990. Bar: Oreg. 1991, Esquire Dist.: Oreg. 1991, atty., counselor: US Ct. Appeals (4th cir.) 2001. Librarian asst. Rockford Pub. Libr., Ill., 1968—69; law internship internat. banking Crédit de Nord, Paris, 1989; atty. Connie Swenson, Atty., Portland, Oreg., 1991—93, 2000—07; art dept. asst. Portland State U. Bookstore, 1993—96, 1997; realtor Century 21, Gresham, Oreg., 1997; student asst. to adminstr. Portland State U., Oreg., 1997—98. Hearings officer Multnomah Animal Ctrl., 2003—07. Arbitrator Better Bus. Bur., Portland, 2006—; adv. council U. Oreg., Eugene, 2004—. Mem.: NW Planned Givers Round Table, Multnomah Bar Assn., Am. Trial Lawyers Assn. (advocate 2005), Oreg. Trial Lawyers Assn. Mem. Evangelical Covenant Ch. Avocations: ice skating, hiking. Office: Connie Swenson Atty 465 NE 181 Ave #149 Portland OR 97230 Business E-Mail: swenson997@mail.com.

SWENSON, JACK G., writer, consultant; b. Crookston, Minn., Nov. 28, 1926; s. Gilbert Edward and Ruth Newcomb Swenson; m. Mavis Lucille Smith, Jan. 26, 1945; children: Janet, Joanne, David, Suzanne. Grad. high sch., Blackduck, Minn. Copy boy Mpls. Star-Jour., 1943—44; news reporter WDAY Radio, KVNJ, Fargo, ND, 1944—49; news anchor KFYR Radio, TV, Bismarck, ND, 1949—56; congrl. asst. Rep. Otto Kreuger, Washington, 1956—58; mgr. ND Petroleum Coun., Bismarck, 1958—72; regional mgr. Am. Petroleum Inst., Chgo., 1972—75; exec. v.p. Rocky Mt. Oil & Gas Assn., Denver, 1975—86; dir. Beltrami Elec. Co-op., Bemidji, Minn., 2001—. Author: Uncle Ross, 1999; contbr. columns in newspapers. With USN, 1945—47.

SWENSON, KATHLEEN SUSAN, music educator, art educator; b. Reno, Oct. 23, 1938; d. Harold Ruthaford McNeil and Hollyce Margaret (Scruggs) McNeil Biggs; m. James Michael Phalan, 1956 (div. 1974); children: David Michael, Jeanine Louise Phalan Lawrence, Gregory Sean; m. Gerald Allen Swenson, Nov. 1976 (div. 1987); stepchildren: Craig Allen, Sarah Ann, Eric Sander. Student, U. Nev., Reno, 1956-58, Foothill Coll., 1966-68; AA, West Valley Coll.; BA, U. Calif., Santa Cruz, 1983. Concert pianist, Nev.,Calif, 1950-64; pvt. piano instr. various locations, 1963—; pvt. art instr., 1970—; pvt. astrology instr., 1973—; founder, pres. AAM Triple Arts, Aptos, Calif., 1974—; founder, owner Aptos (Calif.) Acad. Music, 1991—. Producer, instr. art instrn. videos, music instrn. films, books. Mem. Soc Western Artists, Calif. Piano Tchrs. Assn., Los Gatos Art Assn. (pres. 1985-86), Saratoga Contemporary Artists (v.p. 1984-85), Nat. League Am. Pen Women (honorarian 1985), Soroptomists, Phi Beta Kappa. Republican. Episcopalian. Address: AAM Triple Arts Brentwood TN 37027 Home: 416 Springer Ct Brentwood TN 37027-4453 Office Phone: 615-309-0818. Personal E-mail: aamtriplearts@aol.com.

SWENSON, MARK GREGORY, architect; b. Mpls., Nov. 29, 1949; s. Stanley S. and Linnea Marie (Anderson) S.; m. Marcy Gayle Stevenson, Apr. 6, 1974; 1 child, Gregory Peter. B in Environ. Design, U. Minn., 1971, MArch, 1973. Registered architect, Minn., Colo., Ariz., Ohio, Fla., Ill., Iowa, La., Nev., Tex., N.J., Ga., S.D., Wis., Kans., Va. Project planner Ellerbe, Inc., Bloomington, Minn., 1972-78; prin., pres. BRW Architects, Inc., Mpls., 1978-96, also bd. dirs.; prin., pres., bd. dirs. Elness Swenson Graham Architects Inc., Mpls., 1996—. Lectr. architecture U. Minn., Mpls., 1974-82. Bd. edn. Minnehaha Acad., Mpls., 2000—04. Evans scholar, Western Golf Assn., 1968—71. Mem.: AIA (lectr. profl. devel. 1983—87, bd. dirs. Minn. chpt. 2001—07, pres. Mpls. chpt. 2002, pres. elect Minn. chpt. 2005, pres. Minn. chpt. 2006), Urban Land Inst., Lambda Alpha. Home: 5501 Dever Dr Edina MN 55424-1641 Office: Elness Swenson Graham Architects Inc 500 Washington Ave S Minneapolis MN 55415-1130 Office Phone: 612-373-4625. E-mail: mark.swenson@esgarch.com.

SWENSON, WILLIAM W., retired dean, aerospace engineer, consultant; b. Feb. 22, 1922; BS in Engring., U. Mich., Ann Arbor, 1943; MBA, U. Buffalo, 1962. Lic. profl. engr., NY, 1948. Chief engr. instrumentation, chief labs., mktg. mgr. Johnson Space Ctr. Bell Aerospace Corp., 1943—74; asst. dean engring. SUNY U. Buffalo, 1985—2000; dean emeritus, 2000—. Named to Hall of Fame, Niagara Aerospace Mus., NY, 2005; recipient Engring. Educator award, NY State Soc. Profl. Engrs., 1991, Disting. Svc. award, 1992. Mem.: ASME, Am. Rocket Soc., Nat. Soc. Profl. Engrs. (state dir. 1974—2007), Rotary (pres. 1977). Home: 102 Foxcroft Ln Buffalo NY 14221-3204

SWENSSON, EARL SIMCOX, architect; b. Nashville, July 28, 1930; s. Earl Ebenezer and Viola Lazelle (Simcox) Swensson; m. Suzanne Dickenson, June 6, 1953; children: Krista, Lin, Kurt. BS in Bldg. Design, Va. Poly. Inst. and State U., 1952, MSArch, 1953, U. Ill., 1955. Registered 28 states. Founder, prin. Earl Swensson Assocs., Inc., Nashville, 1961—. Adj. prof. Va. Poly. Inst. and State U., Blacksburg, 1971—72, Auburn U., 1976—83; lectr. in field; apptd. chairholder Jennings and Rebecca Jones Chair of Excellence in Urban and Regional Planning, Mid. Tenn. State U., 1999. Contbr. articles to profl. jours.; author (with Richard L. Miller): (books) New Directions in Hospital and Healthcare Facility Design, 1995; author: (book) Hospital and Healthcare Facility Design 2d edit., 2002. Mem. arch. program adv. coun. Auburn U., 1990—94; bd. dirs. Metro Arts Commn., 1979—86; Middle Tenn. Health Systems (pres. 1972) AIA, 1973—78; Leadership Nashville Alumni Groups, 1984—; bd. advisors U. Tenn. Sch. Arch., 1982, chmn., 1985—88. Named Outstanding Nashvillian of Yr., Downtown Kiwanis Club, 1992, One of Top 100 Alumni of Greatest Distinction Throughout 128-yr. History, Va. Poly. Inst. and State U., 2001; recipient Jefferson award, Am. Inst. Pub. Svc. (Nashville chpt.), 1985. Fellow: AIA. Presbyterian. Achievements include patents for on systamodule for pharmacies. Office: Earl Swensson Assocs 2100 W End Ave Ste 1200 Nashville TN 37203-5239

SWENSSON, EVELYN DICKENSON, conductor, composer, librettist; b. Woodstock, Va., Sept. 18, 1928; d. Glenn Gilmer and Evelyn Christine (Ring) Dickenson; m. Sigurd Simcox Swensson, June 9, 1949; children: Lisë, Karen, Erik, Jon. Cert. in piano, Ward-Belmont Coll., Nashville, 1946; BA in Piano and Voice, Hollins Coll., Roanoke, Va., 1949; MusM, West Chester U., Pa., 1972. Condr. Aldersgate Meth. Ch., Wilmington, Del., 1969—2002, Brandywiners Ltd., Kennett Sq., Pa., 1973—2004, Opera Del., Wilmington, 1974—, Bi-Centennial Chorus, Wilmington, 1976; guest condr. Del. Symphony Orch., Wilmington, 1977; condr. Ardensingers, Wilmington, 1978-80; condr. 200th Anniversary Meth. Ch. Am., Balt., 1984. V.p. Opera for Youth Inc.; dir. family opera theater Opera Del., Wilmington, 1974—. Condr.: inaugural concert for Gov. P.S. duPont IV, 1977, Sleeping Beauty (Respighi), 1977, The Zoo (Sullivan and Rowe), 1980, The Lion, the Witch and the Wardrobe (John McCabe), 1980, celebration of Swedes Landing, 1988, The Boy Who Grew Too Fast (Menotti), 1982, Charlotte's Web (Strouse), 1989, A Wrinkle in Time (Larsen), 1992, composer, condr.: The Enormous Egg, 1993, The Adventure of Beatrix Potter, 1994, The Jungle Book, 1995, Anne of Green Gables, 1996, The Homecoming, 1997, The Legend of Redwall Abbey, 1998, All Through the Night, 1999, The Trumpet of the Swan, 2000, The Mixed-Up Files of Mrs. Basil E. Frankweiler, 2002, Billy Lee's Washington, 2003, The Secret of NIMH, 2004, What Child is This?, 2005. Recipient W. W. Laird Music award, Opera Del., Wilmington, 1987, Internat. Reading Coun. Literacy award, 1989, Disting. Alumna award, West Chester U., 1989, 5 composition awards, Nat. League Am. Pen Women, 2000, Outstanding Svc. award, Nat. Opera Assn., 2004. Mem.: Am. Guild Organists (choir master). Home: 166 Heyburn Rd Chadds Ford PA 19317

SWERDLOFF, ILEEN POLLOCK, lawyer; b. Bronx, NY, July 15, 1945; d. Seymour Pollock and Selma (Goldin) Feinstein; m. Mark Harris Swerdloff, Dec. 24, 1967; 1 child, Jonathan Edward. BA, SUNY, 1967; JD, Western New Eng. Sch. of Law, 1978. Bar: Conn. 1979, U.S. Dist. Ct. Conn. 1981, U.S. Supreme Ct. 1985. Mng. ptnr. Swerdloff & Swerdloff, West Hartford, Conn., 1980—. Sec. Chrysalis Ctr., Hartford, Conn., 1988-91, pres., 1991-92. Mem.: ABA, Hartford County Bar Assn., Conn. Bar Assn. Jewish. Avocations: knitting, aerobics. Home: 9 Beacon Heath Farmington CT 06032-1524 Office: Swerdloff & Swerdloff 61 S Main St West Hartford CT 06107-2486 Office Phone: 860-521-8882.

SWERDLOFF, MARK HARRIS, lawyer; b. Buffalo, Sept. 7, 1945; s. John and Joan (Harris) S.; m. Ileen Pollock, Dec. 24, 1967; 1 child, Jonathan Edward. BA, SUNY, Buffalo, 1967; JD, U. Conn., 1975. Bar: Conn. 1975, U.S. Dist. Ct. Conn. 1975, U.S. Ct. Appeals (2d cir.) 1983, U.S. Supreme Ct. 1985, Fla. 1977. Assoc. Wilson, Asbel & Channin, Hartford, Conn., 1975-78; ptnr. Swerdloff & Swerdloff, West Hartford, Conn., 1978—. Pres. Arpus Enterprises, Old Saybrook Conn., 1993—; trial fact finder Superior Ct., Hartford, 1990—; arbitrator Dispute Resolution Inst., Hartford, 1990—. Mem. ABA, Conn. Bar Assn., Conn. Trial Lawyers Assn. Democrat. Jewish. Avocations: photography, travel, cooking. Home: 9 Beacon Heath Farmington CT 06032-1524 Office: Swerdloff & Swerdloff 61 S Main St West Hartford CT 06107-2486 E-mail: mhsips@mindspring.com.

SWERDLOFF, RONALD S., physician, educator, researcher; b. Pomona, Calif., Feb. 18, 1938; s. Julius Lewis and Eva (Kelman) S.; m. Christina Wang; children: Jonathan Nicolai, Peter Loren, Paul Im, Michael Im. BS, U. Calif., 1959, MD, 1962. Diplomate Am. Bd. Internal Medicine, Am. Bd. Endocrinology. Intern U. Wash., Seattle, 1962-63, resident, 1963-64; rsch. assoc. NIH, Bethesda, Md., 1964-66; resident UCLA Sch. Medicine, 1966-67; rsch. fellow Harbor-UCLA Med. Ctr., Torrance, Calif., 1967-69, asst. prof., 1969-72, assoc. prof. divsn. Endocrinology, 1972-78, chief divsn. Endocrinology, 1973—, prof., 1978—, assoc. chair dept. medicine, 1997—; dir. UCLA Population Rsch. Ctr., Torrance, 1986-92, Mellon Found. Ctr. in Reproductive Medicine, 1997—. Dir. WHO Collaborating Ctr. Reproduction, Torrance, NIH Contraceptive Clin. Trials Ctr., 2005—, Torrance; cons. WHO Geneva, 1982-90, NIH, Bethesda, 1982—, UN Fertility Planning Assn., Geneva, 1983—, Am. Bd. Internal Medicine, Phila., 1989—; inaugural lectr. Australian Soc. Reproductive Biology, Perth, 1990; mem. tech. adv. com. Contraceptive R & D Agy. (CONRAD, AID), 1992—. Editor: 3 books; contbr. chapters to books 100, articles 250 to profl. jours. Bd. dirs., vice chair Harbor-UCLA Rsch. and Edn. Inst; bd. dirs. Scaplanes Corp. Recipient Sherman Mellinkoff award, UCLA, 1998. Fellow: ACP; mem.: We. Soc. Clin. Rsch. (pres. 1983—84, Sherman Mellinkoff award UCLA, Mayo Soley award 2000), Endocrinology Soc., Pacific Coast Fertility (pres. 1984, Outstanding Rsch. award 1976, 1984, Wyeth award 1984, Squibb award), Am. Soc. Clin. Rsch. (pres. we. sect. 1972—73), Am. Assn. Physicians, Am. Soc. Andrology (pres. 1992—93, Serono award 1986, Disting. Andrologist award 2004). Office: Harbor UCLA Med Ctr Divsn Endocrinology 1000 W Carson St Torrance CA 90502-2004 Office Phone: 310-222-1867. Business E-Mail: swerdloff@labiomed.org.

SWERDLOW, AMY, historian, educator, writer; b. NYC, Jan. 20, 1923; d. Joseph and Esther (Rodner) Galstuck; m. Stanley H. Swerdlow, Nov. 27, 1949 (dec. Sept. 1991); children: Joan Swerdlow-Brandt, Ezra, Lisa, Thomas. BA, NYU, 1963; MA, Sarah Lawrence Coll., 1973; PhD, Rutgers U., 1984. Prof. emerita Sarah Lawrence Coll., Bronxville, NY, 1981-95, dir. grad. studies in women's history, 1983-95, dir. women's studies program, 1983-95. Mem. adv. bd. Feminist Press, 1973-90. Editor: Memo, Women Strike for Peace, 1969—73; editor, co-author Families in Flux, 1980, (reprint), 1989; author: Women Strike for Peace, Traditional Motherhood and Radical Politics in the 1960s, 1993; editor: Feminist Perspective on Homework and Childcare, 1978; co-editor: Class, Race, and Sex: The Dynamics of Control, 1983, Rethinking Women's Peace Studies, 1995; co-author: The Readers Companion to U.S. Women's History (anon.), 1998, Ella Tulin: Fully Empowered, 2007; contbr. chapters to books, book reviews and essays to history jours. Peace History Soc. non-govtl. rep. to UN, 1994—; panelist Bronx Mus. History, NY, 1995; bd. dir. Bella Abzug Leadership Inst., 2005—08. Rutgers U. fellow, 1977-81, Woodrow Wilson Dissertation fellow, 1980. Mem. Berkshire Conf. in Women's History (program com.).

SWERDLOW, MARTIN ABRAHAM, pathologist, educator; b. Chgo., July 7, 1923; s. Sol Hyman and Rose (Lasky) Swerdlow; m. Marion Levin, May 19, 1945; children: Steven Howard, Gary Bruce. Student, Herzl Jr. Coll., 1941—42; BS, U. Ill., 1945; MD, U. Ill., Chgo., 1947. Diplomate Am Bd Pathology. Intern Michael Reese Hosp. and Med. Center, Chgo., 1947-48, resident, 1948-50, 51-52, mem. staff, 1974—, chmn. dept. pathology, v.p. acad. affairs, 1974-90; pathologist Menorah Med Ctr, Kansas City, Mo., 1954—57. Asst prof, pathologist Univ Ill Col Med, Chicago, 1957—59, assoc prof, 1959—60, clin prof, 1960—64, prof, pathologist, 1966—72, assoc dean, prof pathology, 1970—72; prof pathology, chmn Univ Mo, Kansas City, 1972—74; prof pathology Univ Chicago, 1975—89, Geever prof, head pathology emeritus, 1993—; mem comt standards Chicago Health Sys Agency, 1976—. With MC US Army, 1944—45. Recipient Alumnus of the Yr Award, Univ Ill Col Med, 1973, Instructorship Award, Univ Ill, 1960, 1965, 1968, 1971, 1972. Mem.: Inst. of Medicine, Am. Soc. Dermatopathology, Internat. Acad. Pathology, Coll. Am. Pathologists, Am. Soc. Clin. Pathologists, Chgo. Pathology Soc. (pres 1980—). Jewish. Office Phone: 847-831-2983. Business E-Mail: maswerdl@uic.edu. *My credo these years has been to care about patients, students, colleagues, employees, my institution and the many publics I serve. Honesty and thoroughness has been a basic life style, irrespective of the cost. With all, competence is a necessity and ongoing. Continuous responsibility for my education and learning is my way of living.*

SWETCHARNIK, WILLIAM NORTON, visual artist, instructor, consultant; b. Phila., Oct. 18, 1951; s. Charles Jacob Swet and Emily Wharton Nell; m. Sara Morris, Aug. 2, 1981. Student, R.I. Sch. Design, U. Calif, San Diego, Md. Inst. Art, Towson State U., Schuler Sch. Fine Arts, Art Students League, NYC. Instr. Swetcharnik Studio, Mt. Airy, Md., 1980—; workshop instr. Md. Coll. Art and Design, Silver Spring; instr. Smithsonian Instn., Washington, 1986—; fellow, resident Yaddo, Saratoga Springs, N.Y., 1987, 92; resident Ragdale Found., Lake Forest, Ill., 1990. Instr. Art League Sch., Alexandria, Va., 1983-85; juror numerous art exhbns.; art critic, Frederick (Md.) News-Post, 1979-82. Works exhibited in group shows at CatepetL Gallery, Frederick, Md., 1977-81, Nat. Arts Club, N.Y.C., 1980-84, Washington County Mus. Art, Hagerstown, Md., 1981, Lever House Gallery, N.Y.C., 1982, Cork Gallery of Lincoln Ctr., N.Y.C., 1982, City Hall Courtyard Gallery, Balt., 1983, Md. Artists Exhbn. (first and third place awards), Balt., 1983, Md. State Legislature Bldg., Annapolis, 1976-83, Salmagundi Club (Dumond Meml. award 1981), N.Y.C., 1981-83, Harbor Gallery, 1982-83, Cold Spring Harbor, N.Y., 1982-83, Butler Inst. Am. Art, Youngstown, Ohio, 1982-83, Nat. Cathedral, Washington, 1984, N.J. Inst. Tech., 1984, Weinberg Ctr. Arts, Frederick, 1984, The Hermitage Mus., Norfolk, Va., 1984, Four Arts Soc., Palm Beach, Fla., 1984, Springville (Utah) Mus. Art., 1985. Fellow Millay Colony for Arts, Austerlitz, N.Y., 1983, Cintas Found., N.Y.C., 1985-86; grantee Stacey Found., Quemado, N.Mex., 1983; Fulbright scholar to Spain, 1987-88, 88-89; recipient Juror's and Dir.'s award, Springville (Utah) Mus. Art, 1987. Mem. Pastel Soc. Am. Home: 7044 Woodville Rd Mount Airy MD 21771-7934 Personal E-mail: swetcharnik@aol.com. Business E-Mail: william@swetcharnik.com.

SWETLAND, DAVID WIGHTMAN, real estate company executive, investment company executive; b. Cleve., Apr. 13, 1916; s. Fredrick L. and Pauline (Wightman) S.; m. Mary Ann Sears, May 15, 1943 (dec. Aug. 1969); children: David S., Ruth Swetland Eppig, Polly Swetland Jones; m. Jean Thomas, Sept. 23, 1971 (dec. Jan. 2005); stepchildren: Christine Anderson, Dane Anderson, Carol Juliano, Chace Anderson. AB, Williams Coll., 1938. Mgr. Swetland Co./Park Investment Co., Cleve., 1939-60; owner Park Investment Co., Cleve., 1960—2002, David W. Swetland Bldg. Co. Ltd., Cleve., 2002—. Life trustee Cleve. Mus. Natural History, Holden Arboretum, Vocat. Guidance Svcs., Cleve. Soc. for the Blind; trustee emeritus Western Res. Acad., Shaker Lakes Nature Ctr., Univ. Circle, Inc.; hon. trustee Cleve. Garden Ctr., Ohio chpt. Nature Conservancy. Capt. USAF, 1942-46. Mem. Cleve. Assn. Bldg. Owners and Mgrs. (life trustee), The Pepper Pike Club, Rowfant Club (Cleve.), Biscayne Bay Yacht Club, Wiscasset Yacht Club, Union Club. Home: 1 Peaslee Rd Alna ME 04535-0108 Office: David W Swetland Bldg Co Ltd 140 Public Sq Ste 907 Cleveland OH 44114-2213

SWETLIK, WILLIAM PHILIP, orthodontist; b. Manitowoc, Wis., Jan. 31, 1950; s. Leonard Alvin and Lillian Julia (Knipp) S.; m. Cheryl Jean Klein, June 30, 1973 (div.); children: Alison Elizabeth, Lindsey Ann, Adam William; m. Joyce M. Caris, Mar. 10, 1995. Student, Luther Coll., Decorah, Iowa, 1968-70; DDS, Marquette U., 1974; MS in Dentistry, St. Louis U., 1977. Diplomate Am. Bd. Orthodontics. Resident in gen. dentistry USPHS, Norfolk, Va., 1974-75; practice dentistry specializing in orthodontics Green Bay, Wis., 1977—. Instr. oral pathology NE Wis. Tech. Coll., Green Bay, 1979-86. Author: (with others) Orthodontic Headgear, 1977. Mem. Prevention Walking Club, Family Crisis Ctr. of Green Bay. Served as lt. USPHS, 1974-75. Fellow Coll. Diplomates Am. Bd. Orthodontics; mem. ADA, Am. Assn. Orthodontists, Wis. Dental Assn. (Continuing Edn. award 1986), Wis. Soc. Orthodontists, Orthodontic Edn. and Research Found., Brown Door Kewaunee Dental Soc. (program chmn. 1985-86, sec., treas. 1986-87, v.p. 1987-88, pres. 1988-89), Shawano County Dental Soc. (sec.-treas. 2005-06, pres. 2006—07), St. Louis U. Orthodontic Alumni Assn. (pres. 1988-89), Acad. Gen. Dentistry, Violet Club of Am. Roman Catholic. Avocations: skiing, running, fitness training, raising violets, bicycling. Home: 2160 Greenleaf Rd De Pere WI 54115-8621 Office: 115 Alpine Ct Shawano WI 54166-2041 Office Phone: 715-526-2544. Personal E-mail: wswetlik@earthlink.net, jayecars@earthlink.net.

SWETMAN, GLENN ROBERT, literature and language professor, poet; b. May 20, 1936; s. Glenn Lyle and June (Read) S.; m. Margarita Ortiz, Feb. 8, 1964 (div. 1979); children: Margarita June, Glenn Lyle Maximilian, Glenda Louise. BS, U. So. Miss., 1957, MA, 1959; PhD, Tulane U., 1966. Instr. U. So. Miss., 1957-58, asst. prof., 1964-66; instr. Ark. State U., 1958-59, McNeese U., 1959-61; instr. English Univ. Coll. Tulane U., 1961-64, spl. asst. dept. elec. engring., 1961-64; assoc. prof. La. Inst. Tech., 1966-67; prof., head dept. langs. Nicholls State Coll., Thibodaux, La., 1967-69, head dept. English, 1969-71, prof., 1971-91; prof. emeritus William Carey Coll., Gulfport, Miss., 1991—. Writer in residence, prof. English William Carey Coll., Gulfport, 1991—; ptnr. Breeland Pl., Biloxi, 1960—; stringer, corr. Shreveport Times, La., 1966—; ptnr. Ormuba, Inc., 1975—; cons. tech. writing Union Carbide Corp., Am. Fedn. Tchrs. State v.p. Nat. Com. to Resist Attacks on Tenure, 1974—. Book reviewer Jackson State Times, Miss., 1961; contbr. poetry to various publs. including Poet, Prairie Schooner, Trace, Ball State U. Forum, Film Quar., Poetry Australia, numerous others worldwide; author: (books of poems) Tunel de Amor, 1973, Deka #1, 1973, Deka #2, 1979, Shards, 1979, Concerning Carpenters, 1980, Son of Igor, 1982, Poems of the Fantastic, 1990; contbr. numerous articles to encys.; cons. editor (poetry) Paon Press, 1974—, Scott-Foresman, 1975; mem. editl. bd. Scholar and Educator, 1980—. Subdivsn. coord. Rep. Party, Hattiesburg, Miss., 1964. With AUS, 1957. Recipient Poetry awards KQUE Haiku contest, 1964, Coll. Arts contest, LA, 1966, Black Ship Festival, Yoqosuka, Japan, 1967, Green World Brief Forms award Green World Poetry Editors, 1965. Mem. MLA, S. Cen. MLA, So. Literary Festival Assn. (v.p. 1975-76, 82-83, pres. 1984-85), Coll. Writers Soc. La. (pres. 1971-72, exec. dir. 1983—), IEEE, Am. Assn. Engring. Edn., La. Poetry Soc. (pres. 1971-74, 86—), Internat. Boswellian Inst., Nat. Fedn. State Poetry Socs. (2d v.p., nat. membership chmn. 1972-74, pres. 1976-77), Nat. Soc. Scholars and Educators (bd. dirs. 1982—, sec. exec. bd. 1986—, sec. bd. dirs. 1968—, sec. soc. 1989—, exec. edn. 2001-), Am. Fedn. Tchrs. (chpt. pres. 1973-78), Nat. Fedn. State Poetry Socs. (1st v.p. 1975-76, exec. bd. 1972—), Phi Eta Sigma, Omicron Delta Kappa. Home: PO Box 146 Biloxi MS 39533-0146 Office: William Carey Coll 1856 Beach Dr Gulfport MS 39507-1508

SWETNAM, DANIEL RICHARD, lawyer; b. Columbus, Ohio, Dec. 22, 1957; s. Joseph Neri and Audrey Marguerite (Mason) S.; m. Jeannette Deanna Dean, June 7, 1980; children: Jeremiah Daniel, Laura Janelle, Andrew Michael. BA, Ohio State U., Columbus, 1979; JD, U. Cin., 1982. Bar: Ohio 1982, U.S. Dist. Ct. (so. dist.) Ohio 1982, U.S. Ct. Appeals (6th cir.) 1986, U.S. Supreme Ct. 1986. Assoc. Schwartz, Warren & Ramirez, Columbus, 1982-88, ptnr., 1989-96; prin. Schottenstein, Zox & Dunn, Columbus, 1997—. Deacon Grace Brethren Ch., Worthington, Ohio, 1989—; mem. Grace Brethren Christian Schs. Commn., 1993-98. Mem. ABA, Ohio State Bar Assn., Columbus Bar Assn., Comml. Law League Am., Order of Coif. Republican. Avocations: golf, tennis. Home: 2178 Stowmont Ct Dublin OH 43016-9563 Office: Schottenstein Zox & Dunn 250 West St Columbus OH 43215 Home Phone: 614-761-2253; Office Phone: 614-462-2225. Business E-Mail: dswetnam@szd.com.

SWETNAM, MICHAEL S., think-tank executive; b. Espanola, N.Mex., Aug. 18, 1952; s. Fred R. and Grace M. (Thompson) S.; m. Karen T. Swetnam, June 15, 1971; children: Kelly M., Kevin M.; 1 foster child, Gerry Wild. BSEE, U. Okla., 1979. Program mgr. Nat. Security Agy., Ft. Meade, Md., 1980-83; R&D mgr. RAF Edzell, Scotland, 1983-86; dir. ctrl. intelligence staff CIA, Washington, 1986-90; mgr. strategic investments GTE Corp., Rockville, Md., 1990-92, dir. info. sys., 1992-94; co-founder Potomac Inst. for Policy Studies, Washington, 1994, chmn., 1994—; v.p. Pacific-Sierra Rsch. Corp. Spl. cons. Pres.' Fgn. Intelligence Adv. Bd., Washington, 1990—92; mem. Tech. Adv. Group to US Senate Spl. Select Com. on Intelligence, Washington; bd. dirs. Space and Defense Sys. Inc., Gov. Bd. of Potomac Inst. of New Zealand, Dragon Hawk Entertainment Inc. Co-editor: Cyber Terrorism and Information Warfare: Threats and Responses, 1999; co-author: ETA: Profile of a Terrorist Group, 2001, Usama bin Laden's al-Qaida: Profile of a Terrorist Network, 2001; contbr. articles to profl. jours. Bd. dirs. Boy Scouts UK, Scotland, 1982-83; No. UK Scout Master, 1984-85; mem. Canyon (N.Mex.) Sch. Bd., 1970; pres. Pershinghill PTA, Ft. Meade, 1982-83, Cockroaches, Washington, 1992-95, Corp. Vol. Coun., Montgomery, Md., 1992-94; candidate from 5th dist. Md. for U.S. Ho. of Reps., Bowie, 1992; chmn. P.G. County Tax Referendun, Bowie, 1992. Comdr. USN, 1972-90. Recipient Presdl. Unit citation Naval Rsch. Lab., 1991. Mem.: Term Limits Referendum Com. (chmn. 1992—93), Armed Forces Comms. and Electronics Assn., Security Affair Svc. Assn., Md. Bus. Roundtable (pres. 1993), Montgomery County Corp. Vol. Coun. (pres. 1993), Montgomery County Corp. Partnership for Managerial Excellence (pres. 1993), Old Crows. Republican. Roman Catholic. Achievements include invention of of glucose tape tester. Office: Potomac Inst for Policy Studies 901 N Stuart St, Ste 200 Arlington VA 22203 Office Phone: 703-525-0770. Office Fax: 703-525-0299.

SWETS, JOHN ARTHUR, psychologist, researcher; b. Grand Rapids, Mich., June 19, 1928; s. John A. and Sara Henrietta (Heyns) Swets; m. Maxine Ruth Crawford, July 16, 1949; children: Stephen Arthur, Joel Brian. BA, U. Mich., 1950, MA, 1953, PhD, 1954. Instr. psychology U. Mich., Ann Arbor, 1954—56; asst. prof. psychology MIT, Cambridge, 1956—60, assoc. prof. psychology, 1960—63; v.p. Bolt Beranek & Newman Inc., 1964—69, sr. v.p., 1969—74, gen. mgr. rsch., devel. and cons., dir., 1971—74; chief scientist BBN Labs., 1975—98, chief scientist emeritus, 1998—, sr. rsch. assoc. dept. radiology Brigham and Women's Hosp., 1997—. Lectr. dept. clin. epidemiology Harvard Med. Sch., 1985—88, dept. health care policy, 1988—; mem. corp. Edn. Devel. Ctr., Newton, Mass., 1971—75; Regent's prof. U. Calif., 1969; advisor vision com., com. on hearing and bioacoustics NAS-NRC, 1960—96; mem. Commn. on Behavioral Social Scis. and Edn., NRC, 1988—92, vice chair, 1992—93, chmn., 1993—96; ex-officio mem. governing bd. NRC, 1994—96, mem. various coms., 1960—. Author: Signal Detection Theory and ROC Analysis in Psychology and Diagnostics, 1996; co-author (with D.M. Green): Signal Detection Theory and Psychophysics, 1966; co-author: (with R.M. Pickett) Evaluation of Diagnostic Systems: Methods From Signal Detection Theory, 1982; editor: Signal Detection and Recognition by Human Observers, 1964; editor: (with L.L. Elliott) Psychology and the Handicapped Child, 1974; editor: (with D. Druckman) Enhancing Human Performance, 1988; mem. editl. bd. Med. Decision Making, 1980—85, Psychol. Sci., 1989—94, 1999—2002, Psychol. Rev., 1995—97, Jour. Exptl. Psychology: Applied, 1995—97, Human Factors, 1997—2001; contbr. articles to profl. jours. Mem. bd. dirs. German-Am. Rsch. Coun. Found., 1999—2001; mem. corp. Winchester Hosp., Mass., 1981—84. Fellow vis. rsch. fellow, Philips Labs., The Netherlands, 1958. Fellow: APA (Disting. Sci. Contbn. award 1990), AAAS (coun. 1986—89), Am. Psychol. Soc., Soc. Exptl. Psychologists (chmn. 1986, exec. com. 1986—89, Howard Crosby Warren medal 1985), Am. Acad. Arts and Scis., Acoustical Soc. Am. (exec. coun. 1968—71); mem.: NAS (chmn., Troland award com. 1991, chair psychology sect. 1998—2001, nominating com. 2001), Soc. Math. Psychology, Psychometric Soc., Psychonomic Soc., Tequesta Country Club, Sigma Alpha Epsilon, Sigma Xi. Congregationalist (Moderator). Home: 10411 SE Terrapin Pl 103-C Tequesta FL 33469-1827 E-mail: swets@bbn.com.

SWETT, RICHARD NELSON (DICK SWETT), diplomat, former congressman; b. Bryn Mawr, Pa., May 1, 1957; s. Philip Eugene Sr. and Ann (Parkhurst) S.; m. Yvonne Katrina Lantos, Aug. 29, 1980; children: Chelsea, Sebastian, Keaton, Chanteclaire, Kismet, Atticus, Sunday. BA in Architecture, Yale U., 1979. Lic. contractor, Calif.; lic. architect, Calif., N.H. Arch. Skidmore Owings & Merrill, San Francisco, 1979-82; pres. Bastion Group, Inc., San Mateo, Calif., 1982-87; project mgr. Grosvenor Properties, San Francisco, 1986-87; pres. Veritas Group Inc., Gilford, NH, 1987-90; mem. 101st-102d Congresses from 2nd dist. N.H., Washington, 1991—95; mem. pub. works and transp. com. U.S. Ho. of Reps., Washington, 1991-95, mem. sci., space, and tech. com., 1991-95, mem. select com. on aging, 1991-95; amb. to Denmark Am. Embassy, Copenhagen, 1998-2001; pres. Swett Assocs., Bow, NH, 2001—. State chmn. U.S. Olympic Com., 1992—98; founding mem. adv. bd. European Ctr. of Calif., 2001—06; sr. counselor APCO Worldwide, 2001—; mem. U.S. Govt. Gen. Svcs. Adminstrn. Archtl. Peer Rev. Bd., 2000—; bd. dirs. AeroSat Corp., Amherst, NH, 2001—. Author: Leadership by Design: Creating an Architecture of Trust; contbg. author: A Nation Reconstructed. Bd. advisors Hans Christian Andersen Found., Denmark, 2001—, Architects for Humanity, NYC, 2001—, Abildsø Found., Oslo, 2002—, Project for Pub. Spaces, NYC, 2003—. Presented 1st Comdr. Order of Danabrog, Queen Margrethe II of Denmark, 2001; named as one of Top Ten Outstanding Young Ams., U.S. Jr. C. of C., 1993. Fellow AIA, Design Futures Coun. (sr.); mem. Nat. Hist. Preservation Soc., Ind. Power Producers N.H. Assn., Yale Club N.H., Sierra Club, Winnipesaukee Yacht Club. Democrat. Avocations: athletics, piano, art, sailing. Home Phone: 603-774-0314; Office Phone: 603-774-1072. Business E-Mail: rnswett@swettassociates.com. E-mail: info@swettassociates.com.

SWETT, STEPHEN FREDERICK, JR., artist, educator; b. Englewood, NJ, Sept. 14, 1935; s. Stephen Frederick and Frances (Gulotta) S.; m. Annette Palazzolo, Nov. 18, 1961; children: Susan, Kimberly Ann, Stephen Laurence. BA, Montclair State Coll., 1959, MA, 1965; EdD in Ednl. Adminstrn., Rutgers U., 1976; grad., North Light Art Sch., 1995. Tchr. Long Branch (N.J.) H.S., 1961-62, Roselle Park (N.J.) H.S., 1962-73; rsch. asst. Rutgers U., New Brunswick, NJ, 1973-74; instrnl. supr. Elmwood Park (N.J.) Schs., 1974-76, Morris Hills Regional Schs., Denville, NJ, 1976-77; asst. prin. Lawrence H.S., Lawrenceville, NJ, 1977-79; prin. Stafford Intermediate Sch., Manahawkin, NJ, 1979-94; recreation and art cons., 1994—. Participant NSF Inst. in physics, chemistry and math. Seton Hall U., 1964, Newark Coll. Engring., 1965, Stevens Inst. Tech., summers 1966-68; rschr. sch. fin. Exhibited in group shows at Sheldon Meml. Art Gallery, 1998, Period Gallery, Omaha, 1998, 99, Montserrat Gallery, N.Y.C., 2000, The Looking Glass Art Gallery, Hawley, Pa., 2000, Annette Howell Turner Ctr. for the Arts, Valdosta, Ga., 2004, Schacknow Mus. Fine Arts, Plantation, Fla., 2005, 06. With AUS, 1959-61. Mem. Roselle Park Edn. Assn. (pres. 1971-73), Nat. Soc. Study Edn., Am. Assn. Physics Tchrs., Am. Inst. Physics, Am. Assn. Sch. Adminstrs., N.J. Assn. Sch. Adminstrs., Nat. Assn. Elem. and Mid. Sch. Adminstrs., N.J. Assn. Elem. and Mid. Sch. Adminstrs., Nat. Assn. Secondary Sch. Prins., Phi Delta Kappa (sec. Rutgers chpt. 1977-80, v.p. 1980-82, pres. 1983-84). Home: 306 Tenth Ave Belmar NJ 07719-2313

SWHIER, CLAUDIA VERSFELT, lawyer; b. Mineola, NY, Jan. 15, 1950; d. William Holly and Ruth (Gerland) Versfelt;; children: James Robert, Jeffrey William. BA in Philosophy magna cum laude, Yale U., 1972; JD cum laude, Harvard U., 1975. Bar: Ind. 1975. Assoc. Barnes & Thornburg, Indpls., 1975-82, ptnr., 1982—. Mem. editor Thrift Law in Rev., Banking Law in Rev., 1989—. Mem. ABA, Ind. Bar Assn., Indpls. Bar Assn. Republican. Presbyterian. Avocations: skiing, swimming, aerobics. Office: Barnes & Thornburg 11 S Meridian St Indianapolis IN 46204 Office Phone: 317-231-7231. Office Fax: 317-231-7433. Business E-Mail: claudia.swhier@btlaw.com.

SWIBEL, HOWARD JAY, lawyer; b. Chgo., July 9, 1950; s. Charles Robert and Seena (Minkus) S.; m. Sheryl Siegel, June 19, 1973; children: Matthew, Brian, Justin, Alison. BA cum laude, Harvard U., 1972, JD cum laude, 1975. Bar: Ill. 1975, US Dist. Ct. (no. dist. Ill.) 1975, US Ct. Appeals (7th cir.) 1978. Ptnr. Kirkland & Ellis, Chgo., 1975-83, Arnstein & Lehr, Chgo., 1983—, mem. exec. comm., 1983—2005. Mem. Nat. Conf. Commrs. on Uniform State Laws, Chgo., 1976— (pres.); vice chair Midwest Regional Bd. Anti-Defamation League; v.p. Holocaust Meml. Found. Ill., 2002—; arbitrator, NASD Contbr. articles to law jours. Mem. instl. rev. bd. Ill. Cancer Coun., Chgo., 1986-90; pres. Cmty. Found. Jewish Edn. Met. Chgo., 2000-02. Mem. ABA, Ill. Bar Assn., Chgo. Bar Assn., Harvard Club (bd. dirs. Chgo. 1975-85). Jewish. Avocations: investments, tennis, skiing, travel. Office: Arnstein & Lehr LLP 120 S Riverside Plz Ste 1200 Chicago IL 60606-3910 Office Phone: 312-876-7164. E-mail: hjswibel@arnstein.com. *

SWIBEL, STEVEN WARREN, lawyer; b. Chgo., July 18, 1946; s. Morris Howard and Gloria Swibel; m. Leslie Swibel; children: Deborah, Laura. BS, MIT, 1968; JD, Harvard U., 1971. Bar: Ill. 1971, U.S. Dist. Ct. (no. dist.) Ill. 1971, U.S. Tax Ct. 1973, U.S. Ct. Appeals (7th cir.) 1981. Assoc. Sonnenschein Carlin Nath & Rosenthal, Chgo., 1971-78, ptnr., 1978-84, Rudnick & Wolfe, 1984-93, Schwartz, Cooper, Chartered, Chgo., 1993—. Adj. prof. taxation Ill. Inst. Tech. Kent Coll. Law, Chgo., 1989—2001; lectr. in field. Contbr. articles to profl. jours. Ednl. counselor MIT, 1979—; bd. dirs. MIT Alumni Fund, 1992—95, MIT Enterprise Forum, Chgo., 2002—, Kids in Danger, 1998—, Ragdale Found., 1987—2000, treas., 1987—92. Recipient Lobdell Disting. Svc. award, MIT Alumni Assn., 1989. Mem.: ABA (com. partnerships sect. taxation), Chgo. Bar Assn. (mem. exec. subcom. 1984—2004, chmn. subcom. real estate and partnerships 1986—87, vice-chmn. 1988—89, chmn. 1990, mem. fed. taxation com.), Ill. Bar Assn., MIT Club (sec. 1980—87, dir. Chgo. chpt. 1980—91, pres. 1987—89, dir. Chgo. chpt. 1996—), Met. Club, Sigma Xi, Eta Kappa Nu, Tau Beta Pi. Office: Schwartz Cooper Chartered 180 N La Salle St Ste 2700 Chicago IL 60601-2757 Office Phone: 312-346-1300. Business E-Mail: sswibel@schwartzcooper.com.

SWIBINSKI, EDWARD THOMAS, internist, endocrinologist, educator; b. Jersey City, Jan. 26, 1950; s. Stanley Adolph and Celina Frances (Szymanski) S. BA, Rutgers U., 1972; MD, N.Y. Med. Coll., 1975. Diplomate Am. Bd. Internal Medicine, Am. Bd. Endocrinology and Metabolism. Resident in medicine N.Y. Med. Coll., NYC, 1975-78; gen. internist Nat. Health Svcs. Corp., Camden, NJ, 1978-79; fellow in endocrinology Hosp. of U. Pa., Phila., 1979-80; fellow in endocrinology -R.W. Johnson Med. Sch. U. Medicine and Dentistry N.J., Piscataway, NJ, 1980-81, clin. prof. medicine R.W. Johnson Med. Sch.; divsn. chief endocrinology Our Lady of Lourdes Ctr. Mem. ACP, Phila. Endocrinology Soc. (v.p. 1993-94, bd. dirs. 1991-96, pres. 1994-95), Camden County Med. Soc., Phi Beta Kappa, Alpha Omega Alpha. Roman Catholic. Office: 1210 Brace Rd Cherry Hill NJ 08034-3213 Home Phone: 856-424-2052; Office Phone: 856-795-3597. Personal E-mail: marvoor@aol.com.

SWIBOLD, GRETCHEN ANN, librarian, writer; b. Holland, Mich., May 3, 1933; d. Jan B. and Margaret Ann (Raak) Vanderploeg; m. Richard Edward Swibold, Aug. 15, 1955; children: Katharine Margaret, Edward Jan. AB, Bryn Mawr Coll., 1955; postgrad., U. Ill., Urbana, 1958—59; MS, So. Conn. State Coll., 1970; postgrad., Cen. Conn. State Coll., 1973—82. Editl. asst. Our Wonderful World, Urbana, 1955—57; editor Spencer Press, Urbana, 1957—58; rsch. asst. U. Ill., Urbana, 1958—59; libr. Yale U. Polit. Sci. Rsch. Libr., New Haven, 1967—71, Canton (Conn.) Elem. Schs., 1971—97. Editor: Animals in Action, 1958, Rolling Wheels, 1959; contbr. articles to newspapers and profl. jours. Women's com. Yale U. Art Gallery, New Haven, 1967—71; active Canton Creative Arts Coun., 1980—97, v.p., 1987—88, treas., 1989—92; chmn., sec. Bd. Assessors, 1975—79; active Dem. Town Com., Canton, 1973—92, Charter Commn., Canton, 1983—84; bd. dirs. Creative Arts Workshop, New Haven, 1967—71. Mem.: LWV (bd. dirs. Canton chpt. 1992—2004, Conn. chpt. 1997—2000, pres. Canton chpt. 2000—04), ALA (com. on libr. svc. to children with spl. needs 1992—94), Bryn Mawr Coll. Alumnae Assn. Democrat. Home: PO Box 306 North Canton CT 06059-0306 Personal E-mail: swibold@comcast.net.

SWICK, TODD J., medical association administrator; b. NYC, Feb. 8, 1950; s. Adele Hantman; m. Marilyn L. Farkas, June 22, 2002; m. Lisa C. Bleiweiss, Apr. 14, 1973; children: Jennifer P., Blair J., Chad M. Ruoff. B, and MD, SUNY, Stony Brook, NY, 1974. Med. dir. Houston Sleep Ctr., 1999—; sect. chief divsn. sleep medicine Meth. Neurol. Inst., Houston, 2006—. Fellow: Am. Acad. of Sleep Medicine, Am. Acad. of Neurology (life). Office: Houston Sleep Ctr Ste 525 7500 San Felipe Houston TX 77063 Office Phone: 713-465-9282. Office Fax: 713-465-9248. E-mail: tswick@houstonsleepcenter.com.

SWID, STEPHEN CLAAR, communications executive, director; b. NYC, Oct. 26, 1940; s. David and Selma (Claar) S.; m. Nan Goldman, Mar. 1, 1963; children: Robin, Scott, Jill. BS, Ohio State U., 1962. Mgmt. trainee Alside Aluminum Co., Akron, Ohio, 1962-63; securities analyst Dreyfus Fund, NYC, 1963-66; sr. investment officer Oppenheimer Fund, NYC, 1966-67; gen. ptnr. City Associates, 1967-69, Swid Investors, NYC, 1970-78; co-chmn. bd. Gen. Felt Industries Inc., Saddle Brook, NJ, 1974-86, Knoll Internat., 1977-86; chmn. bd., CEO SBK Entertainment World, Inc., NYC, 1986-89; chmn., CEO SCS Comm., NYC, 1989—2007, SESAC, 1992—. Trustee Solomon R. Guggenheim Mus., New Sch. U.; mem. vis. com. 20th century art Met. Mus. Art; past trustee Horace Mann Sch., NYC.; former exec. vp. bd. dirs. Lenox Sch. NY; dir. Mcpl. Art Soc. Mem.: Coun. Fgn. Rels. Office: SESAC Inc 152 W 57th St New York NY 10019-3310

SWIDARSKI, THOMAS W., manufacturing executive; B in Mktg., U. Dayton, Ohio; M in Bus. Mgmt., Cleve. State U. With various financial firms; mgr. PNC Bank; joined Diebold, Inc., Canton, Ohio, 1996—, sr. v.p., financial self-svc. group, pres., COO, 2005, pres., CEO, 2005—. Bd. dir. Diebold, Inc., Canton, Ohio, 2003—. Office: Diebold Inc 5995 Mayfair Rd PO Box 3077 Canton OH 44720-8077 *

SWIENTON, GREGORY T., transportation company executive; BBA in Mktg., Loyola U., Chgo., 1971; MBS in Bus. Admin., U. Chgo. Various sales and mktg. positions Ill. Bell and AT&T, Chgo., Mpls., 1971-82; former v.p., gen. mgr. DHL Airways, Inc., Chgo. and Houston; mng. dir. We. & Ea. Europe DHL Worldwide Express, Brussels, 1988—90, exec. dir. Europe and Africa, 1991—94; exec. v.p. Intermodal Bus.Unit Burlington No. Railroad, 1994—95; sr. v.p. Industrial Bus. Unit Burlington No. Santa Fe Corp., 1995—99; pres., COO Ryder System, Inc., Miami, 1999—2000, chmn., CEO, 2000—. Mem. bd. dir. St. Thomas Univ. Bd. Trustees. Office: Ryder System Inc PO Box 20816 Miami FL 33102-0816 *

SWIERINGA, ROBERT JAY, dean, accounting educator; BA in Econs., Augustana Coll., 1964; MBA in Acctg. and Econs., U. Denver, 1965; PhD in Acctg. and Complex Orgns., U. Ill., 1969. Asst. prof. acctg. Grad. Sch. Bus., Stanford U., Calif., 1968-74; assoc. prof. acctg. Johnson Grad. Sch. Mgmt., Cornell U., Ithaca, NY, 1974-81, prof. acctg., 1981-85, 1997—, Anne and Elmer Lindseth Dean, 1997—; mem. Fin. Acctg. Standards Bd., Norwalk, Conn., 1986—96; prof. in practice acctg. Yale Sch. Mgmt., 1996—97. Bd. dirs. GE, 2002—; adv. bd. mem. Columbia Bus. Sch. Ctr. for Excellence in Fin. Reporting and Security Analysis, 2003—; mem. editl. bd. Jour. Acctg. Rsch., 1975—97, Acctg. Horizons, 1996—. Co-author: (with R.T. Sprouse) Essentials of Financial Statement Analysis, 1972, (with R.H. Moncur) Some Effects of Participative Budgeting on Managerial Behavior, 1975; (with T.R. Dyckman) Cases in Financial Accounting, 1980, rev. 1981, 3rd edit. 1989; (with H. Bierman Jr.) Financial Accounting: An Introduction, 1987. Grantee Nat. Assn. Accts., 1970, Peat, Marwick, Mitchell & Co. Found., 1976; Recipient Justice Found. Award for Outstanding Teaching, Cornell U., 1976, PhD Alumni of Yr. Award, Accountancy Dept. U. Ill., 1988, Alumni Outstanding Achievement Award, Augustana Coll., 1989, Alumnus of Yr. Award, Sch. Accountancy U. Denver, 1994. Mem. Am. Acctg. Assn. (inducted into Northeast Regional Hall of Fame, 1996), Beta Gamma Sigma, Beta Alpha Psi, Assn. to Advance Collegiate Schs. of Bus. (peer review teams mem., 2001-), Grad. Mgmt. Admissions Coun. (bd. dirs., 2001-05, vice chair, 2002-03, chair, 2003-04). Office: Johnson Grad Sch of Management Cornell University 207 Sage Hall Ithaca NY 14853-6201 Office Phone: 607-255-6418. Office Fax: 607-255-5117. E-mail: rjs22@cornell.edu.

SWIFT, CALVIN THOMAS, electrical and computer engineering educator; b. Quantico, Va., Feb. 6, 1937; s. Thomas and Elsie (Hill) S.; m. Joanne Taylor, Sept. 5, 1959; children: Pamela, Janet. BS, MIT, 1959; MS, Va. Poly. Inst., 1965; PhD, William and Mary Coll., 1969. Research engr. N. Am. Aviation Co., Downey, Calif., 1959-62; aerospace technologist NASA, Hampton, Va., 1962-81; prof. elec. and computer engring. U. Mass., Amherst, 1981—2001, prof. emeritus, 2001—. Cons. engring. Amherst, 1981—; co-founder ProSensing (formerly Quadrant Engring., Inc.), Amherst, 1982; v.p. spl. projects team Limited Liability Corp., 2006. Editor: Transactions on Geoscience and Remote Sensing, 1980-84; assoc. editor: Jour. Oceanic Engring., 1980-84. F.L. Thompson fellow NASA, 1977; faculty fellow U. Mass., 1997. Fellow IEEE (life); mem. Internat. Union Radio Sci. (chmn. Commn. F 1988-91), Antennas and Propagation Soc. (adminstrv. com. 1974-77, 80-85), Geosci. and Remote Sensing Soc. (adminstrv. com. 1978-86, pres. 1985, Disting. Achievement award 1994). Office: U Mass Dept Elec & Computer Engring Amherst MA 01003 Personal E-mail: calswift@comcast.net.

SWIFT, CHARLES D., career military officer, lawyer, educator; b. Franklin, NC, 1962; married. Grad., US Naval Academy, 1984; JD cum laude, Seattle U. Sch. Law, 1994, LLM in Trial Advocacy; LLM with honors, Temple U., 2006. Advanced through grades to lt. comdr. USN; damage control asst. USS Niagara Falls, Agana, Guam, 1985—87; navigator USS Rathburne, Pearl Harbor, Hawaii, 1988—90; asst. internat. training Surface Warfare Dept. Head Sch., Newport, RI, 1990—91; atty. JAGC, USN, 1994—, defense counsel Office Mil. Commns., 2003—. Vis. assoc. prof. internat. humanitarian law, criminal law, evidence and military law Emory U. Sch. Law, Atlanta, 2007—, acting dir. Internat. Humanitarian Law Clinic, 2007—. Assigned USS Niagara Falls (AFS-3) USN, 1985—87, Agana, Guam, assigned USS Rathburne (FF-1057) USN, 1988—90, Pearl Harbor, Haw., assigned Surface Warfare Dept Head Sch. USN, 1990—91, Newport, RI, assigned USN, 1995—97, Naval Legal Svc. Office Northwest, assigned Nava Station Roosevelt Roads USN, 1997—2000, Puerto Rico, assigned Naval Legal Svc. Detachment USN, 2000—03, Mayport, Fla. Decorated Surface Warfare Officer's pin USN, Navy Commendation Medal (2), Navy Achievement Medal (6), Navy Expeditionary Medal, Humanitarian Svc. Medal, Sea Svc. Ribbon (4); named one of 100 Most Influential Lawyers, Nat. Law Jour., 2006. Office: Emory U Sch Law 201 Dowman Dr Atlanta GA 30322 E-mail: cdswift@emory.edu. *

SWIFT, CONSTANCE REDMOND, special education educator; b. Cleve., Aug. 31, 1950; d. Charles Clovis and Sally McMahon Redmond; m. Robert Jeffrey Swift, Sept. 17, 1977 (div. Aug. 1, 1990); children: Robert J., Michael F., J. Patrick, Sally M., Terrence M. BS in Psychology, Loyola U., Chgo., 1972; postgrad., Sam Houston State U., Houston, 1991—93; MA in Counseling Psychology, Sam Houston State U., Huntsville, Tex., 1997. Cert. tchr., spl. edn., tchr., master reading and ESL Tex. Pre-trial coun. Harris County Criminal Ct., Houston, 1990—91; spl. edn. tchr. Houston Ind. Sch. Dist., 1991. Psychology prof. Kingwood Coll., Houston, 1998—; guided studies prof. Houston CC, 2001—03; mem. attendance com. Houston Ind. Sch. Dist., 2004—06, mem., shared decision making com., 2005—; v.p. Swift Entertainment, 2004—06. Social dir. United Way, Houston, 1990—91; active Centre Stage Theatre, Kingwood, 1995—2006. Mem.: Houston Fedn. Tchrs. Democrat. Roman Catholic. Avocations: tennis, reading, working out. Home: 40-22 60th St Woodside NY 11377 Office Phone: 713-805-5966. E-mail: constance_swift@hotmail.com.

SWIFT, DAVID A., lawyer; b. Piqua, Ohio, Nov. 4, 1952; s. Charles Joseph and Margaret Clara Swift; m. Karen Ann Zelenka, June 23, 1979; children: Matthew, Nicole, Daniel. BA, Miami U., Oxford, Ohio, 1975; JD, Ohio State U., Columbus, 1978. Bar: Ohio 1978. Assoc. ptnr. Porter, Wright, Morris and Arthur, Columbus, 1978—90; counsel, ptnr. Vorys, Sater, Seymour, Pease LLP, Columbus, 1990—. Bd. dirs. Boys & Girls Club Columbus, Columbus, 1998—2005; pres. Worthington Youth Boosters, Ohio, 2000—01. Fellow: Am. Coll. Trust and Estate Coun. (Best Lawyers in Am.); mem.: Am. Bar Assn., Ohio Bar Assn., Columbus Bar Assn. Roman Catholic. Avocations: golf, sports. Office: Vorys Sater Seymour Pease LLP 52 E Gay St Columbus OH 43215

SWIFT, DAVID L., manufacturing executive; B in Math. and Physics, Amherst Coll., Mass.; M in Electronics Engring., Dartmouth Coll., Hanover, NH; MBA, Harvard Bus. Sch. Chmn., pres. Greater Asia Region Eastman Kodak Co., Shanghai, pres. Kodak Profl. Group; exec. v.p. N.Am. region Whirlpool, 2001—06, pres. N.Am., bd. dirs., 2006—. Office: Whirlpool Corp 2000 N M-63 Benton Harbor MI 49022-2692 Office Phone: 269-923-5000.

SWIFT, EDWARD FOSTER, III, investment banker; b. Chgo., Nov. 1, 1923; s. Theodore Philip I and Elizabeth (Hoyt) S.; m. Joan McKelvy, July 2, 1947; children: Theodore Philip II, Edward McKelvy, Lockhart McKelvy, Elizabeth Hoyt; m. Carol Coffey Whipple, June 21, 1968. Grad., Hotchkiss Sch., 1941; BA, Yale U., 1945. With Esmark, Inc. (formerly Swift & Co.), 1947-75, asst. to v.p. charge meat packing plants, 1958, asst. v.p., 1958-59, v.p. for provisions, fgn., casings and storage, 1959-64, exec. v.p., 1964-75; vice-chmn. Chgo. Corp., 1975-79; vice chmn. Bacon, Whipple & Co., Chgo., 1980-84; mng. dir. A.G. Becker Paribas Inc., Chgo., 1984-85; with E.F. Hutton and Co., Chgo., 1985-87; mng. dir. Shearson Lehman Hutton Inc, Chgo., 1987-92. Bd. dirs. Santa Fe Pacific Pipelines, Inc. Chmn. So. Ind. chpt. United Negro Coll. Fund, 1956; trustee Northwestern U., Evanston, Ill.; bd. dirs. Northwestern Meml. Hosp., Chgo. Served to capt. U.S. Army, 1942-46. Mem. Chgo. Assn. Commerce and Industry (bd. dirs.), Scroll and Key, Chgo. Club, Racquet Club, Econ. Club, Valley Club, Comml. Club, Onwentsia Club, Old Elm ClubBirnam Wood Golf Club, Aurelian Honor Soc. Home: 1100 Pembridge Dr Apt 129 Lake Forest IL 60045

SWIFT, FRANK MEADOR, lawyer; b. NYC, Dec. 27, 1911; s. Frank Meador and Alberta (Rankin) S.; m. Harriet Elizabeth Simpson, May 30, 1944 (dec. Jan. 2003); children: Frank Meador (dec.), Thomas Lamar. Student, Emory U., 1930-32; LL.B., U. Ga., 1935. Bar: Ga. 1935. Partner Swift, Currie, McGhee & Hiers, Atlanta, 1965-82, of counsel, 1982—. Served to comdr. USNR, 1942-46. Mem. Am., Ga. bar assns., Lawyers Club Atlanta, Clubs: Piedmont Driving. Republican. Presbyterian. Office: Swift Currie McGhee & Hiers 1355 Peachtree St NE Ste 300 Atlanta GA 30309-3238 Home: 12 Renegar Way Apt 220 Saint Simons Island GA 31522

SWIFT, GREGORY, physicist; b. Omaha, July 7, 1952; BS in physics and math., U. Nebr., 1974; PhD in physics, U. Calif., Berkeley, 1980. Dir. postdoctoral fellow condensed matter and thermal physics group Los Alamos Nat. Lab., J. Robert Oppenheimer fellow condensed matter and thermal physics group, tech. staff mem. condensed matter and thermal physics group, lab. fellow condensed matter and thermal physics group. Author: Thermoacoustics: A Unifying Perspective for Some Engines and Refrigerators. Recipient Los Alamos Disting. Performance award, "Thermoacoustic natural-gas liquefier", 1996, R&D-100 award, "Acoustic Stirling Heat Engine", R&D mag., 1999, World Oil's New Horizons Idea award, "Thermoacoustics for gas liquefaction", 2003, Ernest and Orlando Laurence award, US Dept Energy, 2004, Los Alamos Disting. Patent award, 2004, Los Alamos Disting. Licensing award, 2004. Fellow: Am. Physical Soc., Los Alamos Nat. Lab., Acoustical Soc. Am. (Silver Medal in Physical Acoustics 2000). Achievements include 24 patents. Office: Los Alamos Nat Lab PO Mail Stop K764 Los Alamos NM 87545

SWIFT, JOHN FRANCIS, retired health care advertising company executive; b. NYC, June 15, 1935; s. John F. and Mary Veronica (Kehoe) S.; m. Eleanor H. Cunniff, Oct. 10, 1964; children— John Francis, Sharon Ann. BS in Bus. Adminstrn, Seton Hall U., 1960, postgrad., 1960-61. Mktg. research mgr. Lederle Labs. div. Cyanamid Internat., 1960-63; account exec. Robert A. Becker Advt. Agy., NYC, 1963-66; mgr. new products Chesebrough Ponds Co., NYC, 1966-68; v.p. Frohlich Intercon Co., NYC, 1968-72; pres., CEO, Lavey/Wolff/Swift, Inc., NYC, 1972-91, chmn., CEO, 1991-94; pres., CEO, BBDO Health & Med. Comms. Inc., 1977-91; chmn., CEO Health & Med. Comm. Inc., 1991-95, chmn. emeritus, 1995—, ret., 1995; vice-chmn. Lyons Lavey Nickel Swift, Inc., 1995—. Bd. govs. Cathedral Healthcare Systems, 1991-2004; chmn. emeritus Cathedral Healthcare Found., 1994-2004. Served with USN, 1955-57. Named to, Med. Advt. Hall of Fame, 2004. Mem. Pharm. Advt. Coun. (pres. 1979), Bio-Med. Mktg. Assn., Canoe Brook CC (Summit, N.J.), Manasquan River Golf Club, Skytop Club (Pa.), Royal Palm Yacht and Country Club, Boca Raton Resort and Club, N.Y. Athletic Club. Home: 12 Melrose Ln Green Village NJ 07935 also: 600 S Ocean Blvd Boca Raton FL 33432-6265 also: 76 Bay Point Harbour Point Pleasant NJ 08742-5509

SWIFT, JONATHAN, television personality, educator; b. Glasgow, Scotland, Apr. 26, 1932; arrived in U.S., 1948, naturalized, 1954; s. John Francis and Catherline Little (McGowan) S. MA, Wayne State U., 1957; postgrad., Ecole Normale Superieure, Paris, 1954-55; studied with Georges Jouatte, 1954-56; cert., Conservatoire Nat. de Musique, France, 1955; postgrad., U. Mich., 1959, Cambridge U., 1981; PhD, Mich. State U., 1983. On-camera tchr. French Sta. WTVS, Detroit, 1955-56, tchr. Am. lit., 1960-62; instr. French Wayne State U., Detroit, 1955-60; tchr. English, French and social studies Detroit Pub. Schs., 1957-64; tchr. English and history Glasgow Corp. Schs., 1967; tchr. English and French Livonia (Mich.) Pub. Schs., 1967; chmn. English dept. Stevenson H.S., Livonia, 1970-78, dir. Sch. Global Edn., 1978-98; dir. Ctr. Internat. Studies Madonna U., Mich., 1998—. Sr. lectr. Mich. State U. Debut in opera as Alfredo in La Traviata, 1961; host PBS TV and cmty. TV series Global Connections, Time Out for Opera, Dining Out With Jonathan Swift; leading tenor with Detroit Piccolo Opera Co., 1981-96, Detroit Grand Opera Assn., 1965, Mich. Opera Co., 1961-64; concert soloist with major symphonies in U.S., Can., Europe, Australia, 1961-81; appeared as tenor soloist in various radio and TV programs, 1961-81; rec. artist with Scotia and Andis, U.K.; contbr. articles and poems to profl. and lit. jours. Mem. adv. bd. Am. Mid.-East Christian Congress, 2003—. Named Fulbright scholar, 1954—55; named to Hall of Fame, Mich. Model UN, 1999; recipient French Govt. medal, 1954, tribute, Mich. State Legislature, 1984, NEA Applegate-Dorros award, 1987, MEA Siddall Internat. award, 1987, Philo Farnsworth award, Alliance Cmty. Media, 1990, 1994, 1995, 1998, 1998, 1999, 2000, Hometown award, Nat. Fedn. Local Cable Programmers, 1994, 1999, 2001, Nat. TV award, Nat. Assn. Telecomm. Officers and Advs., 1995, Human Rels. award, Livonia, 1999, Multi-Cultural award, Birmingham, Mich., 2000, 2004. Mem.: Confrerie de la Chaine des Rotisseurs, Descs. Knights of Garter, Soc. Friends of St. George. Roman Catholic. also: 4200 Telegraph Rd # 489 Bloomfield Hills MI 48302-2038 Office Phone: 248-734-5669. E-mail: jswift@madonna.edu.

SWIFT, MICHAEL RONALD, internist, educator; b. NYC, Feb. 5, 1935; s. Herbert Allen and Estelle (Clafter) S.; m. Ronnie Elaine Gorman, Nov. 27, 1971; children— Melissa, Amy, Laura. BA, Swarthmore Coll., 1955; MA in Math., U. Calif.-Berkeley, 1958; MD, NYU Sch. Med., 1962. bd. cert. Am. Bd. Internal Medicine, 1969, Am. Bd. Med. Genetics, 1987. Intern med. Coll. Physicians and Surgeons, NY, 1962—63; asst. resident med. NYU Bellevue Hosp., 1963—64; Instr., then asst. prof. NYU Sch. Medicine, NYC, 1966-70; asst. prof. med., 1970; assoc. prof., then prof. U. N.C., Chapel Hill, 1972-92, also chief genetics div.; prof. pediatrics, dir. Inst. for Genetic Analysis Diseases N.Y. Med. Coll., NYC, 1992—2001, prof. med., pathology, 1998. Dir. Inst. Genetic Analysis Common Diseases, 1994—2001, Disease Insight Rsch. Found., 2004—; CEO Sci. dir. Life Testing LLC (now GenDex LLC), 2001—. Author: Malignant Neoplasms in the Families of Patients with Ataxia Telangiectasia, 1976, Breast Cancer and other Cancers in Ataxia-Telangiectasia Families, 1987, Incidence of Cancer in 161 Families affected by Ataxia-Telangiectasia, 1991, Molecular Genotyping shows that Ataxia Telangiectasia Heterozygotes are Predisposed to Breas Cancer, 1996. Mem. AAAS, Am. Soc. Human Genetics, Alpha Omega Alpha. Achievements include discovery of Mutations in the A-T gene predispose carriers in the general population to cancer, particularly female breast cancer. Avocations: hiking, fishing, travel, theater. Office: Disease Insight Rsch Found 410 Saw Mill River Rd Ardsley NY 10502 Office Phone: 914-693-1123. Personal E-mail: msuriftmd@gmail.com.

SWIFT, PEGGY LYNETTE, elementary school educator; b. Forrest City, Ark., Aug. 6, 1969; d. Paul Edward Tabron and Willean Hicks; m. Leonard Terrell Swift, July 3, 1993; 1 child, Symone Sydnee. BS, U. Ark., Pine Bluff, 1992; MS in Edn., Ark. State U., Jonesboro, 2003. Cert. reading specialist Ark. 6th grade classroom tchr. Ector County Ind. Sch. Dist., Odessa, Tex., 1992—93; 4th grade classroom tchr. Marion Sch. Dist., Ark., 1993—2001; literacy coach Earle Sch. Dist., Ark., 2003—. Named Master Edcuator, Reading Renaissance /Accelerated Reading. Mem.: Memphis RAW Readers and Writers Sistaz, Alpha Kappa Alpha (life). Democrat. Baptist. Home: 601 Charles Wood Dr Marion AR 72364 Office: Earle Sch Dist PO Box 637 Earle AR 72331 Home Phone: 870-739-2711; Office Phone: 870-792-7816. Office Fax: 870-735-1704. Business E-Mail: leonardswift@aol.com.

SWIFT, ROBERT J., lawyer; b. Wilmington, Del., Jan. 17, 1948; BA, U. Del., 1972; JD, South Tex. Coll. Law, 1977. Bar: Tex. 1977. Assoc. Fulbright & Jaworski L.L.P., Houston, ptnr., 1985—, and co-head health law-litig. and adminstrn. dept. Mem. ABA, Am. Soc. Healthcare Risk Mgmt., State Bar Tex. (mem. health litigation/med. malpractice com.), Tex. Assn. Def. Counsel, Houston Bar Assn., Greater Houston Soc. Healthcare Risk Mgmt. Office: Fulbright & Jaworski LLP 1301 McKinney St Ste 5100 Houston TX 77010-3031 Office Phone: 713-651-5151. Office Fax: 713-651-5246. Business E-Mail: rswift@fulbright.com.

SWIFT, RONNIE GORMAN, psychiatrist, educator; b. NYC, Sept. 13, 1948; d. Joseph Harry Gorman and Mollie Samuels; m. Michael Ronald Swift, Nov. 27, 1971; children: Melissa, Laura, Amy. BS, CCNY, 1969; MD, U. N.C., Chapel Hill, 1975. Lic. physician N.Y., N.C. Resident U. N.C., Chapel Hill, 1978; pvt. practice psychiatry Chapel Hill, 1979—92; psychiatrist, dir. divsn. psychiatry genetics N.Y. Med. Ctr., Valhalla, 1992—97; chief psychiatry Met. Hosp. Ctr., NYC, 1998—, assoc. med. dirs., 1999—. Clin. assoc. prof. dept. psychiatry U. N.C., Chapel Hill, 1982—83, 1990—92, rsch. scientist Biol. Sci. Rsch. Ctr., 1988—92; assoc. prof. dept. psychology NY Med. Coll., Valhalla, 1992—2005, assoc. chmn. dept. psychiatry, 2004—, First Sidney E. Frank vis. prof., 2005; dir. outpatient svcs., dept. psychiatry Westchester County Med. Ctr., NY, 1995—98; network chief psychiatry and behavioral health svcs. Generations+/No. Manhattan Health Network, Health and Hosps. Corp. Orgn., NYC, 2001—; med. dir. Open Gate Residential Ctr., Somer, NY, 1992—; chief psychiatry Westchester Inst. Human Devel., N.Y. Med. Coll. Orgn., Valhalla, 1999—2001; cons., spkr. in field; mem., chairperson CME adv. bd. Neurosci. Edn. Inst., Carlsbad, Calif., 2006—; v.p. med. bd. Met. Hosp. Ctr., 2006—; psychiat. commentator various programs Fox 5 News. Contbr. articles to profl. jours. Fellow Falk fellow, Am. Psychiat. Assn., 1979. Mem.: Am. Psychiat. Assn., World Psychiat. Assn. (hon.), Alpha Omega Alpha. Avocations: cooking, reading, travel. Office: Metropolitan Hospital Center 1901 First Ave New York NY 10029

SWIFT, STEPHEN CHRISTOPHER, lawyer; b. NYC, Jan. 7, 1954; s. James Stephen and Rhoda Emma Jean (Howd) Swift. AA, Lansing CC, 1980; BA, Mich. State U., 1983; JD, Wayne State U., 1988. Bar: Mich. 1988, Hawaii 1989, U.S. Dist. Ct. Hawaii 1989, U.S. Ct. Fed. Claims 1990, U.S. Ct. Appeals (fed., DC and 9th cirs.) 1990, DC 1991, U.S. Supreme Ct. 1992, Va. 1995, U.S. Dist. Ct. (ea. and we. dists.) Va. 1995, U.S. Bankruptcy Ct. (ea. and we. dists.) Va. 1995, U.S. Ct. Appeals (4th cir.) 1995, U.S. Dist. Ct. DC 1997, U.S. Tax Ct. 1997, Md. 1998, U.S. Dist. Ct. Md. 1998, U.S. Ct. Internat. Trade 2000, U.S. Dist. Ct. (ea. dist.) Mich. 2002, registered: (patent atty.) 1994. Pvt. practice, Honolulu, 1989—94, Arlington, Va., 1995—2003, Alexandria, 2003—. Mem.: ABA, Prince George's County Bar Assn., Bar Assn. Montgomery County, Md., Alexandria Bar Assn., Bar Assn. DC, Am. Intellectual Property Law Assn., Fed. Cir. Bar Assn., Fed. Bar Assn. Office: Swift Law Office 1800 Diagonal Rd Ste 600 Alexandria VA 22314-2840 Office Phone: 703-418-0000. Business E-Mail: steve@swift.law.pro.

SWIFT, STEPHEN JENSEN, federal judge; b. Salt Lake City, Sept. 7, 1943; s. Edward A. and Maurine (Jensen) S.; m. Lorraine Burnell Facer, Aug. 4, 1972; children: Carter, Stephanie, Spencer, Meredith, Hunter. BS, Brigham Young U., 1967; JD, George Washington U., 1970. Trial atty. US Dept. Justice, Washington, 1970-74, asst. US atty. tax divsn. San Francisco, 1974-77; v.p., sr. tax counsel Bank Am. N.T. & S.A., San Francisco, 1977-83; judge US Tax Ct., Washington, 1983—98, 2000—, sr. judge, 1998—2000. Adj. prof. Golden Gate U., San Francisco, 1976-83, 2005—, U. Balt., 1987— Mem. ABA, Calif. Bar Assn., DC Bar Assn. Office: US Tax Ct 400 2nd St NW Washington DC 20217-0002 Office Phone: 202-521-0760.

SWIGER, ELINOR PORTER, lawyer; b. Cleve., Aug. 1, 1927; d. Louie Charles and Mary Isabelle (Shank) Porter; m. Quentin Gilbert Swiger, Feb. 5, 1955; children: Andrew Porter, Calvin Gilbert, Charles Robinson. BA, Ohio State U., 1949, JD, 1951. Bar: Ohio 1951, Ill. 1979. Sr. assoc., now of counsel Robbins, Schwartz, Nicholas, Lifton & Taylor, Ltd., Chgo., 1979—. Author: (book) Mexico for Kids, 1971, Europe for Young Travelers, 1972, The Law and You, 1973 (Literary Guild award), Law in Everyday Life, 1977, Careers in the Legal Professions, 1978, Women Lawyers at Work, 1978. Mem. Glenview (Ill.) Fire and Police Commn., 1976—86; chmn. Glenview Zoning Bd. Appeals, 1987—97. Mem.: Chgo. Bar Assn. (chmn. legis. exec. com. 1990—92), Women Bar Assn. Ill., Ill. Coun. Sch. Attys. (past chmn.), Ohio State U. Coll. Law Alumni Coun., Soc. Midland Authors. Republican. Home: 1933 Burr Oak Dr Glenview IL 60025 Office: Robbins Schwartz Nicholas Lifton & Taylor 20 N Clark St Ste 900 Chicago IL 60602-4115

SWIGER, ELIZABETH DAVIS, chemist, educator; b. Morgantown, W Va, June 27, 1926; d. Hannibal Albert and Tyreeca Elizabeth (Stemple) Davis; m. William Eugene Swiger, June 2, 1948 (dec.); children: Susan Elizabeth Swiger Knotts-Case, Wayne William; m. James E. Coleman, Dec. 11, 2004. BS in Chemistry, W.Va. U., 1948, MS in Chemistry, 1952, PhD in Chemistry, 1964. Instr. math. Fairmont State Coll., 1948-49, instr. math. and phys. sci., 1956-57, instr. chemistry, 1957-60, from asst. prof. to assoc. prof., 1960—66, prof., 1966-92, chmn., divsn. sci., math. and health careers, 1991-92; NSF fellow rsch. W.Va. U., Morgantown, 1963-64, prof. emerita, 1992. Advisor Am. Chem. Soc. student affiliates, 1965-88. Author: Morton Family History, 1984-2004, Davis-Winters Family History, 1994—, Civil War Letters and Diary of Joshua Winters, 1991, 2d edit., 1996; contbr. articles to profl. jour. Chmn. Blacks Chapel Meml. Found., 1993—; rep. adv. coun. to Bd. Regents Fairmont State Coll., Charleston, W.Va., 1977—78, rep. instl. bd. advisors, 1990—92. NSF grantee, 1963; named Outstanding Prof. W.Va. Legislature, Charleston, 1990. Mem.: Am. Chem. Soc. (advisor student affiliates 1965—88, sec. chmn. North W.Va. 1975—83), W.Va. Acad. Sci. (life; pres. 1978—79, exec. com. edn. chmn. 1990—93), Nature Conservancy (bd. dir. W.Va. chpt. 1970—86, chmn. 1980—82), Prickett's Fort Meml. Found. (life; bd. dir. 1988—2000, chmn. elect 1990—92, chmn. 1992—96, bd. dir 2002—), Marion County Hist. Soc. (life), Fairmont Lions Club, Morning Gardeners Garden Club (pres. 1999—2003). Republican. Methodist. Avocations: local history, genealogy, gardening, computers, quilting. Home: 1599 Hillcrest Rd Fairmont WV 26554-4807 Home (Winter): 242 Laird Dr Freeport FL 32439

SWIGERT, JAMES MACK, lawyer; b. Carthage, Ill., Sept. 25, 1907; s. James Ross and Pearl (Mack) S.; m. Alice Francis Titcomb Harrower, July 7, 1931 (dec. 1990); children: Oliver, David Ladd, Sally Harper (Mrs. Hamilton). Student, Grinnell Coll., 1925-27; SB, Harvard U., 1930, LLB, 1935. Bar: Ill. 1935, Ohio 1937. With Campbell, Clithero & Fischer, Chgo., 1935-36, Taft, Stettinius & Hollister, Cin., 1936—, ptnr., 1948-79, sr. ptnr. and chmn. exec. com., 1979-85, of counsel, 1985—. Dir., mem. exec. com.

Union Cen. Life Ins. Co., 1963-79; dir., chmn. audit com. Philips Industries, 1975-82. Author articles on labor rels. and labor law. Bd. dirs. Cin. Symphony Orch., 1976-78; trustee, chmn. exec. com. Am. Music Scholarship Assn., 1987-92. Recipient Lifetime Achievement in Law award, Cin. Bar Fund, 2002, Great Living Cincinnatian award, 2004. Mem.: Harvard Law Club (past pres.), Recess Club (past pres.), Tennis Club (past pres.), Queen City Club, Queen City Optimists Club (past pres., psat bd. dirs.), Cin. Country Club (past v.p., dir.). Republican. Presbyterian. Home: 2121 Alpine Pl Cincinnati OH 45206-2690 Office: 425 Walnut St Ste 1800 Cincinnati OH 45202 Home Phone: 513-221-4983; Office Phone: 513-357-9360. Business E-Mail: swigert@taftlaw.com.

SWIGGER, KEITH, library and information scientist, educator; b. Hutchinson, Kans., Feb. 3, 1943; s. Paul Clarke and Loneta (Miller) S.; children: Jessica, Nathaniel; m. Cindy Johnson Potter, Nov. 29, 1997. BA, U. Chgo., 1965, MA, 1975, Ind. U., 1967; PhD, U. Iowa, 1973. Sketch-writer Marquis Who's Who, Chgo., 1963-67; teaching asst. Ind. U., Bloomington, 1967, U. Iowa, Iowa City, 1968-73, lectr., 1973-74, libr., 1976-77; asst. prof. East Tex. State U., Commerce, 1977-81; asst. prof. libr. scis. Tex. Woman's U., Denton, 1981-85, assoc. prof., 1985-89, prof., 1989—, interim dean Sch. Libr. Sci., 1991-92, dean Sch. Libr. and Info. Studies, 1992-2000, dir. Sch. Libr. and Info. Studies, 2001—02, dir. Ctr. for Consulting and Planning, 1997—, dean Coll. Profl. Edn., 2000—03, dir. Gear Up fed. grant program, 2002—03. Mem. adv. com. continuum libr. edn. We. Coun. State Librs., 2003—; cons. in field. Co-editor Jour. of Youth Svcs., 1997-2000; contbr. numerous articles to profl. jours. Bd. dirs. ACLU, Denton, 1990-92, Emily Fowler Pub. Libr., Denton, 1995-97, vice chair, 1997; mem. Tex. Edn. Tech. Coord. Coun., 2000-03; delegate Tex. Dem. Party state convention, 2004. Rsch. grantee OCLC, Inc., 1990-91, Career Tng. grantee U.S. Office Edn., 1990-98; postdoctoral fellow Coun. on Libr. Resources U. Chgo., 1974-75; recipient Svc. award Nat. Story-telling Assn., 1998. Mem. ACLU, Am. Studies Assn., ALA, Assn. Coll. and Rsch. Librs., Nat. Wildlife Fedn., Sierra Club, World Wildlife Fund, Audubon Soc., Ft. Worth Botanical Soc. Democrat. Office: Tex Womans U Sch Libr Info Studies PO Box 425438 Denton TX 76204-5438 Personal E-mail: keithswigger@charter.net.

SWIHART, JAMES W., JR., diplomat; b. Washington, July 25, 1946; s. James Wilbur and Ruth (Inge) S.; m. Ellen Jane Cendo Mar. 30, 1968; children: Jennifer Anne, Christopher John; m. Kimberly Ann Mack, May 12, 2001. BA, Columbia Coll., 1968. Vice consul Am. Embassy, Belize, Brit. Honduras, 1970-72, 2nd sec., polit. officer Belgrade, Yugoslavia, 1972-74; ops. officer ops. ctr. Dept. State, Washington, 1974-75, country officer for Italy and the Vatican, 1975-78, polit./mil. officer for U.S. Mission Berlin, 1978-82, officer C.S.C.E. Bur. European Affairs Washington, 1982-83, officer for Fed. Republic of Germany, 1983-84; consul gen., prin. officer U.S. Consulate Gen., Zagreb, Yugoslavia, 1984-1988; mem. sr. seminar Dept. State, Washington, 1988-89, dir. Bur. for Ea. European and Yugoslavia Affairs, 1989-1991; min. counselor, deputy chief of mission Am. Embassy, Vienna, Austria, 1991-94, Chargé d'Affaires ad interim, 1993, amb. to Lithuania Vilnius, 1994-97; sr. fellow Inst. for Strategic Studies/Nat. Def. U., Washington, 1997-99; polit. advisor U.S. Space Command, Colorado Springs, Colo., 1999—. Avocations: piano, harpsichord, jogging, classical music. Office: US Space Command Peterson AFB 250 S Peterson Blvd Ste 116 Colorado Springs CO 80914-3285

SWIMMER, ROSS OWEN, federal official; b. Oklahoma City, Oct. 26, 1943; s. Robert Otis and Virginia Marie (Pounder) S.; m. Margaret Ann McConnell, June 30, 1965; children— Joseph Ross, Michael David. BA, U. Okla., 1965, JD, 1967. Bar: Okla. 1967. Partner firm Hanson, Peterson, Thompkins, Oklahoma City, 1967-72; counsel Cherokee Nation, Tahlequah, Okla., 1972-74, prin. chief, 1975-85; exec. v.p. 1st Nat. Bank, Tahlequah, 1974, pres., 1974-84; asst. sec. Indian Affairs Dept. Interior, 1985-89; of counsel Hall, Estill, Hardwick, Gable, Golden & Nelson, Tulsa, 1989—92; spl. trustee Am. Indians US Dept. Interior, Washington, 2003—. Mem. ABA, Okla. Bar Assn., Cherokee Nat. Hist. Soc. (pres. 1979-80), Okla. Hist. Soc. Republican. Office: US Dept Interior 1849 C St NW Rm 5140 Washington DC 20240 Personal E-mail: rswimmer@sbcglobal.net.

SWINAND, ANDREW, advertising executive; b. 1968; m. Laura Swinand; children: Tanner, Georgia. BS economics, U. of Pa., 1990. Account supervisor BBDO, Los Angeles; brand mgr. Procter & Gamble Co., Cincinnati; gen. mgr. Starcom USA, San Francisco, 2000—02, Chicago, 2002—05, exec. v.p., 2005—. Reserve 3rd infantry div USAR, 1990—94. Named one of the best 40 under 40 in business, Crain's Chicago Business, 2005; scholar Reserve Officers' Training Corps, U.S. Army. Office: c/o Starcom 35 W Wacker Dr Chicago IL 60601 *

SWINBURN, CAROL DITZLER, retired state and municipal agency administrator; b. Washington, July 9, 1945; d. John Nevin and Mildred Peterman Ditzler; m. Charles Swinburn, Dec. 16, 1972; children: Ann Elizabeth, Catherine Knowles. BA, Ursinus Coll., Collegeville, Pa., 1967. Founder, dir. The Healthy Gourmet, West Chester, Va., 1990—95; campaign exec. United Way, Alexandria, 1994—95; acting dir., counselor Women's Empowerment Program, Alexandria, 1995—97; dir., coord. Alexandria Cmty. Criminal Justice Svcs., Va., 1997—2004, sr. staff, 1997—2004. Author: (cookbook) Recipes from the Healthy Gourmet Cooking Classes. Shelter staff vol. Domestic Violence Program, Alexandria, 1995—97; shelter staff vol. teen runaway shelter This Way House, Alexandria, 1994—95; parent edn. chair PTO, Alexandria, 1994—96, mem., fundraising chair Chadds Ford, Pa., 1986—90; bd. dirs. Delray Beach Condo Assn., 2006—07. Named Woman of Yr., Alexandria Commn. on Women, 1997. Mem.: NOW, Planned Parenthood, Emily's List, Boca Raton Resort & Club. Democrat. Avocations: travel, beachwalking, yoga. Home Phone: 561-266-0756.

SWINBURN, CHARLES, retired rail transportation executive; b. Bowness on Windermere, Cumbria, Eng., Apr. 11, 1942; came to U.S., 1949; s. Joseph and Myra (Sullivan) S.; m. Carol Ann Ditzler, Dec. 16, 1972; children: Ann Elizabeth, Catherine Knowles. BA in Psychology, Princeton U., NJ, 1963; MBA, Harvard U., Cambridge, Mass., 1971; JD, U. Pa., Phila., 1993. Industry analyst US Dept. Transp., Washington, 1971-73, chief Industry Analysis Div., 1973-76, dep. asst. sec., 1979-83; assoc. adminstr. fed. assistance Fed. R.R. Adminstrn., Washington, 1976-79; v.p. FS Rollins Environ. Svcs. Inc., Wilmington, Del., 1983-90; atty. Morgan, Lewis & Bockius, Washington, 1993—2004; CEO RailAmerica, Inc., Boca Raton, Fla., 2004—07; ret. Capt. USMC, 1963-69; major USMCR, 1970-75. Decorated DFC (2), Air medal (35); recipient Presdl. Disting. Exec. award, 1980, Dept. Transp. Meritorious Achievement award, 1976, 78, 81

SWINDELL, ARCHIE CALHOUN, JR., statistician, consultant; b. Sept. 26, 1936; s. Archie Calhoun and Louise Evelyn (Ellis) S.; m. Dolores Dyer Holland, Dec. 28, 1962; children: Randy Zidick, Matthew Earle. BS in Chemistry, So. Meth. U., 1958; M in Nutritional Sci., Cornell U., 1965, PhD in Biochemistry, 1968. NIH postdoctoral fellow Duke U. Med. Ctr., Durham, NC, 1968-70; rsch. sci. positions in biochemistry, pharmacology, stats. Pfizer, Inc., Groton, Conn., 1970-95; statis. cons., 1995—. Contbr. articles on cholesterol metabolism, hormone action, cell culture, actions of drugs, data analysis, stats. to profl. jours., 1968-2004; patentee several anti-atherosclerosis agts. Active Town Coun., Groton, 1991-95, Bd. of Edn., 1997—; bd. dirs. LEARN, 2001-07. With US Army, 1958—61. Mem. AAAS, Am. Statis. Assn., Am. Heart Assn., Am. Assn. Artificial Intelligence, Sigma Xi, Conn. Botanical Soc., Math. Assn. Am. Avocations: nature photography, hiking, botany. Home and Office: 192 Monument St Groton CT 06340-3915 Home Phone: 860-449-8658; Office Phone: 860-449-8658. Personal E-mail: swindellac@tvcconnect.net.

SWINDELLS, SUSAN, HIV specialist; b. Manchester, Eng., Apr. 11, 1954; came to US, 1979; d. Charles Hubert and Nanette May S.; m. Timothy A. Galbraith, Apr. 22, 1983; children: Emily, Charles. MB, BS, U. Coll., London, 1977. Med. house officer Univ. Coll. Hosp., London, 1977-78; surg. house officer Royal No. Hosp., London, 1978-79; resident family medicine U. Wash., Seattle, 1979-80; staff physician N.W. Emergency Physicians, Seattle, 1980-81; trainee gen. practitioner U. Manchester, England, 1981-82; resident psychiatry St. Bernard's Hosp., London, 1982-83; staff physician Cmty. Physicians, Inc., St. Louis, 1983-84; primary physician Southside Family Health Ctr. Columbus Health Dept., Ohio, 1988-91; clin. asst. prof. dept. medicine Ohio State U. Hosps., Columbus, 1988—91; preceptor dept. family medicine Grant Med. Ctr., Columbus, 1988—91; HIV clinic med. dir., asst. prof. medicine dept. internal medicine U. Nebr. Med. Ctr., Omaha, 1991—96, HIV clinic med. dir., assoc. prof., 1996—2000, co-dir. Ctr. Neurovirology and Neurodegenerative Disorders, 1998—, assoc. prof., 2000—02, Terry K. Watanabe Disting. Chair HIV/AIDS Rsch. and Care, 2001—, prof., 2002—; prin. investigator AIDS Clin. Trial Grp. Subunit, 1992—; dir. Nebr. AIDS Edn. and Tng. Ctr., 1992—; asst. clin. prof. depts. med. microbiol. and medicine Creighton U. Sch. Medicine, Omaha, 1994—96. Cons. Columbus Health Dept., 1988—91, chair pharmacy rev. com., 1988—91; mem. AIDS tech. adv. com. Nebr. State Health Dept., 1991, chair drug utilization rev. com., 92, mem. care options subcommittee, 92, mem. health care workers and invasive procedures subcommittee, 92; mem. systemic mycoses pathogen study grp. AIDS Clin. Trials Grp., Rockville, Md., 1994—96. Contbr. articles to profl. jours., chapters to books; co-editor: Mountain-Plains Regional AIDS Edn. and Tng. Ctr., 5th edit., 1994, Neurology of AIDS, 1998. Vol. Columbus Free Clinic, Ohio, 1989-91; med. cons. AIDS Coalition for Empowerment, 1992; co-chair Nebr. Walk for AIDS; mem. adv. bd. Wellness Ctr., 1994; bd. dirs. Nebr. AIDS project 1996; mem. adv. com. Hospice House, 1997. Recipient Caregiver award, AIDS Interfaith Network Omaha, 1999. Mem.: Royal Coll. Gen. Practitioners, UK, Nebr. Med. Assn., Am. Acad. Family Practitioners, AMA, Internat. Soc. NeuroVirology (founding mem. 1998). Office: Dept Internal Medicine Sect Infectious Disease 985400 Nebr Med Ctr Omaha NE 68198-5400 E-mail: sswindells@unmc.edu.

SWINDLE, RALPH WILSON, JR., research psychologist; b. Palo Alto, Calif., Nov. 17, 1951; s. Ralph Wilson and Jewel Marie Swindle; m. Renee Marie Pobuda, May 8, 1983; children: David Michael, Jeremy Christopher, Natalie Diane. BA Magna Cum Laude in social ecology, U. Calif., Irvine, 1973; PhD in clin. cmty psychology, Ind. U., 1983. Cert. Psychologist, Health Svcs. Provider Ind. Health Svcs. Profl. Bur., 1984. Psychol. intern Quinco Cons. Ctr., Columbus, Ind., 1977—78; program evaluator So. Ctrl. Cmty. Mental Health Ctr., Bloomington, Ind., 1978—87; rsch. psychologist VA Health Svcs. R&D, Stanford U., Palo Alto, Calif., 1987—94, VA Health Svcs. R&D, Ind. U., Indpls., 1994—99; mgr., outcomes rsch., us med. divsn. Eli Lilly & Co., Indpls., 1999—2005, sr. rsch. scientist, 2005—07, rsch. advisor, 2007—. Contbr. chapters to books, more than 50 articles to profl. jours. Recipient Nicolas Aeberhardt award, Outstanding Freshman, U. Calif., Irvine, 1969; fellow Clin. Traineeship in Alcoholism Rsch., NIAAA, 1975-1977; grantee NIMH Rsch. Grant (Heller & Swindle), NIMH, 1995-1998; Summer fellow in Evaluation Rsch., 1975, Pre-Doctoral Clin. Tng. fellowship, 1973-1975. Office: Outcomes Rsch USMD DC 4113 Lilly Corp Ctr Indianapolis IN 46285 Home Phone: 317-843-9447. Office Fax: 317-276-8268. Personal E-mail: pobudaswindle@earthlink.net. Business E-Mail: swindle@lilly.com.

SWINDLE, SHANNON, chef; Asst. pastry chef Star Canyon, Mansion at Turtle Creek; pastry chef Abacus, Dallas, Craft, Dallas. Named one of Dallas' Rising Stars, StarChefs.com, 2007. Office: Craft 2440 Victory Park Ln Ste 100 Dallas TX 75219 Office Phone: 214-397-4111. *

SWING, ELIZABETH SHERMAN, education educator; b. Boston, June 29, 1927; d. James Beatty and Hilda (Ford) Sherman; m. Peter Gram Swing, May 27, 1948; children: Pamela, Timothy (dec.), Bradford. AB cum laude, Harvard U., 1949, MA, 1952; PhD, U. Pa., 1979. Tchr. English Marple Newtown High Sch., Newtown Sq., 1966-73; rsch. asst. U. Pa., Phila., 1973-75; asst. prof. West Chester State U., Pa., 1975-77, St. Joseph's U., Phila., 1978-84, assoc. prof., 1984-89, prof. edn., 1989—99, prof. emeritus, 1999—. Co-coord. commn. V, World Congress of Comparative Edn. Socs., Prague, 1992, co-coord. European commn., 1996. Author: Bilingualism and Linguistic Segregation in the Schools of Brussels, 1980; Editor: Inside Dunwoody, 2005; co-editor: Problems and Prospects in European Education, 2000; mem. editl. bd. European Edn., 1983—; contbr. articles to profl. jours. Collaborative com. Phila. Schs. and Colls., 1983-90; bd. dirs. Orchestra 2001, 1997-2003. Decorated knight Order of Crown (Belgium), 1989; recipient Legion of Honor award Chapel of Four Chaplains, 1984; grantee NEH Summer Seminar, 1981, U.S. Dept. Edn., 1984-87, Fulbright Found., 1989-90; vis. fellow U. London Inst. Edn., 1989-90. Mem. AAUP, Comparative Edn. Soc. Europe, Comparative and Internat. Edn. Soc. (bd. dirs. 1988-91, historian 1999-, hon. fellow 2000). Home: 3500 West Chester Pike Newtown Square PA 19073-4101 Personal E-mail: eswing1@verizon.net.

SWING, WILLIAM LACY, ambassador; b. Lexington, NC, Sept. 11, 1934; s. Baxter Dermot and Mary Frances (Barbee) S.; m. Yuen Fong Cheong; children: Brian Curtis, Gabrielle. AB, Catawba Coll., 1956, LLD (hon.), 1980; BD, Yale U., 1960; postgrad., Oxford U., Eng., U. Tuebingen, Germany, 1961, Hofstra U., LLD (hon.), 1994. Vice consul Am. Consulate, Port Elizabeth, Republic of South Africa, 1963-66; internat. economist Bur. Econ. Affairs US Dept. State, 1966-68; consul, chief consular sect. Am. Consulate Gen., Hamburg, Germany, 1968-72; internat. rels. officer, desk officer Fed. Republic Germany US Dept. State, Washington, 1972-74; dep. chief of mission, counselor Am. Embassy, Bangui, Ctrl. African Republic, 1974-76; fellow Ctr. for Internat. Affairs Harvard U., 1977-79; US amb. to People's Republic of Congo US Dept. State, 1979-81, US amb. to Republic of Liberia Monrovia, 1981-85, US amb. to South Africa, 1989-92, US amb. to Fed. Republic of Nigeria, 1992-93, US amb. to Haiti Port-au-Prince, 1993-98, US amb. to Dem. Republic of the Congo (formerly Zaire), Kinshasha, 1998—2001; spl. rep. of Sec-Gen. for Western Sahara UN, 2001—03, spl. rep. of Sec.-Gen. for Democratic Republic of Congo, 2003—. Dir. Fgn. Svc. Career Devel. and Assignments, 1985-87; sr. dep. asst. sec. state for pers., 1987-89. Co-editor: Education for Decision, 1963, U.S. African Policy and the Case of South Africa: Dilemas and Priorities, 1977, Haiti: In Physical Contact with History, 1995; chpt. chpts. to books. Bd. dirs. Outward Bound Found. South Africa. Recipient Meritorious Honor award USIA, 1971, Superior Honor award Dept. State, 1985, Presdl. Disting. Svc. award, 1985, Presdl. Meritorious Svc. award, 1987, 90, 94, Equal Employment Opportunity award Dept. State, 1988, Disting. Honor award, 1994, Valor award, 1995, Disting. Svc. award, 1996, Disting. Pub. Svc. award USCG, 1998, U.S. Presdl. Cert. of Commendation, 1998, Disting. Alumnus award, Yale U. Divinity Sch., 1995. Mem. Am. Acad. Diplomacy, Army and Navy Club. Yale Club (Washington and N.Y.C.), Harvard Club, Internat. Club, Lions. Mem. United Ch. of Christ. Home: 6002 Paradise Point Dr Miami FL 33157 Office: MONUC-HQ Kinshasa PO Box 4653 Grand Central Sta New York NY 10163-4653 Office Phone: 011-243-81-890-7646. E-mail: swing@un.org, swingwl@yahoo.com, ywswing@bellsouth.net.

SWINNEY, CAROL JOYCE, secondary school educator; Langs. tchr. Hugoton (Kans.) High Sch., 1972-98; dir. distance learning S.W. Plains Regional Svcs. Ctr., Kans., 1998—. Named Kans. Tchr. of Yr., Disney for Lang. Tchr. of Yr., 1993, Milken Nat. Educator, 1992. Office: PO Drawer 1010 Sublette KS 67877-1010

SWINNEY, HARRY LEONARD, physics professor; b. Opelousas, La., Apr. 10, 1939; s. Leonard Robert and Ethel Ruth (Bertheaud) S.; m. Gloria Luyas, Oct. 21, 1967 (dec. Oct. 1997); 1 child, Brent Luyas (dec.); m. Lizabeth Kelley, Aug. 12, 2000. BS in Physics, Rhodes Coll., 1961; PhD in Physics, Johns Hopkins U., 1968. Vis. asst. prof. Johns Hopkins U., 1970-71; asst. prof. physics NYU, 1971-73; assoc. prof. CCNY, 1973-77, prof., 1978; prof. physics U. Tex., Austin, 1978—, Trull Centennial prof., 1984-90, Sid Richardson Found. regents chair, 1990—, dir. Ctr. Nonlinear Dynamics, 1985—. Morris Loeb lectr. Harvard U., 1982. Editor: Hydrodynamic Instabilities and the Transition to Turbulence, 1985; contbr. articles to profl. jours. Regents chair Sid Richardson Found., 1990—. Grantee NSF, Dept. Energy, NASA, Office Naval Rsch., Welch, others; Guggenheim fellow, 1982-83. Fellow AAAS, Am. Phys. Soc. (exec. bd. 1992-94, Fluid Dynamics prize 1996); mem. NAS, Am. Acad. Arts and Scis., Am. Assn. Physics Tchrs. Democrat. Methodist. Office: U Tex Dept Physics Ctr Nonlinear Dynamics Austin TX 78712 E-mail: Swinney@physics.utexas.edu.

SWINSON, SARA HOPE, writer, chaplain; b. Denver, Sept. 10, 1964; d. Honey Constance Harriet Shulman and Thomas Stanley Swinson. BA in Bible and Religion, Montreat, NC, 1993; MA in Exegetical Theology, Covenant Theol. Sem., Mo., 1996. Social worker MERS, Goodwill Industries, St. Louis, 1998—2005; media coord. Zip for Senate, Jefferson County, Mo., 2005; with hosp. chaplaincy, clin. pastoral edn. St. Louis U. Hosp., 2005—06; vocat. evaluator, social worker Lakes Country Resource Ctrs., St. Louis, 2005—06; hosp. chaplain, resident in clin. pastoral edn. St. Luke's Hosp., St. Louis, 2006—. Columnist St. Louis Suburban Jours., 2004—05; staff writer, music journalist Nighttimes.com, St. Louis, 2005—; freelance writer. Writer (humor columns, social critiques, revs.) Opinion Shaper's Columnist, archaeological (byzantine mosaic floor) Abila of the Decapolis; exhibit, Prophetic Self-Portrait. Staff writer New City Fellowship's Mainliner, St. Louis, 2001—. Mem.: St. Louis Writer's Guild, St. Mary's Hosp. Bioethics Com. (com. mem. representing patient's rights 2001—03), Ctr. for Culture and Bioethics. Independent. Avocations: travel, painting, acting, collecting globes and pens. Home: 10331 Oxford Hill Dr Apt 3 Saint Louis MO 63146 Personal E-mail: shswinson@yahoo.com.

SWINT, KERWIN, political science professor; s. Harvey and Ann Swint; m. Sandy Stratton, Dec. 5, 1987; children: Jacob, Zach, Matthew. BA, U. Ga., Athens, 1985; MEd, U. Ga., 1990; PhD, Ga. State U., Atlanta, 1995. Confidential asst. US Dept. Commerce, DC, 1985—87; staff asst. US Commn. Civil rights, DC, 1987—88; account exec. Cohn & Wolfe Pub. Rels., Atlanta, 1988—89; tchg. asst. Ga. State U., 1990—92; prof. Kennesaw State U., Ga., 1992—. Campaign cons. SE Polit. Grp., Marietta, Ga., 1996—2004. Author: (book) Mudslingers: The Top 25 Negative Political Campaigns of All Time. Named one of Forty Under Forty, Ga. Trend, 1998; recipient Disting. Svc. award, Kennesaw State U., 2006. Avocations: hiking, tennis.

SWINTON, JEFFREY CHEEVER, lawyer; b. Salt Lake City, June 22, 1947; s. Kenneth Perry and Venice (Cheever) S.; m. Heidi Sorensen, Apr. 14, 1972; children: Cameron, Daniel, Jonathan, Ian. BA, U. Utah, 1971, JD, 1974. Bar: Utah 1974, U.S. Ct. Appeals (10th cir.) 1985, U.S. Supreme Ct. 1985. Ptnr. Stringham, Larsen, Mazuran & Sabin, Salt Lake City, 1974-79; sr. v.p. Ruti-Sweetwater, Inc., Salt Lake City, 1979-84; ptnr. Larsen, Mazuran & Verhaaren, Salt Lake City, 1984-85, Jensen & Swinton, Salt Lake City, 1986-87; ptnr., v.p., bd. dirs. Woodbury, Jensen, Kesler & Swinton, Salt Lake City, 1988-91; ptnr. Stoker & Swinton, Salt Lake City, 1991—. Assoc. editor Utah Bar Jour., 1973-74; editor Summation: Jour. Utah Law, 1973. Chmn., v.p., del. Salt Lake City Rep. Com., 1975-88; trustee Bus. Industry Cmty. Edn. Partnership, Salt Lake City, 1979-80; mem. panel judges Utah Pub. Employees Assn., 1980-83, 85-87; bd. dirs., pres. Work Activities Ctr. for Handicapped Adults, Salt Lake City, 1987-93; chair Utah state bd. svcs. People with Disabilities, 1993-99, govs. coun., 1996; dist. chmn. Boy Scouts Am., Salt Lake City, 1987-94, coun. exec. bd., 2004—; bd. dirs. Homeless Youth Resource Ctr., 1998-2000, Cmty. Devel. Corp. Utah, 2002—; exec. dir. Salt Lake Inner City Project, 1996-2003; chmn. Pioneer Region Welfare Com., 1998-2003; bishop Mormon Ch., 1977-85, stake pres., 1994-2003, Area Seventy, 2002-06, LDS mission pres. in England, 2006—. Mem. ABA, ATLA, Utah State Bar Assn. (chair franchise law sect. 1997-98, 2003-06), Nat. Futures Assn. (arbitrator 1991), U. Utah Law Sch. Alumni Assn. (treas., trustee 1979-83), Young Alumni Assn. U. Utah (pres. 1981-83), Soc. Bar and Gavel (pres. 1976-78), Beehive, Owl and Key, Skull and Bones, Rotary (pres. 1993). Mem. Lds Ch. Avocations: tennis, golf, singing. Office: 311 S State St Ste 400 Salt Lake City UT 84111-2382 Office Phone: 801-359-4000. Business E-Mail: JCSwinton@gmail.com.

SWINTON, STEPHEN P., lawyer; b. Charles City, Iowa, Sept. 25, 1951; BS, Iowa State Univ., 1973; JD with honors, Drake Univ., 1982. Bar: Calif. 1982, US Dist. Ct. (so., no., ctrl. dist. Calif.), US Ct. Appeals (9th, Fed. cir.), US Patent & Trademark Office, US Supreme Ct. Process & mfg. engr. Proctor & Gamble; extern Judge Roy L. Stephenson, US Ct. Appeals, 8th cir.; ptnr., bus. litigation Cooley Godward LLP, San Diego, 1994—, chmn. Intellectual Property Litigation practice. Faculty mem. Nat. Inst. Trial Advocacy. Served surface line officer USN. Mem.: ABA, State Bar Calif., San Diego Bar Assn., Order of the Coif. Office: Cooley Godward LLP 4401 Eastgate Mall San Diego CA 92121-1909 Office Phone: 858-550-6028. Office Fax: 858-550-6420. Business E-Mail: swintonsp@cooley.com.

SWIONTKOWSKI, MARC FRANCIS, orthopedist; b. Elizabeth, NJ, Sept. 15, 1951; s. William Robert and Agnes Eileen (Baker) S.; m. Beth Ellen, Sept. 2, 1972. BA, Calif. State U., 1973; MD, U. So. Calif., 1979. Gen. surgeon Univ. Wash., Seattle, 1979-80, orthopaedic residence, 1980-84; orthopedic cons. Kllimanjoro Christian Med. Ctr., Moshi, Tanzania, 1984; research assoc. Lab. for Experiment, Davos, Swit.; asst. prof. Vanderbilt Univ. Surgery, Nashville, 1985-86; assoc prof. Vanderbilt Univ., Nashville, 1986-88; assoc. prof. Univ. Wash., Seattle, 1988-91, prof., 1991-97; prof., chair dept. orthop. surgery U. Minn., Mpls., 1997—. Fellow Am. Acad. Orthopaedic Surgery, Soc. Internat. Chgo., Chirurgie Orthopaedic Traumatology, Am. Coll. Surgery, Am. Bd. Orthopaedic Surgery (bd. dirs. 1999—). Democrat. Avocations: bicycle riding, carpentry. Office: U Minn Dept Ortho Surgery 2450 Riverside Ave Minneapolis MN 55454

SWIRNOFF, LOIS, artist, educator; b. Bklyn., May 9, 1931; d. Harold and Fannie (Goldstein) Swirnoff; m. Richard Boyce (dec.); 1 child, Dr. Joshua Avram Boyce; m. J. G. Charney (dec.). Cert. of graduation, Cooper Union Art Sch., NYC, 1951; BFA, Yale U., 1953, MFA summa cum laude, 1956; studied with Josef Albers. Instr. art Wellesley (Mass.) Coll., 1954-58; from asst. prof. to prof. emerita UCLA, 1965—90, prof. emerita, 1990—; lectr. Harvard U., Cambridge, Mass., 1968-75; assoc. prof., chmn. art dept. Skidmore Coll., Saratoga Springs, N.Y., 1977-81; guest artist Cooper Union Art Sch., 1990-91, adj. prof., 1991—; Feltman chair Cooper Union, NYC, 2000—02. Author: Dimensional Color, 1989, Van Nostrand Reinhold, 1992, paperback edit., 1992, The Color of Cities, 2000 (Honorable Mention Best Book on Arch. and Urban Studies, Assn. Am. Pubs.); one-woman shows include Farnsworth Mus., 1958, Swetzoff Gallery, Boston, 1962, Inst. Internat. Edn., N.Y.C., 1978—79, NAS, Washington, 1982—83, The Woman's Bldg., L.A., Bradford Coll. Laura Knott Gallery, 1988, Wellesley Coll., Gallery BAI, N.Y.C., 1996, N.Y. Sch. of Interior

Design, 2000—01, Parson's Sch. Design, 2005, exhibited in group shows at City Art Mus., St. Louis, 1951, Bklyn. Mus., 1951, Munson-Williams Proctor Inst., Unica, N.Y., 1956, Swetzoff Gallery, 1963—65, Inst. Contemporary Art, Boston, 1961, LaJolla (Calif.) Mus., 1968, L.A. County Mus., 1968, Represented in permanent collections Addison Gallery Am. Art at Andover, Wellesley Coll., Mary I. Bunting Inst., Radcliffe Coll, UCLA, Parsons Sch. Design, also pvt.collections;: 2d edit., 2003. Fulbright fellow, Florence, Italy, 1951-52, Yale-Norfolk summer fellow, 1953, fellow Mary I. Bunting Inst., Radcliffe Coll., 1961-63, Yaddo fellow, 1985, 1987; Mellon faculty grantee Skidmore Coll., 1981, grantee Graham Found., 1988, 98, Internat. Interior Design Assn., 2004-05. Studio: 80 Monmouth St Brookline MA 02446-5607 Office Phone: 617-731-5071. Personal E-mail: lswirnoff@earthlink.net.

SWISHER, CHARLES FRANCIS, electrical engineer, consultant; b. Schenectady, NY, Mar. 8, 1934; s. Thomas Hyer and Frances Hannan Swisher. BSEE, U. Ill., 1956. Elec. engr. Dukane Corp., St. Charles, 1956—58; product mgr. Ampex Corp., Redwood City, Calif., 1958—65; v.p. Vega Electronics Corp., Cupertino, Calif., 1965—68; sr. cons. Jaffe Holden Acoustics, Inc., Norwalk, Conn., 1968—72; sound designer San Francisco Opera, 1974—79; v.p. Atlantic City Conv. Hall Organ Soc., Inc., Annapolis, Md., 1980—; exec. dir. The Am. Pipe Organ Mus., Lauderhill, Fla., 1994—. Pres. TBG Prodns., Lauderhill, 1971—. Artist, designer (outdoor symphonic sound sys) NY Philharm. Summer Parks Concerts; prodr.: (CD) The Auditorium Organ, John Balka Plays The Great Organ of St. Mary's Cathedral, San Francisco, (cassette recording) A Treasury of Hymns; dir., designer (music edn. and listening ctr.) The Sound Gallery, prodr., designer (opera and symphony audience expansion) Electronic Standing Rm. Chmn. Arts Commn., Springfield, Oreg., 1992—96. Fellow: Audio Engring. Soc. Achievements include discovery of technique to restore master audio tape recordings; first ever to record in a courtroom trial (1960); co-designer and operator of first PLAT (Pilot Landing Aid Television System), now installed on all US aircraft carriers (1961). Home: 3910 Inverrary Blvd B-608 Lauderhill FL 33319 Personal E-mail: cswisher@comcast.net.

SWISHER, STEPHEN G., thoracic surgeon; BA in Hist., Stanford U., 1982, BS in Biology, 1982; MD, U. Calif., 1986. Diplomate Nat. Bd. Med. Examiners, AM. Bd. Surgery, Am. Bd. Thoracic Surgery, lic. Tex. State Bd. Med. Examiners, Calif. State Bd. Med. Examiners. Intern U. Calif., Los Angeles Med. Ctr., 1986—87, resident, 1987—88, fellow surgical oncology, 1988—90, resident gen. surgery, 1990—93; clin. instr. gen. surgery U. Calif. Los Angeles Med. Ctr., 1993—94; registrar gen. surgery Nottingham, England, 1991; prof. surgery U. Tex., M.D. Anderson Cancer Ctr., fellow cardiothoracic surgery, 1994—96, jr. faculty assoc. to asst. prof. to assoc. prof. to prof., dept. throacic and cardiovascular surgery, 1995—; chmn., prof. surgery, dept. thoracic and cardiovasc. surgery St. Luke's Episc. Hosp., Tex. Heart Assn., 1994—96. Dir. esophageal cancer program, dept. thoracic and cardiovascular surgery U. Tex., M.D. Anderson Cancer Ctr., 2002—05, APN/PA dept. liaison, dept. thoracic and cardiovascular surgery, 2003—, dep. chair academic affairs, dept. thoracic and cardiovascular surgery, 2004—; reviewer various profl. jours.; speaker various nat. and internat. confs. Contbr. articles various profl. jours. and abstracts, chapters to books. Mem. ACS, 1982—86, 1996—98, assoc. fellow to fellow, 1998—2000; mem. Am. Med. Student Assn., 1982—86, Western Student Rsch. Med. Com., 1983—86, AMA, 1986—98. Nominee Clin. Scientist award in translational rsch., Burroughs Wellcome, 2000; named one of Best Doctors in Am., 2005; recipient Yale Book award, Menlo Sch., 1977, Fairclough award, Stanford U., 1982, Lange Publ. award, UCSD Med. Sch., 1986, Pres. award, Soc. Leukocyte Biology, 1989, Golden Scalpel Chief award, UCLA Med. Ctr. Resident, 1993; numerous rsch. grants. Mem.: Denton A. Cooley Cardiovascular Soc., Harris County Med. Soc., Tex. Med. Assn., Longmire Surgical Soc., Am. Assn. Thoracic Surgery, Am. Coll. Surgeons Oncology Group, Soc. U. Surgeons, Internat. Soc. Gastointestinal Cancer, Am. Soc. Gastrointestinal Oncology, Am. Radium Soc., Am. Assn. Cancer Rsch., So. Thoracic Surgical Assn., Soc. Thoracic Surgeons, Am. Bd. Thoracic Surgery, Internat. Soc. Diseases Esophagus, Am. Soc. Clin. Oncology, Internat. Assn. Study Lung Cancer, Soc. Surgical Oncology, Soc. Thoracic Radiology (hon.), Peruvian Soc. Med. Oncology (hon.), Gen. Thoracic Surgical Club, Phi Beta Kappa. Achievements include patents for induction of apoptotic or cytotoxic gene expression by adenoviral mediated gene codelivery; patents pending for methods of enhancing immune induction involving MDA7; proapoptotic adenoviral vectors and methods of use thereof; multigene vectors; compositions and methods involving MDA7 for the treatment of cancer. Office: Thoracic Cardiovascular Surgery 1515 Holcombe Blvd Unit 445 FC9 2044 Houston TX 77030

SWISTEL, DANIEL GEORGE, surgeon; b. Mar. 4, 1953; AB, Harvard Coll., 1975; MD, Rutgers U., 1979. Intern/resident gen. surgery St. Lukes/Roosevelt, 1979—84; resident in cardiovasc. surgery Albert Einstein/Montefiore Hosp. Med. Ctr., 1984—86; chief divsn. cardiothoracic surgery St. Luke/Roosevelt Hosp. Ctr., NYC, 1998—, co-dir. hypertrophic cardiomypathy program. Assoc. prof. surgery Columbia U. Coll. Physicians and Surgeons, 1996—; co-dir. Hypertrophic Cardiopathy Program, 2000—; bd. dirs. Ukrainian Inst. Am., NYC. Home: 25 E 86th St Apt 13D New York NY 10028-0553 Office Phone: 212-523-2705. E-mail: dwistel@chpnet.org.

SWITLO, JANICE GEORGINA ALICE E., barrister, solicitor, mediator, consultant; b. Vancouver, BC, Can., Jan. 10, 1959; d. Alexander Donald and Mary (Shutka) Switlo; married; 1 child. LLB, Osgoode Hall Toronto, 1986; B.Commerce, U. B.C., 1981. Mgmt. cons. Control Data Can. Ltd., Vancouver, 1981—83; articled student Ladner Downs, 1986—87; barrister, solicitor Aydin & Co., Vancouver, 1987—88; legal counsel Dept. Justice of Can., Vancouver, 1989—93; gen. counsel Westbank Indian Band, Westbank, BC, 1993—94; barrister, solicitor, cons. Switlo & Co., Peachland, BC, 1993-97; candidate fed. election Okanagan-Coquihaila, 1997; legal advisor Ministry Aboriginal Affairs Govt. N.W.T., 1999—2000. Mem. adv. coun. on multiculturalism, adv. coun. to Minister of Multiculturalism, B.C., 1996-98; presenter in field. Author: (book/screenplay) Sookinchute, 2001, (treatise) Trick or Treaty?, 1995, Apple Cede: First Nations Land Management Regime, 1999, In A Perfect World: Modern day colonialism in Canada, 2001, The River Forks Here: Canada's attempt to execute the 1969 White Paper and Indigenous Peoples, 2002, Ockham's Razor: Cutting Down a Worn Out Scarecrow, 2005, (book) Gustafsen Lake: Under Seige, 1997. Dir. B.C. Parents in Crisis Soc., Vancouver, 1991—93, Orpheum Kids Club Soc., Vancouver, 1991, Vancouver Youth Theatre, 2001. Scholar, Univ. Mem. Internat. Bar Assn., Internat. Commn. Jurists (Can. sect.), Can. Counsel on Internat. Law, York U. Alumni Assn., U. B.C. Commerce Alumni Assn., Phi Delta Phi. Office: Switlo & Co 141-6200 McKay Ave Ste 955 Burnaby BC Canada V5H 4M9 Office Phone: 800-332-1191. E-mail: janice@switlo.com.

SWITZ, ROBERT E., telecommunications executive; BS in Mktg. and Econs., Quinnipiac Coll., 1969; MBA in Fin., U. Bridgeport, 1973. Sr. fin. mgmt. staff PepsiCo., AMF, Olin Corp.; v.p. European ops., ventures and fin. Burr-Brown Corp., Tucson, 1988-94; CFO ADC Telecom., 1994—2003, sr. v.p. to exec. v.p., 1997—2003, pres. broadband access & transport group, 2000—01, pres., CEO, 2003—. Bd. dirs. Hickory Tech. Corp., Mpls. Youth Trust. Office: ADC Telecommunications 13625 Technology Dr Eden Prairie MN 55344 E-mail: bob_switz@adc.com.

SWITZER, CAROLYN JOAN, artist, educator; b. Petoskey, Mich., Apr. 20, 1931; d. Eugene Constant and Burnis Hazel (Lower) S. Student, Wayne State U., 1954-55, St. John's Coll., Santa Fe, N.Mex., 1993; BA, Mich. State U., 1953, MA, 1964. Cert. tchr., Mich. Art tchr. Ferndale Bd. of Edn., 1953-56, Birmingham Bd. of Edn., Mich., 1956-96; pvt. tchr. drawing and painting. Cons. Girl Scouts U.S., Birmingham, Petoskey, Mich.; mem. Crooked Tree Arts Coun., Petoskey; deacon, mem. choir First Presbyn. Ch. of Petoskey. Recipient Recognition award Birmingham Edn. Assn. Coun., 1967, Outstanding Sr. Woman, Lantern Night MSU, 1953. Mem. AAUW (scholar, Mich. State U., 1962), PEO, Nat. Art Edn. Assn., Mich. Art Edn. Assn., Mich. Edn. Assn., Detroit Inst. Art, Nat. Mus. for Women in Arts, Mich. Coun. for Arts, Art Study Club of Petoskey, Zonta Internat., Crooked Tree Arts Ctr. Petoskey, Little Traverse Hist. Soc. Avocations: music/singing, reading, exercise class, walking, photography. Home: 805 Lindell Ave Petoskey MI 49770-3159

SWITZER, FREDERICK MICHAEL, III, lawyer, arbitrator, mediator; b. St. Louis, Sept. 7, 1933; s. Frederick Michael Jr. and Viola Marie (Bardenheier) S.; m. Suzanne Elizabeth Reichardt, Aug. 28, 1970. BA cum laude, U. Notre Dame, 1956; JD, Washington U., 1959, LLM, 1972. Bar: Mo. 1959, US Ct. Mil. Appeals 1960, US Supreme Ct. 1962, US Dist. Ct. (ea. dist.) Mo. 1993, US Tax Ct. 1974, US Ct. Appeals (8th cir.) 1978, US Dist. Ct. (we. dist.) Mo. 1992, US Ct. Appeals (4th cir.) 1994, US Dist. Ct. (so. dist.) Ill. 1999, US Dist. Ct. (ctrl. dist.) Ill. 2002. Assoc. Switzer, Barnes & Toney, St. Louis, 1963-65, ptnr., 1965-75, Fordyce & Mayne, St. Louis, 1975-87, Coburn Croft, St. Louis, 1987-92, Danna, McKitrick, P.C., St. Louis, 1992—. Dir. Bardenheier Wine Co., St. Louis, 1983-85; instr. St. Louis U., 1971-72. Pres., dir. St. Louis Industry Adv. Group, 1971-90; dir. St. Louis Abbey Sch. Soc., 1975—; bd. dirs. Citizens for Mo.'s Children, St. Louis, 1986-91; adv. bd. Am. Youth Found., St. Louis, 1989—99, pres. Friends of Am. Youth Found., 2000—. Capt. USNR, 1959-63. Recipient Mitchell award for playwriting, U. Notre Dame, 1959. Mem. ABA (labor employment section, equal employment opportunity law com., litig. section, gen. practice section), ATLA, Assn. Atty. Mediators, Mo. Bar Assn. (labor law com., chmn. mil. law com. 1969-71, bar jour. com.), St. Louis Bar Assn. (labor law com., anti-trust com.), Phi Delta Phi. Republican. Roman Catholic. Avocations: sailing, hiking, equestrian activities, tennis. Office: Danna McKitrick PC 150 N Meramec Ave Fl 4 Saint Louis MO 63105-3779 Office Phone: 314-889-7131. Business E-Mail: fswitzer@dmfirm.com.

SWITZER, JO YOUNG, college president; b. Huntington, Ind., Mar. 4, 1948; d. John Frederick and Miriam Lucile (Kindy) Young; children: Sarah Kate Keller, John Christian Keller. BA, Manchester Coll., 1969; MA, U. Kans., 1977, PhD, 1980; postdoctoral, Ind. U., 1983, Harvard U., 1995. Asst. instr. U. Kans., Lawrence, 1977-79; asst. prof. Ind. U.-Purdue, Ft. Wayne, Ind., 1979-82; assoc. prof. Manchester Coll., North Manchester, Ind., 1982-87, Ind. U.-Purdue, Ft. Wayne, Ind., 1987-93; v.p., dean for acad. affairs and prof. comm. studies Manchester (Ind.) Coll., 1993—2004, pres., 2004—. Bd. dirs. BCA Study Abroad Consortium, Indpls. Peace Inst. Recipient E. C. Buehler award U. Kans., 1978; grantee NEH, 1983. Mem. Central States Comm. Assn. (Outstanding Young Educator award 1982), Coun. of Ind. Colls., Am. Coun. on Edn., Am. Assn. Colls. and Univs. Office: Manchester Coll Office of Pres 604 E College Ave North Manchester IN 46962-1276 Home: Tall Oaks 1408 East St North Manchester IN 46962 Office Phone: 260-982-5050. Office Fax: 260-982-5042. Business E-Mail: jyswitzer@manchester.edu.

SWITZER, JON REX, architect; b. Shelbyville, Ill., Aug. 22, 1937; s. John Woodrow and Ida Marie (Vadalabene) S.; m. Judith Ann Heinlein, July 7, 1962; 1 child, Jeffrey Eric. Student, U. Ill., 1955-58; BS, Millikin U., 1972; MA, U. Ill., Springfield, 1981. Registered architect Ill., Mo., Ohio, Colo.; registered interior designer, Ill. Arch. Warren & Van Praag, Inc., Decatur, Ill., 1970-72; prin. Decatur, 1972-81, Bloomington, Ill., 1981-83; arch. Hilfinger, Asbury, Cufaude, Abels, Bloomington, 1983-84; ptnr. Riddle/Switzer, Ltd., Bloomington, 1984-86; with bldg., design and constrn. divsn. State Farm Ins. Cos., Bloomington, 1986-89; arch. The Riddle Group, Bloomington, 1989-91; prin. J. Rex Switzer, Arch., Bloomington, 1991—. Elder Presbyn. Ch., 1996. With U.S. Army, 1958-61. Mem. AIA (pres. Bloomington chpt. 1983, Decatur chpt. 1976, v.p. Ill. chpt. 1986-87, sec. 1985, treas. 1984), Am. Archtl. Found., Chgo. Architecture Found., Nat. Trust Hist. Preservation, Frank Lloyd Found., Decatur C. of C. (merit citation 1974, merit award 1979), Am. Legion, Masons (32d degree). Republican. Presbyterian. Avocations: swimming, hunting, fishing, reading, drawing. Home: 9 Mary Ellen Way Bloomington IL 61701-2014 Office: 2412 E Washington St Ste 6A Bloomington IL 61704-1613

SWITZER, MAURICE HAROLD, journalist; b. Toronto, Ont., Can., Mar. 28, 1945; s. Harold Switzer and Ruby (Marsden) Hicks; m. Mary Helene Pavlik; children: Andrea Zimperi, Adin, Lisa Doracka. Student, Trent U., Peterborough, Ont., 1964-65. Journalist Belleville (Ont.) Intelligencer, Canada, 1965-67, sports editor, 1967-72, mng. editor, 1972-79, Oshawa (Ont.) Times, 1979-81; pub. Timmins (Ont.) Daily Press, 1981-86, Sudbury (Ont.) Star, 1986-92, Winnipeg (Man.) Free Press, 1992-94; owner Media Help Svcs., 1994—. Mem. faculty Aboriginal Media First Nations Tech. Inst., 1996—97; dir. comm. Assembly of First Nations, Ottawa, 1997—2000, Union Ont. Indians, North Bay, 2000—; mem. faculty Aboriginal Leadership and Mgmt. program Banff Ctr., 1998—; prof. comms. Huntington U., Sudbury, Ont., Canada, 2001—. Author: Bruno Cavallo a Conversation, 1991. Mem. elders coun. Mississaugas of Alderville First Nation. Office Phone: 705-497-4127. Personal E-mail: swimau@anishinabek.ca.

SWITZER, ROBERT LEE, biochemistry professor; b. Clinton, Iowa, Aug. 26, 1940; s. Stephen and Elva Delila (Allison) S.; m. Bonnie George, June 13, 1965; children: Brian, Stephanie. BS, U. Ill., 1961; PhD, U. Calif., Berkeley, 1966. Research fellow Lab. Biochemistry, Nat. Heart Inst., Bethesda, Md., 1966-68; asst. prof. biochemistry U. Ill., Urbana, 1968—73, assoc. prof., 1973—78, prof. biochemistry and basic med. scis., 1978—2002, prof. emeritus, 2002—, dept. head, 1988—93. Mem. biochemistry study sect. NIH, 1985-89, chmn., 1987-89; guest prof. U. Copenhagen, 1995; mem. microbial physiology and genetics study sect., NIH, 1998-2000. Author: (with Liam F. Garrity) Experimental Biochemistry, 3rd rev. edit., 1999; mem. bd. editors Jour. Bacteriology, 1977-82, 1985—2002, Archives Biochemistry and Biophysics, 1977-98, Jour. Biol. Chemistry, 1980-85; contbr. articles to profl. jours. NSF predoctoral fellow, 1961-66; NIH postdoctoral fellow, 1966-68; Guggenheim fellow, 1975. Fellow Am. Acad. Microbiology; mem. Am. Soc. for Biochemistry and Molecular Biology, Am. Soc. Microbiology, Am. Chem. Soc., AAAS, Sigma Xi. Home: 404 W Michigan Ave Urbana IL 61801-4948 Office: U Ill Dept Biochemistry 600 S Mathews Ave Urbana IL 61801-3602 Office Phone: 217-333-3940. Business E-Mail: rswitzer@uiuc.edu.

SWITZER, SHARON CECILE, language educator, researcher; PhD, Lesley U., Cambridge, Mass., 2003. Dir. of ESL Martha's Vineyard Sch. Dist., Martha's Vineyard, Mass., 2000—04; asst. prof. East Stroudsburg U., Pa., 2004—. Bd. dirs. Pa. TESOL E., Phila., 2004—. Bd. dirs. Pocono Svcs.s for Family and Children, East Stroudsburg, 2005—06. Grantee Head Start Rsch. scholar, Adminstrn. Children Youth and Families, 1999—2001. Mem.: TESOL. Avocations: painting, travel, yoga. Office: East Stroudsburg University 200 Prospect St East Stroudsburg PA 18301 Home Phone: 570-422-6726; Office Phone: 570-422-3368.

SWITZER, TERI REYNOLDS, library association executive; b. Tucson, Ariz., May 1, 1949; d. Ernest William and Lois Myrtle (Jensen) Reynolds; m. Ralph Vincent Switzer, Jr., June 30, 1973 (div. June 1989); children: Lois, R. Vincent III; m. Gene Joseph Luthman, July 17, 1993. BA, U. Ill., 1971, MS, 1973; MBA, Colo. State U., 1977. Instr. Colo. State U., Ft. Collins, 1973-77, asst. prof., 1988-95, assoc. prof., 1995—; media specialist St. Joseph Elem., Ft. Collins, 1985-88; assoc. dean, rsch., ops. & document delivery services U. Colo. Health Services Ctr., Auraria Libr., Denver. Author: Telecommuters, 1997, Safe at Work?, 1999. Mem. ALA (treas., 2004-2007), Fedn. Info. and Documentation, Colo. Libr. Assn. Avocations: skiing, hiking. Office: U Colo Auroria Libr Denver CO 80204

SWOAP, DAVID BRUCE, government and state agency administrator, consultant, art director; b. Kalamazoo, Aug. 12, 1937; s. Orlo Frederick and Aileen Esther (Hempy) S. BA in Govt. with honors, Denison U., 1959; MA in Govt., Claremont Grad. Sch., 1961; DSc (hon.), U. Osteo. Medicine and Health Scis., Des Moines, 1981. Asst. sec. Calif. State Pers. Bd., Sacramento, 1972-73; chief dep. dir., acting dir. Calif. State Dept. Social Welfare, 1973, dir., 1973-74, Calif. State Dept. Benefit Payments, 1974-75; sr. rsch. asso. Rep. Study Com., U.S. Ho. of Reps., Washington, 1975-76; profl. staff mem. U.S. Senate Com. on Fin., 1976-79; legis. dir. U.S. Senator William L. Armstrong, 1979-81; dep. sec. HHS, 1981-83; sec. health and welfare State of Calif., Sacramento, 1983-85; ptnr. Franchetti & Swoap, San Francisco, 1985-90; owner Mana Olana Farms, Hakalau, Hawaii, 1989—97; vice chmn. Sacramento Advs., 1991-98; owner The David Bruce Gallery, Carlsbad, Calif., 1995-97. Chmn. bd. Hope Unltd. for Children, Los Alamitos, Calif., 1991—96, bd. mem., 2007—, mem. adv. bd., 1996—2007, chmn. adv. bd., 1996—2003. Elder Presbyn. Ch.; bd. dirs. Friends of SOS Children's Villages, 1989-91; bd. regents John F. Kennedy U., 1990-93; mem. Healthy Families Dorchester adv. bd., 2002-05, Md. State Bd. of Physicians, 2003-05. Rotary Club Found. fellow, 1961-62 Mem. Wycliffe Assocs., Phi Beta Kappa, Delta Upsilon. Republican.

SWOAP, THOMAS FRANK, JR., history educator; m. Rebecca R. Swoap; children: Victoria, Lindsey, Tamasin. BA in Polit. Sci., Emory and Henry Coll., Emory, Va. Tchr. history Hanover County Sch. Bd., Ashland, Va., 1976—95, Bluestone Sr. H.S., Skipwith, Va., 1995—. Republican. Baptist. Avocations: reading, camping, farming, church activities.

SWOFFORD, BETH, agent; Motion picture agent Creative Artists Agency (CAA), Beverly Hills. Trustee Mus. of Contemporary Art, LA. Named one of Top 200 Collectors, ARTnews Mag., 2004, 2005, 2007, 100 Most Powerful Women in Entertainment, Hollywood Reporter, 2004, 2005, 2006, 2007. Avocation: Collector of Contemporary Art. Office: Creative Artists Agy 2000 Ave of the Stars Los Angeles CA 90067

SWOFFORD, ROBERT LEE, editor, journalist; b. Berryville, Ark., Aug. 22, 1949; s. Andrew Madison and Verna Mae (England) S.; m. Karan King, Jan. 24, 1969 (div. 1977); children: Teri, Toby; m. Sandra Dunn, 1978 (div. 1979); m. B. Joanna Rongren, Feb. 14, 1981 (div. 2001); 1 child, Tyler. AA, Coll. of the Sequoias, 1969; student, Calif. State U., 1969-71. Photographer, reporter, news editor The Advance-Register, Tulare, Calif., 1965-78; city editor The Record Searchlight, Redding, Calif., 1978-81; suburban editor, Neighbors editor The Sacramento Bee, 1981-86; assoc. metro. editor, cmty. editor The Orange County Register, Santa Ana, Calif., 1986-89; exec. news editor The Press Democrat, Santa Rosa, Calif., 1989-90, mng. editor, 1990—. Mem. Am. Soc. Newspaper Editors, Calif. Soc. Newspaper Editors (bd. mem., past pres.). Office: The Press Democrat 427 Mendocino Ave Santa Rosa CA 95401-6385 Business E-Mail: bob.swofford@pressdemocrat.com.

SWONGER, THOMAS K. H., JR., insurance company executive; s. Thomas K. H. and Mary Helen Swonger; m. Claudia Maria Arteaga, Feb. 6, 2004; children: Richard Thomas, Karli Elizabeth, Thomas K. H. III. BS in Bus. Mgmt., U. Phoenix, Orlando, Fla., 2001—04, MBA, 2004—05. Cert. in workers compensation WCCP, Fla., 1996. Mil. police US Army, Karlsruhe, Germany, 1987—92; police officier Daytona Beach Police Dept., Fla., 1992—93; claims examiner Exec. Risk Cons., Longwood, Fla., 1993—97; sr. claims examiner, claims supr. Gallagher Bassett Svcs., Orlando, Fla., 1997—2004; claims mgr. Sedgwick Claims Mgmt. Svcs., Lake Mary, Fla., 2004—. Youth instr. St. Issac Joques, Orlando, 2003—05. Specialist US Army, 1987—92, Germany, paratrooper US Army, 1988. Decorated Good Conduct medal US Army, Drivers medal, Forgien Svc. medal, Combat citation. Mem.: WCCP (assoc.). Office: Sedgwick CMS 255 Primera Blvd Ste 400 Lake Mary FL 32746 Home Phone: 407-592-4051. Office Fax: 407-833-4111. Business E-Mail: tswonger@sedgwickcms.com.

SWOOPES, SHERYL DENISE, professional basketball player; b. Brownfield, Tex., Mar. 25, 1971; d. Louise Swoopes; m. Eric Jackson, June 7, 1995 (div. 1999); 1 child, Jordan Eric Jackson. Student, South Plains Jr. Coll., Tex.; grad., Tex. Tech. U., 1993. Basketball player South Plains Jr. Coll., 1989—91, Tex. Tech U., 1991—93; profl. basketball player Houston Comets, WNBA, 1997—. Founder Sheryl Swoopes Found. for Youth. Named Nat. Player of Yr., USA Today, Sports Illustrated, others, 1993, Most Outstanding Player, NCAA Final Four, 1993, Most Valuable Player, WNBA, 2000, 2002, Defensive Player of Yr., 2000, 2002, 2003, Female Athlete of Yr., AP, 1993; named to First Team All-WNBA, 1998—2000, 2002, WNBA All-Star Team, 1999, 2000, 2002, 2003; recipient Coll. Performer of Yr. Award, ESPY award, 1994, Women's Pro Basketball Player of Yr. Award, 2001, Best WNBA Player, 2006. Achievements include mem., Texas Tech NCAA Championship Team, 1993; mem., US Women's Basketball Gold Medal Team, World Championships, 2002; mem., US Women's Basketball Gold Medal Team, Atlanta Olympics, 1996; mem., US Women's Basketball Gold Medal Team, Sydney Olympics, 2000; mem., US Women's Basketball Team, Athens Olympics, 2004; first woman to have a Nike shoe, the Air Swoopes, named after her. Office: Houston Comets 1510 Polk St Houston TX 77002-1099

SWOPE, DONALD DOWNEY, retired banker; b. Martinsville, Ill., Feb. 26, 1926; s. Roy V. and Dorothy Irene (Downey) S.; m. Earla Long Markert, Aug. 16, 1960. BS, Ind. State U., 1950. With Ill. Savs. and Loan Commn., Springfield, Ill., 1950-77, chief dept. commr., 1971-77; exec. v.p. Bank for Savs. & Loan Assn., Chgo., 1977-81, pres., 1981-90. Bd. dirs. Country Fair White Elephant, Green Valley, Ariz., 1981—, treas., 1981-84. With USNR, 1944-63. Mem. VFW (life), Nat. Assn. State Savs. and Loan Suprs. (pres. 1972-73), Am. Legion (life), C. C. Green Valley, Kiwanis (pres. Crete, Ill. 1977-78, treas. Green Valley, Ariz. 1994, 95), Elks (life, treas.).

SWOPE, JEFFREY PEYTON, lawyer; b. Evanston, Ill., June 11, 1945; s. Oliver P. and Elspeth E. (Cahill) S.; m. Linda Lee, Aug. 26, 1967; children: Matthew, Gregory, Timothy. AB, Harvard U., 1967, JD, 1970. Bar: Mass. 1970, U.S. Dist. Ct. Mass. 1971, U.S. Ct. Appeals (1st cir.) 1973, U.S. Ct. Claims 1974, U.S. Supreme Ct. 1979. Assoc. Edwards Angell Palmer & Dodge, Boston, 1970-76, ptnr., 1977—. Treas. Social Law Libr., Boston, 1984-2003, pres., 2003-. Treas. Ella Lyman Cabot Trust, Holliston, Mass., 1979-. Home: 54 Hyde St Newton MA 02461-1206 Office: Edwards Angell Palmer & Dodge LLP 111 Huntington Ave Boston MA 02199-7613

SWOPE, RICHARD MCALLISTER, retired lawyer; b. West Chester, Pa., Apr. 19, 1940; s. Charles Seigel and Edna McPherson (McAllister) S.; m. Karen Diane Glass, Aug. 24, 1963 (div. 1972). BS in Edn., Bucknell U., 1962; LLB cum laude, Washington and Lee U., 1968. Bar: Va. 1968. Ret., 1998. Instr. Nat. Inst. Trial Advocacy, 1982-86. Mem. Virginia Beach Beautification Commn.; bd. dirs. Virginia Beach Orchestral Assn., 1982-88; pres., bd. dirs. Swope Found., West Chester, Pa., 1961—; v.p. Swope Scholarship Found. Capt. USMC, 1962-65. Mem. Va. Assn. Def. Attys. (bd. dirs. 1975-78, 88-90), Va. State Bar Assn., Norfolk/Portsmouth Bar

Assn., Virginia Beach Bar Assn., Virginia Beach C. of C., Rotary (pres. 1982, Paul Harris fellow). Avocation: golf. Home: 936 Poquoson Cir Virginia Beach VA 23452-4646 E-mail: swopy@cox.net.

SWYGERT, HAYWOOD PATRICK, academic administrator; b. Phila., Mar. 17, 1943; s. LeRoy and Gustina (Rogers) Huzzy; children: Haywood Patrick Jr., Michael Branson. AB in History, Howard U., 1965, JD cum laude, 1968. Bar: D.C. 1968, Pa. 1970, N.Y. 1970. Law clk. to chief judge U.S. Ct. Appeals (3d cir.), Phila., 1968—69; assoc. Debevoise, Plimpton, Lyons & Gates, NYC, 1969—70; adminstrv. asst. to Congressman Charles B. Rangel NY, 1971—72; spl. asst. dist. atty. Phila., 1973; from asst. prof. to prof. law Temple U., 1972—90, v.p. adminstrn., 1982—88, exec. v.p., 1988—90; pres. SUNY, Albany, 1990—95, Howard U., Washington, 1995—. Bd. dirs. United Tech. Corp., Hartford Fin. Svcs. Group, Fannie Mae; adv. bd. Nat. Security Agency, 2002; chmn. HBCU Capital Fin., 2002—. Gov.'s rep. Southeastern Pa. Transp. Authority, 1987—90; bd. trustees Inst. Pub. Adminstrn., 1992—99; exec. com. Pub. Law Ctr., Phila., 1980—88; bd. dirs. NY State Coun. on Humanities, 1991—95; chmn. ednl. structure, policies and practices NY State Spl. Commn., 1993—95; co-chmn. joint task force grad. edn. Nat. Assn. State Univs. and Land Grant Colls./Am. Assn. State Coll. and Univs., 1993—95; chmn. capital financing program adv. bd. Historically Black Colls. and Univs., 2002—06; mem. founding coun. Smithsonian Instn.'s Nat. Mus. of African Am. History and Culture, 2004; mem. DC Emancipation Commemoration Commn., 2004, Brown vs. Board Edn. Commemoration Commn., 2002, US Nat. Commn. UNESCO, 2004; bd. dirs. New Cmty. Devel. Corp., HUD, 1980—82, Nat. Pub. Radio, 1995—96; mem. Commn. Presdl. Debates. Recipient Bldg. Industry Assn. Achievement award, DC, Spl. Friend award, Am. Friends of Lubavitch, 2003, Edn. award, Nat. Conf. Cmty. & Justice, 2003, Chmn. award, Congl. Black Caucus 34th Ann. Legis. Conf., 2004, Legend award for outstanding leadership in edn., Nat. Urban League, 2005. Mem.: ABA, Victory Funds (trustee 1994—2002), Middle States Assn. Colls. and Schs. (commn. on higher edn. 1992—95). Office: Howard U Office of Pres 2400 6th St NW Ste 402 Washington DC 20059-0002 Office Phone: 202-806-2500. *

SYDOW, MICHAEL DAVID, lawyer; b. Dec. 12, 1950; m. Kelli McDonald; children: Kristen, David, Wyatt. BA, Southwestern U., 1973; JD with honors, U. Tex., 1976. Bar: Tex. 1976, U.S. Ct. Claims 1977, U.S. Ct. Appeals (5th cir.) 1977, U.S. Dist. Ct. (so. dist.) Tex. 1977, U.S. Dist. Ct. (ea. dist.) Tex. 1979, U.S. Supreme Ct. 1980, U.S. Dist. Ct. (no. dist.) Tex. 1985, U.S. Dist. Ct. (we. dist.) Tex. 1986; cert. in civil trial law Tex. Bd. Legal Specialization. Trial atty. Office Gen. Counsel USN, Arlington, Va., 1976-77; mem. firm Eastham, Watson, Dale & Forney, Houston, 1977-84, Hagans & Sydow, LLP, Houston, 1985-90, Reynolds & Sydow, LLP, Houston, 1993-94; pvt. practice, 1990-93; with Sydow & McDonald, LLP, 1995-97; shareholder Verner, Liipfert, Bernhard, McPherson & Hand, Houston, 1997—2002, Sydow, Kormack Carrigan & Eckerson, 2002—04, Sydow, McDonald, Kaiser & Ahmed, LLP, 2005—. Fellow Tex. Bar Found., Houston Bar Found.; mem. Houston Bar Assn. (chmn. jud. liaison com. 1988-90, Pres.'s award 1990), Maritime Law Assn. U.S. (mem. com. on gen. average 1977-88, practice and procedures com. 1988—), State Bar Tex., Phi Delta Phi. Address: Sydow McDonald Kaiser & Ahmed LLP 2000 Bering Dr Ste 700 Houston TX 77057 Home: 5773 Woodway Dr Houston TX 77057-1501 Office Phone: 713-355-4200. E-mail: msydow@smkalaw.com.

SYED, ELIZABETH CHANCE, health facility administrator, critical care nurse; b. Clermont, Fla., Oct. 18, 1958; d. Brooker Lawson and Beulah Catharine (Lord) Chance; m. Mohsin M. Syed, Dec. 30, 1993; children: Adam, Jibran. B in Gen. Studies, Howard Payne U., 1981; MA in Comm. without thesis, SW Bapt. Theol. Sem., 1985; ADN, E. N.Mex. U., 1988. Cert. CCRN, program nurse sr. options, med. office mgr. Critical care nurse Meml. Hosp. & Med. Ctr., Midland, Tex., 1990—94, Angelo Cmty. Med. Ctr., San Angelo, Tex., 1992; staff nurse ICU Med. Ctr. Hosp., Odessa, Tex., 1998; mental health nurse Glenwood Hosp., Midland, Tex., 1998—99; practice adminstr. Family Care Clinic and Med. Spa of Midland, 1998—. Instr. ACLS. Mem. Cmty. Chorale, Farmington, N.Mex., 1981, Roswell, N.Mex., 1989-90. Mem. AACN (rsch. assoc. Thunder Project 1991-92). Avocation: music. Office: Family Care Clinic 4506 Briarwood Ave Midland TX 79707-2642 Office Phone: 432-689-6818. Business E-Mail: elizabeth@medicalspaofmidland.com.

SYED, IBRAHIM BIJLI, medical educator, physicist; b. Bellary, India, Mar. 16, 1939; came to US, 1969, naturalized, 1975; s. Syed Ahmed Bijli and Mumtaz Begum (Maniyar) S.; m. Sajida Shariff, Nov. 29, 1964; children: Mubin, Zafrin. BS with honors, Veerasaiva Coll., Bellary U., Mysore, 1960; MS with honors and distinction, Bangalore U., Mysore, 1962; diploma, U. Bombay, 1964; DSc, Johns Hopkins U., Balt., 1972; PhD (hon.), Malta, 1985. Cert. hazard control officer, 1980, internat. health care safety profl., 1980; diplomate Am. Bd. Radiology, Am. Bd. Health Physics. Lectr. physics Veerasaiva Coll., Bellary U., Mysore, 1962-63; med. physicist, radiation safety officer Victoria Hosp., India, 1964-67, Bowring and Lady Curz on Hosp. & Postgrad. Med. Rsch. Inst., Bangalore, India, 1964-67; cons. med. physicist, radiation safety officer Ministry of Health, Govt. of Karnataka, India, 1964-67, Bangalore Nursing Home, India, 1964-67; med. physicist, radiation safety officer Baystate Med. Ctr., Springfield, Mass., 1973-79; assoc. prof. Springfield Tech. C.C.; also adj. prof. radiology Holyoke C.C., Mass., 1973-79; asst. clin. prof. nuclear medicine U. Conn. Sch. Medicine, Farmington, 1975-79; cons. med. physicist Mercy Hosp., Springfield, 1973-79, Wing Meml. Hosp., Palmer, Mass., 1973-79; med. physicist, radiation safety officer VAMC, Louisville, 1979—, exec. officer radiation safety com., 1979—; prof. medicine U. Louisville Sch. Medicine, 1979—, dir. nuclear med. scis., 1980—; mem. Instl. Review Bd. Veterans Admin. Medical Ctr., Louisville, 2000—. Guest lectr. religious studies program U. Louisville, 1979—; vis. prof. Bangalore U., 1987—88, Gulbarga U., India, 1987—88; vis. scientist Bhabha Atomic Rsch. Ctr., Bombay; invited spkr. Veerasaiva Coll., Bellary, India, 1996, Vijayanagar Coll., Hospet, 1996, Vajayanagar Inst. Med. Scis., Bellary, 1996, Deccan Coll. Med. Scis., Hyderabad, India, Bhabha Atomic Rsch. Ctr., Bombay, 1997, 15th Ann. Islamic Conf. New Eng., Islamic Coun. New Eng., 1999, Coun. for a Parliament of the World's Religions, Cape Town, South Africa, 1999, Garden City Coll. Bangalore, 2000, Veerasaiva Coll., Bellary, 2000, Islamic Rsch. Found., Mumbai, India, 2001, Islamic Assn. of Essex, England, 2001, Assn. Muslim Social Scientists, Detroit, 2001, Darus Salam, Bangalore, India, 2005; invited faculty Assn. Muslim Social Scientists, Dallas, 2005; invited spkr. Islamic Orgn. Med. Scis., Cairo, 2002; PhD thesis examiner Allahabad U., 1996—; course dir. licensing for nuclear cardiologists U. Louisville, 1980—, mem. admissions com. nuclear medicine program, 1980—; guest relief examiner Am. Bd. Radiology, 1991, 2005; examiner in radiol physics, 1995, 97, 98, 2000; examiner in radiol. physics, 03, 05, 06; mem. panel of examiners Am. Bd. Health Physics; PhD thesis examiner U. Delhi, Internat. Inst. for Advanced Study, Clayton, Mo., 1985—, Allahabad (India) U., 1996—2005; faculty mem. Med. Physicists of India Ann. Meeting, 1987; IAEA tchr. expert in nuclear medicine on mission to People's Republic of Bangladesh, 86; to Guatemala, 94; founder, pres. Islamic Rsch. Found. Internat., Louisville, 1988—; convener Internat. Conf. on Islamic Renaissance: Action Plan for the 21st Century, Chgo., 1995; cons. Coun. Sci. and Indsl. Rsch., Govt. India, 0809—, Am. Coun. Sci. and Health, 1980—; cons. gastroenterology and urology divsn. FDA, HHS, 1988—, cons. radiopharm. divsn., 1989—; cons. Govt. India in nuclear medicine, diagnostic radiol. physics, therapeutic radiol. physics and radiation safety, 1992; cons. radiol. and med. nuc. physics Govt. India, Un Devel. Program, 1992; convenor Internat. Conf. on Islamic Renaissance, Chgo., 1995; guest spkr. Muslim Cmty. Ctr., Chgo., 1988; invited spkr. objective studies and Islamic voice, Bangalore, 96, Parliament of World Religions, Chgo., 1993, Cape Town, South Africa, 99, Cooper Mosque, Mississauga, Ont., Canada, 2002; invited faculty Assn. of Muslim Social Scientists, Dallas, 2005; invited spkr. Darus Salam, Bangalore, India, 2005. Author: Radiation Safety for Allied Health Professionals, Radiation Safety Manual, 1979, Intellectual Achievements of Muslims, 2002; contbg. editor Jour. of Islamic Food and Nutrition Coun. of Am., 1986—, health and sci. column Muslim Jour., 1989—; freelance writer Minaret Biweekly, NYC, 1975—, Islamic Voice, India, 1988—, Al-Balaagh, Lenasia, South Africa, 1989—, AL'FURQAN Internat., Norcross, Ga., 1990, Message Internat., Jamaica, NY, 1990, Minaret Monthly Mag., LA, 1995—, The Message, London, 1998—, The Minaret, Botswana, 1998—; editor: Science and Technology for the Developing World, 1988; mem. editl. bd. Jour. Islamic Med. Assn., 1981—; regular contbr. Pres.'s Page; manuscript reviewer for sci. and med. jours., 1973; assoc. editor AAlim, 1998—; contbr. more than 100 articles to sci. jours.; pub. internat. more than 300 articles on various topics of Islam in jours. and mags. Moderator fgn. policy workshop U.S. Dept. State, Louisville, 2000; spkr. Dayton Islamic Ctr., Dayton, 2000, Muslim Student Assn. U. Cin., 2000, Muslim Cmty. Ctr., Chgo., 2001; invited spkr. Muslim Assn. of Cleve. East, 2002; bd. dir. Nur Islamic Sch., Louisville, 2003, Am. Muslim Assn. Louisville, 2003—; bd. dirs. Islamic Ctr. of Louisville, 1992—; founder, mgr., trustee Bijli Found. Charitable Trust, Bellary, India, 2005—. Recipient Disting. Cmty. Svc. award India Cmty. Found., 1982, Hind Rattan Jewel of India Title award Govt. India, 1994; WHO fellow, Govt. India scholar Bhabha Atomic Rsch. Ctr., Bombay, 1963-64; USPHS fellow Johns Hopkins U., 1969-72. Fellow Inst. Physics (UK), Am. Inst. Chemists, Royal Soc. Health, Am. Coll. Radiology, Internat. Acad. Med. Physics; mem. Am. Assn. Physicists in Medicine, Am. Coll. Nuclear Medicine, Health Physics Soc., Am. Acad. Health Physics, Soc. Nuclear Medicine (faculty mem. ann. meeting 1987, convenor internat. conf. 1995), Nat. Assn. Ams. of Asian Indian Descent (chmn. state pub. rels. com. 1982—), Islamic Med. Assn. N.Am. (life, faculty 1994, 96, 98), Internat. Inst. Islamic Medicine (faculty Orlando, Fla. 1996, 97, Birmingham, UK 1998), Islamic Soc. N.Am. (faculty Chgo. 1998), Islamic Soc. Balt. (founding mem.), Islamic Cultural Ctr.(sec. 1999-), Louisville, Islamic Assn. Maritime Provinces Can., Halifax, N.S. (asst. sec. 1967-69), Health Physics Soc. (chmn. med. health physics com. 1989—, affirmative action com. 1984—), Am. Assn. Physicists in Medicine (biol. effects com.), Assn. Muslim Scientists and Engrs. N.Am. (program chmn. ann. conf. 1987, treas. 1987-88, sec. 1988—), AAUP, Soc. Nuc. Medicine India (life, faculty mem. ann. meeting 1987, invited spkr. and faculty ann. meeting 1996), Assn. Med. Physicists India (life, invited spkr. and faculty ann. meeting Madras 1996), Med. and Biol. Physics (divsn. Can.) Assn. Physicists, Hosp. Physicists Assn., NY Acad. Scis., Islamic Assn. Maritime Provinces of Can., Ky. Med. Assn., Jefferson County Med. Soc. (assoc.), Am. Muslim Assn. Louisville (bd. dirs. 2003—), Assn. Muslim Social Scientists, Sigma Xi Islamic. Home: 7102 W Shefford Ln Louisville KY 40242-4642 Office: 800 Zorn Ave Louisville KY 40206-1499 Office Phone: 502-287-6262. Business E-Mail: irfi@iname.com.

SYED, YASSER FOUAD KHADERI, electrical engineer; b. Halifax, Nova Scotia, Can., Sept. 9, 1968; s. Asif Syed, Amtul Syed; m. Romana Yasser Shahdad; 1 child, Arva Hanan. BS cum laude, Rensselaer Polytechnic Inst., 1990; MS Elec. Engring., U. So. Calif., LA, 1992; DPhil Elec. Engring., U. Tex., 1999. Sr. systems engri. SpectraPoint Wireless, Richardson, Colo., 1996—2000; project dir. emerging digital video tech. CableLabs, Louisville, 2000—. Assoc. mem. INCITS, Washington, 2000—; del. MPEG USA; chmn, adv. codes Drafting Group SCTE, 2005—. Named Dean's List, Rensselaer Polytechnic Inst., 1986—90; grantee, Tex. Instruments, 1998; scholar, Hewlett-Packard, 1990. Mem.: IEEE (sr.), Greater Dallas Indo- Am. C. of C. (bd. dirs. 1999—2000), Alpha Phi Omega, Eta Kappa Nu, Tau Beta Pi. Office: Cable Television Laboratories Inc 400 Centennial Pkwy Louisville CO 80027 Home Phone: 720-565-9189; Office Phone: 303-661-3319. Personal E-mail: yasser_syed@ieee.org.

SYGALL, SUSAN E., international educational exchange director; b. NYC, June 4, 1953; d. Michael and Lisa S. BS, U. Calif., Berkeley, 1975; MS, U. Oreg., 1981. Co-founder, dir. Berkeley Outreach Recreation Program, 1975-78, Mobility Internat. USA, Eugene, Oreg., 1981—. Mem. exec. bd. Mobility Internat., London, 1989-92. Co-author: A World of Options, 1991, Global Perspectives on Disability, 1992; co-prodr. (videos) Look Back-Looking Forward, 1990, Emerging Leaders, 1992. Named Disabled Oregonian of the Year, 1994; recipient Rotary grad. fellow Rotary Found., 1978, Kellogg Nat. Leadership fellow, Kellogg Found., 1988, MacArthur Fellow, MacArthur Found., 2000, Humanitarian award, Jewish Fedn., Women to Watch award, Jewish Woman Mag., President's award from Pres. Bill Clinton, 1995. Jewish. Office: Mobility Internat USA 132 E Broadway Ste 343 Eugene OR 97401 *

SYHABOUT, JAMES, chef; Grad., Calif. Culinary Acad., 1999. Sous chef Manresa; stage The Fat Duck, Bray, England, 2004; chef de partie Alkimia, Barcelona, Mugaritz, Errenteria, Spain; commis El Bulli, 2005; chef de partie Coi, San Francisco; exec. chef PlumpJack Café, San Francisco. Named one of San Francisco's Rising Stars, StarChefs.com, 2007. Office: PlumpJack Cafe 3127 Fillmore St San Francisco CA 94123 Office Phone: 415-563-4755. *

SYKES, DIANE S., federal judge, former state supreme court justice; b. Milw., Dec. 23, 1957; 2 children. BA, Northwestern U., 1980; JD, Marquette U., 1984. Reporter Milw. Jour.; law clk. to Hon. Terence T. Evans US Dist. Ct. (ea. dist.) WI, 1984—85; assoc. Whyte & Hirschboeck S.C., 1985—92; judge Milw. County Ct., 1992—99, Wis. Supreme Ct., Madison, 1999—2004, US Ct. Appeals (7th cir.), 2004—. Mem.: St. Thomas More Soc., Milw. Lawyers Chpt., Federalist Soc., Fairchild Inn, Am. Inns of Ct., Assn. for Women Lawyers, Seventh Cir. Bar Assn., Milw. Bar Assn., Wis. Bar Assn. Office: US Ct Appeals 7th Cir 371 US Court House 517 E Wisconsin Ave Milwaukee WI 53202 also: Dirksen Fed Bldg Rm 2742 219 S Dearborn St Chicago IL 60604 Office Phone: 414-727-6988. *

SYKES, GRESHAM M'CREADY, sociologist, educator, artist; b. Plainfield, NJ, May 26, 1922; s. M'Cready and Beatrice (Evans) S.; m. Carla Adelt, July 13, 1946. AB summa cum laude, Princeton U., 1950; PhD (Woodrow Wilson fellow 1950-51, Univ. fellow 1951-52), Northwestern U., 1953; MA (hon.), Dartmouth Coll., 1961. Instr. sociology Princeton U., 1952-54, asst. prof., bicentennial preceptor, 1954-58; assoc. prof. Northwestern U., Evanston, Ill., 1958-60; prof. sociology Dartmouth Coll., Hanover, NH, 1960-63, chmn. dept., 1961-63; exec. officer Am. Sociol. Assn., 1963-65; research prof. law and sociology, dir. adminstrn. of justice program U. Denver, 1965-72; chmn. dept. sociology U. Houston, 1973; prof. sociology U. Va., Charlottesville, 1974-88, chmn. dept., 1978-81, emeritus prof., 1988—. Chmn. Salzburg (Austria) Seminar in Am. Studies, summer 1965; working as artist, with frequent group and one-man exhbn., 1988—. Author: Crime and Society, rev. edit., 1967, The Society of Captives, 1958, Law and the Lawless, 1969, Social Problems in Am., 1971, Criminology, 1978, rev. edit., 1992, The Future of Crime, 1980; criminology editor Jour. Criminal Law, Criminology and Police Sci., 1959-64; assoc. editor Rev. Am. Sociol. Assn., 1960-62, Contemporary Sociology, 1977-80, Criminology, 1980-84; contbr. articles and revs. to Ency. Britannica, profl. jour. Served to capt., C.E. AUS, 1942-46, ETO. Recipient Edwin H. Sutherland award Am. Soc. Criminology, 1980. Home: 2197 Shepherds Ridge Road Charlottesville VA 22901

SYKES, GWENDOLYN, academic administrator, former federal agency administrator; b. West Point, NY; B in Acctg., Cath. U.; MPA, Am. U., 2001. Cert. govt. fin. mgr. With Def. Contract Audit Agy.; legis. correspondent to Senator Ted Stevens US Senate; sr. program analyst, Office Under Sec. US Dept. Def.; dep. CFO NASA, 2002—03, CFO, 2003—07, Yale U., New Haven, 2007—. Lectr. in field. Named one of 50 Most Powerful Women in Bus., Black Enterprise mag.; recipient Exceptional Achievement medal, NASA, 2003. Office: Yale U CFO 265 Church St New Haven CT 06511 E-mail: gwendolyn.sykes@yale.edu. *

SYKES, JOHN, communications company executive; BS in Comm., Syracuse U. Staff CBS Records, 1977-80; mem. start-up team to v.p. programming MTV, 1980-86; agt. Creative Artists Agy., 1986-88; pres. Champion Entertainment, 1988—92; exec. v.p. talent acquisition and mktg. EMI Mus. Pub. Worldwide, 1992—94; pres. VH1, NYC, 1994—2004; chmn., CEO Infinity Radio ops. Viacom Inc., 2004—05, with MTV Networks, 2005—. Bd. mem. The Robin Hood Found., T.J. Martell Cancer Found., The City of Hope, Rock and Roll Hall of Fame; mem. adv. bd. Syracuse U. S.I. Newhouse Sch. Office: VH1 Viacom International 1515 Broadway Fl 20 New York NY 10036-8901

SYKES, LINDA DIANE, elementary school educator, music educator; b. Indpls., Aug. 23, 1950; d. Theodore Ross and Mary Elizabeth Willits; m. Gregory Allen Sykes, Nov. 29, 1946; children: Amanda Ruth, Bryan Paul. MusB in Edn., U. Evansville, Indi., 1972; MusM, Butler U., Indpls., 1976. Tchr. elem. music Jac-Cen-Del Schs., Osgood, Ind., 1972—73; tchr. music grades k-12 NHJ United Sch. Corp., Trafalgar, 1974—86; tchr. elem. music MSD Warren Twp., Indpls., 1986—. Indpls. Alumnae chpt. pres. Sigma Alpha Iota, 1984—88, 1999—2000; vestry mem. St. Matthews Episcopal Ch., Indpls., 2006—; pres., bd. mem. Sounds Hope Alumni Assn., North Webster, Ind. Mem.: Ind. Kodaly Educators (founding pres. 1993—99), Orgn. Am. Kodaly Educators (midwest divsn. pres. 2003—05). Episcopalian. Avocations: travel, reading, needlecrafts, scrapbooks. Home: 5619 Allan Ct Indianapolis IN 46239 Office: Lowell Elementary School 2150 Hunter Rd Indianapolis IN 46239 Home Phone: 317-862-6713; Office Phone: 317-532-3945. Personal E-mail: lsykes4188@aol.com. E-mail: lsykes@warren.k12.in.us.

SYKES, MEGAN, immunologist; b. Toronto, Can., 1958; MD, Univ. Toronto, 1982. Cert. Am. Bd. Internal Medicine. Resident, medicine Montreal Gen. Hosp., Univ. Toronto, 1982—85; joined Mass. Gen. Hosp., Boston, 1990—, chief, bone marrow transplantation sect., Transplantation Biology Rsch. Ctr., and head, Cellular Immunology Lab; also prof., surgery and medicine Harvard Med. Sch., Boston. Served on Immunobiology Study Sect. NIH, 1996—2000; sci. adv. bd. Biotransplant, Inc., Immerge; trustee Roche Biomedical Rsch. Found. Author: 216 sci. jour. articles, book chapters. Recipient Jr. Faculty Rsch. award, Am. Cancer Soc., 1991, Wyeth-Ayerst Young Investigator award, Am. Soc. Transplantation, 1998, Astellas Basic Sci. Established Investigator award (Prof. Level), 2007. Office: Transplantation Biology Rsch Ctr MGH-East, Bldg 149-9019- 13th St Boston MA 02119 Office Phone: 617-726-4065. Office Fax: 617-726-4067. Business E-Mail: Megan.Sykes@tbrc.mgh.harvard.edu. *

SYKES, MELVIN JULIUS, lawyer; b. Balt., Jan. 9, 1924; s. Philip Louis and Sara (Klein) S.; m. Judith Janet Konowitz, Sept. 24, 1950; children: David K., Rachel A. (dec.), Daniel E., Israel J. Grad., Balt. City Coll., 1940, Balt. Hebrew Coll., 1941; AB with honors, Johns Hopkins U., 1943; LLB magna cum laude, Harvard U., 1948. Bar: Md. 1949, U.S. Ct. Appeals (4th cir.) 1949, U.S. Dist. Ct. Md. 1950, U.S. Supreme Ct. 1955. Law clk. to Judge Morris A. Soper U.S. Ct. Appeals (4th cir.), 1948-49; pvt. practice Balt., 1949—. Draftsman Md. Dept. Legislative Reference, 1949—50; rsch. cons. Md. Commn. Adminstrv. Orgn., 1951—52, reporter Md. Commns. to Study Judiciary, 1953, Md. commns. to revise law relating to pub. svc. commn., 1953—55; mem. standing com. on rules of practice, procedure Md. Ct. Appeals, 1954—72, 1978—; mem. legis. coun. Commsn. on Revision Condemnation Laws, 1961—63; mem. Balt. Charter Revision Com., 1962—63; pres. Bar Libr. Balt., 1962—63; mem. Md. Constl. Conv. Commn., 1966—67; cons. Gov. Md. Commn. to Revise Testamentary Laws, 1967—69; mem. Gov. Md. Commns. to study state aid to nonpub. edn., 1969—71, Md. Code Revision Commn., 1970—78. Co-author: West's Maryland Procedural Forms, 1964, Jewish Law (Mishpat Ivri), Cases and Materials, 1999; co-translator Elon, Jewish Law--History, Principles, Sources, 1994. Mem. governing coun. Am. Assn. Jewish Edn., 1968—81; hon. bd. dirs. Balt. Jewish Coun., 1970—72; bd. dirs. Balt. chpt. Am. Jewish Com.; bd. dirs. Inst. for Christian and Jewish Studies; former mem. and chmn. bd. trustees Balt. Hebrew U.; hon. bd. dirs. Balt. Neighborhoods. With USAF, 1943—45. Fellow Am. Coll. Trial Lawyers, Am. Acad. of Appellate Lawyers, Am. Coll. Trust and Estate Counsel, Am. Bar Found., Md. Bar Found. (chmn. 1981-83), Balt. City Bar Found.; mem. ABA, Am. Law Inst., Md. Bar Assn., Balt. City Bar Assn., Am. Jewish Congress, Balt. Zionist Dist., B'nai B'rith, Phi Beta Kappa Democrat. Home: 3811 Fords Ln Baltimore MD 21215-2804 Office: Ste 1701 120 E Baltimore St Baltimore MD 21202-6701 Home Phone: 410-358-6765; Office Phone: 410-727-3078. Business E-Mail: msykes@mjsykes.com.

SYKES, PLUM, writer; b. London, 1969; married. BA in Modern History, Oxford U. Fashion writer Vogue (British), 1993—97; contbg. editor Vogue (Am.), 1997—. Author: (novels) Bergdorf Blondes, 2004 (Publishers Weekly Bestseller lists), The Debutante Divorcee, 2006. Office: c/o Janklow & Nesbit 445 Park Ave New York NY 10022

SYKES, RICHARD NESBIT, retired history professor, department chairman; b. Charlotte, NC, Jan. 11, 1942; s. Richard Nesbitt and Sarah Elizabeth (Hovis) Sykes. AB in History and English summa cum laude, So. Wesleyan U., 1964; MA in Social Sci. and Reading Spec., Appalachian State U., 1965; PhD in History, Greenwich U., 2001. Cert. educator S.C., N.C. Instr. history and polit. sci. Gordon Coll., Barnesville, Ga., 1965—67; asst. prof. history and reading Gardner-Webb Coll., Boiling Springs, NC, 1967—69; instr. history and reading Ctrl. Piedmont C.C., Charlotte, 1969—70; coordinator secondary reading Chester County Schs., 1971—73; reading specialist Williamsburg County Schs., 1973—74; reading diagnostician Chesterfield County Schs., 1974—79; tchr., reading specialist Buford HS, Lancaster, SC, 1979—90; prof. history Aiken Tech. Coll., 1990—2005, dept. chair, 2001—05, ret., 2006. Nominee Gov.'s Disting. Prof. award, S.C. Commn. on Higher Edn., 2000; named Faculty Mem. of Yr., Aiken Tech. Coll., 1999; recipient medal, Nat. Inst. Staff and Orgnl. Devel., 2000. Mem.: S.C. State Employees Assn., S.C. Tech. Edn. Assn. (Educator of Yr. 1991—92, Nominee State Educator of Yr. 1991—92), Nat. Geog. Soc., Smithsonian Instn. Avocations: reading, walking, fishing. Home: 838 Osbon Dr Aiken SC 29801-4154

SYKES, WANDA, comedienne, actress; b. Portsmouth, Va., Mar. 7, 1964; BS, Hampton U. Actor: (TV series) Best of Chris Rock, 1999, Larry David: Curb Your Enthusiasm, 1999, Crank Yankers, 2003—, Wanda Does It, 2004; (films) Tomorrow Night, 1998, Nutty Professor II: The Klumps, 2000, Down to Earth, 2001, Pootie Tang, 2001, Monster-in-Law, 2005, Clerks II, 2006, My Super Ex-Girlfriend, 2006, (voice) Over the Hedge, 2006, Barnyard: The Original Party Animals, 2006; actor, writer (TV series) The Chris Rock Show, 1997—2000 (Emmy award for outstanding writing, 1999), The Downer Channel, 2001, writer, creator, actor, prodr. Wanda at Large, 2003, writer The Keenen Ivory Wayans Show, 1997, guest appearances include The Drew Carey Show, Chappelle's Show; author: Yeah I Said It, 2004; appears on (TV series) Inside the NFL, 2002—. Recipient Am. Comedy award for Funniest Female Stand-Up Comic, 2001. Office: Creative Artists Agy 9830 Wilshire Blvd Beverly Hills CA 90212

SYKIOTIS, GERASIMOS, biomedical researcher; US, 2003; MD, U. Patras, 1997, PhD, 2003. Resident internal medicine Patras U. Hosp., 1998—2000; postdoctoral rsch. assoc. U. Rochester Med. Ctr., NY, 2003—07; investigator Novartis Insts. for Biomed. Rsch., Cambridge, Mass., 2007—. Contbr. articles to med. jours. Mem.: AAAS, Hellenic Bioscientific Assn. USA, Hellenic Med. Assn., Nat. Postdoctoral Assn., Soc. Free Radical Biology and Medicine, Genetics Soc. Am., Am. Assn. Cancer Rsch.

SYKORA, PETR, professional hockey player; b. Plzen, Czechoslovakia, Nov. 19, 1976; m. Reynata Sykora. Center Cleve. Lumberjacks, 1993—94, Detroit Vipers, 1994—95, Albany River Rats; right wing NJ Devils, 1995—2002, Anaheim Mighty Ducks, 2002—06, NY Rangers, 2006, Edmonton Oilers, 2006—07, Pitts. Penquins, 2007—. Mem. Czech Republic Nat. Hockey Team, World Cup of Hockey, 1996, 2004, Czech Republic Nat. Hockey Team, Olympic Games, Salt Lake City, 2002. Named to All-Rookie Team, NHL, 1996. Achievements include being a member of Stanley Cup Champion NJ Devils, 2000. Office: Pitts Penguins 66 Mario Lemieux Pl Pittsburgh PA 15219

SYLK, LEONARD ALLEN, manufacturing executive, real estate developer; b. Phila., Feb. 25, 1941; s. Harry S. and Gertrude (Bardy) S.; m. Barbara Ann Lovenduski, Dec. 1, 1975; children: Tristan, Tyler, Galen. BS in Econs., U. Pa., 1963; MBA, Columbia U., 1965. Cert. comml. property builder. Founder, chmn. bd., CEO Shelter Systems Corp., Hainesport, NJ, 1965-99; ret.; prin. and CEO Property Mgmt. Svcs., Hainesport, 1996—. Vice chmn. USA Bancshares, Inc., 1998-2000; chmn., bd. govs. Mid. East Forum; trustee Nat. Bldg. Sys. Coun., 1986—; presdl. advisor on housing trade with Soviet Union, 1990; bldg. industry advisor US Dept. Commerce, 1997-99; mem. leadership coun. Franklin and Marshall Coll., 2006—; mem. bd. advisors Columbia U., 2006; mem. adv. bd. Hosp. U. Pa., 2006. Contbr. articles to industry publs. Chmn. ann. awards dinner Jewish Nat. Fund, Phila., 1987, v.p., bd. dir.; bd. dirs. Phila. Orch. Assn., 1990-98, emeritus, 1999—; trustee Roman Cath. HS, Phila., 2003—; bd. dir. Pa. Ballet, 1994-99, exec. com., 1996-99, vice-chmn., pres., 1998; bd. dir. Resources for Childrens' Health, 1993-96, Acad. Music, Phila., 1990-96, Rock Sch. of Pa. Ballet, 1995-98, Young Scholars Charter Sch., 2000—; bd. dir. Jewish Nat. Fund, 1987—, v.p., 2000—; trustee Hahnemann U. and Hosp., 1991-96; vice chmn., trustee St. Christopher's Hosp. Children, Phila., 1994-2002, chmn. St. Christophers Found. Children, 1999, v.p., bd. dirs., 1999-2002; chmn. 1999, bd. dirs., vice chmn. St. Peter's Sch, Phila., 1995-03; trustee Allegheny U. Hosps., 1999—; bd. dirs. Hosp U. Pa. Cancer Ctr., 2004-; NJ chmn. Builders Bush, 1988; mem. Phila. Coun. for Excellence in Edn., 2006; mem. adv. bd. Columbia U. Grad. Sch. Bus., 2006—. Named Man. of Yr., 1988, Man of Yr., NJ C. of C., 2002, 2001; recipient Tree of Life award presented by R. Hon. Margaret Thatcher, 1995, Leadership award, Roman Cath. Sch. Sys., 2006. Mem. Nat. Assn. Homebuilders (com. chmn., nat. bd. dir. 1984—, mem. exec. com. 1990, 97, fundraising chmn. 1991, Man of Yr. in Industrialized Housing 1990), Wood Truss Coun. Am. (bd. dir. 1983—, pres. 1987, named to Hall of Fame 1990), Builders League South Jersey (v.p., bd. dir. 1984-94), NJ Builders Assn. (bd. dir., com. chmn., exec. com. 1990-96), Merion Civic Assn. (bd. dir. 1999-2001), Le Club (NYC), Atlantic City Country Club, Vesper Club, Union League, Capitol Club (Washington), Masons, United Way Million Dollar Roundtable. Republican. Home: 350 N Highland Ave Merion Station PA 19066-1708 Office: Property Mgmt Svcs PO Box 9 Hainesport NJ 08036-0009 Office Phone: 609-261-4300. Business E-Mail: info@hainesport.us.

SYLLA, CASEY J., insurance company executive; m. Delores Sylla; 4 children. BS, Univ. Wis., Eau Claire, 1966; MS, Univ. Mo., 1969. Investment dept. positions through v.p. Northwestern Mutual Life Ins. Co., 1971—89, v.p., head securities dept. to sr. v.p., 1989—95; chief investment officer, then pres. Allstate Investments LLC, 1995—2002; chmn., pres. Allstate Financial, 2002—07; sr. v.p. Allstate Ins. Co., Northbrook, Ill.; chmn., pres. Allstate Life Ins. Co. Bd. dir. GATX Corp., Spirit Fin. Corp., Am. Council Life Insurers, Ins. Marketplace Standards Assn. Mem.: Assn. for Investment Mgmt. & Rsch., Investment Analysts Soc. Chgo. Office: Allstate Corp 2775 Sanders Rd Northbrook IL 60062 *

SYLLA, RICHARD EUGENE, economics professor; b. Harvey, Ill., Jan. 16, 1940; s. Benedict Andrew and Mary Gladys (Curran) S.; m. Edith Anne Dudley, June 22, 1963; children: Anne Curran, Margaret Dudley. BA, Harvard U., 1962, MA, 1965, PhD, 1969. Prof. econs. and bus. N.C. State U., Raleigh, 1968-90; Henry Kaufman prof. history fin. insts. and markets NYU, NYC, 1990—, prof. econs., 1990—, acting chmn. dept. econs., 2002—03. Cons. Citibank NA, N.Y.C., 1979-82, Chase Manhattan Bank, N.Y.C., 1983-85; vis. prof. U. Pa., Phila., 1983, U. N.C., Chapel Hill, 1988; rsch. assoc. Nat. Bur. of Econ. Rsch., 1983—; trustee Am. Mus. Fin., 2002—. Author: The American Capital Market, 1975; co-author: Evolution of the American Economy, 1980, 2d edit., 1993, A History of Interest Rates, 1991, 4th edit., 2005; co-editor: Patterns of European Industrialization, 1991, Anglo-American Financial Systems, 1995, The State, The Financial System, and Economic Modernization, 1999; editor Jour. Econ. History, 1978-84. Study fellow NEH, 1975-76; Rsch. grantee NSF, 1985-94, 98-02, Sloan Found., 1995-97. Mem. Am. Econs. Assn., Econ. History Assn. (v.p. 1987-88, trustee 1977-88, Arthur H. Cole prize 1970, pres. 2000-01), Bus. History Conf. (trustee 1991-94, 2002-04, pres. 2005-06), So. Econ. Assn. (v.p. 1981-82), Cliometrics Soc. (trustee 1997-2000, trustee chair 1998-2000). Avocations: golf, hiking, stamp collecting/philately, arts. Home: 110 Bleecker St Apt 23D New York NY 10012-2106 Office: NYU 44 W 4th St New York NY 10012-1106 Home Phone: 212-673-2131; Office Phone: 212-998-0869. Business E-Mail: rsylla@stern.nyu.edu.

SYLVESTER, DENNIS MICHAEL, electrical engineer, educator; BSEE, U. Mich., Ann Arbor, 1995; PhD in Elec. Engring., U. Calif., Berkeley, 1999. Assoc. prof. U. Mich., Ann Arbor, 2005—. Vis. assoc. prof. Nat. U. Singapore, 2006—07; cons. in field. Contbr. over 150 articles to profl. jours. Recipient David Sakrison Meml. award, U. Calif., Berkeley, 2000, Henry Russel award, U. Mich., 2006. Mem.: IEEE. Office: Univ Michigan 1301 Beal Ave Ann Arbor MI 48109-2122 Home Phone: 734-222-9184; Office Phone: 734-615-8783.

SYLVESTER, JOHN ANDREW, social studies educator; b. Springfield, Mass., Dec. 20, 1935; s. Andrew Armour Sylvester and Stella Elizabeth Davies. AB cum laude, Harvard U., 1957; MA, U. Wis., 1959, PhD, 1967. Assoc. prof. history Okla. State U., Stillwater, 1970—95, asst. prof. history, 1966—70. Contbr. articles to profl. jours. Staff sgt. US Army, 1958—62. Mem.: The Soc. for Historians of Am. Fgn. Rels., Orgn. of Am. Historians. Avocations: classical music, films, philately. Home: O4 Belden Ct Agawam MA 01001-3803

SYLVESTER, ROBERT, dean, musician; b. NYC; Dir. cultural affairs Western Wash. U., dean Sch. Fine & Performing Arts; pres. Portland State U., 1997—. Cofounder Chamber Music at Guggenheim Festival, NYC, Cape & Island Festival, Cape Cod, Mass., Bellingham Festival Music. Avocation: cello. Office: Office of the Dean Sch Fine & Performing Arts Portland State U 349 Lincoln Hall Portland OR 97207-0751 Office Phone: 503-725-3105. E-mail: sylvesterr@pdx.edu.

SYLVESTRE, JEAN GUY, former national librarian; b. Sorel, Que., Can., May 17, 1918; s. Maxime Arthur and Yvonne Marie (Lapierre) S.; m. Francoise Poitevin, Feb. 27, 1943; children: Marie, Jean, Paul. BA, U. Ottawa, 1939, B.Ph., 1940, MA, 1942, D.L.S. (hon.), 1969, D.Litt. (hon.), 1970, LL.D. (hon.), 1974, 75, 82. Translator Dept. Can. Sec. of State, 1942-44; editor Wartime Info. Bd., 1944-45; asst. pvt. sec. to minister of justice, 1945-47; pvt. sec. to sec. of state for external affairs, 1947-48; pvt. sec. to prime minister, 1948-50; adminstrv. officer Dept. Resources and Devel., 1950-53; asst. librarian Library of Parliament, Ottawa, Ont., 1953-56, asso. parliamentary librarian, 1956-68, nat. librarian, 1968-83; pres., chmn. bd. Can. Inst. for Hist. Microprodns., 1983-86; chmn. Ottawa Valley Book Festival, 1988-92; hon. chmn., 1993—. Author: Louis Francoeur, journaliste, 1941, Situation de la poésie canadienne, 1941, Anthologie de la poésie canadienne-française, 1943, 58, 64, 66, 68, 74, Poétes catholiques de la France contemporaine, 1944, Sondages, 1945, Impressions de théâtre, 1950, Amours, délices et orgues, 1953, Panorama des lettres canadiennes-francaises, 1964, Canadian Writers, 1964, Literature in French Canada, 1967, A Century of Canadian Literature, 1967, The Future of the National Library of Canada, 1980, Guidelines for National Libraries, 1987 French, Spanish and Arabic edits., 1988; also articles in profl. jours., encys.; editor: A Canadian Errant (J.P. Manion), 1960; editor: Canadian Universities Today, 1961, Structures sociales du Canada francais, 1967. Chmn. Gov. Gen.'s Lit. Awards, 1960-62; organizer, chmn. World Poetry Conf., Expo 1967; chmn. Can. Council Com. on Aid-to-Publs., 1960-68; lectr. U. Ottawa Library Sch., 1954-71; v.p. Can. Library Week Council, 1965-67; Bd. dirs. Can. Writers Found., pres., 1960-61. Decorated comdr. Ordre International du Bien Public, officer Order of Can.; comdr. Order of Merit of Poland; recipient Centennial medal., Outstanding Pub. Service award, Internat. Fedn. Libr. Assn. medal. Fellow Royal Soc. Can. (hon. sec. 1959-62, pres. sect. I 1963-64, hon. libr. 1969-91, pres. 1973-74); mem. Can. Libr. Assn. (life), Ont. Libr. Assn. (hon. life), Can. Assn. Info. Sci. (pres. 1971-72), Assn. Scis. et Techniques de la Documentation (life). Home: 2286 Bowman Rd Ottawa ON Canada K1H 6V6

SYLVIA, DENNIS ASHTON, geologist; b. New Bedford, Mass., Sept. 29, 1951; s. Leonard Earl and Mildred Agnes Sylvia; m. Lavenia Rumiko Mace, June 22, 2000. BS in Geology, Ariz. State U., Tempe, 1978; MS in Geoscis., U. Ariz., Tucson, 1985; MS in Civil Engring., U. Tex., San Antonio, 1993; PhD, U. Tex., Austin, 2002. Cert. profl. geologist Tenn., 1996, basic meteorology Tex. A&M U., 1979. Post doctoral rsch. fellow U. Tex. Inst. Geophysics, Austin, Tex., 2002; natural resources planner US Forest Svc., Thorne Bay, Alaska, 2002—. Chmn. Planning and Zoning Comm., Thorne Bay, Alaska, 2003—04. Capt. US Air Force, 1986—95. Mem.: Soc. Sedimentary Geology, Am. Geophys. Union, Geol. Soc. Am., Phi Kappa Phi. Home: Pob 19461 Thorne Bay AK 99919-0461 Office: US Forest Service 1312 Federal Way Thorne Bay AK 99919 Home Phone: 907.828-395; Office Phone: 907-828-3226. Personal E-mail: dennis_sylvia@hotmail.com. E-mail: dennissylvia@fs.fed.us.

SYMCHOWICZ, SAMSON, retired biochemist; b. Krakow, Poland, Mar. 20, 1923; came to U.S., 1954; s. Chiel and Esther M. S.; m. Sarah R. Nussbaum, May 24, 1953; children: Esther, Beatrice, Caren. Chem. engr., Poly. Inst. Prague, Czechoslovakia, 1950; MS in Chemistry, Bklyn. Poly. Inst., 1956; PhD in Biochemistry, Rutgers U., 1960. Asst. biochemist McGill U., Montreal, Que., Can., 1951-54, SUNY, 1954-56; biochemist Schering-Plough Corp., Bloomfield, N.J., 1956-73, assoc. dir. biol. rsch., 1973-80, dir. drug metabolism, 1980-92; ret. Editorial bd. Drug Metabolism and Disposition; contbr. over 90 sci. papers to profl. pubs. Mem. Internat. Soc. Study of Xenobiotics, Am. Chem. Soc., N.Y. Acad. Sci., Soc. Pharmacology and Exptl. Therapeutics.

SYME, DANIEL BAILEY, rabbi, institution executive; b. Sharon, Pa., Feb. 6, 1946; s. Monte Robert and Sonia (Hendin) S.; m. Jill Susan Young; 1 child, Joshua. BA, U. Mich., Ann Arbor, 1967; BHL, MAHL, Hebrew Union Coll.-Jewish Inst. Religion, Cin., 1972; MEd, Columbia U., 1977, EdD, 1980. Ordained rabbi, 1972. Asst. dir. Nat. Fedn. Temple Youth, 1972-73; rabbi Stamford (Conn.) Fellowship for Jewish Learning, 1973-77; asst. nat. dir. edn. Union of Am. Hebrew Congregations, NYC, 1973-77, dir., 1977—; asst. dir. Commn. Jewish Edn. for Reform Movement, NYC, 1973-77, dir., 1977—, Union of Am. Hebrew Congregations TV Inst., NYC, 1982-83, exec. asst. to pres., 1983-85, v.p., 1985-91, sr. v.p., 1991-96; sr. rabbi Temble Beth El, Bloomfield Hills, Mich., 1996—. Chmn. coalition for Alternatives in Jewish Edn., N.Y.C., 1978-80; mem. Nat. Assn. Temple Educators, 1972-91, Commn. on Teaching of Israel and Zionism, World Zionist Orgn., 1980-84; dir.-at-large Jewish Nat. Fund, Jewish Fedn. Met. Detroit, 2000—, internat. bd. Meml. Found. for Jewish Culture; nat. cabinet mem. Am. Zionist Movement, v.p. Am. Zionist Youth Movement; bd. dirs. United Israel Appeal, Ecumenical Inst., Jewish Nat. Fund. Author: 100 Essential Books for Jewish Readers, Finding God, My Body is Something Special, Prayer Is Reaching, I'm Growing, I Learn About God, Books Are Treasures, Jewish Home, What Happens After I Die?, Why I Am a Reform Jew, Drugs, Sex and Integrity, The Jewish Wedding Book, The Book of the Jewish Life; exec. prodr. T.V. programs A Conversation with Menachem Begin, 1981, Choosing Judaism, 1981, To See the World Through Jewish Eyes, 1983, A Conversation with Yitzchak Navon, 1983, You Can Go Home Again, Jewish Youth and Cults, 1984; contbr. articles to religious publs. Mem. Rabbinic Adv. Coun., United Jewish Appeal, Nat. Religious Edn. Assn. (exec. bd.), Nat Coun. Jewish Edn. (exec. bd.), Econ. Club Detroit (bd. dirs.), Jewish Nat Fung (bd. dir.) Office: 7400 Telegraph Rd Bloomfield Hills MI 48301-3876

SYMES, LAWRENCE RICHARD, computer science educator, university dean; b. Oliver Lawrence and Maybell Melita Blanche Symes; m. Evelyn Jean Hewett, Apr. 3, 1964; children: Calvin Richard, Michelle Louise, Erin Kathleen. BA, U. Sask., Saskatoon, Can., 1963, postgrad. in math., 1964; MS, Purdue U., 1966, Phd, 1969. Asst. prof. Purdue U., West Lafayette, Ind., 1969-70; assoc. prof. computer sci. U. Regina, Sask., Canada, 1970-74, prof. Sask., 1974—, dir. computer ctr. Sask., 1970-75, head dept. computer sci. Sask., 1972-81, dean of sci. Sask., 1982-92, dean grad. studies, assoc. rsch. v.p. Sask., 1997-99, dir. info. svcs. Sask., 1999—. Dir. tng. Software Tech. Ctr., 1993-94; exec. dir. postsecondary svcs. br. Saskatchewan Edn. Tng. and Employment Govt. of Saskatchewan, 1994-95, exec. dir. multimedia learning, 1995-96; invited lectr. Xian Jiaotong U., 1983; invited lectr., Shandong Acad. Sci., China, 1987, guest prof.; vis. prof. Ednl. Inst. Jilin Province, Shandong U., Jinan, China; co-chair IT cluster Regina Regional Econ. Authority, 2002—. Contbr. articles to profl. jours. Bd. dirs. Hosp. Sys. Study Group, Saskatoon, 1978-94, chmn. bd., 1980-83; dir. SSTA Computer Svcs., Regina, 1972-89; mem. adv. coun. Can./Sask. Advanced Tech. Agreement, 1985-87; mem. Sask. Agrl. Rsch. Found. Bd., 1987-88; mem. steering com. IBM/Sask. Agreement, 1990-92; mem. adv. bd. Plant Biotech. Inst., NRC. Can. Fed. Govt. grantee, 1977-84. Mem. Assn. Computing Machinery, Can. Info. Processing (pres. 1979-80, accreditation com. 1988-94), IEEE Computer Soc., Sask. ADA Assn. (bd. dirs. 1990-93), Software Tech. Ctr. (bd. dirs. 1993-98), Regina Regional Econ. Authority (IT cluster co-chair). Office: U Regina Info Svcs 3737 Wascana Pkwy Regina SK Canada S4S 0A2

SYMINGTON, TOBY, foundation administrator; b. Washington, Jan. 20, 1943; s. Arthur Lloyd Symington and Nancy Everett Glover. BA, Princeton U., NJ, 1964; MA, Oxford U., England, 1966. Astrological cons. pvt. practice, San Anselmo, Calif., 1980—; exec. dir. Lloyd Symington Found., San Anselmo, 1986—. Liberal. Avocations: music, hiking, travel, reading. Home and Office: 33 Knoll Rd San Anselmo CA 94960

SYMLAR, JESSE LEE, finance executive; b. Cleve., Aug. 4, 1959; s. Jesse Lee and Willa Leeann S. BA in Pub. Adminstrn., Christopher Newport U., 1982; MBA. MS in Tech. Mgmt., U. Md., 2001. Project mgr. VYCOR Corp., Washington, 1986-90; multimedia tng. Multimedia Tng. Inst., Washington, 1987-88; program analyst Det. Vets. Affairs, Washington, 1990; program mgmt. U.S. Dept. Agrl., Washington, 1990-93; program analyst Dept. Vets. Affairs, Washington, 1993-99; bus. process engr. Multimedia, Upper Marlboro, Md., 1998-2000; CEO Kyi Internat., Upper Marlboro, Md., 2000—. Author of poems. Mentor Each-One-Teach-One, Upper Marlboro, 1997-99. Sgt. USAF, 1975-79. Mem. Amherst Soc., Internat. Soc. Poets (disting.). Avocations: art, poetry, music, chess, sports, computers. Home: 3311 Old Largo Rd Upper Marlboro MD 20772-7811 E-mail: jsymlar@msn.com.

SYMONE, RAVEN (RAVEN-SYMONÉ CHRISTINA PEARMAN), actress, singer; b. Atlanta, Dec. 10, 1985; d. Christopher B. Pearman and Lydia Gaulden. Actor: (TV series) The Cosby Show, 1989—92, A Different World, 1989, The Fresh Prince of Bel-Air, 1992, Hangin' with Mr. Cooper, 1994—97, Happily Ever After: Fairy Tales for Every Child, 1998, My Wife and Kids, 2001, (voice) Kim Possible, 2002—07, That's So Raven, 2003—07 (Blimp Award for Favorite TV Actress, Kids' Choice Awards, 2004, 2005, Outstanding Performance, Children's Program, NAACP Image Awards, 2004, 2005, 2006, 2007), Fillmore!, 2004, Higglytown Heroes, 2005; (films) The Little Rascals, 1994, Doctor Dolittle, 1998, Dr. Dolittle 2, 2001, The Princess Diaries 2: Royal Engagement, 2004, (voice) Fat Albert, 2004, Everyone's Hero, 2006, (video) Kim Possible: The Secret Files, 2003, That's So Raven: Supernaturally Stylish, 2004, That's So Raven: Raven's Makeover Madness, 2006, Raven Symone: Raven's Postcards from Spain, 2006; (TV films) The Cheetah Girls, 2003, (voice) Kim Possible: A Sitch in Time, 2003, Kim Possible: So the Drama, 2005, Zenon: Z3, 2004, For One Night, 2006; prodr.: (TV series) That's So Raven, 2006; actor, co-prodr.: (TV films) The Cheetah Girls 2, 2006; singer: (soundtrack) Ella Enchanted, 2004, That's So Raven, 2004, The Princess Diaries 2: Royal Engagement, 2004. Former amb. Children First program; spkr. for Nat. Safe Kids Campaign. Home: c/o Internat Creative Mgmt 8942 Wilshire Blvd Beverly Hills CA 90211-1934 *

SYMONS, EDWARD LEONARD, JR., lawyer, educator, investment advisor; b. Pitts., Dec. 21, 1941; s. Edward Leonard and Lillian Mae (Daniel) S.; m. Louise Quinn, July 18, 1970; children: Amy, Colin. BA, Cornell U., 1963; JD summa cum laude, U. Pitts., 1969. Assoc., ptnr. Reding, Blackstone, Rea & Sell, Pitts., 1969-72; asst. atty. gen., chief counsel Pa. Dept. Banking, Harrisburg, 1972-74; prof. law U. Pitts. Sch. Law, 1974-98; chmn. Symons Capital Mgmt., Inc., 1983—. Tax cons., Wash., 1987, Del., 95; exec. v.p. investments Smithfield Trust Co., 1996—2000; mem. adv. coun. Conflict Resolution Ctr. Internat., 1994—2004; mem. bd. internat. scholars Ctr. for Comml. Law Studies, Queen Mary and Westfield Coll., U. London, 1993—2004. Co-author: Pennsylvania Professional Corporations, 1974, Banking Law Teaching Materials, 1984, 3d edit., 1991, Regulation of Financial Institutions, 1998; contbr. articles to profl. jours. Commr., Mt. Lebanon, Pa., 1976—80; chmn. St. Clair Hosp. Found., Pitts., 1996—2006; bd. dirs. Performing Arts for Children, Pitts., 1980—84, Mt. Lebanon Hosp. Authority, 1993—2004, St. Clair Hosp., 1995—. 1st. lt. arty., AUS, 1964—66. Mem.: Order Coif. Office: Symons Capital Mgmt Inc 250 Mount Lebanon Blvd Ste 301 Pittsburgh PA 15234-1248 Home Phone: 412-854-1977; Office Phone: 412-344-7690.

SYMONS, ROBERT SPENCER, electronics engineer; b. San Francisco, July 3, 1925; s. Spencer W. and Avesia (Atkins) S.; m. Alice Faye Smith, Dec. 21, 1960; children: Julia Ann, Robert Spencer Jr. BS, Stanford U., 1946, MS, 1948. Engr. Eitel-McCullough, Inc., San Bruno, Calif., 1947, Heinz & Kaufman, South San Francisco, 1948, Pacific Electronics Co., Los Gatos, Calif., 1949; sr. engring. mgr. Varian Assocs., Palo Alto, Calif., 1950-83; tech. dir. CTO Litton Sys., Inc., San Carlos, Calif., 1983—. Patentee in field. 1st lt. AUS, 1950-53. Recipient Charles B. Thornton award for Advanced Tech. Achievement, 1991, 99. Fellow IEEE (assoc. editor Transactions on Electron Devices jour. 1980-83); mem. Commonwealth of Calif. Club, Phi Beta Kappa, Tau Beta Pi. Home: 290 Surrey Pl Los Altos CA 94022-2180 Office: Litton Industries 960 Industrial Rd San Carlos CA 94070-4194

SYMONS, VAN JAY, humanities educator; b. Logan, Utah, June 5, 1945; s. Joseph Nathaniel Symons and Vivian Lavon Burrup; m. Ruth Alene Thomson; children: Amy Marie Ettore, Brandt Nathaniel, Cherilyn Andrea, Diana Christine, Karl Woodruff. AB, Brigham Young U., Provo, Utah, 1970; PhD, Brown U., Providence, RI, 1974. Asst. prof. Whittier Coll., Calif., 1974—78; prof. Augustana Coll., Rock Island, Ill., 1978—. Dir. ASIANetwork Consultancy Adv. Program, Bloomington, Ill., 1998—99; exec. dir. ASIANetwork, Bloomington, 1999—2005; mem. editl. adv. bd. EastBridge Press, Norwalk, Conn., 2001—; sr. editl. adv. bd. Edn. About Asia, Ann Arbor, Mich., 2003—05; vis. prof. Brigham Young U., Provo, 1982—83; vis. Mansfield prof. of modern Asian affairs Maureen and Mike Mansfield Ctr., U. Mont., Missoula, 1990—91. Author: (book) Ch'ing Ginseng Management: Ch'ing Monopolies in Microcosm; co-author (with Sechin Jagchid): Peace, War, and Trade Along the Great Wall: Nomadic Chinese Interaction through Two Millennia; co-editor: Asia in the Undergraduate Curriculum: A Case for Asian Studies in Liberal Arts Education. Vice-chair, chair ASIANetwork, Bloomington, 1995—99. Fellow, NEH, Summer Insts., 1978, 1980, 1994, 1995. Lds Ch. Home: 123 Fernwood Ave Davenport IA 52803 Office: Augustana Coll 639 - 38th St Rock Island IL 61201 Home Phone: 563-355-2821; Office Phone: 309-794-7413. Office Fax: 309-794-7702. Business E-Mail: vanjsymons@augustana.edu.

SYNCLAIR, LARRY ROSS, news correspondent, educator, advocate; b. Fresno, Calif., June 27, 1960; s. Emily C. and Larry R. Griffith; m. S.E. Stinson, July 30, 1980 (div. Sept. 1981); m. S.V. Gavrilova, June 4, 1994 (div. Jan. 23, 2003); children: Jason, Larry Jr. AA, N. Idaho Coll., Coeur d'Alene, 1984; BA, Wash. State U., Pullman, 1986; MA, Calif. State U., Chico, 1990. Cert. grant writing Portland C.C., 2005. U. instr. Wash. State U., Pullman, Wash., 1986—86; ops. dir. KCHO-FM, Chico, Calif., 1987—90; assoc. prof. Calif. State U., Chico, 1991; radio prodr., announcer Radio Moscow, 1991—92; fgn. news corr. USA Radio Network, Moscow, 1991—94; news dir., morning show co-host Radio 7, Moscow, 1992—94; fgn. news corr. substitute NBC Radio News, Moscow, 1994; founder, pres. Synclair & Assoc., Moscow, 1994—98; state corr. Westwood One, Portland, Oreg., 2004—05; freelance writer, legal rschr. Portland, 1998—. Instr. Oreg. State U., Corvallis, 2007. Mem. Parental Abduction Prevention Work Group, Oreg. Commn. Children and Families), Salem, 2006; author Synclair-Cannon Child Abduction Prevention Act of 2003, Calif. family code sect. 3048. Recipient Spl. Recognition, Delta Kappa Gamma, 1990; KCPQ scholar, Kelly Broasdcasting, 1985, Athletic scholar, N. Idaho Coll., 1980.

SYNEK, MIROSLAV, physicist, chemist, world affairs consultant; b. Prague, Czech Republic, Sept. 18, 1930; came to U.S., 1958, naturalized, 1963; s. Frantisek and Anna (Kokrment) S.; children: Mary Rose, Thomas Robert. Cert., Indsl. Chemistry Tech. Sch., Prague, 1946-50; cert. in liberal arts, Prague, 1951; MS in Physics with distinction, Charles U., Prague, 1956; PhD in Physics, U. Chgo., 1963. Analytical chemist Indsl. Medicine Inst., Prague, 1950-51; rsch. physicist Acad. Scis., Prague, 1956-58; from asst. to assoc. prof. De Paul U., Chgo., 1962-67; prof. Tex. Christian U., Ft. Worth, 1967-71; lectr., rschr. U. Tex., Austin, 1971-75; tenured faculty U. Tex., San Antonio, 1975-95. Sci. advisor Tex. Edn. Agy., Austin, 1971-73, U. Tex., 1971-73; advisor Student Physics Soc., active numerous univ. coms. Contbr. numerous articles to sci. jours., abstracts to presentations. Campaigner United Way, San Antonio, 1975-95; judge Alamo Sci. Fairs and Tex. Acad. of Sci. Fairs, annually; grand award judge Internat. Sci. and Engring. Fairs, 1998, 99. Rsch. grantee Robert A. Welch Found., 1968-71, 76-83, 93-95. Fellow AAAS, Am. Phys. Soc. (life), Tex. Acad. Sci., Am. Inst. Chemists; mem. NEA, Tex. State Tchrs. Assn., AAUP, DAV Comdrs. Club, Am. Assn. Physics Tchrs., Am. Acad. Polit. Sci., Am. Mus. Natural

History, Libr. Congress, Smithsonian Instn., Nat. Trust Hist. Preservation, N.Y. Acad. Scis., Am. Chem. Soc. (San Antonio edn. com. chmn.), Czechoslovak Nat. Coun. Am. (dist. sec. Chgo. 1961-63, chmn. 1967), Czechoslovak Soc. Arts and Scis. Am., Internat. Soc. Poets (disting. mem.), Sheriffs' Assn. Tex. (assoc.), San Antonio Astron. Assn., World Affairs Coun. San Antonio (diplomat mem.), Bexar County Czech Heritage Soc. of Tex., Sigma Xi (life), Sigma Pi Sigma (sustaining). Roman Catholic. Achievements include research in atomic structure calculations of laser-active lanthanides, analytical relativistic self-consistent field theory, approximate estimate of the extra-terrestrial intelligence probability, nuclear age requiring free elections, main dangers of our times, suggested priorities for human society. Home and Office: Independent Consultant PO Box 5937 San Antonio TX 78201-0937 Personal E-mail: m.synek@juno.com.

SYNNOTT, AIDAN JOHN, lawyer; b. Cork, Ireland, July 1, 1964; arrived in U.S., 1987; s. Edward Christopher Synnott and Nora Mary Angela Walsh; m. Elizabeth Lauren Grayer, May 11, 2002; 1 child, Catherine Eve. B of Civil Law, Univ. Coll. Cork, 1985; LLM, U. Mich., 1989. Bar: Ireland 1987, NY 1989, US Dist. Ct. (so. and ea. dists.) NY 1989, US Ct. Appeals (2nd cir.) 1992, US Supreme Ct. 1993, US Dist. Ct. (no. dist.) Calif. 1993, US Dist. Ct. (no. dist.) NY 2001, US Ct. Appeals (9th cir.) 2003, US Ct. Appeals (3rd cir.) 2005, US Ct. Appeals (6th cir.) 2006, Barrister at Law: Hon. Soc. of King's Inns, Dublin 1987. With Paul, Weiss, Rifkind, Wharton & Garrison LLP, NYC, 1988—2000, ptnr., 2000—. Assoc. editor: Antitrust Law Jour., 2000—07. Named Alumnus of Yr. in Law, Univ. Coll. Cork, 2004. Fellow: Am. Bar Found.; mem.: ABA (mem. leadership antitrust sect. 2000—), NY State Bar Assn. (chair com. on antitrust 1999—2002), Bar Assn. City NY (mem. pro bono com. 2002—05). Home: 124 Hudson St New York NY 10013 Office: Paul Weiss Rifkind Wharton & Garrison LLP 1285 Avenue of the Americas New York NY 10019-6064

SYNNOTT, MARCIA GRAHAM, history professor; b. Camden, NJ, July 4, 1939; d. Thomas Whitney and Beatrice Adelaide (Colby) S.; m. Willard Edwin Sharp, June 16, 1979; children: Willard Sharp, Laurel Beth Sharp. AB, Radcliffe Coll., 1961; MA, Brown U., 1964; PhD, U. Mass., 1974. History tchr. MacDuffie Sch., Springfield, Mass., 1963-68; instr. U. S.C., Columbia, 1972-74, asst. prof., 1974-79, assoc. prof. history, 1979-97, dir. grad. studies history dept., 1990-92, prof. history, 1997—. Author: The Half-Opened Door, 1979; contbr. essays to books, articles to profl. jours. Active university-wide cmty. svc. projects. Grantee, Am. Coun. Learned Socs., 1981; Fulbright scholar, 1988. Mem. Am. Hist. Assn., So. Hist. Assn., Orgn. Am. Historians (membership com. 1990-93), S.C. Hist. Assn. (pres. 1994-95), History of Edn. Soc. (mem. editl. bd. 1996, 97, 98, bd. dirs. 2000-02). Avocations: history, skiing, walking. Office: U SC Dept History Columbia SC 29208-0001 Office Phone: 803-777-2585. Business E-Mail: synnott@gwm.sc.edu.

SYNNOTT, WILLIAM RAYMOND, retired management consultant; b. Fall River, Mass., Dec. 29, 1929; s. William Joseph and Marie Aurore (Labrie) S.; m. Suzanne Pauline Moseley, Oct. 21, 1967; children—Dianne, Mark, Amy Grad. cert., Rutgers U., 1958; BS summa cum laude, Boston U., 1973; grad. advanced mgmt. program, Harvard Bus. Sch., 1973. Sr. v.p. Bank of Boston, 1967-87; sr. dir. The Yankee Group, Boston, 1987-88; dir. Nolan Norton & Co., Lexington, Mass., 1988-91; pres. W.R. Synnott Assocs., Wellesley Hills, Mass., 1990-94; ret., 1994. Lectr., seminar leader on info. technology worldwide. Author: The Information Weapon, 1987; co-author: Information Resource Management, 1981. Served as sgt. U.S. Army, 1951-53, Korea. Avocations: skiing, tennis, golf. Home (Summer): 6 Iron Mountain Rd Jackson NH 03846 Home: Po Box 608 Jackson NH 03846-0608 Personal E-mail: wilsyn@aol.com.

SYNOLAKIS, COSTAS E., engineering educator; b. Athens, Greece, Sept. 21, 1956; BS in Engring. and Applied Sci., Calif. Inst. Tech., 1978, MS in Civil Engring., 1979, PhD in Civil Engring., 1986. Asst. prof. civil and environ. engring. U. So. Calif., LA, 1985-91, assoc. prof. civil, environ. and aerospace engring., 1991-97, prof. civil, environ., mech. and aerospace engring., 1997—. Prime Minister's adv. sci. and tech., Greece, 1993; vis. prof. U. Calif., Berkeley, 1994. Contbr. articles to sci. jours., chapters to books; co-author: Long Wave Runup Models, 1997, Furious Earth: The Sci. of Earthquakes, Volcanoes and Tsunamis, 1999. Recipient Presdl. Young Investigator award, 1989—94; grantee Alexander Onassis Pub. Benefit Found. fellowship, 1981—83. Mem.: Internat. Assn. Hydraulic Rsch., NY Acad. Scis., Armenian Acad. Scis., Soc. Theoretical and Applied Mechanics, Assn. Asphalt Paving Technologists, Am. Geophys. Union, Am. Phys. Soc., AAUP, AAAS, ASCE, Chi Epsilon, Sigma Xi. Office: Dept Civil Engring U So Calif Los Angeles CA 90089-2531 E-mail: costas@usc.edu.

SYPHER, FRANCIS J., writer, editor, educator; s. Francis J. and Mildred A. Sypher; m. Marie-Claire Cournand, 1966 (div. 1969); m. Eleanor C. Kramer, 1970 (div. 1983); 1 child, Eleanor H. AB, Columbia U., NYC, 1963, AM, 1964, PhD, 1968. Prof. Columbia U., 1965—68, U. NY, Albany, 1968—75. Author: (books) Saint Agnes Chapel of the Parish of Trinity Church, 2002, Frederick L. Hoffman, His Life and Works, 2002, Letitia Elizabeth Landon, 2004, New York Society of the Cincinnati: Biographies of Original Members and Other Continental Officers, 2004, Landon Bibliography, 2005; editor: Landon's Works, 1990, 15th vol., 2007; contbr. articles to profl. jours. Rsch. grant, NY State Regents Fellowship, 1963—65, SUNY Rsch. Found., 1974, Mellon Found. Pub., 1974, Fulbright Sr. Lectureship Am. Lit., 1981—83, 1986—88. Mem.: Huguenot Soc. Am., St. Nicholas Soc. City NY (editor), NY State Soc. Cin., Cosmos Club. Office: FDR Station PO Box 1125 New York NY 10150-1125 Personal E-mail: fjsypher@usa.net.

SYPOLT, DIANE GILBERT, retired judge; b. Rochester, NY, June 14, 1947; d. Myron Birne and Doris Isabell (Robie) Gilbert; m. Dwight Douglas Sypolt; children: Andrew, David Weinstein. BA, Smith Coll., Northampton, Mass., 1969; postgrad., Stanford U., 1977-78, Georgetown U., 1978; JD, Boston U., 1979. Bar: D.C. 1979, Mass. 1979. Law clk. to judge D.C. Ct. Appeals, Washington, 1979-80; assoc. Peabody, Lambert & Meyers, Washington, 1980-83; asst. gen. counsel Office of Mgmt. and Budget, Washington, 1983-86; dep. gen. counsel U.S. Dept. Edn., Washington, 1986-88, acting gen. counsel, 1988-89; legal counselor to V.P. of U.S., White House; counsel Pres.'s Competitiveness Coun., Washington, 1989-90; judge U.S. Ct. Fed. Claims, Washington, 1990—2005; ret., 2005. Recipient Young Lawyer's award Boston U. Law Sch., 1989. Mem. Fed. Am. Inn of Ct. (Master), Federalist Soc. Home Phone: 410-685-6097. Personal E-mail: dgsypolt@yahoo.com.

SYPOLT, SHIRLEY RAE, elementary school educator; b. Farmville, Va., Sept. 9, 1953; d. Benifield and Ruth Bethel Burnett; m. Russell Eugene Sypolt, Jr., Sept. 1, 1974; children: Russell Eugene III, Jason Michael, Ryan Alexander. AS, Southside Va. CC, Keysville, 1973; BS in Edn., U. Nebr., Omaha, 1991; MSc in Tchg. Environ. Edn., Christopher Newport U., Newport News, Va., 2001. Lic. early childhood k-4, mid. grades 4-8 Va. Bd. Edn., cert. mid. childhood generalist Nat. Bd. Profl. Tchg. Stds., 2005. Pre-sch. tchr. Greenfield Childhood Devel. Ctr., Bossier City, La., 1986—88; sub. tchr. Bossier Parish Sch. Dist., 1988—89, Omaha Pub. Schs., Nebr., 1992; 5th grade tchr. Hampton City Schs., Va., 1992—; k-5 sci. instrnl. leader Cooper Elem. Schs., 1999—. State facilitator, project learning tree Va. Dept. Forestry, Richmond, 1999—; state facilitator, project WET Va. Dept. Environ. Quality, Richmond, 1999—; state facilitator, project WILD Va. Dept. Game, Richmond, 2000—; adj. prof. Christopher Newport U., 2002—05; edn. adv. panel Nat. Wildlife Fedn., 2002—; exec. adv. com. Gov.'s Environ. Edn., 2001; adv. com. Project Learning Tree, 2000—. Author: (poem) Earth's Rock Cycle, 2002, project WILD k-12 curriculum & activity guide. Chair Sch. Pride in Action Com., Hampton, 1998—, Hampton Clean City Commn., 2004—. Recipient Pres.' Coun. Environ. Quality Tchr. Tng. award, NEETF, 2001, Outstanding Educator award, Nat. Project Learning Tree, 2001, Presdl. award for Excellence in Math. & Sci. Tchg., Nat. Sci. Found., 2003. Mem.: NSTA (Disting. Tchg. award 2003), Nat. Wildlife Fedn. Leaders Club, Soc. Elem. Presdl. Awardees, Assn. Presdl. Awardees in Sci. Tchg. Republican. Protestant/Methodist. Avocations: gardening, reading. Home: 6 Enscore Ct Hampton VA 23666 Office: Cooper Elem Magnet Sch 200 Marcella Rd Hampton VA 23666 Office Phone: 757-825-4645. Personal E-mail: shirleysyp@aol.com.

SYRDAHL, RICKELLE LYN, biology professor; b. Encino, Calif., Sept. 1, 1964; d. Richard Preston and Marilyn Ann Johnson; m. Leif Frederick Syrdahl, July 14, 1990; 1 child, Kaelyn Ann. BA, U. Calif., Santa Barbara, 1986; MS, Calif. State U., Chico, 1993. Rsch. asst. Calif. State U., Chico, 1991—92, tchg. asst., 1992—93; instr. Upward Bound, Chico, 1993; rsch. asst. Jean Hubbell, Chico, 1993—94; lab mgr. Pepperdine U., Malibu, 1994—97; assoc. prof. Porterville (Calif.) Coll., 1997—. Adj. faculty Butte Coll., Oroville, Calif., 1994. Mem.: Nat. Assn. Biology Tchrs., Phi Kappa Phi. Avocations: camping, hiking, reading, photography. Office: Porterville Coll 100 E College Ave Porterville CA 93257 Office Phone: 559-791-2347. Business E-Mail: rsyrdahl@portervillecollege.edu.

SYRON, RICHARD F. (RICHARD FRANCIS SYRON), finance company executive, economist; b. Boston, Oct. 25, 1943; s. Dominick Richard and Elizabeth (McQuire) S.; m. Margaret Mary Garatoni, Oct. 21, 1972; children: Erin Elizabeth, Brendan Paul. BS in Econs.-Acctg. with high honors, Boston Coll., 1966; MA in Econs., Tufts U., 1969, PhD in Econs., 1971. Dep. dir. budget Commonwealth of Mass., 1973-74; v.p., economist Fed. Res. Bank of Boston, 1974-82, sr. v.p., econ. advisor, 1982-85; exec. asst. to sec. U.S. Dept. Treasury, Washington, 1979-80, dep. sec. for econ. policy, 1980-81; asst. to Chmn. Volcker Fed. Res. Sys., Washington, 1981-82; pres., CEO Fed. Home Loan Bank of Boston, 1986-88; pres., chief exec. officer Fed. Res. Bank of Boston, 1989-94; chmn. Am. Stock Exch., NYC, 1994-99; chmn., CEO Thermo Electron, Waltham, Mass., 1999—2002, exec. chmn., 2002—03; chmn., CEO Fed. Home Loan Mortgage Corp. (Freddie Mac), McLean, Va., 2003—. Bd. trustees Boston Coll.; past chmn. Boston Pvt. Industry Coun.; bd. dirs. McKesson Corp., Nabors Industries. Author: Urban Fire Insurance, 1972; contbr. articles to profl. jours. Mem. Fed. Open Market Com., 1989—94. Teaching fellow Tufts U., 1966-69. Mem.: Comml. Club Boston, Boston Econ. Club, Clover Club Boston. Office: Freddie Mac 8200 Jones Branch Dr Mc Lean VA 22102-3110 *

SYTSMA, FREDRIC A., lawyer; b. Grand Rapids, Mich., Jan. 12, 1944; BA, Mich. State U., 1964; JD, U. Mich., 1968. Bar: Mich. 1968. Mem. Varnum, Riddering, Schmidt & Howlett, Grand Rapids. Fellow Am. Coll. Trust and Estate Counsel; mem. ABA, State Bar Mich. (mem. coun. probate and estate planning sect. 1977—, chmn. 1986-87), Grand Rapids Bar Assn. Office: Varnum Riddering Schmidt & Howlett PO Box 352 333 Bridge St NW Grand Rapids MI 49501-0352 Office Phone: 616-336-6000. Business E-Mail: fasytsma@varnumlaw.com.

SYVERTSON, CLARENCE ALFRED, management consultant, engineer; b. Mpls., Jan. 12, 1926; s. Alfred and Esther Louise (Goertemiller) S.; m. Helen Hammond Gonnella, May 4, 1953 (dec. May 1981); 1 child, Marguerite Louise.; m. JoAnn Mary Caruso, May 8, 1982; 1 stepchild, Lynn S. Sechrest. B. Aero. Engring., U. Minn., 1946, MS, 1948, DSc (hon.), 2004; postgrad., Stanford U., 1950—57; grad., Advanced Mgmt. Program, Harvard U., 1977. Research scientist Ames Aero. Lab., NACA, Moffett Field, Calif., 1948-58; exec. dir. Joint Dept. Transp./NASA Civil Aviation Research and Devel. Policy Study, 1970-71; with Ames Research Center, NASA, Moffett Field, 1958-84, dep. dir., 1969-78, dir., 1978-84. Adv. bd. Coll. Engring., U. Calif., Berkeley, 1980-85; cons. prof. Stanford U., 1985-88; hon. prof. Northwestern Poly. U., Xian, China, 1998. Served with U.S. Army, 1946-47. Recipient invention and contbn. award NASA, 1964, Exceptional Svc. medal, 1971, Disting. Svc. medal, 1984, Outstanding Achievement award U. Minn., 1982, Comdrs. award for civilian service U.S. Army, 1984 Fellow AIAA (Lawrence Sperry award 1957), Am. Astronautical Soc., Calif. Coun. Sci. and Tech.; mem. Nat. Acad. Engring. Home: 14666 Springer Ave Saratoga CA 95070-5748 Personal E-mail: syvertson@comcast.net.

SYVERUD, KENT DOUGLAS, dean, law educator; b. Rochester, NY, Oct. 23, 1956; s. Warren Lukken and Janet (Thatcher) S.l; m. Ruth Chi-Fen Chen, May 22, 1982; children: Steven, Brian, David. BSFS, Georgetown U., 1977; JD, U. Mich., 1981, MA, 1983. Bar: D.C. 1982, Mich. 1993. Law clk. to Judge Oberdorfer U.S. Dist. Ct. D.C., Washington, 1983-84; law clk. Justice O'Connor Supreme Ct. U.S., Washington, 1984-85; assoc. Wilmer, Cutler & Pickering, Washington, 1985-97; exec. sec. Mich. Law Revision Commn., Lansing, 1993-95; prof. U. Mich. Law Sch., Ann Arbor, 1987-97; dean, Garner Anthony prof. Vanderbilt U. Law Sch., Nashville, 1997—2005; dean, Shepley prof. Wash. U. Law Sch., St. Louis, 2005—. Visiting prof. U. Tokyo, 1993, U. Pa., 1997; chair exec. com. Inst. CLE, Ann Arbor, 1995-97; chair, bd. trustees Law Sch. Admissions Coun., 2005-. Editor: Journal of Legal Education, 1998—2004. Mem. Am. Law Inst., Law and Soc. Assn. Office Phone: 315-935-6420, 314-935-6420. Business E-Mail: syverud@wulaw.wustl.edu.

SZABLYA, HELEN MARY, writer, language educator; b. Budapest, Hungary, Sept. 6, 1934; came to U.S., 1963; d. Louis and Helen (Bartha) Kovacs; m. John Francis Szablya, June 12, 1951; children: Helen, Janos, Louis, Stephen, Alexandra, Rita, Dominique-Mary. Diploma in Sales, Mktg., U.B.C., 1962; BA in Fgn. Lang., Lit., Wash. State U., 1976. Freelance writer, translator, 1967—; columnist Cath. News, Trinidad, West Indies, 1980-91; adult educator TELOS Bellevue (Wash.) C.C., 1987-89; adult educator Pullman-Spokane (Wash.) C.C., 1976-80; faculty Christian Writers' Conf., Seattle, 1983-88, Pacific N.W. Writers' Conf., Seattle and Tacoma, 1987—92; hon. consul for Wash., Oreg., Idaho Republic of Hungary, 1993—. Lectr. Washington Commn. for Humanities, 1987-89. Author (with others): Hungary Remembered, 1986 (Guardian of Liberty award, 1986, George Washington Honor medal, Freedoms Found. award, 1988); author: 56-os Cserkészcsapat, 1986; author: (with others) The Fall of the Red Star, 1996, Hungarian transl., 1999 (1st prize Wash. Press Assn., 1st prize Nat. Fedn. Press Women); pub., editor Hungary Internat. newsletter, 1990—93, columnist Hungarian Bus. Weekly, 1994—95; translator: Emlèkezünk, 1986, Mind Twisters, 1987, A vörös csillag lehull, 1999. Recipient Nat. 1st place editl. Nat. Fedn. Press Women, 1987, Senator Tom Martin Meml. award Pacific N.W. Writers Conf., 1979, Pro Auxilio Civium Hungarorum, Min. Fgn. Affairs, Republic of Hungary, 2003, Order of Merit, Republic of Hungary, 2005, Pro Communitate, City of Pecs, Hungary, 2006; grantee Hungarian Am. Assn. Wash., 1986, Wash. Com. for Humanities, 1986; named Cmty. Woman of Yr. Am. Bus. Women Assn., 1990. Mem. AAUW, Wash. Press Assn. (pres. 1987-88, 1st and 2nd place awards, several editl. and profile awards 1983, 87, 89, 90, 91, 92, 96, Communicator of Achievement award 1987), Nat. Fedn. Press Women (Affiliate Pres.' award 1988, bd. dirs. edn. fund N.W. quadrant, mem. 21st century planning com.), Authors Guild, Am. Translators Assn., Arpad Acad. (Gold medal 1987), Nat. Writers Club, Internat. PEN Club, Sigma Delta Chi (editl. award 1989), Hungarian-Am. Coalition (bd mem. 1992—, chair bd. 2007), Am.-Hungarian Fedn. Avocations: children, reading, dance, swimming, travel. Home and Office: PO Box 578 Kirkland WA 98083-0578 Home Phone: 425-576-8997; Office Phone: 425-739-0631. Personal E-mail: szablyahj@aol.com.

SZABO, BARNA ALADAR, engineering educator; b. Martonvasar, Hungary, Sept. 21, 1935; arrived in US, 1967, naturalized, 1974; s. Jozsef and Gizella (Ivanyi) S.; m. Magdalin Gerstmayer, July 23, 1960; children: Mark, Nicholas. BASc., U. Toronto, Ont., Can., 1962; MS, SUNY, Buffalo, 1966, PhD, 1968; D. honoris causa, U. of Miskolc, Hungary, 1998. Registered profl. engr., Mo. Mining engr. Internat. Nickel Co. Can., 1960-62; engr. Acres Cons. Services Ltd., Niagara Falls, Can., 1962-66; instr. SUNY, Buffalo, 1966-68; from mem. faculty to sr. prof. Washington U., St. Louis, 1968—2006, sr. prof. mech. engring., 2006—; chmn. Engring. Software R&D, Inc., St. Louis, 1989—. Author: (with Ivo Babuska) Finite Element Analysis, 1991; contbr. articles to profl. jours. Fellow, St. Louis Acad. Sci. Fellow: Hungarian Acad. Sci., US Assn. Computational Mechanics (founding mem.). Office: PO Box 1129 Saint Louis MO 63188-1129 Office Phone: 314-935-6352. Business E-Mail: szabo@wustl.edu.

SZABO, DANIEL, federal official; b. Budapest, Hungary, Mar. 23, 1933; came to U.S., 1950, naturalized, 1954; s. Alexander and Maria (Berger) S.; m. Corinne Holiber, July 3, 1955; children— Nancy Beth, Peter Stuart. BA, CCNY, 1957; MA, Johns Hopkins U., 1959. Internat. economist U.S. Tariff Commn., 1959-60; desk officer for Vietnam, Cambodia and Laos U.S. Dept. Commerce, 1960-63; spl. asst. to U.S. Senator Jacob K. Javits, 1963-69; dep. asst. sec. state for Inter-Am. Affairs, Washington, 1969-74; sr. adviser Inter-Am. Devel. Bank, Washington, 1974-95. Bd. dirs. Washington chpt., chmn. Md. legis. task force Am. Jewish Com.; Am. Jewish Com. advocate Md. Interfaith Legis. Com., 1999—. With US Army, 1954—56. Home: 11600 Danville Dr North Bethesda MD 20852-3716 Personal E-mail: ds3693@verizon.net. *In approaching life I want my work to represent a service to our society. I am attracted to new ideas and new ways of solving old problems.*

SZABO, DENIS, criminologist, educator; b. Budapest, Hungary, June 4, 1929; arrived in Can., 1958; s. Jenö and Catherine (Zsiga) Szabo; m. Sylvie Grotard; children: Catherine, Marianne. D in Social and Polit. Sci., U. Louvain, Belgium, 1956; diploma in Criminology, Sorbonne U., Paris, 1958; Doctorate (hon.), U. Sienna, Italy, 1983, U. Budapest, Hungary, 1985, U. Aix Marseille, 1992, Panteios U., 1996, U. Bucarest, 2004. Asst. in sociology U. Louvain, 1951—56; lectr. sociology Cath. Univ., Paris, Lyon, 1956—58; mem. rsch. group Ctr. Nat. de la Recherche Scientifique, Paris, 1954—58; asst. prof. to assoc. prof. U. Montreal, Canada, 1958—66, founder, dir. dept. criminology, 1960—70, prof., 1966—95; founder, dir. Internat. Ctr. Comparative Criminology, Canada, 1969—84; prof. emeritus U. Montreal, Canada, 1995—. Emeritus prof. law U. Ecuador, Quito, 1984. Author, editor: book Can. Criminal Justice Sys., 1977, Criminologie et Politique Criminelle, 1978, La Criminologie Empirique au PQ, 1985, Sci. et Crime, 1986, De L' Anthropologie a la Criminologie Comparee, 1993, La Criminologie: Ses Fondements et sa Fondation, 1998; author (with Marc LeBlanc): Le Traité de Criminologie Empirique, 1993, The Criminal Justice Sys., 2001. Decorated officer Order Can.; named Comdr., Nat. Order Merite Hungarian Republic, 1996; recipient Beccaria Award, German Soc. Criminology, 1970, Chevalier Des Arts et des Lettres, France, 1996. Fellow: Am. Soc. Criminology (exec. coun., Sutherland award 1968), Am. Sociol. Soc., Royal Soc. Can.; mem.: Acad. Sci. Morales et Politiques, Quebec Soc. Criminology (founder, 45 Yrs. Svc. award 2005), Can. Soc. Criminology (v.p. 1962—64), Hungarian Acad. Sci., Inst. France (corr.; corres. mem.), Basque Inst. of Criminology San Sebastian (hon.), Romanian Soc. Criminology (hon.; elected hon. mem. 2003), Medaille de l' Institut Basque de Criminology (hon.), Nat. Order Merit (comdr. Ivory Coast 1987), Internat. Assn. Sociology, Order Nat. du Que. (officer 1998—), Soc. de Criminology du Que. (sec.-gen. 1960—70), Soc. Criminology (v.p. 1962—64), Internat. Soc. Criminology (pres. 1978—85, hon. pres.). Roman Catholic. Avocations: swimming, gardening, travel. Home: 66 Carré Copp Georgeville PQ Canada J0B 1T0 Office: U Montreal Internat Ctr Com Criminology CP 6128 succursale Centre-ville Montreal PQ Canada H3C 3J7 Business E-Mail: denis.szabo@umontreal.ca.

SZABO, JOHN F., library director; b. Orlando, Fla., 1968; BA in Telecommunication and Film, U. Ala.; M in Info. and Libr. Studies, U. Mich. Announcer WUAL/WQPR; map cataloger U. Mich. Map Libr.; dir. U. Mich. Residential Coll. Libr., Robinson Pub. Libr. Dist., Ill., Palm Harbor Pub. Libr., Fla., Clearwater Pub. Libr. Sys., Fla., 1999—2005, Atlanta-Fulton Pub. Libr. Sys., 2005—. Pres. Fla. Libr. Assn., 2003—04, Gulfcoast Libr. Orgn.; pres. bd. dirs. Tampa Bay Libr. Consortium, 2004. Mem. pub. libr. adv. coun. Ga. Bd. Regents; mem. pub. arts adv. com. Fulton County Arts Coun.; bd. trustees Cherokee Garden Libr./Ctr. Study of So. Garden Hist. Recipient Alexander J. Skrzypek award for Libr. Svc. to the Blind and Visually Impaired, Ill. Libr. Assn., 1994. Office: Atlanta Fulton Pub Libr Sys One Margaret Mitchell Sq Atlanta GA 30303 Office Phone: 404-730-1972. Office Fax: 404-730-1990. E-mail: john.szabo@fultoncountyga.gov.

SZADOKIERSKI, CINDY, air transportation executive; b. 1959; BA French, Edn., Randolph Macon Coll.; MEd., MBA, James Madison U. High school french teacher; joined United Airlines Inc., 1985, variety of positions in reservations, airport ops., sales, human resources and United Express; gen. mgr. Washington Dulles Internat. Airport; mng. dir. United Express; v.p. Corp. Real Estate United Airlines Inc., v.p. O'Hare Internat. Airport Ops., 2006—. Named a Woman to Watch, Crain's Chgo. Bus., 2007. Office: United Air Lines Inc 1200 E Algonquin Rd Elk Grove Village IL 60007 *

SZAKAL, ANDRAS KALMAN, immunologist, anatomist, educator; s. Andor Viktor and Maria Szakal; m. Norma Elisabeth Skinner; children: Andras Robert, Tamas Kalman. BA in Zoology, U. Colo., 1961, MA in Biology, 1963; PhD, U. Tenn., 1972. Rsch. biologist for immunology of carcinogenesis group divsn. biology Oak Ridge (Tenn.) Nat. Labs., 1972—74; prin. scientist Meloy Labs., Springfield, Va., 1974—79; assoc. prof. dept. anatomy, divsn. immunobiology Va. Commonwealth Univ./Med Sch., Richmond, 1979—91, prof. dept. anatomy and neurobiology and The Immunology Group, 1991—. Cons. electron microscopist in exptl. biology Oak Ridge Nat. Lab., 1969—70; cons. electron microscopist Lunar Receiving Lab., NASA Manned Spacecraft Ctr., Houston, 1969; cons. on electron micros. autoradiography Nat. Cancer Inst., NIH, Bethesda, Md., 1974. Contbr. articles to profl. jours. Grantee, NIH, Nat. Inst. on Aging, 1985—88, 1991—94, 1999—2004. Mem.: AAAS, Va. Acad. Sci., Am. Assn. Immunologists, Am. Assn. Anatomists. Achievements include discovery of Antigen Transport Cell; ICCOSOMEs and the role of follicular dendritic cells (FDCs) in aging. E-mail: aszakal@hsc.vcu.edu.

SZAKY, TOM, agricultural products executive; b. Budapest, Hungary, 1982; Stud., Princeton U. Founder, pres. Flyte Design; worked with Werehome.com, piority.com, studentmarks.com; founder, CEO TerraCycle, Inc., 2002—. Named one of 40 under 40, Advt. Age, 2007. Office: TerrCycle Inc 121 NY Ave Trenton NJ 08638 Office Phone: 609-393-4252. Office Fax: 609-393-4259. *

SZALAPSKI, ROBERT FRANCIS, theoretical physicist; b. St. Paul, Dec. 21, 1964; s. Edward William and Judith Mary (Raines) S.; m. Jeanne Therese Larson, Sept. 17, 1985 (div. Feb. 2005); children: Jacob Daniel, Maxwell Martin, Damien Alexander. BS in Physics, U. Minn., 1988; PhD in Physics, U. Wis., 1994. Rsch. assoc. Nat. Lab. for High Energy Physics, Tsukuba, Japan, 1994-96, rsch. fellow, 1996-98; mem. physics faculty U. Rochester, N.Y., 1998-99; sr. rschr. R & D Synopsys, Inc., 1999—2004; sr. dynamics analyst ITT Industries Space Systems Divsn., Rochester, NY, 2004—. Adj. physics faculty SUNY Brockport, 2000; scientist Lab. for Laser Energetics, U. Rochester, 2004. Contbr. articles to profl. jours.

Fellowship NSF, 1996-97, postdoctoral fellowship Japan Soc. for the Promotion of Sci., 1996-97, grad. fellowship Dept. of Edn., 1989-93 Avocations: tennis, running, skiing, ballroom dancing, tango. Office: ITT Industries Space Sys Divsn PO Box 60488 Rochester NY 14606-0488

SZALKOWSKI, CHARLES C., lawyer; b. Amarillo, Tex., Apr. 14, 1948; s. Chester Casimer and Virginia Lee Szalkowski; m. Jane Howe, Dec. 28, 1971; children: Jennifer Lee, Stephen Claude. BA, BS in Acctg., Rice U., 1971; MBA, JD, Harvard U., 1975. Bar: Tex. 1975. Assoc. Baker Botts L.L.P., Houston, 1975-82, ptnr., 1983—, gen. coun., 2006—. Speaker in field. Chmn. ann. fund campaign Rice U., Houston, 1991-93, chmn. Fund Coun., 1995-96; chmn. adminstrv. bd. St. Luke's United Meth. Ch., Houston, 1994, chmn. bd. trustees, 1997, 2003; chmn. DePelchin Children's Ctr., Houston, 2002-04; bd. dirs. Meth. Children's Home, Waco, 1998-2001, 03—. Mem.: ABA (fed. regulation of securities com.), Assn. Corp. Growth, Tex. Bus. Law Found. (mem. exec. com. 1988—, chmn. 1998—2000, bd. dirs.), Harvard Law Sch. Assn. Tex. (pres. 1983—84), Houston Bar Assn. (corp. counsel sect. 1989—90, chmn.), State Bar Tex. (chmn. bus. law sect. 1991—92), Am. Law Inst., Assn. Rice U. Alumni (bd. dirs. 1999—2002, pres. 2007—), HBS Club (Houston) (bd. dirs. 2000—04, 2006—). Office: Baker Botts LLP 1 Shell Plz 910 Louisiana St Ste 3000 Houston TX 77002-4991 Office Phone: 713-229-1480.

SZAMOSFALVI, JOZSEF, corporate financial executive, consultant; arrived in US, 1994; s. Jozsef Szamosfalvi and Iren Hornyak. BS in Econs. and Internat. Politics, Brigham Young U., 2001. Chartered fin. analyst candidate level 2. V.p. Summit Ventures Internat. and Interlink Capital Strategies, Falls Church, Va., 2002—; mng. dir. New Europe Capital Mgmt., LLC, Va., 2003—, CAPPA FUND I, LLC, Falls Church, 2006—; intern divsn. programs coord. and evaluation Internat. Atomic Energy Agy., Vienna, 1998; rsch. asst. Brigham Young U., Provo, Utah, 1999—2001; CFO Rustico, Inc., Orem, Utah, 1999—2001; dir. of fin. Summit Ventures, LLC, Washington, 2003—. Vol. rep. Ch. of Jesus Christ of Latter-day Saints, Tirana, Albania, 1995—97. Mem.: NY Soc. Security Analysts, Nat. Assn. Bus. Econs. Conservative. Avocations: guitar, soccer, ballroom dancing. Office: Summit Ventures LLC 1101 30th St NW Washington DC 20007 Home Phone: 703-786-9000; Office Phone: 202-333-9055. Office Fax: 202-478-5111. Personal E-mail: jozsef@summit-ventures.com.

SZÁRA, STEPHEN ISTVÁN, pharmacologist, consultant; b. Budapest, Hungary, Mar. 21, 1923; arrived in U.S., 1957; s. János Szára and Mária Katona; m. Madeleine Gadányi, Sept. 5, 1959 (div. June 1980); 1 child, Christopher. D of Natural Scis., Petrus Pázmány U., Budapest, 1950; MD, Med. U. Budapest, 1951. Asst. prof. dept. biochemistry Med. U. Budapest, 1950—53; chief biochemistry lab. State Inst. for Nervous Disorders, Budapest, 1953—56; vis. scientist Clin. Sci. Lab. NIMH, Bethesda, Md., 1957—61, sect. chief Washington, 1961—71; br. chief NIDA NIH, Rockville, Md., 1971—90; sci. cons. Kensington, Md., 1990—. Assoc., clin. prof. psychiatry George Washington U., Washington, 1966—75; mem. adv. bd. Heffter Rsch. Inst., Santa Fe, 1993—. Co-author (with H. Weil-Malherbe): Biochemistry of Functional and Experimental Psychoses, 1971; co-editor (with M. Braude): The Pharmacology of Marihuana, 1976; co-editor: (with J.P Ludford) Benzodiazepines: A Review of Research Results, 1980; editor: Neurobiology of Behavioral Control of Drug Abuse, 1986; contbr. articles to profl. jours. Recipient Meritorious Achievement award, ADAMHA/PHS/DHHS, 1984, Kovats Freedom medal, Am. Hungarian Fedn., 2005. Fellow: Coll. Internat. Neuro-Psychopharmacologicum, Am. Coll. Neuro-Psychopharmacology; mem.: AAAS, Am. Soc. Pharmacol. Exptl. Therapy. Achievements include discovery of hallucinogenic effects of NN-Dimethyltryptamine in man. Avocations: sailing, computer programming. Home: 10901 Jolly Way Kensington MD 20895-1111 Personal E-mail: siszara@earthlink.net.

SZAREK, STANISLAW JERZY, mathematics professor; b. Ladek Zdroj, Poland, Nov. 13, 1953; arrived in US, 1980, naturalized, 1994; s. Mieczyslaw and Bronislawa (Brzezinska) S.; m. Malgorzata Chwascinska, June 22, 1980 (separated 1996, div. 2002); children: Martina, Natalia; 1 stepchild, Olga; m. Margaretmary Daley, May 15, 2004; 1 child, Emily; stepchildren: Blake, Devin. M in Math., Warsaw U., Poland, 1976; PhD in Math. Scis., Polish Acad. Scis., Warsaw, 1979. Rsch. asst. Math. Inst. Polish Acad. Scis., Warsaw, 1976-79, rsch. fellow, 1979-83; asst. prof. Case Western Res. U., Cleve., 1983-87, prof., 1987—, chair math. dept., 1994-96; prof. U. Paris, 1996—. Vis. positions U. Ill., Urbana, 1980, Ohio State U., Columbus, 1981, U. Tex., Austin, 1981-83, Inst. des Hautes Etudes Scientifiques, Bures-Sur-Yvette, France, 1986-89, U. Paris, 1990, 92, 95, Math. Scis. Rsch. Inst., Berkeley, Calif., 1996; invited spkr. Internat. Congress of Math. Madrid, 2006. Contbr. articles to profl. jours. Recipient Prize of Sci. Sec., Polish Acad. Scis., 1979, Langevin prize Acad. Scis., France, 2007; Rsch. grantee NSF, 1983—, U.S.-Israel Binat. Sci. Found., 1993-97, 2003—; Sloan fellow Alfred P. Sloan Found., 1986-88. Mem.: Am. Math. Soc. Avocations: skiing, sailing, diving, bridge, travel. Office: Case Western Res U Dept of Math Cleveland OH 44106 Home Phone: 216-283-0303; Office Phone: 216-368-2880. Business E-Mail: szarek@cwru.edu.

SZAREK, WALTER ANTHONY, chemist, educator; b. St. Catharines, Ont., Can., Apr. 19, 1938; s. Anthony and Sophia (Kania) S. BSc, McMaster U., 1960, MSc, 1962; PhD, Queen's U., 1964. Postdoctoral fellow in chemistry Ohio State U., Columbus, 1964-65; asst. prof. biochemistry Rutgers U., New Brunswick, N.J., 1965-67; asst. prof. chemistry Queen's U., Kingston, Ont., 1967-71, assoc. prof., 1971-76, prof., 1976—2003, emeritus prof., 2003—, dir. Carbohydrate Research Inst., 1976-85; founding mem., prin. investigator Neurochem, Inc., 1993—. Cons. to govt. and industry; mem. Premier's Coun. Tech. Fund., Queen's Chemistry Innovation Coun., 2006-. Mem. editl. adv. bd. Carbohydrate Rsch. jour., 1973-97, Jour. of Carbohydrate Chemistry, 1994-2001; contbr. articles to profl. jours. Recipient Tchg. Excellence award Queen's U. Arts and Sci. Undergrad. Soc., 1988-89, Tchg. Excellence in Chemistry award, 1993, 2000, 2002. Fellow Chem. Inst. Can.; mem. AAAS, Am. Chem. Soc. (chmn. divsn. carbohydrate chemistry 1982-83, councilor 2002—, Claude S. Hudson award in carbohydrate chemistry 1989, Melville L. Wolfrom award 1992), Inst. Theol. Encounter with Sci. and Tech., Royal Soc. Chemistry, N.Y. Acad. Scis., Soc. Glycobiology. Roman Catholic. Office: Dept Chemistry Queens Univ Kingston ON Canada K7L 3N6 Home Phone: 613-544-4358; Office Phone: 613-533-2643. Fax: 613-533-6532. Business E-Mail: szarekw@chem.queensu.ca.

SZASZ, THOMAS STEPHEN, psychiatrist, educator, writer; b. Budapest, Hungary, Apr. 15, 1920; came to U.S., 1938, naturalized, 1944; s. Julius and Lily (Wellisch) S.; m. Rosine Loshkajian, Oct. 19, 1951 (div. 1970); children: Margot Szasz Peters, Susan Marie Szasz Palmer. AB, U. Cin., 1941, MD, 1944; DSc (hon.), Allegheny Coll., 1975, U. Francisco Marroquin, Guatemala, 1979; LHD (hon.), Towson U., 1999; D Sc(hon.), SUNY, 2001. Diplomate: Nat. Bd. Med. Examiners, Am. Bd. Psychiatry and Neurology. Intern 4th Med. Service Harvard, Boston City Hosp., 1944-45; asst. resident medicine Cin. Gen. Hosp., 1945-46, asst. clinician internal medicine div. out-patient dispensary, 1946; asst. resident psychiatry U. Chgo. Clinics, 1946-47; tng. research fellow Inst. Psychoanalysis, Chgo., 1947-48, rsch. asst., 1949-50, staff mem., 1951-56; practice medicine, specializing in psychiatry, psychoanalysis Chgo., 1949-54, Bethesda, Md., 1954-56, Syracuse, NY, 1956—; prof. psychiatry SUNY Health Sci. Ctr., Syracuse, 1956-90, prof. psychiatry emeritus, 1990—. Vis. prof. dept. psychiatry U. Wis., Madison, 1962, Marquette U. Sch. Medicine, Milw., 1968, U. N.Mex., 1981; holder numerous lectureships, including C.P. Snow lectr. Ithaca Coll., 1970; E.S. Meyer Meml. lectr. U. Queensland Med. Sch.; Lambie-Dew orator Sydney U., 1977; Mem. nat. adv. com. bd. Tort and Med. Yearbook; cons. com. mental hygiene N.Y. State Bar Assn.; mem. research adv. panel Inst. Study Drug Addiction; adv. bd. Corp. Econ. Edn., 1977— Author: Pain and Pleasure, 1957, The Myth of Mental Illness, 1961, Law, Liberty and Psychiatry, 1963, Psychiatric Justice, 1965, The Ethics of Psychoanalysis, 1965, Ideology and Insanity, 1970, The Manufacture of Madness, 1970, The Second Sin, 1973, Ceremonial Chemistry, 1974, Heresies, 1976, Karl Kraus and the Soul-Doctors, 1976, Schizophrenia: The Sacred Symbol of Psychiatry, 1976, Psychiatric Slavery, 1977, The Theology of Medicine, 1977, The Myth of Psychotherapy, 1978, Sex by Prescription, 1980, The Therapeutic State, 1984, Insanity: The Idea and its Consequences, 1987, The Untamed Tongue: A Dissenting Dictionary, 1990, Our Right to Drugs: The Case for a Free Market, 1992, A Lexicon of Lunacy, 1993, Cruel Compassion, 1994, The Meaning of Mind, 1996, Fatal Freedom, 1999, Pharmacracy: Medicine and Politics in America, 2001, Liberation By Oppression: A Comparative Study of Slavery and Psychiatry, 2002, Words to the Wise: A Medical-Philosophical Dictionary, 2004, Faith in Freedom: Libertarian Principles and Psychiatric Practices, 2004, Szasz Under Fire: The Psychiatric Abolitionist Answers His Critics, 2004, My Madness Saved Me: The Madness and Mariage of Virginia Woolf, 2006, Coercion as Cure: A Critical History of Psychiatry, 2007, The Medicalization of Everyday Life, 2007; editor: The Age of Madness, 1973; cons. editor of Psychiatry and Psychology: Stedman's Medical Dictionary, 22d edit, 1973; contbg. editor: Reason, 1974—, Libertarian Rev., 1986—; mem. editl. bd. Psychoanalytic Rev, 1965—, Jour. Contemporary Psychotherapy, 1968—, Law and Human Behavior, 1977—, Jour. Libertarian Studies, 1977—, Children and Youth Services Rev, 1978—, Am. Jour. Forensic Psychiatry, 1980—, Free Inquiry, 1980—. Comdr. M.C., USNR, 1954-56. Recipient Stella Feiss Hofheimer award U. Cin., 1944, Holmes-Munsterberg award Internat. Acad. Forensic Psychology, 1969; Wisdom award honor, 1970; Acad. prize Institutum atque Academia Auctorum Internationalis, Andorra, 1972; Distinguished Service award Am. Inst. Pub. Service, 1974; Martin Buber award Midway Counseling Center, 1974, Thomas S. Szasz award Ctr. Ind. Thought, 1990, Alfred R. Lindesmith award for achievement in field of scholarship and writing Drug Policy Found., 1991, Rollo May award APA, 1998; others; named Humanist of Year Am. Humanist Assn., 1973; Hon. fellow Postgrad. Center for Mental Health, 1961, Mencken award, 1981, Humanist Laureate, 1984, Statue of Liberty-Ellis Island Found. Archives Roster, 1986, George Washington award Am. Hungarian Found., 2003. Fellow Am. Psychiat. Assn. (life), Am. Psychoanalytic Assn., Internat. Psychoanalytic Soc., Western N.Y. Psychoanalytic Soc. Home: 4739 Limberlost Ln Manlius NY 13104-1405 Office: 750 E Adams St Syracuse NY 13210-2306 Personal E-mail: tszasz@aol.com.

SZAUTER, KAREN, gastroenterologist; b. Youngstown, Ohio, Apr. 23, 1957; m. Michael Ainsworth, Jan. 4, 1997; 1 child, Lindsay. BA in Psychology, Case Western Res. U., Cleve., MD, 1983. Med. dir., standardized patient program U. Tex. Med. Br., Galveston, 2000—. Office: Univ Tex Med Br 301 Univesrity Blvd Galveston TX 77555 Office Phone: 409-772-6300. Office Fax: 409-772-6301. Business E-Mail: kszauter@utmb.edu.

SZCZERBIAK, WALLY, professional basketball player; b. Mar. 5, 1977; Grad., U. Miami, Ohio, 1999. Basketball player Minn. Timberwolves, 1999—2006, Boston Celtics, 2006—. Named Mac Player Yr., 1999; named to Second Team All-Am., AP, 1999, All-Rookie Team, NBA, 1999—2000; recipient MVP Rookie Challenge, 2001. Office: Boston Celtics Fourth Fl 226 Causeway St Boston MA 02114-4714

SZCZUBLEWSKI, WENDY SUE, small business owner, musician, freelance/self-employed writer; b. Dunkirk, NY; d. Bernard and Rosemary Dougherty; m. Michael Szczublewski, June 26, 1999; 1 child, Preston Thomas. BA in polit. sci. cum laude, SUNY Coll. at Fredonia, 1987—91. Project mgr. Vanstar Corp., Vienna, Va., 1996—97; proposal mgr. RS Info. Systems, Inc., McLean, Va., 1997—98; writer/editor Computer Assoc. Internat., Inc., Herndon, Va., 1999—2002; pres. and ceo WoBop Music, Columbia, Md., 2002—; owner Szczublewski Music, Fairfax Station, Va., 2005—. Mem.: Nat. Guild of Piano Teachers, Am. Coll. of Musicians, MENSA. Avocations: baking, gardening, reading, bicycling, hiking. Mailing: PO Box 131 Fairfax Station VA 22039 Office Phone: 410-772-1097. Business E-Mail: wszczub@szczublewski.com.

SZCZYRBA, IGOR NICHOLAS, mathematical physicist, consultant; b. Prague, Czech Republic, May 20, 1946; s. Mikolaj and Rozalia Szczyrba; m. Halina Agnieszka Kocewiak; children: Rafal W, Anna P. MS, Warsaw U., 1969, PhD, 1973, Dr. Habilitatis, 1983. Tchg. and rsch. asst. Warsaw U., 1969—73, tenured prof., 1973—84; vis. prof. Warsaw Sch. Econs., 1973—77; rsch. fellow Inst. Theoretical Physics, Trieste, Italy, 1975; vis. prof. U. Heidelberg, Germany, 1977—81; asst. prof. U. No. Colo., Greeley, 1986—88, assoc. prof., 1988—90, full prof., 1990—. Linguistic cons. Internat. Lang. Engring., Boulder, Colo., 1988—99, LionBridge, Boulder, Colo., 2000—, Bowne Global Solutions, Montreal, Canada, 2003—; polit. scis. cons. U. No. Colo., Greeley, 1986—. Contbr. articles to profl. jours. Recipient Scholar of Yr. award, U. No. Colo., Coll. Arts and Scis., 1989, 2002—03. Mem.: Math. Assn. Am. Office: U No Colo Ross Hall Greeley CO 80639 Home Phone: 970-667-9948; Office Phone: 970-351-2011. Office Fax: 970-351-1225. E-mail: igor.szczyrba@unco.edu.

SZE, MICHAEL MING-CHIH, actuary, consultant; b. Shanghai, June 1, 1940; came to US, 1968; m. Elsie Sim-Yee Chin, Aug. 19, 1972; children: Benjamin, Samuel, Timothy. BS, U. Hong Kong, 1964; MS, Calif. State U., Hayward, 1969; PhD in Math., Ohio State U., 1975. CFA. Internat. pension and ins. cons., ptnr. Hewitt Assocs., Lincolnshire, Ill., 1975-96; pres., fin. planner Sze Assocs., Toronto, Canada, 1996—. Adj. prof. U. Mich., Ann Arbor, 1998—99; tech. panel adv. bd. Social Security Adminstrn., Washington, 1994—96, Washington, 1999; cons. in field. Mem. editl. bd. Jour. Actuarial Practice, 1996—; co-author: Carswell's Benefits Manual, 1999-2002. Fellow Soc. Actuaries (bd. govs. 1994-97), Can. Inst. Actuaries (com. on investment practice 1994-96); mem. Acad. Social Scis., NY Acad. Scis. Roman Catholic. Avocations: bridge, fitness workouts. Office: Sze Assocs 45 Francine Dr Willowdale ON Canada M2H 2G5 Office Phone: 416-756-2181. Business E-Mail: msze@szeassociates.com.

SZE, SARAH, sculptor; b. Boston, 1969; BA magna cum laude, Yale U., 1991; MFA, Sch. of Visual Arts, NYC, 1997. One-woman shows include, Mus. of Fine Arts, Boston, Inst. of Contemporary Art, London, The Found. Cartier, Paris, Walker Art Ctr., Mpls., 2002, The Whitney Mus. Am. Art, N.Y.C., 2003, Mus. of Contemporary Art, Chgo, Marianne Boesky Gallery, NY, 2000, 2005, exhibited in group shows, The Whitney Mus. of Am. Art, N.Y.C., The Carnegie Mus. of Art, Pitts., Mus. Modern Art, San Francisco, 48th Venice Biennial, The L.A. (Calif.) Mus. Contemporary Art, 1999. Recipient Paula Rhodes Meml. award, 1997, award, Louis Comfort Tiffany Found., 1999, Lotus Club Found. Prize, 2003; fellow John D. and Catherine T. MacArthur Found. 2003.

SZEFLER, STANLEY JAMES, pediatrics and pharmacology educator; b. Buffalo, Aug. 24, 1948; s. Stanley and Bernice Laura (Platt) Szefler; m. Christine M. Drezek, Dec. 26, 1970; children: David, Paul. BS, SUNY, Buffalo, 1971, MD, 1975. Resident pediat. Children's Hosp. Buffalo, 1975—77; postdoctoral fellow in clin. pharmacology and allergy immunology SUNY, Buffalo, 1977—79, asst. prof. pediat. and pharmacology, 1979—82; assoc. prof. pediat. and pharmacology U. Colo., Denver, 1982—90, prof. pediat., pharmacology, 1990—. Dir. clin. pharmacology Children's Hosp., Buffalo, 1979—82, Nat. Jewish Ctr. for Immunology and Respiratory Medicine, Denver, 1982—. Contbr. articles to profl. jours. Mem. steering com., Asthma Camp for Children Am. Lung Assn., Denver, 1987—96. Maj. USAR, 1979—88. Grantee NIH, 1980—84, 1990—, FDA, Denver, 1988—91. Fellow: Am. Acad. Pediat. (liaison mem. com. drugs), Am. Acad. Allergy, Asthma and Immunology (chmn. asthma, rhinitis and respiratory disease interest sect. 1995—97). Avocations: literature, history, reading. Office: Nat Jewish Med & Rsch Ctr Dept Pediat 1400 Jackson St Denver CO 80206-2761 Business E-Mail: szeflers@njc.org.

SZEGO, CLARA MARIAN, cell biologist, educator; b. Budapest, Hungary, Mar. 23, 1916; arrived in U.S., 1921, naturalized, 1927; d. Paul S. and Helen (Elek) S.; m. Sidney Roberts, Sept. 14, 1943. AB, Hunter Coll., 1937; MS, U. Minn., 1939, PhD, 1942; DSc (hon.), CUNY, 2007. Instr. physiology U. Minn., 1942-43; Minn. Cancer Rsch. Found. fellow, 1943—44; rsch. assoc. OSRD, Nat. Bur. Stds., 1944-45, Worcester Found. Exptl. Biology, 1945-47; rsch. instr. physiol. chemistry Yale U. Sch. Medicine, 1947-48; mem. faculty UCLA, 1948—, prof. biology, 1960—. Contbr. articles to profl. jours., book chapters and revs. Garvan fellow U. Minn., 1939; Guggenheim fellow, 1956; named Woman of Year in Sci. Los Angeles Times, 1957-58; named to Hunter Coll. Hall of Fame, 1987. Fellow AAAS; mem. Am. Physiol. Soc., Am. Soc. Cell Biology, Endocrine Soc. (CIBA award 1953), Soc. for Endocrinology (Gt. Britain), Biochem. Soc. (Gt. Britain), Internat. Soc. Rsch. Reproduction, Phi Beta Kappa (pres. UCLA chpt. 1973-74), Sigma Xi (pres. UCLA chpt. 1976-77). Home: 1371 Marinette Rd Pacific Palisades CA 90272-2627 Office: U Calif Dept Molecular Cell & Devel Biology Los Angeles CA 90095-1606 Business E-Mail: cmszego@ucla.edu.

SZELENYI, IVAN, adult education educator; b. Budapest, Apr. 17, 1938; came to the U.S., 1981; s. Gusztav and Julianna (Csapo) S.; m. Valeria Vanilia Majoros; children: Szonja, Lilla, Balazs. PhD, Hungarian Acad. Scis., Budapest, 1973, DSc, 1990; doctorate (hon.), Budapest U. Econs., 1992; DLitt (hon.), Flinders U., 1997; dr. rer.pol. h.c. (hon.), Friedrich-Alexander U., 2003. Rsch. fellow Hungarian Acad. Scis., Budapest, 1963-75; found. prof. Flinders U., Adelaide, Australia, 1975-80; prof. U. Wis., Madison, 1981-86; disting. prof. CUNY Grad. Ctr., 1986-88; prof. UCLA, 1988-99; William Graham Sumner prof. sociology Yale U., New Haven, 1999—. Author: Urban Inequalities under State Socialism, 1983, Socialist Entrepreneurs, 1988 (C. Wright Mills award 1989); co-author: Intellectuals on the Road to Class Power, 1979, Making Capitalism without Capitalists, 1998, Theories of New Class, 2004, Patterns of Exclusion, 2006. Mem. Hungarian Acad. Scis; fellow Am. Acad. Arts and Sci. Business E-Mail: ivan.szelenyi@yale.edu.

SZELIGA, VICTORIA L., retired social studies educator; b. Williamsport, Pa., Nov. 29, 1950; d. George E. Mayer and Dorothy M. Thomas; m. Martin A. Szeliga, Jan. 24, 1972; children: Christopher M., Bryan J. MA, U. No. Colo., Greeley, 1975. Tchr. Dist. #11, Colorado Springs, Colo., 1973—83, Acad. Dist. #20, 1983—2006. Author: (ednl. materials) Book Bridges #1. Blood donor Penrose Hosp., Colorado Springs, Colo., 1976—. Named Tchr. of Yr., Rockrimmon Elem., 1986; grantee, Pikes Peak Coalition Ctr., 1985, 1987, Colo. Endowment Humanities, 1991, Colo. Geog. Alliance, 1992, Acad. Dist. #20, 2001; scholar, Nat. Geog. Soc., 1997, Econ. Tchr. award, Found. Tchg. Econ., 2001. Achievements include development of science, social studies and technology curricula. Avocations: reading, hunting, fishing, hiking. Home Phone: 719-598-2764.

SZERLAG, CHESTER THEODORE, health care executive; MBA, U. Chgo., 1984. Exec. adminstr. U. Chgo., 1980—. Contbr. articles to profl. jours.; mem. editl. bd.: ADVANCE Jour. for Imaging and Oncology Adminstrs. Bd. trustee Village of Woodridge, Ill., 1997—2005; vice chmn. U. Chgo. Credit Union, Ill., 2001—. Recipient Gold medal, Soc. Radiation Oncology Adminstrs., 1991. Fellow: Am. Coll. Healthcare Execs.; mem.: Healthcare Fin. Mgmt. Assn., Radiol. Soc. N.Am. (chair assoc. sci. consortium), Am. Coll. Med. Practice Execs. (cert. med. practice exec. 2004), Soc. Radiation Oncology Adminstrs. (pub. chair, past treas., past. pres., past chmn.), Rotary Internat. (Woodrige chpt. sec. 2002—, pres.-elect 2005, pres. 2005—). Office: Univ Chgo 5758 S Maryland Ave MC 9006 Chicago IL 60637 Office Phone: 773-702-3311. Business E-Mail: cszerlag@radonc.uchicago.edu.

SZIGETI, JÁNOS, physicist; b. Budapest, Hungary, Oct. 11, 1936; s. György and Zsuzsanna (Ziffer) S.; m. Boglárka Gulyás, Aug. 7, 1967; children: Andrea, Zsófia. Diploma, Roland Eötvös U., 1960; PhD, U. Leningrad, 1972. With Ctrl. Rsch. Inst. for Physics, 1960—91; sr. scientist Rsch. Inst. for Particle and Nuc. Physics, 1991—96, sci. advisor, 1996—, head dept. laser spectroscopy, 1991—. Asst. scientific co-worker, 1960-66; scientific co-worker Acad. of Sci., 1966-72, sr. scientist, 1972-96, head dept. laser spectroscopy, 1993—, sci. advisor, 1996—; head of dept. Rsch. Inst. of Particles and Nuclear Physics, 1991—. Contbr. numerous articles to profl. jours. Mem. Roland Eötvös Phys. Soc., European Phys. Soc. Avocation: rowing on the danube. Home: Erzsebet u 27 app 40 1043 Budapest Hungary Office: Rsch Inst Particle & Nuc Physics PO Box 49 H-1525 Budapest Hungary Office Phone: 36-1-392-27-52. Business E-Mail: szigeti@rmki.kfki.hu.

SZINI, ISTVAN JANOS, electronics engineer; s. Istvan and Alice Vidal Szini; m. Luciana Rocha Silva, Feb. 20, 1988; children: Ferenc Janos, Lilla Katalin. BSEE, Mogi Das Cruzes U., 1989; MSEE, Sao Paulo U., 1998; postgrad., U. SC, 2005—. Sr. engr. NEC of Brazil, Sao Paulo, 1989—98; prin. staff engr. Motorola Inc., Libertyville, Ill., 1998—. Mem.: IEEE. Achievements include research in handsets internal and external antennas. Office: Motorola 600N US 45 Libertyville IL 60048 Office Phone: 847-523-8780. E-mail: istvan.szini@motorola.com.

SZKUTAK, TOM, corporate financial executive; married; 2 children. BS in Fin. magna cum laude, Boston U. Fin. mgmt. positions through exec. v.p. fin. GE Investments, CFO GE Lighting GE, 1982—2002; sr. v.p., CFO Amazon.com, Seattle, 2002—. Office: Amazon.com 1200 12th Ave S Seattle WA 98144 *

SZOKA, EDMUND CASIMIR CARDINAL, archbishop; b. Grand Rapids, Mich., Sept. 14, 1927; s. Casimir and Mary (Wolgat) Szoka. BA, Sacred Heart Sem., 1950; JCB, Pontifical Lateran U., 1958, JCL, 1959. Ordained priest Roman Catholic Ch., 1954, elevated to cardinal 1988. Asst. pastor St. Francis Parish, Manistique, Mich., 1954—55; sec. to bishop Marquette, 1955—57, 1959—62; chaplain St. Mary's Hosp., Marquette, 1955—57; tribunal, defender of bond Marquette, 1960—71; asst. chancellor Diocese of Marquette, 1962—69, chancellor, 1970—71; pastor St. Pius X Ch., Ishpeming, Mich., 1962—63, St. Christopher Ch., Marquette, 1963—71; bishop Diocese of Gaylord, Mich., 1971—81; archbishop of Detroit, 1981—90. Sec.-treas. Mich. Cath. Conf., Lansing, 1972—77; chmn. region VI Nat. Conf. Cath. Bishops, 1972—77; treas., adminstrv. bd. and adminstrv. com., budget and fin. com. Nat. Conf. Cath. Bishops/U.S. Cath. Conf., 1981—84; pres. Prefecture for Econ. Affairs of the Holy See, 1990—97, Pontifical Commn. Vatican City State, 1997—2006; mem. Secretariat of State 2d sect. Coun. for Rels. with States; pres. Governatorato Vatican City State, 2001—06. Trustee Nat. Shrine of the Immaculate Conception, Washington, 1981—90; chmn. bd. trustees Cath. Telecomm. Network Am., 1984—90; trustee, exec. com., chmn. com. for univ. rels. Cath. U. Am, 1981—90. Mem.: Congregation for Clergy, Congregation for Evangelization of Peoples, Congregation for Bishops, Congregation for Causes of Saints, Congregation for Insts. Consecrated Life and Socs. Apostolic Life. Roman Catholic. Address: Governatorato 00120 Vatican City Italy

SZOKODY, ANIKO, pianist, educator; b. Szeged, Hungary, Apr. 24, 1973; arrived in U.S., 1997; d. Fedor Sandor Szokody and Zsuzsanna Szlovak; m. Willis Dee Ottery III, Mar. 1, 2002; 1 child, Willis David. MusB, Zoltan Kodaly Spl. Musical Secondary Sch., Kecskemet, Hungary, 1991; Piano Performer Artist Degree, tchrs. diploma, Franz Liszt Acad. Music, Budapest, Hungary, 1997; MusM in Piano Performance, Ind. U., 2000; artist diploma (hon.), Conservatorio Beethoven, Buenos Aires, 1997. Assoc. instr. piano Ind. U., Bloomington, 1998—2000; instrumental accompanist, chamber music coach Chautauqua Instn., 1999—2002, head instrumental accompanist, chamber music coach, 2002—06. Guest instr. piano Conservatorio Beethoven, Buenos Aires, 1996—97; studio pianist for cellist Janos Starker Ind. U., Bloomington, 1998—2000; pvt. piano instr., Albany, NY, 2000—; mem. piano faculty Luzerne Music Ctr., NY, 2007; piano faculty Union Coll., Schenectady, NY, 2007; organist Hist. St. George's Ch., Schenectady, NY, 2007—. Musician (pianist): (solo performances) Europe, North and South America. Grantee, Hungarian Nat. Cultural Found., 1996, Conservatorio Beethoven, 1996—97, for profl. career documentary, Hungarian Pub. TV, 2002; scholar, studio of Prof. Gyorgy Sebok, Ind. U., 1998—2000. Mem.: Luzerne Chamber Players, Am. Fed. Musicians, Capitol Chamber Artists, Adirondack Ensemble, N.Y. State Music Tchrs. Assn., Coll. Music Soc., Music Tchrs. Nat. Assn., Upper Hudson Musical Arts, Schenectady Musical Union, Albany Symphony Orch. Home: 819 Woodland Ave Schenectady NY 12309

SZOLNOKI, JOHN FRANK, special education educator, administrator; b. NYC, Apr. 16, 1956; s. Jacob and Anna (Reinwald) S.; m. Kathleen Bascetta, Dec. 28, 2004; children: Melissa Beth, David Jacob, Elizabeth, Eric. BS, Manhattan Coll., 1978; MS, Coll New Rochelle, 1981; MEd, Columbia U., 1983, EdD, 1988. Cert. tchr. spl. edn., sch. adminstr., supr., dist. adminstr., N.Y. Therapy aide Office Mental Health, N.Y. State Bronx Psychiat. Ctr., 1978; tchr. sci. 6th-8th grades Sts. Philip and James Sch., Archdiocese of N.Y., 1978-79; program supr. occpl. edn. classes St. Mary's Habilitation Inst. Inst. Applied Human Dynamics, Bronx, 1979-83; sch. supr. Assn. for Help of Retarded Children Bronx Habilitation Ctr., NYC, 1983-87; spl. educator Mt. Pleasant-Blythedale Union Free Sch. Dist., Valhalla, NY, 1987-88; spl. edn. educator Bd. Coop. Ednl. Svcs. So. Westchester, White Plains, NY, 1988—, Dobbs Ferry (N.Y.) H.S., 1995-96, Harrison (N.Y.) H.S., 1996-97, Hommocks Mid. Sch., Larchmont, NY, 2002—05, West Lake H.S., Valhalla, 2005—. Adj. prof. Western Conn. State U., Danbury, 1988-89, St. Thomas Aquinas Coll., Sparkill, N.Y., 1990, 91, Coll. New Rochelle, N.Y., 2001-, CUNY Hunter, 1994-99; team leader Bd. Coop. Ednl. Svcs., So. Westchester, 1989-93, site coord. extended sch. yr. program Rye Lake campus, 1991-95; presenter in field; Ctr. Spl. Edn. and Tng. Resource Ctr., workshop presenter supts. day, 1995; mem. So. Westchester Bd. coop. Ednl. Svcs. Vol. firefighter, sec. hook & ladder Harrison (N.Y.) Fire Dept., 1993-95, lt., 1996-97 capt., 1998-99 (Firefighter of Yr. 1990); mem. com. Very Spl. Arts,White Plains, N.Y., 1990; parent rep. exec. bd. Harrison Children's Ctr., 1991-93, 95—; lector, tchr. catechism St. Gregory the Gt. Roman Cath. Ch., 1994-95, Secular Franciscan Order, Roman Cath. Ch., 2002—; sec. St. Francis Fraternity, N.Y., 2003—; EMT vol. Harrison Ambulance Corps, 1993-94; aux. police officer N.Y.C. Police Dept., 1975-77; mem. Ctrl. Westchester Vicariate Coun., Archdiocese of N.Y., 1998—99; mem. parish coun. St. Gregory the Great, 1998—99; panel mem. surrogate decision making com. N.Y. State Commn. on Quality Care for the Mentally Disabled, 1999—. Grantee: Readers Digest Found., Westchester Edn. Coalition, 1990, Innovation Network, Westchester, Rockland Impact II, Adaptor award, 1991, 92, 93, 94, 95, 97, 98, 2000 Mem. Am. Assn. on Mental Retardation (rsch. project norming examiner adaptive behavior scale 1991), Coun. for Exceptional Children (pres. Hunter Coll. chpt. 1997-2000, regional rep. to bd. dirs. N.Y. State Fedn. 1990-93, treas. 1993-96, exec. bd. dirs. 1993-96, del. Nat. conv. 1998, co-chair N.Y. state conv. 1997, sec. 2002—, co-chmn. promotion/publicity subcom. local arrangements com. nat. annual conv. 2002, v.p. NY State Fedn. Chpts. Coun. Exceptional Children, 2003-04, pres.-elect, 2004-05, NY State CEC pres. 2005-), Kappa Delta Pi, Phi Delta Kappa. Avocation: marathon running. Office: Bd Coop Ednl Svcs So Westchester 1606 Old Orchard St White Plains NY 10604-1049 Home: 51 Holmes Ave Hartsdale NY 10530-1339 Office Phone: 914-948-7271. Personal E-mail: johnszolnoki@aol.com.

SZOLOVITS, PETER, computer scientist; BS, PhD, Calif. Inst. Tech. Prof. computer sci. & engring. MIT, Cambridge, Mass., 1974—, prof. health sciences & tech., head of Clin. Decision-Making Group, Computer Sci. & Artificial Intelligence Lab. (CSAIL). Contbr. articles, scientific papers. Fellow: Am. Coll. Med. Informatics, Am. Assn. Artificial Intelligence; mem.: Inst. Medicine. Office: MIT 32-254 EECS 77 Mass Ave Cambridge MA 02139-4307 Office Phone: 617-253-3476. E-mail: psz@mit.edu.

SZOSTAK, JACK WILLIAM, molecular biologist, educator; b. London, Nov. 9, 1952; s. William J. and Viola (Munford) S.; m. Terri-Lynn McCormick, May 29, 1993. BS in Cell Biology, McGill U., Montreal, Can., 1972; PhD in Biochemistry, Cornell U., Ithaca, NY, 1977. Rsch. assoc. in biochemistry Cornell U., Ithaca, NY, 1977-79; asst. prof. dept. biol. chemistry Harvard Med. Sch./Sidney Farber Cancer Inst., Boston, 1979-83; assoc. prof. dept. biol. chemistry Harvard Med. Sch./Dana Farber Cancer Inst., Boston, 1983-84; assoc. prof. dept. genetics Harvard Med. Sch., Boston, 1984-87, prof., 1988—; assoc. molecular biologist, dept. molecular biology Mass. Gen. Hosp., Boston, 1984-87, molecular biologist, dept. molecular biology, 1988—, Alex Rich Disting. Investigator, dept. molecular biology, 2000—; investigator Howard Hughes Med. Inst., 1998—. Cons. Genetics Inst., 1980-87; mem. site visit team, NIH, 1982; mem. Presdl. Young Investigator Review Panel, 1984; mem. Nat. Sci. Found. Review Panel, 1985, NASA Exobiology Study Sect., 1997; NATO Advanced Study Course on RNA, Spetses, Greece, 1994; program dir., Genetics Cancer and Inherited Disease Tng. Grant, Harvard Med. Sch., 1986-92; mem. sci. adv. bd. Gilead Scis., Inc., 1990-98, Trans-Karyotic Therapies, Inc., 1990—, Cubist, Inc., 1993-97; ad hoc mem., NIH Molecular Biology Study Sect., 1992; mem. Subcommittee of Professors, Harvard Med. Sch., 1992-94, preliminary qualifying exam com., 1996-97, com. on postdoctoral fellow, 1997-98; mem. com. on sr. appointments, Mass. Gen. Hosp., 1992-97; co-chair, Nucleic Acids Gordon Conf., 1993, Keystone Symposium on RNA, 1996; Can. reallocation exercise external reviewer, NRC, 1998, mem. workshop on size limits of microorganisms, 1998, co-chair com. on the origin and evolution of life, 2003-; mem. partners com. on sr. appointments, 1997-; mem. bd. tutors, biochemical sciences, Harvard U., 2000-; mem. NIH Intramural Review Panel, 2001; invited lectr., Agouron Inst. Sponsored Geobiology Course, Catalina Island, 2002; vis. fellow, Brasenose Coll. and Astor Lectr., Oxford U., 2005; tchr. Introductory Lecture, RNA World Quarter Course, 2005. Contbr. articles to sci. jours. Recipient Louis Vuitton-Moet Hennesey 'Vinci of Excellence' award, 1996, Hans Sigrist prize U. Bern, Switzerland, 1997, Genetics Soc. Am. medal, 2000, Harrison Howe award, Am. Chemical Soc., Rochester sect., 2003; co-recipient Albert Lasker award for Basic Med. Rsch., Lasker Found., 2006 Fellow NY Acad. Scis.; mem. NAS (award in molecular biology, 1994), Am. Acad. Arts & Sciences. Achievements include patents in field. Office: Howard Hughes Med Inst Mass Gen Hosp Dept Molecular Biology Boston MA 02114 also: CCIB 7215 Simches Research Ctr 185 Cambridge St Boston MA 02114 Address: Mass Gen Hosp 32 Fruit St Boston MA 02114 Business E-Mail: szostak@molbio.mgh.harvard.edu.

SZUCS, ANDREW ERIC, freelance/self-employed writer; b. Cleve., Apr. 25, 1946; s. Andrew Elmer and Katherine (Krizsak) S.; m. Laura Jean Nyhan, June 4, 1971; children: Andrew Edward, Eric Stephen. BA, U. Dayton, 1968; diploma, Cleve. Inst. Electronics, 1972; MBA, Wright State U., 1984. Pub. affairs specialist USAF, Laughlin AFB, Tex., 1968-70; exhibit rschr., writer USAF Orientation Group, Wright-Patterson AFB, Ohio, 1970-73; cmty. rels. dir. Wright-Patterson AFB, 1973-77; publ. mgr. Air Force Logistics Command, Wright-Patterson AFB, 1977-85, chief pub. officer, 1985-90; civilian command tng. mgr./adminstrn. Air Force Materiel Command, Wright-Patterson AFB, 1990-2001; program mgr. Materiel Sys. Group Supply Logistics Wright-Patterson AFB, 2001—04; freelance writer The Arts & Sci. of Commn., 2004—. Contbr. articles to profl. jours. (AWA Jour. award 1986). Staff sgt. USAF, 1968—73. Named Disting. Alumnus, St. Ignatius High Sch., Cleve., 1994. Mem. Soc. Aerospace Communicators, Nat. Press Club (Silver Owl), Am. Radio Relay League, Amateur Satellite Corp., U.S. Soccer Fedn. (referee), Ohio High Sch. Athletic Assn. (referee), Wright State U. Bus. Alumni Assn. (rec. sec. 1985-89), Nat. Assn. Sports Ofcls. Roman Catholic. Avocations: amateur radio, writing. Home and Office: 1135 Mint Springs Dr Fairborn OH 45324-5728

SZUGDA, SHARON A., elementary school educator; b. Nashua, NH, Mar. 8, 1971; d. Chester and Judith Szugda. BS in Elem. Edn., Keene State Coll., NH, 1995, BA in Social Sci., 1995. 7th grade math/geography tchr. Epping Mid. HS, NH, 1998—2002, Paul Sch., Sanbornville, NH, 2002—. Home: 97 Dulko Cir Sanbornville NH 03872 Office: Paul Sch 60 Taylor Way Sanbornville NH 03872 Home Phone: 603-522-8622. Personal E-mail: sszugda064@mac.com.

SZULIK, MATTHEW J., information technology executive; With Sapiens Internat., MapInfo Corp.; pres. Relativity Technologies, 1997—98; COO Red Hat, Inc., Raleigh, NC, 1998—99, CEO, 1999—, pres., 1999—, dir., 1999—, chmn., 2002—. Chmn. sci. and tech. bd. State NC Econ. Develop. Bd. Recipient 20/20 Vision award, CIO mag. Mem.: NC Electronics and Information Technologies Assn. (past chmn. and exec. dir.). Office: Red Hat Inc 1801 Varsity Dr Raleigh NC 27606-2072 Office Phone: 919-754-3700. Office Fax: 919-754-3701.

SZUWALSKI, ANDRE MICHAEL, lawyer; b. Buffalo, Aug. 16, 1964; m. Angela Fontana. BS in Elec. Engring., U. Miss., 1987; JD cum laude, Tulane U., 1990. Bar: Tex. 1990, registered: US Patent & Trademark Office. Assoc. Jenkens & Gilchrist, P.C., Dallas, 1990—97, shareholder, 1997—, firm co-leader intellectual property practice group. Mem.: ABA, Am. Intellectual Property Law Assn., Dallas Assn. Young Lawyers, Dallas/Ft. Worth Patent Law Assn., Dallas Bar Assn., Tex. State Bar Assn. Office: Jenkens & Gilchrist PC Ste 3200 1445 Ross Ave Dallas TX 75202-2799 Office Phone: 214-855-4795. Office Fax: 214-855-4300. Business E-Mail: aszuwalski@jenkens.com.

SZWERC, MICHAEL FRANCIS, thoracic surgeon; b. Mar. 24, 1966; BA, Washington U., 1992; MD, Washintong U. Sch. Medicine, 1988. Chief thoracic surgery Leighiy Valley Hosp., Allentown. Fellow: Am. Coll. Physicians; mem.: So. Thoracic Surg. Assn., Soc. Thoracic Surgeons, Gen. Thoracic Club. Office: 1240 S Cedar Crest Blvd Ste 403 Allentown PA 18103

SZYDLOWSKI, JOSEPH EDWARD, music librarian; b. Wyandotte, Mich., July 13, 1955; s. Joseph Victor and Hedwig Szydlowski. MusB, Ea. Mich. U., 1979; MusM, San Francisco State U., 1985; M in Info. and Libr. Studies, U. Mich., 1993. Libr. clk. U. Mich. Music Libr., Ann Arbor, 1991—93; libr., gen. reference Chgo. Pub. Libr., 1993—94, music libr., 1994—. Musician (classical guitarist) Spanish and Polish music concerts. Union trustee AFSCME, Chgo., 2001—02. Scholar Robert Guthrie Master Class, So. Meth. U., 1999. Mem.: Guitar Found. Am., Chgo. Classical Guitar Soc., Music Libr. Assn. (reviewer 2003—04). Roman Catholic. Avocations: politics, ecology, renaissance and baroque music, architecture, art. Office: Chgo Pub Libr - Main 8th Fl 400 S State St Chicago IL 60605 Home Phone: 312-949-1490; Office Phone: 312-747-4823. Office Fax: 312-747-4832. Personal E-mail: joszyd@onshore.net. Business E-Mail: szydlows@chipublib.org.

SZYGENDA, RALPH J., automotive executive; b. McKeesport, Pa., Sept. 6, 1948; BS in Computer Sci., U. Mo., 1970; MEE, U. Tex., 1975; ED (hon.), U. Mo. With Tex. Instruments Inc., 1972—93; v.p., chief info. officer Bell Atlantic Corp., Arlington, Va., 1993—96, GM Corp., 1996—2000, group v.p., chief info. officer, 2000—. Bd. dir. Handleman Co. Mem.: GM Automotive Stratey Bd., U. Mo. Sch. Mgmt. Info. Sys. (chmn. advisory bd.), InformationWeek Mag. (editl. bd.), Rsch. Bd. Office: GM Corp 300 Renaissance Ctr PO Box 300 Detroit MI 48265-3000

SZYGENDA, STEPHEN A., electrical and computer engineering educator, researcher; b. McKeesport, Pa., Oct. 5, 1938; s. Stephen A. Sr. and Elizabeth B. (Zolczer) S.; m. Marie A. Deli, Apr. 2, 1960; children: Stephanie Burden, Diana Easton, Mark. BS, Fairleigh Dickinson U., 1965; MS, Northwestern U., 1967, PhD, 1968. Registered profl. engr., Tex. Engr. Comprehensive Design, NJ, 1959-62; mem. tech. staff Bell Tel. Labs., NJ, Ill., 1962-68; assoc. prof. elec. engring. and computer engring. U. Mo., Rolla, 1968-70; prof. elec. engring. and computer engring. So. Meth. U., Dallas, 1970-73, U. Tex., Austin, 1973-86, dir. Ctr. for Tech. Tng., 1986-89, Clint Murchison Sr. Chair of Free Enterprise prof., 1986-96, chmn. elec. and computer engring. dept., 1993-96; dean Sch. Engring. U. Ala., Birmingham, 1996-2000, So. Meth. U., Dallas, 2000—04, Cecil H. Green chair, 2004—. Pres. CCSS, Austin, 1972-81, Comsat Gen. Internat. Sys., Austin, 1981-83, SBI, Inc., Austin, 1985—; pres., CEO Rubicon Group, Austin, 1983-85; active Tex. Gov. Coun. for Sci. and Tech., 1984-87. Contbr. articles to profl. jours. Dir. Laguna Gloria Mus., Austin, 1981-83; pres. bd. Austin Ballet, 1983. With USN, 1956-59. Fellow IEEE (bd. dirs. 1973-75 Svc. awards 1977, 79, 83, 87, 96), IC2, Soc. for Design and Process Sci.; mem. Assn. Computing Machinery (Svc. award 1975, 79, 87, 88, Disting. lectr. 1991-95). Roman Catholic. Achievements include pioneering in CAD, simulation, fault tolerant computing, telecommunications, entrepreneurship, and software engineering. Home: 5227 Beckington Ln Dallas TX 75287 Office: Southern Methodist Univ Sch of Engring Dallas TX 75275 Office Phone: 214-768-3959. Personal E-mail: szygenda@msn.com.

SZYMANCZYK, MICHAEL E., tobacco products executive; BS in Finance, Indiana U., 1972. Various sales and gen. mgmt. positions Procter & Gamble, 1971-87; v.p. sales Kraft Inc., Glenview, Ill., 1987-88, v.p retail ops., 1988; sr. v.p. Swift-Eckrich Inc., 1989; sr. v.p. sales Philip Morris USA (now divsn. of Altria Grp., Inc.), NYC, 1990-97, pres., CEO, 1997—, chmn., 2002—. Mem.: Indiana U. Kelley Sch. of Bus. Dean's Adv. Council (chmn.), bd. trustees Va. Found. for Independent Coll. Office: Philip Morris USA 120 Park Ave New York NY 10017-5592

SZYMANSKI, BOLESLAW KAROL, computer scientist, educator, entrepreneur; b. Paslek, Poland, Apr. 22, 1950; arrived in U.S., 1982; s. Kazlmierz and Aniela Marta (Langer) Szymanski; m. Emilia Haraf, Dec. 15, 1973; children: Peter Rafal, Witold Andrew. M in Engring. Electronics, Warsaw Poly. Inst., Poland, 1973; PhD in Computer Sci., Nat. Acad. Scis., Warsaw, 1976. Asst. prof. Warsaw Poly. Inst., 1973-75; rschr. Inst. Sci. Technol. and Econ. Info., Warsaw, 1975-78, divsn. head, 1979-82; postdoctoral fellow Aberdeen U., England, 1978; vis. asst. prof. U. Pa., Phila., 1982-85, assoc. prof. computer sci., 1985-89, prof. computer sci., 1990—, acting chmn., 1993—94; assoc. dean info. tech. Rensselaer Poly. Inst., Troy, NY, 1997—2001, dir. Ctr. for Pervasive Computing and Networking, 2003—; founder/chmn. bd. dirs. Premonitia, Inc., Boston, 2000; founder, pres., CEO Optimaret, Inc., Latham, NY, 2004. Chief sci. officer Computer Command & Control Co., Phila., 1984—87; cons. GE R & D Ctr., Schenectady, 1987—90, IBM Corp., Poughkeepsie, NY, 1992—96, Cardiomag, Inc., Schenectady, NY, 2001—, Internat. Med. Programs, Albany, 2003—; EPL parallel computer lang. expert witness U.S. Congress, Washington, 1987; expert UN Indsl. Devel. Office, Vienna, 1990—96. Author: Parallel Functional Languages and Compilers, 1993; editor-in-chief Sci. Computing IOS Press, Amsterdam, 2000—; editor: Languages, Compilers & RT Systems, 1996, Advances in Pervasive Computing and Networking, 2004. Recipient Wiley Disting. Faculty award, 2003, Tech. Innovation award, NASA, 1996, SuPaCup '93, German Computer Soc., Mannheim, 1993; Rsch. grantee, IBM, Lucent, CISCO, DARPA, ARO, NSF, ONR, 1966—. Fellow: IEEE; mem.: Assn. Computing Machinery (nat. lectr. 1987—88). Avocations: history, bridge. Home: 6 Hollow Rd Newtonville NY 12110-5100 Office: Rensselaer Poly Inst 110 8th St Troy NY 12180-3590 Home Phone: 518-421-1787; Office Phone: 518-276-2714. Personal E-mail: bkszym@yahoo.com. Business E-Mail: szymab@rpi.edu.

SZYMANSKI, EDNA MORA, provost; b. Caracas, Venezuela, Mar. 19, 1952; came to U.S., 1952; d. José Angel and Helen Adele (McHugh) Mora; m. Michael Bernard, Mar. 30, 1973. BS, Rensselaer Poly. Inst., Troy, NY, 1972; MS, U. Scranton, Pa., 1974; PhD, U. Tex., 1988. Vocat. evaluator Mohawk Valley Workshop, Utica, NY, 1974-75; vocat. rehab. counselor NY State Office Vocat. Rehab., Utica, 1975-80, sr. vocat. rehab. counselor, 1980-87; rsch. assoc. U. Tex., Austin, 1988-89; asst. prof. U. Wis., Madison, 1989-91, assoc. prof., 1991-93, assoc. dean sch. edn., 1993—97, dir. rehab. rsch. and tng. ctr., 1993-96, prof. rehab. psychology and spl. edn., 1993—99, chair dept. rehab. psychology and spl. edn., 1997-99, fellow tchg. acad., 1997; dean Coll. Edn. U. Md., College Park, 1999—2006; sr. v.p. acad. affairs, provost U. Maine, Orono, 2006—. Cons. Rsch. Assocs. Syracuse, NY, 1988-90. Author/co-author various book chpts.; co-editor: Rehabilitation Counseling Basics and Beyond, 1992, 98, 2005; co-editor Work and Disability, 1996, 2003, Rehabilitation Counseling Bull., 1994-2000; contbr. articles to profl. jours. Recipient Rsch. award Am. Assn. Counselor Edn. and Supr., 1991. Mem. ACA (chair rsch. com. 1992-94, Rsch. awards 1990, 93, 95), Am. Rehab. Counseling Assn. (pres. 1985-86, rsch. award 1989, 94, Disting. Profl. award 1997, James F. Garrett award for disting. career in rehab. rsch. 1999), Coun. Rehab. Edn. (chair rsch. com. 1990-95, v.p. 1993-95, 97), Nat. Coun. Rehab. Edn. (chair rsch. com. 1992-99, Rehab. Edn. Rschr. of Yr. 1993, New Career in Rehab. Edn. award 1990). Office: U Maine Office of Provost 201 Alumni Hall Orono ME 04469 Personal E-mail: emszy@aol.com.

SZYMANSKI, PATRICK JOSEPH, lawyer; b. Detroit, Jan. 18, 1949; s. Frank S. and Lillian F. (Mikula) S. Student, MIT, 1966-69; BA, Wayne State U., Detroit, 1973, JD, 1976. Bar: Mich. 1976, US Ct. Appeals (DC, 1st, 2nd and 4th cirs.) 1977, US Ct. Appeals (9th cir.) 1978, Calif. 1979, DC 1979, US Dist. Ct. (no. dist.) Calif. 1979, US Ct. Appeals (10th cir.) 1984, US Supreme Ct. 1985, US Dist. Ct. DC 1988, US Dist. Ct. Md. 1988, US Dist. Ct. Mich. (ea. dist.) 1991, US Ct. Appeals (3rd cir.) 1991. Appellate ct. br. NLRB, Washington, 1976-78, 83-88; assoc. Beeson, Tayer & Bodine, San Francisco, 1978-83, Baptiste & Wilder, P.C., Washington, 1988—2003. Mem. editl. bd. Wayne State U. Law Rev., 1975-76. Gen. counsel Internat. Brotherhood Teamsters, 1999—2006, Change to Win, 2006—. Democrat. Roman Catholic. Office: Change to Win 1900 L St NW Ste 900 Washington DC 20036 Office Phone: 202-721-6035. Business E-Mail: patrick.szymanski@changetowin.org.

SZYMCZAK, EDWARD JOSEPH, mechanical engineer; b. Anderson, Tex., Sept. 28, 1938; s. Harold and Verna (Walkoviak) S.; m. Lorena Jane Sharp, Sept. 26, 1964; children: Denise, Lisa, Brian. Student, U. St. Thomas, Houston, 1958; BSME, Tex. A&M U., College Station, 1961; MBA, U. Houston, 1970. Registered profl. engr., Tex. Engr. trainee to engring. mgr. Cameron Iron Works, Houston, 1961-90; dir. engring. Ea. hemisphere Cooper Oil Tool Div./Cooper Industries, London, 1990-91, dir. engring. Houston, 1991-95, Cameron div. Cooper Cameron Corp., Houston, 1995-97; mgr. design process tech. ABB Vetco Gray, Houston, 1998—2003; pvt. practice Spring, Tex., 2004—. Past chmn. indsl. adv. bd. U. La., Lafayette (formerly U. Southwestern La.), 1991—; trustee Tex. A&M U. Rsch. Found., College Station, 1994—; mech. engring. adv. bd. U. Tenn., Knoxville, 1996-2000; cons. in field. Patentee (8) on oil tool equipment. Bd. dirs. Polish Home, Houston, 2004—05. Recipient Disting. Svc. award, U. La. Lafayette Mech. Engring., 2006. Mem. ASME, Tex. A&M Former Students Assn., Tex. A&M 12th Man Found., Tex. A&M Mech. Engring. Acad. Disting. Grads., Soc. Petroleum Engrs., Nat. Assn. Corrosion Engrs., Tau Beta Pi. Republican. Roman Catholic. Avocations: ranching, farming, design process technology, investing. Home and Office: 4002 Cypress Hill Dr Spring TX 77388-5717

TA, TAI VAN, lawyer, researcher; b. Ninh Binh, Vietnam, Apr. 16, 1938; came to U.S., 1975; s. Duong Van and Loan thi (Pham) T.; m. Lien-Nhu Tran, Oct. 26, 1967; children: Becky, John, Khuong Virginia, Dora. LLB, U. Saigon, Vietnam, 1960; MA, U. Va., 1964, PhD, 1965; LLM, Harvard U., 1985. Bar: Mass. 1986, U.S. Dist. Ct. Mass. 1987. Prof. U. Saigon Law Sch., 1965-75, Nat. Sch. Adminstrn., 1965-75; ptnr. Tang thi Thanh Trai & Ta Van Tai, 1968-75; legal rschr. Reed Smith Shaw & McClay, Pitts., 1975; rsch. assoc. Harvard U. Law Sch., Cambridge, Mass., 1975—, adj. lectr., 1998; pvt. practice, Brookline, Mass., 1986—; rsch. scholar NYU Law Sch., NYC, 1990-94. Lectr. in field; cons. in field. Co-author: The Laws of Southeast Asia, 1986, The Le Code: Law in Traditional Vietnam, 1987, Investment Law in Vietnam, 1990, Histoire de La codification Juridique au Vietnam, 2001; author: Vietnamese Tradition of Human Rights, 1988; contbr. articles to profl. jours. Commr. Mass. Govs. Asian-Am. Coun., 1992—. Fulbright scholar 1960-62; grantee Asia Found., 1972, Ford Found., 1975-76, Aspen Inst. 1993. Avocations: piano, swimming, foreign languages. Home and Office: 145 Naples Rd Brookline MA 02446-5748 Office: E Asian Legal Studies Program Harvard U Law Sch 1563 Mass Ave Cambridge MA 02138-2903 Home Phone: 617-734-1315; Office Phone: 617-216-3873. Personal E-mail: taivanta@yahoo.com.

TAATI, POOPAK, media director; d. Abdol Ali Taati and Mahin Dokht Farzan. PhD in Sociology, U. Tex., Austin, 1988. Asst. prof. of sociology Minn. State U., Moorhead, 1988—92; prof. sociology Georgetown U., Washington, 1995—96; prof. social scis. Montgomery Coll., Germantown, Md., 1999—2003; freelance journalist BBC, 2003—05; dir. Media for Thought, 2004—06. Vis. prof. anthropology & sociology Wittenberg U., Springfield, Ohio, 1987—88. Prodr.: (documentary film/video) When Authorities Turn Violent, (educational film/video) When Different is Beautiful. Treas. Ctr. Iranian Rsch. and Analysis, 1988—89; mem. tchg. com. Am. Sociol. Assn., 1997—98; mem. Iranian Professionals Assn., Washington, 1993—94, Iranian-American Cultural Assn., 1996—97. Recipient Tchg. and Svc. award, Montgomery Coll., 2002; fellow, NEH, 1991, 1997; grantee, MIT, Cambridge, 1990, U.S. Inst. Peace, 1996. Mem.: Gulf 2000. Independent. Spiritual Moslem. Avocations: participation in cultural activities, movies, travel, exercise, sauna. Home Phone: 202-903-6321.

TABACHNICK, NORMAN DONALD, psychiatrist, educator; b. Toronto, Ont., Can., Feb. 21, 1927; BS, U. Ill., 1947, MD, 1949; PhD in Psychoanalysis, So. Calif. Psychoanalytic Inst., 1977. Diplomate Am. Bd. Med. Examiners, Am. Bd. Psychiatry and Neurology. Intern Michael Reese Hosp., 1949-50; resident in psychiatry U.S. VA Hosp., Bedford, Mass., 1950-51, U.S. AFB, Biloxi, Miss., 1951-52, L.A. County Gen. Hosp., 1953-54; staff psychiatrist Sepulveda VA Hosp., 1976-78; pvt. practice LA; mem. staff Resthaven Sanitarium, U. So. Calif. Med. Ctr., L.A. County, Westwood Hosp., Edgemont Hosp., Cedars-Sinai Med. Ctr.; mem. staff Neuropsychiatric Inst. UCLA; clin. prof. psychiatry U. So. Calif., LA, 1970-75, UCLA, 1975—. Hon. mem. med. staf. Resthaven Cmty. Med.

Health Ctr., 1973; guest lectr. Cedars-Sinai Med. Ctr., 1985; mem. adv. bd. divsn. psychoanalysis Nassau County Med. Ctr.; mem. faculty Calif. Sch. Profl. Psychology, L.A. Ctr. Group Psychotherapy, Grad. Ctr. Child Devel. and Psychotherapy; cons. L.A. County Coroner's Office, 1963-70, Bur. Vocat. Rehab., Jewish Family Svc., profl. adv. bd. Resthaven Sanitarium, Marianne Frostig Sch. Ednl. Therapy, W. Valley Ctr. Edl. Therapy. Author: Accident or Suicide?, 1973; mem. edtl. bd. Jour. Acad. Psychoanalysis, book rev. editor, 1978; mem. edtl. bd. Internat. Jour. Psycho-analytic Psychotherapy, 1979-83; reviewer Am. Jour. Psychiatry, 1983—, Jour. Neuropsychiatry and Clin. Neuro Scis., 1988-90; contbr. articles to profl. jours.; cons. (film) Suicide Prevention: The Physician's Role, 1967, Highlights of the 1964 American Psychiatric Association; cons., participant The Thin Edge--Guilt., 1975; author book revs. Assoc. chief psychiatrist L.A. Suicide Prevention Ctr., 1968-76, prin. investigator; adv. com. Walter Briehl Human Rights Found., 1984; v.p., bd. dirs. Suicide Prevention Ctr., Inc.; bd. dirs. Inst. Suicide Prevention, L.A., 1996, chmn. funding a crisis line com., 1997; bd. dirs. We. divsn. Am. Found. Suicide Prevention, 1998, chair program com., 1999-2002. Recipient award for disting. creativity and leadership, Am. Found. for Suicide Prevention, 2003; rsch. grantee, Founds. Fund Rsch. Psychiatry, 1963, NIMH, 1970. Fellow Am. Psychiatric Assn. (life), Am. Acad. Psychoanalysis (pres. 1974, chmn. nominating com. 1975, trustee, chmn. com. on rsch., mem. editl. bd. The Acad., presdl. citation 1975); mem. Internat. Psychoanalytic Assn., Internat. Assn. Suicide Prevention, Am. Psychoanalytic Assn. (cert., mem. com. liason with AAAS 1977-80), Am. Assn. Suicidology, (founder, mem. editl. bd. Life-Threatening Behavior, cert. recognition 1996) Inst. Contemporary Psychoanalysis (founding mem., trustee 1990-93), So. Calif. Psychoanalytic Inst. (pres., tng. and supervising analyst, selection rsch. clin. assocs. com., dir. rsch. divsn. 1970-81, chief investigator 1976-88, chmn. com. rsch. award stds. 1979, pres.-elect 1980, 86, pres. 1981, 87-90, mem. tng. and supr. analyst, new ctr. for psychoanalysis), Am. Coll. Psychiatrists, Med. Rsch. Assn. So. Calif., So. Calif. Psychiat. Soc. (consultation and violence panel), L.A. County Med. Assn. Office: 505 N Bonhill Rd Los Angeles CA 90049-2325 Office Phone: 310-472-5044. Personal E-mail: ndtmd@aol.com.

TABAK, LAWRENCE A., federal agency administrator, dentist; b. Bklyn., Dec. 15, 1951; BS in biology and chemistry, City Coll., CUNY, 1972; DDS, Columbia U., 1977; PhD in oral biology, SUNY, Buffalo, 1981. Certificate of Proficiency in Endodontics SUNY, Buffalo, 1985. Asst. prof. oral biology SUNY, Buffalo, 1980—81, asst. prof. endodontics and oral biology, 1981—85, assoc. prof., 1985—86; assoc. prof. dental rsch. and biochemistry Sch. Medicine and Dentistry, U. Rochester, 1986—92, prof., 1992—96, prof. dental rsch. and biochemistry and biophysics, 1996—97, prof. dentistry and biochemistry and biophysics, 1998—2000, chair dept. dental rsch., 1995—97, sr. assoc. dean for rsch., 1998—2000; dir. Nat. Inst. Dental and Craniofacial Rsch., NIH, 2000—; sr. investigator Nat. Inst. Diabetes and Digestive and Kidney Diseases, NIH, 2000—. Vis. scientist Nat. Inst. Dental Rsch., NIH, 1982—83. Named Alumnus of Yr., Sch. Dental and Oral Surgery, Columbia U., 1997. Fellow: AAAS; mem.: Inst. Medicine, Soc. Glycobiology, Am. Assn. for Dental Rsch., Internat. Assn. for Dental Rsch. (Disting. Scientist Award 1996). Office: Nat Inst Dental and Craniofacial Rsch Bldg 31 Rm 2C39 31 Center Dr MSC 2290 Bethesda MD 20892 Office Phone: 301-496-3571. Office Fax: 301-402-2185. E-mail: lawrence.tabak@nih.gov.

TABAK, STEVEN WILLIAM, cardiologist; b. LA, May 7, 1952; MD, Johns Hopkins U., 1977. Intern Cedars-Sinai Med. Ctr., LA, 1977-78, resident in internal medicine, 1978-81, fellow in cardiovascular disease, 1981-83; assoc. clin. prof. medicine UCLA; clin. chief of cardiology, chmn. cardiac catheterization com. Cedars-Sinai Med. Ctr., 1996-98. Pvt. practice., interventional cardiologist, Cardiovascular Med. Group So. Calif.; chmn. cardiology divsn., Brotman Med. Ctr. Cardiovascular med. surgery featured Extreme Makeover, 2007. Fellow Am. Coll. Cardiology; mem. AMA, ACP Avocations: fishing, skiing. Office: 414 N Camden Dr Ste 1100 Beverly Hills CA 90210-4532 Office Phone: 310-278-3400. E-mail: tabak@evang.com. *

TABAKA, SANDRA LEE, retired medical/surgical nurse; d. Elmer William and Elaine Verba Viehmann; m. John Lawrence Tabaka, Oct. 8, 1960 (div. Nov. 1985); children: James Lawrence, Anthony Michael, Theresa Lynn. ADN, St. Mary's Coll., O'Fallon, Mo., 1978; BSN, Webster U., 1993. RN Mo. Staff nurse St. Luke's Hosp., Chesterfield, Mo., 1978—82, assoc. head nurse, 1982—94, staff nurse, 1994—2004, ret., 2004. Founding mem. St. Charles Countians Against Hazardous Waste, 1982—84; bd. mem. Cedar Groves Townhomes Assn., St. Charles, 1999—2002. Mem.: Oncology Nursing Soc. (oncology cert. nurse). Home: 244 Cedar Grove Dr Saint Charles MO 63304

TABASSUM, SHAKIL MAHMUD, financial executive; b. Pakistan, Feb. 13, 1962; came to U.S., 1975; s. Ahmed Mahmud and Nasreen Tabassum; m. Nabeela Mahmud Saeed, Dec. 31, 1988; children: Hamza, Batool, Junaid, Khizer. BS, L.I. U., 1985, MBA, 1986. Acct. Actax Svcs. Ltd., NYC, 1985-88; program asst. USAID, Peshawar, Pakistan, 1988-89, project mgmt. asst., 1989-90; fin. mgr. CARE Internat., Pakistan and Afghanistan, 1990-92, contr. Lusaka, Zambia, 1992-93; asst. contr. Clin. Diagnostic Svcs., Queens, NY, 1994-96; cons. Robert Half Internat., NYC, 1996; CFO LEAD Internat., NYC, 1996—. Office: LEAD Internat 3d Fl 700 Broadway Fl 3D New York NY 10003-9536 Home: 20D Kings Cir Newark DE 19702-1462 E-mail: shakil@lead.org.

TABATABAI, M. ALI, chemist, biochemist; b. Karbala, Iraq, Feb. 25, 1934; BS, U. Baghdad, 1958; MS, Okla. State U., 1960; PhD in Soil Chemistry, Iowa State U., 1965. Rsch. assoc. soil biochemistry Iowa State U., Ames, 1966-72, from asst. prof. to assoc. prof., 1972-78, prof. soil chemistry and biochemistry, 1978—. Cons. Electric Power Rsch. Inst., Palo Alto, 1978-83. Fellow AAAS, Am. Inst. Chemists, Am. Soc. Agronomy (Soil Sci. rsch. award 1992), Soil Sci. Soc. Am., Iowa Acad. Sci. (Disting. scientist, Disting. fellow); mem. Coun. Agrl. Sci. and Tech., Am. Chem. Soc., Am. Soc. Microbiology, Am. Soc. Agronomy, Soil Sci. Soc. Am., Assn. Univ. Profs., Iowa Acad. Sci., Gamma Sigma Delta (Alumni award of merit Iowa Beta chpt. 1993), Sigma Xi, Phi Kappa Phi. Achievements include research in soil enzymology and chemistry of sulfur, nitrogen and phosphorus in soils, nutrient cycling in the environment. Office: Iowa State U Sci & Tech Dept Agronomy Ames IA 50011-0001 E-mail: malit@iastate.edu.

TABATZNIK, BERNARD, retired cardiologist; b. Mir, Poland, Jan. 8, 1927; came to U.S., 1959, naturalized, 1966; s. Max and Fay (Ginsberg) T.; m. Marjorie Turner, Jan. 8, 1956; children: Darron Mark, Keith Donald, Ilana Wendy; m. Charline Edwards Harmon, Aug. 7, 1992. BSc, U. Witwatersrand, South Africa, 1945, MB, BChir, U. Witwatersrand, South Africa, 1949. Intern Baragwanath Hosp., Johannesburg, 1950-51, Hillingdon Hosp., Ashford Hosp., also rsch. unit Can. Red Cross Meml. Hosp., Taplow, England, 1951-54; med. registrar Ashford Hosp., 1954-56, Johannesburg Gen. Hosp., 1956-58; physician Baragwanath Hosp., 1958-59; fellow in medicine Sch. Medicine Johns Hopkins U., Balt., 1959-60, fellow in cardiology, 1960-61, asst. prof. medicine, 1966-97, ret., 1997; head cardiopulmonary divsn. Sinai Hosp., Balt., 1961-72, assoc. chief medicine, 1964-72; chief cardiology dept. North Charles Gen. Hosp., Balt., 1972; also dir. med. edn., dir. Postgrad. Inst., coord. ambulatory svcs.; med. dir. Nurse Practitioner-Physician Asst. Program Ch. Hosp., Balt., 1987-90. Contbr. articles to profl. jours. Recipient Save-A-Heart Humanitarian award, 1977, Maimonides award, 1983, Shaarei Zion Humanitarian award, 1987. Fellow Royal Coll. Physicians (London); mem. South African Cardiac Soc., Am. Heart Assn., Md. Heart Assn. (chmn. health careers 1964-66), Am. Coll. Cardiology. Home: 63 Oakridge Dr Monterey VA 24465-2350 Office Phone: 540-474-2343. Personal E-mail: btabatznik@aol.com.

TABAZADEH, AZADEH, environmental scientist, researcher; b. Tehran, Iran, Feb. 17, 1965; came to U.S., 1982; d. Modjtaba and Fatema (Beigi) T.; m. Mark Z. Jacobson, Aug. 30, 1993; children: Dionna Shelly Jacobson, Daniel Forest Jacobson. BS in Chemistry, UCLA, 1988, MS in Chemistry, 1990, PhD, 1994. Rsch., tchg. asst. UCLA, 1989-94; postdoctoral NASA, Moffett Field, Calif., 1994-97, rsch. sci., 1997—. Lectr. in field. Contbr. articles to profl. jours. including Jour. Geophys. Rsch., Geophys. Rsch. Letters, Sci. NASA fellow, 1991-94, 94-97; recipient Presdl. Early Career award for Scientist and Engrs., 1998; named to Brilliant 10, Popular Science Mag., 2002. Mem. Am. Chem. Soc., Am. Geophysical Union (James B. Macelwane medal, 2001), Am. Assn. Aerosol Rsch., Air and Waste Mgmt. Assn., UCLA Chemist Assn. Achievements include discovery of narrow rings of cold air over the Earth's poles that help to form clouds which contribute to the destruction of the ozone layer. Fax: 650-604-3625. Business E-Mail: azadeh.tabazadeh-1@nasa.gov.

TABB, VANDOSTER LANGFORD, SR., retired military officer; b. Williamsburg, Va., June 4, 1935; s. George Edward and Mary Alice (Parker) Tabb; m. Evangelyn Maria Darby, May 26, 1965; m. Julia Spain (div. Oct. 2, 1961); children: Yolanda Agnes West Jenkins, Vandoster Langford Jr., Jacinda Lynn, Larticia Ann, Myrtinia Alores. BS in Acctg., Va. State U., Petersburg, 1959; MA in Mgmt. and Pub. Adminstrn., Webster U., St. Louis, 1978. Commd. 2d lt. US Army, 1959, detachment comdr. adv. group, 1968—69, post comptr. Ft. Holabird Balt., 1969—72, with adv. group, 1973—76, civic action officer 18th Airborne Corps, 1976—80; fin. mgmt. officer US Dept. of State, Washington, 1981—2000; ret., 2000. Career counselor, cons. US Dept. of State, 2000—. Budget officer Assoc. Md. Africa Societies, Inc, Ft. Washington, Md., 2004—07. Decorated Vietnam Campaign medal US Army, Combat Inf. Badge, Bronze Star medal, Bronze Medal for Meritorious Svc., Army Commendation Medal, Legion of Merit, Joint Svc. Commendation medal, Meritorious Svc. medal US Dept. of State, Washington, Superior Honor award. Mem.: NAACP, Rock, Inc, Am. Fgn. Svc. Assn., Mil. Officers Assoc. Am. (life). Democrat. Baptish. Avocations: bowling, travel, golf, movies, reading. Home: 1806 Williamsburg Ct Fort Washington MD 20744-4259 Office: US Dept State C St NW Washington DC 20522-4201 Office Phone: 703-302-7407. Office Fax: 703-302-7416. Personal E-mail: lank69@verizon.net. Business E-Mail: tabbvl@state.gov.

TABB, WALLER CROCKETT, retired allergist, immunologist; b. Richmond, Va., 1935; MD, U. Va., 1959. Diplomate Am. Bd. Internal Medicine, Am. Bd. Allergy and Immunology. Intern U. Va. Hosp., Charlottesville, 1959-60, resident in internal medicine, 1964-66, fellow in allergy/immunology and pulmonary medicine, 1966-67; mem. staff Lakeland (Fla.) Regional Med. Ctr., 1967—; pvt. practice Watson Clinic, Lakeland, ret., 1997. Fellow ACP, Am. Acad. Allergy and Immunology, Am. Coll. Chest Physicians; mem. Alpha Omega Alpha. Address: PO Box 178 Ware Neck VA 23178-0178 Home: 6102 WAre Neck Rd Ware Neck VA 23178

TABB, WINSTON, library director; b. Tulsa, Okla. BA magna cum laude, Okla. Baptist U., 1963; MA in Am. Lit., Harvard U., 1964; MLS, Simmons Coll., Boston, 1972. Various positions with Libr. of Congress, Washington, 1972—2002, asst. chief Gen. Reading Room, 1978—84, chief Copyright Info. & Reference Dvsn., 1984—88, dir. Rsch. Svc., 1988—89, acting dep. libr., 1989—92, assoc. libr., 1992—2002; Sheridan Dean of Univ. Libr. Johns Hopkins U., Baltimore, 2002—, dir. Sheridan Libraries, 2002—, vice provost for arts, 2006—, dir. historic houses. Mem. Nat. Digital Libr. Fedn. Policy Com., Coun. Libr. & Info. Resources; mem. vis. com. Harvard Libr.; rsch. libr. adv. com. Online Computer Libr. Ctr. Past bd. mem. Soros Found. Served with US Army, in Thailand. Recipient Ainsworth Rand Spofford President's award, District of Columbia Libr. Assn., 2002. Mem.: ALA (Melvil Dewey Medal 1998, Joseph W. Lippincott award 2007), Internat. Fedn. of Libr. Assns. & Insts. (chmn. IFLA Profl. Com. 2001—, vice chmn. profl. bd., chmn. Nat. Libr. Sect., chmn. Coordinating Bd. Divsn. Rsch. Libr.). Office: Milton S Eisenhower Libr Johns Hopkins Univ 3400 N Charles St Baltimore MD 21218 Office Phone: 410-516-8328. Office Fax: 410-516-5080. E-mail: wtabb@jhu.edu. *

TABBAL, NICOLAS G., plastic surgeon; b. Beirut, 1946; MD, Am. U., Beirut, 1972. Diplomate Am. Bd. Plastic Surgery, Am. Bd. Surgery. Intern Am. U. Med. Ctr., Beirut, 1971—72, resident in surgery, 1972—76; resident in plastic surgery Akron City Hosp., Ohio, 1977—79; fellow in gen. surgery Upstate Med. Ctr., Syracuse, NY, 1976—77; fellow in plastic reconstructive surgery NYU, 1979—80; pvt. practice plastic surgery NYC, 1980—; attending plastic surgeon Manhattan EET Hosp. Clin. instr. plastic surgery NYU Med. Ctr. Office: 521 Park Ave New York NY 10021-1840 Office Phone: 212-644-5800. Business E-Mail: mail@tabbal.us.

TABBERT, JAMES LEE, music educator; b. LaCrosse, Wis., Jan. 20, 1956; s. Wayne Gordon and Patricia Agnes Tabbert; m. Cheryl Lea Jones, Aug. 9, 1980; children: Marcus John, Molly Jane. Grad., Mil. Sch. Music, Little Creek, Va., 1975; MusB Edn., U. Wis., Eau Claire, 1984; EdM in Profl. Devel., U. Wis., Lacrosse, 2002. Lic. tchr. Dept. Pub. Instrn., Wis., 1989, Dept. Pub. Instrn., Minn., 1984. Music instr. Mountain Lake Pub. Schs., Minn., 1984—87; h.s. band instr. Arcadia Pub. Schs., Wis., 1987—; educator Hayward Cmty. Schs., Wis., 1989—. Choir dir. First Luth. Ch., Hayward, 1990—2003; ch. choir dir. Grace Luth. Ch., Hayward, 2003—, ch. pianist, 2003—. Musician: (profl. trumpet performer) several cmty. orchs. Accompanist Grace Luth. Ch., Hayward, 2003—07; exec. com. Artist Series U. Wis., Eau Claire, 1982. Recipient Excellence In Edn. award, Hayward Cmty. Schs., 1994—95, 2000—02, 2004. Mem.: Wis. Sch. Music Assn. (licentiate). Home: 10751 N Wittwer Hayward WI 54843 Office: Hayward Community Schools PO Box 860 Greenwood Ln Hayward WI 54843 Office Phone: 715-634-2619 1544. Office Fax: 715-634-2761. Business E-Mail: jtabbert@hayward.k12.wi.us.

TABEA, EMILE VICTOR, health facility administrator; b. Abidjan, Ivory Coast, June 6, 1959; arrived in US, 1982; s. Leon Kobe and Jeannette Saoua Tabea; m. Melanie Ayere Gbangninan, Dec. 20, 1990; children: Joel Victor, Eunice Victoire. MS, U. Mass., 1992. Cert. human svcs. profl. Mass. Instr. French and ESL U. Mass., Lowell, 1984—97; coord. Tewksbury Hosp., Mass., 1989, discharge planner dept. pub. health, 1989. Deacon Bethel Internat. Ch., Everett, Mass., 2003—05. Recipient Performance Recognition award, Commonwealth of Mass., 2000. Mem.: Internat. Reading Assn., Mass. Tchr. Assn. (assoc.). Mem. Independent Thinkers. Avocations: soccer, reading, travel. Home: 46 Barclay St Lowell MA 01851 Office: Tewksbury Hosp Dept Pub Health 365 East St Tewksbury MA 01876 Home Phone: 978-337-1449; Office Phone: 978-851-7321. Office Fax: 978-851-6743; Home Fax: 978-851-6743. Personal E-mail: emile_tabea@uml.edu. Business E-Mail: emile.tabea@state.ma.us.

TABER, DAVID O., urological surgeon; b. Panama City, Panama, June 30, 1938; s. Alden Pugh and Virginia (Kresler) Taber; m. Rebecca M.; children: Sharon Taber Silverman, Jeffrey, Andrew, Richard; m. Rebecca M. Taber, Dec. 20, 1987. BA, Syracuse U., 1959; MD, George Washington U., 1963. Diplomate Am. Bd. Urology. Urologic surgeon in pvt. practice, El Paso, Tex., 1972—. Chief med. staff Columbia West Hosp., El Paso, 1975-76, chief of urology, 1998-99; chief of surgery Sierra Med. Ctr., El Paso, 1977-78, chief of urology, 1995-97; prof. urology Tex. Tech Sch. Medicine, El Paso, 1998—. Mem. state com. on prostate cancer Am. Cancer Soc., Austin, 1998-99, bd. dirs. El Paso unit, 1999; mem. Tex. Rangers Found., Waco, 1998-2005; judge Santa Fe Indian Market; med. exec. com. El Paso County; founder Am. Mus. Served to lt. U.S. Army, 1963-72. Lt. col. US Army. Fellow ACS; mem. AMA, Urol. Soc. Internat., Urostomy Assn. (adv.), Tex. Urol. Soc., Am. Urol. Assn., Tex. Med. Assn., Am. Fertility Soc., Am. Lithotripsy Soc., El Paso Med. Soc. (exec. com. 2004— sec. 2006—, pres. elect, 2007, named in Best Doctors in Am., Best Doctors in Tex.), Mason (32 degree), Elmaida Shrine, Rotary, Alpha Epsilon Delta, Pi Sigma. Episcopalian. Avocations: photography, diving instructor. Office: 2201 N Stanton St El Paso TX 79902 Office Phone: 915-533-0800. Personal E-mail: dotabarmd@yahoo.com.

TABER, GEOFFREY ALEXANDER, industrial engineer, quality assurance professional; s. Richard Allen Baldwin and Trudy Diane Drwenski; 1 child, Alexis Renee. BA in Psychology, U. Colo., Denver, 2001; MBA, U. Phoenix, Lonetree, Colo., 2004. Cert. six sigma black belt Tyco Internat., 2006. Quality assurance mgr. ADT Security Svcs. Inc., Aurora, Colo., 2001—03, bus. analyst, 2003—04, project mgr., 2004—04, six sigma black belt, 2004—07, six sigma mgr., 2007—. Mem.: Am. Soc. of Quality, Inst. Industrial Engrs. Democrat. Episcopalian. Avocations: swimming, coaching, travel. Home Phone: 303-400-6884; Office Phone: 303-306-5524.

TABER, KENNETH W., lawyer; b. Nov. 28, 1956; BS summa cum laude, Univ. Pa., 1977; JD, Yale Univ., 1980. Bar: NY 1981, US Dist. Ct. (so., ea. dist. NY) 1981. Ptnr. Pillsbury Winthrop Shaw Pittman, NYC, litigator employment, co-chmn. nat. litig. practice. Founder Interfaith Legal Outreach, Westchester County, NY. Office: Pillsbury Winthrop Shaw Pittman 1540 Broadway New York NY 10036 Office Phone: 212-858-1813. Office Fax: 212-858-8405. Business E-Mail: kenneth.taber@pillsburylaw.com.

TABER, MARGARET RUTH, retired engineering technology educator; b. St. Louis, Apr. 29, 1935; d. Wynn Orr and Margaret Ruth (Feldman) Gould Stevens; m. William James Taber, Sept. 6, 1958 B of Engring. Sci., Cleve. State U., 1958, BEE, 1958; MS in Engring., U. Akron, 1967; EdD, Nova Southeastern U., 1976; postgrad., Western Res. U., 1959-64. Registered profl. engr., Ohio; cert. engring. technologist. From engring. trainee to tng. dir. TOCCO divsn. Ohio Crankshaft Co., Cleve., 1954-64; from instr. elec.-electronic engring. tech. to prof. Cuyahoga C.C., Cleve., 1964-79, chmn. engring. tech., 1977-79; assoc. prof. elec. engring. tech. Purdue U., West Lafayette, Ind., 1979-83, prof., 1983-2000, prof. emeritus, 2000—. Lectr. Cleve. State U., 1963-64; mem. acad. adv. bd. Cleve. Inst. Electronics, 1981—; cons. in field. Author: (with Frank P. Tedeschi) Solid State Electronics, 1976; (with Eugene M. Silgalis) Electric Circuit Analysis, 1980; (with Jerry L. Casebeer) Registers, 1980; (with Kenneth Rosenow) Arithmetic Logic Units, 1980, Timing and Control, 1980, Memory Units, 1980; 6809 Architecture and Operation, 1984, Programming I: Straight Line, 1984; contbr. articles to profl. jours. Bd. dirs. West Blvd. Christian Ch., deaconess, 1974-77, elder, 1977-79; deacon Federated Ch., 1981-84, 86-89, Stephen Leader, 1988—2002; mem. Cancer Support Group; vol. Lafayette Adult Resource Acad., 1992—; vol. ednl. resource, vol. tchr. Sunburst Farm/Rainbow Acres, Ariz., 1988—. Recipient Helen B. Schleman Gold Medallion award Purdue U., 1991, The Greater Lafayette Cmty. Survivorship award, 1994, Outstanding Alumni award U. Akron Coll. Engring., 1994, Disting. Alumni award, Cleve. State U., 2002; Margaret R. Taber Microcomputer Lab. named in her honor Purdue U., 1991; NSF grant, 1970-73, 78; Rainbow Acres Computer Lab named The Marge Taber Computer Lab., 2002. Fellow Soc. Women Engrs. (counselor Purdue chpt. 1983-94, Disting. Engring. Educator award 1987); mem. IEEE (life sr.), Am. Cancer Soc. (co-chair svc. and rehab com. 1992-94, vol. coord. CanSurmount 1993-98, chair Cmty. Connections, mem. Resource, Info. and Guidance CoreTeam, 1994-98, v.p. Tippecanoe bd. dirs. 1996-98, relay for life hon. chair 1999), Am. Bus. Women's Assn. (ednl. chmn. 1964-66), Am. Soc. Engring. Edn., Am. Tech. Edn. Assn., Tau Beta Pi (hon.), Phi Kappa Phi. Avocations: robotics, computers. Home: 3036 State Rd 26 W West Lafayette IN 47906-4743 Office: Purdue U Elec Engring Tech Dept Knoy Hall Tech West Lafayette IN 47907

TABER, RODMAN EASTMAN, thoracic surgeon; b. Sept. 25, 1919; BA, St. U. Iowa, Iowa City; MD, State U. Iowa, Iowa City. Physician thoracic surgery divsn. Henry Ford Hosp., Detroit; assoc. prof. thoracic surgery divsn. Wayne State U., Detroit; physician thoracic dept. surgery State U. Iowa Coll. Medicine. Contbr. more than 85 articles to med. jours. Mem.: AMA, AOA, ACS, Mich. State Soc. Thoracic Surgeons (pres. 1980—82), Am. Assn. Thoracic Surgeons, Soc. Thoracic Surgeons. Home: 3924 S Cook Valley Dr Grand Rapids MI 49546 Personal E-mail: rtabe@comcast.net.

TABIN, CLIFFORD S., geneticist, educator; PhD in Biol. Scis., MIT, 1984. Postdoctoral fellow, dept. biochemistry Harvard U.; postdoctoral fellow, dept. molecular biology Mass. Gen. Hosp.; with Harvard Med. Sch., Boston, 1989—, prof. dept. genetics. Bd. dir. Am. Napal Med. Found., 2002—; adj. prof. health scis. and tech. MIT; co-dir., grad. program Harvard Med. Sch. Contbr. articles to profl. jours. Mem.: NAS (award in molecular biology 1999). Office: Dept Genetics Harvard Med Sch New Research Bldg 3rd Fl 77 Ave Louis Pasteur Boston MA 02115 Office Phone: 617-432-7618. Office Fax: 617-432-7595. Business E-Mail: tabin@genetics.med.harvard.edu. *

TABIN, JULIUS, lawyer, physicist; b. Chgo., Nov. 8, 1919; s. Sol and Lillian (Klingman) T.; m. Johanna Krout, Sept. 7, 1952; children: Clifford James, Geoffrey Craig. BS, U. Chgo., 1940, PhD in Physics, 1946; LLB, Harvard U., 1949. Bar: Calif., D.C. 1949, Ill. 1950. Jr. physicist metall. lab. U. Chgo., 1943-44; physicist Los Alamos Sci. Lab. (U. Calif.), N.Mex., 1944-45, Argonne Nat. Lab., AEC, Chgo., 1946; staff mem., group supr. Inst. Nuc. Studies, MIT, 1946-49; patent examiner U.S. Patent Office, Washington, 1949-50; assoc. firm Fitch, Even, Tabin & Flannery, Chgo., 1950-52; mem. firm Fitch, Even, Tabin & Flannery, Chgo., 1952—. Lectr. U. Chgo., 1959. Mem. Am., D.C., Calif., Ill., Chgo. bar assns., Sigma Xi. Home: 162 Park Ave Glencoe IL 60022-1352 Office: 120 S La Salle St Chicago IL 60603-3403 Office Phone: 312-577-7000. E-mail: jtabin@fitcheven.com.

TABLER, BRYAN G., lawyer; b. Louisville, Jan. 12, 1943; s. Norman Gardner and Sarah Marie (Grant) T.; m. Susan Y. Beidler, Dec. 28, 1968 (div. June 1987); children: Justin Elizabeth, Gillian Gardner; m. Karen Sue Strome, July 24, 1987. AB, Princeton U., 1969; JD, Yale U., 1972. Bar: Ind. 1972, U.S. Dist. Ct. (so. dist.) Ind. 1972, U.S. Dist. Ct. (no. dist.) Ind. 1976, U.S. Ct. Appeals (7th cir.) 1976, U.S. Supreme Ct. 1976. Assoc. Barnes & Thornburg, Indpls., 1972-79, ptnr., chmn. environ. law dept., 1979-94; v.p., gen. counsel, sec. IPALCO Enterprises, Inc., 1994—; sr. v.p., gen. coun., sec. Indpls. Power & Light Co., 1994—. Mem. exec. com. Environ. Quality Control, Inc., Indpls., 1985-97. Mem. Indpls. Mus. of Art, 1972—; bd. dirs. Indpls. Symphony Orch., 1995—. 1st lt. U.S. Army, 1964-68, Vietnam. Mem. ABA, Ind. Bar Assn., Bar Assn. of the 7th Cir., Indpls. Bar Assn. Avocation: golf. Home: 137 Willowgate Dr Indianapolis IN 46260-1471 Office: Indpls Power & Light Co One Monument PO Box 1595 Indianapolis IN 46206-1595

TABLER, NORMAN GARDNER, JR., lawyer; b. Louisville, Oct. 15, 1944; s. Norman Gardner and Marie (Grant) T.; m. Dawn Carla Martin, May 6, 1989; 1 child, Rachel Ann Tabler. BA, Princeton U., 1966; MA, Yale U., 1968; JD, Columbia U., 1971. Bar: Ind. 1971, U.S. Dist. Ct. (so. dist.) Ind. 1971. Assoc. Baker & Daniels, Indpls., 1971-77, ptnr., 1978-96; sr. v.p. corp. affairs, gen. counsel, chief compliance officer, sec. Clarian

Health Ptnrs., Inc., Indpls., 1996—. Adj. prof. Ind. U. Law Sch., Indpls., 1984-88; mem. adv. com. Ctr. for Law and Health, Ind. U., Indpls., 1987-91; mem. antitrust task force Ind. Dept. Health, 1993-94; lectr. Ind. U. Law Sch., 1992-96; chmn. bd. dirs. CH Assurance Ltd., 2002-, Clarian Health Risk Retention Group, Inc., 2004—, Emergency Medicine Group, Inc., 2004—. Bd. dirs. Ind. Repertory Theatre, Inc., Indpls., 1984-97, 2005-06, Indpls. Art Ctr., 1988-93, 2006—, chmn., 1989-92; bd. dirs. Indpls. 500 Festival, 1992-98, Brickyard 400 Festival, 1993-98, Found. of Indy Festivals, 1995-98, Indy Festivals, 1995-98; bd. dirs. Indpls. Pub. Broadcasting, 1992—, chmn., 1997-2001, 05-; mem. Ind. Sec. of State's Com. on Revision of Ind. Nonprofit Corp. Act, 1989-92, Ind. Ednl. Fin. Authority, 1989-93; mem. Ind. Recreational Devel. Commn., 1993—, vice chmn., 2002—; mem. Medicaid Task Force Ind. Commn. Health Policy, 1990-92, Ind. Commn. on CLE, 1999-2005; mem. nat. bd. lay reps. PBS, 1997-2003. Mem. ABA (health care com. sect. antitrust law, health law sect.), Ind. Bar Assn. (health law sect.), Indpls. Bar Assn. (health law sect.), Am. Health Lawyers Assn. (com. on antitrust, com. on fraud and abuse, self-referrals and false claims, in-house counsel com. and tchg. hosps., acad. med. ctrs. com.), Ind. Health and Hosp. Assn. (com. on hosp. governance 1999—), Ind. U. Parents Assn., Ind. U. Parents Ann. Fund (nat. chmn. 1995-98), U.S., Squash Racquets Assn., Princeton Alumni Assn. Ind. (pres. 1988-97), Indpls. Athletic Club (bd. dirs. 1994-2000), Skyline Club (bd. govs. 1992—), Princeton Club N.Y., Lawyers Club (Indpls., pres. 2007—), Highland Golf & Country Club (Indpls.), Carmel Racquet Club (Ind.). Methodist. Avocations: reading biographies, squash, kayaking. Office: General Counsel & Sr VP Legal Dept Clarian Health Ptnrs Inc PO Box 1367 Indianapolis IN 46206-1367

TABOR, CURTIS HAROLD, JR., retired librarian, minister; b. Atlanta, July 3, 1936; s. Curtis Harold and Gerturde Olive (Casey) Tabor; m. Dorothy May Corbin, June 30, 1957 (dec. June 1996); m. Paulene C Pennington, July 12, 1997; children: Timothy M, John M. AA, Fla. Coll., Temple Ter., 1957; BA, Harding Coll., Ark., 1960; MA, Butler U., Indpls., 1969; MDiv, Bapt. Missionary Assn. Theol. Sem., Jacksonville, Tex., 1974; MLS, Tex. Woman's U., Denton, Tex., 1977. Min. Ch. of Christ, Bowling Green, Ky., 1960-61, Hamilton, Ont., Canada, 1961-64, Indpls., 1964-67, Nacogdoches, Tex., 1967-75, Dallas, 1976-77, Columbus, Miss., 1977-79, Tampa, Fla., 1993-97, Maryville, Tenn., 1997—; reference libr. Blount County Pub. Libr., 1998—2006; ret., 2006. Tchr. Great Lakes Christian Coll., Beamville, Ont, Canada, 1961—64; Bible chair dir Stephen F Austin State U., Nacogdoches, Tex., 1967—75; participant archeological excavations, Tell Gezer, Israel, 1969, Tell Lachish, Israel, 80; profl. libr. sci. Fla. Coll., Temple Terrace, 1979—85, libr. dir., 1985—97; prin., owner Tabor Properties, Inc., 2005. Author (with others): (book) Resurrection, 1973, Biblical Authority, 1974, The Lord of Glory, 1980, Making A Difference: Florida College, the First Fifty Years, 1996. Cub master Boy Scouts Am, Nacogdoches, 1970—75; pres Nacogdoches Baseball Asn, 1974—75; vol driving instr 55 Alive AARP, 1998—2001. Recipient Scouters Key, Cub Scouts Ams, 1975. Mem.: SAR, Tampa Bay Libr. Consortium (treas 1986—89), Beta Phi Mu, Eta Beta Rho. Republican. Mem. Ch. Of Christ. Avocations: amateur radio (KC4XS), locksmithing. Home: 1906 Raulston View Dr Maryville TN 37803-2868 Personal E-mail: haltabor@yahoo.com.

TABOR, EDWARD, medical researcher; BA, Harvard U., Cambridge, Mass., 1969; MD, Columbia U., NYC, 1973. Intern and resident Columbia-Presbyn. Med. Ctr., NYC, 1973-75; rsch. investigator Bur. Biologics, Bethesda, Md., 1975-83; dir. divsn. anti-infective drug products FDA, Rockville, Md., 1983-88; assoc. dir. for biol. carcinogenesis Nat. Cancer Inst./NIH, Bethesda, 1988-95; dir. divsn. transfusion transmitted diseases FDA, Bethesda and Rockville, Md., 1995-99; assoc. dir. med. affairs Office Blood Rsch. and Rev., FDA, Rockville, 1999—2005; exec. dir. Regulatory Consulting, Quintiles, Inc., Rockville, 2005—06; head regulatory affairs Americas L'Quintiles, Inc., Rockville, 2006—. Author: Infectious Complications of Blood Transfusion, 1982; editor: Viruses and Liver Cancer, 2002, Emerging Viruses in Human Populations, 2007,(with others) Etiology, Pathology, and Treatment of Hepatocellular Carcinoma in North America, 1991, Hepatitis C Virus and its Involvement in the Development of Hepatocellular Carcinoma, 1995, Liver Cancer, 1997; contbr. more than 300 articles to profl. jours. Capt. USPHS, 1975-05. Achievements include formulation of US regulatory policy on antibiotics, anti-viral drugs, and blood transfusion safety, research in hepatitis viruses, hepatocellular carcinoma. Office: Quintiles Inc 1801 Rockville Pike Ste 300 Rockville MD 20852 Business E-Mail: edward.tabor@quintiles.com.

TABUENCA-CORDOBA, MARIA-SOCORRO, education educator, researcher; b. El Paso, Tex., Dec. 9, 1955; d. Manuel Tabuenca-Gutierrez and Socorro Cordoba De Tabuenca. BA, U Tex., El Paso, 1976; MA, U. Tex., El Paso, 1979; PhD, SUNY, Stony Brook, 1997. Instr. El Paso CC, 1992—98; lectr. U. Tex., El Paso, 1993—, tchr. asst., 1996—98; regional dir. El Colegio de la Frontera Norte, Ciudad Juarez, Chihuahua, Mexico, 1995—99, dean NW region, 1999—2007. Vis. prof. N.Mex. State U., Las Cruces, 1998, U. Tex., El Paso, 2007—. Regional dir. Hunger Project Mex., Ciudad Juarez, 1984—85; adv. bd. Techo Comunitario Found., Ciudad Juarez, 1993—2006; mem. Immigration Mus., U. Tex., El Paso, 2002—04; bd. advisors folklife festival Rio Bravo/Rio Grande exhibit Smithsonian Instn., Washington/Ciudad Juarez, 1999—2003; student rep. Turner Fellows, SUNY, Stony Brook, 1990—92. Recipient Pres. Selection Com. for Nat. Poetry award, Instituto Sonorense De Cultura, 1995; W.B Turner fellow, Suny, Stony Brook, 1990—94, Transl. Of Chicana Authors grantee, Fideicomiso Para La Cultura Mexico-estados Unidos, 1996—97, Nat. Rsch. scholar, Consejo Nacional De Ciencia Y Tecnologia, 1998—, Cooperation US/Spain Latinos in Spain fellow, Instituto De Cooperacion Iberoamericana, Paso Del Norte Region Bldg. Project grantee, William and Flora Hewlett, 2001—03, Student Mobility Project grantee, Secretaria De Educacion Publica, 2004—. Mem.: MLA (assoc.), Latin Am. Studies Assn. (assoc.), Raza Assn. (assoc.). Roman Catholic. Achievements include research in methodology for study of borders' literatures between the US and Mexico. Avocations: reading, swimming, walking, travel, movies. Office: El Colegio de la Frontera Norte Ave Insurgentes # 3708 Chihuahua Ciudad Juarez Mexico Home Phone: 915-566-1866; Office Phone: 915-747-5462. Business E-Mail: tabuenca@colef.mx.

TACAL, JOSE VEGA, JR., retired public health official, veterinarian; b. Ilocos Sur, Philippines, Sept. 5, 1933; arrived in US, 1969; s. Jose Sr. and Cristina (Vega) T.; m. Lilia Caccam, 1959; children: Joyce, Jasmin, Jose III. DVM, U. Philippines, Quezon City, 1956; diploma, U. Toronto, 1964. Diplomate Am. Coll. Vet. Preventive Medicine; lic. vet., Calif. Provincial veterinarian Philippine Bur. Animal Industry, Manila, 1956-57; instr. vet. medicine U. Philippines, Quezon City, 1957-64, asst. prof., chmn. dept. vet. microbiology, pathology and pub. health, 1965-69; pub. health veterinarian San Bernardino (Calif.) County Dept. Pub. Health, 1970-83, sr. pub. health veterinarian, program mgr., sect. chief, 1984-2000. Zoonotic diseases lectr. Calif. State U., San Bernardino, 1984; lectr. U. Calif. Ext., Riverside, 1985; vis. prof. vet. pub. health U. Philippines at Los Banos, Laguna, 1988; participant 1st Internat. Conf. on Emerging Zoonoses, Jerusalem, 1996; presenter 4th Internat. Symposium on Ectoparasites of Pets, U. Calif., Riverside, 1997; presenter 8th Ann. Rabies in the Ams. Conf., Kingston, Ont., Can., 1997; rabies and ferret adv. group Calif. Dept. Health Svcs., 1998; presenter 48th Western Poultry Disease Conf., Vancouver, B.C., Can., 1999, 10th Rabies in Ams. Meeting, San Diego, 1999. Columnist LA Free Press, 1991, Pilipinas Times, 1993, Mabuhay Times, 1994-95; panelist Filipino-Ams. TV series The Many Faces of San Bernardino, California; contbr. more than 50 articles to profl. jours. Pres. Filipino Assn. of San Bernardino County, Highland, Calif., 1979; charter mem. Greater Inland Empire Filipino Assn., Highland, 1986—; del. First Filipino Media Conf. N.Am., LA, 1993; active San Bernardino County Africanized Honey Bee Task Force, 1993-2000, City of Highland Historic and Cultural Preservation Bd., 2007; v.p. Friends of the Highland Libr., 2006. Named Vol. of Yr., Friends of Highland Libr., 2007; recipient Donald T. Fraser Meml. medal, U. Toronto, 1964, cert. of merit, Philippine Vet. Med. Assn., 1965, cert. of appreciation, Calif. State Bd. Examiners in Vet. Medicine, 1979, 1984, cert. of recognition, Congressman George E. Brown Jr., 42d Congl. Dist. Calif., 1994, Assemblyman Joe Baca, 62d Assembly Dist., Calif. State Legis., 1994, Vet. Medicine/Journalism award, Greater Inland Empire Filipino Assn., 1999, cert. appreciation, San Bernardino County Libr., Highland Br., 2005—06; Colombo Plan Study fellow, Can./Philippine Govts., 1963—64, hon. fellow, Philippine Coll. Vet. Pub. Health, 2002. Mem.: ACLU, AVMA, AAAS, Highland Area Hist. Soc., Calif. Rare Fruit Growers (Inland Empire chpt.), Soc. for Advancement of Rsch., Western Poultry Disease Conf., Am. Vet. Med. History Soc., U. Philippines Alumni Assn. (life), Phi Sigma, Phi Kappa Phi. Office: PO Box 1023 Highland CA 92346-1023

TACCONE, JORMA, writer, director; b. Berkeley, Calif., Mar. 19, 1977; s. Tony. Grad., U. Calif. LA. Co-founder, mem. The Lonely Island, NYC, 2001—. Writer MTV Movie Awards, 2004, 2005, G-Phoria, 2004, Saturday Night Live, 2005—; actor(appearances): Saturday Night Live, 2005—06; guest appearances (TV Specials) 40 Most Awesomely Bad Dirrty Songs...Ever, 2004. Recipient WIRED Rave Award - TV, 2006. Office: United Talent Agency Inc 9560 Wilshire Blvd Ste 500 Beverly Hills CA 90212 Office Phone: 310-273-6700. Office Fax: 310-247-1111.

TACHA, ATHENA, sculptor, artist, educator; b. Larissa, Greece, Apr. 23, 1936; arrived in U.S., 1963; MA, Nat. Acad. Fine Arts, Athens, Greece, 1959; MA in Art History, Oberlin Coll., 1961; PhD, U. Paris, 1963. Curator modern art Allen Art Mus., Oberlin, Ohio, 1963-73; prof. art Oberlin Coll., 1973-2000; adj. prof. art U. Md., College Park, 1999—. One-woman shows include Zabriskie Gallery, NY, 1979, 81, Max Hutchinson Gallery, NY, 1984, High Mus. Art, Atlanta, 1989, Cleve. Ctr. Contemporary Art, 1989, Franklin Furnace, NY, 1994, Found. for Hellenic Culture, NY, 2001, Marsha Mateyka Gallery, Washington, 2004, Am. Univ. Mus., Washington, 2006, Kouros Gallery, NYC, 2007, others; prin. pub. commns. include sculptures at Am. Airlines Ctr., Dallas., City of Phila., Dept. Environ. Protection, Trenton, NJ, Case-Western Res. U., Cleve., Low Water Dam Riverfront Pk., Tulsa, Dept. of Transp., Hartford, Conn., Metrorail, Miami, Fla., Ecology Dept. U. Minn., St. Paul, Strathmore Music Ctr., Bethesda, Md., Metro Morgan Sta., Washington, Light Rail Sta., Newark, NY, Light Rail Stas., Newark; collections include Hirshhorn Mus., Washington, Albright-Knox Art Gallery, Buffalo, Mus. Fine Arts, Houston, Nat. Coll. Fine Arts, Washington, Cleve. Mus. Art, Munson-Williams-Proctor Inst., Uttica, Nelson-Atkins Mus. Art, Kansas City, Allen Art Mus., Oberlin, Speed Art Mus., Louisville; author: (as A. T. Spear) Rodin Sculpture in the Cleveland Museum of Art, 1967, Brancusi's Birds, 1969; contbr. articles to profl. jours.; subject of book Cosmic Rhythms: Athena Tacha's Public Sculpture (E. McClelland), 1998, Dancing in the Landscape: The Sculpture of Athena Tacha, 2000. Recipient 1st prize May Show, Cleve. Mus. Art, 1968, 71, 79; NEA grantee, 1975; Bogliasco Found./Liguria Study Ctr. fellow, 2003, Bellagio Study Ctr. fellow, 2007. Home: 3721 Huntington St NW Washington DC 20015-1817 E-mail: atacha@umd.edu.

TACHA, DEANELL REECE, federal judge; b. Goodland, Kans., Jan. 26, 1946; m. John Allen Tacha; children: John Reece, David Andrew, Sarah Nell, Leah Beth. BA, U. Kans., 1968; JD, U. Mich., 1971. Spl. asst. to US Sec. of Labor, Washington, 1971—72; assoc. Hogan & Hartson, Washington, 1973, Thomas J. Pitner, Concordia, Kans., 1973—74; dir. Douglas County Legal Aid Clinic, Lawrence, Kans., 1974—77; assoc. prof. law U. Kans., Lawrence, 1974—77, prof., 1977—85, assoc. dean, 1977—79 assoc. vice chancellor, 1979—81, vice chancellor, 1981—85; judge US Ct. Appeals (10th cir.), Denver, 1985—2001, chief judge, 2001—; mem. US Sentencing Commn., 1994—98; nat. pres. Am. Inns. of Ct., 2004—. Office: US Ct Appeals 643 Massachusetts St Ste 301 Lawrence KS 66044 *

TACHNA, RUTH C., retired lawyer; b. NYC; d. Max and Rose (Rosenblatt) T.; m. Paul Bauman (dec.); children: Leslie Levy, Lionel Bauman. BA, Cornell U., 1935; LLB cum laude, Bklyn. Law Sch., 1937. Bar: N.Y. 1938, Calif. 1978, U.S. Dist. Ct. (so. dist.) N.Y. 1966, U.S. Ct. Appeals (2d cir.) 1966, U.S. Supreme Ct. 1956. Founding atty. Legal Aid, Westchester, N.Y., 1960-64; sr. ptnr., of counsel Tachna & Krassner, White Plains, NY, 1964—2001; ret. Prof. law Northrop U. Sch. Law, L.A., 1977-85; speechwriter for many office holders including Franklin D. Roosevelt. Group mng. editor Matthew Bender, N.Y.C., 1968-77; editor law rev. Bklyn. Law Sch. Staff atty., founder Legal Aid for Srs., Santa Monica, Calif., 1980-83. Mem. Calif. Bar Assn., L.A. County Bar Assn. Home: 5400 Eagles Point Cir Apt 106 Sarasota FL 34231-9154

TACHNER, LEONARD, lawyer; b. Bklyn., Jan. 18, 1944; BEE, CCNY, 1965; MSEE, Calif. State U., Long Beach, 1969; JD, Western State U., Fullerton, Calif., 1973. Bar: Calif. 1973, US Patent Office 1972. Supr. electronic counter measures sect. Ford Aerospace Corp., Newport Beach, Calif., 1969—73; patent atty. Reed C. Lawlor, LA, 1973—76, Rockwell Internat. Corp., Anaheim, Calif., 1976—78; ptnr. Fischer, Tachner & Strauss, Newport Beach, 1978—84; pvt. practice Irvine, Calif., 1984—. Instr. intellectual property Calif. State U., Long Beach, 1979—82; com. maintenance profl. competence Calif. State Bar, 1978—81. Mem. editl. bd. Western State U. Law Rev., 1972—73, columnist Interface Age mag., 1979—82, Bus.-to-Bus. mag., 1983—85. Mem.: Orange County Patent Law Assn., Calif. Bar Assn., Greater Irvine Indsl. League, Phi Kappa Phi. Office: 17961 Sky Park Cir Ste 38-E Irvine CA 92614 Home Phone: 949-786-7767; Office Phone: 949-752-8525. Personal E-mail: ltachner@aol.com.

TACK, THERESA ROSE, women's health nurse; b. Lunenburg, Vt., Nov. 10, 1940; d. Gustave L. and Blanche Rose Fournier; m. Dennis M. Tack, Sept. 2, 1961; children: Lynelle Scullard, Karyn Terry, LeAnn Gomez. Diploma, Cen. Maine Gen. Hosp., 1961. Cert. ACLS, neonatal resuscitation Am. Heart Assn. Staff nurse neurosurgery unit Hillcrest Med. Ctr., Tulsa, 1961-62; staff nurse cardiovascular unit Meth. Hosp., Houston, 1962-65; staff nurse St. John's Hosp., Red Wing, Minn., 1979-85, Wasatch County Hosp., Heber City, Utah, 1985-97. Columnist, Nurses Notes in Wasatch Wave, Heber City, Utah, 1990-97.

TACKER, WILLIS ARNOLD, JR., medical educator, researcher; b. Tyler, Tex., May 24, 1942; s. Willis Arnold and Willie Mae (Massey) T.; m. Martha J. McClelland, Mar. 18, 1967; children: Sarah Mae, Betsy Jane, Katherine Ann. BS, Baylor U., 1964, MD, PhD, 1970. Lic. physician, Ind., Alaska, Tex. Intern Mayo Grad. Sch. Medicine Mayo Clinic, Rochester, Minn., 1970-71; pvt. practice Prudhoe Bay, Alaska, 1971; instr. dept. physiology Baylor Coll. Medicine, Houston, 1971-73, asst. prof. dept. physiology, 1973-74; clin. prof. family medicine Ind. U. Sch. Medicine, West Lafayette, Ind., 1981—; vis. asst. prof. Biomed. Engring. Ctr., Purdue U., West Lafayette, 1974-76, assoc. prof. Sch. Vet. Medicine, 1976-79; assoc. dir. William A. Hillenbrand Biomed. Engring. Ctr., Purdue U., West Lafayette, 1980-93, prof. Sch. Vet. Medicine, 1979—, acting dir., 1991-93; exec. dir. Hillenbrand Biomed. Engring. Ctr., 1993-95. Vis. rsch. fellow Sch. Aerospace Medicine, Brooks AFB, San Antonio, 1982; with Corp. Sci. and Tech., State of Ind., 1985-88; presenter, cons. in field. Author: Some Advice on Getting Grants, 1991; co-author: Electrical Defibrillation, 1980; author: (with others) Handbook of Engineering and Medicine and Biology, 1980, Implantable Sensors for Closed-Loop Prosthetic Systems, 1985, Encyclopedia of Medical Devices and Instrumentation, 1988, (with others) Defibrillation of the Heart, 1994; contbr. numerous articles to profl. jours. Chmn. bd. dirs. Assn. Advancemnt Med. Instrumentation Found., Arlington, Va., 1987-95. Mem. Am. Heart Assn. (bd. dirs. Ind. affiliate 1975-81, med. edn. com. 1975-81, pub. health edn. com. 1975-81, chmn. ad hoc com. CPR tng. for physicians 1976-77, rsch. review com. 1988-90), Am. Physiol. Soc., Ind. State Med. Assn., Tippecanoe County Med. Soc., Assn. Advancement Med. Instrumentation (chmn. various coms., bd. dirs. 1981-84, pres. 1985-86), Am. Men and Women Sci., Alpha Epsilon Delta, Beta Beta Beta, Soc. Sigma Xi. Achievements include research in biomedical engineering, cardiovascular physiology, medical education, emergency cardiovascular care, motor evoked potentials, skeletal muscle ventricle; patents for an apparatus and method for measurement and control of blood pressure, electrode system and method for implantable defibrillators, pressure mapping system with capacitive measuring pad. Office: Purdue U Basic Med Scis 625 Harrison St West Lafayette IN 47907-2006 E-mail: tacker@vet.purdue.edu.

TACKETT, STEPHEN DOUGLAS, retired education services specialist; b. Waverly, Ohio, Apr. 27, 1939; s. James Elbert and Zelma Iola (Manahan) T.; m. Magdalena Schneider, Jan. 4, 1958; children: Doris, Janice, Jerry, Suzanne. AA, El Paso C.C., 1974; BS, SUNY, Albany, 1976; MA, Ball State U., 1979. Nat. cert. counselor; lic. profl. clin. counselor. Enlisted US Army, 1955, advanced through grades to Command Sgt. Maj., 1973, ret., 1982; instr. Mt. Wachusett CC, Gardner, Mass., 1979-81; asst. dir. Evaluation US Army Sgts. Maj. Acad., Ft. Bliss, Tex., 1981-82; dir. substance abuse treatment Sun Valley Hosp., El Paso, Tex., 1982-84; from guidance counselor to ednl. svcs. officer US Army, Germany, 1984-86, 88-90; edn. advisor US Army Sgts. Maj. Acad., Fort Bliss, 1990-92; edn. svcs. specialist Mil. Entrance Processing Sta., El Paso, 1992—2002; ret., 2002. Mem. adv. bd. for Counselor Edn. U. Tex., El Paso, 1983. Cubmaster Boy Scouts Am., Ft. Leonard Wood, Mo., 1970-71, com. mem., Frankfurt, Germany, 1972-73, asst. scoutmaster, Kaiserslautern, Germany, 1976-79. Mem. ACA, Assn. for Career and Tech. Edn., Nat. Assn. Secondary Sch. Prins., Tex. Assn. Secondary Sch. Prins., Tex. Counseling Assn.

TACKETT, VITI LEE, writer; d. Clarence James and America Jane (Mason) Hunt; m. Floyd Vernon Tackett, July 2, 1953; children: Floyd Randall, Terry Lynn, Lucinda Gail Tackett/Hines. Diploma, Inst. Children's Lit., West Redding, Conn. Author: (novel series) Roseanna, Belle's Restless Heart, Beyond the Tempest, Rainbow's End, Girl on the Run, Two Roads, Summer's Dream, Betrayal; contbr. poems to anthology. Home Phone: 870-572-7587; Office Phone: 870-572-7587. Personal E-mail: goviti@hotmail.com. E-mail: vititackett6@yahoo.com.

TACOPINA, JOSEPH, lawyer; b. Bklyn., Apr. 14, 1966; s. Cosmo Michael and Josephine (Oliva) T.; m. Patricia Ann MacDonald, Dec. 29, 1991; children: Morgan Elizabeth, Christopher Joseph. BA, BS, Skidmore Coll., 1988; JD, U. Bridgeport, 1991. Bar: NY 1992, US Dist. Ct. (so. and ea. dists.) NY 1994. Assoc. Law Office of Bruce Cutler, NYC, 1980-92; asst. dist. atty. Kings County Dist. Atty.'s Office, Bklyn., 1992-95; ptnr. Altchiler & Tacopina, NYC, 1995-97; founder Law Offices of Joseph Tacopina, P.C., NYC, 1994—. TV commentator Fox News, NYC, 1996—, Court TV, NYC, 1995—, also MSNBC, CNBC. Mem. Fed. Bar Coun., NY Counsel Def. Lawyers, NY State Assn. Criminal Def. Lawyers, (dir., chair legis. com. 1995—), Nat. Assn. Criminal Def. Lawyers (coord. legis. com. 1995—). Office: Law Offices of Joseph Tacopina PC 275 Madison Ave 35th Fl New York NY 10016 E-mail: jtacopina@tacopinalaw.com. *

TADDEI, LOIS ANNETTE MAGOWAN, artist, interior designer; b. Phila., Sept. 17, 1935; d. Frank Rue Magowan and Grace Gloria (Valentino) Weinstein; m. Robert Matthew Taddei, May 21, 1960; 1 child, Robyn Grace. Degree, Pierce Coll. Represented by Phila. Mus. of Art. Watercolor botanicals shown at Phila. Mus. Art; one-woman shows include Pa. Hort. Soc., Phila, La Grande Gallery, Moorestown, N.J., Camden County Libr.; group shows include Art at Armory, Phila, Great Galleries, New Hope, Pa., Hardcastle Gallery, Wilmington, Del., Hockessin, Del., Gallery I, Chadds Ford, Pa., Rhoads Gallery, Gwynedd Valley, Pa., Festival Arts, Cape May, N.J., Ocean City (N.J.) Arts Festival; designer Vassar Designers Showcase House, 1991-92, Haddonfield Design Showcase House, 1992, Barry Decorators Haddonfield & Cherry Hill, Interiors by Marilouise, West Chester, Pa., Rocco Marianni & Assoc. Interior Design, Haddonfield. Mem. Graphic Artist Guild, United Visual Artists, Burlington Country Art Guild. Avocations: gardening, needlepoint, ballet, museums.

TADEPALLI, SRIKANTH, mechanical engineer, researcher; s. Sitharamanjaneya Sastry and Syamala Tadepalli. BME, Jawaharlal Nehru Technol. U., Hyderabad, India, 2001; MSE in Mfg. Sys. Engring., U. Tex., Austin, 2003, postgrad. in Mech. Engring., 2004—. In-plant trainee Indian Space Rsch. Orgn., Bangalore, 2000; project trainee Def. R&D Orgn., Hyderabad, 2001; tchg. asst. U. Tex., Austin, 2002—03, 2006—07, grad. rsch. asst., 2003—06; use condition devel. intern Intel Corp., Chandler, Ariz., 2005. Recipient Excellence in Tchg. Fellowship award, H. Grady Rylander Longhorn Mech. Engring. Club, 2003; grantee NSF, 2003—06. Mem.: ASME (assoc.), Soc. Mfg. Engrs. (assoc.). Hindu. Achievements include development of mathematical basis and the foundation principles for the systematic evolution of an innovative similitude method in empirical domain; research in enhancement of the novel similarity process through the use of numerical procedures by incorporating the non-linearities of a mechanical system and the associated response parameters; designing, developing and prototyping an assistive bowling device using mechanical design methodology tools. Avocations: reading, puzzles, chess. Business E-Mail: tsrikanth@mail.utexas.edu.

TADESSE, MESFIN, botanist, consultant, biology professor, researcher; s. Tadesse Woldemeskel and Askale Ayetaged; m. Hirut Girma, Oct. 18, 1986; children: Sofonias Mesfin, Brook Mesfin. BSc, Haile Selassie 1st U., Addis Ababa, 1973; MSc, U. Minn., Mpls., 1976; PhD, Uppsala U., Sweden, 1984. Grad. asst. Haile Sellasie 1st U., Addis Ababa, 1973—74; asst. lectr. Addis Ababa U., 1976—77, dir., nat. herbarium, 1976—92, lectr., 1977—80, asst. prof., 1984—89, assoc. prof., 1989—93; adj. prof. Columbus State CC, 2001—; vis. prof., lectr. Ohio State U., Columbus, 1993—2002, curator vascular plants, 2003—. Cons. Ethiopian Toursim Orgn., Addis Ababa, 1989—92; external examiner botany Moi U., Eldoret, Kenya, 1990—92; external examiner in botany Dar-Es-Saalam U., Tanzania, 1991. Author: (booklet) Some Endemic Plants of Ethiopia, 1991, (book) Asteraceae of Ethiopia, 2004; contbr. articles to profl. jours. Chmn. Ethiopian Cmty. Orgn., Inc., Columbus, 2003—06. Recipient Leadership award, Ethiopian Cmty. Orgn., Inc., 2006; grantee, SAREC, Sweden, 1981—92, Young Scientist Rsch. award, UNESCO, 1989, Ministry Coffee & Tea Devel., Ethiopia, 1990; scholar, USAID, 1974—76. Mem.: Assn. pour l'etude de la Flore Taxonomique d'Afrique Tropicaux (assoc.). Achievements include research in scientific names of plants. Avocations: reading, writing, exercise. Office: Ohio State Univ 1315 Kinnear Rd Columbus OH 43212 Home Phone: 614-436-9542; Office Phone: 614-292-3296.

TADESSE, TSEGAYE, climatologist, researcher; arrived in US, 1998; s. Tadesse Yifru and Tenagnework Merine; m. Betleham B Konjit, Dec. 19, 1998; children: Betselot (King) Tsegaye, Bemnet (Kate) Tsegaye. BSc in Physics, Addis Ababa U., Ethiopia, 1982; MSc, Internat. Space U., France, 1998; PhD, U. Nebraska-Lincoln, 2002—02. Meteorologist, team leader meteorol. comm. Nat. Meteorol. Svcs. Agy. Ethiopia, Addis Ababa, Ethiopia, 1984—97; rsch. assoc. Nat. Drought Mitigation Ctr., Lincoln, Nebr., 1998—; climatologist, asst. geoscientist, mem. faculty U. Nebr., Lincoln, 2006—. Contbr. articles to profl.jours. V.p. Ethiopian Cmty. in Lincoln (Nebr.) Area, 2001—04. Mem.: Nat. Geog. Soc., Am. Meteorol. Soc. Achievements include research in modern drought monitoring tools.

Home: 2201 Gunnison Dr Lincoln NE 68521 Office: National Drought Mitigation Center University of Nebraska Lincoln NE 68503 Home Phone: 402-435-8724; Office Phone: 402-472-3383. Personal E-mail: ttadesse2@unl.edu.

TADROS, FAWZI M., educator; b. Mar. 12, 1934; came to U.S. 1967; BA in Library & Info. Scis., Cairo U., 1960; MA, U. Utah, 1972, Ind. U., 1973; MLS, U. Mich., Ann Arbor, 1974; PhD in Library & Info. Scis., Cairo U., 1979. Expert in libr. sci. Inspector Egyptian Nat. Libr., 1960-67; mem. faculty U. Utah, 1967-69, Ind. U., 1969-76; Arab area specialist Library of Congress, 1976—; mem., expert libr. sci. UNESCO, 1981-83. Cons. U. Libr. Saudi Arabia, Oman, Qatar, Bahrain, Kuwait, United Arab Emirates, Alexandria Libr. Com.; cons. for edn. and info. scis. UNESCO; vis. prof. Cairo U., U. Qatar, U. Bahrain, U. Oman; supr. World Global Gate Way between Libr. of Congress and Nat. Libr. Egyp; acting field dir. Cairo office Libr. of Congress. Pub. bibliography on the Holy Koran (among the best 60 Am. pub., 1994), others; contbr. articles to profl. jours. Mem. Congl. Del. State Qatar. Recipient Fulbright Sr. Awd., Univ. Qatar, 1990. Mem. AAUP, Middle East Studies Assn., Middle East Libr. Assn., Fulbright Assn. Achievements include first to exhibit in Qatar on the Holy Koran Manuscripts. Office Phone: 202-707-7311. Business E-Mail: ftad@loc.gov.

TAFLOVE, ALLEN, electrical engineer, educator, researcher, consultant; s. Harry and Leah T.; m. Sylvia Hinda Friedman, Nov. 6, 1977; children: Michael Lee, Nathan Brent. BS with highest distinction, Northwestern U., 1971, MS, 1972, PhD Cabell Fellow, 1975. Assoc. engr. IIT Rsch. Inst., Chgo., 1975-78, rsch. engr., 1978-81, sr. engr., 1981-84; assoc. prof. Northwestern U., Evanston, Ill., 1984-88, prof., 1988—, Charles Deering McCormick prof., 2000—03; master Lindgren/Slivka Residential Coll. Sci. & Engring., 2000—05. Author: Computational Electrodynamics: The Finite-Difference Time-Domain Method, 1995, 3rd edit., 2005; co-author: Computational Electromagnetics: Integral Equation Approach, 1993; editor: Advances in Computational Electrodynamics: The Finite-Difference Time-Domain Method, 1998. Fellow: IEEE. Achievements include pioneer of finite-difference time-domain method in computational electrodynamics. Office: Northwestern U Dept Elec Engring and Computer Sci 2145 Sheridan Rd Evanston IL 60208-0834 Home Phone: 847-674-0597; Office Phone: 847-491-4127. Business E-Mail: taflove@ece.northwestern.edu.

TAFOYA, JOE, school system administrator; BA, MA, San Diego State U.; D, Northern Ariz. U., 1983. Various San Diego City Schools, 1969—90; asst. supt. Santa Ana Unified Sch. Dist., 1990—94, dep. supt. of curriculum, 1994—99; dir. Dept. Def. Edn. Activity, 2000—. Recipient Exceptional Civilian Svc. award, Office of Sec. of Def., 2001, 2003 Presdl. Rank Award, 2004. Office: Dept of Def Edn Activity Webb Bldg 4040 N Fairfax Dr Arlington VA 22203 Office Phone: 703-696-4236. *

TAFT, BOB (ROBERT ALPHONSO TAFT II), former governor; b. Conn., Jan. 8, 1942; great grandson of William Howard Taft, 27th President of US; m. Hope Taft; 1 child, Anna. BA in Govt., Yale U., 1963; MA, Princeton U., 1967; JD, U. Cin., 1976. Budget officer, asst. dir. Ill. Bur. Budget, 1967—73; mem. Ohio Ho. of Reps., Columbus, 1976-80; commr. Hamilton County, Ohio, 1981-90; sec. of state State of Ohio, Columbus, 1991-99, gov., 1999—2007. Vol. Peace Corps., Tanzania, 1963—65. Republican. Protestant.

TAFT, DAVID DAKIN, chemicals executive; b. Cleve., Mar. 27, 1938; s. Kingsley A. and Louise D. T.; m. Sararose Leonard, July 8, 1961; children: Amy Rose, Kingsley Leonard, Elisabeth. AB, Kenyon Coll., 1960; PhD in Chemistry, Mich. State U., 1963. Sr. rsch. chemist Archer-Daniels Midland, 1964-67; mgr. polymer rsch. Ashland Chem., 1967-72; dir. comml. devel. Gen. Mills Chems., 1972-74; v.p., dir. R&D, Henkel Corp., 1973-78, group v.p. consumer and splty. products, 1978-81, exec. v.p. chem. products div., dir., 1981-82; gen. mgr. materials div. Raychem Corp., Menlo Park, Calif., 1983-84; gen. mgr. Telecom group, 1983-86; v.p. Raychem Corp., 1984-93, v.p. manufacuturing, 1986-93; COO Landec Corp., Menlo Park, Calif., 1993—2001, 2005—; pres. Dock Resins Corp., Guadalupe, 2002—05. Author: Fundamentals of Powder Coatings; bd. editors: Rsch. Mgmt. Jour.; patentee in field. Trustee Mpls. Soc. Fine Arts, 1981-83, Kenyon Coll., 1990—2002; vice chmn. Mem. Comml. Devel. Assn., Indsl. Research Inst., Am. Chem. Soc., Kenyon Alumni Assn. (pres. 1978), Circus Club. Republican. Office: Landec Corp 3603 Haven Ave Menlo Park CA 94025-1010 Office Phone: 650-261-3695. E-mail: dtaft@landec.com.

TAFT, SHELDON ASHLEY, retired lawyer; b. Cleve., Mar. 2, 1937; s. Kingsley Arter and Louise Parsons (Dakin) T.; m. Rebecca Sue Rinehart, Dec. 26, 1962; children: Mariner R., Ashley A., Curtis N. BA, Amherst Coll., 1959; LLB, Harvard U., 1962. Bar: Ohio 1962. Assoc. Vorys, Sater, Seymour & Pease, Columbus, Ohio, 1965-69, 71-73; chief legal counsel Pub. Utilities Commn. Ohio, 1969-71; ptnr. Vorys, Sater, Seymour & Pease, Columbus, Ohio, 1974—2001, of counsel, 2002—04, ret., 2005. Ohio bd. advisors Chgo. Title Ins. Co., 1967-98. Rep. candidate for justice Ohio Supreme Ct., 1974; trustee Opera Columbus, 1989—, pres., 1991-93, life trustee, 1995—; trustee Columbus Bach Ensemble 2002—, pres. 2002-06; trustee Chamber Music Columbus, 2006—; councilor New England Hist. and Geneal. Soc., 2005—. 1st lt. USAF, 1963-65. Mem. Ohio State Bar Assn. (pres. pub. utilities com. 1984-87), Columbus Bar Assn., Ohio Camera Collectors Soc. (pres. 1985-87), Rocky Fork Hunt and Country Club, Hillsboro Club, 41 Club, Review Club. Congregationalist. Avocation: camera collecting. E-mail: staft@columbus.rr.com.

TAFT, TIMOTHY NED, orthopedist, surgeon, sports medicine physician; s. Samuel Milton and Helen Taft; m. Judith Ann Huffman, Sept. 13, 1971; children: Todd Daniel, Rebecca Lynn Fecher. AB, Princeton U., NJ, 1964; MD, U. Mo., Columbia, Mo., 1969. Diplomate Am. Bd. Orthopaedic Surgery, 1978, lic. physician N.C., 1978. Intern, resident in orthopedics U. N.C., NC, 1969—74, prof., 1974—, dir. sports medicine, 1991—2006. Mem. Red Cross, Chapel Hill, NC, 1999—2006. Mem.: Red Cross, Spl. Olympics N.C. Office: University of North Carolina 3154 Bioinformatics CB 7055 Chapel Hill NC 27599 Office Phone: 919-966-3340. Office Fax: 919-966-6730; Home Fax: 919-966-6730. Business E-Mail: ttaft@med.unc.edu.

TAFT, WILLIAM HOWARD, IV, lawyer; b. Washington, Sept. 13, 1945; s. William Howard and Barbara Hoult (Bradfield) T.; m. Julia Vadala, May 4, 1974; Maria Consetta, William Howard V, Julia Harris. BA, Yale U., 1966; JD, Harvard U., 1969. Bar: D.C. 1969. Assoc. Winthrop, Stimson, Putnam & Roberts, NYC, 1969-70; atty.-advisor to chmn. FTC, Washington, 1970; prin. asst. to dep. dir. Office Mgmt. & Budget, Exec. Office of the Pres., Washington, 1970-72, exec. asst. to dir., 1972-73; exec. asst. to sec. US Dept. Health Edn. & Welfare, Washington, 1973-76, gen. counsel, 1976-77; ptnr. Leva, Hawes, Symington, Martin & Oppenheimer, Washington, 1977-81; gen. counsel US Dept. Def., Washington, 1981-84, dep. sec., 1984—89, acting sec., 1989; perm. rep. U.S. Mission to NATO, Brussels, 1989—92; legal adviser U.S. Dept. State, Washington, 2001—05; ptnr. Fried Frank Harris Shriver & Jacobson LLP, Washington, 1992—2001; of counsel Fried Frank Harris Shriver & Jacobson, 2005—; Warren Christopher prof. practice of internat. law and diplomacy Stanford Law Sch., 2007—. Recipient Disting. Service award HEW, 1975 Mem. D.C. Bar Assn., Lit. Soc. (Washington) Clubs: Cosmos (Washington), Leo (Washington). Republican. Office: Fried Frank Harris Shriver & Jacobson LLP 1001 Pennsylvania Ave NW Washington DC 20004 Office Phone: 202-639-7164. Business E-Mail: taftwi@ffhsj.com.

TAGATZ, GEORGE ELMO, retired obstetrician, gynecologist, educator; b. Milw., Sept. 21, 1935; s. George Herman and Beth Elinore (Blain) T.; m. Susan Trunnell, Oct. 28, 1967; children: Jennifer Lynn, Kirsten Susan, Kathryn Elizabeth. AB, Oberlin Coll., 1957; MD, U. Chgo., 1961. Diplomate Am. Bd. Obstetricians and Gynecologists, Am. Bd. Reproductive Endocrinology (examiner, bd. reproductive endocrinology 1976-79). Rotating intern Univ. Hosps. of Cleve., 1961-62, resident in internal medicine, 1962-63; resident in ob-gyn U. Iowa, 1965-68; sr. research fellow in endocrinology U. Wash. dept. obstetrics and gynecology, 1968-70; from asst. prof. ob-gyn to prof. emeritus Med. Sch. U. Minn., 1970—2000, prof. emeritus Med. Sch., 2000—. Fertility and maternal health adv. com. FDA, USPHS, HHS, 1982-86; cons. in field. Ad hoc editor: Am. Jour. Ob-Gyn, Fertility and Sterility; contbr. articles to profl. publs. Served with M.C. U.S. Army, 1963-65. Mem. AMA, Minn., Hennepin County med. socs., Minn. Obstet. and Gynecol. Soc., Am. Coll. Ob-Gyn (subcom. on reproductive endocrinology 1979-82), Endocrine Soc., Am. Fertility Soc., Central Assn. Obstetricians and Gynecologists, U. Iowa Ob-Gyn Alumni Soc. Home: 5828 Long Brake Trl Edina MN 55439-2622 Home Phone: 952-941-7930. Personal E-mail: getagatz@comcast.net.

TAGGARSE, JYOTSNA SHARAD, mathematics educator; b. Dharwad, India, Sept. 18, 1942; arrived in US, 1986; d. Narayan Sheshgin Kaikini and Sushila Ganesh Arur; m. Sharad Prabhakar Taggarse, May 27, 1960; children: Ajanta S. Vinekar, Akash S. BA, Karnataka U., 1963; BE, Meerut U., United Providence, 1972. Tchr. Indian Schs., 1968—86; math. and sci. tchr. St. Jude's Sch., Houree, Conn., 1986—90, St. Peter's Sch., Olney, Md., 1990—98, math. tchr., 1998—. Author: (textbook) Onward English Series, 1984. Mem.: NCTM. Avocations: quilting, knitting, crocheting. Home: 3230 Spartan Rd #66 Olney MD 20832 Office: St Peter's Sch 2900 Sandy Spring Rd Olney MD 20832

TAGGART, BRUCE M., library administrator; BS in Pub. Adminstrn., Nichols Coll., Mass.; M in Pub. Adminstrn., U. Conn., PhD in Edn., 1993. Past assoc. dir. Computing Ctr. U. Conn.; exec. dir. Info. Tech. Portland State U., Oreg.; vice provost Libr. and Tech. Svc. Lehigh U., Pa., 2000—. Mem. Educause, Gov.'s Telecom. Adv. Com., Oreg., N.W. Academic Computing Consortia, Lehigh Valley Econ. Devel. Corp. Office: Libr and Tech Svc Lehigh U 8A E Packer Ave Bethlehem PA 18015 Office Phone: 610-758-3025. E-mail: bmt2@lehigh.edu. *

TAGGART, GANSON POWERS, management consultant; b. Albany, NY, Aug. 16, 1918; s. Ralph Cone and Ruth Harriett (Townsend) T.; m. Paulett Long, June 30, 1945; children: H.Tee, Paulett Long, Cornelia V.C. BSChE, U. Mich., 1940, MSChE, 1941; postgrad., NE Sch. Advanced Mgmt., 1964. Registered engr., Mass. Mng. dir. Badger N.V., The Hague, Netherlands, 1965—70; v.p. world sales Badger Co., Cambridge, Mass., 1970—71; sr. v.p., dir. Badger Co. Inc., Cambridge, 1978—82; mgmt. cons. Devel. Scis. Inc., Sandwich, Mass., 1972—77; chmn. bd. Serapis Energy Inc., Boston, 1982—85, dir.; pres. Mgmt. Sys. Inc., 1984—. Chmn. bd. dirs. William K. Stout Pub. Co., 1995—; bd. dirs. E.F. Schumacher Soc. Contbr. articles to mags. Oil mem. Energy Facilities Siting Coun. Mass., Boston, 1979-82; mem. Winchester (Mass.) Planning Bd., 1971-77, Winchester Town Meeting, 1960-64; mem. exec. com. Internat. Sch. The Hague, 1965-70; trustee Ledges Condominium Assn., 1992-98, chmn., 1998; trustee USS Constn. Mus., 1989-95, treas. 1991-92; moderator Winchester Unitarian Soc., 1983-93; active Mus. Sci., Boston, Found. Global Cmty. Lt. (j.g.) USNR, 1944-48. Mem. AIChE (chmn. Boston sect. 1955, Order of Xiphias), Soc. Chem. Industry (London), Conservation Law Found., Am. Chem. Soc., World Bus. Acad., Inst. Noetic Scis., Chemists Club (N.Y.C.), Annisquam Yacht Club (Gloucester, Mass.), Harvard Club (Boston). Office: PO Box 516 7 Church St Winchester MA 01890-0516 *Hard work and flexibility in doing and thinking pays big dividends, as long as you are honest with yourself and others. I have always tried to see things from the other person's point of view, to give them the benefit of the doubt. I strive always to do the best I can and I do not spend a lot of time analyzing or criticizing what is wrong with others. And most important is a wonderful wife who accepts constructively life as it is dealt to you.*

TAGGART, HELEN M., adult education educator, nurse; b. Savannah, Ga., Dec. 6, 1946; d. Thomas Anthony and Ruth Elizabeth (Sisson) McKenzie; m. Thomas Robert Taggart, Mar. 9, 1968; children: Kathleen Taggart Swanner, Thomas Robert Jr. BSN, Armstrong State Coll., 1978; MSN, Ga. So. U., 1992; postgrad., U. Ala., Birmingham, 1995—. Staff nurse St. Joseph's Hosp., Savannah, 1967-68, 77-89, head nurse Ga., 1971-74, St. Mary's Hosp., Athens, Ga., 1968-71; instr. Armstrong State Coll., Savannah, 1989-92; asst. prof. Armstrong Atlantic State U., Savannah, 1992—. Profl. adv. com. Nat. Multiple Sclerosis Soc., Atlanta, 1992-96; bd. mem. Ga. Bd. Nursing, Atlanta, 1994—; mem. Clin. Simulation Task Force Nat. Coun. State Bds. Nursing, Chgo., 1996-99. Editor, contbr.: Adult Nursing in Acute Community, 1998; contbr. articles to profl. jours. and chpts. to books. Counselor Multiple Sclerosis Support Group, Savannah, 1989-97. Nat. Assn. Orthop. Nurses rsch. grantee, 1996, U. Ala. (Birmingham) traineeship grantee, 1997, Armstrong Atlantic State U. rsch. grantee, 1997-98. Mem. Nat. League Nurses (exec. bd. 1996-98), Assn. Bus. Women Am. (exec. bd. 1994-96), Nat. Assn. Orthop. Nurses (rsch. com. 1995-99), Ga. Nurses Assn. (exec. bd. 1992-96). Avocations: gardening, swimming, skiing. Home: 6 Mulberry Bluff Dr Savannah GA 31406-3226 Office: Armstrong Atlantic State Univ 11935 Abercorn St Savannah GA 31419-1989

TAGGART, JENNIFER T., lawyer; b. Hammond, Ind., Oct. 8, 1968; d. William E. and Mary Beth (Silvian) T. BS, Calif. Polytechnic State Univ., 1990; JD cum laude, Southwestern Univ., 1995. Cert. engr., Ca. Environ. engr., Rocketdyne div. Rockwell Internat.; ptnr., environ. law practice Demetriou, Del Guercio, Springer & Francis LLP, LA. Contbr. articles to profl. jours. Commr. LA City Environ. Affairs Commn., 1996—2000, 2004—05, v.p., 2003—04, pres., 2000—02. Recipient GM Spirit award/Pres.'s award Calif. Poly., 1990, Rocketdyne Leadership award, 1991, Am. Jurisprudence Book award Constitutional Law I, 1992, Acad. Excellence Juvenile Law, 1993, Acad. Excellence in Environ. Law, 1994; named Outstanding Contbr. to Goals & Pub. Image of Sch. Engring., 1990; Paul Wildman scholar Southwestern U., 1991. Mem. ABA, ASME, Air & Waste Mgmt. Assn., Tau Beta Pi (pres. 1989-90). Home: Demetriou Del Guercio Springer & Francis 10th Fl 801 S Grand Ave Los Angeles CA 90017-4613 Office Phone: 213-624-8407. Office Fax: 213-624-0174. Business E-Mail: jtaggart@ddsffirm.com.

TAGGART, RICHARD J., forest products company executive; BS, U. Wyo., 1967, MS in Agrl. Econs., 1970; grad. exec. mgmt. program, U. Wash. CPA. With ops. rsch. and systems devel. depts. Ford Motor Co., 1970—74; with Weyerhaeuser Co., Federal Way, Wash., 1974—, dir. investor rels., 1994—96, v.p. investor rels., 1996—98, v.p., treas., 1998—2001, v.p. fin., 2001—03, exec. v.p., CFO, 2003—. Office: Weyerhaeuser Co 33663 Weyerhaeuser Way S Federal Way WA 98063-9777 *

TAGGART, THOMAS MICHAEL, lawyer; b. Sioux City, Iowa, Feb. 22, 1937; s. Palmer Robert and Lois Allette (Sedgwick) T.; m. Dolores Cecilia Baroway Renfro, Jan. 4, 1963; children: Thomas Michael Jr., Theodore Christopher; m. Mary Ann Gribben, Feb. 7, 1976. BA, Dartmouth Coll., 1959; JD, Harvard U., 1965. Bar: Ohio 1965, U.S. Dist. Ct. (so. dist.) Ohio 1967, U.S. Dist. Ct. (no. dist.) Ohio 1981, U.S. Supreme Ct. 1997. Ptnr. Vorys, Sater, Seymour & Pease, Columbus, Ohio, 1965—, now of counsel. Lectr. Ohio Legal Ctr. Inst., Ohio Mfrs. Assn., Capital U. Ctr. for Spl. and Continuing Legal Edn. Capt. USMC, 1959-63. Mem. ABA, Ohio Bar Assn. (bd. govs. 1991-99, liability ins. com. 1996-, pres. 1997-98, trustee Found. 1996-98, 2000—, pres 2005—, chair commn. on jud. evaluations 2000, Ohio Bar medal 1999), Columbus Bar Assn. (bd. govs., pres. 1989-90), Am. Bd. Trial Advocates, Columbus Area C. of C. Methodist. Home: 145 Stanbery Ave Columbus OH 43209-1465 Office: Vorys Sater Seymour & Pease 52 E Gay St Columbus OH 43215-3161 Office Phone: 614-464-6252. E-mail: tmtaggart@vssp.com.

TAGIURI, CONSUELO KELLER, child psychiatrist, educator; b. San Francisco; d. Cornelius H. and Adela (Rios) Keller; m. Renato Tagiuri; children: Robert, Peter, John. BA, U. Calif.-Berkeley; MD, U. Calif.-San Francisco. Diplomate Am. Bd. Psychiatry and Neurology. Resident psychiatry Mass. Gen. Hosp., Boston; staff psychiatrist Children's Hosp., Boston, 1951-59; med. dir. Gifford Sch., Weston, Mass., 1965-85; chief psychiatrist Cambridge (Mass.) Guidance Ctr., 1961-84; mem. faculty dept. psychiatry Harvard Med. Sch., 1965—2002; cons. early childhood program Children's Hosp., 1985—. Contbr. articles in field to books. Fellow Am. Orth. Psychiat. Assn., Mass. Med. Soc., New Eng. Coun. Child Psychiatry.

TAGLIABUE, PAUL JOHN, retired national football league commissioner; b. Jersey City, Nov. 24, 1940; s. Charles and Mary Tagliabue; m. Chandler M. Minter, Aug. 28, 1965; children: Drew, Emily. BA, Georgetown U., 1962; JD, NYU, 1965; PhD. Humane Letters (hon.), Northeastern Univ., 1990; PhD of Laws (hon.), Colgate Univ., 2001. Bar: N.J. 1965, D.C. 1969. Atty. to sec. def. Dept. Def., Washington, 1966—69; assoc. Covington & Burling, Washington, 1969—74, ptnr., 1969—89; commr. NFL, NYC, 1989—2006. Bd. dir. Pro Football Hall of Fame; bd. dirs. Nat. Urban League; bd. govs. United Way of Am., 1998—99. Contbr. articles to profl. jours. Cofounder NFL Teacher of the Yr. Program, 1990. Co-recipient Stay Close Individual Leadership award, PFLAG, 2005; named Sports Industrialist of the Yr., Sports Business Daily, 2000, Sports Executive of the Yr., Sports Business Journal, 2001, Most Powerful Person in Sports, The Sporting News, 2001; recipient Humanitarians of the Yr. award, Comty. Anti-Drug Coalitions of Am., 2004, Ellis Island Family Heritage award, 2004; Gordon Grand Fellow, Yale U., 2001. Mem.: ABA (chmn. sports and entertainment industry com. antitrust sect. 1986), D.C. Bar Assn.

TAGLIAFERRI, LEE GENE, investment banker; b. Mahanoy City, Pa., Aug. 14, 1931; s. Charles and Adele (Cirilli) Tagliaferri; m. Maryellen Stanton, Apr. 29, 1962; children: Mark, John, Maryann. BS, U. Pa., 1957; MBA, U. Chgo., 1958. Div. comptroller Campbell Soup Co., Camden, NJ, 1958—60; securities analyst Merrill, Lynch, Pierce, Fenner & Smith, Inc., NYC, 1960—62; asst. v.p. US Trust Co. of NY, 1962—71; v.p. corp. fin. div. Laidlaw & Co., Inc., NYC, 1972—73; pres. Everest Corp., NYC, 1973—. Dir. Fairfield Communities Inc., UEC, Inc., LRA, Inc., Industrialized Bldg. Systems, Inc. Past pres. West Windsor Cmty. Assn.; trustee Schuyler Hall, Columbia, Madison Sq. Boys Club. With AUS, 1953—55. Mem.: Princeton Club (NYC), U. Pa. Club, K.C. Home: 77 Lillie St Princeton Junction NJ 08550-1307 Office: 1 Penn Plz New York NY 10119-0002

TAGLIAPIETRA, ROBERT, apparel designer; Grad., Parsons Sch. of Design. Co-owner, designer (with Jeffrey Costello) Costello Tagliapietra, 2004—. Work featured in Metropolitan Museum of Art's Costume Inst., Vogue, Elle, Bazaar, Style.com, Gloss, Maxim, Black Book. Recipient Ecco Domani Fashion Found. award, 2005. Office: Costello Tagliapietra 97 Second Pl 3Fl Brooklyn NY 11231

TAGLIENTE, JOSEPHINE MARLENE, artist; b. Chisholm, Minn., Nov. 28, 1939; d. Joseph and Carmela (DeLuca) T.; m. Wayne W. Brown, May 28, 1960 (div. 1972); children: Michael Anthony, Troy Tagliente, Roben Tagliente, Angela Monique, Ninon Terese, Anina Maria (dec.). Student, Mpls. Coll. Art and Design, 1957-59, Mankato State Coll., 1966, Kansas City Art Inst., 1972; MFA, U. Guanajuato, Mex., 1974. Artist-in-residence Jewish Cmty. Ctr., Wilmington, 1969; illustration chairperson, mem. faculty Ray Coll. of Design, Chgo., 1980-87; adj. faculty Paradise Valley C.C., Phoenix; spkr. in field. One-woman exhbn. Natalini Gallery, Chgo., 1986; group exhbns. include Windbell Gallery, Wilmington, Del., Newark (Del.) Gallery, Galeria San Miguel, Mex., Galeria Osman, Mex., Galeria Condor, Mex., Torres Gallery, Albuquerque, Dartmouth Gallery, Albuquerque, Edith Lampert Gallery, Santa Fe, La Luna Nueva, Santa Fe, Herberger Theatre, Phoenix Little Theatre, Artesimo Gallery, Scottsdale, Ariz., Del. Art Mus., Wilmington, Sky Harbor Airport, 1994, Westaff, UK-Ariz., Canticles: Sight and Sound, 2002, others; represented in corp. collections Collins, Miller & Hutchins, Chgo., Mt. Sinai Hosp., N.Y.C.; also pvt. and pub. permanent collections; represented by Artisimo Gallery, Scottsdale; illustrations published in books; poetry published in anthologies; inventor garden products, office implements. Vol. art educator St. Anne's Intercity, Wilmington, 1967-68, Recreation Intercity, Chgo., 1978-79; cultural advocate for homeless Cultural Labor Party, Chgo., 1980-87, cultural advocate for minority concerns, 1985-88. Recipient Fine Art award Artist's Guild of Chgo., 1977, Print Drawing award, 1978, Educator/Svcs. award Sauk Area Career Ctr., 1984. Mem. Nat. Mus. Women in Arts, The Drawing Soc., Soc. Children's Book Writers and Illustrators, Statue of Liberty-Ellis Island Found. Social Democrat. Avocations: writing, digital painting, raising turtles and studying their habitat. E-mail: joyfulsunrise@qwest.net.

TAGUE, CHARLES FRANCIS, retired engineering company executive, real estate company executive, construction executive; b. NYC, Aug. 16, 1924; s. Charles and Isabelle (Carey) T.; m. Alicia Patricia Murtha, Aug. 6, 1949; children: Patrick, Charles, Thomas, Mary Alicia Haberman, James, Beth Anne Giuliano BS, Fordham U., 1952. Auditor Scovell, Wellington & Co., NYC, 1951-57; comptroller Chem. Constrn. Corp., NYC, 1957-75; contr. Burns and Roe, Inc., Oradell, NJ, 1975-81; fin. dir. Alfred Sanzari Enterprises, Hasbrouck Heights, NJ, 1981-84; v.p. fin. Alexander Summer Co., 1984-93; ret., 1993. Fin. advisor Cath. Cmty. at Seabrook Village. Mem. Colts Neck (N.J.) Sports Found.; active Boy scouts Am.; mem. Lacawac Sanctuary Steering Com.; pres. parish coun. Ch. of Presentation; mem. pastoral coun. St. Thomas More Cath. Ch. With USNR, 1943-46, PTO, ETO, NATOUSA. Mem. Controllers Inst., Nat. Contract Mgmt. Assn., Assn. Govt. Accts., Scranton Club. Democrat. Roman Catholic. Address: 4 Appleby Ct Jackson NJ 08527

TAGUE, JOHN PATRICK, air transportation executive; married; 2 children. Dir., then sr. v.p. Midway Airlines, 1985—91; with ATA Holdings, 1991—95; co-chmn., CEO The Pointe Group, 1995—97; pres., CEO ATA Holdings, 1993—2002; exec. v.p., customer United Airlines Corp., 2003—04, exec. v.p. mktg., sales and revenue, 2004—06, exec. v.p., chief revenue officer, 2006—.

TAHA, ASSAD M., surgeon; b. Nabatieh, Lebanon, Dec. 12, 1955; came to U.S. 1980; s. Muhyddin S. and Hind (Jaber) T. BS, Am. U. Beirut, 1976, MD, 1980; PhD, Med. Coll. Ohio, Toledo, 1992. Diplomate Am. Bd. Surgery, Am. Bd. Surg. Critical Care. Surgery resident Good Samaritan Hosp., Cin., 1980-82, Med. Coll. Ohio, Toledo, 1982-85, attending surgeon, 1985-94, Am. U. of Beirut, 1994—, assoc. prof. surgery and physiology, 1994—. Dir. hyperbaric medicine Med. Coll. Hosp., Toledo, 1987—94, dir. surg. intensive care, 1988—94, assoc. prof. surgery; vis. surgeon surg. critical care Brigham & Women's Hosp., Harvard Med. Sch., Boston, 2000—01; vis. assoc. prof. Harvard U., 2000—01; vis. scholar trauma Ryder Trauma Ctr., U. Miami Sch. Medicine, Fla., 2003—04. Mem. editl. bd. European Jour. Emergency Surgery and Intensive Care; contbr. articles to profl. jours. Recipient AMA Physician Recognition award, 1987,

1991, 1997, 2000; grantee, Ohio Lions, 1987—92, Am. U.- Beirut U. Rsch. Bd., 1993—2000. Fellow ACS, AMA, Am. Heart Assn., Am. Physiologic Soc., Am. Soc. Gastrointestinal Endoscopy, European Assn. Trauma and Emergency Surgery, Royal Coll. Surgeons Can., Soc. Critical Care Medicine, Undersea and Hyperbaric Med. Soc., Am. Soc. Laser Medicine and Surgery, Am. Coll. Nutrition, Internat. Coll. Surgeons, Assn. Acad. Surgery, Shock Soc., European Soc. Intensive Care Medicine, World Assn. Disaster and Emergency Medicine, Soc. Am. GI Endoscopic Surgeons, World Med. Assn., Laser Inst. Am., Royal Soc. Medicine, Am. U. Beirut Alumni Assn., Am. Trauma Soc., Crit. Care Club, Disaster Med. Asst. Team; mem. AMA, AAUP. Avocations: chess, bridge. Office: Am U Beirut 3 Dag Hammarskjold Plz 8th Fl New York NY 10017-2303 Home Phone: 305-490-3682; Office Phone: 011-9613628627, 305-468-2810. Office Fax: 212-583-7650, 011-961-1363291. Business E-Mail: at03@aub.edu.lb.

TAHBAZ, CHRISTOPHER K., lawyer; b. Dec. 29, 1964; BA cum laude, Columbia U., 1986, JD, 1990. Bar: NY 1991. Assoc. Donovan Leisure Newton & Irvine; mem. Debevoise & Plimpton LLP, NYC, 1994—, ptnr. litig. dept., mem. Mem.: ABA (mem. Litig. & Antitrust Sects.), Urban Justice Ctr. (bd. dirs.), NY Lawyers Pub. Interest, Inc. (vice chair, bd. dirs.), Internat. Bar Assn., Assn. Bar City NY. Office: Debevoise & Plimpton LLP 919 Third Ave New York NY 10022 Office Phone: 212-909-6543. E-mail: cktahbaz@debevoise.com.

TAHERI, MARSHALL M., lawyer, educator; b. Iran, Dec. 29, 1934; came to U.S., 1963; children: Tara, Sara, Dara Jon. BBA, U. Houston, 1968; JD, So. Tex. Coll. Law, 1973; PhD of Law, Ministry Scis. and Higher Edn. Iran, 1974. Bar: Tex. 1974, N.Y. 1999, U.S. Supreme Ct. 1981, D.C. 1982, U.S. Ct. Internat. Trade 1989, U.S. Dist. Ct. (so. dist.) 1975, U.S. Ct. Appeals (5th cir.) 1975, U.S. Ct. Appeals (11th cir.) 1981, U.S. Ct. Appeals (9th cir.) 1986, U.S. Ct. Appeals (fed. cir.) 1991. Pvt. practice, Houston, 1974—. Adj. prof. internat. civil litig. South Tex. Coll. Law, Houston, 1980—; participant internat. bus. litig. and arbitration conf., N.Y.C., 2002. Fellow Houston Bar Found.; mem. ABA, ATLA, Tex. Bar Assn., State Bar Tex. (vice chmn. com. laws relating to immigration and nationality), Houston Bar Assn., Tex. Trial Lawyers Assn., Houston C. of C. (internat. bus. com., ad hoc immigration task force 1982, 87), World Trade Assn., Inst. Internat. Edn., Internat. Lawyers Assn., South Tex. Coll. Law Alumni Assn. (past pres.), Iran-Am. C. of C. (founder), Forum Club Office: PO Box 460001 Houston TX 77056-8001 Office Phone: 713-871-0000. Business E-Mail: taheri@marshalltaheri.com.

TAI, ELIZABETH SHI-JUE LEE, library director; b. Si-Ann, China, Aug. 12, 1942; arrived in U.S., 1965; d. Jun-Yee Lee and Fang-Yee Liu; m. Hsiang Tai, Dec. 29, 1969; children: Alan C., Victoria C., Brian C. BA in English Lang. and Lit., Nat. Cheng Kung U., Taiwan, 1965; M in Libr. and Info. Sci., Tex. Woman's U., 1967. Sr. libr. Queens (N.Y.) Borough Pub. Libr., 1967-73; asst. regional libr. Cin. Pub. Libr., Libr. for Blind and Physically Handicapped, 1973-75; libr. Ga. State Libr., Atlanta, 1975-78; dir. Poquoson (Va.) Pub. Libr., 1979—. Vol. ARC York County chpt., Va., 1980—; mem. York County Sch. Sys. Extend Program Coun., 1997; mem. Va. social svcs. bd. York County/City of Poquoson, 2002—; vice chmn. Peninsula Ret. Sr. Vol. Program Coun., Newport News, Va., 1994—99, chmn., 2000; bd. dirs. Peninsula Ret. Sr. Vol. Program, 2001—, sec., 2002—05. Named City Employee of Yr., City of Poquoson, Va., 1989; recipient Letter of Commendation, Va. Gov. James Gilmore III, 2001, Unsung Hero/Heroine award Nat. Cheng Kung U. N.Am. Alumni and Found., 2003. Mem. ALA, Va. Libr. Assn., Va. Pub. Libr. Dirs. Assn. (region 3 rep. 2003-05, treas., 2004—, Outstanding Pub. Rels. award 1998, 2001, 02, 04, 06, 07, Outstanding Facility award 1998, Outstanding Young Adult Program award 1999, Outstanding Children's Program award 1999, Outstanding Libr. Staff award 2003, Outstanding Va. Pub. Libr. Dir. award 2004), Va. Peninsula Chinese Am. Assn. (bd. mem. 2004—, pres. 2006—), Tidewater Area Libr. Dirs. Coun.,Kiwanis Club (charter mem. Tabb chpt., chmn. youth program 2005—). Avocations: reading, gardening, swimming, tennis. Home: 129 Loblolly Dr Yorktown VA 23692-4254 Office: 500 City Hall Ave Poquoson VA 23662-1996 Office Phone: 757-868-3066. Business E-Mail: etai@poquoson-va.gov.

TAI, TSZE CHENG, aerodynamicist, researcher; b. Shaoxing, Chekiang, China, Apr. 29, 1933; arrived in U.S., 1963, naturalized, 1972; m. Shih Lin Sun, Aug. 27, 1965; children: Kuangheng, Kuangkai, Kuangshin. Diploma, Air Tech. Inst., Taiwan, Republic of China, 1957; MS, Clemson U., 1965; PhD, Va. Poly. Inst. and State U., 1968. Aircraft insp. Taoyuan Air Base, Taiwan, 1958—63; rsch. asst. Clemson U., 1963—65; grad. asst. Va. Poly. Inst. and State U., 1965—67, instr., 1967—68; sr. rsch. scientist Carderock divsn. Naval Surface Warfare Ctr., Bethesda, Md., 1968—2005. Chmn. panel US Navy Aero ballistics Com., Washington, 1978—81; Lectr. von Karman Inst. Fluid Dynamics, Belgium, 1980. Prin. Potomac Chinese Sch., Md., 1981—82; sci. officer fluid mechanics Office Naval Resch., 1985—86. Recipient Eugene Brooks award, Naval Ship R&D CTR., 1979. Fellow: AIAA (assoc.); mem.: Sigma Xi (pres. David Taylor chpt. 1989—90). Achievements include obtained world's first numerical solution to full inviscid transonic flow equations that detects the effect of entropy on the shock wave in 1970; research in aeodynamic development of US Navy's V-22 tilt-rotor aircraft in areas of tail buffet alleviation, aerodynamic drag reduction, and fuel dumping. Home: 10705 Tara Rd Potomac MD 20854-1356 Personal E-mail: tszetai@yahoo.com.

TAIEBAT, MAHDI, civil engineer; s. Jalal Taiebat and Masumeh Sobhieh. BS in Civil Engring., Sharif U. Tech., Tehran, Iran, 2001, MS in Civil Engring., 2003; postgrad., U. Calif., Davis, 2004—. EIT Calif. Bd. Profl. Engrs. and Land Surveyors, 2007. Rschr. and tchg. asst. Sharif U. Tech., Tehran, 2001—03, U. Calif., Davis, 2004—. Structural engr. Energy Industries Engring. & Design Cons. Engrs., Tehran, 2001—02; geotech. engr. Tehran Engring. and Tech. Consulting Org., Tehran, 2002—04, Tarh-e-NowAndishan Consulting Engrs. Co., Tehran, 2002—04, Qeshm Fish Process Complex, Tehran, Iran, 2004; session chair 7th World Congress Computational Mechanics, LA, 2006. Reviewer Internat. Jour. Solids and Structures, 2006—; contbr. articles to profl. jours. Recipient Travel award, Johns Hopkins U., Md., 2004, Excellence in Geotech. Engring. prize, U. Calif. Davis, 2007; grantee, U. Calif., Davis, 2006—; Rsch. fellow, 2005. Mem.: US Assn. Computational Mechanics. Achievements include research in numerical study of sand behavior during earthquake loading using advanced constitutive models in a fully coupled finite element framework. Business E-Mail: mtaiebat@ucdavis.edu.

TAIGANIDES, E. PAUL, agricultural and environmental engineer, consultant; b. Polymylos, Macedonia, Greece, Oct. 6, 1934; s. Pavlos Theodorou and Sophia ((Elezidou) T.; m. Maro Taiganides, Dec. 25, 1961; children: Paul Anthony, Tasos E., Katerina. BS in Agri. Engring., U. Maine, 1957; MS in Soil and Water Engring., Iowa State U., 1961, D of Environ. Engring., 1963. Cert. engr., Iowa, Colo. Rsch. assoc., asst. prof. Iowa State U., Ames, 1957-65; prof. Ohio State U., Columbus, 1965-75; mgr., chief tech. adviser UN, FAO, Singapore, Singapore, 1975-84, mgr., chief engr., 1984-85, mgr., chief tech. adviser Kuala Lumpur, Malaysia, 1985-87; mgr., owner EPT Cons., Columbus, 1987—. Cons. EPD/Hong Kong, 1988-92, WHO, UN, Denmark, Poland, Czechoslovakia, 1972-75, Internat. Devel. Rsch. Ctr., Can., China, Asian, 1984-89, NAE, Thailand, 1990, FAO, Malaysia, Foxley & Co., Nu-Tek Foods; environ. advisor to Bertam Devel. Corp., Kuala Lampur, Malaysia, 1992—; waste cons. to U.S. Feed Grains Coun., Taiwan, Malaysia, 1992, Venezuela, 1993; pres. Fan Engring., (US) Inc., 1991—, Red Hill Farms, Ohio, 1992—. Author: (video) Waste Resources Recycle, 1985, Pig Waste Treatment and Recycle, 1992; editor: Animal Wastes, 1977; co-editor Agricultural Wastes/ Biological Wastes, 1979; contbr. articles to profl. jours. Bd. govs., v.p. Singapore Am. Sch., Singapore, 1978-83; clergy-leity congress Greek Orthodox Ch., Houston, 1974. Recipient rsch. awards EPA, 1971-75, Water Resources Inst., 1968-73; rsch. grantee UNDP, FAO, IDRC, GTZ, Asean, 1975-88. Fellow Am. Soc. Agrl. Engrs. (chmn. dept., A.W. Farral award 1974), Am. Assn. Environ. Engrs. (diplomate); mem. Am. Soc. Engring. Edn. (div. chmn.), Singapore Lawn Tennis Assn. (v.p. 1980-84), Am. Club (mgmt. com. 1980-85), Sigma Xi. Greek Orthodox. Avocations: tennis, classical music, folk dancing.

TAILLON, ARMAND PHILIP, mechanical engineer; b. Sydney, New South Wales, Australia, June 6, 1964; s. Denis Philip Taillon and Geraldine Irene O'Connell; m. Stephanie Weiwei Wang, Sept. 6, 1997; children: Audrey Anyi-Wang, Gigi Anran-Wang. BS in Mech. Engring., U. Kans., Lawrence, 1987; M Mgmt., Northwestern U., Evanston, Ill., 1997. Registered profl. engr., Ill., 2001. Sr project engr. Std. Car Truck Co., Park Ridge, Ill., 1988—98, dir. R & D, 1998—2004, regional mgr. sales and tech. support, 2004—. Contbr. tech. papers to profl. publs. Evans scholar, Evans Scholarship Found. - Western Golf Assn., 1983—87. Mem.: ASME, Rlwy. Supply Inst., Air Brake Association, Can. Rlwy. Club, Toronto Rlwy. Club, Pi Tau Sigma (pres. 1986—87). Achievements include patents for friction wedge optimized for high warp low damping; rail car truck pedestal shear pad; roller bearing adapter stabilizer bar; rail car truck dumping system; roller bearing adapter stabilizer bar; pad of rigid resin for a friction wedge; stabilized roller bearing adapter; wheel chock for a aotor vehicle container. Home: 386 Beverly Rd Barrington IL 60010 Office: Std Car Truck Co 865 Busse Highway Park Ridge IL 60068 Home Phone: 312-391-1549; Office Phone: 847-692-6050 ext. 2241. Personal E-mail: ataillon@stdcar.com.

TAI-SEALE, MING, science educator, consultant; d. Jianzhong Tai and Xiouhua Zhao; m. Thomas Scott Seale, July 23, 1988; children: Sahar Marguerite, Arin Minghua. MPH, Emory U., Atlanta, Ga., 1988; PhD, UCLA, 1995. Asst. prof. Tex. A&M Health Sci. Ctr., College Station, 2001—02, assoc. prof., 2002—. Cons. to grant reviewers NIH, Bethesda, Md., 2001—. Recipient Mentored Scientist Career award, NIH, 2002—07. Mem.: Am. Soc. Health Economists, Internat. Health Econs. Assn., Acad. Health (mem. adv. bd. health econs. interest group 2005—). Office: Taxes A&M Health Sci Ctr TAMU 1266 College Station TX 77843 Office Phone: 979-845-2387.

TAIT, C. DOWNING, JR., (COLUMBUS DOWNING TAIT JR.), physician, medical educator; b. Valdosta, Ga., Sept. 3, 1923; s. C. Downing Sr. and Mary Lucretia (Jacobs) T.; m. Nancy Reep, Aug. 25, 1956; children: Carl, Jennifer. BA in Philosophy, U. Va., 1943, MD, 1947; cert. in psychoanalytic medicine, Columbia U., 1957. Diplomate Am. Bd. Psychiatry and Neurology; cert. in adult psychoanalysis. Intern Bellevue Hosp., NYC, 1947-48; resident in psychiatry Compton (Calif.) Sanitarium, 1948-49, N.Y. State Hosp., Orangeburg, 1950-51; psychoanalytic trainee Columbia U., NYC, 1950-51, 53-57; pvt. practice NYC, 1953-64; assoc. prof. Emory U. Sch. of Medicine, Atlanta, 1964-67, prof. psychiatry, 1967-81; pvt. practice NYC, 1953-64, Atlanta, 1977—. Geographical tng. and supervising psychoanalyst Emory Columbia U. Psychoanalytic Tng., Atlanta, 1966-78; dir. rsch. Ga. Mental Health Inst. Emory U. and State, Atlanta, 1965-71. Co-author: Delinquents, Their Families, and the Community, 1962; contbr. articles to profl. jours. Cons. to juvenile ct. judges Atlanta, 1966-71; Lt. USNR, 1951-53. Rsch. fellowship Atomic Energy Commn., Duke U., 1949, Yale U., 1950. Fellow Ga. Psychiat. Assn., Am. Psychiat. Assn.; mem. AMA, Atlanta Med. Assn., Ga. Med. Assn., Internat. Psychoanalytic Assn., Am. Psychoanalytic Assn., Atlanta Psychoanalytic Assn. (pres. 1979-81). Avocations: travel, music. Home and Office: 3895 Chaucer Wood NE Atlanta GA 30319-1687 Office Phone: 770-454-9247.

TAIT, JOHN REID, lawyer; b. Toledo, Apr. 7, 1946; s. Paul Reid and Lucy Richardson (Rudderow) T.; m. Christina Ruth Bjornstad, Mar. 12, 1972; children: Gretchen, Mary. BA, Columbia U., 1968; JD, Vanderbilt U., 1974. Bar: Idaho 1974, U.S. Dist. Ct. Idaho 1974, U.S. Ct. Appeals (9th cir.) U.S. Supreme Ct., Nez Perce Tribal Ct. Assoc. Keeton & Tait, Lewiston, Idaho, 1974-76, ptnr., 1976-86, 89—, Keeton, Tait & Petrie, Lewiston, 1986-88. Chmn. bd. No. Rockies Action Group, Helena, Mont., 1985-86, bd. dirs., 1981-88; active Lewiston Hist. Preservation Commn., 1975-94, chmn., 1988-94; bd. dirs. Idaho Legal Aid Svcs., Boise, 1975-99, Idaho Housing Agy., Boise, 1984-91, St. Joseph Regional Med. Ctr. Found., Inc., 1989-94, Lewiston Ind. Found. for Edn., Inc., 1996—; Dem. precinct committeeman, 1976-86, state committeeman, 1977-94, 2000—; del. Dem. Nat. Conv., 1980, 84; regional coord. Idaho State Dem. Party, 1996-99; treas. Larry LaRocco for Congress, 1990, 92. With U.S. Army, 1968-71. Recipient Pro Bono Svc. award Idaho State Bar, 1988, Cmty. Recognition award Lewiston Intergovtl. Coun., 1992, Spl. Recognition award Idaho Legal Aid Svcs., 1993. Mem. ABA, Am. Assn. Justice, Idaho Trial Lawyers Assn. (regional dir. 1976-77, 86-88, 97-03), Idaho State Bar (worker's compensation sect. 2002—, chmn. 2004-06), Clearwater Bar Assn. (sec. 1974-76, pres. 1984-86), Consumer Attys. Calif., Workers Injury Law and Litig. Group (bd. dirs. 2002-). Office: Keeton & Tait PO Drawer E 312 Miller St Lewiston ID 83501-1944 Office Phone: 208-743-6231. Office Fax: 208-746-0962. Business E-Mail: lewlawus@lewiston.com.

TAIT, ROBERT E., lawyer; b. Lima, Ohio, Sept. 3, 1946; s. Robert and Helen (Smith) T.; m. Donna G. Dome, June 22, 1968; children: Heather, Jennifer, Robert. BA, Kenyon Coll., Gambier, Ohio, 1968; JD, U. Mich., Ann Arbor, 1973. Bar: Ohio 1973, US Dist. Ct. (so. dist.) Ohio. 1976, US Dist. Ct. (no. dist.) Ohio 1976, US Dist. Ct. Md. 1980, US Ct. Appeals (6th cir.) 1981, US Supreme Ct. 1982. Ptnr. Vorys, Sater, Seymour & Pease, LLP, Columbus, Ohio, 1973—. Staff counsel Govs. Select Com. on Prevention Indsl. Accidents, Columbus, 1977-78. Served with US Army, 1969-70. Fellow Ohio Bar Found., Columbus Bar Found.; mem. ABA (litigation sect., products liability com.), Ohio Bar Assn. (worker's compensation com.), Columbus Bar Assn. (workers compensation and professionalism coms.), Def. Rsch. Inst. (workers compensation com.), Am. Bd. Trial Advocates, Assn. Def. Trial Attys. (exec. com. 1991-94, treas., 2002-07, v.p. 2007-), Dept. Energy and Contractors Attys. Assn., Fedn. Def. and Corp. Counsel (toxic torts com). Home: 2045 Wickford Rd Columbus OH 43221-4223 Office: Vorys Sater Seymour & Pease PO Box 1008 52 E Gay St Columbus OH 43215-3161 Home Phone: 614-488-4003; Office Phone: 614-464-6341. Business E-Mail: retait@vssp.com.

TAITT, EARL PAUL, psychiatrist, military officer; b. LA, Nov. 6, 1956; s. Earl and Mary (Freitas) T.; m. Puruca Estepa, May 11, 1985; children: Anamaria, Earl. AA, East L.A. Coll., 1976; BS, U. Calif., Irvine, 1978; MD, Northwestern U., Chgo., 1984. Commd. capt. U.S. Army, 1984, advanced through grades to maj., 1991; intern in psychiatry Tripler Army Med. Ctr., Honolulu, 1984-85; resident in psychiatry Eisenhower Army Med. Ctr., Ft. Gordon, Ga., 1985-88; staff psychiatrist Community Mental Health Ctr., Ft. Gordon, Ga., 1988; div. psychiatrist, chief mental health 10th Mountain Div., Ft. Drum, N.Y., 1988-90; staff psychiatrist Community Mental Health Ctr., Ft. Meade, Md., 1990—; chief resident in psychiatry U.S. Army Hosp., Ft. Gordon, Ga., 1988. Cons. Army Drug and Alcohol Program, Ft. Drum, 1988-90, Installation Detention Facility, Ft. Meade, 1990—. Mem. San Gabriel (Calif.) Mission Parish Coun., 1975-76; pres. Medical Soc., L.A., 1976. Mem. Assn. U.S. Army, Order of Green Key. Republican. Roman Catholic. Home: 14403 Altamaha Ct Orlando FL 32837-5425 Office Phone: 407-931-3001. Business E-Mail: valenciaoffice@yahoo.com.

TAK, TAHIR, cardiologist, researcher; b. Lahore, Punjab, Pakistan, July 18, 1951; arrived in U.S., 1985; s. E. Tak. BS, Govt. Coll. Lahore, 1971; MD, U. Nijmegen, 1980; PhD, U. Maastricht, 1989. Diplomate in internal medicine and in cardiovasc. diseases Am. Bd. Internal Medicine. Cardiology fellow U. Amsterdam, 1982—85; resident in internal medicine U. So. Calif., LA, 1988—89, asst. prof. medicine, 1989—96; assoc. prof. medicine U. Nev., Las Vegas, 1996—98; cardiologist Scott and White Clinic, Temple, Tex., 1998—2001; assoc. prof. Tex. A&M U. HSC, Temple, 1998—2001; cardiologist Marshfield Clinic, Wis., 2001—04; clin. prof. medicine U. Madison Sch. Medicine, Wis., 2001—04; prof. medicine U. North Tex., Ft. Worth, 2004—07; cardiologist Mayo Clinic, Rochester, Minn., 2007—. Fellow: ACP, Am. Coll. Cardiology, Am. Coll. Chest Physicians, Am. Heart Assn., European Soc. Cardiology. Home: 4685 Brickyard Ln La Crosse WI 54601 Office: Mayo Clinic 200 First St SW Rochester MN 55905 Office Phone: 608-796-1170. Business E-Mail: tak.tahir@mayo.edu.

TAKAHASHI, MASATO, pediatric cardiologist, educator; b. Tokyo, Feb. 10, 1933; came to U.S., 1952; s. Noboru and Fujiko (Tarumoto) T.; m. Marcia Parnell, Jan. 16, 1966; children; Rumi Anne, Yuki Lynn. AB, Wabash U., 1956; MD, Ind. U., 1960. Attending physician Children's Hosp., LA, 1968—; prof. pediatrics,, Keck Sch. Medicine U. So. Calif., LA, 1986—2005, prof. pediat. emeritus, 2005—. Chmn. 4th Internat. Kawasaki Disease Symposium, 1991. Vol. Habitat for Humanity, San Fernando Valley, Calif., 1993-94, Am. Heart Assn. L.A., 1982-85, com. mem. 1991-93 (Disting. Achievement award 1983). Mem. Am. Acad. Pediatrics, Am. Coll. Cardiology, Meth. Avocations: long distance running, wood working. Office: Divsn Cardiology Children's Hosp LA MS#34 4650 Sunset Blvd Los Angeles CA 90027 Office Phone: 323-669-4634. Business E-Mail: mtakahashi@chla.usc.edu. *

TAKAHASHI, TAKAMUNE, medical researcher, educator; b. Odawara, Kanagawa, Japan, Nov. 30, 1962; s. Makio and Kuniyo Takahashi; m. Keiko Miyake, Mar. 31, 1996. MD, Jikei U., Tokyo, 1988, PhD (hon.), 1994. Med. residency Saitama Med. U., Kawagoe, Japan, 1988—90; med. staff Jikei U., Tokyo, 1994—96; rsch. fellow Vanderbilt U., Nashville, 1996—99, rsch. asst. prof., 1999—2003, asst. prof., 2003—. Recipient Young Investigator award, Nat. Kidney Found., 1999—2000; grantee, Juvenile Diabetes Found., 2000—05, NIH, 2000—04, Collaborative Rsch. Grant, Vanderbuilt/Immunex, 2001—02. Mem.: Am. Soc. Nephrology (assoc.). Achievements include patents for CD148 monoclonal antibody. Office: Vanderbilt U 21st Ave S MCN S3223 Nashville TN 37232-2372 Home Phone: 615-353-9849; Office Phone: 615-343-4312. Office Fax: 615-343-7156.

TAKEI, GEORGE HOSATO, actor; b. LA, Apr. 20, 1937; s. Takekuma Norman and Fumiko Emily Takei; life ptnr. Brad Altman. BA, UCLA, 1960, MA, 1964. Dir., chmn. Golden Security Bancorp, Alhambra, Calif., 1981-. Appeared in films, including Green Beret, 1967, Star Trek I-VI, 1979-91, Return from the River Kwai, 1989, Blood Oath, 1990, Prisoners of the Sun, 1990, Live by the Fist, 1993, Oblivion, 1994, Chongbal, 1994, Oblivion 2: Backlash, 1996, Trekkies, 1997, Bug Buster, 1998, Mulan, 1998, Who Gets the House, 1999; plays include Equus, 2005, The Wash, 1990, Undertow, 1988, Year of the Dragon, 1974, Macbeth, 1972; TV shows include, Star Trek, 1966-69, Playhouse '90, 1959, Hercules, 1998; (TV movie) Kissinger and Nixon, 1995, The Best Bad Thing, 1997; announcer, radio personality, The Howard Stern Show, Sirius Satellite Radio, 2006-. Trustee, Japanese Am. Nat. Mus., L.A. Theatre Ctr., 1984—; dir., v.p. So. Calif. Rapid Transit Dist., L.A., 1973-84. Mem. Nat. Japanese-Am. Citizens League (cultural affairs chmn. 1970-73), SAG, Assn. of Asian Pacific Am. Artists, Am. Pub. Transit Assn. (v.p. 1978-80). Democrat. Buddhist. Avocations: running, architecture, historic preservation. Mailing: Hosato Enterprises Inc PMB 82 419 N Larchmont Blvd # 41 Los Angeles CA 90004-3013

TAKENAKA, TOSHIKO, lawyer, educator; b. Tokyo, July 10, 1958; LLB, Seikei Univ., Tokyo, 1981; LLM, Univ. Wash., 1990, PhD, 1992. Bar: N.Y. 1993. Patent preparation analyst Texas Instruments Japan, 1981—86; assoc. Yamasaki Law & Patent Office, Tokyo, 1987—89; vis. rsch. assoc. U. Tokyo, 1999; adj. prof. George Washington U., 1998; vis. scholar US Ct. Appeals Fed cir., 1998; assoc. prof. U. Washington Sch. Law, 1993—2003, W. Hunter Simpson prof., 2003—, dir. Ctr. Advanced Study & Rsch. Intellectual Property; vis. scholar Max Planck Inst., Munich; vis. prof. Wasenda U., Tokyo, 2003—. Contbr. articles to prof. jour. Mem.: Internat. Assn. for Advancement of Tchg. & Rsch. in Intellectual Property, Am. Intellectual Property Law Assn. (mem. exec. com., Intellectual Property sect.), N.Y. State Bar Assn., Assn. Am. Law Sch. Office: University of Washington Law School 1100 NE Campus Pky Seattle WA 98118 *

TAKESH, FAHI, lawyer; b. Teheran, Iran, Sept. 12, 1969; BA magna cum laude, UCLA, 1992; JD, Loyola Law Sch., 1996. Bar: Calif. 1996. Ptnr., family law practice Harris Ginsberg LLP, LA. Bd. dir., v.p., pres.-elect Harriet Buhai Ctr. for Family Law. Contbg. editor: Calif. Evidence for the Family Law Lawyer, LA County Bar Assn., 1998. Named a Rising Star, So. Calif. Super Lawyers, 2006. Mem.: ABA, State Bar Calif., LA County Bar Assn., Santa Monica Bar Assn., Phi Beta Kappa. Office: Harris Ginsberg LLP Ste 1870 6500 Wilshire Blvd Los Angeles CA 90048 Office Phone: 310-444-6333. Office Fax: 310-444-6330. Business E-Mail: ftakesh@harris-ginsberg.com.

TAKETOMI, SUSAMU, physicist, researcher; b. Chiba City, Japan, Sept. 25, 1950; s. Manjiro and Kimie (Kida) T. B of Engring., U. Tokyo, 1975; DSc, Keio U., Yokohama, Japan, 1989. Rschr. Ctrl. Rsch. Lab. Fuji Elec. Co. Ltd., Yokosuka City, Japan, 1975-85; rschr. Matsumotoyushi Seiyaku Co. Ltd., Yao City, Japan, 1985—; vis. rschr. Keio U., Yokohama, Japan, 1985-89, Seikei U., Tokyo, 1990-95, U. Ctrl. Fla., 1995-96, U. Wash., Seattle, 1996-98, Kans. State U., Manhattan, 1998-2000, Nat. Inst. Stds. and Tech., Gaithersburg, Md., 2001—03, Matsumoto Yeshi-Seiyaku Co. Ltd., Yao City, Japan, 2004—. Lectr. in field. Author: (book) Magnetic Fluids: Principle and Application, 1988, Magnetic Fluid Handbook, 1995. Mem. Am. Phys. Soc., Japan Phys. Soc., Japan Applied Phys. Soc. Avocation: playing violin. Office: Matsumoto Yushi-Seiyaku Co Ltd Shibukawa-Cho 581-0075 Japan Home: 1-1-4 # 201 Osakabe Yao City Osaka 581-0015 Japan also: PMB 1042 6600 NE 78th Ct Ste A3 Portland OR 97218-2821 Office Phone: 81-72-992-5268. Personal E-mail: staketomi@hotmail.com.

TAKEUCHI, ESTHER SANS, chemist; Chemist, rschr. Wilson Greatbatch, Ltd., Clarence, NY, v.p. battery rsch. and devel. Named to Western NY Women's Hall of Fame, 1998; recipient Jacob F. Schoeffjopf medal, 1998. Mem.: NAE, Am. Inst. for Med. and Biological Engring., Am. Chem. Soc. Office: Wilson Greatbatch Ltd 9645 Wehrle Dr Clarence NY 14031-2090

TAKHAR, BONNIE, apparel executive; Sales dir. Nicole Farhi Grp.; sales mgr. Donna Karan; CEO Earl Jean Europe, London, 1999—2002; global pres. Earl Jean, Inc., 2002—04; adv. to CEO bus. devel. Jimmy Choo Ltd., NYC, 2004—06, chief comml. officer, 2006—07; pres., CEO Halston Co., NYC, 2007—. Office: Halston Co 1350 Ave of Americas Ste 2025 New York NY 10019 Office Phone: 212-282-1200. Office Fax: 212-786-6775. *

TAKIS, STEPHANIE, retired state senator; Dem. rep. dist. 36 Colo. Ho. of Reps., 1996-2000; Dem. senator dist. 25 Colo. State Senate, 2000—; fin. specialist FEMA, Denver, 1992—94; rep. AtLarge City Coun., Aurora, Colo., 1989—93; mgmt. analyst U.S. Army, Aurora, Colo., 1983—92; congl. rels. Dept. Commerce, Washington, 1980—82; asst. to sen. Housing & Urban Devel. Com., Washington, 1979—80; ret. Mem. bus. affairs and labor and fin. coms. Colo. Ho. of Reps.; mem. legis. audit coms. Colo. State Senate, bus., labor com.; chair Trans com. Office: Colo State Senate State Capitol 200 E Colfax Denver CO 80203 Business E-Mail: stephanie.takis.senate@state.co.us.

TAKKE, KARYN COPPOCK, social worker, educator; b. Sacramento, June 13, 1961; d. Arthur Clifton Coppock and June Marie Betz; m. Vince Takke, Sept. 15, 1991; children: Jake Taylor, Kyle Hunter, Chad Brigham, Joshua Spencer. BS in Social Work, Brigham Young U., 1982; MSW, U. Tex., Austin, 1989. LCSW Utah. Dir. The Adoption Ctr., Orem, Utah, 2001—; med. social worker Intermountain Health Care-Home Care, Orem, 2002—05; pediat. continuum care mgr. Primary Children's Med. Ctr., Salt Lake City, 2005—. Adj. faculty Brigham Young U., Provo, Utah, 2003—, Utah Valley State Coll., Orem, 2003—. Mem., tchr. The Relief Soc., 1979—; vol. Sun Porch Group Home, Palo Alto, Calif., 1983—86; Sunday sch. tchr. LDS Ch., Calif. and Utah, 1990—; bd. dirs. LDS Family Svcs., Fresno, Calif., 1999. Republican. Avocations: reading, gardening, needlework, baking. Office: Utah Valley State Coll Behavioral Sci Dept 800W University Pky #MC Orem UT 84058 Office Phone: 801-718-4375. Fax: 801-302-7301. E-mail: karyn.takke@intermountainmail.org.

TAKUMI, ROY MITSUO, state legislator; b. Honolulu, Oct. 13, 1952; m. Wanda A. Kutaka; children: Aisha, Jaron. BA, Friends World Coll., 1991; MPA, U. Hawaii, 1993. Cmty. organizer, Osaka, Japan, 1977-83; program dir. Am. Friends Svc. Com., Honolulu, 1984-90; polit. dir. Hawaii State AFL-CIO, Honolulu, 1990-92, comms. dir., 1992—. Rep. Ho. of Reps., Honolulu, 1992—. Office: State Ho Reps State Capitol Honolulu HI 96813 Home Phone: 808-456-2665; Office Phone: 808-586-6170. E-mail: reptakumi@capitol.hawaii.gov.

TAKYAR, MIR SHAHROUZ, electrical engineer, researcher; b. Langeroud, Iran; s. Shahrokh Takyar and Touba Ahmadi. BEE, Sharif U. Tech., Tehran, 2000; MSEE, Sharif U. Tech., 2002; PhD in Elec. Engring., U. Minn., Mpls., 2003—. Rsch. asst. U. Minn., 2003—. Mem.: IEEE. Office: Univ Minn EE/CSci Bldg 200 Union St South E Minneapolis MN 55455

TAL, JACOB, electronics executive; b. Tiberias, Israel, Nov. 29, 1940; s. Refael and Seriora Tboul; m. Rivka Barlev; 1 child, Tomer. BS, Technion, Haifa, Israel, 1966; MS, U. Minn., 1968, PhD, 1970. Rsch. fellow U. Minn., Mpls., 1970-71; prof. elec. engring. U. Utah, Salt Lake City, 1971-78; rsch. engr. Hewlett Packard, Palo Alto, Calif., 1978-81; founder, owner Motion Control Seminar, Mountain View, Calif., 1981—90; founder, chmn. bd. dirs. Galil Motion Control, Mountain View, 1983—. Cons. Control Data, Mpls., 1970—75, Electro Craft, Mpls., 1970—78, Ford Motor Corp., Detroit, 1976—78, Burroughs Corp., Westlake, Calif., 1981—82. Author: Motion Control by Microprocessors, 1984, Motion Control Applications, 1989; author: (with others) Incremental Motion Control, 1978; contbr. articles to profl. jours. Mem.: IEEE, Electronic Motion Control Assn. Avocations: folk dancing, hiking, windsurfing. Office: Galil Motion Control 3750 Atherton Rd Rocklin CA 95765 Office Phone: 916-626-0101. E-mail: jacobt@galilmc.com.

TALALAY, PAUL, pharmacologist, educator; b. Berlin, Mar. 31, 1923; arrived in U.S., 1940, naturalized, 1946; s. Joseph Anton and Sophie (Brosterman) Talalay; m. Pamela Judith Samuels, Jan. 11, 1953; children: Antony, Susan, Rachel, Sarah. SB, MIT, 1944; student, U. Chgo. Sch. Medicine, 1944—46; MD, Yale U., 1948; DSc (hon.), Acadia U., 1974. House officer, asst. resident surg. services Mass. Gen. Hosp., Boston, 1948—50; asst. prof. surgery U. Chgo., 1950—51, asst. prof. biochemistry, 1955—57, assoc. prof., then prof., 1957—63; asst. prof. Ben May Lab. Cancer Research, 1951—57, assoc. prof., then prof., 1957—63; John Jacob Abel prof., dir. dept., pharmacology and exptl. therapeutics Johns Hopkins Sch. Medicine, 1963—75, John Jacob Abel Distinguished Service prof., 1975—. Am. Cancer Soc. prof., 1958—63, 1977—. Sr. asst. surgeon USPHS, 1951—53; vis. prof. Guy's Hosp. Med. Sch., London, 1970, London, 1974—76; nat. adv. cancer coun. USPHS, 1967—71; vis. com. dept. biology MIT, 1964—67; bd. sci. advisers Jane Coffin Childs Meml. Fund for Cancer Rsch., 1971—80; bd. sci. consultants Sloan-Kettering Inst. Cancer Rsch., 1971—81. Hon. editl. adv. bd. Biochem. Pharmacology, 1963—68, editl. bd. Jour. Biol. Chemistry, 1961—66, Molecular Pharmacology, 1965—68, 1971—80, editor-in-chief, 1968—71. Recipient Premio Internationale la Madonnina Milan, 1978, Med. Alumni Disting. Svc. award, U. Chgo., 1978; fellow Guggenheim Meml., 1973—74; scholar Am. Cancer Soc., 1954—58. Fellow: Am. Acad. Arts and Scis.; mem.: NAS, AAAS (Theobald Smith award med. scis. 1957), Am. Soc. Pharm. and Exptl. Therpeutics, Am. Chem. Soc., Biochem. Soc., Am. Soc. Clin. Investigation, Am. Soc. Biochem. Molecular Biology, Am. Philos. Soc., Alpha Omega Alpha, Sigma Xi, Phi Beta Kappa. Home: 5512 Boxhill Ln Baltimore MD 21210-2039 Office: Johns Hopkins U Sch Medicine 725 N Wolfe St Baltimore MD 21205 Office Phone: 410-955-3499. Fax: 410-502-6818. Business E-Mail: ptalalay@jhmi.edu.

TALAMO, JONATHAN HASKELL, ophthalmologist, educator; b. Boston, Sept. 25, 1960; Student, Cornell U., Ithaca, NY, 1978-80; AB, Johns Hopkins U., Balt., Md., 1982, MD, 1986. Diplomate Am. Bd. Ophthalmology. Intern in medicine Children's Hosp. San Francisco-U. Calif., 1986—87; resident in ophthalmology Wilmer Ophthal. Inst., Johns Hopkins Hosp., Balt., 1987—90; clin. fellow ophthalmology, cornea and external disease Mass. Eye and Ear Infirmary-Harvard U. Med. Sch., Boston, 1990—91, asst. surgeon, 1992—95, sr. surgeon, 1995—, dir. gen. eye and cataract consultation svc., 1992—94, dir. keratorefractive surgery unit, 1992—95, acting dir. cornea svc., 1994—95, dir. cornea and external disease fellowship program, 1994—95; pvt. practice Providence, 1991—92, Boston, 1995—. Rsch. fellow in ophthalmology Harvard U. Med. Sch., 1984-85, clin. fellow in ophthalmology, 1990-91, instr. ophthalmology, 1992-94, asst. prof., 1994-95, asst. clin. prof., 1995-2005, assoc. clin. prof., 2005—; clin. fellow in ophthalmology Johns Hopkins U. Med. Sch., 1987-90; asst. clin. prof. dept. surgery Brown U. Sch. Medicine, Providence, 1991-93; attending surgeon Miriam Hosp., Providence, 1991-93, R.I. Hosp., Providence, 1991-93; med. adv. bd. Intralase Corp., 2003—. Author: The Excimer Manual: A Clincians Guide to Excimer Laser Surgery,1996; asst. editor jour. Refractive Surgery, 1994-99; mem. editl. bd. Ophthalmology Times, 1995—; contbr. 70 articles to profl. jours., chpts. to books. Tng. grantee USPHS, 1984, travel grantee Assn. for Rsch. in Vision and Ophthalmology, 1985, N.E. Corneal Transplant Rsch. Fund, 1993-94, Coherent Med., Inc., 1994-95; fellow Fight for Sight, 1985, Heed Ophthalmic Found., 1990. Mem. Am. Acad. Ophthalmology (Honor award 1998), Internat. Soc. Refractive Surgery (bd. dirs. 1995-2001), Am. Soc. Cataract and Refractive Surgery, Soc. Heed Fellows, New Eng. Ophthal. Soc., Mass. Soc. Eye Physiciand and Surgeons. Home Phone: 617-899-7233; Office Phone: 781-890-7797. Business E-Mail: jtalamo@lecb.com.

TALAREK, NICOLAS, geneticist, researcher; b. Marmande, France, Apr. 25, 1978; s. George Stanislas and Anne-Marie Elisabeth Talarek. BS in Molecular Cell Biology, U. Bordeaux, France, 1998, MS in Genetic Molecular Biology, 2001, PhD, 2004. Postdoctoral rschr. Dana Farber Cancer Inst., Boston, 2005—. Fellowship, French Ministry Rsch., 2001—04. Achievements include discovery of of Antiprion drugs; research in conservation of the Prion Mecanisms through evolution. Avocations: squash, movies, cooking, hiking. Office: Dana Farber Cancer Institue 44 Binney St Boston MA 02115 Home Phone: 617-331-9663; Office Phone: 617-632-4340.

TALBERT, CHARLES HAROLD, theologian, educator; b. Jackson, Miss., Mar. 19, 1934; s. Carl E. and Audrey (Hale) T.; m. Betty O'Neal Weaver, June 30, 1961; children: Caroline O'Neil, Charles Richard. BA, Samford U., 1956, LittD (hon.), 1990; BD, So. Bapt. Theol. Sem., Louisville, 1959; PhD, Vanderbilt U., 1963. Asst. prof. Wake Forest U., Winston-Salem, NC, 1963-68, assoc. prof., 1968-74, prof., 1974-89, Wake Forest prof., 1989-96; disting. prof. religion Baylor U., Waco, Tex., 1996—. Author: Reading Luke, 1982, Reading Corinthians, 1987, Learning Through Suffering, 1991, Reading John, 1992, The Apocalypse, 1994, Reading Acts, 1997, Romans, 2002, Reading Luke-Acts in its Mediterranean Milieu, 2003, Reading the Sermon on the Mount, 2004, Literary Patterns, Theological Themes and the Genre of Luke-Acts, 2005, Paldeia: Ephesians and Colossiana, 2007. Postdoctoral fellow U. N.C., 1968-69, Soc. for Values in Higher Edn., 1971-72. Mem. Soc. Bibl. Lit. (editor SBL Dissertation Series, N.T. 1984-86, 87-89, editorial bd. jour. 1984-89), Cath. Bibl. Assn. (assoc. editor Cath. Bibl. Quar. 1991-98, pres. 1999-00), Nat. Assn. Bapt. Profs. Religion (pres. 1985), Studiorum Novi Testamenti Societas. Independent. Baptist. Home: 9602 Old Farm Rd Waco TX 76712-6402 Office: Baylor Univ Dept Religion PO Box 97284 Waco TX 76798-7284 Business E-Mail: charles_talbert@baylor.edu.

TALBERT, DEBRA KAISER, elementary school educator, artist; b. Louisville, May 14, 1970; d. John Richard and Gwen Richter Kaiser, Rochelle Weaver Kaiser (Stepmother); m. John Matthew Talbert, June 20, 1992; 1 child, Alyssa Rose. BFA, Murray State U., Ky., 1994, MA in Edn., 2001. Cert. tchr. Ky. Itinerant art tchr. Massac County Schs. Unit #1, Metropolis, Ill., 1994—97; art tchr. Reidland Elem. Sch., Paducah, Ky., 1997—. Webmaster, tech. leader Reidland Elem. Sch., 2001—, coord. sch. tech., 2006—; mem. Sch. Based Decision Making Coun., Paducah, 2000—03; mem. dist. decision making coun. McCracken County Schs., Paducah, 2002. Mem. Kentuckiana Girl Scouts, Louisville, 1976—87, unit mgr. Paducah, 1994—96; youth leader First Presbyn. Ch., Paducah, 2001—04. Named Outstanding Young Am., 1997. Mem.: McCracken County Edn. Assn., Ky. Edn. Assn. Office: Reidland Elem Sch 5741 Benton Rd Paducah KY 42003 Home Phone: 270-444-8482; Office Phone: 270-538-4180. Personal E-mail: jtalbert0001@comcast.net. E-mail: debra.talbert@mccracken.kyschools.us.

TALBERT, KENT DEAN, federal agency administrator, lawyer; b. Greenwood, SC, 1960; BA magna cum laude, Erskine Coll., 1982; JD, USC, 1985. Staff mem., com. edn. and the workforce US Ho. of Reps.; staff mem., com. health edn. labor and pensions US Senate; staff mem. Office US Senator Strom Thurmond; atty. Columbia, SC; dep. gen. counsel, Divsn. Bus. Adminstrv. Affairs & Divsn. Legis. Counsel US Dept. Edn., Washington, 2001—06, acting gen. counsel, 2005—06, gen. counsel, 2006—. Republican. Office: US Dept Edn Office of Gen Counsel 400 Maryland Ave SW Rm 6E313 Washington DC 20202 Office Phone: 202-401-6000. E-mail: kent.talbert@ed.gov. *

TALBOT, DAVID LYLE, online magazine publisher, former editor; b. LA, Sept. 22, 1951; s. Lyle and Margaret (Epple) T.; m. Camille Marie Peri, Dec. 9, 1989; children: Joseph, Nathaniel. Student, Univ. Calif., 1973. Staff writer Environ. Action Found., Washington, D.C., 1979-81; sr. editor Mother Jones Mag., San Francisco, 1981-85, San Francisco Examiner Image Mag., 1985-86, editor in chief, 1990-93, features editor, 1993-95; founder, chmn. Salon Mag., San Francisco, 1995—, editor-in-chief, 1995—2005. Author: Brothers: The Hidden History of the Kennedy Years, 2007; Co-author: Burning Desires: Sex in America, 1989, Creative Differences: Profiles of Hollywood Dissidents, 1978 Recipient Best Web Site award Time Mag., 1997, Best Web Mag. award Webby Awards, 1998, 99. Office: Salon Mag 22 4th St Fl 16 San Francisco CA 94103-3148 *

TALBOT, DONALD ROY, management consultant; b. Bridgeport, Conn., Jan. 23, 1931; s. Grant Edward and Elvera (Gilbert) T.; m. Beverly Rinebold, Aug. 15, 1953; children: Donna, Randall, Theodore, Timothy, Thomas. B in Marine Engring., N.Y. State Maritime Coll. Project engr. atomic power equipment div. GE, San Jose, Calif., 1952-58; mgr. nuclear labs., nuclear div. Martin Marietta Corp., Balt., 1958-62, project dir. nuclear div., 1962-67, dir. spl. studies Friendship, Md., 1967-71, project dir. environ. programs Balt., 1971-74, dir. environ. tech. ctr. Relay, Md., 1974-83, gen. mgr. environ. systems div. Columbia, Md., 1984-87; corp. v.p. Versar, Inc., Springfield, Va., 1987-89; pres. R.E. Mgmt. Svc., Inc., Towson, Md., 1989—. Recipient Antarctica Svc. medal Civil Engrs. Corps USN, 1965, Cert. of Appreciation Sec. Dept. Commerce, 1975 Avocation: outdoor activities. Home: 712 Hickory Lot Rd Baltimore MD 21286-1427 Office: R E Mgmt Svcs Inc PO Box 10614 Baltimore MD 21285-0614 Office Phone: 410-583-1334.

TALBOT, EMILE JOSEPH, French language educator; b. Brunswick, Maine, Apr. 12, 1941; s. Joseph Emile and Flora Talbot; m. Elizabeth Mullen, Aug. 6, 1966; children: Marc, Paul. BA, St. Francis Coll., Biddeford, Maine, 1963; MA, Brown U., 1965, PhD, 1968. From instr. French to prof. U. Ill., Urbana, 1967—86, prof., 1986—2004, prof. emeritus, 2004—, head dept. French, 1988-94. Editor: (book) La Critique Stendhalienne, 1979; author: Stendhal and Romantic Esthetics, 1985, Stendhal Revisited, 1993, Reading Nelligan, 2002; rev. editor: The French Rev., 1979—82, Quebec Studies, 1988—93, mem. editl. bd.:, 1993—96; mem. editl. bd. Quebec Studies, 2003—05; mem. editl. bd.: Nineteenth-Century French Studies, 1986—2003, La Revue Francophone, 1990—96, Etudes Francophones, 1996—2004, Nouvelles Etudes Francophones, 2004—; editor: Quebec Studies, 2004—. Decorated chevalier Ordre des Palmes Académiques (France); recipient prize, Quebec, 2006; fellow, Ctr. Advanced Study U. Ill., 1973, Assoc., 1988, NEH, 1973—74, Camargo Found., France, 1976. Mem.: MLA, Am. Coun. Que. Studies (v.p. 1995—97, pres. 1997—99), Assn. Can. Studies in U.S., Am. Assn. Tchrs. French. Roman Catholic. Office: U Ill Dept French 707 S Mathews Ave Urbana IL 61801-3625 Home Phone: 217-351-6039; Office Phone: 217-244-2728.

TALBOT, FRANIS, writer; b. Salem, Mass., July 17, 1929; s. Herbert Hersey Talbot and Priscilla Gove Affeld; m. Ellika Elisabet Linden, July 17, 1988; m. Emmy Rainwalker (div.); children: Tokeem, Tashin. BA, Cornell U., Ithaca, NY, 1954; MEd, Lexington U., Ky., 1974; PhD, Am. Coll. Metaphys. Theology, Mpls., 2002. Mem. adv. bd. Nature Sch., Greenville, NH, 2000—, Keepers of the Lore, Milford, NH, Hawkwind, Ala.; spkr. UN Meml. Editor: Akwesasne Notes, 1976, Heritage, 1997. Bd. dirs. Mettanokit Native Prisoner Program, 1985—. With US Army, 1951—53, ETO. Home: 167 Marriam Hill Rd Greenville NH 03048

TALBOT, LEE MERRIAM, ecologist, educator, director; b. New Bedford, Mass., Aug. 2, 1930; s. Murrell Williams and Zenaida (Merriam) T.; m. Martha Walcott Hayne, May 16, 1959; children: Lawrence Hayne, Russell Merriam. BA, U. Calif., Berkeley, 1953, MA, PhD, U. Calif., Berkeley, 1963. Biologist Arctic Research Lab., Point Barrow, Alaska, 1951; staff ecologist Internat. Union for Conservation, Brussels, 1954-56; ecologist, dir. East African ecol. research project Nat. Acad. Scis., Govts. of Kenya and Tanzania, 1959-63; wildlife advisor UN Spl. Fund, Africa, 1963-64; dir. S.E. Asia project Internat. Union for Conservation, 1964-65; resident ecologist, field rep. for internat. affairs Smithsonian Instn., Washington, 1966-70; sr. scientist, dir. internat. activities Pres.'s Council on Environ. Quality, Washington, 1970-78; sr. sci. advisor Internat. Council Sci. Unions, Paris, 1978-83; dir. conservation, spl. sci. advisor World Wildlife Fund Internat., Switzerland, 1978-80; dir. gen. Internat. Union for Conservation of Nature and Natural Resources, Gland, Switzerland, 1980-83; resident fellow Environ. and Policy Inst., East West Ctr., 1983-87; vis. fellow World Resources Inst., Washington, 1984-89; sr. environ. advisor World Bank, 1984—; pres. Lee Talbot Assocs. Internat., 1991—; sr. prof. environ. scis., internat. affairs and pub. policy George Mason U., Va., 1994—, affiliate prof. geography, 2007—. Cons. UNESCO, World Bank, Asian Devel. Bank, Nat. Geog. Soc., Inter-Am. Devel. Bank, The Nature Conservancy, U.S. Govt., U. Calif., UN Spl. Fund, WHO, UN Environment Program, UN Univ., UN Devel. Programme, African and Asian Govts.; conservation coord. Internat. Biol. Program, 1965-70; bd. dirs. Defenders of Wildlife; mem. corp. NY Bot. Gardens; mem. sci. adv. coun. Nat. Pks. Conservation Assn., Bailey Wildlife Compensation Trust; founding trustee Inst. Ecosys. Studies, NY, 2006; mem. pres.'s coun. Population Reference Bur., 2007—. Author 17 books and monographs; contbr. more than 270 articles to profl. jours. Active Boy Scouts Am., Geneva, 1980-82, Washington, 1987-95. With USMC, 1953-54. Decorated officer Order of Lion (Senegal); recipient Regents Lectureship award U. Calif., Santa Barbara, 1986, Pierre Chaleur prize French Acad. Scis., 1993, Festschrift Career Accomplishments award George Mason U., 2003, World Commn. Protected Areas East Asia award, 2005; named Disting. Alumnus, 1953 Officer Candidate Sch., USMC, 2003; Centenary Symposium named in his honor Bombay Natural History Soc., 2003 Fellow Royal Geog. Soc., Royal Soc. Arts, AAAS, N.Y. Zool. Soc.; mem. Am. Inst. Biol. Scis. (Disting. Scientist award 1979), Acad. Medicine, World Conservation Union (hon.), Am. Assn. for Club of Rome, Am. Soc. Mammalogists, Ecol. Soc., Wildlife Soc. (Outstanding Publ. award 1963), Soc. for Conservation Biology, Internat. Soc. for Ecol. Econs., Boone and Crockett Club (N.Y.C.), Explorers Club (N.Y.C.), Cosmos Club (Washington), Sigma Xi, Phi Kappa Sigma. Achievements include incorporation of ecological principles in international development; development of new principles for management of wild resources; biodiversity conservation; definition of ecosystem dynamics of tropical savannahs including role of fire, feeding habits and migrations of wild herbivores; development and negotiation of national legislation and international agreements for environmental protection. Home: 6656 Chilton Ct Mc Lean VA 22101-4422 *My career is based on two premises: first, that our most important challenges are environmental issues which determine the earth's carrying capacity for human life and, equally important, the quality of that life; and second, that it is important to obtain direct experience in as much of the world as possible to understand the human ecological setting as a basis for action to improve it.*

TALBOT, MARTHA HAYNE, conservationist, biologist; b. San Francisco, Aug. 3, 1932; d. Francis Bourn and Anna (Walcott) Hayne; m. Lee Merriam Talbot, May 16, 1959; children: Lawrence Hayne, Russell Merriam. BA, Vassar Coll., 1954. Co-founder, asst. dir. student conservation program U.S. Nat. Parks, 1955-59; co-dir. East African Ecol. Rsch. Project, Kenya and Tanzania, 1959-63; asst. dir. S.E. Asia Project, Internat. Union for Conservation of Nature/Natural Resources, 1964-65; asst. coord. Internat. Biol. Programme, London, 1966; rsch. assoc. Smithsonian Instn., Washington, 1966-75; mem., treas. Fairfax County Park Authority, Fairfax, Va., 1973-77; sec.-treas. Talbot Racing Assocs., McLean, Va., 1983—; owner, dir. Talbot Hayne Vineyard, St. Helena, Calif., 1988—; sec.-treas. Lee Talbot Assocs. Internat., McLean, 1991—. Bd. dir. Student Conservation Assn., 1966-78, 83-87, hon. dir., 1987— (Svc. Honor award), Defenders of Wildlife, 1974-77, Audubon Naturalist Soc., 1975-78, Rachel Carson Coun., 1975-94, treas., 1994-98, v.p., 1998—. Co-author: Introduction to the Landscape, East Africa, 1961; co-editor: Conservation in Tropical South East Asia, 1968; contbr. articles to profl. jours. Leader Boy Scouts Am., Geneva, 1978-83, transp. coord., McLean, 1989-95; mem. Woman's Nat. Dem. Club. Recipient Outstanding Pub. award The Wildlife Soc., 1963, Cinema Golden Eagle award Documentary Film, 1968, Disting. Alumna award Katharine Branson Sch., 1981, Conservation Svc. award U.S. Dept. Interior, 1986, Bd. Tribute to co-founder, Student Conservation Assn., 1984, Resolution of Honor, 1999; N.Y. Zool. Soc. grantee, 1961; co-recipient World Comm. on Protected Areas East Asia award, 2005 Mem. Soc. Woman Geographers (bd. dir. 1972-75, treas. 1984-89, treas. Washington group 1990-96), Napa Valley Grape Growers Assn., Rachels Network, Explorers Club, Woman's Nat. Dem. Club. Avocations: backpacking, hiking, bicycling, travel, swimming. Home: 6656 Chilton Ct Mc Lean VA 22101-4422

TALBOT, MARY LEE, minister; b. Cleve., Apr. 18, 1953; d. Richard William and Mary Helen (Jacobs) T. BA, Coll. Wooster, 1975; MDiv, Andover-Newton Theol. Sch., 1979; MPhil, Tchrs. Coll. Columbia U., 1990; PhD, Columbia U., 1997. Ordained to ministry Presbyterian Ch. (U.S.A.), 1981. Asst. in ministry Grace Congl. Ch., Framingham, Mass., 1975-78; resources coord. Women's Theol. Coalition, Boston, 1977-79; assoc. editor Youth Mag., Phila., 1979-80; co-dir. youth and young adult program Presbyn. Ch. U.S.A., NYC, 1981-88; cons. in religious edn. NYC, 1988-90; dir. continuing edn. Pitts. Theol. Sem., Pitts., 1990—2001; interim pastor Hebron U.P. Ch., Clinton, 2002—03, supply pastor, 2004—. Bd. dirs. Christian Assn., U. Pa., 1979-81; mem. religion com. Chautauqua Inst., 1988-91. Author, editor Suicide and Youth, 1981, (newsletter) Trackings, 1986—88; editor: Racism and Anti-Racism, 1982, One Fantastic Book, 1982, My Identity: A Gift from God, 1987, A Guidebook for Presbyterian Youth Ministry, 1988, God's Gift of Sexuality, 1989, Celebrate Bible Study, 1990, The C.L.S.C. Banner Book, 2004; contbr. articles to popular mags., profl. jours. Bd. dirs. Christian Assn., U. Pa., 1979-81. Recipient English award Bus. and Profl. Women, 1971. Mem. Assn. Presbyn. Ch. Educators, Assn. Presbyn. Clergywomen, Religious Edn. Assn. (bd. dirs. 1986-91), History of Edn. Soc., Kappa Delta Pi. Democrat. Office: 1767 Rte 30 Clinton PA 15026 Office Phone: 724-899-2620. Personal E-mail: mltalbot@aol.com.

TALBOT, NYNA LUCILLE, psychologist, writer; b. Warrington, Eng., May 24, 1954; d. John Robert Talbot and Lois June Snow. MA, Calif. Inst. Integral Studies, 1997, PhD, 2000; BA, Elmhurst Coll., 1976. Sr. tech. writer Hitachi Data Sys., Santa Clara, Calif., 1986—2006; clinical psychologist Royal Cornhill Hosp., Aberdeen, Scotland, 2007—. Clin. psychology intern San Mateo County Emergency Response Team, 1990—91, San Mateo County Mental Health Svcs., Half Moon Bay, 2000—01. Clin. psychology intern mem. Red Cross, San Mateo, 1990—91. Mem.: Internat. Coun. Psychologists, Assn. Transpersonal Psychology, APA. Achievements include research in the relationship of companionship coupling in two significant populations. Avocations: painting, poetry. Home: Dogshillock Aberchirder by Huntly Aberdeenshire AB547PS Scotland Home Phone: 01466 780 291. Personal E-mail: drnyna@yahoo.com. Business E-Mail: ntalbot@nhs.net.

TALBOT, PAMELA, public relations executive; b. Chgo., Aug. 10, 1946; BA in English, Vassar Coll., 1968. Reporter Worcester, Mass. Telegram and Gazette, 1970—72; account exec. Daniel J. Edelman, Inc., Chgo., 1972—74, account supr., 1974—76, v.p., 1976—78, sr. v.p., 1978—84, exec. v.p., gen. mgr., 1984—90; pres. Edelman West, Chgo., 1990—95; pres., CEO Edelman U.S., 1995—. Named a Pub. Rels. All Star, PR Mag.; recipient Silver Anvil award, Publicity Club Chgo., Golden Trumpet award. Mem.: PRSA, Chgo. Network, Execs. Club Chgo. Office: Edelman Pub Rels 200 E Randolph Dr Ste 6300 Chicago IL 60601-6436 Business E-Mail: pam.talbot@edelman.com.

TALBOT, PHILLIPS, retired Asian affairs specialist; b. Pitts., June 7, 1915; s. Kenneth Hammet and Gertrude (Phillips) T.; m. Mildred Aleen Fisher, Aug. 18, 1943 (dec. June 20, 2004); children: Susan Talbot Jacox, Nancy, Bruce Kenneth (dec.). BA, U. Ill., 1936, BS in Journalism, 1936; student, London Sch. Oriental Studies, 1938—39, Aligarh Muslim U., India, 1939—40; PhD, U. Chgo., 1954; LLD (hon.), Mills Coll., 1963, Elmhurst Coll., Ill., 2007. Reporter Chgo. Daily News, 1936-38, corr. India and Pakistan, 1946-48, 49-50; assoc. Inst. Current World Affairs, 1938-41,

46-51; instr. U. Chgo., 1948-50, Columbia U., NYC, 1951; exec. dir. Am. Univs. Field Staff, 1951-61; asst. sec. Near Eastern and S. Asian affairs Dept. State, 1961-65; U.S. amb. to Greece, 1965-69; pres. Asia Soc., NYC, 1970-81, pres. emeritus, 1981—. Phi Beta Kappa vis. scholar, 1973-74. Author: (with S.L. Poplai) India and America, 1958, India in the 1980s, 1983; editor: South Asia in the World Today, 1950, An American Witness to India's Partition, 2007. Life trustee Aspen Inst., US-Japan Found.; counselor United Bd. for Christian Higher Edn. in Asia; elder Presbyn. Ch. 2d lt. cav. Officers Res. Corps, 1936; 1st lt. NG, 1937-38; lt. comdr. USNR, 1941-46. Recipient Padma Shri honors, India, 2002, Bharatiya Shiromani Purskar award, 2006. Mem. Am. Acad. Diplomacy, Coun. Am. Ambs., Coun. Fgn. Rels., Century Assn., Cosmos Club. Address: 200 E 66th St New York NY 10065-9178 Personal E-mail: talbotp@pipeline.com.

TALBOT, PIERRE JOSEPH, microbiologist, researcher; b. Quebec City, Que., Can., July 11, 1956; s. Arthur and Suzanne (Hudon) T.; m. France Ouellet, July 29, 1977; children: Natalie, Benoit, Dominic. BSc in Biochemistry, Laval U., Ste-Foy, Que., 1977; PhD in Biochemistry, U. B.C., Vancouver, 1981. Rsch. assoc. Scripps Clinic and Rsch. Found., La Jolla, Calif., 1981-84; asst. prof. Inst. Armand-Frappier U. Que., Laval, 1984-89; assoc. prof. Inst. Armand-Frappier, Laval, Que., 1989-92, prof., 1992—, dir. Human Health Rsch. Ctr., 1998—2001; dir. INRS Inst. Armand-Frappier, 2002—. Com. reviewer Med. Rsch. Coun., Ottawa, Ont., Can., 1989-96, 98-2000, Multiple Sclerosis Soc., Toronto, Ont., 1993-96, Nat. Sci. Engring. Res. Coun., Ottawa, 1999-2002, Can. Inst. Health Rsch., 1998—. Mem. editl. bd. Viral Immunology, San Antonio, 1990-99; contbr. articles to Virology, Jour. Virology, Annals Neurology, Jour. Immunology. Fonds de la Recherche en Santé du Que. scholar of exceptional merit, 1992-97. Mem. AAAS, Am. Soc. Virology, Am. Soc. Microbiology, Can. Soc. Microbiologists (Fisher Sci. award 1987, Roche Diagnostics award 2002), Can. Soc. Immunology, Assn. Can.-Francaise Pour L'Avancement des Scis., Internat. Soc. Neuroimmunology, Internat. Soc. Neurovirology. Achievements include research in immuno- and molecular biology of neurotropic coronaviruses and possible involvement in neurologic disease. Office: INRS Inst Armand-Frappier 531 Boul Des Prairies Laval PQ Canada H7V 1B7 Home: 92 ch du Grand Moulin Deux Montagnes PQ Canada J7R 3C7 Home Phone: 450-623-3268; Office Phone: 450-687-5010. Business E-Mail: pierre.talbot@iaf.inrs.ca.

TALBOTT, BEN JOHNSON, JR., lawyer; b. Louisville, May 2, 1940; s. Ben Johnson and Elizabeth (Farnsley) Talbott; m. Sandra Riehl, Oct. 19, 1963; children: Elizabeth, Betty, John, Ben, Sandra. AB magna cum laude, Xavier U., Cin., 1961; LLB, Harvard U., 1964. Bar: Ky. 1965, U.S. Ct. Appeals (6th cir.) 1967. Law clk. to presiding justice U.S. Dist. Ct. Ky., Louisville, 1964-65; assoc. Middleton, Reutlinger & Baird, Louisville, 1965-68, ptnr., 1968-80, Westfall, Talbott & Woods, Louisville, 1980-2000, Talbott & Talbott, PLLC, Louisville, 2000—04, Bardenwerper, Talbott & Roberts, PLLC, Louisville, 2004—. Atty. Stitzel-Weller Distillery, 1970—72, Louisville Gen. Hosp., 1974—83, Louisville and Jefferson County Bd. Health, 1974—80, U. Louisville, 1980—95. Mem. adv. bd. Louisville 15, Sta. WKPC-TV, bd. dirs., 1972—74, pres., 1974; past bd. dirs. U. Louisville Found., U. Louisville Med. Sch. Fund Orgn.; bd. dirs. Louisville Theatrical Assn., 1971—, pres., 1975—76, chmn., 1977—78; bd. dirs. Def. Enterprise Fund, 1994—2006, Macauley Theatre, 1975, TARC Adv. Com., 1971, Jefferson County Capital Constrn. Com., 1971, Louisville Orch., 1976—86, pres., 1979—81; bd. dirs. Ky. Ctr. Arts, 1983—2006, Louisville Lung Assn., 1974—75, treas., 1975; bd. dirs. Hist. Homes Found., 1972—78, 1995—97, 2000—01, 2002—06, v.p., 1978, 2002—06, advisor, atty., 1978—98; bd. regents Whitehall, 1993—2001; trustee U. Louisville, 1970—79, sec., 1974, vice chmn., 1975, chmn. fin. com., 1976. Named an Outstanding Young Man of Louisville, Louisville Jaycees, 1976. Mem.: SAR, ABA, Louisville Bar Assn. (past mem. exec. com.), Def. Rsch. and Trial Lawyers Assn., Ky. Bar Assn. (chmn. 1989, Gen. Practice Session of CLE), Alden Kindred Am., Inc., Mayflower Soc., Soc. Colonial Wars, St. Andrews Club, Big Sand Lake Club, Louisville Boat Club, Pendennis Club, Harvard Law Sch. Assn. Ky. (sec. 1965, pres. 1989—), Filson Hist. Soc., Louisville Country Club, U. Louisville Club, Gulf Stream Bath and Tennis Club, Country Club Fla., Phi Kappa Phi (bd. dirs., treas. Louisville chpt. 1990—). Avocations: golf, tennis, skiing, fishing. Home: 566 Blankenbaker Ln Louisville KY 40207-1167 Office: Bardenwerper Talbott & Roberts PLLC 8311 Shelbyville Rd Louisville KY 40222 Home Phone: 502-895-8251; Office Phone: 502-426-6688. Business E-Mail: lynn@bardlaw.net.

TALBOTT, CLOYCE A., energy executive; BS in Petroleum Engring., Tex. Tech U., Lubbock. Co-founder, bd. dirs. Patterson-UTI Energy, Inc. (formerly Patterson Drilling Co. and then Patterson Energy before merging with UTI Energy in 2001), Snyder, Tex., 1978—; v.p. Patterson-UTI Energy, Inc. (formerly Patterson Drilling Co. and then Patterson Energy before merging with UTI Energy), 1978—83, chmn., 1983—2001, CEO, 1983—, pres., 2006—. Office: Patterson-UTI Energy Inc PO Box 1416 Snyder TX 79550 Office Phone: 325-574-6300. Office Fax: 325-574-6390. *

TALBOTT, FRANK, III, lawyer; b. Danville, Va., Mar. 26, 1929; s. Frank and Margaret (Jordan) Talbott; m. Mary Beverley Chewning, July 11, 1952; children: Beverley, Frank IV. BA, U. Va., 1951, LLB, 1953. Bar: Va. 1952. With firm Meade, Talbott & Tate, Danville, 1956—59, Talbott, Wheatley & Talbott, Danville, 1959—66; with Dan River Inc., 1966-76, v.p., gen. counsel, 1968-76; ptnr. firm Clement, Wheatley, Winston, Talbott & Majors, Danville, 1977-78; individual practice law Danville, 1979-92; gen. counsel Va. Mfrs. Assn. Inc., 1983-92; of counsel Woods, Rogers PLC, Danville, Va., 1992—. Chmn. adv. bd. NationsBank, Danville, 1984-94. Vice-chmn. Danville Sch. Bd., 1964-70; trustee Va. Student Aid Found., 1963-68; bd. dirs. United Fund Danville, 1959-63, Meml. Hosp., Danville, 1977-90. Served with AUS, 1953-56. Decorated Commendation medal. Fellow Am. Bar Found. (life); mem. Va. Bar Assn. (v.p. 1965-66, exec. com. 1967-70), Danville Bar Assn. (pres. 1965-66), Am. Judicature Soc., Newcomen Soc., U. Va. Alumni Assn. (bd. mgrs.), Danville Golf Club, Farmington Country Club, Country Club Va., Country Club of North Carolina, Delta Psi, Phi Alpha Delta. Methodist. Home: 221 Salisbury Cir Danville VA 24541-5571 Office: 341 Main St Danville VA 24541

TALBOTT, STROBE, think-tank executive; b. Dayton, Ohio, Apr. 25, 1946; s. Nelson S. and Josephine (Large) T.; m. Brooke Lloyd Shearer, Nov. 14, 1971; children: Devin Lloyd, Adrian Nelson. BA, Yale U., 1968, MA (hon.), 1976; MLitt, Oxford U., Eng., 1971. East european corr. Time Mag., 1971-73, U.S. state dept. corr., 1973-75, white house corr., 1975-77, diplomatic corr., 1977-84, chief Washington bur. & fgn. affairs columnist, 1984-89, editor at large, 1989-94; amb. at large & spl. advisor to the Sec. of State on the new independent states U.S. Dept. State, Washington, 1993—94, dep. sec. state, 1994—2001; pres. Brookings Instn., Washington, 2002—. Editor, translator: Khrushchev Remembers, 1970, (with Edward Crankshaw) Khrushchev Remembers: The Last Testament, 1974, The Age of Terror: America & The World After September 11, 2001; author: Endgame: Inside Story of SALT II, 1979, Deadly Gambits: Reagan Administration & Arms Controls, 1984, The Russians and Reagan, 1984, Reagan and Gorbachev, 1987, The Master of the Game: Paul Nitze and the Nuclear Peace, 1988, (with Michael Beschloss) At the Highest Levels: The Inside Story of the End of the Cold War, 1993, The Russia Hand: A Memoir of Presidential Diplomacy, 2002, (with Robert L. Suettinger) Beyond Tiananmen: The Politics of U.S.-China Relations 1989-2000, 2003, Engaging India: Diplomacy, Democracy, and the Bomb, 2004. Trustee Yale U. 1976-82, Hotchkiss Sch., 1982-87; bd. dirs. Carnegie Endowment Internat. Peace; Council on Fgn. Relations. Recipient Edward Weintal Prize for Disting. Diplomatic Reporting Georgetown U., Overseas Press Club award, Stanley Hillman award. Office: Brookings Instn 1775 Massachusetts Ave NW Washington DC 20036 *

TALENT, JAMES MATTHES, former senator, congressman, lawyer; b. Des Peres, Mo., Oct. 18, 1956; m. Brenda Lyons, 1984; children: Michael, Kathleen Marie, Christine. BA in Polit. Sci., Washington U., 1978; JD, U. Chgo. Law Sch., 1981. Law clk. to Hon. Richard A. Posner US Ct. Appeals (7th Cir.), 1982—83; adj. prof. law Washington U. Sch. Law, 1984—86; mem. Mo. State Ho. Reps., 1985—93, minority leader, 1989-93; mem. US Congress from 2nd Mo. Dist., 1993—2001, mem. edn. and the workforce com., armed svcs. com., chmn. small bus. com., 1993—2001; US Senator from Mo., 2002—07. Legislative Achievement award Mo. Hosp. Assn., 1989, Legis. of Yr. award Dept. Mo. Veterans Fgn. Wars, Spirit Enterprise award, Mo. C. of C., 1990, Nat. Public Policy award Nat. Assn. Women Bus. Owners, Lifetime Achievement award Vietnam Veterans of Am. 2000, Lawmaker of Yr. award Independent Electrical Contractors, Inc., 2004 Mem. Mo. Bar Assn. (Award for significant contbns. to adminstrv. justice 1989), Mo. C. of C. (Spirit of Enterprise award 1990), Order of the Coif. Republican. Presbyterian. *

TALESE, GAY, writer; b. Ocean City, NJ, Feb. 7, 1932; s. Joseph Francis and Catherine (DiPaola) T.; m. Nan Ahearn, June 10, 1959; children—Pamela, Catherine. BA in Journalism, U. Ala., 1953. Staff writer N.Y. Times, NYC, 1955-65; writer Esquire mag., NYC, 1960. Author: New York - A Serendipiter's Journey, 1961, The Bridge, 1964, The Overreachers, 1965, The Kingdom and the Power, 1969, Fame and Obscurity, 1970, Honor Thy Father, 1971, Thy Neighbor's Wife, 1980, Unto the Sons, 1992, A Writer's Life, 2006; co-author: (with Barbara Lounsberry) The Literature of Reality, 1995; editor: Italians in America: A Celebration, 2001, The Gay Talese Reader, 2003; contbr. articles to Esquire mag., The New Yorker, others. Served to 1st lt. AUS, 1954-56. Mem. P.E.N. (v.p. 1984-87, bd. dir. 1980—), Phi Sigma Kappa. Home: 109 E 61st St New York NY 10065-8101 also: 154 E Atlantic Blvd Ocean City NJ 08226-4511 Office Phone: 212-753-3820.

TALESE, NAN AHEARN, freelance/self-employed publishing executive; b. NYC, Dec. 19, 1933; d. Thomas James and Suzanne Sherman (Russell) Ahearn; m. Gay Talese, June 10, 1959; children: Pamela Frances, Catherine Gay. BA, Manhattanville Coll. of Sacred Heart, 1955; LHD (hon.), Manhattanville, 2003. Fgn. exchange student 1st Nat. City Bank, London and Paris, 1956; editorial asst. Am. Eugenics Soc., NYC, 1957-58, Vogue mag., NYC, 1958-59; copy editor Random House Pub., NYC, 1959-64, assoc. editor, 1964-67, sr. editor, 1967-73, Simon & Schuster Pubs., NYC, 1974-81, v.p., 1979-81; exec. editor, v.p. Houghton Mifflin Co., NYC, 1981-83, v.p., editor-in-chief, 1984-86, v.p., pub., editor-in-chief, 1986-88; sr. v.p. Doubleday & Co., NYC, 1988—; pres., pub., editorial dir. Nan A. Talese Books, 1990—.

TALESNICK, STANLEY, lawyer; b. Indpls., June 4, 1927; s. Louis and Rose (Galerman) T.; m. Joan Goldstone, Mar. 16, 1952 (div. Feb. 1967); children: Jill Wilkins, Jane Talesnick, Kay Gilmore; m. Claudia Jean Ferrell, Nov. 28, 1969 (dec.). AB, Ind. U., 1948, LLB, 1950, JD, 1967. Bar: Ind. 1950, US Dist. Ct. (no. and so. dists.) Ind. 1950, US Dist. Ct. (ea. dist.) Wis. 1991, US Ct. Appeals (7th cir.) 1961, US Supreme Ct. 1980. Ptnr. Dulberger, Talesnick, Claycombe & Bagal, Indpls., 1952-57, Bagal & Talesnick, Indpls., 1957-67, Talesnick & Kleiman, Indpls., 1967-74, Dann Pecar Newman Talesnick & Kleiman, Indpls., 1974-94; bankruptcy and creditor's rights counsel Leagre, Chandler & Millard, Indpls., 1995-1999; of counsel Ancel & Dunlap, LLP, 2000—01, Sommer Barnard PC (merger), 2002—. Asst. city atty. City of Indpls., 1959-67; instr. bus. law Butler U., Indpls., 1981-82. Chmn. Ind. bd. NCCJ, 1974-76; v.p. Jewish Fedn. Greater Indpls., 1985-89, pres. 1989-91; bd. dir. Coun. Jewish Fedns. (now United Jewish Cmtys.), 1986-90; treas. Indpls. Hebrew Congregation, 1967-70; v.p. Indpls. Hebrew Congregation Found., 1992-96. With USN, 1945-46, USNR. Disting. fellow Ind. Bar Assn.; recipient Liebert I. Mossler Cmty. Svc. award outstanding & enduring vol. svcs. Jewish Fedn. Greater Indpls. Inc., 1997. Fellow Comml. Law Found., Internat. Bar Found.; mem. Ind. State Bar Assn. (ho. of dels. 1985-2005, past chair sr. lawyer sect., 2006—), Indpls. Bar Assn. (v.p. 1989-90, chmn. comml. and bankruptcy sect. 1985, bd. mgr. 1994-96), Comml. Law League Am., B'nai Brith (local pres. 1957-58). Democrat. Jewish. Office: One Indiana Sq Ste 3500 Indianapolis IN 46204 Office Phone: 317-713-3500. Office Fax: 317-715-4546. Business E-Mail: stalesnick@sommerbarnard.com.

TALIAFERRO, PHILIP, III, lawyer; b. Cin., July 10, 1937; s. Philip II and Shirley (Denny) T.; children from previous marriage: Greg, Gina, Laura Elizabeth, Morgan; m. Diana Perryman, Nov. 12, 1989; 1 child, Philip IV. BA in Bus., Centre Coll., Danville, Ky., 1959; JD, U. Ky., 1962. Bar: Ky. 1962, US Dist. Ct. (ea. dist.) Ky. 1966, US Dist. Ct. (so. dist.) Ohio 1966, US Ct. Appeals (6th cir.) 1968, US Supreme Ct. 1970, Ohio 1991. Assoc. Ware, Bryson, Nolan & West, 1966-69; ptnr. Davies, Nelson & Taliaferro, 1969-72; sr. ptnr., founder Taliaferro, Smith, Mann, Wolnitzek & Schachter, 1972-86; sr. ptnr. Taliaferro and Mann, 1986-92, Taliaferro and Mehling, Covington, Ky., 1993—96; ptnr. Taliaferro, Mehling, Shirooni, Carran & Keys, PLLC, 1996—2006; sr. ptnr. Taliaferro, Shirooni, Carran & Keys, PLLC, Covington, 2007—. Bd. editors U. Ky. Law Jour., 1960-62; asst. prosecutor Kenton County, Ky., 1967-72; personnel bd. Commonwealth Ky., 1972-87; chmn. emeritus 1988; adj. prof. Salmon P. Chase Coll. Law No. Ky. U., 1984-2001; spl. justice Ky. So. Ct., 1994; lectr. in field. Mem. Greater Cin. Tall Stacks Commn., Inc., 1989-92, sec., 1990-92, trustee, 1990-92; mem. pres.'s coun. Dan Beard Coun. Boy Scouts Am., 1990—; chmn. Kenton County, Ky. Bicentennial Commn., 1990-92; trustee Covington Ladies Home, Inc., 1991-93; bd. dirs. Common Cause Ky., 1991-2001, No. Ky. Bd. Regents, 1987-90, 92-98; vice chmn. bd. regents No. Ky. U., 1992-93; founding trustee No. Ky. Leadership Found.; Master of Bench Salmon P. Chase Inn of Ct., 1993-. Lt. (JAG) USNR, 1962-66, Vietnam, with USNR, 1966-69. Recipient Outstanding Dedication and Svc. to State Employees award Ky. Assn. State Employees, 1983, Outstanding Leadership, Accomplishments and Kinship to Career Employees, Ky. State Tenure Club, 1984, Award of Merit, Transitions, 1985, Silver Beaver award Boy Scouts Am., 1996; named Boss of Yr., No. Ky. Legal Secs. Assn., 1991. Fellow: Internat. Acad. Trial Attys.; mem. ABA, Am. Arbitration Assn. (arbitrator), Assn. Trial Lawyers Am., Cin. Bar Assn., Ky. Bar Assn., No. Ky. Bar Assn. (Disting. Svc. award 1995), Ky. Acad. Trial Attys. (regional v.p. 1981, 82, treas. 1983, sec. 1984, v.p. 1986, bd. govs. 1987-, Outstanding Trial Lawyer of Yr. award 1996), Louisville Bar Assn., Centre Coll. Alumni Assn. (dir., Disting. Alumnus award 2002), Am. Legion, Navy League US (no. Ky. chpt.), Mil. Order Fgn. Wars, VFW, Omicron Delta Kappa, Phi Delta Phi. Office Phone: 859-291-9900. Business E-Mail: ptaliaferro@tmsck.com.

TALIAFERRO, ROBERT See **BROOKE, TAL**

TALIS, ESTHER R., educator, writer; b. NYC, Feb. 20; d. Louis Rogoff and Ida Fishman; m. Harold Talis (dec.); children: Stephen, George, Richard. BA, Hunter Coll., NYC; MA, PhD, Columbia U., NYC. Substitute tchr. Hunter Coll. H.S., NYC; instr. Hunter Coll., NYC, asst. prof., assoc. prof., prof., dept. chmn. Chmn. Temple Beth El, San Pedro, Calif. Recipient Zebulon award, Temple Beth El, San Pedro. Mem.: Omicron Delta Epsilon.

TALL, SUSAN PORTER, music educator; b. NYC, Apr. 16, 1942; m. Alan R. Tall, July 27, 1979; 1 child, Alexander A.; m. Burton F. Porter (div.); 1 child from previous marriage, Anastasia Porter. BA, Montclair State U., 1965; MA in Musicology, NYU, 1973; postgrad., U. Ill., 1978—80. Instr. music Am. Sch. London, 1966—68; instr. music, dir. inst. music Russell Sage Coll., Troy, NY, 1971—74; grad. asst. in conducting U. Ill., Champagne-Urbana, 1978—79; mem. faculty music Tenafly Sch. Sys., NJ, 1980—. Dir. music, condr. Presbyn. Ch., Tenafly, 1980—90, 1995—2005, North Jersey Symphony Orch., Tenafly, 1984—89, Concerto Orch. N.J., Tenafly, 1986—88; guest condr. in field. Organizer, dir. Fanfare for Humanity, Tenafly, 2001, 2005, THS Chorus and Orch. Benefit, Tenafly, 2005. Nominee Disting. Secondary Sch. Tchg. award, Princeton U., 1990; named Tchr. of Yr., Tenafly Sch. Dist., 2002; recipient Disting. Tchg. award, Tenafly H.S., 2002, Tchr. Recognition award, Gov., N.J., 2002, Disting. Leadership in Arts Edn. award, Gov. of N.J., 1997. Mem.: N.J. Music Educators Assn. (Master Tchr. award 1997). Avocation: classical guitar. Home: PO Box 104 Cresskill NJ 07626 Office: Tenafly Sch Dist Dept Music 19 Columbus Dr Tenafly NJ 07626 Office Phone: 201-816-6621. Business E-Mail: stall@tenafly.k12.nj.us.

TALLACKSON, JEFFREY STEPHEN, lawyer; b. Washington, May 10, 1943; s. John Robert and Betty Marcelle (Crockett) T.; m. Christine Ann Johnson, Aug. 10, 1974. BA, Yale U., 1965; LLB, Columbia U., 1968. Bar: N.Y. 1968. Law clk. to judge US Dist. Ct. (so. dist.) NY, 1968-70; assoc. Milbank, Tweed, Hadley & McCloy, NYC, 1970-78, ptnr., 1979-87; exec. v.p., gen. counsel, sec. Am. Savs. Bank, White Plains, NY, 1987-92; ptnr. Lowy & Tallackson, NYC, 1993-96; pvt. practice, 1996-2000, 2007—; counsel Brauner, Baron, Rosenzweig & Klein, LLP, NYC, 2000—06. Mem. exec. com. N.Y. Law Inst., N.Y.C., 1980-87; bd. dirs., exec. v.p., gen. counsel, sec. Riverhead Savs. Bank., 1988-92; chmn. com. on banking law and regulation Community Banking Assn. N.Y. State, 1990-92; sec. banking law com. of the Assn. of Bar of City of N.Y., 1997-2000. Mem. ABA, N.Y. State Bar Assn., Assn. Bar City N.Y. Republican. Home: 1060 New Forge Rd II Ancram NY 12502-5005 Office: 2 Penn Plaza Ste 1910 New York NY 10121 Home Phone: 518-851-7212; Office Phone: 212-292-4978. Business E-Mail: tallacksonlaw@hughes.net, jtallackson@hughes.net.

TALLENT, STEPHEN EDISON, lawyer; b. Columbus, Nebr., Aug. 10, 1937; s. William E. and Helen Tallent; m. Martha Sutcliffe, Apr. 6, 1971; 1 child, Jennifer Diane. BA, Stanford U.; JD, U. Chgo.; LLD (hon.), Lincoln U. Bar: Calif. 1963, U.S. Dist. Ct. (so. and cen. dists.) Calif. 1965, U.S. Dist. Ct. (so. and ea. dists.) N.Y. 1989, U.S. Ct. Appeals (D.C. cir. 1981), U.S. Ct. Appeals (2d cir.) 1987, U.S. Ct. Appeals (3d. cir.) 1980, U.S. Ct. Appeals (4th cir.) 1982, U.S. Ct. Appeals (9th cir.) 1968, U.S. Ct. Mil. Appeals 1965, U.S. Supreme Ct. 1973. Ptnr. Gibson, Dunn & Crutcher, LA, 1962-96; pvt. practice Washington, 1997—. Former adj. prof. Loyola Law Sch., L.A.; mem. vis. com. U. Chgo. Law Sch.; former mem. Calif. Atty. Gen.'s adv. com. for Evaluation of Anti-Organized Crime Programs; mem. L.A. Town Hall, L.A. World Affairs Council; mem. bd. visitors Stanford Law Sch.; founding dir. Am. Employment Law Coun., 1993—. Fellow Coll. Labor and Employment Lawyers (founding, pres. and gov. 1995—); mem. ABA (chair labor and employment law sect. 1998-99), Indsl. Rels. Rsch. Assn. Home: PO Box 512 Reedville VA 22539-0512 Office: 1050 Connecticut Ave NW Ste 900 Washington DC 20036-5320 Home Phone: 804-453-6832; Office Phone: 202-955-8552.

TALLET, JORGE ANTONIO, philosopher, writer; b. Havana, Cuba, Feb. 3, 1928; came to the U.S., 1956; s. José Zacarías Tallet and Judith Martínez; m. Elena Villazón, Oct. 13, 1958; children: Julio, Lourdes María. PhD, U. Havana, 1953; grad., Havana Inst. Secondary Edn., 1945. Columnist Newspaper El Mundo, Havana, 1950-55; writer, editor AP, NYC, 1956-59, Fgn. News Svc., NYC, 1961-64, UPI, NYC, 1964-71, Editl. Am., Miami, Fla., 1971-76, The Miami Herald, 1976-90. Lectr. philosophy SUNY, Purchase and Mount Vernon, 1970-71. Author: Perspectivas Actuales de la Filosofía, 1954, The Absolute Being, 1955, 58, The Possible Universe, 1990, 97; author of essays. Avocations: reading, music listening, meditating, walking, travel.

TALLETT, ELIZABETH EDITH, biopharmaceutical company executive; b. London, Apr. 2, 1949; d. Edward and Edith May (Vickers) Symons; m. James Edward Wavle Jr.; children: James Edward Tallett, Alexander Martin Tallett, Christopher Andrew Wavle. BS with honors, Nottingham U., Eng., 1970. Ops. rsch. analyst So. Gas Bd., 1970-73; mgmt. svcs. mgr. Warner-Lamber (UK), Eastleigh, England, 1973-77, strategic planning mgr., 1977-81; internat. dir. strategic planning Warner-Lambert, Morris Plains, NJ, 1981-82, corp. dir. strategic planning, 1982-84; dir. mktg. ops. Parke-Davis, Morris Plains, 1984-87; exec. v.p. therapeutic products Centocor, Malvern, Pa., 1987-89, pres. pharms. div., 1989-92; pres., CEO Transcell Techs., Inc., Monmouth Junction, NJ, 1992-96, Dioscor, Inc., Stockton, 1996—2003; prin. Hunter Ptnrs. LLC, 2002—. Bd. dirs. Prin. Fin. Group, Inc., Varian, Inc., Coventry Health Care, Inc., IntegraMed Am. Inc., Immunicon Inc., Varian Semi Conductor Equipment Assoc. Inc.; dir. Biotech. Coun. N.J., NJ Ctr. Life Sci. Contbr. articles to profl. jours. Avocations: acting, badminton, travel, skiing. Personal E-mail: dioscor@comcast.net.

TALLEY, ANDRÉ LEON, Editor-At-Large (Periodical); b. Washington, 1949; BA in French Lit., NC Ctrl. U.; M in French Lit., Brown U. Worked for Andy Warhol, 1975; reporter Women's Wear Daily, 1977; apprentice to Diana Vreeland, Costume Inst. NY's Met. Mus.; fashion editor Ebony mag., 1982; fashion news dir. Vogue mag., NYC, 1983—88, creative dir., 1988—95, editor-at-large, 1998—; Paris fashion editor W mag., 1995, Paris bur. chief, 1995—98. Amb. Vogue mag., Moscow, 2004; trustee Savannah Coll. Arts and Design, SC; curator Ann. Oscar fashion show, 2007. Columnist Life with André, Vogue mag.; author: (books) A.L.T.: A Memoir, 2003, A.L.T. 365+, 2005. Recipient Eugenia Sheppard award, Coun. Fashion Designers of Am., 2003. Office: Vogue Conde Nast Publications 4 Times Sq Ste 17 New York NY 10036-6518 *

TALLEY, CHARLES RICHMOND, retired bank executive; b. Richmond, Va., Dec. 23, 1925; s. Charles Edward and Marie (Thorckmorton) Talley; m. Anne Marie Smith, June 4, 1948 (dec. Feb. 16, 2007); children: Laurie Anne, Charles Richmond Jr. BA in Econs, U. Richmond, 1949; postgrad., Rutgers U., 1959-61, Northwestern U., 1954-55; grad. exec. program, U. Va., 1974. Asst. cashier 1st & Mchts. Nat. Bank, Richmond, 1955-57, asst. v.p., 1957-63, v.p., 1963-69, sr. v.p., 1969-73, exec. v.p., 1973-84; corp. exec. officer Sovran Bank N.A., 1984-86, ret., 1986, 1986. Bd dirs Security Atlantic Life Ins Co; vpres, bd dirs Security Atlantic Ins Agency; bd dirs Sovran Properties Inc; vice chmn bd dirs Va Educ Loan Authority, 1983—87, chmn, 1988—91; vpres, mem exec comt Richmond Eye and Ear Hosp, pres, 1988—91. Pres Richmond Jr Cof C, 1960—61; treas Richmond chpt Nat Found, 1956—; pres Baptist Extension Bd Va, 1973—75; bd dirs Commonwealth Eye and Ear, 1986—89, Richmond Symphony Orchestra, Richmond Better Bus Bur. With USNR, 1944—46. Mem.: Richmond Clearing House Asn (pres 1977), Richmond Metropolitan CofC (bd dirs 1979—89), The Tartan Golf Course (Irvington, Va), Bull and Bear Club, Willow Oaks Country Club Richmond (pres 1971), Rotary (bd dirs Richmond 1981—83). Home: 4301 Stratford Rd Richmond VA 23225-1060 also: Bldg 2 Unit 2 The Green At Tides Lodge Irvington VA 22480

TALLEY, HAYWARD LEROY, communications executive; b. Nov. 3, 1923; s. Roy and Reta (Hayward) T.; m. Emma Mae Chandler, Sept. 2, 1950; children: Brian, Kevin. BS, U. Ill., 1948. Chief engr. Sta. WOKZ-AM-FM, Alton, Ill., 1948-50; pres., gen. mgr. Talley Broadcasting Corp.

(sta. WSMI AM and FM), Litchfield, Ill., 1950—; pres. Talley Broadcasting Co. (sta. KBKB AM and FM), Ft. Madison, Iowa, 1960-99, North Cen. Iowa Broadcasting Co. (stas. KLSS, KSMN), Mason City, 1963-83, Talley Broadcasting Corp. (sta. WAOX), Staunton, Ill., 1999—. Chmn. ofcl. bd. Meth. Ch., 1961-63, 65-66, chmn. ch. coun., 2003-05; adv. bd. Lewis & Clark Coll., 1978—; adv. coun. St. Francis Hosp., 1992—. With Signal Corps, U.S. Army. Recipient Vincent T. Wasilewski Broadcaster of Yr. award, Ill. Broadcasters Assn., 2002. Mem.: Ill. Broadcasters Assn., Nat. Assn. Broadcasters, Am. Legion, Masons, Rotary (pres. Litchfield Club 1989—90). Home: 1414 N Harrison St Litchfield IL 62056-1209 Office: Sta WSMI PO Box 10 Litchfield IL 62056-0010

TALLEY, JOSEPH EUGENE, psychologist; b. Springfield, Mass., May 27, 1949; s. Joseph Addison and Miriam Louise (Ayers) T.; m. Vibeke Absalon, Jan. 3, 1981; children: Kirsten, David, Jonathan. BA, U. Richmond, 1971; MA, Radford Coll., 1973; PhD, U. Va., 1978. Diplomate Am. Bd. Profl. Psychology; lic. psychologist, NC; cert. health svc. provider, NC. Faculty Duke U. Med. Ctr., Durham, NC, 1977—2005, clin. prof. med. psychology, 2005—, with counseling and psychol. svcs., 1977—, asst. dir., 2006—; gen. practice psychotherapy Durham, 1980—. Author: Study Skills, 1981, Performance Prediciton of Law Enforcement Personnel, 1990, The Predictors of Successful Very Brief Psychotherapy, 1992, Seeking Something Sacred: Managing Our Frustrations, Losses and Fears, 2001; author, editor: Counseling and Psychotherapy Services, 1985, Counseling and Psychotherapy with College Students: A Guide to Treatment, 1986, Multicultural Needs Assessment with College and University Populations, 1995; contbr. articles to profl. jours. Bd. deacons Hillsborough Presbyn. Ch., NC, 1983-85, chmn., 1985, bd. elders, 1987-94, 2002—, v.p. bd. trustees, 1992-94; bd. dirs. Orange County Mental Health Assn., Chapel Hill, NC, 1982-83, mem. legis. com., 1983, site visitor for accreditation. Fellow APA (awards com. divsn. 17, 2002-05, chair awards com. 2006-07), Am. Acad. Clin. Psychology, Am. Acad. Counseling Psychology, Am. Acad. Counseling Psychology (pres. 1995-97, Disting. Svc. award 2002); mem. Am. Bd. Profl. Psychology (sec., treas. coun. of pres.'s psychology splty. acads. 1997-98, chmn., CEO 2000-03, spl. liaison to related groups 2003—, past chmn., CEO 2003-05, exec. bd. and spl. liaison to congress and related profl. groups, 2005—, Disting. Contbns. award 2002), NC Psychol. Assn., Nat. Soc. Clin. Hypnosis (cert. and approved cons., supr. and practitioner, ethics com. 1995-97), Phi Kappa Phi, Omicron Delta Kappa, Psi Chi, Phi Kappa Sigma. Democrat. Presbyterian. Home: 134 E Tryon St Hillsborough NC 27278-2550 Office: Duke U Counseling & Psychol Svcs PO Box 90955 214 Page Bldg Durham NC 27708-0955 Office Phone: 919-660-1000. Business E-Mail: jtalley@duke.edu.

TALLEY, MELVIN GARY, academic administrator; b. West Chester, Pa., Feb. 26, 1945; s. Melvin G. and Alberta M. (Faddis) T.; m. Jolene Keller (div.); children: Kristin Jolene, Mark Gary. BS, Pa. State U., 1967; D (hon.), Bristol (Tenn.) Coll., 1988; MBA, U. Mo., 1998. Registered rep. DeHaven & Townsend, Phila., 1967-68; dir. Brown Mackie Coll., Salina and Overland Park, Kans., 1968-72, pres., 1972—94, emeritus, also bd. chmn.; mng. ptnr. ETG Partnership, LP, 2002—. Pres. Realty Mgmt. Investment Co., Salina, 1976—94; advisor region VI HEW, 1976-86, chmn. Region VII Adv. Proprietary Coun., 1989; mem. adv. bd. U.S. Office of Edn., 1988; chmn. region VII Coun. for Pvt. Career Colls. and Schs., 1989. Author: Reassessing Values in Postsecondary Edn., 1977. Bd. dirs. St. Francis Boys Home, Salina, 1975; trustee duPont, Hagley Mus. and Libr., 2004—. Mem. Pvt. Edn. Research Council, Inner Circle, Assn. Ind. Colls. and Schs. (bd. dirs. Washington chpt. 1968-78), Claymont Savings and Loan Assn. (bd. dirs.), Hagley Mus. and Libr. (trustee, 2004—). Home: 4609 W 113th Terr Brittany Ct Leawood KS 66211 Office: ETG Partnership LP 4609 W 113th Terr Leawood KS 66217 Office Phone: 913-491-9348.

TALLEY, MICHAEL FRANK, lawyer; b. Chesterfield, SC, Aug. 14, 1945; s. Frank and Rosena A. Talley; m. Dianne Wright, May 24, 1980; children: Michanna, Michael. BA, S.C. State U., 1966; MA, Howard U., 1971, JD, 1976. Bar: S.C. 1976, U.S. Dist. Ct. S.C. 1976, U.S. Ct. Appeals (4th cir.) 1976, U.S. Ct. Appeals (11th cir.) 1994. French instr. S.C. State U., Orangeburg, 1970-71, Tenn. State U., Nashville, 1971-73; staff atty. Presdl. Clemency Bd., White House, Washington, 1975; atty. Bishop Law Firm, Greenville, S.C., 1976-77, Talley, Green & Lewis, Greenville, 1977-87, Talley Law Firm, Greenville, 1987—. French lab. instr. Howard U., Washington, 1973-76. Bd. dirs. Legal Svcs. for Western S.C., Greenville, 1978-82. Earl Warren Legal fellowship NAACP Legal Def. Fund, 1973-76; recipient Cert. of Appreciation S.C. Bar Pro Bono Program, 1991. Mem. S.C. Bar Assn., Nat. Bar Assn., Greenville C. of C., Kappa Alpha Psi. Avocations: fishing, travel, swimming, reading. Home: 208 Boling Rd Greenville SC 29611-7604 Office: Talley Law Firm 206 Green Ave Greenville SC 29601-3436 Office Phone: 864-233-6229. Personal E-mail: talleylaw@aol.com.

TALLEY, NICHOLAS JOSEPH, medical educator, research scientist, physician; b. Perth, Australia, Jan. 9, 1956; arrived in U.S., 2002; s. Nicholas Alexander and Irene Mary Talley; m. Catherine Elizabeth Davies, Dec. 30, 2004; children: Nicholas Stephen, Matthew Jonathon, Nicole Sarah, Luke James. MB, BS, U. NSW, 1979; PhD, U. Sydney, 1987; MD, U. NSW, 1993, M in Med. Sci., 2003. Resident med. officer/registrar Prince of Wales Hosp., Sydney, 1979—83; rsch. fellow, prof. registrar Royal North Shore Hosp., Sydney, 1983—87; rsch. fellow Mayo Clinic, Rochester, Minn., 1987—88, asst. prof. medicine, 1988—91, assoc. prof., 1991—93; head divsn. medicine, prof. medicine Nepean Hosp., Sydney, 1993—2001; area dir. medicine Westworth Area Health Svc., Nepean Hosp., Sydney, 2001—02; prof. medicine, cons. Mayo Clinic Coll. Medicine, Rochester, 2003—, prof. epidemiology, 2007—; chair dept. internal medicine Mayo Clinic, Jacksonville, 2007—. Author: Examination Medicine, 1985, 5th edit., 2006, Clinical Examination, 1988, 5th edit., 2006, Internal Medicine, 1990, 2d edit., 2000, Clinical Gastroenterology, 1996, 2d edit., 2006, Multiple Choice Questions in Clinical Examination, 1996, Pocket Clinical Examination, 1998, 2d edit., 2002, Conquering Irritable Bowel Syndrome, 2006, GI Epidemiology, 2007; asst. editor Am. Jour. Gastroenterology, 1992-97; co-editor-in-chief, Am. Jour. Gastroenterology, 2004—; mem. editl. bd. Gastroenterology, 1993-98, Jour. Clin. Gstroenterology, 1994—, Alimentary Pharmacology and Therapeutics, 1995-03, Jour. Gastroenterology and Hepatology, 1994-98, editor, 1998-03; contbr. articles and revs. to profl. jours., chpts. to books. Pres. Miranda br. Young Liberals, Sydney, 1976; wing comdr. Royal Australia Air Force, 2000. Postgrad. rsch. scholar Nat. Health and Med. Rsch. Coun., Australia, 1984-85. Fellow ACP, Royal Australasian Coll. Physicians, Am. Coll. Gastroent., Australian Faculty Pub. Health Medicine (founding mem.), Royal Coll. Physicians (London and Edinburgh); mem. Am. Gastroent. Assn., Gastroent. Soc. Australia, Brit. Soc. Gastroenterology, Functional Brain Gut Rsch. Group (pres.). Avocations: tennis, writing, travel, jogging, martial arts. Office: Mayo Clinic 200 First St SW PL-6 Rochester MN 55905 Business E-Mail: talley.nicholas@mayo.edu.

TALLEY, RICHARD BATES, lawyer; b. Oklahoma City, Mar. 19, 1947; s. Olin Jack and Betty Lee (Bates) T.; m. Joan Walker, Sept. 15, 1992; children from a previous marriage: Richard Bates Jr., Samuel Logan, Bradley Dale, Rachel Alexandra. BBA, Okla. U., 1969, JD, 1972. Bar: Okla. 1972, U.S. Dist. Ct. (we. dist.) Okla. 1972, U.S. Ct. Appeals (10th cir.) 1973, U.S. Dist. Ct. (no. dist.) Tex. 1987, U.S. Tax Ct. 1987.; CPA, Okla. Atty. Talley, Crowder & Gallagher (and predecessor firm), Norman, Okla., 1995—. Bd. dirs. Bacchus Enterprises, Inc., Norman, The Top of the Center, Inc. Pres. Cleveland Co. YMCA. Mem. ABA, Okla. Bar Found., Okla. Bar Assn., Okla. Trial Lawyers Assn., Okla. Soc. CPAs, Cleve. County Bar Assn., Soc. CPAs. Democrat. Methodist. Avocations: clock collecting, motorcycling, golf, boating. Home: 1819 Joe Taylor Cir Norman OK 73072-6650 Office: Talley Crowder and Gallagher 219 E Main St Norman OK 73069-1304 Home Phone: 405-364-1841; Office Phone: 405-364-8300. Personal E-mail: rtalley1@cox.net.

TALLEY, RICHARD WOODROW, accountant; b. Birmingham, Ala., Sept. 10, 1941; s. Alton Woodrow and Alta O. (Tittle) T.; m. Anita Marcell Moses, Jan. 14, 1966; children: Richard Woodrow Jr., Leah Michelle. BS in Commerce and Bus. Adminstrn., U. Ala., 1964. CPA Ala. Pres. Talley, Maulding & Peete, PC, Decatur, Ala., 1964—. Officer Boy Scouts Am., Decatur, Austin Band Boosters, Decatur, PTA, Decatur; mgr., coach Dixie Youth Baseball, Decatur; deacon Ch. of Christ. Served as sgt. USAR, 1964-70. Named Boss of Yr. Decatur Jaycees, 1980. Mem. AICPA, Tenn. Soc. CPAs, Ala. Soc. CPAs, Commerce Execs. Soc. U. Ala., Lions (sec. 1982-83, treas. 1985-86, sec.-treas. 1994-95). Avocations: genealogy, photography. Home: 1266 Brandywine Ln SE Decatur AL 35601-4582 Office: Talley Mauldin & Peete PC PO Box 2067 Decatur AL 35602-2067 Home Phone: 256-355-1264; Office Phone: 256-353-1421. Business E-Mail: richard@tmpcpa.com.

TALLEY, ROBERT COCHRAN, academic administrator, cardiologist; b. May 26, 1936; m. Katherine Ann Plocar; children: Andrew, Katherine, David. BS, U. Mich., 1958; MD, U. Chgo., 1962. Diplomate Nat. Bd. Med. Examiners (mem. medicine com. 1984-88, com. chair 1988-93). Asst. prof., dept. physiology and medicine U. Tex. Med. Sch., San Antonio, 1969—71, head, sect. cardiovascular diseases, 1971—75, assoc. prof., dept. medicine, 1971—75; acting chief medicine VA Hosp., San Antonio, 1974, chief cardiology svc., 1973—75; chmn. dept. internal medicine U. SD Sch. Medicine, Sioux Falls, 1975—87, Freeman prof. medicine, 1984—87, interim v.p., dean, 1986—87, v.p., dean, 1987—2004, dir. residency program, 2004—. Mem. liaison com. med. edn., 1998—. Contbr. articles to med. jours. Surgeon USPHS, 1966—68. Tchg. scholar, Am. Heart Assn. U. Chgo., 1972—75. Fellow: ACP, Am. Coll. Cardiology; mem.: AMA, Liaison Com. on Med. Edn., Assn. Am. Med. Coll. (mem. coun. deans new dean mentoring program, mem. adminstrn. bd. coun. deans 1999—2004), Am. Fedn. Clin. Rsch., Am. Heart Assn. (bd. dirs. Dakota affiliate). Home: 1305 Cedar Ln Sioux Falls SD 57103-4512 Office: U SD Sch Medicine 1400 W 22nd St Sioux Falls SD 57105-1505 Business E-Mail: rtalley@usd.edu.

TALLEY, STEVEN K., lawyer; b. May 5, 1962; BS in Physics, Harvey Mudd Coll., 1984; JD, Univ. Calif., Berkeley, 1991. Former mgr., mgmt. info. systems for a mfg. co.; ptnr., corp. transactions and securities Gibson Dunn & Crutcher LLP, Denver, 2000—, and ptnr.-in-charge Denver office. Articles editor High Technology Law Jour., 1990—91. Mem.: Order of Coif. Office: Gibson Dunn & Crutcher LLP Ste 4100 1801 California St Denver CO 80202 Office Phone: 303-298-5775. Office Fax: 303-313-2840. Business E-Mail: stalley@gibsondunn.com.

TALLEY, TRUMAN MACDONALD, publisher, editor; b. NYC, Feb. 3, 1925; s. Truman Hughes and Helen Nicholson (Macdonald) T.; m. Madelon DeVoe, Oct. 17, 1953 (dec. 1997); children: Melanie, Macdonald, Marina. Student, Buckley Sch., Deerfield Acad., Sorbonne, 1945—46; grad. cum laude, Princeton U., 1949. Assoc. editor New Am. Libr. of World Lit., NYC, 1949-59, editl. v.p., 1959-64; pres., editl. dir. Weybright & Talley, NYC, 1966-78; pub. Truman Talley Books with Times Books, 1978-82; with E.P. Dutton, 1983-98, St. Martin's Press, NYC, 1998—. Trustee Clinton Hall Assn. Merc. Libr., N.Y.C. With AUS, 1943-46, ETO. Decorated Purple Heart. Mem.: PEN. Office: Truman Talley Books St Martin's Press 175 5th Ave New York NY 10010-7703

TALLEY, VERNON ANDREW, museum administrator; b. Balt., Feb. 13, 1968; s. Kenneth Franklyn Talley; m. Nancy Rae Gerhart, Dec. 30, 1988; 1 child, Rhiannon Victoria. BA in Art History, Calif. State U., LA, 1996; MA in Mus. Studies, U. Okla., Norman, 2007. Exhibit tech. Calif. African Am. Mus., LA, 1995—98, registrar interpretive collections, 1998—. Presenter ann. meeting Associated Hist. Socs. LA County, 2003—03; presenter ann. conf. Packing, Art Handling & Crating Info. Network, Portland, 2003—03. Mem. NAACP, Balt., 2004—06. Sgt. US Army, 1989—91. Decorated Army Achievement medal US Army, Army Commendation medal; Joseph Uribe Meml. scholar, Calif. State U., LA, 1994, MA Alumni scholar, U. Okla., 2007. Mem.: Packing, Art Handling & Crating Info. Network, Am. Assn. Museums (registrar's com.), Am. Legion, Phi Kappa Phi, Golden Key Nat. Honor Soc. Independent. Office: Calif African Am Mus 600 State Dr Exposition Pk Los Angeles CA 90037 Office Phone: 213-744-2023. Office Fax: 213-744-2050. E-mail: dtalley@caamuseum.org.

TALLMAN, AMI RENEE, artist; b. Camarillo, Calif., June 5, 1979; d. Michael and Claire Tallman. BFA in Interdisciplinary Fine Arts, San Francisco Art Inst., 1999; MFA, Art Ctr. Coll. Design, Pasadena, Calif., 2006. Resident artist Painting's Edge, Idyllwild Arts ctr., Calif., 2003, Atlantic Ctr. for Arts, New Smyrna Beach, Fla., 2006. Exhibitions include Wight Gallery, UCLA, 2004, See Line Gallery, LA, 2006, Cirrus Gallery, 2006, High Energy Constructs, 2006, Barnsdall Mpcl. Art Gallery, 2006, High Energy Constructs, 2006, Jack Hanley Gallery, 2007, Bklyn. Fireproof, 2007; contbr. revs. to Flash Art Mag. Atlantic Ctr. for Arts scholar, Joan Mitchell Found., 2006. Progressive. Avocations: reading, history, drums, horseback riding, travel.

TALLMAN, ANN MARIE, lawyer; b. Iowa; BS in Psychology and Polit. Sci., with distinction and spl. honors, U. Iowa; JD, U. Calif. Berkeley, Boalt Hall Sch. Law. Atty. Kutak Rock, Denver; dep. dir. & head Planning and Community Develop. Agy. City and County of Denver; with Fannie Mae, Pasadena, Calif., 1994—2004; pres., CEO Fannie Mae Found., Washington, 1998—99; pres., gen. counsel MALDEF (Mexican Am. Legal Def. and Edn. Fund), LA, 2004—06. Bd. mem. MALDEF (Mexican Am. Legal Def. and Edn. Fund), 1998—2006; bd. dirs. J. C. Penney Company, Inc., 2006—. Founding bd. mem. Hispanic PAC USA; exec. dir. Colo. Hispanic League, 1990.

TALLMAN, DENNIS EARL, chemistry professor, research scientist; b. Bellefontaine, Ohio, Apr. 23, 1942; s. Maurice Earl and Mary Elizabeth Tallman. PhD, Ohio State U., Columbus, 1968. Postdoctoral rsch. assoc. Cornell U., Ithaca, NY, 1968—70; asst. prof. chemistry N.D. State U., Fargo, 1970—73, assoc. prof. chemistry, 1973—78, prof. chemistry, 1978—2006, rsch. prof. dept. coatings and polymeric materials, 2007—. Co-dir. Corrosion/Coatings Rsch. Ctr. N.D. State U., Fargo, 2000—. Contbr. articles to profl. jours. (Fred Waldren Award for Outstanding Rsch., 2000); N.Am. editor: Jour. Solid State Electrochemistry, 1997—. Recipient postdoctoral fellowship, NIH, 1968—70, numerous rsch. grants, NSF, Dept. of Def., NIH, and EPA, 1970—. Mem.: Nat. Assn. of Corrosion Engrs., Electrochem. Soc., Am. Chem. Soc. (lobbied Congress for increases in fed. rsch. funding 2000—03), Soc. for Electroanalytical Chemistry (life; bd. dirs. 1998—2002), Phi Kappa Phi, Sigma Xi, Phi Lambda Upsilon. Avocations: four-wall handball, skiing, canoeing, biking, backpacking. Office: ND State U Dept Coatings and Polymeric Materials Fargo ND 58105-5376 Business E-Mail: dennis.tallman@ndsu.edu.

TALLMAN, EVE, library director; Dir. Grand County Pub. Libr., Moab, Utah. Recipient Merit award, Utah Humanities Coun., 2005, Best Small Libr. in Am., Libr. Jour., 2007. Mem.: Utah Libr. Assn. (vice-chair pub. com.). Office: Grand County Pub Libr 257 E Ctr St Moab UT 84532 Office Phone: 435-259-1111. Office Fax: 435-259-1380. E-mail: eve@moablibrary.org.

TALLMAN, RICHARD C., federal judge, lawyer; b. Oakland, Calif., 1953; s. Kenneth A. and Jean M. Tallman; m. Cynthia Ostolaza, Nov. 14, 1981. BSc, U. Santa Clara, 1975; JD, Northwestern U., 1978. Bar: Calif. 1978, Wash. 1979, US Dist. Ct. (no. dist.) Calif. 1979, US Dist. Ct. (we. dist.) Wash. 1979, US Dist. Ct. Hawaii 1986, US Ct. Fed. Cl. 1999, US Ct. Appeals (9th cir.) 1979, US Dist. Ct. (ea. dist.) Wash. 1998, US Supreme Ct. 1997. Law clk. to Hon. Morrell E. Sharp US Dist. Ct. (we. dist.) Wash., Seattle, 1978—79; trial atty. US Dept. Justice, Washington, 1979—80; asst. US atty. (we. dist.) Wash., Seattle, 1980—83; assoc., then ptnr. Schweppe, Krug & Tausend, PS, Seattle, 1983—89; mem. Bogle & Gates, PLLC, Seattle, 1990—99; ptnr. Tallman & Severin, LLP, Seattle, 1999—2000; apptd. US cir. judge US Ct. Appeals (9th cir.), 2000—. Chmn. western dist. Wash. Lawyer Reps. to Ninth Cir. Jud. Conf., 1996—97. Instr. Nat. Pk. Svc. Seasonal Ranger Acad., Everett and Mt. Vernon, Wash., 1983—93; chmn. Edmonds C.C. Found., Lynnwood, Wash., 1990—92; gen. counsel Seattle-King County Crime Stoppers, 1987—99; mem. exec. bd. Chief Seattle coun. Boy Scouts Am., 1997—; chmn. US Jud. Conf. Adv. Com. Crime Rules, 2007—. Mem.: Fed. Judges Assn. (bd. dirs. 2002—06), King County Bar Assn., Fed. Bar Assn. (we. dist. trustee 1992—93, v.p. 1994, pres. 1995), Wash. Athletic Club, Rainier Club. Office: Park Place Bldg 1200 Sixth Avenue 21st FL Seattle WA 98101-3123 *

TALLMAN, SEAN DALE, anthropologist; b. Seattle, Feb. 15, 1978; s. Dale F. and Tina D. Tallman. AA, Shoreline C.C.; BA in Anthrop., U. Wash., Seattle, 2000; MA in Anthrop., SUNY, Binghamton, 2005. Tchg. asst., anthropology SUNY, Binghamton, NY, 2002—04; osteologist NW Archaeological Assocs., Inc., Seattle, 2005—07; Oak Ridge Inst. for Sci. and Edn. postgrad. fellow, anthropologist, lab. technician JPAC/CIL, Hickam AFB, Hawaii, 2007—. Osteological cons. Slater Mus. Natural History, U. Puget Sound, Tacoma, 2005—; adj. instr. anthropology Tacoma C.C., 2005—07; presenter in field. Mem. Seattle King County Dental Soc. Forensic Com., 2006—06. Fellow, SUNY, 2002—04. Mem.: Am. Soc. for Forensic Odontology, Am. Acad. Forensic Scis., Assn. Wash. Archaeology, Paleopathology Assn., Soc. Am. Archaeology, Am. Assn. Phys. Anthropologists. Liberal. Avocations: photography, movies, jogging, hiking, travel. Home: 1103 3d Ave Honolulu HI 96816 Office: JPAC/CIL 310 Worchester Ave Hickam Afb HI 96853 Home Phone: 206-328-2732; Office Phone: 808-448-1765. Personal E-mail: sean.tallman@gmail.com. Business E-Mail: sean.tallman@jpac.pacom.mil.

TALLMER, MARGOT SALLOP, psychologist, gerontologist, psychoanalyst; b. NYC, Sept. 8, 1925; d. Harry and Mildred (Schifrin) Sallop; m. Jonathan Tallmer, Apr. 12, 1949 (dec.); children: Mary, Megan, Jill, Andrew. MS, NYU, 1948; MA, Yeshiva U., 1962, PhD, 1967; cert. in psychotherapy and psychoanalysis, NYU, 1976. Faculty dept. psychol. founds. Hunter Coll., NYC, 1969-76, assoc. prof., 1976-79, prof., 1979—94, prof. emeritus; staff psychologist Mt. Sinai Hosp., NY, 1967-68; pvt. practice NYC, 1979—; faculty NY Ctr. for Psychoanalytic Tng., NY. Lectr. N.Y. Ctr. Psychoanalytic Tng. Author: Sex in Later Life, 1996; editor: Sex and Life Threatening Illness, HIV Testing Positive, The Child and Death, Sexuality and the Older Adult; co-author: Suicide in the Elderly; mem. editl. bd. Current Issues in Psychoanalysis, Psychoanalytic Rev.; contbr. chpts. to textbooks, articles to profl jours. Mem. APA, Boston Soc. Gerontologic Psychiatry, N.Y. State Psychol. Assn. (past pres. divsn. adult devel. and aging), Nat. Psychol. Assn. for Psychoanalysis (trustee 1972-2005, bd. dir. 1972—). Address: 515 E 85th St New York NY 10028-0246 Personal E-mail: mamadoc4@n.y.c.rr.om. E-mail: mamadoc4@gmail.com.

TALLON, DALE, professional sports team executive; b. Oct. 19, 1950; m. Meg Tallon; 2 children. Player Vancouver Canucks, 1970—73, Chicago Blackhawks, 1973—78, Pittsburgh Penguins, 1978—80; color analyst Chicago Blackhawks, 1981—97, dir. of Player Personnel, 1998—2002, color analyst, 2002—03, asst. gen. mgr., 2003—05, gen. mgr., 2005—. Named to NHL All-Star Team, 1971, 1972. Office: c/o Chicago Blackhawks 1901 W Madison St Chicago IL 60612

TALLON, EDWARD JOSEPH, social studies educator; b. Peoria, Ill., Dec. 6, 1962; s. Edward Joseph and Dorothy Margaret Tallon; m. Ellen Ruth Eason. BBA in Accountancy, U. Notre Dame, Ind., 1985; MS in History, Ill. State U., Normal, 2005. CPA Ill. Acct. Price Waterhouse, Seattle, 1985—88, Newark Electronics, Chgo., 1988—91; tchr. Peoria Notre Dame H.S., 1991—2001, Ill. Valley Ctrl. H.S., Chillicothe, 2001—. Office: Ill Valley Ctrl HS 1300 W Sycamore Chillicothe IL 61523

TALLON, MICHAEL, language educator; b. San Antonio, Apr. 8, 1968; s. Eugene Michael and Shirley Ann Tallon. BA, U. Tex., San Antonio, 1991; MS in Spanish Linguistics, Georgetown U., Washington, 1994; PhD in Fgn. Lang. Edn., U. Tex., Austin, 2006. Substitute tchr. Harlandale Ind. Sch. Dist, San Antonio, 1991—92; lectr. Georgetown U., Washington, 1993—94, U. Tex., San Antonio, 1994—2002, U. Incarnate Word, San Antonio, 1994—2002, instr. Spanish, 2002—07, 2007—. Mem. editl. and rev. com. Tex. Papers in Fgn. Lang. Edn., 2003—06, editor in chief, 2006—. Contbr. articles to profl. jours. Named mem., Fechter's Finger Flicking Frolic Magic Conv., Best Close-Up Magician, Tex. Assn. Magicians, 2000, Outstanding Grad., U. Tex. Austin, 2006; recipient Amber award, U. Tex. San Antonio, 1999; grantee, UTOPIA U. Tex.; scholar, U. Tex. Austin, 2005; South Tex. Grad. fellow, 2003—04, Alexander Caswell Ellis fellow, 2005—06. Mem.: Computer Assisted Lang. Instrn. Consortium, Nat. Fedn. Modern Lang. Tchg. Assns., Alamo Lang. Assn., Am. Coun. Tchg. Fgn. Langs., Am. Assn. Tchrs. Spanish and Portuguese, Soc. Am. Magicians San Antonio Assembly 52, Internat. Brotherhood Magicians San Antonio Ring 18 (Magician of Yr. 1997), Pi Lambda Theta. Roman Catholic. Avocations: magic, reading, sports. Home: 419 Northstar Dr San Antonio TX 78216-4414 Office: Univ Incarnate Word Fgn Lang Dept 4301 Broadway CPO 353 San Antonio TX 78209 Office Phone: 210-805-5891. Personal E-mail: tallon@satx.rr.com.

TALLY, LURA SELF, state legislator; b. Statesville, NC, Dec. 9, 1921; d. Robert Ottis and Sara (Cowles) Self; m. J.O. Tally Jr., Jan. 30, 1943 (div. 1970); children: Robert Taylor, John Cowles. AB, Duke U., 1942; MA, NC State U., 1970. Tchr., former guidance counselor Fayetteville (NC) city schs.; mem. NC Ho. of Reps. from 20th Dist., 1971—83, chmn. com. higher edn., 1975, 1980—83, vice-chmn. com. appropriations for edn., 1973—86; state senator from 12th Dist. NC, 1983—95; chmn. NC Senate Com. of Natural Resources, Cmty. Devel. and Wildlife, 1987, Environment and Natural Resources, 1989—94. Past pres. Cumberland County Mental Health Assn., NC Historic Preservation Soc.; trustee Fayetteville Tech. Inst., 1981—94; active Legis. Rsch. Com. Mem.: Am. Pers. and Guidance Assn., Fayetteville Woman's Club (past pres.), Fayetteville Bus. and Profl. Women's Club, Kappa Delta, Delta Kappa Gamma. Methodist. Office: W Jones St Raleigh NC 27601

TALMADGE, PHILIP ALBERT, retired judge, state senator; b. Seattle, Apr. 23, 1952; s. Judson H., Jr. and Jeanne C. Talmadge; m. Darlene L. Nelson, Sept. 6, 1970; children: Adam, Matthew, Jessica, Jonathan, Annemarie. BA magna cum laude, Yale U., 1973; JD, U. Wash., 1976. Bar: Wash. 1976. Atty. Karr Tuttle Campbell, 1976—89; pres. Talmadge &

Cutler, P.S., 1989—95; senator State of Wash., 1979—94; justice Supreme Ct. Wash., 1995—2001; ptnr. Talmadge Law Group PLLC, 2001—. Author: The Nixon Doctrine and the Reaction of Three Asian Nations, 1973; editor: Law Rev., 1975—76; contbr. articles to profl. jours. Chair Senate Judiciary Com., 1981, 1983—87, Senate Health and Human Svcs. Com., 1992—95, Wash. Senate, 1978—94, ways and means com. Fellow: Am. Assn. Appellate Lawyers; mem.: Wash. Appellate Lawyers Assn., King County Bar Assn., Wash. State Bar Assn. Office: Talmadge Law Group PLLC 18010 Southcenter Pkwy Tukwila WA 98188

TALMAGE, DAVID WILSON, retired microbiologist, educator, dean; b. Kwangju, Korea, Sept. 15, 1919; s. John Van Talmage and Eliza (Emerson) Talmage; m. LaVeryn Marie Hunicke, June 23, 1944; children: Janet, Marilyn, David, Mark, Carol. Student, Maryville Coll., Tenn., 1937—38; BS, Davidson Coll., NC, 1941; MD, Washington U., St. Louis, 1944. Intern Ga. Baptist Hosp., 1944—45; resident medicine Barnes Hosp., St. Louis, 1948—50, fellow medicine, 1950—51; asst. prof. pathology U. Pitts., 1951—52; asst. prof., then assoc. prof. medicine U. Chgo., 1952—59; prof. medicine U. Colo., 1959—, prof. microbiology, 1960—86, disting. prof., 1986—, chmn. dept., 1963—65, assoc. dean, 1966—68, dean, 1969—71; dir. Webb-Waring Lung Inst., 1973—83, assoc. dean for rsch., 1983—86. Mem. nat. council Nat. Inst. Allergy and Infectious Diseases, NIH, 1963—66, 1973—77. Author (with John Cann): Chemistry of Immunity in Health and Disease; editor: Jour. Allergy, 1963—67; editor: (with M. Samter) Immunological Diseases. With M.C. AUS, 1945—48. Scholar Markle, 1955—60. Mem.: Am. Assn. Immunologists, Am. Acad. Allergy, Inst. Medicine, NAS, Alpha Omega Alpha, Phi Beta Kappa. Home Phone: 303-388-1898. Home Fax: 303-388-6955.

TALMAGE, KENNETH KELLOGG, consumer products company executive; b. Morristown, NJ, Jan. 16, 1946; s. Edward Taylor Hunt Jr. and Dorothy Rogers Talmage. BA, Claremont Men's Coll., 1968; MBA, Boston U., Brussels, 1976. Aide to U.S. ambassador to Austria, Vienna, 1969-72; asst. to chmn. Fin. Com. to Re-elect Pres. Nixon, 1972-73; assoc. Hon. Leonard K. Firestone, LA, 1973-74; attaché Am. Embassy, Brussels, 1974-77; mgmt. cons. strategic planning and fin. Arthur D. Little, Inc., Cambridge, Mass., 1977-80; pres. Boston Co. of New Orleans, 1980—81; sr. v.p. Boston Safe Deposit & Trust Co., 1980-87; pres. Lloyd's, Inc., Denver, 1987-92. Pres. Sprague Corp., Cape Elizabeth, Maine, 1978-79; bd. dirs. Monterey Water Co., pres., 1995-97, chmn., CEO, 1997—; bd. dirs. Pure West Industries, Inc., vice-chmn., 1993-95. Mem. exec. com. Outward Bound, U.S.A., 1980—85; dir. Vols. for Outdoor Colo., 1988—94, Breckenridge Outdoor Edn. Ctr., 1989—92; advisor Hurricane Island Outward Bound Sch., Maine, 1987—2005, bd. trustee, 1979—87, chmn. bd. trustees, 1980—83; bd. trustee Colo. Outward Bound Sch., 1990—96, vice chmn., 1995—96, bd. govs., 1996—2005; bd. trustees Outward Bound Profl., 2005—. With USNR, 1968—69. Home: PO Box 1526 Carmel CA 93921-1526 Office: Monterey Water Co 1158 S Main St Manteca CA 95337-9505 Personal E-mail: kktalm@aol.com.

TALMAGE, LANCE ALLEN, obstetrician, gynecologist, military officer; b. Vandergrift, Pa., Feb. 23, 1938; s. Guy Wesley and Martha Lois (Bradstock) T.; m. Diana Elizabeth Heywood, June 23, 1962; children: Tamara, Lance Jr., Tenley. BS in Chem. Engring., U. Toledo, Ohio, 1960; MD, U. Mich., 1964. Flight surgeon 24th Infantry Divsn. US Army, 1966-69; resident U. Mich. Med. Ctr., Ann Arbor, 1969-73; clin. prof. Med. Univ. Ohio, Toledo, 1987—; med. dir. Ctr. for Women's Health, Toledo, 1987—2003. Brigadier gen. 112th Med. Brigage Ohio Army Nat. Guard, Columbus, 1995-97; pres. med. staff Toledo Hosp., 1989-91, chair dept. Ob-gyn., 1979-86; pres. Toledo Lucas County Acad. Medicine, 1994-95; mem. Toledo Hosp. Found. Bd., 2000-05, Ohio State Med. Bd., 1999—, supervising sec., 2003—. Cabinet mem. United Way, Toledo, 1994-96; hon. chmn. March of Dimes Mothers-March, Toledo, 1989; pres. Ottawa Hills Athletic Boosters, Ohio, 1986-88, team physician, 1981-2003; trustee U. Toledo Found., 1999—. Decorated Legion of Merit; named to, Ohio Vets. Hall Fame, 2001; recipient Disting. Alumni award, Waite H.S., 1996, Garde Nationale Trophy, N.G. Assn. U.S., 1998, Outstanding Team Physician, Ohio H.S. Athletic Assn., 2002, Blue T award, U. Toledo, 2002, Outstanding Chem. Engr. Grad. award, 2002—03. Fellow ACS, ACOG (dist. chair 1996-99, v.p. 2000-01, Disting. Dist. Svc. award, 2004), Fedn. State Med. Bds. (editl. com.); mem. AMA (mem. ho. of dels.), Am. Soc. Reproductive Medicine, Ohio State Med. Assn. (pres. 1998-99), Pi Kappa Phi Alumni Assn. (Beta Iota chpt. Hall of Fame), U. Toledo Alumni Assn. (trustee 1996-2002, pres. 2000-01, athletic com., 2005—), Res. Officers Assn., Soc. Med. Cons. to Armed Forces, Am. Legion Post 335, Mil. Officers Assn. Am. (life), Assn. Mil. Surgeons US (life), Nat. Guard Assn. US (life). Republican. Lutheran. Office: The Toledo Hosp 2150 W Ctrl Ave Toledo OH 43606 Office Phone: 419-291-2193. Personal E-mail: latalmage@bex.net.

TALMI, YOAV, conductor, composer; b. Kibbutz Merhavia, Israel, Apr. 28, 1943; m. Erella Gottesmann; 2 children. Diploma, Rubin Acad. Music, Tel Aviv; postgrad., Julliard Sch. Music; D (hon.), Laval U., 2001. Artistic dir., condr. Gelders Symphony Orch., Arnhem, 1974-80; prin. guest condr. Munich Philham. Orch., 1979-80; artistic dir. Israel Chamber Orch., 1984-88; music dir. New Israeli Opera, 1985-89, San Diego Symphony Orch., 1990-96, Waterloo Festival, NJ, 1994-95, Que. Symphony, Can., 1999—, Hamburg (Germany) Symphony, 2000—04. Guest condr. Berlin Philharm., Munich Philharm., London Philharm., Philharmonia, Royal Philharm., Concertgebouw, Paris Orch. Nat., Israel Philharm., NHK Symphony, Tokyo, New Japan Philharm., Vienna Symphony, St. Petersburg Philharm., Pitts. Symphony, Detroit Symphony, St. Louis Symphony, Houston Symphony, Dallas Symphony, Montreal Symphony, N.Y. Chamber Symphony, LA Chamber Orch., Oslo Philharm., Tonhalle Orch., Zurich, others. Composer: Dreams for choir a capella, Music for Flute and Strings; Overture on Mexican Themes (recorded), 3 Monologues for Flute Solo (pub.), Inauguration Fanfare, Elegy for Strings, Timpani, and Accordion, 1997, Suite on Israeli Songs, The Double Marriage of Figaro; recs. include: Bruckner 9th Symphony (Oslo Philharm.), Tchaikovsky 1st Symphony (Quebec Symphony), Gliere 3d Symphony, Brahms Sextet/4 Serious Songs, Rachmaninov's Isle of the Dead, Berlioz: Symphonie Fantastique, Overtures, Harold in Italy, Romeo and Juliette, (San Diego Symphony), Tchaikowsky/Schoenberg, Bloch/Barber/Grieg/Puccini (Israel Chamber Orch.); (with Erella Talmi) works for flute and piano. Recipient Boskovitch prize for composition, Israel, 1965, Koussevitzky Meml. Conducting prize, Tanglewood, 1969, Ruppert Found. Condr. competition award, London, 1973, Ahad Ha'am award L.A. Ctr. Jewish Culture and the Am.-Israel Cultural Found., 1997. Home: PO Box 1384 Kefar Sava 44113 Israel Office: Michal Schmidt Artists Internat 59 E 54th St Ste 83 New York NY 10022 Office Phone: 212-421-8500. Home Fax: 972-9-765-6553. E-mail: talmi@netvision.net.il.

TALUKDER, JAMIL, physiologist, researcher; b. Bogra, Bangladesh, May 31, 1967; s. Abdul Hamid Talukder and Rashida Begum; m. Jubairun Nessa, Dec. 18, 1992; 1 child, Antara Jaima. DVM, Faculty Vet. Scis., Mymensingh, Bangladesh, 1991; MS, Dept. Physiology, Mymensingh, Bangladesh, 1995; PhD, Yamaguchi U., Japan, 2003. Lectr. Bangladesh Agrl. U., Mymensigh, Mymensingh, 1992—95, asst. prof., 1995—2003, assoc. prof., 2003—05. Presenter in field. Fellow, U. Rochester, NY, 2003—04, U. W.Va., Morgantown, 2004—07; scholar, Japanese Govt., 1998. Home: 418 Med Ctr Dr Apt # A-304 Morgantown WV 26505 Office: U WVa One Med Ctr Dr HSC Medicine Morgantown WV 26506-9161 Home Phone: 304-293-4518; Office Phone: 304-293-6582. Office Fax: 304-293-2135; Home Fax: 304-293-4518. Personal E-mail: jrtalukder@yahoo.com. E-mail: jtalukder@hsc.wvu.edu.

TALWALKAR, ABHI Y. (ABHIJIT Y. TALWALKAR), computer company executive; b. Pune, India, 1965; BEE, Oreg. State Univ., 1985. Sr. engring., mktg. mgmt. Sequent Computer Sys. (now part of IBM), Bipolar Integrated Tech. Inc., Lattice Semiconductor Inc.; with Intel Corp., Santa Clara, Calif., 1993—2005, various positions including v.p., gen. mgr., enterprise platform group, v.p., co-gen. mgr., digital enterprise group; pres., CEO, dir. LSI Logic Corp., Milpitas, Calif., 2005—. Office: LSI Logic Corp 1621 Barber Ln Milpitas CA 95035 Office Phone: 408-433-8000. *

TALWANI, MANIK, geophysicist, educator; b. Patiala, India, Aug. 22, 1933; came to U.S., 1954; m. Anni Fittler, Apr. 3, 1958; children: Rajeev Manik, Indira, Sanjay. BSc with honors, Delhi U., India, 1951, MSc, 1953; PhD, Columbia U., 1959; PhD (hon.), Oslo U., 1981. From rsch. scientist to assoc. prof. Lamont-Doherty Geol. Obs., Columbia U., NYC, 1959-70, dir. obs., 1972-81; prof. Columbia U., NYC, 1970-82; dir. Ctr. for Crustal Studies Gulf R & D Co., Pitts., 1981-83, chief scientist exploration div. Houston, 1983-85; Schlumberger prof. geophysics Rice U., Houston, 1985—; pres. Integrated Ocean Drilling Program-Mgmt. Internat., 2004—. Cons. Govt. of Iceland, 1982-92, Lockheed Martin, 1998-2000; dir. Geotech. Rsch. Inst., Houston Advanced Rsch. Ctr., Woodlands, 1985-98; Sackler disting. lectr. U. Tel Aviv, 1987; prin. investigator Apollo 17 first gravity measurements on moon. Co-author: Geophysical Atlas of the Norwegian Sea; editor 12 books on earth sci., Maurice Ewing Meml. Symposium; co-editor: Geophysical Atlases of Indian, Atlantic and Pacific Oceans; contbr. over 150 papers to profl. jours. Recipient Krishnan award Indian Geophys. Union, 1964, Exceptional Sci. Achievement award NASA, 1973, Guggenheim award, 1974, Alfred Wegener medal European Union Geoscis., 1993; Fulbright-Hays fellow, 1974. Fellow: AAAS, Geol. Soc. Am. (George P. Woollard award 1984), Am. Geophys. Union (James B. Macelwane award 1964, Maurice Ewing award 1981), Geol. Soc. India (hon.); mem.: Houston Philos. Soc., Acad. Nat. Scis. Russian Fedn., Petroleum Club, Houston Geophys. Soc. (hon.), Norwegian Acad. Scis., Am. Assn. Petroleum Geologists, Soc. Exptl. Geophysicists, Cosmos Club, Sigma Xi. Home: 1111 Hermann Dr Apt 10 D Houston TX 77004-6929 Office: Rice U PO Box 1892 Houston TX 77251-1892 also: IODP-MI 815 Connecticut Ave NW Ste 210 Washington DC 20006 Home Phone: 713-529-6344.

TAM, ALICE OI-LAI, entrepreneur, director; d. Tommy Wee Hong Hom and Fong Chan. BTh, Can. Mennonite Bible Coll., Canada, 1984; MDiv, Alliance Theol. Seninary, Nyack, NY, 2001; BA, U. Man., Canada, 2003. Prodr., v.p. Createvision Prodns., Inc., NYC, 1987—90; prodr. Apple TV, NYC, 1990—92, Chinese Comm. Channel, NYC, 1992—94; prodr., scriptwriter Sil-Met Corp., Hong Kong, 1994—96; exec. asst. Bank China Customer Svc., Hong Kong, 1996—97; mgr. Acts Trading Co., NYC, 1996—98; founder, exec. dir. Creator's Voice, Inc., NYC, 2005—. Prodr. Christian Chinese Song Writing Competition Concerts, 2005—; editor-in-chief Creator's Voice, Inc., NYC, 2006—. Prodr., dir. (numerous films & videos). Pastor Chinese ministries Grace Faith Ch., NYC, 2002—; pres. Cancer Survivor Coll. Fund Found., NYC, 2004. Recipient Jury award, NY Short Film & Video Awards, 1990. Office: Creator's Voice Inc PO Box 162 128 E Broadway New York NY 10002 Office Phone: 917-846-6363. Business E-Mail: alice@creatorvoice.org.

TAM, SUNNY WING YEE, physicist; s. Yin-Tso Tam and Yuk-Ying Sham Tam; m. Miho Ujimoto, Jan. 14, 1998; 1 child, Laurence Yoshina Ka-Ming. BA, U. of Calif., 1985—89; PhD, MIT, 1989—96. Rsch. asst. MIT, Cambridge, Mass., 1989—96, postdoctoral assoc., 1996—2000, rsch. scientist, 2000—06, rsch. affiliate, 2006—; assoc. rsch. prof. Plasma and Space Sci. Ctr., Nat. Cheng Kung U., Tainan, Taiwan, 2006—. Prin. investigator of federally funded rsch. project NASA, 2003—07, NSF, 2003—06; co-investigator of federally funded rsch. project NASA, 2000—03; co-principal investigator of federally funded rsch. projects NSF, 1996—2002; manuscript reviewer Geomagnetism and Aeronomy, 1996, Geophys. Rsch. Letters, 1996—; invited lectr., solar & stellar physics seminar Harvard U., Cambridge, Mass., 1995; invited lectr. 1995 Cambridge Workshop on Multiscale Phenomena in Space Plasmas, Bermuda, 1995; invited mem., internat. team on polar wind rsch. Internat. Space Sci. Inst., Bern, Switzerland, 2000; manuscript reviewer Jour. of Geophys. Rsch., 2001—; rsch. proposal reviewer NASA, 2002—, NSF, 2002—, Natural Sciences and Engring. Rsch. Coun. of Can., 2003; guest editor, spl. issue on most recent advances in the new polar wind theory and observations Jour. of Atmospheric and Solar-Terrestrial Physics, 2004—; manuscript reviewer Multiscale Coupling of Sun-Earth Processes (Elsevier Pub.), 2004; prin. investigator Nat. Ctr. for High-Performance Computing, Taiwan, 2007—; spkr. in field. Contbr. scientific papers. Grantee, Nat. Ctr. for High-Performance Computing, Taiwan, 2007—; Edward Frank Kraft scholar, U. Calif., Berkeley, 1986, James Monroe McDonald scholar, Physics Dept., U. Calif., Berkeley, 1988, Solar and Heliospheric Rsch. grantee, NASA, 2003—06, Magnetospheric Physics Rsch. grantee, NSF, 2003—05. Mem.: Am. Geophys. Union (co-convener spl. session Fall mtg. 2005), Golden Key, Phi Beta Kappa Soc., Sigma Pi Sigma. Avocations: soccer, Scrabble, backgammon, fencing.

TAMADDON, SINA, information technology executive; b. Aug. 27, 1957; V.p. Advanced Tech. Software Alliance Inc.; v.p. profl. svcs. NeXT, 1994—96, v.p. Europe, 1996—97; sr. v.p. worldwide svc. and support Apple Computer Inc., v.p. and gen. mgr. Newton Group, sr. v.p. applications Cupertino, Calif., 1997—. Office: Apple Computer Inc 1 Infinite Loop Cupertino CA 95014 Office Phone: 408-996-1010.

TAMARELLI, ALAN WAYNE, venture capitalist; b. Wilkinsburg, Pa., Aug. 13, 1941; s. John Adam Tamarelli and Florence Eleanor (Heacock) T.; m. Carol Ann Crawford, Aug. 3, 1963; children: Robin Carol, Alan Wayne. BS, Carnegie Mellon U., 1963, MS, 1965, PhD, 1966; MBA, NYU, 1972. Engr. Exxon Corp., Linden, NJ, 1966, project leader, 1968-70; corp. planner Engelhard Minerals & Chem. Corp., Newark, 1970-71, asst. to exec. v.p., 1971-74, gen. mgr., 1974-77, v.p., 1977-79, group v.p., 1979-81; sr. v.p. Engelhard Corp., Iselin, NJ, 1981-83; chmn., chief exec. officer Dock Resins Corp, Linden, NJ, 1983—2000; pres. AWT Private Investments, 2000—. Mem. exec. com. nat. adv. coun. for environ. policy and tech. U.S. Dept. Environment Protection, Gov's. Econ. Task Force, N.J.; mem. exec. com. Alliance for Union County; chmn. Jumpstart N.J., Joseph Priestley Soc. Capt. U.S. Army, 1966-68. NSF fellow, 1963-66 Mem. Synthetic Organic Chems. Mfrs. Assn. (chmn., vice chmn., bd. govs.), Am. Chem. Soc., N.Y. Paint and Coatings Assn. (chmn., pres., v.p., sec., treas., bd. dirs.), Chem. Industry Coun. (chmn., bd. dirs., exec. com.), N.J. Energy Rsch. Inst. (founding trustee), Am. Mgmt. Assn., N.Y. Acad. Scis., Scabbard and Blade, Rotary (pres., v.p., sec. Linden Club), Linden Indsl. Assn. (pres.), Joseph Priestley Soc. (chmn.), Shakespeare Theater of N.J. (bd. dirs.), Sigma Xi, Tau Beta Pi, Phi Kappa Phi, Omicron Delta Kappa. Home: 49 Wexford Way Basking Ridge NJ 07920-2432 Office Phone: 908-581-4308.

TAMAREN, MICHELE CAROL, spiritual director, writer, presenter, personal coach, retired special education educator; b. Hartford, Conn., Aug. 2, 1947; d. Herman Harold and Betty (Leavitt) Liss; m. David Stephen Tamaren, June 8, 1968; 1 child, Scott. BS in Elem. Edn., U. Conn., 1969; MA in Spl. Edn., St. Joseph Coll., West Hartford, Conn., 1976; student, Claritas Inst. for Interspiritual Inquiry, Boulder, Colo., 2005—. Cert. elem. and spl. edn. tchr. Conn., Mass. Tchr. N.Y. Inst. Spl. Edn., Bronx, 1971-74; ednl. cons. Renbrook Sch., West Hartford, 1975-78; grad. instr. St. Joseph Coll., 1978; elem. tchr. Acton (Mass.) Pub. Schs., 1969-70, tchr. spl. edn., 1978-94, inclusion and behavioral specialist, 1996-2000; learning specialist and writer Educators Pub. Svc., Cambridge, Mass., 1994-96. Personal coach; cons., presenter in field. Author: (book) I Make a Difference, 1992; contbr. articles to profl. jours. Bd. dirs. United Way, Acton-Boxborough, 1996—99. Grantee, Mass. Gov.'s Alliance Against Drugs, 1992; Horace Mann grantee, Mass. Dept. Edn., 1987, 1988. Mem.: Kappa Delta Pi, Phi Kappa Phi. Avocations: travel, writing, reading, yoga, swimming. Home and Office: 34 Constitution Way Apt D Marblehead MA 01945-4652 Personal E-mail: to_life@earthlink.net.

TAMARGO, MAURICIO J., federal agency administrator; b. Cuba; arrived in U.S., 1961; m. Tara Tamargo; 2 children. BA in History, U. Miami, 1985; JD, Samford U., 1989. Bar: Fla., D.C., U.S. Supreme Ct. Adminstrv. asst. Fla. State Rep. Ileana Ros-Lehtinen; legis. dir. Congresswoman Ileana Ros-Lehtinen; staff dir., counsel subcom. on internat. econ. policy and trade House Internat. Rels. Com., staff dir., counsel subcom. on Africa, staff dir. internat. ops. and human rights subcom.; chief of staff, legal counsel Congresswoman Ileana Ros-Lehtinen; chmn. Fgn. Claims Settlement Commn. U.S. Dept. Justice, Washington, 2002—. Republican. Office: US Dept Justice Fgn Claims Settlement Commn 600 E St NW Rm 6002 Washington DC 20579

TAMARGO, RAFAEL J., neurological surgeon, educator; b. Havana, Cuba, Mar. 22, 1958; AB magna cum laude, Princeton U., NJ, 1980; MD, Columbia U., NYC, 1984. Diplomate Am. Bd. Neurol. Surgery. Intern Columbia Coll. Physicians and Surgeons, NYC, 1984—85; resident in neurosurgery Johns Hopkins Hosp., Balt., 1985—92, active staff, 1992—, from assoc. prof. neurosurgery to Walter E. Dandy prof., 1998—2004, Walter E. Dandy prof., 2004—, assoc. prof. of otolaryngology, 2002—04, prof. otolaryngology, 2004—. Fellow ACS; mem. Am. Assn. Neurol. Surgeons. Office: Johns Hopkins Hosp 600 N Wolfe St Meyer 8-181 Baltimore MD 21287-0001 Office Phone: 410-614-1533. Business E-Mail: rtamarg@jhmi.edu.

TAMARO, GEORGE JOHN, retired consulting engineer; b. Weehawken, NJ, Mar. 16, 1937; s. Giorgio Angelo and Giacomina T; m. Rosemary Ann Volta, June 24, 1961; children: Peter Louis, Jean Marie, Paul Anthony, Mark Joseph. BCE, Manhattan Coll., 1959; MCE, Lehigh U., 1961; M of Archtl. Tech., Columbia U., 1969. Profl. engr., N.Y., N.J., D.C., Md., Pa., Calif., Ill., Tex., La., Wis., Wash., R.I., Ark., Idaho; structural engr., Ill., Mass.; geotech. engr., Calif.; chartered engr., U.K.; registered European engr. Staff engr. Port Authority NY & NJ, NYC, 1961—71; v.p., chief engr. ICOS Corp. Am., NYC, 1971—80; sr. ptnr. Mueser Rutledge Cons. Engrs., NYC, 1980—2006; ret., 2007. Patentee in field; author tech. papers. Chmn. Bergen County Planning Bd., N.J., 1978-82; vice-chair Leonia (N.J.) Planning Bd., 1971-89; mem. Bd. Adjustment, Leonia, 1974-76; councilman Borough Governing Body, Leonia, 1972. Recipient Lynn Beedle award, Lehigh U., 2005, NSPE award, 2006. Mem. ASCE (hon., Martin S. Kapp Found. Engr. award 1987, Homer Gage Balcom award 2002, Ralph B. Peck medal 2003, Friedman Profl. Recognition award 2003, OPAL award for engring. design 2004, Ernest E. Howard award 2006), NSPE (Annual award 2006), Am. Assn. Engring. Socs. (John Fritz medal 2005), Lehigh U.(Lynn Beedle award), Nat. Acad. Engring., Internat. Soc. Soil Mechs. and Found. Engrs., Deep Found. Inst. (Disting. Svc. award), The Moles (past pres., Outstanding Achievement in Constrn. award 2003, Beavers' award for outstanding achievement in heavy engring. constrn. 2004), Coun. on Tall Bldgs. and Urban Habitat, Chi Epsilon (hon. mem. award 1990), Tau Beta Pi. Avocations: sailing, photography.

TAMBAKERAS, MARKOS I., machine tool manufacturer; BS, U. Witwatersrand, Johannesburg, South Africa. Various positions Honeywell Inc., 1984-92, v.p. mktg. and bus. ops., pres. indsl. automation and control bus., 1995-99; pres. Honeywell Asia Pacific, 1992-94; pres., CEO Kennametal Inc., Latrobe, Pa., 1999—2005, chmn., 1999—. Office: Kennametal Inc PO Box 231 1600 Technology Way Latrobe PA 15650-0231

TAMBLYN, AMBER ROSE, actress; b. Santa Monica, Calif., May 14, 1983; d. Russ and Bonnie Tamblyn. Actor: (TV series) General Hospital, 1995—2001, Joan of Arcadia, 2003—05; (films) Live Nude Girls, 1995, Rebellious, 1995, Johnny Mysto: Boy Wizard, 1996, The Ring, 2002, The Sisterhood of the Traveling Pants, 2005, Stephanie Daley, 2006, The Grudge 2, 2006, (guest appearances): Buffy the Vampire Slayer, 2001, Boston Public, 2002, Twilight Zone, 2002, CSI: Miami, 2002, Without a Trace, 2003, Punk'd, 2003. Office: 8383 Wilshire Blvd Ste 530 Beverly Hills CA 90211 *

TAMBOLI, AKBAR RASUL, consulting engineer; b. Babhulgon, India, July 20, 1942; s. Rasul M. and Chandbi T.; m. Rounkbi A. Tamboli, May 21, 1969; children: Tahira, Ajim, Alamgir. BS, U. Poona, India, 1965; MS, Stanford U., 1967. Sr. engr. Miller Assocs., Pottsville, Pa., 1967-69; assoc. Edwards & Hjorth, NYC, 1970-76; sr. project engr. Engrs. Inc., East Orange, NJ, 1977-80; v.p. Office of Irwin G. Cantor PC, NYC, 1981-91; cons. engr. CUH2A Inc., Princeton, NJ, 1992-98; sr. v.p. Thornton-Tomasetti Group, NYC, 1999—. Editor: Steel Design LFRD Method Handbook, 1996, Handbook of Structural Steel Connection Design and Details. Vol. Cancer Fund Drive, N.J., 1986. Fellow ASCE; mem. Am. Steel Constrn., Am. Soc. Welding. Avocations: golf, boating. Home: 10 Davenport Dr Princeton Junction NJ 08550-3001 Office: Thornton-Tomasetti Group 641 Ave of the Americas New York NY 10011-2014

TAMBOR, JEFFREY, actor, theater director, educator; b. San Francisco, July 8, 1944; m. Kasia Ostlun, Oct. 6, 2001; children: Gabriel Kasper, Eve Julia. BA, San Francisco State; MFA, Wayne State U. Acting tchr. Milton Katselas' Acting Workshops, Beverly Hills, Calif. Actor (theatre) Sly Fox, 1976 (Broadway and L.A.), Measure for Measure, The Hands of the Enemy, Flea in Her Ear, American Mosaic; (films) ...And Justice For All, 1979, Saturday the 14th, 1981, Dreamchasers, 1982, The Man Who Wasn't There, 1983, Mr. Mom, 1983, No Small Affair, 1984, Desert Hearts, 1985, Three O'Clock High, 1987, Brenda Starr, 1989, Lisa, 1990, City Slickers, 1991, Life Stinks, 1991, Pastime, 1991, Article 99, 1992, Crossing the Bridge, 1992, The Webbers, 1993, A House in the Hills, 1993, Radioland Murders, 1994, Heavyweights, 1995, My Teacher's Wife, 1995, Big Bully, 1996, Dr. Dolittle, 1998, There's Something About Mary, 1998, Meet Joe Black, 1998, Muppets From Space, 1999, Teaching Mrs. Tingle, 1999, Girl Interrupted, 1999, Pollock, 2000, How the Grinch Stole Christmas, 2000, Never Again, 2001, Get Well Soon, 2001, Scorched, 2002, The Freshman, 2002, Malibu's Most Wanted, 2003, My Boss's Daughter, 2003, Nobody's Perfect, 2004, Hellboy, 2004, Funky Monkey, 2004, (voice) The SpongeBob SquarePants Movie, 2004; (TV series) The Ropers, 1979-80, Hill Street Blues, 1981-87, 9 to 5, 1982, Mr. Sunshine, 1986, (voice) Jonny Quest, 1986, Max Headroom, 1987-88, Studio 5-B, 1989, American Dreamer, 1990, The Larry Sanders Show, 1992-98 (Emmy award nominee 1993), Me & George, 1998, (voice) The Lionhearts, 1998, Everything's Relative, 1999, The Lot, 1999, (voice) Sammy, 2000, That Was Then, 2002, 3-South, 2002, Hollywood Squares (announcer), 2002-03, Arrested Development, 2003—; (TV episodes) M*A*S*H, Barney Miller, L.A. Law, The Golden Girls, Empty Nest, Who's The Boss, Doogie Houser, M.D., Equal Justice, Murder She Wrote, Tales From The Crypt (Dead Right) (TV movies) Eddie and Herbert, 1977, Alcatraz: The Whole Shocking Story, 1980, A Gun in the House, 1981, The Star Maker, 1981, Pals, 1981, The Awakening of Candra, 1981, Take Your Best Shot, 1982, The Zertigo Diamond Caper, 1982, Cocaine: One Man's Seduction, 1983, Sadat, 1983, The Three Wishes of Billy Grier, 1984, Wildfire, 1986, A Quiet Little Neighborhood, a Perfect Little Murder, 1990, The Burden of Proof, 1992, 1775, 1992, (voice) Jonny's Golden Quest, 1993, Another Midnight Run, 1994, (voice) Jonny Quest vs. the Cyber Insects, 1995, The Man Who Captured Eichmann, 1996, Weapons of Mass Distraction, 1997, Eloise at the Plaza, 2003, Eloise at the Plaza, 2003, Eloise at Christmastime, 2003, The Muppets' Wonderful Wizard of Oz, 2005; (TV spls.) Living and Working in Space: The Countdown Has Begun; (TV miniseries) Robert Kennedy and His Times, 1985; dir. for numerous theatre companies including Seattle Repertory Theatre, Actors Theatre of Louisville, Milw. Repertory Theatre, Acad. Festival Theatre, Chgo., San Diego Shakespeare Festival, South Coast Repertory Theatre, Loeb Drama Ctr., Cambridge, Mass., Sky Light Theatre, L.A. Office: Care The Gersh Agency c/o Leslie Siebert 232 N Canon Dr Beverly Hills CA 90210-5302

TAMBORLANE, WILLIAM V., JR., pediatrician, educator; b. NYC, Aug. 25, 1946; s. William and Eleanor (Bernabo) T.; m. Kathleen Mary Blinn, Dec. 27, 1969; children: Melissa, Amy, James. BS, Georgetown U., 1968, MD, 1972. Diplomate Am. Bd. Pediatrics, Am. Bd. Pediatric Endocrinology. Attending physician Yale New Haven Hosp., 1977—. Asst. prof. pediatrics Yale U., New Haven, 1977-81, dir. Children's Diabetes Ctr., 1977-2004; assoc. prof. pediatrics Sch. Medicine, New Haven, 1982-83; chief pediatric endocrinology and diabetes Yale Sch. Medicine, 1985-, prof. pediatrics, 1986-; program dir. Yale Children's Clin. Rsch. Ctr., N.H., Conn., 1986-2004; chmn. Lawson Wilkens Diabetes Com., 1988-89; dir. Yale Pediatric Pharmacology Rsch. Unit, 1999-2004; chair steering com. Diabetes Rsch. Children Network, 2001-; dep. dir. Yale Ctr. Clin. Investigation, 2006-. Editor: Yale Guide to Children's Nutrition, 1997. Recipient Jonathan May award, Charles Best award Am. Diabetes Assn., 1979, Clin. Investigator award NIH, 1979-82, Juvenile Diabetes Rsch. Found. award for excellence in clin. rsch., 2006. Mem. Am. Fedn. Clin. Rsch., Am. Soc. Clin. Investigation, Endocrine Soc., Soc. Pediatric Rsch., Phi Beta Kappa. Office Phone: 203-785-4646. Business E-Mail: william.tamborlane@yale.edu.

TAMBS, LEWIS ARTHUR, diplomat, historian, educator; b. San Diego, July 7, 1927; s. Fred B. and Marguerite Johanna (Tambs) Jones; m. Phyllis Ann Greer, 1982. BS, U. Calif., Berkeley, 1953; MA, U. Calif., Santa Barbara, 1962, PhD, 1967. Plant engr. Std. Brands, San Francisco, 1953—54; pipeline engr. Creole Petroleum Co., Caracas, Maracaibo, Venezuela, 1954—57; gen. mgr. Cacyp, Maracaibo, 1957—59; instr. Creighton U., 1965—67, asst. prof., 1967—69; prof. history Ariz. State U., Tempe, 1969—82, 1987—2002, dir. Ctr. L.Am. Studies, 1972—76; cons. NSC, 1982—83; U.S. amb. to Colombia, 1983—85; U.S. amb. to Costa Rica, 1985—87; ret., 2002. Author: East European and Soviet Economic Affairs, 1975, Historiography, Method and History Teaching, 1975, Hitler's Spanish Legion, 1979; editor: United States Policy Toward Latin America, 1976, Inter-American Policy for the 80's; co-editor: Santa Fe IV, 2000, English translation of Karl Haushofer's Geopolitics of the Pacific, 2002; co-author periodical guides; contbr. articles to profl. jours. Bd. dirs. Ariz.-Mex. Commn., 1974-82, Coun. Inter-Am. Security, 1979-90. With U.S. Army, 1945-47, 50-51. Faculty grantee, Ariz. State U., 1970, 1971, 1974, 1978, 1979. Roman Catholic. E-mail: lewtambs@aol.com.

TAMBURINE, JEAN HELEN, sculptor, painter, illustrator; b. Meriden, Conn., Feb. 20, 1930; m. Eugene E. Bertolli. Student, Art Students League, NYC, 1948-50; student of Jon Corbino, John Groth, Carlo Ciampaglia, Elisabeth Gordon Chandler. Exhibited group shows Rockport Art Assn., Mass., North Shore Arts Assn., Gloucester, Mass., George Walter Vincent Mus., Springfield, Mass., Hudson Valley Art Assn., NY, Pearl S. Buck Found., Phila., Am. Artists Profl. League, NY, Acad. Artists Assn., Springfield, Pen and Brush, NY; heritage bronze commd. by Wallingford Pub. Library, 1986, Conn.; represented in permanent collections Conn. State Library, Middletown, Nashville Pub. Library, Strong Sch., Hartford, Conn., L'Heure Joyeux, Paris; also pvt. collections; author, designer, illustrator: Almost Big Enough, 1963, I Think I Will Go to the Hospital, 1965, How Now, Brown Cow, 1967. Recipient Assoc. Members prize Acad. Artists, Founders prize Pen and Brush, 1981, 1st prize for sculpture Arts and Crafts Assn. of Meriden, Conn.; named to Meriden Hall of Fame. Mem. Rockport Art Assn. (Martha Moore Meml. award 1983), North Shore Arts Assn., Acad. Artists Assn., Salmagundi Club, Am. Artists Profl. League, Am. Medallic Sculpture Assn., FIDEM, Authors Guild. Home and Office: The Bertolli Studio 73 Reynolds Dr Meriden CT 06450-2532

TAMBURRO, PETER JAMES, JR., secondary school educator; b. Hoboken, NJ, Jan. 20, 1947; s. Peter James and Rose Catherine (Verta) Tamburro; m. Andrea Everitt Huber, Aug. 21, 1976 (div. 1998); children: Peter James III, Christopher Harding, Matthew Everitt. BA in Polit. Sci, Dickinson Coll., 1969; MAT in Social Studies, Trenton State Coll., 1973. Cert. secondary sch. tchr., social studies N.J. Tchr. Morris Sch. Dist., NJ, 1973-76, Hanover Park Regional HS Dist., East Hanover, NJ, 1976—2005, Frisch HS, 2005—. Cross country coach Hanover Park HS, 1983—2003, volleyball coach, 1990—98, asst. basketball coach, 1994—2001; judge Bicentennial Com., NJ; asst. basketball coach Caldwell Coll., 1989—93; cons. Hist. Commn., East Hanover, 1989—92; cons. for developing Advanced Placement history programs, reader Advanced Placement exams ETS; mem. hist. com. Washington Twp., 1994—97, curriculum adv. com., 1996—97; adj. prof. William Paterson U., NJ, 1999—; chess coach Frisch HS, 2005—, table tennis coach, 2006—; spkr. in field. Author: (book) Gateway to Morris, 1993, Learn Chess from the Greats, 2000; editor (with Dale Brandreth): The Chess Diary of Rudolph Spielmann; editor: Atlantic Chess News, 1973—76, 2000—02, Teaching Chess Step by Step, 2006; contbr. articles to chess mags.; nationally syndicated columnist: U.S. Chess Fedn., 1994—2001, columnist: Chessmates, Newark Star Ledger, 1997—, feature writer: Chess Life for Kids; host internet radio show Openings for Amateurs, www.chess.fm. Mem. Hist. Commn., Washington Twp., NJ, 1994—96; scoutmaster Boy Scouts Am., 1994—97; team capt. Rep. Nat. Conv., 2000; Rep. County Committeeman Hanover Twp., NJ, 1984—88; legis. aide Assemblyman Robert Martin, Trenton, 1985—89; Rep. County Committeeman Morristown, NJ, 2002—03. Named N.J.'s Outstanding Tchr. History, DAR, 1990, Cross Country State Section Champions, 1987, 2000, 2001, 2002, Morris County Coach of the Yr., Cross Country, 2000; fellow Taft Inst. Two Party Govt., Fairleigh Dickinson U., 1984, Woodrow Wilson Found., 1991, Nat., Coun. Basic Edn., Washington, 1993; grantee, NSF, 1978, Dodge Found., Madison, N.J., 1987. Mem.: Chess Journalists Am. (v.p. 1990—99, pres. 1999—2003, awards 1995, 1996, 1997, 2002, 2003, Journalist of Yr. 2006, awards 2006), US Chess Fedn. (nat. chmn. hist. com. 1994—99), NJ Edn. Assn., Hanover Park Regional Ednl. Assn. (v.p. 1994—95, pres. 1995—2001, chief negotiator 2003—05), Morris County Hist. Soc., Nat. Coun. Social Studies. Avocations: rare books, chess. Home: 22 Budd St Morristown NJ 07960-5304 Office: Frisch Sch Paramus NJ 07652

TAMEN, HARRIET, lawyer; b. Yonkers, NY, May 17, 1947; d. Saul and Lily (Balglau) T. AB, Bryn Mawr Coll., 1969; JD, George Washington U., Washington, 1973. Bar: N.Y. 1974, U.S. Dist. Ct. (so. dist.) N.Y. 1975. Atty. W.T. Grant, NYC, 1974-76, City of N.Y. Office Econ. Devel., divsn. Real Property, NYC, 1977-81, Credit Lyonnais Bank, NYC, 1981-86, Chase Manhattan Bank, 1986-89; v.p., counsel internat. corp. fin. Citibank, 1989-92; ptnr. Claugus Tamen & Orenstein, 1992-93; pvt. practice NYC, 1994—. Bd. dirs. Dromenon Theatre, N.Y., 1980-86, Nat. Dance Inst., N.Y., 1982, chmn. bd. dirs., 1984-87; chmn. bd. dirs. Theatre & Dance Alliance, 1989-90; del. exch. program Women in Law, South Am., 1987—; mem. campaign staff Ed Koch for Mayor, N.Y.C., 1977; mem. steering com. Soviet Am. Banking Law Working Group, 1991—; guest lectr. Moscow Conf. on Banking, 1992, Ulaan Baatar, Mongolia, 1993-94, 96, Harriman Inst. of Columbia U., 1994; co-chair N.Y. Lawyers Com. for Clinton-Gore; mem. adv. coun. U.S. Export Import Bank, 2000. Mem. ABA, Assn. of Bar of City of N.Y. Office Phone: 212-284-5260.

TAMIR, THEODOR, electrophysics researcher, educator; b. Bucharest, Romania, Sept. 17, 1927; came to U.S., 1958, naturalized, 1968; s. Martin and Helena (Hart) Berman; m. Hadassah Cohen, Oct. 5, 1949; children: Jonathan, Yael. BS Technion, Israel Inst. Tech., 1953, Dipl. Ingenieur, 1954, MS, 1958; PhD, Poly. Inst. Bklyn., 1962. Instr. Technion Israel Inst. Tech., Haifa, 1956-58; mem. rsch. staff Poly. Inst., Bklyn., 1958-62; mem. faculty Poly. Univ., Bklyn., 1962—, head dept. elec. engring., 1974—79, prof. electrophysics, 1969—92, Univ. prof., 1992—. Sci. and engring. cons. to indsl. and govtl. labs. Editor, author: Integrated Optics, 1975 (transl. into Russian and Chinese), Guided Wave Optoelectronics, 1988 (transl. into Russian); co-editor: Springer Series in Optical Sciences, 1979-96; contbr. chpts. to books, articles to profl. jours. Served with Israeli Army, 1947-49. Awarded Instn. Premium, 1964, Electronics Premium, 1967, Instn. Elec. Engrs., London; citation for disting. research Polytechnic chpt. Sigma Xi, 1978. Fellow IEEE, Optical Soc. Am.; mem. Internat. Union Radio Sci., Sigma Xi. Home: 981 E Lawn Dr Teaneck NJ 07666-6604 Office: Polytechnic Univ Elec & Comp Engring Dept 5 MetroTech Ctr Brooklyn NY 11201 Office Phone: 718-260-3320. Business E-Mail: ttamir@duke.poly.edu.

TAMKE, GEORGE WILLIAM, venture capitalist; b. Beacon, NY, May 16, 1947; s. George William and Josephine Edna (Carbone) Tamke; m. Christine Barbara MacLeod, June 28, 1969; children: Kara Lee, Shannon. BSChemE, Vanderbilt U., 1969; MS in Mgmt. Sci., Stanford U., 1979. With IBM, NY, Fla., Calif., Ga., Minn., 1969—86, dir. orgn. planning and sec. to corp. mgmt. com. White Plains, NY, 1981—82, v.p. mfg. Communication Products div., 1982—83, v.p. display products Communication Products div., 1983—84, asst. group exec. Info Systems, Products Group, 1984—86; pres. Cullinet Software, Inc., Westwood, Mass., 1986—87, COO, 1987—88; exec. v.p. Emerson Electric Co., St. Louis, 1989—; principal Clayton, Dubilier & Rice, 2000—; CEO Kinkos, 2001, chmn., 2001—04, Culligan Internat., 2004, Hertz Corp., 2005—06, Servicemaster Co., 2007—. CEO Astec (BSR) Plc, Hong Kong, 1989—; bd. dir. Target Corp. Contbr. articles to profl. jours. Avocations: tennis, golf. Office: Clayton Dubilier & Rice 375 Park Ave 18th Fl New York NY 10152-1899 *

TAMKIN, CURTIS SLOANE, real estate development company executive; b. Boston, Sept. 21, 1936; s. Hayward and Etta (Goldfarb) T.; m. Priscilla Martin, Oct. 18, 1975; 1 child, Curtis Sloane. BA in Econs., Stanford U., Calif., 1958. V.p., treas., dir. Hayward Tamkin & Co., Inc., mortgage bankers, LA, 1963-70; mng. ptnr. Property Devel. Co., LA, 1970-82; pres. The Tamkin Co., 1982—2000; chmn. Tamkin Capital Group L.L.C., 1999—. Mem. bd. govs. Music Ctr. LA, 1974—98; pres. LA Master Chorale Assn., 1974—78; mem. vis. com. Stanford U. Librs., 1982—86; vice-chmn. bd. dirs., mem. exec. com. LA Philharm. Assn., 1985—2006, vice chmn. bd., 2004—06, chmn. bd. overseers, 2001—07. Lt. (j.g.) USNR, 1960—63. Mem.: Nat. Coun. World Wildlife Fund, Pacific Council Internat. Policy, L.A. Jr. C. of C. (dir. 1968—69), Founders League L.A. Music Ctr. (pres. 1988—98, chmn. emeritus 1998—), Hillcrest Country Club, Burlingame Country Club. Home: 1230 Stone Canyon Rd Los Angeles CA 90077-2920 Office: 9460 Wilshire Blvd Beverly Hills CA 90212-2732

TAMKIN, S. JEROME, manufacturing executive, consultant; b. LA, Apr. 19, 1926; s. William W. and Thelma (Brandel) T.; m. Judith Deborah, Mar. 23, 1963; children: Steven Marc, Windy Lynn, Gary William, Sherry Dawn. BS, U. So. Calif., 1950; MA, Fremont Coll., 1951, PhD, 1952; LL.D., St. Andrews U., London, 1954. Rsch. staff chemistry dept. U. Calif., LA, 1943; rsch. chemist, analyst supr. synthetic rubber div. U.S. Rubber Co., 1943-44; rsch. engr. Coll. Engring., U. So. Calif., 1946-48; gen. mgr. Pan Pacific Oil Co., Long Beach, Calif., 1948-55; plant mgr. indsl. sales and mfg., 1953-55; v.p., sales mgr. Wilco Co., LA, 1948-55, v.p. charge indsl. sales and mfg., 1953-55; v.p., sales mgr. Unit Chem. Corp., LA, 1955-56; pres. Phillips Mfg. Co. (merger Instl. Food Equipment Corp.), LA, 1957-62, Waste King Corp. (subs. Instl. Food Equipment Corp.), 1962-67; also dir.; v.p., dir. Dyna Mfg. Co., LA, 1962-68; pres., dir. Profl. Rsch. Inc., LA, 1965-73; exec. v.p. Am. Med. Internat., Inc., Beverly Hills, Calif., 1966-71, dir., 1966-89; sec., dir. Rodger Young, Inc., LA, 1971-77; pres., chmn. bd. TGT Petroleum Corp., Wichita, 1972—; pres., dir. Tamkin Cons. Corp., 1978—; owner, operator Tamkin Securities Co., 1979-86; vice chair bd., dir. Integrated Voice Solutions Inc., Chattanooga, 1991-96; bd. dirs. CAPP Care Inc., Newport Beach, Calif., 1991-99. Tech. cons. Daylin Inc., Beverly Hills, 1973-75; bd. dirs. Healthcare Decisions, Inc., Newport Beach, Calif., 1996-99. Contbr. articles to profl. jours.; patentee electronic gas detector, circuits for automatic control hazardous vapors. Cmty. warden W. Adams-Baldwin Hills Cmty. CD, 1950—52; bd. govs. West LA County coun. Boy Scouts Am., 1977—; bd. govs. Technion-Israel Inst. of Tech., 2001—; dep. sheriff L.A. County, 1949; city commr. L.A. Bd. Environ. Quality, 1972—73; bd. dirs. Sunair Home Asthmatic Children, Recovery Found., Fund for Higher Edn., U. of Judaism, 1999—, UCLA Brain Mapping Found., 1999—, UCLA Ctr. on Aging, LA, 2005—; bd. visitors UCLA Sch. Medicine, 1990—; exec. com. adv. coun. crime prevention LA Police, 1985—; trustee, bd. visitors U. Calif.-Irvine Coll. Medicine, 1989—; trustee Morehouse Sch. Medicine, 1995—2005, Scripps Found. for Medicine and Sci., 1996—. Officer USNR, 1944—46. Mem. AIM, Am. Mgmt. Assn., Inst. Aero. Scis., Am. Soc. Naval Engrs., Soc. Am. Mil. Engrs., Am. Chem. Soc., IEEE, Soc. Motion Picture and TV Engrs., Am. Inst. Chem. Engrs., Soc. Advancement Mgmt., U.S. Naval Inst., Calif. Scholarship Fedn. (life), Nat. Eagle Scout Assn., Sunrise Country Club, The Springs Country Club, Malibu Riding and Tennis Club, Alpha Eta Rho. Office: 2100 Sawtelle Blvd Ste 201 Los Angeles CA 90025-6264 Office Phone: 310-479-2555.

TAMKUS, DANIEL, writer, advertising executive; b. Scranton, Pa., Feb. 8, 1934; s. Stanley Ambrose Tamkus and Bernice Eva Levinskas; m. Edith Neil Russell, Apr. 30, 1955 (div.); life ptnr. Ellen Brown Cutler; children: Michele Anne, Denise Holenstein. AB, Johns Hopkins U., Balt., 1953, MA, 1954. Editor U.S. Govt. Proving Ground, Aberdeen, Md., 1955—61; writer N.W. Ayer, Phila., 1961—74; owner, pres. Daniel Tamkus Inc., Phila., 1974—. Mem. adv. com. writing seminars Johns Hopkins U., 2002—. Author: (novel) The Much Honored Man, 1959; author under pen-name L. J. Key: novel The Spawn, 1983; screenwriter (film) The Way We Live Now, 1969, story credit Cloud Dancer, 1979. Recipient Best Comml. award, Clio Awards, 1972. Mem.: NARAS, ASCAP, Writer's Guild of Am., Phi Beta Kappa. Avocations: reading, gardening, travel, painting. Personal E-mail: dtamkus@jhu.edu.

TAMMARO, KELLY ANN, pharmacist, researcher; b. Methuen, Mass., Mar. 9, 1978; s. Joseph Peter and Sheila Ann DiBurro; m. Daniel Pasquale Tammaro, Aug. 10, 2003. PharmD, Mass. Coll. Pharmacy and Allied Health Scis., Boston, 2002. Cert. pharmacist NH, 2002, Mass., 02. Pharmacy practice resident Boston VA Healthcare Sys., 2002—03, clin. oncology pharmacist, 2003—, clin. trials heme/oncology rsch. coord., mgr., 2005—. Mem.: Am. Soc. Hosp. Pharmacist. Achievements include research in effects of oxaliplatin induced neurotoxicity. Office: Boston VA Healthcare Sys 150 South Huntington Avenue Boston MA 02130 Home Phone: 978-664-5515; Office Phone: 857-364-5033. Business E-Mail: kelly_tammaro_va@yahoo.com.

TAMMEUS, WILLIAM DAVID, journalist, columnist; b. Woodstock, Ill., Jan. 18, 1945; s. W. H. and Bertha H. (Helander) T.; m. Marcia Bibens, Nov. 29, 1996; children: Lisen Tammeus Mann, Kate Tammeus Willaredt; stepchildren: Christopher L. Johnston, Daniel Bednarczyk, Kathryn B. Dandino, David Bednarczyk. BJ, U. Mo., Columbia, 1967; postgrad., U. Rochester, 1967-69. Reporter Rochester (N.Y.) Times-Union, 1967-70; reporter Kansas City (Mo.) Star, 1970-77, columnist, 1977—; syndicated columnist N.Y. Times News Svc., 1989-99, Knight Ridder/Tribune Info. Svcs., 2000—06; ret., 2006. Author: A Gift of Meaning, 2001; editor-at-large Presbyn. Outlook, 1993; contbg. editor Mo. Life mag., 1980-81; commentator Sta. KCPT-TV, 1979-90. Co-recipient Pulitzer prize for gen. local reporting of Hyatt Regency Hotel disaster, 1982; recipient 1st pl. opinion-editl. divsn. Heart of Am. award Kansas City Press Club, 1991, 93, 1st pl. column divsn., 1994, 1st pl. award best column/humor divsn. Mo. Press Assn., 1997, 2002, Best In-Depth Reporting on Religion award Am. Acad. Religion, 2001, David Steele Disting. Writer award Presbyn. Writers Guild, 2003, 1st pl. religion coverage Kans. Press Assn., 2004, Wilbur Column Writing award, Religion Communicators Coun., 2005, 1st pl. best feature column divsn. Mo. Press Assn., 2006. Mem. Nat. Soc. Newspaper Columnists (v.p. 1990-92, pres. 1992-94, 1st pl. items divsn. Writing award 1992, 3d place humor writing, 1999, 2000), Soc. Profl. Journalists. Presbyterian. Personal E-mail: wtammeus@kc.rr.com.

TAMPAS, JOHN P., radiologist; married; children: Jessica, Peter, Andrea, Christiana. BS, U. Vt., 1951, MD, 1954. Diplomate Am. Bd. Radiology. Radiology resident U. Vt., Burlington, 1957—60; teaching fellow pediat. radiology L.A. Children's Hosp., 1960—61; NIH Nat. Heart Inst. resident fellow cardiovascular radiology U. Ind., Indpls., 1961—62; attending radiology Med. Ctr. Hosp. Vt., Burlington, 1962—; asst. prof. radiology Coll. Medicine U. Vt., 1962—70; prof. & chmn. dept. radiology Med. Ctr. Hosp. Vt., Burlington, 1970—96. Contbr. articles to profl. jours. Recipient Karl Jefferson Thompson Meml. Excellence in Tchg. award, 1969, 1975; scholar, James Picker Found./NRC, 1962—65. Fellow: Am. Coll. Radiology (pres. 1987—88, bd. chancellors, emergency radiology com., accreditation com., chmn. mem. ins. com., adminstrv. affairs commn., radiologic practice commn., Gold medal 1996); mem.: AMA, Vt. Med. Soc., Vt. Radiol. Soc., Assn. Univ. Radiologists, Soc. Chmn. Acad. Radiology Depts., New Eng. Roentgen Ray Soc., Radiol. Soc. N.Am., Am. Roentgen-Ray Soc. (pres. 1982—83, Gold medal 1992), Soc. Pediat. Radiology, Alpha Omega Alpha. Office: Fletcher Allen Health Ctr 111 Colchester Ave Burlington VT 05401-1416 also: Hosp Vt Med Ctr Dept Radiology Burlington VT 05401

TAMTE-HORAN, MICHAEL WILLIAM, music educator, conductor; b. Webster City, Iowa, Dec. 27, 1949; s. William Eugene Horan and Rosalie Anabelle May; m. Deborah Elsie Tamte-Horan, Sept. 8, 1979; children: Chelsea Lynn, Kirsten Marie. BS in Music Edn., Luther Coll., Decorah, Iowa, 1972; MFA in Choral Conducting, U. Minn., Mpls., 1978; EdD in Music Edn., U. Ill., Champaign, 1988. Dir. choral activities U. West Ala., Livingston, 1980—82; dir. glee clubs and music edn. U. NC, Chapel Hill, 1982—88; dir. choral music Triton Coll., Chgo., 1995—98; dir. choral activities DePaul U., Chgo., 1997—99, St. Cloud State U., Minn., 1999—2004; dir. choral music Marywood U., Scranton, Pa., 2005—. Condr. guest choral performances Minn. Music Educators State Conf., NC Music Educators State Conf., Am. Choral Directors Assn. Minn. State Conf., Am. Choral Directors Assn. NC State Conf.; guest condr., adjudicator and/or clinician, Ala., 1975—, Colo., 1975—, Ill., 1975—, Minn., 1975—, NC, 1975—, Ohio, 1975—, Pa., 1975—, Va., 1975—, Wash., 1975—; founder, artistic dir. Cantatica, Chamber Choir and Website; mem., soloist Dale Warland Singers. Dir. music United Meth. Ch. Named condr. Vancouver Chamber Choir, Can. Nat. Choral Conducting Symposium, 2005; scholar, Luther Coll., U. Minn., U. Ill. Mem.: Music Educators Nat. Conf., Nat. Assn. Tchrs. of Singing, Chorus Am., Am. Choral Dirs. Assn. (life; bd. mem. (Minn. chpt.) 2002—04, Creative Programming and Excellence in Choral Performance award 2005), Phi Delta Kappa. Home Phone: 610-871-0542; Office Phone: 570-348-6268.

TAMULONIS, FRANK LOUIS, JR., lawyer; b. Pottsville, Pa., Sept. 26, 1946; s. Frank Louis Sr. and Cecelia Florence T.; m. Jane Alice Troutman, June 26, 1976; children: Kathryn Lydia, Frank Louis III. AB, Cornell U., 1968; JD, Villanova Law Sch., 1971. Bar: Pa. 1971, U.S. Supreme Ct. 1975, U.S. Ct. Appeals (3d cir.) 1981. Law clk. to dist. judge U.S. Dist. Ct. (ea. dist.), Phila., 1971—74; assoc. Kassab, Cherry & Archbold, Media, Pa., 1974—76, Zimmerman, Lieberman & Derenzo, Pottsville, 1976—2001; ptnr. Zimmerman, Lieberman, Tamulonis & Crossen, Pottsville, 2001—04, Zimmerman, Lieberman & Tamulonis, Pottsville, 2004—. Contbr. articles to profl. jours. Mem. ATLA, Def. Rsch. Inst., Pa. Def. Inst., Inst. Pa. Trial Lawyers Assn., Pa. Bar Assn., Schuylkill County Bar Assn. Republican. Roman Catholic. Office: Zimmerman Lieberman & Tamulonis PO Box 238 111 E Market St Pottsville PA 17901 Office Phone: 570-622-1988. Personal E-mail: ftamulonis@comcast.net.

TAMURA, CARY KAORU, consultant; b. Honolulu, Jan. 9, 1944; s. Akira and Harue T.; m. Denise Jeanne Mitts, Oct. 17, 1987; children: Jennifer Joy, Matthew D. Student, U. Hawaii, 1961—63; BA in Philosophy, Nyack Coll., 1966; MA in Theology, Fuller Sem., 1986. Dir. svc. tng. ops. Fin. Adv. Clinic of Hawaii, Honolulu, 1972—76; dir. planned giving The Salvation Army, Honolulu, 1976—78, Portland, Oreg., 1981—85; cons. planned giving InterVarsity Christian Fellowship, Portland, 1978—80; account exec. Am. Income Life, Portland, 1980—81; dir. devel., planned giving U. So. Calif., 1985—90; dir. gift planning UniHealth America, Burbank, Calif., 1990—94; pvt. practice Brea, Calif., 1995—. Adv. com., adj. faculty UCLA Extension; lectr. in field. Bd. dirs. Nat. Com. on Planned Giving, Indpls., 1991-93, sec. exec. com., 1993; bd. dirs. Japanese Evang. Missionary Soc., 1990-95, 2003—, Simpson U., 1998—; deacons Evang. Free Ch., 1992-95. With U.S. Army, 1969-72. Mem. Planned Giving Round Table So. Calif. (pres. 1989-91, Pres.'s award 1992), Assn. of Fundraising Profls. (bd. dirs. Greater L.A. chpt. 1990-97, v.p. 1993, 95, treas. 1996-97, Profl. Fund Raiser of Yr. award 1995). Republican. Avocations: photography, golf, travel. Office: PO Box 908 Brea CA 92822 Personal E-mail: visionkeeper1@yahoo.com.

TAN, AMY RUTH, writer; b. Oakland, Calif., Feb. 19, 1952; d. John Yueh-han and Daisy Ching (Tu) T.; m. Louis M. DeMattei, Apr. 6, 1974. Student, Linfield Coll., McMinnville, Oreg., San Jose City Coll., Calif.; BA in Linguistics and English with honors, San Jose State U., Calif., 1973, MA in Linguistics, 1974; LHD (hon.), Dominican Coll. San Rafael, 1991. Specialist lang. devel. Alameda County Assn. for Mentally Retarded, Oakland, 1976-80; project dir. M.O.R.E. Project, San Francisco, 1980-81; mng. editor Emergency Medicine Reports newsletter, San Francisco; freelance writer, 1981-88; literary editor West mag. LA Times. Author: (novels) The Joy Luck Club, 1989 (Nat. Book Critics Cir. award for best novel nomination 1989, LA Times Book award nomination 1989, Gold award for fiction Commonwealth Club 1990, Bay Area Book Reviewers award for best fiction 1990), The Kitchen God's Wife, 1991, The Hundred Secret Senses, 1995, The Bonesetter's Daughter, 2001, The Opposite of Fate: A Book of Musing, 2003, Saving Fish from Drowning, 2005; (children's books) The Moon Lady, 1992, The Chinese Siamese Cat, 1994; also numerous short stories and essays; screenwriter, prodr.: (film) The Joy Luck Club, 1993. Recipient Best Am. Essays award, 1991. Office: c/o Putnam Publicity 375 Hudson Street New York NY 10014 *

TAN, ENG MENG, immunologist, biomedical researcher; b. Seremban, Malaysia, Aug. 26, 1926; arrived in US, 1950; s. Ming Kee and Chooi Eng (Ang) T.; m. Liselotte Filippi, June 30, 1962; children: Philip, Peter. BA, Johns Hopkins U., 1952, MD, 1956. Intern Duke U., Durham, NC, 1956-57; resident, fellow Case-We. Res. U., Cleve., 1957-62; rsch. assoc. Rockefeller U., NYC, 1962—65; asst. prof. Washington U. Sch. Medicine, St. Louis, 1965—67; assoc. mem. and mem. Scipps Rsch. Inst., LaJolla, Calif., 1967—77; prof. Scripps Rsch. Inst., LaJolla, Calif., 1982—2006, prof. emeritus, 2006—; prof. U. Colo. Sch. Medicine, Denver, 1977-82. Chmn. allergy & immunology rsch. com. NIH, Bethesda, Md., 1982-84;

mem. nat. arthritis adv. bd. HHS, Washington, 1981-85; hon. prof. Shanghai Jiao Dong U., Zhengzhou U., China. Contbr. chapters to books, articles to profl. jours. Named to Nat. Lupus Hall Fame, 1984; recipient US Sr. Scientist award, Humboldt Found., Germany, 1986, Ciba-Giegy-Internat. League against Rheumatism award, 1989, Carol Nachman award, Wiesbaden, Germany, 1989, Lee Howley Sr. award, Arthritis Found., 1989, Paul Klemperer award and medal, NY Acad. Medicine, 1993, City Medicine award, Durham, NC, 1996, Disting. Med. Alumnus award, Duke U., 2000, Mayo Soley award, Western Soc. Clin. Investigation, 2002, Japan Rheumatism Found. Internat. prize, 2003, Meritorious Svc. award, European League Against Rheumatism, 2005, Lifetime Achievement award, 8th Internat. Lupus Congress, China, 2007. Fellow AAAS; mem. Am. Coll. Rheumatology (pres. 1984-85, chmn. Blue Ribbon com. Future Acad. Rheumatology 1997-98, Disting. Investigator award 1991, Gold medal award 1998), Assn. Am. Physicians, Am. Soc. Clin. Investigation, Western Assn. Physicians (v.p. 1980-81), Am. Assn. Immunologists, Brazilian Soc. Rheumatology (hon.), Australian Rheumatism Assn. (hon.), Brit. Soc. Rheumatology (hon.), Mex. Nat. Acad. Medicine (hon.). Achievements include research on antibodies and antigens in cancer and in autoimmune diseases, systemic lupus erythematosus, scleroderma, Sjogren's syndrome, myositis and mixed connective tissue disease; relationship of autoantibodies to pathogenesis. Home: 8303 Sugarman Dr La Jolla CA 92037-2224 Office: Scripps Rsch Inst 10550 N Torrey Pines Rd La Jolla CA 92037-1000 Office Phone: 858-784-8686. Business E-Mail: emtan@scripps.edu.

TAN, LIQIN, artist, educator; arrived in US, 2000, permanent resident, 2003; s. Hong Jun Tan and Bing Xi Xian; m. Kuan Dong; children: Ju, Shelly. Diploma in Fine Arts, Hengyang Tchrs. Coll., Hengyang, China, 1981; cert. in Art History, Ctrl. Acad. Fine Arts, Beijing, 1984; BA, Hunan Normal U., ChangSha, China, 1987; MA, Concordia U., Montreal, Can., 1993; cert. in Animation, Sharidan Coll., Ont., Can., 1995, cert., 1996; cert. in Softimage/XSI, Nat. Animation and Design Ctr., Can., 2000; cert. in Softimage/XSI Character Animation, Mesmer Animation Lab., Seattle, 2003. Cert. in advanced Softimage instrn. AVID Tech. Inc., Can., 1999. Instr. art Hengyang Tchrs. Coll., China, 1981—85; exec. art editor Hunan Art Pub. Ho., ChangSha, China, 1985—87; dir. art 12 Sources Arts Inc., Mississauga, Ont., Canada, 1991—96; lectr. Ngee Ann Poly., Singapore, 1997—2000; prof. Rutgers U., Camden, NJ, 2000—. Juror Nat. Traveling Art Show, Zhuhai, GuangDong, China, 1986; curriculum external examiner Ngee Ann Poly., Singapore, 2007—; adj. prof. digital media ctr. Seneca Coll., Toronto, Canada, 2000. Exhibitions include Butler Inst. of Am. Art, Ohio, 1996 (First Pl. 5th Ann. Digital Art and Computer Animation Juried Competition award, 2006), Hopkins Ho. Gallery, Hadden, 2002 (Best of Show award, 2002), Int'l Digital Media & Arts Assn., 2004 (Best of Show award iDEAa Exhbn., 2004), Da Vinci Art Alliance, Phila., 2004 (Gold medal, 2004), Ctr. Digital Art, LA, 2004 (Second Pl. award, 2004), Gallery Internat., Balt., 2004 (Excellence award, 2004), Period Gallery, Omaha, 2004 (Excellence award, 2004). Grantee, Rutgers U., 2001—06, Lindback Found., 2002, Bildner Family Found., 2003—05; John W. O'Brien Grad. fellowship, Concordia U., 1987. Mem.: AAUP, ACM (assoc.; chmn. IT animation graphics program internat. conf. 2004, juror art gallery 2006, students' print/animation competition 2007—), Internat. Media and Arts Assn. Office: Rutgers Univ 314 Linden St Camden NJ 08102 Home Phone: 856-857-9858; Office Phone: 856-225-6247. Office Fax: 856-225-6330. Personal E-mail: liqintan@gmail.com. Business E-Mail: ltan@camden.rutgers.edu.

TAN, LI-SU LIN, accountant, insurance company executive, consultant; b. Keelung, Taiwan, Republic of China, Mar. 7, 1956; arrived in US, 1985; d. I-Chang and Sung-Mei (Chen) Lin; m. Bert T. Tan, Aug. 19, 1985; children: Patricia Tan, Peter Puwen Tan, Lotus Tan. BBA, Nat. Taiwan U., 1978; MBA, Ill. Inst. Tech., Chgo., 1991. CPA, Ill., Taiwan; lic. ins. agt., Ill.; registered investment advisor. Asst. mgr. T.N. Soong & Co. (mem. firm Arthur Anderson & Co., SC), Taipei, 1978—85; practitioner Li-Su Lin, CPA, Taipei, 1981—85, Li-Su Lin Tan, CPA, Naperville, Ill., 1988—90; pres. Lisu L. Tan & Co., Ltd., CPAs, Naperville, 1990—; agt. Mut. Omaha Co., Lombard, Ill., 1991—94, Met. Life and Affiliated Cos., Bloomingdale, Ill., 1993—98, GE Fin. Assurance, Schaumburg, Ill., 1999—. Chair family Naperville Chinese Assn., 1990. Mem.: AICPA (tax divsn., quality control program), Ill. Soc. CPA, Chinese Women's League Chgo. Assn. (bd. dir. 2006—), Amitabha Buddhist Libr. Chgo. (pres. 2003—, bd. dir.), Buddha's Light Internat. Assn. (pres. Chgo. chpt. 2002—04, bd. dir.), Chinese Am. Culture Found. (pres. 2001—, bd. dir.), Nat. Taiwan U. Alumni Assn. Greater Chgo. (bd. dir. 1999—2003), World Taiwanese C. of C. (dep. treas. 1998—99), Taiwanese C. of C. N.Am. (treas. 1998—99, bd. dir.), Greater Chgo. Area Taiwanese Am. C. of C. (bd. dir. 1995—2006), Taipei First Girls High Alumni Assn. (treas. 1990—94). Buddhist. Avocations: travel, art, photography. Office: Lisu L Tan & Co Ltd CPAs 6S235 Steeple Run Dr #200 Naperville IL 60540-3754 Home Phone: 630-305-7206; Office Phone: 630-416-9422. Business E-Mail: lisu@lisutancpas.com.

TAN, MING, research scientist; s. Huagang Tan and Jinying Xie; m. Dawn Song, July 5, 1986; 1 child, Wenjun (Tony). BS, Zhongshan U., Guangzhou, China, 1982, MS, 1986; PhD, U. Muenster, Germany, 1997. Asst. engr. Guangzhou Chicken Form, Guangdong province, China, 1982—83; tchg., rsch. asst. Zhongshan U., 1986—88, instr., 1988—92; rsch. scientist U. Muenster, 1997—99; rsch. assoc. Cin. Children's Hosp. Med. Ctr., 2002—05, instr., 2005—. Contbr. articles to profl. jours. Fellow, U. Nebr., Lincoln, 1999—2000, U. Cin., 2000—02; grantee, Cin. Children's Hosp. Med. Ctr., Rsch. Found., 2006—07; scholar, Edn. Commn. China, 1992—96. Mem.: Congl. Liaison Com., Am. Soc. Virologists. Achievements include patents pending for novel norovirus particles as an antiviral or vaccine. Home: 2177 Budwood Ct Cincinnati OH 45230 Office: Cin Childrens Hosp 3333 Burnet Ave Cincinnati OH 45229 Home Phone: 513-233-0889; Office Phone: 513-636-0510. Office Fax: 513-636-7655; Home Fax: 513-636-7655. Business E-Mail: ming.tan@cchmc.org.

TAN, ROBERT C., music educator; b. Singapore, Oct. 8, 1936; arrived in U.S., 1959; s. Chin Khin and Lena Tan. BA, Union Coll., Lincoln, Nebr., 1963. Lic. tchg. Royal Sch. Music London, 1957, performance Royal Sch. Music London, 1958. Tchr. music Fortune Jr. Acad., Calif., 1965—68, Pleasant Hill Jr. Acad., 1968—82, Lodi Acad., 1982—2005; founder and dir. Lodi Children's Chorus, 1983—. Dir. English Oaks Seventh Day Adventist Ch. Choir, Lodi, Calif., 1983—, Zion Ref. Ch. Choir, 1983—. Recipient Instr. of Yr., Lodi Arts Commn., 1992, Tchr. of Yr., Lodi Acad., 1999, Mayor's Cmty. Svc. award, Lodi, Calif., 2002. Mem.: Am. Choral Dir. Assn., Twin Arbors Athletic Club. Republican. Adventist. Avocations: swimming, skiing, tennis, bodybuilding. Home: 1853 Songbird Pl Lodi CA 95240-7827

TAN, SOO CHUEN, financial analyst, researcher; arrived in US, 1999; s. See Boon Tan and Oi Ling Wong. MA in Jurisprudence, Oxford U., Eng., 1999; MBA, Harvard Bus. Sch., Boston. Bar: NY 2001. Analyst McKinsey & Co., NYC, 1999—2002; investment analyst Halcyon Asset Mgmt., NYC, 2004—05, The Baupost Group, Boston, 2005, Deccan Value Advisors, Greenwich, Conn., 2005—. Adv. bd. mem. Harvey Fellowship, Washington, 2004—06. Recipient Wronker prize, Oxford U., 1999; scholar, Jarding Found., Hong Kong, 1996; Baker scholar, Harvard Bus. Sch., 2006. Mem.: NY Bar Assn., Am. Mensa Soc. Roman Catholic. Avocation: chess. Office Phone: 203-983-7251.

TAN, TJIAUW-LING, psychiatrist, educator; b. Pemalang, Java, Indonesia, June 2, 1935; came to U.S., 1967; naturalized, 1972; s. Ping-Hoey and Liep-Nio (Liem) T.; m. Esther Joyce Kho, June 2, 1961; children: Paul Budiman, Robert Yuling, Alice Ayling. BS, U. Indonesia Faculty Medicine, 1957, MD, 1961; postgrad., U. Indonesia, Jakarta, 1961-65, UCLA, 1967-71, Pa. State U., 1971-72. Diplomate Am. Bd. Psychiatry and Neurology, Gen. Psychiatry, Bd.Psychiatry & Neurology, Geriat. Psychiatry. Lectr. psychiatry U. Indonesia, Jakarta, 1965-67; psychiat. cons. Ctrl. Gen. Hosp., Jakarta, 1965-67; postdoctoral fellow UCLA Brain Rsch. Inst., 1967-69; asst. rsch. psychiatrist, dept. psychiatry Neuropsychiat. Inst., UCLA, 1969-70; asst. prof. psychiatry Pa. State U., 1972-87, assoc. prof. psychiatry, 1987-99, prof. psychiatry, 1999—. Chief inpatient psychiatry Univ. Hosp. Milton S. Hershey Med. Ctr., 1972-2005, dir. Behavioral Medicine Clinic, co-dir. Biofeedback Lab., 1975—2005; cons. psychiatry Family and Children's Svc. Lebanon County, Lebanon, Pa., 1971-79. Contbr. articles to profl. jours. Bd. dir. Retarded Children's Assn. Dauphin County, Inc., 1971—73. Fellow Am. Psychiat. Assn. (disting. life), Pa. Psychiat. Soc.; mem. Ctrl. Pa. Psychiat. Soc., Assn. Advancement Behavior Therapy, Assn. Applied Psychophysiology and Biofeedback, Soc. Behavioral Medicine, Assn. Psychophysiol. Study of Sleep, Am. Assn. for Geriat. Psychiatry, Am. Geriat. Soc. Democrat. Presbyterian. Home: 1478 Bradley Ave Hummelstown PA 17036-9143 Office: Pa State U Coll Medicine Dept Psychiatry 500 University Dr Hershey PA 17033-2390 Home Phone: 717-566-3009; Office Phone: 717-531-8207. Business E-Mail: lingtan@psu.edu.

TANABE, CHARLES Y., lawyer; b. Denver, Nov. 27, 1951; BA cum laude, U. Colo., 1973; JD, U. Calif., Berkeley, 1976. Bar: Colo. 1976. Atty. Sherman & Howard LLC, Denver; gen. counsel Liberty Media Corp., Englewood, Colo., 1999—2001, sr. v.p., sec., gen. counsel, 2001—07, exec. v.p., sec., gen. counsel, 2007—. Bd. dir. FUN Technologies Inc. Mem. ABA, Phi Beta Kappa. Office: Liberty Media Corp 12300 Liberty Blvd Englewood CO 80112 *

TANAKA, J(EANNIE) E., lawyer; b. LA, Jan. 21, 1942; d. Togo William and Jean M. Tanaka. BA, Internat. Christian U., Tokyo, 1966; MSW, UCLA, 1968; JD, Washington Coll., 1984. Bar: Calif. 1984, U.S. Dist. Ct. (cen., no. dists.) Calif. 1985, U.S. Ct. Appeals (9th cir.) 1985, D.C. 1987. Instr. Aoyama Gakuin, Meiji Gakuin, Sophia U., Tokyo, 1968-75; with program devel. Encyclopedia Britannica Inst., Tokyo, 1976-78; instr. Honda, Mitsubishi, Ricoh Corps., Tokyo, 1975-80; with editorial dept. Simul Internat., Tokyo; assoc. Seki and Jarvis, LA, 1984-86, Jones, Day, Reavis & Pogue, LA, 1986-87, Fulbright, Jaworsky and Reavis, McGrath, LA, 1987-89; asst. counsel Unocal, LA, 1989-91; pvt. practice LA, 1991—; counsel Calif. Dept. Corps., LA, 1993—. Active Japan-Am. Soc., L.A., 1984-95, Japanese-Am. Citizens League, L.A., 1981, 92—, Japanese Am. Cultural and Cmty. Ctr., 1986-89; vol. Asian Pacific Am. Legal Ctr. So. Calif., 1985-86. Mem. Japanese-Am. Bar Assn., Mensa. Democrat. Mem. Foursquare Meth. Ch. Avocations: languages, martial arts. Office Phone: 310-712-1947.

TANAKA, KOUICHI ROBERT, hematologist, educator; b. Fresno, Calif., Dec. 15, 1926; s. Kenjiro and Teru (Arai) T.; m. Grace Mutsuko Sakaguchi, Oct. 23, 1965; children: Anne M., Nancy K., David K. BS, Wayne State U., 1949, MD, 1952. Cert. in internal medicine Am. Bd. Internal Medicine, 1961, recertified in internal medicine Am. Bd. Internal Medicine, 1974, cert. in hematology Am. Bd. Internal Medicine, 1972. Intern Los Angeles County Gen. Hosp., 1952—53; resident, fellow Detroit Receiving Hosp., 1953—57; instr. Sch. Medicine UCLA, 1957—59, asst. prof. medicine, 1959—61, assoc. prof. medicine, 1961—68, prof. Sch. Medicine, 1968—97, prof. emeritus, 1998—. Chief hematology divsn. Harbor-UCLA, Torrance, Calif., 1961—97, chief hematology, 1998—2000. Author 137 rsch. publs. Served US Army, 1946—48. Recipient Disting. Alumni Svc. award, Wayne St. U. Sch. Med. Alumni Assn., Med. Alumni Assn. Disting. Svc. award, UCLA. Master ACP (gov. So. Calif. region I 1993-97); mem. Am. Fedn. Med. Rsch., We. Soc. Clin. Investigation, Am. Soc. Hematology, Internat. Soc. Hematology, We. Assn. Physicians, Am. Soc. Clin. Investigation, Assn. Am. Physicians, Sigma Xi, Alpha Omega Alpha. Achievements include research on red cell metabolism. Home: 4 Cayuse Ln Rancho Palos Verdes CA 90275-5172 Office: Dept Med Box 400 Harbor-UCLA Med Ctr Torrance CA 90509 Home Phone: 310-377-7687; Office Phone: 310-222-3695.

TANAKA, PATRICE AIKO, public relations executive; b. Hawaii; BA, U. Hawaii, 1974. Editor Hawaii Press Newspapers, 1974-77; dir. pub. rels. Hotel Inter-Continental Maui, 1977-79; acct. exec. to sr. v.p. and creative dir. Jessica Dee Comm., NYC, 1979-87, exec. v.p., gen. mgr., 1987-90; CEO, creative dir. PT&Co., NYC, 1990—2005, CRT/tanaka, 2005—. Featured in books: American Dreamers, Visionaries and Entrepreneurs, 1995, The Art of Public Relations, 2002. Bd. dirs. Greater NY coun. Girl Scouts US, US Fund for UNICEF, Family Violence Prevention Fund, Asian Pacific Am. Women's Leadership Inst. Named one of nation's 500 Most Influential Asian Ams., Avenue mag., 1996; recipient Mothering That Works award, Working Mother mag., 1994, Women Mean Bus. award, Bus. and Profl. Women U.S.A., 1999, Paul M. Lund award for pub. svc., Pub. Rels. Soc. Am., 2002. Mem.: Asian Women in Bus. (bd. dirs.), Coun. Pub. Rels. Firms (founding bd. dirs.), Women Execs. in Pub. Rels., NY Women in Comm. (pres. 2001—02, 2002—03, Matrix award for pub. rels. 1996), Asian Pacific Am. Women's Leadership Inst. (founding bd. dirs.), Women's Forum NY, U. Hawaii Alumni Assn. (bd. dirs. NY chpt.). Office: CRT/tanaka 320 W 13th St Fl 7 New York NY 10014-1200

TANAKA, RICHARD I., computer company executive; b. Sacramento, Dec. 17, 1928; s. G. and Kei Tanaka; m. Edith M. Arita, Aug. 18, 1951; children: Steven Richard, Jean Elizabeth, John Richard, Anne Mariko. BS with highest honors, U. Calif., Berkeley, 1950, MS, 1951; PhD, Calif. Inst. Tech., 1958. Sr. rsch. engr. N.Am. Aviation, Inc., 1951-54; mem. tech. staff Hughes Aircraft Co., 1954-57; dept. mgr., sr. mem. computer rsch. Lockheed Missiles & Space Co., Palo Alto, Calif., 1957-65; sr. v.p. Cal Comp (Calif. Computer Products, Inc.), Anaheim, 1966-77; pres. Internat. Tech. Resources Co., Tustin, Calif., 1977-80; pres., CEO Systonetics, Inc., Fullerton, Calif., 1980-86; pres. Lundy Electronics & Sys., Inc., Glen Head, NY, 1986-89; chmn., CEO, pres. Scan-Optics, Inc., Manchester, Conn., 1989-97; chmn., CEO V-Sys., Inc., San Juan Capistrano, Calif., 1999-2000; pres. ITR Co., Santa Ana, Calif., 2000—. Vis. prof. U. Calif., Berkeley, 1962 Author: Residue Arithmetic and Its Applications to Computer Technology, 1967. Hughes fellow Calif. Inst. Tech., 1955-57 Fellow IEEE (pres. computer soc. 1965-66, centennial medal, Golden Core award 1996); mem. Internat. Fedn. Info. Processing (pres. 1974-77, hon. life mem., U.S. del.), Am. Fedn. Info. Processing Socs. (pres. 1969-71, disting. service award 1983), Phi Beta Kappa, Tau Beta Pi, Eta Kappa Nu. Home: 10321 Shadyridge Dr Santa Ana CA 92705-1568 Personal E-mail: ritanaka@cox.net.

TANAKA, RICHARD KOICHI, JR., architect, planner; b. San Jose, Calif., Oct. 16, 1931; s. Richard Inoru and Mae Yoshiko (Koga) T.; m. Barbara Hisako Kumagai, Oct. 7, 1961; children: Craig, Todd, Sandra, Trent. BArch, U. Mich., Ann Arbor, 1954; M in Urban Planning, Calif. State U., San Jose, 1978. Arch., planner Steinberg Group, San Jose, L.A., 1954. Chair, bd. dirs. Happi House Restaurants, Inc., 1972—. Author: American on Trial, 1988. Dir. Human Rels. Com., San Jose, 1969-73; past pres., trustee East Side HS Dist., San Jose, 1971-92, Japanese Am. Citizens League, San Jose; dir., pres. Bicentennial Com., San Jose, 1974-77; past pres. Tapestry and Talent, 1976-80; mem. bd. govs. NCCJ, San Jose, 1976—, Boy Scouts Am., San Jose, 1978—; bd. dirs. Santa Clara County Sch. Bd. Assn., 1980—, Calif. CC Trustees, 1993-2002, pres., 1997-98; pres. Internment of Local Japanese Ams., San Jose, 1984—; trustee San Jose/Evergreen CC, 1992—, pres., 1993-94, 97-98, 2001-02, 07—. Mem. AIA, Am. Planning Inst., Constrn. Specification Inst., Rotary. Avocations: golf, painting. Home: 14811 Whipple Ct San Jose CA 95127-2570 Office: 60 Pierce Ave San Jose CA 95110-2819 Office Phone: 408-251-6371. Personal E-mail: rktanaka@sbcglobal.net.

TANANBAUM, HARVEY D., astrophysicist; BA in Physics, Yale U., 1964; PhD in Physics, MIT, 1968. Staff scientist Am. Sci. & Engring. Inc.; project scientist UHURU (SAS0A) X-ray Satellite, 1969—73; astrophysicist Smithsonian Astrophysical Observatory, 1973—, sci. program mgr. HEAO-2/Einstein mission, 1972—81, prin. investigator and dir. Einstein Data Ctr., 1981—94, dir. High Energy Astrophysics Divsn., 1981—93. Recipient Exceptional Sci. Achievement medal, NASA, 1980, Pub. Svc. award, 1988, Medal for Outstanding Leadership, 2000. Fellow: AAAS; mem.: NAS, Am. Astronomical Soc. (v.p., Bruno Rossi prize- High Energy Astrophysics Divsn. 2004). Office: Chandra X-Ray Observatory Smithsonian Rsch Inst 60 Garden St Mailstop 8 Cambridge MA 02138-1516 Office Phone: 617-495-7248. Office Fax: 617-495-7356. E-mail: htananbaum@cfa.harvard.edu.

TANANBAUM, JAMES, medical engineering company executive; b. NYC, May 5, 1963; s. David J. and Elizebeth Zelda (Belfer) T. BS cum laude, Yale U., 1985; postgrad. health scis., tech. program, Harvard U., Cambridge, 1985-89; postgrad., Harvard Bus. Sch., Boston, 1989—. Rsch. asst. MIT, Cambridge, 1986—; chmn. Med. Engring. Devices, Inc., Boston, 1987—. Computer cons. Nat. Retirement Programs, Inc., N.Y.C., 1981—, Software Engring., Inc., N.Y.C., 1985, Clin. Computing Ctr., Inc., Boston, 1985—; student pres. Health, Scis., and Tech. Program, Harvard U. and MIT, 1986—. Mem. Sigma Xi. Office: Advanced Medical Inc 901Gateway Blvd South San Francisco CA 94080

TANANBAUM, STEVEN ANDREW, investment consultant; b. NYC, June 26, 1965; s. David Jay and Elizabeth (Belfer) Tananbaum. BA in Econs., Vassar Coll., 1987. Analyst Kidder, Peabody & Co., NYC, 1987-89; investment specialist MacKay Shields, NYC, 1989—91, head high yield grp., 1991—97, lead portfolio mgr. hedge fund area, 1997; sr. mng. mem., founding ptnr. GoldenTree Asset Mgmt., LP, NYC, 2000—, CEO, chief investment officer. Cons. Nat. Retirement Progs., 1987—89. Bd. dirs. Citymeals-on-Wheels, NYC; mem. corp. fund bd. John F. Kennedy Ctr. Performing Arts. Named one of Top 200 Collectors, ARTnews mag., 2006. Republican. Office: GoldenTree Asset Mgmt LP 300 Park Ave 21st Fl New York NY 10022

TANCER, EDWARD F., lawyer, utilities executive; b. 1961; BA in Polit. Sci., U. Fla., Gainesville, JD. Bar: Fla. 1985. Atty. FPL Energy, Juno Beach, Fla., 1988, v.p., gen. counsel, 2001—05; asst. sec. FPL Group Inc., Juno Beach, Fla., 1997—, assoc. gen. counsel, 2003—05, v.p., gen. counsel, 2005—; asst. sec. Fla. Power & Light Co., 1997—, sr. v.p., gen. counsel, 2005—. Office: FPL Group Inc 700 Universe Blvd PO Box 14000 Juno Beach FL 33408 Office Phone: 561-694-4644. Office Fax: 561-694-4640. *

TANCREDI, JAMES J., lawyer; b. Hartford, Conn., Apr. 1, 1954; s. Joseph I. and Angelina C. (Lanza) T.; children: Lauren, Jamie, Brian. BA in Urban Studies and Polit. Sci., Coll. Holy Cross, Worcester, Mass., 1976; JD, U. Conn., Storrs, 1979. Bar: Conn. 1979, US Dist. Ct. Conn. 1979, US Ct. Appeals (2d cir.) 1982, US Dist. (so. dist.) NY 1988, US Supreme Ct., 1991; cert. comml. bankruptcy specialist. From assoc. to ptnr. Day Pitney LLP, Hartford, Conn., 1979—, chmn. fin. restructuring group, 1996—2007. Editor: CT Bankruptcy Desk Book. Bd. dirs. Conn. Mental Health Assn., Hartford, 1986-89, 2001-04. Mem. ABA (bus. sect.), Am. Bankruptcy Inst., Conn. Bar Assn. (exec. com. mem. bankruptcy section), Hartford County Bar Assn. (dir., chair cmty. comml. law 1997-2004), Conn. Turnaround Mgmt. Assn. (dir. 2004—). Office: Day Pitney LLP 242 Trumbull St Hartford CT 06103 also: 875 Third Ave New York NY 10001 Home Phone: 860-404-0253; Office Phone: 212-829-3600. Business E-Mail: jjtancredi@daypitney.com.

TANCREDI, LAURENCE RICHARD, medical educator, psychiatrist; b. Hershey, Pa., Oct. 15, 1940; s. Samuel N. and Alvesta (Pera) T. AB in English, Franklin and Marshall Coll., 1962; MD, U. Pa., 1966; JD, Yale U., 1972. Diplomate Am. Bd. Neurology and Psychiatry; Bar: N.Y. 1982. Sr. profl. assoc. Inst. Medicine, NAS, Washington, 1972-74; fellow in psychiatry Columbia U. Coll. Physicians and Surgeons, NYC, 1974-75; postdoctoral fellow in psychiatry Yale U. Med. Sch., New Haven, 1975-77; assoc. prof. psychiatry Med. Sch. NYU, New Haven, 1977-84; Kraft Eidman prof. medicine and law U. Tex. Health Sci. Ctr., Houston, 1984-92, dir. health law program, 1983-92; clin. prof. psychiatry NYU, 1992—; clin. prof. health care scis. U. Calif., San Diego, 1993—2003; mem. staff Brookhaven Nat. Labs. Clin. Ctr., 1994-96; pvt. practice NYC, 1994—. V.p. bd. dirs. Internat. Acad. Law and Mental Health, 1987—95, bd. dirs., 2002—07, v.p., 2003—07; mem. adv. com. on transplantations Health Care Fin. Adminstrn., Dept. Health and Human Svcs., 1981—84; mem. nat. adv. bd. NIMH Ctr. Study of Pub. Mental Health N.Y. State Office Mental Health, 1994—99; cmty. svcs. bd. Dept. Mental Health, Mental Retardation and Alcohol Svcs., City of N.Y., 1995—2001; mem. sci. adv. com. Am. Suicide Found., 1995—; cons. Commn. on Med. Profl. Liability; co-prin., investigator study ABA, 1978—80; cons. in field. Fellow: Am. Coll. Psychiatry, N.Y. Acad. Med. Office: 129B E 71st St New York NY 10021-4201 Office Phone: 212-288-5197. Personal E-mail: lrtancredi@yahoo.com.

TANCREDO, THOMAS G., congressman; b. North Denver, Dec. 20, 1945; m. Jackie Tancredo; 2 children. BA, U. North Colo., 1968. Mem. Colo. State Ho. Reps., 1977-81; regional rep. U.S. Dept. Edn., 1981-93; mem. U.S. Congress from 6th Colo. dist., 1999—; mem. edn. and workforce, internat. rels., and resources coms.; mem. Ho. Budget Com. Republican. Office: US Ho Reps 1130 Longworth Ho Office Bldg Washington DC 20515-0606 also: Dist Office Ste 200 6099 S Quebec St Centennial CO 80111-4547 *

TANCS, LINDA ANN, lawyer; b. Elizabeth, NJ, Sept. 27, 1963; d. Tibor Louis and Rose Tancs. Student, U. Warwick, Coventry, Eng., 1984; BA magna cum laude, Rutgers U., 1985; JD cum laude, Seton Hall U. Sch. Law, 1993. Bar: N.J. 1993, N.Y., 1994, U.S. Dist. Ct. (N.J.) 1993, U.S. Ct. Appeals (fed. cir.) 2001. Paralegal Fox and Fox, Counsellors at Law, Newark, 1985-88, Vol. Lawyers for Arts, NYC, 1988; corp. paralegal Wilentz, Goldman & Spitzer, Woodbridge, N.J., 1988-90, assoc., 1993-96; staff atty. Muze, Inc., NYC, 1996-97; atty. IMS Health, Inc., Totowa, NJ, 1997—99; sr. assoc. Norris, McLaughlin & Marcus, Somerville, NJ, 2000—05, ptnr., 2005—. V.p. Pro Agents, Inc., 1995-96; adj. prof. acctg. and legal studies dept. Middlesex County Coll., Edison, N.J., 1998-99; adj. prof. paralegal studies Fairleigh Dickenson U., 1999; councilwoman Borough of Roselle Park, 1999-2001. Assoc. editor Seton Hall Law Rev. Mem. ABA, N.J. Bar Assn., N.Y. State Bar Assn. (chair young entertainment lawyers com. 1994-96, co-chair motion pictures com. 2005-), Phi Beta Kappa, Phi Sigma Iota, Delta Phi Alpha. Office Phone: 908-252-4231. Business E-Mail: latancs@nmmlaw.com.

TANDBERG, GERILYN GAY, theater educator, costume designer; b. Rugby, ND, Aug. 23, 1942; d. Otto and Edna Tandberg; m. Maurice Berger, Aug. 2, 1980. BS in English, Minot State U., ND, 1963, BS in French, 1963, BS in Edn., 1963; PhD, U. Minn., Mpls., 1973. Cert. in tchg. State ND. Asst. prof. Minot State U., ND, 1966—73; costume designer and historian, dept. theatre La. State U., Baton Rouge, 1973—. Critic Am. Coll. Theatre Festival, 1975—79; state chair La. Coll. Theatre Festival, 1976—80; costume designer Ctrl. State U., Okla., 1981—82; mem., theatre advisory bd. La. State Arts Coun., 1981, 82; costume designer U. Tulsa, Okla., 1986—87; reviewer Dress Jour. Am. Costume Soc., 1991—2003; co-chair, region 6 conf. Costume Soc. Am., New Orleans, 1996, bd. dir., region 6 conf., 96; v.p. Theatres La.; lectr. in field. Author: General Learning Press; state chair: National American Coll. Theatre Festival, 1976, 1991, 1997; Theatre Crafts, 1987; contbr. articles to profl. jours.; designed costumes for over 100 plays, musicals, operas at La. State U. Officer pub. rels. flotilla 4-10 and regional divsn. iv Coast Guard Aux., Baton Rouge, New Orleans, 1980—2006. Recipient Outstanding Svc. citation, S.W. Theatre Assn., Gold Medallion, Am. Coll. Theatre Festival, 1984; grantee, Women's and Gender Studies Program, La. State U., 1995, Manship Found., 1996, The Student Tech. Fee Grant, 2000—02. Mem.: Costume Soc. Am. (mem. bd. 1988—91, v.p. 1988—91). Democrat. Unitarian Universalist. Avocations: boating, reading, vintage clothing, vintage jewelry. Office: Theatre La State Univ Hatcher Hall Rm 249 Baton Rouge LA 70836 Mailing: PO Box 2083 Baton Rouge LA 70821 Home Phone: 225-753-9808; Office Phone: 225-578-9808. Personal E-mail: gtandbergl@cox.net. Business E-Mail: gtandb1@lsu.edu.

TANDLER, BERNARD, cell biology educator; b. Bklyn., Feb. 18, 1933; s. Arthur and Pauline (Solomon) T.; m. Helen Weisman, Dec. 25, 1955 (dec. Aug. 14, 1986); children: Janice Dena, Evan Charles. BS, Bklyn. Coll., 1955; AM, Columbia U., 1957; PhD, Cornell U., 1961; DMD (hon.), U. Cagliari, 1997. Instr. anatomy NYU, NYC, 1962-63; assoc. Sloan Kettering Inst., 1963-67; asst. prof. cell biology Cornell U., NYC, 1965-67; assoc. prof. Case Western Res. U., Cleve., 1967-72, prof. oral biology, 1972-91, acting chmn. dept. oral biology, 1987-89. Affiliate prof. oral biology U. Wash., Seattle, 1993—; vis. prof. U. Copenhagen, 1973, U. Cagliari, 1983, Kyushu Dental Coll., 1994-98, bio. sci. Case We. Res. U., 2003—; sr. rsch. scientist Tex. Tech U., Lubbock, 1999-01; cons. NIH, NSF, VA. Author: (with C.L. Hoppel) Mitochondria, 1972; assoc. editor: Anatomical Record, 1974-98; guest editor: Microscopy Rsch. and Technique, 1993-94, European Jour. Morphology, 1995-2000, 02—; contbr. chpts. to books, articles to profl. jours. Recipient Disting. Alumnus award Bklyn. Coll., 1981, Robert E. Kennedy award for Acad. Freedom, Ohio chpt. AAUP, 1992, Disting. Scientist award Am. Assn. Dental Rsch., 1999; USPHS fellow, 1957-62. Mem. Am. Assn. Anatomists, Am. Soc. Cell Biology, Electron Microscopy Soc. Am., Japanese Soc. Oral Biology, Japanese Assn. Anatomists, Internat. Assn. Dental Rsch. (Disting. Scientist award 1999) Am. Soc. Mammalogists, Italian Soc. Anatomy (hon.), Sigma Xi. Office Phone: 216-368-0563. Business E-Mail: bernard.tandler@case.edu.

TANDON, NARENDRA NATH, research scientist, director; b. Moradabad, Uttar Pradesh, India, Sept. 20, 1946; arrived in US, 1976; s. Prakash Narain and Kamla Tandon; m. Ranjana Mehrotra, Jan. 28, 1974; children: Nandita, Nitin. BS, Agra U., Lucknow, India, 1965, MS, 1967, PhD in Organic Chemistry, 1975. Assoc. prof. clin. biochemistry King George Med. Coll., Lucknow, India, 1968—76; vis. scientist NIH, Bethesda, Md., 1976—78, FDA, Washington, 1978—80; sr. scientist ARC, Rockville, Md., 1980—96; dir. thrombosis rsch. Otsuka Md. Medicinal Labs., 1996—. Mem. editl. bd. Thrombosis Rsch. (jour.). Recipient Fujii award, Otsuka Pharm. Co., Japan, 2005. Mem.: Internat. Soc. Thrombosis and Hemostasis (corr.). Achievements include patents for Glycoprotein VI and its uses; patents pending for antithrombotic antibodies to GPVI. Office: Otsuka Md Medicinal Labs 9900 Med Ctr Dr Rockville MD 20850 Business E-Mail: narendrt@otsuka.com.

TANDON, RAJIV, psychiatrist, educator; b. Kanpur, India, Aug. 3, 1956; arrived in US, 1984, naturalized, 1988; s. Bhagwan Sarup and Usha (Mehrotra) T.; m. Chanchal Nammi Vohra; children: Neeraj, Anisha, Gitanjali. Student, St. Xavier's Coll., Bombay, India, 1974; BS, All India Inst., New Delhi, 1980; MD, Nat. Inst. of MH, India, 1983. Sr. resident Mental Health and Neuro-Scis., India, 1983-84; resident U. Mich. Hosps., Ann Arbor, 1984-87, attending psychiatrist, 1987-2000. Dir. schizophrenia program, dir. hosp. svcs. divsn. U. Mich., Ann Arbor, 1987—2000, assoc. prof., 1993—99, prof., 1999—2004; cons. Lenawee County Cmty. Mental Health, Adrian, Mich., 1985—99. Author: Biochemical Parameters of Mixed Affective States; Negative Schizophrenic Symptoms: Pathophysiology and Clinical Implications; contbr. over 250 articles to profl. jours. Recipient Young Scientist's award Biennial Winter workshop on Schizophrenia, 1990, 92, Travel award Am. Coll. Neuropsychopharmacology/Mead, 1990, Rsch. Excellence award Am. Assn. Psychiatrists from India, 1993, Sci. award, Best Drs. in Am. award, 1994-98, Gerald Klerman award for outstanding rsch. by a Nat. Alliance for Rsch. in Schizophrenia and Depression young investigator, 1995, FuturPsych award CINP, 1997. Mem. Am. Psychiat. Assn. (Wisniewski Young Psychiatrist Rschr. award 1993), World Fedn. Mental Health, Soc. for Neurosci., N.Y. Acad. Scis., Soc. Biol. Psychiatry, Mich. Psychiat. Soc. Independent. Hindu. Business E-Mail: rtandon@umich.edu.

TANDON, RAJIV, training company executive; b. Allahabad, India, May 9, 1944; came to U.S., 1969; s. Jagdish Bihari and Vimla Devi (Mehrotra) T.; m. Priti Khanna, Sept. 1969; children: Ribhu Dev, Veeti. BTech with honors, Indian Inst. of Tech., 1966, MS in Ops. Rsch., 1972; MBA, U. Minn., 1972, PhD, 1987. Trainee Kumardhubi (India) Engring. Works, 1966-67, prodn. control officer, 1967-69; ops. rsch. analyst Nat. Car Rental, Mpls., 1971-72, mgr. ops. rsch., 1972-75, dir. fin. analysis, 1975-77, corp. v.p., MIS, 1977-81, corp. v.p., gen. mgr. car rental, 1981-86; dir. venture mgmt. U. St. Thomas, Mpls., 1988-93, dir. corp. venturing, 1993-95; pres., CEO Learning Byte Internat. (formerly Inst. for Advanced Tech.), Mpls., 1995—2001, Adayana, Inc., Mpls., 2001—. Mgmt. cons., 1986-95 Exec. editor New Venture Rev., 1985-90; contbr. articles to profl. jours. Pres. Planners League, 1978. Mem. Am. Mgmt. Assn., Inst. of Noetic Sci., Inst. of Mgmt. Scis. (sec. upper Midwest chpt. 1975-76, v.p. 1976-77, pres. 1977-78). Avocations: reading, news. Home: 8109 Rhode Island Ave S Bloomington MN 55438-1146 Office: 4444 W 76th St Minneapolis MN 55435 E-mail: rtandon@adayana.com.

TANDY, CARLA M., dancer, educator; b. Redlands, Calif., July 21, 1923; d. Charles Raymond and Alice Vilora Lane Weaver; m. Henry Cecil Taylor (div.); children: Kim Michael Taylor, Craig Alan Taylor, Kelye Anette Taylor Allen; m. Robert Tandy (dec.). BA, U. Redlands, 1945; MA, Mills Coll., Oakland, Calif., 1978. Dancer Christopher Beck's Theater Co., San Francisco, 1975—89, Am. Dance Therapy Assn., 1977—2007. Pvt. tchr.; dance therapist Calif. Sch. Blind and Deaf, Palo Alto, 1976—78, Stanford U., Palo Alto, 1978, Altenheim, Oakland, 1976—78, Ctr. of Elders Independence, Oakland, 1991—2006; instr. Religious Soc. Friends, Palo Alto, Calif. Author: Rhythm, A Guide for Creative Movement, 1974, 1975. Mem.: NAACP. Democrat. Home: 1010 Chelsea Hercules CA 94547

TANDY, KAREN P., federal agency administrator; b. Ft. Worth; married; 2 children. Grad., Tex. Tech. U., Tex. Tech. Law Sch., 1977. Law clk. No. Dist. Tex.; asst. U.S. atty. ea. dist. Va., 1979—90; asst. U.S. atty. western dist. Wash., 1979—90; supr. dept. drug and forfeiture litig. Criminal Divsn. of Dept. Justice, 1990—99; assoc. dep. atty. gen., dir. Organized Crime Drug Enforcement Task Forces, 1999—2003, mgr., 2001—03; adminstr. Drug Enforcement Adminstrn., 2003—. Chief asset forfeiture unit U.S. Attys. Office Western Dist., Wash., 1988—90; clk. Chief Judge of No. Dist., Tex.; dep. chief Narcotics and Dangerous Drug Sect.; lectr. in field. Recipient Atty. Gens. award for disting. svc., Award for Extraordinary Achievement, Dept. Justice, Award for Superior Svc., U.S. Atty. Dir. Office: Drug Enforcement Adminstrn Mailstop AXS 2401 Jefferson Davis Hwy Alexandria VA 22301 *

TANE, SUSAN JAFFE, retired manufacturing company executive; b. NYC; d. Irving and Beatrice (Albert) J.; m. Irwin R. Tane; children by previous marriage: Robert Wayne, Stephen Mark. BS, Boston U., 1964; postgrad., Hofstra U., C.W. Post U. Elem. sch. tchr., Long Beach, NY, 1964-67; pres. Fashions by Appointment, Glen Cove, NY, 1967-71; adminstrv. asst. Peerless Sales Corp., Elmont, NY, 1967-71; from sales mgr. to mktg. dir. United Utensils Co., Inc., Port Washington, NY, 1973-78; v.p. ops. and control United Molded Products divsn. United Utensils Co., Inc., Port Washington, 1978-80; v.p. mktg. Utensco, Port Washington, 1980-88. Bd. dirs. Peerless Aerospace Corp. Co-inventor plastic container and handling assembly. Life mem. Ronald McDonald House; friend N.Y. Pub. Libr.; pres. Susan Jaffe Tane Found., Am. Jewish Congress, sr. v.p.; life mem. Hadassah; chair Commn. for Women's Equality/Am. Jewish Congress; bd. dirs. Poe Found. Mem. Boston U. Alumni Assn., Cornell Weil Med. Coll., Ptnrs. in Leadership, Shareholder ASsn. Rsch. and Edn. Leadership Coun., Poe Studies Assn. (sponsor), Boston U. (sponsor poetry workshop), Lotos Club, Grolier Club.

TANENBAUM, ALLAN JAY, lawyer; b. Savannah, Ga., Aug. 9, 1946; s. Nathan and Gertrude Sadie (Palefsky) T.; m. Elaine Kruger, Aug. 8, 1971; children: Louis, Sharon, Stephen, Eric. BS in Econs., U. Pa., 1967; JD, U. Va., 1971. Bar: Ga. 1972. Ptnr. Frankel, Hardwick, Tanenbaum, Fink, P.C., Atlanta, 1972-96, Cohen Pollock Merlin Axelrod & Tanenbaum, 1996-2001; gen. counsel AFC Enterprises, Inc., 2001—; mng. dir. Lawyer Reference Svc. of Atlanta, 1977-87. Trustee Congregation B'nai Torah; sec., exec. com., bd. dirs. Jewish Family and Career Svcs., Inc. With USAR, 1968-74. Fellow Am. Bar Found.; mem. ABA (ho. of dels., chair gen. practice sect., spkr. young lawyers divsn., lawyer referral and info. svc., chair pub. edn. divsn., chair com. on scope and correlation of work, chair fellows young lawyers divsn., chair coun. fund for justice and edn. 2003—, nominating com. 2003—, Ga. state del. to ho. dels.), Atlanta Bar Assn. (past sec., del.), Lawyers Club Atlanta, Atlanta Council Younger Lawyers (past pres.). Office: Afc Enterprise Inc 5555 Glenridge Connector NE Ste 300 Atlanta GA 30342-4741 Office Phone: 770-353-3321. Business E-Mail: atanenbaum@afce.com.

TANENBAUM, BASIL SAMUEL, engineering educator; b. Providence, Dec. 1, 1934; s. Harry Milton and Rena Ada (Herr) Tanenbaum; m. Carol Binder, Aug. 26, 1956; children: Laurie, Stephen, David. BS summa cum laude, Brown U., 1956; MS, Yale U., 1957, PhD in Physics, 1960. Staff physicist Raytheon Co., Waltham, Mass., 1960—63; prof. engring. Case We. Res. U., Cleve., 1963—75; prof. Harvey Mudd Coll., Claremont, Calif., 1975—2003, dean faculty, 1975—93, Norman F. Sprague, Jr. prof. life scis., 1996—2003, prof. emeritus, 2003—; interim assoc. dean joint sci. dept. The Claremont Colls., 2003—05, adj. prof., 2005—. Vis. scientist Arecibo (P.R.) Obs. Cornell U., 1968—69; vis. assoc. prof. Northwestern U., Evanston, Ill., 1970; mem. sci. adv. com. Nat. Astronomy and Ionosphere Ctr., 1972—77; dir. Minority Engrs. Indsl. Opportunity Program, 1973—75; mem. sci. adv. com. Calif. Poly. Inst., Pomona, 1976—87; mem. engring. and sci. adv. com. Calif. State U., Fullerton, 1976—87; dir. summer sci. program Thacher Sch., Ojai, Calif., 1977—82; vis. scholar Beckman Laser Inst. U. Calif., Irvine, Calif., 1993—94, 1998, 2006—, mem. biomed. engring. adv. com., 2000—05; mem. nat. adv. com. Rowan Coll., Glassboro, NJ, 1993—2000; mem. Eisenhower adv. com. Calif. Postsecondary Edn. Com., 1993—97; pres.'s adv. coun. Olin Coll. Engring., Needham, Mass., 2001—, vice chmn., 2001, chmn., 2002—06; cons. in field. Author: Plasma Physics, 1967. Trustee Western U. Health Scis., Pomona, 1997—2004. Recipient Witke Tchg. award, Case We. Res. U., 1973; Woods Hole Oceanog. Inst. fellow, 1959, NSF fellow, Yale U., 1956—60, Sr. Sterling fellow, 1959. Mem.: AAUP, IEEE, AAAS, Am. Soc. Engring. Edn., Am. Phys. Soc., Sigma Xi (Rsch. award 1969). Home: 611 W Delaware Dr Claremont CA 91711-3458 Office: Harvey Mudd Coll 301 E Platt Dr Claremont CA 91711-5901 Office Phone: 909-607-0716. Business E-Mail: sam_tanenbaum@hmc.edu.

TANENBAUM, EDWARD, lawyer; b. NYC, May 12, 1949; BA magna cum laude, Queens Coll., 1971; JD, Fordham Univ., 1974; LLM in Taxation, NYU, 1980. Bar: NY 1975. Ptnr., chmn., internat. tax group, mem., fed. income tax group Alston & Bird LLP, NYC. Mem.: ABA, Bar Assn. City NY, NY Bar Assn., Internat. Tax Inst. (past pres.), Nat. Coun., Internat. Fiscal Assn. Office: Alston & Bird LLP 90 Park Ave New York NY 10016-1387 Office Phone: 212-210-9425. Office Fax: 212-210-9444. Business E-Mail: edward.tanenbaum@alston.com.

TANENBAUM, JAY HARVEY, lawyer; b. NYC, Nov. 17, 1933; s. Leo Aaron and Regina (Stein) T.; m. Linda Goldman, May 28, 1961; children: Susan Hillary, Steven Eric. BA, Hobart and William Smith Colls., 1954; LLB, Union U., 1957, JD, 1961. Bar: N.Y. 1957, U.S. Dist. Ct. (so. dist.) N.Y. 1961, U.S. Supreme Ct. 1967. Internat. trader Associated Metals and Minerals Corp., NYC, 1960-64; pvt. practice, NYC, 1964—. Corp. counsel Internat. Gate Corp., Gen. Gate Corp. Named to Knighthood, His Royal Highness The Prince of Cittanova and His Royal Highness The Prince of Trabzon, 2001. Mem. N.Y. State Bar Assn., N.Y. Trial Lawyers Assn., Bronx County Bar Assn. Clubs: St. James (London), Le Club (N.Y.).

TANENBAUM, JEFFREY L., lawyer; b. NYC, Apr. 2, 1952; BA cum laude, SUNY, Binghamton, 1973; JD with honors, SUNY, Buffalo, 1976. Bar: N.Y. 1977, U.S. Dist. Ct. (so., ea., and we. dists.) N.Y. 1977, U.S. Ct. Appeals (4th cir.) 1983, U.S. Ct. Appeals (11th cir.) 1984, U.S. Supreme Ct. 1986. Law clk. Appellate Divsn. 4th Dept., NY, 1976-78; joined Weil, Gotshal & Manges, NYC, 1978, ptnr. Tech. editor Buffalo Law Review, 1975-76. Mem. ABA, Am. Bankruptcy Inst., N.Y. State Bar Assn. (banking, corporation, bus., bankruptcy and antitrust sects., com. on bankruptcy of the banking, corporation and bus. sect.), Phi Beta Kappa. Office: Weil Gotshal & Manges 767 5th Ave New York NY 10153-0119

TANENBAUM, JOEY, real estate developer; m. Toby Tanenbaum. PhD (hon.), Ryerson U., 2003. Chmn., CEO Jay-M Enterprises Ltd., Jay-M Holdings Ltd. Trustee Royal Ontario Mus., Art Gallery of Ontario; hon. chmn. Can. Psychiat. Rsch. Found. Named one of Top 200 Collectors, ARTnews mag., 2003—06; recipient Order of Can. Avocation: Collector of 19-century European art; Cycladic and Neolithic art. Address: 317 Dundas St W Toronto ON M5T 1G4 Canada

TANENBAUM, RICHARD HUGH, lawyer; b. Washington, July 10, 1947; m. Cindy Marks, Mar. 22, 1996; children: Brian J., Drew S. BS, Bradley U., 1969; JD, Cath. U. Am. Sch. Law, 1974. Bar: Md. 1974, D.C. 1975, U.S. Ct. Claims 1975, U.S. Ct. Appeals (D.C. cir.) 1975, U.S. Ct. Appeals (4th cir.) 1982, U.S. Tax Ct. 1982, U.S. Supreme Ct. 1982. Consumer edn. developer, tchr. Peoria (Ill.) Pub. Sch. System, 1969-71; legal asst. Pay Bd., Exec. Office of Pres., Washington, 1971-72; acct. Alexander Grant & Co., Washington, 1972; assoc. Jones, Day, Reavis & Pogue, Washington, 1973-78; ptnr. Lerch, Early & Brewer, Bethesda, Md., 1978-85; atty. pvt. practice, Bethesda, Md., 1985—; chmn. Am. Masterworks Devel. Co., 2002—. Chmn. Am. Masterworks Devel. Co., 2002—, 2002—. Mng. editor Cath. U. Law Rev., Washington, 1974. Recipient Superior Performance award Exec. Office of Pres., Washington, 1972. Mem. ABA, Montgomery County Bar Assn., D.C. Bar Assn., Bethesda-Chevy Chase C. of C. (bd. dirs. 1980-83), Bethesda Country Club, Rotary (charter mem., bd. dirs. 1980—). Office: 6259 Executive Blvd Rockville MD 20852 Office Phone: 301-560-0838. Personal E-mail: rht775n@aol.com.

TANENBAUM, WILLIAM ALAN, lawyer; b. Rochester, NY, Feb. 16, 1954; s. Burton David and Millicent (Kroll) T.; m. Judy Ellen Hertz, June 15, 1986. BA with highest honors, Brown U., 1976; JD, Cornell U., 1979. Ptnr. Kenyon & Kenyon, NYC, Rogers & Wells, NYC. Lectr. in field. Co-author A Guide to European Data Protection and Privacy Laws for U.S. Companies, contbr. articles to profl. jours. Mem. ABA, NY State Bar Assn. (litigation com., intellectual property litigation com.), Intellectual Property Law Assn., Computer Law Assn. (founding co-chmn. ann. outsourcing conf., pres. 1995-96), NY Intellectual Property Law, Copyright Soc. USA, Am. Arbitration Assn. (panel arbitrators), Phi Beta Kappa. Avocation: sailing. Office: Kaye Scholer LLP 425 Park Ave New York NY 10022 Home Phone: 212-570-0871; Office Phone: 212-836-7661. Business E-Mail: wtanenbaum@kayescholer.com.

TANENHAUS, SAM, editor; m. Kathryn Bonomi; 1 child. BA in English, Grinnell Coll., 1977; MA in English Lit., Yale U., 1978. With publicity Farrar, Straus and Giroux; with trade, acad., and crossover books Oxford Univ. Press, Chelsea House; contbg. editor Vanity Fair, 1999—2004; asst. editor op-ed page N.Y. Times, 1997—99, editor book rev., 2004—. Juror on biography Pulitzer Prize Com., 2000; affiliated writer Sch. Journalism NYU, 2002—03. Author: Literature Unbound: A Guide for the Common Reader, 1984, Louis Armstrong: Biography of a Musician, 1989, Whittaker Chambers: A Biography, 1997 (L.A. Times Book prize for biography, 1997, finalist Nat. Book award for nonfiction, 1997, finalist Pulitzer prize for biography, 1998); contbg. author: Wall St. Jour., Washington Post; contbg. author Boston Globe, LA Times, N.Y. Times Mag., Nat. Rev., New Criterion, N.Y. Rev. Books, New Republic, Am. Scholar, Commentary. Recipient award, John M. Olin Found., Bradley Found.; grantee, NEH, 1997; Media fellow Hoover Instn., Stanford U., 2000, 2002. Mem.: Soc. Am. Historians (mem. exec. bd.). Office: The NY Times 229 W 43rd St New York NY 10036 Business E-Mail: tanenhaus@nytimes.com.

TANEY, FRANCIS XAVIER, JR., lawyer; b. Camden, NJ, Aug. 31, 1970; s. Francis Xavier Sr. and Clara Mary Taney; m. Sheila Ann FitzPatrick, Oct. 26, 1996; children: Patrick Francis, Bridget Ann. BA in Econs. summa cum laude, Drew U., 1992; JD, U. Pa., 1995. Bar: Pa. 1995, NJ 1995, US Dist. Ct. (ea. dist.) Pa. 1995, US Dist. Ct. (NJ) 1995, US Ct. Appeals (3d cir.) 1996. Assoc. Klehr, Harrison, Harvey, Branzburg & Ellers, Cherry Hill, NJ, 1995—96, Piper & Marbury LLP, Phila., 1996—97, Saul, Ewing, Remick & Saul LLP, Phila., 1997—2001, Buchanan Ingersoll and Rooney, P.C., Phila., 2001—03, shareholder, 2004—. Guest lectr. Pa. State U. Gt. Valley Campus, Malvern, 2004—; spkr. in field. Contbr. articles to profl. jours., chpt. to book.; editor: U. Pa. Law Sch. Law Rev., 1994—95. Recipient Pa. Rising Star (atty.) award, Law and Politics Mag. and Phila. Mag., 2005—06. Mem.: ABA, Friendly Sons of St. Patrick, Drew U. Phila. Area Alumni Club (pres. steering com. 1999—2002), Phi Beta Kappa, Omicron Delta Epsilon. Avocations: tennis, music. Office: Buchanan Ingersoll and Rooney PC 1835 Market 14th Fl Philadelphia PA 19103 Home Phone: 856-354-9623; Office Phone: 215-665-3846. Office Fax: 215-665-8760. Business E-Mail: francis.taney@bipc.com.

TANG, C. MARK, investment banker, venture capitalist; b. Jiangyin, China, June 21, 1964; s. J. H. Tang and R. F. Kong; m. S. Sharon Guo, Jan. 20, 1994; children: Alexander, Gloria. BS in Biochemistry, Nanjing U., China, 1985; PhD in Biochemistry and Molecular Biol., U. Calif., 1993; MBA in Fin., NYU, 2000. Postdoctoral rsch. assoc. Rockefeller U., NYC, 1993-96; assoc. v.p. biotech., merchant banking and venture capital DH Blair Investment Banking Corp., NYC, 1996-98; co-founder, CFO, vice chmn. Aegisoft Corp. (acquired by RealNetwork Inc.), Rockville, Md., 1998-2000; investment advisor UBS PaineWebber, Inc., NYC, 1998-2000, Morgan Stanley, Jersey City, 2001—02; pres. World Tech. Ventures, LLC, 2002—. Author: The Essential Biotech Investment Guide, 2002; founding mng. editor, biotech. analyst Bio/Med. Tech. Stock Newsletter, 1994—98; contbr. articles to profl. jours. Mem.: Soc. Chinese Bioscientists Am. Avocations: tennis, golf, volleyball, reading, writing. Home: PO Box 212 Jersey City NJ 07303 Office: World Tech Ventures 14 Wall St 20th Fl New York NY 10005 Personal E-mail: c.mark.tang@gmail.com.

TANG, CHING WAN, research scientist; BS, U. BC, 1970; PhD in Physical Chemistry, Cornell U., 1975. Disting. rsch. fellow rsch. and devel. Eastman Kodak Co., Rochester, NY. Recipient Industrial Innovation Award, Am. Chem. Soc., 2001. Mem.: NAE.

TANG, CHRISTOPHER S., finance educator; BSc, U. London, 1978—81; MSc, Yale U., New Haven, Conn., 1981—83, PhD, 1981—85. Edward Carter prof. bus. adminstrn. UCLA Anderson Sch., 1985—; dean Nat. U. Singapore, 2002—04. Sr. advisor to vice-chancellor Nat. U. Singapore, 2000—02. Contbr. articles to profl. jours. Recipient Citibank Tchg. of Yr. award, UCLA Anderson Sch., 1999, Neidorf's Best Tchr. of Decade award, 2000; grantee Standford Supply Chain Forum fellowship, Stanford Bus. Sch., 1997. Office: UCLA Anderson Sch 110 Westwood Plz Los Angeles CA 90095 Business E-Mail: ctang@anderson.ucla.edu.

TANG, CYRUS, investment company executive; b. Chiangsu Province, China, 1930; arrived in US, 1950; married; 2 children. Attended, Widener U., Ill. Inst. Tech. CEO, pres., chmn. Tang Industries, Mt. Prospect, Ill. Office: 1650 W Jefferson Ave Trenton MI 48183-2136 Address: Tang Industries 3773 Howard Hughes Pkwy Ste 350N Las Vegas NV 89109

TANG, ESTHER DON, real estate developer, consultant, social worker; b. Tucson, Mar. 5, 1917; d. Don Wah and Yut (Gnan) Don; m. David W. Tang, June 14, 1942; children: Patricia Karen Tang Crowley, Diana Cheryl Tang Simoes, David. Jr., Elizabeth Carol. Student, Draughn's Bus. Sch., San Antonio, 1936, U. Ariz., 1938-41, DHL, LHD, U. Ariz., 1992. Owner, operator supermarket, Tucson, 1940-66; exec. dir. Pio Decimo Ctr., Cath. Diocese, Tucson, 1966-85; cons., ptnr., vice chmn. bd. Netwest Devel. Corp., Tucson, 1985—. Prodr.: (video) Tapestry of Tucson (award winning). Mem. Tucson Airport Authority, 1975—, Pima County Crime and Pub. Safety Coun., 1999; chmn. Tucson-Taichung Sister Cities, 1979-91; chmn. Tucson Sister Cities Steering Com., 1984—, Sister Cities Assn. Tucson, 1990, Ariz. Pers. Bd.; chmn. bd. dirs. Pima Community Coll., 1975-85; pres. bd. dirs. Pima Coun. on Aging, 1986-90; coord. US Bicentennial, Tucson; mem. adv. bd. Ariz. Dept. Econ. Security; master of ceremonies to welcome Pres. Clinton, City of Tucson, 1999. Named Woman of Yr., City of Tucson, 1955, Woman of Yr. in Adminstrn., 1968, Lady Comdr. the Holy Sepluchre Jerusalem; recipient Disting. Friend of the Humanities award Nat. Adv. Bd., 1989, Jefferson award Ariz. Daily Star, 1987, Svc. award Pima Coun. on Aging, 1987-89, Disting. Svc. award U. Pima CC Found., 1988, Roots and Wings Cmty. award, 1988, Rosie award So. Ariz. Ctr. Against Sexual Assault, 1990, Lifetime Achievement award YWCA, 1992, 93, La Doña de los Descendientes del Precido de Tucson, 1997-98, centennial alumni award U. Ariz., 1998, Pan-Asian Cmty. Leadership award, 1999, Arthritis Humanitarian award, 1999, Altrusa Women in Svc. award, 2000, Asia Am. Times Devel. Mgmt. Excellence award, 2000, Voices into the Millennium award Ariz. Border Patrol, Dynamic Duo—Pointing Lives in New Directions award Compass Health Care, Congl. Recognition, 2002, Lulac Nat. Presdl. citation, 2002, award Agave Ariz. Hist. Tape TV, 2002, Lifetime award U. Ariz. Coll. Agr. and Life Sci., 2002; Learning Svc. Bldg. and Gallery named in her honor, U. Ariz., 2001; named Ariz. History Maker State of Ariz. Hist. League, 2003, 15th annual Cath. Found. Honoring Esther Don Tang, 2004; featured as an active activist Foothills Publ., 2005; named to Hall of Fame Tucson H.S. Badger Found., 2006. Mem. Soroptimist (hon., Women Who Helped Build Tucson award), Rotary Club Tucson (4 way test award 1998) Cath.

Found. Diocese of Tucson (honorable mention, honoree Corner Stone Gala, 2004). Roman Catholic. Avocations: travel, cooking, golf. Home: 701 E Camino De Los Padres Tucson AZ 85718-1921

TANG, GEORGE CHICKCHEE, investment company executive; b. Hong Kong, Nov. 8, 1964; came to U.S., 1984; s. George and Margaret Tang. BS, Case Western Res. U., 1987; MS, Northwestern U., 1989. Registered securities rep., commodity rep., ins. agt., Ill.; CFA, CFP, portfolio mgr. sr. investment mgmt. cons., fin. planning specialist. With AT&T Bell Labs., Naperville, Ill., 1989-92; fin. advisor Smith Barney, Oakbrook, Ill., 1992—, 2d v.p. for investments, 1998-2000, v.p. for investments, 2000-01, 1st v.p. investments, 2001—05, 1st v.p. wealth mgmt., 2006—. Spkr., lectr. in field. Contbr. fin. columns to Chgo. Chinese Daily News, 1993—, Chinese Am. News, 1993—, China Jour., 1994-97. Writer ARC, Cleve., 1985-86; spkr. on environ. protection City Coun. Hong Kong, 1982. Recipient Champion of Wildlife Conservation award Hong Kong Std., 1982. Mem. Inst. CFA's (chartered), Assn. for Investment and Rsch., Orgn. Chinese Ams. (internal v.p. Chgo. chpt. 1994-95, pres. 1995-97). Avocations: tennis, swimming, bridge, art. Office: Smith Barney One Lincoln Ctr Ste 1300 Oakbrook Terrace IL 60181

TANG, JOHN, network technician, information scientist, educator; b. Hong Kong, Oct. 21, 1959; s. Chew Sang and Miu King Tang; m. Juana Teresita Enriquez, Mar. 15, 1990; 1 child, Jonathan Alexander. BA, San Francisco State U., 1981; MA, San Francisco State Univeristy, 1983; PhD, U. of Va., 1991. MIS mgr. Oakland Pvt. Industry Coun., Oakland, Calif., 1991—95; IT mgr. Western Human Nutrition Rsch. Ctr., San Francisco, 1995—98; network analyst Shaman Pharms., South San Francisco, Calif., 1995—98; instr. The Computer Learning Ctr., San Francisco, 1997—2001; adj. prof. City Coll. of San Francisco, 2000—; prof. DeVry U., Fremont, Calif., 2002—. Founder/pres. easyRE.net, Fremont, Calif., 2003—; founder, CEO Home Opportunities Inc., Oakland, Calif., 2003—. Contbr. articles to profl. jours., chpts. to books. Pres. Dance for Power, Oakland, 1993—98; mem. of bd. of advisors American-Viet League, Oakland, 1991—2003. Recipient Dupont fellow, U. of Va., 1984—88, Grad. Achievement award, San Francisco State U., 1983. Roman Catholic. Avocations: creative writing, travel. Home: 6651 Gunn Dr Oakland CA 94611 Office: DeVry Univ 6600 Dumbarton Cir Fremont CA Personal E-mail: jltang@sbcglobal.net. Business E-Mail: jtang@fre.devry.edu.

TANG, KAIZHI, research scientist; s. Yingwu Tang and Youyuan Jiang; m. Xuequn Ding, Apr. 30, 2000; 1 child, Esther. BS, Tsinghua U., Beijing, 1996; MS, Pa. State U., State Coll., 2001; PhD, Pa. State U., 2005. Rsch. scientist Intelligent Automation Inc., Rockville, Md., 2004—. Logistics expert Allexpert.com. Deacon State Coll. Alliance Ch., 2001—02, Christian Life Ch. Wash. DC, Rockville, Md., 2005—07; pres. Chinese Student, Scholar, Family Ministry, State Coll., 2001—03. Grantee Rsch. grant, NASA, 2004—06, SBIR Army Rsch. grant, US Army Rsch. Lab., 2005—06, Rsch. grant, USAF, 2006—07, US Office Sec. Def., 2007. Achievements include research in operations research related to prediction and optimization. Avocations: tennis, ping pong/table tennis. Office: Intelligent Automation Inc 15400 Calhoun Dr Ste 400 Rockville MD 20855 Business E-Mail: ktang@i-a-i.com.

TANG, MAN-CHUNG, civil engineer, company executive; b. Xiao Qing, China, Feb. 22, 1938; came to U.S., 1968; s. Yu-Fung and Jing Tse Tang; m. Yee-Yun Fung, Aug. 26, 1966; children: Chin-Chung, Chin-Ning. BSc, Chu-Hai Coll., Hong Kong, 1959; DLitt (hon.), Chu-Hai U., Hong Kong, 1997: MS. Tech. U. Darmstadt, Germany, 1964, PhD, 1965; D of Engring. (hon.), Kassel U., Germany, 2001. Registered profl. engr., N.Y., Mass., Fla., Ill., Wash., others. Bridge engr. GHH, Germany, 1965-68; sr. engr. Severud & Assocs., NYC, 1968-70; v.p., chief engr. Dyckerhoff & Widmann, NYC, 1970-78; pres. DRC Cons. Inc., NYC, 1978—; chmn. bd. T.Y. Lin Internat., San Francisco, 1995—. Contbr. more than 100 articles to profl. jours. Recipient Leadership award Am. Segmental Bridge Inst., 1991, Roebling Life Achievement award Internat. Bridge Conf., 1998. Mem. ASCE (hon.), named N.Y. Civil Engr. of Yr. 1989, Roebling award 1999, Nat. Acad. Engring. (life), Chinese Acad. Engring. (life mem.). Achievements include pioneer work in design and construction of cable-stayed and segmental bridges. Office: TY Lin Internat Two Harrison St Ste 500 San Francisco CA 94105 Office Phone: 415-291-3707. E-mail: mtang@tylin.com.

TANG, PAUL C., lawyer; b. Hong Kong, Oct. 4, 1952; arrived in US, 1958, naturalized, 1964; m. Shirley Tang; children: Elizabeth, Margaret. BA, Harvard U., 1974; JD, Columbia U., 1977, MBA, 1978. Bar: NY 1981, NJ 1994. Tax acct. Deloitte & Touche, 1978—80; mem. Phillips Nizer, 1980—85, ptnr., 1985—87; co-founder law firm, 1987—89; ptnr. Reid & Priest, 1989—93; exec. v.p., gen. counsel, sec. Burlington Coat Factory Warehouse Corp., NJ, 1993—. Bd. dirs. NJ Retail Merchants Assn., 2006—. Mem.: ABA, NJ State Bar Assn., NY State Bar Assn. Office: Burlington Coat Factory 1830 Rt 130 Burlington NJ 08016-3020 Business E-Mail: paul.tang@coat.com.

TANG, TERRY, editor, lawyer; BA, Yale Univ., 1980; JD, NYU, 1983. Atty. Preston Thorgrimson Ellis & Holman, Seattle, 1983; staff writer Seattle Weekly, 1984—89; editl. writer Seattle Times, 1989—97; mem. editl bd. New York Times, 1997—2000, Op-Ed page editor, 2000—03, dep. tech. editor, 2003—. Editor (mng.): Rev. of Law & Social Change, 1982—83. Nieman fellow, Harvard Univ., 1992—93. Office: New York Times 229 W 43d St New York NY 10036 Office Phone: 212-556-7745. Office Fax: 212-556-1448. Business E-Mail: tang@nytimes.com.

TANG, YAO LIANG, medical educator, researcher, surgeon; b. Shanghai, July 14, 1970; s. HaiChuan Tang and MeiJuan Liang; m. Yan Shen, Oct. 27, 2000; 1 child, SongTing. MD, Shanghai 2nd Med. U., 1993; PhD, Fudan U., Shanghai, 2002. Diplomate physician Ministry of Health P.R. China, 2000. Cardiac surgeon Shanghai Inst. of Cardiovasc. Diseases, Shanghai, Shanghai, 1997—2002; postdoctoral fellow Univeristy of South Fla., St. Petersburg, 2003—04; asst. prof. U. of South Fla., Tampa, 2004—; postdoctoral fellow U. of Fla., Gainesville. Ad hoc reviewer Can. Inst. of Health Rsch. (CIHR), Ottawa, Ont., 2005—, Nat. Med. Rsch. Coun. (NMRC), Singapore, 2005—. Contbr. articles to profl. jours. Recipient Outstanding Postdoctoral Fellow Rsch. award, Am. Heart Assn. (Fla./Puerto Rico Affiliate), 2003, Young Investigator award, Am. Coll. of Cardiology Found., 2004, Dr. Jeff Isner Young Investigator award, Mass. Gen. Hosp., 2004, Melvin L. Marcus award, Am. Heart Assn., 2004. Mem.: Am. Heart Assn., Sigma Xi (Outstanding Postdoctoral Fellow award 2004). Buddhism. Achievements include patents pending for vigilant cell system for enhancing grafted cell survial in ischemic myocardium; stem cell beacon system for targeting stem cells to ischemic myocardium for repair; vigilant vector for cardioprotection; invention of adult cardiac stem cells for heart repair. Avocations: swimming, travel. Home: 2870 N Towne Apt 13 Pomona CA 91767 Office: Keck Grad Inst Applied Life Scis 535 Watson Dr Claremont CA 91711 Home Phone: 727-366-8298. E-mail: tangyl888@hotmail.com.

TANG, YUE, financial analyst; s. Xiangrong Tang and Jiayin Zhang. BS in Genetics, Fudan U., Shanghai, 1998; M.S. in Molecular Pharmacology and Toxicology, U. So. Calif., 2001; MBA, U. Notre Dame, 2003. Cert. NASD. Founder BioRoad Gene Devel. Ltd. (now United Gene Ltd.), Shanghai, 1997—99; equity analyst Needham & Co., NYC, 2003—05; equity analyst, portfolio mgr. BB Biotech, Boston, 2005—. Provost scholar, U. Notre Dame, 2001—02. Mem.: NY Acad. of Scis., Oxygen Club Calif. Achievements include research in metabolic pathways to dopamine mediated by nitric oxide in dopaminergic neurons.

TANGHERLINI, FRANK ROBERT, physics educator; b. Boston, Mar. 14, 1924; s. Emiliano Francesco Tangherlini and Rosa (Robinson) Leclaire; m. Jane Kjaergaard Kjems, Jan. 2, 1960 (div. 1979); children: Arne E.(dec.), Timothy R., Daniel M., Niels L. SB in Physics with honors, Harvard U., Cambridge, Mass., 1948; MS in Physics, U. Chgo., 1952; PhD in Physics, Stanford U., Calif., 1959. Rsch. engr. Convair-Gen. Dynamics, San Diego, 1952—55; postdoctoral fellow NSF, Copenhagen, Naples, 1958—60; rsch. assoc. U. NC, Chapel Hill, 1960-61; asst. prof. Duke U., Durham, 1961-64; assoc. prof. George Washington U., Washington, 1964-66; sci. assoc. Danish Space Rsch. Inst., Lyngby, Denmark, 1966-67; assoc. prof. Coll. of the Holy Cross, Worcester, Mass., 1967-94. Vis. scientist Internat. Ctr. Theoretical Physics, Trieste, Italy, 1973—74. Author: Introduction to the General Theory of Relativity, 1961, (book of poetry) Love is not Always Commutative, 2004; contbr. articles to profl. jours. Chmn. Cub Scouts Am., Auburn, Mass., 1975—77. With US Army, 1943—46, with US Army, 1944—45, ETO. Vis. scholar, Harvard U., 1988—89; Travel grantee, NSF, 1980, 1984. Mem.: AAUP, Am. Phys. Soc., Balboa Tennis Club, Stanford Club San Diego, Harvard Club San Diego, U. Chgo. Club San Diego, Sigma Xi. Achievements include research in dimensionality of space, the classical electron, Snell's law, relativity, gravitation and cosmology. Avocations: poetry, history, philosophy. Office Phone: 858-638-7362. Personal E-mail: frtan96@sbcglobal.net.

TANGNEY, MICHAEL J., consumer products company executive; With Colgate, 1971, various US and internat. mgmt. positions in L.Am. and Europe; pres. Colgate-Mex. Colgate-Palmolive Co., pres. Colgate-L.Am., exec. v.p., pres. Colgate-L.Am., 2000—. Office: Colgate Palmolive Co 300 Park Ave New York NY 10022-7499 Office Phone: 212-310-2000. Office Fax: 212-310-3284. *

TANGORA, ANTHONY JOSEPH, director; b. Urbana, Ill., Feb. 6, 1974; s. Paul Anthony and Sally Melahn Tangora. BA, U. Ill., Urbana-Champaign, 1998. Student supr. U. Ill., Urbana, 1996—97, asst. dir. club programs, alumni assn., 2001—05, assoc. dir. devel. Chgo., 2005—; dir. alumni devel. Tau Kappa Epsilon Frat. Inc., Indpls., 1999—2001. Co-chair Young Leaders Fund Chgo. Cmty. Trust, 2006—07; vol. Tau Kappa Epsilon Frat., Indpls., 2001—07. Fellow Jerry F. Tarty Young Profl. award, Coun. Alumni Assn. Execs., 2002. Mem.: Assn. Fundraising Profls. (assoc.). R-Conservative. Roman Catholic. Avocations: travel, sailing, exercise. Office: Illini Ctr 200 S Wacker Dr Chicago IL 60606 Business E-Mail: atangora@uiuc.edu.

TANGORA, MARTIN CHARLES, mathematician, educator; b. NYC, June 21, 1936; s. Albert and Virginia T.; m. Linda Perry, June 17, 1973; children: Charles, Elizabeth. BS, Calif. Inst. Tech., 1957; MS, Northwestern U., 1958, PhD, 1966. Instr. Northwestern U., Evanston, Ill., 1966—67, U. Chgo., 1967—69; asst. prof. U. Ill., Chgo., 1970—72, assoc. prof., 1972—2002, assoc. prof. emeritus, 2002—. Temp. lectr. U. Manchester, Eng., 1969-70; sr. vis. fellow U. Oxford, Eng., 1973-74. Author: Computing the Homology of the Lambda Algebra, 1985; co-author: Cohomology Operations and Applications in Homotopy Theory, 1968; editor: Computers in Algebra, 1988, Computers in Geometry and Topology, 1989, Algebraic Topology Oaxtepec 1991 (conf. proc.), 1993. Bd. dirs. Landmarks Preservation Coun. Ill., Chgo., pres., 1976, v.p. 1997-99; bd. dirs. Uptown Theatre and Ctr. for the Arts, chmn. bd., 2003-2005; bd. dirs. Civic Ballet of Chgo., 2005—. Mem. Math. Assn. Am., Am. Math. Soc. Office: U Ill Chgo Math M/C 249 851 S Morgan St Chicago IL 60607-7045 Business E-Mail: tangora@uic.edu.

TANGUAY, JEANNE MARIE, social worker; b. Flint, Mich., Sept. 1, 1939; d. Charles Frank and Mary Stella Ocenasek; m. Ray Tanguay (div.); children: Ray Eric, Michele Lynne. AA with high honors, Flint Jr. Coll., 1966; BA with high distinction, U. Mich., 1976. Mem. reservation dept. TWA Airlines, Los Angeles, 1980—81; travel agent Cardillo Travel, Commerce, Calif., 1982—83; sales agent Threshold, Scotts Valley, Calif., 1990—93; social worker Develop. Ctr., Ft. Walton Beach, Fla., 1995—96, Bridgeway, Ft. Walton Beach, Fla., 0196—1998; ret., 1998. Bd. mem. Tulsa Human Svcs., Okla., 1977. Polit. worker Dem. Party, Flint, Mich., 1962; council mem. Holy Name Ch., Niceville, Fla., 2005, 2006; worker Dem. Party for John Kerry, Niceville, 2004. Mem.: Twin Cities Sr. Club, Pi Alpha. Democrat. Roman Cath. Avocations: reading, movies, Bingo.

TANGUAY, PETER EUGENE, child and adolescent psychiatry educator; b. Quebec City, Que., Can., Nov. 6, 1935; came to U.S., 1960, naturalized, 1971; s. Oscar E. and Marion L. (Grady) T.; m. Margaret Fife, Dec. 22, 1960; children: Heather Louise, Gretchen Marie. BA, U. Ottawa, Ont., Can., 1956, MD, 1960. Diplomate Am. Bd. Psychiatry and Neurology (com. for cert. in child and adolescent psychiatry 1981-87, written exam. com. for child and adolescent psychiatry 1981-87, chmn. 1985-87, dir. 1990—). Intern Harper Hosp., Detroit, 1960-61; resident in psychiatry UCLA Med. Ctr.-Harbor Gen. Hosp., 1961-64; registrar in psychiatry Kingsway Hosp., Derby, Eng., 1966-68; fellow in child psychiatry UCLA Ctr. for Health Scis., 1968-70, from asst. prof. to assoc. prof., 1970-8076, prof., 1980-94, dir. child psychiatry clin. rsch. ctr., 1977-87, assoc. chief div., 1984-91, acting chief, 1992-94; Ackerly prof. child psychiatry U. Louisville Sch. Medicine, 1994—2004, emeritus, 2004—. Tech. advisor Rainman, 1988; vis. prof. U. Tours, France, 1982, U. Hawaii, 1987, 90; Roy Grinker vis. prof. Michael Reese Hosp., Chgo., 1984; mem. gen. assembly Am. Bd. Med. Specialists, 1990—, rep. to Accreditation Coun. on Continuing Med. Edn., 1993—, mem. exec. com., 1994-96; bd. advisors Rieger Found., Santa Barbara, Calif., 1992—; mem. psychol. scis. rev. com. NIMH, 1976-80; lectr., presenter in field; editl. cons. EEG and Clin. Neurophysiology, 1979-85; numerous others. Author: (with Margaret Tanguay) Travel Adventure in Europe with Tent, Van or Motorhome, 1970; editor-in-chief Psychiat. Residents Tng. Program, 2007—; contbr. over 60 articles, abstracts and book revs. to sci. jours., over 20 chpts. to books. Mem. Clinton-Gore Nat. Leadership Coun., 1991-93. Recipient career sci. devel. award NIMH, 1970-75; grantee USPHS, 1977-87, 84-89, NIMH, 1980-95, MacArthur Found., 1983-88. Fellow Am. Psychiat. Assn. (coun. on rsch. 1980-95, vice chmn. 1981-94, mem. com. on chronically ill-emotionally handicapped child 1990-94), Am. Acad. Child and Adolescent Psychiatry (assoc. editor Jour. 1988—, co-chmn. task force on universal access to health care 1991—), Am. Coll. Psychiatry; mem. AMA, AAAS, Group for Advancement Psychiatry (chmn. child com. 1988—), Soc. for Rsch. in Child and Adolescent Psychopathology, Royal Coll. Psychiatry (Gt. Britain, affiliate). Democrat. Avocations: microcomputers, vegetable gardening, travel. Home: 1129 Cardinal Dr Louisville KY 40213-1363 Office: U Louisville Bingham Child Guidance Ctr 200 E Chestnut St Louisville KY 40202-1822 Personal E-mail: ptanky@aol.com.

TANI, LLOYD YASUO, pediatrician, educator; b. LA, Aug. 6, 1956; s. Lorraine Hiroko Tani; m. Yvette Friede Tani, May 30, 1990; children: Ryan Yasuo, Jaclyn Christine. BA in Biology, UCLA, 1978; MD, U. Calif., LA, 1982. Diplomate Nat. Bd. Med. Examiners, 1986, Am. Bd. Pediatrics, 1987, pediatric cardiology Am. Bd. Pediatrics, 1991, lic. Utah, 1989. Internship and residency pediat. Baylor Coll. Medicine, 1982—86, fellowship pediat. cardiology, 1986—89; pediat. cardiologist Sch. Medicine U. Utah, 1989—, prof. pediat. Sch. Medicine, 1989—, assoc. dir. divsn. pediat. cardiology, 2002—07, dir. divsn. pediat. cardiology, 2007—. Mem.: Utah Med. Assn., Am. Acad. Pediatrics, Am. Soc. Echocardiography, Am. Heart Assn. Office: University of Utah School of Medicine 100 N Medical Drive Salt Lake City UT 84113 Office Phone: 801-662-5400. Office Fax: 801-662-5404.

TANICK, MARSHALL HOWARD, lawyer, educator; b. Mpls., May 9, 1947; s. Jack and Esther (Kohn) T.; m. Cathy E. Gorlin, Feb. 20, 1982; children: Lauren, Ross. BA, U. Minn., 1969; JD, Stanford U., 1973. Bar: Calif. 1973, Minn. 1974. Law clk. to presiding justice U.S. Dist. Ct., Mpls., 1973-74; assoc. Robins, Davis & Lyons, Mpls., 1974-76; ptnr. Tanick & Heins, P.A., Mpls., 1976-89, Mansfield & Tanick, Mpls., 1989—. Prof. constrn., real estate and media law U. Minn., Mpls., 1983—, Hamline U., St. Paul, 1982—; prof. constl. law William Mitchell Coll. Law, 1994. Editor: Hennepin Lawyer, Bench, Bar and Litigation mag.; contbr. articles to mags. Avocation: writing. Home: 1230 Angelo Dr Minneapolis MN 55422-4710 Office: Mansfield Tanick Cohen Pa 220 S 6th St Ste 1700 Minneapolis MN 55402-4511 Office Phone: 612-339-4295. Business E-Mail: mtanick@mansfieldtanick.com.

TANIGUCHI, TADATSUGU, biology professor, researcher; b. Wakayama-ken, Japan, Jan. 1, 1948; s. Takashi and Tomiko Taniguchi; m. Yoko Tsuchihashi, Apr. 30, 1977; 1 child, Masanori. BS, Tokyo U., 1971; PhD, U. Zurich, 1978. Chief Japanese Found. for Cancer Rsch., 1983—84; prof. Inst. Molecular and Cellular Biology Osaka U., Japan; prof. Dept. Immunology, Grad. Sch. Medicine U. Tokyo. Recipient Hammer prize, 1985, Hideyo Nguchi Meml. award, 1985. Mem.: Am. Assn. Cancer Rsch. (co-chmn. internat. affairs com. 2003—07), NAS. Mailing: Am Assn for Cancer Rsch Internat Affairs Committee 615 Chestnut St 17Th Fl Philadelphia PA 19106 *

TANIS, JAMES ROBERT, library director, history professor, clergyman; b. Phillipsburg, NJ, June 26, 1928; s. John Christian and Bertha Marie (Tobiasson) T.; m. Florence Borgmann, June 26, 1963 (dec. June 2006); children Justin Edward, James Tobiasson. BA, Yale, 1951; B.D., Union Theol. Sem., NYC, 1954; Dr. Theol., U. Utrecht, Netherlands, 1967; LittD (hon.), Dickinson Coll., Carlisle, Pa., 1994. Ordained to ministry Presbyn. Ch., 1954. Co-pastor Greystone Presbyn. Ch., Elizabeth, NJ, 1954-55; librarian, mem. faculty Harvard Div. Sch., 1956-65; univ. librarian Yale U., 1965-68; mem. faculty Yale Div. Sch., 1968-69; dir. libraries, prof. history Bryn Mawr (Pa.) Coll., 1969-97; guest curator Phila. Mus. Art, 1997—2002; parish assoc. Valley Forge Presbyn. Ch., King of Prussia, Pa., 1973—2005. Author: Calvinistic Pietism in the Middle Colonies, 1967; co-author: Bookbinding in America, 1983, Images of Discord/De Tweedracht Verbeeld, 1993, Fantasy and Fashion, 1996, Leaves of Gold: Manuscript Illumination from Philadelphia Collections, 2001. Decorated officer Order Orange-Nassau. Home: 11302 Shannondell Dr Audubon PA 19403-5616 E-mail: jrtanis@sdlifestyle.com.

TANNA, ANGELO PETER, ophthalmologist, educator, researcher; m. Carola Ann Tanna. BA, Johns Hopkins U., 1989; MD, Columbia U. Coll. of Physicians and Surgeons, 1994. Glaucoma Fellowship Johns Hopkins Hosp. / Md., 1999. Internship Grad. Hosp., Md., 1995; ophthalmology residency Wilmer Eye Inst., Md., 1998; attending ophthalmologist Johns Hopkins Bayview Med. Ctr., Baltimore, Md., 1998—99; dir., glaucoma svc. Northwestern Med. Faculty Found., Chicago, Ill., 1999—; asst. prof. of ophthalmology Northwestern U. Feinberg Sch. of Medicine, Chicago, Ill., 1999—. Dir., glaucoma svc. Northwestern Med. Faculty Found., Chicago, Ill., 1999—; editl. bd. mem. Survey of Ophthalmology, Brookline, Mass., 2000—. Contbr. articles various profl. jours. Named to Best Drs. in Am., Best Drs., Inc., 2005—06; recipient Frey prize in engring., Northwestern U., 2003. Fellow: Am. Acad. of Ophthalmology; mem.: Am. Glaucoma Soc., Alpha Omega Alpha. Office: NW Med Faculty Found 675 N Saint Clair Ste 15-150 Chicago IL 60611 Home Phone: 847-735-7470; Office Phone: 312-908-8152. Business E-Mail: atanna@northwestern.edu.

TANNEN, DEBORAH FRANCES, writer; b. Bklyn., June 7, 1945; d. Eli S. and Dorothy (Rosen) T. BA, SUNY, Binghamton, 1966; MA, Wayne State U., 1970, U. Calif., Berkeley, 1976; PhD, U. Calif., 1979. English instr. Mercer County C.C., Trenton, NJ, 1970-71; lectr. in acad. skills CUNY, Bronx, NY, 1971-74; asst. prof. Georgetown U., Washington, 1979-85, assoc. prof. linguistics, 1985-90, prof. linguistics, 1989-91, univ. prof., 1991—. McGraw disting. lectr. in writing Coun. for Humanities and dept. anthropology Princeton U., fall 1991; visitor Inst. for Advanced Study, Princeton, spring 1992; fellow Ctr. for Advanced Study in Behavioral Scis., Stanford, Calif., 1992-93. Author: Lilika Nakos, 1983, Conversational Style: Analyzing Talk Among Friends, 1984, That's Not What I Meant!: How Conversational Style Makes or Breaks Your Relations With Others, 1986, Talking Voices: Repetition, Dialogue and Imagery in Conversational Discourse, 1989, You Just Don't Understand: Women and Men in Conversation, 1990, Gender and Discourse, 1994, Talking From 9 to 5: Women and Men in the Workplace: Language, Sex and Power, 1994, The Argument Culture: Moving from Debate to Dialogue, 1998, The Argument Culture: Stopping America's War of Words, 1999, You're Wearing That? Understanding Mothers and Daughters in Conversation, 2006; editor: Analyzing Discourse: Text and Talk, 1982, Spoken and Written Language: Exploring Orality and Literacy, 1982, Coherence in Spoken and Written Discourse, 1984, Perspectives on Silence, 1985, Linguistics in Context: Connecting Observation and Understanding, 1988, Gender and Conversational Interaction, 1993, Framing In Discourse, 1993, (play) An Act of Devotion, 1994. Rockefeller Humanities fellow, 1982-83; grantee NEH, 1980, 85, 86; recipient Elizabeth Mills Crothers prize U. Calif., 1976, Dorothy Rosenberg Meml. prize U. Calif., 1977, Joan Lee Yang Meml. Poetry prize U. Calif., 1977, Shrout Short Story prize, 1978, Emily Chamberlain Cook prize, 1978. Office: Georgetown U Lang & Linguistics ICC Bldg Rm 471 37th & O St NW Washington DC 20057-0001 Office Phone: 202-687-5910. Business E-Mail: tannend@georgetown.edu.

TANNEN, RICHARD LAURENCE, nephrology educator; b. NYC, Aug. 31, 1937; s. Harold and Fannie (Rosenberg) T.; m. Elizabeth Whitney Harriman, Aug. 8, 1964 (div. Apr. 1990); m. Vivien Baraban, Nov. 17, 1990; children: Bradford, Whitney, Jennifer, Alison, Julie. Student, Vanderbilt U., 1957; MD, U. Tenn., Memphis, 1960. Rsch. internist Walter Reed Inst. Rsch., Washington, 1966-69; assoc. prof., co-dir. nephrology unit U. Vt., Burlington, 1969-78; prof., chief nephrology divsn. U. Mich., Ann Arbor, 1978-88; prof., chmn. dept. medicine U. So. Calif., LA, 1988-95; vice dean for rsch. U. Pa., Phila., 1995-97, prof. medicine, 1995—, sr. vice-dean, 1997—2002. Established investigator Am. Heart Assn., 1971-76. Co-editor: Fluids and Electrolytes, 1986, 3d edit., 1996; contbr. more than 130 sci. articles to profl. jours. Maj. U.S. Army, 1966-69. Recipient Merit award NIH, 1986-94, Disting. Alumnus award U. Tenn., 1991. Fellow ACP; mem. Am. Soc. Nephrology (pres. 1991-92), Am. Soc. Clin. Investigation, Assn. Am. Physicians, Nat. Kidney Found. (regional v.p. 1984-87, Pres.'s award 1986). Jewish. Avocations: tennis, travel. Office: U Pa Sch of Med 295 John Morgan Bldg Philadelphia PA 19104 Office Phone: 215-898-2270. Business E-Mail: tannen@mail.med.upenn.edu.

TANNENBAUM, BERNARD, lawyer; b. NYC, July 14, 1928; s. Jacob and Lillian (Jupiter) T.; m. Elinor Fried, June 3, 1950; children: Jody, Ilene, Carol, Jeffrey. BA in Edn., NYU, 1950, JD, 1953; MA (hon.), Internat. U. Comm., 1974. Bar: N.Y. 1954, D.C. 1980, U.s. Dist. Ct. (so. and ea. dists.) N.Y. 1961, U.S. Ct. Claims 1964, U.S. Supreme Ct. 1964. Assoc. Halperin, Natanson, Shivitz & Scholar, NYC, 1952-54; sole practice Mineola, N.Y., 1954-60, NYC, 1969-87; mng. ptnr. Fried, Beck, Tannenbaum & Field, NYC, 1960-69; counsel Meltzer, Lippe & Goldstein, Mineola, 1987—. Spl.

counsel U.S. Senate Subcom. on Juvenile Delinquency, Washington, 1965-70, subcom. on Panama Canal U.S. Ho. of Reps., Washington, 1970-71, com. on mcht. marine and fisheries U.S. Ho. of Reps., 1977-80; arbitrator Small Claims Divsn. Civil Ct., N.Y.C., 1975—. Contbr. NYU Law Rev., editor, pub., The Democratic Forum, 1960-73; bd. dirs., trstee, chmn. Daytop Village Inc., N.Y.C., 1983—; bd. advisors Assn. Children with Retarded Mental Devel., N.Y.C., 1984-86. Office: 190 Willis Ave Mineola NY 11501-2693 Home Phone: 516-621-8527. Personal E-mail: Tanbern@aol.com.

TANNENBAUM, BERNICE SALPETER, national religious organization executive; b. NYC; d. Isidore and May Franklin; 1 child, Richard Salpeter. BA, Bklyn. coll. Chmn. Commn. on the Status of Women of the World Jewish Congress; mem. exec. bd. Am. sect. World Jewish Congress; chmn. internat. affairs com.; mem. Zionist Gen. Coun.; active Exec. World Zionist Orgn. Bd. dirs., mem. gen. assembly Jewish Agy.; bd. dirs., v.p. United Israel Appeal; mem. exec. com. Am. Zionist Movement; former chair Hadassah mag.; nat. pres. Hadassah, 1976-80; nat. chmn. Hadassah Internat., 1984-95; liaison Hadassah Found.; sec. Jewish Telegraphic Agy.; bd. govs. Hebrew U. Office: Hadassah 50 W 58th St New York NY 10019-2590

TANNENBAUM, HARVEY, defense technology consultant; b. NYC, June 26, 1923; s. Alfred and Ida (Kolbe) T.; m. Mildred Cohen, July 4, 1946; children: David Bruce, Mark Scott, Lynne Ellen. BS, NYU, 1946; postgrad., George Washington U., 1963-64. Chemist U.S. Army Chem. R & D Ctr., Aberdeen Proving Ground, Md., 1949-62, chief remote sensing, 1962-79; prin. staff engr. Honeywell, Inc., Clearwater, Fla., 1979-84; cons. Reistertown, Md., 1984—85; sr. program dir. SRI, Internat., 1985—88. Cons. EPA, CIA, Arms Control and Disarmament Agy., USAF, 1962-79; group chmn. NATO panel of experts on laser monitoring of atmosphere, Norway, 1976. Contbr. articles to profl. jours.; patentee in field. Served to cpl. USAF, 1942-45, ETO. Mem. Optical Soc. Am., Internat. Soc. Optical Engring., Infrared Symposia, Sigma Xi. Jewish. Achievements include patents in field. Avocations: bridge, photography. Home and Office: 12611 Mt Laurel Ct Reisterstown MD 21136-1801

TANNENBAUM, MICHAEL J(AY), physicist; b. NYC, Mar. 10, 1939; s. Morris and Ann Tannenbaum; m. Barbara C. Moshinsky, July 15, 1973; children: Nina Fay, Lisa Marie. AB magna cum laude, Columbia U., NYC, 1959, MA, 1960, PhD, 1965. Vis. scientist CERN, Geneva, 1965-66, 91, attache scientifique, 1973-84; from asst. prof. to assoc. prof. Harvard U., Cambridge, Mass., 1966-71; assoc. prof. Rockefeller U., NYC, 1971-80; physicist Brookhaven Nat. Lab., Upton, NY, 1980-87, sr. physicist, 1987—, group leader, 2001—. Mem. sci. coun. Lab. Leprince-Ringuet, Ecole Polytechnique, France, 2002—05. Contbr. articles to profl. jours. Ernest Kempton Adams fellow, 1965, NSF fellow, 1959-63, 66, Alfred P. Sloan Found. fellow, 1967-69. Fellow: AAAS, Am. Phys. Soc.; mem.: NY Acad. Scis., Sigma Xi, Phi Beta Kappa. Home: 245 E 93rd St Apt 10F New York NY 10128-3965 Office: Physics Dept Brookhaven Nat Lab Bldg # 510C Upton NY 11973-5000 Office Phone: 631-344-3722. E-mail: mjt@bnl.gov.

TANNENBAUM, MIKE (MICHAEL B. TANNENBAUM), professional sports team executive; b. NYC, 1969; m. Michelle Tannenbaum; 1 child, Ella Morgan. BA in Acctg. & Sports Mgmt., U. Mass., 1991; JD cum laude, Tulane Law Sch. Bar:, Sports Law. Player personnel asst. New Orleans Saints, 1994, Cleve. Browns, 1995; with NY Jets, 1997—, team dir., pro. player devel., 2000, asst. gen. mgr., dir. pro. personnel, 2001—03, sr. v.p., football ops., asst. gen. mgr., 2003—06, gen. mgr., 2006—. Office: NY Jets 1000 Fulton Ave Hempstead NY 11550

TANNENBAUM, STEVEN ROBERT, toxicologist, chemist; b. NYC, Feb. 23, 1937; m. Carol Eigen, Sept. 6, 1959; children: Lisa, Mark. BS in Food Tech, MIT, Cambridge, 1958, PhD in Food Sci. and Tech, 1962. From asst. prof. to co-dir. Biol. Engring. Divsn. MIT, 1964—2002, co-dir. Biol. Engring. Divsn., 2002—03. Vis. prof. Hebrew U. of Jerusalem, 1973-74; BASF vis. prof. U. Kaiserslautern, 1994; mem. adv. com. on biochemistry and chem. carcinogenesis Am. Cancer Soc., 1977-81, Inst. Medicine, Nat. Acad. Sci., 1996; bd. sci. advisors divsn. cancer etiology, NCI, 1994-95, Frederick Cancer Rsch. Facility, 1989—94, Nat. Cancer Inst., 1989-93; mem. cancer spl. program adv. com., 1979-82; mem. peer rev. com. Nat. Toxicology Program, 1983-85; founder, bd. dirs. Vicam, Ltd., Partnership; chmn. rev. homeland security safe bldg. program EPA, 2003; mem. sci. adv. bd. USAF, 1999. Editor: (with R.I. Mateles) Single-Cell Protein, 1968, (with D.I.C. Wang) Single-Cell Protein II, 1975, (with others) The Economics, Marketing and Technology of Fish Protein Concentrate, 1974, (with J.R. Whitaker) Food Proteins, 1977, Nutritional Safety Aspects of Food Processing, 1979, (with others) Gastrointestinal Cancer: Endogenous Factors, 1981, (with R.A. Scanlan) N-Nitroso Compounds, 1981; mem. editl. bd. Japanese Jour. Cancer Rsch., 1986—, Chem. Rsch. Toxicology, 1988-91, 95-98, Cancer Epidemiology, Prevention and Biomarkers, 1990—, Cancer Rsch., 1993-2001; contbr. over 350 articles to profl. jours. Fellow Japan Soc. Promotions Cancer Rsch., AAAS; mem. Nat. Acad. Scis., Inst. Medicine, Am. Chem. Soc., Inst. Food Technologists (sect. councillor N.E. chpt. 1966-69, Samuel Cate Prescott Rsch. award 1970, Babcock Hart award 1980), editorial bd. sci. jour. 1970-73, Am. Inst. Nutrition, Am. Assn. Cancer Rsch., Soc. Toxicology, Oxygen Soc., Sigma Xi. Achievements include 11 US patents. Office: MIT Div Biol Engring 77 Mass Ave Rm 56-731A Cambridge MA 02139-4307 *Motto: Crisis equals danger plus opportunity.*

TANNENBERG, DIETER E.A., retired manufacturing executive; b. Chevy Chase, Md., Nov. 24, 1932; s. E.A. Wilhelm and Margarete Elizabeth (Mundhenk) T.; m. Ruth Hansen, Feb. 6, 1956; 1 child, Diana Sylvia Tannenberg BSME, Northwestern U., 1959. Registered profl. engr., N.Y., Ohio, Ill., Ind., Wis., N.J. Supervising engr. Flexonics div. Calumet & Hecla, Inc., Chgo., 1959-61, chief engr., 1961-63, program mgr. advanced space systems, 1963-65, dir. mfg. services, 1965-67; dir. mfg. engring. SCM Corp., Cortland, NY, 1967-69; tech. dir. internat. Singer Co., NYC, 1969-71; v.p. ops. internat. div. Addressograph-Multigraph Corp., Cleve., 1971-74; mng. dir. Addressograph Multigraph GmbH, Frankfurt/Main, W. Ger., 1974-78; v.p., gen. mgr. Europe, Middle East, Africa AM Internat. Inc., Chgo., 1978-79; pres. AM Bruning div., 1979-82, AM Multigraphics Div., Mt. Prospect, Ill., 1982-86; corp. v.p. AM Internat., Inc., 1981-83, corp. sr. v.p., 1983-86; chmn. bd. dirs., pres., chief exec. officer Sargent-Welch Sci. Co., Skokie, Ill., 1986-89; pres., CEO ExhibitGroup, Inc., Elk Grove Village, Ill., 1990-91, Bell & Howell Document Mgmt. Products Co., Chgo., 1991-94, Bell & Howell Postal Sys. Inc., Chgo., 1994-97; corp. v.p. Bell & Howell Co., Skokie, Ill., 1991-97. Chmn. AM Internat. GmbH, Frankfurt, 1977-86 Contbr. chpts. to handbooks, articles to tech., trade mags.; patentee in machinery field Served with M.I., U.S. Army, 1953-56 Named Man of Yr. Quick Print Mag., 1985 Mem. NSPE, ASME, Assn. Reprodn. Materials Mfrs. (bd. dirs. 1979-82, v.p. 1980-82), Nat. Assn. Quick Printers (bd. dirs. 1982-84), Nat. Printing Equipment and Supplies Mfg. Assn. (bd. dirs. 1983-86, chmn. govt. affairs com. 1985-86), Computer and Bus. Equipment Mfg. Assn. (bd. dirs. 1983-86, 91-93), Soc. Am. Value Engrs. (hon. v.p. 1985—), Value Found. (trustee 1985—), Pi Tau Sigma

TANNENWALD, PETER, lawyer; b. Washington, Apr. 8, 1943; s. Judge Theodore and Selma (Peterfreund) T.; m. Carol B. Baum, May 25, 1969; 1 child, Jonathan Mark. AB, Brown U., 1964; LLB, Harvard U., 1967. Bar: U.S. Dist. Ct. D.C. 1968, U.S. Ct. Appeals (D.C. cir.) 1968, U.S. Supreme Ct. 1972. Assoc. Arent, Fox, Kintner, Plotkin & Kahn, Washington, 1967-74, ptnr., 1975-94; v.p. Irwin, Campbell & Tannenwald, P.C., Washington, 1995—. Columnist The LPTV Report, 1988-92. Mem. cmty. coun. Sta. WAMU-FM, Washington, 1986-93, 94-97, 2003—; dir. Brown Broadcasting Svc., Inc., Providence, 1970—; chmn. maj. law firms divsn. Nat. Capital Area affiliate United Way, 1977-79. Mem. Harvard Law Sch. Assn. D.C. (pres. 1979-80), Harvard Law Sch. Assn. (sec. 1982-84). Avocations: electronics, photography. Office: Irwin Campbell Tannenwald PC 1730 Rhode Island Ave NW Washington DC 20036-3101 Office Phone: 202-728-0400.

TANNER, BRUCE L., aerospace transportation executive; m. Vicki Tanner; 1 child. BBA, Univ. Mich., 1981; MBA, Univ. Tex., Arlington, 1990. Fin. mgmt. positions Lockheed Martin, Bethesda, Md., 1982—97, v.p. bus. mgmt. aeronautics bus. area, 1997—2002, CFO elec. systems bus. area, 2002—06, v.p. fin. & bus ops. aeronautics bus. area, 2006—07, exec. v.p., CFO, 2007—. Office: Lockheed Martin 6801 ROckledge Dr Bethesda MD 20817-1836 *

TANNER, DANIEL, education educator; b. NYC, Sept. 22, 1926; s. Jack and Lillian (Jupiter) T.; m. Laurel Nan Jacobson, July 11, 1948 (div. 1988). BS with honors, Mich. State U., 1949, MS, 1952; PhD, Ohio State U., 1955. Asst. prof. edn. San Francisco State Coll., 1955-60; assoc. prof. edn., coord. Midwest program on airborne TV instrn. Purdue U., 1960-62; assoc. prof. edn., assoc. dir. internat. program for edn. leaders Northwestern U., 1962-64; assoc. prof. rsch. divsn. tchr. edn. CUNY, 1964-66; prof. edn., dir. Ctr. for Urban Edn., U. Wis.-Milw. Sch. Edn., 1966-67; prof. edn., dir. grad. programs in curriculum theory and devel. Grad. Sch. Edn., Rutgers U., New Brunswick, NJ, 1967—, chmn. dept. curriculum and instrn., 1969-72, faculty rsch. fellow, 1974-75, 88-89. Vis. faculty U. Kansas City, 1956, Tchrs. Coll. Columbia, 1966, Emory U., 1968, SUNY, Binghamton, 1968, U. London, 1975, King Abdulaziz U., Saudi Arabia, 1992, U. Iowa, 1996; disting. lectr. ASCD, 1985, 86, Dewey Meml. lectr., 1984, Raths Meml. lectr., SUNY, 1984; Leadership Inst. lectr. U. Del., 1990; disting. lectr. Rider U., 1996; vis. scholar U. London Inst. Edn., 1974-75; rev. bd. coll. work-study program US Office Edn., 1965; mem. symposium on comparative curriculum history Inst. Sci. Edn. Kiel U., Fed. Republic Germany, 1989; del. leader Citizen Amb. Program, People-to-People Internat., Republic of South Africa, 1996, China, 1997, Dem. Citizenship Project Czech Republic, USIA, 1996-98; cons. U. Tex. Med. Ctr., 1961-62, Chgo. Sch. Survey, 1964-65, ctr. Urban Edn., NYC, 1964-65, West Chgo. Sch. Survey, 1963-64, Nat. Ednl. TV Ctr., NYC, 1963, Campbell County Sch. Survey, Va., 1970, Memphis Schs., 1977-78, Perth Amboy Schs., NJ, 1996-97; ASCD Commn. on Gen. Edn., 1980-81, West Orange, NJ, Curriculum Study, 1984, ASCD Commn. on Secondary Sch. Practices, 1985, ASCD Ednl. Policy Task Force, 1985, NASSP Curriculum Coun., 1985-95; SUNY Buffalo External Evaluation, 1988; dir. Nat. Curriculum Inst., Washington, 1987; delivered Founder's Day address Delaware Valley Coll., 1985, keynote address Nat. Conf. Citizen Edn., Palacky U., Czech Rep., 1998. Author: Schools for Youth: Change and Challenge in Secondary Education, 1965, Secondary Curriculum: Theory and Development, 1971, Secondary Education: Perspectives and Prospects, 1972, Using Behavioral Objectives in the Classroom, 1979, Supervision in Education, 1987, History of the School Curriculum, 1991, Crusade for Democracy: Progressive Education at the Crossroads, 1991, 2d edit., 2002; co-author: Teen Talk: Curriculum Materials in Communications, 1971, Curriculum Development Theory Into Practice, 4th edit., 2007, History of the School Curriculum, Chinese rev. edit., 2006; co-editor: Improving the School Curriculum, 1988, Restructuring for an Interdisciplinary Curriculum, 1992, Curriculum Issues and the New Century, 1995; founding editor, contbg. author: Rsch. Rev. for Sch. Leaders, 1996, 98, 2000, Philosophy Edn. Ency., 1996, Ency. Edn., 2d edit., 2003, Curriculum Issues, 87th Yearbook NSSE, 1988, 98th Yearbook, 1999, Ency. Ednl. Rsch., 5th edit., 1982, Readings in Edn. Psychology, 1965, Yearbook of the Assn. for Student Tchg., 1962, Great Debate, Our Schools in Crisis, 1959, Educational Issues in a Changing Society, 1964, Programs, Teachers and Machines, 1964, Views on American Schooling, 1964, Tng. America's Tchrs., 1975, Curriculum and Instruction, 1981, Experiencing Dewey, 2005, Intricate Palette, 2005; contbg. editor: Ednl. Leadership, 1969-74; mem. editl. bd. Tex. Tech. Jour. Edn., 1984-89, Tchg. Edn., 1986-90, Jour. Curriculum Supervision, Edn. and Culture, 2007-; editl. cons.: Ency. of Ednl. Rsch., 5th edit., 1982, Ency. of Edn., 2d edit., 2003, Jour. Ednl. Psychology. Trustee Delaware Valley Coll., Doylestown, Pa., 1981-95; bd. dirs. Ohio State Alumni Assn. N.J., 1990-96. Recipient Excellence award, Edn. Press Am., 1989, Disting. Educator award, Rider U., 1996; grantee, Rutgers Rsch. Coun., 1988—89, 2000—01; Univ. scholar, Ohio State U., 1955. Fellow AAAS, John Dewey Soc. (bd. dirs. 1985-88, archivist 1989-, chmn. lectrs. commn. 1999-2004, pres. 2001-03); mem. AAUP, Am. Ednl. Rsch. Assn. (Lifetime Achievement award 2006), N.Y. Acad. Scis., Am. Polit. Sci. Assn., Am. Ednl. Studies Assn., Nat. Soc. Study Edn., Phi Kappa Phi, Phi Delta Kappa (Svc. award 1957). Home: Highwood Rd Somerset NJ 08873 Office: Grad Sch Edn Rutgers U New Brunswick NJ 08901-1183 Office Fax: 732-932-6803. Personal E-mail: dantan@rci.rutgers.edu. *The essential quality of education and life is growth. Hence problems must be seen as opportunities and not as limitations if solutions are to be found and progress is to be made.*

TANNER, DEE BOSHARD, retired lawyer; b. Provo, Utah, Jan. 16, 1913; s. Myron Clark and Marie (Boshard) T.; m. Jane Barwick, Dec. 26, 1936 (div. Aug. 1962); children: Barry, Diane McDowell; m. Reeta Walker, Dec. 6, 1981. BA, U. Utah, 1935; LLB, Pacific Coast U., 1940; postgrad., Harvard U., 1936, Loyola U., LA, 1937. Bar: Calif. 1943, US Dist. Ct. (so. dist.) Calif. 1944, US Ct. Appeals (9th cir.) 1947, ICC 1964, US Dist. Ct. (ea. dist.) Calif. 1969, US Supreme Ct. 1971. Assoc. Spray, Davis & Gould, LA, 1943-44; pvt. practice LA, 1944; assoc. Tanner and Sievers, LA, 1944-47, Tanner and Thornton, LA, 1947-54, Tanner, Hanson, Meyers, LA, 1954-64; ptnr. Tanner and Van Dyke, LA, 1964-65, Gallagher and Tanner, LA, 1965-70; pvt. practice Pasadena, Calif., 1970-95; ret., 1995. Mem.: LA Bar Assn., World Affairs Assn., LA Sheriff's Star Org., Harvard Law Sch. Assn., Lawyers' Club LA. Home and Office: 1720 Lombardy Rd Pasadena CA 91106-4127 Home Phone: 626-793-0007. Personal E-mail: rpltd@aol.com.

TANNER, DOUGLAS ALAN, lawyer; b. Palo Alto, Calif., Aug. 30, 1953; s. Bernard R. and Caroline (Orris) Tanner; m. Carol Scilacci, May 28, 1977; children: Lauren Elizabeth, Wynn Ann, Leigh Caroline. AB in History, Stanford U., 1974, MBA, JD, Stanford U., 1978. Bar: Calif. 1978, U.S. Dist. ct. (no. dist.) Calif. 1978, U.S. Ct. Appeals (9th cir.) 1979, N.Y. 1987. Law clk. to judge U.S. Ct. Appeals (9th cir.), San Francisco, 1978-79; assoc. Orrick, Herrington & Sutcliffe, San Francisco, 1979-83, San Jose, Calif., 1984-86, NYC, 1986-89, Milbank, Tweed, Hadley & McCloy, LA, 1989-92, Hong Kong, 1992-2001, Palo Alto, Calif., 2001—04, NYC, 2004—, ptnr., head global securities group. Mem.: San Francisco Barristers (chmn. corps. com. 1981—82), Order of Coif, Phi Beta Kappa. Episcopalian. Office: Milbank Tweed Hadley & McCloy LLP 1 Chase Manhattan Plaza New York NY 10021 Home Phone: 212-734-3841. Office Fax: 212-530-5219. Business E-Mail: dtanner@milbank.com.

TANNER, ERIC BENSON, lawyer; b. St. Louis, Aug. 27, 1949; s. Robert H. and Delores (Benson) Tanner; m. Rosalind Grace Tanner, June 23, 1978; children: Jacob, Adam. BA, U. Mo., Columbia, 1971; JD, U. Mo., Kansas City, 1975; cert., Coll. Fin. Planning, Denver, 1988. Bar: Mo. 1975. Instr. paralegal program Avila Coll., Kansas City, Mo., 1982-84; staff atty. Legal Aid Western Mo., Kansas City, 1975-83; pvt. practice Kansas City, 1983-86, 1990—93, 2002—; asst. v.p. trust dept. United Mo. Bank, NA, Kansas City, 1986-90; v.p., trust counsel Commerce Bank, N.A., Kansas City, 1993—2002. CLE lectr. estate planning topics various bar assns. and univs., 1975—. Contbr. articles to profl. jours. Mem. planned giving com. Nat. Kidney Found., Kansas City, 1995—97; vol. Habitat for Humanity, 1997, 1999, 2002, 2004; bd. dirs. Prime Health, 1980—86, Marillac, 2003—, Investor Literacy Co., 2004—06; mem. planned giving coun. Park U., Parkville, Mo., 2005—. Mem.: Estate Planning Soc. Kansas City, Kansas City Corp. Fiduciaries Assn. (pres. 1997), Nat. Acad. Elder Law Attys., Kansas City Met. Bar Assn., Mo. Bar Assn. Office: 1125 Grand Ste 1900 Kansas City MO 64106 Office Phone: 816-931-7878.

TANNER, HAROLD, investment banker; b. NYC, May 7, 1932; s. Irving and Pauline (Steinlauf) T.; m. Estelle Newman, July 6, 1957; children: David, James, Karen. BS, Cornell U., 1952; MBA, Harvard U., 1956. V.p., dir. Blyth & Co. Inc., NYC, 1956-69; exec. v.p. New Court Securities Corp., NYC, 1969-76, Blyth Eastman Dillon & Co., Inc., NYC, 1977-80; ptnr. Salomon Bros. Inc., 1980-81, mng. dir., 1981-87; pres. Tanner & Co., Inc., NYC, 1987—. Co-founder Vol. Urban Cons. Group. Pres. emeritus Am. Jewish Com.; former chmn. Transatlantic Inst.; chmn. Conf. Pres. Major Jewish Orgns.; chmn. bd. trustees emeritus Cornell U.; trustee Russell Sage Found., Revson Found., Classroom Inc. Lt. (j.g.) USNR, 1952—54. Mem. Coun. on Fgn. Rels., Century Country Club, Harmonie Club. Home: 2 Morris Ln Scarsdale NY 10583-6053 Office: Tanner & Co 950 Third Ave New York NY 10022-1029

TANNER, HELEN HORNBECK, historian, consultant; b. Northfield, Minn., July 5, 1916; d. John Wesley and Frances Cornelia (Wolfe) Hornbeck; m. Wilson P. Tanner, Jr., Nov. 22, 1940 (dec. 1977); children: Frances, Margaret Tanner Tewson, Wilson P., Robert (dec. 1983) AB with honors, Swarthmore Coll., 1937; MA, U. Fla., 1949; PhD, U. Mich., 1961. Asst. to dir. pub. rels. Kalamazoo Pub. Schs., 1937-39; with sales dept. Am. Airlines Inc., NYC, 1940-43; tchg. fellow, then tchg. asst. U. Mich., Ann Arbor, 1949-53, 57-60, lectr. ext. svc., 1961-74, asst. dir. Ctr. Continuing Edn. for Women, 1964-68; project dir. Newberry Libr., Chgo., 1976-81, rsch. assoc., 1981-95, sr. rsch. fellow, 1995—. Expert witness in Indian treaty litig., 1963—; dir. D'Arcy McNickle Ctr. for Indian History, 1984-85; mem. Mich. Commn. Indian Affairs, 1966-70; cons. in field Author: Zespedes in East Florida 1784-1790, 1963, 89, General Green Visits St. Augustine, 1964, The Greeneville Treaty, 1974, The Territory of the Caddo Tribe of Oklahoma, 1974, The Ojibwas, 1992; editor: Atlas of Great Lakes Indian History, 1987, The Settling of North America: An Atlas, 1995, Powhatan's Mantle, 2006, Beyond Red Power, 2007. Named to Mich. Women's Hall of Fame, 2006; NEH grantee, 1976, fellow, 1989; ACLS grantee, 1990. Mem. Am. Soc. Ethnohistory (pres. 1982-83), St. Augustine Hist. Soc., Conf. L.Am. History, Soc. History Discoveries, Chgo. Map Soc., Hist. Soc. Mich., Ctr. French Colonial Studies. Home: 5178 Crystal Dr Beulah MI 49617-9618 Personal E-mail: hhtanner@charter.net.

TANNER, JERRÉ E., composer, retired publishing executive; b. Lock Haven, Pa., Jan. 5, 1939; s. Roger P. Tanner and Mildred E. Catté. BA, U. Iowa, 1960; MA, San Francisco State U., 1970. Composer, Kailua-Kona, Hawaii, 1970—2003. Instr. music U. Hawaii, Hilo, 1965—67; West Hawaii arts coord. State Found. Culture and Arts, Hawaii, 1975—76; artistic dir. Opera Players Hawaii, Honolulu, 1978—79; pres., CEO Malama Arts, Inc., Kailua-Kona, Hawaii, 1979—2003. Composer: (opera) The Lei of God Kane, Boy with Goldfish, Heroic Fantasy For Soloists, Chorus, Orchestra, (choral symphony) The Naupaka Floret, (chamber opera) The Kona Coffee Cantata, (comic opera for youth) The Singing Snails, (choral symphony) No. 2: Keepers of the Land, (theme & variations for symphonic band) High Seas to High Shoals, (choral symphony) No. 3: Aumakua - Living Ancestors. Recipient Celia S. Buck award, Am. Composers & Conductors Assn., 1966, Std. Music award, A.S.C.A.P., 1967—2007; fellow Residence fellow, Huntington Hartford Found., 1963—64; Artist Music Composition fellow, Hawaii State Found. Culture & Arts, 1997, Margaret Fairbank Jory Copy Assistance grants, Am. Music Ctr., 1989, 1994, Assistance grants, Hawaii State Found. Culture & Arts, 1974, 1976, 1980, 1986. Mem.: Hawaii Chpt. Am. Choral Dirs. Assn., Iowa Composers Forum, Am. Music Ctr., Am. Composers Forum. Home: 159 La'imi Rd Honolulu HI 96817 Home Phone: 808-595-2963. Personal E-mail: arsmusica@hawaiiantel.net.

TANNER, JIMMIE EUGENE, retired dean; b. Hartford, Ark., Sept. 27, 1933; s. Alford C. and Hazel Ame (Anthony) Tanner; m. Carole Joy Yant, Aug. 28, 1958; children: Leslie Allison, Kevin Don. BA, Okla. Baptist U., 1955; MA, U. Okla., 1957, PhD, 1964. Prof. English Okla. Bapt. U., Shawnee, 1958—64, 1965—72; assoc. prof. Franklin Coll., Ind., 1964—65; v.p. acad. affairs Hardin-Simmons U., Abilene, Tex., 1972—78, La. Coll., Pineville, 1978—80; dean William Jewell Coll., Liberty, Mo., 1980—97, prof., 1997—2003, interm pres., 1993—94; ret., 2003. Contbg. author: The Annotated Bibliography of D. H. Lawrence, Vol. 1, 1982, Vol. 2, 1985. Mem. Shawnee Sch. Bd., 1966—72; edn. commn. So. Bapt. Conv., 1967—72; bd. dirs. Mo. Coun. for Humanities, 2003—. So. Fellowships Fund fellow, 1960—61, Danforth fellow, 1962—63. Mem.: SAR. Democrat. Baptist. Avocations: tennis, photography. Home: 609 Lancelot Dr Liberty MO 64068-1023 *As I reflect on my life, the thought that presses on me is my incredible luck at having been born in America in the 20th century, my good fortune in having the opportunity for education, for a satisfying career, for supportive family, friends, mentors at every stage of my life. I must recognize any accomplishment as communal as well as individual.*

TANNER, JOHN S., congressman, lawyer; b. Halls, Tenn., Sept. 22, 1944; s. E.B. and Edith (Sumners) Tanner; m. Betty Ann Portis, Sept. 2, 1967; children: Elizabeth Tanner Atkins, John Portis. BBA, U. Tenn., Knoxville, 1966; JD, U. Tenn. Sch. Law, 1968. Bar: Tenn. 1968. Mem. Tenn. State Ho. Reps., 1976-88, US Congress from 8th Tenn. dist., 1989—, mem. nat. security com., 1989—97, mem. sci. com., 1989—97, mem. ways and means com., 1997—, mem. Sportsmen's Caucus. V.p. NATO Parliamentary Assembly. Active Obion County Cancer Soc.; bd. visitors US Naval Acad.; former mem. bd. visitors US Mil. Acad., USAF Acad. Lt. USN, 1968—72, col. Tenn. Army N.G., 1974—2000. Recipient Outdoor Life Conservation award, Pub. Svc., Silver Bayonet award, AMVETS. Mem. Obion County C. of C., Obion County Bar Assn., Rotary, Masons (32nd degree) Democrat. Mem. Christian Ch. (Disciples Of Christ). Avocations: golf, hunting. Office: US Ho Reps 1226 Longworth Ho Office Bldg Washington DC 20515-4208 Office Phone: 202-225-4714. *

TANNER, JONATHAN D., educational association administrator; b. Cedar Rapids, Iowa, Apr. 18, 1964; s. Richard Elmer and Jean Ellen Tanner. MusB, Coe Coll., Cedar Rapids, 1982—86; MS in Libr. & Info. Sci., Pratt Inst., New York, 2001—05. Sr. account rep. Weill Cornell Med. Coll., NYC, 1994—97, account adminstr., 1998—2006. Freelance libr. cons. Mem. Archivists Roundtable Met. NY, NYC, 2006, Mid Atlantic Regional Archivists Conf., Vienna, Va. Mem.: Spl. Librs. Assn., Soc. Am. Archivists. Avocations: swimming, tennis, exercise, mountain biking, mountain hiking. Home: 135 W 225th St #6L New York NY 10463 Office: Weill Med Coll Cornell Univ 575 Lexington Ave #640 New York NY 10463 Home Phone: 718-364-5454. Personal E-mail: tannerjonathan@hotmail.com.

TANNER, JOSEPH RICHARD, astronaut; b. Ill., 1950; married; 2 children. BSc in Mech. Engring., U. Ill., 1973, BS, 1973. Commd. ensign USNR, 1973, advanced through grades to comdr., 1988, pilot, 1975—89; astronaut NASA, Houston, 1992—. Astronaut Space Shuttle Atlantis (STS-66), 1994, Svc. to Hubble Space Telescope, Discovery (STS-82), 1997, ISS Assembly Flight 4A Endeavour (STS-97), 2000; astronaut, will perform spacewalks Space Shuttle Atlantis (STS-115), 2006. Recipient Outstanding Alumnus award, U. Ill., NASA Exceptional Svc. medal,

NASA Space Flight medal, NASA Stuart M. Present Flight Achievement award. Avocations: swimming, camping, mountain climbing, time with family. Office: Astronaut Office CB NASA Johnson Space Ctr Houston TX 77058

TANNER, LAUREL NAN, education educator; b. Detroit, Feb. 16, 1929; d. Howard Nicholas and Celia (Solovich) Jacobson; m. Daniel Tanner, July 11, 1948; m. Kenneth J. Rehage, Nov. 25, 1989. BS in Social Sci, Mich. State U., 1949, MA in Edn., 1953; EdD, Columbia U., 1967. Pub. sch. tchr., 1950-64; instr. tchr. edn. Hunter Coll., 1964-66, asst. prof., 1967-69; supr. Milw. Pub. Schs., 1966-67; mem. faculty Temple U., Phila., 1969—, prof. edn., 1974-89, prof. emerita, 1993—; prof. edn. U. Houston, 1989-96. Vis. professorial scholar U. London Inst. Edn., 1974—75; vis. scholar Stanford U., 1984—85, U. Chgo., 1988—89; curriculum cons., 1969—; disting. vis. prof. San Francisco State U., 1987. Author: Classroom Discipline for Effective Teaching and Learning, 1978, La Disciplina en la enseñanza y el Aprendizaje, 1980, Dewey's Laboratory School: Lessons for Today, 1997; co-author: Classroom Teaching and Learning, 1971, Curriculum Development: Theory into Practice, 1975, 4th edit., 2007, Supervision in Education: Problems and Practices, 1987, (with Daniel Tanner) History of the School Curriculum, 1990; editor Nat. Soc. Study Edn. Critical Issues in Curriculum, 87th yearbook, part 1, 1988. Faculty rsch. fellow Temple U., 1970, 80, 81; recipient John Dewey Rsch. award, 1981-82, Rsch. Excellence award U. Houston, 1992, Outstanding Writing award Am. Assn. Colls. Tchr. Edn., 1998; Spencer Found. rsch. grantee, 1992. Mem. ASCD (dir. 1982-84), Soc. Study Curriculum History (founder, 1st pres. 1978-79), Am. Edn. Rsch. Assn. (com. on role and status of women in ednl. R & D 1994-97, Lifetime Achievement award 2007), Profs. Curriculum Assn. (Factotum 1983-84, chair membership com. 1994-95), Am. Ednl. Studies Assn., John Dewey Soc. (bd. dirs. 1989-91, pres. 2000-01), Alumni Coun. Tchrs. Coll. Columbia U. *In my view, America has progressed over the years, and the best days are still to come. We have the single necessary resource to solve our most urgent problems and achieve our deepest moral values — human intelligence.*

TANNER, MARTIN ABBA, statistician, educator; b. Highland Park, Ill., Oct. 19, 1957; s. Meir and Esther Rose (Bauer) T.; m. Anat Talitman, Aug. 14, 1984; 1 child, Noam Ben. BA, U. Chgo., 1978, PhD, 1982. Asst. prof. stats. and human oncology U. Wis., Madison, 1982-87, assoc. prof., 1987-90; dir. lab., prof. and dept. chair biostatistics U. Rochester, 1990-94; prof. dept. statistics Northwestern U., 1994—. Cons. Kirkland & Ellis, 1980-82; mem. Nat. Inst. Allergy and Infectious diseases study sect., 1994-98; reviewer NIH, NSF, VA. Assoc. editor Jour. Am. Stat. Assn., 1987-99; editor Jour. Am. Statis. Assn., 1999-03, Chapman & Hall, 2002-; contbr. articles to profl. jours. Recipient New Investigator Rsch. award NIH, 1984, Mortimer Spiegelman award Am. Pub. Health Assn., 1993; NSF grantee, 1983, 95, NIH grantee, 1986—. Fellow Royal Statis. Soc., Am. Statis. Assn. (Continuing Edn. Excellence award); mem. AAAS, Mensa, Sigma Xi. Avocations: classical guitar, medieval poetry. Office: Northwestern U 2006 Sheridan Rd Evanston IL 60208-0852 Home Phone: 847-491-2700; Office Phone: 847-491-2700. Business E-Mail: mat132@northwestern.edu.

TANNER, W(ALTER) RHETT, lawyer; b. Athens, Ga., May 16, 1938; s. Johnnie Bryson and Walterette (Arwood) T.; m. Carolyn Laverne Watson, Nov. 11, 1967; 1 child, Walter Rhett (dec. 1989). AB cum laude, U. Ga., 1960, JD cum laude, 1962. Bar: Ga. 1961; cert. neutral Ga. Office of Dispute Resolution. With Hansell & Post, Atlanta, 1964—89, Jones, Day, Reavis & Pogue, Atlanta, 1989—99. Panelist Am. Arbitration Assn., 1995—. Bd. dirs. Atlanta Symphony Orch., 1975—95, mem. exec. com., 1977—86, v.p., 1978, chmn. maj. gifts campaign, 1980, bd. counsellors, 1996—; mem. Leadership Atlanta, 1980, Leadership Ga., 1982; mem. bd. visitors Grady Meml. Hosp., 1983—92; trustee Ga. Legal History Found., 1986—, pres., 1996—; hon. chmn. Atlanta Decorators Show House, 2002; bd. dirs., vice chmn. Sr. Citizens Svc. Met. Atlanta, Inc., 2000—; bd. dirs. Sr. Citizens Found., 2005—, Highlands/Cashiers Chamber Music Festival, 2003—. Lt. comdr. USNR, ret. Mem. Atlanta Bar Assn. (bd. dirs. 1982-87, exec. com. 1983-87), State Bar Ga. (vice chmn. bar and media com. 1979-82), Atlanta Bar Found. (trustee 1985-91), U. Ga. Alumni (pres. chpt. 1973-74, chmn. Atlanta/Met. coun. 1975, mem. state bd. mgrs., v.p. 1976-78), Rotary Club, Gridiron, Capital City Club, Peachtree Racket Club, Phi Beta Kappa, Omicron Delta Kappa, Phi Kappa Phi, Phi Delta Phi, Delta Tau Delta. E-mail: wtanner516@aol.com.

TANNO, JOHN W., university librarian; b. Bklyn., Sept. 28, 1939; s. John C. and Hildegarde (Whitaker) T.; children: Maria Elena, Luisa. AA, Phoenix Jr. Coll., 1959; MusB, Ariz. State U., 1963; MusM, U. So. Calif., 1965, MLS, 1970. Music librarian SUNY, Binghamton, 1965-68; order librarian Claremont Colls., Calif., 1970; music librarian U. Calif., Riverside, 1970-72, head monographs sect., 1972-78, asst. univ. librarian, 1978-83, assoc. univ. librarian, 1983—2002, assoc. univ. libr. Davis, 2002—. Mem. ops. com. So. Regional Library Facility, 1984—, task group Intercampus Transp., 1984, negotiating team CLSI, 1981-84, bldg. com. So. Regional Compact Shelving Facility, 1979-82, steering com. Univ. Bibliographic Access System, 1978-82; chair Systemwide Ops. and Planning Adv. Group, 2001-04. Editor Soundboard, 1976-80; contbr. articles to profl. jours. Mem. ALA, The Music Library Assn., Coll. Music Soc., Assn. Recorded Sound Collections, Guitar Found. Am. (exec. com. 1976-80), Beta Phi Mu. Home: 130 Eastbrook Cir Sacramento CA 95835 Office: Gen Libr U Calif Davis 100 NorthWest Quad Davis CA 95616-5292 Office Phone: 530-752-2110. Business E-Mail: jwtanno@ucdavis.edu. *

TANNON, JAY MIDDLETON, lawyer; b. Augusta, Ga., Feb. 24, 1956; BA summa cum laude, Univ. N.C., 1978; JD, U. Va., 1982; MBA cum laude, U. Louisville, 1983. Bar: Ky. 1982, DC. Ptnr. Brown, Todd & Heyburn, Louisville, 1982-2000; exec. committee Frost, Brown, Todd LLC, 2000—04; chmn. Kentucky WorldTrade Ctr., 1999—2004; ptnr., Corp. & Securities, Private Equity, Internat. practices, head DC & no. Va. Corp. & Securities group Pillsbury Winthrop LLP (now Pillsbury Winthrop Shaw Pittman), Washington, 2004—06; ptnr., co-chair Pvt. Equity Group DLA Piper, Washington, 2006—. Chmn., founder Comml. Dispute Resolution Inc., Louisville, 1986—90; chmn. Ky. Export Coun., 2001—04; svcs. adv. com. US Trade Rep., 2002—; internat. studies adv. bd. U. NC; exec. com. Evermore Investments LLC, 2000—04; mem. So. Tech. Coun., 2004—; mem. steering com. Internat. Bus. Exchange Coun., 2004—06. Contbg. author Ky. Bus. Acquisitions; contbr. articles to profl. jours. Bd. dirs. U. Louisville Sch. Bus., 1985-88, Independent Industries, Inc. 1988-95. Hearst Found. scholar, 1974, Johnston scholar U. N.C., 1976, Phillips scholar U. N.C., 1977, du Pont scholar U. Va., 1979; named one of Best Lawyers in Am., Woodward-White, Am.'s Leading Bus. Lawyers Chambers & Ptnrs. Mem. ABA, Internat. Bar Assn., Ky. Bar Assn., D.C. Bar Assn. Office: DLA Piper 1200 19th St NW Washington DC 20036 Office Phone: 202-861-3932. Business E-Mail: jay.tannon@dlapiper.com.

TANNU, NILESH SURESH, medical researcher; b. Pune, Maharashtra, India, Nov. 21, 1974; s. Suresh Vasudeo and Nilima Suresh Tannu; m. Indrayani Nilesh Ganacharya, Dec. 29, 2001. MD, B.J. Med. Coll., Pune, 1998; MS, U. Tenn. Health Sci. Ctr., Memphis, 2003. Clin. intern Nashik Civil Hosp., Nashik, Maharashtra, 1998—99; med. officer in family medicine Primary Health Ctr., Parbhani, Maharashtra, 1999—2000; resident B.J. Med. Coll., 2000—01; grad. rsch. asst. U. Tenn. Health Sci. Ctr., 2001—03, postdoctoral rsch. fellow, 2003—04; proteomics analyst U. Ga., Athens, 2004—05; rsch. assoc. Wake Forest U. Sch. Medicine, Winston Salem, NC, 2005—. Presenter in field. Author rsch. papers in field. Mem.: Sci. Adv. Bd., Soc. Neurosci., Am. Soc. Mass Spectrometry. Achievements include discovery of high-tech research shows Cocaine changes proteins and brain function. Avocations: cricket, badminton. Home: 2311 Cloverdale Ave Apt B Winston Salem NC 27103 Office: Wake Forest U Sch Medicine 115 S Chestnut St Winston Salem NC 27101 Home Phone: 336-793-0759; Office Phone: 336-716-8621. Office Fax: 336-716-8501. Personal E-mail: niltan74@yahoo.com. Business E-Mail: ntannu@wfubmc.edu.

TANOUE, DONNA A., bank executive, former federal agency administrator; BA, U. Hawaii, 1977; JD, Georgetown U., 1981. Spl. dep. atty. gen. Dept. Commerce and Consumer Affairs, Hawaii, 1981-83; commr. financial inst. State of Hawaii, 1983-87; ptnr. Goodsill Anderson Quinn & Stifel, Hawaii, 1987-98; chmn. FDIC, Washington, 1998—2002; vice chmn. Bank of Hawaii, 2002—. Office: PO Box 2900 Honolulu HI 96846-6000

TANOUS, HELENE MARY, radiologist, educator; b. Zanesville, Ohio, Oct. 22, 1939; d. Joseph and Rose Marie (Mokarzel) T.; m. John Camp, 1986 (dec. 1990). BA, Marymount Coll., 1961; MD, U. Tex., 1967. Diplomate Am. Bd. Radiology. Intern County Hosp., LA, 1967-68; resident in radiology Cedars-Sinai Med. Ctr., LA, 1968-69, U. So. Calif. Hosp., LA, 1969-71; pvt. practice medicine specializing in radiology LA, 1972-73; instr. radiology U. So. Calif. Med. Sch., LA, 1971-72; asst. prof. diagnostic radiology Baylor Med. Sch., Houston, 1973-75; dir. med. student elective in diagnostic radiology Ben Taub Hosp., Houston, 1973-75; pvt. practice diagnostic radiology Largo, Fla., 1975—. Chief Radiology Diagnostic Clinic, Largo, Fla.; asst. prof. diagnostic radiology U. South Fla. Med. Sch., 1980—; asst. prof., dir. med. student edn. in diagnostic radiology U. Tex., Galveston, 1988-91. Pres., founder Children's Advs., Inc., 1977-85; bd. dirs. Fla. Endowment for Humanities, 1979-83. Decorated Chevalier des Palmes Academiques Govt. of France, 1988. Mem. AMA, So. Med. Assn., L'Alliance Francaise of Tampa (bd. dirs. 1984—, pres. 1985-87), Fedn. Alliances Francaises U.S.A. (bd. dirs. 1987-89), Houston Com. Fgn. Rels. Home: 661 Bering Dr Unit 108 Houston TX 77057-2137 Office Phone: 713-785-3975. E-mail: helene@tanousladies.com.

TANOUS, JAMES JOSEPH, lawyer, insurance company executive; b. Olean, NY, Sept. 11, 1947; s. Michael F. and Philomena M. (Eade) T.; m. Constance M. Griffin, Nov. 27, 1982; children: James M., Michele P. BA, St. Bonaventure U., 1969; JD, U. Va., 1972. Bar: N.Y. 1973, U.S. Dist. Ct. (we. dist.) 1973, U.S. Ct. Appeals (2d cir.) 1973. Ptnr., chmn. exec. com. Jaeckle Fleischmann & Mugel, LLP, Buffalo, 1973—2007; exec. v.p., sec., gen. counsel Erie Ins. Group, Erie, Pa., 2007—. Served to capt. USAR, 1971-79 Mem. ABA, N.Y. State Bar Assn. Office: Erie Ins Group 100 Erie Ins Pl Erie PA 16530 *

TANOUS, PETER JOSEPH, investment advisor; b. NYC, May 21, 1938; s. Joseph Carrington and Rose Marie (Mokarzel) T.; m. Barbara Ann MacConnell, Aug. 18, 1962; children: Christopher, Helene, William. BA in Econs., Georgetown U., 1960. With Smith Barney & Co., Inc., NYC, 1963-78, 2d v.p., mgr. Paris office, 1967, v.p., 1968-78, resident European sales mgr. in Paris, 1969-71, internat. sales mgr., 1971-78, 1st v.p., 1975-78; chmn. bd. Petra Capital Corp., NYC, 1978-81; pres. Lynx Investment Advisory Inc., Washington, 1992—. Exec. v.p. Bank Audi (USA), NYC, 1984—92; del. U.S.-Saudi Arabian Joint Econ. Commn. Bus. Dialogue; bd. dirs. MPS Group, Inc. (formerly Modis Profl. Svcs., Inc.), Jacksonville, Fla., Christian Children's Fund, Worldcare Ltd., Cambridge, Mass. Author: Investment Gurus, 1997, The Wealth Equation, 1999, Investment Visionaries, 2003. Trustee Browning Sch., NYC, 1987—93. Recipient Nat. Order of Cedar, Govt. of Lebanon, 2002. Office: 1100 Connecticut Ave NW Washington DC 20036-4101

TANOV, ROMIL R., mechanical engineer, researcher; b. Rousse, Bulgaria, July 10, 1962; arrived in U.S.A., 96; s. Rayko I. Tanov and Ekaterina Y. Tanova; m. Nadya T. Georgieva, June 23, 1988; children: Radostin R., Srebrina R. Tanova. MSc, U. for Architecture, Civil Engring. and Geodesy, Sofia, Bulgaria, 1988; PhD, U. Cin., 2000. Asst. prof. U. Rousse, Bulgaria, 1989—96; rsch. asst. U. Cin., 1996—2000; applied mechanics engr. Ctr. Advanced Product Evaluation divsn. Ind. Mills & Mfg. Inc., Westfield, Ind., 2000—04; sr. engr. Abaqus Inc., Cin., 2004—. Reviewer Finite Elements in Analysis and Design, Internat. Jour. of Solids and Structures, AIAA Jour.; contbr. articles to sci. jours. R.T. Davis scholar, U. Cin., 2000. Mem.: ASME, Internat. Assn. for Computational Mechanics, U.S. Assn. for Computational Mechanics, Am. Soc. for Composites, Soc. Automotive Engr. Office: Abaqus Inc Cin Office 9075 Centre Pt Dr Ste 410 West Chester OH 45069 Business E-Mail: rtanov@abaquscentral.com.

TANPHAICHITR, KONGSAK, rheumatologist, allergist, immunologist, internist; b. Bangkok, Feb. 22, 1946; came to U.S., 1971; s. Boonchoo and Hong (Nayakovit) T.; m. Sirirat Tareesung, June 17, 1973; children: Saksiri Marc, Marisa. Student, Mahidol U., Bangkok, Thailand, 1964-66, MD cum laude, 1970. Diplomate Am. Bd. Internal Medicine, Am. Bd. Rheumatology, Am. Bd. Allergy and Immunology; cert. Rheumatologist Royal Coll. Physicians Can. Straight med. intern Detroit Gen. Hosp.-Wayne State U., 1971-72; resident Barnes Hosp.-Washington U., St. Louis, 1972-74, fellow in rheumatology and immunology, 1974-76; instr. in medicine Washington U., 1976-77, asst. prof. medicine, 1977-97, assoc. prof. clin. medicine, 1997—2004, prof. clin. medicine, 2005—; attending physician Barnes Hosp., 1976—, Jewish Hosp. of St. Louis, 1981—. Dir. Allergy, Rheumatology & Immunology Specialists, St. Louis; cons. rheumatology Washington U., St. Louis, 1976—. Author: Amyloid Fibrils in Joint Fluid, 1976, Studies of Tolerance in NZB/NZW Mice, 1977, Vasculitis and Multiple Sclerosis, 1980, Buddhism and Science, 1987, Buddhism: Answers to Common Questions, 1990, Buddhism Answers Life, 1995, 2006, Mindfulness: The Key to Perfect One's Life, 1997, Mind and Universe, Mindfulness and Stress Management, 1998, Awakened Life for the New Millennium, 2000, Ethics and Morality, 2000, Parenting, 2000, Buddhism Beyond Non-Violence, 2001, Mom, 2001, The Best, the Worst and the Horrible of 9/11, 2001, Miracle of the Buddha's Wisdom, 2002, Mindfulness Amidst the Evolving World, 2003, Self-Awareness: The Neglected Essence of Life, 2003, Universal Language, Laws, and Community, 2004, Dharma In Action, 2006; editor: Vipassana 101, 2004, World Peace, 2004, Dependent Arising: Center of all Truths, 2004, Essence of Life: Mindfulness and Self-Awareness, 2005, Buddhism: The Ultimate Self-Improvement System, 2005, Science on Mind & Mindfulness, 2005, Buddhism and Qualia, 2006, Buddhism & Medicine, 2006, How Brain, Mind and Consciousness Work, 2007, PDR on Theravada Buddhism, 2007. Dharma tchr., bd. dirs., sec. Wat Phrasriratanaram Buddhist Temple, St. Louis, 1983—; co-dir. Buddhist Coun., St. Louis, 1985-90; chmn. Buddhist Coun. Greater St. Louis, 1999—. Named Am.'s Top Physician, Consumers' Rsch. Coun. Am., 2003—. Fellow: ACP, Royal Coll. Physicians Can., Am. Coll. Rheumatology, Am. Acad. Allergy, Asthma, and Immunology; mem.: Thai-Am. Physicians Found. (treas., bd. dirs. 2000—), Thai Physicians Assn. Am. (treas. Midwest chpt. 1994, sec. Midwest chpt. 1997, nat. treas. 1998, nat. bd. dirs. 1999—2001, nat. treas. 2000), UN Assn. Greater St. Louis (bd. dirs. 2004—07), UN Assn. U.S.A., Thai Assn. Greater St. Louis (pres.), Thai Temple Karate Shorinryu Club (Black Belt). Avocations: Karate, karaoke, insight meditation. Home: 12413 Ladue Rd Saint Louis MO 63141-8100 Office: Allergy Rheum & Immun Specs 11115 New Halls Ferry Rd Florissant MO 63033-7613 Home Phone: 314-878-1014; Office Phone: 314-839-4339. Personal E-mail: kongsakt@sbcglobal.net.

TANS, PIETER P., research scientist; PhD in Exptl. Physics, Rijksuniversitet Groningen, The Netherlands, 1978. Postdoctoral Scripps Inst. Oceanography, La Jolla, Calif., 1978—79; staff scientist, astrophysics group Lawrence Berkeley Lab., Berkeley, Calif., 1979—85; rsch. assoc. Cooperative Inst. for Rsch. in Environ. Sciences (CIRES), U. Colo., Boulder, Colo., 1985—90, fellow, 1997—; supervisory physicist, climate monitoring and diagnostics lab. Nat. Oceanic and Atmospheric Adminstrn. (NOAA), Boulder, Colo., 1990—96, chief scientist, climate monitoring and diagnostics lab., 1996—. Mem. dept. chemistry & biochemistry U. Colo. at Boulder, 1992—2000; mem. com. on oceanic carbon, ocean studies bd. NRC, 1992—93, mem. Dec-Cen panel, bd. on atmospheric sciences and climate, 1995—97; mem. working group drafting a multi-agy. US Carbon Cycle Sci. Plan, 1998. Assoc. editor Journal of Climate, 1996—, mem. editl. adv. bd. Tellus B, 1997—; contbr. articles to profl. jours. Named ISI Highly Cited, 2002—; recipient Gold medal, Dept. Commerce, 2000—. Fellow: Am. Geophysical Union; mem.: Royal Dutch Acad. Sciences (corr. mem. 1995—). Office: Environ Rsch Lab Climate Monitoring and Diagnositcs Lab Nat Oceanic and Atmospheric Adminstrn 325 Broadway Mail Code R/GMD1 Boulder CO 80303-3328 Office Phone: 303-497-6811, 303-497-6678. Office Fax: 303-497-5590. Business E-Mail: Pieter.Tans@noaa.gov.

TANSELLE, GEORGE THOMAS, language educator, foundation administrator; b. Lebanon, Ind., Jan. 29, 1934; s. K. Edwin and Madge R. (Miller) T. BA magna cum laude, Yale U., 1955; MA, Northwestern U., 1956, PhD, 1959. Instr. Chgo. City Jr. Coll., 1958-60, U. Wis., Madison, 1960-61, asst. prof., 1961-63, assoc. prof., 1963-68, prof. English, 1968—78; v.p. John Simon Guggenheim Meml. Found., 1978—2006; adj. prof. English and comparative lit. Columbia U., 1980—. Mem. Planning Inst. Commn. on English, 1961; exec. com. Ctr. for Edits. Am. Authors, 1970-73; adv. com. for drama for bicentennial Kennedy Ctr., 1974-76; mem. Soviet-Am. symposium on editing Ind. U., 1976; adv. com. Howells Meml., Kittery Point, 1976-78; exec. com. Ctr. for Scholarly Edits., 1976-81; mem. nat. adv. bd. Ctr. for Book, Libr. of Congress, 1978—; adv. bd. Burton's Anatomy of Melancholy, 1978—, Pub. and Printing History, A Guide to Manuscript Resources in the U.S., 1980—; bd. dirs. Lit. Classics of U.S., Inc., 1979—, chmn. editl. standards com., 1979—, corp. sec., 1989—; adv. com. N.Am. imprints program, 1980-92; Hanes lectr. U. NC, 1981; adv. coun. Rosenbach Mus. and Libr., 1980—, Ind. U. Inst. Adv. Study, 1983—; faculty Summer Rare Book Sch., Columbia U., 1984-87; adv. bd. Ctr. for Am. Culture Studies, Columbia U., 1985-94, Blake Archive, 1998—, Ctr. for Renaissance and Baroque Studies, U. Md., 1990—; adv. coun. Am. Trust for the Brit. Libr., 1987—, Am. Literary Manuscripts project, 1988—; Rosenbach lectr. U. Pa., 1987; bd. dirs. 18th Century Short-Title Catalogue/N.Am., Inc., 1988—, chmn., 1994—, Mark Twain Edition Project, 1991—; vis. com. Lilly Libr., 1988-92; adv. com. Writings of J.F. Cooper, 1990—; Sandars lectr. Cambridge U., 1997; bd. dirs. Am. Newspaper Repository, 1999—; faculty Beineke Libr. Master Classes, 1999--; adv. bd. Cambridge edit. of Jonathan Swift, 2002--. Author: Royall Tyler, 1967, Guide to the Study of United States Imprints, 1971, A Checklist of Editions of Moby-Dick, 1976, Selected Studies in Bibliography, 1979, The History of Books as a Field of Study, 1981, Textual Criticism since Greg, 1987, expanded edit., 2005, A Rationale of Textual Criticism, 1989, Parkman Dexter Howe Library, Hawthorne and Melville, 1989, Textual Criticism and Scholarly Editing, 1990, Libraries, Museums, and Reading, 1991, A Description of Descriptive Bibliography, 1992, The Life and Work of Fredson Bowers, 1993, Literature and Artifacts, 1998, Italian transl., 2004, The Pleasures of Being a Scholar-Collector, 2006; co-editor: The Writings of Herman Melville, 1968—, Samuel Johnson's Translation of Sallust, 1993; editor: Library of Am. Melville, 1982-83, Books as a Way of Life: Essays by Gordon N. Ray, 1988, The Art Deco Book in France by Gordon N. Ray, 2005; mem. editorial bd. Contemporary Literature, 1962-91, Abstracts of English Studies, 1964-78, Papers of Bibliog. Soc. Am, 1968-80, Resources for American Literary Study, 1971—, Analytical and Enumerative Bibliography, 1977—, Review, 1978—, Am. Literature, 1979-82, Literary Research, 1986-90, Common Knowledge, 1991—, Book History, 1996—, Leviathan, 1998—, contbr. articles to books and profl. jours. Mem. coun. Friends of Columbia U. Librs., 1990-94; bd. dirs. Friends of Lilly Libr., 1990-92. Recipient Kiekhofer Teaching award U. Wis., 1963, Jenkins award for bibliography, 1973; Guggenheim fellow, 1969-70; Am. Council Learned Socs. fellow, 1973-74; Nat. Endowment for the Humanities fellow, 1977-78, Laureate award Am. Printing History Assn., 1987. Mem. MLA (mem. exec. com. bibliog. evidence group 1974-75, methods of lit. rsch. div. 1979-83, chmn. 1982, mem. Hubbell award Com. Am. lit. sect. 1978-82, chmn. 1982, mem. com. on prize for ind. scholars 1983-87, chmn. 1985-87, chmn. ad hoc com. on future of print record 1993-95), Modern Humanities Rsch. Assn., Bibliog. Soc. London (pres. Am. Friends 1992—), Bibliog. Soc. Australia, Bibliog. Soc. Am. (mem. council 1970-94, vice chmn. publs. com. 1974-76, chmn. 1981-84, sec. 1976-78, chmn. com. on regional groups, 1978-80, 2d v.p. 1978-80, 1st v.p. 1980-82, pres. 1984-88), Bibliog. Soc. U. Va. (pres. 1992—), Oxford, Cambridge, Edinburgh, Birmingham, No. Ill., Can. bibliog. socs. (mem. coun. 1996—), Soc. for Bibliography of Natural History, Printing Hist. Soc. (Am. corr. 1970-84), Am. Printing Hist. Assn. (trustee N.Y. chpt. 1979-85), Pvt. Librs. Assn., Ind. Rsch. Librs. Assn. (com. on standards for rare book cataloging in machine-readable form 1978-79), Fellows Morgan Libr., Manuscript Soc. (bd. dirs. 1974-79), Am. Pub. Libr. Film Project (bd. advisors 1993—), Am. Antiquarian Soc. (mem. publs. com. 1972-81, chmn. com. 1978-81, mem. coun. 1974-92, hon. councillor, 1992—, del. to Am. Coun. Learned Socs. 1978-93, exec. com. dels., 1987-89, chmn. exec. com. program on book in Am. culture 1983-89, com. on edn., 1982-85, chmn., 1983-85, chmn. com. on libr. 1988-91), Soc. Textual Scholarship (adv. bd. 1979—, pres. 1981-83), The Johnsonians (chmn. 1993), Melville Soc. (pres. 1982, Electronic Melville Com. 1997—), Book Club Calif., Typophiles, Guild Book Workers, Wis. Acad. Scis., Arts and Letters, Renaissance Soc. Am., Am. Soc. 18th-Century Studies, Renaissance English Text Soc., Assn. Documentary Editing (chmn. Julian Boyd award com. 1986, Boydston award com. 1995), Soc. Scholarly Pub., Assn. internationale de bibliophilie, Soc. History of Authorship, Reading and Pub. (bd. dirs. 1993—), Century Club, Yale Club, Caxton Club, Grolier Club (publs. com. 1979-82, 83-87, 97—, coun. 1980—, small exhbns. com. 1979-87, chmn. 1980-82, sec. 1982-86, chmn. libr. com. 1985-86, 90-2002, pres. 1986-90), Odd Volumes, Phi Beta Kappa. Home: 420 E 51st St # 10D New York NY 10022

TANSEY, MARK, painter; b. San Jose, Calif., 1949; One-man shows include Grace Borgenicht, 1982, 1984, John Berggruen Gallery, San Francisco, 1984, Contemporary Arts Mus., Houston, Tex., 1984, Curt Marcus Gallery, NY, 1986, 1990, 1993, 1997, 2000, Walker Art Ctr., Minn., 1990, Kohn/Abrams Gallery, 1993, Mus. Fine Art, Boston, 1994, Galleri Faurschou, Copenhagen, 1995, Gagosian Gallery, NY, 2004, Mus. Kurhaus, Kleve, Germany, 2005, exhibitions include Biennial, Whitney Mus. Am. Art, NYC, 1983, Aperto 86, Venice Biennale, Italy, 1986, Color and/or Monochrome, Nat. Mus. Modern Art, Tokyo, 1989, 10+10: Contemporary Soviet & Am. Painters, Corcoran Gallery Art, Washington, DC, 1989, The Charade of Mastery: Deciphering Modernism in Contemporary Art, Whitney Mus. Am. Art, 1990, Mountains of the Mind, Aspen Art Mus., Colo., 1994, Am. Kaleidoscope, Nat. Mus. Am. Art, Washington, DC, 1996, Double Trouble: The Patchett Collection, Mus. Contemporary Art, San Diego, 1998, Reality and Desire, Jóan Miro Found., Barcelona, 1999, The Burbs, DFN Gallery, NY, 2003, Perspectives @ 25: A Quarter Century of New Art in Houston, Contemporary Arts Mus., 2004, Am. Art of the 1980s, Washington U. Gallery Art, St. Louis, 2004.

TANSILL, FREDERICK JOSEPH, lawyer; b. Washington, Feb. 27, 1948; s. Frederick Riker and Mary Eileen (Loftus) T.; m. Joan Louise Trefsgar, July 10, 1971; children: Brendan Frederick, Brooke Charlotte, Charlotte Trefsgar. BA with honors, Brown U., 1970; JD, Georgetown U., 1974, LLM in Taxation, 1982. Bar: D.C. 1974, U.S. Tax Ct. 1976, Va. 1983. Assoc. Cross, Murphy & Smith, Washington, 1974-77; ptnr. Bird & Tansill, Washington, 1977-79; assoc. Ober, Grimes & Shriver, Washington,

1979-81; ptnr. Lewis, Mitchell & Moore, Vienna, Va., 1981-86; counsel Boothe, Prichard & Dudley, McLean, Va., 1986-87; ptnr. McGuire, Woods, Battle & Boothe, McLean, 1987-90; shareholder Verner, Liipfert, Bernhard, McPherson & Hand, Chartered, McLean, 1990-97; owner-mgr. Frederick J. Tansill & Assocs., LLC, McLean, 1997—. Gen. counsel No. Va. Cmty. Found., 1995-98, 1st v.p., 1998-99, pres., 1999-2000; bd. dirs. Children's Mus., Boston, Boston Found.; mem. Estate Planning Coun. Washington, 2007—. Fellow Am. Coll. Trust and Estate Counsel; mem. ABA, Internat. Bus. Bar, Va. Bar Assn. (exec. coun. taxation sect. 1989-92, coun. and legis. com. wills sect. 1993-99—, trusts and estate sect. 1983-99, bd. govs. 1988-96, chmn. bd. govs. 1991-92, co-chmn. spl. task force lawyers as fiduciaries 1993-95), D.C. Bar Assn. (steering com. estates, trusts and probate law sects. 1995-97, co-chair 1997-99), Fairfax County Bar Assn. (will sect. 1986, chmn. tax sect. 1987-88, CLE com. 1988-89), No. Va. Estate Planning Coun. (exec. com. 1987-92, pres. 1990-91), Tower Club (bd. dirs. 1988—). Office: Frederick J Tansill & Assocs 1355 Beverly Rd Ste 215 Mc Lean VA 22101-3654 Home Phone: 703-734-6240; Office Phone: 703-847-1359. Office Fax: 703-847-1357. Business E-Mail: fred@fredtansill.com.

TANSKY, BURTON M., department store executive; b. 1938; married BA, U. Pitts., 1960. With Kaufmann's, 1961-67; from asst. store mgr. to mgr. Filenes, Boston, 1967-71; mdse. mgr. Rikes, Dayton, Ohio, 1971-74; v.p. Forbes and Wallace, Springfield, Ohio, 1974, I. Magnin, San Francisco, 1974-77; from sr. v.p. to exec. v.p. Saks and Co., NYC, 1977-80, pres., 1980—94; chmn., CEO Saks & Co., NYC, 1990—94, Neiman Marcus Stores, Dallas, 1994—98; exec. v.p. Neiman Marcus Group, Dallas, 1998, pres., COO, 1998—2001, pres., CEO, 2001—; interim CEO Bergdorf Goodman, 2004. Bd. dir. Internat. Flavors & Fragrances, 2003—. Named a Chevalier de la Legion d'Honneur, Govt. France, 2002. Office: Neiman Marcus Group One Marcus Sq 1618 Main St Dallas TX 75201-2581 *

TANSY, MARTIN F., dean; m. Margaret Tansy; children: Martin Jr., Margaret, Matthew. BS, Wilkes Coll.; MS, Thomas Jefferson Med. Coll., PhD, 1964. From asst. to assoc. prof. physiology Temple U., Phila., 1964—72, prof., 1972—86, chmn. dept. physiology and biophysics in basic sciences, acting dean Sch. Dentistry, 1986, dean Sch. Dentistry, 1987—. Bd. dirs. Friends of the Nat. Inst. Dental and Craniofacial Rsch. Recipient Alumni Excellence Award in Edn. and Adminstrn., Wilkes U., 2000. Fellow: Internat. Coll. Dentists (hon.), Am. Coll. Dentists (hon.); mem.: Nat. Acad. Practices, Acad. Gen. Dentistry (hon.). Office: Temple U Sch Dentistry 333 Dental Sch Bldg 3223 N Broad St Philadelphia PA 19140 Office Phone: 215-707-2799. Office Fax: 215-707-3192. Business E-Mail: martintansy@temple.edu.

TANT, MARTIN RAY, chemical engineer, biomedical engineer; b. Seneca, SC, Apr. 10, 1953; s. Larry Ray and Doris Jo Anne (Alexander) T. BS, Old Dominion U., 1975; MS, Va. Tech., 1979, PhD, 1986; postgrad. in Biomed. Sci., East Tenn. State U., 2003—. Chemist Naval Mine Engring. Facility, Yorktown, Va., 1975-76; chem. engr. Naval Surface Warfare Ctr., Dahlgren, Va., 1979—82; sr. rsch. engr. Dow Chem. USA, Freeport, Tex., 1986-88; rsch. assoc. Eastman Chem. Co., Kingsport, Tenn., 1988—. Co-editor Ionomers: Synthesis, Structure, Properties and Applications, 1997, High-Temperature Properties and Applications of Polymeric Materials, 1995, Structure and Properties of Glassy Polymers, 1998; contbr. over 50 publs. to books and profl. jours. Cunningham Dissertation fellow, 1985. Mem.: AIChE, Am. Assn. Pharm. Scientists, Am. Chem. Soc., Sigma Xi. Office: Eastman Chem Co PO Box 1972 Kingsport TN 37662-1972 Office Phone: 423-229-2147. Business E-Mail: tant@eastman.com.

TANTILLO, MARY DARLENE, nurse; b. Rochester, NY, July 28, 1960; d. Salvatore Augustus and Constance Tantillo; m. Odysseus Adamides, Oct. 2, 1993; 1 child, Odysseus Alexander Adamides. AAS in Nursing, Monroe C.C., Rochester, NY, 1980; BS in Nursing, Nazareth Coll. Rochester, NY, 1982; MS in Psychiat. Mental Health Nursing, U. Rochester Sch. Nursing, NY, 1986; PhD, Adelphi U., Garden City, NY, 1992. Profl. RN, N.Y., 1980. Nurse mgr. behavioral medicine unit U. Rochester/Strong Meml. Hosp., 1985—86, clinician II clin. nurse specialist cons., 1986—90, assoc. dir. adult ambulatory svcs.-psychiatry, 1990—94, adminstrv. dir. ambulatory svcs.-psychiatry, 1994—98, dir. eating disorder treatment svc., 1997—2000; dir. eating disorders program Unity Health Sys. Dept. Psychiatry and Behavioral Health, Rochester, 2000—, dir. We. N.Y. Comprehensive Care Ctr. for Eating Disorders, 2005—. Chair legis. com. Rochester Area Psychiat. Mental Health Nurse Clin. Specialist Group, 1986—94; chairperson Rochester Consortium on Eating Disorders, 1990—93; coord. Jean Baker Miller Tng. Inst. Rsch. Network, Wellesley, Mass., 1996—; pres., bd. dirs. Mental Health Assn., Rochester, 2002—05; bd. dirs. Acad. Eating Disorders, Northbrook, Ill., 2002—05, chairperson credentialing task force, 2004—; clin. assoc. prof. psychiatry U. Rochester Med. Ctr., 2004—; co-chair Rochester Eating Disorders Cmty. Adv. Bd., 2004—. Mem. mental health outreach Spiritus Christi Ch., Rochester, 2000—. Recipient Ann. Outstanding Nurse award for Excellence in Patient and Family Nursing, U. Rochester Dept. Psychiat. Nursing, 1984, Rsch. award, Sigma Theta Tau Internat. Inc. Epsilon xi Chpt., 1996, Gottschalk Mental Heatlh Rsch. award, Mental Health Assn., 1996, Excellence in the Treatment of Eating Disorders, Excellus, Blue Cross/Blue Shield of Rochester, 2002—, Woman of Influence in Health Care, Girl Scouts Genesee Valley, Inc., 2005; fellow, Acad. Eating Disorders, 2003. Fellow: Acad. Eating Disorders; mem.: Nat. Ctr. Addictions and Substance Abuse, Nat. Alliance for the Mentally Ill, Nat. Eating Disorders Assn., AAUW, Sigma Theta Tau Internat., Wellesley Centers for Women, Nat. Registry Cert. Group Psychotherapists, Jean Baker Miller Tng. Inst., Am. Group Psychotherapy Assn., Rochester Area Group Psychotherapy Soc., Genesee Valley Nurses Assn. Democrat-Npl. Catholic. Avocations: bicycling, hiking, dance, swimming, crafts. Office: Unity Health System Dept of Psychiatry 835 W Main St Rochester NY 14611 Home Phone: 585-703-3403; Office Phone: 585-368-6550 8590. Office Fax: 585-368-6540. Business E-Mail: mtantillo@unityhealth.org.

TANUR, JUDITH MARK, sociologist, educator; b. Jersey City, Aug. 12, 1935; d. Edward Mark and Libbie (Berman) Mark; m. Michael Isaac Tanur, June 2, 1957; children: Rachel Dorothy, Marcia Valerie. BS, Columbia U., 1957, MA, 1963; PhD, SUNY, Stony Brook, 1972. Analyst Biometrics Rsch., NYC, 1955-67; lectr. SUNY, Stony Brook, 1967-71, from asst. prof. to prof. sociology, 1971-94, Disting. tchg. prof., 1994—2006, Disting. tchg. prof. emerita, 2006—. Cons. NBC, NYC, 1976—89, Lang. of Data Project, Los Altos, Calif., 1980—89, Inst. for Rsch. on Learning, 1994—95; mem. com. on nat. stats. NAS, 1980—87, com. on applied and theoretical stats., 1997—2000; trustee NORC, U. Chgo., 1987—; bd. dirs. Social Sci. Rsch. Coun., 2000—06; mem. adv. com. SBE, NSF, 2000—06. Author: The Subjectivity of Scientists and the Bayesian Approach, 2001; editor: Statistics: A Guide to the Unknown, 1972, Internat. Encyclopedia of Statistics, 1978, Cognitive Aspects of Survey Methodology, 1984, Questions About Questions, 1991, Cognition and Survey Research, 1999, Internat. Ency. of Social Scis., 1963—67; contbr. articles to sci., stats., and social sci. jours. Bd. dirs. Vis. Nurse Svc., Great Neck, N.Y., 1970-2000; bd. govs. Gen. Soc. Survey, Chgo., 1989-92. Sr. rsch. fellow, Am. Statis. Assn./NSF/Bur. Labor Stats., 1988—89. Fellow AAAS, Am. Statis. Assn. (Founders award 1997); mem. Internat. Statis. Inst., Phi Beta Kappa. Home: PO Box 280 Montauk NY 11954 Office: SUNY Dept Sociology Stony Brook NY 11794-4356 Office Phone: 631-632-7738. Business E-Mail: jtanur@notes.cc.sunysb.edu.

TAN VAN, See NGO, VAN

TANZI, RONALD THOMAS, artist, educator; b. Brookline, Mass., Mar. 3, 1949; s. Henry Francis and Jennie (Vicenza) T.; m. Patricia Marie Morrill, Mar. 16, 1974 (div. Apr. 1990); children: Jennie Grace, Jacob Thomas. Student, Chapman Coll., Orange, Calif., 1968-70, Ea. Wash. U., Cheney, 1970-72; BFA magna cum laude, U. Wash., 1984; MFA, U. Cin., 1986. Artist self-employed, Spokane, Boston, Seattle, 1970—; art editor Contbr.'s Copy Quar., Spokane, 1970-73; instr., lectr. U. Cin., 1984-86; instr. U. Wash., Seattle, 1986-87, Seattle Cmty. Colls. (North and Ctrl. campuses), 1987—, Edmonds (Wash.) C.C., 1992—96, Bellevue (Wash.) C.C., 1993—. Dir. R's Studio Gallery, Cheney, 1971-73; visual advisor Masque Theater Co., Everett, Wash., 1987-88; lectr. Seattle Art Mus., 1991, Seattle Art League, 1992, Bellevue Art Mus., 1995. Exhibited paintings in shows including Spokane City Arts, 1971, Pacific Northwest Annual, 1976, N.W. Traditions: A Retrospective, 1987, King County Arts Commn., 1988, Seattle Ctrl. CC, 1994-2004, Annual Faculty Art Shows, Bellevue CC, 1994-2005, Philip Howe Gallery, 1998; artist, pub. commn. Metro Bus Shelter Mural Program, 1991, Harborview Med. Ctr. Mural, 1995; represented in pvt. collections in U.S., Japan, Germany, Finland. Sgt. USAF, 1966-70, Vietnam. U. Cin. Grad. scholar, 1984, 85, 86. Mem. Coll. Art Assn., Am. Fedn. Tchrs., Wash. State Fedn. Tchrs., Seattle Art Mus., Phi Beta Kappa. Avocations: swimming, hiking, travel. Home: 5509 5th Ave NE Seattle WA 98105 Personal E-mail: rtanzi@sccd.ctc.edu.

TANZI, RUDOLPH EMILE, neuroscientist, researcher, educator; b. Providence, Sept. 18, 1958; s. Rudolph Anthony and Anne Marie (Macari) Tanzi; m. Dora Marta Kovacs, May 24, 2002. BS in Microbiology, U. Rochester, 1980, BA in History, 1980; PhD in Neurobiology, Harvard U., 1990. Rsch. asst. genetics unit to prof. Mass. Gen. Hosp., Boston, 1980—99, prof. neurology, 1999—, dir. Genetics and Aging Unit, 1999—. Instr. neurology Harvard U. Med. Sch., 1990—92, asst. prof. to prof., 1992—; bd. sci. counselors Nat. Inst. Aging; chmn. sci. adv. bd. Blanchette Rockefeller Neurosciences Inst. Editl. bd. Neuron, 1994—; co-editor: Molecular Mechanisms of Dementia, 1997, Presenilins and Alzheimer's Disease, 1998, Alzheimer's Disease: Advances in Genetics, Molecular and Cellular Biology, 2006; co-author: Decoding Darkness: The Search for the Genetic Causes of Alzheimer's Disease, 2001; contbr. articles to profl. jours. Adv. bd. Lifeboat Found. Recipient Nathan Shock New Investigator award, Gerontology Soc. Am., 1993, Met. Life award, 1995, Potamkin prize, 1995; fellow French Found., 1991, Pew scholar in biomed. scis., 1993. Fellow: AAAS; mem.: Am. Soc. Human Genetics, Am. Soc. for Neurosci. Avocations: skiing, tennis, scuba diving, piano. Office: Mass Gen Hosp - East Genetics and Aging Rsch Unit 114 16th St Charlestown MA 02129 Office Phone: 617-726-6845. Office Fax: 617-724-1949. E-mail: tanzi@helix.mgh.harvard.edu. *

TAO, JING, environmental scientist; arrived in US, 2005; d. XueLi Tao and YuYing Zhang. BS in Geography, E.China Normal U., Shanghai, 1986—91, MS in Geomorphology and Quarternary Geology, 1991—94; PhD in Geosci. and Chemistry, U. Mo., Kans. City, 1998—2005. Rsch. assoc., Inst. Comparative Sedimentology E.China Normal U., 1994—98; tchg., rsch. asst. U. Mo., Kansas City, 1998—2002; environ. scientist Water Svcs. Dept., Kansas City, 2002—. Contbr. articles to profl. jours. Grantee Grad. Rsch. fellowship, Geol. Soc. Am., 2001. Mem.: Sigma Xi. Home Phone: 816-523-4090.

TAO, MARIANO, biochemistry educator; b. Davao, Philippines, Mar. 3, 1938; came to U.S., 1963; s. Bong-Hua and Siu-Hua (Co) T.; m. Pearl Koh, June 3, 1967; children: Stephen, Kevin. BSChemE, Cheng Kung U., Tainan, Taiwan, 1962; PhD in Biochemistry, U. Wash., 1967. Sr. fellow U. Wash., Seattle, 1967-68; guest investigator Rockefeller U., NYC, 1968-70; asst. prof. U. Ill., Chgo., 1970-74, assoc. prof., 1974-78, prof. dept. biochemistry and molecular biology, 1978-98, prof. emeritus, 1998—, acting head, 1979-80. Biochemistry study sect. NIH, 1985-89; established investigator Am. Heart Assn., 1973-78. Mem. Am. Soc. Biochemistry and Molecular Biology, Am. Chem. Soc. Achievements include membrane abnormality and diseases I and II.

TAO, TERENCE CHI-SHEN, mathematics professor; b. Adelaide, South Australia, Australia, July 17, 1975; arrived in US, 1992; s. Billy and Grace Tao; married. BSc with honors in Math., Flinders U., 1991, MSc in Math., 1992; PhD in Math., Princeton U., 1996. Asst. rschr. Flinders Med. Ctr., 1992—94, Princeton U., 1993—94; Hedrick asst. prof. UCLA, 1996—98, acting asst. prof., 1999, asst. prof., 2000, full prof., 2000—. Mem. Math. Scis. Rsch. Inst., 1997; vis. fellow U. NSW, Sydney, 1999—2000, vis. prof., 2000; long-term prize fellow Clay Math. Inst., Boston, 2001—03; hon. prof. Australian Nat. U., 2001—03; mem. sci. adv. bd. Australian Math. Scis. Inst., 2002—; mem. adv. bd. Internat. Math. Rsch. Surveys (IRMS), 2003—. Reviewer Zentralblatt Math., 1998—2005, assoc. editor J. Am. Math. Soc., 2002—04, full editor, 2004—06, assoc. editor Am. Jour. Math., 2002—, Dynamics of Partial Differential Equations, 2003—; author: Solving Mathematical Problems: A Personal Perspective, 1992, 2006, Analysis Vol. I, Analysis Vol. II, 2006. Co-recipient Levi L. Conant prize, Am. Math. Soc., 2005; named one of Brilliant 10, Popular Sci. mag., 2006; recipient Bronze medal, Internat. Math. Olympiad, 1986, Silver medal, 1987, Gold medal, 1988, medal, Flinders U., 1992, Fulbright postgraduate award, Fulbright Assn., 1992—95, Salem prize, Salem Prize Com., 2000, medal, Australian Math. Soc., 2005, Bocher Meml. prize, Am. Math. Soc., 2000, Fields medal, Internat. Math. Union, 2006, SASTRA Ramanujan prize, 2006; Packard Found. fellow, David & Lucille Packard Found., 1999—, Rsch. fellow, Sloan Found., 1999—2001, MacArthur Fellow, John D. and Catherine T. MacArthur Found., 2006. Fellow: Royal Soc. UK; mem.: Australian Acad. Sci. (corr.). Office: UCLA Dept Math Math Sciences 5622 MS 6364 405 Hilgard Ave Los Angeles CA 90095-1555 Office Phone: 310-206-4844. Business E-Mail: tao@math.ucla.edu. *

TAORMINA, CHARLES ANTHONY, writer, editor, artist; b. Johnstown, Pa., Apr. 2, 1948; s. Anthony James and Shirley Ruth (Wagner) T.; m. Brenda Gail Gilbert, Aug. 8, 1970 (div. 1981); 1 child, Angela Loraine. BA in Liberal Arts, Indiana U. of Pa., 1970. Contbg. editor/reporter Times of Charlottesville, Va., 1976-78; editor Blue Ridge Rev., Charlottesville, 1978-79, VIRTU, Uniontown, Pa., 1993—; writer, editor, mgr. The Renaissance Workshop, Uniontown, 1990—. Spkr. World Future Soc., Bethesda, Md., 1989, 93; mem., actor Actors & Artists of Fayette County, Scottdale, Pa., 1993; contbg. author/mem. writing workshop project-Projects, Inc. Author: (novels) Abse & Merdan, Endgames, Karma Bums, Gratuity, Legacy, The Entropy Wars, (novella) Of Rifles & Butterflies, (drama) Freedom One, Tauromenium, Rally!, Catalyst, (nonfiction) Along the Journalistic Path, Infinity, Vision, Ardour, Keystone, Quintessence, Autobiography, (story collections) Early Tales, Moments, Shared Lives, (poetry) Rain Folio, also monographs,(audio cassette) Renaissance: An Introduction; editor: Commercial Book and Story Editing; contbr. fiction to Blue Ridge Rev., Samisdat, Gargoyle, Fool's Jour., William and Mary Rev.; contbr. nonfiction to Daily Progress, The Sun, Harper's Weekly, others; contbr. photography to Washington Post, Gargoyle, others; contbr. on-line arts newsletter PRIVY, Write Advice, poetry to Am. Poetry Ann.; dramas staged Gemini Theater, Pitts., 1998. Freedom writer Amnesty Internat., N.Y.C., 1989—; mem. Regeneration Project, Rodale Press, Emmaus, Pa., 1989; workshop leader VISTA Literacy Project, Ravenna, Ohio, 1988; pub. rels. worker Nat. Road Heritage Park Project, Uniontown, 1993. Recipient Honorable Mention award Soc. for Am. Cuisine, 1987. Mem. Dramatists Guild (assoc.), Am. Christian Writers Assn., Renaissance Soc. Am., Union of Concerned Scientists. Roman Catholic. Avocations: sketching, cosmology, travel, music listening, hiking. Office: The Renaissance Workshop 860 Chalker St Fl 1 Akron OH 44310-2116 also: 103 Camden Ave Johnstown PA 15904-2302 Personal E-mail: CATAORMINA@prodigy.net.

TAPHORN, JOSEPH BERNARD, lawyer; b. Beckemeyer, Ill., Oct. 9, 1921; s. Herman Henry and Marie (Gasser) T.; m. Anna Marie Klinge, June 25, 1944 (dec. Dec. 1991); children: Robert J., Joanne M., John F.; m. Joan Campen Klemmer, July 13, 1996. BS in Agr., U. Ill., 1943; BS in Engring., George Washington U., 1949, LLB, 1950. Bar: N.Y. 1952, D.C. 1952, U.S. Dist. Ct. (so. and ea. dists.) N.Y. 1952, U.S. Dist. Ct. (no. dist.) N.Y. 1991, U.S. Dist. Ct. D.C., 1952, U.S. Ct. Appeals (D.C. cir.) 1961, U.S. Ct. Appeals (fed. cir.) 1996, U.S. Supreme Ct. 1961. Patent examiner U.S. Patent Office, Washington, 1946-49, patent classifier, 1949-50; patent agt. Pollard and Johnston, NYC, 1950-52; patent atty. IBM Corp., NYC, 1952-59, patent mgr., counsel various locations, 1959-70, copyright counsel Armonk, NY, 1970-78, copyright and trademark counsel, 1978-88; pvt. practice Poughkeepsie, NY, 1989—. Chmn. bd. U.S. Dynamics, Yonkers, N.Y. 1975-77. Contbr. articles to profl. jours. Pres. Huntley Civic Assn., Eastchester, N.Y., 1958-59; trustee Copyright Soc. USA, N.Y.C., 1985-88. Capt. U.S. Army, 1943-46, ETO. Mem. ABA (com. chmn. 1983-87), N.Y. State Bar Assn., Dutchess County Bar Assn., Am. Intellectual Property Law Assn., N.Y. Intellectual Property Law Assn. (com. chmn. 1987-89), Ea. N.Y. Intellectual Property Law Assn., Noi Italiani d'Oggi, Dutchess Golf and Country Club, Germania Club. Republican. Roman Catholic. Avocations: golf, hunting, fishing, tennis, skiing. Home and Office: 8 Scenic Dr Poughkeepsie NY 12603-5521 Office Phone: 845-462-3262. Personal E-mail: jbtaphorn@prodigy.net.

TAPIA, RICHARD ALFRED, mathematics professor; b. Santa Monica, Calif., Mar. 25, 1939; s. Amado and Magda Tapia; m. Jean Rodriguez, July 25, 1959; children: Circee (dec.), Richard, Rebecca. BA, UCLA, 1961, MA, 1966, PhD, 1967. Asst. prof. math. rsch. ctr. U. Wis., Madison, 1968-70; asst. prof. math. scis. Rice U., Houston, 1970-72, assoc. prof., 1972-76, prof. math. scis., 1976—, chair dept. math. scis., 1978-83, assoc. dir. minority affairs Office Grad. Studies, 1989—. Vis. assoc. prof. ops. rsch. Stanford (Calif.) U., 1976-77. Author: Nonparametric Density Estimation; contbr. articles to profl. publs. Named one of 20 Most Influential in Minority Math. Edn., NSF, 1990, 50 Most Important Hispanics in Govt., Edn. Hispanic Engineer and Info. Tech. mag., 2005; recipient Nat. Achievement award for Edn. Hispanic Engring. Mag., 1990, A. Nico Habermann award Computer Rsch. Assn., 1994; named Prof. of Yr., Assn. Hispanic Sch. Adminstrs., 1994. Mem. NAE, Am. Math. Soc. (mem. com. on edn.), Soc. for Indsl. and Applied Math. (trustee, lectr. 1988), Math. Assn. Am., Math. Programming Soc., Soc. for Advancement of Chicanos and Native Ams. in Sci. Home: 5723 Portal Dr Houston TX 77096-6010 Office: Rice U Dept Math Scis PO Box 1892 Houston TX 77251-1892

TAPKEN, MICHELLE G., prosecutor; BA in Edn., U. SD, 1967, MA in Ednl. Psychology, 1970, JD, 1989. Bar: South Dakota; lic. Psychologist. Fed. law clerk, Lincoln, Nebr., 1989—90; prosecutor US Atty. Office, Sioux Falls, SD, 1990—2001; interim US atty. Dist. SD US Dept. Justice, 2001, 2002, 1st asst. US atty. Dist. SD, 2005—. Recipient Director's award, US Dept. Justice, 1996, 2006. Office: 325 S 1st Ave Sioux Falls SD 57104 *

TAPLIN, WINN LOWELL, historian, retired federal agency administrator; b. Saint Albans, Vt., Oct. 3, 1925; s. Winn Lowell and Elinor (Cunningham) T.; m. Ellajean Allard, July 16, 1949; children: Leslie Taplin Baumann, Mark Allard. BSCE, U. Mich., 1946, AB, 1948, AM, 1950, PhD, 1956. Oper. officer CIA, Washington, Saigon, Bucharest, Geneva, Bangkok, 1955-81; cons. Stowe, Vt., 1981-94, Sarasota, Fla., 1994—. Author: Secret New England: Spies of the American Revolution, 1991, We Vermonters, 1992. Mem. U.S. del. to UN Commn. on Human Rights, 1969; pres. Vt. Hist. Soc., 1989-93, trustee, 1983-96; mem. Sarasota Geneal. Soc., v.p., 1999-2001, pres., 2001—03; pres. Mansfield View Water Corp., Stowe, 1989-92. 1st lt. USMC, 1943-46, 50-52, Korea. Decorated Bronze Star, Intelligence Medal of Merit. Mem. DAV, Central Intelligence Retirees Assn., Assn. Former Intelligence Officers, First Day Cover Soc., Am. Philatelic Assn., Soc. Mayflower Descendants (Sarasota Tilley chpt., dir. 2005-), Am. Legion, U. Mich. Club Sarasota (dir. 1994-04), Sigma Chi. Avocations: historical research, genealogy, classical music, stamp collecting/philately. Home: 4468 Calle Serena Sarasota FL 34238-5641 Personal E-mail: winn.ej@juno.com.

TAPP, MAMIE PEARL, educator; b. Aiken, SC, July 20, 1955; d. Willie Lee and Nancy (Madison) Garrett; m. Anthony Karl Tapp, Aug. 13, 1983; children: Anthony K. II, Barry Garrett, Myles Jarvis. BA, CUNY, 1977; MA, New Sch. for Social Rsch., 1984; student, Nova Southeastern U., 1994—2000. Flight attendant Capitol Airlines, Jamaica, N.Y., 1976-81; pers. assoc. Cmty. Svc. Soc., NYC, 1982-83; pers. specialist Marriott Hotel, Tampa, Fla., 1983-84; dir. placement Tampa Coll., 1984-86, facility coord., 1986-87, compliance officer, 1987-88; career counselor Alpha House, Tampa, 1988-91; career specialist U. Tampa, 1991-96, adj. prof., 1992-93; career specialist Jr. Achievement Greater Tampa, Inc., Tampa, 1996—, tchr. asst. program adv. com. mem., 1996-98; area mgr. BBBS, Belcamp, Md., 2004—05; mem. faculty U. Phoenix, 2006—. Tchr. asst. program adv. com. Hillsborough H.S., 1996-97; sr. edn. svc. mgr. Jr. Achievement, 1997-2004; faculty U. Phoenix, 2005. Author: Resumes, 1992, Cover Letters, 1991, Thank You Letters, 1992, (poetry) Inner Peace, 1999; co-editor: I Cried, 2001, Life, 2002. Bd. dirs. Children's Mus. Tampa, 1992-94; com. mem. United Way, Tampa, 1994-95; mem. bd. St. Peter Claver Cath. Sch., Tampa, 1995-99, exec. com. Glee Club, 1995; vol. Scout troop leader, 1997-98. Recipient Outstanding Bus. Woman award Am. Bus. Women's Assn., Tampa, 1987, Cmty. Svc. award Tampa Connections, 1993, Editor's Choice award Internat. Libr. of Poetry, 1999. Mem.: AAUW, Fla. Assn. Women in Edn., Am. Vocat. Assn. Roman Catholic. Avocations: reading, sewing. Office: Appollo Group Inc 4324 Marigold Ln Belcamp MD 21017 Personal E-mail: tapptbjpt@earthlink.net.

TAPPÉ, ALBERT ANTHONY, architect; b. Pitts., Aug. 12, 1928; s. Albert Anthony and Martha Ann (McKee) T.; m. Jean Bates, June 27, 1963; children: Eliza Bruce, Albert Anthony III. Student, William and Mary Coll., 1947-48, Fontainebleau Fine Art and Music Sch., 1951; BS, U. Va., 1952; M.Arch., MIT, 1958, M.City Planning. Designer McLeod & Ferrara (Architects), Washington, 1954-55; planner Boston City Planning Bd., 1957-58; architect, planner Architects Collaborative, Cambridge, Mass., 1958-61; ptnr. Huygens & Tappé, Inc. (architects and planners), Boston, 1962-80; pres. A. Anthony Tappé & Assocs., Inc., Boston, 1980—. Instr. dept. city planning MIT, 1959-60; instr. office exec. edn. Harvard U., 1989—; cons. architect Mass. Bur. Library Extension, 1965-76; chmn. bldg. commn., Brookline, Mass., 1977, mem. bd. examiners, Brookline; v.p. Guild Religious Architecture; mem. Back Bay Archtl. Commn.; bd. dirs. Boston Archtl. Ctr., 1980, bd. overseers, 2001-; vis. architect Am. Acad. Rome, 1997. Author: Guide to Planning a Library Building, 1967; important works include: Longy Concert Hall, Cambridge, Mass., Campus NH Coll., Franklin Park Zoo, Boston, Lynn Inst. for Savs., Interfaith Religious Ctr., Columbia, Md., student housing W.Va. Wesleyan Coll., Hotel, Costa Smeralda, Sardinia, Newton Pub. Libr., Beverly Pub. Libr., Am. Coll., Athens, Greece, Morse Inst. Library, Natick, Mass., Newton Public Library, Mass., Ctrl. Sch., Longmeadow, MA.; also residences in US, France, Switzerland, housing projects in New Eng. Served with AUS, 1946-47, 52-54. Recipient Prog. Architecture Design award, 1966, 1st place single family category Plywood Design Awards Program, 1973, award Merit, 1974 Fellow AIA (mem. nat. urban planning design com. 1975, citation, hon. mentions 1969, 1st honor award 1970, honor award New Eng. Regional Council 1976); mem. Mass. Assn. Architects (exec. com.), Boston Soc. Architects (dir., v.p. 1981-82, pres. 1982-83, award 1998), Am. Inst. Planners, Am. Planning Assn., Am. Inst. Cons. Planners, Ecoles D'Art Americanes Fontainebleau (trustee 2003), Harvard Travelers

Club. Clubs: Union Boat (Boston), Eastern Point Yacht (Gloucester, Mass.), Harvard Club (Boston), Bass Rocks Golf Club (Gloucester, Mass.). Office: Tappe Assocs Inc 6 Edgerly Pl Boston MA 02116-5327 Business E-Mail: aatappe@tappe.com.

TAPPONNIER, PAUL, physics professor; Prof. Tectonics Dept. Inst. de Physique du Globe, Paris, dir. Tectonics Dept.; vis. scientist Jet Propulsion Lab. Calif. Tech. Inst., Pasadena, Calif., 1985—. Recipient Knight Legion Honour, France, 1991. Mem.: NAS (corr. 1994, fgn. assoc. 2005). Office: c/o Inst de Physique du Globe 4 place jussieu Case 89 75252 Paris France

TAPSCOTT, WILLIAM KEN, JR., lawyer; b. Anderson, Ind., Feb. 1, 1970; BS/BA, U. Ala., Huntsville, 1992; JD, U. Miami, 1995. Bar: Ala. 1995, Ind. 1997, Tex. 1997, US Dist. Ct. (mid. dist. Ala.), US Dist. Ct. (no. and so. dists. Ind.), US Dist. Ct. (no. dist. Tex.). With Office Hearings and Appeals Social Security Adminstrn.; atty. Baron & Budd, P.C., Dallas, 1997—. Named a Rising Star, Tex. Super Lawyers mag., 2006. Mem.: Ind. State Bar Assn. Office: Baron & Budd PC 3102 Oak Lawn Ave Ste 1100 Dallas TX 75219 Office Phone: 214-521-3605. E-mail: ktapscot@baronbudd.com. *

TAQUETI, VIVIANY R., immunologist; b. Vila Velha, Espirito Santo, Brazil, Aug. 19, 1981; arrived in US, 1989, naturalized, 2004; d. Claudemiro and Izaura Rodrigues Taqueti. AB in Biochem. Scis. summa cum laude, Harvard U., Cambridge, 2002; MD magna cum laude, Harvard Med. Sch., 2007. Tchg. fellow, dept. chemistry & chem. biology Harvard U., 2001—02; internship New Eng. Jour. Medicine, Boston, 2002; Howard Hughes rsch. fellow, dept. patholgoy & vascular biolgoy Brigham & Women's Hosp., Boston, 2003—05; tchg. fellow cellular & molecular immunology, MIT divsn. health scis. & tech. Harvard Med. Sch., 2004—05, tchg. fellow neurobiology of disease, dept. neurosci., 2004—05; Albert Schweitzer fellow Family Van Nonprofit Mobile Health Ctr., 2004—05; resident internal medicine Mass. Gen. Hosp., Boston, 2007—. Co-author (textbook) Review of Immunology; contbr. articles to profl. jours. Vol. clin. interpreter Esperanca Found., Santarem, Brazil, 2001; clin. vol. Gorongosa Nat. Pk. Restoration Project, The Carr Found., Mozambique, 2007—. Recipient Derek Bok Tchg. award, Harvard U., 2002, 45th Internat. Achievement Summit award, Acad. Achievement, 2006; fellow New Ams. fellowship, Paul & Daisy Soros, 2005. Mem.: Am. Assn. Immunologists, Am. Heart Assn., Mass. Med. Soc., Aesculapian Club, Phi Beta Kappa. Business E-Mail: taqueti@post.harvard.edu.

TARAGIN, DAVIRA SPIRO, curator; d. Herman Frank and Edith Mae Spiro; m. Marvin Maynard Taragin, June 22, 1975; 1 child, Charles Steven. BA, Barnard Coll., NYC, 1973; MA, George Wash. U., Washington, 1975. Curator ednl. svcs. and grant rsch. Fayetteville Mus. Art, NC, 1976—77; curator, edn. coord. Mich. Artrain, Detroit, 1977—78; various positions ranging from rsch. assoc. to curator of 20th-century decorative arts and design Detroit Inst. Arts, Detroit, 1978—90; curator 19th and 20th-century glass Toledo Mus. Art, 1990—2002, dir. Ctr. for Glass, 2001—02; dir. exhbns. and programs Racine Art Mus., Wis. Adviser Assn. Israel's Decorative Arts, NYC, 2003—; contbr. to Web site Dale Chihuly Studio, Seattle, 2004—; mem. curatorial adv. panel New Art Forms Internat. Expn., Chgo., 1988—90. Exhbn. and publ., Design in America: The Cranbrook Vision 1925-1950 (Charles F. Montgomery prize, 1983), Contemporary Crafts and the Saxe Collection (Hon. Mention, AAM Publs. award, 1993), Furniture by Wendell Castle, The Alliance of Art and Industry: Toledo Designs for a Modern America (Hon. Mention, AAM Publs. award, 2002), Women's Tales: Four Leading Israeli Jewelers, 2006, exhbn. and brochure, Material Response: Michael James at RAM, 2006, exhbn. and catalog, Automobile and Culture-Detroit Style, 1985, Art to Art: Paley, Dine, Statom Respond to Toledo's Treasures, 1996, Contemporary Directions: The William and Maxine Block Collection, 2002—03, The Artist Responds: Albert Paley and Art Nouveau, 2004, Introducing RAM: Its Building and Collections, 2003, exhbn., Drawing Out The Collection: John McQueen Responds to RAM, 2004. Bd. dirs. Toledo Modern Art Group, 1992—2000. Recipient Legal Issues in Mus. Adminstrn. scholarship, ALI-ABA, 2004, David Lloyd Kreeger award Hon. Mention, 1975, Internat. Partnership Among Museums grant, administered by Am. Assn. of Museums and funded by Dept. of State's Bur. of Ednl. and Cultural Affairs, 2003—05; grantee, Ctr. for Craft, Creativity and Design, U. NC, 2005—08. Mem.: Friends of Fiber Art, Soc. of North Am. Goldsmiths, Glass Art Soc. Office: Racine Art Mus PO Box 187 441 Main St Racine WI 53403 Office Phone: 262-638-8300. Office Fax: 262-898-1045. Business E-Mail: dtaragin@ramart.org.

TARAN, LEONARDO, classicist, educator; b. Galarza, Argentina, Feb. 22, 1933; came to U.S., 1958, naturalized, 1976; s. Miguel and Liuba Taran; m. Judit Sofia Lida, Dec. 10, 1971; 1 child, Gabriel Andrew. Legal degree, U. Buenos Aires, 1958; PhD in Classics, Princeton U., 1962. Jr. fellow Inst. Rsch. in Humanities, U. Wis., 1962-63, Ctr. Hellenic Studies, Washington, 1963-64; asst. prof. classics U. Calif., LA, 1964-67; mem. faculty Columbia U., NYC, 1967—, prof. Greek and Latin, 1971—, Jay prof. Greek and Latin, 1987—, chmn. dept., 1976-79; emeritus, 2004. Mem. Inst. Advanced Study, Princeton, N.J., 1966-67, 78-79; trustee Assn. Mems. Inst. Advanced Study, 1974-79; mem. mng. com. Am. Sch. Classical Studies, 1976-. Author: Parmenides, 1965, Asclepius of Tralles, Commentary to Nicomachus' Introduction to Arithmetic, 1969, Plato, Philip of Opus and the Pseudo-Platonic Epinomis, 1975, Anonymous Commentary on Aristotle's De Interpretatione, 1978, Speusippus of Athens, 1981, Collected Papers (1962-1999), 2001; co-author: Eraclito: Testimonianze e imitazioni, 1972; mem. editl. bd.: Columbia Studies in the Classical Tradition, 1976-80. Am. Coun. Learned Socs. fellow, 1966-67, 71-72, Guggenheim Found. fellow, 1975, NEH fellow, 1986-87; grantee Am. Philos. Soc., 1963, 71, 75, Am. Coun. Learned Socs., 1968, 72, NEH, 1985-87, 88-89. Mem. Am. Philol. Assn., Classical Assn. Atlantic States, Soc. Ancient Greek Philosophy, Assn. Guillaume Bude. Home: 39 Claremont Ave New York NY 10027-6802 Office: Columbia U 615 Hamilton Hall New York NY 10027 Business E-Mail: lt1@columbia.edu.

TARANIK, JAMES VLADIMIR, geologist, educator; b. LA, Apr. 23, 1940; s. Vladimir James and Jeanette Downing (Smith) T.; m. Colleen Sue Glessner, Dec. 4, 1971; children: Debra Lynn, Danny Lee. BSc in Geology, Stanford U., 1964; PhD, Colo. Sch. Mines, 1974. Chief remote sensing Iowa Geol. Survey, Iowa City, 1971-74; prin. remote sensing scientist Earth Resources Observation Systems Data Ctr., U.S. Geol. Survey, Sioux Falls, SD, 1975-79; chief non-renewable resources br., resource observation div. Office of Space and Terrestrial Applications, NASA Hdqrs., Washington, 1979-82; dean mines Mackay Sch. Mines U. Nev., Reno, 1982-87, prof. geology and geophysics, 1982—98, Arthur Brant chair of geophysics, 1998—; pres. Desert Rsch. Inst., Univ. and C.C. Sys. Nev., 1987-98, Regents's prof. and pres. emeritus, 1998—; adj. prof. geology U. Iowa, 1971-79; vis. prof. civil engring. Iowa State U., 1972-74; adj. prof. earth sci. U. S.D., 1976-79; scientist HQ program space shuttle OSTA-1 Payload on STS-2 NASA, 1981—82, large format camera expt. for heat capacity mapping mission and for magnetic field satellite mission; liaison, 1981—82; dir. NOAA Coop. Inst. Aerospace Sci. & Terrestrial Applications, 1986-94; program dir. NASA Space Grant consortium Univ. and C.C. Sys. Nev., Reno, 1991—2005, dir. NASA EPSCOR program, 1998—2005; bd. dirs. NASA Challenger Learning Ctr., Reno, 2006—; dir. Great Basin Ctr. Geothermal Energy, 2000—03; acting dean Mackay Sch. Mines, 2003; dir. Mackay Sch. Earth Sci. and Engring., U. Nev, 2004—. Team mem. Shuttle Imaging Radar-B Sci. Team NASA, 1983-88, NASA space applications adv. com., 1986-88; chmn. remote sensing subcom. SAAC, 1986-88; chmn. working group on civil space commercialization Dept. Commerce, 1982-84, mem. civil operational remote sensing satellite com., 1983-84; bd. dir. Newmont Mining Corp., 1986-; adv. com. NASA Space Sci. and Applications Com., 1988-90, Nat. Def. Exec. Res., 1986-94, AF studies bd., com. on strategic relocatable targets, 1989-91; pre-launch rev. bd., NASA, Space Radar Lab., 1993-94; fed. lab. rev. task force, NASA, 1994-96; prin. investigator Japanese Earth Resources Satellite, 1991-94; environ. task force MEDEA, Mitre Corp., McLean, Va., 1993-98; mapping scis. com. Nat. Rsch. Coun., 2001-04; cons. Jet Propulsion Lab., Calif., Hughes Aircraft Corp., Lockheed-Marietta Corp., Mitre Corp., TRW; developer remote sensing program and remote sensing lab. State of Iowa, ednl. program in remote sensing Iowa univs. and U. Nev., Reno; program scientist 2d space shuttle flight Office Space and Terrestrial Applications Program; mem. terrestrial geol. applications program NASA, 1981-82; co-investigator Can. Radarsat Program, 1995-97; mem. geol. scis. bd., NAS. Contbr. articles to profl. jours. Bd. dirs. Mountain States Legal Found., 2000—, sec., 2006—, Northwest Mining Assn., 2006—. Served with C.E. U.S. Army, 1965-67; mil. intellegence officer Res. Decorated Bronze Star medal; recipient Spl. Achievement award U.S. Geol. Survey, 1978, Exceptional Sci. Achievement medal NASA, 1982, NASA Group Achievement award Shuttle imaging radar, 1990, NASA Johnson Space Ctr. Group Achievement award for large format camera, 1985; NASA prin. investigator, 1973, 83-88, prin. investigator French Spot-1 Program to Evaluate Spot 1986-88; NDEA fellow, 1968-71. Fellow: AAAS, AIAA (assoc.), Am. Soc. Photogrammetry Remote Sensing, Explorers Club, Geol. Soc. Am.; mem.: IEEE (sr.), N.W. Mining Assn. (trustee 2005—), Mining and Metall. Soc. Am., Soc. Econ. Geologists, Am. Geol. Inst. Found. (trustee 1999—), Am. Astron. Soc. (sr.), Am. Inst. Metall. Engrs., Soc. Mining Engrs. Am. (gen. chmn. ednl. sustainability task force 2005—), Am. Assn. Petroleum Geologists (chmn. rsch. com. 2000—), Am. Geophys. Union, Soc. Exploration Geophysicists, Internat. Acad. Astronautics, Bohemian Club San Francisco. Home: PO Box 7175 Reno NV 89510-7175 Office Phone: 775-682-8735. Business E-Mail: jtaranik@mines.unr.edu. *I have always been in awe of the universe in which we live and the little time we have on earth to perceive and understand it.*

TARANTA, ANGELO (VISCA TARANTA), physician, educator; b. Rome, 1927; came to U.S., 1952, naturalized, 1956; MD, U. Rome, 1949. Diplomate Am. Bd. Internal Medicine, also sub-bd. Rheumatology. Intern, dept. internal medicine and pediatrics Univ. Hosp., Rome, 1949-50, resident, 1950-52; resident in medicine St. Mary's Hosp., Rochester, NY, 1952-53; resident in cardiology Irvington (N.Y.) House, 1953-54, research assoc., 1955-59, research dir., 1959-62; assoc. dir. Irvington House Inst., NYC, 1965-71; research fellow in microbiology NYU Sch. Medicine, 1955-56, instr. in microbiology, 1955-58, adj. asst. prof. microbiology, 1958-60, asst. prof. medicine, 1960-65, assoc. prof., 1965-75, on leave of absence, 1975-79; dir. medicine Cabrini Health Care Ctr., NYC, 1973-93; prof. medicine, chief rheumatology and immunology div. N.Y. Med. Coll., 1979-85, chief div. humanities and ethics, 1985-88. Co-chmn. study group on heart disease in the young Inter-Soc. Commn. on Heart Disease Resources, 1972-78; bd. dirs. Am. Heart Assn., 1975-77; chmn. Council on Cardiovascular Disease in the Young, 1975-77; cons. in field. Author: (with M. Markowitz) Rheumatic Fever; editor (with E. Kaplan) Infectious Endocarditis; contbr. numerous articles to profl. publs. and textbooks. Fulbright travel grantee, 1952; recipient Terence Cardinal Cooke medal N.Y. Med. Coll., 1985. Master Am. Coll. Rheumatology; mem. Soc. Clin. Investigation, Am. Assn. Immunologists, N.Y. Acad. Medicine (chmn. sect. medicine 1980-87), Italian Rheumatology Soc. (hon.), Argentine Rheumatology Soc. (hon.). E-mail: angelissimo27@hotmail.com.

TARANTINO, DAVID A., JR., military officer, emergency physician; b. Dec. 17, 1965; MD, Georgetown U., 1992. Surgeon Office Peace Keeping and Humanitarian Affairs, US Dept. Def., Washington; program dir. Civil, Military and Contingency Med. Affairs, Office Asst. Sec. Def. (Health Affairs). Lt. comdr. USN. Decorated medal Navy/Marine Corps; named regional finalist, White House Fellows Program, 2003—04; recipient Washingtonian Yr. award, Washingtonian Mag., 2001, Humanitarian Svc. medal, 2001, Medal Valor, AMA, 2003.

TARANTINO, DOMINIC A., retired professional services firm executive; b. San Francisco, Aug. 1, 1932; m. Leona Lazzareschi, July 24, 1954; children: John Robert, Stephen, Leanne. BS, U. San Francisco, 1954. With Price Waterhouse, 1957-98, mem. policy bd. and mgmt. com., 1979-93, vice chmn. tax svcs., 1982-88, co-chmn. bd., mng. ptnr., 1988-93; chmn. Price Waterhouse World Firm, 1995-98; ret., 1998. Mem. IRS Commr.'s Adv. Group, 1978. Trustee U. San Francisco, 1996—2005, chair bd. trustees, 1999—2003, chair Capital Campaign, 2001—07, chair bd. trustees emeritus, 2005—; treas., bd. dirs. Bus. Opportunities for Leadership Diversity, 1988—. Recipient Delta Sigma Pi Career Achievement award, 1997. Mem. AICPA (bd. dirs. 1988-95, vice chair 1992-3, chmn. 1993-94, Dixon Meml. award 1990, Gold medal for disting. svc. 2000). Address: 549 Indian Field Rd Mead Point Greenwich CT 06830

TARANTINO, LOUIS GERALD, lawyer, management consultant; b. Bridgeport, Conn., Sept. 7, 1934; s. Louis Gerald and Mary Louise (Boyle) T. BA, U. Pa., 1955, LLB, 1958. Bar: Conn. 1958, N.Y. 1960. Assoc. Beekman & Bogue, 1959—67, ptnr., 1968—76; pres., bd. dirs. Berkeley Mgmt. Assocs., Inc., Boston, 1994—2003. Mem. enterprise adv. bd. Photonics Ctr., Boston U., 1999-2004; bd. dirs. Midnight Trader, Inc., Bethesda, Md., Celsene., Inc., Pitts. Mem. Bar Assn. City N.Y., N.Y. Bar Assn., Conn. Bar Assn., Huguenot Soc. Pa., St. Anthony Hall, Knickerbocker Club, India House N.Y.C., St. Anthony Club Phila. Home: One Devonshire Pl Apt PH309 Boston MA 02109

TARANTINO, QUENTIN JEROME, film director, scriptwriter; b. Knoxville, Tenn., Mar. 27, 1963; s. Tony and Connie Tarantino. Co-founder (with Lawrence Baker) A Band Apart Records. Actor: (films) My Best Friend's Birthday, 1987, Eddie Presley, 1993, (voice) The Coriolis Effect, 1994, Sleep With Me, 1994, Somebody to Love, 1994, Destiny Turns on the Radio, 1995, The Anatomy of Horror, 1995, Desperado, 1995, Girl 6, 1996, Steven Spielberg's Director's Chair, 1996, Full Tilt Boogie, 1997, Little Nicky, 2000, Planet of the Pits, 2004, Epreuves d'artistes, 2004; actor, writer & prodr.: From Dusk Till Dawn, 1996, writer (story): Natural Born Killers, 1994, writer & dir.: CSI: Crime Scene Investigation, Episode 5.23, 2003, writer, dir. & prodr.: Kill Bill: Vol. 1, 2003, Kill Bill: Vol. 2, 2004, actor, writer & dir.: Reservoir Dogs, 1992, Pulp Fiction, 1994, actor (voice), writer & dir.: Jackie Brown, 1997, writer & prodr.: Curdled, 1996, actor, writer, prodr. & dir.: (with Alexandre Rockwell, Robert Rodriguez & Allison Anders) Four Rooms, 1995, Grindhouse, 2007; exec. prodr.: God Said, 'Ha!'', 1998, From Dusk Till Dawn 2: Tex. Blood Money, 1999, From Dusk Till Dawn 3: The Hangman's Daughter, 2000; exec. prodr.: Hostel, 2005, Daltry Calhoun, 2005, Freedom's Fury, 2006; prodr.: Siunin Wong Fei-hung tsi titmalau (aka Iron Monkey), 1993, released 2001; TV appearances Golden Girls, 1998, 1990, All-American Girl, The Muppets' Wonderful Wizard of Oz, 2005; dir.: (TV series) ER, episode 'Motherhood', 1994, Jimmy Kimmel Live, episode 5/18/2004. Named one of Time Mag. 100 Most Influential People, 2005; recipient Building Bridges award, Asian Excellence Awards, 2006. Home: 8439 W Sunset Blvd West Hollywood CA 90069-1921 *

TARANTO, BARBARA, library director; Dig. libr. systems coord. NY Pub. Libr., NYC, dir. digital libr. program, 2001—. Mem. Coalition for Networked Info., DLF Developers Forum, Metro. Libr. Assn. Info. Sys. Adv. Council. Office: NY Public Library 5th Ave and 42nd St New York NY 10018

TARAS, PAUL, physicist, researcher; b. Tunis, Tunisia, May 12, 1941; emigrated to Can., 1957, naturalized, 1962; s. Wladimir and Benita (Koort) T.; m. Marja-Leena Malinen, Aug. 3, 1963; children— Lisa Helene, Michele Anne. BASc., U. Toronto, 1962, MA, 1963, PhD, 1965. Asst. prof. physics U. Montreal, Que., Canada, 1965-70, assoc. prof., 1970-76, prof., 1976—. Spokesman U. Montreal in rsch. projects. Helios, SDC, Babar. Rsch. on nuclear and particle physics; co-managed conception and constrn. of 8pi Spectrometer, Chalk River Nuclear Labs, 1984-86; contbr. articles to profl. jours.; presenter papers to profl. confs. U. Toronto, Province of Ont., U.K. Atomic Energy Authority fellowships; France-Que., NRC, Natural Scis. and Engring. Research Council Can. grantee. Mem. Am. Phys. Soc., Can. Assn. Physicists, Soc. Galilée (mem. exec. bd.), Babar Collaboration (bd. dirs.). Home: 1639 Norway Rd Montreal PQ Canada H4P 1Y3 Office: U Montreal Groupe Physique des Particules Montreal PQ Canada H3C 3J7 Home Phone: 514-735-8392. Business E-Mail: taras@lps.umontreal.ca.

TARASI, LOUIS MICHAEL, JR., lawyer; b. Cheswick, Pa., Sept. 9, 1931; s. Louis Michael and Ruth Elizabeth (Records) T.; m. Patricia Ruth Finley, June 19, 1954; children: Susan, Louis Michael III, Elizabeth, Brian, Patricia, Matthew. BA, Miami U., Ohio, 1954; JD, U. Pa., 1959. Bar: Pa. 1960, U.S. Dist. Ct. (we. dist.) Pa. 1960, U.S. Ct. Appeals (3d cir.) 1964, U.S. Supreme Ct. 1969, U.S. Dist. Ct. (we. dist.) Tex. 1988, U.S. Ct. Appeals (5th cir.) 1989, U.S. Ct. Appeals (4th cir.) 1994, U.S. Ct. Fed. Claims 1987, U.S. Dist. Ct. Colo. 1998; cert. civil trial adv. Nat. Bd. Trial Advocacy. Assoc., owner Burgwin, Ruffin, Perry & Pohl, Pitts., 1960-68; ptnr. Conte, Courtney & Tarasi, Beaver County, Pa., 1968-78, Tarasi & Tighe, Pitts., 1978-82, Tarasi & Johnson, P.C., Pitts., 1982-95, Tarasi & Assocs., P.C., Pitts., 1995-99, The Tarasi Lawfirm, P.C., Pitts., 1997-2001, Tarasi & Tarasi, P.C., Pitts., 2001—. Mem. parish coun. St. James Ch., Sewickley, Pa.; active Sewickley Borough Allegheny Coun., 1978-1982. With U.S. Army, 1954-56. Fellow: Internat. Soc. Barristers; mem.: Am. Coll. Barristers (sr. counsel), Am. Bd. Trial Advs., Melvin Belli Soc., St. Thomas More Soc. (award 1991), West Pa. Trial Lawyers Assn. (pres. 1975), Pa. Bar Assn., Allegheny County Bar Assn., Acad. Trial Lawyers Allegheny County, Pa. Trial Lawyers Assn. (pres. 1979—80), Assn. Trial Lawyers Am. (gov., rep.). Democrat. Roman Catholic. Avocations: reading, golf, lecturing. Home: 1 Way Hollow Rd Sewickley PA 15143-1192 Office: Tarasi & Tarasi PC 510 3d Ave Pittsburgh PA 15219-2107 Home Phone: 412-741-8534; Office Phone: 412-391-7135. Business E-Mail: lmt@tarasilaw.com.

TARAVELLA, CHRISTOPHER ANTHONY, lawyer; b. Pueblo, Colo., Sept. 19, 1951; s. Frank Louis and Ann Jean T.; m. Kathleen; children: Nicholas M., John L. BS in Engring. Mechanics, USAF Acad., 1973; JD, U. Colo., 1976; postgrad., Harvard U., 1996. Bar: Iowa 1976, Colo. 1976, U.S. Ct. Mil. Appeals 1976, U.S. Dist. Ct. Colo. 1976, Fla. 1977, U.S. Supreme Ct. 1982, U.S. Ct. Appeals (fed. cir.) 1983, D.C. 1984, U.S. Claims Ct. 1984, Mich. 1985. Commd. 2nd lt. USAF, 1973, legal intern Staff Judge Adv. Lowry AF Base, Denver, 1973-76, advanced through grades to lt. col. Hurlburt Field, Fla., 1976-78, asst. staff judge adv. Zaragoza, Spain, 1978-81, chief cir. trial counsel Washington, 1981-83; chief Constitutional Torts Br. Civil Litigation, Washington, 1983-85; resigned USAF, 1985; asst. gen. counsel Chrysler Motors Corp., Highland Park, Mich., 1985-90; asst. gen. counsel comml. affairs, chief patent counsel Chrysler Corp., Auburn Hills, Mich., 1990-96; v.p., gen. counsel Daimler Chrysler Svcs. N.Am. LLC, Southfield, Mich., 1997—. Mem. governing com. Conf. on Consumer Fin. Law; bd. dirs. Rte. One. Staff Judge Adv. USAFR, 927 Air Refueling Group, Selfridge Air NG Base, Mich., 1985-94. Mem. Am. Fin. Svcs. Assn. (bd. dirs.). Office: Daimler Chrysler Svcs N Am LLC CIMS 405-27-16 27777 Inkster Rd Farmington Hills MI 48334 Office Phone: 248-427-2577. Business E-Mail: cat8@daimlerchrysler.com.

TARBELL, MARK, chef; Degree in Culinary Arts, La Varenne, Paris; studied, l'Academie du Vin, Paris. Chef Boulders Resort, Carefree, Ariz.; owner, exec. chef Tarbell's, Phoenix, 1994—, Barmouche; mng. ptnr. The Oven, Lakewood, Colo. Tchr. Food & Wine Aspen Classic, Greenbrier Cooking Sch. Columnist Ariz. Rep., published in Wine & Spirits, Food Arts, appearances on Good Morning Am., Today Show, contrib. author Chris Carmichael's Fitness Cookbook. Bd. mem. Ariz. Dept. Edn., Phoenix Theatre; judge LA County Fair Wine Competition. Nominee Best Chef: Southwest, James Beard Found., 2001; recipient Best Restaurant award, Food & Wine mag. Mem.: Internat. Assn. Culinary Professionals (bd. mem. culinary trust). Achievements include cooking for various high profile celebrities and world leaders such as the Dalai Lama. Office: Tarbells 3213 E Camelback Phoenix AZ 85018 *

TARBI, WILLIAM RHEINLANDER, secondary education curriculum consultant, researcher; b. San Bernardino, Calif., Feb. 23, 1949; s. William Metro and Sue (Rheinlander) T.; m. Jenny Workman, Apr. 10, 1980 (div. 1985); m. Michele Hastings, July 4, 1990; children: Amy, Melissa. AA, Santa Barbara City Coll., 1969; BA in History, U. Calif., Santa Barbara, 1976; MA, U. Redlands, 1992. Cert. secondary edn. social studies tchr., Calif. Reporter AP, Santa Barbara, Calif., 1976-80, UPI, Seattle, 1980-85, Golden West Radio Network, Seattle, 1980-85; tchr. Redlands (Calif.) Unified Sch. Dist., 1986—. Cons. IMCOM, Redlands, 1985—. Mem. E Clampus Vitus, Phi Delta Kappa. Avocations: painting, photography, writing, gardening, fencing.

TARBUTTON, LLOYD T., hotel executive, consultant; Dr Comml. Sci. in Mktg., Pacific Western U. Grad. Realtors Inst.; cert. franchise exec., La. State U., cert. hotel adminstr. Divsn. sales mgr. Reuben H. Donnelley Corp. (advt. agy.), Norfolk, Va., 1953-58; chmn. bd., dir. Tarbutton Assocs., Inc., Norfolk, 1962—; founder, dir., pres., chmn. bd. Econo Lodges of Am., Norfolk, 1967-83; chmn. bd. emeritus Econo Lodges of Am. (formerly Econ-Travel Motor Hotel Corp.), Norfolk, 1983—. Co-founder, chief judge Franchising Hall of Fame, Washington, 1979-82; co-founder, chmn. Coun. Franchise Suppliers, Washington, 1986-88. Author: Franchising--The How To Book, 1986. Trustee Edn. Found. Old Dominion U., 1979-86, chmn. bd. trustees Ctr. Econ. Edn., Old Dominion U., 1983-84. Recipient Hon. Tchr. award Maury High Sch., Norfolk, 1959. Mem. Internat. Franchise Assn. (hon. life, chmn. bd. dirs., chmn. 1st Asian Symposium on Franchising, Tokyo 1978, 1st European Symposium on Franchising, Amsterdam 1978, 1st So. Pacific Symposium on Franchising, Jakarta 1991), 1st Ea. Europe Franchise Symposiums (Varna, Bulgaria, 2000, inducted into Franchise Hall of Fame 2000), Internat. Coun. Hotel/Motel Mgmt., Realtor's Inst. Norfolk (chmn. 1965), Internat. Sales Execs. Club (Distinguished Sales award 1957), Internat. Platform Assn., Airplane Owners and Pilots Assn., Cavalier Golf and Yacht Club, Town Point Club, Registry Resort Tennis Club, The Club at Pelican Bay. Presbyterian. *I believe the greatest assist to my progress in business and personal life came when I became more aware of the "value of self" and thus others.*

TARDE, JERRY (GERARD TARDE), editor-in-chief; married; 2 children. Grad., Northwestern U. Sch. Journalism, 1978. Asst. editor Golf Digest, assoc. editor, 1979—82, sr. editor, 1982—84, editor, 1984—90; v.p. NY Times Mag. Group, 1990, editl. dir., 1998; editor-in-chief Golf Digest; chmn., editl. dir. Golf Digest Publs., Wilton, Conn., 2000—. Office: Golf Digest 20 Westport Rd Box 850 Wilton CT 06897 Office Phone: 203-761-5225. *

TARDIF, DONNA LYNN, elementary school educator; BS in Elem. Edn., Univ. Maine, Farmington, 1990; MS in Curriculum, Va. Commonwealth Univ.; cert. of Adv. Study in Literacy, Univ. So. Maine. Tchr., 1992—,

Montello Elem. Sch., Lewiston, Maine, 2001—. Named Maine Tchr. of Yr., 2006. Office: Montello Elem Sch 407 East Ave Lewiston ME 04240 E-mail: dtardif@lewnet.avcnet.org. *

TARDIFF, JILL ALEXANDRIA, publishing executive, photographer; b. Morristown, NJ, Apr. 8, 1953; d. Howard James Tardiff and Jean Elizabeth Cook; m. Paul Edward Kozlowski, Feb. 11, 1984. BA in liberal arts, Coll. St. Elizabeth, 1975. Cert. teacher, K-12 NJ, 1975. Mgr. retail Hallmark Cards Inc./Flagship, NYC, 1976—81; mgr./gen. mgr. Doubleday Book Shops/Flagship, NYC, 1981—91; sales mgr./dir. of sales Tiffany & Co., NYC, 1991—93; entrepreneur, self-propr. Bamboo River Assocs., Hoboken, NJ, 1993—; mng. editor/sr. rschr. Lintel Press, NYC, 1993—94; assoc. editor BookWire Online, NYC, 1995—98; contbg. editor/project mgr. Pubs. Weekly, NYC, 1996—; mgr. advt. Persimmon, Asian Lit., Arts, and Culture Mag., NYC, 1999—2002. Profl. spkr./tour facilitator Bamboo River Associates, Hoboken, 1991—; sec./bd. dirs. Contemporary Asian Culture Inc., NYC, 1999—; adv. bd. mem. Women's Ink., NYC, 1999—2004. Contbr. book Bob Vila's Guide to Historic Homes Series; reporter Shinbunka Weekly, Tokyo, 1995—2000. Mem.: AAUW (assoc.), Internat. Women's Writing Guild (hon.), N.Y. Women in Comm. (assoc.), Women's Nat. Book Assn. (assoc.; main rep. UN DPI/NGO 2000—, nat. v.p., pres. elect 2002—04, nat. pres. 2004—06), Women's Nat. Book Assn. (assoc.; newsletter editor/v.p. N.Y.C. chpt. 1997—2000, pres. N.Y.C. chpt. 2000—, immediate past nat. pres. 2006—), Editl. Freelancers Assn. (assoc.), Diev Donné Papermill (assoc.), Japan Soc. (assoc.), Asia Soc. N.Y. (assoc.). Avocations: travel, photography, gardening, architecture, paper making. Office: Bamboo River Associates 625 Madison StSte 2 Hoboken NJ 07030-6305 Personal E-mail: jat-bambooriver@worldnet.att.net.

TARDIO, THOMAS A., public relations executive; V.p. strategic planning and other positions Columbia Pictures Industries, 1979-88; CFO, v.p. adminstrn. Rogers & Cowan, Inc., LA, 1988-89, exec. v.p. entertainment sect., 1989-91, pres., 1991-95; CEO Rogers & Cowan, LA, 1995—; pres. Shandwick, United States, LA, 1998—2000. Mem. IBM mobile computing mktg. adv. bd. Mem. bd. visitors adv. bd. Loyola Law Sch. Mem. Pub. Rels. Soc. Am., Nat. Acad. Recording Arts and Scis., Pub. Communicators L.A., Contry Music Assn. Office: Rogers & Cowan 8687 Melrose Ave 7th Fl Los Angeles CA 90069

TARDOS, EVA, computer scientist, educator; Dipl.Math., Eötvös U., Budapest, Hungary, 1981, PhD, 1984. Mem. faculty to prof., chair dept. computer sci. Cornell U., Ithaca, NY, 1989—. Contbr. articles to profl. jours.; mem. editl. bd.: Jour. Assn. Computing Machinery; co-author: Algorithm Design, 2005. Recipient Fulkerson prize, Math. Programming Soc., 1988, Dantzig prize, 2006. Fellow: Assn. Computing Machinery; mem.: Am. Acad. Arts & Scis., NAE. Office: Dept Computer Sci Cornell U 4130 Upson Hall Ithaca NY 14853 Office Phone: 607-255-0984. Office Fax: 607-255-4428. E-mail: eva@cs.cornell.edu. *

TAREN, JAMES ARTHUR, neurosurgeon, educator; b. Toledo, Nov. 10, 1924; s. Joseph Clarence and Mary Frances (Walker) T. BS, U. Toledo, 1948; MD, U. Mich., 1952. Diplomate Am. Bd. Neurosurgery. Intern U. Mich. Hosp., Ann Arbor, 1952-53, resident in surgery, 1953-54, resident neurosurgery, 1955-57; clin. instr. U. Mich. Med. Sch., Ann Arbor, 1955-57, instr. neurosurgery, 1957-58, asst. prof., 1958-63, assoc. prof., 1963-67, prof. neurosurgery, 1967—, dir. neurobehavioral sci. program, 1975-78, assoc. dean acad. programs, 1978-87, dir. Brain Tumor Lab., 1985-88; dir. Integrated Acad. Info. Mgmt., 1988-89; dir. neuromodulation program U. Mich. Med. Sch., Ann Arbor, 1994-97. Neurosurgeon Wayne County Gen. Hosp., Eloise, Mich., 1957-71, VA Hosp., Ann Arbor, 1957-73, U.S.S. Hope (Project Hope), Peru, 1962, Ecuador, 1963, Guinea, 1965; vis. prof. Hosp. Foch, Paris, 1966-67, St. Anne Hosp., Paris, 1981, Karolinski Inst., Stockholm, 1981, Haukland Sykehus, Bergen, Norway, 1984, Gumma U., Japan, 1989, Nihon U. Sch. Medicine, Tokyo, 1990. Author, co-editor: Correlative Neurosurgery, 1969, 3rd edit., 1982; contbr. articles to profl. jours. Dep. med. examiner Washtenaw County Dept. Health, Ann Arbor, 1962-90; pres. Hawaii Youth New Leadership Forum, 2000. Active U.S. Armed Forces, 1943-46, PTO. Fellow NIH, 1953; rsch. fellow in neurosurgery Boston Children's Hosp., Peter Bent Brigham Hosp., Boston, 1955. Fellow ACS; mem. AMA, Congress of Neuro. Surgeons, Am. Assn. Neuro. Surgery, Am. Assn. Med. Colls., Am. Soc. for Stereotactic and Functional Neurosurgery, Am. Neuromodulation Soc. (treas. 1994-98, v.p. 1998-99), Royal Soc. Medicine (affiliate), Brit. Med. Soc., Internat. Assn. Study of Pain, Ferrari Club Am. Personal E-mail: jtaren@ilhawaii.net.

TARGOFF, MICHAEL BART, space and communications company executive; b. NYC, July 20, 1944; s. Jerome H. and Tillie R. T.; m. Cheri Kamen, June 11, 1966; children: Ramie, Joshua, Jason, Hannah. AB, Brown U., 1966; JD cum laude, Columbia U., 1969. Bar: N.Y. 1969. Law clk. to presiding justice U.S. Dist. Ct. Mass., 1969-70; assoc. Willkie, Farr & Gallagher, NYC, 1970-76; ptnr. Willkie, Fair & Gallagher, NYC, 1976-80; gen. counsel, v.p. Savin Corp., Valhalla, NY, 1980-81; gen. counsel, sr. v.p., sec. Loral Corp., NYC, 1981-92, sr. v.p., 1992—96, also sec.; pres, COO Loral Space and Communications, 1996—98; founder Michael B. Targoff & Co.; vice chmn. Loral Space and Communications, 2005—06, CEO, 2006—. Bd. dirs. Leap Wireless, 1998—, Globalstar Telecommunications Ltd., Infocrossing, Inc., 2001—06, Booksfree.com, ViaSat Inc., 2003—. Harlan Fiske Stone scholar, 1968-69. Mem. ABA, N.Y. State Bar Assn., Assn. of Bar of City of N.Y. Office: Loral Corp 600 3rd Ave Rm 3000A New York NY 10016-1901 Office Fax: 212-338-5662.

TARGOVNIK, SELMA E. KAPLAN, dermatologist; b. NYC, Apr. 22, 1936; d. Harry A. and Helen (Goodstein) Kaplan; m. Jerome H. Targovnik, Dec. 2, 1961; children: Nina Rebecca, Labe Eric (dec.), Diane Michelle. BA, NYU, 1957; MD, Albert Einstein Col. Medicine, 1961. Diplomate Am. Bd. Dermatology. Intern Kaiser Found. Hosp., San Francisco, 1961-62; resident in internal medicine Bellevue Hosp., NYU Med. Ctr., 1962-63, U. Colo. Med. Ctr., Denver, 1963-64; rsch. fellow, resident in dermatology Boston U. Med. Ctr., 1964-66, mem. staff, 1968-69, NYU Med. Ctr., 1966-68, St. Joseph's Hosp., Phoenix, 1969—98, Good Samaritan Hosp., Phoenix, 1969—, Carl Hayden VA Hosp., Phoenix, 1998—. Mem. staff St. Joseph's Hosp., Phoenix, St. Luke's Hosp., Phoenix; chief divsn. dermatology Good Samaritan Hosp., Phoenix, 1985-90; adj. assoc. prof. Midwestern U. Coll. Medicine, Glendale, Ariz., 1998—; clin. assoc. prof. dermatology Kirksville Coll. Osteopathic Medicine, 2000—, clin. assoc. prof. dermatology, 1998; supr. physicians assts., med. students, residents Carl Hayden VA Hosp., Phoenix, 1998-. Bd. dirs. ACLU, Ariz., 1973-78, 83-94, Congregation Beth El, Phoenix, 1971-75, Flagstaff Festival of the Arts, 1984-86; active Jewish Nat. Fund. Fellow Am. Acad. Dermatology, Assocs. for the Weizmann Inst. Sci., Assocs. for the Technion Inst.; mem. Am. Technion Soc. (bd. dirs. 1988-92, pres. Ariz. divsn. 1990-92), Dermatology Found., Sonoran Dermatologic Soc., Southwestern Dermatologic Soc., Pacific Dermatological Soc., Noah Worcester Dermatol. Soc., Phi Beta Kappa, Mu Chi Sigma, Pi Delta Phi, Beta Lambda Sigma. Democrat. Jewish. Home: 3706 E Rancho Dr Paradise Valley AZ 85253 Office Phone: 602-628-8117. Fax: 602-667-6813. Personal E-mail: selmaderm@cox.net.

TARINO, GARY EDWARD, lawyer; b. Jersey City, Oct. 3, 1951; s. Edward G. and Veronica Tarino; m. Maureen Fitzpatrick, May 9, 1987. BA summa cum laude, Rutgers U., 1973, JD, 1976. Bar: N.J. 1976, U.S. Dist. Ct. N.J. 1976, D.C. Ct. Appeals 1978, U.S. Supreme Ct. 1980, N.Y. 1982, U.S. Dist. Ct. (so. dist.) N.Y. 1988, U.S. Dist. Ct. (ea. dist.) N.Y. 1990. Assoc. Winne, Banta, Rizzi & Harrington, Hackensack, N.J., 1976-79; asst. pros. Bergen County Pros. Office, Hackensack, 1979-83, chief organized crime squad, 1981-83; atty. Automatic Data Processing, Inc., Roseland, N.J., 1983—, assoc. gen. counsel, staff v.p., 1994—. Pub. defender Borough of Maywood, N.J., 1978; bd. dirs. N.J. Coun. Econ. Edn., 1990-2000; master Sidney Reitman Employment Law Am. Inn Ct., 1995-2000. Bd. dirs. Am. Heart Assn., N.J., 1976-81, Middlesex County (N.J.) chpt., 1973-81; trustee Integrity, Inc., 1991-97; grad. Leadership N.J., 1989; cubmaster pack III Boy Scouts Am., 2000-04; mem. oper. coun. N.J. Bus. Force, 2003—. Recipient cert. of appreciation U.S. Treasury Dept., 1983, letter of commondation PBA, 1983, Alumni Vol. Leadership award 1st Ann. Leadership N.J., 1991. Office: Automatic Data Processing 1 A D P Blvd Roseland NJ 07068-1786

TARJAN, ROBERT ENDRE, computer scientist, educator; b. Pomona, Calif., Apr. 30, 1948; s. George and Helen Emma (Blome) T.; m. Gail Maria Zawacki, Apr. 22, 1978 (div. June 1992); children: Alice Marisha, Zosia Emma Zawacki, Lily Maxine. BS in Math., Calif. Inst. Tech., 1969; MS in Computer sci., Stanford U., 1971, PhD in Computer sci., minor in Math., 1972. Asst. prof. computer sci. Cornell U., Ithaca, NY, 1972-73; Miller rsch. fellow U. Calif., Berkeley, 1973-75; asst. prof. computer sci. Stanford U., Palo Alto, Calif., 1974—77, assoc. prof. computer sci., 1977-80; mem. tech. staff AT&T Bell Labs., Murray Hill, NJ, 1980-90; adj. prof. NYU, 1981-85; James S. McDonnell Disting. U. prof. computer sci. Princeton U., NJ, 1985—. Fellow NEC Rsch. Inst., Princeton, 1989-97; co-dir. NSF Ctr. for Discrete Math. and Theoretical Computer Sci. (DIMACS) Princeton U. and Rutgers U., 1989-94, 2001-; chief scientist, InterTrust, and sr. rsch. fellow, STAR Labs, Inter Trust Technologies, Corp., Sunnyvale, Calif., 1997-2001; chief scientist Hewlett Packard, Palo, Alto, Calif., 2002-03, sr. fellow, 2003-; vis. scientist, MIT, Cambridge, Mass., 1996; corp. fellow, Compaq Computer Corp., Houston, Tex., 2002; mem. of program com. or organizing com. for confs. and symposiums; mem. Nat. Adv. Bd., Coputer Profl. for Social Responsibility, 1987-. Author: Data Structures and Network Algorithms, 1983; (with G. Polya and D. Woods) Notes on Introductory Combinatorics, 1983; editor, Princeton U. Press Series in Computer Sci., 1985—, Discrete and Computational Geometry, 1985—, others; corr. Mathematical Intelligencer, 1991—. Recipient Honorable mention, Lancaster prize, Ops. Rsch. Soc. Am., 1984, 93, Rolf Nevanlinna prize Internat. Math. Union, 1982, Blaise Pascal medal in Math. and Computer Sci., 2004; Guggenheim fellow, 1978-79. Fellow AAAS, Am. Acad. Arts and Scis., Assn. Computing Machinery (A.M. Turing award 1986, Paris Kanellakis award in Theory and Practice, 1999), NY Acad. of Scis.; mem. NAS (award for Initiatives in Rsch., 1984, mem. class membership com., 1991, 92), NAE (Computer Sci. and Engring. Peer Com., 1989-92), Am. Philos. Soc., Soc. Indsl. and Applied Math.; Found. Fellow, Inst. for Combinatorics and its Applications, 1991. Office: Princeton U Dept Computer Sci 35 Olden St Rm 324 Princeton NJ 08544-2087 Address: Hewlett Packard Corp 1501 Page Mill Rd Mail Stop 3U-1172 Palo Alto CA 94304 Office Fax: 609-258-1771. Business E-Mail: ret@cs.princeton.edu. E-mail: robert.tarjan@hp.com.

TARLIN, SARA-FAY, school psychologist, consultant; b. Boston, May 16, 1938; d. Bernard Solomon and Ruth Gilda (Rosen) Elliott; m. Norman Stanley Tarlin, June 24, 1962; children: Amy Beth, Jonathan Elliott. BS in Edn., Boston U., 1959; MA, Framingham State U., Mass., 1977; cert. advanced grad. study U. Mass., Boston, 1986. Lic. ednl. psychologist Mass. Allied Mental Health Profls. Bd. Registration, cert. Bd. Allied Mental Health Profls., sch. psychologist Mass. Bd. Edn. Sch. psychologist Pembroke Pub. Schs., Mass., 1985—87, Wilmington Pub. Schs., Mass., 1987—90, Woburn Pub. Schs., Mass., 1990—99; cons. Mashpee Pub. Schs., Mass., 2000—06, Charlton Pub. Schs., Mass., 2006. Apptd. mem. Allied Mental Health Profls. Bd. Registration, 1990—98. Mem.: Nat. Assn. Sch. Psychologists (Mass. del. 1999—2005, sch. psychology advocacy network coord. 1999—, nat. cert. sch. psychologist, Cert. Achievement 1996, Sch. Psychology Advocacy Network Coord. of Yr. 2005), Mass. Sch. Psychologists Assn. (legis. chair 1986—, Sch. Psychologist of Yr. 1990). Avocations: reading, knitting, golf, bridge, mahjong. Home: 6 Pine Hill Blvd Mashpee MA 02649

TARLOV, ALVIN RICHARD, foundation administrator, physician, educator; b. Norwalk, Conn., July 11, 1929; s. Charles and Mae (Shelinsky) T.; m. Joan Hylton, June 12, 1956 (div. 1976); children: Richard, Elizabeth, Jane, Suzanne, David. BA, Dartmouth Coll., 1951; MD, U. Chgo., 1956. Intern Phila. Gen. Hosp., 1956-57; resident in medicine U. Chgo. Hosps., 1957-58, 62-63, research assoc., 1958-61; asst. prof. medicine U. Chgo., 1963-68, assoc. prof., 1968-70, prof., 1970-84, prof. medicine, 2006—, chmn. dept. medicine, 1969-81; chmn. grad. med. edn. nat. adv. com. HHS, Washington, 1980; pres. Henry J. Kaiser Family Found., Menlo Park, Calif., 1984-90; sr. scientist New Eng. Med. Ctr., Boston, 1990-99, exec. dir. The Health Inst., 1995-99; prof. pub. health Harvard U., Boston, 1990-99; prof. of medicine Tufts U., 1990-99. Dir. Tex. Program for Soc. and Health, James Baker III Inst. for Pub. Policy, Rice U., 1999-2005. Pres. Med. Outcomes Trust, Inc., 1993-2000; chmn. bd., pres. Mass. Health Data Consortium, 1994-98. Served to capt. U.S. Army, 1958-61. Recipient Research Career Devel. award NIH, 1962-67; John and Mary Markle Found. scholar, 1966-71. Mem. ACP (master), Inst. Medicine of Nat. Acad. Scis. Home: 540 N State St Apt 3801 Chicago IL 60610-7240 E-mail: atarlov@gmail.com.

TARLOWE, JEFFREY L., health products executive; 3 children. BA in Math., Pomona Coll., Claremont, Calif., 1986; MBA in Fin., Columbia U., NY, 1988. V.p. fin. evaluations Merck-Medco Managed Care, Franklin Lakes, NJ, 1988—2000; CFO capital ventures Merck & Co., Inc., Woodcliff Lake, NJ, 2001—. Office: Merck Capital Ventures LLC 50 Tice Blvd Woodcliff Lake NJ 07677 Office Phone: 201-722-5073. Office Fax: 201-722-5041. Business E-Mail: jeff_tarlowe@merck.com.

TARN, NATHANIEL, poet, educator, translator; b. Paris, June 30, 1928; s. Marcel and Yvonne (Suchar) T.; children: Andrea, Marc. BA with honors, Cambridge U., Eng., 1948, MA, 1952; postgrad., U. Sorbonne, U. Paris, 1949-51; MA, U. Chgo., 1952, PhD, 1957; postgrad., London Sch. Econs., 1953-58. Anthropologist, Guatemala, Burma, Alaska, and other locations, 1952—; prof. comparative lit. Rutgers U., 1970-85, prof. emeritus modern poetry, comparative lit, anthropology, 1985. Vis. prof. SUNY, Buffalo and Princeton, 1969-70. Author: Old Savage/Young City, 1964, Where Babylon Ends, 1968, The Beautiful Contradictions, 1969, October, 1969, A Nowhere for Vallejo, 1971, Lyrics for the Bride of God: Section: The Artemision, 1972, The Persephones, 1974, Lyrics for the Bride of God, 1975, The House of Leaves, 1976, Birdscapes, with Seaside, 1978, The Desert Mothers, 1985, At the Western Gates, 1985, Palenque, 1986, Seeing America First, 1989, Flying the Body, 1993, Multitude of One, 1995, Views from the Weaving Mountain: Selected Essays in Poetics and Anthropology, 1991, Scandals in the House of Birds: Shamans & Priests on Lake Atitlan, 1997, The Architextures, 2000, Three Letters From The City: The St. Petersburg Poems 1968-1998, 2000, Selected Poems 1950-2000, 2002, Dying Trees, 2003, Recollections of Being, 2004, The Embattled Lyric, 2007; co-author: (with Janet Rodney) The Forest, 1978, Atitlan/Alashka, 1979, The Ground of Our Great Admiration of Nature, 1978; contbg. author: Penguin Modern Poets No. Seven: Richard Murphy, Jon Silkin, Nathaniel Tarn, 1965, A.P.E.N. Anthology of Contemporary Poetry, 1966, The Penguin Book of Modern Verse Translation, 1966, Poems Addressed to Hugh MacDiarmid, 1967, Music and Sweet Poetry: A Verse Anthology, 1968, Frontier of Going: Anthology of Space Poetry, 1969, Shaking the Pumpkin, 1972, America: A Prophecy, 1973, Open Poetry, 1973, Active Anthology, 1974, Symposium of the Whole, 1983, Random House Book of Twentieth Century French Poetry, 1983, Beneath a Single Moon: Buddhism in American Poetry, 1991, American Poetry since 1950: Innovators and Outsiders, 1993; translator: The Heights of Macchu Picchu (Pablo Neruda), 1966, Stelae (Victor Segalen), 1969, Zapotec Struggles, 1993; editor, co-translator: Con Cuba: An Anthology of Cuban Poetry of the Last Sixty Years, 1969, Selected Poems (Pablo Neruda), 1970; editor Cape Edits. and founder-dir. Cape Goliard Press, J. Cape Ltd., 1967-69. Recipient Guinness prize for poetry, 1963.

TARNACKI, DUANE L., lawyer; b. Detroit, Dec. 21, 1953; s. Leo A. and Dorothy O. (Roginski) T.; m. Sheila Rimmel, July 28, 1994. BA in Psychology with high distinction and high honors, U. Mich., 1976; MBA with honors, JD cum laude, U. Notre Dame, 1980. Bar: Mich. 1980, U.S. Dist. Ct. (so. dist.) Mich., 1980. Ptnr., mem. Clark Hill P.L.C., Detroit, 1980—. Sec. Ctr. for Creative Studies, 1991-96; bd. dirs. Stratford Shakespearean Festival of Am., sec., 1991—; bd. dirs. Detroit Hist. Soc., Juvenile Diabetes Found. Met. Detroit chpt., 1990-95, Acct. Aid Soc., 1990-96; gen. counsel Econ. Club of Detroit, 1995—; vice chmn., exec. com. Planned Giving Roundtable of S.E. Mich., 1992-98. Author: Establishing a Charitable Foundation in Michigan, 1986, 3d edit., 1999, The Responsibilities of Service: A Guide for Directors of Nonprofit Organizations in Michigan, 1997, 99, 2003; co-author: The Michigan Community Foundation Legal Reference, 1993, 2d edit., 1996; assoc. editor Notre Dame Lawyer, 1977-80. Mem. increasing philanthropy and govt. rels. coms., Coun. Mich. Founds., planned giving com., Karmanos Cancer Inst., 1991-94; bd. dirs. Mich Supreme Court Hist. Soc. Inc., 1988-96; mem. legal adv. subcom. to cmty. found. com. Coun. on Founds., IRS Exempt Orgns. Liaison Group; trustee Thompson-McCully Found., 1999-2003, The Futures Found.; mem. adv. coun. Jr. League Detroit. Fellow: Mich. State Bar Found.; mem.: ABA (nonprofit corps. com., bus. law sect., real property, probate and trust law and tax sects., Outstanding Nonprofit Atty. award bus. law sect. 2003), Mich. Bar Assn. (nonprofit corp. com., bus. law sect., probate and estate planning law and tax sects.), Detroit Renaissance (bus. contbns. com.), Detroit Athletic Club (bd. dirs.), Econ. Club. Roman Catholic. Home: 39824 Woodside Dr N Northville MI 48167-3429 Office: 500 Woodward Ave Ste 3500 Detroit MI 48226-3435

TARNOFF, JEROME, lawyer; b. June 22, 1931; s. Meyer and Anne (Soshnick) T.; children: Marcy Jane, Margery Lynne; m. Nancy Radin, 1990. AB, Syracuse U., 1952; JD, Columbia U., 1957. Bar: NY 1957, U.S. Dist. Ct. (so. and ea. dists.) NY 1960, U.S. Ct. Appeals (2d cir.) 1961. Ptnr. Sheldon and Tarnoff, NYC, 1957-78, Feldesman, D'Atri, Tarnoff & Lubitz, NYC, 1978, Baskin and Sears, P.C., NYC, 1979-84, Baskin & Steingut P.C., 1984-85, Berger & Steingut, 1986-92, Morrison, Cohen LLP, NYC, 1993—. Contbr. articles to legal jours. Chmn. policy com. NY Dem. Party, 1975-78, vice chmn. NY County, 1978—, mem. nat. com., 1980-88; mem. Cmty. Planning Bd. #8, 1966-75; bd. dirs. Grand St. Settlement, 1973—1981, Assoc. Y's of NY, 1972-88. With U.S. Army, 1952-54. Recipient Disting. Svc. award NAACP, 1975, Cert. Achievement, El Diario-La Prensa, 1977. Mem. ABA, NY State Bar Assn., Assn. Bar City of NY, N.T. County Lawyers, Am. Arbitration Assn. (nat. panel arbitrators), Phi Alpha Delta, Sunningdale Country Club (Scarsdale, NY), Harmonie Club (NYC), Audubon, Masons. Jewish. Office: Morrison Cohen LLP 909 Third Ave New York NY 10022 Home Phone: 212-988-5842; Office Phone: 212-735-8632. Business E-Mail: jtarnoff@morrisoncohen.com.

TARNOFF, PETER, federal agency administrator, consultant; b. NYC, Apr. 19, 1937; s. Norman Tarnoff and Henrietta (Goldfarb) Laing; m. Daniele Oudinot, Jan. 13, 1962 (div. Oct. 1981); children: Nicholas, Alexander; m. Mathea Falco, Dec. 24, 1981; 1 child, Benjamin. Student, U. Paris, 1956-57, postgrad., 60-61; BA, Colgate U., 1958; postgrad., U. Chgo., 1958-60. Joined Fgn. Svc., Dept. State, 1961; spl. asst. to amb. Am. Embassy, Bonn, Fed. Republic Germany, 1969; trainee Nat. Sch. Adminstrn., Paris, 1970; prin. officer Am. Consulate Gen., Lyon, France, 1971-73; dep. chief of mission Am. Embassy, Luxembourg, 1973-75; dir. Office Rsch. and Analysis for Western Europe Dept. State, Washington, 1975-76, exec. sec. Dept. State, 1977-81, fgn. affairs fellow San Francisco. 1981-82; exec. dir. World Affairs Coun. No. Calif., San Francisco, 1983-86; pres., dir. Coun. on Fgn. Rels., NYC, 1986-93; under sec. state for polit. affairs Dept. State, Washington, 1993-97; pres. Internat. Adv. Corp., San Francisco, 1997—. Office: Internat Adv Corp 2028 Green St San Francisco CA 94123-4813 Home Phone: 415-567-4241; Office Phone: 415-440-7997. Personal E-mail: iacmail@aol.com.

TARNOPOL, MICHAEL LAZAR, bank executive; b. 1936; s. Irving and Charlotte (Weber) T.; m. Lynne Lichtenstein, June 29, 1958; children: Lisa Silverman, Lori Moore. Gen. ptnr., sr. mng. dir., also bd. dirs. Lehman Bros. Inc., 1959-75; with Bear Stearns & Co. Inc., 1975—, vice-chmn., bd. dirs.; chmn. investment banking divsn., bd. dirs. Bear Stearns Internat. Mem. pres.'s coun. Solomon R. Guggenheim Found.; vice chmn. bd. trustees U. Pa., bd. overseers Wharton Sch.; bd. overseers, bd. mgrs. Meml. Sloan Kettering Cancer Ctr.; Bd. dirs. Cap Cure Found., U.S. Polo Tng. Found., Robert Steel Found., Inc. Mem. Palm Beach Country Club, Harmonie Club, East Hampton Tennis Club, Atlantic Golf Club, Quaker Ridge Golf Club, Trump Internat. Golf Club.

TARNOVE, LORRAINE, medical association executive; b. Atlantic City, July 26, 1947; d. Leonard Robert Tarnove and Jeanne Tarnove Yudkin; m. Steven B. Friedman, June 1, 1969; children: K. Brooke, Ari-Benjamin. BA, U. Md., 1969. Pres. Lorraine Tarnove Consulting, Columbia, Md., 1985-93; exec. dir. Am. Med. Dirs. Assn., Columbia. Contbr. chpt. to book. Office: AMDA 10840 Little Patuxent #760 Columbia MO 21044

TAROKH, VAHID, engineering educator; PhD in Elec. Engring., U. Waterloo, 1995; AM (hon.), Harvard U., 2002; DSc (hon.), U. Windsor, 2003. Postdoctoral fellow U. Ill., Urbana-Champaign, 1995—96; tech. staff mem. AT&T Labs-Rsch., Florham Park, NJ, 1996—99, prin. tech. staff mem., 1999—2000, head dept. wireless comm. and signal processing, 2000; assoc. prof. Mass. Inst. Tech., Cambridge, Mass., 2000—02; Gordon-Mckay prof. elec. engring., Vinton Hayes sr. rsch. fellow Harvard U., 2002—. Co-founder Ctr. Comm. and Networking; mem. Harvard Broadband Comm. Lab. Author (with V.K. Bhargava, H. Vincent Poor and S. Yoon): (book) Communications, Information and Network Security, 2002; contbr. articles to profl. jours. Named one of Top 100 Inventors of Yr., Tech. Rev. Mag., 1999—2002; recipient Gold Medal, Gov. Gen. Canada, 1995, Info. Theory Soc. Prize Paper award, IEEE, 1999, Alan T. Waterman award, NSF, 2001. Achievements include invention of space-time coding; design of efficient network protocols, wireless networks and algorithms for scheduling and switching; patents in field. Office: Divsn Engring and Applied Sci Harvard Univ 33 Oxford St Rm MD-347 Cambridge MA 02138 Office Phone: 617-384-5026. Office Fax: 617-496-6404. E-mail: vahid@deas.harvard.edu.

TARONJI, JAIME, JR., lawyer; b. NYC, Nov. 20, 1944; s. Jaime and Ruth T.; m. Mary Taronji, May 16, 1970; children: Ian A., Mark N., Nicole V. BA, George Washington U., 1972; JD, Georgetown U., 1976. Bar: Va. 1977, DC 1978. Asst. to dep. staff dir. U.S. Commn. on Civil Rights, Washington, 1972-76; antitrust enforcement atty. FTC, Washington, 1976-79; antitrust counsel Westinghouse Electric Corp., Pitts., 1979-81; group legal counsel Dana Corp., Toledo, 1982-88; v.p., gen. counsel Packaging Corp. Am. subs. Tenneco, Evanston, Ill., 1988-95; law v.p. NCR Corp., Dayton, 1996-99; v.p., gen. counsel, sec. Dayton Superior Corp., Dayton, 1999—2003; of counsel antitrust practice group Howrey LLP, Washington, 2004—. Mem. adv. bd. Corp. Counsel Inst., Georgetown U. Law Ctr. Author: The 1970 Census Undercount of Spanish Speaking Persons, 1974; editor: Puerto Ricans in the U.S., 1976. Capt. M.I., U.S. Army, 1965-70, Vietnam. Mem. ABA (antitrust sect.), Hispanic Nat. Bar Assn., Hispanic Bar Assn. DC. Democrat. Roman Catholic. Office: Howrey LLP 1299

Pennsylvania Ave NW Washington DC 20004-2402 Office Phone: 202-383-7406. E-mail: taronjij@howrey.com.

TAROY-VALDEZ, LOLITA B., nursing educator, nurse; b. Cogon, Mindanao, Philippines, Sept. 3, 1951; d. Horonio Taroy and Florentina Lucagbo Bequiso; married, May 28, 1990. BSN, Mountain View Coll., Philippines; MN, U. Philippines, Diliman, Quezon City, 1981. Cert. AACN, 1994. Dir. Hongkong Adventist Sch. Nursing, 1985—88; asst. prof. Southwestern Adventist U., Keene, Tex., 1991—. Dean Mountain View Coll. Sch. Nursing, Valencia, Bukidnon, Philippines, 1982—85. Coord. mission trips to Philippines Healing Outreach Profl. Endeavor, Keene, 2004—05, sec., 2000—06. Named one of Gt. 100 Nurses, Dallas /Ft. Worth Hosp. Council-Nurse Exec. Forum and Tex. Nurses Assn., 2002; recipient President's award for svc., Mountain View Coll. Sch. Nursing Alumni Assn., 1997, Leadership award, 1997. Home: 2725 Hill Ln Cleburne TX 76031 Office: Southwestern Adventist U Hillcrest Keene TX 07659 Home Phone: 817-641-9988. Home Fax: 817-641-9988. Personal E-mail: valdezl@swau.edu.

TARPLEY, LEE, botanist, educator; m. Ming-Hsuan Chen; children: William, Lara. BA in Botany with high honors, U. Wyo., 1980; MS in Plant Sci., Calif. State U., 1987; PhD in Plant Physiology, Tex. A&M U., College Station, 1993. Rsch. plant biochemist Tex. A&M U., 1992—93, postdoctoral plant physiologist (sorghum physiology), 1993—96, postdoctoral crop physiologist (cotton physiology), 1996—97; postdostoral rschr. plant biochemistry and physiology USDA Agrl. Rsch. Svc., Mississippi State, Miss., 1997—99; vis. rsch. scientist Miss. State U., 1999—2001; asst. prof. plant physiology Tex. A&M Agrl. Rsch. and Ext. Ctr., Beaumont, 2001—. Mem.: Internat. Chemometrics Soc., Rice Tech. Working Group (chair rice culture panel 2004—06, chair nominations com. 2002—04, exec. com. 2006—), Crop Sci. Soc. Am., Am. Soc. Plant Biologists, Bot. Soc. Am. Achievements include first 'in plant' determination of sugar metabolism in stem of large tropical grass (sorghum, sugarcane, maize); first metabolomic characterization of cereal crop plant branching (major yield component); research in technology to economically increase rice crop yield; separate characterization of the environmental and physiological contributions to a plant reflectance spectrum. Office: Tex Agrl Expt Sta 1509 Aggie Dr Beaumont TX 77713

TARPY, THOMAS MICHAEL, lawyer; b. Columbus, Ohio, Jan. 4, 1945; s. Thomas Michael and Catherine G. (Sharshal) T.; m. Mary Patricia Canna, Sept. 9, 1967; children: Joshua Michael, Megan Patricia, Thomas Canna, John Patrick. AB, John Carroll U., 1966; JD, Ohio State U., 1969. Bar: Ohio 1969, U.S. Dist. Ct. (so. dist.) Ohio 1972, U.S. Dist. Ct. (no. dist.) Ohio 1974, U.S. Ct. Appeals (6th cir.) 1982, U.S. Supreme Ct. 1997. Assoc. Vorys, Sater, Seymour & Pease LLP, Columbus, 1969-76, ptnr., 1977—85, 1985—87, 1987—2005; v.p. Liebert Corp., Columbus, 1985-87. Chmn. Columbus Graphics Commn., 1980; mem. Columbus Area Leadership Program, 1975. With U.S. Army, 1969-75. Fellow Coll. Labor and Employment Lawyers, Ohio Mgmt. Lawyers Assn. (founding mem.); mem. ABA, Ohio Bar Assn., Columbus Bar Assn. Office: Vorys Sater Seymour & Pease LLP PO Box 1008 52 E Gay St Columbus OH 43215-3161 E-mail: tmtarpy@vssp.com.

TARR, CURTIS W., management consultant, educator; b. Stockton, Calif., Sept. 18, 1924; s. F.W. and Esther (Reed) T.; m. Elizabeth May Myers, 1955 (div. 1978); children: Pamela Elizabeth, Cynthia Leigh; m. Marilyn Van Stralen, 1979 (div. 1991); m. Mary Katherine Stegmiller, 1992. BA, Stanford U., 1948, PhD, 1962; MBA, Harvard U., 1950; L.H.D., Ripon Coll., 1965, Grinnell Coll., 1969, Lincoln Coll., 1980; LL.D., Lawrence U., 1974, Ill. Wesleyan U., 1980. Rsch. asst., instr. Harvard U., 1950-52; v.p. Sierra Tractor & Equipment Co., Chico, Calif., 1952-58; staff mem. 2d Hoover Commn., 1954-55; asst. dir. summer session Stanford U., 1961-62, dir., 1962-63, asst. dean humanities and scis., 1962-63, lectr. bus. sch., 1962-63; pres. Lawrence U., Appleton, Wis., 1963-69; asst. sec. for manpower and res. affairs Air Force, 1969-70; dir. SSS, Washington, 1970-72; under sec. state for security assistance, 1972-73; acting dep. under sec. state for mgmt., 1973; from v.p. parts distbn. and matrials mgmt. to v.p. mgmt. devel. Deere & Co., Moline, Ill., 1973—83; dean, prof. Johnson Sch. Mgmt., Cornell U., 1984—89, prof. mgmt., 1989-90, dean emeritus, 1990—; vice chmn. Intermet Corp., 1992-95. Bd. dirs. Phyton Corp., Ithaca, N.Y., 1985-2002, State Farm Ins. Companies, 1985-98, Banta Corp, 1976-95, Intermet Corp., 1984-98; mem. Internat. Rsch. Coun. Ctr. for Strategic and Internat. Studies, Washington, 1989-92; adj. prof. mgmt. Emory U., 1991-93. Author: Private Soldier, 1976, By the Numbers, 1981, Youth, 1994. Trustee Inst. Paper Chemistry, 1963-69, Morehouse Sch. Medicine, Atlanta, 1994—2004; chmn. Task Force on Govt. Orgn., Fin. and Tax Distbn. for State Wis., 1967-69; chmn. Def. Manpower Commn., 1974-76, Ill. State Scholarship Commn., 1978-79, Quad Cities Grad. Study Ctr., 1982-84, Rep. candidate for Congress 2d Dist., Calif., 1958; trustee Am. Coll., Bryn Mawr, Pa., 1989-92; dir. Bethesda Home, Savannah, Ga., 1998-2003, The Mighty 8th Air Force Mus., Savannah, 1999-2004. With AUS, 1943-46, ETO. Recipient Exceptional Civilian Service medal Air Force Dept., 1970; Distinguished Service award SSS, 1975 Mem. Univ. Club (Chgo.), Cosmos Club (Washington). Methodist. Personal E-mail: curtis.tarr@sbcglobal.net.

TARR, DAVID GERALD, economist; b. Phila., Aug. 10, 1943; s. Morris and Esther P. (Martin) T.; m. Linda Haas, June 1971; children— Michael Eli, Adam Haas. B.A., Glassboro (N.J.) State Coll., 1965; M.A., Ohio U., 1967; Ph.D., Brown U., 1970. Instr., U. R.I., Kingston, 1969; asst. prof. Ohio State U., Columbus, 1970-74; sr. economist FTC, Washington, 1974-85; lead economist World Bank, 1985—. Authored over fifty peer reviewed professional journal articles and edited/wrote ten books/monographs. While at the World Bank, provided trade policy advice to governments in twenty countries. Have given seminars in an additional fifteen countries. Speak French well and good Russian. Recipient Disting. Alumnus of Yr. award, Rowan U., 1998. Mem.: Phia Kappa Psi, Pi Gammu Nu. Avocations: tennis. Personal E-mail: dgtarr@yahoo.com.

TARR, JOEL ARTHUR, historian, educator; b. Jersey City, May 8, 1934; s. Max Alfred and Florence (Levin) Tartalsky; m. Arlene Green, Sept. 2, 1956 (dec. June 1969); children: Michael Jay, Joanna Sue; m. Tova Brafman, Aug. 11, 1978; children: Maya Leah, Ilana Ariel. BS, Rutgers U., 1956, MA, 1957; PhD, Northwestern U., Evanston, Ill., 1963. Asst. prof. Calif. State U., Long Beach, 1961-66; vis. prof. U. Calif., Santa Barbara, 1966-67; asst. prof. Carnegie Mellon U., Pitts., 1967-70, assoc. prof., 1969-72, prof. history and pub. policy, 1973-90, Richard S. Caliguiri prof. urban and environ. history and policy, 1990—2004, Richard S. Caliguiri univ. prof. history and pub. policy, 2004—, dir. program in tech. and soc., 1975-87, co-dir. program in applied history and social sci., 1978-86, acting dean Sch. Urban and Pub. Affairs, 1986, assoc. dean Coll. Humanities and Social Sci., 1988-91, acting dean Coll. Humanities and Social Sci., 1991-92, acting head dept. history, 1992-93, Univ. prof., 2004—. Author: A Study in Boss Politics, 1971; co-author: Horses in Cities: Living Machines in the 19th Century, 2007; editor: Patterns of City Growth, 1974, Retrospective Technology Assessment, 1977, Transportation Innovation and Spatial Change in Pittsburgh, 1850-1934, 1978, Pittsburgh-Sheffield: Sister Cities, 1986, Technology and the Rise of the Networked City in Europe and America, 1988, The Search for the Ultimate Sink: Urban Pollution in Historic Perspective, 1996, Devastation and Renewal: An Environmental History of Pittsburgh and Its Region, 2003. Bd. dirs. Action Housing, Pitts., 1983; trustee Hist. Soc. Western Pa., 1993-2000. NEH fellow, 1969-70; grantee NSF, 1975-80, 83-85, 95-98, NOAA, 1982-84; recipient Robert Doherty prize for contbns. to excellence in edn., 1992, Choice Outstanding Acad. Book award, 1997, cert. Commendation Am. Soc. State and Local History, 2005. Mem. AAAS, Pub. Works Hist. Soc. (pres. 1982-83, Abel Wolman prize 1989), Orgn. Am. Historians, Pub. History Assn., Am. Soc. Environ. History, Soc. for the History of Tech., Urban History Assn. (pres. 1999). Democrat. Jewish. Home: 5418 Normlee Pl Pittsburgh PA 15217-1116 Office: Carnegie-Mellon U Schenley Pk Pittsburgh PA 15213 Office Phone: 412-268-2609. Business E-Mail: jt03@andrew.cmu.edu.

TARR, KENNETH J., retired investment company executive; b. 1945; s. Julius and Alice T.; 1 child, Alexandra Jennifer; m. Charlotte Kruesi, 1990 BA, U. Pa., 1967; MBA, Columbia U., 1971. With Chem. Bank, NYC, 1971-72; asst. v.p. Standard and Poors/Inter Capital, NYC, 1972-74; founder, mgr. S&P/Market Insights, NYC, 1974-75; v.p. Kuhn Loeb and Co., NYC, 1975-77; asst. v.p. Bessemer Trust Co., NYC, 1977-80, v.p., 1980-82, sr. v.p., 1982-91, dir. rsch., 1984; pres., dir. Suisse Asset Mgmt., Inc., NYC, 1991-93; mng. prin. Weiss, Peck & Greer, LLC, NYC, 1994-97; exec. v.p., regional head pvt. banking Am.'s Deutsche Bank AG, NYC, 1997-99; ret., 2000. Mem.: NY Yacht Club.

TARR, RALPH WILLIAM, lawyer, former federal government official; b. Bakersfield, Calif., Sept. 29, 1948; BA, Dartmouth Coll., 1970; MPA, Calif. State U., Sacramento, 1973; JD, U. Calif., Hastings, 1976. Staff asst. Calif. Gov. Ronald Reagan, 1971—73; extern to assoc. justice Calif. Supreme Ct., 1976; rsch. atty. to presiding justice Ct. Appeal (5th dist.) Calif., 1976-77; assoc. Baker, Manock & Jensen, Fresno, Calif., 1977-81, dir., mem. exec. com., 1981-82; mem. adminstrv. com. Fed. Register, Washington, 1982-85; dep. asst. atty. gen. US Dept. Justice, Washington, 1982-84, acting asst. atty. gen., 1984-85; solicitor US Dept. Interior, Washington, 1985-89, counselor, 1989-90; pvt. practice LA, 1990—. Home: 24011 Alder Pl Calabasas CA 91302-2394 Office: Andrews Kurth LLP Ste 3700 601 S Figueroa St Los Angeles CA 90017-5742 Office Phone: 213-896-3136. Business E-Mail: rtarr@andrewskurth.com.

TARR, ROBERT JOSEPH, JR., publishing executive, retail executive; b. Freeport, NY, Dec. 7, 1943; s. Robert Joseph and Janet Christman (Laughton) T.; m. Molly Worthington Upton, Feb. 28, 1970; children: William Upton, Robert Joseph, III, David Worthington. BS, U.S. Naval Acad., 1966; MBA, Harvard U., 1973; MA, Fletcher Sch. Law & Diplomacy, 1976. Asst. v.p. corp. fin. Paine Webber Jackson Curtis, Boston, 1973-75; dir. corp. planning, then v.p., treas. Gen. Cinema Corp., Chestnut Hill, Mass., 1976-78, sr. v.p., 1978-83, exec. v.p., COO, 1983-85, pres., COO, 1985—92; pres., CEO, COO Harcourt Gen., Inc. (Gen. Cinema Corp., 1993), Chestnut Hill, Mass., 1991-97; pres., spl. ptnr. Chartwell Investments, NYC, 2002—. CEO, COO The Neiman Marcus Group, Inc., 1987—92, pres., bd. dirs., CEO, COO, 1991—97, pres., 2007; bd. dirs. WESCO Internat., Inc.; chmn., pres., CEO HomeRuns.com, Inc., 1999—2001. Lt. USN, 1966-71. Mem.: Old Sandwich Golf Club, Briar's Creek Club, The Oyster Harbors Club, Wianno Yacht Club, Kiawah Island Club. Home: 58 River Marsh Ln Johns Island SC 29455-5202 Personal E-mail: rjtjr12@aol.com.

TARRANCE, VERNON LANCE, JR., research and development company executive; b. Harlingen, Tex., Dec. 4, 1940; s. Vernon Lance Sr. and Mary Gilmore (Rea) T.; m. Eugenia Aline McCuistion, July 2, 1966; children: Vernon Lance III, Haloway McCuistion, Kyle Rea. BA, Washington & Lee U., 1962; postgrad., U. Mich., 1971; MA, Am. U., 1973; postgrad., Harvard U., 1973-74. Dir. rsch. Tex. Rep. Com., Austin, 1964-67, Rep. Nat. Com., Washington, 1969-70; spl. asst. to dir. U.S. Census Bur., Washington, 1970-73; v.p. Decision Making Info. Inc., Santa Ana, Calif., 1974-77; pres., founder Tarrance, Hill, Newport & Ryan, Houston, 1977-92; pres., mng. dir. Gallup China Ltd., Beijing, 1993-95; vis. prof. polit. sci. Tex. A&M U., College Station, 1995-96; scholar in residence Washington and Lee U., Va., 1996; mng. dir. Burson-Marsteller, Washington, 1997-99. Bd. dirs. Gallup Orgn., 1987-92; cons. Gallup Internat. Rsch. Ctr., Lincoln, Nebr.; co-chmn. adv. adjustment panel U.S. Census, 1990. Co-author: The Ticket Splitter, 1972, Checked and Balanced, 1998; editor: Texas Precinct Votes '66, '68, '70. Sr. strategist Senator John McCain for Pres. 2008. Fellow John F. Kennedy Inst. Politics Harvard U., 1973-74; named one of 150 People Who Influence Fed. Govt. Nat. Jour. Mag., 1986. Mem.: Raleigh Tavern Philos. Soc. (founder), Am. Polit. Sci. Assn., Kappa Sigma. Avocations: mountain trekking, golf, aviculture, travel. E-mail: lanceterrancejr@aol.com.

TARRANT, CHRISTINE GLORIA, music educator; d. Nick and Bessie Boulos; m. Timothy Michael Tarrant, May 1, 2004; children: John Nicholas, Victoria Kathleen 1 stepchild, Joseph John. BS, U. Ill., 1992, MS, 1997. Tchr. choral, music Marquardt Mid. Sch., Glendale Heights, Ill., 1992—98, Timber Ridge Mid. Sch., Plainfield, Ill., 1998—99, Heritage Grove Mid. Sch., Plainfield, Ill., 1999—2002, Drauden Point Mid. Sch., Plainfield, 2002—05. Children's choral dir. Hinsdale (Ill.) Children's Choir, 1997—97, United Meth. Ch., Downers Grove, Ill., 1997—99; youth choral dir. All Saints Greek Orthodox Ch., Joliet, Ill., 2000—03. Recipient Fine Arts award, Bloom Sch. Dist., 1988. Mem.: Am. Choral Dirs. Am., Alpha Delta Pi. Greek Orthodox. Avocations: reading, exercise. Home Phone: 708-258-6953.

TARRANT, RICHARD J(OHN), classicist, educator; b. Bklyn., Apr. 4, 1945; s. John Joseph and Bertha (Slaney) T.; m. Jacqueline Brown, Sept. 14, 1968. BA, Fordham U., 1966; DPhil, Oxford U., 1972; AM (hon.), Harvard U., 1982. P.S. Allen jr. research fellow Corpus Christi Coll., Oxford, England, 1968-70; lectr. Univ. Coll., Toronto, Ont., Canada, 1970-71, asst. prof., 1971-74, assoc. prof., 1974-79; prof. U. Toronto, 1979-82; prof. Greek and Latin Harvard U., Cambridge, Mass., 1982-87, Carl A. Pescosolido prof. Roman civilization, 1987-93, Pope prof. Latin language and Literature, 1993—, Harvard Coll. prof., 1999—2004, chmn. dept., 1988-94, acting dean Grad. Sch. Arts and Scis., 1995-96. Vis. Mellon prof. Inst. for Advanced Study, Princeton, 1991-92; vis. fellow Corpus Christi Coll. U. Oxford, 1992. Author: Greek and Latin Lyric Poetry in Translation: A Bibliographical Survey, 1972, Seneca, Agamemnon, 1976, (with others) Texts and Transmission: A Survey of the Latin Classics, 1983, Seneca's Thyestes, 1985, Ovid's Metamorphoses, 2004; editor Phoenix: Jour. Classical Assn. Can., 1978-82, Harvard Studies in Classical Philology, 1985-88, 93-94; editorial bd. Toronto Medieval Latin Texts, 1977—, Cambridge Classical Texts and Commentaries, 1992—; advisory bd. Text: Transactions of the Soc. for Textual Scholarship, 1994—, Materiali e discussioni comitato scientifico, 2002—; contbr. articles to profl. jours. Cabot fellow, 1993—94, 2004—05, Marshall scholar, 1966—69. Mem. Am. Philol. Assn. (bd. dirs. 1987-89, v.p. publs. 1992-95), Cambridge Philol. Assn., Classical Assn. Can., Classical Assn. New Eng., Phi Beta Kappa. Office: Harvard U Dept Classics Boylston Hall 204 Cambridge MA 02138 Home Phone: 617-864-7919; Office Phone: 617-496-3611. Business E-Mail: tarrant@fas.harvard.edu.

TARRANT, SASHA RANAE ADAMS, history professor; b. Torrington, Wyo., July 20, 1967; d. Bryan Robert Adams and Donna Joy Grimes; m. Glenn Durwood Tarrant, July 2, 1985; children: Sheila Ranae, Margo Elizabeth. BA in History, U. Houston, Clear Lake, 1994, MA in History, 1996. Rschr., tchg. asst. U. Houston, Clear Lake, 1995—96; tchg. asst. Tex. A&M U., College Station, 1997—98; intern U. Space Rsch. Assn., NASA Johnson Space Ctr., Houston, 1998—99; honors program dir., asst. prof. history Brazosport Coll., Lake Jackson, Tex., 1999—. Steering com. Viewing the Past Through Different Lenses: The African Am. Legacy in the Lower Brazos Valley Symposium, Lake Jackson, Tex., 2001; pres. Gulf Coast Intercollegiate Honors Coun., Houston, 2004—05; co-chair com. Nat. Collegiate Honors Coun., Lincoln, Nebr., 2005—. Editor: Antifeminism in America; author: (handbook) Texas Community College Student Day Handbook. Troop leader Girl Scouts of Am., Lake Jackson, 2000—04. Named Orgn. Leader of Yr., U. of Houston, Clear Lake, 1995—96; recipient Tchr. of Excellence award, Nat. Inst. Staff and Orgnl. Devel., 2002—03, 2006—07, Martha Wash. award, SAR, 2006. Mem.: AAUW (expanding your horizons coord. com. 1996), Tex. State Hist. Assn. Home: 1611 McFadden Lake Jackson TX 77566 Office: Brazosport Coll 500 College Dr Lake Jackson TX 77566 Office Phone: 979-230-3504. Office Fax: 979-230-3592.

TARRIO, CHARLES, physicist; b. Middletown, Conn., Dec. 20, 1960; s. Frank R. and Frances Baldwin Tarrio; m. Danielle Partello, Feb. 17, 1995; 1 child, Alyssa Partello Tarrio. BS, Bates Coll., Lewiston, Maine, 1982; PhD, U. of Va., Charlottesville, 1991. Physicist Nat. Inst. of Stds. and Tech., Gaithersburg, Md., 1991—. Recipient Dept. of Commerce Silver medal, U.S. Dept. of Commerce, 2004, Arthur S. Flemming award for applied sci., George Wash. U., 2003, Dept. of Commerce Bronze medal, U.S. Dept. of Commerce, 1994. Mem.: SPIE, Optical Soc. of Am. Office: Nat Inst Stds and Tech Stop 8410 100 Bureau Dr Gaithersburg MD 20899

TARRO, GIULIO, virologist; b. Messina, Italy, July 9, 1938; s. Emanuele and Emanuela (Iannello) Tarro. MD, U. Naples, 1962, postgrad. in nervous diseases, 1968, PhD in Virology, 1971; postgrad. in med. and biol. scis., Roman Acad., 1979; degree in medicine (hon.), U. Pro Deo, Albany, NY, 1989; degree in immunology (hon.), St. Theodora Acad., NY, 1991; degree in bioethics (hon.), Constantinian U., Cranston, RI, 1996. Asst. in med. pathology Naples U., Italy, 1964-66; rsch. assoc. divsn. virology and cancer rsch. Children's Hosp., Cin., 1965-68; asst. prof. rsch. pediat. U. Cin. Coll. Medicine, 1968-69; rsch. fellow Nat. Rsch. Coun., Naples, 1966-74, rsch. chief, 1974; prof. oncologic virology Coll. Medicine U. Naples, 1971-85, prof. microbiology and immunology Sch. Specialization, 1972—2006; chief divsn. virology D. Cotugno Hosp. Infectious Diseases, Naples, 1973—2006, pres. ethic com., 1998—2007, head dept. diagnostic labs., 2003—06, emeritus, 2006—. Sr. scientist Nat. Cancer Inst. Frederick Ctr., Md., 1973; project dir. Nat. Cancer Inst., Bethesda, Md., 1971-75; edn. min. rep. Zool. Sta., Naples, 1975-79; cons. Italian Pharmacotherapic Inst., Rome, 1980-98, med. dir., 2006—; nat. com. on bioethics, 1995-98; ethics com. Basilicata Oncologic Hosp., 2005-; pres. De Beaumont Bonelli Found. Cancer Rsch., Naples, 1978—, European Group Econ. Interest, Rsch. and Devel., Naples, 2003-07, Campania Tech. and Ecology Ctr., 2004—; dean faculty natural and phys. scis. Nobile Accademia di Santa Teodora Imperatrice, 1993-2003; dept. head medicine Naples People U., 2000-05; sci. coord. extracorporeal hyperthermia in HCV patients First Circle Med., Mpls., 2000-03; vice chmn., gen. sec. sci. adv. bd. Unihart Biotech Pharm., London, 2005-; chmn. com. on biotechs. and virusphere World Acad. Biomed. Techs., UNESCO, Paris, 2007; adj. prof. dept. biology Temple U. Coll. Sci. and Tech., Phila., 2007—. Author: Virologia Oncologica, 1979, Patologia dell'AIDS, 1991, Con il Cancro si Puó Vivere, 1992, AIDS Cosa Possiamo Fare Cosa Dobbiamo Sapere, 1994, Pocket File Research Collection, 1997, 6th edit., 2003, To Prevent Is To Win, 1998, Bioethics and Culture of Prevention, 2001, Health Without Borders, 2004, 2d edit., 2007, Safety No Limits, 2007; editor-in-chief: Internat. Jour. Clin. Investigation, 2000—, Cotugno News, 2003—, Fratres, 2004—; contbr. over 360 articles to profl. jours. Pres. Sci. Cultural Com., Torre Annunziata, Italy, 1984, Tumor Prevention Assn., Rome, 1984; mem. acad. senate Constantinian U., Providence, 1990, U. Pro Deo, NY, 1994; hon. acad. U. Sancti Cyrilli, Valletta, Malta, 2001; mem. UNESCO-Hebrew U. Jerusalem Internat. Sch. Molecular Biology and Microbiology, UNESCO-World Acad. Biomed. Techs.; hon. rector Ruggero II U., Fla., 2003. Maj. Italian Navy, 1982-84, lt. col., 1993-95. Decorated comdr. Nat. Order of Merit, Star of Europe, knight grand cross Sovereign Constantinian Order St. George, gt. officer Italian Republic; recipient Internat. Lenghi award Lincei Acad., 1969, Gold Microscope award Italian Health Min., 1973, Knights of Humanity award Internat. Register of Chivalry, Malta, 1978, Gold medal of culture award Pres. Italian Republic, 1975, Culture award, 1985, 1st prize in biomed. rsch., Italian Acad. Arts and Scis., 1987, Castello di Pietrarossa award, Italy, 1991, Gold Cesare award Padova, 1991, 20th Century award in Medicine, 1994, Gold Little Horse, Transnat. European Fedn., Rome 1996, King Manfredi award Manfredonia, 1999, Equestris Ordinis S. Sepulcri of Jerusalem, Rome, 1999, Gold medal of health Pres. Italian Republic, 1999, Saint Catherin award, Siena, 2003, Sorrento in the World award, 2004, Medal of Culture Ministry, 2005, Knight of Solidarity Internat. award Norman Acad., Rome, 2006, Saint Pio for Peace award City of Fiuggi, 2006, Tables of Law award Internat. Assn. Cath. Apostleship, Naples, 2006, others. Fellow: AAAS; mem.: Am. Chem. Soc., European Soc. Clin. Virology, Internat. Sch. for Molecular Biology and Microbiology, NY Acad. Scis., Nat. Order Journalists, AIDS Soc. Asia and the Pacific, Assn. Res. Prevention of Cancer (sci. com. 1995), Italian Assn. Viral Study and Rsch. (pres. 1995—), Italian Soc. Immuno-Oncology (v.p. 1975—, pres. 1990—), Internat. League Drs. for Abolition of Vivisection (pres. 1992—), Internat. Assn. Leukemias, Am. Assn. Cancer Rsch., Am. Soc. Microbiology, Rotary, Lions (pres. Pompei chpt. 1987—89, vice gov. dist. 1991—92, pres. com. fight cancer 1992—94, pres. com. sci. and life 1994—95, pres. com. fight drug addiction and AIDS 1995—97, pres. com. transplant and donations 1998—99, pres. com. oncology 2000—02, pres. com. on stem cells 2002—, dist. dir. operative area health and rsch. 2003, pres. Pompei chpt. 2004—06, dist. dir. operative area health and rsch. 2006—, Melvin Jones fellow 1993, 2004). Roman Catholic. Achievements include patents in field; discovery of RSV virus in infant deaths in Naples and of tumor liberated protein as a tumor associated antigen, 100 kilodalton protein overexpressed in lung tumors and other epithelial adenocarcinomas. Home: 286 Posillipo 80123 Naples Italy E-mail: gitarro@tin.it.

TARR-WHELAN, LINDA, policy center executive; b. Springfield, Mass., May 24, 1940; d. Albert and Jane Zack; m. Keith Tarr-Whelan; children: Scott, Melinda. BSN, Johns Hopkins U., 1963; MS, U. Md., 1967; PhD in Public Svc. (hon.), Chatham Coll. Program dir. AFSCME AFL-CIO, Washington, 1968-74, union area dir., 1974-76; adminstrn. dir. N.Y. State Labor Dept., Albany, N.Y., 1976-79; dep. asst. to pres. Carter White House, Washington, 1979-80; dir. govt. rels. NEA, Washington, 1980-86; CEO, pres. Ctr. for Policy Alternatives, Washington, 1986—2000, bd. dirs., 1985—; mng. dir. Tarr-Whelan Assoc. Inc., St. Helena Island, SC, 2000—. Apptd. U.S. rep. UN Commn. on Status of Women, 1996—. Bd. dirs. Benton Found., Adv. Inst., Ind. Sector; pres. State Issues Forum; mem. Freddie Mac Affordable Housing Adv. Bd. Recipient Disting. Grad. award Johns Hopkins U., 1981, Breaking the Glass Ceiling award, 1996; leadership fellow Japan Soc., 1987-88; named one of 50 Most Powerful Women in Washington, Ladies Home Journal. Democrat. Avocations: walking, travel. Home: Tarr-Whelan Assoc Inc PO Box 1012 Saint Helena Island SC 29920

TARS, ERIC, lawyer, consultant; BA in Polit. Sci., Haverford Coll.; student in Internat. Politics, Inst. European Studies and U. Vienna, Austria; JD, Georgetown U. Law Ctr. Rsch. asst. to Prof. Mari Matsuda Georgetown U. Law Ctr.; legal asst. Inter-Am. Commn. Human Rights; law clk. Harmon, Curran, Spielberg & Eisenberg, LLP; fellow US racial discrimination prog. Global Rights, 2004; cons. Coalition Human Rights at Home, US Human Rights Network; human rights atty. Nat. Law Ctr. Homelessness & Poverty, Washington. Office: Nat Law Ctr Homelessness & Poverty 1411 K St NW Ste 1400 Washington DC 20005 Office Phone: 202-638-2535. Office Fax: 202-628-2737. E-mail: etars@nlchp.org.

TARSES, JAMIE, television producer, former television network executive; b. Pitts., Pa., 1964; d. Jay and Rachel Tarses; m. Dan McDermott (div.). BA in Theater, Williams Coll., 1985. Casting dir. Lorimar Prodns.; mgr. creative affairs NBC, 1987, mgr. current comedy programs, 1987-88, mgr. comedy devel., 1988-89, dir. comedy devel., 1989-94, supr. programming team, 1994-95, sr. v.p. primetime series, 1995-96; pres. ABC Entertainment, 1996—99; founder, owner Untitled Burke-Tarses Project, 2003—05; ptnr. Pariah, 2005—. Consulting prodr. (TV films) Imagine That, 2002; exec. prodr.: (TV films) Tikiville, 2001, Crazy Love, 2003, Americana, 2004, More, Patience, 2006, The Angriest Man in Suburbia, 2006; (films) Primeval, 2007. *

TARTAGLIA, JOHN, actor, puppeteer; b. Maple Shade, NJ, Feb. 16, 1978; Creator & puppeteer (TV series) Johnny and the Sprites, 2005, puppeteer Sesame Street, 1997, Sesame Street: A Is For Asthma, 1998; actor(voice): Sesame English, 1999, Sesame Street: 4-D Movie Magic, 2003, Sesame Street: Three Bears and a New Baby, 2003, Play with Me Sesame, 2002; actor & puppeteer (Broadway plays) Avenue Q, 2003—05 (Tony award nomination best actor in a musical, 2004); actor: (Broadway plays) Hair, 2004, Beauty and the Beast, 2006. Recipient Clarence Derwent award. *

TARTAKOFF, DAVID STEPHEN, mathematics professor, researcher; b. Boston, Aug. 2, 1942; s. Joseph and Helen Herlihy Tartakoff; m. Cheryl Ann Corbin, Jan. 20, 1990; 1 child, Ann Elizabeth. BA, Harvard U., Cambridge, Mass., 1960; PhD, U. Calif., Berkeley, 1969. Vis. mem. Courant Inst. Math. Scis., NYU, NYC, 1969—71; asst. prof. Columbia U., NYC, 1971—75, SUNY, Stony Brook, 1977; mem. Inst. Advanced Study, Princeton, NJ, 1975—77; assoc. prof. U. Ill., Chgo., 1977—81, prof., 1981—. Contbr. articles to profl. jours. Chair, devel. dir. Greenwood Music Camp, Cummington, Mass., 1983—2007. Home: 1216 N Kenilworth Ave Oak Park IL 60302-1237 Office: U Ill Chicago 851 S Morgan St Chicago IL 60607 Home Phone: 708-524-8540; Office Phone: 312-996-2440. Office Fax: 312-996-1491; Home Fax: 708-524-2395. Business E-Mail: dst@uic.edu.

TARTER, CURTIS BRUCE, physicist, science administrator; b. Louisville, Sept. 26, 1939; s. Curtis B. and Marian Turner (Cundiff) T.; divorced; 1 child, Shana Lee; m. Gabriela Odell, 2003. BS, MIT, 1961; PhD, Cornell U., 1967. Tchg. asst. Cornell U., Ithaca, NY, 1961—63, rsch. asst., 1964—67; physicist, summers Lawrence Radiation Lab., Livermore, Calif., 1962—63; staff mem. theoretical physics divsn. U. Calif., Lawrence Livermore Nat. Lab., 1967—69, group leader macroscopic properties of matter, 1969—71, assoc. divsn. leader, 1971—74, group leader opacities, 1972—78, divsn. leader, 1974—84; dep. assoc. dir. for physics Lawrence Livermore Nat. Lab., 1984—88, assoc. dir. for physics, 1988—94, dep. dir., 1994, dir., 1994—2002, assoc. dir. at large, 2002—04, dir. emeritus, 2004—. Sr. scientist Applied Rsch. Labs. Aeronutronic divsn. Philco-Ford Corp.; cons. Hertz Found., field com. study on astronomy in the 80's, NRC, 1980; mem. Army Sci. Bd., Washington, 1989-96; adj. prof. dept. applied sci., U. Calif., Davis, 1999-2002; mem. Calif. Coun. on Sci. and Tech., 1996-2002, Pacific Coun. on Internat. Policy, 1998—, lab. opers. bd. DOE, 1998-2002, Nuc. Energy Rsch. Adv. Bd., 1999-2002, Coun. Fgn. Rels., 1999—; bd. dirs. Draper Lab. Contbr. numerous articles to profl. jours. Recipient Roosevelts Gold Medal award for sci., NNSA Gold medal for disting. svc., U.S. Dept. Energy Exceptional Pub. Svc. award, Sec. of Energy's Gold award. Fellow AAAS (chair nuc. weapons complex assessment com. 2006—), Calif. Coun. Sci. and Tech., Am. Phys. Soc. (phys. policy com. 2002-05); mem. Am. Astron. Soc., Internat. Astron. Union. Avocations: golf, running, music. Office: Lawrence Livermore Nat Lab PO Box 808 Livermore CA 94551-0808 Office Phone: 925-422-4169. Business E-Mail: tarter1@llnl.gov. E-mail: cbtarter@yahoo.com.

TARTER, FRED BARRY, advertising executive; b. Bklyn., Aug. 16, 1943; s. Irving and Edna (Kupferberg) T.; m. Lois; children: Scott Andrew, Heather Michelle, Megan Elizabeth. Attended, CCNY, 1962—68. Pres. Jamie Publ. Hootenanny Enterprises, Inc., 1962-65; mdse. dir. Longines Symphonette Soc., 1965-67; with Universal Comm., Inc., NYC, 1967—, pres., CEO, 1969-74; exec. v.p. Deerfield Comm., Inc., NYC, 1974-87, pres., CEO, 1977-88; pres. Deerfield Books, Inc., NYC, 1988-89; pub. S.E.W. mag., NYC, 1977-88; pres. The Rainbow Group Ltd., NYC, 1988—; chmn. Stagebill Mag., 1997-2001; pres., CEO The Lakeside Group of Co., 2001—. Exec. prodr. Joanne Carson's VIP's Miss Am. Teenager Pageant, 1972—73; prodr. Marriage Counselor, 1994, Spenser: Pale Kings & Princes, 1995, Spenser: A Savage Place, 1995, Spenser Judas Goat, 1995, Hearts Adrift, 1995, Ceremony, 1996, Wounded Heart, 1996, Reasons of the Heart, 1996, Lover's Leap, 1996; chmn. Stagebill Enterprises, LLC, 1997—2001; vice-chmn. Affinity Comm., Inc., 1997—2001, Inscap, LLC; pres., CEO The Telephone Co. LLC, 1999—2003; pres. The Programme Exch., U.K. Ltd.; bd. dir. Asset Mktg. Sys., LLC, Caribbean Internat. News Corp., Boardwalk Entertainment, Ltd., Lakeside Group, Inc., Ace Mortgage LLC, Money Mailer LLC. Home: 578 Westport Tpke Fairfield CT 06430-1670 Office: The Lakeside Group Ltd 210 E 39th St New York NY 10016-2754 Personal E-mail: ftarter@lakesideglobal.com. *An integral part of success is the capacity for failure. Persistence, combined with responsibility, has proven to be the winning combination time and again.*

TARTT, BLAKE, lawyer; b. Houston, Mar. 16, 1929; s. Herbert Blake and Bernice (Schwalm) T.; m. Barbara Jean Moore, Jan. 30, 1960; children: Blake III, Courtnay Elias. BBA, So. Meth. U., Dallas, 1949, JD cum laude, 1959. Bar: Tex. 1959. Assoc. Fulbright & Jaworski, Houston, 1959-70, ptnr., 1970-2000, Beirne, Maynard & Parsons, LLP, Houston, 2000—. Mem. Tex. Commn. on Jud. Conduct, 1996-2001; bd. dirs. Nat. Judicial Coll. Bd. dirs. Mus. Fine Arts, Houston; mem. bd. visitors Nat. Jud. Coll. Served to 1st lt. USAF, 1951-55, Korea. Decorated Air medal. Fellow Am. Bar Found. (chmn. fellows 1987, life), Tex. Bar Found. (chmn. bd. 1974-75, chmn. fellows 1978-79, life), Am. Coll. Trial Lawyers; mem. ABA (ho. of dels. 1976-99, state del. 1990-99, standing com. fed. jud. 1996-99, chair 1997, bd. govs. 2001-04), Am. Bd. Trial Advocates (advocate), Houston Bar Found. (life., chmn., bd. dirs. 1992), Fed. Bar Assn., Internat. Assn. Def. Counsel, Am. Judicature Soc. (bd. dirs. 1984-88), So. Conf. Bar Pres. (pres. 1984), State Bar Tex. (dir. 1972-75, exec. com. 1975-76, pres. elect 1982-83, pres. 1983-84), Houston Bar Assn., Am. Law Inst., Tex. Jud. Commn., Citizens Commn. on the Tex. Judiciary, Tex. Commn. Jud. Conduct, Houston Philos. Soc., Coronado Club, Forest Club, Argyle Club (San Antonio), Reform Club (London), Delta Theta Phi, Alpha Tau Omega. Episcopalian. Office: Beirne Maynard & Parsons 1300 Post Oak Blvd Houston TX 77056-3028 Office Phone: 713-960-7331. Business E-Mail: btartt@bmpllp.com.

TARUI, NORI, economics professor; PhD, U. Minn., Twin Cities, 2004. Asst. prof. dept. econs. U. Hawaii, Honolulu, 2004—. Fellow Earth Inst. fellow, The Earth Inst. at Columbia U., 2004—06; MacArthur fellow, MacArthur Found., 1999. Office: University of Hawaii 2424 Maile Way Saunders 542 Honolulu HI 96822

TARUN, ROBERT WALTER, lawyer; b. Lake Forest, Ill., Sept. 1, 1949; s. Donald Walter and Bonnie Jean (Cruickshank) T.; m. Helen J. McSweeney, May 1, 1987; children: Abigail Esch, Tyler Vincent, Parker Donald, Aimée Dakota. AB, Stanford U., 1971; JD, DePaul U., 1974; MBA, U. Chgo., 1982. Bar: Ill. 1974, Calif. 1975, US Dist. Ct. (no. dist. Ill.) 1974, US Dist. Ct. (we. dist. Ark.) 1986, US Dist. Ct. (so. dist. Ind.) 1995, US Dist. Ct. (no. dist. Calif.) 1995, US Dist. Ct. (ea. dist. Mich.) 1996, US Dist. Ct. (ea. dist. Wis.) 2000, US Dist. Ct. (ctrl. dist. Ill.) 2001, US Ct. Appeals (7th cir.) 1975, US Ct. Appeals (5th cir.) 1992, US Ct. Appeals (3rd cir.) 1993, US Ct. Appeals (fed. cir.) 1995, US Ct. Appeals (9th and 11th cirs.) 1996, US Supreme Ct. 1978. Asst. atty. gen. State of Ill., Chgo., 1974-76; asst. US atty. US Dept. Justice, Chgo., 1976-79, dep. chief criminal divsn., 1979-82, exec. asst. U.S. atty. no. dist. Ill., 1982-85; ptnr. Reuben & Proctor, Chgo., 1985-86, Isham, Lincoln & Beale, Chgo., 1986-88, Winston & Strawn, Chgo., 1988—2003, Latham & Watkins, LLP, Chgo., 2003—07, Baker & McKenzie, San Francisco and Chgo., 2007—. Instr. Atty. Gen.'s Advocacy Inst., Washington, 1980—85, Nat. Inst. Trial Advs., 1990; adj. prof. Northwestern U. Sch. Law, 1999—2001; lectr. in law white collar criminal and bus. litig. U. Chgo. Law Sch., 2001—05. Author (with Dan K. Webb): Corporate Internal Investigations, 1993—2005. Bd. dirs. Chgo. Ctrl. Area Com., 1994—2003. Named one of Best Lawyers in Am., Euroguide's Guide to World's Leading Litigators, Chambers USA Leading Bus. Lawyers, Top 100 Lawyers in Ill. Fellow Am. Coll. Trial Lawyers (chair. fed. criminal procedure com. 2003-2004, admission to fellowship com. 1997-2000), bd. regents, 2004-; mem. ABA (white collar crime inst. 1997—, planning com.), Bar Assn. San Francisco, Chgo. Bar Assn., U. Chgo. Grad. Sch. Bus. Alumni Assn. (bd. dirs. 1986), Racquet Club, Wong Sun Soc. (San Francisco), Kenilworth Club, H.O.G. (Black Hills chpt.), Chgo. Stanford Assn. Presbyterian. Avocations: architecture, writing screenplays, motorcycling. Office: Baker & McKenzie 2 Embarcadero Ctr 1100 San Francisco CA 94111 also: Baker & McKenzie 130 E Randolph St Chicago IL 60601 Office Phone: 415-591-3220, 312-861-2533. Business E-Mail: robert.w.tarun@bakernet.com.

TARUSKIN, RICHARD FILLER, musicologist, educator; b. NY, Apr. 2, 1945; s. Benjamin Joseph and Beatrice Filler Taruskin; m. Cathy Roebuck Taruskin, May 1, 1984; children: Paul Roebuck, Tessa Roebuck. BA, Columbia U., 1965, PhD, 1975; MusD (hon.), Grand Valley State U., 2000. Assoc. prof. music Columbia U., NYC, 1975—86; prof. U. Calif., Berkeley, Calif., 1986—. Author: Opera and Drama in Russia, 1981, Music in the Western World: A History in Documents, 1984, The Latin-Texted Works of Antoine Busnoys, 1990, Text and Act: Essays on Music and Performance, 1993, Stravinsky and the Russian Traditions, 1995 (medal Royal Philharm. Soc, 1997), Musorgsky: Eight Essays and an Epilogue, 1997, Oxford History of Western Music, 2004, 1996, Defining Russia Musically, 1997. Fellow: Am. Acad. Arts & Sciences; mem.: Internat. Musicological Soc., Am. Musicological Soc. (dir. 1983—86), Am. Philos. Soc. Jewish. Avocation: performing music. Home: 815 Galvin Drive El Cerrito CA 94530 Office: University of California at Berkeley Music Department/Morrison Hall Berkeley CA 94720 Home Phone: 510-527-5704; Office Phone: 510-642-2678. Office Fax: 510-642-8480. E-mail: taruskin@berkeley.edu.

TARVER, ANTONIO, professional boxer; b. Orlando, Fla., Nov. 21, 1968; Former Olympic boxer, 1996; profl. boxer Internat. Boxing Fedn., 1997—. Actor: (films) Rocky Balboa, 2006. Named World Light Heavyweight Championship Belt, Internat. Boxing Fedn., World Boxing Assn., 2003, 2004—06. Achievements include standing record of 24-4 with 18 wins coming by way of knockout. *

TARVER, BETTY GAIL, music educator; d. Garland E. and Evelyn J. Schiller; m. Robert D. Tarver, July 20, 1991. AA, Temple Jr. Coll., 1978; B of Music Edn., Sam Houston State U., Huntsville, Tex., 1980. Cert. Kodaly Sam Houston State U. Music tchr. Magnolia Elem. Sch., Tex., 1980—83, Bear Br. Elem. Sch., Magnolia, 1983—. Mem.: Assn. Tex. Profl. Educators (assoc.), Tex. Music Educators Assn. (assoc.). Avocations: travel, piano. Office: Bear Branch Elem Sch 8909 FM 1488 Magnolia TX 77354

TARVER, DAVE L., medical association administrator; Exec. v.p. La. State Med. Soc., Baton Rouge. Bd. dir. La. Health Care Commn., La. Med. Mgmt. Assn. Co. cmdr. 24th Evacuation Hosp. US Army, 1967—68, Long Binh, Vietnam. Recipient Med. Exec. Meritorious Achievement award, AMA, 2006. Office: La State Med Soc Ste 100 6767 Perkins Rd Baton Rouge LA 70808 Office Phone: 225-763-8500. Office Fax: 225-763-6122. Business E-Mail: dave@lsms.org. *

TASH, BILL, state senator; b. Dillon, Mont., Aug. 21, 1932; m. Marlene Tash. Student, Western Mont. Coll., Mont. State U. Rancher; Rep. rep. dist. 34 Mont. Ho. of Reps., 1992-2000; Rep. senator dist. 17 Mont. State Senate, 2000—. Mem. state adminstrn. com. Mont. State Senate, chair natural resources. With USN. Office: 240 Vista Dr Dillon MT 59725-3100 also: Mont State Senate Capitol Station Helena MT 59620

TASH, MARTIN ELIAS, publishing company executive; b. NYC, Jan. 24, 1941; s. David and Esther (Milch) T.; m. Arlene Sue Klein, June 23, 1962; children: Nathan, Faye, Jill. BBA, Baruch Sch. City Coll. N.Y., 1962. C.P.A. Staff accountant S.D. Leidesdorf & Co. (C.P.A.'s), NYC, 1962-66; v.p. fin., dir. LMC Data Inc., NYC, 1966-71; with Plenum Pub. Corp., NYC, 1971-98, chmn. bd., pres., 1977-98; chmn. bd., pres., CEO Gradco Systems, Inc., 1990—. Office: Gradco Systems Inc 3753 Howard Hughes Pkwy Ste 200 Las Vegas NV 89109-0952

TASH, PAUL CLIFFORD, editor, publishing executive; b. South Bend, Ind., July 17, 1954; s. Robert N. and Barbara R. (Eller) T.; m. Karyn E. Krayer, Aug. 19, 1983; children: Kaley Marie, Kendyl Barbara. BA summa cum laude, Ind. U., 1976; LLB, Edinburgh U., Scotland, 1978. Reporter St. Petersburg Times, 1978-83, city editor, 1983-86, metro editor, 1986-89, editor, pub. Fla. Trend Mag., 1990-91, Washington bur. chief, 1991-92, exec. editor, 1992-2000, dep. chmn., 1997—2004, editor & pres., 2000—04, editor, chmn. & CEO, 2004—. Bd. dirs. Times Pub. Co., Newspaper Assn. Am., Com. to Protect Journalists, Mich. Journalism Fellows, Fla. Trend Mag., Congressional Quar., Poynter Inst. Media Studies. Chmn. Fla. First Amendment Found.; mem. adv. bd. Ind. U. Sch. Journalism; bd. govs. Fla. C. of C. Marshall Aid Commemoration Commn. scholar, 1976-78. Mem.: Fla. First Amendment Found., Tampa Bay Area Com. on Fgn. Rels., Am. Soc. Newspaper Editors, Fla. C. of C. Office: St Petersburg Times 490 1st Ave S Saint Petersburg FL 33701-4204 Mailing: PO Box 1121 Saint Petersburg FL 33731-1121 Office Phone: 727-893-8887. Office Fax: 727-892-2328. E-mail: ptash@sptimes.com. *

TASHIMA, ATSUSHI WALLACE, federal judge; b. Santa Maria, Calif., June 24, 1934; s. Yasutaro and Aya (Sasaki) Tashima; m. Nora Kiyo Inadomi, Jan. 27, 1957; children: Catherine Y., Christopher I., Jonathan I. AB in Polit. Sci., UCLA, 1958; LLB, Harvard U., 1961. Bar: Calif. 1962. Dep. atty. gen. State of Calif., 1962—67; atty. Spreckels Sugar divsn. Amstar Corp., 1968—72, v.p., gen. atty. Spreckels Sugar divsn., 1972—77; ptnr. Morrison & Foerster, LA, 1977—80; judge US Dist. Ct. (ctrl. dist.), LA, 1980—96, US Ct. Appeals (9th cir.), Pasadena, Calif., 1996—2003, sr. judge, 2003—. Mem. Calif. Com. Bar Examiners, 1978—80. With USMC, 1953—56. Mem.: ABA, LA County Bar Assn. Democrat. Office: Richard A Chambers US Ct Appeals PO Box 91510 125 S Grand Ave Pasadena CA 91109-1510 *

TASMAN, ALICE LEA MAST, not-for-profit fundraiser; d. Clarence Kurtz Mast and Florence Larue Barkley; m. William S. Tasman, Nov. 8, 1962; children: James B., W. Graham, Alice. BA, Barnard Coll., 1956; postgrad., U. Pa. Tchr. Am. Cathedral, Paris, 1953—54; asst. dir. pub. rels. Phila. Art Mus., 1956—61; pub. rels. exec. WUHY-FM, 1976—77; cons. Franklin Mint, 1991—94. Author: Wedding Album: Customs & Lore Through the Ages, 1981, Adam, A Three Island Cat, 1984. Women's bd. Thomas Jefferson U. Hosp., 1983—; chmn. Art in City Hall, 1995—2003; fundraising com., spl. events Recording for Blind, 1993—95; devel. com., trustee Woodmere Art Mus., 1994—2003; mem. Associated Svcs. for Blind; originator, chmn. annual exhibit Form in Art, 1987—; vol. Phila. Mus. Art, 1984—; annual concert and ball com. Phila. Orch., 1972—75; libr. Chestnut Hill Acad. and Springside Sch., 1977—78; antiques show com. U. Pa., 1972—75; coord. long-term patient care Chestnut Hill Hosp., 1981; fundraising and publicity chair Project Orbis, 1982; fundraiser Am. Diabetes Assn., 1984; vol. Chestnut Hill Hosp., 1978—87; hon. chair fundraising Overbrook Sch. for Blind, 1989; fundraiser Am. Indian Fund, 1989; hon. chair symposium, fundraiser 1st Nat. Inst. Blind Artists, 1990; internat. ambassador City of Phila., 1993; assoc. trustee Sulgrave Manor, London; fundraising, corp. devel. exec. Wills Eye Hosp., 1996—, chair 17th ann. forum art exhbn.; co-organizer Haitian Arts Exhbn. Friends of Hosp. Albert Schweitzer, Haiti; bd. dirs. Chestnut Hill Presbyn. Ch., 1989—93, Nat. Exhibits by Blind Artists, 1987—, Chestnut Hill Women's Com. Phila. Orch., 1965—, Chestnut Hill Cmty. Ctr. and Women's Exchange, 1978—; bd. dirs. coun. visual arts Chestnut Hill Acad., 1997—; bd. dirs. Art in City Hall, 1993—2003, Hitchcock Found., 1982—83. Recipient Cert. of Appreciation, Phila. Arts Fest., 1959, Wills Eye Hosp., 1994, Overbrook Sch. for Blind award, 1989, Louis Braille award, Associated Svcs. for Blind, 1993, Founder's award, Nat. Exhibits by Blind Artists, Disting. Daughters of Pa. award, Gov. and Mrs. Tom Ridge, 1997, Lady of Dumbarton award, Nat. Soc. Colonial Dames, 1999, Lifetime Achievement award, Little Rock Found., 2001. Mem.: Friends Vielles Maisons Francaises, Am. Ophthalmology Soc. (chair pres. dinner 1989—), Am. Bd. Ophthalmology (chair 75th anniversary dinner 1992), Am. Acad. Ophthalmology (chair Christian med. dental luncheon 1991—92, organizer 2nd Ann. Orbital Gala), French Huguenot Soc., Chestnut Hill Hist. Soc. (pres. 1972—74, program chair 1974—75, fundraising and spl. events chair 1981—), Nat. Soc. Colonial Dames Commonwealth Pa. (house com. 1980—89, garden com. 1987, house com. 1993—94, chair program com. 1993—96, first v.p. 1998—2002, co-chair capital campaign fund 1999—2001, pres. 2002—05, Alice Lea Mast Tasman ednl. chair), Rotary, Jr. League. Avocations: travel, skiing, painting, crafts, gardening.

TASMAN, ALLAN, psychiatry educator; b. Louisville, Feb. 8, 1947; s. Goodman and Zelda Tasman; m. Cathy Faye Goldstein, May 24, 1970. BA in Chemistry, Franklin and Marshall Coll., 1969; MD, U. Ky., 1973. Diplomate Am. Bd. Psychiatry and Neurology. Resident in psychiatry U. Ky. Med. Sch., Lexington, 1973—74, U. Cin. Med. Ctr., 1974—76; asst. prof. psychiatry U. Conn. Med. Sch., Farmington, 1976—82, assoc. prof. psychiatry and tenure, 1982—88, prof. psychiatry, 1988—91; prof. psychiatry and behavioral scis., tenure and chmn. U. Louisville Sch. Medicine, 1991—. Editor: Annual Review of Psychiatry, 1989-92, Clinical Challenges in Psychiatry, 1993, Less Time to Do More, 1993; sr. editor: Textbook of Psychiatry, 1997, 2d edit., 2003; assoc. editor Am. Jour. Psychotherapy, 1999—; founding dep. editor Jour. Psychotherapy Practice and Rsch., 1992-99. Recipient Alpha Omega Alpha Faculty award, 2002, NAMI Exemplary Psychiatrist award, 2002, Pres.'s Disting. Faculty award for svc. to the profession, U. Louisville, 2003, St. Clair award, Ky. Psychiat. Assn., 2007. Fellow Am. Psychiat. Assn. (disting., v.p. 1996-98, pres.-elect 1998-99, pres. 1999-2000, Nancy Roeske award for excellence in med. student edn. 1991, Irma Bland award for excellence in resident tchg. 2005), Royal Coll. Psychiatrists, Am. Assn. Dirs. Psychiat. Residency Tng. (pres. 1993-94); mem. Assn. Acad. Psychiatry (pres. 1993-94, Educator of Yr. award 2000), Am. Assn. Chmn. Depts. Psychiatry (pres. 1996-97, 97-98), World Psychiat. Assn. (bd. dirs. 2002—, sec. for edn. 2005—), Pacific Rim Coll. Psychiatrists (pres. 2006—). Office: U Louisville Sch Medicine Dept Psychiatry Behavioral Scis Louisville KY 40292-0001

TASOOJI, MICHAEL B., retail executive; m. Linda Tasooji; 3 children. BS in Internat. Trade and Quantitative Bus. Analysis, U. So. Calif., MBA in Internat. Fin. and Bus. Econs. With Getty Oil Co., Columbia Pictures Studio; v.p. application systems Bergen Brunswig Corp.; v.p. info. svcs. Disneyland, 1995—2000; sr. v.p., chief info. officer Walt Disney Attractions, 2000, Walt Disney Co., 2000—03; exec. v.p., chief info. officer Gap, Inc., 2003—. Office: Gap Inc 2 Folsom St San Francisco CA 94105 Office Phone: 650-952-4400. *

TASSÉ, ROGER, lawyer, former Canadian government official; b. Montreal, Que., Can., 1931; BA, Coll. St. Marie, Montreal, 1952; Lic. in Law, U. Montreal, 1955; diploma d'Etudes Superieures, U. Ottawa, Ont., Can., 1957. Bar: Que. 1956, Ont. 1986; called to Queens Counsel 1971. Joined Dept. Justice, 1956, civil law counsel for Can. govt., from 1957, supt. bankruptcy, 1965-68, asst. dep. min. consumer and corp. affairs, 1968-72; dep. min. Dept. of Solicitor Gen., 1972-77; dep. min. of justice, atty. gen. of Can., 1977-85; ptnr. Land Michener Lash Johnston, Toronto and Ottawa, Noel Décary Aubry & Assocs., Hull, Que., 1985-88; exec. v.p. legal and environ. affairs Bell Can., 1988-91; of counsel Fraser & Beatty, Toronto, 1992-95, Gowling, Lafleur & Henderson, Ottawa, 1995—. Prin. constl. advisor to Spl. Joint Com. of the Senate and the House of Commons on a Renewed Can., 1991-92. Mem. Citizens' Forum on Canada's Future, 1990; co-chair task force Can. Mags., 1993; mem. DTH Panel, 1995. Decorated officer Order of Can. Avocations: skiing, tennis. Office: Gowling Lafleur Henderson LLP 160 Elgin St Ste 2600 Ottawa ON Canada K1P 1C3 Office Phone: 813-786-0208. Fax: (613) 563-9869. E-mail: roger.tasse@gowlings.com.

TASSINARI, MELISSA SHERMAN, teratologist, developmental toxicologist; b. Lawrence, Mass., Sept. 26, 1953; m. R. Peter Tassinari; children: Michael, Emily, Sara. AB, Mt. Holyoke Coll., 1975; postgrad., U. St. Andrews, Scotland, 1973-74; PhD, Med. Coll. Wis., 1979. Diplomate Am. Bd. Toxicology. Rsch. asst. in orthopedic surgery, Lab. Human Biochemistry Children's Hosp. Med. Ctr., Boston, 1981-83; rsch. affiliate in toxicology Forsyth Dental Ctr., Boston, 1983-86, staff assoc. dept. toxicology, 1986-89; asst. prof. cell biology U. Mass. Med. Ctr., Worcester, 1989-91; head reproductive and developmental toxicology Pfizer Global R&D, Groton/New London, Conn., 1991—99, group dir. worldwide safety scis., 2001—04, sr. dir. worldwide regulatory policy and intelligence, 2004—. Rsch. fellow oral biology Harvard Sch. Dental Medicine, Boston, 1978-81, instr. oral biology and pathophysiology, 1981-83; asst. prof. biol. scis. Wellesley Coll., Mass., 1985-91, biology Simmons Coll., Boston, 1986-87. Contbr. abstracts, articles to profl. jours. Mem. Teratology Soc. (coun. mem. 2000-07, v.p. 2004, pres. 2005-06), Neurobehavioral Teratology Soc., Mid. Atlantic Reprodn. and Teratology Assn. (steering com. 1994), Midwest Teratology Assn., Soc. Toxicology, Orgn., Teratogen Info. Svcs., Drug Info. Assn. Office: Pfizer Inc 50 Pequot Ave New London CT 06320

TASSIOPOULOS, APOSTOLOS K., vascular surgeon; b. Trikala, Greece, Oct. 8, 1965; arrived in US, 1992; s. Konstantinos A. Tassiopoulos and Vasiliki D. Tassiopoulou; m. Yianna Darsinos Tassiopoulos, Aug. 23, 2003; 1 child, Vasia. MD, Aristotle U., Thessaloniki, Greece, 1989. Resident gen. surgery Upstate Med. U., Syracuse, 1993—99; fellow vascular surgery Loyola U. Med. Ctr., Haywood, Ill., 1999—2001; sr. attending Cook County Hosp., Chgo., 2001—06; asst. prof. surgery Rush U. Med. Ctr., Chgo., 2002—06, SUNY, 2006—. Contbr. chapters to books. Fellow: Am. Coll. Surgeons; mem.: Am. Assn. Vascular Surgery, European Soc. Vascular Surgeon (assoc.). Home: 5 Bayberry Ct Miller Place NY 11764 Office: SUNY Med Ctr HSC Level T-19 Rm 090 Stony Brook NY 11794

TASSLER, NINA, broadcast executive; married; 2 children. BFA, Boston U. With Roundabout Theatre Co., NYC; dir. TV Triad Artists, Inc.; dir. movies & miniseries, pres. drama devel. Warner Bros. TV, 1990—97; with CBS Corp., 1997—; v.p. drama CBS Prodns., 1997—98; sr. v.p. drama devel. CBS Entertainment, 1998—2003, exec. v.p. drama series devel., 2003—04, pres. Los Angeles, 2004—. Named one of 100 Most Powerful Women in Entertainment, Hollywood Reporter, 2006, America 's Top Women in Bus.-Game Changers, Pink mag. & Forté Found., 2007; recipient Imagen award, 2005. Mailing: CBS Entertainment 5555 Melrose Ave Los Angeles CA 90038 *

TASSONE, GELSOMINA (GESSIE TASSONE), metal products executive; b. NYC, July 8, 1944; d. Enrico and A. Cira (Petriccione) Gargiulo; children: Ann Marie, Margaret, Theresa, Christine; m. Armando Tassone, Mar. 20, 1978. Student, Orange County Community Coll., 1975-79, Iona Coll., 1980—. Head bookkeeper Gargiulo Bros. Builders, NYC, 1968-72; pres., owner A&T Iron Works, Inc., New Rochelle, NY, 1973—. Recipient Profl. Image award Contractors Coun. Greater NYC, 1986; named Businesswoman of Yr., Contractors Coun. Greater NYC, 1985, NY State Small Bus. Person of Yr., 1988, Entrepreneur of Yr., Inc. mag., 1990; company named a Successful Small Bus. Co. Westchester County C. of C./BSBA, 1986-88. Mem. Nat. Ornamental and Miscellaneous Metal Assn., Builders Inst. Westchester and Putnam County, Westchester Assn. Women Bus. Owners, Profl. Women in Constrn., New Rochelle C. of C. Office: A&T Iron Works Inc 25 Cliff St New Rochelle NY 10801-6803 Office Phone: 914-632-8992. Personal E-mail: gesjames@aol.com. Business E-Mail: info@atironworks.com.

TATA, GIOVANNI, publishing executive; b. Taranto, Italy, Apr. 26, 1954; came to U.S., 1974, naturalized, 1982; s. Vito and Angela (Colucci) T.; m. Brenda Susan Smith, Feb. 14, 1978; children: Elizabeth Ariana, Katherine Allison, Margaret Anne, Michael Anthony, Hanna Amelia. BS cum laude, Brigham Young U., 1977, MA, 1980; grad. cert. area studies, U. Utah, 1980, PhD, 1986; postgrad., U. Turin, Italy, 1980-81. Archaeologist Utah State Hist. Soc., Salt Lake City, 1979; instr. dept. langs. U. Utah, Salt Lake City, 1983-85; Mediterranean specialist Soc. Early Hist. Archaeology, Provo, Utah, 1978-91; rsch. fellow Direzione Gen. Cooperazione Sci. Culturale e Technica, Rome, 1980-81; mus. curator Pioneer Trail State Park, Salt Lake City, 1982-83; instr. dept. art Brigham Young U., Provo, 1982-84, dir. creative works, 1996—; rsch. curator Utah Mus. Fine Arts, Salt Lake City, 1985-87; pres. Mus. Info. Sys., 1987-93, Transoft Internat., Inc., 1988—. Chmn. 35th Ann. Symposium on the Archaeology of the Scriptures, 1986, Taras Devel. Corp., 1994—97, MuseMedia, Inc., 1995—2000. Patentee method and system for computerized learning, response, and evaluation. Brigham Young U. scholar. Mem.: Intellectual Property Owners Assn., Assn. Univ. Tech. Mgrs., Nat. Coun. Museums, Am. Assn. Museums. Republican. Mem. Ch. Jesus Christ of Latter-day Saints. Home Phone: 801-224-4973; Office Phone: 801-422-3724. Business E-Mail: giovanni_tata@byu.edu. E-mail: tata@lexinet.com.

TATÁR, ANNA, library director; Grad., DePauw U., Greencastle, Ind.; MLS, U. Mich., Ann Arbor. Dir. San Diego Pub. Libr. Bd. dirs. STAR/PAL (Sports, Tng., Academics and Recreational/Police Athletic League), San Diego. Named one of 50 People to Watch in 2003, San Diego Mag. Mem.: ALA. Office: San Diego Pub Libr Ctrl Libr 820 E St San Diego CA 92101-6478 Office Phone: 619-236-5870. E-mail: atatar@sandiego.gov. *

TATAR, ARNOLD MARSHALL, internist, educator; b. Chgo., June 26, 1933; s. Louis and Rose Goldberg Tatar; m. Marina Deull-Wirszup, Aug. 30, 1959; children: Carolyn Beth, Audrey Michelle, Lauren D. W. BA in Chemistry, U. Ill., 1954; BS in Medicine, U. Ill., Chgo., 1955, MD cum laude, 1957. Lic. physician, Ill.; cert., recert. Am. Bd. Internal Medicine. Resident in internal medicine Michael Reese Hosp. and Med. Ctr., Chgo., 1957-60, chief med. resident, 1960-61, attending physician, 1961—2001; pres. Drs. Tatar Tatar Buchanan Hunt Suh and Lavery, Chgo., 1961—; attending physician Northwestern Meml. Hosp., Chgo., 1991—. Assoc. prof. internal medicine U. Chgo., 1973-91; asst. prof. internal medicine Northwestern U., Evanston/Chgo., 1991—; dir. med. intensive care Michael Reese Hosp., Chgo., 1969-76, dir. investigative hypertension clinic, 1964-76, pres. med. staff, 1988-90, hosp. trustee, 1982-91. Contbr. rsch. articles to profl. jours. Pres. Parent-Tchr. Orgn., John F. Kennedy Sch., Highland Park, Ill., 1970-72. Lt. col. U.S. Army, 1967-69. Named one of Chgo.'s Top Drs., Chgo. Mag., 1997, 2001, 2004, Outstanding Primary Care Physicians in U.S., Town and Country Mag., 1999. Fellow Am. Coll. Chest Physicians, Am. Coll. Angiology, Am. Heart Assn. (coun. on hypertension, coun. on clin. cardiology), Am. Soc. Internal Medicine. Avocations: music, theater, dance, bicycling, photography. Home: Apt 5-East 189 E Lake Shore Dr Chicago IL 60611 Office: Drs Tatar Tatar Buchanan Hunt Suh and Lavery Ste 1801 111 W Washington Chicago IL 60602

TATAR, JEROME F., business products executive; V.p., operating officer Mead Corp., Dayton, Ohio, 1994—96, pres., COO, 1996—97, chmn., CEO, 1997—2002; chmn. MeadWestvaco Corp., 2002. Bd. mem. Robbins & Myers Inc., Nat. City Corp., Bartech Group Inc. Office: Mead Corp Courthouse Plz NE Dayton OH 45463-0001

TATARSKII, VALERIAN IL'ICH, physics researcher; b. Kharkov, USSR, Oct. 13, 1929; s. Il'ya A. and Elizabeth A. (Lapis) T.; m. Maia S. Granovskaia, Dec. 22, 1955; 1 child, Viatcheslav V. MS, Moscow State U., 1952; PhD, Acoustical Inst. Acad. Scis., 1957; DSc, Gorky State U., 1962. Scientific rschr. Geophys. Inst. Acad. Sci. USSR, Moscow, 1953-56, Inst. Atmospheric Physics, Acad. Sci. USSR, Moscow, 1956-59, sr. scientific rschr., 1959-78, head lab., 1978-90; head dept. Lebedev. Phys. Inst. Acad. Sci., Moscow, 1990-91; sr. rsch. assoc. U. Colo. Coop. Inst. for Rsch. in Environ. Sci., Boulder, 1991—2001; sr. rsch. scientist Zel Techs. and NOAA/Phys. Sci. Dept., Boulder, 2001—. Author: Wave Propagation in a Turbulent Medium, 1961, 67, The Effect of the Turbulent Atmosphere on Wave Propagation, 1971, Principles of Statistical Radiophysics, 1989; contbr. articles to profl. jours. Recipient USSR State prize, 1990. Fellow Optical Soc. Am. (Max Born award 1994), Inst. Physics; mem. Russian Acad. Sci., USA Nat. Acad. Engring., NY Acad. Sci., MIT Electromagnetic Soc. Avocations: classical music, fine art, photography. Office: Radio Hydro Physics NOAA Phys Sci Dept Mail Stop ZelTech 325 Broadway St Boulder CO 80305-3328 Office Phone: 303-497-3668. Personal E-mail: vtatarskii@hotmail.com.

TATAVARTHY, APARNA, biologist, researcher; arrived in U.S., 1997; d. Subbarao and Manikyalakshmi Kavuru; m. Viswanadh R. Tatavarthy, Oct. 25, 1997; 1 child, Anjali M. BS, Mrs. A.V.N. Coll., 1995; MS, Andhra U., 1997; PhD, U. South Fla., Tampa, 2005. Tchg. asst. dept. biology U. South Fla., Tampa, 2000—02, rsch. asst. Ctr. for Biol. Def., 2002—. Contbr. articles to profl. jours. Home Phone: 813-907-7579.

TATE, DEBORAH TAYLOR, commissioner; b. Murfreesboro, Tenn. d. Louis Carlton Taylor; m. William H. Tate; children: Will, Taylor, Carlton. BA, JD, U. Tenn.; attended, Vanderbilt U. Cert.: Tenn. Supreme Ct. (Rule 31 Mediator). Atty., sr. policy advisor to Gov. Lamar Alexander and Gov. Don Sundquist, Tenn.; dir. Tenn. Regulatory Authority, 2000—06, chmn., 2003—04; commr. FCC, Washington, 2006—. Former dir. state and local policy ctr. Vanderbilt Inst. for Pub. Policy Studies; guest lectr. Vanderbilt U. Fellow: Nashville Bar Found.; mem.: Lawyer's Assn. for Women, Nashville Bar Assn. Office: FCC 445 12th St SW Washington DC 20554

TATE, HAROLD SIMMONS, JR., lawyer; b. Taylors, SC, Sept. 19, 1930; s. Harold Simmons and Cleone (Clayton) T.; m. Elizabeth Anne Coker, Dec. 22, 1952; children— Mary Elizabeth Anne, Martha Coker, Virginia Clayton. Degree in internat. law and rels. cum laude, Harvard U., 1951, postgrad., 1954, JD, 1956; MA, U. SC, 2005. Bar: S.C. 1956. Ptnr. Haynsworth Sinkler Boyd, PA, Columbia, SC, 1962—. Chmn. adv. com. US Dist. Ct. (SC), 1984-2006; lectr. Am. Law Inst.-ABA seminars; adv. com. on rules and procedures US Ct. Appeals (4th cir.), 1990-95. Co-author: South Carolina Appellate Practice, 1985; bd. editors Federal Litigation Guide Reporter, 1985—; co-draftsman S.C. Rules of Evidence, 1995; contbr. articles and book revs. to profl. jours. Chmn. Richland County Mental Health Ctr., 1965-66; co-chmn. Columbia Hearing and Speech Ctr., 1962-64; mem. admission and scholarship com. Harvard U., 1961—; chmn. subcom. on legislation, legislation and fin. study commn. Gov.'s Adv. Group on Mental Health Planning, 1963-65; chmn. Columbia Bd. Supervisors of Registration, 1961-70; pres. Columbia Philharm. Orch., 1966-67, Town Theatre, 1967-70; bd. trustee Richland County Pub. Libr., 1973-78, Hist. Columbia Found., 1971-75, Caroliniana Soc., 1978—, Bostick Charitable Trust, 1968—, Archaeol. Rsch. Trust, 2000—; bd. mgrs. SC Hist. Soc., 1993-99, 2002—; commr. SC Commn. of Archives and History, 1995—. Capt. US Army, 1951—53. Recipient DuRant award Disting Pub. Svc., 2001. Fellow Am. Coll. Trial Lawyers; mem. ABA, Am. Law Inst., Am. Judicature Soc., SC Bar Assn., Assn. Bar City NY, Richland County Bar Assn., Harvard Law Sch. Assn. SC (sec.-treas. 1968-70, pres. 1988—), Columbia Drama Club (pres. 1963-64), Palmetto Club (sec. 1963-70, pres. 1973-76), Forum Club, Harvard Club NYC, Harvard Club SC, Carolina Yacht Club. Episcopalian. Office: Haynsworth Sinkler Boyd PA Fl 22 1201 Main St Ste 2200 Columbia SC 29201-3232 Home: 41 King St Charleston SC 29401 Office Phone: 803-779-3080. Business E-Mail: state@hsblawfirm.com.

TATE, JAMES VINCENT, poet, English educator; b. Kansas City, Mo., Dec. 8, 1943; s. Samuel Vincent Appleby and Betty Jean Whitsitt. BA, Kans. State Coll., 1965; MFA, U. Iowa, 1967. Instr. U. Iowa, Iowa City, 1966-67; vis. lectr. U. Calif., Berkeley, 1967-68; asst. prof. English Columbia U., NYC, 1969-71; from assoc. prof. to dist. univ. prof. English U. Mass., Amherst, 1971—. Poet-in-residence Emerson Coll., 1970-71; cons. Coord. Coun. Literary Mags., 1971-74, Ky. Arts Commn., 1979; mem. Bollingen Prize Com., 1974-75; poetry editor Dickinson Rev., 1967-76; trustee, assoc. editor Pym-Randall Pr., 1968-80; assoc. editor Barn Dream Pr. Author: (poems) Cages, 1966, The Destination, 1967, The Lost Pilot, 1967 (Yale Younger Poets award 1966), Notes of Woe, 1968, Camping in the Valley, 1968, Mystics in Chicago, 1968, The Torches, 1968, Row with Your Hair, 1969, Is There Anything?, 1969, Shepherds of the Mist, 1969, Amnesia People, 1970, Are You Ready Mary Baker Eddy, 1970, Deaf Girl Playing, 1970, The Oblivion Ha-Ha, 1970, Wrong Songs, 1970, Hints to Pilgrims, 1971, Nobody Goes to Visit the Insane Anymore, 1971, Absences, 1972, Apology for Eating Geoffrey Movius' Hyacinth, 1972, A Dime Found in the Snow, 1973, Hottentot Ossuary, 1974, Marfa, 1974, Suffering Bastards, 1975, Who Gets the Bitterroot?, 1976, Viper Jazz, 1976, Riven Doggeries, 1979, The Rustling of Foliage, the Memory of Caresses, 1979, If It Would All Please Hurray, 1980, Land of Little Sticks, 1981, Constant Defender, 1983, Just Shades, 1985, Reckoner, 1986, Distance from Loved Ones, 1990, Selected Poems, 1991 (Pulitzer Prize for poetry 1992), Worshipful Company of Fletchers, 1993 (Nat. Book Award for Poetry 1994), Shroud of the Gnome, 1997, Return to the City of White Donkeys, 2004, Memoirs of the Hawk, 2005; (novel) Lucky Darryl, 1977. Named Poet of Yr. by Phi Beta Kappa, 1972; recipient Nat. Inst. Arts and Letters award for poetry, 1974; Mass. Arts and Humanities fellow, 1975, Guggenheim fellow, 1976, Nat. Endowment for the Arts fellow, 1980. Office: U Mass Bartlette Hall Dept English Amherst MA 01003-0515

TATE, JOHN TORRENCE, mathematics professor, researcher; b. Mpls., Mar. 13, 1925; BA, Harvard U., 1946; PhD, Princeton U., 1950. Sid W. Richardson chair math. U. Tex., Austin, 1990—. Co-recipient Leroy P. Steele prize Am. Math. Soc., 1995, Cole prize in number theory, 1956, Wolf prize in math. Wolf Found., Israel, 2003. Mem. Nat. Acad. Scis., Academie des Scis. (Paris), mem. London Mathematical Society. Office: Univ Texas at Austin Dept Math 1 University Station C1200 Austin TX 78712-0257 Office Phone: 512-471-7127, 512-471-7711. Office Fax: 512-471-9038. E-mail: tate@math.utexas.edu.

TATE, JOHN WILLIAM, consumer products company executive, former food products executive; BA in Econs., U. Tex., 1972. Various fin. and gen. mgmt. positions Dole Food Co. Inc., Westlake Village, Calif.; CFO fresh vegetables divsn. Dole Food Co., 1993-96, CFO Dole Europe Paris, CFO Westlake Village, Calif., 1998—2000, Krispy Kreme Doughnuts, Inc., Winston-Salem, NC, 2000—02; COO Krispy Kreme Doughnuts Inc., Winston-Salem, NC, 2002—04; exec. v.p., COO Restoration Hardware, Inc., Corte Madera, Calif., 2004—. With USAF, 1973-79. Office: Restoration Hardware Inc 15 Koch Rd Ste J Corte Madera CA 94925

TATE, LARENZ, actor; b. Chgo., Ill., Sept. 8, 1975; Actor: (TV series) The Twilight Zone, 1985, Hunter, 1987, Amen, 1988, 21 Jump Street, 1989, The Wonder Years, 1989, Matlock, 1989, New Attitude, 1990, Family Matters, 1990—91, The Royal Family, 1991, Fresh Prince of Bel-Air, 1992, South Central, 1994, Love Monkey, 2006; (TV films) The Women of Brewster Place, 1989, Seeds of Tragedy, 1991; (films) Menace II Society, 1993, The Inkwell, 1994, Dead Presidents, 1995, Love Jones, 1997, The Postman, 1997, Why Do Fools Fall in Love, 1998, Love Come Down, 2000, Biker Boyz, 2003, A Man Apart, 2003, Crash, 2004 (recipient, Outstanding Performance, SAG awards, 2006), Ray, 2004, Waist Deep, 2006.

TATE, SHEILA BURKE, public relations executive; b. Washington, Mar. 3, 1942; d. Eugene L. and Mary J. (Doherty) Burke; m. William J. Tate, May 2, 1981 (dec. Aug. 1998); children: Hager Burke Patton, Courtney Paige Patton Manzel; m. John K. Youel, Nov. 26, 2005. BA in Journalism, Duquesne U., 1964; postgrad. in mass comm., U. Denver, 1975—76. Rsch. asst. Westinghouse Air Brake Co.; asst. account exec. Falhgren and Assocs.; copywriter Ketchum, MacLeod and Grove, 1964—66; account exec. Burson-Marsteller Assocs., Pitts., 1967, sr. v.p. Washington, 1985—87; pub. rels. mgr. Colo. Nat. Bank, Denver, 1967—70; account exec. Hill and Knowlton, Inc., Houston, 1977—78, v.p. Washington, 1978—81; dep. to the chmn. Hill and Knowlton Inc., Washington, 1987—88; press sec. to First Lady White House, Washington, 1981—85; press sec. George Bush for Pres. Campaign, 1988; press sec. to Pres.-elect George Bush, 1988—89; vice chmn. Cassidy and Assocs. Pub. Affairs, Washington, 1989—91; pres. Powell Tate, Washington, 1991—99, vice-chmn., 1999—. Bd. dirs., former mem. Corp. for Pub. Broadcasting, vice chmn., 1990—92, chmn., 1992—94. Mem. nat. adv. bd. The Salvation Army; adv. bd. Am. Acad. Family Physicians, Kansas City, Kans. Mem.: Nat. Press Club, Belfair Club, Farmington Country Club, Washington Golf and Country Club, Duquesne U. Century Club. Office: Powell Tate 700 13th St NW Ste 1000 Washington DC 20005-5926 Home Phone: 703-536-0477. Business E-Mail: state@webershandwick.com.

TATE, STONEWALL SHEPHERD, lawyer; b. Memphis, Dec. 19, 1917; m. Janet Graf; children: Adele Shepherd, Shepherd Davis, Janet Reid Walker. BA, U. Southwestern (now Rhodes Coll.), Memphis, 1939; JD, U. Va., 1942; LLD (hon.), Samford U., 1979, Suffolk U., 1982, Capital U., 1989, Rhodes Coll., 1993. Bar: Va. 1941, Tenn. 1942. Chmn. bd. Martin, Tate, Morrow & Marston, P.C. (and predecessor firms), Memphis, 1947—. Chmn. pres.'s coun. Rhodes Coll., 1995-96, sec. bd. trustees, 1967-77, 80-84. Pres. Episcopal Churchmen of Tenn., 1961-62; sec. standing com. Episcopal Diocese of Tenn., 1969-71; pres. Chickasaw Coun. Boy Scouts Am., 1967-78. With USNR, 1942-46; comdr. USNR; ret. Decorated Order of Cloud Banner (China); recipient Silver Beaver award Boy Scouts Am., 1963, Disting. Eagle Scout award, 1980, Disting. Svc. medal Rhodes Coll., 1978, Disting. Alumni award, 1991, Lawyers' Lawyer award Memphis Bar Assn., 1990; Memphis Rotary Club Civic Recognition award, 1983, Paul Harris fellow, 1985. Fellow Am. Bar Found., Am. Coll. Trust and Estate Counsel, Internat. Acad. Estate and Trust Law, Coll. Law Practice Mgmt. (hon.), Tenn. Bar Found., Memphis Bar Found. (Benjamin L. Hooks award 2003), Shelby County Bar Found.; mem. ABA (chmn. standing com. on profl. discipline 1973-76, chmn. standing com. on scope and correlation of work 1977, chmn. task force on lawyer advt. 1977, pres. ABA 1978-79, chmn. standing com. on lawyer competence 1986-92, mem. coun. sr. lawyers divsn. 1997-2001, 2004-), Am. Judicature Soc. (past bd. dirs.), Am. Law Inst., Lawyer-Pilots Bar Assn., Tenn. Bar Assn. (pres. 1963-64, recipient of William M. Leech, Jr., Public Svc. award, 2005), Memphis and Shelby County Bar Assn. (pres. 1959-60), Nat. Conf. Bar Pres. (pres. 1972-73, Alumnus of Yr. 1996), U.S. 6th Cir. Jud. Conf. (life), U. Va. Law Sch. Alumni Assn. (mem. exec. coun. 1974-77), Rhodes Coll. Alumni Assn. (pres. 1951-53), Rotary (pres. 1982-83, bd. dirs. 1974, 80-84, 89-90), Raven Soc., Order of Coif, Phi Beta Kappa, Omicron Delta Kappa, Phi Delta Phi, Sigma Alpha Epsilon (highest effort award N.Y.C. Alumni Assn. 1979). Office: Martin Tate Morrow & Marston PC 6410 Poplar Ave Ste 1000 Memphis TN 38119-4843 Home Phone: 901-324-2854; Office Phone: 901-522-9000. Business E-Mail: sstate@martintate.com.

TATE, WENDY K., insurance company executive, risk management consultant; b. Elizabeth, NJ, Nov. 11, 1961; d. William Henry Jr. and Catherine Lillian (Fulton) Knight; 1 child, Faith Corinne. Student, U. Warwick, Eng., 1981—82; BA, Duke U., 1983; M in health admin., U. N.C., 2003. Cert. ins. counselor, assoc. in risk mgmt.; CPCU. V.p., client exect. Marsh, Inc., Charlotte, NC, 2003—05; practice leader risk mgmt. divsn. Hartfort Ins. Group, 2005—06; v.p. ins. svcs. and risk mgmt. So. States Coop., 2006—. Mem. CPCU Soc., Soc. Cert. Ins. Counselors. Democrat. Episcopalian. Avocations: camping, tennis. Home: 9312 Springmount Terr Chesterfield VA 23832 Office Phone: 804-281-1581, 804-281-1000. Business E-Mail: wendy.tate@sscoop.com.

TATEL, DAVID STEPHEN, federal judge; b. Washington, Mar. 16, 1942; s. Howard Edwin and Molly (Abramowitz) Tatel; m. Edith Sara Bassichis, Aug. 29, 1965; children: Rebecca, Stephanie, Joshua, Emily. BA, U. Mich., 1963; JD, U. Chgo., 1966. Bar: Ill. 1966. Instr. U. Mich., Ann Arbor, 1966—67; assoc. Sidley & Austin, Chgo. and Washington, 1967—69, 1970—72; dir. Chgo. Lawyer's Com., 1969—70, Nat. Lawyers Commn. for Civil Rights Under Law, Washington, 1972—74; assoc. Hogan & Hartson, Washington, 1974—77, ptnr., 1979—94; dir. Office for Civil Rights US Dept. Health Edn. & Welfare, Washington, 1977—79; judge US Ct. Appeals (DC cir.), Washington, 1994—. Lectr. Stanford U. Law Sch., 1991—92; co-chmn. Nat. Lawyers Com. for Civil Rights Under Law, Washington, 1989—91; chmn., bd. dirs. Spencer Found., Chgo., 1990—97. Bd. dirs. Carnegie Found. for Advancement in Tchg., Stanford, Calif., 1997—. Office: US Ct Appeals 333 Constitution Ave NW US Courthouse Washington DC 20001-2866 *

TATERA, JAMES FRANK, chemist; b. Milw., June 27, 1946; s. Harry Frank and Agnes Rose (Szymanowski) T.; m. Kaaren Marie Piekarski, Sept. 9, 1972; children: Patrick, Monica, David. BS in Chemistry and Math., U. Wis., Oshkosh, 1968; postgrad., U. Minn., 1968, 71-73; MBA, Cen. Mich. U., 1982. Cert. specialist in analytical tech. Tchg. rsch. assoc. chemistry dept. U. Minn., Mpls., 1968, 71-73; analytical chemist Dow Corning Corp., Midland, Mich., 1973-76, scale up engr. new products commercialization, 1976-78, prodn. bldg. supt. prodn. dept., 1978-80; analytical systems specialist project and plant engring. Dow Corning Ltd., Barry, Wales, 1981-84; analytical systems supr. plant engring. & maintenance Dow Corning Corp., Carrollton, Ky., 1984-85, analytical systems specialist plant engring. and maintenance, 1985-87, sr. analytical and control specialist project engring., 1988-90, sr. analytical systems specialist strategic change program, 1991-98, sr. analytical sys. specialist Process Analysis Expertise Ctr., 1998-2000; ret., 2000; sr. process analysis cons. Tatera & Assocs. Inc., Madison, Ind., 2001—. U.S. nat. com. Internat. Electrotech. Commn., Paris, 1993, Milan, 94, Montreal, 96, Houston, 98, Beijing, 2002, Madrid, 03, Ottowa, Canada, 2005—, Berlin, 2007; session developer, panelist, course instr., presenter in field. Mem. editl. adv. bd.: InTech Jour., 1998—; contbr. articles to profl. jours., chpts. to books; author, presenter: internat. process analysis courses. 1st lt. U.S. Army, 1969-71. Decorated Bronze Star, Bronze Star with oak leaf cluster. Fellow: Instrumentation Sys. and Automation Soc. (various sect. offices 1976—79, pres. N.E. Mich. sect. 1979—80, chmn. SP 76 stds. com. 1991—96, dir.-elect, sec.-treas. analysis divsn. 1994—96, chmn. Louisville sect. del. 1996—, dir. 1996—98, com. mem. 1998—, various divsn. and dept. positions 1998—, dir. on stds. and practices bd. 2005—, v.p.-elect stds. and practices dept. 2007—, Stds. and Practices award 2001); mem.: Air and Waste Mgmt. Assn. (com. on enhanced monitoring 1993—99, optical sensing divsn. indsl. issues and applications), Am. Chem. Soc. (sect. careers program and nat. chemistry week com. 1992—99, Louisville sect. chmn.-elect 1998—99, Louisville sect. chair 1999—2001, sect. careers program and nat. chemistry week com. 2001—, soc. councilor 2003—, soc. com. mem. 2004—, rep. vol. in pub. outreach program), KC, VFW, Elks, Am. Legion, Sigma Iota Epsilon, Phi Lambda Upsilon, Delta Sigma Phi. Roman Catholic. Home and Office: 2038 Ridgewood Dr Madison IN 47250-2729 Office Phone: 812-265-2301. E-mail: jtatera@seidata.com.

TATHAM, DAVID FREDERIC, art historian, educator; b. Wellesley, Mass., Nov. 29, 1932; s. Richard Merton and Florence Elizabeth (Mallette) T.; m. Cleota Reed, Dec. 12, 1979. AB, U. Mass., 1954; MA, Syracuse U., 1960, PhD, 1970. Dean students Syracuse (N.Y.) U., 1966-71, assoc. prof. fine arts, 1972-78, chmn. dept. fine arts, 1980-86, prof., 1978—2002, prof. emeritus, 2002—. Author: The Lure of the Striped Pig, 1973, Prints and Printmakers of New York State, 1986, Winslow Homer and the Art of the Book, 1990, Winslow Homer and the Illustrated Book, 1992, Fishing in the North Woods, 1995, Winslow Homer in the Adirondacks, 1996, Winslow Homer and the Pictorial Press, 2002 North American Prints 1913-47:An Examination, 2006, (exhbn. catalogs) Winslow Homer Drawings, 1979, Art, Artists and Museums, 1980, Bolton Brown, 1981, Abraham Tuthill, 1983, Winslow Homer: Masterworks from the Adirondacks, 2004; contbr. articles to profl. jours. Served with U.S. Army, 1956. Daniels research fellow, 1974; Am. Philos. Soc. grantee, 1980, 86, 98; Am. Art Jour. award for outstanding scholarship, 1984; NEH grantee, 1987-88, Newman Prize, 2004. Fellow Athenaeum of Phila., Royal Soc. Arts; mem. Am. Antiquarian Soc. (rec. sec. 1988-93), Coll. Art Assn. Home: 329 Westcott St Syracuse NY 13210-2107 Office: Syracuse U Dept Fine Arts Bowne Hall Syracuse NY 13244-1200 E-mail: dftatham@syr.edu.

TATLOCK, ANN, writer; married. Author: (novels) A Room of My Own, 1998 (Silver Angel award, Excellence in Media, 1999), A Place Called Morning, 1998, All the Way Home, 2002 (First Place Adult Fiction, Midwest Ind. Publ. Assn., 2002, Christy award Contemporary Fiction, 2003), I'll Watch the Moon, 2003 (First Place Gen. Fiction, Midwest Ind. Publ. Assn., 2003, Best of Genre Christian Fiction, Libr. Jour., 2003), Things We Once Held Dear, 2006. Mailing: Bethany House Publ 11400 Hampshire Ave Minneapolis MN 55438 E-mail: anntatlock@yahoo.com.

TATLOCK, ANNE M., retired trust company executive; b. White Plains, NY, July 1, 1939; d. John and Kathleen (McGrath) McNiff; m. William Tatlock, Apr. 29, 1967; children: Julina, Kerry, Christopher. BA, Vassar Coll., 1961; MA in Econs., NYU, 1968. 1st v.p. Smith Barney Harris Upham, NYC, 1962-84; exec. v.p. Fiduciary Trust Internat., NYC, 1984-94, pres., 1994—99, pres., CEO, 1999—2000, chmn., CEO, 2000—06, ret., 2006. Bd. dirs. Fortune Brands, Deerfield, Ill., Franklin Resources, San Mateo, Calif., Merck, NJ, Fiduciary Trust Internat. Trustee Am. Ballet Theatre, N.Y.C., 1994-, pres., 1998-2001; trustee Vassar Coll., 1994-2006, The Teagle Found., N.Y.C., 1995-2006; trustee Andrew W. Mellon Found., NYC, 1995—, chmn., 2003—; trustee Cultural Instns. Retirement Sys., NYC, 1989-2005, chmn., 1996-2001; trustee Howard Hughes Med. Inst., Md., 2000—, The Conf. Bd., NYC, 2001—, Mayo Found., Minn., 2002—, World Trade Ctr. Meml. Found., 2005—. Fellow: Am. Acad. Arts and Scis. (elected 2004); mem.: Coun. on Fgn. Rels.

TATMAN, DAVID C., state agency administrator; Grad., U. Oreg. Sch. Law, 1981. Bar: Oreg. 1981. With Oreg. Divsn. Fin. & Corp. Securities, 1988—, chief enforcement securities sect., dep. adminstr., 2004—05, acting adminstr., 2005—06, adminstr., 2006—; spl. asst. atty. gen. Oreg. Dept. Justice. Office: Dept Consumer & Bus Svcs Divsn Fin and Corp Securities PO Box 14480 Salem OR 97309-0405 Office Phone: 503-378-4140. Office Fax: 503-947-7862. E-mail: david.c.tatman@state.or.us.

TATREAU, (DOLORES) MAXINE, artist; b. Minden, Iowa, Sept. 6, 1929; d. Charles Ross Teninty and Hester Evaline Peterson Teninty Hadfield; m. Donald Max Tatreau, Aug. 18, 1949; children: Douglas M., Dean M., Kevin L. Student, U. No. Iowa, 1947, Iowa State Tchrs. Coll, U. Nebr., Omaha. Receptionist, typesetter Neola (Iowa) Gazette Newspaper, 1946—47; rural sch. tchr. Neola, 1947—48; office worker Orchard and Wilhelm Furniture Co., Omaha, 1948—50; comptometer operator Western Elec., Omaha, 1950—53; office worker Western Elec. (AT&T Tech.), Omaha, 1969—86; artist Tatreau Studio, 1972—; represented by Wickwire Gallery, Hendersonville, NC, Carolina Gallery Art, Spartenburg, SC. Pres. Art League Henderson County, 2004. Exhibitions include Kans. Watercolor Soc. Competition (Purchase award), Rocky Mountain Nat. Watercolor Soc., Phi Theta Kappa Six State Regional Competition, Brand Libr. and Art Gallery, Glendale, Calif., Passageway Gallery, Omaha, Asheville Gallery of Art, 2000—04, Aberdale, Wales, 2004, many others, invitational exhibitions, Edina Art Ctr., Mpls., Conn Gallery, Landrum, SC, Wichita Art Gallery, Kans., Statehouse Gallery, Lincoln, Nebr., many others, numerous corp. and pvt. collections in US and Europe. Den mother Boys Scouts Am., Omaha; wedding coord. 1st Luth. Ch., Omaha, Sunday sch. tchr., children's summer bible sch. leader, circle leader. Mem.: Kans. Watercolor Soc. (signature) (Purchase award), So. Watercolor Soc., Upstate Visual Arts Greenville, SC, Watercolor Soc. NC, Tryon Painters and Sculptors, Nat. Watercolor Soc., Art League Henderson County, Internat. Soc. Exptl. Artists (signature), Nat. Mus. Women (charter). Lutheran. Avocations: golf, bridge, jewelry making, quilting, church choir. Home and Studio: 2701 Kalmia Ln Hendersonville NC 28791-1838

TATRO, RENÉ P., lawyer; b. Moundridge, Kans., July 2, 1953; BS magna cum laude, Kans. State U., 1974; JD cum laude, Harvard U., 1977. Bar: Calif. 1977, US Dist. Ct. (no., ea., ctrl. dist.) Calif., US Dist. Ct. (ea. dist.) Mich., US Dist. Ct. DC, US Ct. Internat. Trade. Mem. Heller, Ehrman, White & McAuliffe, LA; founding ptnr. Tatro Tekosky Sadwick Mendelson LLP, LA, 2003—. Mem. ABA. Office: Tatro Tekosky Sadwick Mendelson LLP 660 S Figueroa St Ste 1450 Los Angeles CA 90017 Office Phone: 213-225-7171. Office Fax: 213-225-7151. E-mail: renetatro@ttsmlaw.com.

TATSCH, JACKI LYNN, music educator, diversified financial services company executive; b. Willimantic, Conn., Mar. 11, 1971; d. Jack Adrian and Ellen Ann Wallis; m. Clinton Edward Tatsch, Aug. 7, 1993; 1 child, Bryan Edward. BS in Music Edn., Ea. Nazarene Coll., 1993. Cert. tchr. K-9 and 5-12 Mass., 1993. Pvt. music instr., Lynchburg, Va., 1994—99; music tchr. Nazarene Christian Sch., Asheville, NC, 1999—2001, Biltmore Bapt. Sch. Music, Arden, NC, 2000—03; pvt. music instr. Arden, 1999—2001, Asheville, 2001—03, Hendersonville, NC, 2003—; prin., owner Hart Lane Enterprises Inc., 2005—. Music tchr. AIMA Ctrl., Va., 1994—96; saxophonist Land Sky Concert Band, Asheville, 2002—03; saxophonist and clarinetist Bathtub Gin, Little Switzerland, 2002—03, Nouveau-Passe Orch., Hendersonville, 2004—; clarinetist Hendersonville Cmty. Band, 2004—05; freelance musician. Mem.: Internat. Clarinet Assn., Nat. Assn. Music Educators, U.S. Amateur Ballroom Dance Assn. Home: 28 Hart Ln Hendersonville NC 23792 Home Phone: 828-693-7019. Personal E-mail: jackitatsch@hotmail.com.

TATUM, BEVERLY DANIEL, academic administrator, writer, psychology and education educator; b. Tallahaassee, Sept. 27, 1954; d. Robert Alphonse and Catherine Faith (Maxwell) Daniel; m. Travis James Tatum, July 28, 1979; children: Travis Jonathan Daniel, David Alexander Daniel. BA, Wesleyan U., 1975; MA in Psychology, U. Mich., 1976, PhD, 1984; MA in Religious Studies, Hartford Seminary. Lic. clin. psychologist. Asst. prof. Dept. Psychology Westfield State Coll., Mass., 1983—86, assoc. prof. Mass., 1986—89; assoc. prof. Dept. Psychology and Edn. Mt. Holyoke Coll., South Hadley, Mass., 1989—96, prof., 1996—, dept. chair, 1997—98, dean, v.p. student affairs, 1998—2002, acting pres., 2002; pres. Spelman Coll., Atlanta, 2002—. Lectr. dept. black studies U. Calif., Santa Barbara, 1980-83, counseling psychologist, 1979-83; vis. scholar Stone Ctr., Wellesley Coll., 1991-92; chair, bd. dirs. Equity Inst., Emeryville, Calif., 1987-89. Author: Assimilation Blues: Black Families in a White Community, 1987, Why Are All the Black Kids Sitting Together in the Cafeteria?: And Other Conversations About Race, 1997, Can We Talk About Race?: And Other Conversations in an Era of School Resegregation, 2007; contbr. articles to profl. jours. Recipient Brock Internat. Prize in Edn., 2005; fellow APA Minority Program, 1976—79, U. Calif., 1980—81, Ford Found., 1991. Mem. APA, Am. Psychol. Soc., Ea. Psychol. Assn., Mass. Psychol. Assn., Assn. Women in Psychology, Assn. Black Psychologists. Office: Spelman Coll Office of Pres 350 Spelman Lane SW Atlanta GA 30314-4399 *

TATUM, CHRISTINE, editor; b. Wilmington, NC; m. Christian Thurstone; children: Tatum Elizabeth, Christian Asa. Grad., U. NC, Chapel Hill. With News & Record, Greensboro, NC, Daily Herald, Arlington Heights, Ill., Tribune Media Services; reporter, online prodr., tech. commentator Chgo. Tribune; asst. bus. editor Denver Post, 2003—. Mem.: Headline Club (pres. 2002), Soc. Profl. Journalists (bd. mem. 2002—, pres. elect 2005—06, pres. 2006—, President's award 2002). Office: Denver Post 101 W Colfax Ave Denver CO 80202 Office Phone: 303-954-1503. E-mail: ctatum@spj.org, ctatum@denverpost.com. *

TATUM, MARK A., sports association executive; m. Lisa Skeete Tatum; children: Tai Aidan, Kylan Ming. BS in Bus. Mgmt. and Mktg., Cornell U., 1991; MBA, Harvard Bus. Sch., 1998. Sales mgr. Procter and Gamble Co., 1991—95; with sports mktg. dept. Pepsi-Cola Co., 1997; regional sales mgr. Clorox Co., 1995—97; with corp. sponsorship and mktg. dept. Maj. League Baseball, 1999—2000; v.p. bus. devel. NBA, 1999, sr. dir., grp. mgr. mktg. properties, dir. mktg. partnerships, 2001—04, sr. v.p. mktg. partnerships, 2004—. Cornell Black Alumni Assn.; Cornell Alumni Mentor Prog. Named one of 40 Under 40, Sports Bus. Jour., 2006. Office: NBA Olympic Tower 645 5th Ave Fl 10 New York NY 10022 *

TATUM, VALORIE, elementary school educator, pharmacist; d. Louis Joe and Ruth (Gary) Tatum. Cert. in pharmacology, Kennedy King Coll., 1990; BA in Elem. Edn., Nat. Lewis U., 1994. Lic. pharmacist tech. Ill.; cert. tchr. Ill. Pharmacist technician Watson Pharmacies, Chgo., 1987—94; tchr. Chgo. Bd. Edn., Chgo., 1995—. Spl. edn. head tchr. McAuliffe Elem., Chgo., 1997—99. Author: Rita Rabbit and the Runaway Pie, 2006. Adminstrv. coun. Rust Meml. United Meth. Ch., Chgo., 2000—03, Sunday sch. tchr., 2002—, pastor parish rels. com., 2003—. Nominee Golden Apple award, 2003, Tchr. of Yr., Ill., 2006; recipient Wall of Tolerance award, 2004, Poet of the Year, Internat. Library of Poetry, 2004; Bilingual Mini grant, Chgo. Bd. Edn., 2003. Democrat. Methodist. Avocations: reading, writing, movies. Home Phone: 773-778-1460; Office Phone: 773-875-1032.

TATYREK, ALFRED FRANK, retired chemist, environmental engineer; b. Hillside, NJ, Jan. 23, 1930; s. Frank Peter and Frances (Luxa) T. BS, Seton Hall U., 1954; postgrad., Rutgers U., 1956—57. Rsch. chemist Bakelite divsn. Union Carbide, Bloomfield, NJ, 1953—58, U.S. Radium Corp., Morristown, NJ, 1958—62; analytical chemist insp. Chem. Procurement Dist. U.S. Army, NYC, 1962—64, rsch. chemist Picatinny Arsenal Dover, NJ, 1964—73; chem. materials engr. U.S. Army Armament Rsch., Devel. and Engring. Ctr., NJ, 1973—95; ret. Cons. pyrotechnics, polymer materials and environ. chemistry. Patentee pyrotechnic compositions, chemiluminescent compounds and processes, crank case oil vacuum purification sys. for internal combustion engines, method for the removal of thermoset potting compound from the electronics package of a munitions item; lectr., contbr. publ. on mountaineering expdns. and adventures in the great mountain ranges of N.Am., S.Am., Europe and Africa to mags.; contbr. more than 50 sci. and tech. publs. 1st aid instr. ARC, Essex County, NJ, 1969-82; chief 1st aid Maplewood CD, NJ, 1971-91; patrol dir. Nat. Ski Patrol, Phoenicia, NY, 1978-84, sr. status, 1979-, lifetime Nat. Ski patroller So. NY and NJ region, 1993-; life mem. Blood Ctr. NJ. Staff sgt. NJ Air N.G., 1948-57. Decorated Comdr.'s Pub. Svc. award US Army, 1996; recipient 35 Yr. Svc. award Nat. Ski Patrol, 2006, 35 Yr. Svc. awrd, 2006. Mem. Nat. Soc. Inventors, Sci. Rsch. Soc. (pres. Picatinny chpt. 1974-75, 79-80, 85-86), Nat. Assn. Underwater Instrs. (cert. basic and advanced diver and underwater photographer 1971-, cert. Nitrox diving 1999), Magician's Roundtable, Internat. Magicians Soc. (life), Alpine Club Can. (life), N.J. Animal Rights Alliance, Appalachian Mountain Club (life; hiking leader), Sierra Club, Sigma Xi. Roman Catholic. Climbed 15,771 feet Mt. Blanc, highest mountain peak in Europe; climbed to highest summit on Point Uruhu on 19,730 feet on Mt. Kilimanjaro, highest mountain peak in Africa, 1972; leader of climb on Matterhorn and Monte Rosa, Switzerland's highest peak; mountain expdns. in U.S. and Can. including 3 first ascents in No. Cascades of Wash. (S.E. ridge of Mt. Goode, Aug. 1963, Peak 7732 via the Snow Chute, Aug. 1964, East ridge of Bear Mountain Aug. 1964); undersea photography expeditions to Caribbean and South Pacific coral reefs. Home: 27 Orchard Rd Maplewood NJ 07040-1919 Personal E-mail: atatyrek@att.net. *"God has given us a world rich in physical and intellectual beauty as well as intriguing scientific discovery. To earn these rewards we must seek out and meet the challanges of life, not as distasteful burdens, but as true opportunities upon which to build where others have failed or left off, using all the infinite resources that God has given to all of us".*

TAUB, ALAN I., automotive executive, researcher; BS, Brown U.; PhD in Applied Physics, Harvard U., 1979. Exec. dir. rsch. and devel. General Motors Corp., Warren, Mich., 2001—. Mem.: NAE.

TAUB, EDWARD, psychology researcher; b. Bklyn., Oct. 22, 1931; s. Samuel Hart and Ida Pearl (Kimmel) T.; m. Mildred Allen Taub, Aug. 13, 1959. BA, Bklyn. Coll., 1953; MA, Columbia U., 1959; PhD, NYU, 1969. Rsch. asst. Columbia U., NYC, 1956; rsch. asst. dept. exptl. neurology Jewish Chronic Disease Hosp., NYC, 1957-60, rsch. assoc., 1960-68; dir. Behavioral Biology Ctr., Inst. for Behavioral Rsch., 1968-83; assoc. dir. Inst. for Behavioral Rsch., 1978-83; univ. prof. psychology U. Ala., Birmingham, 1986—2000, 2000—; standing guest prof. U. Konstanz, Germany, 1995—; guest prof. U. Jena, Germany, 1996—. Asst. prof. dept. psychiatry Johns Hopkins U., Balt., 1972-82; vis. prof. grad. program dept. psychology CUNY, 1984-85; vis. prof. U. Tuebingen, U. Muenster, Humboldt U., Germany, 1993—2001. Contbr. articles to profl. jours. Recipient Pioneering Rsch. Contbn. award, 1989, Disting. Scientist of 1998 award, Assn. of Applied Psychophysiology and Biofeedback, Ireland prize for scholarly distinction, U. Ala., Birmingham, 1997, Humboldt Rsch. award, 2000; fellow Guggenheim Found., 1983—84. Fellow AAAS, APA (exec. com. divsn. 6, Disting. Sci. award for the applications of psychology 2004), Soc. for Behavioral Medicine, Am. Psychol. Soc. (charter, William James Fellow award 1997); mem. Soc. for Neurosci. (named one of 10 leading translational rsch. projects in neurosci. in the 20th Century 2003), Biofeedback Soc. Am. (pres. 1978-79, Outstanding Rsch. Contbn. award 1988), Am. Physiol. Soc. (exec. com. neurosci. sect. 1988-91). Achievements include invention of technique of thermal biofeedback; Constraint-Induced Movement therapy for rehabilitation for stroke, traumatic brain injury, spinal cord injury, cerebral palsy and other motor disorders due to neurological injury. Office: U Ala at Birmingham 712 CPM 1530 3d Ave S Birmingham AL 35294-0018 Office Phone: 205-934-2471. Business E-Mail: etaub@uab.edu.

TAUB, ELI IRWIN, arbitrator, mediator, lawyer, judicial hearing officer; b. NYC, July 6, 1938; s. Max and Belle (Slutsky) T.; m. Nancy Denese Bell, May 15, 1983; 1 child, Jennifer. BA, Bklyn. Coll., 1960; JD, NYU, 1963. Bar: N.Y. 1964, U.S. Dist. Ct. (no. dist.) N.Y. 1979. Ptnr. Silverman, Silverman & Taub, Schenectady, N.Y., 1971-77; pres. Eli I. Taub, P.C., Schenectady, 1978-2001; judge Schenectady County (N.Y.) Family Ct., 2001; arbitrator, mem. arbitration panel Fed. Mediation and Conciliation Svc., 2001—; jud. hearing officer N.Y. State Supreme and Family Cts., 2005—. Arbitrator Am. Arbitration Assn., NY State Pub. Employment Rels. Bd., 1966-, NY State Employment Rels. Bd., US Postal Svc. and Nat. Letter Carriers; mediator U.S. Dist. Ct.; paralegal adv. com. Schenectady County C.C. Former chmn. trustee Joseph Egan Supreme Ct. Libr., Schenectady; former v.p. Jewish Fedn. Schenectady; surrogate decision making com. NY State Commn. on Quality of Care and Advocacy for the Mentally Disabled; bd. dirs. Jewish Cmty. Ctr., former chair Adolescent Pregnancy Prevention Svcs. Coun.; advocate Nat. Coll. of Advocacy; v.p., legal counsel 440 State St. Arts Ctr. Recipient Vol. of Yr. award Jewish Family Svcs., 1998, Humanitarian of Yr. award Alcohol and Substance Abuse Coun., 2001. Mem.: LERA, AJJA, Nat. Coun. Juvenile and Family Ct. Judges, Assn. Family and Conciliation Cts., Nat. Orgn. Social Security Claimant Reps., Schenectady County Bar Assn., N.Y. State Trial Lawyers Assn., N.Y. State Bar Assn., Am. Judges Assn., B'nai B'rith (pres. 1976—77, Youth Svcs. award 1985). Home Phone: 518-664-5399; Office Phone: 518-664-5440.

TAUB, JESSE J., electrical engineering researcher; b. NYC, Apr. 27, 1927; s. Julius and Ida (Orlansky) T.; m. Eva Pollack, Dec. 24, 1955 (dec. Nov. 1973); children: Richard Lawrence, Jocelyn Cara, Suzanne Mara; m. Naomi Etta Trachtenberg, June 30, 1974. BEE, CCNY, 1948; MEE, Poly. U., 1949. Group leader microwave electronics, Material Lab. USN, Bklyn., 1949-55; engr. Airborne Instruments Lab., Mineola, NY, 1955-58, sect. leader, 1958-61, engring. cons., 1961-75; chief scientist AIL Systems Inc., Melville, NY, 1975-93; cons., 1993—. Mem. engring. adv. bd. N.Y. Tech., Hofstra U. Author: (with others) Microwave Measurements, 1963; contbr. numerous papers to profl. publs.; patentee microwave techniques With USN, 1945-46. Fellow IEEE (Centennial medal 1984, 3rd Millenium medal 2000, C.A. Fowler award 1993, Region 1 awards 2001, 06, adminstrv. com. 1972-74, program chmn. microwave symposium, steering com., chmn. L.I. sect. awards, USAB Divsn. award 2002); mem. Archaeology Inst. Am. Democrat. Jewish. Avocations: classical musician, contract bridge, archaeology. Home and Office: 115 Northgate Cir Melville NY 11747-3045 Personal E-mail: jjtaub@aol.com.

TAUB, RICHARD PAUL, social sciences educator; b. Bklyn., Apr. 16, 1937; s. Martin Glynn and Frances (Israel) T.; m. Doris Susan Leventhal, Aug. 14, 1961 (dec. Feb. 1996); children: Neela Robin, Zachariah Jacob; m. Betty G. Farrell, June 21, 2000. BA, U. Mich., 1959; MA, Harvard U., Cambridge, Mass., 1962, PhD in Social Relations, 1966. Asst. prof. sociology Brown U., Providence, 1965-69; from asst. prof. to Paul Klapper prof. of social scis. U. Chgo., 1969—, assoc. dean Coll. of Univ., 1982-86, chmn. dept. comparative human devel., 2000—. Adv. bd. Neighborhood Preservation Initiative, 1993-2000; chair adv. bd. Nat. Comty. Devel. Initiative, 1991-95; dir. South Ark. Rural Devel. Study, 1988-96; Disting. visitor Mac Arthur Found., 1998. Author: Bureaucrats Under Stress, 1969; (with D. Garth Taylor and Jan Dunham) Paths of Neighborhood Change, 1984, Community Capitalism, 1988; (with Doris L. Taub) Entrepreneurship in India's Small Scale Industries, 1989, Doing Development in Arkansas, 2004; (with William Julius Wilson) There Goes the Neighborhood, 2006; editor: (with Doris L. Taub) American Society in Tocqueville's Time and Today, 1974; contbr. articles to profl. jours. Chmn. bd. St. Thomas the Apostle Sch., Chgo., 1983-86; bd. dirs. Hyde Park Kenwood Cmty. Conf., Chgo., 1972-75; bd. seminary Coop Bookstore, Chgo., 1994—. Angell scholar U. Mich., 1956; Woodrow Wilson fellow Harvard U., 1959-60, W.E.B. DuBois Inst. fellow, 1997-98; grantee Am. Inst. Indian Studies, Ford Found., MacArthur Found., NSF, Wieboldt Found., Nat. Inst. Justice; recipient Quanctrell award U. Chgo., 1976, Outstanding Grad. Tchg. award U. Chgo., 2004. Mem. Am. Sociol. Assn., Midwest Sociol. Soc. Avocations: hiking, music. Office: Univ Chgo 5730 S Woodlawn Ave Chicago IL 60637 Office Phone: 773-702-3971. Business E-Mail: rpt2@uchicago.edu.

TAUB, STEPHEN RICHARD, lawyer; b. NYC, Oct. 5, 1944; s. Irving Robert and Sylvia T.; m. Alyson Zoe Winter, Dec. 23, 1968. BA, Queens Coll., 1965; JD, NYU, 1968. Bar: N.Y. 1969, U.S. Dist. Ct. (ea. and so. dists.) N.Y. 1970, U.S. Ct. Appeals (2nd cir.) 1971, U.S. Supreme Ct. 1972. Asst. dist. atty., bur. chief Kings County Dist. Attys. Office, Bklyn., 1970—77; pvt. practice Garden City, NY, 1977—96; ptnr. Ostrow and Taub, LLP, Garden City, 1996—2000, Schlissel, Ostrow, Karabatos, Poepplein & Taub, PLLC, Mineola, NY, 2000—02; pvt. practice Stephen R. Taub, PLLC, Mineola, NY, 2002—05, Taub, Hametz & Waldman, PLLC, Mineola, NY, 2005—. Matrimonial case neutral evaluator Nassau County Supreme Ct., Mineola, 1997—. Village Justice Village Kensington, Great Neck, N.Y., 1986-98; Acting Village Justice Village Old Brookville, N.Y., 1998-2006. Fellow Am. Acad. Matrimonial Lawyers; mem. ABA, N.Y. Family Law, Am. Inn of Ct. (master), N.Y. State Bar Assn., N.Y. State Magistrates Assn., Nassau County Bar Assn., Nassau County Magistrates Assn. (pres. 1993-94). Avocation: tennis.

TAUB, THEODORE CALVIN, lawyer; b. Springfield, Mass., Jan. 1, 1935; s. Samuel and Sara Lee (Daum) T.; m. Roberta Mae Ginsburg, Aug. 23, 1959; children: Tracy, Andrew, Adam. AB, Duke U., 1956; JD, U. Fla., 1960. Bar: Fla., 1960, U.S. Supreme Ct. Atty. Shumaker, Loop & Kendrick, LLP, Tampa. Asst. city atty. City of Tampa, 1963-67; city atty. City of Temple Terrace, Fla., 1974—; panelist in field. Contbr. articles to profl. jours. Chmn. Tampa-Hillsborough (Fla.) County Expy. Authority, 1974-84; mem. Hillsborough County Charter Commn., 1966-69, Local Govt. Mgmt. Efficiency Com., 1979, State of Fla. Environ. Efficiency Study Commn., 1986-88; founder Tampa Bay Performing Arts Ctr. Fellow: Am. Bar Found; mem. ABA (chmn. real property litigation com. 1981-86, chmn. com. on housing and urban environ. 1989-91), Am. Coll. Real Estate Lawyers (bd. govs.), Am. Land Title Assn. (lenders' counsel group), Fla. Bar Assn. (bd. cert. real estate lawyer), Fla. Jaycees (pres.), Tau Epsilon Phi. Democrat. Jewish. Home: 4937 Lyford Cay Rd Tampa FL 33629-4828 Office: Bank of Am 101 E Kennedy Blvd Ste 2800 Tampa FL 33602-5869 Office Phone: 813-227-2351. Business E-Mail: ttaub@slk-law.com.

TAUBENBERGER, JEFFERY KARL, pathologist, molecular biologist; b. Landstuhl, Germany, Sept. 23, 1961; BS in Biology, George Mason U., 1982; MD, Med. Coll. Va., 1986, PhD, 1987. Diplomate Nat. Bd. Med. Examiners; diplomate in anat. pathology Am. Bd. Pathology, diplomate in molecular genetics Am. Bd. Med. Genetics. Staff surg. pathologist Nat. Cancer Inst., Bethesda, Md., 1991-93; co-dir. molecular diagnostics lab. Armed Forces Inst. Pathology, Washington, 1993, chief divsn. molecular pathology, 1994—. Cons. Nat. Cancer Inst., 1993—; vis. scientist Nat. Inst. Allergy and Infectious Diseases, Bethesda, 1993—; affiliate asst. prof. dept. anatomy Med. Coll. Va., Richmond, 1995—. Contbr. articles to profl. jours.; featured in Secrets of the Dead: Killer Flu, PBS, 2005 Recipient Benjamin Castleman awrd U.S. and Can. Acad. Pathology, 1998, WIRED Rave award-Medicine, 2006 Mem. Assn. for Molecular Pathology. Achievements include being principal investigator on project to genetically characterize the 1918 Spanish Influenza virus. Office: Armed Forces Inst Pathology Annex Dept Molecular Biology Bldg 101 Rm 1057D 1414 Research Blvd Rockville MD 20850 Address: Armed Forces Inst Pathology 6825 16th St NW Washington DC 20306-6000 Office Phone: 301-319-0323. Office Fax: 301-295-9507. Business E-Mail: taubenberger@afip.osd.mil.

TAUBENFELD, HARRY S., lawyer; b. Bklyn., June 27, 1929; s. Marcus Isaac and Anna (Engelhard) T.; m. Florence Spatz, June 17, 1956; children: Anne Gail Weisbrod, Stephen Marshall. BA, Bklyn. Coll., 1951; JD, Columbia U., 1954. Bar: NY 1955, U.S. Supreme Ct. 1965, U.S. Dist. Ct. (so. and ea. dists.) NY 1976. Assoc. Benjamin H. Schor, Bklyn., 1955-58; ptnr. Zuckerbrod & Taubenfeld, Cedarhurst, NY, 1958—. Village atty. Village of Cedarhurst, 1977-88, trustee, 1989-2001; mem. bd. Downtown Cedarhurst Bus. Improvement Dist., 1993; legis. chmn., counsel Nassau County Village Ofcls., 1979-86, v.p., 1991-93, pres., 1993-94, mem. exec. com., 1989-99, chmn. intergovtl. liaison com., 1991-93; mem. legis. com. NY State Conf. Mayors, 1979-87, 92-93; mem. exec. bd. Tri-County Village Ofcls., 1991-95, pres., 1993-94; arbitrator Am. Arbitration Assn. Dist. Ct. Nassau County, 1980—, Assessment Rev. Panel, Supreme Ct., Nassau County, 1981—; mem. Constl. Bicentennial Com., 1987-89; adv. bd. First Am. Title Ins. Co. of N.Y., 2004-. Del. World Zionist Congress, 1977, 82, 87; mem. Zionist Gen. Coun., 1977-83; assoc. chmn. Am. Zionist Fedn., 1985-87; pres. Herut Zionists Am., 1977-79; v.p. Hartman YMHA, 1983-87; hon. trustee Cong. Beth Shalom, Lawrence, N.Y., 1990-2001; nat. bd. dir. Zionist Orgn. Am.; bd. govs. Jewish Agy., 1983-92; mem. exec. com. World Zionist Orgn., 1983-92; trustee United Jewish Appeal, 1986-91; bd. dir. United Israel Appeal, 1986-91; hon. vice chmn., bd. dir. Jewish Nat. Fund, 1987-89; nat. bd. dir. Am. for a Safe Israel; hon. pres. World Coun. Herut Hatzoa, Jerusalem, Internat. Bd. Youthtown of Israel. Recipient Centenial award Jabotinsky Found. 1981, Betar Youth award World Betar 1982, award Internat. League for Repatriation of Russian Jews 1977, Youth Towns of Israel Leadership award 1973, Israel Bonds Leadership award 1976, Life Time Achievement award Israel Bonds 1991, Defender of Jerusalem award 1991, Israel Bonds Menachem Begin Leadership award, 1999. Mem.: Internat. Assn. Jewish Lawyers and Jurists, Beth El Synagogue Ctr. New Rochelle, NY, Zionist Orgn. Am. (nat. bd. 1996—), B'nai B'rith, Jewish War Vets. Home: 21 N Chatsworth Ave Larchmont NY 10538 Office: 575 Chestnut St Cedarhurst NY 11516-2223 Personal E-mail: handf21n@verizon.net.

TAUBER, MARK J., retired lawyer; b. Detroit, Mar. 25, 1949; s. Max M. and Beatrice R. (Roth) T.; m. Anita L. Tilben, June 23, 1970; children: Melissa A., Benjamin M., Allison B. BA with honors, U. Mich., 1970; JD with honors, George Washington U., 1973. Bar: D.C. 1973, Md. 1974, US Dist. Ct. (DC, MD. dist.), US Ct. Appeals (1st, 3d, 4th, 7th, 11th, DC cir.), US Supreme Ct. 1980. From assoc. to ptnr. Pierson, Ball & Dowd, Washington, 1973—82; ptnr., chair comm. practice group Piper & Marbury, Washington, 1982—99; ptnr. Piper, Marbury, Rudnick & Wolfe, Washington, 1999—2002; ptnr., chair comm. practice group Piper Rudnick LLP, Washington, 2002—04; ptnr., chair comm., e-commerce and privacy practice group DLA Piper, Washington, 2005—06; ret., 2007. Assoc. editor: George Washington Law Rev., 1972—73. Home: 110 St Martin Dr Palm Beach Gardens FL 33418 Office Phone: 561-626-4632. Office Fax: 561-626-0174.

TAUBIN, DAWN, film company executive; Staff prodr., cable television programming Warner Amex Cable Comms., Ohio; dir., publicity and promotion Nat. Amusements Inc., Boston, 1983—85; west coast regional publicity/promotion rep. to v.p., publicity MGM, 1985—89; v.p., publicity Warner Bros. Pictures, 1989—93, v.p., advt. and publicity, 1993—96, sr. v.p., advt. and publicity, 1996—99, exec. v.p., mktg., 1999—2001, pres., domestic mktg., 2001—. Named an 100 Most Powerful Women in Entertainment, Hollywood Reporter, 2005; named one of, 2004, 2006. Office: Warner Bros Pictures 4000 Warner Blvd Burbank CA 91522-0001 *

TAUBMAN, A. ALFRED, real estate developer; b. Pontiac, Mich., Jan. 31, 1924; s. Philip and Fannie Ester (Blustin) T.; m. Reva Kolodney, Dec. 1, 1949 (div. July 1977); children: Gayle Kalisman, Robert S., William S.; m. Judith Mazor, June 17, 1982. Student, U. Mich., 1945-48, LLD (hon.), 1991; student, Lawrence Inst. Tech., 1948-49, DArch (hon.), 1985; D in Bus. (hon.), Eastern Mich. U., 1984; D in Edn. (hon.), Mich. State U., 1993; HHD (hon.), No. Mich. U., 1995. Chmn. The Taubman Co., Bloomfield Hills, Mich., 1950—, Taubman Ctrs., Inc., Bloomfield Hills, Mich., 1992—. Prin. shareholder Sotheby's Holdings, Inc., N.Y.C., 1983-2001. Author: Threshold Resistance: The Extraordinary Career of a Luxury Retailing Pioneer, 2007. Trustee Ctr. for Creative Studies, Detroit, Harper-Grace Hosps., Detroit; chmn. emeritus Archives Am. Art Smithsonian Inst., Washington, U. Pa. Wharton Real Estate Ctr., Phila.; pres. Arts Commn. of Detroit; mem. nat. bd. Smithsonian Assocs.; established Taubman Ctr. for State and Local Govt. Harvard U., Cambridge, Mass., chmn. Mich. Partnership for New Edn., Program in Am. Instns., U. Mich., Brown U.'s Pub. Policy and Am. Instns. Program; prin. benefactor A. Alfred Taubman Health Care Ctr. and A. Alfred Taubman Med. Libr., U. Mich.; bd. dirs. Detroit Renaissance, Inc., Friends of Art and Preservation in Embassies, Washington; active State of Mich. Gaming Commn. Recipient Bus. Statesman award Harvard Bus. Sch. Club of Detroit, 1983, Sportsman of Yr. award United Found. Detroit, SE Mich. Chpt. March of Dimes Birth Defects, 1983; named Michiganian of Yr. The Detroit News, 1983; named one of Forbes' Richest Americans, 2006 Mem. Urban Land Inst. (trustee), Nat. Realty Com. (bd. dirs.).

TAUBMAN, JANE ANDELMAN, literature and language professor; b. Boston, Oct. 23, 1942; d. Hyman M. and Esther (Rosenthal) Andelman; m. William Chase Taubman; children: Alexander, Phoebe. BA, Radcliffe Coll., 1964; MA, Yale U., 1968, PhD, 1972. Instr. Russian Smith Coll., Northampton, Mass., 1968-72; asst. prof. Russian Amherst (Mass.) Coll., 1973-83, assoc. prof. Russian, 1983-89, prof. Russian, 1989—. Author: A Life Through Poetry: Marina Tsvetaeva's Lyric Diary, 1989, Russian transl., 2000, Cinetek: Asthenic Syndrome, 2000, Kira Muratova, 2004; co-author: Moscow Spring, 1989; co-editor: Marina Tsvetaeva: One Hundred Years, 1994. Woodrow Wilson Found. fellow, 1964—, Am. Coun. Learned Socs.-SSRC, 1974, trustee-faculty fellow Amherst Coll., 1978, fellow Nat. Def. Title VI, 1965-68; grantee Am. Philos. Soc., 1975, Amherst Coll., 1991, 94, IREX grantee USSR, 1988. Mem. AAUP, Am. Assn. Tchrs. Slavic and East European Langs., Am. Assn. Slavic Studies, Am. Coun. Tchrs. of Russian. Office: Amherst Coll Dept Russian Amherst MA 01002 Office Phone: 413-542-2047. Business E-Mail: jataubman@amherst.edu.

TAUBMAN, MARTIN ARNOLD, immunologist, educator; b. NYC, July 10, 1940; s. Herman and Betty (Berger) T.; m. Joan Petra Mikelbank, May 30, 1965; children: Benjamin Abby, Joel David. BS, Bklyn. Coll., 1961; DDS, Columbia U., 1965; PhD, SUNY, Buffalo, 1970; MA (hon.), Harvard U., 1997. Asst. mem. staff Forsyth Dental Ctr., Boston, 1970—, head immunology dept., 1972—, assoc. mem. staff, 1974-80; sr. staff mem. The Forsyth Inst., 1980—; asst. clin. prof. oral biology and pathophysiology Harvard U. Sch. Dental Medicine, 1976-79, assoc. clin. prof., 1979-97, prof. dept. oral and devel. biology, 1997—2005, prof. dept. devel. biology, 2005—. Mem. oral biology and medicine study sect. NIH, 1980-84. Editor: (with J. Slots) Contemporary Microbiology and Immunology; assoc. editor: Jour. Den Res., 2004-; contbr. articles to profl. jours. chpts. to books. Recipient Rsch. Career Devel. award, 1971-76, Fred Birnberg Alumni award for disting. dental rsch. Columbia U. Assn. Dental Alumni, Disting. Faculty award Harvard Sch. Dental Medicine, 1990, MERIT award NIH, 1991-2000; USPHS fellow, 1962-63; postdoctoral fellow, 1966-70. Mem. Am. Soc. Microbiology, Soc. Mucosal Immunology, Internat. Assn. Dental Rsch. (Oral Biology award 1991), Am. Assn. Immunologists, Am. Assn. Dental Rsch. (v.p. 1987—, pres.-elect 1988, pres. 1989). Office: The Forsyth Inst 140 Fenway Boston MA 02115-3799 E-mail: mtaubman@forsyth.org.

TAUBMAN, NICHOLAS F., ambassador; m. Jenny Taubman. BS in Economics, U. Pa.; degree (hon.), Hollins U., 2005. Dir. Shenandoah Life Ins. Co.; chmn., dir. Advance Auto Parts; pres. Mozart Investments, Roanoke, Va.; US amb. to Romania US Dept. State, Bucharest, 2005—. Mem. Roanoke City Coun., 1976—78. Former dir. of various organizations including Ctrl. YMCA, Roanoke, Va., Va. Coll. Fund, Richmond, Blue Ridge Mountains Coun. Am. Boy Scouts, Roanoke Valley Industries, Roanoke Merchants Assn.; fomer trustee Va. Hist. Soc., Burrell Meml. Hosp. With US Army, 1957—58, with US Army, 1960—61. Recipient Disting. Svc. award, Roaoke Jaycees, 1978, Brotherhood Citation, Nat. Conf. of Christians and Jews, 1981. Office: Am Embassy 5260 Bucharest Pl Washington DC 20521

TAUBMAN, PAUL J., investment banker; b. 1961; BS, U. Pa., 1982; MBA, Stanford U., 1986. Joined Morgan Stanley, NYC, 1982, with mergers and acquisitions dept., 1986—, head, strategic adv. practice, 1994—, mng. dir., co-head global mergers and acquisitions. Recipient Rainmaker award, Dealmaker mag., 2006. Office: Global M & A Morgan Stanley 1585 Broadway New York NY 10036 Office Phone: 212-761-7929. *

TAUBMAN, PHILIP M., editor; b. 1948; s. Howard Taubman; m. Felicity Barringer. BA, Stanford U., 1971. Reporter NY Times, 1979, Moscow bur. chief, 1986—88, Washington (DC) editor, 1989—92, dep. nat. editor, 1993—94, asst. editorial page editor, 1994—2002, dep. editorial page editor, 2002—03, Washington (DC) bur. chief, 2003—07, assoc. editor, nat. security investigative reporter, 2007—. Author: Secret Empire: Eisenhower, the CIA & the Hidden Story of America's Space Espionage, 2003. Recipient George Polk award, 1981, 1983. Office: NY Times Washington Bur 7th Fl 1627 I St Washington DC 20006 Office Phone: 202-862-0300. Office Fax: 202-862-0340. E-mail: taubman@nytimes.com. *

TAUBMAN, ROBERT S., real estate developer; b. Detroit, Dec. 27, 1953; s. A. Alfred and Reva (Kolodney) T.; m. Julie Reyes, Aug. 27, 1999; 1 child, Alexander Alfred. BS in Econs., Boston U., MA. With Taubman Co. Inc., Bloomfield Hills, Mich., 1976—, exec. v.p., 1984—, exec. v.p., chief oper. officer, 1988-90; pres. chief exec. officer, 1990—. Bd. dirs. Taubman Ctrs. Inc., Comerica, Inc., Sotheby's Holdings, Inc., fashionmall.com. Chmn. Mich. campaign drive UNCF; bd. dirs. Beaumont Hosp.; trustee Cranbrook Ednl. Cmty. Mem. Nat. Sssn. Real Estate Investment Trusts (bd. govs.), Real Estate Roundtable (bd. dirs.), Urban Land Inst. (trustee, chmn. Detroit regional dist. coun.). Office: Taubman Co Inc 200 E Long Lake Rd Bloomfield Hills MI 48304-2360

TAUBMAN, WILLIAM CHASE, political science professor, writer; b. NYC, Nov. 13, 1941; s. Howard and Nora (Stern) T.; m. Jane Dea Andelman, May 18, 1969; children: Alexander, Phoebe. AB, Harvard U., 1962; MA, Columbia U., 1965, cert. of Russian Inst., 1965, PhD, 1969; MA (hon.), Amherst Coll., Mass., 1978. Instr. Amherst Coll., 1967-69, asst. prof., 1969-73, assoc. prof., 1973-78, prof. dept. polit. sci., 1978-83, Bertrand Snell prof., 1983—. Mem. planning staff U.S. Dept. State, Washington, 1970-71; mem. bd. Internat. Rsch. and Exch. Bd., N.Y.C., 1971-74, mem. selection com., 1984-85; vis. assoc. prof. Yale U., New Haven, spring 1975; chmn. adv. com. Cold War Internat. History Project, Woodrow Wilson Ctr., Washington, 1993—; mem. Internat. Acad. Adv. Group, Russian Fgn. Ministry Archives, 1992-97; assoc. Davis Ctr. for Russian Studies, Harvard U. Author: The View from Lenin Hills, 1967; Governing Soviet Cities, 1973; Stalin's American Policy, 1982, Khrushchev: The Man and His Era, 2003 (Nat. Book Critics Circle award, 2004, Pulitzer Prize for biography, 2004, Wayne S. Vucinich Book prize Am. Assn. for Advancement of Slavic Studies 2004, Robert H. Ferrell Book prize 2004); co-author: (with Jane Taubman) Moscow Spring, 1989; editor, translator: Khrushchev on Khrushchev (Sergei N. Khrushchev), 1990; editor: Globalism and Its Critics, 1973; co-editor: Nikita Khrushchev, 2000. Named Alumnus of Yr., Harriman Inst., Columbia U., 2003; fellow Woodrow Wilson Nat. Found., 1962, Ford Found., 1963-67, Coun. Fgn. Rels., 1970-71, Rockefeller Found., 1983, Columbia U. Harriman Inst., 1987, Fulbright-Hays Found., 1988, NEH, 1992, Woodrow Wilson Internat. Ctr. for Scholars, 2000, Guggenheim Found., 2006; grantee Nat. Coun. Soviet and East European Rsch., 1984 Mem. Coun. Fgn. Rels., Authors Guild. Home: 43 Hitchcock Rd Amherst MA 01002 Office: Amherst Coll Dept Polit Sci Amherst MA 01002 Home Phone: 413-256-8858; Office Phone: 413-542-2420. E-mail: wctaubman@amherst.edu.

TAUC, JAN, retired physics professor; b. Pardubice, Czechoslovakia, Apr. 15, 1922; arrived in US, 1969, naturalized, 1978; s. Jan and Josefa (Semonska) T.; m. Vera Koubelova, Oct. 18, 1947; children: Elena (Mrs. Milan Kokta), Jan. Ing.Dr. in Elec. Engring., Tech. U. Prague, 1949; RNDr., Charles U., Prague, 1956; Dr.Sc. in Physics, Czechoslovak Acad. Scis., 1956. Scientist microwave research Sci. and Tech. Research Inst., Tanvald and Prague, 1949-52; head semiconductor dept. Inst. Solid State Physics, Czechoslovak Acad. Scis., 1953-69; prof. exptl. physics Charles U., 1964-69, dir. Inst. Physics, 1968-69; mem. tech. staff Bell Telephone Labs., Murray Hill, NJ, 1969-70; prof. engring. and physics Brown U., 1970-83, L. Herbert Ballou prof. engring. and physics, 1983-92, L. Herbert Ballou prof. emeritus, 1992—, dir. material research lab., 1983-88. Dir. E. Fermi Summer Sch., Varenna, Italy, 1965; vis. prof. U. Paris, 1969, Stanford U., 1977, Max Planck Inst. Solid State Research, Stuttgart, Germany, 1982; UNESCO fellow, Harvard, 1961-62 Author: Photo and Thermoelectric Effects in Semiconductors, 1962, also numerous articles; editor: The Optical Properties of Solids, 1966, Amorphous and Liquid Semiconductors, 1974; co-editor: Solid State Communications, 1963-92. Recipient Nat. prize Czechoslovak Govt., 1955, 69; Sr. U.S. Scientist award Humboldt Found., 1981, Silver medal Union of Czechoslovak Mathematicians and Physicists, 1992; Jan Tauc Grad. Fellowship in Engring. at Brown U. in his honor, 2003. Fellow AAAS, Am. Phys. Soc. (Frank Isakson prize 1982, David Adler award 1988); mem. NAS, European Phys. Soc. (founding), Czechoslovak Acad. Scis. (corr. 1963-71, 90-91, fgn. 1991-92, Hlavka medal 1992, de Scientia et Humanitate Optime Meritis medal 2003), Czech Learned Soc. (hon.). Business E-Mail: jan.tauc@brown.edu.

TAUCHER, FRED HORACE, data processing company executive; b. Berlin, Germany, Jan. 29, 1933; came to U.S., 1946, naturalized, 1954; s. Julius and Therese (Gerstel) T.; m. Hisako Kawano, Apr. 25, 1955; children: Walter A., Audrey T. Grad. high sch. Asst. supr. data processing dept. Pacific Hwy. Transport, 1955-60; mgr. data processing dept. Graystone Corp., Seattle, 1960-68, dir. Canal Computer Center, 1962-68; pres. Corporate Mgmt., Inc., Seattle, 1968-86; pres. Corp. Computer, Inc., 1986—. Mem. CAP; bd. dirs. Wash. State U.S. Olympic Com.; treas. Nat Kidney Found., Wash. affiliate. Served with AUS, 1951-54. Recipient Individual Performance award Data Processing Mgmt. Assn., 1968, Mayor's Small Bus. award City of Seattle, 1991. Mem. Data Processing Mgmt. Assn. (dir. Puget Sound chpt. 1962-66, 68-70, treas. 1967-68, sec. 1973-74, internat. dir. Puget Sound chpt. 1968-71, 74-76, div. chmn. Northwestern div. 1971-72, gen. chm. Region 2 conf. 1974), Aircraft Owners and Pilots Assn., DAV (life). Home: 1211 8th Ave S Edmonds WA 98020-6630 Office: Corp Computer Inc 11300 25th Ave NE Seattle WA 98125-6639

TAUKE, THOMAS JOSEPH, telecommunications company executive, former congressman; b. Dubuque, Iowa, Oct. 11, 1950; s. Joseph A. and Esther M. (Reicher) Tauke; m. Beverly Tauke, 2 children. BA magna cum laude, Loras Coll., 1972; JD, U. Iowa, 1974. Bar: Iowa 1974. Mem. Curnan, Fitzsimmons, Schilling and Tauke, Dubuque, 1976-79, Iowa Gen. Assembly, 1975-79, US Congress from 2nd Iowa dist., 1979—91; v.p. govt. affairs NYNEX, Washington, 1991—97, exec. v.p. govt. affairs, 1991—97; sr. v.p. govt. rels. Bell Atlantic Corp., 1997—2000; sr. v.p. pub. policy & external affairs Verizon Comm. Inc., 2000, exec. v.p. pub. affairs, policy and comm., 2004—. Del. Rep. Nat. Conv., 1976; chmn. 2nd Congl. Dist. of Iowa Rep. Party, 1974-77; mem. Iowa Rep. Ctrl. Com., 1974-77; chmn. Dubuque County Rep. Party, 1972-74 Mem. pastoral coun. Roman Catholic Archdiocese of Dubuque, 1971-73; trustee Mt. Mercy Coll., Cedar Rapids, Iowa. Mem. ABA, Iowa Bar Assn., Dubuque County Bar Assn., Dubuque C. of C., Cedar Rapids Area C. of C. Clubs: Rotary, Junipera Serra. Office: Verizon Comm Inc 1095 Ave Americas New York NY 10036 *

TAUPENOT, LAURENT, medical educator, researcher; BS in Cell Biology, Biochemistry and Physiology cum laude, U. Burgundy, Dijon, France, 1988; MS in Physiology cum laude, U. Burgundy, 1989; postgrad. degree in molecular and cellular biology, U. Louis Pasteur, Strasbourg, France, 1990; PhD in Molecular and Cellular Neurobiology summa cum laude, U. Louis Pasteur, 1995. Postdoctoral rsch. fellow U. Calif.-San Diego, La Jolla, 1995—2001, asst. rsch. scientist, 2001—03, asst. prof. medicine, 2003—. Recipient Scholarship award, French Ministry Edn. and Rsch., 1989, Rsch. Scientist Devel. award, NIH, 2001, 2004, Faculty Devel. award, 2003, Young Investigator award, 9th Internat. Symposium on Chromaffin Cell Biology, 1997; grantee, NIH, 2005; predoctoral fellow, Nat. Sci. Rsch. Ctr. (CNRS)/DRET, 1991—95, postdoctoral fellow, Nat. Kidney Found., 1996, 1998. Office: U Calif at San Diego 9500 Gilman Dr # 0838 La Jolla CA 92093-0838 Office Phone: 858-534-0670. Office Fax: 858-534-0626. E-mail: ltaupenot@ucsd.edu.

TAUR, YUAN, physicist, researcher; b. Nanchang, Jiangxi, China, Sept. 27, 1946; arrived in U.S., 1968; s. Tang and Ping-Chung Seh Taur; m. Betty Chu, Apr. 20, 1974; children: Ying, Hsuan. BS in Physics, Nat. Taiwan U., 1967; PhD in Physics, U. Calif., Berkeley, 1974. Postdoctoral fellow U. Calif., Berkeley, 1974—75; rsch. assoc. Goddard Inst. Space Studies NASA, NYC, 1975—79; mem. tech. staff Rockwell Internat. Sci. Ctr., Thousand Oaks, Calif., 1979—81; rsch. staff mem., mgr. T. J. Watson Rsch. Ctr. IBM, Yorktown Heights, NY, 1981—2001; prof. U. Calif., San Diego, 2001—. Co-author: Fundamentals of Modern VLSI Devices, 1998; contbr. articles to profl. jours. Fellow IEEE (subject editor Electron Device Letters 1996-99, editor-in-chief 1999—). Achievements include 14 patents. Office: U Calif San Diego Dept Elec and Computer Engring La Jolla CA 92093 Office Phone: 858-534-3816. Business E-Mail: taur@ece.ucsd.edu.

TAURASI, DIANA LURENA, professional basketball player; b. Glendale, Calif., June 11, 1982; d. Mario Taurasi and Lili. Grad. in Sociology, U. Conn., 2004. Player Phoenix Mercury, Ariz., 2004—. Player USA Sr. Nat. Team, 2004. Named Big East Preseason Rookie of Yr., 2000—01, Most Outstanding Player of NCAA East Region, 2000—01, Big East Championship Most Outstanding Player, 2000—01, Kodak All-Am. and AP Second Team All Am., 2001—02, Naismith Player of Yr., 2001—02, 2003, Big East First Team Performer, 2002—03, NCAA Final Four and East Regional Most Outstanding Player, 2003, Nat. Player of Yr., US Basketball Writers Assn., 2003, Preseason All-Am., 2003, WNBA Rookie of Yr., 2004, WNBA Peak Performer, 2006, Female Athlete of Yr., USA Basketball, 2006; named to Big East All-Rookie Team, 2000—01, NCAA Mideast Region All-Tournament Team, 2001—02, All Big-East First Team, 2002, Big East All-Tournament Team, 2002, 2003, All-WNBA First Team, 2004, 2006, WNBA Western Conf. All-Star Team, 2005—07; recipient Honda award for Women's Basketball Finalist, 2001—02, Honda Trophy Award, 2003, Wade Trophy, 2003, Espy Award for Best Female Coll. Athlete, ESPN, 2003, 2004, Espy Award for Best Female Athlete, 2004, Gold medal, Athens Olympics, 2004. Office: Phoenix Mercury 201 E Jefferson St Phoenix AZ 85004 *

TAUREL, SIDNEY, pharmaceutical executive; b. Casablanca, Morocco, Feb. 9, 1949; came to US, 1986; US citizen, 1995; s. Jose and Marjorie (Afriat) T.; m. Kathryn H. Fleischmann, Mar. 22, 1977; children: Alexis, Patrick, Olivia. BSBA, Ecole des Hautes Etudes Commerciales, Paris, 1969; MBA, Columbia U., NYC, 1971. Mktg. assoc. Eli Lilly Internat. Corp., Indpls., 1971-72, pres., 1986-91, exec. v.p. pharm. divsn., 1991; mktg. planning mgr. Eli Lilly Do Brasil Limitada, Sao Paulo, Brazil, 1972-75, gen. mgr., 1981—83; mgr. pharm. ops. Ea. Europe Eli Lilly und Elanco Gesmbh, Vienna, 1976; sales mgr. pharm. Eli Lilly France SA, Paris, 1977-79, mktg. dir. pharm., 1980-81; v.p. Europe Lilly European ops., London, 1983—85; exec. v.p. Eli Lilly and Co., 1993—98, pres. pharm. divsn., 1993, COO, 1996—98, pres., 1996—2005, CEO, 1998—, chmn., 1999—. Bd. dirs. McGraw-Hill, Cies, IBM, ITT Industries; bd. overseers Columbia Bus. Sch.; mem. Adv. Com. for Trade Policy and Negotiation, 2007-. Bd. dirs. RCA Tennis Championships. Recipient Ellis Island Medal of Honor, 2000; named a chevalier (Knight) of the French Legion of Honor, 2001. Mem. Pharm. Rsch. and Mfrs. Assn.(PhRMA), Bus. Coun., Bus. Roundtable, President's Homeland Security Adv. Coun., 2002, Pres.'s Export Coun., 2003; trustee, Indpls. Mus. Art Avocations: tennis, music. Office: Eli Lilly and Co Lilly Corp Ctr Indianapolis IN 46285 Office Phone: 317-276-2000. E-mail: staurel@lilly.com. *

TAURMAN, JOHN DAVID, lawyer; b. Charleston, W.Va., May 22, 1946; s. Ralph and Mikanna Elizabeth (Clark) T.; m. Donna Jill Naroff, June 13, 1981; children: Devon Elliott, Kyra Justine, Quinn Juliet. BA magna cum laude, Duke U., 1968; JD cum laude, Harvard U., 1971. Bar: D.C. 1971, U.S. Supreme Ct. 1981, Tex. 1984, U.S. Ct. Appeals (D.C., fed., 3d, 5th, 9th and 10th cirs.), U.S. Dist. Ct. D.C., U.S. Dist. Ct. (so., no. and ea. dists.) Tex., U.S. Ct. Fed. Claims. Assoc. Covington & Burling, Washington, 1971-78, Vinson & Elkins, Washington, 1979-82, ptnr. Houston, 1982-90, Washington, 1990—. Lectr. State Bar Inst. Tex., 1983. Editor Harvard Law Rev., 1969-71. Mem. ABA, State Bar Tex., D.C. Bar Assn., Phi Beta Kappa. Office: Vinson & Elkins Willard Office Bldg 1455 Pennsylvania Ave NW Fl 7 Washington DC 20004-1013 E-mail: jtaurman@velaw.com. *Notable cases include: ETSI vs. Burlington No., Ea. Dist. Tex., antitrust jury trial; Bank United v. U.S., Ct. Fed. Claims, breach of contract trial; First Nationwide Bank v. U.S., Ct. Fed. Claims, breach of contract; United Investors v. Waddell & Reed, Ala. state ct., tortious interference jury trial; David's Supermarkets v. Fleming, Tex. state ct., fraud jury trial.*

TAURO, JOSEPH LOUIS, federal judge; b. Winchester, Mass., Sept. 26, 1931; s. G. Joseph and Helen Maria (Petrossi) T.; m. Elizabeth Mary Quinlan, Feb. 7, 1959 (dec. 1978); children— Joseph L., Elizabeth H., Christopher M.; m. Ann Lefavour Jones, July 12, 1980. AB, Brown U., 1953; LLB, Cornell U., 1956; JD (hon.), U. Mass., 1985, Suffolk U., 1986, Northeastern U., 1990, New Eng. Sch. Law, 1992, Boston U., 1997, Brown U., 1998. Bar: Mass. 1956, D.C. 1960. Assoc. Tauro & Tauro, Lynn, Mass., 1958-59; asst. U.S. atty. Dept. Justice, Boston, 1959-60; ptnr. Jaffee & Tauro, Boston and Lynn, Mass., 1960-71; chief legal counsel Gov. of Mass., Boston, 1965-68; U.S. atty. Dept. Justice, Boston, 1972; judge U.S. Dist. Ct., Boston, 1972—; chief judge U.S. Dist. Ct., Mass., 1992-99. Mem. exec. com. Cornell Law Assn., Ithaca, N.Y., 1968-71; mem. adv. coun. Cornell Law Sch., Ithaca, 1975-80; vis. prof. law Boston U. Law Sch., 1977—, mem. Jud. Conf. U.S., 1994-97, mem. com. on operation of jury sys., 1979-86, mem. adv. com. on codes of conduct, 1988-94. Trustee Brown U., 1978—, Mass. Gen. Hosp., Boston, 1968-72, Children's Hosp. Med. Ctr., Boston, 1979-94. 1st lt. U.S. Army, 1956-58. Recipient Disting. Alumnus award Cornell U. Law Sch., 1992, Brown Bear award Brown U., 1993; named one of 10 Outstanding Young Men, Greater Boston Jaycees, 1966. Fellow Am. Bar Found.; mem. Mass. Bar Assn., Boston Bar Assn. (coun. 1968-71), D.C. Bar Assn., Boston Yacht Club (Marblehead, Mass.). Republican. Roman Catholic. Avocations: sports, reading, music, films, theater. Office: 1 Courthouse Way Ste 7110 Boston MA 02210-3009 Office Phone: 617-748-9288.

TAUSAN, CAROL A., music educator; b. Holyoke, Mass., Mar. 14, 1958; d. Eugene A. and Margaret M. Miller; m. Jon Criss Tausan, June 20, 1994. MA, Chapman U., Colorado Springs, Colo., 1994; MusB, Nebr. Wesleyan U., 1980. Cert. tchr. Fla., 1996, Nat. Bd. Profl. Tchg. Stds., 2005. Music tchr. Mary Our Queen Sch., Omaha, 1980—86, Panorama Mid. Sch., Colorado Springs, 1987—94, Turman Elem. Sch., Colorado Springs, 1994—96, Garden Elem. Sch., Venice, Fla., 1996—. Choir dir. Panorama Mid. Sch., Colorado Springs, Colo., 1987—94, gifted and talented coord., 1988—92; mem. authentic assessment com. Harrison Sch. Dist. #2, Colorado Springs, Colo., 1989—90; mem. coun. Curriculum, Instrn. and Assessment Coun., Colorado Springs, Colo., 1990—92; choir dir. Turman Elem. Sch., Colorado Springs, Colo., 1994—96, Garden Elem. Sch., Venice, Fla., 1996—, mem. faculty leadership com., 1996—; team leader Garden Elem., Venice, Fla., 1999—; mem. lang. arts com. Garden Elem. Sch., Venice, Fla., 1999—2002, bldg. rep. Sarasota Classified/Tchrs. Assn., 2001—02, sr. bldg. rep., 2002—; mem. com. Cmty./Schs. Partnership for Arts, Sarasota, Fla., 1997—, Renaissance Com., Venice, Fla., 2001—03; mem.music textbook adoption com. Sch. Bd. of Sarasota County, Fla., 2002—03. Choir dir. (performance) St. Mary's Cath. Ch., Bellevue, Nebr., 1982—84, All-City Eighth Grade Chorus, Sun Fiesta Parade (Best Edn. Entry, 1997), Venetian Holiday Festival. Grantee Sing out for Am., The Edn. Found. of Sarasota, 1997—98, The Magnificent 7, Edn. Found. of Sarasota, 1998—99, Hooray for the Red, White and Blue, 1998—99, All Am. Celebration, 1999—2000, Rockin' and Readin', 2000—01, Young Americans and Proud of It, 2000—01, True to the Red, White, and Blue, 2002—03, Rockin' and Readin', Cmty. Found. of Sarasota County, 2000-2001, The Merry Minstrel, 2002-2003, Recorders - An instrumental Opportunity, 2002-2003, Create and Communicate with Recorders, 2003-2004, You Can BEAT This!, 2003-2004, Got Recorders?, 2004—05; African Artist-in-Residence, Arts for a Complete Edn./Fla. Alliance for Arts Edn., 1998—99. Mem.: Colo. Music Educators Assn., Sarasota Area Music Educators, Fla. Music Educators Assn., Music Educators Nat. Conf. Home: 427 Pebble Creek Ct Venice FL 34285 Office: Garden Elem Sch 700 Center Rd Venice FL 34285 Personal E-mail: candcofppcc@comcast.net.

TAUSCHER, ELLEN O., congresswoman; b. Newark, 1951; 1 child, Katherine. BS in early Childhood Edn., Seton Hall U., 1974. With Bache Securities, NYC, NY Stock Exch.; dir. Tauscher Found.; mem. US Congress from 10th Calif. dist., 1997—; mem. ho. armed svcs. com., ho. transp. com. US Ho. Reps. Founder The ChildCare Registry; bd. regents Seton Hall U.; co-chair Dianne Feinstein, US Senate Campaign, 1994; transp. and infrastructure com., surface transp. and water resources and environ. Author: The ChildCare Sourcebook, 1996. Chair New Dem. Coalition, Bipartisan Freshman Campaign Fin. Reform Task Force, House Cancer Awareness Working Group, Congl. Caucus on the Arts; co-chair Congl. Iraqi Women's Caucus; vice-chair Calif. Dem. Del., Dem. Leadership Coun. Democrat. Roman Catholic. *

TAUSSIG, ANDREW RICHARD, investment banker; b. Abington, Pa., Aug. 27, 1951; s. Ralph J. and Sally G. T.; m. Susan Fierman, June 25, 1978. BA, Trinity Coll., 1973; JD, Georgetown Law Sch., 1976; MBA, Wharton Grad. Sch., 1978. Bar: Pa. 1976, NY 1978. Corp. atty. Willkie, Farr & Gallagher, NYC, 1978-82; investment banker, mng. dir. CS First

Boston, NYC, 1983—2005; head retail investment banking First Boston Corp., NYC, 1988—2005; vice chmn., global head, investment banking Lehman Brothers, NYC, 2005—. Bd. dirs. Big V. Supermarkets, Florida, NY,Pueblo Internat., Pompano, Fla. Named a Top Rainmaker, Retail, Dealmaker mag., 2006. Office: Lehman Brothers 745 Seventh Ave New York NY 10019 Office Phone: 212-526-7000. Office Fax: 212-526-0739. *

TAUSSIG, LYNN MAX, healthcare administrator, pulmonologist, pediatrician, educator; b. Milw., July 19, 1942; m. Lisa Peter; children: Heather, Jennifer. AB cum laude, Harvard U., 1964; MD, Washington U., St. Louis, 1968. Diplomate Am. Bd. Pediat., Nat. Bd. Med. Examiners, Am. Bd. Pediat. Pulmonary. Rsch. asst. dept. neuroanatomy Marquette U., Milw., 1965; intern in pediat. St. Louis Children's Hosp., 1968-69; resident in pediat. U. Colo. Med. Ctr., Denver, 1969-70; clin. assoc. pediat. metabolism br. Nat. Inst. Arthritis, Metabolism, and Digestive Diseases, NIH, Bethesda, Md., 1970-72; pulmonary fellow Montreal (Que., Can.) Children's Hosp., 1972-74; asst. prof. pediat. Ariz. Health Scis. Ctr., Tucson, 1974-77, cystic fibrosis ctr. dir., 1974-85, assoc. chief pulmonary function labs., 1974-85, dir. pulmonary sect., 1974-85, asst. dir. divsn. respiratory scis., 1976-92, assoc. prof. pediat., 1977-81, assoc. head dept. pediat., 1979-84, prof., 1981-93, head dept. pediat., 1985-93, dir. Steele Meml. Children's Rsch. Ctr., 1986-93; prof. pediats. U. Colo. Health Scis. Ctr., Denver, 1993—; pres., CEO Nat. Jewish Med. and Rsch. Ctr., Denver, 1993—. Frank Stevenson vis. prof. U. Con., 1977, 82; Robert Chinnock Meml. lectr. Loma Linda U., Calif., 1983; Jour. Pediats. vis. prof. U. Chgo., 1984; Brennenman lectr. L.A. Pediat. Soc., 1988, 94; Danis Meml. lectr. St. Louis U., 1989; Talamo Meml. lectr. Johns Hopkins U., Balt., 1989; Anna Zager vis. lectr. in pediats. Technion U., Haifa, Israel, 1990; Sir Clavering Fison vis. prof. Inst. Child Health, U. London, 1992; Benjamin Meaker vis. prof. U. Bristol, Eng., 1992; Ben Kagan vis. lectr. Cedars-Sinai Hosp., L.A., 1993. Mem. editl. bd. Chest, 1983-88, Am. Rev. Respiratory Diseases, 1983-89; contbr. articles to profl. jours. Trustee Congregation Anshei Israel, 1978-80; bd. dirs. Jewish Cmty. Ctr., 1982-90, sec., 1984-86, v.p., 1987-89; mem. allocations com. Jewish Fedn. So. Ariz., 1985, 88, Allied Jewish Fedn. Denver, 1996—; bd. dirs. Colo. Biomed. Venture Ctr., 1994—, Congregation Rodef Shalom, 1996—; active Martin Luther King Jr. Minority Scholarship Program, 1994—, Colo. Concern, 1995—. Cystic Fibrosis Found. Clin. fellow, 1972-74, Sr. Internat. fellow Fogarty Internat. Ctr., 1980-81; Young Investigator Pulmonary Rsch. grantee Nat. Heart and Lung Inst., 1974-76, and numerous other med. grants; Pfizer Labs. Med. scholar, 1966; recipient Lange Med. Book award, 1966 Mem. Am. Acad. Pediat. (mem. exec. com. sect. on diseases of chest 1978-80, mem. ad hoc com. for pediat. pulmonary bds., sect. on diseases of chest 1978-85), Am. Pediat. Soc., Am. Thoracic Soc. (mem. com. to advise pres. 1975-76, sec. sci. assembly for pediats. 1975-77, mem. respiratory care com. 1976-78, mem. nominating com. 1977, 84-85, chmn. prograom com. 1979-81, mem. ann. meeting com. 1979-81, mem. rsch. rev. com. 1981-82, chmn. publs. policy com. 1988-89, 90-92, mem. exec. com. 1989-90, sec.-treas. 1989-90, active many other coms.), Am. Coll. Chest Physicians (mem. steering group for com. on cardiopulmonary diseases in children 1977-79), Ariz. Pediat. Soc., Ariz. Lung Assn., Pima County Pediat. Soc., Soc. Pediat. Rsch. (founder Lung Club 1985), Western Soc. Pediat. Rsch. (mem. nominating com. 1979-80, elected to coun. 1994—), Rotary, Harvard Club of So. Ariz. (schs. com. 1982-93, sec.-treas. 1989-93), Harvard Club of Colo., Alpha Omega Alpha. Office: Nat Jewish Med & Rsch Ctr 1400 Jackson St Denver CO 80206-2761

TAUZIN, BILLY, II, (WILBERT JOSEPH TAUZIN II), trade association executive, former congressman; b. Chackbay, La., June 14, 1943; s. Wilbert Joseph and Enola (Martinez) T.; m. Cecile Bergeron, May 29, 1993; children: Kristie René, Wilbert J. III, John Ashton, Thomas Nicholas, Michael James. BA, Nicholls State U., 1964; JD, La. State U., 1967. Bar: La. 1967. Practice, Houma and Thibodaux, La., 1967-80; ptnr. Marcel Marcel Fanguy & Tauzin, 1967-72; mem. firm Tauzin-Sonnier, 1972-80; mem. La. Ho. of Reps., 1971-80, house floor leader, 1974-79, chmn. Teche Clearinghouse Rev. Bd., 1975-78, chmn. house natural resources com., 1975-80; mem. U.S. Congress from 3d La. Dist., 1980—2005; mem. commerce com., mem. resources com.; chmn. energy & commerce com., 2001—04; pres., CEO Pharm. Rsch. & Manufacturers of Am. (PhRMA), Washington, 2005—. Mem. Thibodaux Playhouse, 1967-75; mem. Criminal Justice Inst. Recipient Thibodaux Outstanding Young Man award, 1971, Watchdogs of the Treasury award, Nat. Assn. Broadcasters, 1994, Golden Plow award Nat. Farm Bur.; Named Legis. Conservationist of the Yr. La. Wildlife Fedn., 1979; Named to Hall of Fame, Nicholls State U., 1964 Mem. ABA, La. State Bar Assn., Lafourche Parish Bar Assn. (past pres.), Chackbay-Choupic Jr. C. of C. (past pres.), Nicholls Alumni Council (v.p.) Lodges: Kiwanis; K.C. Republican. Office: Pharm Rsch & Manufacturers of Am 1100 15th St NW Ste 900 Washington DC 20005

TAVAKKOLIZADEH, ALI, surgeon; s. Abdulhossein Tavakkolizadeh and Mehranghiz Saidi. MB, Royal London Hosp. Med. Coll., Eng., 1993. Anatomy demonstrator United Med. and Dental Schools of Guy's and St Thomas's Hospitals, London, 1995—96; basic surg. tng. Wessex Deanary, England, 1996—98; rsch. fellow Brigham and Women's Hosp., Harvard Med. Sch., Boston, 1998—2000; surg. specialist registrar East Anglian Deanary, Cambridge, England, 2000—01; surg. resident Brigham and Women's Hosp., Harvard Med. Sch., Boston, 2001—05, adv. minimally invasive fellowship, 2005—06, assoc. surgeon, 2006—. Instr. surgery Harvard Med. Sch., 2005—. Author: (original paper) American Journal of Physiology, Journal of Surgical Research, Journal for Parentral and Enteral Nutrition, (review article) Transplantation Reviews, (letter) Lancet, (review article) Journal for Parentral and Enteral Nutrition. Recipient Japan Surg. Soc. Travel Grant, Japan Surg. Soc., 2000, AGA Travel Award to World Congress of Gastroenterology, Am. Gastroenterology Assn., 2002, GRG/AGA Fellow Travel Award, Gastroenterology Rsch. Group, 2000. Fellow: Royal coll. of Surgeons of Eng.; mem.: Am. Gastroenterology Assn., Soc. for Surgery of Alimentary Tract. Office: Brigham and Women's Hospital 75 Francis Street Boston MA 02115 Home Phone: 617-734-1927; Office Phone: 617-732-6660. E-mail: atavakkolizadeh@partners.org.

TAVALIN, FERN, educational consultant; b. Plainfield, NJ, Feb. 10, 1953; d. Marian Dorothy Higgins and Lester Amos Pagano; m. Peter Robert Tavalin, Apr. 11, 1981; children: Kuna Leya, Julian Zoe. BA, Franklin and Marshall Coll., Lancaster, Pa., 1976; EdD, U. Mass, Amherst, 1994. Tchr. English and social studies Putney Ctrl. Sch., Vt., 1987—93; grad. asst. U. Mass., Amherst, 1992—93; dir. Vt. Arts Assessment Initiative, Montpelier, 1993—96; exec. dir. The WEB Project, Vt., 1995—; project dir. The Flow of History, Vt., 2002—. Steering com. mem. framework of stds. Vt. Dept. of Edn., Montpelier, Vt., 1993—96; adv. coun. IBM Reinventing Edn. Software Devel., Essex Junction, Vt., 1995—99; cons. Spaulding Cmty. Svc. Learning, Barre, Vt., 2002—; program presenter Tech. Innovation in Edn.; dir. The WEB Exch.: Using Multimedia and Telecomm. to Improve Student Learning; spkr. in field. Contbg. writer: Putney: World's Best Known Small Town; author: (learning guide) Collaborative Learning: A Guide to Inquiry-Based Study Groups; co-author: Improving Student Learning through Multimedia Projects (ASCD book pick, 2002); prodr.(and dir.): (videos) Vt. MIDI Project, Art Responding through Tech., From Inside Out: Creating Dance in a Pub. Sch., We Can Work It Out: Using Students as Mediators, Taking a Stand in Cyberspace; dir.: Artifacts, History, and the World Wide Web; contbr. chapters to books, articles to profl. jours. Founding bd. mem. Strolling of the Heifers, Brattleboro, Vt., 2000—05. Named Promising Tech. Program, U.S. Dept. Edn., Putney Person of Yr., 2004; recipient Gov. and Commr. award Contrbn. to Tech. Avocations: photography, videography, travel, house building, gardening. Personal E-mail: ftavalin@comcast.net.

TAVARES, SAMANTHA, psychologist, educator; b. Bahia, Brazil, Oct. 23, 1968; arrived in U.S., 1984; d. Jose and Clarice Maria Tavares; 1 adopted child, Satyana Lua 1 child, Titus Sol. BA in Chinese Lang. Studies, Taipei, 1988; BA in Asian Studies, UCLA, 1990; M in Psychology, Forest Inst. Profl. Psychology, 1993; MA in Ea. Religion, U. Hawaii, 2000; PhD in Clin. Psychology, Am. Schs. Profl. Psychology, 1995. Lic. psychologist Hawaii, 1996, cert. hypnotherapist 1994, level II cert. Eye Movement Desensitization and Reprocessing. 1998, cert. holistic therapist 2000. Sch. counselor Han Guan Inst., China, 1986—88; pvt. practice clin. psychology Honolulu, Kailua, Hawaii, 1995—; clin. psychologist Dept. Health, Honolulu, 1996—98; clin. supr. Alaka'I Na Keiki, Inc., 1996—; clin. psychologist evaluator Dept. Edn. Dist. Hawaii, 1997—2000; assoc. prof. Holos U. Grad. Seminary, 2000—; faculty staff Inst. for Sci. Med. Intuition, 2000—04. Co-founder Samba Axe Hawaii, 1993—; dance instr., performer, 1993—; project dir. Support Adoption Hawaii, 2005—; exec. dir. Hawaii Hearts Helping Adoptions, 2005. Author: (compact disk, cassette tape) Transformative Liberation, 2005. Avocations: dance, yoga, meditation, running, surfing. Office: 43 Oneawa St Kailua HI Office Phone: 808-261-3731. E-mail: dr.tavaressam@yahoo.com.

TAVARES, SAMIA COSTA, economics professor; BA in Econs. with highest honors, U. Fla., Gainesville, 1996, MA in Econs., 1999, PhD in Econs., 2002. Asst. prof. econs. Rochester Inst. Tech., NY, 2003—. Faculty search com. dept. econs. Rochester Inst. Tech., 2003—04, elections com. mem. Coll. Liberal Arts, 2004—, webmaster dept. econs., 2004—; vis. scholar Carleton U., Ottawa, Canada, 2004, Bar-Ilan U., Ramat Gan, Israel, 2005. Recipient Cert. on Achievement in study of German, German Consulate-General, 1994, 1995, Cert. Academic Excellence, Coll. Bus. Adminstrn., U. Fla., 1996, Walter-Lanzillotti Dissertation award, Robert F. Lanzillotti Pub. Policy Rsch. Ctr., U. Fla., 2000—01, 2001—02; Fla. Academic scholar, State of Fla., 1993—96, Challenger Meml. scholar, 1993—96, Valedictorian scholar, U. Fla., 1993, Fla. AP State scholar, Coll. Bd., 1993, Grad. Rsch. Assistantship, Bur. Econs. and Bus. Rsch., U. Fla., 1997—98, Grad. Assistantship, Dept. Econs., U. Fla., 1998—2002, Travel grantee, Ctr. for Internat. Bus. Edn. and Rsch., U. Fla., 2001. Mem.: European Econ. Assn., European Pub. Choice Soc., Phi Sigma Iota, Phi Kappa Phi, Golden Key, Beta Gamma Sigma, Phi Beta Kappa. Office Phone: (585) 475-4647.

TAVEGGIA, THOMAS CHARLES, management consultant; b. Oak Lawn, Ill., June 15, 1943; s. Thomas Angelo and Eunice Louise (Harris) Taveggia; m. Brigitte I. Adams, Jan. 23, 1965; children: Michaela, Francesca. BS, Ill. Inst. Tech., 1965; MA, U. Oreg., 1968, PhD, 1971. Prof. U. Oreg., Eugene, 1970, U. B.C., Vancouver, Can., 1970-73, U. Calif., Irvine, 1973-74, Ill. Inst. Technology, Chgo., 1974-77; mgmt. cons. Towers, Perrin, Forster, & Crosby, Chgo., 1977-80; ptnr. Manplan Cons., Chgo., 1980-81, Coopers & Lybrand, San Francisco, 1981-86, Touche Ross, San Francisco, 1986-88; prof. Calif. Sch. Profl. Psychology, Berkeley, 1988-98, U. Ariz., Tucson, 2000—05. Author: (with Dubin and Arends) From Family and School to Work, 1967; (with Dubin) The Teaching-Learning Paradox: A Comparative Analysis of College Teaching Methods, 1968; (with Dubin and Hedley) The Medium May Be Related to the Message: College Instruction by TV, 1969; contbr. articles to profl. jours. Grantee, Calif. Sch. Profl. Psychology, 1993—98; NDEA Title IV fellow, 1967—71, U. B.C. faculty rsch. grantee, 1970, 1971, 1973. Home: 3622 Edgewater Dr Enid OK 73703 Personal E-mail: taveg@aol.com.

TAVEL, MARK KIVEY, finance company executive, economist; b. Cambridge, Mass., May 9, 1945; s. Bernard Benjamin and Elizabeth (Rogers) T.; m. Susana Sara Doño, Dec. 14, 1980; children: Sarah Emily, Rachel Florence, Amanda Victoria, Nathaniel Benjamin, Roberto Aaron Doño. BA cum laude, Harvard U., 1967; MBA, Columbia U., 1968. Sr. mng. dir. Rothschild Asset Mgmt., Inc., NYC. Trustee, treas. Trevor Day Sch., N.Y.C. Mem. Harvard Club (N.Y.C.). Home: 110 Riverside Dr New York NY 10024-3715 Office: Rothschild Inc 44th Fl 1251 Ave of the Americas New York NY 10020-1193

TAVELLA, ELISE SHANNON, librarian; b. Galveston, Tex., Feb. 7, 1950; d. William Landless Shannon and Mildred (Erlingheuser) Shannon Cooke; m. John Louis Tavella, May 27, 1972; children: Jennifer, Mark, Molly. BA in English with honors, U. of Pacific, 1971; MLS, San Jose State U., 1977. Asst. libr. San Jose (Calif.) State U., 1977; libr. dept. edn. Planned Parenthood Santa Clara County, San Jose, 1977-81; libr. San Jose Pub. Libr., 1980—. Author: The Ghosts of California: Master's Bibliography, 1977. Mem. Kappa Alpha Theta. Democrat. Episcopalian. Avocations: reading, writing, travel.

TAVERNISE, SABRINA, journalist; Reporter NY Times. Named Honorable Mention Kurt Schork award for Internat. Journalism, 2003. Office: New York Times 229 W 43rd St New York NY 10036 Office Phone: 202-556-1251. Office Fax: 212-556-3690.

TAVISS, PATRICIA ANN, management consultant, library association executive; b. Toronto, Ont., Can., Jan. 11, 1955; came to US, 1984; d. Norman Elward and Catherine (Johnson) Larter; m. Michael L. Taviss, Apr. 28, 1984. BA in English and Psychology, York U., Toronto, 1978; MLS, U. Western Ont., 1980; M in Arts and Orgnl. Mgmt., U. Phoenix Online, 2004. Children's libr. Grande Prairie (Can.) Pub. Libr., 1980-84; reference libr. Memphis-Shelby County Pub. Libr., 1984-86; systems mgr. Lane Pub. Libr., Hamilton, Ont., 1986-89; installation cons. CLSI, Boston, 1989-91; pres. TurboTraining, Carmel, Ind., 1991—2001; pres., chief change catalyst Pat Taviss Consulting, Saddlebrooke, Ariz., 2001—. Mem. C. of C., Rewood City, Calif.; vol. lit. tutor Project READ, Redwood City Pub. Libr., 2000—02. Recipient Pres's. award for outstanding contract instr., LMB Microcomputer, 1992. Mem.: Pub. Libr. Assn., Orgnl. Devel. Network, Continuing Libr. Edn. Network and Exchange Round Table (pres.-elect 2006—07, pres. 2007—), Calif. Libr. Assn., Calif. Assn. Libr. Trustees and Commissioners (prog. co-chair 2003—), Bay Area Orgn. Devel. Network, Am. Mgmt. Assn., ALA. Avocations: travel, reading, gardening. Office: Pat Taviss Consulting 38917 S Casual Dr Saddlebrooke AZ 85739 Office Phone: 520-825-2253. Business E-Mail: pat@taviss.com. *

TAVLIN, MICHAEL JOHN, real estate company and manufacturing executive; b. Lincoln, Nebr., Dec. 16, 1946; BEd, Oklahoma City U., 1970; JD, U. Nebr., 1973; LLM in Taxation, Washington U., St. Louis, 1977. Bar: Nebr. 1973, Mo. 1974. Ptnr. Nelson & Harding, Lincoln, 1973-77; sr. tax. mgr. Deloitte & Touche, Lincoln and Tulsa, 1979-84, PriceWaterhouseCoopers, Tulsa, 1984-86; v.p., treas., sec. Aliant Comm. Inc. and subs., Lincoln, 1986-99; sr. v.p., CFO, treas., sec. Interactive Intelligence, Inc. and subs., Indpls., 1999—2001; CFO, gen. counsel Speedway Motors, Inc. and Speedway Properties, Lincoln, 2001—. Bd. dirs., treas. Cmty. Health Endowment, Lincoln, 1998-2004; bd. dirs. Woods Charitable Fund, Lincoln, 2000-06, pres., 2005-06. Named Disting. Alumnus Oklahoma City U., 1995. Office: Speedway Motors Inc PO Box 81906 Lincoln NE 68501 Office Phone: 402-323-3122.

TAVROW, RICHARD LAWRENCE, lawyer; b. Syracuse, NY, Feb. 3, 1935; s. Harry and Ida Mary (Hodess) T.; m. Barbara J. Silver, Mar. 22, 1972; children— Joshua Michael, Sara Hallie. AB magna cum laude, Harvard U., 1957, LL.B., 1960, LL.M., 1961; postgrad., U. Copenhagen, 1961-62, U. Luxembourg, 1962. Bar: N.Y. bar 1961, U.S. Supreme Ct. bar 1969, Calif. bar 1978. Atty. W.R. Grace & Co., NYC, 1962-66; asst. chief counsel Gen. Dynamics Corp., NYC, 1966-68; chief counsel office of fgn. direct investments U.S. Dept. Commerce, Washington, 1969-71; ptnr. Schaeffer, Dale, Vogel & Tavrow, NYC, 1971-75; v.p., sec., gen. counsel Prudential Lines, Inc., NYC, 1975-78, also bd. dirs.; v.p., sec., gen. counsel Am. Pres. Lines, Ltd., Oakland, Calif., 1978-80, sr. v.p., sec., gen. counsel, 1980-91, also bd. dirs.; sr. v.p., sec., gen. counsel Am. Pres. Cos., Ltd., Oakland, Calif., 1983-91, also bd. dirs.; sr. ptnr. Law Offices of R.L. Tavrow, 1991—; chmn., pres., CEO Diabetes Healthcare & Life Enhancement Ltd., 2000—. Instr. Harvard Coll., 1959-61; lectr. Am. Mgmt. Assn., Practising Law Inst., other assns. Recipient Silver Medal award Dept. Commerce, 1970; Fulbright scholar, 1961-62 Mem. ABA, State Bar Calif., Internat. Bar Assn., Am. Soc. Internat. Law, Am. Corp. Counsel Assn., Am. Soc. Corp. Secs. Inc., Harvard Law Sch. Assn., Harvard Club (N.Y.C.).

TAVSS, JOHN E., lawyer; b. Norfolk, Va., June 6, 1954; BA with distinction, Univ. Va., 1976; JD, Vanderbilt Univ., 1979; LLM in Taxation, NYU, 1984. Bar: NY 1980. Assoc. Seward Kissel, NYC, 1979—88, ptnr., pvt. investment partnerships, tax, securities law, 1988—, mng. ptnr., exec. com., 1998—. Mem.: Internat. Bar Assn., NY State Bar Assn. Office: Seward & Kissel LLP One Battery Park Plz New York NY 10004 Office Phone: 212-574-1261. Office Fax: 212-480-8421. Business E-Mail: tavss@sewkis.com.

TAW, DUDLEY JOSEPH, sales executive, director; b. Cleve., Mar. 11, 1916; s. William C. and Ella (Gedeon) T.; m. Louise E. Forshey, Sept. 10, 1938; children: Judith (Mrs. William W. Beck, Jr.), Dudley Joseph. Student, Hiram Coll., 1938. With McKesson & Robbins, Inc. (pharm. co.), after 1937, sales mgr. Boston, 1947, v.p. sales NYC, 1953-60; v.p. Revlon, Inc., NYC, 1960-64; v.p. mktg. East Ohio Gas Co., Cleve., 1964-74, pres., 1975-81, chmn., 1981-82, Middtaw, Ltd., Inc., 1982. Bd. dirs. No. New England Gas Corp., First Union Mgmt. Co., Biskind Devel. Co., Vt. Gas Systems Inc. Mem. Better Bus. Bur., Cleve., chmn., 1973; trustee Lakewood Hosp.; treas. Salvation Army, Cleve. With USNR, 1946-47. Named Sales Exec. of Year Sales and Mktg. Execs. Cleve., 1966, Man of Year, 1977 Mem. Sales and Mktg. Execs. Cleve. (pres. 1969-70), Westwood Country Club, Union Club, Pepper Pike Club, Rotary (pres. Cleve. 1972-73). Methodist. Home: Apt 302 22500 Lake Rd Cleveland OH 44116-1025

TAW, JAMES S., history professor; b. Mineola, NY, July 4, 1950; s. James F. Taw Jr and Stella M. Taw; m. Brenda S. Swanner, Mar. 19, 1971; 1 child, Shannon T. Zapf. BA in History, Valdosta State U., Ga., 1972, MA in History, 1975. Cert. profl. tchr. T-5 Ga., 1972, svc. profl. S-5 Ga., 1983. Dept. chair, history Valdosta H.S., 1972—2002; prof. history Ga. Mil. Coll., Valdosta, 1974—2002; adminstr. Adult & Pediat. Urology, PC, Valdosta, 2002—06; instr. history Valdosta State U., 2001—. State tchr. evaluator State Ga., 1983—90. Chmn. SSS, Ga., 1981—2001. Recipient Outstanding Secondary Educator award, Nat. Orgn. Tchrs., 1976, Tchr. Yr., DAR, 1988, US army Recruiter's award, US Army, 1989, USAF Recruiter's Cmty. Svc. award, US Air Force, 1992, US Marine Corps Recruiter's Svc. award, US Marine Corps, 1991, Registrar's award, SSS, 1992, Svc. award, 2001. Mem.: AAUP (assoc.), Ga. Assn. Educators (assoc.).

TAWEEL, JANICE M., artist, educator; b. Ennis, Tex., Nov. 24, 1950; d. Josh H. and Evelyn M. Rivers; m. George M. Taweel, Nov. 24, 1973 (dec. Aug. 21, 1996); 1 child, Lorie M. BS, Lamar U., Beaumont, Tex., 1976. Cert. Tchg. Tex. Edn. Agy./Austin, Tex., 1976, Elem. Edn. Tex. Edn. Agy./Austin, Tex., 1990, All Level Art Tex. Edn. Agy./ Austin, Tex., 1976. Florist Designs by Delle Florist, Houston, 1968—69; credit/ billing lead Rogers Enterprises, Beaumont, Tex., 1976—90; owner Jan's Art, Beaumont, Tex., 1980—90; co-owner George's Boot and Shoe Repair, Beaumont, Tex., 1980—90; art educator Dallas Ind. Sch. Dist., Dallas, 1991—; owner The Artist Paper Trail, Dallas, 2004—. Sch. site coord. ArtsPartners, Dallas, 1999—, Crayola Dream-Makers, Dallas, 1999—; academic art sponsor Adamson H.S. Academic Fair, Dallas, 1999—; sch. site coord. Dallas Mus. of Art/ Go Van Gogh, Dallas, 1999—. Prin. works include Mushrooms, Iris, The Villiage, Nature on the Lake, White Whooping Crane, Orchid, Hot Fun Day, The Hummingbird, Our Texas Past, Pink Azalea. Sponsor Future Educators, Dallas, 2005. Grantee, Hispanic Salute North Tex. Ford Dealers, 2001, Jr. League of Dallas, 2002, 2003. Mem.: Dallas Art Educator Assn. (assoc.). Independent. Bapt. Avocations: painting, travel, photography, art, crafts. Office: The Artist Paper Trail 8229 Cr 3823 Murchison TX 75778 Home Phone: 214-417-1386.

TAYLER, IRENE, retired English literature educator; b. Abilene, Tex., July 13, 1934; d. B. Brown Smith and Madeline (Bowron); m. Edward W. Tayler, June 3, 1961 (div. 1971); children: Edward Jr., Jesse; m. Saul Touster, Jan. 14, 1978. BA in Philosophy, Stanford U., 1956, MA in Am. Lit., 1961, PhD in English Lit., 1968. Tchr. Breadloaf Sch. of Eng., Middlebury, Vt., 1970, 71, 75, 76; teaching asst. Stanford U., Calif., 1958-60; lectr. Columbia U., NYC, 1961-71; asst. prof. CUNY, 1971-73, assoc. prof., 1973-76, MIT, Cambridge, 1976-82, prof., 1982-96, sec. of the faculty, 1993-95, retired, 1996. Chair gov. com. The English Inst., 1981. Author: Blake's Illustrations to the Poems of Gray, 1971, Holy Ghosts: The Male Muses of Emily and Charlotte Bronte, 1990; editor: Samuel Bak: Between Worlds, Paintings and Drawings from 1946 to 2001, 2002; contbr. articles to profl. jours.; chpts. to books. Internat. Inst. Edn. fellow U. Munich, 1957-58; Wilson fellow Stanford U., 1961-62; NEH sr. scholar fellow, 1980; Mac Vicar faculty fellow MIT, 1993-2003; ACLS study grantee, 1968-69; Faculty Rsch. Found. grantee CUNY, 1972-73; first occupant Thomas Meloy chair rhetoric MIT, 1979-83. Mem.: St. Botolph Club (Boston) (pres. 2000—03). Personal E-mail: itayler@mit.edu.

TAYLOR, ALLAN BERT, lawyer; b. Cin., June 28, 1948; s. H Ralph and Henrietta Taylor; m. Sally Ann Silverstein, June 6, 1971; children: Rachel Elizabeth, Karen Ruth. AB magna cum laude, Harvard U., 1970, M in Pub. Policy, 1975, JD magna cum laude, 1975. Bar: Conn 1975, US Ct Appeals (DC cir) 1977, US Dist Ct (so dist) NY 1979, US Ct Appeals (2d cir) 1979, US Supreme Ct 1979, US Ct Appeals (1st and 10th cirs) 1991. Law clk. to J. Skelly Wright D.C. Cir., Washington, 1975-76; law clk. to Thurgood Marshall U.S. Supreme Ct., Washington, 1976-77; assoc. Day, Berry & Howard, Hartford, Conn., 1977-83, ptnr., 1983—. Overseer Bushnell Meml Hall Corp, Hartford, 1992—. Bd. dirs. Hartford Infant Action Project, 1990—2006, pres., 1999—2005; elected mem Hartford City Coun, 1981—87; mem. Hartford Bd. Edn., 1989—93, v.p., 1991—93; mem. Conn. State Bd. Edn., Hartford, 1994—2005, chair, 2005—; chmn. charter revision comns. City of Hartford, 1999—2002; bd dirs Conn Asn Bds Educ, Hartford, 1989—93, Hartford Stage Co, 1993—2001. Mem.: ABA, Hartford Bar Asn, Conn Bar Asn, Phi Beta Kappa. Democrat. Jewish. Avocation: reading. Home: 238 Whitney St Hartford CT 06105-2270 Office: Day Pitney LLP 242 Trumbull St Hartford CT 06103-1212 Home Phone: 860-233-8087; Office Phone: 860-275-0225. Business E-Mail: abtaylor@daypitney.com.

TAYLOR, ALLAN RICHARD, retired banker; b. Prince Albert, Sask., Can., Sept. 14, 1932; s. Norman and Anna Lydia (Norbeck) T.; m. Shirley Irene Ruston, Oct. 5, 1957; children: Rodney Allan, Leslie Ann. LLD (hon.), U. Regina, Sask., 1987, Concordia U., Montreal, Can., 1988; DBA (hon.), Laval U., Quebec City, Can., 1990; LLD (hon.), Queen's U., Kingston, Ont., 1991; Doctorate of Univ. (hon.), U. Ottawa, 1992. With Royal Bank of Can., Toronto, Ont., 1949-95, pres., COO, dir., 1983-86, chmn., CEO, dir., 1986-94, chmn., 1994-95, ret., 1995. Bd. dirs. NeuroSci. Can. Found., Montreal; mem. adv. coun. Can. Exec. Svc. Overseas; former chmn. Can. Bankers Assn.; past pres. Internat. Monetary Conf. Former chmn. corp. program IMAGINE; mem. adv. bd. Can. Found. AIDS Rsch.; chmn. hon. adv. bd. Can. Assn. for Cmty. Living. Decorated officer Order of Can. Address: 200 Bay St 29th Fl South Tower Toronto ON Canada M5J 2J5 E-mail: allan.taylor@rbc.com.

TAYLOR, ANDREW C., rental and leasing company executive; b. 1947; BSBA, Denver U., 1970. With RLM Leasing Co., San Francisco, 1970—73, Enterprise Rent-A-Car, St. Louis, 1973—, pres., COO, 1980—91, CEO, 1991—, chmn., 2001—. Dir. Anheuser Busch Co., Commerce Bancshares; pres., CEO Crawford Group. Trustee, conference co-chair National Urban League; trustee Washington U., St. Louis Symphony Orch.; bd. dirs. United Way Greater St. Louis; life trustee Mo. Bot. Garden. Office: Enterprise Rent-A-Car 600 Corporate Park Dr Saint Louis MO 63105-4204 *

TAYLOR, ANDREW T., JR., radiologist, educator; b. Jackson, Tenn., Jan. 14, 1942; MD, Duke U., 1968. Cert. nuclear medicine Splty. Bd. 1, internal medicine Splty. Bd. 2. Resident U. Hosp.-U.C.S.D., San Diego, 1970, 1972—74, intern, 1969; co-dir. nuc. medicine Emory U. Sch. Med., prof. radiology, 2002—. Mem.: Am. Bd. of Nuclear Medicine (past chair). Office: Emory U Sch of Medicine Radiology 1440 Clifton Rd Atlanta GA 30322

TAYLOR, ANGELO, Olympic athlete; b. Albany, Ga., Dec. 29, 1978; Student, Ga. Inst. Tech. Champion 400 meter hurdles NCAA Championship, 1998; 2nd place U.S. Championships, 1998; winner 1st nat. title; co-winner Gold Medal 4X400 relay World Championships, 1999; winner Gold Medal 400 meter hurdles and gold medal 4x400m relay Sydney, 2000; IAAF Grand Prix overall and GP final champion, 2000; Jesse Owens award winner for top U.S. male track and field athlete, 2001; world outdoor champs gold medalist in 4x400m relay, 1999; 3 time US champion, 1999—2001; US indoor 400m champion, 1999; NCAA 400H champion, 1998. Named Collegiate Athlete of the Yr., T&FN, 1998. ranked no. 3 400 meter hurdles. Office: USA Track and Field Team One RCA Dome Ste 140 Indianapolis IN 46225

TAYLOR, ANN, writer, educator; d. Gideon S. and Elizabeth L. Stoltzfus; m. James R. Taylor III, Feb. 18, 1983 (dec. Sept. 1995). BA, Ea. Mennonite U., Harrisonburg, Va., 1966; MEd, Millersville U., Pa., 1979; EdD, Temple U., Phila., 1995. Caseworker Lancaster Welfare Dept., Pa., 1969-72, Rockingham County Welfare Dept., 1966—67, Lancaster County Probation Parole Dept., 1967-69; parole agent Pa. Bd. Probation and Parole, Harrisburg, 1972-85; human resource cons., trainer Taylor Assocs., Lancaster, 1985—2004; psychotherapist, career counslor Greystone Psychol. Ctr., 1990—97; founder Kid Brilliance Program, 2005—. Adj. prof. bus. mgmt. Pa. State U., Lancaster, 1979-2000, continuing edn. dept. Franklin and Marshall Coll., Lancaster, 1979-90; free lance trainer Hamilton Bank, Lancaster, 1985-91, Armstrong World Industries, Lancaster, 1987, 91; adv. com. staff trainer Vantage Drug and Alcohol Facility, Lancaster, 1983-85; trainer, public spkr., 1979-92; instr., field rsch., Kid Brilliance Program, Reynold Mid. Sch., Lancaster, Pa. Co-author: Fire Up Your Brilliance, Kid Brilliance. Vol. Lancaster County Mental Health Ctr., 1983-94; seminar leader Fulton County (Pa.) C. of C., 1985-86, York County C. of C., Pa., 1985-86, Lancaster County C. of C., 1985-88. Mem.: ACA. Democrat. Episcopalian. Avocations: travel, reading, gardening, hiking, walking. Office: 214 E King St Lancaster PA 17602 Office Phone: 717-394-6859. Personal E-mail: brilliance@comcast.net.

TAYLOR, ANNA DIGGS, federal judge; b. Washington, Dec. 9, 1932; d. Virginius Douglass and Hazel (Bramlette) Johnston; m. S. Martin Taylor, May 22, 1976; children: Douglass Johnston Diggs, Carla Cecile Diggs. BA, Barnard Coll., 1954; LLB, Yale U., 1957. Bar: D.C. 1957, Mich. 1961. Atty. Office Solicitor Gen. US Dept. Labor, 1957-60; asst. prosecutor Wayne County, Mich., 1961-62; asst. US atty. (ea. dist.) Mich. US Dept. Justice, 1966; ptnr. Zwerdling, Maurer, Diggs & Papp, Detroit, 1970-75; asst. corp. counsel City of Detroit, 1975-79; judge US Dist. Ct. (ea. dist.) Mich., Detroit, 1979—. Hon. chair United Way, Cmty. Found., S.E. Mich.; trustee emeritus Detroit Inst. Arts; co-chair, vol. Leadership Coun.; vice-chair Henry Ford Health Sys. Mem. Fed. Bar Assn., State Bar Mich., Wolverine Bar Assn. (v.p.), Yale Law Assn. Episcopalian. Office: US Dist Ct 740 US Courthouse 231 W Lafayette Blvd Detroit MI 48226-2700

TAYLOR, ANNE WILKERSON, elementary school educator; b. DeFuniack Springs, Fla., Oct. 10, 1950; d. Coston Ingram Wilkerson and Lelan Irene Blair; m. William Henry Taylor, Nov. 9, 1968; children: Matthew Allen, Randall Henry, William Jason. BS in Elem. Ed., Troy U., Ala., 1979; M in Elem. Ed., U. South Ala., 1991, adminstrv. degree, 2001. Cert. Project CRISS trainer. 6th grade tchr. Escatawpa (Miss.) Elem. Sch., 1985—88; 5th and 6th grade tchr. Castlen Elem. Sch., Grand Bay, Ala., 1988—98; 6th and 8th grade tchr. Grand Bay Mid. Sch., 1998—; 4th grade tchr. Dauphin Island Elem., Ala., 2005—. Title I parenting coord., staff dev. coord. Grand Bay Mid. Sch., 2003—. Named Tchr. of Yr., Castlen Elem. Sch. and Grand Bay Mid. Sch., 1997, 2004. Home: 10428 Knoke Ave Grand Bay AL 36541 Home Phone: 251-865-6304; Office Phone: 251-861-3864. Personal E-mail: wmhbilltaylor@aol.com.

TAYLOR, ANTHONY BALDWIN, civil engineer; b. Nassau, Bahamas, Nov. 25, 1971; came to U.S., 1990; s. Anthony Baldwin Sr. and Ruth Inez (McKenzie) T.; m. Kaaryn Wilaine Rogers, July 2, 1994; children: Anthony Baldwin III, Andrew Benjamin, Antonia Beth. BSCE, NC State U., 1994; PhD, Columbia State U., 1997. Owner, engr. TNT Constn., Nassau, 1992-94; constrn. engr. Greenman Pedersen Inc., Durham, NC, 1994-96; resident engr. Parsons, Butner, 1996—2000, dir. engring. Newport, 2000—03, v.p., program mgr. Atlanta, 2003—. Mem. ASCE, Assn. for Advancement of Cost Engring. Avocations: reading, writing, basketball, sport shooting, fishing. Business E-Mail: tony.taylor@parsons.com.

TAYLOR, AUBREY ELMO, physiologist, educator; b. El Paso, Tex., June 4, 1933; s. Virgil T. and Mildred (Maher) Taylor; m. Mary Jane Davis, Apr. 4, 1953; children: Audrey Jane Hildebrand, Lenda Sue Taylor Brown, Mary Ann. BA in Math. and Psychology, Tex. Christian U., 1960; PhD in Physiology, U. Miss., 1964. Fellow biophysics lab. Harvard U. Med. Sch., Boston, 1965-67; from asst. prof. to prof. dept. physiology U. Miss. Coll. Medicine, Jackson, 1967-77; prof., chmn. dept. physiology U. South Ala. Coll. Medicine, Mobile, 1977—2002, Louise Lenoir Locke eminent scholar disting. prof. emeritus, 2002—. Pulmonary score com. mem. Nat. Heart, Lung and Blood Inst., 1976; with Surgery and Anesthesiology, 1979—82, Manpower Com., 1985—95; chmn. RAP, 1983; spl. lectr. Wu-Ho-Su Meml. Symposium. Mem. editl. bd.: Jour. Applied Physiology, 1994—, Critical Care Medicine, 1991—97, Circulation Rsch., Am. Jour. Physiology, Internat. Pathophysiology, Microcirculatory and Lymphatic Rsch., Chinese Jour. Physiology, Microcirculation, Jour. Biomed. Sci., Am. Rev. Resp. and Critical Care Jour., Internat. Soc. Pathology, author 9 books:; contbr. chapters to books, over 730 articles to profl. jours.; N.Am. editor: Clin. Scis., 1998—. With US Army, 1953—55. Named Disting. Physiologist, Am. Coll. Chest Physicians, 1994; recipient Lederle Faculty award, 1967—70, Philip Dow award, U. Ga., 1984, NIH Merit award, 1987—97, Lucian award, McGill U., 1988, John Whitney award, U. Ark., 1990, Gelen award, Intestinal Shock Soc., 1991, Arthur C. Guyton award, U. Miss Coll. Medicine, 1993, Myerson-De Luzio Lectr., Tulane Sch. Medicine, 1997, Disting. Lectr., La State U., Shreveport, 1997, Med. Student Rsch. Conf., U. Tex. Sch. Medicine, Galveston, 1998, Abreu Meml. Keynote Spkr., 1998, Disting. Alumnus award, Tex. Christian U., 1998, 1998, Disting Svc. award, USA med. Alumni Assn., 2000, Disting. Graduate award, Paschal H.S., 2002; grantee NIH, 1964—. Fellow: Royal Soc. Medicine (bd. dirs.), Am. Heart Assn. (So. regional rev. com. 1977—81, cardiopulmonary, critical care coun. 1977—, chmn. 1979—81, EIA Rev. Com. 1986—95, pulmonary and devel. rev. com. 1987—95, nat. rsch. com. 1990—95, del. assembly 1990—99, chmn. 1993—98, chmn. grant/rev.com 1994—95, coun. affairs com. 1994—98, nominating com. 1998—99, basic sci. com. 1998—, circulation coun., chmn., AALAC bd. trustees rep., Bronze award Miss. AHA 1976, Dickinson W. Richards award 1988, Outstanding Ala. AHA program 1993, Sci. Coun. Achievement award 1995, Disting. Svc. award 1995, Rsch. Achievement award 1997, So. Ala. Dist. Achievement award 2000, Gala honoree 2000, Hall of Fame Spring Hill Hosp. Heart Assn. 2001), AAAS; mem.: European Respiratory Soc. (sec. lung injury group), Am. Thoracic Soc., Fedn. Am. Socs. for Exptl. Biology (bd. dirs. 1988—90, reorganizing com.), Biophys. Soc., N.Y. Acad. Scis., Internat. Pathophysiology Soc. (v.p. 1991—99), N. Am. Soc. Lymphology (pres. 1988—90, Cecil Drinker Rsch. award 1988), Internat. Lymphology Soc., Ala. Acad. Scis. (Ann. State Rsch. award 1988), Micro Circulatory Soc. (coun. 1977—81, pres. 1981—83, Eugene Landis Rsch. award 1985), Assn. Dept. Chairs of Physiology (exec. com. 1996—2001, sec. treas. 1998—2002), Am. Physiol. Soc. (coun. 1984—87, chmn. mem. com. 1985—87, pres. 1987—90, hon. com., chmn. 1993—96, chmn. Perkins fellow com. 1996—98, Cannon lectr. 1999, Wiggers award 1987, Achievement award 2002), NAS (com. for Internat. Union Physiol. Sci.), Sigma Xi, Alpha Omega Alpha. Democrat. Presbyterian. Achievements include research in in cardio-pulmonary physiology, fluid balance, edema, microcirculation and capillary exchange of solute and water and inflammatory processes in the lung. Home: 11 Audubon Pl Mobile AL 36606-1907

TAYLOR, BARBARA ALDEN, public relations executive; b. Dallas, Aug. 21, 1943; d. Harold Earl and Sally Alden (Howard) T. BA, Smith Coll., 1965; MA, Antioch Coll., 1971. Vol. Peace Corps., India, 1966-68; tchr. Upper Merion Sch. Dist., King of Prussia, Pa., 1969-70, Cheltenham Sch. Dist., Elkins Park, Pa., 1970-74; pub. rels. dir. Princess Hotels Internat., NYC, 1974-75; chmn. Taylor & Hammond Ltd., NYC, 1975-84; pres. Doremus/Marketshare, 1984-86; exec. v.p. Porter/Novelli, NYC, 1986-90; sr. v.p. Hill and Knowlton, Inc., NYC, 1990-93; sr. v.p. corp. comm. Lancaster Group Worldwide, 1993-95; sr. v.p. Coty Inc. and Benckiser Group, 1995-97; exec. v.p. Edelman Pub. Rels. Worldwide, NYC, 1997—. Bd. dirs. Madison Square Boys' and Girls' Club N.Y., 1978—, also mem. women's bd. Boys' Club N.Y. Named to Acad. of Women Achievers YWCA, 1985; bd. dirs. Up With People, Tucson, 1990—; trustee Smith Coll., 1999—. Mem. Women in Comms., Pub. Rels. Soc. Am. (counselors acad.), Internat. Women's Forum, Advt. Women N.Y., Cosmetic Exec. Women, Fashio Group, Doubles Internat., Smith Coll. Alumnae Assn. (bd. dirs. 1993-96), Club N.Y., Lyford Cay Club, Jr. League City N.Y. Avocations: tennis, walking. Office: Edelman Pub Rels Worldwide 1500 Broadway Ste 504 New York NY 10036-4048

TAYLOR, BARBARA ANN OLIN, writer, educational consultant; b. St. Louis, Feb. 8, 1933; d. Spencer Truman and Ann Amelia (Whitney) Olin; m. F. Morgan Taylor Jr., Apr. 5, 1954; children: Spencer O., James W., John F., Frederick Morgan. AB, Smith Coll., 1954; MBA, Northwestern U., 1978, PhD, 1984; LHD, U. New Haven, 1995. Mem. faculty Hamden (Conn.) Hall Country Day Sch., 1972-74; cons. Booz, Allen & Hamilton, Inc., Chgo., 1979; program assoc. Northwestern U., Evanston, Ill., 1982; co-founder, exec. dir. Nat. Ctr. Effective Schs. R&D, Okemos, Mich., 1986-89, rsch. assoc., 1987; chmn. Nat. Ctr. for Effective Schs. Resource and Devel. Found., 2002—03; cons. on effective schs. rsch. and reform Nat. Ctr. Effective Schs. R&D U. Wis., Madison, 1990-96; pres. Excelsior! Found., Chgo., 1994—. Mem. exec. com. Hudson Inst. New Am. Schs. Devel. Corp. Design Team, 1990—94; Danforth Disting. lectr. U. Nebr., Omaha, 1993. Co-author: (book) Making School Reform Happen, 1993, Keepers of the Dream, 1994, The Revolution Revisited: Effective Schools and Systemic Reform, 1995; editor: Case Studies in Effective Schools Research, 1990; contbr. articles to profl. jours. Co-chair Coalition Housing and Human Resources, Hartford-New Haven, 1970—73; co-chair steering com. Day Care Conn., Hartford, 1971—73; trustee U. New Haven, 1961—71, Smith Coll., Northampton, Mass., 1984—90, Choate Rosemary Hall Sch., 1973—78, Lake Forest Coll., 1996—, Hudson Inst., 1989—97, Northwestern U., 1998—2002; pres. Jr. League New Haven, 1967—69, NCCJ, New Haven, 1971—73. Recipient Humanitarian award, Mt. Calvary Bapt. Ch., 1988, Oustanding Alumna award, John Burroughs Sch., 1994, Pres.'s award, U. New Haven, 1998, Alumni Merit award, Northwestern U., 2004. Mem.: ASCD, Nat. Staff Devel. Coun., Nat. Commn. Citizens Edn. (bd. dirs. 1980—86), Phi Delta Kappa (Internat. award Outstanding Svc. 2000). Episcopalian. Office: Nat Ctr Effective Schs Rsch & Devel 1124 Lake Rd Lake Forest IL 60045-1723

TAYLOR, BARBARA MAE HELM, artist, educator; b. Salina, Kans., Aug. 4, 1940; d. Wilber John and Mildred Mae (Walters) Helm; m. Walter Luther Taylor, II, Feb. 11, 1957; children: Walter Luther III, Natalie Sue Taylor Estes, Laura Marie, Toby Clark. AA, East Ark. C.C., Forrest City, 1990; BFA, Ark. State U., Jonesboro, 1992, MA, 1994. Portrait painter Barbara Taylor Art Studio, Palestine, Ark., 1992—. Adj. prof. Mid South C.C., West Memphis, Ark., 1996—98, East Ark. C.C., Forrest City, Ark., 1998—2006. Author: Every One and Me; numerous art shows. Country fiddle player Ark. Gospel Assn., Forrest City, 1994—; violin player Midway Bapt. Ch., Palestine, 1988—. Mem.: Smithsonian Soc., Audubon Soc., Little Rock Art Links, Am. Soc. Portrait Artists (assoc.), Ark. Artist Registry (life), Delta Art Soc. (v.p. 1999—2000), Memphis Art Links, St. Francis Art Club (life; founder, pres. 2000—), Gamma Beta Phi (life). Avocation: birdwatching. Home: 523 Saint Francis 867 Palestine AR 72372 Office: Barbara Taylor Art Studio 493 St Francis Co 867 Palestine AR 72372-8936 Home Phone: 870-581-2490; Office Phone: 870-581-3890. Business E-Mail: barbhelmtaylor@arkansas.net.

TAYLOR, BARRY LLEWELLYN, microbiologist, educator; b. Sydney, May 7, 1937; arrived in US, 1967; s. Fredrick Llewelyn and Vera Lavina (Clarke) T.; m. Desmyrna Ruth Tolhurst, Jan. 4, 1961; children: Lyndon, Nerida, Darrin. BA, Avondale Coll., Cooranbong, New South Wales, 1959; BSc with honors, U. New South Wales, Sydney, 1966; PhD, Case Western Res. U., 1973; postgrad., U. Calif., Berkeley, 1973-75. Vis. postdoctoral fellow Australian Nat. U., Canberra, 1975-76; asst. prof. biochemistry Loma Linda (Calif.) U., 1976-78, assoc. prof. biochemistry, 1978-83, prof. biochemistry, 1983—, prof., chmn. dept. microbiology and molecular genetics, 1988-2000, interim dir. Ctr. for Molecular Biology, 1989-94, 96-98, v.p. for rsch. affairs, 2000—. Contbr. articles to profl. publs. Rsch. grantee Am. Heart Assn., 1978-85, NIH, 1981—. Mem. Am. Soc. Microbiology, Am. Soc. Biochemistry and Molecular Biology. Office: Loma Linda U VP Rsch Affairs Loma Linda CA 92350-0001

TAYLOR, BRYCE B., music educator, consultant; b. Edinburg, Tex., Feb. 12, 1925; s. Charles B and Cecile B Taylor; m. Diana Olivia Rodriguez, Apr. 4, 1946; children: Scott Lee, David Kim, Cynthia Diane, Richard Kerry. MusB, Tex. A&I, 1951, M of music edn., 1955. Music band instr. 3 Rivers Tex. Pub. Schools, 1951—61; music supr./band dir. Alice Ind. Sch. Dist., Alice, Tex., 1961—91, music cons., 1991—; music edn. prof. Tex. A&M, Kingsville, 1993—; condr./music dir. Corpus Christi Wind Symphony, 1986—. Music cons. U. Interscholastic League, 1960—; adjudicator Tex. Music Adjudicators Assn., 1958—. Cpl. USMC, 1942—46, Pearl Harbor. Recipient Outstanding Music Educator, Nat. Fedn. Music Assn., 1991, Tchr. of the Yr., 1982, Bandmaster of the Yr., Tex. Bandmasters Assn., 1983. Mem.: Am. Concert Band Assn., Am. Bandmasters Assn. (past pres., bd. mem. 1999—2000), Tex. Music Educators Assn. (past. pres., divsn. chair 1962—64), Tex. Bandmasters Assn. (life), Phi Beta Mu Nat. Band Assn. Independent. Cath. Avocations: golf, auto restoration, guest conducting. Home: 1001 Lincoln Alice TX 78332 Personal E-mail: dbtaylor1001@sbc.global.net.

TAYLOR, BYRON KEITH, industrial engineer; b. Portsmouth, Va., July 9, 1955; s. Robert Lee and Joyce Sue (Cox) T.; m. Barbara Sue Keene, Aug. 27, 1977; 1 child, Joshua Lee. BS in Indsl. Engring., Va. Poly. Inst. and State U., 1980; MBA, Ariz. State U., 2002. Indsl. engr. Deere & Co. (Harvester), East Moline, Ill., 1980-81, 83-84, product engr., 1981-83, prodn. engr., 1984-90, module owner, 1990-93; sr. engr. new product devel., 1993-95; supr. engring. John Deere, Davenport (Iowa) Works, 1995-97; mgr. loader fabrications John Deere, Davenport Works, 1995-97; mgr. header and sheet metal mfg. John Deere Harvester Works, East Moline, Ill., 1998-99, mgr. supply mgmt., 1999—2001, mgr. mfg., 2001—04; dir. quality worldwide agrl. divsn. Deere and Co. World Hdqs., Moline, Ill., 2005—. Mem. engring. curriculum devel. panel Black Hawk Coll., Moline, Ill., 1989; tech. del. conf. Citizen's Amb. program Soviet Union, 1990. Program chmn. Meth. Mens Club, Colona, Ill., 1985; advisor Jr. Achievement, East Moline, 1986-87, cons., 1988; bd. dirs. Handicapped Devel. Ctr., Davenport, 2000—; dir. Deere Harvester Credit Union, East Moline, 2000—. Named Young Engr. of Yr. Quad-Cities Engring. and Sci. Coun., 1989-90. Mem. Inst. Indsl. Engrs. (sr., dir. pub. rels. chpt. 46, 1986-87, pres.-elect 1988-89, pres. 1989-90). Republican. Avocation: golf. Home: 3110 Halcyon Dr Bettendorf IA 52722 Office: Deere & Co World Hdqs One John Deere Pl Moline IL 61265

TAYLOR, CARL ERNEST, preventive medicine physician, epidemiologist, educator; b. Landour, Mussoorie, India, July 26, 1916; s. John C. and Elizabeth (Siehl) Taylor; m. Mary Daniels, Feb. 14, 1943; children: Daniel, Elizabeth, Henry. BS, Muskingum Coll., 1937, DSc, 1962; MD, Harvard, 1941, MPH, 1951, DPH, 1953; LHD (hon.), Towson U., 1974. Diplomate Am. Bd. Preventive Medicine. Intern, resident pathology, surg. staff, tropical disease rsch. Gorgas Hosp., Panama, 1941—44; charge med. service Marine Hosp., Pitts., 1944—46; supt. Meml. Hosp., Fategarh, India, 1947—50; rsch. assoc. Harvard Sch. Pub. Health, Boston, 1950—52, asst. prof. epidemiology, 1957—59, assoc. prof., 1959-61; prof. preventive and social medicine Christian Med. Coll., Ludhiana, Punjab, India, 1953—56; prof. internat. health, chmn. dept. internat. health Johns Hopkins Sch. Hygiene and Pub. Health, Balt., 1961—83, prof. emeritus, 1984—. Cons. AID, 1959—; UNICEF country rep. in China, 1984—87; expert com. WHO, 1963, 1966—67, 1970—73, 1975; mem. Nat. Adv. Commn. Health Manpower; chmn. Nat. Council for Internat. Health. Contbr. articles to profl. jours. Fellow: Am. Pub. Health Assn., Royal Soc. Tropical Medicine and Hygiene, Royal Coll. Physicians; mem.: Nat. Acad. Medicine, Inst. Medicine, Indian Assn. for Advancement Med. Edn., Am. Soc. Tropical Medicine and Hygiene, Assn. Tchrs. Preventive Medicine. Achievements include research in rural health, population dynamics, nutrition, epidemiology of leprosy. Home: Bittersweet Acres 1201 Hollins Ln Baltimore MD 21209-2209 Office: Johns Hopkins Sch Hygiene and Pub Health 615 N Wolfe St Baltimore MD 21205-2103 *The growing complexity of human relationships around this increasingly crowded world presents new challenges to concerned scientists. Solutions to our problems must come from new collaborative styles of work bridging the usual boundaries between people, since the problems we face are mutual.*

TAYLOR, CAROL FAY, education educator; b. Saint Elizabeth, Jamaica, May 9, 1957; d. Isaac Obadiah and Elvera Allen; m. Winford Taylor, Dec. 17, 1983. Diploma, Jamaica Sch. Agr., 1979, Jamaica Inst. Mgmt., 1997, Inst. Children's Lit., 2006. Tchr., guidance counsellor Elim Agrl. Sch., Jamaica, 1992—96; tchr. Heart Trust, Kingston, Jamaica, 1996—2003. Tchr. Alumina Ptnrs. Jamaica, 2000—03; examiner Caribbean Exam. Coun. External Exams. Evangelism & prayer outreach com. Antioch Seventh Day Adventist, Deer Park, NY, 2003—06. Named Instr. of Yr., 2002; scholar, Jamaica Sugar Estate Co., 1977—79. Seventh Day Adventist. Avocation: writing. Home: 35 Hilliard Ave Central Islip NY 11722 Personal E-mail: carolfay@optonline.net.

TAYLOR, CAROLYN ROBERTS, small business owner, chef; b. Washington, Feb. 10, 1946; d. Thomas Edward and Mary Spiawn Taylor; m. James Joseph Maranville, June 25, 1994; m. David R. Williams (div.); children: Nathan J. Williams, Samuel T. Williams. At, Guilford Coll., Greensboro, NC, 1964—67; BS, Ill. Inst. Tech., Chgo., 1969; cert., Cordon Bleu Sch. Cooking, London, 1974. Summer chef Mt. Desert Biol. Lab., Maine, 1981—83; pastry chef Al Forno Restaurant, Providence, 1983; sous chef Jordan's Restaurant, Leesburg, Va., 1984; chef Middleburg Tennis Club and Catering, 1985—88; chef and co-owner Taylor & Fuog Catering, Hamilton, 1988—91; pastry chef ARA at Xerox Tng. Ctr., Leesburg, 1991—93; chef Morningside Ho., 1993—96; owner and operator Taylor Made Cakes, Hamilton, 1997—. Baking instr. Boston Adult Edn., 1976; pvt. cooking instr., Providence, 1976—79; guest tchr. Chef's Co. Sch., Barrington, 1983; cons. Battletown Inn, Berryville, Va., 1985; adv. bd. culinary program Monroe Va. Tech. Sch., Leesburg, 1998—. Tutor and coord. non-tutoring vols. Loudoun Literacy Coun., Leesburg, Va., 1997—98; vol. Loudoun Hosp., 1985. Mem.: Cake and Sugar Artists No. Va., Internat. Cake Exploration Soc., Shenendoah Wedding Profls. Democrat. Mem. Soc. Of Friends. Avocations: scuba diving, snorkeling, country dancing, hiking. Office Phone: 540-338-2324. Personal E-mail: crtbake@aol.com.

TAYLOR, CARROLL STRIBLING, lawyer; b. Port Chester, NY, Jan. 14, 1944; s. William H. Jr. and Anna P. (Stribling) Taylor; m. Nancy S. Tyson, Apr. 7, 1968; children: Heather, Kimberly, Tori, Tiffany, Tacy. AB, Yale U., 1965; JD, U. Calif., Berkeley, 1968. Bar: Hawaii 1969, Calif. 1969, U.S. Dist. Ct. Hawaii 1969, U.S. Dist. Ct. (cen. dist.) Calif. 1975, U.S. Ct. Appeals (9th cir.) 1975. Rschr. Legis. Reference Bur., Honolulu, 1968-70; reporter Jud. Coun. Probate Code Revision Project, Honolulu, 1970-71; assoc. Chun, Kerr & Dodd, Honolulu, 1971-75; ptnr. Hamilton & Taylor, Honolulu, 1975-80; officer, dir. Char, Hamilton, Taylor & Thom, Honolulu, 1980-82, Carroll S. Taylor Atty. at Law, A Law Corp., Honolulu, 1982-86; ptnr. Taylor & Leong, Honolulu, 1986-91, Taylor, Leong & Chee, Honolulu, 1991—. Adj. prof. Richardson Sch. Law U. Hawaii, Honolulu, 1981-86, 88-90, 97; mem. Disciplinary bd. of Supreme Ct. of Hawaii, 1994-2006, vice chair, 1997-99, chair, 2000-03; dir. Am. Nat. Lawyers Ins. Reciprocal, 1997-2000; mem., bd. dirs. Hanahauoli Sch., 1992-97. Fellow Am. Coll. Trust and Estate Counsel; mem. ABA, Calif. Bar Assn., Hawaii State Bar Assn. (Pres.'s award 2002), Hawaii Inst. Continuing Legal Edn. (pres. 1986-88), Pla. Club (Honolulu). Episcopalian. Home: 46-429 Hololio St Kaneohe HI 96744-4225 Office: 737 Bishop St Ste 2060 Honolulu HI 96813-3214 Home Phone: 808-435-1736; Office Phone: 808-528-2222. E-mail: ctaylor@hawaii.rr.com.

TAYLOR, CARSON WILLIAM, retired electrical engineer; b. Superior, Wis., May 24, 1942; s. William Stanley and Elizabeth Marie (Christophersen) T.; m. Gudrun Renate Leistner, Dec. 28, 1966; 1 child, Natasha Marie. BSEE, U. Wis., 1965; M in Engring., Rensselaer Poly. Inst., 1969. Elec. engr. U.S. Bur. Reclamation, Billings, Mont., 1967-68, Bonneville Power Adminstrn., Portland, Oreg., 1969-89, prin. engr., 1989—2006; ret. Prin. Carson Taylor Seminars, Portland, 1986—. Author: Power System Voltage Stability, 1994; contbr. papers to profl. publs.; patentee in field. Lt. U.S. Army, 1965-67. Fellow IEEE (chmn. subcom. 1982—); mem. NAE, Conférence Internationale des Grands Réseaux Électriques a Haute Tension (CIGRE, disting. mem.), Eta Kappa Nu. Lutheran. Avocations: fishing, hunting, woodworking, reading, computers.

TAYLOR, CELIANNA ISLEY, information systems specialist; b. Youngstown, Ohio; d. Paul Thornton and Florence (Jacobs) Isley; divorced; children: Polly, Jerry, Jim. BA in Philosophy, Denison U., 1939; MLS, Western Res. U., 1942. Worked in several pub. libRs. and univ. libRs., 1939-50; head Libr. Cataloging Dept. Battelle Mem. Inst., Columbus, Ohio, 1951-53; head pers. office, assoc. prof. libr. adminstrn. Ohio State U. Librs., Columbus, 1954-65; coord. info. svcs., assoc. prof. libr. adminstrn. Nat. Ctr. for Rsch. in Vocat. Edn., Ohio State U., Columbus, 1966-70; sr.

rsch. assoc., adminstrv. assoc., assoc. prof. libr. adminstrn. dept. computer and info. sci. Ohio State U., Columbus, 1970-86, assoc. prof. emeritus Univ. Librs., 1986—. Mem. Task Force on a Spl. Collections Database, Ohio State U. Librs., Columbus, 1988-89, comm. systems and recs. coord. Ohio State U. Retirees Assn., Columbus, 1992-93, info. specialist, Mac-Forum, Ohio State U., Columbus, 2001-2004; cons. profl. orgns. including Ernst & Ernst CPA's and Oreg. State Sys. of Higher Edn., 1961-82. Author: (with J. Magisos) Guide for State Voc-Tech Edn. Dissemination Systems 1971; editor: (with A.E. Petrarca, and R.S. Kohn) Info. Interaction 1982; Highlights-Coun. for Ethics in Econs., 1997—; contbr. several articles to profl. jours.; designer info. sys.: CALL Sys., 1977-82, Channel 2000 Proj. Home Info. Svc., 1980-81, Continuing Education Info. Ctr., 1989-90, Human Resources (HUR) Sys., 1976-77,1979-82, DECOS, 1975-86, Computer-asst. libr. Sys., Optical Scan Sys., 1972-73, ERIC Clearinghouse for vocat. edn., 1966-70. Chmn. subcom. on design, info. and ref. com. Columbus United Cmty. Coun., 1972-73; bd. dirs. Columbus Reg. Info. Svc., 1974-78, Cmty. Info. Referral Svc., Inc. 1975-81; dir. Computer Utility for Pub. Info. Columbus, 1975-81; acct. coord. Greater Columbus Free-net, 1994-98; info. specialist, coord. LWV Met. Columbus Website Com., 2001-02; judge Laws of Life Ohio Statewide H.S. Essay Contest, 2005—; interprofessional pub. policy panel on tech. and ethics, Interprofessional Commn. Ohio, 2006-07. Mem. ALA, Assn. Computing Machinery (Ctrl. Ohio chpt.), Am. Soc. Info. Sci. and Tech., Assn. Faculty and Profl. Women Ohio State U., Columbus Metro Club, Coun. for Ethics in Econs., World Future Soc., Coun. for Ethical Leadership, Olympic Indoor Tennis Club. Avocations: bird watching, gourmet cooking, tennis, water aerobics. Home and Office: 3471 Greenbank Ct Columbus OH 43221-4724 Office Phone: 614-876-0069.

TAYLOR, CHARLES ELLETT, biologist, educator; b. Chgo., Sept. 9, 1945; s. Stewart Ferguson and Barbara (Ellett) Taylor; m. Minna Glushien, June 22, 1969. AB, U. Calif., 1968; PhD, SUNY, Stony Brook, 1973. Prof. U. Calif., Riverside, 1974-80, UCLA, 1980—. Cons. artificial life and population genetics; dir. UCLA Cognitive Sci. Rsch. Program, 1990—99; mem. adv. bd. Computer Mus. Fishtank. Co-author: Artifical Life II, 1992, Artifical Life VI, 1998; editor: Artificial Life, 1997—2001; assoc. editor: IEEE Transactions on Evolutionary Computing, 1997—99; assoc. editor Artificial Life and Robotics, 1999—, Artificial Life, 2002—; mem. editl. bd.: Internat. Jour. Distributed Sensor Networks, 2004—; contbr. articles to profl. publs. Office: Dept Ecology and Evolutionary Biology UCLA Box 951606 Los Angeles CA 90095-1606 Office Phone: 310-825-6850. E-mail: ctaylor@ucla.edu.

TAYLOR, CHARLES HART, former congressman; b. Brevard, NC, Jan. 3, 1941; m. Elizabeth Owen; 3 children. BA, Wake Forest U., 1963, JD, 1966. Owner-operator Transylvania Tree Farms, Brevard, NC; founder, chmn. bd. Blue Ridge Savings Bank, Asheville, NC; dir. Fin. Guaranty Corp.; mem. NC State Ho. Reps., Raleigh, 1967—73, minority leader, 1969—73; mem. NC State Senate, Raleigh, 1973—75, minority leader, 1973—75; mem. US Congress from 11th NC dist., 1991—2007, mem. appropriations com., chmn. interior, environment and related agencies subcommittee. Bd. visitors US Mil. Acad. West Point. Named to Congl. Honor Roll, Seniors' Coalition; recipient Golden Bulldog award, Watchdogs of the Treasury, 1997—98, Guardian of Small Bus. award, Nat. Fedn. Ind. Bus., 1997—98, Voting Achievement award, Nat. Farmers Union, 1997—98, Friend of the Taxpayer award, Ams. for Tax Reform, Nat. Environ. Edn Leadership award, Nat. Environ. Edn. and Tng. Found., 2005. Mem.: Western NC Environ. Coun. (vice chair), NC Pks. and Recreation Coun. (chair), NC Energy Policy Coun., NC Bd. Transp. Republican. Baptist. Office Phone: 202-225-6401.

TAYLOR, CHARLES HENRY, psychoanalyst, educator; b. Boston, Oct. 2, 1928; s. Charles Henry and Rosamond (Stewardson) T.; m. Diana Burgess, 1950; children: Stephen, Diana Beth, Charles S., Eleanor; m. Patricia Finley, 1988. BA, Yale U., 1950, MA, 1952, PhD, 1955; postgrad., Cambridge U., Eng., 1950-51. From instr. to asst. prof. English Ind. U., 1955-61; from asst. dean to assoc. dean, also assoc. prof. English Yale U., 1961-63, acting provost, 1963-64, provost, prof. English, 1964-72, pres. rep., 1972-76; grad. C.G. Jung Inst., NY, 1979; pvt. practice, 1976—. Bd. dirs. Meridian Audio, Ltd. Author: The Early Collected Editions of Shelley's Poems, 1958, (with Patricia Finley) Images of the Journey in Dante's Divine Comedy, 1997; editor: Essays on the Odyssey, 1963; contbr. articles to profl. jours. Mem. com. on libr. Yale U. Coun., 1990-95; trustee Hampshire Coll., 1988-93, 99—, chair, 2000-04. Mem. Internat. Assn. Analytical Psychology, Archive for Rsch. in Archetypal Symbolism (pres. 1987-93, treas. 1993—), N.Y. Assn. Analytical Psychology, Nat. Assn. for Advancement Psychoanalysis, Phi Beta Kappa.

TAYLOR, CHRISTINE, actress; b. Allentown, Pa., July 30, 1971; d. Skip and Joan Taylor; m. Ben Stiller, May 13, 2000; children: Ella Olivia, Quinlin Dempsey. Actor: (films) Calendar Girl, 1993, Showdown, 1993, The Brady Bunch Movie, 1995, Breaking Free, 1995, The Craft, 1996, A Very Brady Sequel, 1996, Cat Swallows Parakeet and Speaks, 1996, Campfire Tales, 1997, The Wedding Singer, 1998, Overnight Delivery, 1998, Denial, 1998, Kiss Toledo Goodbye, 1999, Desperate But Not Serious, 1999, Zoolander, 2001, Dodgeball: A True Underdog Story, 2004; (TV films) Here Come the Munsters, 1995, To the Ends of Time, 1996, Heat Vision and Jack, 1999. Office: United Talent Agy 9560 Wilshire Blvd Ste 500 Beverly Hills CA 90212

TAYLOR, CINDY B., oil industry executive; BBA, Tex. A&M Univ. CPA. Acctg. mgmt. positions Ernst & Young, 1984—92; v.p., contr. Cliffs Drilling Co., 1992—99; CFO L.E. Simmons & Associates, 1999—2000; sr. v.p., CFO Oil States Internat., Houston, 2000—06, pres., COO, 2006—07, pres., CEO, 2007—. Bd. dir. Boots & Coots Internat. Well Control Inc., Global Industries Ltd. Office: Oil States Internat 333 Clay St Houston TX 77002 *

TAYLOR, CLIFFORD WOODWORTH, state supreme court justice; b. Delaware, Ohio, Nov. 9, 1942; s. Alexander E. and Carolyn (Clifford) T.; m. Lucille Taylor; 2 children. BA, U. Mich., 1964; JD, George Washington U., 1967. Asst. prosecuting atty. Ingham County, 1971-72; ptnr. Denfield, Timmer & Taylor, 1972-92; judge Mich. Ct. of Appeals, 1992-97; justice Mich. Supreme Ct., 1997—, chief justice, 2005—. Mem. standing com. on professionalism Mich. State Bar, 1992. Bd. dirs. Mich. Dyslexia Inst., 1991—, Friends of the Gov.'s Residence, 1991—; mem. St. Thomas Aquinas Ch. With USN, 1967-71. Fellow Mich. State Bar Found.; mem. Mich. Supreme Ct. Hist. Soc., Federalist Soc., Cath. Lawyers Guild, State Bar. Home: 9760 Sunny Point Dr Laingsburg MI 48848 Office: Mich Supreme Ct PO Box 300052 Lansing MI 48909 *

TAYLOR, CORINNA LORRAINNE, artist, small business owner; b. Price City, Utah, Aug. 31, 1964; d. Richard Leroy and Laura Da Cruz Taylor; life ptnr. Frank Myrle Griswold; 1 child, Brianna Nicole Patti. Grad. H.S., Cerritos, Calif. Internat. sales rep. Jordache Jeans, LA, 1989—90; designer, owner Peppermint Patti, Palm Desert, Calif., 1990—. Cartoons, Art for Children (Sugar Plum Creative Art and Design award, 2000). Vol. Niguel Coast Cmty., Laguna Niguel, Calif., 2004—06. Mem.: Plein Air Artists So. Calif. (assoc.). Achievements include design of personalized art for children. Avocations: painting, travel, interior decorating. Home Phone: 949-495-5110. Personal E-mail: corinnataylor@cox.net.

TAYLOR, DANIEL RUSSELL, JR., lawyer; b. Clarksville, Tenn., July 6, 1946; s. Daniel Russell Taylor and Effie Mae Winslow; m. Gwynne Stephens Taylor, May 24, 1975; children: Edward Winslow, William Brinson. Grad., U.S. Mil. Acad., West Point, NY, 1968; JD, Wake Forest U., Winston-Salem, NC, 1976. Sr. ptnr. Kilpatrick Stockton, LLP, Winston-Salem, 1978—. With US Army, 1968—73. Home: 700 Arbor Road Winston Salem NC 27104 Office: Kilpatrick Stockton LLP 1001 W Fourth Street Winston Salem NC 27101 Home Phone: 336-725-9000; Office Phone: 336-607-7330. Business E-Mail: dantaylor@kilpatrickstockton.com.

TAYLOR, DARRELL RICHARD, art gallery director, artist; b. Nashville, Jan. 10, 1961; s. Melvin Richard Taylor and Nancy Ledbetter (Taylor) Briggs; m. Christina Moose Taylor (div.); 1 child, Matthew Harrison; life ptnr. Mark Stephen McCusker. BFA, U. Iowa, 1996, MA, 1998, MFA, 1999. Co-artistic dir. Habeas Corpus, Iowa City, 1997—2007; prodn. asst. dance dept. U. Iowa, Iowa City, 1998—2001; acting dir. UNI Gallery of Art, U. No. Iowa, Cedar Falls, 2001—02, art gallery dir., 2003—. Standing mem. art and architecture com. U. No. Iowa, 2001—, mem. mus. adv. bd., 2004—. Author: (exhbn. catalog) Transformations in the Nervepool: The Rituals and Zoacodes of Ebon Fisher, 2005. Sec. Cedar Valley Cultural Alliance, Cedar Falls, 2005; tenor sect. leader Nashville Symphony Chorus, 1990. Recipient Charles Massey award, Mid. Tenn. State U., 1992; grantee, Iowa Arts Coun., 2002, 2004, Humanities, Iowa Veridian Credit Union, 2007; Mendieta Meml. scholar, U. Iowa, 1997. Mem.: Coll. Art Assn., Cedar Falls Pub Art Com. Democrat. Avocation: dance. Office: UNI Gallery of Art U No Iowa 104 KAB Cedar Falls IA 50614 Home: 4410 University Ave PO Box 1241 Cedar Falls IA 50613 Office Phone: 319-273-6134. Office Fax: 319-273-7333. Business E-Mail: galleryofart@uni.edu.

TAYLOR, DAVE, professional sports team executive, retired professional hockey player; b. Levack, Ont., Can., Dec. 4, 1955; m. Beth Duken, July 11, 1981; children: Jamie, Katie Ann. Attended, Clarkson U. Right wing LA Kings, 1977—94, capt., 1985—89, mem. front office, 1993—97, gen. mgr., 1997—2006, dir. amateur devel., 2006—07; dir. player personnel Dallas Stars, 2007—. Player NHL All-Star Game, 1981, 82, 86, 94. Named NHL Exec. of Yr., Hockey News, 2001; named to Second All-Star Team, 1981; recipient Bill Masterton Meml. Trophy, 1991, King Clancy Meml. Trophy, 1991. Achievements include having his number, 19, retired by LA Kings, 1995. Office: Dallas Stars 2601 Avenue of the Stars Frisco TX 75034 *

TAYLOR, DAVID GEORGE, retired banker; b. Charlevoix, Mich., July 29, 1929; s. Frank Flagg and Bessie (Strayer) Taylor; m. Robyne T. McCarthy, July 28, 1990; children from previous marriage: David, Amy, Jeanine. BS, Denison U., 1951; MBA, Northwestern U., 1953. With Continental Ill. Nat. Bank and Trust Co. Chgo., 1958—86, asst. cashier, 1961—64, 2d v.p., 1964—66, v.p., 1966—72, sr. v.p., 1972—74, exec. v.p., 1974—80, exec. v.p., treas., 1980—83, vice chmn., 1983—84, chmn., CEO, 1984; vice chmn. Irving Trust Co., NYC, 1986—89; group exec. Chem. Bank, NYC, 1989—94; ret., 1994. Mem. Dealer Bank Assn. Com. on Glass-Steagall Reform, 1985—86; bd. dirs. CNA Income Shares. Author: Bajan's Tale. Bd. dirs. Evanston Hosp., Glenbrook Hosp.; trustee Art Inst. Chgo., 1981—86; advisor J.L. Kellogg Grad. Sch. Mgmt., Northwestern U., 1984—. Served to lt. USN, 1953—56. Mem.: Assn. Ret. City Bankers (asset/liability com., govt. rels. com. 1983—), Govt. and Fed. Agys. Securities Com. (chmn. bd. dirs. 1982—83), Pub. Securities Assn. (chmn. 1977, bd. dirs. 1977—78, treas. 1978). Republican. Presbyterian. Personal E-mail: caldave110@aol.com.

TAYLOR, DAVID KERR, international business educator, consultant; b. Oxford, NC, Oct. 11, 1928; s. David Kerr and Myrtle Norman (Shamburger) T.; m. Isabel de Sousa Botelho de Albuquerque, Apr. 23, 1960; children: Anne de Albuquerque Taylor Grave, Katherine Rowena Taylor. BA, Duke U., 1947, JD, 1949. Bar: N.Y., N.C. Atty. Ins. Co. N.Am., NYC, 1949-51, Milbank, Tweed, Hadley & McCloy, NYC, 1954-55; internat. exec. Mobil Corp., NYC, Washington, Can., Portugal, Nigeria, France, others, 1955-86; adj. prof. internat. affairs, sr. fellow intrnat. bus. Georgetown U. Sch. Fgn. Svc., Washington, 1987-2000. Pres. Luso-Am. Bus. Coun., 1987-89; bd. visitors Duke U. Law Sch. 1st lt. U.S. Army, 1951-54, Germany. Mem. Am. Portuguese Soc. (bd. dirs., pres. 1968-70, 76-80), Washington Export Coun., Washington Inst. Fgn. Affairs, Dacor Bacon House, Cosmos Club, Phi Beta Kappa. Avocation: singing. Home: 2737 Devonshire Pl NW Washington DC 20008-3479

TAYLOR, DAVID RANDY, museum staff member, consultant; b. Richmond, Va., July 29, 1950; s. Bobby Herman Taylor and Jane Roseberry Fagan. BFA, U. Ga., Athens, 1972; MEd, Ga. State U., Atlanta, 1980. Edn. dir. Open City Theatre, Atlanta, 1975—99; arts specialist Ga. State U., Child Devel. Ctr., Atlanta, 1984—95; tchg. artist Alliance Theatre, Atlanta, 1992—; curator edn. Mus. Design Atlanta, 2002—; arts edn. cons. Ga. Coun. Arts, Atlanta, 2003—. Arts edn. cons. Randy, Atlanta, 1990—; co-founder Open City Children's Ednl. Theatre. Actor: (one person performance) A Visit with Vincent van Gogh, In the Studio of Leonardo da Vinci; contbr. articles to profl. jours. Founder Artsbusters Summer Arts Camp. Grantee, Young Audiences Atlanta, 1999. Mem.: Met. Atlanta Trainers Edn. Group, Spring Conf., Atlanta Orff Sculwerk Assn., Ga. Schoolage Care Assn. (mem. exec. bd. 1995—2000). Achievements include development of nation-wide training in school-age care with work family directions. Avocations: collecting Japanese art, hiking, collecting arts and crafts movement. Home: 673 Brownwood Ave SE Atlanta GA 30316 Office: Museum of Design Atlanta 285 Peachtree Center Ave Atlanta GA 30303 Home Phone: 404-627-2707; Office Phone: 404-979-6448. E-mail: rtaylor@museumofdesign.org.

TAYLOR, DAVID WYATT AIKEN, retired clergyman; b. Tsingkiangpu, Kiangsu, China, Dec. 13, 1925; s. Hugh Kerr and Fanny Bland (Graham) T.; m. Lillian Ross McCulloch, Aug. 25, 1951; children: Frances Bland, David Wyatt. BA, Vanderbilt U., 1949; B.D. cum laude, Union Theol. Sem. Va., 1952; Th.M., Princeton Theol. Sem., 1953; D.D. (hon.), King Coll., Bristol, Tenn., 1959. Ordained to ministry Presbyn. Ch. U.S., 1952. Pastor chs., Elkton, Va., 1953-55, Bristol, Va., 1955-62; ednl. sec. bd. world missions Presbyn. Ch. U.S., 1962-68, program div. dir., 1968-73, ecumenical officer gen. assembly mission bd. Atlanta, 1973-82; pastor Orange Park Presbyn. Ch., Orange Park, Fla., 1982-86; gen. sec. for strategy and interpretation Consultation on Ch. Union, Princeton, NJ, 1986-88, gen. sec., 1988-93; ret., 1993. Instr. Bible Presbyn. Jr. Coll., Maxton, N.C., 1951; mem. program bd., div. Christian edn. Nat. Council Chs., 1965-69, bd. mgrs., dept. edn. for mission, 1962-68, mem. program bd., div. overseas ministries, 1968-78, mem. governing bd., 1976-80, chmn. governing bd. credentials com., 1978; chmn. Church World Service, Inc., 1973-75; mem. adminstrn. and fin. com. Nat. Council Chs., 1973-75, mem. commn. on faith and order, 1978-93; mem. commn. on interchurch aid World Council Chs., 1973-75; mem. 5th Assembly, 1975; rep. Presbyn. Ch. U.S. to World Alliance Ref. Chs., 1976-82; bd. dirs. Presbyn. Survey mag., 1963-68; mem. Consultation on Ch. Union, 1974-93; chmn. Nat. Ecumenical Officers Assn., 1978-81; exec. coun. NC Coun. Chs., 2003—. Bd. dirs. Abingdon Presbytery's Children's Home, Wytheville, Va., 1958-62. Served with AUS, 1944-46, PTO. Mem. Sigma Chi. Presbyterian. Home: 3113 Glenhope Ct Cary NC 27511 Personal E-mail: taylor3@mindspring.com.

TAYLOR, DIANA LANCASTER, investment company executive, former state official; b. Summit, NJ, Feb. 6, 1955; d. Edwin Douglas and Lois Johnston (O'Neill) T. AB, Dartmouth Coll., 1977; MBA, Columbia U., 1979-81. Analyst N.Y. State Dept. Soc. Service, NYC, 1977-79; assoc. Smith, Barney, Harris, Upham, NYC, 1981-82, Lehman Brothers Kuhn Loeb, NYC, 1982-83, v.p., 1983-84, Donaldson, Lufkin & Jenrette, NYC, 1984-86, sr. v.p., mgr. short-term banking, 1987-88, sr. v.p., mgr. edn. fin. group, 1987-88; founding ptnr. M.R. Beal & Co., 1988—90, pres., 1990—93; exec. v.p., head capital markets Muriel Siebert & Co., 1993—95; sr. v.p. pub. fin. Smith Mitchell Investment Group Inc., 1996—99; asst. sec. for pub. authorities State of NY, 1999; v.p. govtl. & regulatory affairs KeySpan Energy, NYC, 2000—02; CFO LI Power Authority, NY, 2001—02; dep. sec. for state authorities State of NY, 2002—03, dep. sec. for fin. & housing, 2003, supt. banks, 2003—07; mng. dir. Wolfensohn & Co. LLC, NYC, 2007—. Bd. dirs. YMCA Greater NYC, Hudson River Park Trust, The After Sch. Corp., NYC Transit Mus., Bklyn. Acad. Music. *

TAYLOR, DONALD, retired manufacturing executive; b. Worcester, Mass., June 2, 1927; s. John A. B. and Alice M. (Weaver) T.; m. Ruth L. Partridge, June 24, 1950; children: Linda Taylor Robertson, Donald, Mark, John. BSME, Worcester Poly. Inst., 1949; grad., Northeastern U. Mgmt. Devel. Program, 1962, Harvard Bus. Sch. Advanced Mgmt. Program, 1979. Registered profl. engr., Mass. With George J. Meyer Mfg. Co., Milw., 1954-69; pres. mfg. div. A-T-O, Inc., 1969; exec. v.p. Nordberg div. Rex Chainbelt, Inc., Milw., 1969-73; v.p. ops. Rexnord Inc., Brookfield, Wis., pres., chief operating officer, 1978-85, chief exec. officer, from 1985, chmn., 1985-88; pres. Nordberg Machinery Group, Milw., 1973-78. With USNR, 1951—54. Mem. ASME, Milw. Country Club, Milw. Town Club, Univ. Club, Masons. Office: 1 Runnymede Dr North Hampton NH 03862-2328

TAYLOR, DUNCAN PAUL, pharmacologist, researcher; b. Bremerton, Wash., Feb. 4, 1949; s. Alan Earl and Barbara Eleanor (Thiel) T.; m. Jeanne Louise Damgaard, Apr. 8, 1972; 1 child, Jack Xander. BS in Chemistry, Calif. Inst. Tech., 1971; PhD in Biochemistry, Oreg. State U., 1977. Technician analytical svcs. Carnation Co. Rsch. Labs., Van Nuys, Calif., 1967-70; Peace Corps vol. Princess Margaret Secondary Sch., St. Johns, Antigua and Barbuda, 1971-73; grad. tchg. and rsch. asst. biochemistry and biophysics Oreg. State U., Corvallis, 1973-77; rsch. assoc. sect. biochemistry and pharmacology NIMH, Bethesda, Md., 1977-79; scientist, neuropharmacologist, rsch. assoc. Pharm. divsn. Mead Johnson & Co., Evansville, Ind., 1979-80; sr. scientist, group leader Pharm. div. Mead Johnson & Co., Evansville, Ind., 1980-82; sr. scientist, group leader, neuropharmacologist Pharm. R & D divsn. Bristol-Myers Co., Evansville, 1982-83, sr. rsch. scientist, mgr., 1983-85, rsch. fellow preclin. ctrl. nervous sys. rsch., 1985-89; sr. rsch. fellow preclin. ctrl. nervous sys. rsch. Pharm. Rsch. Inst. Bristol-Myers Squibb Co., Wallingford, Conn., 1989-94; dir. pharmacology Symphony Pharms., Malvern, Pa., 1994-95; cons., 1995-96; analyst bus. devel. Pharmacia & Upjohn, Kalamazoo, 1996-98, dir. strategic rsch. assessment, 1998—2003; prin. MT Enterprises, Kalamazoo, 2003—04; dir. strategic rsch. assessment Biovail Techs., Ltd., Bridgewater, NJ, 2004—05; sr. dir. strategic intelligence Biovail Pharms., Inc., Bridgewater, 2005—07; pvt. practice Bridgewater, 2007—. Mem. external adv. bd. dept. chemistry U. So. Miss.; grant reviewer NSF, 1981, 82, Med. Rsch. Coun. Can., 1987, 88; frequent presenter to profl. confs.; cons. in field. Contbr. numerous articles and abstracts to profl. jours. Bd. dirs. Posey County chpt. Am. Cancer Soc., 1983—85; mem. Tri-State Cursillo Cmty.; mentor Horizons Leadership Acad., Evansville-Venderburgh Sch. Corp., 1985; cons. Project Bus. Jr. Achievement, 1988; mem. chancel choir 1st United Meth. Ch., Mt. Vernon, Ind., 1976—86; mem. adult choir South Congl. Ch., Middletown, Conn., 1986—96, deacon, 1987—90, 1995—96, co-chmn., 1989—90, 1996, mem. coun., 1989—90, mem. task force on long-range planning, 1989—90; mem. adult choir 2d Reformed Ch., Kalamazoo, 1997—2004, mem. handbell choir, 1997—2004, mem. worship coun., 1997—99, elder, 1998—2001, consistory mem., 1998—2001, ch. outreach coun., 2000—01; active Grace United Ch. of Christ, Clinton, NJ, 2005—, trustee, 2006—, coun. moderator, 2006—. Scholar Carnation Co., 1967-70, Calif. State scholar, 1967-68, 70; rsch. fellow NSF, 1970, Cold Spring Harbor Labs., 1974. Fellow: Am. Inst. Chemists; mem.: AAAS, Am. Acad. Neurology, Soc. Competitive Intelligence Profls., Internat. Brain Rsch. Orgn.-World Fedn. Neuroscientists, Fedn. Am. Socs. for Exptl. Biology, European Brain and Behavior Soc., Brit. Brain Rsch. Assn, Soc. for Neurosci. (v.p. Conn. chpt. 1989—93), Am. Soc. for Pharmacology and Exptl. Therapeutics, Am. Chem. Soc., Phi Lambda Upsilon, Sigma Xi. Democrat. Achievements include patent for method and treatment of ischemia in the brain; made significant efforts in identification and development of new antipsychotics and antidepressants; identification of potential mechanism of action of the antipsychotic BMY14802; research in receptors, in etiology, expression and pharmacotherapy of psychiatric disorders. Home: 11 Jockey Ln Flemington NJ 08822-1599 Office: Biovail Pharms Inc 700 Route 202/206 North PO Box 6935 Bridgewater NJ 08807 Business E-Mail: duncantaylor@patmedia.net.

TAYLOR, E. JANE, lawyer; b. Niagra Falls, NY, Dec. 16, 1954; BA cum laude, Kent State U., 1977; JD, U. Akron, 1980. Bar: Ohio 1981, U.S. Dist. Ct. No. Dist. Ohio 1981, U.S. Ct. Appeals (6th cir.) 1985, U.S. Dist. Ct. So. Dist. Ohio 2002. Assoc. atty. Guy Lammert & Towne, Akron, Ohio, 1981—90, ptnr., 1990—. Mem. Akron Law Rev., 1979—80. Mem. bd. trustees United Way Summit County, 1995—2002, past chair svc. rev. team, mem. cmty. investment coun., chair portfolio coun. improving health and wellness, past mem. planning and allocations com., co-chair task force multi-yr. funding. Named one of 100 Women of Distinction, Akron Area YWCA, 2001. Mem.: ABA, Comml. Law League Am., Ohio Women's Bar Assn., Nat. Conf. Bar Presidents, Ohio State Bar Assn. (mem. coun. delegates 1996—2003, mem. bd. govs. 2000—03, pres.-elect 2004—, pres. 2005), Akron Bar Assn. (chair bar applicants and students com. 1988—90, mem. bankruptcy and comml. law sect. 1989—, bd. trustees 1990—93, v.p. 1993—94, pres. 1994—95, outstanding com. chairperson 1997—98). Office: Guy Lammert & Towne 2210 First National Tower Akron OH 44308 Office Phone: 330-535-2151. Office Fax: 330-535-9048. E-mail: guylaw2210@aol.com. *

TAYLOR, EDNA JANE, retired employment program counselor; b. Flint, Mich., May 16, 1934; d. Leonard Lee and Wynona Ruth (Davis) Harvey; children: Wynona Jane MacDonald, Cynthia Lee Zellmer. BS, No. Ariz. U., 1963; MEd, U. Ariz., 1967. Tchr. h.s. Sunnyside Sch. Dist., Tucson, 1963—68; employment program counselor employment devel. State of Calif., Canoga Park, 1968—98; ret., 1998. Mem. adv. coun. Van Nuys Cmty. Adult Sch., Calif., 1983-96, steering com., 1989-91, leadership coun., 1991-92; mem. adv. coun. Pierce C.C., Woodland Hills, Calif., 1979-81; first aid instr., recreational leader ARC. Mem. NAFE, Internat. Assn. of Pers. in Employment Security, Calif. Employment Counselors Assn. (state treas. 1978-79, state sec. 1980), Delta Psi Kappa (life). Avocations: writing, tennis, health and fitness, gardening. Personal E-mail: tauchi2@mindspring.com.

TAYLOR, EDWARD A., lawyer; b. SI, Jan. 25, 1958; BA, Fordham U., 1980, JD, 1983. Bar: NY 1984, US Dist. Ct. So. Dist. NY, US Dist. Ct. Ea. Dist. NY. Ptnr. Wilson, Elser, Moskowitz, Edelman & Dicker LLP, NYC. Mem.: ABA (torts & ins. practice sect., govt. & regulatory affairs divsn.), NY State Bar Assn. (ins. practice sect.). Office: Wilson Elser Moskowitz Edelman & Dicker LLP 150 E 42nd St 23rd Fl New York NY 10017-5639 Office Phone: 212-490-3000 ext. 2386. Office Fax: 212-490-3038. Business E-Mail: taylore@wemed.com.

TAYLOR, EDWARD CURTIS, chemistry professor; b. Springfield, Mass., Aug. 3, 1923; s. Edward Curtis and Margaret Louise (Anderson) T.; m. Virginia Dion Crouse, June 29, 1946; children: Edward Newton, Susan Raines. Student, Hamilton Coll., 1942-44, DSc (hon.), 1969; AB, Cornell U., 1946, PhD, 1949. Postdoctoral fellow Nat. Acad. Scis., Zurich, Switzerland, 1949-50; DuPont postdoctoral fellow chemistry U. Ill., 1950-51, faculty, 1951-54, asst. prof. organic chemistry, 1952-54; faculty

Princeton U., 1954—, prof. chemistry, 1964—, A. Barton Hepburn prof. organic chemistry, 1966—, A. Barton Hepburn prof. organic chemistry emeritus, 1997—, chmn. dept. chemistry, 1974-79, sr. rsch. scientist, 1997—, sr. scholar, 2007—. Vis. prof. Technische Hochschule, Stuttgart, Fed. Republic Germany, 1960, U. East Anglia, 1969, 71; Disting. vis. prof. U. Buffalo, 1968, U. Wyo., 1977; Backer lectr. U. Groningen, Holland, 1969; mem. chemistry adv. com. Office Sci. Research, USAF, 1962-73, Cancer Chemotherapy Nat. Service Ctr., 1958-62; mem. internat. adv. bd. Ctr. Medicinal Chemistry, Bar-Ilan U., Israel, 1994—; cons. rsch. divs. Parke-Davis Co., 1951-56, Procter & Gamble, 1953-80, Smith Kline & French, 1956-62, Eastman Kodak Co., 1965-83, Tenn. Eastman Co., 1968-83, Eli Lilly & Co., 1962-2002, Burroughs Wellcome Co., 1983-95, E.I. duPont de Nemours & Co., 1986-90, Polaroid Corp., 1986-2001, Dow Elanco Co., 1989-96, DuPont Merck Pharm. Co., 1990-97, Dow AgroScis., 1997-2003, DuPont Pharms. Co., 1997-2001. Author: (with McKillop) Chemistry of Cyclic Enaminonitriles and o-Aminonitriles, 1970, Principles of Heterocyclic Chemistry: film and audio courses, 1974; editor (with Raphael and Wynberg) Advances in Organic Chemistry, vols I-V, 1960-65, (with Wynberg) Vol VI, 1969, vols. VII-IX, 1970-79 (with W. Pfleiderer) Pteridine Chemistry, 1964, The Chemistry of Heterocyclic Compounds, 1968—, General Heterocyclic Chemistry, 1968—; organic chemistry editl. advisor John Wiley & Sons, Inc., 1968—; mem. editl. adv. bd. Jour. Medicinal Chemistry, 1962-66, Jour. Organic Chemistry, 1971-75, Synthetic Communications, 1971—, Heterocycles, 1973—, Chm. Substructure Index, 1971—, Advances in Heterocyclic Chemistry, 1983—, Pteridines, 1989—. Recipient rsch. awards, SmithKline and French Found., 1955, Hoffmann-LaRoche Foun., 1964—65, Ciba Found., 1971, Disting. Hamilton award, 1977, U.S. Sr. Scientist prize, Alexander von Humboldt Found., 1983, Disting. Alumni medal, Hamilton Coll., 1990, F. Gowland Hopkins medal, 1993, Thomas Alva Edison award, R&D Coun. NJ, 2004; sr. faculty fellow, Harvard U., 1959, Guggenheim fellow, 1979—80. Fellow N.Y. Acad. Scis., Am. Inst. Chemists; mem. Am. Chem. Soc. (award for creative work in synthetic organic chemistry, 1974, chmn. organic chemistry div. 1976-77, Arthur C. Cope scholar award 1994, Heroes of Chemistry award 2006), German Chem. Soc., Royal Soc. London, Internat. Soc. Heterocyclic Chemistry (5th Internat. award 1989), Phi Beta Kappa, Sigma Xi, Phi Kappa Phi. Achievements include patents for Alimta. Home: 288 Western Way Princeton NJ 08540-5337 Home Phone: 609-924-3483; Office Phone: 609-258-3914. Business E-Mail: etaylor@princeton.edu.

TAYLOR, EDWARD MCKINLEY, JR., lawyer; b. Dayton, Ohio, Apr. 19, 1928; s. Edward McKinley and Margaret Helen (Gaessler) T.; m. Mary Joan McMahon; 1 child, Mary Margaret Taylor Neises. JD with distinction, 1951. Bar: Ohio 1951, U.S. Supreme Ct. 1971, U.S. Ct. Mill. Appeals 1973, U.S. Dist. Ct. (so. dist.) Ohio 1959. Ptnr. Taylor & Taylor, Dayton, 1957—; asst. city atty. City of Dayton, 1957-77; solicitor Village of Union (Ohio), 1978-82, law dir., 1982, law dir. emeritus, 1982—. Col. JAGC, USAF. Mem. ABA, Ohio State Bar Assn., Dayton Bar Assn., Judge Advocate Assn., Shriners, Racquet Club (Dayton) Address: 7417 N Main St Dayton OH 45415-2545 Office Phone: 937-278-2723. Personal E-mail: taylore@donet.com.

TAYLOR, EDWARD STEWART, obstetrician, educator; b. Hecla, SD, Aug. 20, 1911; s. Robert Stewart and Sylvia Frances (Dewey) T.; m. Ruth Fatherson, June 15, 1940; children: Edward Stewart, Elizabeth Dewey Taylor Bryant, Catherine Wells Taylor. BA, U. Iowa, 1933, MD, 1936. Diplomate Am. Bd. Ob-Gyn (dir. 1962-69). Intern, Hurley Hosp., Flint, Mich., 1936-37; splty. tng. ob-gyn L.I. Coll. Hosp., 1937-41; prof. ob-gyn, chmn. dept. Sch. Medicine, U. Colo., 1947-76, clin. prof., 1976-81, prof., chmn. emeritus, 1981—. Nat. cons. ob-gyn to surg. gen. USAF, 1958-62. Author: Manual of Gynecology, 1952, Essentials of Gynecology, 4th edit.; editor: Beck's Obstetrical Practice, 10th edit.; editor-in-chief for obstetrics: Obstetrical and Gynecol. Survey, 1967-92. Trustee Denver Symphony Orch., 1979-85. Served to lt. col. AUS, 1942-45. Endowed ob-gyn. chair U. Colo., 1999. Fellow ACS, Am. Coll. Obstetricians and Gynecologists (Disting. Svc. award 1984); mem. AMA, Am. Gynecol. Soc. (v.p. 1974-75), Am. Assn. Obstetricians and Gynecologists (pres. 1970-71), Ctrl. Assn. Obstetricians and Gynecologists, S.W. Obstet. and Gynecol. Soc. (hon.), Am. Gynecol. and Obstet. Soc., Assn. Profs. Ob-Gyn (pres. 1974-75), Western Surg. Soc., Finnish Gynecol. Soc. (hon.), University Club, Alpha Omega Alpha. Congregationalist. Home: 80 S Dexter St Denver CO 80246-1051

TAYLOR, EDWIN R., music director; b. Port Huron, Mich., Sept. 4, 1952; s. Leroy E. and Virgene M. Taylor; m. Faith A. Ferry, Sept. 28, 1996; children: Jenelle F. Ferry, Jordan W. Ferry, Colton W. Ferry. MusB, Westminster Choir Coll., Princeton, NJ, 1975, MusM, 1979; postgrad., UCLA, 1996. Music dir. Covenant Presbyn. Ch., Fort Myers, Fla., 1984—98; co-dir. Gulf Coast Opera Co., Fort Myers, Fla., 1996—2001; chorus master SW Fla. Symphony Chorus, Fort Myers, 1997—98; music dir. Venice United Ch. Of Christ, Fla., 1998—2001; min. music, music dir. The First Congl. Ch., Ridgefield, Conn., 2001—. Adj. prof. Fla. Gulf Coast Univ., Fort Myers, 1999—2001; concert series dir. The First Congl. Ch., Ridgefield, 2001—; guest condr. Wapping Cmty. Ch., South Windsor, Conn., 2004—; singer Yale Camerata, New Haven, 2005—. Composer: (anthem for choir, organ, brass, percussion) Sing Praise To God Who Reigns Above, (anthem for male chorus) In The Bleak Midwinter, (hymntunes) Farmer, Crown Chase, Simpson, Keddy, Faithsong, Sluyter, King's Crown, Harding, Emory, Spring Hill Lane, St. Patrick's, Liberation, Duncan, (for brass quintet) Lo, How A Rose E'er Blooming, Angels We Have Heard On High, (for piano) Songs Of Home; arranger: for choir, organ, brass, percussion O Praise Ye The Lord, for brass, organ, percussion Feierlicher Einzug, for handbells, organ, brass, percussion The Great Gate of Kiev, for brass and organ Processional March, Rigaudon, Trumpet Tune, Prelude, for handbells Jesus Walked This Lonesome Valley. Mem.: Westminster Choir Coll. Alumni Assn. (class agt. 1984—90, alumni coun. mem. 1994—96), Choristers Guild (v.p. 2006), Fairfield-West Chpt. Am. Guild Organists (mem. exec. bd. 2002—05, dean 2006—), Aircraft Owners and Pilots Assn. Achievements include first to Conduct the modern-day premiere of Sousa's The Last Crusade. Avocations: flying, writing, cooking, travel. Home: 34 Spring Hill Ln Bethel CT 06801-2724 Office: The First Congregational Church 103 Main St Ridgefield CT 06877 Home Phone: 203-830-3096; Office Phone: 203-438-8077. Office Fax: 203-438-9678. Personal E-mail: fafert@sbcglobal.net. Business E-Mail: music@firstcongregational.com.

TAYLOR, ELISABETH COLER, retired secondary school educator; b. NYC, Jan. 24, 1942; d. Gerhard and Judith Coler; m. Billie Wesley Taylor II, 1960; children: Letitia Rose, Billie Albert. Student, Wilmington Coll., Del., 1959-60; BS, Wayne State U., Detroit, 1969; MS, Ohio State U., Columbus, 1980; postgrad., Wright State U., Dayton, Ohio, 1989—. Cert. home economist. H.s. tchr. home econs., computer sci. Dayton (Ohio) City Schs., 1972-99. Bd. dirs. Camp Fire Girls, 1970-71, vol. Detroit Mus. of Art, 1970-71, group leader Camp Fire Girls, Boy Scouts, Dayton, 1968-74. Mem. AAUW (life), Am. Mensa Ltd. (life). Avocations: birdwatching, travel, needlecrafts. Home: 131 Snow Hill Ave Dayton OH 45429-1705

TAYLOR, ELIZABETH (DAME ELIZABETH ROSEMOND TAYLOR), actress; b. London, Feb. 27, 1932; d. Francis Lenn and Sara Viola (Warmbrodt) Taylor; m. Conrad Nicholas Hilton Jr., May 6, 1950 (div. Feb. 1, 1951); m. Michael Wilding, Feb. 21, 1952 (div. Jan. 30, 1957); children: Christopher Edward, Michael Howard; m. Michael Todd, Feb. 2, 1957 (dec. Mar. 22, 1958); 1 child, Elizabeth Frances; m. Eddie Fisher, May 12, 1959 (div. Mar. 6, 1964); m. Richard Burton, Mar. 15, 1964 (div. June 26, 1974); 1 adopted child, Maria; m. Richard Burton, Oct. 10, 1975 (div. Aug. 1, 1976); m. John W. Warner, Dec. 4, 1976 (div. Nov. 7, 1982); m. Larry Fortensky, Oct. 6, 1991 (div. Oct. 31, 1996). Student, Byron House, Hawthorne Sch., Metro-Goldwyn-Mayer Sch. Ptnr., cons. House of Taylor Jewelry, Inc, 2005—. Actress: (films) There's One Born Every Minute, 1942; Lassie Come Home, 1943; The White Cliffs of Dover, 1944; Jane Eyre, 1944; National Velvet, 1944; Courage of Lassie, 1946; Cynthia, 1947; Life with Father, 1947; A Date with Judy, 1948; Julia Misbehaves, 1948; Little Women, 1950; Conspirator, 1950; The Big Hangover, 1950; Father of the Bride, 1950; Quo Vadis, 1951; Father's Little Dividend, 1951; A Place in the Sun, 1951; Callaway Went Thataway, 1951; Lover is Better Than Ever, 1952; Ivanhoe, 1952; The Girl Who Had Everything, 1953; Elephant Walk, 1954; Rhapsody, 1954; Beau Brummel, 1954; The Last Time I Saw Paris, 1954; Giant, 1956; Raintree County, 1957; Cat on a Hot Tin Roof, 1958; Suddenly, Last Summer, 1959; Scent of Mystery, 1960; Butterfield 8, 1960 (Acad. award for Best Actress, 1960); Cleopatra, 1963; The V.I.P.'s, 1963; The Sandpiper, 1965; Who's Afraid of Virginia Woolf?, 1966 (Acad. award for Best Actress, 1966); The Comedians, 1967; Reflections in a Golden Eye, 1967; Dr. Faustus, 1967; Boom!, 1968; Secret Ceremony, 1968; Anne of the Thousand Days, 1969; The Only Game in Town, 1970; Under Milkwood, 1971; X, Y and Zee, 1972; Hammersmith is Out, 1972; Night Watch, 1973; Ash Wednesday, 1973; That's Entertainment, 1974; The Driver's Seat, 1974; Blue Bird, 1975; Winter Kills, 1977; A Little Night Music, 1977; The Mirror Crack'd, 1980; Young Toscanini, 1988; The Flintstones, 1994; Actress, prodr. The Taming of the Shrew, 1967; Actress: (TV films) Divorce His-Divorce Hers, 1973; Victory at Entebbe, 1977; Return Engagement, 1979; Between Friends, 1982; Malice in Wonderland, 1986; There Must Be a Pony, 1986; Poker Alice, 1987; Sweet Bird of Youth, 1989; These Old Broads, 2001; (TV miniseries) North and South, 1985; (TV series) General Hospital, 1981; All My Children, 1984; Hotel, 1984; The Simpsons, 1993; The Nanny, 1996; Murphy Brown, 1996; High Society, 1996; theatre appearances include: (Broadway plays) The Little Foxes, 1981; Private Lives, 1983; narrator: (documentaries) Genocide, 1981; exec. prodr.: (films) Number 13, 1962; exec. prodr.: (films) Oz, 1967; assoc. prodr.: (films) The Caretaker, 1963; author: (autobiography) Elizabeth Taylor, 1965, Elizabeth Taylor Takes Off: On Weight Gain, Weight Loss, Self Esteem and Self Image, 1988, Elizabeth Taylor: My Love Affair with Jewelry, 2002; co-author (with Richard Burton): (novels) World Enough and Time, 1964; lic. (fragrances) Elizabeth Taylor's Passion, Passion for Men, White Diamonds/Elizabeth Taylor, Elizabeth Taylor's Diamonds & Emeralds, Diamonds and Rubies, Diamonds & Sapphires, Elizabeth Taylor Black Pearls. Active philanthropic, relief, charitable causes internationally, including Israeli War Victims Fund for the Chaim Sheba Hosp., 1976, UNICEF, various children's hosps., med. clinics, Botswana; initiated Ben Gurion U. - Elizabeth Taylor Fund for Children of the Negev, 1982; supporter AIDS Project, LA, 1985; founder, nat. chmn. Am. Found. for AIDS Rsch. (AmFAR), 1985—, internat. fund, 1985—; founder Elizabeth Taylor AIDS Found., 1991—. Named a Kennedy Ctr. Honoree, John F. Kennedy Ctr. for the Performing Arts, 2002; named Comdr. Arts Letters, France, 1985, an honoree with dedication of Elizabeth Taylor Med. Ctr. Whitman - Walker Clinic, Washington, 1993, Dame Comdr. of Order of British Empire, 1999; recipient Legion of Honor (for work with AmFAR), France, 1987, Aristotle S. Onassis Found., 1988, Jean Hersholt Humanitarian Acad. award (for work as AIDS advocate), 1993, Life Achievement award, Am. Film Inst., 1993, BAFTA Fellowship Award, British Acad. Film and Television Arts, 1999, Presdl. Citizen's Medal, 2001. Address: Elizabeth Taylor AIDS Found PO Box 55995 Sherman Oaks CA 91413

TAYLOR, ELIZABETH JANE, investment advisor, real estate company executive, marketing executive; b. Tiffin, Ohio, Oct. 27, 1941; d. Albert Joseph Lucas and Mary Jane Siebenaller-Swander; m. Gaylen Lloyd Taylor, July 11, 1977. Student, Heidelberg Coll., 1961, Austin CC, Tex., 1983-84; grad., Real Estate Edn. Ctr., 1984, Inst. Real Estate, 1988, Real Estate Inst., 1989; Tex. Realtors Inst., 1989; student, Rockhurst Coll., 1991-92. Dir. regional mktg. Sibrow, Inc., Ottawa, Can., 1981-83; realtor assoc. Alliance Sales, Austin, 1985-88; assoc. Broadway Comml. Investments, 1988-91; prin. Taylor & Assocs. Internat. Mktg. & Bus. Devel., 1980-98. Cons. Hypnosis Conn., Ohio, Tex. and Ariz., 1967—; tchr. mktg. and bus. devel., 1980-96. Author: Letters from Home, 1986, Unfinished Business, 2001, Reflections and Dreams, 2002, Unfinished Business, 2002, Southwest Celebration, 2003, A Dark and Stormy Night, 2003, Soul's Music, 2003, A Christmas Collection, 2003, Sourdough & More, 2003, Joy of Poetry, 2004, A Treasury of Poetry, 2005, Marketing Yourself As a Freelance Writer, 2005; contbr. Best New Poets of 1986, American Poetry Anthology, vol. VI., #3, 1986; columnist Austin Women Mag., 1984-86. V.p. Am. Congress on Real Estate, 1982-83; arbitrator Better Bus. Bur., 1984-89, sr. arbitrator, Austin, 1989-95; spkrs. bur. Austin Womans Ctr., 1985-88; v.p. Austin World Affairs Coun., 1984-94; adv. panel Austin Woman Mag., 1984-86. Nominee to Tex. Womens Hall of Fame, 1984. Mem. NAFE (network dir. 1980-88), Am. Biog. Inst. Rsch. (hon., bd. advisors 1988). Avocations: writing, behavior research. Home: 3926 E Cherokee St Phoenix AZ 85044-3827 Personal E-mail: elizabethlucastaylor@yahoo.com.

TAYLOR, ERROL BANCROFT, lawyer; b. Kingston, Jamaica, Nov. 24, 1955; s. Samuel George and Etta Maud (Champagnie) T.; m. Paula Whitfield, July 8, 1989; children: Bradford Russell, Kyle Bancroft. BA in Biology, SUNY, Oswego, 1977; JD, NY Law Sch., 1987. Bar: NY 1988, US Dist. Ct. (So. and Ea. Dists.) NY 1988, US Ct. Appeals (fed. cir.) 1991, US Supreme Ct. 2006. Sr. rsch. assoc. Squibb Corp., New Brunswick, NJ, 1977-81, asst. rsch investigator, 1981-87; assoc. atty. Fitzpatrick, Cella, Harper & Scinto, NYC, 1987-93, ptnr., 1994—2003, Milbank, Tweed, Hadley & McCloy, LLP, NYC, 2003—. Lectr. in field. Bd. dirs. Oswego Coll. Found., 1997—. Named one of Top 10 Litigators, Nat. law Jour., 2003. Mem. ABA, Am. Intellectual Property Law Assn., Fed. Cir. Bar. Assn., Nat. Bar. Assn., N.Y. Intellectual Property Law Assn., Assn. Bar for the City N.Y. (patent com. 1994-97). Office: Milbank, Tweed, Hadley & McCloy LLP 1 Chase Manhattan Plz New York NY 10005-1413 Office Phone: 212-530-5545. Office Fax: 212-822-5545. Business E-Mail: etaylor@milbank.com.

TAYLOR, ESTELLE WORMLEY, language educator, dean; b. Washington, Jan. 12, 1924; d. Luther Charles and Wilhelmina Wormley; m. Ivan Earle Taylor, Dec. 26, 1953. BS magna cum laude, Miner Tchrs. Coll., 1945; MA, Howard U., 1947; PhD, Cath. U. Am., 1969. Instr. English Howard U., 1947-52; tchr. Langley Jr. H.S., Washington, 1952-55, Eastern Sr. H.S., Washington, 1955-63; from instr. to prof. D.C. Tchrs. Coll., 1963—76; assoc. provost Fed. City Coll., Washington, 1974-75; prof. Howard U., 1976-91, chmn. dept. English, 1976-85, assoc. dean Coll. Liberal Arts, 1985-86, dir. expository writing program Grad. Sch. Arts and Scis., 1988-91, prof. emeritus, 1991. Mem., sec. Edn. Licensure Commn. of D.C., 1993—; mem. Commn. on Higher Edn., Mid. States Assn. Colls. and Schs., 1984-87, 88-90, co-chair steering com. to revise Characteristics of Excellence, 1992-93; mem. ctrl. exec. com. Folger Inst. Renaissance and 18th Century Studies, 1982-91; adv. bd. Humanities Inst. Montgomery Coll., 1997—. Contbg. editor A Howard Reader, 1997. 1st v.p. Order Daus. of King Episc. Ch. Diocese, Washington, 1994-98; commr. Edn. Licensure Com. of D.C., 1993—, also sec., vice chmn., 1995—; trustee U. D.C., 1979-83, vice chmn., 1983; mem. D.C. Cmty. Humanities Coun., 1990-91; co-chmn. planning com. Centennial Celebration of the Andrew Rankin Chapel Howard U., 1994; adv. bd. Coll. Arts and Svcs., Howard U., 2002—; mem. selection bd. Fgn. Agrl. Svc., 2002. Named Disting. Alumni, Howard U., 1995, Alumni award for Disting. Postgrad. Achievement in Edn. and Lit., 1997; So. fellow, 1968-69; Rockefeller/Aspen Inst. fellow, 1978-79. Mem. MLA (del. assembly 1994—), Nat. Assn. for Equal Opportunity in Higher Edn., Coll. Lang. Assn., Shakespeare Assn. Am., Pub. Mems. Assn. Fgn. Svc. Dept. of State, Links (v.p. Capital City chpt. 1979-81, corr. sec. 1989, rec. sec. 1991-93, 95—). Democrat. Home: 3221 20th St NE Washington DC 20018-2421 *Throughout my career I have been climbing a giant ladder, invisible to all but me. The challenging but humbling feature of this ladder is that whenever I get the feeling that I have almost reached the top, several additional rungs attach themselves to my Jacob's Ladder. Thus, that thing called success is for me forever a goal to be reached. As long as I continue to feel a restlessness and a yearning to climb another rung, I shall know that I am alive.*

TAYLOR, FANNIE TURNBULL, art association administrator, educator; b. Kansas City, Mo., Sept. 11, 1913; d. Henry King and Fannie Elizabeth (Sills) Turnbull; m. Robert Taylor, Dec. 2, 1938 (div. 1974); children: Kathleen Muir Taylor Isaacs, Anne Kingston Taylor Wadsack. BA, U. Wis., 1938; LHD (hon.), Buena Vista Coll., Storm Lake, Iowa, 1975. Mem. faculty U. Wis., Madison, 1941—, prof. social edn., 1949—, emerita, 1979—. Dir. Wis. Union Theater, 1946-66, coord. univ. systems arts coun., 1967-70, assoc. dir. Ctr. Arts Adminstrn., 1970-72, coord. Consortium for Arts, 1976-84; cons. in field. Author: The Arts at a New Frontier: The National Endowment for the Arts, Wisconsin Union Theater: Fifty Golden Years (Book award of Merit, State Hist. Soc. Wis. 1990); contbr. articles to profl. jours. Program dir. music Nat. Endowment Arts, 1966-67, program info. dir., 1972-76; bd. dirs. Wis. Arts Coun., 1964-72, Wis. Found. Arts, 1976-91, Madison Civic Music Assn., 1976-84, Madison Children's Mus., 1983-96, Chazen Art Coun., 1976—, chair 1983-86; Madison Civic Ctr. Found., 1981-94; hon. chair Wis. Union Theater Program Endowment Fund, 1985—; bd. dirs. Wis. chpt. Nature Conservancy, 1963-84, chmn. 1976-77; bd. dirs. Shorewood Hills Found., 1976-2002, pres., 1976-81. Recipient Oak Leaf award Nature Conservancy, 1981, Wis. Gov.'s award in Support of the Arts, 1992, Madison Cmty. Found. Asset Builders Leadership award, 2002, Madison Children's Mus. Star Soc. award, 2005; named Woman of Distinction, Madison YWCA, 1994. Fellow Wis. Acad. Scis., Arts and Letters; mem. Assn. Performing Arts Presenters (founder, exec. dir. 1957-72, 1st recipient Fannie Taylor Disting. Svc. award 1972), Am. Assn. Dance Cos. (bd. dirs. 1967-72), Nat. Assn. Regional Ballet (bd. dirs. 1975-77), Nat. Guild Cmty. Music Schs. Arts (bd. dirs. 1977-80), Women in Comm. (Writers' Cup 1980), U. Wis. Found., U. Wis. Alumni Assn. (Disting. Svc. award 1979), Bach Dancing and Dynamite Soc. (bd. dirs. 1993-2004, Big Bang award), Madison Civics Club (pres. 1969-70), Univ. Club (pres. 1982-85), Blackhawk Club. Home: 8301 Old Sauk Rd Apt 303 Middleton WI 53562-4393 Business E-Mail: ftaylor@facstaff.wisc.edu.

TAYLOR, FELICIA, newscaster; BS in Comm., Northwestern U. Prodr., field reporter WLS-TV, Chgo.; anchor, prodr., writer Fin. News Network; anchor bus. shows Fin. Times; London corr. CNBC, Ft. Lee, N.J., 1992-93, co-anchor Today's Bus., anchor This Morning's Bus., 1993—98, co-anchor MarketWatch; co-anchor Weekend Today in New York NewsChannel4, NYC, 1998—2003, co-anchor NewsChannel 4 at 6 and 11, 2003—. Office: NBC News 30 Rockefeller Plaza New York NY 10112

TAYLOR, FOSTER JAY, retired university president; b. Gibsland, La., Aug. 9, 1923; s. Lawrence Foster and Marcia Aline (Jay) T.; m. Lou Kavanaugh; 1 son, Terry Jay. Student, La. Poly. Inst., 1940-42; BA, U. Calif., Santa Barbara, 1948; MA, Claremont Grad. Sch., Calif., 1949; PhD, Tulane U., 1952. Assoc. prof. history, dean men. La. Coll., Pineville, 1952-56, prof., 1956-62, dean coll., 1960-62; pres. La. Tech. U., Ruston, 1962-87, pres. emeritus, 1987—. Past chmn. La. Labor Mediation Bd.; arbitrator Am. Arbitration Assn., Fed. Mediation and Counciliation Svc.; former mem. La. Adv. Coun. on Vocat.-Tecy. Edn.; bd. dirs. First Guaranty Bank. Author: The United States and the Spanish Civil War, 1936-39, 1956, Reluctant Rebel, The Secret Diary of Robert Patrick, 1861-1865, 1959. Served to lt. comdr., aviator USNR, 1942-46. Mem. Am. Hist. Assn., Miss. Valley Hist. Assn., So. Hist. Assn., Nat. Acad. Arbitrators., Phi Alpha Theta. Clubs: Rotary. Home: 500 Audubon Dr Ruston LA 71270-7800 Office Phone: 318-251-1790.

TAYLOR, FRANCIS MICHAEL, auditor, municipal official; b. Munich, 1960; came to the U.S., 1961; BS, Va. Tech., 1982. CPA Va., cert. internal auditor. Pub. acct., Roanoke, Va., 1982-84; controller ARC Roanoke, Inc., Roanoke, 1984-87; audit supr. City of Roanoke, 1987-94; city auditor City of Stockton (Calif.), 1994—. Nat. coord. com. Key Nat. Indicators Initiative. Mem. AICPA, Nat. Assn. Local Govt. Auditors (past pres.), Calif. Soc. CPAs, Inst. Internal Auditors, Govt. Fin. Officers Assn., Info. Sys. Audit and Control Assn., Bay Area Local Govt. Auditors. Office: 22 E Weber Ave Ste 325 Stockton CA 95202-1951

TAYLOR, FRANCIS X., former federal agency administrator, retired military officer; BA in Govt. and Internat. Studies, U. Notre Dame, 1970, MA in Govt. and Internat. Studies, 1974; grad., Squadron Officer Sch., 1975, Air Command and Staff Coll., 1980, Armed Forces Staff Coll., 1984, Air War Coll., 1988. Commd. 2d lt. USAF, 1970, advanced through grades to brigadier gen., 1996, ret., 2001; analyst, Mid. E, Africa, & S Asia divsn., Analysis & Dissemination Branch, Counterintelligence Divsn. Hdqs. Air Force Office of Spl. Investigations, Washington, 1970—72, area supr. Acquisition & Analysis Divsn., Directorate of Personnel, 1974—76; chief counterintelligence acquisition and analysis br. Air Force Office of Spl. Investigations Dist. 69, Ankara, Turkey, 1976-77; comdr. Air Force Office of Spl. Investigations Detachment 411, Bolling AFB, D.C., 1977-79; chief resource career mgmt. divsn. Directorate of Pers. Hdqs. Air Force Office of Spl. Investigations, Bolling AFB, 1979-80, comdr. Hdqs. Squadron sect., asst. exec. to comdr., 1980-83; dep. dir. for ops. Dir. Counterintelligence/Invest. Programs Office of Dep. Under Sec. of Def. for Policy, The Pentagon, Washington, 1984-87; dep. comdr. 487th Combat Support Group, Comiso Air Station, Italy, 1988-90; comdr. Air Force Office of Spl. Investigations Dist. 45, Osan Air Base, South Korea, 1999-92, Air Force Office of Spl. Investigations Region 2, Langley AFB, Va., 1992-94; dir. mission guidance Hdqs. Air Force Office of Spl. Investigations, Bolling AFB, 1994-95; dir. spl. investigations Office of Inspector Gen. Office of Sec. of Air Force, The Pentagon, Washington, 1995-96; comdr. Hdqs. Air Force Office of Spl. Investigations, Bolling AFB, 1996-98, Andrews AFB, Md., 1998—2001; coord. for counterterrorism US Dept. State, Washington, 2001—02, asst. sec. for diplomatic security, dir. Office Fgn. Missions, 2002—05. Decorated Disting. Svc. medal, Def. Superior Svc. medal, Legion of Merit, Meritorious Svc. medal with 3 oak leaf clusters, Air Force Commendation medal with two oak leaf clusters, Air Force Achievement medal with oak leaf cluster; Named Outstanding Advocate for Women, Women in Fed. Law Enforcement, 2000

TAYLOR, FRED, professional football player; b. Belle Glade, Fla., June 27, 1976; m. Andrea Taylor; children: Nataajah, Inari. BS in Sociology, U. Fla. Running back Jacksonville Jaguars, Fla., 1998—. Spokesman Leukemia Soc. Am., Lymphoma Soc. Am., Glades Asthma Project. Achievements include ranks fourth on U. Fla. all-time rushing list; played in 3 college bowl games; team was 14-0 in games in which he had over 100 yards rushing. Office: Jacksonville Jaguars 1 Alltel Stadium Pl Jacksonville FL 32202-1917

TAYLOR, GAIL SINGLETON, education educator; b. NYC, Mar. 18, 1962; d. James Alphonso and Muriel Louise (Clarke) Singleton; m. Andrew Joseph Taylor. BA, Vassar Coll., 1984; MS, Fordham U., 1988; PhD, Tex. A&M U., 1995. Elem. sch. tchr. Bd. Edn., NYC, 1986-89; rsch./asst. tchr. Tex. A&M U., College Station, 1989-93, asst. dir. minorities interested in tchg. conf., summer 1992; asst. prof. edn. curriculum and instrn. Old Dominion U., Norfolk, Va., 1993—, dir. multicultural mentorship project, 1994—. Tchg. workshops children's lit., multicultural edn. Norfolk (Va.) Pub. Schs., 1993—; cons. Acad. TV Svcs., Old

Dominion U., Norfolk, 1994—. Mem. Am. Edn. Rsch. Assn., Nat. Coun. Tchrs. English, Phi Delta Kappa. Office: Old Dominion Univ Darden Coll Edn Norfolk VA 23529

TAYLOR, GENE (GARY EUGENE TAYLOR), congressman; b. New Orleans, Sept. 17, 1953; m. Margaret Gordon; children: Sarah, Emily, Gary. BA, Tulane U., New Orleans, 1976; student, U. So. Miss., Hattiesburg. Sales rep. Stone Container Corp.; city councilman Bay St. Louis, Miss., 1981—83; mem. Miss. State Senate, 1984-89, US Congress from 4th Miss. dist., 1989—, mem. house armed svcs. com., mem. transp. and infrastructure com., chmn. subcommittee on seapower and expeditionary forces, co-chair Shipbuilding Caucus, Nat. Guard and Res. Caucus, Coast Guard Caucus and Expeditionary Warfare Caucus; mem. Conservative Dems.' Blue Dog Coalition. With USCGR, 1971-1984. Mem.: Rotary, Lions, Kappa Sigma. Democrat. Roman Catholic. Office: US House Reps 2269 Rayburn House Office Bldg Washington DC 20515-2405 Office Phone: 202-225-5772. Office Fax: 202-225-7074. *

TAYLOR, GENE, bank executive; m. Kathy Taylor; 3 children. BS in Fin., Fla. State U. Credit analyst Bank Am. Corp., 1969, pres. Florida bank, 1990, pres. NationsBank, 1993, pres. merged NationsBank and Barnett Bank, 1997, head consumer and comml. banking ops. Western US, 1998, pres. consumer and comml. banking, 2001, head global bus. and fin. svcs., 2004, vice chmn., pres. global corp. and investment banking, 2005—. Mem. risk and capital com. Bank Am. Corpn., mem. mgmt. operating com. Office: Bank Am Corp Ctr 100 N Tryon St Fl 58 Charlotte NC 28255-0001

TAYLOR, GEORGE FREDERICK, newspaper publisher, editor; b. Portland, Oreg., Feb. 28, 1928; s. George Noble and Ida Louise (Dixon) T.; m. Georga Bray, Oct. 6, 1951; children— Amelia Ruth, Ross Noble. BS, U. Oreg., 1950. Reporter Astoria (Oreg.) Budget, 1950-52, Portland Oregonian, 1952-54; copy reader Wall St. Jour., 1955-57, reporter, 1957-59, Detroit Bur. chief, 1959-64, Washington corr., 1964-68, asst. mng. editor San Francisco, 1968-69, mng. editor NYC, 1970-77, exec. editor, 1977-86; pub. North Bend (Oreg.) News, 1981-86, Prime Time, 1987—, Coquille Valley Sentinel, 1989-2000. Lt. USAF, 1955-57. Mem. Oregon Newspaper Publishers Assn. (bd. dirs. 1997-2000). E-mail: Ftaylor@harborside.com.

TAYLOR, GEORGE KIMBROUGH, JR., lawyer; b. Atlanta, Aug. 28, 1939; s. George Kimbrough and Helen Whiteside (Shepard) T.; m. Carol Ann McKinney, July 1, 1961 (div. 1976); children: George Kimbrough III, Thomas Haynes; m. Triska Ashley Drake, Oct. 2, 1981. BA, Emory U., 1961; LLB, U. Va., 1964. Bar: Ga. 1964, U.S. Dist. Ct. (no. dist.) Ga. 1964, U.S. Ct. Appeals (11th cir.) 1964. Assoc. Kilpatrick & Cody, Atlanta, 1964-70, ptnr., 1970-96, Kilpatrick Stockton LLP (formerly Kilpatrick & Cody), 1997—. Bd. dirs. Ont. Reins. Co. Ltd., Atlanta; chmn., bd. dirs. MFI Am., Inc., Atlanta, 2003—06. Chmn. bd. dirs. Spl. Audiences, Inc., Atlanta, 1985-87; bd. dirs. Atlanta Symphony Orch., 1986—; trustee Woodruff Arts Ctr., Atlanta, 1997—; bd. dirs. Atlanta Opera, 1995—, Ga. Humanities Coun., Atlanta, 1986-93, Ga. Conservancy, 1979-85; bd. dirs. Ga. Trust for Hist. Preservation, 2002—, vice chair, 2004—; bd. dirs. Ga. Coun. Internat. Visitors, Atlanta, 1987-94, pres., 1993; bd. dirs. Brit.-Am. Bus. Group, 1989-95, pres., 1994; bd. visitors Emory U., Atlanta, 1993-96, Brit.-Am. Bus. Coun., 1997—, chmn. 1997-98; mem. alumni coun. U. Va. Law Sch., 1995-98; active Leadership Atlanta. Woodrow Wilson fellow, 1961. Mem. ABA, Internat. Bar Assn., Atlanta Bar Assn., Order of Coif, Soc. Internat. Bus. Fellows, Capital City Club, Phi Beta Kappa, Omicron Delta Kappa. Democrat. Avocations: sailing, skiing. Office: Kilpatrick Stockton LLP 1100 Peachtree St NE Ste 2800 Atlanta GA 30309-4530 Office Phone: 404-815-6500. Business E-Mail: ktaylor@kilpatrickstockton.com.

TAYLOR, GLEN A., printing, direct mail and technology executive, professional sports team owner; b. Apr. 20, 1941; m. Becky Taylor; children: Terri, Jean, Taylor Moor, Jeff, Kendahl. BS in Math., Physics and Social Sci., Mankato State U., 1962; student, Harvard Grad. Sch. Bus.; D (hon.), Mankato State U., 1997. Chmn., CEO Taylor Corp., North Mankato, Minn., 1975—2001, chmn., 2001—; mem. Minn. State Senate, 1980—90; owner NBA Minn. Timberwolves and Minn. Lynx, Mpls., 1995—. Named Exec. of Yr., Corp. Report mag., 1987; named one of Forbes' Richest Ams., 2006; named to Minn. Hall of Fame, Twin Cities Monthly mag., 2002; recipient Sales Exec. of Yr. award, Sales and Mktg. Execs. Mpls./St. Paul, 1999. Office: Taylor Corp 1725 Roe Crest Dr North Mankato MN 56003-1807 also: Minn Timberwolves Target Ctr 600 1st Ave N Minneapolis MN 55403-1416

TAYLOR, GLORIA A., minister, educator; d. Walter Hedland and Margaret Rose Atkinson; m. Frederic Edward Taylor, Feb. 23, 1947; children: Greg Eugene, Lance Norman, Brett Jack, Scott Frederic, Penny Gay. Ordination, Diocesan Sch. Faith & Ministry, 1989. Ordained Diocese No. Ind., 1989. Chairperson Episcopal AIDS Ministry, South Bend, Ind., 1989—99; deacon St. Paul Episcopal Ch., Munster, Ind., 1989—93, Trinity Ch., Mich. City, Ind., 1993—. Support groups for people with HIV/AIDS and mothers, South Bend, 1988—99; provider pastoral care for women in all walks of life. Conservative. Episcopalian. Achievements include being the first woman ordained in the 100 year old diocese in 1989. Avocations: travel, watercolor. Home: 1809 Holly Lane Munster IN 46321 Home Phone: 219-923-9278; Office Phone: 219-874-4355. Personal E-mail: gataylor89@aol.com.

TAYLOR, GRANT DAVID, urologist; b. Arlington, Tex., Feb. 14, 1974; s. Michael Albert and Lynda Lavelle Taylor; m. Carla Ranee Nedderman, July 5, 1995; children: Benjamin Grant, Sarah Ranee. BS, John Brown U., Siloam Springs, Ariz., 1996; MD, U. Tex. Houston Med. Sch., 2000. Lic. Tex. State Bd. Med. Examiners, 2002, Tenn. State Bd. Med. Examiners, 2005, diplomate Am. Bd. Urology, 2007. Intern MD Anderson Rsch., Houston, 1997; intern gen. surgery U. Tex. Southwestern, Dallas, 2000—01, resident urology, 2001—05; urologist Johnson City Urol. Clinic, Tenn., 2005—. Surg. mentor Rita Med. Sys., Fremont, Calif., 2006—. Contbr. articles to profl. jours., chapters to books. Scholar, John Brown U., 1992—96. Mem.: AMA, Christian Med. and Dental Soc. (internat. med. missionary 2006—), Americal Urol. Assn., Endourological Soc., Tenn. Med. Assn., Alpha Omega Alpha, Alpha Chi (pres. 1994—95). Office: Johnson City Urol Clinic 300 W Watauga Ave Johnson City TN 37604 Home Phone: 423-262-0007; Office Phone: 423-926-6112.

TAYLOR, HAROLD ALLEN, JR., industrial minerals consultant; b. San Jose, Calif., June 27, 1936; s. Harold Allen and Marie Anna (Briody) T.; m. Theresa Josephine Kustritz, Aug. 29, 1963; children: Harold Allen III, Ruth F., Jonathan L.E. BA, Brown U., 1958; MA, U. Minn., 1968. Project leader Office Mineral Supply, U.S. Bur. Mines, Mpls., 1968-70, commodity specialist divsn. ferrous metals Washington, 1970-74; commodity analyst U.S. internat. Trade Commn., Washington, 1974-80; sr. commodity specialist br. indsl. minerals U.S. Bur. Mines, Washington, 1980-95; pres. Basics Mines, Summit Point, W.Va., 1995—. Pub., editor Dimension Stone Advocate News, Graphite Advocate News, Bismuth Advocate News, Indium Advocate News, 2000—; contbr. articles to profl. jours. Pres. Arlington (Va.) Interfaith Coun., 1994, 95. Mem. AIME (sec 1983-84, 1st vice chmn. 1984-85, chmn. 1985-86, exec. adv. bd. mineral econs. subsect. 1981-83, 87-91), ASTM (chmn. subcom. nomenclature of com. on dimension stone 1987-2004, sec. of com. 1990-95), Soc. Govt. Economists (chmn. materials policy panels, 1979-84), Capitol Metals Forum (steering com. 1979-85), Toastmasters (pres. 1978, 81, 87, 91, asst. area gov. 1978-79, area gov. 1979-80, dep. divsn. lt. gov. 1989-90), Sigma Gamma Epsilon Address: PO Box 185 Summit Point WV 25446-0185 Office Phone: 304-725-6619. E-mail: bmhtayl@earthlink.net.

TAYLOR, HARRIS C., endocrinologist, consultant; b. Bklyn., Apr. 30, 1940; s. William and Florence Ruth T.; m. Diana Kahn, Sept. 3, 1962; children: Brian David, Rebecca Lynn. BS, Queens Coll., 1961; MD, U. Chgo., 1965. Diplomate Am. Bd. Internal Medicine, Am. Bd. Endocrinology and Metabolism. Cons. endocrinologist Kaiser Found., Cleve., 1972-86; chief divsn. endocrinology Luth. Med. Ctr., Cleve., 1977-96, dir. endocrinology & radioimmunoassay lab., 1978-96, dir. internal medicine residency, 1985-94, dir. rsch., internal medicine residency program Fairview Health Sys., 1996—. Sr. clin. instr. Case We. Res. U. Sch. Medicine, Cleve., 1977-81, clin. asst. prof., 1981-88, clin. assoc. prof. medicine in endocrinology, 1988-2003, clin. prof., 2003—; prin. investigator NIH, 2006—. Contbr. articles to profl. jours. Chmn. program com. Diabetes Assn. Cleve., 1976-81, exec. com., 1978-85, pres.-elect, 1981-82, pres., 1982-84. Sr. asst. surgeon USPHS, 1966-68. Named One of Best Drs. in Cleve., Cleve. Mag., 1998, 2002, 2004. Fellow: ACP (reviewer Annals of Internal Medicine 1986—, Master Tchr. award 2001), Am. Coll. Endocrinology (editl. bd. Endocrine Practice 1997—2004); mem.: Endocrine Soc., Am. Assn. Clin. Endocrinologists, Phi Beta Kappa. Jewish. Avocations: stamp collecting/philately, classical music. Office: Case Western Reserve Univ Sch of Medicine-Div of Endocrinology 2109 Adelbert Rd Cleveland OH 44106 Home Phone: 216-921-7393; Office Phone: 216-368-6129. Personal E-mail: dkthct62@sbcglobal.net.

TAYLOR, HENRY SPLAWN, retired literature educator, poet; b. Loudoun County, Va., June 21, 1942; s. Thomas Edward and Mary Marshall (Splawn) Taylor; m. Mooshe Taylor, 2002. BA, U. Va., Charlottesville, 1965; MA, Hollins Coll., Va., 1966. Instr. English Roanoke Coll., Va., 1966—68; asst. prof. U. Utah, 1968—71; faculty Am. U., Washington, 1971—2003, prof. lit., 1976—2003, co-dir. MFA program in creative writing, 1982—2003, dir. Am. studies program, 1983—84. Dir. writer's conf. U. Utah, 1970—72; writer-in-residence Hollins Coll., 1978; poet-in-residence Wichita State U., 1994, Randolph-Macon Woman's Coll., 1997; prof. poetry U. Cin., 2002. Author: (poetry) The Horse Show at Midnight, 1966, Breakings, 1971, An Afternoon of Pocket Billiards, 1975, Desperado, 1979, The Flying Change, 1985 (Pulitzer prize, 86), Crooked Run, 2006, Understanding Fiction: Poems 1986-96, 1996, Brief Candles: 101 Clerihews, 2000, Poetry: Points of Departure, 1974; editor: The Water of Light: A Miscellany in Honor of Brewster Ghiselin, 1976; author: Compulsory Figures: Essays on Recent American Poets, 1992, (cassette) Landscape with Tractor, 1985; contbg. editor: Hollins Critic, 1971—78, 1997—; editl. cons.: Magill's Literary Annual, 1972—90, cons. editor: Poet Lore, 1977—84; translator (with others): The Children of Herakles, 1981; translator: Plautus' The Weevil, 1995, Sophocles' Electra, 1998. Recipient Pulitzer Prize, Poetry, 1986, Michael Braude award for light verse, Am. Acad. Arts and Letters, 2002, Aiken Taylor award in Modern Am. Poetry, 2004; fellow, Nat. Endowment Arts, 1978, 1986; grantee, NEH, 1980—81. Mem.: PEN, Fellowship of So. Writers, Am. Lit. Translators Assn. Democrat. Mem.Soc.Of Friends.

TAYLOR, HOLLY ANN, music educator; b. Midland, Tex., Oct. 11, 1978; d. Thomas Woods and Donna Louise Hughston; m. Mark Alan Taylor, July 22, 2006. MusB in Music Edn., George Mason U., Fairfax, Va., 2003, M in Music Performance, 2006. Cert. tchr. Va., 2003. Music/strings tchr. Fairfax County Pub. Schs., 2003—. Freelance performer Haase Quartet, Fairfax, 1999—. Mem.: Music Educators Nat. Conf. Home Phone: 703-250-5098; Office Phone: 703-715-3800. Personal E-mail: holly.taylor@fcps.edu.

TAYLOR, IAN LOGAN, dean; b. Eng. MD, PhD, Liverpool Med. Sch. Fellow in gastrointestinal rsch. UCLA, mem. Wadsworth V.A. Tng. Program, various positions, prof. medicine; chief of gastroenterology Duke U., 1986—89, dir. Sarah W. Stedman Ctr. for Nutritional Studies, 1989—90, prof. physiology, dept. cell biology, 1990—93; prof. and chmn. dept. medicine Med. U. S.C., 1993—2001, pres. U. Med. Assocs., 1999—2001; dean Sch. Medicine Tulane U., 2001—05; dean Coll. Medicine SUNY Health Sci. Ctr., Bklyn., 2006—. Office: Coll Medicine SUNY Health Sci Ctr 470 Clarkson Ave Brooklyn NY 11203

TAYLOR, ISHMAEL JAY, environmental scientist; b. Durham, Aug. 23, 1948; s. Jay Taylor and Aileen Turner. BA, U. Tex., Austin, 1970. Endangered Species and Marine Mammal Observer Nat. Marine Fisheries Svc., 1997. Prin., owner Bookshop, 1973—79; secondary tchr. Ministry Edn., Mongo, Chad, 1971—73; marine surveyor Stott and Ogram, Inc., Norfolk, 1979—82; fgn. fisheries observer Nat. Marine Fisheries Svc., Gloucester, 1983—80; environ. cons. Atlantic Inspection Svcs., New Bedford, 1994—. Vol. Peace Corp., Washington, 1971—73. Mem.: Humiliation Studies Group, Phi Theta Kappa. Avocation: tensile structure. Home: 4327 Millstead St San Antonio TX 78230 Home Phone: 210-363-8289; Office Phone: 508-990-9054. Personal E-mail: ishmael@alumni.utexas.net.

TAYLOR, J. MARY (JOCELYN MARY TAYLOR), museum director, educator, zoologist; b. Portland, Oreg., May 30, 1931; d. Arnold Llewellyn and Kathleen Mary (Yorke) T.; m. Joseph William Kamp, Mar. 18, 1972 (dec.); m. Wesley Kingston Whitten, Mar. 20, 2001. BA, Smith Coll., 1952; MA, U. Calif., Berkeley, 1953, PhD, 1959. Instr. zoology Wellesley Coll., 1959-61, asst. prof. zoology, 1961-65; assoc. prof. zoology U. B.C., 1965-74; dir. Cowan Vertebrate Mus., 1965-82, prof. dept. zoology, 1974-82; collaborative scientist Oreg. Regional Primate Research Ctr., 1983-87; prof. (courtesy) dept. fisheries and wildlife Oreg. State U., 1984-95; dir. Cleve. Mus. Nat. History, 1987-96, dir. emerita, 1996—. Adj. prof. dept. biology Case Western Res. U., 1987-96. Assoc. editor Jour. Mammalogy, 1981-82. Contbr. numerous articles to sci. jours. Trustee Benjamin Rose Inst., 1988-93, Western Res. Acad., 1989-94, U. Circle, Inc., 1987-96, The Cleve. Aquarium, 1990-93, Cleve. Access to the Arts, 1992-96; corp. bd. Holden Arboretum, 1988-98, The Cleve. Mus. Natural History, 1996—, The Catlin Gabel Sch., 1998-2000, The Inst. for the Northwest, 1999—2001. Recipient Lake County Environ. award, Lake county metro parks.; Fulbright scholar, 1954-55; Lalor Found. grantee, 1962-63; NSF grantee, 1963-71; NRC Can. grantee, 1966-84; Killam Sr. Rsch. fellow, 1978-79 Mem.: Rodent Specialist Group of Species Survival Commn. (chmn. 1989—93), Assn. Sci. Mus. Dirs. (v.p. 1990—93), Cooper Ornithol., Australian Mammal Soc. (hon. life), Am. Soc. Mammalogists (1st v.p. 1978—82, pres. 1982—84, hon. life, Hartley T. Jackson award 1993), Soc. Women Geographers, Sigma Xi. Home: 2718 SW Old Orchard Rd Portland OR 97201-1637 E-mail: taylorwhitten@comcast.net.

TAYLOR, JACK CRAWFORD, rental and leasing company executive; b. 1922; With Lindburg Cadillac, St. Louis, 1944-50, Forrest Cadillac, St. Louis, 1951-56; chmn. bd. Enterprise Rent-A-Car, St. Louis, 1980—2001, chmn. emeritus, 2001—. Served with USN. Named one of Forbes Richest Americans, 2006, World's Richest People (with family), Forbes Mag., 2007. Office: Enterprise Rent-A-Car 600 Corporate Park Dr Saint Louis MO 63105-4204 *

TAYLOR, JACKIE A., educational association administrator; 1 child. PhD candidate, U. Tenn. Coll. Edn., Health & Human Sciences. Tchr. Families First welfare reform program, Nashville; rsch. assoc. U. Tenn. Ctr. Literacy Studies, Knoxville, 2001—. Chmn. Assn. Adult Literacy Profl. Developers. Recipient Literacy Leadership award, Nat. Coalition Literacy, 2006. Office: Ctr Literacy Studies Ste 312 600 Henley St Knoxville TN 37996 Office Phone: 865-974-0959. Office Fax: 865-974-3857. E-mail: jataylor@utk.edu. *

TAYLOR, JAMES FRANCIS, marketing professional; b. Detroit, Sept. 5, 1951; s. Harold James and Mary Frances (Law) T.; m. Janet Elizabeth Joss, May 21, 1977; children: Jonathan Harold, Jessica Frances, Jenna Leigh, Jeanette Mary. BA in Polit. Sci., Mich. State U., 1976; postgrad., Thomas Cooley Law Sch., 1979. Product mgr. Gen. Aluminum Products, Charlotte, Mich., 1975-77; sales mgr. Empire Metal Products, Columbus, Ohio, 1978; bus. mgr. Law Offices of Paul Martin, Lansing, Mich., 1978-79; dir. mktg. and sales Feather-Lite Mfg. Co., Troy, Mich., 1979-81; v.p. mktg. and sales Innovative Products Corp., Madison Heights, Mich., 1981-82; pres. J.F. Taylor Assocs., Inc., Durham, N.C., 1982—, Meadowcrest Group, Inc., 1989—; pres., bd. dirs. The Taylor-Grant-Joss Found., Durham, N.C.; COO C.J. Woodmaster, Inc., Durham, 1998—. Corp. sec., bd. dirs., CFO of All Corps. Unfinished Furniture Express, Inc., 1997—, Durham, NC, C.J. Woodmaster of Raleigh, Inc.; CFO C.J. Woodmaster of Cary, Inc., 1999—; CFO, corp. sec. C.J. Woodmaster Devel., Inc., Durham, C.J. Woodmaster of Fayetteville, Inc. Mem.: Hope Valley Country Club, Rotary. Republican. Roman Cath. Home: 4 Roswell Ct Durham NC 27707-5070 Office: PO Box 51280 Durham NC 27717 Business E-Mail: jtaylor@cjwoodmaster.com.

TAYLOR, JAMES GILBERT, protective services official; b. Tupelo, Miss., Feb. 5, 1936; s. Sherman Milton and Fern Laura Taylor; m. Sherry Yvonne Taylor, Apr. 5, 1985; children: Rubby, Doug, Steven, Tammy, Michael, Aaron, Jacet. LLD, London Inst., 1975; PhD, Pepperdine Coll., 1979; LLD, U. Fla., Gainesville, 1980. Dep. sheriff Marion County Sheriff, Salem, Oreg., 1965—68; chief of police Madras Police Dept., Oreg., 1968—80; dir. police U. Oreg. Health Sci., Portland, 1979; dist. comdr. Oreg. Liquer Control Enforcement, Portland, Oreg., 1980—90; investigator Portland, Oreg., 1990—. Author: Illegal Financial Assistance, 1982, Investigatio Techniques, 1982. Sgt. USMC, 1952—57, POW, Korea. Decorated Silver Star medal US Marine Corp, Purple Heart; recipient Outstanding Police Performance, State of Oreg., 1982. Mem.: Internal. Assn. Investigators, Oreg. Police Chiefs, Marine Corps. Assn., Am. Legion, Amvets, VFW (life). Democrat. Protestant. Home: 8181 SE 162nd Ave Portland OR 97236

TAYLOR, JAMES JOHN, finance educator; b. Mpls., July 26, 1940; s. James John and Mary Elizabeth (Mason) T.; m. Margaret Claire Zacha, Dec. 28, 1976; children: Jerry William, John Allen. BA, Oblate Coll. of S.W., 1966; MEd, St. Louis U., 1969, MBA in Fin., 1972; cert. of advanced studies, Harvard U., 1977; PhD in Adminstrn., Curriculum and Instrn, U. Nebr., 2002. Dept. head, tchr. Althoff High Sch., Belleville, Ill., 1966-71; asst. to controller U. of South Fla., Tampa, 1972-79; project mgr. W.Va. Bd. of Regents, Morgantown, 1979-83; prin., project dir. Am. Mgmt. Systems, Arlington, Va., 1983-90; mng. cons. Taylor Mgmt. Group, Arlington, 1990-91; v.p. bus. and fin. Guam C.C., 1991—2005; assoc. prof. fin. and econs. U. Guam, 2005—. Founder, treas. Guam Ednl. Radio Found., KPRG-FM, 1992-99; organizer Chief Bus. Officers of the Pacific, 1997, 98, 99; sec., trustee Govt. Guam Retirement Bd., 2004—; trustee, bd. govs. Guam C.C. Found., 1996-2007. Mem. adv. com. on spl. edn. Arlington Sch. Bd., 1981-83; founder, producer St. Louis High Sch. Film Makers Festival, 1968-72; contbr. articles to profl. jours. Bd. trustees Govt. Guam Retirement Fund, 2004. Founding mem. Harvard Club at Nat. Press Club; mem. Rotary. Avocations: photography, bridge, scuba diving. Home: 180 G Cruz Hts Talofofo GU 96915-3736

TAYLOR, JAMES WALTER, business and management educator; b. St. Cloud, Minn., Feb. 15, 1933; s. James T. and Nina C. Taylor; m. Joanne Syktte, Feb. 3, 1956; children: Theodore James, Samuel Bennett, Christopher John. BBA, U. Minn., Mpls., 1957; MBA, NYU, 1960; DBA, U. So. Calif., LA, 1975. Mgr. rsch. divsn. Atlantic Refining, Phila., 1960-65; dir. new product devel. Hunt-Wesson Foods, Fullerton, Calif., 1965-72; mng. dir. Digital Workbook Internat., LLC, Laguna Beach, Calif., 1975—. Vis. prof. U. Calif., Irvine; cons. Smithkline Beecham Corp., Tokyo, Govt. of Portugal, Lisbon, Austrade, Govt. of Australia, Hagenfeldt-Affarerna AB, Stockholm. Author: Profitable New Product Strategies, 1984, How to Create a Winning Business Plan, 1986, Competitive Marketing Strategies, 1986, The 101 Best Performing Companies in America, 1987, The Complete Manual for Developing Winning Strategic Plans, 1988, Every Manager's Survival Guide, 1989, Developing Winning Strategic Plans, 1990, How to Develop Successful Advertising Plans, 1993, Marketing Planning: A Step by Step Guide, 1997, The Marketing Strategy and Planning Workbook, 2004. Fulbright scholar Ministry of Industry, Lisbon, Portugal, 1986-87, U. We. Sydney, Australia, 1989-90; recipient Merit award Calif. State U., 1986-90. Home: 2719 Via Casa Loma San Clemente CA 92672

TAYLOR, JASON PAUL, professional football player; b. Pitts., Sept. 1, 1974; m. Katina Taylor; 2 children. BA in Polit. Sci. & Criminal Justice, U. Akron, 1997. Defensive End Miami Dolphins, 1997—. Founder Jason Taylor Found., 2004—. Named NFL Defensive Player of Yr., AP, 2006; named to AFC Pro Bowl Team, 2000, 2002, 2004—06, NFL All Pro Team, 2006. Office: c/o Miami Dolphins 7500 SW 30th St Davie FL 33314 *

TAYLOR, JEAN ELLEN, mathematics professor, researcher; d. Richard and Donna Taylor; m. John Mark Guckenheimer, Apr. 18, 1969 (div.); m. Frederick J. Almgren, Oct. 6, 1973 (dec. 1997); 1 child, Karen Taylor Almgren stepchildren: Ann Almgren, Robert Almgren; m. William T. Golden, July 8, 2001 (div.). AB summa cum laude, Mt. Holyoke Coll., 1966, DSc (hon.), 2001; MS in Chemistry, U. Calif., Berkeley, 1968; MS in Math., U. Warwick, Coventry, Eng., 1971; PhD, Princeton U., 1973. Instr. MIT, Cambridge, Mass., 1972-73; asst. prof. Rutgers U., New Brunswick, N.J., 1973-77, assoc. prof., 1977-82, prof., 1982-87, prof. II, 1987—2002, prof. emeritus, 2002—; vis. scholar Courant Inst., NYU, 2002—. Mem. Inst. for Advanced Study, Princeton, N.J., 1974-75, 77-78, 85, 95-96; Miller vis. prof. U. Calif., Berkeley, 1999; vis. scholar Stanford (Calif.) U., 1989; visitor Princeton U., 1980-81; mem. Geometry Computing Group (permanent faculty of the Nat. Sci. and Tech. Ctr. for Computational and Visualization of Geometric Structures); cons. Nat. Bur. Standards, Gaithersburg, Md.; guest expert 3-2-1 Contact program Children's TV Workshop, 1978; mem. exec. com. Conf. Bd. of the Math. Scis., 2000-2002; lectr. in field. Contbr. articles in math., physics and materials sci. to profl. jours. Mem. at large bd. dir. Black Rock Forest Consortium. Recipient Presdl. Pub. Svc. award Rutgers Coll. Class of 1962, 1999; Sloan Found. fellow, 1976-78; NSF grad. fellow, 1966-72, hon. fellow Woodrow Wilson Found.; rsch. grantee NSF, 1973—97, Air Force Office Sci. Rsch., 1987-94; vis. scholar Phi Beta Kappa, 2006—. Fellow: AAAS (bd. dir. 1995—99, chair sect. 2004—05), Assn. for Women in Sci., Am. Acad. Arts and Scis.; mem.: Soc. for Indsl. and Applied Math., Assn. for Women in Math. (pres. 1999—2001, nominating com. chair 2003—04), Math Assn. Am., Materials Rsch. Soc., Am. Math. Soc. (nominating com. 1977—78, coun. 1984—89, exec. com. 1985—88, v.p. 1994—97, trustee 2003—, chair bd. trustees 2006—), Assn. Princeton Grad. Alumni (governing bd. 1999—2003), Phi Beta Kappa. Democrat. Achievements include proof, in the context of Geometric Measure Theory, that the singular set in a mathematical model for soap bubble clusters and soap films on wire frames is what is physcally observed, thereby solving a 100 year old problem; development of mathematical models for treating shapes of surfaces and interfaces for crystalline materials and use of them to model crystal growth. Office: Courant Inst 251 Mercer St New York NY 10012 Business E-Mail: jtaylor@cims.nyu.edu.

TAYLOR, JEFF, Internet company executive; Degree, U. Mass. at Amherst; certificate, Owner/Pres. Mgmt. (OPM) Program, Exec. Edn., Harvard Bus. Sch.; PhD (hon.), Bentley Coll. Head recruitment ad agency Adion; founder, chief monster Monster Board (formerly Monster.com now Monster, purchased by TMP Worldwide Inc. in 1995, now Monster Worldwide, Inc.), 1994—2005; global dir. Interactive for Monster Worldwide, 2005; founder, CEO Eons, Inc., Boston, 2006—; launched Eons People, 2006—, Cranky.com, 2007—. Bd. advisor InternetRealEstate.com; frequent spkr. at tech., advertising and human capital conferences; spkr. at numerous colleges and universities across the country. Co-author: Monster Careers, 2004. Bd. dir. Nat. Jr. Achievement, Mass. Jr. Achievement, Wang Ctr. for Performing Arts, Boston. Achievements include helped pioneer job searching on the internet; created Eons, Inc., a 50+ media company inspiring a generation of boomers and seniors to live the biggest life possible; In March 2000, Taylor became the Blimp Waterskiing World Champion. Office: Eons Inc 31 5th St Boston MA 02129 Office Phone: 617-886-5400. Office Fax: 617-241-0617. *

TAYLOR, JEFFREY A., prosecutor; m. Marcia Taylor. BA, Stanford U.; JD, Harvard Law Sch. Law clk. Hon. John C. Mowbray, Supreme Ct. Nev., 1991—92; asst. US atty. (so. dist.) Calif. US Dept. Justice, 1995—99, US atty. dist. DC, 2006—; counsel to US Senate Com. on Judiciary, 1999—2002; counselor to atty. gen. John Ashcroft and Alberto Gonzales, 2002—06. Office: US Atty's Office 555 4th St NW Washington DC 20530 Office Phone: 202-514-7566. *

TAYLOR, JIM, scriptwriter, film director; MFA, NYU. Dir., writer: Memory Lane, 1995, The Lost Cause, 2004, writer: screenplays Citizen Ruth, 1996, Election, 1999, Jurassic Park III, 2001, About Schmidt, 2002, Sideways, 2004 (Academy award for best adapted screenplay, 2005); dir.: (films) Living Will, 1999.

TAYLOR, JIMMY LYNN, retired family practice physician, administrator; b. Franklin County, NC, May 11, 1936; s. Herman Benjamin and Ruby Lynn (Perry) T.; m. Dorothy Keenum, Sept. 4, 1960; children: Gregory Scott, Sonya Lynn Taylor Loper. AA, Mars Hill Coll., 1956; BS, Wake Forest U., 1958; MD, Wake Forest U. Sch. Medicine, 1962. Postdoctoral fellow Greenville (S.C.) Gen. Hosp., 1962-63; staff physician USPHS Indian Hosp., Pine Ridge, SD, 1963-65, chief of obstetrics, 1964-65; family physician, co-founder Monroe (N.C.) Family Med. Ctr., 1965, family physician, ptnr., 1965-95; student physician Wingate (N.C.) U., 1987-94; med. dir. Brian Ctr. Nursing Facility, Monroe, 1992-95. H.S. team physician, 1965—75. Lt. comdr. USPHS, 1963-65. Recipient Head Start Child Care Achievement award N.C. Head Start Assn., 1990. Fellow Am. Acad. Family Physicians; mem. Am. Bd. Family Practice (diplomate), N.C. Acad. Family Physicians, N.C. Med. Soc., Union County Med. Soc. (pres. 1976-77). Republican. Baptist. Avocations: golf, fishing, gardening, bridge, collecting autographed first edition books. Home: 1657 Pageland Hwy Monroe NC 28112-8737 Office: Monroe Family Med Ctr PA 1420 E Franklin St Monroe NC 28112-5160 Personal E-mail: jtaylor28112@yahoo.com, jtaylorb@carolina.rr.com.

TAYLOR, JOB, III, lawyer; b. NYC, Feb. 18, 1942; s. Job II and Anne Harrison (Flinchbaugh) T.; m. Mary C. August, Oct. 24, 1964 (div. 1978); children: Whitney August, Job IV; m. Sally Lawson, May 31, 1980; 1 child, Alexandra Anne. BA, Washington & Jefferson Coll., 1964; JD, Coll. William and Mary, 1971. Bar: N.Y. 1972, Mass. 2003, U.S. Dist. Ct. (no., so. ea. and we. dists.) N.Y. 1973, U.S. Ct. Appeals (2d cir.) 1973, U.S. Ct. Claims 1974, U.S. Tax Ct. 1974, U.S. Supreme Ct. 1975, U.S. Ct. Appeals (9th cir.) 1976, U.S. Ct. Mil. Appeals 1977, U.S. Ct. Appeals (D.C. and 10th cirs.) 1977, D.C. 1981, U.S. Ct. Internat. Trade 1981, U.S. Ct. Appeals (fed. cir.) 1982, U.S. Dist. Ct. (no. dist.) Calif. 1983, U.S. Ct. Appeals (6th cir.) U.S. Dist. Ct., 1987, U.S. Ct. Appeals (3d cir.) 1990, U.S. Dist. Ct. Conn. 1996. Ptnr. Olwine, Connelly, Chase, O'Donnell & Weyher, NYC, 1971-85, Latham & Watkins, NYC, 1985—. Served to lt. USN, 1964-68. Mem. ABA, Assn. Bar City N.Y., La Confrerie des Chevaliers du Tastevin, Racquet and Tennis Club, Wee Burn Country Club (Darien, Conn.). Republican. Episcopalian. Avocations: squash, tennis, golf, reading. Office Phone: 508-240-3069. Personal E-mail: job.taylor@lw.com.

TAYLOR, JOE CLINTON, judge; b. Durant, Okla., Mar. 28, 1942; s. Luther Clinton and Virena (Parker) T.; m. Margaret Pearl Byers, June 8, 1963; children: Marna Joanne, Leah Alison, Jocelyn Camille. Student, Southeastern State Coll., 1960—62; BA, Okla. State U., 1965; JD, U. Okla., 1968. Bar: Okla. 1968. Pvt. practice, Norman, Okla., 1968-69; apptd. spl. dist. judge Durant, 1969-72; assoc. dist. judge Bryan County, Okla., 1972-76; dist. judge, chief judge 19th Dist. Ct., Bryan County, Okla., 1976-93; presiding judge Southeastern Okla. Jud. Adminstrv. Dist., 1984-92, Choctaw Tribal Ct., 1979-83; pres. Okla. Jud. Conf., 1987-88; chmn. Assembly Presiding Judges, 1989-90; presiding judge trial divsn. Okla. Ct. on the Judiciary, 1991-93, Okla. Ct. of Tax Rev., 1992—; judge Okla. Ct. of Civil Appeals, Tulsa, 1993—. Chmn. bd. dirs. Durant Youth Svcs., 1976-93; bd. dirs. Bryan County Youth Svcs., Inc., 1971-93. Lt. Col. USAR. Mem. Lions, Phi Sigma Epsilon, Delta Theta Phi. Mem. Ch. of Christ. Home: PO Box 329 Durant OK 74702-0329 Office: Ct Civil Appeals 601 State Bldg 440 S Houston Ave Tulsa OK 74127-8922 E-mail: joe.taylor@oscn.net.

TAYLOR, JOEL SANFORD, government agency administrator, retired lawyer; b. Hazleton, Pa., Oct. 8, 1942; s. Robert Joseph and Alice Josephine (Sanford) T.; m. Donna Rae Caron, Mar. 26, 1967; children: Jason, Adam, Jeremy. BA in Polit. Sci. and Internat. Rels., Swarthmore Coll., 1965; LLB, Columbia U., 1968. Bar: NY 1969, US Ct. Appeals (2d cir.) 1970, US Dist. Ct. (no. dist.) Ohio 1974, US Supreme Ct. 1974, US Dist. Ct. (so. dist.) Ohio 1975, US Ct. Appeals (6th cir.) 1975, US Dist. Ct. (ea. dist.) Ky. 1979. Law clk. hon. Constance B. Motley US Dist. Ct., NYC, 1968-69; assoc. Paul, Weiss, Rifkind, Wharton & Garrison, NYC, 1969-72; exec. asst. Ohio Office Budget and Mgmt., Columbus, 1972-74; asst. atty. gen. Ohio Atty. Gen., Columbus, 1974-83, chief counsel, 1983-91; ptnr. Dinsmore & Shohl, Columbus, 1991-2000; dir. fin. and mgmt. City of Columbus, 2000—. Pres. Ohio Sundry Claims Bd., Columbus, 1972-74, Ohio State Controlling Bd., Columbus, 1973-74; mem., bd. trustees Ohio State Tchrs. Retirement Sys., Columbus, 1986-91, Solid Waste Authority Ctrl. Ohio, 2001—. Mem.: Govt. Fin. Officers Assn., Nature Conservancy, Nat. Wildlife Fedn., Columbia Law Alumni Assn. Office: City Hall 90 W Broad St Columbus OH 43215-9000 Home Phone: 614-237-5854; Office Phone: 614-645-7036. E-mail: jstaylor@columbus.gov.

TAYLOR, JOHN BRIAN, economist, educator, former federal agency administrator; b. Yonkers, NY, Dec. 8, 1946; s. John Joseph and Lorraine (Crowley) T.; m. Raye Allyn Price, Dec. 30, 1972; children: Jennifer Lynn, John Andrew. AB in Econs. summa cum laude, Princeton U., 1968; PhD, Stanford U., 1973. Asst. prof. econs. Columbia U., NYC, 1973-77, assoc. prof., 1977-79, prof., 1979-80; prof. econs. and pub. affairs Princeton U., 1980-84; prof. econs. Stanford U., 1984—, dir. Ctr. for Econ. Policy Rsch., 1994-97, dir. Introductory Econs. Ctr., 1997-2001; under sec. for internat. affairs U.S. Dept. Treasury, Washington, 2001—05. Vis. prof. econs. Yale U., 1980; sr. staff economist Pres.'s Coun. Econ. Advisers, 1976—77, mem., 1989—91; econometric cons. Townsend-Greenspan and Co., NY, 1978—81; rsch. advisor Fed. Res. Bank, Phila., 1981—84; rsch. assoc. Nat. Bur. Econ. Rsch., 1980—; rsch. economist Bank of Japan, Tokyo, 1987, hon. adviser, 1994—2001; panel of econ. advisers Congl. Budget Office, 1995—2001; sr. fellow Hoover Instn., 1996—. Author: (non-fiction) Macroeconomics, 1986, Macroeconomic Policy in the World Economy, 1993, Economics, 1995, Unemployment, Inflation, and Monetary Policy, 1998, Monetary Policy Rules, 1999, Handbook of Macroeconomics, 2000, Global Financial Warriors: The Untold Story of International Finance in the Post 9/11 World, 2007; co-editor: Am. Econ. Rev., 1985—89; assoc. editor: Econometrica, 1981—85, Jour. Econ. Dynamics and Control, 1978—85, Jour. Monetary Econs., 1978—83, Jour. Econ. Perspectives, 1997—2001, mng. editor: Internat. Jour. Ctrl. Banking, 2005—; contbr. articles to profl. jours. NSF grantee, 1979-81, 81-83, 83-86, 86-89, 92-95; Guggenheim Found. fellow, 1983-84. Fellow Econometric Soc., Am. Acad. of Arts and Sci.; mem. Am. Econ. Assn. (exec. com. 1991-94, v.p. 2000-01). Office Phone: 650-723-9677. Business E-Mail: johnbtaylor@stanford.edu.

TAYLOR, JOHN CALVIN, dentist; b. Cin., July 22, 1914; s. John Calvin Taylor V and Magdala Elizabeth Siehl; m. Adah Packard Boggs, Mar. 7, 1941; children: Sarah, Margaret, Virginia, John, Frederick, Alison, Carla. BSc, Muskingum Coll., 1937; BD, Cedarville Sem., 1939; DDS, U. Pitts., 1949; cert. excellence in Hindi and Urdu, Lang. Sch., Landour, India, 1940-41. Diploma Acad. Gen. Dentistry. Missionary Reformed Presbyn. Synod, Roorkee, India, 1939-46; moderator, pastor Reformed Presbyn., Pitts., Fairview, Pa., 1946-47; nat. missions missionary Presbyn. Bd. Home Missions, Pitts., Tyre, Pa., 1947-52; missionary dentist United Presbyn., Pitts., Seattle, 1953-59; dir. Meth. Mission Hosp. Dental Clinic, Bariely, India, 1954—55; founder Dental Clinic Landour Cmty. Hosp., Mussoorie, India, 1955-59; pres. Rotary Club Internat., Mount Union, Pa., 1964-65; pastor 3 chs. Mt. Union, Johnsonburg and St. Mary areas, 1964-68; founder Shanta Bhawan Hosp. Dental Clinic, Katmandu, Nepal, 1968, Missionary Dentist, Inc., 1977; dental missionary svc. E.L.W.A. Hosp., Liberia, 1977, Tank Hosp., Pakistan, 1980—81, Sahiwal Hosp., Pakistan, 1981, Shell Clinics, Ecuador, 1983; provider free dental care India, 1978—2001; founder Oral Clinic Ctr., Dera Dun, India, 1981—. Tchr. emergency dentistry Vellore (India) Med. Coll., 1958; dentist Youth With a Mission, Mercy Ship, Hawaii, 1985. Author: Wildlife in India's Tiger Kingdom, 1980, Face the Devil's Roar, 1995, God's Kingdom helps Animal Kingdoms, 2005 Co-founder, life mem. Wildlife Preservation Soc., Dehra-Dun, India, 1954—, organizer, founder Rajpur Wildlife Park, 1954—. Recipient Cert. of Honor for 50 Yrs. of Dedicated Svc. to Dentistry, ADA, 1999. Mem. Herminie Lions Club (fgn. chmn., Lions Hat award 1993), N.Am. Hunting Club, NRA. Republican. Presbyterian. Avocations: zoology, hunting, taxidermy, photography, music. Home Phone: 724-446-7732; Office Phone: 724-446-7732. Personal E-mail: tgrtlr@juno.com.

TAYLOR, JOHN CHESTNUT, III, lawyer; b. NYC, Jan. 7, 1928; s. John Chestnut and Jean Elizabeth (Willis) T.; m. Dolores Yvonne Sunstrom, Nov. 17, 1950; children: Jane Willis, John Sunstrom, Anne Holliday. BA, Princeton U., 1947; LL.B., Yale U., 1950. Bar: N.Y. 1950, D.C. 1972. Assoc. Paul, Weiss, Rifkind, Wharton & Garrison, NYC, 1950, 52-60, ptnr., 1961-85, 87-91, of counsel, 1986-87, 92—; exec. v.p., dir. AEA Investors Inc., NYC, 1985-86, pres., 1986-87. Bd. dirs. AFS Intercultural Programs, Inc., N.Y.C., 1972-80, trustee, 1973-79, chmn., 1975-79; trustee Carnegie Corp. N.Y., N.Y.C., 1975-84, chmn., 1979-84; trustee, mem. exec. com. Devereux Found., 1992-2003, vice chmn., 1994-2003. Served to capt. JAGC, AUS, 1950-52. Mem. Assn. of Bar of City of N.Y., Order of Coif, Phi Beta Kappa, Phi Delta Phi. Democrat. Home: 64 Meadow Lakes Hightstown NJ 08520 Office: Paul Weiss Rifkind Wharton & Garrison 1285 Avenue Of The Americas New York NY 10019-6064 E-mail: budsunny@verizon.net.

TAYLOR, JOHN E., foundation administrator, lawyer; BA, Northeastern U., 1973, JD, 1980. Pres., CEO Nat. Cmty. Reinvestment Coalition. Chmn. Nat. Neighbors; appointed to Cmty. Devel. Fin. Insts. (CDFI) Fund; mem. bd. dirs. Rainbow/PUSH Coalition, Leadership Conf. for Civil Rights; past bd. mem. Consumer Adv. Coun., Fed. Reserve Bank Bd., Fannie Mae Housing Impact Div., Freddie Mac Housing Adv. Bd.; spkr. in field. Guest coor. ABC's Nightline, CBS, Fox news, CNN, CSPAN, Chgo. Tribune, NY Times, Washington Post; contbr. articles to profl. jours. Recipient Martin Luther King, Jr. Peace Award, US Congl. Citation Award, Award for Excellence in Cmty. Econ. Devel., State of Mass. Office: Nat Cmty Reinvestment Coalition Ste 900 727 15th St Washington DC 20005 Office Phone: 202-628-8866. Office Fax: 202-628-9800. E-mail: jtaylor@ncrc.org.

TAYLOR, JOHN JACKSON (JAY TAYLOR), writer, retired diplomat; b. Little Rock, Dec. 4, 1931; s. Alfred Wesley and Annie Laurie (Cain) T.; m. Elizabeth Rose, July 9, 1954; children: John Jr., Laurie, Amy, Cynthia. BA, Vanderbilt U., 1952; MA, U. Mich., 1968. 3d sec. U.S. Fgn. Svc., Accra, Ghana, 1957-59, 2d sec. Taichung and Taipei, China, 1960-65; Chinese affairs analyst Dept. State, Washington, 1966-67; staff assoc. Ctr. for Chinese Studies, U. Mich., Ann Arbor, 1967-68; U.S. consul Sarawak, Sabah and Brunei, Kuching, Malaysia, 1968-70; chief external affairs reporting U.S. Consulate Gen., Hong Kong, 1970-74; officer-in-charge Chinese affairs Dept. State, Washington, 1974-75; staff mem. E. Asian affairs Nat. Security Coun., Washington, 1975-77; polit. counselor U.S. Embassy, Pretoria/Capetown, 1977-80, polit. cons. Peking, 1980-82; rsch. fellow Fairbank Ctr. for East Asian Studies Harvard U., Cambridge, Mass., 1982-83; dir. East Asian analysis Dept. State, Washington, 1983-85; dep. asst. sec. state Bur. Intelligence and Rsch., Dept. State, Washington, 1986-87; chief of mission U.S. Interests Sect., Havana, Cuba, 1987-90; diplomat in residence Carter Presdl. Ctr., Emory U., 1990-92; sr. mem. State Task Force 2000, 1992-93; sr. assoc. Global Bus. Access; assoc. in rsch. Fairbank Ctr. for East Asian Studies, Harvard U.; prodr., writer, dir. ?Why Prodns. Guest faculty Emory U. and Spelman Coll. Author: China and Southeast Asia, 1974, 1976, The Dragon and the Wild Goose, 1987, 1990, The Rise and Fall of Totalitarianism, 1993, The Generalissimo's Son, 2000, (documentary) Ubuntu, African and Afrikaner, 2000; contbr. China and National Security, 1985, columns in newspapers Washington Post, L.A. Times, N.Y. Times. Served as Naval Aviator with USMC, 1953-57. Mem.: Wash. Inst. Fgn. Affairs, Fgn. Svc. Assn. E-mail: jaytaylor888@sprintmail.com.

TAYLOR, JOHN JOSEPH, nuclear engineer, researcher; b. Hackensack, NJ, Feb. 27, 1922; s. John J.D. and Johanna F. (Thibideau) T.; m. Lorraine Crowley, Feb. 5, 1943; children: John B., Nancy M., Susan M. BA, St. John's U., Jamaica, NY, 1942, DSc (hon.), 1975; MS, U. Notre Dame, Ind., 1947. Mathematician Bendix Aviation Corp., Teterboro, NJ, 1946-47; engr. Kellex Corp., NYC, 1947-50; v.p. water reactor divsn. Westinghouse Electric Corp., Pitts., 1950-81; v.p. nuc. power Electric Power Rsch. Inst., Palo Alto, Calif., 1981-95; energy cons., 1995—. Adv. com. Oak Ridge Nat. Lab., Tenn., 1973-83, Brookhaven Nat. Lab., Upton, NY, 1986-92, Inst. for Nuc. Power Ops., 1988-95; adv. com. Argonne Nat. Lab., Ill., 1980-86, bd. dirs.; cons. Office Tech. Assessment, Washington, 1975-93; internat. adv. group IAEA, Vienna, Austria, 1992-95; nuc. rsch. rev. com. NRC, 1995-97; mem. US-Russian Commn. on Weapons Plutonium Disposition, 1996-2001, Nat. Acad. Bd. Radioactive Waste Mgmt., 1998-2001, DOE Nuc. Energy Rsch. Adv. Bd., 1998-2002; co-chair Atoms for Peace Study, Livermore Lab., 2003-04; com. on rev. of Dept. Energy Nuc. Energy R&D, Nat. Acad., 2006. Co-author: Reactor Shielding Manual, 1953, Naval Reactor Physics Manual, 1956, Nuclear Power, Policy and Prospects, 1987, Management and Disposition of Excess Weapons Plutonium, 1995; contbr. articles to profl. jours. Bd. regents emeritus St. Mary's Coll., Moraga, Calif., Bd. of Regents, St. Patrick's U. Calif. Lt. (j.g.) USN, 1942—45. Recipient Order of Merit Westinghouse Electric Corp., 1957, George Westinghouse Gold medal ASME, 1990. Fellow AAAS, Am. Phys. Soc., Am. Nuc. Soc. (bd. dirs., Walter Zinn award 1993); mem. NAE (chair), Elec. Power/Energy Sys. Engrs. Republican. Roman Catholic. Office: Electric Power Rsch Inst PO Box 10412 3412 Hillview Ave Palo Alto CA 94304-1344 Home: 620 Sand Hill Rd Apt 303b Palo Alto CA 94304-2069 Office Phone: 650-855-2030.

TAYLOR, JOHN LOCKHART, retired municipal official; b. NYC, Nov. 4, 1927; s. Floyd and Marian (Lockhart) T.; m. Barbara Becker, July 19, 1952; children: Catherine Fair, Robert, William, Susan. AB, Middlebury Coll., 1952; M.Govtl. Adminstrn., U. Pa., 1956. Reporter Providence Jour.-Bull., 1952-54; adminstrv. intern City of Xenia, Ohio, 1955-56; mcpl. mgr. Borough of Narberth, Pa., 1956-60, Twp. of Lakewood, N.J., 1960-64; asst. city mgr. Fresno, Calif., 1964-65; city mgr., 1965-68, Kansas City, Mo., 1968-74, Berkeley, Calif., 1974-76; lectr. U. Pa., 1957-58, Golden Gate U., 1977; sr. urban mgmt. specialist Stanford Research Inst., 1977-80; dir. Internat. Devel. Center, 1980-82; clk. of bd. suprs. City of San Francisco, 1982-98, spl. asst., 1998—. Pres. Calif. Clks. Bd. Suprs. Assn., 1988-89. Served with USN, 1945-48. Mem. Internat. City Mgrs. Assn., Mcpl. Execs. Assn. (pres. 1991-93, 98). Address: 1005 Creston Rd Berkeley CA 94708-1503 E-mail: misterclerk@sbcglobal.net.

TAYLOR, JOHN MCKOWEN, lawyer; b. Baton Rouge, Jan. 20, 1924; s. Benjamin Brown and May (McKowen) T.; 1 child, John McKowen. BA, La. State U., 1948, JD, 1950. Bar: La. 1950, U.S. Ct. Appeals (5th cir.) 1959, U.S. Supreme Ct. 1960. Assoc. Taylor, Porter, Brooks, Fuller & Phillips, Baton Rouge, 1950-55, Huckaby, Seale, Kelton & Hayes, Baton Rouge, 1955-58; ptnr. Kelton & Taylor, Baton Rouge, 1958-61; pvt. practice, Baton Rouge, 1961—. With AUS, 1943—46, maj. USAR, 1946—, ATO, ETO, PTO. Mem. ABA, AAAS, La. State Bar Assn., Baton Rouge Bar Assn., Mil. Order of World Wars, Am. Radio Relay League, Baton Rouge Country Club, City Club of Baton Rouge, Baton Rouge Amateur Radio Club, Camelot Club, SAR, Sigma Chi, Pi Gamma Mu, Phi Delta Phi. Republican. Presbyterian. Home and Office: 2150 Kleinert Ave Baton Rouge LA 70806-6712 Office Phone: 225-343-1928. E-mail: jmcktaylor@cox.net.

TAYLOR, JOHN READ, JR., financial management company executive; b. NYC, July 16, 1943; s. John Read and Patricia (Green) T.; m. Sandra Shackelford Brown, June 28, 1969 (div. 1988); 1 child, Louise Tiffany; m. Joyce Manis, Jan. 28, 1989; 1 child, John Read III. AB, Princeton U., 1965; postgrad. in polit. sci., U. N.C., 1966-69. Asst. mgr. Chem. Bank, NYC, 1969-73; asst. v.p. First Nat. Bank Chgo., 1973-74; v.p. Citibank, NYC, 1974-78, Gessellschaft fur Trendanalysen, NYC, 1978-79; pres. EMCOR Mgmt., NYC, 1979-81; chmn., CEO, CIO FX Concepts, Inc., NYC, 1981—. Chmn. J3 Biologics, Inc., NYC, 1992-98, US Transgenics, Inc., 1999-02, Am. Integrated Biologics, Inc., 2002-07, Am. Detection Techs., Inc., 2002-, Inspiration Biopharms., Inc., 2005-. Bd. dirs. Franklin Coll. Switzerland, Lugano, 1975—, chmn., 1980-90, vice chmn. 1995-01; dir. Hemophilia Assn. NY, 1990-06; chmn. Coalition Hemophilia B, NY, 1990-07. Home: 45 E 89th St New York NY 10128-1251 Office: FX Concepts Inc 225 W 34th St Ste 710 New York NY 10122-0710

TAYLOR, JOSEPH HOOTON, JR., radio astronomer, physicist; b. Phila., Mar. 29, 1941; s. Joseph Hooton and Sylvia Hathaway (Evans) T.; m. Marietta Bisson, Jan. 3, 1976. BA in Physics, Haverford Coll., 1963; PhD in Astronomy, Harvard U., 1968; DSc (hon., U. Chgo., 1985, U. Mass., 1994. Research fellow, lectr. Harvard U., 1968-69; asst. prof. astronomy U. Mass., Amherst, 1969-72, assoc. prof., 1973-77, prof., 1977-81; prof. physics Princeton U., 1980—, James McDonnell Disting. prof. physics, 1986—, dean of faculty, 1997—2003. Author: Pulsars, 1977. Recipient Dannie Heineman prize in astrophysics, Am. Inst. Physics/Am. Astron. Soc., 1980, prize in gravitation and cosmology, Tomalla Found., 1985, Magellanic Premium award, Am. Philos. Soc., 1990, Einstein prize laureate, Albert Einstein Found., 1993, Wolf prize in physics, Wolf Found., Israel, 1992, Nobel Prize in Physics, Nobel Found., 1993, Carty Award for Advancement of Scis., Schwartzchild Medal; fellow MacArthur fellow, 1981. Fellow: Am. Phys. Soc., Am. Acad. Arts and Scis.; mem.: Internat. Astron. Union, Internat. Sci. Radio Union, Am. Astron. Soc., Am. Philos. Soc., NAS (Draper Medal). Mem. Soc. Of Friends. Achievements include discovery of first binary pulsar - a twin star system that provides a rare natural laboratory in which to test Albert Einstein's prediction that moving objects emit gravitational waves. Home: 272 Hartley Ave Princeton NJ 08540-5656 Office: Princeton U Dept Physics 215 Jadwin Hall PO Box 708 Princeton NJ 08544-0001 Business E-Mail: joe@pulsar.princeton.edu.

TAYLOR, JUNE RUTH, retired minister; b. Annapolis, Md., June 27, 1932; d. Benjamin and Naomi Medora (Dill) Michaelson; m. Thomas Wayne Taylor, Mar. 20, 1954; children: Rebecca Susan Taylor DeLameter, Michael Steven. AB, Goucher Coll., 1952; MRE, Presbyn. Sch. of Christian Edn., Richmond, Va., 1954; MDiv., McCormick Theol. Sem., 1978. Ordained to ministry Presbyn. Ch. (U.S.A.), 1976. Min. Christian Edn. Congl. United Ch. of Christ, Arlington Heights, Ill., 1974-79; dir. pastoral svcs. Presbyn. U. Hosp., Pitts., 1979-89; dir. chaplaincy svcs. Ephrata (Pa.) Community Hosp., 1991-96; ret., 1996; interim pastor Kreutz Creek Presbyn. Ch., Hellam, Pa., 2001; interim parish vis. Highland Presbyn. Ch., Lancaster, Pa., 2004. Chaplain Rush-Presbyn. St. Luke's Med. Ctr., Chgo., 1976-78; chair exec. com. Presbyn. Assn. Specialized Pastoral Ministries, Louisville, 1987-89; bd. dirs. Cocalico Place; parish assoc. Krentz Creek Presbyn. Ch., 2007-. Book reviewer in field. Fellow Assn. Profl. Chaplains (sec. exec. com. 1985-87); mem. Soc. Chaplains, Hosp. Assn. Pa. (pres. 1983), Assn. Profl. Chaplains (cert.), Assn. for Clin. Pastoral Edn. (clin.), Rotary (liaison to Boys and Girls Club S.W. Pitts. chpt. 1990-91, v.p., program chair Denver-Adamstown club 1996-97, pres.-elect 1997-98), York North Rotary Club (chmn. vocation svc. 2003-2005), Mental Health Assn. York County (bd. dirs. 1999—2005), Gamma Phi Beta Alumnae Club (pres. 1990-91).

TAYLOR, KATHLEEN (CHRISTINE TAYLOR), physical chemist, researcher; b. Cambridge, Mass., Mar. 16, 1942; d. John F. and Anna M. T. BA in Chemistry, Douglass Coll., New Brunswick, NJ, 1964; PhD in Phys. Chemistry, Northwestern U., 1968. Postdoctoral fellow U. Edinburgh, Scotland, 1968-70; assoc. sr. rsch. chemist Gen. Motors Rsch. Labs., Warren, Mich., 1970-74, sr. rsch. chemist, 1974-75, asst. phys. chemistry dept. head, 1975-83, environ. sci. dept. head, 1983-85, phys. chemistry dept. head, 1985-96; physics and phys. chemistry dept. head Gen. Motors Global Rsch. & Devel. Operations, Warren, Mich., 1995-98, materials and processes dir., 1998—2002. Recipient Mich. Sci. Trailblazer award Detroit Sci. Ctr., 1986. Fellow AAAS, Soc. Automotive Engrs. Internat., mem. NAE, Am. Chem. Soc. (Garvan medal 1989), Materials Rsch. Soc. (treas. 1984, 2d v.p. 1985, 1st v.p. 1986, pres. 1987), N.Am. Catalysis Soc., Am. Acad. Arts Sci, Sigma Xi.

TAYLOR, KATHLEEN P., hotel executive; married; 3 children. BA, U. Toronto, 1980; MBA, York U., 1984; JD, Osgoode Law Sch. Atty. Goodmans law firm; with Four Seasons Hotels and Resorts, 1989—, v.p., gen. counsel, 1992—93, sec., bd. dirs., 1993, sr. v.p., 1993—95, sr. v.p. corp. planning and devel., 1995—97, exec. v.p., 1997—98, exec. v.p., chief corp. officer, 1998—99, pres. worldwide bus. ops., 1999—. Dir. Royal Bank Canada, mem. audit com., human resources com. Cabinet mem. United Way of Greater Toronto; chair Endowment Giving portfolio; bd. dirs. The Hosp. for Sick Children Found. Mem.: Schulich Sch. Bus. (mem. internat. adv. coun.), Am. Hotel and Motel Assn. (mem. industry real estate financing adv. coun.), World Travel and Tourism Coun. Office: Four Seasons Hotels and Resorts 1165 Leslie St Toronto ON M3C 2K8 Canada

TAYLOR, KATHY, mayor; b. 1955; d. Jim and Lola Taylor; m. Bill Lobeck; 1 child. BA in Journalism, Okla. U., JD, 1981. Atty. pvt. practice; v.p., gen. counsel Thrifty Car Rental, 1988—2003; sec. Dept. Commerce State of Okla., 2003—05; mayor City of Tulsa, 2006—. Bd. mem. Tulsa Airport Authority; mem. Tulsa Parks and Recreation Bd.; bd. mem. Tulsa Energy Authority. Recipient Pinnacle award for community svc., Mayor's Commn. on Status of Women, 2003, Mona Lambird Spotlight award, Okla.

Bar Assn., 2003, Headliners award, Tulsa Press Club, 2004. Office: Office of Mayor City Hall 200 Civic Ctr 11th Fl Tulsa OK 74103 Office Phone: 918-596-7411. Office Fax: 918-596-9010. *

TAYLOR, KENNETH DOUGLAS, stockbroker, finance and computer consultant, educator; b. Topeka, Nov. 21, 1942; s. Olin Orlando and Lola Louise (Conley) T.; AB, George Washington U., 1964, MS in Stats., 1966; MS in Computer Sci. SUNY, 1990, PhD in Math. Eurotech, 1992, (univ. fellow); student of Peter Hilton; postgrad., McGill U., 1974, Bowdoin Coll., U. Montreal; m. Joy Ellen Rice, May 25, 1973 (div. Nov. 1981); m. Elizabeth Flanagan Brunner, May 6, 1995. Registered rep./stockbroker, options principal. Sr. programmer C-E-I-R, Inc., 1963, 69; instr. Army Map Svc., 1964-65; student instr. McGill U., 1966-71; rsch. assoc. U. Va. Med. Sch., 1972; fin. and computer cons., Plymouth, N.Y., 1973-87; computer scientist USAF, 1989-90; broker Russell Hawkes Assoc./Linsco/Pvt. Ledger, 1993-94, LESKO Fin Svcs, 1994—; sec. Richmond (Va.) Computer Club, 1977. Contbr. articles to profl. jours. Summer grantee NSF, Can. Research Council. Mem. ASTM, Am. Math. Soc. Home: PO Box 288 Montrose PA 18801-0288 Office: LESKO Fin Svcs Centre Plz 53 Chenango St Binghamton NY 13901-2820

TAYLOR, LANCE JEROME, economics professor; b. Montpelier, Idaho, May 25, 1940; s. Walter Jerome and Ruth (Robinson) T.; m. Yvonne S.M. Johnsson, May 31, 1963; children: Ian Lance, Signe Marguerite. BS with honors, Calif. Inst. Tech., 1962; PhD, Harvard U., 1968. Instr. econs. Harvard U., Cambridge, Mass., 1967-68, asst. prof., assoc. prof., 1970-74; research assoc. MIT, Cambridge, 1968-70, prof. econs., 1974-93, New Sch. for Social Rsch., NYC, 1993—. Vis. prof. U. Brasilia, 1974, Pontifical Cath. U. Rio de Janeiro, 1981, U. Delhi, 1987-88, Stockholm Sch. Econs., 1990; Marshall lectr. Cambridge U., 1986-87; cons. World Bank, UN, various fgn. govts. Author: Macro Models for Developing Countries, 1979, Models of Growth and Distribution for Brazil, 1980, Structuralist Macroeconomics, 1983, Varieties of Stabilization Experience, 1988, Income Distribution, Inflation, and Growth, 1991, The Market Meets its Match: Restructuring the Economies of Eastern Europe, 1994, Global Finance at Risk, 2000, Restructuring Macroeconomics: Structuralist Proposals and Critiques of the Mainstream, 2004. Fulbright fellow, 1962-63 Mem. Am. Econ. Assn., Royal Econ. Soc. Home: PO Box 378 Washington ME 04574-0378 Office: New School for Social Rsch Grad Faculty 65 5th Ave New York NY 10003-3089 E-mail: lance@blacklocust.com.

TAYLOR, LEIGH HERBERT, dean; b. Chgo., Oct. 23, 1941; s. Herbert and Leona Taylor; m. Nancy E. Young; children: Jennifer, Jeremiah. BA, U. Tulsa, 1964, JD, 1966; LLM, NYU, 1969. Bar: Okla. 1966, Ill. 1976. Trial atty. Civil Rights div. Dept. Justice, Washington, 1966-68; prof. DePaul U. Coll. Law, Chgo., 1969-77, asst. dean, 1972-73, assoc. dean, 1973-77; dean Coll. Law, Ohio No. U., Ada, 1977-78, Sch. Law Southwestern U., LA, 1978—2005, dean emeritus, prof. law emeritus, 2005—. Mem. adv. bd. 1st Woman's Bank of L.A., 1981-85; dir. Law Sch. Admissions Svcs., Inc., 1982-86; chmn. audit com. Law Sch. Admissions Coun., 1989-91, trustee, 1991-98, chair-elect, 1994-95, chair, 1995-97; mem. bd. trustees Coun. on Legal Edn. Opportunity, 1993-96, NALP Found., 1999—, chair-elect, 2002—. Editor-in-chief Tulsa Law Jour., 1966; author: Strategies for Law-Focused Education, 1977; (with others) Law in a New Land, 1972; mem. editorial bd. Family Law Quarterly, 1977-78. Bd. dirs. Criminal Def. Consortium Cook County (Ill.), Inc., 1975-77, L.A. Press Club Found., NALP Found., 1999—. With AUS, 1959. Fellow Am. Bar Found.; mem. ABA (accreditation com. 1991-95), Law in Am. Soc. Found., Ill. Bar Assn., Chgo. Bar Assn. (rec. sec.), L.A. County Bar Assn., Okla. Bar Assn. Office: Southwestern U Sch Law Office of Dean 675 S Westmoreland Ave Los Angeles CA 90005-3905 E-mail: ltaylor@swlaw.edu.

TAYLOR, LELAND BARIDON, lawyer; b. Poughkeepsie, NY, July 5, 1920; s. Alexander J. and Elsie Jane (Van Wyck) T.; m. Rosemary Olcott Coon, June 24, 1945; children: Barry Eugene, Craig Cameron, Mark Alexander, Meg Olcott Taylor Casey. BS, Syracuse U., 1942, JD, 1948. Bar: N.Y. 1948, U.S. Dist. Ct. (no. dist.) N.Y. 1954, U.S. Supreme Ct. 1958. Ptnr. Fitzgerald, Taylor, Pomeroy & Armstrong and predecessor, Cortland, NY, 1948-2000; of counsel Pomeroy, Armstrong & Casullo, Cortland, NY, 2000—. Judge City of Cortland, 1952-57; bd. dirs. First Nat. Bank of Dryden. Trustee Cortland Free Libr., 1950—. With Supply Corps, USNR, 1942-45. Named Cortland County Jr. C. of C. Young Man of Yr., 1952, N.Y. State Young Man of Yr., N.Y. State Jaycees, 1953, Syracuse U. Letterman of Distinction, 1977. Fellow N.Y. Bar Found., Am. Bar Found.; mem. ABA, N.Y. State Bar Assn. (v.p. 1974-76, sec. 1976-79, chmn. fin. com. 1979-84), Cortland County Bar Assn., Rotary (Paul Harris fellow), Masons. Presbyterian. Address: 16 Tompkins St Cortland NY 13045-2541 Home Phone: 607-753-9059.

TAYLOR, LEONARD STUART, engineering educator, consultant; b. NYC, Dec. 28, 1928; m. Lillian Rachel Schlang, Apr. 11, 1954; children: Robin Jolie, Allyn Lise. AB, Harvard Coll., 1951; MSc, N.Mex. State U., 1955, PhD, 1960. Microwave engr. Raytheon Mfg. Co., Bedford, Mass., 1950-55; research physicist Gen. Electric Co., Phila., 1960-63; assoc. prof. Case Western Res. U., Cleve., 1964-67; prof. U. Md., College Park, Md., 1967-96, prof. emeritus, 1996—. Cons. USN, Silver Spring, Md., 1967-96. Contbr. articles to profl. jours; inventor Microwave Scalpel, Implantable Microwave Hyperthermia Applicator and numerous others. With US Army, 1955—57. Recipient Disting. Alumni award, N.Mex. State U., 1975, Outstanding Contbn. award, U. Md. Coll. Engring., 2002. Fellow IEEE (life), Am. Soc. for Laser Medicine and Surgery; mem. Am. Phys. Soc. (life), Optical Soc. of Am., Bioelectromagnetics Soc. Avocations: tennis, music. Office: U Md ECEE Dept College Park MD 20742-0001 Office Phone: 301-405-3741. Business E-Mail: taylor@umd.edu.

TAYLOR, LESLIE GEORGE, mining and finance company executive; b. London, Oct. 8, 1922; arrived in U.S., 1925; s. Charles Henry and Florence Louisa (Renouf) Taylor; m. Monique S. Schuster, May 1964 (div. 1974); children: Leslie G. Anthony II, Sandra J. Mira, Linda S. Marshall-(dec.); m. Wendy Ann Ward, July 4, 1979. BBA, U. Buffalo, 1952. Asst. to pres. Kelsey Hayes Co., 1952—60; pres. Aluminum Industries and Glen Alden Co., Cin., NYC, 1960—63; pres., chmn. bd. dirs. DC Internat. (and European subs.), Denver, 1963—68; prin. Taylor Energy Enterprises, Denver, 1968—, Taylor Mining Enterprises, Denver, 1968—, Leslie G. Taylor and Co., Denver, 1968—; gen. ptnr. Am. Universal Mgmt. Corp., Miami Beach, Fla. Del. Internat. Astronautical Soc., Stockholm, 1968, London, 69, Speditur Conv., 1976; COO Merendon Mining Colo., Inc., Denver, Merendon Mining Nev., Inc., Las Vegas; sr. advisor Spring Hill Capital LLC, Miami Beach, Fla. Mem. USCG Aux. Mem.: Soc. Automotive Engrs., Scottish Rite, Masons, Shriners. Republican. Episcopalian. Office: Am Universal Mgmt Corp 2525 Sunset Dr Miami Beach FL 33140 Office Phone: 541-956-9600. E-mail: LGTaylor@Terragon.com.

TAYLOR, LILI, actress; b. Chgo., Feb. 20, 1967; Appeared in films Mystic Pizza, Say Anything, Born on the Fourth of July, Bright Angel, Dogfight, Watch It, Household Saints, Short Cuts, Rudy, Arizona Dream, Mrs. Parker and the Vicious Circle, Ready to Wear, The Addiction, Cold Fever, I Shot Andy Warthol, Girls Town, Ransom, Cosas Que Nunca te Deve, 1996, Letters Not About Love, 1997, Kicked in the Head, 1997, O.K. Garage, 1998, Pecker, 1998, The Impostors, 1998, Spring Forward, 1999, A Life Slipping Down, 1999, Janis, 1999, The Haunting, 1999, High Fidelity, 2000, Julie Johnson, 2001, Gaudi Afternoon, 2001, Casa de los Babys, 2003, Factotum, 2005; broadway plays include What Did He See, Aven U Boys; regional plays include Mud, The Love Talker, Fun.; TV appearance in (films) Subway Stories: Tales from the Underground, 1997, Deadline, 2000, Anne Frank: The Whole Story, 2001, Live From Baghdad, 2002, (TV series) Six Feet Under, 2002-2005. Office: c/o William Morris Agy 151 S El Camino Dr Beverly Hills CA 90212-2704

TAYLOR, LINDSAY DAVID, JR., healthcare executive, bank executive, federal agency administrator; b. Balt., Dec. 15, 1945; s. Lindsay David Sr. and Lillian Helen (Wagner) T.; children: Sarah Ruth, John David, Margaret Katherine. B in Mech. Engring., Rensselaer Poly. Inst., 1967; MBA, Dartmouth Coll., 1969. Bus. assoc. U.S. Steel Corp., Pitts., 1968-70; spl. asst. to asst. sec. for health HEW, Washington, 1970-71, mgr. operational planning, 1971-74, dep. asst. sec. mgmt., 1977-79; programming officer World Bank, Washington, 1974-76; dir. exams. and supervision Fed. Home Loan Bank Bd., Washington, 1979-81; exec. v.p. Perpetual Bank, Alexandria, Va., 1981-89; pres., CEO Columbia (Md.)-FreeState Health Sys., 1989-91, Preferred Health Network, 1992-96; CEO Alpha Health Plan, 1997-99; COO NPD, LLC, Bethesda, Md., 1999—, Nat. Assn. Cmty. Health Ctrs., Washington, 2001—. Cons. Nat. Acad. Pub. Adminstrn., Washington, 1985—86, Ctr. for Advancement of Health, Washington, 1988—89, Diabetex Corp., Balt., 1996—2003, Latin Am. Youth Ctr., 2003—04; trustee Md. Sci. Ctr., 1996—2000; co-chair Greater Balt. Health Care Coun., 1996—2001, Leadership Md., 1996; mem. bd. advisors Found. for Island Health, 2001—06; mem. adv. bd. WAMU Pub. Radio, 1985—88; bd. dirs. Hospice No. Va., 1984—88; chmn. Washington Employers Coalition on Day Care, 1983—90; chair CHC Funding, LLP, 2002—06; bd. dirs. Capital Link, 2003—06. Recipient Mgmt. Improvement award Pres. U.S., 1973, 77; Edward Tuck scholar. Mem. Ctr. for Excellence in Govt. (prin. 1986-05), Washington Coun. Govts. (devel. policy com. 1986-89, mem. editl. adv. bd. Managed Care 1989-95), Tau Beta Pi, Pi Tau Sigma. Avocations: photography, folk music instruments, travel, wilderness, coaching youth baseball and basketball. Office: 4800 Montgomery Ln Ste 1000 Bethesda MD 20814-3472 also: Ste 210 7200 Wisconsin Ave Bethesda MD 20814 E-mail: LDavidTaylor@yahoo.com.

TAYLOR, LYNDON C., lawyer, energy executive; b. Lawton, Okla., June 9, 1958; s. Clinton Harold and Doris Lee (Nance) T. BS of Indsl. Engring., Okla. State U., 1981; JD, U. Okla., 1984. Bar: Okla. 1984, U.S. Dist. Ct. (we. dist.) Okla. 1985, D.C. 1986. Assoc. Watson & McKenzie, Okla. City, 1984-86; assoc. through mng. ptnr. energy practice Skadden, Arps, Slate, Meagher & Flom LLP, Houston, 1986—2005; dep. gen. counsel Devon Energy Corp., Okla. City, 2005—07, sr. v.p., gen. counsel, 2007—. Republican. Avocation: golf. Office: Devon Energy Corp 20 N Broadway Oklahoma City OK 73102-8260 *

TAYLOR, MARCUS KEENE, physiologist, researcher; b. Springfield, Mo., Apr. 16, 1972; s. Jerry Keene and Criseyde Anne Taylor; m. Deborah Legas, Oct. 21, 1995. PhD, U. NC, Greensboro, 2005. Exercise physiologist Duke U. Med. Ctr., Durham, NC, 2004—05; rsch. physiologist Naval Health Rsch. Ctr., San Diego, 2005—. Contbr. articles to profl. jours. Lt. USN, 2005—07. Rsch. grantee, USN Core Capabilities, 2007. Mem.: Aerospace Med. Assn., Am. Coll. Sports Medicine. Avocation: acting. Home: 2315 Blom St San Diego CA 92109 Home Phone: 919-308-6298; Office Phone: 619-553-0645. Business E-Mail: taylorm@nhrc.navy.mil.

TAYLOR, MARGARET WISCHMEYER, retired language educator; b. Terre Haute, Ind., Aug. 5, 1920; d. Carl and Grace (Riehle) Wischmeyer; m. John Edward Taylor, Sept. 5, 1942 (dec. 1988); children: Deborah Ann, Tobin Edward (dec. 2002), Mary Leesa. BA magna cum laude, Duke U., 1941; MA, John Carroll U., Cleve., 1973. Feature writer Dayton Daily News, Ohio, 1945—53; freelance writer Cleve., 1953—; asst. to Dr. Joseph B. Rhine Duke U. Parapsychology Lab., Durham, NC, 1941; asst. prof. English and journalism Ea. Campus, Cuyahoga CC, Cleve., 1973-92, prof. emeritus, 1992—, advisor campus newspaper, 1973-84, dir. Writers Conf., 1975-90. Writing cons., editor various cos. and pubs., Cleve., 1973—; founder, operator Grammar Hot Line, 1987-92. Author: Crystal Lake Reflections, 1985, English 101 Can Be Fun, 1991, The Basic English Handbook, 1995. Recipient top state honors Ohio Newspaper Women's Assn., 1947, award for best ednl., best overall stories Am. Heart Assn., 1970, Besse award for tchg. excellence, 1980, Profl. Excellence award, 1985, Provost's Pride award, 1987, Nat. Tchg. Excellence award Coun. for Advancement and Support of Edn., 1989; named Ohio Outstanding Citizen, Ohio Ho. Reps., 1987, 89, Innovator of Yr., League for Innovations in C.C.s, 1988, Pres.'s award Cuyahoga C.C., 1992. Mem. Mensa, Phi Beta Kappa, Pi Beta Phi. Presbyterian. Avocations: grammar consulting, reading, writing. Home: 27900 Fairmount Blvd Cleveland OH 44124-4616 Personal E-mail: debbie.taylor@gmail.com.

TAYLOR, MARILYN JORDAN, architectural firm executive; m. Brainerd O. Taylor; children: Brainerd I., Alexis. Degree in govt. and urban affairs, Harvard Coll., 1969; MArch, U. Calif., Berkeley; postgrad., MIT. Joined Skidmore, Owings and Merrill LLP, Washington, 1971, urban designer, dir. design stations program of N.E. Corridor Improvement Project, 1978—85, chief urban design and planning practice NYC, 1985—2001, ptnr., 1987—, chmn., 2001—04. Past pres. N.Y.C. chpt. AIA; chmn. Nat. AIA Regional and Urban Design Com.; vis. prof. Harvard Grad. Sch. Design; David Rockefeller fellow N.Y.C. Partnership, fellows adv. com. Key projects include N.J. Performing Arts Ctr., Newark, Riverside South, Manhattan, NYNEX Hdqs., Battery Park City, Penn Sta. Redevelopment Project, various airports, many others. Chmn. Urban Land Inst., 2005—; bd. dirs. NYC Bldg. Congress (chmn. 2002-04), Comml. Real Estate Women N.Y., Inst. for Urban Design. Named Woman of Yr., Comml. Real Estate Women N.Y., 1998; named one of Most Influential Women in Am. Real Estate, GRID mag., 2001; named to List of Most Influential Women, Crain's N.Y., 1996, 2000; recipient Profl. Leadership award, Profl. Women in Constrn., 2001. Office: Skidmore Owings and Merrill LLP 14 Wall St New York NY 10005

TAYLOR, MARK, former lieutenant governor; b. Atlanta, May 7, 1957; m. Sacha Taylor; 1 child. Degree in polit. sci., Emory U.; degree in law, U. Ga. Exec. Fred Taylor Co., Albany; mem. Ga. Senate, Atlanta, 1987—99; asst. adminstrn. floor leader then adminstrn. floor leader Gov. Zell Miller; sec. transp. com.; mem. appropriations, ethics, ins. and labor, rules coms.; lt. gov. State of Ga., Atlanta, 1999—2007. Mem. bd. dirs. March of Dimes, Albany/Dougherty 2000 Partnership, Thronateeska Heritage Found. Mem. Ga. Bar Assn., Dougherty County Bar Assn., Leadership Albany (charter), Artesian City Sertoma Club (past pres.), Rotary. Democrat. Office: Taylor One Georgia Inc PO Box 250241 Atlanta GA 30325 Office Phone: 404-816-5724. Office Fax: 404-846-8579.

TAYLOR, MARK DOUGLAS, publishing executive; b. Geneva, Ill., Jan. 16, 1951; s. Kenneth Nathaniel and Margaret Louise (West) T.; m. Carol E. Rogers, May 28, 1973; children: Jeremy Peter, Kristen Elizabeth, Margaret Louise, Rebecca Cynthia, Stephen Rogers. BA, Duke U., 1973. Exec. dir. Tyndale House Found., Wheaton, Ill., 1973-78, pres., CEO, 2004—; v.p. Tyndale House Pubs., Wheaton, Ill., 1978-84, pres., chief exec. officer, 1984—. Dir. Living Bibles Internat., Naperville, Ill., 1972-92; trustee Taylor U., 1998—. Author The Complete Book of Bible Literacy, 1992. Mem. Wheaton Liquor Control Commn., 1986—, chmn., 1994—; chmn. bd. dirs. Outreach Cmty. Ctr., 1986-93. Mem. Internat. Bible Soc. (bd. dirs. 1992-96). Office: Tyndale House Publishers Inc PO Box 80 Wheaton IL 60189-0080 *What we accomplish in life is soon forgotten. Our best legacy is to pass on to our children and grandchildren our positive values.*

TAYLOR, MARTHA SUE, librarian; b. Sweetwater, Tex., Aug. 16, 1947; d. John Neville Shipley and Erma Hall Shipley Neeper; m. Linn Bryant Taylor, May 22, 1981; children: Mark Bryant, Melissa Anne. BA in English and Govt., Tex. Tech U., 1969, MA in English, 1971; postgrad. in Libr. Sci., U. Tex., 1973. Tchr. English Sweetwater Ind. Sch. Dist., 1971-73, supr. elem. libr., 1973-78, tchr. govt. and English, 1978-83, libr. high sch., 1983—. Mem. dist. improvement coun. Sweetwater Ind. Sch. Dist., 1991-94, 95—, sec., 1993-94, v.p., 1995-96, mem. H.S. campus improvement com., 1991—; instr. govt. Western Tex. Coll., Snyder, 1983-88; com. to draw up new state libr. standards, 2001-03. Sec. adminstrv. bd. 1st United Meth. Ch., 1978-83, organist, 1979—. Mem. AAUW (pres. 1971-73, 1st v.p. 1985-87, treas. 1989-90), Tex. State Tchrs. Assn. (pres. 1987-88), Tex. Libr. Assn. Methodist. Avocations: organ, piano. Home: 1632 Morris Ave Sweetwater TX 79556-2646 Office: Sweetwater High Sch 1205 Ragland St Sweetwater TX 79556-2438 Office Phone: 325-235-4371. Business E-Mail: mtaylor@sweetwater.esc14.net.

TAYLOR, MARVIN EDWARD, JR., lawyer; b. Smithfield, NC, Oct. 15, 1937; s. Marvin Edward and Ellen Borden Broadhurst T.; m. Karin Gunilla Guggenheim, Nov. 29, 1969; 1 child, Karin Elizabeth Guggenheim. AB, U. NC, 1960, JD with honors, 1965. Bar: NY 1966, NC 1968, US Dist. Ct. (ea. dist.) NC 1973, US Ct. Appeals (4th cir.) 1974, Calif. 1976. Assoc. Nixon Mudge Rose Guthrie Alexander & Mitchell, NYC, 1965-67, Sanford Cannon Adams & McCullough, Raleigh, N.C., 1967-71; atty. pvt. practice, Raleigh, N.C., 1972-75, 1984—; corp. counsel Memorex Corp., Santa Clara, Calif., 1975-80; atty. pvt. practice, Hickory, N.C., 1983. Dept. counsel GE Co., Hickory, NC, 1980—82; mem. staff N.C. Law Rev., 1964, rsch. editor, 65. Dir. Parents' Assn. NC State U., Raleigh, 1989-93, Coun. Entrepreneurial Devel, Research Triangle Park, NC, 1985-88, chmn. pub. com., 1985-88; participant NC Ctr. Nonprofits Pro Bono Program, Raleigh, 1994—. With USAF, 1960-62. Mem.: Swedish-Am. C. of C. NC (co-founder, dir., sec.-treas. 1998—2000), Swedish-Am. C. of C. USA (sec. 1999—2000), NC Bar Assn. (com. comml. banking and bus. law 1970—75, subcom. securities regulation 1972—75, bus. law sect. coun. 1982—90, internat. law com. 1990—92, internat. law and practice sect. coun. 1992—95, pub. info. com. 1995—2000, lawyers in the schs. com. 1999—2005, comm. com. 2000—04), Order of Coif. Democrat. Episcopalian. Avocations: skiing, photography, reading. Office: 119 SW Maynard Rd Cary NC 27511-4472 Home Phone: 919-847-3051; Office Phone: 919-469-8899.

TAYLOR, MICHAEL E., mathematics professor; AB, Princeton Univ., 1967; PhD, Univ. Calif., Berkeley, 1970. William R. Kenan, Jr. prof. math. Univ. NC, Chapel Hill. Fellow: Am. Acad. Arts & Scis.; mem.: Soc. Industrial and Applied Math., Math. Assn. Am., Am. Math. Soc. Office: Math Dept Univ NC Chapel Hill NC 27599-3250 Business E-Mail: met@math.unc.edu. *

TAYLOR, MICHAEL RAY, media specialist, educator; b. Daytona Beach, Fla., Sept. 20, 1959; s. Dan Floyd and Joyce Ann Taylor; m. Kathryn Lee Steadham, May 7, 1983; children: Alexander Ray, Kenneth Daniel, Christopher Dale. BA, Fla. State U., Tallahassee, 1981; MA in English, U. SC, Columbia, 1986; MFA, U. Ark., Fayetteville, 1996. Prof. mass media Henderson State U., Arkadelphia, Ark., 1991—. Author: (book) Caves: Exploring Hidden Realms, Dark Life, Cave Passages. Office: Henderson State Univ 1100 Henderson St Arkadelphia AR 71999 Home Phone: 870-230-5182; Office Phone: 870-230-5182. Office Fax: 870-230-5472.

TAYLOR, MILDRED D., author; b. Jackson, Miss., Sept. 13, 1943; d. Wilbert Lee and Deletha Marie (Davis) Taylor. BA in Edn., U Toledo, 1965; MA, U Colo., 1969. Vol., tchr. English and history Peace Corps, Ethiopia, 1965-67, then recruiter U.S., 1967-68; study skills coord. black edn. program U. Colo., 1969-71. Author: (children's fiction) Song of the Trees, 1975 (Coun. on Interracial Books for Children award 1975), Roll of Thunder, Hear My Cry, 1976 (Newbery medal, 1977), Let the Circle Be Unbroken, 1981, The Gold Cadillac, 1987 (Christopher award), The Friendship and Other Stories, 1987, Mississippi Bridge, 1990 (Christopher award), The Road to Memphis, 1990, The Well, 1995 (winner Jane Addams book award, 1996), The Land, 2001 (Coretta Scott King award, L.A. Times Book award, Scott O'Dell award, Pen USA award). Address: care Dial Books For Young Readers 375 Hudson St New York NY 10014-3658

TAYLOR, MINNA, lawyer; b. Washington, Jan. 25, 1947; d. Morris P. and Anne (Williams) Glushien; m. Charles Ellett Taylor, June 22, 1969; 1 child, Amy Caroline. BA, SUNY, Stony Brook, 1969; MA, SUNY, 1973; JD, U. So. Calif., 1977. Bar: Calif. 1977, U.S. Dist. Ct. (cen. dist.) Calif. 1978. Extern to presiding justice Calif. Supreme Ct., 1977; field atty. NLRB, LA, 1977-82; dir. employee rels., legal svcs. Paramount Pictures Corp., LA, 1982-85, v.p. employee rels. legal svcs., 1985-89; dir. bus. and legal affairs Wilshire Ct. Prodns., LA, 1989-91; sr. counsel Fox Broadcasting Co., LA, 1991-92, v.p. legal affairs, 1992-97, sr. v.p. legal affairs, 1997—. Webmaster www.ifcome.com, 2001—. Editor notes and articles: U. So. Calif. Law Rev., 1976-77. Mentor MOSTE, L.A., 1986-87, 88-89; pres. Beverly Hills chpt. ACLU, LA, 1985; mem. Jr. League LA, 2003-, sec. 2006-07. Fellow ABA, Calif. State Bar (mem. copyright subcom. 1994-95), L.A. County Bar Assn.; mem. Beverly Hills Bar Assn., L.A. Bead Soc. (membership sec. 1992-94, mem. bd. dirs. 1994-95), Order of Coif. Office: Fox Broadcasting Co 10201 W Pico Blvd Los Angeles CA 90064-2606

TAYLOR, NANCY ELIZABETH, lawyer; b. Salt Lake City, Apr. 6, 1956; d. Calvin Walker and Dorothy (Cope) Taylor; m. Christopher Robbins Bowen, Jan. 22, 1978; children: Elizabeth Grant Bowen, Alexandra Taylor Bowen. BS, U. Utah, 1978; JD, Cath. U., 1988. Health policy dir. Senate Com. on Labor and Human Resources, Washington, 1981-91; ptnr. Law Offices of Deborah Steelman, Washington, 1991-93; prin. shareholder, nat. co-chair health law dept. Greenberg Traurig LLP, Washington, 1993—. Testimony presentor Rep. Nat. Conf., 1992. Recipient Commr. award FDA, 1989. Mem. Nat. Health Lawyers, Women & Gov. Rels., Food and Drug Law Inst. Republican. Mem. Lds Ch. Office: Greenberg Traurig LLP Ste 500 800 Connecticut Ave NW Washington DC 20006 Office Phone: 202-331-3100. Office Fax: 202-331-3101. Business E-Mail: taylorn@gtlaw.com.

TAYLOR, NATHALEE BRITTON, retired nutritionist, freelance/self-employed writer; b. Lubbock, Tex., June 8, 1941; d. Nathaniel E. and Dessie Pauline (Moss) Britton; children by previous marriage: Clay H., Bret N. Courtney. BS in Home Econs., Tex. Tech U., 1963. Home economist Pioneer Gas, Lubbock, Tex., 1963-65; dietitian Tex. Tech U., Lubbock, 1966-71; home economist South Plains Electric Co-op., Lubbock, 1986; mgr. quality control Rip Griffins Enterprises, Lubbock, Tex., 1987; sales rep. Time Chem., Lubbock, 1987—2003; with Sentry, Lubbock; mktg. rep. Dodson Group Ins., Lubbock, Farmers Ins., Lubbock, Southwestern Bell Wireless; ret., 2003. Ranch Historian. Co-author: (cookbook) From Our House to Yours, 1975; columnist: Lubbock Lights (mag.) Ranch Record, Nat. Ranching; presenter: (TV show) Southwestern Cooking Sta. KTXT; contbr. articles to profl. publs. Bd. dirs. Am. Heart Assn., Lubbock, 1985-87; mem. Home Economist in Bus., pres. Lubbock chpt., 1985; culinary co-chmn. Lubbock C. of C. Arts Festival, 1982, 83, 84; mem. Write for Nat. Ranching Heritage Ctr., Lubbock., Womens Studies Cmty. Connection. Named Lincoln County Fair Queen. Mem. Tech. Home Econs. Alums (sec./treas.), Am. Home Econs. Assn. (v.p., sec./treas.), Bd.-Cove, Soroptomist (v.p. Lubbock club). Democrat. Avocations: gardening, writing, cooking, horseback riding. Personal E-mail: nathaleet@ranch-horses.com.

TAYLOR, NELLIE RUBY, artist, poet; b. Lundale, W.Va., Apr. 18, 1946; d. John Otis and Blanche L. (Wright) Taylor; m. Ivan Lee Hurt, July 31, 1965 (div. Nov. 1982); children: Ivan Lee Hurt Jr., Bradley Allen Hurt. Student, Gallipolis Bus. Coll, Buckeye Hills Career Ctr., Hocking Tech. Sch., Nelsonville, Ohio; AA, Kans.; MA, Pa., 1995. Agent A.L. Williams Ins., Athens, Ohio, 1984—87; adminstr. Cleve. Sch., 1987—; nursing Mary Farmers Nurses, Cleve. Heights, Ohio, 1987—2002; tchr. Manor-Care, Mayfield Heights, Ohio, 2002—. Involved with Career Ladder Program Cleve. Mcpl. Sch. Adminstrn.; tchr. Head Start Gallia-Meigs Head Start Sch., Cheshire, Ohio, mem. bd. of mental retardation and devel. disabilities; founder, pres. Mean Corp. Author: Mental Education; inventor Hopter-Copter; prodr., dir., host: (television) In Time Like These; Represented in permanent collections Portrait of Bill Clinton, Presdl. Libr., Little Rock, Ark., painting, The Tree of Love, portraits, William Shakespeare, Queen Elizabeth II, Prince Phillip, Pres. Nelson Mandella, Pres. John Zemin, Prince Charles, Princess Diana, Bob Evans, others. Recipient Award of Excellence, Ohio Sch. Bd. Assn, 1985—87, Award of Excellence in speaking, Dr. harris, Black Tellers Assn., Lifetime Congl. award, US Congress 11th Dist., 1998, Plaque of Excellence in Edn., Ohio Sch. Bds. Assn., USA Lifetime Congl. award Humanities, Black Story Tellers award of Excellence. Mem.: Am. Fedn. Tchrs. Achievements include represented as permanent leader, justice, tolerance new civil rights mem. ctr. with Rosa Parks, Montgomery, Ala; The Path of King, The Path of America, The Freedom Journey Continues, a speech telling the history of freedom in the USA until present time (MLK day 2004 in Gallipolis and 2007 in Shaker Heights). Avocations: writing, travel, poetry, drama. Home: 2826 E 130th Unit # 102 Shaker Heights Cleveland OH 44120

TAYLOR, NICOLE RENÉE (NIKI TAYLOR), model, shop owner; b. Miami, Fla., Mar. 5, 1975; d. Ken and Barbara Taylor; m. Matt Martinez (div. 1996); children: Jake Martinez, Hunter Martinez; m. Burney Lamar, Dec. 27, 2006. With Tri Star Sports and Entertainment Group, Brentwood, 2006—; owner Abbie and Jesse's, Cool Springs, Tenn., 2006—, Franklin, Tenn., 2006—. Contracts with L'Oreal, 1990-92, Cover Girl Makeup; appeared in Seventeen (cover girl) 1989, Vogue, Elle, Mademoiselle, Harper's Bazaar; modeled for Yves Saint Laurent, Karl Lagerfeld; modeled swimsuit Sports Illus., 1997, cover Sports Illus. Calendar, 1998. Founder Begin Found. Achievements include appearing on over 320 magazine covers worldwide; youngest model to appear on the cover of Vogue; holds the world record for being the youngest model to receive a six figure deal. Office: TriStar Entertainment Group Suite 200 215 Ward Circle Brentwood TN 37027 Office Phone: 615-309-0969. Business E-Mail: tristar@tristarse.com. *

TAYLOR, NOLAN J., information systems educator; b. Tuskegee, Ala., June 18, 1964; s. Elmer Augustine and Betty Andrews Taylor; children: Byron Derek Powell, Vivian Elizabeth, Donovan Lee, Payton Alexandria. BS, U. Ala., Tuscaloosa, 1986; MBA, Calif. State U., San Bernardino, 1995; PhD, U. Ga., Athens, 2000. Sys. engr. USAF, Dayton, 1986—91, software project mgr. San Bernardino, 1991—95; asst. prof. Ind. U., Indpls., 2001—. Mem.: IEEE, Assn. for Info. Sys., Decision Scis. Inst. Office: Indiana U 801 W Michigan St BS 4030 Indianapolis IN 46202 Home Phone: 317-531-3379; Office Phone: 317-274-0185. Office Fax: 317-274-3312. Personal E-mail: nolanjtaylor@comcast.net. Business E-Mail: notaylor@iupui.edu.

TAYLOR, PALMER W., pharmacology educator; m. Susan Serota; three children. BS in Pharmacy, U. Wis., 1960, PhD in Phys. Pharmacy, 1964. Rsch. assoc. pharmacology-toxicoogy assoc. program Lab. Chem. Pharmacology, 1965-68; NIH fellow molecular pharmacology unit Med. Rsch. Coun., Cambridge, Eng., 1968-70; NIH fellow Max Planck Inst. for Phys. Chemistry, Gottingen, Germany, 1970, asst. prof. divsn. pharmacology dept. medicine U. Calif., San Diego, 1971-74, assoc. prof. divsn. pharmacology dept. medicine, 1974-78, prof. divsn. pharmacology dept. medicine, 1978-87, head divsn. pharmacology dept. medicine, 1979-87, prof., chair dept. pharmacology, 1987—2003, Sandra & Monroe Trout endowed chair pharmacology, 1994—2002, dean Skaggs Sch. Pharmacy and Pharm. Scis., assoc. vice chancellor health scis. Mem. pharmacology study sect. NIH, 1974-78; mem. study sect. on chemotherapeutic agts. Multiple Sclerosis Soc., 1974-86; co-chmn. conf. on membrane receptors and diseases NIH-NIGMS, Bethesda, Md., 1978; participant Nat. Acad. Scis. Pharmacology Symposium, 1979; co-chair ASPET Symposium on Application of Molecular Pharmacology to Therapeutic Considerations, 1980; mem. pharmacol. scis. rev. com. NIH, 1980-85; vis. fellow Darwin Coll., U. Cambridge, 1980-81; Sterling Drug Co. vis. prof. U. Mich., 1985, U. Oreg., 1990; nat. adv. coun. mem. Nat. Inst. Gen. Med. Scis., 1988-92; vice chair, chair Gordon Conf. on Molecular Pharmacology, 1987-89; Krantz Meml. lectr. U. Md., 1989; Harold C. Hodge lectr. U. Rochester Med. Ctr., 1992; vis. prof., lectr. series Coll. de France, 1999, Tyler lectr. series Purdue U.; bd. trustees Gordon Rsch. Confs., 1999—; Rene Couteaux lectr. XI Internat. Symposium on Cholinergic Mechanisms, 2002. Co-editor: (with W.B. Pratt) Principles of Drug Action, 3d edit., 1990, (with A.G. Gilman, T.W. Rall and A.S. Nies) Godoman and Gilman's Pharmacological Basis of Therapeutics, 8th edit., 1990; assoc. editor Molecular Pharmacology, 1971-75; mem. editl. bd. Jour. Biol. Chemistry, 1981-86, 92-98, Molecular Pharmacology, 1983—, Trends in Pharmacol. Scis., 1983-90, Jour. Molecular Medicine, 1992-98, Pharm. News, 1997—; cons. editor Jour. Clin. Investigation, 1992-98; contbr. articles to profl. jours. Recipient Borden award, Phi Lambda Upsilon award in pharm. chemistry, Toral Tollmann award in pharmacology, 2003, 700 Yr. award for rsch. in the cholinesterases Perugia U., Italy, 2004; Fogarty fellow U. Cambridge, 1980-81. Mem. FASEB (fin. com. 2000—), NAS-Inst. Medicine, Internat. Union Pharmacology (del. 1995—), Am. Soc. for Clin. Investigation (hon.), Am. Soc. for Pharmacology and Exptl. Therapeutics (councillor 1987-90, pres.-elect 1994-95, pres. 1995-96), Am. Soc. for Biochemistry and Molecular Biology, Am. Assn. for Med. Sch. Pharmacology, Fedn. Exptl. Biologists (bd. mem. 1995-99), Croatian-Slovenian Biochem. Soc. (hon.). Office: Dept Pharmacology Basic Sci Bldg 9500 Gilman Dr La Jolla CA 92093-0636 Business E-Mail: pwtaylor@ucsd.edu.

TAYLOR, PATRICIA, director; b. Balt., Aug. 30, 1959; d. Roger Kirkbride and Katherine Heller Taylor; m. Augusto Hacthoun, July 10, 1984; 1 child, Katherine Ariadne Hacthoun. BA, Wheaton Coll., Norton, MA, 1982; M of Internat. Affairs, Columbia U., NYC, 1991, MPhil, 1995. Dir. prestigious fellowships Fordham U., Bronx, NY, 1998—2000; grad. sch. and fellowship adv. Marist Coll., Poughkeepsie, NY, 2004—. Internat. Predissertation fellow, Social Sci. Rsch. Coun., 1992—93, Cordier fellow, Columbia U., 1995—96. Mem.: Nat. Assn. Fellowship Advisors, Phi Beta Kappa. Avocations: cooking, reading, travel. Office: Marist Coll 3399 North Rd/Library 332 Poughkeepsie NY 12601 Office Phone: 845-575-3547. Business E-Mail: pat.taylor@marist.edu.

TAYLOR, PAUL B., choreographer; b. Allegheny County, Pa., July 29, 1930; s. Paul B. and Elizabeth (Pendleton) Taylor. Student, Syracuse U., 1949—52, Juilliard Sch. Music, 1952—53; PhD (hon.), Duke U., 1983, Conn. Coll., 1983, Syracuse U., 1986, Juilliard, 1988, SUNY, Purchase, 1988, Calif. Inst. Arts, 1989, Skidmore Coll., 1995. Artistic dir. Paul Taylor Dance Co., 1954. Dancer Merce Cunningham Co., 1954, Martha Graham, 1955—62, Paul Taylor Dance Co., 1954—74. Dancer Paul Taylor Dance Co. has performed in over 450 U.S. cities and 60 countries, PBS TV Dance in Am., Live From the Am. Dance Festival, Two Landmark Dances, Three Modern Classics, The Wrecker's Ball, The Taylor Co.: Recent Dances, Am. Masters, Paul Taylor, Dancemaker, Acts of Ardour, choreographer (partial list) Aureole, 1962, Private Domain, 1969, Esplanade, 1975, Cloven Kingdom, 1976, Airs, 1978, Le Sacre du Printemps (the Rehearsal), 1980, Arden Court, 1981, Mercuric Tidings, 1982, Sunset, 1983, Roses, 1985, Last Look, 1985, Musical Offering, 1986, Ab Ovo Usque ad Mala, 1986, Syzygy, 1987, Speaking in Tongues, 1988, Company B, 1991, Funny Papers, 1994, Offenbach Overtures, 1995, Eventide, 1996, Piazzolla Caldera, 1997, The Word, 1998, Cascade, 1999, Arabesque, 1999, Black Tuesday, 2001, Promethian Fire, 2002, Dante Variations, 2004, Klezmer-bluegrass, 2004, Spring Rounds, 2005, Banquet of Vultures, 2005; author (autobiography): Private Domain, 1987 (Nat. Book Critics Cir. award for biography, 1987). Decorated Chevalier des Arts et Lettres, elevated to Officier France, Comdr. Legion of Honor; named Dancer of Yr., London's Dance and Dancers, 1965; named to Nat. Mus. Dance Hall of Fame, 1995; recipient Internat. Cir. of Criticism for Artistic Rsch. and Cultural Exch. award, Festival Nations, Paris, 1962, Best Fgn. Attraction prize, Critics of Chile, 1966, Capezio Dance award, 1967, Creative Arts award, Brandeis U., 1978, Dance Mag. award, 1980, Samuel H. Scripps Am. Dance Festival award, 1983, Arts award, State N.Y., 1987, Lions of Performing Arts award, N.Y. Pub. Libr., 1989, Emmy award, Speaking in Tongues, 1992, Kennedy Ctr. Honors award, 1992; Guggenheim fellow, 1961, 1966, 1983, MacArthur Found. fellow, 1985. Office: Paul Taylor Dance Co 552 Broadway New York NY 10012-3922 Office Phone: 212-431-5562. *

TAYLOR, PAUL PEAK, pediatric dentist, educator; b. Childress, Tex., May 11, 1921; s. Noah Peak and Lois C. (Vinson) T.; m. LaVerne Countryman, Aug. 11, 1945; chi dren: Scott, Peri Ann. Student, W. Tex. State Coll., 1938-40; DDS, Baylor U., 1944; MS, U. Mich., 1951. Diplomate Am. Bd. Pediatric Dentistry (examining mem. 1977-84, chair 1983). Prof. Baylor U. Coll. Dentistry, Dallas, 1958-86, chmn. grad. pediatric dentistry, 1960-69, chmn. dept. pediatric dentistry, 1969-86, prof. emeritus, 1986—; dir. dental svcs. Children's Med. Ctr., Dallas, 1965-86, dir. emeritus dental svcs., 1986—; dir. dental svcs. Tex. Scottish Rite Hosp. for Children, Dallas, 1965-86, dir. emeritus dental svcs., 1986—. Contbr. articles to Jour. of Dentistry for Children, 1960-82; author (with others) Pediatric Dentistry, 1986, Current Therapy in Pediatric Infectious Disease, 1989; mem. editl. and publs. com. Jour. Dentistry for Children. Capt. U.S. Army, 1951-53. Named to Baylor Coll. Dentistry Hall of Fame, 1999; Mott Found. fellow, 1949-51. Fellow Am. Coll. of Dentists (life); mem. ADA (life), Tex. Dental Assn., Dallas County Dental Assn. (Dentist of Yr. 1999, Lifetime Achievement award 2002), Masons (life, 32d degree, KCCH), Shriners. Episcopalian. Avocation: golf. Home: 2615 Briarcove Dr Plano TX 75074-4905

TAYLOR, PAULETTE ANN, special education educator, educational consultant; b. Plainfield, NJ, June 8, 1948; d. Arthur John and Bess Ealy Taylor. AA, Centenary Coll. for Women, Hackettstown, NJ, 1966—68; BS in Edn., U. Tenn., Knoxville, 1968—70; MEd, Memphis State U., Tenn., 1972—73. Cert. English tchr. (7-12) N.J. Bd. Edn., 1970, English/Psychology tchr. (7-12) Tenn. Bd. Edn., 1970, Spl Edn. tchr. (with endorsements) Tenn. Bd. Edn., 1970, English tchr. (9-12) Minn. Bd. Edn., 1976, Spl. Edn. tchr. (k-12) Minn. Bd. Edn., 1976, Secondary tchr. (with approvals in English, Mental Disabilities Resouce) Iowa Bd. Edn., 1977, Spl. Edn. tchr. (k-12) Iowa Bd. Edn., 1977, Ednl. Cons. Iowa Bd. Edn., 1977. Para-educator Willis Sch. of Ednl. Therapy, Bound Brook, NJ, 1971; English tchr. Marshall County Sr. HS, Lewisburg, Tenn., 1971—72; spl. edn. tchr. Coro Lake Elem. Sch., Memphis, 1973—76, Inver Grove Heights Jr. High, Minn., 1976—77, Black Hawk Jr. HS, Pleasant Valley, Iowa, 1977—88; spl edn./ednl. cons. Miss. Bend Area Edn. Agy., Bettendorf, 1988—. Mem. negotiations team Pleasant Valley Edn. Assn., 1979—85, pres. elect, 1981—82, pres., 1982—84, past pres., 1984—85; pres. elect Miss. Bend UniServ Unit, 1985—86, pres., 1986—87, past pres., 1987—88; exec. bd. mem., profl. staff orgn. Miss. Bend Area Edn. Agy., 1989—, membership co-chair, profl. staff orgn., 1993—, mentor for new cons., 1995; vol. practicum supr. St. Ambrose U., Bettendorf/Davenport. Vol. Homework Hotline, Betttendorf, 1986—96; exec. bd. mem./grant reader Riverboat Devel. Authority, Davenport, 1989—99; bd. dirs. Scott. Co. Hist. Preservation Soc., Davenport, 1980—85, 1991—96, awards com., 1980—85, 1992, 1994, 1996, hist. homes tour organ. com. mem., 1984—95; bd. dirs. Neighborhood Housing Svc., Davenport, 1987—89; mem. organizing/steering com. East Bluff Neighborhood Dist., Davenport, 2004—06. Mem.: NEA (del. to 3 conventions 1982—86), Coun. for Exceptional Children, Iowa State Edn. Assn. (del. to 7 conventions 1981—87), Cornbelt Running Club (vol.), Delta Kappa Gamma (mem. program com., mem. membership com.). Democrat. Meth. Avocations: reading, gardening, exercise, computers. Office: Miss Bend Area Edn Agy 729 21st St Bettendorf IA 52722

TAYLOR, PETER J., diversified financial services company executive; Grad., UCLA; MS in pub. policy analysis, Claremont Grad. U. Mem. staff Calif. State Assembly; exec. dir. Coro Found.; mgr. GTE Calif.; now mng. dir. Lehman Bros., LA. Mem. bd. James Irvine Found., 2000—; mem. bd. trustees J. Paul Getty Trust, LA, 2005—. Office: Lehman Bros 25th Fl 10250 Constellation Blvd Los Angeles CA 90067

TAYLOR, PETER VAN VOORHEES, advertising and public relations consultant; b. Montclair, NJ, Aug. 25, 1934; s. John Coard and Mildred (McLaughlin) T.; m. Janet Kristine Kirkebo, Nov. 4, 1978; 1 child, John Coard III. BA in English, Duke U., 1956. Announcer Sta. WQAM, Miami, Fla., 1956; announcer, music dir. Sta. KHVH, Honolulu, 1959-61; promotion mgr. Sta. KPEN, San Francisco, 1962; with Kaiser Broadcasting, 1962-74, GE Broadcasting Co., 1974-78; program and ops. mgr. Sta. KFOG, San Francisco, 1962-66; mgr. Sta. WXHR-AM-FM, Cambridge, Mass., 1966-67; gen. mgr. Sta. WJIB, Boston, 1967-70; v.p., mgr. FM divsn. Kaiser Broadcasting, 1969-72; v.p., gen. mgr. Sta. KFOG, San Francisco, 1970-78; pres. Taylor Comm., 1978-90, 97—, Baggott & Taylor, Inc., 1990-91, Taylor Advt. & Pub. Rels., 1991-96, No. Calif. Broadcasters Assn., 1974-76, Broadcast Skills Bank, 1975-76. Pres. Roast Host, 1993—96, Taylor Voice & Proofreading Works, 2006—. Trustee WDBS, Inc., Duke U., 1974-80; bd. dirs. San Francisco BBB, 1976-78, 89-94, Calif. Broadcasters Assn., 1982-84, KCRH Chabot Coll., 1982-83, San Francisco Boys and Girls Club, 1991-93, Coast Guard Found., 1991-2000, Leukemia Soc., San Francisco, 1992-93, Duke Devel. Coun., 1992-96; bd. dirs. Commencement Bay Rowing Club, sec., 1997-98, v.p. 1998-99, pres., 1999-2000; mem. exec. bd., sec. Scandinavian Culture Coun., 2001-04, v.p., 2002-03, pres., 2003-04; bd. dirs. Lindquist Children's Dental Clinic, 2004—. Lt. USCGR, 1957—63. Mem. Nat. Radio Club, Internat. Radio Club, Long Wave Radio Club, Worldwide TV-FM Dx Assn., Rotary (bd. dirs. San Francisco, 1988-93, 1st v.p. 1990-91, pres. 1991-92, chmn. pub. rels. dist. 5150 1986-89, conf. chmn. 1990, area rep. 1992-93, dist. gov. nominee 1995-96, pub. rels. chair Tacoma 2002-03, bd. dirs. 2004—, auction chair 2005, pres.-elect 2005-06, pres. 2006-2007, mem. chair 2007-). Home and Office: 6002 Bayview Dr NE Tacoma WA 98422-1227 E-mail: taytac@comcast.net.

TAYLOR, PEYTON TROY, JR., oncologist, educator; b. Tuscaloosa, Ala., July 21, 1941; s. Peyton Troy, Sr. and Frances (Sutter) Taylor; m. Helena Ström, Sept. 23, 1967; children: Annika, Karin, Sarah. BS, U. Ala., 1963, MS, 1968; MD, Med. Coll. Ala., 1968. Intern U. Va. Hosp., Charlottesville, 1968-69, resident, 1969-70, 72-75; asst. prof. ob-gyn. U. Va., Charlottesville, 1976-79, assoc. prof., dir. divsn. ob-gyn. Health Scis. Ctr., 1981-87, Richard N. and Louise R. Crockett prof., 1987—, med. dir. Cancer Ctr., 1996—; clin. assoc. surgery Nat. Cancer Inst., Bethesda, Md., 1970-72. Assoc. prof. U. Ala., Birmingham, 1979—81. Contbr. articles to profl. jours. With USPHS, 1970—72. Recipient Disting. Alumnus, U. Ala. Med. Alumni Assn., 2000. Fellow: ACS, Am. Coll. Obstetricians and Gynecologists; mem.: So. Surg. Assn., Internat. Gynecol. Cancer Soc., Am. Assn. Cancer Rsch., Am. Soc. Clin. Oncology, Soc. Surg. Oncology, Soc. Gynecol. Oncologists, Assn. Acad. Surgeons. Episcopalian. Avocations: sports, travel. Home Phone: 434-971-2886; Office Phone: 434-924-9933. Business E-Mail: ptt9y@virginia.edu.

TAYLOR, PHILIP CRAIG, physics professor; b. Paterson, NJ, Mar. 17, 1942; s. Philip D. and Elizabeth E. Taylor; m. Muriel A. Allison, Dec. 20, 1969; children: Allison T. Severson, Heather M. Porreca. BA, Carleton Coll., 1964; PhD, Brown U., 1969. Postdoctoral rsch. assoc. NAS, Washington, 1969—71; rsch. physicist Naval Rsch. Lab., Washington, 1971—80, supervisory rsch. physicist, 1980—82; prof. physics U. Utah, Salt Lake City, 1982—2001, chmn. Dept. Physics, 1989—98, disting. prof. physics, 2001—05; prof. physics Colo. Sch. Mines, Golden, Colo., 2005—. Dir. Dixon Laser Inst., Salt Lake City, 1998—2005; assoc. dir. Colo. Energy Rsch. Inst., Golden. Recipient Rsch. Publ. award, Naval Rsch. Lab., 1975, Oustanding Profl. Contributions medal, Brown U., 1992, Disting. Rsch. award, U. Utah, 2002. Fellow: Am. Phys. Soc. (chmn. four-corners sect. 2000—02); mem.: AAAS, Materials Rsch. Soc., Am. Assn. Physics Tchrs. Office: Colorado School of Mines 1523 Illinois Street Golden CO 80401-1887 Office Phone: 303-273-3586. Office Fax: 303-273-3919. Business E-Mail: pctaylor@mines.edu.

TAYLOR, PHILIP RAYMOND, lawyer; b. Dublin, Ga., Nov. 1, 1933; s. Evan Augustus and Eula Bush Taylor; m. Elizabeth Lester Taylor (div.); children: Emily Taylor Fendig, Lester Taylor Odachowski. AB, Mercer U., Macon, Ga., 1955, JD, 1957. Bar: Ga. Ptnr. Harris, Watkins, Taylor & Davis, Macon, Ga., 1958—80, Fendig, McLemore, Taylor, Whitworth & Durham, Brunswick, Ga., 1980—2001; sr. ptnr. Taylor, Odachowski, Sperry & Crossland, St. Simons, Ga., 2001—. Bd. visitors Mercer U. Law Sch., Macon, Ga., 1998—2004, chmn. bd. visitors, 2002—04. Mem. editl. bd Mercer Law Rev., 1956—57. Mem. Ga. State Ho. of Reps., Atlanta, 1961—62; chmn. Macon-Bibb County Dem. Exec. Com., Macon, Ga., 1964—68, Macon-Bibb County Bd. of Elections, Macon, Ga., 1969—80. Capt. USAR, 1962—78. Fellow: Am. Coll. Trial Lawyers, Am. Bd. Trial Lawyers; mem.: ABA, Am. Acad. Healthcare Attys., Def. Rsch. Inst., Ga. Soc. Hosp. Attys., Brunswick-Glynn County Bar Assn., Ga. Def. Lawyers Assn. (bd. dirs. 1967), Delta Theta Phi. Avocations: travel, fishing, hunting. Office: Taylor Odachowski Sperry & Crossland 300 Oak St Ste 200 Saint Simons Island GA 31522 Office Phone: 912-634-0955. Business E-Mail: ptaylor@toslaw.com.

TAYLOR, PHYLLIS MILLER, energy executive; m. Patrick F. Taylor (dec. 2004). Grad., U. S.W. La.; LLB, Tulane U. Law clerk for Supreme Ct. La., Orleans Parish Civil Dist. Ct.; in-house counsel for John W. Mecom, Sr., 1972; exec. v.p., bd. mem. Taylor Energy Co. LLC, New Orleans, 1979—2004, chmn., CEO, 2004—. Chmn., pres. Patrick F. Taylor Found. Named an Forbes' Richest Americans, 2006. Office: Taylor Energy Co LLC 1615 Poydras St New Orleans LA 70112 Office Phone: 504-581-5491.

TAYLOR, R. EUGENE, bank executive; B in Fin., Fla. State U. Credit analyst Bank Am. Corp., 1969—86, pres. Fla. bank, 1986—93; pres. NationsBank Mid Atlantic, 1993—97; pres. cons. and comml. banking Bank Am. Corp., 2000—04, pres. global bus. and fin. svcs., 2004—05, vice chmn., pres. global corp. and investment banking, 2005—. Office: Bank of America Corp 100 N Tryon St Charlotte NC 28255 *

TAYLOR, RALPH ARTHUR, JR., lawyer; b. Washington, Jan. 19, 1948; s. Ralph Arthur Sr. and Mary Florence Taylor; m. Joanna Lamb Moorhead, Jan. 30, 1988; children: Alison M., John Duncan. BS in Engring. with honors, Princeton, 1970; JD, U. Va., 1975. Bar: Va. 1975, D.C. 1976, Md. 1989, U.S. Dist. Ct. D.C. 1977, U.S. Dist. Cts. (ea. and we. dists.) Va. 1986, U.S. Dist. Ct. Md. 1988, U.S. Dist. Ct. Colo. 1998, U.S. Ct. Appeals (4th cir.) 1991, U.S. Ct. Appeals (D.C. cir.) 1977, U.S. Ct. Appeals (6th cir.) 1991, U.S. Ct. Claims 1985, U.S. Supreme Ct. 1980. Program advisor US EPA, Boston, 1970-72; assoc. Steptoe & Johnson, Washington, 1975-84, Shaw, Pittman, Potts, & Trowbridge, Washington, 1984-86, ptnr., 1986—2000, leader tech. and intellectual property litigation group, co-leader Yr. 2000 practice group; ptnr. Dorsey & Whitney, LLP, Washington, 2000—05, co-chair intellectual property litig. group, 2000—03, chair intellectual property litig. group, 2003—05; ptnr., litig., intellectual property groups Arent Fox LLP, Washington, 2005—. Assoc. editor Litigation News, 1985-99, exec. editor, 1999-2004; notes editor Va. Law Rev., 1974-75; contbg. author: International Technology Transfers, 1995; co-chair com. newsletters com. ABA Litigation Sect., 2004—. Pres. Cloisters West Homeowners Assn., Washington, 1989, 1990, 1625 Q St. Condo. Assn., Washington, 1982—86; bd. dirs. Am. Liver Found., nat. capital chpt., pres., 2004—; mem. grad. bd. trustees Princeton Quadrangle Club. Lt. USPHS, 1970—72. Mem. Order of the Coif, Met. Club (Washington), Barristers, Princeton Club (Washington), Chevy Chase Club, Lawyers Club Protestant. Avocations: sailing, skiing, tennis, golf. Office: Arent Fox LLP 1050 Connecticut Ave NW Washington DC 20036-5339

TAYLOR, REGINA, actress; b. Dallas, Aug. 22, 1960; d. Nell Taylor. Student, So. Meth. U. TV appearances include (movies) Crisis at Central High, 1981, Howard Beach: Making the Case for Murder, 1989, Children of the Dust, 1995, Hostile Waters, 1997, The Third Twin, 1997, Strange Justice, 1999, Cora Unashamed, 2000, In from the Night, 2006, (TV series) I'll Fly Away, 1991-93 (Emmy award nominee best actress in a drama 1993, Golden Globe award), Feds, 1997, The Education of Max Bickford, 2001-02, The Unit, 2006-; films include Lean on Me, 1989, Losing Isaiah, 1995, Clockers, 1995, The Keeper, 1995, Spirit Lost, 1996, A Family Thing, 1996, Courage Under Fire, 1996, The Negotiator, 1998; stage appearances include Romeo and Juliet, 1986, King Lear, 1987, The Tempest, 1988, one-woman show Escape From Paradise, 1994.

TAYLOR, RENEE, actress, writer; b. NYC, Mar. 19, 1933; m. Joseph Bologna, 1965; 1 child, Gabriel. Grad., Acad. Dramatic Arts; doctorate (hon.), Hofstra U. Actress (films) The Errand Boy, 1961, The Detective, 1968, A New Leaf, 1971, Last of the Red Hot Lovers, 1972, Lovesick, 1983, White Palace, 1990, Delirious, 1991, End of Innocence, 1990, All I Want for Christmas, 1991, Forever, 1992, Love Is All There Is, 1996, Dying on the Edge, 2001, 61*, 2001, Dr. Dolittle 2 (voice), 2001, Returning Mickey Stern, 2002, Lady Killers, 2003, Alfie, 2004, Kalamazoo?, 2005, A-List, 2005, Boynton Beach Club, 2006, Ice Age: The Meltdown, 2006, Kalamazoo?, 2006, (TV series) Dream On, 1992-94, Daddy Dearest, 1993, The Nanny, 1993-99, (stage) Three Sisters, Machinal, Annie Get Your Gun, Li'l Abner, Wish Your Were Here; writer (film) Lovers and Other Strangers (Academy award nomination), (TV) Paradise, (HBO spl.) Bedrooms (Writers Guild award); author: My Life On A Diet. Address: 16830 Ventura Blvd Ste 326 Encino CA 91436-1725

TAYLOR, RICHARD, mathematics professor; b. Eng., May 19, 1962; BA, Cambridge U., 1984; PhD, Princeton U., 1988. Taught Cambridge U., 1989—95; Savilian chair geometry Oxford U., 1995—96; Herchel Smith prof. math. Harvard U., 2002—. Co-recipient Shaw prize, Math. Scis., Shaw Prize Found., Hong Kong, 2007; recipient Fermat prize, 2001, Cole prize, Am. Math. Soc., 2002. Fellow: Royal Soc. London. Office: Dept Math Harvard U One Oxford St Cambridge MA 02138

TAYLOR, RICHARD EDWARD, physicist, researcher; b. Medicine Hat, Alta., Can., 1929; arrived in U.S., 1952; s. Clarence Richard and Delia Alena Taylor; m. Rita Jean Bonneau, 1951; 1 child, Norman Edward. BS, U. Alta., 1950, MS, 1952; PhD, Stanford U., 1962; DHC (hon.), U. Paris-Sud, 1980; DSc, U. Alta., 1991; LLD (hon.), U. Calgary, Alta., 1993; DSc (hon.), U. Lethbridge, Alta., 1993, U. Victoria, B.C., Can., 1995; DHC (hon.), U. Blaise Pascal, 1997; DSc (hon.), Carleton U., Ottawa, Ont.,

1999, U. Liverpool, UK, 1999, Queen's U., Kingston, Ont., 2000. Boursier Lab. de l'Accelerateur Lineaire, Orsay, France, 1958—61; physicist Lawrence Berkeley Lab., Berkeley, Calif., 1961—62; staff mem. Stanford Linear Accelerator Ctr., 1962—68, assoc. prof., 1968—70, prof., 1970—2003, assoc. dir., 1982—86, Lewis M. Terman Prof., 1993—99, emeritus prof., 2003—. Named Companion, Order of Can., 2005; recipient Nobel prize in Physics, 1990; fellow Guggenheim Found., 1971—72, von Humboldt Found., 1982. Fellow: AAAS, Royal Soc. London, Royal Soc. Can., Am. Acad. Arts and Scis.; mem.: NAS (fgn. assoc.), Can. Assn. Physicists, Am. Phys. Soc. (W.K.H. Panofsky prize divsn. particles and fields 1989). Achievements include first to conduct investigations concerning deep inelastic scattering of electrons on protons and bound neutrons, which have been of essential importance for the development of quark model in particle physics. Office: Stanford Linear Accelerator Ctr M/S 43 2575 Sand Hill Rd Menlo Park CA 94025-7015 E-mail: retaylor@slac.stanford.edu.

TAYLOR, RICHARD WILLIAM, investment banker, portfolio manager; b. Toledo, Sept. 16, 1926; s. Everett Ellsworth and Hazel (Broer) T.; m. Lyn Westerlund, Sept. 11, 1954; children: Julie Everett, Richard William, Alison Nichols, Jennifer Broer, Liane Westerlund. BS, U.S. Naval Acad., 1949; postgrad., U. Calif., 1952. Mem. Ohio Ho. of Reps. (100th gen. assembly from 9th Dist.); asst. mgr. Navy sales Martin Aircraft, Balt., 1953-56; with McKinsey & Co. (mgmt. cons.), NYC, 1956-60; asst. to v.p. Cerro Corp., NYC, 1960-62, spl. asst. to pres., 1965; pres. Cerro Aluminum Co., NYC, 1962-65; successively v.p., exec. v.p., pres. and CEO Carter, Walker & Co., Inc., 1967-69; pres., CEO Burton, Dana, Westerlund, Inc., NYC, 1969—; v.p. Sterling, Grace & Co., Inc., 1971-74, sr. v.p. corp. fin., 1980-81; v.p. corp. fin. Moseley, Hallgarten, Estabrook & Weeden Inc., 1975-80; v.p. Kidder, Peabody & Co. Inc., 1981-93; dir. investments, pvt. client divsn. Oppenheimer & Co., 1993—. Bd. dirs., pres., chmn. fin. com. YWCA Retirement Fund, Inc. With USN, 1944-52. Decorated Air medal, Navy Commendation medal. Mem. U.S. Naval Acad. Alumni Assn., U.S. Naval Inst. Home: Apt D 132 Heritage Hill Rd New Canaan CT 06840-4631 Office: Oppenheimer & Co Inc 200 Park Ave New York NY 10166 Home Phone: 203-801-9604; Office Phone: 212-667-4022. E-mail: richard.taylor@opco.com.

TAYLOR, RICHARD WIRTH, retired political science professor; b. Cleve., Jan. 15, 1923; s. Robert and Irmgard (Wirth) T.; m. Sadie White, Sept. 19, 1946; children: Peter, Karla, Mark, Stephen. BA, U. Ill., 1947, MA, 1948, PhD, 1950. Instr. polit. sci. U. Minn., Mpls., 1950-52; asst. prof. polit. sci. Lehigh U., Bethlehem, Pa., 1952-55, Wis. State U., Stevens Point, 1955-56; vis. asst. prof. Northwestern U., Evanston, Ill., 1956-57; assoc. prof. Coe Coll., Cedar Rapids, Iowa, 1957-60, chmn., prof., 1960-67; prof. polit. sci. Kent State U., Ohio, 1967-92, prof. emeritus Ohio, 1992—, chmn. Ohio, 1974-82. Vis. prof. Karl-Marx-Universität, Leipzig, Fed. Republic Germany, 1990. Co-exec. editor Peace and Change, 1986-87. Policy com. Friends Com. Nat. Legis., Washington, 1964-85, exec. com., 1986-87; acad. adv. com., ombudsman com. Internat. Bar Assn., Edmonton Alta., Can., 1980—; active Friends World Com. on Consultation, 1991-98, Am. Friends Svc. Com., 2000—, clk. Lake Erie Yearly Meeting, 1977-79. Home: 115 Kendal Dr Oberlin OH 44074-1905 E-mail: sadiewithers@aol.com.

TAYLOR, ROBERT A., veterinarian; b. Los Alamos, N.Mex. Attended, Southwest Tex. Jr. Coll., Colo. State U.; BS and DVM, Tex. A&M, 1970; MS in Surgery, Colo. State U., 1977. Diplomate Am. Coll. Veterinary Surgery, 1985, cert. Canine Rehabilitation Practitioner. Founder Alameda East Veterinary Hosp., Denver, 1971—. Affiliate faculty mem. Sch. Veterinary Medicine, Colo. State U.; past vis. faculty mem. U. Denver; founding faculty, Canine Rehabilitation Course U. Tenn.; bd. dir. Denver Zoological, Arapahoe County 4H, Colo. Humane Soc., Hospice St. John, Recycled Racers, Denver Zoo, Morris Animal Found., Animal Cancer Ctr.; lectr. in Argentina, Chile, Brazil, US, Mex., and Spain, 2006. Featured on Animal Planet Emergency Vets and E-Vet Interns; author: Manual of Post-operative care, Canine Sports Medicine, Canine Phys. Therapy; contbr. chapters to books; contbr. Canine Phys. Therapy and Rehabilitation-Veterinary Clinics of N.Am. Base veterinarian USNR, Lowry AFB. Mem.: Am. Coll. Veterinary Surgeons Found. (treas., bd. dir.), Am. Canine Sports Medicine Assn. (bd. dir.), Am. Coll. Veterinary Surgeons (treas., bd. dir.). Achievements include being an early teacher and innovator in canine arthroscopy and organized the first Canine Arthroscopy meeting in 1988. Has taught several hundred veterinarians both basic and advanced arthroscopy; implanted the first biological in-growth prosthesis in a dog. Office: Alameda East Veterinary Hosp 9770 E Alameda Ave Denver CO 80247 Office Fax: 303-366-2639, 303-344-8150. *

TAYLOR, ROBERT BROWN, physician, educator, writer; b. Elmira, NY, May 31, 1936; s. Olaf C. Taylor and Elizabeth (Place) Brown; m. Anita Dopico; children: Diana Taylor Root, Sharon Taylor Oliverio. Student, Bucknell U., 1954-57; MD, Temple U., 1961. Diplomate Am. Bd. Family Medicine. Gen. practice medicine, New Paltz, NY, 1964-78; faculty physician Sch. Medicine Wake Forest U., Winston-Salem, NC, 1978-84; prof. dept. family medicine Oreg. Health Scis. U. Sch. Medicine, Portland, 1984—, chmn., 1984-98, prof. emeritus family medicine, 1998—. Mem. comprehensive part II com. Nat. Bd. Med. Examiners, Phila., 1986-91. Author: Common Problems in Office Practice, 1972, A Primer of Clinical Symptoms, 1973, The Practical Art of Medicine, 1974; editor: Family Medicine: Principles and Practice, 1978, 6th edit., 2003, Health Promotion: Principles and Clinical Applications, 1982, Difficult Diagnosis, 1985, Difficult Medical Management, 1991, Difficult Diagnosis II, 1992, Fundamentals of Family Medicine, 1996, 3rd edit, 2003, Manual of Family Practice, 1997, 2d edit., 2002, Taylor's Review of Family Medicine, 1998, Manual of Ten-Minute Diagnosis, 2000, The Clinician's Guide to Medical Writing, 2004, Taylor's Diagnostic and Therapeutic Challenges, 2005, Taylor's Cardiovascular Diseases, 2006, Academic Medicine: A Guide for Clinicians, 2006, Taylor's Musculoskeletal Problems and Injuries, 2006; contbg. editor Physicians Mgmt. Mag., 1972-99; editl. bd. Family Practice Rsch. Jour., 1980-90, Female Patient, 1984-2006, Am. Family Physician, 1990-98, Jour. Family Practice, 1990-93, Med. Tribune, 1993-99. Served as surgeon USPHS, 1961-64. Recipient J. David Bristow MD award, Oreg. Health Scis. U., 1993, F. Marian Bishop Leadership award, Soc. Tchrs. Family Medicine Found., 2007. Fellow Am. Acad. Family Physicians (sci. program com., Thomas W. Johnson award 1998, bd. curators found. archives, John G. Walsh Lifetime Achievement award 2003, Outstanding Sci. Paper award 1982); mem. Soc. Tchrs. Family Medicine (bd. dirs., Excellence cert. 1989), Assn. Am. Med. Colls., Am. Assn. for Study Headache, World Orgn. Family Doctors (chmn. sci. program com.), Portland City Club, Multnomah Athletic Club, Phi Beta Kappa, Alpha Omega Alpha (award 1961). Home: 1414 SW 3rd Ave Apt 2904 Portland OR 97201-6629 Office: Oreg Health Sci U Sch Medicine Mail Code FM 3181 SW Sam Jackson Park Rd Portland OR 97239-3098 Home Phone: 503-241-1826; Office Phone: 503-494-6611.

TAYLOR, ROBERT LARRY, freelance/self-employed writer; b. Abilene, Tex., July 22, 1940; s. Larry Thornton and Virginia (Kerby) T.; life ptnr. Theodore Thomas Nowick, June 22, 1975. BA in Journalism, Tex. Tech U., 1962. Editor NHSC Newsletter, Nat. Home Study Coun., Washington, 1968-72; asst. editor Music Educators Jour., Music Educators Nat. Conf., Washington, 1972-76; editor Transp. USA mag. U.S. Dept. Transp., Washington, 1976-80; dep. text editor Am. Illustrated mag. USIA, Washington, 1980-86; freelance writer and author, 1986—. Affiliate scholar Oberlin Coll., 2004—. Author: (novels) The Innocent, 1997, All We Have Is Now, 2002, Whose Eye Is On Which Sparrow?, 2004 (winner Ind. Pub. Book award, 2005), All We Have Is Now, 2006, A Few Hints and Clews, 2007, (short stories) Revelation and Other Stories, 2002; contbg. author: Gay Pride: Photographs from Stonewall to Today, 1994; contbg. author I Do / I Don't: Queers on Marriage, 2004; contbr. short stories to publs. Mem. nat. coun. Am. Speaks Out, 2001—04; trustee Pierre Monteux Meml. Found., treas., 1994—97, bd. dirs., 1994—, exec. com., 1997—2002, v.p., 2002—06; trustee Bill Long Found., 2005—, sec., 2006—, Kendal at Oberlin Residents Assn., 2007—; bd. dirs. Down East AIDS Network, 2003—04. With US Army, 1962—67. Decorated Bronze Star; recipient Blue Pencil award as 1st place for best mag. Nat. Assn. Govt. Communicators, 1980, Outstanding Alumnus award Tex. Tech U. Sch. Mass Comm., 1986. Mem.: Vets. for Peace, Authors Guild. Democrat. Avocations: singing, making handmade books. Home: Kendal at Oberlin Oberlin OH 44074 Business E-Mail: kailuum@oberlin.net.

TAYLOR, ROBERT LEWIS, management educator; b. Pitts., Dec. 10, 1939; s. Robert William and Elinor (Miller) T.; m. Linda Taylor Shapiro, Oct. 28, 1988; 1 step child, Kara; children by previous marriage: Rob, Mike. AB in Am. Studies, cum laude, Allegheny Coll., 1961; MBA, Ohio State U., 1966; D in Bus. Adminstrn., Mgmt., Ind. U., 1972. Asst. prof., dir. rsch. USAF Acad., Colorado Springs, Colo., 1971-77, assoc. prof., dir. instrn. dept. econ., geography, mgmt., 1977-79, prof. mgmt., head dept. econs., geography, mgmt., 1980-81; assoc. dean Coll. Letters and Sci., head div. Bus. and Econs., Carl N. Jacobs Prof. of Bus. U. Wis., Stevens Point, 1981-84; dean Coll. Bus. Pub. Adminstrn. U. Louisville, 1984—2003, dean emeritus and prof. of mgmt., 2003—. Chmn. bd. dirs. Ky. Wood Floors, Louisville, 1988-98, AACSB: Internat., Tampa, Fla., 1999-2000; bd. advisors Rawlings Co., Louisville; bd. dirs. Stock Yards Bancorp; cons., advisor Kellogg Nat. Fellowship program Kellogg Found., Battle Creek, Mich., 1985-89. Co-editor: Contemporary Issues in Leadership, 1984, 6th edit., 2006, Leadership Challenges for Today's Manager, 1988, Military Leadership: In Pursuit of Excellence, 5th edit., 2005; contbr. articles to profl. jours Chmn. Mayor's Strategic Planning Group, Louisville, 1986—; mem. Gov.'s Econ. Devel. Com., Frankfort, Ky., 1987-89, exec. com. Bus. Advs., 1988-92, task force on econ. devel. Ky. Legis. Rsch. Coun., 1991, Leadership Louisville, 1986, Leadership Ky., 1987; bd. dirs. Metro United Way, 1999—, Ctr. Nonprofit Excellence, 2005—, Pub. Radio Partnership, 2006—; bd. trustees Jewish Hosp. Healthcare Svcs., Louisville, 2000—; active St. Michael Orthodox Ch. Mem. Acad. Mgmt. (proceedings editor 1976-77, newsletter editor 1983-86), Louisville C. of C. (bd. dirs., exec. com 1990-94), Sigma Xi, Beta Gamma Sigma, Pi Gamma Mu. Avocations: travel, walking, stamp collecting/philately, reading. Home: 1516 Sylvan Way Louisville KY 40205-2408 Office: U Louisville 375 College of Bus Louisville KY 40292-0001 Office Phone: 502-852-4786. Personal E-mail: tayl1450@bellsouth.net. Business E-Mail: rltayl01@gwise.louisville.edu.

TAYLOR, ROBERT M., minister; b. Englewood, NJ, Mar. 5, 1932; s. Robert M. and Irene Maude T.; m. Anna Elizabeth Taylor, Dec. 27, 1953 (dec. Sept. 1970); m. Beverly Ann Taylor, Nov. 7, 1971; children: Robert M., William Harrison, Joanne Elizabeth, Susan Ruth. BA cum laude, Lafayette Coll., 1953; MDiv, Princeton Sem., 1956. Ordained min. Presbyn. Ch., 1956. Pastor Mahoning Presbyn. Ch., Danville, Pa., 1956—59; asst. pastor Harundale Presbyn. Ch., Glen Burnie, Md., 1959—62; pastor Ctrl. Presbyn. Ch., Downingtown, Pa., 1962—69; sr. pastor The Presbyn. Ch., New Brunswick, NJ, 1969—75, Rosedale Gardens Presbyn. Ch., Livonia, Mich., 1975—79, Immanuel Presbyn. Ch., Albuquerque, 1979—85; interim pastor Cmty. Presbyn. Ch., Mountainside, NJ, 1985—86; interim sr. pastor First Presbyn. Ch., Matawan, NJ, 1986—88; pastor Christ Ch. on Quaker Hill, Pawling, NY, 1988—94, Hope Presbyn. Ch., Lakewood, NJ, 1994—97; ret., 1997. Commr. Gen. Assembly/Presbyn. Ch., Mpls., 1968; supr. Princeton Sem. Tchg. Ch., New Brunswick, N.J., 1969-75; v.p. Inter-Ch. Coalition on Mission in Southwest, Phoenix, 1984; mem. Monmouth Presbytery, 1994—; mem. ethics com. Harlem Valley Psychiat. Ctr.; mem. Interfaith Clergy Coun.; bd. dirs., v.p. Cmty. Resource Ctr. Pawling, 1988-94. Mem. bd. govs. United Fund, Downingtown, 1969, Citizen's Adv. Com., 1969, Mayor's Youth Adv. Com., East Brunswick, 1973; sec. Coll. Scholarship Found., 1975. Fellow in Pastoral Leadership Devel., Princeton Theol. Seminary, 1973. Mem. Rotary, Alpha Chi Rho (pres. 1952-53). Home: 1500 Bishop Estates Rd Villa 13B Jacksonville FL 32259 *Life is a marvelous journey of caring and sharing with continual opportunities for growth. The challenge is to remain open to God's leading, even when the necessary hurdles are many.*

TAYLOR, ROBERT MORGAN, electronics executive; b. Orange, NJ, May 13, 1941; s. Morgan H. M. Taylor and Grace Anna (Bonynge) Loding; m. Sandra Ruth Cox, Sept. 11, 1965; children; Scott Joseph, Karen Lynne. BA in Chemistry, Williams Coll., 1963; PhD in Chemistry, Pa. State U., 1968; MBA, Drexel U., 1973. Scientist Leeds & Northrup Co., North Wales, Pa., 1968-70, sr. scientist, 1970-72, prin. scientist, 1972-84, corp. scientist, 1984-85, dir. R&D, 1985-92, dir. analytical mktg., 1990-93; v.p. The Capital Controls Group, Colmar, Pa., 1993-99; pres. RMT Cons., Lansdale, Pa., 1999—. Contbr. articles to profl. jours. Chmn. indsl. com. Montgomery County (Pa.) Sci. Rsch. Competition, 1987-99. Mem. IEEE, Electrochem. Soc. (fin. com. 1971-73, controlling mems. com. 1977), Am. Chem. Soc., Instrument Soc. Am. (sr.), Indsl. Rsch. Inst. (rep.). Achievements include patents for for water analysis (5). Personal E-mail: rmtconsulting@comcast.net.

TAYLOR, ROBERT SAXTON, retired dean; b. Ithaca, NY, June 15, 1918; s. James Barnaby and Flora Estelle (Brown) Taylor; m. Leni Reichenberger (dec.); m. Fay Ann Golden, Aug. 22, 1998. BA, Cornell U., 1940; MS, Columbia U., 1950; MA, Lehigh U., 1954. Asst. libr., dir., info. scis. Lehigh U., Bethlehem, Pa., 1950—67; dir., libr. ctr. Hampshire Coll., Amherst, Mass., 1967—72; dean, prof. Syracuse U., Sch. of Info. Studies, Syracuse, NY, 1972—83; ret., 1983; Fulbright lectr. Delft Tekniske Hogeschole, Netherlands, 1956—57. Reviewer Nat. Sci. Found., 1965—77; com. mem. info. sci. Nat. Inst. of Heath, Bethesda, Md., 1965—76; reviewer US Office of Edn., 1970—76. Author: Making of a Library, 1972 (Am. Soc. for Info. Sci. Best Book, 1972), Value Added Processes in Information Systems, 1986. Co-founder, mem. governing com. Chamber Music Society, Bethlehem, Pa., 1952—67. With CIC US Army, 1942—47. Decorated Bronze star. Mem.: Am. Soc. for Info. Sci. (pres. 1968). Home: 5085 Skyline Dr Syracuse NY 13215 E-mail: rtaylor1@twcny.rr.com.

TAYLOR, ROBERT WILSON, military officer, publishing executive; b. Cambridge, Mass., Sept. 7, 1926; s. Walter Denzelo and Lucy Goudie Taylor; m. Shirley Hosmer, Apr. 3, 1948; children: Tobey Lee, David Alan, Stephen Hosmer. AA Polit. Sci., Syracuse U., 1959. With U.S. Army and USAF, 1945; advanced through grades to sgt. maj. USAF, 1965; asst. v.p. Skaneateles Savs. Bank, NY, 1965—78; land and residential appraiser Pomeroy Appraisal Assoc., Syracuse, 1978—88; co-owner Family Rm. Miniatures, Skaneateles, 1980—95; owner Romance Lives Publ. Co., Marcellus, NY, 2004—. Pres. consortium N.Y. savs. banks N.Y. State Savs. Banks Study Group, NYC, 1977—78; instr. Syracuse U. Coll. Liberal Arts, 1954—59. Author: The Memories of a Childhood, 1999, The Secret Life of William Roberts, 2004, The Hosmer Family-Footprints in History, 2005, Twenty Years in Business: Remembering Those Days, 2005, Ancora Per Favore, 2006, Echos-Collection of Writings-Boyle Senior Center, 2006. Fund originator, bd. mgmt. United Ch. of Change Islands, Newfoundland, 2000—; charter pres. Kiwanis Club We. Onondaga County, Skaneateles, 1974—77. Mem.: Small Pub. Assn. N.Am., Syracuse U. Alumni Club NY, Am. Legion. Republican. Presbyterian. Avocations: writing, gardening, literature. Home: 2474 Roman Ave Marcellus NY 13108 Office: Romance Lives Publ Co PO Box 134 Marcellus NY 13108 Office Phone: 315-673-0788. Office Fax: 315-673-0788.

TAYLOR, ROGER LEE, academic administrator, lawyer; b. Canton, Ill., Apr. 6, 1941; s. Ivan and Pauline Helen (Mahr) T.; m. E. Anne Zweifel, June 13, 1964. BA, Knox Coll., 1963; JD cum laude, Northwestern U., 1971. Bar: Ill. 1971, U.S. Dist. Ct. (no. dist.) Ill. 1971, U.S. Dist. Ct. (no. dist.) Tex. 1975, U.S. Ct. Appeals (7th cir.) 1972, U.S. Ct. Appeals (5th and 11th cirs.) 1981, U.S. Supreme Ct. 1975. Assoc. Kirkland & Ellis, Chgo., 1971-78, ptnr., 1978—; pres. Knox Coll., Galesburg, Ill., 2002—. Trustee Knox Coll., pres. 2002; trustee Ill. Hist. Preservation Agy., dir. Assoc. Coll. of Midwest, dir. Assoc. Coll. of Ill. Mem. Order of Coif, Univ. Club, Soangetaha Country Club (Galesburg, Ill.). Office: Knox College Galesburg IL 61401

TAYLOR, RONALD LEE, academic administrator; b. Urbana, Ill., Nov. 11, 1943; s. Lee R. and Katherine L. (Becker) Taylor; m. Patricia D. Fitzimmons, Mar. 10, 1973; children: Jamie, Lara, Meredith, Dana. AB, Harvard U., 1966; MBA, Stanford U., 1971. Asst. contr. Bell & Howell, Chgo., 1971-73; pres., CEO DeVry Inc., Chgo., 1973—2004, CEO, 2004—06, co-founder, sr. advisor, 2006—. Trustee Higher Learning Comm., North Ctrl. Assn. Colls. and Schs., 1985—2006; bd. dirs. La Petite Acad., Inc., 1997—2007. Trustee Rehabilitation Inst. Chgo.; mem. mgmt. bd. Stanford U. Sch. Bus., 2003—06. 1st lt. US Army, 1966—69. Decorated Commendation medal with oak leaf cluster US Army; recipient Outstanding Pub. Svc. medal, Sec. Def., 1998. Achievements include feature in Crain's Mag. Chgo., 2006. Office: DeVry Inc 1 Tower Ln Ste 2350 Oakbrook Terrace IL 60181-4663 Business E-Mail: rtaylor@devry.com.

TAYLOR, RONALD LEWIS, sociology educator; b. St. Petersburg, Fla., Feb. 27, 1941; s. David T. and Lillian (Bell) Miller; m. Bernice E. Chavis, Dec. 24, 1967; children: Kevin, Darryl. BA, Bethune-Cookman Coll., 1962; MA, Howard U., 1964; PhD, Boston U., 1973. Dean of men Bethune-Cookman Coll., Daytona Beach, Fla., 1964-65, dir. fin. aid, 1965-67; instr., lectr. Boston U., 1967-70; rsch. assoc., cons. Army Bur. Rsch., Ft. Devens, Mass., 1971-73; asst. prof. U. Conn., Storrs, 1972-78, assoc. prof., 1978-90, chair dept. sociology, 1981-86, prof. sociology, 1990—, dir. Inst. African-Am. Studies, 1993-99, vice provost multicultural and internat. affairs, 1999—. Nat. adv. bd. Ctr. Nat. Policy, Washington, 1991—; grant review panel Ctrs. for Disease Control, Atlanta, 1991-93. Editor: Black Youth in America, 1990, Minority Families in the U.S., 1994, African-American Youth, 1995; co-editor: The Black Male in America, 1977; mem. editl. bd. Jour. African-Am. Male Studies, 1991-93; editor Race and Soc. Assn. Black Sociologists, 1995-2003 Mem. AAUP (U. Conn. chpt. pres. 1993-94), Am. Sociol. Assn. (com. on coms. 1991-93, nominations com. 1994-96), Eastern Sociol. Soc. (chair elections 1991-93, v.p. 2003-04) Home Phone: 860-872-0596. Business E-Mail: ronald.taylor@uconn.edu.

TAYLOR, RONALD LOUIS, lawyer; b. Memphis, July 18, 1942; s. George Festus and Ina Dell (Sanderson) T.; m. Elsa Juanita Parker, Dec. 28, 1969; children: Anna-Kathryn, Benjamin Louis. BA magna cum laude, Miss. State U., 1964; JD, U. Miss., 1970. Bar: Miss. 1970, U.S. Ct. Appeals (5th cir.) 1976, U.S. Supreme Ct. 1976. Assoc. B.G. Perry, Southaven, Miss., 1970-71; ptnr. Perry & Taylor, Southaven, 1971-73, Perry, Taylor & Whitwell, Southaven, 1973-75, Taylor & Whitwell, Southaven, 1976-85, Taylor, Jones, Alexander, Seale & Ryan, Ltd., Southaven, 1985-89, Taylor, Jones Alexander & Sorrell Ltd., Southaven, 1994—2003, Taylor, Jones & Alexander Ltd., Southaven, 2003—. Mcpl. judge City of Horn Lake, Miss., 1975-77; city atty. City of Southaven, 1982—2003. Vice chmn. Southaven Libr. Bd., 1973-76. Lt. col. USAR, 1964-2002, ret. Fellow Miss. Bar Found.; mem. ATLA, Miss. Trial Lawyers (bd. govs. 1980), DeSoto County Bar Assn. (pres. 1978, 86), Exch. Club (pres. 1973), Lions, Rotary Club (Paul Harris Fellow), Masons (32d degree), Shriner (Al Chymia Shrine Temple), Rotary (chmn. Southhaven Spring Fest). Republican. Baptist. Office: Taylor Jones & Alexander Ltd PO Box 188 961 Main St Southaven MS 38671-0188 Home: 5115 Meadow Pointe Dr Southaven MS 38671 Office Phone: 662-342-1306.

TAYLOR, ROY LEWIS, botanist, educator; b. Olds, Alta., Can., Apr. 12, 1932; s. Martin Gilbert and Crystal (Thomas) T. BSc, Sir George Williams U., Montreal, Que., Can., 1957; PhD, U. Calif., Berkeley, 1962; DSc (hon.), U. BC, Vancouver, Can., 1997. Pub. sch. tchr. Olds Sch. Div., 1949-52; jr. high sch. tchr. Calgary Sch. Bd., Alta., Canada, 1953-55; chief taxonomy sect., research br. Can. Agrl. Dept., Ottawa, Ont., Canada, 1962-68; dir. Bot. Garden, prof. botany, prof. plant scis. U. B.C., Vancouver, 1968-85; pres., CEO Chgo. Hort. Soc., 1985-94; dir. Chgo. Bot. Garden, Glencoe, Ill., 1985-94; exec. dir. Rancho Santa Ana Bot. Garden, Claremont, Calif., 1994-99; prof. botany, chmn. botany program Claremont Grad. U., 1994-99, dir. emeritus, 1999. Pres. Western Bot. Svcs. Ltd. Author: The Evolution of Canada's Flora, 1966, Flora of the Queen Charlotte Islands, Vols. I and II, 1968, Vascular Plants of British Columbia: A Descriptive Resource Inventory, 1977; The Rare Plants of British Columbia, 1985; assoc. editor Pacific Horticulture, 2001—. Mem. State of Ill. Bd. Natural Resources and Conservation, 1987-94; trustee Nature Ill. Found., 1990-94, Elisabeth C. Miller Bot. Garden Trust, Seattle, 1994—, Elisabeth C. Miller Bot. Garden Endowment, 2001—, The Arbor Fund, Seattle, 1997—, chmn., 2002—; bd. dirs. Milner Gardens and Woodland Soc., Qualicum Beach, B.C., Can., 2000—, chmn., 2002—. Fellow Linnean Soc. London (hon.); mem. Can. Bot. Assn. (pres. 1967-68), Biol. Coun. Can. (pres. 1973-74), Am. Assn. Mus. (accreditation com. 1980-85, chmn. 1985-91, chmn. ethics commn. 1991-93, Centennial Honor Roll award, 2006), Am. Assn. Bot. Gardens and Arboreta (hon. life; pres. 1976, 77, award of merit 1987), Am. Soc. Bot. Artists (bd. dirs. 1997—2004), Claremont C. of C. (bd. dirs. 1995-98), Ottawa Valley Curling Assn. (pres. 1968-69), Milner Gardens and Woodland Soc. (bd. dirs. 2000—, chmn. 2002—), B.C. Soc. Landscape Archs. (hon.), U. B.C. Bot. Garden (hon.), Chgo. Hort Soc. (life, medal 1994), Gov. Gen.'s Curling Club Can. (life), Wood Acres Strat Corp (pres., 2005—). Home Fax: 250-390-0860. E-mail: taylor.rl@shaw.ca.

TAYLOR, RUSSELL BENTON, mining executive; b. Eskridge, Kans., May 16, 1925; s. Bayard Charles and Eva May (Russell) T.; m. Arlene Marie Krehbiel, Aug. 14, 1959; 1 child, Bruce Charles. BSBA, U. Kans., 1949; JD, U. Kans, 1951. Asst. cashier Eskridge (Kans.) State Bank, 1951-57, cashier, 1957, pres., 1958-69, chmn., 1969-78; v.p., dir South Standard Mining Co., Salt Lake City, 1978-96. Mayor City of Eskridge, Kans., 1959. Decorated Purple Heart. Mem. Kans. Bar Assn., Kiwanis, Masonic, Arab Shrine. Republican. Methodist. Avocations: travel, ranching. Home and Office: 18213 Sanford Rd Eskridge KS 66423 Personal E-mail: r7b9t@earthlink.net.

TAYLOR, RUTH ARLEEN LESHER, marketing educator; b. Riverton, Iowa, Mar. 7, 1941; d. Clyde Almond and Bernice Emogene (Graves) Lesher; m. Leslie (Milburn) Taylor, Aug. 10, 1963; children: Treg Anthony, John Leslie II. BS in Home Econs. Edn. magna cum laude, U. Houston, 1975; MEd, Tex. Christian U., 1977; PhD, U. North Tex., 1981. Prof. mktg. Tarrant County C.C., Ft. Worth, 1977-78, North Tex. State U., Denton, 1978-81, Southwestern U., Georgetown, Tex., 1982-87, S.W. Tex. State U., San Marcos, 1981-82, 87—; lectr. U. Nat. Mayor de San Marcos, Lima, Peru, 2006—. Dir. travel to China, Japan, Hong Kong, Costa Rica, Morocco, Europe, Eng., Mex., Dominican Republic, Venezuela, Chile, Peru; faculty intern Tex. Dept. Econ. Devel. and Tex. Sec. of State Office; collaborator STAT-USA Internet and Catalog Exhbn. U.S. Dept. Commerce; dir. study program, Washington. Author: Text Maps Study Guides, 1994—; contbg. author: The Psychology of Fashion, 1985, Ethics in Accounting, 1994; contbr. articles to profl. jours. Mem. Lost Creek Garden Club, Austin, Tex., 1985—, v.p.; vol. Bob Bullock State Hist. Mus.

Nominee Gary Woods Rsch. award, 2005; recipient Tchg. award, McCoy Coll. Bus., 2005, award, N.Am. Small Bus. Trade Educators, 2005, Gold medal of honor, U. Nacional Mayor de San Marcos, Lima, 2007; grantee, Merrick Found., 1991; Fulbright sr. specialist grantee, U. Lima, 2006. Mem.: DAR, Am. Soc. for Competitiveness, Winthrop Soc., French Huguenot Soc., Colonial Dames, Internat. Hospitality Coun. (bd. dirs.), Mayflower Soc., Mktg. Mgmt. Assn., Western Mktg. Educators Assn., Am. Mktg. Assn., Alpha Mu Alpha, Alpha Kappa Psi, Phi Delta Kappa, Phi Epsilon Omicron, Beta Gamma Sigma. Avocations: travel, gardening, reading, entertaining. Office: Texas State University 601 University Dr San Marcos TX 78666-4685 E-mail: rt01@txstate.edu.

TAYLOR, S. BROOKE, lawyer; b. Port Angeles, Wash. BA in Polit. Sci., Stanford U., 1965; JD, U. Va., 1968. Bar: Wash. 1968. Dep. prosecuting atty. Clallam County, 1969—70, prosecuting atty., 1970—75; co-owner, ptnr. Taylor & Taylor P.S., Port Angeles, 1975—90, Platt Irwin Taylor, Port Angeles, 1991—. Spkr. in field. Dir., pres. Clallam County Family YMCA; dir. G.M. Lauridsen Found.; dir., pres. Clallam County Cmty. Mental Health Ctr.; mem., dir. Port Angeles C. of C.; mem. Penninsula Coll. Found. Named Citizen of Yr., Clallam County, 1999. Mem.: ABA, Assn. Trial Lawyers Am., Wash. State Trial Lawyers Assn., Clallam County Bar Assn. (pres. 1981), Wash. State Bar Assn. (mem. bd. govs. 2000—02, treas. 2001—02, chmn. facilities com. 2001—, liaison dist. and mcpl. ct. judges assn. 2003—04, pres.-elect 2004, pres. 2005), Kiwanis Club (dir.). Achievements include contributions to the Washington State Bar Association's "Diversity Amendment" (later called the "Taylor Draft") which expanded the Association's definition of diversity and led to the creation of three governor-at-large positions. Office: Platt Irwin Taylor 403 S Peabody Port Angeles WA 98362 Office Phone: 360-457-3327. Office Fax: 360-452-5010. *

TAYLOR, SARA MARIE, former federal official; b. Dubuque, Iowa, 1974; d. Ray Taylor. BA, Drake U., 1997. Pollster Terrence Group, Va., 1996—98; coalitions dir. George Bush Electoral Team, 1999—2000; campaign worker Senator Phil Gramm Pres. Campain, 1995—96; dep. to chief strategist Bush-Cheney 2004 Campaign, 2003—04; dep. asst. to Pres, dir. polit. affairs The White House, Washington, 2005—07. Recipient Young Alumni Achievement award, Drake U., 2006. *

TAYLOR, SARAH ANN, oncologist, educator; b. Wichita, Kansas, July 2, 1950; Grad., Cornell Coll., Iowa; MD, U. Kansas Sch. Medicine, 1975. Cert. Internal Medicine, Med. Oncology. Intern, internal medicine U. Kansas Med. Ctr., 1975—76, resident, oncology, 1976—78, fellow, 1978—80, hosp. appointment, 1980—, med. dir., Palliative Care Svcs., 1987—; prof. internal medicine, divsn. hematology/oncology U. Kansas. Med. dir., hematology.oncology fellowship program and Kendellwood Hospice; prin. investigator, clin. trials grant at U. Kansas Southwest Oncology Group; mentor FDA Oncology Drug Adv. Com. Named one of Kansas City Super Doctor, Kansas City Mag. Office: U Kansas Med Ctr Palliative Care Svcs Mail Stop 1044 3901 Rainbow Blvd Kansas City KS 66160-7353 Office Phone: 913-588-6029. Office Fax: 913-588-4085. *

TAYLOR, SHANNON, lawyer, not-for-profit developer; b. Passaic, NJ, June 14, 1955; s. Michael and Rita Taylor; m. Judith Ann Bernz. BA magna cum laude, Tufts U., 1976; attended, Hebrew U. Law, 1977; JD, Temple U., 1979. Bar: NJ 1979, NY 1980, So. Dist. 1980, US Dist. Ct. 1980, Ea. Dist. 1981. Ct. atty. to Hon. David Follender, Supreme Ct.-Civil Term, Hackensack, NJ, 1979—80; assoc. comml. litigation Goetz & Fitzpatrick, NYC, 1981—85; assoc. Nathan Cyperstein & Paul Gerstner, Bklyn., 1985—90; prin. ct. atty. to Hon. Jerome Hornblass, NY State Supreme Ct.-Criminal Term, 1992—96; ct. atty. NY State Criminal Ct., Housing Ct., Kings County, 1997—. Exec. dir. Blacks and Jews in Conversation, Inc., NYC, 1993—; pub. rels. and press coord., photographer, chronicler Not Just Blacks and Jews in Conversation, 1994—, stand-up comic, 1998—; adminstrv. law judge NYC Taxi and Limousine Commn., 1997—; radio show co-host The Conversation, NYC; guest news commentator/panelist radio and TV news, NYC, 1990—; co-creator, exec. dir. ann. jud. fact-finding missions to Israel Blacks and Jews in Conversation, Inc. Photojournalist (for TV, newspapers, films, and mag.), contbr. columnist. Prodr., promoter comedy-celebrity workshops fundraiser Not-for-Profit Religious and Health Instns., internationally and in NYC, 1990—. Recipient Most Productive Cmty. Assistance Orgn., YWCA, Bklyn., 1999. Mem.: NY Drama Leagye, NYC Bar Animal Rights Divsn., NY Jewish Lawyers Guild, Tufts U. Law Alumni, NY Players Club, NY Friars Club. Avocations: percussionist, table tennis, mineralogy. Home: 225 W 83rd St 5 L New York NY 10024 Office: NYC Criminal Ct Law Dept 120 Schermerhorn St Brooklyn NY 11201 Office Phone: 917-374-3623. E-mail: staylor@nyc.rr.com.

TAYLOR, SHELLEY E., psychology researcher, educator; b. Mt. Kisco, NY, Sept. 10, 1946; d. Charles Fox and Pearl May (Harvey) T.; m. Mervyn Francis Fernandes, May 1, 1972; children: Sara F., Charles F. AB magna cum laude in Psychology, Conn. Coll., 1968; PhD in Social Psychology, Yale U., 1972. Asst. prof. psychology and social rels. Harvard U., Cambridge, Mass., 1972-77, assoc. prof., 1977-79; assoc. prof. psychology UCLA, 1979-81, prof., 1981—. Mem. vis. faculty dept. adminstrv. scis. Yale U., New Haven, 1971-72, vis. Sloane fellow, 1978; mem. basic sociocultural rsch. rev. com. NIH, 1979-83; Katz-Newcomb lectr. U. Mich., 1982; cons. to pub. houses and TV producers. Author: Social Cognition, 1986, 2d edit., 1991, Health Psychology, 1986, 3d edit., 1995, 5th edit., 2002. Positive Illusions: Creative Self-Deception and the Healthy Mind, 1989, The Tending Instinct: How Nurturing is Essential to Who We Are and How We Live, 2002; contbr. numerous articles to sci. publs. Active numerous charitable and fund-raising orgns. including Curtis Sch. PTA and U. So. Calif./Norris Cancer Ctr. Recipient Rsch. Scientist Devel. award NIMH, 1981-86, 86-91, MERIT award, 1987, Donald Campbell award for disting. sci. contbn. to sociology, 1995; numerous rsch. grants in field; Winthrop scholar, 1967; Woodrow Wilson fellow, 1968, NIMH fellow, 1968-72. Fellow APA (Sci. Weekend lectr. 1988, Disting. Sci. award 1980, Outstanding Sci.Contbn. award Divsn. 38, 1994), Brit. Psychol. Soc. (flying fellow), Acad. Behavioral Medicine Rsch., Soc. Psychol. Study Social Issues, Soc. Behavioral Medicine; mem. AAAS, Soc. Exptl. Social Psychology, Western Psychol. Assn. (pres. 1993-94), Inst. Medicine. Office: UCLA Dept Psychology Franz 4611 Box 951563 Los Angeles CA 90095-1563

TAYLOR, SHERRIL WIGHTMAN, broadcast executive; b. Salt Lake City, Jan. 4, 1924; s. Kenneth E. and Florence May (Wightman) T.; m. Josephine Vermillion, May 2, 1970; 1 child by previous marriage, Sarah. Student, U. Utah, 1943-46; BJ, U. Mo., 1947; postgrad., Yale U. Promotion mgr. KSL Radio, Salt Lake City, 1947-51; sales promotion mgr. CBS, Hollywood, Calif., 1951-53, CBS radio sales NYC, 1953-56; dir. sales promotion and advt. CBS Radio, NYC; also v.p. Radio Advt. Bur., NYC, 1956-58; sr. group head J. Walter Thompson, Chgo., 1958-61; ind. TV producer Kukla, Fran, and Ollie Show, NYC, 1961-64; v.p. Nat. Assn. Broadcasters, Washington, 1964-67, dir., 1969-78; v.p. affiliate relations CBS, 1967-79. Cons. Bonneville Internat. Corp., 1979-85; pres. Taylor Co., 1985-91; vice chmn. Coltrin & Assoc., 1991—; pvt. sector coordinator USIA, Washington, 1982, cons., 1982—; chmn. adv. com. Voice of Am., Washington, 1989—; vis. lectr. Brigham Young U., Provo, Utah, 1980—, Emerson Coll., Boston, Mich. Central U., Southern Vt. Coll.; adv. faculty-industry seminar, 1980, 81; bd. dirs. Am. Communications Inc., Utica-Rome TV Svcs. Inc., 1988—. Author: Radio Programming in Action, 1967. Mem. Carnegie Hall com. for Utah Symphony, Park Avenue Preservation Com.; past trustee The Helene Toolen Inst. Med. Rsch., Bennington, Vt., 1985—; mem. futures com. Bennington Mus., 1985—; bd. dirs. Nautical Ventures Inc., N.Y.C., 1987—; chmn. bd. Cmty. Action Network-N.Y., 2000-01. Recipient Nat. Assn. Broadcasters Ann. Conv. Am. Broadcast Pioneer award, 1998. Mem. Internat. Radio and TV Soc. (v.p., bd. dirs., pres., chmn., bd. dirs. found.), Broadcasters' Found. (dir.), Food and Wine Soc. (N.Y. chpt.), Yale Club of N.Y., Sigma Chi (Significant Sig award 2000). Episcopalian. Home: PO Box 4004 Bennington VT 05201 Office: Yale Club of NY 50 Vanderbilt Ave Box 35 New York NY 10017 Office Phone: 727-403-9018. Personal E-mail: swt3@verizon.net.

TAYLOR, STAN, retired state agency administrator; b. Nov. 17, 1951; m. Jill Taylor; children: Nathan, Lora, Kathryn, Lindsey. BA in Sociology, U. Del., 1974. Correctional officer Dept. of Correction, State of Del., 1976-79, correctional counselor, 1979-82, program and staff devel. officer, 1982-83, supt. of security, 1983-84, temporary warden III, 1991, dep. warden, 1983-92, warden, 1992-93, chief of bur. of prisons, 1993-95, commr. of correction, 1995—2007. Recipient Gov.'s award. Home: PO Box 238 Ocean View DE 19970-0238 *

TAYLOR, STEPHEN LLOYD, toxicologist, educator, food scientist; b. Portland, Oreg., July 19, 1946; s. Lloyd Emerson and Frances Hattie (Hanson); m. Susan Annette Kerns, June 23, 1973; children: Amanda, Andrew. BS in Food Sci. Tech., Oreg. State U., 1968, MS in Food Sci. Tech., 1969; PhD in Biochemistry, U. Calif., Davis, 1973. Research assoc. U. Calif., Davis, 1973-74, research fellow, 1974-75; chief food toxicology Letterman Army Inst., San Francisco, 1975-78; asst. prof. food toxicology U. Wis., Madison, 1978-83, assoc. prof., 1983-87; head dept. food sci. technology, dir. Food Processing Ctr. U. Nebr., Lincoln, 1987—2004, prof. dept. food sci. tech., 2004—. Cons. in field. Contbr. articles to profl. jours. Fellow: Inst. Food Technologists (divsn. chmn. 1981—82, sect. chmn. 1984—85, exec. com. 1988—91), Nat. Acad. Scis. (Food Forum); mem.: Soc. Toxicology, Am. Chem. Soc., Am. Acad. Allergy, Asthma and Immunology. Democrat. Presbyterian. Home: 941 Evergreen Dr Lincoln NE 68510-4131 Office: U Nebr Dept Food Sci Tech Lincoln NE 68583-0919 Home Phone: 402-488-6477; Office Phone: 402-472-2833. Business E-Mail: staylor2@unl.edu.

TAYLOR, STEVE HENRY, zoologist; b. Inglewood, Calif., Mar. 18, 1947; s. Raymond Marten and Ardath (Metz) T.; 1 child, Michael Travis; m. Sarah Margaret Young, May 14, 1993. BA in Biology, U. Calif.-Irvine, 1969. Animal keeper Los Angeles Zoo, 1972-75, assoc. curator, 1975-76; children's zoo mgr. San Francisco Zoo, 1976-81; zoo dir. Sacramento Zoo, 1981-88; dir. Cleve. Met. Zoo, 1989—. Bd. dirs. Sacramento Soc. Prevention Cruelty to Animals, 1983-87, Sacramento Red Cross, 1988-89, Conv. and Visitor Bur. of Greater Cleve., 1995-03, 06-, Leadership Cleve. Class 1997; mem. admissions com. United Way, 1999. Recipient Robert P. Bergman Impact award Convention & Visitors Bur. Greater Cleve., 2000. Fellow Am. Assn. Zool. Parks and Aquariums (infant care diet advisor 1979, 85, bd. dirs. 1987-93, pres. 1991-92, chmn. pub. edn. com. 1987-89, bd. regents, mgmt. sch., chmn. accreditation com. 1998, 99, Outstanding Svc. award 1979, 85, 88, 89, 91, 95, 98, 99, 2001); mem. Conservation Breeding Specialist Group, World Assn. Zoos and Aquariums, Sierra Club, Audubon Soc. Democrat. Home: 1265 Elmwood Rd Rocky River OH 44116-2236 Office: Cleveland Metroparks Zoo 3900 Wildlife Way Cleveland OH 44109-3132 Home Phone: 440-333-7564; Office Phone: 216-635-3331. Business E-Mail: sht@clevelandmetroparks.com.

TAYLOR, STEVEN W., state supreme court justice; b. Henryetta, Okla., June 7, 1949; m. Mary Taylor; 1 child. BA in Political sci., Okla. State U., 1971; JD, U. Okla. Coll. of Law, 1974. Atty. Gotcher, Gotcher & Taylor, Okla., 1978—84; councilman McAlester City, 1980—82, mayor, 1982—84; judge Okla. Dist. Ct., 1984—94; dist. judge, chief judge 18th Jud. Dist., 1994—2004; presiding judge E. Ctrl. Jud. Adminstrv. dist., 1997—2003; justice Okla. Supreme Ct., Oklahoma City, 2004—. Pres. Okla. Jud. Conference, 1990. Mem. bd. dirs. Okla. Heritage Assn., Okla. Medical Rsch. Found. Served atty. & judge USMC, 1970—78. Mem.: Pittsburg County Bar Assn., Okla. Bar Assn. (Jud. Excellence award 2003, Outstanding Okla. Judge of Yr. 2003). Office: Okla Supreme Ct Rm 200 State Capital Bldg Oklahoma City OK 73105 Office Phone: 405-521-3844. Business E-Mail: steven.taylor@oscn.net.

TAYLOR, STUART ROSS, geochemist, writer; b. Ashburton, New Zealand, Nov. 26, 1925; s. Thomas Stuart and Anne Grace (Lloyd) T.; m. Noel Elvie White, May 21, 1958; children: Susanna, Judith, Helen. BSc, U. New Zealand, 1948, MSc, 1951; PhD, Ind. U., 1954; DSc, Oxford U., 1978. Lectr. U. Oxford, Eng., 1954-58; sr. lectr. U. Cape Town, South Africa, 1958-60; professorial fellow Australian Nat. U., Canberra, 1961-90, vis. fellow, 1990-99, prof. emeritus, 1997; prof. U. Vienna, 1992, 96. Vis. scientist Lunar and Planetary Inst., Houston, 1969-90. Author: Lunar Science: Post-Apollo View, 1975, Planetary Science, 1982, Solar System Evolution, 1992, (with others) Continental Crust, 1985, Destiny or Chance: Our Solar System and Its Place in the Cosmos, 1998, Solar System Evolution, 2d edit., 2001; contbr. more than 220 articles to profl. jours. Recipient Goldschmidt medal Geochem. Soc., 1993, Gilbert award Geol. Soc. Am., 1994, Bucher medal Am. Geophys. Union, 2002; Asteroid 5670 named Rosstaylor, 1997. Fellow Royal Soc. New Zealand (hon.), Australian Acad. Sci., Geol. Soc. London (hon.), Geol. Soc. India (hon.); mem. NAS (fgn. assoc.), Meteoritical Soc. (pres. 1989-90, Leonard medal 1998). Office: Australian Nat U Dept Geology Canberra 0200 Australia E-mail: ross.taylor@anu.edu.au.

TAYLOR, SUSAN L., magazine editor; b. NYC, Jan. 23, 1946; d. Lawrence and Violet (Weekes) T.; m. William Bowles (div.); 1 child, Shana-Nequai; m. Khephra Burns, 1989-. BA in Sociology, Fordham U., 1991, postgrad.; doctorate (hon.), Spelman Coll., Bennett Coll., Del. State, Fisk U., Lincoln U. Founder, rschr. and developer of a line of customized cosmetics and natural skin care line Nequai Cosmetics, 1970—81; freelance beauty editor to fashion Essence Mag., NYC, 1971-81; editor-in-chief Essence Comm., Inc., NYC, 1981—2000, v.p, 1986—93, sr. v.p., 1993, editl. dir., 2000—, also bd. dir. Host, exec. prodr. weekly tv show Essence, 1983-87; exec. prodr. and driving force behind Essence Awards and Essence Music Festival; served on Comm. on Rsch. in Black Edn. through the Assn. Ednl. Rsch. Assn; spkr. in field. Author: In the Spirit: The Inspirational Writings of Susan L. Taylor, 1993, Lessons in Living, 1995; co-author with husband Confirmation: The Spiritual Wisdom That Has Shaped Our Lives, 1997; co-editor of several books. Co-chair Danny Glover for Shared Interest (to raise money to build housing in rural areas of S. Africa); bd. dir. Joint Ctr. for Polit. and Econ. Studies, Washington; mem. adv. bd. Black Adminstr. in Child Welfare; mem. La. Recovery Authority; committed to serving and empowering the poor and work with disadvantaged women and teenagers to encourage them take charge of their lives. Recipient Henry Johnson Fisher award, 1998, President's award, NAACP Image award, 2006. Mem.: Women in Communications, Am. Soc. Mag. Editors (inducted into Hall of Fame 2002), Nat. Assn. Black Journalists. Office: Essence Comm Inc 135 W 50th St 4th Fl New York NY 10020

TAYLOR, SUZONNE BERRY STEWART, real estate broker; b. Memphis, Sept. 27, 1926; d. Andrew Cleveland and Sue Hodge (Berry) Stewart; m. Robert Allen Taylor, Sr., June 15, 1946; children: Robert A. Jr., Suzonne Stewart Taylor Davids. Student, Rhodes Coll., Memphis, 1948, U. S.C., Columbia, 1969. Cert. residential specialist CRS Coun., 1996; grad. Realtors Inst.; cert. real estate broker; accredited buyer's rep. Am. Bd. Realtors. Sales agt. E. Roy Stone Realtors, Greenville, SC, 1967—69; real estate broker Aven Assoc. Realtors, Dover, Del., 1970—80, Emerson & Co. Realtors, Dover, 1980—2000; realtor ERA Harrington Realty, Dover, 1998—. Active Cresent Music Club, Greenville, 1955, Wildwood Garden Club, Greenville, 1960; mem., costume chmn. Greenville Little Theater, Jr. League Greenville, 1956-66, sustaining mem., 1966—, Jr. League Wilmington, Del., 1999—, dir., 1999. Recipient Beyond Excellence award, ERA, 2004, 2005. Mem. Nat. Bd. Realtors, Del. Bd. Realtors, Kent County Bd. Realtors, Del. Hist. Soc., Biggs Mus., Alpha Omicron Pi. Republican. Episcopalian. Home: 517 Greenhill Rd Dover DE 19901-3766 Office: ERA Harrington Realty 1404 Forest Ave Dover DE 19904 Office Phone: 302-674-4663. Business E-Mail: staylor@harringtonera.com.

TAYLOR, TERESA, telecommunications industry executive; BS, U. Wis., LaCrosse. With US West (now Qwest), 1988—2000; exec. v.p. products and pricing group Qwest Comm. Internat., Inc., Denver, 2000—03, exec. v.p. wholesale markets group, 2003—04, exec. v.p., chief human resources officer, 2004—. Bd. dirs. Colo. Inst. Tech., Colo. Children's Campaign, Colo. Symphony Orch. Office: Qwest Comm Internat Inc 1801 California St Denver CO 80202 Office Phone: 303-992-1400. Office Fax: 303-896-8515. *

TAYLOR, TERRY R., editor, educator; b. Valley Forge, Pa., Oct. 4, 1952; d. Thomas R. and Anna P. (Bystrek) T. BA in Journalism, Temple U., 1974. Reporter gen. assignments, sch. news Charlotte (N.C.) News, 1974-77; supr., writer AP, Phila., 1977-81, supr., writer sports desk NYC, 1981-85, asst. editor sports, 1985-87, dep. editor sports, 1987-91, asst. chief bur., 1991-92, editor sports, 1992—; asst. editor sports N.Y. Times, 1991. Assoc. in journalism Columbia U., N.Y.C., 1991-95; adv. bd. Honda Awards, 1996—06. Mem. Internat. Olympic Com. Press Commn., 2005—. Recipient John A. Domino Meml. award St. Bonaventure U., 1996, Founder's award Temple U., 1999; inductee Delaware County Sports Hall of Fame, 1998. Roman Catholic. Achievements include first woman sports editor at the AP. Office: AP Sports 450 W 33rd St New York NY 10001

TAYLOR, THOMAS WILLIAM, lawyer; b. Columbus, Ind., Feb. 11, 1943; s. Virgil W. and Margaret Emma (Voiles) T.; m. Linda Kay Followell, Jan. 1, 1964; children: Pamela Kay, William Lansing. AB with honors, Ind. U., 1965; LLB cum laude, Harvard U., 1968. Bar: Mass. 1968, U.S. Dist. Ct. Mass. 1969. Assoc. Ropes & Gray, Boston, 1968-78, ptnr., 1978-98, of counsel, 1999—. Lectr. Pres.'s urban policy program seminars U.S. Coun. of Mayors, 1982; chmn. tax panel nat. workshop Coun. of Infrastructure Financing Authorities, 1993; vol. astronomer Chaco Obs., Chaco Culture Nat. Hist. Park, 2000, 2006, prin. astronomer, 2001, 2005. Vol. Wilderness First Responder, 2002—; snowboard instr. Nashoba Valley Ski Area, 1999—2005, staff trainer, 2003—05. Mem. Nat. Assn. Bond Lawyers (opinions com., chmn. securities law panel Washington workshop 1992, lectr. atty.'s workshop Chgo. 1983-97), Am. Coll. Bond Counsel (founding fellow), Appalachian Mountain Club Stewardship Soc. Avocations: rock climbing, orienteering, trumpet playing, canoeing. Office: Ropes & Gray 1 International Pl Fl 4 Boston MA 02110-2624

TAYLOR, TOM, marketing executive; Assoc. Outside Garden Dept. Home Depot, Inc., Miami, dept. head to asst. store mgr. to mgr., dist. mgr., regional v.p. S.W. Divsn., 1996, merchandising v.p. N.W. Divsn., 1999, divsn. pres. N.W., sr. v.p. PRO Bus., 2001—02, pres. Ea. Divsn., 2002—05, exec. v.p. Home Depot stores, exec. v.p. merchandising and mktg. Atlanta, 2005—06, cons., 2006—. Named one of Top 20 Southerners to Watch, The Fin. Times, 2003. Office: Home Depot Inc 2455 Paces Ferry Rd Atlanta GA 30339

TAYLOR, TRENT E., retail executive; BS in information sci., Northeastern Ill. Univ., Schaumburg, Ill., 1984. Sr. programmer, analyst Motorola, Inc., 1984; cons. Ernst & Young, Chgo.; mgr. info sys. Walgreens, 1992—95, dir. infrastructure, architecture, 1995—99, divsn. v.p., CIO, 1999—2002, corp. v.p., CIO, 2000—, sr. v.p., CIO, 2002—05, exec. v.p., CIO, 2005—, pres. Health Services, 2007—. Home: Walgreens 200 Wilmot Rd Deerfield IL 60015 *

TAYLOR, VICTORIA, real estate rehabilitator, sculptor; b. Toronto, Ont., Can., Oct. 18, 1935; arrived in U.S., 1978; d. Alberto A. Equable and Evelyn McLaughlin; children: James R., Joseph J., Sherry L., Vincent A. AA, Fla. Keys C.C., 1989. Owner, operator Spring Dale Nursing Home, Peterborough, Ont., Canada, 1973—78, Sun & Surf Motel, Key West, Fla., 1978—79, Dairy Queen, Key West, 1979—82; real estate salesman/broker Key West, 1983—96. Mem.: Nat. Sculpture Soc. Home: 15A E Circle Dr Key West FL 33040-4013 Office Phone: 305-745-1363.

TAYLOR, WALLACE EDMONDSON, JR., otolaryngologist; b. Corpus Christi, Tex., May 13, 1953; s. Wallace Edmondson and Anne Porter Taylor; m. Lynne Ann Warren, Dec. 26, 1975; children: Timothy Ryan, Jenna Noel. BA in Zoology, U. Tex., Austin, 1974; MD, Southwestern Med. Sch., Dallas, 1978. Diplomate Amer Bd. Otolaryngology, 1983. Med. staff San Luis Valley Regional Med. Ctr., Alamosa, Colo., 2004—; med. dir., owner Ultimate Skin MediSpa, Alamosa, 2006—07. Pres. San Luis Valley Med. Profls. Corp., Alamosa, 2001—04. Chmn. adminstrv. coun. First United Meth Ch., Alamosa, 1998—99. Lt. col. US Army, 1978—87. Decorated Army Achievement medal US Army. Fellow: Amer Acad. Otolaryngology. Methodist. Avocations: golf, camping, gardening, fly fishing. Office: Ultimate Skin MediSpa 319 Ross Ave Alamosa CO 81101 Home Phone: 719-589-6478; Office Phone: 719-587-1901. Office Fax: 719-587-4079. Business E-Mail: info@ultimateskinspa.com.

TAYLOR, WATSON ROBBINS, construction company executive; b. Wetumpka, Ala., Sept. 7, 1925; s. Henry Watson and Helen Robbins Taylor; m. Ernestine Jenkins, Sept. 10, 1949; children: Jane Albright, W. Robbins Jr., George Lewis. BS, U. Ala., 1948; DSc (hon.), Auburn U., Ala., 1986. Estimator Std. Roofing Co., Montgomery, Ala., 1948—52, v.p., 1952—66, pres., CEO, 1966—97, CEO, chmn. bd., 1997—; chmn., pres. Std.-Taylor Industries Inc., Montgomery, 1979—. Chmn. bd. Union Bank and Trust Co., Montgomery, 1980—94. Chmn. bd., founding chmn. Auburn U., Montgomery, 1967-80; dir. Ala. Shakespeare Festival, 1995—, Ala. State Docks, Mobile, 1992—. Lt. j.g. USN, 1943-45. Named Contractor of Yr. RSI mag., 1999; named univ. ctr. in his honor, Watson Robbins Taylor Ctr. Auburn U., 1999. Republican. Episcopalian. Avocations: golf, hunting. Home: PO Box 1 Letohatchee AL 36047-0001 Office: Std Roofing Co 516 N Mcdonough St Montgomery AL 36104-2645 Office Phone: 334-265-1262. Business E-Mail: r.taylor@standardtaylor.com.

TAYLOR, WESLEY BAYARD, JR., retired army officer; b. Covington, Ky., June 5, 1944; s. Wesley B. Sr. and Varina Martha (Morgan) T.; m. Linda L. Taylor, June 2, 1967; children: Kathleen C., Clint C. BS, U.S. Mil. Acad., 1965; MA in Internat. Rels., U. Calif., Santa Barbara, 1973; student, U.S. Army War Coll., 1985-86. Commd. 2d lt. U.S. Army, 1965, advanced through grades to brig. gen., 1990; asst. bn. advisor, sr. bn. advisor Airborne Divsn. Adv. Detachment, U.S. Mil. Assitance Command, Vietnam, 1967-68; staff officer Dept. of Army, Washington, 1980-81; bn. comdr. 3rd Bn., 5th Inf. U.S. Army, Republic of Panama, 1981-83; bn. comdr. 1st Ranger Bn. Hunter Army Airfield, Ga., 1983-85; strategic fellow U.S. Army War Coll., Carlisle Barracks, Pa., 1986-87; regimental comdr. 75th Ranger Regiment, Ft. Benning, Ga., 1987-89; asst. divsn. comdr. 1st Armored Divsn., Germany, 1989-91; dep. dir. ops, readiness and mobilization Dept. of Army, Washington, 1991-92; dep. asst. sec. of def. for policy and missions Office Sec. of Def., Washington, 1992-94; pres., CEO Cal Farley's Boys Ranch & Affiliates, U.S.A., Amarillo, Tex., 1995-99, Family & Childrens Ctr, Mishawaka, Ind., 2000—05, George C. Marshall Found., Lexington, Va., 2006—. Dist. commr. Boy Scouts Am., Germany, 1989-91. Decorated DSM, Def. Superior Svc. medal, Silver Star, Legion of Merit, Def. Meritorious Svc. medal, Bronze Star medal with oak leaf cluster, Air medals. Mem. Assn. U.S. Army, U.S. Army Ranger Assn., 75th Ranger Regiment Assn., Soc. Vietnamese Airborne Advisors, Soc. 173rd Airborne Brigade. Methodist. Avocations: fishing, hunting. Office: George C Marshall Found PO Drawer 1600 VMI Parad Lexington VA 24450 Personal E-mail: trextayl@comcast.net.

TAYLOR, WILLARD B., lawyer; b. NYC, 1940; BA, Yale U., 1962, LLB, 1965. Bar: N.Y. 1966. With firm Sullivan & Cromwell, NYC. Adj. faculty NYU Law Sch. Trustee North European Oil Royalty Trust. Mem. N.Y. State Bar Assn. (chair tax sect. 1983-84), Am. Law Inst. Office: Sullivan & Cromwell 125 Broad St New York NY 10004-2489

TAYLOR, WILLIAM AL, church administrator; b. Danville, Va., Sept. 26, 1938; s. Preston Floyd and Helen Elizabeth (Doss) T.; m. Brenda Flo Owen, June 4, 1961 (dec. 1996); children: Fawnia Rae Ricks, Albert Todd, Athena Dawn Jarman; m. Norma S. Pierce, June 28, 1997. AA, Lee Coll., 1957; postgrad., U. Calif., Santa Barbara, 1980. Br. mgr. Ency. Britannica, Greensboro, NC, 1960-62, divsn. trainer Mpls., 1963, dist. mgr. Omaha, 1964-72; adminstrv. asst. Forward in Faith Internat. Broadcast, Cleveland, Tenn., 1972-80; gen. mgr. Sta. WQNE-FM, Cleveland, 1980—; cons. stewardship Ch. of God Internat. Offices, Cleveland, 1980—2004. Pres. Pathway Credit Union, Cleveland, 1985-2005, Vision Found., Cleveland, 1985—, exec. dir., 1979-80; chmn. Internat. Commn. on Prayer, Cleveland, 1986—. Author: Proving God, 1991, Days of Heaven on Earth, 1993, Stewardship Masterplanning, 1993, The Power of Vision, 2003. Pres. Clean Water Soc., Gastonia, N.C., 1974-75; speaker Citizens Against Legalized Liquor, Bradley County, Tenn., 1973, 75; advisor Mothers on March, Cleveland, 1976; active Nat. Conf. on Drug Abuse, Washington, 1978; master of ceremonies Nat. Religious Leaders Conf. on Alcohol and Drug Abuse, Indpls., 1979; pres. Ch. of God Found., 2002. Recipient Mass Communications award Ch. of God Media Ministries, 1980, Stephen award Ch. of God Lay Ministries, 1990. Mem. Nat. Assn. Evangelicals (bd. adminstrs. 1985-98, chmn. stewardship commn. 1985-89), Christian Stewardship Assn. (bd. dirs. 1990-96, nat. prayer com. 1999—, Best of the Best Faculty award 1999, Outstanding Stewardship Profl. award 2000). Mem. Ch. Of God. Avocations: flying, travel, racquetball. Office: Ch of God Dept Stewardship 2490 Keith St NW Cleveland TN 37311-1309 Business E-Mail: ataylor@cogwm.org. E-mail: stewardcog@mindspring.com. *We are all spending the precious gift of life, and we have been given the privilege to decide upon what we shall spend it. I have found the most worthy and fulfilling investment of life is God's stated purpose, "that we be conformed to the image of His son Jesus Christ.".*

TAYLOR, WILLIAM B., JR., ambassador; married; 2 children. Grad., US Mil. Acad., 1969; MA in Pub. Policy, Harvard U., 1977. Dir. Office Emergency Preparedness Dept. Energy; mem. staff Senator Bill Bradley; dir. Def. Dept., Washington; spl. dep. def. adv. US Amb. to NATO, Brussels, 1987—92; coord. US Assistance to Europe and Eurasia US Dept. State, Washington, 1992—2002, spl. rep. Donor Assistance to Afghanistan Kabul, 2002—03, Afghanistan coord., 2003, dir. Iraq Reconstruction Mgmt. Office Baghdad, Iraq, 2004—05, mem. Quartet Spl. Envoy Jerusalem, 2005—06, US amb. to Ukraine Kiev, 2006—. Infantry officer US Army, 1969—75, Vietnam and Germany. Office: DOS Amb 5850 Kiev Pl Washington DC 20521-5850 *

TAYLOR, WILLIAM COLTON, physician, educator; b. Boston, Jan. 25, 1948; s. Manuel and Marjorie Taylor; m. Julia Katherine Landau, Dec. 4, 1983; children: Rachel, Hannah, Daniel, Benjamin, Jessica. BA, Yale U., New Haven, Conn., 1970; MD, U. Pa., Phila., 1974. Cert. bd. Am. Bd. of Internal Medicine, 1977. Sr. physician Beth Israel Deaconess Med. Ctr., Boston, 1996—; assoc. prof. medicine Harvard Med. Sch., Boston, 2006—.

TAYLOR, WILLIAM IRVING, retired chemicals executive; b. Auckland, New Zealand, July 23, 1923; arrived in US, 1955; s. John Taylor and Irene Irving Miller; m. Giuliana Ermelinda Valsangiacomo, Aug. 14, 1952; children: John Stephen, Frank, Mark. BSc, Auckland U., 1945, MSc, PhD, Auckland U., 1948, DSc, 1967. Assoc. prof. chemistry U. NB, Fredericton, Canada, 1952—55; dir. natural products rsch. Ciba Pharm. Co., Summit, NJ, 1955—68; v.p. R&D, Internat. Flavors and Fragrances, Union Beach, NJ, 1968—78; dir. tech., v.p. E.A.ME. Internat. Flavors & Fragrances, London, 1979—88; ret., 1988. Contbr. articles to profl. jours. Recipient award, Pharm. Assn. Found., 1968. Fellow: New Acad. Scis.; mem.: Am. Chem. Soc. Home: 4 Hickory Rd Radford VA 24141

TAYLOR, WILLIAM JAMES (ZAK TAYLOR), lawyer; b. Milw., Jan. 26, 1948; s. William Elmer and Elizabeth Emily (Lupinski) T.; m. Marlou Belyea, Sept. 20, 1975; children: Danielle Belyea, James Zachary Belyea. BA in Econs., Yale U., 1970; JD, Harvard U., 1976. Bar: Calif. 1976, US Dist. Ct. (cen. dist.) Calif. 1976, US Dist. Ct. (no. dist.) Calif. 1977, US Ct. Appeals (9th cir.) 1977, US Dist. Ct. (ea. dist.) Calif. 1980, US Supreme Ct. 1980, US Tax Ct. 1988. Law clk. to hon. Shirley M. Hufstedler U.S. Ct. Appeals (9th cir.), LA, 1976-77; assoc. Broebeck, Phleger & Harrison, San Francisco, 1977-83; ptnr. Broebeck, Phleger and Harrison, San Francisco, 1983-95; shareholder Taylor & Jenkins, P.C., Oakland, Calif., 1995-96, Chilvers & Taylor, P.C., Oakland, 1996-99; of counsel Brobeck, Phleger & Harrison, LLP, San Francisco, 2000—03, Morgan Lewis & Bockius, LLP, San Francisco, 2003—04, ptnr., 2004—. Bd. dirs. Berkeley (Calif.) Law Found., 1988-91, Legal Svcs. for Children (recipient Jean Waldman Child Advocacy award, San Francisco 1988), 1983-89; co-chmn. Attys. Task Force for Children, San Francisco, 1983-89. Editor-in-chief Harvard Civil Rights, Civil Liberties Law Rev., 1976; bd. editors No. Dist. Calif. Digest, 1978-83; co-author: California Antitrust Law, 1991; contbg. editor: Calif. Bus. Law Reporter, 1995—, Antitrust Law Developments, 1997, 4th edit., 2002. With US Army, 1970—73. Mem. ABA, Bar Assn. San Francisco (bd. dirs. 1986-87, chair antitrust sect. 1987, chair fed. cts. sect. 1995-97; award of merit 1987), Am. Bus. Trial Lawyers Assn., Am. Health Lawyers Assn., Calif. Soc. Healthcare Attys., Barristers of San Francisco (bd. dirs. 1980-82, v.p. 1982-83). Democrat. Office: Morgan Lewis & Bockius LLP 1 Market Spear Tower San Francisco CA 94105-1420 Office Phone: 415-442-1315. Business E-Mail: wtaylor@morganlewis.com.

TAYLOR, WILLIAM JESSE, JR., international security studies educator, research institute senior advisor; b. Florence, SC, Dec. 28, 1933; s. William J. and Dorothy (Byrd) T.; m. Louise Inger Haegerstrom, Apr. 9, 1977; 1 child, Nicolaus; children by previous marriage: Juliana C., William J. III, L. Scott, Christopher B., Helen B. BS, U. Md., 1962; MA, Am. U., 1964, PhD, 1967. Enlisted U.S. Army, commd. 2d lt., 1955, advanced through grades to col., 1976; prof. U.S. Mil. Acad., West Point, N.Y., 1970-81; vis. prof. U.S. Nat. War Coll., 1975-76; ret. col. U.S. Army, 1981; sr. exec. Ctr. for Strategic and Internat. Studies, Washington, 1981—2001, sr. v.p. internat. security programs, 1987—99; pres. Taylor Assocs. Inc., 1984—2006. Internat. lectr., debater, T.V. and radio mil. analyst, 1970—. Author: Future of Conflict: U.S. Interests, 1982, Future of Conflict into the 21st Century, 1987; co-author: American National Security: Policy and Process, 1981, 83, 89, 93, 99; co-editor: Defense Manpower Planning, 1980, The Future of Conflict in the 1980's, 1982, Strategic Requirements for the Army to the Year 2000, 1983, Strategic Responses to Conflict in the 1980's, 1984, Nordic Defense: Comparative Decisionmaking, 1985, Strategic Dimensions of Military Manpower, 1987, The Future of U.S.-Republic of Korea Security Ties, 1989, The Korean Peninsula: Prospects for Arms Control, 1990, Korea 1991: The Road to Peace, 1991, Elvis in The Army, 1995, 97. Mem. Presiding Bishop's Nat. Episc. Roundtable, 1983-86. Decorated Bronze Star with oak leaf cluster, Legion of Merit (2), Air Medal (3), Air medal for valor, Vietnam Cross of Gallantry, Combat Infantry Badge; recipient Pitman Potter Medal Am. U., 1964; named to Infantry Officer Hall of Fame, 1976; named Disting. Alumnus, Episcopal Acad., 1995, Disting. Alumnus, CSIS, 2001. Mem. St. Anthony Club. Republican. Episcopalian. Home: 6010 Maiden Ln Bethesda MD 20817-6261 Office Phone: 202-775-3203. Personal E-mail: wjtaylor44@aol.com. Business E-Mail: wtaylor@csis.org.

TAYLOR, WINNIFRED JANE, psychologist; b. Akron, Ohio, Aug. 27, 1925; d. Edwin Dain and Jessie Pearl (Keeran) Fletcher; B.S., U. Akron, 1962, M.S., 1965, Ph.D., 1971; m. John Idris Taylor, June 22, 1943; children— John Frederick Taylor, Timothy David Taylor, Kathryn Sue Taylor Cline. Tchr., Akron and Barberton, Ohio, 1959-65; sch. psychologist Akron Pub. Sch., 1965-74; pvt. practice family counseling and psychology, Clinton, Ohio, 1969-74; assoc. prof. and coordinator counseling programs U. Wis., Superior, 1974-93, prof. emeritus, 1993—; pvt. practice counseling psychology and family therapy, 1982—; lectr. Sun Am. Seminars, 1993-95. Author: AMP Therapy: Strategies for Anger Management and Violence Prevention, 1996; syndicated columnist; contbr. articles to profl. jours. Recipient Freedom Found. award for Teaching, 1965-66. Mem. Nat. Assn. Sch. Psychologists, Am., Wis. personnel and guidance assns., Am. Soc. Adlerian Psychology, Am. Edn. Research Assn., Am. Sch. Counselors Assn., Assn. Humanistic Psychology, Douglas County Mental Health Assn., Am. Soc. Indiviual Psychology. Home: 1421 E 6th St Superior WI 54880-3315

TAYLOR-ANDERSON, JILL, reading specialist; b. Oakland, Calif., Feb. 21, 1962; d. Allen Isaac and Phyllis Evelyn Taylor; 1 child, Christopher M. Anderson. BA in Liberal Studies, Calif. State Poly. U., 1984, MA in Edn., 1989. Reading specialist credential Calif. 6th grade tchr. Hacienda La Puente Unified Sch. Dist., Calif., 1984—88; kindergarten tchr. Riverside Unified Sch. Dist., Calif., 1988—95; reading specialist Corona-Norco Unified Sch. Dist., Norco, 1995—. Cub scout leader Boy Scouts Am., Grand Terrace, Calif., 1997—. Named Tchr. of Yr., Riverview Elem. Sch., 2003—04; recipient Celebrate Reading award, Inland Empire Reading Assn., 1997—2001, Founders' Day award, Riverview Elem. PTA, 2003. Mem.: Calif. Reading Assn., Internat. Reading Assn. Republican. Avocations: quilting, reading.

TAYLOR CLAUD, ANDREA, retired educational consultant; b. Warrenton, Va., Nov. 5, 1952; d. Andrew Earl and Catherine (Dennis) Taylor. BS, Norfolk State U., 1974, MA, 1983; postgrad., Old Dominion U., 1975-76, 89; MA in Cmty. Counseling, Regent U., 2000. Profl. collegiate cert. in learning disabilities, mentally handicapped, emotionally handicapped and technology stds. Classrm. tchr. Facquier County Sch. System, Warrenton, Va., 1974-75; child devel. specialist, team leader Norfolk Pub. Schs., Norfolk, Va., 1976-82, ednl. diagnostician, 1982-87; ednl. cons. Va. State Dept. Edn., Norfolk, 1987—2004; v.p. A Taylor of Hope, Inc., 2004—; pres. Perfect Storm, L.L.C., 2004—. V.p. DECAA Enterprises, Norfolk, 1983—. Active Nat. Kidney Found. of Va., Hampton Rds., Lindenwood Civic League, Norfolk; coord. bereavement ministry Pleasant Grove Bapt. Ch., Va. Beach, 2003, coun. mem., 2004; troop leader Girl Scouts U.S.A., Norfolk, 1977-79. Named Outstanding Young Women of Am., 1983; recipient Apple for Tchr. award, Iota Sorority, Inc., 1997, Outstanding Renal Healthcare Profl. Yr. award, Nat. Kidney Found. of Va., 1998, Sch. Bell award, Norfolk Pub. Sch., 2003. Mem. AARP, ACA, NEA, NAFE, Va. Edn. Assn., Norfolk Edn. Assn., Coun. Exceptional Children, Assn. Supervision and Curriculum Devel., Nat. Counseling Assn., Commonwealth Va. Notary, Delta Sigma Theta. Democrat. Avocations: travel, reading, listening to music, fishing.

TAYLOR-DUNN, CORLISS LESLIE, marriage and family therapist; d. Hilary Oliver and Sally Wilkins Taylor; m. David Charles Dunn, Aug. 2, 1975 (dec. Apr. 6, 2001). BA in Performing Arts, classically trained dramatic soprano, Ctrl. State U., 1971; MA in Marriage & Family Therapy, Azusa Pacific U., Calif., 1995; student in Counseling for the Ministry, Biola U., 1991—93; DS in Psychology, Calif. Coast Coll., 2006. Lic. marriage & family therapist Bd. of Behavioral Scis., Calif., 2000. Psychotherapist Helicon Youth Ctr., Riverside, Calif., 1998—2001, Genesis Counseling Svcs., San Bernardino, Calif., 2002—02; pvt. practice Fort Garland, Colo., 2003—; pres., CEO, tchr. The Dunn Ctr. of Ft. Garland, Fort Garland, 2002—. Pres., CEO, nationwide safe ho. planter, tchr. www.freudsfunstuff.com, Fort Garland, 2002—; tchr. music, drama and dance Cmty. Ctr.; presenter in field. Author: (plays) (with Sandra Reaves-Phillips) Musical, Opening Night, 1981—82 (nominated for 3 off-Broadway Audelco awards, 1983); composer; dir.: Musical, Opening Night; author: (plays) Sojourner; The Story of an Ex-Slave (The Brody Art award Calif.Commn. Nat. Edn. Arts Assn., 1987); actor: (plays, Broadway) Ella, Bubbling Brown Sugar, 1977, Rockette Spectacular, Pin 'N Needles, Don't Bother Me I Can't Cope, (Broadway tour) Ruth in Raisin, 1976, 1988—89; prodr.: (TV films) Safehouse. Mem. Friends of the Fort support com. Fort Garland (Colo.) Mus.; founder Buffalo Soldiers Essay Contest Colorado Schs.; established David Charles Dunn scholarship Bilola U., 2002; mem. steering com. Rural Philanthropy Days; bd. dirs. Cmty. Revitalization Com., Neighborhood Action Group, Marketing Com. Friends of the Fort. Mem.: Am. Assn. Marriage and Family Therapists (licentiate), Calif. Assn. Marriage and Family Therapists (licentiate), Internat. Fellowship Christians and Jews, Costilla County C. of C. (mktg. com. 2003). Republican. Avocations: gardening, travel, acting, interior decorating, performing. Office: The David Charles Dunn Foundation 611 Macdonald Place Fort Garland CO 81133 Personal E-mail: ctaylordunn@aol.com.

TAYLOR-WHITE-GRIGSBY, QUEEN DELORIS, minister, consultant; b. Oklahoma City, Aug. 21, 1948; d. Barnett C., Sr. and M. Bedell Boles Dewitt Taylor; m. Walter Thomas White II, Nov. 26, 1966 (div. June 1976); children: Walter Thomas III, Robin Orlando; m. James O. Grigsby, Sept. 19, 1976 (dec. Dec. 1976); 1 child, James Jumaané. BS, Howard U., 1970; M in Counseling, Liberty U., 1988. RN Va., 1993; ordained to ministry Ray Deliverance Found., 1989; cert. housing specialist Housing Specialist Inst., 1972. Housing cons. Montgomery County, Rockville, Md., 1971—73; founder, cons., pres. Taylor & Co., Richmond, Va., 1973—; assoc. cons. Trust Inc., Richmond, Va., 1973—80, Orgnl. Devel. Cons., Richmond, 1979—81; founder, pastor Tangible Substance God Is Love Ch., 1985—; founder, min. Man Child Ministries, Phoenix, 1988—. Tchr. nursing J. Sargent Reynolds C.C., Richmond, 1992—93, Richmond Meml. Hosp., 1992—93; cons. in field, 1972—2007. Author: numerous poems. Advocate child and adult welfare Dept. Corrections, Commonwealth Va., 1974-75, Ariz. Dept. Corrections, Phoenix, 1990, Ark. Dept. Corrections, 1994—, Okla. City Dept. Corrections, 1995—, advocate tchr. rights, 1991; active tchr. rights Phoenix Pub. Sch. Sys., 1992; supr. elections County Election Bd., Maricopa County, Ariz., 1987-88; trainer, developer Internat. Transactional Analysis counseling model for abused women and their families in YWCA residential housing programs, 1992; coord. Y-Splash program Maricopa County YWCA, 1992-93, grant writer, 1992; active food programs and ministry Internat. Healing Cathedral/Hall of Deliverance Found. and Desert Moon Mission, 1985-93; active children and youth program Phoenix Women's League, 1991-92; active Las Guias Heard Mus. Guild, 1990-93; docent Okla. Zoo., 2004-07; vol. VA, 2004-07, Column Writers, 2005; planning commn., Md.; dir. children's program United Meth. Ch., Richmond, 1977; grant writer Met. Better Living Ctr., 1993-97. Lucille McMahn scholar, 1965, Nellie Green scholar, 1965, Philip Morris scholar, 1983; recipient Danforth Leadership award, 1965, Golden Poet award, World of Poetry, 1991-92; named Internat. Woman of Yr., 2000-06. Mem. Soc. Tng. and Devel., Friends Libr. Republican. Avocations: reading, swimming, hunting, fishing, camping. Office: Taylor & Co 1138 N Bath Ave Oklahoma City OK 73117-2602

TAYMOR, JULIE, theater, film and opera director, designer; b. Newton, Mass., Dec. 15, 1952; d. Melvin L. and Betty Taymor. BA in folklore and mythology, Oberlin Coll., 1974; attended, L'Ecole Mimet Theatre in Paris, France, Herbert Berghof Studio, NYC. Founder Teatr Loh. Dir. Way of Snow, The Transposed Heads, 1984, The Tempest, 1986, Liberty's Taken, 1985, Juan Darién, 1988, Fool's Fire, 1992, Titus Andronicus, 1994, Oedipus Rex, 1992, The Magic Flute, Salomé, The Flying Dutchman, The Lion King, 1997, (Tony awards for best director and costume design 1998), The Green Bird, 2000, (films) Titus, 1999 (Acad. award nominee), Frida, 2002 (two Acad. awards), Across the Universe, 2007, operas, classical plays and exptl. theater projects; prodr. Shakespeare plays and operas; designer puppets, masks, imaginative costumes and other visual elements. MacArthur grantee, Watson fellow, 1974-79, Obie awards, 1988, Golden Plate award, Acad. Achievement, 2006 Mailing: c/o Bart Walker CAA 2000 Ave of Stars Los Angeles CA 90076 also: CAA 162 Fifth Ave New York NY 10010 *

TAZELAAR, HENRY DALE, physician, educator; s. Henry and Evelyn Teresa Tazelaar; m. Peggy Jean Ritsema, June 6, 1978; children: Andrew, Jeffrey. BA, Calvin Coll, Grand Rapids, Mich., 1978; MD, Rush U., Chgo., 1983. Bd. cert. in anatomic pathology Am. Bd. Pathology. Intern Stanford U. Med. Sch., Calif., 1983—84, resident, 1984—85, fellow, NIH, 1985—86, fellow, 1986—87, instr., 1987—88; asst. to full prof. Mayo Clinic Coll. Medicine, Rochester, Minn., 1988—, cons., 1988—. Vice chair edn. Dept. Lab. Medicine and Pathology, 2002—05; mem. edn. com. US and Can. Acad. Pathology, Augusta, Ga., 2003—; chair anatomic pathology divsn. Mayo Clinic, Ariz., 2006—. Author: Pathology and Genetics of Tumors in the Lung, Pleura, Thymus and Heart, 2004; author, editor Lung Pathology, 2005. Bd. mem. Ransom Fellowship, Rochester, 1990—. Fellow: Am. Coll. Chest Physicians, Coll. Am. Pathologists; mem.: Pulmonary Pathology Soc. (pres. 2004—). Presbyterian. Avocations: hiking, scuba diving, backpacking, classical organ performance, choral arts. Office: Mayo Clinic 13400 E Shea Blvd Scottsdale AZ 85259

TCHAIKOVSKY, LESLIE J., federal judge; b. 1943; BA, Calif. State Univ., Hayward, 1967; JD, Univ. of Calif., Berkeley, 1976. Law clk. to Hon. John Mowbray Nev. Supreme Ct., 1976-77; with Dinkelspiel, Steefel, Leavitt & Weiss, 1977-80, Gordon, Peitzman & Lopes, 1981, Dinkelspiel, Donovan & Reder, 1981-88; bankruptcy judge U.S. Bankruptcy Ct. (Calif. no. dist.), 9th circuit, Oakland, 1988—. Office: US Courthouse 1300 Clay St Oakland CA 94612-1425

TCHANTCHOU, FLAUBERT, medical researcher; arrived in US, 2001; s. Gabriel Tchana and Touwoud Monique; m. Wyllie Christiane Njinou Noupet, Apr. 12, 2003; 1 child, Francesca Gabrielle Tchatch. BSc, Yaounde U., Cameroon, 1992; diploma in tropical med. biology, Inst. Tropical Medicine, Antwerp, Belgium, 1999; MSc, Free U. Brussels, 2001; PhD, U. Mass., Lowell, 2005. Tchr. and rsch. asst. U. Douala, Cameroon, 1996—98; rsch. asst. U. Mass., 2002—05; postdoctoral rsch. fellow So. Miss. U., Hattiesburg, 2005, U. Md., Balt., 2005—. Assoc. rev. editor Jour. Alzheimer's Disease, 2006—. Mem.: AAAS, Am. Physiol. Soc., Am. Assn. Pharm. Sci. Home: 4 Liberty Place Rd # 6 Baltimore MD 21244 Office: U Md Sch Pharmacy 20 N Pine St Baltimore MD 21244

TCHERVIAKOVA, OLGA A., language educator; b. Minsk, Belarus, Sept. 15, 1976; m. Andrei G. Kazlouski, Sept. 26, 1998; 1 child, Ivan A. Charviakou. M, State Linguistic U. Belarus, Minsk. Cert. tchr. Pa. Dept. Edn. Spanish tchr. Nazareth Area H.S., Pa., 1999—. English as a fgn. lang. instr. Adult Literacy Ctr. Lehigh Valley, Allentown, Pa., 2001—04. Mem.: NEA. Home: 188 Shiloh Ct Whitehall PA 18052

TCHOBANOGLOUS, GEORGE, civil engineering educator; b. Patterson, Calif., May 24, 1935; s. Christo and Penelope (Megdani) T.; m. Rosemary Ash, June 16, 1957; children: Kathryn, Lynn, Julianne. BCE, U. Pacific, 1958; MCE, U. Calif., Berkley, 1960; PhD, Stanford U., 1969; D in Engring. (hon.), Colo. Sch. Mines, 2005. Registered profl. engr., Calif. Research engr. U. Calif.-Berkeley, 1960-62; cons. Metcalf & Eddy Engrs., Palo Alto, Calif., 1963-81, Nolte & Assocs., Sacramento, 1981—, Calif. Water Resources Control Bd., 1972-80; assoc. prof. U. Calif.-Davis, 1970-76, prof. engring., 1976—2004, prof. emeritus, 2004—. Prin. author: Wastewater Engineering: Collection, Treatment, Disposal, 1972; author: (with R. Smith and R. Crites) Wastewater Management: A Guide to Information Sources, 1976, (with H. Theisen and R. Eliassen) Solid Wastes: Engineering Principles and Management Issues, 1977, (with Schroeder) Water Quality: Characteristics, Modeling, Modification, 1985, (with Peavy and Rowe) Environmental Engineering, 1985, (with H. Theisen, S.A. Vigil) Integrated Solid Waste Management: Engineering Principles and Management Issues, 1993, (with R. Crites) Small and Decentralized Wastewater Management Systems, 1998; co-author: Wastewater Engineering: Treatment, Disposal, Reuse, 1991, 4th edit., 2002; author, editor: Wastewater Engineering: Collection and Pumping of Wastewater, 1981; co-editor: Pumping Station Design, 1989 (with F Burton and D. Stensel) Wastewater Engineering: Treatment and Reuse, 4th ed., 2002, co-editor: (with F Kreith) Solid Waste Handbook, 2d edit., 2002; contbr. numerous articles to profl. jours. Mem. bd. Calif. Integrated Waste Mgmt.; lectr. T.R. Camp, 1990. Recipient Waste to Energy Rsch. and Tech. Coun. Disting. award, 2004. Mem. AAAS, ASCE, NAE (Wiert Svc. award, 2004, Rsch. Edn. award, 2004), Assn. Environ. Engring. Profs. (bd. dirs., past pres.), Am. Acad. Environ. Engrs., Water Environ. Fedn. (Gordon Maskew Fair medal 1985, Jack Edward McKee medal 1999), Am. Water Works Assn. (Thomas R. Camp lectr. 1991), Nat. Water Rsch. Inst. (Athalie Richardson Irvine Clarke prize, 2003), Nat. Acad. Engring. Home: 662 Diego Pl Davis CA 95616-0123 Office Phone: 530-756-5747.

TCHOUMAK, ADELINA, corporate financial executive; b. Chishinau, Moldovia, Feb. 16, 1974; arrived in U.S., 1990; d. Mercuriu and Olga Ciumac. BBA in Econs. cum laude, U. Anchorage, 1995. Performance analyst Clay Finlay Inc., NYC, 1996—2000, Oppenheimer Capital, 2000—02; asst. v.p., sr. performance analyst Citibank, 2002—04; ret., 2004. Sponsor Children Internat., Honduras, 2002—. Atheist. Avocations: reading, yoga. Home: 5108 Marcadas Rd NW Albuquerque NM 87114 Personal E-mail: tadelina@hotmail.com.

TCHOUNWOU, PAUL BERNARD, environmental health specialist, toxicologist, educator; b. Bangou, Cameroon, Aug. 14, 1960; came to U.S., 1985; s. Maurice and Christine (Kouanang) Seumo; m. Martha Namondo Mondoa, Aug. 3, 1990; children: Christine K., Hervey M., Solange S. BSc, U. Yaounde, Cameroon, 1983, MSc, 1984; MS in Pub. Health, Tulane U., 1986, ScD, 1990. Cert. toxicologist Nat. Environ. Health Assn.; registered sanitarian La. State Bd. Examiners for Sanitarians. Tchg. asst. Tulane Sch. Pub. Health, New Orleans, 1988—90; med. rschr. Inst. Med. Rsch., Yaounde, 1991—94; asst. prof. Faculty Medicine, Yaounde, 1992—94; rsch. assoc. Xavier and Tulane Univs., New Orleans, 1994—96; assoc. prof., dir. environ. sci. PhD program Jackson State U., 1996—; adj. assoc. prof. sch. pub. health Tulane U., 1999—2005; prof., dir. environ. sci. doctoral program Jackson State U., 2001—, dep. dir. Ctr. for Environ. Health, 2003—06, chair dept. biology, 2004—, interim assoc. dean coll. sci., engring. and tech., 2006—. Adj. prof. Tulane U. Sch. Pub. Health, 2005—; environ. health cons. Orstom & UNICEF, Yaounde, 1992-93, U.S. AID, Kaele, 1991-93; rsch. supr. Tulane Sch. Pub. Health, New Orleans, 1994—; tng. and rsch. fellow U.S. AID, Washington, 1985-90; adj. assoc. prof. environ. health scis. Tulane U. Sch. Pub. Health and Tropical Medicine, 1999—. Editor-in-chief: Internat. Jour. of Environ. Rsch. and Pub. Health, 2003—, mem. editl. bd.: Internat. Jour. Environ. Toxicology and Water Quality, 1994—, guest editor: Internat. Jour. Molecular Scis., 2002—, regional editor: USA-Environ. Toxicology, 2002—, mem. overseas editl. bd.: Jour. Environ. Biology, 2002—; contbr. articles to profl. jours.; editor-in-chief: Environmental Toxicology, 2006—, mem. editl. bd.: Revs. on Environ. Health, 2003—. Grantee, Internat. Devel. Rsch. Ctr., 1992—93, Nat. Aeronautics and Space Adminstrn., 1977—99, NIH, 1998—, Nat. Oceanic and Atmospheric Adminstrn., 2001—, Dept. Army, 2002—03. Mem. APHA, AAUP, AAAS, Am. Assn. Cancer Rsch., Water Environ. Fedn., Cameroon Bioscis. Soc., Cameroon Assn. Epidemiology, Nat. Environ. Health Assn., N.Y. Acad. Scis., Miss. Acad. Sci., Soc. Environ. Toxicology and Chemistry, Soc. Toxicology, Delta Omega. Roman Catholic. Avocations: travel, playing tennis, watching tv sport programs. Home: 230 Clark Farms Rd Madison MS 39110-8112 Office: Jackson State U Coll Sci Engring and Tech PO Box 18540 Jackson MS 39217

TEACHOUT, TERRY, writer, critic; b. Cape Girardeau, Mo., Feb. 6, 1956; s. H.H. and Evelyn (Crosno) Teachout. BS in Music and Journalism, William Jewell Coll., 1979. Sr. editor Harper's Mag., NYC, 1985-87; editl. writer Daily News, NYC, 1987-93, classical music and dance critic, 1993-2000; music critic Commentary Mag., NYC, 1995—; contbr. Time Mag., NYC, 1998—2001; arts columnist Washington Post, 1999—2005; drama critic Wall St. Jour., 2003—. Mem. Nat. Coun. on the Arts Nat. Endowment for the Arts, 2005—. Author: City Limits, 1991, The Skeptic: A Life of H.L. Mencken, 2002, A Terry Teachout Reader, 2003, All in the Dances: A Brief Life of George Balanchine, 2004; editor: Ghosts on the Roof: Selected Journalism of Whittaker Chambers, 1989, Beyond the Boom, 1990, A Second Mencken Chrestomathy, 1995. Office: 68 W 82nd St New York NY 10024-4660 Business E-Mail: tteachout@artsjournal.com.

TEAGAN, JOHN GERARD, publishing executive; b. Detroit, Sept. 23, 1947; s. Stanley John and Margaret Suzanne (Sullivan) T.; m. Carla Kay Eurich, Sept. 13, 1975; 1 child, Elizabeth Margaret. BBA, U. Notre Dame, 1969. CPA Mich. Audit supr. Ernst & Whinney (C.P.A.s), Detroit, 1969-73; acctg. mgr. Detroit Free Press, 1973-77, treas., controller, 1977-83, v.p. fin., treas., 1983-89, v.p., bus. mgr., 1989—2005; CFO Duluth News Tribune, 2005—. Adv. bd. Providence Hosp., Southfield, Mich., 1984-93, sec., 1989, vice chmn. 1990, chmn., 1991; trustee Grosse Pointe (Mich.) Acad., 1990-96, Children's Home Detroit, Grosse Pointe, 1997-2005; bd. dirs., treas. Free Press Charities, Inc.; bd. dirs. Providence Hosp. and Med. Ctrs., Southfield, 1998-2005; Metro Detroit bd. dirs. Am. Heart Assn., 1999-2005, chair, 2004-05; bd. dirs. Holy Cross Children's Svcs., 2001-05; mem. cmty. adv. bd. Knight Found., 2002-05. Mem. AICPA, Internat. Newspaper Fin. Execs., Mich. Assn. CPAs, Grosse Pointe Yacht Club. Roman Catholic. Business E-Mail: jteagan@duluthnews.com.

TEAGUE, BERNICE RITA, accountant; b. Lowell, Mass., Nov. 1, 1957; d. Francis Joseph and Agnes Lena (Laferriere) T. Grad. h.s., Lowell, Mass. Student aide Hanscom AFB, Bedford, Mass., 1974; sec. asst. Family Svcs. of Greater Lowell, 1975—, asst. bookkeeper, 1976-86, bookkeeper, 1986, asst. bus. mgr., 1987-88, prin. acct., 1988-89; bus. mgr., 1989-99; acctg. clk., billing rep. Med Life Pharmacy, N. Billerica, Mass., 2000—01. Democrat. Roman Catholic. Avocations: embroidery, crafts, reading, fishing, gardening. Home: 163 A St Lowell MA 01851-4117

TEAGUE, LAVETTE COX, JR., systems educator, consultant; b. Birmingham, Ala., Oct. 8, 1934; s. Lavette Cox and Caroline Green (Stokes) T. Student, Auburn U., 1951-54; BArch, MIT, 1957, MSCE, 1965, PhD, 1968; MDiv with distinction, Ch. Div. Sch. Pacific, 1979. Cert. computer profl. Inst. Cert. Computer Profls. Archtl. designer Carroll C. Harmon, Birmingham, 1957, Fred Renneker, Jr., Birmingham, 1958-59; architect Rust Engring. Co., Birmingham, 1959-62, Synergetics, Inc., Raleigh, NC, 1962-64, Rust Engring. Co., Birmingham, 1964-68; rsch. asst., instr., rsch. assoc. MIT, Cambridge, 1964-68; dir. computer svcs. Skidmore Owings & Merrill, San Francisco, Chgo., 1968-74; postdoctoral fellow UCLA, 1972; adj. assoc. prof. arch. and civil engring. Carnegie-Mellon U., Pitts., 1973-74; archtl. systems cons. Chgo., 1974-75, Berkeley, Calif., 1975-80, Pasadena, 1980-82, Altadena, Calif., 1982—. Lectr. info. systems Calif. State Poly. U., Pomona, 1980-81, prof., 1981-98, prof. emeritus, 1998—, asst. chair, 1990-91, chair, 1991-93, 96-98; Fulbright lectr., Uruguay, 1985; lectr. Peking U., 2004. Author: Event-Based Analysis and Design: An Introduction to Structured Methods, 2000; co-author: Structured Analysis Methods for Computer Information Systems, 1985, Object-Oriented Systems Analysis and Design with UML, 2005, Chinese edit., 2005. Mem. adv. bd. Ch. Div. Sch. of the Pacific. Recipient Tucker-Voss award MIT, 1967; Fulbright scholar, 1985. Mem. AIA (Arnold W. Brunner scholar 1966), Assn. Computing Machinery, Sigma Xi, Phi Eta Sigma, Scarab, Scabbard and Blade, Tau Beta Pi, Chi Epsilon, Beta Gamma Sigma. Episcopalian. Home: 1696 N Altadena Dr Altadena CA 91001-3623 Office: 3801 W Temple Ave Pomona CA 91768-2557 Business E-Mail: lcteague@csupomona.edu.

TEAGUE, RANDAL CORNELL, SR., lawyer; b. Durham, NC, May 19, 1944; s. Roy M. Sr. and Lottie (Rhew) T.; children: R. Cornell, R. Townsend, Mary Robb Durham, James K.B. BA, Am. U., 1967; JD, George Washington U., 1971, LLM with highest honors, 1972; LLD (hon.), Allen U., 1973. Bar: Fla. 1972, D.C. 1972, U.S. Dist. Ct. D.C. 1972, U.S. Tax Ct. 1972, U.S. Ct. Mil. Appeals 1972, U.S. Ct. Appeals (D.C. and fed. cirs.) 1972, U.S. Ct. Appeals (5th cir.) 1973, U.S. Supreme Ct. 1975, Mass. 1979, U.S. Ct. Appeals (1st cir.) 1979, U.S. Dist. Ct. Mass. 1979, U.S. Ct. Internat. Trade. Coord. policy devel. Exec. Office of Pre. of U.S., Washington, 1971-73; chief of staff, legis. counsel to Rep. Jack F. Kemp Ho. of Reps., Washington, 1973-79; div. counsel Cabot Corp., 1979-81; counsel Vorys, Sater, Seymour & Pease LLP, Washington, 1981-83, ptnr., 1984—. Pres. Internat. Exch. Coun., 1984—; trustee Fund Am. Studies, Washington, 1976—, chmn., 1998—; trustee, dir. Air Force Acad. Found., Colorado Springs, Colo., 1983—; chmn. adv. com. voluntary aid U.S. AID, 1987-91; trustee Earth U., Costa Rica, 1987—; councillor Atlantic Coun. of U.S., 1990—; co-founder Am. Inst. on Polit. and Econ. Sys., Charles U., Prague, 1993—; founder Internat. Inst. Polit. and Econ. Studies, Athens, Greece, 1996—; dir. Salzburg Seminar, 1997—. Named one of Outstanding Young Men Am., 1973; recipient George Washington medal Freedoms Found., 1978. Mem. Fla. Bar Assn., Mass. Bar Assn., D.C. Bar Assn., Univ. Club (Washington). Republican. Episcopalian. Office: Vorys Sater Seymour & Pease LLP 1828 L St NW Fl 11 Washington DC 20036-5109 Office Phone: 202-467-8817. Business E-Mail: rcteague@vssp.com.

TEAGUE, ROBERT COLE, physician; b. Waxahachie, Tex., June 13, 1930; s. Isaac Lawson and Frances (Cole) Teague; m. Virginia M. Teague, Nov. 11, 1960 (dec. May 1, 2005); children: Patrick, Michael. BA in Chemistry, Baylor U., Waco, Tex., 1951; MD, U. Tex., Galveston, 1955. Lic. physician Ariz. Intern McLaren Hosp., Flint, Mich., 1955—56; med. officer, active duty USNR, 1956—58; physician family practice LaJolla, Calif., 1958—63, Phoenix, 1963—. Med. dir., pres. Vis. Nurse Svc., Phoenix; chmn. Family Practice Humana Hosp., 1984—86, past chmn.; chmn. Family Practice Good Samaritan Hosp., 1990—91. Fellow Am. Acad. Family Physicians (charter); mem. Ariz. Acad. Family Physicians (pres. 1988). Republican. Episcopalian. Avocations: golf, travel. Office: 6707 N 19th Ave Ste 201 Phoenix AZ 85015-2451

TEAL, ARABELLA W., lawyer, former state attorney general; b. NYC, Jan. 1961; m. Gary Teal; 2 children. BA, Harvard Coll., 1984; JD, Georgetown U. Law Ctr., 1987. Law clerk for sr. judges D.C. Superior Court, 1987—88; section chief General Litigation Section I, 1996—99; acting prin. dep. corp. counsel D.C., 1999—2000, prin. dep. corp. counsel, 2000—02, interim corp. counsel, 2002—03; atty. McCabe & Mack LLP, Poughkeepsie, 2003—. Office: McCabe & Mack LLP 63 Washington St PO Box 509 Poughkeepsie NY 12602-0509

TEAL, GILBERT EARLE, II, lawyer, coast guard officer; b. Lafayette, Ind., May 1, 1959; s. Gilbert Earle and Evangeline Maxine (Piper) T.; m. Mary Anne Liwoch, Oct. 3, 1987. AS, Western Conn. State U., 1979; BS, USCG Acad., 1983; MPA, George Mason U., 1988; JD, Coll. William and Mary, 1991. Bar: Va. 1991, U.S. Mil. Ct. Appeals 1991, U.S. Ct. Appeals (4th cir.) 1991, D.C. 1992, U.S. Ct. Claims 1992, U.S. Ct. Appeals (fed. cir.) 1992, U.S. Tax Ct. 1998, Alaska 1998, U.S. Dist. Ct. Alaska 1998, U.S. Ct. Appeals (9th cir.) 1998, U.S. Supreme Ct. 1998; designated mil. judge, 2001; appellate judge Coast Guard Ct. Criminal Appeals, 2004. Commd. ensign USCG, 1983, advanced through grades to capt., 2004; assigned to USCG Cutter Vigorous (WMEC 627), New London, Conn., 1983-85; intelligence officer COMDT (G-OIS-3) Hdqs. USCG, Washington, 1985-88; law clk. to chief trial judge Capt. Thomas Snook, USCG, NYC, 1989; law clk. USCG RTC Yorktown, 1990; staff atty. Maintenance and Logistics Command Atlantic, Governors Island, N.Y., 1991-94; legal officer USCG Support Ctr., Kodiak, Alaska, 1994-97; br. legal officer 17th Coast Guard Dist., spl. asst. U.S. Atty., Dist. of Alaska, Anchorage, 1997—2001; dep. staff judge adv. Maintenance and Logistics Command Atlantic, Norfolk, Va., 2001—04; chief legal policy and program devel., spl. asst. to the judge adv. gen. USCG Hdqrs., Washington, 2004—06; asst. counsel U.S. Navy Fleet and Indsl. Supply Ctr., Norfolk, 2006—. Recipient Dirs. award for outstanding performance as spl. asst. U.S. atty. Dept. Justice, Exec. Office for U.S. Attys., 1998, Lawrence R. Schneider award U.S. Dept. Transp., 1999, Cert. of Commendation, Dept. of Justice Environ. Natural Resources Divsn., 2000. Mem. ABA, FBA, Va. State Bar, Va. Bar Assn., D.C. Bar, AK Bar Assn., Jud. Advs. Assn. (life), U.S. Naval Inst. (life), Nat. Eagle Scout Assn. (life), Army and Navy Club (Washington), Army-Navy Country Club (Arlington, Va.), Trout Unltd. (life), Coastal Conservation Assn. (life), Fedn. Fly Fishers (life), Masons, Shriners, Phi Delta Phi (life), Phi Delta Kappa. Avocations: fishing, dog sport. Office: Office of Counsel Fleet Indsl and Supply Ctr Norfolk VA 23511-1088 Home: 4769 Bristol Cir Williamsburg VA 23185 Office Phone: 757-443-1088. Business E-Mail: gilbert.teal@navy.mil.

TEARE, JOHN RICHARD, JR., lawyer; b. Phila., Sept. 23, 1954; m. Claire M. Batuk, Jan. 25, 1975 (div. Dec. 1981); 1 child, John III; m. Gale Angela Waters, June 5, 1982; children: Angela, Stephanie. BS in Criminal Justice summa cum laude, Wilmington Coll., 1987; JD cum laude, U. Richmond, 1990. Bar: W.Va. 1990, U.S. Dist. Ct. (so. dist.) W.Va. 1990, U.S. Dist. Ct. (no. dist.) W.Va. 1996, U.S. Ct. Appeals (4th cir.) 1991. Sec. guard U. Del., Newark, 1973-76; police officer City of Dover (Del.), 1976-85; summer assoc. Hirschler Fleischer Weinberg Cox & Allen, Richmond, 1989; ptnr. Bowles Rice McDavid Graff & Love, LLP, Charleston, W.Va., 1990—; mem. exec. com., 2000—03. Counsel Charleston Police Civil Svc. Commn.; instr. Charleston Regional Police Acad., 1999; exec. dir. W.Va. Housing Inst., Inc., 2004-2005, dist. and scouting commr., 2005—; instr. inservice tng. Charleston Police Dept.; spkr. and panelist in field. Cub scout leader Boy Scouts Am., Felton, Del., 1984-88, asst. scoutmaster, Richmond, 1988-89, Charleston, 1991-98; chmn. pub. safety commn. Greater Charleston C. of C., 1991; sec. United Meth. Men, 1993; dir. Charleston Leadership Coun. on Pub. Safety, 1993-97, chmn. police dept. resource task force, 1994-97; dir./sec. Kanawha County Pub. Safety Coun., 2000-02. Mem. Def. Rsch. Inst. (state liaison to govtl. liability com./bus. litigation com.), Def. Trial Counsel W.Va. (v.p. employment law com., 2005—), Nat. Manufactured Housing Atty. Network, W.Va. Manufactured Housing Assn. (interim exec. 2004-05), Fraternal Order of Police, Nat. Eagle Scout Assn., McNeill Law Assn., Greater Charleston C. of C., Delta Epsilon Rho. United Methodist. Avocations: camping, fishing, stamp collecting/philately. Home: 1565 Virginia St E Charleston WV 25311-2416 Office: Bowles Rice McDavid Graff & Love LLP PO Box 1386 Charleston WV 25325-1386 Home Phone: 304-342-2873; Office Phone: 304-347-1724. Business E-Mail: jteare@bowlesrice.com.

TEARE, RICHARD WALLACE, retired foreign service officer; b. Cleve., Feb. 21, 1937; m. Jeanie Walter; 3 children. BA, Harvard U., 1958; diploma, Nat. War Coll., 1978. Joined Fgn. Svc., 1959; vice consul U.S. Consulate, Bridgetown, Barbados, 1960-62; consular officer U.S. Embassy, Manila, 1962-64, polit. officer Saigon, Vietnam, 1965-67, Mexico City, 1971-74, counselor for polit. affairs Vientiane, Laos, 1974-76, dep. chief mission Wellington, New Zealand, 1983-86, Canberra, Australia, 1986-89; dep. and acting prin. officer U.S. Consulate Gen., Nha Trang, Vietnam, 1973; intelligence and rsch. specialist Dept. State, 1967-69, desk officer Vietnam Working Group, 1969-71, spl. asst. to asst. sec. for East Asian and Pacific Affairs, 1976-77, dep. dir. Office Philippine Affairs, 1978-80, dep. and acting U.S. rep. for Micronesian Status Negotiations, 1980-83, dir. Office of Indonesia, Malaysia, Brunei and Singapore Affairs, 1989-92, spl. projects officer Office of Dir. Gen., 1992-93, U.S. amb. to Papua New Guinea, Solomon Islands and Vanuatu, 1993-96; fgn. policy advisor to the Commander in Chief U.S. Pacific Command, Camp Smith, Hawaii, 1996-98; dir. Ctr. Australian and New Zealand studies Sch. Fgn. Svc., Georgetown U., 1998—2004, sr. fellow, 2004—07; ret., 2007. Mem.: Australian and New Zealand Studies Assn. N.Am. (past pres.), U.S.-New Zealand Coun. (bd. dirs.), Am. Fgn. Svc. Assn., Historic Chevy Chase DC. Home: 3111 Oliver St NW Washington DC 20015-1654

TEAS, RICHARD HARPER, lawyer; b. Streator, Ill., Sept. 24, 1930; s. Bert H. and Audrey C. Teas; m. Janice K. Eikenmeyer, July 29, 1960 (dec.); children: Catherine L. Teas-Rogers, Amelia H. AB, U. Ill., 1957, LLB, 1960. Bar: Ill. 1960, U.S. Dist. Ct. (so. dist.) Ill. 1960. Probate adminstr. Continental Nat. Bank and Trust Co. of Chgo., 1960-66; ptnr. Tracy, Johnson, & Wilson Law Offices, Joliet, Ill., 1966—. Comdr. USNR, 1952-69. Mem. Ill. State Bar Assn. (trust and estates sect. coun., chair, 2002-03, standing com. on legislation, task force on unauthorized practice of law), Will County Bar Assn. (probate com.), Am. Coll. of Trust and Estate Counsel, Estate Planning Coun. of Greater Joliet (pres. 1976) Avocations: tennis, golf. Home: 20853 Rock Run Dr Joliet IL 60431-9323 Office: Tracy Johnson & Wilson 2801 Black Rd Fl 2 Joliet IL 60435 Office Phone: 815-723-8500.

TEASDALE, BRENT, sociologist, educator; b. Burlingame, Calif., Aug. 4, 1976; s. Margaret Ann (Colin) and David Grant Teasdale. BA, Calif. State U., Sacramento, 1999; MA, Pa. State U., University Park, 1999, PhD, 2004. Asst. prof. sociology U. Akron, Ohio, 2004—; rsch. assoc. Inst. for Health and Social Policy, Akron, Ohio, 2005—. Contbr. articles to profl. jours. Mem.: Soc. for the Study Social Problems, Am. Sociol. Assn., Am. Soc. Criminology (Gene Carte Student Paper Competition award 2002). Home Phone: 330-928-7283; Office Phone: 330-972-7995.

TEASDALE, KENNETH FULBRIGHT, lawyer; b. St. Louis, Nov. 8, 1934; s. Kenneth and Ann (Fulbright) T.; m. Elizabeth Driscol Langdon, June 13, 1964; children: Caroline, Doug, Cindy. AB, Amherst Coll., 1956; LLB, Washington U., St. Louis, 1961. Bar: Mo. 1961. Atty. antitrust div. U.S. Dept. Justice, Washington, 1961-62; asst. counsel Dem. Policy Com. U.S. Senate, Washington, 1962-63, gen. counsel Dem. Policy Com., asst. to majority leader, 1963-64; assoc. Armstrong, Teasdale, Kramer & Vaughan, St. Louis, 1964-67, ptnr., 1967-86; mng. ptnr. Armstrong, Teasdale, Schlafly & Davis, St. Louis, 1986-93, chmn. of firm, 1993—. Trustee United Way Greater St. Louis, Sci. Ctr. St. Louis, St. Louis Art Mus.; trustee, chmn. bd. regents St. Louis U.; mem. nat. coun. Washington U. Law Sch., 1988—. Mem. ABA, Bar Assn. Mo., Bar Assn. St. Louis, St. Louis Coalition for Plant and Life Scis., Racquet Club, Noonday Club, Old Warson Country Club. Episcopalian. Office: Armstrong Teasdale LLP Ste 2600 One Metropolitan Sq Saint Louis MO 63102-2733 Office Phone: 314-621-5070.

TEATER, DOROTHY SEATH, retired county official; b. Manhattan, Kans., Feb. 11, 1931; d. Dwight Moody and Martha (Stahnke) Seath; m. Robert Woodson Teater, May 24, 1952; children: David Dwight, James Stanley, Donald Robert, Andrew Scott. BS, U. Ky., 1951; MS, Ohio State U., 1954. Home econs. tchr. Georgetown (Ky.) City Schs., 1951-53; extension specialist Ohio Coop. Extension, Columbus, 1967-73; consumer affairs adminstr. City of Columbus, 1974-79, Bank One Columbus NA, 1980-85; councilmember Columbus City Coun., 1980-85; commr. Franklin County, Columbus, Ohio, 1985-2000; ret. Mem. Columbus Met. Area Cmty. Action Orgn.; mem. adv. bd. Ohio Housing Trust; chairwoman Franklin County Children's Cabinet; pub. mem. Ohio Bd. Pharmacy, 2000—. Bd. dirs. BBB;, Silesian Boys and Girls Club, Rickenbacker-Woods Mus.; mem. hon. adv. bd. Girl Scouts. Recipient Outstanding Alumnus award U. Ky., 1989, Women of Achievement award YWCA, 1995, Disting. Svc. award Ohio State U., 1997; named Disting. Alumni, Ohio State U., 1977. Mem. County Commrs. Assn. Ohio (pres. 1994), Columbus Met. Club, Greater Columbus C. of C. (Columbus award 1997). Republican. Methodist. Avocations: gardening, sewing.

TEBBETS, GARY DUANE, music educator; b. Kansas CIty, Mo., Apr. 2, 1948; s. Gilbert Dean and Bernice Ruth (Belk) Tebbets; m. Anna Marie Feagins, May 29, 1999; m. Roxanne Cox (div.); 1 child, Gary Duane Jr. B of Music Edn., U. Mo., Kansas City, 1975, B of Piano Music, 1978, B of Vocal Music, 1980; MusM in Theory, Pittsburg State U., Kans., 1997. Tchr. Jayhawk-Linn High Sch., Mound City, Kans., 2001—04; prof. Allen County C.C., Iola, 2004—. Adj. instr. Ft. Scott C.C., Ft. Scott, Kans.; dir. music First Christian Ch., 1998—. Mem. Jackson Coumty Rep. Com., Kansas City, 1978—84; candidate Mo. State Legis., 1980, 1982; founder, dir. Ft. Scott Cmty. Chorus, Kans., 1997—. Mem.: Am. Choral Dirs. Assn., Music Educators Nat. Conf., Music Tchrs. Nat. Assn., Phi Kappa Phi. Avocations: crossword puzzles, reading. Home: PO Box 128 Fort Scott KS 66701 Office: Allen County CC 1801 N Cottonwood Iola KS 66749 Office Phone: 620-365-5116 258. Business E-Mail: tebbets@allencc.edu.

TEBBS, CAROL ANN, secondary school educator, academic administrator; b. Columbus, Ohio, Sept. 9, 1939; d. John Arthur and Ann Laurie (Wickham) Williams; m. Ronald Daniel Tebbs, Mar. 31, 1957; children: Kimberly Ann, Ronald Dan. BA in English, Whittier Coll., 1963, MA in English and Edn., 1972. Cert. tchr. K-adult Calif. Tchr. art and English Hacienda La Puente Unified Sch. Dist., Hacienda Heights, Calif., 1963-84; tchr. advanced placement English, acad. decathlon advisor, yearbook advisor Glen A. Wilson H.S., Hacienda Heights, 1984—2000. Mentor tchr. Hacienda La Puente Sch. Dist., Hacienda Heights, 1988—2000; reader, tchr. trainer advanced placement English Coll. Bd., 2000—; bd. dirs. Kepler Coll., Lynnwood, Wash., pres., 2003—; tchr. Online Coll., 2000—; pres. Kepler Coll., 2006—. Contbr. articles to profl. jours. Named Tchr. of the Yr., Nat. Walmart Stores Found., 1998; recipient D. Fedderson Cmty. Svc. award, PTA, 1970, Teacher of the Year, 1971, Glen A. Wilson Faculty Tchr. of Yr. award, 1999—2000. Mem.: United Astrology Congress (program chair 1986, 1989, 1992, coord. 1995, bd. chmn. 1995—99, co-founder), Internat. Soc. Astrol. Rsch. (pres. 1988—95, bd. dirs. 1995—2004), Delta Kappa Gamma. Methodist. Home: 56870 Jack Nicklaus Blvd La Quinta CA 92253-5074 Office: 4630 200th St SW Ste A-1 Lynnwood WA 98036 Office Phone: 425-673-4292. Personal E-mail: caroltebbs@aol.com.

TEBEDO, MARYANNE, state legislator; b. Denver, Oct. 30, 1936; m. Don Tebedo; children: Kevin, Ronald, Linda, Thomas, Christine. Profl. registered parliamentarian. Mem. Colo. Ho. of Reps., Denver, 1982-88, Colo. Senate, Denver, 1988—2001; owner, pres. Colo. Mediation and Parliamentary Profls., Colorado Springs. Mediator 4th Jud. Dist. Colo. Mem.: Nat. Assn. Parliamentarians, Colo. Assn. Parliamentarians (pres.). Republican. Office Phone: 719-471-2561. E-mail: matebedo@isp.com.

TEBOH-EWUNGKEM, MIRANDA IJANG, education educator; d. Aaron Bagen and Christiana Enih Teboh; m. Julius Ewungwo Ewungkem, July 31, 1998; 1 child, Julius Jr. Ewungwo Ewungkem. BS in Math., U. Buea, 1996, MS in Math., 1998; PhD in Math., Lehigh U., 2003, MS in Stats, 2003. Tchg. asst. U. Of Buea, Cameroon, 1997—98; dean's fellow Lehigh U., Bethlehem, Pa., 1998—99, tchg. asst., 1999—2003, hsiung vis. asst. prof., 2003—04; vis. post doc U. Mich., 2004—04; vis. asst. prof. Lafayette Coll., Easton, Pa., 2004—. Author: (conference book of abstracts) International Conference for Mathematics in Biology and Medicine, International Conference on Applied Math, International Conference on Mathematical Biology; contbr. articles to jours. Landahl student travel grant, Soc. of Math. Biology, 2002, Travel grant, AWM, 2004, Reidler grant, Lehigh U., 2003, SMB Travel grant, SMB, 2004, Commonwealth scholarship, Commonwealth group, 1998. Mem.: Soc. of Indsl. and Applied Mathematicians, Soc. for Math. Biology, Am. Math. Soc., Assn. for Women in Math. Christian. Avocations: reading, tennis. Office: Lafayette Coll Pardee Hall 225A Easton PA 18042 Home Phone: 610-419-4818; Office Phone: 610 330 5328. Office Fax: 610 330 5721. Business E-Mail: tebohewm@lafayette.edu.

TECCO, ROMUALD GILBERT LOUIS JOSEPH, violinist, concertmaster; b. Toulon, Var, France, May 1, 1941; came to U.S., 1960; s. Raymond Charles and Angele (Cornille) T. Student, Paris Conservatoire, 1954-60; diploma, postgrad. diploma, Juilliard Sch. Music, 1967-68. Mem. N.Y. String Quartet, 1969-72; concertmaster Juilliard Ensemble, NYC, 1969-72, St. Paul Chamber Orch., 1972-98; soloist Chgo. Symphony, Bavarian Radio Orch., Orch. of Mex., Orchestre Colonne, Paris, Rotterdam Philharm.; performer numerous festivals, Sweden, Finland, France, Italy, U.S. Recs. with Aaron Copland and Lou Harrison Chamber Music. Served with French Navy, 1964-65, NATO hdqrs. Recipient first prize in violin Conservatoire Paris; recipient first prize chamber music Conservatoire Paris Mem. St. Paul Univ. Club.

TECHAR, FRANK J., bank executive; b. Minn. BS in engring., Princeton U., 1978; MBA, U. Denver, 1983; exec. program, USC, 1992. Various banking positions First Interstate Bank, Denver; various engring. positions USG Corp., Oakfield, NY; sr. v.p., gen. mgr. BMO Fin. Group, London; acct. officer, corp. banking Bk. of Montreal, Denver, 1984, mgr. dir., corp. banking Houston, 1993—95, exec. v.p., small bus. banking Canada, 1999—2002; pres., CEO Harris Bankcorp, Toronto, Canada, 2002—06; pres., CEO Personal & Comml. Banking Canada BMO Fin. Group, 2006—. Mem.: Northwestern U. Bus. Sch. Adv. Coun., Chicagoland C.of.C. (bd. mem.), Exec. Club Chgo. (bd. mem.), U. Club, Chgo. Club, Econ. Club, Comml. Club of Chgo. Office: BMO Fin Group 1 First Canadian Pl M5X 1H3 Toronto ON Canada

TEDDER, THOMAS FLETCHER, immunology educator, researcher; b. Chateauroux, France, May 14, 1956; came to U.S. 1959; s. Raymond Percy and Barbara (Hagemann) T. AA, Okaloosa-Walton C.C., Niceville, Fla., 1976; BS with honors, U. Fla., 1978, MS, 1980; PhD, U. Ala., Birmingham, 1984. Rsch. fellow in pathology Harvard Med. Sch., Boston, 1984-85, instr. pathology, 1986-88, asst. prof. pathology, 1988-93; assoc. prof. pathology Harvard U. Med. Sch., Boston, 1993; prof. immunology Duke U. Med. Ctr., Durham, NC, 1993—, chmn. dept. immunology, 1993—. Alter Geller prof. rsch. in immunology Duke U. Med. Ctr., 1997—; co-founder Angelica Therapeutics, Inc.; cons. in field. Assoc.

editor Jour. Immunology, 1989-93, sect. editor, 1993-98, dep. editor, 2004-; contbr. numerous articles to med. jours., including Jour. Immunology, Nature, Lancet, Immunity. Recipient LeRoy Collins Disting. Alumnus award Fla. Assn. C.C.'s; named 25th Anniversary Disting. Alumnus, Okaloosa-Walton C.C., 1989; Damon Runyon-Walter Winchell rsch. fellow, 1985-87; scholar Leukemia Soc. Am., 1991-96, Stohlman scholar, 1995-96. Mem. Am. Soc. for Microbiology (Pres. fellow 1982), Am. Assn. Immunologists, Sigma Xi, Phi Kappa Phi. Achievements include identification and determination of structure and function of many human B lymphocyte cell-surface molecules. Office: Duke U Med Ctr Dept Immunology PO Box 3010 Durham NC 27710-0001 Office Phone: 919-684-3578. E-mail: thomas.tedder@duke.edu.

TEDESCHI, GEORGE, labor union administrator; Journeyman newspaper pressman Newsday, Long Island, NY; mem. Graphic Commn. Internat. Union, 1959—; v.p. & sec.-treas. Local 406C Graphic Comm. Internat. Union, pres., Nassau County 406C, 1972—2000; pres. Graphic Comm. Internat. Union (now Graphic Comm. Internat./Internat. Brotherhood Teamsters), 2000—. Mem. from Atlantic region gen. bd. Graphic Comm. Internat. Union, 1983—2000, pres. N.Am. Newspaper Conf., 1979—2000, sec. Ea. Conf.; exec. bd. Long Island Fedn. Labor, AFL-CIO. Dir. and sec. United Way of Long Island; bd. dir. Union Labor Life Ins. Co. (ULLICO). Office: Graphic Comm Internat Union 1900 L St NW Washington DC 20036 Office Phone: 202-462-1400. *

TEDESCHI, JOHN ALFRED, historian, educator, librarian; b. Modena, Italy, July 17, 1931; came to U.S., 1939, naturalized, 1944; s. Caesar George and Piera (Forti) T.; m. Anne Wood Christian, Sept. 8, 1956; children: Martha, Philip, Sara. BA, Harvard U., 1954, MA, 1960, PhD, 1966. Bibliographer European history and lit. Newberry Library, Chgo., 1965-84, curator rare books and manuscripts, head dept. spl. collections, 1970-82, dir. Ctr. Renaissance Studies, 1979-84; curator rare books and spl. collections Meml. Library U. Wis.-Madison, 1984-96; ret., 1996. Lectr. history U. Chgo., 1969—71; vis. prof. U. Ill., Chgo., 1972—73, adj. prof., 1979—84. Co-editor: (series) Corpus Reformatorum Italicorum, 1968-96; editor-in-chief: Bibliographie Internat. de L'Humanisme et de la Renaissance, 1977-82; editor: Italian Reformation Studies in Honor of Laelius Socinus, 1965, (with Anthony Molho) Renaissance Studies in Honor of Hans Baron, 1971, (with Gustav Henningsen) The Inquisition in Early Modern Europe: Studies on Sources and Methods, 1986, The Prosecution of Heresy: Collected Studies on the Inquisition in Early Modern Italy, 1991 (transl. into Italian 1997), Tomasso Sassetti, Il Massacro di San Bartolomeo, 1995, The Italian Reformation of the Sixteenth Century and the Diffusion of Renaissance Culture: A Bibliography of the Secondary Literature (c. 1750-1997), 2000, The correspondence of Roland H. Bainton and Delio Cantimori, 1932-66, 2002; translator: (with Anne Tedeschi) The Cheese and the Worms. The Cosmos of a Sixteenth-Century Miller (Carlo Ginzburg), 1980 (named an Outstanding Acad. Book by Choice mag.), The Night Battles. Witchcraft and Agrarian Cults in the Sixteenth and Seventeenth Centuries (Carlo Ginzburg), 1983, Clues, Myths, and the Historical Method (Carlo Ginzburg), 1989, Hans Urs von Balthasar: A Theological Style (Angelo Scola), 1995, Domenico Scandella Known as Menocchio: His Trials Before the Inquisition (1583-1599) (Andrea Del Col), 1996, The Protestant Reformation in Sixteenth-Century Italy (Salvatore Caponetto), 1999, Books of the Body: Anatomical Ritual and Renaissance Learning (Andrea Carlino), 1999, The Jews in Mussolini's Italy (Michele Sarfatti), 2006; mem. editl. com.: Index des Livres Interdits (Sherbrooke), Collected Works of Erasmus (Toronto); mem. editl. bd.: Studi e Testi per la Storia Religiosa Italiana del '500 (Florence), The Peter Martyr Libr. (Kirksville, Mo.); contbr. articles to profl. jours. Served with U.S. Army, 1954-56. Grantee Am. Philos. Soc., 1961; grantee NEH, 1967; Old Dominion fellow Harvard U. Ctr. Renaissance Studies, Florence, Italy, 1967-68; fellow Inst. Research in Humanities, U. Wis.-Madison, 1976-77; Huntington Library fellow, 1984. Mem. Am. Soc. Reformation Research (pres. 1972), Renaissance Soc. Am. (exec. bd. 1971-96), 16th Century Studies Conf. (pres. 1987), Archive of Congregation for the Doctrine of the Faith (Vatican City; pres. 1999-2002, scholarly adv. com.), Univ. Trieste, Congregation for the Doctrine of the Faith (the Vatican), Gen. Adminstrn. for Archives (Rome; pres. scholarly adv. com. for collaborative project to catalogue electronically dispersed Inquisitorial sources, 2004-; Livorno, Italy scholary adv. com. to plan for 4th centenary of elevation to status of a city, 2004—06), Am. Hist. Assn., Am. Cath. Hist. Assn., Renaissance Soc. Am. Home: 57211 Rush Creek Rd Ferryville WI 54628 E-mail: tede@mwt.net.

TEDESCO, FRANCIS JOSEPH, retired academic administrator, medical educator; b. Derby, Conn., Mar. 8, 1944; s. Lena (Tufano) Tedesco; m. Luann Lee Ekern, Aug. 1, 1970; 1 child, Jennifer Nicole. BS cum laude, Fairfield U., 1965; MD cum laude, St. Louis U., 1969. Asst. instr. Hosp. of U. Pa., Phila., 1971-72; asst. prof. Washington U. Sch. Medicine, St. Louis, 1974-75, U. Miami (Fla.) Sch. Medicine, 1975-77, co-dir. clin. research, 1976-78, assoc. prof., 1977-78, Med. Coll. Ga., Augusta, 1978-81, chief of gastroenterology dept., 1978-88, prof., 1981—, acting v.p. clin. activities, 1984, v.p. for clin. activities, 1984-88, Interim dean Sch. of Medicine, 1986-88, pres., 1988—2001, pres. emeritus, 2001—. Cons. Med.-Letter/AMA divsn. drugs, Dwight D. Eisenhower Army Med. Ctr., Ft. Gordon, Ga., VA Med. Ctr., Augusta, Walter Reed Army Med. Ctr., Washington; mem. gastroenterology spl. study sect. NIH, Washington, 1982—, mem. nat. digestive disease adv. bd., 1985-88, vice chmn., 1986-87, chmn., 1987-88; mem. Ty Cobb Found. Scholarship Bd., 1998—. Contbr. numerous articles to profl. jours. Bd. dirs. Augusta Country Day Sch., 1981-83, Am. Cancer Soc., Augusta, 1985—, v.p., 1986—; bd. dirs., exec. com. Ga. Coalition for Health, 1995-2002; chmn. Gov.'s Health Strategies Coun., 1992-2002; bd. visitors CDC, 1998—; nat. adv. bd. Ga. Acad. Sci., Math. and Engring., 1998—; mem. Ty Cobb Fedn. Bd., 1998—. Recipient Eddie Palmer award for gastrointestinal endoscopy, 1983, cert. of appreciation Am. Cancer Soc., 1986, Outstanding Faculty award Med. Coll. Ga. Sch. Medicine, 1988, Profl. Achievement award Fairfield U., 1993, alumni merit award St. Louis U. Sch. Medicine, 1996; Avalon Found. scholar St. Louis U., 1968-69, Paul Harris fellow Rotary, 1990, Spirit of Ga. award Ga. Econ. Devel. Assn., 1998. Fellow ACP, Am. Fedn. Clin. Investigation, Am. Gastroent. Assn., Am. Soc. Gastrointestinal Endoscopy (treas. 1981-84, pres.-elect 1984-85, pres. 1985-86, Rudolph Schindler award 1993); mem. Am. Coll. Gastroenterology, So. Soc. Clin. Investigation, Richmond County Med. Soc., Med. Assn. Ga. Roman Catholic. Avocations: reading, swimming. Home: 2810 Peachtree Pl Augusta GA 30909 Office: Med Coll Ga Office Pres 1120 15th St Augusta GA 30912-0006 Business E-Mail: frant@mcg.edu.

TEDESCO, PAUL HERBERT, humanities educator; b. Nashua, NH, Dec. 28, 1928; s. Steven R. and Ruth (Weaver) T.; m. Eleanor Martha Hollis, Jan. 24, 1953; children: Steven Anthony, Sara Adams Tagget, James Beattie. AB in History, Harvard Coll., 1952; AM in History, Boston U., 1955, PhD in History, 1970; CAGS in Adminstrn., Northeastern U., Boston, 1974. Instr. humanities Mich. State U., East Lansing, 1955—60; tchr. history Great Neck North H.S., NY, 1960—62; chmn. dept. social studies Canton H.S., Mass., 1962—65; prof., chmn. edn. Northeastern U., Boston, 1965—87; Fulbright prof. history Peking U., Beijing, 1988—89; historian-in-residence City of Haverhill, Mass., 1989—90; asst. dir. bus., history, govt. edn. Asian divsn. U. Md., Korea, Japan, Guam, 1990—94; team leader, lectr. Joint Siberian-Am. Faculty Irkutsk State U., Russia, 1994—95; edn. coord. Asian divsn. U. Md., 1995—97, prof. European divsn., 1997—. Nat. dir. BHelp Bus., History and Econ. Life Program, Boston, 1968—; cons. in field Author: Teaching with Case Studies, 1978, A New England City: Haverhill Massachusetts, 1987, Attleboro, Massachusetts: The Hub of the Jewelry Industry, 1979, Protection, Patriotism and Prosperity: James M. Swank, the AISA, and the Tariff, 1872-1913, 1985; co-author: (with James B. Tedesco) Portable and Prefabricated Houses of the Thirties: The E.F. Hodgson Company 1935 and 1939 Catalogs, 2007; author, editor: The Creative Social Science Teacher, 1970, The Thunder of the Mills, 1981, Images of America: Dover, 2002. Mem. Town Fin. Com., Canton, Mass., 1966-; mem. long-range planning com. St. Dunstan, 1968-70; commr. Dover Hist. Comm., 2001—, Dover Hazardous Waste coord., 2003—. With U.S. Army, 1952-54. Recipient FEI Nat. collegiate award, 1985, Freedoms Found. George Washington medal for econ. edn., 1984. Mem. New Eng. History Tchrs. Assn. (past pres., Kidger award 1975), Dover Hist. Soc. (pres. 2000—). E-mail: pht52@aol.com.

TEDFORD, JACK NOWLAN, III, construction executive, small business owner; b. Reno, Jan. 1, 1943; s. Jack Nowlan Jr. and Elizabeth (Kolhoss) T.; m. Nancy Joanne Stiles, Feb. 27, 1971; children: Jack Nowlan IV, James Nathan. BS, U. Nev., 1966, MBA, 1969. Bus. mgr. Los Angeles Bapt. Coll., Newhall, Calif., 1969-71; v.p. Jack N. Tedford, Inc., Fallon, Nev., 1971-98; owner/broker Tedford Realty, Fallon, 1974-94; owner/mgr. Tedford Bus. Systems, Fallon, 1978-94; pres. JNT, Inc., Incline Village, Nev., 1994—. Pres., Jack N. Tedford, Inc., 1998—. Author numerous computer programs. Mem. Selective Svc. Local Bd., Fallon, 1971-76; chmn. City of Fallon Bd. Adjustment, 1972-95, chmn. Churchill Co. Reps., Fallon, 1976-80; mem. ctrl. com. Nev. Reps., 1976-2002; del. Nat. Conv., Detroit, 1980, Dallas, 1984; former coun. ofcls. Western Nev. Devel. Dist.; former treas. Lahontan Valley Environ. Alliance. Mem. Assn. Gen. Contractors (past pres., former v.p., treas. Nev. chpt., dir.), Nat. Bd. Realtors, State Bd. Realtors, Incline Village Bd. Realtors, CEDA Bus. Coun. (bd. dirs. 1991-97), Rotary (bd. dirs. 1980-81), Master's Coll. (bd. dirs. 1971-95), Slavic Gospel Assn. (bd. dirs.), Nat. Assn. Gen. Contractors (bd. dirs. open shop com., closely held bus. com.), Fellowship of Cos. for Christ Internat. Republican. Baptist. Avocations: computers, golf. Home and Office: 1995 Champion Hills Dr Reno NV 89523 Business E-Mail: jnt@jntinc.com.

TEDFORD, JEFF, college football coach; b. Lynwood, Calif., Nov. 2, 1961; BS in physical edn., Fresno State U., 1983. Profl. football player Hamilton, Calgary, Saskatchewan, and Winnipeg (CFL), 1983—87; volunteer asst. coach Fresno State U., 1987—88; coached Calgary Stampede (CFL), 1989—91; quarterback coach Fresno State U., 1992—97; offensive coord. U. Oregon, 1998—2001; head coach U. Calif. Golden Bears, 2002—. Named Pac-10 coach of the year, 2002. Achievements include winning the Insight Bowl (2003), Las Vegas Bowl (2005); creating a team that earned the school's highest national ranking (No. 4) since 1952 and registered its best regular-season record (10-1) in 54 years. Office: UC Berkeley Intercollegiate Athletics 209 Memorial Stadium Berkeley CA 94720 Office Phone: 510-642-3857.

TEDROW, JOHN CHARLES FREMONT, soils educator; b. Rockwood, Pa., Apr. 21, 1917; s. John Wesley and Emma Grace (Younkin) T.; m. Mary Jane Lough, Mar. 20, 1943 (dec. Mar. 1991); children: John Charles Fremont, Thomas Lough (dec.). BS, Pa. State U., 1939; MS, Mich. State U., 1940; PhD, Rutgers U., 1950. Jr. soil technologist Dept. Agr., 1941-42, soil scientist, 1946-47; instr. Rutgers U., New Brunswick, N.J., 1947-50, asst. prof., 1950-53, assoc. prof., 1953-57, prof. soils, 1957—73, prof. II, soils, 1973—84, prof. emeritus, 1984—. Cons. N.S. Research Found., 1949—; sr. pedologist Boston U., 1953—; prin. investigator Arctic Inst. N.Am., Washington, 1955-68, NSF, 1961-62, Atomic Energy Commn., Washington, 1961-63; cons. to govt. and industry. Author: (with R.C. Murray) Forensic Geology: Earth Sciences and Criminal Investigation, 1974, Soils of the Polar Landscapes, 1977, (with K.A. Linell) Soil and Permafrost Surveys in the Arctic, 1981, Soils of New Jersey, 1986, (with R.C. Murray) Forensic Geology, 1991; editor in chief Soil Science, 1968-79; editor: Antarctic Soils and Soil Forming Processes, 1966. Lt. USN, 1942—46. Recipient Lindback Research award Rutgers U., 1978, Antarctic Service medal. Fellow Am. Soc. Agronomy, Soil Sci. Soc. Am., Arctic Inst. N.Am.; mem. Internat. Soc. Soil Sci., Am. Geophys. Union, Sigma Xi, Alpha Zeta (hon.), Phi Mu Delta. Achievements include investigation of polar soils in Alaska, Can., Greenland, Scandinavia, Siberia and Antarctica. Home: 5 Bluebird Ct Edison NJ 08820-3677 Office: Rutgers U Ecology Evolution and Natural Resources PO Box 231 New Brunswick NJ 08903-0231 Office Phone: 732-932-1588. Business E-Mail: tizzano@aesop.rutgers.edu.

TEEGARDEN, LISA A., psychologist, military officer; d. John F. and Sanka B. Teegarden; m. Gregory R. Gonzalez, Sept. 4, 1993; children: Gunnar, Senia. BS, Colo. State U., Fort Collins, 1988; MS, U. Idaho, Moscow, 1993; D Psychology, Baylor U., Waco, Tex., 1998. Commd. 2d lt. US Army, advanced through grades to maj.; psychology intern Walter Reed Army Med. Ctr., Washington, 1997—98, neuropsychology fellow, 2003—05, chief adult outpatient clinic, 2005—; divsn. psychologist 10th mountain divsn. 710th MSB, Fort Drum, NY, 1998—2001; staff psychologist 902nd MI Group, Fort Meade, Md., 2001—01; chie, behavioral healthcare svcs. Kimbrough Ambulatory Care Clinic, Fort Meade, 2001—02, chief, cmty. mental health svcs., 2002—03. Bd. dirs. Def.-Graduate Psychology Edn. Program, Washington, 2005—06; presenter in field. Co-author: The CVLT-II Forced Choice Recognition Trial as a Measure of Effort in a TBI Population, 2005. Decorated MSM, ARCOM, AAM, NDSM (2), GWOTS, Army Superior Unit award; Health Profl. Scholarship Program scholar, US Army, 1995—98. Mem.: APA. Office: Walter Reed Army Med Ctr 6900 Georgia Ave NW Washington DC 20307-5001 Home Phone: 410-309-1043; Office Phone: 202-782-0065. Office Fax: 202-782-7165. Business E-Mail: lisa.teegarden@amedd.army.mil.

TEEGUARDEN, DENNIS EARL, forest economist, educator; b. Gary, Ind., Aug. 21, 1931; s. Gary Leon and Mary Dessa (Purciful) T.; m. Sally Annette Gleason, Dec. 23, 1954; children: Jason Earl, Julie Annette, Justin Gary. BS in Forestry with honors, Mich. Tech. U., Houghton, 1953; M.Forestry, U. Calif., Berkeley, 1958, PhD in Agrl. Econs. (Bidwell research fellow 1962-63), 1964. Rsch. aid U.S. Forest Service, 1957; asst. rsch. specialist U. Calif., Berkeley, 1958-63, mem. faculty, 1963-91, prof. forestry econs. Sch. Forestry, 1963-91, S.J. Hall prof. forest econs., 1989-91, prof. emeritus, 1991—, chmn. dept. forestry and resource mgmt., 1978-86, acting dir. forest products lab., 1987-88, assoc. dean for acad. affairs, 1990-92, assoc. dean rsch. and extension, 1992-93. Mem. Calif. Commn. on Agr. and Higher Edn., 1993-95, com. scientists Dept. Agr., 1977-80; cons. in field; mem. adv. bd. U. Calif. Forest Products Lab., 1994-98; mem. adv. coun. Alberta Heritage Found. for Sci. and Engring. Rsch., 2001-03. Co-author: Forest Resource Management: Decision-Making Principles and Cases, 1979; contbr. articles to profl. jours. Trustee Mich. Tech. Fund, Mich. Tech. U., Houghton, 1994-2004, life trustee, 2004—. Lt. USNR, 1953-57, Korea. Recipient Outstanding Alumnus award Mich. Tech. U., 1993, Berkeley citation U. Calif., Berkeley, 1994, Outstanding Svc. award Mich. Tech. Alumni Assn., 2007; grantee U.S. Forest Svc., Bur. Land Mgmt.; named to Honor Acad. Sch. Forestry and Wood Products, Mich. Tech. U., 1995. Fellow Soc. Am. Foresters; mem. Western Forest Economists, Calif. Water Fowl Assn. Home: 4732 Westwood Ct Richmond CA 94803-2441 Office: U Calif Coll Natural Resources Berkeley CA 94720-0001

TEEL, JOYCE RALEY, retail executive; b. 1930; m. James Teel. Dir. Raley's, West Sacramento, 1950—; co-chmn. bd. dirs. Raley's, Bel Air Markets, Food Source, Nob Hill Foods, No. Calif., Nev., NMex., 1991—. Dir. non-profit Food for Families. Named one of Forbes' Richest Americans, 2006. Office: Raleys & Belaire 500 W Capitol Ave West Sacramento CA 95605-2696

TEEL, PATRICIA JO, English language educator; d. Joseph Robutz and Mary Ella Rutherford; m. Jerry Leo Turnbull, July 30, 1999; children: Joley Kae Deerman, Sam Cody. BA, Calif. State U., Pomona, 1999, MA, 2000; PhD, Capella U., Mpls., 2006. Owner Triple R, Artesia, N.Mex., 1989—98; lectr. Calif. State U., Pomona, 1999—2000; prof. English Victor Valley Coll., Victorville, Calif., 2001—. Author: (video) A Challenge to the Champions, (presentation) Teachers as Students, Students as Teachers: Or You Are Here, Female and Foreign: Abolishing the Binary, From Biscuit-making to Branding Pen: Women on the Ranch, Adnan's L'Ecriture Feminine: Sensitizing the Insensitive, Crazy Jane as Persona: Madwoman or Ph, Gilbert and Makhaya: Christs in Exile. Chmn. N.Mex State 4-H Rodeo Bd. Dirs., 1986—90, mem., 1985—92, N.Mex., 1990—93; chmn. N.Mex State H.S. Finals, 1990—93; outside resource person N.Mex State U. Coop. Ext. Svc. Western Regional Forum, 1985—92. Mem.: NEA, Calif. Faculty Assn., Sigma Tau Delta. Home Phone: 760-240-6243; Office Phone: 760-245-4271.

TEELEY, KEVIN, educational association administrator; b. Detroit, 1954; BA in Sociology and Elem. Edn., U. Wash., 1978. Tchr. 5th and 6th grade gifted students Lake Washington Sch. Dist., Redmond, Wash., 1978—91, curriculum/staff devel. specialist, 1994—95; pres. Lake Washington Edn. Assn., Redmond, 1991—94, 1996—. Mem.: NEA (mem. profl. stds. and practice com. 1996—2002, del. Edn. Internat. World Congress 1998, 2001, 2004, rep. goodwill mission to Russia 2000), Nat. Bd. for Profl. Tchg. Stds. (bd. mem.). Office: Lake Washington Edn Assn 10628 NE 37t Cir Kirkland WA 98033 Office Phone: 425-822-9898.

TEEM, PAUL LLOYD, JR., bank executive; b. Gastonia, NC, Mar. 10, 1948; s. Paul Lloyd Sr. and Ruth Elaine (Bennett) T. BA, U. N.C., 1970; Cert., Inst. Fin. Edn., Chgo., 1984, Diploma, 1985, Degree of Distinction, 1989. Cert. tchr. N.C., cert. consumer credit exec.; lic. real estate broker; lic. lay Eucharistic minister. Exec. v.p., sec. Citizens South Bank, Gastonia, NC, 1983—; exec. v.p., sec., bd. dirs. Citizens South Fin. Svcs. Inc., Gastonia, 1988—; exec. v.p., sec. Citizens South Holdings, Mut. Holding Co., Gastonia, 1998—2002, Citizens South Banking Corp., Gastonia, 1998—. Bd. dirs. Gastonia Mchts. Assn., Inc., 1981-83; lay reader, lay eucharistic min. Episcopal Ch. Decorated Order Purple Cross, Legion of Honor. Fellow Soc. Cert. Credit Execs.; mem. Nat. Soc. Sons and Daus. of Pilgrims, SAR, Sons of Confederate Vets., Mil. Order of Stars and Bars, Masons (32d degree, bd. dirs., Disting. Svc. award 1987, Gold Honor award 1988, Active Legion of Honor 1989, Order of the Purple Cross of York 1990), Shriners, KT, Royal Order of Scotland, Hon. Order Ky. Cols., Phi Alpha Theta. Democrat. Avocation: genealogy. Home: 1208 Poston Cir Gastonia NC 28054-4634 Office: Citizens South Bank PO Box 2249 Gastonia NC 28053-2249 Office Phone: 704-884-2262. Business E-Mail: paul.teem@citizenssouth.com.

TEEMANT, MELANIE J., middle school educator; BS in Elem Edn., Univ. Nev., Las Vegas; MS student in Ednl. Leadership, Nova Southeastern Univ. Tchr. Clark County Sch. Dist., 1997—, Wengert Elem. Sch., Las Vegas, 1997—2001; reading tchr. Bob Miller Mid. Sch., Henderson, Nev., 2001—. Named Nev. Tchr. of Yr., 2007. Office: Bob Miller Middle Sch 2400 Cozy Hills Dr Henderson NV 89052 E-mail: mteemantx6@msn.com. *

TEEMER, CAREY, physiologist, medical researcher; BS in Physiology, U. Calif., Davis. With Oreg. Health Scis. U.; med. rsch. Oreg. Regional Primate Rsch. Ctr., Cancer Rsch. Ctr.; dir., tech. program mngt., Vulcan Inc., Allen Brain Atlas Project Allen Inst. for Brain Sci., Seattle. Co-recipient Rave award-Science, WIRED Mag., 2007. Office: Allen Inst for Brain Sci 551 N 34th St Seattle WA 98103

TEENER, JAMES W., neurologist, medical educator; b. Washington, Feb. 26, 1963; s. James Wallace and Kathryn Paxton Teener; m. Carol Ann Townley, Aug. 9, 1987; children: Samuel James, Maxwell Steadman, Jackson Townley. BA, Ohio Wesleyan U., Delaware, 1985; MD, U. Mich., Ann Arbor, 1990. Cert. neurology Am. Bd. Neurology and Psychiatry, 1997. Assoc. prof. neurology U. Mich. Med. Sch., Ann Arbor, 1998—; dir. neuromuscular program U. Mich. Health Sys., Ann Arbor, 1998—. Mem.: Am. Acad. Neuromuscular and Electrodiagnostic Medicine, Am. Acad. Neurology (Neurology Tchg. award 2004). Liberal. Achievements include research in mechanism by which people who are critically ill become severely weak. Avocations: tennis, photography, cooking, fishing, camping. Office: University Michigan Health System 1500 E Medical Center Dr Ann Arbor MI 48109 Office Phone: 734-936-8586.

TEEPEN, THOMAS HENRY, editor, journalist; b. Nashville, Jan. 19, 1935; s. Albert George and Elizabeth Blanche (Winfree) T.; m. Nancy Irene Roux, Feb. 2, 1957 (div. 1974); children— Kristina Lynn, Jeremy Roux; m. Sandra Jean Richards, May 14, 1975; 1 stepchild, Jennifer Koerlin BS in Journalism, Ohio U., 1957. Reporter Urbana (Ohio) Daily Citizen, 1957-58; asst. editor Kettering-Oakwood Times, Dayton, Ohio, 1958-59; from reporter to editorial writer Dayton Daily News, 1959-68, editorial page editor, 1968-82, Atlanta Constitution, 1982-92; nat. corr. Cox Newspapers, Atlanta, 1992-2000, columnist, 2000—. Contbg. columnist Liberal Opinion Week. Former pres. Joel Chandler Harris Assn., Atlanta; mem. Atlanta Opera, 1985—, Joint Internat. Observer Group, Ethiopian Elections, 1992; mem. internat. adv. com. The African-Am. Inst., N.Y.C., 1985-97; former bd. trustees Freedom to Read Found., Chgo; former Mayor's Cmty. Cultural Steering Com., Atlanta. Profl. journalism fellow Stanford Univ., 1967 Home and Office: 900 Charles Allen Dr NE Atlanta GA 30308-1722 Home Phone: 404-874-1421; Office Phone: 404-874-1421. E-mail: tteepen@earthlink.net, teepencolumn@coxnews.com.

TEEPLE, BRUCE JEFFERY, historian, writer; b. Phila., Feb. 29, 1952; s. Carlyle Jefferys and Barbara Fields Teeple; m. Michelle Fell Teeple, Mar. 5, 1977; children: Alice Catherine, Jane Christina. BA in History, Pa. State U., University Park, 1975, BA in Polit. Sci., 1975. Curator Aaronsburg Hist. Mus., Pa., 1985—2003; columnist Centre Daily Times, State College, Pa., 2004—. State judge Nat. History Day in Pa., University Park, 2004—. Editor, contbr.: Glimpses of the Past, 1994; co-editor, contributor In Schadde vun Rundkopp, 1999. Sec., treas. Aaronsburg Water Pipes, Inc., 1992—2006. Recipient Outstanding Promotion of Local History award, Centre County Hist. Soc., 2002. Mem.: Pa. Hist. Assn., Am. Assn. for State and Local History (sec. small mus. com. 2004—). Home: Box 37 Aaronsburg PA 16820 Home Phone: 814-349-8276. Personal E-mail: mongopawn44@hotmail.com.

TEERLINK, J. LELAND (JOSEPH LELAND TEERLINK), real estate developer; b. Salt Lake City, July 16, 1935; s. Nicholas John and Mary Luella (Love) T.; m. Leslie Dowdle, Nov. 5, 1975; children: Steven, David, Andrew, Suzanne, Benjamin. Student, U. Utah, Salt Lake City, 1953-55. Sales rep. Eastman Kodak Co., Salt Lake City, 1960-69; founder Graphic Systems, Inc., Salt Lake City, 1969-82, pres., 1969-79, chmn. bd., 1979-82; founder Graphic Ink Co., Salt Lake City, 1973, pres., 1975-79, chmn. bd., 1979-82; founder G.S.I. Leasing Co., Salt Lake City, 1975, pres., 1975-82; chmn. bd. Graphic Sys. Holding Co., Inc., Salt Lake City, 1978-82; dir. leasing and acquisitions Terra Industries, Inc., real estate developers, 1982-86, ptnr., 1986—. Bd. dirs. ARC, Salt Lake City, 1979-82; co-founder, dir. Hope Living Ctr. Found. for Mothers and Children, 1993-99; vice consulate of the Netherlands for Utah, 1977-92; mem. active corps of execs., SBA, 1979-83; adv. bd. House of Hope Mothers and Children Utah Alcoholism Found., 1992-94. Recipient Masters award Salt Lake Bd. Realtors, 1993; named Small Businessman of Yr. for Utah, SBA, 1978 Mem. Graphic Arts Equipment and Supply Dealers of Am. (dir. 1978-82),

Printing Industry of Am., Nat. Assn. Indsl. and Office Parks (pres. Utah chpt. 1986-87), Nat. Fedn. Ind. Businessman, Million Dollar Club (life). Republican. Mem.Lds Ch. Home: 2984 Thackeray Pl Salt Lake City UT 84108-2517 Office: 6925 Union Park Ctr Midvale UT 84047-4135 Office Phone: 801-566-6653. Business E-Mail: receptionist@terrautah.com, leet@terrautah.com.

TEES, RICHARD CHISHOLM, psychology professor, researcher; b. Montreal, Que., Can., Oct. 31, 1940; s. Ralph Charles and Helen Winnifred (Chisholm) T.; m. Kathleen F. Coleman, Sept. 1, 1962; children: Susan M., Carolyn V. BA, McGill U., 1961; PhD, U. Chgo., 1965. Asst. prof. U. B.C., Vancouver, Canada, 1965-67, assoc. prof., 1969-75, prof. psychology, 1975—, head dept. psychology, 1984—94, 1999—2004, U. B.C. Okanogen transition mgmt. exec., 2004—, acting dep. vice chancellor, acad. v.p., 2006—. Rsch. prof. U. Sussex, Brighton, Eng., 1972-73, 77-78; chmn. grant selection panel Nat. Scis. and Engring. Rsch. Coun. Can., Ottawa, 1993-96, B.C. Health Care Rsch. Found., Vancouver, 1984-87; chmn. studentship com. Med. Rsch. Coun., Ottawa, 1985-92; chmn. Can. Coun. Dept. Psychology, 1987-93; mem. B.C. Degree Quality Assessment Bd., 2006—; chair bd. dirs. Cetacea Networks Corp., 2005—. Author: (with Kolb) Cerebral Cortex of the Rat, 1990; mem. editl. bd. Can. Jour. Exptl. Psychology, 1975-84, 87—; contbr. articles to profl. jours., chpts. to books. Rsch. fellow Killam Found., 1972-73, 77-78; Rsch. fellow Can. Coun., 1972-73. Fellow APA, Am. Psychol. Soc., Can. Psychol. Assn.; mem. Soc. for Neurosci., Psychonomic Soc., Can. Soc. Brain, Behaviour, and Cognitive Sci. (pres. 1997-98, Richard C. Tees Leadership award, 2004), U. B.C. Senate, Nat. Ctr. Excellence Can. Stroke Network. Office: U BC Dept Psychology Vancouver BC Canada V6T 1Z4 Home: 4506 W 14th Ave Vancouver BC V6R 2Y4 Canada Home Phone: 604-224-6030; Office Phone: 604-822-3245. Business E-Mail: rtees@psych.ubc.ca.

TEETER, DWIGHT LELAND, JR., journalism educator; b. LA, Jan. 6, 1935; s. Dwight Leland and Ruth Elizabeth (Sauer) T.; m. Letitia Ruth Thoreson, July 7, 1956; children: Susan Letitia Hall, John Thoreson, William Weston. AB in Journalism, U. Calif.-Berkeley, 1956, M.J., 1959; PhD in Mass Communications, U. Wis., 1966. Reporter Waterloo Daily Courier, Iowa, 1957-60; asst. prof. Iowa State U., Ames, 1964-66; asst. to assoc. prof. U. Wis., Madison, 1966-72; assoc.prof. to prof. U. Ky., Lexington, 1972-77, dir. journalism dept., 1975-77; prof. journalism, chmn. dept. journalism U. Tex., Austin, 1977-84, William P. Hobby Centennial prof. communication, 1983-87; prof., dept. mass communications U. Wis., Milw., 1987-91; dean Coll. Communications U. Tenn., Knoxville, 1991—2002; prof. journalism, 2002—. Vis. assoc. prof. U. Wash., Seattle, 1969-70; treas. Journalism Council, Inc., N.Y.C., 1972-81 Author: (with Bill Loving) Law of Mass Communications, 11th edit., 2004, (with Jean L. Folkerts) Voices of a Nation: A History of Media in the United States, 4th edit., 2002, (with Lorman A. Ratner) Fanatics and Fire-Eaters: Newspaper Publications Leading to Civil War, 2003; contbr. articles to legal, hist., comm. jours. Chair Headliners Club of Tex. Media Contest, 1979-83; judge Tex. Bar Assn. Media Contest, 1981-85; mem. pub. affairs com. Tex. State Bar, 1985-87. Recipient Tex. Excellence in Teaching award Tex. Ex-Students' Assn., 1983, Harold L. Nelson award U. Wis., 1985, Outstanding Faculty Rsch. award, Tenn. Coll. Communication Info., 2005. Mem. Assn. for Edn. in Journalism and Mass Comm. (chmn. prof. freedom and responsibility com. 1971-73, pres. 1985-86, Disting. Svc. award 2001, Disting. Rsch. award, 2005), Soc. Profl. Journalists (Disting. Tchr. award 1991), Phi Kappa Phi, Kappa Tau Alpha. Office: U Tenn 430 Communication Knoxville TN 37996-0330 Office Phone: 865-974-5139. Business E-Mail: teeter@utk.edu.

TEETERS, JEFFREY R., lawyer; b. Jackson Ctr., Ohio, July 18, 1968; BA, U. Dayton, 1990; JD, U. Cin., 1993. Bar: Ohio 1993, US Dist. Ct. Southern Dist. Ohio 1993, US Ct. of Appeals Sixth Cir. 1998, US Supreme Ct. 2005, US Dist. Ct. Northern Dist. Ohio 2006. Ptnr. Frost Brown Todd LLC, Cin., chair, Unfair Competition Litig. Practice Grp., mem., Recruiting Com. Mentor U. Cin. Coll. Law, 1997—2003; baseball and basketball coach Mariemont Recreation Assn., 2003—; mentor Sr. High Youth, Lutheran Ch. of Good Shepherd, 1997—2002; ministry, Bd. Trustees U. Cin. Luth. Campus, 2003—. Named one of Ohio's Rising Stars, Super Lawyers, 2005, 2006. Mem.: ABA (co-editor, Bus. Torts Jour. 2004—), Ohio State Bar Assn. (mem., Litig. Sect., Antitrust Sect.), Cin. Bar Assn. Office: Frost Brown Todd LLC 2200 PNC Ctr 201 E Fifth St Cincinnati OH 45202-4182 Office Phone: 513-651-6715. Office Fax: 513-651-6981.

TEETERS, JOSEPH LEE, mathematician, consultant; b. Caney, Kans., Dec. 10, 1934; s. Jesse L. and Marie (Tapper) Teeters; m. Janet L. Hamm, June 18, 1984; children: Jeffrey, Susan, Christopher. Student, Colo. Sch. Mines, 1956, U. Kans., 1957; MA in Math., U. No. Colo., 1960, EdD in Math., 1968. Cert. secondary sch. tchr., Colo., Ill., hazard waste profl., OSHA. Exploration geologist Ohio Oil Co., Rawlings, Wyo., 1956-57; instr. Stout State U., Menomonie, Wis., 1960-62; asst. prof. Baker U., Baldwin City, Kans., 1962-65; temp. instr. U. No. Colo., Greeley, 1965-68; asst. prof. Western State Coll., Gunnison, Colo., 1968-69; prof. U. Wis., Eau Claire, 1969-88; cons. assoc. Delphi Data, Corona, Calif., 1989-98; ind. mathematician and cons., Lake Zurich, Ill., 1998—. Land surveying cons. Donaldson Engring., Menomonie, 1960-62; land boundary cons. ACLU, Eau Claire, 1974; lectr., spkr., cons. in field. Author: Creating Escher-Type Drawings, 1977; designer tessellation art; contbr. cover designs for profl. publs. Active Forest Lake (Ill.) Cmty. Assn., 1990—; sr. citizen trainer Marathon Challenge, St. Louis, 1994; mem. Golden Colo. Civic Orch., 1956; unicyclist Kans. State Sunflower State Games. Grantee NSF, 1965, U. New Orleans, 1987. Mem. Internat. Assn. for Math. Geology, Internat. Platform Assn., Stanton County Kans. Hist. Assn., No Man's Land Hist. Soc., Santa Fe Trail Assn., Kans. Trails Assn., Am. Volkssport Assn. (triathlete), Colo. Sch. Mines Assn., Tiblow Trailblazers (sports cons. 1994—), Sherman County Kans. Hist. Soc., Ill. Running Club, Kappa Kappa Psi, Sigma Gamma Epsilon, Phi Delta Kappa. Achievements include drill site improvisation of a magnetic fishing tool for small sand screen well openings; invention of a multi-function recursive algorithm which yields (with each use) a unique random lottery number ball quick-pick selection result; two successful completions of the Boston Marathon as well as six other 26.2 mile running events; design and development of motion activated vortiginous reflector system(s) for bicycles. Avocations: raising St. Bernards, planning and building full size windmills, designing birdhouses. Home and Office: 8683 Felsview Dr Laurel MD 20723

TEETERS, NANCY HAYS, economist, director; b. Marion, Ind., July 29, 1930; d. S. Edgar and Mabel (Drake) Hays; m. Robert Duane Teeters, June 7, 1952; children: Ann, James, John. AB in Econs., Oberlin Coll., 1952, LLD, 1979; MA in Econs., U. Mich., 1954, postgrad., 1956—57, LLD (hon.), 1983, Bates Coll., 1981, Mt. Holyoke Coll., 1983. Tchg. fellow U. Mich., Ann Arbor, 1954—55, instr., 1956—57, U. Md. Overseas, Germany, 1955—56; staff economist govt. fin. sect. Bd. Govs. of FRS, Washington, 1957—66, mem. bd., 1979—84; economist (on loan) Coun. Econ. Advs., 1962—63; economist Bur. Budget, 1966—70; sr. fellow Brookings Instn., 1970—73; sr. specialist Congl. Rsch. Svc., Library Congress, Washington, 1973—74; asst. dir., chief economist Ho. of Reps. Com. on Budget, 1974—78; v.p., chief economist IBM, Armonk, NY, 1984—90. Author: (with others) Setting National Priorities: The 1972 Budget, 1971, Setting National Priorities: The 1973 Budget, 1972, Setting National Priorities: The 1974 Budget, 1973; contbr. articles to profl. publs. Recipient Comfort Starr award in econs. Oberlin Coll., 1952; Disting. Alumnus award U. Mich., 1980 Mem. Nat. Economists Club (v.p. 1973-74, pres. 1974-75, chmn. bd. 1975-76, gov. 1976-79), Am. Econ. Assn. (com. on status of women 1975-78), Am. Fin. Assn. (dir. 1969-71) Democrat. Home: 77 3rd St C-8 Stamford CT 06905

TEETS, PETER B., former civilian military employee; b. Feb. 1942; BS, U. Colo., 1963, MS in Applied Math., 1965, DSc (hon.), 1990; MS in Mgmt., MIT, 1978. Engr. Martin Marietta Denver Aerospace, Colo., 1963—70, mgr., Titan IIIC inertial guidance system Colo., 1970—75, program mgr. Transtage Project & dir. Space Systems Colo., 1975—80, v.p. bus. devel. Colo., 1980—82, v.p., gen. mgr. aerospace strategic & launch systems divsn. Colo., 1982—85, pres. Colo., 1985—93, Martin Marietta Space Group, Bethesda, Md., 1993—95; pres., COO Lockheed Martin Info. & Services, Bethesda, Md., 1995—97, Lockheed Martin Corp., Bethesda, Md., 1997—99; under sec. Dept. Air Force, US Dept. Def., Washington, 2001—05, acting sec., 2005; dir. Nat. Reconnaissance Office, Washington, 2001—05. Bd. trustees The Aerospace Corp, El Segundo, Calif., 2005—. Recipient Sloan Fellow Award, W. Stuart Symington award, 2004. Fellow: Am. Astronautical Society, Am. Institute of Aeronautics and Astronautics; mem.: Nat. Acad. Engring.

TEETS, WALTER RALPH, accounting educator; b. Boulder, Colo., Oct. 1, 1950; s. Otis E. and Elsie (Purchase) T.; m. Mary Anne Clougherty; stepchildren: Katherine Kuder, Elizabeth Wierman B in Music Edn., U. Colo., Boulder, 1973; MMus, U. Wis., Madison, 1976; MS in Edn., U. Wis., Whitewater, 1981, MS in Acctg., 1985; PhD, U. Chgo., 1989. Asst. prof. Wash. U., St. Louis, 1986-89, U. Ill., Urbana-Champaign, Ill., 1989-94, Gonzaga U., Spokane, Wash., 1994-99, assoc. prof., 1999—. Continuing profl. edn. spkr. Gonzaga U., 1996—2007, Wash. Soc. CPAs, numerous others; vis. assoc. prof. U. Notre Dame, 2000. Editor Fin. Reporting Jour., 1998—2002, spl. guest editor Issues in Acctg. Edn., 2001—03, assoc. editor Jour. Derivatives Acctg., 2003—; contbr. articles to profl. jours. Recipient Outstanding Acctg. Educator award Wash. Soc. CPAs, 1998-99; Acad. acctg. fellow Office of Chief Acct., U.S. SEC, 1997-98. Mem. Am. Acctg. Assn. (editor Fin. Reporting Jour. newsletter Fin. Acctg. and Reporting sect. 1998—02), Wash. Soc. CPAs (bd. dirs. Spokane chpt.), K.C. (fin. sec. 1990-93, 99-2003, treas. 2005—) Avocations: music, cross country skiing, four-wheeling. Office: Gonzaga Univ 502 E Boone Ave Spokane WA 99258-0001 Office Phone: 509-323-3416. Office Fax: 509-323-5811. Business E-Mail: teets@gem.gonzaga.edu.

TEGNELIA, JAMES A., federal agency administrator; b. Monessen, Pa., 1942; BS in Physics, Georgetown U.; MS in Engring., George Washington U., 1975; PhD in Physics, Catholic U. Am. Supr. rsch. physicist to mgr. US Army Night Vision Lab., 1971—76; asst. under sec., acting. dep. under sec. Office Undersecretary Defense Rsch. Engring. US Dept Def., 1982—85; program mgr. and officer dir. Defense Advance Rsch. Projects Agy., 1976, dep. dir., 1985, acting dir.; v.p. engring. Martin Marietta Corp., v.p. bus. devel. Electronics Group; v.p. bus. devel., Energy and Environment Sector Lockheed Martin Corp., 1995, pres., Advanced Environ. Systems, Inc., 1996—98; exec. v.p., dep. dir. Sandia Nat. Lab., 1993, v.p. defense programs; dir. US Strategic Command Ctr. Combating Weapons Mass Destruction, 2004—, Defense Threat Reduction Agy., Ft. Belvoir, Va., 2004—. Mem. exec. coun., bd. dirs. Albuquerque C. of C., 1994—95; bd. dirs. Anderson Sch. U. N.Mex., Sandia Sci. and Tech. Pk., Tech. Ventures Corp., Laguna Industries, Inc.; bd. adv. George Washington U. Sch. Engring.; chmn. Greater Albuquerque US Saving Bond Campaign, 1995; chmn. State N.Mex. US Savings Bond Campaign, 1996; chmn. Army Sci. Bd.; co-chmn. Nat. Lab. Nat. Security Adv. Panel; campaign chmn. United Way Ctrl. N.Mex., 1996. Served with US Army, 1968—71, one yr. tour Vietnam. Recipient Bronze Star Medal, Civilian Meritorious Svc. Medal, Sr. Exec. Svc. Meritorious Svc. award. Mem.: Soc. Sigma Xi. Office: Defense Threat Reduction Agy 8725 John J Kingman Rd Stop 6201 Fort Belvoir VA 22060-6201

TEHRANI, NADER, architect; BFA, RI Sch. Design, Providence, 1985, BArch, 1986; MArch with distinction in Urban Design, Harvard Grad. Sch. Design, Cambridge, 1991. Prin. Office dA, Boston, 1991—. Studio critic, seminar instr. Boston Archtl. Ctr., 1988—89; studio instr. art & architecture dept. Northeastern U., 1992—93; adj./asst. prof. architecture dept. RI Sch. Design, 1993—98; vis. design critic Harvard Grad. Sch. Design, 1994—95, 1996, 97, So. Calif. Inst. Architecture, 2002; adj. prof., assoc. prof., asst. prof. Harvard Grad. Sch. Design, 1998—; Thomas W. Ventulett III Disting. chair archtl. design Ga. Inst. Tech., 2005—06; vis. critic archtl. design MIT, 2005. Contbr. articles to profl. publs.; prin. works include Witte Artist Bldg., Green Bay, Wis., Dais Bldg., Green Bay, Tongxian Art, Beijing, Weston Performing Arts Ctr., Conn., Rose Art Mus., Brandeis U., Waltham, Mass., Carl and Ruth Shapiro Campus Ctr. Stair, Brandeis U., Mills Coll. Art Mus., 25 Morrissey Apt. Bldg., Boston, R+D Biotech Bldg., Iran, Issam Fares Inst., Beirut, Fleet Libr., RI Sch. Design (Adaptive Reuse/Material Conservation/New Design/Instl. award, Providence Preservation Soc., 2006), Bin 26 Enoteca, Boston, Powerstation, LA, Obzee Fashion Hdqs., Seoul, Korea, Carlton Hotel at Collyer Quay, Singapore, Hotel Zemsky, Sungwoo Resort, Korea, Washington Restaurant, Boston, exhibitions include Fabrications, MoMA, 1998, Tensegrity in Rope, So. Calif. Inst. Architecture, LA, 2002, Skin + Bones, Mus. Contemporary Art, LA, 2006—. Mem.: Boston Soc. Archs. Office: Office dA 1920 Washington St #2 Boston MA 02118 Office Phone: 617-541-5540. Office Fax: 617-541-5535. E-mail: nadertehrani@officeda.com. *

TEICH, ALBERT HARRIS, professional society administrator; b. Chgo., Dec. 17, 1942; s. Maurice and Ina (Szuldiner) T.; m. Carolyn R. Richmond, June 3, 1965 (div. 1987); children: Mitchell Craig, Kenneth David; m. Jill H. Pace, Jan. 29, 1989; 1 child, Samantha Lynne. BS, MIT, 1964, PhD, 1969. Rsch. fellow Syracuse (N.Y.) U. Rsch. Corp., 1969-71, dir., sci. and tech. studies, 1971-73; coord. rsch. SUNY, Binghamton, 1973-74; dir. rsch. SUNY Inst. for Pub. Policy Alternatives, Albany, 1974-76; assoc. prof. pub. affairs and dep. dir., grad. program sci. tech. and pub. policy George Washington U., 1976-79; mgr., sci. policy studies AAAS, Washington, 1980-84, head, office of pub. sector programs, 1984-89, dir. sci. and policy programs, 1989—. Cons. NAS., Office of Tech. Assessment, Washington, 1976-95, Orgn. Econ. Cooperation and Devel., Paris, 1994—96, Hertz Found., 2003; chmn. SRS adv. com. NSF, Washington, 1988-90; pres. Technosci. Assocs., Inc., Silver Spring, Md., 1977-82; chair Ga. Inst. Tech., Sch. Pub. Adv. Bd., 2001-2005; mem. bd. govs. US-Israel Binational Sci Found., 2001—, vice chmn., 2004-05, chmn., 2005-06; mem. rsch. adv. bd. U. Calif., Davis, 2003—; mem. rsch. and tech. coord. com. Nat. Rsch. Coun., 2003—. Editor: Science and Technology in the U.S.A., 1986, Technology and the Future, 10th edit., 2005; editor, author: Scientists and Public Affairs, 1974; mem. editl. bd. Science Communication, 1991—, Science, Technology and Human Values, 1994—, Prometheus, 1999—, Renewable Resources Jour., 2005-. Recipient Sci. Achievement award, Wash. Acad. Scis., 2004. Fellow AAAS (chmn. sect. X 1988), Wash. Acad. Scis. (pres.-elect 2007—); mem. Tech. Transfer Soc. (v.p. 1985-91), Soc. for Social Studies of Scis., Washington Acad. Scis. (pres.-elect. 2007), Nat. Press Club, Sigma Xi. Avocations: swimming, photography, travel writing. Office: AAAS 1200 New York Ave NW Washington DC 20005-3941 Home Phone: 301-770-9592; Office Phone: 202-326-6600. Business E-Mail: ateich@aaas.org.

TEICH, HOWARD BERNARD, lawyer, volunteer, public information officer; b. Huntington, NY, Nov. 1, 1946; s. Samuel and Beatrice Ann (Kay) T. AB, U. Pa., 1967; JD, Boston U., 1970. Bar: N.Y., 1971, U.S. Dist. Ct. (so. dist.) N.Y. 1984. Counsel N.Y. State Senator Emanuel Gold, NYC, 1971-72; law sec. N.Y. State Supreme Ct. Justin Martin Evans, NYC, 1972-75; assoc. pub. Firehouse mag., NYC, 1975-79; pub. Midtown South Bus., NYC, 1985-87; prin. Law Offices Howard B. Teich, NYC, 1980—; sr. cons. The Kamber Group, Washington, 1995—; sr. counsel McLaughlin & Stein, P.C., NYC, 1997—. Founder, chair New Dem. Dimensions, N.Y.C., 1981-91, Nat. Task Force on Life Safety for Handicapped, Washington, 1979-81; bd. dirs. Boys Choir of Harlem, N.Y.C., 1983-85, Assn. on Am. Indian Affairs, 1990-97, adv. bd., 1997—; chmn. New Leadership of Israel Bonds, N.Y.C., 1977-79; pres. Am. Jewish Congress Met. Region N.Y.C., 1992—, past nat. v.p.; bd. dirs. Jewish Comty. Rels. Coun., N.Y., 1995—, past v.p., 1995-98; co-chair Jewish Heritage, N.Y.C., 1997—;dep. dir. N.Y. state citizens com. McGovern for Pres., 1972, Samuels for Gov., 1974, Carey for Gov., 1974; dep. dir. N.Y. state primary campaign Carter for Pres., 1980; co-chair N.Y. state citizens com. Glenn for Pres., 1984, Mondale/Ferraro '84, 1984; bd. dirs. Manhattan Playhouse. Recipient Robert Briscoe award Emerald Isle Immigration Soc., 1996, Israel Leadership award Israel Bonds, 1979, Martin Luther King Jr. Living-the-Dream award, Gov. George Pataki, N.Y., 1999. Mem. AJ Congress Met Region (pres. 1992—), U. Pa. Club, Assn. on Am. Indian Affairs (bd. dirs., nat. adv. bd.). Democrat. Jewish. Avocations: softball, tennis, reading, theater, dance. Home: 185 E 85th St New York NY 10028-2140 Office: 260 Madison Ave New York NY 10016-2401

TEICH, MALVIN CARL, electrical engineering educator; b. NYC, May 4, 1939; s. Sidney R. and Loretta K. Teich SB in Physics, MIT, 1961; MSEE, Stanford U., 1962; PhD in Quantum Electronics, Cornell U., 1966. Research scientist MIT Lincoln Lab., Lexington, Mass., 1966-67; prof. engring. sci. Columbia U., NYC, 1967-96, prof. emeritus, 1996—, chmn. dept. elec. engring., 1978-80, mem. Columbia Radiation Lab., faculty applied physics dept. NYC; prof. elec. computer engring., biomed. engring., physics Boston U., 1995—. Mem. Photonics Ctr., Boston U., also Ctr. Adaptive Sys., Hearing Rsch. Ctr.; mem. sci. bd. Inst. Physics, Czech Acad. Scis., Prague. Author: (with B.E.A. Saleh) Fundamentals of Photonics, 1991, (with S.B. Lowen) Fractal Based Point Processes; dep. editor Quantum Optics, 1988-92; bd. editors Jour. Visual Comm. and Image Representation, 1989-92, Jemná Mechanika a Optika, 1994—; contbr. articles to profl. jours.; patentee in field; expert in patent and trade secret litigation. Recipient Citation Classic award Inst. for Sci. Info., 1981; Meml. Gold medal of Palacky U., Czech Republic, 1992; Guggenheim Meml. Found. fellow, 1973. Fellow AAAS, IEEE (Browder J. Thompson Meml. prize 1969, Morris E. Leeds award 1997), Optical Soc. Am. (editl. adv. panel Optics Letters 1977-79), Am. Phys. Soc., Acoustical Soc. Am.; mem. Sigma Xi, Tau Beta Pi. Office: Boston U Dept Elec and Computer Engr 8 Saint Mary's St Boston MA 02215-2421 Office Phone: 617-353-1236. Business E-Mail: teich@bu.edu.

TEICHNER, LESTER, general management executive; b. Chgo., Apr. 21, 1944; s. Ben Bernard and Eva Bertha (Weinberg) T.; m. Barbara Rae Bush, Jan. 30, 1966 (div. Aug. 1969); m. Doris Jean Ayres, Jan. 31, 1980; children: Lauren Ayres, Caroline Ayres. BSEE, U. Ill., 1965; MBA in Mktg. and Fin., U. Chgo., 1969. Sales engr. Westinghouse Electric Corp., Chgo., 1965-69; v.p. ops. Intec Inc., Chgo., 1969-74; pres., CEO The Chgo. Group Inc., 1974—2000, Guttermonster, LLC, 2005—; pres., COO Republic Window & Doors, 2000—05. Bd. dirs. Golub & Co., Inc., Strategic Processing Inc., NYC, Dees Comms. Ltd., Vancouver, B.C., Maxcor Mfg. Co., Colorado Springs; CEO, bd. dirs. Axcess Worldwide Ltd., Coal Gasification, Inc., Chgo.; guest lectr. U. Chgo. Grad. Sch. Bus., 1982-95. Co-inventor U.S. patent electronic marketplace; contbr. articles to profl. publs. Mem. The Chgo. Forum, 1976—; bd. dirs. Am. Israeli C. of C. Mem. Am. Mgmt. Assn., Am. Mktg. Assn., Midwest Planning Assn. (bd. dirs. 1981). Republican. Jewish. Avocations: astronomy, skiing. Home: 2230 N Seminary Ave Chicago IL 60614-3507 Office: The Chicago Group Inc 2230 N Seminary Ave Chicago IL 60614-3507 Office Phone: 773-371-0357. Personal E-mail: lteichner@aol.com.

TEIG, MARLOWE GILMAN, investment banker; b. Fargo, ND, Sept. 13, 1938; s. Julius Berner Teig and Inez (Hedlund) Teig-Erickson; m. Carole Lynne Werner, Nov. 25, 1961; children: Jennifer Lynne, Alan Gilman. BA, U. Mich., 1961; postgrad., CCNY, 1962-64. With Harcourt Brace Jovanovich, 1964-80, Houghton Mifflin Co., 1980-87, Macmillan, Inc., 1987-88; mng. dir. Berkery, Noyes & Co., Newton, Mass., 1990—. Home: 40 Kirkstall Rd Newton MA 02460-2218 Office Phone: 617-969-7935. Business E-Mail: marlowe.teig@berkerynoyes.com.

TEIGER, DAVID, management consultant; b. Newark, June 13, 1929; s. Samuel and Fannie (Ginsburg) Teiger; children: Lauren, Douglas. BS, Cornell U., 1951. Ptnr. Samuel Teiger & Co., Newark, 1953-59, Ira Haupt & Co., NYC, 1959-64, Bache & Co., NYC, 1964-65; exec. v.p. Shearson, Hammill & Co., Inc., NYC, 1965-73; chmn., CEO United Rsch. Co., Morristown, NJ, 1973-90; chmn. Gemini Consulting, Morristown, NJ, 1990-95. Hon. trustee Mus. Modern Art, NYC. Served to lt. US Army, 1951—53. Named one of Top 200 Collectors, ARTnews mag., 2006. Mem.: Meadowood; Mountain Ridge. Office: Teiger Inc 51 Peachcroft Dr Bernardsville NJ 07924-1006

TEILLON, LOUIS PIERRE, JR., lawyer; b. NYC, Nov. 15, 1943; AB, Yale U., 1965; LLB, Columbia U., 1968. Bar: Pa. 1968. Mem. Heckscher, Teillon, Terrill & Sager, P.C., West Conshohocken, Pa. Mem. Am. Coll. Trust and Estate Counsel, Pa. Bar Assn. (real property, probate and trust sects.), Phila. Bar Assn. (past chmn. probate sect.). Office: Heckscher Teillon Terrill & Sager PC 100 Four Falls Corp Ctr Ste 300 West Conshohocken PA 19428 Office Phone: 610-940-4169. Fax: 610-940-6042. E-mail: perry@htts.com.

TEIMAN, RICHARD BARRY, lawyer; b. Bklyn., May 19, 1938; AB, Princeton U., 1959; LLB, Harvard U., 1962. Bar: N.Y. 1963. Ptnr. Winston & Strawn LLP and predecessor Cole & Deitz, NYC, 1968—. Trustee Citizens Budget Commn., 1993—. Mem. Assn. Bar City N.Y. (com. admiralty 1975-78, 87, chair 1988-91, 03-06), Maritime Law Assn. (com. maritime financing 1980—, chmn. subcom. Recodification U.S. Ship Mortgage Act 1986-91, chmn. subcom. USCG, citizenship and related matters 1988-94), Phi Beta Kappa. Home: 5 Pryer Ln Larchmont NY 10538-4012 Office: Winston & Strawn LLP 200 Park Ave Rm 4100 New York NY 10166-4193 Home Phone: 914-834-8827; Office Phone: 212-294-6730. Business E-Mail: rteiman@winston.com.

TEIMOURIAN, BAHMAN, plastic surgeon; b. Tehran, Iran, May 18, 1933; BS, Bethany Coll., 1955; MD, George Washington U., 1958. Cert. Am. Bd. Plastic Surgery. Intern, surgery George Washington U., 1958—59, resident, surgery, 1959—61, resident, plastic surgery, 1961—62, chief resident, gen. surgery, 1962—63, chief resident, plastic surgery, 1963—64; prof. plastic surgery Georgetown U., Washington; private practice Bethesda, Md. Mem.: Montgomery County Med. Soc., Northeastern Soc. Plastic Surgeons, Am. Soc. for Aesthetic Plastic Surgery, Am. Soc. Plastic Surgeons, Internat. Soc. for Aesthetic Plastic Surgery. Office: 5402 McKinley St Bethesda MD 20817-3764 Office Fax: 301-897-5666, 301-897-3385. *

TEITEL, STANLEY, principal, science educator; BA, CCNY, 1971; MS in Sci. Edn., Brooklyn Coll.; MA in Adminstrn. and Supervision, Manhattan Coll. Coord. Coll. Bound program William Howard Taft HS, Bronx; tchr. chemistry and physics Stuyvesant HS, NYC, 1983, asst. prin. Dept. Chemistry and Physics, 1997—99, prin., 1999—. Named Educator of Yr., CCNY Alumni Assn., 2003. Mem.: NSF, Sci. Coun. of NYC, Nat. Consortium of Specialized Secondary Schs. in Math., Sci. and Tech., Sci. Tchrs. Assn. of NY State. Office: Stuyvesant HS 345 Chambers St New York NY 10282 Office Phone: 212-312-4800. *

TEITELBAUM, HERBERT, lawyer; b. Bklyn., June 11, 1943; s. Hyman and Rose Leah Teitelbaum; m. Ruth J. Abram, June 4, 1967; children: Anna Mara, Noah. BA, Brandeis U., 1965; JD, NYU, 1968. Bar: Mass. 1968, N.Y. 1970. Assoc. Widett & Kruger, Boston, 1968-70, Skadden, Arps, Slate, Meagher & Flom, NYC, 1970-72; legal dir. P.R. Legal Def. and Edn. Fund, NYC, 1972-77; ptnr., founder Teitelbaum, Hiller, Rodman, Paded & Hibsher, P.C., NYC, 1977—96; ptnr. Bryan Cave LLP, NYC, 1996—. Cons. EEOC, Washington, 1977-80, US Dept. Health Edn & Welfare, Washington, 1982, exec. dir. NY State Ethics Commn., 2007- Co-author: Changing Schools: The Language Minority Student in the Eighties, 1982. Pres. New Israel Fund, Washington, 1993—; chair lawyers com. Nat. Conf. on Soviet Jewry, N.Y., 1989-90; bd. dirs. N.Y. Civil Liberties Union, N.Y.C., 1991-93. Fellow Aspen (Colo.) Inst. of Humanistic Studies, 1976. Office: Bryan Cave LLP 1290 Ave Americas New York NY 10104 E-mail: hteitelbaum@bryancave.com. *

TEITELBAUM, PHILIP, psychologist; b. Bklyn., Oct. 9, 1928; s. Bernard and Betty (Schechter) T.; m. Osnat Boné; children: Benjamin, Daniel, David, Jonathan, Gideon. BS, CCNY, 1950; MA, Johns Hopkins U., 1952, PhD, 1954. Instr., asst. prof. physiol. psychology Harvard U., 1954-59; assoc. prof. psychology U. Pa., Phila., 1959-63, prof., 1963-73; prof. psychology U. Ill.-Urbana-Champaign, 1973-85, emeritus prof., 1985—, Disting. prof. Ctr. Advanced Studies, 1980-85; grad. research prof. U. Fla., Gainesville, 1984—. Author: Fundamental Principles of Physiological Psychology, 1967; editor: (with E. Satinoff) Motivation: Handbook Behavioral Neurobiology, 1983, (with Osmat Tertelbaum) Does Your Baby Have Austism, 2007; contbr. chpts. to books; contbr. articles to profl. jours. Fellow Ctr. for Advanced Study in Behavorial Scis., Stanford U., 1975-76, Fulbright fellow Tel Aviv U., 1978-79, Guggenheim fellow, 1984-85, Carnegie Found. fellow Inst. Neurol. Scis., U. Pa. Med. Sch., 1958-59. Fellow APA (pres. div. physiol. psychology, disting. sci. contbn. award 1978), Am. Psychol. Soc. (William James fellow); mem. NAS, AAAS, Am. Physiol. Soc., Soc. for Neurosci., Soc. Exptl. Psychology. Home: 2239 NW 17th Ave Gainesville FL 32605-3909 Office Phone: 352-392-0615. Personal E-mail: teitelb@hotmail.com.

TEITELBAUM, STEVEN, plastic surgeon; b. LA, Aug. 22, 1962; AB, U. Calif. Berkeley; MD, UCLA, 1988. Lic. Mass., 1989, Calif., 1993, DEA, 1993, cert. Am. Bd. Plastic Surgery, 1997, Am. Bd. Plastic Surgery, 2006, Am. Bd. Surgery, 1995. Gen. surgery resident, chief resident Harvard/Beth Israel Hosp., Boston, 1988—93; plastic & reconstructive surgery resident U. Southern Calif., 1993—95; at Santa Monica/ULCA Med. Ctr., 1995—2006, St. John's Hosp., Santa Monica, Calif., 1995—, UCLA Ctr. Health Sciences, 2006—; asst. clin. prof. plastic surgery UCLA David Geffen Sch. Medicine, 2006—; pvt. practice Santa Monica, Calif. Guest editor Aesthetic Surgery Jour., 2002—, Plastic & Reconstructive Surgery, 2006—. Chair new leadership div. Israel Bonds; state pres. Am. Jewish Congress; bd. mem. Maestro Found. U. Calif. Presdl. rsch. grant, 1982, Heart Assn. rsch. grant, 1985. Mem.: Internat. Soc. Aesthetic Plastic Surgeons, Internat. Ultrasonic Soc., Am. Coll. Surgeons, Calif. Soc. Plastic Surgeons, Bay Surg. Soc., LA Soc. Plastic Surgery (bd. dirs. 2005—, sec. 2005—), Calif. Soc. Plastic Surgery (ethics com. 2000—, co-chair exhibits com. 2001—04, co-chair legis. com. 2003—, exec. coun. 2006—), Calif. Med. Assn. (alt. del. 2004), Am. Soc. Plastic Surgeons (legis. com. 2002—04, exhibits com. 2004—06, performance metrics task force 2007—), Am. Soc. Aesthetic Plastic Surgery (govt. rels. com. 2001—03, electronic comms. com. 2003—, breast implant task force exhibits com. 2004, practice rels. com. 2004—, emerging trends task force & innovative procedures com. 2005—). Avocations: sailing, triathlon, photography, piano, scuba diving. Office: 1301 20th St Ste 350 Santa Monica CA 90404 Office Phone: 310-315-1121. Office Fax: 310-315-9921. Business E-Mail: steve@drteitelbaum.com. *

TEITELBAUM, STEVEN LAZARUS, pathology educator; b. Bklyn., June 29, 1938; s. Hyman and Rose Leah (Harnick) T.; m. Marilyn Ruth Schaffner; children: Caren Beth, Aaron Michael, Rebecca Lee. BA, Columbia U., NYC, 1960; MD, Washington U., St. Louis, 1964; DSc (hon.), CUNY SI Coll., 2004. Intern Washington U. Sch. Medicine, St. Louis, 1964-65, 3d. yr. asst. resident, ACS clin. fellow, 1967-68; intern NYU, 1965-66, 2d yr. resident, 1966-67; assoc. pathologist Jewish Hosp. at Washington U. Med. Ctr., St. Louis, 1969-89, pathologist-in-chief, 1987-96; assoc. pathologist Barnes-Jewish Hosp., St. Louis, 1986—; pathologist St. Louis Shriners Hosp. for Crippled Children, 1986—; Wilma and Roswell Messing prof. pathology Washington U. Sch. Medicine, St. Louis, 1987—. Mem. Othopedics and Musculoskeletal Study Sect. NIH, 1983-87; adv. counsel NIH, 2003—. Contbr. numerous sci. articles to med. jours., 1965—, 12 chpts. to med. books and texts, 1976—; mem. editorial bd. Calcified Tissue Internat., 1980-85, 89-91, Human Pathology; mem. bd. assoc. editors Jour. Orthopaedic Rsch., Jour. Cellular Biochemistry. Recipient 2nd Century award, Washington U. Sch. Medicine, 2004, Rouse-Whipple award, Am. Soc. Investigative Pathology, 2006. Mem. Am. Soc. Clin. Investigation, Assn. Am. Physicians, Am. Acad. Orthopaedic Surgeons (Ann Doner Vaughan Kappa Delta award 1988), Paget's Disease Found. (adv. panel), Am. Soc. for Bone and Mineral Rsch. (pres. 1993, William F. Neuman award 1998), Fed. Am. Soc. Expl. Biology (bd. dirs. 1997—, pres. 2002—). Office: Washington U Sch Medicine 216 S Kingshighway Blvd Saint Louis MO 63110-1026 Business E-Mail: teitelbs@wustl.edu.

TEITELBAUM, ZALMAN, rabbi; b. 1952; s. Moshe Teitelbaum; married. Ordained Rabbi. Former rabbi Satmar, Jerusalem, Sighet Synagogue, Boro Park, NY; grand rabbi congregation Yetev Lev, Satmar, Williamsburg, Brooklyn, NY, 2006—. Named one of The Top Fifty Rabbis in America, Newsweek Mag., 2007. Office: Yetev Lev Synagogue 13 Hooper St Brooklyn NY 11211 *

TEITELBOIM, CLAUDIO, academic administrator; b. Chile; Grad., U. Chile, Santiago, 1969; PhD in Physics, Princeton U., 1973. Prof. physics Princeton Inst. Advanced Studies, U. Tex.; cofounder & dir. Centro de Estudio Cientificos, Santiago, Chile, 1984, dir. Valdivia, Chile, 2000—. Pres. Presdl. Adv. Com. for Sci. Matters, Chile, 1995—2000. Mem.: NAS (fgn. assoc.). Office: Centro de Estudio Cientificos Arthuro Prat 514 Valdivia Chile

TEITELL, CONRAD LAURENCE, lawyer, writer; b. NYC, Nov. 8, 1932; s. Benson and Belle (Altman) T.; m. Adele Mary Crummins, May 26, 1957; children: Beth Mary, Mark Lewis. AB, U. Mich., 1954; LL.B., Columbia U., 1957; LL.M., N.Y. U., 1968. Bar: N.Y. 1958, D.C., 1968. Mem. Prerau & Teitell, NYC and White Plains, NY, 1964-96, Cummings & Lockwood, Stamford, Conn., 1996—. Dir. Philanthropy Tax Inst., Old Greenwich, Conn., 1964—; adj. prof. U. Miami Law Sch., 1980—. Author: Philanthropy and Taxation, 5 vols., 1993-2007; editor, pub. Taxwise Giving, 1964—; contbr. articles to legal jours. Served with U.S. Army, 1957. Recipient Disting. Svc. to Higher Edn. award Am. Coll. Pub. Relations Assn., 1970, Disting. Svc. award Nat. Com. on Planned Giving, 1990, Harrison Tweed Spl. Merit award Am. Law Inst./ABA, 1992. Fellow Am. Coll. Trust and Estate Counsel; mem. ABA (former co-chmn. com. charitable giving, trusts, founds.), Assn. of Bar of City of N.Y. Home: 16 Marlow Ct Riverside CT 06878-2614 Office: Cummings & Lockwood 6 Landmark Sq Stamford CT 06901 also: PO Box 299 Old Greenwich CT 06870-0299 Home Phone: 203-637-1544; Office Phone: 203-351-4164. Business E-Mail: cteitell@cl-law.com.

TEITELL, MICHAEL ALAN, immunologist; b. L.I., NY, Apr. 6, 1959; s. Philip Lawrence and Phyllis Rita (Henkin) T. BS in Biochemistry magna cum laude, UCLA, 1985, MS in Biochemistry, 1985, MD, PhD, 1993. Auto mechanic BMW Svc. Ctr., Woodland Hills, Calif., 1977-80, Bob Smith BMW, Canoga Park, Calif., 1980-81; chemistry lab. tech. L.A. Pierce Coll., Woodland Hills, Calif., 1978-80, UCLA, 1981-84, chief pediatric pathology, prof. pathology and pediatrics; intern, resident Brigham and Women's Hosp., Boston, 1993—; clin. rsch. fellow pathology Harvard Med. Sch., 1993—. Rsch. assoc. dept. medicine Brigham & Women's Hosp. Contbr. articles to profl. jours. Mem. Am. Assn. Immunologists, Am. Soc. Biochemistry and Molecular Biology, Epigenetics Soc., Biophys. Soc., Sigma Xi, Phi Beta Kappa. Avocations: running, baseball, travel, theater, food. Home: 5945 Beckford Ave Tarzana CA 91356-1104

TEITELMAN, RICHARD B., state supreme court judge; BA in Math., U. Pa., 1969; JD, Washington U., 1973. Bar: Mo. 1974. Pvt. practice, St. Louis, 1974-75; staff atty. Legal Svcs. Ea. Mo., St. Louis, 1975-76, mng. atty., 1976-80, exec. dir., gen. counsel, 1980—; judge Mo. Ct. Appeals (ea. dist.), 1997—2000, Mo. Supreme Ct., 2002—. Bd. dirs. Citizens for Mo.'s Children, St. Louis, 1988—. Recipient Durward K. McDaniel award Am. Coun. of Blind, 1986. Mem. The Mo. Bar, Kansas City Met. Bar Assn., Mound City Bar Assn., Lawyers Assn., St. Louis, Women Lawyers' Assn. Greater St. Louis, St. Louis County Bar Assn., Am. Blind Lawyers Assn., Am. Judicature Soc. (bd. dirs. 1986-2005), St. Louis Bar Found., Leadership St. Louis. Office: Mo Supreme Court PO Box 150 Jefferson City MO 65102 Home Phone: 314-367-5541; Office Phone: 573-751-1004. Business E-Mail: rteitelm@courts.mo.gov.

TEIXEIRA, ARTHUR ALVES, food engineer, educator, consultant; b. Fall River, Mass., Jan. 30, 1944; s. Arthur Araujo and Emelia (Alves) T.; m. Jean E. Lamb, Dec. 26, 1966 (dec. Dec. 1983); children: A. Allan, Scott C.; m. Marjorie St. John, June 28, 1986; 1 stepchild, Craig St. John. PhD, U. Mass., 1971. Registered profl. engr., Fla., Mass. Rsch. engr. Ross Labs., Columbus, Ohio, 1971-73, R&D group leader, 1973-77; sr. cons. Arthur D. Little, Inc., Cambridge, Mass., 1977-82; assoc. prof. U. Fla., Gainesville, 1982-89, prof., 1989—. Sci. advisor Escola Superior de Biotecnologia, Porto, Portugal, 1991-96, FMC Corp., Santa Clara, Calif., 1989-92; internat. cons., Albania, Australia, Belgium, Brazil, Bulgaria, Chile, Cuba, Eng., France, Germany, Hungary, Indonesia, Ireland, Israel, Kenya, Netherlands, Poland, Portugal, Peru, Romania, South Africa, Spain; reviewer USDA, Washington, 1991—. Author: Computerized Food Processing Operations, 1989; contbr. 12 chpts. to books, 70 articles to profl. jours. Judge Internat. Sci. Fair, Orlando, Fla., 1991. Recipient Fulbright scholar award, Portugal, 1990—91, Golden Retort award of Merit, IFTPS, 1994, Sr. Faculty award, U. Fla. chpt. Gamma Sigma Delta, 1996, Tchr. of Yr. award, U. Fla. Coll. Engring., 1996, Fulbright scholar award, Peru, 2000, Disting. Food Engr. award, IAFIS/FPEI/ASAE, 2001, Marvin Tung Achievement award, 2005, Disting. Alumni award, B.M.C. Durfee H.S., 2007. Fellow Am. Soc. Agrl. Engrs. (dir. 1988-90, Paper awards 1988-89, 2001, assoc. editor Transactions of ASAE 1985—); mem. AIChE, Am. Soc. Agr. and Biol. Engrs., Inst. Food Technologists (mem. editl. bd. 1980-83, 2003—), Am. Soc. Engring. Edn., Inst. Thermal Process Specialists, Coun. on Agrl. Sci. and Tech., R & D Assocs., Gamma Sigma Delta (chpt. pres. U. Fla. 1999-2000), Sigma Xi, Alpha Epsilon, Tau Beta Pi. Roman Catholic. Achievements include design of on-line process control system to assure safety of sterilized canned foods; tech. and economic feasiblity for radiation sterilization of disposable feeding devices; research in computer optimization and control of food sterilization processes, mathematical modelling of bacterial spore population dynamics in processed foods, and anaerobic composting for solid waste management on long-term NASA space missions. Office: U Fla Rogers Hall Gainesville FL 32611-0570 Home Phone: 352-335-3608; Office Phone: 352-392-1864. E-mail: aateixeira@mail.ifas.ufl.edu.

TEIXEIRA, MARK CHARLES, professional baseball player; b. Severna Park, Md., Apr. 11, 1980; m. Georgia Williams, Dec. 7, 2002. Student, Ga. Inst. Tech., Atlanta. Draft pick Tex. Rangers, 2001, first baseman, 2003—07, Atlanta Braves, 2007—. Mem. Team USA, World Baseball Classic, 2006. Named to Am. League All-Star Team, 2005; recipient Silver Slugger award, 2004—05, Am. League Gold Glove award, 2005—06. Mailing: Atlanta Braves PO Box 4064 Atlanta GA 30302-4064 *

TEJADA, FRANCISCO, physician, educator; b. Moyobamba, San Martin, Peru, July 25, 1942; s. Francisco Tejada and Semiramis Reatequi; m. Barbara Ann Kotowski, Feb. 1, 1970; children: Anamaria, Semiramis, Barbara Lee, Francisco, James. BS, U. Nacional Mayor de San Marcos, Lima, Peru, 1961; MD, U. Peruana Cayetano Heredia, Lima, 1967. Diplomate Am. Bd. Internal Medicine, Am. Bd. Oncology. Resident in medicine Johns Hopkins U., Balt., 1969-72; sr. cancer rschr. Nat. Cancer Inst., NIH, Bethesda, Md., 1972-75; asst. clin. dir. Comprehensive Cancer Ctr. Fla., Miami, Fla., 1975-80; asst. prof. U. Miami, 1975-79, assoc. prof., 1979-85, prof., 1985—; vis. prof. U. Peruana Cayetano Heredia, Lima, 1994—; sr. ptnr. Oncology Assocs., Miami, 1980-85; chief cancer control Papanicolaou Cancer Ctr., Miami, 1984-86; assoc. dir. AMC Cancer Rsch. Ctr., Denver, 1986-87; pres. Am. Oncology Ctrs., Miami, 1985—; prof. U. San Agustin, Arequipa, Peru, 1992—, U. Peruana Cayetano Heredia, Lima, Peru, 1994—; clin. rsch. scientist UM/Sylvester Comprehensive Cancer Ctr., 2001—; investigator Lovelace Rsch. Svcs., Inc., 2002—. Oncology expert Pan Am. Health Orgn., Washington, 1975-85, Nat. Cancer Inst., Bethesda, Md., 1984-86; dir. Miami Cancer Inst., 1980—; dir. Peruvian-Am. Endowment Inc., 1993-99, v.p., 1995-97; bd. dirs. Integrated Med. Svcs. Fla. Keys, Key West, 1997-2000; dir. oncology dept. Clinica Ricardo Palma, Lima, Peru, 1991-99; med. dir. Fla. Comprehensive Cancer Control Initiative, 2000-03; dir. CureMeDoctor Inc., 2002-2002, Precision Med. Devices, Inc., 2007—. Editor Miami Health Letter, 1986—; inventor cancer risk assessment. Mem. Beacon Coun., Miami, 1984, Latin Am. Cancer Info., Washington, 1976, Hispanic Cancer Rsch. Network, Washington, 1990; chpt. pres. Peruvian Am. Med. Soc., Miami, 1986; trustee Miami-Dade County Pub. Health Trust, 2002-05; bd. dirs. Miami-Dade County Policy Health Authority, 2002-03; dir. Precision Med. Devices, Inc., 2007—. Lt. Peruvian Army, 1966-67. Decorated comendador Orden Sociedad, Peruvian U. Cayetano Heredia; recipient Gold Medal Merit award Ministry of Edn., Lima, 1959, Hipolito Unanue award Hipolito Unanue Inst., Lima, 1968. Fellow ACP, Johns Hopkins U., Nat. Cancer Inst.; mem. Colegio Medico del Perú, Am. Assn. Cancer Rsch., Am. Soc. Clin. Oncology, Am. Soc. Hematology, Bolivian Cancer Soc. (hon.), Peruvian Cancer Soc. (hon.), Chilean Soc. Cancer (hon.), Argentinian Soc. Head and Neck Pathology (hon.) Roman Catholic. Avocations: hiking, photography, reading. Office: Dept Epidemiology and Public Health Clin Rsch Bldg 112 NW 14th St Room 1047 Miami FL 33136 Office Phone: 305-251-4540. Personal E-mail: ftejadamd@gmail.com.

TEJADA, MIGUEL (ODALIS), professional baseball player; b. Bani, Dominican Republic, May 25, 1976; Shortstop Oakland Athletics, Calif., 1997—2003, Balt. Orioles, 2004—. Named Most Valuable Player, Am. League, 2002, MLB All-Star Game, 2005; named to Am. League All-Star Team, 2002, 2004, 2005; recipient Silver Slugger award, MLB, 2005. Achievements include won All-Star home run derby, 2004; led Am. League in RBI's (149), 2004. Office: 333 West Camden St Baltimore MD 21201 *

TE KANAWA, KIRI, opera and concert singer; b. Gisborne, N.Z., Mar. 6, 1944; d. Thomas and Eleanor Te Kanawa; m. Desmond Park, Aug. 30, 1967 (div. 1997); children— Antonia Aroha, Thomas Desmond. Student, St. Mary's Coll., Auckland, New Zealand, 1957-60, London Opera Centre, 1966-69; DMus (hon.), Oxford U., Dundee U., 1983, Warwick U., Auckland U., Waikato U., Nottingham U., Chgo. U., Durham U., Cambridge U. Joined Royal Opera House, London, 1971; appeared in role of Countess in Le Nozze di Figaro, 1971; U.S. debut in Santa Fe Festival, 1971; Met. Opera debut as Desdemona in Otello, 1974; appearances with all major European and Am. opera houses, including Australian opera cos., Royal Opera House, Covent Garden, London, Paris Opera, Munich Opera, La Scala, others; opera appearences include Boris Gudonov, Carmen, Don Giovanni, the Magic Flute, Eugene Onegin, La Boheme, Manon Lescaut, many others; appeared in film Don Giovanni as Elvira, 1979; recs. include Blue Skies, 1986, Kiri Sings Gershwin, 1987, Kiri Te Kanawa: Italian Opera Arias, 1991, Kiri Her Greatest Hits, Ave Maria, Kiri on Broadway, The Kiri Selection, Kiri Side Tracks, My Fair Lady, Maori Songs; PBS appearance: Great Performances: West Side Story, 1985; author: Land of the Long White Cloud, 1989, Opera for Lovers, 1996. Decorated comdr. Order Brit. Empire, 1973, Dame Comdr. Brit. Empire, 1983, Order of Australia, 1990, Order of New Zealand, 1995, Golden Plate award, Acad. Achievement, 2006. Mem.: Royal Acad. Music (hon.). *

TELBAN, ETHEL, retired librarian; b. Renton, Wash., Mar. 31, 1914; d. Blase and Amelia (Podbregar) T. BA, Ctrl. Wash. U., Ellensburg, 1938; M Librarianship, Denver U., 1950. Cert. educator, libr. Elem. tchr. Thorp (Wash.) Sch. Dist., 1935-36, Renton (Wash.) Sch. Dist., 1937-50, libr. supr., 1950-74; libr. Western Wash. U., Bellingham, 1965. Instr. libr. U. Wash., Seattle, summers 1955, 58, 59, 60; libr. Ctrl. Wash. U., Ellensburg, summers 1941, 51, 53, 57; mem. Curriculum Commn., State Dept. Edn., Olympia, Wash., 1954-55. Editor: (history book) From Coal to Jets, 1976. Mem. Mcpl. Arts Commn., Renton, 1973-75; mem. bicentennial com. City of Renton, 1975-76. Named Renton Citizen of Yr., Elks, Renton, 1977, Vol of Yr., Assoc. King County Hist. Assn., Seattle, 1994; recipient Individual Excellence award Wash. Mus. Assn., Richland, 1994, Cert. of Commendation, Am. Assn. State and Local History, Nashville, 1995. Mem. ALA (mem. Newbery-Caldecott com. 1960-61), Sch. Librs. Assn. Wash. State (state pres. 1962-63), Renton Hist. Soc. (pres. 1966-96, editor newsletter 1970-94), Renton Retired Tchrs. (sec. 1950-96), PEO Sisterhood (sec. 1959-96), Soroptimist Internat. (pres. 1951-96), Delta Kappa Gamma. Avocations: local history, travel, reading, gardening, crafts. Home: 17406 N Escalante Lane Surprise AZ 85374

TELEGDI, ANDREW, member of parliament; b. Budapest, Hungary, May 28, 1946; arrived in Can., 1957; s. Alexander Sandor and Elenora Maria (Friedrich) T.; m. Nancy Curtin; 1 child, Erin. Student, U. Waterloo. Mem. Waterloo City Coun., 1985-93, Waterloo Regional Coun., 1988-93; mem. parliament Waterloo Ho. of Commons., 1993—2006, vice chair on human rights com., 1994-95, vice chair pub. accts. com., 1995-96; mem. justice com. Ho. of Commons, 1997-98, mem. caucus com. on postsecondary edn., 1996—, vice chair, regional licensing com., assoc. mem. fin., environ., and industry coms., 1993—2002, M.P. for Kitchener-Waterloo, chmn. standing com. on citizenship and immigration, chmn. liberal caucus SW Ontario, 2004—07, vice chair, 2006—. Exec. dir. Youth in Conflict with the Law, 1976-93; coord. Justice Week, Waterloo, 1979-83; pres. Fedn. of Students, U. Waterloo, 1973-75; advisor to Prime Min., Budapest Conf. on Security and Coop. in Europe, 1994; standing com. on citizenship and immigration, Ho. of Commons, Ottawa, 1998-2000; parliamentary sec. to Minister of Citizenship and Immigration, 1998-2000; parliamentary sec. to Prime Min. with spl. emphasis on aboriginal affairs, 2004; standing com. aboriginal affars, no. devel. and natural resources, standing com. on citizenship and immigration, 2004-. Bd. dirs. The Working Centre and St. John's Soup Kitchen, 1986-93, Kitchener House, 1979—; pres. K.W. Multicultural Centre, 1987-89; chair Conestoga Coll. Basic Job Readiness Tng. Adv. Group, 1980-84; mem. clin. adv. com. Cath. Family Counseling Centre, 1986-87, family violence com.; chair People, Working and Learning Inc., 1984-86; mem. Senate U. Waterloo; mem. bd. govs. Wilfrid Laurier U., 1990-93. Mem. Waterloo Uptown Bus. Assn., Kitchener-Waterloo C. of C. (bus. edn. com.). Libr. Com. Mem. Avocations: fishing, golf, chess, reading. Office: House of Commons 285 Confederation Bldg Ottawa ON Canada K1A 0A6 Business E-Mail: telega@parl.gc.ca.

TELEGEN, ARTHUR G., lawyer; b. Boston, Mar. 11, 1947; AB, Brandeis U., 1968; JD magna cum laude, Harvard U., 1974. Bar: Mass. 1974, US Ct. Appeals (1st, 2nd, 3rd and 4th cir.), US Dist. Ct. Mass., RI and Conn., Supreme Jud. Ct. Mass., US Supreme Ct. Mem. Foley, Hoag & Eliot, Boston; ptnr. Foley Hoag LLP, Boston, 1981—. Bd. dirs. Greater Boston Legal Svcs., 1983—. Editor Harvard Law Rev., 1972-74. Recipient Am.'S Leading Lawyers for Bus., Chambers USA, Best Lawyers in Am., Mass. Super Lawyers. Mem.: ABA, Am. Employment Law Coun., Boston Area Mgmt. Attys. Grp., Greater Boston Legal Svcs., Boston Bar Assn., Mass. Bar Assn. Office: Foley Hoag LLP Seaport World Trade Center W 155 Seaport Blvd Boston MA 02210 Office Phone: 617-832-1161. Office Fax: 617-832-7000. Business E-Mail: atelegen@foleyhoag.com.

TELEMAN, SILVIU, mathematician, educator; b. Corbeni, Romania, Aug. 21, 1931; arrived in U.S., 1986; m. Ecaterina Cioranescu, May 15, 1962; children: Calin Nicolae Stefan, Constantin. BS, M. Eminescu H.S., 1950; MS in Math., U. Bucharest, 1957, PhD of Math., 1968. Editor Inst. Romanian-Soviet Studies Romanian Acad. Sci., Bucharest, 1960—62; reader, chmn., lectr., dean Pedagogical Inst., Pitesti, Romania, 1962—68; rschr. Inst. Math. Romanian Acad. Scis., Bucharest, 1968—86; vis. prof. dept. math. Ind. U., Bloomington, 1986—87; Otto Szasz vis. prof. dept. math. U. Cin., 1987—88; vis. prof. dept. math. U. Mich., Ann Arbor, 1988—89; assoc. prof. Dept. Math. U. P.R., San Juan, 1989—95, prof. Dept. Math., 1995—. Author: Theory of Harmonic Algebras, with Applications to Von Neumann Algebras and Cohomology of Locally Compact Spaces (de Rham's Theorem), 1971 (Gh. Tzitzeica award, 1971), An Introduction to Choquet Theory, with Applications to Reduction Theory, 1980; contbr. articles to profl. jours. Recipient Order of Work 3d Class, Pres. Romania, 1967, Rep. Presdl. Legion of Merit, Rep. Presdl. Legion Exec. Bd., 1997, Rep. Sen. Medal of Freedom, Rep. mems. of U.S. Senate, 1999. Mem.: AAAS, N.Y. Acad. Scis., Math. Assn. Am., Am. Math. Soc. Avocation: music. Personal E-mail: silviu.teleman@gmail.com.

TELENGATOR, ALEXANDER M., engineer; b. Samara, Russia, Jan. 11, 1972; MS with honors, Samara State Tech. U., 1994; PhD, U. Calif., La Jolla, 2000. Rsch. engr. Samara State Tech. U., 1994—96; grad. student rschr. dept. mech. and aerospace engring. U. Calif., La Jolla, 1996—2000; engring. scientist Ctr. for Energy Rsch. U. Calif. San Diego, La Jolla, 2000—. Contbr. articles to profl. jours. Recipient The Stipend of the Pres. of Russia, Russian Ministry of Higher Edn., 1995, Silver Medal for Student Sci. Rsch., 1994; Friends of the Internat. Ctr. scholar, U. Calif. Internat. Ctr., 1999. Mem.: AIAA, The Combustion Inst. Office: Univ Calif San Diego 9500 Gilman Dr La Jolla CA 92093-0417 Home Phone: 858-534-6617; Office Phone: 858-534-6617.

TELESETSKY, WALTER, federal agency administrator; b. Boston, Jan. 22, 1938; s. Keril and Nellie (Krelka) T.; m. Sharron-Dawn Lamp, July 15, 1961; children: Stephanie Ann, Anastasia Marie. BS in Mech. Engring., Northeastern U., 1960; MBA, U. Chgo., 1961; postgrad., Harvard U., 1977. Engr. trainee Chrysler Corp., Detroit, 1956-59; rsch. asst. Microtech Rsch. Co., Cambridge, Mass., 1959-60; engr. Allis Chalmers Mfg. Co., Milw., 1960-61; mem. tech. staff The Mitre Corp., Bedford, Mass., 1962-68; sr. mem. tech. staff Data Dynamics, Inc., Washington, 1969; phys. scientist NOAA, Rockville, Md., 1970-71, U.S. Gate Project coord., 1972-74, dir. U.S. Global Weather Experiment Project Office, 1974, dir. Program Integration Office, 1975-77, dir. Programs and Tech. Devel. Office, 1977-79, dir. Programs and Internat. Activities Office, 1979-81; dep. assoc. dir. for tech. svcs., chief AFOS ops. div. Nat. Weather Svc., Silver Spring, Md., 1981-86, dir. Office of Systems Ops., 1986-2000, dir. Office Operational Sys., 2000—02. Liaison to NAS coms. on atmospheric scis., geophysics studies and internat. environ. programs, 1975-81; U.S. coord. U.S./Japan Coop. Program in Natural Resources, 1980-88; chmn. U.S.-Japan Marine Resources and Engring. Coordination Com., 1980-88; U.S.

del. governing coun. UN Environ. Program and World Meteorol. Orgn.; mem. commn. for Basic Systems World Meteorol. Orgn., 1988-2002; speaker in field. Contbr. articles to profl. publs. Recipient Silver medal Dept. Commerce, 1975, Gold medal Dept. Commerce, 1998. Mem. AAAS, Am. Geophys. Union, Am. Meteorol. Soc., Am. Soc. Mech. Engrs., Marine Tech. Soc. Home: 16 Eton Overlook Rockville MD 20850-3003

TELFER, MARGARET CLARE, internist, hematologist, oncologist; b. Manila, Apr. 9, 1939; came to U.S., 1941; d. James Gavin and Margaret Adele (Baldwin) T. BA, Stanford U., 1961; MD, Washington U., St. Louis, 1965. Diplomate Am. Bd. Internal Medicine, Am. Bd. Hematology, Am. Bd. Oncology; lic. Ill., Mo. Resident in medicine Michael Reese Hosp., Chgo., 1968, fellow in hematology and oncology, 1970, assoc. attending physician, 1970-72, dir. Hemophilia Ctr., 1971—, interim dir. div. hematology and oncology, 1971-74, 81-84, 89—, attending physician, 1972—, Rush-Presbyn. St. Luke's Hosp., 1999—, Olympia Fields (Ill.) Hosp., 1999—2005, Cook County Hosp., Chgo., 2000—, dir. hematology/oncology fellowship, 2004—; asst. prof. medicine U. Chgo., 1975-80, assoc. prof. medicine, 1980-85, assoc. prof. clin. medicine, 1985-89; assoc. prof. medicine U. Ill., Chgo., 1990-2001, Rush U., Chgo., 2001—. Mem. med. adv. bd. Hemophilia Found. Ill., 1971, chmn., 1972—83, lectr. annual symposium, 1978—84; mem. med. adv. bd. State of Ill. Hemophilia Program; dir. hematology-oncology fellowship program Michael Reese Hosp., 1971—75, 1981—84, 1989—2000, dir. Cook County Fellowship Program, 2004—, mem. numerous coms.; lectr. in field. Contbr. articles to profl. jours. Fellow ACP; mem. Am. Soc. Clin. Oncology, Am. Assn. Med. Colls., Am. Soc. Hematology, World Fedn. Hemophilia, Blood Club (Chgo.), Thrombosis Club (Chgo.). Office: Stroger Cook County Hosp Rm 750 Adminstrn Bldg 1900 W Polk Chicago IL 60612 Office Phone: 312-864-7250. Business E-Mail: mtelfer@ccbhs.org.

TELLEGEN, AUKE, retired psychology professor; b. Yogyakarta, Indonesia, July 16, 1930; s. Pieter Helenus and Veronica Tellegen; m. Lysbeth Marijke van der Veen, July 27, 1953; children: Peter Auke, Gwendolyn Antoinette. D in Psychology, U. Amsterdam, 1957; PhD, U. Minn., Mpls., 1962. Emeritus prof. U. Minn., Mpls., 1999—. Recipient Bruno Klopfer award, Soc. Personality Assessment, 2000, Jack Block award, Soc. Personality and Social Psychology, 2001. Fellow: APA, Soc. Clin. and Exptl. Hypnosis, Soc. Personality Assessment. Achievements include research in normal and abnormal personality structure and assessment; dimensional structure of emotions. Office: Univ Minn 75 E River Rd Minneapolis MN 55455

TELLEM, NANCY REISS, broadcast executive; b. Danville, Calif., Dec. 13, 1953; m. Arn Tellem; children: Michael, Matthew, Eric. BA in Polit. Sci., U. Calif., Berkeley, 1975; JD, Hastings Coll. Law, 1979. Intern to Congressman Ron Dullums, Washington, 1974; with legal affairs dept. Lorimar TV; joined Warner Bros. TV, 1987, exec. v.p. bus. and fin. affairs; exec. v.p. bus. affairs CBS Entertainment, exec. v.p. CBS Prodns. CBS, 1997—98, pres. CBS Entertainment, 1998—2004; pres. CBS Paramount Network TV Entertainment Group, 2004—. Bd. dirs. ThirdAge Media. Named one of 100 Most Powerful Women in Entertainment, Hollywood Reporter, 2005—06. Avocations: tennis, yoga, hiking, photography. Office: CBS Entertainment 7800 Beverly Blvd Los Angeles CA 90036 *

TELLERIA, ANTHONY F., lawyer; b. June 6, 1938; s. Carlos E. and Melida (Amador) Telleria; m. Dolores A. Rockey, Nov. 3, 1962; children: Matthew J., Andrea F. LLB, Southwestern U., 1964. Bar: Calif. 1964. Pvt. practice, LA, 1964—71, 1975—; sr. ptnr. Telleria, Townley & Doran, LA, 1971—75. Mem.: Consumer Attys. Assn. of LA, Am. Arbitration Assn. (LA adv. coun. accident claims com.), LA County Bar Assn., Am. Trial Lawyers Assn. Home: 1615 Rose Ave San Marino CA 91108-3001 Office: 150 E Colorado Blvd Ste 210 Pasadena CA 91105-3722 Office Phone: 626-585-0017. E-mail: lawaft@aol.com.

TELLES, CYNTHIA ANN, psychologist; b. El Paso, Tex., Aug. 10, 1952; d. Raymond Lawrence and Delfina Telles; m. David Jimenez (div. Aug. 1991); 1 child, Raymond Jimenez. BA, Smith Coll., Northampton, Mass., 1974; PhD in Clin. Psychology, Boston U., 1982. Cert. psychologist, Calif. Psychologist U. Hosp. Boston U. Med. Ctr., 1977-78; rsch. fellow psychology dept. Spanish Speaking Mental Health Rsch. Ctr. UCLA, 1978-79, co-investigator, rsch. diagnostician dept. psychiatry, 1982-84, investigator and mgr. Spanish instrument tng. Dept. Psychiatry, 1981-87; clin. project dir., co-investigator NIMH, 1984-86, investigator, 1986-90; project dir., co-prin. investigator Calif. State Dept. Mental Health, 1986—; psychologist adult outpatient dept. UCLA Neuropsychiat. Inst., 1979-80; dir. UCLA Spanish Speaking Psychosocial Clinic, 1980—. Media psychologist for TV and radio; cons. Boston City Police, 1975, Boulder County Community Mental Health Ctr., 1978, Spl. Svc. for Groups, LA, 1982, Ministry of Health, Lima, Peru, 1982, NIMH, 1984—, LA County Dept. Mental Health, 1985—, Calif. Sch. Profl. Psychology, 1986—; presenter in field; teaching fellow Boston U. Sch. Medicine, 1975-78; lectr. dept. psychiatry UCLA, 1980-85, asst. clin. prof., 1986-95, assoc. clin. prof., 1996-, mem. faculty adv. com. Chicano Studies Rsch. Ctr., 1988—; bd. dirs. United Calif. Bank, 1994-2002, Kaiser Health Plan and Hosps., 2004-, Calif. Cmty. Found., 2005-. Author: (with others) Psychiatric Epidemiology and Prevention: The Possibilities, 1985, Violence and Homicide in Hispanic Communities, 1988; contbr. articles to profl. jours.; mem. editorial bd. Hispanic Jour. Behavioral Scis., 1978-79; ad hoc reviewer Psychology of Women Quar., 1986-87. Bd. dirs. Coalition Pro-Salud Hispana, Boston, 1977-78, Nat. Hispanic Psychol. Assn., 1984-86, Ctr. for Study of Youth in Groups/Teen Line, Dept. of Psychiatry, Cedars-Sinai Med. Ctr., 1986-88, NCCJ, Southern Calif., 1990—, El Centro Human Svcs. Corp., 1988-90, Calif. Commerce Found., Calif. Endowment, 2001-, bd. chair, 2004-; mem. Nat. Adv. Com. on Hispanic Women and AIDS, Ctrs. for Disease Control and Hispanic Designers Inc., 1989—; pres., founder Hispanic Health Found., 1988-98. Boston U. Grad. scholar, 1975-79, APA Minority fellow, 1975-79; recipient Humanitarian award East LA Coll., 1988, Civic and Cmty. Leadership award Nat. Network of Hispanic Women, 1989, First Annual Achievement award for mental health pub. svc. APA Minority Fellowship Program, 1989, Crystal Eagle award CORO Found., 2006, Pioneer for Justice award Mex. Am. Found., LA, 2006, others. Mem. Nat. Hispanic Psychol. Assn. (charter), APA. Roman Catholic. Office: UCLA Dept Psychiatry 300 Ucla Medical Plz Los Angeles CA 90095-8346 Office Phone: 310-825-4568.

TÉLLEZ KUENZLER, LUIS, former government official, investment banker; b. Mexico City, Mex., 1958; Grad., Inst. Tech.; PhD in Econs., MIT. Gen. dir. fin. & planning Sec. Fin. & Pub. Credit, 1988; undersec. planning Sec. Agrl. & Hydraulic Resources, chief staff of Pres. of Mex., 1996—97; sec. Energy, Mines & Parastatal Industry Govt. Mexico, Mexico, 1997—2000; exec. v.p., CEO Desc, S.A. de C.V., Mexico, 2001—03; mng. dir. The Carlyle Group, S. de R.L. de C.V., Mexico City. Dir. Fomento Economico Mexicano, S.A. de C.V., 2001—. Named Global Leader of Tomorrow, World Econ. Forum, Leader for the New Millennium, Time mag. Office: The Carlyle Group Montes Urales 720 Col Lomas de Chapultepec 11000 Mexico Office Phone: 52 55 52498020. Office Fax: 52 55 52498030. Business E-Mail: mexico@carlyle.com.

TELLIER, HENRI, retired Canadian military officer; b. Montreal, Que., Can., Sept. 1, 1918; s. Henry Joseph and Jeanne (St. Cyr) T.; m. Virginia Wright, July 23, 1945; children: Pierre, Michele, Suzanne, John, Nicole. Student, U. Montreal, 1935-40, U. Ottawa, 1946-47, Canadian Army Staff Coll., 1942-43, Imperial Def. Coll., London, Eng., 1966, Dept. Def. Computer Inst., Washington, 1968; DSc hon. causa, Royal Mil. Coll. Can., 2002. Commd. 2d lt. Canadian Army, 1940, advanced through grades to lt. gen., 1973; asst. mil. sec. to minister Nat. Def., 1945-48; comdg. officer Royal 22d Regt., 1948-51; instr. Canadian Army Staff Coll., 1951-54; army mem. Joint Intelligence Staff, 1954-57; mil. adviser Vietnam, 1957-58; chief of staff Que. Mil. Dist., 1958-60; mil attache Rome, 1960- 63; dir. mil. ops. and plans Army, 1963-64, dir. internat. plans, 1964-65; comdr. Canadian Contingent, Cyprus, 1965-66, dir. gen. plans, 1966—69, chief plans, 1969—71; Canadian mil. rep. to mil. com. NATO Hdqrs., Brussels, 1971-73; ret., 1973. Assoc. nat. commr. Canadian Red Cross Soc., 1973, 75, nat. commr., 1975, 82, sec.-gen., 1982-83, hon. v.p.; pvt. mem. Refugee Status Adv. Com., 1984-88; chmn. Canadian Sect. Mil. Coop. Com. Can.-US; mem. Joint Permanent Bd. Def. Can.-US; commr. Commn. for Strategic and Internat. Studies. Decorated Order of Can., Disting. Svc. Order Can.; comdr. Order of Merit, Italy; companion Order of Red Cross, Can.; recipient Queens Commemoration medal, Netherlands. Mem. Canadian Inst. Internat. Affairs., Assn. Royal 22 Regiment, UN Assn. Can., Adv. Coun. Avocation: aquatic sports. Home: Apt 703 The Redwoods 2604 Draper Ave Ottawa ON K2H 9B1 Canada

TELLIER, RICHARD DAVIS, management educator; b. Darby, Pa., Feb. 18, 1942; s. Joseph Campbell and Jane Grace (Davis) T.; m. Susan Gammon, June 10, 1974; children: John-Jo and Tiekka (twins). BSEE, Drexel U., 1967; MBA, Fla. State U., 1971, DBA, 1973. Elec. engr. Philco-Ford Corp., Phila., 1960-67; aerospace sys. engr. GE, Cape Canaveral, Fla., 1967-70; lectr. Fla. State U., Tallahassee, 1970-73; prof. mgmt. Calif. State U., Fresno, 1973-2000, chmn. dept. mgmt. and mktg., 1979-84, assoc. dean Sch. Bus., 1984-85, asst. dean, 1990-92, assoc. provost acad. resources, 1995-99, prof. emeritus, 2000—. Cons. ops. mgmt., market rsch. orgnl. behavior. Author: Operations Management: Fundamental Concepts and Methods, 1978, Production and Operations Management Test Bank, 1990; contbr. articles to profl. jours. Grantee 1975; recipient Meritorious Performance award, 1987, 88, 90. Mem. Ops. Research Soc. Am., Phi Kappa Phi. Home: 8294 N Academy Ave Clovis CA 93619-9454 Office: Calif State U Shaw and Maple Ave Fresno CA 93740-0001 Business E-Mail: rickt@csufresno.edu.

TELLIS, VIVIAN ANTHONY, transplant surgeon, administrator; b. Calcutta, India, Jan. 2, 1939; s. Vivian Joseph and Monica (Mascarenhas) T.; m. Patricia Joan Gioscio, Apr. 20, 1968 (dec.); children: Audrey, Eileen. MBBS, All-India Inst. Med. Scis., New Delhi, 1960. Diplomate Am. Bd. Surgery; lic. physician, N.Y. Intern Jersey City Med. Ctr., 1963-64; resident Harlem Hosp., 1965-66, Montefiore Med. Ctr., Bronx, NY, 1966-68, fellow in transplantation, 1968-70, attending surgeon, 1970—, dir. transplant program, 1989—. Asst. prof. surgery Albert Einstein Coll. Medicine, Bronx, 1972-78, assoc. prof. surgery, 1978-87, prof. surgery, 1987—; transplant cons., med. rev. bd., end stage renal disease, N.Y., 1998—2001. mem. med. adv. bd. Transplant Recipients Internat. Orgn. (Triangle award 1996); chmn. med. bd. N.Y. Organ Donor Network. Contbr. over 250 articles to profl. jours. Pub. spkr. for increased organ donor awareness, various support and ch. groups, 1980—; mem. bd. trustees Kidney and Urology Found., 1993— (Lester Hoenig award 1994). Mem. ACS, Am. Soc. Nephrology, Transplantation Soc., Internat. Pediat. Transplant Soc., Am. Soc. of Transplantation, Am. Soc. Transplant Surgeons, N.Y. Transplantation Soc. (pres. 1985-86). Democrat. Roman Catholic. Avocations: skiing, origami, music. Office: Montefiore Med Ctr 111 E 210th St Bronx NY 10467-2401 Home Phone: 914-234-7003; Office Phone: 718-920-6158. Business E-Mail: vtellis@montefiore.org.

TELLOCK, GLEN E., manufacturing executive; b. 1961; BBA, Univ. Wis., Madison, 1983. CPA. Audit mgr. Ernst & Whinney; fin. planning mgr. Denver Post Corp.; dir. acctg. The Manitowoc Co., Inc., Manitowoc, Wis., 1991—92, corp. contr., 1992—98, v.p. fin., treas., 1998—99, sr. v.p., CFO, 1999—2002, sr. v.p., pres. Crane segment, 2002—07, pres., CEO, 2007—. Vice-chmn. Assn. Equip. Manufacturers. Office: The Manitowoc Co Inc 2400 S 44th St Manitowoc WI 54221-0066 *

TELOWITZ, MARILYN MARIE, English and social studies educator; b. St. Louis, Oct. 31, 1952; d. Nicholas John and Audrey Mulhern Telowitz. BA, U. Mo., Columbia, 1972; cert. 7-12 in English and social studies, U. Mo., St. Louis, 1975. Tchr. English and social studies Rosary HS, St. Louis, 1977—2003, chairperson English dept., 1982—2003; tchr. English and social studies Trinity Cath. HS, St. Louis, 2003—, dean humanities, 2003—04, chairperson English dept., 2004—06, academic dean, 2006—. Mem. Spanish Lake Cmty. Assn., Mo., 2005—. Mem.: Nat. Coun. for Social Studies, Nat. Coun. Tchrs. English. Democrat. Roman Catholic. Avocation: travel. Home: 804 Vista Pointe Saint Louis MO 63138 Office: Trinity Cath H S 1720 Redman Rd Saint Louis MO 63138

TELUSHKIN, JOSEPH, rabbi; m. Dvorah Menashe; 4 children. Studied Jewish History, Columbia U., NYC. Ordained Rabbi Yeshiva U. Spkr. in field. Author: Jewish Literacy: The Most Important Things to Know About the Jewish Religion, Its People and Its History; actor: Biblical Literacy: The Most Important People, Events and Ideas of the Hebrew Bible, 1997, The Book of Jewish Values: A Day by Day Guide to Ethical Living, 2000, The Ten Commandments of Character: Essential Advice for Living an Honorable, Ethical, Honest Life, 2003, Why the Jews: The Reason for Antisemitism, 2004, Heaven's Witness, 2004, A Code of Jewish Ethics: You Shall be Holy, 2006. Named one of The 50 Most Important Rabbis in America, Newsweek Mag., 2007. *

TEMAM, ROGER M., mathematician, educator; b. Tunis, Tunisia, May 19, 1940; s. Ange M. and Elise (Ganem) T.; m. Claudette Cukorja, Aug. 21, 1962; children: David, Olivier, Emmanuel. M in Math., U. Paris, 1962, DSc, 1967. Asst. prof. math. U. Paris, 1960-67, prof., 1967—2003; dir. Inst. Sci. Computing and Applied Math. Ind. U., Bloomington, 1986—. Prof. Ecole Polytechnique, Paris, 1968-85. Author: Numerical Analysis, 1969, 2d edit., 2001, Navier-Stokes Equations, 1977, rev. edit., 2001, Mathematical Problems in Plasticity, 1983, Infinite Dimensional Dynamical Systems in Mechanics and Physics, 1988, 2nd edit., 1997; co-author: Convex Analysis and Variational Problems, 1976, rev. edit., 1999, Dynamic Multilevel Methods and the Numerical Simulation of Turbulence, 1999, Navier-Stokes Equations and Turbulence, 2001; assoc. editor: profl. jours.; contbr. articles to profl. jours. Recipient several prizes. Mem. AAAS, Am. Math. Soc., Am. Phys. Soc., Soc. Indsl. and Applied Math. (first pres. French chpt. 1983-87), NY Acad. Scis. Office: Ind U Dept Math Rawles Hall Bloomington IN 47405

TEMARES, M. LEWIS, academic administrator; b. NYC, Feb. 5, 1941; s. Nathan and Gertrude (Weiss) T.; m. Eleanor Liebman, Dec. 8, 1962 (div. Mar. 1975); m. Louise Cortinovis Delphus, Jan. 1, 1989; children: Scott, Stacy, Christy, Jennifer. BBA, CCNY; MBA, Baruch Coll.; MS, Columbia U.; PhD, CUNY. Dean Coll. Engring. U. Miami, Fla., 1994—2007, v.p., chief info. officer. Office: U Miami PO Box 248011 Coral Gables FL 33124-4220 Office Phone: 305-284-3962. Office Fax: 305-284-3852. E-mail: mtemares@miami.edu. *

TEMARES, STEVEN H., retail executive; BA, Rutgers U., 1980; JD, U. Pa., 1983. Assoc. Real Estate Group Schulte Roth & Zabel LLP, NYC, 1983—85; counsel Universal Maritime Svc. Corp., NYC, 1986—88; atty. Real Estate Group Riker Danzig Scheler Hyland & Perretti, Morristown, NJ, 1988—92; from dir. real estate, gen. counsel to exec. v.p. Bed, Bath & Beyond Inc., Union, NJ, 1992—97, exec. v.p., COO, 1997—99, pres., COO, 1999—2003, pres., CEO, 2003—. Office: Bed Bath & Beyond Inc 650 Liberty Ave Union NJ 07083 *

TEMBREULL, MICHAEL A., automotive executive; Grad., Stanford U., Calif., 1985. Gen. mgr. PACCAR, Inc., 1985—90, sr. v.p., 1990-92, exec. v.p., 1992-95, bd dirs., 1994—, vice chmn., 1995—; prin. fin. officer, vice chmn. PACCAR Fin. Corp. Office: PACCAR PO Box 1518 Bellevue WA 98009 Office Phone: 425-468-7400. Office Fax: 425-468-8216. *

TEMERLIN, LIENER, advertising executive; b. Ardmore, Okla., Mar. 27, 1928; s. Pincus and Julie (Kahn) T.; m. Karla Samuelsohn, July 23, 1950; children: Dana Temerlin, Lisa Temerlin Gottesman, Sandy Gottesman. BFA, U. Okla., 1950. Assoc. editor Sponsor Mag., NYC, 1950-51; from copywriter to COO Glenn Advt. Inc., Dallas, 1952—74; pres. Glenn, Bozell & Jacobs, Inc., 1974-79; chmn. bd. dirs. Bozell & Jacobs Inc., 1979-86, Bozell, Jacobs, Kenyon & Eckhardt, Dallas, 1986-89; chmn. Bozell, 1989-92, Temerlin McClain, Irving, Tex., 1992—2001; pres. Temerlin Cons., 2001—. Bd. dirs. East/West Inst. Chmn. Winston Churchill Found. award dinner, 1986; chmn. Dallas Symphony Assn., 1986-88, pres., 1984-86, bd. govs., 1982-84, pres. coun., 1989—; mem. Blair House Restoration Com., 1987-88; vice-chmn. Am. Film Inst., 1992-93, trustee, 1992-2000, hon. trustee, 2000; bd. dirs. United Way of Met. Dallas Exec. Com., 1986-89, Dallas Bus. Com. for Arts, 1989, Dallas Citizen's Coun., 1984-86, 92; trustee Southwestern Med. Found., 1988—, mem. adv. com., 2003—; trustee com. univ. devel. So. Meth. U., mem. exec. bd., 1990-91, bd. dirs. Tate lectr. series, 2002—; trustee and chmn. of devel. com. Dallas Mus. Art, 1993-96; steering com. Susan G. Komen Found., 1989-91, art acquisition com. Meyerson Symphony Ctr., 1989-92, exec. coun. Daytop/Dallas, 1989—; chmn. grand opening fortnight Morton H. Meyerson Symphony Ctr., 1989; active Madison Coun. Libr. Congress, Washington, 1991-2002; hon. chair rsch. dinner Am. Lung Assn. Tex., 1996; corp. chmn. Sr. Citizens Greater Dallas for Spirit of Generations Award to Stanley Marcus, 1997; fundraising campaign chmn. Lieberman Rsch. Bldg., Baylor Med. Ctr., 1997; hon. chmn. ann. dinner Make A Wish Found., 1998; exec. bd. Meadows Sch. Arts, So. Meth. U., 2001; co-chair ann. fundraising event Vogel Alcove Child Care Ctr. for the Homeless, 2001; adv. cons. Dallas Ctr. Performing Arts, 2003-; founder, chmn. Am. Film Inst. Dallas Internat. Film Festival, 2007. Lt. field arty. US Army, Korea. Decorated Bronze Star; recipient Bill D. Kerss award Dallas Advt. League, 1983, Brotherhood award NCCJ, 1984, Susan G. Komen Found. for Breast Cancer Rsch. Cmty. award, 1989, Neiman Marcus (formerly James K. Wilson) Silver Cup award, 1990, Linz award 1990, Silver Medal award Dallas Advt. League, 1991, Vol. Fundraiser of Yr. award Nat. Soc. Fundraising Execs., 1991, Inst. Human Rels. award Am. Jewish Commn., Dallas, 2003; named Dallas Father of Yr., 1991, Best Man in Advt. award McCall's Mag., 1992; named Temerlin Advt. Inst. for Edn. and Rsch. in his honor So. Meth. U. Sch. Advt., 2001; inducted into Am. Advt. Hall Fame, 2004. Business E-Mail: connie.beebe@temerlinconsulting.com.

TEMES, GABOR CHARLES, electrical engineering educator; s. Erno and Rozsa (Angyal) Wohl-Temes; m. Ibi Kutasi-Temes, Feb. 6, 1954; children: Roy Thomas, Carla Andrea. Dipl.Ing., Tech. U. Budapest, 1952, DSc (hon.), 1991; Dipl. Phys., Eotvos U., Budapest, 1954; PhD, U. Ottawa, Ont., Can., 1961. Asst. prof. Tech. U. Budapest, 1952-56; project engr. Measurement Engring. Ltd., 1956-59; dept. head No. Electric Co. Ltd., 1959-64; group leader Stanford Linear Accelerator Center, 1964-66; corp. cons. Ampex Corp., 1966-69; prof. elec. engring. UCLA, 1969-90, chmn. dept., 1975-80; dept. head Oreg. State U., Corvallis, 1990—. Cons. Xerox Corp., ANT GmbH Author: (with others) Introduction to Circuit Synthesis and Design, 1977, Analog MOS Integrated Circuits for Signal Processing, 1986; assoc. editor: (with others) Jour. Franklin Inst, 1971-82; co-editor, contbg. author: (with others) Modern Filter Theory and Design, 1973, Oversampling Delta-Sigma Data Converters, 1991. Recipient Western Electric Fund award Am. Soc. Engring. Edn., 1982, Humboldt Sr. Rsch. award, 1991; NSF grantee, 1970— Fellow IEEE (life, editor Transactions on Circuit Theory 1969-71 Best Paper award 1969, 81, 85, Centennial medal 1984, Edn. award 1987, Tech. Achievement award 1989, Grad. Tchg. award 1998, Millenium medal 2000, CAS Golden Jubilee medal 2000, Gustav Robert Kirchhoff award 2006). Home: 7100 NW Grandview Dr Corvallis OR 97330-2708 Office: Oreg State U Dept Elec Engring Corvallis OR 97331 Personal E-mail: temes@ieee.org. Business E-Mail: temes@ece.orst.edu.

TEMIN, MICHAEL LEHMAN, lawyer; b. Phila., July 18, 1933; s. Henry and Annette (Lehman) T.; children: Aaron Lehman, Seth Lehman; m. Anne L. Hearn, 2000. BA magna cum laude, Yale U., 1954; LL.B. cum laude, U. Pa., 1957. Bar: Pa. 1958, Del. 2000, U.S. Ct. Appeals (3d cir.) 1958, U.S. Supreme Ct. 1969, U.S. Ct. Appeals (2d cir.) 1986, U.S. Ct. Appeals (9th cir.) 1992, U.S. Ct. Appeals (11th cir.) 2002. Asst. U.S. atty. U.S. Atty.'s Office, Phila., 1958-59; assoc. Wolf, Block, Schorr and Solis-Cohen, Phila., 1959-66, ptnr., 1966—2006, of counsel, 2006—. Lectr. Law Sch., U. Pa., Phila., 1982-90, adj. prof., 1990-93, 94-95, 2002—; Thomas A. O'Boyle vis. disting. practitioner, 1985, I. Grant Irey lectr., 1988, 2003-04; vice chmn. Ea. Dist. Pa. Bankruptcy Conf., 1994-95, chmn., 1995-96. Editor U. Pa. Law Rev., 1955-57. Vice chmn. Ednl. Nominating Panel, Phila., 1981-83; bd. dirs. Citizens Com. in Pub. Edn., Phila., 1970-96, pres. 1980-82. Fellow: Am. Coll. Bankruptcy (regent 1997—2003, scholar in residence 2005—); mem.: ABA (chmn. rules subcom. 1985—92, vice chmn. chpt. 11 subcom. 1992—96, bus. bankruptcy com. of sect. corp. banking and bus. law), Pa. Bar Assn. (ho. of dels. 1985—89, 1990—, co-chmn. legal ethics and profl. responsibility com. 2004—), Phila. Bar Assn. (mem. sect. corp. banking and bus. law 1979—86, chmn. profl. guidance com. 1985, sec. sect. corp. banking and bus. law 1985, treas. sect. corp. banking and bus. law 1986, vice chmn. sect. corp. banking and bus. law 1987, chmn. sect. corp. banking and bus. law 1988, exec. com.), Order of Coif. Jewish. Office: Wolf Block Schorr & Solis-Cohen LLP 22 Fl 1650 Arch St Philadelphia PA 19103-2097 Office Phone: 215-977-2256. Business E-Mail: mtemin@wolfblock.com.

TEMIRKANOV, YURI KHATUEVICH, conductor, music director; b. Nal'chik, Russia, Dec. 10, 1938; s. Khatu Sagidovich and Polina (Petrovna) Temirkanov; m. Irina Guseva; 1 child. Grad., Leningrad Conservatory, Russia, 1966. Condr. Maly Opera and Ballet Theatre, Leningrad, 1966; chief condr. Leningrad Philharm. Orch., 1967—76, Kirov Opera and Ballet Theatre Orch., 1976—88; prof. Leningrad Conservatory, 1979; artistic dir. Leningrad Symphony Orch. (now St. Petersburg Philharm.), 1988; mus. dir., prin. condr. St. Petersburg Philharm.; condr. Baltimore Symphony Orch., Md., 1992, Md., 1995, Md., 1998—2000, dir. music Md., 2000—06, music dir. emeritus, 2006—. Chief guest condr. London Royal Philharm. Orch., 1992; guest condr. Berlin Philharm., Vienna Philharm., l'Orch. Paris, Dresden Staatskapelle, Amsterdam's Royal Concertgebouw, NY Philharm., Phila. Orch., Boston Symphony, Chgo. Symphony, San Francisco Symphony Orch., LA Philharm., Calif., Danish Nat. Radio Symphony; condr. laureate Royal Philharm., London; Rec. artists BMG/RCA, 1988. Musical dir. (Operas) Peter I (Petrov), 1975, War and Peace (Prokofiev), 1976, Dead Souls (Schedrin), 1978, Pushkin (Petrov), 1979, Queen of Spades (Tchaikovsky), 1979. Vice chmn. bd. All-Russian Theatrical Soc. Named People's Artist of Kabardino-Balkarian Autonomous Republic, People's Artist of Russian Soviet Fed. Socialist Republic; recipient 1st prize, USSR Contest for Condrs., 1967, USSR State Prize, 1976. Office: Balt Symphony Orch Meyerhoff Symphony Hall 1212 Cathedral St Baltimore MD 21201-5545 *

TEMKIN, HARVEY L., lawyer; b. Madison, Wis., Jan. 1, 1952; s. Joe L. and Sylvia Temkin; m. Barbara, June 13, 1976; children: James, Daniel, Eli. BA, U. Wis., 1974; JD, U. Ill., 1978. Bar: Wis. 1978. Assoc. Foley & Lardner, Madison, 1978—83; prof. Tulane Law Sch., New Orleans, 1983-87; ptnr. Foley & Lardner, Madison, 1987—2002; shareholder Reinhart Boerner Van Deuren, s.c., Madison, 2002—. Lectr. U. Wis. Law

Sch., 1990-93; mem. U.S. Senator Feingold's Bus. Adv. Group. First v.p. Hillel Found., Madison, 1982-83, bd. dirs., 1987-95; chmn. edn. com. Beth Israel Synagogue, Madison, 1980-82; chmn. Jewish edn. panel Madison Jewish Cmty. Coun., 1993-98, bd. dirs., 1998-03; bd. dirs. Hospice Care, Inc. Fellow Am. Coll. Real Estate Lawyers (chmn. title insurance coverage subcom.); mem. ABA (real property probate and trust sect., reporter significant legis. panel 1983-85, significant lit. panel 1985-87), Downtown Madison, Inc. (chmn. 1989-91), Hospice Care Inc. (bd. dirs.). Office: Reinhart Boerner Van Deuren 22 East Mifflin St PO Box 2018 Madison WI 53701-2018 Business E-Mail: htemkin@reinhartlaw.com.

TEMKIN, ROBERT HARVEY, accountant; b. Boston, Oct. 21, 1943; s. Max and Lillian (Giller) T.; m. Ellen Phyllis Band, Sept. 25, 1966; 1 child, Aron; m. Debra Gottlieb, Oct. 3, 1998; 1 child, Rachel; m. Douglas Moore, Feb. 28, 1999; 1 child, Joshua. BBA, U. Mass., 1964. CPA, Mass. With Ernst & Young LLP, 1964—72, 1973—2002, ptnr., 1976—2002, nat. dir. auditing standards, 1980-88; prin. Robert H. Temkin, CPA, 2002—. Assoc. prof. NYU, 1982. Bd. dirs. Jewish Home for Elderly of Fairfield County, 1979—, pres., 1985-87; mem. Bd. Edn., Weston, Conn., 1983-87; dir. United Synagogue of Conservative Judaism, 1984-99, 2004—; bd. dirs., chmn. bd. dirs. Jewish Cmty. Ctrs. Greater Boston, 2003-05; mem. exec. com. Combined Jewish Philanthropies of Greater Boston, 1995-99, 2000-06, bd. dir. 1993-2006; treas. Synagogue Coun., Mass., 1988-93; dir. Hillel Found., U. Mass., 1992-99; mem. Town of Barnstable Mass Comprehensive Fin. Adv. Com. Recipient Acctg. Alumni award U. Mass., 1978, Alumnus Award Sch. Mgmt. U. Mass., 1986; Cmtys. of Excellence award Combined Jewish Philanthropies, 2003. Mem. AICPA (staff dir. commn. on auditors responsibilities 1976-78, peer rev. com. 1982-84, auditing stds. bd. 1984-88, chmn. internat. auditing task force 1988-90), Mass. Soc. CPAs (Silver medal 1964), N.Y. State Soc. CPAs, Mass. Bd. Pub. Accountancy (sec. 1996, 2001, chmn. 1997, 2002, 2006-07), Hyannis Yacht Club (assoc.). Home: PO Box 225 Barnstable MA 02630 Office: 275 Millway St PO Box 255 Barnstable MA 02630 Office Phone: 508-362-5518.

TEMKO, STANLEY LEONARD, lawyer; b. NYC, Jan. 4, 1920; s. Emanuel and Betty (Alderman) T.; m. Francine Marie Salzman, Mar. 4, 1944 (dec. Dec. 1998); children: Richard J., Edward J., William D. AB, Columbia U., 1940, LLB, 1943. Bar: N.Y. 1943, D.C. 1951. Practice in, NYC, 1943, 46-47; law clk. Mr. Justice Wiley Rutledge, U.S. Supreme Ct., Washington, 1947-48; legal counsel Econ. Coop. Adminstrn., 1948-49; assoc. Covington & Burling, Washington, 1949-55, ptnr., 1955-90, sr. counsel, 1990—. Editor-in-chief: Columbia Law Rev, 1942-43. Trustee Beauvoir Sch., 1963-69; trustee Columbia U., 1980-91, trustee emeritus, 1991—, mem. bd. visitors Sch. Law, 1961-98, mem. emeritus, 1999—; mem. bd. govs. St. Albans Sch., 1967-73, chmn., 1971-73. 2nd lt. U.S. Army, 1943-46. Decorated Bronze Star; recipient medal for conspicuous alumni svc. Columbia U., 1979, Excellence medal Columbia U. Law Sch., 2004. Fellow Am. Bar Found. (chmn. rsch. com. 1970-72); mem. ABA, Am. Law Inst., D.C. Bar Assn., Columbia U. Sch. Law Alumni Assn. (pres. 1982-84), Met. Club, Nat. Press Club, Phi Beta Kappa. Home: Apt 618 700 New Hampshire AVe NW Washington DC 20037 Office: Covington & Burling 1201 Pennsylvania Ave NW Washington DC 20004-2401 Home Phone: 202-342-0811; Office Phone: 202-662-5514. Business E-Mail: stemko@cov.com.

TEMME, MARCIA E. See **HARDCASTLE, MARCIA E.**

TEMPEL, EUGENE RAYMOND (GENE TEMPEL), foundation administrator, speaker, researcher; b. St. Meinrad, Ind., Mar. 30, 1947; s. Charles Xavier and Bernadette Scholastica (Otto) Tempel; m. Mary Ekerle, May 24, 1969; children: Jonathan, Jason, Zachary. BA, St. Benedict Coll., 1970; MA in English, Ind. U., 1973, EdD in Higher Edn., 1985. Asst. prof. English Vincennes U., Ind., 1970—77; dir. Jasper Ctr., 1973—77; v.p., dean of faculty Three Rivers CC, Poplar Bluff, Mo., 1977—80; dir. external affairs Coll. Arts & Scis. Ind. U., Bloomington, 1980—83; asst. prof. higher edn. Ind. U.-Purdue U. Indpls., 1985, vice chancellor external affairs, 1988; chmn. adv. com. Ind. U. Ctr. on Philanthropy, 1987, exec. dir., 1997—. Bd. dirs. Marian Heights Acad., Ferdinand, Ind., 1973; exec. dir. Indpls. Ind. U. Found., 1983—85, v.p., 1985; devel. cons. Ind. Agrl. Inst., Indpls., 1985. Co-author: Fund Raisers: Their Careers, Stories, Concerns and Accomplishments, 1996; editor: Achieving Excellence in Fund Raising. Vice chmn. bd. overseers St. Meinrad Sem., 1986; bd. dirs. Cath. Cmty. Found., 1988. Mem.: NSFRE, Nat. Soc. Fund Raising Execs., Am. Assn. Higher Edn., Coun. for Advancement and Support Edn., Indpls. C. of C. Roman Cath. Avocations: sailing, soccer. Home: 8079 Heyward Dr Indianapolis IN 46250-4226 Office: Ctr on Philanthropy at Ind U 550 W North St, Ste 301 Indianapolis IN 46202-3272 Office Phone: 317-274-4200.

TEMPELIS, CONSTANTINE HARRY, immunologist, educator; b. Superior, Wis., Aug. 27, 1927; s. Harry and Thelma Marie (Hoff) T.; m. Nancy Louise Foster, Aug. 27, 1955; children: William H., Daniel S. BS, U. Wis.-Superior, 1950; MS, U. Wis.-Madison, 1953, PhD, 1955. Project assoc. immunology U. Wis., Madison, 1955-57; instr. immunology U. W.Va., Morgantown, 1957-58; asst. rsch. immunologist U. Calif., Berkeley, 1958-66, assoc. prof. immunology, 1966-72, prof., 1972-95, prof. emeritus, 1995—, prof. grad. sch., 1996—. Vis. scientist Wellcome Rsch. Labs., Beckenham, Kent, Eng., 1977-78, U. Innsbruck, Austria, 1985, 90, 91; cons. in field. Contbr. articles to profl. jours. Served with USNR, 1945-46. Recipient Rsch. Career Devel. award, 1965-70; Fogarty sr. internat. fellow NIH, 1977-78 Mem. AAAS, Am. Assn. Immunologists, Fedn. Am. Soc. Exptl. Biology, Sigma Xi. Office: U Calif Sch Pub Health Berkeley CA 94720-0001 Home Phone: 510-524-7742. Business E-Mail: chtemp@berkeley.edu.

TEMPLAR, TED MAC, lawyer; b. Arkansas City, Kans., Sept. 27, 1929; s. H. George and Helen Marie (Bishop) T.; m. Maxine Bowman, Feb. 19, 1954; children: Lance Cameron, Kenton Lane, Clayton Neil. BBA, Washburn U., 1951, JD, 1954. Bar: Kans. 1954, U.S. Dist. Ct. Kans. 1954, U.S. Ct. Appeals (10th cir.) 1961. Dep. county lawyer Cowley County, Arkansas City, Kans., 1956-58, judge city ct., 1969-73; state rep. 79th dist. State of Kans., Topeka, 1973-77; pvt. practice Arkansas City, 1954—. 1st lt. USAR, 1951-59. Recipient Certificate Appreciation Kans. Bar Assn., 1973. Mem. Rotary Club Arkansas City, Midian Shrine, Wichita, Legion of Honor Order of DeMolay, Jaycee Internat. (senate). Republican. Avocations: hunting, fishing. Office: PO Box 1002 Arkansas City KS 67005-1002

TEMPLE, DONALD, retired allergist, dermatologist; b. Chgo., May 21, 1933; s. Samuel Leonard and Matilda Eve (Riff) T.; m. Sarah Rachel Katz, Sept. 29, 1957; children: Michael A., Matthew D., Madeline B. AB in Biology cum laude, Harvard U., 1954; MD, U. Chgo., 1958. Diplomate Am. Bd. Allergy and Immunology, Am. Bd. Dermatology, Nat. Bd. Med. Examiners; lic. Intern Michael Reese Hosp., Chgo., 1958-59; resident in dermatology U. Chgo. Hosps., 1959-62; clin. asst., dept. dermatology Boston U. Sch. Medicine, 1963-64; clin. instr. dermatology dept. Stanford U. Med. Sch., 1965; preceptee in allergy Offices of Leon Unger, M.D., and Donald Unger, M.D., Chgo., 1965-69; pvt. practice Des Plaines, Ill., 1969-76; with allergy dept. Glen Ellyn (Ill.) Clinic, 1972-97; ret., 1997. Dermatology and allergy staff Louis A. Weiss Hosp., Chgo., 1965-73, allergy sect. Loyola U. Med. Ctr., Maywood, Ill., 1977-80, exec. and contract medicine coms. Glen Ellyn; clin. asst. prof. dermatology Abraham Lincoln Sch. Medicine, U. Ill., 1972-75; clin. asst. prof. medicine sect. allergy and dermatology, Loyola U., 1977-85; mem. staff Cen. DuPage Hosp., Winfield, Ill., 1973-97, Glen Oaks Med. Ctr., Glendale Heights, Ill., Glendale Heights Cmty. Hosp., 1980-92. Contbr. articles to profl. jours. Bd. dirs. Am. Lung Assn., DuPage, McHenry counties, 1980-91; chmn. Contract Medicine, HMO Com., Glen Ellyn Clinic, 1985, mem. exec. com., 1988-92. Fellow Am. Coll. Chest Physicians, Am. Assn. Cert. Allergists, Am. Coll. Allergists, Am. Acad. Allergy, Ill. Soc. Allergy and Clin. Immunology, Chgo. Dermatol. Soc.; mem. AMA, Ill. State Med. Soc., DuPage County Med. Soc., Chgo. Med. Soc., Fla. Med. Assn. Collier County Med. Soc. Jewish. Avocations: sailing, investing. Home: 6585 Nicholas Blvd Ph 3 Naples FL 34108-7210 E-mail: don.temple@post.harvard.edu.

TEMPLE, DONALD EDWARD, medical association administrator; b. NYC, Nov. 28, 1946; s. James Edward and Helen Louise (Gannon) Temple; m. Lucy Chirinos de Lorentzen, Feb. 23, 1974 (div. 1989); 1 child, Gail Marie. BBA, St. Francis Coll., Bklyn., 1968. Vol. U.S. Peace Corps, Lima, Peru, 1968-72; asst. to pres., gen. mgr. Barrons Ednl. Series, Inc., Hauppauge, NY, 1973-78; dir. supply svc. Am. Lung Assn., NYC, 1978-84; bus. mgr. Am. Jour. Respiratory and Critical Care Medicine, NYC, 1985—, Am. Jour. Respiratory Cell and Molecular Biology, 1989—, Procs. Am. Thoracic Soc., NYC, 2004—; dir. bus. affairs Am. Lung Assn., NYC, 1985-89, dep. mng. dir. bus. affairs, 1990-94; dir. bus. affairs Am. Thoracic Soc., NYC, 1994—2007, dep. exec. dir. bus. affairs, 2007—. Mem. mailers tech. adv. com. U.S. Postal Svc., Washington, 1987—93. Vol. L.I. Assn. AIDS Care, 1994—98. Recipient Merit award, Soc. Tech. Communication, 1990. Mem.: N.Y. Soc. Assn. Execs., Healthcare Mktg. Comm. Coun., Am. Soc. Assn. Execs., Alliance Non-Profit Mailers (bd. dirs., chmn. tech. com. 1986—94, v.p. 1990—94), Soc. Scholarly Pub. Home: 63 Vanderwater St Farmingdale NY 11735-5235 Office: Am Thoracic Soc 61 Broadway New York NY 10006-2755 Business E-Mail: dtemple@thoracic.org.

TEMPLE, LARRY EUGENE, lawyer; b. Plainview, Tex., Dec. 26, 1935; s. Herman Edward and Grace Eileen (Ivey) T.; m. Laura Louann Atkins, Feb. 23, 1963; children: Laura Allison, John Lawrence. BBA, U. Tex., 1957, LLB with honors, 1959; LLD (hon.), Lamar U., 1985. Bar: Tex., U.S. Dist. Ct. (we. dist.) Tex., U.S. Ct. Appeals (5th cir.), U.S. Supreme Ct. Law clk. to justice Tom Clark U.S. Supreme Ct., Washington, 1959-60; assoc. Powell, Rauhut, McGinnis, Reavley & Lochridge, Austin, Tex., 1960-63; legal adminstrn. asst., exec. asst. (chief of staff) Tex. Gov. John B. Connally, Austin, 1963-67; spl. counsel to pres. Lyndon Baines Johnson, Washington, 1967-69; pvt. practice Austin, 1969—. Bd. dirs. Temple-Inland, Inc., Guaranty Bank. Mem. U. Tex. Cancer Found., Houston, 1978-84, U. Tex. Devel. Bd., Austin, 1980-85, 90—, chmn., 1993-95; pres. U. Tex. Ex-Students Assn., 1997-98; mem. Tex. Higher Edn. Coordinating Bd., Austin, 1983-89, chmn., 1983-87; chmn. Select Com. for Higher Edn., Austin, 1985-87; bd. dirs. Lyndon B. Johnson Found., 1986—, vice chmn., 1989-2000, pres., 2000—; trustee U. Tex. Law Sch. Found., 1989-2007. Recipient Faculty award U. Tex. Law Sch., 1987, Humanitarian award Austin region NCCJ, 1988, Santa Rita award U. Tex. System, 1989, Disting. Alumnus award U. Tex., Austin, 1990, Mirabeau B. Lamar medal Assn. Tex. Colls. and Univs., 1990, Pro Bene Meritis award U. Tex., 1991 Outstanding Alumnus award U. Tex. Law Sch., 1999, Presdl. Citation award U. Tex., 2001, Leon Green award Tex. Law Rev., 2003; named a Tex. Super Lawyer, 2003, 04, 05. Fellow: Tex. Bar Found.; mem.: ABA, Tex. Bar Assn. (chmn. legis. com. 1980, 1983—86), Tex. Jr. Bar Assn. (chmn. bd. dirs. 1967), Austin Bar Assn. (pres. 1962—63, Disting. Lawyer award 2004). Democrat. Episcopalian. Home: 2606 Escondido Cv Austin TX 78703-1610 Office: 400 W 15th St Ste 1510 Austin TX 78701-1648 Home Phone: 512-453-7936; Office Phone: 512-477-4467. Business E-Mail: larry@larrytemple.com.

TEMPLE, MIKE, software company executive; BBA in Acctg., U. Portland. With Laventhol & Horwath; v.p., CFO Yoshida Group, Intromedix, Inc., Upright Systems; exec. v.p., gen. mgr. Bioject, Inc.; CFO Open Source Develop. Labs, Inc. (OSDL), Beaverton, Oreg., 2005—06, COO, 2006—. Bd. dir. OTBC. Office: Open Source Develop Labs Inc 12725 SW Millikan Way Ste 400 Beaverton OR 97005 Office Phone: 503-626-2455. Business E-Mail: mtemple@osdl.org. *

TEMPLE, ROBERT, physician, federal agency administrator; b. NYC, July 18, 1941; s. Samuel A. and Judith (Coslow) T.; m. Bonnie Streifer, Oct. 27, 1963; 1 child, James. BA magna cum laude, Harvard U., 1963; MD, NYU, 1967. Diplomate Am. Bd. Internal Medicine, Am. Bd. Clin. Pharmacology. Intern Columbia-Presbyn. Med. Ctr., NYC, 1967-68, resident, 1968-69; clin. assoc. Nat. Inst. Arthritis and Metabolic Disease, NIH, Bethesda, Md., 1969-72; med. officer FDA, Rockville, Md., 1972-74, asst. to dir., bur. of drugs, 1974-76, dir. div. cardio-renal drug products, 1976-82, dir. office drug research and rev., 1982-84, dir. office of drug evaluation I, 1984—. Mem. coop. studies rev. com. VA, 1977-80. Contbr. articles to profl. jours. Served with USPHS, 1969-72. Recipient Disting. Alumni award NYU Sch. Medicine, N.Y. 1987; Pub. HealthSuperior Svc. award HHS, 1986, Disting. Svc. award, 1991; NORD Ann. Tribute, 2001; Outstanding Svc. award Drug Info. Assn., 2001, Disting. Svc. and Leadership award FDLI, 2002. Fellow Am. Coll. Clin. Pharmacology (hon.); mem. Soc. Clin. Trials (bd. dirs. 1983, v.p. 1986, pres. 1987), Am. Soc. Clin. Phrmacology and Therapeutics (bd. dirs. 1987-90, 92—, Rawls-Palmer Progress in Medicine lecture and award 2001), Alpha Omega Alpha. Democrat. Jewish. Avocations: model trains, tennis, gardening, cooking. Home: 3325 Rowland Pl NW Washington DC 20008-3226 Office: FDA 5600 Fishers Ln Rockville MD 20857 Office Phone: 301-443-5296. Business E-Mail: temple@cder.fda.gov.

TEMPLE, WAYNE CALHOUN, historian, writer; b. nr. Richwood, Ohio, Feb. 5, 1924; s. Howard M. and Ruby March (Calhoun) T.; m. Lois Marjorie Bridges, Sept. 22, 1956 (dec. Apr. 1978); m. Sunderine Wilson, Apr. 9, 1979; stepson, James C. Mohn. AB cum laude, U. Ill., 1949, AM, 1951, PhD, 1956. Rsch. asst. history U. Ill., 1949-53, tchg. asst., 1953-54; curator ethnohistory Ill. State Mus., 1954-58; editor-in-chief Lincoln Herald, Lincoln Meml. U., 1958-73, assoc. editor, 1973—, also dir. dept. Lincolniana, dir. univ. press, John Wingate Weeks prof. history, 1958-64; with Ill. State Archives, 1964—, now chief dep. dir. Lectr. U.S. Mil. Acad., 1975; sec.-treas. Nat. Lincoln-Civil War Council, 1958-64; mem. bibliography com. Lincoln Lore, 1958—; hon. mem. Lincoln Sesquicentennial Commn., 1959-60; advisory council U.S. Civil War Centennial Commn., 1960-66; maj. Civil War Press Corps, 1962—; pres. Midwest Conf. Masonic Edn., 1985; mem. adv. com. Abraham Lincoln Bicentennial Commn., 2000—. Author: Indian Villages of the Illinois Country: Historic Tribes, 1958, rev. edits., 1966, 77, 87, Lincoln the Railsplitter, 1961, Abraham Lincoln and Others at the St. Nicholas, 1968, Alexander Williamson-Tutor to the Lincoln Boys, 1971, (with others) First Steps to Victory: Grant's March to Naples, 1977, Lincoln and Grant: Illinois Militiamen, 1981, Stephen A. Douglas: Freemason, 1982, Lincoln as a Lecturer, 1982, By Square and Compasses: The Building of Lincoln's Home and Its Saga, 1984, Lincoln's Connections with the Illinois and Michigan Canal, 1986, Dr. Anson G. Henry: Personal Physician to the Lincolns, 1988, Abraham Lincoln: From Skeptic to Prophet, 1995, Thomas and Abraham Lincoln as Farmers, 1996, Alexander Williamson: Friend of the Lincolns, 1998, By Square and Compass: Saga of the Lincoln Home, 2002, The Taste Is In My Mouth a Little...Lincoln's Victuals and Potables, 2004, Abraham Lincoln and Illinois' Fifth Capitol, 2006, Abraham Lincoln's Travels on the River Queen, 2007; co-author: Illinois's Fifth Capitol: The House that Lincoln Built, 1988; contbg. author: Capitol Centennial Papers, 1988; editor: Campaigning with Grant, 1961, 72, The Civil War Letters of Henry C. Bear, 1961; 71 radio scripts A. Lincoln 1809-1959, Indian Villages of the Illinois Country: Atlas Supplement, 1975; mem. editl. bd. Am. Biog. Inst., 1971—, Ency. Indians of Ams., 1973—; contbr. articles to profl. jours., encys. Sponsor Abraham Lincoln Bay, Washington Nat. Cathedral; mem. Ill. State Flag Commn., 1969—; trustee, regent Lincoln Acad. Ill., 1970-82; bd. govs. St. Louis unit Shriners Hosps. for Crippled Children, 1975-81; commissioning com., hon. crew mem. and plank owner USS Springfield submarine, 1990—; hon. crew mem. USS Abraham Lincoln aircraft carrier, 1989—. With U.S. Army, 1943-46, gen. Res. (ret.). Decorated Bronze Star Medal, Silver Citizenship medal SAR, 1993, Literary Merit Gold medal Ill. Lodge of Rsch., 1993; recipient Order of Arrow Boy Scouts Am., 1957, Scouters award, 1960, Scouter's Key, also medallion, 1967, Lincoln medallion Lincoln Sesquicentennial Commn., 1960, award of Achievement U.S. Civil War Centennial Commn., 1965, Algernon Sydney Sullivan medallion, 1969, Distinguished Service award Ill. State Hist. Library, 1969, 77, I.H. Duval Distinguished Service award, 1971, legion of honor Internat. Supreme Council, Order of De Molay, 1972, Disting. Service award Civil War Round Table of Chgo., 1983, 91, Cert. Excellence Ill. State Hist. Soc., 1985, Archbishop Richard Chenevix Trench award, 1999; Lincoln Diploma Honor, Lincoln Meml. U., Harrogate, Tenn., 1963, Lifetime Achievement award 2001; named Hon. Ky. Col., Marshal of Okla. Territory. Fellow Royal Soc. Arts (life); mem. NRA, KT (Red Cross Constantine), Lincoln Group D.C. (hon.), U. Ill. Alumni Assn., Ill. State Hist. Soc., Board of Advisors, The Lincoln Forum, Ill. Profl. Land Surveyors Assn., Ill. State Dental Soc. (citation plague 1966), Res. Officers Assn., Lincoln Fellowship of Wis., Iron Brigade Assn. (hon. life), Mil. Order Loyal Legion U.S. (hon. companion), Mil. Order Fgn. Wars U.S., Army and Navy Union, Masons (33 degree, Meritorious Svc. award, grand rep. from Grand Lodge of Colo.), Shriners, Kappa Delta Pi, Phi Alpha, Phi Alpha Theta (Scholarship Key award), Chi Gamma Iota, Phi Beta Kappa, Tau Kappa Alpha, Alpha Psi Omega, Sigma Pi Beta (Headmaster), Sigma Tau Delta (Gold Honor Key award for editorial writing), Zeta Psi. Presbyterian (elder). Home: 1121 S 4th Street Ct Springfield IL 62703-2200 Office: Ill State Archives Springfield IL 62756-0001 Office Phone: 217-782-3501. *Only in America could a poor farm boy from Ohio work his way through a great university, like the University of Illinois, and receive a doctor's degree. Life has been kind to me, and I have tried hard and worked hard. I am proud to be an American.*

TEMPLEMAN, LYDIA, retired assistant principal; b. Sydney, Australia, 1913; arrived in U.S., 1946; d. Giuseppe and Maria Concetta Lo Schiavo; m. Bruce Liscum Templeman, May 20, 1950; 1 child, Geoffrey. BA, Sydney U., 1934, diploma in Edn., 1935; grad., Royal Acad. London, 1935; MA, U. Mich., 0950, B of Econs., 1956. Tchr. NSW Dept. Edn., Sydney, Australia, 1936—46, Jackson, Mich. Edn. Dept., 1947—91; asst. prof. Fullerton, Calif. Dept. Edn., 1967—91; ret., 1991. Owner, operator Bren Travel Svcs., Calif., 1965—88. Author: Travel Agency Operation, 1988, Dollars and Sense, 2004; tour dir. Europe, 1956—80. Mem.: Calif. Ret. Tchrs. Assn. Democrat. Roman Catholic. Avocations: sailing, motor boats.

TEMPLETON, ALAN ROBERT, biology professor; b. Litchfield, Ill., Feb. 28, 1947; s. John Smith and Lois Arlene (McCormick) T.; m. Bonnie A. Altman, Dec. 20, 1969; children: Jeremy Alan, Jeffrey Alan. BA, Washington U., 1969; MS in Stats., U. Mich., 1972, PhD in Genetics, 1972. Jr. fellow Mich. Soc. Fellows, Ann Arbor, 1972-74; asst. prof. U. Tex., Austin, 1974-77; assoc. prof. Washington U., St. Louis, 1977-81, prof., 1981—, Charles Rebstock prof. biology, 2001—; prof. Inst. Evolution, Haifa, Israel, 2007—. Cons. St. Louis Zool. Park, 1979—; founding mem., dir. Soc. for Conservation Biology, 1985—. Editor: Theoretical Population Biology, 1981-91; mem. editl. bd. Molecular Phylogenetics & Evolution, 1991—, Brazilian Jour. Genetics, 1991-97, Genetics and Molecular Biology, 1998-2001, Animal Conservation, 2004—, Evolutionary Bioinformatics Online, 2005—; assoc. editor Am. Naturalist, 2002-05; contbr. numerous article to profl. jours. Grantee NSF, 1974-80, 90—, NIH, 1980—, Nixon Griffis Fund for Zool. Rsch., 1986-87, Burroughs Welcome Fund for Functional Genomics, 2000—04. Fellow AAAS; mem. Soc. for Study Evolution (v.p. 1982, pres. 1996-97), Soc. Conservation Biology (bd. dirs. 1985-88), Nature Conservancy (trustee Mo. chpt. 1988—, v.p. 1996-2000). Avocations: hiking, caving, ethnomusicology, scuba diving, flying. Office: Washington U Dept Biology Saint Louis MO 63130-4899

TEMPLETON, ALEXIS S., biogeochemist, educator; AB in Earth Scis., Dartmouth Coll., Hanover, NH, 1993, MS in Geochemistry, 1995; student, Lawrence Berkeley Nat. Lab. Ctr. Isotope Geochemistry, 1995—98; PhD in Geomicrobiology, Stanford U., Calif., 2002. Postdoctoral rschr. marine biology rsch. divsn. Scripps Instn. Oceanography, 2002—05; asst. prof. dept. geol. scis. U. Colo., Boulder, 2005—. Contbr. articles to sci. jours. Named one of Brilliant 10, Popular Sci. mag., 2006; recipient Rosalind Franklin award for Young Investigators, 2004. Office: Dept Geol Scis U Colo Campus Box 399 Boulder CO 80309-0399 Office Phone: 303-735-6069. E-mail: alexis.templeton@colorado.edu.

TEMPLETON, JOHN MARKS, investment counsel, financial analyst; b. Winchester, Tenn., Nov. 29, 1912; s. Harvey Maxwell and Vella (Handly) T.; m. Judith Dudley Folk, Apr. 7, 1937 (dec. Feb. 1951); children: John Marks, Anne Dudley, Christopher Winston; m. Irene Reynolds Butler, Dec. 31, 1958 (dec. Nov. 1993). AB, Yale U., 1934; MA (law) (Rhodes scholar), Balliol Coll., Oxford, Eng., 1936; LLD (hon.), Beaver Coll., 1965, Marquette U., 1980, Jamestown Coll., 1983, Maryville Coll., 1984, Babson Coll., 1992, Rhodes Coll, 1992, U. Rochester, 1992, La. Coll., 1993, Moravian Coll., 1994; D.Litt. (hon.), Wilson Coll., 1974; D.D. (hon.), Buena Vista Coll., 1979; D.C.L. (hon.), U. of South, 1984; DLitt (hon.), Manhattan Coll., 1990; LHD, U. Dubuque, 1992, Fla. Southern Coll., 1992; DLitt (hon.), Campbell U., 1993; LLD, Moravian Coll., 1994; DPhil (hon.), Stonehill Coll., 1995; LHD (hon.), Furman U., 1995; LLD (hon.), Notre Dame U., 1996, Methodist Coll., 1997; LHD (hon.), Brigham Young U., 1998, Queens Coll., 1999; LHD (hon.), Johns Hopkins U., 2006. CFA. Sec.-treas., v.p., dir. Nat. Geophys. Co., Dallas and NYC, 1937-41; pres., dir. Templeton, Dobbrow & Vance, Inc., NYC, 1941-65; chmn. Templeton Damroth Corp., 1959-62; v.p., dir. First Trust Bank Ltd., Bahamas, 1963—; pres., dir. Templeton Funds Inc., 1977-86, Templeton Global Funds Inc., 1981-86, Templeton Growth Fund Can., Ltd., Toronto, 1954-85; chmn Templeton Galbraith & Hansberger Ltd, 1986-92. Author: The Humble Approach, 1981; co-author: The Templeton Touch, 1985, The Templeton Plan, 1987, Global Investing, 1988, The God Who Would Be Known, 1989, Riches for the Mind and Spirit, 1990, Looking Forward, 1993, Discovering the Laws of Life, 1994, Is God the Only Reality?, 1994, Evidence of Purpose, 1994, Future Agenda, 1995; contbr. articles to fin. publs. Past pres. Lyford Cay (Bahamas) Property Owners Assn.; Chmn. YMCA Bergen County, 1952-54; dir., campaign chmn. Englewood Community Chest, 1953-54; trustee Englewood Hosp., 1953-56, Soc. for Promoting Christian Knowledge, 1984-87, Balliol Coll. Endowments (Oxford), Templeton Project Trust (Eng.); chmn. bd. trustees Princeton Theol. Sem., 1967-73, 79-85, trustee for restoration of Westminster Abbey, 1991—; trustee Wilson Coll., 1941-73, Buena Vista Coll., 1981—, Templeton Found. Inc., 1952—, John Templeton Found. Inc., 1987—, council on theol. sems. United Presbyn. Ch. U.S.A., 1946-83; mem. Ctr. Theol. Inquiry, 1979-92, Commn. on Ecumenical Mission, 1961-70; bd. corporators Presbyn. Ministers Fund, Inc., 1960-93; bd. visitors Harvard Div. Sch., 1981-88; adv. bd. Harvard Ctr. for the study of World Religions, 1975-89; bd. mgrs. Am. Bible Soc., 1972-92; mgmt. Council Templeton Coll. (Oxford); pres. Templeton Theol. Sem., Bahamas, 1984-88; hon. rector Dubuque U., 1982-92. Decorated knight Order of Brit. Empire, Knight of St. John; recipient Churchman of Yr. award Religious Heritage Am., 1979, Internat. Churchman of Yr. award, 1981, Ecumenical Patriarch's Hon. Order of Mt. Athos, Free Enterprise award Palm Beach Atlantic Coll., 1984, Centennial medal NY Mayflower Soc., 1987, award USA Today, 1991, award for excellence in investment mgmt., 1991, Benjamin Franklin award Royal Soc. Arts, 1994, Lifetime Achievement award Laymans Nat. Bible Assn., 1995, Nat. Bus. Hall of Fame award Jr. Achievement Assn., 1996, Interfaith gold medallion Internat. Coun. Christians and Jews, 1997,

Abraham Lincoln award, 1997, Ind. award Brown U., 1998, Alexis de Tocqueville award Ind. Inst., Calif., 1998, Faith and Freedom award Action Inst., 2000, Faith and Fredom award Action Inst., 2000; named to Wall Street Week Hall of Fame, 1990. Mem. Soc. Security Analysts, World Pres. Orgn., Chief Execs. Orgn. (pres. 1968-69), Bahamas C. of C. (bd. dirs. 1976-79), Internat. Acad. Religious Scis., Mt. Pelerin Soc., Elihu Club, Elizabethan Club (New Haven), Yale Club, University Club (NYC), Lyford Cay Club of Bahamas (dep. chmn. 1980-86), Lansdowne Club, Royal Overseas League, Athenaeum (Eng.), United Oxford and Cambridge Univs. Club (Eng.), White's Club (Eng.), Rotary (Bahamas), Phi Beta Kappa., Zeta Psi. Office: Box N7776 Nassau The Bahamas Mailing: John Templeton Found 300 Conshohocken State Rd, Ste 500 West Conshohocken PA 19428 Office Phone: 242-362-4904.

TEMPLETON, JOHN MARKS, JR., retired pediatric surgeon, foundation administrator; b. NYC, Feb. 19, 1940; s. John Marks and Judith Dudley (Folk) T.; m. Josephine J. Gargiulo, Aug. 2, 1970; children: Heather Erin, Jennifer Ann. BA, Yale Coll., 1962; MD, Harvard U., 1968; degree (hon.), Beaver Coll., Buena Vista U., Va. Commonwealth U., Alvernia Coll. Intern Med. Coll. Va., Richmond, 1968-69, resident, 1969-73; dir. trauma program U. Pa. and Children's Hosp. Phila., 1989—95, prof. pediat. surgery, 1995. Chmn. bd. Templeton Growth Fund, Ltd. Assoc. editor: Textbook of Pediatric Emergencies, 1993; pub. 6000 Name Geneology, 1997, A Searcher's Life, 1999, Thrift and Generosity, 2004. Chmn. health and safety, exec. bd. Cradle of Liberty coun. Boy Scouts Am.; mem. exec. bd. Eastern U., Fgn. Policy Rsch. Inst., Nat. Recreation Found., Coll. Physicians Phila., Melmark Charitable Found.; nat. bd. dirs., pres. Pa. divsn. Am. Trauma Soc.; bd. dirs. Nat. Bible Assn.; elder Proclamation Presbyn. Ch.; pres. John Templeton Found. With M.C., USNR, 1975-77. Barclay fellow Templeton Coll., Oxford U., Eisenhower Exch. fellow, fellow George H. Gallup Internat. Inst. Mem. ACS, AMA, Am. Pediat. Surg. Assn., Am. Acad. Pediats., Am. Assn. Surgery Trauma, Ea. Assn. Surgery Trauma, Phila. Coll. Physicians, Union League, Order Charlemagne, Lyford Cay Club, Merion Cricket Club, Athenaeum Club London, Rotary Internat., White's London, United Oxford and Cambridge U. Club (London). Republican. Evangelical. Office: 300 Conshohocken State Rd Ste 500 West Conshohocken PA 19428 Home Phone: 610-525-6811. Business E-Mail: bmcgraw@templeton.org.

TEMPLETON, RICHARD K., electronics executive; BSEE, Union Coll., NY, 1980. Various positions Tex. Instruments, Inc., Dallas, 1980—91, v.p. semiconductor group, 1991—94, mgr. worldwide application specific products, 1993—96, sr. v.p. semiconductor group, 1994—96, exec. v.p., pres. semiconductor group, 1996—2004, COO, 2000—04, pres., CEO, 2004—. Bd. dirs. Tex. Instruments, Inc., 2003—, Semiconductor Industry Assn. Mem. Bus. Roundtable, Dallas Chief Exec. Roundtable. Office: Tex Instruments Inc PO Box 660199 Dallas TX 75266-0199 Office Phone: 972-995-2011. Office Fax: 972-995-4360. *

TEMPLETON, RICHARD RAYMOND, special education educator, consultant; s. Gary Franklin Templeton and Cynthia Riggs Calhoun; m. Tonya Nixon Templeton, Dec. 14, 2006. BS, Athens State U., Ala., 2001; MS, U. Ala. A&M, Hunstville, 2005, U. North Ala., Florence, 2006. Cert. essentials course master tchg. Intel Teach to the Future. Tchr. Morgan County Bd. Edn., Decatur, 2001—. Presenter in field. Pub. rels. officer Centurion Club, Athens, 2001. Recipient Cert. Appreciation, Centurion Club, 2001. Mem.: Coun. Adminstrs. Spl. Edn., Coun. for Exceptional Children (v.p. 2001, Cert. Appreciation Student Chpt. 722 2001). Avocation: golf. Office: Falkville HS 43 Clark Dr Falkville AL 35622

TEMPLIN, DONALD C., lawyer; b. Jacksonville, Fla., Nov. 10, 1945; BA, Yale U., 1967; JD, U. Okla., 1970. Bar: Okla. 1970, Tex. 1972, admitted to practice: US Supreme Ct., US Ct. Appeals (Fed. Cir.), US Ct. Appeals (5th Cir.), US Ct. Appeals (9th Cir.), US Ct. Appeals (10th Cir.). Ptnr., Intellectual Property Litig. Group Haynes and Boone LLP, Dallas, head, Litig. Sect. Lectr. in field. Contbr. articles to profl. jours. Chmn., exec. com. March of Dimes Birth Defect Found. of North Tex., 1998—99. Capt. USMC, 1971—73. Fellow: Am. Coll. Trial Lawyers; mem.: State Bar Tex., ABA (Intellectual Property Sect.), Okla. Bar Assn., Am. Bd. Trial Adv., Order of Coif. Office: Haynes and Boone LLP 3100 NationsBank Plz 901 Main St Ste 3100 Dallas TX 75202-3789 Office Phone: 214-651-5590. Office Fax: 214-200-0593. Business E-Mail: don.templin@haynesboone.com.

TEMPLIN, JOHN LEON, JR., healthcare consulting executive; b. New Brunswick, NY, Aug. 5, 1940; s. John Leon and Theresa Veronica (Revolinski) T.; m. Barbara Maria Ribley, Sept. 12, 1970; children: John, Joseph, Kevin, Nan, Danielle, Christopher. BS in Mgmt. Engring., Rensselaer Poly. Inst., 1962, MS in Mgmt., 1969. Cert. healthcare cons. Am. Assn. Healthcare Cons. Mgr. customer svc. Norton Abrasives, Troy, N.Y., 1968-70; cons., sr. cons. Hosp. Assn. N.Y. State, Albany, 1970-79, dir. mgmt. svcs., 1979-80, sr. dir. mgmt. svc., 1981-83; dir. productivity improvement Applied Leadership Technologies, Inc., Greenfield Center, N.Y., 1983-84, v.p., productivity improvement div., 1984-85, pres., 1985-86, Templin Mgmt. Assocs., Inc., Greenfield Center, 1987—, The Northeastern Cons. Alliance, Albany, N.Y., 1995-98. Editor quar. jour. Healthcare Supr., 1983—; mem. editorial com. ann. Manual for Workload Recording, 1978-91. Mem. budget com. Greater Saratoga Sch. Dist., Saratoga Springs, N.Y., 1978-79; mem. energy com. Blue Cross Assn., Chgo., 1978-81; mem. Gov.'s Task Force on Nursing, Albany, 1980; mem. parish coun. St. Joseph's Ch., Greenfield Center, 1981-87. Capt. U.S. Army, 1962-64. Fellow Am. Coll. Healthcare Execs., Healthcare Info. and Mgmt. Sys. Soc. (liaison Coll. Am. Pathologists 1978-91, chair edn. com. 1995-96, 97-98); mem. Am. Hosp. Assn. (seminar spkr. 1980-93), Clin. Lab. Mgmt. Assn. (bd. dirs. 1980-84), Soc. for Health Systems (bd. dirs. 2004-06), Am. Assn. Healthcare Execs. (bd. dirs. 2005—), KC. Republican. Roman Catholic. Avocations: golf, computers, gardening, fishing. Home and Office: Templin Mgmt Assocs Inc 265 Locust Grove Rd Greenfield Center NY 12833-1501 Office Phone: 518-893-7760. E-mail: jtemplinjr@aol.com.

TEMPLIN, KENNETH ELWOOD, paper company executive; b. Mason City, Nebr., Jan. 26, 1927; s. Otto Rudolph and Marianna (Graf) T.; m. Harriet Elaine Ressel, Aug. 24, 1951; children: Steven, David, Daniel, Benjamin, Elizabeth. BSBA, U. Nebr., Lincoln, 1950; MBA, Wayne State U., Detroit, 1981. Fin. analyst Ford Motor Co., 1950-54; fin. analyst, corp. staff Chrysler Corp., 1955-60, div. controller marine engine div., 1961-63, gen. sales mgr., 1964-65; v.p. Marsh and Templin, NYC, 1966-69; v.p., gen. mgr. operating group Saxon Industries, NYC, 1970-79, group v.p., 1979-82, sr. v.p., c.o.o., 1982-85; v.p.-converting Paper Corp. Am., Wayne, Pa., 1985-86; exec. v.p. Quality Park Products Inc., St. Paul, 1986-88, 1986-88, pres., 1988-96, ret., 1996. Mem. exec. com. Single Service Inst., 1971-79 Regional chmn. Minn. devel. com. Nat. Multiple Sclerosis Soc., 1970-71; co-pres. Home and Sch. Assn., Bernardsville, N.J., 1975-76; bd. dirs. West Hennepin Counseling Svcs., Inc., 1996-2000, Brain Injury Assn. Minn., 1997-2001; mem. Svc. Corps Ret. Execs. (SCORE), 1996—, chmn. Mpls. chpt., 1999-2000; bd. dirs. Hennepin History Mus., 2000-06. With U.S. Army, 1945-47, 50-51. Mem. Envelope Mfrs. Assn. Am. (postal affairs com. 1989-96, fin. com. chmn. 1994-95, bd. dirs. 1990-91, 93-95). Presbyterian. Office Phone: 612-339-5200. E-mail: templink@aol.com.

TEMPLIN, ROY W., manufacturing executive; B in Acctg., Ind. U., Bloomington. CPA. With Price Waterhouse, Indpls., NCR Corp., Dayton, Ohio; various positions including dir. corp. acctg. and dir. corp. fin. Cummins Engine Co., Columbus, Ind.; v.p. fin., chief acctg. officer Kimball Internat. Inc.; corp. v.p., contr. Whirlpool Corp., Benton Harbor, Mich., 2003—04, exec. v.p., CFO, mem. exec. com., 2004—. Office: Whirlpool Corp 200 N M-63 Benton Harbor MI 49022-2692 *

TENCER, JOHN G., military officer; b. Chgo., Apr. 23, 1965; s. John G. and Darlene M. Tencer; m. Melissa L. Leitsch, July 27, 1991; children: Emily L., John G. BS in Profl. Aeronautics summa cum laude, Embry-Riddle Aero. U., Daytona Beach, 1993; MBA, Georgetown U., Washington, DC, 2005—. Cpl. USMC, Havelock, NC, 1984—88; lt. comdr. USN, Washington, 1995—. Sunday sch. tchr. Mission Valley Ch. the Nazarene, San Diego, 2003—05, Calvary Ch. the Nazarene, Annandale, Va., 2005. Lt. comdr. USN, 1995. Decorated Commendation medal USN, Achievement medal. Mem.: San Diego Supply Corps. Assn., Wash. Area Navy Supply Corps. Assn., Internat. Mountain Biking Assn. Avocations: bicycling, surfing, travel. Home: 8710 Queen Elizabeth Blvd Annandale VA 22003 Home Phone: 703-272-8380. Personal E-mail: jgt22@georgetown.edu.

TENDLER, DAVID, investment company executive; b. NYC, Jan. 15, 1938; s. Philip and Pearl (Berman) T.; m. Beatrice Weisberg, Oct. 11, 1958; children: Pearl, Karen. BBA in Internat. Econs., CCNY, 1959. With Philipp Bros. Co., 1960—, mgr. Far Eastern ops., 1968-75, pres. NYC, 1975—; dir. parent corp. Engelhard Minerals & Chems. Corp. (name changed to Phibro Corp. 1981), NYC, 1975-85, vice chmn. bd., 1979-81, chmn. bd., CEO, 1981—; co-chmn., co-CEO Phibro-Salomon Inc., NYC, 1983-84; ptnr. Tendler Beretz, L.L.C. Ltd., NYC, 1985—. Chmn. subcom. trade U.S.-German Dem. Rep. Trade and Econ. Coun., 1978—84; bd. dirs., mem. exec. com. U.S./USSR Trade and Econ. Coun., 1979—85, U.S.-China Bus. Coun., 1983—94, 1994—2005; bd. dirs. V.I. Techs., Inc., Watertown, Mass., Savient Pharm., East Brunswick, NJ, Agrifos Fertilizer Inc., Pasadena, Tex. Mem. bd. overseers NYU Grad. Sch. Bus., 1981-85; trustee Lenox Hill Hosp., 1981-94; trustee, mem. exec. com. N.Y. Blood Ctr., 1987—; bd. dirs., mem. exec. com. Fgn. Policy Assn., 1983-96; bd. dirs. Ctr. for the Advancement of Women, N.Y.C., 1999—; mem. adv. coun. Weissman Ctr. for Internat. Bus., Baruch Coll., 2001. Recipient Torch of Liberty award metals and metal products divsn. Anti-Defamation League, 1976, Edith and Herbert Lehman award Henry St. Settlement, 1982; named Man of Yr., Fgn. Trade Soc., Baruch Coll., CUNY, 1985. Office: Tendler Beretz LLC 150 E 52nd St New York NY 10022-6017 Home Phone: 212-421-1211; Office Phone: 212-593-0550. Personal E-mail: tenchan@aol.com.

TENDLER, PAUL MARC, lawyer; b. NYC, Oct. 22, 1943; s. Leonard and Gladys (Steisel) T.; m. Elaine Lynn Isaacson, Mar. 28, 1971; children: Jamie Meredith, Seth Evan. BA, Queens Coll., NYC, 1965; MS, So. Ill. U., Carbondale, 1966; JD, Howard U., 1969; postgrad. U. Pitts., 1969-70. Bar: DC 1980. Press asst to Congressman Begich, Washington, 1971; legis. asst. to Congressman Halpern, Washington, 1972, Congressman Rinaldo, 1973; dir. legis. rsch. Cost of Living Council, Washington, 1973-74; asst. dir. govt. affairs Am. Nurses Assn., Washington, 1974-75; pres. Paul Tendler Assocs., Washington, 1975—; mng. ptnr. Tendler & Biggins, 1982-89; ptnr. Tendler, Goldberg, Biggins & Geltzer, 1989—; adj. prof. Georgetown U., 1980-83, asst. prof., 1975-80; dir. bus. program Trinity Coll., Washington, 1983-86. Author: The Federal Government at Work, 1976; An LPNs Guide to the Federal Government, 1978, 84. Ford Found. scholar, 1967-69. Mem. DC Bar Assn., Am. Arbitration Assn., ABA, Assn. Trial Lawyers Am., Delta Sigma Rho, Tau Kappa Alpha. Democrat. Jewish. Home and Office: 1090 Vermont Ave NW Washington DC 20005-4905

TENENBAUM, ANN G., art association administrator; b. Savannah, Ga., June 1961; m. Thomas H. Lee; children: Stephen Zachary, Robert Schiff. Grad. Sarah Lawrence Coll. Mem. vis. com. dept. photogs. Met. Mus. Art, 1996—2005, trustee, 2005—; vice chmn. bd. trustees Dia Art Found., NYC, 1994—2006. Co-pres. bd. trustees Film Soc. Lincoln Ctr. for Performing Arts; founding mem. bd. govs. Bard Coll. Ctr. Curatorial Studies; bd. dirs. Sarah Lawrence Coll., Channel 13/WNET, Studio Mus., Harlem, Second Stage Theatre, Guild Hall East Hampton; mem. chmn.'s coun. Mus. Modern Art. Named one of Top 200 Collectors, ARTnews mag., 2003—06; recipient Leo award, Ind. Curators Internat., 2003, Child Advocacy award, NYU Child Study Ctr., 2003. Avocation: Collector of Modern and contemporary art; Egyptian art. Office: c/o Met Mus Art 1000 5th Ave New York NY 10028

TENENBAUM, BERNARD HIRSH, entrepreneur, educator; b. Long Beach, NY, Dec. 23, 1954; s. Abraham Benjamin and Helen Pearl (Wahrhaft) T. BA, Columbia Coll., NYC, 1976; postgrad., Stanford U., Calif., 1976-77; MBA, U. Pa., Phila., 1981. Mgr. Lido Beach (N.Y.) Hotel, 1976-77; gen. mgr. Sound Spectrum, Huntington, N.Y., 1977-78; dir. Small Bus. Ctr., Phila., 1980-84; asst. dir. Entre Ctr., Phila., 1984-85, assoc. dir., 1986-88; prof. entrepreneurial studies, dir. Fairleigh Dickinson U., Madison, N.J., 1988-93; v.p. corp. devel. Russ Berrie & Co., Inc., 1993-97; pres. Children's Leisure Products Group, The Jordan Co., NYC, 1997—2003; mng. ptnr. China Cat Capital, LLC, 2006—. Cons. Phila. Phillies, 1984-85; bd. dirs. Syms, Unger Global, Franklin Mint. Del. Securities Exchange Commn. on Small Bus. Capital Formation, 1984-86; vice chmn. Small Bus. Devel. Ctr. adv. bd., Phila., 1983—; bd. dirs. Pvt. Industry Council, Phila., 1983-88; chmn. Small Bus. Fair, Phila., 1983-88. Mem. Phila. C. of C. (vice chmn. small bus. coun. 1982-86, chmn. 1986-88), Venture Assn. N.J. (v.p.). Democrat. Jewish. Avocations: swimming, sports car, music, literature, films. Office: Chldns Leisure Products LLC 71 Tamarack Cir Skillman NJ 08558 E-mail: bernie@btenenbaum.com.

TENENBAUM, INEZ MOORE, former school system administrator; b. Hawkinsville, GA, Mar. 8, 1951; m. Samuel J. Tenenbaum. BS in Edn., U. Ga., Athens, 1972, MSE in Edn., 1974; JD, U. S.C. Law Sch., Columbia, 1986. Tchr. Elementary Sch.; dir. rsch. S.C. House Reps., 1977-83; attorney Sinkler & Boye, P.A., 1986-92; supt. edn. S.C. Dept. Edn., Columbia, 1999—2007. Founder S.C. Ctr. Family Policy. *

TENENBAUM, JEFFREY S., lawyer; b. Boston, Oct. 29, 1968; BA, Univ. Pa., 1990; JD, Catholic Univ. Am., 1996. Bar: DC. Legis. asst. U.S. Ho. Reps., 1990—93; legal sect. mgr., govt. affairs analyst Am. Soc. Assn. Exec., Washington, 1993—95; of counsel Venable LLP, Washington, 1999—2003, ptnr., Nonprofit Assns., Trade & Profl. Assns. practices, 2003—. Spkr. in field. Author: Association Tax Compliance Guide; contbr. articles to profl. jours., magazines, newspapers; mem. editl. adv. bd. Assn. Law & Policy, 2000—, Nonprofit Tax & Financial Strategies, 1996—2002. Bd. dir. Fed. City Club Found. Named a Top Washington Lawyer, Washington Bus. Jour., 2004; named Outstanding Nonprofit Lawyer of Yr., Bus. Law Sect., ABA, 2006; recipient Chairman's award, Greater Washington Soc. Assn. Exec., 1997, Ctr. for Assn. Leadership, 2004. Mem.: Am. Soc. Assn. Exec. Office: Venable LLP 575 7th St NW Washington DC 20004 Office Phone: 202-344-8138. Office Fax: 202-344-8300. Business E-Mail: jstenenbaum@venable.com.

TENENBAUM, JOSEPH, cardiologist; b. Neptune, NJ, Feb. 11, 1946; s. Sol and Marilyn Tenenbaum; m. Marilou Faith Jones, May 19, 1978; 1 child, Mollie Rodriguez. BA, Brandeis U., 1968; MD, Harvard U., 1974. Diplomate Am. Bd. Internal Medicine, Am. Bd. Cardiology. Edgar Leifer clin. prof. medicine Columbia U., NYC, 1979—; attending physician, interim chair dept. medicine Presbyn. Hosp., NYC, 2001—03. Fellow Am. Coll. Cardiology; mem. Columbia Faculty Practice Orgn. (chmn. 2000-03) Office: 161 Fort Washington Ave New York NY 10032-3713 Office Phone: 212-305-5288. Business E-Mail: jt7@columbia.edu.

TENER, CAROL JOAN, retired secondary school educator, consultant; b. Cleve., Feb. 10, 1935; d. Peter Paul and Mamie Christine (Dombrowski) Manusack; m. Dale Keith Tener, Feb. 13, 1958 (div. Aug. 1991); children: Dean Robert, Susan Dawn Tener Belair. Student, Cleve. Mus. Art, 1948-53, Cleve. Art Inst., 1953-54; BS in Edn. cum laude, Kent State U., 1957; MS in Supervision, Akron U., 1974; postgrad., Kent State U., 1964, 81, 88-90, Akron U., 1975-79, John Carroll U., 1982, 83, 85-86, Ohio U., 1987, Baldwin Wallace Coll., 1989. Cert. permanent K-12 tchr., Ohio; cert. vol. counselor for Ohio sr. health ins. Office Dept. Ins. Stenographer Equitable Life Iowa, Cleve., 1953-54; tchr. elem. art Cuyahoga Falls (Ohio) Bd. Edn., 1957-58, 62-63, 65-68, tchr. jr. high sch., 1968-69; tchr. high sch. Brecksville (Ohio)-Broadview Heights Sch. Dist., 1969-94; chmn. dept. art Brecksville-Broadview Heights (Ohio) HS, 1979—94, chmn. curriculum devel., 1982, 1989, quality deployment team employee recognition district-wide bd. level, 1993—94; ret., 1994. Instr. for children Kent State U., 1956; advisor, prodr. cmty. svc. in art Brecksville Broadview Heights Bd. of Edn., 1969-94; former tchr. recreation and adult art edn. City of Cuyahoga Falls, 1967-68; com. mem. North Ctrl. evaluation com. Nordonia H.S., Nordonia City, Ohio, 1978, Solon H.S., Solon City, Ohio, 1989; chmn. north ctrl. evaluation com. Garfield Heights H.S., 1991; chair pilot program curriculum devel. com. in art/econs. Brecksville-Broadview Heights H.S., 1985-86, 86-87; spkr. in field. Contbr. articles to newspapers, brochures, mags.; commd. artist for mural Brecksville City's Kids Quarters, 1994, Christopher Columbus/John Glen portraits in relief commemorating Columbus Day, 1961, Wooster (Ohio) Products Co.; editor Greater Cleve. chpt. Ohio Ret. Tchrs. Assn., 1998-2002; contbr. to Resources for You, 2003, Ohio Sr. Health Ins. Info. Program, Ohio Dept. Ins., 2001—. Chmn. Artmart Invitational Exhibit PTA, 1982-94; active Meals on Wheels program in Brecksville and Broadview Hts., 1995-98, Heart Disease collection, 1995, Stow-Glen Assisted Living Visitations, 1994-95, NCR Assisted Living transp. provision to hosps. and dr. in neighboring county; trustee, sec. Gettysburg Devel. Block Group Parma, 1995-96, Kids Quarters, 1994; Med Save fraud vol. Cuyahoga County Dept. Sr. and Adult Svcs., 2000-2002, spkrs. bur.; sr. health ins. info. program, cert. vol. counselor of OSHIIP under the Dept. of Insurance, Ohio Dept. Ins., 2001-04—, vol. coord. spkr. and healthfair mktg., OSHIIP, 2004-05. Recipient Ohio Coun. on Econ. Edn. award, 1985-86, award for significant svc. to cmty. Ret. and Sr. Vol. Program of USA, 1996, Svc. award Greater Cleve. Chpt./Ohio Ret. Tchrs. Assn., 1998, Outstanding Svc. award Sr. Medicare Patrol Projects, Cert. of Appreciation, U.S. Dept. Health and Human Svcs. Adminstrn. on Aging, 2002; Pres.'s scholar Kent State U., 1954-57; Resolution to thank a Med-Save Project Vol. signed by Cuyahoga County Commrs. Tim McCormack, pres., Jimmy Dimora, v.p., and Peter Lawson Jones, commr. Mem.: NAFE, ASCD, NEA (life), AAUW, S.W. Area Ret. Educators (co-chair 1996—98, program chair 1996—98, program coord. 1999—2000), Nat. Mus. Women in Arts, Cleve. Mus. Art, Acad. Econ. Edn., Brecksville Edn. Assn., Internat. Platform Assn., Nat. Art Edn. Assn., Ohio Ret. Tchrs. Assn. (life; registration chair 1997—98, pres.-elect Cleve. chpt. 1998, program chair 1998, interim editor 1998, circulation mgr. 1998—2002, chpt. pres. 1999, editor 1999—2002, trustee 2000, guest spkr. on newsletter writing and pub. 2000, nominating chair 2000—01, by-law chair 2000—01, Pub. Rels. awards 1999—2002), Phi Delta Kappa Pi. Roman Catholic. Avocations: photography, collecting books on architecture, painting. Home: 7301 Sagamore Rd Parma OH 44134-5732 Home Phone: 440-885-2231; Office Phone: 440-885-2231.

TENET, GEORGE JOHN, diplomacy professor, former CIA director; b. Flushing, NY, Jan. 5, 1953; m. A. Stephanie Glakas; 1 child, John Michael BS in Fgn. Svc., Georgetown U., 1976; MIA, Columbia U., 1978. Legis. asst. to Sen. H. John Heinz III Senate Select Com. on Intelligence, Washington, 1985-86, designee to vice chair Sen. Patrick J. Leahy, 1986-89, dir. oversight of arms control negotiations Soviet Union/US, 1989-93, staff dir. to chmn. Senator David Boren, 1993; mem. presdl. transition team Nat. Security Coun., Washington, 1993-95, spl. asst. to pres., sr. dir. intelligence programs, 1995-97; dep. dir. CIA, Washington, 1995-96, acting dir., 1996-97, dir., 1997—2004; prof. diplomacy Georgetown U., Washington, 2004—. Sr. rsch. assoc. Inst. for the Study of Diplomacy, Washington, 2004—; bd. dir. Viisage, 2005—; ind. non-exec. dir. QinetiQ, 2006—. Author: At the Center of the Storm: My Years at the CIA, 2007 Recipient Presdl. Medal of Freedom, Pres. George W. Bush, 2004. Office: Inst for the Study of Diplomacy 1316 36th St NW Washington DC 20007 Office Phone: 202-687-8209.

TEN EYCK, DOROTHEA FARISS, real estate agent; b. Pulaski County, Va., Dec. 2, 1923; d. Orel Cronk and Esther Mildred (Rexrode) Fariss; m. George Ten Eyck, Jan. 4, 1947 (dec.); m. John S. Kreeger, Aug. 27, 1965 (dec.); m. Robert L. Ten Eyck, Oct. 30, 1994; 6 children Student, Ind. U. Market rsch. Proctor & Gamble, Cin., 1944-47; ptnr. Santee Builders, 1960—63. Pres. women's com. Cin. Art Mus., mem. adv. com., docent emeritus; mem. Elder Indian Hill Ch. Independent. Presbyterian. Avocations: golf, gardening, travel, volunteerism. Home: 3032 Alpine Ter Cincinnati OH 45208-2925

TENGEL, JEFFREY J., bank executive; B in Acctg., Marquette U., Milw.; MBA, Case Western Res. U., Cleve. Corp. mgmt. trainee Nat. City Corp., 1986, various positions in corp. banking, mergers and acquisitions, credit, structured fin. divsn. mid. market corp. banking group, chief credit officer Wholesale Banking, chief credit officer, exec. v.p. comml. banking - nat. Mem. adv. com. Case Western Res. U. Office: Nat City Corp Nat City Ctr 1900 E Ninth St Cleveland OH 44114-3484 Office Phone: 216-222-2000. *

TENGLUND, ANN M., librarian; d. Carl Arnold and Alice Taylor Tenglund. MS in Edn., St. Bonaventure U., NY; MLS, Syracuse U., NY, 1999; postgrad., Nova Southeastern U., Ft. Lauderdale, Fla., 2006—. Cert. K-12 reading tchr. NY, N-6 elem. tchr. NY, 7-12 bus. edn. tchr. NY. Libr. St. Bonaventure U., St. Bonaventure, NY, 1982—. Presenter in field. Treas. Immanuel Luth. Ch., Olean, NY, 1993—2006. Mem.: ALA, Am. Ednl. Rsch. Assn., Assn. Study Higher Edn., Assn. Instl. Rsch., Assn.Coll. and Rsch. Librs. (com. mem. 2003—04). Office: St Bonaventure U 3261 West State Rd Saint Bonaventure NY 14778 Home Phone: 716-372-4085; Office Phone: 716-375-2378. Office Fax: 716-375-2389. Business E-Mail: ateng@sbu.edu.

TENHOEVE, THOMAS, academic administrator; b. Bklyn., Oct. 1, 1935; s. Thomas and Adeline Ruth (Vander Hill) T.; m. Suzanne Underwood, June 7, 1957; children: Thomas III, Carol, Timothy. AB, Hope Coll., 1956; MA, U. Mich., 1957; PhD, U. Toledo, 1965; postgrad., U. Western Mich.; EdD (hon.), Northwestern Coll., 1995. Biology tchr. South Haven, Mich. Pub. Schs., 1957-58; biology instr. Northwestern Coll., Orange City, Iowa, 1958-63; supr. biology student tchrs. U. Toledo, Ohio, 1963-65; acad. dean, acting pres. Northwestern Coll., Orange City, 1965-70; pres. Butler (Pa.) County Community Coll., 1970-84, Oakton Community Coll., Des Plaines, Ill., 1984-95. Dir. CoVest Banc, 1987—99. Bd. dirs. Sister Cities Internat., 1986-95, 1998-2004, nat. v.p., treas., 2001-04; trustee Northwestern Coll., 1988-95; mem. Ill. C.C. State Found. Bd., 1993-95, Ill. Math. and Sci. Acad. Selection Bd., 1986, 87, Cook County Sheriff's Scholarship Panel; exec. com. Golden Corridor, 1986-92; vol. Good Samaritan Ministries, 2001-. Recipient Pacesetter award Nat. Coun. for Community Rels., 1986, Orchard Village award, Skyway Conf. Hall of Fame. Mem. Am. Coun. on Internat. Intercultural Edn. (chmn. 1992-95), Coun. North Ctrl. Two-Yr. Colls. (state rep. 1988-92, exec. bd. 1989-95, 2d v.p. 1990-91, 1st v.p. 1991-92, pres. 1992-93).

TENKOTTE, PAUL ALLEN, history and international studies educator; b. Covington, Ky., June 30, 1960; s. Harry Vincent and Mary Margaret (Meier) T. BA in History, Thomas More Coll., 1982; MA in History, U. Cin., 1983, PhD in History, 1989. Charles P. Taft fellow U. Cin., 1982, 1984, 1985, grad. asst. Carl Blegen Libr., 1983, Lenore McGrane fellow, 1986—87; prof. history Thomas More Coll., Crestview Hills, Ky., 1987—, dir. internat. studies, 1991—2001, 2003—, dir. emeritus internat. studies, 2005—. Regional coord. 3 U.S. Congl. dists for Nat. Bicentennial Competition on the Constn. and Bill of Rights, Ctr. for Civic Edn., 1987-89. Author: A Heritage of Art and Faith; co-editor: The Encyclopedia of Northern Kentucky Project, 2003-, contbr. articles to profl. jours. and encyclopedias. Active Miami Purchase Assn. Historic Preservation, Cin., 1985-92; v.p. governing bd., 1987-89; trustee Internat. Visitors Coun. Greater Cin., 2000-2001; mem. Ky. Underground R.R. Adv. Com., 1997-2002; mem. Ky. Abraham Lincoln Bicentennial Commn. Adv. Coun., 2005—; mem. bd. trustees Behringer-Crawford Mus., 2006—. Groesbeck scholar for historic preservation Nat. Soc. Colonial Dames Am. in Ohio, 1986; Cultural Exch. grantee Japan Travel Bur., 1991; recipient Thomas More Coll. Alumni Assn., 1999. Mem. Dinsmore Homestead Found. (adv. coun. 1989-92), Kenton County Hist. Soc. (v.p. 1981-82, pres. 1982), Phi Alpha Theta (Dr. A.F. Zimmerman scholar 1982, Dr. John Pine scholar 1985). Avocations: photography, architecture, bicycling, travel. Office: Thomas More Coll 333 Thomas More Pky Covington KY 41017-3428 Home Phone: 859-426-1776; Office Phone: 859-426-1776. E-mail: nkyencyclopedia@fuse.net.

TENNANT, JOHN RANDALL, management consultant; b. North Bend, Wash., Aug. 23, 1940; s. Maurice Andrew and Jane Downing (Vinnedge) T.; m. Nikki Mae Priem, July 17, 1965 (div.); children: Ann Elizabeth, Randall Warren; m. Deborah Ann Francis, Oct. 25, 1986 (div.); 1 child, Alyssa Jane; m. Carol A. McDonnell, Feb. 2, 2005. BS in Indsl. Engring., Stanford U., 1962; MBA, U. Wash., 1966. Registered profl. engr., Wash. Sr. rsch. engr. Boeing Co., Seattle, 1962-68; mgr. Price Waterhouse, Seattle, 1968-73, ptnr. Tokyo, 1973-79, Los Angeles, 1979-89; founder, CEO, Manex, Inc., Newport Beach, Calif., 1989—; dir. subs. Price Waterhouse Assocs., Pacific region, 1975-79. Mem. John Tracy Clinic Men's Com., Santa Catalina Island Conservancy, pres., 1985-87; capt. Long Beach Mounted Police. Mem. NSPE, Japan Computer Assn. (founder, pres. 1976-77), Japan Modapts Assn. (founder), Japan Am. Soc., Inst. Mgmt. Cons., Am. Inst. Indsl. Engrs. (pres. Seattle chpt. 1970-71), Data Processing Mgmt. Assn., Tokyo Lawn and Tennis Club, L.A. Country Club, Jonathan Club, Empty Saddle Club, Los Rancheros Visitadores Club, Los Caballeros Club. Home: 332 Sunset Ct Oak View CA 93022 Office Phone: 310-618-0299. Personal E-mail: tennantrjohn@aol.com.

TENNANT, THOMAS MICHAEL, lawyer; b. Anniston, Ala., July 23, 1948; s. Thomas Edward and Mary Eugenia (Warren) T.; m. Sharon Leigh Ebert, Mar. 21, 1970; children: Sharon Michelle, Michael Ebert. BS, Auburn U., 1970; JD, Walter F. George Sch. Law, 1973. Assoc. Webb, Fowler & Tanner, Lawrenceville, Ga., 1973-76, ptnr., 1976-77; mng. ptnr. Tennant, Andersen & Davidson, P.C., Lawrenceville, 1978-81, Tennant, Andersen, Davidson & Edmondson, P.C., Lawrenceville, 1982-85, Tennant, Davidson & Edmondson, P.C., Lawrenceville, 1985-86, Tennant, Davidson & Thompson, P.C., Lawrenceville, 1986-87, Tennant, Davidson, Thompson & Sweeny, Lawrenceville, 1987-89, Tennant, Thompson & Sweeny, 1990; ptnr., environ. land use group Alston & Bird LLP, Atlanta, 1991—. Judge Recorder's Ct., Lawrenceville, 1979-80; mem. State Disciplinary Bd., 1988-91. Chmn. bd. trustees Leadership Gwinnett; bd. dirs. Rsch. Atlanta, Inc., Regional Leadership Found., Cmty. Found. N.E. Ga., Inc., Lawrenceville, 1984—. Served to 1st lt. US Army, 1970—78. Mem. Atlanta Bar Assn., State Bar Ga. (chmn. lawyer ethics com. young lawyers sect. 1979-80, bd. govs. 1986-92), Gwinnett County Bar Assn. (pres. 1978), Atlanta Lawyers Club, Gwinnett County C. of C. (pres. 1986). Presbyterian. Office: Alston & Bird One Atlantic Ctr 1201 Peachtree St Atlanta GA 30309-3400 Office Phone: 404-881-7838. E-mail: mtennant@alston.com.

TENNEN, LESLIE IRWIN, lawyer, consultant; b. Toronto, Aug. 26, 1952; came to U.S., 1961; s. Edward and Elsie (Liberbaum) T.; m. Patricia MargaretSterns. BA with distinction, U. Ariz., Tucson, 1973, JD, 1976; Mount Scopus, Hebrew U., Jerusalem, 1975. Bar: Ariz. 1977, US Dist. Ct. Ariz. 1979, US Ct. Appeals (9th cir.) 2007. Sole practice, Tucson, 1977—79; ptnr. Sterns and Tennen, Phoenix, 1979—. Cons. internat. law and aerospace activities; lectr. univs., colls. and law schs.; mem. Ariz. Space Commn., 1994-2000, also profl. aviation and aerospace congresses and seminars in N.Am., Europe, Asia, S.Am., Australia; judge Jessup Internat. Moot Court Competition, 1982, 83, 85, 92; dir., treas. Assn. US Mems. Internat. Inst. Space Law; com. mem. U. Belarusian Culture Internat. Orgn. Mem. editl bd. Space Regulations Libr.; contbr. Ariz. Law Rev., 1975-76; contbr. articles to profl. jours. Precinct committeeman State Dem. Conv., 1972-73. Received highest score Ariz. Bar Exam., Feb. 1977. Mem. AIAA (sr.), Ariz. Bar Found., Internat. Eurasian Acad. Scis., Internat. Inst. Space Law (Appreciation award 1998, Disting. Svc. award 2006), Internat. Acad. Astronautics, Am. Soc. Internat. Law, Soc. Aerospace Communicators Inc., Internat. Law Assn., Planetary Soc., Fedn. Aerospace Socs. in Tucson (exec. bd.). Office: 849 N 3rd Ave Phoenix AZ 85003-1408 Office Phone: 602-254-5197. Business E-Mail: LTennen@astrolaw.com.

TENNENBAUM, MICHAEL ERNEST, investor; b. St. Petersburg, Fla., Sept. 17, 1935; s. Reubin and Frieda (Miller) T.; m. Suzanne Stockfisch; children by previous marriage: Mark Stephen, Andrew Richard. BS, Ga. Inst. Tech., 1958; MBA with honors, Harvard U., 1962. Assoc. Burnham & Co., NYC, 1962-64, Bear, Stearns & Co., NYC, 1964-69, sr. mng. dir., 1969-96, vice chmn. investment banking divsn., 1988-93; chmn. bd. dirs. Tech. Park, Atlanta, 1978-81; sr. mng. ptnr. Tennenbaum Capital Ptnrs., LLC, LA, 1996—. Bd. dirs. Pemco Aviation Group, chmn.; bd. dirs. Anacomp, Inc.; chmn. LA World Affairs Coun., WinCnp; founder Tennenbaum Inst. Enterprise Transformation, Ga. Tech. Sch. Indsl. and Systems Engring., Tennenbaum Interdisciplinary Ctr. Neuropsychiatric Inst. UCLA. Bd. govs., vice chmn. Boys and Girls Clubs Am.; mem. nat. adv. bd. Ga. Inst. Tech., 1971-77; mem. vis. com. Harvard U. Sch. Bus., Cambridge, Mass., 1986-92, bd. assocs., 1992—; trustee emeritus Ga. Tech. Found., Inc., Atlanta, 1988-96; bd. dirs. Joffrey Ballet, 1990-92, chmn. exec. com., 1991-92; bd. dirs. Music Ctr. LA County Unified Fund Cabinet, 1990-91; bd. vistiors UCLA Sch. Medicine, 2000-; chmn. LA Mayor's Spl. Adv. Com. on Fiscal Adminstrn., 1993-94, Calif. High Speed Rail Authority, 1998-2001; commr. Calif. Intercity HighSpeed Ground Transp. Commn. Home: 118 Malibu Colony Rd Malibu CA 90265-4642 Office: Tennenbaum Capital Partners Llc 2951 28th St Ste 1000 Santa Monica CA 90405-2993 Office Phone: 310-899-4950, 310-566-1001. *The older I get, the luckier I feel.*

TENNEY, DUDLEY BRADSTREET, retired lawyer; b. NYC, July 13, 1918; s. Parker Gillespie and Josephine (Keeler) T.; m. Margaret Carter, June 13, 1941 (div. Oct. 1977); children: Ann, Janet Greene; m. Dorothy Walsh, Jan. 7, 1978 (dec. Sept. 1982); m. Joyce McPherson, Jan. 4, 1986. AB summa cum laude, Oberlin Coll., 1939; JD magna cum laude, Harvard U., 1942. Bar: N.Y. 1948. Assoc. firm Cahill, Gordon & Reindel, NYC, 1946-54, ptnr., 1955-86. Pres.: Harvard U. Law Rev., 1941-42. Served to maj. AUS, 1942-46, CBI. Mem. ABA, Assn. Bar City of N.Y., World Trade Ctr. Club (N.Y.C.), Manhasset Bay Yacht Club (Port Washington, N.Y.). Home: 25 Wood Rd Sands Point NY 11050-2625 Office: Cahill Gordon & Reindel 80 Pine St Fl 17 New York NY 10005-1790

TENNEY, FRANK PUTNAM, marketing executive; b. Orono, Maine, Oct. 6, 1937; s. Carl Bither and Velma May (Williamson) T.; m. Margaret Anne Seymour, Apr. 23, 1960; children: Jane Dossiere, Carl B., Janet M., Alan F., Janice M. Lovell. Cert. notary public, Maine. Nat. sales mgr. Shaw & Tenney Oar & Paddle Co., Orono, 1958—68; sales mgr. George D. Wetherill, Phila., 1968—69; with R.M. Flagg, Veazie, Maine, 1968—69; salesman DuBois Chem., Cin., 1969—76; Maine sales mgr. Rochester Midland Co., NY, 1976—82; with H.A. Manning Co., Bellows Falls, Vt., 1982—86; dist. sales mgr. U.S. West Mktg. Resources, Loveland, Colo., 1986—90; sales mgr. City Directory, Inc., Belmond, Iowa, 1990—92; with RAK Industries, 1993; v.p. Maine Mktg. Resources, Brewer, Maine, 1994—. Adv. bd. Salvation Army. Tech. sgt. Maine ANG, 1955-87, ret. Mem.: KC (past grand knight Pine Cone coun., 4th degree, past faithful navigator Pine Cone assembly), VFW (pub. chmn., sr. vice comdr., past comdr. post 1761), Greater Bangor C. of C., Golden Cir. (Averill plaque), 40/8 (chef de Gare), Profl. Sales Club Bangor, Am. Legion (Americanism officer 1997, post comdr. 1999—2000, ADF 2001—, past vice comdr. II, patriotic instr. VFW). Republican. Roman Catholic.

TENNEY, JANE MORRIS, real estate developer; d. Mendel Morris and Floreine Welch; m. Mark William Tenney, June 1, 1974; m. Daniel Marston Shepherd, Mar. 16, 1957 (div.); children: Daniel Vincent Shepherd, David Morris Shepherd. BS, U. Ky., 1962. Sales rep. IBM, South Bend, 1975—80; pres. Technivest, Inc., South Bend, Ind., 1980—88; mgr. bus. incubator Control Data, South Bend, 1984—89; owner, pres. Tenney Assocs., Inc, Niles, Mich., 1992—. Land developer Longmeadow Residential and Comml. Cmty., Niles, Mich., 1997—. Elected del. White Ho. Conf. of Small Bus., Washington, 1984—84. Recipient Demonstration Project on Watershed Devel. Design, Conservation Fund, 1997, Women of Yr., Four Flags C. of C., 2003. Mem.: Nat. Assn. of Realtor, Nat. Home Builders Assn. Office: Tenney Assocs Inc 126 Churchill Ln Niles MI 49120 E-mail: sales@longmeadow.info.

TENNEY, SARAH G., music educator; b. NYC, Apr. 30, 1948; d. John Wool Griswold and Margaret Brett Tenney. BA, Bennington Coll., 1971; MusM, New Eng. Conservatory, 1976. Founder Spectrum Young Audiences Trio, Boston, 1976-80; marimba, percussion tchr. Rivers Music Sch., Weston, Mass., 1976-80, 85—, St. Ann's Sch., Bklyn., 1980-85; founder, dir. Marimba Magic, Weston, 1987—; tchr. improvisation Northeastern U., Boston, 1991-95. Percussionist on 6 Revel records; percussionist/timpanist in Christmas Revels, 1980—; presenter in field. Composer: (composition/musical) Gamelon Dream, 1989, Mysterious Waltz, 1991, Whole Tone Dream, 1996, Adventures, 1999, Machines, 2000, Jaja Mani Dreams, 2001, Drum Circle, 2002, 3 Canons, 2003, Moving Music, 2004, More Moving Music, 2005. Concert performer Concerts for Children, 1976-80, Cambridge World's Fair, 1997, 98, Clarimba Duo, 2002—03, WCRB Cartoonfest, Symphony Hall, 2005. Recipient Am. Composers Forum grant. Mem. Music Tchrs. Nat. Assn. (conf. presenter 1991), Musicians Union, Music Educators Nat. Conf. (presenter ea. conf. 1992, 96), Percussive Arts Soc. (presenter internat. conv. 1989, 97), Orff Schulwerk Assn. (presenter nat. conf. 1996) presenter European Piano Tchrs. Assn., Internat. Conf., Budapest, 2000, Internat. Marimba Conf., Belgium, 1992. Office: The Rivers Music Sch 337 Winter St Weston MA 02493-1072 Office Phone: 781-235-6840. E-mail: marimba_magic@mac.com.

TENNIES, ROBERT HUNTER, headmaster; b. Bogotá, Colombia, Aug. 19, 1952; s. Leo C. and Ruth (Winston) T.; m. Ruth Ellen Fischer, June 14, 1975; children: Debbie, Julie. BS, Wheaton Coll., Ill., 1973; MA, U. South Fla., 1975; EdS, Fla. Atlantic U., 1978, EdD, 1982. Sci. tchr. Cypress Lake Middle Sch., Ft. Myers, Fla., 1973-77, Boca Raton (Fla.) Christian Sch., 1977-78, asst. adminstr., 1978-84, headmaster, 1984—, min. of children, 1984-90; interim. min. of edn., 1991-93. Spkr. Internat. Conf. Religious Edn., Petrozavodsk, Russia; mem. Nat. Rev. Panel Blue Ribbon Schs., 1999. Recipient Excellence in Edn. award Nat. Assn. Elem. Prins., 1990, 97. Mem. Nat. Sci. Tchrs. Assn., Assn. of Christian Schs. Internat. (chair Fla. accreditation commn.), Nat. Assn. Elem. Sch. Prins. Avocation: camping. Home: 2415 NW 30th Rd Boca Raton FL 33431-6214 Office: Boca Raton Christian Sch 315 NW 4th St Boca Raton FL 33432-3739 Office Phone: 561-391-2727. Business E-Mail: bocachristian@bocachristian.org.

TENNIHILL, SALLY KAY, writer, music educator; b. Columbus, Feb. 14, 1941; d. Wayne Harris and Ruth Anne Downs; m. Jack Tennihill (dec.), Oct. 17, 1961; children: John, Ralph, Myrtle, Joe. Student, Ohio State U., 1959—61; BA in English, Northwest Mo. State U., 1985, MA in English, 1987. Tchr. piano, Maryville, Mo., 1970—; cert. nurse asst. Nodaway Nursing Home, Maryville, Mo., 1982-84; grad. asst. Northwest Mo. State U., Maryville, Mo., 1985-86, tchg. asst., 1986-87; substitute tchr. St. Joseph (Mo.) Sch. Bd., 1988-93; stringer St. Joseph News-Press, 1988-92. Mem. Univ. Players, 1982—85. Actor: Mid Summer Night's Dream, 1982, Texas Trilogy, 1983, Ten Little Indians, 1990, Do Not Disturb, 1994; dir.: Nodaway County Theatre Co., 1991—96, Everybody Loves Opal, 1996; author: (one act musical, romantic comedy) Steak, Potatoes and a Little Romance, 1995; editor: (creative mag.) Envy's Sting, 1985—86; contbr. poems and short stories to books/anthologies. Mem. Coalition Against Domestic Violence, Maryville, Mo., 1987-96, Prison Fellowship, Maryville, 1996, Willa Cather Found., Maryville, 1993-96; head Women's Resource Ctr. Northwest Mo. U., Maryville, 1984-87; pres. M.S. Support Group, Maryville, 1995-96; v.p. Nodaway County Civil War Roundtable, pres. 1996-2002. Recipient Mattie Dykes Creative Writer scholarship, Presdl. Scholar's scholarship. Mem. AAUW, Retired Tchrs. Maryville, Sons and Daus. of the Civil War, NW Mo. Multiple Sclerosis Support Group. Home: 123 Park Ave Maryville MO 64468-1347

TENNIMON, DANNIE EARL, academic administrator, educator; b. Selma, Ala., Mar. 15, 1947; s. Earl and Mary Tennimon; m. Lori Dee Krehbiel, Feb. 7, 1991; m. Kathy Leann McCowan, Aug. 31, 1968 (div. Feb. 1, 1991); children: Tara Lee Faulkner, Shelby Danielle, Brandi Kay Miller, Shandon Earl. BA, Auburn U., Ala., 1970; MEd, Boston U., 1975; MA in Tchg., Troy State U., 1995. Commd. lt. U.S. Army, 1970, advanced through grades to lt. col., 1988, ret., 1994; asst. to pres. Troy State U., Montgomery, Ala., 1996—2004; coord. instl. rsch., effectiveness and planning Troy U., Montgomery, 2004—. Adj. instr. history Troy U., Montgomery, 1998—; presenter in field. Deacon Millbrook Presbyn. Ch., Ala., 1996—2001, ruling elder, 2001—. Decorated Bronze Star with oak leaf cluster U.S. Army, Meritorious Svc. award with 2 oak leaf clusters, Joint Svc. Meritorious Svc. award. Mem.: Soc. Coll. and U. Planning (assoc.), Assn. Instnl. Rsch. (assoc.), So. Assn. Instnl. Rsch. (assoc.), Ala. Assn. Instnl. Rsch. (assoc.; pres. 2003—04), Gamma Beta Phi (assoc.). Avocations: travel, backpacking, military history. Home: 46 Pine Mountain Court Millbrook AL 36054 Office: Troy University PO Drawer 4419 Montgomery AL 36103-4419 Home Phone: 334-285-1257; Office Phone: 334-241-9536. Office Fax: 334-241-8619; Home Fax: 334-285-1257. Personal E-mail: ltennimon@yahoo.com. Business E-Mail: dtennimon@troy.edu.

TENNISON, LYNDEN, rail transportation executive; m. Sue Tennison; 1 child. B. U. Tex., Arlington. Various mgmt. and tech. positions AT&T and Southwestern Bell Tel., 1979—87; with SABRE divsn. Am. Airlines; with Union Pacific Corp., Omaha, 1992—, pres., CEO Nexterna, 1998—2001, v.p. info. techs., chief tech. officer Union Pacific RR, 2001—05, sr. v.p., chief info. officer, 2005—. Bd. dirs. Applied Distbn. Group. Office: Union Pacific Corp 1400 Douglas St Omaha NE 68179 Office Phone: 402-544-5000. *

TENNYSON, PETER JOSEPH, lawyer; b. Winona, Minn., Mar. 18, 1946; s. Richard Harvey and Sylvia Josephine (Jadrich) T.; m. Mary Eileen Fay, Jan. 3, 1970; children: Mark Christian, Rachel Christine, Matthew Patrick, Erica Ruth. BA, Purdue U., 1968; JD, U. Va., 1975. Bar: Calif. Assoc. atty. O'Melveny & Myers, LA, 1975-82; v.p., gen. counsel Cannon Mills Co., Kannapolis, NC, 1982-84; ptnr. Stradling, Yocca, Newport Beach, Calif., 1984-89, Jones, Day, Reavis & Pogue, Irvine, Calif., 1990-95, Paul, Hastings, Janofsky & Walker, Costa Mesa, Calif., 1995—. Mem. Calif. Commn. on Future of Legal Profession and State Bar, 1994; lectr. in field. Mem. adv. bd. St. Joseph Hosp., Orange, Calif., 1987-; bd. dirs. Lincoln Club Orange County, 1991-93, South Coast Symphony, 1989-92; mem. found. bd. Orange County H.S. Arts. Capt. US Army, 1968—72. Named one of Best Lawyers in Am., 2006—07; recipient Attys. of Yr. award, Calif. Lawyer, 2003. Mem.: Orange County Bar Assn., South Coast Repertory Silver Circle, Performing Arts Bus. Alliance. Roman Catholic. Avocations: downhill skiing, swimming. Home: 19 Monaco Newport Beach CA 92660 Office: Paul Hastings Janofsky & Walker LLP 695 Town Center Dr Fl 17 Costa Mesa CA 92626-1924 Office Phone: 714-668-6237. Business E-Mail: petertennyson@paulhastings.com.

TENORIO, PEDRO A., resident representative; b. Saipan; BA in Geology, U. Hawaii, MS in Hydrology. Sen. for Northern Marianas Congress of Micronesia, 1972—74; mem. Northern Marianas Polit. Status Commn., 1973—76; exec. dir. Northern Marianas Office Transition Studies and Planning, 1975—77, Marianas Pub. Land Corp., 1977—81; legis. adv. 1st Commonwealth of Northern Mariana Islands (CNMI) Legislature, 1977—81; lt. gov. CNMI, 1981—89; resident rep. CNMI U.S. Ho. of Reps., Washington, 2001—. Mem. Rep. Nat. Com. and Presdl. Victory Team. Mem.: Nat. Rep. Club Capitol Hill, Lions Club East Manoa. Republican. Office: Resident Rep US Ho of Reps 2121 R St NW Washington DC 20008 also: PO Box 504959 Saipan MP 96950 *

TENPAS, RONALD JAY, federal agency administrator, former prosecutor; b. 1963; m. Kathryn Dunn; children: Nathaniel, William. BA with hons., Mich. State U., 1985; degree in Philosophy, Politics and Econs., Oxford U., Eng., 1987; JD, U. Va., 1990. Law clk. to Hon. Louis H. Pollak U.S. Dist. Ct. (ea. dist.) Pa., 1990—91; law clk. to Chief Justice William H. Rehnquist U.S. Supreme Ct., Washington, 1991—92; law clk. to Hon. Howard Holtzmann Iran-U.S. Claims Tribunal, The Hague, Netherlands, 1992—93; assoc. Carlton Fields, P.A., Tampa, Fla., 1993—97; asst. US atty. (mid. dist.) Fla. US Dept. Justice, 1997—99, asst. U.S. atty. Md., 1999—2003, branch chief Dist. Md. So. Divsn., 2001—03, interim US atty. (so. dist.) Ill., 2003—05, US atty. (so. dist.) Ill., 2005, assoc. dep. atty. gen., 2005—. Editor: Va. Law Rev. Rhodes scholarship, 1985—87, Hardy Cross Dillard scholarship, 1987—90. Office: US Dept Justice 950 Pennsylvania Ave NW Washington DC 20530 E-mail: ronald.tenpas@usdoj.gov. *

TENSER, BETH HILLARY, graphics designer, art director; b. Balt., Nov. 11, 1968; d. David Elliott and Myrna Pruzon Tenser. BA, Adelphi U., 1991; MA, NY Inst. Tech., 1993. Dir. art Island Art & Restoration, Elmont, NY, 1991—96, Bond Distbg. Co., Balt., 1997—. Poster Competition, 1989, Liver Let Die, 1991. Pres. Adelphi's Resident Student Assn., Garden City, NY, 1989—91. Recipient Academic Excellence in Leadership, Provosts, 1991. Mem.: The Babe Ruth Mus. Democrat. Avocations: singing, sports, travel, photography. Home: 2 High Stepper Ct #102 Baltimore MD 21208 Home Phone: 410-484-9616; Office Phone: 443-418-1060. Personal E-mail: btenser@bcpl.net.

TENTZERIS, EMMANOUIL MANOS, engineering educator, researcher; b. Athens, Greece, Mar. 20, 1970; came to U.S., 1992; s. Markos E. Tentzeris and Irene M. Tentzeri. Diploma summa cum laude, Nat. Tech. U. Athens, 1992; MSc, U. Mich., 1993, PhD, 1998. Assoc. prof. Ga. Inst. Tech., Atlanta, 1998—2004. Invited prof. Tech. U. Munich, Germany, 2002; assoc. dir. for RF rsch. and RF Alliance Leader NSF-GT-Packaging Rsch. Ctr., 1998; broadband tech. hardware, subthrust leader Ga. Electronics Design Ctr. Initiative of State of Ga., 2000; chair CEM-TD Symposium, 2005; tech. program co-chair Automatic Radio Frequency Techniques Group, Atlanta, 1999; vice-chair IEEE-Components Packaging and Mfg. Tech. Tech. Com. 16 Radio Frequency/Wireless. Author: (with others) Advances Computational FM, 1998, Electronic Packaging, 2000, The RF and Microwave Handbook, 2001, Microwave and RF Product Applications, 2003, Encyclopedia of RF Microwave, 2004, Si RF Handbook, 2005; reviewer in field. Recipient Best Paper award, Internat. Microelectronics and Packaging Soc. Symposium, 1997, Applied Computational Electromagnetics Soc. Symposium, 2001, 2002, Career award NSF, 2000, Ga. Tech.-ECE Outstanding Jr. Faculty award 2002; Greek Acad. Excellence fellow Greek Dept. Edn., 1988-92; Papastavridios Greek Math Excellence fellow Greek Govt., 1989. Mem. IEEE (sr., Outstanding Young Engr. award 2003, MTT-AP Atlanta chpt., chmn. bd. com. 2002, tech. session chair 1996, 2000-2005, chair steering com.1998), Ga. Tech. Wireless Inst., Tech. Chamber of Greece. Avocations: sports, history books, travel. Home: 195 14th St #1208 Atlanta GA 30309 Office: Ga Inst Tech Sch ECE 777 Atlantic Dr Atlanta GA 30332-0250 Office Phone: 404-385-0378.

TENUTA, LUIGIA, lawyer; b. Madison, Wis., June 4, 1954; d. Eugene P. and Nancy (Gardner) T. AB in Internat. Studies with honors, Miami U., Oxford, Ohio, 1976; JD, Capital U., 1981; postgrad., Pontifical Coll. Josephinum, 1987-88. Bar: Ohio 1981. With internat. mktg. dept. Dresser Industries, Columbus, Ohio, 1976-80, analyst strategic planning, 1980, mgr. internat bus. planning Stratford, Conn., 1981; pvt. practice law Columbus, 1981—. Former mem. devel. com. Miami U. Mem. Ohio Bar Assn., Columbus Bar Assn. Roman Catholic. Office: 6400 Riverside Dr Dublin OH 43017-5197

TEPE, THOMAS M., JR., lawyer; b. Cin., June 16, 1972; BA, Ohio State U., 1995; JD, Mich. State U. Detroit Coll. Law, 1999. Bar: Ohio 1999, US Dist. Ct. Southern Dist. Ohio 1999, US Ct. of Appeals Sixth Cir. 2001. Ptnr. Keating Muething & Klekamp PLL, Cin. Trustee Starfire Coun. Greater Cin., Inc.; com. mem. Bus. Devel. and Permit Ctr. Adv., Cin. Named one of Ohio's Rising Stars, Super Lawyers, 2005, 2006. Mem.: Ohio State Bar Assn., Cin. Bar Assn. Office: Keating Muething & Klekamp PLL One E Fourth St Ste 1400 Cincinnati OH 45202 Office Phone: 513-639-3947. Office Fax: 513-579-6457.

TEPLER, JEFFREY, oncologist; b. Bronx, NY, 1958; BA, Yeshiva U., 1982; MD, Yale U. Sch. Medicine, 1982. Cert. Internal Medicine, Oncology, Hematology. Intern, internal medicine NY Weill Cornell Med. Ctr., 1982—83, resident, hematologic oncology, 1983—85, fellow, 1985—88; mem. staff NY Presbyn. Hosp.-Columbia U. Coll. Physicians & Surgeons & Weill Med. Coll. Cornell U., 1988—; instr. Cornell U. Med. Sch., NYC, 1988—2004, clin. asst. prof. medicine, 2004—. Named Best Oncologist, New York Press. Office: 310 E 72nd St New York NY 10021 Office Phone: 212-650-1780. Office Fax: 212-737-4329. *

TEPLINSKY, JOEL JACK, plastic surgeon; b. Milw., Wis., Apr. 12, 1939; s. George and Dorothy Teplinsky; m. Arleen Green Teplinsky, June 20, 1965; children: David Adam, Aimee Jill. BS, U. Wis., Madison, 1961, MD, 1965. Internship Herrick Meml. Hosp., Berkeley, Calif., 1965—66; residency Langley Porter NPI U. Calif., San Francisco, 1966—67; residency gen. surgery Fresno County Hosp., Calif., 1969—72; resident, chief gen. surgery Kaiser Found. Hosp., Panorama City, Calif., 1972—75; resident, chief plastic surgery Baylor Coll. Medicine, Houston, 1975—77; pvt. practice Encino, Calif., 1977—. Attending staff, plastic surgery dept. U. Calif. LA, 1978—. Editor: Journal International College of Surgeons,

2002—. Chmn. resident tng. Sherman Oaks Burn Ctr., 1983—98. Capt. USAF, 1967—69, Wichita Falls, Tex. Fellow: Internat. Coll. Surgeons (pres. US section. 2003—04), Am. Coll. Surgeons. Avocations: travel, ventriloquist, bible, philatalist. Office: 16161 Ventura Blvd 838 Encino CA 91436

TEPLOW, THEODORE HERZL, retired valve company executive; b. Brockton, Mass., Apr. 14, 1928; s. Edward Abraham and Evelyn (Stone) T.; m. Charlotte Leah Savitz, June 14, 1953; children: Rachel P., David I., Deborah R., Evan S., Jonathan P. BS, U.S. Mcht. Marine Acd., 1950; MBA, Harvard U., 1953; DHL honoris causa, Hebrew Coll., 1999; PhD honoris causa, Weizmann Inst. Sci., 2002. Mgmt. trainee to pres. Crosby Valve Inc. a Tyco Internat. Ltd. Co., Wrentham, Mass., 1953-82, cons., 1982—2001; dir. Emerson Investment Mgmt., Inc., Boston, 1985—. Cons. Firesafe Products Corp., N.Y.C., 1982-96; pres. Gateway Investment Corp., 2003—. Trustee Am. Mcht. Marine Mus. Found., Kings Point, NY, 1988—98, Rofeh Internat., Boston, 1990—, Hebrew Coll., Newton Center, Mass., 1971—, chmn., 1992—99, Hebrew Coll. Bd. Mgrs. of Trust Property, 1999—; trustee Kings Point Challenge, 1997—, US Mcht. Marine Acad., Kings Point, 2002—; v.p., bd. dirs. Internat. Catacomb Soc., Boston, 1982—99; asst. treas., dir. Am. Com. for Weizmann Inst. Sci., NY, 1987—2002, vice chair fin. and adminstrn., dir., 2002—; gov. Weizmann Inst. Sci., Rehovoth, Israel, 1991—; dir. Archives for Hist. Documentation, Boston, 1994—; bd. dirs. Nat. Ctr. Jewish Policy Studies, LA and Boston, 1993—, Cong. Beth El-Atereth Israel, Newton Center, 1975—85, Beth El Cmty. Hebrew Sch., Newton Center, 1965—86, US Mcht. Marine Acad. Alumni Found., Kings Point, 1957—, Stone Charitable Found., 1982—99. Comdr. USNR, ret. Recipient Outstanding Profl. Achievement award U.S. Mcht. Marine Acad. Alumni Assn., 1970, Meritorious Alumni Svc. award, 1990, Disting. Svc. award, 1995. Democrat.

TEPPER, CLIFFORD, allergist, immunologist, educator; b. Schenectady, NY, Oct. 26, 1922; s. Solomon B. and Annette (Lifset) T.; m. Cynthia S. Tepper; children: Stewart, Nancy, Henry, Audrey. Chief allergy dept. Ellis Hosp., Schenectady, 1990—; allergist allergy asthma immunology ctr. Albany (N.Y.) Med. Coll., 1992—, prof. pediats., 1973—. Co-dir. Schenectady Vol. Physicians Free Clinic; cons. in field. Trustee Schenectady Mus., 1987-99, Schenectady Pub. Libr., 1985—; pres. Anti-smoking Acad. Schenectady County; co-dir. Vol. Physician Clinic, Shcenectady County. Mem. Coll. Allergy and Immunology, Am. Acad. Pediatrics, Am. Acad. Allergy and Immunology, New Eng. Soc. Allergy (pres. 1990-92), N.Y. State Allergy Soc. (treas. 1993-95), Eastern Allergy Soc. (exec. com.), Physicians for Social Responsibility. Avocations: bird watching, art history. Home: 2216 Stoneridge Rd Niskayuna NY 12309-5524 Office: Allergy Asthma Immunology Ctr Albany Med Coll 1201 Washihngton Ave Ext Albany NY 12205 Fax: 518 452 2683. E-mail: tepperc@mail.amc.edu.

TEPPER, DAVID ALAN, hedge fund manager; b. Pitts., Sept. 11, 1958; m. Marlene Tepper; 3 children. BA in Economics, with honors, U. Pitts., 1978; MBA, Carnegie Mellon U., 1982. Credit & securities analyst Equibank, Pitts., 1978—80; mem. treas. dept. Republic Steel, Ohio, 1982—84; with Keystone Mutual Funds, Boston, 1984—85; credit analyst Goldman Sachs, NYC, 1985, head trader at high-yield desk, 1985—92; pres. & co-founder Appaloosa Mgmt., Chatham, NJ, 1993—. Mem. bus. bd. advisors Carnegie Mellon U. Tepper Sch. Bus. Named one of 400 Richest Americans, Forbes, 2005, 2006, World's Richest People, 2006. Office: Appaloosa Mgmt 26 Main St Chatham NJ 07928 Office Phone: 973-701-7000. *

TEPPER, LLOYD BARTON, preventive medicine physician, educator; b. LA, Dec. 21, 1931; m. Lamonte Leverage; children: Jeffrey Hamilton, Evan Clothier. AB, Dartmouth Coll., 1954; MD, Harvard U., 1957; MIH, 1960, ScD in Hygiene, 1962. Diplomate Am. Bd. Preventive Medicine (trustee, vice chair, 1986-94), Am. Bd. Occupl. Medicine. Intern U. Calif., San Francisco, 1957—58; resident Harvard Sch. Pub. Health, 1959—62; rsch. fellow Harvard Med. Sch., Boston, 1958-59; clin. fellow Mass. Gen. Hosp., Boston, 1958-60; rsch. assoc. MIT, Cambridge, 1959-61; physician U.S. AEC, Washington, 1962-65; prof. environ. health U. Cin., 1965-72; assoc. dir. Kettering Lab., Cin., 1965-72; assoc. commr. U.S. FDA, Washington, 1972-76; corp. med. dir. Air Products and Chems., Inc., Allentown, Pa., 1976-97; adj. prof. medicine Jefferson Med. Coll., 1998—2001. Adj. prof. emergency medicine occupl. and environ. medicine U. Pa., 2000—. Editor: Jour. Occupl. Medicine, 1979—91. Fellow: Am. Acad. Occupl. Medicine (pres. 1980—81), Am. Coll. Occupl. and Environ. Medicine. Office Phone: 610-527-8918. E-mail: lbtepper@icdc.com.

TEPPER, LYNN MARSHA, gerontologist, educator; b. NYC, Mar. 16, 1946; m. William Chester Tepper, Aug. 27, 1967; children: Sharon Joy, Michelle Dawn. BS, SUNY, Buffalo, 1967; MA, Wayne State U., 1971; MS, Columbia U., 1977, EdM, 1978, EdD, 1980. Instr. John F. Kennedy Sch., Berlin, 1967-68, ednl. counselor, 1968-69; ednl. coordinator Army Edn. Ctr., Berlin, 1969-71; psychologist U.S. Dept. Def., Berlin, 1971-73; prof. gerontology L.I. U., 1979—2000, Mercy Coll., Dobbs Ferry, 1979—, Columbia U., NYC, 1982—. Cons. NATO, Naples, Italy, 1969-71, SHAPE, Brussels, 1969-71, Found. for Long Term Care, 1992—, others; dir. Gerontology Resource Ctr., Ctr. for Geriatrics and Gerontology, Columbia U., NYC, 1980-85, dir. Behavioral Sci. Program, 1982—; del. White House Conf. on Aging, 1980; clin. prof. Columbia U., 1982— Author: (textbooks) Long Term Care, 1993, Respite Care, 1993, Multidisciplinary Perspectives on Aging, 2004; contbr. articles to profl. jours., chpts. to books. Advisor Office on Aging, State of N.Y., Albany, 1980-90; dir. Mercy Coll., Inst. Gerontology, 1990—; trustee, St. Cabrini Nursing Home, 1988-98, Morningside Nursing Home, 1998—; bd. dirs. Found. Long Term Care. Brookdale Inst. on Aging fellow, 1983; rsch. grantee NIH, Nat. Inst. on Aging, Nat. Inst. Gen. Med. Sci., U.S. Dept. Edn., U.S. Bur. Health Professions, interdisciplinary geriat. tng. U.S. Dept. Health Resources Svcs. Adminstrn. Fellow Gerontol. Soc. Am.; mem. Am. Psychol. Assn. Avocations: exercise, hiking. Office: Columbia U Med Campus Box 20 630 W 168th St New York NY 10032-3702

TEPPER, MORRIS, retired health science association administrator, mathematics professor; b. Jerusalem, Mar. 1, 1916; s. Benjamin and Anna Tepper; children: Andrew S., Bradford M. BS, Bklyn. Coll, 1936; MS, Bklyn. Coll., 1938; PhD, Johns Hopkins U., Balt., 1954. With US Geol. Survey, Washington, 1939—40; occupl. analyst US Civil Svc. Com., 1940—43; rsch. meteorologist US Weather Bur., DC, 1945—60; dir. weather satellite program NASA, DC, 1960—79; prof. math and physics Capital Coll., Laurel, Md., 1979—89; ret. Contbr. articles to profl. jours. Capt. USAF, 1943—45, SW Pacific. Avocation: bridge.

TEPPER, R(OBERT) BRUCE, JR., lawyer; b. Long Branch, NJ, Apr. 1, 1949; s. Robert Bruce and Elaine (Ogus) T.; m. Belinda Wilkins, Nov. 26, 1971; children: Laura Katherine, Jacob Wilkins. AB in HIstory, Dartmouth Coll., Hanover, NH, 1971; JD cum laude, St. Louis U., 1976, MA in Urban Affairs, 1976. Bar: Mo. 1976, Calif. 1977, Ill. 1978, US Ct. Appeals (7th cir.) 1978, (8th cir.) 1976, (9th cir.) 1978, US Dist. Ct. (ctrl., no., so. and east dists.) Calif. 1978, US Supreme Ct. 1991. Asst. gen. counsel St. Louis Redevel. Authority, 1976-77; assoc. Goldstein & Price, St. Louis, 1977-78, Loo, Merideth & McMillan, LA, 1978-82; sole practice LA, 1982-84; sr. prin., CFO Kane, Ballmer and Berkman, LA, 1984—2001; with R. Bruce Tepper, ALC, 2002—. Litigation counsel to San Diego, Santa Barbara, Huntington Beach, Anaheim, Culver City, LA, Lynwood, Norwalk, Redondo Beach, Oceanside, Ontario, Oxnard, Pasadena, Moreno Valley, Grover Beach, Glendale, Hawthorne,and Calif. City; spl. counsel Castaic Lake Water Agy., 1993—; Friant Water Authority, Hyundai, 2002-, San Diego State U, 2004; judge pro tempore Los Angeles County Mcpl. Ct., 1983—95; grader State Bar Calif., 1980-84; lectr. in land use and environ. issues Assoc. editor St. Louis U. Law Jour., 1974-76; mem. editl. bd. LA Lawyer; contbr. articles to legal jours. Mem. ABA, LA County Bar Assn. (com. on jud. evaluations), Assn. Bus. Trial Lawyers., So. Calif. Dartmouth Club (bd. dirs. 1980-83), LA Athletic Club. Republican. Jewish. Home: 10966 Wrightwood Ln Studio City CA 91604-3957 Office: 1880 Century Pk E Ste 615 Los Angeles CA 90067-1622 Home Phone: 323-654-1719; Office Phone: 310-551-6590. Business E-Mail: tap@rbtlaw.com.

TEPSTEIN, DANIEL C., lawyer; b. Encino, Calif., May 28, 1971; BA, Loyola Marymount Univ., 1993; JD cum laude, Southwestern Univ., 1997. Bar: Calif. 1997, D.C. 1999, US Dist. Ct. Ctrl. & No. Calif., US Ct. Appeals Ninth Cir., US Supreme Ct. Judicial extern Judge Arthur Alarcon, US Ct. Appeals Ninth Cir., 1997; assoc. Haight, Brown & Bonesteel LLP, Santa Monica, Calif., 1997—99, O'Donnell & Mortimer LLP, LA, 1999—2004, ptnr., 2004—06; ptnr., intellectual property & antitrust litigation Hunton & Williams LLP, LA, 2006—. Adj. assoc. prof. Southwestern Univ. Sch. Law, 2002—04. Editor (in-chief): Southwestern Univ. Law Rev., 1997. Named a Rising Star, So. Calif. Super Lawyers, 2005—06. Mem.: State Bar Calif. Office: Hunton & Williams LLP Ste 2000 550 S Hope St Los Angeles CA 90071-2627 Office Phone: 213-532-2109. Office Fax: 213-532-2020.

TERAKEDIS, JOHN, JR., lawyer; b. Dennison, Ohio, Mar. 30, 1945; s. John C. and H. Kathryn (Wenger) T.; m. Sharon A. McPeek, June 14, 1968; children: J. Troy, Leigh A., Lauren A. BS, Baldwin Wallace Coll., 1967; JD, Harvard U., 1970. Bar: Ohio 1970, U.S. Tax. Ct. 1971, U.S. Supreme Ct. 1974. Assoc. Emens, Kegler, Brown, Hill & Ritter, Columbus, Ohio, 1970-74; prin. Terakedis & Blue, LPA, Columbus, 1974-87; ptnr. Porter, Wright, Morris & Arthur, Columbus, 1987-89; prin. Schittenstein, Zox & Dunn, Columbus, 1990—; ptnr. Schottenstein Zox & Dunn Co., Columbus, Ohio. Adj. prof. sch. law Capital U., Columbus, 1993; guest lectr. coll. law Ohio State U., mem. planning com. and faculty Annual Creative Pension Strategies Conf.; past chmn. Columbus Tax Conf. Contbr. Mem. planning giving com. Baldwin Wallace Coll., Bereo, Ohio, 1993. Recipient Hall of Fame award Baldwin Wallace Coll. 1987, Best Lawyers in Am. Employee Benefits Law and Tax Law 1983-2007, fellow The Best Lawyers in Am. Am. Coll. Trust and Estate Counsel 1983-2006, Ohio Super Lawyer, 2004-2007. Mem. ABA, Ohio State Bar Assn., Columbus Bar Assn. (past chmn. bus. law and tax com.), Omnicron Delta Kappa, com. mem. Estate & Gift Tax Bus. Tax & Employee Benefits, past chmn. & lectr. Columbus Tax Conf., Columbus Estate Planning Coun., mem. Personal Svcs. Orgn. sub-com., legal adv. bd. mem. Columbus Found., Adv. bd. mem. Ohio State U. Coll. of Social and Behavioral Sci., legal adv. bd. mem. Small Bus. Counsel of Am., planning com. mem. OSU Creative Pension and Benefit Seminar. Office: Schottenstein Zox & Dunn Co Arena Dist 250 W St Columbus OH 43215 Office Fax: 614-224-3571. Business E-Mail: jterakedis@szd.com.

TERBURG, BART PAUL, physicist, industrial engineer; b. Leidschendam, Zuid-Holland, Netherlands, July 6, 1969; arrived in US, 1992; s. Antoon Lambertus and Hendriena Maria Terburg. Degree in Engring., Delft U. Tech., The Netherlands, 1992; MS in Physics, U. Ill., 1993, PhD in Physics, 1999. Mgr. global regulations GE Consumer and Indsl. Automotive Lighting, Cleve., 1999—, lead systems engr., 1999—. Chmn. SAE Internat. Lighting Standards Com., Warrandale, Pa., 2004—; vice-chmn. working group Groupe de Travail Bruxelles, 2004—. Contbr. articles to profl. jours. Recipient Thesis prize, S.E. U. Rsch. Assn., 1999; grantee, Netherlands Fulbright Com., 1992; Felix T. Adler fellowship, The U. Ill. Physics Dept., 1999. Mem.: Royal Dutch Inst. Engrs., Soc. Automotive Engrs. (Young Engrs. award 2004). Achievements include patents pending for tungsten halogen lamp with optimized silicon hydride fill; automotive headlamps with improved beam chromaticity. Office: GE Consumer and Industrial - Lighting 1975 Noble Road MD 334D Cleveland OH 44143 Home Phone: 440-473-0013; Office Phone: 216-266-9070. Personal E-mail: terburg@n2net.net.

TEREFENKO, DARIUSZ, music educator; b. Slupsk, Poland, Dec. 18, 1968; s. Kunegunda Danuta and Jan Iwan Terefenko. PhD, U. Rochester, NY, 2004. Asst. prof. music theory and jazz and contemporary media Eastman Sch. Music, Rochester, 2004—07. Home: 254 Wexford Pl Webster NY 14580 Office: Eastman Sch Music 26 Gibbs St Rochester NY 14604 Home Phone: 585-670-0114. Business E-Mail: dterefenko@esm.rochester.edu.

TERESI, JOSEPH, publishing executive; b. Mpls., Mar. 13, 1941; s. Cliff I.A. and Helen Ione (Leslie) (dec.); 1 child, Nicholas (dec.). CEO Jammer Cycle Products Inc., Burbank, Calif., 1968—80, Paisano Pubs. LLC, Agoura Hills, Calif., 1970—; chmn. bd., CEO V-Twin Expo, Agoura Hills, Calif., 1998—. Promoter motorcycle events; prodr. Easyriders Video mag.; owner Teresi Dyno Drags. Pub. (mags.) Easyriders, 1971—, In the Wind, 1974—, Biker, 1986—, Tattoo, 1986—, Am. Rodder, 1987-2001, Womens Enterprise, 1987-89, V-Twin News, 1989—, V-Twin, 1989, Tattoo Flash, 1993—, Tattoo Savage, 1993—, VQ, 1994—, Early-Riders, 1994-96, Quick Throttle, 1995-99, Roadware, 1995—, Tailgate, 2000, Tattoo Industry, 2000, Highbeams, 2003, Street Customs, 2004, Am. Choppers, 2004, Rebel Rodz, 2007; cable TV prodr.: V-Twin TV, 2004. Achievements include holding the world speed record for motorcycles set at 322 miles per hour, 1990-2006. Office: Paisano Pubs LLC PO Box 3000 Agoura Hills CA 91376-3000

TER HORST, JERALD FRANKLIN, public affairs counselor; b. Grand Rapids, Mich., July 11, 1922; s. John Henry and Maude (Van Strien) ter H.; m. Louise Jeffers Roth, Jan. 20, 1945; children: Karen Bayens Morris, Margaret Fulton Robinson, Peter Roth, Martha Morgan Lubin. Student, Mich. State U., 1941-42; AB, U. Mich., 1947. Reporter Grand Rapids Press, 1946-51; mem. staff Detroit News, 1953-74, city and state polit. writer, 1953-57, Washington corr., 1958-60; chief Detroit News (Washington bur.), 1961-74; White House press sec. to Pres., 1974; columnist Detroit News/Universal Press Syndicate, 1974-81; dir. nat. pub. affairs Ford Motor Co., 1981-91; fgn. assignments include Berlin crisis, 1959; assignments in Vietnam, Israel, Germany, USSR, Latin Am. Writer N.Am. Newspaper Alliance, 1958-74 Author: Gerald Ford and Future of the Presidency, 1974, The Flying White House: The Story of Air Force One, 1979; contbr. to mags. and TV documentaries. Bd. dirs. Nat. Press Found., 1982-98, WETA-TV (Channel 26), 1988-99, Brady Campaign to Prevent Gun Violence, 1992-2002; chmn. Gridiron Found., 1978-2005, Grad. Sch. Polit. Mgmt., George Washington U., 1985-96. Officer USMCR, 1943-46, 51-52. Mem. Pub. Rels. Soc. Am., Soc. Profl. Journalists, Psi Upsilon. Presbyterian (elder). Clubs: Gridiron, Nat. Press. Overseas Writers. Office Phone: 703-765-8056. Personal E-mail: jterhorst@aol.com.

TERK, GLENN THOMAS, lawyer; b. Feb. 27, 1949; s. Raymond Arthur and Marguerite Ida (Nichols) T.; m. Mary Ann Michaud, Sept. 25, 1982. BSME, Clarkson Coll. Tech., 1971; JD, U. Conn., 1976. Bar: Conn. 1976, U.S. Dist. Ct. Conn. 1976, U.S. Ct. Appeals (2d cir.) 2002. Engr. Combustion Engring. Co., Windsor, Conn., 1971-76; assoc. Francis, Kroopnick & O'Neil, Hartford, Conn., 1976-78; ptnr. Brignole & Terk, Hartford, Conn., 1993-95; pvt. practice Hartford, Conn., 1995—. Mem. Dem. Town Com., Windsor, 1978-79, Windsor Inland Wetlands Commn., 1978-79, Rep. Town com., Wethersfield, 1997—; chmn. Trinity United Meth. Ch. adminstrv. bd., Windsor, 1982-83, finance chmn. 1997-99. Mem. Conn. Bar Assn. (cmty. subcom. 1981-85, real property exec. com. 1994—; comml. law com. 1994—). Home: 445 Old Reservoir Rd Wethersfield CT 06109-3956 Office: 81 Wolcott Hill Rd Wethersfield CT 06109-1242 E-mail: Gterk@cs.com.

TERKEL, STUDS (LOUIS TERKEL), writer, journalist; b. NYC, May 16, 1912; s. Samuel and Anna (Finkel) T.; m. Ida Goldberg, July 2, 1939; 1 son, Dan. PhB, U. Chgo., 1932, JD, 1934. Disting. Scholar in Residence, Chgo. Hist. Soc., 1998—. Stage appearances include Detective Story, 1950, A View From the Bridge, 1958, Light Up the Sky, 1959, The Cave Dwellers, 1960; moderator: (TV program) Studs Place, 1950-53, (radio programs) Wax Museum, 1945— (Ohio State Univ. award 1959, UNESCO Prix Italia award 1962), Studs Terkel Almanac, 1952—, Studs Terkel Show, Sta. WFMT-FM, Chgo.; actor (films) Beginning to Date, 1953, Eight Men Out, 1988; (TV movies) The Dollmaker, 1984; master of ceremonies Newport Folk Festival, 1959, 60, Ravinia Music Festival, 1959, U. Chgo. Folk Festival, 1961, others; panel moderator, lectr., narrator films; Author: Giants of Jazz, 1957, Division Street: America, 1967, Hard Times: An Oral History of the Great Depression, 1970, Working: People Talk about What They Do All Day and How They Feel about What They Do, 1974 (Nat. Book award nomination 1975), Talking to Myself: A Memoir of My Times, 1977, American Dreams: Lost and Found, 1980, The Good War: An Oral History of World War II (Pulitzer prize for Non-fiction 1985), Chicago, 1986, The Great Divide: Second Thoughts On The American Dream, 1988, Race: How Blacks and Whites Think and Feel About the American Obsession, 1992, Coming of Age, 1995, My American Century, 1997, Spectator, 1999, Will the Circle Be Unbroken, 2001, And They All Sang: Adventures of an Electric Disc Jockey, 2005, The Studs Terkel Reader: My American Century, 2007; (play) Amazing Grace, 1959; also short stories. Named Communicator of Yr. U. Chgo. Alumni Assn., 1969; recipient Nat. Humanities Medal, 1997, Nat. Book Critics Circle Lifetime Achievement award, 2004, Dayton Lit. Peace prize, 2006. Office: Disting Scholar in Residence Chgo Hist Soc Clark St at North Ave Chicago IL 60614 *

TERMAN, LEWIS MADISON, retired electrical engineer, researcher, director; b. San Francisco, Aug. 26, 1935; s. Frederick Emmons and Sibyl (Walcott) T.; m. Barbara Chertok, Aug. 28, 1958. BS in Physics, Stanford U., 1956, MSEE, 1958, PhD, 1961. Mem. rsch. staff T.J. Watson Rsch. Ctr., IBM, Yorktown Heights, NJ, 1961-89, sr. mgr., 1989-91, sr. mem. tech. planning staff, 1991-93; mgr. VLSI processor design IBM Rsch. Ctr., Yorktown Heights, NY, 1993-94, rsch. staff T.J. Watson Rsch. Ctr., 1994—2001, assoc. dir. Sys. Dept., 2003—06, rschr. emeritus, 2006—; pres. IBM Acad. Tech., Yorktown Heights, 2001—03. Co-chmn. Symposium on Very Large Scale Integrated Technology, Systems and Application, Taiwan, 1989, 91, 93, 95, 97, 99, 01, 03, 05, tech. program co-chmn., 1985, 87; tech. program chmn. Internat. Solid State Cirs. Conf., N.Y.C., 1983; chmn. Symposium on Very Large-Scale Integrated Tech., Kobe, Japan, 1985, San Diego, 1986, Symposium on Very Large-Scale Integrated Cirs., Karuizawa, Japan, 1988, Kyoto, Japan, 1989, Symposium on Low Power Electronics, San Diego, 1994; mem. tech. coun. IBM Acad. Tech., 1995-98. Contbr. articles to profl. jours. Pres. Twin Lakes Water Works Corp., S. Salem, N.Y., 1980—. Recipient IEEE Solid-State Cirs. Tech. Field award, 1995. Fellow: IEEE (chmn. tech. mtgs. coun. 1993—94, tech. activites bd. treas. 1995—98, chair strategic planning and rev. com. 1999—2000, v.p. elect tech. activities bd. 2000, v.p. tech. activities bd. 2001, treas. publs., svcs. and products bd. 2003, divsn. one dir., mem. bd. dirs. 2004—05, pres.-elect 2006—, 2007), AAAS; mem.: Nat. Acad. Engring., Circuits and Sys. Soc. of IEEE (adminstrv. com. 1981—83), IEEE Solid-State Circuits Soc. (editor jour. 1974—77, treas. 1988—89, v.p. 1996—97, pres. 1998—99), IEEE Electron Devices Soc. (v.p. 1988—89, pres. 1990—91. Disting. Svc. award 1995), IBM Acad. Tech. (co-chair tech. program com. 1996, chair components and processes com., tech. coun. 1996—98, pres. 2001—03, past pres. 2003—05). Achievements include patents in field. Avocations: music, theater, opera, hiking. Home: 61 Twin Lakes Rd South Salem NY 10590-1012 Office: IBM TJ Watson Rsch Ctr 1101 Kitchawan Rd PO Box 218 Yorktown Heights NY 10598 Home Phone: 914-763-5744.

TERMEER, HENRICUS ADRIANUS, pharmaceutical executive; b. Tilburg, Holland, Feb. 28, 1946; came to U.S., 1971, naturalized, 1999; s. Jacques and Mary (Van Gorp) T. Student, Economisch Hogeschool (Erasmus U.), Rotterdam, The Netherlands, 1969; MBA, Darden Sch., U. Va., 1973; DSc (hon.), U. Mass. Mgr. mgmt. svcs. Norvic Co., Norwich, England, 1969-71; mgr. internat. product planning Baxter Travenol, Inc., Deerfield, Ill., 1973-74, internat. mktg. mgr., 1975-76; gen. mgr. Travenol GMBH, Munich, 1976-79; v.p. Hyland Therapeutics divsn. Baxter Travenol, Glendale, Calif., 1979-81, exec. v.p., 1981-83; pres. Genzyme Corp., Inc., Boston, 1983—, COO, 1983-85, CEO, 1985—, chmn., 1988—. Bd. dir. Abiomed, Inc., Biotech. Industry Orgn., Pharma. Rsch. and Manufactures Am., Mass. High Tech. Coun., Mass. Gen. Hosp., Fed. Res. Bank Boston, MIT Corp; bd. assocs. Whitehead Inst. Biomedical Rsch.; mem. MIT Corp. vis. com. dept. biology; chmn. New England Healthcare Inst., 2002-06. Trustee Boston Mus. Sci., Harvard Med. Sch. Bd. Fellows, Biomedical Sci. Careers Project, 1994., dir. 1995; bd. dir. Project Hope; Served to 1st lt. Netherlands Royal Air Force, 1966-67. Named Entrepreneur of Yr., Merrill Lynch and Ernst & Young, Inc., 1992, Renegade of Yr., Success Mag., 1995, Humanitarian of Yr., Cardinal Cushing Sch. for Exceptional Children, 1997; recipient Torch of Liberty award, Anti-Defamation League, New England Region, 1995, The Governor's New Am. Appreciation award, 1997, Golden Door award, Internat. Inst. Boston, 1999, Genetic Disease Found. Humanitarian award, 1999, Franklin Delano Roosevelt Humanitarian award, March of Dimes, 2003, Cor Vitae award, Am. Heart Assn., 2003. Fellow: Am. Acad. Arts & Sciences, Royal Coll. Physicians (hon.). Office: Genzyme Corp 500 Kendall St Cambridge MA 02142

TERMINI, ROSEANN BRIDGET, law educator; BS magna cum laude, Drexel U., 1975; MEd, Temple U., 1979, JD, 1985, grad. in food and pharmacy law, 1998. Bar: Pa. 1985, U.S. Dist. Ct. (ea. dist.) Pa. 1985, DC 1986. Jud. clk. Superior Ct. Pa., Allentown, 1985-86; atty. Pa. Power & Light Co., Allentown, 1986-87; corp. counsel food and drug law Lemmon Co., Sellersville, Pa., 1987-88; sr. dep. atty. bur. consumer protection plain lang. law (Notable cases include: Waste Conversion case, 1990, violation of Pa. Solid Waste Mgmt. Act.) Office of Atty. Gen., Harrisburg, Pa., 1988-96; prof. Villanova U. Sch. Law, 1996-2000; prof. food and drug law Temple U. Sch. Pharmacy, Phila., 1998—, St. Joseph U., 2000—; prof. food and drug law Grad. Sch. John Hopkins U., 2005—; prof. grad. pharmacy/biotech master program U. Ga., 2005—. Adj. prof. law online life scis. Widener U., 1993—; adj. prof. Dickinson Sch. Law; specialized food, drug, cosmetic and med. device law course dir. pres.'s coun. Immaculata Coll.; on-line distance learning legal issues pharmacy promotion and legal environ. bus. St. Joseph U., 2002—; instr. online exec. MBA program Drexel U., 2002—; mem. adv. bd. RXMD; spkr. Pa. Health Law Inst., 2007—. Author: Food, Drug and Medical Device Law: Topics and Cases, 2001, Health Law: Federal Regulation of Drugs, Biologics, Medical Devices, Foods and Dietary Supplements, 2003, Biologics, 2003, Medical Devices, 2004, Foods and Dietary Supplements, 2003, Statutory Supplement and Teacher's Manual, 2003;: 2d edit., 2004, Life Sciences Law Book and Statutory CD, 2007; contbr. articles to profl. jours. Active Sr. Citizens Project Outreach, Hospice, 1986—; mem. St. Thomas More Law Bd. Mem.: ABA (mem. various coms.), Pa. Bar Assn. (ethics, exceptional children and environ. sects., Plain English award 1999), Bar Assn. DC, Drexel U. Alumni Assn., Temple U. Law Alumni Assn., Phi Alpha Delta, Omicron Nu. Avocations: tap dancing, hiking, cross country skiing. Personal E-mail: rtermini@lawyer.com. Business E-Mail: rtermini@fortipublications.com.

TERNAR, MINE Y., artist, art educator; b. Istanbul, Turkey, Apr. 18, 1961; d. Orhan Ternar and Gulbun Tok; 1 child, Dilara Ilayda Nur Ternar Kal. Student, State Acad. Fine Arts, Istanbul, 1979—80; BA in Liberal Arts, Bennington Coll., Vt., 1984; MA in Painting and Serigraphy, Mimar Sinan U., Istanbul, 1986; MFA in Art Practice, U. Calif., Berkeley, 1991. C.c. instr. credential fine and applied arts Bd. Govs. Calif. Cmty. Colls., tchg. credential adult edn. art Commn. Tchr. Credentialing. Papermaking and painting asst. to artist Sophie Healy Trout Paper, Eagle Bridge, NY, 1980—81; copywriter, illustrator Radar Advt. Agy., Istanbul, 1985—86; curatorial asst., intern Phoebe A. Hearst Mus. Anthropology, U. Calif., Berkeley, 1989—91, intern Berkeley Art Mus., 1990—91; vol. coord. Pro Arts Gallery, Oakland, Calif., 1991—92; mem. adj. faculty Calif. Coll. Arts, Oakland, 1992—93, San Francisco Art Inst., 1992—93; asst. dir. Cartoon Art Mus., San Francisco, 1993—94; cmty. outreach coord. Dean Lesher Regional Ctr. Arts, Walnut Creek, Calif., 1994—97; mem. adj. faculty dept. visual arts Cabrillo Coll., Aptos, Calif., 1994—98; mem. faculty dept. art City Coll. San Francisco, 1996—. Vol. outreach coord. Gilles Peres photo installation New Langton Arts, San Francisco, 1994; freelance designer, computer graphics Golden Touch Design, Berkeley, 1996—2000; intranet webmaster Coherent Laser Co., Santa Clara, Calif., 1997—98; faculty advisor Diego Rivera website City Coll. San Francisco, 1997—98, gallery dir., curator City Arts Gallery, 1998—, mem. works of art sub-com., acad. senate, 2002—. Author, co-prodr., collaborator (film/video) Conversations Across the Bosphorus, 1995; one-man shows include Osman Hamdi Hall, Mimar Sinan U., Istanbul, 1986, exhibitions include Lutfu Gunay Studio, Turkish-Am. Cultural Assn., Ankara, Turkey, 1978, Adnan Coker Studio, Istanbul State Gallery Fine Arts, 1985, Berkeley Art Mus., 1991, Worth Ryder Gallery, U. Calif., Berkeley, 1991, Walter/McBean Gallery, San Francisco Art Inst., 1992—93, KALA Artists Exhbn., 1997—98, Kala Artists' Ann., 1998—99, exhibited in group shows at Harcourts Modern and Contemporary Art Gallery, San Francisco, 1989, Berkeley Art Ctr., 1998, PRO ARTS Open Studios, 1996, Cabrillo College Gallery, 1997. Recipient Winning design, Health Through Art: Signs of Recovery, Alameda County Cmty. Project, 1996—2000; fellow, Calif. Student Aid Commn., 1990—91, KALA Art Inst., Berkeley, 1997; grantee, City Coll. San Francisco, 1997—98, Vt. Studies Ctr., 2007; scholar, Univ. per Stranieri, Perugia, Italy, 1979, Bennington Coll., 1980—84. Mem.: Coll. Art Assn. Am., Turkish-Am. Assn. Calif. (assoc.; bd. dirs., dir. arts and culture 1994—97), U. Calif. Alumni Assn. (life), YMCA. Avocations: reading, swimming, films, music, travel. Office: City Coll San Francisco Art Dept 50 Phelan Ave San Francisco CA 94112 Home Phone: 510-237-7747; Office Phone: 415-239-3157, 415-452-5354. Office Fax: 415-239-3131. Business E-Mail: mternar@ccsf.edu.

TERNBERG, JESSIE LAMOIN, pediatric surgeon, educator; b. Corning, Calif., May 28, 1924; d. Eric G. and Alta M. (Jones) T. AB, Grinnell Coll., Iowa, 1946, ScD (hon.), 1970; PhD, U. Tex., Austin, 1950; MD, Washington U., St. Louis, 1953; ScD (hon.), U. Mo., St. Louis, 1981. Diplomate: Am. Bd. Surgery. Intern Boston City Hosp., 1953—54; asst. resident in surgery Barnes Hosp., St. Louis, 1954-57, resident in surgery, 1958-59; rsch. fellow Washington U. Sch. Medicine, 1957-58; practice medicine specializing in pediatric surgery St. Louis, 1966—; instr., DGMS trainee in surgery Washington U., 1959-62, asst. prof. surgery, 1962-65, assoc. prof. surgery, prof., 1965-71, prof. surgery, 1971-96, chief divsn. pediatric surgery, 1972-90, prof. emeritus, 1996—; mem. staff Barnes Hosp., 1959—90; gen. surgeon in chief Children's Hosp. of St. Louis, 1974-90. Mem. staff Children's Hosp., dir. pediatric surgery, 1972-90. Contbr. numerous articles on pediatric surgery to profl. jours. Trustee Grinnell Coll., 1984—. Recipient Alumni award Grinnell Coll., 1966, Faculty/Alumni award Washington U. Sch. Medicine, 1991, 2nd Century award 2006, 1st Aphrodite Jannopaulo Hofsommer award, 1993, Local Legend Changing the Face of Medicine award AMWA. Fellow AAAS; mem. SIOP, Am. Pediatric Surg. Assn., We. Surg. Assn. (2d v.p. 1984-85), St. Louis Med. Soc., Soc. Surgery of the Alimentary Tract, Am. Acad. Pediatrics, Soc. Pelvic Surgeons (v.p. 1991-92), Brit. Assn. Paediatric Surgeons, Assn. Women Surgeons (disting. mem. 1995), Mo. State Surg. Soc., St. Louis Surg. Soc. (pres. 1980-81), St. Louis Pediatric Soc., Soc. Surg. Oncology, Pediatric Oncology Group (chmn. surg. discipline 1983-96), St. Louis Childrens Hosp. Soc. (pres. 1979-80), Acad. Sci. St. Louis (Trustees award 2002), St. Louis Met. Med. Soc. (hon., councilor, trustee), Barnes Hosp. Soc., Phi Beta Kappa, Sigma Xi, Iota Sigma Pi, Alpha Omega Alpha. Office: St Louis Childrens Hosp 1 Childrens Pl Saint Louis MO 63110-1002 Business E-Mail: ternbergj@wudosis.wustl.edu.

TERNUS, MARSHA K., state supreme court chief justice; b. Vinton, Iowa, May 30, 1951; married; 3 children. BA, U. Iowa, 1972; JD, Drake U., 1977. Bar: Iowa 1977, Ariz. 1984. With Bradshaw, Fowler, Proctor & Fairgrave, Des Moines, 1977—93; justice Iowa Supreme Ct., Des Moines, 1993—, chief justice, 2006—. Former mem. Iowa Jury Instructions Com.; former bd. mem. Polk County Legal Aid Soc.; pres. bd. of counselors Drake U. Law Sch.; former mem. Iowa Supreme Ct. Commn. on Planning for the 21st Century, MultiState Perf. Test Policy Com., Nat. Conf. of Bar Examiners. Editor-in-chief: Drake Law Rev., 1976—77. Mem.: Iowa State Bar Assn. (bd. governors), Polk County Bar Assn. (pres. 1984—85), Order of Coif, Phi Beta Kappa. Office: Iowa Supreme Ct Jud Branch Bldg 1111 E Ct Ave Des Moines IA 50319-0001 *

TERP, THOMAS THOMSEN, lawyer; b. Fountain Hill, Pa., Aug. 12, 1947; s. Norman T. and Josephine (Uhran) T.; m. Pamela Robinson; children: Stephanie, Brian, Adam; step-children: Taylor Mefford, Grace Mefford. BA, Albion Coll., Mich., 1969; JD, Coll. of William and Mary, 1973. Bar: Ohio 1973, US Dist. Ct. (so. dist.) Ohio 1973, US Ct. Appeals (6th cir.) 1973, US Supreme Ct. 1979. Assoc. Taft, Stettinius & Hollister, Cin., 1973-80, ptnr., 1981—, chmn., mng. ptnr., 2007—. Bd. dirs. Starflo Corp., Orangeburg, SC, Attorneys' Liability Assurance Soc., Ltd., Hamilton, Bermuda, ALAS, Inc., Chgo. Editor-in-chief William & Mary Law Rev., 1972-73; mem. bd. editors Jour. of Environ. Hazards, 1988—, Environ. Law Jour. of Ohio, 1989—. Mem. Cin. Athletic Club, Camargo Club, Epworth Assembly (Ludington, Mich.), Lincoln Hills Golf Club (Ludington), Queen City Club. Avocations: tennis, golf, travel. Office Phone: 513-357-9354. Business E-Mail: terp@taftlaw.com.

TERPELUK, PETER G., JR., former ambassador; b. Pa., Feb. 1948; Bachelors Degree, LaSalle Coll.; MPA, Rider Coll. Founder Terpeluk and Assocs., 1986—93; prin. Wojdak and Assocs., Washington, 1989—93; mng. dir. Am. Continental Group, 1994—2002; U.S. amb. to Luxembourg US Dept. State, Washington, 2002—05. Active U.S. SBA, 1981—84; bd. dirs. Pa. Ave. Devel. Commn.; town mgr. Pa., 1972.

TERR, LENORE CAGEN, psychiatrist, writer; b. NYC, Mar. 27, 1936; d. Samuel Lawrence and Esther (Hirsch) Cagen; m. Abba I. Terr; children: David, Julia. AB magna cum laude, Case Western Res. U., 1957; MD with honors, U. Mich., 1961. Diplomate Am. Bd. Psychiatry and Neurology (subspecialty bd. child and adolescent psychiatry). Intern U. Mich. Med. Ctr., Ann Arbor, 1961-62; resident Neuropsychiat. Inst. U. Mich., Ann Arbor, 1962-64, fellow Children's Psychiat. Hosp., 1964-66; from instr. to asst. prof. Case Western Res. U. Med. Sch., Cleve., 1966-71; pvt. practice Terr Med. Corp., San Francisco, 1971—; from asst. clin. prof. to clin. prof. psychiatry Sch. Medicine U. Calif., San Francisco, 1971—. Lectr. law, psychiatry U. Calif., Berkeley, 1971—90, Davis, 1974—88; dir. Am. Bd. Psychiatry and Neurology, 1988—96, chair psychiatry coun., 1996. Author: Too Scared to Cry, 1990, Unchained Memories, 1994, Beyond Love and Work, 1999, Magical Moments of Change, 2007; contbr. articles to profl. jours.; exhibited works in art show at Canessa Gallery, San Francisco, 2002. Named to Cleveland Heights H.S. Disting Alumni Hall of Fame, 2003; recipient Career Tchr. award, NIMH, 1967—69, Child Advocacy award, APA, 1994; grantee project, Rosenberg Found., 1977, William T. Grant Found., 1986—87, Leon Lowenstein Found., 2002; scholar-in-residence, Rockefeller Found., Italy, 1981, 1988. Fellow: Am. Acad. Child and Adolescent Psychiatry (coun. 1984—87), Am. Coll. Psychiatrists (program chair 1991—92, Bowis award 1993), Am. Psychiat. Assn. (Child Psychiatry Rsch. award 1984, Clin. Rsch. award 1987, Marmor Sci. award 2002); mem.: Phi Bet Kappa, Alpha Omega Alpha. Avocations: piano, walking, travel, gardening, needlepoint. Office Phone: 415-433-7800. E-mail: lenoreterrmd@sbcglobal.net.

TERRACCIANO, ANTONIO, psychologist, researcher; b. Napoli, Italy, Apr. 21, 1974; s. Giuseppe Terracciano and Giuseppina Varriale. PhD, Seconda Universita' di Napoli, Italy, 1999. Vis. rsch. fellow NIH, Balt., 1999—2006, staff scientist, 2006—. Cons. editor, ad hoc reviewer several jours. Contbr. articles to profl. jours. Mem.: APA (co-chair program com. 2005), Assn. Psychol. Sci. Radical Party. Achievements include research in personality traits development; accuracy of national character stereotypes; perceptions of Americans' character around the world and influences of the Iraq invasion; personality traits associated with smoking status; cross-cultural differences in personality traits; sex differences across cultures on personality traits and emotions; sequencing human genome and genome wide association analysis for complex traits. Office Phone: 410-558-8358. Business E-Mail: terraccianoa@grc.nia.nih.gov.

TERRACINA, ROY DAVID, entrepreneur; b. Chgo., Aug. 24, 1946; s. Angelo R. and Josephine T.; divorced; children: Joseph, Vincent, Angela, Peter, Paul. BS in Fin., Marquette U., 1968, MBA, 1972. Officer First Wis. Nat. Bank, Milw., 1968-71; account exec. Robert W. Baird Co., Milw., 1971-74; v.p. mktg. Midwest Retail Group, Milw., 1974-76; mgmt. cons. Anderson-Roethle, Milw., 1976-77; v.p., treas. Farm House Foods Corp., Milw., 1977-84; pres. Sterling Foods, Inc., San Antonio, 1984-93, pvt. investor, 1994—. Instr. personal fin. Marquette U.; instr. fin. Trinity U.; bd. dir. US Global Investors, JP Morgan Chase, San Antonio. Roman Catholic. Office: 7900 Callaghan Rd San Antonio TX 78229-2327

TERRANOVA, ELIZABETH (ELISA) JO, artist; b. Monrovia, Liberia, Jan. 15, 1954; (parents Am. citizens); d. Joseph and Joy Alice Terranova; life ptnr. Mark Gerard Domzalski, Oct. 19, 1996; life ptnr. Russell James Sether (div.); m. John Kenneth Mayes (div.). BFA in Art Edn., Ariz. State U., Tempe, 1987, MFA in Painting, 1993. Fine artist, 1980—; founder / pres. Sacred Heart Studios, Folsom, Calif., 1995—. Art film maker Twenty-three Degrees, Sacramento, 2001—; lectr. / guest spkr. colls., univs., fine art galleries. Short animated film, Trompe L'oeil, exhibitions include Orlando (Fla.) Mus. Art, Florence (Italy) Internat. Biennale, 2003, one-woman shows include U. Club Gallery, Winter Park, Fla., Women Image Now Gallery, Ariz. State U., Tempe, 1986, 1987, Harry Wood Gallery, Ariz. State U., Tempe, 1989, Student Union Art Gallery, San Francisco State U., 1993, James Kaneko Galler, Am. River Coll., Sacramento, 1994, Sheppard Fine Arts Gallery, U. Nev., Reno, Ridley Gallery, Sierra Coll., Rocklin, Calif., 2001; artist (invitational group shows) Ctr. Contemporary Art, Sacramento, (internat. juried group shows) Sacramento Fine Arts Ctr. (Excellence award, Merit award), (group shows) Crest Theater, Sacramento, 2002, (video group shows) Gallery Horse Cow, (group shows) Fortezza da Basso, Florence, 2003, Toyroom Gallery, Sacramento, 2004; Exhibited in group shows at Sacramento French Film Festival, 2003, 2004. Phelps Dodge scholar, 1990—91. Achievements include In collaberation with the United Nations and Italy, I have been nominated and accepted as one of the US representatives to display my artwork at the Florence International Biennale 2003, Italy; I was selected to participate in a juried exhibition at the Orlando Museum of art. The exhibit traveled to the Rotunda Building at the US capitol in Washington, D.C; development of my art serves as a visual diary that describes the human condition as told from the perspective of a quadriplegic. Like the works of Frida Kahlo and The Diary of Anne Frank; I hope to inspire this message that great things can be achieved against all odds. Avocations: art history, digital animation, computer animation, gardening. Office: Sacred Heart Studios Folsom CA 95763-6566 E-mail: elisa@elisat.com.

TERRAS, AUDREY ANNE, mathematics professor; b. Washington, Sept. 10, 1942; d. Stephen Decatur and Maude Mae Bowdoin. BS with high honors in Math., U. Md., 1964; MA, Yale U., 1966, PhD, 1970. Instr. U. Ill., Urbana, 1968-70; asst. prof. U. P.R., Mayaguez, 1970-71, Bklyn. Coll., CUNY, 1971-72; asst. prof. math. U. Calif.-San Diego, La Jolla, 1972-76, assoc. prof., 1976-83, prof., 1983—. Prin. investigator NSF, 1974-88; vis. positions MIT, fall 1977, 83, U. Bonn West Germany, spring 1977, Inst. Mittag-Leffler, Stockholm, winter, 1978, Inst. Advanced Study, spring 1984, Math. Scis. Rsch. Inst., Berkeley, Calif., winter 1992, spring 1995, U. Aachen, Germany, 1998, Tsuda Coll., Tokyo, 1999, CRM, U. Montreal, 1999, U. Colo., Boulder, 2006, Newton Inst., Cambridge, Eng., 2007thers; dir. West Coast Number Theory Conf., U. Calif.-San Diego, 1976, AMS joint summer rsch. conf., 1984; lectr. in field. Author: Harmonic Analysis on Symmetric Spaces and Applications, Vol. 1, 1985, Vol. II, 1988, Fourier Analysis on Finite Groups and Applications, 1999; editor: The Selberg Trace Formula and Related Topics, 1986; contbr. chapters to books, articles to profl. jours. Woodrow Wilson fellow, 1964, NSF fellow, 1964-68; NSF grantee Summer Inst. in Number Theory, Ann Arbor, Mich., 1973. Fellow: AAAS (nominating com. math. sect. project 2061); mem.: Assn. for Women in Sci., Assn. for Women in Math. (travel grants com. 1996), Soc. Indsl. and Applied Math., Math. Assn. Am. (program com. for nat. meeting 1988—90, chair joint program com. Am. Math. Soc. and Math. Assn. Am. 1991), Am. Math. Soc. (com. employment and ednl. policy com. on coms., coun., trans. editor, com. for the yr. 2000, western sect. program com., assoc. editor book revs. Bull., assoc. editor Notices). Achievements include research in harmonic analysis on symmetric spaces; number theory; graph theory. Office: U Calif San Diego Dept Math La Jolla CA 92093-0112

TERRELL, G. IRVIN, lawyer; b. Houston, Sept. 28, 1946; s. George I. and Adella (Weichert) T.; m. Karen Steenberg, Jan. 8, 1984; 1 child, Katharine. BA, U. Tex., 1968, JD, 1972. Bar: Tex., US Supreme Ct., US Ct. Appeals (3d and 5th cirs.), US Dist. Ct. (so., no. and ea. dists.) Tex., US Dist. Ct. (we. dist.) Pa, US Dist. Ct. (so. dist.) NY. Assoc. Baker & Botts LLP, Houston, 1972-79, ptnr., 1980—. Mem. ABA, Houston Bar Assn., Internat. Soc. Barristers. Office Phone: 713-229-1231. Business E-Mail: irv.terrell@bakerbotts.com.

TERRELL, HELLENNA L., education educator; d. Ernestine Robinson and Herman L. Terrell. BS, Spelman Coll., Atlanta, 1986; MS, Jacksonville State U., Ala., 1995; EdD, U. Ala., Tuscaloosa, 1999. Dir. alumni affairs/pub. rels. Mary Holmes Coll., West Point, Miss., 1986—88; project dir. U.S. Dept. of Agr., Washington, 1988—91; asst. to exec. v.p. Talladega (Ala.) Coll., 1991—93; dean student life Tex. Coll., Tyler, 1993—95; dean multicultural initiatives U. Tenn., Chattanooga, 1997—2004; v.p. for student affairs St. Augustine's Coll., Raleigh, NC, 2004—07; dept. chair gen. studies U. Md. Ea. Shore, 2007—, dir. honors program, 2007—. Mem. Raleigh Rotary Club, 2006, Chattanooga Area Food Bank, 1997—2004, Chattanooga Theater Ctr., 1997—2004. Mem.: So. Assn. for Coll. Student Affairs, Nat. Assn. of Student Pers. Administrs., Am. Assn. Univ. Pers., Am. Assn. Univ. Women. Office Phone: 410-651-6082. Office Fax: 410-621-3750. Business E-Mail: hlterrell@umes.edu.

TERRELL, J. ANTHONY, lawyer; b. NYC, Sept. 20, 1943; s. Claude M. and Kathleen L. (Prevost) Terrell; m. Karen E. Terrell; 1 child, Elizabeth S. BA, NYU, 1965, LLM in Taxation, 1975; JD, Villanova U., 1968. Bar: NY. With Frueauff, Farrell, Sullivan & Bryan, NYC, 1970—74, ptnr., 1974; assoc. Thelen Reid & Priest LLP, NYC, 1974—76, ptnr., 1977; now ptnr. Dewey Ballantine LLP, NYC. Named one of Am.'s Leading Lawyers for Bus., Chambers USA, 2005, Best Lawyers in Am., 2006. Mem.: ABA, Nat. Assn. Bond Lawyers, Internat. Bar Assn., Coral Beach and Tennis Club, Met. Club, Belle Haven Club. Office: Dewey Ballantine LLP 1301 Avenue of the Americas New York NY 10019-6092 Office Phone: 212-259-7070. Office Fax: 212-259-6333. E-mail: jterrell@deweyballantine.com.

TERRELL, (NELSON) JAMES, physicist; b. Houston, Aug. 15, 1923; s. Nelson James Sr. and Gladys Delphine (Stevens) T.; m. Elizabeth Anne Pearson, June 9, 1945; children— Anne (dec.), Barbara, Jean BA, Rice U., 1944, MA, 1947, PhD, 1950. Rsch. asst. Rice U., Houston, 1950; asst. prof. physics We. Res. U., Cleve., 1950—51; mem. staff Los Alamos Nat. Lab., U. Calif., 1951—89, assoc., 1989—94; affiliate, 1994—2005; ret., 2005. Producer (computer generated movie) The X-Ray Sky, 1969-76; contbr. articles to profl. jours. and encys. Served to 1st lt. AUS, 1944-46 Graham Baker scholar Rice U., 1943-44; fellow Rice U., 1946-48, AEC, 1948-50 Fellow Am. Phys. Soc., AAAS; mem. Am. Astron. Soc., Internat. Astron. Union, Phi Beta Kappa, Sigma Xi Achievements include research in relativity, quasars, x-ray and gamma ray astronomy, nuclear physics, lasers. Home: 85 Obsidian Loop Los Alamos NM 87544-2528

TERRELL, JAMES DANIEL, lawyer; b. Kansas City, Oct. 22, 1956; s. D. Ronald and Bobbie L. (Graham) T.; m. Lori J. McAlister, May 31, 1980; children: Justin Daniel, Christopher James, Alexander Graham. BS, Ctrl. Mo. State U., 1979; JD, U. Mo., 1982. Bar: Mo. 1982, U.S. Dist. Ct. (we. dist.) 1982, U.S. Dist. Ct. (ea. dist.) Mo. 1984. Assoc. Wasinger, Parham & Morthland, Hannibal, Mo., 1982-87; ptnr. Wasinger, Parham, Morthland Terrell & Wasinger, Hannibal, 1987—. Bd. dirs. Marion County Svcs. for the Developmentally Disabled, Hannibal, 1989—. Mem.: 10th Jud. Cir. Bar Assn. (pres. 2001—), Mo. Bar Assn. (family law sect.), U. Mo. Alumni Assn. (life), Phi Delta Phi. Office: Wasinger Parham Morthland Terrell & Wasinger 2801 Saint Marys Ave Hannibal MO 63401-3775

TERRELL, MAURICE L., SR., music educator; b. Orlando, Fla., July 15, 1974; s. Dolores Terrell-Hagan; 1 child, Maurice L. Jr. BA in Music, Rollins Coll., Winter Park, Fla., 2003; MA in Music Edn., U. Ctrl. Fla., Orlando, 2006. Prof. music Seminole C.C., Sanford, Fla., 2004—; asst. violin instr. A Gift for Music, Orlando. Min. music Calvary Temple of Praise, Inc., Sanford, Fla., 2000—. Musician: (albums) Jehud, Heritage Festival, Bernie Mac Comml. Mem.: Percussive Arts Soc., Internat. Assn. Jazz Educators, Delta Epsilon Iota. Democrat. Avocations: running, kick-boxing. Office: Seminole Cmty Coll 100 Weldon Blvd Sanford FL 32773 Home Phone: 321-377-9233; Office Phone: 407-708-2039. Personal E-mail: mastermusician74@aol.com. Business E-Mail: terrellm@scc-fl.edu.

TERRILL, ROSS GLADWIN, writer, educator; b. Melbourne, Australia; arrived in U.S., 1965, naturalized, 1979; s. Frank and Miriel (Lloyd) Terrill. BA with honors, U. Melbourne; PhD, Harvard U., 1970. Tutor in polit. sci. U. Melbourne, 1962-63; staff sec. Australian Student Christian Movement, 1964-65; tchg. fellow Harvard U., 1968-70, lectr. govt., 1970-73, assoc. prof., 1974-78, rsch. assoc. E. Asian studies, 1970—, dir. student programs Ctr. Internat. Affairs, 1974-78; contbg. editor Atlantic Monthly, 1970-84; rsch. fellow Asia Soc., 1977—79. Vis. prof. Monash U., Melbourne, 1994—97, U. Tex., Austin, 1999—2003. Author: China Profile, 1969, China and Ourselves, 1971, 800,000,000: The Real China, 1972, R. H. Tawney and His Times, 1973, Flowers on an Iron Tree, 1975, The Future of China, 1978, The China Difference, 1979, Mao: A Biography, 1980, rev., 2000, White-Boned Demon, 1984, The Australians, 1987, Madam Mao, 1992, rev., 1999, China in Our Time, 1992, The Australians: How We Live Now, 2000, The New Chinese Empire, 2003; contbr. articles to Foreign Affairs, National Geographic, New Republic, Weekly Standard, New York Review of Books, Wilson Quarterly, others. Recipient Sumner prize, 1970, Nat. Mag. award, 1972, George Polk Meml. award outstanding mag. reporting, 1972, Book prize, L.A. Times, 2003. Mem.: PEN, Authors Guild, Harvard Club (N.Y.C.). Avocations: squash, music. Home: PO Box 230772 Astor Station Boston MA 02123-0772 Office Phone: 617-445-2542. Personal E-mail: rt5789@cs.com.

TERRIS, LILLIAN DICK, psychologist, health facility administrator; b. Blooomfield, NJ, May 5, 1914; d. Alexander Blaikie and Herminia (Doscher) Dick; m. Louis Long, Apr. 22, 1935 (dec. Sept. 1968); 1 son, Alexander Blaikie Long; m. Milton Terris, Feb. 6, 1971 (dec. Oct. 2002). BA, Barnard Coll., 1935; PhD, Columbia U., 1941. Diplomate Am. Bd. Examiners in Profl. Psychology. Instr. psychology Sarah Lawrence Coll., Bronxville, NY, 1937-40; jr. pers. tech. SSA, Washington, 1941; sr. pers. clk. OWI, NYC, 1941-43; dir. profl. examination svc. Am. Pub. Health assn., NYC, 1943-70; pres., 1970-79; pres. emeritus, 1979—. Assoc. editor: Jour. Pub. Health Policy, 1979—; contbr. articles to profl. jours. Recipient Nat. Environ. Health assn. award, 1976, Cert. Svc. award Bd. Preventive Medicine, 1979. Fellow Am. Psychol. Assn., Am. Coll. Hosp. Adminstrs. (hon.); mem. Am. Pub. Health Assn., N.Y. State Psychol. Assn., Phi Beta Kappa, Sigma Xi. Office: 475 Riverside Dr New York NY 10115-0122 E-mail: jphpterris@aol.com.

TERRIS, SUSAN, physician, cardiologist, researcher; b. Morristown, NJ, Sept. 5, 1944; d. Albert and Virginia Terris. BA in History, U. Chgo., 1967, PhD in Biochemistry, 1975, MD, 1976. Diplomate in internal medicine, endocrinology and metabolism, cardiovasc. disease Am. Bd. Internal Medicine. Resident in internal medicine Washington U., Barnes Hosp., St. Louis, 1976-78; fellow in endocrinology and metabolism U. Chgo., 1978-80, fellow cardiology, 1980-83, U. Mich., Ann Arbor, 1983-85, instr. cardiology, 1985-86; head cardiac catheterization lab., head cardiology Westland (Mich.) Med. Ctr., 1985. Contbr. articles to Jour. Biol. Chemistry, Am. Jour. Physiology, Am. Jour. Cardiology, Jour. Clin. Investigation, other profl. publs. Grantee Juvenile Diabetes Found., 1978-80, NIH, 1978-79. Mem. AAAS, Am. Heart Assn., N.Y. Acad. Sci. Achievements include rsch. demonstrating dependence of intracellular degradation of insulin upon its prior adsorptive pinocytotic uptake by liver; studies on the electrophysiologic effect of cathecholamimes on sheep Parkinje fibers and on the hemodynamic effects of various drugs on the human circulatory system.

TERRITO, MARY C., health facility administrator, hematologist, educator; BS in Biology, Wayne State U., 1965, MD, 1968. Intern/resident in internal medicine Parkland Hosp., Dallas, 1971-73; fellow in hematology/oncology Harbor-U. Calif., LA, 1973-74, UCLA, 1974-75; rsch. assoc. Wadsworth VA Hosp., LA, 1975-81; asst. prof. dept. medicine UCLA, 1975-81, assoc. prof., 1981-96, prof., 1996—, dir. bone marrow transplant program Ctr. Health Scis., 1981—. Contbr. articles to profl. jours. Office: UCLA Bone Marrow Transplantation Program Ctr 42-121 CHS 10833 Le Conte Ave Los Angeles CA 90095-3075

TERRUSO, LUIGI LEONARDO, artist, educator; b. Oct. 19, 1964; s. John James Terruso and (Ewashenko) Anne. BS with honors, CUNY, Staten Island, 1987; MFA, Yale U., 1994. Tchg. asst. to prof. CUNY, SI, 1987; studio artist, 1987—; instr. art lab. Snug Harbor Cultural Ctr., SI, NY, 1991—96; tchg. asst. Yale U. Sch. Art, New Haven, 1994; instr. Trumbull Coll., Yale Coll., New Haven, 1994; pvt. instr. Santa Fe, 2007—. Vis. artist Am. Acad. Rome, 2003—04, 2006—07; artist in residence Santa Fe Art Inst., 2005—06. One-man shows include Milton Gallery, Washington, 1998, Shneyer and Shsen Anonia Gallery, NYC, 1998, Smith and Thompson, 2000, 55 Mercer Gallery, 2005, exhibited in group shows at Gallery 313, 1990, Frank Bustemante Gallery, 1990, Foundry Gallery, DC, 1991, A.I.R. Gallery, NYC, 1991, Logan Gallery, Chautauqua, NY, 1991, Bklyn Waterfront Artists Coalition, 1992, Montpelier Cultural Arts Ctr., Laruel,

Md., 1992, Yale U. Art and Architecture Gallery, New Haven, 1994, Snug Harbor Cultural Ctr., NYC, 1996, Bklyn. Waterfront Artists Coalition, Bklyn., 1998, Am. Acad. Arts and Letters, NYC, 2001, Nat. Acad. Mus., 2006. Fellow, Vermont Studio Ctr., 1997, 2005; grantee, Santa Fe Art Inst., 2006; scholar, Joan Mitchell Found., 2006; Tenebaum scholar, CUNY, 1983—87. Mem.: Century Assn., Coll. Art Assn., Print Club NY. Avocation: travel. Studio: 526 W 26th St Studio 910 New York NY 10001

TERRY, ANNE CURTIS, lawyer, writer; d. Charles and Florine Curtis; m. Edward H. Terry; children: Edward, Ellyn. BA, Fla. State U., Tallahassee, 1970; MA, U. Tex., Austin, 1972; JD, U. Fla., Gainesville, 1978. Bar: Fla. 1979. Tchg. asst./lectr. dept. geography U. Tex., Austin, 1972—74; appellate law clk. 1st Dist. Ct. of Appeals, Tallahassee, 1978—79; asst. atty. gen. Office of Fla. Atty. Gen., Tallahassee, 1980—86; staff counsel Fla. Legislature, Tallahassee, 1986—89; solo practitioner/firm owner Law Office of Anne Curtis Terry, Tallahassee, 1993—. Author: The Spirit in the South, 2006; contbr. legal opinions to ann. report of atty. gen. Fla. NDEA Title VI fellow, Inst. Latin Am. Studies, U. Tex., 1971-1972. Mem.: Phi Alpha Delta, Phi Kappa Phi. Democrat. Methodist. Achievements include represented Southern Christian Leadership Conference in First Amendment litigation; represented numerous plaintiffs in employment discrimination cases, based on disability, race and gender; and plaintiff-relators in state and federal qui tam litigation. Avocations: travel, photography, poetry, cooking, gardening. Office: Law Office of Anne Curtis Terry 6209 Verdura Way Tallahassee FL 32311

TERRY, CAROLE COSGROVE, retired small business owner, historian, researcher; b. San Francisco, Jan. 5, 1938; d. John Charles and Emile Dohrmann Cosgrove; m. Norman Berkley Terry, Feb. 14, 1970; children: Emilie Terry Meinadier, Brenda Jane. BA, Stanford U., Calif., 1959; MA, U. Nevada, Las Vegas, 2000, PhD candidate, 2001—. Cert. Merit Katherine Gibbs Sch., N.Y., 1960. Sec. asst. Hon. Herbert Hoover, NYC, 1959—60; exec. sec. E.F. Hutton & Co. Inc., LA, 1960—71; interim alumnae dir. Marlborough Sch., LA, 1991—92; owner, v.p., CFO Galleria Travel, Inc., Glendale, 1976—93; ret., 1994. Co-author (with Emilie D. Cosgrove): California Potpourri 1852-1936, 1966; co-author: (pamphlet) The History of Chinatown, 1971; contbr. articles to profl. jour., scientific papers. Treas. bd. mem. Sun City Quilters, 2002—05; stewardship team chair St. Andrew Luth. Ch., 2004—05, stewardship, counting chair, 1996—99; treas. bd. mem. Jr. League Las Vegas Sustainers, 2001—05; sec. bd. mem. Jr. League Las Vegas Endowment Bd., 2002—; bd. mem., treas. Costume Coun., L.A. County Mus. Art, 1992—95. E-mail: terrynandc@cox.net.

TERRY, CLIFFORD LEWIS, journalist; b. Highland Park, Ill., Jan. 19, 1937; s. Clifford Lewis and Isabelle (Marlow) T.; m. Patricia West Dickelman, Sept. 1, 1966; children: Christopher West, Scott Marlow. Student, Carleton Coll., Northfield, Minn., 1954-55; BA, Trinity Coll., Hartford, Conn., 1958; postgrad., Columbia U., 1962-63. Tchr., English and history Mt. Hermon (Mass.) Sch., 1958-59; police reporter City News Bur. Chgo., 1959-60; mem. staff Chgo. Tribune, 1960-94, movie critic, 1965-70; assoc. editor Chgo. Tribune (Sunday mag.), 1970-82, feature writer, 1982-85, TV critic, 1985-89, arts feature writer, 1989-94; ind. writer, 1994—. Author: Chicago: Off the Beaten Path, 2001, 3d edit., 2005. Served with AUS, 1960. Nieman fellow Harvard U., 1969-70 Mem. Phi Beta Kappa.

TERRY, EDWIN WELLINGTON, college librarian; b. Bklyn., Dec. 4, 1918; s. Edwin Wellington Roberts Terry and Ursaline Whittle McClane; m. Natalie Johnston (dec.); children: Brian Paul, Francesca Natalie. BA, Bklyn. Coll., 1941, MA, 1968; BSc with honors, Columbia U., 1946; MA, Columbia Tchrs. Coll., 1948; PhD, St. John's U., 1971. Cert. pub. libr. SUNY Dept. Edn., 1967. Cataloger Columbia U. Libr., NYC, 1946—47; acquisition asst. Queens Coll., Flushing, NY, 1948—59; dir. Dillard U. Libr., New Orleans, 1947—48, Nassau CC Libr., Garden City, 1960—67, Bronx CC Libr., 1967—78, staff mem., 1978—88; adj. libr. Bronx CC, 1988—93, Manhattan CC, NYC, 1993—2000. Chair two yr. coll. chief librs. SUNY, 1965; mem. ad hoc com. Nassau County Ctrl. Libr., 1965—66; pres. Nassau County Lib. Assn., 1965—66; chair profl. status com. Libr. Assn. of CUNY, 1978—80, chair publ. com., 1980—88; mem. adv. com. minority fellowship Queens Coll. Libr. Sch., 1966—90. Editor: Urban Academic Librarian, 1983—88; contbr. articles to profl. jours.; co-author: Core Collection in Nursing and Allied Health Sciences, 1990. Mem. Friends of U. Calif. San Diego Libr., 2004. Staff sgt. US Army, 1943. Recipient Cert. of Svc., Bronx CC Student Coun., 1968, Cert. of Merit, Bronx CC, 1988. Mem.: Archons of Colophon, Beta Phi Mu. Democrat.

TERRY, ELIZABETH HAYS, artist, small business owner; b. Bryn Mawr, Pa., July 29, 1935; d. James Franklin and Mary Ellen (Carmichael) Hays; m. Charles L. Terry, III, Feb. 8, 1958; children: Elizabeth Harllee Carmichael Terry Moran, Charles L. IV. AB, Smith Coll., Northampton, Mass., 1957. Asst. to profs. Harvard U., Cambridge, Mass., 1957-58; art tchr. Exeter Day Sch., NH, 1968-72; asst. editor Phillips Exeter Acad. Alumni Quarterly, 1972-75, dir. alumni records, 1975-85; owner Elizabeth Terry, Calligraphy, Illumination and Needlepoint Design, Exeter, NH, 1980—. Tchr. needlepoint Guild of Strawbery Banke, Portsmouth, NH. Dir. for Town of Exeter-Save Our Shores, 1972. Mem. Smith Coll. Class of 1957 (class fund agt. 1972-77, alumnae fund com. 1977-80, class bequest chair 1982—, com. on deferred giving 1990—), NH Colonial Dames (pres. 1989-92, nat. historian 1992-94, nat. v.p. 1994-2000). Episcopalian. Avocations: tennis, needlepoint, historic preservation. Home and Office: 77 Brookside Dr Stratham NH 03885-2128 Office Phone: 603-772-8942. Personal E-mail: ceterry@verizon.net.

TERRY, FRANCES JEFFERSON, retired psychiatric nurse practitioner; d. Walter Louis and Ruth Williams Jefferson; m. Robert Terry, Sept. 29, 1926; children: Deborah Ella Terry-Hays, Robert David, Michael Duane, William Brian, Walter Louis. BSN, Seattle U., 1951; MSN, U. Wash., Seattle, 1981. Lic. Advanced RN Practitioner, ANCC. Health enhancement-program nurse Ctrl. Area Sr. Ctr., Seattle; staff nurse Providence Hosp., Seattle; prescribing and consulting nurse Cmty. Ho. Mental Health Agy., Seattle; psychiat. mental health practitioner U. of Wash.-Harborview Med. Ctr., Seattle; nursing instr. Shoreline C.C., Seattle; nurse case mgr.-mental health U. of Wash.; nursing instr. Seattle U.; dir. of health svcs. NW Ctr. for Disabled, Seattle; sch. nurse Seattle Pub. Schs.; pub. health nurse Seattle King County Health Dept., Seattle. Diabetes support group vol. facilitator Joslin Diabetes Ctr., Seattle. Auditor/ch. coun. ImmaculateConception Ch., Seattle; mem. Seattle Ctrl. Cmty. Coll. Found.; planning com. Susan G. Komen Breast Cancer Found./Puget Sound, Seattle. Named Outstanding Nurse, U. of Wash.-Harborview Med. Ctr., 1993; named to Hall of Fame, Wash. State Nurses Assn., 2000; recipient Cmty. Svc. Award, Seattle U., 2004. Mem.: Mary Mahoney Profl. Nurses Assn., Am. Nurses' Assn. (life), Alpha Kappa Alpha Sorority (life). Home Phone: 206-325-3944; Office Phone: 206-325-3944. Personal E-mail: bobfrater@comcast.net.

TERRY, FREDERICK ARTHUR, JR., lawyer; b. Buffalo, May 24, 1932; s. Frederick Arthur and Agnes Elizabeth (Tranter) T.; m. Barbara (Anderson). BA, Williams Coll., 1953; LLB, Columbia U., 1956. Bar: N.Y. 1957, U.S. Dist Ct. (so., no., and ea. dist.), N.Y., U.S. Tax Ct., U.S. Supreme Ct. Law clk. to Hon. Sterry R. Waterman U.S. Ct. Appeals (2d cir.), 1956—57; assoc. Sullivan and Cromwell, NYC, 1957—64, ptnr., 1965—99, sr. counsel, 2000—. Trustee Harold K. Hochschild Found.; chmn. Flagler Found.; bd. dir. McIntosh Found., Weinman Found.; trustees coun. Nat. Gallery of Art; hon. trustee Natural Resources Def. Coun.; trustee emeritus Rockefeller U. Recipient David Rockefeller Extraordinary Svc. award, Rockefeller U. Mem. ABA, N.Y. State Bar Assn., Assn. Bar City of N.Y., River Club, Union Club, India House, Maidstone Club, The Bathing Corp. Office: Sullivan and Cromwell 125 Broad St Fl 25 New York NY 10004-2400 Office Phone: 212-558-3923.

TERRY, GARY A., lawyer, director, former trade association executive; b. Ogden, Utah, Apr. 2, 1935; s. Hyrum Aceal and Viola (Sorenson) T.; m. Carole Ann Eitel, June 23, 1962; children— Stephanie Ann, Brendan Gary BA in Polit. Sci., UCLA, 1964; JD, George Washington U., 1968. Bars: Va. 1969 D.C. 1969. Mem. staff U.S. Ho. of Reps., Washington, 1964-65; Washington staff Bethlehem Steel Corp., 1965-69; atty. HUD, Washington, 1969; exec. v.p. Am. Land Devel. Assn. (now Am. Resort Devel. Assn.), Washington, 1969-82, pres., 1982-91, also dir.; with Jones, Waldo, Holbrook & McDonough, Washington, 1991-95, St. George, 1995-97. Dir. Internat. Found. for Timesharing, Washington, 1981-91, mem. consultative council Nat. Inst. Bldg. Scis., Washington, 1982-85; U.S. rep. land use and town planning com. Internat. Real Estate Fedn., Brussels, 1984-91; mem. Found. for Internat. Meetings, Washington, 1984-92; del. Lincoln Inst. Land Policy, Harvard U., 1984, 85 Contbr. articles to profl. jours. Asst. to exec. dir. Presdl. Inaugural Com., 1969-70; mem. adv. bd. NOAA, Washington, 1972; bd. dirs. Zacchaeus Free Med. and Legal Clinics, Washington, 1991-95, co-chair lawyers com., 1992-95; bd. dirs. Celebrity Concert Series, St. George, 1999—2005, pres., 2004-05; chmn. Pioneer Ctr. for the Arts Found., St. George, 2000-02, bd. trustees, 1998-03. Seved with USN, 1953-56. Decorated Am. Spirit of Honor medal. Mem. Va. Bar Assn., D.C. Bar Assn. Mem. Lds Ch. Avocations: music, literature, flying, art, travel. Home: 952 Lizzie Ln Saint George UT 84790-2255 Personal E-mail: gaterry@earthlink.net.

TERRY, JACK CHATTERSON, lawyer; b. Monett, Mo., Nov. 23, 1919; s. Jacob E. and Florence V. (Chatterson) T.; m. Susan W. Terry, June 7, 1941; children: Susan L. Terry Galewaler, Philip C. BA in History and Govt., U. Mo., Kansas City, 1949, JD, 1952. Bar: Mo. 1952, U.S. Supreme Ct. 1961. Sole practice, Independence, Mo., 1952—. Mem. Mo. Legislature, 1955-56; legis. liaison officer Jackson County (Mo.), 1967-68; atty. Inter-City Fire Protection Dist., 1955-74; city atty. City of Blue Summit (Mo.), 1971-76; atty. Jackson County (Mo.) Bd. Election Commrs., 1974—. Pres. Independence Good Govt. League, 1961-63, Jackson County League Better Govt., 1962-66. Served as officer USAAF, 1941-46, PTO. Decorated Purple Heart, Air medal. Mem. ABA, Mo. Bar Assn., Kansas City Bar Assn., Inter-City Kiwanis (pres. 1967), Masons, Shriners. Democrat. Mem. Christian Ch. (Disciples Of Christ). Home: 614 Bellevista Dr Independence MO 64055-1746 Office Phone: 816-254-6070.

TERRY, JAMES JOSEPH, JR., lawyer; b. Yonkers, NY, July 2, 1952; s. James Joseph Sr. and Marie Catherine (O'Boyle) T.; m. Marguerite Mary O'Connor, Sept. 29, 1985; 1 child, James Daniel. BA, NYU, 1974; JD, Columbia U., 1977. Bar: N.Y. 1978, U.S. Dist. Ct. (so. and ea. dists.) N.Y. 1978, U.S. Ct. Appeals (2d cir.) 1981, U.S. Ct. Appeals (3d cir.) 1989, U.S. Supreme Ct. 2000. Assoc. Cole & Deitz, NYC, 1977-89; ptnr. Winston & Strawn (formerly Cole & Deitz), NYC, 1989—2002; v.p., gen. counsel F.J. Sciame Constrn. Co., Inc., NYC, 2002—. Mem. ABA, N.Y. State Bar Assn., N.Y. County Lawyers Assn. Democrat. Roman Catholic. Avocations: fishing, reading. Home: 190 Kneeland Ave Yonkers NY 10705-2713 Office: Sciame Constrn Co Inc 80 South St New York NY 10038 Office Phone: 212-232-2200. E-mail: jterry@fjsciame.com.

TERRY, JOHN ALFRED, judge; b. Utica, NY, May 6, 1933; s. Robert Samuel and Julia Berenice (Collins) T. BA magna cum laude, Yale U., 1954; JD, Georgetown U., 1960. Bar: D.C. 1960. Asst. U.S. atty. for D.C. US Dept. Justice, 1962-67; staff atty. Nat. Commn. Reform of Fed. Criminal Laws, Washington, 1967-68; pvt. practice law Washington, 1968-69; chief appellate divsn. U.S. Atty.'s Office for D.C. US Dept. Justice, 1969-82; judge DC Ct. Appeals, 1982—2006, sr. judge, 2006—. Mem. D.C. Bar (bd. govs. 1977-82), ABA, Phi Beta Kappa. Office: DC Ct Appeals 500 Indiana Ave NW Washington DC 20001-2138

TERRY, JOHN JOSEPH, transportation investor; b. Chgo., July 29, 1937; s. Michael Parnell and Honore (Ryan) T.; m. Terese Rose Mulkern, Dec. 31, 1960; children: Michael P., Gregory, Deirdre BS, Loyola U., Chgo., 1959; postgrad., U. So. Fla., 1967. C.P.A., Ill. With Touche, Ross & Co., 1959-65; v.p. Nat. City Lines, Denver, 1965-71; v.p. fin. Pepsico Transp., Inc., Tulsa, 1971-74; v.p. U.S. Rwy. Assn., Washington, 1974-76; chmn. P.I.E. Transport Europe, 1976-79; exec. v.p. IU Internat. Corp., Wilmington, Del., 1976-85; pres. Transp. Mgmt. Investment Group, Inc., Phila., 1985—. V.p.-at-large Am. Trucking Assn., Washington, 1984-85, chmn., internat. competitiveness task force, 1991, tax policy com., 1987—; bd. dirs. Caldwell Freight Lines, Lenoir, N.C., Basin Western, Inc., Roosevelt; cons. freight transp. World Bank and European Bank for Reconstrn. and Devel., 1986—. Served with U.S. Army, 1960-63 Recipient Best Motor Carrier Rsch. award Transp. Rsch. Forum, 1991. Office: Transp Mgmt Investment Group Inc 210 Locust St Apt 11B Philadelphia PA 19106-3923

TERRY, JOSEPH RAY, JR., retired lawyer; b. Vicksburg, Miss., Aug. 10, 1938; s. Joseph Ray Sr. and Alma Blanche (Smith) T.; m. Louise Caroline Beland, July 17, 1965; children: Kathleen A., Marie L., Bernard R. JD, Loyola U., 1965; degree, Fed. Exec. Inst., Va., 1984. Bar: D.C. 1966, Miss. 1968, U.S. Ct. Appeals (5th cir.) 1971, Ga. 1973, U.S. Dist. Ct. (no. and so. dists.) Ga. 1973, U.S. Ct. Appeals (D.C. cir.) 1973, U.S. Supreme Ct. 1973, U.S. Ct. Appeals (8th cir.) 1974, U.S. Dist. Ct. (we. dist.) Tenn. 1983, U.S. Ct. Appeals (6th cir.) 1989; cert. mediator. Trial atty. civil rights div. U.S. Dept. Justice, Washington, 1966-69; assoc. regional counsel U.S. Dept. HUD, Atlanta, 1969-70; ptnr. Crosland, Myer, Rindskopf & Terry, Atlanta, 1974-76; regional counsel EEOC, Atlanta, 1970-73, supr. trial atty. Litigation Cen., 1976-79, regional atty. Memphis, 1979-96, dep. gen. counsel Washington, 1996-99, cons., lectr., mediator, 1999—2001; ret., 2001. Part-time asst. atty. City of Atlanta, 1975-76; cons. NLRB, Memphis, 1981-82; adj. prof. law Emory U., 1971-75; vis. prof. law St. Louis U., 1973-74, William C. Wefel disting. vis. prof. law, 1998-2000; acting program dir. EEOC, Washington, 1983, acting dist. dir., Memphis, 1984-85; bd. dirs. Fed. Credit Union, 1984-91; mem. adv. com. to U.S. Dist. Ct. for western dist. Tenn., 1990-93, chmn. case mgmt. subcom., 1991-98; mem. faculty Southwestern Legal Found., Dallas, spring 1998; cons. equal employment, 1999—; cert. gen. civil mediator Supreme Ct. Tenn., 2000. Contbr. articles to profl. jours. Appt. by Pres. of US Selective Svc. Bd., Memphis, 2002—03, Amnesty Internat., 2005; cons. Alaska Human Rights Commn., Anchorage, 1981; mem. Leadership Memphis, 1988—2004; bd. dirs. United Meth. Neighborhood Ctr., 1985—88, St. Patrick's Parish Coun., Memphis, pres., 1986—88; bd. dirs. Place of Grace Ministries, Carlisle, Pa., 1997—2005, Nat. Kidney Found. of West Tenn., Memphis, pres., 1984—85. Named Honor Law Graduate U.S. Atty. Gen., 1965. Mem.: FBA (bd. dirs. 1988—89, v.p. West Tenn. chpt. 1991—92, pres. 1993—94, nat. coun. 1996—99, named Younger Fed. Lawyer of Yr. 1973), ABA (EEOC liaison com. 1987—89), St. Thomas More Lawyers Guild, Supreme Ct. Hist. Soc., Sierra Club. Roman Catholic. Avocations: tennis, golf, skiing, hiking, reading. Home and Office: 1560 Harbert Ave Memphis TN 38104-5033 Personal E-mail: terryteam@bellsouth.net.

TERRY, LEE RAYMOND, congressman, lawyer; b. Omaha, Jan. 29, 1962; s. Leland R. Terry; m. Robyn L. Terry, Feb. 14, 1992; children: Nolan E., Ryan, Jack. BA in Polit. Sci., U. Nebr., Lincoln, 1984; JD, Creighton U. Sch. Law, Omaha, 1987. Bar: Nebr. 1987, US Dist. Ct. Nebr. 1987. Staff atty. Schrempp & Salerno, Omaha, 1987-92; ptnr. Schrempp, Salerno & Terry, Omaha, 1992-93, Terry & Kratville, Omaha, 1993-98; mem. City Coun., Omaha, 1991—98, US Congress from 2nd Nebr. dist., 1999—, mem. energy & commerce com. Co-author: Trying the Soft Tissue Case in Nebraska, 1995. V.p. Omaha City Coun., 1993-94, pres., 1995-97; chair elect Am. Diabetes Assn., Great Plains, 1996-97, chair Nebr. area, 1997-99; co-chmn. Impact Aid Coalition. Named One of Ten Outstanding Young Omahans, Omaha Jaycees, 1994, Outstanding Young Nebraskan Nebr. Jaycees, 1997; recipient Spirit of Enterprise award US C. of C., 2002 Mem. Nebr. Assn. Trial Attys. (dir. 1995), Suburban Rotary. Republican. Meth. Avocations: travel, playing, spending time with family. Office: US House Reps 1524 Longworth House Office Bldg Washington DC 20515-2702 Office Phone: 202-225-4155. *

TERRY, LEON CASS, neurologist, educator; b. Dec. 22, 1940; s. Leon Herbert and Zella Irene (Boyd) T.; m. Suzanne Martinson, June 27, 1964; children: Kristin, Sean. Pharm. D., U. Mich., 1964; MD, Marquette U., 1969; PhD, McGill U., 1982; MBA, U. So. Fla., 1994. Diplomate Am. Bd. Psychiatry and Neurology, Am. Bd. Med. Mgmt. Intern U. Rochester, NY, 1969-70; staff assoc. NIH, 1970-72; resident in neurology McGill U., Montreal, Que., Canada, 1972-75; MRC fellow, 1975-78; assoc. prof. U. Tenn., Memphis, 1978-81; prof. neurology U. Mich., Ann Arbor, 1981-89; assoc. prof. physiology, 1982-89; asst. chief neurology VA Med. Ctr., Ann Arbor, 1982-89; chmn. dept. neurology Med. Coll. of Wis., Milw., 1989—2000, prof. neurology and physiology, 1989—2003; chief med. officer Nexostherapeuticals, 2003—; pres., CEO Neurologic Cons., LLP, 2004—, Longevitech, 2004—. Dir. clin neurosci. ctr. and multiple sclerosis clinic, Med. Coll. Wis.; assoc. dean for amb. care, 1996-98; vice chief of staff Froedtert Hosp., 1994-97; chief of staff, 1997-98; chief med. officer cenegenics, 1997-98. Contbr. articles to profl. jours, chpts. to books. Served to lt. comdr. USPHS, 1970-72. NIH grantee, 1981-92; VA grantee, 1980-92; VA Clin. Investigator award, 1980-81. Mem. AMA, Am. Soc. Clin. Investigation, Cen. Soc. Clin. Investigation, Am. Neurol. Assn., Am. Coll. Physician Execs. (vice chmn. academic health ctr. soc. 1994-95, chair, 1995-98, leader forum health care delivery 1995-98), Am. Coll. Healthcare Execs., Endocrine Soc., Am. Acad. Neurology, Internat. Soc. Neuroendocrinilogy, Internat. Soc. Psychoeuroendocrinilogy, Soc. Neurosci., Soc. Rsch. Biol. Rhythms, Milw. Acad. Physicians, Wis. Neurol. Assn., Wis. State Med. Soc. (del.-elect 1995-96), Med. Soc. Milw. County, Milw. Neuropsychiatric Soc. (pres.-elect.). Avocations: pilot, skiing, scuba diving, computers. Office: Neurologic Consultnats LLP Suite 209 1009 W Glen Oaks Lane Mequon WI 53092 Home Phone: 414-234-9207; Office Phone: 262-241-8512. E-mail: cass@cass-terry.com, drcassterry@wi.rr.com.

TERRY, LINDA FAYE, librarian; b. Paducah, Ky., June 26, 1947; d. John Rodman and Frances B. (Clark) Tomlinson; m. Steven Lynn Terry, June 8, 1974; children: Elizabeth Lynn, Matthew Lee. BS, Western Ky. U., 1970, MA in Reading, 1971; MLS, Ind. U., 1991. Cert. tchr., Ky., Ind., libr., Ind. Student asst. Coll. Hgts. Found., Western Ky. U., Bowling Green, 1966-69; tchr. elem. Waddell Ave. Elem. Sch., Madisonville, Ky., 1969-70; bookkeeper asst. City County Hosp., Bowling Green, 1970; grad. asst. reading Western Ky. U., Bowling Green, 1970-71; cons. reading tchr. Greater Clark County Schs., Jeffersonville, Ind., 1971-75; reading tchr. Crittenden (Ky.) Elem. Sch., 1975; children dir., asst. dir. Brownsburg (Ind.) Pub. Libr., 1979-82, bookkeeper, treas., 1984-87, jr. high tchr., 1990; project cons. Ind. State Libr., Indpls., 1991-92, pub. libr. svcs. cons., 1993—. Treas. Floyd-Clark County I.R.A., Jeffersonville, Ind., 1971-73; treas.-pres. Hendricks County I.R.A., Brownsburg, 1980-85, membership com., 1988-92; family involvement com. Ind. State Reading Coun., Indpls., 1985-88. Leader Girl Scouts of Am., Brownsburg, 1982-84; parent support group Brownsburg Jr. High Sch., 1988-90, Brownsburg High Sch., 1990-92, band boosters, 1990—. Named Libr. Employee of Yr., Ind. State, 2006. Mem. ALA, ASCD, Internat. Reading Assn., Am. Assn. Sch. Librs., Pub. Libr. Assn., Hendricks County Reading Coun. (pres. 1980—), Assn. Ind. Media Educators, Ind. Reading Assn. Southern Baptist. Office: Ind State Libr 140 N Senate Ave Indianapolis IN 46204-2207 Office Phone: 317-232-1938. E-mail: fayeterry626@yahoo.com.

TERRY, MARK, art educator; s. Hayes and Carol Terry; m. Melissa Blair, Oct. 10, 1981; children: Kaitlin, Erin. MEd, Western Oreg. U., Monmouth, 1991. Asst. prof. art George Fox U., Newberg, Oreg., 1987—. Numerous exhbns. ceramics. Recipient Undergrad. Tchg. Achievement award, 2005. Office: George Fox Univ 414 North Meridian St Newberg OR 97123 Home Phone: 503-554-8208; Office Phone: 503-554-2636. Office Fax: 503-538-3834.

TERRY, MARSHALL NORTHWAY, JR., language educator, writer; b. Cleve., Feb. 7, 1931; s. Marshall Northway and Margaret Louise (Carpenter) T.; m. Antoinette Barksdale, Sept. 5, 1953; children: Antoinette Terry Bryant, Mary Marshall Terry Benton. Student, Amherst Coll., 1949-50, Kenyon Coll., 1950-51; BA, So. Meth. U., 1953, MA, 1954. Teaching fellow English So. Meth. U., Dallas, 1954, dir. pub. relations, lectr. English, 1957-64, instr. English, 1956, 65-67, asst. dir., 1968, assoc. prof., 1969-71, prof. English, 1972—, chmn. dept., 1971-75, 79-82, dir. creative writing program. Book critic Dallas News, 1970-75; pres. faculty senate So. Meth. U., 1993-94, assoc. provost, 1994-98, E.A. Lilly prof. Eng., 1998—. Author: Old Liberty, 1961, Tom Northway, 1968, Dallas Stories, 1986, Ringer, 1987, My Father's Hands, 1993, Land of Hope and Glory, 1996, Angels Prostate Fall, 2001, Tex Rex, 2003, The Memorialist, 2006; contbr. short stories to various jours. and mags.; editor Prize Stories, 1986. Past trustee Incarnate Word Coll., San Antonio; sec. bd. trustees Fort Burgwin Research Ctr., Ranchos de Taos, N.Mex. Recipient Jesse H. Jones fiction award Tex. Inst. Letters, 1968, Best Short Story award S.W. Rev., 1973, S.W. Writer of Yr. award, 1988, Willis M. Tate award So. Meth. U., 1990, 94, Lon Tinkle award for continuing excellence in Letters, Tex. Inst. Letters, 1991, Disting. Alumnus award, So. Meth. U., 2003. Mem. AAUP (chpt. pres. 1971), Coll. Conf. Tchrs. English, South Central MLA, Tex. Inst. Letters (pres. 1977-79, councilor 1980—) Democrat. Methodist. Home: 2717 Lovers Ln Dallas TX 75225-7905 Office: So Meth Univ Dept English Dallas TX 75275-0001 Office Phone: 214-768-2952. Business E-Mail: mterry@smu.edu.

TERRY, MICKEY THOMAS, music educator, director; b. Greenville, NC, Feb. 29, 1956; s. Thomas Lewis Terry and Beatrice Claudia Chapman. BA, East Carolina U., Greenville, NC, 1977, MA, 1980; PhD, Georgetown U., Washington, 1991. Adminstr. humanities program NEH, Washington, 1991; lectr. history Georgetown U., 1992—93; dir. music St. Rita's Cath. Ch., Alexandria, Va., 1996—2000; lectr. music Howard U., Washington, 1999—2000; dir. music St. Mary's Cath. Ch., Clinton, Md., 2001—; lectr. Howard U., 2007. Vice chair African Heritage Cultural Inst., Mitchellville, Md., 2006. Mem.: Am. Guild Organists (mem. exec. bd. 1994—97, 1988—94). Democrat. Episcopalian. Avocations: reading, antiques.

TERRY, NICHOLAS P., law educator; b. London, Eng., Dec. 5, 1952; BA, Kingston Univ., UK, 1975; LLM, Univ. Cambridge, 1977. Lectr. Univ. Exeter, England; prof. Saint Louis U. Sch. Law, 1980—, co-dir. Ctr. Health Studies, 2000—; prof. Saint Louis U. Sch. Pub. Health, 2003—. Vis. prof. Univ. Mo. Columbia Sch. Law, 1986—87, Washington Univ. Sch. Law, 1986—99; dir. Legal Edn. LEXIS-NEXIS, Dayton, Ohio, 1996—97; sr. fellow Melbourne Law Sch., Australia, 2001—. Co-author: Cases, Materials and Problems in the Law of Torts, 2002, Products Liability, Cases, Material, Problems, 2002; contbr. articles to prof. jour.; co-editor (in-chief): Jour. Health Law, 2000—. Mem. bd. dir. Ctr. for Computer Assisted Legal Instruction, 1998—; mem. editl. bd. Jour. Medical Internet. Rsch., 2000—; mem. internat. bd. adv. Medical Law Rev., Oxford Univ. Press, 1992—; mem. bd. adv. Melbourne Law Sch., Australia, 2001—. Mem.: ABA, Am.

Health Lawyers Assn., Am. Soc. Law & Medicine (mem. bd. dir.), Health Law Tchr. Assn. Office: Saint Louis U Sch Law 3700 Lindell Blvd Saint Louis MO 63108 Office Phone: 314-977-3998. Business E-Mail: terry@slu.edu. *

TERRY, PETER BROWNE, medical educator; b. Peoria, Ill., May 2, 1941; s. Charles and Frances Terry; m. Joan Salim; children: Michael, Norah Smith, Vanessa Smith. BSc, Loyola U., Chgo., 1964; MD, St. Louis U., 1968; MPhil, Georgetown U., 1993. Lic. Mo., 1968. Intern U. Conn., 1968—69, resident, 1969—70, Johns Hopkins U., Balt., 1972—73, fellow pulmonary medicine, 1973—74, Mayo Clin., 1974—75; from asst. prof. to prof. medicine Johns Hopkins U., 1975, prof. medicine, 1993—. Chmn. ethics com. Johns Hopkins Hosp., Balt., 1994—97. Contbr. articles to profl. jours. Vice chmn. sci. and med. adv. bd. Hereditary Hemmorhagic Telangetasia Found., Balt., 2003—07. Maj. US Army, 1970—72. Recipient Roger C. Bone Meml. Lectureship award, Am. Coll. Chest Physicians, 1999. Mem.: Am. Thoracic Soc. Achievements include development of treatment of for rare disease Hereditary Hemorrhagic Telangectasia. Office: The Johns Hopkins Univ 1830 East Monument St Baltimore MD 21210

TERRY, ROBERT BROOKS, food products executive, lawyer; b. Kansas City, Mo., July 7, 1956; s. Frank R. and Susan S. (Smart) T.; m. Penny Susan Kanterman, July 2, 1987; children: Ryan, Kevin, Erin. Student, Vanderbilt U., 1974-75; BS in Acctg., U. Mo., 1978, JD, 1981. Bar: Mo. 1981, U.S. Dist. ct. (we. dist.) Mo. 1981, U.S. ct. Appeals (8th and 10th cirs.) 1983. Assoc. Spencer, Fane, Britt & Browne, Kansas City, Mo., 1981—89; v.p., gen. counsel Farmland Industries, Inc., Kansas City, 1993—, pres., CEO, 2002—. Mem. ABA, Kansas City Mo. Bar Assn., Lawyers' Assn. Kansas City, Order of Coif. Avocation: baseball. Home: 4952 W 132nd Ter Leawood KS 66209-3460

TERRY, ROBERT ELI, physicist, aerospace scientist, educator; b. Port Arthur, Tex., Apr. 28, 1946; s. Gilbert Graydon and Elizabeth Vuylsteke Terry. PhD, Johns Hopkins U., Balt., 1978. Scientist JAYCOR, Alexandria, Va., 1979—84; rsch. physicist Naval Rsch. Lab., Washington, 1985—. Dir. aerospace edn. Md. Wing CAP, Balt., 2005—07. Mem.: Am. Phys. Soc. Home: 10837 Braeburn Rd Columbia MD 21044 Home Phone: 410-531-1643.

TERRY, ROBERT MEREDITH, foreign language educator; b. Danville, Va., Dec. 16, 1939; s. Willard Terry and Martha Willeford; m. Anne Reynolds Beggarly, Jan. 30, 1965; children: Michael Reynolds, Christopher Robert, Meredith Anne. BA in French, Randolph-Macon Coll., Ashland, Va., 1962; PhD in Romance Langs., Duke U., Durham, NC, 1966. Asst. prof. French U. Fla., Gainesville, Fla., 1966-68; assoc. prof. U. Richmond, Richmond, Va., 1968-83, prof., 1983—. Pres. Am. Coun. on Tchg. Fgn. Langs., 1994, mem. exec. coun., 1983-85, 2000-04. Co-author: Accent: Conversational French I, 1980, Vous Y Etes!, 1990, Intersections, 1991; editor Dimension, So. Conf. on Lang. Tchg., 1991-97; assoc. editor ACTFL Foreign Language Education Series, 1994, 96, 98, 99, 2000; editor N.E. Conf. Report, 2000; articles editor NECTFL Rev., 2002—; contbr. articles to profl. jours. Recipient Stephen A. Freeman award N.E. Conf. on Teaching Fgn. Lang., 1990, Robert J. Ludwig Nat. Fgn. Lang. Leadership award, 1995, Florence Steiner award for Leadership in Fgn. Lang. Post-Secondary Edn., 2004. Mem. Am. Coun. on Tchg. Fgn. Langs., Fgn. Lang. Assn. Va., So. Conf. on Lang. Tchg. Home: 1504 Cloister Dr Richmond VA 23238 Office: Univ Richmond PO Box 25 28 Westhampton Way Richmond VA 23173-0025 Home Phone: 804-740-0862. Business E-Mail: rterry@richmond.edu.

TERRY, ROBIN, museum director; b. 1969; Degree in Telecom. and Film, Eastern Mich. U., 1992. Dir., Pub. Rels. Motown Hist. Mus., Detroit, 1992—95, dep. dir., 2002—04, exec. dir., 2004—; worked for D'Arcy Masius Benton & Bowles Inc., Troy, Mich., 1995, Gable Grp.; dir., Pub. Rels. Coll. for Creative Studies; devel. officer Focus: HOPE, 1998—2002. Named one of 40 Under 40, Crain's Detroit Bus., 2006. Office: Motown Historical Museum 2648 W Grand Blvd Detroit MI 48208 Office Phone: 313-875-2264.

TERRY, ROGER, retired pathologist, consultant; b. Waterville, NY, May 8, 1917; s. Orrin and Mary Isabelle (Kennedy) T.; m. Eleanor Virginia Wallace, Dec. 13, 1942; children: Robin, Orrin. AB magna cum laude, Colgate U., 1939; MD, U. Rochester, 1944. Cert. anatomic pathologist. Intern then resident Strong Meml. Hosp., Rochester, NY, 1944-51; asst. prof. U. Rochester Sch. Medicine, 1951-56, assoc. prof., 1956-61, prof. pathology, 1961-69, U. So. Calif. Sch. Medicine, Los Angeles, 1969-82; pathologist San Gabriel (Calif.) Valley Med. Ctr., 1982—2003; ret., 2003. Exec. dir. Calif. Tumor Tissue Registry, L.A., 1969-84. Contbr. articles to profl. jours. Served to capt. USAF, 1954-56. Fellow Am. Soc. Clin. Pathologists, Coll. Am. Pathologists; mem. AMA, Internat. Acad. Pathology (councilor 1973-76), Am. Soc. Investigative Pathology, L.A. Soc. Pathologists (pres. 1974, Lifetime Achievement award 2006), Am. Soc. Cytopathology, Internat. Soc. Dermatopathology, Phi Beta Kappa, Sigma Xi, Alpha Omega Alpha. Republican. Episcopalian. Avocations: ballroom dancing, snorkeling, bicycling. Home: 2841 Shakespeare Dr San Marino CA 91108-2230

TERRY, TIMOTHY P., lawyer; b. Aug. 11, 1965; BA, U. Tex., Austin, 1986; grad. studies in Internat. Transactions, George Mason U., 1993; JD, U. Calif. Hastings Coll. Law, 1999. Bar: Calif. 2000. Worked on Subcom. on Commerce US Ho. of Reps, 1987—88; legis. asst. & press sec. US Rep. Gus Yatron, 1988—90; legis. dir. US Rep. Vic Fazio, 1990—95; prin. Ferguson Co., Washington, 1995—96; law clk./assoc. Abramson & Smith, San Francisco; assoc. Leboeuf, Lamb, Greene & MacRae, LA, Sonnenschein Nath & Rosenthal LLP, LA. Chmn. bd. dirs. The Fed. Tech. Ctr., Sacramento. Mem.: ABA. Office: Sonnenschein Nath & Rosenthal LLP 601 S Figueroa St, Ste 1500 Los Angeles CA 90017 Office Phone: 213-892-5073. Office Fax: 213-623-9924. Business E-Mail: tterry@sonnenschein.com.

TERRY, W. BURKS, lawyer; b. Balt., Dec. 12, 1950; BA in Econ. and Philosophy, U. Calif., Berkeley, 1973; JD, U. Notre Dame, 1976. Bar: Calif. Contracts mgr. George A. Fuller Co., 1976; corp. v.p., asst. gen. counsel Space Electronics Group Northrop Grumman Corp., LA, 1989, v.p., dep. gen. counsel, corp. v.p., gen. counsel, 2000—. Mem.: ABA, Ill. Bar Assn. Office: Northrop Grumman Corp 1840 Century Park E Los Angeles CA 90067-2199 *

TERRY, WAYNE GILBERT, healthcare educator, hospital administrator; b. Plymouth, Mass., Oct. 2, 1932; s. Lawrence Arthur and Betty Frances (Boutemain) Terry; m. Barbara Bromwell, Sept. 20, 1980; children: Karleton Wayne, Dale Duane, Kendrick Shane, Kristen Alayne, Tammye Van Clief, Wade Bromwell Delk. AA in Gen. Adminstrn., Allan Hancock Coll., Santa Maria Calif., 1960; BBA in Bus. Mgmt., U. Hawaii, Honolulu, 1966; MHA, Med. Coll. Va., Va. Commonwealth U., Richmond, 1973; PhD in Health Svcs. Mgmt., LaSalle U., 1999. Commd. 2d lt. USAF Med. Svc. Corps, 1967, advanced through grades to maj., 1976; asst. adminstr. for registrar activities USAF Hosp., Orlando AFB, Fla., 1966-67; assoc. adminstr. aeromed. evacuation activities USAF, Hickam AFB, Hawaii, 1967-71; adminstrv. resident USAF Regional Hosp., Langley AFB, Va., 1972-73; CEO USAF Hosp., Columbus AFB, Miss., 1973-75; nat. health edn. and tng. program advisor Office of Surgeon Gen., Dept. of Air Force, Washington, 1975-78; dir. health professions pers. planning and policy divsn. Office of Asst. Sec. Def. for Health Affairs, The Pentagon, Washington, 1978-80; dep. project mgr./adminstrv. dir. King Faisal U. Teaching Hosp., Al-Khobar, Saudi Arabia, 1980-82; dep. project mgr., hosp. dir. North Yemen Healthcare Project, As-Salem Hosp., Sadah, Yemen Arab Republic, 1982-83; hosp. dir., CEO western area Armed Forces Hosps., Khamis Mushayt, Saudi Arabia, 1983-84; chief adminstr./commissioning team chief Orbit Summit Health, Ltd., Riyadh, Saudi Arabia, 1984-85; hosp. dir., adminstrv. dir. Truk State Dept. Health Svcs., Moen, Federated States of Micronesia, 1985-87; assoc. adminstr. support svcs. King Fahad Hosp., Saudi Arabian N.G., Riyadh, 1987-90; project mgr., CEO N.W. Armed Forces Hosps. Program, Tabuk, Saudi Arabia, 1990-98, cons. in health svcs. mgmt., 1998-99; cons., mediator in health svcs. mgmt. Crozet, Va., 1999-2000; exec. dir., CEO Southside Area Health Edn. Ctr. Longwood U., Farmville, Va., 2000—. Apptd. mil. cons. healthcare planning to the Air Force Surgeon Gen., 1979; apptd. preceptor program in healthcare adminstrn. U. Mich. for adminstrv. residents at N.W. Armed Forces Hosps. Programs, Tabuk, Saudi Arabia, 1993; supervisory bd. Royal Coll. Surgeons in Ireland, Dublin, 1990-98; cert. sr. grant specialist, reviewer, cons.; lectr., cons. in field. Contbr. articles to profl. jours. Warden to Am. Cmty. N.W. Region of Yemen Arab Republic to Am. Embassy in Sanaa, 1982-83, warden to Am. Cmty. N.W. Region of Saudi Arabia to Am. Embassy in Riyadh, 1990-99; mem. Internat. Sch. Sys. Coord. Com., Tabuk, 1990-99; bd. dirs. Taif Sch. Dist. Sys., Saudi Arabia, 1981-82; chmn., exec. com., bd. dirs. Ctrl. Va. Health Planning Agy., Richmond, Va., 2001—; bd. dirs. Va. Tobacco Settlement Found., Regional Adv. Bd., Richmond, Va., 2001—, Southside Area Health Edn. Ctr., Longwood U., Farmville, 2001—; leadership and planning group Nat. Area Health Edn. Ctr. Assn., Balt., 2003-04. Decorated Def. Meritorious Svc. medal, Air Force Meritorious Svc. medal with 3 oak leaf clusters, Air medal with 2 oak leaf clusters, Air Force Commendation medal with 2 oak leaf clusters, Republic of Vietnam Gallantry Cross with palm, Republic of Vietnam Svc. medal with 11 svc. stars, Korean Def. Svc. medal, Sec. of Def. Svc. medal/badge, Air Staff badge Dept. Air Force, Air Force Chief Med. Svc. Corps badge; recipient Citation of Appreciation Nat. Coun. Social Welfare, Seoul, Republic of Korea, 1963, Citation of Appreciation award Suchan Province Gov., Choong Nam, Republic of Korea, 1963, award of merit Pacific Air Forces Command, Hickam AFB, Hawaii, 1965, Outstanding Jr. Officer in 22nd Air Force, USAF, 1970, Outstanding Rsch. award Med. Coll. Va., 1973, Personality of the South award, 1975, Men of Achievement award, Cambridge, Eng., 1982, Citation of Appreciation Gov. Truk State, Federated States of Micronesia, 1987, Citation of Merit Internat. Red Cross Commn., Bern, Switzerland, 1991, N.W. Armed Forces Hosps., Ministry Def. and Aviation, Tabuk, 1991, Citation of Appreciation Presidency of Gen. Staff Hdqs., Ministry of Def. and Aviation, Tabuk, 1992-93, 95-99, Disting. Alumni award Allan Hancock Coll., Santa Maria, 2000, Citation of Appreciation Longwood U., Va., 2006. Fellow Am. Coll. Healthcare Execs., Royal Soc. Health; mem. Am. Hosp. Assn., Am. Mgmt. Assn., Air Force Med. Svc. Corps Assn. (membership and awards com. 2003—, bd. dirs., newsletter editor 2005—), Assn. Mil. Surgeons of U.S., Air Force Assn. Republican. Baptist. Avocations: tennis, coin collecting/numismatics, hiking. Office: Southside Area Health Edn Ctr Longwood Univ 201 High St Farmville VA 23909 Home Phone: 434-392-3226; Office Phone: 434-395-2862. Business E-Mail: terrywg@longwood.edu.

TERRY, WILLIAM B. (BILL), lawyer; b. Chgo., Aug. 31, 1946; BA, U. Nev., 1969; JD, U. San Diego, 1973. Bar: Nev. 1973, US Ct. Appeals (9th cir.) 1974, US Dist. Ct., Nev. 1977, US Ct. Appeals (5th and 10th cir.) 1977, US Supreme Ct. Asst. US atty. Dist. of Nev., 1973—76, alternate mcpl. ct. judge, 1976; mem. Law Offices of William B. Terry, Las Vegas. Lawyer rep. US Ct. Appeals (9th cir.), 1981—84, chmn., 1983—84; mem. Com. to Revise Rules of Practice, US Dist. Ct., Nev. Named one of Best Criminal Defense Attys., Las Vegas Review-Jour., 1999; recipient Justinian Award, 1997. Mem.: ABA, Nev. Attys. for Criminal Justice, Nev. Trial Lawyers Assn., Nat. Assn. Criminal Defense Lawyers, Assn. Trial Lawyers of Am., State Bar Nev., Clark County Bar Assn. (Professionalism Award 1997), Phi Alpha Delta, Phi Beta Kappa, Sigma Chi. Office: 530 S Seventh St Las Vegas NV 89101 Office Phone: 702-385-0799. Office Fax: 702-385-9788. E-mail: info@williamterrylaw.com. *

TERRY, WILLIAM LEAKE, lawyer; b. Little Rock; s. David Dickson and Adolphine Fletcher Terry; m. Elizabeth Kilbury Terry, June 20, 1947; children: Elizabeth Terry Foti, Ellen Fletcher, Susan Terry Borne. Student, Princeton U., NJ, 1941—43; BS in Bus. Adminstrn., U. Ark., Fayetteville, 1948, LLB, 1950. Bar: Ark., US Ct. Mil. Appeals. Law clk. Ark. Supreme Ct. Justice, Little Rock, 1950; atty. Ark. State Hwy. Dept., Little Rock, 1951—53; ptnr. Friday, Eldredge and Clark, Little Rock, 1954—90, of counsel, 1991—. Bd. trustees Ark. Arts Ctr., Little Rock, 1968—72; ombudsman Ark. Com. Employer Support Guard and Reserve; bd. dirs. Ark. River Hist. Soc., Tulsa, MacArthur Mus. Ark., Little Rock, 2000—, Ctrl. Ark. Libr. Sys, Little Rock, 1991—2000, United Way Pulaski County, 1966—79, All Saints Epsicopal. Sch., Vicksburg, Miss., 1968—70. Lt. col. USAF, 1943—45, with USAFR, with JAG. Decorated Disting. Flying Cross with Oak Leaf Clusters. Mem.: Ark. Bar Found. (bd. dirs. 1969—72), Pulaski County Bar Assn. (pres. 1977—78), Kiwanis. Avocations: history, tennis, boating, hunting, travel. Home: 6323 Greenwood Rd Little Rock AR 72207 Office: Friday Eldredge & Clark 2000 Regions Ctr 400 w Capital Ave Little Rock AR 72201

TERSCHAN, FRANK ROBERT, lawyer; b. Dec. 25, 1949; s. Frank Joseph and Margaret Anna (Heidt) T.; m. Barbara Elizabeth Keily, Dec. 28, 1974; 1 child, Frank Martin. BA, Syracuse U., 1972; JD, U. Wis., 1975. Bar: Wis. 1976, U.S. Dist. Ct. (ea. and we. dists.) Wis. 1976, U.S. Ct. Appeals (7th cir.) 1979, U.S. Ct. Appeals (10th cir.) 1989, U.S. Supreme Ct. 1992. From assoc. to ptnr. Frisch, Dudek & Slattery Ltd., Milw., 1975-88; ptnr. Slattery and Hausman Ltd., Milw., 1988-94, Terschan & Steinle Ltd., Milw., 1994-96, Terschan, Steinle & Ness, Milw., 1996—. Chmn. MBA Fee Adminstrn. Com., 2000—; mem. Wis. Jud. Conduct Adv. Com., 2002—. Treas., sec. Ville du Park Homeowners Assn., Mequon, Wis., 1985-86; cubmaster Boy Scouts Am., 1989-90, asst. scoutmaster, 1991-93. Mem. ABA, Am. Bd. Trial Advocates, Wis. Bar Assn., Milw. Bar Assn., Assn. Trial Lawyers Am., Wis. Acad. Trial Lawyers (bd. dirs. 1996—), 7th Cir. Bar Assn., Order of Coif. Republican. Lutheran. Avocations: swimming, coin collecting/numismatics, reading, outdoor activities. Home: 10143 N Lake Shore Dr Mequon WI 53092-6109 Office: 309 N Water St Ste 215 Milwaukee WI 53202 Office Phone: 414-258-1010. Business E-Mail: frt@tsn-law.com.

TERSIGNI, JENNIFER M., not-for-profit fundraiser; BA in Polit. Sci., Indiana U. Pa., Pa., 1996; MA in Women's Studies, U. Ariz., Tucson, 1998. Intern White Ho., Washington, 1995; rsch., tchr. asst. U. Ariz., Tucson, 1996—98; devel. coord. CODAC Behaviorial Health, Tucson, 1998—99; div. devel. Family Counseling Agy., Tucson, 1999—2005; dir. major and planning giving ARC, Tucson, 2005—. Bd. dirs. Pie Allen Neighborhood Assn., Tucson, 2001—. Mem.: Ariz. Women's Polit. Caucus, Assn. Fundraising Profls. (chmn. youth in philanthropy 2005—, bd. dirs. 2005—). Democrat. Office: ARC So Ariz Chpt 5301 E Broadway Blvd Tucson AZ 85711

TERSOFF, JERRY DAVID, physicist; BA in Physics, Swarthmore Coll., 1977; PhD in Physics, U. Calif., Berkeley, 1982. Postdoctoral fellow Bell Labs., Murray Hill, NJ, 1982-84; mem. rsch. staff IBM T.J. Watson Rsch. Ctr., Yorktown Heights, NY, 1984—. Contbr. numerous articles on solid state physics to scholarly and profl. jours. Fellow Am. Physical Soc. (Davisson Germer prize 1997); mem. Materials Rsch. Soc. (MRS medal 1996), Am. Vacuum Soc. (Peter Mark award 1988). Achievements include theoretical advances in the understanding of scanning tunneling microscopy; heterojunction band offsets and Schottky barriers; epitaxial growth and carbon nanotube electronic devices. Office: IBM TJ Watson Rsch Ctr PO Box 218 Yorktown Heights NY 10598-0218

TERTELING-PAYNE, CAROLYN ANN, city official; b. Buhl, Idaho, Dec. 20, 1936; d. Carl Treva and Ann Christine (Witt) Edwards; m. Joseph Loyd Terteling, June 20, 1959 (div. Sept. 1991); children: Joseph Nixon, Steven Loyd, Thomas Edward, Andrew James; m. Frank Adrian Payne, May 13, 1995. BA with highest honors, U. Idaho, Moscow, 1959. Grad. tchg. asst. Ariz. State U., Phoenix, 1959-60; mem. Boise City Coun., 1993—, pres., 1996—2003; mayor City of Boise, Idaho, 2003—. Sustainer Boise Jr. League; mem. Collector's Forum, Boise Art Mus.; trustee, mem. exec. com., mem. bldg. and planning com. St. Lukes Regional Med. Ctr.; pres. Boise Pub. Libr. Found.; dir., past pres. U. Idaho Found.; dir. Fundsy Charitable Found., Boise River Festival; mem. adv. bd. Lit. Lab, Warm Springs Counseling Ctr.; hon. bd. Idaho Zool. Soc.; emeritus dir. Boise Philharmonic; past dir. Boise Mus. Art, Boise Bicentennial Commn., Boise Sch. Vols., Idaho Hist. Preservation Coun., Morriso Ctr. for Arts, Endowment Dr., Women's Life at St. Lukes, Idaho Law Found.; mem. adv. bd. Children at Risk Evaluative Svcs.; past dir. area coun. 11 Western states, Assn. Jr. Leagues Am.; past pres. St. Lukes Hosp. Aux., U. Idaho Found., Boise Jr. League; past chair symposium Albertson Coll. Idaho, Grand Opening of Morrison Ctr. for Arts, Sun valley, Arts and Humanities Benefit, Alternate Mobility Adventure Seekers, Boise State U. Named Idaho Statesman Disting. Citizen, 1979, Woman of Yr., C. of C., 1986; recipient Woman of Today and Tomorrow award Girl Scouts, 1992, Disting. Svc. award Idaho State Bar, 1992, Cultural Heritage award Coll. Letters and Sci. U. Idaho, 1994. Mem. U. Idaho Alumni Assn., Hillcrest Country Club (past dir.), PEO, Phi Beta Kappa, Gamma Phi Beta. Avocations: golf, tennis, gardening, reading. Home: 2050 Table Rock Rd Boise ID 83712-6663 Office: City Hall 150 N Capitol Blvd Boise ID 83702-5920

TERVALON, JOSEPHINE M., psychotherapist, social worker; b. Pender County, NC, Oct. 9, 1939; d. Joseph Samuel and Dorothy Ann (Messick) Merritt; m. William F. Cunningham Jr. (div.); children: Charles F. Cunningham, Steven Troy Cunningham; m. Albert T. Tervalon, Mar. 20, 1999; stepchildren: Albert L. III, Mark, Brett, Tasha. BS, Tuskegee Inst., 1961; MSW, Smith Coll., 1963. Diplomate Am. Bd. Examiners in Clin. Social Work; LCSW Tex. State Bd. Examiners, lic. Registry of Cert. Group Psychotherapists N.Y., cert. profl. coach Grow Tng. Inst. Sr. psychiatric social worker Cmty. Guidance Ctr., San Antonio; dir. outpatient svc., chief social worker San Antonio Children's Ctr.; program coord. adolescent ctr. Houston Internat. Hosp.; dir. social svcs., coord. adolescent unit W.Oaks Hosp., Houston; dir. unit programs Psychiatric Inst. Houston; pvt. practice Houston. Cons., Houston; practicum asst. prof. Worden Sch. Social Svcs., Our Lady of Lake U., 1975—80; clin. instr. Baylor Coll. Medicine, 1981—2006; adj. asst. prof. Smith Coll. Sch. Social Work, 1985—2007; presenter in field. Fellow: Am. Group Psychotherapy Assn. (life); mem.: NAFE (workshop presenter 1990—92), Tex. Soc. Clin. Social Work (keynote spkr. 2001). Office: Cunningham Tervalon Assoc 4801 Woodway Dr Ste 350W Houston TX 77056

TERVEER, JOYCE ANN, academic administrator, English language educator; b. Freeburg, Ill., Aug. 21, 1936; d. Oliver Andrew and Elsa Pearl (Davis) Klopmeyer; m. Russell Benjamin Terveer, Dec. 29, 1973; children: Robert Scott France, Tab France. BA, McKendree Coll., 1957; MA, So. Ill. U., 1974. English tchr., libr. Freeburg HS, Ill., 1957-64; English tchr., adminstr. Althoff Cath. HS, Belleville, Ill., 1965-98. Mem. Nat. Coun. Tchrs., Nat. Assn. Secondary Sch. Prins., Ill. Assn. Tchrs. English, Delta Kappa Gamma. Church of Christ. Home: 33 Fawnlily Dr Belleville IL 62221-4344

TERWILLEGAR, JANE CUSACK, librarian, educator; b. Warsaw, NY, Nov. 7, 1935; d. James Scott and Estella B. (Ackerman) Cusack; m. Gordon H. Terwillegar, July 26, 1958 (div. Mar. 1989); children: Sarah Ann Terwillegar Smedley, Arne Matthew. BA, Elmira Coll., NY, 1957; MLS, SUNY, Geneseo, 1960; EdS, U. Ga., 1977. Cert. tchr., Fla. Instr. U. Ga., Athens, 1975-81; libr. Palm beach County Libr., West Palm Beach, Fla., 1981-83, Palm Beach County Schs., Royal Palm Beach, Fla., 1983-94, dist. libr. media svcs. mgr. West Palm Beach, 1994—2000; dir. Lake Park Public Libr., 2000—. Lectr. Sch. Libr. and Info. Sci., U. South Fla., Tampa, 1987—, Nova U., Ft. Lauderdale, Fla., 1995—; task force mem. SUNLINK project Fla. Dept. Edn., 1995-2000; mem. adv. coun. Fla. Libr. Svcs. and Tech. Act., 1999—. Co-author: Commonsense Cataloging, 3d edit. 1983, 4th edit. 1990; reviewer Sch. Libr. Jour., 1986—; contbr. articles to profl. jours. Pres. Staff Assn. Palm Beach Sch. Dist., 1997-99. Mem. ALA, AAUW (pres. No. Palm Beach br. 2001-05), Am. Assn. Sch. Librs. (exec. bd. 1990-94), Assn. for Libr. Svc. to Children (Newbery com. 1988-89), Fla. Assn. Media in Edn. (sec. 1988-89, bd. dirs. 1997—, pres. 1999-2001), Ednl. Media Assn. Fla. (pres. 1988), Kiwanis Club of Lake Park, Phi Beta Kappa, Phi Delta Kappa. Avocations: scuba diving, sports cars. Home: 911 Oak Harbour Dr Juno Beach FL 33408-2173 Office: Lake Park Public Libr 529 Park Ave West Palm Beach FL 33403- Office Phone: 561-881-3330.

TERWILLIGER, GEORGE JAMES, III, lawyer; b. New Brunswick, NJ, June 5, 1950; s. George James Jr. and Ruth Nancy (Mellilo) T.; m. Carol Anne Hitchings, Dec. 18, 1976; children: Sarah Katherine, George Zachary Grant, Virginia. BA in Communications, Seton Hall U., 1973; JD, Antioch Law Sch., 1978. Bar: D.C. 1978, U.S. Dist. Ct. D.C., 1979, U.S. Ct. Appeals (D.C. cir.) 1979, U.S. Dist. Ct. (so. dist.) Fla. 1980, U.S. Dist. Ct. Vt. 1981, U.S. Ct. Appeals (2d cir.) 1982, Vt. 1983, U.S. Supreme Ct. 1992, U.S. Ct. Appeals (4th cir.) 1993. Asst. US atty. DC dist. US Dept. Justice, Washington, 1978-81, asst. US atty. dist. Vt Burlington, 1981-86, US atty., 1986-91, dep. atty. gen. Washington, 1992-93; ptnr.-in-charge McGuire, Woods, Battle & Boothe, Washington, 1993; ptnr. White & Case LLP, Washington. Named one of 100 Most Influential Lawyers, Nat. Law Jour., 2006. Mem. ABA, Vt. Bar Assn., D.C. Bar Assn., Rep. Nat. Lawyers Assn. (pres. 1994-95). Republican. Congregationalist. Avocations: skiing, tennis, fishing. Office: White & Case LLP 701 Thirteenth St NW Washington DC 20005

TERWILLIGER, J. RONALD, real estate company executive; Grad., US Naval Acad.; MBA (hon.), Harvard U. Pres., COO Sea Pines Plantation Co., Hilton Head (S.C.) Plantation Co.; chmn., CEO Trammell Crow Residential, Atlanta, 1986—. Chmn. emeritus Wharton Real Estate Ctr.; mem. Fannie Mae Adv. Coun. Mem. internat. bd. dirs. Habitat for Humanity; vice chmn. Atlanta Neighborhood Devel. Partnership; dir. Naval Acad. Found. Baker scholar, Harvard Grad. Sch. Bus. Mem.: Real Estate Roundtable, Urban Land Inst. (immediate past chmn.). Office: Trammell Crow Residential Ste 1100 2859 Paces Ferry Rd Atlanta GA 30339

TERWILLIGER, MOLLY, lawyer; b. Wausau, Wisc., Sept. 27, 1972; BA, Northwestern Univ., Chgo., 1994; JD, Univ. Wis., Madison, 1998. Bar: Wis. 1998, Wash. 1998. Assoc. atty., antitrust, trade regulation Heller Ehrman LLP, Seattle. Contbr. articles to numerous profl. jours. Named Wash. Rising Star, SuperLawyer Mag., 2006. Mem.: ABA, Wash. Bar Assn. Office: Heller Ehrman LLP Ste 6100 701 Fifth Ave Seattle WA 98104-7098 E-mail: molly.terwilliger@hellerehrman.com.

TERZA, JOSEPH VINCENT, economics professor; PhD, U. Pitts., 1981. Prof. epidemiology and health policy rsch. U. Fla., Gainesville, 2005—. Mem.: Am. Soc. Health Economists, Internat. Health Econs. Assn. Office: Univ Fla Dept Epidemiology & Health Policies Rsch Gainesville FL 32610 Office Phone: 352-265-0111 85068. Office Fax: 352-265-7221. Business E-Mail: jvt@ichp.ufl.edu.

TERZIAN, GRACE PAINE, communications executive; b. Boston, Oct. 19, 1952; d. Thomas Fite and Grace Hillman (Benedict) Paine; m. Philip Henry Terzian, Oct. 20, 1979; children: William Thomas Hillman, Grace Benedict Paine. BA in Art History, Williams Coll., Williamstown, Mass., 1974. Art dir. The New Republic, Washington, 1976-78; asst. editor The Chronicle of Higher Edn., Washington, 1978-79; rsch. editor Archtl. Digest, LA, 1982-85; pub. The Women's Quar., Arlington, Va., 1994—2004; exec. dir. Allergy and Asthma Network Mothers of Asthmatics, 2004—06; v.p. comm. Hudson Inst., Washington, 2006—. Editor Ex Femina, 1996—2004; sr. v.p. Ind. Women's Forum, 1998-2004. Mem. Soc. Colonial Dames in Am., Phi Beta Kappa. Episcopalian. Home: 10505 Adel Rd Oakton VA 22124-1605 Office: The Hudson Inst 1015 15th St NW 6th Fl Washington DC 20005 Home Phone: 703-938-7321; Office Phone: 202-974-2400. Personal E-mail: gterzian@cox.net. Business E-Mail: gracet@hudson.org.

TERZIAN, PHILIP HENRY, journalist; b. Kensington, Md., July 5, 1950; s. L. A. and Louise (Anderson) Terzian; m. Grace Barrett Paine, Oct. 20, 1979; children: William Thomas Hillman, Grace Benedict Paine. BA in English, Villanova U., 1973; DTS, Episcopal Theol. Sem., Va., 1995; postgrad., Oxford U., Eng., 1976. Desk editor Reuters, Washington, 1973, U.S. News & World Report, Washington, 1973-74; asst. editor The New Republic, Washington, 1974-78; mem. policy planning staff Dept. State, Washington, 1978-79; asst. editor Anniston (Ala.) Star, 1979-80; assoc. editor Lexington (Ky.) Herald, 1980-82; asst. editor of editl. pages L.A. Times, 1982-86; editor of editl. pages Providence Jour., 1986-92, assoc. editor, syndicated columnist, 1992—2005; lit. editor The Weekly Standard, Washington, 2005—. Panelist Washington Wk. in Rev., C-SPAN, Fox News, Nat. Pub. Radio. Contbr. articles to newspapers and jours. Pres. Providence Cm. Fgn. Rels., 1989—92. Named finalist Disting. Commentary, Pulitzer Prize, 1991; recipient Edn. Writers award, Edn. Writers Am., 1981, Svc. to Preservation award, Ida Lee Willis Found., 1982, juror, Pulitzer Prize, 1994—95; Travelling fellow, Am. Journalism Found. Mem.: Nat. Book Critics Cir., Va. Hist. Soc., Am. Coun. on Germany, Assn. Literary Scholars and Critics, Order Hosp. St. John of Jerusalem, Soc. King Charles the Martyr, St. Andrew's Soc. Washington, Sons of Union Vets. of Civil War, Wolver Beagles (hon. whip), Univ. Club, Nat. Beagle Club. Republican. Episcopalian. Home: 10505 Adel Rd Oakton VA 22124-1605 Office: The Weekly Standard 1150 17th St NW Washington DC 20036 Office Phone: 202-293-4900. E-mail: pterzian@weeklystandard.com.

TERZIC, PETAR, mathematician, educator; b. Podgorica, Montenegro, Serbia-Monteneg (Yugoslavia), July 9, 1944; arrived in U.S., 1994; s. Vojin and Koviljka Terzic; m. Slavka Kaludjerovic, Jan. 28, 1950; children: Balsa, Katarina Terzic Conrad. BS, U. of Montenegro, Podgorica, 1974; MS, U. of Belgrade, Yugoslavia, 1985; MA, Liberty Theol. Sem., Lynchburg, Va., 2001; Bible cert., Liberty Bible Inst., Lynchburg, Va., 1996. Math. tchr. Dusan Vlahovic Agrl. H.S., Bar, Montenegro, 1973—74; instr. elec. engring. E. T. C. Nikola Tesla, Belgrade, 1974—80; comm. adminstr. City of Belgrade, 1980—90; prof. of elec. engring. Mil. Acad., Belgrade, Serbia, Yugoslavia, 1990—94; instr. of math. Liberty U., Lynchburg, 1997—. Author: (book) Einstein's Picture of the World, 1996, Philosophy of Nature, 1996, (5-vol. book) Famous Military Leaders of the World, 1992—93 (2nd Pl. award Internat. Book Fair, Belgrade, 1993). Recipient Recognition for excellence in tchg., State of Montengro, 1974, 2nd Pl. award at the European Vet.'s Athletic Competition, European Recreation Assn., 1989, 3rd Pl. award at the amateur chess competition in Belgrade, Chess Assn. of Belgrade, 1977, 1st Pl. award in shot put in the jr. competition, Athletic Assn. of Montenegro, 1961. Mem.: Am. Math. Assn., Nikola Tesla Amateur Radio Club (bd. dirs. 1980—90). Avocation: recreation.

TESAREK, DENNIS GEORGE, retired business consultant, writer, educator; b. Chgo., Jan. 2, 1935; s. George Joseph and Mary (Basl) T.; m. Caroline Arrena Myers, Jan. 1956 (div. Oct. 1968); children: William Paul, Dianne, Peter Bond; m. Kathleen Leigh Holm, Nov. 26, 1969; children: Philip Shawn, Leigh-Anne. BA in Math., U. Mo., 1956; postgrad., Systems Rsch. Inst., 1966, UCLA, 1984, Harvard U., 1985, MIT, 1986. Saleman Conn. Mut. Life Ins. Co., Dallas, 1959-61; systems engr. IBM, Phoenix, 1961-66, instr. LA, 1966-68, mgr. Houston, 1968-74, industry mgr. White Plains, NY, 1974-76, project mgr. LA, 1976-78, planning cons. Houston, 1978-84, cons. in bus. transformation, planning and gen. mgmt., 1984-97; owner Tesarek Enterprises (Consulting and Investments), 1997—. Adj. prof. Ariz. State U., 1963-65; guest lectr. U. Houston, 1980, 81, 83, 87. Author: Distributed Information Systems Planning Methodology, 1982, Information Systems Management Effectiveness Assessment, 1983, Business Systems Planning for Competitive Advantage Methodology, 1986, Executive Strategy Session Methodology, 1987, Management Planning Session Methodology, 1987, Steps in Strategic Investment Methodology, 1989. Tutor Vols. in Pub. Schs., Houston Ind. Sch. Dist., 1972-74, 80-82. 1st lt. USMC, 1956-59. Republican. Mem. Christian Sci. Ch. Avocations: color photography and printing, woodworking, reading, hiking, shooting.

TESCH, PHIIP C., dean, minister; s. Henry C. and Erna M. Tesch; m. Ruth Hoffmann; children: Amy Strickland, Rachel Kintop, David, Banjamin. BA, St. Francis Coll., Fort Wayne, Ind., 1971; MDiv, Concordia Theol. Sem., Springfield, Ill., 1975; JD, U. Houston, Tex., 1984. Pastor Trinity Luth. Ch., Decatur, Ill., 1976—78, Prince of Peace Luth. Ch., Racine, Wis., 1978—81, Christ Luth. Ch., Houston, 1981—85; v.p. student affairs, dean students Concordia U., St. Paul, 1985—2001, prof. applied ethics, 2001—06, dean grad. sch., 2006—07. Office: Concordia Univ 275 Syndicate St N Saint Paul MN 55104 Home Phone: 651-695-1692; Office Phone: 651-641-8861. Personal E-mail: tesch@csp.edu.

TESCHER, DONALD R., lawyer; b. Bklyn., Sept. 26, 1944; s. Harry A. and Irma (Gordon) T.; m. SuAnn Leiken; children: Jennifer L., Jonathan M. BSBA in Acctg., U. Fla., 1966, JD, 1969; LLM in Taxation, NYU, 1973. Bar: Fla. 1969, US Dist. Ct. (so. dist. Fla.), US Tax Ct. 1973. Sr. shareholder Schwartz, Nash, Heckerling & Tescher, Miami, 1973-84, Fine, Jacobson, Schwartz, Nash, Block & England, P.A., Miami, 1984-86, Tescher & Milstein, P.A., 1986-90, Tescher, Gutter, Chaves, Josepher, Rubin, Ruffin & Foreman, P.A., Miami, 1990—. Adj. prof. grad. tax progs. Sch. Law U. Miami, 1974-80, 92-95; spkr. in field. Contbr. articles to profl. jours., chpts. to books. Bd. trustees Found. Jewish Philanthropies of The Gtr. Miami Jewish Fedn., 1985, chmn. profl. adv. com., 1989-91; mem. profl. adv. com. Dade Cmty. Found., 1989-; bd. dirs. Switchboard of Miami, 1986-90, bd. trustees, 1990-95, pres. Beth David Congragation, 1981-83. Named one of Top 100 Attys., Worth mag., 2005—06. Fellow Am. Coll. Trust and Estate Counsel (mem. bus. planning com. 1994, spkr.), Am. Coll. Tax Counsel; mem. ABA (sect. taxation mem. com. fgn. tax problems 1973-74, com. partnerships 1974-75, com. income taxation estates and trusts 1975-77, estate and gift tax com. 1977, charitable transfers subcommittee 1990, bus. planning-chpt. 14 subcommittee, chmn. subcommittee internat. estate and gift taxation 1987-89), Fla. Bar (tax sect. chmn. 1984-85, del. tax sect. S.E. region liaison conf., bd. dirs. tax sect. exec. coun., spkr., real property, probate and trust law sect., mem. estate and trust tax planning com. 1986, chmn. probate and trust problems study com. 1995-98, chair trust law com. 1998), Gtr. Miami Tax Inst., Estate Planning Coun. Gtr. Miami, Dade County Planned Giving Coun., Boca Raton Tax Inst., South Palm Beach County Jewish Fedn. (adv. com.), Planned Giving Coun. Miami-Dade County. Avocations: skiing, tennis, reading. Office: Tescher Gutter Chaves Josepher Rubin Ruffin & Forman PA Boca Corp Ctr 2101 Corporate Blvd Ste 107 Boca Raton FL 33431-7343 Office Phone: 561-998-7847. Office Fax: 561-998-2642. E-mail: dtescher@floridatax.com. *

TESCHER, JENNIFER, bank executive; b. 1971; Grad., Northwestern U.; MA in pub. policy, U. Chgo. With ShoreBank Corp., Chgo., 1996—, ShoreBank Adv. Services, Chgo., 2002—04; dir. Ctr. Fin. Services Innovation, Chgo., 2004—. Pres. bd. Ctr. Econ. Progress, Chgo.; monthly columnist Am. Banker. Named one of 40 Under 40, Crain's Chgo. Bus., 2006. Office: Ctr Fin Services Innovation Ste 200 2230 S Michigan Ave Chicago IL 60616 Office Phone: 312-881-5856. Office Fax: 312-881-5801. E-mail: cfsi@cfsinnovation.com.

TESCHNER, DOUGLASS PAUL, project administrator; b. Cambridge, Mass., Oct. 29, 1949; s. Douglass P. Teschner and Mary Elizabeth (Bernt) Teschner Zeller; m. Martha Weaver, Sept. 26, 1981. BS in Forestry, U. Mass., 1971, EdD in Adminstrn., 1985; MS in Botany, U. Vt., 1978. Land surveyor Lincoln Engring. and Burnell Land Surveying, 1974, 78; tchr. White Mountain Sch., 1976; dir. Inst. Exptl. Studies, various locations, 1984-87; fin. officer Becket Acad., East Haddam, Conn., 1984-85; devel. dir. Riverbend Cmty. Mental Health, Concord, 1987—2002; state rep. N.H. Ho. of Reps., Concord, 1988—98, 2000—02; project dir. Rwanda Parliament Support Project, Kigali, 2002—04; project dir. Morocco Parliament Support Project USAID, 2004—. Co-editor: Wilderness Challenge: Outdoor Education Alternatives for Youth in Need, 1984; contbr. articles to profl. jours. Mem. Haverhill Hist. Soc.; vol. Peace Corps, 1971-73, Haverhill Congl. Ch. Mem.: Appalachian Mountain Club. Avocations: mountain climbing, hiking, rock and ice climbing, skiing. Home: 2100 Brushwood Rd Pike NH 03780-9706

TESELLE, EUGENE ARTHUR, JR., religion educator; b. Ames, Iowa, Aug. 8, 1931; s. Eugene Arthur and Hildegarde (Flynn) TeS.; m. Sallie McFague, Sept. 12, 1959 (div. Oct. 1976); children: Elizabeth, John; m. Penelope Saunders, Mar. 4, 1978; children: William, James, Thomas. BA, U. Colo., Boulder, 1952; BD, Princeton Theol. Sem., NJ, 1955; MA, Yale U., New Haven, Conn., 1960, PhD, 1963. Commr. to gen. assembly Presbyn. Ch. in U.S.A., 1993. Issues analyst Witherspoon Soc., 1987-93, 99-2005, pres., 1996-99; chmn. global missions com. Presbytery Mid. Tenn., 1989-93, mem. nominating com., 2002-05. Author: Augustine, the Theologian, 1970, Augustine's Strategy as an Apologist, 1974, Christ in Context, 1975, Thomas Aquinas: Faith and Reason, 1988, Living in Two Cities: Augustinian Trajectories in Political Thought, 1998, Augustine (Abingdon Pillars of Theology), 2006. Incorporator Belmont-Hillsboro Neighbors, Nashville, 1971, Consumer Coalition for Health, Nashville, 1980, Nashville Local, Dem. Socialists Am., 1983, Cen. Am. Solidarity Assn., Nashville, 1986. Presbyn. Grad. fellow, 1958, Rockefeller doctoral fellow, 1960, Kent fellow, 1961; recipient Thomas Jefferson award Vanderbilt U., 1996. Mem. Am. Acad. Religion, Am. Soc. Ch. History, Soc. for Values in Higher Edn., Workgroup on Constructive Christian Theology, Witherspoon Soc. (pres. 1995—99), Phi Beta Kappa. Home: 1925 19th Ave S Nashville TN 37212-3805 Personal E-mail: teselle@bellsouth.net.

TESMER, NANCY ANN STUTLER, retired librarian; b. Aug. 25, 1934; d. Ernest Lynn and Sophrona Rebecca (Pepper) Stutler; m. John A. Tesmer, Sept. 10, 1980. Student, U. Akron, 1952—54; BA, Kent State U., 1956. Jr. asst. libr. E. Br. Libr., Akron, 1956—59; hosp. libr. VA Hosp., Northampton, Mass., 1959—61, med. libr. Brecksville, Ohio, 1961—65, chief libr., 1965—73, assoc. chief libr. Cleve., 1973—75, chief libr., 1975—. Chief Regional Libr. Svc., 1986—90. Mem.: N.E. Ohio Med. Libr. Assn., Med. Libr. Assn., Zeta Tau Alpha. Home: 8537 SW 90th Pl Unit G Ocala FL 34481-7516 E-mail: nst0825@aol.com.

TESREAU, CYNTHIA LYNN, elementary school educator; b. Jackson, Tenn., Apr. 29, 1960; d. Dewitt Talmadge and Brenda Lynn Coppedge; m. Kevin Paul Tesreau, Mar. 29, 1997; children: Kristen Lynn Burrage, Nick Lee Burrage. BS in Elem. Edn., U. of Houston, 1983; MA in Tchg., Cumberland U., Lebanon, Tenn., 2001. Cert. tchr., adminstr. Tenn., Administration Tenn., 2005. Tchr. Spring Br. Ind. Sch. Dist., Houston, 1984—87, Shelby County Schs., Memphis, 1987—. Women's ensemble leader Trinity Bapt. Ch., Memphis, 2003—06, women's mininstry team mem., 2003—06. Named Tchr. of Yr., Chimneyrock Elem. Sch., 2005, Bailey Station Elem. Sch., 2006, Shelby County Schs., 2006; recipient, Patricia Ashcraft award for outstanding tchg., 2005. Mem.: NEA (assoc.), Tenn. Ednl. Assn. (assoc.), Shelby County Ednl. Assn. (assoc.), Pi Delta Kappa (assoc.), Pi Lambda Theta (life). Baptist. Avocations: needlepoint, quilting, water sports, travel. Office: Bailey Station Elementary 3435 Bailey Station Elementary Collierville TN 38017 Home Phone: 901-755-1288; Office Phone: 901-853-6380. E-mail: ctesreau@scsk12.org.

TESSIER, DENNIS MEDWARD, paralegal, writer; b. Royal Oak, Mich., Sept. 20, 1956; s. Medward James and Marilyn (Pitsos) Tessier; children: Brian Jae, Carson Lee. Cert. paralegal, U. West L.A., 1987, cert. atty. practice, 1990; cert. in epidemiology, U.S. CDC, 1991. Spl. asst. office of the gen. counsel U.S. Jud. Intelligence Agy., Pacific Sta., LA, 1981—; paralegal O'Melveny & Myers, LA, 1986, Haight, Brown & Bonesteel, Santa Monica, Calif., 1987-93, Helsell & Fetterman, Seattle, 1993-94, Nintendo of Am. Inc., Redmond, Wash., 1994-96, Tousley Brain PLLC, Seattle, 1996-98, Kirkpatrick & Lockhart Preston Gates Ellis, LLP, Seattle, 1998—. Family law cons. Helping Svcs., LA, 1990—93, L.A. Clinic, 1990; rschr. Tessier & Assocs. Rsch., Topanga Canyon, Calif., 1983—; assoc. Starlight Found., Redmond, Wash., 1993—. Author: Beauty in Motion, 1983, Champerty and Barratry, 1998, Trial Survival Manual, 1999, 2d edit., 2006, Anonymous Paralegal Survival Manual, 2007; contbr. articles to profl. jours. Mem.: ATLA, ABA (sci. and tech. law sect., jud. adminstrn. sect.), Wash. State Paralegal Assn., Wash. State Trial Lawyers Assn., U.S. Nat. Acad. Scis. Academe Industry Program (spkr. CLE), King County Bar Assn., Judge Advs. Assn., Assn. Investigative Scis., Soc. Epidemiology Rsch., Am. Legion. Democrat. Lutheran. Avocations: music, arts. Home: 21100 Pioneer Way Edmonds WA 98026-6947 Office: Kirkpatric Lockhart Preston Gates Ellis 925 Fourth Ave Ste 2900 Seattle WA 98104-1158 Office Phone: 206-623-7580. Personal E-mail: dtessier@justice.com. Business E-Mail: dennist@prestongates.com, dennis.tessier@klgates.com.

TESSIER-LAVIGNE, MARC TREVOR, neurobiologist, researcher; b. Trenton, Ont., Can., Dec. 18, 1959; arrived in US, 1987; s. Yves Jacques and Sheila Christine (Midgley) Tessier-L.; m. Mary Alanna Hynes, Feb. 4, 1989; children: Christian, Kyle, Ella. BSc, McGill U., 1980; BA, Oxford U., 1982; PhD, U. London, 1986. Exec. dir. Can. Student Pugwash Orgn., Ottawa, Ont., 1982-83; rsch. fellow devel. neurobiology unit Med. Rsch. Coun., London, 1986-87; rsch. fellow Ctr. for Neurobiology, Columbia U., NYC, 1987-91; asst. prof. dept. anatomy U. Calif., San Francisco, 1991-95, assoc. prof. dept. anatomy, 1995-97, prof. dept. anatomy and dept. biochemistry and biophysics, 1997—2000; Susan B. Ford prof. dept. biol. scis. Sch. Humanities and Scis. Stanford U., 2000—03; sr. v.p. rsch. drug discovery Genentech Inc., 2003—. Asst. investigator Howard Hughes Med. Inst., 1994-97; investigator Howard Hughes Med. Inst., 1997—. Contbr. articles on neurobiology to profl. jours. Recipient McKnight Investigator award, 1994, Karl Judson Herrick award for comparative neurology Am. Assn. Anatomists, 1994, Ameritec prize for significant contbn. in basic rsch. towards cure for paralysis, 1995, Ipsen prize for neuronal plasticity, 1996, Viktor Hamburger award in devel. neurobiology Internat. Jour. Devel. Neurosci., Young Investigator award Soc. for Neurosci., 1997, Wakeman award, 1998, Rober Dow award, 2003; Rhodes scholar, 1980, Commonwealth scholar, 1983, Markey scholar, 1989, Searle scholar, 1991, McKnight scholar, 1991; Klingenstein fellow, 1992. Fellow: AAAS, Royal Soc. of Can., The Royal Soc. (London); mem.: NAS, Soc. for Neuroscience (nominating com. 2000—02). Office: Genentech Inc 1 DNA Way South San Francisco CA 94080-4990

TESSING, LOUISE SCIRE, graphic designer; b. Chgo., May 13, 1946; d. Rocco Roy and Ruth Louise (Knueppel) Scire; m. Arvid Victor Tessing, Jan. 18, 1975. BS in Visual Design, Ill. Inst. Tech., 1968; MBA in Mktg., Loyola U., Chgo., 1986. Jr. designer Field Mus. Natural History, Chgo., 1968—69, Charles MacMurray & Assocs., Chgo., 1969—74; designer, art dir. Grant-Jacoby Inc., Chgo., 1974—76, Playboy Enterprises Inc., Chgo., 1976—78, Stevens Biondi Decicco Inc., Chgo., 1978—80; prin., owner Tessing Design Inc., Chgo., 1980—. Lobby treas. Ill. Women's Agenda, Chgo., 1990-92. Mem.: Soc. Typographic Arts (v.p. 2000—05), Internat. Assn. Bus. Communicators (v.p. comm. and design 1998—2002), Am. Ctr. for Design (bd. dirs. 1971—77, pres. 1976—77), Women in Design Chgo. (founder 1977, pres. 1977—78, 1991—93, Friend award 1990, Founder award 1997). Home and Office: Tessing Design Inc 3822 N Seeley Ave Chicago IL 60618-3912 Home Phone: 773-525-7704; Office Phone: 773-525-7704. E-mail: tess46@comcast.net.

TESSLER, SIDNEY, pulmonologist; MD, SUNY, Bklyn., 1970. Diplomate pulmonary disease Am. Bd. Internal Medicine, 1980, critical care medicine Am. Bd. Internal Medicine, 1997, Am. Bd. Internal Medicine, 1977. Dir. divsn. pulmonary and critical care medicine Maimonides Med. Ctr., Bklyn., 1977—. Clin. prof. medicine SUNY, Bklyn., 2002—. Lt. comdr. USPHS, 1972—74. Office: Maimonides Med Ctr 4802 Tenth Ave Brooklyn NY 11219 Office Phone: 718-283-8380. Office Fax: 718-283-7884. Business E-Mail: stessler@maimonidesmed.org.

TESTA, JAMES A., lawyer; b. Newark, Aug. 7, 1948; AB magna cum laude, Princeton U., 1970; JD, Harvard U., 1973. Bar: N.Y. 1974, U.S. Dist. Ct. (so. dist.) N.Y. 1975. Mem. Willkie Farr & Gallagher, NYC; shareholder Buchanan Ingersoll P.C., Princeton, NJ; pvt. practice Princeton, NJ. Mem. ABA (mem. bus. law sect.), N.Y. State Bar Assn., Phi Beta Kappa. Office: 26 Primrose cir Princeton NJ 08540-9415 Office Phone: 732-274-9455.

TESTA, JOSEPH R., geneticist; b. Norwalk, Conn., Apr. 28, 1947; PhD, Fordham U., 1976. Diplomate Am. Bd. Med. Genetics. Geneticist tumor cytogenetics U. Chgo., 1976-80; sr. mem. staff Fox Chase Cancer Ctr., Phila., dir. Human Genetics Program, Weg endowed chair human genetics. Mem. AAAS, ASGH, Am. Assn. Cancer Rsch., Am. Soc. Hematology. Office: Fox Chase Cancer Ctr 333 Cottman Ave Philadelphia PA 19111-2497 Office Phone: 215-728-2610. Fax: 215-214-1623. E-mail: Joseph.Testa@fccc.edu.

TESTA, MICHAEL HAROLD, lawyer; b. NYC, 1939; m. Carol Waldenberg, 1962; 2 children. BS summa cum laude, NYU, 1958, LLB cum laude, 1961, LLM in Taxation, 1967. Bar: NY 1961. Assoc. White & Case, NYC, 1962-71, Skadden, Arps, Slate, Meagher & Flom, NYC, 1971-72, ptnr., 1972-91; conservation lawyer, sole practitioner Michael H. Testa, NYC, 1992—. Advisor U.S. del. to UN Conf. on Straddling Fish Stocks and Highly Migratory Fish Stocks, 1994-95, U.S. del. to Kyoto Internat. Conf. on Sustainable Contribution of Fisheries to Food Security, 1995, to N.W. Atlantic Fisheries Orgn., 1996, 98, to 22d Session of FAO Com. on Fisheries, 1997, to Western and Ctrl. Pacific Fisheries Conf., 1998-2001; adj. assoc. prof. law NYU Law Sch., 1986; mem. consultative com. to secs. state and commerce N.W. Atlantic Fisheries Conv., 1996-2002. Assoc. editor, contbr.: NYU Law Rev., 1960-61; contbr. articles to legal jours. Mem. planning bd. Town of Tuxedo (N.Y.), 1971-76. Served to capt. USAFR, 1961-72. Root-Tilden-Snow scholar, 1958-61. Mem. Order of Coif. Home: 860 UN Plz New York NY 10017 Office: Ste 28-424 4 Times Square New York NY 10036-6522

TESTAVERDE, VINCENT FRANK (VINNY TESTAVERDE), professional football player; b. Bklyn., Nov. 13, 1963; m. Mitzi Testaverde; children: Alicia Marie, Vincent Jr. Student, U. Miami, Fla. Quarterback Tampa Bay (Fla.) Buccaneers, 1987—92, Cleve. Browns, 1993—95, Balt. Ravens, 1996—98, NY Jets, Hempstead, NY, 1998—2004, 2005, Dallas Cowboys, 2004, New England Patriots, 2006—. Named Coll. Football Player of Yr., The Sporting News, 1986; named to NFL Pro-Bowl, 1996, 1998; recipient Heisman trophy, 1986. Achievements include Passing for over 40,000 yards. Office: New England Patriots 60 Washington St Foxboro MA 02035 *

TESTER, JON(ATHAN), senator, former state legislator, farmer; b. Havre, Mont., Aug. 21, 1956; m. Sharla Tester; children: Christine, Shon. BS in Music, U. Great Falls, 1978. Tchr. Big Sandy School District, 1978—80; farmer organic wheat, barley, lentils, peas, millet, buckwheat, alfalfa and hay; mem. Mont. Senate from Dist. 45, Helena, 1998—2005, 2005—06, minority whip, 2001—03, minority leader, 2003—05, pres., 2005—06; US Senator from Mont., 2007—. Mem. Big Sandy Sch. Bd., 1983—91, chmn., 1986—91. Named an Outstanding Agrl. Leader, Coll. Agrl., Mont. State U., 2005. Democrat. Office: US Senate B-40E Dirksen Senate Office Bldg Washington DC 20510 Office Phone: 202-224-3121. E-mail: jontester@yahoo.com. *

TETER, HANNAH, Olympic athlete; b. Belmont, VT, Jan. 27, 1987; Profl. snowboarder Burton Snowboarding team, 2002—; snowboarder US Olympic Team, Torino, Italy, 2006. Named Competitor of the Yr., N.A. Snowsports Journalists Assoc., 2004; recipient Winner Halfpipe Event, World Cup, 2003, 2004, 2005, 2006, Halfpipe award, Vans Triph Crown, 2003, 2004, 2005, ESPY award Best Female Action Sports Athlete, 2006. Achievements include halfpipe Jr. World Champion, 2002; winner, World halfpipe Championship, 2003-2004, Vans Triple Crown halfpipe, 2003, US Snowboard Overall Grand Prix Champion, 2004; winner, Gold Medal, Winter X Games, 2004; winner, Gold Medal, halfpipe, Torino Olympic Games, 2006. Office: c/o USOC 1 Olympic Plaza Colorado Springs CO 80909

TETHER, ANTHONY JOHN, aerospace executive; b. Middletown, NY, Nov. 28, 1941; s. John Arthur and Antoinette Rose (Gesualdo) T.; m. Nancy Engle Pierson, Dec. 27, 1963 (div. July 1971); 1 child, Jennifer; m. Carol Suzanne Dunbar, Mar. 3, 1973; 1 child, Michael. AAS, Orange County C.C., NYC, 1961; BS, Rensselaer Poly Inst., 1963; MSEE, Stanford U., Calif., 1965, PhD, 1969. V.p., gen. mgr. Sys. Control Inc., Palo Alto, Calif., 1968-78; dir. nat. intelligence Office Sec. of Def., Washington, 1978-82; dir. strategic tech. DARPA, Washington, 1982-86; corp. v.p. Ford Aerospace, Newport Beach, Calif., 1986-90, LORAL, Newport Beach, 1990-92; corp. v.p., gen. mgr. Sci. Application Internat., Inc., San Diego, 1992-94; CEO Dynamics Tech. Inc., Torrance, Calif., 1994-96; CEO, pres. Sequoia Group, Newport Beach, Calif., 1996-2001; dir. def. advanced rsch. project agy. Office of Sec. of Def., Washington, 2001—. Bd. dirs. Condyne Tech., Inc., Orlando, Fla., 1990—92, chmn., 1990—92; dir. Orincon, La Jolla, Calif., 1996—99, Evans & Sutherland, Salt Lake City, 2001; mem. def. sci. bd. Army Sci. Bd. Task Forces, 1998—2002; cons. Army Sci. Bd., Def. Sci. Bd. Contbr. articles to profl. jours.; mem. editl. adv. bd. Scientific American. Recipient Nat. Intelligence medal DCI, 1986, Civilian Meritorious medal U.S. Sec. Def., 1986. Mem. IEEE, Cosmos Club, Sigma Xi, Eta Kappa Nu, Tau Beta Pi. Avocations: amateur radio, skiing, golf. Home: 6400 Lyric Ln Falls Church VA 22044 Personal E-mail: ttether@aol.com.

TETI, LOUIS NICHOLAS, lawyer; b. Bryn Mawr, Pa., May 29, 1950; BA, Dickinson Coll., 1972; JD, Temple U., 1976, LLM in Taxation, 1981. Bar: Pa. 1976. Ptnr. MacElree Harvey, Ltd., West Chester and Kennett Square, Pa. Mem. disciplinary bd. Supreme Ct. Pa., 2000-, chair, 2004-05. Fellow Am. Coll. Trust and Estate Counsel; mem. ABA (ho. dels. 1985-91, 99-2001), Pa. Bar Assn. (chmn. young lawyers divsn. 1982-83, bd. govs. 1982-85, 91-94, 97-2001, pres. 1999-2000), Chester County Bar Assn. (sec. 1979-82, 86-88, v.p. 1989, pres.-elect 1990, pres. 1991, chair young lawyers sect. 1977, bd. dirs. 1977-92), Chester County Estate Planning Coun. (pres. 1988-89). Office: MacElree Harvey Ltd 17 W Miner St PO Box 660 West Chester PA 19381-0660 Home Phone: 610-873-5557; Office Phone: 610-840-0300. Fax: 610-429-4486. E-mail: lteti@macelree.com.

TETLIE, HAROLD, soldier, priest; b. Madison, Minn., Aug. 24, 1926; s. H. Ben and Anna (Mauland) T. BA cum laude, St. Olaf Coll., Northfield, Minn., 1951; MBA, U. Denver, 1956; postgrad., Cornell U., 1959—60; MDiv, Luther Sem., St. Paul, 1965. Ordained to ministry Am. Luth. Ch., 1965. Pastor Christ the King Chs. (True Caths.), Alice, Tex., 1965—, congregation supr., 1969—. Cir. parish priest, Nuevo Leon, Tamaulipas, Hidalgo, San Luis Potosi, Mex. Author numerous poems. Coord. Joint Action in Cmty. Svc., Inc., Alice, 1970—. Sgt. U.S. Army, 1945-46, PTO. Recipient Svc. to Mankind award Sertoma Club, Corpus Christi, Regional Vol. of Yr. award Joint Action in Cmty. Svc., 1991, Michael Madhusudan award for poem, Calcutta, 1996; Ky. Col., 1992. Mem. NEA (life), VFW (life), Am. Legion (life), 40 et 8 (life), Family Motor Coach Assn., Sons of Norway, Order of Ky. Col., Internat. Platform Assn., Thousand Trails, WWII Tank Destroyer Soc. (chaplain). Home and Office: Christ the King Chs PO Box 1607 Alice TX 78333-1607 *It is by the Power of Jesus Christ: He tells us in John 13:34: "Love one another, even as I loved you.".*

TETLOW, ELISABETH MEIER, writer, researcher, lawyer; b. Cin., Mar. 26, 1942; d. Carl L. and Margaret (Hersey) Meier; m. L. Mulry Tetlow, July 5, 1970; children: Tania C., Maria A., Sonia M., Sarah A. BA, Columbia U., 1964; MA, Fordham U., 1967, MA, 1970, Columbia U., 1973; STM, Woodstock Coll., 1974; MDiv, Jesuit Sch. Theology, Berkeley, 1979; JD, Loyola U., New Orleans, 1984. Bar: La. 1984. Instr. Coll. of Mt. St. Vincent, Riverdale, NY, 1968-69, Fordham U., 1970, Loyola U., New Orleans, 1979-82; law clk. to Atty. Gen. of La., Dept. Justice, 1983; law clk. La. Supreme Ct., New Orleans, 1984-85; staff atty. U.S. Ct. Appeals (5th cir.), New Orleans, 1985-87; rsch. atty. Kierr, Gainsburgh, Benjamin, New Orleans, 1988; law clk. La. Ct. Appeals (4th cir.), 1989-91. Author: Women and Ministry in the New Testament, 1980, 2d edit., 1984, Partners in Service, 1983, The Spiritual Exercises of St. Ignatius Loyola, 1987, 2d edit., 1996, Women, Crime and Punishment in Ancient Near Eastern Law and Society, 2004, Women, Crime and Punishment in Ancient Greek Law and Society, 2005; contbr. articles to profl. jours. Active Amnesty Internat., Bread for the World, Pax Christi, Oxfam, Spl. Olympics, Sierra Club, Audubon Soc.; bd. dirs. Women's Ordination Conf., 2007—, New Orleans region Dystonia Med. Rsch. Found., Symphony Chorus New Orleans, 1996—2005; v.p., bd. dirs. Greater New Orleans region Nat. Assn. Riding for the Handicapped, 1995—97. Recipient Disting. Svc. award, Alliance for Affordable Energy, 1992, U.S. Gold Medal, USA Karate Fedn., 1989. Mem. ABA, Cath. Bibl. Assn. Am., Cath. Theology Soc. Am., Am. Acad. Religion, Soc. Bibl. Lit., Coll. Theology Soc., La. Bar Assn., La. Karate Assn., Internat. Shotokan Karate Fedn., Symphony Chorus New Orleans (bd. dirs.), Met. Opera Regional Auditions. Democrat. Roman Catholic. Avocations: shotokan karate, choral music, hiking. Home and Office: 16 Fontainebleau Dr New Orleans LA 70125-3452 Business E-Mail: etetlow@loyno.edu.

TETTLEBAUM, HARVEY M., lawyer; m. Ann Safier; children: Marianne, Benjamin. AB, Dartmouth Coll., 1964; JD, Washington U. Sch. Law, 1968, AM in History, 1968. Asst. dean Washington U. Sch. Law, 1969-77; asst. atty. gen., chief counsel Consumer Protection and Anti-Trust Div., 1970-77; pvt. practice Jefferson City, Mo., 1977-90; mem., chmn. health law practice group Husch & Eppenberger, LLC, Jefferson City, Mo., 1990—. Mem. selection com. US Magistrate, 1988; mem. Fed. Jud. Merit Selection Commn., 1991. Contbr. articles to profl. jours. Treas. Mo. Rep. State Com., 1976—2004; v.p. Moniteau County R-1 Sch. Dist. Bd., 1991-95, pres., 1995-96; mem. Calif. R-1 Sch. Bd., 1990-96, v.p., 1993-95, pres., 1995-96. Named Best Lawyers in Am., 2007; named one of, 2005, 2006; recipient Legis. award, Legal Svcs. Ea. Mo., 1999. Mem. Am. Health Lawyers Assn. (bd. dirs. 1993-99, co-chair long-term care and the law program 1993-01, chair 2001—07, chair long-term care and law program 2001—07, former chair long term care practice group 1997-01), Mo. Bar Assn. (health and hosp. law com., chmn. adminstrv. law com., vice chair delivery legal svc. com., Mo. statewide legal svc. com., President's award 2000, 03), Am. Health Care Assn. (legal subcom. 1994—, chair 2004-06), Rep. Nat. Lawyers Assn. (bd. dirs. 1988-, 1st v.p. 2002—, pres. 2003-06, Lawyer of Yr. 2006). Republican. Jewish. Home: 56295 Little Moniteau Rd California MO 65018-3069 Office: Husch & Eppenberger LLC Monroe House Ste 300 235 E High St PO Box 1251 Jefferson City MO 65102-1251 Office Phone: 573-761-1107. Business E-Mail: harvey.tettlebaum@husch.com.

TETZELI, RICK, editor; m. Mari Blecher; 1 child, Jonah. BA in Comparative Lit., Middlebury Coll., Vt. Asst. editor Little, Brown; with FORTUNE Mag., 1990—93, assoc. editor, 1993—93, editor, 1996—97, sr. editor, 1997—99, asst. mng. editor, 1999, exec. dir., 2000, dep. mng. editor, 2001—02; mng. editor Entertainment Weekly, NYC, 2002—. Office: Entertainment Weekly 1675 Broadway New York NY 10019 Office Fax: 212-522-6104, 212-522-8350. *

TETZLAFF, THEODORE R., lawyer; b. Saukville, Wis., Feb. 27, 1944; AB magna cum laude, Princeton U., 1966; LLB, Yale U., 1969. Bar: Ind. 1969, D.C. 1969, Ill. 1974. Legis. asst. to Congressman John Brademas, 1970; exec. dir. Nat. Conf. Police Community Rels., 1970-71; acting dir. US Office Legal Svcs., Office Econ. Opportunity, Washington, 1972-73; counsel, Com. Judiciary US Ho. of Reps., Washington, 1974; v.p., legal and external affairs Cummins Engine Co., 1980-82; gen. counsel Tenneco, Inc., Greenwich, Conn., 1992-99; ptnr. Jenner & Block, Chgo., 1976—80, 1982—2001, McGuireWoods LLP, Chgo., 2002—05, mng. ptnr. Chgo. office; gen. counsel Peoples Energy, 2003—05; ptnr. Ungaretti & Harris LLP, Chgo., 2005—. Bd. dirs. Continental Materials Corp., Chgo. Pres. Chgo. area Found. Legal Svcs., 1983—; commr. Pub. Bldg. Commn. Chgo., 1990-2005; chmn. Met. Pier and Expo Authority, 2005—. Reginald Heber Smith fellow, 1969-70. Mem. ABA (chair sect. litigation 1991-92), Ill. State Bar Assn., Ind. State Bar Assn., D.C. Bar. Office: Ungaretti & Harris LLP 3500 Three First Nat Plz Chicago IL 60602 Office Phone: 312-977-4150. Business E-Mail: tedt@mycingular.blackberry.net. *

TEUBER, WILLIAM J., JR., corporate financial executive; B, Coll. of the Holy Cross; MS in Taxation, Bentley Coll.; MBA, Babson Coll. Ptnr. Audit and Fin. Adv. Svcs. Coopers & Lybrand LLP; v.p., contr. EMC Corp., Hopkinton, Mass., 1995—97, v.p., CFO, 1997—2000, sr. v.p., CFO, 2000—01, exec. v.p., CFO, 2001—06, vice-chmn., 2006—. Bd. dirs. Popular, Inc. Bd. trustees Babson Coll. Office: EMC Corp 176 South St Hopkinton MA 01748 Office Phone: 508-435-1000. *

TEUBNER, FERDINAND CARY, JR., retired publishing executive; b. Phila., Sept. 22, 1921; s. Ferdinand Cary Teubner and Esther Roslyn (Test) Alperstein; m. Ruth May Hazen, Nov. 1, 1953; 1 child, Janell Caron Teubner Crispyn. Student, U. Pa., 1940-41; grad., Charles Morris Price Sch. Advt. and Journalism, 1949. Rep. W.H. Hoedt Studios, Inc., Phila., 1945-52; account exec. Patterson Prodns., Inc., Phila., 1955-56, v.p., 1956-57; staff exec. Am. Assn. Advt. Agys., NYC, 1957-59; rep. W.H. Martin & Co., Inc., NYC, 1959-62; advt. salesman Editor & Pub. Co., Inc., NYC, 1962-65, advt. mgr., 1965-76, gen. mgr., treas., 1976-78, treas., pub., 1978-95, dir., 1969-95; sec.-treas., dir. E & P Research, Inc., NYC, 1985-95, ret., 1995. Served with USAAF, 1942-45, ETO; served with U.S. Army, 1952-55, Korea, ret. maj. AUS, 1981. Decorated Purple Heart; recipient Silver Shovel award Internat. Newspaper Mktg. Assn., 1993, David Paul Hegg II Lifetime Achievement award Episcopal Diocese Newark, 2003. Mem. Sales Execs. Club N.Y.C., Res. Officer Assn. Clubs: Union League, Lake Valhalla Country. Episcopalian.

TEUSCHER, SIMON HANS, history professor, researcher; b. Bern, Switzerland, Apr. 26, 1967; arrived in U.S., 2000; s. Hans Gottfried Teuscher and Denise Claire Lehmann. MA, U. of Zurich, Switzerland, 1995, PhD, 1997, Habilitation, 2005. Asst. prof. U. of Zurich, 1995—99; vis. prof. U. Neuchâtel, Switzerland, 2001—02, Ecole des Hautes Etudes en Scis. Sociales, Paris, 2002; mem. Inst. for Advanced Study, Sch. of Hist. Studies, Princeton, NJ, 2004—05; vis. asst. prof. UCLA, 2000—; univ. prof. U. Zurich, 2006—. Author: (book) Bekannte—Klienten—Verwandte. Soziabilität und Politik in der Stadt Bern um 1500; contbr. articles to profl. jours. Home Phone: 01141442423115; Office Phone: 310-825-8333. Business E-Mail: teuscher@history.ucla.edu.

TEUTSCH, CLIFFORD L., editor-in-chief; b. NYC, 1950; m. Patrice Nelson. BA, Amherst Coll. With Daily Hampshire Gazette, Northampton, Mass., Hartford (Conn.) Courant, 1980—, local news reporter, politics editor, 1987—91, asst. mng. editor, 1991—94, mng. editor, 1994—2006, exec. editor & v.p., 2006—. John S. Knight fellowship, Stanford. U., 1986—87. Office: Hartford Courant 285 Broad St Hartford CT 06115-3785 Office Phone: 860-241-3931. E-mail: cteutsch@courant.com. *

TEUTUL, PAUL, SR., television personality, mechanic; b. Yonkers, NY, May 1, 1949; children: Paul Jr., Michael, Daniel, Kristin. Owner Orange County Iron Works, Inc., 1973—, Orange County Choppers, 1999—. Co-star: (TV series) Amercian Chopper: The Series, 2003—; co-author (with Paul M. Teutul, Michael Teutul, Keith & Kent Zimmerman): (book) Orange County Choppers: The Book, 2006; co-author: (with Paul M. Teutul, Michael Teutul) Orange County Choppers: The Tale of the Teutuls, 2006; actor: (films) Wild Hogs, 2007. Office: Orange County Choppers 10 Factory St Montgomery NY 12549 Office Phone: 845-457-1992. Office Fax: 845-457-4529. *

TEVAULT, DAVID EARL, chemist, researcher; b. Evansville, Ind., July 23, 1948; s. David Earl Tevault and Jo Ann (Jennings) Payne; m. Judy Louise Keith, May 19, 1973; children: Neil, Nancy. BA, U. Evansville, 1970; PhD, U. Va., 1974. Wehr postdoctoral fellow Marquette U., Milw., 1974-76; NRC postdoctoral fellow U.S. Naval Rsch. Lab., Washington, 1976-78, rsch. chemist, 1979-87; supervising rsch. chemist U.S. Army Edgewood Rsch., Devel. and Engring. Ctr., Aberdeen Proving Gound, Md., 1987—. Contbr. numerous articles to profl. jours. Mem. Am. Chem. Soc., Sigma Xi. Avocation: sports.

TEVRIZIAN, DICKRAN M., JR., judge; b. LA, Aug. 4, 1940; s. Dickran and Rose Tevrizian; m. Geraldine Tevrizian, Aug. 22, 1964; children: Allyson Tracy, Leslie Sara. BS, U. So. Calif., 1962, JD, 1965. Tax acct. Arthur Andersen and Co., LA, 1965-66; atty., ptnr. Kirtland and Packard, LA, 1966-72; judge LA Mcpl. Ct., 1972-78, State of Calif. Superior Ct., LA, 1978-82; ptnr. Manatt, Phelps, Rothenberg & Tunney, LA, 1982-85, Lewis, D'Amato, Brisbois & Bisgaard, LA, 1985-86; judge U.S. Dist. Ct., LA, 1986—. Adv. dir. UCLA Sch. Pub. Policy. Recipient Peter the Great Gold Medal of Honor Russian Acad. Natural Scis., 1998, Ellis Island Medal of Honor award, 1999, Disting. Pub. Svc. award Orange County Fed. Bar Assn., 2003. Mem. Calif. Trial Lawyers Assn. (Trial Judge of Yr. 1987), LA County Bar Assn. (Trial Judge of Yr. 1994-95), Malibu Bar Assn. (fed. ct. trial judge of yr. 1998, Maynard Toll award 2002, Jud. Svcs. award DSR Emil Gumpert ADR, 2005, Justice Armand Arabian Leaders in Pub. Svc. award 2005). Office: US Dist Ct Royal Federal Bldg 255 E Temple St Los Angeles CA 90012-3332

TEW, E. JAMES, JR., management services company executive; b. Dallas, July 7, 1933; s. Elmer James and Bessie Fay (Bennett) T.; children: Teresa Annette, Linda Diane, Brian James. Student, Arlington State Jr. Coll., 1955—57; BBA in Indsl. Mgmt., So. Meth. U., 1969; MS in Quality Systems, U. Dallas, 1972, MBA in Mgmt., 1975; EdD in Adult Edn., Nova U., 1986. Registered profl. engr., Calif. Mgr. quality assurance ops. Tex. Instruments Inc., Dallas, 1957-98; chmn. corp. metric implementation com. Texins Credit Union, co-chmn. credit com. Adj. faculty Richland Coll. Mountain View Coll., LeTourneau U.; precinct chmn., election judge, del. several county and state convs.; bus. computer info. systems adv. bd. U. North Tex., bd. dirs. ctr. for quality and productivity U. North Tex.; bd. examiners Malcolm Baldridge Nat. Quality award, U.S. Dept. Commerce, Nat. Inst. Standard and Tech., 1988, 89, 90, 91, 95, 96; chmn. panel judges, fellow Tex. Quality Award, 1993-2001; cons. nat. quality award Govt. Singapore, 1994; spkr. in field; bd. examiners Presdl. Quality Award, 1994-96, judge 1997-2000; quality examiner U.S. Army, 1996—; sr. quality examiner USAF, 1995-98, postdoctoral edn. in mediation and arbitration edn., 1998, 99; vol. mediator for dispute mediation svc., 1998—. Spkr. in field. Contbr. articles to profl jours. Decorated Army Commendation medal with oak leaf cluster, Meritorious Svc. medal, Legion of Merit. Fellow Am. Soc. Quality Control (cert. quality auditor, cert. quality mgr., cert. as quality and reliability engr., chmn. Dallas-Ft. Worth sect. 1974-75). Fellow U.S. Metric Assn. (cert., chmn. cert. bd. 1986-87); mem. U.S. Res. Officers Assn., Dallas C. of C. (chmn. world mfg. com. 1974-77, chmn. spl. tasl force career edn. adv. bd. 1973-74), Mensa (mem. air force blue ribbon commn. on assesments and evaluations 1996-98), Sigma Iota Epsilon, Phi Delta Kappa. Baptist. Clubs: Texins Rod and Gun (pres. 1969-70), Texins Flying, Masons (32 degree). Office Phone: 214-348-0794. Office Fax: 214-349-3686. Personal E-mail: ejtew@swbell.net.

TEWARSON, REGINALD PRABHAKAR, retired mathematics educator, consultant; b. Pauri, Garhwal, India, Nov. 17, 1939; came to U.S., 1957; s. Seth Narottam and Chand (Mani) Tewarson; m. Hedi Thomann, July 1, 1960 (div. Nov. 1990); children: Anita Jasmine, Monique Shanti; m. Ghenwah Albarazi, Apr. 16, 2003. MA, Agra U., 1952; PhD, Boston U., 1961. Lectr. Lucknow U., India, 1951—57; sr. mathematicisn Honeywell EDP, Wellesley Hills, Mass., 1960—64; leading prof. applied math. and stats. SUNY, Stony Brook, 1964—2000, leading prof. physiology and biophysics dept., 1964—2000, leading prof. emeritus, 2001—. Cons. NIH, Washington, 1971-74. Author: Sparse Matrices, 1973; mem. editorial bd. Applied Math. Letters, 1986-2004, Math. Computer Modeling, 1991-2004, Pan. Am. Math. Jour., 1991-2004; contbr. articles to profl. jours. Centenary scholar Govt. of India, 1946-50, Crusade scholar U.S. Coun. Chs., 1957-59; rsch. grantee NIH, 1973-97, Air Force Office Sch. Rsch. Math. and Info. Scis., 1983-85, NSF, 1993-95. Mem. Am. Math. Soc., Soc. Indsl. and Applied Math., Soc. for Math. Biology. Democrat. Achievements include pioneering research on sparse matrices based largely on own research; co-development of mathematical model of kidney concentrating mechanism, of computer model of neuronal function. Home: 22 Night Heron Dr Stony Brook NY 11790-1108 Office: SUNY Dept Applied Math And Stats Stony Brook NY 11794-0001 Office Phone: 631-632-8370. Personal E-mail: tewarson@optonline.net. E-mail: tewarson@ams.sunysb.edu.

TEWELEIT, RUSS, music educator; PhD in Music Edn., U. Okla., 2006. Coord. music edn. W. Tex. A&M U., Canyon, 1999—.

TEWELL, JOSEPH ROBERT, JR., retired electrical engineer; b. Albany, NY, May 19, 1934; s. Joseph Robert and Florence Edna Tewell; m. Barbara Ann Johnson, Nov. 20, 1960; children— Patricia Ann, Donna Lynn, Joseph Robert, III. B.E.E., Rensselaer Poly. Inst., 1955, M.E.E., 1958. Rsch. engr. N.Am. Aviation, Inc., Downey, Calif., 1955; assoc. rsch. engr. Lockheed Aircraft Corp., Burbank, Calif., 1956; instr. Rensselaer Poly. Inst., 1957-64; sr. rsch. scientist Martin Marietta Corp., Denver, 1964-79, mgr. advanced programs Michoud, La., 1979-87, mgr. shuttle-C project, 1988-90, mgr. computer-aided productivity, 1991-93, mgr. sys. engring., 1994-96; ret., 1996. Cons. in field. Contbr. articles to profl. jours. Founding sponsor Challenger Ctr. Served with Army Security Agy., 1957. Recipient NASA Manned Awareness citation, 1970, NASA Skylab Achievement award, 1974, NASA New Tech. award, 1976, Tech. Achievement award Martin Marietta Corp., 1977, Sustained Performance award Martin Marietta Corp., 1981, NASA cert. of recognition, 1977, Author of Yr. award, 1986, also 38 publ. awards, 1965— Fellow Explorers Club; mem. AIAA, Smithsonian Assocs., Air and Space Mus., Unmanned Vehicle Sys., Nat. Audubon Soc., Sigma Xi, Eta Kappa Nu, Tau Beta Pi, Theta Chi. Achievements include invention of dual action single drive actuator; spacecraft docking and retrieval mechanism. Home and Office: 619 Legendre Dr Slidell LA 70460-3427

TEWES, R. SCOTT, lawyer; b. Chgo., Mar. 23, 1956; s. Raymond Henry and Vivian Marie Tewes; m. Marcia Anne King, June 5, 1981; children: Benjamin Scott, Matthew Philip, Madeline Anne Marie, Carrie Elizabeth, Aimee Marie. BS, Bob Jones U., 1978, MS, 1980; JD, U. S.C., 1983. Bar: S.C. 1983, D.C. 1985, Ga. 1987, U.S. Supreme Ct. Assoc. Brown & Hagins, Greenville, S.C., 1983-86; law clk. to Hon. Jean Galloway Bissell U.S. Ct. Appeals Fed. Cir., Washington, 1986-87; assoc., ptnr. Kilpatrick Stockton, Atlanta, 1987—2002; with Tewes Law Group LLC, 2002—. Articles editor S.C. Law Rev., 1982-83; contbr. articles to profl. jours. Active Greenville (S.C.) County Alcohol and Drug Abuse Commn., 1985-86; trustee Killian Hill Baptist Ch., Lilburn, Ga., 1994-2000. Mem. S.C. Bar (practice and procedure com., bar ethics adv. com. 1985-86), Am. Intellectual Property Law Assn., Christian Legal Soc., Federalist Soc., Order of Barristers. Avocations: tennis, biking, skiing. Office: 2180 Satellite Blvd Ste 400 Duluth GA 30097-4927 Office Phone: 678-382-0388. E-mail: STewes@TewesLaw.com.

TEWKSBURY, RUSSELL BAIRD, media consultant, internet strategist, educator; b. Ft. Lauderdale, Fla., 1961; s. Michael King and Barbara T. BS in Bus., U. South Fla., 1986. Mktg. cons., Tampa, Fla., 1988-90; pres. Baird Advt., Tampa, 1990-93, Marketworks Corp., Tampa, Fla., 1993-98; CEO Marketworks LLC, 2004—. Dir. mktg. Angel Flight, Tampa, 1989-94, also bd. dirs.; mem. mktg. and steering com. Paint Your Heart Out Tampa, 1989-93; lectr. Am. Mktg. Assn., 1996; spkr. INET'98 - the Internet Summit, Geneva, 1998, Caribbean Assn. Nat. Telecoms. Orgns., Aruba, 1999, 2000, Internat. Inst. Comm., 2000; exec. prodr. Eye of the Storm in assn. with NASA and The Discovery Channel. Columnist CANCION (quar. publ. CANTO). Mem. mktg. advance Sen. Paul Tsongas Presdl. Campaign, Tampa, 1992; exec. prodr. streaming media U.S. Presdl. Campaign of Gore/Lieberman, 2000; mem. Leadership Fla Clas XXI, 2002; advance lead U.S. Pres. W.J. Clinton, 2004. Mem. Internet Soc., Leadership Fla. Avocation: travel. Home: P O Box 321389 Cocoa Beach FL 32932-1389

TEXTER, JOHN, physical chemist consultant; b. Lancaster, Pa., Aug. 9, 1949; s. Kenneth Raymond and June Eleanor (Hoffman) T.; m. Rose Marie Joan Piotrowski, June 1970 (div. Oct. 1980); m. Melanie Ann Martin, June 1984; children: Kurt Martin, Grace Martin. BSEE, Lehigh U., 1971, MS in Chemistry, 1973, MS in Math., 1976, PhD in Chemistry, 1976. Grad. asst. and Horner fellow Lehigh U., Bethlehem, Pa., 1971-73; instr. chemistry Lafayette Coll., Easton, Pa., 1973-74; Buch fellow Lehigh U., Bethlehem, 1974-76; assoc. physiologist Biophys. Spectroscopy Lab. U. Calif., Irvine, 1976-77; postdoctoral rsch. assoc. SUNY, Binghamton, 1977-78; rsch. assoc. electrochemistry group Eastman Kodak Co., Rochester, N.Y., 1978—. Vice chair Chemistry at Interfaces Gordon Rsch. Conf., 1994, chair, 1996. Editor: Electrochemistry in Colloids and Dispersions, 1992, Amphiphiles at Interrfaces, 1997; mem. editorial rev. bd. Jour. Imaging Sci., 1990; patentee in photog. systems and dispersion tech. Dir. Montessori Sch. Rochester, 1994-96. Recipient CTO Patent award, 1994, Disting. Inventors Gallery award, 1995, MRE Innovation award, 1995; grantee Office Naval Rsch., 1991, Petroleum Rsch. Found., 1991, 95, 97, Army Rsch. Office, 1996, NSF, 1996; Nat. Merit scholar, 1967-71. Mem. IEEE, AIChE, Internat. Assn. Colloid and Interface Scientists, Am. Chem. Soc. (exec. com. divsn. colloid and surface chemistry 1994-95, vice-chair 1996, chair-elect 1997), Am. Phys. Soc., Soc. for Imaging Sci. and Tech., Rochester Yacht Club, U.S. Sailing Assn., Sigma Xi. Avocations: sailboat racing, wilderness camping, travel.

TEXTOR, ROBERT BAYARD, cultural anthropology educator, writer, consultant; b. Cloquet, Minn., Mar. 13, 1923; s. Clinton Kenney and Lillian (Nickles) T.; divorced; children: Alexander Robertson, Marisa Elizabeth. Student, Lafayette Coll., 1940—41, Antioch Coll., 1941—43; BA in Asian Studies, U. Mich., 1945; PhD in Cultural Anthropology, Cornell U., 1960. Civil info. and edn. officer Mil. Govt., Kyoto-Wakayama, Japan, 1946-48; rsch. fellow anthropology and S.E. Asia studies Yale U., 1959-60, assoc., 1960-61; rsch. fellow in stats. Harvard U., 1962-64; assoc. prof. edn. and anthropology Stanford U., 1964-68, prof. edn. and anthropology, 1968-86, prof. anthropology, 1986-90, prof. anthropology emeritus, 1990—; sr. scholar Ctr. to Bridge the Digital Divide, Wash. State U., 2005—. Vis. prof. U. Saar, Saarbrücken, Germany, 1984-85; cons. Motorola, Inc., 1991-2001, Ministry of Planning, Kuwait, 1999; mem. S.E. Asia Coun., 1974-77; cons. cultural anthropology to govt. agys., 1957-58, 61-62. Author: Roster of the Gods: An Ethnography of The Supernatural in a Thai Village, 6 vols., 1973, Austria 2005: Projected Sociocultural Effects of the Microelectronic Revolution, 1983, Anticipatory Anthropology, 1985, (with Sippanondha Ketudat) The Middle Path for the Future of Thailand, 1990; (with others) Uncompromising Integrity: Motorola's Global Challenge, 1998; editor, commentator: Margaret Mead and the World Ahead: An Anthropologist Anticipates the Future, 2005; editor, commentator; assoc. editor Jour. Conflict Resolution, 1965-70; mem. editl. bd. Human Orgn., 1966-71, Jour. Cultural Futures, 1979-87; adv. editor Behavior Sci. Rsch., 1974-86. Bd. dirs. Vols. in Asia, Stanford, Calif., 1968-73; mem. Metro Portland Future Vision Commn., 1993-95; Served with U.S. Army, 1943-46. Fellow Rockefeller Found., 1951-52, fgn. area tng. fellow Ford Found., Thailand 1955-58, Carnegie fellow, 1958-59, Fulbright West Europe rsch. fellow, 1984-85, East-West Ctr. fellow, 1988-90; NSF grantee, Thailand, U.S., 1969-73, Volkswagen Found. grantee, Thailand and Germany, 1984. Fellow Am. Anthrop. Assn. (life, chair resource devel. com. 2003-04), Soc. Applied Anthropology; mem. Siam Soc. (life), Assn. Asian Studies (life), Council on Anthropology and Edn. (pres. 1974-75), AAUP (pres. Stanford chpt. 1975-76), Phi Kappa Phi.

TEYAN, FREDERICK GENE, pediatrician; b. NYC, Sept. 16, 1938; s. Jack H. and Pearl A. (Chernesky) T.; m. Dec. 18, 1965; children: Frederick II, Julie, Jonathan. AB, St. Peter's Coll., 1960; MD, Seton Hall, 1964. Diplomate Am. Bd. Pediatrics. Intern Kings County Hosp., Bklyn., 1964-65, resident in pediat., 1969-70, L.I. Jewish Hosp., New Hyde Park, NY, 1970-71; pvt. practice, Rockville Centre, NY, 1971—. Major U.S. Army, 1966-69. Fellow Am. Acad. Pediatrics; mem. Nassau Pediatric Soc. Roman Catholic. Office: 36 Lincoln Ave Rockville Centre NY 11570-5768 Office Phone: 516-766-2602. Personal E-mail: fgjteyan@ix.netcom.com.

TEZANOS-PINTO, ROSA, Hispanic American literature educator; d. Alfredo Tezanos Pinto and Enriqueta Otiniano Tezanos Pinto; m. Jose L. Vargas Vila, Aug. 6, 1993; children: Sebastian Martin Valverde, Isabel Maria Valverde. BA, U. Miami, 1979, MA, 1994, PhD, 2002. Cons. and test evaluator U. Fla., Tampa, 1985—99; pres. Sigma Delta Pi, Miami, 1988—91; coord. symposia Michel de Certeau Ctr. for Critical Studies, Coral Gables, Fla., 1990—92; lectr. U. Miami, Coral Gables, 1992—99; dir. John Adams Pub. Co., Coral Gables, 1994—97; prof. of hispanic Am. lit. Lebanon Valley Coll., Annville, Pa., 1999—; dir. Alroquema Pub., Miami, 1999—; coord. youth scholars program in Spanish Lebanon Valley Coll., Annville, 2000—, advisor Spanish club, 2001—, advisor Spanish majors and minors, open majors, 2001—; dir. Asociación de Poetas de América, Buenos Aires, 2000—; coord., meeting hispanic authors program Lebanon Valley Coll., Annville, 2001—; advisor Nat. Assn. of Fellowships Advisors, 2002—. Rschr. Alroquema Pub. Co., Miami, 2003—. Editor: Redimiendo la Infancia en la estructura póetica, 2004, Nation and Narration in The LUSO - Hispanic World, 2005. Recipient Jayanca Disting. Visitor Diploma, Chiclayo, Peru, 2002, Comodoro Rivadavia Book Fair Plaque, Comodoro Rivadavia Book Fair (Argentina), 2001; Profl. grant, Lebanon Valley Coll., 2001—03. Mem.: Latin Am. Inst. Pa. (pres.), Assn. Cervantistas, Colloquium Com., Diversity Adv. Com., Círculo Panamericano, Instituto Literario y Cultural Hispánico, Casa del Poeta del Perú, Am. Assn. of Teachers of Spanish and Portuguese, Nat. Assn. of Fellowships Advisors, Grad. Fellowship Com., Sigma Delta Pi, Phi Sigma Iota. Achievements include research in the relationship in form and practice of poetic language and the Freudian psychoanalytic language; the hidden text of Infancy in the Poetic works of Ester de Izaguirre and Loreina Santos Silva and testimonial literature; publications in the USA, France, Spain, Argentina, Peru, Paraguay, Brazil, Puerto Rico, India, etc; presented papers at USA, Chile, Venezuela, Guatemala, Puerto Rico, Australia, Peru, Colombia, Paraguay, Argentina, Spain, France, India, Mexico and Brazil. Office: Lebanon Valley College 101 North College Ave Annville PA 17003 Office Phone: 717-867-6257. E-mail: tezanos@lvc.edu.

THABAULT, PAULETTE J., state agency administrator; A in Nursing, U. Vt.; BSN, U. Wash.; MSN, Simmons Coll.; JD, New Eng. Sch. Law. Bar: Vt., Mass. Dep. commr. health care adminstrn. Vt. Dept. Banking, Ins., Securities and Health Care Adminstrn., Montpelier, 2003—05, commr., 2007—. Mem. devel. com. Alzheimer's Assn. Vt. and NH; bd. dirs. Cmty. Health Ctr. Burlington, Vt. Office: Vt Dept Banking Ins Securities and Health Care Adminstrn 89 Main St Drawer 20 Montpelier VT 05620-3101 Office Phone: 802-828-3307. Office Fax: 802-828-1477. E-mail: pthabault@bishca.state.vt.us.

THACH, WILLIAM THOMAS, JR., neurologist, educator; b. Okla. City, Jan. 3, 1937; s. William Thomas and Mary Elizabeth T.; m. Emily Ransom Otis, June 30, 1963 (div. 1979); children: Sarah Brill, James Otis, William Thomas III. AB in Biology magna cum laude, Princeton U., 1959; MD cum laude, Harvard U., 1964. Diplomate Am. Bd. Psychiatry and Neurology (in Neurology). Intern Mass. Gen. Hosp., Boston, 1964-65, asst. residency, 1965-66; staff assoc. physiology sect. lab. clin. sci. NIMH, Bethesda, Md., 1966-69; neurology resident, clin. and rsch. fellow Mass. Gen. Hosp., 1969-71; from asst. prof. neurology to assoc. prof. neurology Yale U. Sch. Medicine, New Haven, Conn., 1971-75; assoc. prof. neurobiology and neurology dept. anatomy and neurobiology Washington U. Sch. Medicine, St. Louis, 1975-80, prof. neurobiology and neurology dept. anatomy and neurobiology, 1980—, chief divsn. neurorehab. dept. neurology, 1992—. Acting dir. Irene Walter Johnson Rehab. Inst. Washington U. Sch. Medicine, 1989-91, dir., 1991-92; attending neurologist Barnes Hosp., med. dir. dept. rehab.; attending neurologist Jewish Hosp., St. Louis Regional Hosp.; bd. sci. counselors NINCDS, 1988-92; mem. NIH Study Sect. Neurology A, 1981-85. Assoc. editor Somatosenory and Motor Research; contbr. numerous articles to profl. jours. Fulbright grantee U. Melbourne, Australia, 1959-60; NIH grantee, 1971— Mem. Physiol. Soc., Am. Acad. Neurology, Soc. Neurosci., Am. Neurol. Assn., Am. Soc. Neurorehab., Phi Beta Kappa, Sigma Xi, Alpha Omega Alpha. Achievements include research on brain control of movement and motor learning, roles of the basal ganglia and the cerebellum in health and disease. Home: 7520 Clayton Rd Saint Louis MO 63117-1418 Office: Washington Univ Dept Anatomy & Neurobiol 600 S Euclid Ave Dept Anatomy& Saint Louis MO 63110-1010 E-mail: thachw@peg.wustl.edu.

THACKER, CHARLES P., computer engineer, engineering executive; m. Karen Thacker; 2 children. BA, U. Calif., 1967; D (hon.), Swiss Fed. Inst. Tech. Engr. U. Calif., Berkeley, 1967-68; project leader Berkeley Computer Corp., 1969-71; mem. rsch. staff Xerox Palo Alto Rsch. Ctr., Calif., 1971-75, mgr. processor architecture sys. devel. divsn., 1975-77, mgr. digital processor devel. electronics divsn., 1977-79, prin. engr., 1979-80, rsch. fellow, 1980-82, sr. rsch. fellow, 1982-83; sr. cons. engr. Digital Equipment Corp. Sys. Rsch. Ctr., Palo Alto, 1983-89, corp. cons. engr., 1989—97; dir. advanced systems Microsoft Rsch., Cambridge, England, 1997—99; disting. engr., emerging tech. group Microsoft Corp., 1999—. Named a Disting. Alumnus, U. Calif. Fellow: Am. Acad. Arts and Sciences, Assn. Computer Machinery (Software Sys. award 1984); mem.: IEEE (John von Neumann medal 2007), NAE (Charles Stark Draper prize 2004). Achievements include research in in digital computer development. Mailing: c/o Microsoft Research Thames Valley Park Reading RG6 1WG England

THACKER, STEPHEN BRADY, medical association administrator, epidemiologist; b. Independence, Mo., Dec. 30, 1947; m. 1976; 2 children. AB, Princeton U., 1969; MD, Mt. Sinai Sch. Medicine, 1973; MSc, London Sch. Hygiene and Tropical Medicine, 1984. Chief consolidated surveillance and commn. activity epidemiol. program office Ctrs. Disease Control and Prevention, Atlanta, 1978-83, dir. surveillance and epidemiol. studies, 1983-86, dir. epidemiol. program office, 1989—2004, acting dep. dir., 1998, acting dir. Nat. Ctr. Injury Prevention and Control, 1999-2000, acting dir. Nat. Ctr. Environ. Health, 1993-95, dir. Office of Workforce and Career Devel., 2004—; asst. dir. sci. Ctr. Environ. Health and Injury Control, Atlanta, 1986-89. Mem. steering com. Assn. Behavioral Sci. Med. Edn., 1971-74; assoc. Dept. Cmty. Medicine, Med. Ctr. Duke U., Durham, N.C., 1975-76; lectr. Cmty. Ctr. Mt. Sinai Sch. Medicine, N.Y.C., 1978—, Sch. Medicine Emory U., Atlanta, 1985-86; cons. epidemiology Arab Republic Egypt, 1979-91; clin. asst. prof. cmty. health Sch. Medicine Emory U., 1986-91; adj. prof. Emory U. Sch. Pub. Health, 1992—. Editor: Epidemiologic Revs., 1990-2003. Clin. scholar Robert Wood Johnson Found., 1974-75; recipient Mosby Book award for excellence, 1973, Pub. Health Svc. Outstanding Svc. medal, 1987, Pub. Health Svc. Meritorious Svc. medal, 1988, 2002, Saul Horowitz Jr. Meml. award, 1990, Supervisory award for contbr. advantage of women, 1991, Pub. Health Svc. Commendation medal, 1991, Pub. Health Svc. Disting. Svc. medal, 1993, 2006, Pub. Health Svc. Surgeon Gen.'s Exemplary Svc. medal, 1993, Pub. Health Svc. Disting. Svc. medal, 1997, Medal of Excellence William C. Watson, Jr., 1996, Ray E. Brown award Assn. Mil. Surgeons of U.S., 2003. Achievements include rsch. public health surveillance, infectious disease, environ. health, injury prevention, alcohol abuse, health care delivery, meta-analysis, technology assessment. Office: Ctrs for Disease Control and Prevention MS E94 1600 Clifton Rd NE Atlanta GA 30333 Business E-Mail: sbt1@cdc.gov.

THACKER, THOMAS JAMES, surveyor; b. Cin., Aug. 20, 1951; s. James Aryle Thacker and Ruth Mary Blackburn; m. Cynthia Becker, July 31, 1982 (dec. Sept. 25, 2006); children: Timothy Crock, Christopher Salvatore, Carolyn Damato, Jennifer Buell. BA in Polit. Sci., Pa. State U., State College, 1973; AS in Aeronautics, Pitts. Inst. Aeronautics, West Mifflin, Pa., 1978. Office mgr. Brownell & Assocs., Naples, Fla., 1980—84; land surveyor Survicon, Dallas, 1985—88, VRS Greiner, Santa Ana, Calif., 1989—2003. Pres. Monarch Hills Homeowners Assn., Dana Point, Calif., 1998—2003. Mem.: Mensa. Republican. Avocations: motorcycling, golf, tennis.

THACKERAY, JONATHAN E., lawyer; b. Athens, Ohio, July 30, 1936; s. Joseph Eugene and Betty Rutherford (Boright) T.; m. Sandra Ann McMahon; children: Jennifer, Sara, Amy, Jonathan. AB cum laude, Harvard U., 1958, JD, 1961. Bar: Ohio 1961, U.S. Dist. Ct. (no. dist.) Ohio 1961, U.S. Supreme Ct. 1972, U.S. Ct. Appeals (6th cir.) 1973, U.S. Ct. Appeals (9th cir.) 1982, N.Y. 1993. Assoc. Vorys, Sater, Seymour & Pease, Columbus, Ohio, 1961, Baker & Hostetler, Cleve., 1965-72, ptnr., 1973-93; v.p., gen. counsel The Hearst Corp., NYC, 1993—2003; ret., 2003. Served to lt. USNR, 1961-65. Mem. ABA, Ohio Bar Assn., Cleve. Bar Assn., Am. Law Inst. Office: Hearst 959 Eighth Ave New York NY 10019 *Notable cases include: administrative proceedings leading to approval of joint newspaper operating agreements in Cincinnati, Seattle and Las Vegas; litigation of newspaper antitrust cases in Memphis, Trenton and Dallas.*

THACKER-ESTRADA, ELIZABETH LORELEI, librarian, historian; b. Burbank, Calif., Nov. 29, 1957; d. Ernest Wichman and Mariam Lorelei (Ihrig) Thacker; m. Hedwing José Estrada, Nov. 29, 1997. BA summa cum laude, U. Calif., Santa Barbara, 1979; M in Libr. and Info. Studies, U. Calif., Berkeley, 1986. Part-time reference libr. Advanced Info. Mgmt., Mountain View, Calif., 1987—93; head libr. Inst. Transpersonal Psychology, Menlo Park, Calif., 1988—90; part-time faculty Foothill Coll., Los Altos Hills, Calif., 1990; interim campus libr. San Jose (Calif.) State U., Salinas, 1991, part-time reference libr. San Jose, 1994; reference libr. San Francisco (Calif.) Pub. Libr., 1993—95, collection devel. libr., 1995—2000, unit mgr., 2000—02, spl. projects mgr., 2002—04, govt. info. ctr. dir., 2004—. Editl. bd. mem., cons. Nat. First Ladies Libr., Canton, Ohio, 2003—. Mem. editl. bd.: White House Studies; contbr. chpts. to books, encycs., articles to profl. jours. Chair missions and social outreach team Burlingame (Calif.) United Meth. Ch., 2003—. H. W. Wilson Found. scholar, U. Calif., Berkeley, 1985. Mem.: ALA, Inst. Hist. Study, Western Social Sci. Assn. (conf. panelist 2000—02), Govt. Docs. Round Table, Libr. History Round Table, Am. Hist. Assn., Sch. Info. Mgmt. and Systems Alumni Assn. (life), Calif. Alumni Assn. (life), Sierra Club (life), Mortar Bd. / Pi Sigma Alpha (life). Democrat. Methodist. Office: San Francisco Public Library 100 Larkin St San Francisco CA 94102-4733 Home Phone: 650-355-9113; Office Phone: 415-557-4201. Office Fax: 415-557-4475. Business E-Mail: ethacker@sfpl.org.

THACKSTON, EDWARD LEE, civil engineering educator; b. Nashville, Apr. 29, 1937; s. Guy Carleton and Sydney Virginia (Adams) T.; m. Betty Tucker, Mar. 19, 1961; children: Carol Elizabeth Thackston Nixon, Leah Virginia Thackston Hawkins. BE summa cum laude, Vanderbilt U., 1961; MS, U. Ill., 1963; PhD, Vanderbilt U., 1966. Registered profl. engr., Tenn. City engr. City of Lebanon, Tenn., 1959; design engr. City of Nashville, 1961-62; instr. Vanderbilt U., Nashville, 1965-66, asst. prof., 1966-69, assoc. prof., 1969-75, prof. engring., 1975-2000, chmn. dept. civil and environ. engring., 1980-99. Asst. to gov. for environ. affairs, State of Tenn., 1972-74; cons. in field. Author book, tech. reports; contbr. to profl. publs. Bd. dirs. Tenn. Environ. Coun., Nashville, 1971-76; bd. dirs. Tenn. Conservation League, Nashville, 1974-2003, v.p., 1977, pres., 1978-80; trustee Cumberland Mus., Nashville, 1986-92; trustee Cumberland U., Lebanon, 1996—, mem. exec. com., 1996-2002, 04—, sec.-treas., 2000-02, 04-07, chmn. 07—. Recipient Tenn. Lifetime Environ./Conservation Stewardship award State Tenn. 1996, Engr. of Yr. Mid. Tenn. Tenn. Soc. Prof. Engring., 2001, Landmark Paper award Assn. Environ. Engring. and Sci. Profs., 2001; named Tenn. Conservationist of Yr., 1974. Fellow ASCE; mem. Am. Water Works Assn. (life), Water Environ. Fedn. (life), Assn. Environ. Engring. Profs. (emeritus, Landmark Paper award 2001), Tenn. Hist. Soc., Hillwood Country Club, Tau Beta Pi, Chi Epsilon. Republican. Episcopalian. Avocations: genealogy, history, photography, weightlifting. Business E-Mail: elt@vuse.vanderbilt.edu.

THADANI, UDHO, physician, cardiologist; b. Hyderabad, India, Apr. 1, 1941; came to U.S., 1980; s. Vensimal Mulchand and Gopi Thadani; m. Dorothy Ann Thadani, 1974; 1 child, Emma Sarala. MBBS, All India Inst. Med. Scis., New Delhi, 1964. Lic. physician, Okla., Ont., Can., Eng., India; cert. internal medicine, U.K., Can.; cert. cardiology, Can.; diplomate in internal medicine and cardiovasc. diseases Am. Bd. Internal Medicine. Intern All India Inst. Med. Scis., New Delhi, 1964-65, house physician, surgeon, 1965-66; house physician in medicine Joyce Green Hosp., Dartford, Kent, England, 1966-67; sr. house physician in medicine Kingston Gen. Hosp., Hull, England, 1967-69, registrar, rsch. fellow in medicine and cardiology, 1969-71, U. Leeds (Eng.), The Gen. Infirmary at Leeds, 1971-75; sr. rsch. fellow, clin. asst. medicine Queen's U., Kingston Gen. Hosp., Ont., Canada, 1975-78; asst. prof. medicine Queen's U., Kingston, 1978-80; staff physician Kingston Gen. Hosp., 1978-80; assoc. prof. medicine U. Okla. Health Scis. Ctr., Oklahoma City, 1980-83; prof. medicine Okla. U. Health Scis. Ctr., Oklahoma City, 1983—2001, prof. emeritus medicine, 2001, mem. cardiology fellowship com., 1980-82; dir. clin. cardiology Okla. U. Health Scis. Ctr. and VA Med. Ctr., Oklahoma City, 1980-87, cons. cardiologist, 1980—, vice chief cardiovasc. sect., 1981-99, dir. clin. rsch., 1987-99. Vice-chmn. rsch. and devel. com. VA Med. Ctr., Oklahoma City, 1989-92, chmn. physiology-pharmacology categorical rev. com., 1989-94, chmn. rsch. and devel. com., VA Med. Ctr. Oklahoma City, 1992-94, 2003-05; sr. rsch. fellow Ont. Heart Found., 1978-80, rsch. fellow, 1976-78; rsch. fellow dept. medicine Queen's U., Kingston, Ont., 1975-76; rsch. fellow U. Leeds, Pub. Health and Ciba Found., dept. medicine and cardiovasc. sect. Leeds Gen. Infirmary, 1971-75. Editor: Medical Therapy of Ischemic Heart Disease, 1992, Nitrates Updated, 1996; mem. editl. bd. panel Cardiology Drug Facts and Comparison, 1989; contbg. rev. panel Drug Facts and Comparisons, 1989—; mem. editl. bd. Internat. Jour. Cardiology, 1987-93, Cardiovascular Drugs and Therapy, 1987-2004, Heart Diseases, 1999-2004, Am. Jour. Pharmacology, 2000-04, Am. Jour. Cardiovasc. Drugs, 2003—, Cardiology, 2005—; reviewer Circulation, Jour. Am. Coll. Cardiology, Am. Jour. Cardiology, Brit. Heart Jour., Internat. Jour. Cardiology, Can. Jour. Cardiology, European Heart Jour., Annals of Internal Medicine, New Eng. Jour. Medicine, Archives of Internal Medicine, Cardiovasc. Drugs and Therapy, Drugs, European Jour. Pharmacology, Clin. Pharmacology and Therapeutics; contbr. over 200 articles to profl. jours., chpts. to books. Recipient Provost Rsch. award, OUHSC, 1995, James F. Hammarsten award for physicians of excellence award, VA Med. Ctr., Okla., 2003. Fellow: Coun. Clin. Cardiology Am. Heart Assn. (coun. rep. Okla. 1989—2000), Am. Coll. Cardiology (mem. cardiovasc. drug com. 1990—94), Royal Soc. Medicine London; mem.: Can. Cardiovasc. Soc., Royal Coll. Phycisians U.K., Phi Kappa Phi (mem. FDA cardiovasc. and renal drugs adv. com. 1995—99). Avocations: gardening, tennis, travel. Office: Okla U Health Sci Ctr Cardiology Sect 920 SL Young WP 3120 Oklahoma City OK 73104 Office Phone: 405-271-4742. Business E-Mail: udho-thadani@ouhsc.edu.

THADDEUS, PATRICK, physicist, researcher; b. Wilmington, Del., June 6, 1932; s. Victor and Elizabeth (Ross) T.; m. Janice Petherbridge Farrar, Apr. 6, 1963 (dec. Dec. 2001); children: Eva, Michael; m. Valerie McCollom, Nov. 1, 2003. B.Sc., U. Del., 1953; MA, Oxford U., Eng., 1955; PhD, Columbia U., 1960; DSc (hon.), U. Chgo., 2003. Research assoc. Columbia Radiation Lab., 1960-61; research assoc. Goddard Inst. Space Studies, NYC, 1961-63, mem. sci. staff, 1963-86; mem. faculty Columbia U., 1965-86, adj. prof. physics, 1971-86; prof. astronomy and applied physics Harvard U., 1986-2000, Robert Wheeler Willson prof. applied astronomy, 2000—; mem. sci. staff Smithsonian Astrophys. Obs., 1986—. Vis. com. Nat. Radio Astronomy Obs., 1973-76, 91-94; mem. Astronomy Survey Com., 1978-80, 89-90; chair task group on Space Astronomy and Astrophysics, 1996-97; Fairchild Disting. Scholar Calif. Inst. Tech., 1994; Russell Marker lectr. Pa. State U., 1989; vis. fellow Inst. Astronomy, Cambridge, Eng., 1983. Author papers on microwave spectroscopy, optical and radio astronomy. Recipient Exceptional Sci. Achievement medal NASA, 1970, 85; John C. Lindsay Meml. award Goddard Space Flight Center, 1976; Alexander von Humboldt award, 1983; Herschel medal Royal Astron. Soc., 2001; Fulbright fellow, 1953-55. Fellow Am. Phys. Soc.; mem. Am. Astron. Soc., Am. Acad. Arts and Scis., Nat. Acad. Scis., Internat. Astronomical Union, Saturday Club, Sigma Xi. Address: 58 Garfield St Cambridge MA 02138-1802

THADEN, EDWARD CARL, history professor; b. Seattle, Apr. 24, 1922; s. Edward Carl and Astrid (Engvik) T.; m. Marianna Theresia Forster, Aug. 7, 1952. BA, U. Wash., 1944; student, U. Zurich, Switzerland, 1948; PhD, U. Paris, 1950. Instr. Russian history Pa. State U., 1952-55, asst. prof., 1955-58, assoc. prof., 1958-64, prof., 1964-68, U. Ill., Chgo., 1968—92, chmn. dept. history, 1971—73, prof. emeritus, 1992—. Vis. prof. Ind. U., 1957, U. Marburg, 1965, U. Ill., Urbana, 1980, U. Halle, Germany, 1988, U. Helsinki, Finland, 1990; editl. cons. Can. Rev. Studies in Nationalism, 1973—78; vis. rsch. scholar USSR Acad. Scis., 1975, 88, 90; project prin. rschr. Ford Found., 1975—78; U.S. rep. Internat. Congress of Hist. Scis., 1980; project dir. NEH grant, 1980—82. Author: Conservative Nationalism in Nineteenth-Century Russia, 1964, Russia and the Balkan Alliance of 1912, 1965, Russia Since 1801: The Making of a New Society, 1971, Russia's Western Borderlands, 1710-1870, 1984, Interpreting History: collected Essays on Russia's Relations with Europe, 1990, Essays in Russian and East European History: Festschrift in Honor of Edward C. Thaden, 1995, The Rise of Historicism in Russia, 1999; co-author, editor: Russification in the Baltic Provinces and Finland, 1855-1914, 1981; co-author, co-editor: Finland and the Baltic Provinces in the Russian Empire, 1984; mem. editorial bd. Jour Baltic Studies, 1984-93, assoc. editor, 1987-93, East European Quarterly, 1998—. Served to lt. (j.g.) USNR, 1943-46. Carnegie Inter-Univ. Com. travel grantee to USSR, 1956; Fulbright rsch. grantee Finland, 1957-58, Germany, 1965, Poland and Finland, 1968; Soc. Sci. Rsch. Coun. grantee, 1957; Am. Coun. Learned Socs. grantee, 1963, 65-66; fellow Woodrow Wilson Internat. Ctr. for Scholars, 1980 Mem. Am. Hist. Assn. (life), Nat. History Ctr. (founding mem.), Am. Assn. for Advancement Slavic Studies (pres. Midwest br. 1975-76, exec. sec. 1980-82), Chgo. Consortium for Slavic and Ea. European Studies (pres. 1982-84), Baltische Historische Kommission, Göttingen (corr. mem. 1985—), Commn. Internat. des Etudes Historiques Slaves (v.p. 1985-95, pres. 1995-2000, pres.d'honneur 2000—). Office: U Ill Dept History 913 UH (M/C 198) 601 S Morgan St Chicago IL 60607-7100

THAIN, JOHN A., stock exchange executive, former diversified financial services company executive; b. Antioch, Ill., May 26, 1955; m. Carmen M. Ribera; 4 children. BS, MIT, 1977; MBA, Harvard U., 1979. CFO, head of ops., tech. & fin. The Goldman Sachs Group, L.P., 1994—99, co-CEO European ops., 1995—97, pres, co-COO, 1999; co-COO The Goldman Sachs Group, Inc., NYC, 1999—2003, pres., 1999—2004, COO, 2003—04; CEO NY Stock Exch., NYC, 2004—06; CEO, dir. NYSE Group, Inc., NYC, 2006—07, NYSE Euronext, NYC, 2007—. Bd. dirs. The Goldman Sachs Group, Inc., 1998—2004, NYSE Group, Inc., 2006—; mem. MIT Corp., 2000—, MIT Sloan Sch. Mgmt. dean's adv. coun., INSEAD US Nat. Adv. Bd., Fed. Res. Bank NY Internat. Capital Markets Adv. Com., BritishAmerican Bus. Inc. Mem. James Madison Coun. Libr. Congress; gen. trustee Howard U.; trustee NY-Presbyn. Hosp.; gov. NY Presbyn. Found., Inc.; mem. adv. coun. MIT Sloan Sch. Mgmt. Mem.: Trilateral Commn., French Am. Found. Office: NYSE Euronext 11 Wall St New York NY 10005 *

THAKOR, NITISH VYOMESH, biomedical engineering educator; b. Nagpur, India, Feb. 9, 1952; came to U.S., 1976; s. Vyomesh H. and Jayshree V. Thakor; m. Ruchira N. Thakor, Dec. 17, 1983; children: Mitali N., Milan N., Jai N., Vir N. B of Tech., Indian Inst. Tech., Bombay, 1974; PhD, U. Wis., 1981. Engr. Philips India Ltd., Bombay, 1974-76; rsch. asst. U. Wis., Madison, 1977-81; asst. prof. Northwestern U., Evanston, Ill., 1981-83, Johns Hopkins U., Balt., 1984-87, assoc. prof., 1987-94, prof., 1994—. Cons. Biomed. Instrumentation, 1984—. Mem. editl. bd. Jour. Ambulatory Monitoring, Med. Design and Material, 1978—, IEEE Jour. Transactions on Biomed. Engring., IEEE Transactions Info. Tech. Biomedicine, 1988-92, Jour. Biol. Sys., 1993-97; Annals of Biomed. Engring., 2000-05; editor-in-chief IEEE Trans Neural Sys. Rehabilitation Engring. 2006-, Pi Tech, Pan IIT Mag., Indian Inst. Tech.; contbr. over 165 articles to profl. jours.; patentee in field. Recipient Presdl. Young Investigator award 1985, NIH Rsch. Career Devel. award Centennial medal U. Wis. Sch. Engring.; Fulbright scholar 1987; grantee NSF, NIH, Dept. Edn., Defense Rsch. Project Agency Fellow IEEE, Am. Inst. Med. and Biol. Engring., Biomed. Engring. Soc. (founding); mem. Sigma Xi. Achievements include devel. of micro-computer-based ambulatory ECG monitor; techniques for arryhythmia detection in implantable pacemakers and defibrillators, neurological signal processing and monitoring instrumentation, medical microsystems and nanotechnology. Home: 12010 Misty Rise Ct Clarksville MD 21029-1256 Office: Johns Hopkins U Med Sch Biomed Engring Dept 720 Rutland Ave Baltimore MD 21205-2109 E-mail: nthakor@bme.jhu.edu.

THAL, STEVEN HENRY, lawyer, consultant; b. NYC, Nov. 16, 1942; s. Michael and Mildred (Hirsch) T.; 1 child, Eric Alexander. BA, U. Mich., 1964, JD, 1967; postgrad., U. Tubingen, Fed. Republic Germany, 1967-68, New Sch. Social Rsch., NYC, 1971-72. Bar: N.Y., 1968, U.S. Ct. Appeals (2d cir.) 1969, U.S. Dist. Ct. (so. and ea. dists.) N.Y. 1969, U.S. Supreme Ct. 1973; cert. District Ct., Frankfurt, Germany. Assoc. Donovan, Leisure, Newton & Irvine, NYC, 1968-69, Handler, Kleiman & Sukenik, NYC, 1969-72; ptnr. Thal & Youtt, NYC, 1972-84, Kaplan, Russin & Vecchi, NYC, 1984-88, Summit, Rovins & Feldesman, NYC, 1988-90, Oppenheimer Wolff & Donnelly, NYC, 1990-94, LeBoeuf Lamb Greene & MacRae, NYC, 1994—2003, Latham & Watkins, NYC, 2003—. Pres. Export Assist Corp., Ft. Lee, N.J., 1988-94; trusted atty., Consulate Gen. of Fed. Repubic Germany, N.Y.C., 1986—, Austrian Trade Commn., N.Y.C., 1988—; fgn. legal cons., Frankfurt, Germany, 1991; counsel German-Am. Partnership Program, 1998—. Fulbright scholar, 1967-68; grantee Ford Found., 1967-68, Deutsche Akademisches Austauchdienst, 1967-68. Mem. Internat. Bar Assn., N.Y. State Bar Assn. (internat. law com.), Assn. Bar City N.Y., German Am. Lawyers Assn., Gesellschaft fuer Rechtsvergleichung. Avocations: boating, fishing, camping. Office: Latham & Watkins 885 Third Ave Ste 100 New York NY 10022 Home Phone: 917-757-6200; Office Phone: 212-906-1671. Business E-Mail: steven.thal@lw.com. E-mail: stesq17@hotmail.com.

THALACKER, ARBIE ROBERT, lawyer, director; b. Marquette, Mich., Apr. 17, 1935; s. Arbie Otto and Jeanne (Emmett) T.; m. Rita Annette Skaaren, Sept. 11, 1956 (div. July 1992); children: Marc Emmett, Christopher Paul, Robert Skaaren; m. Deborah B. Garrett, Jan. 10, 1998. AB, Princeton U., 1957; JD, U. Mich., 1960. Bar: NY 1961, U.S. Ct. Appeals (2d cir.) 1962. Assoc. Shearman & Sterling, NYC, 1960—68, ptnr., 1968—2000, of counsel, 2001—. Dir. Detrex Corp., Detroit, 1981—, chmn. bd., 1993-96. Leader Rep. Dist. Com., 1966-68; trustee Greenwich Village Soc. for Hist. Preservation; trustee Naropa Univ.; bd. dirs. Meredith Monk House Found., Shambhala Internat. Mem. ABA, N.Y. Bar Assn., Assn. Bar City N.Y. (securities regulatory commn. 1975-78), Wine and Food Soc. (bd. dirs. 1976-78, 85-93, 94-2006), Chevaliers du Tastevin, Commanderie de Bordeaux, Siwanoy Country Club (bd. govs. 1976-79),

Derby Club, Links Club, Verbank Hunting and Fishing Club. Office: Shearman & Sterling 599 Lexington Ave Fl C2 New York NY 10022-6069 Home: 80 Fourth Ave Apt 7A New York NY 10003

THALDEN, BARRY, architect; b. Chgo., July 5, 1942; s. Joseph and Sibyl (Goodwin) Hechtenthal; m. Irene L. Mittleman, June 23, 1966 (div. 1989); 1 child, Stacey; m. Kathryn McKnight, Sept. 1996. BArch, U. Ill., 1965; M in Land Architecture, U. Mich., 1969. Landscape arch. Hellmuth, Obata, Kassebaum, St. Louis, 1969-70; dir. landscape architecture PGAV Archs., St. Louis, 1970-71; pres. Thalden Corp. Archs., St. Louis, 1971—; ptnr. Thalden-Boyd-Emery Archs., St. Louis, 1998—. Prin. works include Rock Hill Park, 1975 (AIA award, 1977), Wilson Residence, 1983 (AIA award), Nat. Bowling Hall of Fame, 1983 (St. Louis RCGA award, 1984), Village Bogey Hills (Home Builders award, 1985, St. Louis ASLA award, 1994), St. Louis U. Campus Mall (St. Louis ASLA award, 1989), Horizon Casino Resort, Lake Tahoe, Nev., St. Louis Airport's Radisson Hotel, Lady Luck, Treasure Bay, Palace Casinos, Biloxi, Miss., Boomtown Casino, New Orleans, Pres. Casino on the Admiral, St. Louis, Plaza of Champions, Busch Stadium, Ho Chunk Casino, Wisconsin Dells (ABC award Best Bldg. in Wis., 2000), Potowatomi Casino, Milw., Terrible's Casino, Las Vegas, Chumash Casino Resort, Santa Ynez, Calif., Casino Morongo, Palm Springs, Calif., Paragon Casino Resort, Marksville, La. Bd. dirs. St. Louis Open Space Coun., 1973—83, St. Louis Art., Ednl. Coun.; bd. trustees Las Vegas Art Mus.; apptd. Mo. Lands Architect Coun., 1990—94. Named Architect of Yr. Builder Architect mag., 1986. Fellow Am. Soc. Landscape Architects (nat. v.p. 1979-81, pres. St. Louis chpt. 1975, trustee 1976-79, nat. conv. chair 1991); mem. AIA, World Future Soc. (pres. St. Louis chpt. 1984-94, keynote conf. spkr. 1995). Avocations: painting, gardening, tennis, guitar. Home: 2204 Chatsworth Ct Henderson NV 89074-5307 Office: Thalden-Boyd Emery Archs 8085 Manchester Rd Saint Louis MO 63144

THALER, LINDA KAPLAN, advertising executive; m. Fred Thaler; children: Michael, Emily. BA magna cum laude, CCNY, MA in music. Former music instr. CCNY; with J. Walter Thompson, most recently as exec. v.p., exec. group creative dir.; exec. v.p., exec. creative dir. Wells Rich Greene BDDP, 1994—97; founder, CEO, chief creative officer Kaplan Thaler Group Ltd., NYC, 1997—. Former mem. comedy improv troupe. Author: (jingle) I Don't Want to Grow Up, I'm a Toys 'R' Us Kid, Eastman Kodak-Because Time Goes By, (book) BANG! Getting Your Message Head in a Noisy World, 2003. Named Advertising Women of Yr., Advertising Women of NY, 2001; recipient 13 Clio awards. Office: Kaplan Thaler Group Ltd 825 Eighth Ave - 34Fl New York NY 10019-7498 Office Phone: 212-474-5000. Office Fax: 212-474-5702. E-mail: kaplanthalergroup@kaplanthaler.com.

THALER, PAUL SANDERS, lawyer, arbitrator, mediator; b. Washington, May 4, 1961; s. Martin S. Thaler and Barbara (Friedman) Mishkin; m. Melinda Ann Frostic, Oct. 12, 1991; children: Rachel Leigh, Daniel Martin. AB, Vassar Coll., Poughkeepsie, NY, 1983; JD, Georgetown U., Washington, DC, 1987. Bar: Md. 1987, DC 1988, US Ct. Appeals (DC and 4th cirs.) 1988, US Dist. Ct. Md. 1988, US Ct. Appeals (fed. cir.) 1989, US Dist. Ct. DC 1989, US Ct. Internat. Trade 1990, US Supreme Ct. 1992. Assoc. Cooter & Gell, Washington, 1987-93; ptnr. The Robinson Law Firm, Washington, 1993-96, Thaler, Liebeler LLP, 1996—; guest lectr. negotiations mediation George Washington U. Law Sch., 1996—. Adj. prof. Kogod Sch. Bus., Am. U. Bus. Ethics, Bus. Law, 1999—. Treas. Montgomery Highlands Estates Homeowners Assn., Silver Spring, Md., 1990-99; mediator Superior Ct. of DC, 1991—; mem. adv. com. Vassar Coll. Fund, 1996-99; trustee Nat. Child Rsch. Ctr., Washington, 1998-2001; mem. implementation com. Montgomery County BRAC, Md., 2007-. Mem. ABA (sect. dispute resolution, vice chmn. ethics 1994-98), DC Bar Assn., Md. Bar Assn. Home: 9429 Locust Hill Rd Bethesda MD 20814-3939 Office: Thaler Liebeler LLP Internat Sq 1825 Eye St NW Ste 400 Washington DC 20006 Home Phone: 301-564-3047; Office Phone: 202-466-4110. Business E-Mail: PThaler@ThalerLiebeler.com.

THALER, RICHARD WINSTON, JR., investment banker; b. Boston, Apr. 9, 1951; s. Richard Winston and Victoria Louise (Sears) T.; m. Mary Alice Gast, June 28, 1980; children: Julia Davis, Sarah Sears, Hannah Warren. BA in Am. Polit. History cum laude, Princeton U., 1973; MBA, Harvard U., 1978. Salesman Media Networks, NYC, 1973-74; banker Bank of Boston, Rio de Janeiro, 1975-77, Boston, 1978-80; mng. dir. investment banking Lehman Bros., NYC, 1980-96; vice chmn. investment banking Deutsche Bank Securities, NYC, 1996—. Spl. gifts solicitor Princeton U. Ann. Giving, NYC, 1987—88, 1997—98, 2002—03, class agt., 1988—93; trustee Daily Princetonian, 1989—, pres. bd., 2004—; trustee Episc. Divinity Sch., Cambridge, Mass., 1995—2004, Plimoth Plantation, Plymouth, Mass., 1995—; del. Dem. Nat. Conv., 1996; active Dem. Leadership Coun.; mem. vestry Chapel of St. James the Fisherman, Wellfleet, Mass. Mem. Mass. Soc. Mayflower Descs., Harvard Club, Siwanoy Country Club, Univ. Cottage Club. Democrat. Episcopalian. Avocations: gardening, sailing, American political history, travel. Personal E-mail: richard.thaler@db.com.

THALL, BURNETT MURRAY, retired newspaper executive; b. Toronto, Ont., Can., Sept. 27, 1922; s. Henry and Selina (Harris) Rosenthal; m. Eleanor Langbord, Sept. 23, 1945; children: Nelson Spencer, Martin Evan BASc., U. Toronto, 1945, MASc., 1947, PhD, 1949. Registered profl. engr., Ont. Spl. lectr. applied sci. and engring. U. Toronto, 1947; cons. engr., then prodn. engr. Toronto Star, 1947-50, v.p., 1958-68, sr. v.p., 1968-96, also dir. Chmn. Toronto Star Newspapers Ltd., elected chmn. bd., 1996-99 Trustee Atkinson Charitable Found.; hon. trustee Women's Coll. Hosp. Urgent Care Ctr.; founding trustee Princess Margaret Hosp. Urgent Care Centre named in his honour Women's Coll. Hosp., 1989 Mem. Assn. Profl. Engrs. Ont. (Citizenship medal 1991) Home: 15 Rosemary Ln Toronto ON Canada M5P 3E7 Office: 16 Yonge St 2111 Toronto ON Canada M5E 2A1

THALLER, SETH RAY, plastic surgeon; b. NYC, June 22, 1949; m. Patricia Thaller; children: Cody, Lexi. BA, Lafayette Coll., 1971; MD, U. Louisville, 1975; DMD, Boston Sch. Dentistry, 1978; resident gen. surgery, St. Vincent's Hosp., 1978-80. Intern in internal medicine SUNY, Buffalo, 1975-76; resident in gen. surgery St. Vincent's Hosp., NYC, 1978-80; resident otalaryngology/head and neck surgery Mass. Eye and Ear Infirmary, 1980-83; resident in plastic surgery Albert Einstein Coll. Medicine Affiliated Hosps., 1983—85; craniofacial fellowship UCLA Sch. Medicine, 1986; clin. instr. NYU Sch. Dentistry, NYC, 1984-86; adj. asst. prof. plastic surgery U. Calif., LA, 1986, asst. prof. plastic surgery, 1987-93, acting chief divsn. plastic surgery, 1989, assoc. prof. plastic surgery Davis, 1993-95; prof. and chief divsn. plastic surgery U. Miami/Jackson Meml. Hosp., 1995—. Mem.: Florida Soc. Plastic Surgeons, Inc, ACS, Am. Assn Plastic Surgeons, Assn. Academic Chmn. Plastic Surgeons, Am. Soc. Maxillofacial Surgeons, Am Soc. Plastic & Reconstructive Surgeons, Am. Cleft Palate Craniofacial Assn., Am. Society for Aesthetic Plastic Surgery, Am. Acad. Pediatrics, AMA. Home: 11010 Paradela St Coral Gables FL 33156-4244 Office: Univ Miami Jackson Meml Hospital PO Box 16960 Miami FL 33101-6960

THAMAN, MICHAEL H., building material systems executive; BSEE, Princeton U., BS in Computer Sci. V.p. Mercer Mgmt. Cons., NYC, 1986—92; dir. corp. devel. Owens Corning, 1992-94, plant mgr. Toronto insulation facility, 1994-96, gen. mgr. OEM solutions group Louisville, 1996-97, v.p., pres. engineered pipe systems bus. Brussels, 1997-99, v.p., pres. exterior systems bus. Toledo, 1999-2000, sr. v.p., CFO, 2000—02, chmn., CFO, 2002—. Bd. dir. FPL Group. Office: Owens Corning One Owens Corning Pkwy Toledo OH 43659 *

THAMES, E. GLENN, JR., lawyer; b. Shreveport, La., Mar. 8, 1968; s. Earl Glenn and Barbara Thames; m. Suzanne LaRa Stephens, July 15, 1989; children: Jeremy, Parker, Dawson. BS in Acctg., U. Ark., Little Rock, 1989; JD cum laude, Baylor U., 1992. Bar: Tex. 1992, US Dist. Ct. (ea. dist. Tex.) 1994, US Ct. Appeals (5th cir.) 1998, US Ct. Appeals (Fed. cir.), US Supreme Ct. Law clk. to Hon. William M. Steger US Dist. Ct. (ea. dist. Tex.), 1992—94; atty. Potter, Minton, Roberts, Davis & Jones, P.C., Tyler, Tex., 1994; shareholder Potter Minton, P.C., Tyler, Tex. Contbr. articles to profl. publs.; notes and comments editor: Baylor Law Rev., 1991, rsch. and topics editor:, 1992. Named a Rising Star, Tex. Super Lawyers mag., 2005, 2006. Mem. ABA (mem. litig. and intellectual property sects., coun. appellate lawyers), Smith County Bar Assn., Phi Delta Phi, Beta Alpha Psi, State Bar Tex. (mem. appellate, litig. and intellectual property sects.), Tex. Bar Assn. (5th fed. cir., ea. dist) Tex., Smith County Young Lawyers Assn. (bd. dirs. 2000-2001), Tex. Young Lawyers Assn., Bar Assn. 5th Fed. Cir., Ea. Dist. Tex. Bar Assn. Avocations: golf, hunting. Office: Potter Minton PC 110 N Coll Ste 500 PO Box 359 Tyler TX 75710 Office Phone: 903-597-8311. Business E-Mail: glennthames@potterminton.com.

THAMES, RICK, publishing executive, editor-in-chief; b. Laurinburg, NC; m. Debbie Thames; children: Nathan, Hunter, Lucy. AB in English, Pfeiffer Coll., Misenheimer, NC; MS in Comm., U. Tenn., Knoxville. Reporter Fayetteville Observer, NC, 1978—80; various positions including mng. editor Miami News, 1980—88; various positions including govt. editor, city editor, assist. mng. editor, public editor Charlotte Observer, NC, 1988—96; editor Wichita Eagle, Kans., 1997—2004; v.p., editor Charlotte Observer, NC, 2004—. Chmn. adv. bd. Elliot Sch. of Comm., Wichita State U. Mem.: Am. Soc. of Newspaper Editors (mem. Freedom of Info. Com.), Kansas Press Assn. (bd. dirs.). Office: The Charlotte Observer PO Box 32188 600 S Tryon St Charlotte NC 28232 Office Phone: 704-358-5000. E-mail: rthames@charlotteobserver.com. *

THAMES, WILLIAM DENNIS, JR., physician; b. Lufkin, Tex., June 25, 1925; s. William Dennis and Claudia King Thames; m. Sarah Jane Brazil, Nov. 6, 1948; children: Ina Jane, Mary Anne Clement. MD, Tulane U., New Orleans, 1947. Lt. USN, 1943—45, lt. USN, 1952—54. Recipient Angelina award, Angelina County C. of C., Lufkin, 1987. Mem.: Nu Sigma Nu, Alpha Omega Alpha. Avocations: hunting, fishing, reading, stamp collecting/philately. Home: 1302 Tom Temple Dr Apt 117 Lufkin TX 75904

THAMM, JOCHEN WALTER, library director; b. Magdeburg, Germany, Jan. 11, 1952; s. Walter and Anna (Goldmann) T.; m. Gabriele Neumann, Apr. 16, 1977; children: Ute, Stephan, Anna. Diplom in math., Tech. U., Merseburg, German Dem. Republic, 1974; Fachbibliothekar, U. Berlin, German Dem. Republic, 1985. Mathematician various cos., 1974-83; dir. libr. Deutsche Akademie der Naturforscher Leopoldina, Halle, 1985—. Office: Dt Akademie Naturforscher Bibliothek A-Bebel-Str 50a D 06108 Halle Sachsen-Anhalt Germany Business E-Mail: thamm@leopoldina-halle.de.

THAMPI, MOHAN VARGHESE, environmental health and civil engineer; b. Kuching, Sarawak, Malaysia, Mar. 25, 1960; s. Padmanabha Ramachandran and Sosamma (Varghese) T. Gen. Cert. Edn., Cambridge U., 1976; B in Tech. with honors, Indian Inst. Tech., Kharagpur, India, 1983; MS in Engring., U. Tex., 1985; DSc (hon.), London Inst. Applied Rsch., 1992. Registered profl. engr., Tex., Fla., registered environ. mgr.; cert. safety tng. OSHA; cert. Nat. Coun. Examiners for Engrs. and Surveyors. Assoc. engr. Brown & Caldwell, Dallas, 1985-87, project mgr. Orlando, 1987-88, Stottler Stagg & Assocs., Cape Canaveral, Fla., 1988-91; sr. project engr. Chastain-Skillman, Inc., Lakeland, Fla., 1991-93; project mgr. Glace & Radcliffe, Inc., Winter Park, Fla., 1993-94; mgr. FDEP, West Palm Beach, Fla., 1995-96; project mgr. Office of Capital Projects Mgmt., Naples, Fla., 1996—2004; projects engring. mgr. Project Mgmt., Bradenton, Fla., 2004—. Author: Ultraviolet Disinfection Studies in a Teflon-Tube Reactor, 1985; contbr. articles to profl. jours. Active Rep. Pres.'s Citizens Adv. Commn., 1992. Recipient Cert. of Cont. Profl. Devel. award Fla. Engring. Soc., 1992. Mem. NRA, NSPE, ASCE (assoc.), Project Mgmt. Inst., Internat. Assn. Water Pollution Rsch. and Control, Am. Mensa, Am. Water Works Assn., Water Pollution Control Fedn. (com. for preparing design practice manuals 1989—), Am. Pub. Works Assn., Internat. Freelance Photographers Assn., Internat. Platform Assn., Internat. Assn. Air Travel Couriers, Am. Mgmt. Assn., Am. Smokers Alliance, Am. Gunsmithing Assn., Smithsonian Instn., Nat. Geog. Soc., Nat. Registry Environ. Profls., U. Tex. Ex-Students Assn., Wine Soc. Am., Nat. Family Opinion, Internat. Deep Purple Appreciation Soc., Wilson Ctr. Assocs., I.I.T. Kharagpur Tech. Found., NASA Tech Briefs Reader Opinion Panel, Chemical Engring. Jour. Product Rsch. Panel, Nat. Rifle Assn., Plant Engring. Editl. Quality Panel, Kharagpur Tech. Alumni Found., N.Am. Hunting Club, Knight Order of Templars (Jerusalem), PC Bug Computer Club. Mar Thoma Syrian Christian. Avocations: photography, music, travel, sports. Home: PO Box 11954 Naples FL 34101-2954 Personal E-mail: thampimv@juno.com.

THAPAR, AMUL R., prosecutor; b. Troy, Mich., 1969; m. Kimberly Ann Thapar; children: Zachary, Carmen, Nicholas. Grad., Boston Coll., 1991; JD, U. Calif. Berkeley, 1994. Law clk. to Hon. S. Arthur Spiegel US Dist. Ct. (so. dist.) Ohio, 1994—96; law clk. to Hon. Nathaniel R. Jones US Ct. Appeals (6th Cir.); assoc. Squire, Sanders & Dempsey, Cin., Williams & Connolly, Washington; asst. US atty. DC US Dept. Justice, Washington, 1999—2001, asst. US atty. (so. dist.) Ohio Cin., 2002—06, US atty. (ea. dist.) Ky. Lexington, 2006—. Founder Street Law Inc., Cin., 1995; adj. prof. law George University Law Ctr., U. Cin. Coll. Law. Office: US Attys Office 110 W Vine St Ste 400 Lexington KY 40507 *

THARALDSON, GARY DEAN, hotel developer, owner; b. Valley City, ND, Oct. 17, 1945; BA in Phys. Edn., Valley City State U.; postgrad., N.D. State U. Tchr., Leonard, N.D.; ins. agt., agy. owner, 1969-89; owner of 350 hotels, Valley City, 1982; pres. Tharaldson Enterprises, Fargo, N.D., 1982—. Office: Tharaldson Enterprises 1202 Westrac Dr Fargo ND 58103-2344

THARNEY, LEONARD JOHN, education educator, consultant; b. New Haven, Nov. 6, 1929; s. Lillian A. Batey; m. Denise A. Gauvin, June 20, 1981; children: Karen L., Linda L. BS, Coll. of NJ, 1954; MEd, Rutgers U., 1959; postgrad., Lehigh U., Bethlehem, Pa., 1963-70, Columbia U.; grad., Command & Gen. Staff Coll., Ft. Leavenworth, Kans., 1972. Cert. secondary math. and sci. tchr., elem. tchr. Tchr. (elem. demonstration) Trenton State Coll., NJ, 1954-60; tchr. (jr. high demonstration) Ewing Twp. Sch., NJ, 1960-63; cons., evaluator Am. Coun. on Edn., Washington, 1975-95, field coord., 1995—2003; cons., evaluator Mid. States Assn., Phila., 1987—; prof. Trenton State Coll., 1963-92, dept. chmn., 1988-92, prof. emeritus, 1993—; cons., evaluator coll. and univ. programs Nat. Assn. Indsl. Tech., Ann Arbor, 2003—. Tchr. grad. courses curriculum and ednl. rsch. overseas sites, Spain, Cyprus, Saudi Arabia, Syria, 1981—; exch. prof. Worcester Coll. Higher Edn., England, 1984—85; presenter sci. edn. workshops AISA Internat. Conf., Nairobi, 1987; rep. Coll. to Prins. Tng. Ctr., London, 1994; mem. accrediting commn. Distance Edn. and Tng. Coun., Washington, 2000—; cons. in field. Co-author: 7 manuals for uniform constrn. codes. Col. US Army, 1947—81. Decorated Meritorious Svc. medal; recipient ACE award for Outstanding Svc. in Mil. Evaluations, 1987, cert. of appreciation, presdl. citation, 1989, spl. plaque award, Outstanding Svc. and Support award, 112th FA Assn., 1998, People to People Internat. Outstanding Leadership award, Seoul, Republic of Korea, 2005, Berlin, 2007, Disting. Svc. award, Coll. NJ, 2005. Mem.: ASCD, Nat. Coun. Social Studies, Assn. for Edn. Tchrs. in Sci., Assn. Tchr. Educators, People to People Internat. (bd. dir. Trenton, NJ chpt. 1995—98, chpt. pres. 1998—, NJ del. various confs., internat. trustee 2000—), Am. Air Mus. in Britain (founding mem.), Torch Club Internat., the Trenton Club (bd. dir. 1998—2001, v.p. 2001—02, pres. 2002—03). Home: 20 Lawrenceville-Penning Rd Lawrenceville NJ 08648-1648 E-mail: ljmt.afa@att.net.

THAROOR, SHASHI, former international organization official, writer; b. London, Mar. 9, 1956; came to the US, 1975; s. Chandran and Lily (Menon) T.; m. Tilottama Mukherii, 1977 (div. 2000); children: (twins) Ishaan, Kanishk; m. Christa Giles, 2007. BA with honors, Delhi U., 1975; MA, Tufts U., 1976, MA in Law and Diplomacy, 1977, PhD, 1978. External affairs officer UN High Commn. for Refugees, Geneva, 1978-81, head sub-office and rep. Singapore, 1981-84, dep. chief of secretariat Geneva, 1984—87, exec. asst. to the dep. high commr., 1987-89; spl. asst. to under-sec. gen. for peace-keeping UN, NYC, 1989—96, prin. officer dept. peace-keeping ops., 1995-96, exec. asst. to the sec-gen., 1997-98, dir. comm. and spl. projects, Office of Sec.-Gen., 1998—2001, interim head of dept. of pub. info., 2001—02, under-sec. gen. for comm. & pub. info., 2002—07; writer Arcade Publishing, NYC. Author: Reasons of State, 1981, The Great Indian Novel, 1989 (Best Book of the Yr., Fedn. Indian Pubs. 1990, Best Book Eurasian region Commonwealth Writers prize 1990), Show Business, 1992, India: From Midnight to the Millennium, 1997, Riot, 2001, (with M.F. Husain) Kerala: God's Own Country, 2002, (short story collection) The Five-Dollar Smile, 1990, 2d edit., 93, Bookless in Baghdad, 2005, The Elephant, the Tiger and the Cellphone, 2007; columnist The Hindu, Times of India; contbg. editor, Newsweek Internat.; book reviewer Washington Post, The NY Times, others; contbr. articles to profl. jours. Mem. adv. bd. Vijay Amritraj Found.; bd. dirs. Fletcher Sch. Law and Diplomacy. Named Global Leader of Tomorrow, World Econ. Forum, Davos, Switzerland, 1998. Fellow NY Inst. of the Humanities; mem. Internat. Inst. Strategic Studies (keynote spkr. 1995), Indian Internat. Ctr. Hindu. Avocations: reading, writing, cricket, theater.

THARP, ROLAND GEORGE, psychology professor; b. Galveston, Tex., June 6, 1930; s. Oswald Roland and Berma Lucille (Keefer) T.; m. Stephanie Dalton; children: Donald Martin, Thomas Roland, David Michael, Julie. Student, Middlebury Coll., 1956-60; BA cum laude, U. Houston, 1957; MA, U. Mich., 1958, PhD, 1961. Cert. Am. Bd. Examiners in Profl. Psychology. Reporter Tex. City Sun, 1946-47; mgr. Tharp Lumber Co., LaMarque, Tex., 1949-54; intern VA Hosp., Menlo Park, Calif., 1960; asst. prof. U. Ariz., Tucson, 1961-65, assoc. prof., 1965-68; prof., dir. clin. studies, dir. multicultural ctr. for higher edn. U. Hawaii, Honolulu, 1968-87; provost and v.p. for acad. affairs U.S. Internat. U., San Diego, 1987-89; prof. edn., psychology U. Calif., Santa Cruz, 1990—; dir. Nat. Rsch. Ctr. for Diversity, 1995—. Dir. Ctr. for Rsch. on Edn., Diversity and Excellence, 1996—; prin. investigator Kamehameha Early Edn. Program, Honolulu, 1969-89; field selection officer Peace Corps, Washington, 1965-67. Author: (poetry) Highland Station, 1978; co-author: Behavior Modification in the Natural Environment, 1969, Self-Directed Behavior, 1980, Rousing Minds to Life, 1988, Teaching Transformed, 2000; writer, producer, dir. film Scenes from the Life, 1981 (Purchase prize The Contemporary Mus. 1981). Mem. Bd. Psychologist Examiners, Ariz., 1964-67; pres. Hawaii Literary Arts Coun., Honolulu, 1982. Robert Frost fellow Middlebury Coll., 1960; recipient Am. Film Mag. award for filmmaking Hawaii Internat. Film Festival, 1990, Grawemeyer award edn., 1993. Mem. Am. Ednl. Rsch. Assn., Am. Anthropol. Assn. Episcopalian. Avocations: tennis, painting. Office: 560 N St SW Apt N702 Washington DC 20024-4621 E-mail: tharp@ucsc.edu.

THARP, STEPHEN JOHN, organist and pianist, artist; b. Chgo., Apr. 12, 1970; s. Michael John and Arlene Erna (Scheer) Tharp; m. Maria Helena Vieira Catarro, Oct. 1, 2004. BA in Music Performance magna cum laude, Ill. Coll., Jacksonville, 1992; MusM in Music Performance, Northwestern U., Chgo., 1994. Cert. performance Internat. Acad. Organists, The Netherlands, 1990. Asst. organist Christ Ch., Des Plaines, Ill., 1984—88; organist The Edgebrook Ch., Chgo., 1984—88, First Presbyn. Ch., Jacksonville, 1988—90, First United Meth. Ch., Springfield, Ill., 1990—93; prin. organist Alice Millar Chapel, Northwest U., 1993—94; organist, choirmaster Holy Trinity Episcopal Ch., Skokie, Ill., 1994—95; organist, dir. concerts St. Patrick's Cathedral, NYC, 1995—97; assoc. organist St. Bartholomew's Ch., NYC, 1998—2004; artist in residence St. Peter's Episcopal Ch., Perth Amboy, NJ, 2006—. Guest tchr. Yale U., New Haven, 2001—; guest instr. Westminster Choir Coll., Princeton, NJ, 2005—06, Bochum U., Germany, 2004. Musician (solo organ): (CD) Stephen Tharp-Debut in Europe, 2001, Stephen Tharp at Sulpice, Paris, France, 2002, Marcel Dupré: The Stations of the Cross, 2005, The Complete Organ Works of Jeanne Demessieux, 2007; composer: (commissioned musical) Easter Fanfares, 2005. Mem.: Am. Guild Organists, St. Wilfred Club (NYC). Episcopal. Avocations: tennis, wine tasting, films, walking. Personal E-mail: stephen.tharp@yahoo.com.

THARP, TWYLA, dancer; b. Portland, Ind., July 1, 1941; m. Peter Young (div.); m. Robert Huot (div.); 1 child, Jesse Huot. Student, Pomona Coll.; BA in Art History, Barnard Coll., 1963; D of Performing Arts (hon.), Calif. Inst. Arts, 1978, Brown U., 1981, Bard Coll., 1981; LHD, Ind. U., 1987; DFA, Pomona Coll., 1987; studied with Richard Thomas, Merce Cunningham, Igor Schwezoff, Louis Mattox, Paul Taylor, Margaret Craske, Erick Hawkins. Dancer Paul Taylor Dance Co., 1963-65; freelance choreographer with own modern dance troupe and various other cos. including Joffrey Ballet and Am. Ballet Theatre, 1965-87; founder, choreographer Twyla Tharp Dance Found., NYC, 1965-87; artistic assoc., resident choreographer Am. Ballet Theatre, NYC, 1987-91; teaching residencies various colls. and univs. including U. Mass., Oberlin Coll., Walker Art Ctr., Boston U. Choreographer White Oak Dance Project. Choreographer Tank Dive, 1965, Re-Moves, 1966, One Two Three, 1966, Forevermore, 1967, Generation, 1968, Medley, 1969, After Suite, 1969, Dancing in the Streets of London and Paris, 1969, The One Hundreds, 1970, The Fugue, 1970, The Bix Pieces, 1971, Eight Jelly Rolls, 1971, The Raggedy Dances, 1972, Deuce Coupe, 1973, As Time Goes By, 1974, Sue's Leg, 1975, Ocean's Motion, 1975, Push Comes to Shove, 1976, Once More Frank, 1976, Mud, 1977, Baker's Dozen, 1979, When We Were Very Young, 1980, Nine Sinatra Songs, 1982, The Catherine Wheel, 1982, Bach Partita, 1984, The Little Ballet, 1984, with Jerome Robbins Brahms Handel, 1988, At the Supermarket, 1984, In the Upper Room, 1987, Ballare, 1987, Stations of the Crossed, 1988, Everlast, 1989, Quartet, 1989, Bum's Rush, 1989, The Rules of the Game, 1990, Brief Fling, 1990, Grand Pas: Rhythm of the Saints, 1991, Deuce Coupe II, 1992, The Men's Piece, 1992, with Mikhail Baryshnikov Cutting Up, 1992—93, Demeter and Persephone, 1993, Waterbaby Bagatelles, 1994, Demeter and Persephone, 1994, Red, White & Blues, 1995, How Near Heaven, 1995, I Remember Clifford, 1995, Jump Start, 1995, Americans We, 1995, Movin' Out, 1998 (Touring Broadway awards, best choreography, 2005), The Times They Are A-Changin', 2006, (films) Hair, 1979, Ragtime, 1981, Amadeus, 1984, White Nights, 1985, Valmont, 1989, I'll Do Anything, 1994, video spls. Making Television Dance, 1977, CBS Cable Confessions of a Corner Maker, 1980, (Broadway plays) Sorrow Floats, 1985, Singin' in the Rain, 1985, TV Baryshnikov by Tharp, 1985 (Emmy award for Outstanding Choreography, 1985, Emmy award for Outstanding Writing of Classical Music/Dance Programming, 1985), The Catherine Wheel, 1982 (Emmy award nomination for Outstanding Choreography, 1982); author (autobiography): When Push Comes to Shove, 1982. Recipient Creative Arts award, Brandeis U., 1972, Dance Mag. award, 1981, Univ. Excellence medal, Columbia U., 1987, Lions of the Performing Arts award, N.Y. Pub. Libr., 1989, Samuel M. Scripps award, Am. Dance Festival, 1990, Best Musical Theatre Choreography award, Nat. Dance Awards Critics' Cir., 2006; fellow MacArthur Found., 1992. *

THARPE, DON I., foundation administrator; b. Jan. 1952; m. Linda Tharpe; children: Justin, Adrienne. BS, Murray State U., 1974, MS, 1975; PhD in Edn. Adminstrn., Va. Polytechnic & State U. Dir. trade and vocational edn. Mo. State Dept. Edn.; with Am. Vocational Assn.; dir. profl. programs Assn. of Sch. Bus. Officials Internat., Reston, Va., 1985—89, acting exec. dir., 1989—90, exec. dir., 1990—2002; exec. v.p., COO Coun. on Founds., Washington, 2002—06; pres., CEO Congl. Black Caucus Found., Inc., Washington, 2005—. Former mem. Nat. Policy Bd. for Ednl. Adminstrn. Contbr. articles to profl. jours. Recipient Disting. Alumnus, Murry State U., 2005. Mem.: Am. Soc. Assn. Execs. (former vice chair, fellow), Greater Washington Soc. Assn. Execs., Alpha Phi Alpha. Office: Congl Black Caucus Found 1720 Massachusetts Ave, NW Washington DC 20036 Office Phone: 202-263-2800. Office Fax: 202-775-0773.

THARPE, FRAZIER EUGENE, journalist; b. Panama City, Fla., Jan. 10, 1941; s. Henry Clayton and Margaret Jane (Jenkins) T.; m. Barbara Ann Hembree, Oct. 30, 1971. BA in Polit. Sci. and History, Vanderbilt U., Nashville, 1963. Reporter Miami (Fla.) News, 1963; reporter U.P.I., Atlanta and Columbia, SC, 1964; pub. relations exec. Atlanta, 1965-69; fin. editor Atlanta Constn., 1969-73. Editl. assoc., columnist, 1974-83, columnist Helpline, ConsumerWatch, 1983-98; editor Homefinder, 1999-2002.

THATCHER, GEORGE ROBERT, banker, writer, journalist, columnist; b. Austin, Pa., Sept. 18, 1922; S. Walter Robert and Roberta Estelle (Bernard) T.; widowed; children: Georgia Anne Thatcher Faneca, Janie Estelle Thatcher Holmes, Walter Wimberly. BA, U. Miss., 1948. Pvt. U.S. Army, 1942, infantry maj., 1948, ret., 1952; ptnr. Rand-Thatcher Advt. Agy., Gulfport, Miss., 1948—67; pres. coast divsn. Magnolia Fed. Bank, Gulfport, 1981-92; councilman City of Gulfport, 1989; hon. canon St. Peter's Cathedral, Likoma Island, Malawi, 1997—; daily columnist The Sun Herald, Biloxi, Miss., 1997—; commentator Pub. Radio Miss., 2006. Trustee U.S. Senate Art Preservation Bd., 2005—. Author: Misrepresentation in MS, 1954, Beach Walks, 1998, 2d edit., 1999, Beach Walks II, 2000, Scenes From the Beach, 2003. Chmn. Miss. Arts Commn., 1991-2000; past chmn. United Way, Harrison County Libr.; past pres. Episcopal Laymen of Miss., Miss. Hist. Assn. Decorated Bronze Star; named Outstanding Citizen Miss. Coast C. of C., 1998. Mem. Gulfport Rotary Club (pres. 1995-96, Citizen of Yr. 1993, Paul Harris fellow), Century Club (pres.), Gulfport Yacht Club, Coast Tennis Club, Great So. Club. Republican. Roman Catholic. Avocations: tennis, chess, reading, classical music. Home: 1302 2nd St Gulfport MS 39501-2219 Office: Regions Bank 2200 14th St Gulfport MS 39501 E-mail: fishcrow@aol.com.

THATCHER, JANET SOLVERSON, financial advisor, writer; b. Sept. 24, 1946; m. John G. Thatcher, Mar. 20, 1976. BA, U. Wis., 1968, MBA, 1976, PhD, 1979. Svc. rep. Wis. Telephone Co., Beloit, 1968-71; trust dept. Baraboo (Wis.) Nat. Bank, 1971-73; pension, profit sharing trust dept. US Bank, Madison, Wis., 1973—74; asst. prof. fin. Va. Tech., Blacksburg, 1978-82, Clarkson U., Potsdam, N.Y., 1982-86; prof. U. Wis., Whitewater, 1986—2001. Contbr. articles to profl. jours. including Jour. Fin., Fin. Mgmt., Jour. Fin. Rsch., Jour. Fin. Rsch., Fin. Rev; columnist Plus Mag. Home: 4546 Wavertree St San Luis Obispo CA 93401-7831

THATCHER, SANFORD GRAY, publishing executive; b. Washington, Aug. 4, 1943; s. Harold Wesley and Genevieve (Harnett) T.; m. Barbara Boal, June 1966 (div.); m. Catherine Dammeyer, May 27, 1980 (div.); m. Robin Glucroft, June 8, 1997; children: Corinne, Christopher; stepchildren: Brian, Mitchell, Mandy. BA summa cum laude, Princeton U., 1965, postgrad., 1966-67, Columbia U., 1965-66. Editor manuscript divsn. Princeton U. Press, NJ, 1967-69, editor social sci. divsn. NJ, 1969-78, asst. dir. NJ, 1978-85, editor in chief NJ, 1985-89; dir. Pa. State U. Press, University Park, 1989—. Author: AAUP Guide to 1976 Copyright Law, 1977; contbr. articles to profl. jours. Active Ch. and Soc. Commn., St. Paul's United Meth. Ch., 1990-92; bd. dirs. The Daily Collegian newspaper, Pa. State U., 1991-99. Mem. Am. Philos. Assn., L.Am. Studies Assn., Assn. Am. Pubs. (copyright com. 1972—, freedom to read com. 1982-86), Assn. Am. Univ. Presses (copyright com. 1972—, bd. dirs. 1995, pres. 2007-), Assn. for Copyright Enforcement (bd. dirs. 1988-93), Copyright Clearance Ctr. (bd. dirs. 1992—). Democrat. Methodist. Avocations: swimming, sailing, tennis, rare book collecting, music. Office: Pa State U Press 820 N University Dr University Park PA 16802-1003 Home: 1051 Teaberry Ln Apt B12 State College PA 16803-2824 E-mail: sgt3@psu.edu. *

THATTASSERY, EMIL GEORGE, cardiologist; b. Washington, Mar. 19, 1977; s. Pious and Jacie Thattassery. BS, Johns Hopkins U., 1997; MD, U. Md., 2003; MPH, Columbia U., 2006. Rsch. intern Walter Reed Army Inst. Rsch., Washington, 1993—97; software engr. Genesis Med. Tech., Balt., 1998—99, Trilogy Software, Austin, Tex., 1999; resident in internal medicine Northwestern Meml. Hosp., Chgo., 2003—06; mem. rapid response team Meml. Sloan Kettering Cancer Ctr., Chgo., 2006—07; cardiology fellow Emory Med. Ctr., Atlanta, 2007—. Contbr. articles to med. jours. Pres. Cir. K, Johns Hopkins U., Balt., 1996—97; pres. student coun. U. Md. Med. Sch., Balt., 2000—01. Mem.: AMA, Tau Beta Pi. Office: Emory Med Ctr Atlanta GA 30308 Office Phone: 212-639-8114. Personal E-mail: ethat001@hotmail.com.

THAU, WILLIAM ALBERT, lawyer; b. St. Louis, June 22, 1940; s. William Albert and Irene Elizabeth (Mundy) T.; m. Jane Hancock, Sept. 7, 1961; children: William Albert, Caroline Jane, Jennifer Elizabeth. BS in Indsl. Mgmt., Ga. Inst. Tech., 1962; JD, U. Tex., 1965. Bar: Tex. 1965. Ptnr., head of real estate sect. Jenkens & Gilchrist, Dallas, 1965—2002. Chmn. real estate developer/builder symposium S.W. Legal Found, 1975-79; bd. dirs. Southwestern Film Archives, So. Meth. U.; lectr. Practicing Law Inst. Author: Negotiating the Purchase and Sale of Real Estate, 1975, Non-Recourse, 2004, The Source Code, 2006; editor Tex. State Bar Assn. Newsletter on Real Estate, Probate and Trust Law, 1978-81; contbr. articles to Real Estate Rev., 1983—. Bd. dirs. St. Philips Sch., Dallas, 1988, So. Meth. U.; trustee Dallas Can. Acad., 1987-88. Mem. ABA, Tex. State Bar Assn. (chmn. real estate, probate, trust law sect.), Am. Coll. Real Estate Lawyers. Republican. Office: 140 Tanglewood Rd Saint Simons Island GA 31522 Personal E-mail: wthau@aol.com.

THAWLEY, MICHAEL, diplomat; b. Eng., 1950; arrived in Australia, 1960; m. Deborah Wilkins; children: Samuel, Thomas, Cosimo. BA with honors, Australian Nat. U., 1971; postgrad. diploma in Russian, Surrey U., Eng., 1980. Joined Australian Fgn. Svc., 1972, first asst. sec. Prime Mins. Dept., 1993-96; nat. security advisor Prime Min. Australia, 1996; dep. sec. dept. fgn. affairs and trade; Australian amb. to the U.S. Washington, 2000—. Avocations: reading, music, gardening. Office: Embassy of Australia 1601 Massachusetts Ave NW Washington DC 20036-2273 Fax: 202-797-3209.

THAXTON, MARVIN DELL, lawyer; b. Electra, Tex., June 1, 1925; s. Montgomery Dell and Ida (Scheurer) T.; m. Carolyn Moore Alexander, Aug. 30, 1949; children: Rebecca Thaxton Henderson, Gail Thaxton Fogleman, Marvin D. Jr. JD, U. Ark., Fayetteville, 1949. Bar: Ark. 1949, US Dist. Ct. (ea. dist.) Ark. 1952, US Dist. Ct. (we. dist.) Ark. 1978, US Dist. Ct. (we. dist.) Okla., US Supreme Ct. 1987. Prin. Thaxton Furniture Co., Newport, Ark., 1949-50; ptnr. Thaxton, Hout & Howard, Attys., Newport, 1950-97; retired, 1997. Spl. assoc. justice Ark. Supreme Ct., 1978, 84; examiner Ark. State Bd. Law Examiners, 1968—73, chmn., 1973. Pres. Newport Sch. Dist. Bd. Edn., 1964; past pres. Ea. Ark. Young Men's Clubs; leader Newport area Boy Scouts Am., 1949-94; active Newport City Planning Commn., 2006-07. Officer US Mcht. Marine, 1945-46, PTO. Named Outstanding Citizen, Jackson County, 2006. Fellow Ark. Bar Found.; mem. ABA, Ark. Bar Assn. (honor cert. 1973), Newport C. of C. (pres. 1956, bd. dirs. 1997-2007), Newport Rotary Club (past pres., Paul Harris fellow 1990, Oustanding Citizen Jackson County 2006), Sigma Chi. Democrat. Methodist. Avocations: hunting, fishing, boating. Home: 12 Lakeside Ln Newport AR 72112-3914

THAYER, CHARLES JAMES, investment banker; b. Abilene, Kans., Feb. 28, 1944; s. Bruce V. and Neoma (Obermeyer) T.; 1 child, Travis J. Grad., U. Kans., 1967. Exec. v.p., CFO Citizens Fidelity Bank, Louisville, 1977—87; exec. v.p. fin. PNC Bank Corp., Pitts., 1987—89; chmn., mng. dir. Chartwell Capital Ltd., Ft. Lauderdale, Fla., 1989—; interim chmn., CEO Sunbeam-Oster, Providence, 1993. Adv. dir. Louisville Cmty. Devel. Bank, 1997—, Keefe Mgrs., Inc., NYC, 1990-02; mem. adv. bd. Am. Assn. Bank Dirs.; bd. dirs. BB&T Bank, Fla., 2004-06, Republic Bank, St. Petersburg, Fla., 1999-04 Trustee Cystic Fibrosis Found., Washington, 1980—; chmn. Cystic Fibrosis Svcs., Washington, 1994-04. Mem. Nat. Assn. Corp. Dirs. (Fla. bd. dirs. 2005). Avocation: sailing. Office: Chartwell Capital Ltd 420 Isle Of Capri Dr Fort Lauderdale FL 33301-2438 Business E-Mail: cjt@chartwellcapital.com.

THAYER, EDNA LOUISE, health facility administrator; b. Madelia, Minn., May 21, 1936; d. Walter William Arthur and Hilda Engel Emily Ann (Geistfeld) Wilke; m. David LeRoy Thayer, Aug. 30, 1958; children: Scott, Tamara, Brenda. Diploma in nursing, Bethesda Luth., 1956; BS in Nursing Edn., U. Minn., 1960; MSN, Washington U., St. Louis, 1966; MS in Counseling, Mankato State U., Minn., 1972. Cert. nursing adminstr. advanced ANA. Nurse Bethesda Luth. Hosp., St. Paul, 1956-58, U. Minn. Hosp., Mpls., 1958; from nurse to asst. head nurse supr., edn. dir. Fairmont (Minn.) Community Hosp., 1959-63; instr. Alton (Ill.) Meml. Hosp., 1963-66; from nursing instr. to assoc. prof. and dean Sch. Nursing Mankato State U., 1966-77; asst. adminstr. Rice County Dist. One Hosp., Faribault, Minn., 1977-89; RN, adminstrv. supr. St. Peter (Minn.) Regional Treatment Ctr., 1990-96; spkr., 1996—. Nurse surveyor Minn. Dept. Tech. Edn., St. Paul, 1980-93; mem. adv. co. LPN and MA programs Tech. Inst., Faribault, 1977-2001. Co-author (with Mary Huntley and Linda Beer): Celebrating the First Fifty Years, 2003; co-author: (with Mary Huntley) A Mirthful Spirit: Embracing Laughter for Wellness, 2007. Mem. Rice County Ext. Bd., Faribault, 1986-91, adult leader 4-H Club, Rice County and St. Paul, 1971-97; advisor Med. Explorers, Faribault, 1977-89; mem. Rep. Rodosovich Health Com., Faribault, 1984-94; coun. mem. Our Savior's Luth. Ch., Faribault, 1984-87; mem. Rep. Boudreau Health Care Adv. Com., 1996-2001. Recipient Alumni award, Nat. 4-H Club, 1983, Disting. Friend of Nursing award, Mankato State U., 1995, Women of Distinction award, Girl Scouts, 2007. Mem. Minn. Orgn. Nurse Execs. (bd. dirs. 1987-89), Dist. F Nursing Svc. Adminstrs. (pres. 1980-82), Minn. Nurses Assn. (bd. dirs. 1982-87, Pres.'s award 1983, pres. 5th dist. 1974, 75, pres. 13th dist. 1984-86), AAUW, Sigma Theta Tau, Delta Kappa Gamma (pres. Pi chptr. 1982-84, Woman of Achievement award 1985, Golden Stipend award 2006), Hosp. Aux., Legion Aux. Republican. Avocations: crafts, volunteer work, theater, plays. Home: 7 Roots Beach Ln Elysian MN 56028-9731 Office Phone: 507-267-4588. Personal E-mail: dethayer@myclearwave.net.

THAYER, GAYLORD BERTRAM, JR., retired electronics executive, private investor; b. Jamestown, NY, July 2, 1944; s. Gaylord Bertram and Marion Brown (Klock) T. BSME, U. Rochester, 1966; MBA, Harvard U., 1968. Asst. to contr. Teradyne, Inc., Boston, 1968-70, mgr. MIS, 1970-72, sales engr., 1972-76, product mgr., 1976-84, divsn. mgr., 1984-91, mktg. dir., 1991-98; pvt. investor, 1998—. Exec.-in-residence entrepreneurship program Babson Coll., 2003—; adv. bd. Lexent Techs., Lexington, Mass., 1999—, Simply Media Inc., Lincoln, Mass.; gubernatorial appt. to Mass. Pub. Health Coun. Policy Bd. State Dept. of Pub. Health, 2003. Bd. dirs. New Eng. divsn. Am. Cancer Soc., Boston; elected town meeting mem., 2003—; bd. trustees Boston Collegiate Charter Sch. Mem.: Nat. Assembly Am. Cancer Soc. Avocations: cooking, reading, travel, flying. Home: 52 Royalston Rd Wellesley MA 02481-1244

THAYER, ROBERT WILCOX, music educator; b. Detroit, Oct. 26, 1927; s. Willard Charles and Eva Stuart (Missildine) T.; m. Norma Jean Boyd, Dec. 19, 1954; children: Douglas Boyd, Stephen Bruce. MusB, U. Rochester, 1949; M of Mus. Edn., Wichita State U., 1955; PhD, U. Iowa, 1971. Elem. and secondary music tchr. pub. and pvt. schs. Waterford Pa., Wichita, Kans., Clearwater, Kans., 1949-53; asst. prof. music Friends U., Wichita, 1953-58; assoc. prof. music Cornell Coll., Mt. Vernon, Iowa, 1958-72; assoc. prof. music SUNY, Potsdam, 1972-73, assoc. dean music, 1973-76, dean music, 1976-82; dean music Coll. Musical Arts Bowling Green State U., Ohio, 1983-93, devel. officer, 1993-96, dean emeritus, trustee prof., 1993, interim dean DePauw U., 2001-02; interim head dept. music U. Conn., 2003-05, dean Lawrence U. Conservatory Music, 2005—; musician French horn and tuben Rochester Philharm. Orch., NY, 1949, French horn Erie Philharm. Orch., Pa., 1949-50; solo French horn Wichita Symphony Orch., Kans., 1950-58, Cedar Rapids Symphony Orch., Iowa, 1958-70; adj. instr. horn Wichita State U., 1955-58; cons. Nat. Assn. Schs. Music, Reston, Va., 1978—, accreditation evaluator, 1975-93, grad. commn., 1979-85, mem. task force on State Certification, 1981-82, chmn. commn. on non-degree granting instns., 1988-93, cons., 1996—, hon. mem., 1995; planner, adminstr. Olympic ceremonial music by Crane Sch. Music 1980 Winter Olympic Games, Lake Placid, NY, 1980; cons. music edn. Republic of China, 1981, 88, 91, 92. Contbr. articles to profl. jours. Mem. Music Educators Nat. Conf., Coll. Music Soc., Torch Club (Toledo), Phi Mu Alpha (sec. Wichita alumni chpt. 1955-58). Democrat. Home Phone: 920-832-7159; Office Phone: 920-832-6614. Business E-Mail: thayerr@bgnet.bgsu.edu.

THAYER, RUSSELL, III, air transportation executive; b. Phila., Dec. 5, 1922; s. Russell and Shelby Wentworth (Johnson) T.; m. Elizabeth Wright Mifflin, June 12, 1947; children: Elizabeth, Dixon, Shelby, Samuel, David. Student, St. George's Sch., 1937-42; AB, Princeton U., 1949. Mgmt. trainee Eastern Air Lines, 1949-52; mgr. cargo sales and service Am. Airlines, Los Angeles, 1952-63; v.p. mktg. Seaboard World Airlines, NYC, 1963-70; sr. v.p. Braniff Airways, Inc., Dallas, 1970-72, exec. v.p., 1972-77, pres., chief oper. officer, 1977-80, vice chmn., 1981-82; dir. (Braniff Airways, Inc.), 1971-82; v.p. Pan Am. World Airways, Inc., NYC, 1982-84, sr. v.p., 1984-88, Airline Econs., Inc., Washington, 1988—, also bd. dirs., 1988—. Dir. Ft. Worth Nat. Bank, 1977-82; vice chmn. Airline Capital Assn; bd. dirs. Kiwi Internat. Airlines, Inc., World Aux. Power Corp. Mem. Trinity Ch. Ushers Guild, Princeton, N.J., 1968—; Trustee Aviation Hall of Fame N.J. Served with USAAF, 1942-45, ETO. Decorated D.F.C., Air medal with 11 oak leaf clusters. Mem. Am. Aviation Hist. Assn., Air Force Assn., Exptl. Aircraft Assn., Nat. Aeros. Assn., Ivy Club (Princeton), Pretty Brook Tennis Club (Princeton), Bay Head (N.J.) Yacht Club, Nassau Club (Princeton), Princeton Club (N.Y.C.), Phila. Club, Delta Psi. Home: Hulfish St Apt 17-I Princeton NJ 08542-3706 Office: Airline Capital Associates Inc 545 5th Ave Rm 1009 New York NY 10017-3655 Office Phone: 609-252-9675.

THAYER, STACY E., research scientist; b. Weymouth, Mass., June 14, 1978; d. Robert I. Thayer and Susan Clark-Thayer; m. Christien Rioux, Oct. 1, 2006. BS in Comm., Suffolk U., Boston, 2000, MA in Psychology, 2002. Elp program mgr. Sullfolk U., Ballotti Learning, Boston, 1997—2004; recruiter Wilmark Group, Wellesley, Mass., 2005—06; rsch. analyst Linkage, Inc, Burlington, Mass., 2005—. Mem.: APA (assoc.), Soc. Consulting Psychology (assoc.), Soc. Indsl. Orgnl. Psychology (assoc.). Office: Linkage Inc 16 New England Executive Office Burlington MA 01803 Home Phone: 781-899-6888; Office Phone: 781-402-5429. Business E-Mail: sthayer@linkageinc.com.

THAYER, THOMAS MANOR, JR., artist; b. Lansing, Mich., Apr. 8, 1958; BFA, U. Mich., 1981. Owner, lead artist Alexander Raymond Thomas Qaulity Fine Art, Camano Island, Wash., 1996—. Instr. Art Workshop, 1999—. One-man shows include Mountlake Terrace Civic Ctr. Gallery, Mountlake Terrace, Wash., 1999, Edmonds C.C., Edmonds, Wash., 1996, PACCAR Corp., Bellevue, Wash., 1995, Mountlake Terrace Libr., 1995, Cascade Estates Winery, Seattle, 1992, exhibited in group shows at The Artist's Mag. Competition, 2001, 2002, Washington State Ducks Unlimited, 1997 (2d pl. award Artist of Yr., 1997), Northwest Color III Exhbn., Seattle, Statements DC 207 Exhbn., 2001, The Colored Pencil Soc. of Am., 2d Ann. Internat. Exhbn., Portland, 1994, 4th Ann. Internat. Exhbn., San Diego, 1996, 8th Ann. Internat. Exhbn., Birmingham, Mich., 2000, 9th Ann. Internat. Exhbn., San Francisco, 2001 (Cippy Best of Show award), 10th Ann. Internat. Exhbn., Dallas, 2002, New Art Internat., 2004, Arts of the Terrace, 2004 (Best Show, 2d pl., 2004), numerous others, including the Points of Color DC 207 Exhbn., Bothell, Wash., 2000; contbr. artwork and articles to mags.; contbr. (books) Best of Colored Pencil, 1994, 1997, Creative Colored Pencil, 1995, Creative Colored Pencil Portraits, 1996, Exploring Colored Pencil, 1999; Exhibited in group shows at Edmonds Art Festival, 2002 (1st pl. award, 2002, 1995, 2d pl. award, 1996, 1st pl. award, 1998), 2003 (1st pl. award, 2003). Mem.: Am. Soc. of Classical Realism, Colored Pencil Soc. of Am. Avocation: collecting and restoring classic cars of the 1960s and 1970s, snow skiing. Home: 1633 Hemlock Dr Camano Island WA 98282

THEALL, DONALD FRANCIS, retired university president; b. Mt. Vernon, NY, Oct. 13, 1928; s. Harold A. and Helen (Donaldson) T.; m. Joan Ada Benedict, June 14, 1950; children: Thomas, Margaret, John, Harold, Lawrence, Michael. BA with honors, Yale U., 1950; MA with 1st class honors, U. Toronto, 1951, PhD with 1st class honors, 1954, DST (hon.), 2006. Teaching fellow U. Toronto, 1950-52, mem. faculty, 1952-65, prof. English, chmn. joint depts. English, 1964-65; dir. communication studies York U., also prof. English and communications, 1965-66; dir. English Atkinson Coll., 1965-66; mem. faculty McGill U., Montreal, Que., Canada, 1966-79, prof. English, 1966-79, chmn. dept., 1966-74, Molson prof., 1972-79, dir. grad. program in communications, 1976-79, adj. prof. grad. comm. Montreal, Que., Canada, 1989-91; pres., vice chancellor, prof. English and cultural studies Trent U., Peterborough, Ont., 1980-87, univ. prof., 1987-94, univ. prof. emeritus, 1994—. Cultural exch. prof. Govt. of Can. and China, 1974; mem. adv. bd. Semiotic Inquiry, 1982—; cons. in field. Author: (with Robinson and Wevers) Let's Speak English, 4 vols., 1960-61, The Medium Is the Rear View Mirror: Understanding McLuhan, 1971, (with G.J. Robinson) Studies in Canadian Communications, 1975, Beyond the Word: Reconstructing Sense in the Joyce Era of Technology, Culture, and Communication, 1995 (short-listed Harold Adams Innis prize 1997), James Joyce's Techno-Poetics, 1997, The Virtual Marshall McLuhan, 2001; mem. editl. bd. Sci. Fiction Studies, 1976—, Can. Jour. Comm., 1979—, Jour. Can. Studies, 1980-87. Mem. Greater Peterborough Econ. Council, 1982-87; mem. fed. adv. council to minister employment and immigration for Peterborough area, 1986-87. Recipient awards Social Sci. and Humanities Rsch. Coun., 1991-94, 94-97, 97-2000, 2000—, Can. Fedn. Humanities-Aid to Scholarly Publs., 1994, 96, 2000; grantee Humanities Rsch. Coun. Can., 1954-56, 73-76, Ont. Dept. Edn., 1956-59, 91, Atkinson Found., 1960, CBC, 1961, Can. Coun., 1966-68, 73-76, Eastman Kodak Corp., Nat. Film Bd. Can., Can. Dept. Industry, Can. Dept. Trade and Commerce, Can. Ctrl. Mortgage and Housing, 1967-69, Que. Ministry Comm., 1977; sr. leave fellow Can. Coun., 1975. Corr. fellow Acad. Medicine (Toronto); mem. Internat. Communications Assn. (dir. 1978-81), Can. Communications Assn. (chmn. com. to investigate formation 1978, pres. 1979-80), MLA, Philol. Soc. Gt. Britain, Can. Assn. Chmn. English (founding chmn. 1971-74), Assn. Can. Univ. Tchrs. English, Internat. Inst. Communications, Soc. Arts Publs. (v.p. 1967-68), Sci. Fiction Research Assn., University Club of Toronto, Yale Club (Toronto), McGill Faculty Club, Elizabethan Club (Yale). Office: Trent Univ Grad Methodologies Program Peterborough ON Canada K9J 7B8 E-mail: dtheall@trentu.ca, dtheall@cogeco.ca.

THE EDGE, (DAVID HOWELL EVANS), musician; b. Ireland, Aug. 8, 1961; children: Holly, Aaron, Blue Angel, Cian. Guitarist U2, 1978—. Albums include U2:3, 1979, Boy, 1980, October, 1981, War, 1983, Under A Blood Red Sky, 1983, Unforgettable Fire, 1984, Wide Awake in America, 1985, Joshua Tree, 1987 (Grammy awards for best rock performance by a duo or group with vocals, album of yr., 1988, MTV Music Video award for viewers choice for With or Without You 1987, best performance music video for Where the Streets Have No Name 1989), Rattle and Hum, 1988 (MTV Music Video award for best video from film for When Love Comes to Town with B.B. King 1989, Grammy award for best rock performance by a duo or group with vocal for Desire 1989), Achtung Baby, 1991 (Grammy award for prodr. yr. 1991, MTV Music Video awards for best group video, best spl. effects in a video for Even Better Than the Real Thing 1992), Zooropa, 1993 (Grammy award for alternative album of yr. 1993), Pop, 1997, All That You Can't Leave Behind, 2000 (Grammy awards: album of the year, best pop performance, best rock performance, best rock album, 2001), The Best of 1990-2000, 2002, How to Dismantle an Atomic Bomb, 2004 (Grammy awards: best rock album, album of yr., best rock group performance & song of yr. for Sometimes You Can't Make it On Your Own, best rock song for City of Blinding Lights, 2006). Co-founder Music Rising initiative, 2005. U2 named Best-Selling Irish Artist of Yr., World Music Awards, 1993, 1998, World's Best-Selling Rock Act, World Music awards, 2006; named to VH1: Greatest Artists of Rock & Roll, 1998; co-recipient (with U2) Ambassador of Conscience award, Amnesty Internat., 2005; recipient Brit. Record Industry award for best internat. group, 1988, 89. Achievements include inducted into Rock and Roll Hall of Fame as mem. U2, 2005. Address: Interscope Records 2220 Colorado Ave Santa Monica CA 90404

THEILMANN, MICHAEL T., human resources specialist; m. Nancy Theilmann; 3 children. Grad., Gustavas Adolphus Coll.; MS, U. Nebr. With human resources dept. Burger King, Grand Metropolitan; various positions in human resources PepsiCo and Yum! Brands, Inc., 1993—2000; v.p. human resources Europe ops. Yum! Brands, Inc., 2000—02, sr. v.p. human resources, chief people officer internat. bus., 2002—05; exec. v.p., chief human resources and adminstrn. officer JC Penney Company, Inc., 2005—. Office: JC Penney Co Inc 6501 Legacy Dr Plano TX 75024-3698 Office Phone: 972-431-1000. Office Fax: 972-431-1362.

THEIN, HLA-HLA, research scientist; d. Thein Maung and Khin Hla Myint. MBBS, Inst. Medicine, Yangon, 1980; MPH, U. Calif., Berkeley, 1997; postgrad., U. New South Wales. Med. officer Dept. of Health Svcs., Yangon, 1982—88, Ministry of Health, Labasa, Northern Division, Fiji, 1991—96, 1997—2000; rsch. asst. Nat. Ctr. HIV Epidemiol/Clin. Rch., Darlinghurst, Australia, 2001—. Fellow, Toronto Gen. Rsch. Inst., U. Health Network, 2005—; scholar, Nat. Centre in HIV Epidemiology and Clin. Rsch., U. New South Wales, 2003—; Population fellow, Internat. Sch. Pub. Health, U. Calif., Berkeley, 1996—97. Mem.: Australasian Soc. HIV Medicine (assoc. Jr. Rsch. award 2003—06). Office: Univ Health Network Toronto Gen Rsch Inst Critical Decision Making and Health Care 200 Elizabeth St Rm 13E 222A Toronto ON M5G 2C4 Canada Office Phone: 416-340-4800 x 3687. E-mail: rthein@uhnres.utoronto.ca.

THEIS, PETER FRANK, engineering executive; b. Chgo., Mar. 21, 1937; s. Frank Victor and Hazel (Ericsson) Theis; m. Jill Anne Pendexter, May 9, 1970; children: Juliana, Ethan. BSEE, Yale U., 1958; MBA in Fin., U. Chgo., 1966; JD, Ill. Inst. Tech.-Kent Coll Law, Chgo., 1974; postgrad., U. Stockholm. Bar: Ill. 1975. Engr. ASEA, Ludvika, Sweden, 1959, Signode Corp., Glenview, Ill., 1959-61; importer Internat. Idea, Inc., Chgo., 1961-62; systems analyst Continental Ill. Nat. Bank and Trust, Chgo., 1963-64; sales rep. Honeywell, Inc., Chgo., 1964-68; exec. Morgan Industries, Inc., Chgo., 1968-87; pres. Conversational Voice Techs. Corp., Chgo., Gurnee, Ill., 1973-91, Theis Rsch., Inc., Gurnee, 1991—; v.p. Conservational Voice Techs. Corp., Chgo., Gurnee, 1997-98. Pres. Conversational Voice Techs. Corp., 1973—91, 1998—; cons. Ill. Tech. Transfer LLC, 1994—; cons., mng. mem. Theis Rsch. & Engring. LLC, 1994—. With N.G. USAF, 1961—66. Mem.: Intellectual Property Creators (bd. dirs. 1993—98), Tech. Exec. Roundtable (bd. dirs. 1992—99). Achievements include patents for voice, telecommunications, speech recognition and turbine engines. Avocations: canoeing, hiking, sailing. Office: Conversational Voice Techs Corp 1914 E Grand Ave Lindenhurst IL 60046 Home Phone: 815-385-5122; Office Phone: 847-265-4901. Personal E-mail: theis@owc.net. Business E-Mail: theis@theisresearch.com.

THEIS, PETER GEORGE, retired classicist; b. Milw., Dec. 18, 1930; s. Peter Joseph and Laura Gertrude (Kornely) T.; m. Jane Elizabeth Grattan, Aug. 12, 1961; children: Peter Leo, Paul Joseph, Mary Ellen Brune, Thomas George. BA magna cum laude, Marquette U., 1952; AM, U. Chgo., 1957. Part-time instr. U. Wis., Milw., 1956; instr. Rockhurst U., Kansas City, Mo., 1960-61; instr., then asst. prof. classics Marquette U., Milw., 1961-90; ret., 1990. Mem. edn. bd. Holy Family Cath. Ch., Whitefish Bay, Wis., 1974-75; troop fundraising chmn. Boy Scouts Am., Whitefish Bay, 1976-77; pres. Post-Polio Resource Group of Southeastern Wis., Wauwatosa, 1987, Milw. Area Latin Tchrs. Assn., 1963-64, Fox River Valley Classical Assn., Milw., 1970-71, Wis. Latin Tchrs. Assn., Milw., 1976-78. Cpl. U.S. Army, 1953-55. NEH grantee, 1973. Mem. AAUP, Am. Classical League, Am. Philological Assn., Classical Assn. of the Mid. West and South, Wis. Assn. Fgn. Lang. Tchrs. (pres. 1980-82, Recognition award 1989), Paralyzed Vets. Am. (life), Disabled Am. Vets. (life), Wis. Latin Tchrs. Assn., Marquette U. Retirees Assn. Avocations: reading, puzzles. Home: 2328 W Apple Tree Rd Milwaukee WI 53209-3312

THEISMANN, JOE (JOSEPH ROBERT THEISMANN), sportscaster, retired professional football player; b. New Brunswick, NJ, Sept. 9, 1949; s. Joseph James and Olga (Tobias) T.; m. Robin Smith, Dec. 5, 1970 (div.); children: Joseph Winton, Amy Lynn, Patrick James. BA in Sociology, U. Notre Dame, 1971. Quarterback Toronto Argonauts, CFL, 1971-74; quarterback, punt returner Washington Redskins, 1974—78, quarterback, 1978—86; analyst NFL broadcasts CBS, 1987-88, ESPN, 1988—, announcer, Monday Night Football, 2006—07. Pres., CEO JRT Assocs.; tchr. Offense-Def. Football Camp; Superstar participant, 1979-80; mem. Pres.'s Athletic Adv. Com., 1975; active Pres. Nat. Svc. Adv. Com., 1993. Author: Quarter Backing. Mem. corp. bd. Children's Hosp. Nat. Med. Center, Washington; participant benefits for Multiple Sclerosis children's hosps., Armed Forces Christmas benefits. High sch. All-Am. Football, 1967; All-Am. Coll., 1971; Acad.-All-Am.; recipient Brian Picollo award, Bert Bell award, 1982, Cable Ace award, Best Sports Commentator-Analyst, 1994; named NFL MVP, 1983; named to Nat. Football Conf. Pro Bowl Team, 1982-83; Coll. Football Hall of Fame, 2003 Mem. Nat. Football Players Assn. Republican. Methodist. mem. Super Bowl XVII Championship Team, 1983. Office: ESPN 935 Middle St Bristol CT 06010 *

THEISS, CYNTHIA C., home economist, educator; d. Scruggs Arnold and Margaret Mae Colvin; m. Michael John Theiss, Dec. 29, 1967 (dec.); children: Viktor, Matthew. BS in Home Econ. Edn., U. Ill., Champaign, 1969, MEd in Home Econ., 1971. Tchr. Babylon Union Free Sch. Dist., NY, 1977—. Life mem. Babylon PTA, 1977—; clk., Sunday sch. tchr. 1st Ch. of Christ, Levittown, NY, 1995—, pianist. Named Tchr. of Yr., Town of Babylon, 1995; recipient Spotlight award, LI Family and Consumer Sci., 1994, Disting. Svc. award, 2003, LI Family and Consumer award, 2004, Woman of Dist., NY State Senate, 2003, Cmty. Svc. award, Suffolk Coalition, 2004. Avocations: gardening, travel, cooking, sewing. Home: 50 W Islip Rd West Islip NY 11795

THEISS, JANE I., music educator; b. Aug. 8, 1930; BA, Carleton Coll., Northfield, Minn., 1952; MA, Eastman Sch. Music, Rochester, NY, 1953. Pvt. instr., 1952—. Instr. Maryville Coll., Tenn., 1953—55, U. Wis., Eau Claire, 1955—56; organist First Presbyn. Ch., Carson City, Nev., 1977—2000. Co-author: Music Hath Power, 1978. Recipient organ scholarship in name, U. Nev. Reno, 2000. Mem.: Am. Guild Organists (treas. 1995—), Carson City Music Club (founder 2001, pres. 2001—). Mailing: 2105 Birch St Carson City NV 89701-5412

THEISS, RICHARD EDWARD, electrical engineer, applications engineer; b. Nyack, NY, July 30, 1965; s. Joseph Francis and Lorraine Anita Theiss; m. Janet Grace Heapes, Apr. 9, 1994; children: Steven Richard, Nicole Grace, Andrew Joseph. BSEE, Boston U., 1987; MBA, Iona Coll. Hagen Sch. of Bus., NYC, 1994. Tech. support engr. IPC Automation, Riverdale, NJ, 1987—92; applications engr. LeCroy Corp., Chestnut Ridge, NY, 1992—95, applications engring. supr., 1995—98, product mgr., 1998—2001; sr. applications engr. Boonton Electronics (Wireless Telecom Group Co.), Parsippany, NJ, 2001—05, product mgr., sr. applications engr., 2005—. Lecroy coprorate rep. PXI Sys. Alliance, San Diego, 2000—01. Author: (web seminar) Wireless OEM Design Expo. Coach Monroe Woodbury PTA Basketball, Central Valley, NY, 2002—06; mgr. Monroe (N.Y.) Woodbury Little League, 2004; coach St. Patricks CYO Basketball, Highland Mills, NY, 2005—06. Liberal. Avocations: coaching, running, travel, baseball, football. Home: 7 Country Hollow Highland Mills NY 10930 Office: Boonton Electronics (Wireless Telecom Group Co) 25 Eastmans Rd Parsippany NJ 07054-3702 Home Phone: 845-928-8013; Office Phone: 973-386-9696. Business E-Mail: rtheiss@boonton.com.

THELEN, BRUCE CYRIL, lawyer; b. St. Johns, Mich., Nov. 24, 1951; BA, Mich. State U., 1973; JD, U. Mich., 1977. Bar: NY 1978, Mich. 1980, Ill. 1992. Assoc. Dewey, Ballantine, Bushby, Palmer & Wood, NYC, 1977-80, Dickinson, Wright, Moon, Van Dusen & Freeman, Detroit, 1981-83; ptnr. Dickinson Wright PLLC, Detroit, 1984—. Mem. US Dept. Commerce-Mich. Dist. Export Coun., 1995—. Contbr. articles to profl. jours. Mem. allocation panel, mem. spkrs. bur., chmn. rsch. and info. svcs. com., mem. strategic planning com. and cmty. leaders coun. United Way Cmty. Svcs., 1987—; mem. Mich. Task Force Internat. Trade, Lansing, 1990, Detroit Com. Fgn. Rels., Greater Detroit-Windsor Japan Am. Soc.; 2000, mem. global partnership Mich. Econ. Devel. Corp.; mem. adv. coun. Ctr. Internat. Bus. Edn., U. Mich. Sch. Bus. Decorated Order of Merit Germany. Mem.: German Am. C. of C. Mich. (pres. Mich. chpt. 1994—2004, chmn. Mich. chpt. 2004—), Internat. Inst. Detroit (bd. dirs. 1997—99, v.p. 1999—2000, adv. coun. 2001—), Ill. Bar Assn. (internat. law sect.), Am. Soc. Internat. Law, Internat. Bar Assn. (chmn. fin. aspects internat. sales subcom. 2003—05, vice chmn. internat. sales com. 2006—07, sr. vice chmn. internat. sales com. 2007—), State Bar Mich. (chmn. internat. law sect. 1990—91), NY Bar Assn. (internat. law sect.), Wayne State U. Internat. Bridge Coun. (bd. vis. internat. programs 2006—, mem. internat. bridge coun.), Greater Detroit C. of C. (mem. Leadership Detroit VIII program 1986—87, chmn. European mission com. 1991, 1992, mem. export com. 1992—95, mem. exec. com. world trade club and internat. bus. coun. 1992—, chmn. European mission com. 1995), Mich. Israel C. of C. (bd. dirs. 1997—2001), German Am. C. of C. Midwest (bd. dirs. 1992—2006), French-Am. C. of C. Detroit, Detroit Athletic Club, Econ. Club Detroit. Office: Dickinson Wright PLLC 500 Woodward Ave Ste 4000 Detroit MI 48226-3416 Office Phone: 313-223-3624. Business E-Mail: bthelen@dickinsonwright.com.

THELEN, EDMUND, research executive; b. Berkeley, Calif, May 8, 1913; s. Paul and Alice (Arnold) T.; m. Helen Naomi Betton, Oct. 30, 1965; children: Nancy Anne, Joan Arnold Thelen Hanson. BS, U. Calif., Berkeley, 1934. Asst. chemist Certain-Teed Products Corp., Richmond, Calif., 1934-35; chemist O. C. Field Gasoline Corp., Santa Maria, Calif., 1936-41; asst. mgr. Eclipse Pioneer divsn. Bendix Corp., Teterboro, NJ, 1946-47; sr. rsch. chemist Franklin Inst. Rsch. Labs., Phila., 1947-51, mgr. colloids and polymers br., 1951-74, v.p., dir. phys. and life scis. dept., 1974-76, Inst. fellow, sec. com. on sci. and the arts, 1976-82, mem., 1982-2001, emeritus, 2001—. Pres. Safety Surface Corp., 1983-88; mem. Coun. for Delivery of Dental Care, 1970-85; bd. govs. Franklin-Hahnemann Inst. Occupl. and Environ. Health, 1975-80, Mayor's Sci. and Tech. Adv. Com. on Environment, 1973-80; instr. dental medicine Hahnemann Med. Coll. and Hosp., 1964-74; v.p., dir. Pa. Environ. Coun., 1974-85; treas. Home Health Svcs. of Chester County and Vicinity, 1981-86. Co-author: (book) Porous Pavement for Runoff Control, 1978; editor Am. Assn. Ret. Persons, Eastern Chester County newsletter, 1994-97; contbr. papers to tech. publs. Bd. dir. Neighborhood Vis. Nurse Assn., 1987-93. With USN, 1941-45; comdr. USNR, 1941-66. Recipient spl. recognition award Am. Soc. Landscape Archs., 1974. Mem. Franklin Inst., Sierra Club (ea. Pa. group chmn. 1968, Atlantic chpt. vice-chmn. 1971-73, founding chmn. Pa. chpt. 1974), Ret. Officers Assn. (treas. Valley Forge chpt. 1980-85, v.p. 1987, pres. 1988-89, sec. 1994-97), Toastmasters Internat. (dist. gov. 1960-61), Sunday Breakfast Spkr. Club (pres. 1960-61), Sigma Xi, mem., Nat. Resources Defense Coun., Southern Poverty Law Ctr. Home: 658 Davis Ln Wayne PA 19087-5418 Office Phone: 610-687-3958. E-mail: ked92@comcast.net.

THELIN, JOHN ROBERT, historian, educator, researcher; b. West Newton, Mass., Oct. 15, 1947; s. George Willard and Rozalija Katherine (Komarec) T.; m. Anna Sharon Blackburn, June 24, 1978. AB cum laude, Brown U., 1969; MA, U. Calif., Berkeley, 1972, PhD, 1973. Rsch. asst. Brown U., Providence, 1968-69; rschr., lectr. U. Calif., Berkeley, 1972-74; asst. prof. U. Ky., Lexington, 1974-77; asst. dean Pomona Coll., Claremont, Calif., 1977-79; from asst. dir. to rsch. dir. Assn. Ind. Calif. Colls. and Univs., Santa Ana, 1979-81; chancellor prof. Coll. William and Mary, Williamsburg, Va., 1981-93, pres. faculty assembly, 1990-91; prof. higher edn. and philanthropy Ind. U., Bloomington, 1993-96; prof. ednl. policy and history U. Ky., Lexington, 1996—, disting. univ. rsch. prof., 2001—. Vis. prof. grad. sch. Claremont U., 1978—81; vis. scholar U. Calif., Berkeley, 1995; curator Marquandia Soc., 1971—2006; essay rev. editor Rev. of Higher Edn., 1979—91; rsch. cons. NSF, Washington, 1991; mem. faculty senate U. Ky., 1997—; guest faculty Coll. Bus. Mgmt. Inst., 1998—2006; chair social sci. com. Grad. Coun., U.K., 1998—2001; cons. Booz, Allen & Hamilton, 2004—05; rsch. cons. Am. Enterprise Inst., 2005—06; keynote spkr.; spkr. NASPA Nat. Conf., 2007. Author: Higher Education and Its Useful Past, 1982, The Cultivation of Ivy, 1976, Higher Education and Public Policy, 1991, Games Colleges Play, 1994, A History of American Higher Education, 2004; author: (with others) The Old College Try, 1989, One Hundred Classic Books About Higher Education, 2001; assoc. editor (jour.) Higher Edn.: Theory and Rsch., 1983—91, guest columnist Lexington Herald-Leader, 2001. Pres., bd. dirs. United Way, Williamsburg, 1987-89; pres. Friends of Williamsburg Libr., 1989. Grantee Spencer Found., 1989-91, 99-2001, Ky. Humanities Coun., 2003-05; Regents fellow U. Calif., 1972; recipient Outstanding Faculty Rsch. award Coll. of Edn., U. Ky., 2000, Great Tchrs. award U. Ky., 2004, Provost's Tchg. award U. Ky., 2006, State Local History Rsch. award Ky. Hist. Soc., 2006. Mem. Assn. for Study of Higher Edn. (bd. dirs. 1988-90, keynote spkr. 1994, pres. 1999-2000), Am. Ednl. Rsch. Assn. (Exemplary Rsch. Higher Edn. award 2007), History of Edn. Soc. (editl. bd. 1988-91), Order of Ky. Cols., Lexington Club, Phi Beta Kappa (Faculty award for advancement of scholarship Alpha of Va. 1986, Alpha of R.I. 1969), Omicron Delta Kappa. Avocations: long-distance running, history of Los Angeles and California, sports history. Home: 1745 Richmond Rd Lexington KY 40502 Office: U Ky Edn Policy Studies Lexington KY 40506-1 Home Phone: 859-269-0125; Office Phone: 859-257-4996. Business E-Mail: jthelin@uky.edu.

THENGUMTHARA, KUNHIKRISHNAN, meteorologist; b. Karivellur Kannur, India, Apr. 26, 1963; arrived in US, 2005; s. Krishnan Nair Thekepariyarath and Devaki Amma Thengumthara; m. Sudha Kiral Kooloth, Mar. 7, 1993; children: Sunand Krishnan, Karthika Krishnan. BS, Calicut U., Payyanur, India, 1983; MS in Math., Calicut U., 1985; B of Edn., Calicut U., 1987; MTech in Atmospheric Scis., Cochin U. Sci. & Tech., India, 1992; PhD, U. Bremen, Mainz, Germany, 2004. Cert. inverse methods in atmospheric scis. Internat. Ctr. Theoretical Physics, Italy, 2001; basic meteorology India Meteorol. Dept., 1989, solar radian theory & instrumentation Radiation Lab., IMD, Pune, 1992, extreme meteorological events World Meteorol. Orgn./IMD, 1997, lecturship in Earth & Planetary scis. UGC/CSIR, Govt. India, 1999, German lang. Goethe Inst., Max Muller Bhavan, India, 1999, meteorology German Weather Svc., Offenbach, Germany, 2000, satellite meteorology EUMETSAT, Darmstadt, Germany, 2000, internat. mgmt. tng. Carl Duisburg Centern, Jansky Inst., Köln, Germany, 2000, data assimilation ENVISAT, European Space Agy., Italy, 2003. Indian meteorol. svcs. India Meteorol. Dept., Pune, Mangalore, Minicoy Island, 1987—2000; rsch. fellow Indian Inst. Tropical Meteorology, Pune, 1992; vis. scientist German Weather Svc., Offenbach, Frankfurt, Germany, 2000; vis. fellow Inst. Geophysics & Meteorology, U. Koeln, Germany, 2000; vis. scientist EUMETSAT, Darmstadt, 2000—01; doctoral fellow Max Planck Inst., Mainz, 2001—04, post doctoral scientist, 2004—05; nat. rsch. coun., post doctoral fellow NASA Langley Rsch. Ctr., Hampton, Va., 2005—. Spkr. in field. Contbr. articles to profl. jours. Recipient Indo-German-CDG (Carl-Duisberg) award, German Govt., 2000—01, Cert. Excellent Grade award, Internat. Sch. Atmospheric Chemistry & Physics, Max Planck Soc., Germany, 2004, Bhavanarayana award, Indian Meteorol. Soc., 1997—98, 2004, NRC Rsch. Associateship award, Nat. Rsch. Coun./NASA, 2005; grantee Post Doctoral Rsch. fellowship, Max Planck Inst., 2004. Mem.: Indian Meteorol. Soc., European Geoscis. Union, Am. Meteorol. Soc., Am. Geophys. Union. Achievements include discovery of recurring NO2 plumes over the central Indian Ocean during monsoon transition periods; development of a theory, called small perturbation tendency, to perform sensitivity studies with NOx emission in a chemical transport model; formulated and tested the theory of non-linear optimum interpolation of mass and wind field for Indian monsoon conditions in NWP model; development of a methodology to estimate soil heat flux for Agrometeorological studies; hypothesis proposed to explain an enhanced tropospheric ozone column induced by NOx chemistry over northern Indian region during summer months as observed by satellites. Home: 201 F Thoreau Cir Yorktown VA 23693 Office: NASA Langley Rsch Ctr 21 Langley Blvd Hampton VA 23681 Home Phone: 757-788-8855; Office Phone: 757-864-5025. Office Fax: 757-864-6326. Personal E-mail: kunhi_krish@yahoo.com. Business E-Mail: kunhi@larc.nasa.gov.

THEOBALD, EDWARD ROBERT, lawyer; b. Chgo., Feb. 10, 1947; BA, So. Ill. U., 1969; JD, Ill. Inst. Tech., 1974. Bar: Ill. 1974, U.S. Dist. Ct. (no. dist.) Ill. 1974. Asst. state's atty. Cook County, Chgo., 1974-79, supr. felony trial divsn., 1980-81; assoc. Conklin, Leahy & Eisenberg, Chgo., 1977; ptnr. Boharic & Theobald, Chgo., 1981-83, owner, ptnr., 1983—. Legal adv. Sheriff of Cook County, Ill., 1986-89; spl. state's atty. U.S. Dist. Ct. no. dist. Ill., 1989-91, Cook County, Ill., 2002-06; apptd. spl. corp. counsel City of Chgo., 1994. Mem. Parent adv. bd. Downers Grove (Ill.) South H.S., 1992-94. Named Number One Trial Atty. in Felony Trial Divsn. of Office of Cook County State's Atty., Felony Trial Divsn. Suprs., 1979. Mem. ABA (sect. on tort and ins. law, sect. on labor and employment law, chmn. com. on sentencing alternatives young lawyers sect. 1982-83, tort and ins. practice sect., labor and employment law sect.), ATLA, Chgo. Bar Assn. (mem. bd. mgrs. 1985-87, mem. labor and employment law com. 1983—2002, mem. com. on coms. 1990-94, mem. membership com. 1990-95, vice chair judicial evaluation com. 1999-2000), Ill. Bar Assn. Roman Catholic. Office: Three First Nat Plaza 70 W Masdison Ste 2030 Chicago IL 60602 Office Phone: 312-346-9246. Personal E-mail: bears51@aol.com.

THEODORE, ARES NICHOLAS, chemist, researcher; b. Kalamata, Greece, Oct. 28, 1933; came to U.S., 1954; s. Nicholas A. and Angeliki (Myseros) Theodoracopulos; m. Peggy Salvarakis, Sept. 3, 1961; children: Nicholas A., Angie A. BA cum laude, Westminster Coll., Salt Lake City, 1958; MS, U. Utah, 1961; postgrad., Case Western Res. U., 1967-68. Asst. prof. chemistry Westminster Coll., 1961-64; sr. rsch. chemist Diamond Shamrock Corp., Cleve., 1964-69; rsch. scientist Ford Motor Co., Detroit, 1969-73, sr. rsch. scientist, 1973-84, prin. rsch. scientist, 1984—2000. Contbr. articles to profl. jours. Mem. ch. bd. Holy Cross Greek Orthodox Ch., Farmington Hills, Mich., 1986-88; campaigner Farmington Hills Dem. Com., 1986-88; mem. bus. coun. Boston Dem. Com., 1988—, Nat. Dem. Com., 1988—. Fellow, NSF, 1964; U. Utah fellow, 1958—61. Mem. Am. Chem. Soc. (treas. 1967), Ahepa (bd. govs. Dearborn, Mich. 1985-86). Achievements include patents in field. Avocations: swimming, golf, photography. Home: 34974 Valley Forge Dr Farmington Hills MI 48331-3210

THEODORE, DAVID, research scientist; MS in Materials Sci. and Engring., Northwestern U., 1986; PhD in Materials Sci. and Engring., Cornell U., 1991. Sun Certified Programmer For Java 2 Platform Sun Microsystems, Inc., 2003. Staff scientist Advanced Custom Technologies Motorola Inc., Mesa, Ariz., 1990—91, sr. staff scientist Advanced Custom Technologies, 1991—92, prin. staff scientist Materials Rsch. & Strategic Technologies, 1992—96, mem. tech. staff, rsch. scientist and tech. mgr. Ctr. for Integrated Systems Devel., 1997—99, mem. tech. staff, tech. mgr. and rsch. scientist Materials Rsch. & Strategic Technologies, 1999—2001, disting. mem. tech. staff, tech. mgr. and rsch. scientist Advanced Products R&D Labs. Tempe, Ariz., 2001—04; disting. mem. tech. staff Freescale Semiconductor Inc., Tempe, 2005—07, mgr. tech., 2005—, rsch. scientist advanced products R&D Labs., 2005—06, rsch. scientist wireless and packaging sys. lab., 2006—. Contbr. articles to profl. jours. Vol. tchr. 5th-6th grade kids, Mesa, 1995—2004. Mem.: Materials Rsch. Soc. Achievements include patents in field; patents pending in field. Office: Freescale Semiconductor Inc Wireless and Packaging Sys Lab 2100 East Elliot Rd Tempe AZ 85284 Personal E-mail: femtophysicist@yahoo.com.

THEODORE, EUSTACE D., educational association administrator, consultant; b. Marietta, Ohio, Aug. 4, 1941; s. Demetrios E. and Nicoletta D. T.; m. Carol Nagy, June 13, 1964; children: Kyle James, Graham Clark. BA, Yale U., New Haven, 1963; MA, Cornell U., Ithaca, NY, 1965, PhD, 1967. Mem. faculty Hollins Coll., Roanoke, Va., 1967-71, Mt. Holyoke Coll., South Hadley, Mass., 1971-72; dean Calhoun Coll., Yale U., New Haven, 1972-81; exec. dir. Assn. Yale Alumni, 1981-97; pres. Coun. for Advancement and Support of Edn., Washington, 1997-2000; prin. eAdvancement.org, 2000—. Mgmt. and ednl. cons., 1965—. Contbr. articles to jours. Office: eAdvancement 1301 21st St NW Washington DC 20036-1503 Home Phone: 202-986-6676; Office Phone: 202-463-7310. Business E-Mail: theodore@eadvancement.org.

THEODORE, JOSE, professional hockey player; b. Sept. 13, 1976; Goalie Montreal Canadiens, 1995—2006, Colo. Avalanche, 2006—. Player NHL All-star game, 2002, 04; mem. Team Can., World Cup of Hockey, 2004. Named Player of Week, Nat. Hockey League, 1999, Fredericton's Player of Yr., Am. Hockey League; named to World Hockey Championship 2nd All-Star team, 2000; recipient Vezina Trophy, 2002, Hart Meml. Trophy, 2002. Achievements include being a member of World Cup Champion Team Canada, 2004. Office: c/o Colorado Avalanche Pepsi Ctr 100 Chopper Circle Denver CO 80204-1743

THEODORESCU, DAN, urologic oncologist, molecular biologist; b. Bucharest, Romania, May 6, 1962; arrived in Can., 1968; s. Radu Amza Serban and Ana Elena (Florescu) T.; m. Diane Louise Causier, June 1, 1991; children: Thomas William, Claire Ana. MD, Queen's U., Kingston, Ont., Can., 1986; PhD, U. Toronto, Ont., Can., 1991. Diplomate Royal Coll. Physicians and Surgeons Can. Intern in surgery U. Toronto, 1986-87, MRC rsch. fellow Mt. Sinai Hosp. Rsch. Inst., 1988-91, resident in urology, 1991-94; clin. fellow urology svc. Meml. Sloan-Kettering Cancer Ctr., NYC, 1995-98; asst. prof. urology, molecular physiology U. Va., Charlottesville, 1995-98, assoc. prof., Paul Mellon chair in urology, 1998—; atending urologic oncologist U. Va. Health Scis. Ctr., Charlottesville, 1995—. Lectr. in field. Reviewer Am. Jour. Pathology, 1996—, Clin. Chemistry, 1996—, Cancer, 1996—, Jour. Urology, 1994—; contbr. over 50 articles to profl. jours. Recipient Career award Am. Cancer Soc., 1996. Fellow Med. Rsch. Coun. Can.; mem. Am. Soc. Clin. Oncology, ACS, Am. Urol. Assn., Am. Assn. Cancer Rsch., Med. Soc. Va., Ea. Coop. Oncology Group. Achievements include research in clinical aspects of prostate and bladder cancer and the elucidation of the molecular signalling pathways of the epidermal growth factor receptor and molecular control of vascular endothelial growth factor expression.

THEODORIDIS, GEORGE CONSTANTIN, biomedical engineering educator, researcher; b. Braila, Romania, Dec. 3, 1935; came to U.S., 1959; s. Constantin George and Anastasia (Haritopoulos) T.; m. Lilly Kate Hyman, Sept. 20, 1975; 1 child, Alexander. BS in Mechanical and Elec. Engring., Nat. Tech. U. Athens, 1959; DSc, MIT, Cambridge, Mass., 1964. Rsch. assoc. MIT, Cambridge, Mass., 1964; sr. scientist Am. Sci. Engring., Cambridge, Mass., 1964-68; assoc. prof. in residence U. Calif., Berkeley, 1968-70; biomedical engring. U. Va., Charlottesville, 1970—; prof. elec. engring. U. Patras, Greece, 1976-83. Cons. Food and Drug Adminstrn., Washington, 1975-76, Applied Physics Lab, Columbia, Md., 1978-79. Author: Applied Math, 1983; contbr. articles to profl. jours. Den leader Boy Scouts Am., Charlottesville, Va., 1984-85. Fulbright fellow U.S. Govt., MIT, 1959-60; Nato fellow NATO, MIT, 1961-64; Spl. fellow NIH, U. Calif., 1968-70; recipient teaching award GE, MIT, 1963. Mem. Inst. Elec. and Electronics Engrs., Sigma Xi. Greek Orthodox. Avocations: history, travel. Home: 1817 Fendall Ave Charlottesville VA 22903-1613 Office: U Va Dept Biomed Engring PO Box 377 Charlottesville VA 22902-0377 Office Phone: 434-924-8885. Business E-Mail: gct@virginia.edu.

THEODOSIUS, retired leader of the Orthodox Church in America; b. Canonsburg, P.A., 1933; Grad., Washington and Jefferson Coll., Washington, PA; M of Divinity, Saint Vladimir Orthodox Theological Seminary, 1960. Ordained to the diaconate & priesthood Orthodox Church in Amer., 1961; bishop Diocese of Sitka and Alaska, 1967—72, Diocese of Pittsburgh, Pa., 1972—77; metropolitan of Amer., Canada Orthodox Church of Amer., 1977—2002; archbishop of Washington, 1977—2002. Office: Orthodox Ch in Am PO Box 675 Syosset NY 11791-0675

THEOHARIDES, THEOHARIS CONSTANTIN, pharmacologist, physician, educator; b. Thessaloniki, Macedonia, Greece, Feb. 11, 1950; s. Konstantinos A. and Marika (Krava) T.; m. Efthalia I. Triarhou, July 10, 1981; children: Niove, Konstantinos. Diploma with honors, Anatolia Coll., 1968; BA in Biology, History of Sci. and Med., Yale U., 1972, MS in

Immunology, 1975, MPhil in Endocrinology, 1975, PhD in Pharmacology, 1978; postgrad., Tufts U., Harvard U. Asst. in rsch. biology Yale U., New Haven, 1968—71, asst. in rsch. pharmacology, 1973—78, spl. instr. modern Greek, 1974, 77, exec. sec. univ. senate, 1976—78, rsch. assoc. faculty clin. immunology, 1978—83; asst. prof. biochemistry and pharmacology Tufts U., Boston, 1983—88, co-dir. med. pharmacology curriculum, 1983—85, 1983—85, dir. med. pharmacology, 1985—93, assoc. prof. pharmacology, biochemistry and psychiatry, 1989—94, dir. grad. pharmacology, 1994—2000, prof. pharmacology and internal medicine, 1995—, prof. biochemistry, 2002—. Vis. faculty Aristotelian U. Sch. Medicine, Thessaloniki, 1979; trustee Anatolia Coll., 1984-85; clin. pharmacologist Commonwealth Mass. Drug Formulary Commn., 1985—; trainee internal medicine and allergy Tufts-New Eng. Med. Ctr., 1986-93; co-chmn. neuro-immunology 2d and 3d World Conf. on Inflammation, Monte Carlo, 1986, 89; mem. internat. adv. bd. 4th, 5th, 6th and 7th World Conf. on Inflammation, Geneva, 1991, 93, 95, 97; spl. cons. Min. of Health, Greece, 1993-95; mem. supreme spl. sci. health coun. Hellenic Republic, 1998—; chmn. Internat. Com. to Upgrade Med. Edn. in Greece, 1994; bd. dirs., spl. cons. Inst. Pharm. Rsch. & Tech., Athens, 1994-2002; mem. Supreme Health Bd.; mem. Nat. Pub. Health Coun. Hellenic Republic, 2003—; vis. prof. Athens U., 2006; spl. advisor Allergy Clin. Rsch. Ctr., Ahikon Hosp., Athens U., 2006—. Author books on pharmacology; mem. editorial bd. numerous jours.; contbr. articles to profl. jours.; patentee in field. Recipient Theodore Buyler award, Yale U., 1972, George Papanicoalou Grad. award, 1977, Med. award, Hellenic Med. Soc. N.Y., 1979, 1983, M.C. Winternitz prize in pathology, Yale U., 1980, Disting Svc. award, Tufts U. Alumni Assn., 1986, Spl. Faculty Recognition award, Tufts U. Med. Sch., 1987, 1988, Boston Mayor Menino Cmty. Svc. award, 1998, Oliver Smith award, 1999, Archon of Ecunemical Patriarchate of Christian Orthodox Ch., 2000, George Papnikolase award, 2003. Mem. AMA, AAUP, AAAS, European Acad. Allergology and Clin. Immunology, Am. Acad. Allergy, Asthma, Immunology, Hellenic Biochem. and Biophys. Soc., N.Y. Acad. Scis., Am. Inst. History Pharmacy, Soc. Health and Human Values, Am. Assn. History Medicine, Am. Soc. Cell Biology, Soc. Neurosci., Am. Fedn. Clin. Rsch., Conn. Acad. Arts and Scis., Am. Soc. Pharmacology and Exptl. Therapeutics, Hellenic Soc. Cancer Rsch., Hellenic Soc. Med. Chemistry, Internat. Soc. Immunopharmacology, Am. Soc. Microbiology, Am. Assn. Immunologists, Internat. Soc. History of Medicine, Mass. Med. Soc., N.E. Hellenic Med. Soc. (sec. 1984-85, v.p. 1985-86, 94-96, pres. 1986-87), Hellenic Sci. Assn. Boston (bd. dirs. 1985), Internat. Anatolia Alumni Assn. (sec. 1984-85), Alpha Omega Alpha, Sigma Xi. Achievements include research on mechanisms of release of secretory products: immunopharmacology, membrane functions of polyamines; pathophysiology of mast cells in neuroimmunoendocrine diseases exacerbated by stress such as irritable bowel syndrome, interstitial cystitis, psoriasis, migraines and multiple sclerosis. Home: 14 Parkman St Apt 2 Brookline MA 02446-3802 Office: Tufts U Sch Med 136 Harrison Ave Boston MA 02111-1817 Office Phone: 617-636-6866. Business E-Mail: theoharis.theoharides@tufts.edu.

THEOLOGIDES, STERGIOS, lawyer, real estate company executive; BA, Princeton U.; JD, Columbia U. Assoc. corp. dept. O'Melveny & Myers, LLP, 1992—96; corp. counsel Wynn's International, Inc., 1996—98; v.p., gen. counsel New Century Fin. Corp., Irvine, Calif., 1999—, corp. sec., 1999—2005, exec. v.p. corp. affairs, 2003—. Exec. v.p. corp. affairs, sr. legal counsel, sec. New Century Mortgage; exec. v.p., dir. NC Capital; corp. sec. Home123, 2004—. Harlan Fiske Stone Scholar, Charles Evans Hughes Fellow. Office: New Century Fin Corp 18400 Von Karman Ste 1000 Irvine CA 92612 *

THEON, JOHN SPERIDON, meteorologist, researcher; b. Washington, Dec. 12, 1934; s. Lewis and Merope Theon; m. Joanne Edens, July 31, 1965; children: Christopher James, Catherine. BS in Aero. Engring, U. Md., 1957; BS in Meteorology, Pa. State U., 1959, MS, 1962; PhD in Engring. Sci. and Mechanics, U. Tenn., 1985. Aero. engr. Douglas Aircraft Co., Santa Monica, Calif., 1957-58; engr. U.S. Naval Ordnance Lab., White Oak, Md., 1962; rsch. meterologist, 1962-74; head meterology br. NASA Goddard Space Flight Center, Greenbelt, Md., 1974-77; asst. chief lab. Atmospheric Scis., 1977-78, Nimbus project scientist, 1972—78; program scientist Global Weather Rsch. Program NASA Hdqrs., Washington, 1978—82, chief atmospheric dynamics and radiation program, program scientist Spacelab 3 missions, 1982—87, mission scientist tropical rainfall measuring program, 1984—95, chief climate process rsch. program, 1987—94, exec. sec. interagency task force on observations and data mgmt., 1994—95. Cons. Orbital Scis. Corp., 1995—96, Inst. Global Environ. Strategies, 1995—2005, Cal Tech Jet Propulsion Lab., 1997—99, George Washington U., Washington, 2005—. Contbr. articles to profl. jours. With USAF, 1958—60. Named Disting. Alumnus, U. Tenn., 1989; recipient Goddard Exceptional Performance award, 1978, Exceptional Performance award, NASA, 1986, Radio Wave award, Ministry of Posts & Telecom. Japan, 1995. Fellow: Am. Meterol. Soc. Presbyterian. Home and Office: 6801 Lupine Ln Mc Lean VA 22101-1518

THERIOT, JULIE, microbiologist, medical educator; BS, MIT, 1988; PhD in Cell Biology, U. Calif. San Francisco, 1993; predoctoral fellow, Howard Hughes Med. Inst., 1988—93; fellow, Whitehead Inst.for Biomedical Rsch., 1993—97. Asst. prof., biochemistry, microbiology and immunology Stanford U. Sch. Medicine, Calif., 1997—. Author: of numerous articles pub. in such acad. jour. as Nature, Proceedings of the Nat.l Acad. of Sci. USA, and Jour. of Cell Biology. Office: Theriot Lab Beckman Ctr Dept Biochemistry Stanford Univ Med Sch Stanford CA 94305

THERNSTROM, ABIGAIL, federal agency administrator, writer; b. NYC, Sept. 14, 1936; d. Ferdinand and Helen Mann; m. Stephan Thernstrom, Jan. 3, 1959; children: Melanie, Samuel. BA, Barnard Coll., NYC, 1958; MA, Harvard U., Cambridge, Mass., 1961; PhD, 1975. Lectr. Harvard U., Cambridge, Mass., 1975-78; project dir. The Twentieth Century Fund, NYC, 1981-86; vis. lectr. Harvard U., Cambridge, Mass., 1988-89, Boston Coll., 1990; stringer The Economist, London, 1988-92; adj. prof. Sch. Edn. Boston U., 1991—93; sr. fellow The Manhattan Inst., NYC, 1993—. Domestic strategy group Aspen (Colo.) Inst., 1992-97; edn. policy com. Hudson Inst., 1994-97; bd. dirs. Inst. for Justice, Washington; adv. bd. Am. Friends the Inst. for Justice, London, 1993-2003; mem. Mass. State Bd. Edn., 1995-2006; commr. US Commn. on Civil Rights, 2001—, vice-chair, 2004—. Author: Whose Votes Count?: Affirmative Action and Minority Voting Rights, 1987, School Choice in Massachusetts, 1991; co-author: (with Stephan Thernstrom) America in Black and White: One Nation Indivisible, 1997, No Excuses: Closing the Racial Gap in Learning, 2003; editor: A Democracy Reader, 1992; co-editor: Beyond the Color Line: New Perspectives on Race and Ethnicity in America, 2002; contbr. articles to profl. jours. Mem. Citizen's Initiative on Race and Ethnicity, 1998—2002; vice chair U.S. Commn. on Civil Rights, 2004—; mem. bd. advisors U.S. Election Assistance Commn., 2006—. Recipient Anisfield Wolf Book award, 1987, Am. Bar Assn. cert. merit, 1988, Best Policy Book award Polit. Studies Orgn., 1987, Benchmark Book award Ctr. for Judicial Studies, 1987, Disting. scholarship on edn. award Fordham Found., 2007, prize for Outstanding Achievement Bradley Found., 2007. Am. Polit. Sci. Assn. Home and Office: 1445 Massachusetts Ave Lexington MA 02420-3810 Office Phone: 781-861-7634. Business E-Mail: thernstr@fas.harvard.edu.

THERNSTROM, STEPHAN, historian, educator; b. Port Huron, Mich., Nov. 5, 1934; s. Albert George and Bernadene (Robbins) T.; m. Abigail Mann, Jan. 3, 1959; children— Melanie Rachel, Samuel Altgeld. BS, Northwestern U., 1956; A.M., Harvard, 1958, PhD, 1962. Instr. history Harvard U., Cambridge, Mass., 1962-66, asst. prof., 1966-67, prof., 1973-81, Winthrop prof., 1981—, chmn. com. on higher degrees in history of Am. civilization, 1985-92; prof. Brandeis U., 1967-69, UCLA, 1969-73; Pitt. prof. Am. history and instns. Cambridge U., 1978-79; dir. Charles Warren Ctr. for Research in Am. History, 1980-83. Author: Poverty and Progress, 1964, Poverty, Planning and Politics in the New Boston, 1969, The Other Bostonians, 1973, History of the American People, 1984, 88; co-author: America in Black and White, 1997, Reflections on The Shape of the River, 1999, No Excuses: Closing the Racial Gap in Learning, 2003; editor: Harvard Ency. Am. Ethnic Groups; co-editor: Harvard Studies in Urban History; Cambridge Interdisciplinary Perspectives on Modern History Series, Beyond the Color Line, 2001. Recipient Bancroft prize, R.R. Hawkins award, Faculty prize Harvard U. Press, Waldo G. Leland prize, Fordham Found. prize, 2007, Bradley prize, 2007; Guggenheim fellow, John M. Olin fellow, ACLS fellow, sr. fellow Manhattan inst., 1998—, Nat. Humanities Coun., 2003. Office: Harvard U Robinson Hall Cambridge MA 02138 Office Phone: 617-495-3035. Business E-Mail: thernstr@fas.harvard.edu.

THERON, CHARLIZE, actress; b. Benoni, South Africa, Aug. 7, 1975; d. Charles and Gerda Theron. Studied dance, Joffrey Ballet, NYC. TV and print ad representative for J'Adore perfume Christian Dior, 2004—. Actor: (films) Children of the Corn III, 1995, 2 Days in the Valley, 1996, That Thing You Do!, 1996, The Devil's Advocate, 1997, Trial and Error, 1997, Celebrity, 1998, Mighty Joe Young, 1998, The Astronaut's Wife, 1999, The Cider House Rules, 1999, Reindeer Games, 2000, The Yards, 2000, Men of Honor, 2000, The Legend of Bagger Vance, 2000, Sweet November, 2001, 15 Minutes, 2001, The Curse of the Jade Scorpion, 2001, Trapped, 2002, Waking Up in Reno, 2002, The Italian Job, 2003, (also prodr.) Monster, 2003 (Golden Globe for best dramatic actress, 2004, Screen Actors Guild Award for best actress, 2004, Acad. Award for best actress, 2004), Head in the Clouds, 2004, North Country, 2005, Aeon Flux, 2005; (TV films) The Life and Death of Peter Sellers, 2004, Hollywood Confidential, 1997, (guest appearance): (TV series) Arrested Development, 2005—. Named one of 50 Most Beautiful People, People Mag., 2000; recipient Best Performance by a Human-Female (In Aeon Flux), Spike TV Video Game awards, 2005, Spirit of Independence award, LA Film Festival, 2006. Address: United Talent Agy Ste 500 9560 Wilshire Blvd Beverly Hills CA 90212

THEROUX, DAVID JON, economist, educator, research and development company executive; b. Lansing, Mich., May 25, 1949; s. Paul Richard and Marjorie Erma (Withrow) Theroux; m. Elaine Laconia Shipp, 1976 (div. 1991); children: Paul Jacques, Drake Emeri; m. Mary Lyn Garvey, 1991. AB in Applied Math., U. Calif., Berkeley, 1973, BSME, 1973, MSME, 1974; MBA, U. Chgo., 1977. Rsch. asst. Richmond Field Sta., U. Calif., Berkeley, 1974, U. Chgo., 1976; project engr. Exxon Co. U.S.A., 1975—76; dir. vis. lectr. program in econ. sci. U. Chgo., 1977; v.p., dir. acad. affairs, dir. pub. policy studies Cato Inst., San Francisco, 1977—79; pres., dir. Pacific Rsch. Inst. Pub. Policy, San Francisco, 1979—86, Ind. Inst., Oakland, Calif., 1986—90; pres., gen. ptnr. LTN Ptnrs., 1986—90; pub., editor LibertyTree Network, 1986—; pub. Independent Review: A Journal of Political Economy. Adv. bd. No. Calif. Econ. Seminars, 1981—; bd. dirs. Grocery Express, Ltd., 1986—; mem. Coun. for Monetary Reform. Sr. editor Policy Report, 1978—79; editor: Cato Papers, 1978—79, The Energy Crisis: Government Policy and the Economy, 1978; editor: (with P. Truluck) Private Rights and Public Lands, 1983; editor: Politics and Tyranny: Lessons in Pursuit of Freedom, 1985. Trustee William Koch Found., 1978—79; mem. Mencken award book com. Free Press Assn., 1990—; exec. com. Templeton Honor Roll for Higher Edn. in a Free Soc. With USAF, 1967—72. Recipient George Washington Honor medal for excellence, Freedoms Found., 1983, Mencken award for Best Book, Free Press Assn., 1988. Mem.: Pub. Choice Soc., Nat. Assn. Bus. Economists, So. Econ. Assn., Western Econ. Assn., Royal Econ. Soc., Am. Econ. Assn., John Randolph Club, Omicron Delta Epsilon, Pi Tau Sigma. Home: 11990 Skyline Blvd Oakland CA 94619-2421 Office: 100 Swan Way Oakland CA 94621-1428

THEROUX, EUGENE, lawyer; b. Medford, Mass., Apr. 29, 1938; s. Albert and Anne (Dittami) T.; m. Phyllis Grissim, Feb. 13, 1963 (div. 1978); children: Christian, Elizabeth, Justin; m. Colleen Marie Pankratz, Feb. 27, 1982; children: Jean-Paul, Alexandra, Sebastien. Student, Harvard U., 1959-60; BID, Pratt Inst., 1961, LittD, 1982; JD, Georgetown U., 1968. Bar: D.C. 1969, Mass. 1982, Va. 1985. Ptnr. Baker & McKenzie, Washington, 1969—, mem. policy com., 1992-94. Spl. counsel joint econ. com. U.S. Congress, Washington, 1972; adv. prof. Fudan U., Shanghai, People's Republic China, 1986—; adv. bd. Fletcher Sch. Law and Diplomacy, 1987—; trustee Monterey Inst. Internat. Studies. Author: (book) Joint Ventures In USSR, 1989, Business Guide To Moscow, 1990, Business Guide to Mongolia, 1996. Trustee Am. Leprosy Found., Washington, 1987—; v.p. U.S.-China Bus. Coun., Washington, 1973-75, dir., vice chair of bd., 1991-95. 1st lt. inf., U.S. Army, 1962-64, MAC/V So. Vietnam, 1968. Mem. ABA (chair Soviet law com. 1989-91), Metro. Club. Roman Catholic. Avocations: drawing, painting, running. Home: Short Hill Mountain Farm Lovettsville VA 20180 Office: Baker & McKenzie 815 Connecticut Ave NW Washington DC 20006-4004 Home: Ox Pasture Sandwich MA 02563 Office Phone: 202-452-7000. Business E-Mail: gene.theroux@bakernet.com.

THEROUX, PAUL EDWARD, author; b. Medford, Mass., Apr. 10, 1941; s. Albert Eugene and Anne (Dittami) T.; m. Anne Castle, Dec. 4, 1967 (div. 1993); children: Marcel, Louis; m. Sheila Donnelly, Nov. 18, 1995. BA, U. Mass., Amherst, DLitt, 1988, Trinity Coll., Washington, 1980, Tufts U., 1980. Lectr. U. Urbino, Italy, 1963, Soche Hill Coll., Malawi, 1963-65; faculty English dept. Makerere U., Uganda, 1965-68, U. Singapore, 1968-71; vis. lectr. U. Va., 1972-73. Author: (fiction) Waldo, 1967, Fong and the Indians, 1968, Girls at Play, 1969, Murder in Mt. Holly, 1969, Jungle Lovers, 1971, Sinning with Annie, 1972, Saint Jack, 1973, The Black House, 1974, The Family Arsenal, 1976, The Consul's File, 1977, Picture Palace, 1978 (Whitbread prize for fiction), A Christmas Card, 1978, London Snow, 1980, World's End, 1980, The Mosquito Coast, 1981, The London Embassy, 1982, Half Moon Street, 1984, O-Zone, 1986, My Secret History, 1988, Chicago Loop, 1990, Millroy and the Magician, 1993, My Other Life, 1996, Kowloon Tong, 1997, Collected Stories, 1997, Collected Short Novels, 1998, Hotel Honolulu, 2001, The Stranger at the Palazzo d'Oro, 2003, Blinding Light, 2005, The Eleghenta Suite, 2007; (nonfiction) V.S. Naipaul, 1973, The Great Railway Bazaar, 1975, The Old Patagonian Express, 1979, The Kingdom by the Sea, 1983, Sailing Through China, 1983, Sunrise with Sea Monsters, 1985, The White Man's Burden, 1987, Riding the Iron Rooster, 1988, The Happy Isles of Oceania, 1992, The Pillars of Hercules, 1995, Sir Vidia's Shadow, 1998, Fresh Air Fiend, 2000, Nurse Wolf and Dr. Sacks, 2001, Dark Star Safari, 2002; (film script) Saint Jack, 1979, Chinese Box, 1998. Recipient Editorial award Playboy mag., 1972, 76, 77, 79, Lit. award AAAL, 1977, James Tait Black award, 1982, Yorkshire Post Best Novel award, 1982, Thomas Cook Travel Book prize, 1989. Fellow Royal Soc. Lit., Royal Geog. Soc.; mem. AAAL.

THERRIEN, FRANCOIS XAVIER, JR., business and tax consultant; b. Amesbury, Mass. June 6, 1928; s. Francis Xavier and Doris Alma (Cote) T.; BS, U.S. Mil. Acad., 1950; MS, U. Ariz., 1962; Cert. tax profl., tax advisor, enrolled agt., environ. inspector, bd. cert. bus. appraiser; m. Yoshiko Kashima, July 22, 1969; children: Francois Xavier, Norman, Sakura, Izumi. Commd. 2d lt., U.S. Army, 1950, advanced through grades to lt. col., 1965, ret., 1970; dist. dir. R. J. Carroll Assoc., Inc., Atlanta, 1970-71; with Treasure Lake, Atlanta, 1971; pres. Identiseal of Fla., Orlando, 1972-74; owner Yoshiko Enterprises, Winter Park, Fla., 1974-79; bd. dirs., pres., 1988—; instr. Seminole Community Coll., 1974-79; regional rep. H.D. Vest Investment Securities, Inc., Irving, Tex., 1989—. Decorated Army Commendation medals (2), Air medal, Bronze Star medal, Silver Star, Croix DeGuerre with palm. Mem. Nat. Assn. Enrolled Agts. Roman Catholic. Office: 2265 Lee Rd Ste 223 Winter Park FL 32789-1858

THERRIEN, MICHEL, professional hockey coach; b. Nov. 4, 1963; m. Genevieve Therrien; children: Elizabeth, Charles. Coach Lvaal Titan, Granby Predateurs; 1st head coach Quebec Citadelles, 1999—2000; head coach Montreal Canadiens, 2000—03, Wilkes-Barre/Scranton Penguins (AHL), 2003—05, Pittsburgh Penguins, 2005—. Office: c/o Pittsburgh Penguins 66 Mario Lemieux Place Pittsburgh PA 15219 *

THEURER, BYRON W., aerospace engineer, business owner; b. Glendale, Calif., July 1, 1939; s. William Louis and Roberta Cecilia (Sturgiss) T.; m. Sue Ann McKay, Sept. 15, 1962 (div. 1980); children: Karen Marie, William Thomas, Alison Lee; m. Patricia Ann Pilcher, Nov. 2, 2002 BS in Engring. Sci., USAF Acad., 1961; MS in Aero. Sci., U. Calif., Berkeley, 1965; MBA, U. Redlands, 1991. Commd. USAF, 1961, advanced through grades to lt. col., ret., 1978; project officer Space Shuttle Devel. Prog., Houston, 1971-76; chief of test F-15 Systems Prog. Office Wright Patterson AFB, Ohio, 1976-78; sr. engr. Veda, Inc., Dayton, Ohio, 1979-81, Logicon Inc., Dayton, 1981-83; project mgr. Support Systems Assocs., Inc., Dayton, 1983-84, CTA Inc., Ridgecrest, Calif., 1985-89; owner, operator The Princeton Rev. of Ctrl. Calif., Ridgecrest, 1989-92, San Luis Obispo, 1993—2002; counselor Svc. Corps. Ret. Execs., 2002—. Cons. in field. Counselor SCORE. Decorated Silver Star, D.F.C., Air Medals (16); named Officer of the Yr., Air Force Flight Test Ctr., Edwards AFB, 1970 Mem. Air Force Assn., Assn. Old Crows, USAF Acad. Assn. Grads. (nat. bd. dirs. 1972-75, chpt. pres. 1981-83), Svc. Corps Ret. Execs. Republican. Episcopalian. Avocation: walking. Home and Office: 387 E 800 S Ivins UT 84738

THEUS, REGGIE WAYNE, professional basketball coach, retired professional basketball player; b. Inglewood, Calif., Oct. 13, 1957; m. Elaine Theus; children: Raquel, Reggie, Rhyan. Student, UNLV, 1975—78. Guard Chgo. Bulls, 1978-83, Kans. City Kings, 1983-85, Sacramento Kings, 1985—88, Atlanta Hawks, 1988—89, Orlando Magic, 1989—90, NJ Nets, 1990—91, Ranger Varese, Italy, 1992—93; NBA analyst Turner Sports, ESPN; head coach Am. Basketball Assn. Las Vegas Slam; vol. asst. Calif. State U., LA, 2002—03; asst. coach U. Louisville, 2003—05; head coach N.Mex. State U., 2005—07, Sacramento Kings, Calif., 2007—. Head coach So. Calif. All-Stars (17-and-under); summer league coach Phila. 76ers, Denver Nuggets. Actor: (TV series) Hang Time, 1995—98; co-star: Best Damn Sports Show Period, 2001. Named to NBA All-Rookie Team, 1979, Ea. Conf. All-Star Team, NBA, 1981, 1983, UNLV Athletic Hall of Fame, 1989. Office: Sacramento Kings ARCO Arena One Sports Pky Sacramento CA 95834 *

THEUT, C. PETER, lawyer; b. Center Line, Mich., July 24, 1938; s. Clarence William and Anna Marie (Martens) T.; m. Judith Fern Trombley, Aug. 4, 1962; children: Elizabeth Anne, Kristin Claire, Peter Christopher, Sarah Nicole. BA, U. Mich., 1960, LLB, 1963. Bar: Calif. 1964, Mich. 1964, U.S. Dist. Ct. (no. dist.) Ohio 1968, U.S. Dist. Ct. (ea. dist.) Mich. 1968. Assoc. Overton, Lyman & Prince, LA, 1963-67; ptnr. Foster, Meadows and Ballard, Detroit, 1968-72, Theut & Schellig, Mt. Clemens, Mich., 1972-80, Hill, Lewis, Mt. Clemens, 1980-88, Butzel, Long, Detroit, 1988—. Stockbroker; chmn. Butzel Long Global Trade Group. Mem. ABA (internat. law sect., TIPS admiralty com.), Mich. State Bar Assn., Detroit Bar Assn., Macomb County Bar Assn., Calif. Bar Assn., Maritime Law Assn. (past chmn. recreational boating com.), Nat. Marine Bankers Assn. (gen. counsel), Mich. Boating Industry Assn. (gen. counsel) Lex Mundi, North Star Sail Club. Republican. Home: 579 Glenmoore Dr Ann Arbor MI 48103-9749 E-mail: theut@butzel.com.

THEVENET, PATRICIA CONFREY, social studies educator; b. Norwich, Conn., Apr. 16, 1924; d. John George and Gertrude Pauline (Doolittle) Confrey; m. Rubén Thevenet, Dec. 15, 1945 (dec. Mar. 1983); chldren: Susanne, Gregory, Richard, R. James. BS, U. Conn., 1944; AM, U. Chgo., 1945; EdM, Columbia U., 1992, EdD, 1994. Cert. elem. tchr., N.J. Counselor testing and guidance U. Chgo., 1945; home economist Western Mass. Electric Co., Pittsfield, 1946; tchr. Unquowa Sch., Fairfield, Conn., 1950-53, Alpine (N.J.) Sch., 1968-86; program asst. soc. studies Tchrs. Coll. Columbia U., NYC, 1987-93; ret., 1993. Historian Borough Northvale, N.J., 1987-94; participant summer seminar Smithsonian Instn., Washington, 1984. Del. 2d dist. rep. Town Mtg., Trumbull, Conn., 1954-56; pres., trustee Northvale Pub. Libr. Assn., 1957-63; trustee Northvale Bd. Edn., 1963-72, pres. Northvale Bd. Edn., 1969-70; exec. bd. dirs. Bergen County (N.J.) County Bds. Edn., 1965-72; mem. Evening Sch. Comm. No. Valley Regional Dist., Bergen County, 1976-83; trustee Voluntown Libr., 1997-2001. Mem. Voluntown Hist. Soc., Friends of Slater Mus., DAR. Home: 88 N Shore Rd # B Voluntown CT 06384-1719

THEVENOT, MAUDE TRAVIS, retired home economist; b. Many, La., Dec. 31, 1914; d. Rennie L. and Fairy D. (Minter) Travis; m. Aubrey J. Thevenot, July 4, 1952 (dec. Sept. 1981); 1 stepchild, Peter A. BA, Northwestern State U., 1939; MS, La. State U., 1963. Tchr. home econs. Bienville Parish High Sch., Jamestown, La., 1940-41; parish home mgmt. supr. Farmers Home Adminstrn., USDA, Natchitoches, Oak Grove, Winnefield, La., 1942-47, state home mgmt. supr. Alexandria, La., 1948-52; social worker La. Dept. Pub. Welfare, New Roads, Alexandria, Marksville, La., 1952-56; home economist La. State U.-La. Coop. Extension Svc., Makrsville, Alexandria, 1957-74, specialist expanded food & nutrition edn. program Baton Rouge, 1975-79. Co-advisor in home econs. Ptnrs. of Am. La./El Savador and La. Home Econs., 1975. Author: Central District Louisiana Home Economics Association, 1984 Louisiana Federation of Chapters of the National Association of Retired Federal Workers, 1989; co-author: A Taste of Yesterday, 1988. Mem. Kent Plantation House, Inc., Alexandria, 1970—, com. mem. for orgn., 1970, exec. bd., 1985-88, cookbook chmn., 1985-90; mem. Friendship House-Adult Day Care Ctr., Alexandria, 1982-90, exec. bd., 1982-88, organizer, pres. vol. orgn., 1978-90; advisor Anchors as Pilot Club of Alexandria Outreach Com., Anchor Club of Pineville (La.) High Sch., 1978-90; mem. La. Avoyelles & Rapides Parish Farm Bur., Marksville, Alexandria, 1967-90, Avoyelles & Rapides Cowbelles, Alexandria, Marksville, 1967-70; mem. Calvary Bapt. Ch., leader Sunday Sch. class, mem. sr. group decoration com. for monthly luncheons, leader Dottie Hayes Bible Study Group. Recipient Plaque for Svc. Rapides Parish Coun. on Aging, Alexandria, 1971, Plaque for Outstanding Leadership & Svc., Rapides Parish Homemakers Coun., Alexandria, 1974, Plaque of Appreciation as Coord., Expanded Food and Nutrition Ednl. Program La. State U., Baton Rouge, 1978, 11 Certs. of Appreciation, Anchor Club of Pineville High Sch., 1980-90, Cert. of Recognition (3) Friendship House-Day Care for Adults, 1983, 84, 85, Plaque for Outstanding Svc., Rapides Coun. on Aging 20th Ann., 1967-87. Mem. Internat. Fedn. Home Econs., Am. Assn. Family and Consumer Sci., La. Home Econs. Assn. (v.p. 1972-73, Disting. Home Economist 1979-80), Am. Assn. Family and Consumer Svcs. (Wiley-Berger award 1995), Cen. Dist. Home Econs. (pres. 1972-73, Disting. Svc. award 1967, hon. mem. 1985), Nat. Assn. Extension Home Economist, La. Assn. Extension Home Economist, AAUW, La. Assn. Nat. Assn. Retired Fed. Employees (past pres., v.p. region VI, Meritorious Svc. plaque and cert. of citation 1988-89, Meritorious Svc. award 1992-93, life), CENLA (past pres.), Am. Assn. Retired Persons, La. State U. Alumni, La. State U. Home Econs. Retiree, Northwestern State U. Alumni, La. Retired Tchrs. Assn. (life), Pilot Club Internat., Epsilon Sigma Phi (life), Gamma Sigma Delta (Extension award of merit 1978). Democrat. Avocations: travel, voluntary activities. Home: 507 Tanglewood Dr Alexandria LA 71303-3354

THÉVENOT, MAXINE RACHAEL, musician, educator; b. Zenon Park, Sask., Can., Oct. 8, 1969; arrived in U.S., 1999; d. Norman Joseph and Annette Jeannine Thévenot; m. Iain James Thomas Quinn, June 19, 2005. MusM in Music Edn. with distinction, U. Sask., 1991; MusM, Manhattan Sch. Music, NYC, 2001, DMA, 2006; degree (hon.), Nat. Coll. Music, London, 2006; assoc. diploma, Royal Conservatory of Music, 1992, Royal Can. Coll. Organists, 1995. Assoc. organist Cathedral Ch. of Redeemer, Calgary, Alta., Canada, 1992—96; dir. music, organist Parkdale United Ch., Calgary, 1996—99, Christ Ch. Episcopal, Manhasset, NY, 2000—03; assoc. organist, choir master Cathedral of Imanation, Garden City, NY, 2003—05; mem. faculty Manhattan Sch. Music, 2002—05, U. N.Mex., Albuquerque, 2006—; assoc. organist, choir dir. Cathedral Ch. St. John, Albuquerque, 2005—; founding dir. Polyphony, Albuquerque, 2006—. Concert organist: Notre Dame, St. Paul's Cathedral, Salisbury Cathedral, Westminster Abbey, Washington Nat. Cathedral, numerous others. Grantee, Alta. Found. Arts, Calgary, 2000. Mem.: Am. Choral Dirs. Assn., Coll. Music Soc., Am. Guild Organists (nat. examiner). Avocations: photography, cooking, gardening. Home: 7311 Tricia Rd NE Albuquerque NM 87113 Office: Cathedral Ch of St John PO Box 1246 Albuquerque NM 87103-1246

THEYS, PHILIPPE PAUL, data quality professional; b. Lille, France, Feb. 20, 1949; came to U.S., 1994; s. Maurice and Paulette (Querleu) T.; m. Odile Marie-Paule Bechere, July 15, 1972; children: Sophie, Cedric, Alban, Alice. Diploma in Engring., Ecole Centrale De Paris, 1971; Lic., Scis. Econs., Assas, France, 1971; grad. in Plasma Physics, U. Paris-Orsay, France, 1972. Rsch. engr. French Atomic Commn., 1971-72; geophys. field engr. Schlumberger, France, Sweden, Germany, U.S., Australia, 1972-77, country mgr. Taiwan, 1978-79, interpretation devel. mgr. Ea. Hemisphere, 1980-81, mktg. mgr. United Arab Emirates, Indonesia, Norway, 1982-89, quality mgr. Worldwide, 1990-94, data quality mgr., 1994—. Vice chmn. Log Characterization Consortium, 1997-99. Author: Log Data Acquisition and Quality Control, 1999; editor (mag.) The Log Analyst, 1994-2000, Petrophysics, 2000—. Lt. French Army, 1971-72. Mem. Soc. Profl. Well Log Analysts (v.p. edn. 1997-98, v.p. tech. 1998-99, pres. 2000—), Am. Soc. for Quality, Soc. Petroleum Engrs. Roman Catholic. Avocations: skydiving, long distance running, photography. Office: Sugarland Product Ctr 110 Schlumberger Dr Sugar Land TX 77478 E-mail: theys5@slb.com.

THIARA, PARVINDER SINGH, chemistry scholar; b. 1985; s. Surjit Singh and Sonia T. BS in Chemistry, Harvard Univ., 2007; MSc. student in Theoretical Chemistry, Oxford Univ., 2007—, MSc. student in Water Sci., Mgmt., Policy, 2007—. Fellow Herschel Smith sci. fellow; Rhodes Scholar. Mem.: Phi Beta Kappa. Achievements include co-founder Found. for Advancement of Water Sanitation Improvement Tech. Avocations: Bhangra dancer, golf, weightlifting, football. *

THIBADEAU, EUGENE FRANCIS, education educator, consultant; b. NYC, May 18, 1933; s. Eugene Servanis and Lillian (Archer) T.; 1 child, Christine. BA, NYU, 1959, MA, 1967, MA, 1968, PhD, 1973. Instr. NYU, NYC, 1968; lectr. in philosophy Dowling Coll., Oakdale, 1968-70; prof. edn. Indiana U. of Pa., 1970—. Vis. assoc. prof. Adelphi U., Garden City, NY, 1974-75; vis. scholar NYU, 1984-85; vis. prof. Hofstra U., Hempstead, 1974-75, 84, 86, Fudan U., Shanghai, China, 2000; cons. Ctrl. Bur. of Ednl. Visits, London, 1980-81, Commonwealth Spkrs. Bur., Harrisburg, Pa., 1983-85, US Dept. Edn., Washington, 1983-85, Pa. Dept. Edn., Harrisburg, 1988—. Author: Opening Up Edn.-In Theory and Practice, 1976, Curriculum Theory, 1988; rev. editor: Focus on Learning, 1973-77, editor, 1977-84; contbg. editor: Internat. Ency. of Edn., 2d edit., Internat. Ency.of Teaching and Tchr. Edn., 2nd edit., Internat. Ency. of Social and Behavioral Scis.; contbr. articles to profl. jours. Active United Way, Indiana, Pa., 1980—, NAACP, Indiana, 1985—, Red Cross, Indiana, 1985—. Fulbright sr. lectr. Thames Polytechnic, London, 1978-79, Fulbright sr. scholar Janus Pannonius U., Peces, Hungary, 1990-91; foreign expert Shanghai (China) Tchrs. U., 1988; designated faculty rsch. assoc. Inst. for Applied Rsch. and Pub. Policy, Indiana U. Pa., 1989; named Commonwealth Teaching fellow and Cert. Excellence in Teaching, Pa. State Colls. and Univ. Disting. Faculty Awards Com., 1976; recipient Founder's Day award, NYU, 1973, Outstanding Prof. award Ind. U. Pa.-Pa. State Edn. Assn., 1993; nom. to Ctr. for Social and Behavioral Sci., Stanford U., Palo Alto, Calif., 2007. Fellow Am. Philosophy Edn. Soc.; mem. AAUP, ASCD, Am. Ednl. Studies Assn., The S.W. Philosophy Edn. Soc. Avocations: travel, skiing, tennis, reading, chess. Home: 534 Chestnut Ridge Rd Penn Run PA 15765 Office: Indiana Univ Pa 131 Stouffer Hall Indiana PA 15705 Office Phone: 724-357-4543. Business E-Mail: eftt@iup.edu.

THIBAULT, GEORGE EDWIN, medical educator, non-profit healthcare organization administrator; b. Sept. 4, 1943; m. Barbara C. Thibault; children: Rebecca L., Adam. Degree, Georgetown U., 1965; MD, Harvard Med. Sch., 1969. Resident internal med. Mass. Gen. Hosp., 1971, 1974, chief med. resident, 1975, fellow cardiology, 1976, dir. med. practices evaluation unit, dept. med., 1977, dir. ICU/CCU, 1977, dir. tng. program internal med., 1978, assoc. chief; fellow cardiology Nat. Heart & Lung Inst., Bethesda, Md., 1973; chief med. svcs. Brockton/West Roxbury VA Med. Ctr., Mass., 1988; vice chmn. med. Brigham and Women's Hosp., 1988—95, chief med. officer, 1995—99; v.p. clin. affairs Partners HealthCare System Inc., Boston, 1999—; prof. med. Harvard Med. Sch., dir. The Academy, 2001—. Chmn. special med. adv. group Dept. Vet. Affairs, Boston. Office: Partners HealthCare Sys Inc Prudential Tower 800 Boylston St Ste 1150 Boston MA 02199-8001 E-mail: george_thibault@hms.harvard.edu. *

THIBAULT, LISE, Canadian lieutenant governor; b. St.-Roch-de-l'Achigan, Apr. 2, 1939; m. Rene Thibault, Nov. 21, 1959; children: Guylaine, Anne-Marie. Diploma, St.-Roch-de-l'Achigan; D of civil law, Bishop's U.; D (hon.), Concordia U., Mass. Anna-Maria Coll. Owner Studio Julie, 1956-60; adult edn. tchr. Mille-Iles and Des Ecores sch. bds., 1973-78; commr. Lang. of Instruction Commn. Que. Dept. Edn., 1977; provincial pres. Can. Day Celebrations, 1983-84; v.p. Rels. with Beneficiaries Que. Worker Health and Safety Bd., 1987-93; pres., dir. gen. Que. Bur. for Handicapped, 1993-95; lt. gov. Govt. of Que., 1997—. Founding sec. La Chaine newspaper, 1972; mg. Jour. des femmes d'aujourd'hui, 1973-76; author: De belles et bonnes choses, Vols. 1 and 2; contbr. articles to profl. jours. Active Can. Red Cross, 1985-87, Que. Pension Bd., 1987-95, Que. Bur. for the Handicapped, 1992-93; v.p. of Pre-Referendum Quebecers for the NO Com., 1980; pres. Laval NO Com., 1980; candidate for Que. Liberal Party, 1981, pres. family sub-com., 1983-84, mem. polit. com., 1981-84, candidate Liberal Party of Can., 1984, pres. of comm. com., 1986-87. Recipient Woman of Merit award Montreal YWCA, 1994, medal, Edouard Montpetit Found. of the Faculty of Social, Economic and Polit. Sci.; named Personality of Yr., Chatelaine Mag. Mem. Marie-Paule de Sainte-Veronique Found., Internat. Assn. of Women and Home Page Journalists, Que. Writers Union, others. Avocations: travel, music, cooking, gardening. Office: Office of Lt Gov 1050 rue des Parlemtaires Quebec City PQ Canada G1A 1A1

THIBAULT, MIKE, professional basketball coach; m. Nanci Thibault; children: Eric, Carly. Grad., St. Martin's U., 1979. Scout NBA LA Lakers, 1978—80, dir. scouting, asst. coach, 1980—82, NBA Chgo. Bulls, 1982—86; gen. mgr., head coach World Basketball League Calgary 88's, 1987—88, Continental Basketball Assn. Omaha Racers, 1989—97; scout NBA Seattle SuperSonics, 1997—98; asst. coach NBA Milw. Bucks, 1998—2002; head coach WNBA Conn. Sun, 2003—. Head coach U.S.A. Nat. team World Championship Qualifying Tournament (gold medal), PR, 1993, Pan Am. Games, 1995; asst. coach U.S.A. Women's Basketball team World Championships, Sao Paolo, Brazil, 2006. Named Coach of Yr., World Basketball League, 1988, Sportsman of Yr., Omaha sportscasters, 1993, WNBA Coach of Yr., 2006. Office: Conn Sun 1 Mohegan Sun Blvd Uncasville CT 06382 *

THIBERT, ROGER JOSEPH, clinical chemist, educator; b. Tecumseh, Ont., Can., Aug. 29, 1929; s. Charles and Violet (Hebert) T.; m. Audrey M. Wissler, July 10, 1954; children: Mark Roger, Robert Francis. BA, U. Western Ont., 1951; MS, U. Detroit, 1954; PhD, Wayne State U., 1958; DSc, U. Windsor, 2004. Diplomate: Am. Bd. Clin. Chemistry (past bd. dirs.). Mem. faculty U. Windsor, Ont., Canada, 1953—, prof. chemistry Ont., 1967-94, dir. clin. chemistry Ont., 1972-94, prof. emeritus Ont., 1994—; prof. pathology Med. Sch. Wayne State U., Detroit, 1972-94; assoc. divsn. head, clin. chemistry Detroit Receiving Hosp., Univ. Health Ctr., 1973-94, mem. med. staff, 1973-94. Cons. med. biochemistry Med. Labs. Windsor, Ont., Can., 1995-2000; sci. dir. Med. Labs., Windsor, 2000-2005. Contbr. articles on chemistry, biochemistry, analytical chemistry, clin. chemistry to profl. jours. Recipient Smith Kline award Am. Assn. Clin. Chemistry, 1980, Tchg. award Ont. Confedn. Univ. Faculty Assns., 1990, Beckman Edn. Excellence award Canadian Soc. Clin. Chemists, 1992, Alumni Tchg. award U. Windsor, 1988, Alumni award of merit, 1994, alumni excellence in mentoring award, 2003; Chem. Inst. Can. fellow, 1968—; Nat. Acad. Clin. Biochemistry fellow, 1978—; grantee Natural Scis. and Engring. Rsch. Coun. Can., award Union Carbide, Chem. Inst., Can., 1978. Fellow AAAS, Can. Acad. Clin. Biochemistry; mem. Am. Chem. Soc., Chem. Inst. Can., Assn. Chem. Profession Ont., Am. Assn. Clin. Chemistry, Nat. Acad. Clin. Biochemistry, Can. Soc. Clin. Chemists (Ames award 1988), Ont. Soc. Clin. Chemists, Am. Soc. for Biochemistry and Molecular Biology, Fedn. Am. Socs. Exptl. Biology, Can. Soc. Biochemistry and Molecular Biology, Can. Fedn. Biol. Scis., Can. Soc. for Chemistry, Sigma Xi. Roman Catholic. Home: 4612 Dali Ct Windsor ON Canada N9G 2M8 Office: U Windsor Dept Chemistry/Biochemistry Windsor ON Canada N9B 3P4

THIBIDEAU, CAROLYN C., musician, educator; d. Emery Spencer and Elizabeth Anne Cartwright; m. Robert James Thibideau, Dec. 28, 1958; children: Stephen Robert, Michael Charles, Richard Dayton, Peter John. BS, Oakland U., 1974; MusM, U. Mich., 1980. Cert. tchr. Mich., registered music educator Music Educators Nat. Conf. Ch. organist, music dir. West Bloomfield Schs., Mich., 1954—, music tchr., 1975—2003. Organizing dir. Cmty. Music Series, Orchard Lake, Mich.; composer, arranger, conductor, performer organ, piano, trumpet. Composer (compositions and arrangements) brass quintet and organ, sch. bands, handbell choirs. Music dir., organist 1st Presbyn. Ch., Pontiac, Mich., 1994—. Finalist Tchr. of the Yr., Mich. Dept. of Edn., 1992. Mem.: Mich. Edn. Assn., Am. Guild English Handbell Ringers (former Mich. chairperson, clinician, condr., Nat. Exemplary Handbells in Edn. award 1992), Am. Guild Organists (assoc.; nat. conv. program com. 1980—86, mem. nat. conv. com. 1982—86, bd. dirs. 1986—89, performer). Avocations: music, opera. Office: Antioch Pub 8593 Cooley Lake Rd Commerce Township MI 48382 Personal E-mail: carolynct1@yahoo.com.

THIBODEAU, GARY A., academic administrator; b. Sioux City, Iowa, Sept. 26, 1938; m. Emogene J. McCarville, Aug. 1, 1964; children: Douglas James (dec.), Beth Ann. BS, Creighton U., 1962; MS, S.D. State U., 1967, MS, 1970, PhD, 1971. Profl. service rep. Baxter Lab., Inc., Deerfield, Ill., 1963-65; tchr., researcher dept. biology S.D. State U., Brookings, 1965-76, asst. to v.p. for acad. affairs, 1976-80, v.p. for adminstrn., 1980-85; chancellor U. Wis., River Falls, 1985-2000; sr. v.p. acad. affairs U. Wis. Sys., 2000—01. Mem. investment com. U. Wis., River Falls Found.; trustee W. Cen. Wis. Consortium U. Wis. System; bd. dirs. U. Wis. at River Falls Found.; mem. Phi Kappa Phi nat. budget rev. and adv. comm., Phi Kappa Phi Found. investment comm., comm. on Agrl. and Rural Devel., steering commn. Coun. of Rural Colls. and Univs., Joint Coun. on Food and Agrl. Scis., USDA. Author: Basic Concepts in Anatomy and Physiology, 1983, Athletic Injury Assessment, 1994, Textbook of Anatomy and Physiology, 2006, Structure and Function of the Body, 2004, The Human Body in Health and Disease, 2005, Anatomy and Physiology, 2006. Mem. AAAS, Am. Assn. Anatomists, Am. Assn. Clin. Anatomists, Human Anatomy and Physiology Soc., Sigma Xi, Phi Kappa Phi, Gamma Sigma Delta, Gamma Alpha. Office: U Wis 116 N Hall River Falls WI 54022

THIBODEAU, THOMAS RAYMOND, lawyer; b. St.Paul, Feb. 5, 1942; m. Mollie Nan Mylor, Sept. 24, 1966; 1 child, Matthew Raymond. BA in Polit. Sci. cum laude, U. St. Thomas, St. Paul, 1964; JD, U. Minn., 1967. Bar: Minn. 1967, U.S. Dist. Ct. Minn. 1967, U.S. Ct. Appeals (8th cir.) 1970, U.S. Supreme Ct. 1982, Wis. 1983, U.S. Dist. Ct. Wis. 1983, N.D. 2000, U.S. Dist. Ct. N.D., 2000; solicitor Supreme Ct. Eng. and Wales, 1996; cert. civil trial specialist Nat. Bd. Trial Advocacy. Ptnr. Johnson, Killen & Thibodeau, Duluth, Minn., 1967-2000, Thibodeau, Johnson & Feriancek PLLP, Duluth, 2000—. Pres. Legal Aid Svc. N.E. Minn., Inc., 1969-74; mem. civil justice reform act adv. com. U.S. Dist. Ct. Minn., revision Civil Jury Instruction Guide IV, 1997—, Minn. jud. selection commn. 6th Dist., 2001—; mem. State of Minn. Jud. Selection Commn., 1999—. Chmn. Duluth City Charter Commn., 1976-78; vol. atty. St. Louis County Heritage and Arts Ctr., Duluth, 1980-87; pres. bd. trustees Marshall Sch., 1990-92. Recipient Disting. Alumni award, U. St. Thomas, 1985. Fellow Internat. Soc. Barristers, Am. Coll. Trial Lawyers; mem. Am. Bd. Trial Advs. (advocate), Minn. Bar Assn. (chmn. specialization com. 1974-78, co-chmn. revision Civil Injury Instrn. Guide III com. 1982-85, 96-99), Minn. Def. Lawyers Assn. (pres. 1988-89), Acad. Cert. Trial Lawyers of Minn. (pres. elect 1993, pres. 1994-95), Internat. Assn. Def. Counsel, Assn. Def. Trial Attys. Avocations: hunting, skiing, scuba diving and other water sports, reading. Office: Thibodeau Johnson & Feriancek PLLP 800 Lonsdale 302 W Superior St Duluth MN 55802-1802 Home Phone: 218-724-4144; Office Phone: 218-722-0073. Business E-Mail: trt@trialgroupnorth.com.

THIE, JOSEPH ANTHONY, nuclear engineer; s. Joseph Aloysius and Veronica Veneranda (Volk) Thie; m. Frances Morris Thie, Dec. 30, 1967. BS in Physics, U. Notre Dame, Ind., 1947; PhD in Nuc. Physics, U. Notre Dame, Notre Dame, IN, 1951; DSc (hon.), U. Indpls., 2004. Registered profl. engr., Wis.; Q-clearance AEC. Chief physicist Argonne (Ill.) Nat. Lab., 1953—60; ind. nuc. reactor and medicine cons. Knoxville, 1960—; adj. prof. nuc. engring. U. Tenn., Knoxville, 1989—. Chmn. nuc. reactor safety rev. com. Dairyland Power, LaCrosse, Wis., 1967—; mem., dir.'s adv. com. Oak Ridge (Tenn.) Nat. Lab., 1974—78; lectr. in field. Author: Power Reactor Noise, 1981, Reactor Noise, 1963, Heavy Water Exponential Experiments using ThO2 and UO2, 1961; mem. editl. adv. bd. Jour. Nuc. Medicine, 2003; contbr. articles to profl. jours. Trustee cath. edn. trust fund Roman Cath. Diocese Knoxville, 2004—06. Postdoc. fellow, US AEC, 1951—52. Mem.: Soc. Nuc. Medicine, Am. Nuc. Soc. (life). Achievements include pioneer in first commercial reactors and in analysis of their random phenomena. Avocation: electronic music.

THIEBAUD, WAYNE MORTON, artist; b. Mesa, Ariz., Nov. 15, 1920; s. Morton J. and Alice Eugenia (LeBaro) T.; m. Betty Jean Carr, Dec. 11, 1959; children: Twinka, Mallary Ann, Paul LeBaron. BA, Sacramento State Coll., 1951, MA, 1952; MFA (hon.), Calif. Coll. Arts and Crafts, 1975. Art dir., NYC; also Hollywood, 1946-49; chmn. art dept. Sacramento City Coll., 1951; design cons. Calif. State Fair and Expn.; guest instr. San Francisco Art Inst., 1958; assoc. prof. art U. Calif. at Davis, now prof., Faculty Research lectr., from 1973. Vis. artist Cornell U., U. Hawaii, U. Wis., U. Utah, U. Ill., Yale U., U. Va., Bradley U.; tchr. Sacramento City Coll., 1951—61, U. Calif., 1960—76. Author: Etching Delights, 1965, Prints, 1970-71, Seven Still Lifes and a Rabbit; one-man shows include Crocker Art Gallery, Sacramento, Calif., 1952, Artists Coop. Gallery, Sacramento, Calif., 1954, DeYoung Mus., San Francisco, 1962, Allan Stone Gallery, N.Y.C., 1962—70, Stanford, 1965, Sao Paulo Biennale, 1966, Galleria Schwarz, Milan, 1963, San Francisco Mus., 1967, Pasadena Mus. Art, 1967—68, Whitney Mus., 1972, Indocumenta, 1972, Boston Inst. Contemporary Art, 1976, Walker Art Ctr., Mpls., 1981, Ft. Worth Art Mus., 1981, Mus. Fine Arts, St. Petersburg, Fla., 1981, museums, U.S., Toronto, The Hague, Vienna, Berlin, Hong Kong, S.Am., Oakland Mus., Phoenix Mus., U. So. Calif., Des Moines Mus., one-man shows include organized by Mus. Modern Art for 50th Ann. Wayne Thiebaud exhibn., Newport, R.I., 1985, Milw., 1985, Columbus, 1985, Kansas City, 1985, exhibited in group shows at Santa Barbara (Calif.) Mus. Art, 1980, Bklyn. Mus., 1980, 1981, Whitney Mus. Am. Art, 1981, San Antonio Mus. Art, 1981, Indpls. Mus. Art, 1981, Inst. Contemporary Art, U. Pa., Phila., 1981, Carnegie Inst., Pitts., 1981, Allan Stone Gallery, N.Y.C., 1982, Represented in permanent collections Mus. Modern Art, Whitney Mus. Am. Art, Albright Knox Mus., Wadsworth Athenaeum, Libr. Congress, Woodward Found., Rose Art Mus., Brandeis U., Stanford, Sheldon Meml. Art Gallery U. Nebr., Fines Arts Mus., San Francisco, Utah Mus. Fine Arts U. Utah, Kemper Mus. Contemporary Art, U. Maine Mus. Art, Spencer Mus. Art U. Kans., Nat. Mus. Am. Art, Washington, Crown Point Press, also numerous pvt. collections, commns. include fountain mobile sculpture Calif. State Fair, 1952, paintings Wimbledon Tennis Tournament, 1968, woodblock prints Crown Point Press, Kyoto, Japan, 1987, Yosemite Ridge Line for Bicentennial Exhibn., 1976, 42 works on paper Arts Club Chgo., 1987; prodr., dir.: 12 ednl. motion pictures (1st prize Art Film Festival, 1956, award for Space Golden Reel Film Festival Calif. State Fair, 1956, named Univ. Art Studio Tchr. of Yr. Coll. Art Assn. Am., 1981, Faculty Rsch. medal U. Calif., Davis., 1984, Award of Distinction Nat. Art Schs. Assn., 1984, Spl. Citation Nat. Assn. Schs. Art and Design, 1984). With USAF, 1942—45. Recipient Cyril Magnin award, San Francisco, 1987, Golden Plate award, Am. Acad. Achievement, 1987, Nat. Medal Arts, 1994. Mem.: Nat. Acad. Design (academician), Am. Acad. and Inst. Arts and Letters. Office: co Paul Thiebaud Gallery 631 Union St San Francisco CA 94133

THIEL, DAVID BRIAN, physician assistant; b. Cin., July 2, 1956; s. Joseph Lee and Mary Jane (Otting) T. BA, Wabash Coll., Crawfordsville, Ind., 1978; AS with honors, Kettering Coll. Med. Arts, 1980. Cert. physician asst. Resident Los Angeles County-U. So. Calif. Med. Ctr., LA, 1985-86; physician asst. in orthopedic surgery Ketchikan, Alaska, 1980-85; physician asst. in phys. medicine and electrodiagnostic medicine New Orleans, 1987—2004; physician asst. USCG, 2004—. In-svc. lectr. Health-South Rehab., Harahan, La., 1990—. Tannenbaum scholar, 1974-78; recipient Orchid award Paphiopedilum Mystic Jewel, David's Dream, Highly Commended Cert. Am. Orchid Soc., 2003. Fellow: Sigma Xi (numerous Orchid awards); mem.: Internat. High IQ Soc. Republican. Avocations: swimming, skiing, sailing, orchid growing, bicycling. Address: 106 Sawmill Crrek Rd Pearl River LA 70452 E-mail: cynicno@hotmail.com.

THIEL, PETER A., investment company executive; b. 1967; BA in Philosophy, Stanford U., JD. Securities law atty. Sullivan & Cromwell; derivatives trader CS Fin. Products; founder, head Thiel Capital Mgmt. LLC; chmn., CEO Confinity, Inc; co-founder PayPal, Inc., 1998, chmn., CEO, 1998—2002; founder, pres., chmn. Investment Com. Clarium Capital Mgmt., LLC, 2003—. Rsch. fellow, bd. dirs. Independent Inst.; bd. dirs. Pacific Rsch. Inst. Co-author: The Diversity Myth, 1998. Bd. visitors Stanford Law Sch.; bd. dir. The Hoover Inst. Avocation: chess. Office: Clarium Capital Mgmt LLC Ste 4360 555 California St San Francisco CA 94104 Office Phone: 415-248-5140. Office Fax: 415-248-5141. *

THIEL, PHILIP, design educator; b. Bklyn., Dec. 20, 1920; s. Philip and Alma Theone (Meyer) T.; m. Midori Kono, 1955; children: Philip Kenji, Nancy Tamiko, Susan Akiko, Peter Akira (dec.) BSc, Webb Inst. Naval Architecture, 1943; MSc, U. Mich., 1948; BArch, MIT, Cambridge, 1952. Registered arch., Wash. Instr. naval architecture MIT, Cambridge, 1949—50; instr. architecture U. Calif., Berkeley, 1954—56, asst. prof., 1956—60; assoc. prof. U. Wash., Seattle, 1961—66, prof. visual design and experiential notation, 1966—91; guest prof. Tokyo Inst. Tech., 1976—78; vis. prof. Sapporo Sch. Arts, Japan, 1992—98. Lectr., US, Can., Japan, Norway, Denmark, Sweden, Eng., Austria, Switzerland, Peru, Bolivia, Korea; cons. FAO, Rome, 1952; co-founder Environment and Behavior, 1969; founder Ctr. for Exptl. Notation, Seattle, 1981 Author: Freehand Drawing, 1965, Visual Awareness and Design, 1981, People, Paths and Purposes, 1997; patentee in field Soc. Naval Architects and Marine Engrs. scholar, 1947; Rehmann scholar AIA, 1960; grantee NIMH, 1967, Nat. Endowment for Arts, 1969, Graham Found., 1995 Mem. Soc. Naval Archs. and Marine Engrs. (assoc.), Phi Beta Kappa, Sigma Xi

THIELE, DWAIN LOUIS, medical educator, department vice chairman; b. Kingsville, Tex., Dec. 22, 1952; s. Louis and Olivia Thiele; m. Elizabeth Crosser, Oct. 30, 1954; children: Alan, Kyle. BA, Rice U., 1974; MD, Baylor Coll. Medicine, 1977. Diplomate Am. Bd. Internal Medicine, 1980, in gastroenterology Am. Bd. Internal Medicine, 1983. Internship, residency Duke U. Med. Ctr., 1977—80; fellow gastroenterology, hepatologn U. Tex. Southwestern Med. Ctr., Dallas, 1980—83, from asst. prof. internal medicine to prof., 1983—95, prof. internal medicine, 1995—, chief hepatology, 1998—2005, interim chief digestive, liver diseases, 2002—05, vice chair internal medicine, 2005—. Mem.: Assn. Am. Physicians, Am. Soc. Clin. Investigation. Office: University of Texas Southwestern Med Ctr 5323 Harry Hines Blvd Dallas TX 75390 Office Phone: 214-648-4570. Office Fax: 214-648-5607. E-mail: dwain.thiele@utsouthwestern.edu.

THIELE, HERBERT WILLIAM ALBERT, lawyer; b. Gananoque, Ont., Can., Apr. 14, 1953; s. Herbert and Bertha (Shields) T.; m. Kathi M. Brown, May 29, 1982; children: Herbert R. R., Eric W. R., Brian A. J., Kelly M. M., Kevin M. H., Karl S. H. BA, U. Notre Dame, 1975; JD, U. Fla., 1978. Bar: Fla. 1978, U.S. Dist. Ct. (so. dist. trial and gen. bars) Fla. 1979, U.S. Ct. Appeals (5th and 11th cirs.) 1981, U.S. Supreme Ct. 1982, U.S. Tax Ct. 1983, U.S. Dist. Ct. (no. dist.) Fla. 1991. Assoc. Law Offices of Roger G. Saberson, Delray Beach, Fla., 1979-81; asst. city atty. City of Delray Beach, 1979-81, city atty., 1981-90; county atty. Leon County, Tallahassee, Fla., 1990—. Bd. dirs. Delray Beach Mcpl. Employees Credit Union, 1985-88; pres. Notre Dame Club of Tallahassee, 2002--. Recipient award of recognition Stetson U. Law Rev., 1989, Ralph A. Marsicano award for Local Govt. Law, Fla. Bar, 1991. Mem. ABA (vice-chmn. urban, state and local govt. com. of gen. practice sect. 1991-95, labor and employment law, litigation, govt. lawyers, gen. practice and trial practice com. sects.), ATLA, FBA, Fla. Bar (exec. coun. local govt. law sect. 1986-87, sec.-treas. 1987-88, chmn., 1989-90, ex-officio officer 1991—, trial, real property, gen. practice and labor and employment law sect., bar com. on individual rights and responsibilities 1986-90, long-range planning com. 1991-93, continuing legal edn. com. 1998-99, vice chair 2d Jud. Cir. bench/bar com. 2003—, Paul S. Buchman award local govt. law sect. 2000), Tallahassee Bar Assn., Fla. Mcpl. Atty. Assn. (steering com. 1985-86, bd. dir. 1980-89, sec.-treas. 1989-90, Fla. Mcpl. Atty. of Yr. 1987), Fla. Assn. Police Atty., Internat. Mcpl. Lawyers Assn. (pers. and labor law com., trial practices and litigation com., legal advocacy com., 11th cir. rep. 1989—, chmn. counties and spl. dists. com. 2005-), Am. Soc. Pub. Adminstrn., Fla. Pub. Employer Labor Rels. Assn., Fla. Assn. County Atty. (chmn. coun. county atty. 1990-91, bd. dir. 1991-93, treas. 1993, sec. 1993-94, v.p. 1994-95, pres. 1995-96, 2007—, chmn. 1996-97, 2007-, bd. dir. 1997-2007, Recognition award 1994, Ethics in Govt. award 1998, 01). Republican. Avocations:

music, sports, stamp collecting/philately. Home: 318 Milestone Dr Tallahassee FL 32312-3574 Office: Office of Leon County Atty Leon County Courthouse Tallahassee FL 32301 Office Phone: 850-606-2500. Business E-Mail: thieleh@leoncountyfl.gov.

THIELE, HOWARD NELLIS, JR., lawyer; b. Dayton, Ohio, June 22, 1930; s. Howard Nellis and Irma Laura (Scheibe) T.; m. Alma Kuhn, Oct. 14, 1995; children: Leslie, Howard III, Craig. AB, Miami U., Oxford, Ohio, 1952; JD with distinction, U. Mich., 1955. Bar: Ohio 1955. Assoc., ptnr. Smith & Schnacke, LPA, Dayton, Ohio, 1957-89; ptnr. Thompson, Hine & Flory, Dayton, 1989-95; ret., 1995. Pres. Dayton Art Inst., 1981-85; bd. dirs. Dayton Area chpt. ARC, 1983—, 1st vice chmn., 1990-91, chmn., 1992-94. Capt. USAF, 1955-57. Mem.: Phi Beta Kappa, Order of the Coif. Republican. Lutheran.

THIEMANN, RONALD FRANK, dean, religious studies educator; b. St. Louis, Oct. 4, 1946; s. Frank Joseph and Marie Magdalene (Graeser) T.; m. Beth Arlene Barkow, June 15, 1968; children: Sarah Elizabeth, Laura Kristen. BA magna cum laude, Concordia Sr. Coll., Fort Wayne, Ind., 1968; MDiv, Concordia Sem., St. Louis, 1972; MA, Yale U., 1973, MPhil, 1974, PhD, 1976; postgrad., Eberhard-Karls Universitat, Tubingen, W.Ger., 1974-75. Asst. prof. dept. religion Haverford Coll., Pa., 1976-82, assoc. prof. dept. religion Pa., 1982-85, prof. dept. religion Pa., 1985-86, acting provost Pa., 1985, acting pres. Pa., 1986; dean Div. Sch. Harvard U., Cambridge, Mass., 1986-98, John Lord O'Brian prof. divinity, 1986-98, prof. theology, religion & soc., 1998—, faculty fellow Hauser Ctr., JFK Sch. Govt. Vis. prof. honors program Villanova U., 1981; vis. asst. prof. Luth. Theol. Sem., Phila., 1977; mem. Ctr. Theol. Inquiry, Princeton, N.J., 1982-83; mem. consultation on Christianity and Marxism, U.S.A. nat. com. Luth. World Fedn., 1979-83, mem. consultation on civil religion, 1983-86, mem. consultation on problem of common good, 1985-88; bd. dirs. Trinity Press Internat.; mem. exec. com. Assn. Theol. Schs., 1994-2000; faculty mem. Hanser Ctr. JFK Sch. Govt. Harvard U., 1998—. Author: Revelation and Theology, 1985, Constructing a Public Theology: The Church in a Pluralistic Culture, 1991, Religion in Public Life: A Dilemma for Democracy, 1995, Who Will Provide? The Changing Role of Religion in American Social Welfare, 2001; editor: The Legacy of H. Richard Niebuhr, 1991, Why Are We Here? Everyday Questions and the Christian Life, 1998, Where Shall My Wandering Soul Begin: The Landscape of Evangelical Piety and Thought, 2000; mem. editl. bd.: Dialog, 1987—; contbr. numerous articles to profl. jours. Mem. bd. trustees Buckingham Browne & Nichols Schs., 1988-90; mem. task force on theol. education, Evang. Luth. Ch. in Am., 1989-91, task force on Luth.-Reformed Conversations, Evang. Luth. Ch. Am., 1988-92. Recipient Disting. Teaching award Lindback Found., 1982, Lilly Scholars award, 1998-99; Mellon Found. fellow, 1982-83; Deutscher Akademischer Austauschdienst fellow, 1974-75. Mem. Am. Acad. Religion, (chmn. narrative interpretation and theology group 1982-86), Soc. Christian Ethics, Am. Theol. Soc. Avocations: tennis, squash, piano. Home: 186 Shadyside Ave Concord MA 01742-2740 Office: Harvard Div Sch 45 Francis Ave Cambridge MA 02138-1911

THIEME, JEAN LOUISE, retired art association administrator; b. Greenville, Ohio, May 9, 1926; d. William Edward and Dorothy Coppock Hole; m. Walter Irving Thieme, June 18, 1948; foster children: Ilona Jekabsons Reif, Gracie Hill Ratliff children: Michael Alan, Rebecca Louise, Susan Kathleen. AB in Chemistry, U. Mich., Ann Arbor, 1947; cert. in mgmt., Radcliffe Coll., Cambridge, Mass., 1948; postgrad., Earlham Coll., Richmond, Ind. Trustee Migrant Health Bd., Greenville Ministerial Assn., Ohio, 1970—73; exec. dir. Migrant Health Clinic (later Family Health Svcs.), Greenville, 1973—81, Darke County Ctr. Arts, Greenville, 1982—90; trustee Ctr. Arts Bd., Jackson, Wyo., 1997—2007. Editor: This is Darke County, 1982. Organizer FISH emergency phone svc., 1975—2006; trustee The Brethren's Home, Greenville, 1982—90, H.O.P.E. Found. of Darke County, 1990—2002; bd. internat. studies U. Wyo., 2001—05; mem. design com. Downtown Greenville, Inc., 2001—06; trustee Offsquare Theatre Co., Jackson, 2006—; organizer design and financing Traffic Cir., Greenville, 2005. Recipient Citizenship award, VFW, Greenville, 1981, Svc. to Mankind award, Greenville Sertoma Club, 1984. Episcopalian. Avocations: family reunions, gardening, reading, travel, performing arts. Home: 3565 Hollansburg Sampson Rd Greenville OH 45331 also: PO Box 3858 Jackson WY 83001 Personal E-mail: thieme@bresnan.net. E-mail: thieme@wesnet.com.

THIEMENS, MARK H., chemistry professor; b. St. Louis, Jan. 6, 1950; m. Nasrin Thiemens; 2 children. BS, U. Miami, 1972; MS, Old Dominion U., 1974; postgrad., Fla. Inst. Technology, 1974-75; PhD, Fla. State U., 1977. Grad. rsch. asst. dept. oceanography Old Dominion U., Norfolk, Va., 1972-74; grad. rsch. asst. dept. physics Fla. Inst. Technology, Melbourne, 1974-75; participant trace element aerosol rsch. program Fla. State U., Tallahassee, 1975-76; researcher dept. atmospheric chemistry Brookhaven Nat. Labs., Upton, N.Y., 1976-77; postdoctoral fellow Enrico Fermi Inst. U. Chgo., 1977-80; vis. prof. dept. chemistry U. Calif., San Diego, La Jolla, 1980-81, asst. prof. step II dept. chemistry, 1981-83, asst. prof. step IV dept. chemistry, 1983-85, assoc. prof. step I dept. chemistry, 1985-87, assoc. prof. dept. chemistry step II, 1987-88, assoc. prof. step III dept. chemistry, 1988-89, prof. step I dept. chemistry, 1989-91, prof. step II dept. chemistry, 1991-93, prof. step III dept. chemistry, 1993-95, prof. step VII dept. chemistry, 1996-2000, prof. step IX dept. chemistry, 2000—, chair dept. chemistry, 1996-99, dean divsn. phys. sci., 1999—. Dir. Cr. Environ Rsch. and Tng. U. Calif., San Diego, 1996—, mem. Ctr. Astrophysicis and Space Sci., 1980—, Scripps Inst. Oceanography, 1996—; mem. workshop panel Origins of Solar Sys. NASA, 1989, mem. panel cosmochemistry divsn. group b isotope geochemistry, 1996—, cosmochemistry rev. panel Johnson Space Ctr., 1997; organizer, convenor 1997 Informal Symposium on Kinetic and Photochemical Processes in the Atmosphere, 1997. Contbr. numerous articles to profl. jours. Alexander von Humboldt fellow Inst. Phys. Chemistry U. Göttingen (Germany), 1990-91, 93; Camille and Henry Dreyfus tchg. scholar, 1984-89; recipient Ernest Orlando Lawrence Meml. award US Dept. of Energy, 1999, Disting. Scientist of Yr. award Am. Chem. Soc., 2002. Fellow Meteoritical Soc.; mem. Am. Acad. Arts Scis., NAS. Achievements include development of analytical capability to measure stable isotope variations at ultra-high precision in sulfur, oxygen, carbon and nitrogen to use in development of experimental programs in varying research fields including atmospheric chemistry, physical chemistry of gas phase photochemical eractions, electrical plasmas, early solar system history, and gas-solid conversion mechanisms; development of the ability to measure sulfur isotopic in meteoritic and lunr material to a precision greater than an order-of-magnitude over previous laboratory determination to determine the nature of pre-solar sulfur chemistry, cosmic-ray-spallation, and nucleosynthetic inputs; development of rocket borne atmospheric sampling and analysis.

THIENEMAN, MICHAEL D., manufacturing executive; b. Louisville; BA in Physics, Bellarmine Coll., 1970; MS, PhD in Physics, U. Ky., 1977; MBA, U. Evansville, 1981. Project engr. Whirlpool Corp., 1977, pres., CEO Inglis Ltd. subs., pres. Whirlpool Compressor Ops. Riva di Chieri, Italy, corp. v.p. global procurement ops., exec. v.p. N.Am. region, 1997—2000, exec. v.p., chief tech. officer, 2000—. Chair fund devel. com. Harbor Habitat for Humanity; trustee Whirlpool Found., 1997—. Office: Whirlpool Corp 2000 N M-63 Benton Harbor MI 49022 Office Phone: 269-923-5000. E-mail: michael_d_thieneman@whirlpool.com. *

THIEN-STASKO, VICKI LYNN, civil engineer; b. Scott AFB, Ill., Apr. 22, 1953; d. Cordell Albert Knepper and Erna Rose (Studnicka) Knepper; m. Michael Lee Stasko, Nov. 19, 1988; stepchildren: Julie Stasko, Elliott Stasko; m. William Frederick Thien, Mar. 12, 1971 (div.); 1 child, Kyle Thien. Associates of Arch., Belleville Area Coll., 1982, Associates of Applied Sci., 1988; BSc cum laude, Greenville Coll., 1998. Civil engr. tech. St. Clair County Hwy. Dept., Belleville, Ill., 1982—; part-time real estate agent Better Homes & Gardens /Strano, Belleville, Ill., 1993—94. Census enumerator U.S. Dept. Commerce, Belleville, 2000—01; co-chmn. Operation Bag-It, Belleville, 1998—2002; owner, designer Bagapalooza Purse Co., 2004—. Exhibitions include Not a Creature was Stirring, 1996 (Best of Show, 1996), Nuts Anyone?, 1997 (Merchant's award, 1997), Frosty the Gingerbread Snowman, 1998 (Downtown Merchant's award, 1998), Crayola Factory, 2002 (first place profl. divsn.), Mr. G. Shops Downtown Belleville, 2000 (Best of Show, 2000). Precinct committeewoman Dem. Party, Belleville, 1978—91; sec. Belleville Dem. Orgn., Belleville, 1979—91; mayoral appointment/mem. Belleville Re-develop. Com., Belleville, 1982—84; member St. Clair County Hist. Soc., Belleville, 2000—02; ch. sch. bd. mem., tchr. Christ United Ch. of Christ, Belleville, 1987—91. Recipient Ill. Gov.'s Hometown award, State of Ill., 1999. Avocations: gardening, remodeling, travel. Office: St Clair County Hwy Dept 1415 N Belt W Belleville IL 62226

THIER, SAMUEL OSIAH, physician, educator; b. Bklyn., June 23, 1937; s. Sidney and May Henrietta Thier; m. Paula Dell Finkelstein, June 28, 1958; children: Audrey Lauren, Stephanie Ellen, Sara Leslie. Student, Cornell U., 1953—56; MD, SUNY, Syracuse, 1960, DSc (hon.), 1987, Tufts U., 1988, George Washington U., 1988, Mt. Sinai Sch. Med., 1989, Hahnemann U., 1989; DSc (hon.), U. Pa., 1994, Dartmouth Coll., 1996; LHD (hon.), Rush U., 1988, Va. Commonwealth U., 1992, Med. Coll. Pa., 1992; LHD (hon.), Brandeis U., 1994. Diplomate Am. Bd. Internal Medicine. Intern Mass. Gen. Hosp., Boston, 1960—61, asst. resident, 1961—62, sr. resident, 1964—65, clin. and research fellow, 1965, chief resident, 1966; clin. asso. Nat. Inst. Arthritis and Metabolic Diseases, 1962—64; from instr. to asst. prof. medicine Harvard U. Med. Sch., 1967—69; prof. medicine, health care policy Harvard Med. Sch., 1994—; asst. in medicine, chief renal unit Mass. Gen. Hosp., Boston, 1967—69; asso. prof., then prof. medicine U. Pa. Med. Sch., 1969—72, vice chmn. dept., 1971—74; assoc. dir. med. svcs. Hosp. U. Pa., 1969—71; David Paige Smith prof. medicine Yale U. Sch. Medicine, 1978—81, Sterling prof. medicine, 1981—85, chmn. dept., 1975—85; pres. Inst. Medicine NAS, Washington, 1985—91; pres., Univ. prof. Brandeis U., Waltham, Mass., 1991—94; pres. Mass. Gen. Hosp., Boston, 1994—97, Ptnrs. HealthCare Sys., Inc., Boston, 1994—96, 1997—2002, CEO, 1996—2002. Chief medicine Yale-New Haven Hosp., 1975—85, trustee, 1978—85; bd. dirs. Conn. Hospice, Inc., 1976—82; dir. Am. Bd. Internal Medicine, 1977—85, exec. com., 1981—85, chmn., 1984—85. Mem. editl. bd.: New Eng. Jour. Medicine, 1978—81; contbr. articles to med. jours. Mem. adv. com. to the dir. NIH, 1980—85. With USPHS, 1962—64. Recipient Christian R. and Mary F. Lindback Found. Disting. Tchg. award, 1971. Mem.: ACP (bd. regents 1982—85), Interurban Clin. Club, Assn. Am. Physicians, Assn. Profs. Medicine, Internat. Soc. Nephrology, Am. Physiol. Soc., Am. Soc. Nephrology, Am. Fedn. Clin. Rsch. (pres. 1976—77), John Morgan Soc., Assn. Am. Med. Colls. (adminstrv. bd. coun. acad. socs.), Alpha Omega Alpha. Home: 99-20 Florence St # 8 Chestnut Hill MA 02467-1927

THIEROLF, RICHARD BURTON, JR., lawyer; b. Medford, Oreg., Oct. 27, 1948; s. Richard Burton Sr. and Helen Dorothy (Rivolta) T. BA, Columbia U., NYC, 1970; JD, U. Oreg., 1976. Bar: Oreg. 1976, U.S. Dist. Ct. Oreg. 1976, U.S. Ct. Appeals (9th cir.) 1977, U.S. Dist. Ct. (no. dist.) Calif. 1980, U.S. Supreme Ct. 1993, U.S. Ct. Fed. Claims 1993. Staff atty. Orgn. of the Forgotten Am., Inc., Klamath Falls, Oreg., 1976-77, exec. dir., 1977-79; ptnr. Jacobson, Thierolf & Dickey, P.C., Medford, 1980—. Author: Timetable for Litigation Matters, 2004. Mem. City of Medford Planning Commn., 1990-92; mem. Jackson County Planning Commn., 2001—; mem. Medford Sch. Dist. 549-C Budget Com., 1991-92, chmn., 1991. Mem. ABA, Fed. Bar Assn., Oreg. State Bar (local profl. responsibility com. 1987-89, mem. fed. practice and procedure com. 1994-97, sec. 1995-97, jud. adminstrn. com. 1998-2001, low income legal svcs. com. 1990-93, house of dels. 1999), Jackson County Bar Assn. (sec. 1988), So. Oreg. Estate Planning Coun. (bd. dirs.2001-06, pres. 2005). Episcopalian. Avocation: violin. Home: 234 Ridge Rd Ashland OR 97520-2829 Office: Jacobson Thierolf & Dickey PC Two N Oakdale Ave Medford OR 97501 Business E-Mail: dthierolf@jtdlegal.com.

THIESSEN, DELBERT DUANE, psychologist; b. Julesberg, Colo., Aug. 13, 1932; s. David and Eva Peters (Wetherby) T.; children: Trevor, Theron, Kendell Courtney. BA in Psychology with distinction, San Jose State Coll., Calif., 1958; PhD, U. Calif., Berkeley, 1963. Extension instr. U. Calif., La Jolla, fall 1964; asst. sect. med. psychology, divsn. psychiatry and neurology Scripps Clinic and Research Found., La Jolla, 1962-65; faculty U. Tex., Austin, 1965-2000, prof. psychology, 1971-2000, prof. emeritus Austin, 2000—. Rsch. cons. NIMH. Author: Gene Organization and Behavior, 1972, The Evolution and Biochemistry of Aggression, 1976, Bitter-Sweet Destiny: The Stormy Evolution of Human Behavior, 1996, Universal Desires and Fears: The Deep History of Sociobiology, 1997, Survival of the Fittest: The Darwinian Diet and Exercise Program, 1998, Night of the Dagger: A Historical Voodoo Novel, 2005; contbr. articles and chpts. to books. With AUS, 1952-54, Korea. Fellow USPHS, 1960-61; recipient Career Devel. award NIMH, 1967-72, grantee, 1967-78; grantee Russel Sage Found., NSF, U. Tex. Rsch. Inst. Fellow AAAS, APA; mem. Alumni Assn. Roscoe B. Jackson Meml. Lab., Am. Genetic Assn., Psychonomic Soc., Animal Behavior Soc., Southwestern Psychol. Assn., Behavior Genetics Assn., Sigma Xi, Phi Kappa Phi, Psi Chi. Business E-Mail: wolf@delthiessen.com.

THIGPEN, ALTON HILL, transportation executive; b. Kinston, NC, Feb. 3, 1927; s. Kirby Alton and Alice (Hill) T.; m. Rebecca Ann Braswell, May 16, 1953; children: David Alton, Jennifer Ann, Steven Roy. BS in Indsl. Engring., N.C. State U., 1950. With Assoc. Transport, Inc., Burlington, NC, 1950-71, engr., 1950-57, asst. terminal mgr. Phila., 1957-58, terminal mgr. Knoxville, Tenn., 1959, regional mgr. Valley region, 1960-62, South region, 1962-68, v.p.,dir. So. divsn., 1968-71; v.p. R.S. Braswell Co. Inc., Kannapolis, NC, 1971-80, pres., 1980—, Hartford Motor Inn Inc., North Myrtle Beach, SC, 1982—, A.T. Developers, Inc., North Myrtle Beach, 1983-97. Pres. Cherokee 2 Inc., Shelby, N.C., 1986-95, bd. dirs.; bd. dirs. Wachovia Bank, Earl Ownsby Studios Inc., Shelby. Bd. regents Berkshire Christian Coll., Lenox, Mass., 1975—; mem. adv. bd. Salvation Army, chmn. adv. bd., 1997-99. Served with USNR, 1945-46. Mem. Motor Carriers Va. (pres. 1967-68), N.C. Motor Carriers Assn. (dir. 1968-), Masons (32d degree), Lions, Sigma Chi, Tau Beta Pi. Mem. Advent Christian Ch. Home: 5395 Mooresville Rd Kannapolis NC 28081-8726 Office: PO Box 1197 Kannapolis NC 28082-1197 Office Phone: 704-933-2269.

THIGPEN, JAMES TATE, oncologist, educator; b. Columbia, Miss., June 6, 1944; m. Louisa Berdie Kessler, June 14, 1969; children: Monroe Tate, James Howard, Samuel Calvin, Richard Allen, David Albert. BS, U. Miss., 1964, MD, 1969. Intern Strong Meml. Hosp., U. Rochester, NYC, 1969-70; resident U. Miss. Sch. Medicine, 1970-71, prof., dir. divsn. med. oncology dept. internal medicine, 1973—. Nat. med. del. from Miss. Am. Cancer Soc., 1983-85, nat. pub. issues com., 1983-85; cancer clin. investigations rev. com. Nat. Cancer Inst., 1990-95, chmn., 1993-95. Nat. bd. govs. ARC, 1981-87. Fellow divsn. hematology/oncology dept. medicine, 1971-73. Fellow ACP; mem. AMA, Miss. Med. Assn., Ctrl. Med. Soc., Jackson Acad. Medicine, Miss. Acad. Scis., SW Oncology Group, Gynecologic Oncology Group (group vice chmn. sci. 1988—), Am. Fedn. Clin. Rsch., Am. Assn. Cancer Edn., Am. Soc. Clin. Oncology, Am. Assn. cancer Rsch., Am. Soc. Hematology, Soc. Gynecologic Oncologists, Soc. Assn. Oncology (pres. 1988-90), Am. Radium Soc., Optimists (internat. v.p. 1983-84, internat. pres. 1990-91). Baptist. (deacon 1978—, Sunday sch. tchr. 1979-85). Home: 3601 Kings Hwy Jackson MS 39216-3322 Office: Miss Oncology Assocs 2500 N State St Jackson MS 39216-4500 Office Phone: 601-984-5590. Personal E-mail: jtthigpen@att.net.

THIGPEN, RICHARD ELTON, JR., retired lawyer; b. Washington, Dec. 29, 1930; s. Richard Elton and Dorathy (Dotger) Thigpen; m. Nancy H. Shand, Dec. 15, 1951; children: Susan B., Richard M. AB, Duke U., 1951; LLB, U. N.C., 1956. Bar: NC 1956, U.S. Ct. Appeals (4th cir.) 1960, U.S. Ct. Appeals (5th cir.) 1960, U.S. Ct. Appeals (10th cir.) 1974, U.S. Tax Ct. 1958, U.S. Ct. Claims 1978, U.S. Supreme Ct. 2003. Lawyer FTC, Washington, 1956-58, Thigpen & Hines, Charlotte, NC, 1958-84, Moore & Van Allen, Charlotte, 1984-88, Poyner & Spruill, Charlotte, 1988-93; gen. counsel Richardson Sports, 1994-98; ret. Bd. dirs. OrthoCarolina Rsch. Inst., 2001—, Charlotte-Mecklenburg YMCA, 1964—88, Heineman Med. Rsch. Ctr., Charlotte, 1970—, Charlotte C. of C., 1982—85. Lt. USNR, 1951—53. Fellow: Am. Coll. Tax Counsel (regent 1989—95, vice chmn. 1992, chmn. 1993—94); mem.: ABA, Sports Lawyers Assn. (bd. dirs. 1995—2007, pres. 2003—05, dir. emeritus 2007—), N.C. Bar Assn. (chmn. tax sect. 1976—80, pres. 1988—89), N.C. State Bar. Avocations: golf, travel. Office: 1100 Kenilworth Ave Ste 200 Charlotte NC 28204-2943 Office Phone: 704-332-8000. Personal E-mail: thigpenhouse@carolina.rr.com.

THIGPEN, STEPHEN P., horticulture products company executive; b. 1956; BS in Plant and Soil summa cum laude, U. Mass.; PhD in Plant Physiology, U. Calif., Davis. Joined Weyerhauser Co., 1981, gen. mgr. Vacaville nursery, 1985; pres., CEO Hines Horticulture, Inc., Irvine, Calif., 1995—, chmn. bd., 2000—. Bd. dirs. Coun. for a Green Environment. Office: Hines Horticulture Inc 12621 Jeffrey Rd Irvine CA 92620 Office Fax: 949-786-0968.

THILL, LINDA SUSAN, secondary school educator; b. Waukegan, Ill., Sept. 25, 1950; d. John Herbert Roos and Dorothy A. Hartwick; m. Keith Ronald Thill, June 28, 1975. BS in Music Edn. with distinction, U. Minn., 1972; MA in Music Edn., U. St. Thomas, 1996. Music specialist Moundsview Schs., New Brighton, Minn., 1972—75, Howard-Suamico Schs., Green Bay, Wis., 1976—89, Einstein Jr. High, Appleton, Wis., 1989—97, Ferber Elem., Appleton, 1990—2004; choral dir. East H.S., Appleton, 2004—. Handbell choir dir. Pilgrim Congl., Green Bay, 1985—2006; artistic dir. Green Bay Girl Choir, 1999—. Big sister Big Bro./Big Sister, Mpls., 1971—72. Tech. grantee, Mielke Found., 1992. Mem.: Am. Choral Dirs. Assn., Brown County Civic Music (exec. bd. 1988—2005, v.p. campaign 1990—2002, talent com. 1990—2005). Avocations: travel, decorating, collecting antique glass and ornaments. Home: 422 Silver Spring Dr Green Bay WI 54303 Office: Green Bay Girl Choir 1678 E Mason St Green Bay WI 54302

THIM, FRANK, physicist, astronomer; b. Immenhausen, Germany, Aug. 5, 1963; s. Josef and Franziska Thim; life ptnr. Christa Heckelmann; 1 child, Wega Heckelmann. MSc in Physics, U. Freiburg, Germany, 1994; Dr., U. Basel, Switzerland, 2001. Customer engr. Applied Materials, Munich, 1995; rsch. assoc. U. Basel, 1995—2001, Nat. Optical Astronomy Obs., Tucson, 2001—04; physicist Software Co., Paderborn, Germany, 2004—. Played in concerts, various cities including Berlin, Munich, Heidelberg, Kassel, Germany; played with bands Paranoid, Paran, others. Grantee, European So. Obs., 2001—02. Achievements include research in distances to spiral galaxies; magnetic structure of solar pores; discovery of new variable stars. Avocations: music, sports, science, reading, travel. Home: Querweg 65 Paderborn 33098 Germany Office: Brandenburg GmbH Technologiepark 19 Paderborn 33100 Germany Home Phone: 0049-5251-8788893; Office Phone: 0049-5251-681644. Personal E-mail: fthim@web.de. E-mail: thim@brandenburg-gmbh.de.

THIMMIG, DIANA MARIE, lawyer; b. Germany, May 5, 1959; BA cum laude, John Carroll U., 1980; JD, Cleve. State U., 1982. Bar: Ohio 1983, U.S. Dist. Ct. (no. dist.) Ohio 1983, U.S. Ct. Appeals (6th cir.) 1983, U.S. Supreme Ct. 1983, U.S. Ct. Appeals (3d cir. 1996); cert. Am. Bankruptcy Bd. for Consumer and Bus. Bankruptcy. Ptnr. Roetzel & Andress, Cleve. Contbr. articles to profl. jours. Trustee Geauga United Way Svcs. Coun., 1992-96, Altenheim, 1992-97, Internat. Svcs. Ctr., 1998-04; trustee Cuyahoga County Bar Assn., 1995-05, pres., 2005-06; trustee Legal Aid Soc., 1998-2006, pres., 2003-05. Named Hon. Consul, Germany, 1988—. Mem. Women's City Club Cleve. (pres. 1995-97). Office: Roetzel & Andress 1375 East Ninth St One Cleveland Ctr Ninth Floor Cleveland OH 44114 Office Phone: 216-696-7078. Business E-Mail: dthimmig@ralaw.com.

THIMOTHEOSE, KADAKAMPALLIL GEORGE, psychologist; b. Karipuza, India, Feb. 11, 1938; came to the U.S., 1976; s. K.G. and Mariamma Varghese; m. Mariamma Thimotheose, May 20, 1968 (div.); children: Geebee, Sonia T. Andrews. MA in Psychology, ME.D 1st class & rank, Kerala U., India, 1967, B in Edn., 1960, MA in Sociology, 1969, MA in History, 1975, PhD in Psychology, 1975; D Therapeutic Philosophy (hon.), World U., 1989. Lic. psychologist, marriage and family therapist, Mich.; diplomate Am. Bd. Med. Psychotherapists, Am. Bd. Psychotherapy, Am. Bd. Sexology, Am. Bd. Forensic Examiners, Am. Bd. Forensic Medicine, Am. Bd. Psychol. Specialities. Lectr., head dept. ednl. psychology S.N. Tchrs. Coll., Trivandrum, India; clin./adminstrv. dir. Alexandrine House, Inc., Detroit, 1976-81; chief exec. officer Cen. Therapeutic Svcs., Inc., Southfield, Mich., 1981—. Adv. bd. Trivandrum Med. Coll. Hosps., 1969-75; edn. faculty mem. U. Calicut, Kerala, India, 1969-75; v.p. forum ednl. rsch. and studies Kerala U., 1969-73. Author: Educational Psychology for B.Ed. Students, 1970; editor Kerala U. Jour. Edn., 1969-73. Fellow Am. Bd. Med. Psychotherapists, Am. Acad. Clin. Sexologists. Am. Coll. Forensic Examiners, Am. Coll. Advanced Practice Psychologists; mem. APA, Am. Coll. Sexologists (sexologist), Am. Bd. Sexology (clin. supr.), Am. Acad. Experts in Traumatic Stress, World U. Round Table (hon. cultural doctorate in therapeutic philosophy), diplomate Am. Bd. Psychological Specialities, Am. Acad. Experts Traumatic Stress. Republican. Avocations: photography, travel, reading, sightseeing. Home: 3048 Brewster West Bloomfield MI 48322-2471 Office: Cen Therapeutic Svcs Inc 17600 W 8 Mile Rd Ste 7 Southfield MI 48075-4316 Home Phone: 248-737-2846; Office Phone: 248-559-4340. E-mail: drtimch@yahoo.com.

THIRLBY, RICHARD COLLER, surgeon; b. Traverse City, Mich., Aug. 30, 1952; s. Richard Leeson Thirlby; m. Patricia Rosso, July 17, 1976; children: Marjorie Rose, David Ryan. BA, Dartmouth U., Hanover, NH, 1974; MD, U. Mich., Ann Arbor, 1978. Contbr. articles to profl. jours. Mem.: ACS (pres. Wash. State chpt. 2003—04), Am. Bd. Surgery (bd. dirs. 2006—), Western Surg. Assn. (pres. 2005—06). Office: Virginia Mason Med Ctr 1100 9th Ave Mailstop C6-GSUR Seattle WA 98111 Office Phone: 206-223-6636.

THIRSK, ROBERT BRENT, astronaut; b. New Westminster, Brit. Columbia, Canada, Aug. 17, 1953; m. Brenda Biasutti; 3 children. BSc in Mech. Engring., U. Calgary, 1976; MSc in Mech. Engring., MIT, 1978; MD, McGill U., 1982; MBA, MIT, 1998. Resident Queen Elizabeth Hosp., Montreal, Canada, 1982—83; astronaut Can. Astronaut Program, 1984—; sabbatical yr. Victoria, B.C., Canada, 1994—95; chief astronaut Can. Space Agy., 1993—94; astronaut NASA, Houston, 1998—. Dir. Can. Found. Internat. Space U., 1992—; crew comdr. CAPSULS mission, 1994; astronaut Space Shuttle mission STS-78, 1996; crew comdr. NEEMO 7 undersea mission, 2004; backup astronaut STS-41G space shuttle mission, 1984, Soyuz 10 S taxi mission, 2005. Recipient Disting. Alumni award, U.

Calgary, 1985. Mem.: Coll. Physicians and Surgeons B.C., Coll. Physicians & Surgeons Ontario, Aerospace Med. Assn., Can. Aeronautics & Space Inst., Can. Coll. Family Physicians, Assn. Profl. Engrs. Ontario (Gold Medal award 1997). Avocations: hockey, squash, playing the piano. Office: Astronaut Office CB NASA Johnson Space Center Houston TX 77058

THIRY, KENT J., health products executive; BA in Polit. Sci., Stanford U., 1978; MBA with honors, Harvard U., 1983. Sr. cons. Andersen Consulting, 1978-81; ptnr., v.p. Bain & Co., 1983—91; pres., COO Vivra, Inc., San Francisco, 1991-92, pres., CEO, 1992-97; chmn., CEO Vivra Holdings Inc., 1997—99, Da Vita Inc., El Segundo, Calif., 1999—. Dir. Oxford Health Plans, 1998—2004, chmn., 2002—04. Bd. dirs. Vol. Ctr. San Mateo County. Mem. Phi Beta Kappa. Office: 601 Hawaii St El Segundo CA 90245-4814 *

THISTED, RONALD AARON, statistician, educator, consultant; b. LA, Mar. 2, 1951; s. Dale Owen and Barbara Jean (Walker) T.; m. Linda Jeane Soder, Dec. 30, 1972; 1 child, Walker. BA, Pomona Coll., 1972; PhD, Stanford U., 1977. Asst. prof. statistics U. Chgo., 1976-82, assoc. prof. statistics, 1982-92, assoc. prof. anesthesia and critical care, 1989-92, prof. stats. and anesthesia and critical care, 1992—, prof. health studies, 1996—, chmn. health studies, 1999—. Co-dir. Clin. Rsch. Training Program, 1999—. Author: Elements of Statistical Computing, 1988; contbr. more than 90 articles to profl. jours. Fellow AAAS, Am. Statis. Assn.; mem. Assn. for Computing Machinery, Inst. for Math. Stats. Office: U Chgo MC 2007 5841 S Maryland Ave Chicago IL 60637-1463 Home Phone: 773-947-9243; Office Phone: 773-834-1242.

THISTLETHWAITE, DAVID RICHARD, architect; b. Burlington, Iowa, Aug. 24, 1947; s. Robert and Nona (Binder) T.; m. Carol Anne Armstrong, Aug. 22, 1970. BArch, Iowa State U., 1971. Registered arch., Calif., 1979, Minn., 1975; registered Nat. Coun. Archtl. Registration Bds., 1978; cert. Health Care arch., Am. Coll. Healthcare Archs., 2000. Designer Morrison Architects, St. Paul, 1971-73, Times Architects, Mpls., 1973-74; project architect Bentz/Thompson Assocs., Mpls., 1974-77; project mgr. Setter Leach Lindstrom, Mpls., 1977-78; project architect Wurster Bernardi Emmons, San Francisco, 1978-79, Strotz & Assocs., Tiburon, Calif., 1979-81, Hood Miller Assoc., San Francisco, 1981-84; prin., ptnr. R S T Architects, San Francisco, 1984-88; prin. Thistlethwaite Archtl. Group, San Francisco, 1988—2007; vice prin. HGA Archs. & Engrs., Inc., 2007—. Contbr. articles to profl. jours. Mem. AIA (nat. profl. devel. com. 1983-86, treas. San Francisco chpt. 1985-86, chmn. Calif. coun. health facilities com. 1994-96, chmn. design com. Acad. Architecture for Health, 1994-96, Calif. coun. ins. bd. trustees 1988-2002, Calif. coun. legis. com. 1996-98) Am. Coll. Healthcare Archs. (mem. pub. rels. com. 2004-05), Am. Soc. Healthcare Engring., Design Profls. Safety Assn. (bd. dirs.). Home Phone: 415-778-0600.

THOM, RICHARD DAVID, retired electronics executive; b. St. Louis, Oct. 4, 1944; s. Reginald James and Vlasta (Koukl) T.; m. Linda Marie Hunt, Sept. 9, 1967; children: Elizabeth Marie, Robert James. BS in Physics, U. Mo., Rolla, 1967; MSEE, UCLA, 1971. Co-op engr. McDonnell Aircraft Corp., St. Louis, 1962-67; head advanced tech. group IR systems dept., aerospace group Hughes Aircraft Co., Culver City, Calif., 1967-72; mem. tech. staff Santa Barbara Rsch. Ctr., Hughes Aircraft Co., Goleta, Calif., 1972-76, asst. mgr. R&D Lab., 1976-80, mgr. advanced applications, 1980-83, chief engr., 1984-86, chief scientist, 1986-90, dir. tech., 1990-95; tech. program exec. Hughes Aircraft Co., Goleta, Calif., 1995-98; asst. mgr. Raytheon Santa Barbara Rsch. Ctr., Goleta, Calif., 1998-99; ret. Contbr. articles to profl. jours.; patentee in field. Recipient Hughes Group Patent award for pioneering contbns. in infrared detector tech., 1990. Mem. IEEE, Tau Beta Pi, Sigma Pi Sigma, Delta Sigma Phi. Republican. Avocations: freelance travel writing and photography, specializing in railway travel around the world. Home: 38 Fawn Run Pl PO Box 326 Coupeville WA 98239-0326 Home Phone: 360-678-1444. Personal E-mail: richthommail@aol.com.

THOMA, RICHARD WILLIAM, chemical safety and waste management consultant; b. Milw., Dec. 7, 1921; s. Joseph Donath and Margaret Mary (Murphy) T.; m. Ida Mary Scharfschwerdt, Mar. 15, 1952; children: Adele, Richard W., Joseph O., John C. AA, U. Chgo., 1941; BS, U. Wis., Madison, 1947, MS in Biochemistry, 1949, PhD, 1951. R&D fermentation E.R. Squibb & Sons, Inc., New Brunswick, NJ, 1951-82; dir. process devel. New Brunswick Sci. Co., Inc., Edison, 1982-84, cons., 1984—. Safety officer Harbor br. Oceanographic Inst. St. Lucie County, Fla., 1988—96. Contbr. articles to profl. jours.; patentee microbiol. transformation of steroids. Commr. Somerset County Bd. Elections, 1981-84; mem. Bridgewater Town Coun., 1975-81, Environ. Commn., 1974-75, Sewerage Authority, 1975-76, Police Commn., 1977-81; chmn. Birdgewater Dem. Mcpl. Com., 1980-87; alderman St. Lucie Village, 1996-98. With AUS, 1942-46. Mem. VFW, Am. Chem. Soc., Am. Soc. Microbiology, Am. Acad. Microbiology, Phi Beta Kappa, Sigma Xi, Phi Lambda Upsilon. Home and Office: 3772 Outrigger Ct Fort Pierce FL 34946-1911 E-mail: rthoma3772@aol.com.

THOMAN, G. RICHARD, corporate financial executive; b. Tuscaloosa, Ala., June 25, 1944; s. Richard S. and Evelyn (Zumwalt) Thoman; m. Wenke Helina Brier, Aug. 25, 1966 (div. Dec. 1987); children: Camille, Alexis; m. Lynn Susan Bendheim, Sept. 16, 1989; children: Kylie, Max, Amy, Eric. BA with honors, McGill U., 1966; MA, Grad. Inst. Internat. Studies, Geneva, 1968; MA in Internat. Econs., Tufts U., 1967, MA in Law and Diplomacy, 1969, PhD in Internat. Econs., 1971. Exec. trainee Citicorp, NYC, 1968-69; sr. fin. analyst Exxon Corp., NYC, 1970-72; sr. assoc. McKinsey and Co., NYC and Paris, 1972-79; exec. v.p., CFO Am. Express Travel Related Svcs., NYC, 1979-85, pres., Travel Related Svcs. Internat., 1985-89, chmn., CEO, 1989-92; pres., CEO Nabisco Internat. RJR Nabisco, Inc., NYC, 1992-94; sr. v.p., group exec. IBM Corp., Somers, NY, 1994-95, sr. v.p., CFO Armonk, NY, 1995-97; pres., COO Xerox Corp., 1997-99, pres., CEO, 1999-2000, also bd. dirs.; pvt. investor; sr. advisor Evercore Ptnrs., NYC, 2001—02; mng. ptnr. Corporate Perspectives, NYC, 2002—; adj. prof. Columbia U., 2003—; vis. prof. Fletcher Sch., 2005—. Bd. dirs. Union Bancaire Privee, Geneva; mem. US adv. bd. INSEAD; mem. adv. bd. Mid Oceanic Capital Ptnrs. Bd. dirs. Americas Soc., NYC, 1990—, French-Am. Found.; bd. advisors Fletcher Sch. Law and Diplomacy, Tufts U., Medford, Mass., 1990—; chmn. Internat. Mgmt. Coun., Fletcher Sch. Law and Diplomacy, Tufts U., Mass.; mem. adv. bd. Sch. Mgmt. McGill U., Montreal, Bus. Coun.; US chair TransAtlantic Bus. Dialogue. Recipient Legion of Honors, Govt. of France, 1992. Mem.: Trilateral Commn., Coun. on Fgn. Rels., River Club, Links Club. Avocations: tennis, reading, jogging, travel. Office: Corp Perspectives 126 E 56th St Fl 9 New York NY 10022 Home Phone: 203-661-9505; Office Phone: 212-813-0323.

THOMAN, HENRY NIXON, lawyer; b. Cin., May 5, 1957; s. Richard B. and Barbara (Lutz) Thoman; m. Anne Davies, May 25, 2002; children: Victoria E., Nicholas B. BA, Duke U., 1979; JD, U. Chgo., 1982. Bar: Ohio 1982, U.S. Dist. Ct. (so. dist.) Ohio, 1982. With Taft, Stettinius & Hollister, Cin., 1982-88; sr. atty. John Morrell & Co., Cin., 1988-90; sr. counsel Chiquita Brands Internat. Inc., Cin., 1990-91, corp. planner, 1991-92; sr. dir. CTP ops. Chiquita Brands, Inc., Cin., 1993-94, chief adminstrv. officer Armuelles divsn., 1994-95; corp. counsel The Loewen Group, Covington, Ky., 1995-97; asst. chief counsel, asst. v.p. The Midland Co., Amelia, Ohio, 1997-99; v.p. orgnl. devel. Kendle Internat. Inc., 1999-2000, v.p. complementary ops., 2000—02; pvt. atty., 2002—05; exec. dir. Madisonville Edn. and Assistance Ctr., 2004—05; dir. acquisitions, corp. counsel Unifund CCR Ptnrs., 2004—. Mem. counselors com. U.S. Swimming, Colo., 1983-89; bd. dirs. Friends of Cin. Parks, 1990-93, 96-98, Starshine Children's Hospice, 1996-99, Cin. Aquatic Club, 1997-2002, Kids Helping Kids, 2000-2001, Summerbridge, Cin., 2006—, Mariemont Aquatic Club, v.p., 1992-93; pres. Club Atletico Y Socialde Chiriqui, 1994-95. Mem. ABA, Ohio State Bar, Cin. Bar Assn. E-mail: thoman.henry@fuse.net.

THOMAN, MARK EDWARD, pediatrician; b. Chgo., Feb. 15, 1936; s. John Charles and Tasula Mark (Petrakis) T.; m. Theresa Thompson, 1984; children: Marlisa Rae, Susan Kay, Edward Kim, Nancy Lynn, Janet Lea, David Mark. AA, Graceland Coll., 1956; BA, U. Mo., 1958, MD, 1962. Diplomate Am. Bd. Pediat., Am. Coll. Toxicology (examiner), 1975-90. Intern U. Mo. at Columbia, 1962—63; resident in pediat. Blank Meml. Children's Hosp., Des Moines, 1963—65; cons. in toxicology USPHS, Washington, 1965—66; chief dept. pediat. Shiprock (N.Mex.) Navajo Indian Hosp., 1966—67; dir. N.D. Poison Info. Ctr.; also practice medicine specializing in pediat. Quain & Ramstad Clinic, Bismarck, ND, 1967—69; dir. Iowa Poison Info. Ctr., Des Moines, 1969—99; mem. pediat. exec. com. Broadlawns Med. Ctr., Des Moines, 1969—2000, pres. med. staff, 2000—01. Accident investigator FAA, 1976—2005, sr. aviation examiner, 1977—2000; lectr. aviation seminars, 1977—; mem. faculty Des Moines U., 1969—2005, dir. cystic fibrosis clin., 1973—82; dir. Mid-Iowa Drug Abuse Program, 1972—76; mem. med. adv. bd. La Leche League Internat., 1965—; chief med. officer Broadlawns Med. Ctr., Des Moines, 2000—02; sci. rev. panel Nat. Libr. Medicine, 2003—; med. cons., expert witness Office Hearings and Appeals Social Security Adminstrn., 2003—; cons. in field. Editor-in-chief AACTION, 1975-90; monthly columnist Aviation Medicine Twin and Turbine Mag., 2005-06. Bd. dirs. Polk County Pub. Health Nurses Assn., 1969-77, Des Moines Speech and Hearing Ctr., 1974-79, Ecumenical Coun. Iowa, 1990-99; bd. govs. Mo. U. Sch. Medicine Alumni, 1988—; pres. parish coun. Greek Orthodox Ch., 2007—. With USMCR, 1954-59; lt. comdr. USPHS, 1965-67; capt. USNR, 1988-96, ret. 1996; dir. Dept. Health Svcs. USNR. Recipient N.D. Gov.'s award of merit, 1969, Cystic Fibrosis Rsch. Found. award, 1975, Am. Psychiat. Assn. Thesis award, 1962. Fellow Am. Coll. Med. Toxicology (diplomate 1996), Acad. Clin. Toxicology; mem. AMA (del. 1970-88), APHA, NRA (life), Assn. Am. Physicians & Surgeons (chief of staff, pres. Broadlawns Polk County Med. Ctr. 2000-02), Polk County Med. Soc., Iowa State Med. Assn., Aerospace Med. Assn., Res. Officers Assn., Civil Aviation Med. Assn., Soc. Adolescent Medicine, Inst. Clin. Toxicology, Internat. Soc. Pediat., Am. Acad. Pediat. (chmn. accident prevention com. Iowa chpt. 1975-2000), Cystic Fibrosis Club, Am. Acad. Clin. Toxicology (trustee 1969-90, pres. 1982-84), Am. Assn. Poison Control Ctrs., Am. Coll. Physician Execs., U.S. Naval Inst., Flying Physicians Club, Aircraft Owners and Pilots Assn, Nat. Pilots Assn. (Safe Pilot award). Republican. Greek Orthodox. Home: 5355 Crane Ave E Port Orchard WA 98366 Office Phone: 360-871-2219. Office Fax: 360-871-4436. Personal E-mail: paro1795@aol.com.

THOMAN, ROY EDWARD, political scientist, educator; b. Evansville, Ind., Mar. 11, 1938; s. Joseph Henry and Nell Yates Thoman; m. Judith Ann Schiff, May 20, 1967 (div. Apr. 18, 1985); 1 child, Mark; m. Jan Brister, May 21, 2005. BA magna cum laude, U. Evansville, 1960; MA, Ind. U., 1964; PhD, U. Ky., 1967. Asst. prof. West Tex. A&M U., Canyon, 1968—70, assoc. prof., 1970—76, prof., 1976—. Contbr. articles to profl. jours.; consulting editor World Affairs, 1979—82. Recipient scholarship medal, Pi Gamma Mu, 2000, endowed scholarship in his name, Phi Eta Sigma, 2000; grantee, Tex. Ednl. Assn., 1972—75. Mem.: KC, Am. Polit. Sci. Assn. Republican. Roman Catholic. Office: West Tex A&M U WT Box 725 Canyon TX 79016 Home: 3816 Doris Dr Amarillo TX 79109-5505 Office Phone: 806-352-6140. Business E-Mail: rthoman@mail.wtamu.edu.

THOMAS, ADRIAN WESLEY, research scientist, director, retired science educator; b. Edgefield, SC, June 23, 1939; s. Hasting Adrian and Nancy Azalena (Bridges) T.; m. Martha Elizabeth McAllister, July 12, 1964; children: Wesley Adrian, Andrea Elizabeth. BS in Agrl. Engring., Clemson U., 1962, MS in Agrl. Engring., 1965; PhD, Colo. State U., 1972. Rsch. scientist USDA-Agrl. Rsch. Svc., Tifton, Ga., 1965-69, Fort Collins, Colo., 1969-72, rsch. leader Walkinsville, Ga., 1972-89, lab. dir. Tifton, 1989-98, retired, 1998. Mem. acad. faculty Colo. State U., Ft. Collins, 1969—72; acad. faculty U. Ga., Athens, 1973—, grad. faculty, 1988—2002, adj. prof., 2004—. Contbr. agrl. rsch. articles to profl. jours. With U.S. Army, 1962-63. Mem. Am. Soc. Agrl. Engrs., Am. Soc. Agronomy, Soil and Water Conservation Soc. Am., Soil Sci. Soc. Am., Sigma Xi, Alpha Epsilon, Gamma Sigma Delta, Phi Kappa Phi. Lutheran. Avocations: reading, gardening, yard care, remodeling home, sports. Personal E-mail: awthomas39@hotmail.com.

THOMAS, ALLEN LLOYD, lawyer, private investor; b. Orange, NJ, Sept. 15, 1939; s. Richard Lloyd and Dorothy (Carr) Thomas; m. Virginia Dehnert, June 24, 1961 (div. 1974); children: Sarah Ann, Anne Marjorie; m. Barbara Singer, Mar. 12, 1978 (div. 2001); 1 child, Allen Lloyd. BA, Wesleyan U., 1961; LLB, Yale U., 1964. Bar: N.Y. 1965, U.S. Ct. Appeals (D.C. cir.) 1981; solicitor, Eng. and Wales, 1996. Ptnr. Paul Weiss Rifkind Wharton & Garrison, NYC, 1973—92; resident ptnr. Hong Kong, 1983-87; dir., gen. counsel Gerard Atkins & Co. Ltd., 1992-94; gen. counsel Gen. Atlantic Group Ltd, 1992-94; chmn. Highway Insurance Holdings, PLC, 1996—2002, Forney, Inc., 2005—. Bd. dirs. Gen. Reins. UK Ltd., non-exec. dir., 2006—; gov. English Nat. Ballet Sch.; chmn. Cathy Marston Project; of counsel Egorov Pugensky Afanasiev & Ptnrs., 2006—. Chmn. Urban Bus. Assis. Corp., N.Y.C., 1971-82; chmn. Hong Kong Ballet, 1985-87; co-chmn. Internat. Com., N.Y.C. Ballet, 1986-91; pres. Internat. Salzburg Assn. Am., 1987-92; dir., mem. exec. com., gen. counsel Child Care Action Campaign, 1990-92. Mem. River Club (NY), Boodle's, Hong Kong Club, Hong Kong Jockey Club, Lenox Club. Home: 3 Chester St London SW1X 7BB England E-mail: allenlloydthomas@hotmail.com.

THOMAS, ALYCE M., nutritionist, consultant; d. Joseph A. and Alfreda G. Drummond; m. Lee A. Thomas, Jr. BSc in Home Economics, Mt. St. Vincent U., Nova Scotia, Canada, 1976. Registered dietitian Am. Dietetic Assn., 1980. Coord., nutritionist Passaic Health Dept., NJ, 1980—83; coord. nutrition svcs. Jersey City Family Health Ctr., 1984—89; perinatal nutrition cons. St. Joseph's Regional Med. Ctr., Paterson, NJ, 1989—; social planning nutritionist City Halifax Social Planning Dept., Nova Scotia. Bd. dirs. Perinatal Nutrition Cons., Trenton, 1996—2003; chair Women's Health & Reproductive Nutrition Dietetic Practice Grp., Chgo., 2002—03; mem. Govs. Coun. Prevention Mental Retardation & Devel. Disabilities, Trenton, 2002—; adv. bd. mem. Black Infant Mortality Reduction Ctr., Paramus, NJ, 2006—. Author: (book) American Dietetic Association Guide to Gestational Diabetes; co-author (book) Medical Nutrition Therapy Saves Health Care Dollars; contbr. diabetes profl. resource book, CD-rom, articles to profl. jours. Chair NJ State WIC Adv. Coun., Trenton, 1992—94. Mem.: NJ Nutrition Coalition (assoc.), NJ Dietetic Assn. (assoc.; bd. dirs. 1993—95, ann. meeting co-chair 1994—95), Am. Dietetic Assn. (assoc.; profl. issues del. 2004—). Independent. Avocations: travel, reading. Office: St Joseph's Regional Med Ctr 703 Main St Paterson NJ 07503 Office Fax: 973-754-4074. Business E-Mail: thomasa@sjhmc.org.

THOMAS, ANDREA B., food products executive; B, U. Utah; MBA, Brigham Young U., Provo, Utah. Dir., new product mktg. Pizza Hut, Inc.; v.p., retail mktg. and promotions, Fritos and Tostitos brands Frito-Lay, Inc., v.p., innovation; v.p. global chocolate Hershey Co., 2006—. Named one of 25 Masters of Innovation, BusinessWeek. Office: Hershey Co 100 Crystal A Dr Hershey PA 17033-0810

THOMAS, ANDREW S.W., astronaut; b. Adelaide, South Australia, Dec. 18, 1951; s. Adrian C. and Mary E. Thomas. B with hon. in Mech. Engring. (with First Class Honors), U. Adelaide, South Australia, 1973; PhD in Mech. Engring., U. Adelaide, 1978. Rsch. scientist Lockheed Aero. Sys. Co., Marietta, Ga., 1977—80, principal aerodynamic scientist, 1980—83, head, advanced flight sciences dept., 1983—87, mgr. flight sci. divsn., 1987—89; with Jet Propulsion Lab., Pasadena, Calif., 1989—92, NASA, Houston, 1992—93, astronaut, mission specialist, 1993—. Payload comdr. Endeavour Space Shuttle STS-77, 1996; bd. engr. 2, STS-89, returned with crew of STS-91 Space Shuttle Endeavor, Russian Space Sta. Mir, 1998; with space flight STS-102, 2001; dep. chief astronaut office NASA, 2001—03; mission specialist 3 (MS-3) STS-114 (Discovery) Return to Flight mission during which the crew will test & evaluate new procedures for flight safety & shuttle inspection & repair techniques, 2005. Fellow: Institution of Engrs. Australia (hon.). Achievements include first Australian citizen in space. Avocations: horseback riding, mountain biking, running, wind surfing, playing classical guitar. Office: Astronaut Office CB NASA Johnson Space Ctr Houston TX 77058

THOMAS, ANN FREDA, lawyer; b. South Bend, Ind., Aug. 4, 1951; d. Raymond Dwight and Sara (Silberman) T.; m. Daniel L. Rabinowitz, Aug. 18, 1974; children: Caleb, Samuel. AB, Harvard U., 1973; JD, Yale U., 1976. Bar: NY 1977, US Dist. Ct. (so. dist.) NY 1977, US Tax Ct. 1980, US Supreme Ct. 1982. Assoc. Fried, Frank, Harris, Shriver & Jacobson, NYC, 1976-83, ptnr., 1983-92; fellow Bunting Inst. Radcliffe Coll., Cambridge, Mass., 1992-93; vis. lectr. Law Sch. Yale U., New Haven, spring 1993-fall 94; vis. scholar Wagner Sch. Pub. Svc. NYU, NYC, 1992-94; assoc. prof. N.Y. Law Sch., NYC, 1995; prof. of law, mng dir.(grad. tax prog.) NY Law Sch., NYC. Contbr. articles to profl. jour. Bd. dirs. Jewish Found. for Edn. of Women, NYC, 1980—. Mem. ABA (tax sect.), NY State Bar Assn. (tax sect., exec. com. 1996—, co-chair com. on tax exempt entities), Assn. of Bar NYC (mem. tax com.)., Fellow Bunting Inst. Radcliffe Coll., 1992. Office: NY Law Sch 57 Worth St New York NY 10013 Office Phone: 212-431-2328. Office Fax: 212-343-2039. Business E-Mail: athomas@nyls.edu.

THOMAS, ANN VAN WYNEN, retired law educator; b. The Netherlands, May 27, 1919; arrived in U.S., 1921, naturalized, 1926; d. Cornelius and Cora Jacoba (Daansen) Van Wynen; m. A. J. Thomas, Jr., Sept. 10, 1948. AB with distinction, U. Rochester, NY, 1940; JD, U. Tex., 1943; degree, So. Meth. U., Dallas, 1952. US fgn. svc. officer, Johannesburg, London, The Hague, Netherlands, 1943-47; rsch. atty. Southwestern Legal Found. So. Meth. U. Sch. Law, Dallas, 1952-67, asst. prof. polit. sci., 1968-73, assoc. prof., 1973-76, prof., 1976-85, prof. emeritus, 1985—. Author: Communism versus International Law, 1953, Non-Intervention - The Law and Its Import in the Americas, 1956, OAS: The Organization of American States, 1962, International Legal Aspects of Civil War in Spain, 1936-1939, 1967, Legal Limitations on Chemical and Biological Weapons, 1970, The Concept of Aggression, 1972, An International Rule of Law - Problems and Prospects, 1974, Presidential War Making Power: Constitutional and International Law Aspects, 1981; author: (with A. J. Thomas, Jr.) International Treaties, 1950. Chmn. time capsule com. Grayson County Commn. Tex. Sesquicentennial, 1986—88; co-chmn. Grayson County Commn. Bicentennial US Constn., 1988—93, Grayson County Commn. Millenium, 1997—; co-chmn. com. Grayson County Sesquicentennial, 1994—97. Recipient Am. medal, Nat. DAR, 1992. Mem.: Grayson County Bar Assn., Am. Soc. Internat. Law, Tex. Bar Assn. Home: Spaniel Hall 374 Coffee Cir Pottsboro TX 75076-3164

THOMAS, ANNE MOREAU, former newspaper owner; b. Trenton, NJ, May 23, 1930; d. Daniel Howard and Lillis Dale (Simmonds) Moreau; m. Henry Seely Thomas, Jr., June 14, 1952 (dec. Aug. 1994); children: Catherine, John Martin II, Howard Moreau. BA, Middlebury Coll., 1951; DHL, Rutgers U., 1999; AA (hon.), Raritan Valley C.C. Tchr. North Hunterdon H.S., Annandale, N.J., 1951-52, Hunterdon Adult Sch., Flemington, N.J., 1953-70; home and food editor Hunterdon County Democrat, Flemington, 1954-99, owner, bd. sec., 1985-94, owner, chmn. bd., 1994—2001. Trustee Rutgers U., New Brunswick, N.J., 1985-2005, bd. govs., 1991-2005, chmn. bd. govs., 1995-98, trustee emerita, 2005—; trustee Bloomfield Coll., 2005—, Hunterdon Med. Ctr. Found.; mem. N.J. Commn. Higher Edn., Trenton, 1995-98. Recipient N.J. Food Communicator of Yr. award N.J. Dept. Agr., 1981, Golden award for cmty. svc. Hunterdon County C. of C., 1990, Eagle Leadership award Ctr./Urban cmty. Leadership, 1996, Hunterdon Disting. Citizen award Ctrl. N.J. Coun. Boy Scouts Am., 1999-2000; named Woman of Yr., Hunterdon County YMCA, 1997. Mem. N.J. Press Assn. (bd. dirs. 1977-85, pres. 1984, chmn. 1985), DAR, Copper Hill Country Club, N.J. Mus. Agr. (trustee). Republican. Presbyn. Avocations: restoration of circa 1750 Cape Cod family homestead, gardening, cooking. Home: 38 Pennsylvania Ave Flemington NJ 08822-1222

THOMAS, ARCHIBALD JOHNS, III, lawyer; b. Jacksonville, Fla., Apr. 27, 1952; s. Archibald Johns and Jean (Snodgrass) T.; m. Martha Ann Marconi, Sept. 1, 1973. BA, U. So. Fla., 1973; JD, Stetson U., 1977. Bar: Fla. 1977, U.S. Dist. Ct. (mid. dist.) Fla. 1977, U.S. Ct. Appeals (11th cir.) 1981, U.S. Supreme Ct. 1981, U.S. Claims Ct. 1990; cert. labor and employment law, Fla. Law clk. to U.S. magistrate U.S. Dist. Ct., Tampa, Fla., 1977-78; 1st asst. fed. pub. defender U.S. dist. Ct., Jacksonville, 1978-84; sr. ptnr. Thomas & Skinner, P.A., Jacksonville, 1984-89; pvt. practice Jacksonville, 1990—. Faculty mem. Stetson U. Coll. Law, 1999—; mem. labor and employment law cert. com. Fla. Bar, 2002—. Mem.: ATLA (employment rights sect.), Jacksonville Bar Assn., Fla. Nat. Employment Lawyers Assn. (pres. 2002), Nat. Employment Lawyers Assn. (co-chmn. Fla. chpt. 1992), Fed. Bar Assn., Fla. Bar Assn. (co-chmn. individual rights com. 2001, exec. coun. labor and employment law sect. 2006—, chmn. current legal events com. 2006—). Democrat. Avocation: sailing. Home: 708 Mccollum Cir Neptune Beach FL 32266-3789 Office: Riverplace Tower 1301 Riverplace Blvd Ste 1640 Jacksonville FL 32207 Home Phone: 904-241-0905; Office Phone: 904-396-2322. E-mail: archibald@job-rights.com.

THOMAS, BETTY, director, actress; b. St. Louis, July 24, 1948; BFA, Ohio U., 1969. Former sch. tchr.; co-star Hill St. Blues, from 1981. Joined Second City Workshop, Chgo.; appeared on Second City TV, 1984; appeared in after sch. spl. The Gift of Love, 1985, Prison of Children, 1986. Appeared in The Fun Factory game show, 1976; (TV films) Outside Chance, 1978, Nashville Grab, 1981, When Your Lover Leaves, 1983, The Late Shift, 1996 (Dirs. Guild Am. dramatic spl. award 1996); star TV series Hill Street Blues, 1981-87 (Emmy nominations 1981, 82, 83), (Emmy award, 1985); dir.: (TV) Hooperman, 1987, Doogie Howser, M.D., 1989, Mancuso, FBI, 1989, Shannon's Deal, 1990, Dream On: "For Peter's Sake" (Emmy award, Outstanding Individual Achievement in Directing in a Comedy Series, 1993), 1993, Parenthood, 1990, Sons and Daughters, 1991, On the Air, 1992, My Breast, 1994, Couples, 1994, The Late Shift, 1996, The Loop, 2006-; (films) Troop Beverly Hills, 1989, The Brady Bunch Movie, 1995, Private Parts, 1997, Doctor Dolittle, 1998, 28 Days, 2000, I Spy, 2002, R3, 2003, John Tucker Must Die, 2006; prodr.: Can't Hardly Wait, 1998, Surviving Christmas, 2004; exec. prodr. (films) Charlie's Angels, 2000, Guess Who, 2005, (TV films) Silicon Follies, 2001. Recipient Women in Film Crystal award, 2001.

THOMAS, BEVERLY IRENE, special education educator, counseling administrator, educational diagnostician; b. Del Rio, Tex., Nov. 12, 1939; d. Clyde and Eve Whistler; m. James Thomas, Jan. 28, 1972; children: Kenneth (dec.), Wade, Robert, Darcy, Betty Kay, James III, Debra, Brenda, Michael. BM summa cum laude, Sul Ross State U., 1972, MEd, 1976, MEd in Counseling, 1992, MEd in Mid. Mgmt., 1996. Cert. music, 1972, elem. edn., 1974, music edn., 1976, learning disabilities, 1976, spl. edn. generic, 1976, ednl. diagnosis, 1976, ednl. counseling, 1996, spl. edn. counseling and mid. mgmt., 1995, anger resolution therapist, 1995; cert. correctional justice addictions profl.; lic. chem. dependency counselor, 2006. Tchr. Pecos-Barstow-Toyah Ind. Sch. Dist., 1974—92, 1999—2000; edn. diagnostician West Tex. State Sch., Tex. Youth Commn.; tchr. spl. edn. and enhanced 5th grade Pecos-Barstow-Toyah Ind. Sch. Dist., 1999-2000; youth counselor Tex. Workforce Ctr., Pecos, 2000; substance abuse counselor Reeves County Detention Ctr., 2001—. Gifted-talented coordinator 5th grade, Pecos-Barstow-Toyah Ind. Sch. Dist., 1999-2000. Mem. AAUW, ASCD, NEA, MENSA, Assn. for Children with Learning Disabilities (local sec. 1974), Tex. State Tchrs. Assn. (treas. 1991-94), Tex. Ednl. Diagnosticians Assn., Tex. Profl. Ednl. Diagnosticians, Reeves County Assn. of Children with Learning Disabilities, Nat. Coun. Tchrs. of Maths., Nat. Coun. Tchrs. English, Learning Disabilities Assn., Nat. Coun. for Geog. Edn., Learning Disabilities Assoc., Tex., Coun. for Exceptional Children, Tex. Counseling Assn., Am. Correctional Assn., Alpha Chi, Kappa Delta Pi, Chi Sigma Iota. Personal E-mail: beverlythomas@valornet.com.

THOMAS, BILL (WILLIAM MARSHALL THOMAS), retired congressman; b. Wallace, Idaho, Dec. 6, 1941; s. Virgil and Gertrude Thomas; m. Sharon Lynn Hamilton, Jan. 1968; children: Christopher, Amelia. Student, Santa Anna CC, 1961; BA, San Francisco State U., 1963, MA, 1965. Mem. faculty Bakersfield (Calif.) Coll., 1965-74, prof. Am. govt., 1965-74; mem. Calif. State Assembly, 1974-78, US Congress from 22nd Calif. dist. (formerly 21st), 1979—2007, chmn. oversight com., 1995-2001, chmn. adminstrn. com., 1995—2001, chmn. ways and means com., 2001—07, chmn. joint com. on taxation, 2001, 2003—07; vis. fellow Am. Enterprise Inst., 2007—; sr. adv. fed. govt. rels. section Buchanan Ingersoll & Rooney PC, 2007—. Mem. del. to Soviet Union, by Am. Council Young Polit. Leaders, 1977; chmn. Kern County Republican Central Com., 1972-74; mem. Calif. Rep. Com., 1972-80; del. Republican Party Nat. Conv., 1980, 84, 88; mem. Rep. Leader's Task Force on Health Care Reform. Recipient James Madison award Am. Library Assn. 1993, Legis. Svc. award, Pharm. Care Mgmt. Assn., 2000, Congl. award, Small Bus. Coun. Am., 2001 Republican. Baptist. Office: Buchanan Ingersoll & Rooney PC 1700 K St NW Ste 300 Washington DC 20006 E-mail: bill.thomas@bipc.com. *

THOMAS, BROOKE C., assistant principal; b. Salinas, Calif., Mar. 12, 1970; d. Craig D. and Mary J. Campbell; m. Michael L. Thomas, Jan. 8, 2005; 1 child, Brody Michael. BA in Liberal Studies, Calif. State U., Fresno, 1994; MS in Instrnl. Leadership, Nat. U., Fresno, 1997, MS in Ednl. Counseling, 2001; student in Edn., U. La Verne, Calif., 2001—. Cert. pupil personnel svcs. Calif., 2000, profl. clear administrv. svcs. Calif., 2004. Asst. prin. Riverdale Unified Sch. Dist., Calif., 2002—05, Modesto City Schs., Calif., 2005—. Recipient Calif. Gold Star Adminstr. award, Future Farmers Am., 2000. Mem.: Phi Mu (life). Avocations: water-skiing, football, travel. Home Phone: 209-869-0202; Office Phone: 209-576-4847.

THOMAS, BROOKS, publishing executive, director; b. Phila., Nov. 28, 1931; s. Walter Horstman and Ruth Sterling (Boomer) Thomas; m. Galen Pinckard Clark, Apr. 15, 1969 (div. 1973); m. Kiono Tucciarone, Oct. 7, 2004. BA, Yale U., 1953, LLB, 1956; grad. Advanced Mgmt. Program, Harvard U., 1973. Bar: Pa. 1957, N.Y. 1960. With law firm Winthrop, Stimson, Putnam & Roberts, NYC, 1960—68; sec., gen. counsel Harper & Row, Pubs., Inc., NYC, 1968—69, v.p., gen. counsel, 1969—73, exec. v.p., 1973—79, COO, 1977—81, pres., 1979—87, CEO, 1981—87, chmn. bd., 1986—87. Chmn. bd. dirs. Harper & Row, Ltd., London, 1973—87; bd. dirs. Harper & Row, Pty. Ltd., Australia, Harla S.A. de C.V., Mexico, Harper & Row Pubs. Asia, Pty. Ltd., Singapore. Trustee Outward Bound USA, 1980—, vice chmn., 1983—84, chmn., 1984—87, Nat. Book Awards, 1984—85, bd. dirs., 1985—87, Outward Bound Internat., 1997—2003, Outward Bound Expenditionary Learning, 2000—; pres., bd. dirs. Butterfield House, 1968—72; trustee, bd. dirs. RADG, Inc., 1987—89; bd. dirs. Thomason Island Outward Bound Edn. Ctr., 1987—96, Colo. Outward Bound Sch., 1990—96, bd. govs., 1996—; bd. dirs. Young Audiences, Inc., 1977—, chmn., 1985—, Vail Valley Inst., 1989—; trustee Episcopal Acad., 2000—, sec., 2002—; mem. devel. bd. Yale U., 1985—89, adv. bd. Sch. Orgn. and Mgmt., 1987—96. Lt. (j.g.) USNR, 1956—59. Mem.: ABA, Assn. Am. Pubs. (bd. dirs. 1980—85, chmn. 1983—85), Assn. Bar City of N.Y., Century Assn. (N.Y.C.), Yale U. Alumni Assn. (law sch. rep. 1980—83), Coun. Fgn. Rels., Essex Yacht Club (Conn.), N.Y. Yacht Club (N.Y.C.), Univ. Club (N.Y.C.), Yale Club (N.Y.C.), Merion Cricket Club (Phila.). Home: 5 Tudor City Pl New York NY 10017-6853 also: 141 Saybrook Rd Essex CT 06426-1412

THOMAS, BYRON ANDREW, lawyer; b. Salem, Oreg., Aug. 31, 1947; s. Byron K. and Mary Barbara (Neidig) T. BA, Tex. Tech. U., 1969, JD, 1976. Bar: Tex. 1976, D.C. 1979, U.S. Ct. Appeals (5th cir.) 1978, U.S. Ct. Appeals (d.C. cir.) 1979. Assoc. Butler, Binion, Rice, Cook & Knapp, Houston, 1976-80; pvt. practice Tyler, Tex., 1980-82; exec. v.p. La. Intrastate Gas Corp., Alexandria, 1982-86; v.p., counsel Celeron Corp., Lafayette, La., 1984—85; v.p. Tenngasco Corp., Houston, 1986-87; pvt. practice Houston, 1987—. Mng. editor Tex. Tech. Law Review, 1976. Chmn. Delia Stewart Dance Co., Houston, 1988. Capt. U.S. Army, 1969-73, Korea. Lutheran. Home and Office: 2407 Wroxton Rd Houston TX 77005-1435

THOMAS, CHARLES ALLEN, JR., molecular biologist, educator; b. Dayton, Ohio, July 7, 1927; s. Charles Allen and Margaret Stoddard (Talbott) T.; m. Margaret M. Gay, July 7, 1951; children: Linda Carrick, Stephen Gay. AB, Princeton U., NJ, 1950; PhD, Harvard U., 1954. Rsch. scientist Eli Lilly Co., Indpls., 1954-55; NCR fellow U. Mich., Ann Arbor, 1955-57; prof. biophysics Johns Hopkins U., Balt., 1957-67; prof. biol. chemistry Med. Sch. Harvard U., Boston, 1967-78; chmn. dept. cellular biology Scripps Clinic & Rsch. Found., La Jolla, Calif., 1978-81; pres., dir. Helicon Found., San Diego, 1981—; founder, CEO The Syntro Corp., San Diego, 1981-82; founder, CEO, now dir. of R & D Pantox Corp., San Diego, 1989—. Mem. genetics study sect. NIH, 1968-72; mem. rsch. grants com. Am. Cancer Soc., 1972-76, 79-85. Mem. editl. bd. Virology, 1967-73, Jour. Molecular Biology, 1968-72, BioPhysics Jour., 1965-68, Chromosoma, 1969-79, Analytic Biochemistry, 1970-79, Biochim Biophys. ACTA, 1973-79, Plasmid, 1977—. With USNR, 1945-46. NRC fellow, 1965-66. Mem. AAAS, Am. Acad. Arts and Scis., Am. Fedn. Biol. Chemists, Genetics Soc. Am., Am. Chem. Soc. Achievements include research in genetic and structural organization of chromosomes and development of a practical assessment of the antioxidant defense system by analytical biochemistry. Home: 1640 El Paso Real La Jolla CA 92037-6304 E-mail: cathomas@pantox.com.

THOMAS, CHERRYL T., former federal agency administrator; b. Oct. 31, 1946; BS Biology & Chem., Marquette U.; MS Physiology, U. Illinois, Chicago. Dir., mgmt. services Dept. Aviation, 1983—89; dir., personnel policy & utilization Dept. Water, 1989—92; deputy chief of staff Mayor Richard M. Daley City of Chgo., 1992—94, commr. Dept. Bldgs., 1994-98, chmn. U.S. Railroad Retirement Bd., 1998—2003. Mem., bd. trustees U. Chgo., 2000—. Home: 5020 S Lake Shore Dr Apt 2716N Chicago IL 60615-3220

THOMAS, CHRISTOPHER YANCEY, III, surgeon, educator; b. Kansas City, Mo., Oct. 27, 1923; s. Christopher Yancey and Dorothea Louise (Engel) T.; m. Barbara Ann Barcroft, June 27, 1946; children— Christopher, Gregg, Jeffrey, Anne Student, U. Colo., 1942-44; MD, U. Kans., 1948. Diplomate Am. Bd. Surgery. Intern U. Utah Hosp., Salt Lake City, 1948-49; resident in surgery Cleve. Clinic Found., 1949-52; pvt. practice specializing in surgery Kansas City, Mo., 1954-89. Mem. staff St. Luke's Hosp., chief surgery, 1969-70; mem. staff Children's Mercy Hosp.; clin. prof. surgery U. Mo., Kansas City Med. Sch.; pres. St. Luke's Hosp. Edn. Found., 1977-83, Med. Plaza Corp., 1977-79; pres. Midwest Organ Bank, 1977-82. Editor IMTRAC investment adv. letter, 1978-2000. Served to capt. M.C., U.S. Army, 1952-54 Fellow ACS; mem. AMA, Southwestern Surg. Congress, Central Surg. Assn., Mo. State Med. Soc., Kansas City Surg. Soc. (pres. 1968), Jackson County Med. Soc. (pres. 1971) Clubs: Kansas City Country. Republican. Methodist. Home: 50 Coventry Ct Shawnee Mission KS 66208-5225 Personal E-mail: christhomas5452@sbcglobal.net.

THOMAS, CLARA MCCANDLESS, retired literature educator; b. Strathroy, Ont., Can., May 22, 1919; d. Basil and Mabel (Sullivan) McCandless; m. Morley Keith Thomas, May 23, 1942; children: Stephen, John. BA, U. Western Ont., London, 1941, MA, 1944; PhD, U. Toronto, 1962; DLitt (hon.), York U., 1986, Trent U., 1991; LLD (hon.), Brock U., 1992. Instr. English U. Western Ont., London, 1947-61, U. Toronto, 1958-61; asst. prof. English York U., Toronto, 1961-68, prof., 1969-84, prof. emeritus, Librs. Can. Studies Rsch. fellow, 1984—; acad. adv. panel Social Scis. and Humanities Research Council, 1981-84; mem. Killam Awards Selection Bd., 1978-81; rsch. fellow York U. Librs. Can. Studies, 1984—. Author biography of Anna Jameson, 1967, of Egerton Ryerson, 1969, of Margaret Laurence, 1969, 75, (with John Lennox) of William Arthur Deacon, 1982; Literary criticism (Can.), 1946, 72, 94, Memoir, 1999; mem. editl. bd. Literary History of Can., 1980—, Collected Works of Northrop Frye, 1993—. Recipient Internat. Coun. of Can. Studies prize No. Telecom, 1989; grantee Can. Coun., 1967, 73, Social Sci. and Humanities Rsch. Coun. Can., 1978-80, Clara Thomas Archives and Spl. Collections, York U., 2005. Fellow Royal Soc. Can.; mem. Assn. Can. Univs., Tchrs. English (pres. 1971-72), Assn. Can. and Que. Lit., Bus. and Profl. Women's Club, Assn. for Can. Studies. New Democratic. Office: York U 305 Scott Libr 4700 Keele St North York ON Canada M3J 1P3 Office Phone: 416-736-2100 22374.

THOMAS, CLARENCE, United States supreme court justice; b. Pin Point, Ga., June 23, 1948; s. M.C. Thomas and Leola Anderson (Williams); m. Kathy Grace Ambush, 1971 (div. 1984); 1 child, Jamal Adeen; m. Virginia Lamp, May 30, 1987. Student, Immaculate Conception Sem., 1967—68; BA, Holy Cross Coll., 1971; JD, Yale U., 1974. Bar: Mo. Asst. atty. gen. State of Mo., Jefferson City, 1974—77; legal counsel Monsanto Co., St. Louis, 1977—79; legis. asst. to Senator John C. Danforth US Senate, Washington, 1979—81; asst. sec. for civil rights U.S. Dept. Edn., Washington, 1981—82; chmn. EEOC, Washington, 1982—90; judge U.S. Ct. Appeals (DC cir.), Washington, 1990—91; assoc. justice U.S. Supreme Ct., Washington, 1991—. Mem. bd trustees Holy Cross Coll.; bd. advisors DC Cases. Mem.: Internat. Churchill Soc. Office: US Supreme Court One First St NE Washington DC 20543-0001 *

THOMAS, CLAUDEWELL SIDNEY, psychiatrist, educator; b. NYC, Oct. 5, 1932; s. Humphrey Sidney and Frances Elizabeth (Collins) T.; m. Carolyn Pauline Rozansky, Sept. 6, 1958; children: Jeffrey Evan, Julie-Anne Elizabeth, Jessica Edith. BA, Columbia U., 1952; MD, SUNY, Downstate Med. Ctr., 1956; MPH, Yale U., 1964. Diplomate Nat. Bd. Med. Examiners, Am. Bd. Psychiatry. From instr. to assoc. prof. Yale U., New Haven, 1963-68, dir. Yale tng. program in social community psychiatry, 1967-70; dir. div. mental health service programs NIMH, Washington, 1970-73; chmn. dept. psychiatry UMDNJ, Newark, 1973-83; prof., chmn. dept. psychiatry Drew Med. Sch., 1983—93, chmn. dept. psychiatry, 1983-93; prof. dept. psychiatry UCLA, 1983-94, vice chmn. dept. psychiatry, 1983-93, prof. emeritus dept. psychiatry, 1994—, med. dir. Tokanui Hosp., TeAwamutu, N.Z., 1996. Cons. A.K. Rice Inst., Washington, 1978—80, SAMSA/PHS Cons., 1991—99, L.A. County Homeless Outreach Program, 2001—04; mem. LA County Superior Ct. Psychol. Panel, 1991—97; cons. psychiatrist L.A. County AB2034 Homeless Outreach Program (Skid Row Dual Diagnoses), 2001—04. Author: (with B. Bergen) Issues and Problems in Social Psychiatry, 1966; editor (with R. Bryce LaPorte) Alienation in Contemporary Society, 1976, (with J. Lindenthal) Psychiatry and Mental Health Science Handbook; mem. editl. bd. Adminstrn. Mental Health. Bd. dirs. Bay Area Found., 1987—. Served to capt. USAF, 1959-61. Fellow APHA, Am. Psychoanalytic Assn. (hon.), Am. Psychiat. Assn. (disting. life), NY Acad. Sci., NY Acad. Medicine; mem. Am. Sociol. Assn., Am. Coll. Mental Health Adminstrs., Am. Coll. Psychiatrists (emeritus), Sigma Xi. Avocations: tennis, racquetball, violin, piano. Office: 30676 Palos Verdes Dr E Palos Verdes Peninsula CA 90275-6354 Personal E-mail: cysid32@ucla.edu, cst240@columbia.edu. *Personal philosophy: Integrity sooner or later calls upon courage. If courage is not home integrity goes away.*

THOMAS, CRAIG DAMON, protective services official; b. Nov. 1, 1965; s. Eugene and Mary Thomas; m. Kimberly Ann James (div.); children: Justin, Arayna, Dorian. Student, Wayne County C.C., Detroit, 1981—82, Highland Park C.C., 1982. Police officer Detroit Police Dept., 1987—, patrolman harbor master, 1987—89, spl. ops., 1992—2000, investigator domestic violence, 2000—07. Author: Jahmo & the Giant, 1999. Named Officer of Yr., Detroit Police Dept., 1993; recipient Meritourius award, 1988, 1990, 1993, 1996, Purple Heart, 1992. Mem.: Nat. Poets Soc. Home: 5095 Farmbrook St Detroit MI 48224

THOMAS, DALE E., lawyer; b. New Rochelle, NY, Jan. 25, 1947; AB summa cum laude, Princeton U., 1969; MDiv, Yale Divinity Sch., 1973; JD, Yale U., 1974. Bar: Ill. 1975, US Ct. Appeals (2nd & DC cir.), US Dist. Ct. (no. dist.) Ill. Law clerk U.S. Ct. Appeals 2d cir., 1974-75; ptnr. Sidley Austin, Chgo., 1980—. Mem. ABA, Ill. State Bar Assn., Chgo. Bar Assn., Phi Beta Kappa. Office: Sidley Austin 1 S Dearborn Chicago IL 60603 Office Phone: 312-853-7787. Office Fax: 312-853-7036. Business E-Mail: dthomas@sidley.com.

THOMAS, DANIEL FOLEY, retired diversified financial services company executive; b. Washington, Aug. 24, 1950; s. Richard Kenneth and Margaret (Foley) T.; m. Barbara Jane Clark, June 30, 1973; 1 child, Alison Clark. BS in Acctg., Mt. St. Mary's Coll., 1972. CPA, Va. Auditor Deloitte & Touche, Washington, 1972-74; various fin. positions Comm. Satellite Corp., Washington, 1974-78, asst. treas., 1984-85, treas., 1986-87, contr., 1987-89, Comsat Telesystems, Washington, 1978-79; mgr. acctg. and taxes Satellite Bus. Systems, McLean, Va., 1979-81, treas., 1981-84; v.p. fin. Comsat Tech. Products, Inc., Washington, 1985-86, Comsat Video Enterprises, Inc., Washington, 1989-90; exec. v.p. Leasetec Corp., Boulder, Colo., 1990—2002; ret., 2002. Instr. acctg. Colo. State U., 2003—, U. Colo., 2003—. Active cmty. svc. activities. Mem. AICPA, Va. Jaycees (life), Great Falls Jaycees (pres. 1978). Roman Catholic. Avocations: running, golf. Home: 36495 Peak to Peak Hwy Nederland CO 80466 Office Phone: 303-808-1181. E-mail: dfthomas@aol.com.

THOMAS, DAVID ALBERT, law educator, director; b. LA, Feb. 4, 1944; s. Albert Rees and Betty Lou (Adams) T.; m. Paula Rasmussen, Aug. 7, 1967; children: Rebecca, David R., John H., Matthew A., Susannah, Amanda, Christina, Erin. BA, Brigham Young U., 1967; JD, Duke U., 1972; MLS, Brigham Young U., 1977. Jud. clk. U.S. Dist. Ct. Utah, Salt Lake City, 1972-73; pvt. practice, 1973-74; asst. prof. Law Sch. Brigham Young U., Provo, 1974-76, dir. law libr. Law Sch., 1974-90, assoc. prof. Law Sch., 1976-79, prof. Law Sch., 1979—, Rex E. Lee endowed chair, prof. law, 2005—. Accreditation site insp. ABA, Chgo., 1978—. Author: Utah Civil Procedure, 1980, (with others) A Practical Guide to Disputes Between Adjoining Landowners, 1989, Utah Civil Practice, 1992, 5th edit., 2006, (with others) Thomas and Backman on Utah Real Property Law, 1999, 2d edit., 2005; prin. author, editor-in-chief: Thompson on Real Property, Thomas Edition, 15 vols., 1994; contbr. articles to profl. jours. With U.S. Army, 1969-71, Vietnam. Mem. ABA (mem. sect. coun., chmn. real property probate and trust sect.) Office: Brigham Young U Law Sch Provo UT 84602 Business E-Mail: david_thomas@byu.edu.

THOMAS, DAVID CLIFTON, music educator; s. Donald and Glenon Thomas; m. Kathie Weeks Thomas. AAS, Onondaga C.C., 1981; B of Music, Syracuse U., 1983; MusM, Ithaca Coll., 1989. Tchr. music Onteora Jr./Sr. High Sch., Boiceville, NY, 1984—. Sgt. USAF, 1990—99. Home: 31 Church St Great Barrington MA 01230 Office: Onteora Jr/Sr High Sch Rte 28 Boiceville NY 12412 Office Phone: 845-657-2373. Business E-Mail: dkthomas31@verizon.net.

THOMAS, DAVID LINDSEY, lawyer, former state senator; b. Washington, Jan. 14, 1962; s. Lindsey Kay and Nancy ruth Thomas; m. Lynn Stosich Thomas, Apr. 21, 1987; children: Tyler, Tristan, Richard, Gwendolyn. BS in Fin., Brigham Young U., Salt Lake City, 1986; JD, Coll. William and Mary, Williamsburg, Va., 1990. Vice chmn. Utah Comm. Agy. Network, West Valley City, Utah, 1996—; chief civil dep. Summit County Atty., Utah; state senator, 2002—06. Mem. Utah Tech. Commn., 2002—06; former chmn. standing commn. edn. Utah State Senate, Salt Lake City, former chmn. judiciary interim com., former chmn. exec. offices and criminal justice appropriations com. Contbr. articles to law jours. Planning commr., South Weber, Utah, 2000; city councilman, 2001—02. Maj. US Army, 1990—99. Recipient Profl. Merit award, ABA, 1991, Exec. Dirs. award, Utah Sheriff's Assn., 2005, Exec. award for merit, Dept. Pub. Safety, 2006. Mem.: Nat. Assn. Bond Attys., Am. Legion.

THOMAS, DAVID LLEWELLYN, physician; b. Clinton, Iowa, June 11, 1948; s. Marvin Llewellyn and Marjorie Emma (Mayer) Thomas; m. Sheryl L. Miller, 2002; children: Tana, Paige, Drew, Aleksandr. BA in Zoology, U. Iowa, 1970, MD, 1974. Diplomate Am. Bd. Family Practice, cert. added qualification in geriatric medicine. Resident in family medicine U. Ill., Rockford, 1977; pvt. practice Marshalltown, Iowa, 1977—; family physician McFarland Clinic, PC, Marshalltown, 1994, also bd. dirs., v.p., 1995—98, treas., 1999—. Clin. lectr. U. Iowa Coll. Medicine, Iowa City, 1981—; med. dir. Iowa Found. Med. Ctr., 1992—. Bd. dirs. Iowa Found. Med. Care, Des Moines, 1986—2001, Iowa Ctrl. Agrl. Safety and Health, 1995—97; trustee Marshalltown Med. and Surg. Ctr., 1998—2003. Mem.: Am. Health Quality Assn. (bd. dirs. 1995—2005, v.p. 1997—2000, pres. 2000—03). Republican. Episcopalian. Office: McFarland Clinic 303 Nicholas Dr Ste 1 Marshalltown IA 50158-4443 Home Phone: 641-752-8551; Office Phone: 641-752-0099. Business E-Mail: dthomas@mcfarlandclinic.com.

THOMAS, DAVID MANNING, secondary school educator; b. Youngstown, Ohio, Nov. 6, 1954; s. Willie J and Willetta H Thomas; children: Ruyshannia, Leandria, Imani. BS in music edn., Case Western Reserve, 1981; M in music, Cleve. State U., 1983. Tchr. E. Cleve. Bd. Edn., 1987—93, Cleve. Bd. Edn., 1993—. Adj. music instr. Cleveland State U., 1989—98; performing musician and music dir. Southeast 7th Day Aventist Ch., 2002—. Co-author: (book) A Child's First Book of African-American Spirituals "All Night All Day", 1991, composer orchestral compositions and choral pieces. Recipient Tchr. of the Yr., East Cleve. Bd. Edn., 1993, Loretta Scott King award, 1992. Mem.: Music Educators Nat. Conf., Phi Delta Kappa Internat. Office: Cleve Bd Edn JFK H S Cleveland OH 44112 Office Phone: 216-371-0500. Business E-Mail: stthomas@en.com.

THOMAS, DAVID SNOW, plastic surgeon; b. Chgo., Feb. 7, 1951; s. Allan Perry and Verna Bea (Snow) T.; m. Becky Williams Thomas, Aug. 25, 1973; children: Nathan David, Abigail, Elizabeth. BA, U. Utah, 1974, MD, 1978. Diplomate Am. Bd. Plastic Surgery, Am. Bd. Surgery. Resident surgery UCLA, 1978-83, resident plastic surgery, 1983-85, fellow craniofacial surgery, 1985; pvt. practice Salt Lake City, 1986—; chief plastic surgery Primary Childrens Med. Ctr., Salt Lake City, 1988-90, LDS Hosp., 1993-99. Clin. asst. prof. U. Utah Plastic Surgeons, Salt Lake City, 1986-89, assoc. prof. surgery, 1990-93, clin. assoc. prof., 1993—. Bd. Dirs. AMICUS, Salt Lake City, Utah, 1990-92. Fellow ACS; mem. Am. Soc. Plastic and Reconstructive Surgery, Am. Soc. Maxillofacial Surgery, Am. Cleft Palate Craniofacial Assn., Am. Soc. Aesthetic Plastic Surgery, Interplast (pres. Salt Lake City, 1992—, bd. dirs. Palo Alto, Calif., 1992—), The Country Club (Salt Lake City), Alta Club (sec.). Office: 370 9th Ave Ste 200 Salt Lake City UT 84103-3185 Home Phone: 801-355-0104; Office Phone: 801-355-0731. Business E-Mail: dst@davidsthomasmd.com.

THOMAS, DEBI (DEBRA J. THOMAS), ice skater; b. Poughkeepsie, NY, Mar. 25, 1967; d. McKinley and Janice Thomas; m. Christopher Bequette, Nov. 1996; children: Christopher Jules II, Luc. BS, Stanford U.; MD, Northwestern U., 1997; grad., Charles R. Drew U., 2005. Competitive figure skater, 1976-88. Winner U.S. Figure Skating Championship, 1986, 88, World Figure Skating Championship, 1986, World Profl. Figure Skating Championship, 1988, 89, 91. Recipient Am. Black Achievement Award, Ebony mag., named Women Athlete of Yr., 1986; winner Bronze medal Olympic Games, 1988; named to U.S. Figure Skating Hall of Fame, San Jose Sports Hall of Fame. Address: Mentor Mgmt 5610 Town Center Dr # 5 Granger IN 46530-

THOMAS, DENE KAY, academic administrator, educator; 3 children. B Lit., S.W. State U., cert. in secondary edn., 1978; PhD English, U. Minn., 1984; course, Bryn Mawr's Women in Higher Edn. Adminstrn. program, 1990. Vice provost acad. affairs to tchr., dept. chmn., dean U. Idaho; pres. Lewis-Clark State Coll., 2001—. Office: Lewis-Clark State Coll 500 8th Ave Lewiston ID 83501 *

THOMAS, DENNIS, retired paper company executive, federal official; b. Balt., Dec. 8, 1943; s. George Crosby and Justa Mae (Witherspoon) T.; m. Dawn Frances Haines, 1965; 1 son, William David. BS, Frostburg State Coll., 1965; MSW., U. Md., 1967. Asst. to Hon. J. Glenn Beall, Jr. U.S. Ho. of Reps., Washington, 1969-71, spl. asst., 1971-73, 1973-77, adminstrv. asst. to Hon. William V. Roth, Jr., 1977-81; asst. sec. legis. affairs Dept. Treasury, Washington, 1981-83; dep. asst. to Pres. for legis. affairs White House, Washington, 1983-85; ptnr. Touche Ross and Co., Inc., 1985; asst. to Pres., The White House, 1985-87; sr. v.p. pub. affairs and comm. Internat. Paper Co., Stamford, Conn., 1987—. Republican. Office: Internat Paper 400 Atlantic St Stamford CT 06921

THOMAS, DEONA LEE, music educator; b. Nashville, Dec. 15, 1955; d. Joseph Benjamin and Frances Lee (Gwaltney) Thomas. BMus in Edn., Belmont Coll., Nashville, 1978; MusM in Edn., Peabody Coll. Vanderbilt U., Nashville, 1980. Cert. tchr. Tenn., 1978. Pvt. practice tchr. music, Carthage, Tenn., 1982—2001. Dir. Women's Missionary Union, 1980—; coord. North Ctrl. Region Children's Bible Drill, 2000—. Mem.: DAR (historian Carey Fork chpt.), Am. Orff Schulwerk Assn., Am. Guild Organists, Am. Coll. Musicians, Hist. and Geneological Soc., Sigma Alpha Iota, Beta Sigma Phi. Baptist. Avocations: sewing, church activities. Home: 220 Jenkins Hill Rd Alexandria TN 37012

THOMAS, DOROTHY, indexing consultant, writer; b. N.Y.C., Mar. 3, 1923; d. Hyman and Clara (Lond) Fisch; student Hunter Coll., 1940-43; cert. N.Y. U. Sch. Bus., 1944; m. Sidney Thomashower, Sept. 2, 1944; children— William Jay, James Evan. Personnel troubleshooter W.P.B., 1943; employment mgr. Emerson Radio & Phonograph Corp., 1943-47;

editor, author, 1947—; indexer, cons., N.Y.C., 1960—; biographer, lectr., radio producer and moderator; specialist in history of women in legal profession; dir. spl. projects Found. Continuing Legal Edn.; dir. Documentation Abstracts Inc., lectr. colls., clubs, orgns. Active legis. reform and women's movement; mem. Nat. Women's Polit. Caucus, NOW. Mem. AFTRA, Am. Soc. Indexers (pres. elect 1982-83, pres. 1983-84, dir.), Coalition of Labor Union Women, Friends of Columbia Libraries, Friends of Schlesinger Library of Harvard U., N.Y. Hist. Soc. Ind. Democrat. Club: Women's City (N.Y.C.). Author: Women Lawyers in the U.S., 1957; Women, The Bench and The Bar, in preparation; contbr. articles and biographies to Notable American Women, 1607-1950, 1971, Law Book Indexing, 1983; author: Wigmore on Evidence, Vol. XI, 1985, also other indexes and tables. Home and Office: 123 W 74th St New York NY 10023-2209

THOMAS, DWIGHT REMBERT, writer; b. Savannah, Ga., Dec. 8, 1944; s. Huguenin and Alma (Sanders) Thomas. BA in English with honors, Emory U., 1967; PhD in Am. Lit., U. Pa., 1978. Fellow English dept. U. Pa., Phila., 1971-78; writer Savannah, 1979—. Cons. Film Odyssey, Washington, 1988—89. Author: (book) The Poe Log: A Documentary Life of Edgar Allan Poe, 1987. Dir. Edgar Allan Poe Mus., Richmond, 1988—96. With US Army, 1969—71. Mem.: MLA, Am. Med. Writers Assn., Mensa (treas. Savannah area 1985—88, local sec. 1989—90), Phi Beta Kappa. Roman Catholic. Avocations: German language, current cinema, bicycling. Home: 7 E Gordon St Savannah GA 31401-4925

THOMAS, DYNDA A., lawyer; b. Springfield, Ill., 1959; BA magna cum laude, Miami U., 1982; JD, U. Cin., 1986. Bar: Ohio 1986. Ptnr. Squire, Sanders & Dempsey LLP, Cleve., co-chmn., Project Fin. Practice Group. Mem.: ABA (global infrastructure com., Pub. Utility, Comm. & Transp. Law Sect.), Cleve. Bar Assn. (Real Property, Probate & Trust Law Sect.). Office: Squire Sanders & Dempsey LLP 4900 Key Tower 127 Public Sq Cleveland OH 44114-1304 Office Phone: 216-479-8583. Office Fax: 216-479-8780. Business E-Mail: dthomas@ssd.com.

THOMAS, EDDIE, composer, recording industry executive, producer, promoter; b. Chgo., Nov. 5, 1931; s. Edward E. and Lucille Thomas; m. Verlene Lofton, Dec. 7, 1997; children: Alvin, Denise, Parrish, Robert; m. Audrey Ruth Jones, 1968 (dec. Oct. 29, 1996); 1 child, Robert. Founder, owner Dogs of War, Chgo.; founder, mgr. The Impressions, Chgo., 1957—; pres., CEO CurTom Records, Chgo., 1963—70; pres. Thomas Mktg. Pub. Co., Chgo., 1970, Thomas Assocs., Chgo., 1970—90, Thomas First Class Limo, Chgo., 1971—80; pres., CEO Thomas Prodns. LLC, Chgo., 2000—. Cons. Probation Challenge, Chgo., 2003—. Co-writer: songs Otis Redding Anthology Album "Cigarettes & Coffee", 1996, We're The New York Giants, 1987 (Gold Record, 1987); prodr.: (documentary) The Rise and Fall of Vee-Jay, 1994. Recipient Membership award, Chgo. Tourism, 1970, Cert. award, Cook County Sheriff Dept., 1980, award, History Makers, Chgo., 2000, Black Music award, Nat. Newspapers Pubs. Assn., 2005, Hall of Fame Achievement award, Wendell Phillips Acad., Chgo., 2006. Achievements include producer and promoter of many hit records and artists including Ray Charles, Barry White, Quincy Jones, The Stylistics and Johnny Talyor. Avocations: exercise, travel. Office: Thomas Prodns LLC 6348 N Milwaukee Chicago IL 60646

THOMAS, EDWARD DONNALL, internist, hematologist, retired medical educator; b. Mart, Tex., Mar. 15, 1920; m. Dorothy Thomas; 3 children. BA, U. Tex., 1941, MA, 1943; MD, Harvard U., 1946; MD (hon.), U. Cagliari, Sardinia, 1981, U. Verona, Italy, 1991, U. Parma, 1992, U. Barcelona, Spain, 1994, U. Warsaw, Poland, 1996, U. Jagiellonski, Cracow, Poland, 1996. Lic. physician Mass., N.Y., Wash., diplomate Am. Bd. Internal Medicine. Intern in medicine Peter Bent Brigham Hosp., Boston, 1946—47, rsch. fellow hematology, 1947—48; NRC postdoctoral fellow in medicine dept. biology MIT, Cambridge, 1950—51; chief med. resident, sr. asst. resident Peter Bent Brigham Hosp., 1951—53, hematologist, 1953—55; instr. medicine Harvard Med. Sch., Boston, 1953—55; rsch. assoc. Cancer Rsch. Found. Children's Med. Ctr., Boston, 1953—55; physician-in-chief Mary Imogene Bassett Hosp., Cooperstown, NY, 1955—63; assoc. clin. prof. medicine Coll. Physicians and Surgeons Columbia U., NYC, 1955—63; attending physician U. Wash. Hosp., Seattle, 1963—90; prof. medicine Sch. Medicine U. Wash., Seattle, 1963—90, head divsn. oncology Sch. Medicine, 1963—85, prof. emeritus medicine Sch. Medicine, 1990—; dir. med. oncology Fred Hutchinson Cancer Rsch. Ctr., Seattle, 1974—89, assoc. dir. clin. rsch. programs, 1982—89, mem., 1974—. Mem. hematology study sect. NIH, 1965—69; mem. bd. trustees and med. sci. adv. com. Leukemia Soc. Am., Inc., 1969—73; mem. clin. cancer investigation rev. com. NCI, 1970—74; 1st ann. Eugene C. Eppinger lectr. Peter Bent Brigham Hosp. and Harvard Med. Sch., 1974; Lilly lectr. RCP, London, 1977; Stratton lectr. Internat. Soc. Hematology, 1982; Paul Aggeler lectr. U. Calif., San Francisco, 1982; 65th Mellon lectr. U. Pitts. Sch. Medicine, 1984; Stanley Wright Meml. lectr. Western Soc. Pediat. Rsch., 1985; Adolfo Ferrata lectr. Italian Soc. Hematology, Verona, Italy, 1991. Mem. editl. bd. Blood, 1962—75, 1977—82, Transplantation, 1970—76, Proc. of Soc. for Exptl. Biology and Medicine, 1974—81, Leukemia Rsch., 1977—87, Hematological Oncology, 1982—87, Jour. Clin. Immunology, 1982—87, Am. Jour. Hematology, 1985—, Bone Marrow Transplantation, 1986—. With US Army, 1948—50. Recipient A. Ross McIntyre award, U. Nebr. Med. Ctr., 1975, Philip Levine award, Am. Soc. Clin. Pathologists, 1979, Disting. Svc. in Basic Rsch. award, Am. Cancer Soc., 1980, Kettering prize, GM Cancer Rsch. Found., 1981, Spl. Keynote Address award, Am. Soc. Therapeutic Radiologists, 1981, Robert Roesler de Villiers award, Leukemia Soc. Am., 1983, Karl Landsteiner Meml. award, Am. Assn. Blood Banks, 1987, Terry Fox award, Can., 1990, Internat. award, Gairdner Found., 1990, Hong Kong prize, N.Am. Med. Assn., 1990, Nobel Prize in Medicine, 1990, Presdl. medal of sci., NSF, 1990, Lifetime Achievement award, Am. Soc. Blood and Marrow Transplantation, 2004. Mem.: NAS, Soc. Exptl. Biology and Medicine, Western Assn. Physicians, Swiss Soc. Hematology, Internat. Soc. Hematology, Internat. Soc. Exptl. Hematology, Am. Soc. Hematology (pres. 1987—88, Henry M. Stratton lectr. 1975), Am. Soc. Clin. Investigation, Am. Soc. Clin. Oncology (David A. Karnoksky Meml. lectr. 1983), Am. Fedn. Clin. Rsch., Assn. Am. Physicians (Kober medal 1992), Am. Assn. Cancer Rsch., Academie Royale de Medicine de Belgique (corr.), Nat. Acad. Medicine Mex. (hon.), Royal Coll. Physicians and Surgeons Can. (hon.), Swedish Soc. Hematology (hon.). Office: Fred Hutchinson Cancer Ctr 1100 Fairview Ave N D5-100 PO Box 19024 Seattle WA 98109-1024 Home Phone: 425-454-7381; Office Phone: 206-667-4319. Business E-Mail: ethomas@fhcrc.org.

THOMAS, ELIZABETH MARSHALL, writer; b. Boston, Sept. 13, 1931; d. Laurence K. and Lorna (McLean) Marshall; m. Stephen Thomas, 1956; children: Stephanie, Ramsay. Student, Smith Coll.; BA in English, Radliffe Coll., 1954. Writer, 1954—. Author: The Harmless People, 1959, Warrior Herdsmen, 1965, Reindeer Moon, 1987, The Animal Wife, 1990, The Hidden Life of Dogs, 1993, The Tribe of Tiger, 1994, Certain Poor Shepherds, 1998, The Social Lives of Dogs, 2000, The Old Way: A Story of the First People, 2006. Office: 80 E Mountain Rd Peterborough NH 03458-2318

THOMAS, ELLEN LOUISE, school system administrator; b. Doylestown, Pa., Nov. 30, 1940; d. Edward Martin and Evelyn Graham (Axenroth) Happ; m. Eugene Greene Leffever, June 30, 1963 (dec. Nov. 1978); children: Eugene Greene II, Jeanette Ellen Dellaripa; m. William Dewey Thomas, Sept. 15, 1981; 1 child, Jeremiah David. BA in Edn., Immaculata Coll., Pa., 1962; postgrad., Pa. State U., 1962-67. Pvt. practice tutor, Doylestown, 1958-65; tchr. Cen. Bucks Sch. System, Doylestown, 1962-65; adminstr. The Curiosity Shoppe, Doylestown, 1965—, The Toddler Ctr., Doylestown, 1979—; exec. dir. Camp Curiosity, Doylestown, 1984—, Thomas Lea Equestrian Ctr., Doylestown, 1988—. Tchr. trainer Confortunity of Christian Doctrine, Doylestown, 1965-78; cons. early childhood Am. Sch. in Hong Kong, 1981-84; lectr. in early childhood Bucks County Community Ctr., Newtown, Pa., 1978-90; workshop facilitator Head Start, Phila., 1990; cons. day care Cen. Bucks C. of C., Doylestown, 1989-90; ednl. coord. Forest Grove Presbyn. Ch., 1984-90. Mem. U.S. C. of C., Washington, Bucks County C. of C., Doylestown, Nat. Fedn. of Ind. Bus., Washington; children's ministry coord. Jesus Focus Ministry, 1995—; trainer Pa. Child Care, 1995—; past pres. Pa. Day Camp Assn., 1998-2001; Sunday sch. tchr. Hilltown Bapt. Ch., 1995-2000; mem. Am. Camping Assn., 1994-, Plumstead Christian Sch. Bd., 1995-2001; varsity tennis coach Plumstead Christian Sch.-boys, 1998-2004, girls, 2001-2007; children's chmn. Central Bucks Village Fair, 2001-03; mem. Quality Child Care Coun., Pa. Keystone Stars; bd. dirs., ednl. chair Plumstead Christian Sch., 2002-05. Mem. ASCD, Assn. for Childhood Edn. Internat., United Pvt. Acad. Schs. Assn., Bucks County Assn. Edn. Young Children (pres. 1974-78). Office: The Curiosity Shoppe 4425 Landisville Rd Doylestown PA 18901-1134 E-mail: FaxThomdew@aol.com.

THOMAS, ESTHER MERLENE, elementary and adult education educator; b. San Diego, Oct. 16, 1945; d. Merton Alfred and Nellie Lida (Von Pilz) T. AA with honors, Grossmont Coll., 1966; BA with honors, San Diego State U., 1969; MA, U. Redlands, 1977. Cert. elem. and adult edn. tchr.; cert. in crosscultural lang. and acad. devel., English lang. devel. Tchr. Cajon Valley Union Sch. Dist., El Cajon, 1969—; sci. fair coord. Flying Hills Sch. Tchr. Hopi and Navajo Native Americans, Ariz., Utah, 1964-74, Goose and Gander Nursery Sch., Lakeside, Calif., 1964-66; dir., supt. Bible and Sunday schs. various chs., Lakeside, 1961-87; mem. sci. com., math. coun. Cajon Valley Union Sch. Dist., 1990-91, libr. com., 1997-98. Author: Individualized Curriculum in the Affective Domain; co-author: Campbell County, The Treasured Years, 1990; songwriter: songs Never Trouble Trouble, Old Glory, Jesus Is Our Lord, Daniel's Prayer, There Lay Jesus, God's Hands, Washing Machine Charlie, Playmates, The Kid in the Hall, Spring Time on the Blue Ridge, Christ's DNA, If You Need Me, Chances (Four Star award, 2003), Blame, The Star of Bethlehem, Where the Eagle Flies, Born to Win, Happy Birthday Dear Jesus, Christmas Lights, Walk the Line, You Don't Know What Repentance Is, I'm Asking You, Clear the Path Lord, Aqua Forte, In the Volume of the Book, Home is Where the Heart Is, You Don't Even Know Who I Am, No Place to Cry, To Walk With God, Ixnay, If You Never Loved Me, for Columbine Records Corp., Life of A Single Woman, Take This Pain Away, We Can Keep In Touch, Let Me Know, A Letter Is A Letter, The Battle, 2004; contbr. articles to profl. jours., newspapers, chpts. to books. Tem. U.S. Senatorial Club, Washington, 1984—, Conservative Caucus, Inc., Washington, 1988—, Ronald Reagan Presdl. Found., Ronald Reagan Rep. Ctr., 1988, Rep. Presdl. Citizen's Adv. Commn., 1989—, Rep. Platform Planning Com., Calif., 1992, at-large del. representing dist. #45, Lakeside, Calif., 1992, 1995—, Am. Security Coun., Washington, 1994, Congressman Hunter's Off Road Adv. Coun., El Cajon, Calif., 1994, Century Club, San Diego Rep. Century Club, 1995; mem. health articulation com. project AIDS, Cajon Valley Union Sch. Dist., 1988—, Recruit Depot Hist. Mus., San Diego, 1989, Citizen's Drug Free Am., Calif., 1989—, The Heritage Found., 1988—; charter mem. Marine Corps Mus.; life mem. San Diego Aerospace Mus.; mem. Lakeside Centennial Com., 1985-86; hon. mem. Rep. Presdl. Task Force, Washington, 1986; del. Calif. Rep. Senatorial Mid-Term Conv., Washington, 1994; mus. curator Lakeside Hist. Soc., 1992-93, life mem.; mem. Rep. Nat. Com., Washington, 2003 Recipient Outstanding Svc. award PTA, 1972-74, Outstanding Tchr. award KYXY Radio, San Diego, 1999, Dream Classroom award KSWB-TV, San Diego, 2005; recipient Hats Off to Tchr. award, San Diego Bd. Edn., 1989, others. Mem. NRA, Tchrs. Assn., Calif. Tchrs. Assn., Cajon Valley Educators Assn. (faculty advisor, rep. 1980-82, 84-86, 87-88), Nat. Trust for Hist. Preservation, Christian Bus. and Profl. Women, Trust for Hist. Preservation, Nat. WWII Memml. (life, charter), Ridgecrest Golden Terrace Park Assn. (pres. 1998-99), Capitol Hill Women's Club, Am. Ctr. for Law and Justice, Internat. Christian Women's Club (Christian amb. to Taiwan, Korea, 1974), Paul Revere Soc. Independent. Avocations: travel, vocal music, piano, guitar. Office: Flying Hills Elem Sch 1251 Finch St El Cajon CA 92020-1433

THOMAS, ETAN, professional basketball player, poet; b. Harlem, NY, Apr. 1, 1978; BS in Bus. Mgmt., Syracuse Univ., 2000. Profl. basketball player Wash. Wizard, 2001—. Political spkr. and activist. Author: (volume of poetry) More Than an Athlete, 2005. Achievements include hon. mention All-America, AP, 2000; named to first team All-Big East Conf., 2000; two-time Big East Defensive Player Yr. Office: Washington Wizards MCI Ctr 601 F St NW Washington DC 20004

THOMAS, EVELYN B., agricultural products supplier; Sec., treas., bookkeeper Brandt Fertilizer, Pleasant Plains, Ill., 1953—; co-owner Har Brand, 1963-67, Brandt Chem., 1967; sec./treas. Brandt Consol., Pleasant Plains. Office: Brandt Consol PO Box 350 Pleasant Plains IL 62677-0277 Business E-Mail: bcadmin@brandtconsolidated.com.

THOMAS, FAYE EVELYN J., elementary and secondary school educator; b. Summerfield, La., Aug. 3, 1933; d. Reginald Felton and Atlee (Hunter) Johnson; m. Archie Taylor Thomas, Sept. 8, 1960; 1 child, Dwayne Andre. BA, So. U., 1954; student, Tuskegee Inst., 1958, student, 1969, U. Detroit, 1961, student, 1962, student, 1963, Ctrl. Mich. U., 1965; MS, U. Ctrl. Ark., 1971, Cleve. State U., 1979. Tchr. Cullen (La.) Elem. Sch., 1957; tchr. English and social studies Charles Brown H.S., Springhill, La., 1957—70; tchr. English, Upward Bound Program, Grambling State U., 1968; tchr. English, Springhill H.S., 1970; elem. intermediate tchr. Riveredge Elem. Sch., Berea, Ohio, 1971—93; tchr. 7th grade English, Ford Mid. Sch., 1993—94, Tchr. asst. elem. coun. curriculum and instrn. Berea Sch. Dist., 1984—85. Author: When the Time Is Right, Move On, 2002, A Journey to the Mountain Top, 2003. Program dir. teen pregnancy prevention program First Bapt. Ch., Cullen, La., 2003—04, Grantee, EDPA, 1970—71, Internat. Paper Found., 1958, 1960, NDEA, 1965; scholar Martha Holden Jennings scholar, 1984—85. Mem.: ASCD, NEA, N.E. Ohio Tchrs. Assn., Berea Edn. Assn., Ohio Edn. Assn., Ohio Motorists Assn., Charles Brown Soc. Orgn. (trustee 1984—), Black Caucus NEA, People United to Save Humanity, Toastmasters, Order Eastern Star. Democrat. Baptist. Office: 311 Henrietta White Blvd Springhill LA 71075-8407

THOMAS, FRANK EDWARD, professional baseball player; b. Columbus, Ga., May 27, 1968; Student, Auburn U. With Chgo. White Sox, 1990—2006, Oakland Athletics, 2006, Toronto Blue Jays, 2006—. Named Maj. League Player of Yr., Sporting News, 1993, AL Comeback Player Yr., Players Choice Awards, 2006; named to All-Star Coll. All Am. team, Sporting News, 1989, All-Star Team, 1991, 1993—94, Am. League, 1993—95; recipient Silver Slugger award, 1991, 1993, 1994, Most Valuable Player award, Am. League, 1994. Achievements include becoming the 21st player in major league history to hit 500 home runs, June 28, 2007. Office: Toronto Blue Jays Ste 3200 1 Blue Jays Way M5V 1J1 Toronto ON Canada *

THOMAS, FRANKLIN AUGUSTINE, lawyer, consultant; b. Bklyn., May 27, 1934; s. James and Viola (Atherley) T.; div.; children: Keith, Hillary, Kerrie, Kevin. BA, Columbia U., 1956, LL.B., 1963; LL.D. (hon.), Yale U., 1970, Fordham U., 1972, Pratt Inst., 1974, Pace U., 1977, Columbia U., 1979, New School U., 2002. Bar: N.Y. 1964. Atty. Fed. Housing and Home Finance Agy., NYC, 1963-64; asst. U.S. atty. for So. Dist. N.Y., 1964-65; dep. police commr. charge legal matters NYC, 1965-67; pres., chief exec. officer Bedford Stuyvesant Restoration Corp., Bklyn., 1967-77; pres. The Ford Found., 1979-96; atty., cons., 1996—. Bd. dirs. ALCOA, Citigroup, Lucent Techs., PepsiCo, Inc. Trustee Columbia U., 1969-75. Served with USAF, 1956-60. Recipient LBJ Found. award for contbn. to betterment of urban life, 1974, medal of excellence Columbia U., 1976, Alexander Hamilton award Columbia U., 1983 Office Phone: 212-557-3004.

THOMAS, FREDERICK BRADLEY, lawyer; b. Evanston, Ill., Aug. 13, 1949; s. Frederick Bradley and Katherine Kidder (Bingham) T.; m. Elizabeth Maxwell, Oct. 25, 1975; children: Bradley Bingham, Stephens Maxwell, Rosa Macaulay. AB, Dartmouth Coll., 1971; JD, U. Chgo., 1974. Bar: Ill. 1974. Law clk. to hon. judge John C. Godbold U.S. Ct. Appeals (5th cir.), Montgomery, Ala., 1974-75; assoc. Mayer, Brown, Rowe & Maw, LLP, Chgo., 1975—80, ptnr., 1981—. Bd. trustees La Rabida Children's Hosp., 1990—; bd. mgrs. YMCA Met. Chgo., 2002—. Mem.: ABA, Chgo. Coun. Lawyers. Republican. Episcopalian. Office: Mayer Brown Rowe & Maw LLP 71 South Wacker Dr Chicago IL 60606-4637

THOMAS, GARNETT JETT, accountant; b. Farmington, Ky., July 27, 1920; s. Pinkney Madison and Ethel (Drinkard) T.; m. Katherine Gardner, Mary. 26, 1948 (dec. Sept. 1979); m. Nell Penton, May 23, 1981; stepchldren: Vernon Bice, Michael Bice, Gina Black. BS, Lambuth U., 1947; MS, Miss. State U., 1949. Clk., acct. Ill. Cen. R.R., Paducah, Ky., 1941-42; mgr. Coll. Bookstore Lambuth U., Jackson, Tenn., 1946-47; acct. Miss. Agrl. and Forestry Expt. Sta., Mississippi State, 1948-60, chief acct., 1960-75, administrv. officer and chief acct., 1975-85; administrv. officer emeritus, 1985—; pres. PBR Corp., Starksville, Miss., 1974-84. Fin. adminstr. seed tech., rsch. internat. programs Brazil, India, Guatemala, Columbia, Thailand, Kenya, 1958-85; pres. Govt. Employees Credit Union. Mem. adv. bd. Nat. Bank of Commerce of Miss., 1974—; fin. administr. seed tech, research internat. programs Brazil, India, Guatemala, Columbia, Thailand, Kenya, 1958-85; bd. dirs. Govt. Employees Credit Union, 1967-86, pres., 1969-73. With USN, 1942-46. Decorated Bronze Star with oak leaf cluster. Mem. Nat. Assn. Accts., Asn. Govt. Accts., Am. Assn Accts., Acad. Acctg. Historians, So. Assn. Agrl. Scientists, Rotary (pres., 1959-90, dist. 682 gov. 1977-78, adv. com. to pres. 1979-80, dist. chmn. Poloplus, 1987-90). Republican. Methodist. Home: 114 Grand Ridge Rd Starkville MS 39759-4112

THOMAS, GARY L., retired academic administrator; b. Willows, Calif., May 12, 1937; s. Leonel Richard and Myrtle Blanch (Moncur) T.; m. Margaret Anderson, Aug. 11, 1960 (div. 1975); children: Katelin, Elizabeth Ann, Derek Alan. AA, Modesto Jr. Coll., 1958; BS in Elec. Engring., U. Calif., Berkeley, 1960, MA in Physics, 1962, PhD in Elec. and Computer Engring., 1967. Acting asst. prof. U. Calif., Berkeley, 1967; asst. prof. elec. engring. SUNY, Stony Brook, 1967-70, assoc. prof. elec. engring., 1970-73, assoc. dean grad. sch., 1973-74, chairperson, prof. elec. engring., 1975-79; congl. fellow A.A.A.S., Washington, 1974-75; provost, v.p. acad. affairs N.J. Inst. Tech., Newark, 1980-98, prof. elec. and computer engring., 1980—2000; chancellor U. Missouri-Rolla, Rolla, Mo., 2000—05. Student asst. bd. Dept. Higher Edn., N.J., 1980-97; chairperson rsch. adv. bd. PSE & G, Newark, 1986-90, Regional Transp. Rsch. Bd., N.Y. and N.J., 1987-90; bd. dirs. Kessler Inst. for Rehab., West Orange, N.J., 1988—; chair bd. dirs. Kessler Med. Rehab. Rsch. & Edn. Corp., 1997-2002. Author, editor: Fundamentals of Electrical and Computer Engineering, 1983. State of Calif. scholar, 1960, Schumberger scholar, 1961; NSF grantee, 1973-79. Home: 7 Vosseler Ct West Orange NJ 07052-3911

THOMAS, GARY LYNN, information technology executive; b. Port Vue, Pa., May 15, 1942; s. Willis L. and Luella M. (Rorabaugh) T.; m. Sharen A. Gibbons, May 13, 1967; children— Gregory Scott, Tara Elizabeth. BS in Bus. Adminstrn, Pa. State U., 1964; grad., Sch. Bank Adminstrn., U. Wis., 1973. CPA, Pa. Sr. auditor Arthur Andersen & Co., Los Angeles and Pitts., 1964-69; v.p. and dep. comptroller Pitts. Nat. Bank, 1969-77; v.p. and treas. Md. Nat. Corp., Balt., 1977-80; v.p., mgr. corp. fin. div. Md. Nat. Bank, Balt.; exec. v.p. adminstrn. Peterson, Howell & Heather, Hunt Valley, Md., 1980-82; v.p. fin. Am. TeleServices, Inc, a Metromedia co., Balt., 1983-85; chief fin. officer First Cellular Group, Inc., Balt., 1985-88, Schelle, Warner, Murray & Thomas, Inc., Balt., 1988—95. Mng. dir. Schelle Cellular Group, Inc., 1989—; pres. Ruxton Capital Group, Inc., 1989-95; chief fin. officer Am. Personal Communications, Inc., Balt. and D.C., 1990-98; adj. instr. Sch. Bank Adminstrn., U. Wis., 1975-80; speaker 14th ann. Bank Tax Inst., 1978. Mem. adv. bd., fin. com. St. Joseph Hosp., Balt., 1979-1982; bd. dirs. industry luncheon club Towson State U., 1980-1985. Served with USAR, 1965-1971. Inducted into McKeesport H.S. Hall of Fame, 1994. Mem. AICPA, Pa. Inst. CPAs, Md. Assn. CPAs (prior chmn. mems. in industry com.), Greater Naples Leadership Program, Conservancy SW Fla.(bd. dir., treas.). Republican. Methodist. Home: 575 18th Ave S Naples FL 34102-7536

THOMAS, GEOFFREY L., lawyer; b. Lindsay, Calif., May 12, 1944; AB cum laude, Harvard U., 1967; JD, Stanford, 1971. Bar: Calif. 1972. Ptnr. Paul, Hastings, Janofsky & Walker LLP, LA, gen. counsel, chmn. profl. responsibility com. Mem. bd. editors Stanford Law Rev., 1970—71. Contbr. (chapter) Examining Witnesses to Civil Procedure During Trial. Office: Paul Hastings Janofsky & Walker LLP 515 S Flower St Los Angeles CA 90071-2228 Office Phone: 213-683-6149. Office Fax: 213-627-0705. Business E-Mail: geoffreythomas@paulhastings.com.

THOMAS, GLEN R., lawyer; BA, Colgate U., 1991; JD, Dickinson Coll., 1994. Bar: Pa. Ptnr. Blank Rome LLP, Phila. Former chmn. Pa. Utility Commn.; environ. and energy advisor to Pa. Gov. Tom Ridge and Calif. Gov. Arnold Schwarzenegger. Named one of 40 Under 40, Phila. Bus. Jour., 2006. Mem.: Sec. of Energy's Electricity Adv. Com., Nat. Regulatory Rsch. Inst., Nat. Assn. of Regulatory Utility Commrs., Mid-Atlantic Conf. of Regulatory Utilities Commrs. (former pres.), Energy Bar Assn. (bd. dirs.). Office: Blank Rome LLP One Logan Sq 130 N 18th St Philadelphia PA 19103-6998 Office Phone: 215-569-5582. Office Fax: 215-832-5582. E-mail: Thomas@blankrome.com.

THOMAS, GREGG DARROW, lawyer; b. Jacksonville, Fla., July 31, 1951; BA magna cum laude, Vanderbilt U., 1972; JD with honors, U. Fla., 1976. Bar: Fla. 1976, D.C. 1978. Law clk. U.S. Dist. Ct. (mid. dist.) Fla., 1976-79; mem. firm Holland & Knight, Tampa, Fla., 1979—2006, ptnr., 1983—2006, Thomas & LoCicero PC, Tampa, 2006—. Exec. editor U. Fla. Law Rev., 1975-76. Bd. dirs. Vol. Lawyer's Resource Ctr., 1990-95; trustee Tampa Mus. of Art, 1993—, vice chmn., 1998, chair, 1999-2001. Mem. ABA (mem. forum com. comm. law 1983—), Am. Judicature Soc., Fla. Bar (co-chair Fla. bar media and comm. com. 1987-88, mem. grievance com. 1988, chmn. 1989-91), Fla. Bar Found. (mem. legal assistance to poor com. 1988-91), Hillsborough Bar Assn., D.C. Bar, Phi Beta Kappa. Office: Thomas & LoCicero PC 400 N Ashley Dr Ste 1100 Tampa FL 33602 Office Phone: 813-984-3060. Business E-Mail: gthomas@tlolawfirm.com.

THOMAS, HARRY K., JR., federal agency administrator, former ambassador; b. 1956; m. Ericka O. Smith-Thomas; 1 child, Casey Merie Eunice. Grad., Coll. Holy Cross, 1978; postgrad., Columbia U. With U.S. Fgn. Svc., New Delhi, Harare, Kaduna, and Lima, 1984; staff asst. to asst. sec. for African affairs US Dept State; spl. asst. to under sec. polit. affairs US Dept. State; dep. dir. to dir. Ops. Ctr. US Dept State, sr. watch officer;

dir. for South Asia NSC, Washington, 2001—02; US amb. to Bangladesh US Dept State, Dhaka, Bangladesh, 2003—05, exec. sec. Office of the Sec. Washington, 2005—. Office: US Dept State 2201 C St NW Washington DC 20520

THOMAS, HAYWARD, retired manufacturing executive; b. LA, Aug. 9, 1921; s. Charles Sparks and Julia (Hayward) T.; m. Phyllis Mary Wilson, July 1, 1943; children: H. David, Steven T. BS, U. Calif., Berkeley, 1943. Registered profl. engr. Staff engr. Joshua Hendy Corp., Los Angeles, 1946-50; prodn. mgr. Byron Jackson Co., Los Angeles, 1950-55; mgr. mfg. Frigidaire div. Gen. Motors Corp., Dayton, Ohio, 1955-70; group v.p. White Motor Corp., Cleve., 1971-73; sr. v.p. Broan Mfg. Co., Hartford, Wis., 1973-85; pres. Jensen Industries, Los Angeles, 1985-87; retired, 1987. Served to lt. USNR, 1943-46. Mem. Soc. Mfg. Engrs. (chmn. mfg. mgmt. council 1984-86). Republican. Episcopalian. Avocations: tennis, fishing. Home: 1320 Granvia Altamira Palos Verdes Peninsula CA 90274-2006

THOMAS, HAZEL BEATRICE, state official; b. Franklin, Tenn. d. William Henry Fuller and Mattie Betty (Covington) Fuller Young; m. Charles B. Thomas (dec. 1969); children; Charles Bradford Jr., Deborah Carlotta (dec.). BA, Fisk U., 1946; MA, Tenn. State U., 1972. Cert. elem. and secondary tchr., Tenn. Tchr. elem. Met.-Nashville Sch., 1954—87; rsch. assoc. Johns Hopkins U., Balt., 1978—79, Marquette U., Milw., 1979—86; exec. asst. to commr. edn. Tenn. Dept. Edn., Nashville, 1987—. Cons. Peer Mediated Learning System, Nashville, 1980-82; instr. Met. Sch. Tchr. Ctr., Nasvhville, 1985-87; mem. tech. assistance team for high sch. that work, So. Regional Edn. Bd., 1998-99; nat. disseminator student team learning rsch. project, Johns Hopkins U., 1978-1979. Author training modules Substitute Teaching, Tchr. Aides. Pres. Davidson County Dem. Women, Nashville, 1985-87; v.p. Tenn. Fedn. Dem. Women, 1989-91, pres., 2001—; pres. elect Nashville Women's Polit. Caucus, 1991—; pres. Tenn. Women's Polit. Caucus, 1994-95; mem. adminstrv. com. of bd. Nat. Women's Polit. Caucus, 1993-95, v.p., 1995—, v.p. edn. and tng., 2001—; mem. Tenn. Leadership, Inc., 1992—; spkr., polit. trainer U.S. Info. Agy., Nairobi, Kenya, 1997; mem. exec. bd. Citizen's Com. for Ann. Gov.'s Prayer Breakfast, 1992—; mem. exec. com. Tenn. Dem. Party, 2001—; chmn. edn. com. Bellevue C. of C.; pres. Tenn. Fedn. Dem. Women, 2001-03; v.p. Nat. Fedn. Dem. Women, 2002-05, 3d v.p., 2005—; mem. pub. edn. and govt. com. Metro. Govt. Nashville, Tenn., 2002-03; apptd. to pub. ednl. and govtl. access oversight com. Nashville Mayor Purcell, 2003—; apptd. to pub. edn. govt. com. Metro Nashville City Coun., 2002 Recipient Svc. to Edn. and Teaching Profession award Nat. Coun. Negro Women, 1988; Nat. Def. Edn. Act scholar, 1965, 67. Mem. Am. Bus. Womens Assn. (charter), Tenn. Edn. Assn. (pres. dept. classroom tchr. 1974-75, state dept. affiliate, pres. 1988-Ed. c90), Bellevue C. of C. (bd. govs. 1990-91, edn. chair 2002-03), Assn. Classroom Tchrs. (pres. S.E. region 1975-76), Met. Nashville Edn. Assn. (exec. bd. 1971-77), Bellevue Sertoma Club (life, pres. 1990-91), Nat. Women's Polit. Caucus (v.p. 1995—), Nat. Assn. Dem. Women (v.p., 2003-05, named Woman of Distinction for Tenn., 2002, 03), Nat. Fedn. Dem. Women (v.p. 2003). Baptist. Avocations: reading, bridge. Office: Tenn Dept Edn Andrew Johnson Tower 710 James Robertson Pkwy Nashville TN 37243-1219 Office Phone: 615-532-5740. E-mail: hazel.thomas@state.tn.us.

THOMAS, HELEN AMELIA (MRS. DOUGLAS B. CORNELL), editor-in-chief, former White House correspondent; b. Winchester, Ky., Aug. 4, 1920; d. George and Mary (Thomas) T.; m. Douglas B. Cornell. BA, Wayne State U., 1942; BA in Law, Mount Vernon Coll., 1999; LHD, Wayne State U., 1974, U. Detroit, 1979; LLD, Ea. Mich. State U., 1972, Ferris State Coll., 1978; LLD (hon.), Brown U., 1986, St. Bonaventure U., 1988, Franklin Marshall U., 1989, No. Mich. U., 1989, Northeastern U., 1990, Skidmore Coll., 1992, Susquehanna U., 1993, Sage Coll., 1994, U. Mo., 1994, Franklin Coll., 1995, Mich. State U., 1996, Potsdam U., 1998, A. Willenberg Univ., 1999, Milliken U., 2002, Am. U. Beirut, 2003, Western Ky. U., 2005, Cabrini Coll., 2005; LittD (hon.), Ohio Dominican U., 2004; LLD (hon.), Ind. Tech. U., 2007, Sienna Coll., 2007. With United Press Radio, UPI, 1943-2000, wire svc. reporter Washington, 1943-74; White House corr. Washington, 1970; White House bur. chief UPI, Washington, 1974-2000; columnist Hearst Newspapers, 2000—. Author: Dateline White House, Front Row at the White House: My Life and Times, 1999, Thanks for the Memories Mr. President: Wit and Wisdom from the Front Row at the White House, 2002, Watchdogs of Democracy?: The Waning Washington Press Corps and How It Has Failed the Public, 2006; columnist Hearst Newspapers. Named one of 25 Most Influential Women in Am., World Almanac; recipient Woman of Yr. in Comm. award, Ladies Home Jour., 1975, 4th Estate award, Nat. Press Club, 1984, Journalism award, U. Mo., Al Newharth award, 1990, Ralph McGill award, 1995, Lifetime award, Internat. Media Found., Internat. Women's Press Found., 1996, Lowell Thomas award, Marist Coll., 2001, Kahlil Gibran award, 2003, NOW award, 2003, Torch Bearer award, Planned Parenthood award, Physician Social Responsibility award, Utah Am. Women of Yr., 2004, Eleanor Roosevelt Legacy award, 2004, Lifetime Achievement award, Glamour mag., Lifetime award, Washington Press Found., 2007. Mem. Women's Nat. Press Club (pres. 1959-60, William Allen White Journalism award), Am. Newspaper Women's Club (past v.p.), White House Corrs. Assn. (pres. 1976, Helen Thomas Lifetime Achievement award 1998), Nat. Newspaper Assn. (Lifetime award 2002), Gridiron Club (pres. 1993), Sigma Delta Chi (fellow, Hall of Fame), Delta Sigma Phi (hon.). Achievements include research in women's representation in the fields of journalism and politics, and in clubs and organizations; the first women officer of the National Press Club, the White House Correspondents Association, and first women member of the Gridiron Club; has covered nine presidents; only woman print journalist to go on President Nixon's historic trip to China and traveled with presidents Ford, Carter, Reagan, Bush, Sr., Clinton, & Bush; first female White House chief of a wire service in 1974; considered the "dean of Washington press corps" and she was allowed to ask the first question at the presdl. conferences; referred to as "The First Lady of the Press"; covered every presdl. econ. summit until 1999. Office: Hearst Corp 959 8th Ave New York NY 10019 Office Phone: 202-263-6437. Business E-Mail: helent@hearstdc.com.

THOMAS, HOWARD, business educator; b. Jan. 31, 1943; BSc, London U., 1964, MSc, 1965; MBA, U. Chgo., 1966; PhD, Edinburgh U., Scotland, 1970, DSc, 2007. From prof. dept. bus. adminstrn. to dean emeritus U. Ill., Urbana-Champaign, 1980—2001, dean emeritus Commerce and Bus. Adminstrn., 2001—; dean Warwick Bus. Sch. U. Warwick, Coventry, U.K., 2000—. Vis. prof. MIT, 1986-87, Northwestern U., 1990. Office: Warwick Bus Sch U Warwick Coventry CV4 7AL England E-mail: Howard.Thomas@wbs.ac.uk.

THOMAS, HOWARD PAUL, civil engineer, consultant; b. Cambridge, Mass., Aug. 20, 1942; s. Charles Calvin and Helen Elizabeth (Hook) T.; m. Ingrid Nybo, Jan. 4, 1969; children: Kent Michael, Lisa Karen, Karina Michelle. BS in Engring., U. Mich., 1965, MS in Engring., 1966. Registered profl. engr., Calif., 1969, Alaska, 1976, BC, 2007. Engr. Ove Arup & Ptnrs., London, 1966-67; project engr. Woodward-Clyde Cons., San Francisco, 1967-73, assoc. Anchorage, 1975-89; spl. cons. Cowiconsult Cons., Copenhagen, 1973-75; prin. engr. Harding-Lawson Assocs., Anchorage, 1989-90; v.p., chief engr. EMCON Alaska, Inc., Anchorage, 1991-94; gen. mgr. Internat. Tech. Corp., Anchorage, 1994-96; assoc. GeoEngrs., Inc., Anchorage, 1996—2002; prin. engr. CH2M Hill, Anchorage, 2001—; mem. Anchorage Mayor's Geotech. Adv. Commn., 1997—2003. Chmn. Nat. Tech. Coun. Cold Regions Engring., 1988-89, chmn. com. program and publs., 1982-84; chmn. 4th Internat. Conf. Cold Regions Engring., Anchorage, 1986; liaison NAS/Nat. Rsch. Coun. Polar Rsch. Bd., 1989-99. Contbr. articles to profl. jours. Named Alaskan Engr. of Yr., 1986. Fellow ASCE (pres. Anchorage chpt. 1985-86, chair mgmt. group A 1996-97, pres. Alaska sect. 1998-99, mem. nat. policy com. 2005—, named Alaskan Engr. of Yr. 1986, Harold R. Peyton award 2002); mem. Internat. Soc. for Soil Mechanics and Geotech. Engring., Cons. Engrs. Coun. Alaska (pres. 1989-90), Am. Cons. Engrs. Coun. (nat. dir. 1990-91), Project Mgmt. Inst. (v.p. Alaska chpt. 1991-95), Can. Geotechnical Soc., Toastmasters (pres. Anchorage club 1984), Sons of Norway (pres. Anchorage lodge 2000-02). Lutheran. Avocations: french horn, travel, classical music. Mailing: 8880 202d St Ste 320 Langley BC Canada V1M 4E7 Business E-Mail: hthomas@ch2m.com.

THOMAS, HUW FRANCIS, dean, dental educator; BDS, U. London, Guy's Hosp., 1975; MS in Dental Rsch., U. Rochester, 1978; PhD in Biomedical Sci., U. Conn., 1986. Cert. pediatric dentistry Eastman Dental Ctr., U. Rochester, 1978. Postdoctoral fellow. NIH, 1980—84; asst. prof. pediatric dentistry U. Tex. Health Sci. Ctr., San Antonio, 1978—80; assoc. prof. pediatric dentistry dept. U. Conn. Health Ctr., Conn., 1980—92; prof., chmn. dept. pediatric dentistry U. Tex. Health Sci. Ctr., San Antonio, 1992—2003, prof. dept. pediat. & cellular and structural biology; prof., dean Sch. Dentistry, U. Ala., Birmingham, 2004—. Sci. cons. ADA Commn. on Dental Accreditation. Reviewer: American Journal of Anatomy, Archives of Oral Biology, Journal of Dental Education. Recipient New Investigator Research award, NIH, 1985. Fellow: Internat. Coll. Dentists, Am. Coll. Dentists, Am. Acad. Pediat. Dentistry; mem.: AAAS (mem. at large sec. on dentistry and oral health sci.), Am. Assn. Dental Rsch. (mem. nominating com.), Am. Acad. Pediat. (mem. exec. com. pediat. dentistry sect.), Omicron Kappa Upsilon. Office: U Ala Birmingham Sch Dentistry SDB 406 1530 3rd Ave S Birmingham AL 35294-0007 Office Phone: 205-934-4720. Office Fax: 205-975-6544. Business E-Mail: hft@uab.edu.

THOMAS, IRV, writer, journalist; b. San Francisco, Apr. 14, 1927; s. David Goldstein and Minnie Resnick; m. Vivian Laura Allen, Nov. 30, 1956; life ptnr.: Alice Joy (dec. Dec. 2006). BA, U. Wash., 1990. Pub./editor Black Bart Brigade/Yin Times, Canyon, Calif., 1971-83; editor Earthstewards jour./newsletter, Bainbridge Island, Wash., 1985-89; pub./editor Ripening Seasons Jour., Seattle, 1995—2003. Tchr., workshop organizer Finding a Way Out, San Francisco, 1971-75; presenter World Futurist Conf., Toronto, Ont., 1980, Assn. for Humanistic Psychology Conv., Estes Park, Colo., 1976, Calif. Libr. Assn. Conv., Disneyland, 1972. Author, illustrator: Innocence Abroad, 1994, rev. edit., 2001, Derelict Days..., 2004, A Seasoned Life, 2006; contbr. anthology: Alternative Papers, 1982; contbr. articles to profl. jours. Housing activist Seattle Sr. Housing Program Advocates, 1996-99; co-founder Afterlife.org, 2001. Avocation: hitchhiking. Home: 6545 Ravenna Ave NE #307 Seattle WA 98115 Personal E-mail: irvthom1@comcast.net.

THOMAS, ISIAH LORD, III, professional basketball coach, sports team executive, retired professional basketball player; b. Chgo., Apr. 30, 1961; s. Mary Thomas; m. Lynn Kendall, 1985; children: Joshua, Lauren. BA in Criminal Justice, Ind. U., 1987. Profl. basketball player Detroit Pistons, 1981—94; pres. NBA Players Assn., 1989—94; v.p. Toronto Raptors, 1994—97, co-owner, exec. v.p. basketball ops., 1994—98; sportscaster NBC Sports, NYC, 1997—2000; owner, chmn., CEO Continental Basketball Assn., 1999—2001; founder Enlighten Sports, Inc., 1999—; head coach Ind. Pacers, Indpls., 2000—03; pres. basketball ops. NY Knicks, 2003—, head coach, 2006—. Mem. US Olympic Basketball Team (did not compete), 1980. Named Michiganian of the Yr., 1985; named to NBA All-Rookie team, 1982, All-Star Team, 1982—93, All NBA First Team, 1984, 1985, 1986, Basketball Hall of Fame, 2000; recipient All-Star Team MVP award, 1984, 1986, J. Walter Kennedy Citizenship award, NBA. 1987, NBA Playoff MVP award, 1990, NBA Finals MVP, 1990. Achievements include playing on NBA Championship Teams, 1989-90. Office: NY Knicks Two Pennsylvania Plz New York NY 10121-0091 *

THOMAS, J. MARK, sociologist, educator, minister; b. Ft. Worth, Dec. 20, 1947; s. Jacob Gillespie and Eleanor Rose (Geivett) T.; m. Jacquelyn Higby, Sept. 2, 1978; children: Megan Lane, Drew Martin. BA, Tex. Christian U., 1971, MDiv, 1974; PhD, U. Chgo., 1983. Ordained to ministry United Ch. of Christ, 1974. Asst. prof. philosophy and religion, chaplain Drury Coll., Springfield, Mo., 1983-85; adj. asst. prof. religion, chaplain Ripon (Wis.) Coll., 1985-87; vis. asst. prof. philosophy and religion Beloit (Wis.) Coll., 1987-89; sr. rsch. fellow Au Sable Inst. Environ. Studies, Mancelona, Mich., 1989—. Sociology instr., chair dept. social sci. Madison Area Tech. Coll. Author: Ethics and Technoculture, 1987, (with others) Being and Doing, 1987, Philosophy and Technology, Vol. 10, 1990, Religion in the New Millennium, 2001, Encyclopedia of Science, Technology and Ethics, 2005; editor: Paul Tillich, The Spiritual Situation in Our Technical Society, 1988, God and Capitalism, 1991, Religion in the New Millennium, 2001. Chmn. planning com. Congress of Sci., Tech. and Religion for the Parliament of World Religion, 1993. Recipient Disting. Tchr. Yr., Madison Area Tech. Coll., 1999. Mem. Midwest Sociol. Soc., Communitarian Network. Democrat. Mem. United Ch. of Christ. Home: 816 Lincoln St Madison WI 53711-2163 Office: Madison Area Tech Coll Downtown Edn Ctr 211 N Carroll St Madison WI 53703-2211 E-mail: jmarkthomas@charter.net.

THOMAS, JACOB EARL, retired physicist; b. Seattle, Sept. 7, 1918; s. Jacob Earl and Ursula May (Johnson) T.; m. Margaret Louise Johnston, June 15, 1977; children— Richard Bruce, Jacob Earl, John Calvin, James Hayden, Denise May Thomas Pratt, Stillman Jefferson. AB, Johns Hopkins U., 1939; PhD, Calif. Inst. Tech., 1943. Group leader rocket devel. Calif. Inst. Tech., Pasadena, 1942-45; group leader Manhattan Project, U. Calif., Los Alamos, 1945-46; asst. prof. elec. engring. M.I.T., Cambridge, 1946-51; mem. tech. staff Bell Telephone Labs., Murray Hill, NJ, 1951-52; group leader M.I.T. Lincoln Labs., Lexington, 1952-55; prof., chmn. dept. physics Wayne State U., Detroit, 1955-59; dir. research Sylvania Electric, Woburn, Mass., 1959-62; mgr. solid state devel. IBM, Poughkeepsie, NY, 1962-64; mgr. new product devel. Gen. Instrument Co., Newark, 1964-67; v.p. Carman Sapphire Co., Reseda, Calif., 1967-70; cons. Warnecke Electron Tubes, Des Plaines, Ill., 1970-71; dir. components research Victor Comptometer Co., Des Plaines, 1971-75; mgr. advanced devel. NCR Corp., Ithaca, NY, 1975-84. Cons. pvt. cos. and govt. agys. Contbr. articles to sci. jours.; patentee in field. Active S.E. Asian refugee resettlement program. Recipient Service award U.S. Office Sci. Research and Devel., 1946 Fellow: IEEE (Millennium medal), Am. PHys. Soc.; mem.: Tau Beta Pi, Phi Beta Kappa, Sigma Xi. Democrat. Presbyterian. Home: 323 Savage Farm Dr Ithaca NY 14850-6503 E-mail: ethomas4@twcny.rr.com.

THOMAS, JACQUELYN MAY, librarian; b. Mechanicsburg, Pa., Jan. 26, 1932; d. William John and Gladys Elizabeth (Warren) Harvey; m. David Edward Thomas, Aug. 28, 1954; children: Lesley J., Courtenay J., Hilary A. BA summa cum laude, Gettysburg Coll., Pa., 1954; postgrad., U. NC, Chapel Hill, 1969; MEd, U. NH, Durham, 1971. Libr. Phillips Exeter Acad., Exeter, NH, 1971-77, acad. libr., 1977—. Chair governing bd. Child Care Ctr., 1987-91; chair Com. to Enhance Status of Women, Exeter, 1981-84; chair Loewenstein Com., Exeter, 1982—; pres. Cum Laude Soc., Exeter, 1984-86; James H. Ottaway Jr. prof., 1990—; mem. bldg. com. Exeter Pub. Libr., 1986-88; chair No. New Eng., Coun. for Women in Ind. Schs., 1985-87; chmn. Lamont Poetry Program, Exeter, 1984-86. Editor: The Design of the Library: A Guide to Sources of Information, 1981, Rarities of Our Time: The Special Collections of the Phillips Exeter Academy Library; pub.: Memorial Minutes, Phillips Exeter Academy, 1936-2002, Friends of the Academy Library, Collected Letters Book, Class of 1945 special collections brochure, other Phillips Exeter materials. Libr. trustee, treas. Exeter Day Sch., 1965-69; bd. Exeter Hosp. Vols., 1954-59; mem. Exeter Hosp. Corp., 1978—; bd. dirs. Greater Portsmouth Cmty. Found., 1990—; active AAC&U, On Campus with Women, Wellesley Coll. Ctr. for Rsch. on Women; mem. People to People Amb. Program, sch. and youth svcs. libr. del. to People's Rep. China, 1998. Grantee N.H. Coun. for Humanties, 1981-82, NEH, 1982; recipient Lillian Radford trust award, 1989. Mem. ALA, Internat. Assn. Sch. Librs., New Eng. Libr. Assn., NJ, Ednl. Media Assn., New Eng. Assn. Ind. Sch. Librs., Am. Assn. Sch. Librs. (chmn. non-pub. sch. sect.), Phi Beta Kappa. Home: 17 Eagle Dr Newmarket NH 03857 Office: Class of 1945 Libr Phillips Exeter Acad 20 Main St Exeter NH 03833-2460 Office Phone: 603-777-3328. Office Fax: 603-777-4389. Business E-Mail: jthomas@exeter.edu.

THOMAS, JAMES, JR., retired engineering executive, retired military officer; b. Tallahassee, Fla., July 16, 1940; s. James Thomas, Sr. and Mattie B. Thomas; m. Claudia L. Elmore; children: Wallace D., Cassandra M. Hamer, James Thomas, III, Jasper L. BA in Mgmt., St. Leo U., Fla., 1981—85. Lic. general contractor, State Ga., 2001; realtor State Ga., 1995. Non-commd. officer USMC, Parris Island, SC, 1957—60, US Army, 1962—65, commd. officer, 1965—80; mgr. Eckerd Drugs, Inc., Savannah, Ga., 1981—82; US civil svc. real estate officer US Army, Ft. Stewart, Ga., 1982—88; project mgr. engring. US Civil Svc., Ft. Stewart, 2001—; real estate specialist US Army Corps Engrs., Savannah. Contbr. articles to army manuals. Chmn. Hinesville Planning & Zoning Commn., 1987—2005, Liberty County Consol. Planning Commn., Hinesville, Ga., 2005—06; pres./dir. EBM Liberty County Inc., 1991—2006; mem. Liberty County Fin. Authority, Hinesville, 2003—05, Liberty County Hosp. Authority, Hinesville, 2004—06, Hinesville Met. Planning Orgn., 2005—06. Officer US Army, 1957—80, US, Germany, Japan, Italy, Vietnam, Thailand & Taiwan. Recipient Commanders award for civilians, US Army, 1991—92, 1994, 2000, 2006, Commanders award, 1992, Dir. of Yr. award, EBM Liberty County, Inc., 2000, Outstanding Civic Person of Yr. award, Liberty County Emancipation Assn., 2004. Mem.: NAACP (officer 1986—2006), Ga. Assn. Planning & Zoning Adminstrs. (assoc.), INTERTEL (assoc.), Mensa (assoc.), Porsche Club Am. (assoc.). Achievements include design of Warriors Walk, a memorial for soldiers killed during Iraqui Freedom from Ft. Stewart. Avocations: golf, sport car racing, shooting. Home: 947 Fox Haven Ct Hinesville GA 31313 Home Phone: 912-876-5630. Personal E-mail: tylert@clds.net.

THOMAS, JAMES B., dean, management educator; m. Michele Thomas; 3 children. Grad., Pa. State U., 1974; MA in Govt., Fla. State U.; PhD in Strategic Mgmt., U. Tex., Austin, 1988. Dir. info. mgmt. sys. Fla. Dept. State; dir. info. tech. strategic planning Office of Tex. Sec. of State; asst. prof. Pa. State U.; sr. assoc. dean Smeal Coll. Bus., Pa. State U., dean, prof. info. scis. and mgmt., 2006—; founding dean Coll. Info. Scis. and Tech., Pa. State U., 1999—2006. Spkr. in field. Contbr. articles to profl. jours. Office: Pa State U Smeal Coll Bus 210B Business Bldg University Park PA 16802 Office Phone: 814-863-0448. Office Fax: 814-865-7064. E-mail: jthomas@smeal.psu.edu.

THOMAS, JAMES BERT, JR., retired federal agency administrator; b. Tallahassee, Mar. 16, 1935; s. James Bert and Stella E. (Lewis) T.; m. Sharon Mae Kelly, June 16, 1962; children: James Bert III, Mary Elizabeth, John Christopher. BS, Fla. State U., 1957. C.P.A., Fla. Spl. auditor Office State Comptr., Jacksonville, Fla., 1958; jr. auditor J.D.A. Holley & Co., C.P.A.'s, Tallahassee, 1959; sr. auditor Office of the State Auditor, Tallahassee, 1959-60; trainee, audit dir. HUD audit divsn., Washington, 1960-71; asst. dir. Bur. Accounts ICC, Washington, 1972-75, dir. Bur. Accounts, 1977-80; insp. gen. U.S. Dept. HUD, Washington, 1975-77, U.S. Dept. Edn., Washington, 1980-95; dir. auditing Office of the Gov., State of Fla., Tallahassee, 1995—2004; ret., 2004. Mem. Pres.'s Coun. Integrity and Efficiency, chmn. audit stds. subcom., 1984-95, chmn. audit com., 1989-90. Mem. AICPA (strategic planning com. 1987-90, chmn. govt. auditing stds. adv. coun. 1991—), Inst. Internal Auditors (trustee Rsch. Found. 1991-92), Assn. Govt. Accts. (chmn. fin. mgmt. stds. bd. 1985-86), Accts. Roundtable. Roman Catholic. Home: 4737 Tory Sound Ln Unit 601 Tallahassee FL 32309-2266 Office: Exec Office of Governor Rm 2107 The Capitol Tallahassee FL 32399-0001

THOMAS, JAMES EDWARD, JR., brokerage house executive; b. Atlanta, Apr. 23, 1950; s. James Edward and Dortha Jean (White) Thomas; m. Leslie Ann Stagmaier, Sept. 6, 1975; children: Steele Stagmaier, Katherine Mills. BA magna cum laude, U. Ga., 1972, JD cum laude, 1975. Mgr. Genuine Parts Co., Atlanta, 1975-77; v.p. Robinson Humphrey Co., Atlanta, 1977-94; ptnr. J.C. Bradford and Co., Atlanta, 1994—2000; mng. dir. Wachovia Securities, Ga., 2000—02; chmn., CEO Stillpoint Advisors, Inc., 2003—. Bd. dirs. Enstar Comm. Corp., The Kinston Group, Inc., Atlanta, Tophat Soccer Club, Atlanta, Hall's Boathouse, Inc., Lakemont, Ga., Vista Environ. Info., Inc., San Diego. Pres. Castlewood Civic Orgn., Inc., Atlanta; mem. Lake Rabun Homeowners Assn., Lakemont, Ga.; mem. bd. advisors U. Ga., Habitat for Humanity. Mem. Internat. Platform Assn., Ga. Bar Assn., La Societe des Tetes Grandes, Capital City Club, U. Ga. LEADS Adv. Bd., Ga Tennis Found. (treas., trustee). Republican. Episcopalian. Avocations: boating, tennis, golf.

THOMAS, JAMES PATRICK, special education educator; b. Chgo., Sept. 24, 1946; s. Jacque Anthony and Dorothy Lucille (Brown) T.; m. Cathy E. Hanks, Sept. 29, 1979 (div. Aug. 1990); 1 child, Nicholas Jacque. BA in History and Polit. Sci., Drake U., 1973; MS in Pub. Adminstrn., Troy State U., 1983; MS in Spl. Edn., Johns Hopkins U., 1994, cert. advanced grad. studies, 1994. cert. spl. educator. Commd. 2nd lt. USAF, 1973, advanced through grades to maj., 1985; missile launch officer, instr., crew comdr., contr. 91st Strategic Missile Wing, Minot, N.D., 1974-78; exec. officer, asst. ops. officer, resource advisor 6916th Electronic Security Squadron, Hellenikon Air Base, Greece, 1978-81; chief programs br. 6940th Electronic Security Wing, Ft. Meade, Md., 1981-82; program mgr. USAF Ops. Security Hq USAF/XOEO Directorate of Electronic Combat, Washington, 1982-85; intelligence collection activities mgr./chief Hdqrs. U.S. European Command, Stuttgart, Germany, 1986-88; signals intelligence planning staff officer Nat. Security Agy., Ft. Meade, 1988-90; cons. spl. edn. Balt., 1991—. Adj. faculty mem. Catonsville (Md.) C.C., 1991—; spl. educator Howard County Sch. System, Columbia, 1992-94, Boonsborro (Md.) Middle Sch., 1994-96, Hiatt Mid. Sch., Des Moines, 1996-98, Johnston (Iowa) Mid. Sch., 1998-99, Johnston H.S., 1999-2000, Variety Sch., Las Vegas, Nev., 2000-04, spl. edn. instrnl. facilitator Victoria Fertitta Mid. Sch., 2004-05, C.J. Lawrence Mid. Sch., 2005— Author: (pamphlet) Your Rights to Legal Advice, 1994; co-author: The Outcome of a Services Evaluation for Families of Vietnam Vets. with Children with Disabilities in the Balt. Met. Area, 1995. Pres. Cath. Men Parish Athens, Greece, 1979—81, Minot AFB, ND, 1975—78. With USN, 1964—73. Decorated Purple Heart, 2 Def. Meritorious Svc. medals, Meritorious Svc. medals, Air Force Commendation medal, Air medal, Air Force Achievement medal, Navy Combat Action Ribbon, Vietnam Gallantry Cross. Mem.: KC, VFW (life), Swiftboat Sailors Assn. Inc. (pres. 1995—2002), Am. Legion China Post 1, Assn. Air Force Missileers (life), Vets. Vietnam War (life), Navy League (life), Mil. Order Purple Heart (life), Ret. Officers Assn. (life), Air Force Assn. (life), Disabled Am. Vets. (life), Phoenix Soc., Soaring Assn. Am., Phi Delta Gamma. Roman Catholic. Avocations: pilot of sailplanes, sailing, snorkeling, golf, running. Home: 1929 High Mesa Dr Henderson NV 89012-6182

THOMAS, JAMES WILLIAM, lawyer; b. NYC, May 12, 1949; s. Howard and Alice (Brennan) T.; m. Cecilia Coleman Goad, July 7, 1973; children: James William, Brennan McKinney. BS, U. Dayton, 1971; JD, Ohio No. U., 1974. Bar: Ohio 1974, U.S. Dist. Ct. Ohio 1976. Ptnr. Earley

& Thomas, Eaton, Ohio, 1974-89; pvt. practice Eaton, 1989—. Village solicitor Village of Lewisburg (Ohio), 1977-81, Village of Verona (Ohio), 1979-81; asst. pros. atty. Preble County (Ohio), 1980-81. Mem. Preble County Cmty. Corrections Planing Bd. Fellow Ohio State Bar Found.; mem. ABA, Ohio State Bar Assn., Ohio State Bar Coll., Ohio Acad. Trial Lawyers, Ohio Assn. Criminal Def. Lawyers, Preble county Bar Assn. (pres. 1982-84), Comm. Improvement Corp., Eaton Country Club, Rotary (dir. 1980-87, pres. 1987-88). Republican. Roman Catholic. Avocations: boating, tennis. Home: 761 Vinland Cv Eaton OH 45320-2536 Office: 112 N Barron St Eaton OH 45320-1702 E-mail: jthomaslaw@yahoo.com.

THOMAS, JANET Y., political science professor, researcher; d. Ehoch Thornton and Florence Rose Thomas. BA, Norfolk State U., 1991; EdM, Widener U., 1997; PhD, U. Ill., 2000. Rsch. assoc. Hahnemann U., Phila., 1995—97; assoc. rsch. scientist Johns Hopkins U., Balt., 2000—03; with dept. academic support programs Office of Dep Provost, U. Pa., Phila., 2003—. Author: Educating Drug-Exposed Children, 2004. Mem.: Am. Edn. Assn., Am. Edn. Rsch., Kappa Delta Pi, Phi Delta Kappa. Business E-Mail: janety@pobox.upenn.edu.

THOMAS, JEFFREY CONE, financial executive, consultant; b. New Orleans, Oct. 10, 1941; s. Eads Poitevent and Virginia Lee (King) T.; m. Brenda Gayle Ballard, June 7, 1969 (div. Mar. 1972). BA, La. State U., 1965. CLU; ChFC; CFP; CFS. Mgmt. trainee Am. Bank and Trust Co., Baton Rouge, 1965—68; supr. Travelers Ins. Co., Baton Rouge, 1968—71; dist. dir. Conn. Gen. Life Ins. Co., Baton Rouge, 1971—74; pres., CEO Pension & Profit Sharing Cons., Baton Rouge, 1974—77; pres. Fin. Advisor & Cons., Baton Rouge, 1977—. Adj. instr. adult eve. classes Coll. Fin. Planning, 1987-92; cons. Ethyl Corp., Baton Rouge, 1982, Dow Chem., Plaquemine, La., 1986. Vol. ARC, Baton Rouge, 1965—69; mem. adminstrv. bd. First Meth. Ch., Baton Rouge, 1987—89. Avocations: golf, tennis, fishing, gardening. Office: Fin Advisor & Cons PO Box 65238 Baton Rouge LA 70896-5238 Home Phone: 225-925-0912; Office Phone: 225-293-1035.

THOMAS, JENNIE See ORR, JENNIE

THOMAS, JEREMIAH LINDSAY, III, lawyer; b. Wilmington, Del., June 20, 1946; s. Jeremiah Lindsay Jr. and Dorothy Eleanor (Conway) T.; m. Clara Ewing Ruthrauff, Oct. 17, 1981; children: Catherine Ewing, Lindsay Barlow. BA, U. Va., 1968, JD, 1972. Bar: N.Y. 1973. Assoc. Simpson Thacher & Bartlett, NYC, 1972-79, ptnr., 1979—. Mem.: ABA, Met. Golf Assn. (legal counsel 1984—, exec. com. 1992—98, dir. Found. 1992—98), Assn. Bar of City of N.Y., N.Y. State Bar Assn. Office: Simpson Thacher & Bartlett 425 Lexington Ave Fl 28 New York NY 10017-3954 Office Phone: 212-455-7110. Business E-Mail: jthomas@stblaw.com.

THOMAS, JERRY ARTHUR, soil scientist; b. Logansport, Ind., Mar. 5, 1942; s. Purnal Kidd and Dorothy Helen (Smith) T.; m. Virginia Amy York, Oct. 17, 1964; 1 child, Charles Edward. BS in Agronomy and Soil Chemistry, Purdue U., 1965; MS in Soil Fertility, Pa. State U., 1968. Libr. chemistry dept. Purdue Univ., West Lafayette, Ind., 1963, tech. aid USDA, ARS, agronomy dept., 1963-65; grad. teaching asst. agronomy dept. Pa. State U., University Park, 1965-67; soil scientist USDA Soil Conservation Svc., Indpls., 1967-85, Ind. State Bd. Health, Indpls., 1985—. Com. mem. Ind. State 4-H Rabbit com., West Lafayette, 1976-2000. Author publs. in field including Classification of the Sloping Soils of the West Baden Group in Monroe County, Ind., 1978, Soil Survey of Monroe County, Ind., 1981, Soil Survey of Lawrence County, Ind., 1985, Availability of Conservation Tillage Planting Systems for Northwestern Ind., 1985. Asst. scoutmaster Boy Scouts Am., Rensselaer, Ind., 1982-92. Recipient Innovative award Coun. State Govts., 1988; named Environ. Health Specialist of Yr., Environ. Health Assn., 1993. Mem. Am. Soc. Agronomy, Soil Sci. Soc. Am., Soil and Water Conservation Soc. Am., Ind. Acad. Sci., Ind. Assn. Profl. Soil Classifiers, Ind. Environtl. Health Assn., Masons, Eastern Star. Mem. Christian Ch. (Disciples Of Christ). Home: 301 S Park Ave Rensselaer IN 47978-3037 Office: Ind State Bd Health Divsn Sanitary Engring 5E 2 N Meridian St Indianapolis IN 46204-3003 Office Phone: 317-233-7177. Business E-Mail: jthomas@isdh.in.gov.

THOMAS, JIMI ELIZABETH, elementary school educator; b. Kinston, NC, Oct. 15, 1947; d. Charles L. and Mildred Elizabeth; 1 child, Stephanie Elizabeth. BS in Elem. Edn., Old Dominion U., Norfolk, Va., 1970, MS in Elem. Edn., 1977, degree in Adminstrn. and Supervision, 1984, PhD in Urban Svcs., 1986. Cert. elem. edn. tchr. grades K-7 Va., social studies tchr. grades 5-8 Va. Sixth grade tchr. Lindenwood Elem., Norfolk, Va., 1970—71; fifth grade tchr. Bayview Elem., Norfolk, Va., 1974—76; English and reading instr. Wahiawa CC, Wahiawa, Hawaii, 1977—79, St. Louis HS, Honolulu, 1979—80; eighth grade English and history tchr. Dept. Def., Gaeta, Italy, 1982—83; drug intervention specialist VBCPS, Va. Beach, Va., 1986—87, drug edn. coord., 1987—89; eighth grade civics tchr. Brandon Mid. Sch., Va. Beach, Va., 1989—. Va. and US history tchr. Open Campus HS, Va. Beach, Va., 1998; adj. faculty reading edn. Old Dominion U., 2004—; tchr. mentor City of Va. Beach, 2005—, student tchr. supr., 2005—; presenter in field. Recipient Project Citizen award, Va., 2002. Mem.: Nat. Coun. History Educators, Profl. Assn. Tchrs., Longstreet Soc., Civil War Roundtable. Achievements include design of sixth, seventh and eighth grade social studies remedial program with focus on standards of learning in Virginia. Home: 5048 Clairmont Ct Virginia Beach VA 23462 Personal E-mail: jethomas1@verizon.net.

THOMAS, JIMMY LYNN, retired treasurer; b. Mayfield, Ky., Aug. 3, 1941; s. Alben Stanley and Emma Laura (Alexander) T.; m. Kristin H. Kent, Oct. 1986; children: James Nelson, Carter Danforth. BS, U. Ky., 1963; MBA, Columbia U., 1964. Fin. analyst Ford Motor Co., Detroit, 1964-66; asst. treas. Joel Dean Assocs., NYC, 1966-67; asst. contr. Trans World Airlines, NYC, 1967-73; sr. v.p. fin. svcs., treas. Gannett Co., Inc., Arlington, Va., 1973-98. Bd. dirs. HSBC, Rochester, Tremont Ptnrs. Fundraiser United Negro Coll. Fund; bd. trustees, treas. Harley Sch., Rochester, N.Y.; bd. overseers Strong Meml. Hosp., Rochester; bd. govs. Genesee Hosp., Rochester; bd. dirs. Arlington Cmty. Found., Nat. Press Club Bldg., Washington. With U.S. Army, 1966-72. Ashland Oil Co. scholar, 1959-63, McKinsey scholar 1964; Samuel Bronfman fellow, 1963-64. Mem. Nat. Assn. Corp. Treas., U. Ky. Alumni Assn., Columbia U. Alumni Assn., Country Club of Rochester, Genessee Valley Club, Beta Gamma Sigma, Omicron Delta Kappa, Sigma Alpha Epsilon. Democrat. Mem. Christian Ch. (Disciples Of Christ). Home: 9700 Jennings Rd Eden NY 14057-9518 Office Phone: 716-992-9935.

THOMAS, JO, journalist, educator; b. Long Beach, Calif., Dec. 7, 1943; d. Guy O'Neil DeYoung, Jr. and Josephine (Bradley) DeYoung; m. William L. Thomas III, June 12, 1965 (div. Sept. 1969); m. William F. Kelleher Jr., Dec. 19, 1985; children: Susan Elizabeth Kelleher, Kathleen DeYoung Kelleher. BA summa cum laude, Wake Forest U., 1965; MA, U. N.C., 1967. Reporter Cin. Post and Times-Star, 1966—70, Detroit Free Press, 1971—77; from Washington corr. to writer N.Y. Times, 1977—2001, writer, 2001—02; assoc. prof. U. Ill., Urbana, 1987—94, asst. chancellor, 2003—04; assoc. chancellor Syracuse U., NY, 2004—07, prof. journalism, 2004—07. Contbr. articles to newspapers and mags. Recipient Outstanding Reporting award Detroit Press Club, 1974-75, Robert F. Kennedy award, 1973; Nieman fellow Harvard U., 1970-71; mem NY Times staff team winning Pulitzer prize, 2002. Mem. Phi Beta Kappa, Kappa Tau Alpha. Personal E-mail: jothom@gmail.com.

THOMAS, JOAB LANGSTON, retired academic administrator, biologist, educator; b. Holt, Ala., Feb. 14, 1933; s. Ralph Cage and Chamintney Elizabeth (Stovall) Thomas; m. Marly A. Dukes, Dec. 22, 1954; children: Catherine, David, Jennifer, Frances. AB, Harvard U., 1955, MA, 1957, PhD, 1959; DSc (hon.), U. Ala., 1981; LLD (hon.), Stillman Coll., 1987; LHD (hon.), Tri-State U., 1994; LHD (hon.), N.C. State U., 1998. Cytotaxonomist Arnold Aboretum, Harvard, 1959—61; prof. biology U. Ala., University, 1966—76, 1988—91, asst. dean Coll. Arts and Scis., 1964—65, 1969, dean for student devel., 1969—74, v.p., 1974—76, dir. Herbarium, 1961—76, dir. Arboretum, 1964—69, pres. Tuscaloosa, 1981—88; chancellor N.C. State U., Raleigh, 1976—81; pres. Pa. State U., University Park, 1990—95, pres. emeritus, 1995. Intern acad. adminstrn. Am. Coun. on Edn., 1971. Author: A Monographic Study of the Cyrillaceae, 1960, Wildflowers of Alabama and Adjoining States, 1973, The Rising South, 1976, Poisonous Plants and Venomous Animals of Alabama and Adjoining States, 1990. Bd. dirs. Internat. Potato Ctr., 1977—83, chmn., 1982—83; bd. dirs. Internat. Svc. for Nat. Agrl. Rsch., 1985—91. Named Citizen of Yr., City of Tuscaloosa, 1987; recipient Ala. Acad. Honor, 1983, Palmer Mus. Art medal, Coll. Pres.'s award, All-Am. Football Found., 1997, Spl. Recognition award, Assn. for Continuing Higher Edn., 1998. Mem.: Golden Key, Phi Kappa Phi, Omicron Delta Kappa (Laurel Crowned Circle award 2001), Sigma Xi, Phi Beta Kappa. Office: Univ Ala 413 Sci Collections Bldg Tuscaloosa AL 35487-0001 Business E-Mail: jlthomas@dbtech.net.

THOMAS, JOE CARROLL, retired human resources director; b. Belmont, NC, Nov. 2, 1931; m. Ruth Stone, June 17, 1951; children: Joe(dec.), Jerry, Angela. BA, Belmont Abbey Coll., 1954; MS, Cornell U., 1961; postgrad., U. NC, 1985. Diplomate in profl. counseling; cert. Sr. Profl. in Human Resources. Terr. salesman Gen. Foods Corp., Charlotte, NC, 1954—59, adminstrv. asst. to dist. mgr. Atlanta, 1960, mgr. terr. sales San Antonio, 1962; asst. dir. personnel textiles divsn. Kendall Co., Charlotte, NC, 1962-64; dir. personnel S.E. region Gifford Hill & Co., Charlotte, 1964-71; dir. mgmt. svcs. Ervin Industries, Charlotte, 1971-75; v.p. indsl. rels. Crompton & Knowles, Charlotte, 1975-76; exec. v.p., dir. human resources Barclays Group Inc., Charlotte, 1976-97; ret., 1997. Mem. adv. coun. Sch. Bus., Western Carolina U., Cullowhee, NC, 1980-84; mem. bd. arbitrators NASD Dispute Resolution, Inc., 2001; bd. adv. Belmont Abbey Coll., 2005 Vice chmn. bd. trustees Belmont Abbey Coll., 1982-88; chmn. fundraising campaign Charlotte chpt. Am. Heart Assn., 1984; mem. bd. visitors mercy Hosp., Charlotte, 1984-87; bd. dirs. mercy Health Svcs., Charlotte, 1988-96; bd. dirs. Jr. Achievement Charlotte, 1985-88, INROADS divsn. Charlotte, Inc., 1987-88; bd. visitors Johnson C. Smith Univ., 1989-92 Mem. Soc. Human Resource Mgmt., Employers Assn. (bd. dirs. 1993-99, exec. com. 1995-99), Charlotte Athletic Club (pres. 1982-83), Charlotte Rotary, Charlotte C. of C. (bd. advisors 1992-97, Aldersgate bd. advisors 2000—, Aldersgate bd. dirs. 2003—, bd. dirs. chair-elect 2005-2006, chmn. bd. dirs. 2007). Republican. Personal E-mail: carrolleth@aol.com.

THOMAS, JOHN, mechanical engineer, artist; b. Tiruvalla, Kerala, India, Jan. 2, 1946; arrived in U.S., 1974; s. Munnencheril Varghese and Rachel (Mathai) Thomas; m. Mary Parapat Varghese, Apr. 28, 1975; children: Joel George, Sayana Rachel. BSMechE, Birla Inst. Tech., Ranchi, India, 1969; MSMechE, U. Waterloo, Ont., Can., 1974. Registered profl. engr., Wis. Lectr. mech. engring. U. Kerala, 1970-71; design engr. Combustion Engring., Inc., Springfield, Ohio, 1974-76; mech. engr. Ingersoll-Rand Co., Painted Post, NY, 1977-80; engr. Allis-Chalmers Corp., Milw., 1980-82; pvt. practice engring. cons. Milw., 1982-84; sr. technology devel. engr. Cross & Trecker divsn. Kearney & Trecker Corp., Milw., 1984-87; prin. John Thomas & Assocs., Brookfield, Wis., 1988-90; sr. product engr. N.W. Water Group, Pub. Ltd. Corp. (now U.S. Filter Corp.), Waukesha, Wis., 1989-94; pres. Thomas Products Co., Brookfield, Wis., 1995—; staff engr. Milsco Mfg. Co. unit of Jason Inc., Milw., 1997—2003. Mem.: ASME, U. Waterloo Alumni Assn. Achievements include patents in field. Avocations: photography, golf. Home: 18330 Benington Brookfield WI 53045-5419 Office: Thomas Products Co The Nature Arts Gallery PO Box 401 Brookfield WI 53008-0401

THOMAS, JOHN, professional sports team executive; Grad. in Bus., U. Minn. With KSTP-TV, Mpls./St. Paul, KFAN Sports Radio, Maj. League Baseball Seattle Mariners, NHL Minn. North Stars, NBA Minn. Timberwolves, NBA Rockets, WNBA Comets and Arena Football League Thunderbears, Houston, 1994—99; pres. Maloof Sports & Entertainment (NBA Kings, WNBA Monarchs and ARCO Arena), Sacramento, 1999—. Bd. dirs. Sacramento Conv. and Visitors Bur., Sacramento Metro Chamber, Valley Vision's Leadership Coun. Office: Sacramento Kings ARCO Arena 1 Sports Pky Sacramento CA 95834-2301 *

THOMAS, JOHN ARLEN, pharmacologist, educator, science administrator; b. LaCrosse, Wis., Apr. 6, 1933; s. John M. and Eva Hazel (Nelson) T.; m. Barbara A. Fisler, June 22, 1957; children: Michael J., Jane L. BS in Sci. Edn., U. Wis., 1956; MA in Physiology, U. Iowa, 1958, PhD in Physiology, 1961. Diplomate Am. Acad. Toxicologic Sci. Instr. U. Iowa, Iowa City, 1961; asst. prof. U. Va., Charlottesville, 1961-64; assoc. prof. Creighton U., Omaha, 1964-67, W.Va. U., Morgantown, 1968-69, prof. pharmacology, 1970-80; asst. dean W.Va. Sch. Medicine, Morgantown, 1973-75, assoc. dean, 1973-80; v.p. corp. rsch. Baxter Internat. Travenol Labs., Round Lake, Ill., 1980-87; v.p. acad. svcs. U. Tex. Health Sci. Ctr., San Antonio, 1988-99, prof. emeritus pharmacology dept. toxicology, 1988—; prof. Ind. U. Sch. Medicine. Chmn. expert adv. com. Can. Network Toxicol. Ctr., 1999-02; sci. adv. bd. USAF, 2002-05, FDA, 2003—; adj. prof. pharmacology Ind. U. Sch. Medicine, Indpls., 2005; cons. to NIH, Inst. of Medicine, NRC, NAS. Author (with M.G. Mawhinney): Synopsis of Endocrine Pharmacology, 1978; author: (with E.J. Keenan) Principles of Endocrine Pharmacology, 1986; editor (with others): Basic and Clinical Toxicology of Lead, 1985; editor: Endocrine Toxicology, 1985, 1996, Drugs Athletes & Physical Performance, 1988, Biotechnology and Safety Assessment, 1993; editor: (with Laurie A. Myers) Biotechnology and Safety Assessment 2d edit., 1981; editor: (with Roy L. Fuchs) Biotechnology and Safety Assessment, 3d edit., 2002; editor: Endocrine Methods, 1996, Toxic Substances Mechanism Jour.; contbr. articles to profl. jours. Sgt. U.S. Army, 1951-53. Recipient Cert. Svc. US EPA, 1977, Commn. Spl. citation FDA, 2006, Advis Commn. Svc. award FDA, 2007; named Outstanding Tchr., W.Va. U., 1971, 73, 79, Outstanding alumnus U. Wis., La Crosse, 1978, Disting. Alumni, U. Iowa, 1997, Adv. Com. Svc. award FDA, 2007; named to Hall of Excellence-LaCrosse, 2002. Fellow Acad. Toxicol. Sci. (pres. 2001); mem. Endocrine Soc., Soc. Toxicology (councilor, Merit award 1998), Am. Soc. Pharmacology and Exptl. Therapeutics, Am. Coll. Toxicology (councilor, pres., disting. fellow 2004, Disting. Svc. award), Teratology Soc., Am. Acad. Vet. Pharmacology, Am. Chem. Soc. (pres. chem. toxicology pathology), Tex. Soc. Biomed. Rsch. (bd. sci. advisors 1989-99, Disting. Svc. award 1996), Russian Acad. Med. Sci. (fgn. fellow-elect 1995). Home and Office: 7258 Pymbroke Cir Fishers IN 46038 Office Phone: 317-845-5224. Personal E-mail: jat-tox@sbcglobal.net.

THOMAS, JOHN CHARLES, lawyer; b. Norfolk, Va., Sept. 18, 1950; s. John and Floretta V. (Sears) T.; m. Pearl Walden, Oct. 9, 1982; children: John Charles Jr., Ruby Virginia, Lewis LeGrant. BA in Am. Govt. with distinction, U. Va., 1972, JD, 1975. Bar: Va. 1975, U.S. Dist. Ct. (ea. and we. dists.) 1976, U.S. Ct. Appeals (4th cir.) 1976, U.S. Supreme Ct. 1979, U.S. Ct. Appeals (D.C. cir.) 1980, U.S. Ct. Appeals (10th cir.) 1991, U.S. Ct. Appeals (11th cir.) 1992. Assoc. Hunton & Williams, Richmond, Va., 1975-82, ptnr., 1982-83, 89—; justice Supreme Ct. of Va., Richmond, 1983-89. Former mem. adv. con. on appellate rules U.S. Jud. Conf., permanent mem. 4th cir. Hon. dir. U. Va. Law Sch. Found. Fellow Am. Bar Found., Va. Bar Found.; mem. ABA (former co-chair nat. conf. lawyers and reps. of media, coun. appellate lawyers), Ct. Arbitration for Sport, Am. Acad. Appellate Lawyers, Va. State Bar, Va. Bar Assn., Bar Assn. City of Richmond, Old Dominion Bar Assn., Omega Psi Phi Office: Hunton & Williams Riverfront Plz East Tower PO Box 1535 Richmond VA 23218-1535 Office Phone: 804-788-8522. Business E-Mail: jcthomas@hunton.com.

THOMAS, JOHN DAVID, composer, musician, compact disc artist, photographer, music and arts business owner; b. Muncie, Ind., Mar. 30, 1951; s. John Charles and Phyllis Lorraine (Wear) T.; m. Rosalie Faith Baldwin, July 27, 1974 (div. 1990); children: Bethany Carol, Mark David. Student, Purdue U., 1969-71, Jordan Coll. of Music, Indpls., 1961-65; BS in Music Theory and Composition, Ball State U., 1976. Musician, composer, 1955—; digital and film photographer, graphic designer Have Camera Will Travel, 1956—; cellist The Howe String Quartet (with Ann Pinney, Mary Ann Tilford, Anne Wuster), Indpls., 1967-68; keyboardist, vocalist, cellist Fire and The Rebel Kind rock bands, Indpls., 1967-69, Good Conduct rock band, Muncie, Ind., 1972-73; pianist The Pavillion at Olde Towne, Los Gatos, Calif., 1969; radio announcer John David's Late Night Rock Show WCCR-AM, West Lafayette, Ind., 1969-70; photographer Indpls., 1964—84, 1991—2000; budget analyst Office of Comptr. USAFAC, Indpls., 1976-84; co-leader, keyboardist, composer, arranger, vocalist, sound technician Jetstream band, Carmel, Indpls., Kokomo, Columbus, Bloomington, Ind., 1979-83; co-leader, keyboardist, vocalist, sound technician The Thomas Bros., King's Crown Inn, Kokomo, 1979; sound/audio visual technician Valley Cathedral Ch., Phoenix, 1987. Pianist, synthesist Paul Thomas and Night and Day, The Tim Barnett Band, Indpls. Mus. Art, 1992, Radisson Hotel and Broadmoor Country Club, Indpls., 1991, Highland Country Club, Indpls., The Ritz Charles Hotel and Summertrace, Carmel, Ind., Stonehenge Resort, Bedford, Ind., 1991; solo pianist Terranova Mansion, Paradise Valley, Ariz., 1987, Wrigley Mansion, Phoenix, 1988, Boulders Resort, Carefree, Ariz., 1987, Clarion Inn/McCormick's Ranch Resort, Scottsdale, Ariz., 1986, China Gate, Phoenix, 1988, Victor's, Phoenix, 1988, Cascade Club, Everett, Wash., 1990; keyboardist, synthesist, key bassist, The Gulch Gang, Pinnacle Peak Patio, Scottsdale, 1984, Dee Dee Ryan, The Longhorn Saloon, Apache Junction, Ariz., 1984-86, The Last Straw Band, Country City saloon, Mesa, Ariz., 1986; keyboardist, pianist, vocalist with Peter, Paul and John, Anderson Coll., Ind., 1977; CEO, owner, composer, photographer, arranger, prodr., musician, engr., graphic designer, computer operator, John David Thomas Prodns., Indpls., 1993—; CEO, owner JD Thomas Music Co., 1999—, Monolith Records, 1999-2001, The JDT Group, 2000-, JDT Records, 2001—, Serious Bizness Music Co., 2002—, Global Concept Music Co., 2002—, Silky Rd. Music Co., 2002—, Spirit Realm Music Co., 2002—, Mega Modern Music Co., 2002—, Dark House Music Co., 2005-, John David Thomas Photography, 2007-; rec. artist CD label mp3.com., 2000-04, CD label besonic.com, Europe, 2002-05, JDT Records, 2001-. Composer, lyricist of over 350 classical, religious, comml., rock, jazz, popular and avante garde/futuristic compositions, including Infinity, 1970-71, Death of Rock and Roll, 1970, Night Visions, 1972, First Things First, 1972, Two Nudes and a Fire Hydrant, 1972-73, Chant for Orchestra, 1972, 2001, Love Theme in D, 1972, 98, Zeitgeist: The Spirit of the Time, 1974, The Little Prince, 1973, 2001, When We Dead Awaken, 1973, Pray, 1972, Apogee, 1974, Chinese Baby, 1973, Alabama DA (Top Forty recording), 1973, Angel, 1974, Music for French Horn, Cello, and Piano, 1976, Cruising Beyond, 1979, Jetstream Theme, 1979, Chrissy, 1979, Love Theme in B Minor, 1979, In Your Heart, 1983, Future Music, 1987, The Recurrent New Millenium Orchestral Olympic Disco Festival Dance, 1989, Jubilee in F, 1989, Praise Him, The King Liveth, 1989, Love Flowers: Reflections and Meditations on Beauty and Truth, 1990, Sheena's Theme, 1992, I Want You Forever You're My Miracle, 1992, My Pseudo-Erotic, Sensual, Exotic Musical Fantasy and Romance for Our Heavenly Nocturnal Starry-Skied Carpet Ride to Paradise in Istanbul and Constantinople, 1992, I'm in Love with Someone Beautiful, 1992, Improvisations for Sheena, 1992, Musical Essences, 1994, 2002, Mystery World #1, 1994, Mystery World #2, 1994, Orient, 1994, Orchestral #17, 1994, Drums and Percussion Music, 1994, My Renaissance Brass Music, 1994, Postlude, 1994, Music for Baritone Vocal and String Orch., 1995, Meditations for Pipe Organ and Male Choir, 1996, Trumpet Voluntary in F, 1996, Pathway to Love, 1996, Majestic Brass Music in F#, 1997, J.D.'s Theme, 1998, The Road to Tomorrow, 1999, Let Me Be the One, 2000, God and the Everlasting, 2000, Sunshine, 2000, Love Theme, 2000, Dreaming, 2000, Together, 2000, Love You, 2000, The Road of Life, 2000, Desires of the Heart, 2000, The Open Sky, 2000, Just Me and You, 2000, In the Spirit of Mozart, 2001, God and the Everlasting, 2001, From Me to You, 2001, Ostinato for Double Reeds, 2001, God 1, 2001, God 2, 2001, Randy's Theme, 2002, Music for Suzy, 2003, Music for Beautiful Women, 2003, over 140 short piano compositions, 1999-2003; (albums) The Journey of Life, Destiny's Calling: Improvisations, 1994, 2002; (cd's) The Journey of Life, 1994, 2002, Musical Essences, 1994, 2002, Music for Bethany, 2002, The Avant-Garde of John David Thomas, 2002, From Me to You, 2002, Desires of the Heart, 2002, Spirit Music, 2002, The Seen and the Unseen, 2000, John David Thomas at the Piano, 2005, Romantic Abstract for the Modern Woman in Love with this Composer, 2005, Pathway to Love, 2005, Desires of the Heart, 2005, Early Songs and Jazz of John David Thomas: 1970-1987, 2005, Potpourri: Music for the World, 2000, Music for the World, vol. 2, 2000, (broadcast) Hometown Hour, Sta. WFBQ-FM, Indpls., 1979-80, Music for Kelly, Judy, Karyn, and Stacey, 2003; performed orginal composition, Sonebay, WFBM-TV, Indpls., 1969; designer automotive concepts and popular fashions; recordings of over 120 original songs and compositions including Love Theme in D, 1972, 98, Majestic Brass Music in F# for Bethany and Mark, 1997, J.D.'s Theme, 1998; plus over 90 recordings on CD's; author numerous poems. Musician, vocalist, composer Downey Ave. Christian Ch., Indpls., 1961-69, Univ. Presbyn. Ch., West Lafayette, Ind., 1969-71, Castleview Bapt. Ch., Indpls., 1974-84, Valley Cathedral Ch., Phoenix, 1986-87, Edmonds (Wash.) Christian Ch., 1988-90, Edmonds United Meth. Ch., 1989-90; page to speaker Ho. of Reps. Ind. State Legislature, 1963; active All Souls Unitarian Ch., Indpls., 1994-96. GM scholar Purdue U., 1969-70, Hoosier scholar, 1969, Palmer Meml. Music scholar Ball State U., 1971-74; named to Ind. All-State Orch. (cellist), 1968; recipient 1st place award (cellist) Ind. State Music Contest, 1968, God and Country award, 1965, Outstanding Musician award Irvington Music Club, Indpls., 1969, Purdue U. Symphonette, 1970, Hometown Hour award WFBQ-FM Radio Sta., Indpls., 1979. Mem. ASCAP, NARAS, PPA, Mensa. Avocations: reading, computers, music, photography, bridge. Home: PO Box 811804 Los Angeles CA 90081 Office Phone: 877-888-5870, 877-777-2308, 866-999-6479. E-mail: john1951usa@yahoo.com, moderncomposer@hotmail.com, johndavidthomas1@yahoo.com, jdtrecords@yahoo.com, johndavidthomasphotography@yahoo.com, thejdtgroup@yahoo.com.

THOMAS, JOHN HOWARD, astrophysicist, mechanical engineer, educator; b. Chgo., Apr. 9, 1941; s. William Whitney and Dorothy Loretta (Derris) T.; m. Lois Ruth Moffit, Aug. 11, 1962; children: Jeffrey, Laura. BS in Engring. Sci., Purdue U., 1962, MS in Engring. Sci., 1964, PhD in Engring. Sci., 1966. Lic. profl. engr., NY. NATO postdoctoral fellow U. Cambridge, Eng., 1966-67; asst. prof. mech. and aerospace sci. U. Rochester, 1967-73, assoc. prof., 1973-81, prof., 1981—, prof. astronomy, 1986—, assoc. dean for grad. studies Coll. Engring. and Applied Sci., 1981-83, univ. dean grad. studies, 1983-91. Vis. astronomer Nat. Solar Obs., Sunspot, N.Mex., 1971, 81; vis. scientist Max-Planck Inst. for Physics and Astrophysics, Munich, 1973—74, High Altitude Obs., Boulder, Colo., 1985; vis. fellow Worcester Coll., vis. prof. dept. theoretical physics U. Oxford, England, 1987—88; affiliate scientist Nat. Ctr. for

Atmospheric Rsch., Boulder, 1989—; vis. prof. Rsch. Ctr. for Theoretical Astrophysics U. Sydney, 1991, Sch. Math. and Stats., 1993; vis. fellow Clare Hall, vis. prof. dept. applied math. and theoretical physics U. Cambridge, England, 2002, sr. fellow Isaac Newton Inst., 04; prin. investigator NASA, NSF, USAF, Office Naval Rsch. Editor: Physics of Sunspots, 1981, Sunspots: Theory and Observations, 1992; assoc. editor Astrophys. Jour., 1993—96, sci. editor, 1996—2002, author articles on astrophysics, solar physics and fluid dynamics. NSF fellow, 1963-66; Guggenheim fellow, 1993-94. Fellow Am. Phys. Soc.; mem. AAAS, Am. Astron. Soc. (chair solar physics divsn. 1995-97), Internat. Astron. Union, Am. Geophys. Union, Royal Astron. Soc. (UK), Sigma Xi, Tau Beta Pi, Sigma Delta Chi.

THOMAS, JOHN MELVIN, retired surgeon; b. Carmarthen, U.K., Apr. 26, 1933; U.S, 1958; s. Morgan and Margaret (Morgan) T.; m. Betty Ann Mayo, Nov. 3, 1958; children: James, Hugh, Pamela. MB, BChir, U. Coll. Wales, U. Edinburgh, 1958. Intern Robert Packer Hosp., Sayre, Pa., 1958-59, chief surg. resident, 1963, pres. med. staff, 1968; assoc. surgeon Guthrie Clinic Ltd., Sayre, 1963-69, chmn. dept. surgery, 1969-91; vice chmn. Guthrie Healthcare System, 1995—99. Pres. bd. dirs. Guthrie Clinic Ltd., 1972-89; pres. bd. dirs. Donald Guthrie Found., 1983-95; chmn. Chemung Springwater Co.; trustee Robert Packer Hosp.; chmn. exec. com. Guthrie Healthcare Sys., 1990-92, dir., 1994-2001; guest examiner Am. Bd. Surgery, 1979, 81, 85; bd. dirs. Measurement Innovations Corp., Mansfield, Pa., Trianalytics Corp., First Citizens Nat Bank; cons. The Hunter Group, 1993-96; interim pres., Citizen Fin. Bank, 2003—; arbitrator Nat. Assn. Securities Dealers, 2005—. Bd. dirs. Donald Guthrie Found. for Rsch., pres., 1983-94; bd. dirs. Pa. Trauma Sys. Found., 1984-90, pres., 1988, 89; chmn. licensure and accountability Gov.'s Conf., 1974; bd. dirs. Vol. Hosps. Am., 1993-95; trustee Mansfield (Pa.) U. Found., 1991-98; trustee Mansfield Univ. Found., 1991-95. Fellow ACS (gov. 1985-91); mem. AMA, Am. Group Practice Assn., Soc. for Surgery Alimentary Tract, Pa. Med. Soc., Bradford County Med. Soc., Cen. NY Surg. Soc., Internat. Soc. Surgery, Soc. Surgery Alimentary Tract, Ea. Vascular Soc., Ithaca Country Club, Whitchurch Golf Club, Country Club Naples, Tower Club (Ft. Lauderdale). Presbyterian. Home: Cap Ferrat 6597 Nicholas Blvd #701 Naples FL 34108 E-mail: jthoma8422@aol.com.

THOMAS, JOHN THIEME, management consultant; b. Detroit, Aug. 21, 1935; s. John Shepherd and Florence Leona (Thieme) T.; m. Ellen Linden Taylor, June 27, 1959; children: Johnson Taylor, Evan Thurston. BBA, U. Mich., 1957, MBA, 1958. Mfg. dept. mgr. Procter & Gamble Co., Cin., 1958-60, brand mgr., 1960-63; sr. cons. Glendinning Cos. Inc., Westport, Conn., 1964-66, v.p. London, 1967-69, exec. v.p. Westport, 1970-74, also bd. dirs.; exec. v.p., chief operating officer Ero Industries, Chgo., 1974-76; v.p. Lamalie Assocs. Inc., Chgo., 1977-81; pres. Wilkins & Thomas Inc., Chgo., 1981-87; ptnr. Ward Howell Internat., Chgo., 1987—, mng. dir., cons. practice, 1992-98, chief of staff, 1995-98; also bd. dirs.; cons. ret. LAI Ward Howell, Chgo., 1999—, El Jefe, Thomas Ent. Inc., 1989—. Exec. dir. Procter & Gamble Alumni Assn., Chgo., 1981—. Pub. Procter & Gamble Mktg. Alumni directory, 1981—; author articles in profl. jours. Chmn. bd. dirs. Winnetka (Ill.) Youth Orgn., 1986—2005; chmn. United Way Winnetka, 2001—, United Way North Shore; bd. dirs. No. Ill. Girl Scouts Coun., 2002—; mem. planning commn. City Winnetka, 2003—05; selector Winnetka Town Coun., 1978, 1980, 1984, Winnetka Caucus Exec. Com., 1997—2001, Winnetka Zoning Bd., 2002—05; commr. Winnetka Pks., 2005—. Mem. Nat. Assn. Corp. & Profl. Recruiters, Assn. Exec. Search Cons., Am. Soc. Pers. Adminstrn. Clubs: Fairfield (Conn.) Hunt (treas. 1971-74). Avocations: gardening, music, tuba. Home and Office: 525 Ash St Winnetka IL 60093-2601 Office Phone: 847-446-5401. Business E-Mail: pngalumni@aol.com.

THOMAS, JOHN VAL, architect; b. San Diego, Feb. 26, 1943; Grad arch., Rice Univ., Houston; MArch, MCP, U. Pa. Prin. Val Thomas, Inc., Seattle, 1985—; devel. mgr. Pike Pl. Market Preservation and Devel. Authority, Seattle, 1974. Cons. ptnr. Cardwell/Thomas & Assoc., Seattle. Conversion, W. Queen Anne Sch. (Award for Excellence, Nat. Endowment for the Arts). Fellow: Am. Inst. Arch.; mem.: Housing Comm. of the Greater Seattle Chamber of Commerce, Univ. of Wash. Profl. Coun. for the Sch. of Urban Planning, Seattle Planning Commission (chrmn.). Democrat. Episcopalian. Achievements include development of Thomas Incorporated; headed the development team for the new headquarters building of the Fremont Public Association on North 45th Street. Avocations: skiing, aerobics, painting, gardening. Office: Thomas Inc 1221 2nd Ave Ste 480 Seattle WA 98101 Office Phone: 206-621-1221.

THOMAS, JOSEPH FLESHMAN, retired architect; b. Oak Hill, W.Va., Mar. 23, 1915; s. Robert Russel and Effie (Fleshman) T.; m. Margaret Ruth Lively, Feb. 28, 1939 (dec.); children: Anita Carol, Joseph Stephen; m. Dorothy Francene Root, Apr. 29, 1967 (div.); m. Bonnie Abbott Buckley, June 15, 1991 (dec.). Student, Duke U., 1931—32; BArch, Carnegie-Mellon U., 1938. Practice architecture various firms, W.Va., Va., Tenn., Calif., 1938-49; staff arch. Calif. Divsn. Architecture, LA, 1949-52; prin. Joseph F. Thomas, Arch., Pasadena, Calif., 1952-53; pres. Neptune & Thomas (archs.-engrs.), Pasadena and San Diego, 1953-78. Mem. Pasadena Planning Commn., 1956-64, chmn., 1963-64; pres. Citizens Coun. for Planning, Pasadena, 1966-67; steering com. Pasadena NOW, 1970-74; mem. Pasadena Design Com., 1979-86; adv. bd. Calif. Office Architecture and Constrn., 1970-72; archtl. adv. com. Calif. State U. Sys., 1981-84; adv. coun. Sch. Environ. Design Calif. Poly. Inst., 1983-2002; outreach for architecture com. Carnegie Mellon U., 1989-95, pres.'s devel. com., 1991-95. Prin. works include Meth. Hosp., Arcadia, Calif., Foothill Presbyn. Hosp., Glendora, Calif., master plans and bldgs., Citrus Coll., Azusa, Calif., Riverside (Calif.) Coll., Westmont Coll., Monticeto, Calif., Northrop Inst. Tech., Inglewood, Calif, Indian Valley Coll., Marin County, Calif., Pepperdine U., Malibu, Calif., UCLA, U. Calif., San Diego, Long Beach (Calif.) State U., Calif. Inst. Tech., Pasadena, Pacific Tel. Co., Pasadena, LA County Superior Ct. Bldg., U.S. Naval Hosp., San Diego, others Trustee Almansor Edn. Ctr., 1986-92; bd. dirs., co-founder Syncor Internat., 1973-83; founding dir. Bank of Pasadena, 1962-65. Lt. (j.g.) USNR, 1943-46. Recipient Svc. award, City of Pasadena, 1964, Disting. Svc. award, Calif. Dept. Gen. Svcs., 1972, Gold Crown award, Pasadena Arts Coun., 1981. Fellow AIA (dir. Calif. coun. 1966-68, exec. com. 1974-77, pres. Pasadena chpt. 1967, chmn. Calif. sch. facilities com. 1970-72, mem. nat. jud. bd. 1973-74, nat. dir. 1974-77, treas. 1977-79, exec. com., planning com., chmn. finance com., 4 awards honor, 13 awards merit 1957-78, Lifetime Achievement award 2007); mem. Breakfast Forum (chmn. 1983), Annandale Golf Club, Pi Kappa Alpha. Republican. Methodist. Home: 330 San Miguel Rd Pasadena CA 91105-1446

THOMAS, KENNETH GLYNDWR, mining executive; b. Llanelli, Wales, June 25, 1944; arrived in Can., 1980; m. Elizabeth June Hickman, Sept. 25, 1976; children: Louise June, Kelly Jane. BSc in Metallurgy, U. Wales, Cardiff, 1970; MSc in Mgmt. Sci., U. London, 1971; PhD in Tech. Sci., U. of Delft, The Netherlands, 1994. Chartered engr., U.K.; registered profl. engr., Ont., Can. Metallurgist Brit. Steel Corp., Wales, 1959-67, Anglo Am. Corp., Kitwe, Zambia, 1971-75, plant supt. Klerksdorp, South Africa, 1975-80; design metallurgist Kilborn Engring., Toronto, Ont., 1980-85; mill supt. Giant Yellowknife (Can.) Mines Ltd., N.W.T., 1985-87; sr. v.p. metallurgy and constrn. Barrick Gold Corp., Toronto, 1987-95, sr. v.p. tech. svcs., 1995-2001; mng. dir. mining and mineral processing Hatch, Mississauga, Ont., 2001—02; mng. dir. We. Australia, 2002—03; COO, exec. v.p. ops. Crystallex Internat. Corp., Toronto, 2003—05; mng. dir. Hatch, Mississauga, 2006—. Contbr. articles to tech. jours.; co-patentee in field. Fellow Inst. Materials, Minerals & Mining (U.K.), Can. Inst. Mining, Metallurgy and Petroleum (Mill Man of Yr. award 1990, Airey award 1999, Selwyn G. Blaylock medal 2001), Can. Inst. Mining and Metallurgy. Home Phone: 905-896-8608; Office Phone: 905-403-3980. Personal E-mail: kenthomas@rogers.com.

THOMAS, LAWRENCE ELDON, mathematics professor; b. Columbus, Ohio, Mar. 15, 1942; s. Bertram D. and Glorian (Butler) T.; m. Rebecca Nolan, June 13, 1970; children: David Nolan, Kathleen Rebecca. BS, U. Mich., 1964; PhD, Yale U., 1970. Rsch. asst. math. dept. Swiss Fed. Inst. Tech., Zurich, 1970-72; rsch. asst. physics dept. U. Geneva, 1972-74; asst. prof. math. U. Va., Charlottesville, 1974-76, assoc. prof., 1976-82, prof., 1982—, chmn. dept., 1989-93. Contbr. articles on theory of Schrodinger operators, statis. mechanics and stochastic processes to profl. jours. Mem. Am. Math. Soc., Am. Physics Soc., Internat. Nat. Math. Physics, Phi Beta Kappa. Avocations: sailing, tennis. Office: U Va Dept Math Cabell Dr Charlottesville VA 22903

THOMAS, LEE MULLER, forest products company executive, former government official; b. Ridgeway, SC, June 13, 1944; s. Robert Walton and Laura (Muller) Thomas; m. Dixie Gay Smily, June 20, 1981; children: Jordan, Braden; children: Lee, Elliott. BA, U. of South, 1967; M.Ed., U. S.C., 1971. Exec. dir. criminal justice program Office Gov., Columbia, SC, 1972-77, dir. pub. safety programs, 1979-81; ind. cons. Criminal Justice Planning, 1977-79; assoc. dir. state and local programs and support FEMA, Washington, 1981-82, dep. dir., 1982-83; asst. adminstr. EPA, Washington, 1983-85, adminstr., 1985-89; chmn., chief exec. officer Law Environmental Inc., Atlanta, 1989—93; with Georgia Pacific Corp., Atlanta, 1993—, sr. v.p. paper, 1995—96, exec. v.p. paper & chemicals, 1997—2000, exec. v.p. consumer products, 2000—02, pres. bldg. products & distribution, 2002, pres., 2002—03, pres., COO, 2003—05; pres., CEO Rayonier Inc., Jacksonville, Fla., 2007—. Bd. dir. Airgas Inc., Resolve Inc., Rayonier Inc., Regal Entertainment Inc., Fed. Reserve Bank, Atlanta. Bd. dir. World Resources Inst., Washington, Nat. Merit Scholarship Corp., Ga. Environ. Facilities Authority. Mem.: SC Law Enforcement Officers Assn., SC Corrections Assn., Nat. Criminal Justice Assn. (chmn. 1979—81), Sigma Nu. Office: Rayonier Inc 50 N Laura St Jacksonville FL 32202 *

THOMAS, LEONA MARLENE, healthcare educator; b. Rock Springs, Wyo., Jan. 15, 1933; d. Leonard H. and Opal (Wright) Francis; children: Peter, Paul, Patrick, Alexis. BA, Govs. State U., University Park, Ill., 1982, MHS, 1986; cert. med. records adminstrn., U. Colo., 1954. Asst. prof. Chgo. State U., 1984—, acting dir. health info. adminstrn. program, 1991-92; acting dir. health info. Internat. Coll., Naples, Fla., 1994; dir. Chgo. State U., 1994—. Chairperson dept. health info. adminstrn. Chgo. State U., 1994—. Mem. adv. com. Wellness Ctr., mem. adv. com. occupl. therapy program Chgo. State U. Mem. Assembly on Edn., Am. Health Info. Mgmt. Assn., APHA, Chgo. and Vicinity Med. Records Assn., Ill. Assn. Allied Health Profls., Gov.'s State Alumni Assn. Democrat. Methodist. Home: 6340 Americana Dr Apt 1101 Willowbrook IL 60527 Office: Chgo State U Coll Health Scis 95th at King Dr Chicago IL 60628 Personal E-mail: lmthomas@msn.com.

THOMAS, LINDSEY KAY, JR., research ecology biologist, educator, consultant; b. Salt Lake City, Apr. 16, 1931; s. Lindsey Kay and Naomi Lurie (Biesinger) T.; m. Nancy Ruth Van Dyke, Aug. 24, 1956; children: Elizabeth Nan Thomas Cardinale, David Lindsey, Wayne Hal, Dorothy Ann Thomas Brown. BS, Utah State Agrl. Coll., Logan, 1953; MS, Brigham Young U., Provo, Utah, 1958; PhD, Duke U., Durham, NC, 1974. Park naturalist Nat. Capital Pks., Nat. Pk. Svc., Washington, 1957—62, pk. naturalist (rschr.) Region 6, 1962—63, rsch. pk. naturalist Nat. Capital Region, 1963—66; rsch. biologist S.E. Temperate Forest Pk. Areas, Washington, 1966, Durham, NC, 1966—67, Great Falls, Md., 1967—71, Nat. Capital Pks., Great Falls, 1971—74, Nat. Capital Region, Triangle, Va., 1974—93, Washington, 1985—93, Nat. Biol. Svc., Washington, Triangle, 1993—96; resource mgmt. specialist Balt.-Washington Pkwy., Greenbelt, Md., 1996, Nat. Capital Parks-East, 1996—98; rsch. ecologist emeritus and cons. Nat. Capital Region, Nat. Park Svc., 1998—. Bd. dirs. Prince William County Svc. Authority, Va., 1996-2004; adj. prof. George Mason U., Fairfax, Va., 1988—, George Washington U., Washington, 1992-98; instr. Dept. Agr. Grad. Sch., 1964-66; aquatic ecol. cons. Fairfax County Fedn. Citizens Assns., Va., 1970-71; guest lectr. Washington Tech. Inst. (now U. DC), 1976. Contbr. articles to profl. jours. Wildlife mgmt. cons. Girl Scouts Am., Loudoun County, Va., 1958; preservation and mgmt. cons. McAteean Magnolia Bogs, Save Araby, Mattawoman and Mason Springs in Charles County, Md., 2002-06, Nat. Resources Divsn., Arlington County, Va., 2004—; asst. scoutmaster, scoutmaster, merit badges counselor Boy Scouts Am., 1958—, Scouters Tng. award, 1961. Recipient Incentive awards Nat. Park Svc., 1962, Superior Performance award, 1989; rsch. grantee Washington Biologists' Field Club, 1977, 82. Mem.: AAAS, Md. Native Plant Soc., Nat. Trust for Historic Preservation, Washington Biologists' Field Club, So. Appalachian Bot. Soc., Soc. for Early Hist. Archaeology, The Nature Conservancy, George Wright Soc., Ecol. Soc. Am., Bot. Soc. Washington, Sigma Xi. Mem. Lds Ch. Home: 13854 Delaney Rd Woodbridge VA 22193-4654 Office: Prince William Forest Park 18100 Park Hdqrs Rd Triangle VA 22172

THOMAS, LIZANNE, lawyer; BA, Furman U, 1979; JD, Washington & Lee, 1982. Bar: Ga. 1982. Ptnr. mergers and acquisitions practice Jones Day, Atlanta, firmwide adminstrv. ptnr., 2003—. Lectr. corp. fin. U. Calif., Berkeley and Davis; pres. Law Alumni Assn. Washington and Lee U., 2001—02; bd. dirs. Krispy Kreme Doughnuts, 2004—. Recurring panelist Directors' Inst. of the Conf. Bd. Mem. adv. bd. Salvation Army Metro Atlanta; former bd. dirs. Ga. C. of C.; bd. trustees Furman U. Mem.: State Bar of Ga. Office: Jones Day 1420 Peachtree St NE Ste 800 Atlanta GA 30309-3053 Office Phone: 404-581-8411. Office Fax: 404-581-8330. Business E-Mail: lthomas@jonesday.com.

THOMAS, LLOYD BREWSTER, economics professor; b. Columbia, Mo., Oct. 22, 1941; s. Lloyd B. and Marianne (Moon) T.; m. Sally Leach, Aug. 11, 1963; 1 child, Elizabeth. AB, U. Mo., 1963, AM, 1964; PhD, Northwestern U., 1970. Instr. Northwestern U., Evanston, Ill., 1966-68; asst. prof. econs. Kan. State U., Manhattan, 1968-72, assoc. prof., 1974-81; asst. prof. Fla. State U., Tallahassee, 1973-74; prof. Kans. State U., Manhattan, 1983—, head dept., 2004—. Vis. prof. U. Calif., Berkeley, 1981-82, U. Del., 1993, U. Ind., Bloomington, 1997-98, Adelaide U., 2002; prof., chair dept. econs. U. Idaho, 1989. Author: Money, Banking and Economic Activity, 3d edit., 1986, Principles of Economics, 2d edit, 1993, Principles of Macroeconomics, 2d edit, 1993, Principles of Microeconomics, 2d edit, 1993, Money, Banking and Financial Markets, 2006; contbr. articles to profl. jours. Mem. Am. Econs. Assn., Midwest Econs. Assn., Phi Kappa Phi. Avocations: tennis, classical music. Home: 1501 N 10th St Manhattan KS 66502-4607 Home Phone: 785-539-1108; Office Phone: 785-532-4584. Business E-Mail: lbt@ksu.edu.

THOMAS, LOIS C., musician, educator, religious organization administrator, composer; b. Ft. Worth, Oct. 15, 1932; d. Walter Scott and Margaret Alice Dawn Cook; m. Richard Wallace Thomas, Nov. 5, 1988. BA in Organ Performance, Tex. Christian U., 1966; postgrad., SWBT Sem. Cert. profl. instr. piano, organ theory. Organist Western Hills Bapt. Ch., Ft. Worth, 1959-69, 1st Ch. of Christ, Scientist, Ft. Worth, 1969-84, First Congl. Ch., Ft. Worth, 1985-87; organist, dir. Anglican Ch. St. Charles the Martyr, Grand Prairie, Tex., 1989—99; organist, dir., assoc. rector Anglican Ch. St. Raphael, the Archangel, Grand Prairie, 2002—04. Deacon United Cath. Ch., 1996; priest Communion Evang. Episcopal Chs., 1997; fin. officer USCG Aux., Grapevine, Tex., 1989—95, sec., Grand Prairie, Tex., 1995. Commd.: hymnal Diocese St. Paul, the Apostle, 2000. Mem.: Music Tchr.'s Nat. Assn., Tex. Music Tchr.'s Assn., Arlington Music Tchr.'s Assn. (phone com.), Am. Guild Organists (phone com., svc. playing cert.). Home: 1501 Connally Ter Arlington TX 76010-4514

THOMAS, LOWELL, JR., writer, retired military officer, state senator; b. London, Oct. 6, 1923; s. Lowell Jackson and Frances (Ryan) T.; m. Mary Taylor Pryor, May 20, 1950; children: Anne Frazier, David Lowell. Student, Taft Sch., 1942; BA, Dartmouth Coll., 1948; postgrad., Princeton Sch. Pub. and Internat. Affairs, 1952. Asst. cameraman Fox Movietone News, S.Am., 1939, Bradford Washburn Alaskan mountaineering expdn., 1940; illustrated lecturer, 1946—; asst. economist, photographer with Max Weston Thornburg, Turkey, 1947, Iran, 1948; film prodn. Iran, 1949; Tibet expdn. with Lowell Thomas, Sr., 1949; field work Cinerama, S.Am., Africa, Asia, 1951-52; travels by small airplane with wife, writing and filming Europe, Africa, Middle East, 1954-55; mem. Rockwell Polar Flight, first flight around the world over both poles, Nov., 1965; mem. Alaska State Senate, 1967-74; lt. gov. State of Alaska, 1974-79; owner Talkeetna Air Taxi, Inc., air contract carrier, Anchorage, Alaska, 1980-94. Producer series of films Flight to Adventure, NBC-TV, 1956; producer, writer TV series High Adventure, 1957-59; producer documentary film Adaq, King of Alaskan Seas, 1960; producer two films on Alaska, 1962, 63, film on U. Alaska, 1964, South Pacific travel documentary, 1965, film on Arctic oil exploration, Atlantic-Richfield Co., 1969. Author: Out of this World, A Journey to Tibet, 1950, (with Mrs. Lowell Thomas, Jr.) Our Flight to Adventure, 1956, The Silent War in Tibet, 1959, The Dalai Lama, 1961, The Trail of Ninety-Eight, 1962, (with Lowell Thomas Sr.) More Great True Adventures, 1963, Famous First Flights that Changed History, 1968. Past pres. Western Alaska coun. Boys Scouts Am.; bd. dirs. Anchorage unit Salvation Army, Alaska Conservation Found. 1st lt. USAAF, 1943-45. Mem. Nat. Parks and Conservation Assn. (bd. dirs.), Alaska C. of C., Aircraft Owners and Pilots Assn. Clubs: Explorers, Marco Polo, Dutch Treat (N.Y.C.); Rotary, (Anchorage), Press (Anchorage); Dartmouth Outing; American Alpine. Address: 10800 Hideaway Lake Dr Anchorage AK 99507-6139

THOMAS, LUCILLE COLE, librarian; b. Dunn, NC, Oct. 1, 1921; d. Collie and Minnie (Lee) Cole; m. George Browne Thomas, May 24, 1943; children: Ronald C., Beverly G. BA, Bennett Coll., 1941; DHL (hon.), Benentt Coll., 1996; MA, NYU, 1955; MS, Columbia U., 1957. Tchr. Bibb County Bd. Edn., Macon, Ga., 1947—55; libr. Bklyn. Pub. Libr., 1955—56, NYC Bd. Edn., Bklyn., 1956—68, supr. librs., 1968—77, dir. elem. sch. librs., 1977—83; program dir. Weston Woods Inst., Weston, Conn., 1984—85; adj. prof. libr. sci. Queens Coll., CUNY, 1986—89. Founder Sch. Libr. Media Day, NY State, 1973; del. NY Gov's. Conf. on Librs., 1978, 90, White House Conf. Libr. and Info. Svcs., 1979; trustee NY Met. Ref. and Rsch. Libr. Agy., NYC, 1979—83; hon. del. White House Conf. Libr. and Info. Svcs., 1991; coord. UNESCO/Internat. Assn. Sch. Librarianship Book Program for devel. countries, 1980—89; adv. bd. Regents' Adv. Council on Learning Tech., Albany, NY, 1982—88; cons. Putnam Pub. Group, NYC, 1983; 1st v.p. Shomburg Corp., 1983—85; bd. examiners NY City Bd. Edn., 1983—91; founder Nat. Sch. Libr. Media Month, 1985; liaison Freedom to Read Found., 1986—88; prof. libr. sci. St. John's U., 1986; reviewer U.S. Office Ednl. Rsch. & Improvement, 1988—90; prof. libr. sci. Pratt Inst., 1989; mem. libr. sect. Nat. Martin Luther King, Jr. Commn., 1990—95; bd. dirs NY is Book Country, 1991—96; chair seminar for librs. from devel. countries, Barcelona, 1993; trustee Bklyn. Pub. Libr., 1993—, v.p., 2000—03, pres., 2003—06, chair audit com., 2006—. Contbr. articles to profl. jours.; editor: Insight, 1974, Cultural Heritage Through Literature, 1993. Del. World Conf. on Edn. for all in Jamtien, Thailand, 1990; treas. Bklyn. Home for Aged Commn., 1967—2007; adv. bd. Books Kids, 1989—; pres. bd. trustees St. Mark's Day Sch., 2001—, trustee Leroy Merritt Humanitarian Found., 2005—; vestry mem. St. John's Episcopal Ch., Bklyn., 1988—90, chair stewardship com., 1987—90; active St. Mark's Ch., Bklyn., 1960—. Named Woman on the Move, State Sen. Carl Andrews, 2003; recipient Disting. Alumna award, Bennett Coll., 1981, Edn. award, Bus. and Profl. Women's Club, 1983, Achievement award, Columbia U. Sch. Libr. Svcs., 1987, Grolier Found. award, 1988, Disting. Pub. Svc. award, SUNY, Albany, 1989, Cmty. Svc. award, North Queens, NY, 1993, Disting. Svc. award, St. Mark's Ch., 2003, Achievement award, Consortium of Doctors, 2004, NY Black Librs., 2004, citation, Bklyn. Borough Pres., 2005, Letter of Commendation, First Lady Laura Bush, 2005, Faithful Servant award, Concord Bapt. Ch., 2006, Dedicated Svc. honoree, Bklyn. Pub. Libr., 2006, Freedom to Read Found. award, 2007; honoree, Bennett Coll. Alumnae, 2006. Mem.: ALA (hon.; councilor 1980—91, exec. bd. 1984—91, direction and rev. com. 1985—91, chair nominations and spl. assignments com. 1987—88, chair Hqtrs. Libr. Rev. Accountability Com. 1987—88, exec. bd. found. 1987—89, pers. com. 1988—89, chair ALA/AASL disting. svc. award com. 1989—90, disaster relief com. 1989—91, chair rev. com. of office for rsch. 1990—91, AASL/SIRS Disting. Libr. Svc. award sch. adminstrs. com. 1990—91, chair rsch. rev. com. 1990—91, AASL internat. rels. com. 1990—94, internat. com. 1991—95, councilor 1993—2002, mem. intellectual freedom com., assn. trustees 2005—, Disting. Svc. award Black Librs. Caucus 1992, Trailblazer's award Libr. Black Caucus 1995), NY Libr. Assn. (pres. sch. libr. media sect. 1973—74, v.p. 1976—77, pres. 1977—78, appreciation cert. 1983, oustanding achievement award 1984, achievement award 1988), Internat. Assn. Sch. Librarianship (pres. 1989—95), Internat. Fedn. Libr. Assn. (sec. 1985—96, chair sch. librs. sect. 1989—93, ofcl. rep. UN and UNICEF 1991—94, chair planning and implementation com.), NYC Sch. Librs. Assn. (pres. 1970—72, chair sch. librs. of NY Libr. Assn. sect. 1989—93), Bklyn. Hist. Soc. (named one of outstanding women of Bklyn. 1985), Schomburg Commn. (1st v.p. 1986—90), Women's City of NYC Club (bd. dirs. 1986—2000, vice chmn. 1987—89, chair edn. com. 1989—92, v.p. 1992—93), NY Libr. Club (v.p. 1976—77, pres. 1977—78), Alpha Kappa Alpha (Pi Phi Omega chpt. parliamentarian 1990—92, v.p. 1990—94, 1992—94, pres. 1994—98, co-coord. North Atlantic region 1996—2000, mem.-at-large 2004—07). Democrat. Avocation: reading. Home: 1184 Union St Brooklyn NY 11225-1512 Personal E-mail: lucillecthomas@aol.com.

THOMAS, MARCIA MARKOWITZ, library director, educator; b. Fort Worth, Dec. 2, 1944; d. Samuel and Davida Shosid Markowitz; m. Rickard James Thomas, Sept. 1, 1978 (div. July 1982); children: Aaron, James; m. John Katchmarik, Dec. 2, 1994. BA, U. Mo., 1968, MA, 1975. Libr. asst. Kansas City (Mo.) Pub. Libr., 1968—73; libr. dir. Ruth R. Cleveland Meml. Libr., Kansas City, 1976—. Chair instl. rev. bd. Cleve. Chiropractic Coll., Kansas City, Mo., 1979—99, prof. human biology, 1996—, faculty coun. pres., 1993—95, 1997—99, 2001—03, 2005—07. Co-author: Chiropractic: An Annotated Bibliography, 2000; contbr. articles to profl. jours. Rep. Southtown Neighborhood Coun., Kansas City; campus coord. Heart of Am. United Way, 1999—; bd. dirs. Astor Place Homes Assn., Kansas City, pres., 2004—; mem. task force sch. governance Kansas City Consensus; mem. task force Kansas City Wet Weather Solutions, 2006—. Mem.: ALA, MLA (chiropractic librs. sect., chair, program chair, bylaws com.), Chiropractic Libr. Consortium (pres., treas., sec.), Kansas City Libr. Network (treas., archivist), Midwest Bioethics Ctr., Med. Libr. Assn. (sect. coun. rep.). Liberal. Jewish. Avocations: bioethics, music, neighborhood advocacy. Office: Ruth R Cleveland Meml Libr 6401 Rockhill Rd Kansas City MO 64131 Office Phone: 816-501-0142. E-mail: marcia.thomas@cleveland.edu.

THOMAS, MARIANNA, volunteer community activist, writer, speaker; b. Greenville, Ohio, Dec. 9, 1927; d. John Darl and Eva Jane (Hill) Munn; m. Harold D. Krickenbarger, Aug. 31, 1947 (div.); children: Harold Krickenbarger Jr., Jane Krickenbarger, Maryln Krickenbarger, John Krickenbarger; m. Lowell J. Thomas, Jan. 5, 1977 (dec.); 1 stepchild, Lowell J.

Student, Dayton Art Inst., Ohio; MA (hon.), Union (Ky.) Coll., 1978. Farmer Holstein Show Herd, Arcanum, Ohio, 1947-68; advt., broadcasting sta. work and writing positions Arcanum Times; sales and decorating positions Lowe Bros., Greenville, Ohio; exec. dir./fundraising Help for Children in the Holy Land/Spafford Children's Ctr., NYC, 1969-76. Author: Catitudes, 1987, The Second Mrs. Lowell Thomas, 2000; mem. bd. contbrs. Dayton Daily News. Founder Citizens for Moral War peace orgn., 1967—70; mem. coun. Freedoms Found. Valley Forge, 1982—84; founder, chmn. US Civil Responsibilities, Dayton, 1988—93; nat. bd. dirs. Family Svc. Assocs. Am., NYC, 1979—85, Am. Judicature Soc., 1978—80. Mem.: Dayton Engrs. Club (hon.). Avocations: painting, poetry, swimming, cooking. Home: PO Box 626 Dayton OH 45405-0626

THOMAS, MARLIN ULUESS, industrial engineer, educator, academic administrator; b. Middlesboro, Ky., June 28, 1942; s. Elmer Vernon and Helen Lavada (Banks) T.; m. Susan Kay Stoner, Jan. 18, 1963; children: Pamela Claire Thomas Davis, Martin Phillip. BSE, U. Mich., Dearborn, 1967; MSE, U. Mich., Ann Arbor, 1968, PhD, 1971. Registered profl. engr., Mich. Asst. and assoc. prof. dept. ops. rsch. Naval Postgrad. Sch., Monterey, Calif., 1971-76; assoc. prof. systems design dept. U. Wis., Milw., 1976-78; mgr. tech. planning and analysis vehicle quality-reliability Chrysler Corp., Detroit, 1978-79; prof. dept. indsl. engring. U. Mo., Columbia, 1979-82; prof. indsl. engring., chmn. dept. Cleve State U., 1982-88, acting dir. Advanced Mfg. Ctr., 1984-85; prof., chmn. indsl. engring. Lehigh U., Bethlehem, Pa., 1988-93; prof., head Sch. Indsl. Engring. Purdue U., West Lafayette, Ind., 1993-98; dir. Inst. Interdisciplinary Engring. Studies, West Lafayette, 1998—. Program dir. NSF, Washington, 1987-88. Contbr. numerous articles on indsl. engring. and ops. rsch. to profl. jours. With USN, 1958-62; capt. USNR, 1971—. Named Outstanding Tchr., U. Mo. Coll. Engring., 1980, Coll. Man of Yr, Cleve. State U. Coll. Engring., 1985, Disting. Alumnus of Yr., U. Mich.-Dearborn, 1996, Engr. Excell Engagement Svc. award, Purdue U., 2003, IIE Holzman Disting. Educator award, 2004. Fellow Inst. Indsl. Engrs. (past pres., recipient Frank Groseclose Medallion award, 2005), Am. Soc. for Quality, Inst. for Ops. Rsch. and Mgmt. Scis.; mem. Am. Soc. for Engring. Edn., Am. Indian Sci. and Engr. Soc., VFW, Seabee Vet. Am. Office: Sch Indsl Engring Purdue Univ 315 N Grant St West Lafayette IN 47907-2023 Home Phone: 765-497-4586. Office Fax: 765-494-1299. Business E-Mail: muthomas@ecn.purdue.edu.

THOMAS, MARLO (MARGARET JULIA THOMAS), actress; b. Detroit, Nov. 21, 1943; d. Danny and Rose Marie (Cassanti) T.; m. Phil Donahue, May 21, 1980. Ed., U. So. Calif. Theatrical appearances in Thieves, Broadway, 1974, Barefoot in the Park, London, Social Security, Broadway, 1986, The Shadow Box, Broadway, 1994, Two Goldsteins on Acid, 1999; star: TV series That Girl, 1966-71 (Golden Globe award Best TV actress, 1967); appeared in TV films: The Body Human: Facts for Girls (Emmy award Best Performer Children's Program), 1981, The Last Honor of Kathryn Beck, 1984 (also exec. prodr.), Consenting Adults, 1985, Nobody's Child, 1986 (Emmy Best Dramatic Actress), Held Hostage: The Sis and Jerry Levin Story, 1991, Ultimate Betrayal, 1994, Reunion, 1994, A Century of Women, 1994, Playing Mona Lisa, 2000; TV movies: Two Against Time, 2002, Our Heroes, Ourselves, 2002, Deceit, 2004; TV appearances include Friends, 1996, 2002, Roseanne, 1996, Ally McBeal, 2000, Law & Order: Special Victims Unit, 2004; conceived book and record, starred in TV spl. Free to Be... You and Me, 1974 (Emmy for best children's show); films include Jenny, 1963, Thieves, 1977, In the Spirit, 1991, The Real Blonde, 1997, Startucker, 1998; conceived book, record and TV spl. Free to Be A Family (Emmy Best Children's Show). Recipient 4 Emmys, Golden Globe award, George Foster Peabody award, Tom Paine award Nat. Emergency Civil Liberties Com.; inducted into Broadcasting & Cable Hall of Fame. Mem. Ms. Found., Nat. Women's Polit. Caucus. Address: William Morris Agy 151 El Camino Dr Beverly Hills CA 90212 also: Creative Artists Agy 9830 Wilshire Blvd Beverly Hills CA 90211 Office: Kerner Entertainment 8522 National Blvd Ste 109 Culver City CA 90232-2454

THOMAS, MARY ANN MCCRARY, counselor, school system administrator; b. Washington, Feb. 11, 1935; d. Frank Robert and Mary (Davison) McCrary; m. John Ralph Thomas, Sept. 30, 1961; children: Robert Davison, John Shannon, Kristen Aldridge. BA, U. Calif., Berkley, 1956; MA, UCLA, 1959. Cert. tchr., Calif. Supr. Pacific Bell, San Francisco, 1962-67; advisor gifted, talented San Rafael (Calif.) City Schs., 1973—, counselor, 1973—, dir. student affairs, 1982—. Pres. San Rafael PTA Coun., 1981-84, outstanding svc. award, 1983, 86, 89, San Rafael High Sch. Site Coun., 1985; pres. bd. dirs. Marin Wildlife Ctr., 1979-85. Recipient Golden Bell award, Marin Community Found., 1987, Outstanding Student Activities program state award, 1992; named Pub. Schoolmaster of Yr., 1993. Mem. Calif. Assn. Gifted, Calif. Assn. Tchrs. English. Republican. Episcopalian. Avocations: reading, gardening. Office: Davidson Mid Sch 280 Woodland Ave San Rafael CA 94901-5097

THOMAS, MARY LEE, property manager; d. Louis and Virgie Mae Bedford; children: Tamara Simone Times, Bobbi Makeda. A in Liberal Arts, S.W. Ill. Coll., 2003; B in Bus. Adminstrn., Lindenwood U., 2005. Mgmt. intern program East St. Louis Housing Authority, 1992, cert. earned income dissallowance specialist Nan Mckay And Assoc., 2003, pub. housing rent calculation specialist Nan McKay And Assoc., 2004, universal phys. condition stds. specialist Nan McKay & Assocs., 2005. Property mgr. East St. Louis (Ill.) Housing Authority, 1990—2004, asset mgr., 2004—. Mem.: Nat. Assn. Housing Redevelopment Orgn. (cert. pub. housing mgr. 1992). Democrat. Baptist. Achievements include received award for providing inspiration to co-workers and residents by singing at various functions within the housing authority and the community. Avocations: singing, cycling, walking, tae-bo, skating. Home: 718 Country Meadow Ln Belleville IL 62221 Office: E St Louis Housing Authority 700 N 20th St East Saint Louis IL 62205 Home Phone: 618-236-3848; Office Phone: 618-646-7353. Business E-Mail: mthomas@elsha.org.

THOMAS, MELISSA ANN, lawyer; b. San Diego, Aug. 11, 1955; d. Frank H. and Ann (Beyerle) T.; m. John W. Spiegel, Sept. 19, 1987. AB, U. Calif., Davis, 1975; JD, Harvard U., 1978. Bar: Va. 1978, D.C. 1984, Calif. 1988. Assoc. McGuire, Woods & Battle, Richmond, Va., 1978-83; ptnr. Miller & Chevalier, Washington, 1984-87, Pillsbury, Madison & Sutro, LA, 1987—. Legis. atty. U.S. Joint Com. on Taxation, Washington, 1979-80; mem. Tax Coalition, Washington, 1984—. Counsel, bd. dirs. Va. Women's Cultural Project, Inc., Richmond, 1982-87.

THOMAS, NANCY HINCKLEY, special education educator; b. LA, Mar. 7, 1939; d. Barton Armin and Helen (Ferguson) Hinckley; children: Gregory Dean, Garold Daniel, Deanna Nancy, Barton William, Deborah Hinckley, Bryan Joseph. AB, Stanford U., Calif., 1959. Resource Specialist Calif. Dept. head K-Mart Corp., Petaluma, Calif., 1982—89; spl. edn. tchr. R-House, Santa Rosa, Calif., 1994—2005, resource specialist, 1998—, St. Rose Sch., 2005—. Resource specialist St. Rose Sch., Santa Rosa, Calif., 2005—07. Mem.: AAUW (treas. 1965—67), Commonwealth Club, Nat. Trust Hist. Preservation. Avocations: reading, gardening. Home: 724 Bassett St Petaluma CA 94952

THOMAS, ORVILLE C., retired allergist; b. Haynesville, La., Aug. 23, 1915; children— David, Diane, Cody Pre-med. Student, Marian Mil. Inst., 1932-33, Tulane U., 1933, MD, 1939. Diplomate Am. Bd. Pediatrics. Diplomate Am. Bd. Allergy and Immunology. Intern Shreveport Charity Hosp., La., 1939-40; asst. resident in pediatrics Children's Meml. Hosp., Chgo., 1946-47, resident in pediatrics, 1947, chief resident in pediatrics, 1948; sr. staff pediatrics Confederate Meml. Hosp., Shreveport, La., 1948-61; chief pediatrics Schumpert Meml. Hosp., Shreveport, La., 1958-61, chief of staff, 1958; active staff Tex. Children's Hosp., Houston, from 1962, fellow in pediatric allergy, 1963-65, chief allergy sect., 1973-78; fellow in pediatric allergy Baylor Coll. Medicine, Houston, 1963-65; active staff Highland Hosp., Shreveport, La., 1948-61, North La. Hosp., Shreveport, La., 1948-61, Physicians and Surgeons Hosp., Shreveport, La., 1948-61, Ben Taub Gen. Hosp., Houston, from 1962, Hermann Hosp., Houston, 1966-69; hon. staff St. Luke's Hosp., Houston, from 1962; cons. staff Meth. Hosp., Houston, from 1962, St. Joseph Hosp., Houston, from 1966, Bellaire Gen. Hosp., Tex., 1966-86, Rosewood Gen. Hosp., Houston, from 1967, Meml. Bapt. Hosp., Houston, from 1968, Pasadena Bayshore Hosp., Pasadena, Tex., from 1970; instr. pediatrics Northwestern U. Sch. Medicine, Chgo., 1948; assoc. prof. pediatrics La. State U. Postgrad. Sch. Medicine, 1956-61; clin. instr. pediatrics Baylor Coll. Medicine, Houston, 1961-66, asst. clin. prof. pediatrics, 1966-76, assoc. clin. prof. pediatrics, 1977—91; ret., 1991. Assoc. clin. prof. allergy and immunology U. Tex. Grad. Sch. Biomed. Scis., Houston, 1970—. Book reviewer: Venom Diseases; Aspects of Allergy and Applied Immunology. Contbr. articles to profl. jours. Served to maj. USMC AUS, 1942-46. Fellow Am. Coll. Allergy and Immunology (pediatrics com. 1964—, pres. 1978), Am. Acad. Allergy and Immunology, Am. Assn. Cert. Allergists (bd. govs. 1974, pres. 1979); mem. AMA, Am. Acad. Pediatrics, So. Med. Assn. (chmn. allergy sect. 1970-71), Tex. Allergy Research Found. Houston(research and edn. com. 1966-86, chmn. sci. adv. council 1973—), Tex. Pediatric Soc., Harris County Med. Soc., Tex. Med. Assn. (chmn. allergy sect. 1976-77), Am. Assn. for Inhalation Therapy (awards com. 1969-72, spl. edn. com. 1969-72), Greater Houston Allergy Soc. (pres. 1977), Joint Council of Allergy and Immunology, Internat. Assn. of Allergology and Clin. Immunology (U.S. rep. 1981-85). Home: Willis, Tex. Died Apr. 13, 2007.

THOMAS, OUIDA POWER, music educator; b. Louisville, Miss., Nov. 25, 1939; d. Robert Alvin and Mavis (Simpson) Power; m. Charles Victor Thomas, Aug. 4, 1962; children: Karla Victoria, Sylvia Katharine Thomas White, Charles Gregory. BS in Bus. Edn. with highest honors, Miss. State U., Starkville, 1963; M Music Edn., Delta State U., 1993; postgrad., U. Memphis, 1996—. Nat. cert. tchr. of music. Ind. music tchr. piano and organ, Grenada, Miss., 1963—; classroom gen. music tchr. Kirk Acad., Grenada, 1977-87. Adjudicator auditions Federated Music Clubs, Oxford, Miss., 1990—99. Accompanist musical prodns. Grenada Fine Arts Playhouse, 1979-81; organist, choirmaster All Saints' Episcopal Ch., Grenada, 1977—; mem. music and liturgy com. Episcopal Diocese of Miss., 1996-99. Mem. Am. Guild Organists, Nat. Guild Piano Tchrs. (chmn. local auditions 1977—, adjudicator auditions 1993—), Music Tchrs. Nat. Assn. (cert. in piano and organ), Miss. Music Tchrs. Assn. (cert. in piano and organ, exec. bd. 1993-94, state chair pre-coll. student activities 1995-96, chair state cert. 1999-2000, adjudicator auditions 1993—), Grenada Area Music Tchrs. Assn. (v.p. 1995—). Avocations: gardening, needlecrafts. Home: 1985 Wooded Dr Grenada MS 38901-4073 Personal E-mail: opthomas@cableone.net.

THOMAS, PATRICIA ANNE, retired law librarian; b. Cleve., Aug. 21, 1927; d. Richard Joseph and Marietta Bernadette (Teevans) T. BA, Case Western Res. U., 1949, JD, 1951. Bar: Ohio 1951, U.S. Supreme Ct. 1980. Libr. Arter & Hadden, Cleve., 1951-62; asst. libr., libr. IRS, Washington, 1962-78; libr. dir. Adminstrv. Office U.S. Cts., 1978-93; ret., 1993. Mem. Am. Assn. Law Librs., Soc. D.C. (pres. 1967-69), Soc. Benchers (Case Western Res. Law Sch.)

THOMAS, PATRICIA GOODNOW, journalist; b. Framingham, Mass., Dec. 28, 1924; d. Charles Frederick and Dorothy (Eaton) G.; m. Roy Condit Thomas, Oct. 7, 1961. BS, Simmons Coll., 1946; MAT, Rollins Coll., 1971. News reporter-writer Radio Station WCOP, Boston, 1946-52; editorial specialist Central Intelligence Agy., Washington, 1952-54; asst. editor Hood Milk Corp., Boston, 1954-55; sr. writer/editor Voice of America, Washington, 1955-61; writer Orlando Mag., Orlando, Fla., 1964-72; tchr. French, Eng. Oviedo (Fla.) H.S., 1965-66; prof. of journalism Seminole Cmty. Coll., Sanford, Fla., 1972-88; freelance writer Blairsville, Ga., 1988—. Editor: From Sky to Sea, 1993; contbr. articles to profl. jours. Mem. Fla. Freelance Writers Assn., Kappa Delta Pi. Personal E-mail: rpthomas@alltel.net.

THOMAS, PATRICK ROBERT MAXWELL, oncologist, educator, academic administrator; b. Exmouth, Devon, Eng., Feb. 23, 1943; came to U.S., 1976; s. Christopher Codrington and Aileen Daphne (Gordon) T.; m. Linda Sharon Rich, June 23, 1986 (dec. 1987), m. Geraldine M. Jacobson, Mar. 2, 1996 (div. 1999); m. Frances Aquino, Feb. 19, 2005. Diploma in biochemistry, London U., 1965, MB, BS, 1968. Lectr. Inst. Cancer Rsch., London, 1974-76; assoc. chief clinician Roswell Park Meml. Inst., Buffalo, 1976-79; asst. prof. Washington U., St. Louis, 1979-83, assoc. prof., 1983-89, prof., 1989-90; prof., chmn. Temple U., Phila., 1991-98; radiation oncologist Pinellas (Fla.) Radiation Oncology Assocs., 1998—2003; prof. radiation oncology Pa. State U., Pa., 2006—. Extramural bd. PDQ, Bethesda, Md., 1989—; mem. in-svc. exam. com. Am. Coll. Radiology, Reston, Va., 1990-97; examiner Am. Bd. Radiology, Louisville, 1990—. Mem. editl. adv. bd.: Med. and Pediatric Oncology, 2002—. Fellow: Royal Coll. Physicians of London, Am. Soc. Radiation Oncologists, Am. Coll. Radiologists; mem.: Internat. Soc. Pediat. Oncology (sci. com. 2000—). Office: 500 University Dr MC H063 Hershey PA 17033 Business E-Mail: pthomas2@psu.edu.

THOMAS, PAUL D., metal products executive, human resources specialist; V.p. Alcoa, Inc., Pitts., 1998—2004, pres. engineered products, 1998—2001, pres. mill products, 2001—03, group pres. N.Am. fabricated products, 2003—04, exec. v.p., 2004—, exec. v.p people, ABS and culture, 2004—06, exec. v.p., group pres. packaging & consumer products, 2006—. Bd. dirs. Aloca Found., Aluminum Assn., Inc. Office: Alcoa Inc 201 Isabella St Pittsburgh PA 15212-5858 Office Phone: 412-553-4545. *

THOMAS, PAUL LINDSLEY, composer, musician, director; b. NYC, Mar. 18, 1929; s. Richard Banks and Virginia Bartholomew (Carrington) T.; m. Joyce Robertshaw, Sept. 3, 1955; 1 child, Craig Carrington. BA, Trinity Coll., Hartford, Conn., 1950; diploma, Am. Conservatory, Fontainbleau, France, 1954; MusB, Yale U., 1957, MusM, 1958; D of Musical Arts, U. North Tex., 1979. Organist, choirmaster St. George's-by-the-River, Rumson, NJ, 1950-55, St. James Episcopal Ch., West Hartford, Conn., 1955-60; organist Wesleyan U., Middletown, Conn., 1958-60; dir. Apollo Glee Club, Yale U., New Haven, 1958-60; instr. in organ So. Meth. U., Dallas, 1960-65; music dir., organist St. Michael and All Angels Ch., Dallas, 1960-97, composer in residence, music dir. emeritus, 1997—; music dir. Trinity Epis. Ch., Dallas, 1998—. Chmn. liturgy and music commn. Episcopal Diocese of Dallas, 1992—98. Composer (opera) Everyman, 1986; composer ch. anthems and organ music. Named Canon of Ch. Music, Episcopal Diocese of Dallas, 1980; recording grantee Stemmons Found., Dallas, 1995; Joyce and Paul Thomas Music Wing named in his honor St. Michael and All Angels, Dallas, 1994. Fellow Am. Guild Organists (dean Dallas chpt. 1967-69, gen. chmn. nat. conv. 1972, nat. coun. 1972-75); mem. Assn. Anglican Musicians, Am. Choral Dirs. Assn. Republican. Episcopalian. Home: 6822 Northwood Rd Dallas TX 75225-2538 Office: Trinity Episcopal Ch 12727 Hillcrest Rd Dallas TX 75230-2007

THOMAS, PAUL MILTON, retired science educator; b. Sligo, Pa., Dec. 1, 1929; s. Milton Ivan and Maude Hazel Thomas; m. Dorothy Marie McGinnett; 1 child, Mona Lee Callahan. BA, Allegheny Coll., 1958; MEd, U. Mich., 1959, MA, 1962, PhD, 1964; DMin, Drew U., 1980. Instr. biology Houghton Coll., NY, 1959—62; asst. prof. Point Loma Coll., San Diego, 1964—66; rsch. fellow Calif. Inst. Tech., Pasadena, 1967—68; vis. prof. Johns Hopkins U., Balt., 1968; prof., chmn. dept. biology Edinboro U., Pa., 1968—90; pastor United Ch. of Christ, Greensburg, 1995—. Vis. scholar Harvard U., Cambridge, Mass., 1993. Contbr. articles to profl. jours.; author: (books) W. Edwards Deming: Improving Quality in Colleges and Universities, Easter Urges Us to Look at Death, A Christian Looks at Death, Pennsylvania Fish Commission, Fishes of Erie County, Fishes of Pymatuning. Mem. Sch. Bd., Union City, Pa., 1969—75. Mem.: Audubon Soc., Sigma Xi, Phi Kappa Phi. R-Consevative. United Church Of Christ. Avocations: hiking, world traveling. Home: 87 West High St Union City PA 16438-1239 Personal E-mail: pthomas@velocity.net.

THOMAS, PHILIP STANLEY, economist, educator; b. Hinsdale, Ill., Oct. 23, 1928; s. Roy Kehl and Pauline (Grafton) Thomas; m. Carol Morris, Dec. 27, 1950; children: Lindsey Carol, Daniel Kyle, Lauren Louise, Gay Richardson. BA, Oberlin Coll., 1950; MA, U. Mich., 1951, PhD, 1961; postgrad., Delhi U., 1953—54. Instr. U. Mich., 1956-57; asst. prof. Grinnell (Iowa) Coll., 1957-63, assoc. prof., 1963-65; assoc. prof. econs. Kalamazoo Coll., 1965-68, prof. econs., 1968-94, prof. emeritus, 1994—. Econ. advisor Pakistan Inst. Devel. Econs., 1963—64, USAID, 1965—68, 1971, Planning Commn., Pakistan, 1969—70, Ctrl. Bank Swaziland, 1974—75, Ministry Planning, Kenya, 1980—81, 1983—85, 1986—88, Ministry Fin., Swaziland, 1990, Kenya, 91, 92, Ministry Indsl. Devel., Sri Lanka, 1997, Res. Bank Malawi, 1998—99, Jordan-U.S. Bus. Partnership, 2000—01. Contbr. articles to profl. jours. Mem. alumni coun. Oberlin Coll., 1961—63, 1974—76, 1983—86, 1995—2001, treas. alumni coun., 2004—06. With AUS, 1954—56. Fellow Overseas, Ford Found., 1953—54; scholar Fulbright. Mem.: Am. Econs. Assn., Phi Beta Kappa. Home and Office: 313A S Shabwasung St Northport MI 49670-9604 E-mail: pcmthomas@charter.net.

THOMAS, RADFORD, art educator, painter; s. Wilburn Ronald and Rachel Elizabeth Thomas; m. Sue Steele Steele, Jan. 13, 1979. BFA in Studio Art, U. Tex., Austin, PhD, 1967—70; MA in Studio Art, N.Mex. Highlands U. Self-employed, San Antonio, 1982—88; dir. Noel Art Mus. for the Permian Basin, Odessa, Tex., 1988—90; adj. prof. art Va. Western C.C., Roanoke, 1998—, Radford U., Va., 2001—06. Exhibitions include A Whole Childhood of Fantasy Lies Ahead, 1959, Represented in permanent collections Fish Stamp, Oakland, Calif. Mus., Man. Chair visual arts program EXPO '74 Worlds Fair, Spokane, Wash., 1972—74; chair visual arts adv. panel Tenn. Arts Commn., Nashville, 1975—78. Recipient Purchase award, Witte Meml. Mus., San Antonio, 1959, 1st prize, Dallas Mus. Art, 1959. Mem.: Men Art Guild (chair 1959—60), Tex. Fine Arts Assn., Coll. Art Assn. D-Liberal. Avocations: travel, artifact collecting. Home: 4853 Hunting Hills Dr Roanoke VA 24018 Office: Va We CC 3095 Colonial Ave Roanoke VA 24036 Office Phone: 540-857-6070. Personal E-mail: radsue@verizon.net. Business E-Mail: rthomas@vw.vccs.edu.

THOMAS, RALPH CHARLES, III, federal official; b. Roanoke, Va., Apr. 10, 1949; s. Ralph C. Jr. and Dorothy (Easley) T. BA, U. Calif., Berkeley, 1975; JD, Harvard U., 1978. Assoc. Bergson, Borkland, Margolis & Adler, Washington, 1978-80; sr. ptnr. Thomas, John & Everett, Washington, 1980-85; clin. instr. in Law Sch. George Washington U., Washington, 1982-83; exec. dir. Nat. Assn. Minority Contractors, Washington, 1985-92; assoc. adminstr. for small/disadvantaged bus. utilization NASA, Washington, 1992—. Adj. instr. U. Va., Charlottesville, 1989—91; chmn. Fed. Small Bus. Dirs. Interagy. Coun., 2001—03; bd. dirs. Sr. Execs. Assn., 2002—05. Author: Extreme Flashbacks, 1997; contbr. articles to profl. jours. Mem. Pres.'s Interagy. Working Group on Minority Bus. Devel., 1995. Staff sgt. USAF, 1967-71, Vietnam. Recipient Spl. Honor award, World Assn. Small and Medium Enterprises, 1999, Presdl. Rank for Disting. Exec. award, 2001, Minority Bus. Entrepreneur Adv. of Yr. award, Asian Enterprise mag., 2004, Man of Yr. award, Minority Enterprise Adv. Mag., 2005. Mem. Fed. Bar Assn. (chair govt. contracts sect. 2002-03).

THOMAS, RANDALL STUART, lawyer, educator; b. Princeton, NJ, Nov. 25, 1955; s. John Bowman and Eleanor (Graefe) T.; m. Cheri D. Ferrari; children: Cameron Stuart, Cortland Andrew, Colin Duncan, Carson F. Thomas. BA, Haverford Coll., 1977; MA, U. Mich., 1979, PhD, 1983, JD, 1985. Bar: Del. 1987, U.S. Dist. Ct. Del. 1987. Economist U. Mich., Ann Arbor, 1979-83; law clk. Fed. Dist. Ct. (ea. dist.) Mich., Ann Arbor, 1985; assoc. Potter, Anderson & Corroon, Wilmington, Del., 1986, Skadden, Arps, Slate, Meagher & Flom, Wilmington, 1987-90; assoc. prof. law U. Iowa, 1990-94, prof. law, 1994—, Vanderbilt Univ., 2000—, John Beasley prof. law and bus., 2003—. Vis. prof. Boston U. Law Sch., 1995, U. Mich. Law Sch., 1996, Duke U. Sch. Law, 1999. Rackham fellow U. Mich., 1982-83. Mem.: Order of Coif. Democrat. Methodist. Office: Vanderbilt Univ Sch Law 131 21st Ave S Nashville TN 37203-1120 Home Phone: 615-292-0813; Office Phone: 615-343-3814. Business E-Mail: Randall.Thomas@law.vanderbilt.edu.

THOMAS, REGENA L., former state official; b. Clinton, Ky., Oct. 31, 1957; BA in U. Studies, Morehead State U. Cons. Dem. Gov.'s Assn.; legislative analyst Legislative Research Commn., KY State Legislature, 1980—85; prin. IEM Mesage mgmt., Inc.; served Torricelli for Senate, 1996, McGreevey for Gov., 1997, Corzine for Senate, 2000; sec. state State of N.J., Trenton, 2002—06. Prin. liaison non-govtl. orgns., key Dem. constituencies; dep., dir. Constituent Svcs. Govt. Dist. Columbia; legis. analyst Legis. Rsch. Commn. Ky. State Legislature; with Nat. Rainbow Coalition and its founder, Rev. Jesse L. Jackson.

THOMAS, RHONDA CHURCHILL, lawyer; b. 1947; m. J. Regan Thomas; children: Ryan, Aaron, Evan. BA cum laude, Drury Coll., 1969; JD, U. Mo., 1972, Yale U., 1973. Bar: Mo. 1973, Ill. Newswoman Sta. KFRU Radio, Columbia, Mo., 1969-70; law clk. to Hon. Robert E. Seiler Supreme Ct. of Mo., Jefferson City, 1973-74; asst. city counselor City of Columbia, 1974-76, city counselor, chief legal advisor to city coun., dept. heads, 1976-79; assoc. prof. law U. Mo., 1979-82; ptnr. Thompson Cobum, St. Louis, 1985—, Sonnenschein Nath & Rosenthal, Chgo. Past chmn. franchise com. Nat. Inst. Mcpl. Law Officers. Contbr. articles to profl. jours. Past chmn. Boone County Home Rule Charter Commn.; past pres. Boone County Indsl. Devel. Authority, bd. trustees U. Mo. Law Sch. Found., U. Mo. Law Soc., U. Mo. Jefferson Club, Sheldon Arts Found., Dance St. Louis, Chgo. River North Dance Co. Mem. ABA (local govt. law sect., taxation sect.), Mo. Bar Assn. (mem. edn. law com., mem. local govt. law com., mem. med.-legal rels. com., past mem. spl. com. on quality and methods of practice), St. Louis Bar Assn., Nat. Assn. Bond Lawyers, Mo. Mcpl. Attys. Assn. (past pres.). Office: Sonnenschein Nath & Rosenthal 7800 Sears Tower Chicago IL 60606 Office Phone: 312-876-8966. Office Fax: 312-876-7934. Business E-Mail: rthomas@sonnenschein.com.

THOMAS, RICH L., secondary school educator; b. St. Charles, Mo., Feb. 16, 1980; s. Richard and Rebecca Thomas; m. Kristin Thomas. BS, N.W. Mo. State, Maryville, 2003; MA, S.W. Mo. State U., Cape Giradia, 2007. Cert. secondary edn. Mo. Instr. agr. edn. Jefferson City HS, Mo., 2003—04; head instr. agr. edn. Advance HS, Mo., 2004—. Blood dr. coord. ARC; bell ringer Salvation Army. Named one of Top 50 Agr. Tchr., Indpls., 2005, Top 30 Agr. Tchr., Mo., 2005. Mem.: Mo. State Tchr. Assn., Nat. Assn. Agr. Educators, Mo. Agr. Tchr. Assn. (local pres.). Avocations: golf, fishing. Office: Advance Pub Schs 201 E School St Advance MO 63730

THOMAS, RICHARD, actor; b. NYC, June 13, 1951; s. Richard and Barbara (Fallis) T.; m. Alma Gonzalez, Feb. 14, 1975 (div. 1993); children: Richard F., Barbara, Gwyneth and Pilar (triplets); m. Georgiana Bischoff, Nov. 20, 1995; 1 child, Montana; children from previous marriage: Brooke,

Kendra. Student, Columbia U. Owner, prin. Melpomene Prodns. Actor: (broadway debut at age 7 in) Sunrise at Campobello, 1958, A Naked Girl on the Appian Way, 2005; (regular on children's series) One, Two, Three-Go!, 1961-62, regular (TV series) The Waltons, 1972—77 (Emmy award, 1973, Golden Globe nominee); dir.: (TV series) The Waltons, 1972; actor: (films) Strange Interlude, 1962, The Playroom, 1965, Winning, 1969, Last Summer, 1969, You Can't Have Everything, 1970, Red Sky at Morning, 1971, The Todd Killings, 1971, Cactus in the Snow, 1971, You'll Like My Mother, 1972, 9/30/55, 1977, Battle Beyond the Star, 1980, Wonder Boys, 2000, Fortune Hunters, 2000; (stage appearances) Sunrise at Campobello, 1958, Whose Life Is It Anyway?, 1980, The Fifth of July, 1981, The Sea Gull, 1984, The Count of Monte Cristo, 1985, Citizen Tom Paine, 1986, The Front Page, 1986, Hamlet, 1987, Peer Gynt, 1989, Love Letters, 1989-90, Square One, 1990, Lisbon Traviata, 1990, Danton's Death, 1992, Richard II, 1993, Richard III, 1994, Tiny Alice, 1998, 2000, Measure for Measure, 1999, A Midsummer's Night's Dream, 1999, stage appearances ART (West End), 2000, 2001, A Distant Country Called Youth, 2002, The Stendahl Syndrome, 2004, Democracy, 2004; stage appearances: A Naked Girl on the Apian Way, 2005, Twelve Angry Men, 2006—; author: (poems) Poems by Richard Thomas, Vols. I and 2, 1974; actor: (TV dramatic spl. and movies) The Homecoming-A Christmas Story, 1971, The Red Badge of Courage, 1974, The Silence, 1975, All Quiet on the Eastern Front, 1979, The Hank Williams Jr. Story, 1983, Hobson's Choice, 1984, The Master of Ballantrae, 1984, Getting Married, No Other Love, 5th of July, 1981, Common Ground, Glory!, Glory!, 1990, Andre's Mother, 1990, It, 1990, Mission of the Shark, 1991, Yes, Virginia There Is a Santa Claus, 1991, A Walton's Thanksgiving Reunion, 1993, Death in Small Doses, 1993, Linda, 1993, A Walton Wedding, 1995, A Christmas Box, 1995, What Love Sees, 1996, A Walton Easter, 1998, Swiss Family Robinson, 1997, 1,000 Men and a Baby, 1997, Swiss Family Robinson, 1997, 1,000 Men and a Baby, 1997, Flood: A River's Rampage, 1997, Down Out and Dangerous, 1997, Big and Hairy, 1998, Beyond the Prairie, 2000, In the Name of the People, 2000, It's a Miracle, 1999-2000, The Christmas Secret, 2000, Miracle of the Cards, 2001, Beyond the Grave II, 2002, Anna's Dream, 2002, Annie's Point, 2005, Wild Hearts, 2005, Nightmaers and Dreamscapes, 2006, (host children's spl.) H.M.S. Pinafore, 1973; (TV series) Touched By an Angel, 1994, Promised Land, 1996, The Practice, 1997, Law & Order: Special Victims Unit, 1999, Just Cause, 2002—03; host: It's a Miracle. Nat. chmn. Better Hearing Inst., 1987. Office: care Springer Assoc 1501 Broadway Ste 506 New York NY 10036-5601 Office Phone: 212-354-4660.

THOMAS, RICHARD STEPHEN, construction executive; b. Mason City, Iowa, June 5, 1949; s. H. Idris and Mildred (Keen) T.; m. Pamela Jane Chipka, Sept. 11, 1982. AA, No. Iowa C.C., 1969; BA, U. No. Iowa, 1971, BLS, 1991; MBA, U. Calif., Berkeley, 1991. Cost acct. Boise Cascade, Mason City, Iowa, 1971-72, cost acct. mgr. Shippensburg, Pa., 1973-74; staff acct. Grumman Corp., Williamsport, Pa., 1974-76; acctg. mgr. Pullman Power Products, Williamsport, 1976-79; treas, controller Schweizer Dipple Inc., Cleve., 1979-87; treas., corp. controller Langenau Mfg. Co., Cleve., 1987-92, chief fin. officer, 1987-92; sec.-treas. World Trade Wins Inc., Cleve., 1987-92; v.p. fin. and CFO Norris Bros. Co., Inc., Cleve., 1992—. Mem. employer adv. com. Ohio Job Svc., Greater Cleve. Growth Assn., Westlake Ohio Sch. Bd. Mem. Inst. Mgmt. Accts. (contr.'s coun. 1985), Constrn. Fin. Mgmt. Assn. (pres. 1995-2002, state dir., nat. dir.), Am. Coun. for Constrn. Edn. (fin. comm. 1997-98), Constrn. Industry Liason Comm. (chmn.), Cleve. Treas.'s Assn., Cleve. Engring. Soc., Associated Builders and Contractors, Constrn. Employers Assn., Cleve. World Trade Assn., Masons (local treas. 1984), York Rite Bodies, City Club of Cleve., U. Club, Cleve. Athletic Club, Phi Beta Lambda. Republican. Avocations: skiing, photography, sailing. Home: 1663 Settlers Reserve Way Westlake OH 44145-2042 Office: Norris Bros Co Inc 2138 Davenport Ave Cleveland OH 44114-3791 Office Phone: 216-771-2233. Personal E-mail: rsthomas49@sbcglobal.net. Business E-Mail: rthomas@norrisbr.com.

THOMAS, RITCHIE TUCKER, lawyer; b. Cleve., Aug. 12, 1936; s. Myron F. and Marjorie (Ritchie) T.; m. Elizabeth Blackwell Hanes Main, Jan. 1, 1994. BA, Cornell U., 1959; JD, Case-Western Res. U., 1964. Bar: Ohio 1964, U.S. Dist. Ct. (no. dist.) Ohio 1964, U.S. Ct. Appeals (D.C. cir.) 1971, U.S. Ct. Appeals (fed. cir.) 1973, U.S. Ct. Fed. Claims 1973, U.S. Ct. Internat. Trade 1976, U.S. Ct. Appeals (9th cir.) 1985. Assoc. office of gen. counsel U.S. Tariff Commn., Washington, 1964-67; assoc. Squire, Sanders & Dempsey, Cleve., 1967-69, Cox, Langford & Brown, Washington, 1969-74; ptnr. Squire, Sanders & Dempsey, Washington, 1974—. Mem. exec. com. Meridian House Internat., Washington, 1977-94. Assoc. editor Western Res. U. Law Rev., 1964; columnist Commerce Germany; contbr. articles to profl. jours. Mem. Waring Prize Com., Western Res. Acad., 1996—; mem. Bretton Woods Com., Washington, 2003— Recipient Book award West Pub. Co., 1964 Mem. Fed. Bar Assn., D.C. Bar Assn., Belgian American Assn. (v.p. bd. dirs. 1989—), Am. C. of C. (Washington rep. 1984—), Order of Coif. Home: 6700 Bradley Blvd Bethesda MD 20817-3045 Office: Squire Sanders & Dempsey 1201 Pennsylvania Ave NW PO Box 407 Washington DC 20044-0407 Business E-Mail: rtthomas@ssd.com.

THOMAS, ROBERT EGGLESTON, retired manufacturing executive; b. Cuyahoga Falls, Ohio, July 28, 1914; s. Talbott E. and Jane S. (Eggleston) T.; 1 child, Barbara Ann. BS in Econs, U. Pa., 1936. Asst. to gen. mgr., sec., mgr. r.r. investments Keystone Custodian Funds, Boston, 1936-53; v.p. Pennroad Corp., NYC, 1953-59; chmn. exec. com., dir. M.-K.- T. R.R., 1956-65; mem. exec. com. MAPCO Inc., 1960-84, dir., chief exec. officer, 1960-80, pres., 1960-76, chmn. bd., 1973-84. Adv. bd. BancOkla. Corp. Mem.: Newcomen Soc., Nat. Mining Assn. (hon. dir.), Am. Petroleum Inst. (hon. dir.), Desert Horizons Country Club (Indian Wells, Calif.), San Diego Yacht Club, Summit Club (Tulsa), So. Hills Country Club (Tulsa), Chgo. Club. Episcopalian. Office: Williams Cos PO Box 4679 Tulsa OK 74159-0679 Home Phone: 918-749-2113; Office Phone: 918-573-8100. E-mail: Robert.Thomas@williams.com.

THOMAS, ROBERT L., retired manufacturing company executive; b. Atlanta, Aug. 1, 1941; s. Orville Kermit Smith and Ina Evelyn (Farris) Peterson; m. Karen Degenhardt, Dec. 4, 1960 (div. Apr. 1978); children: John Harding, Gregory James, Kristen Ann; m. Mary Ellen Seaman, May 2, 1981; children: Lindsey Marian, Mark Gordon. BA in History, Queens Coll., 1968. Buyer J.C. Penney Co. Inc., NYC, 1964-70; sales mgr. Avon Products Inc., Atlanta, 1970-72; pres. Saul Bros. & Co. Inc., Atlanta, 1973—2002; founder, pres., CEO RLT Enterprises, LLC, Atlanta, 2004—. Bd. dirs. Murphey Candler Little League, Atlanta, 1972, also bd. trustees; bd. dirs. Leukemia Soc., Atlanta, 1988—; mem. Dekalb County Exec. Com. Rep. Party, Atlanta, 1970-74; del. State Convention Rep. Party, Atlanta, 1972. Established scholarship Michael Daniel and Alexander Tyler Smith Scholarship Found., U. S.C., 1995—. Mem. South East Textile and Apparel Mfrs., U.S. Polo Assn., Atlanta Polo Club, Gulfstream Polo Club (West Palm Beach), N.Y. Athletic Club (N.Y.C.), Country Club of the South (Alpharetta, Ga.). Republican. Roman Catholic. Home: 4095 Big Creek Overlook Alpharetta GA 30005-4213 Office Phone: 678-296-6409. E-mail: rthomas93@comcast.net.

THOMAS, ROBERT MCGUFFEY, automotive executive, educator; b. Newcastle, Pa., Jan. 7, 1917; s. Trevor Thomas and Clara Belle Speer; m. Millie Reddy, Jan. 7, 1945 (div. Apr. 11, 1962); children: Trevor, Diane, Robert; m. Natalie Khoranoff, Apr. 10, 1964. Degree in Music (hon.), Music Master, Sharon, Pa., 1938. Exec. stalist Ford Motor Co., Dearborn, Mich., 1965—74; piano tchr. and band leader San Diego, 1975—95; sign painter Penny Co. Sharon. Author: How To Play Piano, 1984, War Is Hell, 1985, Life Is Life, 1995. With US Army, 1940—45, Europe. Mem.: Piano Club. Avocation: piano. Home: 10539 Caminito Pollo San Diego CA 92126

THOMAS, ROBERT MORTON, JR., lawyer, director; b. Kansas City, Jan. 1, 1941; s. Robert Morton Sr. and Arlowyne Edith (Arganbright) T.; m. Rebecca Ann Myers, Aug. 21, 1965; children: Brooke J., Austin B. BA, U. Kans., 1962; LLB, Harvard U., 1966. Bar: NY, 1970, US Dist. Ct. (so. dist.) NY, 1970, US Ct. Appeals (2d cir.), 1970. Local govt. advisor Republic of Botswana, Gaborone, 1966, dist. officer Serowe, 1967, dist. commr. Maun, 1968; assoc. Sullivan & Cromwell, LLP, NYC, 1969-75, ptnr., 1975—2007, ptnr.-in-charge London, 1979-82, Beijing, 2005—07, mng. ptnr. gen. practice group NYC, 1986-91. Mem. exec. bd. Manhattan coun. Boy Scouts Am.; trustee U. Kans. Endowment Assn., Helen Keller Internat.; dir. Sheffield Law Trust, Mass. Mem. ABA, NY State Bar Assn., Assn. Bar City of NY, Internat. Bar Assn., Harvard Club, Mill Reef Club, Verbank Hunting and Fishing Club, Knickerbocker Club, Beijing Am. Club, Confrerie des Chevaliers de Tastevin, Bentley Drivers Club, Vintage Sports Car Club Am. Republican. Presbyterian. Office: Sullivan & Cromwell 125 Broad St New York NY 10004-2498 Office Phone: 212-558-3704.

THOMAS, ROBERT PAIGE, lawyer; b. Columbus, Ohio, July 31, 1941; s. Charles Marion and Elsie (Cavanaugh) T.; children: Paige Cason, Park Cavanaugh. B.A., Vanderbilt U., 1963, M.A., 1965, J.D., 1970. Bar: Tenn. 1970, U.S. Dist. Ct. (mid. dist.) Tenn. 1970, U.S. Ct. Appeals (6th cir.) 1977. Assoc. Boult, Cummings, Conners & Berry, Nashville, 1970-74, ptnr., 1974—, mng. ptnr., 1977-84. chmn. Tenn. Dem. Party; Mem. Bill Clinton's Nat. Fin. Com.; fin. chmn. Sen. Jim Sasser. Mem. ABA, Tenn. Bar Assn., Nashville Bar Assn. Democrat. Episcopalian. Clubs: Yale of N.Y.C.; Belle Meade Country. Office: PO Box 340025 Nashville TN 37203 Home Phone: 615-383-1907; Office Phone: 615-252-2314. Business E-Mail: bthomas@boultcummings.com.

THOMAS, ROBERT R., state supreme court justice; b. Rochester, NY, Aug. 7, 1952; m. Maggie Thomas; 3 children. BA in govt., U. Notre Dame, 1974; JD, Loyola U., 1981. Cir. ct. judge DuPage County, 1988, acting chief judge, 1989—94; judge Appellate Ct. Second Dist., 1994—2000; justice Ill. Supreme Ct., 2000—, chief justice, 2006—. Named to Academic All-Am. Hall of Fame; recipient NCAA Silver Anniversary award, 1999. Mem.: DuPage County Bar Assn., Acad. All-Am. Hall of Fame (life NCAA Silver Ann. Award 1999). Office: Illinois Supreme Ct 160 N LaSalle St Chicago IL 60601 *

THOMAS, ROGER MERIWETHER, lawyer; b. Hartford, Conn., Feb. 28, 1930; s. Frederick Metcalf and Helen Meriwether (Lewis) T.; m. Mary Dorothea Wyman, Dec. 4, 1965; children— Donald Wyman, Helen Dorothea. AB, Princeton U., 1952; LL.B., Va. U., 1957; LL.M., Boston U., 1964. Bar: N.Y. 1958, Mass. 1960, U.S. Dist. Ct. (Mass) 1965, U.S. Tax Ct. 1965, U.S. Supreme Ct. 1967. Assoc. Angulo, Cooney, Marsh & Ouchterloney, NYC, 1957-60; assoc., then ptnr. Gaston & Snow, Boston, 1960-91; counsel Condit & Assocs., P.C., Boston, 1992-94. Outline author and lectr. Mass. Continuing Legal Edn., Inc., Boston; past panelist New Eng. Law Inst. Estate Planning Forums, Boston. Trustee Buckingham Browne & Nichols Sch., Cambridge, Mass., 1967-69. 1st lt. U.S. Army, 1952-54, Korea. Mem. Am. Coll. Trust and Estate Counsel, Boston Bar Assn., Mass. Bar Assn. Avocations: reading, sports, old movies. Home: 40 Byron Rd Weston MA 02493-2229

THOMAS, ROGER WARREN, lawyer; b. South Weymouth, Mass., Sept. 17, 1937; s. Clement Rogers and Beatrice (Merritt) T.; m. Maria Sava Brenner, July 5, 1968; children: Caroline, Andrew, Phillip. BA, U. NH, Durham, 1959; postgrad. (Rotary Internat. fellow), Free U. Berlin, 1960; LLB (Root-Tilden scholar), NYU, 1963, LLM (Ford Found. grantee), 1965; postgrad., U. Chile, Santiago, 1965. Bar: NY 1964. Assoc. Cleary, Gottlieb, Steen and Hamilton, NYC, 1965-66, 69-74, partner, 1974—. Mem. Harvard-Chile Tax Reform Project, 1966-68, head project in Chile, 1968-69; cons. to UN, Santiago, 1969; adj. prof. taxation NYU, 1974-96. Co-author: El Impuesto a la Renta, 1969. Bd. dirs. Spanish Repertory Theatre, Fundacion Chile; chmn. UNH Found. Mem. Am. Fgn. Lawyers Assn., N.Am.-Chilean C. of C. (pres. 1984-96), Am. Soc., Coun. of Am., Knickerbocker Club. Home: 1150 5th Ave New York NY 10128-0724 Office: 1 Liberty Plz New York NY 10006-1404

THOMAS, RONALD ROBERT, English literature educator, writer; b. Orange, NJ, Jan. 29, 1949; s. Robert Louis and Doris Josephine (Rambo) T.; m. Mary Domingo, June 15, 1991. BA in English, Wheaton Coll., 1971; MA in English and Am. Lit., Brandeis U., 1978, PhD in English and Am. Lit., 1983. Asst. prof. English lit. U. Chgo., 1982-90; assoc. prof. Trinity Coll., Hartford, Conn., 1990—2003, chmn. dept. English, 1993—2003, chief of staff, v.p., 1998—2001, acting pre., 2001—02; pres. Univ. Puget Sound, Tacoma, 2003—. Author: Dreams of Authority: Freud and the Fictions of the Unconscious, 1990, Detective Fiction and the Rise of Froensic Science, 1999; co-editor: Nineteenth-Century Geographics: The Transformation of Space from the Victorian Age to the American Century, 2002; contbr. articles to profl. jours., chpt. to Columbia History of Brit. Novel. Andrew Mellon fellow Harvard U., 1991-92. Mem. MLA, Dickens Soc., Soc. for Study of Narrative Lit., N.E. Victorian Assn., Interdisciplinary 19th-Century Studies Assn., Phi Beta Kappa. Office: Univ Puget Sound 1500 North Warner Tacoma WA 98416 Business E-Mail: president@ups.edu.

THOMAS, SARAH E., university librarian; AB, Smith Coll., 1970; MS in Libr. Sci., Simmons Coll., 1973; PhD in German, Johns Hopkins U., 1982; student, U. Hamburg, Germany, 1968—69, Albert-Ludwigs U., 1971, Johann Wolfgang Goethe U., 1977—78. Preliminary cataloger Widener Libr., Harvard U., Cambridge, Mass., 1970—71, catalog intern & reference libr., 1971—73, original cataloger Germanic languages, 1973, head departmental libr. cataloging sect., 1974, head computer-based cataloging, 1974—75; instr. elem. German Johns Hopkins U., Balt., 1976—77, instr. intermediate German, 1978—79, sr. cataloger Eisenhower Libr., 1978—79; libr. coord. Rsch. Libraries Group, Stanford, Calif., 1979—80, mgr. libr. coordination, 1980—83; Coun. Libr. Resources academic libr. mgmt. intern U. Ga., Athens, 1983—84; assoc. dir. tech. services Nat. Agrl. Libr., Beltsville, Md., 1984—92; dir. cataloging Libr. Congress, Washington, 1992—94, acting dir. pub. services and collection mgmt., 1995, acting dir. public svc. collections, 1995—96; Carl A. Korch U. Libr. Cornell U., Ithaca, NY, 1996—2007, adj. prof. German dept. modern languages, 1996—2007; Bodley's Libr. & dir. univ. libr. svcs. Oxford U., England, 2007—. Faculty adv. bd. on info. tech. Cornell U., 1996—2007; corp. vis. com. for the libraries of MIT, 1997—; bd. governors Cornell Inst. for Social and Econ. Rsch., 1997—2007; vis. com. Carnegie Mellon Libr., 1999—; overseers' com. to visit the libr. Harvard U., 1999—; chair exec. com. Smith Coll. Libraries, 2002—; chair adv. bd. Project Euclid, 2002—; ctrl. adv. bd. PubMed, 2003—; adminstrv. bd. Cornell U. Coun. Named Online Computer Libr. Ctr. Disting. Scholar, 2000; recipient Cert. Merit, Nat. Agrl. Libr., 1989, Superior Svc. Award, USDA, 1990; Deutscher Akademischer Austauschdienst Fellowship, 1977—78. Mem.: ALA (life Melvil Dewey medal 2007), Assn. Libr. Collections and Tech. Services, Assn. Coll. & Rsch. Libraries, Assn. Rsch. Libraries (bd. mem. 1999—, pres. 2003—04, membership com. 2003—, chair nominating com. 2003—), Grolier Club. Achievements include becoming first woman, and first non-British, Bodley's Librarian. Office: Bodleian Libr Broad St Oxford OS1 3BG England Office Phone: +44 (0)1865 277166. Office Fax: +44 (0)1865 277187. Business E-Mail: bodleys.librarian@bodley.ox.ac.uk. *

THOMAS, SARAH ELAINE, music educator; b. Little Rock, Aug. 8, 1947; d. William and Madie Murle (Stout) Collins; m. Gary Wayne Thomas Aug. 8, 1970 (dec. Nov. 1991). MusB in Edn., U. N. Tex., 1970; M in Ednl. Adminstrn., Dallas Bapt. U., 1997. Cert. tchr.-all-levels, Tex., prin. Music tchr. Winnetka Elem., Dallas, 1970-82, L. K. Hall Elem., Dallas, 1982-94, Kleberg Elem., Dallas, 1994—2001, Pleasant Grove Elem., 2001—05; supr. elem. fine arts Lincoln Instrnl. Ctr., 2005—. Staff. devel. presenter Dallas Ind. Sch. Dist., 1977-97, 97-2005; workshop presenter Tex. Arts Coun., Austin, 1990-94. Bd. dirs. Dallas PTA, 1980-82; bd. dirs. Dallas All-City Elem. Choir, chair, 1991—, dir., 1999-2004. Named Class Act Teacher, Sta. KDFW-TV, Dallas, 1992. Mem. PTA (life), Am. Fedn. Tchrs., Tex. Music Educators Assn., Dallas Music Educators Assn. (v.p. 1992), Am. Orff-Schulwerk Assn., Music Educators Nat. Conf., Rotary (Svc. Above Self award 2003). Avocations: cooking, sewing, gardening, travel. Home: 2407 Norwich Ct Arlington TX 76015-3262 Office: Lincoln Instrnl Ctr 5000 S Malcom X Blvd Rm 104 Dallas TX 75215 Office Phone: 972-749-2545. Personal E-mail: elainethomas3@tx.rr.co. Business E-Mail: elthomas@dallasisd.org.

THOMAS, SCOTT E., lawyer, former commissioner; b. Buffalo, Wyo., Mar. 5, 1953; s. Ralph E. and Bonnie E. Thomas; m. Elena W. King, Apr. 28, 1984. BA, Stanford U., 1974; JD, Georgetown U., 1977. Bar: D.C. 1977, U.S. Ct. Appeals (9th cir.) 1980, U.S. Supreme Ct. 1981. Atty. Office of Gen. Counsel, Fed. Election Commn., Washington, 1977-80; asst. gen. counsel for enforcement Fed. Election Commn., Washington, 1980-83, exec. asst. to commr., 1983-86, commr., 1986—2006, vice chmn., 1992, 1998, chmn., 1987, 1993, 1999, 2005; of counsel Pub. Policy & Law Group Dickstein Shapiro Morin & Oshinsky LLP, Washington, 2006—. Mem. D.C. Bar Assn. Office: Dickstein Shapiro Morin & Oshinsky LLP 2101 L St NW Washington DC 20037 E-mail: ThomasS@dsmo.com.

THOMAS, SIDNEY, fine arts educator, researcher; b. NYC, Dec. 21, 1915; s. Hyman and Rose (Samilowitz) T.; m. Rae Dinkowitz, May 26, 1940; children: David Phillip, Deborah Rose. BA, CCNY, 1935; MA, Columbia U., 1938, PhD, 1943. Tutor in English CCNY, NYC, 1939-43; instr. English Queens Coll., NYC, 1946-54; self-employed as editor, 1954-58; asst. editor Merriam-Webster, Springfield, Mass., 1958-61; assoc. prof. fine arts Syracuse U. (N.Y.), 1961-66, prof., 1966-85, prof. emeritus, 1985—, dir. humanities doctoral program, 1964-72, chmn. dept. fine arts, 1969-73. Bibliographer Shakespeare Assn., N.Y.C., 1949-54 Author: The Antic Hamlet, 1943; co-editor: The Nature of Art, 1964; editor: Images of Man, 1972. Served to sgt., inf. U.S. Army, 1943-45, ETO. Research fellow Folger Shakespeare Library, Washington, 1947-48 Mem.: AAUP (pres. Syracuse U. chpt. 1974), ACLU, MLA (life), Shakespeare Assn. Am., Phi Beta Kappa. Office: Syracuse U Dept Fine Arts Syracuse NY 13210

THOMAS, SIDNEY R., federal judge; b. Bozeman, Mont., Aug. 14, 1953; m. Martha Sheehy. BA in Speech-Comm., Mont. State U., 1975, JD cum laude, 1978; D (hon.), Rocky Mountain Coll., 1998. Bar: Mont. 1978, US Dist. Ct. Mont. 1978, US Ct. Appeals (9th cir.) 1980, US Dist. Ct. (9th cir.) 1980, US Ct. Fed. Claims 1986, US Supreme Ct. 1994. Shareholder Moulton, Bellingham, Longo and Mather, P.C., Billings, Mont., 1978—96; judge US Ct. Appeals (9th cir.), Billings, 1996—. Adj. instr. Rocky Mountain Coll., Billings, 1982—95. Contbr. articles to profl. jours. Recipient Gov.'s award for Pub. Svc., 1978, Outstanding Faculty award, Rocky Mountain Coll., 1988. Mem.: ABA, Yellowstone County Bar Assn., State Bar Mont. Office: US Ct Appeals Ninth Circuit PO Box 31478 Billings MT 59107-1478 *

THOMAS, STEPHEN JAY, anesthesiologist; b. Washington, 1943; MD, Jefferson Med. Col., 1968. Intern San Francisco Gen. Hosp., 1968-69; resident in anesthesiology Mass. Gen. Hosp., Boston, 1971-73, fellow, 1973-74; assoc. prof. NYU Med. Ctr.; vice chmn., Topkins-Van Poznak prof. dept. anesthesiology N.Y. Presbyn. Weill Cornell Ctr., 1989—. Office: NY Presbyn Weill Cornell Ctr Dept Anesthesiology 525 E 68th St New York NY 10021-4870

THOMAS, STEPHEN PAUL, lawyer; b. Bloomington, Ill., July 30, 1938; s. Owen Wilson and Mary Katherine (Paulsen) T.; m. Marieanne Sauer, Dec. 7, 1963 (dec. June 1984); 1 child, Catherine Marie; m. Marcia Aldrich Toomey, May 28, 1988; 1 child, Ellen Antonia. BA, U. Ill., 1959; LLB, Harvard U., 1962; student in MLA Program, U. Chi, 2005—. Bar: Ill. 1962; cert. naturalist Morton Arboretum, 2001, treekeeper Openlands Found., 2004. Vol. Peace Corps, Malawi, Africa, 1963-65; assoc. Sidley Austin LLP, Chgo., 1965-70, ptnr., 1970-2000. Lectr. on law Malawi Inst. Pub. Adminstrn., 1963-65. Pres. Hyde Park-Kenwood Cmty. Conf., Chgo., 1988-90; life trustee Chgo. Acad. for Arts, chmn., 1992-97; life trustee Union League Civic and Arts Found., Chgo., 1999—. Recipient Paul Cornell award Hyde Park Hist. Soc., 1981. Mem. ABA, Chgo. Bar Assn., Chgo. Fedn. Musicians, Ill. State Hist. Soc., Union League Club Chgo., Chgo. Lit. Club (pres. 2007-), Ill. Geog. Soc. Democrat. Roman Catholic. Avocations: jazz piano playing, naturalist studies. Home: 9756 S Longwood Dr Chicago IL 60643-1610 Office: Sidley Austin LLP One S Dearborn St Ste 900 Chicago IL 60603 Office Phone: 312-853-7516. Business E-Mail: sthomas@sidley.com.

THOMAS, STEVEN ALLEN, lawyer; b. Birmingham, Ala., Mar. 19, 1951; s. Reginald Allen and Billie Ruth (Brewer) T.; m. Rebecca Phillips, Aug. 1972; children: Jennifer Ruth, Matthew Allen. AS, Walker Coll., Jasper, Ala., 1971; BA, U. Ala., Tuscaloosa, 1973; JD, Samford U., Birmingham, Ala., 1976. Bar: Ala. 1977, U.S. Dist. Ct. (no. dist.) Ala. 1986. Law clk. Circuit Ct. Walker Co., Jasper, 1978-83; lawyer Beaird, Thomas, Higgins, Jasper, 1983-91; ptv. practice Jasper, 1991—. Judge Mcpl. Ct., Carbon Hill, Ala., 1983-2004, Nauvoo, Ala., 1985-88, Arley, Ala., 1991—, Oakman, Ala., 1997—; prosecutor, Addison, Ala., 2001-04; atty. City of Jasper Civil Svc. Bd., 2001-03. Legal counsel Ala. Jaycees, 1986-88; pres. Ala. Mining Mus., Dora, 1989—; treas. Jasper Band Boosters, 1993-95; advisor Explorers, 1991-98; bd. dirs. Assn. Ala. Fairs, Inc., 1998-03, 1st v.p. 2000, pres. 2001-02, Blue Ribbon Club (Hall of Fame), 2004. Named Jaycee of Yr., Jasper Jaycees, 1983-84, Officer of Yr., 1984, 88. Mem. Ala. Bar Assn. (elder law section, family law section), Walker County Bar Assn. (pres. 1990-91), Ala. Mcpl. Judges Assn., Ala. Assn. Mcpl. Attys., East Walker C. of C. (pres. 1992-94), Phi Alpha Delta. Methodist. Avocations: fishing, reading, swimming, boating, spectator sports. Home: 1401 9th Ave W Jasper AL 35501-4538 Office: PO Box 1951 Jasper AL 35502-1951 Office Phone: 205-221-3100. Personal E-mail: stevenjd76@aol.com.

THOMAS, TERESA ANN, retired microbiologist, educator; d. Sam Charles and Edna Thomas. BS cum laude, Coll. Misericordia, Dallas, Pa., 1961; MS in Biology, Am. U., Beirut, 1965; MS in Microbiology, U. So. Calif. Med. Sch., LA, 1973; cert. in ednl. tech., U. Calif., San Diego, 1998. Tchr., sci. supr., curriculum coord. Meyers H.S., Wilkes-Barre, 1962-64, Wilkes-Barre Area Pub. Schs., 1961-66; rsch. assoc. Proctor Found. Rsch. in Ophthalmology U. Calif. Med. Ctr., San Francisco, 1966-68; instr. Robert Coll. of Istanbul, Turkey, 1968-71, Am. Edn. in Luxembourg, 1971-72, Bosco Tech. Inst., Rosemead, Calif., 1973-74, San Diego C.C. Dist., 1974-80; prof. microbiology and ecology Sch. Math Sci. and Engring. Southwestern Coll., Chula Vista, Calif., 1980—2005, prof. emeritus, 2005—. Pres. acad. senate, 1984-85, del., 1986-89; chmn., coord., steering com. project Cultural Rsch. Ednl. and Trade Exch., 1991-2000, Southwestern Coll.-Shanghai Inst. Fgn. Trade; coord. great tchg. seminar Southwestern Coll., 1987, 88, 89, coord. scholars program, 1988-90, mem. Vecinos Baja Studies EcoMundo team internat. program, mem. steering com.; exec. com. Acad. Senate for Calif. C.C.s, 1985-86, Chancellor Calif. C.C.s Adv. and Rev. Coun. Fund for Instrnl. Improvement, 1984-86; co-project dir. statewide, coord. So. Calif. Biotech. Edn. Consortium, 1993-95, steering com., 1993-98; adj. asst. prof. Chapman Coll., San Diego, 1974-83, San Diego State U., 1977-79; chmn. Am. Colls. Istanbul Sci. Week, 1969-71; adv. bd. Chapman Coll. Cmty. Ctr., 1978-81; cons. sci. curriculum Calif. Dept. Edn., 1986-89; pres. Internat. Rels. Club, 1959-61; mem. San Francisco World Affairs Coun., 1966-68, San Diego World Affairs Coun., 1992—; v.p. Palomar Palace Estates Home Owners Assn., 1983-85, pres., 1994-99, 2003-2004, v.p., 1999—; mem. Rsch. Conf. on Undergrad. Microbiology Edn., Conn. Coll., 1999; bd. dirs. US Orgn. Med. Ednl. Needs, US Internat. Boundary and Water Commn. Citizens Forum Bd., 2001—; mem. South Bay Networking Group, 2006—; dir. South Bay Irrigation Dist., 2006—, Sweetwater Authority, 2006—. Emeritus mem. edilt. rev. bd.: Jour. of Coll. Sci. Tchg. Commr. Internat. Friendship Commn., Chula Vista, 1985-95, vice chmn., 1989-90, chmn., 1990-92; mem. US-Mex. Sister Cities Assn., nat. bd. dirs., 1992-94, gen. chair 30th nat. conv., 1993; founding pres. Chula Vista-Odawara Sister Cities Assn., 1993—; mem. City of Chula Vista Resource Conservation Commn., 1996-05, chmn. 2002-04; mem. Chula Vista Bd. Ethics, 1999-2000, County San Diego Solid Waste Hearing Panel, 2000-05; co-organizer Chula Vista People-to-People Sister City Dels. to Odawara City, Japan, 1991, 94, 99; cmty. adv. com. San Diego Mus. Man, 2000-03; citizens forum bd. US Internat. Boundary & Water Commn., 2001—; steering com. Chula Vista Gen. Plan Update, 2002-05; com. mem. Chula Vista Environ., Open Space & Sustainable Devel., 2002-05; del. citizens adv. com. Port of San Diego & City Chula Vista Bayfront Master Plan, 2003—; mem. Calif. Local Govts. Commn., 2005—; docent Bonita Mus. & Cultural Ctr., 2006—. Grantee Pa. Heart Assn., 1962; fellow NSF, 1965, USPHS, 1972-73; recipient Nat. Tchg. Excellence award Nat. Inst. Staff and Orgnl. Devel., 1989; named Southwestern Coll. Woman of Distinction, 1987, Hon. Coach Southwestern Coll. Ladies Basketball Apaches, 2001, Jaguars Basketball Team, 2003, Chula Vista Environmentalist of Yr., 2005, 50th Anniversary Cir. Dist. Vol. award Sister Cities Internat., 2006. Mem.: NIH (mentor Bridges to the Future program Southwestern Coll. and San Diego 1993—98, steering com.), NEA (life), Bonita Bus. Profl. Assn., Southwest Chula Vista Civic Assn. (founding steering com. mem. 2006—), Faculty Assn. Calif. CC's (state policy com. 2003—05), Am. Soc. Microbiology (So. Calif. MicrobeDiscovery Team 1995—99), Northwest Chula Vista Civic Assn. (assoc.), San Diego Yokohama Sister City Soc. (life), Calif. Sci. Tchrs. Assn. (life), Calif. Tchrs. Assn. (life), Nat. Assn. Biology Tchrs. (life), Nat. Sci. Tchrs. Assn. (life; coord. internat. honors exch. lectr. competition 1986, internat. com.), Chula Vista N.W. Civic Assn., Chula Vista-Odawara Sister Cities Assn. (founding pres. 1993—), San Diego Zool. Soc., Am.-Lebanese Assn. San Diego (1st v.p. 1984—91, pres. 1988—93, chmn. scholarship com.), Am. U. Beirut Alumni and Friends of San Diego (1st v.p. 1984—91), Chula Vista C. of C., Chula Vista Nature Ctr. (life), Japan Soc. San Diego and Tijuana (life), Japanese Am. Hist. Soc. (life), Am. Lebanese Syrian Ladies Club (life; pres. 1982—83), Lions Internat. (bull. editor 1991—93, 2d v.p. 1992—93, 1st v.p. 1993—94, editor Roaring Times Newsletter 1993—94, chmn. dist. internat. rels. and cooperations com. 1993—95, pub. rels. 1997—98, S.W. San Diego County v.p. 2006—07, Best Bull. award 1992—93, Southwest San Diego County Lion of Yr. award 2002, 2006), Delta Kappa Gamma (Gamma Omicron chpt. corr. sec. 2006—, Outstanding Pub. Svc. award, Gamma Omicron chpt. 2003, liaison Learning Is For Everyone), Phi Theta Kappa, Sigma Phi Sigma, Kappa Gamma Pi (pres. Wilkes-Barre chpt. 1963—64, pres. San Francisco chpt. 1967—68), Alpha Pi Epsilon (life; advisor Southwestern Coll. chpt. 1989—90, founder). Personal E-mail: terrytom@ix.netcom.com. Business E-Mail: tthomas@sweetwater.org.

THOMAS, TOM, retired plastics company executive; b. Malang, Java, Indonesia, Feb. 15, 1932; arrived in Can., 1954; s. Ferdinand and Elfrieda Emma (Macht) T.; m. Jannie Chine Sneep, Jan. 19, 1956; children: Gregory John, Renée Sonja Elfrieda, Michael Grant, Thomas. Grad. high sch., The Hague, Holland. Jr. mgr. Lever Bros. Ltd., Toronto, Ont., Canada, 1954-60; sr. mgr. Impac & Somerville Plastics, Toronto, Ont., Canada, 1960-64; founder, C.E.O. Can. Cup Inc., Toronto, Ont., Canada, 1964—, also bd. dirs., 1964-93; ret., 1993. Inventor in field. Trustee Fraser Inst., Vancouver, B.C., Can., 1977-93; gov. Massey and Roy Thomson Hall, Toronto, 1991-92; bd. dirs. Toronto Symphony, 1986-92, mem. Maestro's Club, 1984, mem. pres.'s coun. Can. Opera Co., 1980, adv. coun. Toronto Symphony, 1995-2000, pres. Coun. Can. Opera, 1980-95. Avocations: sailing, history, classical music, chess.

THOMAS, TRACEY WILLIAMS, researcher; b. Birmingham, Ala., Nov. 14, 1971; d. Donald Randolph and Mary Hunter Williams; m. Stephen Wesley Thomas, Feb. 18, 1971. BA, Hampton U., 1994; PhD, Howard U., 2000. Postdoctoral rsch. fellow Johns Hopkins Sch. of Medicine, Balt., 2000—03; aaas sci. policy fellow U.S. EPA, Washington, 2003—. Founder, CEO TWThomas Solutions, LLC, Wash., DC; officer Postdoctoral Assn., Johns Hopkins Sch. of Medicine, Balt., 2001—03; rsch. supr. BioTechnical Inst. of Md., Balt., 2002—; sr. bioscience cons. Booz Allen Hamilton, Abingdon, Md., 2004—06. Contbr. articles various profl. jours. Team leader Greater DC Cares, Youth Impact, Wash., DC, 1995—98; mem. Joint Steering Com. for Pub. Policy, Bethesda, Md., 2002—04. Recipient Predoctoral and Postdoctoral Travel awards, Am. Soc. of Cell Biology, 1998-2000, XIV Internat. Conf. on AIDS Young Sci. Investigator award, Conf. Com., 2002; Postdoctoral fellowship Funding, NIH, 2001-2003, Sci. Policy fellowship, AAAS, 2003-2004. Mem.: AAAS, Am. Soc. of Cell Biology, Assn. of Women in Sci. (assoc.). Democrat. Roman Catholic. Achievements include research in calcium release mechanism in eggs of a protostome; posttranslational modification mutation of a G-Protein coupled receptor involved in HIV. Avocations: travel, reading. Home: 105 Autumnwood Ave York PA 17404 Personal E-mail: twthomas20@hotmaill.com. Business E-Mail: tracey.thomas@twthomassolutions.com.

THOMAS, VIOLETA DE LOS ANGELES, real estate broker; b. Buenos Aires, Dec. 21, 1949; came to U.S., 1967; d. Angel and Lola (Andino) de Rios; m. Jess Thomas, Dec. 23, 1974; 1 child, Victor Justin. Student, Harvard U. and U. Buenos Aires, 1967—73. Mgr. book div. Time-Life, NYC, 1985—93; real estate broker First Marin Realty, Inc., Mill Valley, Calif., 1996-97; assoc. broker Trump Corp., NYC, 1995—97, Brown Harris Stevens, NYC, 1997—. Rep. N.Y.C. Bd. dirs. Alliance Francaise, St. Louis, 1995-96, City of Tiburon, Calif., 1987-93, Art and Heritage Commn., Tiburon. Named Woman of Yr., City of Buenos Aires, 1977, Broker of Yr., Marin County and San Francisco, 1987-92. Mem. Principia Coll. Club. Office: Brown Harris Stevens 60 Windmill Ln Southampton NY 11968 Office Phone: 631-204-2437.

THOMAS, WALTER DILL, JR., retired forest pathologist, consultant; b. St. Louis, July 3, 1918; s. Walter D. and Helen (Gardner) T.; m. Dolores B. Thomas, Dec. 31, 1939 (div. May 1984); children: Sandra Thomas Bosworth, Arthur D; m. Nancy McCarthy, Feb. 15, 1985. BS, Colo. State U., 1939; MS, U. Minn., 1943, PhD, 1947. Diplomate Am. Bd. Forensics Examiners. Prof. plant pathology Colo. State U., Ft. Collins, 1947-55; supr. biol. research Chevron Chem. Co., Richmond, Calif., 1955-70; v.p. rsch. Nat. Resource Mgmt., Eureka, Calif., 1970-72; pres. Forest Ag Corp., Lafayette, Calif., 1972-86; ret., 1999. Coord. bd. forest stewardship Calif. Dept. Forestry and Fire Control, 1990-94; cons. in field, 1986-97. Author: Field Manual of Forest and Shade Tree Diseases, 1947, Not Long Apart, 1965, Mauget Field Manual: Insects and Diseases of Shade Trees, 1995. Commr. Park and Recreation Com., Ft. Collins, 1949-54, Concord, Calif., 1959-65; city forester, Ft. Collins, 1950-55. Comdr. USNR, 1944-80. Fellow AAAS (life); mem. Am. Phytopathol. Soc., Soc. Am. Foresters, Foresters Assn. (Calif. lic.), Pesticide Applicators Profl. Assn., Internat. Soc. Arboriculture, Nat. Forensic Soc., Bd. Forensics Examiners, Assn. Cons. Foresters, Am. Soc. Cons. Arborists, Soc. Tech. Comms. (sr. mem.), VFW, Lions. Democrat. Avocations: swimming, writing, music. Home: 2435 Heatherleaf Ln Martinez CA 94553-4337 *It is better to fail humbly while trying to succeed than to never even try.*

THOMAS, WAYNE LEE, lawyer; b. Sept. 22, 1945; s. W. M. and June F. Thomas; m. Patricia H. Thomas, Mar. 16, 1968; children: Brigitte Elisabeth Williams, Kate Adelaide Culpepper. BA, U. Fla., 1967, JD cum laude, 1971. Bar: Fla. 1971, U.S. Supreme Ct. 1975, U.S. Ct. Appeals (5th cir.) 1975, U.S. Ct. Appeals (11th cir.) 1981, U.S. Ct. Claims 1976, U.S. Dist. Ct. (mid. dist.) Fla. 1973, U.S. Dist. Ct. (so. dist. trial bar) Fla. 1975; cert. mediator and arbitrator. Law clk. U.S. Dist. Ct. (mid. dist.) Fla., 1971—73; assoc. Trenam, Simmons, Kemker, Scharf, Barkin, Frye & O'Neill, PA, Tampa, 1973—77, ptnr., 1978—81; founder, pres. McKay & Thomas, PA, Tampa, 1981—89; ptnr. Carlton, Fields, Ward, Emmanuel, Smith & Cutler, PA, 1989—95; pvt. practice Tampa, 1995—. Bd. mem. State of Fla. 13th Jud. Cir. Indigent Svcs. Com., 2006—07. Mem. ABA, Fla. Bar (chmn. sect. gen. practice 1981-83, ethics com., vice chmn. unauthorized practice law com. 1994-98, 2000-04, chmn. 2004-06, vice chmn. fed. practice com. 1995-96, chmn. 1996-97, bd. bar examiners 1986-91, chmn. 1990-91, chmn. unauthorized practice law com. 13A 1998-2001), Nat. Conf. Bar Examiners (multistate profl. responsibility exam. policy com. 1994-2004), Hillsborough County Bar Assn. (chmn. grievance com. 1985-86), J.C. Cheatwood Am. Inn of Ct. (pres. 2007-), Order of Coif, Fla. Blue Key, Phi Kappa Phi, Omicron Delta Kappa. Democrat. Office: 707 N Franklin St Fl 10 Tampa FL 33602-4430

THOMAS, WILLIAM GRIFFITH, lawyer; b. Washington, Nov. 1, 1939; s. Henry Phineas and Margaret Wilson (Carr) T.; m. Suzanne Campbell Foster, June 7, 1960. Student, Williams Coll., 1957-59, Richmond Coll., 1960; JD, U. Richmond, 1963. Bar: Va. 1963. With Hazel & Thomas (combined with Reed Smith in 1999), 1973—99; ptnr. Reed Smith LLP, Falls Church, Va., 1999—, mem. exec. com. Dir. Va. Electric and Power Co.; mem. 4th circuit judicial conf. Sec. Va. Dem. Com., 1968-70, chmn., 1970-72. Named Administrative Law Super Lawyer, Va. Super Lawyers Mag., 2006. Mem. ABA, Va. State Bar Assn., Am. Law Inst., Am. Coll. Real Estate Lawyers. Office: Reed Smith LLP 3110 Fairview Park Dr Ste 1400 Falls Church VA 22042-4503 Home Phone: 804-994-0040; Office Phone: 703-641-4238. Business E-Mail: wthomas@reedsmith.com.

THOMAS, WILLIAM SCOTT, lawyer; b. Joliet, Ill., Aug. 16, 1949; AB, Stanford U., Calif., 1971; JD, U. Calif., Hastings, 1974; LLM in Taxation, Golden Gate U., 1981. Bar: Calif. 1975, US Dist. Ct. (no. dist. Calif.) 1975, US Tax Ct. 1982. Tax editor Internat. Bur. Fiscal Documentation, Amsterdam, Netherlands, 1974-75; tax atty. Chevron Corp., San Francisco, 1975-77; assoc. to ptnr. Brobeck, Phleger & Harrison, San Francisco, 1978—2003; ptnr. Morgan Lewis & Bockius, San Francisco, 2003—. Named one of Top 100 Attys., Worth mag., 2005—06. Mem. ABA (taxation sect.), Calif. Bar Assn. (exec. com. taxation sect. 1984-89, chmn. 1987-88). Office: Morgan Lewis & Bockius 1 Market Plz Ste 2900 San Francisco CA 94105 Office Phone: 415-442-1211. Office Fax: 415-442-1001. E-mail: wthomas@morganlewis.com.

THOMAS, ZACH MICHAEL, professional football player; b. Pampa, Tex., Sept. 1, 1973; BS in Exercise Science, Tex. Tech, 1996. Linebacker Miami Dolphins, 1996—. Opened health and fitness club Zach's Club 54, Amarillo, Tex. Mem. Crunch on Paralysis team. Named First Team All-American, 1995; named to Pro-Bowl, 1999—2003, 2005, NFL All Pro Team, 2006. Avocations: weightlifting, basketball. Office: Miami Dolphins Tng Facility 7500 SW 30th St Davie FL 33314

THOMASCH, ROGER PAUL, lawyer; b. NYC, Nov. 7, 1942; s. Gordon J. and Margaret (Molloy) T.; children: Laura Leigh, Paul Butler. BA, Coll. William and Mary, 1964; LLB, Duke U., 1967. Bar: Conn. 1967, Colo. 1974. Assoc. atty. Cummings & Lockwood, Stamford, Conn., 1967-70; trial atty. U.S. Dept. Justice, Washington, 1970-73; ptnr. Roath & Brega, Denver, 1975-87; mng. ptnr. Denver office of Ballard, Spahr, Andrews & Ingersoll LLP, 1987—, chmn. litigation practice, 2005—. Vis. assoc. prof. of law Drake U. Sch. Law, Des Moines, 1973-74; frequent lectr. in field, U.S. and Can.; adj. faculty mem. U. Denver Coll. Law, 1976-80. Recipient Leland Forrest Outstanding Prof. award, Drake U. Sch. Law, 1973. Fellow Am. Coll. of Trial Lawyers, Am. Bar Found., Colo. Bar Found.; mem. ABA, Colo. Bar Assn., Denver Country Club, Univ. Club. Office: Ballard Spahr Andrews & Ingersoll LLP 1225 17th St Ste 2300 Denver CO 80202-5535 Home Phone: 303-744-8434; Office Phone: 303-299-7301. E-mail: Thomasch@BallardSpahr.com.

THOMAS-HARRIS, YVONNE ANITA, writer, poet; b. Millington, Tenn., Aug. 27, 1964; d. William Albert and Romelia Louise (Rich) Thomas; m. Gregory Harris; children: Antonio Dewayne James, Trishanna Renea, Chantell S. Harris, Ashley K. Harris, Gregory Juwan Harris. Cert., Morris & McDaniel Sch., Memphis, 1987, ITT Career Tng. Ctr., 1991; diploma, Jefferson Bus. Coll., Memphis, 1988; attended, Southwest Tenn. C.C., 2005; atneded, World Harvest Bible Coll., 2006. Security guard Ringling Bros. and Barnum Bailey, Washington, 1986; mental health tech. S.E. Mental Health Ctr., Memphis, 1987; nursing asst. St. Peters Villa, Memphis, 1987; profl. model Memphis, 1990; housekeeper Econo Inn, Millington, 1990; med. asst. Primary Med. Care, Inc., Memphis, 1991; receptionist, supr. H & R Block, Memphis, 1991—; adminstrv. asst. Perea Presch., Memphis, 2006; prin., sec. UT Health Sci. Ctr., Coll. of Dentistry, 2006. Med. office asst./receptionist psychiatry dept. U. Tenn. Med. Group, 1996. Contbr. poems to World Treasury of Golden Poems, 1990, Poetic Voices of America, 1992, Shadows and Light, 1996; songwriter Cream High Records, Blue Time Blues, 1986, A Surrender to the Moon, 2005. Sec. Project Amos, Memphis, 1989; vol. Dept. Human Svcs., Memphis, 1988. Mem.: ADEA. Democrat. Avocations: quilting, photography, drawing, crafts. Home: 3815 Kerr Rd Millington TN 38083 Home Phone: 901-873-0614; Office Phone: 901-527-8344. Personal E-mail: yvonneharris64@yahoo.com. Business E-Mail: yvonhrr5@aol.com.

THOMASHOW, LINDA SUZANNE, microbiologist; b. Norwood, Mass. d. John Michael and E. Jean (Cole) Ravinski. BS, U. Mass., 1968; PhD, UCLA, 1979. Asst. prof. Wash. State U., Pullman, 1983-84; rsch. geneticist USDA Agrl. Rsch. Svc., Pullman, 1985—. Adj. prof. dept. plant pathology Wash. State U. Editorial bd. Applied & Environ. Microbiology, Washington, 1990-98; contbr. articles to profl. jours. Mem. Am. Soc. Microbiology, Am. Phytopathol. Soc. (Ruth Allen award 1997), Internat. Soc. for Molecular Plant-Microbe Interactions. Achievements include research in production of antibiotics by beneficial bacteria that live in association with the roots of plants, structure, function and regulation of genes involved in antibiotic synthesis by bacteria, the ecological significance of antibiotic production in natural environments. Office: Wash State Univ PO Box 646430 Dept Plant Pathology Pullman WA 99164-6430

THOMASHOW, STEVEN ROY, military officer, intelligence officer; b. Bronx, NY, Jan. 27, 1957; s. Isaac Tom and Dorothy (Cuillino Bodsky) T. Accredited, U.S. Mil. Acad. Commd. United States of the World, adm., with spl. ops., 1988—; served with Israeli War USN, served with Gulf War. Recipient Pres. Nat. Medal of Patriotism; named to Am. Police Hall of Fame, 1996. Fellow Nat. Law Enforcement Acad. (hon.); mem. Am. Fedn. Police. Avocations: Karate (black belt), torah studies, boxing, reading. Home and Office: United States of the World Recon One 4644 Myrtle Ln West Palm Beach FL 33417-5316 Fax: 561-640-4359.

THOMAS-LÖWE, CHRISTINE L., small business owner; d. Alfred Joseph Thomas and Loyce Mae Argo (Thomas); m. Scott H. Lowe, Feb. 8, 1997. BA Edn., Western Ky. U., Bowling Green, 1972; MPS in Pub. Adminstrn., Western Ky. U., 1982; MS in Data Processing & Mgmt. & Info. Sys., Amber U., Garland, Tex., 1985. Bus. analyst and ISO internal auditor ADP, Coppell, Tex., 2000—03; prin., owner CLL Consulting & Documentation Svcs., Owensboro, Ky., 2003—. Software QA tester and documentation specialist IBM, Dallas, 1997—2000. Composer: (opera) Soldato Del Destino (Soldier of Destiny), 2003—06; author: (screenplay) Soldato Del Destino; performer: (opera excerpts) Lyon Cmty. Orch., 2004, Owensboro Youth Symphony, 2007, Lyon Cmty. Orch. Mem.: Am. Mensa (assoc.). Roman Catholic. Home: 2020 York Dr Owensboro KY 42301-3436 Office: CLL Consulting & Documentation Services 2020 York Dr Owensboro KY 42301-3436 Home Phone: 270-926-0605; Office Phone: 270-926-5336. Personal E-mail: lowes@bellsouth.net.

THOMASON, SANDRA LEE, elementary school educator; d. Eugene LeRoy Ducat and Jean Frances Miller-Ducat; 1 child, Eric Christopher. EdB, U. Toledo, 1968, MEd, 1974. Permanent Tchg. Cert. Ohio State Dept. Edn., 1993, Reading Cert. K-12 Ohio State Dept. of Edn., 1993. Primary edn. tchr. Wash. Local Schs., Toledo, 1968—75, Sylvania (Ohio) schs., 1985—2000; vis. prof. U. Toledo, 1999—2003; reading instr. Ohio State Dept. of Edn., Perrysburg, Ohio, 1999—2003, Sylvania, 1999—2003, Toledo, 1999—2003; guest tchr. Lourdes Coll., Sylvania, Ohio, 2000; literacy specialist Sylvania Schs., 2000—03; reading cons., tchr., trainer NW Ohio Regional Profl. Devel. Ctr., Toledo, 2000—03; literacy support tchr., mid. sch. Olentangy Local Schs., Powell, Ohio, 2003—. Program adminstr. Summer Fun Summer Play Sch., Toledo, 1979; literacy specialist Ohio State Dept. of Edn., 1999—2003; counseling support group leader U. Toledo Counseling Ctr., 1982—84; youth enrichment seminar tchr. Sylvania Schs., Sylvania, 1996—97, 1996—97; spkr. Lourdes Coll., 1997—98; presenter, integrated curriculum with a lit. base, k-4 Patrick-Henry Local Schs., Deshler, Ohio, 1995—96; cons. in field. Dir.: (exhbn.) Developmentally Appropriate and Integrated Activities Across the Curriculum; contbr. articles to popular mags. Sect. leader Toledo 20/20 City Initiative. Mem.: ASCD, Ohio Coun. of the Tchrs. Lang. Arts, Internat. Reading Assn., Pi Lambda Theta (hon.), Phi Delta Kappa (hon.). Achievements include development of curriculum for primary grade children, balanced literacy curriculum for elementary and middle school students; design of edn. programs for summer sch. students in presch. and primary grades. Office: Olentangy Local Schs 814 Shanahan Rd Ste 300 Lewis Center OH 43035 Home Phone: 614-891-3096; Office Phone: 740-657-4050. Business E-Mail: sandra_thomason@olentangy.k12.oh.us.

THOMASOS, DENYSE, artist; b. Trinidad, 1964; BA in Painting and Art History, U. Toronto, 1987; student, Skowhegan Sch., 1988; MFA in Painting and Sculpture, Yale U., 1989. Asst. prof. painting Tyler Sch. Art Temple U., Phila., 1990—95; asst. prof. painting visual and performing arts Rutgers U., Newark, 1995—. One-woman shows include Fleisher Art Meml. Gallery, Phila., 1993, Olga Korper Gallery, Toronto, Ont., Can., 1994, 1998, Queens (N.Y.) Mus. Art, Bulova Corp. Ctr., 1997, Lennon, Weinberg Gallery, N.Y.C., 1997, 1999, exhibited in group shows at Alpha Gallery, Boston, 1989, A Space, Toronto, 1992, Vox Populi, Phila., 1993, Mercer Union, Toronto, 1994, Ottawa (Ont.) Art Gallery, 1994, Lennon, Weinberg Gallery, N.Y.C., 1996, 1998, Newhouse Ctr. Contemporary Art, Snug Harbor Cultural Ctr., S.I., 1997, Art Gallery North York, N.Y., 1997, Fine Arts Ctr. Galleries, U. R.I., Kingston, 1999, Works on Paper, Global Art Source, Zurich, Switzerland, 2002—03, others; curator (exhibitions) Art in Gen., Gallery 6, N.Y., 1998; one-woman shows include St. Vincent Univ. Gallery, Halifax, NS, 2004. Recipient Joan Mitchell Found. award, 1998; grantee Exploration grantee, Can. Coun., 1990, "B" Nat. grantee, 1994, Visual Arts fellow in painting, Pa. Coun. on Arts, Phila., 1994, Mid-Atlantic Regional grantee, NEA, 1994; Pew fellow in Arts, Phila., 1995, Guggenheim Found. fellow, 1997. Office: Lennon Weinberg Inc 514 W 25th St New York NY 10001-5585 Fax: 212-941-0098.

THOMAS-RAZZA, CONSTANCE, retired elementary school educator; b. Balt., Dec. 28, 1935; d. Arthur and Bertha Crippen Thomas; m. Joseph C. Razza, Jr., Oct. 29, 1969; children: Joseph C. Razza III, Constance Miriam Razza, Renata Joy Razza; m. Garnett George Adams, 1962 (div. 1968). BA, Coppin State Tchrs. Coll., Balt., 1957, U. Mich., Ann Arbor, 1962. Cert. tchr. Balt., Md., 1957, Washington, DC, 1962. Tchr. Balt. City Pub. Schs., 1957—62, DC Pub. Schs., 1962—96; tchr. ESL Peace Corps, Cape Verde, West Africa, 2000—02. Lectr. Am. U., Washington, 1973. Author: (book) My Mother's Love Life, 1998; prodr.: (theatre) Spedjo, 2001. Sec. LeDroit Park Civic Assn., Washington, 1990, 2005; vol. Smithsonian Instn., Washington, 1996—98; protestor No War on Cuba, 2002—. Named Outstanding Newsletter Publisher, DC Fedn. Civic Assns., 1986, Outstanding Educator, Potomac LINKS, 2005. Democrat. Buddhist. Avocations: beading, writing, gardening. Home: 501 T St NW Washington DC 20001 Personal E-mail: ctrazza05@verizon.net.

THOMAS-ROBINSON, GREGORY LEON, sales executive; b. Portland, Oreg., Nov. 13, 1964; s. Raydell and Catherine Ann Robinson; m. Martha Ann Moncrief, Aug. 25, 1996; children: Tieavsha Robinson, Lakeisha Harris, Gregory Robinson, Donta Harris, Mia Robinson. Student, Western Oreg. State U., 1983—86; AS, Chemeketa C.C., Salem, Oreg., 1987; AA, United Theol. Sem., 2001. Mgr. Nordstrom, Gaithersburg, Md., 1988—92; sales mgr. Polo Meier & Frank, Portland, 1992—94; customer rep. Wash. Mutual FSB, Vancouver, 1994—96; adminstrv. coord. Legacy Emanuel Hosp., Portland, 1996—97; health svc. rep. Oakdale (La.) Cmty. Hosp., 1997—98; owner Around Town Sounds, Oakdale, 1997—. Coord. G&T Bus. and Consultant, Oakdale, 1997—. Male mentor Urban League, Portland, 1993—; pres. Young Minister's Alliance, Portland, 2001—; pastor Dominion and Power House of Prayer, Portland, Mount Olive Bapt. Ch., 1998—2001; elder New Generation Revival, 2002—. Republican. Avocations: weightlifting, reading, Biblical research and writing. E-mail: greg46162003@yahoo.com.

THOMASSEN, PAULINE FRANCES, medical and surgical nurse; b. Cleve., Jan. 19, 1939; d. Henry Clifford and Mabel Pauline (Hill) Nichols; m. Ruben Thomassen, Nov. 10, 1979; children: Rhonda, Terry, Diana, Philipp, Jody, Barbara. AA in Nursing, So. Colo. State Coll., 1974, BA in Psychology with distinction, 1975; BSN magna cum laude, Seattle Pacific U., 1986. RN Wash. Staff nurse III orthopedic unit, clin. spine educator Swedish Hosp. Med. Ctr., Seattle, 1975—, preceptor orientation of RNs and student RNs, 1975—, clin. spine educator, 1998—2002; ret., 2002. Mem. planning task force and faculty Nat. Nurses Conf., The Nurse and Spinal Surgery, Cleve.; lectr. Coll. of Nursing, Raleigh Fitkin Meml. Hosp., Manzini, Swaziland, South Africa, 1999, St. Petersburg, Russia, 2003; mem. med. mission to assist in clinic for street children, Satipo, Peru, 00, Honolulu Police Dept., 2001; mem. med. mission, Philippines, 04, 06, Mexico, 06, Miss.-Katrina Relief, 2006; med. mission ofcl. Camp Nurse Camp Li-WA, Fairbanks, Alaska, 2002, Fairbanks, 06, Mexico, 06; guest spkr. degenerative lumbar spinal techniques, cadaver workshop U. Wash., Seattle, 2001; guest spkr. Am. Acad. Orthop. Surgeons, Dallas, 2002, Dallas, 02. Author: Spinal Disease and Surgical Interventions, 1995; author: (contbg. author) Making Sense of Minimally Invasive Spine Surgery, 1998. Mem.: Nat. Assn. Orthop. Nurses. Office: Swedish Health Ctr 747 Broadway Seattle WA 98122-4379

THOMASSON, DAN KING, newspaper executive, columnist; b. Shelbyville, Ind., Dec. 22, 1933; s. Hubert Lee and Mary Margaret (King) T.; m. Laqueta Forducey, Sept. 7, 1958; children: Scot, Lisa, Sean, Patrick. BS, Ind. U., 1956; postgrad., Colo. U., 1959. Reporter, editor Indpls. Star, 1956; reporter Lawton (Okla.) Constitution, 1957-58, The Rocky Mountain

News, Denver, 1959-64; corr. Scripps Howard Newspapers, Washington, 1964-74, asst. mng. editor, 1974-76; mng. editor Scripps Howard News Svc., Washington, 1976-80, editor, 1980—; v.p. news Scripps Howard Newspapers, Cin., 1986—; v.p. E.W. Scripps Co., 1996—. Weill vis. prof. Ind. U., 1999; vis. prof. Hampton U., 2000. Pres. Raymond Clapper Found., Washington, 1980-2004; bd. dirs. Scripps Howard Found., Cin., 1987-2003, v.p., 1994; trustee Franklin Coll., 1990—; mem. nat. adv. com. E.W. Scripps Sch. Journalism, 1990, Ohio U., 1990, Nat. Pub. Affairs Coun., Ind. U., 1990—; bd. visitors Inst. Polit. Journalism Georgetown U., 1990—. With U.S. Army, 1956-58. Named Man of Yr., Shelbyville, Ind. C. of C., 1970, Washington Journalism Hall of Fame, 1993; elected Ind. Acad., 1993; named to Ind. Journalism Hall of Fame, 1997; Presdl. fellow Trinity Coll., Hartford, 2000; media fellow Hoover Instn., 2001, 2002, 2003 Mem. Am. Soc. Newspaper Editors, White House Corrs. Assn., Gridiron Club of Washington, Overseas Press Club, Nat. Press Club, Univ. Club of Washington, Washington Golf and Country Club (Arlington, Va.), Bohemian Club (San Francisco), Sigma Delta Chi. Home: 3729 Morningside Dr Fairfax VA 22031-3317 Office: Scripps Howard 1090 Vermont Ave NW Ste 1000 Washington DC 20005-4906 Business E-Mail: thomassondan@aol.com.

THOME, DENNIS WESLEY, lawyer; b. Yakima, Wash., Feb. 1, 1939; s. Walter John and Vareta Lucille (Voris) T.; m. Penelope Lee Freeman, Aug. 27, 1961; children: Christopher, Geoffrey. BSBA, U. Denver, 1961, JD, 1967. Bar: Colo. 1967, U.S. Dist. Ct. Colo. 1967, Calif. 1971, U.S. Dist. Ct. (cen. dist.) Calif. 1971, U.S. Supreme Ct. 1971, U.S. Ct. Appeals (9th cir.) 1972. Assoc. Pehr & Newman, Westminster, Colo., 1967-69, Juggert, VaVerka & Wayman, Costa Mesa, Calif., 1975-77; house counsel Wycliffe Bible Translators, Inc., Huntington Beach, Calif., 1969-73; pvt. practice Newport Beach, Calif., 1973-75, Denver, 1977—. Bd. dirs. First Fruit, Inc., Newport Beach, MOPS Internat., Inc., Denver; mem. Centennial Estate Planning Coun., 1977—. Treas. Gibson for Mayor Com., Denver, 1967; bd. dirs. Christian Eye Ministry, Inc., San Diego, 1983-91, World Eye Care, Inc., 1990-91, Christian Legal Soc. Metro Denver, Inc., 1994-98; pres., bd. dirs. LOGOS Ministries USA, 2004-07; chmn. Arvada (Colo.) Covenant Ch., 1993-94; bd. dirs., sec. Wycliffe Bible Translators, Inc., Huntington Beach, Calif., 1977-83 Mem. Colo. Bar Assn. (Bill of Rights com. 1992-2005), State Bar Calif., Omicron Delta Kappa Office: 1510 Glen Ayr Dr #9 Lakewood CO 80215-2876

THOMLINSON, RALPH, demographer, educator; b. St. Louis, Feb. 12, 1925; s. Ralph and Ora Lee (Barr) T.; m. Margaret Mary Willits, Dec. 21, 1946; children: Elizabeth Barr, William Lockwood. BA, Oberlin Coll., 1948; postgrad., U. Pitts., 1943-44, Harvard U., 1948; MA, Yale U., 1949; PhD, Columbia U., 1960. Asst. town planner, Montclair, N.J., 1949-50; asst. city planner Paterson, N.J., 1950; research asst. Bur. Applied Social Research, NYC, 1952; med. statistics asst. actuarial dept. Met. Life Ins. Co., NYC, 1952-53; instr. statistics and population U. Wis., 1953-56; instr. sociology and anthropology Denison U., Granville, Ohio, 1956-59; asst. prof. sociology Calif. State U., LA, 1959-62, assoc. prof., 1962-65, prof., 1965-88, prof. emeritus, 1988—, chmn. dept. sociology, 1967-69; vis. prof. sociology U. Alta., Can., 1966; vis. prof. biostatistics U. N.C., Chapel Hill, 1972-73; demographic adviser Inst. Population Studies, Chulalongkorn U., Bangkok, Thailand, 1969-71; cons. Nat. Family Planning Program, Thailand, Census of Thailand, 1970-71, Population/Food Fund, 1977-79, also various research centers abroad, 1969-73. Cons. to fourteen book pubs., 1965—; field assoc. Population Coun., N.Y.C., 1969-71; rsch. adviser Ctr. for Rsch. and Demographic Studies, Rabat, Morocco, 1972-73; acad. visitor Population Investigation Com., London Sch. Econs., 1973; vis. scholar Nat. Inst. Demographic Studies, Paris, 1973-74 Author: A Mathematical Model for Migration, 1960, Population Dynamics. 2d edit. 1976 Sociological Concepts and Research, 1965, Demographic Problems, 2d edit, 1975, Urban Structure, 1969, Thailand's Population, 1971, (with others) The Methodology of the Longitudinal Study of Social, Economic and Demographic Change, 1971; editor: (with Visid Prachuabmoh) The Potharam Study, 1971; adv. editor: Sociol. Abstracts, 1963-67, Sociology Quar, 1978-84; cons. editor: As-Soukan, 1972-73; assoc. editor: Pacific Sociol. Rev, 1976-83; Sociol. Perspective, 1983-85; chmn. editorial bd. Calif. Sociologist, 1981-84; cons.: Dictionary of Modern Sociology, 1969; contbr. to: Dictionary of Demography, 5 vols., 1985-86; books, profl. jours. Served with AUS, 1943-45, ETO. Mem. Population Assn. Am., Internat. Union for Sci. Study Population, Am. Sociol. Assn., Internat. Assn. Survey Statisticians, Assn. Asian Studies. Home: 201 Chadbourne Ave Apt 218 Millbrae CA 94030

THOMLINSON, VIVIAN AYTES, literature and language professor; married. BS in English and Polit. Sci., Tex. A&M U., Commerce, 1976; MA in English, Tex. Women's U., Denton, 1982, PhD in English, 1986. Tchr. North Tex. Coll., Gainseville, Prince George's CC, Largo, Md., US Army's Command and Gen. Staff Coll., Ft. Leavenworth, Kans.; faculty mem. Cameron U., Lawton, Okla., 1986—94, faculty mem. to assoc. prof. English, 1998—. Dir. composition Dept. English, Fgn. Langs. and Journalism Cameron U., 1987—94, 1999—2001, campus coord. writing across the curriculum. Contbr. articles to profl. jours. Recipient US Prof. of Yr. award, Carnegie Found. for Advancement of Tchg. and Coun. for Advancement and Support of Edn., 2006. Mem.: Okla. Coun. Tchrs. of English (coll. chair Exec. bd.). Office: Cameron U Dept English & Fgn Langs 637 S Shepler 2800 W Gore Blvd Lawton OK 73505-6377 Office Phone: 580-581-2545. Office Fax: 580-581-2572. E-mail: viviant@cameron.edu. *

THOMOPOULOS, MICHAEL, music educator; b. Lowell, Mass., Apr. 24, 1953; s. George and Doris Thomopoulos. MusB, The New Eng. Conservatory of Music, Boston, 1975; MusM, The Juilliard Sch., NYC, 1977. Founder, music dir. Palisades Chamber Players, Ft. Lee, NJ, 1979—. Founder, dir., tchr. Palisades Sch. Music. Recipient Morris Loeb Meml. prize, Internat. Concert Artist Guild, 1977. Avocations: private piloting, scuba diving, politics, travel. Office: The Palisades Sch of Music 196 Washington Ave Fort Lee NJ 07024 Home Phone: 212-933-0275; Office Phone: 201-944-1311. Office Fax: 201-944-1311. Personal E-mail: mthomopoulos@yahoo.com.

THOMOPULOS, GREGS G., consulting engineering company executive; b. Benin City, Nigeria, May 16, 1942; s. Aristoteles and Christiana E. (Ogiamien) Thomopulos; m. Patricia Walker, Sept. 4, 1966 (div. 1974); 1 child, Lisa; m. Mettie L. Williams, May 28, 1976; children: Nicole, Euphemia. BSCE with highest distinction, U. Kans., 1965; MS in Structural Engrng., U. Calif., Berkeley, 1966; PhD (hon.), Teikyo Marycrest U., 1996. Sr. v.p. internat. div. Stanley Cons., Inc., Muscatine, Iowa, 1978-84, sr. v.p. project divsn., 1984-87; pres., CEO Stanley Consultants, Inc., Muscatine, Iowa, 1987—; exec. v.p. SC Co., Inc., Muscatine, 1992-98; pres., COO, 1998-99; pres., CEO, 2000—; also bd. dirs. SC Co., Inc., Muscatine; chmn., CEO Stanley Environ., Inc., Chgo., 1991—, also bd. dirs.; chmn., CEO SC Power Devel., Inc., 1992—. Chmn., CEO Stanley Design-Build, Inc., 1995—; bd. dirs. Stanley Cons., Inc., Muscatine, Wellmark, Inc., Blue Cross Blue Shield Iowa and S.D., 1999—; mem. adv. bd. U. Kans. Sch. Engrng., 2002—; mem. industry adv. panel US Dept. State, 2006—07. Mem. adv. bd. Coll. Engrng. U. Iowa, 1992-2000, Hydraulics Inst., 2000-06. Fellow ASCE, Am. Coun. Engrng. Cos. (exec. com.); mem. NSPE, Internat. Fedn. Cons. Engrs. (exec. com.), 33 Club (pres. 1987), Rotary. Presbyterian. Avocations: tennis, computers, music. Home: 75 Shagbark Ct Iowa City IA 52246-2786 Office: Stanley Cons Inc 225 Iowa Ave Muscatine IA 52761-3765 Personal E-mail: thomopulos@home.com. Business E-Mail: thomopulosg@stanleygroup.com.

THOMPSON, ALAN ERIC, economics professor; b. Sept. 16, 1924; s. Eric Joseph and Florence Thompson; m. Mary Heather Long, 1960; 4 children. MA, U. Edinburgh, 1949, MA with 1st class honors, 1951, PhD, 1953. Asst. in polit. econ. U. Edinburgh, 1952-53, lectr. econs., 1953-59, 64-71; prof. econs. of govt. Heriot-Watt U., Edinburgh, 1972—. Adviser to Scottish TV, 1966-76; Scottish gov. BBC, 1976-79; vis. prof. Grad. Sch. Bus., Stanford U. (Calif.), 1966, 68; chmn. adv. bd. econs. edn. Esmee Fairbairn Rsch. Project, 1970-76. Author: (with others) Development of Economic Doctrine, 1980; contbr. articles to profl. jours. M.P. Labour Party, Dunfermline, 1959-64; mem. Scottish Com. Pub. Schs. Commn., 1969-70; mem. Joint Mil. Edn. Com. Edinburgh and Heriot-Watt Univs., 1975—, local govt. boundary commn. for Scotland, 1975-82; chmn. No. Offshore Resources Study, 1974-84; chmn. bd. govs. Newbattle Abbey Coll., 1980-82; bd. govs. Leigh Nautical Coll., 1981-87; trustee Bell's Nautical Trust, 1981-87; parliamentary adviser Pharm. Gen. Coun., 1985-2000; bd. dirs. Scottish AIDS Rsch. Found., 1992; adv. Robert Burns Meml. Trust, 1995—99; advisor Robert Burns Meml. Trust, 1995-2000. With Brit. Army, WWII. Carnegie Rsch. scholar, 1951-52. Fellow Royal Soc. Arts, Soc. Antiquaries (Scotland); mem. Assn. Nazi War Camp Survivors (v.p. 1960—), Edinburgh Amenity and Transport Assn. (pres. 1970-75), New Club, Loch Earn Sailing Club.

THOMPSON, ANDREA, television personality, retired newscaster, actress; b. Dayton, Ohio, 1959; m. David Guc, 1987 (div. 1990); m. Jerry Doyle, 1995 (div. 1997); 1 child, Alec. Correspondent KRQE-TV, Albuquerque, 2000—01; news anchor, Headline News CNN, 2001—02. Films include Wall Street, 1987, Doin' Time on Planet Earth, 1988, Delirious, 1991, Lost Valley, 1998, A Gun, A Car, A Blonde, 1998, Rocket's Red Glare, 2000; TV series include Falcon Crest, 1989-90, Babylon 5, 1994-95, JAG, 1995-96, NYPD Blue, 1996-2000; host: Court TV, Saturday Night Line Up, 2002.

THOMPSON, ANNE KATHLEEN, entertainment journalist; b. NYC, Aug. 10, 1954; d. Charles Torrington Thompson and Eleanor Josephine (Callahan) Dekins; m. David Christopher Chute, Oct. 23, 1983; 1 child, Nora Thompson Chute. BA in Cinema Studies, NYU, 1976. Asst. mgr. Bleecker St. Cinema, NYC, 1975—76; publicist United Artists, NYC, 1976—79; account exec. P/M/K Pub. Rels., NYC, 1979—81; assoc. editor Film Comment Mag., NYC, 1981-82, west coast editor, 1982-96; publicity dir. Twentieth Century Fox Pictures, 1983-85; wrote column Risky Bus. LA Weekly, LA Times Syndicate, 1985-93; columnist Inside Film, 1988-90; U.S. editor Empire Mag., London, 1989-91; sr. writer Entertainment Weekly, 1993-96; west coast editor Premier Mag., 1996—2002; contbr. Premiere, Filmmaker, Wired, NY Times, Washington Post, NY mag., London Observer; dep. film editor The Hollywood Reporter, LA, 2005—. Mem. Nat. Writer's Union, Women in Film. Office: The Hollywood Reporter 5055 Wilshire Blvd Los Angeles CA 90036-4396

THOMPSON, ANNIE FIGUEROA, retired academic administrator; b. Río Piedras, PR, June 7, 1941; d. Antonio Figueroa-Colón and Ana Isabel Laugier; m. Donald P. Thompson, Jan. 23, 1972; 1 child, John Anthony. BA, Baylor U., 1962; MSLS, U. So. Calif., 1965; AMD, Fla. State U., 1978, PhD, 1980. Educator Mayan Sch., Guatemala City, Guatemala, 1962-63; cataloger libr. sys. U. P.R., Río Piedras, 1965-67, head music libr., 1967-81, assoc. prof. librarianship, 1981-85, dir. grad. sch. libr. info. sci. Rio Piedras, 1986-93, prof., 1986-96; ret., 1996. Author: An Annotated Bibliography About Music in Puerto Rico, 1975; co-author: Music and Dance in Puerto Rico from the Age of Columbus to Modern Times, An Annotated Bibliography, 1991; contbr. articles to profl. jours.; performed song recitals Inst. of P.R. Culture and U. P.R. Artist Series, 1974-78; soloist with P.R. Symphony Orch., San Juan, 1978; performed in opera, on radio and TV, San Juan, 1968-81. Sec. P.R. Symphony Orch League, San Juan, 1982-84; mem. pub. libr. adv. com. Adminstrn. for Devel. of Arts and Culture, P.R., 1982-84, Pub. Libr. Adv. Bd., 1989-94. Recipient Lauro a la Instrucción Bibliotecaria Sociedad de Bibliotecarios de P.R., 1985, Lauro a la Bibliografía Puertorriqueña, 1993. Mem. Sarasota Rotary (bd. dirs. 2000-02), Sociedad de Bibliotecarios de P.R. (pres. 1994-96), Music Libr. Assn. (bd. dirs. 1982-84, asst. conv. mgr. 2002-04, conv. mgr. 2004-06), Sarasota Rotary Found. (bd. dirs.), Sigma Delta Kappa, Mu Phi Epsilon, Beta Phi Mu. Episcopalian. Home: 435 S Gulfstream Ave Sarasota FL 34236-6736 Personal E-mail: annietmla@aol.com.

THOMPSON, ANTHONY WAYNE, metallurgist, educator, consultant; b. Burbank, Calif., Mar. 6, 1940; s. William Lyman and Mary Adelaide (Nisbet) T.; m. Mary Ruth Cummings, Aug. 24, 1963; children: Campbell Lyman, Michael Anthony. BS, Stanford U., 1962; MS, U. Wash., 1965; PhD, MIT, 1970. Research engr. Jet Propulsion Lab., Pasadena, Calif., 1962-63; mem. tech. staff Sandia Labs., Livermore, Calif., 1970-73, Rockwell Sci. Ctr., Thousand Oaks, Calif., 1973-77; assoc. prof. Carnegie Mellon U., Pitts., 1977-79, prof., 1980-94, dept. head, 1987-90; staff scientist Lawrence Berkeley Lab., Berkeley, Calif., 1994-99; rsch. engr. U. Calif., Berkeley, Calif., 1995—. Vis. scientist U. Cambridge, Eng., 1983, Risø, Denmark, 1987, U. Calif., 1991; cons. Sandia Labs., 1977—1998, GE, 1988-2000. Editor: Work Hardening, 1976, Metall. Transactions, 1983-88, Signature Press Book Pubs., 1993-; co-editor: Hydrogen in Metals, 1974, Hydrogen Conf. Proc., 1976, 81, 89, 94, 2002; mem. editl. bd. Internat. Metals Revs., 1980-88; contbr. articles to profl. jours. Overseas fellow Churchill Coll. Cambridge U., 1982 Fellow Am. Soc. Metals; mem. Clubs: Sierra, Nat. Model R.R. Assn. Democrat. Home: 2906 Forest Ave Berkeley CA 94705

THOMPSON, B. LOLANA, archivist; b. Harlingen, Tex., Dec. 8, 1953; d. John M. and Betty E. Lummus; m. Foye Lynn Thompson, May 15, 1976; children: Jay Alan, Amy Kay. BA in History, U. Tex., Austin, 1975; MA in History, Tex. Tech U., Lubbock, 1982. Cert. archivist Acad. Cert. Archivists, 2005, in archival adminstrn. U. Tex., 1999. Archival asst. SW Collection, Tex. Tech U., Lubbock, 1976—79; libr. asst. Tex. Tech U. Libr., 1983—84; acquisitions asst. Dallas Theol. Sem., 1992—2001, archivist, 2003—. Local program spkr. SW Area Theol. Libr. Assn., 2004. Mem.: Soc. SW Archivists, Soc. Am. Archivists. Office: Dallas Theol Seminary 3909 Swiss Ave Dallas TX 75204

THOMPSON, BARBARA ELLEN, occupational therapist, educator; b. Mineola, NY, July 25, 1952; d. William Creighton Thompson and Wilma Esther Lewis; m. George Elliot Ruta, Jan. 31, 1987. BS in Occupl. Therapy, U. Fla., Gainesville, 1975; MSW, SUNY, Albany, 1996; postgrad., Creighton U., Omaha, 2004—. Cert. in advanced grad. studies expressive arts European Grad. Sch., 2003. Supervising occupl. therapist Sunnyview Hosp., Schenectady, NY, 1976—81; hospice day care coord. St. Peter's Hospice, Albany, 1981—88; coord. ALS Regional Ctr. St. Peter's Hosp., Albany, 1988—98; assoc. prof. Sage Colls., Troy, NY, 1998—. Contbr. chapters to books, articles to profl. jours. Coord. meditation group Shambhala Internat., Troy, 2005—07; coord. thresholds program Mary McClellan Hosp., Cambridge, NY, 1989—90; adv. bd. Hospice of Wash. County, Cambridge, 1992—2000. Mem.: NASW, Am. Occupl. Therapy Assn. (Svc. award 1985). Democrat. Buddhist. Avocations: sea kayaking, painting, gardening. Office: The Sage Colleges 45 Ferry St Troy NY 12180 Home Phone: 518-274-1975; Office Phone: 518-244-3112. Business E-Mail: thompb@sage.edu.

THOMPSON, BARBARA STORCK, state official; b. McFarland, Wis., Oct. 15, 1924; d. John Casper and Marie Ann (Kassabaum) Storck; m. Glenn T. Thompson, July 1, 1944; children— David C., James T. BS, Wis. State U., 1956; MS, U. Wis., 1959, PhD, 1969; L.H.D. (hon.), Carroll Coll., 1974. Tchr. pub. schs., West Dane County, Mt. Horeb, Wis., 1944-56; instr. Green County Tchrs. Coll., Monroe, Wis., 1956-57; coordinator curriculum Monroe Pub. Schs., 1957-60; instr. U. Wis., Platteville, 1960; supr. schs. Waukesha County Schs., Wis., 1960-63, supt. schs., 1963-65; prin. Fairview Elem. Schs., Brookfield, Wis., 1962-64; adminstrv. cons. Wis. Dept. Pub. Instrn., Madison, 1964-72, state coordinator, 1971-72; instr. U. Wis., Madison and Green Bay, 1972; supt. pub. instrn. Madison, Wis., 1973—81. Mem. Wis. State Bd. Vocat. Edn., 1973-81, Wis. Edn. Comm. Bd., 1973-81, Univ. Wis. Sys. Bd. Regents, 1973-1981. Author: A Candid Discussion of Critical Issues, 1975; mem. editorial bd.: The Education Digest, 1975—; contbr. articles to profl. jours. Mem. White House Conf. Children, 1970, Gov.'s Com. State Conf. Children and Youth, 1969-70, Manpower Council, 1973-81; bd. dirs. Vocational, Tech. and Adult Edn., 1973-81, Ednl. Communications, 1973-81, Higher Edn. Aids, 1973-81, Agy. Instructional TV, 1975-81; mem. nat. panel on SAT score decline; bd. regents U. Wis., 1973-81, U.S. office f Edn. Visiting Sch. Team - England, GErmany, Sweden, Poland, Iran, Syria, India, and Japan. Recipient State Conservation award Madison Lions CLub, 1956; Waukesha Freeman award, 1961 Mem. ASCD, NEA, Nat. Coun. Adminstrv. Women in Edn. (named Woman of Year 1974), Nat. Coun. State Cons. in Elem. Edn. (pres. 1974-75), Wis. Assn. Sch. Dist. Adminstrs., Wis. ASCD, Southwestern Wis. ASCD, Southeastern Wis. ASCD (mem. exec. coun. 1972-73), Dept. Elem. Sch. Prins., Wis. Elem. Sch. Prins. Assn., Wis. Edn. Assn. (pres. local chpt. 1970-71); life mem. So. Wis. Edn. Assn., Wis. Ednl. Rsch. Assn., Dept. Elem.-Kindergarten-Nursery Edn., Assn. Childhood Edn. Internat., Assn. Childhood Edn., Coun. Chief State Sch. Officers, Edn. Commn. States, Nat. Coun. State Cons. in Elem. Edn. (pres. 1974-75), Am. Assn. Sch. Dist. Adminstrs. (chmn. policy com. 1963-81), Madison Ctrl. Internat. Lions Club, U. Wis. Alumni Orgn. (Sarasota, Fla. and Madison), U. Wis. League (Madison chpt.), Delta Kappa Gamma, Pi Lambda Theta. Office: Apt 123 325 S Yellowstone Dr Madison WI 53705-4301

THOMPSON, BENNIE G., congressman; b. Bolton, Miss., Jan. 28, 1948; m. London Johnson; 1 child, BendaLonne. BA in Polit. Sci., Tougaloo Coll., Miss., 1968; MS in Ednl. Adminstrn., Jackson State U., Miss., 1972; grad., U. So. Miss. Alderman, Bolton, Miss., 1969—73; mayor, 1973—79; supr. Hinds County, Miss., 1980-93; mem. US Congress from 2nd Miss. dist., 1993—, former mem. budget com., agr. com. and small bus. com., ranking mem. homeland security com. Presdl. appointee Nat. Coun. Health Planning and Devel. Bd. trustees Tougaloo Coll.; bd. dirs. So. Regional Coun., Housing Assistance Coun. Named one of 100 Most Influential Black Americans, Ebony mag., 2006. Mem.: Miss. Assn. Black Suprs. (founding mem.), Miss. Assn. Black Mayors (founding mem.). Democrat. Methodist. Original plaintiff in 1975 Ayers case. Office: US House Reps 2432 Rayburn House Office Bldg Washington DC 20515-0001 Office Phone: 202-225-5876. Office Fax: 202-225-5898. E-mail: thompsonms2nd@mail.house.gov. *

THOMPSON, BERNIDA LAMERLE, principal, consultant, educator; b. Tuskeegee, Ala., July 5, 1946; d. Berry James Sr. and Doris LaMerle (Askey) T.; m. Rolando Amerson, June 15, 1968 (div. Aug. 1988); children: Afriye Amerson, Mwando Amerson. BS in Elem. Edn., Cen. State U., 1968; MEd in Adminstrn. and Curriculum, Miami U., Oxford, Ohio, 1971; EdD in Early and Mid. Childhood Edn., Nova U., 1992. Classroom elem. sch. tchr. Dayton Pub. Schs.; asst. prin., intern St. James Cath. Sch., Dayton, Ohio; tchr. St. Augustine Cath. Sch., Washington; sci. resource tchr. D.C. Pub. Schs., Washington; founding tchr., prin. Roots Activity Learning Ctr., Washington, 1977—, Roots Pub. Charter Sch., 1999—. Multicultural advisor HBJ 1992 Reading Textbook. Author: Black Madonnas and Young Lions a Rite of Passage for African American Adolescents, 1992, rev. edit., 1998, Africentric Interdisciplinary Multi-Level Hands On Science, 1994, rev. edit., 2001; contbr. articles to profl. jours. Mem. Nat. Assn. Edn. Young Children, World Coun. Curriculum Instrn., Coun. Ind. Black Inst., Inst. Ind. Edn., Nat. Black Child Devel. Inst. Office: Roots Pub Charter Sch 15 Kennedy St NW Washington DC 20011-5201 Home Phone: 202-829-5941; Office Phone: 202-882-8073. Business E-Mail: bthompson@rootspcs.org.

THOMPSON, BERT ALLEN, retired librarian; b. Bloomington, Ind., Dec. 13, 1930; s. James Albert and Dorothy Fern (Myers) T.; m. Martha Ellen Palmer; children— John Carter II, Anne Palmer, Paul Julian. BS, Ball State Tchrs. Coll., 1953; AM, Ind. U., 1960; certificate in archival adm., U. Denver, 1967. Tchr., libr. Ind. pub. schs., 1953-55; ref. asst. Indpls. Pub. Libr., 1956-59; head ref. svc. Mankato (Minn.) State U., 1959-61; instr. Grad. Libr. Sch. No. Ill. U., Dekalb, 1961-63; dir. libs., asst. prof. ednl. media U. Nebr. at Kearney, 1963-69; dir. libr. svc. Benedictine U., Lisle, Ill., 1969-90, spl. collections libr., 1990-92. Mem. exec. bd. Ill. regional Libr. Coun., 1976-79. Recipient 1st Melvin R. George LIBRAS award for Outstanding Svc. to Libr. Cooperation, 1993. Mem. Ill. (de Lafayette Reid Research scholar 1976), Cath. Libr. Assn. (treas. Ill. chpt. 1973-75, nat. sec.-treas. coll./univ. sect. 1981-85, nat. bd. dirs. 1987-93), Nebr. Libr. Assn, chmn. coll. and univ. sect. 1963-64) Episcopalian. Home: 1808 Caxton Dr Wheaton IL 60187-6140

THOMPSON, BERTHA BOYA, retired education educator; b. New Castle, Pa., Jan. 31, 1917; d. Frank L. and Kathryn Belle (Park) Boya; m. John L. Thompson, Mar. 27, 1942; children: Kay Lynn Thompson Koolage, Scott McClain. BS in Elem. and Secondary Edn., Slippery Rock State Coll., Pa., 1940; MA in Geography and History, Miami U., Oxford, Ohio, 1954; EdD, Ind. U., Bloomington, 1961. Cert. elem. and secondary edn. tchr. Elem. tchr., reading specialist New Castle Sch. Sys., Pa., 1940—45; tchr., chmn. social studies Talawanda Sch. Sys., Oxford, Ohio, 1954—63; assoc. prof. psychology and geography, chair edn. dept. Western Coll. for Women, Oxford, 1963-74; assoc. prof. edn., reading clinic Miami U., Oxford, 1974-78, prof. emeritus, 1978—. Contbr. articles to profl. jours. Folk art com. Miami U. Art Mus., Oxford, 1974—76; adv. com. Smith libr., Oxford Pub. Libr., 1978—81. Mem. AAUP, Nat. Coun. Geographic Edn. (exec. bd. dirs. 1966-69), Nat. Soc. for Study Edn., Assn. Am. Geographers, Soc. Women Geographers, Nat. Coun. for the Social Studies, Pi Lambda Theta, Zeta Tau Alpha, Pi Gamma Mu, Gamma Theta Upsilon, Kappa Delta Pi. Avocations: antiques, reading, travel, tennis. Home: 6073 Contreras Rd Oxford OH 45056-9708

THOMPSON, BETTY JANE, retired small business owner; b. Ladysmith, Wis., Nov. 18, 1923; d. Edward Thomas and Mayme Selma (Kratwell) Potter; m. Frederick Sturdee Thompson, Apr. 19, 1945 (div. Apr. 1973); children: Denise Alana, Kent Marshall; m. J.R. Critchfield, Feb. 14, 1977 (div. 1989). Student, Jamestown Coll., ND, 1946-47, U. Calif., Long Beach, 1964-69; AA, Orange Coast Coll., 1976; postgrad., Monterey Peninsula Coll., 1979-80; SBA Cert., Hartnell Coll., 1982. Cert. fashion cons. Owner, mgr., buyer Goodview (Minn.) Food Mart, 1947-50; dist. mgr. Beauty Counselor of Minn., Winona County, 1951-61; Boy Scout liaison J.C. Penney Co., Newport Beach, Calif., 1969-72; dept. mgr. and buyer boyswear At Ease, Newport Beach, 1972-77; mgr. Top Notch Boys Wear, Carmel, Calif., 1977-83, buyer, 1984-88; owner, mgr. Top Notch Watch, Sun City, Ariz., 1989-95; editor H&R Block, 1995-98; employee Wells Fargo and Co., 1998—2004; ret., 2004. V.p., chmn. Don Loper Fashion Show, 1967, pres., 1968, bd. dirs., 1969. Co-editor Aux. Antics mag., 1965. Vol. fundraising leadership Family Svc. Assn., Orange County, Calif., 1962-68, other orgns.; chmn. publicity, study group, Sunday sch. tchr., Congl. Ch., Winona, Minn., 1956-58, fellowship pres., Santa Ana, Calif., 1963-65; pres. Goodview Civic Club, 1948; mem. Wells Fargo and Co. Bank Silver Bullets, Sr. Citizens of the Sun Cities, Phoenix, 1998-2000; counselor AARP Tax Aide, 1997—; moderator Congl. Christian Fellowship, 1999-2001; sec. Tont Ct. Condominium, 1998-2004. Recipient Athena award Panhellenic Assn. Orange City, Calif., 1968, El Camino Real Dist. Svc. award Orange Empire coun. Boy Scouts Am., Baden-Powell award, Outstanding Leadership award, El Camino Real Dist., Calif., 1972.

Ringling North award, 1949; named Outstanding Svc. Vol. Family Svc. Assn., 1969. Mem. Carmel Bus. Assn. Avocations: genealogy, photography, ballroom dance, bicycling, skiing. Home and Office: 10048 W Hawthorn Dr Sun City AZ 85351-2829 E-mail: tbjtonto@aol.com.

THOMPSON, BIRGIT DOLORES, civic worker, writer; b. Jamestown, NY, Apr. 7, 1930; d. Oscar Einar and Karin Johanna (Videll) Wolff; m. William Andrew Thompson, Jan. 26, 1952 (div. June 1978); children: William A., Christina A., Michael J., Timothy A., Kathleen S., Jeffrey B. AB summa cum laude, SUNY, Fredonia, 1974. Exec. dir. Fenton Hist. Ctr., Jamestown, 1975-82; fin. dir. Amicae, Inc., Fredonia, 1983-90; office mgr. JEM Counseling Ctr., Jamestown, 1990-93; resource/info. person Audubon Nature Ctr., Jamestown, 1993—. Author: Illustrated History of Jamestown and Chautauqua County, 1983, Jamestown Audubon Society 50th Year History; musician Jamestown String Quartet, violist local orchestras, 1970-2000; contbr. articles to newspapers. Historian City of Jamestown, 1978—; bd. dirs., chair scholarship com. Mozart Club, 2001—05; play selection com. Lucille Ball Little Theatre of Jamestown, 1976—, pit orch.; mem. steering and fin. coms. Underground Railroad Tableau Project; v.p., bd. trustees Unitarian Universalist Congregation Jamestown; bd. dirs. Jamestown YWCA, Chautauqua Regional Youth Symphony, pres., 1996—2001; com. mem. Jamestown Audubon Soc., newsletter editor, 1982—98. Recipient Women of Achievement award in civic category, YWCA, 2004, Friend of Edn. award, Delta Kappa Gamma Internat. Kappa Chpt., 2006. Mem. AAUW (chmn. What's New Fair Jamestown 1988-94, legislative breakfast 1995—, bd. dirs., pres. 1988-92, co-pres. 2000-06, v.p. membership 2006—, named gift award 1987), Interclub Coun. Jamestown (treas. 1998—, Woman of Yr. award 1992). Avocations: museums, concerts, reading, gardening. Home: 13 Lamont St Jamestown NY 14701-2021 Personal E-mail: musicat2@gmail.com.

THOMPSON, BRADFORD, chef; b. Wilmington, Del., 1969; Grad., U. Rochester, NY. Garde mgr. Max on Main, Hartford, Conn., line cook, pastry chef; chef Camelback, Phoenix, Café Boulud, NYC, DB Bistro Moderne, NYC; mgr. private dinning Daniel, NYC; exec. chef Mary Elaine's, The Phoenician, Scottsdale, Ariz. Author: two cookbooks. Named one of Top 10 Best New Chefs in Am., Food & Wine Mag., 2004; recipient Best Chef: Southwest award, James Beard Found., 2006. Achievements include cuisine featured on Today Show and Food Network. Office: The Phoenician Mary Elaine's 6000 E Camelback Rd Scottsdale AZ 85251 Office Phone: 480-423-2530. *

THOMPSON, BRIAN JOHN, academic administrator, optics scientist, educator; b. Glossop, Eng., June 10, 1932; came to U.S., 1962; s. Alexander William and Edna May (Gould) T.; m. Joyce Emily Cheshire, Mar. 31, 1956; children: Karen Joyce, Andrew Derrick. B of Sci. Tech., U. Manchester, Eng., 1955, PhD, 1959. Demonstrator in physics dept. tech. U. Manchester, 1955-56, asst. lectr. dept. tech., 1957-59; lectr. physics U. Leeds, England, 1959-62; sr. physicist Tech. Optics, Inc., Burlington, Mass., 1963-65, dir. dept. optics, 1966-67; mr. tech. ops. west, tech. dir. Beckman and Whitley, Mountainview, Calif., 1967-68; prof. Inst. Optics U. Rochester, NY, 1968-94, dir. Inst. Optics NY, 1968-75, dean Coll. Engring. and Applied Scis. NY, 1975-84, Wm. F. May prof. engring. NY, 1982-85, provost NY, 1984-94, provost emeritus, prof. of optics emeritus, Disting. U. prof. NY, 1994—. Editor Optics and Laser Tech., 1969-96; assoc. editor: Optical Engring., 1972-76, Optics Comm., 1978-86; editor Optica Acta, 1981-85, Optical Scis. and Engring. Series, vols. 1-124, 1980—; mem. editl. bd. Laser Focus, 1970-84, Particle Characterization, 1984-95, Optics and Lasers in Engring., 1985, Milestone Series of Selected Papers, vols. 1-182, 1985-2006, Optical Engring., 1991-98; chmn. adv. bd. Marquis Who's Who Directory Optical Scientists and Engrs., 1983-86; contbr. articles to profl. jours. With Brit. Army, 1950-52. Fellow: Inst. Physics and Phys. Soc. (Gt. Britain), Optical Soc. Am. (bd. dirs. 1969—72, exec. com. 1970—73, assoc. editor jour. 1966—77), Soc. Photo-Optical Instrumentation Engrs. (life; pres. 1974—76, editor jour. 1991—98, Pres.'s award 1967, Pezzuto award 1978, Kingslake medal 1978, Gold medal 1986, Dir. award 1998); mem.: AAAS, Am. Phys. Soc. Home and Office: 9 Esternay Ln Pittsford NY 14534-1014 Office Phone: 585-461-0739.

THOMPSON, BUZZ (BARTON H. JR.), law educator; b. 1951; AB in Economics, Stanford U., 1972, MBA, JD, Stanford U., 1976. Law clk. to Judge Joseph T. Sneed US Ct. Appeals 9th Cir., San Francisco, 1976—77; law clk. to Justice William H. Rehnquist US Supreme Ct., 1977—78; assoc. O'Melveny & Myers, LA, 1978—83, ptnr., 1984—86; mem. faculty Stanford Law Sch., 1986—, Robert E. Paradise fellow, 1993—95, Robert E. Paradise prof. natural resources law, 1996—, vice dean, 2000—04; co-dir. Stanford Inst. for the Environment, 2004—. Instr. water resources UCLA, 1980—83; vis. fellow Hoover Instn. for War, Revolution, and Peace Stanford U., 1999. Bd. dirs. Nat. Heritage Inst. Office: Stanford Law Sch Crown Quadrangle 559 Nathan Abbott Way Stanford CA 94305-8610 Office Phone: 650-723-2518. Office Fax: 650-725-8509. Business E-Mail: buzzt@stanford.edu.

THOMPSON, CARLYNN JEAN, information scientist; b. San Saba, Tex., Nov. 8, 1952; d. Joe Paul and Andragene Grumbles; m. David John Thompson, May 27, 1972; children: Lessa Anne, Kira Jo. MLS, U. of Md., 1976. Libr. in phys. sciences and engring. Def. Tech. Info. Ctr., Ft. Belvoir, Va., 1976—79, adminstrv. libr., 1979—82, tech. info. specialist, 1982—85, divsn. chief info. rsch. and tech., 1986—91, dir. component info. support, 1991—. Chmn. World Wide Web Fed. Consortium, Arlington, Va., 1996—98; def. sci. bd. summer study on roles and missions in homeland security Dept. Def., Arlington, 2003; sr. advisor Fed. Web Content Stds. Working Group, Washington, 2004; elected mem. Internat. Coun. Sci. and Tech. Info., Paris, 2004—06. Comtemporary music dir. Village Bapt. Ch., Bowie, Md., 1999—2006. Named Fed. Libr. of Yr., 2001; recipient Leadership award, Assn. for Fed. Info. Resources Mgmt., 1998, Exceptional Civilian Svc. award, Def. Info. Sys. Agy., 2003, Svc. citation, L. Paul Bremer, III, Coalition Provisional Authority, Iraq, 2004, Fed. Computer Week Fed. 100 award, 1999. Mem.: Am. Soc. for Info. Sci. and Tech. Bapist. Office: Def Tech Info Ctr 8725 John J Kingman Rd Fort Belvoir VA 22060 Office Fax: 703-767-9174. Business E-Mail: cthompson@dtic.mil.

THOMPSON, CHARLES MURRAY, lawyer; b. Childress, Tex., Oct. 13, 1942; s. Walter Lee and Lois S. (Sheehan) T.; children: Murray, McLean. BS with honors, Colo. State U., Ft. Collins, 1965; JD cum laude, U. SD, Vermillion, 1969, LLD (hon.), 1995. Bar: SD 1969, US Dist. Ct. SD 1969, US Ct. Claims 1989, US Ct. Appeals (8th cir.) 1972, US Supreme Ct. 1973. Ptnr. May, Adam, Gerdes & Thompson, Pierre, SD, 1969—. Bd. dirs. Bank West, Pierre, SD; past pres., dir. Delta Trust, Pierre; spkr. in field. Editor S.D. Law Rev., 1969 Pres. SD Coun. Sch. Attys., 1984-86. Fellow Am. Bar Found. (chmn. 1991-92, bd. dirs. 1989-92), Coll. Law Practice Mgmt., Am. Coll. Trial Lawyers; mem. ABA (ho. of dels. 1978-2002, bd. govs. 1983-86, standing com. on fed. judiciary 2004-06), ATLA, Am. Bd. Trial Advs., Am. Counsel Assn., Am. Judicature Soc. (bd. dirs. 1981-85), Am. Bar Endowment (bd. dirs. 1991-2006, dir. emeritus 2006-, pres. 2000-02), Nat. Conf. Bar Pres.'s (exec. coun. 1986-94, pres. 1992-93), State Bar S.D. (pres. young lawyers sect. 1974-75, pres. 1986-87), SD Bar Found. (pres. 1991), SD Trial Lawyers Assn. (pres. 1980-81), Jackrabbit Bar Assn. (chancellor 1981-82, ABA, Am. Bar Endowment, Am. Bar Found., Nat. Jud. Coll. pension bd., 1987-90, adminstrv. com., 2005-), SD Cmty. Found., Kiwanis (pres. local club 1977). Democrat. Avocations: flying, ranching. Home and Office: PO Box 160 Pierre SD 57501-0160 Office Phone: 605-224-8803.

THOMPSON, CHARLES WILLIAM SYDNOR See THOMPSON, SYDNOR JR.

THOMPSON, CHARLOTTE ELLIS, pediatrician, educator, writer; d. Robert and Ann Ellis; divorced; children: Jennifer Ann, Geoffrey Graeme. BA, Stanford U., 1950, MD, 1954. Diplomate Am. Bd. Pediat. Intern Children's Hosp., San Francisco, 1953-54; resident UCLA, 1960-61, L.A. Children's Hosp., 1962-63; pvt. practice La Jolla, Calif., 1963-75; dir. Muscle Disease Clinic Univ. Hosp.-U. Calif. Sch. Medicine, San Diego, 1969-80, asst. clin. prof. pediat., 1969—; founder, dir. Ctr. for Handicapped Children and Teenagers, San Francisco, 1981—2004. Cons. U.S. Naval Hosp., San Diego, 1970-91; dep. dir. Santa Clara County Child Health and Disability, Santa Clara, Calif., 1974-75; dir. Ctr. for Multiple Handicaps, Oakland, Calif., 1976-81; co-dir. Muscle Clinic Children's Hosp., San Diego, 1963-69; dir. muscle program U. Rochester, 1957-60. Author: Raising a Handicapped Child: A Helpful Guide for Parents of the Physically Disabled, 1986, 4th edit., 1991, rev., expanded edit., 2000, Allein leben: Ein umfassendes Handbuch für Frauen, 1993, Making Wise Choices: A Guide for Women, 1993, Raising a Child with a Neuromuscular Disorder, 1999, Raising A Handicapped Child, 1999, 101 Ways To The Best Medical Care, 2006; contbr. articles to med. jours., including Clin. Pediat., New Eng. Jour. Medicine, Neurology, Jour. Family Practice, Mothering, Jour. Pediatric Orthopedics, Pediatrician, Am. Baby, Pediatric News, also chpts. to books. Mem. Calif. Children's Svc. Com., 1977—. Fellow: Am. Acad. Pediat. Avocations: tennis, ice skating, opera. Office: 8070 La Jolla Shores Dr # 514 La Jolla CA 92037-3296 Personal E-mail: cetmd@earthlink.net.

THOMPSON, CLAIRE LOUISA, nurse, educator, consultant, human services manager; b. Columbus, Ohio, Sept. 29, 1938; d. Harry Edgar and Clara Etta (Brackenbusch) McKeever; m. Roger Lee Thompson, Dec. 20, 1958 (div. 1988); children: Jeffrey, Michael. Diploma, Bethesda Hosp. Sch. Nursing, Cin., 1959; student, Ball State, 1970, Ind. U., 1981, Purdue U., 1982-83. RN, Ohio, Ind., Calif.; cert. ins. rehab. specialist, case mgr.; cert. health occupl. level tchr., Ind. Oper. rm./emergency rm. nurse Greene Meml. Hosp., Xenia, Ohio, 1959-60; med.-surg. nurse, charge nurse Bethesda Hosp., 1960-64; med.-surg. nurse Porter Meml. Hosp., Valparaiso, Ind., 1965-66; staff and charge nurse Mercy Hosp., Elwood, Ind., 1968-74; gen. practice nurse W. A. Scea, MD, Elwood, 1970-74; exec. dir. Vis. Nurse Assn., Elwood, 1974-78; analyst Blue Cross/Blue Shield of Indpls., 1978; supr. Meth. Hosp. Clinic, Indpls., 1979-80; DON Upjohn Health Care, Indpls., 1980; staff nurse Americana Health Care Ctr., Indpls., 1981; instr. health occups. Washington Twp. Schs., Indpls., 1981-84; br. mgr. health & rehab. Crawford & Co., Indpls., 1984-88, regional med. svcs. advisor western region San Francisco, 1988-92; br. mgr. Crawford & Co., Health Care Mgmt., Modesto, Calif., 1992-94; ret., 1994. Developer in case mgmt. nursing svcs., 1974-94. Founder Meals on Wheels, Elwood, 1975, Vis. Nurses Assn., Elwood, 1976; mem. altar guild, lay eucharist min. Episcopal Ch.; vol. H.E.B. Hosp., 2004-07; vol. adv. Good Shepherd Hosp., 2007—. Mem. NLN, Assn. Rehab. Nurses (pres. Ind. chpt. 1987-88), Nat. Ins. Womens Assn., Case Mgmt. Soc. Am., San Francisco Ins. Womens Assn., Rehab. Ins. Nurses Group. Avocations: the arts, photography, antique collect glass.

THOMPSON, CLIFTON C., retired chemistry professor, academic administrator; b. Franklin, Tenn., Aug. 16, 1939; s. Clifton C. and Ruby M. Thompson; m. Sarah Ellen Gaunt, Dec. 1, 1978; children: Brenda Kay, Victoria Lea. BS, Middle Tenn. State U., 1961; PhD, U. Miss., 1964. Asst. prof. Rutgers U., New Brunswick, NJ, 1965, Marshall U., Huntington, W.Va., 1965-66; assoc. prof. Middle Tenn. State U., Murfreesboro, 1966-68, U. Memphis, 1968—74; prof. chemistry, dept. head, dean Coll. Sci. and Math., dir. Ctr. for Sci. Rsch., assoc. v.p. for grad. studies and rsch. Mo. State U., Springfield, 1974-96, prof. emeritus, 1996—; prof. chemistry Cen. Mich. U., Mt. Pleasant, 1996-98. Rsch. assoc. U. Tex., Austin, 1964-65; rschr. Oak Ridge Nat. Lab., 1968; cons. Mid-South Research Assocs., Memphis, 1969-71; mem. med. tech. rev. com. Nat. Accrediting Agy. for Clin. Lab. Sci., Chgo., 1974-80; vis. prof. So. Ill. U., Carbondale, 1995. Author: Ultraviolet-Visible Absorption Spectroscopy, 1974; contbr. articles to profl. jours. Mem. health care com. Springfield C. of C., 1978-79, mem. econ. devel. com., 1983-89; bd. dirs. United Hebrew Congregation, Springfield, 1983-86, United Hebrew Found., Inc., 1994-96. NSF fellow, 1961-64; Sigma Xi grantee-in-aide, 1970; NSF sr. fgn. scientist grantee, 1971; NSF coop-coll. sch. sci. grantee, 1972; Higher Edn. Applied Projects grantee, 1987-90. Mem. Am. Chem. Soc., Royal Soc. Chemistry, Sigma Xi, Phi Kappa Phi. Office: Mo State U Dept Chemistry Springfield MO 65804

THOMPSON, CRAIG B., physician; b. Cambridge, Mass., Feb. 9, 1953; m. Tullia Lindsten; children: Kajsa, Nicklas. AB summa cum laude, Dartmouth Coll., 1973, BS with honors, 1975; MD, U. Pa., 1977. Asst. prof. Uniformed Svcs. U. Health Scis., Bethesda, Md., 1982-87; asst. investigator Howard Hughes Med. Inst., Ann Arbor, Mich., 1987-89; asst. prof. U. Mich., Ann Arbor, 1987-89, assoc. prof., 1989-92; assoc. investigator Howard Hughes Med. Inst., Ann Arbor, 1989-93, investigator, 1993; prof. U. Chgo., 1993—99; scientific dir. Abramson Family Cancer Rsch. Inst., 1999—; chair dept. cancer biology U. Pa. Recipient Clinical Investigator award, Am. Soc. Clinical Investigation, 2003, Mosby Book award, Merck award, Med. Sci. award, Alpha Omega Alpha. Mem.: Am. Acad. Arts Sciences, IOM, NAS. Office: Abramson Inst 451 BRB II/III 421 Curie Blvd Philadelphia PA 19104-6160

THOMPSON, CRAIG SNOVER, corporate communications executive; b. Bklyn., May 24, 1932; s. Craig F. and Edith (Williams) T.; m. Masae Sugizaki, Feb. 21, 1957; children: Lee Anne, Jane Laura. Grad., Valley Forge Mil. Acad., 1951; BA, Johns Hopkins U., 1954. Newspaper and radio reporter Easton (Pa.) Express, 1954-55, 57-59, Wall St. Jour., 1959-60; account exec. Moore, Meldrum & Assocs., 1960; mgr. pub. relations Cen. Nat. Bank of Cleve., 1961-62; account exec. Edward Howard & Co., Cleve., 1962-67, v.p., 1967-69, sr. v.p., 1969-71; dir. pub. relations White Motor Corp., Cleve., 1971-76; v.p. pub. relations No. Telecom Inc., Nashville, 1976-77, White Motor Corp., Farmington Hills, Mich., 1977-80, v.p. corp. communications, 1980-81; dir. exec. communications Rockwell Internat. Corp., Pitts., 1981-86, El Segundo, Calif., 1986-91, Seal Beach, Calif., 1992-97, sr. communications exec., 1997; pres. Craig S. Thompson. Inc., 1997—. Bd. dirs. Shaker Lakes Regional Nature Center, 1970-73. Served to 1st lt., inf. U.S. Army, 1955-57. Mem. Pub. Rels. Soc. Am. (accredited), Alumni Assn. Valley Forge Mil. Acad. (bd. dirs. 1988-94).

THOMPSON, DANIEL EMERSON, vending machine service company executive; b. Fairbanks, Alaska, Jan. 24, 1947; s. George Edmond and Emma Jean (Burns) T.; m. Yvette Clarice Brazeau, Aug. 16, 1980. Student, U. Notre Dame, 1965-67. Vice-pres. Music Inc., Fairbanks, 1965—67; pres. Music Inc. (doing bus. as Alaska Music Co.), Fairbanks, 1967—81, 1987—; sec. Music Inc. (doing bus. as Vend Alaska-Fairbanks), Fairbanks, 1984—87; pres. Vend Inc. (doing bus. as Vend Alaska-Anchorage), Anchorage, 1984—. Bd. dirs. Music Inc., Fairbanks, Vend Inc., Anchorage, Denali State Bank, Fairbanks; ptnr. Thompson Investment Co., Fairbanks, 1976—. Trustee Hi Pow, Fairbanks, 1972—; pres. Fairbanks Downtown Assn., 1987-88, bd. dirs., 1984-94; bd. dirs. Alaska State Devel. Corp., Juneau, 1971-82, Monroe Found., Fairbanks, 1991-2000, North Star Dance Found., 2002—; vocatonal edn. adv. com. Fairbanks North Star Borough Sch. Dist., 1993—. Mem. Amusement Music Operators Am., Nat. Automatic Merchandising Assn., N.W. Automatic Vending Assn. (bd. govs. 1983—), Rotary, Fairbanks C. of C. Roman Catholic. Office: 1810 Burgess Ave Fairbanks AK 99709-5516

THOMPSON, DARLENE BENNETT, realtor, musician; b. Simpson, La., June 28, 1931; d. Odis Pharon and Carrie Josephine (Knight) Blackwell; m. Elmo Bennett (dec.); children: Debra Kathleen Bennett, Eric Blane Bennett, Denise Darlene Bennett; m. Mitchell Glenn Thompson, Dec. 28, 1990. BS, Northwestern State U., Natchitoches, La., 1952, EdM, 1959, MusM, 1963, EdD, 1981. Tchr. K-12 Vernon Parish Sch. Bd., Leesville, La., 1952—82; dir. alternative sch. Vidor (Tex.) Ind. Sch. Dist., 1982—85; reading specialist Burkville (Tex.) Ind. Sch. Dist., 1986—2000; realtor ERA Broker, Leesville, 2003—. Dir. music Simpson Ch. of God, Simpson Assembly of God; organist Pok Episcopal Ch., St. Michael's Cath. Ch. Mem.: Ret. Tchrs. La., Piano Tchrs. La., Music Educators La., Pilot Club Leesville, Phi Delta Kappa. Home: 554 Alexandria Hwy Leesville LA 71446

THOMPSON, DAVID, publishing executive; m. Jane Thompson; children: Kathryne, Jeffrey, Robyn. Grad., U. Ctrl. Okla., 1973. Mem. retail adv. sales staff Oklahoman, Oklahoma City, 1974, mgr. phone room classified adv. dept., asst. adv. dir., 1986, dir. adv., 1987—2001, pres., pub., 2003—; mgr. adv. Colo. Springs Sun, 1977—86; v.p. adv. Charlotte Observer, 2001—03. Mem. bd. Carolina Regional Partnership; mem. Mecklenburg Coun., exec. bd. dirs. Last Frontier Coun. Boy Scouts Am., pres. Last Frontier Council, 2006; with Charlotte C. of C.; chmn. elect YMCA, Oklahoma City; mem. bd. Ind. Coll. Found.; chmn. econ. develop. dept. C. of C.; mem. bd. Oklahoma City C. of C., State C. of C., Okla. Health Ctr. Found., Allied Arts, State Fair of Okla., Oklahoma City Pub. Schs. Found., Okla. Bus. Roundtable, Okla. Bus. & Edn. Coalition. Mem.: So. Newspaper Pubs. Assn., Newspaper Assn. Am., Kiwanis (pres.). Office: Oklahoman PO Box 25125 Oklahoma City OK 73125 *

THOMPSON, DAVID ALFRED, industrial engineer; b. Chgo., Sept. 9, 1929; s. Clifford James and Christobel Eliza (Sawin) T.; children: Nancy, Brooke, Lynda, Diane, Kristy. B.M.E., U. Va., 1951; BS in Indsl. Engring, U. Fla., 1955, MS in Engring, 1956; PhD, Stanford U., 1961. Registered profl. engr., Calif; cert. profl. ergonomist; bd. cert. diplomate in forensic engring. Research asst. U. Fla. Engring. and Industries Exptl. Sta., Gainesville, 1955-56; instr. indsl. engring. Stanford U., 1956-58, acting asst. prof., 1958-61, asst. prof., 1961-64, asso. prof., 1964-72, prof., 1972-83, prof., asso. chmn. dept. indsl. engring., 1972-73, prof. emeritus, 1983—; clin. faculty occupational medicine U. Calif. Med. Sch., San Francisco, 1985—; pres., chief scientist Portola Assocs., Palo Alto, Calif., 1962—97, Incline Village, Nev., 1997—; prin. investigator NASA Ames Rsch. Ctr., Moffatt Field, Calif., 1974-77. Cons. Dept. State, Fed. EEO Commn., maj. U.S. and fgn. cos.; cons. emergency commn. ctr. design Santa Clara County Criminal Justice Bd., 1974, Bay Area Rapid Transit Control Ctr., 1977, Govt. of Mex., 1978, Amadahl Corp., 1978-79, Kerr-McGee Corp., 1979, Chase Manhattan Bank, 1980, St. Regis Paper Co., 1980-82, Pacific Gas & Electric, 1983-85, Pacific Bell, 1984-86, 89-93, IBM, 1988-91, Hewlett-Packard, 1990-91, 98-99, Reuter's News Svc., 1990-92, Safeway Corp., 1992-94, New United Motors Mfg., 1993-95, Sun Microsys., 1993-94, Microsoft, 1995-00; mem. com. for office computers Calif. OSHA. Dir., editor: documentary film Rapid Answers for Rapid Transit, Dept. Transp., 1974; mem. editorial adv. bd. Computers and Graphics, 1970-85; reviewer Indsl. Engring. and IEEE Transactions, 1972-86; contbr. articles to profl. jours. Served to lt. USNR, 1951-58. HEW grantee, 1967-70 Fellow Nat. Assn. Forensic Engrs.; mem. IEEE, Am. Inst. Indsl. Engrs., Human Factors and Ergonomics Soc., Am. Soc. Safety Engrs., Soc. Forensic Engrs. and Scientists, Am. Assn. Forensic Scientists. Home: PO Box 6685 Incline Village NV 89450-6685 Address: PO Box 6088 Incline Village NV 89450-6088 Office Phone: 775-833-3304. Personal E-mail: davidthompson@pyramid.net. Business E-Mail: davidthompson@humanfactors.org.

THOMPSON, DAVID O'NEAL, retired basketball player; b. Shelby, NC, July 13, 1954; BS in Sociology, N.C. State U., 1975. With Denver Nuggets, 1975-82, Seattle SuperSonics, 1982-84. Named Athlete of Yr., ACC, 1973, 75, Player of Yr., ACC, 1973-75, Most Valuable Player, NCAA Tournament, Player of Yr., Naismith, 1975, Rupp, 1975, AP, 1975, UPI, 1975, Eastman Kodak, 1975, The Sporting News, 1975, Most Valuable Player ABA All-Star, 1976, MBA Rookie of Yr., 1976, N.C. Sports Hall of Fame, 1982, Most Valuable Player, 1979 All-Star Game, Basketball Hall of Fame, 1996, Colo. Sports Hall of Fame, 1996, Sport Mag. Performer of Yr./Basketball, 1978; voted to Best 5 in History of Coll. Basketball, AP Coll. Player of Yr., 1974, 75; recipient Joe Mallamo Humanitarian award 1994, others; Naismith Basketball Hall of Fame inductee, 1996, voted All Time ABA top 30 team, 1997. Achievements include three-time First-Team All-Am., Three-time All-ACC selection; mem. Championship Team, 1974, NCAA All-Decade Team, 1970's; First Team All-NBA selection, 1977, 78, four-time NBA All-Star.

THOMPSON, DAVID RENWICK, federal judge; b. 1930; BS in Bus., U. So. Calif., 1952, LLB, 1955. Pvt. practice Thompson & Thompson (and predecessor firms), 1957—85; judge US Ct. Appeals (9th cir.), 1985—98, sr. judge, 1998—. With USN, 1955—57. Mem.: ABA, Am. Bd. Trial Lawyers (sec. San Diego chpt. 1983, v.p. 1984, Pres. 1985), San Diego County Bar Assn. Office: US Ct Appeals 940 Front St Rm 2193 San Diego CA 92101-8919 *

THOMPSON, DAVID RUSSELL, engineering educator, dean; b. Cleve., Apr. 4, 1944; s. Dwight L. and Ella Caroline (Wolff) T.; m. Janet Ann Schall, Aug. 27, 1966; children: Devin Mathew, Colleen Michelle, Darin Michael. BS in Agrl. Engring., Purdue U., 1966, MS in Agrl. Engring., 1967; PhD in Agrl. Engring., Mich. State U., 1970. Asst. prof. agrl. engring., food sci. and nutrition depts. U. Minn., St. Paul, 1970-75, assoc. prof., 1975-81, prof., 1981-85; prof. agrl. engring., head dept. Okla. State U., Stillwater, 1985-91, assoc. dean Coll. Engring., Architecture and Tech., 1991—. Engr. ops. dept. Green Giant Co., La Sueur, Minn., 1978-79; reviewer Colo. State U., Coop. State Rsch. Svc., USDA, Ft. Collins, 1989, foods, feeds and prodn. cluster U. Mo., Columbia, 1989, 93, dept. agrl. engring. Pa. State U., University Park, 1990, Tex. A&M U., College Station, 1992, Utah State U., Logan, 1993, USAF, Tyndall, Fla. and San Angelo, Tex., 1994-95, 97, Wash. State U., Pullman, 1995, U. Ga., Athens, 1996, S.D. State U., 1997, U. Fla., 1998, U. Del., 1998, U. Neb., 1999, U. Wis., 2000, U. Idaho, 2001, Rutgers U., 2003, Lake Superior State U., Sault St. Marie, 2003, Auburn U., 2004, U. Tenn., 2005, Western New Eng. Coll., 2005, So. Ill. U., Carbondale, 2006, St. Petersburg Coll., 2006, U. of the Pacific, 2006, others; reviewer USDA, 1983; vis. scholar Va. Poly. Inst. and State U., Blaksburg. Author: The Influence of Materials Properties on the Freezing of Sweet Corn, 1984, Mathematical Model for Predicting Lysine and Methionine Losses During Thermal Processing of Fortified Foods; contbr. over 50 articles to profl. jours. including Jour. Food Sci. Fellow Am. Soc. Agrl. Engrs. (divsn. chmn. 1976-77, bd. dirs. 1981-84, 87-89, v.p. 1994-98, stds. coun. chmn. 1997-98, Farm and Indsl. Equip. Inst., Young Rschr. award 1983, Pres.'s citation 1989, 98); mem. ASHRAE, NSPE (chair Okla. mid-north sect. 1994-95), Okla. Soc. Profl. Engrs. (v.p. 2000-01), Inst. Food Technologists (program com. 1982-85, state officer 1987-89), Am. Soc. Engring. Edn. (chair Midwest sect. 1994-95), Engring. Accreditation Commn. Accreditation Bd. Engring. and Tech., Sigma Xi, Phi Kappa Phi, Tau Beta Pi, Alpha Epsilon, Phi Eta Sigma, Gamma Sigma Delta. Office: Okla State U Coll Engring Arch & Tech 201 Adv Tech Rsch Ctr Stillwater OK 74078-5010 Home Phone: 405-377-5263; Office Phone: 405-744-5140. Business E-Mail: dthomps@okstate.edu.

THOMPSON, DAVID WALKER, astronautics company executive; b. Phila., Mar. 21, 1954; s. Robert H. and Nancy S. (Walker) T.; m. Catherine K. Ahulii, April 16, 1983. BS in Aeronautics and Astronautics, MIT, 1976; MS, Calif. Inst. Tech., 1977; MBA, Harvard U., 1981. Project engr. Jet

Propulsion Lab., Pasadena, Calif., 1976; aerospace engr. NASA, Houston, 1977, project mgr. Huntsville, Ala., 1977-79; spl. asst. to pres. Hughes Aircraft Co., Los Angeles, 1981-82; co-founder, pres., chief exec. officer Orbital Scis. Corp., Dulles, Va., 1982—. Cons. Rockwell Internat., Thousand Oaks, Calif., 1980-81, Rand Corp., Santa Monica, Calif., 1982. Recipient Nat. award Space Found., Houston, 1981, Nat. Medal Tech. U.S Dept. Commerce Tech. Adminstrn., 1991, Nat. Air and Space Mus. Trophy, 1990, George M. Low Space Transportation award, Am. Inst. Aeronautics and Astronautics, 1994, World Tech. award for Space, Economist Mag.; fellow Hertz Found., 1976, NSF fellow, 1976, Rockwell Internat. fellow, Harvard U. fellow, 1979; named Va. Industrialist Yr., 1991, Satellite Exec. of Yr., Satellite Mag., 1990, High-Tech. Entrepreneur Yr. Fellow AIAA (assoc., Young Engr./Scientist Yr. award 1984, George M. Low Space Trans. award 1994), Am. Astronautical Soc., Royal Aeronautical Soc.; mem. Nat. Space Club, Internat. Acad. Astronautics, NAE. Office: Orbital Sciences Corp 21839 Atlantic Blvd Sterling VA 20166-6850 *

THOMPSON, DAVID W.J., atmospheric scientist, educator; BS in Aerospace Engring., U. Colo., Boulder, 1994; MS in Atmospheric Scis., U. Wash., Seattle, 1998, PhD in Atmospheric Scis., 2000. Asst. prof. Colo. State U., Ft. Collins, 2001—06, assoc. prof., 2006—. Contbr. articles to sci. jours.; assoc. editor: Jour. Climate, 2004—. Named one of Brilliant 10, Popular Sci. mag., 2006; recipient CAREER award, NSF, 2001. Fellow: Am. Geophys. Union (Macelwane medal 2004). Achievements include one of the first to identify the Arctic Oscillation. Office: Colo State U Dept Atmospheric Sci Fort Collins CO 80523 Office Phone: 970-491-3338. Office Fax: 970-491-8449. E-mail: davet@atmos.colostate.edu. *

THOMPSON, DEAN ALLAN, cattleman; b. Peru, Ind., Jan. 29, 1934; s. Paul Franklin and Pauline St. Clair (Thrush) T.; m. Shirley Roach Anerson, May 25, 2003. Student Purdue U., 1952-54. Mgr. Thompson Farms, breeders registered Hereford cattle, Peru, 1956-69; owner Thompson Farms, Wartrace, Tenn. and Peru, 1970-87, Dean Thompson Prodns., Wartrace, Wartrace Records; chmn. bd. Instant Copy and Printing, Inc., Monterey, Calif., 1976-86, Trenton Energy Inc., 1977-83, Bloomfield, Ind.; v.p., dir. 5B Cattle Co., Twin Bridges, Mont., 1986-87; ptnr., Brann-Thompson Ltd.; internat. beef cattle judge; dir. Maine Manna, Gorham, Met. Bd. Fair Commrs. Bd. dirs. Thrush-Thompson Found. (formerly H.A. Thrush Found.), Peru; trustee Middle Tenn. State U. Found., 1981-83, 85-89, chmn. fin. com., 1982-83, 85-87, exec. com., 1983-89, sec. 1988, pres.-elect, 1989; precinct committeeman, chmn. Miami County (Ind.) Young Republican Com., 1962-67; elder Presbyn. Ch., 1986-88. With U.S. Army, 1955-56. Mem. Nat. Western (dir.), Ind. (dir. 1958-68, pres. 1960) Polled Hereford Assns., Ind. Cattleman's Assn. (founding dir.), Ind. Livestock Breeders Assn., Am. Hereford Assn. (v.p. pres.'s coun. 1981, pres. 1982), Tenn. Hereford Assn. (dir. 1977-81, 93-97, v.p. 1979, pres. 1980-81, 97), Toastmasters (pres., area gov.), Columbia Club. Home and Office: 900 19th Ave S Apt 1201 Nashville TN 37212-2155

THOMPSON, DEAN M., II, marketing executive; BA, U. NC, Greensboro. Dir. mktg. and MIS Stockton Bates LLP, Phila., 1992—99; chief mktg. officer, co-founder MoveMedia, Inc., Norristown, Pa., 1999—2000; v.p. strategic devel. Wired Vines, Inc., Plymouth Meeting, Pa., 2000; dir. mktg. and comm. Cmty. Options, Inc., Princeton, NJ, 2003—. CEO Knowledge Shark, Trenton, NJ, 2000—; bd. adv. Practice Devel. Inst., Inc., Pub. Interest Law Ctr., Phila.; internet initiative project mem. Rutgers U., NJ. Mem.: Legal Mktg. Assn., Assn. Acctg. Mktg., Am. Mktg. Assn.

THOMPSON, DENNIS FRANK, political science professor, consultant; b. Hamilton, Ohio, May 12, 1940; s. Frank and Florence (Downs) T.; m. Carol Thompson, June 22, 1963; children: Eric, David. BA, Coll. William and Mary, Williamsburg, Va., 1962, LHD (hon.), 1990; BA, Oxford U., 1964, MA, 1968; PhD, Harvard U., Cambridge, Mass., 1968. Instr. govt. Harvard U., Cambridge, Mass., 1967-68, Alfred North Whitehead prof., 1986—, dir. univ. ctr. for ethics, 1986—2007, assoc. provost, 1996—2002, sr. advisor to the pres., 2002—05; prof. politics Princeton U., NJ, 1968—75, prof., 1975—86, chmn. dept. politics, 1976—79, 1982—83. Cons. to spl. counsel U.S. Senate Select Com. on Ethics, 1990-91, U.S. Dept. HHS, 1980, FDA, 1993. Author: The Democratic Citizen, 1970, John Stuart Mill and Representative Government, 1976, Political Ethics and Public Office, 1987, Ethics in Congress, 1995, (with A. Gutmann) Democracy and Disagreement, 1996, Ethics and Politics: Cases and Comments, 4th edit., 2005, Just Elections, 2002, (with A. Gutmann) Why Deliberative Democracy, 2004, Restoring Responsibility, 2005; mem. editl. bd. Polit. Theory, 1974—, Philosophy and Pub. Affairs, 1971—, Am. Polit. Sci. Rev., 1985-88. Trustee Smith Coll., 1994-2004. Fellow Am. Acad. Arts and Scis.; mem. Am. Soc. Legal and Polit. Philosophy (v.p. 1977-80, pres. 1986-89). Home: 9 Shady Hill Sq Cambridge MA 02138-2035 Office: Harvard U Dept Govt C915 N422 1737 Cambridge St Cambridge MA 02138-5801

THOMPSON, DENNIS PETERS, plastic surgeon; b. Chgo., Mar. 18, 1937; s. David John and Ruth Dorothy (Peters) T.; m. Virginia Louise Williams, June 17, 1961; children: Laura Faye, Victoria Ruth, Elizabeth Jan. BS, U. Ill., 1957, BS in Medicine, 1959, MS in Physiology, 1961, MD, 1961. Diplomate Am. Bd. Surgery, Am. Bd. Plastic Surgery. Intern Presbyn.-St. Lukes Hosp., Chgo., 1961—62; resident in gen. surgery Mayo Clinic, Rochester, Minn., 1964—66, fellow in gen. surgery, 1964—66; resident in gen. surgery Harbor Gen. Hosp., LA, 1968—70; resident in plastic surgery UCLA, 1971—73, clin. instr. plastic surgery, 1975—82, asst. clin. prof. surgery, 1982—97, assoc. clin. prof. plastic surgery, 1998—. Practice medicine specializing in plastic and reconstructive surgery, LA, 1974-78, Santa Monica, Calif., 1978—; chmn. plastic surgery sect. St. John's Hosp., 1986-91; staff Olive View Hosp., 1982—, St. John's Hosp., 1982-; chmn. dept. surgery Beverly Glen Hosp., 1978-79; pres. Coop. of Am. Physicians Credit Union, 1978-80; bd. dirs. Coop. Am. Physicians, 1980-97, chmn. membership devel. com., 1983-97, treas., 1985-97. Contbr. articles to med. jours. Moderator Congl. Ch. of Northridge (Calif.), 1975-76, chmn. bd. trustees, 1973-74, 80-82; bd. dirs. L.A. Bus. Coun., 1987-90. Am. Tobacco Inst. rsch. grantee, 1959-60. Fellow ACS; mem. AMA (Physicians Recognition award 1971, 74, 77, 81, 84, 87, 90, 93, 96, 99, 2002, 05), Calif. Med. Assn., L.A. County Med. Assn. (chmn. bylaws com. 1979-80, chmn. ethics com. 1980-81, 2000-01, sec.-treas. dist. 5 1982-83, program chmn. 1983-84, pres. 1985-86, councilor 1988-96, 2001-03, councilor-at-large 2004—,, v.p. 1999-2000), Pan-Pacific Surg. Assn., Am. Soc. Plastic Surgeons, Calif. Soc. Plastic Surgeons (chmn. bylaws com. 1982-83, chmn. liability com. 1983-85, councilor 1988-91, sec. 1993-95, v.p. 1995-96, pres.-elect 1996-97, pres. 1997-98), L.A. Soc. Plastic Surgeons (sec. 1980-82, pres. 1982-97), Lipoplasty Soc. N.Am., UCLA Plastic Surgery Soc. (treas. 1983-84, v.p. 1996-98, pres. 1998-2005, 03-05), Am. Soc. Aesthetic Plastic Surgery, Internat. Soc. Clin. Plastic Surgeons (bd. dirs. 1999-2006, pres. 2004-06), Am. Assn. Accreditation of Ambulatory Surg. Facilities (bd. dirs. 1995-97, 2002-, ofcl. observer to AMA ho. of dels. 1999—), Western L.A. Regional C. of C. (bd. dirs. 1981-84, 86-89, chmn. legis. action com. 1978-80), Phi Beta Kappa, Alpha Omega Alpha, Nu Sigma Nu, Phi Kappa Phi, Delta Sigma Delta, Omega Beta Pi, Phi Eta Sigma. Republican. Office: 1301 20th St # 460 Santa Monica CA 90404-2102 Office Phone: 310-829-6876. Business E-Mail: dthompso@ucla.edu.

THOMPSON, DON, food products executive; m. Elizabeth Thompson; children: Xavier, Maya. BSc in elec. engring., Purdue U. Engr. specialist, def. systems divsn. Northrop Corp., Rolling Meadows, Ill.; restaurant systems engr. McDonald's Corp., 1990—91; project mgr., 1991—93, staff dir., then dir. ops. for Denver region, 1993, regional v.p., San Diego region, 1998, sr. v.p., restaurant support officer, Midwest divsn., 1998—2000; pres., Midwest divsn. McDonald's USA, 2000—01; pres., West divsn. McDonald's Corp., 2001—04, exec. v.p. restaurant Solutions, 2004—05, exec. v.p., COO McDonald's USA, 2005—06, pres. McDonald's USA, 2006—. Office: McDonald's Corp McDonald's Plaza Oak Brook IL 60523

THOMPSON, DONALD RAYMOND, film producer, playwright; b. Long Beach, Calif., Oct. 19, 1956; s. Norman Allen and Margie Ann Thompson; m. Diana Misa Takata, June 24, 1984. BA, MA, U. Calif., LA, 1984. Dir.(prodr., writer): (films) Clouds (Best New Dir. award Bklyn. (N.Y.) Internat. Film Festival, 1999); co-prodr.: Singing The Bones (named Ofcl. Selection, Montreal (Can.) Internat. Film Festival, 2001), Through The Hollow Bamboo: Tibet In Song; author: (plays) Democracy: A Work In Progress, Tibet Does Not Exist, L.A. Book Of The Dead; co-editor: Your Life Is A Movie: The Best of SolPix, 2002-2005. Mem.: Ind. Feature Project. Democrat. Office: nextPix Productions LLC 295 Greenwich Street #348 New York NY 10007 Home Phone: 301-371-8034; Office Phone: 212-465-3125. Office Fax: 212-658-9627; Home Fax: 212-658-9627. Business E-Mail: don@nextpix.com.

THOMPSON, EARL ALBERT, economics professor; b. LA, Oct. 15, 1938; s. Hyman Harry and Sue (Field) T.; m. Velma Montoya, June 9, 1961; 1 son, Bret. BA, UCLA, 1959; MA (fellow), Harvard U., 1961, PhD, 1961. Asst. prof. econs. Stanford (Calif.) U., 1962-65, UCLA, 1965-68, assoc. prof., 1968-70, prof., 1970—. Grantee NSF, Lily Found., Found. Rsch. in Econs. and Edn. Mem. Am. Econ. Assn. Home: 6970 Los Tilos Rd Los Angeles CA 90068-3107 Office Phone: 310-825-4387. E-mail: thompson@econ.ucla.edu.

THOMPSON, EDWARD IVINS BRADBRIDGE, biological chemistry and genetics educator, endocrinologist; b. Burlington, Iowa, Dec. 20, 1933; s. Edward Bills and Lois Elizabeth (Bradbridge) T.; m. Lynn Taylor Parsons; children: Elizabeth Lynn, Edward Ernest Bradbridge. BA with distinction, Rice U., 1955; postgrad., Cambridge U., 1957-58; MD, Harvard U., 1960. Intern The Presbyn. Hosp., NYC, 1960-61, asst. resident internal medicine, 1961-62; rsch. assoc. Nat. Inst. Mental Health, NIH, Bethesda, Md., 1962-64; rsch. scientist Nat. Inst. Arthritis and Metabolic Diseases, NIH, Bethesda, Md., 1964-68, Lab of Biochemistry, Nat. Cancer Inst., NIH, Bethesda, Md., 1968-73, sect. chief, 1973-84; prof., chmn. dept. human biol. chemistry and genetics U. Tex. Med. Br., Galveston, 1984—2003, I.H. Kempner prof., 1984—2005, prof. internal medicine, 1984—, interim dir., Sealy Ctr. for Molecular Sci., 1996—2003, prof., dept. biochem. & molecular biology, 2003—, J.P. Saunders prof., 2006—. UNESCO vis. expert Inst. Genetics, Hungarian Acad. Sci., Szeged, Hungary, 1976; attending physician Nat. Naval Med. Ctr., Bethesda, 1978-80; chmn. hormones and cancer task force NIH, Bethesda, 1978-80; co-chmn. Gordon Rsch. Conf., 1980; mem. adv. com. on Biochem. and Chem. Carcinogenesis, Am. Cancer Soc., 1982-86; mem. revision com. Endocrinology adv. panel U.S. Pharmacopoeial Conv., Inc., 1980-85; mem. coun. for clin. investigation and rsch. awds., Am. Cancer Soc., 1989-93; bd. sci. overseers Pennington Nutrition Rsch. Ctr. La. State U., 1991-98; Fulbright prof., Marburg, Germany. 1992-93; mem. edn. bd. Am. Med. and Grad. Depts. Biochemistry, 1999-2003; co-organizer FASEB Summer Conf., 2006. Co-editor Gene Expression and Carcinogenesis in Cultured Liver, 1975, Steroid Receptors and the Management of Cancer, 1979, DNA: Protein Interactions and Gene Regulation; other vols. in field; assoc. editor Cancer Rsch. jour., 1976-86; corr. editor Jour. Steroid Biochemistry, 1977-85; founding editor-in-chief Molecular Endocrinology Jour., 1985-92; editor-in-chief Endocrine Reviews, 2001-05; mem. editl. bd. Steroids, 1995—, Molecular Endocrinology, 1998; sect. editor: Handbook of Cell Signalling, 2004, 05; contbr. over 250 sci. articles to profl. jours. Mem. troop com. Girl Scouts U.S., Rockville, Md., 1970-76; mem. PTA. Rockville, 1967-77, Wilderness Soc., Washington, 1964-75; initiator sci. edn. liaison program Galveston Pub. Schs., 1991; mem. pres.'s cabinet U. Tex. Med. Br. Served as med. dir. USPHS, 1962-84. Grantee NIH, Walls Rsch., Nat. Inst. Diabetes and Digestive and Kidney Diseases, Nat. Cancer Inst.; Am. Cancer Soc. scholar, 1992-93; Fulbright scholar; named Disting. alumnus Rice U., 2001; honored Signalling Life and Death Symposium, 2004; recipient J.G. Sinclair award Sigma Xi, 1997, Educator award Endocrine Soc., 2004; finalist 4th Pl. age group triathlon Sr. Olympics, 2005, fellow Am. Assn. Advi Sci., 2005. Mem.: SW Environ. Mutagen Soc., Am. Coll. Med Genetics (affiliate), Am. Soc. Microbiology, Endocrine Soc., Am. Soc. Biol. Chemists, Am. Assn. Cancer Rsch., Am. Soc. Cell Biology, Pres.'s Clubs of Rice U. and U. Tex. Med. Br., Harvard Club, Bar Harbor Yacht Club, Phi Kappa Phi, Alpha Omega Alpha, Phi Beta Kappa. Achievements include patent on anti-tumor activity of a modified fragment of glucocorticoid receptor. Office: U Tex Med Br Dept Biochem & Molecular Biology Galveston TX 77555-1068 Office Phone: 409-772-3367. Business E-Mail: bthompso@utmb.edu.

THOMPSON, ELLEN ANN, elementary school educator; b. Newton, Mass., Mar. 23, 1955; d. Arthur Malachi and Eva Louise (Harris) T.; m. John A. Rasys, Nov. 30, 1980 (div. Apr. 1987); 1 child, Christopher Michael Rasys; m. James E. Holzschuh, July 1, 1995. BS in Edn., U. Vt., 1977, MEd, 1986, postgrad. Cert. elem. tchr., spl. edn. tchr., Vt.; nat. bd. cert. tchr. early childhood generalist. Title I tchr. remedial reading grades 1-3 Colchester (Vt.) Sch. Dist., 1977-78; title I readiness rm. tchr. Union Meml Sch., Colchester, 1978-79, tchr. grade 2 transitional grade, 1979-81, classroom tchr. grades 1-3 multiage, 1981-99; adj. instr. dept. grad. edn. U. Vt., Burlington, 1987—; adj. instr. undergrad. edn. program Trinity Coll., Burlington, 1992-94. Presenter N.E. Whole Lang. Conf., Johnson (Vt.) State Coll., 1987-97, resource agt. tchr. insvc. programs Vt. Dept. Edn., 1988—, resource cons. Vt. Writing Portfolio Assessment Program, 1990—, network leader # 16, 1991-95; conf. presenter, adj. instr. Am. Inst. for Creative Edn., Augusta, Maine, 1988-92; art cons. Within the Forest, Sci. Rsch. Assocs., 1991—; ednl. cons., presenter Soc. for Devel. Edn., Peterborough, N.H.; teaching fellow regional lab. Rural Small Sch. Network, 1991-92; pres. Ellen A. Thompson, Inc., 1999—; reading lang. arts cons., Vt. Dept. Ed., 1999-2000; adj. prof. U. Vt., Undergrad. Sch. Edn., literacy cons. Reading Excellence Award Grant Program, Winooski, Vt., Gloucester, Mass., 2000—. Author: (videos) The Nuts and Bolts of Multiage Classrooms, 1994, How to Teach in a Multiage Classroom, 1994, (book) I Teach First Grade!, 2001. Recipient State Teacher of the Yr. awd., Vermont, Coun. of Chief State School Offices, 1993. Mem. ASCD, Nat. Coun. Tchrs. English (presenter 1991, 92), Internat. Reading Assn. (presenter annual conf. 1991, Leaders of Readers award 1990), Vt. Coun. on Reading (newsletter editor and conf. presenter 1988—, pres. 1991-92), Vt. Tchrs. Applying Whole Lang., Colchester Edn. Assn. (internal newsletter 1987-89, newsletter editor 1988-89, 96-98), Phi Delta Kappa. Mailing: Univ Vermont Education Dept Waterman Bldg Burlington VT 05405 Office Phone: 802-656-3356. E-mail: Ellen.Thompson@uvm.edu.

THOMPSON, EMMA, actress; b. London, Apr. 15, 1959; d. Eric Thompson and Phyllida Law; m. Kenneth Branaugh, Aug. 20, 1989 (div. Oct. 1995); m. Greg Wise, July 29, 2003, 1 child Gaia Romilly Wise. Student of English, Cambridge U., Eng. Performances include: (films) Henry V, 1989, The Tall Guy, 1989, Dead Again, 1991, Impromptu, 1991, Howard's End, 1992 (Acad. award for best actress 1993), Peter's Friends, 1992, Much Ado About Nothing, 1993, The Remains of the Day, 1993 (Acad. award nominee for best actress 1993), In the Name of the Father, 1993 (Acad. award nominee for best supporting actress 1993), My Father, the Hero, 1994, Junior, 1994, Carrington, 1995 (Best Actress award Nat. Bd. Rev. 1995), Sense and Sensibility, 1995 (Golden Globe award nominee for best actress in film 1996, Acad. award nominee for best actress 1996), Winter Guest, 1996, Primary Colors, 1998, Judas Kiss, 1998, Maybe Baby, 2000, Treasure Planet (voice), 2002, Love Actually, 2003, Imagining Argentina, 2003, Harry Potter and the Prisoner of Azbakan, 2004, Nanny McPhee, 2005, Stranger Than Fiction, 2006; (TV films) Al Fresco, Up For Grabs (a.k.a. Sexually Transmitted), Tutti Frutti, Fortunes of War, 1987, Cheers, 1991, Wit, 2001; (miniseries) Angels in America, 2003; (London stage) Me and My Girl, Look Back in Anger; also writer screen adaptation: Sense and Sensibility (Jane Austin), 1995 (Best Screenplay award N.Y. Film Critics 1995, L.A. Film Critics 1995, Boston Film Critics 1995, Golden Globe award for best adapted screenplay 1996, Acad. award for best adapted screenplay 1996, BAFTA Best Actress award 1996), Nanny McPhee, 2005. Active in Footlights Theatrical Group, Cambridge, Eng. Office: William Morris Agy 151 S El Camino Dr Beverly Hills CA 90212-2775 *

THOMPSON, EUGENE CEBRON, III, lawyer; b. Warsaw, NC, Feb. 15, 1936; s. Eugene Cebron and Lydia (Briscoe) T.; m. Mary Sue Kennedy, Mar. 30, 1969; children: Eugene Cebron IV, Kennedy Lee. AB in Econs., U. N.C., 1959; JD, Wake Forest U., 1966. Bar: N.C. 1966, U.S. Dist. Ct. (ea. dist.) 1967. Ptnr. Thompson & Mikitka, Warsaw, 1966—. Served to capt. USMC, 1959-63. Mem. ABA, N.C. Bar Assn. (sec., treas. 1971-72), Duplin County Bar Assn. (v.p. 1969, pres. 2003), Am. Trial Lawyers Assn., N.C. Trial Lawyers Assn., N.C. Mcpl. Attys. Assn. (bd. dirs. 1973-75, v.p. 1976, state pres. 1977). Methodist. Avocations: skiing, handball, tennis, swimming, coaching. Home: 714 Forrest Rd Warsaw NC 28398-2211

THOMPSON, EWA M., foreign language educator; b. Kaunas, Lithuania; came to U.S., 1963; d. Jozef and Maria Majewski; m. James R. Thompson. BA in English and Russian, U. Warsaw, Poland, 1963; MFA in Piano, Sopot Conservatory Music, 1963; MA in English, Ohio U., 1964; PhD in Comparative Lit., Vanderbilt U., 1967. Instr. Vanderbilt U., Nashville, Tenn., 1964-67; asst. prof. Ind. State U., Terre Haute, 1967-68, Ind. U., 1968-70, Rice U., Houston, 1967-73, assoc. prof., 1974-79, prof., 1979—, chair, 1987-90; assoc. prof. U. Va., Charlottesville, 1973-74. Cons. NEH, 1973—, The John D. and Catherine T. MacArthur Found., The John Simon Guggenheim Found., U.S. Dept. Edn.; vis. cons. Tex. A&M U.; seminar dir. NEH Summer Inst., Southeastern La. U., 1990; chair Russian lit. conf. Rice U., 1989; lectr. various colls. and univs. Author: Russian Formalism and Anglo-American New Criticism: A Comparative Study, 1971, Witold Gombrowicz, 1979, Polish transl., 2002, Understanding Russia: The Holy Fool in Russian Culture, 1987, Chinese transl. 1995, 2nd Chinese edit. 1998, The Search for Self-Definition in Russian Literature, 1991, Imperial Knowledge: Russian Literature and Colonialism, 2000, Polish transl., 2000, Ukrainian transl., 2006; editor the Sarmatian Rev., 1988—; contbr. articles to profl. jours., chpts. to books. Recipient Silver Thistle award Houston's Scottish Heritage Found, 1988; Mellon grantee, 1990, Rice U. grantee, 1990, Internat. Rsch. and Exchanges Sr. Scholar grantee, 1991; Hoover Inst. fellow, 1988; Vanderbilt U. scholar, 1964-67, Will Herberg award, ISI, 2003. Roman Catholic. Personal E-mail: sarmatianreview@yahoo.com.

THOMPSON, FRANCES MCBROOM, mathematics professor, writer; BS in Edn., Abilene Christian U., Tex., 1963; MA, U. Tex., Austin, 1967; EdD, U. Ga., Athens, 1973. Math. cons., tchr., 1963—84; math. prof. Tex. Woman's U., Denton, 1984—. Author: (tchr. resource books) Hands on Math for Grades 4-8, 1994, Hands on Algebra for Grades 7-12, 1998, Math Proficiency Lessons and Activities, Fourth Grade, 2003, Math Essentials, Middle School Level, 2005, Math Essentials, High School Level, 2005, Math Essentials, Elementary School Level, 2007. Bible class coord.; tchr., 1982—95. Recipient Mary Mason Lyon Jr. Faculty award, Tex. Woman's U., 1992, Alumni Citation for achievement, Abilene Christian U., 1998, Grover C. Morlan Outstanding Educator award, 2005, Distinction in Svc. award, Tex. Woman's U., 2006. Mem.: Rsch. Coun. for Math. Learning, Tex. Coun. Tchrs. Math., Tex. Assn. Suprs. Math., Math. Assn. Am., Nat. Coun. Tchrs. Math. Office: Tex Woman's U PO Box 425886 Denton TX 76204-5886 Home Phone: 972-681-4184; Office Phone: 940-898-2157. Business E-Mail: fthompson@twu.edu.

THOMPSON, FRANK JOSEPH, political science professor; b. New Ulm, Minn., Mar. 21, 1944; s. Joseph Mariem and Alice Louise (Lindquist) T.; m. Benna Miriam, June 15, 1944; children: Samuel, Aliza, Elizabeth. BA in Polit. Sci., U. Chgo., 1966; MA in Polit. Sci., U. Calif., Berkeley, 1967, PhD in Polit. Sci., 1973. Asst. prof. polit. sci. Calif. State U., Long Beach, 1971-72; asst. prof. U. Ga., Athens, 1972-78, assoc. prof., 1978-83, prof., 1983-88, head dept., 1982-87; prof. pub. adminstrn., policy, polit. sci. and pub. health SUNY, Albany, 1987—, dean Grad. Sch. of Pub. Affairs, 1988—97, assoc. provost, 1990-97, interim provost, 1998—2000; dean Rockefeller Coll., 2000—. Analyst HEW, Washington, 1968, City Govt. Oakland, Calif., 1968-71; cons. USPHS, 1976-79, 82, U.S. Pres.'s Commn. for Nat. Agenda for 80's, 1980, Am. Pub. Welfare Assn., 1981-83; publ. cons. U.S. Adv. Commn. on Intergovtl. Rels., 1983; mem. task force on exec. and mgmt. devel. U.S. Office Pers. Mgmt., 1990; exec. dir. Nat. Commn. on the State and Local Pub. Svc., 1991-97. Author: Personnel Policy in the City, 1975, Health Policy and the Bureaucracy, 1981, Public Administration: Challenges, Choices, Consequences, 1990; editor: Classics of Public Personnel Policy, 1979, 3d edit., 2003, Revitalizing State and Local Public Service, 1993, Medicaid and Devolution: A View from the States, 1998; contbr. articles to profl. jours. Bd. dirs. Upper Hudson Planned Parenthood, 1990-96, Albany-Tula Alliance, 1998-2003. Pub. adminstrn. fellow U.S. Pub. Health Service, 1975-76, NSF fellow, 1970-71; recipient Simon award Internat. Jour. Pub. Adminstrn., 1981. Fellow Nat. Acad. Pub. Adminstrn.; mem. Assn. for Pub. Policy Analysis and Mgmt., Am. Soc. for Pub. Adminstrn. (publs. com. 1982-84, William E. Mosher award 1983), Am. Polit. Sci. Assn. (chmn. departmental services com. 1985-87, exec. com. sect. pub. adminstrn. 1985-87, 89, 91, 96—98, chair sect. pub. adminstrn. 1990-91, chair Gaus award com. 1991-92), Nat. Assn. Schs. Pub. Affairs and Adminstrn. (peer rev. com. 1984-86, 1st chmn. commn. on peer rev. and accreditation 1986-87, chmn. task force on revitalizing the pub. svc., v.p. 1990-91, pres. 1991-92, chmn. com. advancement of pub. adminstrn. 1996-98), N.Y. State Acad. Pub. Adminstrn. (bd. dirs. 1994—98). Home: 9 Harvard Ave Albany NY 12208-2019 Office: SUNY Rockefeller Coll Milne 102 Albany NY 12222-0001 E-mail: thompson@albany.edu.

THOMPSON, FRANKIE MAZIE, school psychologist; b. Montgomery County, Ga., Dec. 17, 1944; d. Freeman Franklin and Emmer May Fountain Thompson; children: Ursula Fran Tyson, Elizabeth Louise Boswell. BS in Edn., Ga. So. U., 1966, MEd, 1970, EdS, 1972; postgrad., U. S.C., 1987, Valdosta State U., 2004. Lic. sch. psychology Ga., sch. counselor Ga., spl. edn. tchr. Ga., dir. spl. edn. Ga., gifted edn. Ga. Tchr. mid. grades Savannah Christian Sch., Ga., 1966—67; tchr. reading Baxterville Attendance Ctr., Miss., 1967—68; tchr. mid. grades math. Petal Jr. HS, 1968—69; head resident counselor Ga. So. U., Statesboro, 1969—72; tchr. of gifted, counselor Wadley HS, Ga., 1972—76; tchr. spl. edn. S. Madison Mid. Sch., Colbert, 1978—79, Brookley Mid. Sch., 1976—78; tchr. h.s. spl. edn. Appling County HS, Baxley, 1979—81; tchr. spl. edn. Claxton HS, 1981—86, Glennville Mid. Sch., 1986—91, Hinesville Mid. Sch., 1991—96; sch. psychologist Liberty County Sch. Sys., Hinesville, 1996—98; sch. psychologist dept. def. Diamond Elem. Sch., Ft. Stewart, 1998—. Author: (bi-weekly newspaper column) Frankly Speaking (Outstanding Educators of Am. award, 1972). Ct.-apptd. spl. advocate CASA, Hinesville, 2006. Named Tchr. of Yr., Glennville Mid. Sch., 1988. Mem.: NEA (life), Ga. Assn. of Educators (life), First Families of Ga. (life; libr. gen. 1992—2000). Methodist. Avocations: Scrabble competitions, sewing, gardening, travel, cooking. Home: 815 Barrington Dr Hinesville GA 31313

Office: Diamond Elem Dept Def 482 Davis Avenue Fort Stewart GA 31315 Office Phone: 912-876-5798. Office Fax: 912-876-8350. Personal E-mail: fmthompson84@coastalnow.net. E-mail: frankie.thompson@am.dodea.edu.

THOMPSON, FRED DALTON, actor, former senator; b. Sheffield, Ala., Aug. 19, 1942; s. Fletcher and Ruth Thompson; m. Sarah Elizabeth Lindsey, Sept. 12, 1959; children: Tony, Daniel, Elizabeth Betsy Panici(dec.); m. Jeri Kahn, June 29, 2002; 1 child, Hayden Victoria. BS, Memphis State U., 1964; JD, Vanderbilt U., 1967. Asst. U.S. atty. (mid. dist.) Tenn. US Dept. Justice, 1969-72; minority counsel US Senate Select Com. on Presdl. Campaign Activities (Watergate Com.), 1973-74; pvt. practice, 1975-94; spl. counsel to Gov. State of Tenn., 1980; spl. counsel US Senate Fgn. Rels. Coms., 1980—81, US Senate Intelligence Com., 1982; atty. Arent, Fox, Kintner, Plotkin & Kahn, 1991-94; US Senator from Tenn., 1994—2003. Chmn., US Senate Govtl. Affairs Com., 1997-2001; vis. fellow Am. Enterprise Inst., mem. US-China Econ. & Security Review Commn. Actor: (films) Marie: A True Story, 1985, No Way Out, 1987, Feds, 1988, Fat Man and Little Boy, 1989, The Hunt for Red October, 1990, Days of Thunder, 1990, Die Hard 2: Die Harder, 1990, Flight of the Intruder,1991, Class Action, 1991, Necessary Roughness, 1991, Curly Sue, 1991, Cape Fear, 1991, Aces: Iron Eagle III, 1992, Thunderheart, 1992, White Sands, 1992, Born Yesterday, 1993, In the Line of Fire, 1993, Baby's Day Out, 1994, Download This, 2002, (voice only) Racing Stripes, 2005; (TV movies) Unholy Matrimony, 1988, Bed of Lies, 1992, Stay the Night, 1992, Day-O, 1992, Keep the Change, 1992, Barbarians at the Gate, 1993,(voice only) Rachel and Andrew Jackson: A Love Story, 2001, Evil Knieval, 2004, Looking for Comedy in the Muslim World, 2005; (TV series) Law & Order, 2002-07; (TV appearances) Wiseguy, 1988, China Beach, 1989, Roseanne, 1989, Matlock, 1989, Sex & the City, 2000, Law & Order: Special Victims Unit, 2003-2006, Law & Order: Trial By Jury 2005-2006, Law & Order: Criminal Intent, 2005, Conviction 2006; author: At That Point in Time: The Inside Story of the Senate Watergate Committee, 1975. Mem.: Coun. Fgn. Rels. Republican. Address: PO Box 143 Hermitage TN 37076-0143 *

THOMPSON, G. KENNEDY (KEN THOMPSON), bank executive; b. Rocky Mount, NC, Nov. 25, 1950; s. Maynard and Stacy Kennedy Thompson; m. Kathylee B. Thompson; 3 children. BA in Am. Studies, U.N.C., Chapel Hill, 1973; MBA, Wake Forest U., 1975. With First Union Corp., Charlotte, NC, 1976—, head S.E. divsn., mgr. mid. market dept., mgr. N.Y. loan prodn. office, pres. First Union-Ga., sr. v.p., head human resources, pres. First Union-Fla., vice chmn. corp., head global capital markets, 1998—99, pres., CEO, 1999—2001, Wachovia Corp. (merger of First Union and Wachovia Corp.), 2001—, chmn., 2001—. Bd. dirs. Hewlett Packard Co., 2006-, N.Y. Clearing House; mem. Fin. Services Roundtable Fin. Svcs. Forum, chmn.-elect. Bd. visitors U. N.C., Chapel Hill, Babcock Grad. Sch. Mgmt., Wake Forest U.; bd. dirs. N.C. Blumenthal Performing Arts Ctr., Charlotte Latin Sch., United Way, Charlotte, Teach for Am., Carolinas Healthcare Sys., Charlotte Inst. Tech. Innovation; mem. met. bd. YMCA Morehead scholar U. N.C. Office: Wachovia Corp 301 S College St Charlotte NC 28288 *

THOMPSON, GEORGE ALBERT, geophysicist, educator; b. Swissvale, Pa., June 5, 1919; s. George Albert Sr. and Maude Alice (Harkness) T.; m. Anita Kimmell, July 20, 1944; children: Albert J., Dan A., David C. BS, Pa. State U., 1941; MS, MIT, 1942; PhD, Stanford U., 1949. Registered profl. geophysicist Calif., profl. geologist Calif. Geologist, geophysicist U.S. Geol. Survey, Menlo Park, Calif., 1942-49; asst. prof. Stanford (Calif.) U., 1949-55, assoc. prof., 1955-60, prof. geophysics, 1960—, chmn. geophysics dept., 1967-86, chmn. geology dept., 1979-82, Otto N. Miller prof. earth scis., 1980-89, dean sch. earth scis., 1987-89. Part-time geologist U.S. Geol. Survey, Menlo Park, 1949-76; cons. adv. com. on reactor safeguards Nuclear Regulation Commn., Washington, 1974-94; mem. bd. earth sci. NRC, 1986-88, vice chmn. Yucca Mountain Hydrology-tectonics panel NRC, 1990-92; mem. exec. com. Inc. Rsch. Inst. for Seismology, Washington, 1990-92; mem. sr. external events rev. com. Lawrence Livermore Nat. Lab., 1989-93; mem. Coun. on Continental Sci. Drilling, 1990-94; cons. Los Alamos Nat. Lab. on volcano-tectonic processes, 1993-96, S.W. Rsch. Inst., 1993; chair com. to review sci. issues NRC, Ward Valley, Calif., 1994-95, 2004-; mem. panel on probabalistic volcanic hazard analysis Geomatrix Cons., Inc., 1995-96, 2005— Author over 100 research papers. With USN, 1944—46. Recipient John Wesley Powell award US Geol. Survey, 1999; NSF postdoctoral fellow, 1956-57, Guggenheim Found. fellow, 1963-64 Fellow AAAS, Geol. Soc. Am. (coun. mem. 1983-86, George P. Woollard award 1983, v.p. 1995, pres. 1996), Am. Geophys. Union; mem. NAS (chair geology sect. 2000-03), Seismol. Soc. Am., Soc. Exploration Geophysicists. Avocation: forestry. Home: 421 Adobe Pl Palo Alto CA 94306-4501 Office: Stanford U Geophysics Dept Stanford CA 94305-2215 Home Phone: 650-493-3230; Office Phone: 650-723-3714. Business E-Mail: thompson@pangea.stanford.edu.

THOMPSON, GEORGE FLETCHER, editor, publishing executive; b. Denver, Jan. 4, 1954; s. Richard Potter and Alasee Payne Thompson; m. Cynthia Ann Roberts, Sept. 2, 1978; 1 child, Haley Ellen. Student, U. Pa., Phila., 1971—73; BA in English, U. Ala., 1977; MA in Landscape Architecture, U. Wis., Madison, 1990. Acquisitions editor Johns Hopkins U. Press, Balt., 1984—89; founder and pres. Ctr. for Am. Places, Santa Fe and Staunton, Va., 1990—2007; dir. Ctr. Am. Places Columbia Coll., 2007—. Editor: Landscape in America (Notable Book of 1995); co-editor: Ecological Design and Planning, 1997, 2007; co-author: Registered Places of New Mexico, 1995, Beyond the Great Divide, 1992; editor, curator: Chicago Portfolio: Where Geography and Photography Meet, 2006. Recipient Publs. award, Assn. Am. Geographers, 2000, Publs. citation, Vernacular Architecture Forum, 2002, Comms. award, Coun. Educators in Landscape Architecture, 2005. Mem.: Sigma Lamda Alpha. Independent. Avocations: reading, gardening, travel, photography, music. Office: Columbia Coll Chgo 600 S Michigan Ave Chicago IL 60605-1996 Office Phone: 540-885-1180. Office Fax: 540-886-5263. Business E-Mail: editors@americanplaces.org.

THOMPSON, GEORGE LEE, retail executive, consultant; b. Denver, June 12, 1933; s. George H. and Frances M. (Murphy) Thompson; m. Patricia M. Mackenzie, Sept. 25, 1993; children: Shannon, Tracy, Bradley. BS in Bus., U. Colo., 1957; degree in Advanced Mgmt., NYU, 1969. With GTE Sylvania, Danvers, Mass., 1957-65, nat. sales mgr., 1965-67, mktg. mgr., 1967-68; v.p. sales entertainment products Batavia, NY, 1968-73; dir. corp. mktg. Stamford, Conn., 1973-74; v.p. mktg. Servomation Corp., NYC, 1974-76, exec. v.p., 1976-78, Singer Co., Edison, NJ, 1978-81, pres., 1981-83; pres. consumer products SCM Corp., NYC, 1983-86; pres., CEO Smith-Corona Corp., New Canaan, Conn., 1986-89, chmn., CEO, 1989-95; chmn. Mackenzie-Thompson Assocs., Essex, Conn., 1995—. Bd. dirs. Vol. Products, Inc.; chair Sweet P's, Essex, Conn., 1998—; dir. Conn. State Tourism Coun., 2003-. Chmn. Standards Com. U.S. Dept. Commerce; mem. bus. alumni adv. coun. U. Colo., 1989—94; mem. bd. overseers Sch. Bus. U. Conn., 1993—96; mem. Pres.'s Export Coun., 1991—93; mem. bd. advisors Jr. League; vice chmn. Essex Econ. Devel. Commn., Conn., 2003—; chmn. Main Street renovation com. City of Essex; bd. dirs. Internat. Tennis Hall of Fame, Am. Jr. Golf Found., 1986—89, Am. Jr. Golf Assn., 1986—2000, United Way of New Canaan, 1989—93; pres. Essex Bd. Trade, 2005—. Recipient Disting. Bus. Alumni award, U. Colo., 1990. Mem. Computer and Bus. Equipment Mfg. Assn. (bd. dirs. 1992-94), Sales and Mktg. Execs. Internat. (trustee), Am. Mgmt. Assn. (trustee, exec. com. chmn., gen. mgmt. coun. 1989-99), St. John Assn. (bd. dirs., pres. 1983-93), Woodway Country Club, Club at Seabrook Island, Wilton Riding Club (bd. govs. 1980-83), Navesink Country Club (bd. govs. 1983-86), Harbour Ridge Yacht and Country Club, Essex Yacht Club, Chi Psi. Episcopalian. Office: Mackenzie Thompson Assocs 51 Main St Essex CT 06426-1150 also: Sweet P's LLC Griswold Sq Essex CT 06426 Home Phone: 860-767-8201. Personal E-mail: leethompson51@sbcglobal.net.

THOMPSON, GERALDINE KELLEHER RICHTER, retired orthopedist; b. Tokyo, Aug. 22, 1948; (parents Am. citizens); d. Edward Elkins and Marguerite Geraldine Kelleher; m. Wayne Wray Thompson, Dec. 30, 2000; m. Paul S. Richter (div.); children: Karl Kelleher Richter, Brian Kelleher Richter, Kelly Kelleher Richter. BA with high honors, Wellesley Coll., Mass., 1969; MD, Georgetown U., Washington, 1973. Intern internal medicine Georgetown U. Hosp., Washington, 1973—74, residency orthop. surgery, 1974—78; pvt. practice orthop. surgery Fairfax and Manassas, Va., 1978—2002; assoc. prof. orthop. surgery Georgetown U., Washington, 1978—2002; fellow Am. Acad. Orthop. Surgery, 1981—2001. Pres. Prince William Med. Soc., 1999—2000. Parent leader Boy Scouts Am., 1990—99; mem. parents assn. St. Albans Sch., Washington, Nat. Cathedral Sch. Girls. Fellow: Am. Acad. Orthop. Surgeons; mem.: Wellesley Literary Cir., AOA, Sigma Xi, Phi Beta Kappa. Avocations: art history, literature, cultural history, history of medicine. Home: 2720 N Quincy St Arlington VA 22207-5055 *three successful children-Karl 27- St. Albans and MIT, capt. MIT crew team - current micro chip analysts San Francisco; Brian 24, MS fron UCSD-internat. econs. and Asian studies, currently at Fed Reserve; Kelly 21 will graduate from U. Chgo. this June in three years Dean's List plans to go in to med. sch.*

THOMPSON, GORDON, JR., federal judge; b. San Diego, Dec. 28, 1929; s. Gordon and Garnet (Meese) T.; m. Jean Peters, Mar. 17, 1951; children— John M., Peter Renwick, Gordon III. Grad., U. So. Calif., 1951, Southwestern U. Sch. Law, Los Angeles, 1956. Bar: Calif. 1956. With Dist. Atty.'s Office, County of San Diego, 1957-60; partner firm Thompson & Thompson, San Diego, 1960-70; U.S. dist. judge So. Dist. Calif., San Diego, 1970—, chief judge, 1984-91, sr. judge, 1994—. Mem. ABA, Am. Bd. Trial Advocates, San Diego County Bar Assn. (v.p. 1970), San Diego Yacht Club, Delta Chi. Office: US Dist Ct 940 Front St San Diego CA 92101-8994

THOMPSON, GREGORY LEE, social sciences educator; b. Huntington Park, Calif., June 14, 1946; s. Karl Windsor and Virginia Alice (Hanna) T. AB in Geography, U. Calif., Davis, 1968; M of City Planning, U. Calif., Berkeley, 1970; PhD in Social Scis., U. Calif., Irvine, 1987. Transp. planner City of Edmonton (Alberta) Transit Sys., 1970-72; transp. analyst Can. Transport Commn., Ottawa, Ontario, 1972-73; transp. coord. City of Berkeley (Calif.) Planning Dept., 1973-74; sr. transp. planner San Diego County, 1974-77, Met. Transp. Devel. Bd., San Diego, 1977-80; sr. cons. Mass Transit, Calif. Assembly, Sacramento, 1980-81; rsch. fellow Hagley Mus. & Libr., Wilmington, Del., 1987-88; asst. prof. Fla. State U., Tallahassee, 1988-94, assoc. prof., 1994—2003, prof., 2003—. Author: The Passenger Train in the Motor Age: California 1910-1941, 1993; contbr. articles to profl. jours. Organizer, pres. Citizens of Rail Calif., San Diego, 1976—80. Named Advanced Rsch. fellow Andrew W. Mellon/NEH, 1987-88, Disting. Student scholar Sch. Engring. U. Calif., Irvine, 1983. Mem. Am. Planning Assn. (sect. dir. San Diego), Soc. for History of Technology, Econ. History Assn., Bus. History Assn., Planning History Assn., Am. Inst. Cert. Planners. Democrat. Avocations: photography, swimming. Home: 418 E Georgia St Tallahassee FL 32301 Office: Fla State U Dept Urban Regional Pl Tallahassee FL 32306 Office Phone: 850-644-8514.

THOMPSON, HAROLD LEE, lawyer; b. Dayton, Ohio, Feb. 17, 1945; s. Harold Edward Thompson and Johnita Dorothy (Cox) Metcalf; children: Aishah T., Aliya S. BS in Acctg., Cen. State U., Wilberforce, Ohio, 1967; JD, U. Conn., 1972. Bar: Ohio 1975, US Dist. Ct. (so. dist.) Ohio 1975, DC 1976, US Ct. Appeals (4th cir.) 1990, US Supreme Ct. Acct. Communication Satellite Corp., 1968-69; atty. Ohio State Legal Service, Columbus, Ohio, 1972-74; of counsel Ohio Indsl. Commn., Columbus, 1974-76; sole practice Columbus, 1976—; ptnr. Jones & Thompson, Columbus, 1984-88; prin. H. Lee Thompson Co. L.P.A., Columbus, 1988—; pres. toys and clothing H. Lee Toy Co., Columbus, 1988—. Adj. prof. law Columbus State Coll., 1989; instr. Acad. Ct. Reporting, 1989; adj. prof. tax and prins. of acctg. Bliss Coll., 1990-91. 2nd v.p. NAACP, Columbus, Ohio. Reginald Heber Smith fellow U.S. Fed. Ct., 1972. Mem. Inst. (exec. mem. birth trauma litig. group), Ohio Bar Assn., Am. Coll. Legal Medicine, Ohio Acad. Trial Lawyers (trustee, mem. exec. com.), Am. Bd. Forensic Examiners, Franklin County Trial Lawyers Assn., Trial Lawyers Pub. Justice, Am. Assn. for Justice (chair profl. negligence sect. 2000), Frontiers Internat., Univ. Club, Columbus Met. Club. Roman Catholic. Avocations: reading, music, jogging. Office: 85 E Gay St Ste 810 Columbus OH 43215-3118 Office Phone: 614-461-9000. Personal E-mail: thomlaw@msn.com.

THOMPSON, HERBERT ALDEN, microbiologist, public health scientist; s. Otto Anous and Carmen Louise Thompson; m. Donna Rae Burrhus, June 13, 1964; 1 child, Bradley Alden. BA, Drake U., Des Moines, 1964; MA, Drake U., 1966; PhD, U. Kans., Lawrence, 1971. From asst. to full prof. W.Va. U., Morgantown, 1976—2000; microbiologist Ctrs. for Disease Control and Prevention, Atlanta, 2000—02, chief viral and rickettsial zoonoses br., 2002—06; retired, 2006. Contbr. articles to profl. jours. Pres., treas., newsletter editor Trout Unlimited, Morgantown, 1982—88. Named Outstanding Tchr., W.Va. U., 1980; recipient MacLachlan award, W.Va. U. Sch. Medicine; grantee, NIH, 1997—99, NSF, 1980—86. Mem.: Am. Biol. Safety Assn. (corr.), Am. Soc. Rickettsiology (corr.), Soc. Gen. Microbiology (corr.), Sigma Xi (corr.). Avocations: physical fitness, physical rehabilitation, fly fishing, carpentry, astronomy.

THOMPSON, HOLLEY MARKER, lawyer, consultant, marketing professional; b. Jamestown, NY, Jan. 30, 1947; d. Burdette James and Mary Marker; m. Lawrence D. Thompson; children: Jennifer Kristen Simos, Kendra Elise Blair, Jennifer Lynn, Stephanie Lynn. AAS, Jamestown C.C., 1966; BS, Ohio U., 1969; MA, W.Va. U., 1974, JD, 1980. Bar: W.Va. 1980, U.S. Dist. Ct. (so. dist.) W.Va. 1980, Pa. 1982, U.S. Dist. Ct. (we. dist.) Pa. 1982. Tchr. math. various pub. schs., Santa Ana (Calif.), Lakewood (NY) and Morgantown (W.Va.), 1970-77; atty. for students W.Va. U., Morgantown, 1980; assoc. libr., lectr. W.Va. U. Coll. Law, Morgantown, 1980-83; assoc., libr. Jackson, Kelly, Holt & O'Farrell, Charleston, W.Va., 1983-86; cons. Hildebrandt, Inc., Somerville, NJ, 1986—94; sr. v.p. mktg. and preference markets LexisNexis, Dayton, Ohio, 1994—2006; ptnr. Sterling Group 925, Springboro, Ohio, 2006—. Spkr. in field. Contbr. articles to profl. jours. Mem.: Am. Assn. Law Librs., Phi Delta Phi. Business E-Mail: holleymthompson@tsg925.com.

THOMPSON, HORACE A., III, (TOPPER THOMPSON), commissioner, lawyer; b. New Orleans, 1942; m. Susan Thompson; children: Clarke, Jeffery. BA, Tulane U., 1965, JD, 1968. Bar: La. 1968, Miss. 1998, Ark. 1988, U.S. Ct. Appeals (5th cir.) 1979, U.S. Supreme Ct. 1977, U.S. Dist. Ct. (ea., we. and mid. dists.) La. 1968. Adminstrv. leader labor and employment law sect. Jones, Walker, Waechter, Poitevent, Carrere & Denegre LLP; founding ptnr. McCalla, Thompson, Pyburn, Hymowitz & Shapiro, LLP, 1976—2001; ptnr., co-chair labor and employment law practice group Watkins Ludlam Winter & Stennis, P.A., 2001—06; commr. Occupational Safety and Health Rev. Commn., Washington, 2006—. Fellow: Am. Coll. Labor Rels. and Employment Lawyers; mem.: ABA, La. Bar Assn., Miss. Bar Assn., New Orleans Met. Safety Coun., La. Assn. Bus. and Industry, La. Restaurant Assn. Office: One Lafayette Ctr 1120 20th St 9th Fl Washington DC 20036-3457 Office Phone: 202-606-5390, 228-864-3094. Office Fax: 202-606-5050, 228-864-0516. E-mail: tthompson@watkinsludlam.com.

THOMPSON, HUGH P., state supreme court justice; b. Montezuma, Ga., July 7, 1943; married; 2 children. JD, Mercer U., 1969. Bar: Ga. 1970. Pvt. practice, Milledgeville, Ga., 1970—71; judge Recorder's Ct. of Milledgeville, 1971—79, Baldwin County Ct., 1973—78, Superior Ct. of Ga., 1979—94; chief judge Ocmulgee Jud. Cir., 1987—94; justice Ga. Supreme Ct., Atlanta, 1994—. Instr. bus. law Ga. Coll., 1971—72; pres. Coun. Superior Ct. Judges, 1993—94. Communicant St. Stephen's Episcopal Ch. Named Outstanding Young Man of Baldwin County, 1972; recipient Disting. Svc. award, Baldwin County Jaycees, 1972, Outstanding Alumnus award, Mercer U. Law Sch., 1994, Disting. Svc. award, Ga. Coll. and State U., 2002. Mem.: ABA, Bleckley Inn of Ct., Ga. Bar Found., State Bar Ga., Charles Longstreet Weltner Family Law Inn of Ct., Old War Horse Lawyers Club, Lawyers Club Atlanta. Avocations: hunting, gardening, golf, fishing. Office: Supreme Ct Ga State Judicial Bldg 244 Washington St SW Rm 572 Atlanta GA 30334-9007 *

THOMPSON, J. ANDY, bank executive; b. Ft. Worth, Sept. 21, 1943; s. Fredrick Dickson and Mary Alice (Rhea) T.; m. Nancy Sealy, Jan. 15, 1966; children: J. Andrew Jr., Christopher Sealy. BBA, U. Tex., 1965. Exec. v.p. Internat. Svc. Ins. Co., Ft. Worth, 1968-83, Ctrl. Bancorp. Inc., Ft. Worth, 1984-86, pres., 1986-88, chmn., chief exec. officer, 1988-97, Cen. Bank & Trust, Ft. Worth, 1988-97, North Ft. Worth Bank, 1988-92. Adv. bd. Policy Mgmt. Systems, Columbia, S.C., 1975-83; bd. dirs. Ft. Worth C. of C., 1989-91; chmn., trustee Tex. Health Resources. Mem. adminstrv. bd. First Meth. Ch.; trustee, chmn. Harris Meth. Hosp., Ft. Worth, Harris Meth. Health System, Harris Meth. Health Found.; bd. dirs. Lena Pope Home for Children, James L. West Presbyn. Spl. Care Ctr.; vice chair Ft. Worth Mus. Sci. & History; bd. trustees Lean Pope Home Found. Capt. U.S. Army, 1966-68, Vietnam. Mem. Tex. Banker's Assn., Am. Banker's Assn., Ft. Worth Club (pres. 1993-96, mem. bd. govs.), Rotary Internat. Republican. Methodist. Avocations: tennis, sailing, golf.

THOMPSON, JACK EDWARD, mining company executive; b. Central City, Nebr., Nov. 17, 1924; s. Ray Elbert and Bessie Fay (Davis) T.; m. Maria del Carmen Larrea, May 8, 1948; children: Jack Edward, Ray Anthony, Robert Davis. Student, Northwestern U., 1942-43, Colo. Sch. Mines, 1943-45, D of Engring. (hon.), 1993. V.p. Cía. Química Comercial de Cuba S.A., 1946-60, Cía. de Fomento Químico S.A., 1946-60; with Newmont Mining Corp., NYC, 1960-86, asst. to pres., 1964-67, v.p., 1967-71, dir., 1969-86, exec. v.p., 1971-74, pres., 1974-85, vice chmn., 1985-86, cons., 1986-90. Chmn. bd. trustees Minerals Industry Ednl. Found. Recipient Distinguished Achievement medal Colo. Sch. Mines, 1974 Mem. AIME, Mining and Metall. Soc. Am., Mining Found. of S.W. (past pres., bd. govs.), Tucson Country Club. E-mail: rayonera@aol.com.

THOMPSON, JAMES ALEXANDER, JR., lawyer; b. Providence, July 18, 1945; s. James Alexander and Agnes Florence (Bainton) T.; m. Cheryl Ann Martin, Mar. 6, 1971; children: Scott Alexander, Jeffrey Martin. BA, U. Pa., 1967; JD, George Washington U., 1973. Bar: Mass. 1974, D.C. 1983, Conn. 1989. Atty.-advisor Region 1 U.S. EPA, Boston, 1974-76, asst. regional counsel Region 1, 1976-79, regional counsel Region 8 Denver, 1979-82; ptnr. Wickwire, Gavin & Gibbs, P.C., Washington, 1982-86, Pepe & Hazard, Hartford, Conn., 1986-94, LeBoeuf, Lamb, Greene & MacRae, LLP, Conn., 1994—. Mem. exec. com. LeBoeuf, Lamb, Greene & MacRae, LLP, co-chmn. nat. and internat. environ. health and safety practice group. Contbg. author: Environmental Law and Planning, 1973. Soccer coach Hartwell Sports Club, Glastonbury, Conn., 1986—89; basketball coach Youth Basketball Assn., Glastonbury, 1990; chmn. bd. trustees Talcott Mountain Sci. Ctr., Avon, Conn., 1991—2003. 1st lt. US Army, 1969—73. Mem. ABA (natural resources sect.), Conn. Bar Assn. (environ. quality sect.). Avocations: running, skiing, tennis, architecture. Office Phone: 860-293-3507. Office Fax: 860-293-3555. Business E-Mail: jthompso@llgm.com.

THOMPSON, JAMES E., lawyer; BA, U. Mich., 1983, JD, 1986. Bar: Ill., DC. Law clk. stagiaire Court of Justice of European Communities, Luxembourg; atty. Jones, Day, Reavis & Pogue, 1987—95; chief legal officer innovations bus. unit Alticor, Inc., assoc. gen. counsel internat. legal dept.; group v.p., gen. counsel, sec. McLeodUSA Inc.; sr. v.p., gen. counsel, sec. Chiquita Brands Internat., Inc., 2006—. Office: Chiquita Brands Internat Inc Chiquita Ctr 250 E Fifth St Cincinnati OH 45202 Office Phone: 513-784-8000. Office Fax: 513-784-8030.

THOMPSON, JAMES HOWARD, historian, librarian; b. Memphis, Aug. 20, 1934; s. Curtis Barnabas and Clara (Terry) T.; m. Margareta Ortenblad, Nov. 24, 1961; children— Ralph, Anna, Howard. BA in History, Rhodes Coll., Memphis, 1955; MA, U. N.C., Chapel Hill, 1957, PhD in History, 1961; MS in LS, U. Ill., 1963. Teaching fellow U. N.C., Chapel Hill, 1955-56, departmental asst., 1956-57, reference asst., 1959-61, dir. undergrad. library, lectr. in history, 1968-70; circulation asst. U. Ill., 1961-63; asst. Center for Russian Area and Lang. Studies, 1962-63; cataloger Duke U., 1963-65; asst. prof. history U. S.W. La., 1965-66; asst. prof. U. Colo., 1966-68; dir. libraries, prof. history U. N.C., Greensboro, 1970-94; ret., 1994. Bd. dirs. Southeastern Library Network, 1979-82, treas., 1981-82 Contbr. articles, revs. to profl. jours. Ford Found. research fellow, 1957-58; U. Colo. grantee, 1967; U. N.C. at Greensboro grantee, 1977-78, 89. Mem. Phi Beta Kappa (chpt. pres. 1979-80), Beta Phi Mu, Phi Alpha Theta, Chi Beta Phi. Episcopalian. Home: 4020 Crown Hill Dr Durham NC 27707-5393 Personal E-mail: jaytee34@earthlink.net.

THOMPSON, JAMES LEE, lawyer; b. LI, NY, Sept. 9, 1941; s. Robert Luther and Marjorie Emma (Jones) T.; m. Diana Dill Stevenson, June 29, 1963; children: James C., Thomas J. BA, Yale U., 1963; JD, U. Va., 1966. Bar: Va. 1966, Md. 1966, U.S. Ct. Mil. Appeals 1968, U.S. Dist. Ct. Md. 1972, U.S. Supreme Ct. 1978. Ptnr. Miller & Canby, Rockville, Md., 1970—, head litigation, 1975—. Mem. jud. conf. U.S. Ct. Appeals (4th cir.). Mem. Thousand Acres Assn., Deep Creek Lake, Md., 1985-87. Capt. JAGC, USMC, 1966-70. Decorated D.S.M. Fellow Am. Coll. Trial Lawyers; mem. ABA, Md. State Bar Assn. (bd. govs. 1975, 78, 79, 83, 89, 94, sec. 1995, pres. 1999-00), Montgomery County Bar Assn. (pres. 1987-88, Cert. of Merit 1985), Nat. Conf. Bar Pres., Md. Bar Found., Montgomery County Bar Found. (pres. 1988-89), Loophole Club (pres. 1978-79), Phi Delta Phi. Democrat. Episcopalian. Avocations: sailing, skiing, tennis, golf, gardening. Home: 419 Russell Ave Apt 110 Gaithersburg MD 20877-2836 Office: Miller & Canby 200 Monroe St Ste B Rockville MD 20850-4423 Home Phone: 301-216-5591; Office Phone: 301-762-5212. Business E-Mail: jlthompson@mmcanby.com.

THOMPSON, JAMES NICHOLAS, medical association administrator; b. Cin., Oct. 20, 1944; m. Carol Washburn; children: Carrie, David, Victoria, Deborah. BA, DePauw U., 1966; MD, Ohio State U., 1971. Lic. otolaryngologist NC, diplomate Am. Bd. Otolaryngology. Intern Mercy Hosp., Pitts., 1971—72, resident in gen. surgery, 1972—73, resident in otolaryngology, 1973—76; fellow in otolaryngology U. Calif., Irvine, 1976—77; asst. prof. surg. scis., otolaryngology Bowman Gray Sch Medicine, Winston-Salem, NC, 1979—81, assoc. prof. surg. scis., otolaryngology, 1981—88, dep. assoc. dean, 1986—87, assoc. dean, 1987—94, prof. surg. scis., otolaryngology, 1988—2002, assoc. sports medicine, 1989—2002, assoc. pediat., 1991—2002, dean, 1994—97; v.p., dean Wake Forest U. Sch. Medicine, 1997—2001, spl. adv. to exec. v.p. for health affairs, 2001—02, dean emeritus, 2002—, prof. emeritus, 2002—; pres., CEO Fedn. of State Med. Bds. of U.S., Inc., Dallas, 2002—. Libr. and learning resources com. Wake Forest U. Sch. Medicine, 1981—82, clin. skills workshops and rev., 1982, 84, admissions and pre-med. rels. com., 1984—86, clin. faculty adv. coun., 1985—2001, chair dept. clinics computer adv. com., 1985—87, faculty exec. coun., 1986—2002, vice chair, 1993—94, chair, 1994—2001, clin. svcs. coord. com., 1988—89, chair clin. scis. bldg. com., 1988; profl. ins. com. Risk and Ins. Mgmt. Adv. Coun., 1989—2001, affirmative action com., 1990—2001, 50th anniversary com., 1990—91, compliance com., 1999—2001; acad. coun. Wake Forest U., 1987, adminstrv. coun., 87, affirmative action com., 90, long range planning standing com., 93, intra-univ. ops. com., 2001, exec. coun., 1994, univ. ofcl. for animal care, 97, audit and compliance com., 99; clin. prof. otolaryngology U. Tex. S.W. Med. Ctr., Dallas, 2002; composite com. U.S. Med. Licensing Exam., 2002—, budget com., 2002—. Contbr. chapters to books, articles to profl. jours. Chair med. adv. com. Wake Forest U. Sch. Medicine/VA Med. Ctr., Salisbury, NC, 1995—2001; med. audit/utilization rev. com. NC Bapt. Hosp., 1982—84, capital equipment com., 1984—92, chiefs of profl. svcs. com., 1984—2001; bd. trustees The Med. Found., 1984—2001, Wake Forest Sch. Medicine, 1984—2001, NC Bapt. Hosp., 1984—2001, Arts Coun. Winston-Salem and Forsyth County, 1992; bd. visitors Wake Forest U. Bapt. Med. Ctr., 1997—2001; internat. med. edn. cons. to China China Med. Bd. N.Y., Inc., 2000; bd. govs. Bermuda Run Country Club, 1982—84; disting. citizens dinner steering com. Old Hickory Coun. Boy Scouts Am., 1994, 1997, 2000; indsl. devel. and econ. authority City of Winston-Salem, 1998—99; mem. planning com. Crosby Golf Classic, Bermuda Run, NC, 1987; bd. advisors Here's Life Winston-Salem, 1985—87; corp. recruitment chair Juvenile Diabetes Found. Winston-Salem, 2000; mem. Leadship Winston-Salem, 1987—88, health and human svc. day com., 1988—89, co-chair health and human svc. day com., 1991—92; dinner of champions com. Nat. Multiple Sclerosis Soc., Ctrl. NC chpt., 1999; campaign coord. surgery dept., otolaryngology sect. United Way Forsyth County, 1983—84, mem. med. ctr. com., 1987, health care campaign divsn. chair, 1989, vice chmn. divsn. III, 1992, mem. campaign cabinet, 1997—99, cmty. chair Forsyth County Cmty. Campaign, 2001—02, bd. dirs. Forsyth County, 2001—02; bd. dirs. Forsyth County Day Sch., 1987—90, Greater Winston-Salem C. of C., 1995—97. With USAR, 1972—78. Mem.: Tex. Med. Assn., Dallas County Med. Soc., Am. Acad. Med. Ethics, Am. Coll. Physician Execs., Am. Acad. Med. Dirs., Am. Laryngological, Rhinological and Otological Soc., Am. Acad. Otolaryngology, Head and Neck Surgery, So. Med. Assn., Christian Soc. Otolaryngology, Head and Neck Surgeons, Christian Med. and Dental Assns., Bapt. Med./Dental Fellowship. Office: Fedn State Med Bds of the US Inc PO Box 619850 Dallas TX 75261-9850 Office Phone: 817-868-4000. E-mail: jthompson@fsmb.org.

THOMPSON, JAMES ROBERT, JR., lawyer, former governor; b. Chgo., May 8, 1936; s. James Robert and Agnes Josephine (Swanson) Thompson; m. Jayne Carr, 1976; 1 child, Samantha Jayne. Student, U. Ill., Chgo., 1953-55, Washington U., St. Louis, 1955-56; JD, Northwestern U., 1959. Bar: Ill. 1959, US Supreme Ct. 1964. Asst. state's atty., Cook County, Ill., 1959-64; assoc. prof. law Northwestern U. Law Sch., 1964-69; asst. atty. gen. State of Ill., 1969-70; chief criminal divsn., 1969; chief dept. law enforcement and pub. protection, 1969-70; 1st asst. U.S. atty. (No. dist.) Ill. US Dept. Justice, 1970-71, U.S. atty., 1971-75; counsel Winston & Strawn LLP, Chgo., 1975-77, ptnr., 1991—, chmn., CEO, 1993—2006, chmn. exec. com., 1991—2006, head gov. rels. practice; gov. State of Ill., Springfield, Ill., 1977-91. Chmn. Rep. Govs. Assn., 1982, Nat. Govs. Assn., Midwest Govs. Assn., Coun. Gt. Lakes Govs., 1985, Pres.' Intelligence Oversight Bd., 1989—93; adv. bd. Fed. Emergency Mgmt. Agy., 1991—93; bd. govs. Chgo. Bd. Trade; mem. ABA Commn. on Separation of Powers & Jud. Independence, 1996—97; commr. The Nat. Commn. on Terrorist Attacks Upon the U.S. (The 9-11 Commn.), 2002—04; bd. dirs. FMC Tech., Inc., Navigant Cons. Inc., Maximus, Inc. Co-author: Cases and Comments on Criminal Justice, 1974, Criminal Law and Its Administration. Bd. dirs. Civic Com., Comml. Club Chgo. Mem.: ABA, Chgo. Bar Assn., Ill. Bar Assn. Republican. Office: Winston & Strawn LLP 35 W Wacker Dr Ste 4200 Chicago IL 60601-9703 Home Phone: 312-640-0420; Office Phone: 312-558-7400. Office Fax: 312-558-5700. Business E-Mail: jthompson@winston.com.

THOMPSON, JAMES WILLIAM, lawyer; b. Dallas, Oct. 22, 1936; s. John Charles and Frances (Van Slyke) Thompson; m. Marie Hertz, June 26, 1965 (dec. 1995); children: Elizabeth, Margaret, John; m. Linda Ball Dozier, May 2, 1998. BS, U. Mont., 1958, JD, 1962. Bar: Mont. 1962; CPA, Mont. Acct. Arthur Young & Co., NYC, 1959; instr. bus. adminstrn. Ea. Mont. Coll., Billings, 1959-60, U. Mont., Missoula, 1960-61; assoc. Cooke, Moulton, Bellingham & Longo, Billings, 1962-64, James R. Felt, Billings, 1964-65; asst. atty. City of Billings, 1963-64, atty., 1964-66; ptnr. Felt, Speare & Thompson, Billings, 1966-72, McNamer, Thompson & Cashmore, 1973-86, McNamer & Thompson Law Firm PC, 1986-89, McNamer, Thompson, Werner & Stanley, P.C., 1990-93, McNamer Thompson Law Firm PC, 1993-98, Wright Tolliver Guthals Law Firm PC, Billings, 1999—2003, Guthals Hunnes Reuss Thompson PC, Billings, 2004—07, Thompson Law Firm PLLC, Billings, 2007—. Bd. dirs. Associated Employers of Mont., Inc., 1989—98; mem. adv. coun. Sch. Fine Arts, U. Mont., 1997—2001. Mem. Billings Zoning Commn., 1966—69; v.p. Billings Cmty. Action Program (now Dist. 7 Human Resources Devel. Coun.), 1968—70, pres., 1970—75, bd. trustees, 1975—; mem. Yellowstone County Legal Svcs. Bd., 1969—70, City-County Air Pollution Control Bd., 1969—70; pres. Billings Symphony Soc., 1970—71; bd. dirs. Billings Studio Theater, 1967—73, United Way Billings, 1973—81, Mont. Inst. Arts Found., 1986—89, Downtown Billings Assn., 1986—90, Billings Area Bus. Incubator, Inc., 1991—94, Found. of Mont. State U, Billings, 1992—98, Our Mont., Inc., 1997—, pres., 2000—; bd. dirs. Rimrock Opera Co., 1998—, treas., 1998—2002; mem. Billings Transit Commn., 1971—73, City Devel. Agy., 1972—73; bd. ethics City of Billings, 2001—06, chmn., 2006; Diocesan Exec. Coun., 1972—75. Mem. ABA, Am. Acad. Estate Planning Attys., Nat. Acad. Elder Law Attys., State Bar Mont., Yellowstone Area Bar Assn. (bd. dirs. 1983-87, pres. 1985-86), Elks, Kiwanis (pres. Yellowstone chpt. 1974-75), Sigma Chi (pres. Billings alumni assn. 1963-65). Episcopalian. Home: 123 Lewis Ave Billings MT 59101-6034 Office: Thompson Law Firm PLLC Business Ctr and 32nd Ste 4 Billings MT 59102-6848 Office Phone: 406-294-4230. Personal E-mail: jwtldt@aol.com.

THOMPSON, JANE, writer; b. Oklahoma City, Mar. 8, 1945; d. George Harry Thompson and Mary Agnes Angonand. BA, U. Okla., Norman, 1967, MA, 1968. Cert. paralegal Southea. Paralegal Sch., 1988. Rschr., writer Polit. Rsch., Dallas, 1991—93; writer Primedia, Dallas, 1994—2001. Author: Sugar and Salt: My Life with Bipolar Disorder, 2006. Canvasser Tony Sanchez for Gov., Dallas, 2001. Mem.: Mensa (assoc.; sec., mem.-at-large 2000—01). Democrat. Personal E-mail: jtokc@yahoo.com.

THOMPSON, JAYNE CARR, public relations and communications executive, lawyer; b. Oak Park, Ill., Apr. 7, 1946; d. Robert Edward and Laurette (Rentner) Carr; m. James R. Thompson, June 19, 1976; 1 child, Samantha Jayne. BA, U. Ill., Chgo., 1967; JD, Northwestern U., 1970; degree (hon.), Lincoln Coll., Ill., 1990, St. Xavier U., Chgo., 1995, Ill. Coll., 1995. Assoc. in litigation McDermott, Will & Emery, Chgo., 1970; asst. atty. gen. State of Ill., Chgo., 1970-77, chief of criminal appeals divsn., 1972-77, dep. chief prosecution assistance bur., 1975-76, dep. chief criminal divsn., 1976-77, acting chief criminal divsn., 1977; of counsel Brown, Hay & Stephens, Springfield, Ill., 1977-78, Silets & Martin, Chgo., 1983-84; house counsel and v.p. devel. Nat. Coll. Edn., Evanston, Ill., 1984-85; atty. Lydon & Griffin, Chgo., 1989-91; prin. Dilenschneider Group Inc., Chgo., 1999-2000, mng. prin., 2000—02; CEO, pres. Jayne Thompson and Assocs. Ltd., 2002—. Contbr. chpt. to book, articles to profl. jours. First Lady of Ill., Springfield, 1977-91; mem. Ill. Commn. on Status of Women, 1997-2001; pres. bd. dirs. Chgo. Pub. Libr., 1998—; mem. women's bd. Northwestern U., 1978—; bd. dirs. Chgo. Pub. Libr. Found., 1998—; mem. adv. bd. for Ill. Treas. for Women's Issues, 2002—; mem. chmn.'s adv. coun. Lincoln Pk. Zoo, 2002—; mem. Met. Planning Coun., 2002--. Mem. Ill. State Bar Assn., Execs. Club (Chgo.), Coun. on Fgn. Rels. (Chgo. com.), Econ. Club (Chgo.). Avocations: reading, cooking, tennis. Office: Jayne Thompson & Assocs Ltd 33 N Dearborn St Ste 2200 Chicago IL 60602 E-mail: jthompson@jaynethompson.com.

THOMPSON, JEAN TANNER, retired librarian; b. San Luis Obispo, Calif., June 15, 1929; d. Chester Corey and Mildred (Orr) T.; 1 child, Anne Marie Miller Student, Whitworth Coll., Spokane, Wash., 1946-49; AB, Boston U., 1951; postgrad., U. Wis., Eau Claire, 1964-67; MSL.S., Columbia U., 1973; Ed.M., U. Va., Charlottesville, 1978. Asst. social sci. librarian Univ. Libraries Va. Polytechnic Inst. and State U., Blacksburg, 1973-77, head social sci. dept. Univ. Libraries, 1977-83; head reference dept. Meml. Library U. Wis., Madison, 1983-86, asst. dir. reference and info. svcs., 1986-91, ret. Contbg. editor: ALA Guide to Information Access, 1994; mem. editorial bd. RQ, 1984-89. Mem. ALA, Assn. Coll. and Research Libraries (edn. and behavioral sci. sect. vice chmn. 1985-86, chmn. 1986-87), Wis. Library Assn., Wis. Assn. of Acad. Librarians. Presbyterian. Home: 4929 High Grove Rd Tallahassee FL 32309-2957

THOMPSON, JENNIFER B., Olympic swimmer; b. Dover, NH, Feb. 26, 1973; BS in Human Bio., Stanford Univ., 1995; student in Med. Sch., Columbia U. Mem. U.S. Olympic Swim Team, Barcelona, 1992, Atlanta, 1996, Sydney, 2000, Athens, 2004. Active Swim Across Am. Named Sportswoman of Yr., Women's Sports Found., 2000, Swimmer of Yr., USA Swimming, 1993, 1998, 10-time USA Swimming All-Star; recipient Spring Nationals Kiphuth award, 1993, Performance of Yr. award, USA Swimming, 1999. Achievements include being the most decorated olympic female athlete in U.S. history; winning gold medal in 4x100m medley relay, 4x100m free relay, Olympic Games, 1992, 1996, 2000, 4x200m free relay, 1996, 2000; winnning 8 career Olympic Gold medals, 3 Silver, 1 Bronze; being World Champion in 4x100m free relay, winning World Championships in 1991, 1998, 2003, 4x100m medley relay, 1991, 1998, 100m butterfly, 1998, 2003, 100m free, 1998; winning 36 career Pan Pacific titles; winning 26 US National titles.

THOMPSON, JEROME LAFAYETTE, curator; b. Ames, Iowa, Apr. 30, 1952; s. Louis Milton Thompson, Sr and Margaret Stromberg Thompson; m. Gretchen Lynn Mlinar, June 28, 1975; 1 child, Grant Lafayette. BA, Iowa State U., 1974; MA, Tex. Tech. U., Lubbock, 1977. Site adminstr. Ter. Hill, Des Moines; hist. sites coord. State Hist. Soc. of Iowa, Des Moines, 1982—86, mus. dir., 1986—2004, state curator, 2004—. Recipient Disting. Svc. award, Art Educators of Iowa, 1993. Mem.: Ter. Hill Soc., Iowa Mus. Assn. (pres. 1991—93, bd. dirs. 1994—). Avocations: Tae Kwon Do, hunting, fishing, cooking, travel. Office: State Hist Soc of Iowa 600 E Locust Des Moines IA 50319 Office Phone: 515-281-4221. Office Fax: 515-281-6975. Business E-Mail: jerome.thompson@iowa.gov.

THOMPSON, JEROME WALTER, otolaryngologist; b. Blytheville, Ark., Jan. 8, 1950; MD, UCLA, 1976, MBA, 1994. Prof., chmn. ear, nose and throat dept. U. Tenn. Health Sci. Ctr., Memphis; pediat. ear, nose and throat surgeon LeBonhowe Children's Med. Ctr., Memphis. Chmn. Meth. Hosps., 2004—. Fellow: Am. Acad. Pediat.; mem.: Am. Acad. Otolaryngology (mem. audit com. 2006—). Office: 956 Court Ave B 226 Memphis TN 38163

THOMPSON, JERRY E., oil industry executive; BS, Colo. Sch. Mines. V.p. refining CITGO Petroleum Corp., 1987—98, sr. v.p., 1998—2003, COO, 2003—06; pres., CEO TEPPCO Partners LLP, Houston, 2006—. V.p., past chmn. Nat. Petrochemical & Refiners Assn. Office: TEPPCO Partners 2929 Allen Pkwy Houston TX 77019 *

THOMPSON, JEWEL TAYLOR, music educator; b. Kinsale, Va., Oct. 27, 1935; d. Waverly Edward and Ella Joyce (Holman) Taylor; m. Leon Everette Thompson, June 10, 1961 (dec. June 1983); children: Sonca Patrice, Miya Kateri. BS, Va. State U., 1956; MA, Eastman Sch. of Music, 1960, PhD, 1982. Asst. prof. Va. State U., Petersburg, 1960-62, W.Va. State Coll., Institute, 1967-68, W.Va. Inst. Tech., Montgomery, 1968-72; adj. asst. prof. Hunter Coll., CUNY, 1972-85, asst. prof., 1985-90, assoc. prof., 1990-96, prof., 1997—. Organist Abyssinian Bapt. Ch., N.Y.C., 1978-83, minister of music, choirmaster, 1983—; ea. area music dir. Links, Inc., 1995-2003, nat. music dir., 2004—. Author: Samuel Coleridge-Taylor, 1994; composer and arranger numerous compositions; contbr. Internat. Dictionary of Black Composers, 1999. Scholarship selection com. United Negro Coll. Fund; chair art program Links, Inc., 1989-93; music dir. at area and nat. levels; mem. Am. Music Ctr., Inc. Named Dame of Honour, Knights of Malta, 1982; recipient Hunter Coll. Presdl. award for excellence in svc., 1998, Outstanding Ministry award, Coun. Chs. of NYC, 2005; Hattie M. Strong Found. fellow, 1959—60, Ford Found. fellow, 1974—77, Prince Hall Masons grantee, 1977—78. Mem. ASCAP, Am. Women Composers, Inc., Music Theory Soc. N.Y. State. Avocations: travel, art. Office: CUNY Hunter Coll 695 Park Ave New York NY 10021-5024 Office Phone: 212-650-3608.

THOMPSON, JO(AN), anthropologist; b. Colo. B in Psychology and Sociology, Wittenberg Univ., Ohio, 1978; M in Anthropology, Univ. Colo., 1992; PhD in Biological Anthropology and Primatology, Univ. Oxford, Eng., 1997. Founder, dir. Lukuru Wildlife Research Project, Democratic Republic of Congo, 1992—98; fund-raiser LWRP, Colo. (due to unrest in DRC). Named an assoc. laureate, Rolex award for Enterprise, 2004. Achievements include 13 years of conducting biological field rsch., community-based conservation and wildlife edn. in the Dem. Republic of the Congo on behalf of human and primate populations, particularly bonobos. Office: Lukuru Wildlife Rsch Found PO Box 1284 La Grande OR 97850-6284 Business E-Mail: jat434@aol.com.

THOMPSON, JOCELYN PHARR, organist, director, music educator; b. Peekskill, NY, Mar. 30, 1956; d. Ernest Eugene and Jonsie (Crawford) Pharr; m. Sherman Bradford Thompson, Oct. 12, 1985. MusB, U. NC, Greensboro, 1978, MusM in Edn., 1980, M in Spl. Edn., 1986. Cert. K-12 music, K-12 in spl. edn. Tchrs. aide Clay St. Elem., Gastonia, NC, 1980—81; tchr. Eckerd Family Youth Alternatives, Candor, NC, 1981—85, ednl. coord., 1985—89; choral tchr. Providence Sr. HS, Charlotte, NC, 1989—94; asst. dir., prin. accompanist Carolina Voices, 1994—2001, dir. mainstage choir, 2001—02; asst. dir. music Meml. Presbyn. Ch., 1990—96, dir. music, organist, 1996—; choral tchr. West Charlotte Sr. HS, 1992—. Asst. dir., accompanist Charlotte Contemporary Ensemble, Charlotte, 2002—; dir. Martin Luther King Mass Choir, Gaston County Orgn. for Cmty. Concern, 1997—. Mass choir dir. Nat. Bapt. Conf., Charlotte, 2001, World Gathering Presbyn. Women, Louisville, 2003—. Recipient Cmty. Svc. award, Black Women's Caucus, Charlotte, 2002, Heritage award, Cultural Calendar, Charlotte, 2001, Person of Year, Gaston County Orgn. for Cmty. Concern, NC, 2005. Mem.: Am. Music Choral Dirs. Assn., Music Educators Nat. Conf., Links Inc., Alpha Kappa Alpha. Democrat. Avocations: reading, tennis, piano, movies. Office: West Charlotte Sr HS 2219 Senior Dr Charlotte NC 28216

THOMPSON, JOE D., physicist; BS in Physics, 1969, PhD in Physics, 1975. Postdoctoral Cryogenics Group Los Alamos Nat. Lab., N.Mex., 1975—77, tech. staff mem. Condensed Matter and Thermal Physics Group, 1977—2001, dep. group leader, 1989—92, group leader, 1992—2001, Lab. fellow, 2001—. Fellow: AAAS, Am. Phys. Soc. Office: Los Alamos Nat Lab MSK-764 PO Box 1663 Los Alamos NM 87545

THOMPSON, JOE FLOYD, aerospace engineer, researcher; b. Grenada, Miss., Apr. 13, 1939; s. Joe Floyd and Bernice Thompson; m. Emilie Kay Wilson, June 1, 1974; children: Mardi, Douglass. BS, Miss. State U., 1961, MS, 1963; PhD, Ga. Inst. Tech., 1971. Aerospace engr. NASA Marshall, Huntsville, Ala., 1963-64; prof. Miss. State U., Starkville, 1964—, Disting. prof. aerospace engring., 1995—. Mem. tech. rev. bd. Army Rsch. Lab., Adelphi, Md., 1993-95; dir. computer code Nat. Grid Project 1993-96; dir. NSF Engring. Rsch. Ctr. for Computational Field Simulation, 1990-95; dir. acad. team Dept. of Def. Cewes Major Shared Resource Ctr., 1996—; mem. Pres.'s Info. Tech. Adv. Com., 1997—. Author: Numerical Grid Generation, 1985, (computer code) Eagle Grid System, 1987; sr. assoc. editor Applied Math. and Computation, 1985-94; assoc. editor Numerical Heat Transfer, 1989—; mem. edit. bd. Computational Fluid Dynamics Jour., 1993—, Jour. Computational Physics, 1995—. Recipient Commdr.'s award Army Waterways Exp. Sta., Vicksburg, Miss., 1992. Mem. IEEE Computer Soc., AIAA (Aerodynamics award 1992), Assn. for Computing Machinery. Presbyterian. Achievements include establishment of NSF Engineering Research Center; pioneering work in field of numerical grid generation; led academic team in winning competition for programming environment and training support at three of the four Dept. of Defense Major Shared Resource Center. Home: Miss State U PO Box 255 Mississippi State MS 39762-0255 Office: Miss State U PO Box 9627 Mississippi State MS 39762

THOMPSON, JOEL ERIK, lawyer; b. Summit, NJ, Sept. 15, 1940; s. Maurice Eugene and Charlotte Ruth (Harrington) T.; m. Bonnie Gay Ransa, June 15, 1963 (div. Dec. 1980); m. Deborah Ann Korp, Dec. 24, 1980 (div. Jan. 1987); children: Janice Santiesteban, Amber; m. Shandae EmLaw, Apr. 21, 2002. Student, Va. Poly. Inst., 1958, Carnegie Inst. Tech., 1960-61; BSME cum laude, Newark Coll. Engring., 1966; JD, Seton Hall, 1970. Bar: N.J. 1970, Ariz. 1975, U.S. Tax Ct. 1972, U.S. Ct. Claims 1972, U.S. Customs Ct., 1972, U.S. Ct. Mil. Appeals, 1972, U.S. Ct. Customs and Patent Appeals 1972, U.S. Dist. Ct. N.J. 1970, Ariz. 1975, U.S. Ct. Appeals (9th cir.) 1975, U.S. Supreme Ct. 1975; cert. specialist criminal law Ariz. Bd. Legal Specialization; lic. profl. engr., N.J. Sr. technician Bell Tel. Labs., Inc., Murray Hill, NJ, 1965-67, patent agent, 1967-70, staff atty., 1970-73; sr. trial atty. N.J. Pub. Defender's Office, Elizabeth, NJ, 1973-74; assoc. Cahill, Sutton and Thomas, Phoenix, 1974-76; trial lawyer Maricopa County Pub. Defender's Office, Phoenix, 1976-80; trial lawyer, criminal law specialist Henry J. Florence, Ltd., Phoenix, 1980-86; pvt. trial lawyer Phoenix, 1987—. Judge Superior Ct. Ariz., Phoenix, 1987-95; instr. Phoenix Regional Police Acad., 1976-80, Glendale C.C., 1977, Ariz. State U. Sch. Law, 1978, Am. Inst., 1990; pres., CEO Eagle Master Corp., Phoenix, 1995—; pres. Joel Erik Thompson, Ltd., Phoenix, 1987—; bd. dirs. Am. Loans, Inc., San Diego; presenter in field. Contbr. articles to profl. jours. Mem. planning com. Camelback East Village, Phoenix, 1992-98, chmn., 1993-96; mayor's select com., Phoenix, 1997, blue ribbon com. Maricopa Assn. Govs., 1996-97. Mem. Ariz. Bar Assn., Nat. Assn. Criminal Def. Lawyers, Ariz. Attys. Criminal Justice (charter), Ariz. Assn. Pvt. Investigators (hon.), Internat. Assn. Identification (hon.), Tau Beta Pi, Pi Tau Sigma. Office: 3104 E Camelback Rd 521 Phoenix AZ 85016-4502 E-mail: joel.thompson@azbar.org.

THOMPSON, JOHN, III, men's college basketball coach; b. Mar. 11, 1966; s. John Thompson; m. Monica Thompson; children: Morgan, John Wallace, Matthew. Grad. in Politics, Princeton U., NJ, 1988. Asst. coach Princeton U., NJ, 1995—2000, head coach, 2000—04, Georgetown U., Washington, 2004—. Recipient Fritz Pollard Male Coach of Yr. award, Black Coaches Assn., 2006. Achievements include leading the Princeton Tigers to three Ivy League Championships as head coach. Office: Men's Basketball Georgetown U Athletic Dept McDonough Gym Washington DC 20057 *

THOMPSON, JOHN ALBERT, JR., dermatologist; b. Austin, Tex., June 5, 1942; s. J. Albert Sr. and Elizabeth (Brady) T. BA, Georgetown U., 1963; MD, Bowman Gray Sch. Medicine, 1967; Dermatology Fellowship, U. N.C., 1971-73. Diplomate Am. Bd. Dermatology. Resident in internal medicine N.C. Baptist Hosp., Winston-Salem, NC, 1967-69; resident in dermatology N.C. Meml. Hosp., Chapel Hill, NC, 1971-73; pvt. practice Charlotte, NC, 1974—; clin. prof. dermatology Dept. Dermatology, U. N.C. Sch. Medicine, Chapel Hill, 1974—. Author profl. papers. Lt. comdr. USNR, 1969-71, Vietnam. Mem. Am. Acad. Dermatology (chmn. subcom. for sch. health edn. 1976-79, task force--nat. health ins.), Carolinas-Va. Dermatology Assn. (adv. bd. council rep. 1976-79), Charlotte Dermatology Assn., Mecklenburg County Med. Soc., N.C. Med. Soc., North Am. Clin. Dermatology Soc. Southern Med. Assn., Southeastern Consortium for Continuing Dermatol. Edn. (steering com. 1983—2003), South Cen. Dermatol. Congress (organizing com. 1982-86), Am. Soc. Dermatol. Surgery, Am. Dermatol. Soc. Allergy and Immunology, Am. Soc. Laser Medicine and Surgery, Inc. Democrat. Episcopalian. Home: 2633 Richardson Dr Apt 8A Charlotte NC 28211-3346 Office: Dermatol Laser Ctr Dermatologic Laser Ctr 2310 Randolph Rd Charlotte NC 28207-1526 Office Phone: 704-376-9849.

THOMPSON, JOHN DOUGLAS, corporate financial executive; b. Montreal, Que., Can., Sept. 28, 1934; s. William Douglas and Anne F. (Whebby) T.; children: Jacqueline, Catherine, Peter, Anne Marie, Francois. B, McGill U., 1957; MBA, U. We. Ont., 1960. Dep. chmn. bd. Montreal Trustco Inc. Past chmn. bd. dirs. Trust Cos. Assn. of Can.; bd. dir. Air Transat, Shermag Inc., Nat. Trust Co., Scotia Mortgage Corp., Scotia Life Ins. Co., Scotia Gen. Ins. Co., The Bank of N.S. Trust Co., The Mortgage Ins. Co. of Can, Victoria and Grey Corp. Bd. dirs. MacDonald Stewart Found., Windsor Found., mem. audit com. McGill U.; past pres. St. Mary's Hosp. Found.; gov., past pres. St. Mary's Hosp. Ctr. Mt. Royal Club, Montreal, Royal Montreal Golf Club, Mt. Bruno Country Club, Inc., The Forest and Stream Club. Roman Catholic. Office: Montreal Trust 4th Fl 1002 Sherbrooke West Montreal PQ Canada H3A 3L6 Office Phone: 514-499-5517.

THOMPSON, JOHN W., information technology executive; b. Ft. Dix, NJ, Apr. 24, 1949; s. John H. and Eunice Thompson; m. Sandi Thompson; children: John E., Ayanna. BBA, Fla. A&M U., 1971; MBA in Mgmt. Sci., MIT's Sloan School of Mngmt., 1982. Sales rep. IBM, 1971—75, branch office mgr., 1975—79, regional adminstrv. asst., regional mktg. dir., 1980—84, asst. to CEO, 1984, dir. Midwest ops., 1990—93, head mktg. US ops., 1993, gen. mgr. personal software products, 1994—98; gen. mgr. IBM Americas, 1997—99; chmn., CEO Symantec Corp., Cupertino, Calif., 1999—. Bd. dirs. UPS, 2000—, NiSource, Inc., Seagate Tech., 2004—, Crystal Decisions; appt. mem. Nat. Infrastructure Adv. Com., Washington, 2002—; chair Silicon Valley Blue Ribbon Task Force on Aviation Security & Tech.; mem., Worldwide Mgmt. Coun. IBM; spkr. in field. Chmn. Fla. A&M U. Cluster; Ill. Gov.'s human resource adv. coun. Named one of 50 Who Matter Now, CNNMoney.com Bus. 2.0, 2006. Office: Symantec Corp 20330 Stevens Creek Blvd Cupertino CA 95014 *

THOMPSON, JON L., retired oil industry executive; BS in Geology, MS in Geology, U. Fla. Geologist Exxon Co. U.S.A., New Orleans, 1962; v.p. Exxon Corp., 1992—99; pres. Exxon Exploration Co., 1992—99; v.p. ExxonMobil Corp., 2000—; pres. ExxonMobil Exploration Co., 2000—. Office: ExxonMobil Exploration Co Ste 1241 233 Benmar St Houston TX 77066-3105

THOMPSON, JONATHAN SIMS, business executive; b. Ft. Benning, Ga., Nov. 19, 1947; s. Donald Frederick and Gene Elizabeth (Pierce) T.; m. Dinetha Lynn Richards, Aug. 26, 1979; children: Tracy A., Terry A., Jonathan S. II, Tiffany A. BSME, Tex. A&M U., 1970, M Indsl. Engring., 1978; M Bus. Mgmt., Ctrl. Mich. U., 1980; diploma in program mgmt., Def. Sys. Mgmt. Coll., 1987. Registered profl. engr., Tex. Commd. 2d. lt. U.S Army, 1971, advanced through grades to col., engr. platoon leader 27th Engr. Battalion Ft. Bragg, NC, 1971-72, staff engr. 5th Spl. Forces Group, 1973-74, engr. instr. Spl. Forces Sch., 1974-75, co. comdr. 2d Engr. Battalion Camp Castle, Korea, 1976-77, project dir. Engr. Strategic Studies Ctr. Rockville, Md., 1978-81, plans and ops. officer 317th Engr. Battalion Eschborn, Germany, 1982-84, engr. staff officer Office of Chief of Staff Washington, 1985-87, ops. rsch. analyst Office of Sec. of Army, 1987-88, battalion comdr. 2d Engr. Battalion Camp Castle, 1989-90, dep. chief of staff Corps. of Engrs. Washington, 1991-92, exec. dir. Office of Chief of Engrs., 1992-93, fellow Ctr. Stratetic/Internat. Studies U.S. Army War Coll., 1993-94, brigade comdr. 20th Engr. Brigade Ft. Bragg, NC, 1994-96; sr. fellow U.S. Dept. State, 1996-97; chief of staff U.S. Army Criminal Investigations Command, 1997-99; CEO, chmn. Attventure Ltd., 1999—. Editor: Peacetime Defensive Preparations in Europe, 1981 (deMarche award 1985); author govt. study, article in field. Adult leader, asst. scoutmaster Boy Scouts Am., Dale City, Va., 1990-92, chmn. troop advancement com., Ft. Bragg, 1994-96; coun. rep. Recreation Ctr. Bd., Dale City, 1985-89. Decorated Legion of Merit with 2 oak leaf clusters, DSM; fellow, Govt. Affairs Coun. for Excellence in Govt., 1991—92. Fellow Soc. Am. Mil. Engrs. (nat. bd. dirs. 1990-92, post pres. 1994—); mem. NSPE, Army Navy Club, Shriners (life mem., Noble), Masons (Companion, Sir Knight). Presbyterian. Achievements include leading the world's largest military engineering task force into Haiti during Operation Uphold Democracy to restore the government and rebuild the infrastructure; principal deputy to engineer commander of 24th infantry "Hail Mary" task force during Operation Desert Storm and the liberation of Kuwait. Personal E-mail: jack@attventure.com.

THOMPSON, JOSEPH T., JR., health facility administrator; b. Cranston, RI, Jan. 13, 1946; s. Joseph T. Thompson Sr. and Frances R. (Marshall); m. Sidney Carla Lopez, June 22, 1986; children: Endre J., Paige Nicole. BS, La Salle U., 1999. Cert. CCFC, LADAC, S.A.P. Case mgr. San Juan Youth Shelter, Aztec, N.Mex., 1998—99; DWI counselor San Juan County DWI Detention/Treatment Facility, Farmington, N.Mex., 1999—2001; intake coord. Four Winds Recovery Ctr., Farmington, N.Mex., 2001—; dir., owner White Eagle Counseling & Edn. Svc., Farmington, N.Mex., 2001—; with dept. behavioral health svcs. Navajo Nation, 2001. Adj. faculty San Juan Coll., Farmington, N.Mex., 1999—; prin. substance abuse counselor Dept. Behavioral Health Navajo Nation, 2001—. Chief petty officer USN, 1964—86. Mem.: Am. Coll. Cert. Forensic Counselors, NAADAC. Avocations: fishing, hunting, camping. Office: White Eagle Counseling 605 N Butler Ave Farmington NM 87401

THOMPSON, JOSIE, nurse; b. Ark., Apr. 16, 1949; d. James Andrew and Oneda Fay (Watson) Rhoads; m. Mark O. Thompson, Feb. 14, 1980. Diploma, Lake View Sch. Nursing, 1970; student, Danville C.C., 1974-75, St. Petersburg Jr. Coll., 1979. RN Ill., Wyo., cert. Devel. Disabilities Divsn., N.Y. Staff nurse St. Elizabeth Hosp., Danville, Ill., 1970-78, Osteo. Hosp., St. Petersburg, Fla., 1980-81, Wyo. State Hosp., Evanston, 1981-83, Wyo. Home Health Care, Rock Springs, 1984—, adminstr., 1986-95; pres. Home Health Care Alliance Wyo., 1991-92; staff nurse home health Interim Health Care, Cheyenne, Wyo., 1996-97; staff nurse Rocky Mountain Home Health Care, Green River, Wyo., 1997—, dir. nursing, 2000-01; staff nurse Sageview Care Ctr., 2001, S.W. Wyo. Rehab. Ctr. for Mentally and Physically Handicapped Persons, Rock Springs, Wyo., 2001—03, SW Rehab. Ctr., 2006; pvt. practice Wyo., 2004—. Mem. nursing program adv. bd. Western Wyo. C.C.; mem. Coalition for the Elderly, Spl. Needs Com. Sweetwater County, 1992-93. Home: PO Box 1154 Rock Springs WY 82902-1154

THOMPSON, JUDITH KASTRUP, nursing researcher; b. Marstal, Denmark, Oct. 1, 1933; arrived in US, 1951; d. Edward Kastrup and Anna Hansa (Knudsen) Pedersen; m. Richard Frederick Thompson, May 22, 1960; children: Kathryn Marr, Elizabeth Kastrup, Virginia St. Claire. BS, RN, U. Oreg., Corvallis, 1958; MSN, U. Oreg., 1963. RN Calif., Oreg. Staff nurse U. Oreg. Med. Sch., Eugene, 1957-58, Portland, 1958-61, head staff nurse, 1960-61; instr. psychiat. nursing U. Oreg. Sch. Nursing, Portland, 1963-64; rsch. asst. U. Oreg. Med. Sch., Portland, 1964-65, U. Calif., Irvine, 1971-72; rsch. assoc. Stanford (Calif.) U., 1982-87; rsch. asst. Harvard U., Cambridge, Mass., 1973-74; rsch. assoc. U. So. Calif., LA, 1987—. Contbg. author: Behavioral Control and Role of Sensory Biofeedback, 1976; contbr. articles to profl. jours. Treas. LWV, Newport Beach, Calif., 1970-74; scout leader Girl Scouts Am., Newport Beach, 1970-78. Named Citizen of Yr. State of Oreg., 1966. Mem. Soc. for Neurosci., Am. Psychol. Soc. (charter), ANA, Oreg. Nurses Assn. Republican. Lutheran. Avocations: art collecting, travel, tennis. Home: 28 Sky Sail Dr Corona Del Mar CA 92625-1436 Office: U So Calif University Park Los Angeles CA 90089-0001 Office Phone: 213-740-7350. Business E-Mail: judith@usc.edu.

THOMPSON, KARLEEN, professional basketball coach; children: Ayesha, Keisha. Student, Contra Costa Coll., Calif.; grad. in Psych. and Sociology, U. So. Calif., 1996. Position in sports mktg. dept. Gatorade; with LA Sparks, 1997—2005, asst. coach, 2002—05, interim co-head coach, 2004; asst. coach Houston Comets, 2005—07, head coach, gen. mgr., 2007—. Asst. coach WNBA Western Conf. All-Star Team, 2002, 03; asst. coach WNBA Select Team Internat. Basketball Fedn. Women's World Cup, 2003. Office: Houston Comets Toyoto Ctr 1510 Polk St Houston TX 77002-1099 *

THOMPSON, KATHERINE GENEVIEVE, lawyer; b. Bklyn., May 11, 1945; d. George Otway and Marie (Burke) T. BS, Good Counsel Coll., 1966; JD, Bklyn. Law Sch., 1970; LLM, NYU, 1981. Bar: N.Y. 1971, U.S. Dist. Ct. (so. and ea. dists.) N.Y. 1978, U.S. Supreme Ct. 1981. Editor Matthew Bender Pub. Co., NYC, 1970-71; atty. juvenile rights div. Legal Aid Soc., NYC, 1971-76, asst. atty. in charge juvenile rights div. N.Y. County office, 1976-77; sole practice NYC, 1977-78; ptnr. Rothenberg, Sherman, Thompson & Halpin, NYC, 1978-84, Sherman, Thompson & Halpin, NYC, 1984-87, Beldock, Levine & Hoffman, NYC, 1987—. Mem. appellate div. 1st Dept. Screening Panel, 1981-82, appellate div. 1st Dept. Family Ct. Adv. Com., 1983-90, chmn., 1986-89. Co-author: Adoption Law and Practice, 1988; contbg. editor: Bender's Federal Practice Forms, 1971, Bender's Forms of Discovery, 1971. Bd. dirs. August Aichorn Resdl. Ctr., N.Y.C., 1979-94. Fellow Am. Bar Found., N.Y. State Bar Found.; mem. ABA (family law sect.) N.Y. State Bar Assn. (spl. com. on juvenile justice 1980-87, family law sect. 1980—), Assn. of Bar of City of N.Y. (family ct. and family law com. 1977-80, chmn. 1980-83, lectures and continuing edn. com. 1984-85, matrimonial law com. 1985-88), Womens Bar Assn., N.Y. County Lawyers Assn. (family ct. com. 1978-79). Office: Beldock Levine & Hoffman 99 Park Ave Fl 16 New York NY 10016-1508 Office Phone: 212-490-0400. Business E-Mail: kthompson@blhny.com.

THOMPSON, KEITH F. MACKECHNIE, geochemist, consultant; b. Romford, Eng., Mar. 16, 1933; arrived in US, 1960; s. Alexander William and Rose Mary Thompson; m. Carol J. Hinkley, Oct. 7, 1961 (div. July 21, 1979); children: Kathryn, Gregory, Rebecca, Gwendolynne, Monica; m. E. Jo Jones, Oct. 3, 1981. BSc, U. Manchester, Eng., 1955; PhD, MIT, Cambridge, Mass., 1966. Geologist Iraq Petroleum Co., Basrah, 1955—59; geochemist Sinclair Rsch. Inc., Tulsa, 1966—69; rsch. assoc. geochemist ARCO Oil and Gas Co., Plano, Tex., 1969—85; assoc. rsch. scientist Tex. A&M U., College Station, 1985—89; rsch. geochemist Brit. Petroleum Co., Ltd., Houston, 1989—93; rsch. geochemist, cons. Petroleum Geochem. Data, Dallas, 1993—. Owner, pres. Petrosurveys, Inc., Dallas, 1992—2002; guest scientist Geoforschungszentrum, Potsdam, Germany, 2002; cons. in field. Contbr. 22 papers to profl. publs. Recipient Energy Related Inventions award, US Dept. Energy, 1995—97. Fellow: Geol. Soc. London; mem.: European Assn. Organic Geochemists. Roman Catholic. Achievements include research in light hydrocarbons; elucidation of petroleum generative reactions; described evaporative fractionation (generation of gas-condensates); patents for offshore petroleum exploration system. Home: 7747 Royal Ln Dallas TX 75230 Office: Petroleum Geochemical Data PO Box 671264 Dallas TX 75367-1264

THOMPSON, KENNETH, software engineer; b. New Orleans, 1943; BSEE, U. Calif., Berkeley, 1965, MSEE, 1966. With Computer Scis. Rsch. Ctr. Bell Labs/Lucent Technologies, Murray Hill, NJ, 1966—2000; disting. mem. tech. staff Bell Labs/Lucent Techs, Murray Hill, NJ; fellow Entrisphere, Inc. Vis. prof. U. Calif., Berkeley, 1975—76, U. Sydney, Australia, 1988. Co-recipient U.S. Nat. Medal of Tech., 1999, C&C prize, NEC, 1989; named Bell Labs Fellow, 1983; recipient Fellow award, Computer History Mus., 1997, Emmanuel R. Piore award, IEEE, Richard Hamming medal, Harold Pender Award, Sch. Engring. and Applied Sci., U. Pa., 2003. Mem.: Assn. Computing Machinery (Turing award and software sys. award 1983), NAE, NAS, IEEE Computer Soc. (Tsutomu Kanai award 1999). Achievements include patents for computer technology; research in operating systems, programming languages, software for voice and data communications, security, computer games and digital music distribution; co-developer of UNIX operating system in 1969; with J.H. Condon was involved with the development of Belle, a chess computer, which won the US and World Computing Chess Championships in 1980.

THOMPSON, KENNETH W(INFRED), educational association administrator, writer, editor, social sciences educator; b. Des Moines, Aug. 29, 1921; s. Thor Carlyle and Agnes (Rorbeck) T.; m. Betty Bergquist (dec.); m. Beverly Bourret (dec.); children: Kenneth Carlyle, Paul Andrew, James David, Carolyn Cordry. AB, Augustana Coll., 1943, LHD, LLD, Augustana Coll., 1986; MA, U. Chgo., 1948, PhD, 1950; LLD, U. Notre Dame, Ind., 1964, Bowdoin Coll., Brunswick, Maine, 1972, St. Michael's Coll., 1973, St. Olaf Coll., Northfield, Minn., 1974, U. Denver, 1983; L.H.D., W.Va. Wesleyan U., 1970; LHD, Nebr. Wesleyan Coll., 1971. Lectr. social scis. U. Chgo., 1948, asst. prof. polit. sci., 1951-53; from asst. prof. to assoc. prof. polit. sci. Northwestern U., 1949-55, chmn. internat. relations com., 1951-55; asst. dir. social scis Rockefeller Found., 1955-57, from assoc. dir. social scis. to v.p., 1957-73; dir. higher edn. for devel. Internat. Council for Ednl. Devel., 1974-76; Commonwealth prof. govt. and fgn. affairs U. Va., 1975-78, White Burkett Miller prof. govt. and fgn. affairs, 1979-86; J. Wilson Newman prof. govt. and fgn. affairs, 1986—2006; dir. White Burkett Miller Ctr. Pub. Affairs, 1978-98; dir. emeritus Miller Ctr., 1999—. Riverside Meml. lectr. Riverside Ch., NYC, 1958; Lilly lectr. Duke, 1959; James Stokes lectr. NYU, 1962; Rockwell lectr. Rice U., 1965; Ernest Griffith lectr. Am. U.; Andrew Cecil lectr. U. Tex., 1983; Stuber lectr. U. Rochester, 1984; Morgenthau Meml. lectr., NYC, Mike Mansfield Ctr. lectr., U. Mont.; dir. Inst. Study World Politics, NYC, 1975-01; cons. in field. Author, editor: Principles and Problems of International Politics, 1951, 82, Man and Modern Society, 1953, Christian Ethics and the Dilemmas of Foreign Policy, 1959, 81, Conflict and Cooperation Among Nations, 1960, Political Realism and the Crisis of World Politics, 1960, 82, American Diplomacy and Emergent Problems, 1962, 82, Foreign Policies in a World of Change, 1964, The Moral Issue in Statecraft, 1966, Reconstituting the Human Community, 1972, Foreign Assistance: A View From Private Sector, 1972, 82, Higher Education for National Development, 1972, Understanding World Politics, 1975, Higher Edn. and Social Change, 1976, World Politics, 1976, Truth and Tragedy, 1977, Ethics and Foreign Policy, 1978, Interpreters and Critics of the Cold War, 1978, Foreign Policy and the Democratic Process, 1978, Ethics, Functionalism and Power, 1979, Morality and Foreign Policy, 1980, Masters of International Thought, 1980, The Virginia Papers, vols. 1-30, 1979-96, The President and the Public Philosophy, 1981, Cold War Theories: World Polarization, 1944-53, Vol. I, 1981,91. Winston S. Churchill's World View, 1983, 89, Toynbees's World Politics and History, 1985, Moralism and Morality, 1985, Ethics and International Relations, 1985, Theory and Practice of International Relations, 1987, Arms Control and Foreign Policy, 1990, Traditions and Values in Politics and Diplomacy, 1992, Fathers of International Thought, 1994, Schools of Thought in International Relations, 1996, Politics Among Nations, expanded and updated, 2005; editor: Am. Values Series, Vols. I-XX, Presdl. Nominating Process, Vols. I-IV, Portraits of American Presidents, Vols. I-IX, Herbert Butterfield: The Ethics of History; The American Presidency, Vols. I-XVI, 1982-83, Ethics and International Relations, 1985, Moral Dimensions of American Foreign Policy, 1985, 94, The Credibility of Leadership and Institutions, Vols. I-XX, 1983-86, Rhetoric and Political Discourse, Vols.I-XX, Governance, Vols. I-VII, 1990-97, Constitutionalism, Vols. I-VII, 1989-91, Presidency and Science Advising, Vols. I-VIII, 1986-90, Political Transitions and Foreign Policy, Vols. I-IX, 1985-91, A World in Change, Vols. I-XI, 1989-96, Presidential Disability, Vols. I-IV, 1989-96, A New World Order, Vols. I-VI, 1991-97, Great American Presidents, 1994, Defeated Presidential Candidates, 1994, Statesmen Who Were Never President, 1996; bd. editors Society, Ethics and International Affairs, Interpretation, The Rev. of Politics; contbr. articles to profl. jours. Pres. Dist. of Scarsdale and Mamaroneck Bd. Edn., NY, 1965-68; trustee Union Theol. Sem., 1967-71, Dillard U., 1975-96, Social Sci. Found., U. Denver, 1974-94, Compton Found., 1975-98. 1st lt. AUS, 1943-46. Named Va. laureate, 1981; recipient Phi Beta Kappa and Va. Coll. Stores prizes, Va. Social Sci. Assn. ann. award, English Speaking Union award.Spl. Edward Weintal prize Georgetown U. Acad. Diplomacy, 1999. Fellow Soc. Religion Higher Edn., Am. Acad. Arts and Scis.; mem. Century Club, Scarsdale Town Club, Raven Soc. (ann. award U. Va.), Phi Beta Kappa (pres.), Omicron Delta Phi. Home Phone: 434-971-6649. Business E-Mail: kwt.8b@virginia.edu.

THOMPSON, KIRK, transportation executive; CPA, Ark. With J.B. Hunt Transport Svcs., Inc., Lowell, Ark., 1973-78, v.p. fin., 1979-84, exec. v.p., CFO, 1984-85, pres., COO, 1986-87, pres., CEO, 1987—. Office: JB Hunt Transport Svcs Inc 615 JB Hunt Corporate Dr Lowell AR 72745 *

THOMPSON, LARRY ANGELO, film and television producer, lawyer, motivational speaker, writer; b. Clarksdale, Miss., Aug. 1, 1944; s. Angelo and Ann (Tuminello) T.; m. Kelly Ann LeBlanc, 1999; children: Taylor Ann, Trevor Lorenzo. BBA, U. Miss., 1966, JD, 1968. Bar: Miss. 1968, Calif. 1970. In-house counsel Capitol Records, Hollywood, Calif., 1969-71; sr. ptnr. in entertainment law Thompson, Shankman, Bond and Moss, Beverly Hills, Calif., 1971-77; pres. Larry A. Thompson Orgn., Inc., 1977—. Co-owner New World Pictures, 1983-85; lectr. in entertainment bus. UCLA, U. So. Calif., Southwestern U. Law Sch., The Learning Annex; founder Project Rise and Shine, 2004. Author: How to Make a Record Deal and Have Your Songs Recorded, 1975, Prime Time Crime, 1982, Shine: A Powerful 4-Step For Becoming a Star in Anything You Do, 2005; prodr.: (TV) Jim Nabors Show, 1977 (Emmy nominee), Mickey Spillane's Margin for Murder, 1981, Bring 'Em Back Alive, 1982, Mickey Spillane's Murder Me, Murder You, 1982, The Other Lover, 1985, Convicted, 1986, Intimate Encounters, 1986, Eagle and My Bear, 1987, The Woman He Loved, 1988 (Emmy nominee, Golden Globe nominee), Original Sin, 1989, Class Cruise, 1989, Little White Lies, 1989, Mann in the Middle, 1989, Lucy and Desi: Before The Laughter, 1990 (Emmy nominee), Broken Promises, 1993, Separated By Murder, 1994, Face of Evil, 1996, Replacing Dad, 1998, Tonight @ House of Blues, 1998, The Beat Goes On: The Sonny and Cher Story, 1999 (Emmy nominee), Murder in the Mirror, 2000, Iron Chef USA: Showdown in Las Vegas, 2001, Iron Chef USA: Holiday Showdown, 2001, Celebrity Home Video, 2003, A Date with Darkness: The Trial of Andrew Luster, 2003, Little Girl Lost: The Delimar Vera Story, 2005; (film) Crimes of Passion, 1984, Fraternity Vacation, 1985, Quiet Cool, 1987, My Demon Lover, 1987, Breaking the Rules, 1992. Co-chmn. Rep. Nat. Entertainment Com.; apptd. by Gov. of Calif. to Calif. Entertainment Commn.; mem. Inauguration of Thompson Ctr. for Fine Arts in Clarksdale, 1986. Served with JAGC, U.S. Army, 1966-72. Recipient Show Bus. Atty. of Yr. award Capitol Records, 1971, Vision award, 1993; named Showman of Yr., U.S. TV Fan Assn., 1997. Mem. ABA, Miss. Bar Assn., Calif. Bar Assn., Inter-Am. Bar Assn., Hon. Order Ky. Cols., Am. Film Inst., Nat. Acad. Rec. Arts and Scis., Acad. TV Arts and Scis. Republican. Roman Catholic. Office: Larry A Thompson Orgn 9663 Santa Monica Blvd Ste 801 Beverly Hills CA 90210-4303 Home: 1348 Club View Dr Los Angeles CA 90024-5304 Office Phone: 310-288-0700. E-mail: ltbeverlyhills@aol.com.

THOMPSON, LARRY DEAN, lawyer, former federal agency administrator; b. Hannibal, Mo., Nov. 15, 1945; s. Ezra W. and Ruth L. (Robinson) T.; m. Brenda Anne Taggart, June 26, 1970; children: Larry Dean, Gary E. BA cum laude, Culver-Stockton Coll., Canton, Mo., 1967; MA, Mich. State U., 1969; JD, U. Mich., 1974. Bar: Mo. 1974, Ga. 1978. Indsl. rels. rep. Ford Motor Co., Birmingham, Mich., 1969-71; atty. Monsanto Co., St. Louis, 1974-77, King & Spalding, Atlanta, 1977-82, ptnr., 1986—2001; U.S. atty. (no. dist.) Ga. U.S. Dept. Justice, 1982-86; dep. atty. gen. U.S. Dept Justice, Washington, 2001—03; sr. fellow Brookings Instn., Washington, 2003—04; sr. v.p. govt. affairs, gen. counsel, sec. PepsiCo, Inc., Purchase, NY, 2005—. Mem. 11th Cir. Commn. on Lawyer Qualifications and Conduct; ind. counsel HUD investigation, 1995, visiting prof., U. Ga Sch. of Law, 2004; mem. Ga. Bd. Bar Examiners; bd. dirs. Delta Air Lines Inc., 2003-. Editor: Jury Instructions in Criminal Antitrust Cases 1976-80, 1982. Chmn. Atlanta Urban League; mem. Ga. Bd. Edn., 1997; bd. dirs. Ga. Rep. Found. Recipient Outstanding Achievement award FBA, 1992. Mem. ABA, Nat. Bar Assn. Republican. Presbyterian. Office: PepsiCo Inc 700 Anderson Hill Rd Purchase NY 10577 *

THOMPSON, LARRY JAMES, retired gifted and social studies education educator; b. Savannah, Ga., May 14, 1948; s. James Howell and Dorothy (Hendley) T. BA, Armstrong Atlantic State U., 1970; MAT, Tulane U., 1974; EdD, U. Ga., 1986. Cert. tchr., instrnl. supr., adminstr., Ga. Tchr. social studies Chatham County Bd. Edn., Savannah, 1970-71, 75-87, adminstrv. coord. social studies, 1987-97, gifted, talented educator, 1997-2001; ret., 2001. With USNR, 1971-73. Mem. Nat. Coun. Social Studies, Ga. Ret. Educators Assn., Ga. Hist. Soc., Chatham Ret. Educators Assn., Armstrong Atlantic State U. Alumni Assn. (bd. dirs.), Phi Delta Kappa. Home: 18 E Deerwood Rd Savannah GA 31410-3171

THOMPSON, LAWRENCE HYDE, retired federal agency official; b. Hamilton, Ohio, Oct. 6, 1943; s. William Hayton and Evelyn (Covault) T.; m. Catherine Crosby, Feb. 3, 1973; children: Bradford Stephen, Sarah Catherine. BS, Iowa State U., 1964; MBA, U. Pa., 1966; PhD, U. Mich., 1971. Economist Office Sec. Health, Edn. and Welfare, Washington, 1974-77, dir. Soc. Security Planning, 1977-79; assoc. commr. Social Security Adminstrn., Washington, 1979-81, dir. rsch., 1981-83; prin. dep. commr. Social Security Adminstrn., 1993-95; chief economist Gen. Acctg. Office, Washington, 1983-89, asst. comptroller gen., 1989-93; sr. fellow The Urban Inst., Washington, 1996—2007; ret., 2007. Contbr. articles to pubs., books. Mem. Am. Economic Assn., Nat. Acad. Social Ins. (dir. 1985-96, sec. 1997-99, pres. 1999-2003, bd. chair 2006—). Avocations: racquetball, choral singing. Office: The Urban Inst 2100 M St NW Ste 401 Washington DC 20037-1264 Business E-Mail: lthompso@ui.urban.org.

THOMPSON, LEE (MORRIS THOMPSON), lawyer; b. Hutchinson, Kans., Nov. 29, 1946; s. Morris J. and Ruth W. (Smith) T.; m. M. Susan Morgan, May 26, 1974; children: Deborah, Erin, Andrew, Christopher. BA, Wichita State U., 1968; MA, Emporia State U., 1970; JD, George Washington U., 1974. Bar: Kans., 1974, U.S. Dist. Ct. Kans., 1974, U.S. Ct. Appeals (10th cir.) 1976, U.S. Supreme Ct., 1978. Instr., lectr. Emporia State U., Kans., 1969-70; lctr. in speech George Washington U., Washington, 1970-71; asst. to Senator James Pearson Washington, 1971-75; assoc. Martin, Pringle, et al., Wichita, Kans., 1976-78, ptnr., 1979-89; U.S. atty. for dist. of Kans., Dept. Justice, Wichita, 1990-93; ptnr. Triplett, Woolf & Garrets, LLC, Wichita, 1993—2001; mng. mem. Thompson Law Firm, LLP (previously Thompson Stout & Goering LLC), Wichita, 2001—. Treas. Kansans for Kassebaum, Wichita, 1978-88; mem. Kans. State Rep. Cen. Com., Topeka, 1978-79, 88-90; candidate U.S. Ho. of Reps., Kans., 1988; chmn. civil issues subcom. Atty. Gen.'s Adv. Com. of U.S. Attys., 1992-93. Mem. Kans. Bar Assn. (pres. criminal law sect. 1994-95). Methodist. Office: Thompson Law Firm 106 E 2nd St Wichita KS 67202 Office Phone: 316-267-3933. Office Fax: 316-267-3901. E-mail: lthompson@tslawfirm.com.

THOMPSON, LOHREN MATTHEW, oil company executive; b. Sutherland, Nebr., Jan. 21, 1926; s. John M. and Anna (Ecklund) T.; children: Terence M., Sheila M., Clark M. Ed., U. Denver. Spl. rep. Standard Oil Co., Omaha, 1948-56; sales mgr. Frontier REF. Co., 1956-67, v.p. mktg., 1967-68; mgr. mktg. U.S. region Husky Oil Co., Denver, 1968-72; v.p. Westar Stas., Inc., Denver, 1967-70; chmn. bd. Colo. Petroleum, Denver, 1971—. Served with USAAF, 1944-46 Mem. Colo. Petroleum Council, Am. Petroleum Inst., Am. Legion Clubs: Denver Petroleum, Denver Oilman's,. Lodges: Lions. Lutheran. Home: 2410 Spruce Ave Estes Park CO 80517-7146 Office: Colo Petroleum 4080 Globeville Rd Denver CO 80216-4906

THOMPSON, LONNIE G., glaciologist, educator; b. Gassaway, W.Va., July 1, 1948; m. Ellen Mosley-Thompson. BS in Geology, Marshall U., 1970; MS in Geology, Ohio State U., 1973, PhD in Geology, 1976. Rsch. sci. Byrd Polar Rsch. Ctr. Ohio State U., 1976, assoc. prof., dept. geological sciences, 1991, prof., dept. geological scis., 1994, univ. disting. prof., dept. geological scis., 2002. Field team leader and other roles of several field rsch. expeditions, 1973—; mem. US Ice Core Working Group, 1986—89; mem. sci. adv. panel for the climate change data and detection program NOAA Climate and Global Change Program, 2001—04; co-dir. academics Tibetan Palteau Rsch. Inst., Beijing, 2005; mem. review com. Canadian Found. for Climate and Atmospheric Scis., 2004—05; mem. exec. review com. Canadian Polar Climate Stability Network, 2005—; chmn., external review com. Environ. Sciences Grad. Prog., Sch. Natural Resources, 2005; sci. advisor, climate and water initiative Ohio State U., Coll. Math & Phys. Scis., 2005. Contbr. articles to profl. jours.; mem. internat. editl. adv. bd. Interdisciplinary Journal-The Holocene, 1990—, mem. editl. bd. Geology, 1994—, Quaternary Science Review, 2000—. Co-recipient (with wife) Disting. Explorer award, Roy Chapman Andrews Soc., Beloit Coll., Wis., 2007; named one of America's Best in Sci. and Medicine, CNN and Time Mag., 2001; recipient John Marshall medal for Civic Responsibility, Marshall U., 2002, Vega medal, Swedish Soc. for Anthropology and Geography, 2002, Common Wealth award for Sci. and Invention, 2002, Dr. A.H. Heineken Prize for Environ. Sciences, Royal Netherlands Acad. Arts and Scis., 2002, Tyler prize, The World prize for environ. achievement, 2005, 2005 Nat. Medal Sci., NSF, 2007; several grants from NSF, NASA, NOAA and Nat. Geodetic Survey. Fellow: AAAS, Am. Geophysical Union; mem.: Internat. Glaciological Soc. (mem. adv. bd. 1999—), Am. Philos. Soc., NAS, Phi Beta Kappa (Epsilon of Ohio, elected alumni mem.), Phi Kappa Phi. Office: Ohio State U Sch Earth Scis 275 Mendenhall Lab 125 S Oval Mall Office SC 082C & OR 102 Columbus OH 43210 Office Phone: 614-292-6652. Office Fax: 614-292-4697. E-mail: thompson.3@osu.edu. *

THOMPSON, LORAN TYSON, lawyer; b. NYC, Dec. 23, 1947; s. Kenneth Webster and Mary (Tyson) T.; m. Meera Eleanora Agarwal, Apr. 2, 1976. BA magna cum laude, Amherst Coll., 1969; MA, Harvard U., 1970, JD, 1976. Bar: N.Y. 1977, U.S. Tax Ct. 1977. Assoc. Breed, Abbott & Morgan, NYC, 1976-83, ptnr., 1983-93, Whitman Breed Abbott & Morgan LLP, NYC, 1993-2000, Winston & Strawn LLP, NYC, 2000—. Mem. ABA, N.Y. State Bar Assn. (exec. com., tax sect. 1991-98, co-chmn. com. on nonqualified employee benefits 1991-95, co-chmn. com. on qualified plans 1995-98), Assn. Bar of City of N.Y., Phi Beta Kappa. Home: 79 W 12th St Apt 12G New York NY 10011-8510 Office: Winston & Strawn LLP 200 Park Ave New York NY 10166-4193 Office Phone: 212-294-2667. Business E-Mail: lthompson@winston.com.

THOMPSON, LORING MOORE, retired academic administrator, writer; b. Newton, Mass., Feb. 17, 1918; s. Henry E. and Ella (Gould) T.; m. Pearl E. Judiesch, Dec. 30, 1949 (dec. May 2002); children: Bruce C., Douglas P. (dec.). BS in Indsl. Engring, Northeastern U., 1940; MS, U. RI, 1947; PhD, U. Chgo., 1956. Instr. U. RI, 1946; asst. to pres. Assn. Colls. Upper NY, 1947-49; assoc. prof. U. Toledo, 1952-59, asst. dean acad. adminstrn., 1958-59; dir. univ. planning Northeastern U., Boston, 1959-63, dean adult programs, 1964-66, v.p. planning, 1967-80, emeritus, 1980—; faculty assoc. continuing edn. Ariz. State U., 1982-84. Cons. in field. Author: (with others) Business Communication, 1949; contbr. articles to profl. jours. Bd. dirs. Back Bay Assn., Boston, 1961-63, v.p., 1963; trustee Huntington Gen. Hosp., Boston, 1970-80; mem. Fenway Project Area Com., 1973-76; mem. Mass. conf. ch. and edn. com. United Ch. of Christ, 1972-78, chairperson, 1973-74, mem. task force on ch. growth, 1978-80; mem. Chandler Area Coun., 1988-89; sec. Interfaith Coun. Greater Sun Lakes, 1993-96. Lt. USNR, 1942-45. Mem. Inst. Noetic Scis., Tau Beta Pi. Home: 25408 S Sedona Dr Sun Lakes AZ 85248-6636

THOMPSON, LOUIS MILTON, agronomy educator, researcher; b. Throckmorton, Tex., May 15, 1914; s. Aubrey Lafayette and Lola Terry (Frazier) T.; m. Margaret Stromberg, July 10, 1937 (dec. Nov. 1972); children: Louis Milton, Margaret Ann, Glenda Ray (dec.), Carolyn Terry, Jerome Lafayette; m. Ruth Hiatt Phipps, July 7, 1990. BS, Tex. A&M U., 1935; MS, Iowa State U., 1947, PhD, 1950. Soil surveyor, Tex., 1935-36, 39-40; instr. Tex. A&M U., 1936-39, 40-42; asst. prof. soils Iowa State U., Ames, 1947-50, prof. soils, head farm operation curriculum, 1950-58, assoc. dean agr. charge resident instrn., 1958-83, emeritus prof. agronomy, 1983—, assoc. dean emeritus, 1984—. Author: Soils and Soil Fertility, rev. edit., 1957; co-author: rev. edit., 1978, 1983; contbr. articles on weather-crop yield models and climate change to profl. jours. Elder Presbyn. Ch. With AUS, 1942-46; col. Res. (ret.). Recipient Henry A. Wallace award for Disting. Svc. to Agr., 1982, Faculty citation Iowa State U. Alumni Assn., 1990, Disting. Achievement citation, 1993, Alumni Recognition medal, 1996, Disting. Iowa Scientist award Iowa Acad. Sci., 1991, Agr. Innovator award Iowa State U. Agr. Alumni Soc., 1992, Friends of Agrl. award Iowa Dept. Agr. and Nat. Agrl. Mktg. Assn., 1993, Disting. Svc. to Iowa Agr. award Iowa Farm Bur., 1995, Disting. Svc. to Agr. award Iowa chpt. Am Soc. Farm Mgrs. and Rural Appraisers, 2000; named one of 150 Iowans Who Made a Difference, Iowa Farm Bur., 1996. Fellow AAAS, Am. Soc. Agronomy, Soil Sci. Soc. Am., Soil and Water Conservation Soc. (pres.'s citation); mem. Farm House (hon.), Rotary (past local pres., Paul Harris fellow), Sigma Xi, Alpha Zeta (Tall Corn award 1957), Gamma Sigma Delta (nat. pres. 1956-58), Phi Kappa Phi (chpt. pres. 1961, Centennial medal 1997). Home: 2214 Hamilton Dr Ames IA 50014-8287 *To succeed in an academic community one must become an authority on a subject and be able to communicate it.*

THOMPSON, LOUIS MILTON, JR., investment company executive, consultant; b. Bryan, Tex., Sept. 21, 1938; s. Louis Milton and Margaret (Stromberg) T.; m. Anne Strand, Aug. 5, 1961 (div. Feb. 1992); children: Louis Milton III, Eric Norman, Christopher Scott, Mary Margaret, Mary Elizabeth; m. Laura Russell, Nov. 28, 1992; children: Emily Allan, Helen Aubrey. BS, Iowa State U., 1961, MS with honors, 1969. News editor, anchor Sta. WOI-TV-AM-FM, Ames, Iowa, 1960-61; commd. 2d lt. U.S. Army, 1961, resigned, 1974; advanced through grades to lt. col. USAR, 1981; asst. press sec. The White House, Washington, 1974-75; asst. to pres. Am. Enterprise Inst., Washington, 1975-76; dir. pub. affairs Nonprescription Drug Mfrs. Assn., Washington, 1976-78; sr. v.p. Nat. Assn. Home Builders, Washington, 1978-82; pres., CEO, Nat. Investor Rels. Inst., Vienna, Va., 1982—. Individual investor adv. com. NY Stock Exch., NYC, 1990—92, NYC, 2004—; new founds. working group Harvard U. John F. Kennedy Sch., Cambridge, Mass., 1992—94; consumer affairs adv. com. SEC, Washington, 1996—99; chmn. adv. coun. Greenlee Sch. Journalism and Comm., Iowa State U., Ames, 2005—, liberal arts and scis. dean's coun., 2001—. Author: The Handbook of Investor Relations, 1989; contbr. articles to profl. jours. Va. chmn. U.S. Equestrian Team, Gladstone, NJ, 1978—82; dressage judge Am. Horse Shows Assn., Lexington, Ky., 1979—86; bd. dirs. Nat. Coun. Econ. Edn., 2001—04. Recipient Disting. Svc. award, Investment Edn. Inst., 1987, Investor Rels. Mag. and Barron's lifetime achievement award, 2000, J.W. Schwartz award, Iowa State U., 2001. Mem. Investor Rels. Assn., Internat. Investor Rels. Fedn., Am. Hanoverian Soc. (disting. mem., pres. 1988-94), Univ. Club, Phi Kappa Phi. Avocations: equestrian sports, golf, wine collecting, breeding horses. Home and Office: Home Again Farm 11539 Spicers Mill Rd Orange VA 22960-2103 Home Phone: 540-672-0485.

THOMPSON, MACK EUGENE, historian, educator; b. Burley, Idaho, Feb. 24, 1921; s. Eugene and Nora (McFate) T.; m. Helen Goldhamer, Oct. 30, 1945. AB, Queen's Coll., CUNY, 1948; MA, Brown U., 1951, PhD, 1955. Instr. history Brown U., 1954-55; asst. prof. Calif. Inst. Tech., 1955-56, U. Calif. at Riverside, 1956-62, asso. prof., 1962-66, prof., 1966-77; emeritus prof., 1977—; chmn. div. humanities U. Calif. at Riverside, 1961-63, asso. univ. dean acad. planning, 1965-66, dean, div. undergrad. studies, 1971-74; exec dir. Am. Hist. Assn., Washington, 1974-81. Chmn. editorial bd. Experiment and Innovation: New Directions in Edn., U. Calif., 1966-68 Author: The Ward-Hopkins Controversy and the American Revolution in Rhode Island: An Interpretation, 1959, Moses Brown, Reluctant Reformer, 1962, Causes and Circumstances of the Du Pont Family's Emigration, 1969. Bd. dirs. Harry S. Truman Libr. Inst., 1974-81. With AUS, 1942-45. Home: 1378 River Oaks Ct Oldsmar FL 34677-4828

THOMPSON, MARGARET M., physical education educator; b. Merrifield, Va., Aug. 1, 1921; d. Lesley L. and Madeline (Shawen) T. BS, Mary Washington Coll., 1941; MA, George Washington U., 1947; PhD, U. Iowa, 1961. Tchr., supr. phys. edn. Staunton (Va.) City Schs., 1941-44; tchr. jr. high sch. phys. edn. Arlington County, Va., 1944-47; instr. women's phys. edn. Fla. State U., Tallahassee, 1947-51; instr., asst. prof., assoc. prof. phys. edn. Purdue U., Lafayette, Ind., 1951-65, dir. gross motor therapy lab., 1963-65; assoc. prof. phys. edn. U. Mo., Columbia, 1965-68, prof., 1968-71, dir. Cinematography and Motor Learning Lab. Dept. Health and Phys. Edn., 1965-71; prof. phys. edn. U. Ill., Champaign-Urbana, 1971-87, prof. emeritus, 1987—. Vis. prof. Escola de Educacão Fisica, U. de Saõ Paulo, Brazil, 1985; vis. prof. phy. edn. Inst. Bioscis. de Rio Claro, U. Estadual Paulista, Brazil, 1991. Author: (with Barbara B. Godfrey) Movement Pattern Checklists, 1966, (with Chappelle Arnett) Perceptual Motor and Motor Test Battery for Children, 1968, (with Barbara Mann) An Holistic Approach to Physical Education Curriculum: Objectives Classification System for Elementary Schools, 1977, Gross Motor Inventory, 1976, revised edit., 1980, Developing the Curriculum, 1980, Setting the Learning Environment, 1980, Sex Stereotyping and Human Development, 1980; also film strips, articles. Mem.: AAHPER. Home and Office: 1311 Wildwood Ln Mahomet IL 61853-9770

THOMPSON, MARK K., lawyer; b. St. Paul, Aug. 1, 1967; BA in Polit. Sci., U. St. Thomas, St. Paul, 1996; JD, William Mitchell Coll. Law, St. Paul, 1999. Bar: Minn. 1999, US Dist. Ct. (dist. Minn.) 2000, US Ct. Appeals (8th cir.) 2001, US Dist. Ct. (we. dist. Wis.) 2003. Assoc. Dudley & Smith, P.A., St. Paul, 1999—. Co-founder, pres. Computer Legal Internet Com. William Mitchell Law Sch. Contbr. articles to profl. publs. Named a Rising Star, Minn. Super Lawyers mag., 2006. Mem.: Minn. Trial Lawyers Assn., ABA, Minn. State Bar Assn., Ramsey County Bar Assn. Office: Dudley & Smith PA 2602 US Bank Ctr 101 E 5th St Saint Paul MN 55101 Office Phone: 651-291-1717. E-mail: mkt@dudleyandsmith.com. *

THOMPSON, MARK S., electronics executive; BS in Chemistry, SUNY; PhD in Inorganic Chemistry, Univ. NC. V.p. OEM group Raychem Electronics; v.p., gen. mgr. power components divsn. Tyco Electronics; CEO Big Bear Networks, 2001—04; exec. v.p. mfg. and tech. group Fairchild Semiconductor Internat., Portland, Maine, 2004—05, pres., CEO, dir., 2005—. Bd. dir. Big Bear Networks. Office: Fairchild Semiconductor 82 Running Hill Rd South Portland ME 04106 Office Phone: 207-775-8100. *

THOMPSON, MARTIN CHRISTIAN, retired news executive; b. Council Bluffs, Iowa, Oct. 25, 1938; s. Ross Kenneth and Mary Ellen (Pierce) T.; m. Janet Ann Morrow, Aug. 4, 1962; children: Chris Michael, Sean Martin. BA in Comms., U. Wash., 1960. Newsman Sta. KEDO, Longview, Wash., 1960-61; news dir. Sta. KREW, Sunnyside, Wash., 1961-66; newsman AP, Seattle, 1966-68, corr. Reno, 1968-70, newsman San Francisco, 1970-72, news editor, 1972-75, chief of bur. San Francisco, 1975-86, Los Angeles, 1986-88, mng. editor NYC, 1989-92, dir. state news, 1992—2003; ret., 2003. Methodist.

THOMPSON, MARTYN PHILIP, political and literary studies educator, translator; b. Hitchin, Gt. Britain and No. Ireland, Nov. 13, 1945; arrived in U.S., 1991; s. Philip John and Doris Primrose Thompson; m. Penelope Ann Burden, Jan. 15, 1972; 1 child, Daniel. BS in Econs., London Sch. Econs., 1967; PhD, London U., 1974; Dr. phil. habil., Tübingen (Germany) U., 1984. Lectr. in polit. studies London U., 1971-74; lectr. Tübingen, 1974-76, asst. prof., 1976-85, assoc. prof., 1985-87, prof. lit. and intellectual history, 1987-91; prof. polit. theory Tulane U., 1991—. Founder, mem. exec. com. German Soc. Study of Polit. Thought, Münster, 1989; vice chmn. Conf. for Study of Polit. Thought, 1991-96, chmn., 1996; mem. nat. screening com. for Fulbright Awards, Inst. Internat. Edn., N.Y.C., 2000—. Author: Ideas of Contract in the Age of John Locke, 1987; editor: Locke and Kant: Historical Reception and Contemporary Relevance, 1991, co-editor Yearbook of German Political Thought, 11 vols., 1991—; contbr. articles to profl. jours. Huntington Libr. and Art Gallery fellow, 1980; fellow commoner Churchill Coll., Cambridge U., Eng., 1985—; recipient Mellon fellowship William Andrews Clark Meml. Libr., UCLA, 1981. Mem. Am. Polit. Sci. Assn., Polit. Studies Assn. Gt. Britain, Inst. Hist. Rsch. U.K., Collingwood Soc. UK (hon. life), Deutsche Gesellschaft zur Erforschung des politischen Denkens (exec. com. 1989-2001). Avocations: travel, chess, non-pedigree dogs. Office: Tulane Univ Dept Polit Sci St Charles Ave New Orleans LA 70118-5698 E-mail: martynpt@aol.com. mpt@tulane.edu.

THOMPSON, MARY CECILIA, nurse midwife; b. Georgetown, Guyana; came to the U.S., 1977; d. John Alexander and Monica Eileen (Thorne) T. RN, Southend-on-Sea Sch. Nursing, Essex, Eng., 1973; cert. midwife, Basildon & Thurrock Sch., Essex, Eng., 1975; perinatal nurse practitioner, Cmty. Gen. Hosp., Syracuse, NY, 1986; cert. nurse midwife, Frontier Sch. Midwifery, Hyden, Ky., 1990. Cert. nurse midwife. Staff nurse pediatric unit Rochford Hosp., Essex, 1973-74; staff midwife Basildon & Orsett Maternity Units, Essex, 1975-76, St. Peter's Hosp. Chertsey, Surrey, Eng., 1976-78; staff nurse pediatric critical care SUNY Health Sci. Ctr., Syracuse, 1978-82; staff nurse pvt. duty nursing Med. Pers. Pool, Syracuse, 1982-83; staff nurse labor and delivery Cmty. Gen. Hosp., Syracuse, 1983-86, perinatal nurse practitioner, 1986-90; pvt. practice cert. nurse midwife Syracuse, 1990—. Mem. AWHONN, Am. Assn. Nurse Practitioners, Am. Coll. Nurse Midwives. Roman Catholic. Avocations: embroidery, reading, tennis, music, travel. Home: 4904 Razorback Run Syracuse NY 13215-1347 Office: Choices West Med Ctr West W Genesee St Camillus NY 13031-2238

THOMPSON, MARY ELIZABETH, application developer; d. William Reid Jones and Mildred Faye King; 1 child, Barbara Chancee Craig. MA, St. Mary Coll., 1995; BFA, U. of Kans., 1963. Cert. Computer Programming and Operations Ga., 1980; supr. devel. program for higher edn. Art dir. Quantico Va. Dependents Sch. Sys., Quantico, Va., 1964—65, Camp LeJeune NC Dependents Sch. Sys., Camp Lejeune, NC, 1965—67; computer programmer analyst Bank of the South, Atlanta, 1980—82, Hanes Corp., Atlanta, 1982—82; computer programming instr. Cobb County Cmty. Sch. Sys., Marietta, Ga., 1983—83; computer info. sys. instr. Johnson County C.C., Overland Park, Kans., 1987—88; computer info. sys. sr. prof. DeVry U., Kansas City, Mo., 1988—, suprv. devel. program, 2005—. Kansas designer craftsman show, (Charles Rombold Art Award, 1963), philharmonic showhouse book. Mem. Jr. Women's Philharm. Assn., Kansas City, Mo., 1970—73; chairperson Alpha Phi Help Lick Heart Disease, Kansas City, Mo., 1974; mem. Jr. League of Johnson County, Overland Park, Kans., 1998—99. Recipient New Prof. Prime Addition award, DeVry U., 1988, Mo. Governor's award for Excellence in Tchg. and Performance Excellence in Edn., The State of Mo., 2004. Mem.: Kans. City Profl. Devel. Coun., Micro Focus User Group, Assn. of Info. Tech. Profls., Alpha Phi Sorority (life; alumni rep. 1963—63). Achievements include development of faculty adv. for portfolio devel; exploring teamwork in the classroom seminar; textbook selection chairperson; assessment faculty adv. com; development of mentor to new faculty. Home: 10801 W 115th St Overland Park KS 66210 Office: DeVry U 11224 Holmes Rd Kansas City MO 64131 Home Phone: 913-909-5522; Office Phone: 816-941-0430. E-mail: mbthompson@kc.devry.edu.

THOMPSON, MARY KOLETA, small business owner, not-for-profit developer; b. Portsmouth, Va., Dec. 27, 1938; m. James Burton Thompson, May 5, 1957 (dec. 2006); children: Burt, Suzan, Kate, Jon. BFA, U. Tex., 1982; postgrad., Boston U.; MA in Philanthropy and Devel., St. Mary's U. Minn., 1999. Cert. non-profit mgmt. Pres., CEO The Planning Resource People, Burnet, Tex., 1990—; Tex. fin. devel. specialist ARC Tex., 1994-98; devel. dir. Very Spl. Arts Tex., 1991-92; dir. devel. ARC, Austin, 1992-94; pub. affairs adminstr. Pink Palace Mus. and Memphis Mus. Inc., Memphis, 1998; CEO Lamapasas C. of C., Lampasas, TX, 1998-99; pres., CEO Assn. Non-Profit Orgns., 1998—, Tex. Assn. Bed and Breakfast Innkeepers, 1998; pres. A Little Cottage B&B, 1999—2004; owner Heritage Sta. Antiques, 1999—, Heritage Country Realty, 1999—2006. Dir. Tex. Children's Mus., Fredericksburg, 1987-88, Internat. Hdqrs. SHAPE Command Arts and Crafts Ctr., 1985-86; com. chmn. Symposium for Encouragement Women in Math. and Natural Sci., U. Tex., Austin, 1990; instr. nonprofit mgmt., fin. devel., bd. leadership, grant proposal writing Ctrl. Tex. Coll., 2002—. Sculptor portrait busts. Bd. dirs. Teenage Parent Coun., Austin, 1990-92, ARC; lay speaking minister, First United Methodist Ch., 2000-. Named U.S. Vol. of Yr., NATO-Shape Belgium Cmty. Svcs., 1986; grantee, NEA, 1988. Mem.: AAUW (life; pres. 1990—92), Women in Comm. (co-chmn. SW regional conf.), Lometa Lions Club (pub. rels. com. 1999—2003), Heritage Station Antique Vehicle Show (founder), Heritage Station Antiques Show and Sale (founder), Leadership Tex. (life), U. Tex. Ex-Student Assn. (life), Heritage Station Antiques Forum (founder), Raleigh Tavern Soc. (founder), Leadership Tex. Alumnae Assn. (bd. dir.), Tex. Hist. Found (life). Avocations: writing, lecturing, meeting and strategic planning. Personal E-mail: heritagecountryrealty@pegabusbb.com.

THOMPSON, MICHAEL, lawyer; b. Des Moines, Aug. 2, 1951; s. Harold L. and Carolyn Annette (Yacinich) T.; m. Barbara Ann Haafke, Oct. 29, 1977 (div. Oct. 1984). BA, U. No. Iowa, 1973; JD, U. Iowa, 1976, MA, 1977. Bar: Iowa 1976, N.Y. 1979, Mo. 1980, Tex. 1994, Ill. 1999, U.S. Ct. Appeals (2d cir.) 1980, U.S. Ct. Appeals (7th cir.) 1982, U.S. Ct. Appeals (D.C. cir.) 1981, U.S. Ct. Appeals (fed. cir.) 1988, U.S. Ct. Internat. Trade 1988, U.S. Supreme Ct. 1984. Asst. atty. gen. Iowa Dept. Justice, Des Moines, 1976; economist Iowa Commerce Commn., Des Moines, 1976-77; spl. asst. N.Y. Pub. Svc. Commn., Albany, 1977-80; commerce counsel Mo. Pacific R.R., St. Louis, 1980-83; atty. Southwestern Bell Corp., St. Louis, 1983—86; exec. v.p., gen. counsel SBC Internat. Devel. Corp., 1986—2000; pvt. practice Chgo., 2000—. Adj. instr. corp. fin. Drake U., Des Moines, 1977; lectr. U. Chgo. Law Sch., 2006—. Mem.: ABA, Caxton Club (pres. 2003—05), Union League Club, Arts Club Chgo., Grolier Club, Houston Yacht Club, Chgo. Yacht Club. Republican. Office: 401 N Michigan Ave Ste 1200 Chicago IL 60611 E-mail: michaelthompsonlaw@earthlink.net.

THOMPSON, MICHAEL DAVID, physician; b. Toronto, Canada, July 3, 1961; s. Samuel John Thompson and Dorothy Gwendolyn Armstrong; m. Angela Mary Nervi, June 7, 1996; children: Mary Claire, Matthew Christopher. BS in Engring., U. Mass., 1983; MSEE, Univ. So. Calif., LA, 1985; MD, U. Mass., 1993. Diplomate Nat. Bd. of Med. Examiners, 1995, Am. Bd. of Surgery, 1999, Am. Bd. of Plastic Surgery, 2002. Systems engr. Hughes Aircraft Corp., LA, 1983—88; physician New Eng. Plastic Surgery, Fallon Clinic, Worcester, Mass., 2001—. Author: (abstract presentation) Internat. Ultrasonic Imaging Conf. Vol. Canton Youth Hockey, Canton, Mass., 2005—06. Recipient Ann. Housestaff Tchg. award, Dartmouth Med. Sch., 1997, Outstanding Med. Educator, Worcester Med. Ctr., 2003, 2004; Fellowship, Howard Hughes Found., 1983—85. Mem.: Mass. Med. Soc., ACS, New Eng. Soc. of Plastic and Reconstructive Surgeons, Am. Soc. of Plastic Surgeons, Am. Soc. for Aesthetic Plastic Surgery (assoc.). Roman Catholic. Avocations: airplane pilot, hockey, travel. Office: Thompson Plastic Surgery Assocs LLC 18 Washington St Foxboro MA 02035 Home Phone: 781-828-2776; Office Phone: 508-698-0888. Office Fax: 508-368-3902.

THOMPSON, MICK, state agency administrator; BA, Southeastern Okla. State U., Durant; MEd, Northeastern State U., Tahlequah, Okla.; grad. in Banking, U. Colo., Boulder. Exec. v.p. Ctrl. Nat. Bank, Poteau, Okla., 1977—90; dir. legis. and govtl. rels. Okla. Gov.'s Office; commr. Okla. State Banking Dept., Oklahoma City, 1992—. Mem. Okla. House Reps., Poteau, 1976—84, chmn. banking and fin. com., mem. appropriations and budget com., majority floor leader, 1983—84; pres. Okla. Cmty. Bankers Assn., 1988—90; bd. dirs. UICI, North Richland Hills, Tex., 2004—. Mem. adv. coun. Southeastern Okla. State U. Bus. Sch., Durant; adv. to bd. trustees U. Colo. Grad. Sch. Banking, Boulder. Mem.: Conf. State Bank Suprs. (chmn. 2003). Office: Okla State Banking Dept 4545 N Lincoln Blvd Ste 164 Oklahoma City OK 73105-3403 Office Phone: 405-521-2782. Office Fax: 405-522-2993. E-mail: rmt1@onenet.net.

THOMPSON, MIKE (C. MICHAEL THOMPSON), congressman; b. St. Helene, Calif., Jan. 24, 1951; s. Charles Thompson and Beverly (Forni) Powell; m. Janet Thompson, Mar. 8, 1982; children: Christopher, Jon. BA in Political Sci., Calif. State U., Chico, 1982, MA in Public Admin., 1996. Owner, maintenance supr. Beringer Winery; mem. Calif. State Senate, 1991—98, U.S. Congress from 1st Calif. dist., 1999—; mem. armed svcs. com., agr. com. Former chair select com. on Calif.'s Wine Industry; former chair Calif. Senate budget com.; former vice chair Calif. Senate natural resources com; lectr. San Francisco State U., Calif. State U., Chico. Co-founder, co-chair Congl. Wine Caucus; co-vice chair Congl. Sportsmen's Caucus; mem. New Dem. Coalition, Blue Dog Coalition. Staff sgt. US Army, Vietnam. Decorated Purple Heart. Named Freshman Legislator of the Yr. Calif. Sch. Bds. Assn., 1990, Legislatorof the Yr. Calif. Abortion Rights Action League, Legislator of the Yr. Calif. Assn. Persons with Handicaps, Legislator of the Yr. Police Officers Rsch. Assn. Calif., Legislator of the Yr. Disabled in State Svc., 1994, Senator of the Yr. Calif. Assn. Homes and Svcs. for Aging, 1995; Recipient Disting. Svc. award Calif. State Assn. Counties, Disting. Svc. award Calif. Assn. Hosps., Legis. Leadership award Calif. Assn. Health Svcs. Home, 1994, Disting. Svc. award Aids Project L.A., 1995, Outstanding Senator award Planned Parenthood Affiliates Calif., 1996, Outstanding Senator of the Yr. award Calif. Sch. Bds. Assn., 1996, Outstanding Senator of the Yr. award Calif. Profl. Firefighters, 1996 Democrat. Roman Catholic. Office: US Ho Reps 231 Cannon Ho Office Bldg Washington DC 20515-0501 *

THOMPSON, NEIL DANIEL, retired lawyer; b. Calexico, Calif., Feb. 21, 1935; s. Francis Marion Thompson and Leah Harriet Howell. AB with honors, UCLA, 1957; PhD, Columbia U., 1963; LLB, Harvard U., 1963. Bar: NY 1964, US Dist. Ct. (so. dist.) NY 1965, US Customs Ct. 1967, US Ct. Appeals (2d cir.) 1971, US Supreme Ct. 1973. Assoc. Jas. Maxwell Fassett, NYC, 1964-65, Doman & Ablondi, NYC, 1965-69, Pollack & Kaminsky, NYC, 1969-80; pvt. practice NYC, 1980-86; rsch. cons. Salt Lake City, 1986—. Author: Family of Bartholomew Stovall, 1993; editor The Genealogist, 1980-96; contbr. articles to profl. jours. Trustee Bd. for Cert. of Genealogists, 1977-89, pres., 1983-86. Fellow Am. Soc. Genealogists (pres. 1992-95), Soc. Genealogists (London), Utah Geneal. Assn. (bd. dirs. 1988-89); mem. Phi Beta Kappa, Phi Mu Alpha. Democrat. Mem. Lds Ch. Avocations: music, stamp collecting/philately, book collecting. Home: 255 N 200 W Salt Lake City UT 84103-4545 Office Phone: 801-521-4732. Personal E-mail: gryphon801@aol.com.

THOMPSON, N(ORMAN) DAVID, insurance company executive; b. Rockville Centre, NY, July 30, 1934; s. Norman J. and Laurel H. (Johnson) T.; m. Joyce L. Angeletti, June 7, 1958; children: John L., Jennifer L., Sarah S. BA with distinction, Wesleyan U., 1956; LLB, Columbia U., 1959; postgrad., Harvard U., 1973. Bar: N.Y. Pvt. practice law, NYC, 1961-62; corp. sec. Gen. Reins. Corp., NYC, 1964-69, v.p. Greenwich, Conn., 1969, v.p., gen. counsel, sec., 1976-77; exec. v.p. N.Am. Reins. Corp., NYC, 1977-78, pres., 1978-92; chmn., CEO Swiss Reins. Am. Corp. (formerly N.Am. Reins.), 1992-95, chmn. Swiss Re Am. Holding Corp. (formerly SwissRe Holding Co.), 1992-97; chmn. SwissRe Group Cos. (U.S.), 1992-95. Dir. Nat. Legal Ctr. for Pub. Interest, chmn., 1992-95; trustee Coll. Ins., 1992, 98. With U.S. Army, 1959-60. Mem. Reins Assn. Am. (chmn. 1982-83), Nat. Assn. Casualty and Surety Execs. (pres. 1986-87), Am. Arbitration Assn. (bd. dirs., chmn. fin. com. 1992-93), Am. Inst. Property and Casualty Underwriters (trustee, 1992-98), Univ. Club (N.Y.C.), Saugatuck Harbor Yacht Club (Westport, Conn.). Home: 47 Kettle Creek Rd Weston CT 06883-2208

THOMPSON, NORMAN WINSLOW, surgeon, educator; b. Boston, July 12, 1932; s. Herman Chandler and Evelyn Millicent (Palmer) T.; m. Marcia Ann Veldman, June 12, 1956; children: Robert, Karen, Susan, Jennifer. BA, Hope Coll., Holland, Mich., 1953; MD, U. Mich., 1957; MD (hon.), U. Linköping, Sweden, 1995. Diplomate Am. Bd. Surgery. From intern to prof. emeritus surgery U. Mich., Ann Arbor, Mich., 1957—2001, prof. emeritus surgery, 2001—. Contbr. articles to profl. jours. Trustee Hope Coll., 1973-88. Fellow Royal Australasian Coll. Surgeons (hon.), Royal Coll. Physicians and Surgeons of Glasgow; mem. ACS (gov. 1979-85), Ctrl. Surg. Assn., Western Surg. Assn. (1st v.p. 1992-93, pres. 1994-95), F.A. Coller Surg. Soc. (pres. 1986), Am. Surg. Assn., Am. Thyroid Assn., Soc. Surg. Alimentary Tract, Internat. Assn. Endocrine Surgeons (pres. 1989-91), Internat. Soc. Surgeons (v.p. 1995—), Am. Assn. Endocrine Surgeons (pres. 1980-81, 81-82), Royal Soc. Medicine, Brit. Assn. Endocrine Surgeons, Spanish Assn. Surgeons (hon.), Assn. French Endocrine Surgeons, Scandanvian Surg. Soc., Soc. Surg. Oncology, Turkish Assn. Endocrine Surgeons, European Soc. Endocrine Surgeons (hon.), Spanish Soc. Surgeons (hon.), Alpha Omega Alpha. Home: 465 Hillspur Rd Ann Arbor MI 48105-1048 Office: Surgery Emeritus Faculty 1327 Jones Dr Ste 201 Ann Arbor MI 48105 Office Phone: 734-998-0167. Office Fax: 774-998-0173. Business E-Mail: normant@med.umich.edu.

THOMPSON, OTHO M., lawyer, former solicitor; b. Md., Sept. 4, 1945; BA, Morgan State U., 1967; JD, U. Md., 1971. Bar: Md. 1972, Md. Ct. Appeals, US Dist. Ct. (Md.), US Ct. Appeals (4th cir.), US Supreme Ct. Asst. solicitor City of Balt., 1975—93, dep. city solicitor, 1993—96, city solicitor, 1996-2000; ptnr., State & Local Govt. practice Venable LLP, Balt., 2000—. Chmn. authored com. report Citizens' Ad Hoc Com. for Children at Risk, Anne Arundel County Public Schools, 1988—90; mem. Anne Arundel County Pub. Sch. Parents Council, 1988—90, Anne Arundel County Children's Council, 1988—90. Served to major USAR, 1972—81. Mem.: Nat. Bar Assn., Md. Volunteer Lawyers Assn., Internat. Mcpl. Lawyers Assn., Md. State Bar Assn., Anne Arundel County Bar Assn., Saltworks Cmty. Assn., Balt. Assn. for Retarded Citizens, Anne Arundel County YMCA. Office: Venable LLP 1800 Mercantile Bank & Trust Bldg 2 Hopkins Plaza Baltimore MD 21201 Office Phone: 410-244-7452. Office Fax: 410-244-7742. Business E-Mail: omthompson@venable.com.

THOMPSON, PAMELA PADWICK, public relations executive; b. Columbus, Ohio, June 13, 1943; d. Frank John and Tiami Judith (Padwick) T.; stepfather, James William Bampton; m. Fairman Rogers Thompson, Jan. 10, 1942; children: Ryder McNeal, Darby McNeal. BA, U. Louisville, 1994; MA, U. Dayton, 1998. Ptnr. Crutcher, Kelly and Assocs., Louisville, 1979-83; owner Transl. Co., Louisville, 1981-83, Technigraphics, Louisville, 1984-87; v.p. dir. individual support Grtr. Louisville Fund for the Arts, Louisville, 1989-92; v.p. comms. John Templeton Found., Radnor, Pa., 1997—. Adj. prof. U. Louisville, 1997. Contbr. articles to profl. jours. including Small Group Behavior. Chair pub. rels. com. Keene Valley Libr., 2000-01; bd. dirs. Louisville Nature Ctr., 1996-97; mem. ad hoc com. State Ky. Biodiversity Coun., Louisville, 1996-97; city commr. City of Rolling Fields, Louisville, 1991-94; alliance bd. dirs. J.B. Speed Art Mus., Louisville, 1986-92. Mem. APA, Soc. for Consumer Psychology, Pub. Rels. Soc. Am., Jr. League Phila., Cosmo. Club Phila., Ausable Club. Episcopalian. Avocations: hiking, gardening, tennis, travel. Home: 4 Porter Ln Rose Valley PA 19086 Office: John Templeton Foundation 300 Conshohocken State Rd Ste 500 Conshohocken PA 19428-3801 Office Phone: 610-941-5194. Fax: (610) 687-8961. Business E-Mail: pthompson@templeton.org.

THOMPSON, PATRICK S., lawyer; b. Muskegon, Mich., July 24, 1967; BA with high honors, U. Mich., 1989; JD, Harvard Law Sch., 1992. Bar: Calif. 1992. Ptnr., antitrust, telecom., complex litig. Pillsbury Winthrop LLP, San Francisco; ptnr. Goodwin Procter LLP, 2006—. Editor: Antitrust Law Jour., 1996—2002. Vice chair, conservatory com. Am. Conservatory Theater; sec., bd. trustees Grace Cathedral; chmn. bd. dirs. Calif. Pacific Med. Ctr., 2003—04, dir., 1996—2004; sec., bd. trustees Am. Conservatory Theater; bd. dirs. Francis of Assisi Cmty. Named one of Am. Top Black Attys., Black Enterprise, 2003, Top 20 Lawyers Under Age 40, Daily Jour., Calif., 2004, N. Calif. Super Lawyers, 2004—05. Mem.: ABA (mem. antitrust section, mem. editl. bd. Antitrust Source, liaison to commn. racial and ethnic diversity in legal profession), State Bar Calif. (vice chair, exec. com. antitrust and unfair competition section 2005). Office: Goodwin Procter LLP 101 Calif St San Francisco CA 94111 Office Phone: 415-733-6068. Office Fax: 415-677-9041. Business E-Mail: pthompson@goodwinprocter.com. *

THOMPSON, PAUL A., business consultant, performance improvement expert; b. Orpington, Kent, Eng., Nov. 16, 1942; came to U.S., 1970; s. William John and Jean Inez Thompson; m. Sarah Jean Erskine, July 15, 1972; 1 child, Alastair Stewart. BA in Econs. with honors, Cambridge U., Eng., 1965, MA in Econs., 1969. Sr. analyst Shell Oil, London, 1966-70; bus. analyst Westinghouse Electric, Pitts., 1970-76, site mgr. Richmond, Va., 1976-79; founder Westinghouse Productivity & Quality Ctr., 1979; productivity improvement mgr. Westinghouse Electric, Pitts., 1980-94; internat. bus. cons. Delmont, Pa., 1995—. Advisor to U.S. Congress and fgn. govts., 1980—; cons. to airlines, auto. corps., banks, ins., oil and gas, engring., power, healthcare, postal, comms., armed forces, higher edn., and govt. depts.; founder, chmn. Reengring. Users Group, Pitts., 1992-2002, dir. productivity & leadership consortium, 1996-2001; vis. lectr. Carnegie Mellon U., Oakland, Pa., 1992-2002; lectr. United Arab Emirates Higher Colls. of Tech., 1995-2001; internat. author and seminar leader on productivity and quality, 1995—. Editor Forum mag.; mem. editorial bd. Focus on Change Mgmt., 1994—; contbr. articles to profl. jours. Pres. Children's Festival Chorus, Pitts., 1991-96; program dir. Pitts. Folk Festival, 1980-96; chmn. strategic planning Redstone Presbytery, Westmoreland, Pa., 1990-92; tchr. Royal Scottish Country Dance Soc. Republican. Presbyterian. Avocations: golf, travel, horseback riding, dance, music/theatre. Home and Office: 127 Surrey Dr Delmont PA 15626-1539 Home Phone: 724-468-5800; Office Phone: 724-468-5800. Business E-Mail: pthompson@tqconsultants.com.

THOMPSON, PAUL C., labor union administrator; m. Roberta Thompson; 2 children. Fireman Atchison, Topeka & Santa Fe Railway, 1959; with Kans. City Southern; pres. Local 298, United Transp. Union, 1968—70, chairperson, 1970—82; internat. v.p. United Transp. Union, 1983—99, gen. sec., treas., 1999—2001, asst. pres., 2001—04, internat. pres., 2004—. Labor rep. to Pres. Clinton's Sch./Work program com., 1993. Office: UTU 14600 Detroit Ave Cleveland OH 44107-4250 Office Phone: 216-228-9400. Business E-Mail: President@utu.org.

THOMPSON, PAUL MATTHEW, neuroscientist; b. York, Eng., June 13, 1971; s. Derek and Cynthia (Jenkinson) T.; m. Lynn Lee Hodges, Sept. 9, 1995. BA in Classical Langs., Oxford U., Eng., 1991, MA in Math., 1993; PhD in Neurosci., UCLA, 1998. Rsch. scholar Oxford U., 1989-93; Fulbright scholar Brain Mapping divsn. UCLA, 1993-98; fellow Howard Hughes Med. Inst., Bethesda, Md., 1993-98; prof. neurology UCLA Brain Rsch. Inst., 1998—. Cons. Nathan Kline Inst., N.Y.C., 1998—; sci. investigator NIH Neuro-Imaging Resource, L.A., 1998—, NSF, Bethesda, 1998—. Contbr. over 70 articles to profl. jours. Recipient SPIE Medical Imaging award, 1997, Outstanding Grad. Student of the Yr., UCLA Chancello's Svc. award, 1998, Eiduson award for Neuroscience Rsch., 1998, Di Chiro Outstanding Scientific Paper award, 1998; Rsch. grantee Nat. Ctr. for Rsch. Resources, 1998—, NIH, 1998—, NINDS, 1998—, NSF, 1998—. Mem. U. Calif. Alumni Assn. Achievements include design of new algorithms for brain image analysis and pathology detection; developed new strategies for analyzing brain image data bases and for brain mapping in large human populations; creation of systems to detect and map alterations in brain structure and function; developed system to map growth patterns in brain development. Office: Lab of Neuro Imaging UCLA Sch Med 635 Charles E Young Dr S Ste 225E Los Angeles CA 90095 E-mail: thompson@loni.ucla.edu.

THOMPSON, PAUL MICHAEL, lawyer; b. Dubuque, Iowa, Aug. 30, 1935; s. Frank W. and Genevieve (Cassutt) T.; m. Mary Jacqueline McManus, Jan. 30, 1960; children: Anne, Tricia, Paul, Tim, Jim. BA magna cum laude, Loras Coll., 1957; LLB, Georgetown U., 1959. Bar: Iowa 1959, DC 1959, Va. 1966. Atty. appellate ct. br. NLRB, Washington, 1962-66; assoc. Hunton & Williams, Richmond, Va., 1966-71, ptnr., 1971—. Adj. prof. The T.C. Williams Sch. Law U. Richmond; adj. prof. law sch. Coll. William and Mary Sch. Law. Served with JAGC, USAF, 1960-62. Mem. ABA, Va. State Bar, Va. Bar Assn., Internat. Bar Assn., Commonwealth Club. Roman Catholic. Office: The TC Williams School Law University of Richmond Richmond VA 23173 Office Phone: 804-289-8856. Personal E-mail: thompmerrypoint@comcast.net. Business E-Mail: pthomps3@richmond.edu.

THOMPSON, PETER L., lawyer; s. David D. and Lynn P. Thompson; m. Amy A. Aldredge, Sept. 12, 1987; children: Elizabeth R., Bennett D., Miles M. BS, Bowdoin Coll., 1991; JD, U. Maine, 1994. Cert.: Maine 1994. Atty. Law Offices of Peter L. Thompson, Portland, Maine, 1994—. Dir. Consumer Health Law Program, Augusta, Maine, 1997—. Active Million Dollar Advocates Forum, 2004—; bd. dirs. Brain Injury Assn. Maine, Augusta, 2001—, Disability Rights Ctr., Augusta, 2004—. Mem.: Assn. Trial Lawyers Am., Maine Employment Lawyers Assn., Maine Bar Assn., Maine Trial Lawyers Assn. Office: Law Offices of Peter L Thompson 92 Exchange St Portland ME 04101 Office Phone: 207-874-0909. Business E-Mail: peter@ptlawoffice.com.

THOMPSON, PETER LAYARD HAILEY, SR., landscape and golf course architect, architectural firm executive; b. Modesto, Calif., Apr. 26, 1939; BS in East Asian Studies, U. Oreg., 1962, B in Landscape Architecture, 1971, M in Urban Planning, 1971; postgrad., U. Calif., Berkeley, 1975, Nat. U. Registered landscape arch., Calif., Oreg., Wash., Nev. With Oreg. Planning Commn., Lane County, 1965-70, commr. Eugene, 1981-83; sr. assoc. Ruff, Cameron, Lacoss, Eugene, 1971-75; prin. Peter L. H. Thompson & Assocs., Eugene, 1975-83, John H. Midby & Assocs., Las Vegas, Nev., 1983-86, Thompson-Wihlborg, Ltd., Corte Madera, Calif., 1982-89, Thompson Planning Group (now Thompson Golf Planning), Ltd., Novato, Calif., 1989—. With Oreg. Planning Commn., commr., 1981-83, Novato, Calif. Planning Commn., commr. 1989-93, pres. 1989-93; spkr. Oreg. Home Builders Conf., 1980, Pacific Coast Builders Conf., 1984, Tacoma Country Club Pro-Pres. Tournament, 1991, Madrona Links Men's Golf Club, 1991, Twin Lakes Country Club Pro-Pres. Tournament, 1992, Golf Expo, Palm Springs, Calif., 1993, 95, Golf Expo, Nashville, 1993, Golf Expo, Monterey, Calif., 1994, others. Contbr. articles to mags. Mem. citizen's adv. bd. City of Eugene, Oreg., City of Las Vegas. Mem. USGA, Am. Soc. Landscape Archs., Am. Assn. Planners, Nat. Golf Found., Urban Land Inst., Rotary Internat. Office: Thompson Golf Planning Ltd 1510 Grant Ave Ste 305 Novato CA 94945-3146 Office Phone: 415-878-2020.

THOMPSON, PHILIP C., lawyer, investment advisor, educator; b. Balt., Oct. 21, 1945; s. Earl Clinton and Virginia (Baugh) Thompson; m. Julie Ann Young, June 10, 1948; children: Kathryn Adair, Julia Hamilton, Philip Clinton Jr. BA, Washington and Lee U., 1967, BS, 1968, JD, 1971. Bar: Ga. 1973, US Dist. Ct. (ea. dist.) Ga. 1973. Ptnr. Jones, Day, Reavis & Pogue, Atlanta, 1973—86, Dow, Lohnes & Albertson, Atlanta, 1986—94, Arnall, Golden, Gregory LLP, Atlanta, 1994—2004, Duane Morris LLP, Atlanta, 2004—. Adj. prof. Emory U., Atlanta, 2003—; guest adj. prof. Ga. State, Atlanta, 2007, Robertson Bus. Coll., Atlanta, 2007. Capt. US Army, 1972—73. Mem.: Capital City Club. Republican. Reformed Anglican. Avocations: youth programs, gardening, running, tennis, chess. Office Phone: 404-253-6920. Business E-Mail: pcthompson@duanemorris.com.

THOMPSON, PHYLLIS D., judge, lawyer; b. Washington, Oct. 1, 1952; BA in Anthropology, with distinction, George Washington U., 1974; MA in Religion (focus in Ethics), Princeton U., 1976; JD with high honors, George Washington U., 1981. Bar: DC 1981. Instr., lectr. Georgetown U., Washington, 1977-81; joined Covington & Burling, Washington, 1982—, now ptnr., fed. benefits programs practice group; assoc. judge DC Ct. Appeals, Washington, 2006—. Instr. & lectr. - Theology Dept. Georgetown U., Washington, 1977—81. Co-author (with Susan L. Burke): Analysis Has Its Privileges: Compliance Rev. May Be Protected From Discovery, 1999. Mem.: Am. Health Lawyers Assn., DC Bar Assn. (steering com. affairs divsn.). Office: DC Ct of Appeals Moultrie Courthouse 500 Indiana Ave NW Washington DC 20001 Office Phone: 202-662-5668, 202-897-2781. Office Fax: 202-662-6291. Business E-Mail: pthompson@cov.com. *

THOMPSON, RALPH GORDON, federal judge; b. Oklahoma City, Dec. 15, 1934; m. Barbara Irene Hencke, Sept. 5, 1964; children: Lisa, Elaine, Maria. BBA, U. Okla., 1956, JD, 1961. Bar: Okla. 1961. Spl. agt. Office of Spl. Investigations, USAF, 1957—60; ptnr. Thompson, Thompson, Harbour & Selph (and predecessors), Oklahoma City, 1961-75; judge U.S. Dist. Ct. for Western Dist. Okla., Oklahoma City, 1975—; chief judge U.S. Dist. Ct. (we. dist.) Okla., 1986-93. Mem. Okla. Ho. of Reps., 1966-70, asst. minority floor leader, 1969-70; spl. justice Supreme Ct. Okla., 1970-71; tchr. Harvard Law Sch. Trial Advocacy Workshop, 1981—; apptd. by chief justice of U.S. to U.S. Fgn. Intelligence Surveillance Ct., 1990-97; elected to jud. conf. of the U.S., 1997; apptd. to Edward J. Devitt Disting. Svc. Justice award selection com., 1997-99; apptd. by chief justice of U.S. to exec. com. of Jud. Conf. of the U.S., 1998-2000; coord. Long Range Planning for Fed. Judiciary, 1999-2000. Co-author: Bryce Harlow: Mr. Integrity, Bob Burke and Ralph G. Thompson, 2000. Rep. nominee for lt. gov., Okla., 1970; chmn. bd. ARC, Oklahoma City, 1970-72; chmn., pres. Okla. Young Lawyers Conf., 1965; mem. bd. visitors U. Okla., 1975-78, U. Okla. Honors Coll., 2007—. Lt. USAF, 1957-60, col. Res., ret. Decorated Legion of Merit; named Oklahoma City's Outstanding Young Man, Oklahoma City Jaycees, 1967, Outstanding Young Oklahoman, Okla. State Jr. C. of C., 1968, Outstanding Fed. Trial Judge, Okla. Trial Lawyers Assn., 1980; recipient Regents Alumni award U. Okla., 1990, Disting. Svc. award, 1993, Jour. Record Pub. Co. award for Disting. Svc., 2001, Humanitarian award Oklahoma City Pub. Schs. Found., 2003; inducted Okla. Hall of Fame, 1995, Fellow Am. Bar Found.; mem. ABA, Fed. Bar Assn., Okla. Bar Assn. (chmn. sect. internat. law and gen. practice 1974-75), Oklahoma County Bar Assn. (Jud. Svc. award 1988), Jud. Conf. U.S. (com. on ct. adminstrn. 1981-89, com. on fed.-state jurisdiction 1988-91), U.S. Dist. Judges Assn. 10th Cir. (pres. 1992-94), Rotary (hon.), Order of Coif, Am. Inns of Ct. (pres. XXIII 1995-96), Phi Beta Kappa (pres. chpt. 1985-86, Phi Beta Kappa of Yr. 1991), Beta Theta Pi, Phi Alpha Delta. Episcopalian. Office: US Dist Ct 200 NW 4th St Oklahoma City OK 73102-3027

THOMPSON, RALPH NEWELL, former chemical corporation executive; b. Boston, Mar. 4, 1918; s. Ralph and Lillian May (Davenport) T.; m. Virginia Kenniston, Jan. 31, 1942; children: Pamela, Nicholas, Diana. BS, MIT, 1940. Research engr. Middlesex Products Co., Cambridge, Mass., 1940-42; tech. dir. Falulah Paper Co., Fitchburg, Mass., 1945-48; staff engr. to v.p., div. gen. mgr. Calgon Corp., Pitts., 1948-70; v.p. mktg., corp. devel. Pa. Indsl. Chem. Corp., Clairton, 1970-74; gen. mgr. chem. div. Thiokol Corp., Trenton, NJ, 1974-76, group v.p.-chem. Newtown, Pa., 1976-82; marine artist, specializing in lighthouses and historic sailing vessels, 1982—. Dir. Mulford Co. Inc., Mass., 1956-82, Thiokol Can. Ltd., 1975-82, Thiokol Chems., Ltd., Eng., 1976-82, Toray Thiokol Co. Ltd., Japan, 1976-82, Nisso-Ventron K.K., Japan, 1977-82, S.W. Chem. Services Inc., Tex., 1978-82, S.W. Plastics Europe (S.A.), Belgium, 1978-82, Dynachem. Corp., Calif., 1979-82, Carstab Corp., Ohio, 1980-82 Patentee in field. Mem. Mt. Lebanon (Pa.) Civic League, 1950-74. Served with USNR, 1942-45. Recipient Goodreau Meml. Fund medal in chemistry, 1936 Fellow Am. Inst. Chemists; mem. TAPPI (contributor monograph series 1950-65), N.Y. Acad. Scis., Soc. Chem. Industry, Nat. Maritime Soc., Am. Soc. Marine Artists, Mil. Order World Wars, Pa. Soc., Soc. Descs. Colonial Clergy. Republican. Presbyterian. E-mail: thompsonrn@verizon.net.

THOMPSON, RAYMOND HARRIS, retired anthropologist, educator; b. Portland, Maine, May 10, 1924; s. Raymond and Eloise (MacIntyre) T.; m. Molly Kendall, Sept. 9, 1948; children: Margaret Kelsey Luchetta, Mary Frances. BS, Tufts U., 1947; A.M., Harvard U., 1950, PhD, 1955. Fellow div. hist. research Carnegie Instn., Washington, 1950-52; asst. prof. anthropology, curator Mus. Anthropology, U. Ky., 1952-56; faculty U. Ariz., 1956-97, prof. anthropology, 1964—, Riecker Disting. prof., 1980-97, head dept., 1964-80; emeritus, 1997; dir. Ariz. State Mus., 1964-97; emeritus, 1997. Mem. adv. panel program in anthropology NSF, 1963-64, mem. mus. collections program, 1983-85; mem. NSF grad. fellowship panel Nat. Acad. Scis.-NRC, 1964-66; mem. research in nursing in patient care rev. com. USPHS, 1967-69; com. on social sci. commn. edn. in agr. and natural resources Nat. Acad. Scis., 1968-69; mem. anthropology com. examiners Grad. Record Exam., 1967-70, chmn., 1969-70; mem. com. recovery archaeol. remains, 1972-77, chmn., 1973-77; collaborator Nat. Park Service, 1972-76; mem. Ariz. Hist. Adv. Commn., 1966-97, chmn., 1971-74, chmn. hist. sites rev. com., 1971-83; mem. editl. bd. Science, 1972-77; chmn. Ariz. Humanities Council, 1973-77, mem., 1979-85; adv. bd. Ariz. Hist. Recors, 1976-84; mem. research review panel for archaeology NEH, 1976-77, mem. rev. panel mus., 1978, Ariz. Archaeology Adv. Commn., 1985-97; cons. task force on archaeology Adv. Council on Historic Preservation, 1978; editl. advisor, Jour. of the Southwest. Author: Modern Yucatecan Maya Pottery Making, 1958; editor: Migrations in New World Culture History, 1958, When is a Kiva, 1990. Trustee Mus. No. Ariz., 1969-84, 86-90; bd. dirs. Tucson Art Mus., 1974-77; cons. Nat. Mus. Act Coun., 1984-86. Served with USNR, 1944-45, PTO. Named Raymond H. Thompson award in his name, Dept. Anthrop., U. Ariz., 2006; recipient Pub. Svc. award, Dept. Interior, 1990. Fellow AAAS (chmn. sect. H 1977-78), Tree-Ring Soc., Am. Anthrop. Assn. (Disting. Svc. award 1980); mem. Soc. Am. Archaeology (editor 1958-62, exec. com. 1963-64, pres. 1976-77, disting. svc. award 1998), Am. Soc. Conservation Archaeology (Conservation award 1980), Seminario de Cultura Maya, Am. Assn. Museums (accreditation vis. com. 1972, 82-90, cons. mus. assessment program 1983-89, repatriation task force 1987, steering com. mus. data collection program 1988-93), Internat. Coun. Museums (assoc.), Coun. Mus. Anthropology (dir. 1978-79, pres. 1980-83), Assn. Sci. Mus. Dirs. (sec.-treas. 1978-80), Ariz. Acad. Sci., Ariz. Archaeol. and Hist. Soc. (Byron Cummings award 1993), Mus. Assn. Ariz. (pres. 1983, 84), Phi Beta Kappa, Sigma Xi. Office: Univ Ariz Ariz State Museum Tucson AZ 85721-0026

THOMPSON, RICHARD DICKSON, lawyer; b. Lexington, Ky., Aug. 14, 1955; s. Lawrence Sidney and Algernon Smith (Dickson) T.; m. Bobbi Dale Magidoff, Aug. 3, 1980; children: Anne Katherine, Harrison Asher, Tracey Ruth. AB, Harvard U., 1977; JD, Stanford U., 1980. Bar: Calif. 1980, U.S. Dist. Ct. (so. dist.) Calif. 1980. Assoc. Rosenfeld Meyer & Susman, Beverly Hills, Calif., 1980-83, Silverberg Rosen Leon & Behr, LA, 1983-86, assoc. ptnr., 1986-89; ptnr. Silverberg Katz Thompson & Braun, LA, 1989-95, Bloom, Hergott, Diemer, & Cook, Beverly Hills, Calif., 1995—2000; sr. v.p., corp. devel. then COO The Brodia Group, San Francisco, 2000—02; of counsel Bloom, Hergott Diemer Rosenthal & LaViolette, LLP, Beverly Hills, Calif., 2002—. Former bd. trustees L.A. Copyright Soc. (former pres.). Mem. Order of the Coif, Phi beta Kappa. Office: Bloom Hergott et al 150 S Rodeo Dr Beverly Hills CA 90212 Office Phone: 310-859-6839. E-mail: rdt@bhdrl.com.

THOMPSON, RICHARD ELLIS, secondary school educator; b. Gary, Ind., May 5, 1935; s. Elijah and Roberta (May) T. AA, Ind. U., 1956; BA, Roosevelt U., 1963, MA, 1966; EdM, De Paul U., 1973. Cert. tchr., adminstr., Ill., Ind. Psychiatric aide Beatty Meml. Hosp., Westville, Ind., 1955-58; counselor child care Lake County Children's Home, Gary, 1958-59, 62-63; tchr., counselor Harlan HS, Chgo., 1963-70; instr. City Colls. Chgo., 1966-70, registrar, adminstrv. asst., 1973-79; employment counselor Ill. Dept. Labor, Chgo., summers 1966, 67; asst. prin. Harlan Cmty. Acad., Chgo., 1970—97; cons. CPS, 1998—2003; ret. Contbr. articles to profl. jours. Sgt. US Army, 1959—62. Named Fort Leonard Wood Soldier of the Month, 1960; named to Hall of Fame, Harlan HS, 2003; recipient Good Conduct medal, US Army, 1961, Cert. outstanding svc., Fort Leonard Wood, 1962. Mem. Chgo. Asst. Prins. Assn. (trustee 1973—, Outstanding Secondary Educator of Am. 1975, Disting. Educator Achievement award 1990), Ill. Notaries Assn., De Paul U. Club, Roosevelt Club, Phi Delta Kappa, Kappa Delta Pi. Democrat. Avocations: silent movies, travel. Home: 500 E 33rd St Apt 1601 Chicago IL 60616-4036 Personal E-mail: rellistlm500@webtv.net.

THOMPSON, RICHARD FREDERICK, psychologist, neuroscientist, educator; b. Portland, Oreg., 1930; s. Frederick Albert and Margaret St. Clair (Marr) T.; m. Judith K. Pedersen, May 22, 1960; children: Kathryn M., Elizabeth K., Virginia St. C. BA, Reed Coll., 1952; MS, U. Wis., 1953, PhD, 1956. Asst. prof. med. psychology Med. Sch. U. Oreg., Portland, 1959-63, assoc. prof., 1963-65, prof., 1965-67; prof. psychobiology U. Calif., Irvine, 1967-73, 75-80; prof. psychology Harvard U., Cambridge, Mass., 1973-74, Lashley chair prof., 1973; prof. psychology, Bing prof. human biology Stanford U., Palo Alto, Calif., 1980-87; Keck prof. psychology and biol. scis. U. So. Calif., LA, 1987—, dir. neuroscience program, 1989—. Author: Foundations of Physiological Psychology, 1967, (with others) Psychology, 1971, Introduction to Physiological Psychology, 1975; Psychology editor (with others), W.H. Freeman & Co. publs., chief editor, Behavioral Neurosci., 1983—; editor: Jour. Comparative and Physiol. Psychology, 1981-83; regional editor: (with others) Physiology and Behavior; contbr. (with others) articles to profl. jours. Fellow AAAS, APA (Disting. Sci. Contbn. award 1974, governing coun. 1974—), Soc. Neurosci. (councilor 1972-76); mem. NAS, Am. Acad. Arts and Scis., Internat. Brain Rsch. Orgn., Nat. Sci. Bd., Am. Philos. Soc., Psychonomic Soc. (gov. 1972-77, chmn. 1976), Am. Psychol. Soc. (pres. 1994-96), Western Psychol. Assn. (pres. 1994-95), Soc. Exptl. Psychology (Warren medal). Office: Univ of So Calif Neuroscis Program HNB 122 Univ Park Los Angeles CA 90007 Office Phone: 213-740-7350. Business E-Mail: thompson@usc.edu.

THOMPSON, RICHARD LEON, pharmaceutical executive, lawyer; b. Rochester, NY, Dec. 5, 1944; s. Leslie L. and Marion (Cosad) T.; m. Catherine Jean Terry, July 6, 1974; children: Kristin Anne, Catherine Elizabeth. AB cum laude, SUNY, Albany, 1966; MA, Syracuse U., 1967; JD, Cath. U., 1975. Staff dir., counsel U.S. Ho. of Reps., Washington, 1973-78; dir. Abbott Labs., Washington, 1978-83; v.p. Squibb Corp., Washington, 1983-89, Bristol-Myers Squibb Corp., Washington, 1989—2001, sr. v.p. policy and govt. affairs, 2001—. Chmn. legis. adv. com. Proprietary Assn., Washington, 1984; bd. dirs. Bus. Govt. Rels. Coun. Mem. com. on changing enrollments Fairfax (Va.) County Pub. Sch., 1983-84, supts. adv. com., 1984-85, mem., 1988-98; mem. Fed. City Coun., 1992; chmn. legis. com. P.R.-U.S.A. Found., 1985-95; co-chair Edn. in 2010; bd. dirs. D.C. Hospice, Bryce Harlow Found., 1990-95; bd. dirs. Ford Theater, 2000—, chmn., 2000-06; chmn. governance com. Meridian Internat. Ctr., 2000-02 1st lt. U.S. Army, 1968-69, Vietnam. Named one of

Outstanding Young Men of Am., Jaycees, 1976. Mem. ABA, D.C. Bar Assn., Pharm. Mfrs. Assn. (chmn. Washington reps. com.1988), Congl. Country Club, City Club. Office Phone: 202-783-8609.

THOMPSON, RICHARD LLOYD, retired pastor; b. Lansing, Mich., May 8, 1939; s. Lloyd Walter and Gladys V. (Gates) T.; m. Dianne Lee Tuttle, Nov. 14, 1958; children: Matthew, Beth Anne, Douglas. BA, Azusa Pacific U., 1969; MDiv, Concordia Theol. Sem., 1973; DD, Concordia U., Mequon, Wis., 1997. Aerospace industry test engr. Hycon Mfg. Co., Monrovia, Calif., 1961-69; pastor Trinity Luth. Ch., Cedar Rapids, Iowa, 1973-84, Billings, Mont., 1984-94, Good Shepherd Luth. Ch., Watertown, Wis., 1994—2001; ret., 2001. Chmn. mission com. Iowa E. dist. Luth. Ch. Mo. Synod, 1979-81, 2nd v.p. Iowa dist. E, Cedar Rapids, 1981-84, cir. counselor so. cir. and 2d v.p. Mont. dist., bd. mgr. Concordia plans, St. Louis, 1983-86, bd. dirs., St. Louis, 1986-98, chmn. bd. dirs., 1992-98, mem. commn. on theology and ch. rels., 2001; chmn. bd. dirs. Ambs. and Reconciliation, 2005-; served on various task forces and coms. dealing with structure and vision setting for chs. at local, dist. and nat. level, 1975—. Mem. Nat. Exch. Club, Cedar Rapids, 1982-84, Billings, 1986; pro tem com. structure Commn. Doctrinal Rev., 2001—. With USN, 1957—61. Mem. Kiwanis. Lutheran. Avocations: attending auctions, yard work, travel, exercise activity. Home Phone: 406-656-0006. Personal E-mail: diarich39@msn.com, rlt50@hotmail.com.

THOMPSON, RICHARD S., lawyer, former prosecutor; b. Jacksonville, Fla., Nov. 26, 1957; m. Jennifer Darby; children: Loree Ann, Darby. BA cum laude, Mercer U., 1979, JD, 1982. Bar: Ga. Asst. dist. atty. Douglas County, Ga.; asst. atty. gen. State of Ga., 1986—88; pvt. practice Statesboro and Vidalia, 1989—95; ptnr. McNatt, Greene & Thompson, Vidalia, Ga., 1995—2001; U.S. atty. so. dist. Ga. US Dept. Justice, 2001—04; ptnr. Weidner & Thompson, LLC, Clarksville, Ga., 2004—. Mem.: Ga. Def. Lawyers Assn. Office: So Dist Ga PO Box 8999 Savannah GA 31412 also: Weidner & Thompson LLC 146 Professional Park Dr PO Box 2017 Clarkesville GA 30523 Office Phone: 706-754-9000. Office Fax: 706-754-0098.

THOMPSON, RICHARD STEPHEN, management consultant; b. Des Moines, Oct. 14, 1931; s. Richard Stephen and Mary Ellen (Dailey) T.; m. Nancy Ann Jensen, Apr. 17, 1954; children— Traci Nan, Gregory Christian, Jonathan Richard BSc, State U. Iowa, 1953; MBA, Ind. U., 1960. Regional dir. Bristol Myers Co., NYC, 1969-75; regional dir. Warner Lambert Co., Morris Plains, NJ, 1975-78; exec. v.p. Milton Bradley Co., Milton Bradley Internat., Inc., Springfield, Mass., 1979-83, pres., 1983-84; sr. v.p. internat., dir. Hasbro, Inc., Pawtucket, RI, 1984-89; pres. Richard Thompson Assocs., London, 1989—. Served to 1st lt. USAF, 1954-55 Mem.: Chatham Beach Tennis (Mass.); Pilgrims (London and N.Y.); American (London); Roehampton (London). Independent. Avocations: tennis, hiking, skiing, reading.

THOMPSON, RICHARD THOMAS, academic administrator; b. Buffalo, Oct. 11, 1939; m. Nancy A. Streeter, July 29, 1959; children: Elizabeth Thompson Grapentine, Richard Thomas Jr., David Bryant. BA, Ea. Mich. U., 1961, MA, 1963; LLD (hon.), Walsh Coll., 2000. Cert. tchr. Mich. Tchr. Warren Consol. Sch., Mich., 1961—66; dean, pres. Highland Lake campus Oakland C.C., Union Lake, 1966—75, pres. Orchard Ridge campus Farmington, 1975—84, v.p. Bloomfield, 1984—88, vice chancellor, 1988—91, chancellor, 1996—2004, pres. Auburn Hills campus, 1995—96, chancellor emeritus, 2004. Arbitrator Better Bus. Bur., Detroit, 1987—; bd. dirs., past chair Providence Hosp., Southfield; cons. examiner North Ctrl. Assn. Commn. Higher Learning, 1988—2004. Contbr. articles to profl. jours. Pres. Oakway Symphony Orch., Livonia, Mich., 1981—85; chair Oakland Literacy Coun., Pontiac, 1988—2002. Recipient Leadership award, Oakland County C. of C., 1987, Tricounty Disting. Svc. award, Detroit Coll. Bus., 1996, Shirley B. Gordon award Distinction, Phi Theta Kappa Internat., 2001. Mem.: Phi Delta Kappa. Home: 6868 W Harbor Dr Elk Rapids MI 49629

THOMPSON, ROBERT ALLAN, aerospace engineer; b. Cleve., June 10, 1937; s. Roy Henry and Viola Alverta (Nehls) T.; m. Louise Alberta Saari, Nov. 27, 1970. BSEE, Case Western Reserve U., 1958; postgrad. studies, Cleve. State U., 1959, John Marshall Law Sch., 1970; PhD, Union Inst., 1979. Registered profl. engr., Ohio, Wis., Conn., R.I. Tchr. Cleve. Bd. Edn., 1958-65; rsch. engr. Sohio Satellite Tracking Sta., Standard Oil Rsch. Lab., Cleve., 1958-63, acting dir., 1964-65; dir. Warrensville Hghts. (Ohio) Planetarium and Space Sci Program, 1964-65; tchr. spl. programs faculty Case Inst. Tech., Cleve., 1965; dir. planning phase sci. divsn. Cleve. Supplementary Edn. Ctr., 1965-66; dir. James A Lovell Regional Space Ctr., Milw., 1967-73; engring. and edn. cons. Chgo., 1973-78, Mystic, Conn., 1978—; pres., chmn. bd. Spatialworld Corp., 1982—. Chmn. secondary math. curriculum com. Cleve. Pub. Schs., 1963-64; mem. Wis. Aerospace Edn. Com., 1968-71; lectr. U. Wis., Milw., 1968-71; sec. Friends of Space Ctr., 1968-75. Author: The New Egoshell: An Individualized Space Age Realty; co-author (with L. Thompson) Egoshell-Planetary Individualism Balanced within Planetary Interdependence, 1987; contbr. articles to profl. jours. Kiwanian faculty adv. Collinwood Key Club, 1959—64. Recipient Leadership award, NE Cleve. Kiwanis, 1961; Goodwin Watson fellow, Union Inst., 1978—79. Fellow: Brit. Interplanetary Assn.; mem.: AIAA (chmn. Wis. sect. 1969—70, sr. mem. Conn. sect., coun. 1984—85, disting. lectr. 1987—89), AAAS, IEEE (sr. life) (chmn. membership com. Cleve. sect. 1965—66, exec. com.), Cleve. Astron. Soc. (exec. com. 1966—67), Cleve. Engring. Soc., Inst. Planetary Egology (pres. 1988—), Union Inst. Alumni Assn., Case Alumni Assn. Home: PO Box 624 Mystic CT 06355-0624 Office: PO Box 2001 Mystic CT 06355-0624 Office Phone: 860-572-0145. Personal E-mail: egoshell@aol.com.

THOMPSON, ROBERT CHARLES, lawyer; b. Council, Idaho, Apr. 20, 1942; s. Ernest Lavelle and Evangeline Montgomery (Carlson) T.; m. Marilyn Anne Wilcox, Jan. 17, 1960 (dec. Mar. 1962); m. Patricia Joan Price, June 1, 1963 (div. 1969); m. Jan Nesbitt, June 29, 1973 (dec. May 1998); m. Shari Lewis, Feb. 7, 1999; children: Christopher, Eric, Tanya, Carrie AB, Harvard U., Cambridge, Mass., 1963, LLB, 1967. Bar: Mass. 1967, Calif. 1983, US Dist. Ct. (ea. dist.) Mass. 1975, US Ct. Appeals (1st cir.) 1976, US Ct. Appeals (9th cir.) 1984, US Dist. Ct. (no. dist.) Calif. 1983, US Dist. Ct. (ea. dist.) Calif., 1996. Assoc. Choate, Hall & Stewart, Boston, 1967-73; asst. regional counsel EPA, Boston, 1973-75, regional counsel, 1975-82, assoc. gen. counsel, 1979-82, regional counsel San Francisco, 1982-84; ptnr. Graham & James, San Francisco, 1984-91, LeBoeuf, Lamb, Greene & MacRae LLP, San Francisco, 1992—99, of counsel, 2000—. Co-author: Crime and Conflict, 2006; contbr. articles to profl. jours. Bd. dirs. Peninsula Indsl. and Bus. Assn., Palo Alto, Calif., 1986-98, chmn. Cambridge Conservation Commn., Mass., 1972-74; co-chmn. The Clift Confs. on Environ. Law, 1983-98; assoc. mem. Bay Conservation and Devel. Commn., 1998-2000. John Russell Shaw traveling fellow Harvard Coll., 1963-64; recipient Regional Administrs. Bronze medal EPA, 1976, 84. Mem. ABA (chmn. natural resources sect., chmn. com. native Am. natural resources law, spl. com. mktg.), HumanRights Watch, Internat. Pub. What You Pay Campaign, Human RightsFirst, OxFan Am., Phi Beta Kappa. Democrat. Episcopalian. Avocations: yoga, antiques, cooking, gardening, opera. Office: LeBoeuf Lamb Greene & MacRae One Embarcadero Ctr San Francisco CA 94111 E-mail: thomps925@aol.com.

THOMPSON, ROBERT LEE, agricultural economist, educator; b. Canton, NY, Apr. 25, 1945; s. Robert M. and Esther Louise (Weatherup) T.; m. Karen Hansen, Aug. 9, 1968; children— Kristina Marie, Eric Robert. BS, Cornell U., Ithaca, NY, 1967; MS, Purdue U., West Lafayette, Ind., 1969, PhD, 1974; LLD, Dalhousie U., 1999; DSc honoris causa, Pa. State U., 1999. Vol. agriculturalist Internat. Vol. Service, Pakse and Vientiane, Laos, 1968-70; vis. prof. Fed. Univ. Vicosa, Brazil, 1972-73; prof. Purdue U., West Lafayette, Ind., 1974-93, dean of agr., 1987-93; rsch. scholar Internat. Inst. for Applied Systems Analysis, Laxenburg, Austria, 1983; sr. staff economist Coun. Econ. Advisers, Washington, 1983-85; asst. sec. econs. U.S. Dept. Agr., Washington, 1985-87; pres., CEO Winrock Internat. Inst. Agrl. Devel., 1993-98; sr. advisor World Bank, Washington, 1998-99, dir. rural devel., 1999—2002; sr. advisor Ctr. for Strategic and Internat. Studies, 1998—99, Nat. Ctr. for Food and Agr. Policy, Washington, 2003—; Gardner endowed chair agr. policy U. Ill., Urbana, 2004—. Vis. prof. Econ. Rsch. Svc., USDA, 1979-80; chmn. adv. coun. Nat. Ctr. Food and Agrl. Policy, Washington, 1987-92; mem. Ind. Commn. on Agr. and Rural Devel., 1989-93, Nat. Commn. on Agrl. Trade and Export Policy, 1985-86, Nat. Commn. Internat. Trade, Devel., and Cooperation, 1996-97; mem. bd. agr. NRC, 1987-92; mem. Internat. Policy Coun. on Agr. and Trade, 1987—, chmn., 2000-06; mem. USDA Joint Coun. on Food and Agrl. Scis., 1994-96; bd. dir. Land O'Lakes, Cordell Hull Inst., Washington; advisory bd. mem. Rabobank N. Am. Agribus., 1998-2003; mem. agrl. policy adv. coun. trade, USDA and US Trade Rep., 2005-. Contbr. numerous articles to profl. publs. Author monographs, book chpts. Bd. dirs. Ind. 4-H Found., Ind. Inst. Agr. Food and Nutrition, 1987-93, Inst. for Sci. in Soc., 1991-93, USDA Grad. Sch., Washington, 1985-87; mem. nat. adv. coun. Minorities in Agr., Natural Resources and Related Sci.; bd. dirs. Farm Found., 1987-92, chmn. 1991-92. Recipient Agrl. Rsch. award Purdue U., 1983, Outstanding Alumni award Cornell U., 1988, Superior Svc. award USDA, 1989, Justin Smith Morrill award, 1995, Nat. 4-H Alumni award, 1992, Chgo. Farmers Agriculturalist of Yr. award, 1992, Bob Pim Agrl. Vision award Nat. Forum Agr., 1997; named Humanitarian of Yr., Am. Coll. Nutrition, 1999. Fellow AAAS, Am. Agrl. Econs. Assn. (editl. coun. 1983-85, quality com. award 1979, 91, 93); mem. Internat. Agribus Mgmt. Assn., Am. Econ. Assn., Internat. Assn. Agrl. Economists (pres. 1993-96), Coun. Fgn. Rels., Chgo. Coun. on Global Affairs, Bretton Woods Com., Royal Swedish Acad. Agr. and Forestry (fgn.), Ukrainian Acad. Agrl. Scis., Cosmos Club (Washington), Sigma Xi, Alpha Gamma Rho, Alpha Zeta (Centennial Honor Role award 1997), Gamma Sigma Delta. Republican. Avocation: foreign language study. Office: 412 Mumford Hall MC-710 1301 W Gregory Dr Urbana IL 61801-3608 Office Phone: 217-333-1313. Business E-Mail: rlt@uiuc.edu.

THOMPSON, ROBERT SAMUEL, retired lawyer; b. Cleve., Nov. 2, 1930; s. Wayne Charles Thompson and Cornelia Irene (Anderson) Thompson Baker; m. JoAnne Courtney; children: Robert Dale, Richard Wayne. BA, Hamilton Coll., 1953; JD, U. Mich., 1956; postgrad., Air Command and Staff Coll., Montgomery, Ala., 1967-68. Bar: Mich. 1956, Ohio 1962, U.S. Supreme Ct. 1962, Oreg. 1973. Judge advocate USAF, 1956-77; pvt. practice McMinnville, Oreg., 1977—2003; ret., 2003. Judge mcpl. ct. 1977-2003. Mem. Oreg. Soc. SAR (pres. 1989-90), Oreg. Mcpl. Judges Assn. (pres. 1992-93), Rotary (bd. dirs. McMinnville chpt. 1989), Am. Legion, Masons. Home and Office: 127 NW 19th St Mcminnville OR 97128-2611

THOMPSON, ROBY CALVIN, JR., orthopedic surgeon, educator, department chairman; b. Winchester, Ky., May 1, 1934; s. Roby Calvin and Mary Davis (Guerrant) T.; m. Jane Elizabeth Searcy, May 2, 1959; children: Searcy Lee, Roby Calvin, III, Mary Alexandra. BA, Va. Mil. Inst., 1955; MD, U. Va., 1959. Diplomate Am. Bd. Orthopaedic Surgery (mem. bd. 1983). Intern Columbia Presbyn. Med. Center, NYC, 1959-60, asst. resident, then resident in orthopedic surgery, 1963-67; instr. orthopaedic surgery Coll. Phys. and Surg. Columbia U., 1967-68; mem. faculty Med. Sch. U. Va., 1968-74, prof. orthopaedic surgery, vice chmn. dept. Med. Sch., 1973—94; prof., chmn. dept. Med. Sch. U. Minn., 1974—94; chief med. officer U. Minn. Health Sys., 1995-96, v.p. clin. and acad. affairs, 1996—2001; sr. assoc. dean clin. affairs U. Minn. Sch. Medicine, 1996—. Merit rev. bd. VA, 1977-80; study sect. on applied physiology and orthopedics NIH, 1980-83; adv. coun. NIH, Nat. Inst. Arthritis, Musculoskeletal Disease and Skin, 1987-91; chmn. bd. dirs. U. Minn. Physicians, 2001-05, CEO, 2001—. Trustee Jour. Bone and Joint Surgery, 1988-94, chmn. bd. trustees, 1991-94; contbr. articles to med. jours. Capt. M.C. USAR, 1960-61. Grantee John Hartford Found., NIH Mem. ACS, Orthopaedic Rsch. and Edn. Found. (bd. trustees 1990-96), Am. Acad. Orthopaedic Surgeons (bd. dirs. 1975-76, 83-90, pres. 1986), Orthopaedic Rsch. Soc. (pres. 1978), Am. Orthopaedic Assn., Musculoskeletal Tumor Soc. (pres. 1988-89), U. Va. Med. Alumni Assn. (bd. dirs. 1979-84), Woodhill Club (Wayzata). Republican. Presbyterian. Office: U Minn MMC 293 420 Delaware St SE Minneapolis MN 55455-0374

THOMPSON, RONALD EDWARD, lawyer; b. Bremerton, Wash., May 24, 1931; s. Melville Herbert and Clara Mildred (Griggs) T.; m. Marilyn Christine Woods, Dec. 15, 1956; children: Donald Jeffery, Karen, Susan, Nancy, Sally, Claire BA, U. Wash., 1953, JD, 1958. Bar: Wash. 1959. Asst. city atty. City of Tacoma, 1960—61; pres. firm Thompson, Krilich, LaPorte, West & Lockner, P.S., Tacoma, 1961—99. Judge pro tem Mcpl. Ct., City of Tacoma, Pierce County Dist., 1972—, Pierce County Superior Ct., 1972—. Chmn. housing and social welfare com. City of Tacoma, 1965-69; mem. Tacoma Bd. Adjustment, 1967-71, chmn., 1968; mem. Tacoma Com. Future Devel., 1961-64, Tacoma Planning Commn., 1971-72; bd. dirs., pres. Mcpl. League Tacoma; bd. dirs. Pres. Tacoma Rescue Mission, Tacoma Pierce County Cancer Soc., Tacoma-Pierce County Heart Assn., Tacoma Grand Cinema, Tacoma-Pierce County Coun. for Arts, Econ. Devel. Coun. Puget Sound, Tacoma Youth Symphony, Kleiner Group Home, Tacoma C.C. Found., Pierce County Econ. Devel. Corp., Wash. Transp. Policy Inst.; Coalition to Keep Wash. Moving, precinct committeeman Rep. party, 1969-73. With AUS, 1953-55; col. Res. Recipient Internat. Cmty. Svc. award Optimist Club, 1970, Patriotism award Am. Fedn. Police, 1974, citation for cmty. svc. HUD, 1974, Disting. Citizen award Mcpl. League Tacoma-Pierce County, 1985; named Lawyer of the Yr. Pierce County Legal Secs. Assn., 1992. Mem. ATLA, Am. Arbitration Assn. (panel of arbitrators), ABA, Wash. State Bar Assn. (Local Hero award 2002), Tacoma-Pierce County Bar Assn. (sec. 1964, pres. 1979, mem. cts. and judiciary com. 1981-82), Wash. State Trial Lawyers Assn., Tacoma-Pierce County C. of C. (bd. dirs., exec. com., v.p., chmn.), Downtown Tacoma Assn. (com. chmn., bd. dirs. exec. com., chmn.), Variety Club (Seattle), Lawn Tennis Club, Tacoma Club, Optimist (Tacoma, internat. pres. 1973-74), Phi Delta Phi, Sigma Nu. Roman Catholic. Home: 3101 E Bay Dr NW Gig Harbor WA 98335-7610 Office: PO Box 2091 4411 Point Fosdick Dr Ste 207 Gig Harbor WA 98333-4091 Office Phone: 253-853-7449. Personal E-mail: retpllc@att.net.

THOMPSON, RONELLE KAY HILDEBRANDT, library director; d. Earl E. and Maxine R. (Taplin) Hildebrandt; m. Harry Floyd Thompson II, Dec. 24, 1976; children: Clarissa, Harry III. BA in Humanities magna cum laude, Houghton Coll., 1976; MLS, Syracuse U., 1976; postgrad., U. Rochester, 1980-81; cert., Miami U., 1990. Libr. asst. Norwalk (Conn.) Pub. Libr., 1977; elem. libr. Moriah Ctrl. Schs., Port Henry, NY, 1977—78; divsn. coord. pediat. gastroenterology and nutrition U. Rochester (N.Y.) Med. Ctr., 1978—81, cons., pediat. housestaff libr. com., 1980—81; dir. Medford Libr. U. S.C., Lancaster, 1981—83; dir. Mikkelsen Libr., Libr. Assocs., Ctr. for Western Studies, mem. libr. com. Augustana Coll., Sioux Falls, SD, 1983—, adminstrv. pers. coun., 1989—94, 1997—2004. Presenter in field. Contbr. articles to profl. jours. Mem. S.D. Symphony; advisor pers. dept. City of Sioux Falls. Recipient leader award YWCA, 1991; Gaylord Co. scholar Syracuse U., 1976; named S.D. Libr. of Yr., 1998. Mem. ALA, AAUW, Assn. Coll. and Rsch. Librs. (nat. adv. coun. coll. librs. sect. 1987—), Mountain Plains Libr. Assn. (chair acad. sect., nominating com. 1988, pres. 1993-94), S.D. Libr. Assn. (chair interlibr. coop. task force 1986-87, pres. 1987-88, chair recommended minimum salary task force 1988, chair local arrangements com. 1989-90, 2002-03), S.D. Libr. Network (adv. coun. 1986—, exec. com. 1992-96, 1998-2000, 2006-, chair adv. coun. 1994-96, 98-2000, 2006-). Office: Augustana Coll Mikkelsen Libr 29th & Smt Sioux Falls SD 57197-0001 Office Phone: 605-274-4921. Business E-Mail: ronelle.thompson@augie.edu.

THOMPSON, SALLY ANN, editor; b. Hillsboro, ND, Apr. 10, 1943; d. C. Hilman and Blanche E. (Bjerkan) Swenson; m. Arthur G. Thompson, July 1, 1965 (dec. Mar. 1990); 1 child, Laurie Kate Beth. Student, Concordia Coll., Moorhead, Minn., 1961-65. Reporter Valley Jour., Halstad, Minn., 1979-84; contbg. editor Prairie West Publs., Wahpeton, ND, 1982-84; editor Hillsboro Banner, Hillsboro, ND, 1984-95, Sun Newspapers, Eden Prairie, Minn., 1995—. Lectr. Career Day Mayville State U., ND, 1985—92. Bd. dirs. Trail County Hist. Soc., 1979—95, Hillsboro Forestry Bd., 1990—93; mem. commns. com. Eastern N.D. Synod ELCA, 1990—93. Recipient numerous journalism awards. Lutheran. Avocations: photography, collages, reading, history. Home: 1805 Highway 101 Apt 203 Plymouth MN 55447-2715 Office: Sun Newspapers 10917 Valley View Rd Eden Prairie MN 55344 Office Phone: 952-392-7668. Personal E-mail: sally_thompson@hotmail.com.

THOMPSON, SAMUEL DONALD, assemblyman; b. Mobile, Ala., July 31, 1935; m. Jacqueline Thompson; children: Shaun, Vanessa, Richard. BS in Chemistry and Math, U. of Ark., 1960; PhD in Phys. Chemistry, La. State U., 1965. Del. Rep. Nat. Con., 1988, 1992, 1996, 2000, alt. del., 2004; dir. planning, analysis, and govt. rels. N.J. Turnpike Authority, 1994—97; assemblyman N.J. Gen. Assembly, 1998—; chmn. Old Bridge Rep. County Com., 2001. Rsch. scientist E.I. duPont de Nemours, 1965—68, J.P. Stevens and Co., 1968—71; dir. clin. lab improvement svc. N.J. State Dept. of Health, 1972—94; chmn. Middlesex County Rep. Com., 1986—94; mem. Old Bridge Twp. Environ. Commn., 1983, Old Bridge Twp. Planning Bd., 1983, U.S. Armed Forces Epidemiological Bd., 1983—90; co-chair Govs. Edn. Task Force, 1994. Mem. Task Force on Adolescent Violence, 1983, Commn. on Elder Care, 1999—2001. Republican. Baptist. Office: 725 Hwy 34 Matawan NJ 07747 Home Phone: 732-679-4391; Office Phone: 732-583-5558. Business E-Mail: AsmThompson@njleg.org.

THOMPSON, SANDRA GUERRA, lawyer, educator; BA, Yale U., 1985, JD, 1988. Asst. dist. atty. NY County Dist. Atty.'s Office, 1988—90; prof. U. Houston Law Ctr., 1990—, dir. Mexican Legal Studies Program, 2000; dir. Criminal Justice Inst., Univ. Houston. Co-author: The Law of Asset Forfeiture; contbr. articles to prof. jour. Mem.: Assn. Am. Law Sch. (chair, Criminal Justice sect. 2001), Hispanic Bar Assn. (mem. bd. dir.), Houston Bar Assn., Am. Law Inst. (mem. bd. adv. Model Penal Code: Sentencing project). Office: Criminal Justice Institute 100 Law Ctr 4800 Calhoun Rd Houston TX 77204 Office Phone: 713-743-2134. E-mail: sgthompson@Central.uh.edu. *

THOMPSON, SANDRA LEE, library administrator; b. Dover, Ohio, Jan. 23, 1968; d. Robert Leonard and Gwendolyn Ruth Stewart; m. Alan McKinney Thompson, Sept. 9, 1990; children: LeeAnna, Alisha, James. BS in Edn., Ohio U., 1989; M of Libr. Info. Sci., U. S.C., 2001. Tchr. Harrison Hills City Sch. Dist., Hopedale, Ohio, 1989-90; asst. dir. Puskarich Pub. Libr., Cadiz, Ohio, 1990-97, dir., 1998—. Mem. Ohio Libr. Coun., Columbus, 1994—; bd. dirs. Southeastern Ohio Libr. Orgn., Caldwell, 1997-07, Ohio Pub. Libr. Info. Network. Mem.: Cadiz Rotary Assocs. (trustee), Am. Libr. Assn. Office: Puskarich Pub Libr 200 E Market St Cadiz OH 43907-1200 E-mail: sthompson@oplin.org.

THOMPSON, SHIRLEY WILLIAMS, mathematics professor; b. Laurens, SC, Oct. 12, 1941; d. Spellman and Lula Mae S.R. Williams; m. Joseph Earl Thompson, Nov. 27, 1969; children: Shirley Elizabeth Thompson Marshall, Joseph Earl Jr., Amber Gale Thompson Ramsey. BS, Johnson C. Smith U., Charlotte, NC, 1963; MEd, U. NC, 1971; MS, Atlanta U., 1988; PhD, Ga. State U., Atlanta, 1980. Adminstrv. specialist Ga. State U., Atlanta, 1976—77; asst. prof. math. Morehouse Coll., Atlanta, 1980—84, assoc. prof. math., 1984—. Bd. dir. Nat. Assn. Mathematicians, Balt., 1996—2000, Excellence in Edn. Barry Goldwater Scholarship, Phoenix, 1990—; program rev. com. Presdl. Scholars, Washington, 1995—. Field reader Jack Kent Cooke Found., Washington, 2002—. Mem.: Math. Assn. Am., Beta Kappa Chi, Pi Mu Epsilon, Kappa Delta Psi. Presbyterian. Achievements include first to receive master's degree in mathematics from U. NC. Avocations: travel, reading, art history. Home: 4793 Carlene Way SW Lilburn GA 30047 Office: Morehouse Coll 830 Westview Dr Atlanta GA 30314 Business E-Mail: sthompson@morehouse.edu.

THOMPSON, SYDNOR, JR., (CHARLES WILLIAM SYDNOR THOMPSON JR.), lawyer, mediator, arbitrator; b. Balt., Feb. 18, 1924; s. Charles William Sydnor Thompson and Helen Josephine Layne; m. Harriette Line, June 2, 1947; children: Darcy T. Howard, Charles William Sydnor III, Harriet T. Moore, Brenneman L., Mary Katherine Line T. Kelly. AB, Syracuse U., 1947; LLB, Harvard U., 1950; student, St. Andrews U., Scotland, 1945, Manchester U., Eng., 1950, London Sch. Econs., 1951. Cert.: NC Dispute Resolution Commn. (mediator), EEOC, Am. Arbitration Assn. (arbitrator), Nat. Assn. Securities Dealers. Assoc. Davis Polk & Wardwell, NYC, 1951—54; ptnr. Parker Poe Thompson Bernstein Gage & Preston, Charlotte, NC, 1954—94; judge NC Ct. Appeals, Raleigh, NC, 1994; of counsel Parker, Poe, Adams & Bernstein, LLP, Charlotte, 1995—; prin. Mediation, Inc., Winston-Salem, NC, 1995—. Author: The Sydnor Family Saga, 2000, A Collection of Ad Hominem Verse, 2002, Sydnor Knows the Answer: A Memoir, 2006; contbr. articles to law revs. Pres. Charlotte Symphony Orch., 1958—61, Charlotte Opera Assn., 1971—75; vice chair NC Arts Coun., Raleigh, 1981—84; pres. Mecklenburg Ministries, 1987—89, Wing Haven Found., 2001—02; chmn. Mecklenburg County Dem. Party, 1977—81. With US Army, 1943—46, ETO. Decorated Bronze star; Fulbright scholar, 1950, 1951. Master: William H. Bobbitt Inn of Ct.; mem.: ABA (chmn. circuits subcom. 1977—95), Mecklenburg Bar Assn. (pres. 1990), NC Bar Assn. (chmn. appellate rules study com. 1989—91, chmn. local bar svcs. com. 1991—93), Old Catawba Soc., Horace Williams Philosophy Club, English Speaking Union, Charlotte City Club, Sporadic Book Club, Charlotte Country Club. Avocations: genealogy, writing, tennis, acting. Office: Parker Poe Adams & Bernstein LLP Ste 3000 401 S Tryon St Charlotte NC 28202 Office Phone: 704-372-9000. Business E-Mail: sydnorthompson@parkerpoe.com.

THOMPSON, TERENCE WILLIAM, lawyer; b. Moberly, Mo., July 3, 1952; s. Donald Gene and Carolyn (Stringer) T.; m. Caryn Elizabeth Hildebrand, Aug. 30, 1975; children: Cory Elizabeth, Christopher William, Tyler Madison. BA in Govt. with honors and high distinction, U. Ariz., 1974; JD, Harvard U., 1977. Bar: Ariz. 1977, U.S. Dist. Ct. Ariz. 1977, U.S. Tax Ct. 1979. Assoc. Brown & Bain P.A., Phoenix, 1977-83, ptnr., 1983-92, Gallagher and Kennedy, P.A., Phoenix, 1992—. Legis. aide Rep. Richard Burgess, Ariz. Ho. of Reps., 1974; mem. bus. adv. bd. Citibank Ariz. (formerly Great Western Bank & Trust, Phoenix), 1985-86. Mem. staff Harvard Law Record, 1974-75; rsch. editor Harvard Internat. Law Jour.,1976; lead author, editor-in-chief: Arizona Corporate Practice, 1996—; contbr. articles to profl. jours. Mem. Phoenix Mayor's Youth Adv. Bd. 1968-70, Phoenix Internat.; active 20-30 Club, 1978-81, sec. 1978-80, Valley Leadership, Phoenix, 1983-84, citizens task force future financing needs City of Phoenix, 1985-86; exec. coun. Boys and Girls Clubs of Met. Phoenix, 1990-2000, sr. coun. 2000—; bd. dirs. Phoenix Bach Choir, 1992-94; deacon Shepherd of Hills Congl. Ch., Phoenix, 1984-85; pres. Maricopa County Young Dems., 1982-83, Ariz. Young Dems., 1983-84, sec. 1981-82, v.p. 1982-83; exec. dir. Young Dems. Am., 1985, exec. com. 1983-85; others. Recipient Best of Ariz. State Bar, Ariz. Bus. Jour., 2004.

Fellow Ariz. Bar Found.; mem. State Bar Ariz. (vice chmn. internt. law sect. 1978, sec. securities law sect. 1990-91, vice chmn. sect. 1991-92, chmn.-elect 1992-93, chmn. 1993-94, exec. coun. 1988-96, sec. bus. law sect. 1992-93, vice chmn. 1993-94, chmn. 1994-95, exec. coun. 1996-98, 07-), Nat. Assn. Bond Lawyers, Nat. Health Lawyers, Selden Soc., Greater Phoenix Black C. of C. (bd. dirs. 1999-2001), Blue Key, Phi Beta Kappa, Phi Kappa Phi, Phi Eta Sigma. Home: 202 W Lawrence Rd Phoenix AZ 85013-1226 Office: Gallagher & Kennedy PA 2575 E Camelback Rd Phoenix AZ 85016-9225 Home Phone: 602-248-8237; Office Phone: 602-530-8515. Business E-Mail: twt@gknet.com.

THOMPSON, THELMA BARNABY, university president, classical languages educator; b. Balaclava, Jamaica, West Indies, July 22, 1940; d. Claude Noel and Elaine Jordan (Robertson) Barnaby; m. Winston Lloyd Thompson, June 15, 1976; 1 child, Lisa Valdeen. BA, Howard U., DC, 1970; MA, Howard U., 1972, PhD, 1978; diploma, Bethlehem Tchrs. Coll., Malvern, Jamaica, West Indies, 1960. Lectr. CUNY, 1972—74; asst. prof. Bowie (Md.) State Coll., 1974—76; assoc. prof., asst. chmn. English dept. U. DC, Washington, 1976—88, assoc. dean, 1988—90; dean Sch. Arts and Letters Norfolk State U., 1990—98, v.p. acad. affairs, 1998—2002; pres. U. Md. Ea. Shore, Princess Anne, 2002—. Author: The Seventeenth Century English Hymn; also articles. Named one of Md.'s 100 Outstanding Women, 2004, Women Shaping the World, Essence Mag., 2005; recipient Bethlehem Coll. Medal of Distinction, scholarship and grad. fellowship, award for outstanding accomplishment in field of edn., Howard U., 2005, Best of St. Bess award, Jamaica, West Indies, 2003. Mem. MLA, Coll. Lang. Assn., South Atlantic MLA, Middle Atlantic Writers, Phi Beta Kappa, Phi Delta Kappa (award for disting. svc. and commitment to excellence in edn. 1991). Achievements include extensive outreach work in Africa and the Caribbean. Office: U Md Eastern Shore JT Williams Hall Rm 2107 Princess Anne MD 21853 Office Phone: 410-651-6101. Business E-Mail: tbthompson@umes.edu.

THOMPSON, THEODORE ROBERT, pediatric educator; b. Dayton, Ohio, July 18, 1943; s. Theodore Roosevelt and Helen (Casey) J.; m. Lynette Joanne Shenk; 1 child, S. Beth. BS, Wittenberg U., 1965; MD, U. Pa., 1969. Diplomate Am. Bd. Pediatrics (Neonatal, Perinatal Medicine). Resident in pediat. U. Minn. Hosp., Mpls., 1969—72, chief resident in pediat., 1971—72, fellow neonatal, perinatal, 1974—75, asst. prof., 1975—80, dir. divsn. neonatology and newborn intensive care unit, 1977—91, assoc. prof., 1980—85, prof., 1985—, co-dir. Med. Outreach, 1988—91, med. dir. med. outreach, 1991—2000, assoc. chief pediat. svcs., 1988—2003, assoc. head pediat. edn. and cmty. programs, 2003—04, assoc. head cmty. affairs, 2004—; med. dir. outreach, bd. dirs. U. Minn. Physicians, 1992—. Med. exec. com., sec.-treas. U. Minn. Med. Ctr., Fairview, 2002—04, chief of staff elect, 2004—07, chief of staff, 2007. Editor: Newborn Intensive Care: A Practical Manual, 1983. Bd. dirs. Life Link III, St. Paul, 1987—; cons. Maternal and Child Health, Minn. Bd. Health, 1975-94; bd. dirs. Minn. Med. Found., 1995-99. With USPHS. 1972-74. Recipient Advocacy award, U. Minn. Med. Sch., Pres.'s award for outstanding svc., U. Minn., Alumni Catalogs award, Wittenberg U., 2005. Fellow: Am. Acad. Pediats.; mem.: Acad. Med. Educators, Gt. Plains Orgn. for Perinatal Health Care (Sioux Falls, SD Kunshe award 1989). Lutheran. Office: MMC 39 420 Delaware St SE Minneapolis MN 55455-0374 Office Phone: 612-626-2841. Business E-Mail: thomp005@umn.edu.

THOMPSON, THOMAS MARTIN, lawyer; b. Albion, Pa., Jan. 7, 1943; s. Donald C. and Mabel Louise (Martin) T.; m. Judith E. Daucher; children: Reid, Chad, Matthew, Molly. AB, Grove City Coll., 1965; JD cum laude, Harvard U., 1968. Bar: Pa. 1968. Ptnr. Buchanan Ingersoll & Rooney, Pitts., 1968—. Adj. prof. law U. Pitts.; past chairperson, dir. Pa. Lawyer Trust Acct. Bd. Past pres., bd. dir. Neighborhood Legal Svcs. Assn.; trustee emeritus Pitts. Pub. Theater. Mem. ABA (program chiar, Negotiated Acquisition Com.), Pa. Bar Assn. (chair bus. law sect., Pro Bono award 1989), Allegheny County Bar Assn. (past chmn. pub. svc. com., past chmn. bus. law coun., past chair PBA legal opinion steering com.), Assn. for Corp. Growth (past pres. Pitts. chpt.). Democrat. Home: 1142 Dartmouth Rd Pittsburgh PA 15205-1705 Office: Buchanan Ingersoll & Rooney One Oxford Ctr 301 Grant St Fl 20 Pittsburgh PA 15219-1410 Office Phone: 412-562-8855. Business E-Mail: thomas.thompson@bipc.com.

THOMPSON, TIMOTHY LEWIS, lawyer; b. Stamford, Conn., Feb. 28, 1948; s. Elbert Paul and Carol Lewis Thompson; m. Elizabeth Anne Wasik, June 3, 1973; children: Andrew Austin, Charles Erling, Nicholas James, Daniel Raymond. Diploma, Phillips Acad., Andover, Mass., 1967; BA, Columbia U. Columbia Coll., NYC, 1971; JD, George Washinton U., DC, 1974. Bar: NY 1975. Assoc. McCanliss & Early, NYC, 1974—82, ptnr., 1982—. Dir. Adirondack Explorer, Saranac Lake, NY, 2005—07; trustee Harding Ednl. and Charitable Found., NYC, 1990—; pres., trustee Montauk Club, Bklyn., 2004—; sec., trustee Down Town Assn., NYC, 1996—. Mem.: ABA, NY State Bar Assn., Oneita Boat Club. Avocations: sailing, viola, violin. Office: McCanliss & Early 88 Pine St New York NY 10005 Office Phone: 212-943-0280. Business E-Mail: tthompson@mccanliss.com.

THOMPSON, TINA MARIE, professional basketball player; b. LA, Feb. 10, 1975; 1 child. B in Sociology, U. So. Calif., LA, 1997. Forward Houston Comets, 1997—; forward (off-season) Rovereto Basket, Italy, 2001—02, Women's Korea Basketball League Kumho Falcons, Republic of Korea, 2003, Nat. Women's Basketball League Houston Stealth, 2003. Named All-Star Game MVP, WNBA, 2000; named to All-WNBA First Team, 1997, 1998, Western Conf. All-Star Team, WNBA, 1999, 2000, 2001, 2002, 2003, 2006, 2007. Achievements include becoming the number 1 draft pick in 1997, the first WNBA draftee in the history of the league; member, Houston Comets WNBA Championship Teams, 1997, 98, 99, 2000; member, US Women's Basketball Team, Athens Olympics, 2004. Mailing: Houston Comets 1510 Polk St Houston TX 77002 *

THOMPSON, TOMMY (THOMAS GEORGE), lawyer, former secretary of health and human services; b. Elroy, Wis., Nov. 19, 1941; s. Allan and Julia (Dutton) T.; m. Sue Ann Mashak, 1969; children: Kelli Sue, Tommi, Jason. BS in Polit. Sci. and History, U. Wis., 1963, JD, 1966. Polit. intern U.S. Rep. Thomson, 1963; legis. messenger Wis. State Senate, 1964-66; sole practice Elroy and Mauston, Wis., 1966-87; mem. Dist. 87 Wis. State Assembly, 1966-87, asst. minority leader, 1972-81, floor leader, 1981-87; self-employed real estate broker Mauston, 1970—; gov. State of Wis., 1987-2001; sec. U.S. Dept. Health & Human Services, Washington, 2001—05; pres. Logistics Health Inc., 2005—; ptnr. Akin Gump Strauss Hauer & Feld LLP, 2005—; independent chmn, sr. advisor Deloitte Ctr for Health Solutions Deloitte & Touche USA LLP, 2005—. Alt. del. Rep. Nat. Conv., 1976; chmn. Intergovtl. Policy Adv. Commn. to U.S. Trade Rep.; chmn. Nat. Govs. Assn., 1995-96, mem. nat. govs. assn. exec. com., AGA Med. Corp.; chmn. bd. dirs., Amtrak, 1998-2001; mem. bd. dirs. C.R. Bard, Inc., 2005-, Certere Corp., 2005-; pres. Logistics Health, 2005-. Served with USAR. Recipient med. award for Legis. Wis. Acad. Gen. Practice, Thomas Jefferson Freedon award Am. Legis. Exchange Coun., 1991, Most Valuable Pub. Official award City and State Mag., 1991, Governance award Free Congress Found., 1992, Governing Mag. Public Ofcl. of the Year, 1997, recipient Horatio Alger award, 1998, USA Mex. C of C, Good Neighbor award., 1999. Mem. ABA, Wis. Bar Assn., Rep. Govs. Assn., Phi Delta Phi. Republican. Roman Catholic. Office: Akin Gump Robert Stauss Bldg 1333 New Hampshire Ave NW Washington DC 20036-1564

THOMPSON, WADE FRANCIS BRUCE, manufacturing executive; b. Wellington, New Zealand, July 23, 1940; came to US, 1961, naturalized, 1990. m. Angela Ellen Barry, Jan. 20, 1967; children: Amanda and Charles (twins). B in Commerce, Cert. Acctg., Victoria U., Wellington, 1961; MSc, NYU, 1963; PhD of Commerce (hon.), Victoria U., 2007. Dir. diversification Sperry & Hutchinson, NYC, 1967-72; v.p. Texstar Corp., NYC, 1972-77; chmn. Hi-Lo Trailer Co., Butler, Ohio, 1977—2003; chmn., pres., CEO Thor Industries Inc., Jackson Center, Ohio, 1980—. Trustee Mystic Seaport Mus., Conn., 1984—; trustee Wade F.B. Thompson Charitable Found. Inc., 1985—, Mcpl. Art Soc., NYC, 1993—, Seventh Regiment Armory Conservancy, NYC, 1997—; founder The Drive Against Prostate Cancer. Recipient Oliver R. Grace award for Disting. Svc., Cancer Rsch. Inst., 2007, Jacqueline Kennedy Onassis award for Oustanding Contbn. to NYC, Mcpl. Art Soc., 2007. Mem. Union Club, NY Yacht Club (NYC). Avocations: tennis, collecting contemporary art. Office: Thor Industries Inc PO Box 629 Jackson Center OH 45334-0629

THOMPSON, WAYNE WRAY, historian; b. Wichita, Jan. 30, 1945; s. Clarence William and Elaine Maxine (Wray) T.; m. Lillian Evelyn Hurlburt, June 28, 1969 (div. 1999); m. Geraldine Kelleher Richter, Dec. 30 2000. BA, Union Coll., Schenectady, 1967; student, U. St. Andrews, Scotland, 1965-66; PhD, U. Calif., San Diego, 1975. Historian USAF, 1975—2004, Checkmate Air Campaign Planning Group, 1990—2004; sr. hist. advisor Gulf War Air Power Survey, 1991-93. Contbr. Congress Investigates (Arthur M. Schlesinger Jr. and Roger Bruns, editors), 1975; editor Air Leadership, 1986; contbr. War in the Pacific (Bernard Nalty, editor), 1991; contbr.: Winged Shield, Winged Sword, 1997; author: To Hanoi and Back, 2000. Served with AUS, 1971-72. Mem. Am. Hist. Assn., Orgn. Am. Historians, Air Force Hist. Found., Air Force Assn., Soc. Historians Am. Fgn. Rels., Soc. Mil. History, US Commn. Mil. History, World History Assn., Phi Beta Kappa, Cosmos Club (Washington). Home: 2720 N Quincy St Arlington VA 22207

THOMPSON, WILLIAM C., JR., school system administrator; b. Bklyn. BA in Polit. Sci., Tufts U., 1974; LHD (hon.), Mercy Coll., 1998. Chief of staff Congressman Fred Richmond, Bklyn.; dep. borough pres. Borough of Bklyn., 1983—92; Bklyn. rep. NYC Bd. Edn., 1994—96, pres., 1996; comptroller NYC, 2002—. Cons. investment banking svcs. to states, muncipalities and pub. benefit corps. in N.Y., Health Care industry, non-profit orgns. Bd. dirs. Bedford Stuyvesant Restoration Corp., City Parks Found., Bklyn. Union Gas Co; trustee Tufts U. Office: Office of the Comptroller c/o Karen Crowe 1 Centre St Room 526 New York NY 10007 Fax: 718-935-3157.

THOMPSON, WILLIAM DAVID, minister, educator; b. Chgo., Jan. 11, 1929; s. Robert Ayre and Mary Elizabeth (McDowell) T.; m. Linda Brady Stevenson, Nov. 2, 1968; children: Tammy, Kirk, Lisa, Rebecca, Gwyneth. AB, Wheaton Coll., Ill., 1950; BD, No. Bapt. Sem., 1954; MA, Northwestern U., 1955, PhD, 1960. Ordained to ministry Am. Baptist Ch., 1954. Instr. speech Wheaton Coll., 1952-55; pastor Raymond Baptist Ch., Chgo., 1956-58; assoc. prof. homiletics No. Bapt. Sem., Chgo., 1958-62; mem. faculty Eastern Bapt. Sem., Phila., 1962-87, prof. preaching, 1969-87; minister 1st Bapt. Ch., Phila., 1983-90. Pres. Thompson Comm., 1988-98, prin. The Spirited Workplace, 1998—, Thompson Properties, 1999-. Author: A Listener's Guide to Preaching, 1966, Recent Homiletical Thought, 1967, Dialogue Preaching, 1969, Preaching Biblically, 1981, Listening on Sunday for Sharing on Monday, 1983, Philadelphia's First Baptists, 1989, Public Speaking for Pleasure and Profit, 1997, On the Job Prayers, 2005; editor Abingdon Preachers Libr., 12 vols., Essence of Public Speaking series, 10 vols. Mem. Phila. Hist. Commn., 1984-92, Ctr. for Baptismal Living Bd., 1999-, Singing City Bd., 2003-. Vis. fellow Cambridge U., 1968-69. Mem. Nat. Speakers Assn., Mid-Atlantic Speakers Assn. (pres. 1995), Acad. Homiletics (pres. 1973, Lifetime Achievement award 2005), Religious Speech Comm. Assn. (v.p. 1983, pres. 1984), Union League Club, Wheaton Coll. Scholastic Honor Soc. Democrat. Home: 765 Ormond Ave Drexel Hill PA 19026-2417 Personal E-mail: Thompcom@aol.com.

THOMPSON, WILLIAM IRWIN, writer, educator; b. Chgo., July 16, 1938; s. Chester Andrew and Lillian Margaret (Fahey) Thompson; m. Gail Joan Gordon, Feb. 3, 1960 (div. Jan. 1979); children: Evan Timothy, Hilary Joan, Andrew Rhys; m. Beatrice Madeleine Rudin, Mar. 1, 1979. BA in Philosophy, Pomona Coll., 1962; MA (Woodrow Wilson fellow), Cornell U., 1964, PhD (Woodrow Wilson dissertation fellow), 1966. From instr. to asst. prof. humanities MIT, Cambridge, 1965—67, assoc. prof., 1968, Old Dominion fellow, 1967; assoc. prof. York U., Toronto, Ont., Canada, 1968-72, prof., 1973; founding dir. Lindisfarne Assocs., 1972—97; curriculum designer, faculty cons. Ross Sch., East Hampton, NY, 1995—2005. Vis. prof. religion Syracuse (N.Y.) U., 1973; vis. scholar in polit. sci. U. Hawaii, 1981, vis. prof., 85; vis. prof. Celtic studies U. Toronto, 1984; mentor, cons. Ross Sch., East Hampton, NY, 1995—; Lindisfarne scholar-in-residence Crestone Mt. Zen Ctr. Author: (book) Imagination of an Insurrection: Dublin, Easter 1916, 1967, (books) At the Edge of History, 1971, Passages about Earth, 1974, Evil and World Order, 1976, Darkness and Scattered Light, 1978, The Time Falling Bodies Take to Light, 1981, From Nation to Emanation, 1981, Blue Jade from the Morning Star, 1983, Islands Out of Time, 1985, Pacific Shift, 1986, GAIA: A Way of Knowing, 1987, Imaginary Landscape, 1989, GAIA TWO: Emergence, the New Science of Becoming, 1991, Reimagination of the World, 1991, The American Replacement of Nature, 1991, Coming into Being, 1996, Worlds Interpenetrating and Apart, 1997, Transforming History, 2001, Self and Society, 2004, (poems) A Diary of Sorts and Streets, 2006. Hon. colleague, Lindisfame scholar Cathedral St. John the Divine, NYC, 1972—97. Recipient Obstfelder prize, Oslo Internat. Poetry Festival, 1986; grantee, Laurance S Rockefeller, 1992—98; Rockefeller scholar, Calif. Inst. Integral Studies, 1992—95. Mailing: PO Box 5202 Portland ME 04101 Personal E-mail: towit@williamirwinthompson.org.

THOMPSON, WILLIAM MOREAU, radiologist, educator; b. Phila., Oct. 20, 1943; s. Charles Moreau and Aileen (Haddon) T.; m. Judy Ann Seel, July 27, 1968; children: Christopher Moreau, Thayer Haddon. BA, Colgate U., 1965; MD, U. Pa., 1969. Diplomate Am. Bd. Radiology. Intern Case Western Res. U., Cleve., 1969-70; resident in radiology Duke U., Durham, NC, 1972-75, from asst. prof. Med. Ctr. to prof., 1975—2001, prof. radiology Med. Ctr., 2001—, The Reed and Martha Rice Disting. prof. radiology Med. Ctr., 2004—; chmn. Dept. Radiology U. Minn. Hosp. and Clinic, Mpls., 1986-2000, Vilhelmina and Eugene Gedgared chair radiology, 1986—2001, prof. radiology, dir. imaging rsch., 2000-01. Contbr. chpts. to books and articles to profl. jours. Served with USPHS 1970-72. Recipient James Picker Found. Scholar in Acad. Medicine award, 1975-79, Disting. Scientist award, Armed Forces Inst. Pathology, Washington, 2001-02; R & D grantee VA, 1977-86. Fellow Am. Coll. Radiology; mem. AMA, Radiology Soc. N.Am. (program chmn. 1994-97), Minn. Med. Soc., Am. Roentgen Ray Soc., Assn. Univ. Radiologists (pres. 1989-90, Gold medal 2001), Soc. Gastrointestinal Radiology (pres. 1994-95, Cannon medal 2001), Assn. Program Dirs. (pres. 1995, Achievement award 2001), Soc. Chairs of Acad. Radiology Depts. (pres. 1997-98), Sigma Xi. Republican. Presbyterian. Office: PO Box 3808 Durham NC 27702-3808 Home: 1033 Marilee Glen Ct Durham NC 27705 Office Phone: 919-684-7443. Business E-Mail: thomp132@nc.duke.edu.

THOMPSON, WINSTON MARK OBED, entomologist, consultant, writer; s. Samuel Frendo and Iris Agatha Thompson. BSc, U. Guyana, S.Am., 1989; M of Agr., Oreg. State U., 1994; PhD, U. Greenwich, Eng., 2001. Rsch. asst. Nat. Agrl. Rsch. Inst., Georgetown, Guyana, 1989—92, rsch. scientist virology, 1994—98, rsch. scientist, 2001—03; rsch. fellow Internat. Inst. for Biol. Control, Curepe, Trinidad and Tobago, 1991, Caribbean Agrl. R&D Inst., Bridgetown, Barbados, 1991; lectr. entomology Guyana Sch. Agr., Georgetown, 1995—98; pvt. cons. and author Bellevue, Wash., 2004—. Keynote spkr. Ministry of Agr., Guyana, 1989—90; nat. agrl. rsch. inst.'s rep. Guyana's Vegetable Quality Assurance Com., Georgetown, 1996—98; mem. rev. team Caribbean Jour. Agr. and Natural Resources, Georgetown, 1997—98, Internat. Jour. Tropical insect Sci., 2005—. Contbr. articles to profl. jours. V.p. Ebenezer Luther League, New Amsterdam, Berbice, Guyana, 1983—83; music dir. Ebenezer Music Group, New Amsterdam, Berbice, Guyana, 1995—98. Recipient Pub. Svc. Ministry award, Govt. Guyana, 1985-1989, 9 Acad. awards, U. Guyana, 1986-1989; Commonwealth scholar, Assn. of Commonwealth Univs., 1998-2001, FAO of UN fellow, 1992-1994. Mem.: Guyana Assn. Profl. Agriculturists, Entomol. Soc. Am., Internat. Soc. for Pest Info. (corr.). Achievements include research recognized by other professionals; research recognized by the United States Dept. of Justice as an Alien of Extraordinary Ability for the O visa; a visa category exclusive for nobel prize winners or persons of international acclaim; research recognized by the Food and Agricultural Organization of the United Nations in 1995 as the only Plant Virologist In Guyana, South America; research recognized and selected by the Inter-American Institute for Cooperation on Agriculture to participate in a Caribbean Regional Workshop on Citrus Budwood Certification. Avocations: reading, guitar, piano. Office: PO Box 7226 Bellevue WA 98008 Personal E-mail: winston_thompson@hotmail.com.

THOMPSON, ZACHARY, city health department administrator; AS, El Centro Coll.; BS in Social Work, U. Tex., Arlington; MS, Amberton U., Garland, Tex. With W. Dallas Cmty. Ctr.; dep. dir. Dallas Co. Dept. Health and Human Svcs., Dallas, 1997—2004, dir., 2004—. Office: Dallas Co Dept Health and Human Svcs 2377 N Stemmons Fwy Dallas TX 75207-2710

THOMPSON CORNWALL, LONIETA AURORA, music educator, consultant; b. Newark, June 13, 1944; d. Wilmore and Hattie Stewart Thompson; children: Arminta Morant Cornwall, Ronald Pearson Cornwall Jr. MusB, Manhattan Sch. Music, NYC, 1962, MusM, 1966; M of Sacred Music, Union Theol. Sem., Sch. of Sacred Music, NYC, 1973; EdD in Coll. Tchg. of Music, Teachers Coll., Columbia U., NYC, 2006. Music tchr. Bd. Edn., NYC, 1966—70; instr. music Shaw U., Raleigh, NC, 1984—. Organist Abyssinian Bapt. Ch., NYC, 1965—68; dir. music Holy Trinity Luth. Ch., Hollis/Queens, NY, 1970—75; min. music First Bapt. Ch., Raleigh, NC, 1981—95; organist Christian Faith Bapt. Ch., Raleigh, 1999—2001; dir. music First Ref. Ch. of Cary, Cary, NC, 2001—. Composer: (musical score) Canticles for the Soul, Hebrews 25 Let us Encourage One Another, 2004, The African American Art Song: A Continuum In the Art of Song, 2006; presentor Nat. Assn. Negro Mus., 2006; contbr. scientific papers. Participant US EPA, Raleigh, NC, 2002, NC State Workers/ Dr. Martin Luther King Holiday Observance, Raleigh, NC, 2000—04; missionary to Zambia, South Africa Operation Reachback, Redlands, Calif., 2000; chair Gethsemane Seventh-day Adventist Ch. Sch., Raleigh, NC, 1995—2000; musical cons. Dr. Martin Luther King Celebration Com., Raleigh, 1995—2004. Recipient H.B. Caple Humanitarian award, The Shaw Players/Shaw U., 1997—98, The Crystal award, Women's Ministries/South Atlantic Conf. of Seventh-day Adventists, 1999, Lamplighter -Music Outreach award, Radio One-Hunter Industries, 2002. Mem.: Nat. Assn. Study Performance of African Am. Music, Nat. Assn. Tchrs. of Singing, Nat. Assn. Negro Musicians, Raleigh Chamber Music Guild (bd. dirs. 1994—95, 2006—), N.C. Bach Festival (bd. dirs. 1990—94), Am. Guild of Organists, Alpha Chi. Seventh-Day Adventist. Avocations: writing (liturgies), walking, travel. Home: 2304 Foxtrot Rd Raleigh NC 27610 Office: Shaw Univ 118 East South St Raleigh NC 27601 Office Phone: 919-546-8412. Personal E-mail: lonieta@aol.com.

THOMPSON-DRAPER, CHERYL L., electronics and real estate company executive; b. Houston, Dec. 11, 1950; d. J. R. and Mary Claude Thompson; m. John T. Draper, Aug. 17, 1991; children: Mary-Catherine, John M., Tom. Student, Houston C.C., Massey Bus. Coll. Various positions Warren Electric Group hdqrs., 1970—85; mgr. Warren Electric Co., 1985-89, v.p., bd. dirs., sec., 1990-92; chmn. bd., CEO, owner Warner Electric Co., Del Caribe, Dominican Republic, LA, Tex., 1992—; mgr., CEO, owner Warren Electric Telecomms.-Utility Co., 1995—; chmn., pres., CEO, owner Warren Electric Group Ltd., 1995—; chmn. bd., CEO, pres., owner Thompson Real Estate Ltd., 1995—. Cons. in field. Contbr. articles to profl. jours. Bd. dirs., v.p. San Jacinto coun. Girl Scouts U.S., chmn. fundraiser Urban Campout 1995-96, Houston Sports Found.; vice chmn. Theatre Under the Stars, 1997-2001, chmn. bd., 2001—; bd. dirs. Houston Livestock Show and Rodeo, 1994—; mem. spkrs. and internat. com. All Those Texans, pres., 1997; bd. dirs., mem. exec. com. Greater Houston Partnership, 1996—; mem. Tex Fedn. of Rep., Montgomery County Fair Adv. Bd., 1996—; bd. dirs. Nat. Edn. Found.; mem. med. adv. coun. and vet. med. adv. coun. Tex. A&M U., mem. tech. adv. coun. Coll. Engring.; chmn. indsl. distbn. adv. coun. U. Houston Coll. Engring.; mem. Am. Leadership Forum-Houston, 2000. Recipient Texan of Yr. award All Those Texans, 1994, Mktg. Excellence award-Indsl. Sales, Affiliated Distbrs., 1994, Woman on the Move award City of Houston, 1995, Outstanding Family Owned Bus. award State of Tex., 1995, 1st Largest Woman-Owned Bus. award Houston Bus. Jour., 1998, 99, 2000, 01, Warner Cable's Hometown Hero award, 1996, 3rd Largest Woman-Owned Bus. award State of Tex, Woman Enterprise Mag., 1996, 1997, Disting. Svc. award Houson Elec. League, 1996, Leadership Tex 1997 Class, Cora Bacon Foster award, 1997, 1998, Cmty. Svc. award Houston Bus. Jour., 1997, Indsl. Distbn. award of Distinction, Texas A&M U., 1997, Honeywell's Supplier of Yr. award, 1998. Fellow Paul Harris Rotary Club of Houston (bd. dirs.); mem. Nat. Assn. Elec. Distbrs. (bd. dirs., v.p. 1999-00); mem. NAFE, U.S. C. of C. (internat. com.), Am. Alliance of Family Bus., Nat. Assn. Corp. Dirs., Tex. Exec. Women, Exec. Women Internat., DAR, Petroleum Club of Houston, Pasadena C. of C., Women's C. of C. of Tex., Women's Contractor Assn. Republican. Methodist. Office: Warren Electric Group PO Box 67 Houston TX 77001-0067 Fax: 713-236-2188. E-mail: cherylitd@warrenelectric.com.

THOMS, DAVID MOORE, lawyer; b. NYC, Apr. 28, 1948; s. Theodore Clark and Elizabeth Augusta (Moore) T.; m. Susan Rebecca Stuckey, Dec. 16, 1972. BA, Kalamazoo Coll., 1970; M in Urban Planning, Wayne State U., 1975, LLM in Taxation, 1988; JD, U. Detroit, 1979. Bar: Mich. 1980, NY 1995. Planner City of Detroit, 1971-75; atty. Rockwell and Kotz, P.C., Detroit, 1980-87; pvt. practice David M. Thoms & Assocs., P.C., Detroit, 1987—2002, Miller Canfield Paddock and Stone, P.L.C., 2002—. Adj. assoc. prof. Madonna U., 1993—; presenter NYU Tax Inst. Editor Case and Comment U. of Detroit Law Rev., 1978-79. Mem. program com. Fin. and Estate Planning Coun. Detroit, 1980—; mem. adv. bd., chmn. nominating com., mem. exec. com. Met. Detroit Salvation Army, 1980—, sec.-treas., vice chmn., 1994-95, chmn., 1995-96; bd. dirs. bylaws and property com., mem. nominating com., devel. com., exec. com. Mich. chpt. ARC; bd. dirs. L'Alliance Française de Grosse Pointe, 1980-2004, 05—, pres., 1985-88, 94-95; bd. dirs. French Festival of Detroit, Inc., 1986-89, 91-94, pres.; bd. dirs. Fedn. of Alliances Françaises, 1989-95, 97-2002, 2007—, past treas., v.p., chmn. fin. com., pres., 2000-01; bd. dirs. Vis. Nurse Assn., 2003—, sec., 2004—; bd. dirs. Detroit Symphony Orch. Hall, Inc., 1996-97; trustee Kalamazoo Coll., 1993-97, mem. exec. com., 1995-97; trustee Henry M. Seldon Charitable Trust, 2003—, Mich. Colls Found., 2004-, Whitney Fund, Henry M. Seldon Chairtable Trust, 2004 (sec. 2006-); dir. vis. com. European art DIA, 1995-97. Decorated officier Ordre des Palmes Academiques, knight Order of Salvador (Salvador Dali Mus.); recipient Prix Charbonnier; Burton scholar U. Detroit, 1979; named to Best Lawyers in Am., 2005, 06, 07. Mem. ABA (chmn. subcom. on probate and estate planning, mem. charitable trust com.), Fed. Bar Assn., Oakland County Bar Assn., Detroit Bar Assn., State Bar Mich., NY Bar Assn., Bar Assn. of City of NY, Am. Planning Assn. (Mich. chpt.), The Grosse Pointe Club. Mem.

United Church of Christ. Avocations: tennis, architecture, music, travel, art history. Office: 840 W Long Lake Rd Ste 200 Troy MI 48098 Office Phone: 248-267-3242. Business E-Mail: thoms@millercanfield.com.

THOMS, JANNET, rapid transit executive; BBA in Mgmt. Info. Systems, U. Memphis; MS in Bus., Ctrl. Mich. U.; PhD in Info. Systems, pending dissertation, Nova Southeastern U. Sr. v.p. info. tech. Tech. Plus Corp.; dir. info. tech. dept. BellSouth Corp., assoc. dir. E-Directory; dir. info. tech. dept. Halo Solutions; dir. info. tech. mgmt. and planning Met. Atlanta Rapid Transit Authority (MARTA), 2002—05, asst. gen. mgr. tech. and customer svc. delivery, 2005—, chief information officer, 2005—, mem. smart card automated fare collection exec. steering com., chair info. tech. working group., Bus. Transformation Program. Mem. leadership program Am. Pub. Transp. Assn., 2004—05. Named Woman of Yr. Tech. (not for profit/public sector), (WIT) Women in Tech., 2006; named one of Next Generation of Bus. Leaders Under 40, Minority MBA, 2004. Mem.: Nat. Black MBA Assn., Inc. (Atlanta chpt. pres. 2004, Atlanta chpt. dir. econ. devel.), Am. Profl. Transit Assn., Conference Minority Transp. Officials, Women's Transp. Seminar, Coalition of 100 Black Women (Metro Atlanta chpt.). Office: MARTA Attn: CIO 2424 Piedmont Rd NE Atlanta GA 30324-3311

THOMS, JEANNINE AUMOND, lawyer; b. Chgo. d. Emmett Patrick and Margaret (Gallet) Aumond; m. Richard W. Thoms; children: Catherine Thoms, Alison Thoms. AA, McHenry County Coll., 1979; BA, No. Ill. U., 1981; JD, Ill. Inst. Tech., 1984. Bar: Ill. 1984, U.S. Dist. Ct. (no. dist.) Ill. 1984, U.S. Ct. Appeals (7th cir.) 1985; cert. mediator 19th Jud. Cir. Ill. Assoc. Foss Schuman Drake & Barnard, Chgo., 1984-86, Zukowski Rogers Flood & McArdle, Crystal Lake and Chgo., 1986-92, ptnr., 1992—2006; pvt. practice, 2007—. Arbitrator 19th Jud. Ct. Ill., 1991—. Mem. women's addv. coun. to Gov. State of Ill.; mem. adv. coun. McHenry County Mental Health Bd., 1991—98, v.p., 1993—94, pres., 1995—98; mem. governing coun. Advocate Good Shepherd Hosp., Barrington, Ill., 2001—; mem. adv. com. Adv. Found., 2003—, McHenry County Cmty. Found., 2004—, mem. grant com. Named one of Ill. Super Lawyers, 2005. Mem.: LWV, ABA, Acad. Family Mediators (cert.), Am. Trial Lawyers Assn., McHenry County Bar Assn., Chgo. Bar Assn., Ill. State Bar Assn. (coun. trust and estates sect. 2000—01, Ill. legis. dist. scholarship com. 2001, 2002—05), Phi Alpha Delta. Office: 101 N Virginia St Ste 150 Crystal Lake IL 60014-4126

THOMSEN, LINDA CHATMAN, federal agency administrator; b. 1954; d. William C. Chatman; m. Steuart Hill Thomsen, Oct. 16, 1982. BA, Smith Coll., 1976; JD, Harvard U. Atty. Davis Polk & Wardwell, Washington, NYC; asst. U.S. atty. Dist. Md. US Dept. Justice; asst. chief litigation counsel SEC, Washington, 1995—97; asst. dir. Divsn. Enforcement, SEC, Washington, 1997—2000, assoc. dir., 2000—02, dep. dir., 2002—05, dir., 2005—. Named one of 50 Women to Watch, Wall St. Jour., 2005, 2006. Office: SEC 450 Fifth St NW Washington DC 20549 *

THOMSON, BASIL HENRY, JR., lawyer; b. Amarillo, Tex., Jan. 17, 1945; m. Margaret Shepard, May 4, 1985; children: Christopher, Matthew, Robert. BBA, Baylor U., 1968, JD, 1973. Bar: Tex. 1974, U.S. Ct. Mil. Appeals 1974, U.S. Supreme Ct. 1977, U.S. Dist. Ct. (we. dist.) Tex. 1988, U.S. Ct. Appeals (fed. cir.) 1990. Oil title analyst Hunt Oil Co., Dallas, 1971-73; atty., advisor Regulations and Adminstrv. Law divsn. Office of Chief Counsel USCG, Washington, 1973-77; dir. estate planning devel. dept. Baylor U., Waco, Tex., 1977-80, gen. counsel, 1980—2002; ret., 2002; assoc. gen. counsel So. Meth. U., Dallas, 2002—. Adj. prof. law Baylor U.; lobbyist legis. Ind. Higher Edn., 71st Session of Tex. Legislature; mem. legis. com. Gov.'s Task Force on Drug Abuse; dir. govtl. rels. Baylor U.; spkr. at meetings of coll. and univ. adminstrs.; assisted in drafting legis. for Texan's War on Drugs Tex. Legislature; mem. legal adv. com. United Educators Ins. Risk Retention Group, 1994-96. Active Longhorn Coun. Boy Scouts of Am.; mem. planning and zoning commn. City of Woodway, 2004—, mem. bd. adjustment, 1998—2004; bd. dirs. Heart of Tex. Coun. on Alcohol and Drug Abuse, 1987—91. Recipient Pres.'s award Ind. Colls. and Univs. of Tex., 1994, Dist. award of merit Boy Scouts Am. Fellow Coll. State Bar Tex.; mem. ABA, FBA, Nat. Assn. Coll. and Univ. Attys. (fin., nominations and elections coms. 1994-95, bd. dirs. 1988-91, 2000—, pres. 2004-05), Nat. Assn. Ind. Colls. and Univs. (mem. legal svcs. rev. panel), Tex. Bar Assn., Waco Bar Assn., McLennan County Bar Assn., Owners Assn. of Sugar Creek, Inc. (bd. dirs. 1991-95). Baptist. Avocations: backpacking, running, environmental concerns, historical reinactment. Home: 100 Sugar Creek Pl Waco TX 76712-3410 Office: So Meth U PO Box 750132 Dallas TX 75275-0137 Home Phone: 254-772-7706; Office Phone: 214-768-3233. Business E-Mail: bthomson@smu.edu.

THOMSON, CAROLINE HELEN, artist; b. Takapuna, New Zealand, Jan. 12, 1945; d. William Harvey Thomson and Phyllis Alwyn Morgan. Artist Provincetown Art Assn. and Mus. One-woman shows include Eye of Horus Gallery, Provincetown, 1993-94, Bangs St. Gallery, Provincetown, Mass., 1995-99; exhibited in group shows at Bangs St. Gallery, Provincetown, 1995-99, David Armstrong, Susanna Coffey, Jack Pierson, Caroline Thomson, 2000, two person exhbn., Susanna Coffey, Caroline Thomson, 1996-99, Provincetown Art Assn. and Mus., 1999, selections from the permanent collection, juried exhbn., Provincetown Art Assn. and Mus., 1989-97, Invitational exhbns., PAAM, 1989-98. Exhbn. include Charles Hawthorne, Varujan Boghosian, Lily Harmon, Provincetown Art Assn. and Mus. Documentary film based on the life of Caroline Thomson, London, 1967, directed by Sheldon Rochlin and Diane Rochlin. Avocations: singer-song writer, wildlife rehabilitation. Home Fax: 508-349-7922. Personal E-mail: dmschachter2000@yahoo.com.

THOMSON, DAVID KENNETH ROY, publishing executive; s. Kenneth Thomson; 3 children. Grad., Upper Can. Coll.; MA in hist., Selwyn Coll., Cambridge, 1978. With Hudson's Bay Co.; pres. Zellers and Simpsons, 1980—90; dep. chmn. Woodbridge Co. Ltd., 1990—; mem. bd. dirs. The Thomson Corp., Toronto, 1988—, chmn., 2002—. Named one of Top 200 Collectors, ARTnews Mag., 2004, World's Richest People (with family), Forbes, 2007. Avocation: Collector of Constable; Italian Futurism; Contemporary art. Office: Thomson Corp Toronto-Dominion Bank Tower, 66 Wellington St W Toronto ON M5K 1A1 Canada Office Phone: 416-360-8700. *

THOMSON, GERALD EDMUND, physician, educator; b. NYC, 1932; s. Lloyd and Sybil (Gilbourne) T.; m. Carolyn Webber; children: Gregory, Karen. MD, Howard U., 1959; DSc (hon.), Morehouse Med. Coll., 1997. Diplomate Am. Bd. Internal Medicine (bd. govs. 1985-92, exec. com. 1988-91, chmn.-elect 1990-91, chmn. 1991-92). Resident in medicine SUNY-Kings County Hosp. Center, 1959-62, chief resident, 1962-63, NY Heart Assn. fellow in nephrology, 1964-65, asst. vis. physician, 1963-70, clin. dir. dialysis unit, 1965-67; practice medicine specializing in internal medicine NYC, 1963-64; attending physician SUNY Med. Bklyn. Hosp., 1966-70; instr. in medicine SUNY, Bklyn., 1963-68, clin. asst. prof. medicine, 1968-70; assoc. chief med. services Coney Island Hosp., Bklyn., 1967-70; attending physician Presbyn. Hosp., 1970—; dir. nephrology Harlem Hosp. Center, NYC, 1970-71, dir. med. services, 1971-85, pres. med. bd., 1976-78; assoc. prof. medicine Columbia Coll. Physicians and Surgeons, 1970-72, prof., 1972—, Samuel Lambert prof. medicine, 1980—, Robert Sonneborn prof. medicine, 1997—; exec. v.p. for profl. affairs, chief of staff Columbia-Presbyn. Med. Ctr., 1985-90; sr. assoc. dean Coll. Physicians and Surgeons, Columbia U., NYC, 1990—93. Mem. Health Rsch. Coun. City NY, 1972-75; mem. med. adv. bd. NY Kidney Found., 1971-82; mem. Health Rsch. Coun., State NY, 1975-81; mem. hypertension info. and edn. adv. com. NIH, 1973-74, NY State Adv. Com. on Hypertension, 1977-80; com. on non-pharm. treatment of hypertension Inst. of Medicine, Nat. Acad. Scis., 1980; mem. med. adv. bd. Nat. Assn. Patients on Hemodialysis and Transplantation, 1973-83; mem. adv. bd. Sch. Biomed. Edn., CUNY, 1979-83, Med. News Network, 1993-95; mem. com. on mild hypertension Nat. Heart and Lung Inst., 1976, mem. clin. trials rev. com., 1980-85, mem. rev. panel, 1979; bd. dirs. NY Heart Assn., 1973-81, chmn. com. high blood pressure, 1976-81; bd. dirs. Primary Care Devel. Corp.; chmn. com. hypertension NY Met. Regional Med. Program, 1974-76; mem. adv. com. Heart and Hypertension Inst. of NY State, 1984; mem. NY Gov.'s Health Adv. Coun., 1981-84, pub. Health Coun., NY, 1983-95, Joint Nat. Com. High Blood Pressure NIH, 1983-84, 87-88, mem. rev. panel hypertension detection and monitoring bd. study cardiovasc. risk factors in young Nat. Heart, Lung and Blood Inst., 1984-90; mem. panel on receiving and withholding med. treatment ACLU, 1984-88; mem. Grad. Med. Edn. Commn., State of NY, 1984-86, mem. Commn. on End-State Renal Disease, 1985, 89-90; pres. Washington Heights-Inwood Ambulatory Care Network Corp., 1986-91; bd. dirs. Primary Care Devel. Corp., 1993-98. Mem. adv. bd. Jour. Urban Health, 1974-80, Med. News Network, 1993-94. Chmn. ad hoc com. on access to nursing homes Pub. Health Coun. State of NY, 1982-96; pres. Washington Heights-Inwood Ambulatory Care Network Corp., 1986-91; mem. Mayor's Commn. Health and Hosps. Corp.; dir. Harlem Ctr. for Health Promotion and Disease Prevention, 1993-95. Recipient Nat. Med. award Nat. Kidney Found., NY, 1984, Outstanding Alumnus award Howard U., 1987, Disting. Alumnus award, 1998, Dean's Outstanding Tchg. award Coll. Physicians and Surgeons Columbia U., 1986, Columbia U. Pres. award Outstanding Tchg., 2002, Nickens award, Soc. General Internal Med., 2004. Mem: AAAS, ACP (master, Gov.'s coun. downstate region 1982-89, chmn. com. health pub. policy NY chpt. 1982-89, health care professions com. 1987-90, bd. regents 1990-97, chmn. nat. health and pub. policy com. 1993-94, pres.-elect 1994-95, pres. 1995-96), NY Acad. Medicine (mem. com. medicine in soc. 1974-76, chmn. com. medicine in soc. 1997-98, bd. trustees, 2000-, sec., 2003-07), NY Soc. Nephrology (pres. 1973-74), Am. Fedn. Clin. Rsch., Federated Coun. for Internal Medicine (chmn. 1991-92, 95-96), Soc. Urban Physicians (pres. 1972-73), Am. Soc. Artificial Internal Organs (adv. bd., 1998-2002, chmn. bd. trustees, 2002-), Assn. Program Dirs. in Internal Medicine, Pub. Health Assn. NYC (dir. 1983-86), Physicians for Social Responsibility of NY (dir. 1983), Physicians Human Rights (bd. trustees, 2005-) Assn. Acad. Minority Physicians (pres. 1988-90), Inst. Medicine, Nat. Acad. Scis. (chmn. com. on review of NIH strategic plan on health disparities, 2004-06). Home: Premium Pt New Rochelle NY 10801-5327 Office: Coll Physicians & Surgeons Columbia U New York NY 10032 Business E-Mail: get1@columbia.edu.

THOMSON, HELEN LOUISE, artist; b. Lewiston, Ill., Nov. 28, 1928; d. Clyde Arthur Pomeroy and Myrtle Lynch Cluney; m. William Edward Thomson, 1950; children: Persephone Ann, Lucinda Renee, Cynthia Louise. Student, Western Ill. U., Macomb, 1972, 78, 85, U. Ill., 1972; diploma, North Light Art Sch. Artist, Table Grove, Ill., 1970—. Adj. prof. Wester Ill. U., Macomb, 1985—94; mem. spkrs. roster Spoon River Coll., Canton, Ill., 1986—94; exec. dir. Two Rivers Arts Coun., Macomb, 1985—94. Exhibitions include in numerous one woman and group exhbns.; contbr. art to calendars. Officer PTA, Table Grove, 1957—85; pres. Fulton County Arts Coun., Canton, 1973—83, Spoon River Coll. Found., Canton, 1979—85; mem. adv. panel Ill. Arts Coun., Chgo., 1980—83; bd. dirs. regional arts adv. coun. Western Ill. U., 1978—85. Recipient Ruth Watts Svc. award, Performing Arts Soc., Western Ill. U., 1994, award, Two Rivers Arts Coun., 1994. Mem.: Chgo. Art Inst., Galesburg Civic Art Ctr. (exhbn. awards), Ill. Watercolor Soc., Ill. Art League (exhbn. awards), PEO Sisterhood (pres., sec., chaplain, v.p.). Avocations: antiques, antique dolls, family history, travel. Home: 404 S Broadway St PO Box 163 Table Grove IL 61482-0163

THOMSON, IAIN DONALD, philosopher, educator; s. Captane Peter and Helen McLeod Thomson; m. Kirsten Millinor Krebs, Apr. 27, 1996; 1 child, Darian Skye. PhD in Philosophy, U. Calif. San Diego, La Jolla, Calif., 1999; BA magna cum laude, with highest honors in polit. scis., high honors in philosophy, U. Calif., Berkeley, 1991. Asst. prof. Dept. Philosophy U. N.Mex., Albuquerque, 2000—05, assoc. prof. Dept. Philosophy, 2005—. Author: Heidegger on Ontotheology: Technology and the Politics of Education, 2005. Recipient Gunter Starkey Tchg. Excellence award, U. N.Mex. Coll. Arts and Scis., 2003. Fellow: Phi Beta Kappa. Office: University of New Mexico Department of Philosophy — MSCO3 2140 Albuquerque NM 87131-0001 Home Phone: 505-277-4149. Personal E-mail: ithomson@unm.edu.

THOMSON, JAMES ALAN, think-tank executive; b. Boston, Jan. 21, 1945; s. James Alan and Mary Elizabeth (Pluff) T.; m. Darlene Thomson; children: Kristen Ann, David Alan. BS, U. NH, 1967, DSC (hon.), 2007; MS, Purdue U., 1970, PhD, 1972, DSc (hon.), 1992; LLD (hon.), Pepperdine U., 1996. Research fellow U. Wis., Madison, 1972-74; systems analyst Office Sec. Def. US Dept. Def., Washington, 1974-77; staff mem. Nat. Security Council, The White House, Washington, 1977-81; v.p. The RAND Corp., Santa Monica, Calif., 1981-89, pres., CEO, 1989—. Bd. dirs. L.A. World Affairs Coun., AK Steel Holding Corp., Encysive Pharms., Object Reservoir. Contbr. articles to profl. jours. and chpts. to books. Mem. Internat. Inst. for Strategic Studies (coun. 1985-99), Coun. Fgn. Rels. Office: The RAND Corp 1776 Main St Santa Monica CA 90401-3297 Office Phone: 310-451-6936. Business E-Mail: thomson@rand.org.

THOMSON, JAMES ALEXANDER, molecular biologist, educator; b. Oak Park, Ill., Dec. 20, 1958; married; 2 children. BS in Biophysics, U. Ill., 1981; DVM magna cum laude, U.Pa., 1985, DS in molecular biology, 1988. Cert. Am. Coll. Veterinary Pathologists. Joined U. Wis., Madison, 1991, assoc. veterinarian; chief pathologist Wis. Regional Primate Rsch. Ctr., dir., 1999—; John D. McArthur Prof., dept. anatomy U. Wis.-Madison Med. Sch., 2002—. Contbr. articles to profl. sci. jours. Named a finalist for World Tech. award in health and medicine, The Economist, London, 1999; named one of The Most Intriguing People, People Mag., 2001; recipient Ill. Gen. Assembly award, 1978, Eastman Kodak award in Biol. Scis., 1979, Golden Plate award, Am. Acad. Achievement, 1999, Man of the Year, Madison Mag., 2001, World Tech. Award, 2002, LIFE Internat. Rsch. Award, 2002, Frank Annunzio award, Christopher Columbus Fellowship Found., 2003, Outstanding Achievement Award, Am. Coll. of Veterinary Pathologists, 2003, Disting. Service Award for Enhancing Edn. through Biol. Rsch., The Nat. Assn. of Biology Teachers, Inc., 2005, Nathan R. Brewer Sci. Achievement Award, Am. Assn. for Lab. Animal Sci. (AALAS), 2006; fellow Undergrad. Rsch. Participation, Princeton U., N.J., 1979, Wis. Acad. of Sciences, Arts, and Letters, 2002; scholar Nat. Merit, 1977. Mem.: Soc. for Devel. Biology, Internat. Soc. for Stem Cell Rsch., Am. Coll. of Veterinary Pathologists, Phi Zeta, Phi Beta Kappa. Achievements include first to isolate and culture nonhuman primate embryonic stem cells in 1995, and human ES cells in 1998. Office: Univ Wisconsin Genome Ctr of WI 425 Henry Mall Rm 4420 Madison WI 53706 E-mail: thomson@primate.wisc.edu. *

THOMSON, JOHN ANSEL ARMSTRONG, biochemist; b. Detroit, Nov. 23, 1911; s. John Russell and Florence (Antisdel) T.; m. June Anna Mae Hummel, June 24, 1938; children: Sheryll Linn, Patrisha Diane, Robert Royce. AA, Pasadena City Coll., Calif., 1935; AB cum laude, U. So. Calif., 1957; BGS (hon.), Calif. Poly. State U., 1961; MA, PhD, Columbia Pacific U., 1978-79; DA, Internat. Inst. Advanced Studies, Clayton, Mo., 1979. Cert. secondary tchr., Calif. Chemist J.A. Thomson Bio-Organic Chemist, LA, 1938, Vitamin Inst. (formerly J.A. Thomson Bio-Organic Chemist), L.A. and North Hollywood, Calif., 1939—. Vocat. edn. instr. U.S. War Manpower Commn., 1943-44; chmn. activities coun. World Coun. of Youth, L.A., 1932; pres. Coun. of Young Men's Divsns. Athletic Commns., YMCA Pasadena area, 1931, chmn. exec. coun., 1932; dist. officer Boy Scouts Am., San Fernando Valley coun., 1954-64, del. to nat. conf., 1959, and others. Author: (booklets) Whose Are the Myths?, 1949, Open Eyes, Illegalize Agency Abuses, 1968, Non-toxic Vitamins-hormones Answers to Environmental, Public Problems, 1972, Lobby Interest Goals to Sequester Nutrients Among Those Rarely Educated in Them, 1973, Support of Pressures to Homeostasis, Normality, 1990, Minimization of Toxics in Agriculture, 1991, Need for Recognition and Reversal of Rapid Decline of Heritage of American and World Children 1995, 1996; contbr. articles to jours. Instr. United Methodist Ch. nat. seminar for profls., Nashville, Tenn., 1983; chmn. commn. ch. and soc., 1986—, First United Meth. Ch., North Hollywood; mem. Rep. county ctrl. com. L.A. County, 1941-50, chmn. 63d assembly dist., 1948-50, Rep. state ctrl. com., Calif. 1948-50. Recipient Sci. and Industry award San Francisco Internat. Expn., 1940, various scouting leadership awards Boy Scouts Am., Civic Svc. award State of Calif., 1949, others. Mem. AAAS (life), Am. Inst. Biol. Scis., NY Acad. Scis., Am. Hort. Soc., Am. Chem. Soc., Internat. Acad. Nutrition and Preventive Medicine, Am. Forestry Assn., Garden Writers Assn. Am., Profl. Grounds Mgmt. Soc., Internat. Soc. Hort. Sci., Nat. Recreation and Parks Assn., Nat. Nutritional Foods Assn. (Pioneer Svc. award 1970), Nat. Health Fedn. (life), Nat. Resources Def. Coun., Lawn and Garden Mktg. and Distbn. Assn. (Lifetime Achievement award 2006), Am. Nursery and Landscape Assn., Calif. Assn. Nurseries and Garden Ctrs., China Soc. So. Calif. (pres., 1990-1991), Com. for Nuc. Responsibility, Inst. for Health Freedom, Internat. Union of Pure and Applied Chemistry, Perennial Plant Assn., So. Calif. Pub. Health Assn., Tree Care Industry Assn., Universal City-North Hollywood C. of C., Sierra Club, Soc. Colonial Wars (life), Kiwanis (projects panelist internat. confs. 1987, 91, pres. N. Hollywood club 1996-97), Friends of the Earth, Negative Population Growth, Amnesty Internat., U. So. Calif. Gen. Alumni Assn. (life), Life Extension Found., Am. Assn. for Health Freedom, Union of Concerned Scientists, US C. of C., Am. Acad. of Anti-Aging, United Meth. Men (hon., life, conf. program leader 1982, pres. 1979-80, adminstv. bd., 1952—). Republican. Achievements include origination of a high proportion of known uses for horticultural hormones, with first products, many of them via solely-invented and produced Horms 4, 1 and 2, Superthrive, Cutstart and Seedyield, multiple vitamins-hormones, distributed worldwide; development of highest known efficacies in plant activating, reviving, transplanting, growing, perfecting, rooting and seed invigoration; creation of water-miscible multiple vitamins powder Auzon, for humans; creation of more than 300 other formula products. Office: Vitamin Inst 12610 Saticoy St S North Hollywood CA 91605-4313

THOMSON, KEITH STEWART, biologist, author; b. Heanor, Eng., July 29, 1938; s. Ronald William and Marian Adelaide (Coster) T.; m. Linda Gailbreath Price, Sept. 27, 1963; children: Jessica Adelaide, Elizabeth Rose. B.Sc. with honors, U. Birmingham, Eng., 1960; A.M., Harvard U., 1961, PhD (NATO fellow), 1963. NATO postdoctoral fellow Univ. Coll., London U., 1963-65; asst. prof. to prof. biology Yale U., 1965-87, dean Grad. Sch., 1979-87; dir. Peabody Mus. Natural History, 1976-79; pres. Acad. Natural Scis., Phila., 1987-95; distinguished scientist-in-residence New Sch Social Rsch., NYC, 1996-98; prof., dir. Mus. Natural History Oxford U., 1998—2003, prof. emeritus, 2003—; sr. rsch. fellow Am. Philos. Soc., Phila., 2003—. Dir. Sears Found. Marine Rsch. and Oceanographic History; hon. rsch. fellow Australian Nat. U., 1967; trustee, mem. corp. Woods Hole Oceanographic Inst.; bd. dirs. Wistar Inst., Ctrl. Phila. Devel. Corp., Wetlands Inst., Phila. Cultural Alliance, Charles Darwin Trust; rschr. in vertebrate evolution. Mem. editl. bd. Paleobiology, Jour. Morphology, 1988, Aspects of Lower Vertebrate Evolution, 1968, Origin of Terrestrial Vertebrates, 1968, Saltwater Fishes of Conn., 1971, 88, Priorities and Needs in Systematic Biology, 1981, Morphogenesis and Evolution, 1988, Living Fossil, 1991, The Common But Less Frequent Loon and Other Essays, 1993, HMS Beagle, 1995, 2003, Treasures on Earth, 2002, Before Darwin: Reconciling Science and Religion, 2005, Fossils, A Very Short Introduction, 2005. Fellow Linnean Soc. London, Zool. Soc. London; mem. Soc. Vertebrate Palaeontology, Sigma Xi.

THOMSON, PAUL RICE, JR., lawyer; b. Syracuse, NY, Dec. 28, 1941; s. Paul Rice and Marcella Elizabeth (Shea) T.; m. Elizabeth Ann Cutcliff, Aug. 21, 1965; children: Paul R. III, Pamela Judeth. BA in History, Va. Mil. Inst., 1963; JD, Washington and Lee U., 1966. Bar: Va. 1966, US Dist. Ct. (we. dist.) Va. 1966, US Ct. Mil. Appeals 1967, US Ct. Appeals (4th cir.) 1972, US Ct. Appeals (11th cir.) 2004. Assoc. Clement, Wheatley, Winston & Ingram, Danville, Va., 1969-71; asst. US atty. Western Dist. Va., Roanoke, 1971-75, US atty., 1975-79; gen. counsel natural resources The Pittston Co., Lebanon, Va., 1980—87; dep. asst. adminstr. EPA, Washington, 1987—90; ptnr. Woods Rogers PLC, Roanoke, Va., 1990—. Pres. Roanoke Valley Law Enforcement Coun., 1975-76; mem. Fed.-State Law Enforcement Coun., 1975-79; trustee Ea. Mineral Law Found., Pitts., 1980-82; adj. prof. Washington & Lee U., 1981-99. V.p. Danville Jr. C. of C., 1971. Capt. JAGC USMC, 1966—69. Recipient Spl. Achievement award Dept. Justice, 1974, Silver Beaver award, Boy Scouts Am., Blue Ridge Mountains Coun., 2004. Mem. ABA, Va. Bar Assn., NRA, Trout Unltd. Roman Catholic. Avocations: fly fishing, bird hunting, raising labrador retreivers. Office: Woods Rogers PLC 10 S Jefferson St Roanoke VA 24011 Office Phone: 540-983-7742. Business E-Mail: thomson@woodsrogers.com.

THOMSON, RICHARD MURRAY, retired bank executive; b. Winnipeg, Man., Can., Aug. 14, 1933; s. H.W. and Mary Thomson. BASC in Engring., U. Toronto, 1955; MBA, Harvard U., 1957; fellow course in banking, Queen's U., 1958. From mem. staff to pres., CEO Toronto Dominion Bank, Ont., Canada, 1957—77, pres., CEO, 1977—78, chmn., 1978—98, CEO, 1978—97, ret., 1998. Bd. dirs. S.C. Johnson & Son Inc., Thomson Corp., Nexen, Inc. Office: The Toronto Dominion Bank 66 Wellington St W 10th Fl TD Bank Tow POB 1 Toronto Dominion Ctr Toronto ON Canada M5K 1A2

THOMSON, ROGER F., lawyer; b. Detroit, Apr. 4, 1949; m. Carol M. Barger. BA, Miami U., Oxford, OH, 1971; JD, So. Meth. U., Dallas, 1974. Bar: Tex. 1974, US Dist. Ct. No. Dist. Tex., US Ct. Appeals 5th Cir. Legal counsel S&A Restaurant Corp., Dallas, 1978—80, corp. counsel, 1980—82, v.p., gen. counsel, 1982—83, v.p., gen. counsel, sec., 1983—84, sr. v.p., gen. counsel, sec., 1984—85, exec. v.p., gen. counsel, sec., 1985—88; sr. v.p., gen. counsel Burger King Corp., Miami, Fla., 1988—93; sr. v.p., gen. counsel, sec. Brinker Internat. Inc., Dallas, 1993—94, dir., 1993—95, exec. v.p., gen. counsel, sec., 1994—, chief adminstrv. officer, 1996—. Mem.: State Bar Tex. Office: Brinker Internat Inc 6820 LBJ Fwy Dallas TX 75240 *

THOMSON, THYRA GODFREY, former state official; b. Florence, Colo., July 30, 1916; d. John and Rosalie (Altman) Godfrey; m. Keith Thomson, Aug. 6, 1939 (dec. Dec. 1960); children— William John, Bruce Godfrey, Keith Coffey. BA cum laude, U. Wyo., 1939. With dept. agronomy and agrl. econs. U. Wyo., 1938-39; writer weekly column Watching Washington pub. in 14 papers, Wyo., 1955-60; planning chmn. Nat. Fedn. Republican Women, Washington, 1961; sec. state Wyo. Cheyenne, 1962-86. Mem. Marshall Scholarships Com. for Pacific region, 1964-68; del. 72d Wilton Park Conf., Eng., 1965; mem. youth commn. UNESCO, 1970-71, Allied Health Professions Council HEW, 1971-72; del. U.S.-Republic of China Trade Conf., Taipei, Taiwan, 1983; mem. lt. gov.'s trade and fact-finding mission to Saudi Arabia, Jordan, and Egypt, 1985 Bd. dirs. Buffalo Bill Mus., Cody, Wyo., 1987—; adv. bd. Coll. Arts and Scis., U. Wyo., 1989, Cheyenne Symphony Orch. Found., 1990—. Recipient Disting. Alumni award U. Wyo., 1969, Disting. U. Wyo. Arts and Scis. Alumna award, 1987, citation Omicron Delta Epsilon, 1965, citation Beta Gamma Sigma, 1968, citation Delta Kappa Gamma, 1973, citation Wyo. Commn. Women, 1986; named Internat. Woman of Distinction, Alpha Delta Kappa, Keith and Thyra Honors Convocation in her honor Coll. of Arts and Scis. U. Wyo., 1997. Mem. N.Am. Securities Adminstrs. (pres. 1973-74), Nat. Assn. Secs. of State, Council State Govts. (chmn. natural resources com. Western states 1966-68), Nat. Conf. Lt. Govs. (exec. com. 1976-79) Republican. Home: 3102 Sunrise Rd Cheyenne WY 82001-6136

THOMSON, TODD STUART, former diversified financial services company executive; b. Stanford, Calif., Jan. 30, 1961; s. Scott Dayton and Margaret Elaine (Guice) T.; m. Melissa Kay McKeithen, May 22, 1988. BA in Econs., Davidson Coll., 1983; MBA with distinction, U. Pa., 1987. With Barents Group LLC; cons., sr. cons. Booz Allen & Hamilton, Bethesda, Md., 1983-85; cons., mgr. Bain & Co., Boston, 1986-91; sr. v.p. strategic planning & bus. devel. GE Capital Sevices; sr. v.p.-global devel. Travelers Group, NYC, 1998; sr. v.p. strategy & bus. devel. Citigroup Inc., NYC, 1998—2000, exec. v.p. fin., ops. & strategy, CFO, 2000—04, chmn., CEO, Citigroup Global Wealth Mgmt. Divsn., 2004—07. *

THOMSON, VIRGINIA WINBOURN, humanities educator, writer; b. Oakland, Calif., Aug. 6, 1930; d. Harry Linn and Jennie Cook (Vineyard) Thomson. AA, San Mateo Coll., 1949; BA, San Jose State Coll., 1951; MA, U. Calif., Berkeley, 1952. Cert. secondary tchr. Calif. Tchr. social sci. Capuchino H.S., San Bruno, Calif., 1952—54, Watsonville H.S., Calif., 1954—87. Saleswoman, storyteller Home Interiors, San Mateo, 1963—64. Author: The Lion Desk, 1965, Short Talks Around the Lord's Table, 1985, Lawson's Castle, 2001, numerous poems. Mem.: AAUW (life), Nat. Geog. Soc. (life), Calif. Alumni Assn. (life), Calif. Writer's Club (life), Homer Honor Soc., Internat. Poets, Phi Alpha Theta. Republican.

'T HOOFT, GERARDUS (GERARD 'T HOOFT), physicist, researcher; b. Den Helder, The Netherlands, July 5, 1946; s. Hendrik 't Hooft and Margaretha Agnes (van Kampen) t' Hooft; m. Albertha Anje Schik, July 1, 1972; children: Saskia Anne, Ellen Marga. Student, Utrecht U., The Netherlands; doctoraalexamen Theoretical Physics, Rijksuniversiteit Utrecht, The Netherlands, 1969, PhD, 1972; DSc (hon.), U. Chgo., 1981, U. Louvain, 1996, U. Bologna, 1998, Eurasian U., Astana, Kazakjstan, 2000, U. Western Cape, South Africa, 2001; D Humane Letters honoris causa, Hofstra U., 2001; Doctorat de Scences honoris causa, U. Mediterranee, 2001; Dsc honoris causa, Ohio State U., 2003; Doctorate (hon.), U. Sci. and Tech. China, 2004. Fellow European Ctr. Nuc. Rsch., Geneva, 1972—74; lectr., asst. prof. physics U. Utrecht, The Netherlands, 1974—77, prof., 1977—. Loeb lectr. Harvard U., Cambridge, Mass., 1976; Fairchild disting. scholar Calif. Inst. Tech., Pasadena, 1981; assoc. etranger Acad. des Scis., Paris, 1995; guest prof. Boston U., 1998, Duke U., 1989; hon. prof. Nanjing U., China, 2002, Zhejiang U., China, 2004. Assoc. editor Nuc. Physics B; contbr. articles to profl. jours. Decorated officer Legion of Honor France, comdr. Order Ned. Leeuw; recipient Dannie Heineman prize, Am. Phys. Soc., 1979, Am. Inst. Physics, N.Y.C., 1979, Wolf prize in physics, Wolf Found., Israel, 1981, Piou XI medal, Pontifica Accademia delle Sci. John Paul II, Vatican City, 1983, Spinoza premium, NWO, 1995, Franklin medal, Phila., 1995, Gian Carlo Wick commn. medal, Lausanne, 1997, HEP prize, European Phys. Soc., 1999, Nobel prize in physics, 1999, Osker Kein Silver medal, Royal Acad. Sweden, 1999, Hon. medal, Astana, Kazakhstan, 2000. Mem.: Academie des Scis. Paris, Koninlijke Nederlandse Academie voor Wetenschappen (Lorentz medal 1986), Am. Acad. Arts and Scis. (hon.), U.S. Nat. Acad. Scis. (assoc.). Office: Spinoza Inst Leuvenlaan 4 PO Box 80 195 NL3508TD Utrecht Netherlands E-mail: g.thooft@phys.uu.nl.

THOPPIL, CECIL KOSHEY, pediatrician, consultant, educator; b. Trivandrum, India, Aug. 4, 1961; m. Jennifer Carrol Gallego, Apr. 25, 1992; children: Cecilia Ruth, Andrew Obed. Pre-degree, Mar Ivanios Coll., 1979; MB, BS, Med. Coll. Hosp., 1984. Diplomate Am. Bd. Pediat.; cert. instr. neonatal advanced life support, pediat. advanced life support, BLS. Compulsory rotating internship Med. Coll. Hosp., Trivandrum, Kerala, India, 1985—86; postgrad. tng. pediat. medicine dept. child health S.A.T. Hosp., Trivandrum, 1986—87; postdoctoral rsch. assoc. dept. perinatal pediat. U. Tex. Med. Br., Galveston, 1987—89; pediat. internship U. Hosps. Cleve. Rainbow Babies and Children's Hosp., 1989—90; pediat. residency dept. pediat. Scott & White Meml. Hosp./Tex. A&M U. Coll. Medicine, Temple, 1990—92; pediatrician Surry County Health Dept., Dobson, NC, 1992—94, Med. Assocs. of Surry, Novant Health Physicians Divsn. Triad Region, Mt. Airy, NC, 1994—2002; asst. chief of staff No. Surry Hosp., 2002—04, chief of staff, 2005—06. Physician cons. Mount Airy Sch. Health Adv. Coun., Surry Pre-sch. Interagy. Coun., Surry County Day Care Assn.; pediat. cons. Surry Smart Start Task Force; mem. Vision Steering and Implementation Com. Forsyth Med. Group, Med. Exec. Com. No. Surry Hosp.; affiliate staff Forsyth Med. Ctr., mem. physician leadership bd., 2005—; corp. faculty Novant Health. Contbr. articles to profl. jours. Recipient Father Kuncheria Goldmedal for First Rank in Loyola Sch. for Matriculation. Fellow Am. Acad. Pediat.; mem. AMA, N.C. Med. Soc., N.C. Pediat. Soc., Surry-Yadkin Med. Soc. Home: 151 Cross Creek Dr Mount Airy NC 27030-9229 Office: Med Assocs of Surry 865 W Lake Dr Mount Airy NC 27030-2157 Office Phone: 336-719-6100. Office Fax: 336-719-7935. Personal E-mail: cthoppil@triad.rr.com. Business E-mail: ckthoppil@novanthealth.org.

THOR, IRA P., sports director; b. Paterson, NJ, Jan. 20, 1977; s. Hilary S. and Karen B. M. Thor; m. Kathryn J. Boal, July 9, 2000. BA in Com., William Paterson U., 2001. Promotions asst. Sta. WQHT-FM, NYC, 1997—2000; staff writer Bergen Record, Hackensack, NJ, 1999—2000; sports writer Worrall Cmty. Newspapers, Union, NJ, 2000; sports info. dir. N.J. City U. Athletics, Jersey City, 2000—. Sports info. dir. N.E. Collegiate Volleyball Assn., Mahwah, NJ, 2002—; divsn. II/III coord. N.J. Collegiate Baseball Assn., New Brunswick, NJ, 2004—. Bd. trustees Camelot at Woodhaven Homeowners Assn., Old Bridge, NJ, 2003—. Recipient 2d pl. Outstanding Sports Writing Weekly Newspapers, Soc. Profl. Journalists, N.J. chpt., 2000, 1st pl. Outstanding Sports Writing Weekly Newspapers, 2000, V.P.'s Excellence in Svc. award, N.J. City U., Divsn. Student Affairs, 2003—04, Grant Burger Media award, Region SID of Yr., Am. Volleyball Coaches Assn., 2004—06. Mem.: Eastern Coll. Athletic Conf. Sports Info. Dirs. Am., Coll. Sports Info. Dir. Am. Independent. Jewish. Avocations: golf, tennis, beach volleyball, collecting/listening to music, travel. Home: 36 Cannon Rd Old Bridge NJ 08857-4247 Office: New Jersey City Univ Athletics 2039 Kennedy Blvd Jersey City NJ 07305-1597 Office Phone: 201-200-3301. Office Fax: 201-200-2365. Personal E-mail: iraphor@optonline.net. E-mail: ithor@njcu.edu.

THOR, LINDA M., college president; BA, Pepperdine U., 1971, EdD, 1986; MPA, Calif. State U., LA, 1980. Dir. pub. info. Pepperdine U., Los Angeles, 1971-73; pub. info. officer L.A. C.C. Dist., 1974-75, dir. comm., 1975-81, dir. edn. svcs., 1981-82, dir. high tech., 1982-83, sr. dir. occupl. and tech. edn., 1983-86; pres. West Los Angeles Coll., Culver City, Calif., 1986-90, Rio Salado Coll., Phoenix, 1990—. Contbr. articles to profl. jours. Active Continuous Quality Improvement Network for Cmty. Colls., 1991—; mem. Ariz. Gov.'s Adv. Coun. on Quality, 1992—97; pres. Ariz. Cmty. Coll. Pres.'s Coun., 1995—96; bd. dirs. Coun. for Adult and Experiential Learning, 1990—2005, C.C. Baccalaureate Assn., 2000—, Ariz. Town Hall, 2005—, Nana's Children Mental Health Found., 2003—, Friends of Pub. Radio Ariz. Named Woman of the Yr., Culver City Bus. and Profl. Women, 1988, Pacesetter of Yr., Nat. Coun. Mktg. and Pub. Rels., 1998; recipient Delores award, Pepperdine U., 1986, Alumni Medal of Honor, 1987, Outstanding Achievement award Women's Bus. Network, 1989, Shirley B. Gordon award of distinction, Phi Theta Kappa Internat. Honor Soc., 2000, Paul A. Elsner Excellence in Leadership award, Chair Acad., 2003. Office: 2323 W 14th St Tempe AZ 85281-6950 Business E-Mail: linda.thor@riomail.maricopa.edu.

THORBECKE, ERIK, economics professor; b. Berlin, Feb. 17, 1929; s. William and Madelaine (Salisbury) T.; m. Charla J. Westerberg, Oct. 17, 1954; children: Erik Charles, Willem, Jon. Student, Netherlands Sch. Econs., Rotterdam, 1948-51; PhD, U. Calif., 1957; doctorate (hon.), U. Ghent, 1981. Asst. prof. econs. Iowa State U., 1957-60, assoc. prof., 1960-63, prof., 1963-73, Cornell U., 1974—, chmn. dept. econs., 1975-78, H.E. Babcock prof. econs. and food econs., 1978—. Econ. adviser Nat. Planning Inst., Lima, Peru, 1963-64; asso. asst. adminstr. for program policy AID, Washington, 1966-68, mem. research advisory com., 1976-81; sr. economist world employment program Internat. Labor Office, Geneva, 1972-73; vis. prof. Erasmus U., Rotterdam, 1980-81; mem. com. on internat. nutritional programs NRC-NAS, 1979-81; dir. program on comparative econ. devel., Cornell U., 1988—; sr. rsch. fellow USAID Inst. Policy Reform, 1990—. Author: The Tendency Towards Regionalization in International Trade, 1960, (with Irma Adelman) Theory and Design of Economic Development, 1966, (with K. Fox, J. Sengupta) Theory of Quantitative Economic Policy, 1968, Role of Agriculture in Economic Development, 1968, (with G. Pyatt) Planning Techniques for a Better Future, 1976; (with J. Defourny) Structural Path Analysis and Multiplier Decomposition within a Social Matrix, 1984, (with J. Foster, J. Greer) A Class of Decomposable Poverty Measures, 1984, (with J. Lecaillon, C. Morrisson) Economic Policies and Agricultural Performance of Low Income Countries, 1987, Planning Techniques for Social Justice In: The Balance between Industry and Agriculture in Economic Development, vol. 4, 1989, (with I. Adelman) The Role of Institutions in Economic Development, Special Issue of World Development, 1989, (with others) Adjustment and Equity in Indonesia, 1992, (with D. Berrian) Budgetary Rules to Minimize Societal Poverty in a General Equilibrium Context, 1992, (with T. van der Pluijm) Rural Indonesia: Socio-economic Development in a Changing Environment, 1993, (with A. de Janvry and E. Sadoulet) Impact of State and Civil Institutions on the Operation of Rural Market and Non-Market Configurations In: State, Market and civil Organizations: New Theories, New Practices, and Their Implications for Rural Development, 1995, (with A. Parikh) Impact of Rural Industrialization on Village Life and Economy: A Social Accounting Matrix, 1996, (with H-S Jung) A Multiplier Decomposition Method to Analyze Poverty Alleviation, 1996, (with others) Methods of Interregional and Regional Analysis, 1998, (with H. Wan) Taiwan's Development Experience: Lessons on Roles of Government and Market, 1999, (with C. Charumilind) Economic Inequality and its Socio-economic Impact, 2002, (with M. Nissanke) Impact of Globalization on the World's Poor; contbr. articles to profl. jours. Mem. Am. Econ. Assn., Am. Assn. Agrl. Econs. (Nat. award for best pub. research 1970) Office: Cornell U 3M11 MVR Ithaca NY 14853 Office Phone: 607-255-2066. Business E-Mail: et17@cornell.edu.

THORBURN, DAVID, literature educator; b. NYC, Aug. 14, 1940; s. Frank and Claire (Feller) T.; m. Barbara Ellen Levitan, June 30, 1963; children: Daniel, Adam, Rachel. AB, Princeton U., 1962; MA, Stanford U., 1966, PhD, 1968. Instr., asst. prof., then assoc. prof. dept. English, Yale U., New Haven, 1966-76; prof. lit., dir. film and media studies MIT, Cambridge, 1976—, dir. cultural studies project and comm. forum, 1985—. Vis. appointments include U. Calif., Santa Barbara, U. Ill. Author: Conrad's Romanticism, 1974; contbr. articles to profl. jours.; editor scholarly collections; gen. editor Media and Popular Culture, 1986-90, Media in Transition, 2001— (book series). Fulbright fellow, Morse fellow, Woodrow Wilson fellow and Rockefeller fellow, 1966-77. Mem. MLA, Popular Culture Assn., Am. Studies Assn., Soc. for Cinema Studies. Democrat. Avocation: basketball. Office: MIT 14N-335 Lit Faculty Cambridge MA 02139

THORDARSON, WILLIAM, retired hydrogeologist; b. NYC, Mar. 14, 1929; s. William and Lillian (Hirsch) T. BA, Columbia U., 1950; postgrad., U. Kans., 1953—55; MA, U. Colo., 1987. Hydrogeologist U.S. Geol. Survey, Denver, 1955—94; ret., 1994. Author: Perched Groundwater, Nevada, 1965, Hydrogeology of Test Wells, 1975, Hydrogeology of South-Central Great Basin, 1983, Hydrogeologic Monitoring, Nevada, 1985, Hydrogeology of Anhydrite, 1989. Served with U.S. Army, 1950-52. Mem. Nat. Geog. Soc., Colo. Ground Water Assn., Colo. Sci. Soc., Geol. Soc. Wash. Home: 1453 Belcourt Lane Mount Pleasant SC 29466-8103

THOREEN, MARY LOUISE, elementary school educator, consultant; b. Fort Walton Beach, Fla., Oct. 3, 1959; d. James Leonard and Norma Jean Thoreen; m. James L. Young, June 14, 1997. BS in Math., Fla. State U., 1981, MS in Higher Edn., 1982. Cert. early adolescence math. Nat. Bd. for Profl. Tchg. Stds., 1999, math. grades 6-12 Fla., 2002, math. grades 5-9 Fla., 2002, gifted edn. Fla. Dir. student activities Mars Hill (N.C.) Coll., 1982—84; program dir. Va. Tech, Blacksburg, 1984—87; asst. dir. U. Ctr. U. South Fla., Tampa, 1987—89; consulting analyst The Omnia Group, Tampa, 1989—94; math. tchr. Sch. Dist. Hillsborough County, Tampa, 1994—. On-air tutor math. homework hotline The Edn. Channel, Tampa, 2004—. Finalist Dist. Tchr. of Yr., Sch. Dist. Hillsborough County, 1999; recipient Nat. Educator award, Milken Family Found., 2003. Mem.: Nat. Coun. Tchrs. Math., Phi Delta Kappa. Lutheran. Avocations: hiking, bicycling, music. Home Phone: 813-880-9267; Office Phone: 813-215-3327. Personal E-mail: tampathor@aol.com.

THORELLI, SARAH V., economist, researcher; b. Atlanta, Dec. 30, 1922; m. Hans B. Thorelli; children: Irene, Tom. AB, U. Ga., 1944; MA, U. Ala., 1945; Ph.Lic., U. Stockholm, 1954. Free-lance researcher and scholar; v.p. Intopia, Inc. Cons. FTC, NSF, Sears, Roebuck and Co.; ofcl. translator legal documents Swedish Fgn. Office, Stockholm; intelligence rsch. analyst U.S. Dept. State; overseas rep. Equifax Co.; account exec. J. Walter Thompson Advt. Agy., NYC. Co-author: Consumer Information Handbook: Europe and North America, Consumer Information Systems and Consumer Policy; contbr. articles to profl. jours. Mem. Ind. U. Women's Club, AAUW, Network Career Women, Local Coun. Women, Psi Iota Xi. Home and Office: 2604 E 2nd St Apt F Bloomington IN 47401-5351 Office Phone: 812-333-3174.

THOREN-PEDEN, DEBORAH SUZANNE, lawyer; d. Robert Roy and Marguerite Natalie (Geoghegan) Thoren; m. Steven E. Peden, Aug. 10, 1985. BA in Philosophy, Polit. Sci./Psychology, U. Mich., 1978; JD, U. So. Calif., 1982. Bar: Calif. 1982. Assoc. Bushkin, Gaines & Gaims, LA, 1982-84, Rutan & Tucker, Costa Mesa, Calif., 1984-86; sr. counsel First Interstate Bancorp, LA, 1986-96; ptnr. Pillsbury Winthrop LLP, LA, 1996—; asst. gen. counsel CarsDirect.com; gen. counsel CD1 Financial-.com; gen. counsel, sr. v.p., chief privacy officer PayMyBills.Com, 2000; ptnr. Pillsbury Winthrop LLP, 2000—; (Pillsbury Winthrop LLP merged with Shaw Pittman LLP, 2005); ptnr., corp. & securities dept., co-chair, consumer and retail industry team Pillsbury Winthrop Shaw Pittman LLP, Los Angeles, 2005—. Lectr. on e-commerce, privacy Bank Secrecy Act and Ethics, Office of Fgn. Assets Control. Supervising editor U. So. Calif. Entertainment Law Jour., 1982-83, Entertainment Publishing and the Arts Handbook, 1983-84; contbr. articles to profl. jours. Mem. ABA (past vice-chmn. compliance exec. com., money laundering task force, privacy task force, co chmn. BSA staff commentary com.), Calif. Bankers Assn. (regulatory compliance com., co-chmn. regulatory compliance conf., past ex-officio mem. state govt. rels. com., co-vice chmn., vice-chmn., Regulatory Compliance Profl. award 1997, Frandzel award for outside counsel 2001, award 2001), Calif. State Bar Assn. (chmn., consumer fin. com.). Avocations: horseback riding, travel, reading, skiing. Office: Pillsbury Winthrop Shaw Pittman LLP Ste 2800 725 S Figueroa St Los Angeles CA 90017-5443 Office Phone: 213-488-7320. Office Fax: 213-629-1033. Business E-Mail: deborah.thoren-peden@pillsburylaw.com.

THORESON, RYAN R., social anthropology scholar; s. Sue T. BA in Govt., Studies of Women, Gender, and Sexuality, Harvard Univ., 2007; MPhil student in Social Anthropology, Oxford Univ., 2007—. Sr. editor Perspective mag. Rhodes Scholar. Achievements include conducting rsch. S. Africa; interned at MTV where he worked on social and ednl. initiatives; working at Internat. Lesbian and Gay Assn., Brussels, Belgium, 2006. Avocations: playwriting, blogger. *

THORIN, SUZANNE E., dean, university librarian; BA in music edn., N. Park Coll., Chgo., 1963; MA in music history, lit., Univ. Mich., 1964, MLS, 1968. With Libr. Cong., Washington, 1980—96, chief of staff, 1992—96; Ruth Lilly univ. dean of univ. libr. and assoc. v.p. digital libr. devel. Ind. Univ., 1996—2005; univ. libr., dean of libr. Syracuse Univ., 2005—. Office: Dean of Libr Syracuse Univ 223 D S Bird Libr 2573 Syracuse NY 13244 Office Phone: 315-443-2573. Business E-Mail: sethorin@syr.edu. *

THORMODSGARD, DIANE L., bank executive; b. 1950; m. Gaylord Thormodsgard. BA in Math., Econ. & Acctg., Luther Coll.; MBA, U. Minn. Controller, asst. treas. First Bank System (now US Bancorp), 1978, sr. v.p. Regional Cmty. Banking, 1985—89, sr. v.p. ops., 1989—93, sr. v.p., treas., chief adminstr. officer, 1993—95, sr. v.p., chief adminstr. officer Corp. Trust, 1995—99, pres. Corp. Trust., Inst. Trust and Custody Svcs., 1999—2007, vice chmn., head wealth mgmt., 2007—. Bd. mem. St. Paul C of C, St. Paul Chamber Orch., Minn. Church Found., Central Corridor Partnership. Named one of The Top 15 Women in Fin., Finance & Commerce, 2005, 25 Most Powerful Women in Banking, US Banker, 2006. Mem.: Am. Inst. of Certified Pub. Accountants, Minn. Soc. of Certified Pub. Accountants, Lutheran Social Services Fin. Com. Office: US Bancorp US Bancorp Ctr 800 Nicollet Mall Minneapolis MN 55402 Office Phone: 612-303-7936. E-mail: diane.thormodsgard@usbank.com. *

THORN, RODNEY KING, professional sports team executive, retired professional basketball player; b. Princeton, W.Va., May 23, 1941; m. Peggy Thorn; children: Jonathan, Amanda, Jessica. Student, W.Va. U.; BA in Polit Sci., U. Wash., Seattle; degree (hon.), W.Va. U. Player NBA Balt. Bullets, 1963—64, NBA Detroit Pistons, 1964—65, NBA St. Louis Hawks, 1965—67, NBA Seattle SuperSonics, 1967—71, asst. coach, 1971—73, Am. Basketball Assn. NY Nets, 1973—75, NBA NY Nets, 1976—78; head coach Am. Basketball Assn. St. Louis Spirits, 1975—76; gen. mgr. NBA Chgo. Bulls, 1978—85, interim head coach, 1982; v.p. basketball ops. NBA, NYC, 1985—2000; pres. NBA NJ Nets, East Rutherford, 2000—. Chair Sr. Men's Basketball com. USA Basketball, 1992—2000. Bd. dirs. W.Va. U. Named NBA Exec. of Yr., 2002. Office: NJ Nets Nets Champion Ctr 390 Murray Hill Pky East Rutherford NJ 07073-2109 Office Phone: 201-935-8888. Office Fax: 201-935-1088. *

THORN, STUART WALLACE, marketing and financial executive; b. Glen Cove, NY, Mar. 20, 1956; s. Benjamin Chessman and Nancy Elizabeth (Libby) T.; m. Jean Marie Gillis, Oct. 7, 1979 (div.); children: Alexander Chessman, Jason Keane, Tyler Steven; m. Sharon Elizabeth Foreman, June, 2003. BS in Econs. magna cum laude, U. Pa., 1978, MBA in Fin., 1979. Market rsch. intern People's Savs. Bank, Bridgeport, Conn., 1987-88; fin. analyst, corp. control S.C. Johnson & Son, Inc., Racine, Wis., 1979-80, cost mgmt. analyst, prodn. support, 1980-81; project supr. Johnson Worldwide Assocs., S.C. Johnson & Son, Racine, 1982-83; fin. mgr. Porelon, Inc., Cookeville, Tenn., 1983-86; corp. acquistions dir. S.C. Johnson & Son, Inc., Racine, 1986-87, regional controller Africa and Nr. East Frimley, Eng., 1987-90, internat. mktg. assoc. Racine, 1990-91, dir. fin. N.Am. consumer products, 1991-94; v.p. internat. fin. Campbell Soup Co., 1994—; CFO Beaulieu of Am., 1995—2001; pres., CEO Southwire Co., Carrollton, Ga., 2001—. Solicitor United Way, Racine; bd. dirs. Explorers, Boy Scouts Am., 1986-87; bd. dirs. Racine County Opportunity Ctr., 1991—. Named Nat. Champion Nat. Collegiate Racing Assoc. Avocations: tennis, windsurfing, golf. Office: Southwire Co 1 Southwire Dr Carrollton GA 30119

THORN, SUSAN HOWE, interior designer; b. Washington, Apr. 22, 1941; d. James Bennett Cowdin and Lois (Fiesinger) Howe; m. William D. Thorn, June 22, 1963; children: Melissa Ann, William David. Cert. lighting design, Parsons Sch. Design, NYC, 1975—77; BA, Syracuse U., NY, 1962; AB, NY Sch. Interior Design, NYC, 1995. Owner, designer Susan Thorn Interiors, Inc., Cross River, NY, 1965—. Designer total bldg. Cooper Labs, Bedford Hills, NY, 1973, total redesign Nycrest Corp., Cold Spring, NY, 1973-75, showrooms, model rooms stylist and coordinator France Voiles Co. Inc., NYC, 1976, total design new corp. hdqrs. in Gen. Dynamics Bldg. (with Marjorie Borradaile Helsel), Robert E. Eastman Co., NYC, 1967, Cummin & Friedland Capital Corp., 1982; designer offices, stores, employee areas comml., public, residential clients, including Waccabuc Country Club, NY, 1969, S. Salem Libr., NY, St. Vincent's Hosp., NYC, 1996; instr. adult edn. dept. John Jay High Sch.; spkr. civic orgns. Mem. Am. Soc. Interior Designers (profl.), Internat. Assn. Lighting Designers (assoc.), Decorators Club, Club of NY, Waccabuc Country Club. Episcopalian. Home: 88 N Salem Rd Cross River NY 10518 Office Phone: 914-763-1210. Personal E-mail: thorninteriors@earthlink.net.

THORN, TERENCE HASTINGS, energy executive, consultant, writer; b. Takoma, Md., July 6, 1946; s. John Hastings and Norine R. (Freytag) T.; m. Judith Carol Bailey, Aug. 15, 1970; children: Kristin Lynn, Matthew Hastings. BA, U. Md., 1969, MA, 1973. Dir. congl. rels. Am. Gas Assn., Arlington, Va., 1975-79; dir. govt. rels. J. Walter Thompson Co., Washington, 1979-81; v.p. govt. rels. Houston Natural Gas Co., Washington, 1981-85; exec. v.p., chmn. bd. Mojave Pipeline Co., Houston, 1986-89; pres., CEO Transwestern Pipeline Co., Houston, 1993—; sr. v.p., exec. mgmt. com. bd. Enron Corp., Houston, 1993-98, exec. v.p. internat. govt. rels. and environ. affairs, 1998—2001, mng. dir. Middle East, 2001; cons. Houston Tex. Energy, Environment, Tech.; pres. JKM Cons., Houston, 2001—. Cons. in field. Contbr. articles to profl. jours. Bd. dirs. Houston Pops, 1989-90, Pin Oak Charities, Houston, 1991-93, Greater Houston chpt. YMCA, 1994; city alderman, 1992-93; mem. Hermann Soc., 1993—, Energy Industry Sector Adv. Com. U.S. Dept. Commerce; prin. liason Pres.'s Coun. Sustainable Devel.; chmn. internat. com. Bus. Coun. of Sustainable Devel.; mem. adv. com. Commn. for Environ. Cooperation; trustee Tomas Rivera Policy Inst.; chmn. Internat. Gas Ctr. Mem. Pacific Coast Gas Assn. (chmn. 1994-95), Internat. Gas Union (chmn. com. 9), U.S. C. of C. (mem. internat. policy com.), Coun. of the Ams. (adv. com.), Wildlife Conservation Soc. (trustee), Nature Conservancy (trustee). Avocation: international energy development writing.

THORNBERRY, MAC (WILLIAM MCCLELLAN THORNBERRY), congressman; b. Clarendon, Tex., July 15, 1958; m. Sally Thornberry; 2 children. BA summa cum laude in Hist., Tex. Tech U., Lubbock, 1980; JD, U. Tex. Law Sch., 1983. Legis. coun. Staff of US Rep. Tom Loeffler of Tex., 1983-85; chief of staff Staff of US Rep. Larry Combest of Tex., 1985-88; dep. asst. sec. legis. affairs US State Dept., 1988-89; def. atty. Peterson, Farris, Doores & Jones, Amarillo, Tex., 1989-94; mem. US Congress from 13th Tex. dist., 1995—. Mem. armed svcs. com. US Congress, mem. permanent select com. on intelligence, chair oversight subcommittee. Mem. Tex. and Southwestern Cattle Raisers Assn. Republican. Presbyterian. Office: US Ho Reps 2457 Rayburn Ho Office Bldg Washington DC 20515-4313 Office Phone: 202-225-3706. *

THORNBRO, WILLIAM GRADEN, writer; b. Muncie, Ind., July 8, 1952; s. William Wesley Thornbro and Bonnie Ather Marcum; m. Janice Kay Waters, Aug. 7, 1976; children: Christopher Wesley, Nicholas Dale. BS, Ball State U., 1978. Author: (book) An Uncertain Justice, A Question of Conspiracy, numerous poems. Mem.: Acad. Am. Poets, Environ. Def., Planetary Soc., Sierra Club. Democrat. Avocations: reading /research, gardening. Home: 212 S Pasture Ln Muncie IN 47304-4120 Personal E-mail: wmthornbro@sbcglobal.net.

THORNBURG, FREDERICK FLETCHER, lawyer, educator; s. James F. and Margaret R. (Major) T.; children: James Brian, Charles Kevin, Christian Sean, Christopher Herndon; m. Patricia J. Malloy, Dec. 4, 1981. AB, DePauw U., 1963; postgrad., U. Notre Dame, 1965; JD magna cum laude, Ind. U., 1968. Bar: Ind. 1968, U.S. Tax Ct. 1970, U.S. Ct. Appeals (7th cir.) 1970, U.S. Supreme Ct. 1971. Tchr., coach U.S. Peace Corps, Colombia, 1963-65; law clk. to chief judge U.S. Ct. Appeals (7th cir.), 1968-69; assoc. Thornburg, McGill, Deahl, Harman, Carey & Murray, South Bend, 1969-75, ptnr., 1975-80; v.p. systems and svcs. group The Wackenhut Corp., Coral Gables, Fla., 1981-82, sr. v.p. adminstrn., 1982-86, exec. v.p., 1986-88, also bd. dirs.; pres. Wackenhut Internat. Corp. and Wackenhut Svcs., Inc.; v.p., legal counsel St. Thomas U., 1988-90, adj. prof. law, 1989-90; pres., CEO PropServ, Inc., 1991-94; CEO Practice Resources Corp., 1996-97; CEO, of counsel Stephens, Lynn, Klien & McNicholas, P.A., 1998-2000; dean CAU Bus. Sch., 2006—. Cons. MSC, Am. Tel. Corp.; legal and mgmt. cons., mem. bd. advisors Publix Supermarkets, Inc., 1994—95, St. Thomas U., 1990—95, 2001—06; bd. dirs., mem. exec. com., trustee RFBD, Inc.; bd. dirs. YEI, Inc., Carlos Albizu U. Found., 2002—; trustee U. Cmty. Hosp. Found., 1991—94; adj. prof. bus. St. Mary's Coll., 1975—78; vis. prof. CTA, 1985—95; vice chmn., pvt. sec. adv. coun. Fla. Sec. of State, 1985—90; chair ethics com. Miami-Dade County Pub. Schs., 2002—; legal and mgmt. cons., mem., chair bd. advisors WLRN-PBS Radio and TV, 2003—; adj. prof. bus. St. Thomas U. Law Sch., 1999—2000, Carlos Albizu U., 2004, chair Bus. Sch. Adv. Bd., 2003—04. Assoc. editor in chief Ind. Law Jour., 1967-68; contbr. articles to legal and bus. jours. Mem. Civic Ctr. Found., 1976—80; pres. Jaycees, 1974; trustee RFD&D, Inc.; former bd. dirs. Michiana YMCA, Channel 34, Symphony Orch. Assn., 1974—80, Boy Scouts of U.S.A., 2000—02; bd. dirs., mem. exec. com. Doral and West Airport C. of C.; bd. dirs. Miami-Dade (Fla.) County Ethics Coalition. Fulbright selectee, Halleck scholar. Mem. ABA, Ind. Bar Assn., Greater Miami C. of C. (former corp. rep. trustee), Doral Park Golf and Country Club (bd. dirs., pres. 2004-06), Order of Coif, Phi Delta Phi, Alpha Delta Sigma, Lambda Phi Gamma Delta (Disting. Alumni award) Office: 10005 NW 52nd Ter Miami FL 33178-2608 Office Phone: 305-987-2402. Office Fax: 305-591-6560.

THORNBURG, GARRETT, JR., finance company executive; BA, Williams Coll.; MBA, Harvard Univ. CFO NY State Urban Develop. Corp.; limited ptnr., founding mem. pub. fin. dept. Bear Stearns & Co., NYC; sole dir. Thornburg Investment Mgmt. Inc., 1982—, Thornburg Securities Corp.; founder, chmn., CEO Thornburg Mortgage Inc., Santa Fe, 1993—. Bd. gov. Investment Co. Inst., Nat. Assn. REIT Inc. Bd. mem. Nat. Dance Inst. N. Mex.; trustee Coll. Santa Fe. Office: Thornburg Mortgage Inc Ste 302 150 Washington Ave Santa Fe NM 87501 *

THORNBURG, LACY HERMAN, federal judge; b. Charlotte, NC, Dec. 20, 1929; s. Jesse Lafayette and Sarah Ann (Ziegler) T.; m. Dorothy Todd, Sept. 6, 1953; children— Sara Thornburg Evans, Lacy Eugene, Jesse Todd, Alan Ziegler. AA, Mars Hill Coll., 1950; BA, U. N.C., 1951, JD, 1954. Bar: U.S. Dist. Ct. (we. dist.) N.C. Practiced law, Webster, NC, 1954-67; superior ct. judge State of N.C., 1967-83, atty. gen Raleigh, 1985-92; emergency judge N.C. Superior Ct., Webster, 1993-94; mem. Nat. Indian Gaming Commn., 1994-95; judge U.S. Dist. Ct. for N.C., Asheville, 1995—. Mem. staff Congressman Taylor, Sylva, NC, 1960, Congressman David Hall, Sylva, 1959-60; mem. N.C. Ho. of Reps., 1961-65; mem. NC Cts. Commn., NC Criminal Code Commn., Capital Planning Commn., Raleigh Chmn. Jackson County Bd. of Health, Sylva, 1965-84; commr. Tryon Palace, New Bern, N.C. Served with U.S. Army, 1947-48. Mem. Lions, Masons, Shriners. Democrat. Avocations: fly fishing, skeet shooting. Office: US Dist Ct 200 US Courthouse 100 Otis St Asheville NC 28801-2611 Office Phone: 828-771-7250. Business E-Mail: lacythornburg@ncwd.uscourts.gov.

THORNBURGH, DANIEL ESTON, retired university administrator, journalism educator; b. Terre Haute, Ind., Sept. 17, 1930; s. Lester D. and Dorothy (Green) T.; m. Adrianne Ames, Aug. 11, 1956; children: Debra Kay Thornburgh Considine, Stewart Beckett, Malcolm Noble. BS, Ind. State U., 1952; MA, U. Iowa, 1957; EdD, Ind. U., 1980. Reporter Terre Haute Star, 1952; publicity dir. Simpson Coll., Indianola, Iowa, 1955; info. dir. Marshall U., Huntington, W.Va., 1957—59, Ea. Ill. U., Charleston, 1959—65, chmn., prof. journalism, 1965—84, dir. univ. rels., 1992; ret. Vis. prof. U. Hawaii, 1982—83, U. Fla., 1993—94, Millikin U., 1996; mem. Gov.'s Coun. Health and Phys. Fitness, 1987—2003; pub. Casey Banner Times, Ill., 1967—69. Editor: (with others) Interpretative Reporting Workbook, 1982. Mem. Charleston City Coun., 1973-77; active Ill. Recreation Coun., Springfield, 1979-85; pres. Coles Hist. Soc., Charleston, 1972-74, 1992, trustee, 2004—; pres., trustee Five Mile House Found., 1998—; trustee Lincoln and Sargent Farm Found., 1999-2004; chmn. higher edn. and campus min. com. Meth. Ch., 2000-02. With US Army, 1952—54. Named Outstanding Advisor, Coun. Coll. Publs. Advisors, 1971. Mem. Charleston C. of C. (Area Man of Yr. award 1971), Assn. Edn. Journalism and Mass Comm., Pub. Rels. Soc. Am., Soc. Profl. Journalists, Coun. Advancement and Support Edn. (Ea. Ill. U. PRSSA chpt.), Assn. Preservation Hist. Coles County (Merit award 2003), Masons (Cmty. Builder award 1997), Elks, Rotary (pres. Charleston 1976-77, dist. gov. 6490 2000-01, dist. Hall of Fame 2004, pres. chpt. Charitable Found. 2004-06), Ea. Ill. U. Found., Charleston Country Club. Methodist. Avocation: writing. Home: 1405 Buchanan Ave Charleston IL 61920-2924 Personal E-mail: adthorn@consolidated.net.

THORNBURGH, DICK (RICHARD L.), lawyer, former United States attorney general; b. Pitts., July 16, 1932; s. Charles Garland and Alice (Sanborn) T.; m. Virginia Walton Judson, Oct. 12, 1963; children: John, David, Peter, William. B in Engring., Yale, 1954; LLB, U. Pitts., 1957; 31 degrees (hon.). Bar: Pa. 1958, US Supreme Ct. 1965, DC 1998. Atty. Kirkpatrick, Lockhart, Preston, Gates, Ellis, LLP, Pitts., 1959-69, 77-79, 87-88, 91-92, 94—, counsel Washington; US atty. (we. dist.) Pa. US Dept. Justice, Pitts., 1969-75, asst. atty. gen. criminal divsn. Washington, 1975-77; gov. State of Pa., Harrisburg, 1979-87; dir. Inst. Politics John F. Kennedy Sch. Govt., Harvard U., 1987-88; atty. gen. US Dept. Justice, Washington, 1988-91; under-sec.-gen. for adminstrn. & mgmt. UN, NYC, 1992-93. Del. Pa. Constl. Conv., 1967-68; vice-chair World Com. on Disability; bd. dirs. Nat. Mus. Indsl. History, Gettysburg Found. Author: (autobiography) Where the Evidence Leads: The Autobiography of Dick Thornburgh, 2003. Trustee U. Pitts. Recipient Spl. Medallion award, Drug Enforcement Adminstrn., 1973, DSM, Am. Legion, 1992, Lifetime Achievement award, Am. Lawyer mag., 2006. Fellow Am. Bar Found.; mem. Am. Judicature Soc., Coun. Fgn. Rels., Am. Law Inst. Republican. Office: Kirkpatrick Lockhart Preston Gates Ellis LLP 1601 K St NW Washington DC 20006-1600 Office Phone: 202-778-9080. Office Fax: 202-778-9100.

THORNBURGH, RON E., state official; b. Burlingame, Kans., Dec. 31, 1962; m. Annette Thornburgh; 2 children. BA in Criminal Justice, Washburn U., 1985. Dep. asst. sec. state to asst. sec. state State of Kans., Topeka, 1985-87, asst. sec. state, 1991-95, sec. state, 1995—. Vice chairperson blue ribbon panel on ethical conduct State of Kans., 1989. Mem. Kids Voting Kans. Exec. Com.; mem. adv. com. United Way. Toll fellow Henry Toll Fellowship Prog., 1995, Digital Govt. Agent of Change award, MIT, 2002, Lee Ann Elliott Election Excellence award, Kids Voting USA, 2004. Mem. Washburn U. Alumni Bd., 20/30 Club Internat. Republican. Methodist. Office: Office Sec State Memorial Hall First Floor 120 SW 10th Ave Topeka KS 66612-1504 Office Phone: 785-296-4575. Office Fax: 785-368-8033. *

THORNBURY, JOHN ROUSSEAU, radiologist, physician; b. Cleve., Mar. 16, 1929; s. Purla Lee and Gertrude (Glidden) T.; m. Julia Lee McGregor, Mar. 20, 1955; children: Lee Allison, John McGregor. AB cum laude, Miami U., Oxford, Ohio, 1950; MD, Ohio State U., 1955. Diplomate: Am. Bd. Radiology. Intern Hurley Hosp., Flint, Mich., 1955-56; resident U. Iowa Hosps., Iowa City, 1958-61; instr., asst. prof. radiology U. Colo. Med. Center, Denver, 1962-63; practice medicine specializing in radiology Denver, 1962-63, Iowa City, 1963-66, Seattle, 1966-68, Ann Arbor, Mich., 1968-79, Albuquerque, 1979-84, Rochester, NY, 1984-89, Madison, Wis., 1989-94. Mem. staff U. Wis. Hosp., Madison; prof. radiology, chief sect. body imaging, U. Wis. Med. Sch., 1989-94, prof. emeritus, 1994—; asst. prof. radiology U. Iowa Hosps., 1963-66, U. Wash. Hosp., Seattle, 1966-68; assoc. prof. radiology U. Mich. Med. Ctr., 1968-71, prof., 1971-79, chief uroradiology sect., 1971-79; prof. radiology, chief divsn. diagnostic radiology Sch. Medicine, U. N.Mex., 1979-84; prof. radiology U. Rochester Sch. Medicine, 1984-89, acting chmn., 1985-87; chmn. sci. com. on efficacy studies Nat. Coun. on Radiation Protection, 1980-95; rapporteur/mem. sci. group on indications/limitations of x-ray diagnostic procedures WHO, 1983; cons. com. on efficacy of magnetic resonance nat. health tech. adv. panel Australian Inst. Health, 1986; invited U.S. cons. MRI program, U. Med. Ctr., Nijmegen, The Netherlands, 1992; mem. planning group Low Back Pain Collaboratives and Nat. Congress, Inst. for Health Care Improvement, 1997-98; mem. methodologic rsch. issues working group NIH and Pub. Health Svc.-Office of Women's Health, 1998; cons., spkr. Royal Australasian Coll. Radiologists, Melbourne, Australia, 1997; cons. tech. assessment and outcomes rsch., 1994—; cons. in tech. assessment and outcomes rsch. to dept. neuroradiology Loma Linda Med. Ctr., 2002-; cons. to Am. Soc. Neuroradiology, 1995-2000; lectr. in field. Co-author/cons. Clin. Efficacy Assessment Project, Am. Coll. Physicians, 1986-89; assoc. editor: Yearbook of Radiology, 1971-82; mem. editl. bd.: Contemporary Diagnostic Radiology, 1977-84, Urologic Radiology, 1977-84 Bd. dirs. Sally Jobe Found., Denver, 1996—. Capt., M.C. USAF, 1956-58. Recipient Dist. Svc. award Am. Bd. Radiology, 2000, Alumni Achievement award Ohio State U. Coll. Medicine, 2000, Gold medal Assn. Univ. Radiologists, 2002, Gold medal Soc. Uroradiology, 2005; grantee Agy. Health Care Policy and Rsch., 1986-91, U. Rochester, 1986-89, U. Wis., Madison, 1989-91 Fellow Am. Coll. Radiology (mem. emeritus); mem. Am. Coll. Radiology Imaging Network (outcomes and quality of life subcom., urology com., NIH, 1999-2002), Soc. Uroradiology (pres. 1976-77, dir. 1977-79, gold medal 2005), Assn. Univ. Radiologists (pres. 1980-81), Radiol. Soc. N.Am., Am. Roentgen Ray Soc. (Caldwell medal 1993), Soc. for Health Svcs. Rsch. in Radiology (adv. com. to bd. dirs. 1998—), Colo. Radiol. Soc., Phi Beta Kappa, Delta Tau Delta, Omicron Delta Kappa, Phi Chi. Episcopalian. Home: 1340 Forest Park Cir #16 Lafayette CO 80026 *"Mooring Post" relationships and sharing have been essential to success and achievements in my multi-disciplinary research. "Mooring Post" persons range from expert mentors and stellar colleagues, to the bedrock of a loving and supportive family. Further, to me, Rule One in medicine has always been, "The patient comes first.".*

THORNDIKE, EDWARD HARMON, physicist; b. Pasadena, Calif., Aug. 2, 1934; s. Edward Moulton and Louise (Harmon) T.; m. Elizabeth H. Wenger, Sept. 8, 1955; children: Susan Lee, Patricia Lynn, Edward Harmon Jr. AB, Wesleyan U., Middletown, Conn., 1956, MS, Stanford U., 1957; PhD, Harvard U., 1960. Rsch. fellow Harvard U., Cambridge, Mass., 1960-61; mem. faculty U. Rochester, NY, 1961—, asso. prof. physics, 1965-72, prof., 1972—. Vis. prof. U. Geneva, 1969-70; vis. scientist CERN, Geneva, 1969-70; mem. adv. coun. Ctr. Environ. Info., Rochester, 1974-93; mem. adv. com. Stanford Linear Accelerator Ctr. Exptl. Program, 1987-89; mem. vis. com. for Fermilab, Univs. Rsch. Assn., 1993-95. Author: Energy and Environment, a Primer for Scientists and Engineers, 1976; contbr. articles to profl. jours. Recipient W.K.H. Panofsky prize, 1999; NSF fellow, 1970, Guggenheim fellow, 1987-88. Fellow Am. Phys. Soc. Office: U Rochester Dept Physics/Astronomy Rochester NY 14627

THORNE, CARL F., gas industry executive; b. 1940; BS in Petroleum Engring., U. Tex.; JD, Baylor U. Bar: Tex. 1967. Dir. Sedco Inc., Dallas, 1986—, pres., CEO, 1987—, chmn. bd. dirs., 1987—; dir. Crescent Op., Inc., chmn. compensation com.; CEO, dir. Blocker Energy Corp., 1987—; ptnr. BEC Ventures; former pres. Sedco-Forex; pres., CEO ENSCO Internat. Inc., Dallas, 1987—, chmn. bd., 1987—. Mem. Nat. Ocean Industries Assn. (dir.). Office: ENSCO 500 N Akard St Ste 4300 Dallas TX 75201-3331

THORNE, CHARLES HEDGES MCKINSTRY, plastic surgeon; b. Oakland, Calif., Oct. 27, 1952; BA in Biophysics and Biochemistry, Yale Coll., 1974; MD, UCLA Sch. Medicine, 1976—81. Cert. Am. Bd. Surgery, 1987, Am. Bd. Plastic Surgery, 1991. Residency tng. Mass. Gen. Hosp., 1981—86, NYU Med. Ctr., 1986—88, fellowship, Craniofacial Surgery, 1988—89, dir., Plastic Surgery Residency Prog., 1989—98, dir., Ctr. for Ear Anomalies, 1990—; exec. chief resident Inst. Reconstructive Plastic Surgery, 1987—88; co-dir. Ctr. for Craniofacial Prosthetics, 1992—; chief, Plastic Surgery Svc. Bellevue Hosp., 1992—; prog. dir., Cosmetic Surgery Manhattan Eye and Ear Hosp., 1998—99; assoc. prof., Dept. Surgery NYU Sch. Medicine. Mem. exec. com., NYU Med. Bd., 1994—96, Surgical House Staff Com., 1989—97, Oper. Rm. Com., NYU, 1990—98, Oper. Rm. Com., Bellevue Hosp., NYU, 1993—98, Exec. Com., NYU Assn. Attending M.D.'s, 1995—98; mem., Credentials Com. Manhattan Eye, Ear and Throat Hosp., 1998—99, mem., Quality Assurance Com., 1998—99, bd. mem., Surgeon Directors, 2000—; mem. LCME Faculty Com., NYU Sch. Medicine, 1999, Curriculum Com., NYU Sch. Medicine, 2002, Adv. Bd., Forward Face. Assoc. editor (journals) Journal of Cranio-Maxillofacial Trauma, 1995—2001, Journal of Plastic and Reconstructive Surgery, 2000—. Vol. Peace Corps, Ghana, 1974—76. Recipient First prize, Am. Soc. Maxillofacial Surgeons, 1990, 1992, NY Regional Soc. Plastic Surgery, 1990, Tchr. of Yr. award, Inst. Reconstructive Plastic Surgery, NYU Med. Ctr., 1993—94, 1997—98, 1999—2000. Mem.: Northeastern Soc. Plastic Surgeons (prog. chmn. 2000, parliamentarian 2000—01, bd. mem.-at-large 2001—03, pres. 2002—03), Internat. Soc. Craniomaxillofacial Surgeons, Forum for Academic Plastic Surgeons (pres. 1996—97), Am. Soc. Plastic Surgeons, Am. Soc. Craniofacial Surgery, Am. Soc. Aesthetic Plastic Surgery, AMA, Am. Coll. Surgeons, Am. Cleft Palate Assn., Am. Assn. Plastic Surgeons. Office: NYU Medical Ctr 812 Park Ave New York NY 10021 Office Phone: 212-794-0044. Office Fax: 212-772-1326. Business E-Mail: thornc01@popmail.med.nyu.edu. *

THORNE, FRANCIS, composer; b. Bay Shore, NY, June 23, 1922; s. Francis Burritt and Hildegarde (Kobbé) T.; m. Ann Cobb, Dec. 9, 1942; children: Ann Boughton (Mrs. William F. Niles), Wendy Oakleigh (Mrs. William H. Forsyth, Jr.), Candace Kobbé (Mrs. Anthony M. Canton). BA in Music Theory, Yale U., 1942. Founder, pres. Thorne Music Fund, Inc., 1965-75; pub. Edward B. Marks Music Corp., 1963—, Gen. Music Pub. Co., 1971—, G. Schirmer/AMP, 1985—, Theodore Presser Co., 1989—. Exec. dir. Lenox Arts Ctr., 1972-76, Am. Composers Alliance, 1975-85; co-founder, pres. Am. Composers Orch., 1976—. Composer: Elegy for Orch., 1964, Burlesque Overture, 1966, Lyric Variations for Orch., 1967, Symphony No. 1, 1963, No. II, 1966, No. III, 1970, No. IV, 1977, Fortuna, 1961-62, Liebesrock, 1969, Sonar Plexus, 1969, Six Set-Pieces, 1969, Contra Band Music, 1970, Antiphonies, 1970, Simultaneities, 1971, Quartessence, 1971, Fanfare, Fugue and Funk, 1972, Lyric Variations II, 1972, Piano Sonata, 1972, Lyric Variations III, 1973, Cantata Sauce, 1973, Evensongs, 1973, Cello Concerto, 1974, Piano Concerto, 1974, Violin Concerto, 1975, String Quartet 1, 1960, 2, 1967, 3, 1976, 4, 1983, Spoon River Overture, 1976, Grand Duo, 1976, Five Set Pieces, 1976, Love's Variations, 1976, Pop Partita, 1978, The Eternal Light for Soprano and Orchestra, 1979, Divertimento for Flute, Strings and Percussion, 1979, Lyric Variations IV for Solo Violin, 1980, Divertimento 2 for Bassoon and Stringed Instruments, 1980, Eine Kleine Meyermusik, 1980, Gems From Spoon River, 1980, Lyric Variations No. 6 for solo clarinet, 1981, Divertimento No. 3, 1982, Praise and Thanksgiving, 1983, Lyric Variations No. 5 for Orch., 1980-81, Symphony No. 5, 1984, Concerto Concertante, 1985, Rhapsodic Variations, No. 2, 1985, Humoresque for Orch., 1985, Rhapsodic Variations No. 3 for Oboe and Strings, 1986, The Affirming Flame for Soprano and Chamber Ensemble, 1987; seven simple syncopations for Piano solo, 1987, Rhapsodic Variations No. 4 For Viol Solo, 1987, Rhapsodic Variations No. 5 for Violins and Piano, 1988, Money Matters for Tenor and Chamber Ensemble, 1988, Piano Concerto No. 3, 1989, Remembering Dizzy for Brass Quintet, 1990, Pop Partita No. 2 for woodwinds and strings, 1991, Mario and The Magician, opera after Thomas Mann, in Prologue and 1 Act, 1991, Symphony No. 6 for Strings, 1992, Symphony No. 7 Along the Hudson for chorus and orch., 1994, Cello Concerto No. 2, 1995, Echo for Soprano and Mixed Chorus, 1996, Clarinet Concerto, 1997, Rhapsodic Variations No. 7 for Solo Piano, 1998, Lyric Variations No. 8, 1999, Flash Dances for Orchestra, 1999, Oboe Concerto, 1999-2000, SONG To Mark Stand's Poem, 2000, Concerto for Orchestra, 2000-01, The Four Seasons, for mezzo and string trio, 2002, Triple Concerto for English Horn, Bass Clarinet, Viola and Orchestra, 2004, Lyric Variations No. 9 for Solo Piano, 2004, Songs and Dances for Orchestra, 2005, The Four Seasons, 2006, Three Poems of Robert Fitzgerald, 2007; recs. on Composers' Recs., Inc., Serenus, Owl, Louisville Opus One and New World Trustee Am. Symphony Orchestra League, Manhattan Sch. Music, Am. Music Center, MacDowell Colony, Walter W. Naumburg Found., Contemporary Music Soc., Theater Devel. Fund, Group for Contemporary Music., Am. Brass Quintet. Lt. USNR, 1942-45. Nat. Endowment Arts grantee, 1966, 73; fellow, 1976, 79; Nat. Inst. Arts and Letters grantee, 1968; N.Y. State Arts Council ballet commn., 1973 Mem. AAAL, BMI, Contemporary Music Soc. (bd. dirs.), Am. Composers Alliance, League Composers. Clubs: Century Assn. (N.Y.C.). Home: Geer Village #104 77 S Canaan Rd Canaan CT 06018 Business E-Mail: aco@americancomposers.org. *Having spent ten years as a businessman, I have been privileged to serve my composer colleagues as an administrator for musical organizations. The practical experience has also served me well as a creative artist in having instilled the virtues of discipline. Serving music as composer and administrator gives the highest sense of satisfaction, from participating in this life-giving world in a total comprehensive way.*

THORNE, JOHN REINECKE, finance educator, venture capitalist; b. Pitts., Mar. 25, 1926; s. John Mueller and Louise (Reinecke) T.; m. Barbara Siebert, Aug. 31, 1951 (dec. Feb. 1995); children: John S., Barbara L., Richard W.; m. Helen L. Totzke, Dec. 29, 1999. BS, Brown U., 1947; MSEE, U. Pitts., 1949; MS in Indsl. Adminstrn., Carnegie Mellon U., 1952. Devel. engr. Westinghouse Elec. Corp., Pitts., 1947-50; mgr. fin. analysis Hughes Aircraft Co., LA, 1952—57; dir. computer systems lab. Litton Industries, LA, 1957—63; founder, chmn., pres. The Scionics Corp., LA, 1963—69; cons., LA, 1969-72; prof. bus. Carnegie-Mellon U., Pitts., 1972—2003, Morgenthaler prof. entrepreneurship, 1987—2003, Morgenthaler emeritus prof. entrepreneurship, 2003—, dir. Donald H. Jones Ctr. for Entrepreneurship, 1990—2000; founder, chmn. Enterprise Corp. Pitts., 1983-98; gen. ptnr. Pitts. Seed Fund, 1985—2000. Contbr. articles to profl. jours. Named Fin. Svcs. Adv. of Yr., SBA, 1988. Mem.: Rolling Rock Club, Duquesne Club. Unitarian Universalist. Home: 137 Furnace Run Ln Laughlintown PA 15655-0369 Office: Tepper Sch Bus Carnegie-Mellon U Pittsburgh PA 15213 Office Phone: 412-268-2263. Business E-Mail: thorne@andrew.cmu.edu.

THORNE, JOHN WATSON, III, advertising and marketing executive; b. Washington, Jan. 16, 1934; s. John Watson, Jr. and Mary Washington (Tucker) T.; m. Joan Kramer Vail, Mar. 2, 1957; children: Vail Tucker, Tracy Tucker, John Watson, IV. BA in Polit. Sci., George Washington U., 1955; MA in Sociology, The New Sch. U., NYC, 1974. Asst. account exec. Young & Rubicam, Inc., NYC, 1957-59; advt. mgr. GE, Decatur, Ill., 1959-63; dir. advt. promotion Brand Names Found., NYC, 1963-66; account exec. Tatham-Laird & Kudner (advt.), NYC, 1966-67; v.p., mgmt. supr. Wells, Rich, Greene, Inc., NYC, 1973-76; v.p., account supr. Batten, Barton, Durstine & Osborn, Inc., NYC, 1967-73, sr. v.p., mgmt. supr., 1976-81, exec. v.p., 1981-87, also dir., mem. oper. com.; chmn. Thorne & Assocs., Newtown, Pa., 1987—; pres., CEO Telerx Mktg., Spring House, Pa., 1991-95; chmn., CEO Alliance Mktg. Svcs. Group, Inc., Jamison, Pa., 1995—2004, Alliance Healthcare Info., Inc., Ivyland, Pa., 2004—. Mem. bus. program com. Proprietary Assn., Washington; adj. prof. advt. Syracuse (N.Y.) U. Pres. Hastings-on-Hudson (N.Y.) Bd. Edn.; bd. dirs. Young Concert Artists, N.Y.C.; mem. comm. coms. Nat. Urban League, Carnegie Hall. Served as 1st lt. USMCR, 1955-57. Mem.: Lotos Club (NYC), Buckingham Racquet Club. Republican. Roman Catholic. Home: 100 Stoney Brook Rd Newtown PA 18940-2506 Office: Alliance Healthcare Info Inc One Ivybrook Blvd Ste 100 Warminster PA 18974

THORNE, KIP STEPHEN, physicist, researcher; b. Logan, Utah, June 1, 1940; s. David Wynne and Alison (Comish) T.; m. Linda Jeanne Peterson, Sept. 12, 1960 (div. 1977); children: Kares Anne, Bret Carter; m. Carolee Joyce Winstein, July 7, 1984. BS in Physics, Calif. Inst. Tech., 1962; A.M. in Physics (Woodrow Wilson fellow, Danforth Found. fellow), Princeton U., 1963, PhD in Physics (Danforth Found. fellow, NSF fellow), 1965, postgrad. (NSF postdoctoral fellow), 1965-66; D.Sc. (hon.), Ill. Coll., 1979; Dr.h.c., Moscow U., 1981; D.Sc. (hon.), Utah State U., 2000, U. Glasgow, 2001; D.H.L. (hon.), Claremont Grad. U., 2002. Research fellow Calif. Inst. Tech., 1966-67, assoc. prof. theoretical physics, 1967-70, prof., 1970—, William R. Kenan, Jr. prof., 1981-91, Feynman prof. theoretical physics, 1991—. Fulbright lectr., France, 1966; vis. assoc. prof. U. Chgo., 1968; vis. prof. Moscow U., 1969, 75, 78, 82, 83, 86, 88, 90, 98; vis. sr. rsch. assoc. Cornell U., 1977, A.D. White prof.-at-large, 1988-92; adj. prof. U. Utah, 1971-98; mem. Internat. Com. on Gen. Relativity and Gravitation, 1971-80, 92-01, Com. on U.S.-USSR Coop. in Physics, 1978-79, Space Sci. Bd., NASA, 1980-83; co-founder, chair steering com. LIGO, 1984-87. Co-author: Gravitation Theory and Gravitational Collapse, 1965, Gravitation, 1973, Black Holes: The Membrane Paradigm, 1986, Black Holes and Time Warps: Einstein's Outrageous Legacy, 1994. Alfred P. Sloan Found. Rsch. fellow, 1966-68; John Simon Guggenheim fellow, 1967; recipient Sci. Writing award in physics and astronomy Am. Inst. Physics, 1969, 94, P.A.M. Dirac Meml. lectureship Cambridge U., 1995, Karl Schwarzschild medal Astron. Soc. Germany, 1996, J. Robert Oppenheimer Meml. lectureship U. Calif., 1999, Charles Darwin Meml. Lectureship Royal Astron. Soc., 2000, Arthur Holly Compton Meml. lectureship Washington U., 2001, Herzberg Meml. Lectureship Can. Assn. Physicists, 2001; recipient Common Wealth award, Sci. Invention, 2005; Robinson Prize in Cosmology, U. Newcastle, 2002; named Calif. Scientist of Yr., 2004. Fellow Am. Phys. Soc. (Julius Edgar Lilienfeld prize 1996, chair topical group in gravity 1997-98); mem. Am. Philosophical Soc., Nat. Acad. Scis., Am. Acad. Arts and Scis., Am. Astron. Soc., Internat. Astron. Union, AAAS, Russian Acad. Scis., Ligo Sci. Collaboration, Lisa Internat. Sci. Team, Sigma Xi, Tau Beta Pi. Office: California Inst Tech 130-33 Theoretical Astrophysics 1200 E California Blvd Pasadena CA 91125

THORNE, NATHAN C., investment company executive; BA, Yale Univ. Joined Merrill Lynch, NYC, 1984, head high yield fin. & restructuring group, head corp. fin., high yield fin. & real estate, head. internat pvt. equity, vice chmn. global pvt. equity, sr. v.p., pres. global pvt. equity, 2002—. Office: Merrill Lynch 4 World Fin Ctr 250 Vesey St New York NY 10080 *

THORNE, RICHARD MANSERGH, physicist; b. Birmingham, Eng., July 25, 1942; s. Robert George and Dorothy Lena (Goodchild) T.; children: Peter Baring, Michael Thomas, Thomas Mansergh. BSc, Birmingham U., 1963; PhD, MIT, 1968. Grad. asst. M.I.T., 1963-68; asst. prof. dept. atmospheric scis. UCLA, 1968-71, asso. prof., 1971-75, prof., 1975—, chmn. dept., 1976-79. Vis. fellow St. Edmund's Coll., Cambridge (Eng.) U., 1986-87, 92; cons. NATO Adv. Group for Aerospace R&D, 1973, Jet Propulsion Lab., Aerospace Corp. Contbr. articles to profl. jours. Recipient numerous grants NSF, NASA, NATO, Jet Propulsion Lab.; Fulbright scholar, 1963-70; fellow Royal Norwegian Coun. for Sci. and Indsl. Rsch., 1973, sr. vis. fellow U. Sussex, 1979-80, rsch. fellow Royal Soc. London, 1986-87. Fellow Am. Geophys. Union; mem. Internat. Union Radio Scis. Home: 10390 Caribou Ln Los Angeles CA 90077 Office: UCLA Dept Atmospheric and Oceanic Scis Los Angeles CA 90095-1565 Business E-Mail: rmt@atmos.ucla.edu.

THORNE, WILLIAM ALBERT, retired lawyer; b. Chgo., Feb. 20, 1924; s. William A. and Irma J. Thorne; m. Elizabeth Lee Douglas, June 19, 1948; children: Deborah, Elizabeth Ann, Margaret, Doulgas. JD, Valparaiso U., 1949. Bar: Ind. 1949, U.S. Dist. Ct. (no. and so. dists.) Ind. 1949, U.S. Supreme Ct. 1960. Pvt. practice, Elkhart, Ind., 1949-63; ptnr. Thorne Grodnik, LLP, Elkhart, 1963-95; of counsel Thorne.Grodnik, LLP and predecessor, Elkhart, 1995—2002; ret., 2002. Chmn. City of Elkhart Pks. and Recreation Bd., 1971—75, Elkhart Bd. Water Works, 1975—83, No. Ind. Conf. United Meth. Ch., Bd. Higher Edn. and Campus Ministry, 1994—2000; bd. vis. Valparaiso U. Law Sch., 1990—96; trustee Meth. Theol. Sch., Ohio, 1993—2003. With US Army, 1943—46. Named a Disting. Hoosier, Gov. Joseph Kernan, 2005. Fellow: Ind. State Bar Assn. (chmn. bankruptcy sect. 1985—86, bd. govs. 1987—88). Democrat. Avocations: golf, reading. Personal E-mail: thollaw@msn.com.

THORNELL, PATRICIA L., elementary school educator; d. John Raymond and Dora Bond Thornell. Degree in edn., Adelphi U., Garden City, NY, 1968; degree in edn. and reading, LI U., Greenvale, 1971. Tchr. 2d grade Brentwood Elem. Sch., NY, 1969; tchr. Sachem Sch., Holbrook, 1970—95, tchr. math., 1995—96, tchr. remedial math., 1995—2006; tchr. sewing Seams Straight To Me, Great River, 1995—2007; ret., 2007. Mem.: Am. Sewing Guild, Nat. Coun. Tchrs. Math. Avocations: music, sewing. E-mail: buttonsandbows@optonline.net.

THORNER, JEREMY W., biology professor; Prof., molecular and cell biology, William V. Power chair, biology Univ. Calif., Berkeley. Med. sci. adv. bd. Lowe Syndrome Assn. Fellow: Am. Acad. Arts & Scis.; mem.: Am. Soc. Biochemistry and Molecular Biology, Am. Soc. For Cell Biology. Office: Dept Molecular & Cell Biology Univ Calif MC 3202 526 Barker Berkeley CA 94720 Office Phone: 510-642-2558. Business E-Mail: jthorner@berkeley.edu. *

THORNER, MICHAEL OLIVER, medical educator; b. Beaconsfield, Eng., Jan. 14, 1945; came to U.S., 1977; s. Hans and Ilse T.; m. Prudence Maria Ross, July 7, 1966; children— Benjamin Bruno, Anna Rosa MB, BChir, U. London, 1970. Intern, resident Middlesex Hosp., St. Bartholomew's Hosp., London; lectr. chem. pathology St. Bartholomews Hosp., London, 1974, research fellow, 1974-75, lectr. medicine, 1975-77; assoc. prof. medicine U. Va., Charlottesville, 1977-82, prof. medicine, 1982-90, head div. endocrinology and metabolism, 1986-98, dir. Clin. Research Ctr., 1984-97, assoc. dir. CRC, 1981-84, Kenneth R. Crispell prof. in internal medicine, 1990-98, chmn. dept. internal medicine, 1998—2006, Henry B. Mulholland prof. internal medicine, 1998—2006, David C. Harrison prof. internal medicine, 2006—. Contbr. articles to profl. jours. Recipient Albion O. Bernstein award, 1984, Virginia Scientist of Yr. award, 1985, Gen. Clin. Rsch. Ctrs. program award, 1995, The Pituitary Soc. Annual award for contbns. to understanding pituitary disease, 1995, Theodore E. Woodward Award 1996. Master Am. Coll. Physicians; fellow ACP (John Phillips Meml. award 1999), AAAS, Royal Coll. Physicians, Soc. Endocrinology, Endocrine Soc. (Edwin B. Astwood award 1992), Assn. Am. Physicians, Am. Soc. Clin. Investigations. Office: U Va Health Sys Dept Internal Medicine Endocrinology PO Box 801411 Charlottesville VA 22908 Home: 906 Fendall Terr Charlottesville VA 22903 Fax: 434-982-0147. E-mail: mot@virginia.edu.

THORNHILL, ARTHUR H., JR., retired publishing executive; b. Boston, Jan. 1, 1924; s. Arthur Horace and Mary Josephine (Peterson) T.; m. Dorothy M. Matheis, Oct. 28, 1944; children: Sandra Susanne Thornhill Brushart, Arthur Horace. AB magna cum laude, Princeton U., 1948. With Little, Brown & Co., Inc., Boston, 1948-88, v.p., 1955-58, gen. mgr., 1960-87, chief exec. officer, pres., 1962-87, chmn. bd., 1970-87; chmn., pres., dir. Little, Brown & Co. (Can.), Ltd., 1955-84; v.p. Time, Inc., 1968-87; vice chmn. Time-Life Books, Inc., 1976-86. Mem. adv. council history dept. Princeton U., 1964-85; trustee, treas. Princeton U. Press, 1972-85; chmn. N.Y. Graphic Soc., 1974-79. Trustee Bennington Coll., 1969-76; fellow emeritus Ctr. for Creative Photography U. Ariz.; bd. dirs. Am. Book Pubs. Council, 1964-67. Served to 1st lt. USAAF, World War II. Decorated Air medal; recipient Princeton U. Press medal, 1985, Disting. Alumni award Dwight-Englewood Sch., 1998. Mem. Assn. Am. Pubs. (bd. dirs. 1978-81), Edgartown Yacht Club, Edgartown Reading Room (pres. 1990-92), Union Club (N.Y.C.), Princeton Club (N.Y.C.), Century Club (N.Y.C.), Publs. Lunch Club (N.Y.C.), Union Club (Boston), St. Botolph (Boston). Home: Apt 5303 250 Pantops Mountain Rd Charlottesville VA 22911-8703

THORNHILL, HARLEN WEBSTER, retired aircraft engineer; b. Syracuse, NY, June 10, 1932; s. Harlan Alva and Golda Doan Thornhill; m. Earlene Allday Thornhill, Aug. 11, 1956 (div. Feb. 22, 1977); children: Sheryl, David(dec.), Mark, James, Patricia; m. Patricia Scott Hayes Thornill, Aug. 20, 1977; stepchildren: Henry, Patricia, William. BS in Profl. Aeronautics, Embry Riddle Aero. U., Daytona Beach, Fla., 1978, MS in Aviation Mgmt., 1985. Airframe and powerplant lic. FAA. Aircraft maintenance staff Syracuse Aircraft Sales, 1950—51; flight mechanic Carrier Corp., Syracuse, 1961—64; aircraft mechanic, foreman Ea. Airlines, various locations, 1964—87; aircraft maintenance/engring. staff Continental Airlines, Houston, 1987—97; aircraft maintenance staff British Internat. Aviation, Conroe, Tex., 2000—. Vice comdr. Am. Legion, The Woodlands, Tex., 1987. With USN, 1951—59, ETO, with USAF, 1959—73, Korea. Mem.: AARP, AACP, NRA, VFW, Continental Airlines Retiree Assn., Ea. Airlines Retiree Assn., Am. Mil. Soc., Tex. State Rifle Assn., Nat. Assn. Uniform Svcs., Air Force Sgts. Assn., Non-Commd. Officers Assn., Air Force Assn., Ret. Enlisted Assn., 174th Alumni Assn., Embry Riddle Aero. Univ. Alumni Assn., Am. Legion, N.Am. Hunting Club, Alpha Eta Rho. Republican. Avocations: hunting, fishing, bowling.

THORNLOW, CAROLYN, law firm administrator, consultant; b. Kew Gardens, NY, May 25, 1954; 1 child, Johanna Louise Ramm. BBA magna cum laude, Baruch Coll., 1982. Gen. mgr. Richard A. Ramm Assocs., Levittown, N.Y., 1972-78; adminstr. Tunstead Schechter & Torre, NYC, 1978-82, Cowan Liebowitz & Latman, P.C., NYC, 1982-84, Rosenberg & Estis, P.C., NYC, 1984-85; contr. Finkelstein, Borah, Schwartz, Altschuler & Goldstein, P.C., NYC, 1986-92; pres. Concinnity Svcs., Hastings, N.Y., 1984—. Instr. introduction to law office mgmt. seminars Assn. Legal Adminstrs., NYC, 1984. Editor: The ABA Guide to Professional Managers in the Law Office, 1996; contbr. numerous articles to profl. jours. Mem. ABA (bd. dirs. law practice mgmt. div. 2000-01), N.Y. Assn. Legal Adminstrs. (v.p. 1982-83), Internat. Assn. Legal Adminstrs. (asst. regional v.p. 1983-84, regional v.p. 1984-85), Nat. Soc. Tax Profls. (cert. tax profl.), Am. Mgmt. Assn., Inst. Cert. Profl. Mgrs. (cert.), ABA, Inst. Cert. Mgmt. Accts., Mensa, Beta Gamma Sigma, Sigma Iota Epsilon. Home and Office: Concinnity Svcs 109 Washington Ave Hastings On Hudson NY 10706 Home Phone: 914-478-4545; Office Phone: 914-478-9000. Business E-Mail: cthornlow@concinnityservices.com, lawbucks@aol.com, crtinny@aol.com.

THORNSBERRY, CLYDE, microbiologist; b. Pippa Passes, Ky., June 20, 1930; s. Columbus B. and Ollie Mae (Sparkman) T.; m. Glenda L. Martin, May 13, 1952; children: Teresa, David, Robert. BS, U. Ky., Lexington, 1958, PhD, 1966. Chief Antimicrobial Investigations Br. Ctrs. for Disease Control, Atlanta, 1966-89; dir. Inst. for Microbiol. Rsch., Franklin, Tenn., 1989-93, Focus BioInova, Inc., Franklin, 1993—; dirt. Eurofins Medinet, Inc., Franklin. Lectr. in field; chmn., vice-chmn. Intersci. Conf. Anti-Agts., Washington, 1989-94; adv. bd. several pharm. cos., 1980—. Contbr. articles to profl. jours. Recipient awards USPHS, Washington, 1982, 87. Fellow Infectious Disease Soc. of Am.; mem. Am. Soc. Microbiology (BD award for Rsch. in Clin. Microbiology 2003), Am. Acad. Microbiology, NY Acad. Scis., WHO Coms. on Antibiotics, Nat. Com. Clin. Lab. Stds. Democrat. Achievements include patent-use of antimicrobial agts. to sterilize tissue for implanting; study of antimicrobials, antimicrobial resistance, and in vitro testing of antimicrobial activity; lab. was designated a WHO lab. for antimicrobial agts. Home: 5182 Waddell Hollow Rd Franklin TN 37064-9436 Office: Eurofin Medinet Inc 5182 Waddell Hollow Rd Franklin TN 37064 Office Phone: 615-794-7011. Business E-Mail: clyde.thornsberry@eurofinsmedinet.com.

THORNSBERRY, WILLIS LEE, JR., chemist; b. Sturgis, Ky., Aug. 10, 1940; s. Willis Lee and Jane (Hall) T.; m. Mary Elizabeth Gaswint, June 19, 1965; children: Brian, Michele. BS, Murray State U., 1963; MS, U. Ark., 1967; PhD, Tulane U., 1974. Rsch. chemist Freeport-McMoRan Inc., Belle Chasse, La., 1967—74, sr. rsch. chemist, 1974—82; pres. Tech. Devel. Svcs. Inc., Sturgis, Ky., 1995—. Contbr. articles to profl. jours. Coach, leader for youth groups Jefferson Parish Playgrounds, Gretna, La., 1970-84, Boy Scouts Am., Gretna, 1975-82. 1st lt. U.S. Army, 1963-65. Mem. Am. Chem. Soc. (sect. chmn. 1982), Sigma Xi. Democrat. Achievements include numerous patents for process for uranium recovery from phosphoric acid, recovery of silica from hydrofluorosilicic acid, stabilization of gypsum for construction purposes, preparation and use of fertilizer additives. Office: 1024 N Main St Sturgis KY 42459-1245 Office Phone: 270-333-2243. Personal E-mail: mwthorns@bellsouth.net.

THORNTON, BILLY BOB, actor, film producer; b. Hot Springs, Ark., Aug. 4, 1955; s. Billy Ray and Virginia Thornton; m. Melissa Lee Gatlin, 1978 (div. 1980); 1 child; m. Toni Lawrence, 1986 (div. 1988); m. Cynda Williams, 1990 (div. 1992); m. Pietra Dawn Cherniak, Feb. 18, 1993 (div. Apr. 1997); 2 children; m. Angelina Jolie, May 5, 2000 (div. May 27, 2003); 1 child. Actor: (films) For the Boys, 1991, Indecent Proposal, 1993, Tombstone, 1993, On Deadly Ground, 1994, Floundering, 1994, Dead Man, 1995, The Winner, 1996, A Gun, A Car, A Blonde, 1997, U-Turn, 1997, A Thousand Miles, 1997, The Apostle, 1997, Primary Colors, 1998, Homegrown, 1998, Armageddon, 1998, A Simple Plan, 1998, Pushing Tin, 1999, The Last Real Cowboys, 2000, South of Heaven, West of Hell, 2000, Monster's Ball, 2001, Bandists, 2001, The Man Who Wasn't There, 2001, Waking up in Reno, 2002, The Badge, 2002, Intolerable Cruelty, 2003, Love Actually, 2003, Levity, 2003, Bad Santa, 2003, The Alamo, 2004, Friday Night Lights, 2004, Bad News Bears, 2005, The Ice Harvest, 2005, School for Scoundrels, 2006, The Astronaut Farmer, 2007; dir., actor, writer (films) Sling Blade, 1996 (Acad. award Best Adapted Screenplay), Daddy and Them, 2001, dir., prodr. All the Pretty Horses, 2000, actor, writer One False Move, 1992, The Gift, 2000, (screenplays) Trouble Bound, 1993, Some Folks Call It a Slingblade, 1994, A Family Thing, 1996; actor: (TV films) The Man Who Broke 1,000 Chains, 1987, Circus, 1988, Out There, 1995, Don't Look Back, 1996; (TV series) The Outsiders, 1988, Hearts A Fire, 1992; TV appearances include Matlock, 1987, Evening Shade, 1990, Knots Landing, 1990, Ellen, 1997, (voice) King of the Hill, 1998; musician: (albums) Private Radio, 2001, The Edge of the World, 2003, Hobo, 2005, Beautiful Door, 2007. Office: Rogers Cowan 8687 Melrose Ave Ste G700 West Hollywood CA 90069-5721 *

THORNTON, CAMERON MITCHELL, financial planner; b. LA, Sept. 30, 1954; s. H. Walter and Naomi L. (Brown) T.; m. Jane Kubasak, June 18, 1978; children: Mitchell, Kathryn, Andrew. BA, U. So. Calif., LA, 1976; MBA, U. La Verne, 1983. CFP, cert. wealth cons. Planner Lockheed Calif. Co., Burbank, 1980-84; adv. assoc. Fin. Network Investment Corp., Burbank, 1983—, fin. cons., 1983—, prin., br. mgr., 1997—; prin. Cameron Thornton Assocs., Burbank, 1982—; prin. lic. charitable gift planner Renaissance Inc., 1992-99. Author: (manual) Computer Aided Planning System, 1982-83. Vice chair St. Joseph Med. Ctr. Found., 1988-92, chmn. planned giving dept., 1991-92; mem. planned giving dept. Mater Dolorosa Passionist Retreat Ctr., Sierra Madre, Calif., 2000—; chair Burbank Police Commn., 1981-85, Burbank Planning Commn., 1989-93; active ARC, Burbank, 1984-88, chmn. 1985-87; asst. scoutmaster Boy Scouts of Am., Burbank, 1994-97, 2001—05, scoutmaster, 1997-2000. Named Friend of Campfire, Camp Fire Coun., Pasadena, Calif., 1989; named to Bloomberg's Top Wealth Mgr. List, 2001-07; Fin. Advisor Top RIA Ranking, 2006-07. Mem. Fin. Planning Assn., Cert. Fin. Planner Bd. Standards, Burbank C. of C. Republican. Roman Catholic. Avocations: reading, fishing, skiing, travel, sports. Office: Cameron Thornton Assocs 290 E Verdugo Ave Ste 205 Burbank CA 91502-1342

THORNTON, CHARLES VICTOR, metals executive; b. Salt Lake City, Feb. 8, 1915; s. Charles Victor and Winnie May (Fitts) T.; m. Margaret Louise Wiggins, Apr. 17, 1937; children: Charles Victor III, Carolyn Louise (Mrs. John J. Moorhouse), David Frank. BS in Civil Engring., U. Utah, 1935; HHD, Ind. Inst. Tech., 1972. Registered profl. engr., Ohio, Tex. Engr. Truscon Steel Co., Youngstown, Ohio, 1935-37, dist. engr. Washington, 1937-40; chief engr. So. Iron Works, Inc., Alexandria, Va., 1940-45; pres. Thornton Industries, Inc., Ft. Worth, 1945-75, chmn. bd., 1975-88. Bd. dirs. Bank Commerce and Comml. Fin. Corp.; chmn. bd. dirs. Southview Corp. Author: American Association of Private Railroad Car Owners Roster of Private R.R. Cars, 1991, Autobiography, 1993, Charlie, 1994, Winnie, 1994. Chmn. bd. Southview Corp., 1980—, chmn. emeritus Shriners Hosps. for Children; mem. nat. adv. coun. U. Utah, 1985-96; chmn. investment com. Longhorn coun. Boy Scouts Am., 1985-88; v.p. campaign chmn. Ft. Worth Arts United, 1989; v.p. Tarrant County Arts Coun., 1989; pres. Tarrant County Water Bd., 1984-88; mem. policy com. Dallas-Ft. Worth Railtran, 1991-98; pres. Ft. Worth chpt. Internat. Good Neighbor Coun., 1991-92; bd. dirs. Ft. Worth Opera, 1997—; mem. World Affairs Coun. Ft. Worth, 1996, bd. dirs., 1997—, treas., 1998. Recipient Salesman of Yr. award Ft. Worth Sales and Mktg. Execs., 1984, Good Neighbor of Yr. award Internat. Good Neighbor Coun., 1984, Merit of Honor award U. Utah, 1986; holder airplane speed record Dallas to Wichita, Kans., 1969. Mem. ASCE (life) (Tex. sect. Svc. to People award 1995), Tex. Assn. Bus. (life), Ft. Worth C. of C. (pres. 1960), Am. Assn. Pvt. R.R. Car Owners (pres. 1982-83), Petroleum Club, Fort Worth Club, City Club, Exch. Club of Fort Worth (past pres.), La Cima Club, Oxford Club, Grand Coun. (Fort Worth chpt. Confrerie Saint Etienne), Masons (33 degree s.r.), Shriners (past imperial potentate), Kiwanis (past pres.), Elks, Petroleum Club, Tau Beta Pi. Home: 5301 Bryant Irvin Rd Fort Worth TX 76132-4030 Home Fax: 817-237-0100.

THORNTON, CHARLES VICTOR, lawyer; b. Takoma Park, Md., July 18, 1942; s. Charles Victor and Margaret Louise (Wiggins) T.; m. Suzanne Thorne, May 16, 1970; children: Christopher, Matthew, Joshua, Jeremy. AB, Cornell U., 1964; JD, U. Mich., 1967. Bar: Calif. 1969, US Dist. Ct. (ctrl. dist.) Calif. 1969. Instr. U. Pa. Law Sch., Phila., 1967-68; assoc. Paul, Hastings, Janofsky & Walker, LA, 1968-74, ptnr., 1975—, mng. ptnr. L.A. office, 1992-96, mng. ptnr. San Francisco office, 1997-2000. Contbr. articles to publs. Pres. Info. and Referral Fedn. LA County, 1988-95; mem. exec. com. LA County United Way, 1988-92; chmn. bd. dir. San Francisco YMCA, 2006-. Named Bd. Vol. of Yr. United Way, 1986, Bd. Vol. of Yr. YMCA, 2004. Mem. Calif. Club, LA Country Club, San Francisco YMCA (bd. dirs., 1998—, chmn. bd., 2006-). Avocations: running, golf. Office: Paul Hastings Janofsky & Walker 24th Flr 55 Second San Francisco CA 94105 Office Phone: 415-856-7001. Business E-Mail: charlesthornton@paulhastings.com.

THORNTON, CHARLIE MAE, secondary school educator; b. Idabel, Okla., Oct. 7, 1947; d. Juanita Cotton; children: Kimberly, Joel. BA in English Edn., East Cen. State U., Ada, Okla., 1968; MEd, Northeastern State U., Tahlequah, Okla., 1979. Cert. reading specialist Okla. Tchr. 6th grade reading Tulsa Pub. Schs., Okla., 1973—. 6th grade team leader, coord. mid. years program coord. Tulsa Pub. Schs. Contbr. articles to profl. jours. Named Tchr. of Yr., Wilson Mid. Sch., 2006—07, Tchr. of Today, Masonic Fraternity of Okla.; recipient Excellence Edn. award, Wilson Mid. Sch., 2002—03. Mem. NEA, Internat. Reading Assn., Okla. Reading Assn., Okla. Edn. Assn., Tulsa County Reading Coun., Tulsa Classroom Tchrs. Assn., Alpha Kappa Alpha, Phi Delta Kappa Democrat. Mem. Ch. Of Christ. Avocation: reading. Home: 2205 W Reading Pl Tulsa OK 74127-2238 Office: Wilson Mid Sch 1127 S Columbia Tulsa OK 74104 Business E-Mail: thornch@tulsaschools.org.

THORNTON, CLARENCE GOULD, electronics executive, civilian military employee; b. Detroit, Aug. 3, 1925; s. Lorenzo C. and Violet (Gould) T.; m. Gloria Fuchs, June 18, 1949; children: Susan Carol, Richard Scott. BS, U. Mich., 1949, MS, 1950, PhD, 1952. Project engr. Sylvania Electric Co., Woburn, Mass., 1951-52; sect. head to dir. Semiconductor div. Philco Corp., Lansdale, Pa., 1952-60; dir. R&D Philco Corp., Blue Bell, Pa., 1960-72; dir. Electronics Technology and Devices Lab., U.S. Army, Fort Monmouth, NJ, 1972-92; directorate exec. Army Rsch. Lab., 1992-95. Mem. Commn. on Engring. and Tech. Sys. Bd. on Army Sci. and Tech., Nat. Rsch. Coun., 1995—; sci., tech., bus. cons. 1995—; vol. lab. dir. emeritus U.S. Commn. Electronics Rsch., Devel. and Engring. Ctr., 2003-05. Contbr. articles to profl. jours.; patentee in field of electronics. Mem. Colts Neck Bd. Health, 1974-79. Served with USN, 1944-46. Recipient Local Svc. award Boy Scouts Am., 1963, Sci. Conf. award Dept. Army, 1976, Rsch. and Devel. Achievement award, 1976, Lab. of Yr. award, 1980, 83, 88, Lab. Excellence award, 1981, 85, 86, Sr. Exec. award, 1980-93, Gold medal Armed Forces Comms. and Electronics Assn., 1983, Handicapped Adv. Coun. award of achievement, 1985, Exceptional Civilian Svc. medal Dept. Army, 1985, Presdl. Rank award of Meritorious Svc., 1986, Presdl. Rank award of Disting. Sr. Exec., 1987, Crozier award, 1990, Superior Civilian Svc. medal, 1995, Exceptional Civilian Svc. medal, 1995. Fellow IEEE (Centennial medal 1994, Third Millennium medal 2000, Engring. Leadership Recognition award 1994, Joint Logistics Comdrs. award 1994); mem. AAAS, Nat. Def. Indsl. Assn., Assn. U.S. Army, Armed Forces Electronics Assn., Sr. Execs. Assn. (Exec. Achievement award 1994), Am. Defense Preparedness Assn., Alpha Chi Sigma, Phi Kappa Phi, Phi Lambda Upsilon. Mem. Reformed Ch. Home: 28 Glenwood Rd Colts Neck NJ 07722-1015 Office: AMSRL-EP Fort Monmouth NJ 07703

THORNTON, D. MCCARTY (MAC), lawyer; b. Wilmington, Del., Sept. 6, 1947; m. Molly F. Carr, July 7, 1996. BA, Stanford U., 1969, JD with high honors, 1972. Bar: Calif. 1973, DC 1973, US Supreme Ct. 1977. Trial atty. Bur. Consumer Protection FTC, Washington, 1972-78, dep. asst. dir., 1978; prosecutor fraud sect., criminal divsn. US Dept. Justice, Washington, 1978-82; assoc. Cole & Corette, Washington, 1982-83; chief of litigation Office of Insp. Gen., US Dept. HHS, Washington, 1983-90, chief counsel to Insp. Gen., 1990—2002; ptnr., health care group Sonnenschein Nath & Rosenthal LLP, Washington, 2003—. Founder, chmn. bd. W.Va. Rivers Coalition, Elkins, 1989-97. Mem. The Potomac Conservancy (founder, chair 1992-95, vice chair 1995-99), Am. Health Lawyers Assn. (bd. dirs. 1991-97), Health Care Compliance Assn. Avocation: whitewater kayaking. Office: Sonnenschein Nath & Rosenthal LLP Ste 600 East Tower 1301 K St NW Washington DC 20005 Office Phone: 202-408-6432. Office Fax: 202-408-6399. Business E-Mail: mthornton@sonnenschein.com.

THORNTON, EDMUND B., philanthropist; b. Chgo., Mar. 9, 1930; s. George A. and Suzanne W. Thornton; children from previous marriage: Thomas, Jonathan, Susan, Amanda; m. Susan Feldhaus; 1 child, Taylor. BA, Yale U., 1954. With No. Trust Co., Chgo., 1957-59; asst. sec., asst. treas. Ottawa Silica Co., Ill., 1959-61, v.p. corp. devel. Ill., 1961-62, pres., CEO Ill., 1962-75, chmn. bd., CEO Ill., 1975-83, chmn. bd. Ill., 1983-86; dir., v.p. Ottawa Nat. Bank, 2007—. Contbr. articles to profl. jours. Del. Rep. Nat. Conv., 1964-88, precinct committeeman, 1978-92; chmn. LaSalle County Rep. Ctrl. Com., 1980-92, Ill. and Mich. Canal Nat. Heritage Commn., 1985-2004; pres. Ottawa Silica Co. Found., Edmund B. Thornton Found., Ottawa, 1986— 1st lt. USMC, 1954—56. Recipient Conservation Svc. award U.S. Dept. Interior, 1973. Mem. NRA (life), Nat. Assn. Mfrs., U.S. C. of C., Nat. Indsl. Sand Assn. (dir. 1968-73), Ill. Mfrs.' Assn. (dir. 1969-75, chmn. 1975), Ill. State C. of C. (dir. 1972-78), Explorers Club, Univ. Club (Chgo.), Elks. Republican. Congregationalist. Home: PO Box 1 Ottawa IL 61350-0001 Office: PO Box 949 Ottawa IL 61350-0949 Office Phone: 815-434-6664.

THORNTON, ELAINE SERETHA, oncology clinical nurse specialist; b. NYC, Mar. 25, 1967; d. Jerry Richard and Shelia (Beckford) T. BS, Syracuse U., 1990; MSN, Columbia U., 1997. Cert. in gerontology. Staff nurse, clin. nurse I New Rochelle Hosp. Med. Ctr., NY, 1990-92, staff nurse, clin. nurse II, 1993-96, staff nurse drug and alcohol detoxification unit, 1996-97, oncology clin. nurse specialist, 1997-99; breast svc. coord. Robert and Helen Appell Comprehensive Breast Svc., 1997-99; nurse educator III Dept. Vets. Affairs/NY Harbor Health Care Sys., NYC, 1999—; oncology clin. nurse specialist Wyckoff Heights Med. Ctr., 2002—, also assoc. dir. nursing medicine oncology, nurse adminstr., 2004—. RN lab. asst. Sch. Nursing Coll. New Rochelle, 1992-97; adj. prof. Coll. New Rochelle, Borough Manhattan CC, NYC, 1995-97, adj. asst. prof. Iona Coll. Sch. Nursing, New Rochelle, adj. assoc. prof., 1998; vol. Am. Cancer Soc.; with Novartis Pharm. Sprks. Bureau, 1997-. Vol. Cancer Info. Svc., NYC, 1991-92, Clinton/Gore Presdl. campaign, 1992; mem. Sen. John McCain NY State Adv. Com., 2007; vol. providing cancer screening, blood pressure screening Pelham Sr. Ctr., NY, 1992; pub. info. rep. to economically disadvantaged Am. Cancer Soc., bd. dirs. Westchester divsn., 1993-95, 95-97, pres. So. unit; organizer 1st & 2d ann. Cmty. Health Fair, New Rochelle. Recipient Orthobiotech. Spkrs. Bur. Quality of Life award, Pub. Educator award Westchester divsn. Am. Cancer Soc. Mem. Oncology Nursing Soc. (Hudson Valley chpt., nominating com. 1992-93, treas. 1993-94, pres. elect Hudson Valley chpt. 1995-97), Oncology Nursing Soc. (corr., pres. Hudson Valley chpt. 1998-2000), CTME (nat. membership). Republican. Home: 77 Lime Kiln Rd Apt 3d Tuckahoe NY 10707-3063

THORNTON, FELICIA D., food service company executive; BSc Econs., Santa Clara U.; MBA Corp. Fin., Mktg., U. So. Calif. V.p., corp. planning and acctg. Ralphs Grocery Co., v.p., admin., 1998, group v.p., fin. and adminstrn., 1999—2001; group v.p. retail ops. Kroger Co., 2000—01; exec. v.p., CFO Albertson's, Inc., 2001—.

THORNTON, GIRARD B., JR., (JERRY), elementary school educator; m. Susan Thornton; 1 child, Katee. BA, Wash. Univ., St. Louis, 1970; MA, 1996. Cert. in early and mid. childhood/phys. edn. Nat. Bd. Tchg. Standards, 2004. Tchr., 1970—75; owner summer camp, 1975—95; phys. edn. tchr. Francis Howell Sch. Dist., Mo., 1995—. Named Mo. Tchr. of Yr., 2006; recipient The I CAN Learn-NEA Foundation awards for Teaching Excellence, 2007. Mem.: Mo. Nat. Edn. Assn. Office: Warren Elem Sch 141 Weiss Rd Saint Peters MO 63376 Business E-Mail: Jerry_Thornton@fhsd.k12.mo.us. *

THORNTON, J. DUKE, lawyer; b. Murray, Ky., July 11, 1944; s. Arthur Lee and Ruth Maxine (Billings) T.; m. Carol Caceres, Dec. 26, 1966 (dec.); children: Jennifer, Carey. BBA, U. N.Mex., Albuquerque, 1966, JD, 1969. Bar: N.Mex. 1969, U.S. Ct. Appeals (10th cir.) 1969, N.Y. 1985, U.S. Supreme Ct. 1992. With Butt, Thornton & Baehr, P.C., Albuquerque, 1971—, now chmn. bd. Legal counsel N.Mex. Jaycees, 1972; clk. N.Mex. Supreme Ct., Santa Fe, 1969; mem. com. N.Mex. Uniform Jury Instructions, 1987-88. Author: Trial Handbook for New Mexico Lawyers, 1992. Bd. dirs. N.Mex. Bd. of Dentistry, Santa Fe, 1987-88; commr. N.Mex. Racing Commn., Albuquerque, 1988-95. Mem. ABA, Am. Bd. Trial Advs., Albuquerque Bar Assn. (bd. dirs. 1978-79), Nat. Collegiate Athletic Assn. (agt.). Avocation: pilot. Office: Butt Thornton & Baehr PC PO Box 3170 Albuquerque NM 87190-3170

THORNTON, J. RONALD, technology consultant; b. Fayetteville, Tenn., Aug. 19, 1939; s. James Alanda and Thelma White (McGee) T.; m. Mary Beth Packard, June 14, 1964 (div. Apr. 1975); 1 child, Nancy Carole; m. Martha Klemann, Jan. 23, 1976 (div. Apr. 1982); 1 child, Trey; m. Bernice McKinney, Feb. 14, 1986; 1 child, Paul Leon. BS in Physics and Math., Berry Coll., 1961; MA in Physics, Wake Forest Coll., 1964; postgrad., U. Ala., 1965-66, Rollins Coll., 1970. Rsch. physicist Brown Engrng. Co., Huntsville, Ala., 1963-66; sr. staff engr. Martin Marietta Corp., Orlando, Fla., 1966-75; dep. dir. NASA, Washington, 1976-77; exec. asst. Congressman Louis Frey, Jr., Orlando, 1978; pres. Tens Tec, Inc., Orlando, 1978-79; dir. So. Tech. Applications Ctr. U. Fla., Gainesville, Fla., 1979—2002. Bd. dirs., treas. North Fla. Tech. Innovation Ctr., 1994—2004; mem. light wave tech. com. Fla. High Tech. and Indsl. Coun., Tallahassee, 1986—93, NASA Tech. Transfer Exec. Com., Washington, 1987—, Javits Fellowship Bd., Washington, 1986—91, Gov.'s New Porduct Award Com., Tallahassee, 1988—94, Fla. K-12 Math., Sci. and Computer Sci. Edn. Quality Improvement Adv. Coun., 1989—94, Fla. Sci. Edn. Improvement Adv.Com., 1991—92; bd. dirs. North Fla. Enterprise Corp., 2001—04. Pres. Orange County Young Rep. Club, Orlando, 1970-71; treas. Fla. Fedn. Young Reps., Orlando, 1971-72; chmn. Fla. Fedn. Young Reps., Orlando, 1972-74; pres. Gainesville Area Innovation Network, 1988-89; mem. Berry Coll. Alumni Coun., 2006—. Named Engr. Exhibiting Tech. Excellence and Accomplishment ctrl. Fla. chpt. Fla. Engrng. Soc., 1975, Achievement award NASA, 1977; named to Berry Coll. Hall of Fame, 2005. Mem. IEEE, Soc. Mfg. Engrs., Tech. Transfer Soc. (pres. 1999, bd. dirs. 1996—2001, Thomas Jefferson award 1999), Nat. Assn. Mgmt. and Tech. Assistance Ctrs. (bd. dirs. 1988, pres. 1992). Republican. Avocations: music, travel, reading, golf. Home and Office: 17829 NW 20th Ave Newberry FL 32669-2143 Office Phone: 352-472-6026. Personal E-mail: ronthornton@cox.net.

THORNTON, JOE, professional hockey player; b. London, Ont., Can., July 2, 1979; Player Boston Bruins, 1997—2005, HC Davos, Switzerland, 2004—05, San Jose Sharks, 2005—. Mem. Team Can., World Championships, 2001, 05, Team Can., World Cup of Hockey, 2004, Team Can. Olympic Games, Torino, Italy, 2006; player NHL All-Star Game, 2002, 03, 04, 07. Named to Second All-Star Team, NHL, 2003, First All-Start Team, 2006; recipient Art Ross Trophy, 2006, Hart Meml. Trophy, 2006. Achievements include being a member of World Cup Champion Team Canada, 2004. Office: c/o San Jose Sharks 525 W Santa Clara St San Jose CA 95113 *

THORNTON, JOHN L., former diversified financial services company executive; AB in History, Harvard U., 1976; BA, MA in Jurisprudence, Oxford U., 1978; MPPM, Yale U., 1980. With Goldman Sachs Group, Inc., 1980—88, ptnr., 1988—95, co-CEO Goldman Sachs Internat., 1995—96, chmn. Goldman Sachs Asia, 1996—98, pres., co-COO, 1999—2003, sr. adv., 2003—; spl. adv. on China to Pres. Richard C. Levin Yale U., 2003; prof., dir. Global Leadership prog. Tsinghua U., Beijing, 2003—. Bd. dirs. Ford Motor Corp., 1996—, Pacific Century Group, Intel Corp., 2003—, News Corp., 2004—, China Netcom, 2004—; mem. adv. bd. Yale Univ. Sch. Mgmt. Trustee Brookings Institution, 2000—, chmn., 2003—; trustee, bd. pres. Hotchkiss Sch.; trustee Asia Soc., China Inst., Eisenhower Fellowships, Morehouse Coll., Tsinghua U. Sch. Econ. & Mgmt., The Hotchkiss Sch. Mem.: Asia Soc., Coun. Fgn. Rels. Office: Tsinghua U Beijing 100084 China *

THORNTON, JOSEPH SCOTT, research and development company executive, materials scientist; b. Sewickley, Pa., Feb. 6, 1936; s. Joseph Scott and Evelyn (Miller) T.; divorced; children: Joseph Scott III, Chris P. BSME, U. Tex., 1957, PhD, 1969; MSMetE, Carnegie Mellon U., 1962. Engr. Walworth Valve Co., Boston, 1958; metall. engr. Westinghouse Astronuclear Lab., Large, Pa., 1962-64; instr., teaching assoc. U. Tex., Austin, 1964-67; group leader Tracor Inc., Austin, 1967-69, dept. dir., 1973-75; dept. mgr. Horizons Rsch., Inc., Cleve., 1969-73; chmn., chief exec. officer Tex. Rsch. Internat., Inc. (formerly Tex. Rsch. Inst., Inc.), Austin, 1975—. Contbr. numerous tech. papers to profl. publs.; editor: WANL Materials Manual, 2 vols., 1964; patentee in field. Founder, chmn., program dir. Vols. at the Creek, Austin. Recipient IGS award, 2002; fellow Alcoa, Austin, 1964, RC Baker Found., 1967. Mem.: ASTM, Internat. Geosynthetics Soc. (award 2002), Adhesion Soc., Am. Soc. Metals Internat. (exec. com. 1965—66). Office: Tex Rsch Internat Inc 9063 Bee Caves Rd Austin TX 78733-6201 Office Phone: 512-263-2101. E-mail: jst@tri-intl.com.

THORNTON, MICHAEL ALBERT, information technology manager; b. Morgan, Ala., Feb. 19, 1970; s. Malcolm Albert Thornton and Marsha Marie Pullen; m. Melda Elaine Garrison; children: Zion Thomas, Michael Hebreux, Isaac James, Zion Thomas. B in Mech. Engrng., Auburn U., Ala., 1994; M in Ocean Engrng., Tex. A&M U., College Station, 2000. Registered profl. engr., Calif., 2001. Project mgr. Space and Naval Warfare Systems Ctr., San Diego, 2004—. Lt. comdr. USN, 1989—2007. Home Phone: 858-565-1766. Personal E-mail: michael.a.thornton@navy.mil.

THORNTON, MICHAEL B., federal judge; b. Hattiesburg, Miss., Feb. 9, 1954; BS in Acctg., So Miss U., 1976, MS in Acctg., 1977; MA in English Lit., U. Tenn., 1979; JD, Duke U., 1982. Bar: DC 1982. Law clk. to Hon. Charles Clark US Ct. Appeals (5th cir.), 1983—84; assoc. Sutherland, Asbill & Brennan, Washington, 1982—83, Miller & Chevalier, Washington, 1985—88; tax counsel US Ho. Com. on Ways & Means, Washington, 1988—93, chief minority tax counsel, 1995; atty. adv. US Dept. Treasury, Washington, 1995, dep. tax legis. counsel Office Tax Policy, 1995—98; judge US Tax Ct., Washington, 1998—. Mem. editl. bd. Duke U. Law Joun., 1981—82. Recipient Treasury Sec.'s Ann. award, US Dept. Treasury, 1997, Meritorious Svc. award, 1998. Mem.: Order of the Coif. Office: US Tax Ct 400 2nd St NW Washington DC 20217-0001

THORNTON, RITA LOUISE, environmental scientist, lawyer; d. Donald Everett Thornton and Itasker Frances Edmonds-Thornton. BS, Monmouth U., 1973; JD, Seton Hall U., 1993; PhD, N.J. Inst. Tech., 2006. Cert.: (conflict resolution negotiator); pub. mgr. NJ. Toxicologist Johnson & Johnson Ethicon, Somerville, NJ, 1973—81; distributor ednl. film MGM/United Artists Entertainment, NYC, 1981—83; chmn. Dept. Sci. Vail-Deane Sch., Mountainside, NJ, 1983—88; rschr. Reheis Chem. Co., Berkeley Heights, NJ, 1988—90; specialist hazardous site mitigation NJ Dept. Environ. Protection, Trenton, 1990—97, environ. justice adminstr., rule mgr., 1997—99, supr. environ. specialist, 1999—, sect. chief, waste mgmt., 2005—. Founder, CEO Thornton Sisters Found., Inc., Atlantic Highlands, 1991—; exec. dir. Environ. Justice and Equity Cmty. Based Teamwork, Inc, Atlantic Highlands, 1999—; adj. prof. NJ Inst. Tech., Newark, 2003. Co-author: A Suitcase Full of Dreams, 1996; author (editor): New Jersey Solid and Hazardous Waste Transporter Quick Access Guide Book, 2000—05. Nominee Nat. Minority Role Model in Sci., Nat. Sci. Inst. and Minority Access, Inc., 2006; fellow, Alliance Grad. Edn. and Professorale, 2001—06; grantee, U.S. Environ. Protection Agy., 1998, 2000. Mem.: Soc. Women Environ. Profls., Nat. Honor Soc., Alpha Epsilon Lambda. Business E-Mail: rita.thornton@dep.state.nj.us.

THORNTON, ROLAND, telecommunications industry executive; married; 3 children. BSBA, Ind. U.; grad. student in Info. Systems, U. Ill. Co-founder Acquired Knowledge, Ltd.; v.p. customer ops. Ameritech; v.p. interconnection svcs. SBC; sr. v.p. customer svc. ops. Wholesale Markets Qwest Comm. Internat., Inc., exec. v.p. wholesale markets, 2004—. Bd. dirs. Rotary Internat., 2007—, Food Bank of the Rockies, Colo. Black C. of C. Mem.: Rotary Club Denver (mem. world coun. com.). Office: Qwest Comm Internat Inc 1801 California St Denver CO 80202 Office Phone: 303-992-1400. Office Fax: 303-896-8515. *

THORNTON, THOMAS NOEL, former publishing executive; b. Marceline, Mo., Apr. 23, 1950; s. Bernard F. and Helen F. (Kelley) T.; m. Cynthia L. Murray, Nov. 26, 1971; children: T. Zachary, Timothy. B.J., U. Mo., 1972. Asst. to editor Universal Press Syndicate, Kansas City, Mo., 1972, v.p., 1974, dir. mktg., 1976; v.p., dir. mktg. Universal Press Syndicate and Andrews McMeel Pub., Kansas City, 1976-87; pres., COO Andrews McMeel Pub., 1987—2002, pres., CEO, 2003—05. Bd. dirs. Andrews McMeel Universal. Office Phone: 816-932-6700. Business E-Mail: tthornton@amuniversal.com.

THORNTON, YVONNE SHIRLEY, obstetrician, writer, musician; b. NYC, Nov. 21, 1947; d. Donald E. and Itasker F. (Edmonds) T.; m. Shearwood McClelland, June 8, 1974; children: Shearwood III, Kimberly Itaska. BS in Biology, Monmouth Coll., 1969; MD, Columbia U., 1973, MPH, 1996; DSc (hon.), Tuskegee U., 2003. Diplomate Am. Bd. Ob-gyn. Resident in ob-gyn Roosevelt Hosp., NYC, 1973-77; fellow maternal-fetal medicine Columbia-Presbyn. Med. Center, NYC, 1977-79; commd. lt. comdr. M.C. USN, 1979; asst. prof. ob-gyn Uniformed Svcs. U. Health Scis., 1979-82; assoc. prof. Cornell U. Med. Coll., NYC, 1989-92; dir. clin. svcs. dept. ob-gyn N.Y. Hosp.-Cornell Med. Center, 1982-88; asst. attending N.Y. Lying-In Hosp., 1982-89; assoc. clin. prof. ob-gyn. Columbia P&S, 1995-98, assoc. clin. prof., 2001—02; clin. prof. ob-gyn. U. Medicine and Dentistry N.J., 1998-2000; prof. clin. ob-gyn. Med. Coll. Cornell U., 2003—05. Dir. Chorionic Villus Sampling Program, 1984-92; dir. perinatal diagnostic testing ctr. Morristown Meml. Hosp., 1992-2000, divsn. maternal-fetal medicine St. Luke's Roosevelt Hosp. Ctr., 2000-02; vice chair ob-gyn, dir. maternal-fetal medicine, Jamaica Hosp. Med. Ctr., 2002-05; staff Nat. Naval Med. Ctr., Bethesda, Md.; saxophonist Thornton Sisters ensemble, 1955-76; vis. assoc. physician The Rockefeller U. Hosp., 1986-96; prof. clinical OB/GYN Cornell U. Med. Coll., 2003-05; examiner Am. Bd. Ob-Gyn, 1997—; vice chmn. Dept. Ob-Gyn. Jamaica Hosp. Med. Ctr.; bd. dirs. Integra Med Am., 2006. Author: The Ditchdigger's Daughters, 1995, (named best books for young adults ALA, Excellence in Lit. award, NJ Edn. Assn., One Book NJ, NJ Libr. Assn., 2006, nominated Pulitzer Prize 1995) Primary Care for the Obstetrician and Gynecologist, 1997, Woman to Woman, 1997. Bd. dirs. Fair Housing Coun. Northern NJ, 1985—. Recipient Excellence in Literature award, NJ Edn. Assn., 1996, winner Daniel Webster Oratorical Competition, Internat. Platform Assn., 1996; nominated Pulitzer Prize, 1995. Fellow: ACOG, ACS; mem.: AMA, Am. Fedn. Musicians, Soc. Maternal-Fetal Medicine, Assn. Women Surgeons, NY Acad. Medicine. Democrat. Baptist. Office Phone: 201-570-8181. Business E-Mail: thornton@carroll.com.

THORP, BENJAMIN A., III, retired paper company executive; b. Albany, NY, May 31, 1938; s. Benjamin A. Jr. and Anna C. (Head) T.; m. Barbara Sue Tellock, Aug. 1, 1964 (div. Mar. 1986); 1 child, Benjamin A. IV; m. Laurie Diane Murdock, Oct. 25, 1987. Student in elec. engrng., Rensselaer Poly. Inst., 1956-61, postgrad. in mgmt., 1967-68; BS in Physics, U. Md., 1964; postgrad. in engrng., U. Bridgeport, 1966; postgrad. in mktg., U. Tenn., 1970. Product devel. mgr. Huyck Formex div. Huyck, Greenville, Tenn., 1969-71, mktg. mgr., 1971-73, v.p., gen. mgr., 1973-75, Huytech Systems div., Wake Forest, NC, 1975-78; v.p., dir. research Huyck Corp., Rensselaer, NY, 1978-80; pres. Benjamin A. Thorp Inc., Albany, 1980-82, POYRY-BEK Inc., Raleigh, NC, 1982-84; v.p. engrng. BE&K Inc., Birmingham, Ala., 1984-85, James River Corp., Richmond, Va., 1984-95; v.p. mfg. tech. Chesapeake Corp., Richmond, Va., 1996-97; dir. pulp and paper engring. Ga. Pacific, Atlanta, 1998—2004, ret., 2004; pres. Flambeau River Biorefinery, 2006—. Mem. exec. com. Pulp and Paper Found. Bd., Ga. Inst. Tech., 1991-95, pres., 1993-95; mem. indsl. adv. bd. Forest Web.com, 2000—, MTCI, Balt., 2001-03, Flambeau River Paper, 2006-, Peregrine Energy, Greenville, SC, 2002—; chmn. bd. Besicorp.-Empire Newsprint LLC, 2004—; bd. dirs. K.P. Products; pres. Flambeau River Biorefinery, 2006-. Co-author: Pulp and Paper Energy Best Practice Guidebook, 2d edit., 2006; tech. editor Paper Machine Operations, Vol. 7, 3d edit., 1991; contbr. more than 100 articles to profl. jours.; patentee in field. Bd. dirs. Richmond Math. and Sci. Ctr., 1987-93, Sic. Mus. of Va. Found., 1989-98; chmn. papermaking project adv. com. Inst. Paper Sci. and Tech., 1990-94. Fellow TAPPI (chmn. papermakers com. 1984-86, vice chmn. paper and bd. divsn. 1988-90, chmn. 1990-92, bd. dir., Leadership award 1994); mem. Paper Industry Mgmt. Assn. (pres. 1996-97, chmn. bd. trustees 1999—2003, Glen T. Rinnegar award 1999), PIMA-CPBIS Mgmt. Excellence award 2003, Exptl. Aircraft Assn., Meadowbrook Estates Civic Assn. (bd. dirs. 1996-98, pres. 2003-04), Meadowbrook Country Club (bd. dirs. 2005—). Presbyterian. Personal E-mail: bathorp@comcast.net.

THORP, EDWARD OAKLEY, investment management company executive; b. Chgo., Aug. 14, 1932; s. Oakley Glenn and Josephine (Gebert) T.; m. Vivian Sinetar, Jan. 28, 1956; children: Raun, Karen, Jeffrey. BA in Physics, UCLA, 1953, MA, 1955, PhD in Math., 1958. C.L.E. Moore instr. MIT, Cambridge, Mass., 1959—61; asst. prof. N.Mex. State U., 1961—63, assoc. prof. math., 1963—65, U. Calif., Irvine, 1965—67, prof. math., 1967—77, prof. fin., 1977—82, regents lectr., 1992—93; gen. ptnr. Edward O. Thorp & Assocs., LP, Newport Beach, 1989—. Vis. prof. UCLA, 1991; chmn. Oakley Sutton Mgmt. Corp., Newport Beach, Calif., 1972-91; mng. gen. ptnr. Princeton/Newport Ptnrs., Newport Beach, 1969-91, OSM Ptnrs., MIDAS Advisors, Newport Beach, 1986-89; gen. ptnr. Ridgeline Ptnrs., Newport Beach, 1994-2002; portfolio mgr., cons. Glenwood Investment Corp., Chgo., 1992-94; prin., cons. Grosvenor Capital Mgmt., Chgo., 1992-93; pres. Noesis Corp., 1994-2002, UCI Found. Bd., 2004—. Author: Beat the Dealer: A Winning Strategy for the Game of Twenty-One, 1962, rev. edit., 1966, Elementary Probability, 1966, The Mathematics of Gambling, 1984; co-author: Beat The Market, 1967, The Gambling Times Guide to Blackjack, 1984; columnist Gambling Times, 1979-84, Wilmott 2002—. Grantee NSF, 1954-55, 62-64, Air Force Office Sci. Rsch., 1964-73. Fellow NSF, Inst. Math. Stats.; mem. Phi Beta Kappa, Sigma Xi. Avocation: astronomy. Office: Edward O Thorp & Assocs LP 610 Newport Center Dr Ste 1240 Newport Beach CA 92660-6436

THORPE, GEOGORY B., lawyer; b. LA, 1953; BA cum laude, U. Calif., Santa Barbara, 1977; JD cum laude, Loyola Marymount U., 1982. Bar: Calif. 1982. Ptnr., real estate and natural resources practice O'Melveny & Myers LLP, Santa Barbara, Calif., 1982—, chair, project development and fin. practice group. Staff mem. and chief article editor Loyola LA Law Review, 1980—82. Mem.: LA County Bar Assn. (mem. general real property subsection), ABA (mem. real property sect.), St. Thomas More Law Soc. Office: O'Melveny & Myers LLP 400 S Hope St Los Angeles CA 90071-2899 Office Phone: 213-430-6593. Office Fax: 213-430-6407. Business E-Mail: gthorpe@omm.com.

THORPE, JAMES, retired researcher; b. Aiken, SC, Aug. 17, 1915; s. J. Ernest and Ruby (Holloway) T.; m. Elizabeth McLean Daniells, July 19, 1941; children: James III (dec.), John D., Sally Jans-Thorpe. AB, The Citadel, 1936, LL.D., 1971; MA, U. N.C., 1937; PhD, Harvard U., 1941; Litt.D., Occidental Coll., 1968; L.H.D., Claremont Grad. Sch., 1968; H.H.D., U. Toledo, 1977. Instr. to prof. English Princeton, 1946-66; dir. Huntington Libr., Art Gallery and Bot. Gardens, San Marino, Calif., 1966-83; sr. research assoc. Huntington Libr., San Marino, Calif., 1966-99; ret., 1999. Author: Bibliography of the Writings of George Lyman Kittredge, 1948, Milton Criticism, 1950, Rochester's Poems on Several Occasions, 1950, Poems of Sir George Etherege, 1963, Aims and Methods of Scholarship, 1963, 70, Literary Scholarship, 1964, Relations of Literary Study, 1967, Bunyan's Grace Abounding and Pilgrim's Progress, 1969, Principles of Textual Criticism, 1972, 2d edit., 1979, Use of Manuscripts in Literary Research, 1974, 2d edit., 1979, Gifts of Genius, 1980, A Word to the Wise, 1982, John Milton: The Inner Life, 1983, The Sense of Style: Reading English Prose, 1987, Henry Edwards Huntington: A Biography, 1994, H.E. Huntington: A Short Biography, 1996, A Pleasure of Proverbs, 1996, Proverbs for Friends, 1997, Proverbs for Thinkers, 1998, The Gutenberg Bible, 1999, Poems Written at the Huntington Library, 2000, Proverbs for Our Time, 2003, Proverbs for the Future, 2004. Served to col. USAAF, 1941-46. Decorated Bronze Star medal.; Guggenheim fellow, 1949-50, 65-66. Fellow Am. Acad. Arts and Scis., Am. Philos. Soc.; mem. MLA, Am. Antiquarian Soc., Soc. for Textual Scholarship. Democrat. Episcopalian. Home: 20 Loeffler Rd Apt T320 Bloomfield CT 06002-2277

THORPE, JANE FUGATE, lawyer; b. Hazard, Ky., 1954; BA, Univ. Ga., 1976, JD, 1979. Bar: Ga. 1979. Ptnr., food, drug, device products liability group Alston & Bird LLP, Atlanta. Frequent contbr. to profl. journals, frequent lectr. on scientific evidence; co-author: Court-Appointed Experts and Technical Advisors, 2000, Science and Expert Opinion: A Response to the Attack Upon Judge Jones and the Hall Opinion. Mem.: Internat. Assn. Defense Counsel. Office: Alston & Bird LLP One Atlantic Ctr 1201 W Peachtree St NW Atlanta GA 30309-3424 Office Phone: 404-881-7822. Office Fax: 404-881-7777. Business E-Mail: jthorpe@alston.com.

THORPE, JANET CLAIRE, judge; b. Bklyn., Dec. 8, 1953; d. Burton Walter and Phyllis Claire (Read) T.; m. David Frank Palmer, Aug. 26, 1978 (div. Aug. 1988); children: Katherine Elaine, Jennifer Claire; m. James Francis Box, June 29, 1991; children; Melissa Richelle, Maergrethe Cashel. Student, Boston U., 1972-74; BA in Polit. Sci. & History with honors, Union Coll., 1975; postgrad., Western New Eng. Sch. Law, 1975-76; JD, Emory U., 1978. Bar: Ga. 1978, U.S. Ct. Appeals (5th and 11th cirs.) 1978, 80, Fla. 1987, U.S. Dist. Ct. (mid. dist.) Fla. 1987. Law clk. to judge U.S. Dist. Ct., Atlanta, 1978; regional atty. Comptroller of Curency, Atlanta, 1978-80; assoc. corp. counsel Trust Co. Ga., Atlanta, 1980-86; dir. Trusco Properties, Inc., Atlanta, 1981-86; gen. counsel, corp. sec. SunTrust Banks Fla., Inc., Orlando, 1986-2000; gen. counsel SunTrust Bank N.A., Orlando, 1986-2000; group v.p. SunTrust Banks, Inc., 1995-2000; cir. ct. judge State of Fla. (9th cir.), Orlando, Fla., 2000—. Mem. Coun. Battered Women, Atlanta, 1983-86, bd. dirs., 1986; bd. visitors Cornell Mus. Fine Art, Rollins Coll., 1990-96; mem. bd. zoning variances City of Orlando, 1996-99; bd. dirs. Orange County Cmty. Alliance, 2000-03. Mem. Ga. Bar Assn., Fla. Bar Assn., Assn. Bank Holdings Cos (lawyers com. 1983-90), Am. Corp. Counsel Assn. (bd. dirs. ctrl. Fla. chpt. 1991-99), Am. Diabetes Assn. (bd. dirs. Fla. chpt. 1989-97), Leadership Orlando. Episcopalian. Avocations: gardening, child rearing, house renovation, photography. Office: Orange County Courthouse 425 N Orange Ave Orlando FL 32801

THORPE, JASON M., non-profit organization director; b. 1982; Dir., cmty. edn. and outreach Open-Inn Inc. Bd. co-chair Western States Youth Services Network; mem. Ariz. Statewide Devel. Taskforce, Wingspan award com.; co-chair, bd. of incorporators Porch Light Found. Nat. Safe Place adv. bd. mem. YMCA; official organizer Tucson V-Day. Named one of 40 Under 40, Tucson Bus. Edge, 2006. Office: Open Inn 630 E 9th St Tucson AZ 85705 Office Phone: 520-670-9040.

THORPE, NORMAN RALPH, lawyer, automotive executive, retired military officer; b. Carlinville, Ill., Oct. 17, 1934; s. Edwin Everett and Imogene Midas (Hayes) T.; m. Elaine Frances Pritzman, Nov. 1, 1968; children: Sarah Elizabeth Chisholm, Carrie Rebecca Keough. AB in Econs., U. Ill., 1956, JD, 1958; LLM in Pub. Internat. Law, George Washington U., 1967. Bar: Ill. 1958, Mich. 1988, U.S. Supreme. Ct. 1969. Commd. 2d lt. USAF, 1956, advanced through grades to brig. gen., 1983; legal advisor U.S. Embassy, Manila, 1969-72; chief internat. law hdqrs. USAF, Washington, 1972-77; staff judge adv. 21st Air Force, McGuire AFB, N.J., 1977-80, USAF Europe, Ramstein AB, Fed. Republic Germany, 1980-84; comdr. Air Force Contract Law Ctr., Wright-Patterson AFB, Ohio, 1984-88; mem. legal staff, group counsel GM Def. and Power Products Gen. Motors Corp., Detroit, 1988—98; counsel GMR&D Planning and Fuel Cell Activity, 1998—2003; ret., 2003. Legal advisor Dept. of Def. Blue Ribbon Com. on Code of Conduct, 1975; USAF del. Internat. Aero. and Astronautical Fedn., Budapest, 1983; adj. prof. U. Dayton Sch. Law, 1986-87; partnership counsel U.S. Advanced Battery Consortium, Legal Advisor U.S. Coun. Automotive Rsch., Chrysler Corp., Ford Motor Co., GM, 1990—. Contbr. articles to profl. jours. Mem. staff Commn. on Police Policies and Procedures, Dayton, 1986; trustee Dayton Philharm. Orch., 1987-88; mem. bd. visitors U. Ill. Law Sch., 2002-; bd. dirs. Friends of Ctrl. European and Eurasian Law Inst., 2003—. Recipient Disting. Svc. medal Legion of Merit. Mem. ABA (chmn. com. internat. law sect. 1977-80, coun. mem. pub. contract law sect. 1986-88, chmn. com. pub. contract law sect. 1988-95, sec. pub. contract law sect. 2000-01, vice chair 1999-2000, chair-elect 2000-01, chair 2001-02), Air Force Assn., Dayton Coun. on World Affairs, Army/Navy Club, Detroit Econ. Club, Renaissance Club. Republican. Avocations: music, piano, gardening. Home: 498 Abbey Rd Birmingham MI 48009-5618 Home Phone: 248-644-8105; Office Phone: 248-644-8105. Business E-Mail: nthorpe@ameritech.net.

THORSEN, MARIE KRISTIN, radiologist, educator; b. Milw., Aug. 1, 1947; d. Charles Christian and Margaret Josephine (Little) T.; M. James Lawrence Troy, Jan. 7, 1978; children: Katherine Marie, Megan Elizabeth. BA, U. Wis., Madison, 1969; MBA, George Washington U., Washington, 1971; MD, Columbia Coll. Physicians and Surgeons, 1977. Diplomate Am. Bd. Radiology. Intern. Columbia-Presbyn. Med. Ctr., NYC, 1977-78, resident dept. radiology, 1978-81; asst. prof. radiology Med. Coll. Wis., 1982-84, assoc. prof., 1984-89, prof., 1989-94; dir. computed tomography Waukesha Meml. Hosp., 1994—, Oconomowoc Meml. Hosp., 1994—.

Contbr. articles to profl. jours. Fellow, Med. Coll. Wisc., Milw., 1981—82. Fellow Am. Coll. Radiology, Radiol. Soc. N. Am., Wis. Radiologic Assn. (v.p., 2005, pres.-elect, 2006). Home Phone: 262-567-4532. Personal E-mail: mkthorsen@aol.com.

THORSEN, NANCY DAIN, real estate broker; b. Edwardsville, Ill., 1944; d. Clifford Earl and Suzanne Eleanor (Kribs) Dain; m. David Massie, 1968 (div. 1975); 1 child, Suzanne Dain Massie; m. James Hugh Thorsen, May 30, 1980. BSc in Mktg., So. Ill. U., 1968, MSc in Bus. Edn., 1975; grad., Realtor Inst., Idaho, 1983. Cert. residential and investment specialist, fin. instr., luxury home mktg. specialist, 2004; designated real estate instr. State of Idaho; accredited buyer rep. Personnel officer J.H. Little & Co. Ltd., London, 1969-72; instr. in bus. edn. Spl. Sch. Dist. St. Louis, 1974-77; mgr. mktg./ops. Isis Foods, Inc., St. Louis, 1978-80; asst. mgr. store Stix, Baer & Fuller, St. Louis, 1980; assoc. broker Century 21 Sayer Realty, Inc., Idaho Falls, Idaho, 1981-88, RE/MAX Homestead Realty, 1989—. Spkr. in field; real estate fin. instr. State of Idaho Real Estate Commn., 1994; founder Nancy Thorsen Seminars, 1995; pres. S.E. Idaho Women's Coun. of Realtors, 2006 Bd. dirs. Idaho Vol., Boise, 1981-84, Idaho Falls Symphony, 1982; pres. Friends of Idaho Falls Libr., 1981-83; chmn. Idaho Falls Mayor's Com. for Vol. Coordination, 1981-84; power leader Power Program, 1995; mem. Mtn. River Valley Red Cross, chair capital campaign, cmty. gifts chair ARC. Recipient Idaho Gov.'s award, 1982, cert. appreciation City of Idaho Falls/Mayor Campbell, 1982, 87, Bus. Women of the Yr. award C. of C., 1998; named to Two Million Dollar Club, 1987, 88, Four Million Dollar Club, 1989, 90, Top Investment Sales Person for Eastern Idaho, 1985, Realtor of Yr. Idaho Falls Bd. Realtors, 1990, Outstanding Realtors Active in Politics, Women of Yr. Am. Biog. Inst., 1991, Profiles of Top Prodrs. award Real Estate Edn. Assn., Above the Crowd award 1997; named Western Region Power Leader, Darryl Davis Seminars. Mem. Nat. Spkrs. Assn., Idaho Falls Bd. Realtors (chmn. Orientation 1982-83, chmn. edn. 1983, chmn. legis. com. 1989, 95—, chmn. program com. 1990, 91), Idaho Assn. Realtors (pres. Million Dollar Club 1988-2001, edn. com. 1990-93, Mem. of Yr. 1991), Women's Coun. Realtors (Mem. of Yr. 2006), Am. Bus. Women's Assn., So. Ill. U. Alumni Assn., Idaho Falls C. of C. (Bus. Woman of the Yr.-Professions, 1997), newcomers Club, Civitan (pres. Idaho Falls chpt. 1988-89, Civitan of Yr. 1986, 97, Outstanding Pres. award 1990, Hall of Fame 1998), Real Estate Educators Assn. Office: RE/MAX Homestead Inc 1301 E 17th St Ste 1 Idaho Falls ID 83404-6273 E-mail: thorsen@srv.net.

THORSON, ALAN GLEN, surgeon; b. Omaha, June 20, 1952; s. E. Wallace and Vendela Marie (Havenstein) T.; m. Nancy Lois Maricle, Apr. 18, 1981; children: Alicia Marie, Scott Alan, Katherine Elizabeth. BS in Agrl. Econs., U. Nebr., 1974, BA in Internat. Rels., 1976; MD, U. Nebr., Omaha, 1979, cert. gen. surgery, 1984. Diplomate Am. Bd. Med. Examiners, Am. Bd. Surgery, Am. Bd. Colon and Rectal Surgery. Intern gen. surgery U. Nebr. Hosp., Omaha, 1979-80, resident gen. surgery, 1980-84; fellow colon and rectal surgery U. Minn., Mpls., 1984-85; sec. Colon and Rectal Surgery, Inc., Omaha, 1987-89, v.p., 1989—; clin. asst. prof. surgery U. Nebr. Coll. Medicine, Omaha, 1985-93, clin. assoc. prof. of surgery, 1993—; clin. asst. prof. surgery Creighton U. Sch. Medicine, Omaha, 1986-88, asst. prof. surgery, 1989-92, assoc. prof. surgery, 1992—2002, program dir. sect. colon and rectal surgery, 1988—, clin. assoc. prof. surgery, 2002—. V.p. Todd Valley Farms, Inc., Mead, Nebr., 1988—; med. advisor United Ostomy Assn., Omaha chpt., 1986—; assoc. examiner Am. Bd. Colon and Rectal Surgery, 1993-96, mem 1998-2005, pres. 2004-05. Contbr. articles to profl. jours., chapters to medical textbooks. Trustee Nebr. satellite Crohn's Colitis Found. of Am., 1992—93, med. adv. bd. Nebr. satellite, Rocky Mt. chpt., 2007—; pres. Met. Omaha Montreal Soc., 1999—2000, Nebr. Med. Assn., 2003—04; mem. adminstrv. bd. Faith Westwood United Meth. Ch., Omaha, 1988—92; active health ministries St. Andrews United Meth. Ch., Omaha, 2006—; bd. dirs. Nebr. divsn. Am. Cancer Soc., 1991—96, pres. Nebr. divsn., 1996—2005, sec. Heartland divsn., 1998—99, vice chair Heartland divsn., 1999—2000, chmn. Heartland divsn., 2000—03, chief med. office High Plains divsn., 2005—, nat. bd., 2000—, pres. Cancer Action Network, 2004—06, 2d v.p. Nat. Bd., 2007—. Fellow ACS, Am. Soc. Colon and Rectal Surgeons (treas. 2007—), Southwestern Surg. Congress (sec.-treas. 1999-2005, v.p 2005-06, pres. elect., 2006-07, pres. 2007—), Soc. Surg. Oncology; mem. AMA, Am. Soc. Gastrointestinal Endoscopy, Soc. Surgery Alimentary Tract, Soc. Am. Gastrointestinal Endoscopic Surgeons, Wilderness Med. Soc., Nebr. Med. Assn. (pres. 2003-04), Omaha Med. Clin. Soc., Assn. Program Dirs. for Colon and Rectal Surgery (pres. 1996-99), Am. Assn. Clin. Anatomists, Met. Omaha Med. Soc. (pres. 1999-2000, sec., treas. found. 2005—). Avocations: swimming, backpacking, landscape painting in oil. Office: Colon and Rectal Surgery 9850 Nicholas St Ste 100 Omaha NE 68114 Home Phone: 402-496-2490; Office Phone: 402-343-1122. Personal E-mail: agthorson@msn.com.

THORSON, CONNIE CAPERS, library educator; b. Dallas, July 25, 1940; d. Ewing Ashby and Constance (Romberg) Capers; m. James Llewellyn, June 6, 1970. BA, U. Ark., 1962, MA, 1964; PhD, U. N.Mex., 1970; MS in Library Sci., U. Ill., 1977. Instr. English S.E. Mo. State U., Cape Girardeau, 1963-67; with U. N.Mex., Albuquerque, 1970-71, 79-95, acquisitions libr., 1980-94, head reference, 1994-95, assoc. prof. libr., 1984-90, prof., 1990-95, prof. emerita, 1995—; prof., libr. dir. Allegheny Coll., Meadville, Pa., 1995—2000, ret., 2000—; Fulbright sr. scholar Belarus, 2005—06. Author: The RFP Process: Effective Management of the Acquisition of Library Materials, 1998; editor: A Million Stars, 1981, Pocket Companion for Oxford, 1989. Scholar, Fulbright Found., 2005—. Mem. South Cen. Soc. for 18th Century Studies (pres. elect 1988-89, pres. 1989-90, 2002-2003), Modern Lang. Assn. Am., Am. Soc. for 18th Century Studies, ALA. Avocations: travel, reading, walking.

THORSON, ERIC M., federal agency administrator; BS, USAF Acad. Chief investigator permanent subcom. U.S. Senate, spl. asst. to Rep. leader; sr. advisor U.S. Office Personnel Mgmt.; inspector gen. Small Bus. Adminstrn., 2006—. Served with USAF. Office: Small Bus Adminstrn 409 Third St SW Rm 7150 Washington DC 20416 Office Phone: 202-205-6586.

THORSON, STEVEN GREG, lawyer; b. Van Nuys, Calif., Feb. 7, 1948; s. Robert G. and Ruth C. T.; m. Patricia Lynn LaPointe, Aug. 3, 1974; 1 child, Kai Johannes. BA, St. Olaf Coll., Northfield, Minn., 1977; JD, Hamline U., St. Paul, Minn., 1980. Bar: Minn. 1980, US Dist. Ct. Minn. 1980, US Tax Ct. 1980, US Ct. Appeals (8th cir.) 1980, US Supreme Ct. 2003. Pres. Thorson & Berg, Maple Grove, Minn., 1990—99; shareholder Barna, Guzy & Steffen, Ltd. Attys. at Law, Mpls., 1999—. Lectr. continuing legal edn., 1986—; apptd. to Minn. State Bar Assn. Commn. on Unauthorized Practice of Law, 1990-92; atty. for Columbus Twp. (Anoka County), 1981-96; mem. residential real estate com. Minn. State Bar Assn., 1992—. Mem. ch. coun. Peace Luth. Ch. Named a Super Lawyer, Minn. Law and Politics Mag., 2000—07; named one of Minn. Super Lawyers, Mpls./St. Paul mag., 1998, 2000—07, Minns. Top 40 Real Property Attys., Minn. Law & Politics, 2004, 2005. Mem. Minn. State Bar Assn. (real property coun., chair publs. com. 2001—), Hennepin County Bar Assn. (chmn. purchase agreement com. 1986-88), Anoka County Bar Assn. (pres. real estate sect. 1988). Avocation: skiing. Office: 400 Northtown Fin Plz 200 Coon Rapids Blvd NW Ste 400 Minneapolis MN 55433-5894 Office Phone: 763-783-5124. Business E-Mail: sthorson@bgs.com.

THORSTEINSSON, GUDNI, physiatrist; b. Vestmannaeyjar, Iceland, Aug. 5, 1941; came to U.S., 1971; s. Thorstein and A. G. Einarsson; m. Elin Klein, Apr. 10, 1965; children: Arnar Karl, Asdis Thora. BS, Reykjavik (Iceland) Coll., 1961; candidatus med. et chirurg., U. Iceland, Reykjavik, 1968; MS, U. Minn., 1976. Diplomate Am. Bd. Phys. Medicine and Rehab. Dist physician Icelandic Govt., Djupivogur, 1970-71; resident dept. phys. medicine and rehab. Mayo Found., Rochester, Minn., 1972-75, mem. consulting staff, 1975-80; chair dept. Nat. Hosp., Reykjavik, 1980-81; dir. rehab. Mayo Clinic/St. Mary's Hosp., Rochester, 1981-85; dir. out-patient rehab. Mayo Clinic, Rochester, 1985-88, chair dept., 1987-91, chair dept. phys. medicine and rehab. Jacksonville, Fla., 1991-99. Physiatrist cons. Mayo Clinic, Rochester, 81-91, Jacksonville, 1991—. Author: (with others) Efficacy of Transcoutaneous Electrical Stimulation, 1977, Placebo Effect of Transcoutaneous Electrical Stimulation, 1978, Electrical Stimulation for Anagesia, 1983, Management of Post Polio Syndrome, 1997. Mem. Am. Acad. Phys. Medicine and Rehab. Office: Mayo Clinic Jacksonville 4500 San Pablo Rd S Jacksonville FL 32224-1865

THORSTENBERG, (JOHN) LAURENCE, oboe and English horn player; b. Salt Lake City, Dec. 6, 1925; s. Laurence Nathaniel and Alys Josephine (Blomquist) T. MusB, Curtis Inst. Music, Phila., 1951. Instrumental tchr., 1975-96, New Eng. Conservatory, Boston U., 1980-96; mem. Symphony Orch. Balt., 1951-52, Dallas Symphony Orch., 1952-54, Chgo. Symphony Orch., 1954-63, Boston Symphony Orch., 1964-93. Appeared summers, Marlboro (Vt.) Music Festival, 1952-54. With U.S. Army, 1944-46, ETO. Mem. Internat. Conf. Symphony and Opera Musicians (emeritus). Personal E-mail: larrythor@earthlink.com.

THORUD, JEFFREY SCOTT, lawyer, legal studies director; b. Natrona Heights, Pa., Sept. 14, 1964; s. Carol Jean Guman. BA in Speech Comm., Edinboro U., Pa., 1989; MPA, Marywood U., Scranton, Pa., 1993; JD, Thomas Jefferson Sch. Law, San Diego, 1998; cert. in Intl. Human Rights Law, Oxford U., England, 1996. Prof. Kelsey-Jenney Coll., San Diego, 1998—2002; acquisitions assoc. Teligent Comm., 1999—2000; acquisitions mgr. Qwest Comm., 2000—02; pres. Oxford Pacific Lending, 2002—. Dir. Utility Incentive Corp., San Diego; adv. bd. mem. Kelsey-Jenney Coll., 2000—01; dir. legal studies Maric Coll., 2003—, adv. bd. mem., 2003—; pres. Oxford Holdings, LLC, 2004—. Contbr. articles to profl. jours. Mem.: Pi Kappa Delta, Alpha Phi Sigma. Office: Maric Coll 9055 Balboa Ave San Diego CA 92123 Home Phone: 619-847-5883; Office Phone: 858-654-3618. Business E-Mail: jthorud@mariccollege.edu.

THORUP, SHAWNA SAAVEDRA, librarian; b. Torrance, Calif., Mar. 29, 1969; d. Larry Dean and Sylvia Louise (Saavedra) Westphal; m. John Lindstrom Thorup, Dec. 1, 1995; child, Sean. AA in English, El Camino Coll., Torrance, 1989; BA in English, U. Calif., Berkeley, 1991; MLS, UCLA, 1993; grad. transition into mgmt., Calif. State Libr., Sacramento, 1995. Children's libr. L.A. Pub. Libr., Venice, Calif., 1993-96, children's libr. III LA, 1996; sr. libr. Torrance Pub. Libr., 1996—2005; asst. dir. Fayetteville Pub. Libr., Ark., 2005—. Christian Fiction columnist Libr. Jour., 2002—03. Chmn. awards com. Friends of Children and Lit., 1995—. Named one of the Movers & Shakers, Libr. Jour., 2007. Mem. ALA, AAUW, NOW, Calif. Libr. Assn. (chmn. minority students scholarship 1995—, minority scholar 1992), So. Calif. Coun. on Lit. for Children and Young People (awards com. 1995—), Libr. Adminstrn. and Mgmt. Assn. Office: Fayetteville Public Library 401 W Mountain St Fayetteville AR 72701 Office Phone: 479-571-2222. Office Fax: 479-571-0222. E-mail: sthorup@faylib.org.

THOULESS, DAVID JAMES, retired physicist, educator; b. Bearsden, Scotland, Sept. 21, 1934; arrived in U.S., 1979, naturalized, 1994; s. Robert Henry and Priscilla (Gorton) T.; m. Margaret Elizabeth Scrase, July 26, 1958; children: Michael, Christopher, Helen. BA, U. Cambridge, Eng., 1955, ScD, 1986; PhD, Cornell U., 1958. Physicist Lawrence Berkeley Lab., Calif., 1958-59; rsch. fellow U. Birmingham, England, 1959—61, prof. math. physics, 1965—78; lectr., fellow Churchill Coll. U. Cambridge, England, 1961—65; prof. physics Queen's U., Kingston, Ont., Canada, 1978; prof. applied sci. Yale U., New Haven, 1979-80; prof. physics U. Wash., Seattle, 1980—2003; ret. Author: Quantum Mechanics of Many Body Systems, 2d edit., 1972, Topological Quantum Numbers in Nonrelativistic Physics, 1998. Recipient Maxwell medal Inst. Physics, 1973, Holweck prize Soc. Francaise de Physique-Inst. Physics, 1980, Fritz London award for Low temperature physics, Fritz London Meml. Fund, 1984, Wolf prize in physics, Wolf Found., Israel, 1990, Paul Dirac medal Inst. Physics, 1993, Lars Onsager prize Am. Phys. Soc., 2000; Edwin Uehling disting. scholar U. Wash., 1988-98. Fellow: Royal Soc.; mem.: NAS. Office: U Wash PO Box 351560 Seattle WA 98195-1560 Business E-Mail: Thouless@u.washington.edu.

THOYER, JUDITH REINHARDT, lawyer; b. Mt. Vernon, NY, July 29, 1940; d. Edgar Allen and Florence (Mayer) Reinhardt; m. Michael E. Thoyer, June 30, 1963; children: Erinn Thoyer Rhodes, Michael John. AB with honors, U. Mich., 1961; LLB summa cum laude, Columbia U., 1965. Bar: N.Y. 1966, D.C. 1984. Law libr. U. Ghana, Accra, Africa, 1963-64; assoc. Paul, Weiss, Rifkind, Wharton & Garrison, NYC, 1966-75, ptnr., 1975—. Mem. TriBar Opinion Com., 1995—. Bd. visitors Law Sch. Columbia U., N.Y.C., 1991—; bd. dirs. Women's Action Alliance, N.Y.C., 1975-89, pro bono counsel, 1975-97; mem. Women's Coun. Dem. Senatorial, campaign com., 1993-97; organizing com. Alumnae Columbia Law Sch., 1996—. Recipient medal for excellence, Columbia Law Sch., 2003. Mem. N.Y. County Lawyers Assn. (mem. securities and exchs. com. 1976-98), Assn. of Bar of City of N.Y. (mem. securities regulation com. 1976-79, mem. recruitment of lawyers com. 1980-82, mem. com. on mergers, acquisitions and corp. control contests 1996—). Home: 1115 5th Ave Apt 3B New York NY 10128-0100 Office: Paul Weiss Rifkind Et Al 1285 Ave of Americas New York NY 10019-6028

THRAILKILL, DANIEL B., lawyer; b. Sept. 21, 1957; BSBA, U. Ark., 1979; JD, Univ. Ark., 1981. Bar: Ark. 1982, Tex. 1988, U.S. Dist. Ct. (eas. and we. dists.) Ark. 1982, U.S. Dist. Ct. (ea. dist.) Okla. 1995, U.S. Ct. Appeals (8th cir.) 1983, U.S. Supreme Ct. 1985. Ptnr. Page, Thrailkill & McDaniel, P.A., Mena, Ark., 1981—. Assoc. prof., lectr. rich Mountain C.C.; assoc. justice Ark. Supreme Ct., 1996—; city atty. Cities of Mena and Hatfield. Mem.: ABA, ATLA, Ark. Trial Lawyers Assn., Ark. Bar Assn. (bd. govs., tenured del., exec. coun.), Lions Club, Sigma Phi Epsilon, Phi Alpha Delta. Methodist. Home: 200 Craig St Mena AR 71953-2427 Office: Page Thrailkill & McDaniel 311 DeQueen St Courthouse Sq W Mena AR 71953 Office Phone: 479-394-3091. Business E-Mail: danny@arklawyer.com.

THRALL, ARTHUR ALVIN, artist, educator; b. Milw., Mar. 18, 1926; s. Irving and Helen (Fabich) T.; m. Winifred Rogers, 1960; children: Grant, Wade, Sara, Jay. BS, Milw. State Tchrs. Coll., 1950; MS, U. Wis., Milw., 1954; postgrad. (fellow), U. Ill., 1954-55. Tchr. art Lincoln Jr. High Sch., Kenosha, Wis., 1951-54; asst. prof. SUNY, Geneseo, 1955-56; assoc. prof. Milw.-Downer Coll., 1956-64; prof., Farrar-Marrs prof. fine arts Lawrence U., Appleton, Wis., 1964-90, prof. emeritus, 1990—. One-man shows include Smithsonian Instn., 1960, U. Dubuque, Iowa, 1993, Mt. Mary Coll., Milw., 1994, St. Norbert Coll, De Pere, Wis., 1995, Cardinal Stritch U., Milw., 1998, also others; group shows include Corcoran bienials, Washington, 1951, 53, 55, 57, 62, Bklyn. Mus. annuals, Mus. Modern Art, N.Y.C., NAD, N,Y,C, Audubon Artists, N.Y.C., 1985, S.A.G.A., N.Y.C., 1985, Charles Allis Art Mus., Milw., 1996, Miller Art Ctr., Sturgeon Bay, Wis., 1997, Elvehem Mus. Art, Madison, Wis., 1998, 99, Fairfield Gallery, Sturgeon Bay, Wis., 2001; represented in permanent collections Tate Gallery, Victoria and Alberta Mus., Brit. Mus., all London, Phila. Mus., Seattle Mus., Art Inst. Chgo., Bklyn. Mus., others. Served with U.S. Army, 1944-46, ETO. Recipient Bklyn. Mus. print awards 1952, 64; Pa. Acad. Arts award 1960; NAD awards 1956, 68); Louis Comfort Tiffany fellow, 1963 Mem. AAUP, Boston Printmakers (awards 1963, 65), Soc. Am. Graphic Artists (awards 1951-52, 60, 78, 2000), Audubon Artists Inc. (award 1977) Home: 4225 N Woodburn St Milwaukee WI 53211-1504 Office Phone: 414-265-8601.

THRALL, GORDON FISH, publishing executive; b. Jamestown, NY, July 28, 1923; s. Clyde Lowell and Beulah Mae (Fish) T.; m. Betty Jane Roberts, Sept. 24, 1964 (dec. May 28, 2005); 1 dau., Jenifer Jane. A.B. in History and Polit. Sci., Alfred U., 1949; JD, Baylor U., 1953. Bar: Tex. 1953, US Supreme Ct. 1957, DC 1958, US Ct. Appeals (DC cir.) 1958, US Ct. Mil. Appeals 1958, US Dist. Ct. (ea. dist.) Tex. 1976, US Ct. Appeals (5th cir.) 1986. Law clk. US Dist. Ct. (ea. dist.) Tex., 1953-54; asst. prosecutor Dallas County Dist. Atty., 1954-55; assoc. firm Phinney & Hallman, Dallas, 1955-56; asst. Tex. Atty. Gen., 1957; adviser, examiner ICC, Washington, 1957-59; asst. gen. counsel Tex. State Bar, Austin, 1959-61; county atty. Reagan County, Big Lake, Tex., 1961-72; ptnr. Norman, Thrall, Angle, Guy & Day, LLP, Jacksonville, Tex., 1972—2002; v.p. Heflin & Thrall Lang. Publs., Inc., 2002-. Mem. exec. com. Tex. Baptist Gen. Conv., 1965-70, adminstrv. bd., 1991-95; deacon So. Bapt. Ch.; chmn. Permian Basin dist. Concho Valley council Boy Scouts Am., Big Lake, 1965-66; chmn. Jacksonville United Fund Drive, 1987, pres., 1989; pres. Cherokee County Health Facilities Devel. Corp., 1982—; v.p., bd. dirs. Travis Towers Retirement Facility, Jacksonville, 1980-2003; co-trustee Summers A. Norman Found., 1988-2002; mem. Nan Travis Meml. Hosp. Found. Bd., 1994—; pres. bd. visitors Jacksonville Coll., 1998—2003. Mem. Tex. State Bar, Tex. Bar Found. (vice chmn. UPL com. 1964), Big Lake C. of C. (pres. 1963, 67), Jacksonville C. of C. (pres. 1979), Cherokee Country Club, (dir. 1981-83), Kiwanis (pres. 1978, lt. gov. div. 34 1982), Big Lake Lions (pres. 1969), Masons (32 degree). Republican. Home: 702 Fort Worth St Jacksonville TX 75766-2610 Office: Heflin and Thrall Lang Publs Inc PO Box 1724 Jacksonville TX 75766 Office Phone: 903-586-2445. Business E-Mail: jheflin@language-publications.com.

THRALL, RICHARD CAMERON, JR., broadcast executive; b. Delaware, Ohio, Nov. 13, 1929; s. Richard Cameron and Pauline (Taylor) T.; m. Nancy Burrows, June 7, 1952 (div. Jan. 1962); children: Vallerie E. Alm, Cynthia L. Graser; m. Shirley Annette Sturgeon, Oct. 6, 1962; children: Laurie Jo Woodward, James W. Hochberg. BA, Miami U., Oxford, Ohio, 1951. Producer, dir. Sta. WBNS-TV, Columbus, Ohio, 1951-57, Sta. KDKA-TV, Pitts., 1957-59, pub. affairs dir., 1959-63, asst. program dir., 1963-67; program mgr. Sta. WLWC, Columbus, 1967-68; mgr. corp. TV Avco Broadcasting, Cin., 1968-70, mgr. TV programming, 1970-76; v.p. programming Multimedia Broadcasting., Cin., 1976-82; sr. v.p. Multimedia Entertainment, Cin., 1982-84; sr. v.p., gen. mgr. Multimedia Entertainment of Tenn., Nashville, 1984-88; sr. v.p. ops. and adminstrn. Multimedia Entertainment, NYC, 1988-94, sr. v.p. programming, 1994-96; ret., 1996. Freelance prodr., writer, program cons., 1996—. Writer numerous TV scripts and songs. Served with USN, 1947-48. Recipient Outstanding Country Special award Music City News, Nashville, 1983-87; named to Hon. Order Ky. Cols. Mem. Country Music Assn., NATAS (pres. Columbus/Dayton/Cin. chpt. 1980-83, bd. govs. MidSouth chpt. 1985-87, chmn. nat. awards com. 1989-2002, winner regional Emmys and Emmy cert.). Congregationalist. Avocations: fishing, boating, skiing, travel.

THRASH, PATRICIA ANN, retired educational association administrator; b. Grenada, Miss., May 4, 1929; d. Lewis Edgar and Weaver (Betts) T. BS, Delta State Coll., 1950; LHD, Delta State U., 2007; MA, Northwestern U., Evanston, Ill., 1953, PhD, 1959; cert. Inst. Edn. Mgmt., Harvard U., Cambridge, Mass., 1983; EdD, Vincennes U., Ind., 1997; LHD, Drake U., Des Moines, 1997, Adrian Coll., Mich., 1998. Tchr. high sch. English, Clarksdale, Miss., 1950-52; head resident Northwestern U., 1953-55, asst. to dean women, 1955-58, asst. dean women, 1958-60, lectr. edn., 1959-65, dean women, 1960-69, assoc. prof. edn., 1965-72, assoc. dean students, 1969-71; asst. exec. sec. Commn. on Instns. Higher Edn., North Central Assn. Colls. and Schs., 1972-73, assoc. exec. dir., 1973-76, assoc. dir., 1976-87, exec. dir., 1988-96; exec. dir. emeritus, 1997—. Adv. panel Am. Coun. on Edn., MIVER program evaluation mil. base program, 1991-94; nat. adv. panel Nat. Ctr. Postsecondary Tchg., Learning & Assessment, 1991-95. Author (with others): Handbook of College and University Administration, 1970; editor Jour. Northwestern U. Inst. for Learning in Retirement, 2000-02, course coord., 2000—; contbr. articles to ednl. jours. Bd. dirs. Delta State U. Found., 2000-02. Mem. Nat. Assn. Women Deans and Counselors (v.p. 1967-69, pres. 1972-73), Ill. Assn. Women Deans and Counselors (sec. 1961-63, pres. 1964-66), Am. Coll. Pers. Assn. (editl. bd. jour. 1971-74), Coun. Student Pers. Assns. in Higher Edn. (program nominations com. 1974-75, adv. panel Am. Coll. Testing Coll. Outcome Measures project 1977-78, staff Coun. on Postsecondary Accreditation project for evaluation nontraditional edn. 1977-78, mem. editl. bd. Jour. Higher Edn. 1975-80, guest editor Mar.-Apr. 1979, co-editor NCA Quar. 1988-96, vice-chair regional accrediting dirs. group 1993, exec. com. Nat. Policy Bd. for Higher Edn. Inst. 1993-95), Mortar Bd. (hon.), Phi Delta Theta, Pi Lambda Theta, Alpha Psi Omega, Alpha Lambda Delta. Methodist. Home: 2337 Hartrey Ave Evanston IL 60201-2552 Personal E-mail: patsy1941@comcast.net.

THRASHER, DIANNE ELIZABETH, mathematics educator, computer scientist, consultant; b. Brockton, Mass., July 11, 1945; m. George Thomas Thrasher, Jan. 28, 1967; children: Kimberly Elizabeth, Noelle Elizabeth. BA in Math., Bridgewater State Coll., Mass., 1967, postgrad., 1987. Cert. secondary math., history tchr. Tchr. math. Plymouth/Carver Regional Schs., Plymouth, Mass., 1976-78, Alden Sch., Duxbury, Mass., 1980-82, Marshfield H.S., Mass., 1982-84; computer cons. TC2I-Thrasher Computer Cons. and Instrn., Duxbury, Mass., 1988—; dir., owner Internat. Ednl. Franchise, 1991-95; owner Duxbury Math. Ctr. K-Adult, 1995—. Owner New Eng. Regional Kumon Ednl. Franchise, 1991-95, 2000—; Mass. State approved profl. point devel. provider for tchr. cert., 1996. Active US Figure Skating Assn., Colorado Springs, 1978-85; 2d reader First Ch. Christ Scientist, Plymouth, 1971-73; bd. govs. Skating Club of Hingham, Mass., 1978-85, pres., 1983-85, dir. Learn to Skate program, 1983-85; active First Ch. Christ Scientist, Boston, 1964—; with New Eng. Regional Kumon Franchise Owners, 1991-95; charter mem. Nat. Adv. Coun. of the US Navy Meml. Found., 1992, Mary Baker Eddy Libr. for the Betterment of Humanity, Boston, 2002. Recipient Presdl. Nomination for Excellence in Tng. Math., NSF, 1992, Ed Taylor Meml. Vol. Svc. award Skating Club Hingham, 1995, Amateur Photo award Internat. Libr. Photography, 1999. Mem. NAFE, AAUW, Math. Assn. Am., Am. Math. Soc., Am. Nat. Coun. Tchrs. Math, Nat. Hist. Trust and Preservation Soc., Smithsonian, Internat. Soc. Photographers (Amateur Photo award 1999). Avocations: antiques, bicycling, skating, sailing. Home: 140 Toby Garden St Duxbury MA 02332-4945 Office Phone: 781-934-6997. Personal E-mail: sumizumi@aol.com.

THRASHER, FAY C., clinical psychologist; b. Wynne, Ark., Dec. 17, 1935; d. Andrew J. and Joy M. (Charles) Thrasher; children: Jeffrey K. Mitchell, Sidney J. Guidroz Jr. MEd, McNeese State U., 1963; MA, La. State U., 1967, PhD, 1970. Lic. psychologist. Chief psychologist Cmty. Mental Health, Lake Charles, La., 1970-73; clin. psychologist VA Hosp., Salisbury, NC, 1973-76; chief psychologist VA Opt Clinic, San Antonio, 1976-77, Alvin C. York VA Med. Ctr., Murfreesboro, Tenn., 1977-87; clin. psychologist VA Med. Ctr., Alexandria, Va., 1990-95, chief psychologist, 1995—. Bd. dirs. Oasis Ministry, Pineville, La.; cons. to freedom cons., 1996—; bd. dirs. New Beginning Acad., Alexandria, treas., 1997—; cons. Bunkie Adolexcent Ctr., Bunkie Gen. Hosp., 1993—97. Chmn. Combined Fed. Campaign, Murfreesboro, 1985—86. Mem.: APA, Am. Coll. Forensic

Examiners, Nat. Register. Avocations: bridge, antiques, art, music. Home: 303 Rain Tree Pl Pineville LA 71360-5472 Office: Freedom Counseling Ctr 2809 Donahue Ferry Rd Pineville LA 71360-4513 Personal E-mail: drfay@suddenlink.net.

THRASHER, MARY AHLF MARCROFT, educator, social worker; b. St. Louis, Apr. 25, 1923; d. Gustave and Florence Regina (Froelich) Ahlf; m. Keith R. Marcroft, Mar. 23, 1946 (div. 1969); children: Joanne Marcroft Williamson, Karen A. Marcroft; m. Hugh Riley Thrasher, June 28, 1989 (dec. Jan. 2006). BS, Ind. U., 1944; postgrad., U. Md., 1968-69, U. Evansville, 1971-72. Lic. tchr., Ind., Ky. Office mgr. U. Utah, Salt Lake City, 1946-48; sec. Brown Shoe Co., St. Louis, 1948-52; sch. tchr. Prince George's County Schs., Bowie, Md., 1965-70, Troy Twp. Sch. Corp., Tell City, Ind., 1970-73; sec. Perry County Extension Svc., Cannelton, Ind., 1973-75; caseworker Perry County Dept. Pub. Welfare, Cannelton, 1975—86. Composer, lyricist (musical play) ON MAIN STREET, 1988. Pres. Am. Legion Aux., 1986-87, Tell City Hist. Soc., 1987-89. Mem. AAUW, Order of Eastern Star. Mem. United Ch. of Christ. Avocations: choir member, church organist, accompanist to vocal and instrumental soloists, painter, gardener. Home: 225 11th St Tell City IN 47586-1907

THRASHER, ROSE MARIE, critical care and community health nurse; b. Urbana, Ohio, Jan. 19, 1948; d. Jesse and Anna Frances (Clark) T. Student, Mercy Med. Ctr. Sch. Med. Tech., 1966—67, Wittenberg U., Springfield, Ohio, 1969—70; BSN, Ohio State U., 1974, BA in Anthropology, 1994, BA in Art History, 1997, BA in Geography, 2002, postgrad., 2005—. RN, Ohio; bd. cert. cmty. health nurse ANA; cert. provider BCLS and ACLS, Am. Heart Assn., CCRN, AACN; cert. asthma mgmt. edn. Am. Lung Assn. Ohio. Critical care nurse Staff Builders Health Care Svc., Oakland, Calif., 1975—76, 1981—85; supr., case mgr. and home health nurse passport and intermittent care programs Interim Health Care, Columbus, Ohio, 1976—77, 1985—2004; pub. health nurse Columbus Health Dept., 1977—78; critical care nurse VA Med. Ctr., San Francisco, 1981; chart reviewer Interim Health Care Support Svc., Columbus, 1996—98; IRP nurse Ohio State U. Hosps. East, 1999—2003; ind. home health nurse, provider med. svcs. State of Ohio Dept. Human Svcs., 1999—2005; home health nurse Interim Health Care, Newark and Pataskala, Ohio, 2004—, case mgr., 2007—. Acad. scholar Wittenberg U., Ohio State U. Mem. AACN, ANA (coun. cmty. health nursing), AAUW, AAAS, Internat. Union Anthrop. and Ethnol. Scis., NY Acad. Scis., Ohio Nurses Assn., Intravenous Nurses Soc., Ohio State U. Alumni Assn., Am. Anthrop. Assn., Midwest Art History Soc., Coll. Art Assn., Nat. Mus. Women in Arts, Nat. Women's Hall of Fame, Ohio Acad. Sci., Ohio State U. Coll. of Nursing Alumni Soc. Business E-Mail: thrasher.2@osu.edu.

THRASHER, TODD, bar chef; b. Va. Grad., Va. Commonwealth U.; studied first level, Ct. of Sommeliers, 1997. Bartender Carlyle Grand Café, Gabriel, 1996; bar mgr. Café Atlantico; bar chef Restaurant Eve, Alexandria, Va., The PX. Named one of Washington DC's Rising Stars, StarChefs.com, 2006. Office: Restaurant Eve 110 S Pitt St Alexandria VA 22314 Office Phone: 703-706-0450. *

THREEDY, DEBORA LYNN, law educator; b. Chgo., June 10, 1951; d. Edward Clarence and Irene Frances (Palenik) T. BA, Beloit Coll., 1973; JD, Loyola U., 1980. Bar: Ill. Law clk. to Hon. Getzendanner U.S. Dist. Ct. (no. dist.) Ill., Chgo., 1980-82; assoc. Mayer Brown & Platt, Chgo., 1982-86; assoc. prof. law U. Utah, Salt Lake City, 1986—, prof. law, assoc. dean academic affairs, acting dean, 2004—. Contbr. articles to profl. jours. Bd. dirs. ACLU, Salt Lake City, 1990; trustee Theater Works West, Salt Lake City, 1990. McCormick Scholar Loyola U., 1980, Owens Scholar, 1980. Mem. Phi Beta Kappa. Office: U Utah Coll Law 332 South 1400 East Salt Lake City UT 84112-1107

THREEFOOT, SAM ABRAHAM, physician, educator; b. Meridian, Miss., Apr. 10, 1921; s. Sam Abraham and Ruth Frances (Lilienthal) Threefoot; m. Virginia Rush, Feb. 6, 1954; children: Barbara Jane Stockton Mattingly, Ginny Ruth Threefoot Lindberg, Tracyann Threefoot Esenstad, Shelley Ann Cowan. BS, Tulane U., New Orleans, 1943, MD, 1945. Diplomate: Am. Bd. Internal Medicine. Intern Michael Reese Hosp., Chgo., 1945-47; asst. vis. physician Charity Hosp. New Orleans, 1947-50, vis. physician, 1950-57, sr. vis. physician, 1957-69, cons., 1969-70, 76-91; clin. asst. dept. medicine Touro Infirmary, New Orleans, 1953-56, jr. asst., 1956-60, sr. asst., 1960-63, dir. med. edn., 1953-63, dir. research, 1953-70, sr. dept. medicine, 1963-70; fellow dept. medicine Tulane U., 1947-49, instr., 1948-53, asst. prof., 1953-59, asso. prof., 1959-63, prof., 1963-70, 76-91, prof. emeritus, 1991—, asst. dean, 1979-91, adj. prof. emeritus Sch. Pub. Health & Tropical Medicine, 1993—; chief of staff VA Hosp. (Forest Hills div.), Augusta, Ga., 1970-76; assoc. chief staff VA Hosp., New Orleans, 1976-79, chief of staff, 1979-91, cons., 1991—97; asst. dean Med. Coll. Ga., 1970-76, prof. medicine, 1970-76. Cons. physician Lallie Kemp Charity Hosp., Independence, La., 1951-53 Editor: Lymphology, 1967-70, sr. mem. editl. bd.; Contbr. articles profl. jours. Served with AUS, 1943-45. La. Heart Assn. grantee, 1953-55; John A. Hartford Found. grantee, 1956-74; Am. Heart Assn. grantee, 1959-61; USPHS grantee, 1953-66 Fellow ACP, Am. Coll. Cardiology, NY Acad. Sci.; mem. Am. Heart Assn. (v.p. 1970, fellow council on circulation), Central Soc. Clin. Research, So. Soc. Clin. Investigation (pres. 1967), AAAS, Internat. Soc. Lymphology, Soc. Exptl. Biology and Medicine, Soc. Nuclear Medicine, Microcirculatory Conf., Inc., Am. Fedn. Clin. Research, La. Heart Assn. (pres. 1967), Nat. Assn. VA Chiefs of Staff (pres. 1987-88), Phi Beta Kappa, Sigma Xi. Jewish. Home: 1750 St Charles Ave Unit 616 New Orleans LA 70130 Office Phone: 504-524-3668. Personal E-mail: threefoot@bellsouth.net. *I am one of those fortunate individuals who has been able to approach goals set early in life. Although my achievements are far short of my aspirations, at least I have had the opportunity. In dealing with both people and things, I have always felt that no detail was too small to receive attention.*

THRELKELD, RICHARD DAVIS, retired broadcast journalist; b. Cedar Rapids, Iowa, Nov. 30, 1937; s. Robert M. and Lou Jane (Davis) T.; m. Sharon A. Adams, June 11, 1960 (div. 1983); children: Susan Anne, Julia Lynn; m. Betsy Aaron, May 15, 1983. BA, Ripon Coll., 1959, LHD (hon.), 1989; MS in Journalism, Northwestern U., 1961. Editor Sta. WHAS-TV, Louisville, 1961; reporter Sta. WMT-TV, Cedar Rapids, Iowa, 1961-66; corr. CBS News, NYC and San Francisco, 1966-82, nat. corr., 1989-96, Moscow corr., 1996-98, ret., 1998; chief corr. ABC News NY, NYC, 1982-89. Author: Dispatches From the Former Evil Empire, 2001; corr.: TV news report Rhodesia Remembered, 1980 (Overseas Press Club Award), Lebanon-Grenada, 1983 (Overseas Press Club Award), Vietnam Remembered, 1985 (Emmy Award); TV news documentary Defense of America, 1981 (Emmy Award); TV news series Status Reports, 1984 (Alfred I. Dupont-Columbia U. Award). Named to Hall of Achievement, Medill Sch. Journalism, Northwestern U., 2004; CBS News Fellow, 1964. Mem.: Soc. Profl. Journalists. Personal E-mail: threlkeldr@aol.com.

THRESHER, MARK R., insurance company executive; B in Acctg., Otterbein Coll., Westerville, Ohio. With KPMG LLP; v.p., treas. Nationwide Fin. Svcs., Inc., 1996, sr. v.p., CFO, pres., COO Fin., 2004—. Trustee Otterbein Coll., mem. investment and audit coms.; mem. Ctr. of Sci. and Industry (COSI) Columbus Adv. Coun. Mem.: AICPA, Fin. Svcs. Roundtable, Am. Coun. Life Insurers (mem. exec. roundtable com., mem. retirement & fin. security steering com.), Assn. Ohio Life Ins. Cos. Office: Nationwide Fin Svcs Inc One Nationwide Plz Columbus OH 43215-2220 *

THRO, WILLIAM EUGENE, lawyer; b. Elizabethtown, Ky., Nov. 8, 1963; s. Ernest Guernsey and Joan (Young) T.; children: Sandra Lucinda Grace Edwards-Thro, William Thomas Daniel Edwards-Thro, Noah Christopher James Edwards-Thro.; m. Julie Urback, Sept. 04, 2004. BA, Hanover Coll., Ind., 1986; MA, U. Melbourne, Australia, 1988; JD, U. Va., Charlottesville, 1990. Bar: Ky. 1990, Colo. 1991, Va. 1998, US Dist. Ct. (we. dist.) Ky. 1990, US Dist. Ct. Colo. 1991, US Ct. Appeals (6th and 10th cirs.) 1991, US Ct. Appeals (3d cir.) 1993, US Supreme Ct. 1993, US Ct. Appeals (4th cir.) 1997, US Dist. Ct. (ea. dist.) Va. 1998, US Dist. Ct. (we. dist.) Va. 1998, US Ct. Appeals (DC cir.) 1999, US Bankruptcy Ct. (ea. and we. dists.) Va. 1999, US Dist. Ct. (ea. dist.) Ky. 2003, US Dist. Ct. (no. dist.) Ill. 2003, US Ct. Appeals (7th cir.), 2005, US Ct. Appeals (8th cir.), 2006. Jud. clk. Judge Ronald E. Meredith, US Dist. Ct. (we. dist.) Ky., Louisville, 1990-91; asst. atty. gen. State of Colo., Denver, 1991-97, Commonwealth of Va., Richmond, 1997—99; gen. counsel Christopher Newport U., Newport News, 2000—04; dep. state solicitor gen. Commonwealth Va., 2002—04, state solicitor gen., 2004—. Author: Why You Cannot Sue State U: A Guide to Sovereign Immunity, 2001, 2d edit., 2007; co-author: Race Conscious Admissions and Financial Aid After the University of Michigan Decisions, 2004; co-editor: The NACUA Handbook for Lawyers New to Higher Education, 2003, 2d edit., 2007; mem. editl. bd. Coll. and Univ. Law, 2000—, vice chair, 2004-05, chair, 2005—; mem. editl. bd. Encyclopedia of Law, 2005—; mem. author's com. West's Edn. Law Reporter, 1992-2007, mem. editl adv. com., 2007-; contbr. articles to profl. jours. Mem. LaCrosse Presbyn. Ch.; elder Presbyn. Ch. USA, 2007—; gen. counsel adv. bd. NCAA, 2001—04. Recipient Best Brief award, Nat. Assn. of Attys. Gen., 2003—04, Hardin County Sch. Disting. Alumni award, 2004; scholar U.S. Senate Youth scholar, Hearst Found., 1982, Harry S Truman scholar, Truman Scholarship Found., 1984, Rotary Internat. Ambassadorial scholar, Melbourne, 1987. Fellow: Nat. Assn. Coll. and Univ. Attys.; mem.: South Africa Edn. Law Assn., Am. Inns Ct., Edn. Law Assn., Nat. Assn. Coll. and U. Attys., Ky. Bar Assn., Va. Bar Assn., Federalist Soc., Nat. Eagle Scout Assn., Hon. Order of Ky. Cols. Republican. Presbyterian. Office: Office of Atty Gen 900 E Main St Richmond VA 23219 Office Phone: 804-786-2436. Personal E-mail: withro@cox.net. Business E-Mail: wthro@oag.state.va.us.

THROCKMORTON, DOUGLAS CARL, federal agency administrator; b. Hasting, Nebr., Jan. 11, 1959; Degree in Eng. and Chemistry, Hastings Coll.; MD, U. Nebr. Coll. Medicine, 1985. Cert. Internal Medicine, Nephrology. Intern, internal medicine Case Western Reserve Univ. Hosp., Cleve., 1985—86, resident, 1986—88; fellow Yale U., New Haven, 1988—93; asst. prof. Med. Coll. Ga. and VA Med. Ctr., Augusta, Ga.; hosp. appointment FDA, Rockville, Md., med. officer, 1997—2000; dep. dir. Divsn. Cardiovascular and Renal Drug Products, Ctr. for Drug Evaluation and Rsch., FDA, Rockville, Md., 2000—02, dir., 2002—04; acting dep. dir. Ctr. for Drug Evaluation and Rsch., FDA, Rockville, Md., 2004—05, dep. dir., 2005—. Office: FDA 1451 Rockville Pike Rockville MD 20852 also: FDA Divsn Drug Information 5600 Fischers Lane HFD-240 Rockville MD 20857

THROCKMORTON, REX DENTON, lawyer; b. Lima, Ohio, June 4, 1941; s. Francis and Jane (Corwin) T.; m. Barbara Catherine Poore, July 21, 1962; children: Scott, John. BS, Denison U., 1963; JD, Ohio State U., 1965. Bar: Ohio 1966, N. Mex. 1971, U.S. Dist. Ct. N. Mex. 1971, U.S. Ct. Appeals (10th cir.) 1973. Assoc. Squire, Sanders & Dempsey, Cleve., 1965-66; shareholder, bd. dirs. Rodey, Dickason, Sloan, Akin & Robb, P.A., Albuquerque, 1971—, ptnr., pres., mng. dir., 1999—2004. Editor Ohio State Law Jour., 1965. Pres. Albuquerque Civic Light Opera Assn., 1985; sec. Accion, N.Mex. Capt. JAGC, USAF, 1966-71. Named one of best lawyers in Am., 2003—04. Mem. ABA, N.Mex. Bar Assn. (bd. of bar commrs. 1990-98, sec.-treas. 1994, v.p. 1995, pres.-elect 1996, pres. 1997), Albuquerque Bar Assn. (pres. 1982). Republican. Avocations: golf, running. Office: Rodey Dickason Sloan Akin & Robb PO Box 1888 Albuquerque NM 87103-1888 Office Phone: 505-765-5900. Office Fax: 505-768-7395. Business E-Mail: rthrockmorton@rodey.com.

THRODAHL, MARK CRANDALL, medical products executive; b. Charleston, W.Va., Mar. 31, 1951; s. Monte Cordon and Josephine (Crandall) T.; m. Sudie Kenton, Oct. 21, 1978; children: Mary Elizabeth, Anne Katherine, Andrew Kenton. AB, Princeton U., 1973; MBA, Harvard U., Boston, 1975. Various positions Mallinckrodt, Inc., St. Louis, 1975-88; dir. corp. planning Becton Dickinson & Co., Franklin Lakes, NJ, 1988-91, pres. Nippon Becton Dickinson Tokyo, 1991-94, sector pres. Franklin Lakes, 1994-95, sr. v.p., 1995-2001; CEO Bespak Plc, London, 2001—. Mem. Old Warson Country Club, Ivy Club. Republican. Episcopalian. Home: 38 Carteret Rd Allendale NJ 07401-1850 Office: Bespak Plc Blackhill Dr Wolverton Mill So Milton Keynes MK12 5TS England Office Phone: 44 (0) 1908-525200. Business E-Mail: mark.throdahl@bespak.co.uk.

THRONER, GUY CHARLES, JR., aerospace engineering executive, scientist, inventor, consultant; b. Mpls., Sept. 14, 1919; s. Guy Charles and Marie (Zechar) T.; m. Jean Holt, Dec. 5, 1943; children— Richard, Carol Anne, Steven. BA, Oberlin Coll., 1943; postgrad., UCLA, 1960-61. Registered profl. engr., Calif. Br. head Naval Weapon Ctr., China Lake, Calif., 1946-53; mgr. ordnance div. mgr. weapon systems div. Aerojet Gen. Corp., Azusa, Calif., 1953-64; v.p., div. mgr. FMC Corp., San Jose, Calif., 1964-74; research dir. Vacu Blast Corp., Belmont, Calif., 1976-78; v.p., devel. mfg. Dahlman, Inc., Braham, Minn., 1978-79; mgr. ordnance systems & tech. Battelle Meml. Inst., Columbus, Ohio, 1979-85; pres. Guy C. Throner & Assocs., tech. and mgmt. cons., 1985—. Dir. Omron Corp. Am., Chgo., 1976-77 Inventor, patentee indls., med. and mil. systems design. Served as officer USNR, World War II Recipient Am. Order St. Barbara medal U.S. Army Arty, 1983, IR-100 award Indsl. Rsch. Mag., Chgo., 1971, Congl. Commendation, 1985, Commendation, State of Ohio Ho. of Reps., 1995, also various commendations. Mem. AIAA, Am. Def. Preparedness Assn. (Bronze medal 1974, Simon Silver medal 1985), Lake Wildwood Country Club, Sigma Xi. Republican. Avocations: astronomy, photography, golf. Home and Office: 3939 Walnut Ave #152 Carmichael CA 95608 Personal E-mail: jeannguy@comcast.net.

THROWER, RANDOLPH WILLIAM, lawyer; b. Tampa, Fla., Sept. 5, 1913; s. Benjamin Key and Ora (Hammond) T.; m. Margaret Munroe, Feb. 2, 1939; children: Margaret MacCary, Patricia Barmeyer, Laura (Mrs. David T. Harris, Jr.), Randolph William, Mary (Mrs. George B. Wickham). Grad., Ga. Mil. Acad., 1930; BPh, Emory U., 1934, JD, 1936. Bar: Ga. bar 1935, D.C. bar 1953. Partner Sutherland, Asbill & Brennan, Atlanta, Washington, 1947-69, 71—. Commr. internal revenue, 1969-71; Lectr. bar, legal meetings; spl. agt. FBI, 1942-43; mem. Arthur Andersen & Co. Bd. of Rev., 1974-80, Nat. Council on Organized Crime, mem. exec. com., 1970-71 Past pres. Ga., Met. Atlanta mental health assns.; chmn. City of Atlanta Bd. Ethics 1981-93; past trustee Emory U., Clark Coll.; past chmn., trustee Wesleyan Coll.; bd. govs. Woodward Acad.; past chmn. bd. visitors Emory U. Served as capt. USMCR, 1944-45. Mem. Atlanta Legal Aid Soc. (past pres.), Emory U. Alumni Assn. (past pres.), ABA (chmn. spl. com. on survey local needs 1971-78, past chmn. sect. taxation, mem. ho. of dels. 1964-66, 74-89), Ga. Bar Assn., Atlanta Bar Assn. (past pres.), Am. Bar Found. (dir. 1980-88, pres. 1986-88, medal 1993), Am. Law Inst., Atlanta Lawyers Club (past pres.), U.S. Claims Ct. Bar Assn. (pres. 1987-88), Phi Delta Phi. Clubs: Commerce (Atlanta), Capital City (Atlanta), Piedmont Driving (Atlanta). Republican. Methodist. Home: 2240 Woodward Way NW Atlanta GA 30305-4043 Office: Sutherland Asbill & Brennan Ste 2300 999 Peachtree St NE Atlanta GA 30309 Office Phone: 404-853-8149. Business E-Mail: randolph.thrower@sablaw.com.

THRUN, SEBASTIAN BURKHARD, computer science educator, researcher; b. Solingen, Germany, May 14, 1967; s. Winfried and Kristin (Grüner) T.; m. Petra Dierkes, July 1, 1995. BSc in Computer Sci., Econs. and Medicine, U. Hildesheim, Germany, 1988; MSc in Computer Sci. and Stats., U. Bonn, Germany, 1993, PhD summa cum laude in Computer Sci. and Stats., 1995. Rsch. asst. German Nat. Rsch. Ctr. for Info. Tech., Sankt Augustin, Germany, 1989-91; project scientist Carnegie Mellon U., Pitts., 1991-92, rsch. computer scientist, 1995-98, asst. prof. computer sci., 1998-2001, assoc. prof., 2001—03; rsch. assoc. U. Bonn, 1993-95; assoc. prof. computer sci. Stanford U., Calif., 2003—, assoc. prof. elec. engring., 2006—; dir. Stanford Artificial Intelligence Lab., 2004—. Cons. Daimler Benz Rsch., Berlin, 1995, Real World Interface, Inc., Jaffrey, NH, 1996; v.p. devel. Neural Info. Processing Systems Found., 2003-. Author: Explanation-Based Neural Network Learning: A Lifelong Learning Approach, 1996; editor: Recent Advances in Robot Learning, 1996, Learning to Learn, 1997; co-author: Principles of Robotic Motion: Theory, Algorithms, and Implementation, 2004, Probabilistic Robotics, 2005; contbr. articles to profl. jours., chpts. to books. Named one of Brilliant 10, Popular Sci., 2005; recipient CAREER award, NSF, 1999—2003, Olympus award, German Soc. Pattern Recognition, 2001. Fellow: European Coordinating Com. Artificial Intelligence, Am. Assn. Artificial Intelligence (2nd place in autonomous mobile robot competition 1994, 1st place in autonomous mobile robot competition 1996), World Tech. Network (World Tech. award 2006); mem.: NAE. Achievements include leading the development of the robotic vehicle Stanley, which won the Def. Advanced Rsch. Projects Agy. Grand Challenge in 2005. Avocations: singing, connoisseur. Office: Stanford Artificial Intelligence Lab Gates Bldg 154 353 Serra Mall Stanford CA 94305-9010 Office Phone: 650-723-2797. Office Fax: 650-725-1449. E-mail: thrun@stanford.edu.

THUEME, WILLIAM HAROLD, secondary school educator, counselor, travel coordinator; b. St. Clair, Mich., Sept. 4, 1945; s. Harold Arthur and Delphine Betty (Buhl) Thueme; m. Katheen Koning, May 8, 1971; children: Benjamin William, Rebecca Kathleen, Jeffery William, Sarah Kathleen; m. Nora Thueme. Student, Port Huron Jr. Coll., 1963-64; BA, Mich. State U., 1967, MA, 1969; PhD in Counseling, Progressive Universal Life Ch., 1993, PhD in Motivation, 1997, PhD in Paranormal Psychology, 1997, PhD in Psychometrics, 1999; postgrad., Oakland U., 1971, San Francisco State U., 1975, U. Hawaii, 1975; student, Spring Arbor Coll., 1968; PhD in Reading Edn., U. Mich., 1977; PhD (hon.), Aspen U., 2003. Cert. tchr., Mich. Ordained min. Universal Life Ch. Tchr. pub. schs., Charlotte, Mich., 1967-69, Ann Arbor, Mich., 1969—. Fgn. travel coord.-Ambs. Abroad Program, Amsterdam, The Netherlands, 1968—; regional driver coord. for Southeastern Mich. Avis Rent-a-Car, 1983—; travel coord. domestic and fgn. Go Ahead Tours; worldwide travel coord. Air, Land and Sea Cruises. Active UN Children's Found., Mich. Sheriffs Ednl. Found., Feed the Children, Woods Rd. Assn., Normal Pk. Neighborhood Assn., US Legal Found., Found. for Nicaraguan Democracy, Habitat for Humanity Internat. (charter), Carter Ctr., Nat. Coun. Better Edn., participant Skyhook II Project; coord. Mich. Fraternal Order of Police BBB, Ea. Mass.; elections coord. Eaton County (Mich.) Rep. Party, 1968, nat. com., 1968—, nat. senatorial com.; troop com. Coun. Boy Scouts Am., Ypsilanti, merit badge counselor, 1988-89, cub scout summer camp instr.; Internat., Incorp. (life mem.). Shore Nat. Network of Poet's Soc. Wolverne Coun., 1987; coach of the angels Ypsilanti Am. Little League, 1988; parent adv. bd. The Childrens Devel. Lab. Ea. Mich. U., 1988-89; active Mich. United Conservation Clubs, Big Bros. Am., Charlotte, Mich., Human Rights Watch, Nat. Security Caucus US, 1988—, Heritage Found., 1988—, ofcl. sponsor Mandate for Leadership III, Policy Strategies for 1990's Project, Project Save Our Schs., 1988—, Citizens United for Better Edn., World Awareness, Inc., Group 61 Amnesty Internat., Legal Affairs Coun., Coun. for Inter-Am. Security, Am. Inst. for Econ. Rsch., Nicaraguan Resistance Edn. Found., Nat. Right to Work Legal Def. Found., Citizens Against Govt. Waste, Citizens Commn. for Ethics in Govt., Citizens for Decency Through Law, Inc., Nat. Consumers League, Participating Parents for Progress in Ypsilanti Pub. Schs.; parents adv. bd. Chapelle Elem. Sch., Ypsilanti, 1989-90, West Mid. Sch., Ypsilanti, 1991-92, Ypsilanti Pub. Schs., 1990—, Ypsilanti HS; charter sponsor Victory over Communism Project; nominated charter mem. Presdl. Task Force; participant Imperial Congress: Crisis in the Separation of Powers Project, line-item veto project Heritage Found., 1989, campaign to revise medicare catastrophic coverage law project Nat. Assn. Uniformed Svcs., 1989, repeal of catastrophic coverage act program Conservative Caucus Inc., 1989, Srs. Coal. Against the Tax, 1989; nat. adv. coun. Citizens Com. for Right to Bear Arms; jr. and sr. choir, Sunday sch. tchr. St. Paul's Luth. Ch., 1959-64 (Perfect Attendance award 8 yrs.), Marine city, Mich., 1960-63; youth Sunday sch. tchr., dir. youth min. coun. Lawrence Ave. Meth. Ch., Charlotte, Mich., 1967-69; assoc. mem. for Gentlemen of All Ages Second Amendment Sisters, 2003, Internat. Amb. Goodwill World Peace and Diplomacy Forum, founding cabinet, life mem., 2003, amb., 2004; senator seat for lifetime term World Nations Congress; mem. concert choir Mich. Mormon; vol. The Ctrl. Intelligence Agy., The USA, 1967-06, Homeland Security USA, 2005-; vol. missionary The Ch. of Jesus Christ of LDS, 1973-06; Sunday sch. sec., Mich.; Elder's Quorum instr., exec. sec., sec., High Priests Quorum Group Ypsilanti, Mich., Ann Arbor Stake Sunday Sch. sec.; Sunday sch. tchr. youth age grades 7-12. Recipient Spl. Recognition award Richard Nixon, 1968-79, Gerald Ford, 1974-76, Ronald Reagan, 1971-88, George Bush, 1988-92, Spl. Recognition award Reagan Presdl. Campaign, 1981, Bush Presdl. Campaign, 1988, Citizen of Yr. award Citizens Com. for Right to Bear Arms, 1988, cert. recognition US Justice Found., 1991, Hale Found., Am. Security Coun. 30th Anniversary Spl. Recognition cert., cert. appreciation 2d Amendment Found., 1988, Appreciation of Devoted and Valuable Svc. award Chapelle Elem. Sch., 1988-89, Merit Badge, Wolverine Coun.; Internat. Peace prize, United Cultural Conv., 2002, Outstanding contbns. to Literacy, Edn., Humanitarians and Peace, 2002, World medal of Freedom for hope, freedom and peace, 2006; letters from First Lady Nancy Reagan, First Lady Barbara Bush, Mich. Gov. John Engler, Nelson Mandella, Tchg. Excellence award, Cmty. Svc. award, Global Rels. award, 2002, others. Mem. NEA, NRA (life, endowment), Am. Inst. for Econ. Rsch., Lincoln Inst. for Rsch. Edn., United Conservatives of Am. (participant citizens against the catastrophic health act tax 1989), Mich. Edn. Assn., Internat. Reading Assn., Mich. Sheriffs Assn. (assoc.), Police Marksmanship Assn., Washtenaw Reading Coun., Southeastern Mich. Reading Assn., Mich. Reading Assn., Mich. ASCD, Ann Arbor Edn. Assn., Am. Security Coun., Am. Def. Inst., Found. for Christian Living, Am. Family Assn., Nat. Geog. Soc., Am. Film Inst., Internat. Freelance Photographers Orgn. (life, profl. photographer), Taxpayers Edn. Lobby, Gun Owners Am., Nat. Assn. Federally Lic. Firearms Dealers, Nat. Consumers League, Conservative Caucus, Inc., Ams. for Freedom, Tri-County Sportsman League, Mich. United Conservation Clubs, Mich. State U. Alumni Assn. (Blue Water chpt.), Mich. State U. Coll. Comm. Arts Alumni Assn., Cruise Lines Internat. Assn., Internat. Air Transport Assn., US Tour Operators Assn. of One Million Dollar Consumer Protection Plan, Mich. State U. Coll. Social Sci. Alumni Assn., Inventors Assistance League (life), San Francisco State U. Alumni Assn., Shore Nat. Network Poets Soc. (life), Group Leaders Am., Group Travel Bus. Inst., Ft. Gratiot, Lions Club (v.p. 1998—), Lions Club Internat., Washtenaw Sportsmen's Club (Ypsilanti), Internat. Optimist Club (v.p. Ann Arbor chpt., bd. dirs. 1975-78), Port Huron Noon Optimist Club, Judo Black Belt Fedn. Am., Sigma Alpha Eta. Evangelican Lutheran. Office Phone: 800-381-5111. Personal E-mail: whthueme@yahoo.com.

THUESEN, GERALD JORGEN, industrial engineer, educator; b. Oklahoma City, July 20, 1938; s. Holger G. and Helen S. T.; m. Harriett M. Thuesen; children: Karen T. Hannah, Dyan T. Jacobus. BS, Stanford U., 1960, MS, 1961, PhD, 1968. Engr. Pacific Tel. Co., San Francisco,

1961-62, Atlantic Richfield Co., Dallas, 1962-63; asst. prof. indsl. engring. U. Tex., Arlington, 1963, 67-68; assoc. prof. indsl. and sys. engring. Ga. Inst. Tech., Atlanta, 1968-76, prof., 1976-96, prof. emeritus, 1996—. Author: Engineering Economy, 4th edit., 1971, 9th edit., 2001, Economic Decision Analysis, 1974, 3rd edit., 1998; assoc. editor: The Engring. Economist, 1974-80, editor, 1981-91. NASA/Am. Soc. Engring. Edn. summer faculty fellow, 1970. Fellow Inst. Indsl. Engrs. (dept. editor Trans. 1976-80, v.p. publs. 1979-80, divsn. dir. 1978-80, Wellington award 1989, Publs. award 1990, bd. trustees 1979-81), Am. Soc. Engring. Edn. (bd. dirs. 1977-79, Eugene L. Grant award 1977, 91); mem. Sigma Xi. Office: Ga Inst Tech Sch Indsl & Sys Engring Atlanta GA 30332-0205 Office Phone: 770-693-9291. Business E-Mail: gthuesen@isye.gatech.edu.

THUESON, DAVID OREL, pharmaceutical executive, researcher, writer, educator; b. Twin Falls, Idaho, May 9, 1947; s. Orel Grover and Shirley Jean (Archer) T.; m. Sherrie Linn Lowe, June 14, 1969; children: Sean, Kirsten, Eric, Ryan, Todd. BS, Brigham Young U., 1971; PhD, U. Utah, 1976. Postdoctoral fellow U. Tex. Med. Br., Galveston, 1976-77, asst. prof., 1977-82; sr. rsch. assoc. Parke-Davis Pharms., Ann Arbor, Mich., 1982-88; dir. pharmacology Immunetech Pharms., San Diego, 1988-90; dir. immunopharmacology Tanabe Rsch. Labs., San Diego, 1990-92; v.p. discovery Cosmederm Techs., San Diego, 1992-97. Contbr. articles to profl. jours.; patentee in field. Scout leader Boy Scouts Am., Mich., Tex. and Calif., 1979—. NIH grantee, 1978-81. Mem. Am. Acad. Allergy and Clin. Immunology, Am. Assn. Immunologists, Am. Thoracic Soc. Republican. Mem. Lds Ch. Avocations: water-skiing, tennis, scuba diving. Home: 1356 Winchester Ave Mckinleyville CA 95519-8801 Office: 2330 Central Ave Ste 3 Mckinleyville CA 95519-3696 Home Phone: 707-839-4935; Office Phone: 707-840-0623. Business E-Mail: thueson@reninet.com.

THULEAN, DONALD MYRON, symphony conductor; b. Wenatchee, Wash., June 24, 1929; s. Elmer Edward and Mary (Myron) T.; m. Meryl Mary Parnell, Mar. 17, 1951; children— Dorcas Marie, Mark Myron, William Norton. BA, U. Wash., 1950, MA in Music, 1952; Mus.D. (hon.), Whitworth Coll., 1967. Faculty Pacific U., 1955-62; dean Pacific U. (Sch. Music), 1957-62. Assoc. conductor Portland (Ore.) Symphony, 1961-62, conductor, music dir. Spokane Symphony, 1962-84; v.p. profl. and artistic svcs. Am. Symphony Orch. League, 1983-99, condr. emeritus, 1998—; asst. conductor Seattle Symphony, 1966-69, chorus master, Aspen Music Festival, 1957-61; artistic cons. Title III project in performing arts, Wash., 1966-68, music dir. Tamarack Music Festival, 1971. Bd. dirs. Seattle Symphony, 2000-06, Seattle Youth Symphonies, 2002--; mem. vis. com. U. Wash. Sch. Music, 2000—. Served with AUS, 1953-55. Unitarian (trustee). Personal E-mail: thulean2@comcast.net.

THULL, TOM (JOHN THOMAS THULL), state agency administrator; m. Shelley Thull. Grad. in Agr. Edn., Kans. State U., 1975. Loan specialist; v.p. Midland Nat. Bank, Ctrl. Bank & Trust; pres. Ctrl. Nat. Bank, Newton, Kans.; mayor Town of North Newton; mem. Kans. House Reps. from Dist. 72, 2003—07; commr. Office of State Bank Commr., Kans., 2007—. Pres. Harvey County Bankers Assn., Harvey County Econ. Devel. Coun.; dir. Newton C. of C.; mem. adv. bd. Bethel Coll. Democrat. Office: Office of State Bank Commr 700 Jackson Ste 300 Topeka KS 66603 Office Phone: 785-296-2266. Office Fax: 785-296-0168. E-mail: tom.thull@osbckansas.org.

THUMMA, SAMUEL ANDERSON, lawyer; b. Emmetsburg, Iowa, May 2, 1962; s. H. Russell and Lanore Ava (Anderson) T.; m. Barbara J. Dawson. BS, Iowa State U., 1984; JD, U. Iowa, 1988. Bar: Iowa 1988, Ill. 1990, D.C. 1990, Ariz. 1992. Broadcaster Sta. WOI-AM, Ames, Iowa, 1982-84; print journalist Iowa Dept. Agr., Des Moines, 1985; law clk. to Hon. David R. Hansen, U.S. Dist. Ct. for No. Dist. Iowa, Cedar Rapids, 1988-90; assoc. Arnold & Porter, Washington, 1990-92; law clk. to Hon. Stanley G. Feldman, Ariz. Supreme Ct., 1992-93; mem. Brown & Bain, P.A., Phoenix, 1996, Perkins Coie Brown & Bain, P.A., Phoenix, 2004—07; judge Ariz. Superior Ct. Maricopa County, 2007—. Adj. prof. Ariz. State U. Coll. Law, 2000. Contbr. articles to profl. jours. Western area Svc. Coun. Mem., American Red Cross, 2004-; ex officio bd. mem. and spl. transp. svcs. com. chair Grand Canyon chpt. ARC, 1998-99, bd. dirs., 1999-2004, chmn. bd., 2002-2004; bd. dirs., nat. conv. cabinet vice chair blood related activities ARC, 2000-2002; bd. dirs., purchasing coord. Gifts for Homeless, Inc., Washington, 1991-93; mem. study affairs devel. adv. coun. Iowa State U., 1993-96; mem. Paradise Valley Village Planning Com., 1994-96, sec., 1995-96; judge Nat. Chpt. award and Proficiency award Ariz. FFA, 1996-99, 2001. Harry S. Truman Found. scholar, 1982-87. Mem. ABA, Fed. Bar Assn., Am. Law Inst., State Bar of Ariz. (fee arbitration com. 1994—, chair 1997-2002, civil practice and procedure com. 1997—, vice chair 2001-2002, chair 2002—), Maricopa County Bar Assn. (task force on recruitment and retention of women and minorities 1999—, CLE com. 1995-99, barristers ball com. 1997-99), Ill. Bar Assn., D.C. Bar Assn., Iowa Bar Assn., Ariz. Bar Assn., Order of Coif. Republican. Methodist. Avocations: photography, travel, cooking.

THUMS, CHARLES WILLIAM, designer, consultant; b. Manitowoc, Wis., Sept. 5, 1945; s. Earl Oscar and Helen Margaret (Rusch) T. B. in Arch., Ariz. State U., 1972. Ptnr., Grafic, Tempe, Ariz., 1967-70; founder, prin. I-Squared Environ. Cons., Tempe, Ariz., 1970-78; designer and cons. design morphology, procedural programming and algorithms, 1978—. Author: (with Jonathan Craig Thums) Tempe's Grand Hotel, 1973, The Rossen House, 1975; (with Daniel Peter Aiello) Shelter and Culture, 1976; contbg. author: Tombstone Planning Guide, 5 vols., 1974. Office: PO Box 3126 Tempe AZ 85280-3126

THUNE, JOHN RANDOLPH, senator; b. Murdo, SD, Jan. 7, 1961; m. Kimberley Jo Weems, 1984; children: Brittany, Larissa. BBA, Biola U., Calif., 1983; MBA, U. SD, 1984. Legis. asst. to Senator James Abdnor US Senate, 1985-87; dep. staff dir. to the ranking rep. Senate Small Bus. Com., 1987-89; exec. dir. South Dakota Rep. Party, 1989-91; dir. railroad divsn. State of SD, 1991-93; exec. dir. SD Mcpl. League, 1993-96; founder The Thune Group LLC; mem. US Ho. Reps. from SD, 1997—2003; US Senator from SD, 2005—. Mem. com. armed services US Senate, com. environment and public works, com. small bus. and entrepreneurship, com. veterans affairs. Republican. Protestant. Avocations: basketball, pheasant hunting. Office: US Senate 383 Russell Senate Office Bldg Washington DC 20510 also: District Office 320 North Main Ave Sioux Falls SD 57104-6056 Office Phone: 202-224-2321, 605-334-9596. Office Fax: 202-228-5429, 605-334-2591. *

THURBER, PETER PALMS, lawyer; b. Detroit, Mar. 23, 1928; s. Cleveland and Marie Louise (Palms) T.; m. Ellen Bodley Stites, Apr. 16, 1955; children: Edith Bodley, Jane Chenoweth, Thomas, Sarah Bartlett. BA, Williams Coll., 1950; JD, Harvard U., 1953. Bar: Mich., 1954. With Miller, Canfield, Paddock and Stone, Detroit, 1953-93, of counsel, 1994—. Trustee McGregor Fund, Detroit, 1979-2003. Bd. dirs. Detroit Symphony Orch., Inc., 1974-93; trustee Community Found. for Southeastern Mich., 1990-2000, Coun. Mich. Founds., 1991-2000. With U.S. Army, 1953-55. Fellow Am. Bar Found.; mem. Clubs: Country of Detroit (Grosse Pointe Farms, Mich.). Roman Catholic. Avocations: reading, travel, sports. Home: 28 Provencal Rd Grosse Pointe Farms MI 48236-3038

THURBER, SHARON LEE, elementary resource educator; d. Donald Lee and Alka Mae Shears; m. Donald Lee Thurber, Mar. 30, 1983. BE, Ind. State U., Terre Haute, 1971; MEd, Ind. U., Bloomington, 1976. Cert. in tchg. Alaska, Ind., Tex., Fla. Elem. tchr. grade 3 Martinsville Ind. Sch. Dist., 1971—81; elem. tchr. grade 6 Galena Pk. Sch. Dist., Houston, 1981—82; elem. tchr. grades 1 and 2 Burton Ind. Sch. Dist., Tex., 1982—84; elem. tchr. grades 4-6 Archer City Ind. Sch. Dist., Tex., 1984—88; elem. resource tchr. South Elem. Sch., Okeechobee, Fla., 1988—89, Ocala Springs Elem. Sch., Fla., 1989—90, Russian Jack Elem. Sch., Anchorage, 1991—. Named Highly Qualified Tchr., Anchorage Sch. Dist., 2004; named to Career Ladder Excellent Tchrs. Tex., 1984—88. Mem.: NEA, Educators Social Responsibility, Anchorage Edn. Assn. (bldg. rep. 1994—96). Office: Russian Jack Elem Sch 4420 E 20th Ave Anchorage AK 99508 Office Phone: 907-742-1300. Business E-Mail: thurb2r_sharon@asdk12.org.

THURM, DAVID AARON, lawyer, publishing executive; b. Winslow, Ariz., Dec. 5, 1953; s. Richard Henry and Evelyn Joyce (Boches) T.; m. Andrea Granoff, Mar. 29, 1981; children: Amanda Margot, Matthew Charles, James Richard. AB, Harvard U., 1975; JD, NYU, 1978. Bar: NY 1979, US Dist. Ct. (So. and Ea. Dists.) NY 1979. Assoc. Rogers & Wells, NYC, 1978-81; atty. The NY Times Co., NYC, 1982-87, sr. atty., 1988-89, dir. adminstrn., 1988—90, exec. dir. project devel., 1991—95, v.p. prodn., 1995—99; v.p. real estate develop. The NY Times Co. and NY Times, NYC, 2000—, chief information officer, 2004—; COO NY Times Digital, NYC, 1999—2000. Home: 10 Sherman Ave Bronxville NY 10708-4219 Office: The New York Times Co 229 W 43rd St New York NY 10036-3959

THURMAN, ANDREW EDWARD, lawyer; b. Raleigh, NC, May 11, 1954; s. William Gentry and Peggy Lou (Brown) T.; m. Patricia Thurman, May 19, 1979 (dec. 1989); children: Gentry Brown, Harrison Beauchamp, Andrew Guilford; m. Tracy Fletcher, Nov. 16, 1991; 1 child, Spencer Lee. BA, Columbia U., 1976; JD, Coll. William and Mary, 1979; MPH, U. Okla., 1984. Bar: Va. 1979, Okla. 1980, US Ct. Appeals (10th cir.) 1981, US Supreme Ct. 1985, Pa. 1988. Staff atty. Dept. of Human Svcs., Oklahoma City, 1979—80; counsel State of Okla. Tchg. Hosps., Oklahoma City, 1980—84; mem. Miller, Dollarhide, Dawson & Shaw, Oklahoma City, 1984—87; ptnr. Berkman, Ruslander, Pohl, Lieber & Engel, Pitts., 1988—89; of counsel Buchanan Ingersoll, Pitts., 1989; sr. v.p. and gen. counsel Forbes Health Sys., Pitts., 1989—96; sr. counsel Allegheny Health Edn. & Rsch. Found., Pitts., 1997—98; dep. gen. counsel Allegheny U. Hosps. West, 1998—99; asst. gen. counsel We. Pa. Allegheny Health Sys., 1999—2002; assoc. prof. Carnegie-Mellon U., 2000—; pvt. practice, 2002—; assoc. prof. U. Pitts., 2003—, assoc. dir. consortium ethics program, 2004—; asst. prof. Am. U. Caribbean, 2003—06. Pres. Coun. Neighborhood Assns., Oklahoma City, 1984, Lincoln Terr. Neighborhood Assn., Oklahoma City, 1984; trustee Rader Trust, Oklahoma City, 1980—; treas. Bd. dirs. State Okla. Tchg. Hosps. Found., Oklahoma City, 1984-87, Newman Meml. Hosp., 1983-87, Willowview Hosp., Spencer, Okla., 1985-87, Allegheny U. Med. Ctrs., Allegheny U. Med. Ctr./Cannonsburg Ambulance Svc., 1997—, Allegheny U. Hosps. West, 1998—, Diversified Health Group, 1998-99, Allegheny Med. Practices Network, 1999—, Allegheny Speciality Practice Network, 1999—; chair Hosp. Coun. Western Pa. Ethics Task Force, 1993-2000. Fellow Am. Health Lawyers Assn.; mem. St. Anthony Hall Club NYC (pres. 1976), Pitts. Athletic Assn. Democrat. Presbyterian. Avocation: reading detective novels. Home: 910 N Megly Ave Pittsburgh PA 15206 Office: 1151 Freeport Rd # 391 Pittsburgh PA 15238 Office Phone: 412-567-2106. E-mail: andy@thurmanhealthlaw.com, andy@thurmans.net.

THURMAN, CYNTHIA DENISE, human services administrator; b. Ft. Myers, Fla., Mar. 14, 1970; children: Asia Naikee Garcia, Jai'ya Ja'V-ae Armani. Grad. high sch. Residential care coord. Sandy Pk. Redevelopment Ctr., North Fort Myers, Fla., 2001—; human services worker Gulf Coast Ctr., Ft. Myers, 2003—. Author: (poems) Soon. Recipient Shakespare Trophy of Excellence, Famous Poets Soc., 2004. Home: 4926 Gary Dr Fort Myers FL 33905 Office: Gulf Coast Center 5820 Buckingham Rd Fort Myers FL 33905 Office Phone: 239-694-2151 226. Personal E-mail: cind33905@aol.com.

THURMAN, ROBERT A.F., theology studies educator, philosopher; m. Nena von Schlebrugge. BA, MA, PhD, Harvard Univ. Co-founder Am. Inst. Buddhist Studies, 1973—; founder Tibet House, NY, 1987—; scholar, activist, chair religion dept. Columbia U., NYC, 1988—, prof. religion dept., now Jey Tsong Kappa Prof., Indo-Tibetan Studies. Author: The Central Philosophy of Tibet, 1991, Inner Revolution, 1999, Anger, the Seven Deadly Sins, 2004, Infinite Life: Seven Virtues for Living Well, 2004, The Jewel Tree of Tibet: The Enlightenment Engine of Tibetan Buddhism, 2005. Named One of the Most Influential Americans, Time Mag., NY Influentials, NY Mag., 2006. Buddhist. Office: Rm 203 80 Claremont Columbia U New York NY 10027-7003 Office Phone: 212-851-4133. E-mail: tbt7@columbia.edu. *

THURMAN, ROBERT KENNETH, retired military officer; b. Cashmere, Wash., July 9, 1914; s. Robert LeRoy and Lucille May Thurman; m. Mary Frederick Steber, Jan. 3, 1997 (dec.); children: Julie Goss, Bill Steber, Michael Steber 1 stepchild, Mark Steber; m. Vera Mary Marotta, Nov. 13, 1994; 1 adopted child, Robert LeRoy 1 child, Frank J. (dec.). With USN, 1927—35, comdr., 1941—63, Salvage Diving Sch., Bayonne, NJ, 1954—57; sailor Second Mate Merchant Marine, 1935—41; ops. mgr. Merret, Chapman and Scott, NYC, 1963—95. Operational boss Antarctic Operation, 1960—63. Master: Watchmaker Riverside Lodge, Aaron Lodge; mem.: Sabbar Shriners (noble 2003—06), Wally Byam Caravan Club Internat. Republican. Roman Catholic. Avocations: amateur radio, travel. Home: 1008 E Simmons St Tucson AZ 85719

THURMAN, UMA KARUNA, actress; b. Boston, Apr. 29, 1970; d. Robert and Nena (von Schlebrugge) T.; m. Gary Oldman, Oct. 1990 (div. 1992); m. Ethan Hawke, May 1, 1998 (div. July 20, 2004); children: Maya Ray, Roan. Spokesperson Lancome cosmetics, 2000. Appeared in films Kaze no tani no Naushika, 1984, Kiss Daddy Good Night, 1988, Johnny Be Good, 1988, Dangerous Liaisons, 1988, The Adventures of Baron Munchausen, 1988, Where the Heart Is, 1990, Henry and June, 1990, Final Analysis, 1992, Jennifer Eight, 1992, Mad Dog and Glory, 1993, Even Cowgirls Get the Blues, 1993, Pulp Fiction, 1994 (Acad. award nom. Best Supporting Actress), A Month By the Lake, 1995, The Truth About Cats and Dogs, 1996, Beautiful Girls, 1996, Batman & Robin, 1997, Gattaca, 1997, Avengers, 1998, Les Miserables, 1998, Vatel, 1999, Sweet and Lowdown, 1999, Vatel, 2000, Tape, 2001, Chelsea Walls, 2001, Kill Bill: Volume 1, 2003, Paycheck, 2003, Kill Bill: Volume 2, 2004, Be Cool, 2005, Prime, 2005, The Producers, 2005, My Super Ex-Girlfriend, 2006; TV movies include Robin Hood, 1991, Duke of Groove, 1996, The Golden Bowl, 2000, Hysterical Blindness, 2002 (also exec. prodr., Golden Globe for Best Performance by an Actress). Bd. dirs. Room to Grow. Named a knight in the Order of Arts & Letters, France, 2006. Office: Creative Artists Agy care Brian Lourd 9830 Wilshire Blvd Beverly Hills CA 90212-1804

THURMOND, GEORGE MURAT, judge; b. Del Rio, Tex., Oct. 22, 1930; s. Roger H. and Day (Hamilton) T.; m. Elsiejean Davis, June 27, 1959; children: Carolyn Day, Georganna, Sarah Gail. BA, U. of the South, 1952; JD, U. Tex., 1955. Bar: Tex. 1955. Ptnr. Montague & Thurmond, Del Rio, 1955-69; judge Tex. Dist. Ct. (63rd dist.), Del Rio, 1970-2000, sr. judge, 2000—. Presiding judge 6th Adminstrv. Region, Del Rio, 1983-87; chmn. jud. sect. State Bar Tex., 1988-89. Staff: U. Tex. Law Review, 1955. Rep. Tex. Ho. of Reps., 1955-58. Mem.: ABA, Fifth US Ct. Appeals, Tex. Bar Assn. Republican. Anglican. Avocations: exercise, traditional jazz, model railroading. Office Phone: 830-775-3710. Business E-Mail: gthurmand@stx.rr.com.

THURMOND, J. STROM, JR., lawyer, former prosecutor; b. SC, Oct. 18, 1972; s. Strom and Nancy Thurmond; m. Heather Holland, 1998; 1 child, Strom III. BA in English, U. S.C., 1995, grad. in Law, 1998. Bar: S.C. Ptnr. Strom, Young & Thurmond, LLP, Columbia, SC, 1998—99; asst. solicitor S.C. 2d Jud. Cir., 1999—2001; U.S. atty. Dist. SC US Dept. Justice, 2001—05; ptnr. Smith, Massey, Brodie, and Thurmond LLP, 2005—. Chmn. dist. law enforcement coordinating com. Dist. S.C., mem. atty. gen.'s adv. coun. violent crime subcom.

THURMOND, JOHN PETER, II, bank executive, rancher, archaeologist; b. Elk City, Okla., Apr. 22, 1955; s. Arthur Leslie and Dorothea Jean (Lee) Thurmond; m. Susan Ide Smith, June 7, 1979; children: Katherine Anne, Allison Lee, Patrick Andrew. BA, U. Tex., 1976, MA, 1979. Pres., chmn. First Nat. Bank Leedey, Okla., 1984-92, Leedey Bancorporation, Inc., 1984-92, Thurmond Ranch, Inc., Cheyenne, Okla., 1982—. Pres., chmn. Dempsey Divide Rsch. Found., Inc., 2001—05; vis. rsch. assoc. Sam Noble Okla. Mus. Natural History, U. Okla., 2001—05; vice chmn. 1st Nat. Bank & Trust Co., Elk City, 1992—. Author: Archeology of the Cypress Basin, NE Texas, 1981, Late Paleoindian Utilization of the Dempsey Divide, 1990. EMT, sec. Leedey Ambulance Svc., Inc., 1981—88. Recipient Hist. Preservation award, Okla. Hist. Soc., 1991, 1997, Goodyear Conservationist award, 2000. Mem.: Okla. Hist. Soc. (dir. we. chpt. 2004—), Okla. Cattlemen's Assn., Geol. Soc. Am., Am. Quaternary Assn., Plains Anthrop. Soc., Tex. Archeol. Soc., Okla. Anthrop. Soc. (sec., treas. 1988—2006, Disting. Svc. award 1999), Cum Laude Soc., Phi Beta Kappa, Phi Kappa Phi. Personal E-mail: dempseydiv@aol.com.

THURSBY, JERRY GILBERT, economics professor, consultant, department chairman; b. Camp Le Jeune, NC, Aug. 6, 1947; s. Gilbert Earl and Mary Kathleen (Bailey) T.; m. Marie Sloan Currie, Mar. 11, 1972; children: James, Mary. AB, U. N.C., 1969, PhD, 1975. Asst. prof. Syracuse (N.Y.) U., 1975-78; from asst. to assoc. prof. Ohio State U., Columbus, 1978-88; prof. Purdue U., West Lafayette, Ind., 1988-01; prof. econs., chmn. dept. Emory U., Atlanta, 2001—, now Goodrich C. White prof. econs. Contbr. articles to profl. jours. With U.S. Army, 1969-71. Home: 910 Springdale Rd NE Atlanta GA 30306-4620 Office: Emory U Dept Econs Rich Meml Bldg Atlanta GA 30322 Office Phone: 404-712-8688. Business E-Mail: jthursb@emory.edu.

THURSFIELD, FRED FALCONER, II, foundation administrator; b. Rochester, NY, Mar. 13, 1950; s. Richard Emmons and Alice (Hedges) T.; m. Kathi Suzanne Heathcote, Jan. 22, 1972 (div. Dec. 1996); children: Amy Christine Humphreys, Jennifer Anne Swain; m. Sara Garland Barr, Sept. 2, 1997; 1 stepchild, Shelby Blair Oktar. BA, U. Md., 1972. Cert. fund raising exec. Sales rep. Life of Va. Ins. Co., 1972-78; dir. alumni fund Johns Hopkins Med. Instns., Balt., 1978-82; major gift officer, dir. acad. programs Duke U., Durham, NC, 1982-92, asst. dir. devel. Sch. Environ, 1992-94; dir. ann. and capital programs Geisinger Found., Danville, Pa., 1994-95; assoc. dir. devel. Washington Hosp. Ctr. Found., 1995-97; exec. dir. Peninsula Regional Found., Salisbury, Md., 1997—2001, Health First Found., Melbourne, Fla., 2001—04, Upper Chesapeake Health Found., Inc., 2004—. Mem. coun. Wildlife Preservation Trust, Internat., 1994-99; bd. dirs. Harford County Econ. Devel., 2005—, bd. mem. Susquehanna Workforce Network, 2007—. Mem.: Harford County C. of C. (bd. mem. 2004—), Assn. Fund Raising Profls., Assn. Healthcare Philanthropy (regional sec. treas. 1998—99, chair elect 1999—2000, chair 2000—01, mem. Brevard County Zoo bd. 2002—04), U. Md. Alumni Assn. and Terrapin Club, Rotary. Republican. Methodist. Avocations: golf, reading, philately, art. Home: 1014 Hazel Ln Bel Air MD 21014 Office: 520 Upper Chesapeake Dr Bel Air MD 21014 Office Phone: 443-643-3460. Personal E-mail: ffalconert@aol.com.

THURSTON, BONNIE BOWMAN, religious studies educator, minister, poet; b. Bluefield, W.Va., Oct. 5, 1952; d. Ernest Venoy and Eleanor Sabina (King) Bowman; m. Burton Bradford Thurston, May 29, 1980 (dec. Nov. 1990). BA summa cum laude, Bethany Coll., 1974; MA, U. Va., 1975, PhD, 1979; postgrad., Harvard Div. Sch., 1983, Eberhard Karls U., Germany, 1983—84, Ecole Biblique, Jerusalem, 1993. Ordained to ministry Disciples of Christ Ch., 1984. Instr., asst. dean U. Va., Charlottesville, 1979—80; adj. prof. Wheeling Coll. (now Wheeling Jesuit U.), W.Va., 1980—81, assoc. prof., chair dept. theology, 1985—95; asst. prof. Bethany Coll., W.Va., 1981—83; assoc. prof. N.T. Pitts. Theol. Sem., 1995—99, William F. Orr prof., chair, 1999—2002. Vis. scholar Harvard U. Div. Sch., Cambridge, Mass., 1983; tutor Inst. Study of Christian Origins, Tubingen, Germany, 1983—85. Author: (books) The Widows, 1989, Wait Here and Watch, 1989, Spiritual Life in the Early Church, 1993, Women in the NT, 1998, To Everything a Season, 1999, Preaching Mark, 2002, Philippians and Philemon, 2005, (books of poetry) The Heart's Land, 2001, Hints and Glimpses, 2004; contbr. articles to profl. jours., poetry to jours. Mem.: Soc. for the Study of Christian Spirituality, Disciples Hist. Soc., Soc. for Buddhist-Christian Studies, Internat. Thomas Merton Soc., Soc. Bibl. Lit., Cath. Bibl. Assn. Avocations: gardening, music, cooking. Office: PO Box 2258 Wheeling WV 26003

THURSTON, DONALD ALLEN, broadcast executive; b. Gloucester, Mass., Apr. 2, 1930; s. Joseph Allen and Helen Ruth (Leach) T.; m. Oralie Alice Lane, Sept. 9, 1951; children: Corydon Leach, Carolie Lane. Grad., Mass. Radio and Telegraph, 1949; HHD (hon.), North Adams State Coll., Mass., 1977; LHD (hon.), Emerson Coll., 1995. Announcer, engr. Sta. WTWN, St. Johnsbury, Vt., 1949-52; v.p., gen. mgr. Sta. WIKE, Newport, Vt., 1952-60; v.p., treas., gen. mgr. Sta. WMNB, North Adams, 1960-66; pres., treas. Berkshire Broadcasting Co., Inc., North Adams, 1966—2003. Bd. dirs. Broadcast Capital Fund, Inc., 1980-96, chmn. bd., 1981-89; bd. dirs. Broadcast Music, Inc., N.Y.C., 1990-2005, chmn. bd., 1994-97. Pres. No. Berkshire Indsl. Devel. Corp., 1965-67; commr. Mass. Cmty. Antenna TV Commn., 1972-74; trustee Mass. Coll. Liberal Arts, 1991-2001, vice chmn. bd. trustees, 1993-96, chmn., 1996-2001. Recipient Laymen's award Vt. Tchrs. Assn., 1958; Laymen's award Mass. Tchrs. Assn., 1962; Abe Lincoln Merit award So. Baptist Radio and TV Commn., 1975; named Man of Yr. Vt. Assn. Broadcasters, 1978 Mem. North Adams C. of C. (Hayden award 1967, pres. 1964-67), Nat. Assn. Broadcasters (dir. 1965-69, 73-77, chmn. radio 1976-77, chmn. bd., chmn. exec. com. 1977-79, Disting. Svc. award 1980), Mass. Broadcasters Assn. (pres. 1964, Disting. Svc. award 1964, 71, 78), Taconic Golf Club (Williamston, Mass.; bd. dirs. 1975-89). Republican. Methodist. Office: 61 Main St PO Box 386 North Adams MA 01247-0386 *My goals have been to better my community, profession and life in general because I was a positive participant, and to provide independence, a sense of responsibility and a love of humanity for my family.*

THURSTON, GEORGE BUTTE, mechanical and biomedical engineering educator; b. Austin, Tex., Oct. 8, 1924; s. Rudolph D. and Olivia Ruth (Lester) T.; m. Carol A. McWharter, Apr. 5, 1947; children— John Douglas, Mary Elizabeth. BS, U. Tex., Austin, 1944, MA, 1948, PhD, 1952. Registered profl. engr., Tex. Supr. hydroacoustics sect. Def. Rsch. Lab., U. Tex., Austin, 1949-52; asst. prof. physics U. Wyo., Laramie, 1952-53, U. Ark., Fayetteville, 1953-54; physicist Naval Ordnance Test Sta., Inyokern, Calif., 1954-55; assoc. prof. Okla. State U., Stillwater, 1954-59; rsch. physicist U. Mich., Ann Arbor, 1958-59; prof. Okla. State U., 1959-68; vis. scientist Centre de Recherche sur les Macromolecules, Strasbourg, France, 1963-64; prof. mech. engring. and biomed. engring. U. Tex., Austin, 1968—; pres. Vilastic Scientific, Inc. Vis. prof. Helmholtz Inst. fur Biomedizinische Technik, Aachen, West Germany, 1975-76; cons. for govt., industry. Contbr. articles to profl. jours. Recipient Brown U. Calculus prize, 1942; Alexander von Humboldt Found. Sr. U.S. Scientist award, 1975; NSF faculty fellow, 1963-64; numerous grants. Fellow Am.

Phys. Soc., Acoustical Soc. Am.; mem. ASME, Soc. Rheology, Internat. Soc. Biorheology, Brit. Soc. Rheology, Sigma Xi, Sigma Pi Sigma. Home: 1000 Madrone Rd Austin TX 78746-4320 Office: U Tex Dept Mech Engring Austin TX 78712

THURSTON, SALLY A., lawyer; b. Glens Falls, NY, 1961; BS, Cornell U., 1983; JD, Harvard U., 1986. Bar: N.Y. 1987. Ptnr. Skadden, Arps, Slate, Meagher & Flom, NYC; v.p., tax counsel NBC, Inc., NYC, 1994—. Office: Skadden Arps Slate Meagher & Flom LLP 4 Times Sq New York NY 10036-6595 Business E-Mail: sthursto@skadden.com.

THURSTON, STEPHEN JOHN, pastor; b. Chgo., July 20, 1952; s. John Lee and Ruth (Hall) T.; m. Joyce DeVonne Hand, June 18, 1977; children: Stephen John II, Nicole D'Vaugh, Teniece Rael, Christian Avery Elijah. BA in Religion, Bishop Coll., 1975; Hon. degree, Chgo. Baptist Inst., 1986. Co-pastor New Covenant Missionary Bapt. Ch., Chgo., 1975-79, pastor, 1979—; pres. National Baptist Convention, Inc. Third v.p. Nat. Bapt. Conv. Am., mem. exec. com. Christian Edn. Congress; pres. Ill. Nat. Bapt. State Conv.; mem. Christian Fellowship Dist. Assn.; lectr. various orgns.; instr. New Covenant Bapt. Ch., Fellowship Bapt. Ch. Co-chmn. religious affairs div. People United to Save Humanity (PUSH); bd. dirs. nat. alumni assn. Bishop Coll.; active NAACP; trustee, fin. chmn. Chgo. Bapt. Inst. Named one of 100 Most Influential Black Americans, Ebony mag., 2006. Mem. Broadcast Ministers Alliance, Bapt. Ministers Conf. Chgo. (Ministerial Pioneer award). Clubs: Bishop Coll. (Chgo.). Office: New Cov Miss Baptist Church 740 E 77th St Chicago IL 60619-2553

THURSWELL, GERALD ELLIOTT, lawyer; b. Detroit, Feb. 4, 1944; s. Harry and Lilyan (Zeitlin) T.; m. Lynn Satovsky, Sept. 17, 1967 (div. Aug. 1978); children: Jennifer, Lawrence; m. Judith Linda Bendix, Sept. 2, 1978 (div. May 1999); chldren: Jeremy, Lindsey. LLB with distinction, Wayne State U., 1967. Bar: Mich. 1968, N.Y. 1984, D.C. 1985, Colo. 1990, Ill. 1992, U.S. Dist. Ct. (ea. dist.) Mich. 1968, U.S. Ct. Appeals (6th cir.) 1968, U.S. Supreme Ct. 1994, U.S. Dist. Ct. (western dist.) Mich. 2004. Student asst. to U.S. Atty. Eas. Dist. Mich., Detroit, 1966; assoc. Zwerdling, Miller, Klimist & Maurer, Detroit, 1967-68; st. prnt. The Thurswell Law Firm, Southfield, Mich. Arbitrator Am. Arbitration Assn., Detroit, 1969—; mediator Wayne County Cir. Ct., Mich., 1983—, Oakland County Cir. Ct. Mich., 1984—, also facilitator, 1991; twp. atty. Royal Oak Twp., Mich., 1982—; lectr. Oakland County Bar Assn. People's Law Sch., 1988. Pres. Powder Horn Estates Subdivsn. Assn., West Bloomfield, Mich., 1975, United Fund, West Bloomfield, 1976. Arthur F. Lederly scholar Wayne State U. Law Sch., 1965; Wayne State U. Law Sch. grad. profl. scholar, 1965, 66. Mem. ATLA (treas. Detroit met. chpt. 1986-87, v.p. 1989-90, pres. 1991-93), Mich. Bar Assn. (investigator/arbitrator grievance bd., atty. discipline bd., chmn. hearing panel), Mich. Trial Lawyers Assn. (legis. com. on govtl. immunity 1984, exec. bd. 2004-, PAC 2004), Detroit Bar Assn. (past panel pub. adv. com. jud. candidates), Oakland County Bar Assn. Office: The Thurswell Law Firm 1000 Town Ctr Ste 500 Southfield MI 48075-1221 Office Phone: 248-354-2222.

THWAITES, CHRISTIAN WILLIAM, investment company executive; b. Woking, Eng., Dec. 6, 1957; s. Peter Thwaites and Ellen Theresa King; children: Erik, Matthew. BA with honors, U. London, 1981; MBA, Harvard U., Cambridge, Mass., 1988. Fund mgr. Samuel Mortgage, London, 1981—86; mktg. exec. Aetna Inc., Hartford, Conn., 1988—96; chief mktg. officer Am. Skandia, Shelton, Conn., 1996—2001; pres., CEO Skandia Global Funds, London, 2001—04, Sentinal Asset Mgmt., Montpellier, Vt., 2005—. Dir. Sentinel Funds, Boston, 2005—. Mem.: Soc. Investment Analysts. Office: Sentinel Asset Mgmt 1national Life Dr Montpelier VT 05604

THYDEN, JAMES ESKEL, diplomat, educator, lecturer; b. LA, Apr. 10, 1939; s. Eskel A. and Mildred Aileene (Rock) T.; m. Patricia Irene Kelsey, Dec. 15, 1959; children: Teresa Lynn, Janice Kay, James Blaine. BA in Biology, Pepperdine U., 1961; MA in Scandinavian Area Studies, U. Wash., 1992. Tchr. Gompers Jr. High Sch., LA, 1962-64; fgn. svc. officer U.S. Dept. State, Washington, 1964-90; rschr. U. Wash., Seattle, 1992-93; exec. dir. Seattle chpt. UN Assn., 1993-96; affiliat prof. internat. studies Jackson Sch. U. Wash., 2006—. Travel lectr. Cunard Lines' Royal Viking Sun, 1995, and Royal Caribbean's Splendour of the Seas, 1997. Editor govt. report, ann. human rights reports, 1983-86; author, editor in-house govt. reports, documents. Dir. Office of Human Rights, 1983-86; counselor Embassy for Polit. Affairs, Am. Embassy, Oslo, Norway, 1986-90. Named to Outstanding Young Men Am., 1969, Alumnus of Yr., Pepperdine U., 1984. Mem.: Soc. Advancement of Scandinavian Studies, World Affairs Coun. Seattle, Am. Fgn. Svc. Assn. Avocations: travel, reading. Home: 5631 153rd Pl SW Edmonds WA 98026-4239

T.I., See **HARRIS, CLIFFORD JR.**

TIAHRT, TODD (W. TODD TIAHRT), congressman, former state senator; b. Vermillion, SD, June 15, 1951; s. Wilbur E. and Sara Ella Marcine (Steele) T.; m. Vicki Lyn Holland, Aug. 14, 1976; children: Jessica, John, Luke. Student, SD Sch. Mines & Tech., Rapid City, 1969-72; BA, Evangel Coll., 1975; MBA, S.W. Mo. State U., 1989. Property estimator Crawford & Co., Springfield, Mo., 1975-78; project engr. Zenith Electronics, Springfield, 1978-81; cost engr. Boeing, Wichita, Kans., 1981-94, proposal mgr., 1991-94; state senator State of Kans., Topeka, 1993—95; mem. US Congress from 4th Kans. dist., Washington, 1995—; mem. appropriations com., 1997—. Chmn. 4th dist. Rep. party, 1990-92; exec. com. Kans. Rep. party, 1990-92, nat. security com., sci. com. Mem. Pachyderm (bd. dirs. 1991-92), Delta Sigma Phi. Republican. Office: US Ho Reps 2441 Rayburn Ho Office Bldg Washington DC 20515-1604 *

TIAN, FEI-RAN, mathematician, educator; BS in Math., Jinan U., China, 1984; MS in Math., Clarkson U., 1987; PhD in Math., Courant Inst., 1991. Assoc. prof. math. Ohio State U., 2002—; Dicikson instr. math. U. Chgo., 1991—93; postdoctoral staff MSRI, 1993—94; vis. mem. Courant Inst., 1994—95; asst. prof. math. Ohio State U., 1995—2002, assoc. prof. math., 2002—. Fellow, John Simon Guggenheim Meml. Found., 2003. Office: Ohio State Univ Dept Math 231 W 18th Ave Columbus OH 43210

TIAN, HANQIN, ecologist, educator; b. Jinyun, China, May 7, 1962; arrived in USA, 1991, permanent resident, 2006; s. Chen Tian and QiaoRui Chen; m. Shufen Pan, Dec. 14, 1988; children: Tina, Alex. BS, Zhejiang U., Hangzhou, China, 1982; MS, Chinese Acad. Agrl. Scis., Beijing, China, 1986; PhD, SUNY, Syracuse, 1996. Rsch. asst. Zhejiang Jinyun Inst. Agrl. Scis., Jinyun, 1982—83; asst. prof. China Nat. Rice Rsch. Inst., Hangzhou, 1986—88; rsch. asst. Beijing Forestry Inst., 1988—91; postdoctoral scientist Marine Biol. Lab., Woods Hole, Mass., 1995—98, staff scientist, 1998—2001; assoc. prof. The U. Kans., Lawrence, Kans., 2001—03; prof. Auburn U., Ala., 2003—. Mem.: Am. Assn. for Advancement Sci., Am. Geophysical Union, Ecological Soc. Am. Office: Auburn Univ 602 Duncan Dr Auburn AL 36849 Home Phone: 334-821-7249; Office Phone: 334-844-1059. Office Fax: 334-844-1084. Business E-Mail: tianhan@auburn.edu.

TIAN, HONGQI, application developer, researcher; arrived in U.S., 2001; s. Tao Tian and Fengkun Li; m. Yan Li; children: Annie Miao, Tony Run. BS, Huazhong U. Sci. Tech., Wuhan, 1982, Master, 1984, PhD, 1989. Rschr. Chiba (Japan) U., 1991—94; sr. rsch. engr. Seiko Instruments Inc., Chiba, 1994—96; sr. software engr. Digital Dispatch Sys., Richmond, BC, Canada, 1997—2000, Digital Control Inc., Kent, Wash., 2001—. Author: (book) Sliding Mode Control, 1994. Mem.: NY Acad. Sci. Achievements include patents for sliding mode control of magnetic bearing sys. Home: 14245 60th St SE Bellevue WA 98006 Personal E-mail: hongqi_tian@hotmail.com.

TIAN, LI, computer company executive, educator; arrived in U.S., 1996; m. Min Shi, Apr. 20, 2001. B in Engring., Tsinghua U., Beijing, 1993; M in Engring., Beijing U. Aeronautics & Astronautics, 1996; MS in Info. Sys., George Mason U., 1999; MBA, U. Chgo., 2006—. Cert. sys. engr., database adminstr., solution developer Microsoft; project mgmt. profl. Project Mgmt. Inst. Gen. mgr. multimedia tech. Beijing Feitian Inst. New Tech., 1993—96; software engr. GTSI Corp., Chantilly, Va., 1998; project cons. MCI Comm. Corp., Pentagon City, Va., 1998; supr. systems/infrastructure Airlines Reporting Corp., Arlington, Va., 1998—; faculty U. Phoenix, 2002—; founder, CEO Dcom Solutions, Llc, Fairfax, Va., 2001—. Industry advisor and virtual mentor Mgmt. Leadership Tomorrow, NYC, 2005—; dir. Internat. Rsch. Assn., Cambridge, Mass., 2005—; treas. Fairfax Ctr. Recreation Assn., Inc., 2005—; team leader beta program Microsoft, 2001—; v.p. project mgmt. Inst. Diversity SIG, Newtown Sq., Pa., 2005—. Vol. Ctr. Internat. Disaster Info., Arlington, 2003—; pres. Washington organizing com. U.S.-China People Friendship Assn., Fairfax, 2005—. Recipient Software Excellence award, 1996. Mem.: IEEE (sr.), Project Mgmt. Inst., Assn. Computing Machinery (Spl. Interest Group MIS), PA SQL Server, IEEE Control Sys. Soc. (sr.), IEEE Info. Theory Soc. (sr.), IEEE Engring. Mgmt. Soc. (sr.), IEEE Edn. Soc. (sr.), IEEE Computer Soc. (sr.), IEEE Comm. Soc. (sr.). Achievements include development of GTSI.COM, GTSIEXPRESS.COM and MCI ISC Online; C/C++ class libraries for modeling and operation of dimensions and tolerances; computer aided road design system; multimedia general information management software system. Personal E-mail: ltian01@gmail.com.

TIANO, ANTHONY STEVEN, television producer, publishing executive; b. Santa Fe, Mar. 27, 1941; s. Joseph A. and Marian (Adlesperger) T.; m. Kathleen O'Brien, Dec. 29, 1972; children: Mark A., A. Steven. BA, U. N.Mex., 1969, MA, 1971; LittD (hon.), Calif. Sch. Profl. Psychology, 1985. Dir. programming Sta. KNME-TV U. N.Mex., Albuquerque, 1968-72; sta. mgr. Sta. WHA-TV U. Wis., Madison, 1972-76; exec. dir. Sta. KETC-TV, St. Louis, 1976-78; pres., CEO KQED, Inc., San Francisco, 1978-93; chmn., CEO Santa Fe Ventures, Inc., San Francisco, 1993—2003; CEO Santa Fe Prodns., Inc., Albuquerque, 2003—. Vice-chair bd. dirs. Calif. Sch. Profl. Psychology, San Francisco, 1985-90. Mem. Nat. Assn. Pub. TV Stas. (vice chair bd. dirs. 1986).

TIANO, LINDA V., lawyer, insurance company executive; b. 1957; BA summa cum laude, U. Cin.; JD cum laude, Boston U. Assoc. Epstein Becker and Green, P.C., 1981—90, ptnr., stockholder, 1990—92; v.p. for legal and govt. affairs, gen counsel MVP Health Plan, 1992—95; sr. v.p., gen. counsel Empire BlueCross BlueShield, 1995—2002, WellChoice, Inc., NYC, 2002—05; v.p., dep. gen. counsel for Ea. region & nat. accounts WellPoint, Inc., Indpls., 2005—07; sr. v.p., gen. counsel, sec. Health Net, Inc., Woodland Hills, Calif., 2007—. Office: Health Net Inc 21650 Oxnard St Woodland Hills CA 91367 *

TIBBLE, DOUGLAS CLAIR, lawyer; b. Joliet, Ill., May 26, 1952; BA, DePaul U., 1974; JD, Syracuse U., 1977. Bar: Ill., US Dist. Ct. (no. dist.) Ill., US Ct. Appeals (7th cir.), US Supreme Ct. Ptnr. McDermott, Will & Emery, 1977—95, McBride, Baker & Coles, Oakbrook Terrace, Ill., 1996—2003, Brooks, Adams and Tarulis, Naperville, Ill., 2003—. Mem. ABA, DuPage County Bar Assn., Illinois State Bar Assn. Office: Brooks Adams and Tarulis 101 N Washington St Naperville IL 60540-4511 Office Phone: 630-355-2101. Business E-Mail: dtibble@naperville.com.

TIBBS, MARTHA JANE PULLEN, civic worker, retired social worker; b. Memphis, Feb. 12, 1932; d. John Thomas Jr. and Martha Frances (Gragg) Pullen; m. Eugene Edward Tibbs; children: Martha Katherine, Eugene Edward Jr. BSBA, U. Tenn., 1953; MA Edn., U. Memphis, 1958. Cert. tchr., social worker, Tenn. Tchr. Lausanne Sch., Memphis, 1954-55, Millington H.S., Memphis, 1955-56, Presbyn. Day Sch., Memphis, 1956-57, St. Mary's Episcopal Sch., Memphis, 1958-60; social worker Tenn. Dept. Pub. Welfare, Memphis, 1962-63. Author geneal. works. Mem. Memphis Vol. Svc. Bd., 1963-64; mem. Shelby County Hist. Comm., 1983-97, commr., 1983—; block worker Cancer, Kidney and Heart Fund, Memphis, 1984—; sec., treas. Eastland Presbyterian Ch. Mem.: DAR (past chpt. regent, sec.-treas. regents coun.), AAUW, NEA, Tenn. Geneal. Soc., Tenn. Tchrs. Assn., Colonial Dames of Am., Memphis Scottish Soc., Sovereign Colonial Soc. Ams. Royal Descent, Tenn. State Dames of Ct. of Honor (pres. 2003—05, historian, 1st v.p., nat. def. chmn.), Cleve. Med. Aux. (sec./treas.), West Tenn. Hist. Soc., Chicasaw Dist. DAR Sch. (Tenn. state vice chmn. DAR schs., parliamentarian Zachariah Davies chpt., chmn. Zachariah Davies chpt.), Nat. Registrar Daus. of Founders and Patriots Am. (past Tenn. state registrar 2006—, v.p. Tenn. chpt.), Tenn. State Registrar Founders and Patriots (pres. 2003—), Nat. Soc. Colonial Dames XVII Century (1st v.p., pres. 2003—, 2d v.p. past treas. Chucaqua chpt.), Nat. Soc. So. Dames Am. (historian 2001—02, sec. 2002—, past pres. Memphis chpt., past state pres.), Colonial Dames Am., Tenn. State DAR (transp. chmn. 2001—), Cleve. Jr. Aux., Colonial Order of Crown, Soc. Descendants of Knights Most Noble Order of Garter, Family of Bruce Soc., Planetgenet Soc., Am. Clan Donald Soc., Am. Clan Gregor Soc., Tenn. Soc. Pres. Founders and Patriots of Am., Nat. Soc. Magna Charta Dames and Barons (past state sec. 2000—02, past Magna Carta sec. West Tenn. chpt. 2001—02, treas. West Tenn. chpt. 2002—04), Cleve. Garden Club (past pres.), U. Club Memphis, Early Settlers Shelby County (registrar 1988, bd. dirs. 1992—, sec. 1998—, pres. 2002—), Nineteenth Century Club (newsletter editor 1985—88, sec. 1993—95, corr. sec. 1999—), Racquet Club, Cleve. Women's Club, Alpha Omega Pi. Republican. Presbyterian. Avocations: art, genealogy, computers, dance, tennis. Home: 2008 Massey Rd Memphis TN 38119-6404 Personal E-mail: mtptmem@aol.com.

TIBERI, PATRICK JOSEPH, congressman, former state legislator; b. Columbus, Ohio, Oct. 21, 1962; m. Denice Tiberi; 1 child. BA in Journalism, Ohio State U., 1985; HHD (hon.), Capital U., 2005. Realtor ReMax Achievers; asst. dist. mgr. Staff of US Rep. John Kasich; mem. Ohio State Ho. Reps. from Dist. 26, 1993—2001, majority leader; mem. ins. and vets. affairs coms. Ohio Ho. Reps.; mem. US Congress from 12th Ohio dist., 2001—, mem. ways and means com. Mem. adv. bd. Columbus chpt. ARC, Columbus Italian Cultural Ctr.; pres., co-founder Windsor Terrace Learning Ctr. Recipient Pres.'s award Northland Cmty. Coun., Vet. Admin Commendation award, Svc. award ARC, Watchdog of Treas. award United Conservatives of Ohio, Giving from the Heart award Alzheimer's Assn. Ctrl. Ohio Chpt. Mem. Sons of Italy. Republican. Roman Catholic. Office: 3000 Corporate Exchange Dr Ste 310 Columbus OH 43231-7689 Office Phone: 614-523-2555, 202-225-5355. Office Fax: 614-818-0887. *

TIBI, RIGOBERT, seismologist, researcher; MS in Geophysics, U. Mining and Tech., Freiburg, Germany, 1995; PhD in Geophysics, Free U. Berlin, 2000. Rsch. asst. GFZ Potsdam, 1997—2000; rsch. assoc. Wash. U., St. Louis, 2000—04, rsch. scientist, 2004—. Contbr. rsch. articles to profl. jours. Grantee, NSF, 2003—. Mem.: German Geophys. Soc., Am. Geophys. Union. Achievements include discovery of deep-faults interaction and deep earthquakes triggering; ground-breaking research on the origin of deep earthquakes, and the structure and sharpness of upper mantle seismic discontinuities near subduction zones. Avocation: soccer. Office: Washington Univ Dept Earth and Planetary Scis One Brookings Dr CB 1169 Saint Louis MO 63130 Office Phone: 314-935-7965. Business E-Mail: tibi@wustl.edu.

TIBURZI, PAUL A., lawyer; b. Balt., May 28, 1955; BA, Loyola Coll., 1977; JD with honors, Univ. Md., 1980. Bar: Md. 1980. Law clk. Chief Judge Harrison L. Winter, US Ct. Appeals 4th cir.; ptnr., mng. ptnr. Balt. office DLA Piper US LLP, Balt., chmn. state legis. and pub. policy practice group. Editor in chief Md. Law Rev., 1980; legis. counsel and rep. Md. Tort Reform Coalition, 1992—; mem. Coun. Mgmt. and Productivity; adminstrv. law expert, adv. bd. Rev. Md. Laws. Contbr. articles to profl. jours. Chmn. Md. C. of C. Task Force Md. Public Ethics Law, 0200—; mem. transition team Md. Gov. William Donald Schaefer, 1986; chmn. Commn. to Revise Md. Adminstrv. Procedure Act, 1991—92, Md. State Adv. Coun. Adminstrv. Hearings; mem. Md. Governor's Task Force Self-Insurance, 1987, Md. Governor's Task Force Animal Testing, 1989, Md. Governor's Task Force Procurement Law, 1995—96, Md. Governor's Task Force Regulatory Reform, 2000—01, Md. Gen. Assembly Code Revision Com. Public Ethics Law, 1995, Md. Gen. Assembly Code Revision Com. Pub. Svc. Commn. Law, 1998; bd. dir. Greater Balt. Com., 2006—; corp. sec. and chair governance com. Camden Yards Sports and Entertainment Com., Balt., 2006—. Named one of Balt.'s Legal Elite, Balt. SmartCEO mag., 2006, Best Lawyers in Am., 2006; recipient Leadership in Law award, The Daily Record, 2005. Mem.: Wranglers Law Club, Council on Mgmt. & Productivity, Order of the Coif. Office: DLA Piper US LLP 6225 Smith Ave Baltimore MD 21209-3600 Office Phone: 410-580-4273. Office Fax: 410-580-3001. Business E-Mail: paul.tiburzi@dlapiper.com.

TICE, BRADLEY SCOTT, humanities educator; b. Palo Alto, Calif., Oct. 6, 1959; s. Lilburn Trent and Paula Nanette (Osborne) T. AA, De Anza Coll., Cupertino, Calif., 1983, AA, 1995; student continuing edn. program, Stanford U., Calif., 1988, student continuing edn. program, 1991; AA in Liberal Arts, West Valley Coll., 2003; BA in History, San Jose State U., 1987; postgrad., San Francisco State U., 1991—94; PhD in Chemistry, Fairfax U., Baton Rouge, 1996; Diploma in Ayurvedic Medicine, The Ayurvedic Inst.; Diploma in Stress therapy, Internat. Yoga Sch.; LittD in Tchg., St. Clements Univ., The Carribean, 1998; PhD in Elec. Engring., Cambridge State U., 2001, Northwestern Internat. U., Denmark, 2003, PhD in Math., 2003, PhD in Telecomm., 2003, PhD (hon.) in Physics, 2003; M in Law, Northwestern Internat. U., 2003; JD, Northwestern Internat. U., Denmark, 2002; MBA, Suffield U., Twin Falls, Idaho, 2006, PhD in Molecular Biology, 2006. Cert. Cmty. Emergency Response Tng., Cupertino, Calif. Mem. staff Stanford Linear Accelerator Ctr., 1981-87, intern archives dept. Menlo Park, Calif., 1991; prof. Pacific Lang. Inst., Cupertino, Calif., 1992—; dir. rsch. Advanced Human Design, Cupertino, 1992—; CEO Tice Pharms., San Jose; intern Ames Rsch. Ctr. NASA, Moffett Field, Calif., 1997-98, mission specialist astronaut candidate, 2001—04; substitute instr. Palo Alto Unified Sch. Dist., Calif., 2001; assoc. Ames-NASA Rsch. Ctr., Moffett Field, Calif., 2003; instrnl. student asst. Calif. State U. Stanislaus, Turlock, 2004—05. Substitute libr. Robert Crown Law Libr. Stanford U., 1989; substitute instr. San Jose Unified Sch. Dist., 2002; adj. prof. Sch. Arts and Scis. Nat. U., San Jose, 2000—01; adj. prof. Nat. Hispanic U., San Jose, 2000—03, mem. faculty senate; grand awards judge engring. Intel Internat. Sci. and Engring. Fair, Louisville, 2002; mem. staff San Jose Giants Baseball Club, 2002; substitute tchr. Turlock Unified Sch. Dist., 2004—05; instrnl. student asst. Calif. State U., Turlock, 2005. Editor: Jour. Pacific Lang. Inst., 1995—96; mem. editl. bd. The Story of Life.; prodr.: (musical works) HillTop Records, Hollywood, Calif., 1995, 1996; contbr. articles to profl. jours. Troop libr. Boy Scouts Am., 1972—75; vol. De Young Mus., San Francisco, 1990, Mus. Modern Art, San Francisco, 1990, Calif. Acad. Scis., San Francisco, 1990, Nat. Steinbeck Ctr., Salinas, Calif.; vol. guide Monterey Bay Aquarium, 1990; elected mem. Cupertino Pub. Safety Commn., 2000—02; apptd. mem. Turlock City Arts Commn., 2004—06; candidate Office of Pres. San Jose State U., 2004; res. firefighter candidate Turlock Fire Dept., 2006; candidate for bd. trustees Foothill-De Anza CC Dist., Los Altos Hills, Calif., 2002; Democratic candidate Office of the Gov. of State of Calif., 2003 Spl. Elections; candidate Civil Grand Jury Stanislaus County, 2007—; candidate select Civil Grand Jury; grand awards judge in chemistry Intel Internat. Sci. and Engring. Fair, San Jose, 2001; investor in preservation Computer History Mus., Moffett Field, Calif., 2001. Recipient Pres.'s award Nat. Author's Registry, 1996, editor's choice award (3), The Nat. Libr. of Poetry, 1995, (2), 1996, Cert. Merit for essay, Pharmacia Biotech and Sci. prize for young scientists, 1997, Commemorative Medal Honor, Hallmark, 2000, Jr. Engr. award A.G. Spalding and Bros., 1965; elected Order of Internat. Ambs., 1999, Internat. Man of the Year (medal of hon.), 1996, 97, Man of the Year (commemorative medal award), 1997, Internat. Order Merit, 2000, Commemmorative medal of honor Hallmark, 2000, Noble Prize Outstanding Achievement and Contbns. to Humanity, United Cultural Conv., Raleigh, NC, 2001, Order of Am. Ambassadors, Raleigh, NC, 2006, Da Vinci Diamond for Math., Cambridge, Eng., 2006, Diploma of Achievement for Neurosci., Cambridge, Eng., 2006, 2007. Fellow Am. Coll. Metaphys. Theology; em. ACS, IEEE, AIAA, COSPAR (mem. com. space rsch.), Am. Physical Soc., NY Acad. Scis., Assn. Computing Machinery, Am. Soc. Microbiology, Internat. Assn. Tchrs. English as a Fgn. Lang., Internat. Soc. Poets, Mars Soc. (found. mem.), Calif. Assn. for Health, Phys. Edn., Recreation and Dance (v.p. elect for recreation 1999), Internat. Pankration Assn. (founder), Kurt Godel Soc. Avocations: weight training, fencing, bicycling, swimming, scuba diving.

TICE, CAROL HOFF, intergenerational specialist, consultant; b. Ashville, NC, Oct. 6, 1931; d. Amos H. and Fern (Irvin) Hoff; m. (div.); children: Karin E., Jonathan H. BS, Manchester Coll., North Manchester, Ind., 1954; MEd, Cornell U., 1955. Cert. tchr., Mich., N.Y., N.J. Tchr. Princeton (N.J.) Schs., 1955-60, Ann Arbor (Mich.) Schs., 1964—; dir. intergenerational programs Inst. for Study Children and Families Eastern Mich. U., Ypsilanti, 1985-96. Founder, pres. Lifespan Resources, Inc., Ann Arbor, 1979—; presdl. appointee to U.S. Nat. Commn. Internat. Yr. of the Child, Washington, 1979-81; del. to White House Conf. on Aging, Washington, 1995; founder, bd. mem. Tchg.-Learning Community. Innovator; program, Tch. Learning Intergenerational Communities, 1971; author: Guide Books and articles, Community of Caring, 1980; co-producer, Film, What We Have, 1976 (award, Milan, Italy Film Festival 1982). Trustee Blue Lake Fine Arts Camp, Twin Lake, Mich., 1975—; dir. Visual Arts Colony, 1990—. Recipient Program Innovation award, Mich. Dept. Edn., 1974—80, C.S. Mott Found. award, 1982, Nat. Found. Improvement in Edn. award, Washington, 1986, Disting. Alumni award, Manchester Coll., 1979, A+ Break the Mold award, U.S. Sec. of Edn., 1992, Ann Arbor Sch. Supts. Golden Apple award, 1999, Disting. Svc. award, Mich. Art Edn. Assn., 2001; fellow Ford Found. fellow, Ithaca, N.Y., 1955. Mem. AAUW (agt. 1979, Agent of Change award), Generations United (hon. com. for Margaret Mead Centennial 2001, 1998—, Pioneer award 1989), Mich. Edn. Assn. (hon. mention Program Innovation 2000), Optimist Club (Humanitarian award). Democrat. Presbyterian. Office: Scarlett MS 3300 Lorraine St Ann Arbor MI 48108-1970

TICE, DOUGLAS OSCAR, JR., federal bankruptcy judge; b. Lexington, NC, May 2, 1933; s. Douglas Oscar Sr. and Lila Clayton (Wright) T.; m. Janet N. Capps, Feb. 28, 1959 (div. Sept. 1976); children: Douglas Oscar III, Janet E.; m. Martha Murdoch Edwards, June 8, 1996. BS, U. N.C., 1955, JD, 1957. Bar: N.C. 1957, U.S. Ct. Appeals (4th cir.) 1964, Va. 1970, U.S. Dist. ct. (ea. dist.) Va. 1976, U.S. Bankruptcy Ct. (ea. dist.) Va. 1976. Exec. sec. N.C. Jud. Coun., Raleigh, 1958-59; assoc. Baucom & Adams, Raleigh, 1959-61; trial atty. Office Dist. Coun., IRS, Richmond, Va., 1961-70; corp. atty. Carlton Industries, Inc., Richmond, 1970-75; ptnr.

Hubard, Tice, Marchant & Samuels, P.C., Richmond, 1975-87; judge U.S. Bankruptcy Ct. (ea. dist.), Richmond, Norfolk, Alexandria, Va., 1987-99, chief judge, 1999—. Co-author: Monument & Boulevard, Richmond's Grand Avenues, 1996; contbr. articles to profl. jours. Vice pres. Richmond Pub. Forum, 1976-80, com. chmn. Richmond Forum, Inc., 1986-2001; past pres. Richmond Civil War Roundtable, mem., 1965—; bd. dirs. Epilepsy Assn. Va., Inc., 1976-87. Capt. USAR, 1957-66. Fellow Am. Coll. Bankruptcy; mem. ABA, Va. Bar Assn., City of Richmond Bar Assn., Am. Bankruptcy Inst., Nat. Conf. Bankruptcy Judges (bd. govs. 2005—), So. Hist. Assn., Va. Hist. Soc., Old Dominion Sertoma (pres. Richmond chpt. 1967), Comml. Law League Am., Supreme Ct. Hist. Soc., State-Fed. Jud. Coun. Va., Am. Inn of Ct., Hist. Soc. of U.S. Dist. Ct. for Eastern Va. (asst. sec., bd. dir. mem. 2006—). Home: 5 Foxmere Dr Richmond VA 23238 Office: US Bankruptcy Ct 1100 E Main St Ste 339 Richmond VA 23219-3538 Home Phone: 804-740-1265; Office Phone: 804-916-2460. Personal E-mail: thetices2@comcast.net. Business E-Mail: douglas_tice@vaeb.uscourts.gov.

TICE, GEORGE A(NDREW), photographer; b. Newark, Oct. 13, 1938; s. William S. and Margaret T. (Robertson) T.; m. Joanna Blaylock, 1958; m. Marie Tremmel, 1960; children: Christopher, Loretta, Lisa, Lynn, Jennifer. DHL (hon.), William Paterson U., 2003. Instr. photography New Sch. Social Research, 1970-98. Photographer (one-man shows) Met. Mus. Art, 1972, Internat. Ctr. Photography, 2002, Newark Mus., 2006, (group shows) Whitney Mus. Am. Art, 1974, Mus. Modern Art, 1979, J. Paul Getty Mus., 2006, (permanent collections) Mus. Modern Art, Met. Mus. Art, Art Inst. Chgo., Bibliotheque Nationale, Nihon U., Tokyo, books include Fields of Peace, 1970, Fields of Peace, reissued, 1998, Goodbye River, Goodbye, 1971, Paterson, 1972, Seacoast Maine, 1973, George A. Tice Photographs, 1953-73, 1975, Urban Landscapes, 1975, Artie Van Blarcum, 1977, Urban Romantic, 1982, Lincoln, 1984, Hometowns, 1988, Stone Walls, Grey Skies, 1991, George Tice: Selected Photographs, 1953-1999, 2001, George Tice: Urban Landscapes, 2002, Common Mementos, 2005, Paterson II, 2006. Served with USN, 1956-59. Recipient Grand prix for best photography book of Year Arles, France, 1973; Guggenheim Found. fellow, 1973-74, Nat. Endowment for Arts fellow, 1973—; Bradford fellow, Eng., 1990-91, N.J. State Coun. on the Arts fellow, 1998. Address: 581 Kings Hwy East Atlantic Highlands NJ 07716-2825 Office Phone: 732-706-3585.

TICE, RAPHAEL DEAN, military officer; b. Topeka, Dec. 4, 1927; s. Arthur Taylor and Mamie (McDonald) T.; m. Eunice Miriam Suddarth, Dec. 23, 1946; children: Karen Ann Tice Claterbos, William Dean. BS in Mil. Sci., U. Md., 1963; MSBA, George Washington U., 1970. Served as enlisted man U.S. Army, 1946-47; commd. 2d lt., 1947; advanced through grades to lt. gen., 1981; platoon leader and co. comdr. 1st Inf. div., W.Ger., 1949-52; co. comdr., regimental adj. 8th Inf. divsn., 1955-56; tng. advisor Vietnam, 1956-57; mem. staff Office of Dep. Chief of Staff for Pers., Dept. Army, 1960-63; chief pers. mgmt. divsn. Office of Under Sec. of Army, 1963-64; plans Officer So. Command, Panama, 1965-67; dep. comdr. 3rd Brig., 4th Inf. Divsn., 1967; comdr. 2nd Bn., 12th Inf. of 25th Inf. divsn., Vietnam, 1968; exec. for pers. procurement Office of Sec. Def. for Manpower and Res. Affairs, 1968-69; comdr. 1st Brig., 1st Inf. divsn., 1970, chief of staff, 1971; dep. dir. mil. pers. mgmt. Dept. Army, 1972-73; comdg. gen. Berlin Brigade, 1974-76; dep. chief of staff personnel U.S. Army Europe, 1976-77; comdg. gen. 3rd. Inf. divsn., 1977-79; dep. asst. sec. def. for mil. pers. and force mgmt. Dept. Def., 1979-85; exec. dir. Nat. Recreation and Pk. Assn., 1986—2001; ret., 2001. Spl. adviser Pres.'s Coun. on Phys. Fitness and Sports; bd. dirs. Sports Pub. LLC, Class 6 Kayak, Inc. Decorated Silver Star, Legion of Merit with 2 oak leaf clusters, Air medal with V and 7 oak leaf clusters, Bronze Star with V, Vietnam Cross of Gallantry with Palm, Purple Heart., Def. Disting. Service medal, Army Disting. Service medal Mem. Assn. U.S. Army, Am. Chess Found. (hon. pres.) Home: 18077 Clendenning Cir Round Hill VA 20141-2580 Home Phone: 540-338-7194. Personal E-mail: ticepunky@aol.com.

TICHENOR, CHARLES BECKHAM, III, operations research analyst; b. Balt., Mar. 10, 1950; s. Charles Beckham II and Suzanne Nelson (Stevens) T.; m. Alison P. Walton, May 29, 1971; 1 child, Charles Beckham IV. BSBA, Ohio State U., 1972; MBA, Va. Tech., 1990; PhD in Bus., Berne U., 1999. Asst. prodn. supr. Champale Products, Norfolk, Va., 1977—80; ops. rsch. analyst IRS, Washington, 1989—93, tech. adv. info. sys. performance mgmt. office, 1999—2000; ops. rsch. analyst Dept. Def., Alexandria, Va., 2000—. Adj. prof. Strayer U., Balt. Lt. col. USAR, ret. Mem. Mensa. Roman Catholic. Avocations: Tae Kwon Do, astronomy. Home: 6207 Cardinal Brook Ct Springfield VA 22152-1516 Office: Def Security Coop Agy 201 12th St S Ste 203 Arlington VA 22202 Personal E-mail: charley_tichenor@hotmail.com.

TICKNOR, CAROLYN M., computer company executive; BA in Psychology, U. Redlands, Calif.; MA in Indsl. Psychology, San Francisco State U.; MBA, Stanford U. From programming, ops. mgr. to pres., CEO Hewlett-Packard Co., Palo Alto, Calif., 1977-94, pres., CEO laser jet imaging sys., 1994—. Office: Hewlett Packard Co 300 Hanover St Palo Alto CA 94304

TIDBALL, CHARLES STANLEY, computer scientist, educator; b. Geneva, Apr. 15, 1928; (parents Am. citizens); s. Charles Taylor and Adele (Desmaison) T.; m. Mary Elizabeth Peters, Oct. 25, 1952. BA, Wesleyan U., Middletown, Conn., 1950; MS (Univ. scholar), U. Rochester, NY, 1952; PhD, U. Wis., Madison, 1955; MD (Shattuck fellow, Van Noyes scholar), U. Chgo., 1958; LHD (hon.), Wilson Coll., Chambersburg, Pa., 1994; DSc (hon.), Hood Coll., Frederick, Md., 1999. Rotating intern Madison Gen. Hosp., 1958-59; physician I Mendota State Hosp., Madison, 1959; asst. rsch. prof. physiology dept. George Washington U. Med. Center, Washington, 1959-63, USPHS spl. fellow, 1960-61, asso. prof., acting chmn. dept., 1963-64, prof., 1964-65, chmn. dept., 1964-71, Henry D. Fry prof., 1965-84, research prof. med., 1972-80; dir. Office Computer Assisted Edn. George Washington U. Med. Ctr., Washington, 1973-75, dir. Office Computer Assisted Edn. and Svcs., 1975-78; Lucie Stern disting. vis. prof. natural scis. Mills Coll., 1980; prof. edn. George Washington U., 1982-84, dir. ednl. computing tech. program Sch. Edn., 1982-84, prof. computer medicine Med. Ctr., 1984-92, prof. emeritus computer medicine, 1992, prof. neurol. surgery, 1990-92, prof. emeritus neurol. surgery, 1992; civil surgeon Immigration and Naturalization Svc., Dept. Justice, Washington, 1986-89; disting. rsch. scholar, co-dir. Tidball Ctr. for Study Ednl. Environments Hood Coll., Frederick, Md., 1994—. Trustee in residence Skidmore Coll., 1995. Co-author: Consolidated Index to For Thy Great Glory, 1993, Taking Women Seriously, 1999, Jesus, Lazarus, and the Messiah, 2005; editor: (with M. C. Shelesnyak) Frontiers in the Teaching of Physiology: Computer Literacy and Simulation, 1981; mem. editorial bd. Jour. Applied Physiology, 1966-69, Jour. Computer-Based Instrn., 1974-89, Am. Jour. Physiology; assoc. editor The Physiologist, 1979-85; contbr. articles to profl. jours. Trustee Cathedral Choral Soc., 1976-79, Wilson Coll., 1983-92, Everitt-Pomeroy, 1993-96, Population Reference Bur., 1987-94, 1996-2002, chmn. bd. trustees, 1992-94, sec., 1994-97; lay reader St. Albans Parish, 1965-67, Washington Nat. Cathedral, 1967-94, lay eucharist minister, 1994—, clergy asst., 1968—, homilist, 1977—, info. sys. specialist, 1986-93, vol. mgr. info. sys. program, 1993—; mem. commn. Episcopal Diocese Washington, 1964—; mem. com. mgmt. YMCA Camp Letts, 1968-96, chmn., 1972-75, dir., chmn. Endowment Fund, 1977-96; bd. dirs. Met. YMCA, Washington, 1972-84, trustees coun., 1984-91, fin. com., 1972-93, v.p. internat. program, 1974-75, asst. treas., 1975-77, v.p., treas., 1977-79, vice chmn., 1979-80, chmn., 1980-82, pres. of found., 1991-93; bd. dirs., treas. Woodley Ensemble, 1993-2003; bd. dirs. Mid-Atlantic Region YMCA, 1974-83; bd. dirs., vice-chmn. Cathedral West Condo., 1983-84, chmn., 1984-87, 91-93, fin. com., 1979-94; bd. dirs. Buckingham's Choice Residents' Assn., 2000-02, chmn. resident svcs. com., 2000-02, mem. fin. com., 2004—. Recipient award Washington Acad. Scis., 1967, Leader of Yr. award Met. YMCA, Washington, 1974, Red Triangle award, 1976, Service award, 1979; Dakota Indian name Am. Youth Found., 1976, Found. Anniversary award Cathedral Choral Soc., 2007; Rsch. Career Devel. awardee USPHS, 1961-63. Mem. Am. Physiol. Soc. (emeritus). Home: 3200 Baker Cir #I-235 Adamstown MD 21710 Business E-Mail: ctidball@gwu.edu.

TIDBALL, LEE FALK, elementary school educator, writer; b. Waukon, Iowa, Feb. 26, 1955; s. John Harlow and Katherine Jane (Falk) T.; m. Catherine Susan Cooper, June 14, 1975 (div. Aug. 1982); children: Aaron Matthew, Jonathan Michael. BS, Le Tourneau U., Longview, Tex., 1979. Cert. elem. tchr., Calif. Youth dir. Centenary Meth. Ch., Modesto, Calif., 1979-80; recreation dir. Crestwood Manor Hosp., Modesto, Calif., 1980; substitute tchr. Modesto City Schs., 1981-83; 7th grade tchr. Orangeburg Christian Sch., Modesto, 1983-84; 5th & 6th tchr. Bret Harte Elem., Modesto, 1984-91, gifted edn. tchr., 1991-97; tchr. 6th grade Beard Elem. Sch., Modesto, 1997—. Author: (juvenile fiction) Windfork Secrets, 1998, Hidden Talents: Ginah's Journals #2, 2000, (screenplays) Atlanta From Alimpis, 2003, Monkey Biz, 2003, Maid Maryn, 2003, Eter(mi)nal, 2003. Head coach Silverwings Track Club, Modesto, 1982—2000, pres., 1982—2000; actor Modesto Performing Arts, 1994—98; founder Modesto Kids on Stage (non-profit children's theater co.), 2000—. Named Outstanding Young Religious Leader, Mason City (Iowa) Jaycees, 1976. Mem.: NEA, Soc. Children's Book Writers and Illustrators, Modesto Tchrs. Assn. Avocations: writing, performing arts, exercise. Office: Beard Elem Sch 915 Bowen Ave Modesto CA 95350-3096 Home: Apt 1 501 Rose Ave Modesto CA 95355-4336 E-mail: leesius@netzero.net.

TIDBALL, M. ELIZABETH PETERS, physiologist, educator; b. Anderson, Ind., Oct. 15, 1929; d. John Winton and Beatrice (Ryan) Peters; m. Charles S. Tidball, Oct. 25, 1952. BA, Mt. Holyoke Coll., 1951, LHD, 1976; MS, U. Wis., 1955, PhD, 1959; MTS summa cum laude, Wesley Theol. Sem., 1990; DSc (hon.), Wilson Coll., 1973, Trinity Coll., 1974, Cedar Crest Coll., 1977, U. of South, 1978, Goucher Coll., 1979, St. Mary-of-The-Woods Coll., 1986; LittD (hon.), Regis Coll., 1980, Coll. St. Catherine, 1980, Alverno Coll., 1989; HHD (hon.), St. Mary's Coll., 1977, Hood Coll., 1982; LLD (hon.), St. Joseph Coll., 1983; LHD (hon.), Skidmore Coll., 1984, Marymount Coll., 1985, Converse Coll., 1985, Mt. Vernon Coll., 1986. Tchg. asst. physiology dept. U. Wis., 1952—55, rsch. asst. physiology dept., 1958—59; rsch. asst. anatomy dept. U. Chgo., 1955-56, rsch. asst. physiology dept., 1956-58; USPHS postdoctoral fellow NIH, Bethesda, Md., 1959-61; staff pharmacologist Hazleton Labs., Falls Church, Va., 1961, cons., 1962; assoc. in physiology George Washington U. Med. Ctr., 1960-62, asst. rsch. prof. dept. pharmacology, 1962-64, assoc. rsch. prof. dept. physiology, 1964-70, rsch. prof., 1970-71, prof., 1971-94, prof. emeritus, 1994—; asst. dir. M of Theol. Studies program Wesley Theol Sem., 1993-94; disting. rsch. scholar Hood Coll., Frederick, Md., 1994—, co-dir. Tidball Ctr. for Study of Ednl. Environments, 1994—. Lucie Stern Disting. vis. prof. natural scis. Mills Coll., 1980; scholar in residence Coll. Preachers, 1984, Salem Coll., 1985, Wesley Theol. Sem., 1992; Disting. scholar in residence So. Meth. U., 1985; vis. trustee prof. Skidmore Coll., 1995; cons. FDA, 1966-67, assoc. sci. coord. sci. assocs. tng. programs, 1966-67; com. on NIH tng. programs and fellowships NAS, 1972-75; faculty summer confs. Am. Youth Found., 1967-78; founder, dir. Summer Seminars Women Am. Youth Found., 1987-95; cons. for instl. rsch. Wellesley Coll., 1974-75; exec. sec. com. on edn. and employment women in sci. and engring. Commn. on Human Resources, NRC/NAS, 1974-75, vice-chmn., 1977-82; cons., staff officer NRC/NAS, 1974-75; cons. Woodrow Wilson Nat. Fellowship Found., 1975-99, NSF, 1974-91; bd. mentor Assn. Governing Bds. Univs. and Colls., 1991-2000, Gale Fund for the Study of Trusteeship Adv. Comm., 1992-98; cons. Women's Coll. Coalition Rsch. Adv. Com., 1992-2000; Single Gender Schooling Working Group, US Dept. Edn., 1992-94, Women's Colls. Roundtable, 1998; rep. to DC Commn. on Status of Women, 1972-75; nat. panelist Am. Coun. on Edn., 1983-90; panel mem. Congl. Office Tech. Assessment, 1986-87; fellows selection com., fellows mentor Coll. Preachers, 1992-05. Lead author: Taking Women Seriously: Lessons and Legacies for Educating the Majority, American Council on Education Higher Education Series, 1999; columnist Trusteeship, 1993-95; mem. editl. bd. Jour. Higher Edn., 1979-84, cons. editor, 1984—; mem. editl. bd. Religion and Intellectual Life, 1983—; contbr. articles to profl. jours. Trustee Mt. Holyoke Coll., 1968-73, vice chmn., 1972-73, trustee fellow, 1988—; trustee Hood Coll., 1972-84, 86-92, exec. com., 1974-84, 89-92, trustee emerita, 1997—; overseer Sweet Briar Coll., 1978-85, dir. emerita, 2003—; trustee Cathedral Choral Soc., 1976-90, pres. bd. trustees, 1982-84, hon. trustee, 1991—; trustee Skidmore Coll., 1988—, exec. com., 1993—, trustee Bishop Claggett Ctr., 2003—; governing bd. Cathedral Coll. of Preachers, 1979-85, chmn., 1983-85; governing bd. Protestant Episcopal Cathedral Found., 1983-85, exec. com., 1983-85; bd. vis. Salem Coll., 1986-93; ctr. assoc. Nat. Resource Ctr., Girls Club Am., 1983-90; governing bd. Buckinham's Choice Residents' Assn., 1999-2002; cathedral vol. coun. Washington Nat. Cathedral, 2006—. Named Outstanding Grad., The Penn Hall Sch., 1988; recipient Alumnae medal Honor, Mt. Holyoke Coll., 1971, Outstanding Svc. award, Am. Youth Found., 1975, Valuable Contbns. Gen. Alumni Assn. award, George Washington U., 1982, 1987, Pres.'s medal, 1999, Chestnut Hill medal Outstanding Achievement, Chestnut Hill Coll., 1987, Lifetime Svc. and Scholarship award, Bd. Women's Coll. Coalition and Nation's Women's Coll. Presidents, 1998, Order of Merit, Cathedral Choral Soc., 2000; Shattuck fellow, 1955—56, Mary E. Woolley fellow, Mt. Holyoke Coll., 1958—59, postdoctoral fellow, USPHS, 1959—61. Mem. AAAS, Am. Physiol. Soc. (chmn. task force on women in physiology 1973-80, com. on coms. 1977-80, mem. emeritus 1994—), Am. Assn. Higher Edn., Mt. Holyoke Alumnae Assn. (dir. 1966-70, 76-77), Histamine Club, Sigma Delta Epsilon, Sigma Xi. Episcopalian. Home: 4100 Cathedral Ave NW Washington DC 20016-3584 also: 3200 Baker Cir I-235 Adamstown MD 21710 Personal E-mail: ctidball@gwu.edu.

TIDMORE, BRYCE WILLIAM, retired secondary school educator; b. Arab, Ala., May 8, 1932; s. Robert Grover and Julia Mary Tidmore; m. Beatrice Marie Kimbrough, Dec. 23, 1956; children: Susan Tidmore, Donald Glenn. AA, Snead Jr. Coll., Boaz, Ala., 1952; BS, Florence State Tchrs. Coll., Ala., 1954; MA, Florence State Coll. (now U. North Ala.), 1960. Ordained deacon Ala. Bapt. Ch., 1961; cert. tchr. Ala., 1956. Tchr. Fairview H.S., Cullman County, Ala., 1956—57, Deshler H.S., Tuscumbia, Ala., 1957—58, Colbert County H.S., Leighton, Ala., 1958—59, New Bethel Jr. H.S., Tuscumbia, 1959—72, Leighton Mid. Sch., Ala., 1972—86; ret. Air quality rsch. asst. Tenn. Valley Auth., Sheffield, Ala., 1978—81; bd. dirs. N.W. Ala. Reading Aides, Florence, 2005—. Cub scout master Boy Scouts Am.; chmn., deacon First Bapt. Ch., Tuscumbia, 1970—72, 2000—02. Sp-2 US Army, 1954—56, US, Germany. Decorated Legion Honor medal US Army, Cold War Svc. Commemorative medal US Sec. Def.; recipient Ala. Korean Legion Honor award, Gov. Ala. Mem.: Nat. Geog. Soc., Am. Legion (post chaplain 2004—), Colbert County Ret. Edn. Assn. (v.p. 2004—06), Colbert County Edn. Assn. (treas. 1980—86), Tuscumbia Lions Club. Avocations: gardening, woodworking, genealogy.

TIDSWELL, MARK, medical researcher; m. Stephanie Osiecki; children: Ben K., Anna J. BA, Reed Coll., Portland, Oreg., 1982. Asst. prof. U. Calif., San Francisco, 1994—98, Tufts U. Sch. Medicine, Boston, 1998—; critical care physician Baystate Med. Ctr., Springfield, 1999—. Rsch. Baystate Med. Ctr., Springfield, Mass., 2001—. Mem.: Soc. Critical Care Medicine, Am. Thoracic Soc. Achievements include research in acute lung injury and ARDS. Office Phone: 413-794-5439.

TIDWELL, JAMES, Sommelier; BS in Internat. Trade and Fin., La. State U.; grad., Culinary Inst. Am. Cert. Wine Educator Soc. Wine Educators. Sommelier Restaurant Serenade, Chatham, NJ, Erna's Elderberry House, Oakhurst, Calif., Cafe on the Green, Dallas. Co-founder Tex. Sommelier Conf. Named one of Dallas' Rising Stars, StarChefs.com, 2007. Mem.: Tex. Sommelier Assn. (co-founder), Soc. Wine Educators (mem. bd. dirs. 2005, Banfi award 2003). Office: Cafe on the Green 4150 N MacArthur Blvd Irving TX 75038 Office Phone: 972-717-2420. *

TIEDE, TOM ROBERT, journalist; b. Huron, SD, Feb. 24, 1937; s. Leslie Albert and Rose (Allen) T.; children: Kristina Anne, Thomas Patrick. BA in Journalism, Wash. State U., 1959. Mem. staff Kalispell (Mont.) Daily Interlake, 1960-61, Daytona Beach (Fla.) News Jour., 1961-63; war corr. Newspaper Enterprise Assn., NYC, 1964—. Lectr. in field. Author: Your Men at War, 1965, Coward, 1968, Calley: Soldier or Killer?, 1971, Welcome to Washington, Mr. Witherspoon, 1979, The Great Whale Rescue, 1986, American Tapestry: Eye Witness Accounts of the 1900's, 1988, The Man Who Discovered Pluto, 1990, Fosser, 1994, Self Help Nation, 2001; permanent collections Boston U. Libr. Served as lt., inf. AUS, 1960. Recipient Ernie Pyle Meml. award, 1965; Freedoms Found. award, 1966; George Washington medal, 1972 Mem. Internat. Platform Assn., Sigma Delta Chi, Lambda Chi Alpha. Clubs: Overseas Press, National Press, Nat. Headliners (award 1966 Atlantic City). Roman Catholic. Office: NEA 1090 Vermont Ave NW Washington DC 20005-4905 Personal E-mail: ttiede@mindspring.com.

TIEDEMANN, CHARLES WELCH (CHAD), lawyer; b. Bronxville, NY, Jan. 30, 1956; AB, U. Notre Dame, 1978; JD, Catholic U. Am., 1981. Bar: DC 1981. Nat. chair, real estate sect. Holland & Knight LLP, Washington; former chmn., nat. real estate practice development task force; ptnr. Holland & Knight LLP, Washington, chair, United Way Campaign, chair, Christmas in April House Sponsorship. Mem.: Bldg. Industry Assn. (mem. real estate group, Washington, DC), ABA, DC Bar, U. Notre Dame Alumni Club (Washington, DC). Office: Holland & Knight LLP 2099 Pennsylvania Ave NW Ste 100 Washington DC 20006 Office Phone: 202-955-3000. Business E-Mail: chad.tiedemann@hklaw.com.

TIEDJE, JAMES MICHAEL, microbiologist, educator, ecologist; b. Newton, Iowa, Feb. 9, 1942; married, 1965; 3 children. BS, Iowa State U., 1964; MS, Cornell U., 1966, PhD in Soil Microbiology, 1968. From asst. prof. to prof. Mich. State U., 1968-78, disting. prof., 1991—; dir. sci. and tech. ctr. microbial ecology NSF, 1988—. Vis. assoc. prof. U. Ga., 1974-75; cons. NSF, 1974-77; vis. prof. U. Calif. Berkeley, 1981-82; mem. biotech. sci. adv. com. EPA, 1986-89, chair sci. adv. coun. GPA, 1988-90. Editor: Applied Microbiology, 1974—, editor-in-chief, 1980-86. Recipient Carlos J. Finley prize, UNESCO, 1993. Mem. AAAS, Am. Soc. Agronomy (Soil Sci. award 1990), Internat. Inst. Biotech., Am. Soc. Microbiology (award in applied and environ. microbiology 1992), Soil Sci. Soc. Am., Ecol. Soc. Am., Internat. Soc. Soil Sci. (chair soil biology divsn.). Achievements include research in dentrification, microbial metabolism of organic pollutants, and molecular microbiol. ecology. Office: Michigan State U Microbial Ecology Ctr 540 Plant & Soil Scis Bldg East Lansing MI 48824-1325

TIEFEL, VIRGINIA MAY, librarian; b. Detroit, May 20, 1926; d. Karl and June Garland (Young) Brenkert; m. Paul Martin Tiefel, Jan. 25, 1947; children: Paul Martin Jr., Mark Gregory. BA in Elem. Edn., Wayne State U., 1962; MA in Library Sci., U. Mich., 1968. Librarian Birmingham Schs., Mich., 1967-68; librarian S. Euclid-Lyndhurst Schs., Cleve., 1968-69; acquisitions-reference librarian Hiram Coll., Ohio, 1969-77; head undergrad. libraries Ohio State U., Columbus, 1977-84, dir. library user edn., 1978-95, faculty outreach coord., 1995-98. Contbr. articles to profl. jours. Recipient Disting. Alumnus award, U. Mich. Sch. Info. and Libr. Studies, 1993. Mem. ALA (v.p. Ohio sect. 1973-74, pres. 1974-75, Miriam Dudley Bibliographic Instrn. Librarian of Yr. 1986), Acad. Library Assn. Ohio (Outstanding Ohio Acad. Librarian 1984), Assn. Coll. and Research Libraries (chmn. bibliographic instrn. sect. com. on research 1983-84, chmn. com. on performance measures 1984-90). Lutheran. Achievements include Excellence in Teaching award at Ohio State University Libraries established in her honor in 2004. Home: 4711 Oak Bluff Ct Eau Claire WI 54701 E-mail: vtiefel1@aol.com.

TIEFEL, WILLIAM REGINALD, hotel company executive; b. Rochester, NY, Mar. 30, 1934; s. William Reginald and Mary Hazel (Cross) T.; m. Vada Morell, Dec. 30, 1985 (dec. Apr. 1999); m. Norma Gewirz Kline, Nov. 25, 2000. Student, Williams Coll., 1952-54; BA with honors, Mich. State U., 1956; postgrad., Harvard Bus. Sch.; DBA in Hospitality Mgmt. (hon.), Johnson and Wales U. Gen. mgr. Marriott Hotels, Arlington, Va., 1964-65, Saddle Brook, NJ, 1966-69, Newton, Mass., 1969-71, regional v.p. Washington, 1971-80; corp. v.p. Marriott Corp., Washington, 1976-89; exec. v.p. Marriott Hotels and Resorts, Washington, 1980-88; pres. Marriott Hotels, Resorts and Suites, 1988-92; exec. v.p., mem. exec. and growth coms. Marriott Corp., 1988—2002; pres. Marriott Lodging Group, 1992-98; vice chmn. Marriott Internat., 1998—2002; chmn. Ritz-Carlton Hotel Co, 1998—2002, chmn. emeritus, 2002—; dir. Bulgari Hotels and Resorts, 2001—. Bd. dir. CarMax Inc., 2002—, chmn., 2007—; dir. Lydian Pvt. Bank, 2005—. Bd. visitors Valley Forge Mil. Acad. and Jr. Coll., 1976-79, chmn., 1979, trustee, 1982-92; chmn. Campaign Valley Forge, 1985-88, chmn. com. on trustees, 1989-91, hon. life trustee; trustee Johnson and Wales U., 2002—, Norton Mus. Art, 2004—, advancement com. chair, v.p., 2006-; adv. coun. Wilmer Eye Inst., Johns Hopkins U.; trustee Town Palm Beach United Way. Mem. Am. Hotel and Lodging Assn. (dir. Ednl. Inst., Arthur Landstreet award 1997), Soc. of the Four Arts (Palm Beach), Kennedy Ctr. Internat. Com. on the Arts (Washington), Cosmos Club (Washington), Tavern Club (NYC). Independent. Roman Catholic. Home: 236 Via Las Brisas Palm Beach FL 33480-1643 E-mail: william.tiefel@ritzcarlton.com.

TIEFENBRUN, JONATHAN, surgeon; b. NYC, Feb. 5, 1943; s. Joseph and Helen (Henkin) Tiefenbrun; m. Susan Kissil, June 19, 1966; children: Michele, Jeremy, Gregory. MD, SUNY, Bklyn., 1966. Diplomate Am. Bd. Surgery. Med. intern Kings County Hosp., Bklyn., 1966—67; resident in surgery Mt. Sinai Hosp., NYC, 1967—73, chief resident in surgery, 1972—73, attending surgeon, 1973, Beth Israel Hosp., NYC, 1981; sr. attending surgeon St. Luke's Roosevelt Hosp., NYC, 1981; dir. clin. rsch. Lifescore Global Network, San Diego, 2001—03; dir. Balboa Nephrology Ultrasound Lab., San Diego, 2003—. Asst. prof. Mt. Sinai Sch. Medicine, NYC, 1973; clin. prof. surgery U. Calif., San Diego, 2003; mem. nat. ultrasound faculty Am. Coll. Surgeons. Contbr. articles to profl. journals. Fellow NIH, 1968—70. Fellow: Nat. Ultrasound Faculty of ACS (instr. clin. ultrasound, dialysis access surgery); mem.: NY Cardiovasc. Soc. Achievements include patents in field; invention of catheters; endovascular grafts; ultrasonic and laser devices; gen. and vascular medicine and surgery diagnostic ultrasound. Avocation: classical guitar. Personal E-mail: susant@tjsl.edu.

TIEFENBRUNN, ALAN JAMES, medical educator; b. St. Louis, Aug. 26, 1948; s. Kenneth Sylvester and Margaret Ann (Smith) T.; m. Sharon Kay Frost, June 3, 1972; children: Theresa, Curtis. AB cum laude, Washington U., St. Louis, 1970, MD, 1974. Intern, resident U. Calif., San Diego, 1974-77; fellow in cardiology Washington U., St. Louis, 1977-79, asst. prof. medicine, 1980-86, assoc. prof. medicine, 1986—, asst. prof. radiology, 1980—; assoc. physician Barnes Hosp., St. Louis, 1980—. Mem. adv. bd. Nat. Registry Myocardial Infarction, 1991—; cons. in field. Contbr. articles to profl. jours. Fellow Am. Coll. Cardiology, Am. Heart Assn. (coun. clin.cardiology), Alpha Omega Alpha. Avocations: skiing, scuba diving, shotgun sports. Home: 6255 Wydown Blvd Saint Louis MO

63105-2306 Office: Washington U Box 8086 660 S Euclid Ave Saint Louis MO 63110-1093 E-mail: atiefenb@im.wustl.edu.

TIEKEN, ROBERT W., relocation services company executive, retired tire manufacturing company executive; b. Decatur, Ill., May 6, 1939; married; 2 children. BS, Ill. Wesleyan U., 1961. With GE Co., mem. corp. audit staff; mgr. fin. ops. GE Nuclear Energy, GE Transp. Sys.; with GE Aerospace, v.p. fin. and info. tech.; corp. v.p. GE Co., 1988; v.p. fin. Utah Internat., Inc., Martin Marietta Corp., Bethesda, Md., 1993—94; exec. v.p., CFO Goodyear Tire & Rubber Co., Akron, Ohio, 1994—2004; interim CEO SIRVA, Inc., Westmont, Ill., 2007, pres., CEO, 2007—. Bd. dir. Graphic Packaging Corp. Office: SIRVA Inc 700 Oakmont Ln Westmont IL 60559 *

TIELMAN, ROB A.P., social sciences educator; b. Hilversum, The Netherlands, Aug. 19, 1946; s. Albert Tielman and Tine Angenent. MA in Sociology, U. Utrecht, Netherlands, 1971; PhD in Social Sci., U. Utrecht, 1982. Mem. acad. staff U. Utrecht, 1971—, head Gay and Lesbian Studies dept., 1982—92, prof. humanist studies, 1987—. Chmn. adv. bd. WHO, Geneva, 1989—93; head humanist tchr. tng. Humanist Ethical Edn., Utrecht, 1993—99; sec. Study Ctr. Pub. Edn., Utrecht, 1994—; sr. advisor pub. edn. Gen. Pedagogic Ctr., Utrecht, 1994—2005; pres. ethics commn. Dutch Inst. Mental Health, Utrecht, 1975—97; pres. Pub. Schs. in the Netherlands, Utrecht, 1989—; v.p. European Platform on Edn., Alkmaar, 1994—2006; rep. of Internat. Humanist Ethical Union UNESCO, Paris, 1989—99, Coun. of Europe, Strasbourg, 1989—; rep. of European Humanist Fedn. EU, Brussels, 1991—99. Author: Homoseksualiteit in Nederland, 1982; editor: Bisexuality and HIV/AIDS, 1991, Third Pink Book, 1993. Sec.-gen. Dutch Gay and Lesbian Assn., Amsterdam, 1971—75; pres. Dutch Humanist Assn., Utrecht, 1977—87, Internat. Humanist Ethical Union, London, 1986—98, Humanist Archives, Utrecht, 1996—, Ctr. for Inquiry in the Low Countries, 2006—, Jopie Huisman Mus., 2006—. Named Knight, Queen of the Netherlands, 1987. Fellow: Internat. Acad. Humanism; mem.: Dutch Gay and Lesbian Profs. (sec. 1998—), European Humanist Profls. (pres. 1993—2000). Dutch Labor Party. Humanist. Avocation: historical topography of the low countries and former Dutch colonies. Office: Universiteit Utrecht Heidelberglaan 2 3584 CS Utrecht Netherlands Business E-Mail: r.tielman@aps.nl.

TIEMESSEN, JOHN J., lawyer; b. Fairbanks, Alaska, Jan. 21, 1966; BS magna cum laude, Ariz. State U., 1987; JD, Willamette U., 1991. Bar: Alaska 1991. Ptnr. Clapp, Peterson, Van Flein, Tiemessen & Thorsness LLC, Fairbanks, Alaska. Mem. Def. Rsch. Inst. Mem.: ABA, Alaska Bar Assn. (pres. 2006—07), Tanana Valley Bar Assn., Order of Barristers. Office: Clapp Peterson Van Flein Tiemessen & Thorsness LLC Ste 300 411 4th Ave Fairbanks AK 99701 Office Phone: 907-479-7707. Office Fax: 907-479-7966. E-mail: jjt@cplawak.com.

TIEMEYER, KAYLA SUE, music educator; b. Superior, Nebr., Aug. 12, 1967; d. Roland Vernon and Norman Lee Doering; m. David Wayne Tiemeyer, July 31, 1993; children: Dylan, Colton, Jordyn. B, Bethany Coll., 1989. Cert. tchr. State of Kans. Vocal music tchr. Norton (Kans.) Jr. Sr. H.S., 1989—91; show choir dir. Atwood (Kans.) Elemo H.S., 1991—99; music tchr. Rawlins County Elem. Sch., Atwood, 2003—; vocal music dir. Rawlins County Jr. Sr. H.S., Atwood, 2004—. Show choir dir. Atwood H.S., 2002—; presch. tchr. God's Little St. Presch., Atwood, 1999—2004. Organist, choir accompanist Redeemer Luth. Ch., Atwood, 1991—. Mem.: Kans. Music Educators Assn., Music Club. Lutheran. Avocations: walking, scrapbooks, crocheting, singing, piano. E-mail: tiemeyer@ruraltel.net.

TIEMSTRA, JOHN PETER, economics professor; b. Chgo., July 15, 1950; s. Peter John and Margaret T.; m. Suzanne Spicer, Dec. 28, 1985; 1 child: Remi Spicer Rakipi. *Wife, Suzanne T. is founder and director of Grand Rapids Cantata Choir and an authority on Latin American Choral music. Daughter, Remi Rakipi, CSW, MSW, is a clinician at Pine Rest Christian Mental Health Services in Grand Rapids.* AB, Oberlin Coll., 1971; PhD, MIT, 1975. Asst. prof. econs. Calvin Coll., Grand Rapids, Mich., 1975-81, assoc. prof., 1981-85, prof., 1985—. Vis. prof. Potchefstroom U., South Africa, 1992. Author: Economics: A Developmental Approach, 1999; editor, co-author: Reforming Economics, 1990; contbr. articles to profl. jours. Dean Grand Rapids Am. Guild of Organists, 1990-91; pres. West Mich. Irish Heritage Soc., Grand Rapids, 1988-91, Forest Hills Condo Assn., Cascade, Mich., 1988—; organist St. Paul's Episcopal Ch., Grand Rapids, 1990-06, Working Group on Ethics and the Earth, Reformed Ch. in Am., 2002-04. Mem. Assn. Social Econs. (v.p. 2005, pres.-elect 2006, pres. 2007), Assn. Christian Economists, Am. Econ. Assn. Avocation: music. Office: Calvin Coll 1740 Knollcrest Cir SE Grand Rapids MI 49546-4301 Office Phone: 616-526-6192. Business E-Mail: tmst@calvin.edu.

TIEN, JAMES M., dean, engineering educator, consultant; b. NYC, Mar. 27, 1945; s. Yu-Shih Tien and Tien-Lun Li; m. Ellen S. Weston, Aug. 27, 1981; children: Lee, Rex. BEE, Rensselaer Poly. Inst., 1966; SM, MIT, 1967, PhD, 1972. Mem. tech. staff Bell Labs., Holmdel, NJ, 1966-69; rsch. project dir. Rand Corp., NYC, 1970-73; area dir. Urban Sys. Rsch. & Engring., Cambridge, Mass., 1973-75; prin., v.p. Structured Decisions Corp., Cambridge, 1975—; prof. Dept. Elec., Computer, and Sys. Engring. Rensselaer Poly. Inst., Troy, NY, 1977—2007, Yamada Corp. prof., acting chair, 1986—87, founding chair Dept. Decision Scis. and Engring. Sys., 1988, acting dean engring., 1992—94, 1998—99; dean Coll. Engring. U. Miami, 2007—. Fellow AAAS, INFORMS, IEEE (Joseph G. Wohl Oustanding Career award 1998, Major Ednl. Innovation award 2000, Norbert Weiner award), NAE. Office: U Miami Coll Engring PO Box 248294 Coral Gables FL 33124

T'IEN, JAMES SHAW-TZUU, engineering educator; b. Santai, China, Mar. 8, 1942; s. Keh-Ming and Yuan-Chin Tien; m. Sibyl Si-Juang Yang, June 24, 1967; children: Matthew Hua Tien, Joseph Hua Tien. BS in Engring., Nat. Taiwan U., Teipei, 1963; MS, Purdue U., West Lafayette, Ind., 1966; PhD, Princeton U., NJ, 1970. From asst. prof. to full prof. Case Western Res. U., Cleve., 1971—2006, Leonard Case Jr. prof. engring., 2007—; chief scientist on combustion Nat. Ctr. Microgravity Rsch., Cleve., 1998—2005, Nat. Ctr. Space Exploration, Cleve., 2005—06. Co-dir. Case-OAI-NASA Summer Faculty Fellowship Program, Cleve., 1992. Recipient Pub. Svc. medal, NASA, 2000, Silver Snoopy award, 2004; Daniel and Florence Guggenheim fellow in jet propulsion, Guggenheim Found., 1969. Mem.: Combustion Inst. (hon.). Office: Case Western Res U Dept Mech and Aerospace Engring Cleveland OH 44106 Home Phone: 440-449-1858; Office Phone: 216-368-4581.

TIENKEN, ARTHUR T., retired foreign service officer; b. Yonkers, NY, Aug. 5, 1922; BA, Princeton U., 1947, MA, 1949. With U.S. Fgn. Svc., 1949-87, dep. chief mission Tunis, Tunisia, 1973-75, Addis Ababa, Ethiopia, 1975-77; Ambassador to Gabonese Republic and Democratic Republic of Sao Tome and Principe, Libreville, Gabon, 1978-81; dir. Fgn. Svc. Assignments and Career devel. Dept. State, 1981-85, sr. insp., 1985-87, ret., 1987. Diplomat-in-residence Marquette U., 1972-73 Served with U.S. Army, 1943-46. Mem. Diplomatic and Consular Officers Ret. (bd. govs. 1999—2005).

TIERNEY, BRIAN PATRICK, publishing executive, former advertising and public relations executive; b. Bryn Mawr, Pa., Feb. 21, 1957; s. James Richard and Claire Ella (Springfield) T.; married; 2 children. BA, U. Pa., 1979; JD, Widener U., 1987. Field person Rep. Nat. Com., Washington, 1979-82, dir. incumbent programs, 1979-81, dep. dir. edn., 1981-82; polit. dir. GOPAC, Washington, 1982-83; asst. regional adminstr. Small Bus. Adminstrn., Bala Cynwyd, Pa., 1983-84; pres. Tierney & Co., Phila., 1984-86; pres., CEO Lewis, Gilman & Kynett Pub. Rels., Phila., 1986-89, Tierney Communications (formerly The Tierney Group), Phila., 1989—2000, Tierney & Ptnrs., Phila., 1994—98; chief mktg. officer Advanta Corp., 2004—05; CEO Phila. Media Holdings LLC, 2006—. Entrepreneur in resident Wharton Sch. Bus., 2002—03. Ann. giving chmn. Ingis House for Disabled Persons, Phila.; bd. dirs. Wilma Theater, Phila., Moore Coll. Art and Design, Phila., Sch. Bd. Archdiocese of Phila., Ave. of Arts, Inc., Phila. Police Athletic League, Phila. coun. Boy Scouts Am., fund for Phila., Phila. Festival of Arts; chmn. Marian Anderson award City of Phila.; bd. dirs. Phila. Zool. Soc.; mem. bd. regional Performing Arts Ctr., Phila. Mem. ABA, Pa. Bar Assn., Phila. Bar Assn., Pub. Rels. Soc. Am., St. Anthony Club, Union League. Roman Catholic. Avocations: skydiving, gardening.

TIERNEY, GORDON PAUL, real estate broker, genealogist; b. Ft. Wayne, Ind., Oct. 17, 1922; s. James Leonard and Ethele Lydia (Brown) T.; m. Carma Lillian Devine, Oct. 17, 1946; 1 child, Paul N Student, Ind. U., 1940—41, Cath. U. Am., 1941—42. Br. mgr. Bartlett-Collins Co., Chgo., 1956—84; prin., broker Kaiser-Tierney Real Estate, Inc., Palatine, Ill., 1984—89; pres. Tierney Real Estate, Newburgh, Ind. Author: Burgess/Bryan Connection, 1978; assoc. editor Colonial Genealogist Jour., 1976-85 With US Army, 1943—45, China. Named Ky. Col Fellow Am. Coll. Genealogists (pres. 1977-2000); mem. SAR (life, v.p. gen. 1984-85, genealogist gen. 1981-83, Silver and Bronze medals 1978-80, Patriot medal 1976, Meritorious Svc. award 1983, Minutemen award 1984), Huguenot Soc. Ill. (state pres. 1978-80), Huguenot Soc. S.C., Nat. Huguenot Soc., Huguenot Soc. Ind. (pres. 1993-95), Nat. Geneal. Soc., Ind. Hist. Soc., Soc. Ind. Pioneers, First Families Ohio, Ohio Geneal. Soc., Va. Geneal. Soc., Md. Geneal. Soc., Augustan Soc., Gen. Soc. War 1812 (state pres. 1985), Sons and Daus. Pilgrims, Descs. Old Plymouth Colony, Mil. Order Stars and Bars, Soc. Descs. Colonial Clergy, Sons Union Vets., Sons Confederate Vets., Pioneer Wis. Families, Welcome Soc. Pa., Pa. Geneal. Soc., Nat. Soc. Archivists, Soc. Colonial Wars in Ill. (life), Soc. Colonial Wars in Ind. (gov. 1992-94), Soc. Colonial Wars in Commonwealth Ky. (life), Sons Am. Colonists (nat. v.p. 1971-74), Mil. and Hospitalier Order St. Lazarus of Jerusalem, Clan Johnston/e in Am., Order Descs. Ancient Planters, Hump Pilots Assn., Nat. Bd. Realtors, Ill. Bd. Realtors, Sword Bunker Hill, Tri-State Geneal. Soc., Jamestowne Soc., Baronial Order Magna Charta, Royal Order Scotland, Masons, Shriners, Rolling Hill Country Club, Legion of Honor (comdr. 2001-02, decorated) Republican. Presbyterian. Home and Office: 8766 Hanover Dr Newburgh IN 47630-9327 Office Phone: 812-858-9838.

TIERNEY, JAMES EDWARD, law educator, former state attorney general; b. Bklyn., Apr. 12, 1947; s. Charles J. and Agnes V. (Quinn) T.; m. Susan Webster, Jan. 26, 1969; children: Adam, Josie, Matthew, Daniel, Kate. BA with highest honors, U. Maine, 1969, JD, 1974. Bar: Maine 1974. Mem. Maine State Ho. Reps., 1972-80, majority leader, 1976-80; atty. gen. State of Maine, 1980-90; cons. state attys. gen., 1994—; lectr. Columbia Law Sch., NYC, 2000—, dir. Nat. State Atty. Gen. Program, 2004—. Bd. dirs. People for the Am. Way, Topsham, Maine, 1991-93; spl. prosecutor investigate Pa. Supreme Ct., 1992-93; mem. bd. commentators Courtroom TV Network. Wasserstein fellow Harvard Law Sch., 1992-93. Mem. Am. Judicature Soc. (bd. dirs.). Office: Columbia Law Sch 435 W 116 St Box B-26 New York NY 10027 E-mail: jtiern@law.columbia.edu.

TIERNEY, JOHN F., congressman, lawyer; b. Salem, Mass., Sept. 18, 1951; m. Patrice Tierney. BA, Salem State Coll., 1973; JD, Suffolk U., 1976. Ptnr. Tierney, Kalis, and Lucas, North Shore, Mass.; mem. US Congress from 6th Mass. dist., 1997—, mem. com. edn. and workforce, com. gov. reform, permanent select intelligence com. Pres. Salem C. of C. Democrat. Office: US Ho Reps 120 Cannon Ho Office Bldg Washington DC 20515-2106 Office Phone: 202-225-8020. Office Fax: 202-225-5915. *

TIERNEY, JOHN MARION, journalist, columnist, reporter; b. Elgin, Ill., Mar. 25, 1953; s. John William and Patricia Anne (O'Neill) Tierney; m. Dana Groseclose, June 10, 1995; 1 child. BA in Am. Studies cum laude, Yale U., 1976. Reporter Bergen Record, Bergen County, NJ, 1976-78, Washington Star, 1978-80; staff writer Science 81-85 mag., Washington, 1981-85; freelance writer, 1985-90; reporter NY Times, Washington, 1990—, Washington correspondent, 2002—03, 2003—05, Baghdad correspondent, 2003, op-ed columnist, 2005—. Staff writer, columnist N.Y. Times Mag., 1995—; contbr. articles to numerous mags. and newspapers including Atlantic, Discover, Esquire, Hippocrates, National Geographic Traveler, Newsweek, Outside, New York, N.Y. Times Mag., Playboy, Rolling Stone, Washington Monthly, The Wall Street Jour., Washington Post, Vogue; co-author, God Is My Broker; author, The Best-Case Scenario Handbook, 2002. Recipient Washington Monthly Journalism award, 1982, Am. Inst. of Physics-U.S. Steel Found. Sci. Writing award, 1984, AAAS/Westinghouse Sci. Journalism award, 1988; fellow Freedom Forum Media Studies Ctr., Columbia U., 1993-94. Office: NY Times 1627 I St NW Washington DC 20006

TIERNEY, KEVIN ALLEN, elementary school educator; b. Castro Valley, Calif., Sept. 23, 1958; s. Robert James and Jacqueline Elizabeth Tierney; m. Karen Naomi Zimmer, Aug. 23, 1987. BA in History, San Francisco State U., 1990; MA in Edn. Curriculum and Instrn., Sacramento State U., Calif., 2002. Cert. profl.clear multiple subject tchg. credential Calif. Tchr. grade 4 Wagner Holt Elem. Sch., Stockton, Calif., 1991—92; tchr. grade 5 Silva Valley Elem. Sch., El Dorado Hills, 1992—98; tchr. history grade 7-8 Rolling Hills Mid. Sch., 1998. Trainer El Dorado County Office Edn., Placerville, Calif., 2001—; mentor trainer Buckeye Union Sch. Dist., Shingle Springs, 2000—. Com. mem. Cemetery Advisor Com., El Dorado County, 2002—. Named Most Influential Tchr., Oak Ridge H.S. students, 1999, Tchr. of Yr., Rolling Hills Mid. Sch., 2001, 2004, 2005; fellow, Colonial Williamsburg Tchr. Inst., 2001, Eurasia Excellence Tchg. fellow, U.S. Dept., 2004, Japan Fulbright Meml. Fund, 2005. Mem.: ASCD, Nat. Coun. Soc. Studies. Avocations: banjo, golf, fly fishing. Home: 5001 Gold Crest Ct Camino CA 95709 Office: Rolling Hills Mid Sch 7141 Silva Valley Pkwy El Dorado Hills CA 95762-7862 Office Phone: 530-676-2490 x 377. E-mail: katierne@mindspring.com.

TIERNEY, MICHAEL JOHN, mathematics professor; b. St. Louis, Feb. 19, 1947; s. John Thomas and Alice Marie (Krieger) T.; m. Edith L. Echelmeyer, Nov. 21, 1975 (div. Sept. 1984); 1 child, John E.; m. Virginia Lee Christian, Apr. 6, 1985. BS, St. Louis U., 1969, MS, 1971, PhD, 1974; MS, U. Va., 1995. Prof. math. and actuarial sci. Maryville Coll., St. Louis, 1974-83; prof. math. and computer sci. Va. Mil. Inst., Lexington, 1983—, dept. chair, 1995—2004. Mem. AAUP, AAAS, Am. Math. Soc., Math. Assn. Am., Soc. Indsl. and AppliedMath., Assn. Computing Machinery, Sigma Xi. Presbyterian. Avocations: tennis, landscaping. Home: 819 Gwynne Ave Waynesboro VA 22980-3342 Office: Va Mil Inst Lexington VA 24450

TIERNEY, THOMAS J., social entrepreneur; b. San Francisco, Mar. 5, 1954; s. Ralph Thomas and Eleanor Faye (Walker) T.; m. Joy Karen McGee, Sept. 23, 1984; children: Colin McGee, Braden Thomas. BA in Econs. with distinction, U. Calif., Davis, 1976; MBA with distinction, Harvard, 1980. Field engr. Bechtel Internat., Azrew, Algeria, 1976-78; cons. Bain & Co., San Francisco, 1980-82, mgr., 1982-83, v.p., 1983-87, mng. ptnr., 1987-92; pres. Bain & Co. Worldwide, San Francisco, 1992-2000, CEO, 1993-2000; founder & chmn. Bridgespan Group, 2000—; bd. dirs. eBay, Inc. Co-author: Aligning the Stars, 2002; contbr. articles to profl. jours., chapters to books. Trustee Woods Hole Oceanographic Inst., The Hoover Inst., Harvard Bus. Sch. Social Enterprise; former bd. dirs. Nature Conservancy, Cath. Charities, WGBH, U. Calif.-Davis Alumni Assn., Bay Area United Way, United Way Mass. Bay, Stanford Bus. Sch.; bd. dirs. Inst. for Higher Edn., Nat. Acads. Recipient Winslow Meml. award U. Calif. Davis, 1976. Roman Catholic. Avocations: fishing, politics, non-profit sector. Home: 45 Old Farm Rd Wellesley MA 02481-1423 Office Phone: 617-572-3015. Business E-Mail: thomas.tierney@bridgespangroup.org.

TIERNO, JOEL THOMAS, philosopher, educator; b. Bethpage, NY, Apr. 23, 1958; s. Joseph Anthony Tierno and Dolorus Patricia Pesce; m. Gina Sully, Nov. 25, 2001. BA, SUNY, Oswego, 1981; MA, SUNY, Brockport, 1982; MD, PhD, SUNY, Buffalo, 1991. Instr. SUNY, Buffalo, 1984—86, 1993, Elmira Coll., NY, 1993—94; asst. prof. Erie CC, NY, 1994—2000; prof. Coll. So. Nev., Henderson, 2000—; instr. Buffalo State Coll., 1995—2000. Reviewer Sophia, Melbourne, 2000—06. Author: Descartes on God and Human Error, 1997, Epistonic Evil, 2007; contbr. numerous articles to profl. jours. Mem.: ACLU, So. Poverty Law Ctr., Am. Philos. Assn., Phi Theta Kappa. Green Party. Avocations: writing, drawing, hiking. Office: Coll So Nev 700 College Dr Henderson NV 89015

TIERNO, PHILIP MARIO, JR., microbiologist, educator, researcher; b. Bklyn., June 5, 1943; s. Philip M. and Phyllis (Tringone) T.; m. Josephine Martinez, Apr. 2, 1967; children: Alexandra Lorraine, Meredith Anne. BS, Bklyn. Coll. Pharmacy, 1965; MS, NYU, 1974, PhD, 1977. Microbiologist Luth. Med. Ctr., Bklyn., 1965-66; chief rsch. microbiologist hemodialysis unit VA Hosp., Bronx, NY, 1966-70; dir. microbiology divsn. NYU Med. Ctr. Goldwater Meml. Hosp., F.D. Roosevelt Island, 1970-81; assoc. and cons. microbiologist Maimonides Med. Ctr., Bklyn., 1970-79; dir. microbiology dept. Tisch-Univ. Hosp., NYU Med. Ctr., 1981—. Adj. asst. prof. CUNY, 1974—76, Bloomfield (NJ) Coll., 1975—82; assoc. prof. microbiology and pathology NYU Med. Sch., 1981—; cons. Office Atty. Gen. NY State, NIH, Coll. of Am. Pathologists, Dept. Health City of NY, 1981—; mem. Mayoral Task Force on Bioterrorism, NYC. Author: The Secret Life of Germs: Observations and Lessons from a Microbe Hunter, 2001, Protect Yourself Against Bioterrorism, 2002, Nuclear, Chemical and Biological Terrorism: Emergency Response and Public Protection, 2003, The Secret Life of Germs: What They Are, Why We Need Them, and How We Can Protect Ourselves Against Them, 2004; contbr. articles to profl. jours., chapters to books. Pres. Flushing Taxpayers Assn., 1973-77; bd. dirs. Comprehensive Health Planning Agy. City of NY, 1974-75, Norwood Bd. Adjustment, NJ, 1978-83, 86-98, Norwood Bd. Edn., 1983-86; chmn. Norwood Environ. Commn., 1986-98; co-founder, bd. dirs. Found. Sci. Rsch. in Pub. Interest, S.I., NY, 1985—. Recipient Leone de San Marcos award, 2005. Mem. AAAS, NY Acad. Scis., Am. Acad. Microbiology, APHA, Am. Soc. Microbiology, Am. Soc. for Clin. Pathology, Optimists (v.p. Norwood 1978-95), Knights of Malta (Knighthood). Office: Tisch Hosp-Microbiology Dept NYU Med Ctr 560 1st Ave New York NY 10016-6402 Office Phone: 212-263-5905. Business E-Mail: philip.tierno@nyumc.org.

TIESENGA, MARVIN FRANCIS, surgeon; b. Slayton, Minn., Apr. 3, 1929; s. Edward Tiesenga and Sieka Drenth-Tiesenga; m. Ardythe Rae Noorlag, Aug. 19, 1955; children: Jane, Edward, Mary, Frederick, Anne. BS, Roosevelt U., 1950; MD, U. Ill., 1954. Diplomate Am. Bd. Surgery. Intern Cook County Hosp., Chgo., 1954, resident gen. surgery, 1957—61; pres. med. staff West Suburban Hosp., Oak Park, Ill., 1986—88, chief surgery, 1989—. Contbr. articles to profl. jours. Mem. Elmhurst Christian Ref. Ch., 1971—. Capt. US Army, 1955—57, Korea. Named Number one Dr., Crane's Chgo. Mag., 2000, 2001, 2002, 2003; recipient, 2004, Ken Douglas award for excellence, Citizens of Oak Park, 2000. Fellow: ACS; mem.: AMA, SAGES, Chgo. Med. Soc., Ill. Med. Soc., Am. Soc. Breast Surgeons, Am. Soc. Bariatric Surgery, Aux Planes Med. Soc., Christian Med. and Dental Assn. Avocations: boating, travel, history, collecting antique tractors. Office: 7411 Lake St Ste 2100 River Forest IL 60305 Office Phone: 708-386-1078.

TIESI, JOSEPH A., corporate financial executive; Grad., St. Francis Coll., 1980. With PricewaterhouseCoopers, 1980—86; sr. fin. analyst Altria Corp. Svcs., Inc., 1986—90, mgr. fin. reporting and analysis, 1990—95, dir. fin. reporting and analysis, 1995—98, asst. contr. fin. reporting and consolidation, 1998—99, v.p., contr., 1999—. Office: Altria Corp Svcs Inc 120 Park Ave New York NY 10017

TIETZ, DIETMAR JUERGEN, website engineer, scientist; b. Berlin, Jan. 19, 1951; s. Alfred Georg Paul and Gertrud Klara (Schulz) T. m. Angelina (Osorio Ugalde). PhD, Hamburg U., 1982. Lectr. U. Hamburg, 1977-82; sr. scientist macromolecular analysis NIH, Bethesda, Md., 1983-93; pres., CEO, chmn. mktg. Forty Plus Greater Washington, 1992-93; sci. project mgr. dept. biostats. Justus-Liebig U., Giessen, Germany, 1993-95; web engring. team lead, software arch. Aerotek Md., NASA EOSDIS govt. project Raytheon Systems, 1996-99; dir. product devel. Dynamic Diagrams subs. Cadmus Profl. Comm., 1999—. Editor: Nucleic Acid Electrophoresis Lab Manual, 1998; mem. editl. bd. Electrophoresis Jour., VCH Weinheim, Germany, 1994-96. Mem. Am. Chem. Soc., Assn. German Naturforscher and Aerzte. Lutheran. Avocations: nature, computers, photography, electronic keyboard. Office: Cadmus 8621 Robert Fulton Dr # 100 Columbia MD 21046-2278 E-mail: djt@his.com.

TIFFANY, JOSEPH RAYMOND, II, lawyer; b. Dayton, Ohio, Feb. 5, 1949; s. Forrest Fraser and Margaret Watson (Clark) T.; m. Terri Robbins, Dec. 1, 1984. AB magna cum laude, Harvard U., Cambridge, Mass., 1971; MS in Internat. Relations, London Sch. Econs., 1972; JD, U. Calif., Berkeley, 1975. Bar: US Dist. Ct. (no. dist.) 1975, US Dist. Ct. (ea. dist.) 1977, US Ct. Appeals (9th cir.) 1982, US Ct. Appeals (fed. cir.) 2004. Assoc. Pillsbury, Madison & Sutro, San Francisco, 1975-82, ptnr., 1983-2001, Pillsbury Winthrop LLP, Palo Alto, Calif., 2001—05, Pillsbury Winthrop Shaw Pittman LLP, 2005—. Mem. ABA (antitrust sect.), Calif. Bar Assn. (antitrust and unfair competition sect.). Office: Pillsbury Winthrop Shaw Pittman LLP 2475 Hanover St Palo Alto CA 94304-1115 Office Phone: 650-233-4644. Business E-Mail: joseph.tiffany@pillsburylaw.com.

TIFFORD, JOHN MARK, lawyer; d. Harry A. and Rose K. Tifford. BA, CCNY, NYC, 1962; LLB, Cornell U., Ithaca, NY, 1965. Bar: D.C. 1978, N.Y. 1965, Va. 1977. Atty. Fed. Trade Commn., Washington, 1975—88; ptnr. DLA Piper LLP, Washington, 1988—2006; mng. ptnr. Plave Koch PLC, Reston, Va., 2007—. Presenter in field. Contbr. articles to profl. jours. With USAR, 1965—71. Mem.: ABA, D.C. Bar Assn., Va. Bar Assn., N.Y. State Bar Assn. Office: Plave Koch PLC 11250 Roger Bacon Dr Reston VA 20190 Office Phone: 703-774-1204. Business E-Mail: jtifford@plavekoch.com.

TIFFT, WILLIAM GRANT, retired physics professor, scientist; b. Derby, Conn., Apr. 5, 1932; s. William Charles and Marguerite Howe (Hubbell) T.; m. Carol Ruth Nordquist, June 1, 1957 (div. July 1964); children: Jennifer, William John; m. Janet Ann Lindner Homewood, June 2, 1965; 1 child, Amy, stepchildren: Patricia, Susan, Hollis. AB, Harvard Coll., 1954; PhD, Calif. Inst. Tech., 1958. Postdoctoral fellow Australian Nat. U., Canberra, 1958-60; rsch. assoc. Vanderbilt U., Nashville, 1960-61; astronomer Lowell Obs., Flagstaff, Ariz., 1961-64; assoc. prof. U. Ariz., Tucson, 1964-73, prof., 1973—2002, prof. emeritus, 2002—; prin. scientist Sci. Assn. Study of Time in Physics and Cosmology, 2000—. Joint author: Revised New General Catalog, 1973; joint editor: Modern Mathematical Models of Time and Their Applications to Physics and Cosmology, 1997;

contbr. over 100 articles to profl. jours. NSF Predoctoral fellow, 1954-58, NSF Postdoctoral fellow, 1958-60; grantee NASA, NSF, ONR, Rsch. Corp. Fellow Am. Astron. Soc.; mem. Internat. Astron. Union, Sci. Assn. Study of Time in Physics and Cosmology (prin. scientist 2000-). Achievements include discovery of redshift quantization and correlations relating to it, including variability; first to detect voids in mapping of large scale supercluster structure; investigations of three-dimensional time in cosmology and particle physics. Office: U Arizona Dept Astronomy Tucson AZ 85721-0001

TIFT, MARY LOUISE, artist; b. Seattle, Jan. 2, 1913; d. John Howard and Wilhelmina (Pressler) Dreher; m. William Raymond Tift, Dec. 4, 1948. BFA cum laude, U. Wash., 1933; postgrad., Art Ctr. Coll., LA, 1945-48, U. Calif., San Francisco, 1962-63. Art dir. Vaughn Shedd Advt., LA, 1948; asst. prof. design Calif. Coll. Arts & Crafts, Oakland, Calif., 1949-59; coord. design dept. San Francisco Art Inst., 1959-62. Subject of cover story, Am. Artist mag., 1980, studio article, 1987; one-woman shows, Gumps Gallery, San Francisco, 1977, 1986, 90, Diane Gilson Gallery, Seattle, 1978, Oreg. State U., 1981, Univ. House, Seattle, Frye Art Mus., Seattle, 2000; exhibited in group shows including Brit. Biennale, Yorkshire, Eng., 1970, Grenchen Triennale, Switzerland, 1970, Polish Biennale, Crakow, 1972, Nat. Gallery, Washington, 1973, Madrid Biennale, 1980, U.S.-U.K. Impressions, Eng., 1988; represented in permanent collections, Phila. Mus. Art, Bklyn. Mus., Seattle Art Mus., Library Congress, Achenbach Print Collection, San Francisco Palace Legion of Honor, San Diego Mus. Art, U.S. Art in Embassies. Served to lt. USNR, 1943-45. Mem. Print Club Phila., World Print Council, Calif. Soc. Printmakers, Phi Beta Kappa, Lambda Rho. Christian Scientist. Studio: 4400 Stone Way N Apt 521 Seattle WA 98103-7487

TIGAR, MICHAEL EDWARD, law educator; b. Glendale, Calif., Jan. 18, 1941; s. Charles Henry and Margaret Elizabeth (Lang) T.; m. Pamet Ayer Jones, Sept. 21, 1961 (div. Mar. 1973); children: Jon Steven, Katherine Ayer; m. Amanda G. Birrell, Feb. 16, 1980 (div. Aug. 1996); 1 child, Elizabeth Torrey; m. Jane E. Blanksteen, Aug. 22, 1996. BA in Polit. Sci., U. Calif., Berkeley, 1962, JD, 1966. Bar: D.C. 1967, U.S. Ct. Appeals (2d, 4th, 5th, 6th, 7th, 8th, 9th, 10th, 11th, fed. and D.C. cirs.), U.S. Tax Ct., U.S. Supreme Ct. 1972, N.Y. 1993. Assoc. Williams & Connolly, Washington, 1966-69; editor-in-chief Selective Svc. Law Reporter, Washington, 1967-69; acting prof. law UCLA, 1969-71; pvt. practice law Grasse, France, 1972-74; assoc. William & Connolly, Washington, 1974, ptnr., 1975-77, Tigar & Buffone, Washington, 1977-84; prof. law U. Tex., Austin, 1984-87, Joseph D. Jamail Centennial prof. law, 1987-98; of counsel Haddon, Morgan & Foreman, Denver, 1996-98; prof. law, and Edwin A. Mooers, Sr., Scholar Am. U. Washington Coll. Law, Washington, 1998—; mem. Tiger Law Firm. Reporter 5th Cir. Pattern Jury Instrns., Austin, 1988-90. Author: Practice Manual Selective Service Law Reporter, 1968, Law and the Rise of Capitalism, 1977, (with Jane B. Tigar) Federal Appeals: Jurisdiction and Practice, 3d edit., 1999, Examining Witnesses, 1993, Persuasion: The Litigator's Art, 1999; contbr. articles to profl. jours. Mem. ABA (vice chair 1987-88, chair elect 1988-89, chair 1989-90 sect. litigation). Avocations: sailing, cooking. Office: Washington Coll Law 4801 Massachusetts Ave NW Washington DC 20016-8196 Office Phone: 202-549-4229. *

TIGER, IRA PAUL, retired lawyer; b. Bklyn., Jan. 31, 1936; s. Sidney and Rebecca (Frankel) T.; m. Rosalind Silverman, July 4, 1957 (dec. Nov. 1972); children: Ruth, Lori; m. Ann Mae Gersh, May 5, 1974; stepchildren: Jimmie, Randy, Richard Riesenberg. BS in Econs., U. Pa., 1956, JD magna cum laude, 1959. Bar: Pa. 1960, U.S. Dist. Ct. (ea. dist.) Pa. 1960, U.S. Ct. Appeals (3d cir.) 1960, U.S. Supreme Ct. 1971, U.S. Ct. Appeals (7th cir.) 1996. Law clk. 3d cir., 1959-60; assoc. Schnader, Harrison, Segal & Lewis, Phila., 1960-67, ptnr., 1968—2002, chmn. litigation dept., 1986-90, chmn. standing com. on profl. conduct, 1992—2003, sr. counsel, 2003—04. Judge pro tem Phila. Ct. Common Pleas, 1994—2003; mediator U.S. Dist. Ct. (ea. dist.) Pa., 1991—2003. Rsch. editor U. Pa. Law Rev., 1958-59. Pres. Temple Sinai Synagogue, 1989-91, Elkins Park House Coun., 1996-98; mem. Planning Adv. Bd. Upper Dublin Twp., 1982-87, mem. ednl. adv. com., 1976-78; legal counsel Phila. Jr. C. of C., 1963-64, bd. dirs., 1962-66, sec. Jewish campus activities bd., 1971-73; mem. citizens' adv. com. Cheltenham Twp., 2004—, vice-chmn., 2006—. Mem. ABA, Am. Judicature Soc., Inst. Jud. Adminstrn., Phila. Bar Assn. (chmn. fed. cts. com. 1985), Lawyers Club Phila., Order of Coif (exec. com. Pa. chpt. 1981-83), Beta Alpha Psi, Beta Gamma Sigma. Democrat. Office: Schnader Harrison 1600 Market St Ste 3600 Philadelphia PA 19103-7286 Business E-Mail: itiger@schnader.com.

TIGER, LIONEL, social scientist, anthropology consultant; b. Montreal, Que., Can., Feb. 5, 1937; s. Martin and Lillian (Schneider) T.; 1 child, Sebastian Benjamin. BA, McGill U., 1957, MA, 1959; PhD, U. London, 1963. Instr. anthropology U. Ghana, Accra, 1960; asst. prof. dept. anthropology and sociology U. B.C., Vancouver, Canada, 1963—68; assoc. prof. anthropology Rutgers U., New Brunswick, NJ, 1969—74, prof. anthropology, 1974—, Charles Darwin prof. anthropology, 1990—. Cons., rsch. dir. Harry F. Guggenheim Found., N.Y.C., 1972-84; chmn. bd. social scientists U.S. News and World Report, 1986-88; sci. adv. bd. Am. Wine Inst., San Francisco; sr. rsch. assoc. Nat. Inst. Pub. Policy; mem. bd. advisors George Polk Awards, 2004—. Author: Men in Groups, 1969, 3d edit., 2004, (with Robin Fox) The Imperial Animal, 1971, 3d edit., 1998, (with Joseph Shepher) Women in the Kibbutz, 1975, Optimism: The Biology of Hope, 1979, 2d edit., 1994, China's Food, 1985, The Manufacture of Evil: Ethics, Evolution and the Industrial System, 1987; editor: Female Hierarchies, 1978, 2nd edit. 2007, (with Michael Robinson) Man and Beast Revisited, 1992, The Pursuit of Pleasure, 1992, 2d edit., 2000, The Decline of Males, 1999, The Apes of New York, 2003; series editor: Anthropology and Human Nature, 2005; mem. editl. bd. Social Sci. Info., Ethology and Sociobiology jour., Jour. of Social Distress and the Homeless Cultural laureate N.Y.C. Landmarks Found., 1999. Recipient W.I. Susman award for excellence in tchg., 1985, McNaughton prize for creative writing; Guggenheim fellow, 1969, rsch. fellow ASDA Found., 1985, Can. Coun., fgn. area tng. fellow Ford Found., Can. Coun.-Killam fellow for interdisciplinary rsch., Rockefeller fellow Aspen Inst., 1979, H.F. Guggenheim Found. fellow, 1988-89; Inst. for Law and Behavioral Rsch. fellow; Govt. of Que. fellow, 2005-06. Mem. PEN (mem. exec. bd., treas. 1988-91, v.p. 1991-94), Am. Anthrop. Assn., Internat. Humanist Assn. (humanist laureate), Can. Humanists Assn. (hon.), Soc. for Study of Evolution, Century Assn. Home: 248 W 23rd St Fl 4 New York NY 10011-2304 also: PO Box 965 Millbrook NY 12545 Office: Rutgers U 131 George St New Brunswick NJ 08901-1414 Business E-Mail: ltiger@anthropology.rutgers.edu.

TIGERMAN, STANLEY, architect, educator; b. Chgo., Sept. 20, 1930; s. Samuel Bernard and Emma Louise (Stern) T.; m. Margaret I. McCurry; children: Judson Joel, Tracy Leigh. Student, MIT, Cambridge, 1948-49; BArch, Yale U., New Haven, 1960, MArch, 1961. Archtl. draftsman firm George Fred Keck, Chgo., 1949-50, Skidmore, Owings and Merrill, Chgo., 1957-59, Paul Rudolph, New Haven, 1959-61, Harry Weese, Chgo., 1961-62; ptnr. firm Tigerman & Koglin, Chgo., 1962-64; prin. firm Stanley Tigerman & Assos., Chgo., 1964-82; ptnr. Tigerman Fugman McCurry, Chgo., 1982-88, Tigerman McCurry Archs., Chgo., 1988—. Prof. architecture U. Ill.-Chgo., 1967-71, 80-93, dir. Sch. Architecture, 1985-93; vis. lectr. Yale U., 1974, Cornell U., Ithaca, N.Y., 1963, Cooper Union, 1970, U. Calif. at Berkeley, 1968, Cardiff (Wales) Coll., 1965, Engring. U., Bangladesh, 1967; chmn. AIA com. on design, coordinator exhbn. and book Chicago Architects, 1977; Charlotte Shepherd Davenport prof. architecture Yale U., 1979; architect-in-residence Am. Acad. in Rome, 1980; vis. prof. architecture Harvard U., 1982; William Henry Bishop Chair. prof. architecture Yale U., 1984, Sarrinen prof., 1993; dir. post-professional grad. program U. Ill.-Chgo.; co-founder Archeworks, Design Lab., Chgo., 1993; mem. adv. com. Princeton U., 1997. Prin. works include Ounce of Prevention Educare Ctr., Chgo., Fukuoka Apt. Complex, Japan, Power House, Zion, Ill., Chgo. Children's Adv. Ctr., Holocaust Mus. and Edn. Ctr., Skokie, Ill., Pacific Garden Mission, Chgo.; author: Versus, 1982, Architecture of Exile, 1988, Stanley Tigerman: Buildings and Projects, 1966-89, 1989; contbr. Design of the Housing Site, 1966, Chicago on Foot, 1969, Art Today, 1969, New Direction in American Architecture, 1969, Contemporary Jewelry, 1970, Urban Structures for the Future, 1972, Spaces for Living, 1973, Chicago 1930-70, 1974, Interior Spaces Designed by Architects, 1976, 100 Years of Architecture in Chicago, 1976, 100 Years of Architecture in Chicago, 1986, Mies Reconsidered, 1986, Chicago Architecture 1872-1922, 1988, articles; exhibitions include Venice Biennale, 1976, 1980, Calif. Condition, 1982;, author essay; exhibitions include Chicago Architecture, The New Zeitgeist: In Search of Closure, 1989; author: (catalog) Chicago Architecture, The New Zeitgeist: In Search of Closure, 1989. Pres. Yale Arts Assn., 1969-70; bd. dirs. Bangladesh Found.; adv. com. Yale Sch. Architecture, 1976-2006. Served with USN, 1950-54. Recipient Alpha Rho Chi medal, Yale, 1961, Archtl. Record award, 1970, Masonry award, 1974, Masonry gold medal, 1974, Alumni Art award, Yale U., 1985, Design award for Art Inst. Chgo. Schinkel Exhbn., Am. Soc. Interior Designers, 1995, Humanitarian award, Holocaust Meml. Found. Ill., 2001, Grand award of Excellence, NAHB, 2001, 2003, Recognition award, World Trade Ctr. Meml., 2004, Cultures Achievement award, Univ. Club Chgo., 2004; grantee Advanced Studies in Fine Art, Graham Fedn., 1965. Fellow AIA (chmn. com. design 1976-77, adv. com., Disting. Svc. award Chgo. chpt. 1983, Chgo. Honor awards 1977-79, Nat. Honor award 1982, 84, 87, 91, 98, Nat. Modern Income Housing award 1970, Nat. Homes for Better Living award 1974, 75, Ill. award 1976, Nat. award of Merit 1970, 74, 75, named to Hall of Fame 1990, Disting. Bldg. award for pvt. residence Chgo. chpt. 1991, Chgo. Interior Archtl. Award of Excellence 1981, 83, 87, 91, 92, Nat. Interior Archtl. Award of Excellence 1992-93, Chgo. Disting. Bldg. award 1971, 73, 75, 77, 79, 81, 82, 84, 85, 86, 91, 94, Italian Ceramic Tile Design award 1995, Fukuoka Urban Beautification award 1995, 6 citations of merit Chgo. chpt. 1994, Interior Design award for A.I.C. Schinkel Exhibit 1996, Chgo. Interior Architecture award 1997, Chgo. Chpt. Arch. award 1998, Nat. Interior Architecture award 1998, Louis Sullivan award 2000), Ill./Ind. Masonry Coun. (Silver Award for Excellance in Masonry 2003); mem. Arts Club of Chgo., Yale Club of N.Y.C., Phi Kappa Phi. Office: Tigerman McCurry Archs 444 N Wells St Ste 206 Chicago IL 60610-4522 Office Phone: 312-644-5880. E-mail: tma@tigerman-mccurry.com.

TIGHE, MARY ANN, real estate company executive; m. David Hidalgo; 1 child from previous marriage, Aaron. BA in Art Hist., Cath. U.; MA in Art Hist., U. Md. Staff mem. Smithsonian Instn.; arts adv. to v.p. Walter Mondale; dep. chmn. Nat. Endowment Arts; v.p. ABC; sales assoc. Edward S. Gordon Inc. (name changed to Insignia/ESG Inc. 1997), 1984, exec. mng. dir. NYC, 1993—99; vice chmn. Insignia/ESG Inc., NYC, 1999—2002; pres., CEO NY Tri-State Region CB Richard Ellis, NYC, 2002—. Dir. Imperial Parking Corp. Bd. dirs. NYC Ballet, Parrish Art Mus., The New 42nd St., Joan's Legacy: The Joan Scarangello Found. to Conquer Lung Cancer. Recipient Woman of Yr., Comml. Real Estate Women NY, 2001, NJ Deal of Yr. award, Nat. Assn. Indsl. and Office Properties, 2002, NY Deal of Yr. award, 2003, Rising Exec. award, Comml. Property News, 2004. Mem.: Real Estate Bd. NY (mem. exec. com. bd. govs. 2001—, Robert T. Lawrence Meml. award 1992, Henry Hart Rice Achievement award 1997, Robert T. Lawrence Meml. award 1998, Henry Hart Rice Achievement award 2002, Louis Smadbeck Meml. Broker Recognition award 2004, Most Creative Retail Deal of Yr. 2002). Office: CB Richard Ellis Grp Inc 200 Park Ave New York NY 10166 Office Phone: 212-984-8128. Office Fax: 212-984-8322. E-mail: maryann.tighe@cbre.com. *

TIGHE-MOORE, BARBARA JEANNE, electronics executive; b. Wadsworth, Ohio, Jan. 12, 1961; d. Norton Raymond and Laura Alida (Frank) Tighe; m. Derek William Moore, June 26, 1982. Student summa cum laude, Hocking Tech. Coll., Nelsonville, Ohio, 1981; student, Sinclair Coll., 1986; BBA magna cum laude, Kent State U., Ohio, 1988; postgrad. of Info. Tech. Program Mgmt.Q, Capella U. Lic. amateur radio operator. Tech. writer computer dept. Sinclair Coll., Dayton, Ohio, 1983; project mgr. O'Neil & Assocs., Dayton, 1983-84; biomed., bio-acoustic real-time flight simulation tempest developer Systems Rsch. Labs., Dayton, 1984-86; computer specialist Kent State U. Press, 1987-88; mgmt. analyst Electronic Warfare Frontier Engring. Inc., 1988-89; supr. computer tech. svcs. Frontier Engring., Inc., 1989-90, project engr., 1990-92; ptnr., bd. dirs. MKCC, Dayton, 1990—, SDCC, Dayton, 1992—; regional mgr. User Tech. Assocs., Dayton, 1993-96; pres., owner Lida Ray Techs., Dayton, 1978—; prof. dept. computer sci. Nat. Coll. Bus. and Tech.; prof. bus. and computer depts. Nat. Coll. Graphics steering com., mem. sanctioned UNIX software adv. team Aero. Sys. Divsn.; program chair IEEE Internat. Wireless LAN Conf.; pres. Engring. Application Support Environ. Security Working Group, 2000; proceedings chmn. Nat. Aerospace & Electronics Conf., 1995—97, pres., 2000; bd. dirs. MKCC, Dayton, Cin. Digital Women; spkr. in field. Author: Job Search Strategies for the 90's, 1993, Through the Glass Ceiling, 1997, Riding the 5:15, 2000, Convergence of Socio-Economic and Technology Factors, 2001; co-author: Women on a Wire, 1996, vol. 2, 2001; editor: Graphics Directions, 1990—91; pub.: Team Advisor, SDCC Learning Times, IEEE Update; author: numerous poems; contbr. articles to profl. jours. Counselor Kwam's Kinder Kamp; tchr. Bible Sch.; cook Meals on Wheels; organizer/cook funeral Svcs. Dinners. Recipient Vol. Citizen award Wadsworth C. of C, 1979, Ohio Essayist award, 1979, Virginia Perryman award, 1979, Disting. Leadership award, 1990-91 Mem.: IEEE (former treas., sec. Dayton sect., bd. dirs. 1995—97, chmn. bd. dirs. Dayton sect. 1999, region 2 chpt. coord. 2000—, 3d Millennium award, Extended Svc. award 2007), Equestrian Team (point rider 1977—87), Armed Forces Comms. and Electronics Assn. (judge sci. fair western dist. 1992—), Internat. Film Soc. (pres. 1986—88), Assn. Internat. Students Econs. & Commerce (pres. 1986—87), Def. Planning Analysis Soc. (exec. bd.), Assn. Computer Machinery, Data Processing Mgmt. Assn., Tech. and Soc. of IEEE, Engring. Mgmt. Soc. of IEEE, Computer Soc. of IEEE (sec. 1991—92, vice chmn. 1992—93, chmn. 1994—95), Mortar Bd., Fencing Club, Beta Gamma Sigma, Omicron Delta Kappa, Phi Theta Kappa. Avocations: travel, investing, equestrian show jumping, soccer, painting. Home: 729 Kyle Dr Tipp City OH 45371-1435 Office Phone: 937-667-4972. Business E-Mail: bjmoore@lidaray.com.

TIGHIOUART, MOURAD, statistician, researcher; b. Algiers, Algeria, Dec. 21, 1964; s. Laid Tighiouart and Rezkia Djaballah; m. Leila Benbahmed, Dec. 20, 2000; children: Rayan, Tara. BS in Math., USTHB, Algiers, 1987; MS in Math., U. Ctrl. Fla., Orlando, 1991; MS in Stats., Fla. State U., Tallahassee, 1998, PhD, 1998. Asst. prof. Utah State U., Logan, 1998—2003; rsch. biostatistician Fox Chase Cancer Ctr., Phla., 2003—04; asst. prof. Emory U., Atlanta, 2004—. Co-dir. biostatistics Winship Cancer Inst., Atlanta, 2004—. Contbr. articles to profl. jours. Mem.: Internat. Bayesian Soc., Soc. Clin. Trials, Am. Statis. Assn. (corr.). Home: 6394 Mimosa Cir Tucker GA 30084 Office: Emory Univ 1365 Clifton Rd Room B 4111 Atlanta GA 30322 Home Phone: 770-931-3724; Office Phone: 404-778-4157. Business E-Mail: mourad.tighiouart@emoryhealthcare.org.

TILAAR, HENRY A.R., social sciences educator; b. Tondano, Indonesia, June 16, 1932; s. Kilala and Engelien (Mamuaya) T.; m. Martha Handana, Jan. 12, 1964; children: Bryan, Pingkan, Wulan, Kilala. MA in Edn., U. Indonesia, Jakarta, 1961; MSc in Edn., Ind. U., 1967, EdD, 1969. Prof. State U. Jakarta, 1969—97; mem. staff Nat. Devel. Office (Bappenas), Jakarta, 1970—93, asst. min., 1986-93; prof. U. Jakarta, 1987-98, prof. emeritus, 1997—. Dir. Inst. Mgmt. Devel. U. Jakarta, 1991—; mem. adv. bd. Indonesian Tchrs. Assn.; cons. in field. Author: Education in National Development, 1990, National Education Management, 1992, Indonesian Education Development, 1945-1995, A Policy Study, 1995, Human Resources Development, Vision and Mission for 2020, 1997, Agenda for Education Reform for 21st Century, 1998, Education, Culture, and Civil Society, 1999, New Paradigms of National Education, 2000, National Education Reconstruction, 2001, Social Change and Education, A Transformative Pedagogy for Indonesia, 2002, Power and Education, A Cultural Studies Perspective, 2003, Multicultural Education, 2004, National Education Manifesto, 2005. Chmn. bd. advisors Cath. U., Jakarta, 1995-99; mem. bd. advisors Acad. Mgmt., Jakarta, 1996. Recipient Grand medal of merit Republic of Indonesia, 1998. Mem. Nat. Rsch. Coun., Indonesian Soc. for Advancement of Social Scis., Indonesian Lectrs. Assn. Democrat. Roman Catholic. Avocations: gardening, jogging, watching soccer. Home: Jl Patra Kuningan Utara Blok L-VII No 4 Jakarta Indonesia Office: LPMP State U Jakarta Jl Rawamangun Muka Jakarta DKI Indonesia Business E-Mail: hartilaar@martinaberto.co.id.

TILDEN, BRADLEY DOUGLAS, air transportation executive; b. Houston, Tex., 1960; Degree, Pacific Luth. U., Tacoma, Wash., 1983, U. Wash., Seattle, 1997. From mem. staff to exec. v.p., CFO Alaska Air Group, Inc., Seattle, 1991—2000, CFO, 2000—, exec. v.p. fin., 2002—. Office: Alaska Air Group Inc 19300 Pacific Hwy South Seattle WA 98188

TILDEN, WESLEY RODERICK, writer, retired application developer; b. Saint Joseph, Mo., Jan. 19, 1922; s. Harry William and Grace Alida (Kinnaman) T.; m. Lorraine Henrietta Frederick, June 20, 1948 (dec. Mar. 1999). Grad., Navy Supply Corps Sch., 1945; BS, UCLA, 1948; BA, Park Coll., Mo., 1990. Purchasing agent Vortox Co., Claremont, Calif., 1951-61; lang. lab. dir. Mount San Antonio Coll., Walnut, Calif., 1962-65; computer programmer, operator General Dynamics, Pomona, Calif., 1967-70; ret., 1970. Author: Scota, The Egyptian Princess, 1994, Merit-Sekhet: Foster Mother of Moses?, 1996; photographer, textbooks, mags., newspaper, catalogs. Historian Claremont Sister City Assn., 1963-66. Lt. USNR, 1942-46 PTO. Recipient with Lorraine Tilden People to People award Reader's Digest Found., 1963-65; named Hon. Citizen Guanajuato, Mexico, 1963. Mem. Soc. Mayflower Descendants, Scottish Clans, UCLA Alumni Assn., Park Coll. Alumni Assn., Univ. Club of Claremont, The Scituate Hist. Soc. (Mass.). Republican. Avocations: history, genealogy, photography, gardening. Home: 351 Oakdale Dr Claremont CA 91711-5039

TILESTON, JACKIE, artist, educator; b. Manila, Philippines, Dec. 11, 1960; arrived in U.S., 1979; d. Peter Ayer and Margaret Doreen Tileston. BA in fine arts (painting) summa cum laude, Yale U., New Haven, Conn., 1983; MFA in painting, Ind. U., Bloomington, 1988. Faculty Glassell Sch. Art Mus. Fine Arts, Houston, 1990—98; asst. prof. painting U. N.Mex., Albuquerque, 1998—2000; assoc. prof. fine arts U. Pa., Phila., 2000—. Adj. faculty mem. U. Houston, 1993—98; adj. faculty Rice U., 1997. One-woman shows include W.A. Graham Gallery, Houston, 1990, 1992, Mus. Art, Longview, Tex., 1994, Lawing Gallery, Houston, 1997, Satellite Space, U. Tex., San Antonio, 1998, U. N.Mex., Albuquerque, 2000, Barbara Davis Gallery, Houston, 2003, 2006, Phila. Art Alliance, 2003, Zg Gallery, Chgo., 2005, Holly Johnson Gallery, Dallas, 2005, Not Always So, Barbara Davis Gallery, Houston, 2006, Chromatopia, Rowan U. Gallery, Glassboro, NJ, 2006, Pentimenti Gallery, Phila., Pa., 2007, Zg Gallery, Chgo., 2007, numerous group shows, Represented in permanent collections JP Morgan Chase, Mus. Fine Arts, Houston (Catalog), Dallas Mus. Fine Arts. Named Bellagio resident, Rockefeller Found., 2005; recipient Fellowship Award in Painting, Mid-Am. Arts Alliance/Nat. Endowment for the Arts, 1994; fellow, John S. Guggenheim Meml. Found., 2006; Academic fellow, Ind. U., Bloomington, 1986—88, Core Fellowship resident, Mus. Fine Arts, Houston, 1988—90, PEW Found. fellow, Phila., 2004. Mem.: Coll. Art Assn., Phi Beta Kappa. Office: Fine Arts Univ Pa 100 Morgan Bldg 205 S 34th St Philadelphia PA 19104 Business E-Mail: tileston@design.upenn.edu.

TILEWICK, ROBERT, lawyer; b. NYC, Jan. 16, 1956; s. David and Helen (Fogel) T.; m. Susan Dara Tilewick; children: Naomi Seana, Benjamin Solomon. BA, Columbia U., 1977; JD, Temple U., 1985. Bar: N.Y. 1986, Ct. 1993, U.S. Dist. Ct. (so. and ea. dists.) N.Y. 1988, U.S. Ct. Appeals (2d cir.) 1989, U.S. Dist. Ct. Conn. 1991. Systems analyst, cons. Personnelmetrics, Inc., NYC, 1977-80, 81-82; assoc. Cravath, Swaine & Moore, NYC, 1985-87, Paul, Weiss, Rifkind, Wharton & Garrison, NYC, 1987-91, 96-97, Wiggin & Dana, New Haven, Conn., 1991-96, Kalow, Springut & Bressler, NYC, 1997-99, Graham & James, NYC, 1999—. Co-designer race timing system for N.Y.C. Marathon, 1977-82. NIH grantee Marine Biol. Lab., Woods Hole, Mass, 1980. Mem. ABA, N.Y.C. Bar Assn., Conn. Bar Assn., Supreme Ct. Hist. Soc. Avocation: music. Office: 885 3rd Ave New York NY 10022-4834

TILFORD, TERRY TRENT, translator; b. St. Louis, Oct. 21, 1940; s. Winslow Otis Tilford and Arlye June Twombley; m. Louisa Jane Pringle (div.); 1 child, Heather Elaine. BA in English, Creighton U., Omaha, 1964. Tchr. English Nebr. Pub. Schs., Melbeta, 1964—65; instr. English U. Nebr., Lincoln, 1968—69; regular distbn. clerk US Post Office, Omaha, 1969—78; self employed translator, editor San Francisco, 1979—. Mem.: Internat. Campaign Tibet, Defenders Wildlife, Sierra Club, Eta Sigma Phi, Alpha Sigma Nu. Avocations: reading, linguistics, history.

TILGHMAN, RICHARD CARMICHAEL, JR., lawyer; b. Balt., July 6, 1947; s. Richard Carmichael and Mary Donnell (Singer) T.; m. Beverly Oliver Wheeler, Sept. 11, 1975; 1 child, Elizabeth Lloyd. BA, Union Coll., 1969; JD with honors, U. Md., 1975. Bar: Md. 1975, U.S. Dist. Ct. Md. 1976. Law clk. to presiding justice Md. Ct. Appeals, Annapolis, 1975-76; assoc. Piper & Marbury, Balt., 1976-83, ptnr., 1983—2004; ptnr., co-chmn. Pub. Co. & Corp. Governance practice group DLA Piper Rudnick Gray Cary, Balt., 2005—. Asst. editor U. Md. Law Rev., 1975. Trustee Gilman Sch., Balt., Balt. City Life Mus.; bd. mem. Ruxton Country Sch., bd. mem. & past pres. Roland Park Country Sch.; served with USN, 1969-72. Mem. ABA, Md. Bar Assn., Md. Hist. Soc., Order of Coif. Clubs: Md., Elkridge (Balt.). Democrat. Episcopalian. Avocations: golf, squash. Office: DLA Piper Rudnick Gray Cary 6225 Smith Ave Baltimore MD 21209-3600 Office Phone: 410-580-4274. Office Fax: 410-580-3274. Business E-Mail: richard.tilghman@dlapiper.com.

TILGHMAN, SHIRLEY MARIE, academic administrator, biology professor; b. Toronto, Can., Sept. 17, 1946; 2 children. BSc in Chemistry with honors, Queen's U., Kingston, Ont., 1968, DSc (hon.), 2002; PhD in Biochemistry, Temple U., Phila., 1975; DSc (hon.), Oxford U., 2002, NYU, 2005; postgrad., NIH. Secondary sch. tchr., West Africa, Sierra Leone, 1968—70; Fogarty internat. fellow NIH, Bethesda, Md., 1975—77; investigator Inst. Cancer Rsch., Phila., 1979—86, Howard Hughes Med. Inst., Chevy Chase, 1988—2001; asst. prof., Fels Rsch Inst. Temple U., Phila., 1978—79; prof. molecular biology Princeton U., NJ, 1986—, Howard A. Prior prof. life scis., 1986—2001, chair Coun. Sci. and Tech., 1993—2000, pres., 2001—. Founding dir. Lewis-Sigler Inst. Integrative Genomics, 1998—2003; adj. assoc. prof. human genetics and biochemistry and biophysics U. Pa., 1980—86; adj. prof. Robert Wood Johnson Med. Sch., 1988—2001; mem. sci. adv. bd. Whitehead Inst. for Biomed. Scis., MIT, 1995—2001; founding mem. Nat. Adv. Coun. Human Genome Project Initiative NIH; founder Princeton Postdoc. Tchg. fellowship. Trustee The Jackson Lab., 1994—, Carnegie Endowment Internat. Peace, 2005—, Google Inc., Rockefeller U., Cold Spring Harbor Lab.; mem. Pew

Charitable Trusts Scholars Prog., Biomedical Scis. Selection Com., Lucille P. Markey Charitable Trust Scholar Selection Com. Recipient Pres.'s award disting. tchg., Princeton U., 1996, L'Oréal-UNESCO Internat. Women in Sci. award, 2002, Lifetime Achievement award, Soc. Devel. Biology, 2003, Radcliffe Inst. medal, Harvard U., 2004, Presdl. Medal of Honor, Dillard U., 2006. Mem.: NAS, Am. Acad. Arts and Scis., Royal Soc. London, Inst. Medicine, Am. Philos. Soc. Achievements include first to identify the H19 gene in mice, an early example of parental imprinting; research in cloning the first mammalian gene. Office: Princeton U Office of Pres One Nassau Hall Princeton NJ 08544-0001 Office Phone: 609-258-6101.

TILL, JAMES EDGAR, medical educator, researcher; b. Lloydminster, Sask., Can., Aug. 25, 1931; s. William and Gertrude Ruth (Isaac) T.; m. Marion Joyce Sinclair, June 6, 1959; children: David William, Karen Sinclair, Susan Elizabeth. BA, U. Sask., 1952, MA, 1954; PhD, Yale U., 1957; DSc (hon.), U. Toronto, Can., 2004, U. Lethbridge, 2007. Mem. physics divsn. Ont. Cancer Inst., Toronto, 1957-67, with divsn. biol. rsch., 1967-89, divsn. head, 1969-82, with divsn. epidemiology and stats., 1989—; assoc. dean U. Toronto, 1981-84, univ. prof., 1984-97, univ. prof. emeritus, 1997—. Contbr. articles to profl. jours. Recipient Gairdner Found. Internat. award, 1969, Order of Can., 1994, Albert Lasker award for Basic Med. Rsch., Lasker Found., 2005; named to Canadian Med. Hall Fame, 2004. Fellow Royal Soc. Can., Royal Soc. London. Achievements include research in biophysics, cell biology and cancer control research. Home: 182 Briar Hill Ave Toronto ON Canada M4R 1H9 Office: Princess Margaret Hosp 9th Fl Rm 416 610 University Ave Toronto ON Canada M5G 2M9 Office Phone: 416-946-2948. Business E-Mail: till@oci.utoronto.ca. *Albert Einstein said: "The most beautiful thing we can experience is the mysterious. It is the source of all true art and science." He also believed that concern for humanity must always form the chief interest of all technical endeavors— "in order that the creations of our mind shall be a blessing and not a curse to mankind." Is there a more eloquent summary of standards for the scientist than this?.*

TILLER, OLIVE MARIE, retired church worker; b. St. Paul, Dec. 13, 1920; d. Otto William and Myrtle Alice (Brougham) Foerster; m. Carl William Tiller, June 21, 1940; children: Robert W., Jeanne L. Peterson; m. Edward J. Alo, Dec. 15, 2001. BS, U. Minn., 1940. Spl. edn. tchr., Prince Georges County, Md., 1955-63; spl. asst. for profl. svcs. Kendall Demonstration Elem. Sch., Gallaudet Coll., Washington, 1971-78; spl. asst. for program Ch. Women United, NYC, 1979-80; exec. asst. to gen. sec. Nat. Coun. Chs. of Christ in U.S.A., NYC, 1981-87; dep. gen. sec. for coop. Christianity Am. Bapt. Chs. of U.S.A., Valley Forge, Pa., 1987-88. Author (with Carl W. Tiller): At Calvary, 1994. Mem. Human Rels. Commn. Prince George's County, 1967—73; bd. dirs. Am. Leprosy Missions, Greenville, SC, 1981—95, Bapt. Peace Fellowship of N.Am., Charlotte, NC, 1984—95; mem. Nat. Interreligious Svc. Bd. for Conscientious Objectors, 1991—98, treas., 1994—98, sec., 1997—98; mem. nat. coun. Fellowship of Reconciliation, 1985—88, 1996—97; mem. Study Commn. on Human Rights Bapt. World Alliance, 1995—2000, mem. Study Commn. on Freedom and Justice, 2000—05, mem. World Aid com., 2000—05; v.p. Am. Bapt. Chs. U.S.A., Valley Forge, 1976—77. Named to Hall of Fame, St. Paul Ctrl. H.S., 1993; recipient Dahlberg Peace award, Am. Bapt. Chs., 1991, Valiant Woman award, Ch. Women United, 1978, Meeker award, Ottawa U., 1995, Luke Mowbray Ecumenical award, Am. Bapt. Chs., 1999, Girls Dormitory at Ulaya Secondary Sch. in Tanzania named for Olive Marie Tiller. Baptist. Home: 283 Norman Dr Cranberry Township PA 16066-4235 Personal E-mail: olivet@zoominternet.net.

TILLER, THOMAS C., manufacturing executive; BA, MIT, 1983; MBA, Harvard U., 1991; M in Mech. Engring., U. Vt. Engr. GE, 1983; mgr. GE Appliances; v.p., gen. mgr. GE Silicones; pres., COO Polaris Industries Inc., Mpls., 1998—99, pres., CEO, 1999—2005, CEO, 2005—. Bd. dir. KTM Power Sports AG. Office: Polaris Industries Inc 2100 Highway 55 Medina MN 55340 *

TILLERSON, REX W., oil company executive; b. Wichita Falls, Tex., Mar. 23, 1952; m. Renda St. Clair. BS in Civil Engring., U. Tex., Austin. Joined Exxon Co., U.S.A., 1975, various positions, prodn. dept., 1975—87, bus. devel. mgr., natural gas dept., 1987—89, gen. mgr., ctrl. prodn. divsn., 1989—92; prodn. adv. Exxon Corp., Dallas, 1992; coord., affiliate gas sales Exxon Co. Internat., Florham Park, NJ, 1992—95; pres. Exxon Yemen Inc., Esso Exploration and Prodn. Khorat Inc., 1995—98; v.p. Exxon Ventures Inc., 1998—99; pres. Exxon Neftegas Ltd., 1998—99; exec. v.p. Exxon-Mobil Devel. Co., 1999—2001; sr. v.p. Exxon Mobil Corp., 2001—04, pres., 2004—06, chmn., CEO, 2006—. Mem. adv. coun. Engring. Found., U. Tex. at Austin; bd. dirs. Exxon Mobil Corp., 2004—. Bd. trustee Ctr. Strategic and Internat. Studies; mem. nat. exec. bd. Boy Scouts Am.; mem. exec. bd. Circle Ten Coun.; mem. engring. found. adv. coun. U. Tex. Austin. Mem.: U.S.-Russia Bus. Coun. (dir.), Soc. Petroleum Engrs., Am. Petroleum Inst. Office: ExxonMobil Corp 5959 Las Colinas Blvd Irving TX 75039-2298 *

TILLERY, STEPHEN M., lawyer; b. Wood River, Ill., Mar. 9, 1950; BA, Ill. Coll., 1972; JD cum laude, St. Louis Univ., 1976. Bar: Ill. 1976, Mo. 1990. Law clk. to Hon. George J. Moran 5th Dist. Ct. Appeals, Ill., 1976—77; ptnr. Korein Tillery, St. Louis, Swansea, Ill. Adj. prof. law St. Louis Univ., 1977—88; co-dir., Advanced Trial Advocacy Program St. Louis Univ. Sch. Law, 1983—88; designated counsel United Transp. Union. Staff mem. St. Louis Univ. Law Jour., 1975—76; contbr. articles to profl. journals. Mem.: Assn. Trial Lawyers of Am., St. Louis Met. Bar Assn., Mo. Assn. Trial Lawyers, Ill. Trial Lawyers Assn. (amicus curiae com. 1983—, chmn., civil practice and rules com. 1986—, bd. mgrs. 1987—), Mo. Bar., Ill. State Bar Assn., St. Clair County Bar Assn., Order of Woolsack, Phi Alpha Delta, Phi Beta Kappa. Office: Korein Tillery 10 Executive Woods Ct Swansea IL 62226 also: Korein Tillery 505 N 7th St Ste 3600 Saint Louis MO 63101-1820 Office Phone: 314-241-4844, 618-277-1180. Office Fax: 314-241-3525, 618-222-6939. Business E-Mail: stillery@koreintillery.com.

TILLETT, BARBARA ANN BARNETT, librarian, director; b. Galveston, Tex., Sept. 29, 1946; d. Stephen Burney and Phyllis Jean Stewart Barnett; m. Stephen Earl Tillett, June 1, 1970. BA in Math., Old Dominion Coll., Norfolk, 1968; MLS, U. Hawaii, Honolulu, 1970; PhD, U. Calif., LA, 1987. Cert. MEDLINE Tng. Nat. Libr. Medicine, 1973, Lifetime Instr. Credential Calif. CC, 1990. Bibliographic analyst and programmer, tsunami document retrieval sys. U. Hawaii, Honolulu, 1969—70; reference libr. sci. and tech., dir. ocean sci. info. ctr., head serials editing and conversion project Hamilton Grad. Rsch. Libr., U. Hawaii, Honolulu, 1970—73; head tech. svcs. Scripps Instn. Oceanography Libr., U. Calif., San Diego, 1973—76, dir. tech. svcs., 1977—87; OCLC sys. coord. U. Librs., U. Calif., San Diego, 1976—77; co-cons. on planning a libr. for the proposed Lewes Marine Studies complex U. Del., Newark, 1979; vis. asst. prof. Grad. Sch. Libr. & Info. Sci., U. Calif., LA, 1987; head catalog dept. Ctrl. U. Libr., U. Calif., San Diego, 1987—94; instr. AJ Seminars, San Diego, 1989; adj. prof. Palomar CC, San Marcos, Calif., 1990—91; cons. on authority control sys. specifications Colo. Alliance Rsch. Librs., Denver, 1992; co-cons. on functional requirements for bibliographic records Internat. Fedn. Libr. Assn. Standing Com. for the Sect. on Cataloguing, Study Group on Functional Requirements for Bibliographic Records, The Hague, Netherlands, 1992—97; cons. on designing courseware database and record format U. the World, San Diego, 1993; cons. on cataloging process and orgn. U. Librs., U. Iowa, Iowa City, 1993; chief Cataloging Policy and Support Office Libr. Congress, Washington, 1994—, dir. integrated libr. sys. program, integrated libr. sys., 1997—2001, interim dir. for electronic resources, 2000—01, acting chief Cataloging Distbn. Svc., 2006—. Cons. tech. svc. ops. for librs. Escuela Superior de Ciencias Marinas & CICESE Universidad Autonoma de Baja Calif., Ensenada, Mexico, 1974—86; cons. on OCLC implementation U. Calif., U. Libr., Riverside, 1977—78, Santa Barbara, 1979, San Diego State U., U. Libr., 1979; referee Libr. Resources & Tech. Svcs., Chgo., 1988—97; reviewer Coll. & Rsch. Librs., Chgo., 1992—97; chair task group on authorities Coop. Cataloging Coun., Washington, 1993—94; rep. to joint steering com. for revision Anglo-Am. Cataloguing Rules Libr. Congress, Washington, 1994—, co-chair metadata policy group, 2001—, rep. to standing com. the Classification and Indexing Sect., 2002—; mem. Standing Com. on Stds. Program for Coop. Cataloging, Washington, 1995—96; mem. adv. com. OCLC, Inc., Dublin, 2002—04; tech. advisor on Redlight Green Project Rsch. Librs. Group, Mountain View, Calif., 2002—04; advisor Arabic Union Catalogue, King Abdulaziz Pub. Libr., Riyadh, Saudi Arabia, 2006—, Arabic Union Authority File, Bibliotheca Alexandria, Egypt, 2006—. Mem. editl. bd. Cataloging and Classification Quar., Binghamton, NY, 1990—, ACRL Publications in Librarianship, Chgo., 1992—94, Advances in Librarianship, NY, 2000—02, Bibliografija, Vilnius, Lithuania, 2005—. Recipient Arthur S. Flemming award for adminstrn., US Fedn., 2001; fellow Spring Grad. Rsch. Fellowship, U. Calif., LA, 1985; grantee Intramural Rsch. Grant, U. Hawaii, 1971—72, Fed. Sea Grant, 1971, 1972, 1973, Rsch. Grant, Librarians Assn. U. Calif., San Diego, 1985—86, 1987—88, Statewide Rsch. Grant, Librarians Assn. U. Calif., 1986, 1987. Mem.: Assn. Rsch. Librs. (Cataloging Description and Access com. rep. 1989—91, Cataloging in Publication adv. com. rep. 1989—91), Libr. Info. and Tech. Assn. (founder, chair 1984—86, mem. Auth. Control Interest group), Assn. Libr. Collections and Tech. Svcs. (chair Cataloging and Classification Sect. 1991—94, Libr. Congress rep. 1994, dir. at large 1994—97), Internat. Fedn. Libr. Assns. and Instns. (chair standing com. Sect. on Cataloguing 1999—2003, sec. and treas. Divsn. IV 2001—03, Divsn. IV rep. 2003—, governing bd. 2003—07, profl. com. mem. 2003—07, sec., treas. standing com. Classification and Indexing Sect. 2003—07, chair, treas. 2003—07), Spl. Libraries Assn. (So. Calif. chpt.) (network liaison officer 1973—89), Spl. Libraries Assn. (Hawaiian/Pacific chpt.) (charter mem., sec. 1972—73), Online Audiovisual Catalogers, Libr. Congress Pa., Assn. Coll. and Rsch. Librs., Internat. Assn. Marin Sci. Librs. & Info. Ctrs., DC Libr. Assn., Calif. Libr. Assn. (Palomar Chpt. pres. 1977—78), Am. Soc. for Info. Sci. (sec., treas. 1983—85, Spl. Interest Group/User Online Interaction), ALA (Cataloging Sect. standing com. rep. 1993—2003, Libr. Collections and Tech. Svc. rep. 1994—2003, Margaret Mann Citation 2004), Beta Phi Mu. Achievements include development of taxonomy of bibliographic relationships; first to coordinate the move to OCLC for the southern California campuses of the University of California; led the implementation of the first integrated library system for the Library of Congress. Office: Library Congress 101 Independence Ave SE Washington DC 20540-4305 Office Phone: +1 (202) 707-4714. Office Fax: +1 (202) 707-6629. E-mail: btil@loc.gov.

TILLETT, SAMUEL RAYMOND, lawyer; b. Akron, Ohio, May 4, 1951; AB, Hamilton Coll., 1973; JD, Case Western Res. U., 1977. Bar: Ohio 1977, DC 1978, Ill. 1988. Ptnr. Mayer, Brown & Platt, Chgo.; gen. counsel ITI Grp., Poland; internat. counsel Debevoise & Plimpton LLP, Moscow, 2007—. Adj. prof. law DePaul U. Coll. Law, Chgo., 1992; trustee Village of Glencoe, Ill. Libr. Bd., 1995. Bd. dirs. Chgo. Metro History Edn. Ctr., 1989-94. Mem. ABA, Nat. Assn. Bond Lawyers, D.C. Bar Assn., Chgo. Bar Assn. Office: Debevoise & Plimpton Business Ctr Mokhovaya Ulitsa Vozdvizhenka 4/7 125009 Moscow Russia *

TILLEY, CAROLYN BITTNER, information scientist; b. Washington, July 29, 1947; d. Klaud Kay and Margaret Louise (Hanson) Bittner; m. Frederick Edwin Dudley, June 18, 1985 BS, Am. U., 1975; M.L.S., U. Md., 1976. With NIH, 1965-71; statis. research asst. Health Manpower Edn., Bethesda, Md., 1971-72; tech. info. specialist Nat. Libr. Medicine, Bethesda, Md., 1972-81, head medlars (med. lit. analysis and retrieval sys.) mgmt. sect., 1981—2002, advisor for UMLS support, 2002. Mem. editl. bd. Med. Reference Svcs. Quar. Recipient Merit award NIH, 1984, Rogers award Nat. Libr. Medicine, 1991. Mem. Med. Libr. Assn., IEEE Libr. Adv. Coun. Presbyterian. Avocation: horseback riding. Office: Nat Libr Medicine 8600 Rockville Pike Bethesda MD 20894-0002

TILLEY, DAVID ROGERS, engineering educator, researcher; b. Greensboro, NC, Jan. 31, 1969; s. Lloyd Cabol and Wilma Tilley; m. Catherine Mai-Khuhn Nguyen, Oct. 3, 1998; children: I., M. BS, NC State U., Raleigh, 1992; M in Engring., U. Fla., Gainesville, 1999, PhD, 1999. Asst. prof. Tex. A&M U., Kingsville, 1999—2001, U. Md., College Park, 2001—. Contbr. articles to profl. jours. Mem.: Am. Ecol. Engring. Soc. (assoc.; com. chair 2001—04). Avocations: carpentry, gardening, bicycling. Office: University of Maryland 1421 Animal Sci/Agricultural Eng Bldg College Park MD 20742 Office Phone: 301-405-8027. Office Fax: 301-314-9023. Business E-Mail: dtilley@umd.edu.

TILLEY, NORWOOD CARLTON, JR., federal judge; b. Rock Hill, SC, 1943; s. Norwood Carlton and Rebecca (Westbrook) Tilley. BA, Wake Forest U., 1966, JD, 1969. Bar: NC 1969, admitted to practice: US Dist. Ct. (Mid. Dist.) NC 1971. Law clk. to Hon. Eugene A Gordon, U.S. Dist. Judge US Dist. Ct. (Mid. Dist.) NC, 1969-71; ptnr. Osteen, Adams, Tilley & Walker, Greensboro, 1977-88; asst. US atty. US Dist. Ct. (Mid. Dist.) NC, Greensboro, 1971-73, US atty., 1974-77, dist. judge Durham, 1988—2000, chief judge, 2000—. Instr. Wake Forest U. Sch. Law, 1980. Office: US Dist Ct PO Box 3443 Greensboro NC 27402-3443

TILLINGHAST, CHARLES CARPENTER, III, retired marketing company executive; b. NYC, Nov. 16, 1936; s. Charles Carpenter, Jr. and Lisette (Micoleau) T.; m. Cynthia Branch, Sept. 28, 1974; children by previous marriage: Avery D., Charles W., David C. BS in Mech. Engring., Lehigh U., 1958; MBA, Harvard U., 1963. Asst. to dir. devel. Lehigh U., Bethlehem, Pa., 1958-61; adminstrv. asst. Boise Cascade Corp., Portland, Oreg., 1963; asst. to v.p. Boise (Idaho) Cascade Corp., 1964-65, gen. mgr. office supply divsn., 1965-67, gen. mgr. paper distbn. divsn., 1966, v.p. bus. products, 1967-69, sr. v.p. housing group, 1969-71, sr. v.p., 1971-73; pres. CRM divsn. Ziff-Davis Pub. Co., Inc., Del Mar, Calif., 1971-75; pres., treas. Value Communications, Inc., La Jolla, Calif., 1975-76; pres. Oak Tree Publs., Inc., San Diego, 1976-81; co-founder, pres. Advanced Mktg. Svcs. Inc., San Diego, 1982-94, chmn., 1994—2004, pres., CEO, 2004; ret., 2004. Served to 2d lt. AUS, 1959. Home: PO Box 503 207 Morning Star Rd Sun Valley ID 83353-0503 Personal E-mail: ctillinghast@cox.net.

TILLINGHAST, DAVID ROLLHAUS, lawyer; b. NYC, Feb. 25, 1930; s. Charles Carpenter and Josephine Dorothy (Rollhaus) T.; m. Phyllis Van Horn, Sept. 24, 1955 (div. Jan. 1984); m. Lisa Sewell, Feb. 25, 1984; children: Gregory Barrett Sewell, Lauren Alexa. AB cum laude, Brown U., 1951; LLB cum laude, Yale U., 1954. Bar: N.Y. 1955, Oreg. 1956, U.S. Supreme Ct. 1978. Assoc. Hughes, Hubbard & Reed, NYC, 1954-55, 57-61, ptnr., 1961-62, 65-90; assoc. King, Miller, Anderson, Nash & Yerke, Portland, Oreg., 1955-57; spl. asst. for internat. tax affairs U.S. Dept. Treasury, Washington, 1962-65; ptnr. Chadbourne & Parke, NYC, 1990-99, Baker & McKenzie, NYC, 1999—. Adj. prof. Sch. Law, NYU, 1977-87; cons. UN Ctr. on Transnat. Corps., 1978-87; reporter Am. Law Inst. Project on Internat. Aspects of U.S. Income Taxation, 1982-91; cons. to reporters Am. Law Inst. Revision of Restatement of Fgn. Relations Law of U.S., 1982-83. Author: Tax Aspects of Internat. Transactions, 1978, 2d edit., 1984; co-author: Income Tax Treaty Arbitration, 2004; contbr. articles to profl. publs. Mem. transition team Sec. of Treasury W. Michael Blumenthal, 1977. Established David R. Tillinghast lectureship on internat. taxation NYU Sch. Law. Mem.: Tax Forum, Internat. Bar Assn. (vice chmn. com. on taxation bus. law sect. 1984—86), Internat. Fiscal Assn. (v.p. U.S. br. 1983—2000, permanent sci. com. 1983—2000, vice chmn. 1993—95, chmn. 1995—2000), Assn. of Bar of City of N.Y. (chmn. com. on taxation 1981—83). Democrat. Avocation: swimming. Office: Baker & McKenzie 1114 Avenue of the Americas New York NY 10036 Office Phone: 212-891-3526. Business E-Mail: david.r.tillinghast@bakernet.com.

TILLINGHAST, EDWARD HUDSON, III, lawyer; b. Annapolis, Md., July 18, 1958; s. Edward H. Jr. and Eugenia (Cheshire) T.; m. Dorri Elaine Berry. BA with honors, Lake Forest Coll., 1980; JD, Chgo. Kent Coll. Law, 1983. Bar: Ill. 1983, N.Y. 1985, U.S. Dist. Ct. (so., and ea. dist.) N.Y., U.S. Dist. Ct. (no. dist.) N.Y. 1990, U.S. Ct. Appeals (3d cir.) 1987, U.S. Ct. Appeals (2d cir.) 1988, U.S. Supreme Ct. 1989. Asst. county atty. Suffolk County Dept. Law, Hauppauge, N.Y., 1984-86; assoc. Dreyer and Traub, NYC; ptnr., head Global Fin. Restructuring & Insolvency practice & mem. exec. bd. Coudert Bros. LLP, NYC. Mem. Chgo.-Kent Law Rev., 1981-83; contbr. articles to profl. jours. Mem. ABA, N.Y. State Bar Assn., Assn. of Bar of City of N.Y., Am. Bankruptcy Inst., INSOL, Univ. Club N.Y. Avocations: sailing, yachting, skiing. Office: Coudert Bros LLP 1114 Ave of the Americas New York NY 10036 Office Phone: 212-626-4744. Office Fax: 212-626-4120. Business E-Mail: tillinghaste@coudert.com.

TILLINGHAST, JOHN AVERY, utilities executive; b. NYC, Apr. 30, 1927; s. Charles C. and Dorothy J. (Rollhaus) T.; m. Mabel Healy, Sept. 11, 1948; children: Katherine Brickley, Susan Trainor, Abigail Ryan. BSME, Columbia U., 1948, MS, 1949. With Am. Elec. Power Service Corp., NYC, 1949-79, exec. v.p. engring. and constrn., 1967-72, sr. exec. v.p., vice chmn. engring. and constrn., 1972-79; sr. v.p. tech. Wheelabrator-Frye Inc., Hampton, NH, 1979-83, Signal Advanced Tech. Group, The Signal Cos., Hampton, NH, 1983-85; sr. v.p. Allied-Signal Internat., Hampton, 1985-86, Sci. Applications Internat. Corp., San Diego, 1986-88; pres. TILTEC, Portsmouth, NH, 1987—; CEO, Great Bay Power Corp., Dover, NH, 1994-97; CEO BayCorp Holdings, Ltd., Dover, 1997-98, chmn. bd. Portsmouth, 1998—99. Patentee generating unit control system. Elder Reformed Ch., 1976-79. Served with USN, 1944-46. Fellow ASME; mem. IEEE, NAE, Sigma Xi, Tau Beta Pi. Office Phone: 603-964-7454. E-mail: jtillinghast@comcast.net.

TILLINGHAST, NANCY, library director; b. Buckhannon, W.Va., Mar. 2, 1946; children: Beth Norman, Mark. BS, W.Va. Univ., 1969; MLIS, Univ. SC, 1991. Asst. libr. Roane County Libr., Spencer, W.Va., 1982—90; children's & pub. services libr. Thomas County Pub. Libr. Sys., Thomasville, Ga., 1991—94, asst. dir., 1994—96, dir., 1996—. Chmn. Libr. Council SW Ga. Tech. Coll., mem. Literacy Council; chmn. Certified Literate Cmty. Prog. Thomas County. Chmn. United Way Thomas County; mem. Family Connections, Hands on Thomas County. Named Woman of the Yr., Thomasville-Thomas County C. of C., 2007; recipient Libr. award, NY Times, 2006, Cmty. Svc. award, Zion Christian Bible Inst. Mem.: ALA, Pub. Libr. Assn., Ga. Libr. Assn., Rotary. Avocations: gardening, cross stitch, reading. Office: Thomas County Pub Libr Sys 201 N Madison St Thomasville GA 31792 Office Phone: 229-225-5252. Office Fax: 229-225-5258. Business E-Mail: nancy@tcpls.org.

TILLMAN, AUDREY BOONE, insurance company executive; married; 3 children. BA in Polit. Sci., U. NC, Chapel Hill; JD, U. Ga. Law clk. to Judge Richard C. Erwin US Dist. Ct. NC; assoc. Smith, Helms, Mulliss and Moore, Greensboro, NC, 1990—93; assoc. prof. NC Ctrl. U. Sch. Law; mem. legal dept. AFLAC Inc., Columbus, Ga., 1996—97, second v.p., 1997—2000, v.p., sr. assoc. counsel legal divsn., 2000—01, sr. v.p., dir. human resources, 2001, sr. v.p., dir. corp. svcs. Dir.-at-large Soc. Human Resource Mgmt. Mem. Workforce Devel. Task Force State of Ga. Named one of Top 100 Blacks in Corp. Am., Black Profls. mag.; recipient Corp. Governance award, Celebrating Excellence in Leadership Orgn., Office Depot Visionary award, 2007. Mem.: Bar DC, NC State Bar, State Bar Ga. Office: AFLAC Inc 1932 Wynnton Rd Columbus GA 31999 Office Phone: 706-323-3431. *

TILLMAN, EUGENE, lawyer; b. LA, Oct. 9, 1950; BA in anthropology with honors, UCLA, 1973, JD, 1976. Bar: Calif. 1976, DC 1979. Staff atty. Office of Gen. Counsel, 1976—79; dep. dir. Office of Regulation Mgmt., Health Care Financing Adminstrn. HHS, 1979—80; with Reed Smith LLP, 1980—, now ptnr. DC office, dir. legal personnel, mem. exec. com. & mgmt. com. Mem.: DC Bar Assn., Calif. Bar Assn., Am. Health Lawyers Assn. (pres. 1996—97). Office: Reed Smith LLP 1301 K St NW, Ste 1100 Washington DC 20005-3317 Office Phone: 202-414-9244. Office Fax: 202-414-9299. Business E-Mail: etillman@reedsmith.com.

TILLMAN, MARY NORMAN, urban affairs consultant; b. Atlanta, Jan. 31, 1926; d. Mary Nellie Shehee; m. James A. Tillman Jr., Apr. 11, 1952; children: James A., Gina G. BA, Morris Brown Coll., 1947; postgrad., U. Minn., 1964, Old Dominion U., 1975—. Asst. bus. mgr. Morris Brown Coll., Atlanta, 1947-53; race rels. and urban affairs cons. Tillman Assocs. Cons. Social Engrs., Atlanta and Syracuse, NY, 1963—, sr. ptnr., treas., from 1965, now pres. Bd. dirs. The Tillman Inst. of Human Rels., Inc.; clin. prof. United Theol. Sem., New Brighton, Minn.; adj. prof. Gordon-Conwell Theol. Sem., South Hamilton, Mass. Author: What is Your Racism Quotient?, 1964, A Common Sense Approach to Racism and Other Exclusivities, 1998, (with James A. Tillman, Jr.) Why America Needs Racism and Poverty, 1972, Black Intellectuals, White Liberals and Race Relations: An Analytic Overview, 1973; What is your Exclusivity Quotient, 1978, A Common Sense Approach to Racism and Other Exclusivities, 2001; contbr. articles to profl. jours. Adv. coun. to urban ministries dept. So. Bapt. Conv., Cmty. Rels. Commn., Atlanta; bd. dirs. Christian Coun. Met. Atlanta, Tillman Inst. Human Rels. Mem. Tidewater Assn. Pub. Adminstrs. (dir.), Am. Acad. Cons., Nat. Black Writers Consortium (v.p.), Joint Ctr. for Polit. Studies. Office: 1765 Glenview Dr SW Atlanta GA 30331-2307 Office Phone: 404-349-3668.

TILLMAN, MASSIE MONROE, mediator, arbitrator, art gallery owner, retired judge; b. Corpus Christi, Tex., Aug. 15, 1937; s. Clarence and Artie Lee (Stewart) T.; m. Karen Wright, July 2, 1993; children: Jeffrey Monroe, Holly. BBA, Baylor U., 1959, LLB, 1961. Bar: Tex. 1961, U.S. Dist. Ct. (no. dist.) Tex. 1961, U.S. Ct. Appeals (5th cir.) 1969, U.S. Supreme Ct. 1969, formerly bd. cert. personal injury trial law: Tex., cert.: Tex. Edn. Agy (hearing examiner). Pvt. practice, Ft. Worth, 1961—87; U.S. bankruptcy judge Ft. Worth divsn. No. Dist. Tex., 1987—2001; mediator, arbitrator, 2001—. Author: Tillman's Trial Guide, 1970,-1990, comments editor, case notes editor; mem. editl. bd. Baylor Law Rev., 1960-61. Fellow Am. Bd. Trial Advocates, Tex. Bar Found.; mem. Ft. Worth/Tarrant County Bar (bd. dirs. 1969-70, v.p. 1970-71), Trial Attys. Am., Coll. State Bar Tex. Baptist. Avocation: quail hunting. Address: PO Box 20213 Fort Worth TX 76102 Personal E-mail: tillmanmediator@yahoo.com.

TILLMAN, MERCIA V., musician; b. Chatham, Eng. Singer Sid Mills Band, London, 1932—39; club hostess, catering mgr. U.S. Mil. Officer Clubs, 1955—69; owner Mercia Tillman Wedding Cons. & Catering, Manassas, Va., 1972—73; dir. svcs. Innisbrook Resort, Tarpon Springs, Fla., 1975—76; columnist West Coast Publs., Largo, Fla., 1977—78; owner Mercia Tillman Prodns., 1996—. Author: (songs) Florida, My State of Dreams, 1996, Walk Around the Mall, 1996, Goodbye Little Princess, 1998, Hello, My Love, Hello, 2000; author and pub.: Little Gems, 2004. Named Ms. Fla. Sr. Am., 1996; recipient Vol. Woman of Yr., Soroptimist Internat., Fla., 1997, Blue Cross/Blue Shield Ageless Hero award, State of

Fla., 1999, 2000, Inductee Sr. Hall of Fame, City of St. Petersburg, Fla., 2000, KFC Col.'s Way award, State of Fla., 2000. Mem.: WWII Meml. Soc. (charter), Ms. Sr. Am. Fla. Cameo Club. Personal E-mail: merciatillman@att.com.

TILLMAN, VICKIE A., financial information company executive; BA in comm., U. Pitts., MPA in fin. With Standard & Poor's, 1977—, exec. mng. dir. pub. fin. ratings dept., exec. v.p. structured fin. ratings, 1994—99, exec. v.p., 1999—, mem. exec. com. Office: Standard & Poor's 55 Water St New York NY 10041

TILLSON, ALBERT HOLMES, JR., history educator; b. Arlington, Va., Nov. 12, 1948; s. Albert Holmes and Louise Williams (Bragg) T.; m. Barbara Kaye Uzenoff, July 2, 1988. BA with distinction, George Mason U., 1971; MA, Johns Hopkins U., 1974; PhD, U. Tex., Austin, 1986. Part-time lectr. No. Va. Cmty. Coll., Alexandria and Sterling, Va., 1975—76, 1985; tchg. asst., asst. instr. U. Tex., 1977—79, 1981—83; instr. history St. Norbert Coll., De Pere, Wis., 1984—85, Pan Am. U., Edinburg, Tex., 1986; asst. prof. history U. Tampa, Fla., 1986—92, assoc. prof. Fla., 1992—. Author: (book) Gentry and Common Folk, 1991; contbr. articles to profl. jours. Walter Prescott Webb fellow, 1977, Univ. fellow U. Tex., 1980-81, Andrew Mellon Rsch. fellow Va. Hist. Soc., 1991, 92; Faculty Devel. grantee Dana Found., 1987-94. Mem.: Va. Hist. Soc., So. Hist. Assn., Am. Hist. Assn., Inst. Early Am. History and Culture (assoc.). Avocation: bicycling. Office: U Tampa 400 W Kennedy Blvd Tampa FL 33606-1413

TILLY, JENNIFER, actress; b. Harbor City, Calif., Sept. 16, 1958; m. Sam Simon, 1984 (div., 1991). Grad., Stephens Coll., 1979. TV series include: Shaping Up, 1984, Key West, 1993, Out of Practice, 2005-; TV movies include: Heads, 1994; films include: No Small Affair, 1984, Moving Violations, 1985, He's My Girl, 1987, Inside Out, 1987, Rented Lips, 1988, High Spirits, 1988, Johnny Be Good, 1988, Remote Control, 1988, The Fabulous Baker Boys, 1989, Let It Ride, 1989, Far From Home, 1989, Scorchers, 1991, Shadow of the Wolf, 1992, Made in America, 1993, At Home With the Webbers, 1993, Double Cross, 1994, Bullets Over Broadway, 1994 (Academy award nomination best supporting actress 1994), The Getaway, 1994, The Pompatus of Love, 1996, Liar, Liar, 1996, House Arrest, 1996, Edie & Pen, 1996, Bound, 1996, American Strays, 1996, Bride of Chucky, 1998, Music From Another Room, 1998, The Muse, 1999, Goosed, 1999, Do Not Disturb, 1999, (voice) Bartok the Magnificent, 1999, (voice) Stuart Little, 1999, Play It to the Bone, 1999, Bruno, 2000, Cord, 2000, The Crew, 2000, The Cat's Meow, 2001, Monsters, Inc. (voice), 2001, Jericho Mansions, 2003, The Haunted Mansion, 2003, Home on the Range (voice), 2004, El Padrino, 2004, St. Ralph, 2004, Deluxe Combo Platter, 2004, Seed of Chucky, 2004, Bailey's Billion$, 2005, Lil' Pimp (voice), 2005, The Civilization of Maxwell Bright, 2005, Tideland, 2005. Achievements include won Ladies No-Limit Texas Hold'Em World Series of Poker Tournament, Las Vegas, 2005, World Poker Tour Ladies Night III, 2005. Home: Care Carrol Gettko 118 S Beverly Dr Beverly Hills CA 90212-3003

TILLY, JONATHAN L., obstetrician, gynecologist, reproductive biologist; BS in Animal Scis., Rutgers U., 1984, MS in Animal Scis., 1987, PhD in Animal Scis., 1990. Postdoctoral tng., molecular biology Stanford U. Med. Ctr., Calif., 1993; asst. prof. reproductive biology John Hopkins U., Balt., 1993—95; assoc. dir. Vincent Ctr. for Reproductive Biology, Mass. Gen. Hosp., Boston, 1995—98, dir., 1998—; biologist Vincent Obstetrics and Gynecology Svc., Boston, 1995—, chief, divsn. rsch., 1998—; assoc. prof., obstetrics, gynecology, and reproductive biology Harvard Med. Sch., Boston, 1995—; adj. assoc. prof., pathology and lab. medicine Boston U. Sch. Medicine, 1996—2003; investigator Dana-Farber/Harvard Cancer Ctr., 1999—. Mem. rsch. coun. Mass. General Hosp., 1995—98, mem. subcommittee on review of rsch. proposals, 1995—2003, exec. com. mem., dept. obstetrics/gynecology, 1997—2003, mem. small animal users group subcommittee, 2002—; organizer, chair Serono Symposium on Cell Death in Reproductive Physiology, Chgo., 1996, Symposium on Apoptosis in Reproduction and Infertility, 16th World Congress on Fertility and Sterility, San Francisco, 1998; ad-hoc reviewer Reproductive Biology Study sect., 96, 2001; site reviewer, population coun. NIH, 1996; scientific advisor Fed. Dist. Ct. Judge Richard G. Stearns, 1996—2000; panel mem. Internat. Life Sciences Inst. Workshop on the Evaluation and Interpretation of Reproductive Endpoints for Human Health Risk Assessment, Washington, 1997; lectr., apoptosis lab. course dir. NICHD/MBL Tng. Course on Frontiers in Reproduction, Marine Biological Lab., Wood Hole, Mass., 1998—2001; mem., Development-1 (DEV-1) study sect., 2004—. Editl. bd. mem. Endocrinology, 1996—99, Journal Endocrinology, 2000—, Cell Death & Differentiation, 2001—, editl. bd. adv. com. mem. Endocrine Journal, contbg. editor SAGE-KE; contbr. articles to peer-reviewed pubs. Nominee Rave award in Medicine, WIRED, 2005; recipient Boston Coalition award for Disting. Achievement in Rsch., 2002, Richard E. Weitzman Meml. award, Endocrine Soc., 2002. Mem.: Am. Fedn. for Aging Rsch. (mem. Nat. Scientific Adv. Coun. 2003—). Office: Mass General Hosp The Vincent Ctr for Reproductive Biology 55 Fruit St VBK 137 Boston MA 02114 Office Phone: 617-724-2182. Office Fax: 617-726-7548. Business E-Mail: tilly.jonathan@mgh.harvard.edu.

TILSON, DANIEL, elementary school educator; Tchr. Eastwood Elem. Sch., Roseburg, Oreg., 1985—2003, Jo Lane Mid. Sch., Roseburg, Oreg. Recipient Excellence in Sci. Tchg. award, 1990, Milken Nat. Edn. award, 1992, State Tchr. of Yr. elem. award Oreg., 1992; Christa McAuliffe fellow, 1988. Office: Jo Lane Mid Sch 2153 NE Vine Roseburg OR 97470 Business E-Mail: dtilson@roseburg.k12.or.us.

TILSON, DOROTHY RUTH, word processing executive; b. Bloomsburg, Pa., Mar. 24, 1918; d. Roy Earl and Mary Etta (Masteller) Derr; m. Irving Tilson, Sept. 1949. BS, Bloomsburg U., 1940. Tchr. Madison Consol. Sch., Jerseytown, Pa., 1940-42; gage checker Phila. Ordinance Gage Lab., 1942-43; tabulating asst. Remington Rand, Phila., NYC, 1943-46; copy writer Sears Roebuck, Phila., NYC, 1946-48; statis. asst. Ford Internat., NYC, 1949-56; word processing adminstrv. asst. Coopers & Lybrand, NYC, 1956-91; ret. Life mem. Rep. Senatorial Inner Circle, Washington, 1987—. Mem. Am. Movement for World Govt. (sec. 1991—), N.Y. Theosophical Soc. (libr. 1969—), UN Assn.-USA (mem. global policy project which includes internat. econ. governance and human rights). Home: 435 W 119th St # 9G New York NY 10027-7110 Personal E-mail: dotttilson@netscape.net.

TILSON, M(ARTIN) DAVID, III, surgeon, scientist, educator; b. Texarkana, Tex., Aug. 25, 1941; s. M. David and Leta (Martin) Tilson; 3 children. BA, Rice U., 1963; MD, Yale U., 1967. Diplomate Am. Bd. Surgery, Nat. Bd. Med. Examiners. Surg. intern Yale U., New Haven, 1967-68; resident in surgery U. New Haven, 1968-72; asst. to assoc. prof. Yale U., New Haven, 1974-83, prof., 1983-89; Ailsa Mellon Bruce prof. surgery Columbia U., NYC, 1989—. Contbr. articles to profl. jours. Maj. USAF, 1972-74. Rsch. grantee, NIH, 1983—94, 1999—2003. Mem. ACS, Soc. Univ. Surgeons, Am. Surg. Assn., Soc. Vascular Surgery, Internat. Soc. Cadiovasc. Surgery, Halsted Soc. Home: 105 Garth Rd B2 Scarsdale NY 10583-2714 Office: St Lukes Roosevelt Hosp 1000 10th Ave New York NY 10019-1192 E-mail: mdt1@columbia.edu.

TILSON, WHITNEY R., investment company executive; b. 1966; married; 3 children. BA in govt., Harvard Coll., 1989; MBA, Harvard Bus. Sch., 1994. Founding mem. Teach for America; co-founder, exec. dir. Initiative for a Competitive Inner City; cons. Boston Consulting Group; founder, mng. partner T2 Partners LLC, 1999—, Tilson Mutual Funds, 1999—. Co-founder ICV Partners; co-founder, chmn., co-editor-in-chief Value Investor Insight; co-founder, chmn. Value Investing Congress; teacher, fin. statement analysis and bus. valuation The Dickie Grp.; mem. bd. Cutter & Buck, Fistula Found.; vice-chmn. KIPP Acad., Thorn Tree Project. Author: (writes regular column) Fin. Times, (articles) Motley Fool and TheStreet.com; co-author: (novels) Poor Charlie's Almanack. Named one of five top investors, SmartMoney's Power 30. Mem.: Young Presidents' Orgn. Achievements include has appeared on CNBC, Bloomberg TV, Lou Dobbs Moneyline and Wall $treet Week, profiled by the Wall Street Journal and the Washington Post, spoken widely on the topics of value investing and behavioral fin. Office Phone: 800-773-3863. *

TILSON THOMAS, MICHAEL, conductor, music director; b. LA, Dec. 21, 1944; s. Theodor and Roberta Tilson Thomas. Studies with, Ingolf Dahl, U. So. Calif., others; student conducting, Berkshire Music Festival, Tanglewood, Mass.; student conducting (Koussevitsky prize 1968); LL.D., Hamilton Coll.; L.H.D. (hon.), D'Youville Coll., 1976. Asst. condr. Boston Symphony Orch., 1969, assoc. condr., 1970-72, prin. guest condr., 1972-74; also Berkshire Music Festival, summer 1970, 74; music dir., condr. Buffalo Philharmonic Orch., 1971-79; prin. guest condr. LA Philharm., 1981—85; music dir., prin. condr. Great Woods Ctr. for Performing Arts, 1985-88; founder, artistic dir. New World Symphony, Fla., 1988—; prin. condr. London Symphony Orch., 1988—95, prin. guest condr., 1995—; music dir. San Francisco Symphony, 1995—. Chief condr. Ojai Festival, 1967, condr., dir. NY Philharm. Young People's Concerts CBS-TV, 1971—77, vis. condr. numerous orchs., US, Europe, Japan, dir. Ojai Festival, 1972—77, rec. artist Sony Classical/CBS Masterworks, 1973—, opera debut, Cin., 1975, condr. Am. premiere Lulu, Santa Fe Opera, 1979, prin. guest condr. Gershwin Festival London Symphony Orch., Barbcan Ctr., 1987; composer: Grace-A Song for Leonard Bernstein, 1988; composer: (for Empire Brass Quintet) Street Song, 1988; composer: (for orch. and narator Audrey Hepburn and New World Symphony) From the Diary of Anne Frank, 1990; co-artistic dir. Pacific Music Festival, 1990—, commd. for Concerts for Life's European premiere UNICEF, 1991, conducted Mozart Requiem, —. Named Musician of Yr., Musical Am., 1970, Condr. of Yr., 1994; recipient Koussevitsky prize, 1968, Grammy award, Carmina Burana with Cleve. Orch., 1976, Gershwin Live with LA Philharm., 1983, Ditson award, 1994, Am. Music Ctr. award, 2001, Grammy award, Mahler Symphony No. 3 with San Francisco Symphony Orch., 2004, Classic FM Gramophone award for Artist of Yr., 2005, Grammy awards for Best Classical Album and Best Orchestral Performance, Mahler Symphony No. 7 with San Francisco Symphony Orch., 2007. Fellow: Am. Acad. Arts and Sciences. Office: 888 7th Ave Fl 37 New York NY 10106-3799 Mailing: Van Walsum Mgmt 4 Addison Bridge Pl London W14 8XP England Office Phone: 212-246-7726. *

TILTON, DAVID LLOYD, savings and loan association executive; b. Santa Barbara, Calif., Sept. 21, 1926; s. Lloyd Irvine and Grace (Hart) T.; m. Mary Caroline Knudtson, June 6, 1953; children: Peter, Jennifer, Michael, Catharine. AB, Stanford U., 1949, MBA, 1951. With Santa Barbara Savs. & Loan Assn., 1951-90, pres., 1965-84; now pres. Fin. Corp., Santa Barbara. Trustee, chmn. Calif. Real Estate Investment Trust, 1988. Served with USNR, World War II. Mem. Calif. Savs. and Loan League (dir. 1980), Delta Chi. Home: 630 Oak Grove Dr Santa Barbara CA 93108-1402 Office: Fin Corp Santa Barbara 311 E Carillo St Santa Barbara CA 93101-2761 E-mail: dtilton@earthlink.net.

TILTON, GLENN F., air transportation executive; b. Washington, Apr. 9, 1948; BA in Internat. Rels., U. S.C., 1970. Sales trainee U.S. mktg. ops. Texaco Inc., Washington, 1970, various assignments, 1970—76, div. supr. mktg. East Brunswick, NJ, 1976—78, area mgr. resale N.Y. div. NYC, 1978, asst. to gen. mgr. northeastern region, 1978—79, mktg. mgr. resale Phila. div., 1979—81, staff coord. corp. planning and econs. dept. Harrison, NY, 1981—83; asst. gen. mgr. sales Texaco Europe, 1983—84, gen. mgr. mktg., 1984—87; v.p. mktg. Texaco U.S.A., Houston, 1984—88; pres. Texaco Refining and Mktg. Inc., Houston, 1988—91; v.p. Texaco Inc., 1989; chmn. Texaco Ltd., 1991—92; pres. Texaco Eruope, 1992—94, Texaco USA, Houston, 1994—2002; sr. v.p. Texaco Inc., 1995—2002; pres. Texaco Global Bus. Unit; CEO Texaco, White Plains, NY, 2001; chmn., pres., CEO UAL Corp. and United Airlines, 2002—. Mem.: bd. dirs., Chevron Texaco (chmn., 2002). Office: UAL PO Box 66100 Chicago IL 60666 *

TILY, STEPHEN BROMLEY, III, retired bank executive; b. Phila., July 7, 1937; s. Stephen Bromley Jr. and Edith Helen (Straub) T.; m. Janet Anita Walz, July 10, 1965; children: Deborah Powell, Stephen Bromley IV, James Charles II. BS in Econs., Washington and Jefferson Coll., Pa., 1960; postgrad., Temple U. Sch. Law, Phila., 1963. Trust officer Indsl. Valley Bank & Trust Co., Phila., 1968—71; v.p. Farmers Bank Del., Wilmington, 1971—77; exec. officer G&T, Inc., Ltd., Wilmington, 1977—80; pres., COO DCG&T Co., Wilmington, 1977—91, chmn., CEO, 1991—93, chmn. emeritus, 1993—. Chmn. The Declaration Group, Conshohocken, Pa., 1985-97; trustee Declaration Fund, 1988-99; tchr. Am. Inst. Banking, 1970-79. Capt. USAR, 1960-61. Mem. Fin. Analysts of Phila., Barnegat Light Yacht Club (commodore 1988-89, trustee 1989-92), Kimberton Fish and Game Assn., Waynesborough Country Club, John's Island Golf Club, Merion Golf Club, Ducks Unltd., The 200 Club. Republican. Episcopalian.

TIMBALAND, (TIMOTHY Z. MOSLEY), recording industry executive, rap artist; b. Norfolk, Va., Mar. 10, 1971; Mem. Timbaland & Magoo; founder, pres. Mosely Music Group/Geffen. Singer: (albums) Welcome to Our World, 1997, Tim's Bio, 1998, Indecent Proposal, 2001, Under Construction, Part II, 2003, Shock Value, 2007; prodr. (Jodeci) Diary of a Mad Band, 1993, The Show, The After Party, The Hotel, 1994, (Aaliyah) One in a Million, 1996, Aaliyah, 2001, I Care 4 U, 2002, (Ginuwine) The Bachelor, 1996, 100% Ginuwine, 1999, The Life, 2001, (Missy Elliot) Supa Dupa Fly, 1997, Miss E: So Addictive, 2001, Under Construction, 2002, This is Not a Test!, 2003, The Cookbook, 2005, (Jay-Z) Vol. 2: Hard Knock Life, 1998, Vol. 3: Life & Times of S Carter, 1999, The Blueprint, 2001, The Blueprint 2: The Gift & the Curse, 2002, The Black Album, 2003, (Beck) Mutations, 1998, (Nas) I Am, 1999, Nastradamus, 1999, (Snoop Dogg) The Last Meal, 2000, (Ludacris) Word of Mouf, 2001, Red Light District, 2004, (Limp Bizkit) New Old Song, 2001, (Destiny's Child) This is the Remix, 2002, (Justin Timberlake) Justified, 2002, FutureSex/LoveSounds, 2006, (TLC) 3D, 2002, (Fabolous) Ghetto Fabolous, 2001, Street Dreams, 2003, (Bubba Sparxxx) Dark Days, Bright Nights, 2001, Deliverance, 2003, The Charm, 2006, (Alicia Keys) The Diary of Alicia Keys, 2003, (Lil Kim) La Bella Mafia, 2004, (Brandy) Afrodisiac, 2004, (LL Cool J) The DEFinition, 2004, (Jennifer Lopez) Rebirth, 2005, (Black Eyed Peas) Monkey Business, 2005, (Jamie Foxx) Unpredictable, 2005, (Nelly Furtado) Loose, 2006, (soundtracks) Sprung, 1996, Money Talks, 1997, Dr. Doolittle, 1998, Why Do Fools Fall in Love, 1998, The PJs, 1999, Austin Powers: The Spy Who Shagged Me, 1999, Romeo Must Die, 2000, Nutty Professor II: The Klumps, 2000, Exit Wounds, 2000, Lara Croft: Tomb Raider, 2001, Shark Tale, 2004. Co-recipient award for Most Performed Song from Motion Picture, ASCAP, 1999, 2001, 2002; recipient Grammy award for Best Dance Recording, 2007. Office: Mosley Music Group LLC c/o Interscope Geffen A&M Records 2220 Colorado Ave Santa Monica CA 90404 also: c/o Blackground Entertainment 23460 Hatteras St Woodland Hills CA 91367 Office Phone: 818-884-8526.

TIMBERLAKE, CHARLES EDWARD, historian, educator; b. South Shore, Ky., Sept. 9, 1935; s. Howard Ellis and Mabel Viola (Collier) T.; m. Patricia Alice Perkins, Dec. 23, 1958; children: Mark Brewster, Daniel Edward, Eric Collier BA, Berea Coll., 1957; Calif. State Teaching Credential, Claremont Grad. Sch., 1958, MA, 1962; PhD, U. Wash., 1968. Tchr. Barstow H.S., Calif., 1959-60, Claremont City Sch., Calif., 1960-61; tchg., rsch. asst. U. Wash., Seattle, 1961-64; asst. prof. history U. Mo., Columbia, 1967-73, assoc. prof., 1973-81, prof. history, 1981—, Byler disting. prof., 1996, chmn. dept., 1996—2000, asst. dir. Honors Coll., 1988-90. Exch. prof. Moscow State U., 1985, U. Manchester, England, 1987—88; hon. prof. history Lanzou U., China, 1991; dir. edn. svcs. Leisure Voyages, 1992—2000; vis. prof. Joensuu (Finland) U., 1996, 98, 2000, 03, adj. prof., 2005—. Author: The Fate of Russian Orthodox Monasteries and Convents Since 1917, 1995; editor: Essays on Russian Liberalism, 1972, Detente: A Documentary Record, 1978, Religious and Secular Forces in Late Tsarist Russia, 1992, Profiles of Finland series, 1991-94, (microfiche) The St. Petersburg Collection of Zemstvo Publs., 1992—; contbr. chpts. to books, articles to profl. jours. Mem. Citizens Alliance for Progress, Columbia, Mo., 1969—75, pres., 1969—70; founding mem. High Edn. Rescue Operation, Mo., 1983—91; mem. Columbians Against Throw-Aways, 1980—83, Friends of Rock Bridge State Park, 2005—, Friends of Mus. Russian Art, 2005—; assoc. Mus. Art and Archaeology, 2006—. Recipient Disting. Alumnus award Berea Coll., 2002; Fgn. Area fellow, 1965-66, fellow Internat. Rsch. and Exchs. Bd., 1971, 95, 2001, Am. Coun. Learned Socs., 1978-79, Fulbright-Hays fellow, 1995; grantee NEH, 1972, 79, 87; Am. Couns. for Internat. Edn. grantee, 2005. Mem. Am. Assn. Advancement Slavic Studies (bd. dirs. 1980-82, 84-86, chmn. council regional affiliates 1981-82, 85-86, chmn. permanent membership com. 1981-84), Western Slavic Conf., Am. Hist. Assn. (exec. council Conf. on Slavic and East European History 1987-89), Central Slavic Conf. (sec.-treas. 1967-68, pres. 1968-69, 76-77, 83-84, 88-89, 2001-02, exec. bd. 1972—, custodian archive 1972—), Mo. Conf. History (pres. 1992, sec.-treas. 1996-2000), State Hist. Soc. Mo., Fulbright Assn. (pres. Mo. chpt. 1997-2000). Avocations: hiking, travel, theater. Home: 9221 S Rt N Columbia MO 65203-9312 Home Phone: 573-442-4580. Business E-Mail: timberlakec@missouri.edu.

TIMBERLAKE, JUSTIN, singer; b. Memphis, Jan. 31, 1981; s. Randy Timberlake and Lynn Harless. Singer, performer 'N Sync, 1996—2002; solo vocalist, 2002—; chmn. & CEO Tennman Records, LA, 2007—. Launched William Rast clothing line (with Trace Ayala), 2005; restaurant co-owner (with Eytan Sugarman) Destino's, 2006. Singer (with 'N Sync): (albums) N Sync, 1998, Home for Christmas, 1998, No Strings Attached, 2000, Celebrity, 2001; singer: (solo albums) Justified, 2003 (Grammy award, Best Pop Vocal Album, 2003), FutureSex/LoveSounds, 2006, (songs) Cry Me a River, 2003 (Grammy award, Best Male Pop Vocal Performance, 2003), Sexy Back, 2006 (Favorite R&B Song, People's Choice awards, 2007, Grammy award for Best Dance Recording, 2007), My Love, 2006 (Grammy award for Best Rap/Sung Collaboration, 2007); actor: (films) Longshot, 2000, Edison, 2005, Alpha Dog, 2006, Southland Tales, 2006, Black Snake Moan, 2006; (films, voice) Shrek the Third, 2007; (TV films) Model Behavior, 2000. Founder J. Timberlake Found. Named one of The World's Most Influential People, TIME mag., 2007; recipient Best Pop Artist & Best Male Artist awards, MTV Europe Music Awards, 2006, Internat. Male Solo Artist, BRIT Awards, 2007. Office: Jive Records 137-139 W 25th St 9th Floor New York NY 10012 also: Tennman Records PO Box 18765 Beverly Hills CA 90209 *

TIMCENKO, LYDIA TEODORA, secondary school educator, biochemist; b. Beograd, Yugoslavia, July 4, 1951; arrived in U.S., 1975; d. Teodor Pavle and Branislava (Spasojevic) Timcenko; m. Ghazi Youssef, June 16, 1980 (div. Oct. 1989); children: Ali Alexander Youssef, Kareem Misha Youssef; m. Peter Porzio, Mar. 11, 1996. BS in Chemistry, U. Belgrade, Yugoslavia, 1975; MS, Wayne State U., 1977, PhD, 1984. Grad. asst. Wayne State U., Detroit, 1976-78, 81-84, rsch. assoc., 1986—88, lectr. in chemistry, 1989; postdoctoral fellow Mich. Cancer Found., Detroit, 1985; postdoctoral fellow Sch. Medicine Wayne State U., 1986—88; lectr. in chemistry Lawrence Tech. U., Southfield, Mich., 1989, 90-91; biochemist Strohtech, Inc., Detroit, 1990—91; prof. chemistry Sussex County Coll., Newton, NJ, 1997—99; asst. prof. chemistry N.Y. Techol. Coll., City U. Bklyn., 1999—; sci. tchr. New Milford (NJ) H.S., 2002, Newton (N.J.) H.S., 2002—; adj. assoc. prof. organic chemistry Pace U., NYC, 2004—05; tchr. chemistry, physics, biology Dwight Morrow HS, Englewood, NJ, 2004—; sci. tchr. Jonathon Dayton HS, Springfield, NJ, 2005—06, Kinnelon HS, NJ, 2006—. Prin. investigator, rsch. scientist ICN Galenika Inst., Clin. Ctr. Serbia, Belgrade, 1991—96; rsch. scientist, mktg. cons. Huet Biol., Birmingham, Mich., 1987—91; adj. prof. chemistry Kean Coll.; adj. prof. dept. chemistry and chem. biology Stevens Inst. Tech., Castle Point on Hudson, Hoboken, NJ; adj. assoc. prof. organic chemistry Pace U., NYC, 2002—06; adj. prof. in organic and biochemistry CUNY, 2004. Contbr. articles to profl. jours. Mem.: Am. Chem. Soc., Am. Soc. Microbiology, Phi Lambda Upsilon. Achievements include research in shigella toxin in shigella and E. coli; mitoch GPO in advenal cortex; liberation of labile sufur from ferredoxins; adhesion shigella to HCTH and HELA; localization of GST and GP in adrenal. Home: 306 State Route 94 Columbia NJ 07832-2771 Personal E-mail: pjp@eclipse.net.

TIMKEN, WARD J., JR., manufacturing executive; BA, Georgetown Univ.; MBA, Univ. Va. Mgr., Washington office McGough & Assoc. govt. affairs. cons.; with Timken Co., Canton, Ohio, 1992—, corp. v.p., 2000—03, bd. dir., 2002—, exec. v.p., pres. steel group, 2003—05, vice chmn., 2005, chmn., 2005—. Bd. mem. Am. Iron & Steel Inst.; bd. dir. Team NEO, Stark Devel. Bd., Henry & Louise Timken Found.; mem. Ohio Bus. Develop. Council. Bd. dir. Firestone Country Club. Office: Timken Company 1835 Dueber Ave SW Canton OH 44706-0932 Office Phone: 330-438-3000. *

TIMKEN, WILLIAM ROBERT, JR., ambassador, former manufacturing executive; b. 1938; m. Sue Timken; 6 children. BA, Stanford U., Calif., 1960; MBA, Harvard U., 1962. With Timken Co. (formerly The Timken Roller Bearing Co.), Canton, Ohio, 1962—2005, asst. v.p. sales, 1964-65, dir. corp. devel., 1965-68, v.p., 1968-73, vice-chmn. bd., chmn. fin. com., 1973-75, chmn. bd., chmn. fin. com., 1975—2003, non-exec. chmn., 2004—05, also dir.; chmn. Securities Investor Protection Corp., Washington, 2003—05; US amb. to Germany US Dept. State, Berlin, 2005—. Named Ohio Bus. Statesman of Yr., Chevalier French Legion of Honor, Hon. Citizen, Colmar, France; recipient Henry Laurence Gantt medal, ASME, 2003, Woodrow Wilson award, Corp. Citizenship, Adam Smith award, Ellis Island Medal of Honor, Ohio Govs. award. Office: DOS Amb 5090 Berlin Pl Washington DC 20521 *

TIMLIN, JAMES CLIFFORD, bishop; b. Scranton, Pa., Aug. 5, 1927; s. James C. and Helen E. (Norton) T. AB, St. Mary's Sem., Balt., 1948; STB, Gregorian U., Rome, 1950. Ordained priest Roman Cath. Ch., 1951. Asst. pastor St. John the Evangelist Ch., Pittston, Pa., 1952—53, St. Peter's Cathedral, Scranton, 1953—66; asst. chancellor, sec. Diocese of Scranton, 1966—71, chancellor, 1971—77, aux. bishop, vicar gen., 1976—84, bishop, 1984—2003, bishop emeritus, 2003—; pastor Ch. of Nativity, Scranton, 1979—84. Roman Catholic. Address: 1600 Green Ridge St Dunmore PA 18509 Office Phone: 570-343-6170.

TIMLIN, ROBERT J., judge; b. 1932; BA cum laude, Georgetown U., 1954, JD, 1959, LLM, 1964. Atty. Douglas, Obear and Campbell, 1960-61, Law Offices of A.L. Wheeler, 1961; with criminal divsn. U.S. Dept. Justice, 1961-64; atty. U.S. Atty. Office (crtl. dist.) Calif., 1964-66, Hennigan, Ryneal and Butterwick, 1966-67; city atty. City of Corona, Calif., 1967-70; prin. Law Office of Robert J. Timlin, 1970-71, 75-76; ptnr. Hunt, Palladino and Timlin, 1971-74, Timlin and Coffin, 1974-75; judge Mcpl. Ct., Riverside, Calif., 1976-80, Calif. Superior Ct., Riverside, 1980-90; assoc.

justice Calif. Ct. Appeals, 1990-94; judge U.S. Dist. Ct. (ctrl. dist.) Calif., LA, 1994—. Part-time U.S. Magistrate judge Ctrl. Dist. Calif., 1970-74. Served U.S. Army, 1955-57. Mem. Calif. Judges Assn. Office: US Dist Ct Central Distric Calif Western Divsn 312 N Spring St Los Angeles CA 90012 Home Phone: 805-566-0756; Office Phone: 213-894-5272.

TIMM, ROGER K., lawyer; b. Bay City, Mich., May 21, 1947; BS, U. Mich., 1969; JD, Harvard U., 1972. Bar: Mich. 1972. Mem. Dykema Gossett, Detroit. Mem.: ABA, State Bar Mich. Office: Dykema Gossett 400 Renaissance Ctr Detroit MI 48243-1668 Office Phone: 313-568-6597. E-mail: rtimm@dykema.com.

TIMMCKE, ALAN EDWARD, colon and rectal surgeon; b. Madison, Wis., July 7, 1949; s. Wesley Eugene Timmcke; m. Teresa Ann Watkins, Dec. 31, 1977; children: Gretchen Kristine, Alan Edward Jr. BS, Dickinson Coll., 1971; MD with honors, Temple U., 1975. Diplomate Am. Bd. Surgery, Am. Bd. Colon and Rectal Surgery; lic. physician, Pa., Maine, La., Fla. Intern in surgery Nat. Naval Med. Ctr., Bethesda, Md., 1975-76, resident in gen. surgery, 1976-79; rsch. fellow in colon and rectal surgery Jewish Hosp./Washington U. Med. Ctr., St. Louis, 1985-86, clin. fellow in colon and rectal surgery, 1986-87; asst. in surgery Washington U. Sch. Medicine, St. Louis, 1985-87; staff colon and rectal surgeon Ochsner Clinic, New Orleans, 1987—. Staff surgeon Nat. Naval Med. Ctr., Bethesda, 1979, Naval Regional Med. Ctr., Newport, R.I., 1979-82, dept. colon and rectal surgery Lahey Clinic Med. Ctr., Burlington, Mass., 1984-85; staff surgeon Rumford (Maine) Community Hosp., 1982-84, med. staff v.p., 1983-84; instr. surgery Uniformed Svcs. U. of Health Scis., Bethesda, 1978-79; lectr. in field. Assoc. editor Diseases of the Colon and Rectum, 2002—; contbr. articles and abstracts to profl. jours. Lt. comdr. M.C., USN, 1975-82. Recipient Harry E. Bacon Found. award for best original paper, 1987; NIH Summer Rsch. fellow, 1972. Fellow ACS, Am. Soc. Colon and Rectal Surgeons; mem. New Orleans Surg. Soc., Surg. Assn. of La., Internat. Soc. Univ. Colon and Rectal Surgeons, Soc. of Am. Gastrointestinal Endoscopic Surgeons, Am. Soc. Gastrointestinal Endoscopy, Alpha Omega Alpha. Office: Ochsner Clinic Dept Colon/Rectal Surgery 1514 Jefferson Hwy New Orleans LA 70121-2483 Office Phone: 504-842-4060. Personal E-mail: atimmcke@aol.com.

TIMMER, BARBARA, state agency administrator; b. Holland, Mich., Dec. 13, 1946; d. John Norman and Barbara Dee (Folensbee) T. BA, Hope Coll., Holland, Mich., 1969; JD, U. Mich., 1975. Bar: Mich. 1975, U.S. Supreme Ct. 1995. Assoc. McCrosky, Libner, VanLeuven, Muskegon, Mich., 1975-78; apptd. to Mich. Women Commn. by Gov., 1976-79; staff counsel subcom. commerce, consumer & monetary affairs Ho. Govt. Ops. Com., U.S. Ho. of Reps., 1979-82, 85-86; exec. v.p. NOW, 1982-84; legis. asst. to Rep. Geraldine Ferraro, 1984; atty. Office Gen. Counsel Fed. Home Loan Bank Bd., 1986-89; gen. counsel Com. on Banking, Fin. and Urban affairs U.S. Ho. of Reps., Washington, 1989-92; asst. gen. counsel, dir. govt. affairs ITT Corp., Washington, 1992-96; sr. v.p., dir. govt. rels. Home Savs. of Am., Irwindale, Calif., 1996-99; ptnr. Manatt, Phelps & Phillips, Washington, 1999—; gen. counsel MyPrimeTime, Inc., San Francisco, 2000-01; asst. sec. U.S. Senate, 2001—02, asst. sgt. at arms, 2003; chief info. officer Calif. Dept. Transp., Sacramento, 2003—. Mem. info. tech. coun. Women's Transp. Seminar, Calif., 2004—. Editor: Compliance With Lobbying Laws and Gift Rule Guide, 1996. Mem. Calif. State CIO Coun., 2004—05; bd. dirs. Women's High Tech Coalition. Named to Acad. of Women Achievers, YWCA, 1993; recipient Affordable Housing award, Nat. Assn. Real Estate Brokers, 1990, Disting. Alumni award, Hope Coll., 2003. Mem.: FBA (chair exec. coun. banking law com.), ABA (bus. law sect., electronic fin. svcs. subcom.), Bar of D.C., Mich. Bar Assn., Supreme Ct. Hist. Soc., Supreme Ct. Bar Assn., Women in Housing and Fin. (bd. dirs. 1992—94, gen. counsel 1994—98), Exchequer Club. Episcopalian. Office: 2629 Main St PMB 115 Santa Monica CA 90405 E-mail: btimmerdc@earthlink.net.

TIMMERHAUS, KLAUS DIETER, chemical engineering professor; b. Mpls., Sept. 10, 1924; s. Paul P. and Elsa L. (Bever) T.; m. Jean L. Mevis, Aug. 3, 1952; 1 dau., Carol Jane. BS in Chem. Engring, U. Ill., 1948, MS, 1949, PhD, 1951. Registered profl. engr., Colo. Process design engr. Calif. Rsch. Corp., Richmond, 1952-53; extension lectr. U. Calif., Berkeley, 1952; mem. faculty U. Colo., Boulder, 1953-95, prof. chem. engring., 1963—86, assoc. dean engring., 1963—86, dir. engring. rsch. ctr. coll. engring., 1983—86, chmn. aerospace dept., 1983—86, chmn. chem. engring. dept., 1986-89, Patten Chair Disting. prof., 1986-89, presdl. tchg. scholar, 1989—95; ret., 1995. Chem. engr. cryogenics lab. Nat. Bur. Standards, Boulder, summers 1955,57,59,61; lectr. U. Calif. at L.A., 1961-62; sect. head engring. div. NSF, 1972-73; cons. in field. Bd. dirs. Colo. Engring. Expt. Sta., Inc., Engring. Measurements Co. Editor: Advances in Cryogenic Engineering, vols. 1-25, 1954-80; co-editor: Internat. Cryogenic Monograph Series, 1965-. Served with USNR, 1944-46. Recipient Disting. Svc. award Dept. Commerce, 1957, Samuel C. Collins award for outstanding contbns. to cyrogenic tech., 1967, Meritorious Svc. award Cryogenic Engring. Conf., 1987, Disting. Pub. Svc. award NSF, 1984, Exemplary Contbr. award Cryogenic Engring. Conf., 2005; named CASE Colo. Prof. of Yr., 1993, Disting. Lectr., L-T Fan, 2001. Fellow AAAS (v.p. 1985, pres. 1986, Southwestern and Rocky Mountain divsn. Pres.'s award 1989), AIChE (v.p. 1975, pres. 1976, Alpha Chi Sigma award for chem. engring. rsch., 1968, Founders award 1978, Eminent Chem. Engring. award 1983, W.K. Lewis award 1987, F.J. Van Antwerpen award 1991, Inst. Lecture award 1995), Am. Soc. for Engring. Edn. (bd. dirs. 1986-88, George Westinghouse award 1968, 3M Chem. Engring. divsn. award 1980, Engring. Rsch. Coun. award 1990, Delos Svc. award 1991), Cryogenic Soc. Am.; mem. Internat. Inst. Refrigeration (v.p. 1979-87, pres. 1987-95, US nat. commn. 1983-2006, W.T. Pentzer award 1989, hon. co-chair, IIR World Congress, 2003); mem. NAE, Am. Astron. Soc., Austrian Acad. Sci., Cryogenic Engring. Conf. (chmn. 1956-67, bd. dirs. 1967-), Internat. Cryocooler Conf. (bd. dirs. 1980-2006), Soc. Automotive Engrs. (Ralph Teetor award 1991), Sigma Xi (v.p. 1986-87, pres. 1987-88, bd. dirs. 1981-89), Verein Deutscher Ingenieure, Sigma Tau, Tau Beta Pi, Phi Lambda Upsilon. Home: 905 Brooklawn Dr Boulder CO 80303-2708 Business E-Mail: klaus.timmerhaus@colorado.edu.

TIMMERMAN, WILLIAM B., utilities executive, accountant; b. Columbia, SC, Nov. 12, 1946; s. William Bledsoe and Helen (Speissegger) T.; m. Janet Russell, Sept. 15, 1971; children: William III, Catherine Lucille. BA in Pub. Acctg., Duke U., 1968; postgrad., Harvard U., 1990. CPA, N.C. Auditor Arthur Andersen & Co., Charlotte, NC, 1968-78; sr. v.p. Carolina Energies, Inc., Columbia, 1978-82; v.p. S.C. Electric & Gas Co., Columbia, 1982-83, v.p., group exec., 1983-84; chief fin. officer, sr. v.p. SCANA Corp., Columbia, 1984—94, exec. v.p., CFO, contr., 1994—95, pres., 1995—97, COO, 1996—97, chmn., pres., CEO, 1997—. Exec. adv. com. Edison Electric Inst.; acctg. and fin. exec. com. Southeastern Electric Exchange; bd. dir. SCANA Corp., Liberty Corp., Preholding Inc., Palmetto Bus. Forum; past dir. Powertel Inc., SouthernNet/Telecom USA, Wachovia Bank SC, Palmetto Seed Corp.; chmn. bd. Standard Fed. Savs. Bank, Columbia; past chmn. SC Rsch. Authority. Trustee United Way of Midlands, Columbia, 1985—; vice chmn. fin. ARC, Columbia, 1986—; adv. bd. Sch. Bus. U. SC, 1985—, Duke Neighbordhood Partnership; bd. dir. Duke U., the Fuqua Sch.; past dir. Benedict Coll., SC State Ports Authority. Served with USN, 1968-72. Office: SCANA Corp 1426 Main St Ste 100 Columbia SC 29201-2834 *

TIMMERMANN, ALLAN GILLING, management and economics professor; b. Skovlund, Denmark, Oct. 9, 1964; came to U.S., 1994; son of Viggo Nielsen and Gyda (Gilling) T.; m. Solange Maria Ferreli Fortes, Feb. 1, 1992; 1 child: Henry. MS, London Sch. Econs., 1988; degree in Econs., U. Copenhagen, Denmark, 1991; PhD, U. Cambridge, England, 1992. Lectr. fin. econs. U. London, 1991-94; asst. prof. U. Calif., San Diego, 1994-98, assoc. prof., 1999—2001, prof., 2001—, Atkinson/Epstein Chair mgmt. leadership, 2007—. Cons. Barclay's Global Investors, 1998, IMF, Fed. Res. Bd., European Ctrl. Bank; prof. fin. London Sch. Econs., 1998-99. Dept. editor Jour. of Forecasting, 2000-05; assoc. editor Jour. Bus. and Econ. Stats., 2001—, Jour. Fin. Econometrics, 2003—; contbr. articles to profl. jours. Hellman Faculty fellow, U. Calif., San Diego, 1997; British Coun. scholar, London, 1987; recipient Tress prize U. London, 1993. Mem. Am. Fin. Assn., Ctr. Econ. Policy Rsch. (rsch. fellow), Econometric Soc. Avocations: long distance running, tennis. Office Phone: 858-534-4860, 858-534-0894. Business E-Mail: atimmerm@ucsd.edu.

TIMMINS, EDWARD PATRICK, lawyer; b. Denver, June 8, 1955; s. M. Edward and Elizabeth Jean (Imhoff) T.; m. Mary Joanne Deziel, Dec. 27, 1985; children: Edward Patrick Jr., Joan Deziel. BA with honors, Harvard U., 1977; JD magna cum laude, U. Mich., 1980. Bar: Colo. 1981, U.S. Ct. Appeals (D.C. and 9th cirs.) 1982, U.S. Dist. Ct. Colo. 1984, U.S. Ct. Appeals (10th cir.) 1984. Law clk. to cir. justice U.S. Ct. Appeals (7th cir.), Chgo., 1980-81; trial atty. U.S. Dept. Justice, Washington, 1981-84; asst. U.S. atty. Denver, 1984-88; dir. Otten, Johnson, Robinson, Neff & Ragonetti P.C., Denver, 1985-96; pres. Timmins & Assocs., LLC, Denver, 1996—. Sr. editor U. Mich. Law Rev., 1979-80. Bd. dirs., vice chair Colo. Easter Seals; bd. dirs., chair Denver Pub. Schs. Found.; bd. dirs., chmn. career exploring com. Boy Scouts Am.; bd. dirs. March of Dimes, Am. Ireland Fund. Harvard Nat. scholar, 1976. Mem. ABA, Colo. Bar Assn. (bd. govs., exec. coun. jud. sect.), Colo. Bar Found., Denver Bar Assn., Order of Coif, Friends of Harvard Rowing. Avocations: skiing, golf. Office: Timmins & Assocs LLC 1625 Broadway Ste 300 Denver CO 80202-4739 Office Phone: 303-592-4502.

TIMMONS, EVELYN DEERING, pharmacist; b. Durango, Colo., Sept. 29, 1926; d. Claude Elliot and Evelyn Allen (Gooch) Deering; m. Richard Palmer Timmons, Oct. 4, 1952 (div. 1968); children: Roderick Deering, Steven Palmer. BS in Chemistry and Pharmacy cum laude, U. Colo., 1948. Chief pharmacist Meml. Hosp., Phoenix, 1950—54; libr. med. lit. rsch. Hoffman-LaRoche, Inc., Nutley, NJ, 1956—57; staff pharmacist St. Joseph's Hosp., Phoenix, 1958—60; relief mgr. various ind. apothecaries, Phoenix, 1960—68; asst. then mgr., dir. compounding Profl. Pharmacies, Inc., Phoenix, 1968—72; mgr. Mt. View Pharmacy, 1972—76, owner/mgr., 1976—; pres. Ariz. Apothecaries, Ltd., 1976—. Mem. profl. adv. bd., bereavement counselor Hospice of Valley, 1983-96; mem. profl. adv. bd. Upjohn Health Care and Svcs., Phoenix, 1984-86; bd. dirs. Am. coun. on Pharm. Edn., Chgo., 1986-92, v.p., 1988, 89, treas., 1990-91; mem. expert adv. bd. compounding pharms. U.S. Pharmacoepial Conv., 1992—; preceptor U. Ariz., 1965—, Midwestern Coll. Pharmacy, Ariz. Campus, 1998—; chief cons. bioidentical hormone replacement therapy and safety; disease mgmt. specialist; lectr. on NHRT and BHRT. Mem. editl. adv. bd. Internat. Jour. Pharm. Compounding, 1997-2000; author poetry; contbr. articles to profl. jours. Mem. Scottsdale (Ariz.) Fedn. Rep. Women, 1963-68; various other offices Rep. Fedn.; mem. platform com. State of Ariz., Nat. Rep. Conv., 1964; asst. sec. Young Rep. Nat. Fedn., 1963-65; active county and state Rep. coms.; adv. bd. Internat. Jour. of Pharm. Compounding, 1996-2001; fin. chmn. Internat. Leadership Symposium: Women in Pharmacy, London, 1987; treas. Leadership Internat. Women Pharmacy, 1991-2001; mem. founders circle Gladys Taylor McGarey Med. Found., 1996—. Named Outstanding Young Rep. of Yr., Nat. Fedn. Young Reps., 1965, Preceptor of Yr., U. Ariz./Syntex, 1984; recipient Disting. Pub. Svc. award Maricopa County Med. Soc., 1962, Disting. Alumni award Wasatch Acad., 1982, Career Achievement award Kappa Epsilon, 1983, Leadership and Achievement award Upjohn Labs., 1985-86, Outstanding Achievement in Profession award Merck, Sharp & Dohme, 1986, award of Merit Kappa Epsilon, 1988, Disting. Coloradoan award U. Colo., 1989, Vanguard award Kappa Epsilon, 1991, Unicorn award Kappa Epsilon, 1993, Compounding Pharmacist of the Yr. award Profl. Compounding Corp. of Am., 1994, 96, Healing Heart award Gladys Taylor McGarey Found., 1998, 50 Yr. Certificate U. Colo., 2000. Fellow Am. Coll. of Apothecaries (v.p. 1982-83, pres. elect 1983-84, pres. 1984-85, chmn. bd. dirs. 1985-86, adv. coun. 1986-92, Chmn. of Yr. 1980-81, Victor H. Morganroth award 1985, J. Leon Lascoff award 1990), Internat. Acad. of Compounding Pharmacists (bd. dirs. 1993-2000, hon. life fellow 2005); mem. Ariz. Soc. of Hosp. Pharmacists, Am. Pharm. Assn. (Daniel B. Smith award 1990), Ariz. Pharmacy Assn. (Svc. to Pharmacy award 1976, Pharmacist of Yr. 1981, Bowl of Hygeia 1989, 1st Innovative Pharmacy award 1994, 50 Yr. Practice and Membership award 2001), Maricopa County Pharmacy Assn. (pres. 1977, Svc. to Pharmacy award 1977), Am. Soc. of Hosp. Pharmacists, Am. Aircraft Owners and Pilots Assn., Air Safety Found., Nat. Assn. of Registered Parliamentarians, Civinettes (pres. Scottsdale chpt. 1960-61), Kappa Epsilon (recipient Career Achievement award 1986, Vanguard award 1991, Unicorn award 1993). Avocations: flying, skiing, swimming, hiking, writing. Office: Mt View Pharmacy 10565 N Tatum Blvd Ste B-118 Scottsdale AZ 85253-1095 Office Phone: 480-948-7065. Personal E-mail: evelyntimmons@cox.net.

TIMMONS, GERALD DEAN, pediatric neurologist; b. Rensselaer, Ind., June 1, 1931; s. Homer Timmons and Tamma Mildred (Spall) Rodgers; m. Beverly J. Bruneau; children from previous marriage: Jane Christina Timmons Mitchell, Ann Elizabeth, Mary Catherine, Deanna Lynne. AB, Ind. U., 1953, MD, 1956. Diplomate Am. Bd. Psychiatry and Neurology. Intern Lima (Ohio) Meml. Hosp., 1956-57; resident Ind. U. Hosp., Indpls., 1957-59, 61-62; instr. neurology dept. Ind. U., Indpls., 1962-64; practice medicine specializing in psychiatry and neurology Indpls., 1962-64; practice medicine specializing in pediatric neurology Akron, Ohio, 1964—; chief pediatric neurology emeritus Children's Hosp. Med. Ctr., Akron, 1964—2000; chmn. neurology subcouncil Coll. Medicine Northeastern Ohio Univs., Rootstown, 1978-99. Sr. examiner Am. Bd. Neurology and Psychiatry. Contbr. articles to profl. and scholarly jours. Served to capt. USAF, 1959-61. Mem. Summit County Med. Soc., Ohio Med. Soc., AMA, Am. Acad. Pediatrics, Am. Acad. Neurology (practice com. 1980-86, sec. child neurology sect. 2000—), Child Neurology Soc. (chmn. honors and awards com. 1978-88), Am. Soc. Internal Medicine, Am. Electroencephalographic Soc. Republican. Methodist. Office: Akron Pediatric Neurology 300 Locust St Ste 460 Akron OH 44302-1804 Home Phone: 331-686-8600; Office Phone: 330-253-2113.

TIMMONS, GORDON DAVID, economics professor, farmer; b. Elbert, Tex., May 21, 1919; s. Walter James and Ella Mae (McCarson) T.; m. Jean Betty Kulhanek, Feb. 11, 1947; children: Kathy, Linda, Scott, Jim, Tamara, Dallas, Timothy, Kelly, Susanna. Student, U. Tex., 1937-40, U. Mont., 1961-64; BS, Utah State U., 1955; MS, Mont. State U., 1958. Enlisted USAF, 1939, advanced through grades to col., ret., 1961; instr. Columbia Basin Coll., Pasco, Wash., 1966-86. Pres. Assn. Higher Edn., 1969-72. Decorated Legion of Merit, Croix de Guerre (France). Mem. Acad. Polit. Sci., N.W. Econ. Conf. Democrat. Avocation: horse breeding. Home and Office: Star Rte Box 39-A Olney TX 76374-0039 Office Phone: 940-862-5614. Business E-Mail: timmons@brazosnet.com.

TIMMONS, ROBBIE, news anchor; m. Jim Brandstatter. Grad., Ohio State U. Anchor WILX-TV, Lansing, Mich., 1972—76, WJBK-TV, Detroit, 1976—82, WXYZ-TV, Detroit, 1982—. Recipient numerous Emmy awards, Silver Cir. award, Nat. Acad. TV Arts and Scis., 1998, Most Powerful Woman in Mich., 2002. Achievements include being the first woman in the US to anchor TV news at 6 & 11pm. Office: WXYZ-TV 20777 W Ten Mile Rd Southfield MI 48037 Office Phone: 248-827-9413. Business E-Mail: rtimmons@wxyz.com.

TIMMONS, SEAN ABBOTT, lawyer; b. Washington, Aug. 4, 1967; s. James Donald and Anita Abbott Timmons; m. Sheri Lynn Outlaw, June 8, 1996; children: Elizabeth Kelly Ross, Sean Abbott. BA, Williams Coll., 1989; JD, Duke U. Sch. Law, 1994. Bar: NC 1998, US Dist. Ct. (ea. dist.) NC 1998, US Ct. Appeals (4th cir.) 2001. Atty. Smith, Anderson, Blount, Dorsett, Mitchell & Jernigan, LLP, Raleigh, 1998—2006, ptnr., 2006—. Author: Proposed Changes to the Reassignment Rules and the Stark Regulations, 2006, New Stark Exceptions and Anti-Kickback Safe Harbors for Electronic Prescribing and Electronic Health Records, 2006; contbr. articles to profl. jours. Mem.: NC Bar Assn., Am. Health Lawyers Assn., ABA. Avocation: trombone. Home: 2902 Everett Ave Raleigh NC 27607 Office: Smith Anderson Blount Dorsett Mitchell & Jernigan LLP 2500 Wachovia Capitol Ctr PO Box 2611 Raleigh NC 27602-2611 Office Phone: 919-821-1220. Office Fax: 919-821-6800. Business E-Mail: stimmons@smithlaw.com.

TIMMONS, SHARON L., retired elementary school educator; b. South Kansas City, Mo., July 25, 1949; d. Clyde George and Sarah Ethyl (Thrift) Manley; m. Joseph D. Timmons, June 6, 1970; children: Stacia, Matt. BSE, U. Kans., 1972; MA, U. Mo., Kansas City, 1980. Cert. elem., jr. high tchr., Mo; elem. tchr., Kans. Team tchr. elem. Loretto Acad., Kansas City, Mo., 1976—80; team tchr. lead mid. sch. and block schedule programs, 8th grade, Ctr. Sch. Dist. 58, Kansas City, Mo., 1980—94; ret., 1994. Author: (Title II grants) For Indivdualized Math Program, Kansas City Rep. for Scientific Literacy. Mem. Sigma Kappa.

TIMMONS, WILLIAM EVAN, consulting firm executive; b. Chattanooga, Dec. 27, 1930; s. Owen Walter and Doris (Eckenrod) T.; m. Mimi Bakshian, Sept. 28, 1966; children: Karen Leigh, Kimberly Anne, William Evan. Grad., Baylor Mil. Acad., Chattanooga, 1949; BS in Fgn. Svc., Georgetown U., 1959; postgrad., George Washington U., 1959-61. Aide to U.S. Senator Alexander Wiley, 1955-62; adminstrv. asst. to U.S. Rep. William Brock, 1963-69; dep. asst. to Pres. Richard M. Nixon, 1969-70, asst., 1970-74; asst. to Pres. Gerald R. Ford, 1974; pres. Timmons & Co. Inc., 1975-86, chmn. exec. com., 1986—2002, chmn. emeritus, 2002—. Mem. Fed. Property Rev. Bd., 1972-75, Pres.'s Trade Adv. Com., 1975-80; U.S. del. to Internat. Conf. on Viet Nam, Paris, 1973. Presdl. appointee U.S.-Japan Adv. Commn., 1983—85; nat. conv. dir. Reagan for Pres. Com., Detroit, 1980, Dallas, 1984, nat. polit. dir., 1980; exec. dir. Tenn. Rep. Com., 1962; mgr. Brock campaigns, 1962, 1964, 1966, 1968; dir. congl. rels. Nixon-Agnew campaign, 1968; coord. Nixon for Pres.; active Rep. Nat. Conv., Miami, Fla., 1968, 1972, dir. Pres. Ford com. Kansas City, 1976; mem. adv. com. Rep. Nat. Com. Conv., New Orleans, 1988, San Diego, 1996; mem. exec. com. Nat. Young Reps., 1965—67; dep. dir. for transition Office of Pres.-Elect, 1980—81; mem. faculty Nat. REp. campaign workshops, 1963—69; sr. adviser Bush for Pres. Com., New Orleans, 1988, Dole for Pres. Com., 1996; mem. adv. com. Bush for Pres., Rep. Nat. Conv., Phila., 2000; adviser Bush-Cheney Transition, 2000—01; bd. dirs. Radio Free Europe/Liberty, 1975—82, Georgetown U. Ctr. Strategic and Internat. Studies, 1982—85. With USAF, 1951—55. Named Outstanding Young Rep. of Year Nat. Rep. Com., 1965; recipient 170 Ann. Achievement award Georgetown Alumni Club; citation for Disting. Service Baylor Mil. Acad. Alumni Assn., 1970 Mem. SCV, SAR, Soc. of the Cin., Columbia Country Club, George Towne Club, City Club, St. Alban's Tennis Club, Masons (33d degree). Home: 4426 Garfield St NW Washington DC 20007-1142 Office: Timmons & Co 1875 Eye St NW Ste 400 Washington DC 20006 Office Phone: 202-331-1760. Personal E-mail: BTimmons@aol.com.

TIMMONS-GOODSON, PATRICIA, state supreme court justice; b. Florence, SC, Sept. 18, 1954; d. Edward and Beulah Timmons; m. Ernest J. Goodson; 2 children. BA, U. NC, Chapel Hill, 1976, JD, 1979. Dist. mgr. U.S. Census, 1979—80; asst. dist. atty. Twelfth Prosecutorial Dist., NC, 1981—83; staff atty. Lumbee River Legal Services, Inc., Fayetteville, 1983—84; dist. ct. judge Twelfth Judicial Dist., NC, 1984—97; judge NC Ct. of Appeals, 1997—2005; assoc. justice NC Supreme Ct., 2006—. Former co-host and co-prodr. television program Dimensions of Justice. Mem. central selection com. Morehead Scholarship; bd. dirs. alumni assn. U. NC. Mem.: ABA (mem. appellate judges conference exec. com.), NC Assn. of Black Lawyers, NC Bar Assn. Office: NC Supreme Ct PO Box 2448 Raleigh NC 27602 Office Phone: 919-733-3723. *

TIMONEY, PETER JOSEPH, veterinarian, educator, virologist, consultant; b. Dublin, June 5, 1941; came to U.S., 1983; s. John Francis and Evelyn Norah (Whittle) T.; m. Katherine Mary Murphy, Sept. 11, 1971; children: Peter, Caroline, Sarah, David. MVB, Nat. U., Dublin, 1964; MS, U. Ill., 1966; PhD, U. Dublin, 1974. Rsch. assoc. U. Ill., Urbana, 1964-66; rsch. officer Vet. Rsch. Lab., Abbotstown, Ireland, 1966-72; sr. rsch. officer equine diseases sect. Veterinary Rsch. Lab., Abbotstown, Ireland, 1972-79; assoc. prof. diagnostic lab., dept. microbiology Cornell U., Ithaca, NY, 1979-81; sci. dir. Irish Equine Ctr., Johnstown, Ireland, 1981-83; assoc. prof. virology vet. sci. dept. U. Ky., Lexington, 1983-87, prof. virology, assoc. chair for rsch., 1987-89, Frederick Van Lennep chair, 1988—, acting chair, 1989-90, chair, 1990-99, 2002—. Cons. Daryl Labs., Inc., Santa Clara, Calif., 1981-86, Ft. Dodge (Iowa) Animal Health Lab., 1986-92, 94—. Fellow Royal Coll. Vet. Surgeons, World Equine Vet. Assn. (pres. 1995-99); mem. Am. Assn. Equine Practitioners, Am. Soc. Microbiology, Am. Soc. Virology, U.S. Animal Health Assn. Avocations: reading, gardening. Office: Gluck Equine Rsch Ctr 108 Gluck Ctr Lexington KY 40506-0099 Business E-Mail: ptimoney@uky.edu.

TIMONI, STEPHEN ANTHONY, lawyer, accountant; b. Elizabeth, NJ, July 15, 1954; s. Vincent A. and Jean E. (Petrone) T.; m. Cynthia A. Yarusi, May 24, 1987; children: Christina Marie, John Anthony. BS in Bus./Econs., Wagner Coll., 1976; JD, Seton Hall U., 1982. Bar: N.J. 1982, U.S. Dist. Ct. N.J. 1982, U.S. Tax Ct., U.S. Ct. Appeals (3d cir.) 1991; CPA, N.J., N.Y. Audit staff Touche Ross & Co. CPA's, Newark, 1976-78; tax assoc. Reydel Perier & Neral CPA's, Westfield, N.J., 1978-82, Price Waterhouse CPA's, NYC, 1982-84; pvt. practice law Clark, N.J., 1984-87; ptnr. Galfy & Timoni, Clark, 1987-90, Galfy, Timoni, Rubino & Huttle, Clark; ptnr. & pro bono coord. Kirkpatrick & Lockhart Nicholson Graham LLP, Newark. Bd. govs. Rahway (N.J.) Hosp.; mem. N.J. Tech. Council Fellow N.J. Soc. CPAs; mem. ABA, N.J. Bar Assn. (real property and trust sect.), Catholic Health Assn. U.S., Am. Health Lawyers Assn., Union County Bar Assn., Assn. Trial Lawyers Am., N.J. Assn. Trial Lawyers, AICPA, Union County C. of C., Builders Assn. Met. N.J. Roman Catholic. Avocations: reading, travel, golf. Office: Kirkpatrick & Lockhart Nicholson Graham LLP 10th Fl 1 Newark Ctr Newark NJ 07102-5252 Office Phone: 973-848-4020. Office Fax: 973-848-4001. Business E-Mail: stimoni@klng.com.

TIMOSHCHUK, VICTOR ARKADYEVICH, research scientist; b. Mary, Turkmenistan, Sept. 20, 1946; s. Arkady and Raisa Timoshchuk; m. Margarita Sergievsky, Feb. 16, 1990; m. Ludmila Gumenyuk, Aug. 10, 1979 (div. Feb. 13, 1990); children: Vladislav, Kirill, Sergey. MS in Organic Chemistry, St. Petersburg State U., Russia, 1964—69; PhD in Organic Chemistry, Rsch. Inst. Bio-organic Chemistry, Belarus Acad. Scis., Minsk, 1971—75. Sr. rschr. Rsch. Inst. Bio-organic Chemistry, Minsk, Belarus, 1976—81, Rsch. Inst. Peat, Minsk, 1981—84; head, lab. Rsch. Inst. Microbiology and Epidemiology, Minsk, 1984—88; sr. rschr. Rsch. Inst. Radiation Medicine, Minsk, 1988—90; chief rschr. Belarus State U., Minsk, 1990—96; vis. rschr. Brigham Young U., Provo, Utah, vis. scientist, 1996—99; scientist TriLink Biotechnologies, Inc., San Diego, 1999—. Contbr. articles to profl. jours. Mem.: Internat. Soc. for Nucleosides, Nucleotides and Nucleic Acids. Achievements include discovery of a new type of isomery; patents for the syntheses of nucleosides of different types.

Office: TriLink BioTechnologies Inc 9955 Mesa Rim Rd San Diego CA 92121 Office Phone: 858-546-0004. Personal E-mail: vatimoshchuk@yahoo.com. Business E-Mail: vtimoshchuk@trilinkbiotech.com.

TIMOTHY, DAVID HARRY, retired biology professor; b. Pitts., June 9, 1928; s. David Edgar and Harriett P. (Stein) T.; m. Marian Claire Whiteley, Sept. 5, 1953; children: Marjory J., M. Elisabeth, David W. BS, Pa. State U., 1952, MS, 1955; PhD, U. Minn., 1956. Asst. geneticist Rockefeller Found., Bogota, Colombia, 1956-58, assoc. geneticist, 1958-61; assoc. prof. N.C. State U., Raleigh, 1961-66, prof., 1966-93, prof. crop sci., botany and genetics emeritus, 1993—; ret. Cons. to fgn. and U.S. govts., also U.S. and internat. sci. orgns.; mem. USDA crop adv. com. on grasses, 1983-87, mem. policy adv. com., sci. and edn. grants program, 1982-84, chief scientist USDA Sci. and Edn. Competetive Rsch. Grants Office, 1985, 86; with Nat. Plant Genetic Resources Bd., 1984-91, vice chmn., 1991; bd. dirs., treas. Genetic Resources Comms. Sys., Inc., 1985-91, pres., 1991-93; mem. bd. on agr. NAS-NRC, work group on U.S. Nat. Plant Germplasm Sys., 1987-89. Co-author monographs; contbr. chpts. to books; contbr. articles to profl. jours. With AUS, 1946-48, PTO. Grantee NSF, 1965, 78, Rockefeller Found., 1968, 69, Pioneer Hi-Bred Internat., 1982, 83. Fellow AAAS (electorate nominating com., sect. O, Agr. 1988-90), Am. Soc. Agronomy, Crop Sci. Soc. Am. (editl. bd. 1982-84, assoc. editor Crop Sci. 1982-84, Frank N. Meyer medal for plant genetic resources 1994). Home: 101 Wee Loch Dr Cary NC 27511

TIMPA, VICKI ANN, government health program administrator; b. Houston, Aug. 20, 1955; d. Edmund Burke and Helen Kanosky Huber; m. John Gerrard Fewel, May 27, 2000; children: Julie Marie Fecht, Anthony Alan. BSN, U. Tex., 1977; MSN in Edn. Adminstrn. and Rsch., Tex. Woman's U., 1990, advanced nurse practitioner degree, 1993. Cert. ACLS, domestic preparedness for biol.-radiol.-chem. VA, neurosurg. cert., cert. prevention inst. instr.; critical care nurse; cert. Covey trainer, antiques and collectibles appraiser. Team leader cardiopulmonary shock trauma emergency ctr., nurse Ben Taub Emergency Ctr., Harris County Hosp. Dist., Houston, 1977; peritoneal dialysis nurse Parkland Meml. Hosp., Dallas County Hosp. Dist.; emergency rm. and GI lab staff nurse Mesquite Hosp., Tex., 1978—80; nurse Baylor U. Med. Ctr. Hosp. Sys., Dallas, 1980—90; rsch. nurse coord. VA, Dallas, 1990—93; dept. of edn. mgr. Meth. Hosps. of Dallas, 1993; patient health and continuing med. edn. coord., chief ethics cons. VA North Tex. Health Care Sys., Dallas, 1993—. Coord. nat. rsch. studies VA, Dallas, 1990—92, nat. liaison for Nat. Ctr. for Health Promotion and Disease Prevention, Durham, NC, 2002—05, congl. legis. cons., Washington, 2000—; ICU mock code creator and trainer Baylor U. Hosp. Sys., Dallas, 1980—90; cardiopulmonary resuscitation instr. Am. Heart Assn., Dallas, 1989—94; Plain Lang. Act cons. Exec. Br., Washington, 1995—. Contbr. articles to profl. pubs. Sr. v.p. Miracle Wish Found., 2006—. Named Most Valuable Person, VA Rsch., 1992; named one of Great 100 Nurses award, 1997; recipient Unsung Hero award, VA, 1993, Plank award, Nat. Ctr. Health Promotion, 2002—05, Customer Svc. award, VA North Tex. Healthcare Sys., 2007; Pub. Health grant, 2007. Mem.: Sigma Theta Tau (fin. and fund raising com. 1993—2001, vice chairperson of bd. dir., Miracle Wish Found. 2006—, Academic Excellence and Rsch. Excellence awards 1993, 2001, Public Health Grant award 2007—). Roman Catholic. Avocations: travel, antiques and collectibles appraising. Home: 1307 High Ridge Dr Duncanville TX 75137 Office: VA 4500 S Lancaster Rd (141P) Dallas TX 75216 Office Phone: 214-857-1163. Home Fax: 972-572-5525. Personal E-mail: vickiern7@netzero.net. Business E-Mail: vicki.timpa@med.va.gov.

TIMPERLAKE, EDWARD THOMAS, writer; b. Perth Amboy, NJ, Nov. 22, 1946; s. James Elwood Timperlake Jr. and Joan Dorothy (Conkling) Maurer; m. Barbette Runckel, Aug. 10, 1969 (div. 1993); children: Tara, Kimberly; m. Cathryn Porcelli Gekas, Apr. 8, 2000. BS, U.S. Naval Acad., 1969; MBA, Cornell U., 1977. Commd. 2d lt. USMC, 1969, advanced through grades to lt. col., ret., 1993; asst. venture mgr. Exxon Enterprise, NYC, 1977-78; sect. mgr. T.A.S.C., Arlington, Va., 1978-81; dep. dir. Nat. Dir. Vietnam Vets. Leadership Program, Action Agy., Washington, 1981-83; dir. mobilization plans and requirements Office of Sec. Def., Washington, 1984; campaign staff George Bush for Pres., 1988; asst. sec. Dept. Vets. Affairs, Washington, 1989-93; pres. T-9 Group, 1993-95; profl. staff rules com. U.S. House of Reps., Washington, 1996—99; dir. tech. assessment internat. tech. security Office of the Sec. of Def., The Pentagon, Washington, 2003—. Author: Year of the Rat, 1998, Red Dragon Rising, 1999, Showdown, 2006; contbr. articles to profl. jours. Mem.: Naval Acad. Alumni Assn., N.Y. Yacht Club, Army-Navy Club. Home: 1027 22d St Arlington VA 22202

TIMS, ROBERT AUSTIN, data processing official, pilot; b. Seattle, Dec. 21, 1942; s. Robert Mitchell Tims and Winifred Eileen (Dorgan) Bristol; m. Jane Moore, June 6, 1980. Student, Pacific Union Coll., 1960—61, Alpha Aviation Sch., 1976—77; BS in Computer Info. Sys. with honors, Ark. State U., 1998. Lic. comml. and instrument pilot; cert. flight instr. Engring. technician Tex. Instruments, Inc., Ridgecrest, Calif., 1966-67, various projects, Conn., N.Y. and N.J., 1967-70; homesteader Leslie, Ark., 1970-77; chief pilot/flight instr. Sharp Aviation Co., Jonesboro, Ark., 1977-79; chief pilot Pizza Inn of Ark., Jonesboro, 1979-83; data processing mgr., chief pilot Realty Assocs. Brokerage, Inc., Jonesboro, 1983-91, microanalyst, 1991-94. Pres., owner ABS Logic, Inc., computers and programming cons., Jonesboro, 1985—2005; programmer Jimco Lamp Mfg., Bono, Ark., 1998—99; programmer, analyst TEK Systems, Memphis, 2000—02; software engr. Northrop Grumman, Little Rock, 2003—04, Nextech, Memphis, 2003—04, Nucor Steel, Hickman, Ark., 2004—05, JD Resources, Memphis, 2004—05; sr. software engr. Rural Sourcing, Inc., Jonesboro, Ark., 2006—. Served with USN, 1962-66. Recipient Nat. Collegiate Bus. Merit award. Mem. CAP (squadron comdr. Jonesboro 1986-93), NRA, Am. Philatelic Soc., Planetary Soc., Nat. Space Soc., SETI Inst., Second Amendment Found., Gun Owners Am., Beta Gamma Sigma. Avocation: philately. Home and Office: 1616 Alonzo St Jonesboro AR 72401-4802 Office Phone: 870-680-4164. Business E-Mail: rtims@abslogic.com.

TINAGLIA, MICHAEL LEE, lawyer; b. Chgo., Dec. 21, 1952; s. Michael Leo and Josephine (Esposito) T.; m. Lucia Yolanda Guzzo, Oct. 14, 1978; children: Laura, Lisa, Elena. BA, Northwestern U., 1974; JD, DePaul U., 1977. Bar: Ill. 1977, U.S. Dist. Ct. (no. dist.) Ill. 1978, U.S. Dist. Ct. (ea. dist.) Wis. 1986. Assoc. Arnold & Kadjan, Chgo., 1977-79; ptnr. Leader & Tinaglia, Chgo., 1979-86; assoc. Laser, Schostok, Kolman & Frank, Chgo., 1987-92; prin. Law Office of Michael Lee Tinaglia Ltd., Chgo., 1992-93, 2000—; equity ptnr. DiMonte & Lizak, Park Ridge, Ill., 1994-99. V.p., corp. counsel Tiara Med. Sys., Inc., Oak Forest, Ill. Contbr. articles to profl. jours. Alderman City Coun., Park Ridge, 1997-2005, chmn. pub. safety com., 2003-2005, mem. fin. and budget com. Mem. Ill. Bar Assn., Chgo. Bar Assn. Roman Catholic. Avocations: skiing, guitar. Office: Law Offices Of Michael Lee Tinaglia Ltd 9700 Higgins Rd Ste 1015 Rosemont IL 60018 Office Phone: 847-692-0421. Business E-Mail: mlginaglia@tinaglialaw.com.

TINDALL, ROBERT EMMETT, lawyer, educator; b. NYC, Jan. 2, 1934; s. Robert E. and Alice (McGonigle) T.; children: Robert Emmett IV, Elizabeth. BS in Marine Engring., SUNY, 1955; postgrad., Georgetown U. Law Sch., 1960—61; LLB, U. Ariz., 1963; LLM, NYU, 1967; PhD, City U., London, 1975. Bar: Ariz. 1963. Mgmt. trainee GE, Schenectady, NY, Lynn, Mass., Glens Falls, NY, 1955-56, 58-60; law clk. Haight, Gardner, Poor and Havens, NYC, 1961; prin., mem. Robert Emmett Tindall & Assocs., Tucson, 1963—; prof. mgmt. U. Ariz., Tucson, 1969—2003; prof. emeritus, 2003. Vis. prof. Grad. Sch. of Law, Soochow U., China, 1972, Grad. Bus. Ctr., London, 1974, NYU, 1991-96, UCSD, 2005—; dir. MBA program U. Ariz., Tucson, 1975-81, dir. entrepreneurship program, 1984-86; investment cons. Saudi Arabia, 1981—; lectr. USIA, Eng., India, Mid. East, 1974; lectr. bus. orgn. and regulatory laws Southwestern Legal Found., Acad. Am. and Internat. Law, 1976-80. Actor cmty. theatres, Schenectady, 1955-56, Harrisburg, Pa., 1957-58, Tucson, 1961-71; appeared in films Rage, 1971, Showdown at OK Corral, 1971, Lost Horizon, 1972; appeared in TV programs Gunsmoke, 1972, Petrocelli, 1974; author: Multinational Enterprises, 1975; contbr. articles on domestic and internat. bus. to profl. jours. Served to lt. USN, 1956-58. Fellow Ford Found., 1965-67; grantee Asia Found., 1972-73. Mem. Strategic Mgmt. Soc., State Bar Ariz., Acad. Internat. Bus., SAG, Honourable Soc. of Mid. Temple (London), Phi Delta Phi, Beta Gamma Sigma, Assn. Corp. Growth, Royal Overseas League (London). Home: PO Box 42196 Tucson AZ 85733-2196

TING, ALBERT CHIA, biomedical engineer, researcher; b. Hong Kong, Sept. 7, 1950; came to U.S., 1957; s. William Su and Katherine Sung T.; m. Shirley Roung Wang, July 30, 1988. BA, UCLA, 1973; MS, Calif. State U., LA, 1975, Calif. Inst. Tech., 1977; PhD, U. Calif., San Diego, 1983. Rsch. asst. Calif. Inst. Tech., Pasadena, 1975-77, U. Calif., San Diego, 1982-83; sr. staff engr. R&D Am. Med. Optics, Irvine, Calif., 1983-86; project engr., rsch. Allergan Med. Optics, Irvine, Calif., 1987-89, sr. project engr., rsch., 1989-92, sr. project engr., engring., 1993-94; bioengr. cons. Pharmacia Iovision, Inc., Irvine, Calif., 1995-97; sr. engr. D & E, 1997, sr. engr., project mgr., 1998-99; rsch. and devel. mgr., surg. Bausch & Lomb, Irvine, 1999—2001; R & D mgr. Visiogen, Inc., Irvine, 2001—02, sr. R & D mgr., 2002—. Contbr. articles to profl. jours. Mem. AAAS, Biomed. Engring. Soc., Assn. for Rsch. in Vision and Ophthalmology, Biomed. Optics Soc. Achievements include invention of med. and optical devices. Office: Visiogen Inc 4 Jenner St # 180 Irvine CA 92618 Office Phone: 949-341-0700.

TING, DAVID, information technology executive; Sci. staff BNR/INRS Labs, Montreal; with Lexidata, Inc., Delphax Sys. (now Xerox subs.); mgr. Atex System's Imaging Dept.; tech. mgr., Boston Tech. Ctr. Eastman Kodak; biometric applications developer govt. sys.; chief architect eCopyIt; founder, chief tech. officer Imprivata, Lexington, Mass. Named one of Top 25 Chief Tech. Officers, InfoWorld mag., 2006. Achievements include holding six patents in field. Office: Imprivata Inc Bldg 4 10 Maguire Rd Lexington MA 02421-3120 Office Phone: 781-674-2700. *

TING, JOHN M., dean, engineering educator; BEng, McGill U., Montreal, 1975; MS, Calif. Inst. of Tech., Pasadena, 1976; ScD, MIT, Cambridge, Mass., 1981. Registered profl. engr., Calif. Mem. faculty Calif. Inst. Tech., 1981—83, U. Toronto, 1983—90, U. Mass., Lowell, 1990—, dean engring., 2003—. Commr. Lowell Arena and Stadium Commn. Recipient Pres. Public Svc. award, U. Mass., 2006. Office: U Mass Lowell One University Ave Lowell MA 01854 Home: Groton MA 01450

TING, KWUN-LON, engineer, educator, consultant; b. Huwei, Taiwan, Oct. 1, 1948; s. Yin and Swei (Lin) T.; m. Rebecca Sun, May 10, 1975; children: Lilian, Daniel. BS, Nat. Taiwan U., Taipei, 1972; MS, Clemson U., 1977; PhD, Okla. State U., 1982. Instr. Army Ordnance Acad., Taiwan, 1972-74; mech. engr. Taiwan Polymer Chemicals Co., Taipei, 1974-75; rsch. asst. Clemson (S.C.) U., 1975-77; teaching asst. Okla. State U., Stillwater, 1977-80, rsch. assoc., 1980-82; asst. prof. Tenn. Tech. U., Cookeville, 1982-87, assoc. prof., 1987-92, prof., 1992—. Dir. Nat. Conf. on Applied Mechanisms and Robotics, 1989, 91. Editor: Jour. Applied Mechanisms & Robotics, 1993—97; assoc. editor: Jour. Mech. Design, 2005—; contbr. articles to profl. jours. Recipient Kinslow Outstanding Engring. Rsch. award, 1992, 97, B. Roth award, 1993, South Pointing Chariot award Nat. Applied Mechanisms and Robotics Conf., 1999, NSF grantee, 1991—. Fellow: ASME. Baptist. Office: Tenn Tech U PO Box 5077 Cookeville TN 38505-0001 Business E-Mail: kting@tntech.edu.

TING, SAMUEL CHAO CHUNG, physicist, researcher; b. Ann Arbor, Mich., Jan. 27, 1936; s. Kuan H. and Jeanne (Wong) Ting; m. Susan Carol Marks, Apr. 28, 1985; children: Jeanne Min, Amy Min, Christopher M. BS in Engring., U. Mich., 1959, MS, 1960, PhD in Physics, 1962, ScD (hon.), 1978, Chinese U. Hong Kong, 1987, U. Bologna, Italy, 1988, Columbia U., 1990, U. Sci. and Tech., China, 1990, Moscow State U., 1991, U. Bucharest, Romania, 1993, Nat. Tsinghua U., Taiwan, 2002, Nat. Jiaotong U., 2003, Hong Kong Bapt. U., 2003, Rheinische Westfalsich Technische Hochschule, Aachen, Germany, 2004, Nat. Ctrl. U., 2005, Hong Kong U. Sci. and Tech., 2005. Ford Found. fellow CERN (European Orgn. Nuc. Rsch.), Geneva, 1963; instr. physics Columbia U., 1964, asst. prof., 1965—67; group leader Deutsches Elektronen-Synchrotron, Hamburg, Germany, 1966; assoc. prof. physics MIT, Cambridge, 1967—68, prof., 1969—, Thomas Dudley Cabot Inst. prof., 1977—. Program cons. divsn. particles and fields Am. Phys. Soc., 1970; hon. prof. Beijing Normal Coll., 1987, Jiatong U., Shanghai, 1987, U. Bologna, Italy, 1988. Assoc. editor Nuc. Physics B, 1970, editl. bd. Nuc. Instruments and Methods, Mathematical Modeling; contbr. articles to profl. jours. Recipient Nobel prize in Physics, 1976, De Gasperi prize in Sci., Italian Republic, 1988, Ernest Orlando Lawrence award, U.S. Govt., 1976, Gold medal in Sci., City of Brescia, Italy, 1988, Golden Leopard award, Town of Taormina, 1988, Forum Engelberg prize, 1996, Pub. Svc. medal, NASA, 2001; fellow Am. Acad. Arts and Scis., 1975; hon. fellow, Tata Inst. Fundamental Rsch., Mumbai, India. Fellow: Inst. Fundamental Rsch. Mumbai India (hon.); mem.: NAS, Spanish Acad. Sci. (fgn. mem.), Royal Spanish Acad. Sci. (fgn. mem.), Chinese Acad. Sci. (fgn. mem.), Hungarian Acad. Sci., Deutsche Acad. Naturforscher Leopoldina (fgn. mem.), Russian Acad. Sci., Acad. Sinica, Pakistani Acad. Sci. Achievements include the discovery of a heavy elementary particle of a new kind.

TINGELSTAD, JON BUNDE, retired pediatrician, educator; b. McVille, ND, Jan. 15, 1935; s. Sophus B. and Mabelle (Bunde) T.; m. Marcia Ayers, Dec. 17, 1960; children: Paul, Catherine, David. BA, U. N.D., 1957, BS, 1958; MD, Harvard U., 1960. Diplomate Am. Bd. Pediatrics. Intern Children's Hosp. Med. Ctr., Boston, 1960-61, resident, 1961-62, U. Colo. Med. Ctr., Denver, 1962-63; fellow in pediatric cardiology Children's Hosp., Buffalo, 1965-67; asst. prof. pediatrics Med. Coll. Va., Richmond, 1967-71, assoc. prof., 1971-76; prof., vice chmn. pediatrics East Carolina U. Sch. Medicine, Greenville, NC, 1976-77, prof., chmn. pediatrics, 1977-2000. Mem. Greenville City Bd. Edn., 1978-82, chmn., 1981-82. Served to capt. USAF, 1963-65. Fellow Am. Acad. Pediatrics, Am. Coll. Cardiology; mem. Am. Bd. Pediatrics (emeritus), Phi Beta Kappa, Phi Eta Sigma. Home: 103 Providence Pl Chocowinity NC 27817-8940 Office: E Carolina U Sch Med Dept Pediatrics Greenville NC 27858-4354 E-mail: JonBTing1@msn.com.

TINGLE, JAMES O'MALLEY, retired lawyer; b. NYC, June 12, 1928; s. Thomas Jefferson and Mercedes (O'Malley) T. BS, U. Mont., 1950, BA, LL.B., U. Mont., 1952; LL.M., U. Mich., 1953, S.J.D, 1958. Bar: Calif. 1959, Mont. 1952, N.Y. 1961. Asst. prof. law U. Mont., Missoula, 1955-56; atty. Shell Oil Co., NYC, 1957-62; assoc. Pillsbury, Madison & Sutro, San Francisco, 1962-68, ptnr., 1969-2000. Author: The Stockholder's Remedy of Corporate Dissolution, 1959; editor: State Antitrust Laws, 1974. Served to 1st lt. USAF, 1953—55. William W. Cook fellow U. Mich. Mem. Mont. Bar Assn., Calif. Bar Assn., ABA Democrat.

TINGLER, MARLENE JOHANNSEN, music educator, insurance agent; b. St. Louis, Aug. 22, 1948; d. Otto August and Charlotte (Sachse) Johannsen; m. Charles E. Tingler, June 19, 1971; 1 child, Matthew Johannsen. BS in Edn., William Jewell Coll., 1970; studied with Max Rabinovitsj, 1970—73; postgrad., Ctrl. Mo. State U., U. Mo., Kansas City. Cert. ins. Mo.; tchr. Mo. Pvt. violin tchr., St. Louis, Kansas City, 1971—; orch. dir., head dept. Berkeley (Mo.) Sch. Dist., 1971—73, Luth. Sch. Sys., Kansas City, 1989—2002; orch. dir. Parkway Schs., St. Louis, 1974—75; office mgr. Pa. Life Ins., Kansas City, 1976—84; mgr. Liberty (Mo.) Symphony Orch., 1977—85, BTI Ins. Co., Kansas City, 1985—88; v.p. Harry Loves Bess, Kansas City, 1999—. Instr. William Jewell Coll., Liberty, 1978—79; world judge, coach State Bd. Odyssey of the Mind. Musician: Jacksonville (Ill.) Symphony, St. Joseph (Mo.) Symphony, St. Louis Philharm. Recipient Outstanding Svc. award, Liberty Symphony, Hickman Mills, Mo. Sch. Dist. Mem.: Music Educators Nat. Conf., Delta Zeta (music dir. 1968—71), Sigma Alpha Iota (sec. 1968—71). Lutheran. Avocations: computers, travel. Personal E-mail: sniffer4@earthlink.net.

TINGLEY, FLOYD WARREN, retired internist; b. Charlotte, NC, Nov. 22, 1933; s. Floyd Warren Sr. and Janie (Suggs) T.; m. Sandra Carpenter, Aug. 20, 1955 (div. Dec. 1984); children: Sheryl Tingley Hagen, David Alan; m. Johnette Hill, Apr. 5, 1985. BA in English, Emory U., 1955, MD, 1959. Diplomate Am. Bd. Internal Medicine (bd. govs. 1986-92). Intern USAF Hosp., Lackland AFB, Tex., 1959-60; resident in internal medicine Parkland Meml. Hosp., Dallas, 1963-65, fellow in cardiology, 1965-66; pvt. practice specializing in internal medicine Arlington, Tex., 1966-88; med. dir. southwestern region Met. Life Ins. Co., Irving, Tex., 1988-90; regional practice leader William M. Mercer Inc., 1990-91; v.p., sr. med. dir. Provident Life and Accident Co., Chattanooga, 1991-92; v.p., nat. med. dir. Travelers Ins. Cos., Hartford, Conn., 1992-94; sr. v.p., chief med. officer Kemper Nat. Svcs., Plantation, Fla., 1995-2000; med. dir. Mednet Connect, 2005—07, Fairpay Solutions, 2007—. Apptd. Tex. Commn. on Health Care Reimbursement Alternatives, 1987; bd. dirs. Riverside Nat. Bank, Grand Prairie, Tex. Contbr. articles to profl. jours. Pres. Arlington YMCA, 1971; chmn. budget com. Family Services, Ft. Worth, 1973; participant Health Policy Agenda for Am. People, Chgo., 1984-87; trustee Tex. Med. Liability Trust, Austin, 1987-88. Capt. USAF, 1958-63. Fellow ACP (pres. Tex. chpt. 1981); mem. AMA (chmn. sect. coun. internal medicine, 1979-88), Am. Soc. Internal Medicine (pres. 1986-87), Tex. Med. Assn. (treas. 1978-85, alt. del. to AMA 1985-91, commendation 1985), Tarrant County Med. Soc. (pres. Arlington br. 1974, del. to Tex. Med. Assn., Community Svc. award 1983). Presbyterian. Avocations: photography, sailing, gardening, computer hobbies. Home: 2709 Park Place Ct Arlington TX 76016-5891

TINGLEY, TYLER C., headmaster; m. Marcia Tingley; children: Chase, Morgan. AB cum laude, Harvard U., EdM, EdD, Harvard U. Former headmaster Kingswood-Oxford Sch., W. Hartford; head of sch. The Blake Sch., Minneapolis, 1991—97; headmaster Phillips Exeter Acad., Exeter, NH, 1997—. Former pres. Conn. Assn. of Independent Schools, Minn. Assn. of Independent Schools; former vice chmn. Minn. Independent Schools Fund; dir. Secondary Sch. Admissions Testing Bd. Mem.: Headmaster's Assn. (v.p.), Nat. Assn. of Independent Schools. Office: Phillips Exeter Acad 20 Main St Exeter NH 03833 *

TINGUS, STEVEN JAMES, physiologist, researcher; b. Sacramento, Aug. 19, 1963; s. James George and Joanne Fotene (Kamilos) Tingus. BS in Biol. Sci., U. Calif., Davis, 1985, MS in Physiology, 1990, C.Phil. in Physiology, 1994. Dir. Nat. Inst. on Disability and Rehab. Rsch. US Dept. Edn., Washington, 2001—. Mem.: AAAS, Am. Assn. Polit. Cons. Republican. Greek Orthodox. Office: Nat Inst on Disability and Rehab US Dept Edn 400 Maryland Ave SW Washington DC 20202 Office Phone: 202-245-7549. Personal E-mail: stingus@earthlink.net.

TINKELMAN, JOAN, lawyer; b. St. Louis, Apr. 25, 1952; d. Philip and Elizabeth (Cohen) I.; m. David Tinkelman, Jan. 24, 1999. Student, Fleming Coll., Lugano, Switzerland, 1969-70, U. Colo., 1970-71; BS, RN, U. Mo., 1974; BS/RN, St. Louis U., 1976, JD cum laude, 1980. Bar: Mo. 1981, U.S. Dist. Ct. (ea. dist.) Mo. 1981, U.S. Ct. Appeals 1981, Ill. 1981, Colo. 1984, U.S. Dist. Ct. Colo. 1984. RN St. Louis Children's Hosp., 1976-77; assoc. Shepherd, Sandberg & Phoenix, St. Louis, 1980-82; risk mgr. Luth. Med. Ctr., Wheat Ridge, Colo., 1983-91; v.p. risk mgmt. Rose Health Care Systems, Denver, 1991—96; dir. risk mgmt. Denver Health and Hosp. Authority, 1997—99; ind. practice, 1999—. Named Outstanding Young Woman Am., 1984. Mem. ABA, Mo. Bar Assn., Colo. Bar Assn., Denver Bar Assn., Am. Acad. Hosp. Attys., Am. Soc. Healthcare Risk Mgmt., Colo. Health Lawyers Assn. (bd. dirs. 1984-85), Colo. Hosp. Assn. Risk Mgrs. (founder, pres. 1985). Jewish. Office Phone: 303-466-6744.

TINKER, JOHN HEATH, anesthesiologist, educator; b. Cin., May 18, 1941; s. Leonard Henry and Georgia (Reeves) T.; m. Martha Iuen (div. Jan., 1989); children: Deborah H. Lynne, Karen Sue, Juliette Kay; m. Bonnie Howard, Mar. 18, 1989. BS magna cum laude, U. Cin., 1964, MS summa cum laude, 1968. Diplomate Am. Bd. Anesthesiology (sr. examiner 1976—). Surg. intern, resident Harvard Med. Sch., Peter Bent Brigham Hosp., Boston, 1969-70, resident in anesthesiology, 1970-72; cons. anesthesiology Mayo Clinic, Rochester, Minn., 1974-83, chief cardiovascular anesthesiology, 1978-83; prof. anesthesiology U. Iowa Coll. Medicine, Iowa City, 1983-97, chmn. dept., 1983-97; prof., chmn. anesthesiology U. Nebr., Med. Ctr., Omaha, 1997—. Mem. pharm. scis. rev. com., NIH, Bethesda, Md., 1986—; dir. Matrix Med. Inc., Orchard Park, N.Y., 1988—; frequent guest lectr. Author: Controversies in Cardiopulmonary Bypass, 1989 (monograph award Soc. Cardiovascular Anesthsiologists); editor: Anesthesia and Analgesia, Jour. Internat. Anesthesiology Rsch. Soc., 1983—; contbr. over 185 articles to profl. jours. Maj. U.S. Army, 1972-74. NIH grantee, 1977-87. Fellow Royal Coll. Surgeons Australia; mem. Am. Soc. Anesthesiologists (active numerous coms. 1972—), Soc. Cardiovascular Anesthesiologists, Assn. Univ. Anesthetists. Avocations: fishing, golf, modeling ships and airplanes. Office: U Nebr 984455 Nebr Med Ctr Omaha NE 68198-0001

TINKER, THOMAS EATON, retired headmaster; b. Providence, May 24, 1941; s. George Milan and Ruth (Eaton) T.; m. Roslyn May Silverman, Dec. 21, 1968. BA, Columbia U., 1963; MA, Brown U., 1968. English instr. Tabor Acad., Marion, Mass., 1964-66; history instr. Wheeler Sch., Providence, 1967-77; headmaster Broadmeadow Sch., Middletown, Del., 1977-82, St. Paul's Sch., Garden City, N.Y., 1982-89, The Barnard Sch., NYC, 1989-93; assoc. head sch. Trevor Day Sch., NYC, 1993—2003, head sch., 2003—05, ret., 2005. Evaluator Mid. State Assn. Colls. and Schs., Phila., 1978—. Trustee Barnard Sch. Found., 1993—; bd. dirs. Univ. Club L.I., 1984-86. With USAR, 1963-69. Mem. Nat. Assn. Ind. Schs., N.Y. State Assn. Ind. Schs., L.I. Episcopal Sch. Assn. (v.p./treas. 1984-89), Del. Assn. Ind. Schs. (sec. 1978-82). Episcopalian. Avocation: sailing. Home: Box 504 Jamestown RI 02835-0504

TINKHAM, MICHAEL, physicist, researcher; b. Green Lake County, Wis., Feb. 23, 1928; s. Clayton Harold and LaVerna (Krause) T.; m. Mary Stephanie Merin, June 24, 1961; children: Jeffrey Michael, Christopher Gillespie. AB, Ripon Coll., Wis., 1951, Sc.D. (hon.), 1976; MS, MIT, 1951; PhD, 1954; MA (hon.), Harvard, 1966; DSc (hon), ETH Zurich, 1997. NSF postdoctoral fellow at Clarendon Lab., Oxford (Eng.) U., 1954-55; successively research physicist, lectr., asst. prof., asso. prof., prof. physics U. Calif. at Berkeley, 1955-66; Gordon McKay prof. applied physics Harvard U., 1966—, prof. physics, 1966-80, Rumford prof. physics, 1980—, chmn. physics dept., 1975-78. Cons. to industry, 1958—; participant internat. seminars and confs.; mem. commn. on very low temperatures Internat. Union Pure and applied Physics, 1972-78; vis. Miller rsch. prof. U. Calif.-Berkeley, 1987; vis. prof. Technical Univ., Delft, The Netherlands, 1993. Author: Group Theory and Quantum Mechanics, 1964, Superconductivity, 1965, Introduction to Superconductivity, 1975, 2d edit.,

1996; contbr. articles to profl. jours. Served USNR, 1945-46. Recipient award Alexander von Humboldt Found. U. Karlsruhe, W. Ger., 1978-79, Fred E. Saalfeld award for lifetime achievement in sci., Office Naval Rsch., 2005; NSF sr. postdoctoral fellow Cavendish lab.; vis. fellow Clare Hall Cambridge (Eng.) U., 1971-72; Guggenheim fellow, 1963-64 Fellow Am. Phys. Soc. (chmn. div. solid state physics 1966-67, Buckley prize 1974, Richtmyer lectr. 1977), AAAS; mem. Am. Acad. Arts and Scis., Nat. Acad. Scis. Home: 98 Rutledge Rd Belmont MA 02478-2633 Office: Harvard Univ Physics Dept Lyman Lab of Physics 326 Cambridge MA 02138 Business E-Mail: tinkham@RSJ.harvard.edu.

TINKHAM, THOMAS W., lawyer; b. Milw., June 29, 1944; s. Richard Perry and Helen (Savage) T.; m. Jackie Hauser; children: Tamara, Liza, Taylor. BS with honors, U. Wis., 1966; JD with honors, Harvard U., 1969. Bar: Minn. 1969. Ptnr. Dorsey & Whitney, Mpls., 1974—, now ptnr.-in-charge Mpls. off, chmn., comml. contract. litig. Mem. Minn. State Bar (pres. 1991), Hennepin County Bar Assn. (pres. 1980). Office: Dorsey & Whitney Ste 1500 50 S 6th St Minneapolis MN 55402-1498 Office Phone: 612-340-2829. Office Fax: 612-340-2868. Business E-Mail: tinkham.tom@dorsey.com.

TINSLEY, ADRIAN, former college president; b. NYC, July 6, 1937; d. Theodore A. and Mary Ethel (White) Tinsley. AB, Bryn Mawr Coll., 1958; MA, U. Wash., 1962; PhD, Cornell U., 1969. Asst. prof. English U. Md., College Park, 1968-72; dean William James Coll., Grand Valley State, Allendale, Mich., 1972-80; assoc. vice chancellor acad. affairs Minn. State U., St. Paul, 1982-85; exec. v.p., provost Glassboro (N.J.) State Coll., 1985-89; pres. Bridgewater (Mass.) State Coll., 1989—2002, pres. emerita, 2002—. Coord. women higher edn. adminstrn. Bryn Mawr & Hers Summer Inst., Bryn Mawr, Pa., 1977—. Editor: Women in Higher Education Administration, 1984. Office: Boyden Hall Bridgewater State Coll Bridgewater MA 02325-0001 Office Phone: 508-697-9656. Business E-Mail: atinsley@bridgew.edu.

TINSLEY, BARBARA V., lawyer; BA magna cum laude, Emory U., 1971, JD with distinction, 1975. Asst. US atty. US Dept. Justice; with Ga.-Pacific, 1987—92, chief counsel distbn. divsn., 1992—98; corp. compliance officer Home Depot, 1998—2000; asst. gen. counsel Mitsubishi Electric and Electronics USA, Inc., 2000—02; assoc. gen. counsel Cendian Corp., 2002—04; gen. counsel, sec. BlueLinx Holdings, Atlanta, 2004—. Office: BlueLinx Corp 4300 Wildwood Pky Atlanta GA 30339 *

TINSLEY, NIKKI LEE RUSH, federal agency administrator; b. Apr. 23, 1948; BS in Bus. Admistrn., Ohio State U./Va. Commonwealth U., 1970; MS in Bus. Admistrn., U. Colo./U. No. Colo., 1981. Ednl. program asst. Office of Edn., Wash., 1971; bookstore mgr. U.S. Govt. Printing Office, Denver, 1971-76; auditor U.S. GAO, Denver, 1976-82; supervisory auditor Dept. of Interior, Minerals Mgmt. Svc., Lakewood, Colo., 1982-90; divsnl. insp. gen. EPA, Kansas City, Kans., 1990—95, dep. insp. gen. Washington, 1995-96, acting insp. gen., 1997-98, insp. gen., 1998—. Chair human resources com. Pres.'s Coun. on Integrity and Efficiency, 2002—04; mem. Adv. Coun. on Govt. Auditing Stds., Comptroller Gen.'s Domestic Working Group. Recipient Bronze medal for commendable svc. EPA, 1995. Mem.: Colo. Soc. CPAs, Inst. Internal Auditors, Assn. Govt. Accts. (Disting. Fed. Leadership award 2004). Office: EPA MC 2410 1200 Pennsylvania Ave NW Washington DC 20460-0001 Office Phone: 202-566-0847. E-mail: tinsley.nikki@epa.gov.

TINTLE, CARMEL JOSEPH, public relations executive; b. Paterson, NJ, Sept. 25, 1924; s. Herbert J. and Agnes (Merna) T.; m. Alice M. Hayes, Sept. 1, 1948; children: Joseph, Alice Maureen. BS, Fordham U., 1951; postgrad., NYU. Editl. asst. Newsweek mag., NYC, 1946-50; news editor Beverage Retailer Weekly, NYC, 1950-52; city editor Paterson Sunday Eagle, 1950-52; staff writer Carl Byoir & Assocs., Inc., NYC, 1952-59, asst. account exec., 1959-64, assoc. account exec., 1964; account supr. Grey Pub. Rels., Inc., NYC, 1964; v.p. Schenley Affiliated Brands Corp., subs. Schenley Industries, NYC, 1964-72, sr. v.p., 1972-74; v.p. corp. affairs Am. Distilling Co., 1974—80; v.p. Banfi Vintners, Old Brookville, NY, 1980—90; CEO Vinum Comm., Inc., Old Brookville, NY, 1980-90; cons. corp. comm. Banfi Vintners, 1990—2002. Publicity dir., Jumby Bay Island, a Banfi resort property, Antigua, 1985-95. Vol. publicist Assumption Coll. Sis., Mendham, NJ, 2001—. Seaman, officer US Mcht. Marine, 1943-46. Mem. NY Press Club, SAR, KC, St. Patrick Guard of Honor NJ, US Mcht. Marine Vets., Irish-Am. Cultural Inst., Fordham Univ.'s Golden Rams. Home: 14 Potter Ct Upper Montclair NJ 07043-1514

TIO, CELINA, chef; BS, Drexel U. Hotel and Restaurant Mgmt. Chef The Grill Room, Ritz-Carlton Hotel, Phila.; opening chef Spoodles, Walt Disney World, Citricos, Walt Disney World; task force chef Palothe, Walt Disney World's M.S. Magic; chef Narcoosee's; exec. chef The American Restaurant, Kansas City. Host James Beard Dinner, 1995—. Named Chef of Yr., Chef mag., 2005, Best Chef: Mid-West, James Beard Found., 2007; named one of 13 Chefs to Keep Your Eye On, Esquire Mag. Office: The American Restaurant 200 E 25th St Kansas City MO 64108 Office Phone: 816-545-8001. *

TIPLER, FRANK JENNINGS, III, physicist; b. Andalusia, Ala., Feb. 1, 1947; s. Frank Jennings Jr. and Anne (Kearley) T.; m. Jolanta Rokicka; children: Allison Anne, Caroline Nicole. S.B., MIT, 1969; PhD, U. Md., 1976. Rsch. mathematician U. Calif., Berkeley, 1976-79; sr. rsch. fellow Oxford (Eng.) U., 1979; rsch. assoc. U. Tex., Austin, 1979-81; assoc. prof. physics and math. Tulane U., New Orleans, 1981-87, prof., 1987—. Vis. sr. scientist Max-Planck Inst. Astrophysics, Munich, 1987; vis. fellow U. Sussex, Brighton, Eng., 1987; vis. prof. Inst. Astrophysics, Liege, Belgium, 1988, U. Bern, Switzerland, 1988, U. Vienna, Austria, 1992. Author: l'Homme et le Cosmos, 1984, The Anthropic Cosmological Principle, 1986, The Physics of Immortality, 1994, The Physics of Christianity, 2007; editor: Essays in General Relativity, 1980; contbr. articles to profl. jour. Rsch. grantee NSF, 1984, 86. Libertarian. Office: Tulane Univ Physics Dept St Charles ave New Orleans LA 70118 Office Phone: 504-862-3449. Business E-Mail: tipler@tulane.edu.

TIPPETT, DAVE, professional hockey coach; m. Wendy Tippett; children: Nicole, Natalie. Player Hartford Whalers, Wash. Capitals, Pitts. Penguins, Phila. Flyers, 1984—95; capt. Can. Olympic Team, Sarajevo, 1984, mem. Albertville, France, 1992; player, asst. coach Houston Aeros, IHL, 1995—99, gen. mgr., head coach, 1999; asst. coach LA Kings, 1999—2002; head coach Dallas Stars, 2002—. Achievements include being a member of silver medal Canadian Hockey team, Albertville Olympic Games, 1992. Office: Dallas Stars 2601 Ave Of The Stars Ste 100 Frisco TX 75034-9016

TIPPING, HARRY A., lawyer; b. Bainbridge, Md., Nov. 2, 1944; s. William Richard and Ann Marie (Kelly) Tipping; m. Kathleen Ann Palmer, July 12, 1969; 1 child, Christopher A. BA, Gannon U., Erie, Pa., 1966; JD, U. Akron, Ohio, 1970. Bar: Ohio. Asst. law dir. City of Akron, Ohio, 1971—72, chief asst. law dir., 1972—74; ptnr. Gillen, Miller & Tipping, Akron, 1974—77, Roderick, Myers & Linton, Akron, 1977—87; prin., COO Harry A. Tipping Co. L.P.A., Akron, 1987—2003; COO Tipping Co. L.P.A., Akron, 2003—; of counsel Stark & Knoll Co., L.P.A., 2006—. Mem. Fairlawn Charter Rev. Commn., Ohio, 1990—; chmn. bd. Assessment Equalization for the City of Fairlawn, 1989, 1990, 1997; chmn. Bd. of Tax Appeals, City of Fairlawn, 1979—81, mem. merger com., 1980—82. With USCGR, 1966—72. Mem.: Am. Arbitration Assn., Fedn. Ins. and Corp. Counsel, Def. Rsch. Inst., Akron Bar Assn., Am. Bd. Trial Advocates (adv.), Firestone Country Club, Catawaba Island Club, Fairlawn Country Club. Republican. Roman Catholic. Office: Stark & Knoll Co LPA 3475 Ridgewood Rd Akron OH 44333-3163 Office Phone: 330-376-3300. Business E-Mail: htipping@stark-knoll.com.

TIPPING, WILLIAM MALCOLM, social services administrator; b. Oak Park, Ill., Mar. 31, 1931; s. William McKinley and Evelyn Amelia (Freier) T.; m. Lois A. Grife, Sept. 18, 1954 (dec. May 1986); children: William, Barbara, Robert; m. Babette J. Cumming, Oct. 10, 1987; children: Christopher Cumming, Courtney Barone. BA, Carleton Coll., Northfield, Minn., 1954. Sales rep. Gen. Mills, Inc., Mpls., 1954-56; account exec. Campbell Mithun, Inc., Mpls., 1956-63, v.p. mgmt., supr. Mpls. and Chgo., 1965-76; account supr., v.p. Lennen & Newell, Inc., NYC, 1963-65; ptnr., mgr. Heidrick & Struggles, Inc., Chgo., 1976-88; exec. v.p., chief exec. officer Am. Cancer Soc., Atlanta, 1988-91; pres. Tipping and McRae, Inc., Atlanta, 1991-93; mng. dir. Ward Howell Internat., Inc., Atlanta, 1993-97. Trustee Carleton Coll., 1986-90; bd. dirs. Nat. Health Coun., N.Y.C., Ga. Conservancy, Families First; mem. fin. com. UICC, Geneva, 1990-91. Recipient Disting. Svc. award Carleton Coll., 1984. Mem. Capital City Club (Atlanta), Quechee (Vt.) Club, Commerce Club (Atlanta). Republican. Episcopalian.

TIPRE, DNYANESH NISHIKANT, pharmacist, researcher; arrived in US, 2002; s. Nishikant and Sandhya Tipre. BS in Pharmacy, Govt. Coll. Pharmacy, Karad, India, 1995; MS in Pharmacy, Nagpur U., India, 1998; PhD in Pharmacy, U. Mumbai, India, 2002. Rsch. fellow NIH, Bethesda, Md., 2002—06; sch. assoc. scientist Howard U. Hosp., Washington, 2006—. Cons. NIH. Vol. adminstrn. Shiva Vishnu Temple, Greenbelt, Md. Fellow, Fogarty Internat. Ctr., 2002—05. Mem.: Acad. Molecular Imaging (assoc. award 2006). Peace And Freedom. Hindu. Achievements include research in successful inhibition of defluorination of 18F-FCWAY radiotracer in a rat model. Avocations: travel, music. Home: 4604 Crekshore Dr Rockville MD 20852 Office: Howard Univ Hospital 2041 Georgia Ave NW Washington DC 20060 Home Phone: 301-768-3329. Personal E-mail: dnyanesht@yahoo.com.

TIPSORD, MICHAEL L., insurance company executive; b. Ill. B in Acctg., Ill. Wesleyan U.; JD, U. Ill., Urbana-Champaign. CPA; CLU 1991, CPCU 1995. Asst. tax counsel, 1988; with State Farm Ins. Cos., 1988—, dir. acctg., 1995—96, asst. contr., 1996—97, exec. asst., 1997—98, v.p., asst. treas., 1998—2001, v.p., treas., 2001—02, sr. v.p., CFO, 2002—04, vice chmn., CFO, 2004—. Bd. dir. State Farm Lloyds, Inc., Ins. Placement Svc., Inc., State Farm Investment Mgmt. Corp., State Farm V.P. Mgmt. Corp., State Farm Bank, FSB; trustee State Farm Mutual Fund Trust, State Farm Variable Product Trust, State Farm Assoc.'s Funds Trust, State Farm Ins. Co. Employee Retirement Trust, State Farm Ins. Co. Savings and Thrift Trust for US Employees; prof., dept. accountancy U. Ill., Urbana-Champaign. Bd. trustees Ill. Wesleyan U. Mem.: Ill. State Bar Assn., ABA. Office: State Farm Ins Cos 1 State Farm Plz Bloomington IL 61710-0001 *

TIPTON, CLYDE RAYMOND, JR., communications and resources development consultant; b. Cin., Nov. 13, 1921; s. Clyde Raymond and Ida Marie (Molitor) Tipton; m. Marian Gertrude Beushausen, Aug. 6, 1942 (dec. Aug. 2, 2000); children: Marian Page Ashley, Robert Bruce. BS, U. Ky., Lexington, 1946, MS, 1947. Rsch. engr. Battelle Meml. Inst., Columbus, Ohio, 1947-49, sr. tech. adviser, 1951-62, coord. corp. comm., 1969-73, v.p. comm., 1973-75, asst. to pres., 1978-79, v.p., corp. dir. comm. and pub. affairs, 1979-86; staff mem. Los Alamos Sci. Lab., 1949-51; dir. research Basic, Inc., Bettsville, Ohio, 1962-64; asst. dir. Battelle Pacific N.W. Labs., Richland, Wash., 1964-69; pres., trustee Battelle Commons Co. for Cmty. Urban Redevel., Columbus, 1975-78; cons. bus. comm. and devel. Columbus, 1986—. Secretariat US del. 2d Internat. Conf. Peaceful Use Atomic Energy, Geneva, 1958; cons. U.S. AEC in Atoms for Peace Program, Tokyo, 1958, New Delhi, 1959—60, Rio de Janeiro, 1960. Author: (book) How to Change the World, 1982; editor: Jour. Soc. Nondestructive Testing, 1953—57, The Reactor Handbook, Reactor Materials, vol. 3, 1955, vol. 1, 1960, Learning to Live on a Small Planet, 1974. Past pres. Pilot Dogs, United Way Franklin County, Greater Columbus Arts Coun.; bd. dirs., treas. Pilot Guide Dog Found.; pres. emeritus Arhcs. Soc. Ohio Found.; bd. dirs., treas. Torch Club of Columbus; dir. Episc. Retirement Homes, Inc. With USAAF, 1943. Named to U. Ky. Engring. Hall of Distinction, 1997; Haggin fellow, U. Ky., 1947, Sr. fellow, Otterbein Coll., 1978. Fellow: NSPE (past pres., Outstanding Svc. award 1992); mem.: Ohio Soc. Profl. Engr. (past pres., award of distinction, Uncommon Man award, Outstanding Svc. award 1993, 1998), Am. Soc. Metals, Lions, Sigma Xi, Alpha Chi Sigma. Episcopalian. Achievements include patents in field. Home and Office: 2218 Aschinger Blvd Columbus OH 43212-4620 Office Phone: 614-424-6077.

TIPTON, JAMES D., retired military officer, education educator; b. Greeneville, Tenn., Jan. 8, 1937; s. P.H. and Ruby Tipton; 1 child, Dennis R. BA in Biology, Tusculum Coll., Tenn., 1958; MS in Logistic Mgmt., Air Force Inst. Tech., Dayton, Ohio, 1973; MS in Edn., Jacksonville State U., Ala., 1994. Cert. tchr. secondary edn. State of Ala., 1994. Commdg. officer U.S. Army, Washington, 1958—91. Adj. faculty Gadson State C.C., Anniston, Ala., 1994—98, Troy State U., Ft. Benning Campus, Ga., 2000—02, Columbus Tech. Coll., Ga., 2004—. Deacon, 1974—76. Col. (o6) US Army, 1984—91, Ft. McClellan, Ala. Decorated Joint Superior Svc. medal, Bronze Star U.S. Army, Legion of Merit, Meritorious Svc. medals (5), Army Commendation medal U.S. Army Chem. Sch. Home: 1800 Lakewood Dr Apt F-1 Phenix City AL 36867 Office: Columbus Tech Coll Manchester Expressway Columbus GA 39104 Home Phone: 334-448-3365; Office Phone: 706-641-5282.

TIPTON, KENNETH WARREN, retired agricultural administrator, researcher; b. Belleville, Ill., Nov. 14, 1932; s. Roscoe Roy and Martha Pearl (Davis) T.; m. Barbara Adds, Mar. 2, 1957; children: Kenneth Warren Jr., Nancy Tipton O'Neal. BS, La. State U., 1955, MS, 1959; PhD, Miss. State U., 1969. Asst. prof. Agrl. Ctr., La. State U., Baton Rouge, 1959-70, assoc. prof., 1970-75, prof., 1975—, supt. Red River Rsch. Sta., La. Agrl. Expt. Sta. Bossier City, 1975-79, assoc. dir. La. Agrl. Expt. Sta. Baton Rouge, 1979-89, dir. La. Agrl. Expt. Sta., vice chancellor, 1989-96, vice chancellor, dir. emeritus, 1996—; ret., 1996. Com. nine USDA/Coop. State Rsch. Svc., 1986-88; Expt. State Com. Orgn. Policy, 1988-91. Contbr. articles to Agronomy Jour., Jour. Econ. Entomology, Grain Sorghum Conf. Coach baseball program Am. Legion, 1969-74; scoutmaster Boy Scouts Am., Baton Rouge, 1970-75. Capt. USAF, 1955-58. Mem. Am. Soc. Agronomy, Crop Sci. Soc. Am., Coun. Agrl. Sci. Tech., Alpha Zeta, Phi Kappa Phi, Gamma Sigma Delta, Sigma Xi. Achievements include research on inheritance of fiber traits in cotton, resistance of grain sorghum hybrids to bird damage, tannin content of grain sorghum and effects of phosphorus on growth of sorghum. Home: 732 Baird Dr Baton Rouge LA 70808-5916 Personal E-mail: barkentip@aol.com.

TIPTON, MARGARET ANN, religious organization administrator, writer; b. Covington, Tenn., Sept. 25, 1937; d. Hurtell Tipton and Jennie Anna Williams; 1 child, Cheryl Ann Brown-Dunbar. BA, Trinity Coll., Deerfield, Ill., 1985; postgrad., Moody Grad. Sch., Chgo., 1996. Underwriter Motors Ins. Corp., Chgo., 1963—70; youth coord. Monument of Faith Ch., Chgo., 1964—70, pres. personal evang. ministry, 1964—; pres., founder Effectual Door Bible Coll., Chgo., 1982—; editor, writer Beautiful for Him mag., Chgo., 1986—92; Christian edn. dir. Hope Tabernacle Ch., Chgo., 1988—91; pres., founder Jennie Williams Davis Found., Chgo., 2001—. Author: Personal Evangelism, 1-5, 1989, Mission, 2004, Most Misinterpreted Biblical Truths, 2004; host (cable TV program) The Margaret Tipton Show, Effectual Door Bible Coll. Radio Program, host (radio program) The EDBC Radio Teacher's Forum, 1985. Sec. Beat 322 Chgo. Alternative Policing Strategy Chgo. Police Dept., 1999—; pres. Bapt. Midwest Youth Conf., 1961—64; class leader Moody Bible Inst. Sch. Recipient Outstanding Svc. award, Midwest Youth Conf., 1982, Outstanding Cmty. Svc. award, Chgo. Police Dept., 2001. Mem.: NAACP, Nat. Black Evangel. Assn., Evangel. Tng. Assn., Nat. Urban League. Office: Effectual Door Bible Coll PO Box 20350 Chicago IL 60620

TIPTON, NOEL MARTIN, JR., musician, writer, composer; b. Bastrop, La., May 20, 1932; s. Noel Martin Sr. and Agnes (Holt) Tipton; m. Elizabeth Ann Hughes, Sept. 6, 1958; children: Lisa, Noel Martin III, Jennifer Dooling. MusB, Centenary Coll. La., Shreveport, 1950—54; BS, Juilliard Sch. Music, NYC, 1956, MS, 1957; postgrad., Columbia Tchrs. Coll., 1972—73. Cert. group tchg. for piano Columbia Tchrs. Coll., 1983. Founder, co-dir. Tipton Music Studios, Westfield, NJ, 1958—88; assoc. organist, choir dir. St. Paul's Episcop. Ch., Westfield, 1960—86; organist 1st Congl. Ch., Yarmouthport, Mass., 1987—88; mem. piano faculty Cape Cod Conservatory Music and Art, Hyannis, Mass., 1988—95; organist, choirmaster St. Peter's Luth. Ch., Harwich, Mass., 1989—93; dir. music Dennis Union Ch., Mass., 1993—2007; founder, artistic dir., emeritus Eventide Arts, Dennis, 1996—2007; min. music Wellfleet United Meth. Ch., 2007—. Condr. festival Episcop. Ch. Girls Choirs, Trenton, NJ, 1970; founder vol. adult choir St. Paul's Ch., Westfield, 1980—86. Composer: (folk opera) Ballad of Ferdinan', 1972, I Ain't Gonna Dance Alone, 1974, (choral anthme) Christmas Prayer, 1981, (chancel drama) Sassy, 1996, (ballet) The Dance Goes On, 1999, (chancel drama) Anna Howard Shaw Meets Harriet Tubman, 1998; author: Anna Howard Shaw meets Anne Bradstreet, 1998, (plays) G!, 2003; composer, author: (plays) Hymns and Emily Dickinson, 1997, We Are The People, 1992, Stephen Foster's Dear Friends & Gentle Hearts, 1996;; composer Amherst Sabbath, 2007. Recipient award, Ella Lyman Cabot Trust, 1995; grantee, Union County Coun. Arts, 1974, Mass. Found. Humanities, 1996, Cmty. Found. Cape Cod, 1996. Mem.: Am. Guild Organists (sr.). Democrat. Episcopalian. Avocations: writing, painting, poetry. Home: 25 Nickerson Rd Eastham MA 02642 Office: PO Box 1266 Eastham MA 02642 Home Phone: 508-240-0850. Personal E-mail: netipton@comcast.net.

TIRADOR, GABRIEL, insurance company executive; Asst. contr. Mercury Ins. Group, LA, 1994—96; v.p., contr. Automobile Club Calif., 1997—98; v.p., CFO Mercury Gen. Corp., LA, 1998—2001, pres., COO, 2001—06, pres., CEO, 2007—. Office: Mercury Gen Corp 4484 Wilshire Blvd Los Angeles CA 90010 *

TIRANA, BARDYL RIFAT, lawyer; b. Geneva, Dec. 16, 1937; s. Rifat and Rosamond English (Walling) T.; m. Anne Prather, June 22, 1985; children by previous marriage: Kyra, Amina. AB, Princeton U., 1959; LL.B., Columbia U., 1962. Bar: DC 1962, Md. 1986, NY 1986, Va. 1986, Pa. 1992. Trial atty. Dept. Justice, 1962-64; assoc. Amram, Hahn & Sundlun, Washington, 1965-68, ptnr., 1969-72; dir., sec. Exec. Jet Aviation, Inc., Columbus, Ohio, 1970-77, Technics, Inc., Alexandria, Va., 1971-77; ptnr. Sundlun, Tirana & Scher, Washington, 1972-77; dir. def. civil preparedness agy. Dept. Def., Washington, 1977-79, mem. armed forces policy coun., 1977-79; chmn. bd. Technics, Inc., San Jose, Calif., 1979-85; of counsel Silverstein and Mullens, Washington, 1982-84, ptnr., 1984-90; pvt. practice law Washington, 1991—. Mem.-at-large DC Bd. Edn., 1970-74; trustee Jimmy Carter Inaugural Trust, Washington, 1977-87; co-chmn. 1977 Presdl. Inaugural Com., 1976-77; mem. exec. adv. coun. Calif. Commn. Indsl. Innovation, 1981-82; pres. China/USA Edn. Fund, Inc., Washington, 1981-2002; trustee The Waltz Group of Washington, 2000-07; dir. Rocky Mountain Inst., Snowmass Colo., 1982-95. Recipient medal for disting. pub. svc. Dept. Def., 1979, Fuess award Phillips Acad., 1991, Svc. Commendation award YWCA of Nat. Capital Area, 1991. Mem. NYC Racquet and Tennis Club, DC Met. Club, Century Assn. (NYC), Nyack Field Club (NY). Home: 3 Washington Ave Nyack NY 10960-4713 Office Phone: 845-358-0007. Personal E-mail: btirana@aol.com.

TIRAVANIJA, RIRKRIT, sculptor; b. Buenos Aires, 1961; Student, Ont. Coll. Art, Toronto, Can., 1981, Banff Ctr. Sch. Fine Arts, Can., 1984, Whitney Ind. Studies Program, NYC, 1986, Sch. Art Inst. Chgo., 1985. Adj. asst. prof. Columbia U. Sch. Arts, NYC. One-man shows include Paula Allen Gallery, N.Y.C., 1990, Randy Alexander Gallery, N.Y.C., 1991, 303 Gallery, N.Y.C., 1992, 95, Randolph St. Gallery, Chgo., 1993, Jack Hanley Gallery, San Francisco, 1994, Schipper & Krome, Koln, Germany, 1994, Kunsthalle St. Gallen, Switzerland, 1996, Kolnischer Kunstverien, Cologne, Germany, 1996, Mus. Modern Art, N.Y.C., 1997, Mus. for Gegenwartskunst, Zurich, 1998, Phila. Mus. Art, 1998, L.A. County Mus. Art, 1999, Gavin Brown's Enterprise, N.Y.C., 1999, Wexner Ctr. for the Arts, Columbus, Ohio, 1999, la Caixa, Barcelona, 1999, Galleria Emi Fontana, Milan, 2000, Galaria Salvador Diaz, Madrid, 2000; group shows at The New Mus. Contemporary Art, N.Y.C., 1991, Jack Tilton Gallery, N.Y.C., 1991, Ctr. Contemporary Arts, Ujazdowski Castle, Warsaw, Poland, 1991, 303 Gallery, N.Y.C., 1992, Goethe House, N.Y.C., 1992, Holly Solomon Gallery, N.Y.C., 1993, Aldrich Mus. Contemporary Art, Conn., 1993, Inst. Contemporary Arts, London, 1993, Musee d'Art Moderne de la Ville de Paris, 1994, Galerie Jennifer Flay, Paris, 1994, Whitney Mus. Am. Art, 1995, The Carnegie Mus. Art, Pitts., 1995, Walker Art Ctr., Mpls., 1995, CAPC Bordeaux, France, 1997, Wexner Ctr., Columbus, Ohio, 1999, The Ikon Gallery, Birmingham, Eng., 2003-04, Peace Tower, Day for Night, Whitney Biennial, 2006; film exhbns. include The New Film Maker, The Collective for Living Cinema, N.Y.C., 1985, Video Event, Tom Cugliani Gallery, N.Y.C., 1991; sculpture projects Munster, Germany, 1997, Venice Biennial, Italy, 1999. Fax: 212-941-9828.

TIRICO, MIKE, sportscaster; b. Whitestone, NY, Dec. 13, 1966; married, 2 children. BA in Polit. Sci. and Broadcast Journalism, Syracuse U., 1988. Sports dir. WTVH-TV (affil. CBS), Syracuse, NY, 1987-91; reporter ESPN, Bristol, Conn., 1991—, host NFL Prime Monday, co-host GameDay ESPN Sports Radio, anchor SportsCenter, 1993—, announcer, Monday Night Football, 2006—; studio host, NBA broadcasts ABC, 2002—06. Spkr. in field All-American Talent & Celebrity Network. Actor: (films) Jerry Maguire, 1996. Named top local sportscaster Syracuse Jour., 1989; recipient A.P. N.Y. Broadcasters award. Office: ESPN Inc Comms Dept Espn Plz Bristol CT 06010-1099

TIRONE, BARBARA JEAN, retired health insurance administrator; b. Celina, Ohio, Nov. 19, 1943; d. Vincent James and Theresa Barbara (Goettermoeller) G. BA, Miami U., 1965; MBA, U. Chgo., 1977. Asst. dir. for internat. trade State of Ill., Chgo., Brussels, Hongkong and Sao Paulo, Brazil, 1973-76; dir. office of mgmt. and planning Office Human Devel. Svcs., Chgo., 1976-79; dep. regional adminstr. Health Care Financing Adminstrn., Chgo., 1979-82, regional adminstr., 1982-87, dir. bur. of prog. ops. Balt., 1987-92; dir. health stds. and quality bur. Health Care Fin. Adminstrn., Balt., 1992-96; pres., CEO AdminaStar, Inc., Indpls., 1996-2001; ret., 2002. Recipient Presdl. Disting. Rank award 1988, 94, Presdl. Meritorious Rank award 1987, 92; named Fed. Exec. of Yr., 1987. Home: 11212 Appaloosa Dr Reisterstown MD 21136 Office Phone: 410-833-5570. Personal E-mail: bgagel@comcast.net.

TIROZZI, GERALD N., educational association administrator; BS in Elem. Edn., So. Conn. State U., MA in Guidance and Counseling; 6th Yr. Cert. in Ednl. Adminstrn., Fairfield U., Conn.; PhD in Ednl. Adminstrn., Mich. State U.; DHL (hon.), Quinnipiac Coll., Conn., 1996; D in Pedagogy (hon.), Nova Southeastern U., Fla., 1997. Sci. tchr. Notre Dame HS, West Haven, Conn., 1959; prin., guidance counselor, tchr. New Haven Pub. Schs., supt., 1977—83; commr. Conn. Dept. Edn., Hartford, 1983—91;

pres. Wheelock Coll., Boston, 1991—93; prof. dept. edn. leadership U. Conn., 1993—95; asst. sec. elem. and secondary edn. US Dept. Edn., 1996—99; exec. dir. Nat. Assn. Secondary Sch. Prins., Reston, Va., 1999—. Mem. bd. Nat. Bd. Profl. Tchg. Stds., Edn. Commn. States, Jobs for the Future, Ednl. Testing Svc. Contbr. articles to profl. jours. Recipient Disting. Alumni award Mich. State U., awards Conn. Legislature, NAACP, Conn. chpt., Southwestern Conn. Urban League, Middlesex County C. of C. Mem. PTA (hon. life). Office: Nat Assn Secondary Sch Prins 1904 Association Dr Reston VA 20191-1537 Office Phone: 703-860-0200. *

TIRRELL, DAVID A., research scientist, educator; b. Jan. 10, 1953; BS in Chemistry, MIT, 1974; MS in Polymer Sci. and Engring., U. Mass., 1976, PhD in Polymer Sci. and Engring., 1978; D honoris causa (hon.), Tech. Univ. Eindhoven, 2001. Rsch. assoc. Kyoto U., 1978; asst. prof. chemistry Carnegie-Mellon U., 1978-82, assoc. prof. chemistry, 1982-84; assoc. prof. polymer sci. and engring. U. Mass., 1984-87, prof. polymer sci. and engring., 1987-92, Barrett prof. polymer and sci. and engring., 1992-98; Ross McCollum-William H. Corcoran prof. Calif. Inst. Tech., 1998—, chair chemistry divsn. & chem. engring., 1999—. Mem. molecular and cellular biology faculty, 1990—; adj. prof. chemistry U. Mass., 1991; dir. NSF materials rsch. lab., 1991, NSF materials rsch. sci. and engring. ctr., 1994—; vis. prof. chemistry Queensland U., Australia, 1987, Inst. Charles Sadron, Strausbourg, Austria; mem. materials rsch. adv. com. NSF, 1988—91; chmn. com. on synthetic hierarchical structures Nat. Rsch. Coun., 1990—94, mem. panel on biomolecular materials, 1991—; mem. polymers in biosystems com. Naval Rsch. Lab., Oxnard, 1994; co-chmn. grad. polymer rsch. conf., State Coll., Pa., 1994; co-chmn. program com. IUPAC Macromolecular Symposium, 1994; chmn. Gordon Rsch. Conf. on Chemistry of Supramolecules and Assemblies, 1995; Fellow American Association for the Advancement of Science, 2003, 2003. Editor: (profl. jours.) Jour. of Polymer Sci., 1988—99; assoc. editor: New Polymeric Materials, 1986—87, editl. bd.: Indsl. and Engring. Chemistry, Product Rsch. and Devel., 1983—86, Jour. Bioactive and Compatible Polymers, 1986—, Biomaterials, 1986—, New Polymeric Materials, 1987, Jour. of Macromolecular Sci-Chemistry, 1990—, Progress in Polymer Sci., 1992—, Macromolecular Reports, 1992, Materials Sci. and Engring., 1993—, Chem. and Engring. News, 1995—; contbr. articles to profl. jours. Recipient Presdl. Young Investigator award, 1984—89, Fulbright Sr. scholar award, 1987, Chancellor's medal, Univ. Mass., 1997; fellow Univ., 1974—77, Alfred P. Sloan Rsch., 1982—84, Rothschild, Curie Inst., 1995—97. Fellow: Am. Inst. Med. & Biol. Engring., AAAS; mem.: NAS, Phi Lambda Upsilon, Materials Rsch. Soc., NY Acad. Scis., Am. Chem. Soc. (Carl S. Marvel Polymer Chem. award 1991, Harrison Howe award 1996, Polymer Chem. award 2001, Arthur C. Cope Scholar award 2007), Sigma Xi. Office: Calif Inst Tech Divsn Chemistry Mail Code 164-30 Pasadena CA 91125 *

TIRRELL, JOHN ALBERT, organization executive, consultant; b. Boston, Feb. 11, 1934; s. George Howard and Helen Sarah (Hitchings) T.; m. Helga Ruth Eisenhauer, Jan. 29, 1966; children: Steffanie Ruth, Sabina Lisette, Monica Susanne. BA in Psychology, King's Coll., Briarcliff Manor, NY, 1961; MEd, U. Ariz., Tucson, 1975. Various positions for several orgns., 1962-68; analyst instrnl.-ednl. systems GE, Daytona Beach, Fla., 1969-72; dir. curriculum and program devel. Brookdale CC, Lincroft, NJ, 1972; dir. learning and faculty resources Pima CC, Tucson, 1972-76; dir. human resources planning and devel. Miami divsn. Cyprus Copper Co., Claypool, Ariz., 1976-79; exec. dir. Calvary Missionary Fellowship, Tucson, 1983-85; interim pastor Sagauro Evang. Ch., Tucson, 1985-86; pastor Midvale Evangelical Ch., Tucson, 1986-87; founder, pres. The Jethro Consultancy, Birmingham, Mich., 1979—88, Tucson, 1979—; v.p. mgmt. svc. AA Gage, Ferndale, Mich., 1987; pastor Desert Hills Bapt. Ch., Tucson, 1993-95. Mem. adv. bd. UIM Internat., Greeley, Colo., 1983-92, mem. fin. com., 1983-94, sec. support svcs. field bd., 1993-01, sec. bus. and devel. field bd., 2002-, sec., chmn. pers. com., 1997—, sec., 1998—, bd. dirs., 1993—, mem. policy revision com., 2004-, v.p. internat. bd., 2005-, mem. search com., 2005-, vice pres., sec. 2005—, mem. bus. and devel. bd., chmn. nominating com., 2005-; assoc. faculty mem. Gila Pueblo Campus Ea. Ariz. Coll., Globe, 1978; adj. prof. Montclair State Coll., NJ, 1972; chmn. mgmt. and pers. com. Wildwood Ranch, Inc., Howell, Mich., 1989-92; interim pres., v.p. programs, v.p. devel. Detroit Rescue Mission Ministries, 1990-92; v.p. corp. planning, tng., productivity George Instrument Co., Royal Oak, 1988-89; faculty mem. mgmt., comm., sociology, psychology So. Ariz. and Phoenix campuses U. Phoenix, Tuscon and Phoenix, 1997—, area chair for social scis., 2001-04; adj. faculty mem. psychology Pima County CC, 1999-2002. Contbr. articles to profl. jours. Mem. Ariz. Coun. for Econ. Conversion, 1992-94; mem. facilities task force Grace Evang. Free Ch., Birmingham, 1989-90, chmn. bylaws revision com., 1989-90, chmn. property devel. com., 1990-92; interim pastor Desert Hills Bapt. Ch., Tucson, 1992-93; elder 1st Evang. Free Ch., Tucson, 1979-81, 86-87, 97, supt. Sunday sch., 1981-84, supr. adult Sunday sch., 1992-93, chmn. gen. bd., elder bd., 1979-82, short-term missions coord., missions bd., 1992-93; bd. dirs. S.W. Border dist. Evang. Free Ch. Am., 1996-00, mem. comm. com., 1996-01, chmn. comm. com., 1998-99; bd. dirs. Clearing House of Operational Resources for Christian Orgns., Royal Oak, Mich., 1991; bd. dirs. Shadow Roc Homeowners Assn., 1996-98, treas., 1997; v.p. parent-tchr. fellowship Palo Verde Christian Sch., Tucson, 1980-81. Staff sgt. USAF, 1952-56. Mem. ASTD (treas., Old Pueblo chpt. 1982, bd. dirs.-at-large 1983, Human Resources Devel. award Valley of the Sun chpt. 1977), Birmingham-Bloomfield C. of C. (mem. profl. devel. edn. com. 1987-91, mem. pub. rels. mktg. com. 1989), King's Coll. Alumni Assn. (class gov. 1988-95, 2000-03). Independent. Avocation: Bible teaching. Home and Office: 1205 E Deer Canyon Rd Tucson AZ 85718-1069 Office Phone: 520-544-9750. Personal E-mail: jack.tirrell@comcast.net.

TIRRELL, MATTHEW V., engineering educator; b. Phillipsburg, NJ, Sept. 5, 1950; s. Matthew Vincent Tirrell Jr. and Loraine (Wier) Gonsky; m. Pamela LaVigne, Aug. 1993. BS in chem. engring., Northwestern U., 1973; PhD in polymer sci. and engring., U. Mass., 1977. Mem. coop. edn. program Cin. Milacron Chem. Inc., 1970-72; tchg. and rsch. asst. U. Mass., Amherst, 1973-77; asst. prof. U. Minn., Mpls., 1977-81, assoc. prof., 1981-85, prof. chem. engring. and materials sci., 1985—99, Shell disting. chair. chem. engring., 1986-91, Earl E. Bakken Prof. Biomed. Engring., 1993—97, head chem. engring. and materials sci., 1995-99; dir. Biomed. Engring. Inst., 1995-98; dean Coll Engring. U. Calif., Santa Barbara, 1999—, Richard A. Auhll Prof., 1999—, also prof. materials engring.; venture ptnr. NGEN Partners, LLC. Mem. adv. panel Grad. Sch. Integrative Sciences and Engring. Nat. U. Singapore, 2003—05, vis. com. chem. and environ. engring., 2003—05; cons. Institut Francais du Petrole, 1982—, Kimberly-Clark Corp., 2000—, Edwards Lifesciences, 2000—, Santa Barbara Tech. Group, 2000—, bd. mem.; editl. adv. bd. Jour. Polymer Sci., Polymer Physics Edit., 1986—2000, Macromolecules, 1987—90, McGraw-Hill Chem. Engring. Series, 1987—98, Jour. Rheology, 1990—, Progress in Polymer Sci., 1992—97, Polymerica Acta, 1992—, Jour. Adhesion Sci. and Tech., 1993—96, Langmuir, 1995—, Current Opinion in Colloid and Interface Sci., 1996—, Oxford Univ. Press, Chem. Engring. Series, 1998—2000, Chemistry of Materials, 1998—, Gordon and Breach, 2000—; editl. bd. Jour. Chem. Physics, 1991—93; US editor Chem. Engring. Sci., 1988—91; assoc. editor Reviews in Macromolecular Sci., 1992—2000, editor, 2000—; Sci. and Tech. Panel U. Calif. Pres.'s Coun. for Nat. Lab. Adminstrn., 2000—; bd. dirs. Cottage Health Sys., Santa Barbara, 2000—; US Chair German-Am. Frontiers of Engring., 1999—. Author: Modeling of Polymerization Processes, 1995. Advisor Camille and Henry Dreyfus Found., 1998—. Named Outstanding Young Chem. Engr. of Minn., 1981; recipient Camille and Henry Dreyfus Tchr.-Scholar Award, 1980, George Taylor/IT Alumni Soc. Disting. Rsch. Award, U. Minn. Inst. Tech., 1981, Gordon Starr Outstanding Contribution Award, U. Minn., 1981, Presdl. Young Investigator Award, NSF, 1984, Chancellor's Medal, U. Mass. Amherst, 1987, Alumni Merit Award, Northwestern U., 1997; Alfred P. Sloan Found. Fellowship, 1982, John Simon Guggenheim Meml. Found. Fellowship, 1986. Mem. NAE, AIChE (editor jour. 1991—2001, inst. lectr. 2001, Allan P. Colburn award 1985, Profl. Progress award 1994, Charles M.A. Stine Award 1996), Am. Chem. Soc., Materials Rsch. Soc., Biomed. Engring. Soc., Controlled Release Soc., Soc. Biomaterials, Soc. Polymer Sci. Japan, Soc. Rheology; fellow AAAS, Am. Inst. Med. and Bio. Engineers, Am. Phys. Soc. (John H. Dillon Medal 1987). Avocations: gourmet cooking, movies, distance running. Office: U Calif Dean's Office Coll Engring Santa Barbara CA 93106-5080

TIRRO, FRANK PASCALE, music educator, composer, writer; b. Omaha, Sept. 20, 1935; s. Frank and Mary Carmela (Spensieri) T.; m. Charlene Rae Whitney, Aug. 16, 1961; children: John Andrew, Cynthia Anne. B.M.E., U. Nebr., 1960; M.M., Northwestern U., 1961; PhD, U. Chgo., 1974. Chmn. lab. sch. U. Chgo., Ill., 1961—70; fellow of Villa I Tatti Harvard U., Florence, Italy, 1971—72; lectr. U. Kans., Lawrence, Kans., 1972—73; asst. prof. music Duke U., Durham, NC, 1973—74; dir. Southeastern Inst. Medieval and Renaissance Studies, Durham, NC, 1978—80; chmn., assoc. prof. music Duke U., Durham, NC, 1973—80; prof. Yale U., New Haven, 1980—, dean, 1980—89. Reader, cons. several univ. presses; jurist Parisot Internat. Cello Competition, Sao Paolo, Brazil, 1981. Author: Historia del Jazz Clásico, 2001, Historia del Jazz Moderno, 2001, Jazz: A History, 1977, rev. edit., 1993, Renaissance Choirbooks in the Archive of San Petronio in Bologna, 1986, Living With Jazz, 1996, (with others) The Humanities: Cultural Roots and Continuities, 1980, 7th edit., 2004; editor: Medieval and Renaissance Studies No. 9, 1982; mem. editl. bd. Am. Music, Wittenberg Rev.; composer American Jazz Mass, 1960; assoc. editor Am. Nat. Biography, 1994—. Bd. dirs. New Haven Symphony, 1980-89, Neighborhood Music Sch., New Haven, 1982-89, Chamber Orch. New Eng., 1980-82, Ctr. for Black Music Rsch., 1985-91. Recipient Standard Composer award Am. Soc. Composers, Authors and Pubs., 1966, 99, 2000-05, Gustavus Fine Arts medal, 1988, Duke Ellington Fellow medal, 1989, Disting. Alumnus award, U. Nebr., 2006; travel grantee Am. Coun. Learned Socs., 1967; rsch. grantee Duke U., 1978; named to Omaha Ctrl. H.S. Hall of Fame, 2002. Mem. Am. Musicol. Soc. (council 1978-80), Coll. Music Soc. (council 1980-82, mem. exec. bd. 1984-86), Nat. Assn. Schs. of Music, Internat. Soc. Jazz Research, Renaissance Soc. Am., Mory's Club, Yale Club (NYC). Republican. Lutheran. Office: Yale U Sch Music PO Box 208246 New Haven CT 06520-8246 Office Phone: 203-432-5989. E-mail: frank.tirro@yale.edu.

TIRUMALA, VIJAYA RAGHAVAN, materials scientist; arrived in USA, 1999; s. Ranganathan and Kowsalya Tirumala; m. Veena S. Mellarkod, May 13, 2004. BTech in Chem. Engring., Jawaharlal Nehru Technol. U., Anantapur, India, 1999; PhD, Mich. Technol. U., Houghton, 2003. Cert. engring. prins. neutron diffraction, Oakridge Nat. Lab., 2001. Rsch. asst. Mich. Technol. U., Houghton, 1999—2002; guest grad. student Argonne (Ill.) Nat. Lab., 2001—02, rsch. aide, 2002—03, post-doctoral rschr., 2003—05; chem. engr. polymers divsn. Nat. Inst. Standards and Tech., Gaithersburg, Md., 2005—. Vis. scholar polymer sci. and engring. U. Mass., Amherst, 2005—. Recipient Grad. Rsch. award, Exptl. Facilities Divsn., Argonne Nat. Lab., 2002—03, Travel award, Neutron Scattering Soc. Am., 2004; Grad. fellow, Oakridge Associated U., 2002. Mem.: AIChE, AAAS (assoc.), Am. Phys. Soc. (chair polymer gels and networks session March meeting 2006), Am. Chem. Soc. (assoc.). Achievements include patents for procedure by which polymers of any shape or size can be synthesized; invention of novel way to fabricate environmentally responsive nanostructures. Office: NIST 100 Bureau Drive Stop 8541 Gaithersburg MD 20899-8541 Home Phone: 630-776-5661; Office Phone: 301-975-6840. Personal E-mail: vijay.tirumala@nist.gov.

TISCH, ANDREW HERBERT, diversified holding company executive; b. Asbury Park, NJ, Aug. 14, 1949; s. Laurence Alan and Wilma Zelda (Stein) T.; 2 children. BS, Cornell U., Ithaca, NY, 1971; MBA, Harvard U., 1977. Brand mgr. Lorillard Co., NYC, 1971-75; mgr. operational analysis Loews Corp., NYC, 1977-79, chmn. exec. com., 1998—, co-chmn. (with Jonathan Tisch), 2006—; pres. Bulova Corp., Woodside, NY, 1979—90, bd. dirs., past chmn.; chmn., CEO Lorillard Tobacco Co., NYC, 1990—95. Bd. dir. CNA Fin. Corp., 2006—. Contbr. articles to profl. jours. Mem. fgn. affairs com. Am. Jewish Com., NYC, 1983; bd. dirs. Outward Bound, Inc., Greenwich, Conn., 1983-88; trustee Ctrl. Synagogue, NYC, 1984; gen. chmn. United Jewish Appeal Fedn. Jewish Philanthropies NY, vice chmn. United Jewish Appeal, chmn. Prime Min.'s Coun.; bd. dirs. NY Shakespeare Festival, K12; chmn. Children's Hearing Inst., 1988; bd. mem. NYC Sports Commn.; mem. vis. com. Harvard Bus. Sch.; pres. City Pks. Found.; trustee Wildlife Conservation Soc., PENCIL Inc., NY City Police Found. Mem. 24 Karat Club NY, Century Country Club, Harmonie Club, Plumb Club, Achilles Track Club (bd. dirs.). Avocations: tennis, running. Office: Loews Corp 667 Madison Ave New York NY 10021-8087 Office Phone: 212-521-2000. *

TISCH, JAMES SOLOMON, diversified holding company executive; b. Atlantic City, Jan. 2, 1953; s. Laurence A. and Wilma (Stein) T.; m. Merryl Hiat; children: Jessica, Benjamin, Samuel. BA, Cornell U., Ithaca, NY, 1975; MBA, U. Pa. Wharton Grad. Sch., 1976. With Loews Corp., NYC, 1977—, exec. v.p., 1987-94, pres., COO, 1994-99, pres., CEO, 1999—. Chmn., CEO Diamond Offshore Drilling, Inc.; bd. dirs. CNA Fin., Vail Resorts, Inc., Loews Corp. Bd. dirs. Fedn. Employment and Guidance Svc., NYC, 1985; trustee Edn. Broadcasting Corp. 2003-, chmn. 2006; trustee NY Pub. Libr., Mt. Sinai Med. Ctr./NYU Med. Ctr., NYC, 1988—; past pres., UJA Fedn. NY; past chmn. Conf. Presidents Major Am. Jewish Orgns., United Jewish Communities; mem. bd. overseers, U. Pa. Wharton Sch. Bus.; mem. exec. com. Partnership for NYC. Mem.: Coun. Fgn. Rels., Phi Beta Kappa. Office: Loews Corp 667 Madison Ave Fl 7 New York NY 10021-8087 Office Phone: 212-521-2000. *

TISCH, JONATHAN MARK, hotel company executive; b. Atlantic City, Dec. 7, 1953; s. Preston Robert and Joan (Hyman) T. BA in Polit. Sci., Tufts U., 1976. Cinematographer, prodr. WBZ-TV, Boston, 1976-79; sales mgr. Loews Hotels, NYC, 1980-81, dir. devel., 1981-82, v.p., 1982-85, exec. v.p., 1985-86, pres., 1986, CEO, 1989—, chmn.; co-chmn. (with Andrew Tisch) Loews Corp., 2006—. Mem. mgmt. com. Loews Corp.; bd. dirs. NY Giants, 1991—. Author (with Karl Weber): The Power of We: Succeeding Through Partnerships, 2004. Trustee Robert Steel Found., NYC, Gunnery Sch., Washington, Conn., 1983, Tufts U., Medford, Mass., 1986-, Vice Pres.'s Residence Found., 1994; chmn. NYC host com. for Grammys, 1988, 92, 94; bd. dirs. Pediatric AIDS found.; vice chair econ. devel. com. NYC Partnership, 1994—; chmn. NYC & Co. Recipient Disting. Alumni award, Tufts U., 1996. Mem. Am. Hotel and Motel Assn. (officer 1994-97), Travel Bus. Roundtable (chmn. 1995—, conf. chmn. 1995—), Friars Club. Avocations: golf, tennis, skiing. Office: Loews Hotels 667 Madison Ave New York NY 10021-8087 Office Phone: 212-521-2801. *

TISCH, WILMA STEIN, foundation administrator; b. Asbury Park, NJ, June 25, 1927; d. Joseph F. and Rose E. (Liebesman) Stein; m. Laurence A. Tisch (dec. 2003); children: Andrew H., Daniel R., James S., Thomas J. BS, Skidmore Coll., Saratoga Springs, NY, 1948, LHD (hon.), 1990, Mt. Sinai Med. Sch. CUNY, NYC, 1990, NYU, 2006. Trustee Blythedal Children's Hosp., Valhalla, NY, 1964-71, Fedn. of Jewish Philanthropies, NYC, 1971—, pres., 1980-83. Trustee Coun. Jewish Fedns., NYC, 1980-87, Jewish Communal Fund, NYC, Am. Jewish Joint Distribution Com., NY, 1986-94, United Way NYC, 1986—, Skidmore Coll., 1994—, Carnegie Corp., NYC, 1994-98, WNYC Radio, NYC, 1984—, pres., 1988-93; trustee coun. advisors Hunter Coll. Sch. Social Work, NYC, 1986-97. Mem. NY State Gov.'s Select Com. on Capital Health Care Needs, NYC, 1983, Mayor's Transition Coun., NYC, 1993, Carnegie Coun. on Adolescent Devel., NYC, 1987—97; co-chmn. Task Force on Youth Devel. and Cmty. Programs, NYC, 1990—94; chmn. transition adv. team Parks and Recreation Cultural Affairs, NYC, 1993; mem. policy bd. Sept. 11th Fund, 2001—04. Recipient Louis D. Marshall medal Jewish Theol. Sem., 1980; Milender fellow Brandeis U., 1982. Fellow: Am. Acad. Arts & Sciences. Jewish.

TISCHFIELD, JAY ARNOLD, genetics educator; b. NYC, June 15, 1946; s. Max and Ethel Barbara (Smith) T.; m. Donna Marie Mitchell, Aug. 29, 1978; children: Max Alexander, Samuel Eli, David James. BS, Bklyn. Coll., 1967; MPH, Yale U., 1969, PhD, 1973. Diplomate Am. Bd. Med. Genetics. Asst. prof. Case Western Reserve U., Cleve., 1972-78; assoc. prof., prof. Med. Coll. of Ga., Augusta, 1978-87; prof., dir. div. molecular genetics Ind. U. Sch. Medicine, Indpls., 1987—98; Duncan and Nancy MacMillan prof. and endowed chair, dept. of Genetics Rutgers U., 1999—. Prof. of Pediat. and Psychiatry Robert Wood Johnson Med. Sch., 1998—; mem., Sci. Adv. Bd. Genome Inst. of Singapore; mem. scientific adv. bd. Cancer Inst. NJ; dir., Cell and DNA Repository Rutgers U., NJ, dir., Human Genetics Inst., NJ; dir. Ctr. for Collaborative Genetics Rsch. on Mental Disorders, NJ Ctr. for Excellence for the treatment of Tourette Syndrome and Associated Disorders; chmn. scientific adv. bd. Motif Biosciences, NYC; invited lectr. in field. Contbr. articles to profl. jours. Named Disting. Alumnus, Bklyn. Coll., 1990; NIH postdoctoral fellow, 1967-72; grantee NIH, 1972—, NSF, 1983-85; Elliot Osserman award for Disting. Svc. in Support of Cancer Rsch., Israel Cancer Rsch. Fund, 1994. Mem. Am. Soc. for Human Genetics, Am. Soc. for Microbiology, AAAS, Sigma Xi, Yale Club of Ind. Achievements include patents in field. Office: Dept Genetics Rutgers State Univ NJ Human Genetics Inst LS136 145 Bevior Rd Piscataway NJ 08854-8000 Office Phone: 732-445-1027. Office Fax: 732-445-1147. Business E-Mail: jay@biology.rutgers.edu.

TISCHKAU, SHELLEY ANN, physiologist, educator; d. Joe and Helen Elizabeth Tischkau. BS in Biology with honors, Truman State U., Kirksville, Mo., 1986; PhD, U. Ill., Urbana, 1990—95. Asst. prof. U. Ill., 2006—. Office: Univ Ill Dept Vet Biosci 2001 S Lincoln Ave Urbana IL 61801 Home Phone: 217-840-6724.

TISCHLER, GARY LOWELL, psychiatrist, educator; b. NYC, Oct. 30, 1935; s. Louis and Dorothy (Green) T.; m. Judith Post, Aug. 18, 1957; children: Laurie Dee, Marc David, Rachel Mara. AB, Hamilton Coll., 1957; MD, U. Pa., 1961; MS, Yale U., 1975. Intern Kings County Hosp., Bklyn., 1961-62; resident in psychiatry Yale U. Sch. Medicine, New Haven, 1962-65, asst. prof., 1967-70, assoc. prof., 1970-75, prof. psychiatry, 1975-90, chmn. dept. psychiatry, 1986-87; prof., chmn. dept. psychiatry and biobehavioral scis., dir. Neuropsychiatric Inst. UCLA Sch. Medicine, 1990-95; dir. Yale Psychiat. Inst., New Haven, 1978-87; chief psychiatry Yale-New Haven Hosp., 1986-87; clin. dir. Hill-West Haven divsn. Conn. Mental Health Ctr., New Haven, 1968-70, dir., 1970-77; prof. psychiatry UCLA, 1990-95, prof. emeritus, 1996—; prof., exec. vice chair dept. psychiatry, dir. Cornell U. Med. Coll., 1994—2002; dir. Westchester divsn., dir. mental health programs N.Y. Hosp., 1994-99, dir. Payne Whitney Clinic, 1996-97. Study dir. Pres.'s Commn. on Mental Health, Washington, 1977-79; cons. Arthur D. Little Inc., Boston, 1973-75, IBM Corp., Armonk, N.Y., 1986-87; mem. profl. adv. com. Am. Med. Internat., L.A., 1984-86; mem. bd. mental health and behavioral medicine Inst. Medicine, Washington, 1986—, com. on clin. evaluation, 1990-94. Author: Quality Assurance Thru Utilization and Peer Review, 1982; editor: Patient Care Evaluation in Mental Health, 1985, Diagnosis and Classification in Psychiatry, 1987; contbr. articles to profl. jours. Mem. Gov.'s transition staff on mental health, Conn., 1975; vice chmn. Bd. Mental Health State of Conn., 1986. Served to capt. U.S. Army, 1965-67, Vietnam. Fellow Am. Psychiat. Assn., Am. Coll. Mental Health Adminstrn., Am. Assn. for Social Psychiatry, Am. Coll. Psychiatry. Home: 36 Rock Hill Rd Bedford NY 10506-1522 E-mail: glt35@netscape.net.

TISCHMAN, MICHAEL BERNARD, lawyer; b. Elizabeth, NJ, Oct. 8, 1937; s. Nathan and Ann (Goldberg) T.; m. Elinor Cohen, Aug. 16, 1959; children: David F., Susan F. BA, U. Pa., 1959; LLB, Harvard U., 1963; LLM in Taxation, NYU, 1968. Bar: N.J. 1964, Fla. 1979, N.Y. 1984. Law sec. Judge Walter J. Freund N.J. Appellate Div., 1963-64; assoc. Schiff, Cummis & Kent, Newark, 1964-67; ptnr. Cummis, Kent, Radin & Tischman, Newark, 1968-70, Sills, Beck, Cummis, Radin & Tischman, Newark, 1971-87, Sills, Cummis, Radin, Tischman, Epstein & Gross, Newark, 1988—2003; sr. counsel Sills, Cummis, Epstein & Gross, Newark, 2004—. Panel chmn. fee arbitration com. N.J. Supreme Ct. Dist. Essex County, 1987-91; mem. health law and policy program adv. bd. Seton Hall Law Sch., 1997—. Mem. Mayor's Performing Arts Ctr. Task Force, Newark, 1988-96. Mem. N.J. Bar Assn. (com. on ltd. partnership act revisions 1983-88), Phi Beta Kappa. Home: 8 Wedgewood Way Scotch Plains NJ 07076-2727 Office: Sills Cummis Epstein & Gross One Riverfront Pla Newark NJ 07102 Office Phone: 973-643-7000. Business E-Mail: mtischman@sillscummis.com.

TISCH SUSSMAN, LAURIE, art gallery director; d. Preston Robert Tisch; 2 children from previous marriage. B, Duke U.; MFA, Catholic U. Chmn. Ctr. Arts Edn. Inc., Children's Mus. Manhattan; pres. Laurie Tisch Found.; cmmnr. NY City Dept. Cultural Affairs. Sec. Whitney Mus. Am. Art, bd. dir.; dir. Mattel Entertainment, FAO Schwartz. Mem.: NY State Coun. Arts. Mailing: c/o Whitney Mus Am Art 945 Madison Ave New York NY 10021

TISDALE, DOUGLAS MICHAEL, SR., lawyer; b. Detroit, May 3, 1949; s. Charles Walker and Violet Lucille (Battani) Tisdale; m. Patricia Claire Brennan, Dec. 29, 1972 (dec. Jan. 2004); children: Douglas Michael Jr, Sara Elizabeth, Margaret Patricia, Victoria Claire. BA in Psychology with honors, U. Mich., 1971, JD, 1975. Bar: Colo. 1975, U.S. Dist. Ct. Colo. 1975, U.S. Ct. Appeals (10th cir.) 1976, U.S. Supreme Ct. 1979. Law clk. to chief judge U.S. Dist. Ct. Colo., Denver, 1975-76; ptnr. Brownstein Hyatt & Farber, P.C., 1976—92; shareholder Popham, Haik, Schnobrich & Kaufman, Ltd., 1992—97, dir., 1995—97; ptnr. Baker & Hostetler LLP, Denver, 1997—2002; owner Tisdale & Assocs., Denver, 2002—. Chmn. bd. dirs. Eagle Health Care Ctr., Inc., Colo. Neurol. Inst.; treas. Vail Valley Med. Ctr. City councilman Cherry Hills Village, 2000—; mayor pro-tem, 2006—. Roman Catholic. Home: 4662 S Elizabeth Ct Cherry Hills Village CO 80113-7106 Office: Tisdale and Assocs LLC Colo State Bank Bldg Ste 2600 1600 Broadway Denver CO 80202-4989 Office Phone: 303-832-1800. Business E-Mail: doug@tisdalelaw.com.

TISE, LARRY EDWARD, historian, cultural organization administrator; b. Winston-Salem, NC, Dec. 6, 1942; s. Russell Edward and Lena Irene (Norman) T.; children: Larry Edward, Nicholas Allen, William Zane. AB, Duke U., 1965, M.Div., 1968; PhD (Ford Found. fellow, 1970, Research Triangle fellow, 1971), U. N.C., 1974. Part-time editor John Fries Blair, Pub., Winston-Salem, 1969-72; teaching fellow history dept. U. N.C., Chapel Hill, 1971, instr., 1972-73; dir. hist. publs. N.C. Bicentennial Com., 1973-74; asst. dir. N.C. Div. Archives and History, Raleigh, 1974-75, dir., 1975-81, N.C. State Hist. Preservation officer, 1975-81; exec. dir. Pa. Hist. and Mus. Commn., 1981-87; Pa. State Hist. Preservation officer, 1981-87; dir. Am. Assn. for State and Local History, Nashville, 1987-89; exec. dir. Benjamin Franklin Nat. Meml., Phila., 1989-97; pres., CEO Internat. Congress of Disting. Awards, 1997—. Adj. prof. grad. sch. fine arts U. Pa., 1984-87; vis. prof. Vanderbilt U., 1988-89, Temple U., 1989-91; Willbur

Orville Wright vis. disting. prof. E. Carolina U., 2000-; mem. Nat. Hist. Publs. and Records Commn., 1982-88 Author, co-author writings in fields of archives, hist. preservation, hist. sites and museums, history, society, religion; author: The Southern Experience in the American Revolution, 1978, The Monitor: Its Meaning and Future, 1978, Writing North Carolina History, 1979, A House Not Made with Hands, 1966, The Yadkin Melting Pot: Methodism and the Moravians in the Yadkin Valley, 1750-1850, 1968, Proslavery: The Defense of Slavery in America, 1987, A Book About Children, 1992, The American Counterrevolution, 1998, Keep on Running, 1998, Benjamin Franklin and Women, 2000, The Soaring Place: The Untold Story of Kitty Hawk, 2003, Benjamin Franklin, 2004, Hidden Images in the Wright Brothers Photographs, 1900-1911, 2005; gen. editor: writings in fields of archives, hist. preservation, hist. sites and museums, history, society, religion including Winston-Salem in History, 13 vols, 1976; edit. bd. The Public Historian, 1980-86; editor N.C. Hist. Rev., 1974-81, Pa. Heritage, 1981-87, History News, 1987-89, Franklin Gazette, 1989-97; contbr. articles to books, newsletters, publs. Recipient William R. Davie History award, 1979, Herbert L. Feis award, Am. Hist. Assn., 1989, Benjamin Franklin Nat. Meml. awards 1990, Best New Book in History, Ind. Book Pubs., 1999; Nat. Endowment for the Humanities fellow, 1992-93; faculty fellow NASA-Langley Rsch. Ctr., 2000-03. Mem. Am. Hist. Assn. (various coms.), Orgn. Am. Historians (chmn. coms.), So. Hist. Assn., Am. Assn. State and Local History (mem. coun. and coms.), Nat. Assn. State Archives and Records Adminstrs. (pres. 1980-81), Nat. Conf. State Hist. Preservation Officers (bd. dirs. 1976-79, pres. 1979-81), Nat. Coun. on Pub. History (bd. dirs., exec. com. 1979-83, pres. 1983-85), N.C. Hist. Commn. (sec. 1975-81), N.C. Lit. and Hist. Assn. (sec., treas. 1977-81), Pa. Fedn. Hist. Socs. (sec. 1981-87), Friends of Franklin, Inc. (exec. sec. 1989-97). Methodist. Office Phone: 215-765-1311. E-mail: ltise@attglobal.net.

TISHER, CHARLES CRAIG, nephrologist, educator, dean; MD, Wash. U., St. Louis, 1961. Resident Barnes Hosp., St. Louis, U. Wash. affiliated Hosps., Seattle; fellow in nephrology U. Wash., Seattle; positions at Walter Reed Hosp. and Walter Reed Army Inst. Rsch., Washington; joined faculty Duke U. Sch. Medicine, 1969; prof. medicine and pathology U. Fla. Coll. Medicine, Gainesville, Fla., 1980—, chief divsn. nephrology, hypertension and transplantation, 1980—87, named Ctrl. Fla. Kidney Ctr. Eminent Scholar Chair in Nephrology, 1989, prof. anatomy and cell biology, sr. assoc. dean, 1998—2002, Folke H. Peterson Disting. Professorship, 1999—, dean, 2002—; dir. Ctr. Clin. Trials Rsch U. Fla. Founding asst. editor Kidney Internat. jour.; chmn. med. adv. board Bioavailability Systems Inc., Cocoa Beach, Fla. Recipient Faculty Rsch. Prize in Clin. Scis., U. Fla., 1985. Mem.: Internat. Soc. Nephrology, Am. Soc. Nephrology (pres. 1990—91, jour. editor 1996—2001, John P. Peters Award 2001). Office: U Fla Divsn Nephrology Box J224 JHMHC Gainesville FL 32610 also: U Fla PO Box 100215 Gainesville FL 32610-0215 Office Phone: 904-392-3859, 352-846-2473. Business E-Mail: tisher@dean.med.ufl.edu.

TISHER, SHARON S., lawyer; b. York, Maine, Aug. 8, 1951; d. Frederick Fengar and Anna Veronka Shurts; m. Paul Winslow Tisher, June 8, 1974; children: Annya, Jacob. BA, Harvard U., 1973, JD, 1977. Bar: Conn. 1977. Ptnr. Day, Berry & Howard, Hartford, Conn., 1977; instr. & lectr. U Marin (Dept. of Resource Econ. and Policy), Orono, Maine. Bd. dirs. Legal Aid Soc. Hartford. Contbr. articles to profl. jour. Mem. ABA, Conn. Bar Assn., Maine Environ. Priorities Coun., Maine Toxics Action Coalition, bd. of Natural Resources Coun. of Maine, bd & chair Maine Organic Farmers and Gardeners Assn. (pub. policy com.). Office: U Marin (Dept of Resource Econ & Policy) 307Winslow Hall Orono ME 04469 Office Phone: 207-581-3158. Office Fax: 207-581-4278. Business E-Mail: sharon_tisher@apollo.umenfa.maine.edu.

TISHLER, RICHARD NORMAN, lawyer; s. Jack Murray Allen Tishler and Dorothy Tishler Ziff; m. Jean Lawrence Tishler, Oct. 13, 1996; children: Amy, David. BS in Acctg., U. Ala., Tuscaloosa, 1986, JD, 1989; LLM in Taxation, NYU, NYC, 1990. Bar: Ala. 1989, Mo. 1992. Atty. Lange Simpson, Birmingham, Ala., 1990—91, Riezman Berger, P.C., St. Louis, 1992—. Bd. trustees B'nai Amoona, 1999. Named to Ala. Law Rev., U. Ala. Law Sch., 1987; recipient Charles Parker Yarbrough award; Prime F. Osborn scholar, 1987, Hugo Black scholar. Mem.: ABA (coord. subcom. valuation issues sm. bus. 1993), Bar Assn. Met. St. Louis, Order of Coif. Avocation: exercise. Office: Riezman Berger PC 7700 Bonhomme 7th Fl Saint Louis MO 63105 Office Phone: 314-727-0101. Office Fax: 314-727-6458. Business E-Mail: tishler@riezmanberger.com.

TISHLER, WILLIAM HENRY, landscape architect, educator; b. Baileys Harbor, Wis., June 22, 1936; s. William John and Mary Viola (Sarter) T.; m. Betsy Lehner, Sept. 23, 1961; children: William Phillip, Robin Elizabeth. BS in Landscape Architecture, U. Wis., 1960; M in Landscape Architecture, Harvard U., 1964. Urban planner City of Milw., 1961-62; mem. faculty dept. landscape architecture U. Wis., Madison, 1964—; assoc. Hugh A Dega & Assocs. (Landscape Archs.), 1964-66; prin. Land Plans Inc. (Land and Hist. Preservation Planning Cons.), Madison, 1966—. Advisor emeritus Nat. Trust for Hist. Preservation; bd. dirs. The Hubbard Ednl. Trust. Author: American Landscape Architecture: Designers and Places, 1989, Midwestern Landscape Architecture, 2000, Door County's Emerald Treasure: A History of Peninsula State Park, 2005; contbr. articles to profl. jours. With C.E., U.S. Army, 1960. Recipient Design Arts Program award NEA, 1981, Hawthorn award Friends of The Clearing, 1997, Outstanding Educator award Coun. Educators in Landscape Architecture, 1998; Attingham (Eng.) Program fellow Soc. Archtl. Historians, 1980; Dumbarton Oaks sr. fellow, 1990. Fellow Am. Soc. Landscape Archs. (Horace Cleve. vis. prof. U. Minn. 1993, nat. merit award 1971, 97, 99, honor award 1980, 89, Wis. chpt. Lifetime Achievement award 2000), Coun. Educators Landscape Arch.; mem. Assn. Preservation Tech., Wis. Acad. Arts, Letters and Scis., Pioneer Am. Soc. (Henry Douglas award), Hist. Madison (hon.), Vernacular Architecture Forum (past pres.), Madison Trust for Hist. Preservation, Alliance for Hist. Landscape Preservation (founder), The Clearing Landscape Inst. (founder, dir.), Phi Kappa Phi, Sigma Lambda Alpha, Gamma Sigma Delta, Sigma Nu. Meth. Home: 3925 Regent St Madison WI 53705-5222 Office: U Wis Dept Landscape Architecture Madison WI 53706

TISHMAN, DANIEL R., construction executive; b. July 1955; s. John L. and Suzanne Weisberg Tishman; m. Sheryl C. Tishman. BS in Ecology and Planning, Evergreen State Coll., Olympia, Wash.; MS in Environ. Studies, Lesley Coll., Cambridge, Mass. With Tishman Realty and Constrn. Corp., 1990, exec. v.p., head NE ops., 1994; chmn., CEO Tishman Constrn., Interiors and Techs. Corp. Vice chair bd. trustees Natural Resources Def. Coun.; mem. adv. coun. Ctr. Biodiversity and Conservation Am. Mus. Natural History; mem. bd. governing trustees Jackson Labs., Bar Harbor, Maine; chmn. NY divsn. Israel Bonds; mem. exec. com. United Jewish Appeal, NY Bldg. Congress; gov. Real Estate Bd. NY. Named one of 40 Under 40, Crain's NY Bus., 1995; recipient Zeckendorf award, LI U. (C.W. Post campus), 2003, Humanitarian award, Albert Einstein Coll. Medicine of Yeshiva U., 2003. Office: Tishman Constrn Corp 666 Fifth Ave New York NY 10103-0256 Office Phone: 212-399-3600. Office Fax: 212-397-1317. *

TISHMAN, JOHN L., realty and construction company executive; b. NYC, Jan. 24, 1926; s. Louis and Rose F. (Foreman) T.; m. Suzanne Weisberg; children: Daniel R., Katherine T. BS, U. Michigan. Chmn. bd. dirs., pres. Tishman Realty & Constrn. Co., Inc., NYC, 1976—, CEO. Mem. bd. execs. Ronald McDonald House, NYU Med. Ctr., Pratt Inst., Carnegie Hall, Central Park Conservancy; chmn. bd. trustees New Sch. Univ., NYC. Home: Mianus Riv Rd Bedford NY 10506 Office: Tishman Realty Const Corp NY 666 5th Ave Fl 36 New York NY 10103-0256

TISHMAN, LYNN P., psychologist, psychoanalyst; b. Yonkers, NY, Apr. 3, 1951; d. Neal and Olga Petrucci; m. Peter V. Tishman, May 31, 1992; stepchildren: Steven, Linda, Anita. AAS in Acctg., Westchester CC, 1971; BA in Psychology summa cum laude, Hunter Coll., 1993; MSW, LCSW with honors, Hunter Sch. Social Work, 1995; PhD in Clin. Psychology, Columbia U., 2007. Lic. massage therapist Swedish Inst., NY, 1980, cert. biofeedback therapist BCIA, 1985, psychoanalyst, psychotherapist, and rschr., adult and child cert. psychoanalyst Psychoanalytic Inst. Postgrad. Ctr., NYC, 2002. Child devel. specialist and rschr. Pacella Parent Child Ctr., NY Psychoanalytic Inst. Mem.: NASW, APA, NY State Psychol. Assn., Assn. Applied Psychophysiology and Biofeedback, Postgrad. Psychoanalytic Soc. Avocations: running, weightlifting, bicycling, sailing.

TISINGER, CATHERINE ANNE, retired history professor; b. Winchester, Va., Apr. 6, 1936; d. Richard Martin and Irma Regina (Ohl) T. BA, Coll. Wooster, 1958; MA, U. Pa., 1962, PhD, 1970; LLD (hon.), Coll. of Elms, 1985. Provost Callison Coll., U. of Pacific, Stockton, Calif., 1971—72; v.p. Met. State U., St. Paul, 1972—75; v.p. academic affairs Southwest State U., Minn., 1975—77, interim pres., 1976—77; mem. gov.'s office staff State of Minn., 1979; dir. Ctr. for Econ. Edn., R.I. Coll., Providence, 1979—80; v.p. acad. affairs Ctrl. Mo. State U., Warrensburg, 1980—84; pres. North Adams State Coll., Mass., 1984—91; dean arts and scis. Shenandoah U., Winchester, Va., 1991—2001, prof. history and econs., 2001—04, disting. prof., 2001—, prof. emerita, 2004—, acting dean continuing edn., 2006. Cons. North Cen. Assn. Colls. and Schs., 1980-84, New Eng. Assn. Schs. and Colls., 1978-79, 85-91, Minn. Acad. Family Physicians, 1973-77; mem. adv. bd. First Agrl. Bank, North Adams, 1985-91; pres. No. Berkshire Cooperating Colls., 1986-91; v.p. Coll. Consortium for Internat. Studies, 1989-90; cons. Inst. for Experiential Learning, 2002—; dean arts and scis. Zayed U., UAE, 2001-02. V.p. Med. Simulation Found., 1986-88; cons. historian, curator Shenandoah Ctr. for Heritage and Environment, 2002—, bd. dirs. 2004—; bd. dirs. Williamstown Concerts, 1988-91, Shawnee coun. Girl Scouts U.S.A., 1992-93, Parents' Choice, 1997-98, Parents Guide to Children's Media, Inc., 1998-2004, pres. 2004—. Mem. No. Berkshire C. of C. (bd. dirs. 1984-89, v.p. 1986-89). Avocations: fiber and textile arts, photography. Office: Shenandoah U 1460 University Dr Winchester VA 22601-5195 E-mail: ctisinge@su.edu.

TITCOMB, CALDWELL, music and theatre historian; b. Augusta, Maine, Aug. 16, 1926; s. Samuel and Lura Elizabeth (Smith) T. AB summa cum laude, Harvard U., 1947, MA, 1949, PhD, 1952. Univ. organist Brandeis U., Waltham, Mass., 1953-70, dir. undergrad. studies music, 1956-84, curator creative arts, libr., 1961-64, co-chmn. music dept., 1977-84, from instr. to prof. music, 1953-88, prof. emeritus, 1988—. Drama critic Harvard Crimson, 1953-82, Bay State Banner, 1975-2006, This Month on Stage, 1996-99, Totaltheater.com, 2000—, Kay Bourne Arts Report, 2006—; trustee Charles Playhouse, Boston, 1966-71 Editor: The Art of Fine Words, 1965, The Furies (Lucien Price), 1988; co-editor: Varieties of Black Experience at Harvard, 1986, Blacks at Harvard: A Documentary History of African-American Experience at Harvard and Radcliffe, 1993; contbr. articles to profl. jours., ency.; composer stage and film music scores. Bd. dirs. Cambridge (Mass.) Civic Symphony Orch., 1959-70; exec. bd. Mus. Fine Arts Friends Music, Boston, 1959-65; panelist Mass. Commn. Arts and Humanities, 1981-83; mem. selection com. Theater Hall of Fame, 1980—; juror Elliot Norton awards, 1985—; pres. Boston Theater Critics Assn., 1994—. With U.S. Army, 1944-46, PTO; with Mil. Intelligence Res., 1946-50. Mem. AAUP, Coll. Music Soc., Am. Theatre Critics Assn. (charter), New Eng. Theatre Conf. (adv. coun. 1961-81, coll. fellows 1981—), Am. Guild Organists, Am. Musicol. Soc. (coun. 1965-67), Soc. for Ethnomusicology, Eugene O'Neill Soc., Hist. Brass Soc., Signet Soc., Soc. for Am. Music, Phi Beta Kappa (sec. Mu chpt. Mass. 1984—). Avocations: philology, afro-american history and culture. E-mail: caldwell67@aol.com.

TITELBAUM, DANIEL E., lawyer; b. Chgo., Sept. 4, 1946; AB, U. Calif., Berkeley, 1968; JD magna cum laude, Harvard U., 1973. Bar: Calif. 1973. Law clk. to Hon. Matthew O. Tobriner Calif. Supreme Ct., 1973-74; mem. Heller, Ehrman, White & McAuliffe, San Francisco; shareholder Heller Ehrman LLP, San Francisco, 1974—. Mem. ABA, State Bar of Calif., San Francisco Bar Assn., Phi Beta Kappa. Office: Heller Ehrman LLP 333 Bush St San Francisco CA 94104 Office Phone: 415-772-6134. Office Fax: 415-772-6268. Business E-Mail: dan.titelbaum@hellerehrman.com.

TITLE, ALAN M., astrophysicist; BA in Math., UCLA, 1960; PhD in Physics, Calif. Inst. Tech., 1996. Rsch. assoc. Harvard U., 1967—71; scientist, sr. fellow Lockheed Martin Corp., 1971—; prin. investigator TRACE solar telescope project Lockheed Martin Space Systems Advanced Tech. Ctr., Palo Alto, prin. investigator Atmospheric Imaging Assembly, Solar Dynamics Observatory. Prof. physics Stanford U. Recipient Public Svc. award, NASA, Hale prize, Am. Astronomical Soc.; Nat. Acad. Scis. Rsch. fellow, Smithsonian Astrophysical Observatory. Mem.: Internat. Acad. Astronauts, Nat. Acad. Engring., NAS. Achievements include research in techniques and development of optical systems for observing the sun from orbiting spacecraft. Office: Lockheed Palo Alto Rsch Lab Dept 91-30 Bldg 252 3251 Hanover St Palo Alto CA 94304-1191

TITLEY, SPENCER ROWE, geology educator; b. Denver, Sept. 27, 1928; m. Clara Helen Ruxton, May 1951; children: Ronald, Jane, Jennifer. Geol. Engr., Colo. Sch. Mines, 1951; PhD in Geology, U. Ariz., 1958. Ops. geologist N.J. Zinc Co., Gilman, Colo., 1951, 53-55; instr. U. Ariz., Tucson, 1955-58; regional geologist S.W. N.J. Zinc Co., 1958-60; from asst. to full prof. geology U. Ariz., 1960—. Panel mem. NSF, Divsn. Biol., Math. and Geophysical Scis. and Engring., 1978-81; sec. Soc. Econ. Geologists Found., 1972-83; mem. Apollo Field Geology Investigation Team, U.S. Geol. Survey, 1969-72; pres. Ariz. Geol. Soc., 1973-74. Mem. editl. bd. Econ. Geology, 1970-75, Ore Geology Reviews, 1984-2003; editor 5 books; contbr. over 85 articles to profl. jours. Pres. Mining Found. SW, 2007. With U.S. Army Corps Engrs., 1951-53, Korea. Decorated Bronze Star; recipient Disting. Achievement medal Colo. Sch. Mines, 1975, Excellence in Tchg. award Burlington No. Found., 1985, Creative Tchg. award U. Ariz. Found., 1986, D.C. Jackling award Soc. Mining, Mettalurgy and Exploration of AIME, 1997, Merit medal Am. Mining Hall of Fame, 1997; Fulbright Sr. lectr. Fed. U. Para'Brazil, 1986, Phoebe Apperson Hearst Disting. lectr. U. Calif., Berkeley, 1988. Fellow Geol. Soc. Am., Soc. Econ. Geologists (councilor 1980-83, Thayer Lindsley lectr. 1985, Disting. lectr. 1995, Penrose medal 1996), Mineral. Soc. Am., Australasian Inst. Mining and Metallurgy; mem. Nat. Acad. Engring., Soc. Applied Geology Home: 6920 E Taos Pl Tucson AZ 85715-3343 Office: Univ Ariz Dept Geosciences Simpson Bldg Tucson AZ 85721-0001 Office Phone: 520-621-6018. Business E-Mail: stitley@geo.arizona.edu.

TITO, DENNIS ANTHONY, former aerospace engineer, financial advisor; b. Queens, NY, Aug. 8, 1940; m. Suzanne Tito (div.); 3 children. BS in Astronautics and Aeronautics, NYC, 1962; MA in Engring., Rensselaer Polytechnic Inst., Troy, NY, 1964; DEng (hon.), Rensselaer Polytechnic Inst., 2002. Former engr. NASA, Jet Propulsion Lab., 1960—72; founder, CEO Wilshire Associates, Santa Monica, Calif., 1972—. Bd. commr. LA Dept. Water and Power, 1990. Achievements include being the world's first private space tourist to fly in space aboard the Soyuz TM32 to the International Space Station from the Baikonur Cosmodrome in Kazakhstan, Russia in April, 2001; first to pay for a trip to space. Office: Wilshire Associates 1299 Ocean Ave Ste 700 Santa Monica CA 90401

TITTMANN, BERNHARD RAINER, engineering science and mechanics educator; b. Moshi, Tanganjika, East Africa, Sept. 15, 1935; came to U.S., 1950, naturalized, 1956; s. Gustav and Hermine Marie (Polland) T.; m. Katharine Shower, Dec. 17, 1966; children: Christine M., Heidi E., Raymond J., Monica M., Brian P.F. BS, George Washington U., 1957; MS, UCLA, 1961, PhD, 1965. Mem. staff Hughes Aircraft Co., Culver City, Calif., 1957-65; asst. prof. UCLA, 1965-66; mem. staff Rockwell Internat., Thousand Oaks, Calif., 1966-79, dept. mgr., 1979-89; Schell prof. engring. Pa. State U., University Park, 1989—. Co-author 6 books; contbr. over 300 articles to profl. jours.; patentee in field. George Washington fellow George Washington U., 1953, Howard Hughes fellow Hughes Aircraft Co., 1957, Fulbright fellow, 1998. Fellow IEEE (life, adminstrv. com. for ultrasonics, ferrolectrics, frequency control, major awards chmn. 1999—, disting. lectr. 1998-99), Acoustical Soc. Am., Am. Soc. Materials, KC (4th degree); mem. Phi Beta Kappa. Home: 2466 Sassafras Ct State College PA 16803-3366 Office: Pa State U 212 Earth Engring Sci Bldg University Park PA 16802-6804 Home Phone: 814-238-2582; Office Phone: 814-865-7827. Business E-Mail: brt4@psu.edu.

TITUS, BRUCE EARL, lawyer; b. NYC, June 5, 1942; BA, Coll. William and Mary, 1964, JD, 1971. Bar: Va. 1971, D.C. 1972, Md. 1984. Asst. dir. torts br., civil divsn. U.S. Dept. Justice, 1971-82; mem. Jones, Waldo, Holbrook and McDonough, Washington; ptnr. Venable, Baetjer and Howard, LLP, McLean, Va., 1986—97; prin. Rees, Broome & Diaz P.C., Vienna, Va., 1997—. Exec. editor William & Mary Law Review, 1970-71. Mem. ABA, Va. State Bar, D.C. Bar, Fairfax Bar Assn. (pres. 1999-2000), Md. State Bar, Phi Delta Phi, Omicron Delta Kappa. Office: Rees Broome & Diaz PC 9th Fl 8133 Leesburg Pike Vienna VA 22182-2706 Office Phone: 703-790-1911.

TITUS, CHRISTINA MARIA, lawyer; b. Phila., Oct. 31, 1950; BA, NYU, 1972; JD, Georgetown U., 1977. Bar: N.Y. 1978, U.S. Dist. Ct. N.Y. (so. and ea. dists.) 1979. Assoc. Trubin Sillcocks Edelman & Knapp, NYC, 1977-80; v.p., counsel Merrill Lynch, Hubbard Inc., NYC, 1980—. Recipient 1st prize Drexel Keyboard Competition, 1968. Mem. Assn. of Bar of City of N.Y.

TITUS, JEFFREY BYRON, pediatric neuropsychologist; b. St. Louis, Aug. 10, 1974; s. Robert Edmond and Janet L. (Elliott) Titus. BS, Evangel U., Springfield, Mo., 1997; MA, U. No. Colo., 1999; PhD, Ball State U., Muncie, Ind., 2002. Neuropsychology fellow Henry Ford Hosp., Detroit, 2002—04; pediat. neuropsychologist St. Louis Children's Hosp./Washington U. Sch. Medicine, St. Louis, 2004—. Contbr. articles to profl. jours., chapters to books. Profl. adv. bd. Epilepsy Found., St. Louis. Recipient Thelma Hunt Rsch. award, Psi Chi, 2000. Mem.: APA, Am. Epilepsy Soc., Nat. Acad. Neuropsychology, Internat. Neuropsychol. Soc.

TITUS, ROGER WARREN, judge; b. Washington, Dec. 16, 1941; s. George R. and Margaret Titus; m. Catherine Mary Gaughen, Aug. 16, 1961; children: Paula Titus Laboy, Richard Roger, Mark William. BA, Johns Hopkins U., 1963; JD, Georgetown U., 1966. Bar: Md. 1966, D.C. 1966, U.S. Dist. Ct. Md. 1966, D.C. Dist. 1966, U.S. Ct. Appeals (4th cir.) 1966, U.S. Supreme Ct. 1970. Ptnr. Titus & Glasgow, Rockville, Md., 1966-88, Venable, Baetjer & Howard, Rockville, 1998—2003; judge U.S. Dist. Ct. for the Dist. of Md., Greenbelt, Md., 2003—. Asst. city atty. City of Rockville, 1966-69, city atty., 1970-82; spl. asst. Md. State Bd. of Law Examiners, 1969-72; adj. prof. law Georgetown U., Washington, 1972-78; mem. inquiry com. Atty. Grievance Commn., Annapolis, Md., 1975-80; mem. Trial Cts. Judicial Nominating Commn. Montgomery County, 1979-91; mem. standing com. on rules of practice and procedure Ct. of Appeals of Md., 1989-2003; mem. Appellate Jud. Nominating Commn., 1991-99 Trustee Suburban Hosp., Inc., Bethesda, Md., 1986-2000, chmn. bd., 1997-2000. Fellow: Am. Acad. Appellate Lawyers, Md. Bar Found. (bd. dirs. 1987—93, v.p. 1990—91, pres. 1991—93), Am. Bar Found., Am. Coll. Trial Lawyers; mem.: ABA (del. 1987—95), Montgomery County Bar Assn. (exec. com. 1983—84), Md. Mcpl. Attys. Assn. (pres. 1975), Am. Judicature Soc. (bd. dirs. 1995—2001), Md. Bar Assn. (sec. 1984—87, pres. 1988—89), Nat. Conf. Bar Pres. (mem. exec. coun. 1990—93). Office: US Dist Ct for Dist of Md 6500 Cherrywood Ln Greenbelt MD 20770

TITUS, VICTOR ALLEN, lawyer; b. Nevada, Mo., Sept. 2, 1956; s. Charles Allen and Viola Mae (Cliffman) T.; m. Laraine Carol Cook, Oct. 13, 1974 (div. Feb. 1982); 1 child, Matthew; m. Deborah Diane Carpenter, Apr. 10, 1984; 1 child, Jacquelynn. BS, BA, Ctrl. Mo. State U., 1978; JD, U. Mo., 1981. Bar: N.Mex. 1981, U.S. Dist. Ct. N.Mex. 1981, Mo. 1982, U.S. Ct. Appeals (10th cir. 1983), U.S. Supreme Ct. 1986, Colo. 1989, Ariz. 1995. Lawyer Jay L. Faurot, P.C., Farmington, N.Mex., 1981-83; ptnr. Faurot & Titus, P.C., Farmington, N.Mex., 1983-85; lawyer, sole proprietor Victor A. Titus, P.C., Farmington, N.Mex., 1985—. Arbitrator in civil disputes Alternative Dispute Resolution-Arbitration; liquor lic. hearing officer City of Farmington, 1989-94. Contbr. articles to profl. jours. Adult Behind Youth, Boys & Girls Club, Farmington, 1987—; mem. hosp. adv. bd. San Juan Regional Med. Ctr., Farmington, 1988-93. Recipient San Juan County Disting. Svc. award N.Mex. Bar Assn., 1984; named one of Best Lawyers in Am., 1995-96, 97—. Mem. ATLA, Am., N.Mex. Trial Lawyers (bd. dirs. 1983—, pres. 1993-94), State Bar of N.Mex. (disciplinary bd. 1997—2002, specialization com. 1992-98, legal advt. com. 1990), San Juan County Bar Assn. (pres. 1984), Nat. Assn. Criminal Def. Lawyers (life), Colo. Trial Lawyers. Democrat. Avocation: sports. Office: Victor A Titus PC 2021 E 20th St Farmington NM 87401-2516 Home: 6040 Bayhill Dr Farmington NM 87402-5078 Office Phone: 505-326-6503. Business E-Mail: victor@titusmurphylawfirm.com.

TITZE, INGO ROLAND, physics professor; b. Hirschberg, Silesia, Germany, July 8, 1941; came to U.S. 1955; s. Kurt Herrmann and Marta Emma (Bettermann) T.; m. R. Katherine Pittard, July 19, 1969; children: Karin, Michael, Jason, Gregory BSEE, U. Utah, 1963, MS in Elec. Engring. and Physics, 1965; PhD in Physics, Brigham Young U., 1972. Rsch. engr. N. Am. Aviation, Tulsa, 1965-66, Boeing Co., Seattle, 1968-70; lectr. Calif. State Poly. U., Pomona, 1973-74; asst. prof. U. Petroleum and Minerals Dhahran, Saudi Arabia, 1974-76, Gallaudet Coll., Washington, 1976-79; disting. prof. speech sci. and voice U. Iowa, Iowa City, 1979—. Cons. Bell Labs., Murray Hill, N.J., 1977-78; exec. dir. Wilbur James Gould Voice Rsch. Ctr., Denver Ctr. Performing Arts, 1983—; pres. Voice Cons. Inc., 1985—; panelist, site visitor NRC-NAS, 1984—; regular cons. divsn. rsch. grants NIH, 1986—; chmn. task force on voice Nat. Inst. Deafness and Other Comm. Disorders, 1989; adj. prof. Westminster Choir Coll., Princeton, N.J., 1989-94; dir. Nat. Ctr. for Voice and Speech, 1990—. Author: Principles of Voice Production, 1993, The Myoelastic Aerodynamic Theory of Phonation, 2006; editor: Vocal Fold Physiology: Biomechanics, Acoustics and Phonatory Control, 1985, Vocal Fold Physiology: Frontiers in Basic Science, 1992; assoc. editor Jour. of Voice; contbr. articles to profl. jours. Adv. bd. Voice Found., N.Y.C., 1980—; young men's pres. Latter Day Saints Ch. and Boy Scouts Am., Iowa City, 1982—Jacob Javits Neurosci. Investigator grantee NIH, 1984; recipient William and Harriot Gould Found. award, 1983, Claude Pepper award, 1989, Quintant award Voice Found., 1990, U. Iowa Regents award, 1995; ASHA fellow, 1992. Fellow Acoustical Soc. Am. (tech. coun., awards com. 1989), Am. Laryngological Assn. (hon.; award 1996); mem. Am. Speech-Hearing-Lang. Assn., Nat. Assn. Tchrs. Singing (rsch. coun. 1977—, editl. bd. 1986—), Internat. Assn. Rsch. Singing (dir. publs. 1982—), Am. Assn.

Phonetic Scs., Internat. Assn. Logopedics and Phoniatrics, Collegium Medicorium Teatri. Republican. Avocations: singing, tennis, home building. Office: Nat Ctr for Voice & Speech Univ of Iowa 330 Wjshc Iowa City IA 52242-1012 Home: 1551 Larimer St No 2301 Denver CO 80202

TIWARI, ATUL, chemist, researcher; b. Itawah, Uttar Pradesh, India, Jan. 28, 1975; s. Devaki Nandan and Savitri Devi Tiwari; m. Anupama Chaturvedi, May 4, 2005. MSc in Chemistry, Kanpur U., 1997; PhD, Macromolecular Rsch. Ctr., 2003. Polymer Scientist R.D.university Jabalpur, 2003. Rsch. fellow Macromolecular Rsch. Ctr., Jabalpur, Madhya Pradesh, India, 1999—2004; asst. rschr. Hawaii Corrosion Lab, Honolulu, 2005—. Postdoctoral rschr. U. Hawaii, Honolulu, 2005—. Fellow, Def. Rsch. Devel. Orgn., 1999, Dept. Sci. and Tech., India, 2001, Hawaii Corrosion Lab., 2004; rsch. assoc., Coun. for Sci. and Indsl. Rsch., India, 2004. Mem.: Materials Rsch. Soc., Electron Microscope Soc. India (life), Soc. Polymer Sci. India (life). Achievements include research in high performance polymers for advance applications. Office: Hawaii Corrosion Lab U Hawaii 2540 Doles St Holmes Hall Rm 302 Honolulu HI 96822 Home: Rainbow Pl 2102 2754 Kuilei St Honolulu HI 96826 Office Phone: 808-956-7565. Office Fax: 808-956-2373. Personal E-mail: atulmrc@yahoo.com. Business E-Mail: tiwari@hawaii.edu.

TIWARI, SANDIP, electrical and computer engineering educator; s. Anandilal and Lakshmi Tiwari; m. Mari Lee Wallner; children: Nachiketa Wallner, Kunal Landon. PhD, Cornell U., Ithaca, NY, 1980. Sr. mem. tech. staff MA/COM Inc., Burlington, Mass., 1980—83; rsch. staff mem., mgr. exploratory devices and modeling IBM Rsch. Ctr., Yorktown Heights, NY, 1983—99; prof. elec. and computer engring. Cornell U., 1999—2005, Charles N. Mellowes prof. engring., 2005—. Tech. activity bd. Anvik Corp., Hawthorne, NY, 2000—; adv. bd. DANCHIP - Tech. U. Denmark, Bygning, 2003—; tech. adv. bd. ADC Inc., Lansing, NY, 2004—; nat. adv. com. EECS Dept., U. Mich., Ann Arbor, 2004—; adv. bd. Wireless Integrated Microsys. Engring. Rsch. Ctr., Ann Arbor, 2004—, Nanoscale Informal Sci. Edn. Network, Boston, 2004—. Recipient Young Scientist award, Internat. Symposium on GaAs & Related Compounds, 1991, Disting. Alumnus award, Indian Inst. Tech., Kanpur, 2003, Cledo Brunetti award, IEEE, 2007; fellow, 1994, Am. Phys. Soc., 1998. Achievements include invention of nanocrystal memory; research in explanation of surface recombination in compound semiconductor transistors; refractory contacts for compound semiconductors; ultra-low threshold current quantum wire lasers; patents for 32 issued patents. Office: Cornell U 410 Phillips Hall Ithaca NY 14853 Home Phone: 607-257-4228; Office Phone: 607-254-6254.

TIZZIO, THOMAS RALPH, brokerage house executive; b. Elmont, NY, Jan. 9, 1938; s. Anthony Thomas and Ann Marie (Pascale) T.; m. Mary Ann Gentile, Aug. 26, 1962; children: Anthony, Vincent, Thomas. BBA, Bklyn. Coll., 1962. Underwriter W.J. Roberts & Co., NYC, 1957-65; sr. underwriter Atlantic Mut. Ins. Co., 1965-67; various positions AIG Am. Home Assurance Co., NYC, 1967-74, sr. v.p. property underwriting, 1974-78; exec. v.p. AIG Transatlantic Reins. Co., NYC, 1978-80, pres., bd. dirs., 1980-82; sr. v.p. reins. Am. Internat. Group, Inc., NYC, 1982-85, pres. domestic brokerage divsn., 1985-91, pres. Brokerage divsn., 1986-91, pres., 1991-97, sr. vice chmn., 1997—2006, honorary dir. and adviser, 2006—. Bd. dir. 21st Century Ins. Group, 2006—. Recipient Lifetime Achievement award, Nat. Italian American Found., 2003. Mem. Am. Inst. for Property and Liability Underwriters (trustee), Ins. Inst. Am. (trustee). Office: Am Internat Group Inc 175 Water St New York NY 10038-4918

TJOFLAT, GERALD BARD, federal judge; b. Pitts., Dec. 6, 1929; s. Gerald Benjamin and Sarita (Romero-Hermoso) Tjoflat; m. Sarah Marie Pfohl, July 27, 1957 (dec.); children: Gerald Bard, Marie Elizabeth; m. Marcia Penman Parker, Feb. 21, 1998. Student, U. Va., 1947—50, U. Cin., 1950—52; LLB, Duke U., 1957; DCL (hon.), Jacksonville U., 1978; LLD (hon.), William Mitchell Coll., 1993. Bar: Fla. 1957. Pvt. practice, Jacksonville, Fla., 1957—68; judge 4th Jud. Cir. Ct., Fla., 1968—70, US Dist. Ct. Mid. Dist., Jacksonville, 1970—75, US Ct. Appeals (5th cir.), Jacksonville, 1975—81, US Ct. Appeals (11th cir.), Jacksonville, 1981—, chief judge, 1989—96. Mem. Adv. Corrections Coun. U.S., 1975—87, Jud. Conf. U.S., 1989—96, mem. com. adminstrn. probation sys., 1972—87, chmn., 1978—87; mem. Fed. Jud. Ct. Com. on Sentencing, Probation and Pretrial Svcs., 1988—90; U.S. del. 6th and 7th UN Congress for Prevention of Crime and Treatment of Offenders. Hon. life mem., bd. visitors Duke U. Law Sch., 2000; pres. North Fla. coun. Boy Scouts Am., 1976—85, 2000—01, chmn., 1985—90; trustee Jacksonville Marine Inst., 1976—90, Episc. H.S., Jacksonville, 1975—90; mem. vestry St. Johns Cathedral, Jacksonville, 1969—71, 1973—75, 1977—79, 1981—83, 1985—87, 1993, 1995—96, sr. warden, 1975, 1983, 1987, 1991, 1992. With US Army, 1953—55. Recipient Merit award, Duke U., 1990, Fordham-Stein prize, 1996. Mem.: ABA, Am. Judicature Soc., Am. Law Inst., Fla. Bar Assn. Episcopalian. Office: US Courthouse 300 N Hogan St Ste 14-200 Jacksonville FL 32202-4257 Office Phone: 904-301-6570. *

TKACHEV, SERGEY NIKOLAYEVICH, geophysicist; b. Izmail, Odessa Region, Ukraine, July 19, 1964; arrived in US, 1994; s. Nikolay Yefimovich and Liliya Ivanovna Tkachev; m. Maria Sarah Simmons, June 19, 1999. MS in Physics, Moscow State U., Russia, 1991; MS in Geology, U. Ill., Urbana, 1997; PhD in Geology and Geophysics, U. Hawaii, Honolulu, 2005. Rsch. physicist Inst. Exptl. Mineralogy Russian Acad. Scis., Chernogolovka, Russia, 1991—2001; rsch. asst. dept. geology U. Ill., Urbana, 1994—96, tchg. asst., 1996—97; rsch. scientist Hawaii Inst. Geophysics and Planetology, Honolulu, 1997—98; rsch. asst. dept. geology and geophysics U. Hawaii, 1998—99, tchg. asst., 2000, rsch. asst., 2000—05; postdoctoral rschr. dept. physics Colo. State U., Fort Collins, 2005—06; postdoctoral assoc. Geophys. Lab., Carnegie Instn., Washington, 2006—. Contbr. scientific papers, articles to profl. jours. Guard platoon sgt. Soviet Air Forces, 1982—84. Recipient Tuition Waiver award, Dean Grad. Divsn. U. Hawaii, 1999; J. Watumull Merit scholar, Dept. Geology and Geophysics U. Hawaii, 2002—03. Mem.: Am. Geophys. Union. Achievements include first to characterize elastic moduli of the novel bulk superhard cubic BC2N phase (the hardest crystalline material after Diamond) by Brillouin scattering; research in situ Brillouin spectroscopic study of a pressure-induced apparent second order transition in a Silicate glass; Brillouin scattering study of pentane at high pressure; new experimental data on ice VI, ice VII and liquid water phase boundaries; characterization of current nonlinearity in semiconductors in weak electric fields; characterization of elastic properties of nc-TiN/a-Si3N4 nanocomposites films by surface Brillouin scattering; micro-Raman spectroscopy and X-ray diffraction studies of atomic-layer-deposited ZrO2 and HfO2 thin films; elastic and structural properties of Alkaline-Calcium Silica Hydrogels; hydrated and anhydrous Na2O-2SiO2 liquid and also glass to 8 GPa using Brillouin scattering; Characterization of Elastic Properties of Superhard Amorphous Carbon Pressure-Synthesized from C60 by Surface Brillouin Scattering; Brillouin spectroscopy studies of surface modes in thin-film Si3N4 on GaAs; determination of sound velocity and attenuation in stable and metastable liquid water to 1.2 GPa by Brillouin spectroscopy. Avocations: racquetball, tennis, hiking, swimming, camping. Home: 12053 Cherokee Park Rd Livermore CO 80536 E-mail: stkachev@soest.hawaii.edu.

TKACHUK, KEITH, professional hockey player; b. Melrose, Mass., Mar. 28, 1972; m. Chantel Oster; children: Matthew, Braeden, Taryn. Attended, Boston U., 1990—91. Left wing Winnipeg Jets, 1992—96, Phoenix Coyotes (formerly Winnipeg Jets), 1992—2001, St. Louis Blues, 2001—07, 2007—, Atlanta Thrashers, 2007. Mem. Team USA, World Cup of Hockey, 1996, 2004, USA Olympic Hockey Team, Nagano, Japan, 1998, Salt Lake City, 2002, Torino, Italy, 06. Named NHL Second Team All-Star, 1995, 1998; named to NHL All-Star Game, 1997—99, 2004. Achievements include being a member of World Cup Champion Team USA, 1996; being a member of silver medal winning USA Hockey Team, Salt Lake City Olympics, 2002. Office: St Louis Blues Hockey Club Scottrade Ctr 1401 Clark Ave Saint Louis MO 63103 *

TLAPA, RICHARD JOSEPH, retired priest; b. Cicero, Ill., Feb. 20, 1920; s. Francis Richard Tlapa and Josephine Rose Burianek. BA, U. St. Mary of the Lake, Mundelein, Ill., 1941, MA, 1944; PhD, Calif. Christian U., LA, 1976, Columbia U., San Rafael, Calif., 1986. Ordained priest 1944; lic. radiotelephone and ship radar FCC. Pastoral adminstrn. Archdiocese of Chgo., 1944—89; ret., 1989. Tech. cons. Maritime Electronics, Inc., Chgo., 1955—85. Author: The New Apostles, 1977, The Priest in the Pew, 1986, Jubilate Deo, 1989; contbr. articles to religious and secular publs. Mem.: Am. Radio Relay League (life), Internat. Soc. for Philos. Enquery (life; diplomate), Mensa (life). Avocations: electronics, Latin-Greek biblical research, photography. Home: 6350 Taft St Merrillville IN 46410

TLOU, JOSIAH S., education educator; b. Zimbabwe, Dec. 31, 1935; s. Litsila and Mothateho T.; m. Litha T., Sept. 3, 1959; children: Lee, Hla, Joy B., Leeto. BA, Luther Coll., 1968; MA, Ill. State U., 1969; EdD, U. Ill., 1976. Cons. curriculum Glencoe (Ill.) Pub. Schs.; specialist social studies USAID U. Botswana, Gaborone; prof. Va. Tech., Blacksburg; civic curriculum planner for U.S. AID project Creative Assocs. Internat./Harvard Inst. Internat. Devel., Malawi, 1996-98; dir. USAID/Malawi Govt. Projects UPIC, 1998—. Cert. tchr., Zimbabwe. Contbr. articles to profl. jours. Recipient Disting. Svcs. award Luther Coll.; Luce-Bergeson rsch. grantee, African-Am., Scholars Coun. grantee, Creative Univ. Rsch. grantee, 1991-92, 94-95. Mem. ASCD, WCCI, Nat. Coun. Social Studies, ASA, AAPRDTW, Botswana Edn. Rsch. Assn., Phi Delta Kappa. E-mail: tlou@vt.edu.

TLSTY, THEA DOROTHY, research scientist, educator; b. Mobile, Ala., Jan. 28, 1952; d. Theodore H. and Josepine M. Tlsty. BS in zoology, U. South Fla., 1973; PhD in molecular biology, Washington U., 1980. Asst. prof. pathology U. NC, Chapel Hill, 1985-92, mem. Lineberger Comprehensive Cancer Ctr., 1985—95, assoc. prof. pathology, 1992—95, U. Calif., San Francisco, 1995—96, dir. molecular pathology, 1995—96, mem. Cancer Rsch. Inst., 1995—96, prof. pathology, 1996—, dir. Ctr. for Translational Rsch. in the Molecular Genetics of Cancer, 1996—, dir. program cell cycling and signaling, Comprehensive Cancer Ctr., 1996—. Predoctoral fellow cellular and molecular biology program, Wash. U., St. Louis, 1976-80, postdoctoral fellow dept. microbiology and immunology, 1980-81; postdoctoral fellow/sr. rsch. assoc. dept. biological sciences, Stanford U., 1981-85; vis. scientist U. Geneva, 1982; vis. scholar U. Zimbabwe, 1992; cons. Bristol-Meyers Co., 1987, Glaxo, 1990—94, Geron, 1993—95, Oncormed, 1995-97, Onyx, 1997-98, Day Casebeer, 1999-2000, Pennie and Edmonds, 2001-02; mem. editl. bd. Molecular Carcinogenesis, 1992-, Carcinogenesis, 1993-, Cancer Rsch., 1995-, Environ. Health Perspectives, 1996-, Am. Jour. Pathology, 1997-; mem. adv. coun., GM Cancer Rsch. Found. Contbr. numerous articles to sci. jours. Recipient Gold Key Honor Soc. Award; Starter Grant Award, Pharmaceutical Mfrs. Assn.; Avon Scholar, 2001-. Mem. AAAS, Am. Soc. Microbiology, Am. Assn. Cancer Rsch., Am. Soc. Biological Chemists and Molecular Biologists, Assn. for Women in Sci., Women in Cancer Rsch., Women in Cell Biology, Calif. Soc. Pathologists, Assn. Molecular Pathologists, Am. Soc. Investigative Pathology, Am. Soc. Cell Biology, Am. Soc. Biochemistry and Molecular Biology. Avocations: bicycling, sculpting, swimming. Office: U Calif Box 0506 San Francisco CA 94143-0506

TO, STEPHEN EDWARD, editor, writer; b. NYC, July 5, 1963; s. Cho To and Lilly Fong Yee. BA in Biology, Purchase Coll., SUNY, 1985; MBA, Fordham U. Technician specialist Cornell U. Med. Coll., NYC, 1986—88; rsch. biologist Rockefeller U., NYC, 1988—97; mng. med. editor, writer IntraMed Ednl. Group, NYC, 1999—2006; with Hoffman-La Roche, Inc., Nutley, NJ, 2006—. Freelance editor Nature Am., NYC, 1998—99. Mem.: Drug Info. Assn., Am. Med. Writers Assn. Avocations: sailing, travel. Home: 1539 Lexington Ave Apt 3E New York NY 10029 Office: Hoffmann-La Roche Inc PDR Drug Reg Affairs 340 Kingsland St Nutley NJ 07110 Personal E-mail: sto1967@aol.com. Business E-Mail: stephen.to@roche.com.

TOAL, JAMES FRANCIS, academic administrator; b. NYC, June 7, 1932; s. John Joseph and Catherine (Whyte) T. MA, St. John's U., 1966; PhD, Fordham U., 1976. Cert. elem. tchr., N.Y. cert. supt., adminstrn. and supervision, English 7-12. Athletic dir., tchr. English St. Francis Prep. High Sch., NYC, 1957-60; tchr. Bishop Ford High Sch., NYC, 1960-66, chmn. dept. English; prin. St. Francis Central Summer High Sch., NYC, 1966-73, St. Francis Prep. High Sch., NYC, 1966-73; exec. v.p., assoc. prof. dept. edn. adminstrn. and supervision Grad. Sch. St. Bonaventure U., NY, 1976-83; pres., prof. Quincy U., Ill., 1983-97; v.p. Siena Coll., Loudonville, NY, 1997—; also bd. trustees. Mem. Springfield Diocesan Bd. of Edn., Provincial Bd. of Edn., Franciscan Friars of Chgo. and St. Louis. Trustee Siena Coll., Loudonville, N.Y., 1977-83; bd. advisors Jamestown Community Coll., Olean, N.Y., 1979-83; bd. dirs. Am. Cancer Soc., Olean, 1981-83; mem. Mental Health Assn., 1981-83; mem. state legis. com. Commn. of Ind. Colls. and Univs., Albany. N.Y., 1980-83; mem. bd. trustees Padua Franciscan High Sch. Grantee Colgate U., 1967; grantee SUNY-Plattsburg, 1968, St. Bonaventure U., 1980 Mem. Am. Coun. on Edn., Associated Colls. of Ill., Ill. Bus. and Edn. Forum, Assn. of Governing Bds., West Ctrl. Ill. Ednl. Telecomm. Corp. (bd. dirs. exec. com., fin. com., pers. com.), Fedn. Ind. Ill. Colls. and Univs. (pub. rels. com.), Mid. States Accrediting Assn. (assoc., evaluation team for higher edn.), Nat. Assn. Secondary Sch. Prins., North Ctrl. Accrediting Assn. (evaluation team for higher edn., chair evaluation team 1986—), Soc. Coll. and U. Planning, Quincy C. of C. (transp. com. 1985-96, computer com. 1996—), Rotary, Univ. Club, KC, Phi Delta Kappa. Office: Siena Coll Office of VP Loudon Rd Loudonville NY 12211

TOAL, JEAN HOEFER, state supreme court chief justice; b. Columbia, SC, Aug. 11, 1943; d. Herbert W. and Lilla (Farrell) Hoefer; m. William Thomas Toal; children: Jean Toal Eisen, Lilla Patrick. BA in Philosophy, Agnes Scott Coll., 1965; JD, U. S.C., 1968; LHD (hon.), Coll. Charleston, 1990; LLD (hon.), Columbia Coll., 1992, The Citadel, 1999, Francis Marion U., 1999, U. S.C., 2000. Bar: S.C. Assoc. Haynsworth, Perry, Bryant, Marion & Johnstone, 1968—70; ptnr. Belser, Baker, Barwick, Ravenel, Toal & Bender, Columbia, 1970—88; assoc. justice S.C. Supreme Ct., Columbia, 1988—2000, chief justice, 2000—. Mem. S.C. Human Affairs Commn., 1972-74; mem. S.C. Ho. of Reps., 1975-88, chmn. house rules com., constitutional laws subcom. house judiciary com.; mem. parish coun. and lector St. Joseph's Cath. Ch.; chair S.C. Juvenile Justice Task Force, 1992-94; chair S.C. Rhodes Scholar Selection Com., 1994; bd. dirs. Nat. Ctr. State Cts., 2005-; pres. Conf. Chief Justices, 2007—. Mng. editor S.C. Law Rev., 1967—68. Bd. visitors Clemson U., 1978; trustee Columbia Mus. Art, 1980-85; bd. trustees Agnes Scott Coll., 1996—. Named Outstanding Legislator of Yr., Greenville News, 1976, Woman of Yr., U. S.C. Mortar Bd., 1989; named one of Top 25 Doers, Dreamers & Drivers, Govt. Tech. Mag., 2002; recipient Disting. Svc. award, S.C. Mcpl. Assn., 1980, U. Notre Dame award, 1991, Algernon Sydney Sullivan award, U. S.C., 1991, Agnes Scott Coll. Outstanding Alumna award, 1991, John W. Williams award, Richland County Bar Assn., 1995, Jean Galloway Bissell award, S.C. Women Lawyers Assn., 1995, Margaret Brent Women Lawyers of Achievement award, 2004. Mem. ABA, S.C. Women Lawyers Assn., S.C. Bar Assn., John Belton O'Neall Inn of Ct., Phi Beta Kappa, Mortar Bd., Order of the Coif Office: Supreme Ct SC PO Box 11330 Columbia SC 29211-2456 Business E-Mail: jtoal@sccourts.org.

TOALE, THOMAS EDWARD, school system administrator, minister; b. Independence, Iowa, Aug. 30, 1953; s. Francis Mark and Clara R. (DePaepe) T. BS in Biology, Loras Coll., 1975, MA in Ednl. Adminstrn., 1986; MA in Theology, St. Paul Sem., 1980; PhD in Ednl. Adminstrn., U. Iowa, 1988. Ordained priest Roman Cath. Ch., 1981; cert. tchr., prin., supt., Iowa. Tchr. St. Joseph Key West, Dubuque, Iowa, 1975-77, Marquette High Sch., Bellevue, Iowa, 1981-84, prin., 1984-86; assoc. supt. Archdiocese of Dubuque, 1986-87, supt. schs., 1987—2006, vicar for edn., 2002—. Assoc. pastor St. Joseph Ch., Bellevue, 1981-84; pastor Sts. Peter and Paul Ch., Springbrook, Iowa, 1984-86, St. Peter, Temple Hill, Cascade, Iowa, 1986—. Mem. Nat. Cath. Edn. Assn. (past pres., chief adminstrn. Cath. edn.). Office: Archdiocese of Dubuque 1229 Mount Loretta Ave Dubuque IA 52003-7826

TOAN, BARRETT A., former health products executive; s. Winthrop A. and Edith Byrne Toan; m. Polly O'Brien; children: Elliot, Frannie. BA in history, Kenyon Coll., 1969; MBA, U. Pa., 1974. With budget bur. State of Ill., Springfield; positions with State of Pa.; cons. PriceWaterhouse, Washington; commr. divsn. social svcs. State of Ark., 1979—81; dir. dept. social svcs. State of Mo., 1981—85; exec. dir., COO Sanus Health Plan of St. Louis, 1985—91; pres. Express Scripts Inc., Maryland Heights, Mo., 1990—2002, CEO, 1992—2005, chmn., 2000—06. Bd. dirs. Pharm. Care Mgmt. Assn., Sigma-Aldrich Corp. Mem. bd. dirs., treas. Mentor St. Louis. Named Entrepreneur of Yr. Inc. Mag., 1994. *

TOAY, THELMA M., columnist, poet; b. Anamosa, Iowa, Feb. 22, 1915; d. Frank Leroy and Edna May Stoughton; m. John S. Toay; 3 children. Student, St. Lukes Sch. Nursing, Davenport, IA, 1933, Highland Coll., 1966—67; AA in Journalism, N.E. Iowa C.C., Peosta, 1995—97; student, U. Iowa, 2001—03. Contbr. newspapers, Freeport, Ill., 1962—; contbr. Julien's Jour., Dubuque, Iowa, 1995—. Author: Bittersweet, 1979, Places for the Heart - Profiles of Life, 2001. Avocations: theater, music, reading, flower gardening.

TOBACH, ETHEL, retired curator; b. Miaskovka, USSR, Nov. 7, 1921; arrived in U.S., 1923; d. Ralph Wiener and Fanny (Schechterman) Wiener Idels; m. Charles Tobach, 1947 (dec. 1969). BA, Hunter Coll., 1949; MA, NYU, 1952, PhD, 1957; DSc (hon.), LI U., 1975. Lic. psychologist N.Y. Rsch. fellow Am. Mus. Natural History, NYC, 1958-61, assoc. curator, 1964-69, curator, 1969-90, emerita curator; rsch. fellow NYU, NYC, 1961-64, ret., 1990. Adj. prof. psychology and biology CUNY, NYC, 1964—; disting. cons. faculty Saybrook Inst., San Francisco, 1998—. Co-editor: (series) T. C. Schneirta Conference Series, 1981, Genes & Gender Series, 1975; editor: Internat. Jour. Comparative Psychology, 1987—93; assoc. editor: Peace and Conflict: Jour. Peace Psychology, 1994—. Recipient NIHH Career Devel. award, 1964—74, Disting. Sci. Career, Assn. Women in Sci., 1974, Disting. Sci. Publ., Assn. Women in Psychology, 1982, Kurt Lewin award, Soc. Psychol. Study Social Issues, 1993, Gustavus Myers award for Outstanding Pub. Human Rights in N.Am., 1996, Lifetime Achievement Psychology in Pub. Interest Gold Medal award, Am. Psychol. Found., 2003. Fellow: APA (pres. comparative psychology divsn. 1985, peace psychology divsn. 2003, Leadership award Com. in Women in Psychology 2005); mem.: Soc. Study Peace, Conflict and Violence (pres. 2003, Lifetime Peace Activity award 1999), Psychologists for Social Responsibility, N.Y. Acad. Scis. (v.p. behavioral scis. 1973—76), Eastern Psychol. Assn. (pres. 1987, bd. dirs. 2001—, mem. exec. com. 2002—), Internat. Soc. Comparative Psychology (hon.; sec. 1988—92, pres.). Office: Am Mus Natural History Central Pkwy 79th St New York NY 10024-5192 Business E-Mail: tobach@amnh.org.

TOBACK, PAUL A., recreational facility executive; Atty. Katten Muchin & Zavis, Chgo.; dir. adminstrn. City of Chgo.; exec. asst. to Chief Staff The White House, Washington; COO Globetrotters Engring. Corp.; from exec. v.p., COO to pres., CEO Bally Total Fitness Holding Corp., Chgo., 1997—2002, pres., 2002—, CEO, 2002—, chmn. bd. dirs. Office: Bally Total Fitness Holding Corp 8700 W Bryn Mawr Ave Chicago IL 60631

TOBE, BARBARA GAINES, information technology executive; d. Gartrell Jerome and Rosa Lee Gaines; m. Gerome Tobe; children: Erika Monique, Alexis Stephanie. BS, Howard U., DC, 1967. Cert. sys. profl. 1985. Physicist Vitro Labs., Silver Spring, Md., 1967—68; programmer, analyst Control Data Corp., Rockville, Md., 1969—72; computer systems analyst Dept. Health, Edn. & Welfare, DC, 1972—80; computer specialist Nat. Weather Svc., Silver Spring, 1980—2002, info. tech. leader, 2002—. NOAA sch. visitation & Saturday acad. lectr. Nat. Weather Svc., 1980—2000, student intern coord., 1980—2007, EEO coord., 1993—96. Sec. 16th St. Heights Civic Assn., DC, 1996—2002. Recipient EEO Essay Contest Coord. award, NOAA EEO Office, 1996, Adminstr. award, Dept. Commerce/NOAA, 1997, Sustained Superior Performance awards, Dept. Commerce, NOAA. Episc. Achievements include design, development and implementation of the replacement primary and backup telecommunication centers; monitoring and supervising in the design and development of a case tracking system; development of an event tabulation program for a submarine system. Avocations: ballroom dancing, travel, genealogy, movies, reading. Office: National Weather Svc 1325 East West Hwy Silver Spring MD 20910 Personal E-mail: bgwtobe@aol.com.

TOBE, STEPHEN SOLOMON, zoology educator; b. Niagara-on-the-Lake, Ont., Can., Oct. 11, 1944; s. John Harold and Rose T. (Bolter) T.; m. Martha Reller. BSc, Queen's U., Kingston, Ont., 1967; MSc, York U., Toronto, Ont., 1969; PhD, McGill U., Montreal, Que., Can., 1972. Rsch. fellow U. Sussex, Eng., 1972-74; asst. prof. U. Toronto, 1974-78, assoc. prof., 1974-78, prof., 1982—, assoc. dean scis., faculty arts and sci., 1988-93, vice dean faculty arts and sci., 1995-96. Vis. prof. U. Calif., Berkeley, 1981, Nat. U. Singapore, 1987, 1993-94, U. Hawaii, 1988; mem. animal biology grant selection com. Natural Scis. and Engring. Rsch. Coun. Can., 1986-89, chair, 1988-89; lectr. Internat. Congress Entomology, Vancouver, B.C., Can., 1988; cons. in hydroponics. Editor Insect Biochemistry, 1987; mem. editl. bd. Jour. Insect Physiology, 1980—, Physiol. Entomology, 1985—, Life Scis. Advances, 1987—, Gen. and Comparative Endocrinology, 1995—; contbr. chpts. to books and articles to profl. jours. Recipient Pickford medal in comparative endocrinology, 1993; E.W.R. Steacie fellow Natural Scis. and Engring. Rsch. Coun. Can., 1982-84. Fellow Royal Soc. Can., Royal Entomol. Soc.; mem. AAAS, Entomol. Soc. Can. (C. Gordon Hewitt award 1982, gold medal 1990), Soc. Exptl. Biology. Avocations: amateur radio, gardening, hydroponics. Home: PO Box 695 Virgil ON Canada L0S 1T0 Office: U Toronto Dept Cell and Systems Biology 25 Harbord St Toronto ON Canada M5S 3G5 Business E-Mail: stephen.tobe@utoronto.ca.

TOBEN, BRADLEY J. B., dean, law educator; m. Beth Toben; children: John, Sarah Beth. BA in Polit. Sci. with honors, U. Mo., St. Louis; JD with honors, Baylor U., 1977; LLM, Harvard U., 1981. Bar: Tex., Mo. Tchr. Ind. U. Sch. Law, Indpls.; of counsel Dawson & Sodd (Dallas and Corsicana); with faculty Baylor Law Sch., 1983—, dean Law Sch., 1991—, Gov. Bill and Vara Faye Daniel prof. law, 1991—. Participant in accreditation and membership inspection of law schs. ABA, Assn. Am. Schs. Gov. apptd. Tex. commr. Nat. Conf. of Commrs. on Uniform State Laws. Named a Outstanding Young Alumnus, Baylor U., Disting. Alumnus, U. Mo.-St. Louis; recipient Disting. Alumni Polit. Sci. Award. Fellow Am. Bar Found.,

Tex. Bar Found.; mem. State Bar of Tex. (active in bankruptcy specialization cert. program). Office: Baylor U PO Box 97288 Waco TX 76798-7288 Business E-Mail: Brad_Toben@baylor.edu. *

TOBEN, DOREEN A., telecommunications industry executive; b. Curacao; m. Ed Toben; 2 children. AB in Polit. Sci., Rosemount Coll.; MBA in Fin. and Mktg., Fairleigh Dickinson U. Dir. corp. planning AT&T, 1972; exec. dir. mktg. Bell Atlantic Enterprises Internat., Inc., 1989; various positions equipment engring., ops., and small bus. and consumer market mgmt. Bell Atlantic Inc., Pa., dir. fin., 1983, divsn. mgr. strategic planning, 1984, asst. v.p.-comptr., 1992, CFO, 1993, v.p. corp. fin., mem. com., v.p., CFO telecom. network, 1997—99; v.p., contr. Verizon Comm. Inc., 1999—2000, sr. v.p., CFO telecom. group, 2000—02, exec. v.p., CFO, 2002—. Bd. dirs. NY Times Co., 2004—. Named one of 50 Most Powerful Women in Bus., Fortune mag., 2005, 2006, 10 Most Powerful Women in NJ Bus., Star-Ledger, 2006. Office: Verizon 1095 Avenue of Americas New York NY 10036 *

TOBER, BARBARA D. (MRS. DONALD GIBBS TOBER), editor; b. Summit, NJ, Aug. 19, 1934; d. Rodney Fielding and Maude Starkey; m. Donald Gibbs Tober, Apr. 5, 1973. Student, Traphagen Sch. Fashion, 1954-56, Fashion Inst. Tech., 1956-58, N.Y. Sch. Interior Design, 1964. Copy editor Vogue Pattern Book, 1958-60; beauty editor Vogue mag., 1961; dir. women's services Bartell Media Corp., 1961-66; editor-in-chief Bride's mag., NYC, 1966-94; chmn. Mus. Arts and Design; pres. Acronym, Inc., NYC, 1995—, The Barbara Tober Found., 1995—. Sec.-treas., dir. Sugar Foods Corp.; adv. bd. Traphagen Sch.; coord. SBA awards; Am. Craft Coun., 1983—, benefit food com. chmn., 1984-87. Author: The ABC's of Beauty, 1963, China: A Cognizant Guide, 1980, The Wedding...The Marriage...And the Role of the Retailer, 1980, The Bride: A Celebration, 1984 Mem. Nat. Council on Family Relations, 1966; nat. council Lincoln Center Performing Arts, Met. Opera Guild; mem. NYU adv. bd. Women in Food Service, 1983; NYU Women's Health Symposium: Steering Com., 1983—. Recipient Alma award, 1968, Penney-Mo. award, 1972, Traphagen Alumni award, 1975, Diamond Jubilee award, 1983, Disting. Women award Northwood U., 1997. Mem. Fashion Group, Internat. Furnishings and Design Assn. (v.p., program chmn.), Am. Soc. Mag. Editors, Am. Soc. Interior Designers (press mem.), Intercorporate Group, Women in Communications (60 yrs. of success award N.Y. chpt. 1984), Nat. Assn. Underwater Instrs., Pan Pacific and S.E. Asia Women's Assn., Asia Soc., Japan Soc., China Inst., Internat. Side Saddle Orgn., Millbrook Hounds, Golden's Bridge Hounds, Wine and Food Soc., Chaines des Rotisseurs (chargée de press) (bd. dirs.), Dames d'Escoffier, Culinary Inst. Am. Home and Office: 620 Park Ave New York NY 10021-6591

TOBER, STEPHEN LLOYD, lawyer; b. Boston, May 27, 1949; s. Benjamin Arthur Tober and Lee (Hymoff) Fruman; m. Susan V. Schwartz, Dec. 22, 1973; children: Cary, Jamie. Grad., Syracuse U., 1971, JD, 1974. Bar: N.H. 1974, U.S. Dist. Ct. N.H. 1974, U.S. Supreme Ct. 1978, N.Y. 1981. Assoc. Flynn, McGuirk & Blanchard, Portsmouth, NH, 1974-79; pvt. practice Portsmouth, 1979-81, 1992—; ptnr. Aeschliman & Tober, Portsmouth, 1981-91. Lectr. Franklin Pierce Law Ctr., Concord, N.H., 1978-80. Contbr. articles to profl. jours. Mem. Portsmouth Charter Commn., 1976, Portsmouth Planning Bd., 1977-81; del. N.H. Constl. Conv., Concord, 1984; city councilman, Portsmouth, 1977-81. Fellow: Internat. Acad. Trial Lawyers, Am. Bar Found. (chmn. ea. region 2003—); mem.: ATLA (gov. 1980—86), ABA (chmn. standing com. on fed. judiciary 2005—06, state del., chmn. tech. and comms. com., chmn. credentials and admissions com.), N.H. Bd. Bar Examiners, N.H. Trial Lawyers Assn. (pres. 1977), N.H. Bar Assn. (pres. 1988—89, chmn. com. to redraft code of profl. responsibility, Disting. Svc. award 1986, 1994), New Eng. Bar Assn. (bd.dirs. 1988—91). Democrat. Jewish. Avocations: reading, tennis. Home: 55 T J Gamester Ave Portsmouth NH 03801-5871 Office: PO Box 1377 Portsmouth NH 03802-1377 Home Phone: 603-436-4231; Office Phone: 603-431-1003. Business E-Mail: stober@toberlaw.com.

TOBEY, MARTIN ALAN, cardiologist; b. Dallas, Sept. 24, 1947; s. Nathan Gene and Rose Marcus T.; m. Judith Helane Ross, Mar. 10, 1974; children: Daniel, Rachel. BS with highest distinction, Pa. State U., 1968; MD, Jefferson Med. Coll., 1970. Diplomate Am. Bd. Internal Medicine, Am. Bd. Cardiovascular Diseases, Am. Bd. Interventional Cardiology. Intern Phila. Gen. Hosp., 1970-71; resident in internal medicine Parkland Meml. Hosp., Dallas, 1971-74; fellow in cardiology U. Tex. Southwestern Med. Sch., Dallas, 1976-78; cardiologist Fort Worth Heart, 1978—. Mem. med. bd. Harris Hosp. Meth., Ft. Worth, 1988-90, chmn. cardiology divsn., 1988-90. Author (software) Workshops in Coronary Angioplasty, 1984, Revolution: The New Practice of Medicine, 2006, The Torch, 2007. Major U.S. Army, 1974-76. Fellow Am. Coll. Cardiology (regional rep. Tex. chpt. 1996-98); mem. Am. Heart Assn., Sc. Cardiovasc. Computed Tomography, Torch Club (Ft. Worth), Soc. Cardiovascular Computed Tomography, Alpha Omega Alpha. Avocations: classical music, computers, photography. Office: Ft Worth Heart 1300 W Rosedale St Fort Worth TX 76104-2802 E-mail: mjtob@charter.net.

TOBEY, WILLIAM HAYWARD, federal agency administrator, former investment banker; b. Decatur, Ill., Aug. 2, 1959; s. William Robert Jr. and Beverly Joy (Nilson) T.; m. Elizabeth Ness, Oct. 28, 1989; 1 child, Emma Channer. BS, Northwestern U., 1981; M of Pub. Policy, Harvard U., 1984. Presdl. mgmt. intern US Dept. Def., Washington, 1984-85; adv. U.S. Delegation to Nuclear and Space Talks, Geneva, 1985-86; dir. def. policy NSC, Washington, 1986-93; v.p. Smith Barney, NYC; gen. ptnr. Embryon Venture Capital, LLC, 1996; dir. counterproliferation strategy NSC, Washington; dep. adminstr. for def. nuclear nonproliferation Nat. Nuclear Security Adminstrn., US Dept. Energy, Washington, 2006—. Republican. Lutheran. Avocations: golf, squash, oenology. Office: Nat Nuclear Security Adminstrn US Dept Energy 1000 Independence Ave SW Washington DC 20585

TOBIAS, ANDREW PREVIN, columnist, educator; b. NYC, Apr. 20, 1947; s. Seth D. and Audrey J. (Landau) T. BA, Harvard U., 1968, MBA, 1972. Pres. Harvard Agys. Inc., Cambridge, Mass., 1967-68; v.p. Nat. Student Mktg. Corp., NYC, 1969-70; contbg. editor N.Y. Mag., 1972-77, Esquire mag., 1977-83; columnist Playboy mag., 1982-86; contbr. Time mag., 1989-94, Worth mag., 1995—. Co-host Beyond Wall Street, PBS series, 1997; daily internet columnist, 1996-. Author: The Funny Money Game, 1972, (under pen name John Reid) The Best Little Boy in the World, 1973, Fire and Ice, 1976, The Only Investment Guide You'll Ever Need, 1978, rev. edit., 1996, Getting by on $100,000 a Year and (Other Sad Tales), 1980, The Invisible Bankers, 1982, (software) Managing Your Money, 1984-94, Money Angles, 1984, The Only Other Investment Guide You'll Ever Need, 1987, Kids Say Don't Smoke, 1991, Auto Insurance Alert!, 1993, My Vast Fortune, 1997, the Best Little Boy in the World Grows Up, 1998. Treas. Dem. Nat. Com., 1999—; co-founder Alliance to Revitalize Calif.; bd. mem. Human Right's Campaign. Recipient Gerald Loeb award, 1984, Consumer Fedn. of Am. Media Svc. award, 1993, GLSEN Valedictorian award, 1997, Smith-Weld prize Harvard Mag., 1998.

TOBIAS, GEOFFREY, otolaryngologist, plastic surgeon; b. Paterson, NJ, Dec. 20, 1947; MD, Tufts U., 1973. Intern Tufts New England Med. Ctr., 1973—76; resident Mt. Sinai Hosp., NYC, 1976—78; attending surgeon and instr. Mt. Sinai Hosp. and Sch. Medicine, NYC; assoc. chief head and neck surgery Englewood Hosp., NJ. Mem. sci. adv. bd. Longevity mag. Named one of Top Doctors in NY, NY Mag., 2004. Mem.: Am. Acad. Otolaryngology - Head and Neck Surgery, Am. Acad. Facial Plastic Surgery. Office: 214 Engle St Englewood NJ 07631-2418 also: 815 Park Ave New York NY 10021-3276 Office Phone: 201-567-7966. Office Fax: 201-567-6770.

TOBIAS, JOSEPH DREW, pediatric anesthesiologist; b. St. Louis, Mo., Dec. 16, 1958; s. Sherwin Larue and Georgia Xenos Tobias; m. Julie Ann Turpin, Nov. 3, 2001. BA, U. Mo., Kansas City, 1981, MD, 1983. Diplomate Am. Bd. Pediat., Am. Bd. Anesthesiology, Am. Bd. Pediat. Critical Care, Am. Bd. Anesthesiology Critical Care Medicine, Am. Bd. Anesthesiology Pain Mgmt., cert. Am. Acad. Pain Mgmt. 1990. Chief pediatric anesthesiology, attending pediatric ICU St. Jude Children's Hosp., Memphis, 1990—91; assoc. dir., divsn. pediatric anesthesiology/critical care; assoc. prof. anesthesiology and pediat. Vanderbilt U., Nashville, 1991—95; chief, pediatric anesthesiology/pediatric critical care, prof. anesthesiology and pediat. U. Mo., Columbia, 1995—, vice-chmn., dept. anesthesiology, 2001—. Home: 4112 Compton Rd Columbia MO 65203 Office: U Missouri One Hospital Dr - 3W27G HSC Columbia MO 65212 Office Phone: 573-882-7168. Business E-Mail: tobiasj@health.missouri.edu.

TOBIAS, PAUL HENRY, lawyer; b. Cin., Jan. 5, 1930; s. Charles H. and Charlotte (Westheimer) T.; 1 child, Eliza L. AB magna cum laude, Harvard U., 1951, LLB, 1958. Bar: Mass. 1958, Ohio 1962. Assoc. Stoneman & Chandler, Boston, 1958-61, Goldman & Putnick, Cin., 1962-75; ptnr. Tobias, Kraus and Torchia, Cin., 1976—. Instr. U. Cin. Law Sch., 1975-77. Author: Litigating Wrongful Discharge Claims, 1987; co-author: Job Rights and Survivor Strategies, a Handbook for Terminated Employees, 1997; contbr. articles to profl. jours. Mem. Cin. Bd. of Park Commrs., 1973-81, Cin. Human Rels. Commn., 1980-84, Cin. Hist. Conservation Bd., 1990-91. With U.S. Army, 1952-54. Mem. ABA, Nat. Employment Lawyers Assn. (founder), Nat. Employee Rights Inst. (chmn.; editor-in-chief Employee Rights quar. 2000-02), Ohio State Bar Assn., Cin. Bar Assn. (past chmn. legal aid com.), Phi Beta Kappa. Home: 15 Hill And Hollow Ln Cincinnati OH 45208-3317 Office: Tobias Kraus Torchia 911 Mercantile Libr Bldg Cincinnati OH 45202 Office Phone: 513-241-8137. Business E-Mail: tkt@tktlaw.com.

TOBIAS, RANDALL LEE, former federal agency administrator, retired pharmaceutical company executive; b. Lafayette, Ind., Mar. 20, 1942; m. Marilyn Jane Salyer, Sept. 2, 1966 (dec. May 1994); children: Paige Noelle, Todd Christopher; m. Marianne Williams, July 15, 1995; stepchildren: James Russell Ullyot, Kathryn Lee Ullyot. BS in Mktg., Ind. U., 1964; LLD (hon.), Galuedette U.; D of Engring. (hon.), Rose Hulman Inst. Tech., Sagamore of the Wabash, Ind.; LLD (hon.), Ind. U., 1997. Numerous positions Ind. Bell, 1964-77, Ill. Bell, 1977-81; v.p. residence mktg. sales and service AT&T, 1981-82, pres. Am. Bell Consumer Products, 1983, pres. Consumer Products, 1983-84, sr. v.p., 1984-85, vice chmn. NYC, 1986-93; chmn., CEO AT&T Comm., NYC, 1985-91, AT&T Internat., Basking Ridge, NJ, 1991-93, Eli Lilly & Co., Indpls., 1993-98, chmn. emeritus, 1999—; coord., US Govt. Activities to Combat AIDS Globally US Dept. State, Washington, 2003—06, dir. US Fgn. Assistance, 2006—07; adminstr. US Agy. Internat. Devel., Washington, 2006—07. Bd. dirs. Kimberly-Clark, 1994-2003, ConocoPhillips Petroleum Co., 2002-03, Knight-Ridder, Inc. Co-Author: Put The Moose On The Table, 2003 Chmn. bd. trustees Duke U.; trustee Colonial Williamsburg Found.; bd. govs. Indpls. Mus. Art; bd. dirs. Indpls. Symphony Orch., Ind. U. Found. (hon.), Econ. Club Indpls. Named one of Top 25 Mgrs. of Yr., Bus. Week, 1997, Family Champion, Working Mothers Mag., 1997. Mem. Bus. Coun., Indpls. Corp. Cmty. Coun., Coun. Fgn. Rels., Meridian Hills Country Club (Indpls.), Woodstock Club (Indpls.), Columbia Club (Indpls.), Athletic Club (Indpls.), Univ. Club (Indpls.), Amwell Valley Conservancy (N.J.), Theta Chi. Avocations: skiing, fly fishing, shooting. *

TOBIAS, ROBERT MAX, labor leader, lawyer; b. Detroit, Aug. 4, 1943; BA, U. Mich., 1965, MBA, 1968; JD, George Washington U., 1969. Lawyer Nat. Treasury Employees Union, Washington, 1968-70, gen. counsel, 1970-79, exec. v.p. and gen. counsel, 1979-83, pres., 1983-99; disting. adj. prof. pub. adminstrn., dir. Inst. for Study of Pub. Policy Implementation, Am. U., Washington, 1999—, dir. pub. sector exec. edn., 2005—. Lectr. George Washington U. Law Sch., Washington, 1970-90; mem. IRS oversight bd., 2000—. Contbr. articles to law revs. Pres. Fed. Employee Edn. and Asst. Fund, Washington, 1986—. Fellow Nat. Acad. Pub. Adminstrn.; mem. ABA, Soc. for Labor Relations Profls. (1st Annual Union Leader award, 1987), Fed. Bar Assn. Democrat. Episcopalian. Office: Am U Sch Pub Affairs 4400 Massachusetts Ave Washington DC 20016-8070 E-mail: rtobias@american.edu.

TOBIAS, STEPHEN C., rail transportation executive; b. Bogota, Colombia, Dec. 11, 1944; BA in History, Citadel, 1967; postgrad., Harvard U., 1986. Jr. engr. Pocahontas divsn. Norfolk and Western Rlwy. Co., 1969-70, asst. roadmaster Scioto divsn., 1970, asst. trainmaster Pitts. divsn., 1970-71, gen. yardmaster Pitts. divsn., 1971-73, traimaster Bellevue terminal, 1973-74, asst. supt. Bellevue terminal, 1974-79, supt. Pitts. divsn., 1979-81, asst. gen. mgr. lake region, 1981, asst. gen. mgr. supt. eastern region, 1981-84; gen. mgr. eastern region Norfolk (Va.) So. Corp., 1984, gen. mgr. western lines, 1984-89, v.p. transp., 1989-92, v.p. strategic planning, 1992-93, sr. v.p. ops., 1993-94, exec. v.p. ops., 1994-98, vice chmn. and COO, 1998—. Trustee Norfolk Acad.; prin. Va. Bus. Coun.; bd. dirs. Plum Creek Timber Co., TTX Co., Inc. Dir. Va. law Enforcement Found.; mem. exec. adv. coun. Commonwealth Musical Stage. Capt. U.S. Army, 1967-69. Mem. Assn. Am. R.R.s. Office: Norfolk So Corp 3 Commercial Pl Norfolk VA 23510-2108

TOBIASSEN, BARBARA SUE, systems analyst, consultant, volunteer; b. Bklyn., Feb. 22, 1950; d. Vincent and Esther Alice (Hansen) M. BA in Math Edn., Rider Coll., 1972; postgrad., Montclair State U., 1973. Cert. secondary tchr., NJ. Math tchr. Westwood (NJ) H.S., 1973-80; programmer Prudential Ins. Co., Roseland, NJ, 1980-81; programmer, analyst Grand Union, Paramus, NJ, 1981-82; cons. Five Techs., Montvale, NJ, 1987-90; project mgr. Info. Sci., Inc., Montvale, 1982-84, cons., project mgr., 1987-90; pres. B. Maxwell Assoc., Inc., Westwood, 1990—; vol. Peace Corps; mem. Peace Corps., 2001—02; tchr. St. Paul's Luth., Accra, Ghana, 2002—03. Guest spkr. Info. Sci., Best of Am., Computer Assocs. B.A.C.; tchr. in Ghana, 2002-07; math tchr. Woodclif Lake, NJ. Contbr. articles to profl. jours. Vol. Peace Corps, 2001—02. Mem.: APA (v.p. N.J. chpt. 1996), NAFE, Am. Payroll Assn., N.J. Info. Republican. Lutheran. Avocations: travel, reading, gardening, hiking.

TOBIN, BARBARA KAY, minister; b. Davenport, Iowa, Oct. 9, 1943; d. Robert Thomas Myers and Frances Louella Davis; m. Richard James Tobin, Feb. 12, 1966; 1 child, Mary Beth Tobin Peter. B.Humanities, Social Sci. and Edn., Purdue U., 1966; BEd, Ball State U., 1968; MDiv, Colgate Rochester Div. Sch., 1994. Cert. tchr. N.Y., ordained to ministry Presbyn. Ch., 1994. Fgn. lang. tchr. West Irondequoit Schs., Rochester, NY, 1968—93; chaplain Strong Meml. Hosp., Rochester, 1993—94; pastor of visitation First Presbyn. Ch., Pittsford, NY, 1994—96; assoc. pastor Perinton Presbyn. Ch., Fairport, NY, 1995—2000; pastor Irondequoit Presbyn. Ch., Rochester, 2000—. Sec., bd. dirs. Irondequoit Sr. Transp. Ministry, Rochester, 2002—; mem. com. on prep. ministry Genesee Valley Presbytery, 2005—; leader internat. study tours West Irondequoit Schs., 1983—88; leader student mission trips Perinton Presbyn. Ch., 1991—99. Mem. Irondequoit Youth Bureau Adv. Bd., 2004—06. Mem.: N.Y. State Ret. Tchrs. Assn., Purdue U. Alumni Assn. (life; pres.'s coun. 1993—). Presbyterian. Avocations: reading, travel, sailing. Office: Irondequoit Presbyn Ch 2881 Culver Rd Rochester NY 14622 Home Phone: 585-872-5284; Office Phone: 585-266-3370. Personal E-mail: pastorbobbi@rochester.rr.com.

TOBIN, BRUCE HOWARD, lawyer; b. Detroit, July 17, 1955; s. Marshall Edward and Rhoda Maureen (Milman) Tobin; m. Kathleen Tobin; children: Benjamin Stewart, Jenna Rose, Lainie Nicole. BA in Social Sci., Mich. State U., 1978; JD, Detroit Coll. Law, 1982; LLM in Taxation, NYU, 1983. Bar: Mich. 1982, Fla. 1982, U.S. Dist. Ct. (ea. dist.) Mich. 1982, Nebr. 1983, U.S. Tax Ct. 1983. Assoc. Kutak, Rock & Campbell, Omaha, 1983-85; ptnr. Lebow and Tobin PLLC, West Bloomfield, Mich., 1985—2002; pvt. practice West Bloomfield, 2002—. Treas. West Bloomfield Sch. Bd. Mem.: ABA, Nebr. Bar Assn., Mich. Bar Assn. (tax. com. 1985—), Fla. Bar Assn. Jewish. Office: 7001 Orchard Lake Rd Ste 312 West Bloomfield MI 48322-3607 Office Phone: 248-851-4300. Fax: (248) 851 4303. E-mail: btobin@tobinplc.com.

TOBIN, CALVIN JAY, retired architect; b. Boston, Feb. 15, 1927; s. David and Bertha (Tanfield) T.; m. Joan Hope Fink, July 15, 1951; children— Michael Alan, Nancy Ann. B.Arch., U. Mich., 1949. Designer, draftsman Arlen & Lowenfish (architects), NYC, 1949-51; with Samuel Arlen, NYC, 1951-53, Skidmore, Owings & Merrill, NYC, 1953; architect Loebl, Schlossman & Bennett (architects), Chgo., 1953-57, v.p., 1953-57, Loebl, Schlossman & Hackl, 1957—; ret., 1998. Chmn. Jewish United Fund Bldg. Trades Div., 1969; chmn. AIA and Chgo. Hosp. Council Com. of Hosp. Architecture, 1968-76; archtl. cons. Resurrection Healthcare Corp., 1998-. Archtl. works include Michael Reese Hosp. and Med. Ctr., 1954—, Prairie Shores Apt. Urban Redevel., 1957-62, Louis A. Weiss Meml. Hosp., Chgo., Chgo. State Hosp., Ctrl. Cmty. Hosp., Chgo., Gottlieb Meml. Hosp., Melrose Park, Ill., West Suburban Hosp., Oak Park, Ill., Thorek Hosp. and Med. Ctr., Chgo., Water Power Pl., Chgo., Christ Hosp., Oak Lawn, Greater Balt. Med. Ctr., Shriners Hosp. for Crippled Children, Chgo. Hinsdale (Ill.) Hosp., South Chgo. Cmty. Hosp., Chgo., Mt. Sinai Med. Ctr., Chgo., Alexian Bros. Med. Ctr., Elk Grove Village, Ill., Luth. Gen. Hosp., Park Ridge, Ill., Evanston (Ill.) Hosp., Resurrection Med. Ctr., Chgo., New Cook County Hosp., Chgo., also numerous apt., comml. and cmty. bldgs. Chmn. Highland Park (Ill.) Appearance Rev. Commn., 1972-73; mem. Highland Park Plan Commn., 1973-79; mem. Highland Park City Coun., 1974-89, mayor pro-tem, 1979-89; mem. Highland Park Environ. Control Commn., 1979-84, Highland Park Hist. Preservation Commn., 1982-89; bd. dir. Highland Park Hist. Soc., Young Men's Jewish Coun., 1953-67, pres., 1967; bd. dirs. Jewish Community Ctrs. Chgo., 1973-78, bd. dirs., 1989-93; Ill. Coun. Against Handgun Violence, 1989-94; trustee Ravinia Festival Assn., 1990-98; bd. govs. Highland Park Cmty. House, 1994—. With USNR, 1945-46. Recipient Boys Club Medallion award, Boys Club Am., 1968, Disting. Alumni award, Taubman Coll. Architecture and Urban Planning, U. Mich., 2004. Fellow AIA (2d v.p. Chgo. chpt.); mem. U. Mich. Alumni Soc. Coll. Architecture and Urban Planning (bd. govs. 1989-95), U. Mich. Alumni Assn. (bd. govs. 1990-95, v.p. 1993-95, pres. 1997-99, Disting. Alumni Svc. award 1996), Std. Club, Ravinia Green Country Club, Pi Lambda Phi. Jewish. Home: 814 Dean Ave Highland Park IL 60035-4749

TOBIN, GORDON ROSS, surgery educator; b. Twin Falls, Idaho, Jan. 6, 1943; s. Gordon Ross and Garnet Othalia (Peterson) T.; m. Elisabeth Ann Pelcher, Dec. 21, 1968; children: Christopher Ross, Anne-Elise. AB, Whitman Coll., 1965; MD, U. Calif., San Francisco, 1969. Prof. surgery U. Louisville, 1977—. Co-prin. investigator, craniomaxillofacial, hand and composite allograft transplant team U. Louisville/Jewish Hosp., 1999—; chmn., program dir. divsn. plastic surgery U. Louisville, 1994—; pres. Ky. Soc. Plastic and Reconstructive Surgeons, 1985-86, Louisville Soc. Plastic and Reconstructive Surgeons, 1990-92. Author: Muscle and Myocutaneous Flaps, 1986, Refinements in Flap Reconstruction, 1990. Co-founder, med. co-dir. Louisville Burn Project, 1992. Grantee Jewish Hosp. Heart and Lung Inst., 1992—. Fellow ACS; mem. Am. Assn. Plastic Surgeons, Am. Soc. Plastic and Reconstructive Surgeons, Soc. Univ. Surgeons, Jefferson County Med. Soc. (pres., 2003—04, chmn. bd. govs. 2004-). Presbyterian. Avocations: fly fishing, skiing, outdoor cooking. Home: 1505 Northwind Rd Louisville KY 40207-1636 Office: U Louisville Dept Surgery Acb Fl 2 Louisville KY 40292-0001 Home Phone: 502-893-6630; Office Phone: 502-852-6880. E-mail: gordon.tobin@louisville.edu.

TOBIN, JAMES MICHAEL, lawyer; b. Santa Monica, Calif., Sept. 27, 1948; s. James Joseph and Glada Marie (Meisner); m. Kathleen Marie Espy, Sept. 14, 1985; children: Kristina Claire, Victoria Elizabeth Joy. BA with honors, U. Calif., Riverside, 1970; JD, Georgetown U., DC, 1974. Bar: Calif. 1974, Mich. 1987. From atty. to gen. atty. So. Pacific Co., San Francisco, 1975-82; v.p. regulatory affairs So. Pacific Comm. Co., Washington, 1982-83; v.p., gen. counsel Lexitel Corp., Washington, 1983-85; v.p., gen. counsel, sec. ALC Comm. Corp., Birmingham, Mich., 1985-87, sr. v.p., gen. counsel, sec., 1987-88; of counsel Morrison & Foerster, San Francisco, 1988-90, ptnr., 1990—2005, Law Office of James M. Tobin, 2006—. Mem. ABA, Calif. Bar Assn., Fed. Comm. Bar Assn. Republican. Unitarian Universalist. Avocations: carpentry, travel. Home: 3134 Baker St San Francisco CA 94123-1805 Office: Two Embarcadero Ctr Ste 1800 San Francisco CA 94111 Office Phone: 415-732-1700. Business E-Mail: jim@tobinlaw.us.

TOBIN, JAMES ROBERT, biomedical device manufacturing company executive; b. Lima, Ohio, Aug. 12, 1944; s. J. Robert and Doris L. (Hunt) T.; m. Janet Trafton, Dec. 30, 1971; children: James Robert III, Amanda Trafton. BA in Govt., Harvard U., 1966; MBA, Harvard U. Bus. Sch., 1968. Fin. analyst Baxter Internat., Inc., Deerfield, Ill., 1972-73, internat. contr., 1973-75, mng. dir. Japan, 1975-77, mng. dir. Spain, 1977-80, pres. IV Sys. Divsn., 1981—86, group v.p., 1984-88, exec. v.p. Deerfield, 1988-92, pres., COO, 1992-94, Biogen Inc., 1994-97, pres., CEO, 1997-98, Boston Sci. Corp., Natick, Mass., 1999—, also bd. dirs. Bd. dirs. BioMedical Sci. Career Program, Applera, Inc., Curis, Inc. Served to lt. USN, 1968—72. Republican. Office: Boston Scientific 1 Boston Scientific Pl Natick MA 01760-1537

TOBIN, STEVE ROBERT, artist; b. Phila., Feb. 10, 1957; B in Theoretical Mathematics, Tulane U., 1976—79. Rsch. asst. to Dr. Campbell Laird U. Pa., 1975; tchr. glass sculpture Tokyo Glass Art Inst., Japan, 1985—86. One-man shows include Sculptured Glass, Bienville Gallery, New Orleans, 1979, Glasscapes, Spring Street Enamels Gallery, NY, 1980, Glass Portraits, Hanson Gallery, New Orleans, 1980, Glass Sculpture, Gallery 10, NY, 1982, Manhattan Bowls, Snyderman Gallery, Phila., 1985, Wheaton Ware, LaVaggi Gallery, NY, 1986, Glass for Tea Ceremony, Tazawa Gallery, Kyoto, Japan, 1987, The Glass Garden, Coll. Art & Design, Levy Gallery for Arts, Phila., 1988, Cocoons, Moore Coll. Art & Design, Phila., 1988, Transformations: Three Installations in Glass, Lehigh U., Wilson and Hall Gallery, Bethlehem, Pa., 1992, Retretti Art Centre, Punkaharju, Finland, 1993, Sanske Galerie, Zurich, Switzerland, 1994, Reconstructions, Philip and Muriel Berman Mus. Art, Ursinus Coll. Pa., 1995, Matzoh House, Gallery BAI, NY, 1996, Broadway River, NYU, 1997, Earth Bronzes, OK Harris, NY, 1998, Earth Bronze Trilogy-Part I, Buschlen-Mowatt Gallery, Vancouver, Can., 2001, Naked Earth, George C. Page Mus., LA, 2003; Lantern House, George Eastman House, Rochester, NY, 2002, Kouros Gallery, NYC, 2006. Fellowship, Wheaton Village, Millville, NJ, 1983—84. Included in Guinness Book of World Records for blowing world's largest glass bottle, 1995; speaks Spanish, Japanese, and Venetian dialect. Mailing: c/o Kouros Gallery 23 East 73rd St New York NY 10021

TOBIN, THOMAS J., bishop; b. Pitts., Apr. 1, 1948; Grad., St. Mark. Sem. HS, Erie, Pa., St. Francis Coll., Loretto, 1969, PhD (hon.), 1997; studied, Gannon Coll., Erie, North Am. Coll., Rome, Gregorian U., Pontifical Liturgical Inst. of San Anselmo. Ordained priest, 1973; asst. pastor St. Vitus Parish, New Castle, Pa., 1973—79, St. Sebastian Parish, Ross Twp., Pa., 1979—84; adminstrv. sec. to bishop Diocese of Pitts., 1984—87, assoc. gen. sec., 1987—90, vicar gen. & gen. sec., 1990—92; ordained bishop, 1992; Auxiliary Bishop of Pitts., 1992—95; Bishop of Youngstown Ohio, 1996—2005; Bishop of Providence RI, 2005—. Trustee Pontifical Coll. Josephinum, Columbus, Ohio; mem. episcopal adv. bd. Catholics United for the Faith. Mem.: US Conf. Cath. Bishops (mem. adminstrv. com.). Roman Catholic. Office: Diocese of Providence One Cathedral Sq Providence RI 02903

TOBIN, VINCENT MICHAEL, professional football coach, former sports team executive; b. Burlington Junction, Mo., Sept. 29, 1943; BE, U. Mo., 1965, M in Guidance and Counseling, 1966. Def. ends coach Missouri, 1967-70, def. coord., 1971-76, Brit. Columbia Lions CFL, 1977-82, Phila./Balt. Stars USFL, 1983-85, Chgo. Bears NFL, 1986-92, Indpls. Colts NFL, 1994-95; head coach Ariz. Cardinals, 1996—2000.

TOBIN, WILLIAM JOSEPH, newspaper editor; b. Joplin, Mo., July 28, 1927; s. John J. and Lucy T. (Shoppach) Tobin; m. Marjorie Stuhldreher, Apr. 26, 1952; children: Michael Gerard, David Joseph, James Patrick. BS, Butler U., 1948; LLD (hon.), Gonzaga U., 2006. Staff writer AP, Indpls., 1947-52, news feature writer NYC, 1952-54, regional membership exec. Louisville, 1954-56, corr. Juneau, Alaska, 1956-60, asst. chief bur. Balt., 1960-61, Helena, Mont., 1961-63; mng. editor Anchorage Times, 1963-73, assoc. editor, 1973-85, gen. mgr., 1974-85, v.p., editor-in-chief, 1985-89, editor editl. page, 1990, asst. pub., 1991; sr. editor Voice of the Times, 1991—. Mem. devel. com. Anchorage Winter Olympics, 1984-91, bd. dirs. Anchorage organizing com., 1985-91; bd. dirs. Alaska Coun. Econ. Edn., 1978-84, Boys Clubs Alaska, 1979-83, Anchorage Symphony Orch., 1986-87, Blue Cross Wash. and Alaska, 1987—, chmn., 1990-91; chmn. Premera Corp., 1994-99; mem. adv. bd. Providence Hosp., Anchorage, 1974-91, chmn., 1980-85. Sgt. U.S. Army, 1950-52. Mem. Alaska AP Mems. Assn. (pres. 1964), Anchorage C. of C. (bd. dirs. 1969-74, pres. 1972-73), Alaska World Affairs Coun. (pres. 1967-68), Alaska Press Club (pres. 1968-69), Commonwealth North Club (Anchorage). Home: 2130 Lord Baranof Dr Anchorage AK 99517-1257 Office: Anchorage Times PO Box 100040 Anchorage AK 99510-0040 Office Phone: 907-264-8193. Personal E-mail: wjt@alaska.life.net.

TOBIS, JEROME SANFORD, physician; b. Syracuse, NY, July 23, 1915; s. David George and Anna (Feinberg) T.; m. Hazel Weisbard, Sept. 18, 1938; children: David, Heather, Jonathan. BS, CCNY, 1936; MD, Chgo. Med. Sch., 1943. Diplomate Am. Bd. Phys. Medicine and Rehab. Intern Knickerbocker Hosp., 1943-44; resident Bronx VA Hosp., 1946-48; med. dir. state fever therapy unit USPHS, Brookhaven, Miss., 1944-46; practice medicine NYC, 1948-70; prof. dir. dept. phys. medicine and rehab. N.Y. Med. Coll., Flower and Fifth Av. Hosps., 1948-61; prof. rehab. medicine Albert Einstein Coll. of Medicine, 1963-70; chief div. rehab. medicine Montefiore Hosp., 1961-70; dir. vis. physician Met., Bird S. Coler hosps., 1952-61; prof., chmn. dept. phys. medicine and rehab. Calif. Coll. Medicine, U. Calif. at Irvine, 1970-82, prof., dir. program in geriatric medicine and gerontology, 1980-86; mem. adv. com. Acad. Geriatric Resource program, 1984-86, 95—. Expert med. com. Am. Rehab. Found., 1961-70; cons. Dept. Health, NYC, Long Beach VA Hosp., 1970—, Fairview State Devel. Ctr., 1976—; adv. coun. phys. medicine and rehab. for appeals com. Calif. Med. Assn., 1971-74, adv. com. U. Calif. Acad. Geriatric Resource Program, 1995—; NIH Internat. Fogarty fellow, hon. lectr., dept. geriat. medicine U. Birmingham, 1979-80; rev. panel musculoskeletal diseases NIH, 1996; rsch. prof. dept. phys. medicine & rehab. U. Calif., Irvine, 1986—, chair med. ethics com., 1986—; mem. Ctr. Health Policy Rsch. U. Calif., Davis, 1996—. Mem. editorial bd.: Heart and Lung, 1973-76, Geriatrics, 1975-80, Archives of Phys. Medicine and Rehab, 1958-73. Named Physician of the Year, 1957; recipient Distinguished Alumnus award Chgo. Med. Sch., 1972, Acad. award Nat. Inst. on Aging, 1981-86; named hon. faculty mem. Calif. Zeta chpt. Alpha Omega Alpha, 1981; Leavitt Meml. lectureship Baylor Coll. Medicine, 1983, Griffith Meml. lectureship Am. Geriatric Soc., 1984; Australian Coll. Rehabilitation Medicine, 1984; Jerome S. Tobis Ann. Conf. on Geriatric Medicine established in his name, U. Calif. at Irvine, 1986. Fellow ACP, Am. Coll. Cardiology, Am. Congress Rehab. Medicine (hon.); mem. AMA (mem. residency rev. com. Coun. Med. Edn. 1973), AAAS, Am. Acad. Cerebral Palsy, Am. Acad. Phys. Medicine and Rehab. (Disting. Clinician award 1993), Am. Congress Rehab. Medicine (pres. 1962), Calif. Coun. Gerontology and Geriatrics (bd. dirs. 1980-86, pres. 1985), N.Y. Acad. Medicine, N.Y. Acad. Sci., Orange County Med. Soc., Assn. U. Calif. Irvine (chair emeritae/i 1996-97). Home: 1115 Goldenrod Ave Corona Del Mar CA 92625-1508 Home Phone: 949-644-8908. Personal E-mail: jstobis@uci.edu.

TOBISMAN, STUART PAUL, lawyer; b. Detroit, June 5, 1942; s. Nathan and Beverly (Porvin) T.; m. Karen Sue Tobisman, Aug. 8, 1965; children: Cynthia Elaine, Neal Jay. BA, UCLA, 1966; JD, U. Calif., Berkeley, 1969. Bar: Calif. 1969. Assoc. O'Melveny & Myers, LA, 1969-77, ptnr., 1977—2006, Loeb & Loeb LLP, LA, 2006—. Contbr. articles to profl. jours. Trustee L.A. County Bar Assn., 1983-84. With USN, 1961-63. Fellow Am. Coll. Trust and Estate Counsel; mem. Phi Beta Kappa, Order of Coif. Office: Loeb & Loeb LLP 10100 Santa Monica Blvd Los Angeles CA 90067-4120

TOBY, JACKSON, sociologist, educator; b. NYC, Sept. 10, 1925; m. Marcia Lifshitz, Aug. 1, 1952 (dec. Jan. 1997); children: Alan Steven, Gail Afriat (dec.). BA, Bklyn. Coll., 1946; MA in Econs, Harvard U., 1947, MA in Sociology, 1949, PhD in Sociology, 1950. Rsch. assoc. Lab. Social Relations, Harvard, 1950-51; mem. faculty Rutgers U., 1951—2002, prof. sociology, chmn. dept., 1961-68, prof. sociology emeritus, 2002, dir. Inst. for Criminological Rsch., 1969-94; vis. scholar Am. Enterprise Inst., 2004—. Cons. Youth Devel. Program, Ford Found., 1959-63 Author: (with H.C. Bredemeier) Social Problems in America, 1960, 2d edit., 1971; Contemporary Society, 1964, 2d edit., 1971; contbr. numerous articles to profl. jours., pub. policy jours., N.Y. Times, Wall St. Jour., L.A. Times, Chgo. Tribune, Washington Post, The Weekly Standard, Nat. Rev., Sociol. Rsch. Cons., Pres.'s Commn. Law Enforcement and Adminstrn. Justice, 1966; trustee NAMI-N.J., 1997-2000. Recipient Rsch. Excellence award, Rutgers U. Bd. Trustees, 1984, numerous research grants. Mem. Am. Sociol. Assn., Sociol. Rsch. Assn., Am. Soc. Criminology, Nat. Assn. Scholars. Achievements include spl. research adolescent delinquency in U.S., Sweden, Japan, other countries, on violence and dropouts in Am. public schools. Home: 17 Harrison Ave Highland Park NJ 08904-1813 Office: Rutgers U Dept Sociology Lucy Stone Hall Livingston Campus New Brunswick NJ 08903 Home Phone: 732-545-2615. Business E-Mail: jtoby@rci.rutgers.edu.

TOCCO, JAMES, pianist; b. Detroit, Sept. 21, 1943; s. Vincenzo and Rose (Tabbita) T.; 1 child, Rhoya. Prof. music Ind. U., Bloomington, 1977-91; prof. Musikhochschule, Lübeck, Germany, 1990—2006, Manhattan Sch. Music, 2002—; eminent scholar, artist-in-residence U. Cin. Coll.-Conservatory Music, 1991—; artistic dir. Great Lakes Chamber Music Festival, 1994—. Debut with orch., Detroit, 1956, since performed with Chgo. Symphony, LA Philharm., Cin. Symphony, Detroit Symphony, Nat. Symphony, Balt. Symphony, Atlanta Symphony, Denver Symphony, Montreal Symphony, Philharm. Orch., London Symphony, London Philharm., BBC Orch., Berlin Philharm., Moscow Radio-TV Orch., Amsterdam Philharm., Munich Philharm., Bavarian Radio Orch., Royal Concertebouw Orch., also recitals, US and abroad, and performances, CBS and NBC networks; guest performer, White House; Recs. include the complete preludes of Chopin, collected piano works of Leonard Bernstein, complete piano works of Charles Tomlinson Griffes, 4 piano sonatas of Edward MacDowell, selected piano works of Aaron Copland, complete Bach-Liszt organ transcriptions, piano works of John Corigliano. concertos of Igor Stravinsky, Leonard Bernstein, and John Corigliano. Recipient Bronze medal Tchaikovsky Competition, Moscow 1970, Queen Elisabeth of Belgium Competition, Brussels 1972, Salzburg Festival, 1st prize Piano Competition of Americas, Rio de Janeiro 1973, Munich Internat. Competition 1973. Office: U Cin Coll Conservatory Musi Cincinnati OH 45221-0001 Business E-Mail: toccojv@ucmail.uc.edu.

TODARO, GEORGE JOSEPH, pathologist, researcher; b. NYC, July 1, 1937; s. George J. and Antoinette (Piccinni) Todaro; m. Jane Lehv, Aug. 12, 1962; children: Wendy C., Thomas M., Anthony A. BS, Swarthmore Coll., 1958; MD, NYU, 1963. Intern NYU Sch. Medicine, NYC, 1963—64, fellow in pathology, 1964—65, asst. prof. pathology, 1965—67; staff assoc. Viral Carcinogenesis br. Nat. Cancer Inst., Bethesda, Md., 1967—70, head molecular biology sect., 1969—70; chief Viral Carcinogenesis br. Nat. Cancer Inst. (Lab. Viral Carcinogenesis), 1970—83; sci. dir., pres. Oncogen, Seattle, 1987—90; sr. v.p. exploratory biomed. rsch. Bristol-Myers Squibb Pharm. Rsch. Inst., 1990; pres., CEO Cytokine Networks, Inc., Seattle, 1998—; now prof. pathobiology U. Wash., Seattle. Adj. prof. pathology U. Wash., Seattle, 1983—, past chmn. dept. pathobiology; sr. v.p., sci. dir. Pathogenesis Corp., Seattle, 1992—95; mem. Fred Hutchinson Cancer Rsch. Ctr., Seattle, 1991—93. Editor: Cancer Rsch., 1973—86, Archives of Virology, 1976—, Jour. Biol. Chemistry, 1979; contbr. articles to profl. jours. Med. officer USPHS, 1967—69. Named Walter Hubert lectr., Brit. Cancer Soc., 1977; recipient Borden Undergrad. Rsch. award, 1963, Career Devel. award, USPHS, 1967, HEW Superior Svc. award, 1971, Gustav Stern award for virology, 1972, Parke-Davis award in exptl. pathology, 1975. Mem.: Am. Soc. Clin. Investigation, Am. Soc. hemists, Soc. Exptl. Biology and Medicine, Am. Assn. Cancer Rsch., Am. Soc. Microbiology, NAS. Home: 1940 15th Ave E Seattle WA 98112-2829 Office Phone: 206-336-5572. E-mail: gtodaro@targetedgrowth.com.

TODARO, JULIE BETH, libraries dean, association executive; BS, Sch. Edn., U. Tex., Austin, 1971; MLIS, Grad. Sch. Libr. and Info., U. Tex., Austin, 1972; PhD, Sch. Libr. Sci., Columbia U., NYC, 1984. Children and young adult specialist Looscan Br. Libr., Houston Pub. Libr., 1972—75; adj. faculty sch. libr. sci. Sam Houston State U., 1977; children's and young adult specialist, libr. III Jungman Br. Libr., Houston Pub. Libr., 1975—79; tchg. asst. sch. libr. svc. Columbia U., NYC, 1979—80; asst. prof. sch. info. and libr. studies U. Mich., Ann Arbor, 1980—85; dean of libraries Austin Cmty. Coll., Faculty Devel. Learning Resource Services, 1985—; adj. faculty grad. sch. libr. and info. sci. U. Tex., Austin, 1986—; pres., mem. bd. dirs. Connections Resource Ctr., 1996—. Mem. libr. services and constrn. act bd. Tex. State Libr. and Archives Commn., 1993—96, chair libr. services and tech. act bd., 1996—98, chair sch. libr. standards, 1996—98; commr. adv. commn. Austin Pub. Libr., 1994—98, mem., 1998—; co-chair pub. rels. com. Austin Cmty. Coll., Faculty Devel. Learning Resource Services, co-chair devel. com. Mem. steering com. on first lady of Tex. Tex. Book Festival, 1995—. Recipient Edn. award, Nat. Assn. Women in Bus., Austin/Tex. Chpt., 1997. Mem.: Assn. Coll. & Rsch. Libraries (mem. steering com. Info. Lit. Inst. 1997—, pres.-elect 2006—07, pres. 2007—), Tex. Libr. Assn. (co-chair legis. day 1993—, pres. 2000—01, chair Tex. book festival grant com., mem. exec. bd., Libr. of Yr. award 1996), ALA (mem., chair human resources adv. com.). Office: Austin Cmty Coll Rio Grande Campus 1212 Rio Grande Austin TX 78701-1710 Office Phone: 512-223-3071. Office Fax: 512-223-3431. Business E-Mail: jtodaro@austincc.edu. *

TODARO, PETER M., lawyer; b. Easton, Pa., July 20, 1970; s. James M. and Bernice P. Todaro; m. Tanya M. Masri, Sept. 23, 1995; children: Isabella Marie, James Michael, Sofia Grace. BA in Econs. and Fgn. Affairs, U. Va., Charlottesville, 1992, JD, 1996. Bar: Va. 1996, US Ct. Appeals (4th cir.) 1996, DC 1997, US Ct. Appeals (DC cir.) 1998, US Ct. Appeals (7th cir.) 2001, US Ct. Appeals (3rd cir.) 2001, US Supreme Ct. 2002. Assoc. King & Spalding LLP, Washington, 1996—2004; ptnr. King & Spalding LLP, Washington, 2005—. Mem. editl. bd.: Va. Law Rev., 1994—96. Vol. Make-A-Wish Found. of Mid-Atlantic, 2006—, spkr., 2006—. Mem.: ABA (antitrust sect.), Va. Bar Assn., Order of the Coif. Avocation: skiing. Office: King & Spalding 1700 Pennsylvania Ave NW Washington DC 20006 Office Phone: 202-626-5518. Business E-Mail: ptodaro@kslaw.com.

TODD, CAROL, music educator; b. Paulding, Ohio, Apr. 2, 1942; d. Merle and Glendine Jeffery; m. Larry Todd, Aug. 15, 1964; children: Tara Michelle Lineweaver, Trista Lynn Todt. BS, Bowling Green State U., Ohio, 1963; MA, Ohio State U., 1968. Cert. music tchr. Ohio Edn. Dept., elem. tchr. Ohio Edn. Dept., kindergarten tchr. Ohio Edn. Dept. Music tchr. grades 1-12 Licking Heights Sch. Dist., Summit Station, Ohio, 1964—67; music tchr. grades 7-12 Hilliard City Schs., Ohio, 1967—69; music tchr. grades 9-12 Clark-Shawnee Local Schs., Springfield, Ohio, 1982—98; asst. prof. music Cedarville U., Ohio, 1998—2006, Wittenberg U., Springfield, 2000—. Dist. rep. curriculum course study Clark County, Ohio, 1988, Ohio, 93; guest condr. Springfield Symphony All-County Choir, 1992, Ohio Music Educators All-Dist. XII Women's Choir, Dayton, 1997, Clark County All-County Choir Festival, Springfield, 2001; adj. prof. music Clark State C.C., Springfield, 1996—2002; clinician Ohio Music Educators' State Conf., Columbus, Ohio, 2004, Cin., 05. Campaign collector March of Dimes, Springfield, 2000—; min. music Maumee United Meth. Ch., Ohio, 1972—74; leadership coun. Asbury United Meth. Ch., North Hampton, Ohio, 2000—04; active High Street United Meth. Ch., Springfield, 2004—. Recipient Tchr. Achievement award, Ashland Oil Co., 1993, 1995, 1997, Excellence in Tchg. award, Clark County News Assn., 1997. Mem.: Ohio Ret. Tchrs. Assn., Ohio Music Educators' Assn. (Ohio Music Educator 25+ Years award 1999), Am. Choral Dirs. Assn., Music Educators' Nat. Conf. (student chpt. advisor). Republican. Avocations: tennis, musical theater, singing, camping, bridge. Home: 3985 St James Ct Springfield OH 45502 Office: Wittenberg Univ Music Dept PO Box 720 Springfield OH 45501 Office Phone: 937-327-7341. Office Fax: 937-327-7347. Business E-Mail: ctodd@wittenberg.edu.

TODD, CATHERINE JACKSON, writer; b. LA, Jan. 31, 1947; d. Hubert Edward and Carolyn Arden (Laws) Jackson; m. Timothy Gordon Todd, Aug. 24, 1968. AB cum laude, Occidental Coll., 1968; MA, Stanford U., 1969. Cert. tchr., Calif. Tchr. English, French Sequoia Union H.S., Redwood City, Calif., 1968-73, Country Day Sch., San José, Costa Rica, 1970-72; tchr. English Grossmont Union H.S., La Mesa, Calif., 1991-93; bus. svcs. writer San Diego, 1993—. Author: Bond of Honor, 1981, Mariam, 1991, (as Elizabeth Jackson) A Brilliant Alliance, 1993, (as Elizabeth Jackson) Galatea's Revenge, 1993, (as Elizabeth Jackson) Rogue's Delight, 1995, Making Waves, 1997, Staying Cool, 1997, Exit Strategies, 2002, Secret Lives of Second Wives, 2003; contbr. articles to profl. jours. Mem. Authors Guild, Romance Writers Am., Phi Beta Kappa. E-mail: cathetoddbooks@aol.com.

TODD, CHRISTOPHER MICHAEL, marketing executive, consultant; b. Waukesha, Wis., Aug. 16, 1970; s. Michael Burgess Todd and Billie Jeanette Koepke. BA in Journalism and Mass Comm., Drake U., Des Moines, 1992. Lic. capt. USCG, 2006, registered Notary Public Fla., 2002. Account mgr. Schneider Comm., Milw., 1993—96; account exec. Entertainment Publs., Deerfield Beach, Fla., 1996—98; sr. mgr. interactive mktg. CBS SportsLine.com, Ft. Lauderdale, Fla., 1998—2000; analyst Jupiter Rsch., NYC, 2000—01; pres. Christopher Todd, Inc., Miami Beach, Fla., 2002—. Mktg. cons. PartyPoker.com, Santo Domingo, Dominican Republic, 2001—06. Flotilla staff officer USCG Aux., Miami, 2006; mem. City of Miami Beach Marine Authority Bd., Fla., Rep. Nat. Com., Washington, 2006. Mem.: US Boating Assn., Miami Beach Yacht Club, Pi Kappa Phi (Beta Delta chpt., pres. 1990—91). Office: Christopher Todd Inc 1521 Alton Rd #628 Miami Beach FL 33139 Business E-Mail: ct@christophertodd.us.

TODD, EWEN CAMERON DAVID, food safety director; b. Glasgow, United Kingdom, Dec. 25, 1939; s. David Macnair and Viva Macdonald Jane (Young) Todd; m. Zora Isobel Carson Third, Sept. 18, 1943; children: Andrew John Cameron, Amanda Jean, Natasha Jane, Alexander Richard. BSc in Bacteriology with honors, Glasgow U., 1963, PhD in Bacterial Systematics, 1968. Rsch. scientist Health Can., Ottawa, Ontario, Canada, 1968—2001; dir., nat. food safety & toxicology ctr. Mich. State U., E.Lansing, 2001—06, dir., food safety policy ctr., 2005—. Contbr. chapters to books, articles to prof. jours. Pres. Citizens for Safe Cycling, Ottawa, 1988—92; adminstrv. clk. of session St. Andrew's Ch., Ottawa, 1995—2001; chair rsch. table bargaining team Profl. Inst. Pub. Svc. Can., Ottawa, 1997—2001; pres. Ottawa Field-Naturalists' Club, Ottawa, 1974—75. Recipient Citation award, Internat. Assn. Milk, Food & Environ. Sanitarians, 1992, Excellence in Sci. award, Health Can., 1998, Conservation award, Ottawa Field-Naturalists Club, 1999, Dep. Minister's Team Excellence award, Health Can., 1999, Fellows award, Internat. Assn. Food Protection, 2001, Gold Medal award, Profl. Inst. Pub. Svc. Can., 2001. Fellow: Internat. Assn. Food Protection (com. control foodborne illness chair 2000—07); mem.: Soc. Risk Analysis (chair biostressors grp. 2003—05), Inst. Food Technologists (assoc. editor 2006—07), Ottawa Field-Naturalists Club. Presbyterian. Achievements include research in food safety, microbiology, safety policy and surveillance. Avocations: history, gardening. Home: 4183 Indian Glen Dr Okemos MI 48864 Office: Nat Food Safety & Toxicology Ctr Mich State Univ 165 NFST Bldg East Lansing MI 48824 Office Fax: 517-432-2310. Business E-Mail: toddewen@cvm.msu.edu.

TODD, JAMES DALE, federal judge; b. Scotts Hill, Tenn., May 20, 1943; s. James P. and Jeanette Grace (Duck) T.; m. Jeanie M. Todd, June 26, 1965; 2 children. BS, Lambuth Coll., 1965; M Combined Scis., U. Miss., 1968; JD, Memphis State U., 1972. Bar: Tenn. 1972, U.S. Dist. Ct. (we. dist.) Tenn. 1972, U.S. Ct. Appeals (6th cir.) 1973, U.S. Supreme Ct. 1975. Tchr. sci., chmn. sci. dept. Lyman High Sch., Longwood, Fla., 1965-68, Memphis U. Sch., 1968-72; ptnr. Waldrop, Farmer, Todd & Breen, P.A., 1972-83; cir. judge div. II 26th Jud. Dist., Jackson, Tenn., 1983-85; judge US Dist. Ct. (we. dist.) Tenn., Jackson, 1985-2001, chief judge, 2001—. Recipient Lifetime Achievement award Lambuth U., 2001; named Alumnus of Yr. Lambuth Coll. Alumni Assn., 1985. Fellow Tenn. Bar Found.; mem. Fed. Judges Assn. (bd. dirs. 1998-2002), Fed. Bar Assn., Jackson Madison County Bar Assn. (pres. 1978-79), Dist. Judges Assn. of 6th Cir. (pres. 2000-2001). Methodist. Office: US Dist Ct 111 S Highland Ave Jackson TN 38301-6107

TODD, JAMES MARION, retired lawyer; b. Paris, Ky., May 13, 1929; s. Thomas Marion and Ida Saxton (Estes) T.; m. Marjorie Ann Vance, Aug. 22, 1959; children: Thomas Melvin, James M. Jr. AB, U. Ky., Lexington, 1952, JD, 1956. Bar: Ky. 1956. Assoc. S.J. Stallings, Louisville, 1956-57; sole practice Lexington, Ky., 1957-65, 1982-86; ptnr. Todd & Compton, Lexington, 1965-73, Todd & Sherrow, Lexington, 1973-82, Todd & Todd, Lexington, 1986-88, Todd, Hicks & Todd, Lexington, 1988-92, Todd, Bradley & Hicks, Lexington, 1992-93; pvt. practice Lexington, 1993—2002. Vice mayor Lexington-Fayette County Govt., 1978-82; ch. elder. Served in Korean War, ret. as maj. USAF, 1952-54. U. Ky. Fellow. Fellow Ky. Bar Found. (charter, life); mem. Lions (pres. breakfast club 1965-66). Republican. Home: 395 Redding Rd # 28 Lexington KY 40517 Home Phone: 859-263-5502. E-mail: toddyhot@aol.com.

TODD, JOHN DICKERSON, JR., retired lawyer; b. Macon, Ga., June 30, 1912; s. J.D. and Hazel (McManus) T.; m. Mellicent McWhorter, Mar. 7, 1943; children— Rosalind (Mrs. Jack Harding Tedards, Jr.), John D. Student, Va. Mil. Inst., 1930-32; LLB, U. Ga., 1935. Bar: S.C. 1935. With firm Hingson & Todd, 1935-51; partner firm Leatherwood, Walker, Todd & Mann, Greenville, SC, 1952-2000; sr. partner; judge Greenville City Ct., 1939; atty. County of Greenville, 1948-56; mem. bd. bar examiners State of S.C.; ret. Chmn. S.C. Judicial Study Commn., 1995. Served to maj. AUS, 1941-45. Mem.: ABA, Greenville County Bar (past pres.), Greenville Jr. C. of C. (pres.), S.C. Bar Assn. (bd. govs., pres. 1978—), 4th U.S. Cir. Jud. Conf., Am. Bar Found., Am. Coll. Trial Lawyers, Poinsett Club, Greenville Country Club (past pres.), Greenville Kiwanis (past pres.), Sigma Nu, Phi Delta Phi. Baptist. Home: 200 Riverside Dr Greenville SC 29605-1133 Office Phone: 864-232-6440.

TODD, JOHN EDWARD, retired farmer; b. Waynesboro, Va., Feb. 8, 1924; s. Andrew James Todd and Clare Elizabeth Kennedy; m. Jessica Frances Swisher, June 8, 1946; children: John Jr., Cheryl, Jeffrey S., Darcel(dec.), Michell L. BS, U. Md., 1965; MEd, U. Va., 1973, D of Edn., 1976. Commd. lt. U.S. Army, 1952, advanced through grades to capt., 1957, sgt. air crew, 1942—47; sgt. supply specialist USAF, 1948—51; lt. airborne US Army, 1952—64, lt. spl. forces A team, 1956—57, capt. spl. forces 1st lt. team A, 1956—57, capt. spl. forces, 1957—64, ret., 1964; owner beef cattle farm, 1966—98. Mem.: Reserve Officers Assn., Military Officer Assn. Am., Nat. Assn. Uniformed Svcs., Disabled Am. Vets., VFW, Am. Legion. Republican. Presbyterian. Home: 368 Poor Creek Ln Greenville VA 24440-1809

TODD, JOHN JOSEPH, lawyer; b. St. Paul, Mar. 16, 1927; s. John Alfred and Martha Agnes (Jagoe) Todd; m. Dolores Jean Shanahan, Sept. 9, 1950; children: Richard M., Jane E., John P. Student, St. Thomas Coll., 1944, 46-47; BSc and Law, U. Minn., 1949, LLB, 1950. Bar: Minn. 1951. Practice in, South St. Paul, Minn., 1951-72; partner Thuet and Todd, 1953-72; asso. justice Minn. Supreme Ct., St. Paul, 1972-85; sole practice West St. Paul, 1985-92; of counsel Brenner & Glassman Ltd., Mpls., 1992—99, Orme & Assoc., Eagan, Minn., 1999—. With USNR, 1945—46. Mem.: VFW. Home: 6689 Argenta Trl W Inver Grove Heights MN 55077-2208 Office: Orme & Assocs 4040 Nicols Rd Saint Paul MN 55121 Home Phone: 651-454-1113; Office Phone: 651-688-7646. Personal E-mail: jjbtodd@comcast.net. Business E-Mail: jtodd@ormelaw.com.

TODD, LEE TROVER, JR., academic administrator, electrical engineer; b. Earlington, Ky., May 6, 1946; s. Lee T. Todd; m. Patricia Brantley; children: Troy, Kathryn. BSEE, U. Ky., 1968; MS, MIT, 1970, PhD in Elec. Engring., 1973. IBM postdoctoral fellow MIT, 1973-74; asst. prof. engring. U. Ky., Lexington, 1974-78, assoc. prof., 1978-87, pres., 2001—; chmn., chief exec. officer DataBeam Corp., Lexington, 1983—2000; v.p. Hughes Display Products, Lexington, 1993—93; sr. v.p. pres. Lotus Devel. Corp., 2000—01. Chmn. Ky. Sci. & Tech. Coun., Lexington, 1987—; mem. Ky. Epscor Com., 1985—, Ky. Acad. Sci., 1988; chair Southeastern Conf. Com. on Academic Initiatives; mem. Cou. of Edn. Commn. Contbr. articles to profl. jours. Chmn., deacon Calvary Bapt. Ch., Lexington, 1989; bd. dirs. Ky. Econ. Devel. Corp., Frankfort, Georgetown Coll., Ky. Named Entrepreneur of Yr., INC mag., 1989; recipient Outstanding Alumnus award U. Ky. Coll. Engring., 1989, Small Bus. of Yr. award Lexington C. of C., U.S. Gt. Tchr. award, 1983; Hertz Found. fellow, 1968-73. Mem. NSF, Ky. Soc. Profl. Engrs. (Award of Achievement 1990), U. Ky. Alumni Assn., Leadership Ky., Louisville Adv. Tech. Coun. Baptist. Achievements include patents in field. Office: Pres Office U Ky 101 Main Building Lexington KY 40506-0032 Office Phone: 859-257-1701. Office Fax: 859-257-1760. E-mail: ltodd@email.uky.edu. *

TODD, LINDA MARIE, nutrition researcher, circulation manager, financial consultant, pilot; b. LA, Mar. 30, 1948; d. Ithel Everette and Janet Marie Fredricks; m. William MacKenzie Cook, Jan. 11, 1982 (div. Oct. 1989); m. Robert Oswald Todd, Apr. 8, 1990; 1 child, Jesse MacKenzie Todd. BA in Psychology and Sociology, U. Colo., 1969; student in Psychology, U. No. Colo., 1970; ins. and estate planning courses, 1990—, mgmt. tng. programs, 2001—. Pilot lic., weather cert., FCC lic., Calif. life ins. lic., coll. teaching credential; registered with Nat. Assn. Securities Dealers. Counselor Jeffco Juvenile Detention Ctr., Golden, Colo., 1969-71; communications Elan Vital, Denver, 1971-81; legal sec. Fredman, Silverberg & Lewis, San Diego, 1980-82; escrow supr. Performance Mktg. Concepts, Olympic Valley, Calif., 1982-85; mgmt. commn. instr. Sierra Coll., Truckee, Calif., 1986-87; regional mgr. Primerica Fin. Svcs., Reno, 1987-91; air traffic, weather advisor Truckee Tahoe Airport Dist., Calif., 1986-96; circulation mgr. Sierra Sun and Tahoe World Newspapers, 2001—. Student tour leader, air show organizer Truckee (Calif.) Tahoe Airport, 1986-96; fin. cons. Primerica Fin. Svcs., Truckee, 1987-91; gen. agt. TTS Fin., 1992—; co-founder Todd Nutrition, 1995—; co-owner Todd Aero, 1990—; bd. dirs. Pacific Crest Fin. Corp., 1996—. Editor: (newsletter) Communications, 1975. Chorus mem. operas and musicals, 1960s-70s; prodn. crew Lake Tahoe Summer Music Festivals, 2000-03; sec. gen. Arapahoe H.S. Model UN, Littleton, Colo., 1965; del. State Model UN, Colo., 1966; conv. del. Elan Vital, The Ninety-Nines, Inc.; pub. affairs officer CAP. Univ. scholar Littleton (Colo.) Edn. Assn., 1966, flight scholar The Ninety-Nines Inc., Reno, 1990; named Recruiter of Month, Al Williams Primerica, Reno, 1987. Mem. CAP (lt.), Elan Vital, Plane Talkers, The Ninety Nines, Planetary Soc. Avocations: hiking, skiing, swimming, flying, soaring. Home and Office: PO Box 1303 Truckee CA 96160-1303 Personal E-mail: toddaero@sbcglobal.net.

TODD, MARGARET DONNELLAN, library director; MLS, U. So. Calif., LA; MBA, Pepperdine U., Malibu, Calif. Sr. libr. mgr. Orange Pub. Libr., Calif.; dir. Whittier Pub. Libr., Calif., 1989—2001; county libr. County of LA Pub. Libr., 2001—. Mem.: Calif. Libr. Assn. (pres. 2006—07). Office: County of LA Pub Libr 7400 E Imperial Hwy Downey CA 90241-7011 Office Phone: 562-940-8400. E-mail: mdtodd@gw.colapl.org. *

TODD, MARY BETH, oncologist, researcher; b. Tulsa, Okla., June 10, 1951; d. Earl K. and Edith (Beaty) T. BA, Okla. City U., 1972; postgrad., U. Tulsa, 1973-74; DO, Okla. State U., 1978. Assoc. rsch. scientist Yale Sch. Medicine, New Haven, 1984-86; dir. outpatient svc. Yale Medical Sch., New Haven, 1986-93; asst. prof. Sch. Medicine Yale U., New Haven, 1986-91, assoc. prof., 1991-93; assoc. prof. medicine UMDNJ-RWJMS, New Brunswick, 1993—2002, prof. medicine, 2002—; deputy dir. The Cancer Inst. N.J., New Brunswick, NJ, 1993—, COO, chief med. officer, 2005—. Scientific adv. panel for immunology svcs. Food & Drug Adminstrn., Washington, 1991-95; scientific adv. bd. HEM Pharmeceuticals Corp., 1991-93; external medical adv. bd. Conn. Hospice, 1990-92; co-chair N.J. Working Group to Improve Outcomes in Cancer Patients. Recipient grants Nat. Inst. Health, 1989-98. Mem. Am. Coll. Physicians, Am. Fedn. Clinical Rsch., Am. Soc. Clinical Oncology, Am. Assn. Cancer Rsch., Am. Soc. Hematology, Internat. Soc. Interferon and Cytokine Rsch. Office: The Cancer Inst NJ 195 Little Albany St New Brunswick NJ 08903-2681

TODD, MURRAY, retail executive; B, Boise State U, Idaho. With Super Thrift Drugstores, 1974—79; store mgr., dist. mgr. to v.p. ops. PayLess Drug Stores, 1979—89; v.p. procurement Thrifty PayLess, 1994; group v.p. store svcs. and procurement Fred Meyer Stores, 1997—2000; sr. v.p. store ops. and procurement Rite Aid Corp., 2000—. Office: Rite Aid Corp 30 Hunter Ln Camp Hill PA 17011 Office Phone: 717-761-2633. *

TODD, ROBERT FRANKLIN, III, oncologist, educator; b. Granville, Ohio, Apr. 16, 1948; m. Susan Erhard, 1977; children: Currier Nathaniel, Andrew Joseph. AB, Duke U., 1970, PhD, 1975, MD, 1976. Diplomate Am. Bd. Internal Medicine. Intern Peter Bent Brigham Hosp., Boston, 1976-77, resident, 1977-78; fellow in oncology Sidney Farber Cancer Inst., Boston, 1978-80; clin. fellow in medicine Harvard Med. Sch., Boston, 1978-81; postdoctoral fellow divsn. tumor immunology Sidney Farber Cancer Inst., Boston, 1979-81; asst. prof. medicine Harvard Med. Sch., Boston, 1981-84; assoc. prof. internal medicine U. Mich., Ann Arbor, 1984-88, assoc. prof. cellular and molecular biology, 1985-88, assoc. dir. divsn. hematology-oncology internal medicine, 1987-91, prof. internal medicine, 1988—, assoc. chair for rsch. dept. internal medicine, 1989-91, assoc. chair dept. internal medicine, 1991-93, chief divsn. hematology-oncology dept. internal medicine, 1993—2007, assoc. v.p. rsch., 1999—2005, Frances and Victor Ginsberg prof. hematology/oncology, 1999—, interim chair, dept. internal medicine, 2007—. Attending physician U. Mich. Hosps., 1984—. Contbr. numerous articles to profl. jours.; patentee in field. Mem.: Assn. Am. Physicians, Am. Soc. Clin. Investigation, S.W. Oncology Group, Ctrl. Soc. Clin. Rsch. (councilor 1997—, pres. 2001—02), Am. Fedn. Clin. Rsch. (councilor midwest chpt. 1986—89), Am. Soc. Hematology (councilor 2005—), Soc. Leukocyte Biology (councilor 1996—99), Am. Soc. Clin. Oncology, Am. Assn. Cancer Rsch., Am. Assn. Immunologists, ACP, Alpha Omega Alpha, Phi Beta Kappa. Office: U Mich Med Sch 1500 E Med Ctr Dr 3101 Hartman Ctr Ann Arbor MI 48109-5368 Business E-Mail: robtodd@umich.edu.

TODD, RONALD GARY, lawyer; b. Spokane, Wash., Dec. 12, 1946; s. Theodore H. and Dorothea I. (Swanson) T.; m. Natalie A., June 16, 1973; children: Russell E., Brian N., David E. AB, Cornell U., 1969; JD, Columbia U., 1972. Bar: NY 1973, US Dist. Ct. (so. and ea. dists.) NY 1975, US Ct. Appeals (2d cir.) 1975, US Supreme Ct. 1976, DC 1993. Atty. Dewey Ballantine, NYC, 1973-79, Simpson Thacher & Bartlett, NYC, 1980-82; atty., ptnr. Golenbock & Barell, NYC, 1982-89; ptnr. Reid & Priest (now Thelen Reid Brown Reysman & Steiner LLP), NYC, 1989-2000; chief counsel J.P. Morgan Title Agy. LLC, 2000—05; v.p., asst. gen. counsel JP Morgan Chase & Co., 2000—05; v.p., Nat. Underwriting Counsel First Am. Title Ins. Co. NY, NYC, 2005—. Instr., guest lectr. NYU Sch. Continuing Edn., 1983-90; adv. bd. Commonwealth Land Title and TransAm. Title Ins. Co., NYC, 1992-97. Contbr. articles to profl. jours. Pres., bd. dirs. Seven Bridges Field Club, 1982—85. Mem. ABA (real property sect. 1973—), NY Bar Assn. (real property sect. 1973—), DC Bar Assn. (real property sect. 1992—2006). Avocations: instrumental music, tennis. Office: First Am Title Ins Co NY 633 Third Ave New York NY 10017 Business E-Mail: rgtodd@firstam.com.

TODD, STEPHEN MAX, retired lawyer; b. Kansas City, Mo., Oct. 22, 1941; s. Louis O. and A. Maxine (Mittag); m. Carlene Harre; children: Stephanie A., Louis P. BA, Kans. State U., 1963; JD, U. Kans., 1966. Bar: Kans. 1966, U.S. Dist. Ct. Kans. 1966, U.S. Ct. Appeals (10th cir.) 1967, U.S. Supreme Ct. 1971, Mo. 1973. Assoc. Schroeder, Heeney, Groff & Spies, Topeka, 1966-72; office counsel Chgo. Title Ins. Co., Kansas City, Mo., 1973-78, regional counsel, 1978—2006, ret., 2006. Author: Missouri Foreclosure Manual, 2007; contbr., editor books. Mem. Kans. Bar Assn., Mo. Bar (chmn. property law com. 1990-92), Am. Coll. Real Estate Lawyers, Kiwanis (pres. Topeka Downtown Club 1971-72, lt. gov. Mo.-Ark. dist. 1976-77, pres. Kansas City South Platte Club 1979-80), Phi Delta Phi. Home: 137 NW Pointe Dr Kansas City MO 64116-4616 Personal E-mail: stoddinkc@kc.rr.com.

TODD, VIRGIL HOLCOMB, clergyman, theology studies educator; b. Jordonia, Tenn., June 22, 1921; s. George Thurman and Nellie Mai (Dutton) T.; m. Irene Rolman, Sept. 21, 1941; 1 child, Donald Edwin. BA, Bethel Coll., 1945; BD, Cumberland Presbyn. Sem., 1947; MA, Scarritt Coll., 1948; PhD, Vanderbilt U., 1956. Ordained to ministry Presbyn. Ch., 1944. Minister Cumberland Presbyn. Chs., Tenn. and Ky., 1943-52; assoc. prof. Bethel Coll., McKenzie, Tenn., 1952-54; prof. of Old Testament Memphis Theol. Sem., 1954-2001, ret., 2001. Interim minister Presbyn. chs. in Tenn., Ky. and Miss., 1952—; vice-moderator Gen. Assembly Cumberland Presbyn. Ch., 1984-85, moderator, 1985-86. Author: Prophet Without Portfolio (2d Isaiah), 1972, A New Look at an Old Prophet (Ezekiel), 1977, Biblical Eschatology, 1985. Active Shelby (County) United Neighbors, Memphis, 1973-74, United Way of Greater Memphis, 1974-82. Mem. Soc. Bibl. Lit., Memphis Ministers' Assn. Lodges: Civitan (chaplain, bd. dirs. local chpt.). Democrat. Presbyterian. Avocations: travel, golf. Home: 3095 E Glengarry Rd Memphis TN 38128-2911

TODD, WILLIAM MICHAEL, lawyer; b. Cleve., Dec. 13, 1952; s. William Charles and Jennie Ann (Diana) T. BA with hon., U. Notre Dame, 1973; JD cum laude, Ohio State U., 1976. Bar: Ohio 1976, U.S. Dist. Ct. (so. dist.) Ohio 1977, U.S. Supreme Ct. 1987. Assoc. Porter, Wright, Morris & Arthur, Columbus, Ohio, 1976-82, ptnr., 1983-93, Squire, Sanders & Dempsey, Columbus, 1993—2006; of counsel Benesch Friedlander, Columbus, 2006—. Trustee Callvac Svcs., Columbus, Ohio, 1985—91, pres., 1988; trustee Opera Columbus, 2004—. Mem. ABA (governing com. forum on health law 1988-91), Ohio Bar Assn., Columbus Bar Assn., Am. Soc. Med. Assn. Counsel, Am. Bd. Trial Advocates, Ohio Soc. Healthcare Attys. (pres. 1999-2000), Am. Health Lawyers Assn., Rep. Nat. Lawyers Assn. (chmn. Ohio chpt. 2005—), Columbus Athletic Club. Roman Catholic. Avocations: music, recreational sports. Office: Benesch Friedlander et al 41 S High St Columbus OH 43215-6101 Office Phone: 614-223-9348, 614-885-7136. Business E-Mail: wtodd@bfca.com.

TODD, ZANE GREY, retired utilities executive; b. Hanson, Ky., Feb. 3, 1924; s. Marshall Elvin and Kate (McCormick) T.; m. Marysnow Stone, Feb. 8, 1950 (dec. 1983); m. Frances Z. Anderson, Jan. 6, 1984. Student, Evansville Coll., 1947-49; BS summa cum laude, Purdue U., 1951, DEng (hon.), 1979; postgrad., U. Mich., 1965; DHL, U. Indpls., 1993. Fingerprint classifier FBI, 1942-43; electric system planning engr. Indpls. Power & Light Co., 1951-56, spl. assignments supr., 1956-60, head elec. system planning, 1960-65, head substation design div., 1965-68, head distbn. engring. dept., 1968-70, asst. to v.p., 1970-72, v.p., 1972-74, exec. v.p., 1974-75, pres., 1975-81, chmn., chief exec. officer, 1976-89, dir., chmn. exec. com., 1989-94, chief exec. officer, 1981-89; chmn., pres. IPALCO Enterprises, Inc., Indpls., 1983-89, dir., chmn. exec. com., 1989-94; chmn. bd., chief exec. officer Mid-Am. Capital Resources, Inc. subs. IPALCO Enterprises, Inc., Indpls., 1984-89, also bd. dirs., 1984-94. Gen. mgr. Mooresville (Ind.) Pub. Svc. Co., Inc., 1956-60; bd. dirs. Nat. City Bank Ind. (formerly Mchts. Nat. Corp.), 1975-94, Am. States Ins. Co., 1976-94; hon. dir. 500 Festival Assocs., Inc., pres. 1987. Originator probability analysis of power system reliability; contbr. articles to tech. jours. and mags. Past pres. adv. bd. St. Vincent Hosp.; past chmn., bd. trustees Ind. Cen. U. (now U. Indpls.); Nat. and Greater Indpls. adv. bds. Salvation Army, 1984-96; bd. govs. Associated Colls. of Ind., 1979-92. Sgt. AUS, 1943-47. Recipient William Booth award Salvation Army, 1994; named Disting. Engring. Alumnus Purdue U., 1976, Outstanding Elec. Engr. Purdue U., 1992, Knight of Malta, Order of St. John of Jerusalem, 1986. Fellow IEEE (past chmn. power sys. engring. com.); mem. ASME, NSPE, Power Engring. Soc., Ind. Fiscal Policy Inst. (bd. govs.), Ind. C. of C., Indpls. C. of C., Mooresville C. of C. (past pres.), PGA Nat. Country Club, Ulen Country Club, Indpls. Athletic Club (past bd. dirs.), Meridian Hills Country Club (past bd. dirs.), Skyline Club (bd. govs.), Newcomen Soc. (past chmn. Ind.), Rotary, Lions (past pres.), Eta Kappa Nu, Tau Beta Pi.

TODD COPLEY, JUDITH A., engineering educator; b. Wakefield, West Yorkshire, Eng., Dec. 13, 1950; arrived in US, 1978; d. Marley and Joan Mary (Birkinshaw) Booth; m. David Michael Todd, June 17, 1972 (div. June 1981); m. Stephen Michael Copley, Aug. 3, 1984; 1 child, Amy Elizabeth. BA in Materials Sci., Cambridge U., Eng., 1972, MA, PhD in Metall./Materials Sci., 1976. Rsch. asst. Imperial Coll. Sci. and Tech., London, 1976-78; rsch. assoc. SUNY, Stonybrook, 1978; rsch. engr. U. Calif., Berkeley, 1979-81; asst. prof. materials sci. and mech. engring. U. So. Calif., LA, 1982—90; assoc. prof. metall. and materials engring. Ill. Inst. Tech., Chgo., 1990-97, assoc. chair mech. materials and aerospace engring., 1995—2001, prof. materials and mech. engring., 1997—2002, assoc. dean rsch. Armour Coll. Engring. and Sci., 2001—02; P.B. Breneman dept. head chair chair dept. engring. sci. and mechanics Pa. State U., University Park, 2002—. Mem. task force Materials Property Coun., NYC, 1979—89; prof. Iron and Steel Soc., 1996—2002; mem. editl. bds. Contbr. articles to profl. jours.; patentee in field. Recipient Brit. Univs. Student Travel award, 1972, Brit. Fedn. Univ. Women award, 1972, Faculty Rsch. award Oak Ridge (Tenn.) Nat. Lab., 1986, Vanadium award British Inst. Materials, 1990; Kathryn Kingswell Meml. scholar, 1972, Julia Beveridge Award, IIT, 1998, Cert. Appreciation Am. Soc. Mech. Engrs., 1995, 97, Forging Industry Ednl. Rsch. Found., 1993, Booz-Allen and Hamilton Award for Tchg. and Svc., Ill. Inst. Tech., 1996, Mary Ewart Traveling Scholarship, Cambridge Univ., 1972, Sci. Rsch. Coun. Fellowship and Overseas Travel Award, 1972. Fellow ASM Internat., ASME Internat. (chmn. materials and fabrication com. 1993-97, pressure vessel and piping divsn. membership chair PVP divsn., 1997-2001, assoc. editor Jour. Pressure Vessel and Piping Tech. 1994-2001, exec. com. and publs. chair PVP divsn. 2001-05, v.p. mfg. group 2002-05, tech. program chair, 2004-05, tech. conf. chair 2005—, bd. on women and miniorites award 1997), Soc. Engring. Sci. (bd. dirs. 2006—), Assn. Women in Sci., ASM Internat. (chmn. LA chpt. 1986-87, coun. mem. materials sci. divsn. 1984-89); mem. AIME (Rsch. award 1983), ASTM, AAUW, Soc. Women Engrs. (sr.), Electron Microscopy Soc., Electrochem. Soc., Hist. Metallurgy Soc., Nat. Soc. Corrosion Engrs. (Seed grant award 1983), Microbeam Analysis Soc., Soc. Mfg. Engrs. (sr.), Instn. Materials, Chartered (sr.) Engr. Status, Minerals, Metals, Materials Soc. of the Am. Inst. Mining, Metall. Petroleum Engrs., Am. Ceramics Soc., Ill. Microscopical Soc., Soc. Engring. Sci. (mem. bd. dirs.). Avocation: archaeology. Office: Pennsylvania State Univ Dept Engring Sci and Mechanics 212 Earth-Engring Sci Bldg University Park PA 16802-6812 Home Phone: 814-237-2556; Office Phone: 814-863-0771. E-mail: jtodd@psu.edu.

TODHUNTER, JOHN ANTHONY, toxicologist, consultant; b. Cali, Valle, Colombia, Oct. 9, 1949; s. John Arthur and Teresa Maria (Torres) T.; divorced, 1986; children: Jennifer, Julia; m. Holli Wilson, Apr. 19, 1986; 1 child, Jacqueline Rose. BSc, UCLA, 1971; MSc, Calif. State U., 1973; PhD, U. Calif., Santa Barbara, 1976. Diplomate Am. Bd. Toxicology, Am. Bd. Forensic Examiners. Instr. Calif. State U., LA, 1972-73; rsch. asst. U. Calif., Santa Barbara, 1973-76; fellow Roche Inst. Molecular Biology, Nutley, NJ, 1976-78; asst. prof. Cath. U. Am., Washington, 1978-81, chmn. Biochemistry Program, 1980-81; asst. adminstr. U.S. EPA, Washington, 1981-83; cons. Sci. Regulatory Svcs. Internat., Washington, 1983-91; pres. SRS Internat. Corp., 1991—, SRS Internat. Health Care Group, 1995—; CEO Assura Pharmaceuticals, 2006—. Expert advisor European regional office WHO, Stockholm, 1984; mem. Hazardous Waste Siting Bd., Annapolis, Md., 1980-81. Contbr. articles to profl. jours. Bd. dirs. Reagan Alumni Assn., Washington, 1985—; vol. Am. Cancer Soc., Washington, 1988-93; mem. Presdl. Transition Team, Washington, 1980. U. Calif. Bd. Regents fellow, 1975, B.R. Baker Meml. fellow dept. chemistry U. Calif., Santa Barbara, 1976. Fellow Am. Inst. Chemists (dir. at large 1989-92, vice chmn. bd. 1992); mem. Soc. of Toxicology, Am. Chem. Soc., Soc. for Risk Analysis, N.Y. Acad. Sci. Office Phone: 703-821-3221. Business E-Mail: jtodhunter@assurapharm.com.

TODMAN, MICHAEL A., manufacturing executive; b. St. Thomas, US VI; BSBA, Georgetown U. With Price Waterhouse and Co., Wang Labs., Inc.; dir. fin. UK Whirlpool, 1993—95, gen. mgr. No. Europe to v.p. consumer svcs. Whirlpool Europe, 1993—95, contr. N.Am., 1995—96, v.p. product mgmt., 1996—97, v.p. Sears sales and mktg., 1997—99, sr. v.p. sales and mktg. N.Am., 1999—2001, exec. v.p. N.Am., mem. corp. exec. com., 2001, corp. exec. v.p., pres. Whirlpool Europe, 2001—05, pres. Whirlpool Internat., bd. dirs., 2006—. Office: Whirlpool Inc 2000 N M-63 Benton Harbor MI 49022 *

TODREAS, NEIL EMMANUEL, nuclear engineering educator; b. Peabody, Mass., Dec. 17, 1935; s. David and Anna (Gendleman) T.; m. Carol S. Schonberg, June 19, 1958; children: Timothy, Ian. BSM.E., MS, Cornell U., 1958; ScD in Nuc. Engring., MIT, 1966. Asst. prof. dept. nuc. engring. MIT, Cambridge, Mass., 1970-71, assoc. prof., 1971-75, prof., 1975—, Kepco prof. nuc. engring. and prof. mech. engring., 1992—, head dept. nuc. engring., 1981-89. Served to lt. (j.g.) USN, 1958-62. Named Disting. Tchr., Ruth and Joel Spira award MIT Sch. Engring., 1995. Fellow: ASME, Am. Nuc. Soc. (Tech. Achievement award for outstanding contbns. to thermal hydraulics 1994, Arthur Holly Compton award for outstanding educators in nuc. engring. 1995, Henry DeWolf-Smyth award 2005); mem.: Internat. Nuc. Energy Acad., Nat. Acad. Engring., Sigma Xi, Tau Beta Pi, Pi Tau Sigma. Office: MIT Bldg 24 Rm 205 77 Massachusetts Ave Cambridge MA 02139-4307 E-mail: todreas@mit.edu.

TOEDT, D(ELL) C(HARLES), III, lawyer; b. Maxwell AFB, Ala., Nov. 17, 1954; m. Maretta A. Comfort. BA with high honors, U. Tex., 1973, JD, 1981. Bar: Tex. 1982, U.S. Patent and Trademark Office 1983, U.S. Dist. Ct. (so. dist.) Tex. 1984, U.S. Ct. Appeals (fed. cir.) 1984, U.S. Supreme Ct. 1991, Calif. 1996. Atty. Schlanger, Cook, Cohn, Mills & Grossberg, Houston, 1982-83, Arnold, White & Durkee, Houston, 1983-99; v.p., gen. counsel BindView Corp., Houston, 1999—2006. Adj. prof. S. Tex. Coll. Law, 1988—90. Assoc. editor: Tex. Law Rev., 1981—82, author, editor: Licensing Law Handbook: Computer Software Issues, 1987; editor: Law and Bus. Computer Software, 1989—2002; contbr. articles to profl. jours. Served to lt. USN, 1974—79. Mem.: ABA (chmn. computer-related coms. 1985—96, elected mem. coun. sect. intellectual property law 1999—2000). Home Phone: 713-665-2901; Office Phone: 713-893-3925. Personal E-mail: dc.toedt@toedt.com.

TOEDTMAN, JAMES SMITH, journalist, editor; b. Dayton, Ohio, Dec. 1, 1941; s. James Christian and Ella Barnes (Smith) T.; m. Haydee N. Sicart, Aug. 23, 1969; children: Eric, Kristen AB, Coll. Wooster, 1963; postgrad., U. Queensland, Brisbane, Australia, 1964; MSc in Journalism, Columbia U., 1967. Pub. dir. Coll. Wooster, Ohio, 1963, 1965; reporter, city editor, Sunday news editor, mng. editor, Washington Bur. chief Newsday, LI, NY, 1967—79, 1986—2005; exec. editor Boston Herald Am., 1979—82; editor Balt. News Am., 1982—86, AARP Bulletin, 2005—. Co-author: Good Roots, 2006. Adv. bd. comm. dept. Flagler Coll., 2003—. Recipient shared award Silurian Soc., Polk award, Pulitzer Prize, 1970, 92, 97, spl. citation Inter-Am. Press Assn., 1979, Best Editl. award Md.-Del.-D.C. Press Assn., 1984, 86; Rotary Found. fellow, 1964, Internat. fellow Columbia U., 1966-67. Mem.: Coll. Wooster Alumni Assn. (pres. 1980—81). Methodist. Home: 2604 Geneva Hill Ct Oakton VA 22124-1534 Office: AARB Bulletin 601 E St NW Washington DC 20049 Home Phone: 703-319-8914; Office Phone: 202-434-3357. Business E-Mail: jtoedtman@aarp.org.

TOELLE, JENNIFER M., museum staff member; d. Richard and Anita Meek (Stepmother), Cheyenne and J. Greg Duncan (Stepfather); m. David Toelle, June 22, 2002; 1 child, Trae. Student, Washington State C.C., Marietta, Ohio, 1997—98, Ohio State U., Columbus, 1998—2000, Kans. Wesleyan U., Salina, 2000—01. Mus. asst., collections mgr. McPherson County Old Mill Mus., Lindsborg, Kans., 2000—; coord. Kans. Museums Assn., Salina, 2002—. Office: Kansas Museums Assn PO Box 1946 Salina KS 67402-1946 Home Phone: 785-309-0244; Office Phone: 785-309-0244. Business E-Mail: info@ksmuseums.org.

TOENNIES, JAN PETER, research chemical physicist; b. Phila., May 3, 1930; arrived in Fed. Republic Germany, 1957; s. Gerrit and Dita (Jebens) T.; m. Monika Elisabeth Zelesnick; children: Susanne, Annette. BA in Physics, Amherst Coll., Mass., 1952; PhD in Chemistry, Brown U., Providence, 1957; PhD (hon.), U. Gothenburg, 2000; DSc (hon.), Amherst Coll., Mass., 2007. Rsch. asst. Bonn (Fed. Republic Germany) U., 1957-65, dozent, 1965-68; dir., sci. mem. Max Planck Inst. Fluid Mechanics, Göttingen, 1969—98. Adj. prof. Bonn U., 1971—; assoc. prof. Göttingen U., 1971—; vis. Miller Prof. Chemistry and Physics, U. Calif., Berkeley, 2005-06; cons. Uranit GmbH, Jülich, Fed. Republic Germany, 1977-89. Author: Chemical Reactions in Shock Waves, 1964; adv. editor Jour. Chem. Physics, 1973-78; editor monograph series, Springer Series in Chem. Physics, 1979—. Recipient Gold Heyrovsky medal Czechoslovak Acad. Scis., 1991, Alumni citation Brown U., 1988, Hewlett-Packard Europhysics prize for outstanding achievement in condensed matter rsch., 1992, Max Planck prize Deutsche Forschungsgemeinschaft and Alexander Humboldt Soc., 1992, Kotos medal Polish Chem. Soc., 2005, Benjamin Franklin medal in Physics, Franklin Inst., 2006. Fellow Am. Phys. Soc., World Innovation Found.; mem. European Phys. Soc., German Phys. Soc. (sect. chmn. 1977-80, Stern-Gerlach medal 2002, mem. atomic physics sect.), Göttingen Acad. Scis. (corr., Physics award 1964), Coun. European Phys. Soc., Acad. Sciences Czech Republic, World Cultural Coun. (hon.), Deutsche Akademie der Naturforscher Leopoldina. Home: Ewaldstrasse 7 D-37085 Göttingen Germany Office: Max Planck Inst for Dynamics and Self Orgn Bunsenstr 10 D-37073 Göttingen Germany Office Phone: 011 49 551 5176600. Business E-Mail: jtoenni@gwdg.de.

TOENSING, VICTORIA, lawyer; b. Colon, Panama, Oct. 16, 1941; d. Philip William and Victoria (Brady) Long; m. Trent David Toensing, Oct. 29, 1962 (div. 1976); children: Todd Robert, Brady Cronon, Amy Victoriana; m. Joseph E. diGenova, June 27, 1981. BS in Edn., Ind. U., 1962; JD cum laude, U. Detroit, 1975. Bar: Mich. 1976, D.C. 1978. Tchr. English, Milw., 1965-66; law clk. to presiding justice U.S. Ct. Appeals, Detroit, 1975-76; asst. U.S. atty. U.S. Atty.'s Office, Detroit, 1976-81; chief counsel U.S. Senate Intelligence Com., Washington, 1981-84; dep. asst. atty. gen. criminal div. Dept. Justice, Washington, 1984-88; spl. counsel Hughes Hubbard & Reed, Washington, 1988-90; ptnr. Cooter and Gell, Washington, 1990-91; ptnr., co-chmn. nat. white collar group Manatt, Phelps and Phillips, Washington, 1991-95; founding ptnr. diGenova & Toensing, Wasington, 1996—. Mem. working group on corp. sanctions U.S. Sentencing Commn., 1988-89; co-chairperson Coalition for Women's Appts. Justice Judiciary Task Force, 1988-92; spl. counsel for Teamsters investigation, U.S. Ho. of Reps., Subcom. on Oversight and Investigations of com. on Edn. and the Workforce, 1997-98. Author: Bringing Sanity to the Insanity Defense, 1983, Mens Rea: Insanity by Another Name, 1984; contbg. author: Fighting Back: Winning The War Against Terrorism, Desk Book on White Collar Crime, 1991; contbr. articles to profl. jours. Founder, chmn. Women's Orgn. To Meet Existing Needs, Mich., 1975-79; chmn. Republican Women's Task Force, 1979-81; bd. dirs. Project on Equal Edn. Rights, Mich., 1980-81, Nat. Hist. Intelligence Mus., 1987-95, America's Talking Legal Analyst, 1995; MSNBC legal analyst, 1998-99. Recipient spl. commendation Office U.S. Atty. Gen., 1980, agy. seal medallion CIA, 1986, award of achievement Alpha Chi Omega, 1992; featured on cover

N.Y. Time Mag. for anti-terrorism work, April 1991. Mem. ABA (mem. standing com. on law and nat. security, mem. coun. criminal justice sect., mem. adv. com. complex crimes and litigation, vice chmn. white collar crime com., chmn. subcom. on corp. criminal liability). Office: Ste 737 1776 K St NW Washington DC 20006 Home Phone: 301-951-6142; Office Phone: 202-289-7701.

TOEPFER, SUSAN JILL, editor-in-chief; b. Rochester, Minn., Mar. 9, 1948; d. John Bernard and Helen Esther (Chapple) Toepfer; m. Lorenzo Gabriel Carcaterra, May 16, 1981; children: Katherine Marie, Nicholas Gabriel. BA, Bennington Coll., 1970. Mng. editor Photoplay Mag., NYC, 1971-72; freelance writer NYC, 1972-78; TV week editor N.Y. Daily News, NYC, 1978-79, leisure editor, 1979-82, features editor, 1982-84, arts and entertainment editor, 1984-86, exec. mag. editor, 1986-87; sr. writer People Mag., NYC, 1987-89, sr. editor, 1989-91, asst. mng. editor, 1991-94, exec. editor, 1994—2000, dep. mng. editor, 2000—02; editor-in-chief Rosie Mag., 2002, Devel. G+J USA, NYC, 2003—04, Quick & Simple, NYC, 2005—. Home: 225 7th Ave #10X New York NY 10001

TOERGE, LYNN, athletic trainer; b. Pitts., Nov. 11, 1955; d. John Elmer and Mary Ruth Toerge. BS, Ind. State U., Terre Haute, 1981. Athletic trainer, phys. ed. tchr. Hampton Sch. Dist., Allison Park, Pa., 1983—87, cert. athletic trainer, 1983—. EMT, paramedic Ross/West View EMS, Pitts., 1987—97. Mem.: Nat. Athletic Trainers Assn. (licentiate athletic trainer cert.). R-Consevative. Avocations: golf, drawing, weightlifting. Home: 203 Monroe Dr Pittsburgh PA 15229 Office: Hampton Sch Dist 2929 McCully Rd Allison Park PA 15101 Home Phone: 412-367-0322; Office Phone: 412-486-6000. Office Fax: 412-486-7050. Personal E-mail: itoerge@comcast.net.

TOFEL, RICHARD JEFFREY, foundation administrator; b. NYC; s. Robert Leonard and Carol T.; m. Jeanne Helen Straus, Feb. 26, 1983; children: Rachel Straus, Colin Straus. AB, Harvard U., 1979; MPP, JFK Sch. Govt., 1983; JD, Harvard U., 1983. Bar: N.Y. 1984, U.S. Dist. Ct. (so. and ea. dists.) N.Y. 1984, U.S. Ct. Appeals (2d cir.) 1987, U.S. Dist. Ct. (no. dist.) N.Y. 1988, U.S. Supreme Ct. 1990. Assoc. Patterson, Belknap, Webb & Tyler, NYC, 1983—86; exec. dir. Mayor's Commn. Human Svcs. Reorganization, NYC, 1984—85; assoc. Gibson, Dunn & Crutcher, NYC, 1986—89; counsel Dow Jones & Co., NYC, 1989—91, asst. gen. counsel, 1991—92; asst. mng. editor Wall Street Jour., NYC, 1992—95; dir. internat. devel. and adminstrn. Dow Jones & Co., NYC, 1995—97, v.p. corp. comm., 1997—2000, v.p., asst. to publ. Wall Street Jour., 2000—02, v.p., asst. publ. Wall Street Jour., 2002—04; pres. The Internat. Freedom Ctr., World Trade Ctr. site, NYC, 2004—05; v.p., gen. counsel The Rockefeller Found., NYC, 2006—. Bd. dirs. Wildcat Svc. Corp. Author: A Legend in the Making: The New York Yankees in 1939, 2002, Vanishing Point: The Disappearance of Judge Crater, and the New York He Left Behind, 2004, Sounding the Trumpet: The Making of John F. Kennedy's Inaugural Address, 2005; contbr. articles to profl. jours. Democrat. Jewish. Office: The Rockefeller Found 420 Fifth Ave New York NY 10018 Home Phone: 718-549-4545. Business E-Mail: rtofel@rockfound.org. E-mail: dick_tofel@yahoo.com.

TOFIAS, ALLAN, retired accountant; b. Boston, Apr. 13, 1930; s. George I. and Anna (Seidel) T.; m. Arlene Shube, Aug. 30, 1981; children: Bradley Neil, Laura Jean Silver. BA, Colgate U., 1951; MBA, Harvard U., 1956. CPA, Mass. Sr. acct. Peat, Marwick, Mitchell & Co., Boston, 1956—60; mng. ptnr. Tofias, Fleishman, Shapiro & Co., P.C., Boston, 1960-96, chmn. bd., 1996-97. Bd. dir. Rowe Cos.; trustee Gannett, Welch & Kotler Mut. Funds, 1996-2002. Mem. Brookline (Mass.) Town Meeting, 1970-77, mem. fin. adv. bd., 1975-81; mem. New Eng. Bapt. Health Care Corp., 1985—, trustee, 1998-, chmn. fin. com., 1998-2002; bd. dir. West Newton YMCA, 1986-89; mem. exec. com. Boston Aid to Blind, bd. dir., 1988-97, pres., 1993-94. Lt. USNR, 1951-54. Mem. AICPA (coun. 1995-99), Mass. Soc. CPA's (pres. 1995-96), Nat. CPA Group (exec. com. 1983-88, vice chmn. 1985-88), BKR Internat. (world bd. dirs. 1988-97, chmn. 1994-96), Wightman Tennis Club (treas. 1974-76), Newton Squash and Tennis Club (bd. dirs. 1966-99), Masons. Home: 33 Glen Oak Dr Wayland MA 01778 Office: 167 Worcester St Wellesley MA 02481

TOGASAKI, SHINOBU, computer scientist; b. San Francisco, Aug. 17, 1932; s. Kikumatsu and Sugi (Hida) T.; m. Toshiko Kawaguchi, Nov. 24, 1959; children: John Shinobu, Ann Mariko. BS in Math., Duke U., 1954; postgrad., Stanford U., 1954—56. Math. programmer IBM, 1956—69, DB/DC arch., 1969—72, sr. programmer Palo Alto, Calif., 1970—87, mgr. Palo Alto sys. ctr., 1972—74, risk OS mgr., 1974—82, DB/DC mktg. cons., 1982—87; mgr. applications devel. Service Bur. Corp., Palo Alto, 1961—64, sr. analyst, 1964—68, systems architect devel. lab. San Jose, Calif., 1968-70; CFO. Robin Hood Ranch, Inc., 1976—86; mgr. architecture & strategy Hewlett Packard Corp., Cupertino, Calif., 1987-89, mgr. strategic planning, 1989—93; chief architect MFA Hewlett Packard, 1993—2002; strategic cons., 2002—. Mem. Am. Mgmt. Assn., AAAS, Am. Statis. Assn., Assn. Computing Machinery, Inst. Mgmt. Sci., Sigma Pi Sigma. Home: 2367 Booksin Ave San Jose CA 95125-4705 E-mail: togasaki@alumni.duke.edu.

TOGNINO, JOHN NICHOLAS, diversified financial services company executive; b. NYC, Sept. 20, 1938; s. Gennaro and Catherine (Barbieri) T.; m. Norma Lucille Borrelli, Nov. 7, 1959; children: Katherine Ann, John Nicholas Jr., Michael A. BA in Econs. summa cum laude, Fordham U., 1975. Instnl. sales trader A.G. Becker & Co., NYC, 1970-72; trader Merill Lynch, NYC, 1957-69, instnl. salesman, 1972-74, mgr. over-the-counter sales trading, 1974-83, dir. over-the-counter dept., 1983-87, dir. unlisted trading, 1987-88, mng. dir. non-dollar equities London, 1988-91, mng. dir. global equities, ret. NYC, 1991-93; exec. v.p. Charles Schwab & Co., Inc., Jersey City, 1993-96; pres., CEO Security Traders Assn., NYC, 1996-99, EVP NASDAQ, 1999—2001; chmn., CEO Pepper Fin. Group, 2001—. Bd. dirs. Nat. Assn. Security Dealers Automated Quotations Inc. Contbg. author: Market Maker Sponsorship: A Synergistic Package of Services, 1987. Mem. Ardlsey Bd. Edn., 1977—84, pres., 1979; v.p. Ardsley Sch. Dist. Bd., 1978, 1981; trustee, vice chmn. St. Barnabas Hosp., Bronx, 1996—; mem. health sci. adv. coun., Coll. of Phys. and Surgeons Columbia Presbyn. Med. Ctr., 1998—; pres. Ardsley Rep. Club, 1967—68; mem. exec. com. of laity Archdiocese of N.Y.C., 1988; trustee Fordham U., 2000—, chmn. bd. trustees, 2004—; dir. Muscular Dystrophy Assn., 2000—05; bd. dirs. Bus. Coun. for Internat. Understanding, 2000—01. Named Trader of Yr., Security Traders Monthly mag., 1984, Over-the-Counter Man of Yr., Equities mag., 1986; recipient lifetime achievement award Chgo. Stock Exch., 1997. Mem. Nat. Security Traders Assn. (various offices 1981-88, chmn. fin. com. Found. 1992—), Nat. Assn. Security Dealers (bus. conduct com. 1984-86), Security Traders Assn. N.Y. (various offices 1973-83, pres. 1980-81), St. Andrews Golf Club (Hastings, N.Y.), Alpha Sigma Lambda, Alpha Sigma Nu. Republican. Roman Catholic. Avocations: jogging, tennis, golf. Home: Two Stoneleigh Plz Apt 4H Bronxville NY 10708 Office: Pepper Fin Group PO Box 395 Waccabuc NY 10597 Home Phone: 914-966-6016; Office Phone: 914-234-4580. Personal E-mail: jntog@aol.com.

TOGNOLI, ERA M., performing company executive, artistic director; married. M in Voice, La Scala, Milan, Italy. Gen. mgr., artistic dir., founder Metro Lyric Opera, Allenhurst, NJ, 1959—. Singer: (Operas) Puccini's Turandot, 1948, Verdi's La Traviata, Puccini's Madame Butterfly. Office: Metro Lyric Opera PO Box 35 Allenhurst NJ 07711-0035 *

TOI, ZANG, apparel designer; b. Kelantan, Malaysia, June 11, 1961; US, 1980; BFA, Parsons Sch. of Design, 1985. Apprenticed with Mary Jane Marcasiano and Ronaldus Shamask; owner, designer House of Toi, 1989—; launched Zang Toi Couture Collection. Owner Zang Toi Boutiques, Malaysia. Decorated Knight Malaysia; recipient Mouton-Cadet Young Designers award, 1990. Office: House of Toi 30 W 57th St New York NY 10019

TOIBIN, COLM, writer, journalist; b. Enniscorthy, County Wexford, Ireland, 1955; s. Michael Tobin. BA, U. Coll. Dublin, 1975. Tchr. Dublin Sch. English, Barcelona, 1975—78; (returned to Ireland, 1978); writer Hibernia, The Sunday Tribune, In Dublin, features editor, 1981—82; editor Magill, 1982—85; journalist, columnist Dublin Sunday Ind., 1985—. Fellow Ctr. for Scholars and Writers NY Pub. Libr., 2000. Author: (fiction) The South, 1990, The Heather Blazing, 1992, The Story of the Night, 1996, Finbar's Hotel (collaborative novel), 1999, The Blackwater Lightship (made into TV film, 2004), 1999, The Master, 2004 (Internat. Impac Dublin Literary award, 2006), (non-fiction) Seeing is Believing: Moving Status in Ireland, 1985, The Trial of the Generals, 1990, Dubliners, 1990, Homage to Barcelona, 1990, The Sign of the Cross, 1994, Bad Blood, 1994, The Kilfenora Teaboy, 1997, The Irish Famine, 1999, Love in a Dark Time: Gay Lives from Wilde to Almodovar, 2001, Lady Gregory's Toothbrush, 2002, (plays) Beauty in a Broken Place, 2004; editor: SOHO Square VI: New Writing from Ireland, 1997, Enniscorthy: History & Heritage, 1998, The Modern Library: The 200 Best Novels in English since 1950, 1999, The Penguin Book of Irish Fiction, 2001. Recipient E.M. Forster Award, AAAL, 1995. Mem.: Aosdána.

TOKARZ, MICHAEL THEODORE, merchant banker; b. Chgo., Nov. 3, 1949; s. Ted and Lorraine Tokarz; m. Nancy C. Tokarz, Sept. 20, 1975; children: Andrew M., Justin T. BA in Econs., U. Ill., 1971, MBA, 1973. CPA, N.Y. Various exec. positions Continental Ill. Nat. Bank and Trust Co., NYC and Miami, Fla., 1973-85; from assoc. to mem. Kohlberg Kravis Roberts & Co., NYC, 1985—2002; with The Tokarz Group LLC, Purchase, NY, 2002—; non-exec. chmn. Walter Industries, Tampa, Fla., 2006—. Bd. dirs. Evenflo Co., Inc., Vandalia, Ohio, IDEX Corp., Northbrook, Ill., KAMAZ, Inc., Naberezhnye Chelny, Tatarstan, Russia, Spalding Holdings Cpr., Chicopee, Mass., Walter Industries, Inc., Tampa, Fla., Nexstar Fin. Corp., St. Louis, Lomonosov Porcelain Corp., St. Petersburg, Russia., U.F. Holdings, Inc., Niles, Mich. Trustee Rye (N.Y.), YMCA, 2001—; bd. dirs. U. Ill. Found., Champaign, 1997—, bd. mgrs. U. Ill. I-Venture LLC, 2000—. Office: The Tokarz Group LLC 287 Bowman Ave Purchase NY 10577 *

TOKATLIOGLU, THERESA DIAZ LOPEZ, elementary school educator; b. Joliet, Ill., Dec. 26, 1938; d. Emilio Jimenez and Vicenta (Salazar) Diaz; m. Pilar Lopez, Oct. 5, 1957 (dec. May 1971); children: Amanda-(dec.), Armand; m. Bernabe Oscar Lopez Argentina, Aug. 19, 1972 (div.); children: Arturo, Adrianna; m. L. Tokatlioglu. AA in Acctg., Joliet Jr. Coll., 1971; BA in Elem. Edn., U. of St. Francis, Joliet, 1974; post grad., Nat. U. Edn., 1974—75. Cert. elem. edn. tchr., high sch. Spanish tchr., bilingual K-l2 tchr. Typist Boy Scouts Am., Joliet, 1955-56; office worker Shepley Motor Express, Joliet, 1956-57; dictaphone operator N.Am. Accident Ins. Co., Chgo., 1957-59; elem. edn. tchr. Harlingen (Tex.) Consol. Schs., 1978—79; tchr. Joliet Pub. Schs. Dist. 86, 1974—. Vice-pres. Parks Sch. PTA, Joliet, 1969-70; vol. Rialto Square Theatre, Joliet,JTHS Choir Alumni Assn. Recipient Life Mem. award PTA, 1989, Book of Recognition award PTA, 1991. Mem.: Nat. Hawaiian Steel Guitar Assn., League United Latin Am. Citizens (sec. 1971—74, Joliet Woman of Yr. award 1975, state conv. Woman of Yr. award 1985), Am. Italian Cultural Soc., Alpha Delta Kappa, Kappa Delta Pi Internat. Democrat. Avocations: reading, dance, art, travel, opera. Office: Pershing Sch Midland and Campbell Joliet IL 60435 Personal E-mail: tere57@aol.com.

TOKUHATA, GEORGE K., retired medical educator, epidemiologist, consultant; b. Matsue, Japan, Aug. 25, 1924; arrived in U.S., 1951; s. Yujiro and Hama Tokuhata; m. Sumiko Matsui, June 10, 1949. BA, Keio U., 1950; MA, Miami U., Oxford, Ohio, 1952; PhD, U. Iowa, 1955; Dr.PH, Johns Hopkins U., 1962. Chief epidemiology chronic disease divsn. USPHS, Washington, 1961—64; assoc. prof. preventive medicine U. Tenn., Memphis, 1965—67; dir. rsch. Pa. Dept. Health, Harrisburg, 1968—89; prof. behavioral sci. Pa. State U. Coll. Medicine, Hershey, 1970—95; prof. epidemiology U. Pitts., 1970—90; ret., 1990. Cons. product safety U.S. FDA, Washington, 1970—73; cons. maternal child health rsch. U.S. Children's Bur., 1974—77; cons. rsch. grant svcs. Nat. Cancer Inst., 1982—86. Contbr. chapters to books, articles over 100 articles to profl. jours. Grantee, USPHS, U.S. FDA. Fellow: APHA, Am. Coll. Epidemiology; mem.: Fgn. Policy Assn. (bd.dirs. 1995—2000), Torch Club Internat. (bd.dirs. 1999—2002). Achievements include first to find genetic role played in lung cancer; research in radiation, stress and health; first to new method of finding familial aggregation of chronic diseases; design of and execution of long-term cohort study of health effects of the Three Mile Island accident - first major episode among all commercial nuclear plants in the U.S. Avocations: classical music, landscape design, gardening. Home: 410 Rupley Rd Camp Hill PA 17011

TOKUNAGA, EMIKO, dancer; b. San Francisco, Sept. 28, 1939; d. Shigao and Utako (Seiki) T. BFA, U. Utah, 1961; MA, NYU, 1966. Co-dir. Tokunaga Dance Ko, NYC, 1967—; faculty, artistic dir. summer dance Boston Conservatory, 1971—; dance program coord. Harvard U. and Radcliffe Coll., 1995—98. Over 40 residencies in U.S., Japan and Norway. Choreographer 60 modern and Japanese dances; dancer: over 2000 performances in theaters and ednl. instns. in U.S., Norway and Japan. Nat. Endowment for the Arts grantee, Japan-U.S. Friendship Commission, N.Y.C. Dept. of Cultural Affairs; fellow Harvard U., 1995-96. Achievements include research in solar physics. Office: Tokunaga Dance Ko 1 Sheridan Sq New York NY 10014-6825 Home Phone: 212-929-8937. Personal E-mail: emitokunaga@aol.com.

TOLAR, ANNE MELTON, minister, music educator; b. Geneva, Ala., Jan. 17, 1937; d. Ernest Lester and Lovie Hewett Melton; m. Robert F. Tolar, Apr. 21, 1966; children: Robert Jr., William, Sharon Tolar Stone, Ginny Tolar Knight. BA in English & Psychology, U. Ala., 1959; BA in Music/Piano, U. W. Fla., 1960. Teller/bookkeeper 1st Bank & Trust, Pensacola, Fla., 1952—56, collections & loan officer Atlanta; br. office asst. mgr. 1st Fed. Savings & Loan Assn., Atlanta, 1970—73; evangelist, musician, tchr. Fountain of Praise Ministries, St. Pauls, NC, 1972—; presbyter, min. Missionary Ch. Internat., Columbia, SC, 1985—; music tchr. St. Pauls; tchr., musician, pastor Fountain of Praise Ch., Lumberton, NC, 2001—. Judge Mountain Gospel Music; v.p. Fountain of Praise Ministries, Missionary Ch. Internat., Lumberton, NC, 2001—; spkr. in field. Author: (book) Wilt Thou Be Made Whole?, 1988; songwriter: 106 songs and cantatas. Named Internat. Savings & Loan Speech Contest, Atla., 1972; recipient Mother of Yr. award, Fountain of Praise Ch., St. Pauls, N.C., 1998. Republican. Mem. Christian Ch. Office: Fountain of Praise Ministries Cedar St Lumberton NC 28358

TOLBERT, BERNARD, sports association executive; married; 3 children. Student, SUNY, Buffalo. Spl. agt. FBI, Buffalo and NYC, 1980—85, supervisory spl. agt. Intelligence Divsn. Washington, 1985—87, supr. fgn. counterintelligence, counterterrorism and civil rights investigations Western NY area Buffalo, 1987—90, chief counterintelligence and counterterrorism tng. unit Washington, 1990—92, asst. spl. agt. in charge Phila. office, 1992—97, insp. Inspection Divsn. Washington, 1997—98, spl. agt. in charge Buffalo divsn., 1998—2001; security mgr. Coca-Cola Co.; sr. v.p., dir. corp. security HSBC Bank; sr. v.p. security NBA, NYC, 2002—. Bd. mem. United Way, Western NY Pub. Broadcasting, Erie County Youth Bd., Medaille Coll., U. Buffalo Alumni Assn., 100 Club Buffalo and Western NY. Named to SUNY Buffalo Athletic Hall of Fame, 1998; recipient Black Achievers in Industry award, Heroes of Pub. Housing award, Ebony and Ivory award, Presdl. Rank award for Meritorious Achievement, The White House, 2001. Office: NBA Olympic Tower 645 5th Ave Fl 10 New York NY 10022-5986 *

TOLBERT, BERT MILLS, biochemist, educator; b. Twin Falls, Idaho, Jan. 15, 1921; s. Ed. and Helen (Mills) T.; m. Anne Grace Zweifler, July 20, 1959; children— Elizabeth Dawn, Margaret Anne, Caroline Joan, Sarah Helen. Student, Idaho State U., 1938-40; BS, U. Calif., Berkeley, 1942, PhD, 1945; postgrad., Fed. Inst. Tech., Zurich, Switzerland, 1952-53. Chemist Lawrence Radiation Lab., Berkeley, 1944-57; faculty U. Colo., Boulder, 1957-89, prof., 1961-89, prof. emeritus, 1989—, assoc. chmn. dept. chemistry and biochemistry, 1980-88. Bd. dirs. Hauser Chem. Rsch., Boulder, 1983-99; dirs. Hauser Inc., Boulder, 1983-99, vis. prof. IAEA, Buenos Aires, Argentina, 1961-62; Biophysicist U.S. AEC, Washington, 1967-68; cons. pvt. cos, govt. agys. Author: (with others) Isotopic Carbon, 1948; contbr. (with others) articles to profl. jours. Fellow AAAS; mem. Am. Chem. Soc., Am. Soc. Biochemistry and Molecular Biology, Radiation Rsch. Soc., Soc. for Exptl. Biology and Medicine. Achievements include rsch. on organic chemistry, including use of isotopes in chemistry and biochemistry, radiation chemistry, radiation effects in protein, intermediary metabolism, metabolism of ascorbic acid, nutritional biochemistry, instrumentation in radioactivity. Home: 444 Kalmia Ave Boulder CO 80304-1732 Personal E-mail: bert.tolbert@colorado.edu.

TOLBERT, CLINTON JAME, army officer, machinist; b. Auburn, Ala., Dec. 22, 1953; s. Clinton and Rosia Love (Fillmore) T.; m. Gloria Jean Fitzpatrick, Sept. 23, 1974; children: Christopher, Mark, Marcella. BS, Tukegee U., 1983; MBA, Troy State U., 1987, MS, 1990; AS in Applied Sci., So. U., Opelika, Ala., 1996. EMT U.S. Army, Fort Benning, Ga., 1972-75; machine operator West Point Pepperll, Inc., Valley, Ala., 1975-82; 1st lt. Army Nat. Guard, Roanoke, Ala., 1982-86, capt., 1986-92, major Montgomery, Ala., 1992-96; machinist Falk Corp., Auburn, Ala, 1996—. Elder Methodist Ch., Auburn, Ala., 1996— Named All- Am. Scholar, U.S. Achievement Acad., Lexington, Ky., 1996; recipient Minority Leadership award, U.S. Achievement Acad., Lexington, 1996. Mem. Nat. Guard Assn. Democrat. Avocations: reading, golf. Home: 989 Fitzpatric Rd Auburn AL 36830

TOLBERT, CORNELIA EMMA, music educator; b. St. Louis, Sept. 15, 1954; d. Cornelius and Morzell Tolbert. BA, St. Louis U., 1977. Cert. instrumental and vocal music tchr. grades K-12 Mo., 1982. Substitute tchr. St. Louis Pub. Schs., 1975—83, piano and voice tchr., 1976—78, vocal music tchr., 1985—95, asst. music tchr., 1997—2001, instrumental music asst. tchr., 2001—; pvt. piano and organ tchr. Ludwig Aeolian Music Store, 1982—85. Music choral dir. Meth. Ch., St. Louis, 1972—, asst. orgn., 1977—2003, pianist, 2003—. Vol. phone bank St. Louis Tchrs. Union, 2004; coord. for United Way St. Louis Pub. Schs., 2004, coord. William L. Clay Scholarship fund, 2004. Recipient Editor's Choice award, Internat. Soc. Poets, 2001. Mem.: St. Louis Univ. Alumni Assn., Internat. Soc. Poets, Am. Fedn. Tchrs., St. Louis Tchrs. Union Local 420, Nat. Music Educators Assn., Mo. Music Tchrs. Assn. Democrat. Methodist. Avocations: bowling, tennis, ping pong/table tennis, writing songs, gardening.

TOLBERT, MARGARET A., geochemistry educator; AB in Chemistry, with honors, Grinnell Coll., 1979; MS in Chemistry, U. Calif., Berkeley, 1985; PhD in Chemistry, Calif. Inst. Tech., 1986. Postdoctoral fellow Stanford Rsch. Inst., 1986—87; rsch. asst. U. Calif., Berkeley, 1979—83, Calif. Inst. Tech., 1983—86; staff scientist, Chemistry Lab. SRI Internat., 1986—91, leader Atmospheric Chemistry Group, 1990—91; assoc. prof. Dept. Chemistry and Biochemistry U. Colo., 1991—98, prof., 1998—. Author: Stratispheric Ozone Depletion, 2000. Recipient James B. Macelwane Young Investigator medal Am. Geophys. Union, 1993. Fellow: Am. Geophysical Union (James B. Macelwane Young Investigator medal 1993); mem.: NAS. Office: U Colo CIRES 166 Campus Box 216 Boulder CO 80309-0216 Office Phone: 303-492-3179. Fax: 303-492-1149. Business E-Mail: tolbert@colorado.edu.

TOLCHIN, JOAN GUBIN, psychiatrist, educator; d. Harold and Bella (Newman) Gubin; m. Matthew Armin Tolchin, Sept. 1, 1966; 1 child, Benjamin. AB, Vassar Coll., 1964; MD, NYU, 1972. Diplomate Am. Bd. Gen. Psychiatry, Am. Bd. Child Psychiatry. Rsch. asst. Albert Einstein Coll. Medicine, NYC, 1964-68; instr. psychiatry med. coll. Cornell U., NYC, 1977-78, clin. instr., 1978-86, clin. asst. prof., 1986—2004, clin. assoc. prof., 2004—. Contbr. articles to profl. jours., chapters to books. Fellow: Am. Acad. Psychoanalysis and Dynamic Psychiatry (sec. 1998—2001, pres. elect 2007—), Am. Acad. Child and Adolescent Psychiatry; mem.: N.Y. Coun. Child and Adolescent Psychiatry (bd. dirs. 1992—96, pres. 1994—95, bd. advisors 2001—), Alpha Omega Alpha. Office: 35 E 84th St New York NY 10028-0871

TOLCHIN, MARTIN, journalist, writer; b. NYC, Sept. 20, 1928; s. Charles T. and Evelyn (Weisman) Tolchin; m. Susan Jane Goldsmith, Dec. 23, 1965; children: Karen. Student, U. Utah, 1947-49; LL.B., N.Y. Law Sch., 1951. Reporter N.Y. Times, NYC, 1954—94; pub., editor-in-chief The Hill, Washington, 1994—2002; sr. pub., editor The Politico, 2006—. Author (with Susan Jane Tolchin): To The Victor, 1971; author: Clout-Woman Power and Politics, 1974, Dismantling America-The Rush to Deregulate, 1983, Buying Into America: How Foreign Money is Changing the Face of Our Nation, 1988, Selling Our Security-The Erosion of American's Assets, 1992, Glass Houses: Congressional Ethics and the Politics of Venom, 2001, A World Ignited: How Apostles of Ethnic, Religious and Racial Hatred Torch the Globe, 2006. Served with U.S. Army, 1951-53. Recipient Schaeffer Gold Typewriter award E.M. Schaeffer Co., 1967; recipient Page One award Newspaper Guild N.Y., 1967, 69, 73, Citizens Budget Commn. award, 1967, Sigma Delta Chi award, 1973, Everett M. Dirksen award for disting. reporting of Congress, 1983; named to Journalism Hall Fame, Soc. Profl. Journalists, 2004. Mem. Nat. Press Club (Washington), Univ. Club. Jewish. Home: 3525 Winfield Ln NW Washington DC 20007-2378 Home Phone: 202-625-7782. Personal E-mail: mtolchin@aol.com.

TOLCHIN, SUSAN JANE, political science professor, writer; b. NYC, Jan. 14, 1941; d. Jacob Nathan and Dorothy Ann (Markowitz) Goldsmith; m. Martin Tolchin, Dec. 23, 1965; 1 child, Karen Rebecca. BA, Bryn Mawr Coll., 1961; MA, U. Chgo., 1962; PhD, NYU, 1968. Lectr. in polit. sci. CCNY, NYC, 1963-65, Bklyn. Coll., 1965-71; adj. asst. prof. polit. sci. Seton Hall U., South Orange, NJ, 1971-73; assoc. prof. polit. sci., dir. Inst. for Women and Politics, Mt. Vernon Coll., Washington, 1975-78; prof. pub. adminstrn. George Washington U., Washington, 1978-98; prof.sch. pub. policy George Mason U., Fairfax, Va., 1998—. Disting. lectr. Indsl. Coll. Armed Forces, 1994. Author: The Angry American: How Voter Rage is Changing the Nation, 1996, 2d edit., 1998; author: (with Martin Tolchin) To the Victor: Political Patronage from the Clubhouse to the White House, 1971, Clout--Womanpower and Politics, 1974, Dismantling America--The Rush to Deregulate, 1983, Buying Into America--How Foreign Money Is Changing the Face Of Our Nation, 1988, Selling Our Security--The Erosion of America's Assets, 1992, Glass Houses--Congressional Ethics and the Politics of Venom, 2001, A World Ignited: How Apostles of Ethnic, Religions and Racial Hatred Torch the Globe, 2006. Bd. dirs. Cystic Fibrosis Found., 1982-98; county committeewoman Dem. Party, Montclair, N.J., 1969-73. Recipient Founder's Day award NYU, 1968, Trachtenberg award for rsch. George Washington U., 1998; named Tchr. of Yr., Mt.

Vernon Coll., 1978; Dilthey fellow George Washington U., 1983, Aspen Inst. fellow, 1979. Fellow Nat. Acad. Pub. Adminstrn.; mem. Am. Polit. Sci. Assn. (pres. Women's Caucus for Polit. Sci. 1977-78), Am. Soc. Pub. Adminstrn. (chair sect. natural resources and environ. adminstrn. 1982-83, Marshall Dimock award 1997). Democrat. Office: Sch Pub Policy George Mason U 3401 Fairfax Dr Arlington VA 22201 Home Phone: 202-625-7782.

TOLCHINSKY, PAUL DEAN, organization design psychologist; b. Cleve., Sept. 30, 1946; s. Sanford Melvin and Frances (Klein) T.; m. Laurie S. Schermer, Nov. 3, 1968 (div. Jan. 1982); m. Kathy L. Dworkin, June 19, 1988; children: Heidi E., Dana M. BA, Bowling Green State U., 1971; PhD, Purdue U., 1978. Asst. br. mgr., tng. instr. Detroit Bank and Trust, 1971-73; mgr. tng. and devel. nuclear divsn. Babcock and Wilcox Co., Barberton, Ohio, 1973-75; internal cons. food products divsn. Gen. Foods Corp., West Lafayette, Ind., 1975-77; grad. tchg. asst. Krannert Grad. Sch. Mgmt. Purdue U., West Lafayette, 1975-78; asst. prof. mgmt. Coll. Bus. Adminstrn. Fla. State U., Tallahassee, 1978-79, U. Akron, Ohio, 1979-81; pres. Performance Devel. Assocs., Cleve., 1975—; ptnr. Dannemiller Tyson Assocs., Cleve., 1994-99; mng. ptnr. Performance Devel. Assocs., 2000—. Sr. lectr. Case Western Res. U., 2002—. Contbr. articles to profl. publs. Bd. dirs. Temple Tiferth Israel, Cleve., 195, Cleve. Jewish News, Jewish Family Svcs. Assn. Cleve. With U.S. Army, 1966-69, Vietnam. Mem. APA, Acad. Mgmt. Democrat. Jewish. Avocations: running, travel. Office: Performance Devel Assocs 50 Fox Glen Rd Moreland Hills OH 44022 Home Phone: 440-349-1441; Office Phone: 440-349-1990. Personal E-mail: kdtpdt@aol.com.

TOLEDO, BOB, college football coach; b. San Jose, Calif., June 4, 1946; m. Elaine Barras; children: Demetra, Christa, Alissa. BS in Phys. Edn., San Francisco State U., 1968. Asst. football coach Riordan H.S., San Francisco, 1969-70, head coach, 1970-72; offensive coord. U. Calif., Riverside, 1973; head football coach U. Calif. Golden Bears, Riverside, 1974-75; secondary coach U. So. Calif. Trojans, 1976-78; head football coach U. Pacific Tigers, 1979-82; asst. head coach, offensive coord., quarterbacks coach U. Oreg. Ducks, 1983-88; offensive coord., quarterbacks coach Tex. A&M U. Aggies, College Station, 1988-93; offensive coord. UCLA Bruins, 1994-96, head coach, 1996—2002; asst. head coach, offensive coord. U. N. Mex. Lobos, 2006; head football coach Tulane U. Green Wave, New Orleans, 2006—. Office: Tulane U 6823 St Charles Ave New Orleans LA 70118

TOLEDO, FREDERICO GRANCHI STEIDEL, physician, scientist; b. Rio de Janeiro, Jan. 21, 1972; s. Jose Augusto Toledo and Francisca Granchi. MD, U. Fed. Rio de Janeiro, 1996. Rsch. trainee U. Fed. Rio de Janeiro, 1990-93; spl. project assoc. Mayo Clinic, Rochester, Minn., 1994, rsch. fellow, 1996—98; resident in internal medicine U. Miami, Fla., 1999—2002; endocrinology fellow U. Pitts., 2002—04, clin. instr. of medicine, 2004—07, asst. prof., 2007—. Mem.: Am. Diabetes Assn., European Assn. for Study of Diabetes, Endocrine Soc.

TOLEDO, ISABEL, apparel designer; b. Cuba, 1961; m. Ruben Toledo. Grad., Fashion Inst. of Tech., NYC, Parsons Sch. of Design. Launched collection Isabel Toledo, 1985—; opened first store The Lab, NYC, 2004—; creative dir. Anne Klein Jones Apparel Group, 2006—. Collaborator (with Ruben Toledo) on various art exhibits including A Marriage of Art and Fashion; designs shown in Victoria & Albert Museum, London, Mode Museum, Antwerp, Fashion Inst. of Tech., Kent State U. Museum, Ohio, Gallery of Museum of Otis Coll. of Art and Design, Los Angeles. Recipient Cooper Hewitt Design award, 2005, Fashion Design award, Nat. Design Museum. Office: Anne Klein 1411 Broadway New York NY 10018 *

TOLENDINO, LAWRENCE FRANCIS, electrical engineer; b. Rahway, NJ, Mar. 5, 1945; s. Lawrence F. and Anna E. Tolendino; m. Christina Doris Chapman; children: Erik Justin, Gregory Lars. BSEE, Newark Coll. Engring., NJ, 1967; MSEE, U. N.Mex, Albuquerque, 1969. Grad. asst. U. N.Mex., Albuquerque, 1973—76; mem. tech. staff Sandia Nat. Labs., Albuquerque, 1976—. Cons. in field. Contbr. articles to profl. jours. Advisor sci. advisors program Sandia K-12, Los Lunas, N.Mex., 1992—93; judge mid. sch. sci. fair Queen Heaven Sch., Albuquerque, 1996—2001. Capt. USAF, 1969—73. Fellow, NDEA, 1967—69. Mem.: IEEE, Eta Kappa Nu. Avocations: hiking, bicycling, travel, photography. Office: Sandia National Labs PO Box 5800 MS 0806 Albuquerque NM 87185 Home Phone: 505-865-6073; Office Phone: 505-845-8587. Business E-Mail: lftolen@sandia.gov.

TOLER, PENNY, former professional basketball player, sports team executive; b. Mar. 24, 1966; B in Psychology, Long Beach State U., 1989. Guard, Montecchio, Italy, 1989—91, Pescara, Italy, 1991—94, Sporting Flash, Greece, 1994—96, Ramat HaSharon, Israel, 1996—97, Los Angeles Sparks, (WNBA), 1997—99; gen. mgr. L.A. Sparks, 1999—. Mem. U.S. Basketball Olympic Com., 1999—. Founder Points from Penny Program, 1998. Named All-Am. & Co-Player of Yr./Big West, 1988, 1989. Achievements include scored first ever basket in WNBA history. Avocations: ping pong/table tennis, tennis, craps. Office: LA Sparks Great Western Forum 555 N Nash St El Segundo CA 90245-2818

TOLES, THOMAS GREGORY, editorial cartoonist; b. Buffalo, Oct. 22, 1951; s. George Edward and Rose Elizabeth (Riehle) Toles; m. Gretchen Amanda Saarnijoki, May 26, 1973; children: Amanda Laurel, Seth August. BA in English, SUNY, Buffalo, 1973. Artist Buffalo Courier-Express, NY, 1973—80, cartoonist NY, 1980—82, Buffalo News, NY, 1982—2002, UPS, 1982—, US News & World Report, 1994—99, The New Republic, 2000—02, Washington Post, Wash., DC, 2002—. Author: My School Is Worse than Yours, 1997; cartoon collection, The Taxpayer's New Clothes, 1985, Mr. Gazoo: A Cartoon History of the Reagan Era, 1987, At Least Our Bombs Are Getting Smarter: A Cartoon Preview of the 1990's, 1991, My Elected Representatives Went to Washington, 1993, Duh, 1996, comic strip, Curious Avenue, 1992—94, Randolph Itch, 2a.m., 2000—02. Recipient John Fischetti Editorial Cartoon award, Columbia Coll., Chgo., 1984, Pulitzer Prize for editl. cartooning, 1990, Editl. Cartoonist of the Yr., 2002. Mem.: Am. Assn. Editorial Cartoonists. Office: Washington Post 1150 15th St NW Washington DC 20071

TOLF, ROBERT WALTER, writer; b. Chgo., Aug. 3, 1929; s. Carl Oscar and Margaret Emilia (Zeltner) T.; m. Nancy Ellen List, Aug. 9, 1952; 1 child, Carolyn Anne. BA cum laude, Harvard U., 1951; PhD, U. Rochester, 1957. Attache, 2d sec. U.S. Dept. State, various locations, 1957-70; editor Fla. Trend, St. Petersburg, 1973—; columnist, critic Sun-Sentinel, Ft. Lauderdale, Fla., 1975—; sr. sch. fellow Hoover Instn., 1976—77; exec. dir. Phileas Soc., Ft. Lauderdale, 1988—; producer, writer, narrator Columbus Documentaries, Ft. Lauderdale, 1989-92. Sr. rsch. fellow Hoover Inst., 1977. Author: The Russian Rockefellers, 1976, Addison Mizner, 1983, Chicago Sketch Book, 1988, Paris Sketch Book, 1990, Discover Florida, 1982, Country Inns of the Old South, 1978, 83, Country Inns of New York State, 1984, Country Inns of the Mid-Atlantic, 1986, Florida Weekends, 1990, 94, Florida's Best Beach Vacations, 1992, Florida Country Inns, 1993, 96, Destination Florida--Sanibel and Captiva, 1993, Destination Florida--South Beach Miami, 1993, 17 Florida Restaurant Guides, 1973-96, Trumpy, 1996, others; editor: Columbus Documents, 1992; author, prodr. narrator 15 videos in The Great Explorers Series. Lt. U.S. Army, 1954-57. Mem. Harvard Varsity Club, Fox Club, Harvard Club Broward County. Office: 3100 S Ocean Blvd Apt 422 Highland Beach FL 33487

TOLIA, VASUNDHARA K., pediatric gastroenterologist, educator; b. Calcutta, India; came to U.S., 1975; d. Rasiklal and Saroj (Kothari) Doshi; m. Kirit Tolia, May 30, 1975; children: Vinay, Sanjay. MBBS, Calcutta U., 1968-75. Intern, resident Children's Hosp. Mich., Detroit, 1976-79, fellow, 1979-81, dir. pediat. endoscopy unit, 1984-90, dir. pediat. gastroenterology and nutrition, 1990—2005. Instr. Wayne State U., Detroit, 1981—83, asst. prof., 1983—91, assoc. prof., 1991—97, prof., 1997—2005. Mem. editl. bd. Inflammatory Bowel Diseases, 1999-2005 Am. Jour. Gastroenterology, 1999-2005, Rev. of World Lit. in Pediatrics, 1999—, AAP Grand Rounds and Therapy, 2006—; contbr. articles to profl. jours. Named Woman of Distinction, Mich. chpt. Crohn's and Colitis Found. Am., 1991. Fellow Am. Coll. Gastroenterology (chair ad-hoc com. pediat. gastroenterology 1998-2000), Am. Acad. Pediats.; mem. Am. Gastroenterology Assn., N.Am. Soc. Pediat. Gastroenterology and Nutrition, Soc. Pediat. Rsch. Office Phone: 248-737-8793.

TOLINS, ROGER ALAN, lawyer; b. Bklyn., Jan. 25, 1936; s. Albert and Claire (Rothstein) T.; m. Doris Levine, May 15, 1960; children: Fran, Jonathan. AB with distinction, Dartmouth Coll., 1956; LLB, NYU, 1959, LLM in Taxation, 1961. Bar: N.Y. 1959. Assoc. Brennan, London & Buttenwieser, NYC, 1961-67; ptnr. Goldfeld, Charak, Tolins & Lowenfels, NYC, 1967-74, Tolins & Lowenfels, NYC, 1975—. Guest lectr. in securities law Seton Hall U. Sch. Law, 1989—. With U.S. Army, 1959-60. Mem. ABA (sect. on taxation), N.Y. State Bar Assn. Office Phone: 212-421-1965. E-mail: roger@tolinslowenfels.com.

TOLIVER, LEE, mechanical engineer; b. Wildhorse, Okla., Oct. 3, 1921; s. Clinton Leslie and Mary (O'Neall) T.; m. Barbara Anne O'Reilly, Jan. 24, 1942 (dec. Jan. 1999); children: Margaret Anne, Michael Edward. BSME, U. Okla., 1942. Engr. Douglas Aircraft Co., Santa Monica, Calif., 1942, Oklahoma City, 1942-44, Los Alamos Sci. Lab., N.Mex., 1946; instr. mech. engring. Ohio State U., Columbus, 1946-47; engr. Sandia Nat. Labs., Albuquerque, 1947-82; instr. computer sci. and math. U. N.Mex., Valencia County, 1982-84; number theory researcher Belen, N.Mex., 1982—. Author: Relations Between Prime and Relatively Prime Integers, 1998, Prime Number Problems: Solved, 2006. With Manhattan Project (Atomic Bomb) U.S. Army, 1944-46. Home: 206 Howell St Belen NM 87002-6225

TOLKACHEVA, ELENA, physicist, researcher; b. Minsk, Belarus, Feb. 10, 1970; arrived in US, 2001; d. Georgii Zabrodskii and Galina Zabrodskaya; m. Arkadzi Talkachou, Oct. 2, 1969; children: Kate Talkachova, Iryna Talkachova. MS, Belarussian State U., Minsk, 1992; PhD (hon.), Nice U., France, 2003. Postdoctoral assoc. Duke U., Durham, NC, 2001—04; rsch. asst. prof. SUNY Upstate Med. U., Syracuse, NY, 2005—. Recipient Scientist Devel. grant, Am. Heart Assn., 2006—10, Young Investigator award, Upstate NY Cardiac Electrophysiology Soc., 2005. Mem.: Heart Rhythm Soc. (Young Investigator award 2004, fellowship 2004, 2005). Office: SUNY Upstate Medical U 750 E Adams St Syracuse NY 13210 Home Phone: 315-254-4737; Office Phone: 315-464-7958. Personal E-mail: elenatolkacheva@yahoo.com.

TOLL, BARBARA ELIZABETH, art gallery director; b. Phila., June 8, 1945; d. Joseph M. and Evelyn Toll BA, Goucher Coll., 1967; MFA, Pratt Inst., 1969. Asst. dir. jr. coun. Mus. Modern Art, NYC, 1969-70; dir. Hundred Acres Gallery, NYC, 1971-76; curator David Rockefeller Collection, NYC, 1975-81; pres., dir. Barbara Toll Fine Arts, NYC, 1981-94, dir., 1994—. Bd. dirs. Corp. Yaddo; curator Focus: Donald Judd Furniture, Parrish Art Mus., Southampton, NY, 1996, Friendships in Arcadia: Writers and Artists at Yaddo in the 90s, 2000, Follies: Fantasy in the Landscape, Parrish Art Mus., 2001, Reconfiguring Space: Blueprints for Art in Gen., 2003. Trustee Ind. Curators Internat.; nat. bd. dirs. ArtTable, 2001—04. Avocation: gardening. Office: 138 Prince St New York NY 10012-3135

TOLL, BRUCE ELLIOT, real estate developer; b. Phila., Apr. 29, 1943; s. Albert Arthur and Sylvia Toll; m. Robbi Stern; children: Michelle, Elizabeth, Wendy, Jennifer. BA in Acctg., U. Miami, 1965. Pres., dir., COO Toll Brothers Inc., Horsham, Pa., 1967—98, vice chmn., 1998—; founder, principal BET Investments. Bd. dir. UbiquiTel Inc., Home Builders Assn. Bucks & Montgomery Counties. Twp. commr. Abington Twp., Pa., 1985-87; bd. dirs. Abington Meml. Hosp., Pa. Nursing Home Loan Agy., 1983-91; chmn., past pres. Abington Indsl. Devel. Authority; bd. mem. Ben Franklin Tech Ctr. SE Pa., Phila. Mus. Art. Mem. Nat. Homebuilders Assn., Philmont Country Club, Equity. Republican. Office: Toll Brothers Inc 250 Gibraltar Rd Horsham PA 19044 *

TOLL, HENRY WOLCOTT, JR., pathologist; b. Denver, Dec. 20, 1923; s. Henry Wolcott Toll and Cyrena Van Syckel Martin; m. Lydia Brewster Toll, Sept. 17, 1948; children: H. Wolcott, William Brewster, Ellen Toll, Lois Toll, Edward Wolcott. BA, Williams Coll., Williamstown, Mass., 1945; MD, U. Colo., Denver, 1950; JD, U. Denver, 1956. Diplomate Am. Bd. Anatomic Pathology, Clinical Pathology, Forensic Pathology. Fellow internal medicine Lahey Clinic, Boston, 1952—53; assoc. pathologist Denver Gen. Hosp., 1953—59, 1969—79, Presbyn. Hosp., Denver, 1959—69; asst. clin. pathology U. Colo., 1959—95. Bd. dirs. Webb Waring Lung Inst., 1970—73, Bell Bonfils Blood Bank, 1975—92. Lt. USNR, 1943—46. Recipient Silver and Gold award, U. Colo. Med. Alumni Assn. Mem.: Denver Colo. Med. Soc. (pres. 1976), Denver Athletic Club, Cactus Club, Denver Cath. Club, Denver Country Club. Home: 777 Vine St Denver CO 80206

TOLL, JOHN SAMPSON, retired academic administrator, physics professor; b. Denver, Oct. 25, 1923; s. Oliver Wolcott and Merle d'Aubigne (Sampson) T.; m. Deborah Ann Taintor, Oct. 24, 1970; children: Dacia Merle Sampson, Caroline Taintor. BS with honors, Yale U., 1944; AM, Princeton U., 1948, PhD, 1952; DSc (hon.), U. Md., 1973, U. Wroclaw, Poland, 1975; LLD (hon.), Adelphi U., 1978; PhD (hon.), Fudan U., Peoples Republic China, 1987; LHD (hon.), SUNY, Stony Brook, 1990; LLD (hon.), U. Md., Eastern Shore, 1993. Mng. editor, acting chmn. Yale Sci. mag., 1943-44; with Princeton U., 1946-49, proctor fellow, 1948-49; Friends of Elementary Particle Theory Research grantee for study in France, 1950; theoretical physicist Los Alamos Sci. Lab., 1950-51; staff mem., assoc. dir. Project Matterhorn, Forrestal Rsch. Ctr., Princeton U., 1951-53; prof., chmn. physics and astronomy U. Md., 1953-65; pres., prof. physics SUNY, Stony Brook, 1965-78, U. Md., 1978-88, chancellor, 1988-89, chancellor emeritus, prof. physics, 1989—; pres. Univs. Rsch. Assn., Washington, 1989-94, Washington Coll., Chestertown, Md., 1995—. 1st dir. chancellor's panel on univ. pruposes SUNY, 1970; physics cons. to editl. staff Nat. Sci. Tchrs. Assn., 1957—61; U.S. del., head scientist, secretariat Internat. Conf. High Energy Physics, 1960; mem.-at-large U.S. nat. com. Internat. Union Pure and Applied Physics, 1960—63; chmn. rsch. adv. com. on electrophysics NASA, 1961—65; mem. gov. Md. Sci. Resources Adv. Bd., 1963—65; mem., chmn. adv. panel for physics NSF, 1964—67; mem. N.Y. Gov.'s Adv. Com. Atomic Energy, 1966—70; mem. commn. plans and objectives higher edn. Am. Coun. Edn., 1966—69; mem. Hall of Records Commn., 1979—88; mem., chmn. adv. coun. Princeton Plasma Physics Lab., 1979—85; mem. adv. coun. pres.'s Assn. Governing Bds., 1980—88, So. Regional Edn. Bd., 1980—90; mem. exec. com. Washington/Balt. Regional Assn., 1980—89, Nat. Assn. State Univs. and Land Grant Colls., 1980—88, Ctr. Study of the Presidency, 1983—84; mem. univ. programs panel of energy rsch. bd. Dept. Energy, 1982—83; mem. adv. com. SBHE, 1983—89, Md. Gov.'s Chesapeake Bay Coun., 1985; mem. resource com. state trade policy coun. Gov.'s high tech roundtable Md. Dept. Econ. Devel., 1986—89; chmn. marine divsn. NASULGC, 1986; bd. trustees Aspen Inst. Humanities, 1987—89; mem. commn. higher edn. Middle States Assn. Colls. and Schs., 1987; chmn. adv. panel on tech. risks and opportunities for U.S. energy supply and demand U.S. Office Tech. Assessment, 1987—91, chmn. adv. panel on internat. collaboration in def. tech., 1989—91; mem. Sea Grant rev. panel U.S. Dept. Commerce, 1992—, chair, 1996—97; mem. com. financing higher edn. Nat. Assn. Ind. Colls. and Univs., 1996—98; bd. govs. Chesapeake Bay Maritime Mus., 1996—; dir. Md. Gov.'s Blue Ribbon Citizens Pfiesteria Action Commn., 1997; mem. governing coun. Wye Faculty Seminar, 1997—; dir. Eastern Shore Assn. Coll. Pres., 1998—; mem. bd. dirs. Md. Ctr. Agro-Ecology, Inc., 1999—; vis. prof. Nordic Inst. Theoretical Physics, Niels Bohr Inst., Denmark, U. Lund, Sweden, 1975—76; mem. math. scis. edn. bd. NAS; mem. Higher Edn. Heritage Action Com., 2002—. Contbr. articles to profl. jours. Mem. adv. coun. Del-Mar-Va coun. Boy Scouts Am., 1999—; mem. Higher Edn. Heritage Action Com., 2002—; bd. dirs. Hodson Scholarship Found., 1996, Mid-Shore Cmty. Found., 2002—. Recipient Benjamin Barge prize in math. Yale U., 1943, George Beckwith medal for Proficiency in Astronomy, 1944, Outstanding Citizen award City of Denver, 1958, Outstanding Tchr. award U. Md. Men's League, 1965, Copernicus award govt. of Poland, 1973, Stony Brook Found. award for disting. contbns. to edn., 1979, Disting. Svc. award State of Md., 1981, Silver medal Sci. U. Tokyo, 1994, Internat. Landmark award U. Md., 1994, first recipient Lifetime Achievement award Md. Assn. for Higher Edn., 2000, Chief Exec. Leadership award Coun. for Advancement and Support Edn., 2000; named Washingtonian of Yr., 1985, Citizen of Yr. Chestertown Optimist Club, 1997, John S. Toll Physics Bldg., Univ. Md., 2001; John Simon Guggenheim Meml. Found. fellow Inst. Theoretical Physics U. Copenhagen, U. Lund, Sweden, 1958-59. Fellow AAAS, Am. Phys. Soc., Washington Acad. Scis. (pres. 1995-96), N.Y. Acad. Scis.; mem. NSTA, Am. Coun. Edn. (bd. dirs. 1986-89, NAACP (life), Am. Assn. Physics Tchrs., Fedn. Am. Scientists (chmn. 1961-62), Philos. Soc. Washington, Assn. Higher Edn., Yale U. Sci. and Engring. Assn. (award for disting. contbns. 1996), Cosmos Club, Hamilton St. Club, Baltimore, Univ. Club (Washington and N.Y.), Phi Beta Kappa, Phi Kappa Phi (disting., Marylander of Yr. 2000 award), Sigma Xi (Sci. Achievement award 1965), Omicron Delta Kappa (hon.), Sigma Pi Sigma. Achievements include research on elementary particle theory, scattering. Office: U Md Dept Physics College Park MD 20742-4111 also: Washington Coll Pres's Office Chestertown MD 21620 E-mail: johntoll@physics.umd.edu, jtoll2@washcoll.edu. *Throughout my life I have tried mainly to do whatever seemed most important and useful.*

TOLL, PERRY MARK, lawyer, educator; b. Kansas City, Mo., Oct. 28, 1945; s. Mark Irving and Ruth (Parker) T.; m. Mary Anne Shottenkirk, Aug. 26, 1967; children: Andrea Lynne, Hillary Anne. BS in Polit. Sci. and Econs., U. Kans., 1967, JD, 1970. Bar: Mo. 1970 1970, U.S. Dist. Ct. (we. dist.) Mo. 1970, U.S. Tax. Ct. 1979, U.S. Supreme Ct. 1979. With Shughart, Thomson & Kilroy P.C., Kansas City, 1970—, pres., 1995—2006, past chmn. bus. dept. Asst. prof. deferred compensation U. Mo., Kansas City, 1979-83; bd. dirs., pres. Heart of Am. Tax Inst., Kansas City, 1975-87. Mem., chmn. Prairie Village (Kans.) Bd. Zoning Appeals, 1977-95. Mem. ABA, Mo. Bar Assn., Am. Health Lawyers Assn., Am. Agr. Law Assn., Mo. Merchants and Mfrs. Assn., Greater Kansas City Med. Mgrs. Assn., Lawyers Assn. Kansas City, East Kans. Estate Planning Coun. (bd. dirs., pres.), Phi Kappa Tau (bd. dirs. Beta Theta chpt.). Office: Shughart Thomson & Kilroy 12 Wyandotte Plz 120 W 12th St Ste 1500 Kansas City MO 64105-1929

TOLL, ROBERT IRWIN, home construction company executive; b. Elkins Park, Pa., Dec. 30, 1940; s. Albert A. and Sylvia (Steinberg) T.; m. Norma (div.); children: Laurie, Deborah; m. Jane Snyder; children: Rachel, Jacob; stepson, Joshua Goldfein. AB, Cornell U., 1963; LLB cum laude, U. Pa., 1966. Bar: Pa. 1967. Atty. Wolf, Block Schorr Solis-Cohen, Phila., 1966-67; founder Toll Bros. Inc., Huntingdon Valley, Pa., 1967, chmn., CEO, 1967—. Mem. Mayor's Coun. on Housing in Phila.; mem. bd. overseers U. Pa. Law Sch.; mem. real estate coun. Cornell U. Real Estate Coun. Bd. dirs. Pa. Campaign for Choice, Phila., Beth Sholom Synagogue, Elkins Park, Southeastern chpt. ARC, Seeds of Peace, NYC; sponsor Say Yes to Edn., Phila.; mem. bd. trustees Abington Meml. Hosp. Found. Named Profl. Builder of Yr., Builder Mag., 1988, America's Best Builder, Nat. Assn. Homebuilders and Builder Mag., 1996, Ernst & Young's Master Entrepreneur of Yr. Award, 1996; recipient Nat. Housing Quality Award, Nat. Assn. Home Builders, 1995, Bronze Award, CEO of Yr., Fin. World, 1996, Residential Building Industry's CEO Silver Award, Wall Street Transcript, 1996. Mem. Nat. Assn. Home Builders, Philmont Country Club (Huntingdon Valley), Equity Lodge 591. Avocations: racing j/35 sailboats, tennis, skiing. Office: Toll Brothers Inc 250 Gibraltar Rd Horsham PA 19044-2323 *

TOLL, SHELDON SAMUEL, lawyer; b. Phila., June 6, 1940; s. Herman and Rose (Ornstein) T.; m. Roberta Darlene Pollack, Aug. 11, 1968; children: Candice Moore, John Maitland, Kevin Scott. BA, U. Pa., 1962; MA, Oxford U., Eng., 1964; JD, Harvard U., 1967. Bar: Pa. 1967, Mich. 1972, Ill. 1990, Tex. 1990, U.S. Dist. Ct. (ea. dist.) Pa. 1968, U.S. Ct. Appeals (3d cir.) 1970, U.S. Supreme Ct. 1971, Mich. 1972, U.S. Dist. Ct. (ea. dist.), U.S. Ct. Appeals (6th cir.) 1973, U.S. Ct. Appeals (5th cir.) 1978, U.S. Dist. Ct. (no. dist.) Calif. 1986, U.S. Ct. Appeals (9th cir.) 1987, U.S. Dist. Ct. (ea. dist.) Wis. 1989. Assoc. Montgomery, McCracken et al, Phila., 1967-72; sr. ptnr. Honigman Miller Schwartz and Cohn, Detroit, 1972—2003; prin. Sheldon S. Toll PLLC, Southfield, Mich., 2003—. Panelist Bankruptcy Litigation Inst., N.Y.C., 1984-94. Author: Toll's Pennsylvania Crime Code, 2005, Bankruptcy Litigation Manual, 2004. Bd. dirs. Southeastern Mich. chpt. ARC, Detroit. Mem. Fed. Bar Assn. (past pres. Detroit chpt.), ABA, Pa. Bar Assn., Phila. Bar Assn., Franklin (Mich.) Hills Country Club, Mar-a-Lago Club (Palm Beach, Fla.), Phi Beta Kappa. Democrat. Jewish. Office: Sheldon S Toll PLLC 2000 Town Ctr Ste 2550 Southfield MI 48075 Office Phone: 248-358-2460. Business E-Mail: lawtoll@comcast.net.

TOLLEFSON, BEN C., state legislator, retired utilities executive; b. Minot, ND, June 14, 1927; s. Ben K. and Hannah G. (Espeseth) T.; m. Lila R. Adams, Apr. 11, 1949; children: Robb, LuAnn, David, Richard. Student, Minot State U., 1946-48. Advt. salesman Minot Daily News, 1956-57; utility salesman No. States Power Co., Minot, 1957-72, sales mgr., 1972-89; retired, 1989; advisor Ctrl. Venture Capital, Minot, 1990-95; mem. N.D. Ho. of Reps., Bismark, 1984-99, N.D. Senate from 38th dist., Bismark, 2001—. Pres. Minot Jaycees, 1957. Served with USN, 1945-47. Recipient Clara Barton Svc. award Am. Red Cross, 1969; named one of Outstanding Young Men Am., Minot Jaycees, 1958, State Ofcl. Yr., Nat. Assn. Home Builders, 1992. Mem. Kiwanis (Minot lt. gov. 1973, Outstanding Lt. Gov. 1973). Republican. Lutheran. Avocations: hunting, public speaking. Home: 500 Twenty Fourth St NW Minot ND 58701

TOLLEFSON, TERRENCE ALFRED, education educator, consultant; b. Pontiac, Mich., May 1, 1938; s. Alfred and Iva Denice Tollefson; m. Bonnie Lou Bradley, 1961 (dec. 1990); children: Katherine Marie, Michelle Suzanne Miller, Bradley Alfred. BA in Edn. and Soc. Studies, U. Mich., Ann Arbor, 1961; PhD, U. Mich., 1975; MBA in Mktg., Mich. State U., East Lansing, 1963. Assoc. prof. dept. adult and CC edn. NC State U., Raleigh, 1986—93; prof., interim chair dept. ednl. leadership and policy analysis East Tenn. State U., Johnson City, 1993—. Office: East Tennessee State Univ Box 70550 Johnson City TN 37614-1707 Home: 4100 Prescott Dr Johnson City TN 37601 Home Phone: 423-202-7093; Office Phone: 423-439-7617.

TOLLENAERE, LAWRENCE ROBERT, retired industrial products company executive; b. Berwyn, Ill., Nov. 19, 1922; s. Cyrille and Modesta (Van Damme) T.; m. Mary Elizabeth Hansen, Aug. 14, 1948; children: Elizabeth, Homer, Stephanie, Caswell, Mary Jennifer. BS in Engring., Iowa State U., 1944, MS in Engring., 1949; MBA, U. So. Calif., 1969; LLD (hon.), Claremont Grad. Sch., 1977. Specification engr. Alumninum Co. Am., Vernon, Calif., 1946-47; asst. prof. indsl. engring. Iowa State U., Ames, 1947-50; sales rep. Am. Pipe and Constrn. Co. (now AMERON), South Gate, Calif., 1950-53, spl. rep. S.Am., 1952-54, 2nd v.p., mgr. Columbian divsn. Bogota, S.Am., 1955-57, divsn. v.p., mgr. Calif., 1957-63, v.p. concrete pipe ops. Monterey Park, Calif., 1963-65, pres. corp. hdqrs., 1965-67; pres., CEO Ameron Inc., Monterrey Park, Calif., 1967-89, CEO, pres. Pasadena, 1989-93, chmn. bd. dirs., 1989-94, ret., 1994. Trustee The Huntington Library, Art Gallery and Bot. Gardens; emeritus mem. bd. fellows Claremont U. Ctr.; bd. gov.'s Iowa State U. Found. Mem. Calif. C. of C. (bd. dirs. 1977-92), Calif. Club (past pres.), Jonathan Club, Bohemian Club, San Francisco Club, Beavers Club (past pres., hon. dir.), Alpha Tau Omega. Republican. Avocations: fishing, hunting, horseback riding, stamp collecting/philately. Home: 650 Harrison Ave Claremont CA 91711-4538 Office: PO Box 910 Claremont CA 91711-0910

TOLLES, BRYANT FRANKLIN, JR., retired history and art professor; b. Hartford, Conn., Mar. 14, 1939; s. Bryant Franklin and Grace Frances (Ludden) T.; m. Carolyn Coolidge Kimball, Sept. 15, 1962; children: Thayer Coolidge, Bryant Franklin III. BA, Yale U., 1961, MA in Tchg., 1962; PhD, Boston U., 1970. Instr. history King Sch., Stamford, Conn., 1962-63; tchr. history St. George's Sch., Newport, RI, 1963-65; instr., asst. dean Tufts U., Medford, Mass., 1965-71; asst. dir., libr., editor publs. N.H. Hist. Soc., Concord, 1972-74; exec. dir., libr. Essex Inst., Salem, Mass., 1974-84; dir. mus. studies program, prof. history and art history U. Del., Newark, 1984—2005, prof. emeritus, 2005—, chmn. art conservation dept., 1997-2000. Mem. Com. for a New Eng. Bibliography, Inc. Author: New Hampshire Architecture, 1979, Architecture in Salem, 1983, The Grand Resort Hotels of the White Mountains: A Vanishing Architectural Legacy, 1998, Summer Cottages in the White Mountains: The Architecture of Leisure and Recreation, 1870-1930, 2000, Resort Hotels of the Adirondacks: The Architecture of a Summer Paradise, 1840-1940, 2003; editor: Leadership for the Future, 1991; contbr. articles and book revs. to profl. jours. Trustee Mt. Washington Obs., NH, NH Hist. Soc., Squam Lakes Nat. Sci. Ctr., NH. Ford. Found. fellow Yale U., 1962. Mem. Am. Antiquarian Soc., Colonial Soc. Mass., Orgn. Am. Historians, Soc. Archtl. Historians, Soc. Indsl. Archaeology, Am. Assn. Mus., New Eng. Mus. Assn., Mid-Atlantic Mus. Assn., Am. Assn. for State and Local History, Wilmington Rowing Club, Appalachian Mountain Club. Home: 1002 Kent Rd Wilmington DE 19807-2820 Business E-Mail: bftolles@udel.edu.

TOLLEY, AUBREY GRANVILLE, psychiatrist, health facility administrator; b. Lynchburg, Va., Nov. 15, 1924; married. Student, Duke U., 1942—43, U. Va., 1946—48, MD, 1952. Diplomate Am. Bd. Psychiatry and Neurology. Intern St. Elizabeths Hosp., Washington, 1952-53; asst. resident psychiatry U. Va. Hosp., Charlottesville, 1953-54; resident psychiatry VA Hosp., Roanoke, Va., 1955-56; instr. U. N.C. Sch. Medicine, 1956-61, asst. prof., 1961-66, clin. asst. prof. psychiatry, 1966-72, clin. assoc. prof., 1972-76, clin. prof., 1976—; dir. psychotherapy Dorothea Dix Hosp., Raleigh, NC, 1962-67, dir. hosp., 1973-88. Dir. resident tng. John Umstead Hosp., Butner, N.C., 1966-67; dir. profl. tng. and edn. N.C. Dept. Mental Health, Raleigh, 1967-72, asst. dir., 1972-73; prin. investigator USPHS grant, 1957-59; cons. VA Hosp., Fayetteville, N.C., 1957-78; sr. cons., supervising faculty, cmty. psychiatry sect. dept. psychiatry U. N.C. Sch. Medicine, 1971-88; exec. sec. Multiversity Group, 1968-73 Trustee Found. Hope, Raleigh, 1984—. Served with USNR, 1943-46. Recipient The Order of the Long Leaf Pine, State of N.C., 1982. Fellow Am. Psychiat. Assn. (disting. life; assembly rep. N.C. Dist. br. 1969-82, 86-2000, mem. joint commn. on pub. affairs 1984-87, mem. constl. membership com. 1990-96, mem. commn. on subspecialization 1990-94, Warren Williams award 1987), Am. Coll. Psychiatrists (life); mem. AMA, N.C. Med. Soc. (life), Durham-Orange County Med. Soc., N.C. Psychiat. Assn. (pres. 1984-85, Lifetime Disting. Svc. award 1999), N.C. Hosp. Assn. (life), George C. Ham Soc. (Disting. Alumni award 1992). Home and Office: 110 Laurel Hill Rd Chapel Hill NC 27514-4323

TOLLEY, B. CARY, III, lawyer; b. Washington, July 17, 1949; BA in Polit. Sci., Yale Univ., 1972; JD summa cum laude, Washington & Lee Univ., 1975; LLM in Taxation, Univ. Fla., 1978. Bar: Va. 1975, Fla. 1977, NY 1988. Ptnr., tax & ERISA practice Hunton & Williams LLP, NYC, and mem. exec. com. Exec. editor Washington & Lee Law Rev., 1974—75. Trustee Presbyn. Ch. USA Found., Presbyn. Investment Loan Program. Lt. JAG USNR, 1975—78. Mem.: ABA, Order of Coif. Office: Hunton & Williams LLP 43rd Fl 200 Park Ave New York NY 10166-0136 Office Phone: 212-309-1180. Office Fax: 212-309-1100. Business E-Mail: ctolley@hunton.com.

TOLLEY, EDWARD DONALD, lawyer; b. San Antonio, Jan. 31, 1950; s. Lyle Oren and Mary Theresa Tolley; m. Beth Dekle Tolley; 1 child, Edward Spencer. BBA, U. Ga., 1971, MBA, 1974, JD, 1975. Bar: Ga. 1975, U.S. Dist. Ct. (5th cir.) 1976, U.S. Supreme Ct. 1978, U.S. Ct. Appeals (11th cir.) 1981. Ptnr. Cook, Noell, Tolley Bates and Michael and predecessor firms, Athens, Ga., 1975—. Lectr. various colls., univs., civic and profl. groups. Mem. Family Counseling Assn. of Athens, Inc., mem. Gov.'s Commn. on Criminal Sanctions and Correctional Facilities, 1988-90; past bd. dirs. Am. Cancer Soc.; pres. Clarke County Bd. Edn., 1992-93. Recipient award for cmty. svc. Chief Justice Ga. Supreme Ct., 2000. Fellow Ga. Bar Found., Am. Bd. Criminal Lawyers (bd. dirs. 1987, pres. 1996); mem. Fed. Bar Assn. (sec. 1983, treas. 1985, pres. Macon chpt. 1997-98), State Bar Ga. (chmn. law office and econ. com., bd. govs. 1985—, formal adv. opinion bd., Professionalism award 2002), Ga. Trial Lawyers (v.p.), Ga. Assn. Criminal Def. Lawyers (pres. 1985, Indigent Def. award 1983, 88), Athens Bar Assn. (past pres.), Am. Judicature Soc., Order of Barristers (Cmty. Svc. award Chief Justice Ga. Supreme Ct., 2000). Office: Cook Noell et al 304 E Washington St Athens GA 30601-2751 Home Phone: 706-546-9972; Office Phone: 706-549-6111.

TOLLEY, JERRY RUSSELL, academic administrator; b. Goldsboro, NC, Nov. 6, 1942; s. Elva Russell Tolley and Clara (Smith) Tolley-Bunch; m. Joan Morrison, June 8, 1965; children: Jerry R. Jr., Justin Clay. BS, East Carolina U., 1965, MEd, 1966; EdD, U. NC, Greensboro, 1982; exec. mgmt. courses, Duke U. Tchr., coach Fayetteville Sr. HS, NC, 1966; asst. football coach, head track and tennis coach Elon Coll., NC, 1967-77, head football coach, 1977-81, dir. athletic sholarship fund, 1982, dir. corp. and ann. resources, 1983, coordinator Pride II Capital Campaign, 1984, assoc. dir. devel., 1985, officer corp. and major gifts, maj. gifts officer, 1999, dir. ann. giving, 2003; asst. v.p. tng., nat. dir. tng. & pub. affairs Lab. Corp. of Am., Burlington, NC, 1986—. Author: Intercollegiate History of Athletics and Elon College, 1982, American Football Coaches Guidebook to Championship Football Drills, 1985, 101 Winning Football Drills -From the Legends of the Game, 2003, The Complete Book of Defensive Football Drills, 2005, The Complete Book of Offensive Football Drills, 2005; co-author: 101 Winning Plays, 1977, Leadership Education: A Source Book, 1989; contbr. articles. Treas. Town of Elon Coll., 1984-87, mayor protem, 1988, mayor, 1990-98, 2006, mayor emeritus, 1998-2006, chmn. recreation commn.; mayor Town of Elon, 2006; convenor City County Govt. Assn., 1987-98, 2006-, Alamance County, NC, 1986—; mem. exec. bd. dir. Cherokee Coun. Boy Scouts Am., 1986, Thomas E. Powell Jr. Biology Found.; pres. Alamance Found.; exec. bd. NC Health & Fitness Found.; bd. visitors Elon Coll.; mem. exec. com. Alamance County Ptnrs. in Edn.; bd. govs. 2 Those Who Care; dir. Alamance Edn. Alliance; bd. dir. Cmty. Found. Greensboro; chmn. Citizens for Schs.; mktg. advisory com. Village of Brookwood; bd. advisors Randolf Bank. Named one of Outstanding Young Men Am., 1980, Internat. Men of Achievement, 1990, Cmty. Leaders Am., 1990, Mayors Hall of Fame, 1995; recipient Dwight D. Eisenhower award Nat. Football Hall of Fame, 1980, 81, Nat. Collegiate Football Championship award Eastman Kodak, Meritorious Svc. award Tom Sawyer-Huck Finn Tennis Classic, 1986, Order of the Long Leaf Pine, 1997, Laurel Wreath award State of NC, 2002, Old North State award, 2007; named Nat. Football Coach of Yr., Nat. Assn. Intercollegiate Athletics, 1980, Elon Coll. Sports Hall of Fame, East Carolina U. Athletic Hall of Fame, 1991. Mem.: All-Am. Football Found. (Lifetime Achievement award 2003), Coun. Advancement of Edn., Am. Football Coaches Assn. (life), Omicron Delta Kappa, Phi Delta Kappa, Sigma Delta Psi. Avocations: writing, racquet sports, jogging. Home: 1322 Westbrook Ave Elon NC 27244-9358 Office: Elon Univ 2600 Campus Box # 2600 Elon NC 27244-2010 Office Phone: 336-278-7447. Business E-Mail: tolleyj@elon.edu.

TOLLIFSON, THOMAS GERALD, retired art education consultant, educator; b. Albert Lea, Minn., Feb. 4, 1925; s. Virgil Irving and Lucile Katherine Tollifson; m. Jeannine May Dill, Aug. 10, 1952. BS in Art Edn., U. Minn., 1950; MA in Art Edn., Ohio State U., 1952. Art tchr. Columbus (Ohio) State Sch. for Mentally Retarded, 1951-52; art helping tchr. Arlington (Va.) Elem. Schs., 1952-54; art tchr. Washington Lee H.S., Arlington, 1954-56; art edn. instr. Am. U., Washington, 1953-54; art tchr. Jones Jr. H.S., Upper Arlington, Ohio, 1956-66; state art edn. cons. Ohio Dept. Edn., Columbus, 1966-94; ret., 1994. Art edn. instr. Ohio State U., 1950-51, 59-60, U. Va., Arlington, 1954-55—. Author (art edn. TV series guides) Images and Things, Nat. Instrn. TV, 1971, The Big A, Sta. KCTS-TV, Seattle, 1986, In Touch, Tollifson's Art Attack (series) in Art Line, Ohio Edn. Assn., 1978-94 co-author, actor (TV program) What's an Art Curriculum for Anyway?", 1980; editor (art curriculum guide) Planning a Balanced Comprehensive Art Curriculum, Ohio Dept. Edn., 1970, 87, 92; co-prodr.: (ednl. TV program) Making Connections, 1995; co-author: Comprehensive Arts Education Curriculum Framework for Ohio Schools, 1991, Ohio Plan for Comprehensive Arts in Education, 1978; art exhbn. Fitton Art Ctr., Hamilton, Ohio, 1997, Michelle's Gallery, Columbus, Ohio, 2002, Shremshock Gallery, Westerville, Ohio, 2004, MacWorthington Gallerie, Columbus, 2004, Ursus Gallery, Upper Arlington, Ohio, 2004, Soho Gallery, Worthington, Ohio, 2004, High Roads Gallery, Worthington, 2005. Founder Ohio Gov.'s Youth Art Exhbn., Columbus, 1969—, Ohio Alliance for Arts Edn., 1974, Ohio Youth Art Month, 1973, Ohio Arts Criticism Invitational and Open, 1989; advisor Getty Ctr. for Arts in Edn., L.A., 1987, Joint Coun. State Bd. Regents and State Bd. Edn., 1999—, Coalition for Equity and Adequacy, Columbus, 1999—, Winning America's Wars, 2002-, Support for Talented Students, 2002-; art judge, Ohio PTA. Sgt., U.S. Army Inf., 1943-45, ETO; adv. com. art curriculum Ohio Dept. Edn., 2004—. Named Gov.'s Arts Educator of Yr., Ohio Arts Coun., 2000; recipient Grand Nat. Youth Art Month award, 1974; Jerry Tollifson Ohio Mid. Sch. Art Criticism Open Contest named in his honor, 2000. Fellow: Ohio Art Edn. Assn. (adv. com. 1994—, advisor Ohio arts edn., art exhib. chmn. 2000, Outstanding Ohio Art Educator of Yr. 1984); mem.: Columbus Mus. Art, WWII Roundtable, Nat. Assn. State Dirs. Art Edn. (founder, chmn. 1967—70), Nat. Art Edn. Assn. (nat. art adminstr./supr. award 1995, Disting. Svc. award 1990), PBS, Columbus Torch Club. Avocations: drawing, painting, sculpture, architecture, landscape design. Home: PO Box 24352 Columbus OH 43224-0352 Office Phone: 614-475-0470.

TOLLIN, GORDON, retired chemistry professor; b. NYC, Dec. 26, 1930; s. Albert and Evelyn Tollin; children: Allen, Steven, Deborah Alter, Amina Livingston. PhD, Iowa State U., Ames, 1959; doctorate (hon.), Umea U., 2005. Prof. U. Ariz., Tucson, 1959—96, regents prof., 1996—. Contbr. over 350 sci. articles to profl. jours. Achievements include 4 patents in plasmon-waveguide resonance. Office: Univ Ariz 1041 E Lowell St Tucson AZ 85721 Office Phone: 502-621-3447.

TOLLISON, COURTNEY L., history professor; b. Greenville, SC, Aug. 26, 1977; d. Charles David and Linda Surett Tollison. BA, Furman U., 1999; MA, U. SC., 2001, PhD, 2003. Rsch. asst. Smithsonian Instn., Nat. Mus. of Am. History, Washington, 1998—98; instr. history Columbia Coll., SC, 2001—01, Dalton State Coll., Ga., 2003—03; vis. adj. asst. prof. history Furman U., Greenville, SC, 2004—; dir. oral history project Office of Pres. David E. Shi, Furman U., Greenville, SC, 2004—. Advanced placement reader for us history advanced placement exam Ednl. Testing Svc., Princeton, NJ, 2004—05. Author: Furman University, 2004 (Matrix award Nat. Assn. Women in Comms., 2005); contbr. chapters to books. Head agt. class of 1999 Furman U. Devel. Office, Greenville, SC, 2004—05, class agt., coll. graduating class, 1999—2004; reunion com. co-chair Furman U., 2004. Named Communicator of Yr. award, Assn. Women in Comm., 2005; named one of 35 and Under Best and Brightest, Greenville Mag.; recipient Young Profl. Yr., Greenville, SC C. of C., 2006, Head Agy Yr. award, Furman U., 1999, 2005—06. Mem.: So. Assn. of Women Historians, SC. Hist. Assn., Orgn. of Am. Historians, Am. Hist. Assn., Phi Alpha Theta, Alpha Delta Pi (life; stds. chair 1997—98). Avocations: reading, swimming, travel, ballet. Home Phone: 864-242-6410; Office Phone: 864-294-2377. Personal E-mail: courtneytollison@yahoo.com. Business E-Mail: courtney.tollison@furman.edu.

TOLLISON, JOSEPH W., family practice physician; BS, Citadel Mil. Col., SC, 1963; MD, Med. Univ. S.C., 1967. Pres. Am. Bd. Family Practice, Lexington, Ky., 1997, dep. exec. dir., 1999—. Prof. Med. Coll. Ga. Office: Am Bd Family Practice 2228 Young Dr Lexington KY 40505-4219

TOLLIVER, DOROTHY, librarian; b. NYC, Apr. 10, 1937; d. Morris and Rose (Poliner) Lamm; m. Robert F. Tolliver, Sept. 3, 1956; children: Craig Lee, Marc Alan. BA, Ind. U., 1958; MSLS, U. Ill., Champaign-Urbana, 1973. Inter-libr., reference libr. L.A. County Libr., 1958-59; dir. libr. Temple City (Calif.) Pub. Libr., 1959-60; reference, young adult libr. Burbank (Calif.) Pub. Libr., 1960-62; PTA libr. Roselawn Elem. Sch., Danville, Ill., 1970-72; reference libr. Danville Area C.C., 1970—72, head libr., 1973—88; libr. dir. Kahului Pub. Libr., 1988—89; head libr. UH Maui C.C., Kahului, 1989—, unit head for outreach and acad. support, 2004—. Cons. Ill. Office Edn., 1980-88, Hawaii Dept. Edn., 1992—. Mem. Commn. Status of Women, 1992—98; sec. Maui County Com. Status of Women, 1991—96; dir. Jewish Arts and Edn. Coun. Maui, 1996—99; mem. Hawaii Book Acad., judge Ka Pala Pala Po'okela awards, 2002—; chair Maui County Women's Conf., 1993; vice chair Maui County Commn. Persons with Disabilities, 1996—2001; pres. S&M Katz Jewish Libr. of Maui, 1996—, Hawaii Ctr. for the Book, 2002—; bd. dirs. Congregation Gan Eden, 1990—, pres., 1991—95; bd. dirs. Congregation Israel, pres., 1983—87; bd. dirs. Maui Cmty. Theater, 1997—; actor, dir. Voices on the Wind Readers' Theater, 1992—. Recipient Little Red Schoolhouse award Danville Schs. Citizens Com., 1972, Hawaii State award for leadership in promoting postive soc. change, edu. and womens equity, 1997. Mem.: AAUW (pres. Maui chpt. 1993—97, state bd. dirs. 1993, Hawaii State award), ALA, Am. Coll. and Rsch. Librs., Maui County Libr. Assn. (pres. 1990—96), Hawaii Libr. Assn. (bd. dirs.), Phi Beta Mu (alpha chpt.). Jewish. Avocations: reading, theater, travel. Office: Maui Community Coll 310 W Kaahumanu Ave Kahului HI 96732-1617 Home Phone: 808-242-5047; Office Phone: 808-984-3583. E-mail: tolliver@hawaii.edu.

TOLMACH, JANE LOUISE, community activist, municipal official; b. Havre, Mont., Nov. 12, 1921; d. Robert Francis and Veronica (Tracy) McCormick; m. Daniel Michael Tolmach (Dec.), Sept. 9, 1946; children: James, Richard, Eve Alice, Adam, Jonathan. AB, UCLA, 1943; M in Social Scis., Smith Coll., 1945; JD, S. We. U., LA, 1981. Social worker ARC Field Svcs. Corona Naval Hosp., Norco, Calif., 1945-46; chmn. bd. dirs. Camarillo (Calif.) State Hosp., 1959-68; trustee Oxnard (Calif.) Union High Sch. Dist., 1965-72; mem. state reclamation bd. Calif., 1981-82; mem. bd. govs. Calif. C.C., 1982-87; mem. bd. St. John's Regional Hosp., Oxnard, 1986-89; mem. bd. of assessment appeals County of Ventura, Ventura, Calif., 1992—2002, transp. commr., 2002—05, mem. campaign fin. ethics commn., 2005—, mem. fin. ethics commn., 2006—. Chmn. fin. com. Ventura County Grand Jury, 1958; mem. Oxnard (Calif.) Planning Commn., 1957-62; exec. mem. So. Calif. Assn. Govts., L.A., 1975-76. Author: Smith Studies, 1945. Chmn. dem. com., Ventura County, 1959-62; alternate or del. Dem. Nat. Convs., 1960, 68, 76, 88, 92, alt. 1956, 64; Women'schm. S. Calif. Dem. Com., 1966-70; nominee state assembly, 36th dist., Ventura, Calif., 1976; elected Oxnard City Coun. 1970-78, mayor, 1973-74. Home: 656 Douglas Ave Oxnard CA 93030-4614 Personal E-mail: jane.tolmach@adelphia.net.

TOLMAN, BRETT L., prosecutor; b. Provo, UT; BA, Brigham Young U., 1994, JD, 1998. Chief counsel for crime & terrorism, Judiciary com. US Senate, Salt Lake City, 2004—05; asst. US atty. Dist. UT US Dept. Justice, Salt Lake City, 2000—03, US atty., 2006—. Office: US Attys Office 185 S State St Ste 300 Salt Lake City UT 84111 *

TOLMAN, PHILIP D., lawyer, corporate financial executive; s. G. T. and E. F. Tolman. BA, Syracuse U., NY; JD, Suffolk U. Law Sch., Boston; MA, Harvard U., Cambridge, Mass. Bar: Mass. 1991. V.p. legal and contracts Infinium Software, Hyannis, Mass.; gen. counsel Access Tech (formerly Davox Corp.); lawyer, specialist Perot Sys. Corp., Providence. CAO, prin. CSS. Prodr.(broadcaster): (radio program) Life, Law and the Word; program host, author, prodr. (radio broadcasting) Life Skills. Dir., advisor Lighthouse Ministries. Mem.: ABA, Assn. Corp. Counsel, Wilderness Soc., Harvard Club. Avocations: travel, hiking, horseback riding. Home Phone: 978-758-9916; Office Phone: 401-459-1471. Personal E-mail: tolman@fas.harvard.edu. Business E-Mail: philip.tolman@ps.net.

TOLMIE, KENNETH DONALD, artist, writer; b. Halifax, NS, Can., Sept. 18, 1941; s. Archibald and Mary Evelyn (Murray) T.; m. Ruth MacKenzie, Aug. 11, 1962; children: Sarah Katherine, Jane Marianna. B.F.A., Mt. Allison U., 1962. Owner Tolmie Film Prodns., Kendog Films, Tolmie Gallery, Toronto. Chmn. Visual Arts Ottawa, 1975-76; founding mem. Bridgetown and Area Hist. Soc., James House Mus. Author: (children's book) Tale of an Egg, 1974, (art book) A Rural Life: An Artist's Portrait, 1986; 3 TV documentary films produced on his work by CBC and by TV-Ont., producer, Tolmie films prodn. in assn. with CBC, 2002 (aired nat. on CBCTV, 2002); one-man shows include Dorothy Cameron Gallery, Toronto, 1963, Beckett Gallery, Hamilton, 1986, Kaspar Gallery, Toronto, 1988; Mt. Allison Univ. solo cross Can. touring exbn. Bridgetown Series, 1982-84; group shows include Banfer Gallery, N.Y.C., 1963, Nat. Gallery Can., Watercolors Prints and Drawing, 1964, 66, London Art Mus., Ont., 1966, Can. Soc. Graphic Art, 1973, Art Gallery N.S., 1980, 81, N.S. Art Bank, 1981; represented in permanent collections Nat. Gallery Can., Ottawa, Montreal Mus. Fine Arts, N.S. Art Bank, Art Gallery N.S., Confedn. Centre for Arts, Hirshhorn Collection, Washington, Owens Art Gallery, Mt. Allison U., Dofasco Ltd., Husky Oil Ltd., Procter & Gamble Ltd., Slater Steels Ltd., Crownx Ltd., Moving Products, Inc. Bd. dirs. Art Gallery N.S., 1979-81. Recipient prodn. grant Nova Scotia Film Devel. Corp., 1999. Mem. Visual Arts N.S., Visual Arts Ont., Visual Arts Ottawa (chmn. 1975-76), Bridgetown Hist. Soc. (hon. life) Address: 39 Kenneth Ave Toronto ON Canada M6P 1J1 E-mail: ken@kentolmie.com.

TOLO, VERNON THORPE, orthopedist, educator; b. Onawa, Iowa; MD, Johns Hopkins U., 1968. Diplomate Am. Bd. Orthopaedic Surgery. Intern Johns Hopkins Hosp., Balt., 1969—70, resident orthop. surgery, 1972—75; fellow pediat. orthop. Hosp. Sick Children, Toronto, Canada, 1975—76; asst. prof. Johns Hopkins U. Sch. Medicine, Balt., 1976—82, assoc. prof., 1982—87; prof. orthop. surgery U. So. Calif., LA, 1987—; and head, divsn. orthop surgery Children's Hosp., LA. Attending physician Johns Hopkins Hosp., Balt., 1976—87, Children's Hosp., LA, 1987—. Mem.: Calif. Orthop. Assn., Scoliosis Rsch. Soc. (past pres.), Pediat. Orthopedics Soc. N. Am. (past pres., bd. dir. 1989—97), Am. Acad. Pediatricians, Am. Orthop. Assn., Am. Acad. Orthop. Surgeons (1st v.p. 2001—02, pres. 2002—03). Office: Children's Hosp MS 69 4650 W Sunset Blvd Los Angeles CA 90027-6062 Office Phone: 323-442-5860. Business E-Mail: vtolo@chla.usc.edu. *

TOLOR, ALEXANDER, psychologist, educator; b. Vienna, Oct. 21, 1928; s. Stanley and Josephine (Kellner) T.; m. Belle Simon, Sept. 2, 1951; children: Karen Beth, Lori Ann, Diana Susan. BA, NYU, 1949, MA, 1950, PhD, 1954. Diplomate Am. Bd. Profl. Psychologists. Grad. asst. NYU, 1950-52; intern Neurol. Inst., NYC, 1952-53, clin. psychologist, 1953-55; sr. clin. psychologist Inst. of Living, Hartford, Conn., 1957-59; dir. psychol. services Fairfield Hills Hosp., Newtown, Conn., 1959-64; clinic dir. Kennedy Center, Bridgeport, Conn., 1964-65; dir. Inst. Human Devel., Fairfield U., 1965-77, assoc. prof. psychology, 1965-68, research prof. psychology, 1968-75, prof. psychology, 1975-89, dir. school psychology div., 1975-77, dir. sch. and applied psychology program, 1982-86, prof. emeritus, 1989—; practice psychology Danbury, Conn., 1960-96; clin. instr. psychology Yale U., 1963-67. Cons. West Haven VA Hosp., 1962-66, Bridgeport Bd. Edn., Silver Hill Found., 1972-75, Fairfield Hills Hosp., 1973-94, Hallbrooke Hosp., 1975-92. Author: (with H.C. Schulberg) An Evaluation of the Bender-Gestalt Test, 1963, (with G.G. Brannigan) Research and Clinical Applications of the Bender-Gestalt Test, 1980, (with M. Deignan) Adjustment Problems in Children, 1984; editor: Effective Interviewing, 1985; adv. editor Jour. Cons. and Clin. Psychology; cons. editor Personality: An Internat. Jour.; contbr. articles to profl. jours. Served to 1st lt. USAF, 1955-57. Fellow Am. Psychol. Assn., Soc. Personality Assessment, Conn. Psychol. Assn. (mem. council 1964, pres. 1984); mem. Eastern Psychol. Assn., Psi Chi, Delta Phi Alpha, Beta Lambda Sigma, Phi Delta Kappa Home: 6 Brittania Dr Danbury CT 06811-2606 Personal E-mail: atbt51@aol.com.

TOLOZA, ERIC M., thoracic surgeon; BS, U. Calif., LA, 1984, MD, PhD, U. Calif., LA. Lic. thoraici surgeon Am. Bd. Thoracic Surgery, 2002, gen. surgeon Am. Bd. Surgery, 1999. Staff surgeon Durham VA Med. Ctr., NC, 2000—; asst. prof. surgery Duke U. Med. Ctr., Durham, NC, 2000—. Office: Duke Univ Med Ctr Box 3048 Durham NC 27710 Office Phone: 919-681-2979.

TOLSTEDT, CARRIE L., bank executive; BS in Bus. Adminstrn., U. Nebr.; degree in Banking, U. Wash. From credit tng. program to corp. banking officer United Bank Denver, corp. banking officer; from v.p. corp. banking to sr. v.p. downtown Omaha (Nebr.) retail banking Norwest Bank Nebr., Omaha, 1986—95; sr. v.p. corp. retail FirstMerit Corp., Akron, Ohio, 1995—96, pres., CEO Citizens Nat. Bank and Peoples Nat. Bank, 1996—98, exec. v.p., 1996—98; with Norwest Corp., 1998; regional pres. Ctrl. Calif. Wells Fargo & Co., San Francisco, 1998—2001, exec. v.p. regional banking, 2001—. Bd. dirs. The Cmty. Coll. Found. Named one of 25 Most Powerful Women in Banking, US Banker, 2006. Mem.: Consumer Bankers Assn. (bd. dirs.), U. Nebr. Alumni Assn. (bd. dirs.), Calif. C. of C. (bd. dirs.). Office: Wells Fargo & Co 420 Montgomery St San Francisco CA 94163 *

TOLSTOY, MAYA, marine seismologist; b. Nyack, NY, Apr. 20, 1967; d. Ivan and Margie Tolstoy. BSc with honors, U. Edinburgh, 1988; PhD, Scripp Instn. Oceanography, La Jolla, Calif., 1994. Postgrad. rschr. Scripps Instn. Oceanography, 1994—. Mem. Am. Geophys. Union. Democrat. Avocations: skiing, acting.

TOLVA, JOHN, information technology manager; b. Chgo., 1972; m. Robyn Tolva; 3 children. BA, Vanderbilt U.; MA in Eng. Lit., Washington U.; MS in Info. Design & Tech., Georgia Inst. Tech. Prodr., events webcasting group IBM Corp., Atlanta, 1997—2000; global program. mgr. cultural strategy & programs IBM Corp. Comty. Relations, Chgo., 2000—; creative dir. Ctr. IBM e-Bus. Innovation, Chgo. Named one of 40 Under 40, Crain's Chgo. Bus., 2006. Home Phone: 773-755-2563; Office Phone: 312-529-2840. E-mail: jtolva@us.ibm.com, john@ascentstage.com.

TOM, JAMES ROBERT, accountant; b. Odessa, Tex., Apr. 21, 1939; s. George Ellison and Mattie Inez (Zimmerman) T.; m. Frances Kay Mackey, Sept. 16, 1961; children: Susan Kay, James Robert Jr., Emily Christian. Student, Tex. A&M U., 1957; BBA in Acctg., Tex. Tech. U., 1961; postgrad., Colo. State U., 1961—62. CPA Tex. Jr. acct. Peat, Marwick, Mitchell & Co., Midland, Tex., 1965; asst. trust officer 1st City Nat. Bank, Midland, 1966-67, v.p., trust officer, 1969-72; sr. acct. Main Hurdman, Midland, 1967-68; pres. Gibson Mfg. Co., Midland, 1972-73; exec. v.p., CEO Teraco, Inc., Midland, 1974-75, fin. cons., 1975-76, acct., 1976—. Bd. dirs. Am. Heart Assn., Midland, 1966, Arthritis Found., Midland, 1971-72, 75, Midland County Livestock Assn., Midland, 1966-72, ARC, Midland, 1970-80, Boys Club, Midland, 1971-72. 1st lt. U.S. Army, 1963-65. Mem.: AICPA, Permian Basin CPA, Tex. Soc. CPA. Republican. Roman Catholic. Avocations: fishing, hunting, reading. Home: 605 Sandy Oaks Dr Boerne TX 78015 Office: 130 Medical Dr Boerne TX 78006 Office Phone: 830-336-3978.

TOM, LAUREN, actress, singer; b. Chgo., Aug. 4, 1959; d. Chan and Nancy (Dare) T.; m. Curt Kaplan, Oct. 1999; 1 child. Student, Northwestern U., 1977; BA, NYU. Actress (Broadway plays) A Chorus Line, 1978—79, Doonesbury, 1983—84, Hurlyburly, 1985, (plays) The Music Lessons, 1980, Family Devotions, 1981, (one woman show) 25 Psychics (Dramalogue awards, best performance), (films) Nothing Lasts Forever, 1982, Joy Luck Club, 1993, Mr. Jones, 1993, When a Man Loves a Woman, 1994, With Friends Like These, 1998, Catfish in Black Bean Sauce, 1999, Manhood, 2003, Bad Santa, 2003, God's Waiting List, 2006, (TV series) The Facts of Life, 1982, Grace Under Fire, 1993, DAG, 2000, Max Steel, 2001—02, Men in Trees, 2006, actress (voice) Superman, 1996—99, King of the Hill, 1997—2006, Batman, 1999, Futurama, 1999—2003, Rocket Power, 1999—2004, Samurai Jack, 2001—04, Codename: Kids Next Door, 2002, Fillmore, 2002—04, Clifford's Puppy Days, 2003—, Teacher's Pet, 2004, W.I.T.C.H., 2004—06, Kim Possible, 2005, American Dragon, 2005. Supporter Asia Inst., Washington. Mem. Actors' Equity Assn., Screen Actors Guild, AFTRA.

TOM, LAWRENCE, technology executive; b. LA, Jan. 21, 1950; BS, Harvey Mudd Coll., 1972; JD, Western State U., San Diego, 1978; spl. diploma, U. Calif., San Diego, 1991. Design engr. Rockwell Internat., LA, 1972-73, Goodrich Corp. (formerly Rohr, Inc.), Chula Vista, Calif., 1973-76, sr. design engr., 1980, computer graphics engring. specialist, 1980-83, chief engring. svcs., 1989-91, chief engring. quality, 1991-93, project mgr., 1993-98, info. tech. specialist, 1998—2002. Sr. engr. Rohr Marine, Inc., Chula Vista, 1977-79; chief exec. officer Computer Aided Tech. Svcs., San Diego, 1983-87; software cons. Small Systems Software, San Diego, 1984-85; computer graphics engring. specialist TOM & ROMAN, San Diego, 1986-88; dir. Computervision Users Group, 1986-88, vice chmn. 1988-91, pres., 1991-93, exec. chmn., 1992-94; bd. dirs. Exec. Program for Scientists and Engrs.-Alumni Assn. U. Calif., San Diego, 1991—; CFO Global Peregrine Users Group, 2001-03; pres. Art to Art, San Diego, 1994-99; pres. SGL Computer Profls., San Diego, 1999—; ptnr. San Diego Tech. Movers, 2007—; cons. in field. George H. Mayr Found. scholar, 1971, Bates Found. Aero. Edn. scholar, 1970-72. Mem. Nat. Mgmt. Assn. (chpt. v.p.), Aircraft Owners and Pilots Assn., Infiniti Club. Office: 7770 Regents Rd Ste 113-190 San Diego CA 92122-1967 Home Phone: 858-546-9090; Office Phone: 619-985-9850. Business E-Mail: larry.tom@sglpro.com.

TOM, RANDOLPH L., corporate financial executive, lawyer; s. Bell Kam and Choy Mee Tom; m. Linda K. Wong, May 28, 1988; children: Gwendolyn L., Jarrett L. BS, MBA, NYU, 1974, JD, MBA, 1978. Bar: N.Y. 1978, Calif. 1994, DC 1994. Atty. Fulbright & Jaworski, NYC, 1978—85; gen. counsel AT&E Corp., San Francisco, 1985—91; chmn., CEO Dynasty Capital Svcs. LLC, Moraga, Calif., 1988—; pres. Asia Pacific AT&E Corp., San Francisco, 1989—91; securities ptnr., head Asia Pacific practice Oppenheimer Wolff & Donnelly LLP, Palo Alto, Calif., 1998—2000. Adj. prof. sch. law New Coll. Calif., 2007—. Editor: Dynasty Perspectives; author: (nat. law jour. spl. report) Internet May Offer Access to US Cash; columnist Contra Costa Times/Sun, 2005—06; contbr. bus. plans handbook. Bd. dirs. Cmty. Tech. Found. of Calif., San Francisco, 2004—, U. of San Francisco Ctr. for the Pacific Rim, San Francisco, 2004—. Recipient Gary scholarship, NYU, Book scholarship, Mgmt. Assn., N.Y.C., univ. scholarship, NYU, Law Ctr. scholarship, NYU. Sch. of Law, Marcus Nadler fellowship, Stern Grad. Sch. of Bus., George Baker scholar. Mem.: Beta Gamma Sigma, Phi Alpha Kappa. Office: Dynasty Capital Svcs LLC One Madsen Ct Moraga CA 94556 Office Phone: 925-377-5300. Business E-Mail: dynasty@dynastycap.com.

TOM, WILLARD KEN, lawyer; b. Honolulu, Aug. 11, 1952; s. Hing Yee and Marian (Chun) T.; m. Natalie G. Lichtenstein, June 10, 1979; children: Alexander, Joshua. AB cum laude, Harvard U., 1975, JD cum laude, 1979. Bar: DC 1979, US Dist. Ct. DC 1979, US Ct. Appeals (DC cir.) 1983, US Supreme Ct. 1986. Trial atty. U.S. Dept. Justice, Washington, 1979-81; assoc. Sutherland, Asbill & Brennan, Washington, 1981-86, ptnr., 1986-93; counselor to asst. atty. gen. U.S. Dept. Justice, Washington, 1993-95; asst. dir. for policy and evaluation FTC, Wash., 1995—; ptnr. Morgan, Lewis & Bockius, Wash., DC. Editl. chair ABA Antitrust Sects. reference work, contbr. articles to various profl. journs. Recipient Am.'s Leading Lawyers for Bus., Chambers USA, 2006, Best Lawyers in Am., 2005—07. Mem. ABA (mem. coun., antitrust sect. 1992-95, DC Bar (nominations com. 1993), Asian-Pacific Am. Bar Assn. Greater Wash. (bd. dirs. 1983). Office: Morgan Lewis & Bockius 1111 Pennsylvania Ave NW Washington DC 20004 Office Phone: 202-739-5389. Office Fax: 202-739-3001. Business E-Mail: wtom@morganlewis.com.

TOMAIN, JOSEPH PATRICK, law educator, retired dean; b. Long Branch, NJ, Sept. 3, 1948; s. Joseph Pasquale and Bernice M. (Krzan) T.; m. Kathleen (Corcione), Aug. 1, 1971; children: Joseph Anthony, John Fiore. BA, U. Notre Dame, 1970; JD, George Washington U., 1974. Bar: NJ, Iowa. Assoc. Giordano and Halleran, Middletown, NJ, 1974-76; asst. to prof. law Drake U. Sch. Law, Des Moines, 1976-83; prof. law U. Cin., 1983—, acting dean, 1989—90, dean, 1990—2004, Nippert prof. law, 1990—, dean emeritus, 2004. Vis. prof. law U. Tex., Austin, 1986—87. Author: Energy Law in a Nutshell, 1981, Nuclear Power Transformation, 1987; co-author: Energy Decision Making, 1983, Energy Law and Policy, 1989, Energy and Natural Resources Law, 1992, Regulatory Law and Policy, 1993, 2d edit., 1998, 3rd edit., 2003, Energy, The Environment and the Global Economy, 2000. Trustee Ctr. for Chem. Addictions Treatment, Cin., Vol. Lawyers for Poor, Cin.; mem. steering com. BLAC/CBA Round Table, Cin.; chair Knowledge Works Found.; trustee Ohio State Bar Found., Ohio Legal Assitance Found.; gov. Greater Cin. Found. Served in USAR, 1970-76. Mem. ABA, Am. Law Inst., Ohio State Bar Assn. (del.), Mercantile Libr. Assn. (v.p.). Roman Catholic. Home: 3009 Springer Ave Cincinnati OH 45208-2440 Office: U Cin Coll Law Office Dean PO Box 210040 Cincinnati OH 45221-0040 Home Phone: 513-871-3800; Office Phone: 513-556-0067. Business E-Mail: joseph.tomain@uc.edu.

TOMAINO, JOSEPH CARMINE, former retail executive, former postal inspector; b. Danbury, Conn., Dec. 12, 1948; s. Joseph and Lena Marie (LaCava) T.; m. Eileen M. Pulver (div. Feb. 1978); m. Ann C. Underriner, Sept. 20, 1986; children: Joseph Richard, Robert John. BS, Western Conn. State U., 1970; MBA, Roosevelt U., 1978, MS in Acctg., 1986. Cert. fraud specialist; cert. fraud examiner; diplomate Am. Bd. Law Enforcement; expert, lic. pvt. investigator, Ill. Post office clk. U.S. Postal Svc., Ridgefield, Conn., 1970-71, postal inspector Chgo., 1971-80, supervisory postal inspector, 1980-93; mgr. we. ops. loss prevention dept. Walgreen Co., Deerfield, Ill., 1993-96; sr. mgr. litigation svcs. Altschuler, Melvoin & Glasser CPAs, Chgo., 1996-98; dir. litigation svcs. Altschuler, Melvoin & Glasser/Am. Express Co., Chgo., 1999-2000; ptnr. Altschuler, Melvoin & Glasser CPAs, Chgo., 2000—; mng. dir. Am. Express Tax and Bus. Svcs., Chgo., 2000—02; sr. mng. dir. Chgo. region Citigate G.I., 2002—05; ptnr. Smarts & Assocs., LLP, Chgo., 2005—07, Blackman Kallick CPAs, Chgo., 2007—. Fellow Am. Coll. Forensic Examiners; mem. Am. Soc. Indsl. Security, Fed. Law Enforcement Officers Assn., Nat. Assn. Chiefs Police, Ill. Chiefs Police, Spl. Agts. Assn., Ill. Police Assn., Nat. Soc. Pub. Accts., Assn. Cert. Fraud Examiners, Assn. Cert. Anti-Money Laundering Specialists, Ill. Soc. CPAs. Office: Blackman Kallick LLP 10 S Riverside Plz 9th Fl Chicago IL 60606

TOMAN, MARY ANN, federal official; b. Pasadena, Calif., Mar. 31, 1954; d. John James and Mary Ann Zajac T.; m. Milton Allen Miller, Sept. 10, 1988; 1 child, Mary Ann III. BA with honors, Stanford U., Calif., 1976; MBA, Harvard U., Cambridge, Mass., 1981. Mgmt. cons. Bain and Co., Boston, 1976—77; mgr. brand Procter & Gamble Co., Cin., 1977—79; summer assoc. E.F. Hutton, NYC, 1980; head corp. planning Burton Group, PLC, London, 1981—84; pres., founder Glenclair Ltd., London, 1984—86; pres. London Cons. Group, London, Beverly Hills, Calif., 1987—88; mem. U.S. Presdl. Transition Team, Bus. and Fin., 1988—89; dep. asst. sec. commerce, automotive affairs, consumer goods U.S. Dept. Commerce, Washington, 1989—93; commr., chmn. L.A. Indsl. Devel. Authority, 1993—95; dep. treas. State of Calif., Sacramento, 1995—99. Bd. dirs. US Coun. of Devel. Fin. Agencies, 1994-97. Founder, chair Stanford U. Fundraising, London, 1983-88; chair Reps. Abroad Absentee Voter Registration, London, 1983-88; bd. dirs. Harvard Bus. Sch. Assn., London, 1984-87; vol. Bush-Quayle Campaign, 1988; trustee Bath U., Eng., 1988—; apptd. by Gov. Wilson to State of Calif. Econ. Devel. Adv. Coun., 1994-97, Jobs Tng. Coordinating Coun., 1998-2000; first vice chmn. Rep. Party L.A. County, 1996-99, chmn., 1999—; mem. exec. bd. Coun. Calif. County Chairmen, 1999—; mem. US Presdl. Transition Team, 2000-2001; Rep. candidate for Calif. State Treas., 2002. Named Calif. Mother of Yr., 1997. Mem. Stanford Club U.K. (pres. 1983-88), Harvard Club NY, Harvard Club Washington, Harvard Club Boston, Nat. Assn. of Urban Rep. County Chmn. Roman Catholic. Home: 604 N Elm Dr Beverly Hills CA 90210-3421 Office: PO Box 71483 Los Angeles CA 90071-0483 Home Phone: 310-550-5799; Office Phone: 310-274-4822. Business E-Mail: tomanmail@aol.com.

TOMAR, RICHARD THOMAS, lawyer; b. Camden, NJ, Mar. 4, 1945; s. William and Bette (Brown) T.; children: Lindsay, Leanne Meryl, Daniel Gregory. BA, Columbia U., 1967; JD, U. Pa., 1970. Bar: D.C. 1971, N.J. 1971, Md. 1976. Pvt. practice, Washington, 1971-73; ptnr. Philipson, Mallios & Tomar, P.C., Washington, 1973—89, Margolius, Mallios, Davis, Rider & Tomar, LLP, Washington, 1989—2002; chair comml. litigation Karp, Frosh, Lapidus, Wigodsky & Norwind, PA, Rockville, Md., 2002—. Mem. D.C. Trial Lawyers Assn. (bd. dirs. 1980-89). Office: Karp Frosh Lapidus Wigodsky & Norwind PA 2273 Research Blvd Ste 200 Rockville MD 20850-3283 Home: 4801 Hampden Ln Apt 304 Bethesda MD 20814-6556 Home Phone: 301-718-0663; Office Phone: 301-948-3800. Office Fax: 301-948-5449. Business E-Mail: rtomar@karpfrosh.com.

TOMAR, RUSSELL HERMAN, pathologist, educator, researcher; b. Phila., Oct. 19, 1937; s. Julius and Ethel (Weinreb) T.; m. Karen J. Kent, Aug. 29, 1965; children: Elizabeth, David. BA in Journalism, George Washington U., 1959, MD, 1963. Diplomate Am. Bd. Pathology, Am. Bd. Allergy and Immunology, Am. Bd. Pathology, Immunopathology. Intern Barnes Hosp., Washington U. Sch. Medicine, 1963-64, resident in medicine, 1964-65; asst. prof. medicine SUNY, Syracuse, 1971-79, assoc. prof., 1979-88, assoc. prof. microbiology, 1980-84, prof., 1984-88, asst. prof. pathology, 1974-76, assoc. prof., 1976-83, prof., 1983-88, dir. immunopathology, 1974-88, attending physician immunodeficiency clinic, 1982-88, acting dir. microbiology, 1977-78, 82-83, interim dir. clin. pathology, 1986-87; prof. pathology and lab. medicine U. Wis. Ctr. for Health Scis., Madison, 1988—2003; dir. div. lab medicine U. Wis., Madison, 1988-95, dir. immunopathology and diagnostic immunology, 1995-98, prof. population health scis., 1999—2003, vis. prof. population health scis., 2003—07; chair dept. pathology Stroger Hosp. Cook County, Chgo., 1999—; prof. pathology Rush U., 1999—. Past mem. numerous coms. SUNY, Syracuse, U. Wis., Madison; mem. exec. com., chair and med. cons. AIDS Task Force Cen. N.Y., 1983-88. Assoc. editor Jour. Clin. Lab. Analysis; contbr. articles, rev. to profl. jours. Mem. pub. health com. Onondaga County Med. Soc., 1987-88. Lt. comdr. USPHS, 1965-67. Allergy and Immunology Div. fellow U. Pa. Fellow Coll. Am. Pathologists (diagnostics immunology rsch. com. 1993-2003, stds. com. 1995-97, commn. on clin. pathology 1997-2003), Am. Soc. Clin. Pathology (com. on continuing edn. immunopathology 1985-91, pathology data presentation com. 1976-79, pathology rep. coun. med. subspecialty socs. 2004—), Am. Acad. Allergy (penicillin hypersensitivity com. 1973-77); mem. AAAS, Am. Assn. Immunologists, Am. Assn. Pathology (chmn. 2002—), Acad. Clin. Lab. Physicians and Scientists (com. on rsch. 1979-81, chairperson immunology 1979), Clin. Immunology Soc. (clin. lab. immunology com., chair coun. 1991-96, pathology rep. to Coun. Med. Subspecialty Socs. 2003—). Office: Stroger Cook County Dept Pathology 1901 W Harrison St Chicago IL 60612 Personal E-mail: rtomar@comcast.net. Business E-Mail: russell.tomar@hektoen.org.

TOMASETTI, RICHARD L., structural engineer; BS, Manhattan Coll., 1963, DSc (hon.), 2001; MS in Civil Engring., NYU, 1963. Chmn. Thorton-Tomasetti Group Inc., NYC. Adj. prof. Columbia U. Recipient Engr. of Yr. Award, NY Assn. Consulting Engrs., 2002, Industry Honoree, NY Building Congress, 2003. Mem.: NAE, AIA (hon.). Office: Thornton-Tomasetti Group 51 Madison Ave New York NY 10010 Office Phone: 917-661-7800. Office Fax: 917-661-7801.

TOMASH, ERWIN, retired computer company executive; b. St. Paul, Nov. 17, 1921; s. Noah and Milka (Ehrlich) T.; m. Adelle Ruben, July 31, 1943; children: Judith Sarada Tomash Diffenbaugh, Barbara Ann Tomash Bussa. BS, U. Minn., 1943; MS, U. Md., 1950. Instr. elec. engring. U. Minn., 1946; assoc. dir. computer devel. Univac div. Remington Rand Corp., St. Paul, 1947-51; dir. West Coast ops. Univac div. Sperry Rand Corp., LA, 1953-55; pres. Telemeter Magnetics, Inc., LA, 1956-60; v.p. Ampex Corp., LA, 1961; founder, pres. Dataproducts Corp., LA, 1962-71, chmn. bd., 1971-80, chmn. exec. com., 1980-89; chmn. bd., dir. Newport Corp., Irvine, Calif., 1982-94. Founder, trustee, dir. Charles Babbage Found., U. Minn.; dir. and nat. gov. Coro Found., L.A. Served to capt. Signal Corps AUS, 1943-46. Decorated Bronze Star; recipient Outstanding Grad. award U. Minn., 1983. Mem. IEEE (sr., computer entrepeneur award 1988), Am. Soc. for Technion, History of Sci. Soc., Soc. for History of Tech., Assn. Internationale du Bibliophile. Home: 3918 Mainsail Pl Soquel CA 95073 Personal E-mail: etomash@ieee.org.

TOMASI, DONALD CHARLES, architect; b. Sacramento, Oct. 24, 1956; s. Thomas M. and Anita (Migliavacca) T.; m. Loretta Elaine Goveia, Feb. 1, 1986; children: Jeffrey, Genna, Michael. AB in Architecture with honors, U. Calif., Berkeley, 1979; MArch, U. Wash., 1982. Registered architect, Calif. Project mgr. Robert Wells and Assocs., Seattle, 1982-84, Milbrandt Architects, Seattle, 1984, T.M. Tomasi Architects, Santa Rosa, Calif., 1984-86; prin. Tomasi Architects, Santa Rosa, 1986-93, sr. prin.; prin. TLCD Architecture, Santa Rosa, 1993—. Grad. Leadership Santa Rosa, 1992; mem. design rev. com. Sonoma County, 1988-90; chmn. Santa Rosa Design Rev. Bd., 1990-97. Recipient Honor award Coalition for Adequate Sch. Housing, 1991, 93, 96, 99, 2000, 02, 04, Merit award, 1991. Mem. AIA (chpt. bd. dirs. 1990-91, 98, v.p. 1999, pres. 2000, Calif. Coun. bd. dirs. 2002-03, Merit award 1986). Avocations: skiing, wine, travel. Office Phone: 707-525-5600. E-mail: don.tomasi@tlcd.com.

TOMASKO, EDWARD A., financial planner; b. Stafford Springs, Conn., Sept. 18, 1943; s. Edward A. Sr. and Gertrude Ann (Burr) T.; m. Helen F. Flanagan, Oct. 18, 1969; children: Felicia, Joy. BA, Quinnipac Coll., 1966; MBA, Am. U., 1968. CFP. Direct mktg. & sales Iroquois Brands, Stamford, Conn., 1979-81; owner Tomasko Bus. Cons., Bethel, Conn., 1981-82; v.p. mktg. & consulting Excell Mktg., New Canaan, Conn., 1982; market mgr. Stauffer Chem., Westport, Conn., 1982-85; direct mktg. & sales Folz Vending, LI, NY, 1986; registered rep. Moseley Securities, New Haven, 1987-88, Fahnestock & Co. Inc., Danbury, Conn., 1988-90; prin. Titan Value Equities, Hamden, Conn., 1990—. V.p. bd. govs. Quinnipac Coll.; chmn. pension and ins. commn. Town of Bethel, Conn. Mem.: FPA (pres. So. Conn. chpt. 1993—96, chmn. state conf. 1992—93, adv. coun. 1997—). Republican. Avocations: photography, choir singing. Home: 20 Spring Hill Ln Bethel CT 06801-2726 E-mail: edward_a_tomasko@sbcglobal.net.

TOMASKY, SUSAN, electric power industry executive; b. Morgantown, W.Va., Mar. 29, 1953; m. Ron Ungvarsky; 1 child, Victoria. BA cum laude, U. Ky., Lexington, 1974; JD with honors, George Washington U., 1979. Staff mem. House Com. Interstate and Fgn. Commerce, Washington, 1974—76; with Office Gen. Counsel FERC, Washington, 1979—81, gen. counsel, 1993—97; assoc. Van Ness, Feldman & Curtin, Washington, 1981—86; ptnr. Van Ness, Feldman & Curtis, Washington, 1986—93, Hogan & Harts, Washington, 1997-98; sr. v.p., gen. coun., sec. Am. Electric Power Svc. Corp., Columbus, Ohio, 1998—2000, exec. v.p., gen. counsel, sec., 2000—01, exec. v.p., CFO, 2001—06, exec. v.p. Shared Svcs., 2006—. Staff mem. George Washington U. Law Rev., 1979. Trustee Columbus Symphony Orch., Columbus Sch. for Girls; co-chair Keystone Energy Bd. Mem. Greater Columbus C. of C., Phi Beta Kappa. Office: Am Electric Power Svc Corp 1 Riverside Plz Columbus OH 43215-2373 Office Phone: 614-716-1600. *

TOMASSI LINDMAN, SARAH, television producer; b. 1970; married. BA, Yale U. Paralegal Warner Bros. Animation; dir. programming Kids' WB; v.p. programming & prodn. Noggin, 2000—02, The N, 2002—06, gen. mgr., 2006—. Named one of 40 Under 40, Crain's NY Bus., 2007. Office: The N 1633 Broadway New York NY 10019 *

TOMASSON, HELGI, dancer, choreographer, company executive; b. Reykjavik, Iceland, 1942; m. Marlene Rizzo; children: Kristinn, Erik. Student, Sigridur Arman, Erik Bidsted, Vera Volkova, Sch. Am. Ballet, Tivoli Pantomime Theatre, Copenhagen. With Joffrey Ballet, 1961-64; prin. dancer Harkness Ballet, 1964-70, NYC Ballet, 1970-85; artistic dir. San Francisco Ballet, 1985—, also dir. Dancer debut Tivoli Pantomime Theatre, 1958, A Season of Hell, 1967, Stages and Reflections, 1968, La Favorita, 1969, The Goldberg Variations, 1971, Symphony in Three Movements, 1972, Coppelia, 1974, Dybbuk Variations, 1974, Chansons Madecasses, 1975, Introduction and Allegro, 1975, Allegro, 1975, Union Jack, 1976, Vienna Waltzes, 1977, choreographer Theme and Variations, Polonaise, Op. 65, 1982, Ballet d'Isoline, 1983, Menuetto, N.Y.C. Ballet, 1984, Beads of Memory, 1985, Swan Lake, 1988, Handel-a Celebration, 1989, Sleeping Beauty, 1990, Romeo and Juliet, 1994, Prism, 2000, Bartok Divertimento, 2002, Chi-Lin, 2002, Concerto Grosso, 2003, 7 for Eight, 2003. Decorated Knight Order of Falcon Iceland, Comdr. Order of Falcon; recipient Silver medal, Internat. Moscow Ballet Competition, 1969, Golden Plate award, Am. Acad. Achievement, 1992, Dance Mag. award, 1992, Disting. Citizen, Commonwealth Club Calif., 1991. Office: San Francisco Ballet 455 Franklin St San Francisco CA 94102-4438 *

TOMASULO, VIRGINIA MERRILLS, retired lawyer; b. Belleville, Ill., Feb. 10, 1919; d. Frederick Emerson and Mary Eckert (Turner) Merrills; m. Nicholas Angelo Tomasulo, Sept. 30, 1952 (dec. May 3, 1986); m. Harrison I. Anthes, Mar. 5, 1988. BA, Wellesley Coll., 1940; LLB (now JD), Washington U., St. Louis, 1943. Bar: Mo. 1942, U.S. Ct. Appeals (D.C. cir.) 1958, Mich. 1974, U.S. Dist. Ct. (ea. dist) Mo. 1943, U.S. Supreme Ct. 1954, U.S. Tax Ct. 1974, U.S. Ct. Appeals (6th cir.) 1976. Atty. Dept. of Agr., Office of Solicitor, St. Louis and Washington, 1943-48; chief counsel's office IRS, Washington and Detroit, 1949-75; assoc. Baker & Hostetler, Washington, 1977-82, ptnr., 1982-89, of counsel, 1989, ret., 1989. Sec. S.W. Day Care Assn., Washington, 1971—73; state bd. mem., dir. region IV Fla. Life Care Residents Assn., 2002—04; mem. adv. bd. Brede-Wilkins Scholarship Found., 2002—. Mem.: ABA, Mo. Bar, Fla. Life Care Residents Assoc. chpt. 125, Village on the Green Residents Assn. (mem. coun. 1998—2000, chair health care com. 1999—2001, chair fin. com. 2004—07, mem. fin. com.), Wellesley Club (Ctrl. Fla.). Episcopalian. Home: 570 Village Pl Apt 300 Longwood FL 32779-6037 Office Phone: 401-788-6698.

TOMASZEWSKI, RICHARD PAUL, market representation executive; b. Flushing, NY, Jan. 8, 1958; s. Francis Richard and Agatha Jean (Corsaro) T.; m. Joann L. Turone, Aug. 2, 1980; children: Elizabeth Jean, Annamaria Concetta. BA in Econs. and Polit. sci. cum laude, Union Coll., Schenectady, NY, 1980; MBA in Mktg., Fin., Syracuse U., 1982. Grad. asst. Syracuse (N.Y.) U., 1981; field ops. analyst Ford Motor Co., Charlotte, N.C., 1982-83, zone mgr., 1983-93, mkt. representation specialist Atlanta, 1993-98, nat. employee involvement rep. Atlanta region, 1994-98, mkt. representation mgr., 1998—. Mem. Ford Motor Co. Polit. Action Com., Atlanta, 1993, Cmty. Rels. Com., 1999-2002. Tidmarsh scholar Union Coll., Schenectady, 1977; co-recipient Total Market Representation award, 1997, 99-2005. Mem. Union Coll. Alumni Assn., Syracuse U. Alumni Assn., U.S. Tennis Assn., Atlanta Lawn Tennis Assn., Wynterhall Swim and Tennis Club (chmn. tennis com. 2003-05, co-capt., 2002—), Omicron Delta Epsilon, Alpha Mu Alpha. Republican. Roman Catholic. Avocations: tennis, swimming, chess, walking. Office: Ford Motor Co 1455 Lincoln Pkwy E Ste 550 Atlanta GA 30346-2288 Home Phone: 770-522-0630. Business E-Mail: rtomasze@ford.com. E-mail: rjhobbit@bellsouth.net.

TOMAZI, GEORGE DONALD, retired electrical engineer; b. St. Louis, Dec. 27, 1935; s. George and Sophia (Bogovich) T.; m. Lois Marie Partenheimer, Feb. 1, 1958; children: Keith, Kent. BSEE, U. Mo., Rolla, 1958, Profl. EE (hon.), 1970; MBA, St. Louis U., 1965, MSEE, 1971. Registered profl. engr., Mo., Ill., Wash., Ohio, Calif. Project engr. Union Electric Co., 1958-66; dir. corp. planning Gen. Steel Industries, 1966-70; exec. v.p. St. Louis Research Council, 1970-74, Hercules Constrn. Co., St. Louis, 1974-75; dir. design and constrn. div. Mallinckrodt, Inc., St. Louis, 1975-93; ret., 1993. Author: P-Science: The Role of Science in Society, 1972, The Link of Science and Religion, 1973. Active Nat. Kidney Found.; bd. dirs. U. Mo. Devel. Council, St. Louis Artists Coalition, Citizens for Modern Transit; elder Luth. Ch.; v.p. Coun. Luth Chs., St. Louis; adv. com. grad. sch. U. Mo., Columbia, mem. pres.'s role and scope commn.; dir. Coun. Luth. Chs. Greater St. Louis; bldg. com. Humane Soc. Mo.; pres. coun. Luth. Ch. of the Living Christ; bd. dirs. Humane Soc. Mo., 2005; bd. trustees Acad. Sci. St. Louis, 2005. Served with U.S. Army, 1959-61.

Recipient award Acad. Elec. Engrs., U. Mo., Rolla, Achievement award Humane Soc. of Mo., Spl. award, 1998, Achievement award Order of the Golden Shillaleagh, U. Mo., Rolla, 2004, Legacy Cir. award U. Mo., Columbia, 2004, Connaway Soc. U. Mo., Columbia, 2005. Mem. NSPE (life), IEEE (life, chmn. state govt. activities com. 1990-93), Japan-Am. Soc., AAAS, Profl. Engrs. in Industry, Mo. Soc. Profl. Engrs. (pres. St. Louis chpt., Profl. Engr. in Industry 1989, named to Hall Fame 2005), Profl. Engrs. and Land Surveyors (chmn. Mo. bd. for architects 1989-95), Am. Def. Preparedness Assn., U. Mo. Alumni Assn. (bd. dirs. 1972-78), Engrs. Club (pres. 1985-86, Achievement award 2002), Mo. Athletic Club, Rotary, Sigma Pi. Address: #44 Jamestown Farm Dr Florissant MO 63034-1405 Office: 44 Jamestown Farm Dr Florissant MO 63034-1405

TOMBAUGH, DOROTHY ELVE, retired secondary school educator, author, lecturer; b. Newark, NY, Mar. 19, 1917; d. John E. and Edith Deming Elve; m. Roy Wilson Tombaugh, Aug. 10, 1940; children: Sandra Tombaugh Ehrman, Karen Tombaugh Dean. BS, Alfred U., 1938, DSc, 1983; MAT, Siena Heights U., 1965, DHL (hon.), 1982. Cert. med. technologist, Am. Soc. Clin. Pathologists. Med. technologist Rochester (N.Y.) Gen. Hosp., 1938-39, Sage Meml. Hosp., Ganado, Ariz., 1940, Cedars of Lebanon Hosp., LA, 1941; spectographer, rsch. asst. Applied Rsch. Labs., Glendale, Calif., 1942-44; tchr. chemistry and biology Euclid (Ohio) H.S., 1963-79; lectr. NSF Grant, 1979-81, mainstreamed blind students in biology classes and labs, 1970-75. Judge for state and internat. sci. fairs N.E. Ohio, So. Ariz., 1965-98; lectr. NSF Chatauqua for Coll. Tchrs., 1977-80; lectr. in field. Author: Biology for the Blind, 1973; contbr. articles to profl. jours. Troop leader Girl Scouts, Eagle Rock, Calif., 1943-44, Bethel Park, Pa., 1954-55, Dayton, Ohio, 1957-59; deacon Presbyn. Ch., North Elmonte, Calif., 1947-50, Tucson, 1990-93, 1998-2002; fin. com. YWCA, Pitts., 1954-56. Named Outstanding Biology Tchr., Nat. Assn. Biology Tchrs., Ohio, 1975. Presbyterian. Home: Aspen Village at Lowry 150 Quebec St Apt 201 E Denver CO 80230 Office Phone: 303-364-0484.

TOMBLIN, EARL RAY, state legislator, lieutenant governor; b. Logan County, W.Va., Mar. 15, 1952; s. Earl and Freda (Jarrell) T.; m. Joanne Jaeger, Sept. 8, 1979; 1 child, Brent Jaeger. BS, W.Va. U.; MBA, Marshall U.; postgrad., U. Charleston. Former sch. tchr.; businessman; mem. W.Va. Ho. Dels., 1974-80, W.Va. State Senate, 1980—, pres., 1995—; lt. gov. State of W.Va., Charleston, 2000—. Chmn. So. Legis. Conf. Former pres., bd. dirs. Appalachia Ednl. Lab., Inc.; mem. Logan County Devel. Authority. Mem. Kappa Alpha. Democrat. Presbyterian. Office: Capitol Bldg Rm 229M Charleston WV 25305 Address: PO Box 116 Chapmanville WV 25508-0116

TOMBLINSON, JAMES EDMOND, architect; b. Flint, Mich., Feb. 12, 1927; s. Carl and Edna Ethel (Spears) T.; m. Betsy Kinley, Sept. 26, 1959; children: Amy Lisa, John Timothy (dec.). B.Arch., U. Mich., 1951. Draftsman firms in, Detroit, 1951-53, Flint, 1953-54, 56-57, San Francisco, 1955-56; field engr. Atlas Constructors, Morocco, 1952-53; architect Tomblinson, Harburn, & Assocs., Inc. (and predecessors), Flint, 1958—, pres., 1969-95; chmn. bd. Tomblinson, Harburn & Assocs., Inc. (and predecessors), 1995—2001; chmn. Mich. Bd. Registration Architects, 1975-77; sec. Mundy Twp. Planning Commn., 1974-85, Grand Blanc Planning Commn., City of Mich., 1985—; chmn., 1988—. Pres. Flint Beautification Commn., 1968-69; bd. dirs. Grand Blanc Beautification Commn., 1969-84; founding mem. bd. dirs. Flint YMCA, 1969-75, chmn. camp com., 1971-75; founding mem. bd. dirs. Flint Environ. Action Team, 1971-77, v.p., 1971-73; elder First Presbyn. Ch. Flint, 1983, trustee, 1986-99; exec. com. Tall Pine council Boy Scouts Am., 1975—; bd. dirs. New Paths, 1994-2004, pres., 1985-86, 94—; trustee Grand Blanc Cmty. Found., 1997-2004; mem. vestry St. Christopher's Ch., 2004—. Served with AUS, 1945-46. Recipient various civic service awards. Fellow AIA; mem. Mich. Soc. Architects, Flint Area C. of C. Clubs: Greater Flint Jaycees (dir. 1957-63, v.p. 1963), Flint City, U. Mich. (pres. Flint chpt. 1980—). Lodges: Rotary (pres. 1984-85). Home: 686 Applegate Ln Grand Blanc MI 48439-1669 Office: THA Architects Engrs 817 E Kearsley St Flint MI 48503-2076 Office Phone: 810-767-5600. Personal E-mail: jetomblinson@aol.com. E-mail: jtomblinson@tha-flint.com.

TOMBRELLO, THOMAS ANTHONY, JR., physics professor; b. Austin, Tex., Sept. 20, 1936; s. Thomas Anthony and Jeanette Lilian (Marcuse) T.; m. Esther Ann Hall, May 30, 1957 (div. Jan. 1976); children: Christopher Thomas, Susan Elaine, Karen Elizabeth; m. Stephanie Carhart Merton, Jan. 15, 1977; 1 stepchild, Kerstin Arusha. BA in Physics, Rice U., Houston, 1958, MA, 1960; PhD, Rice U., 1961; PhD (hon.), Uppsala U., Sweden, 1997. Rsch. fellow in physics Calif. Inst. Tech., Pasadena, 1961-62, 64-65, asst. prof. physics, 1965-67, assoc. prof., 1967-71, prof., 1971—, William R. Kenan Jr. prof., 1997—, tech. assessment officer, 1996—, chair divsn. physics, math. and astronomy, 1998—; asst. prof. Yale U., New Haven, 1963. Cons. in field; disting. vis. prof. U. Calif.-Davis, 1984; v.p., dir. rsch. Schlumberger-Doll Rsch., Ridgefield, Conn., 1987-89; mem. US V.P.'s Space Policy Adv. Bd., 1992; mem. sci. adv. bd. Ctr. of Nanoscale Sci. and Tech., Rice U., 1995—; bd. dirs. Schlumberger Tech. Corp., Schlumberger Found., 1987-89. Assoc. editor Nuc. Physics, 1971-91, Applications Nuc. Physics, 1980-89, Radiation Effects, 1985-88, Nuc. Instruments and Methods B, 1993-96; mem. editl. bd. Blue Origin, 2003—, Applied Minds, 2004—, Arrowhead Rsch., 2005—, Form Factor, 2005—, Trilience Rsch., 2005— Recipient Alexander von Humboldt award von Humboldt Stiftung, U. Frankfurt, Germany, 1984-85; named Disting. Alumnus, Rice U., 1998; NSF fellow Calif. Inst. Tech., 1961-62, A.P. Sloan fellow, 1971-73. Fellow Am. Phys. Soc.; mem. AAAS, Phi Beta Kappa, Sigma Xi, Delta Phi Alpha. Democrat. Avocations: reading, jogging. Office: Calif Inst Tech Dept Physics Mail Code 200 36 Pasadena CA 91125-0001 Office Phone: 626-395-4241. Business E-Mail: tat@caltech.edu.

TOMBROS, PETER GEORGE, pharmaceutical executive; b. Oak Hill, W.Va., June 12, 1942; s. George P. and Mary Jane (Boliski) T.; m. Ann Riblett Cullen, June 12, 1965. BS, Pa. State U., 1964, MS, 1966; MBA, U. Pa., 1968. Mktg. asst. Pfizer Labs. div. Pfizer Inc., NYC, 1968; asst. product mgr. Pfizer Inc., NYC, 1969, product mgr., 1970-71, group product mgr., 1972-74, v.p. mktg., 1975-80; sr. v.p., gen. mgr. Roerig div. Pfizer Inc., NYC, 1980-86; exec. v.p. Pfizer Pharms. div. Pfizer Inc., NYC, 1986-90, v.p. corp. strategic planning, 1990-94; also corp. officer Pfizer Inc., NYC; ret. pres., CEO Enzon, Inc., Piscataway, 1994—2001, also bd. dirs.; chmn., CEO VivoQuest Inc., 2001—05; dir. Cambrex Corp., East Rutherford; prof., exec. in residence Pa. State U., 2005—. Alumni fellow Pa. State U., 1993; bd. dirs. Alpharma Inc., Bridgewater, NJ, chmn. bd.; bd. dirs. NPS Pharm., Inc., Parsippany, NJ, lead dir.; Protalex, Inc., New Hope, Pa., Pharma Net Devel., Inc. Bd. dirs. Dendrite Internat., Bedminster, NJ, 2006-07, Am. Found. Pharm. Edn., North Plainfield, NJ, 1980-01, past chmn.; trustee Fisk U., Nashville, 1986-96, Dominican Coll., Orangeburg, NY, 1987-02; trustee Bklyn. Borough Hall Restoration, 1987-92; mem. corp. devel. com. Cen. Park Conservancy, NYC, 1986-94; bd. dirs. Vote America, 1990; bd. dirs. Cancer Care; chmn. bd. dirs. NJ Tech. Coun., 2001-03. Recipient Disting. Alumnus award, Pa. State U., 2006. Mem. Pharm. Mfrs. Assn. (past chmn. mktg. steering com., 1986-1992), Links Club, Blind Brook Club, Masons. Avocations: marathon running, golf, tennis, skiing, bridge. Business E-Mail: put10@psu.edu.

TOMCZAK, PATRICIA ANN, dean, archivist; b. Detroit, June 8, 1957; d. Raymond and Veronica Tomczak. BA in History, Wayne State U., 1979; MS in Libr. Sci., Wayne State U., Detroit, 1982. Ref. libr. Quincy Pub. Libr., Quincy, Ill., 1986—88; reference libr. Quincy U., Quincy, Ill., 1988—2000, dean of libr. and info. resources, 2000—. Contbr. digitized, online exhibit, digitized online exhibit. Mem.: Soc. of Am. Archivists, Ill. Libr. Assn., ALA, Colonial Williamsburg Found. Roman Catholic. Avocations: travel, visiting historical sites, reading, theater. Office: Quincy University 1800 College Ave Quincy IL 62301 Home Phone: 217-222-6788; Office Phone: 217-228-5351. Business E-Mail: tomczpa@quincy.edu. E-mail: Tomczakp@aol.com.

TOMCZAK, RODNEY LOUIS, retired surgeon, medical educator; b. Toledo, Sept. 14, 1948; s. Louis and Lucille Tomczak; m. Gretchen Ann Ryan, Mar. 17, 1972; children: Meghan Elizabeth, Lauren Marie. BA, Niagara U., Niagara Falls, NY, 1971; D of Podiatric Medicine, Ohio Coll. Podiatric Medicine, Cleve., 1977; EdD, Drake U., Des Moines, 1991. Diplomate Am. Bd. Podiatric Surgery, 1981. Prof. Des Moines U., Albania, 1986—95; asst. prof. Ohio State U., Columbus, 1995—2002; chair edn. dept. Everest Inst., Gahanna, Ohio, 2006—. Med. cons. HSPharm, Greenville, SC, 2005—. Fellow: Am. Coll. Foot and Ankle Surgeons; mem.: Columbus Cath. Med. Assn. (founding pres. 2006—), Cath. Med. Assn. (pres. 2006—). Achievements include research in unexplained foot fracture predicting undiagnosed osteoporosis. Office: Everest Institute 825 Tech Center Dr Columbus OH 43230 Home Phone: 614-841-1314; Office Phone: 614-322-3414. Personal E-mail: rtomczak@cci.edu.

TOMCZYK, FREDRIC J., brokerage house executive; B in Sci., Applied Econs. and Bus. Mgmt., Cornell U., Ithaca, NY. Chartered acct., 1982. Pres., CEO London Life; head retail br. network and wealth mgmt. ops. TD Bank Fin. Group, vice chmn. corp. ops.; exec. v.p., COO TD Ameritrade. Bd. dirs. Robarts Rsch. Inst., Meloche Monnex, Inc., Symcor, Inc.; mem. exec. com. Can. Bankers Assn. Mem. undergraduate bus. program adv. coun. Cornell U. Office: TD Ameritrade 4211 S 102nd St Omaha NE 68127 Office Phone: 402-331-7856. *

TOME, CAROL B., consumer home products company executive; b. Jackson, Wyo., Jan. 8, 1957; BS in Comm., U. Wyo.; MBA in Fin., U. Denver. Comml. lender United Bank Denver (now Wells Fargo); dir. banking Johns-Manville Corp.; v.p., treas. Riverwood Internat. Corp., 1992—95, Home Depot, Atlanta, 1995—2000, sr. v.p. fin., 2000—01, exec. v.p., CFO, 2001—07, CFO, exec. v.p. corp. svcs., 2007—. Bd. dirs. United Parcel Svc., 2003—. Bd. dirs. Girls Inc.; trustee Ga. Substance Abuse Adv. Coun., Home Fund; chair adv. bd. Met. Atlanta Arts Fund. Named one of Next 20 Female CEOs, Pink Mag. & Forté Found., 2006. Office: Home Depot Inc 2455 Paces Ferry Rd Atlanta GA 30339-4029 *

TOMEI, CAROLYN, state representative; m. Gary Michael. BS in Psychology, Portland State U., MSW. State rep., dist. 41 Oreg. House Rep., Salem, 2001—; mayor City of Milwaukie, Oreg.; child devel. specialist Portland Pub. Schs. Vice-chair House Transport. Com.; chair Human Svcs. and Women's Wellness Com.; vice chair Joint Ways and Means Transport., and Econ. Devel. Subcom.; instr. Portland C.C. Democrat. Office: 900 Court St NE H-286 Salem OR 97301 Office Phone: 503-986-1441. E-mail: rep.carolyntomei@state.or.us.

TOMEI, MARISA, actress; b. Bklyn., Dec. 4, 1964; d. Gary and Patricia Tomei. Attended, Boston U. TV appearances include (series) As the World Turns, 1983-88, A Different World, 1987, Only Love, 1998, My Own Country, 1998, Since You've Been Gone, 1998, (films) The Flamingo Kid, 1984, Playing for Keeps, 1986, Parker Kane, 1990, Oscar, 1991, Zandalee, 1991, My Cousin Vinny, 1992 (Acad. award best supporting actress 1993), Chaplin, 1992, Untamed Heart, 1993, Equinox, 1993, The Paper, 1994, Only You, 1994, The Perez Family, 1994, Four Rooms, 1995, Unhook the Stars, 1996, What Women Want, 2000, Dirk and Betty, 2000, Driven, 2000, King of the Jungle, 2000, In the Bedroom, 2001 (ShoWest award best supporting actress, 2002), Someone Like You, 2001, The Guru, 2002, The Wild Thornberrys Movie (voice), 2002, Anger Management, 2003, Loverboy, 2004, Alfie, 2004, Marilyn Hotchkiss Ballroom Dancing and Charm School, 2005, Factotum, 2005, Danika, 2006, Wild Hogs, 2007; theatre appearances include Slavs! Thinking About the Longstanding Problems of Virtue and Happiness, 1994, Welcome to Sarajevo, 1997, This Is How It Goes, 2005. Office: United Talent Agy 9560 Wilshire Blvd Ste 500 Beverly Hills CA 90212 *

TOMEK, WILLIAM GOODRICH, agricultural economist; b. Table Rock, Nebr., Sept. 20, 1932; s. John and Ruth Genevieve (Goodrich) T. BS, U. Nebr., 1956, MA, 1957; PhD, U. Minn., 1961. Asst. prof. Cornell U., Ithaca, NY, 1961-66, NSF fellow, 1965, assoc. prof. agrl. econs., 1966-70, prof., 1970-99, grad. sch. prof., 2000—, chmn. dept. agrl. econs., 1988-93. Vis. econ. USDA, 1978-79; vis. fellow Stanford U., 1968-69, U. New Eng., Australia, 1988; mem. adv. panel Rev. Agrl. Econs., 1996-98; mem. adv. bd. Rev. Futures Markets, 2005-. Author: Agricultural Product Prices, 2003; editor: Am. Jour. Agrl. Econs., 1975-77; co-editor: Chgo. Bd. Trade Rsch. Symposia, 1993-2001; mem. editl. bd. Jour. Futures Markets, 1992-95; contbr. articles to profl. jours. Served with U.S. Army, 1953-55. Recipient Earl Combs Jr. award Chgo. Bd. Trade Found. Mem. Am. Agrl. Econs. Assn. (pres. 1985-86), Am. Econ. Assn., Econometric Soc., Northeastern Agrl. Econs. Assn., Am. Agrl. Econs. Assn. (awards 1981, 89, 97, fellow), Gamma Sigma Delta (rsch. award 1994). Democrat. Methodist. Office: Cornell U Warren Hall Ithaca NY 14853-7801 Home Phone: 607-257-1753; Office Phone: 607-255-2189. E-mail: wgt1@cornell.edu.

TOMICH, LILLIAN, lawyer; b. LA; d. Peter S. and Yovanka P. (Ivanovic) T. AA, Pasadena City Coll., 1954; BA in Polit. Sci., UCLA, 1956, cert. secondary tchg., 1957, MA, 1958; JD, U. So. Calif., 1961. Bar: Calif., U.S. Ct. Appeals (9th Cir.) 1978, 2002. Sole practice, 1961-66; house counsel Mfrs. Bank, LA, 1966; assoc. Hurley, Shaw & Tomich, San Marino, Calif., 1968-76, Driscoll & Tomich, San Marino, Calif., 1976—2005, Conway & Tomich, San Marino, Calif., 2005—. Dir. Continental Culture Specialists Inc., Glendale, Calif. Trustee St. Sava Serbian Orthodox Ch., San Gabriel, Calif. Recipient Episcopal Gramata award Serbian Orthodox Met. of Midwestern Am., 1993, Episcopal Gramata award Serbian Orthodox Bishop of Western Am., 1996, 2002; Charles Fletcher Scott fellow, 1957; U. So. Calif. Law Sch. scholar, 1958. Mem.: ABA, ATLA, Women Lawyers Assn., Los Angeles County Bar Assn., Calif. Bar Assn., Order Mast and Dagger, San Marino C. of C., UCLA Alumni Assn., Town Hall and World Affairs Coun., Pi Kappa Delta, Alpha Gamma Sigma, Iota Tau Tau. Office: 2460 Huntington Dr San Marino CA 91108-2643 Office Phone: 626-287-1248. E-mail: lilliantomich@yahoo.com.

TOMICKI, STEPHEN G., engineer; s. Victor George and Marilyn Cecilia Tomicki; m. Mary Lynne Gliem, May 28, 1994; children: Shawn T. Gliem, Breana Lynne. BSME, Villanova U., Pa., 1981; MBA, UAR, Hilo, Hawaii, 2006. EIT NJ, 1981, BioPharm equipment specialist and trainer, UN Peacekeeping Force, 1999; CPE PA, 1983, CTA PA, 1985. Design project engr., sports facility designer Athletic Facilities and Sports Complex Designers, Conshohocken, Pa., 1981—94; process equipment specialist, sales engr. Process Equipment and Plant Designers, Robbinsville, NJ, 1994—99; engring. sales, global mktg. Power, Process Svcs. and Facilities Svcs., Houston, 1999—2004; mktg. mgr., bus. devel. T&M Assocs. Consulting Engrs., Middletown, NJ, 2004—. Planning bd. devel. com. Bristol Borough, Pa., 1983—89; pres. Sigit Svcs., Bristol, 1981—; mentor Jr. Achievement, 1981—, dir., 1981—91; sec., treas. Kenilworth Mfgs. Assn., NJ, 2004—. Recipient Nat. Ranked Racquetball Champion award, URA, 1982—88, Excellence award, Trump Investments. Mem.: ISPE (assoc.; com. chair 1988—). Office: T&M Assocas Consulting Engrs 11 Tindall Rd Middletown NJ 07748 Home Phone: 609-426-1929; Office Phone: 732-671-6400. Office Fax: 732-671-6107. Personal E-mail: stomicki@optonline.net. Business E-Mail: stomicki@tandmassociates.com.

TOMITA, MASARU, engineering educator, researcher; b. Kitakyushu, Fukuoka, Japan, Mar. 10, 1965; s. Hiroshi and Yoko Tomita; m. Yoko Aikawa Tomita, Oct. 22, 1995; children: Yutaka, Kana C. B in Mgmt., Kyushu Inst. Tech., Fukuoka, 1987, B in Engring., 1991, M in Engring., 1993; PhD in Engring., U. Tokyo, 2003. Sr. rschr. Railway Tech. Rsch. Inst., Tokyo, 1993—; chief rsch. scientist Superconductivity Rsch. Lab. ISTEC, Tokyo, 1998—2002; rsch. scientist MIT, Cambridge, Mass., 2004—. Vis. prof. Keio U., Yokohama, Japan, 2005, Tokyo Women's Med. U., 2005—. Author: Nature 421, 2003. Recipient Director's award, ISTEC, 2000, Nat. Minister's award Edn. and Culture, Sports, Sci. and Tech., 2004, Nat. Minister's award Economy, Trade and Industry, 2004. Mem.: Japan Soc. Applied Physics (program com. applied superdonductivity conf.), Cryogenic Assn. Japan. Achievements include research in Bulk superconducting materials for improvement of properties and application of superconductivity; discovery of World record data of trapped field of high temprature superconductors. Avocations: basketball, baseball, tennis, ping pong/table tennis, travel. Office: MIT NW14-3209 170 Albany St Cambridge MA 02139 Home Phone: 781-646-5344. Fax: 617-253-5405. Business E-Mail: tomita@mit.edu. E-mail: tomita@rtri.or.jp.

TOMIYASU, KIYO, retired consulting engineer; b. Las Vegas, Nev., Sept. 25, 1919; s. Yonema and Toyono (Kawamura) T.; m. Eiko Nakamizo, Aug. 31, 1947. BS, Calif. Inst. Tech., Pasadena, 1940; MS, Columbia U., NYC, 1941; M.E.S., Harvard U., Cambridge, Mass., 1947, PhD, 1948. Instr. Harvard U., 1948-49; head engring. sect. Sperry Gyroscope Co., Gt. Neck, N.Y., 1949-55; with GE, 1955-93; cons. engr. microwave techniques GE Valley Forge Space Ctr., Phila., 1969-93; with Martin Marietta Corp., Phila., 1993-95, Lockheed Martin Corp., Phila., 1995—2005; ret., 2005. Author: The Laser Literature-An Annotated Guide, 1968; articles; patentee in field. Exec. bd. Friendship Hill Civic Assn., Paoli, Pa., 1972-73, pres., 1973. Recipient Steinmetz award Gen. Electric Co., 1977; Mgmt. and Data Systems fellow Martin Marietta Corp., 1993; Locheed Martin fellow, 2004; established Tomiyasu Meml. ann. scholarship Calif. Inst. Tech., 1977. Fellow IEEE (life, hon. life mem. Microwave Theory and Techniques Soc. 1973, tech. activities bd., awards bd., publs. bd., bd. dirs. div. IV 1985-86, ednl. activities bd. 1987-88, Microwave Career award, 1981, Centennial medal 1984, Millennium medal 2000, established Kiyo Tomiyasu award 2000), Geosci. and Remote Sensing Soc. (hon. life; Geosci. and Remote Sensing Outstanding Svc. award 1986, Microwave Disting. Svc. award 1987); mem. Am. Phys. Soc. Home: 890 E Harrison Ave Apt 30 Pomona CA 91767-2075

TOMKA, PETER, diplomat, arbitrator, judge, lawyer; b. Banská, Bystrica, Slovakia, June 1, 1956; s. Ján and Kornélia (Plai) T.; m. Zuzana Halgasová, June 30, 1990. Grad., Charles U., Prague, Czechoslovakia, 1979; PhD in Internat. Law, Charles U., 1985. Lectr. Law Sch., Charles U., Prague, 1980-86, assoc. lectr. in internat. law, 1986-91; asst. legal advisor Fed. Ministry of Fgn. Affairs, Czechoslovakia, 1986-90, head pub. internat. law divsn., 1990-91; counsellor, legal advisor Permanent Mission to UN, NYC, 1991-92, amb., dep. permanent rep. of Slovakia, 1993-97, charge d'affaires, 1994-97; legal advisor Ministry Fgn. Affairs, Bratislava, Slovakia, 1997-98, dir. gen. legal and consular affairs, 1998-99; permanent rep. of Slovakia to UN, NYC, 1999—2003; judge Internat. Ct. of Justice, The Hague, Netherlands, 2003—; arbitrator Iron Rhine Case, Belgium/Netherlands, 2003—05. Former agt. of Slovakia Internat. Ct. Justice in Gabcikovo-Nagymaros Project Case, Hungary/Slovakia; mem. Permanent Ct. Arbitration, 1994—; chmn. UN Legal Com., 1997; vice chair com. legal advisors Coun. of Europe, 1998—99, chmn. com. legal advisors, 2001—02; mem. UN Internat. Law Commn., 1999—2003, vice chmn., 2000; arbitrator UN Law of the Sea Conv., 2004—, World Bank Internat. Ctr. for Settlement Investment Disputes, 2005—. Office: Internat Ct Justice Peace Palace 2517 KJ The Hague Netherlands Office Phone: (31-70) 3022323. *

TOMKINS, CALVIN, writer; b. Orange, NJ, Dec. 17, 1925; s. Frederick and Laura (Graves) T.; m. Grace Lloyd Fanning, Sept. 11, 1948; children: Anne Graves, Susan Temple, Spencer; m. Judy Johnston, Nov. 11, 1961 (div. Feb. 1981); m. Susan Cheever, Oct. 1, 1981; 1 child, Sarah Liley Cheever; m. Dodie Kazanjian, May 28, 1988. BA, Princeton U., 1948. Assoc. editor Newsweek mag., NYC, 1955-57, gen. editor, 1957-59; staff writer The New Yorker, NYC, 1960—. Author: The Bride and The Bachelors, 1965, Merchants and Masterpieces, 1970, Living Well Is the Best Revenge, 1971, Off the Wall, 1980, Post- to Neo-, 1988, (with Dodie Kazanjian) Alex: The Life of Alexander Liberman, 1993, Duchamp: A Biography, 1997. Bd. dirs. Cunningham Dance Found., N.Y.C., 1963-90. With USN, 1944-46. Guggenheim fellow, 1978 Mem. Authors League Am. Inc., Pen Am. Ctr. Clubs: Century (N.Y.C.). Home: 145 E 74th St New York NY 10021-3225 Office: New Yorker Mag 4 Times Sq New York NY 10036-6561 Business E-Mail: dodietad@aol.com.

TOMLIN, CLAIRE J., aeronautical engineer, educator; b. Southampton, Eng., 1969; BASc in Elec. Engring., U. Waterloo, 1992; MSEE, Imperial Coll., London, 1993; PhD in Elec. Engring. and Computer Sci., U. Calif., Berkeley, 1998. Assoc. prof. dept. aeronautics and astronautics Stanford U., Calif. Courtesy assoc. prof. elec. engring. Stanford U.; assoc. prof. dept. elec. engring. and computer sci. U. Calif., Berkeley. Contbr. articles to sci. jours., chapters to books; co-editor: Hybrid Systems: Computation and Control, 2002. Named one of Top 100 Innovators, MIT Tech. Rev., 2003; recipient Zonta Amelia Earhart awards for Aeronautics Rsch., 1996—98, Career award, NSF, 2000—03, Donald P. Eckman award, Am. Automatic Control Coun., 2003; MacArthur Fellow, John D. and Catherine T. MacArthur Found., 2006. Office: Stanford U Dept Aeronautics and Astronautics Durand Bldg 496 Lomita Mall Stanford CA 94305-4035 E-mail: tomlin@stanford.edu.

TOMLIN, LILY, actress; b. Detroit, Sept. 1, 1939; Student, Wayne State U.; studied mime with Paul Curtis, studied acting with Peggy Feury. Co-founder Lily Tomlin Jane Wagner Cultural Arts Ctr., LA. Appearances in concerts and colls. throughout U.S.; TV appearances include The Music Scene, 1969-70, Laugh In, 1970-73, Lily Tomlin, CBS Spls., 1973, 81, 82; 2 ABC Spls., 1974, 75, Edith Ann Animated Specials, ABC, 1994, The Magic School Bus, 1994 (voice), Murphy Brown, 1996-98, The West Wing, 2002-06; motion picture debut in Nashville, 1975 (N.Y. Film Critics award); also appeared in The Late Show, 1977, Moment by Moment, 1978, The Incredible Shrinking Woman, 1981, Nine to Five, 1980, All of Me, 1984, Big Business, 1987, Shadows and Fog, 1992, The Player, 1992, Short Cuts, 1993, The Beverly Hillbillies, 1993, And the Band Played On, HBO, 1993 (Best Supporting Actress Emmy nominee - Special, 1994, Emmy nominations guest appearance Homicide, 1996), Getting Away with Murder, 1995, The Celluloid Closet, 1995, Blue in the Face, 1995, Flirting With Disaster, 1996, Reno Finds Her Mom, 1997, Get Bruce, 1999, Krippendorf's Tribe, 1998, Tea with Mussolini, 1999, Picking Up the Pieces, 2000, The Kid, 2000, Orange County, 2002, I Heart Huckabees, 2004, A Prairie Home Companion, 2006, (voice) The Ant Bully, 2006; exec. prodr. TV series Citizen Reno, 2001; one-woman Broadway show Appearing Nitely, 1977 (Spl. Tony award), The Search for Signs of Intelligent Life in the Universe, 1985 (Drama Desk award, Outer Critics Circle award, Tony award 1986, Cable Ace award); recs. include This is a Recording, And That's The Truth, Modern Scream, On Stage. Recipient Grammy award 1971, 5 Emmy awards for CBS Spl. 1973, 81, Emmy award for ABC Spl. 1975, Emmy award Magic Sch. Bus, 1995, Peabody award Celluloid Closet, 1997, Peabody Edith Ann's Christmas, 1997, Mark Twain Prize for Am. Humor, Kennedy Center, 2003. Office: Lily Tomlin Jane Wagner Cultural Arts Ctr Village at Ed Gould Plz 1125 N McCadden Pl Los Angeles CA 90038-1212

TOMLIN, MIKE, professional football coach; b. Hampton, Va., Mar. 15, 1972; m. Kiya Tomlin; children: Dino, Mason, Grad., William and Mary Coll., 1994. Wide receivers coach Va. Mil. Inst., 1995; grad. asst. Memphis U., 1996; wide receivers coach Ark. State U., 1997, defensive backs coach, 1998, U. Cin., 1999—2000, Tampa Bay Bucaneers, 2001—05; defensive coord. Minn. Vikings, 2006; head coach Pitts. Steelers, 2007—. Office: Pitts Steelers 3400 S Water St Pittsburgh PA 15203-2349 *

TOMLIN-HOUSTON, LISA, management consultant; b. Bklyn. d. George L. and Joan J. Tomlin; m. Anthony D. Houston, Feb. 2, 1991. BA in Psychology, Oberlin Coll., Ohio, 1987; MEd in Counseling Psychology, Rutgers U., 1990. Career counselor U. Pa., Phila., 1990-93; dir. career svcs. H. John Heinz III Sch. of Public Policy and Mgmt., Carnegie Mellon U., Pitts., 1993-95; mgmt. cons. Ford Found., 1995—97; mgr. undergrad. and MBA recruitment Barclays Capital, 1998—2000; pres. Creative Solutions Strategies, LLC, 2000—02; dir. career svcs. Baldwin-Wallace Coll., Berea, Ohio, 2002—06; pres., owner Houston St. Clair Careers, Cleve., 2006—. Mem.: Soc. Human Resources Profls., Pub. Rels. Soc. Am., Nat. Assn. Coll. and Employers. Avocations: reading, travel, woman's issues.

TOMLINSON, ALEXANDER COOPER, investment banker, consultant; b. Haddonfield, NJ, May 13, 1922; s. Alexander Cooper and Mary (Buzby) T.; m. Elizabeth Anne Brierley, Jan. 10, 1953 (div.); children: William Brierley, Deborah T. Marple, Alexander Cooper III; m. Margaret L. Dickey, Nov. 15, 1986. BS, Haverford Coll., 1943; postgrad., London Sch. Econs. and Polit. Sci., 1947-48; MBA, Harvard U., 1950; LLD (hon.), Haverford Coll., 1995. With Morgan Stanley & Co., NYC, 1950-76, ptnr., 1958-76, mng. dir., 1970-76; dir., pres. Morgan Stanley Can. Ltd. div., Montreal, Que., 1972-76; chmn. exec. com. First Boston, Inc., NYC, 1976-82, dir., 1976-88; pres. Nat. Policy Assn., Washington, 1982-85; exec. dir. Ctr. for Privatization, Washington, 1985-88; pres. Hungarian-Am. Enterprise Fund, Washington, 1990-93; chmn. Fund for Arts and Culture in Ctrl. and Ea. Europe, 1994-97. Mem. U.S. adv. bd. Que. Hydro, 1984-95. Trustee Incorp. Village, Cove Neck, N.Y., 1958-72, 76-82, Cold Spring Harbor Lab., 1976-87, N.Y. Infirmary-Beekman Downtown Hosp., 1968-82, East Woods Sch., Oyster Bay, N.Y., 1962-70, Nature Conservancy, L.I., N.Y., 1970-82, Salisbury Sch., Conn., 1976-87, Carnegie Found. for Advancement Tchg., 1984-90; bd. mgrs. Haverford Coll., 1979-01; bd. dirs. Nat. Bldg. Mus., 1987-94, Nat. Policy Assn., 1982-90, Decatur House Coun., 1990-94; chmn. Am. Friends Can., Inc., 1982-91, Harvard Bus. Sch. Fund, 1981-83. Lt. USNR, 1943-46. Mem. Coun. on Fgn. Rels., Metropolitan Club (Washington), Links (N.Y.). Home: 3314 P St NW Washington DC 20007-2701

TOMLINSON, HERBERT WESTON, lawyer, defender; b. Upland, Pa., Feb. 11, 1930; s. Herbert Elmer and Hilda Josephine (Schlosbon) Tomlinson; m. Mary Jean Litwhiler, Oct. 27, 1961. BS, Pa. State U., 1952, BA with highest distinction, 1994; JD, Dickinson Sch. Law, 1960; postgrad., Temple U. Law Sch., 1969-73; grad. in bus. mgmt. summa cum laude, Widener U., 2006. Bar: Pa. 1961, U.S. Supreme Ct. 1968; lic. pilot. Law clk., pres. Delaware County Bar Assn., 1960-61; assoc. DeFuria Larkin Defuria, Chester, Pa., 1960-62, Hodge & Balderston, Chester, 1962-65, Edward McLaughlin, Chester, 1965-67; exec. dir. Legal Svcs. Program, Delaware County, 1967-69; pvt. practice Media, Pa., 1969—; sr. staff atty. Delaware County Pub. Defender's Office, 1969—. Prof. bus. law Pa. State U., 1969—75, Widener U., 1971—76, 1978—80, Delaware County CC, 1971—75. Actor: TV commls., 1998—. Legal counsel Disabled Vets. Am.; county dir. Delaware County March of Dimes, 1966—71; rep. candidate U.S. Ho. Reps., 1976; Rep. committeeman, 1966—; treas. 168th Legis. Dist., 1975—81; chmn. Media Rep. Com., 1975—76; nat. dir. US Jaycees, 1965—66; chmn. Media Borough Auditor, 1975—79. Capt. USMCR, 1952—56. Named Outstanding Young Man Am., U.S. Jaycees, 1966. Mem.: SAG, ATLA, ABA, AAUP, Delaware County Med. Soc. (dir. pub. health fund 1967—), Delaware County Real Estate Bd., Delaware County Bar Assn., Pa. Trial Lawyers Assn., Pa. Bar Assn., Am. Arbitration Assn. (arbitrator), Nat. Assn. Securities Dealers, Aircraft Owners and Pilots Assn., Rotary, Kiwanis, Shriners, Masons, Beta Gamma Sigma, Alpha Sigma Lambda, Phi Kappa Phi, Phi Theta Kappa (past pres.). Presbyterian. Office: 247 N Middletown Rd Media PA 19063-4535 Office Phone: 610-627-4131. Personal E-mail: herbtomlinson@msn.com.

TOMLINSON, J. RICHARD, retired engineering services company executive; b. Newtown, Pa., Mar. 26, 1930; s. Robert K. and Margaret (Wright) T.; m. Barbara Elizabeth Brazill, Apr. 30, 1955; children: Karin Kathleen Tomlinson Pizzitola, Kimberly Ann Tomlinson Donahue. BA, Swarthmore Coll., 1952; postgrad., George Washington U., 1952-53, U. Mich., 1955-57, Drexel Inst. Tech., 1954-57, Am. U., 1965. Mgmt. analyst Dept. State, Washington, 1952-53; with Old Republic Life Ins. Co., Washington, 1953-54; supr. financial analysis Ford Motor Co., Detroit, 1954-61; cons. McKinsey & Co., Washington, 1961-65; v.p. finance, dir. passenger svcs. Reading Co., Phila., 1965-69; v.p. finance Rollins Internat., Inc., 1969-71; exec. v.p. Amtrak, Washington, 1972-74; ptnr. L.T. Klauder and Assocs., 1974-75, 79-83; exec. v.p. Penn Central Transp. Co., 1975-78; pres. LTK Engring. Svcs., 1984-95. Named Man of Month, Phila. C. of C., 1967 Mem. Union League, Aronimink Golf and Country Club, Phila. Aviation Country Club. Home: 451 Inveraray Rd Villanova PA 19085-1139 E-mail: jrt77@aol.com.

TOMLINSON, JAMES FRANCIS, retired news agency executive; b. Long Beach, Calif., Oct. 18, 1925; s. Lilburn Jesse and Margaret (Roemer) T.; m. Sally JoAnne Ryan, Aug. 12, 1967; children— Elizabeth Anne, Victoria Alexandra. BA, U. Va., 1950; student, Harvard U., Grad. Sch. Arts and Scis., 1950-51; grad., Advanced Mgmt. Program, Harvard U., 1977. With A.P., 1951-92, chief bur. Newark, 1957-63, bus. news editor NYC, 1963-67, dep. treas., 1967-68, treas., 1968-87, v.p., 1972-92, sec., 1978-92, asst. to pres., 1987-92. Served with AUS, 1943-46, ETO. Mem. SAR, N.Y. Athletic Club (N.Y.C.), Harvard Club (N.Y.C.), Phi Beta Kappa, Phi Eta Sigma. Home: 222 E 71st St New York NY 10021-5164

TOMLINSON, JAMES LAWRENCE, mechanical engineer; b. Detroit, Sept. 12, 1935; s. James Emmet and Ethel Pearl (Williams) T.; m. Marilyn Joyce Peterson, Aug. 24, 1957; children: James, Mary, Robert, Susan. BSME, Mich. Tech., 1957. Registered profl. engr., Mich. Design engr. Buick Motor div. GMC, Flint, Mich., 1960-61, project engr., 1961-66, sr. project engr., 1966-71; staff analysis engr. GM Corp., Warren, Mich., 1971-82, sr. staff analysis engr., 1983-88; pres. Eastport (Mich.) Engring., 1989—. Mayor City of Grand Blanc, 1985-89, city councilman, 1969-84, police liaison/commr., 1971-82, planning adv. bd., 1978-80, planning commn., 1985-89; nat. coun. mem. Boy Scouts Am., 1979-90, 93—, regional bd. mem., 1995—, coun. commr., 1979-84, coun. v.p., 1984—, nat. camp sch. staff, 1986-88, regional camp inspector/accreditation team, 1988-2004, subcamp chief nat. jamboree, 2001, 05; vice chmn. Genesee County Sml. Cities and Villages Assn., 1986, chmn., 1987; bd. dirs. Three Lakes Assn., Inc., 1997-2003. Capt. USAF, 1958-60. Recipient Silver Beaver Tall Pine coun. Boy Scouts Am., 1980, Silver Antelope Ctrl. region, 1996. Mem. NSPE (treas. Flint chpt. 1968-72, Engr. of the Yr. Flint chpt. 1990), SAE (mem. com. 1992-94, 96-98), ASME (exec. bd. Saginaw Valley chpt. 1968-70), Friends of Torch Lake Twp., Inc. (pres. 1994—). Mem. Congl. Ch. Home: PO Box 25 Eastport MI 49627-0025

TOMLINSON, LADAINIAN, professional football player; b. Rosebud, Tex., June 23, 1979; s. Oliver Tomlinson and Loreane Chappell; m. LaTorsha Tomlinson. BA in Gen. Studies, Tex. Christian U., Ft. Worth, 2001. Running back San Diego Chargers, 2001—. Founder Tomlinson Touching Lives Found., 2005—. Named NFL All-Pro, 2004—07, Player of Yr., NBC, 2006, NFL Offensive Player of Yr., AP, 2006; named to AFC Pro Bowl team, 2002, 2004—07; recipient Doak Walker award, 2000, NFL MVP award, AP, 2006, Espy award, Male Athlete of Yr., 2007, Espy award, Best NFL Player, 2007, Espy award, Record-Breaking Performance, 2007, Espy award, Like Nothing Else award, 2007. Achievements include being the fifth overall pick in the 2001 NFL Draft, led NFL in rushing touchdowns (17), 2004; reached 100 career touchdowns faster than any other player in NFL history, 2006; holds the NFL record for most rushing touchdowns scored in a single-season (28), 2006; holds the NFL record for touchdowns scored in a single-season (31), 2006. Office: c/o San Diego Chargers 4020 Murphy Canyon Rd San Diego CA 92123 *

TOMLINSON, MARGARET LYNCH, lawyer; b. Cleve., June 21, 1929; d. John Joseph and Margaret (Stevenson) Lynch; m. Alexander C. Tomlinson. AB, Smith Coll., 1950; JD, N.Y. Law Sch., 1963. Bar: N.Y. 1963, D.C. 1971, U.S Ct. Appeals (D.C. cir.) 1971. Staff officer Dept. of State, 1950-55; U.S. Del. UN Gen. Assembly, NYC, 1964-68; asst. legal adviser U.S. Mission to the UN, 1963-69; asst. to Sen. Claiborne Pell, Washington, 1969-71; sr. adviser U.S. Del. to the Law of the Sea Conf., 1972-78; ptnr. Dickey, Roadman & Dickey, Washington, 1978-82; cons. office gen. counsel CIA, Washington, 1987-93. Cons. Law of the Sea; bd. dirs. Coun. Ocean Law, Washington, 1984—, vice-chmn., 1994—; U.S. del. spl. session UN Gen. Assembly, 1994. Contbr. articles to profl. jours. Mem. ABA (internat. law sect., chmn. law of the sea com.), Am. Soc. Internat. Law, Internat. Law Assn., D.C. Bar Assn., Nat. Press Club, Sulgrave Club. Home: 3314 P St NW Washington DC 20007-2701

TOMLINSON, WILLIAM HOLMES, management educator, retired military officer; b. Thornton, Ark., Apr. 12, 1922; s. Hugh Oscar and Lucy Gray (Holmes) T.; m. Dorothy Payne, June 10, 1947 (dec.); children: Jane Axtell, Lucy Gray, William Payne; m. Florence Mood Smith, May 1, 1969 (div.); m. Suzanne Scollard Gill, Mar. 16, 1977. Student, Centenary Coll., Hackettstown, NJ, 1938—39; BS, US Mil. Acad., West Point, NY, 1943; grad., Field Arty. Sch., 1951, Air Command Staff Coll., 1958; MBA, U. Ala., 1960; MS in Internat. Affairs, George Wash. U., Washington, DC, 1966; grad., US Army War Coll., 1966, Indsl. Coll. Armed Forces, 1968; PhD in Bus. Adminstrn., Am. U., Washington, DC, 1974; grad. Advanced Mgmt. Program, Harvard Bus. Sch., Cambridge, Mass., 1968-69; BAS, U. North Fla., Jacksonville, 1988. Commd. 2d lt. US Army, 1943, advanced through grades to Col., Field Arty., 1966; combat svc. in Leyte and Cebu Philippines 246 Field Arty. Bn. Americal Divsn., 1945; aide de camp to comdg. gen. Robert Eichelberger 8th US Army, Japan, 1945-48; comdr. Btry A, 319th FA Bn and Btry A, 39th FA Bn, 3d Divsn., Ft. Benning, Ga., 1948—50; exec. officer 34 FA Bn, ops. officer 9th Divsn. Arty. Germany and Ft. Carson, Colo., 1954-57; with ODCSPER, 1960—61, Office of Undersec. Army, The Pentagon, Washington, 1961-64; comdr. 2d Bn. 8th Arty. and 7th Divsn. Arty. UN Comd. South Korea, 1964-65; faculty Indsl. Coll. Armed Forces, Ft. McNair, Washington, 1966-72, U. North Fla., Jacksonville, 1972—2002, prof. mgmt., prof. emeritus, 2002—. Vis. prof. U. Glasgow, Scotland, 1987; vis. lectr. Moscow Linguistics U., Plekhanov Econ. Acad., Ulyanovsk U., Russia, 1993; mem. Nat. Def. Exec. Res., Fed. Emergency Mgmt. Agy., 1976—. Author: Assessment of the National Defense Executive Reserve, 1974; co-author: International Business, Theory and Practice, 1991, Business Policy and Strategy, 2000; contbr. articles to profl. jours. Mem. exec. bd. Jacksonville Campus Ministry, 1991—, pres., 2002-04. Decorated Bronze Star, Legion of Merit, Philippine Liberation medal, Japanese Occupation, Asiatic Pacific with Invasion Arrow; recipient Freedom Found. award, 1967-71, Lifetime Sr. Profl. in Human Resources, Tchg. Incentive award State Univ. Sys., 1994-95. Fellow Soc. Antiquaries Scotland; mem. SAR, Sons Confederate Vets., Soc. Human Resource Mgmt., Acad. Mgmt., Indsl. Rels. Rsch. Assn., Acad. Internat. Bus., European Internat. Bus. Assn., Internat. Trade and Fin. Assn., Exec. Svc. Corp. Bd., Co. Mil. Historians, Nat. Eagle Scout Assn., N.E. Fla. Employee Svcs. Mgmt. Assn. (charter pres. 1987-89), Stewart Soc. Edinburgh (regional commr.), West Point Soc. North Fla. (pres. 1976-77), Mil. Order Stars and Bars (comdr. 1980-90), Army Navy Club, Fla. Yacht Club, Masons, Shriners, Rotary, Beta Gamma Sigma (pres. 1988-89), Kappa Alpha. Presbyterian (elder, trustee). Office: 1890 Shadowlawn St Jacksonville FL 32205-9430 Office Phone: 904-388-1148. Personal E-mail: 1shadow@comcast.net.

TOMLINSON-KEASEY, CAROL ANN, academic administrator; b. Washington, Oct. 15, 1942; d. Robert Bruce and Geraldine (Howe) Tomlinson; m. Charles Blake Keasey, June 13, 1964; children: Kai Linson, Amber Lynn. BS, Pa. State U., University Park, 1964; MS, Iowa State U., Ames, 1966; PhD, U. Calif., Berkeley, 1970. Lic. psychologist, Calif. Asst. prof. psychology Trenton (NJ) State Coll., 1969-70, Rutgers U., New Brunswick, NJ, 1970-72; prof. U. Nebr., Lincoln, 1972-77, U. Calif., Riverside, 1977-92, acting dean Coll. Humanities and Social Scis., 1986-88, chmn. dept. psychology, 1989-92, vice provost for acad. planning and pers. Davis, 1992-97, vice provost for acad. initiatives, 1997-99, chancellor, 1996—2006. Author: Child's Eye View, 1980, Child Development, 1985, numerous chpts. to books; contbr. articles to profl. jours. Recipient Disting. Tchr. award U. Calif., 1986. Mem. APA, Soc. Rsch. in Child Devel., Riverside Aquatics Assn. (pres.). Office: PO Box 2039 Merced CA 95344 Home Phone: 404-321-7433. Personal E-mail: caroltk@yahoo.com.

TOMLISON, RONDAL SCOTT, music educator; b. Somerset, Ky., June 17, 1965; s. Donald Franklin and Retta B. Tomlison; m. Amy Elizabeth Bixler, Dec. 28, 2002. B Music Edn., Ea. Ky. U., Richmond, 1988; M Music Edn., Murray State U., Ky., 1994; PhD, U. Mo., Columbia, 1999. Cert. tchr. Ky., Ohio, Tenn., Mo. Asst. band dir. Miami East Local Schs., Casstown, Ohio, 1988—90, Grant County Pub. Schs., Dry Ridge, Ky., 1990—91; band dir. Gallatin County Pub. Schs., Warsaw, Ky., 1991—93; grad. asst. Murray State U., 1993—94; band dir. Poplar Bluff R1 Schs., Mo., 1996—2000; asst. prof. music Manchester Coll., North Manchester, Ind., 2000—04, McPherson Coll., Ky., 2004—, head music edn. Adjudicator Kans. HS Activities Assn., Wichita, 2004—, Judges Assn. Mid-Am., Lawrence, Kans., 2006—; guest condr. Heart of Plains League Band, NE Hoosier Conf. Honors Band, All-Region Jr. High Honors Band, numerous others; brass instr., brass capt. head Ltd. Edition Drum and Bugle Corps, 1989—91; presenter in field; adjudicator numerous music competitions. Mem.: Judges Assn. Mid Am., Coll. Music Soc., Kans. Music Educators Assn., Coll. Band Dirs. Nat. Assn., Music Educators Nat. Conf., Kans. Bandmasters Assn., Phi Mu Alpha Sinfonia. Home: 1609 E Kansas Ave Mcpherson KS 67460 Office: McPerson Coll PO Box 1402 Mcpherson KS 67460

TOMLJANOVICH, ESTHER M., retired judge; b. Galt, Iowa, Nov. 1, 1931; d. Chester William and Thelma L. (Brooks) Moellering; m. William S. Tomljanovich, Dec. 26, 1957; 1 child, William Brooks Tomljanovich. AA, Itasca C.C., 1951; BSL, St. Paul Coll. Law, 1953, LLB, 1955. Bar: Minn. 1955, U.S. Dist. Ct. Minn. 1958. Asst. revisor of statutes State of Minn., St. Paul, 1957-66, revisor of statutes, 1974-77, dist. ct. judge Stillwater, 1977-90; assoc. justice Minn. Supreme Ct., St. Paul, 1990—98, ret., 1998. Adv. bd. women offenders Minn. Dept. Corrections, 1999—; leadership com. So. Minn. Legal Svcs. Corp., 1999—. Former mem. North St. Paul Bd. Edn., Maplewood Bd. Edn., Lake Elmo Planning Commn.; trustee William Mitchell Coll. Law, 1995—2004, Legal Rights Ctr., 1995—2004, pres., 1999; bd. dirs. Itasca C.C. Found., 1996—, Medica Health Ins. Co., 2001—, vice chair, 2003—. Recipient Centennial 2000 award William Mitchell Coll., Disting. Alumna award, First Ann. Esther Tomljanovich Lifetime Achievement award, 2005; named one of One Hundred Who Made a Difference William Mitchell Coll. Law, One of 100 Most Influential Lawyers of All Time, Law & Politics Mag., 2007. Mem. Minn. State Bar Assn., Bus. and Profl. Women's Assn. St. Paul (former pres.), Minn. Women Lawyers (founding mem.). Home and Office: 8533 Hidden Bay Trail Lake Elmo MN 55042 Home Phone: 612-777-5970; Office Phone: 612-777-5970.

TOMMASINI, ANTHONY, music critic, writer, musician; b. Brooklyn; BA, Yale U., 1970, MusM; DMA, Boston U.; studied with pianists Donald Currier and Leonard Shure. Former critic Boston Globe; chief classical music critic NY Times, NYC. Author: Virgil Thomson's Musical Portraits, 1986, Virgil Thomson: Composer on the Aisle, 1997 (ASCAP-Deems Taylor award, 1998), The New York Times Essential Library: Opera A Critic's Guide to the 100 Most Important Works and the Best Recordings, 2004; pianist: Portraits and Self-Portraits, Mostly About Love: Songs and Vocal Works. Avocation: bicycling. Office: NY Times Culture Desk 229 W 43rd St New York NY 10036 Office Phone: 212-556-4543. Office Fax: 212-556-1516.

TOMMEY, CHARLES ELDON, retired surgeon; b. Nashville, Ark., Jan. 13, 1922; s. William Robert and America Anna (Compton) T.; m. Clara Blair Newman, Aug. 28, 1948; children: Robert, Jean, Phillip, Dale, Scott. Student, Henderson State Tchrs. Coll., 1940-42; BSM, U. Ark. Sch. Medicine, 1944, MD, 1945. Diplomate Am. Bd. Surgery. Intern City Hosp., Columbus, Ga., 1945-46; surg. resident Bapt. Hosp., Little Rock, 1948-49, VA Hosp., Cleve., 1950-54; pvt. practice surgery El Dorado, Ark., 1954-95; ret., 1995. Asst. clin. instr. surgery U. Ark. Coll. Medicine. Capt. U.S. Army Med. Corps, 1943-45, 46-48. Fellow ACS. Baptist. Avocations: golf, photography. Home: 123 Glenridge Pky El Dorado AR 71730-3117

TOMNITZ, DONALD J., construction executive; V.p. RepublicBank Dallas, N.A., Crow Devel. Co.; v.p. various divsns. D.R. Horton, Inc., Fort Worth, Tex., 1983—94, v.p. western region, 1994, pres. homebuilding divsn., 1996—98, exec. v.p., 1998, vice chmn., CEO, 1998—, pres., 2000—. Capt. US Army. Office: DR Horton Inc DR Horton Tower 301 Commerce St Ste 500 Fort Worth TX 76102 *

TOMOMATSU, HIDEO, chemist; b. Tokyo, June 8, 1929; arrived in U.S., 1959, naturalized; s. Shinsai Natsu and Suma Tomomatsu; m. Yuko Ito, Nov. 12, 1967; 1 child, Tadao. BSChemE., Waseda U., 1952; MS in Chemistry, U. of the Pacific, 1960; PhD in Chemistry, Ohio State U., 1964. Registered profl. engr., Tex.; cert. U.S. Patent Agt. Chemist Hodogaya Chem. Co., Tokyo, 1952—59, Texaco Chems. Co., Austin, Tex., 1964—72; Quaker fellow Quaker Oats Co., Barrington, Ill., 1972—96; cons. Functional Food Resources, Inc., Escondido, Calif., 1996—. Contbr. articles to profl. jours.; patentee in field. Mem.: Inst. Food Technologists, Am. Assn. Cereal Chemists, Am. Chem. Soc. Home: 2555 Seascape Gln Escondido CA 92026-3862 Personal E-mail: hitomoyuko@earthlink.net.

TOMPERT, JAMES EMIL, lawyer; b. Battle Creek, Mich., July 21, 1954; s. James Russell and Marjorie Mary (Storkan) T. BA, Duke U., 1976; JD, U. Mich., 1981. Bar: D.C. 1981, Md. 1985, Va. 1986. Legis. asst. to congressman U.S. Ho. of Rep., Washington, 1977—78; assoc. Baker & Hostetler, Washington, 1981—84, Cooter & Gell, Washington, 1984—86, ptnr., 1987—94, Cooter Mangold Tompert & Karas L.L.P., Washington, 1995—. Mem. D.C. Bar Assn., Univ. Club Washington. Office: Cooter Mangold Tompert & Karas LLP 5301 Wisconsin Ave NW Washington DC 20015-2015 Business E-Mail: jtompert@cootermangold.com.

TOMPKINS, ALAN W., lawyer; b. Ky., 1961; m. Julie R. Tompkins. B in Economics, Ind. State U. (now U. So. Ind.), 1983; MBA, So. Methodist U., 1983; M in Acctg., U. Tex., Dallas, 1990; JD, So. Methodist U., 1993. CPA 1988. Pvt. practice Malouf Lynch Jackson Kessler & Collins, Weil, Gotshal & Manges, Secore & Waller; assoc. gen. counsel Richmont Corp., 1997—2001; pvt. practice Hance, Scarborough, Wright, Ginsberg & Brusilow, 2002—03; v.p., gen. counsel Unity Hunt, 2003—. Adj. prof. bus. law Edwin L. Cox Sch. Bus. Southern Meth. U., 1991—97, lectr. acctg., 1991—97. Bd. dirs. Pegasus Theatre, 1995—2005, USA Film Festival, 1999—2006, For The Love of the Lake Found., 1999—2003, AFI-Dallas Internat. Film Festival, 2006—; mem City of Dallas Judicial Nominating Commn., 1997—2005. Office: Unity Hunt Inc 1601 Elm St Dallas TX 75201 Office Phone: 214-720-1600. Office Fax: 214-720-1612.

TOMPKINS, ALICE ANGELINE, artist; b. Detroit, Mich., June 14, 1939; d. Jesse Stephen and Linda Sophie Blandino; m. Kenneth Tompkins (dec.); m. Robert Lee Caskey (div.); children: Lisa Nicholas, Christopher Caskey, Morgan Beilfuss. BA, Oakland U., Auburn Hills, 1968; MFA, Wayne State U., Detroit, 1976. Sec. Manufacturers Nat. Bank, Detroit, 1962—65; substitute tchr. Detroit Bd. Edn., 1970—75; drawing instr. Wayne State U., 1976—78, Macomb C.C., Warren, Mich., 1977—78; clerk CPHA, Ann Arbor, Mich., 1978—85; proof operator Kelly Svcs., Brighton, Mich., 1995—2000; ret., 2000. Exhibitions include All Mich. II Exhibition, Flint, 1973, People's Art 200+1, 1977; photographer Seen and Unseen, Toronto, 2005 (Purchase award, 2005), A Resting Place, NY, 2005 (Honorable Mention, 2005). Mem. St.Philip Luth. Ch. Recipient Gertrude Kasle award, Wayne State U., 1976. Mem.: Ann Arbor Art Ctr., Shiawasee Art Ctr. Luth. Home: 1573 N Hickory Rd Apt 5 Owosso MI 48867

TOMPKINS, CHRISTOPHER PAUL, researcher; b. Providence, Dec. 1, 1955; s. Charles Bryant and Eloise Phylida Tompkins; m. Heather J. Moodie, Aug. 23, 1980; children: Sarah Elizabeth, Matthew Christopher, Caitlin Ruth. BA, Northeastern U., 1979; MM, Brandeis U., 1982, PhD, 1990. Sr. rsch. assoc. Brandeis U., Waltham, Mass., 1990—96, assoc. prof., 1996—. Chair instl. rev. bd. Brandeis U., Waltham, 2004—, chair, privacy bd., 2004—. Office Phone: 781-736-3913. Office Fax: 781-736-3905. Business E-Mail: tompkins@brandeis.edu.

TOMPKINS, CURTIS JOHNSTON, government agency administrator; b. Roanoke, Va., July 14, 1942; s. Joseph Buford and Rebecca (Johnston) T.; m. Mary Katherine Hasle, Sept. 5, 1964; children: Robert, Joseph, Rebecca. BS, Va. Poly. Inst., 1965, MS, 1967; PhD, Ga. Inst. Tech., 1971. Indsl. engr. E.I. DuPont de Nemours, Richmond, Va., 1965-67; instr. Sch. Indsl. and Systems Engring., Ga. Inst. Tech., Atlanta, 1968-71; assoc. prof. Colgate Darden Grad. Sch. Bus. Adminstrn., U. Va., Charlottesville, 1971-77; prof., chmn. dept. indsl. engring. W.Va. U., Morgantown, 1977-80, dean Coll. Engring., 1980-91; pres. Mich. Technol. U., Houghton, 1991—2004, pres. emeritus, univ. prof., 2004—; dir., mem. sr. exec. svc. John A. Volpe Nat. Transp. Sys. Ctr., U.S. Dept. Transp., 2004—. Mem. engring. accreditation commn. Accreditation Bd. for Engring. and Tech., 1981-86; mem. exec. bd. Engring. Deans Coun., 1985-89, vice chmn., 1987-89; mem. engring. adv. com., chmn. of planning com. NSF, 1988-91, chm. Mich. Univs. pres. coun., 1996-98; Pres. Coun. Assn. Governing bds. 1996-2004, Gov's. Workforce Commn., 1996-2002; mem. engring. adv. bd. U. Cin., 1996-99 Author: (with L.E. Grayson) Management of Public Sector and Nonprofit Organizations, 1983, (with others) Maynard's Industrial Engineering Handbook, 1992; contbr. chpt. to Ency. of Profl. Mgmt. 1978, 83. Co-chmn. W.Va. Gov.'s Coun. on Econ. Devel.; bd. dirs. Pub. Land Corp. W.Va., 1980-89, Mich. C. of C., 1997—, vice chmn., 2002—; mem. faculty Nat. Acad. Voluntarism, United Way Am., 1976-91; mem. Morgantown Water Commn., 1981-87, Morgantown Utility Bd., 1987-91, steering com. W.Va. Conf. on Environ., 1985-89, Coun. on Competitiveness, 1998-2004, Mich. Higher Edn. Assistance Authority, The Mich.

Higher Edn. Student Loan Authority, 2002-04; chmn. Monogalia County United Way, 1989-90; campaign chmn. Copper Country United Way, 1995-96. Named to Com. of 100 Va. Tech. Coll., Disting. Alumni Acad. dept. indsl. engring, hon. alumnus Mich. Technol. U., 2004; recipient Frank and Lillian Gilbreth Indsl. Engring. award Inst. Indsl. Engrs., 1998. Fellow Inst. Indsl. Engrs. (life mem., trustee 1983-90, pres. 1988-89), Nat. Soc. Profl. Engrs., Am. Soc. Engring. Edn. (pres. 1990-91), Mich. Soc. Profl. Engrs.; mem. Am. Assn. Engring. Soc. (bd. govs. 1987-90, exec. com. 1987-90, sec.-treas. 1989-90), Jr. Engring. Tech. Soc. (bd. dirs. 1988-91), Nat. Soc. for Sci., Tech. and Society (bd. dirs. 1991-94), Internat. Hall of Fame of Sci. and Engring. (hon. trustee), Ga. Tech. Coll. Engring. Disting. Alumni Acad., Ga. Tech. Sch. Indsl. and Sys. Engring. Disting. Alumni Acad., W.Va. U. Dept. Indsl. Engring. Disting. Alumni Acad. (hon.), Mich. C. of C. (bd. dirs 1997-2004), Blue Key (hon.), Sigma Xi, Phi Kappa Phi, Tau Beta Pi, Alpha Pi Mu. Methodist. Home: 199 Coolidge Ave #111 Watertown MA 02472 Home Phone: 617-744-0283; Office Phone: 617-494-2222. E-mail: curtisj42@yahoo.com.

TOMPKINS, ELLEN BETH, retired elementary school educator; b. Waco, Tex., Mar. 2, 1933; d. Richard Curtis and Amanda Hazel (Gunn) Cobb; m. Robert Edward Tompkins, May 24, 1952 (dec. 2006); children: Donna Lynne Keller, Karen Elaine Palmer, Robert Curtis. BS, Stephen F. Austin U., Nacogdoches, Tex., 1968, MEd, 1976. 1st grade tchr. Pine Tree Ind Sch. Dist., Longview, Tex., 1968—90, 1st grade lead tchr., 1990—93; ret. Numerous oil painting;, author math and reading curriculum guides. Ongoing vol to dem and rep. election campaigns. Named to Outstanding Elem. Tchr. Am., Washington, 1973; recipient Outstanding Elem. Regional Conservation Tchr., Tex. Assn. Consservation Dists., 1985. Mem.: PTA, Longview HIst. Mus. Republican. Ch. Of Christ. Avocations: art, writing, gardening.

TOMPKINS, EMIL, chiropractor; b. 1975; Degree in Chiropractic, Iowa State U.; grad., Palmer Coll. of Chiropractic. Owner, pres. Tompkin Family Chiropractic. Organized Hoops for Hope basketball camp; foster and adoptive parent Christian Family Care Agy. Mem. Marana Chamber of Commerce, Tucson Black Chamber of Commerce, Palmer Student Alumni Found.; organizer Marana Sch. Dist. Thanksgiving food drive, Marana Sch. Dist. Christmas toy drive, Picture Rocks Intermediate Sch. donation drive; mem. Marana Wellness Coun.; mem., sponsor Marana Healthy You Initiative. Named one of 40 Under 40, Tucson Bus. Edge, 2006; recipient Humanitarian Svc. award, Palmer Coll. of Chiropractic. Mem.: Am. Black Chiropractic Assn., Am. Chiropractic Assn., Internat. Chiropractic Assn., Vogt Leadership Soc. Office: Tompkins Family Chiropractic 7620 N Hartman Ste 124-2 Tucson AZ 85743 Office Phone: 520-572-2596.

TOMPKINS, JOSEPH BUFORD, JR., lawyer; b. Roanoke, Va., Apr. 4, 1950; s. Joseph Buford and Rebecca Louise (Johnston) T.; children: Edward Graves, Claiborne Forbes. BA in Politics summa cum laude, Washington and Lee U., 1971; M Pub. Policy, JD, Harvard U., 1975. Bar: Va. 1975, U.S. Ct. Appeals (D.C. cir.), U.S. Ct. Appeals (5th cir.), 1977, U.S. Supreme Ct. 1977, U.S. Dist. Ct. D.C. 1982, U.S. Ct. Appeals (11th cir.) 1982, U.S. Ct. Appeals (3d cir.) 1983, U.S. Ct. Appeals (6th cir.) 1985, U.S. Ct. Appeals (7th cir.) 1991, U.S. Ct. Appeals (4th cir.) 1993, U.S. Ct. Internat. Trade 1996. Assoc. Sidley & Austin (now Sidley Austin LLP), Washington, 1975-79, ptnr., 1982—; assoc. dir. Office Policy and Mgmt. Analysis criminal divsn. U.S. Dept. Justice, Washington, 1979-80, dep. chief fraud sect. criminal divsn., 1980-82. Contbr. articles to profl. jours. Mem. Va. Bd. Health Professions, Richmond, 1984-92, vice chmn., 1984-86, chmn., 1986-88, 90-91. Mem. ABA (white collar crime com. criminal justice sect. 1980—, chmn. task force on computer crime 1982-92), Va. Bar Assn., D.C. Bar Assn., Phi Beta Kappa, Home: 8146 Wellington Rd Alexandria VA 22308-1214 Office: Sidley Austin LLP 1501 K St NW 8th Fl Washington DC 20005 Fax: 202-736-8711. E-mail: jtompkins@sidley.com.

TOMPKINS, P. KELLY, lawyer, manufacturing executive; BA, Mercyhurst Coll.; JD, Cleveland-Marshall Law Sch., 1981. Bar: Ohio, Tex., US Supreme Ct. Corp. atty. Reliance Electric Co., 1981—85; litigation atty. Exxon Corp., 1985—87; various positions including sr. corp. counsel, dir. corp. devel., dir. investor relations Reliance Electric Co., 1987—96; asst. gen. counsel RPM Internat., 1996—98, v.p., 1998—2002, gen. counsel, sec., 1998—, sr. v.p., 2001—. Mem.: ABA, Defense Rsch. Inst., Am. Corp. Counsel Assn., Nat. Paint & Coatings Assn. (chair corp. adv. group), Cleveland Bar Found. (trustee), Cleveland Bar Assn. (trustee 2000—03, v.p. 2003, pres.-elect 2004—, mem. fiscal policy, planning, capital & exec. comm.). Office: RPM Internat 2628 Pearl Rd PO Box 777 Medina OH 44258

TOMPKINS, RAYMOND EDGAR, lawyer; b. Oklahoma City, July 13, 1934; s. Charles Edgar and Eva Mae (Hodges) T.; m. Sue Anne Sharpe, June 10, 1963; children: Matthew Stephen, Christopher T., Katherine Anne. BS, Okla. State U., 1956; JD, U. Okla., Norman, 1963. Bar: Okla. 1963, US Dist. Ct. (no. dist.) Okla. 1963, US Dist. Ct. (we. dist.) Okla. 1964, US Ct. Appeals (10th cir.) 1965, US Supreme Ct. 1968, US dist. Ct. (ea. dist.) Okla. 1969, US Ct. Appeals (9th cir.) 1981, US Ct. Appeals (4th cir.) 1986. Adminstrv. asst. U.S. Congress, 1966-68; ptnr. Linn & Helms, Oklahoma City, 1980-90, Daughery, Bradford, Haught & Tompkins, P.C., Oklahoma City, 1990-94; shareholder Conner & Winters, P.C., Oklahoma City, 1994—2003; sole practitioner Oklahoma City, 2003—. Past chmn. bd. trustees Okla. Ann. Methodist Conf., St. Luke's United Meth. Ch.; past chmn. adminstrv. bd.; mem. Okla. Bur. Investigation Commn., past chmn.; past gen. counsel Rep. State com., Interstate Oil Compact. Maj. USAR. Recipient award of Honor Oklahoma City Bi-Centennial Commn., 1976. Fellow Am. Coll. Civil Trial Mediators; master William S. Holliway Am. Inns of Ct. (emeritus), Robert J. Turner Am. Inn of Ct. (pres.); mem. ABA, Okla. County Bar Assn. (Pres.'s award 1988), Okla. Bar Assn. (chmn. bench and bar com. 1995-97, chmn. ADR sect., Law Day award), Nat. Arbitration Forum, Am. Arbitration Assn. (mediator/arbitrator), NASD (mediator, arbitrator), NYSE (mediator, arbitrator), Am. Judicature Soc., Assn. Atty.-Mediators (past pres. Okla. chpt., nat. dir. and sec., Nat. President's award 2000), Blue Key, Lions (pres. Oklahoma City chpt.). Home: 3148 Birch Bark Ln Oklahoma City OK 73120 Office: PO Box 20898 Oklahoma City OK 73156-0898 Home Phone: 405-751-5583; Office Phone: 405-607-8303. Personal E-mail: raytompkins@coxinet.net.

TOMPKINS, RONALD GARY, surgeon, educator, biomedical investigator; b. Many, La., Sept. 24, 1951; s. Horace and Ruby (McFerrin) T.; m. Denise Marie Clougherty, Mar. 7, 1985; children: Megan Elizabeth, Ryan Coleman, Caitlin Maureen. BS in Chemistry summa cum laude, Tulane U., 1972, MD, 1976; SM in Chem. Engring., MIT, 1983, ScD in Med. and Chem. Engring., 1983. Diplomate Am. Bd. Surgery (bd. dirs. 1994—), Am. Bd. Surg. Critical Care. Intern in surgery Mass. Gen. Hosp., Boston, 1976-77, asst. resident, then resident, 1977-79, 83-85, asst. in surgery, 1985-87, asst. surgeon, 1988-90, assoc. chief trauma and burn svcs., 1987-90, chief, 1990—, assoc. vis. surgeon, then vis. surgeon, 1991—; clin. fellow in surgery Harvard Med. Sch., Boston, 1977-79, 92-85, instr., then asst. prof. surgery, 1985-90, assoc. prof., 1990-96, John F. Burke prof. surgery, 1996—. Rsch. assoc. MIT, Cambridge, Mass., 1985-86; asst. in surgery Shriners Burns Inst., Boston, 1987-88, asst. surgeon, 1988-90, chief staff, 1990—; numerous presentations in field at regional, nat. and internat. orgns. Mem. editl. bd. Critical Care Medicine, 1991—, Jour. Tissue Engring., 1994—, Jour. Am. Soc. Artificial Internal Organs, 1994—; contbr. over 217 articles and revs. to med. jours., chpts. to books; patent for culturing liver cells. DuPont fellow MIT, 1979-80, E.R. Gilliland fellow, 1980-81, William Prince fellow, 1981-83; Edward D. Churchill rsch. fellow Mass. Gen. Hosp., 1981-82, fellow Am. Surg. Assn. Found., 1987-88; grantee Link Found., 1985—, NIH, 1987-91, Whitaker Found., 1988-91, Nat. Inst. Gen. Med. Scis., 1992—, Nat. Inst. Digestive Diseases and Kidney, 1987-94, Shriners Hosps., 1988—. Fellow ACS; mem. AMA, AAAS, AIChE, Assn. for Acad. Surgery, Am. Chem. Soc., Am. Burn Assn., Am. Fedn. for Clin. Rsch., Soc. Critical Care Medicine, Surg. Infection Soc., Am. Soc. for Artificial Internal Organs, Shock Soc., Am. Assn. for Surgery of Trauma, Am. Soc. for Laser Medicine and Surgery, Soc. for Cryobiology, Soc. Univ. Surgeons, Am. Assn. for Study Liver Diseases, Am. Trauma Soc., New Eng. Surg. Soc., Cell Transplant Soc., Phi Beta Kappa, Alpha Omega Alpha, numerous others. Office: GRB1302 Mass Gen Hosp 55 Fruit St Boston MA 02114-2622 Home: 2 Hawthorne Pl Apt 8N Boston MA 02114-2309

TOMPKINS, RONALD K., retired surgeon, educator; b. Malta, Ohio, Oct. 14, 1934; s. Kenneth Steidley and Mildred Lillian (Loomis) T.; m. Suzanne Colbert, June 9, 1956; children: Gregory Alan, Teresa Susan, Geoffrey Stuart. BA, Ohio U., 1956; MD, Johns Hopkins U., 1960; MS, Ohio State U., 1968; DSc (hon.), U. Bordeaux, 1995. Diplomate Am. Bd. Surgery. Intern in surgery Ohio State U., 1960-61, resident in surgery, 1964-68, adminstrv. chief resident in surgery, 1968-69, NIH trainee in acad. surgery, instr. physiol. chemistry, 1966-69; asst. prof. surgery UCLA, 1969-73, assoc. prof., 1973-79, prof., 1979-2001, prof. emeritus, 2001—, chmn. basic surg. tng. program, 1970-79, asst. dean student affairs, 1979-82, chief divsn. gen. surgery, 1982-88, chief gastrointestinal surgery, 1986-97, assoc. dean, 1988-91, dir. surg. edn., 1996—2004; ret., 2004. Cons. VA Hosps. Editor-in-chief World Jour. Surgery, 1993-2004. With M.C. USAF, 1961-64. Recipient Disting Alumni award, Ohio U. Arts & Scis., 2001; fellow, Royal Soc. Medicine Eng., 1976—77; grantee, NIH, 1968—70, John A. Hartford Found., 1970—79. Fellow ACS (So. Calif. chpt. pres. 1987); mem. Am. Surg. Assn., Am. Gastroenterol. Assn., Am. Fedn. Clin. Rsch. Am. Inst. Nutrition, AMA, Assn. Acad. Surgery, Pacific Coast Surg. Assn. (recorder 1986-91, pres. 1995), Japan Surgical Soc. (hon.), Soc. Clin. Surgery, Soc. Surgery Alimentary Tract (sec. 1982-85, pres.-elect 1985, pres. 1986, chmn. bd. trustees 1987), Soc. Univ. Surgeons, Societe Internationale de Chirurgie (U.S. chpt. sec. 1990-94, pres. 1996-98), Internat. Biliary Assn. (pres. 1979-81), Internat. HepatoPancreato-Biliary Assn. (hon.), Bay Surg. Soc., LA Surg. Soc. (pres. 1981), Robert M. Zollinger/Ohio State U. Surg. Soc. (pres. 1988-90), Longmire Surg. Soc. (pres. 1997-99), Phi Beta Kappa, Sigma Xi, Alpha Omega Alpha, Delta Tau Delta. Achievements include research numerous publs. in gastrointestinal surgery and gastrointestinal metabolism and biochemistry. Home: 309 20th St Santa Monica CA 90402

TOMPSON, MARIAN LEONARD, professional society administrator; b. Chgo., Dec. 5, 1929; d. Charles Clark and Marie Christine (Bernardini) Leonard; m. Clement R. Tompson, May 7, 1949 (dec. 1981); children: Melanie Tompson Kandler, Deborah Tompson Frueh, Allison Tompson Fagerholm, Laurel Tompson Davies, Sheila Tompson Doucet, Brian, Philip. Student public and parochial schs., Chgo. and Franklin Park, Ill. Co-founder La Leche League (Internat.), Franklin Park, 1956, pres., 1956-80, dir., 1956—, pres. emeritus, 1990—; exec. dir. Alternative Birth Crisis Coalition, 1981-85; founder, pres., CEO AnotherLook, Inc., 2001—. Cons. WHO; bd. dirs. N.Am. Soc. Psychosomatic Ob-Gyn, Natural Birth and Natural Parenting, 1981-83; mem. adv. bd. Nat. Assn. Parents and Profls. for Safe Alternatives in Childbirth, Am. Acad. Husband-Coached Childbirth; mem. adv. bd. Fellowship of Christian Midwives; mem. profl. adv. bd. Home Oriented Maternity Experience; guest lectr. Harvard U. Med. Sch., UCLA Sch. Pub. Health, U. Antioquia Med. Sch., Medellín, Columbia, U. Ill. Sch. Medicine, Chgo., U. W.I., Jamaica, U. N.C., Nat. Coll. of Chiropractic, Am. Coll. Nurse Midwives, U. Parma, Italy, Inst. Psychology, Rome, Rockford (Ill.) Sch. Medicine, Northwestern U. Sch. Medicine, NGO Forum/4th World Conf. on Women, Beijing; mem. family com. Ill. Commn. on Status of Women, 1976-85; mem. perinatal adv. com. Ill. Dept. Pub. Health, 1980-83; mem. adv. bd. Internat. Nutrition Comm. Svc., 1980—; bd. cons. We Can, 1984—; exec. adv. bd. United Resources for Family Health and Support, 1985-86; mem. internat. adv. coun. World Alliance of Breast Feeding Action, 1996; mem. US Breastfeeding Com., 2006— Author: (with others) Safe Alternatives in Childbirth, 1976, 21st Century Obstetrics Now!, 1977, The Womanly Art of Breastfeeding, 6th edit., 1997, Five Standards for Safe Childbearing, 1981, But Doctor, About That Shot..., 1988, The Childbirth Activists Handbook, 1983; author prefaces and forwards in 11 books; columnist La Leche League News, 1958-80; columnist People's Doctor Newsletter, 1977-88, mem. adv. bd., cons., 1988-92; assoc. editor Child and Family Quar., 1967—; mem. med. adv. bd. East West Jour., 1980—; also articles. Mem. adv. bd. Shelters for Healthy Environments, 1998—2002. Recipient Gold medal of honor Centro de Rehabilitacao Nossa Senhora da Gloria, 1975, Night of 100 Stars III Achiever award Actors Fund Am., 1990, N.Y. Soc. Ethical Culture Ethical Humanist award, 1999, 100 Women Making a Difference Today's Chgo. Woman, Health Humanity award Svc. Humanity, 2007. Mem. Nat. Assn. Postpartum Care Svcs. (adv. bd.), Chgo. Cmty. Midwives (adv. bd.), World Alliance for Breast Feeding Action (mem. internat. adv. coun. 1997). Office: 957 N Plum Grove Dr Schaumburg IL 60173 Office Phone: 847-869-1278. Personal E-mail: m.tompson@comcast.net. E-mail: mt@anotherlook.org.

TOMS, KATHLEEN MOORE, nurse; b. San Francisco, Dec. 31, 1943; d. William Moore and Phyllis Josephine (Barry) Stewart; m. Benjamin Peskoff (dec. Aug. 2002); children from previous marriage: Kathleen Marie Toms Myers, Kelly Terese Toms Shaver. AA, City Coll., San Francisco, 1963; BPS in Nursing Edn., Elizabethtown Coll., Pa., 1973; MS in Edn., Temple U., 1977; MS in Nursing, Gwynedd Mercy Coll., 1988; grad., US Army War Coll., 1999. RN, Calif. Med.-surg. nurse St. Joseph Hosp., Fairbanks, Alaska, 1963-65, emergency rm. nurse Lancaster, Pa., 1965-69, blood, plasma and components nurse, 1969-71; pres. F.E. Barry Co., Lancaster, 1971—; dir. insvc. edn. Lancaster Osteo. Hosp., 1971-75; coord. practical nursing program Vocat. Tech. Sch., Coatesville, Pa., 1976-77; dir. nursing Pocopson Home, West Chester, Pa., 1978-80, Riverside Hosp., Wilmington, Del., 1980-83; assoc. Coatesville VA Hosp., 1983-89, chief nurse, 1984-89; with VA Ctrl. Office; supr. psychiat. nursing Martinez (Calif.) VA Med. Ctr., 1989-94; assoc. chief nursing svc. edn. VA Ho. Calif. Sys. Clinics, Pleasant Hill, 1994—; nurse mgr. VA Ctr. Rehab. and Extended Care, Martinez, 1996—; patient health edn. coord. VA No. Calif. Health Care Sys., Martinez, 2000—. Trainee assoc. chief Nursing Home Care Unit, Washington; mem. Pa. Gov.'s Coun. on Alcoholism and Drug Abuse, 1974-76; mem. Del. Health Coun. Med.-Surg. Task Force, 1981-83; dir. Lancaster Cmty. Health Ctr., 1973-76; lectr. in field. Col. Nurse Corps, USAR. Decorated Army Commendation medals (6), Meritorious Svc. medals (2); recipient Cmty. Svc. award Citizens United for Better Pub. Rels., 1974; award Sertoma, Lancaster, 1974; Outstanding Citizen award Sta. WGAL-TV, 1975; U.S. Army Achievement award, 1983. Mem. Elizabethtown U. Alumni Assn., Temple U. Alumni Assn., Pa. Nurses Assn. (bd. dirs. 1972-76), Sigma Theta Tau, Beta Gamma. Achievements include invention of auto-infuser for blood or blood components. Home: 208 Sea Mist Dr Vallejo CA 94591-7748 E-mail: ktoms007@aol.com.

TOMSIC, PEGGY A., lawyer; b. Price, Utah, Mar. 16, 1953; d. Marjorie R. and Edward L. Tomsic; life ptnr. Lucinda Bateman. JD, U. Utah, Salt Lake City, 1982. Bar: Utah 1982. Mng. shareholder Berman, Tomsic & Savage, Salt Lake City, 1984—2005; mgr., sr. atty. Tomsic & Peck LLC, Salt Lake City, 2005—07. Adj. prof. U. Utah Coll. Law, Salt Lake City, 2002—07. Chmn. fin. com. Caroon for Salt Lake County Maj., 2004. Mem.: David K. Watkiss Inns of Ct. (life). Democrat. Avocations: skiing, golf, hiking, poetry, travel. Office: Tomsic & Peck LLC 136 E South Temple Ste 800 Salt Lake City UT 84111 Home Phone: 801-582-2215; Office Phone: 801-532-1995. Office Fax: 801-532-4202. Business E-Mail: ptomsic@tomsiclaw.net.

TOMSON, MASON B., environmental engineer, educator; BS in Chemistry and Math., Southwestern Okla. State U., 1967; PhD in Chemistry, Okla. State U., 1972. Lic. profl. engr., 2003. Prof. civil and environ. engring. Rice U., Houston. Mem. sci. adv. com. U. Tulsa Internat. Petroleum Environ. Ctr., 2003—04; rsch. adv. Brita Water Inst., 2004—. Contbr. articles to profl. jours., chapters to books; book rev. editor: Soc. Petroleum Engrs., 2002—, mem. editl. bd.: Jour. Environ. Sci. and Health, 2003—. Mem.: Soc. Petroleum Engrs. (mem. steering com. 2003—04, mem. materials sci. com. 2002—03, mem. editl. rev. com. 2002—03). Achievements include patents for a nano-material that removes arsenic from water. Office: Dept Civil and Environ Engring Rice U MS-318 6100 Main St Houston TX 77005 Office Phone: 713-348-6048. E-mail: mtomson@rice.edu. *

TON, PAUL, investor, educator; b. Buffalo, Apr. 30, 1926; s. Edward Cornelius Ton and Laura Delia Slotboom; m. Joan Karen Marshall, June 18, 1951; children: Scott, Elizabeth, Robert, John. BS, Union Coll., Schenectady, NY, 1949; MA, Stanford U., Palo Alto, Calif., 1951, U. Denver, 1958, PhD, 1969. Instr. electronics USAF, Denver, 1951—52; tchr. history Denver Pub. Schs., 1952—89; adj. prof. history Metro State Coll., Denver, 1990—2003. Dept. head, Driver Edn. Am. Auto Assn., Denver, 1957—64; dept. chair South H.S., Denver, 1972—77; history cons. Am. Frontier TV series, 1985—87; mng. dir. Westton Prodns., 1995—. Contbg. author (book) The Mining Frontier, 1967, Henry M. Porter, Empire Builder, 1991. Cpl. US Army, 1944—46, PTO. Mem.: Western Hist. Assn., Orgn. of Am. Historians, Am. Hist. Assn. Republican. Presbyterian. Avocation: photography. Home: 390 Lansing St Aurora CO 80010 Personal E-mail: forpton@comcast.net.

TONCHI, STEFANO, editor; b. 1959; Classic studies, Liceo Classico Forteguerri, Pistoia, Italy; studied polit. sci., U. Florence, Italy, 1979—84. Co-founder, editor, art dir. Westuff mag., 1984—87; fashion dir. L'Uomo Vogue, 1987—94; creative dir. Self, 1994—96; creative cons. J. Crew, 1996—98; fashion creative dir. Esquire, 1998—2003; style editor NY Times mag., 2003—; head style dept. T: The NY Times Style mag., 2004—. Co-curator (exhibition) & co-editor (book) Excess: Fashion & the Underground in the 80s, 2004; co-editor: Total Living: Art, Fashion, Design, Architecture, Communication, 2002; co-curator (exhibition) & co-editor (book) Uniform: Order & Disorder, 2001. Office: NY Times 229 W 43rd St New York NY 10036 Office Phone: 212-556-3830, 212-556-7596. Office Fax: 212-556-7618, 212-556-7596. E-mail: tonchi@nytimes.com.

TONDEL, LAWRENCE CHAPMAN, lawyer; b. NYC, Apr. 9, 1946; s. Lyman Mark and Jean (Basch) Tondel; m. Sharyn A. Smith, Aug. 3, 1974; children: Michael Lawrence, Kathryn Chapman. Student, The Lawrenceville Sch., 1964; AB, Wesleyan U., 1968; JD, U. Mich., 1971. Bar: N.Y. 1972. Assoc. Brown & Wood LLP, NYC, 1971-79, ptnr., 1980-97, sr. ptnr., 1997-2001; ptnr. Sidley Austin LLP, NYC, 2001—. Chmn. Internat. Bus. Commn. Ann. Internat. Forum Offshore Funds, 1993—2000. Trustee Elisabeth Morrow Sch., Englewood, NJ, 1988—93; mem. exec. com. parents com. Washington U., St. Louis, 2000—02. Mem.: ABA, Assn. Bar City of N.Y., Am. Bar Found., Am. Law Inst. Republican. Roman Catholic. Office Phone: 212-839-5399. Business E-Mail: ltondel@sidley.com.

TONDEUR, PHILIPPE MAURICE, mathematician, educator; b. Zurich, Switzerland, Dec. 7, 1932; came to U.S., 1964, naturalized, 1974; s. Jean and Simone (Lapaire) T.; m. Claire-Lise Ballansat, Dec. 20, 1965. PhD, U. Zurich, 1961. Rsch. fellow U. Paris, 1961-63; lectr. math. U. Zurich, 1963-64, U. Buenos Aires, 1964, Harvard U., Cambridge, Mass., 1964-65, U. Calif., Berkeley, 1965-66; asso. prof. Wesleyan U., Middletown, Conn., 1966-68; assoc. prof. U. Ill., Urbana, 1968-70, prof., 1970—2002, prof. emeritus, 2002—, chair dept. math., 1996-99. Vis. prof. Auckland U., 1968, Eidg. Techn. Hochschule U. Heidelberg, 1973, U. Zurich, 1987, U. Rome, 1984, Ecole Poly., Paris, 1987, U. Santiago de Compostela, Spain, 1987, Max Planck Inst., 1987, U. Leuven (Belgium), 1990, Keio U., Yokohama, Japan, 1993; assoc. mem. Ctr. Advanced Study U. Ill., 1977—78, 1991—92; dir. divsn. math. sci. NSF, 1999—2002. Contbr. articles to profl. jours. Recipient Divsn. Math. Scis. Govtl. Math. award; fellow Swiss Nat. Sci. Found., Harvard U., U. Ill. Mem.: Math. Assn. Am., Soc. Indsl. and Applied Math. (Frederick A. Howes pub. svc. award), Soc. Math. France, Schweiz Math. Gesellschaft, Am. Math. Soc. Office: U Ill Math Dept Urbana IL 61801 Business E-Mail: tondeur@math.uiuc.edu.

TONEGAWA, SUSUMU, biology professor; b. Nagoya, Japan, Sept. 6, 1939; arrived in U.S., 1963; s. Tsutoma and Miyoko T. (Masuko) Tonegawa; m. Mayumi Yoshinari, Sept. 28, 1985; children: Hidde, Hanna, Satto. BS, Kyoto U., Japan, 1963; PhD in Molecular Biology, U. Calif., San Diego, 1968. Rsch. asst. U. Calif., San Diego, 1963—64, teaching asst., 1964—68; mem. Basel (Switzerland) Inst. Immunology, 1971—81; Whitehead prof. biology MIT, Cambridge, 1981—94, Picower prof., depts. Brain and Cognitive Scis. and of Biology, 1994—. Investigator Howard Hughes Med. Inst., 1988—; founding dir. Picower Inst. for Learning and Memory, 1994—2006; professorship Amgen, Inc., 1994; dir. RIKEN-MIT Neuroscience Rsch. Ctr. Mem. editl. bd. Immunity; contbr. articles to profl. jours. Decorated Order of Culture Emperor of Japan; co-recipient Albert Lasker Med. Rsch. award, 1987; named Person with Cultural Merit, Japanese Govt., 1983; recipient Cloetta prize, Switzerland, 1978, Warren Triennial prize, Mass. Gen. Hosp., 1980, Genetics Grand prize, Genetics Promotion Found., Japan, 1981, Avery Landsteiner prize, Gesellschaft fur Immunologie, West Germany, 1981, Asahi prize, Asahi-Shimbun (Asahi Press), Tokyo, Japan, 1982, Louisa Gross Horwitz prize, Columbia U., 1982, V.D. Mattia award, Roche Inst. of Molecular Biology, Nutley, NJ, 1983, Gardiner Found. Internat. award, Toronto, Ont., Can., 1983, Robert Koch Found. prize, Bonn, Germany, 1986, Nobel prize in physiology or medicine, 1987, Bristol-Myers award for Disting. Achievement in Cancer Rsch., 1986. Mem.: NAS (fgn. assoc.), Scandinavian Soc. Immunology (hon.), Am. Assn. Immunologists (hon.). Office: MIT Dept Biology Room 46-5285 31 Ames St Cambridge MA 02139 Office Phone: 617-253-6459. E-mail: tonewaga@mit.edu. *

TONELLO-STUART, ENRICA MARIA, political scientist, economist; b. Monza, Italy; d. Alessandro P. and Maddalena M. (Marangoni) Tonello; m. Albert E. Smith; m. Charles L. Stuart. BA in Internat. Affairs, Econs., U. Colo., 1961; MA, Claremont Grad. Sch., 1966, PhD, 1971. Sales mgr. Met. Life Ins. Co., 1974-79; pres., CEO, ETS R&D, Inc., Palos Verdes Peninsula, Calif., 1977—2004; ret. Pub., editor Tomorrow Outline Jour., 1963—, The Monitor, 1988; pub. World Regionalism-An Ecological Analysis, 1971, A Proposal for the Reorganization of the United Nations, 1966, The Persuasion Technocracy, Its Forms, Techniques and Potentials, 1966, The Role of the Multinationals in the Emerging Globalism, 1978; developed the theory of social ecology and econosociometry. Organizer 1st family assistance program Langley FB Tactical Air Command, 1956-58. Recipient vol. svc. award VA, 1956-58, ARC svc. award, 1950-58. Mem. Corp. Planners Assn. (treas. 1974-79), Investigative Reporters and Editors, World Future Soc. (pres. 1974-75), Soc. Environ. Journalists, Chinese Am. Assn. (life), Palos Verdes C. of C., L.A. Press Club (bd. dirs.), Zonta (chmn. internat. com. South Bay), Pi Sigma Alpha. Avocations: writing, collecting old books and maps, community service, travel, pediatric activist. Office Phone: 310-377-7608. Personal E-mail: stuarteix@netcom.com, stuarte@cox.net.

TONER, MICHAEL E., lawyer, former commissioner; BA with distinction, U. Va, 1986; MA in polit. sci., Johns Hopkins U., 1989; JD cum laude, Cornell Law Sch., 1992. Bar: DC, Va., US Supreme Court, 4th US Circuit Court of Appeals, US Dist. Courts, DC and Eastern Dist. Va. Assoc. atty. Wiley, Rein, & Fielding, Washington, 1992—96; counsel Dole-Kemp Presidential Campaign, 1996; deputy counsel Rep. Nat. Com., 1997—99, chief counsel, 2001; gen. counsel Bush-Cheney Transistion, 2000, Bush-Cheney 2000 Presidential Campaign, 2000; mem. Fed. Election Commn., 2002—07, chmn., 2006—07; ptnr. Bryan Cave Strategies LLC, 2007—, sr. adv., 2007—. Office: Bryan Cave Strategies LLC 700 13th St NW Ste 500 Washington DC 20005 *

TONER, MICHAEL F., journalist; b. LeMars, Iowa, Mar. 17, 1944; s. Francis F. and Mary Ann (Delaney) Toner; m. Patricia L. Asleson, Aug. 28, 1966; children: Susan Michelle, Sharon Lynn. BA cum laude, U. Iowa, 1966; postgrad., U. Okla., Peru; MS cum laude, Northwestern U., 1967. Reporter UPI, Chgo., 1966—67; bur. chief Miami Herald, Key West, Fla., 1967—68, reporter, 1968—69, asst. city editor, 1970—72; sci./environ. writer Miami (Fla) Herald, 1973—84; sci. editor Atlanta Jour. and Constrn., 1984—91, sci. writer, 1991—. Co-author: Florida by Paddle and Pack, 1979; contbr. articles to mags. Recipient Pulitzer Prize for explanatory journalism, 1993. Stanford U. Profl Journalism fellow, 1973. Avocations: photography, swimming, cooking, stamp collecting/philately. Office: Atlanta Jour and Constrn 72 Marietta St NW Atlanta GA 30303-2804

TONEV, THOMAS (TOMA) V., mathematics professor; b. Sofia, Bulgaria, Apr. 5, 1945; children: Daniela, Vassilena. MS, Sofia U., 1969; PhD, Moscow State U., 1973. Adj. prof. Sofia U. - Kliment Ohridski, 1974—88; lectr. Banach Ctr., Warsaw, 1982; sr. rsch. assoc. Inst. Math. and Informatics Bulgarian Acad. Scis., Sofia, 1983—2006; vis. mathematician Internat. Ctr. for Theoretical Physics, Trieste, Italy, 1988—89; vis. prof. U. Toledo, 1989—91; prof. math. U. Mont., Missoula, 1991; vis. prof. Kent State U., Ohio, 1999, U. Wash., Seattle, 2000. Senator Faculty Senate U. Mont., Missoula, 2002—05. Author: Big Planes, Boundaries and Function Algebras, 1992, (textbooks) Function Algebras and Function Spaces, 1995, Topics in Analysis - Banach Algebras of Continuous Functions, 2005; co-author (with E. Lyubenova-Toneva): Continued Fractions, 1989; co-author: (with S. Grigoryan) Shift-Invariant Uniform Algebras on Groups, 2006; editor: Pliska, Studia mathematica bulgarica, vol. 10, 1989, Ctrl. European Jour. Math., 2004, Far East Jour. Math. Scis., 2004, Rocky Mountain Jour. Math., 2006; contbr. over 75 articles to profl. jours. Recipient Rsch. award for Young Mathematicians, Balkan Math. Union, 1975; grantee, NSF, 1992—, IREX, NRC, EPSCOR, Mathematisches Forschungsinstitut, Oberwolfach (Germany), Banach Ctr. (Poland), U. Mont. Fellow: Deutsche Mathematiker-Vereinigung, Union Scientists in Bulgaria; mem.: Union Bulgarian Mathematicians, European Math. Soc., NY Acad. Scis., Mont. Acad. Scis., Math. Assn. Am., Am. Math. Soc., Phi Kappa Phi, Pi Mu Epsilon. Office: U Mont Dept Math 32 Campus Dr Missoula MT 59812 Home Phone: 406-721-0962; Office Phone: 406-243-4850. Office Fax: 406-243-2674. Business E-Mail: tonevtv@mso.umt.edu.

TONEY, ANITA KAREN, printmaker; b. NYC; d. Anthony and Edna Greenfield Toney. BFA, Syracuse Univ.; MA, San Francisco State Univ. Instr. printmaking City Coll. San Francisco, 1979—. Exhibited in group shows at Nancy Dodds Gallery, Carmel, Calif., Le Celle Gallery, San Anselmo, Calif., Andrea Schwartz Gallery, San Francisco, Images Gallery, Briarcliff, NY, exhibitions include with father, Anthony Toney, Coll. of Marin, 2003. Mem.: Calif. Soc. Printmakers, NAD (academician 1995—). Office: Printmaking City Coll San Francisco 50 Phelan Ave San Francisco CA 94112 Office Phone: 415-239-3000.

TONG, JOHN, plastic surgeon, educator, ophthalmic surgeon; Bd. cert. Faculty Jule Stein Eye Inst., LA, 2000; asst. clin. prof. Davis Med. Ctr., Sacramento, 2001—. Faculty mem. UCLA Jule Stein Eye Inst., 2000; lectr. in field. Contbr. chapters to books, articles to profl. jours. Fellow: Am. Acad. Ophthalmology, Am. Assn. Pediat. Ophthalmology and Strabismus, Am. Acad. Cosmetic Surgery, Am. Soc. Ophthalmic Plastic Surgery; mem.: ACS. Office: 1700 Alhambra Blvd Ste 202 Sacramento CA 95816

TONG, KAITY, anchor; m. Patrick Callahan; 1 child. BA, Bryn Mawr Coll.; MA, Stanford U. Street reporter various West Coast radio/tv networks; anchor KCRA, Sacramento, WABC Eyewitness News, WB-11 News at 10/WPIX-TV, NYC. Recipient Exceptional Achievement award, Disting. Woman award, Star award, Edward R. Murrow award, 3 Emmy awards Acitve United Cerebral Palsy, Children's Mus. of Manhattan, Juvenile Diabetes Found., Friends for Life, League for the Hard of Hearing. Office: WPIX-TV/Tribune Co 220 E 42d St New York NY 10017 Business E-Mail: ktong@tribune.com.

TONG, LOUIS LIK-FU, information scientist; b. Kowloon, British Hong Kong, June 15, 1962; arrived in U.S., 1980, naturalized, 1994; s. Yu-Tung and Chen (Yao) T. BS, U. Houston, 1985; M Libr. and Info. Sci., U. North Tex., 1992. Info. asst. Houston Acad. Medicine, Tex. Med. Ctr. Libr., Houston, 1990-93; rsch. libr. svc. specialist Internat. Facility Mgmt. Assn., Houston, 1993-98; knowledge and info. mgr. Brown & Root Svc., Houston, 1998-99; web content adminstr. Halliburton Co., Houston, 1999—2005, web mktg. specialist, 2005—. Mem.: Tex. Bldg. Energy Inst. (exec. com. 1997—98), Japan-Am. Soc. Houston, Spl. Librs. Assn. (Houston local planning chair 2000—03, sec. Tex. chpt. 2001—03), Med. Libr. Assn. (minority scholar 1992), Internat. Facility Mgmt. Assn. (chmn. codes and regulations com. 1994—98, founding dir. environ., health and safety coun. 1998—2002), Tex. State Rifle Assn. (life), NRA (life). Republican. Office: PO Box 230453 Houston TX 77223 E-mail: louis@louistong.com.

TONG, ROSEMARIE, humanities educator, philosopher; b. Chgo., July 19, 1947; d. Joseph John and Lillian (Nedued) Behensky; m. Paul Ki-King Tong, Aug. 15, 1971 (dec. Apr. 1988); children: Paul Shih-Mien Tong, John Joseph Tong; m. Jeremiah Putnam, Aug. 1, 1992. BA, Marygrove Coll., 1970; MA, Cath. U., 1971; PhD, Temple U., 1978; LLD (hon.), Marygrove Coll., 1987; LHD (hon.), SUNY, Oneonta, 1993. Asst. and assoc. prof. philosophy Williams Coll., Williamstown, Mass., 1978-88; vis. disting. prof. humanities Davidson (N.C.) Coll., 1988-89, Thatcher Prof. in med. humanities and philosophy, 1989-99; prof. humanities and philosophy U. N.C., Charlotte, 1999—; dir. Ctr. for Profl. and Applied Ethics, Charlotte, 2002—. L. Stacy Davidson vis. chair in liberal arts U. Miss., Oxford, 1998; Louise M. Olmstead vis. prof. philosophy and women's studies, Lafayette Coll., Easton, Pa., 1993; disting. prof. health care ethics U. N.C., Charlotte, 1999—; manuscript reviewer Wadsworth Pub. Co., 1985-92; curriculum reviewer philosophy dept. Carlton and Bowdoin Colls., 1986; honors examiner Hobart and William Smith Colls., 1990; dissertation dir., adj. faculty The Union Inst., 1992-93; cons., judge, panelist, organizer and speaker in field; mem. numerous U. coms. Author: Women, Sex and the Law, 1984, Ethics in Policy Analysis, 1985, Feminist Thought: A Comprehensive Introduction, 1989, Feminist Philosophies: Problems, Theories, and Applications, 1991, Feminine and Feminist Ethics, 1993, Feminist Thought: A More Comprehensive Introduction, 1998, (with Larry Kaplan) Controlling Our Reproductive Destiny, 1994, Feminist Philosophy: Essential Readings in Theory, Reinterpretation and Application, 1994, Feminist Bioethics, 1997, Feminist Thought: A More Comprehensive Ethics, 1998, Globalizing Feminist Bioethics: Crosscultural Perspectives, 2000; editor: (with Anne Donchin and Susan Dodds) Linking Visions: Feminist Bioethics, Human Rights, and the Developing World, 2004; contbr. numerous articles to profl. jours.; mem. various editl. bds. Project reviewer Annenberg/CPB Project, Washington, 1986; policy writer dvsn. health svcs. rsch. and policy U. Minn., 1988, Frank Graham Porter Early Childhood Ctr., U. N.C. Chapel Hill, 1988; mem. Charlotte task force Congl. Task Force Health Care, Congressman Alex McMillan, 1991, standards and ethics com. Hospice N.C., 1991, resource and ethics coms. McMillan-Spratt Task Force Health Care Policy, 1992, pastoral care com. Carolinas Med. Ctr., 1990—, ethics com. Presbyn. Hosp., 1990—, N.E. Regional Hosp., 1991, Nat. Adv. Bd. Ethics in Reproduction, Washington, 1993; active Hastings Ctr. Project Undergrad. Values Edn., Briarcliff Manor, N.Y., 1993, N.C. Found. Humanities and Pub. Policy; mem. bioethics Resource Group, 1992—; mem. feminist approaches to bioethics network, 1996—; dir. med. humanities program Davidson Coll., 1988-98. Named Prof. of Yr., Carnegie Found. and Coun. Advancement and Support of Edn., 1986. Mem. Internat. Assn. for Feminist Approaches to Bioethics Network (coord. 1999—), Internat. Assn. Bioethics (chair 2003—), Am. Assn. for Bioethics and Humanities, Am. Cath. Philos. Assn., Am. Philos. Assn. (ad hoc com. computers, pub. and role of Am. Philos. Assn. 1984, adv. com. to program com. 1986-88, nomination com. 1989-91, nat. com. on status of women 1989-93, 2003—), Am. Legal Studies and Assn., Am. Soc. Pol. and Legal Philosophy, Am. Soc. Law and Medicine, Nat. Coun. Rsch. on Women, Nat. Women Studies Assn., Internat. Assn. Philosophy Law and Social Philosophy, Assn. Practical and Profl. Ethics, Society Christian Ethics, Soc. Women in Philosophy, Soc. Philosophy and Tech., Soc. Philosophy and Pub. Affairs, Soc. Study of Women Philosophers, Network Feminist Approaches to Bioethics, The Hastings Ctr., Triangle Bioethics Group, So. Soc. Philosophy and Psychology. Avocations: aerobics, boating, hiking. Office Phone: 704-687-2850. Business E-Mail: rotong@email.uncc.edu.

TONG, SIU WING, computer programmer; b. Hong Kong, May 20, 1950; came to U.S., 1968; BA, U. Calif., Berkeley, 1972; PhD, Harvard U., 1979; MS, U. Lowell, 1984. Rsch. assoc. Brookhaven Nat. Lab., Upton, N.Y., 1979-83; software engr. Honeywell Info. Systems, Billerica, Mass., 1984-85; sr. programmer, analyst Hui Computer Cons., Berkeley, Calif., 1985-88; sr. v.p. devel., chief fin. officer Surgicenter Info. Systems, Inc., Orinda, Calif., 1989-94; sr. sys. specialist Info. Sys. Divsn. Contra Costa County Health Svcs., Martinez, Calif., 1995-97, info. tech. supr. Info. Sys. Divsn., 1997—. Vol. tchr. Boston Chinatown Saturday Adult Edn. Program of Tufts Med. Sch., 1977-79. Muscular Dystrophy Assn. fellow, 1980-82. Mem. AAAS, IEEE, Assn. Computing Machinery, N.Y. Acad. Scis. Home: 17 Beaconsfield Ct Orinda CA 94563-4203 Office: Contra Costa County Health Svcs 595 Center Ave Ste 210 Martinez CA 94553-4634 E-mail: swtong@hsd.cccounty.us.

TONG, TOMMY R., surgeon, pathologist; M.B., B.S.(HK), U. of Hong Kong Med. Sch., Pokfulam, Hong Kong, 1976—81. Diplomate Am. Bd. of Pathology. Surgeon St. Teresa's Hosp., Kowloon, Hong Kong, 1988—; sr. pathologist Princess Margaret Hosp., 1996—2006; with Alumnus Pathology Depts. U. Sask., Mt. Sinai Hosp., Meml. Sloan Kettering Cancer Ctr., NY; pathologist AW Pathology Med. Group, Bakersfield, Calif., 2006—. Vis. prof. Mt. Sinai Pathology, 1999; invited spkr. Vanderbilt U. Pathology, 2004. Reviewer: Jour. Clin. Microbiology, Jour. Infectious Diseases, Open Microbiol. Jour., Open Microbiol. Revs., Open Microbiol. Letters; mem. editl. bd. Jour. Clin. Microbiology; mem. editl. bd.: Open Microbiol. Jour., Internat. Jour. Biol. Scis., assoc. editor: Internat. Jour. Diagnosis Molecular Microbiology; contbr. articles to profl. jours. Grantee, Princess Margaret Hosp., 2001, 2001, Innovation and Tech. Commn., the Govt. of the Hong Kong Spl. Adminstrv. Region, 2001, 2003, 2004. Fellow: Am. Soc. of Clin. Pathologists, Coll. of Surgeons of Hong Kong, Royal Australasian Coll. of Surgeons, Coll. of Am. Pathology, Royal Coll. of Surgeons of Edinburgh; mem.: Am. Soc. of Cytopathology, US and Can. Acad. of Pathology, NY Acad. of Sciences, Assn. for the Advancement of Sci., Papanicolaou Soc. of Cytopathology. Achievements include patents for electromolecular diagnosis; molecular diagnosis; patents pending for cervical cancer screening; novel biochip microarrays; novel tracer; method of collection of upper respiratory clinical sample. Office Phone: 661-325-2640. Personal E-mail: tommy.tong@electrobiochip.com, tommyrtongmd@gmail.com.

TONGUE, PAUL GRAHAM, financial executive; b. Phila., Dec. 30, 1932; s. George Paul and Florence Amelia (Kogel) T.; m. Marjorie Joan Meyers, May 26, 1954; children: Suzanne Marjorie, Douglas Paul BS in Commerce, Drexel U., 1957; MBA, NYU, 1965. With Chase Manhattan Bank, NYC, 1957-87; chmn. Plus Systems Inc., Denver, 1985; pres. Eppley-Tongue Assocs., Inc., Towson, Md., 1988—; exec. v.p. Veritas Venture Inc., Scotch Plains, NJ, 1990-91. Pres. Our Saviour Luth. Ch., Manhasset, N.Y., 1984; pres. 1st Night of Williamsburg, Inc.; bd. dirs. Ford's Colony Homeowners' Assn., Williamsburg Area Civic and Cultural Ctr., Inc., Sr. Exec. Resource Corps, Coll. William and Mary; v.p. Williamsburg Symphonia League; mem. Williamsburg Area Arts Commn. Mem. Ford's Colony Country Club. Avocations: golf, classical music. E-mail: pgtongue@cox.net.

TONGUE, WILLIAM WALTER, economics and business consultant, educator; b. Worcester, Mass., May 24, 1915; s. Walter Ernest and Lena (Brown) T.; m. Beverly Harriet Cohan, Dec. 26, 1936; children— Barbara Tongue Duggan, Kathleen Tongue Alligood. AB, Dartmouth, 1937, M.C.S., 1938; PhD, U. Chgo., 1947. Jr. acct. Price, Waterhouse & Co. (C.P.A.'s), NYC, 1938; instr. Coe Coll., Cedar Rapids, Iowa, 1941-42; spl. cons. OSS, 1942; fin. economist Fed. Res. Bank Chgo., 1942-44; economist Jewel Companies, Inc., Chgo., 1944-64; prof. econs. and finance U. Ill. Chgo., 1965-80. Prof. emeritus, 1980—; econ. cons. LaSalle Nat. Bank, Chgo., 1968-91; mem. com. CNA Fin. Separate Fund B., 1997-2003; dir. St. Joseph Light & Power Co., Mo., 1965-86; trustee Signode Employees' Savs. and Profit Sharing Trust Fund, 1980-89. Author: articles; contbr.: to books including How We Can Halt Inflation and Still Keep Our Jobs, 1974. Bd. dirs., v.p. rsch. and stats. Chgo. Assn. Commerce and Industry, 1968-69; bd. dirs. Luther Village Owners Corp., v.p., 2002-05 Mem. Nat. Assn. Bus. Economists (pres. 1962-63), Conf. Bus. Economists, Am. Statis. Assn. (pres. Chgo. chpt. 1951-52), Econ. Club Chgo., Investment Analysts Assn. Chgo., Inst. Chartered Fin. Analysts (chartered fin. analyst 1963), Midwest Fin. Assn. (pres. 1972-73). Home and Office: 1220 Village Dr Apt 427 Arlington Heights IL 60004-8123 Office Phone: 847-670-7836. Personal E-mail: williamtongue@yahoo.com.

TONIETTE, SALLYE JEAN, physician; b. Sulphur, La., 1929; d. Eugene Augusta and Sallye (Tanner) T. Student, John McNeese Jr. Coll., 1946-47; BS, La. State U., 1949, tchrs. cert., 1950, MD, 1955. Intern Crawford W. Long Meml. Hosp., Emory U., Atlanta, 1955-56, resident in ob-gyn., jr., sr., chief residencies, 1956-59; practice in ob-gyn. Sulphur, La., 1959—. Mem. med. staff West Calcasieu Cameron Hosp., 1959—. Dir. Calcasieu Parish Cancer Soc., 1963-67. Named Woman of Distinction, Calcasieu Parish Police Jurors, also Bus. and Profl. Women's Club of West Calcasieu, 1969; Queen of Krewe of Cosmos, 1963, Mardi Gras. Fellow Am. Coll. Ob-Gyn.; mem. La. Med. Assn., Calcasieu Parish Med. Soc., La. Wildlife Fedn., Am. Quarter Horse Assn., Assn. Am. Physicians and Surgeons, Bayou Oaks Country Club (v.p., bd. dirs. 1974—), Krewe de Bon Coer, Krewe of Cosmos, Alpha Chi Omega, Beta Tau Mu, Iota Sigma Pi, Phi Theta Kappa, Beta Sigma Phi. Republican. Methodist. Home: 4917 La Paix Dr Sulphur LA 70665 Office: 521 Cypress St Sulphur LA 70663-5049 Personal E-mail: sassy29@xspedius.net.

TONJES, MARIAN JEANNETTE BENTON, education educator; b. Rockville Center, NY, Feb. 16, 1929; d. Millard Warren and Felicia E. (Tyler) Benton; m. Charles F. Tonjes (div. 1965, dec.); children: Jeffrey Charles, Kenneth Warren. BA, U. N.Mex., 1951, cert., 1966, MA, 1969; EdD, U. Miami, 1975. Dir. recreation Stuyvesant Town Housing Project, NYC, 1951—53; tchr. music., phys. edn. Sunset Mesa Day Sch., Albuquerque, 1963—64; tchr. remedial reading Zia Elem. Sch., 1965—67; tchr. secondary devel. reading Rio Grande H.S., 1967—69; rsch. asst. reading Southwestern Coop. Ednl. Lab., 1969—71; assoc. dir., vis. instr. Fla. Ctr. Tchr. Tng. Materials U. Miami, 1971—72; asst. prof. U.S. Internat. U., San Diego, 1972—75; prof. edn. Western Wash. U., Bellingham, 1975—94, prof. emerita, 1994—; dir. summer study at Oriel Coll. Oxford U., England, 1976—93. Reading supr. Manzanita Ctr., 1968; vis. prof. adult edn. Palomar (Calif.) Jr. Coll., 1974; vis. prof. U. Guam, Mangilao, 1989-90; adj. prof. U. N.Mex., 1995—; invited guest Russian Reading Assn., Moscow, 1992; internat. travel adv. Vantage Deluxe Travel, 2002-05; spkr. European Conf. reading, Tallinn, Estonia, 2003, symposium chair World Congress, Manila, 2004; cons. in field. Author: (with Miles V. Zintz) Teaching Reading/Thinking Study Skills in Content Classroom, 3rd edit., Secondary Reading, Writing and Learning, 1991, Integrated Content Literacy, 1999, (with Ray Wolpow) Integrated Content Literacy, 5th edit., 2006. Trustee White Mountain Sch., 2000—06; tour dir. In the Footsteps of Dickens, England, 2001; hon. trustee Lomonosov Sch., Moscow; read by three com. Albuquerque Bus. and Edn. Compact, 1999—2002. Named Alumnae Vol. of Yr., White Mountain Sch., 2006; recipient Vol of Yr. award White Mt. Sch., 2006; Tng. Tchr. Trainers grantee, 1975; NDEA fellow Okla. State U., 1969; nominated Profl. Outstanding Alumna McDaniel Coll., 2005. Mem.: Am. Reading Forum, Internat. Reading Assn., PEO (past chpt. pres.), World Congress in Reading Buenos Aires, European Coun. Internat. Schs., European Conf. in Reading, UK Reading Assn., Internat. Reading Assn. (non-print media and reading com. 1980—83, workshop dir. S.W. regional confs. 1982, travel, interchange and study tours com. 1984—86, com. internat. devel. N.Am. 1991—96, Outstanding Tchr. Educator award 1981), Am. Reading Forum (chmn. bd. dirs. 1983—85), Oxonian and Friend of Oriel Coll. (Oxford) (hon.), Circumnavigators, Internat. Soc. Rwy. Travelers, Albuquerque Tennis Club, Delta Delta Delta. Presbyterian. Avocations: miniatures, tennis, bridge, art, travel. Business E-Mail: mtonjes@unm.edu.

TONKIN, HUMPHREY RICHARD, academic administrator, educator; b. Truro, Cornwall, Eng., Dec. 2, 1939; arrived in U.S., 1962; s. George Leslie and Lorna Winifred (Sandry) T.; m. Sandra Julie Winberg, Mar. 9, 1968 (div. 1981); m. Jane Spencer Edwards, Oct. 1, 1983; 1 child, Sebastian George. BA, St. John's Coll., Cambridge, Eng., 1962, MA, 1966; AM, PhD, Harvard U., 1966; DLitt (hon.), U. Hartford, 1999. Asst. prof. English U. Pa., Phila., 1966-71, assoc. prof., 1971-80, prof., 1980-83, vice-provost undergrad. studies, 1971-75, coord. internat. programs, 1977-83, master Stouffer Coll. House, 1980-83; pres. State Univ. Coll., Potsdam, NY, 1983-88, U. Hartford, Conn., 1989-98, prof. humanities, pres. emeritus, 1998—; vis. fellow Whitney Humanities Ctr. Yale U., 1998-99. Vis. prof. English Columbia U., N.Y.C., 1980-81; exec. dir. Ctr. Rsch. and Documentation on World Lang. Problems, Rotterdam and Hartford, 1974—. Editor: (journal) Language Problems and Language Planning; author: (bibliography) Sir Walter Raleigh, 1971, Spenser's Courteous Pastoral, 1972, Esperanto and International Language Problems, 4th edit., 1977, The Faerie Queene, 1989, Lingvo kaj Popolo 2006, (with Jane Edwards) The World in the Curriculum, 1981; editor: Esperanto, Interlinguistics and Planned Language, 1997, Service Learning Across Cultures, 2004, (with Allison Keef) Language in Religion, 1989, (with Timothy Reagan) Language in the 21st Century, 2003; editor, translator Esperanto: Language, Literature and Community (Pierre Janton), 1993, Maskerado: Dancing Around Death in Nazi Hungary (Tivadar Soros), 2000; contbr. articles to profl. jours. Pres. Pa. Coun. Internat. Edn., 1980-81; bd. dirs. World Affairs Coun. Phila., 1979-83, Zamenhof Found., 1987-94, Hartford Symphony Orch., 1989-98, World Affairs Coun. Conn., 1989-2003, Greater Hartford Arts Coun., 1989-99, Can.-U.S. Found. Ednl. Exchange, 1997-2003, chmn. 1999-2000; bd. dirs. World Learning, 1998—2007; chmn. Coun. Internat. Exch. Scholars, 1988-94, Esperantic Studies Found., 1991—, Internat. Partnership for Svc.-Learning, 1991-96, v.p., 2001-05; bd. dirs. Am. Forum, 1985—, chmn., 1998-2003. Recipient Lindback award for disting. teaching, 1970; Frank Knox fellow Harvard U., 1962-66; Guggenheim fellow, 1974; Cassandra Pyle Award, NAFSA: Assn. Internat. Educators, 2006. Fellow Acad. Esperanto; mem. Universal Esperanto Assn. (pres. 1974-80, 86-89, rep. to UN 1974-83, hon. com. 1995—), Internat. Spenser Soc. (pres. 1983-84, former dir.), Internat. Acad. Scis. San Marino, Conn. Acad. Arts and Scis., Cosmos Club. Home: 279 Ridgewood Rd West Hartford CT 06107-3542 Office: U Hartford Mortensen Libr 200 Bloomfield Ave West Hartford CT 06117-1599 Office Phone: 860-768-4448. Business E-Mail: tonkin@hartford.edu.

TONKIN, INA LYNN DYER, physician, cardiovascular radiologist, educator; b. Louisville, Apr. 26, 1944; d. Robert S. and Nancy E. (Camp) Dyer; m. Allen K. Tonkin, June 29, 1968; children: Allison Elizabeth-Ann, Kieth Allen. BA, DePauw U., 1966; MD, U. Louisville, 1970. Diplomate Am. Bd. Radiology, 1974; Am. Bd. Vascular Interventional Radiology, 1994; Am. Bd. Pediatric Radiology, 1996. Pediatric intern U. Fla., Gainesville, 1970-71, resident in radiology, 1971-73, fellow in cardiovasc. radiology, 1974-75; asst. prof. U. Ariz. Health Sci. Ctr., Tucson, 1975-77, U. Ala.-Birmingham, 1977-79; assoc. prof. radiology U. Tenn., Memphis, 1979-84, prof., 1984—, prof. pediat., 1985—. Exec. com. LeBonheur Children's Med. Ctr., Memphis, 1981-85, chief med. staff, 1987; disting. scientist Armed Forces Inst. Radiologic Pathology, Washington, 1992-93; prof. radiology & pediat. U. Tenn. Hlth. Sci. Ctr., Memphis; lectr. nat. and internat. Editor: Pediatric Cardiovascular Imaging, 1992; contbr. chpts. to books, rsch. articles to profl. jours. Recipient Disting. Alumnus award U. Louisville Med. Sch., 1999. Fellow Soc. Interventional Radiology, Am. Coll. Radiology, Cardiovasc. Coun. Am. Heart Assn.; mem. Soc. Pediat. Radiology (treas.), Jour. Rev. Club Memphis (sec. 1984, pres. 1985), Soc. Interventional Radiology, N.Am. Soc. Cardiac Imaging (pres.). Methodist. Home: 3415 Chambers Chapel Rd Lakeland TN 38002-9573 Office: LeBonheur Children's Med Ctr 50 N Dunlap St Memphis TN 38103-4909 also: Univ Tenn Health Sci Ctr Prof Radiology and Pediat 50 N Dunlap St Memphis TN 38103-4909 Personal E-mail: drs.tonkin@mindspring.com.

TONKIN, LEO SAMPSON, educational association administrator; b. Suffern, NY, Apr. 2, 1937; s. Leo S. and Ann (Petrone) T. AB, Johns Hopkins, 1959; postgrad., Sch. Advanced Internat. Studies, 1962-63; JD, Harvard, 1962; Dr. Pedagogy, SUNY, 1973. Legis. asst. to US Congressman; then Sen. Charles McC. Mathias, Jr., Md., 1962-63; asso. counsel US Ho. of Reps. Select Com. on Govt. Research, 1964; spl. cons. Ho. Spl. Subcom. on Edn., 1965-66; exec. dir. Commrs. Council on Higher Edn., Washington, 1965-66; pres. Leo S. Tonkin Assos., Inc., 1966—; founder, dir., chmn. bd. Washington Workshops Found., 1967—; pres. Travel Seminars, Ltd., 1999—. Mem. White House Conf. on Edn., 1965, White House Conf. on Youth, 1971; spl. asst. to chmn. U.S. Ho. of Reps. Select Com. on Crime, 1972; mem. bd. plebe sponsors U.S. Naval Acad., 1977—; v.p. London Fedn. Boys' Clubs, 1980—; mem. adv. panel Nat. Commn. for Protection of Human Subjects of Biomed. and Behavioral Research, HEW, 1976-77; bd. dirs. Star Sci., Inc., 1998-2007; nat. adv. coun. Retinitis Pigmentosa Found., 1999—. Contbr. articles to mags. Bd. dirs. Washington Choral Arts Soc., 1971-73, Nat. Coordinating Council on Drug Edn., 1973, Nat. Student Ednl. Fund, 1974—76; chmn. Wall Street Seminar Found., 1978—; chmn. bd. trustees St. Thomas Aquinas Coll., 1966-73, continuing trustee, 1973-78, trustee, chmn. emeritus, 1978—; chmn. bd. trustees City of Phila. Govt. Honors Program; trustee Southeastern U., 1966-73; asso. bd. trustees Immaculata Coll., 1966-73; mem. advisory bd. Pub. Affairs and

Govt. Degree Program, Mt. Vernon Coll., 1971-74; bd. dirs. YMCA, Washington, 1969-71. Recipient Americanism award, Freedoms Found. at Valley Forge, 1973. Mem. Johns Hopkins Alumni Assn. Washington (pres. 1969-72), Harvard Law Sch. Alumni Assn. Washignton (exec. com.), Georgetown Club (Washington), City Tavern Club (Washington), Nat. Press Club (Washington), Capitol Hill Club (Washington), Capitol Yacht Club (Washington), Harvard Club (N.Y.C.). Home: 4368 Sunset Ct Warrenton VA 20187-3584 Office: 3222 N St NW Washington DC 20007-2849 Office Phone: 202-965-3434.

TONKONOGY, JOSEPH MOSES, physician, neuropsychiatrist, researcher; b. Belaya Tserkov, Kiev, Ukraine, Oct. 22, 1925; came to U.S., 1979, naturalized, 1985; s. Moysey Iosifovich and Beyla (Gdalievna (Schvachkina) T.; married; children: Vitaly, Milla, Bella. MD, Military Med. Acad., Leningrad, USSR, 1947; PhD, All Union Acad. Med. Sci., Moscow, 1956; DSc, 1st Med. Inst., Leningrad, 1966. From asst. to prof. The Bechterev Inst., Leningrad, 1956-66, prof., chmn., 1966-78; assoc. Boston U. Sch. Medicine, 1980-81; physician VA Med. Ctr., Northampton, Mass., 1981-87; assoc. prof. U. Mass. Med. Ctr., Worcester, 1987-95, prof., 1995—. Dir. neuropsychiatry svc. Worcester State Hosp., Mass., 1989—. Author: Introduction to Clinical Neuropsychology, 1973, Vascular Aphasia, 1986, The Brief Neuropsychological Cognitive Examination, 1997; editor: Problems of Contemporary Psychoneurology, 1966, Psychological Experiment in Psychiatry and Neurology, 1969, Mathematical Methods in Psychiatry and Neurology, 1971, Current Problems of Clinical Psychology, 1975; cons. (book) Soviet Military Psychiatry, 1986; contbr. numerous articles to profl. jours. Capt. Med. Corps, Germany, 1947-48. Recipient The Bechterev Prize, All Union Acad. Med. Scis., Moscow, 1974. Fellow: The Royal Soc. Medicine (U.K.); mem.: Internet Psychogeriatric Soc., Soc. Neurosci., Internat. Neuropsychol. Soc., Am. Acad. Neurology, Am. Neuropsychiat. Assn. Jewish. Office: U Mass Med Ctr Dept Psychiatry 55 Lake Ave N Worcester MA 01655-0002

TONKS, ROBERT STANLEY, pharmacologist, educator, retired dean; b. Aberystwyth, Wales; emigrated to Can., 1973; s. Robert Patrick Dennis and Prudence Violet (Williams) T.; m. Diana Mary Cownie; children: Pamela Mary, Julia Rosalind, Robert Michael, Sara Katharine. Student, U. Coll. of South Wales, Welsh Coll. Pharmacy; B.Pharm., PhD, Welsh Nat. Sch. Medicine, Cardiff. Organon postdoctoral fellow Med. Sch., Cardiff, Nat. Health Service postdoctoral fellow; Nat. Health Service sr. fellow Cardiff and Nevill Hall Hosp., Abergavenny; lectr. pharmacology U. Wales, Cardiff, 1958-72; vis. fellow Claude Bernard Research Assn., Faculté de Medicine, Paris, 1959; sr. lectr. pharmacology and therapeutics Med. Sch. and U. Wales Hosp., Cardiff, 1972-73; dir., prof. Coll. Pharmacy, Dalhousie U., Halifax, N.S., Canada, 1973-77, dean Faculty of Health Professions, 1977-88, prof. geriatric pharmaco-therapeutics, 1988—, acting head divsn. geriatric medicine, 1991-94. Cons. pharm. industry in U.K., Govt. of N.B., Can., Health and Welfare Dept. Can.; advisor health manpower Govt. of N.S.; coordinator N.E. Can./Am. Health Coun. co-chmn., 1974-91; emeritus chmn., mem. Health and Welfare Personnel Career Rev. Com., 1977-91; pharm. scis. grants com. Med. Rsch. Council Can., chmn.; rev. com. health protection br. fed. govt. div. pharm. chemistry, Can.; chmn. advisory com. N.B. Minister of Health; mem. joint com. on devel. rsch. in nursing Med. Rsch. Coun.-Nat. Health Rsch. Devel. Program; mem. nat. adv. panel on risk/benefit mgmt. of drugs.; adv. com. on restructuring Health Canada's Personnel Career Awards; trustee Lakeridge Health Corp., Oshawa, Ont., 2001-02, Lakeridge Health Whitby Found., Ont., 2003-04, coord. drug and med. supplies Ethiopia airlift, 1984. Contbr. articles on pharmacology and pathology to profl. jours. Mem.: Welsh Cultural Soc. (past pres.), Med. Soc. N.S. (task force on pharmacare), N.S. Pharm. Soc. (cert. of merit), Can. Geriatrics Soc., Am. Soc. Clin. Pharm. and Therapeutics, Canadian Soc. Clin. Investigation, Brit. Pharmacol. Soc., N.B. Pharm. Soc. (hon.), Can. Soc. Hosp. Pharmacy (hon.). Anglican. Mailing: 6 Tom Edwards Dr Whitby ON Canada L1R 2R4 Office: Dalhousie U Coburg Rd Halifax NS Canada Home Phone: 905-579-2667. Business E-Mail: bobtonks@dal.ca.

TONN, ELVERNE MERYL, pediatric dentist, dental benefits consultant, forensic odontologist; b. Stockton, Calif., Dec. 10, 1929; s. Emanuel M. and Lorna Darlene (Bryant) T.; m. Ann G. Richardson, Oct. 28, 1951; children: James Edward, Susan Elaine Tonn. AA, La Sierra U., Riverside, Calif., 1949; DDS, U. So. Calif., 1955; BS, Excelsior Coll., 1984; grad., Citizens Police Acad., Manteca, 2003. Lic. dentist Calif., 1955, diplomate Am. Bd. Quality Assurance and Utilization Rev. Physicians, Am. Bd. Forensic Dentistry, Am. Bd. Spl. Care Dentistry, Am. Bd. for Cert. in Homeland Security, cert. dental cons., forensic cons. Am. Coll. Forensic Examiners, 2004, med. investigator Am. Coll. Forensic Examiners, 2004; in Homeland Security Am. Bd., 2006. Pediatric dentist, assoc. Walker Dental Group, Long Beach, Calif., 1957-59, Children's Dental Clinic, Sunnyvale, Calif., 1959-61; pediatric dentist in pvt. practice Mountain View, Calif., 1961-72; pediatric dentist, ptnr. Pediatric Dentistry Assocs., Los Altos, Calif., 1972-83; pediatric dentist, ptnr. Valley Oak Dental Group, Manteca, Calif., 1987—2003; from clin. instr. to assoc. prof. Sch. Dentistry, U. Pacific, San Francisco, 1964-84; assoc. prof. Sch. Dentistry, U. Calif., San Francisco, 1984-86. Pediat. dental cons. Delta Dental Plan, San Francisco, 1985—2002; chief dental staff El Camino Hosp., Mountain View, Calif., 1964—65, 1984—85; dental cons. Interplast program Stanford U. Sch. Medicine, 1973; cert. physician adv. Physicians' Review Network, Phoenix, 2004—. Weekly columnist Manteca Bull., 1987-92; producer 2 teaching videos, 1986; contbr. articles to profl. jours. Capt. US Army, 1955—63. Fellow Am. Coll. Dentists, Internat. Coll. Dentists, Am. Acad. Pediatric Dentistry, Royal Soc. Health, Acad. of Dentistry for Handicapped, Pierre Fauchard Acad., Acad. Dental Materials, Am. Soc. Dentistry for Children (mastership award 2001), Am. Acad. Forensic Scis., Am. Coll. Forensic Examiners; mem. ADA, Internat. Assn. Pediatric Dentistry, Internat. Assn. Dental Rsch., Am. Soc. Forensic Odontology, Fedn. Dentaire Internationale, Am. Assn. Dental Cons., Calif. Dental Assn., Calif. Soc. Dentistry for Children (pres. 1968), Calif. Soc. Pediatric Dentistry, NY Acad. Scis., Calif. Acad. Sci., Rotary Internat., Manteca Police Dept. (Badge 2003), Nat. Disaster Med. Svc., Disaster Mortuary Org. Response Team (DMORT region 9), Am. Coll. Med. Quality, Manteca Cert. Emergency Response Team. Republican. Avocations: photography, travel, medieval history, anthropology. Home and Office: Tonn Forensic Cons Svcs 2420 Bellchase Dr Manteca CA 95336-5108 Office Phone: 209-815-4824. Personal E-mail: emtonn@comcast.net.

TONN, ROBERT JAMES, retired entomologist; b. Watertown, Wis., June 23, 1927; s. Harry James and Elise (Foogman) Tonn; m. Noemi C. Tonn; children: Sigrid M., Monica E. BS, Colo. State U., 1949, MS, 1950; MPH, Okla. Med. Sch., 1963; PhD, Okla. State U., 1959. Rsch. assoc La. State U., Costa Rica/New Orleans, 1961-63; dir. Taunton (Mass.) Field Sta., 1963-65; chief PMO unit WHO, various locations, 1965-87; ret., 1987. Adj. prof. parasitology U. Tex., El Paso, 1988—; cons. USAID/VBC, 1987—. Contbr. articles to profl. jours. Mem.: Royal Soc. Tropical Medicine and Hygiene, US/Mex. Border Health Assn., Am. Mosquito Control Assn., Soc. Vector Ecology (pres. 1984), Am. Soc. Tropical Medicine, Masons. Congregationalist. Home: 4247 Winchester Rd Las Cruces NM 88011 also: PO Box 772 Cloudcroft NM 88317 Personal E-mail: tonnapollo@aol.com.

TONTIRUTTANANON, CHANNARONG, electrical engineer, researcher; b. Muang, Surin, Thailand, 1971; B in Engring., Chulalongkorn U., Bangkok, 1992; MS, Auburn U., 1997, PhD, 1998. Instr. Assumption U., Bangkok, 1992—95; grad. rsch. asst. Auburn (Ala.) U., 1995—98; postdoctoral rsch. fellow U. Iowa, Iowa City, 1999; sr. mem. sci. staff Nortel Networks Inc., Richardson, Tex., 1999—. Contbr. articles to profl. jours. Mem.: IEEE, Am. Math. Soc., Phi Kappa Phi, Eta Kappa Nu. Achievements include patents for overload control system and method for a telecommunication system. Office Phone: 972-685-4924. E-mail: ctont@nortel.com.

TONYUSHKIN, ALEXEY ALEXEYEVICH, physicist, researcher; arrived in US, 1999; s. Alexei Tonyushkin and Margarita Tonyushkina; m. Ksenia Barkhatova, Aug. 10, 2001; 1 child, Maksim. BS, Nizhny Novgorod State U., Russia, 1998; MS, NYU, 2001, PhD, 2006. Tchg. asst. NYU, 1999—2005, rsch. asst., 1999—2006; rsch. assoc. Los Alamos Nat. Lab., N.Mex., 2006—. Contbr. articles to profl. jours. Recipient Margaret and Herman Sokol Rsch. Travel award, NYU, 2004. Mem.: Am. Phys. Soc. Achievements include research in generation of periodic atomic structures and their imaging by optical tools.

TOOBIN, JEFFREY ROSS, writer, legal analyst; b. NYC, May 21, 1960; s. Jerome and Marlene Sanders T.; m. Amy Bennett McIntosh, May 31, 1986; children: Ellen Frances, Adam Jerome. AB, Harvard U., 1982, JD magna cum laude, 1986. Bar: N.Y. 1987. Law clk. Hon. J. Edward Lumbard, NYC, 1986—87; assoc. counsel Indep. Counsel Lawrence Walsh, Washington, 1987—89; asst. U.S. atty. (ea. dist.) NY US Dept. Justice, Bklyn., 1990—93; legal analyst ABC News, NYC, 1996—2002; staff writer The New Yorker, NYC, 1993—; sr. legal analyst CNN, NYC, 2002—. Author: Opening Arguments: A Young Lawyer's First Case-United States v. Oliver North, 1991, The Run of His Life: The People v. O.J. Simpson, 1996, A Vast Conspiracy: The Real Story of the Sex Scandal that Nearly Brought Down a President, 2000, Too Close To Call: The Thirty Six Day Battle To Decide the 2000 Election, 2001, The Nine: Inside the Secret World of the Surpeme Court, 2007; contbr. articles to The New Yorker.; editor Harvard Law Review. Recipient Emmy award for coverage of Elian Gonzales custody saga, 2000. Office: The New Yorker 4 Times Sq New York NY 10036-6592 Office Phone: 212-286-5886.

TOOGOOD, JAMES STEPHEN, artist, educator; b. Camden, NJ, Sept. 26, 1954; s. James William and Margaret B. Toogood; m. Eileen Frances Monaghan. Student, Pa. Acad. Fine Arts, Phila., 1973—76. Bd. dirs., exhbn. chair Phila. Watercolor Club, 1985—88; instr. Mainline Art Ctr., Haverford, Pa., 1994—2000, Perkins Ctr. for the Arts, Moorestown, NJ, 1998—, Somerset Art Assn., Bedminster, NJ, 2000—04, Pa. Acad. Fine Arts, 2002—, Nat. Acad. Design, NYC, 2007—; artist-in-residence Masterworks Found., Hamilton, Bermuda, 2002. Author: Incredible Light and Texture in Watercolor, 2004; one-man shows include Rosenfeld Art Gallery, Phila., 1981—2005, Woodmere Art Mus., 1986, Masterworks Mus. of Bermuda Art, Hamilton, 1996, 2002. Named Best in Show, Phila. Sketch Club, 2005, NJ Watercolor Soc., 2006. Mem.: Nat. Watercolor Soc., Am. Watercolor Soc. (Artists Mag. award 1990), Pa. Acad. Fellowship Alumni. Home: 920 Park Dr Cherry Hill NJ 08002 Personal E-mail: jtoogood@snip.net.

TOOHEY, BRIAN FREDERICK, lawyer; b. Niagara Falls, NY, Dec. 14, 1944; s. Matthew and Marilyn (Hoag) T.; m. Mary Elizabeth Monihan; children: Maureen Elizabeth, Matthew Sheridan, Margaret Monihan, Mary Catherine, Elizabeth Warner. BS, Niagara U., 1966; JD, Cornell U., 1969. Bar: N.Y. 1969, N.Mex. 1978, Ohio 1980. Ptnr. Jones Day, Cleve., 1981—. Lt. JAG Corps, USNR, 1970-73. Mem. ABA, N.Y. State Bar Assn., State Bar N.Mex., Ohio State Bar Assn., Greater Cleve. Bar Assn. Roman Catholic. Home: 25 Pepper Creek Dr Cleveland OH 44124-5279 Office: Jones Day N Point 901 Lakeside Ave E Cleveland OH 44114-1190 Office Phone: 216-586-7246. E-mail: bftoohey@jonesday.com.

TOOHEY, JAMES KEVIN, lawyer; b. Evanston, Ill., July 16, 1944; s. John Joseph and Ruth Regina (Cassidy) T.; m. Julie Marie Crane, Nov. 1, 1969 (div. Aug. 1977); children: Julie Colleen, Jeannne Christine; m. Anne Margaret Boettingheimer, May 28, 1983; children: James Robert, Kevin John, Casey Anne. BBA, U. Notre Dame, 1966; JD, Northwestern U., 1969. Bar: Ill. 1969, U.S. Dist. Ct. (no. dist.) Ill. 1971, U.S. Dist. Ct. (ctrl. dist.) Ill. 1991, U.S. Ct. Appeals (7th cir.) 1973, U.S. Ct. Appeals (8th cir.) 1975, U.S. Supreme Ct. 1988. Assoc. Taylor, Miller, Magner, Sprowl & Hutchings, Chgo., 1970-71; asst. U.S. Atty. Office U.S. Atty., Chgo., 1971-74; assoc. Ross, Hardies, O'Keefe, Babcock & Parsons, Chgo., 1974-77; ptnr. Ross & Hardies, Chgo., 1978—2003, McGuire Woods, LLP, 2003—05, Johnson & Bell, Ltd., 2005—. Mem. St. Mary of the Wood Parish Coun., 1999-2002 Mem. Ill. State Bar Assn., Soc. Trial Lawyers, Assn. Advancement of Automotive Medicine, Ill. Assn. Def. Attys., Trial Lawyers Club Chgo., Edgebrook Sauganash Athletic Assn. (bd. dirs., commr. 1993-96; softball, baseball, and basketball coach), Evanston Golf Club. Office: Johnson & Bell Ltd 33 W Monroe St Chicago IL 60603 Office Phone: 312-984-0280.

TOOKER, GEORGE, artist; b. Bklyn., Aug. 5, 1920; s. George Clair and Angela Montejo (Roura) Tooker. BA, Harvard U., 1942; student, Art Students League, NYC, 1943-44. Instr. Art Students League, NY, 1965-68. One-man shows include Edwin Hewitt Gallery, 1951, 1955, Robert Isaacson Gallery, 1960, 1962, Durfacher Bros., 1964, 1967, Hopkins Ctr. Dartmouth Coll., 1967, Fine Arts Mus., San Francisco, 1974, Mus. Contemporary Art, Chgo., 1974, Whitney Mus., N.Y.C., 1975, Indpls. Mus. Art, 1975, DC Moore Gallery, 1997, 1998, 2000, exhibited in group shows at Whitney Mus., 1947—50, 1953, 1955—58, 1961, 1964, 1965, 1967, 1975, Venice Biennale, 1956, Art Inst. Chgo., 1951, 1952, 1954, 1959, Inst. Contemporary Arts, London, 1950, Va. Mus., 1954, 1962, Pa. Acad., 1966, Marisa Del Re Gallery, 1985, 1988, 1992, Spoleto Festival, Gibbes Mus. Art, Charleston, S.C., 1987, Robert Hall Fleming Mus., U. Vt., 1987, Marsh Gallery, U. Richmond, Va., 1989, Addison Gallery Am. Art, 1994, Represented in permanent collections Smithsonian Nat. Mus. Am. Art, Smithsonian Hirshorn Mus., Whitney Mus., Dartmouth Coll., Met. Mus., Walker Art Ctr., Mus. Modern Art, S.C. Johnson & Sons, Inc., Art, U.S.A., Sara Roby Fund Collection Am. Art, Addison Gallery, Ariz. State U. Gallery, Bklyn. Mus., Columbus (Ohio) Mus. Recipient Vt. Gov.'s award for Excellence in Arts, 1983, E. Isenbeurger prize, Nat. Acad., 2005; grantee, Nat. Inst. Arts and Letters, 1960. Mem.: NAD, Acad. Arts and Letters. Address: PO Box 385 Hartland VT 05048-0385 Office: care DC Moore Gallery 724 5th Ave New York NY 10019-4106

TOOKER, JOHN PHILLIP, internist, educator, medical association administrator; b. Denver; m. Nancy Tooker; 2 children. MD, U. Colo., 1970; MBA, Temple U. Diplomate Am. Bd. Internal Medicine, Am. Bd. Critical Care Medicine, Am. Bd. Pulmonary Disease. Intern Bellevue Hosp. Ctr., NYC, 1970—71, resident in medicine, 1971—72, U. Colo., 1972—73; fellow Maine Med. Ctr., Portland, 1975—76; fellow internal medicine U. Wash., Seattle, 1976—77; asst. chief dept. internal medicine, program dir. Maine Med. Ctr., Portland; CEO, exec. v.p. ACP, Phila., 2002—. Assoc. prof. medicine U. Vt.; adj. prof. U. Pa. Named one of 50 Most Powerful Physician Execs. in Healthcare, Modern Physician, 2005. Fellow: Coll. Physicians Phila., Am. Coll. Chest Physicians; mem.: AMA, Am. Thoracic Soc., Alpha Omega Alpha. Address: ACP 190 N Independence Mall W Philadelphia PA 19106-1572

TOOLE, JAMES FRANCIS, medical educator; b. Atlanta, Mar. 22, 1925; s. Walter O'Brien and Helen (Whitehurst) T.; m. Patricia Anne Wooldridge, Oct. 25, 1952; children: William, Anne, James, Douglas Sean, Lauren, James, Robert, Dean, Tyler, Kyle, Kaitlin, Grace. BA, Princeton U., 1947; MD, Cornell U., 1949; LLB, LaSalle Extension U., 1963; Dr. Honoris Causa, U. Targu Mures, Romania, 1998. Intern, then resident internal medicine and neurology U. Pa. Hosp., London, 1949—55, Nat. Hosp., London, 1955—56; mem. faculty U. Pa. Sch. Medicine, 1959—61; prof. neurology, chmn. dept. Sch. Medicine Wake Forest Bapt. Hosp., 1962—83. Vis. prof. neuroscis. U. Calif., San Diego, 1969—70; vis. scholar Oxford U., 1989; mem. Nat. Bd. Med. Examiners, 1970—76; mem. task force arteriosclerosis Nat. Heart Lung & Blood Inst., 1970—81; chmn. 6th and 7th Princeton confs. cerebrovascular diseases; cons. epidemiology WHO, Japan, 1972, 73, 93, USSR, 68, Switzerland, 74, Côte d'Ivoire, 77; mem. Lasker Awards com., 1976—77; chmn. neuropharmacologic drugs com. FDA, 1979; chair Commn. on Presdl. Disability, 1994—97; cons. NASA, 1966. Author: Cerebrovascular Diseases, 5th edit., 1999; editor: Current Concepts in Cerebrovascular Disease, 1969—73, Jour. Neurol. Sci., 1990—97; mem. editl. bd. Annals Internal Medicine, 1968—75, Stroke, 1972—74; mem. editl. bd. Jour. AMA, 1975—77; mem. editl. bd. Ann. Neurology, 1980—86, Jour. of Neurology, 1985—89. Pres. N.C. Heart Assn., 1976-77. Served with AUS, 1950-51; flight surgeon USNR, 1951-53. Decorated Bronze Star with V, Combat Med. badge. Master: ACP (licentiate); fellow: AAAS (life), Royal Coll. Physicians; mem.: AMA, Am. Acad. Neurology Rsch. Found., Am. Chem. Soc., Soc. for Neurosci., Hungarian Neurol. Soc., Polish Neurol. Soc., N.C. Stroke Assn. (pres. 1999—2001), Nat. Stroke Assn. (bd. dirs. 1993—, exec. com. 1994—, chmn. Commn. on U.S. Presdl. Disability 1994—), Russian Acad. Neurology (hon.), Am. Clin. and Climatol Assn. (life), Assn. Brit. Neurologists (hon.), German Neurol. Soc. (hon.), Austrian Soc. Neurology (hon.), Irish Neurol. Assn. (hon.), Internat. Stroke Soc. (exec. com. 1989—97, program chmn. 1992, pres. 1999—2004), Am. Soc. Neuroimaging (pres. 1992—94), Am. Acad. Neurology, World Fedn. Neurology (sec.-treas. 1982—89, mgmt. com. 1990—98, pres. 1998—2001, chmn. Rsch. and Edn. Found. 1999—2004), Am. Neurol. Assn. (sec.-treas. 1978—82, pres. 1984—85, historian 1988—, archivist 2004), Am. Physiol. Soc., Am. Heart Assn. (chmn. com. ethics 1970—75), Bohemian Club. Home: 1836 Virginia Rd Winston Salem NC 27104-2316

TOOLE, JOAN TRIMBLE, financial consultant; b. Ipswich, Mass., Apr. 3, 1923; d. Dana Newcomb and Barbara (Campbell) T.; m. John R. Marchi, Dec. 28, 1943 (div. Aug. 1959); children: Jon, Jael, Charis, Peter; m. Kenneth Ross Toole, Apr. 22, 1960 (dec. Aug. 1981); children: Dana O'Keefe, David Campbell. BA, Antioch Coll., Yellow Springs, Ohio, 1946; MS in Fin., U. Mont., 1976; MPA, Harvard U., 1985. Rancher J/J and KJ Ranches, 1955-82; Mont. legis. asst., researcher, 1981-83; cons. Mont. Dept. Revenue, 1985-87, U. Mont. Biol. Sta., 1987-89; pvt. practice, 1987—. State coord. Cranston for Pres., 1983-84; lobbyist Office Pub. Instrn., 1989-90; tax appeals bd. Ravalli County, 1981-84; active Mont. Bd. Natural Resources and Conservation, 1986-90, LWV, Mont. Environ. Info. Ctr., No. Plains Resource Coun.; bd. dirs. Mont. Conservation Voters, 1992—; mem. Lewis & Clark City County Health Bd., 1994-98, treas. Montanans for Coal Trust, 1999-2005, Montanans for Common Sense Mining, 1998-, Mont. Property Owners; bd. dirs. Forever Wild Endowment; vol. money mgmt. Rocky Mountain Devel. Co. Mem. AARP (vol. income tax preparer 1993—), Harvard Club (bd. dirs. ch. schs. and scholarships), Mont. Dem. Womens Club (regional dir.) Democrat. Episcopalian. Home and Office: 536 5th Ave Helena MT 59601-4358

TOOLSON, KAY, transportation executive; Exec. positions with two major motor coach co., 1973—86; pres. Monaco Coach Corp., 1986—95, 1997—2000, CEO, 1986—, chmn., 1993—. Office: Monaco Coach 91320 Coburg Industrial Way Eugene OR 97408 Office Phone: 541-686-8011. Office Fax: 541-681-8899. *

TOOMAJIAN, WILLIAM MARTIN, lawyer; b. Troy, NY, Sept. 26, 1943; s. Leo R. Tooomajian and Elizabeth (Gundrum) Toomajian; children: Andrew, Philip. AB, Hamilton Coll., 1965; JD, U. Mich., 1968; LLM, NYU, 1975. Bar: N.Y. 1968, Ohio 1978. Mem. firm Cadwalader, Wickersham & Taft, NYC, 1971—77, Baker Hostetler LLP, Cleve., 1977—. Lt. U.S. Coast Guard, 1968—71. Mem.: ABA, Cleve. Tax Club, Cleve. Bar Assn., Ohio Bar Assn. Home: 3582 Lytle Rd Cleveland OH 44122-4908 Office: Baker Hostetler LLP 3200 National City Ctr 1900 E 9th St Ste 3200 Cleveland OH 44114-3475 Business E-Mail: wtoomajian@bakerlaw.com.

TOOMBS, KENNETH ELDRIDGE, librarian; b. Colonial Heights, Va., Aug. 25, 1928; s. Garnett Eldridge and Susie W. (Bryant) T.; m. Ada Teresa Hornsby, Aug. 29, 1949; children— Susan Elizabeth Shealy, Cheri Lynn Morris, Teresa Ann Heilman. AA, Tenn. Wesleyan Coll., 1950; BS, Tenn. Poly. Inst., 1951; MA, U. Va., 1955; MLS, Rutgers U., 1956; student, La. State U., 1961-63. Reference asst. Alderman Library, U. Va., 1954-55; research asst. Grad. Sch. Library Sci., Rutgers U., 1955-56; mem. staff and faculty La. State U., 1956-63, asst. dir. charge pub. services, 1962-63; dir. libraries, prof. library sci. U. Southwestern La., 1963-67; dir. libraries U. S.C., Columbia, 1967—88; bd. dirs. Southeastern Library Network, 1967-88; disting. dir. of librs. emeritus U. S.C., Columbia, 1988—; vice chmn. Southeastern Library Network, 1973-74, 83-84, chmn., 1974-75, treas., 1984-85. Libr. cons. for bldgs. and adminstrn. for 60 colls. and univs. in past 30 yrs.; chmn. librarians sect. La. Coll. Conf., 1965-67; mem. Bd. La. Libr. Examiners, 1966-67; participant Libr. Mgmt. Inst., U. Wash., Seattle, 1969, Libr. Bldg. Problems Inst., UCLA, 1970; co-founder Southeastern Libr. Network with John Gribbin. Contbr. articles to profl. jours.; editor: Bull. La. Library Assn, 1959-62; mng. editor: SW La. Jour, 1963-67; adv. bd.: Linguistic Atlas Am. Treas. Wesley Found.; v.p. Am. Field Services Internat. Scholarships; bd. dirs. U. S.C. Ednl. Found., 1975-82; Danforth assoc., 1967—; AIA/ALA Bldg. Awards Jury, 1987. Served to 1st lt. AUS, 1946-47, 51-53. Mem. ALA (life), La. Library Assn. (parliamentarian 1962-63, 66-67), Southeastern Library Assn. (Life mem., exec. bd. 1981-85, Rothrock award 1978), Southwestern Library Assn., S.C. Library Assn. (Life mem., pres. 1976, exec. bd. 1981-85), Assn. Southeastern Research Libraries (chmn. 1973-75, adv. com. to OCLC 1979-84), AAUP (sec.), La. Hist. Assn., La. Tchrs. Assn., Soc. Tympanuchus Cupido Pinnatus, South Caroliniana Soc., Nat. Library Bldg. Consultants List (chmn. 1981-84), Tenn. Squire (Ky. col.), Assn. of S.C. Retirees (bd. dirs. 1995—), Omicron Delta Epsilon. Clubs: Mason (Shriner), Kiwanis, Torch Club. Methodist. Home: 16 Garden Springs Rd Columbia SC 29209-1716

TOOMER, AMANI, professional football player; b. Berkeley, Calif., Sept. 8, 1974; m. Dabrowski Yola Toomer (div. Feb. 28, 2007). Student, Univ. Mich., 1996. Wide receiver NY Giants, 1996—. Founder The Amani Toomer Found., NYC, 2001. Achievements include holding NY Giants franchise records for yards gained in a single season (1343 in 2002). Office: NY Football Giants Giants Stadium East Rutherford NJ 07073

TOOMEY, JEANNE ELIZABETH, animal activist; b. NYC, Aug. 22, 1921; d. Edward Aloysius and Anna Margaret (O'Grady) Toomey; m. Peter Terranova, Sept. 28, 1951 (dec. 1968); children: Peter Terranova (dec.), Sheila Terranova Beasley. Student, Hofstra U., 1938-40; student law sch., Fordham U., 1940-41; BA, Southampton Coll., 1976; postgrad., Monmouth Coll., 1978-79. Reporter, columnist Bklyn. Daily Eagle, 1943-52; with The Fitzgeralds, NBC Radio, NYC, 1952-53; reporter, writer King Features Syndicate, NYC, 1953-55; reporter, columnist N.Y. Jour.-Am., NYC, 1955-61; newsman AP, NYC, 1963-64; stringer; columnist News Tribune, Woodbridge, NJ, 1976-86; editor Calexico (Calif.) Chronicle, 1987-88; editor community sect. Asbury Park (N.J.) Press, 1988; pres., dir. Last Post Animal Sanctuary, Falls Village, Conn., 1989—. Author: Murder in the Hamptons, 1994, Assignment Homicide, 1998. Chmn. com. to establish Wildlife Preserve Hackensack Meadows, NJ, 1968—69. Named Woman of the Yr. N.Y. Women's Press Club, 1960. Mem. Newswomen's Club of N.Y., Overseas Press Club, N.Y. Press Club, Silurians. Roman Catholic. Office: Last Post Sanctuary PO Box 259 Falls Village CT 06031-0259 Office Phone: 860-824-0831. Office Fax: 860-824-5460.

TOOMEY, PATRICK JOSEPH, former congressman; b. Providence, Nov. 17, 1961; m. Kris.; children: Bridget, Patrick. BA cum laude, Harvard U., 1984. Investment banking Chem. Bank N.Y.; v.p., dir. U.S. subsidiary British merchant bank; co-founder internat. fin. svcs. consulting firm; founder Toomey Enterprises, Inc., Allentown, Pa.; mem. U.S. Congress from 15th Pa. dist., 1999—2005. Serves on Banking and Fin. Svcs., Budget and Small Bus. coms. Elected to Allentown Govt. Study Commn., 1994. Elected in 1998 to U.S. Ho. Reps. seat vacated by retiring Rep. Paul McHale. Served an internship with Sen. John Chafee (R-R.I.). Republican. Achievements include Toomey Enterprises, Inc., a family restaurant bus., operates 2 Rookies Restaurants located in Allentown and Lancaster, Pa.

TOOMEY, RICHARD ANDREW, JR., lawyer; b. Portsmouth, NH, Oct. 21, 1944; s. Richard Andrew and Elizabeth Neal (Rylander) T.; m. Jeanne Zurmuhlen; 1 child, Samuel Van Pelt. BA, U. N.H., 1966; JD, NYU, 1969. Bar: N.Y. 1969, Mass. 1989. Atty. VISTA, Mpls., 1969-71; assoc. Carter, Ledyard & Milburn, NYC, 1971-77; v.p., sr. assoc. counsel Chase Manhattan Bank, NYC, 1977-89; gen. coun. Shawmut Bank NA, Boston, 1989-94; dep. gen. coun. Shawmut Nat. Corp., Boston, 1995; group sr. counsel Fleet Fin. Group, Boston, 1996-2000; gen. counsel Fleet Bank NA, Jersey City, 1996—2000; asst. gen. counsel Sovereign Bank, Boston, 2000—05, gen. counsel, 2006—. Mem.: Boston Bar Assn. E-mail: rtoomey@sovereignbank.com.

TOOMEY, SISTER STEPHANA, liturgical consultant, designer; b. Wilmington, Del., Nov. 19, 1930; d. Hugh Jeremiah and Ellen (Vahey) Toomey. BS in Art Edn., Moore Coll. Art, 1952; MEd in Art, Temple U., Phila., 1960; cert., Internat. Ctr. Glass-Mosaics, Ravenna, Italy, 1975; postgrad., Paros Sch. Fine Arts, 1975. Lic. lic. liturgical cons. and designer; joined Dominican Order, Roman Cath. Ch., 1956. Tchr. art pub. schs., Camden, NJ, 1952—54, Oak Grove, Del., 1954—56; founder, pres. Efharisto Studio Inc., Balt., 1976—. Cons., mem. liturgical adv. com. Archdiocese of Balt., 1986—91. Contbr. articles and photogs. to various publs.; 5 nat. TV documentaries produced on her work; Represented in permanent collections Nat. Mus. Women in Arts. Mem. New Ventures. Named Top Winner for stained glass in chs., Bene Internat. Competition, San Jose, 2000—01; recipient hon. mention for stained glass in chs., 1991, 1993, 1998. Mem.: AIA (mem. interfaith forum on religion, art and architecture), Assn. Cons. Liturgical Designers (prof.), Dominican Order's Internat. Inst. Arts (founder Dominican Inst. Arts 1997, Fra Angelico Lifetime Achievement award 1999), Balt. Writers Alliance, Form Reform, Constrn. Specifications Inst. Avocations: being with nature, classical music, doing all religious traditions in design of worship space, liturgical appointments, stained glass. Office: 4 East Rolling Crossroads Ste 303 Catonsville MD 21228 Office Phone: 410-719-1043. Office Fax: 410-719-0995. Personal E-mail: fharisto@charm.net.

TOOMRE, ALAR, applied mathematician, theoretical astronomer; b. Rakvere, Estonia, Feb. 5, 1937; came to US, 1949, naturalized, 1955; s. Elmar and Linda (Aghen) T.; m. Joyce Stetson, June 15, 1958; children: Lars, Erik, Anya. BS in Aero. Engring., BS in Physics, MIT, 1957; PhD in Fluid Mechanics, U. Manchester, Eng., 1960. C.L.E. Moore instr. math. dept. MIT, Cambridge, 1960-62, asst. prof. applied math., 1963-65, assoc. prof., 1965-70, prof., 1970—; fellow Inst. for Advanced Study, Princeton, NJ, 1962-63. Contbr. articles to profl. jours. Guggenheim fellow, 1969-70, MacArthur fellow, 1984-89; Fairchild scholar, 1975, Marshall scholar, 1957-60 Fellow AAAS; mem. Am. Astron. Soc. (Dirk Brouwer award 1993), Internat. Astron. Union, Am. Acad. Arts and Scis., Nat. Acad. Scis. Office: MIT 77 Massachusetts Ave Rm 2-371 Cambridge MA 02139-4307 Office Phone: 617-253-4326. Business E-Mail: toomre@math.mit.edu.

TOON, MALCOLM, former ambassador; b. Troy, NY, July 4, 1916; s. George and Margaret Harcomb (Broadfoot) T.; m. Elizabeth Jane Taylor, Aug. 28, 1943; children: Barbara, Alan, Nancy. AB, Tufts U., 1937, LL.D. (hon.), 1977; MA, Fletcher Sch. Law and Diplomacy, 1938; student, Middlebury Coll., 1950, Harvard U., 1950-51; LL.D. (hon.), Middlebury Coll., 1978, Drexel U., 1980, Am. Coll. Switzerland, 1985, Grove City Coll., 1990. Fgn. service officer, 1946-79; assigned successively Warsaw, Budapest, Moscow, Rome, Berlin, Washington, 1946-60; assigned Am. embassy, London, 1960-63, counselor political affairs Moscow, 1963-67; with Dept. of State, Washington, 1967-69; ambassador to Czechoslovakia, 1969-71; to Yugoslavia, 1971-75; to Israel, 1975-76; to USSR, 1976-79. Mem. U.S. del. Nuclear Test Conf., Geneva, 1958-59, Four Power Working Group, Washington, London, Paris, 1959, Fgn. Ministers Conf., Geneva, 1969, Ten Nation Disarmament Com., Geneva, 1960; mem. SALT II del., 1977-79, U.S.-Soviet Summit Conf., Vienna, 1979; Brennen prof. U. N.C., Asheville, 1981; Finch prof. Miami U., Oxford, Ohio, 1982; Allis-Chalmers chair Marquette U., Milw., 1982 Trustee emeritus Tufts U.; bd. overseers Fletcher Sch. Law and Diplomacy, 1992; former chmn. U.S. Delegation to Joint U.S. Russian Commn. on POW's, MIA's. Served from ensign to lt. comdr. USNR, 1942-46. Decorated Bronze Star with combat V; recipient Freedom Leadership award Hillsdale Coll., 1980, Valley Forge Freedom award, 1981, Disting. Honor award Dept. State, 1980, Wallace award, 1984, Gold medal Nat. Inst. of Social Scis., 1987, Degree of Prof., Acad. Natural Scis. of the Russian Fedn., 1996, Silver medal, 1996. Home: 375 Pee Dee Rd Southern Pines NC 28387-2118

TOOTHE, KAREN LEE, elementary and secondary school educator; b. Seattle, Dec. 13, 1957; d. Russell Minor and Donna Jean (Drolet) McGraw; m. Edward Frank Toothe, Aug. 6, 1983; 1 child, Kendall Erin. BA in Psychology with high honors, U. Fla., 1977, MEd in Emotional Handicaps and Learning Disabilities, 1979. Cert. behavior analysis Fla. Dept. Profl. Regulation, behavior analyst Nat. Behavior Analyst Bd. Alternative edn. self-contained tchr. grades 2 and 3 Gainesville Acad., Micanopy, Fla., 1979; emotional handicaps self-contained tchr. Ctr. Sch. Alternative Sch., Gainesville, Fla., 1979-80; learning disabilities resource tchr. grades 2 and 3 Galaxy Elem. Sch., Boynton Beach, Fla., 1980-81, learning disabilities self-contained tchr. grades 1-3, 1981, varying exceptionalities self-contained tchr. grades 3-5, 1981-83, chpt. one remedial reading tchr. grades 3 and 4, 1982-83; sec. and visual display unit operator Manpower, London, 1983-84; dir. sci./geography/social studies program Fairley House Sch., London, 1984-86, specific learning difficulties self-contained tchr. ages 8-12, dir. computing program, 1984-89; specific learning difficulties resource tchr. ages 8-16 Dyslexia Inst., Sutton Coldfield, Eng., 1990; behavior specialist, head Exceptional Student Edn. dept. Gateway High Sch., Kissimmee, Fla., 1990, behavior specialist, head ESE dept., 1991, resource compliance specialist, head ESE dept., 1991-93, tchr. summer youth tng. and enrichment program, 1993, Osceola High Sch., Kissimmee, 1992; resource compliance specialist, program specialist for mentally handicapped, physically impaired, occupational and phys. therapy programs St. Cloud (Fla.) Mid. Sch., 1993-96, local augmentative/assistive tech. specialist, 1995—; resource compliance specialist, program specialist physically impaired occupl./phys. therapy programs, local augmentative/assistive tech. specialist Hickory Tree Elem. Sch., 1996-97, program specialist assistive tech., occpl., and phys. therapy, physically impaired programs, 1997-99, program specialist assistive tech., 1999—. Sch. rep. CREATE, Alachua County, Fla., 1979-80, Palm Beach County South Area Tchr. Edn. Ctr. Coun., 1980-83, chmn., 1982-83; mem. writing team Title IV-C Ednl. Improvement Grant, Palm Beach County, Fla., 1981; mem. math. curriculum writing team Palm Beach County (Fla.) Schs., 1983; mem., co-dir. Fairley House Rsch. Com., 1984-90; co-founder, dir. Rsch. Database, London, 1984-89; co-chmn. computer and behavior/social aspects writing teams Dyslexia Inst. Math., Staines, Eng., 1990; lectr., course tutor Brit. Dyslexia Assn., Crewe, Eng., 1990; mem. Vocat.-Exceptional Com., 1991-93; mem. Osceola Reading Coun., 1991-98; mem. sch. adv. com. Gateway High Sch., 1991-93, St. Cloud Mid. Sch., 1993-96; mem. sch. adv. com. Hickory Tree Elem. Sch., 1999-2000, Ctr. for Ind. Living Assitance for Tech. Divsn.; presenter in field. Mem. bd. assistive tech. divsn. Ctr. for Ind. Living. Named Mid. Sch. Profl. of Yr. Osceola chpt. Coun. Exceptional Children, 1995, 96, Profl. Recognized Spl. Educator, 1997; winner Disney's Teacherific Spl. Judges award, 1997; recipient Outstanding Svcs. to Coun. for Exceptional Children award, 2002, 2003, Outstanding Related Svcs. Tchr. of Yr., 2003, Outstanding Support Svcs. award, 2003. Mem. CEC (exec. com. 1997-2002, C.A.N. rep. 1997-99, pres.-elect 1999-2000, 06, pres. 2000-01, 07, named local chpt. Mid. Sch. Profl. of Yr. 1995, 96, Outstanding Svcs. to CEC award 2002, 03, Outstanding Related Svcs. Tchr. of Yr. 2003, Outstanding Support Svcs. award 2003, 25 Yrs. Svc. award 2006, Hall of Fame 2005-06), Fla. Soc. for Augmentative and Alt. Comm., Phi Beta Kappa. Avocations: travel, reading, exercise, scuba diving, crafts. Home: 2175 James Dr Saint Cloud FL 34771-8830 Office: Osceola Dist Schs ESE Adminstrv Annex 805 Bill Beck Blvd Kissimmee FL 34744-4492 Office Phone: 407-518-8147. Business E-Mail: toothek@osceola.k12.fl.us.

TOPACIO, ANGELA, marketing executive; b. Germany, 1968; m. Matt DiDio. Brand mgr. Saks Inc.; project mgr. Gyro Creative Grp., Detroit, 1999, majority owner. Named one of 40 Under 40, Crain's Detroit Bus., 2006. Office: Gyro Creative Group 400 Grand River Ave Ste 200 Detroit MI 48226 Office Phone: 313-964-0100. Office Fax: 313-964-0101.

TOPAZI, ANTHONY J., utilities executive; b. 1950; BSEE, Auburn U., Ala. Coop. edn. student Ala. Power Southern Co., 1969, various positions including Western divsn. v.p. and Birmingham divsn. v.p. Ala. Power, sr. v.p. Southern Power, exec. v.p. Southern Co. Generation and Energy Mktg., pres., CEO Miss. Power, 2004—. Bd. dirs. Hancock Bank. Mem. steering com., co-chair econ. devel. work group Blueprint Miss.; chmn. Momentum Miss.; vice chmn. Miss. Partnership for Econ. Devel.; mem. Miss. Gulf Coast Econ. Devel. Coun., Miss. Gulf Coast C. of C., DeToqueville Soc. of United Way of Am.; bd. trustees Nature Conservancy Miss.; bd. dirs. Miss. Econ. Coun., Gulf Coast Cmty. Found., Miss. World Trade Ctr. Office: Miss Power Co 2992 W Beach Blvd Gulfport MS 39501 Office Phone: 866-251-1943. *

TOPEL, DAVID GLEN, agricultural studies educator; b. Lake Mills, Wis., Oct. 24, 1937; BS, U. Wis., 1960; MS, Kans. State U., 1962; PhD, Mich. State U., 1965; DSc (hon.), Szent Istvan U., Godallo, Hungary, 2002. Assoc. prof. animal sci. and food tech. Iowa State U., Ames, 1967-73, prof. animal sci. and food tech., 1973-79, dean Coll. Agr., 1988-2000, dir. agr. and home econs. experiment sta., 1988-2000; prof., head dept. Auburn U., Ala., 1979—88, M.E. Ensminger endowed chair animal sci., 2000—. Cons., presenter, lectr. in field; mem. Gov. of Iowa's Sci. Adv. Coun., 1990-2000, Gov. of Iowa's Livestock Revitalization Task Force, 1993-98; chair Gov.'s Environ. Agr. Com., 1994; mem. Iowa Corn Promotion Bd.; mem. faculty Royal Vet. and Agrl. U., Denmark, 1971-72; vis. prof. Nat. Taiwan U., 1972. Author: The Pork Industry - Problems and Progress, 1968. Secretariat World Food Prize, Iowa State U., Ames, 1991-96. Fulbright-Hays scholar Royal Vet. and Agrl. U., 1971-72; recipient award of merit Knights of Ak-Sar-Ben, 1973, Commr.'s award Agrl. Commr. Republic of China, 1977, disting. Achievement award Block and Bridle Club, 1979, Ala. Cattlemen's Assn.,1 984, Hon. State Farmer Degree, Ala., 1986, Harry L. Rudnick Educator's award Nat. Assn. Meat Purveyors, 1989, USDA Honor award, 1999, Hon. Prof. award Gyöngyös Coll., Hungary, 2000; named hon. prof. Ukrainian State Agrl. U., 1993. Fellow Am. Soc. Animal Sci. (Disting. Rsch. award in meat sci. 1979, Bouffault Internat. Agr. award 2002); mem. Am. Meat Sci. Assn., Inst. Food Tech., Iowa Crop Improvement Assn., Extension and Tchg. (pres. North Ctrl. Region 1992), Nat. Assn. State Univs. and Land-Grant Colls. (chair bd. agr. 1993, mem. commn. on food, environ. and renewable resources 1992-99), Ukrainian Acad. Agrl. Scis., Sigma Xi (Outstanding Achievement award Iowa chpt. 1993), Alpha Zeta, Gamma Sigma Delta (Internat. award). Presbyterian. Avocations: fishing, golf. Office: Iowa State U Coll Agriculture 2374 Kildee Hall Ames IA 50011-0001 Home: 4108 Laura Ct Ames IA 50010 Home Phone: 515-292-7543; Office Phone: 515-294-6304.

TOPINKA, JUDY BAAR, state official, political organization worker; b. Riverside, Ill., Jan. 16, 1944; d. William Daniel and Lillian Mary (Shuss) Baar; 1 child, Joseph Baar. BS, Northwestern U., 1966. Features editor, reporter, columnist Life Newspapers, Berwyn and LaGrange, Ill., 1966-77; with Forest Park (Ill.) Rev. and Westchester News, 1976-77; coord. spl. events dept. fedn. comm. AMA, 1978-80; rsch. analyst Senator Leonard Becker, 1978-79; mem. Ill. Ho. of Reps., 1981-84, Ill. Senate, 1985-94; treas. State of Ill., Springfield, 1995—; chmn. State Rep. Party, 2002—; candidate Gov. Ill., 2006. Former mem. judiciary com., former chmn. senate health and welfare com.; former mem. fin. instn. com.; former co-chmn. Citizens Coun. on Econ. Devel.; former co-chmn. U.S. Commn. for Preservation of Am.'s Heritage Abroad, serves on legis. ref. bur.; former mem. minority bus. resource ctr. adv. com. U.S. Dept. Transp.; former mem. adv. bd. Nat. Inst. Justice. Founder, pres., bd. dirs. West Suburban Exec. Breakfast Club, from 1976; chmn. Ill. Ethnics for Reagan-Bush, 1984, Bush-Quayle 1988; spokesman Nat. Coun. State Legislatures Health Com.; former mem. nat. adv. coun. health professions edn. HHS; mem., GOP chairwoman Legis. Audit Commn. of Cook County; chmn. Riverside Twp. Regular Republican Orgn., 1994—. Recipient Outstanding Civilian Svc. medal, Molly Pitcher award, Abraham Lincoln award, Silver Eagle award U.S. Army and N.G. Office: Office of Ill State Treasurer 100 W Randolph St Ste 15-600 Chicago IL 60601-3232 *

TOPLIN, ROBERT BRENT, history professor, television producer; b. Phila., Sept. 26, 1940; s. Maurice Cunningham and Janet Rachel (Belsinger) T.; m. Karin Bendel, Dec. 26, 1996; children: Cassandra, Jennifer. BS, Pa. State U., 1962; MA, Rutgers U., 1965, PhD, 1968. Asst. prof. Denison U., Granville, Ohio, 1968-74, assoc. prof., 1976-78; assoc. prof. and program dir. U. Houston-Clear Lake City, 1974-76; assoc. prof. U. N.C. at Wilmington, 1978-80, prof. history, 1980. Vis. prof. U. N.C.-Chapel Hill, 1983; media advisor NEH; lectr. in field. Project dir.: A House Divided (TV series) U.S.A.; A Television history, Pres.'s in Crisis, The Am. Frontier; author: The Abolition of Slavery in Brazil, 1972, Unchallenged Violence: An American Ordeal, 1975, Freedom and Prejudice: The Legacy of Slavery in the United States and Brazil, 1982, History By Hollywood: The use and Abuse of the American Past, 1996; author: Reel History: In Defense of Hollywood, 2002, Michael Moore's Fahrenheit 9/11: How One Film Divided a Nation, 2006, Radical Conservatism: The Right's Political Religion, 2006; editor: Slavery and Race Relations in Latin America, 1974; editor anthology: American History Through Film, 1983, Ken Burns's The Civil War: Historians Respond, 1996, Oliver Stone's USA: Film, History and Controversy, 2000; contbg. editor: Jour. Am. History, 1986—, Perspectives, Am. Hist. Assoc., 1995 - 2000, 2007-; contbr. articles to profl. jours.; book reviewer various jours.; project dir.: (PBS TV) Denmark Vesey's Rebellion 1982, Solomon Northup's Odyssey, 1984; Charlotte Forten's Mission, 1985; (films) The War to End All Wars, 1985, Lincoln and the War Within, 1992; broadcast appearances on PBS TV, CBS TV, The History Channel, Turner Classic Movie Channel, C-SPAN. Pres. Williston Jr. H.S. PTA; v.p. New Hanover County PTA, New Hanover County Bd. Edn. Grantee or fellow Ford Found., 1967, NEH, 1970, 77-80, 82-89, 90-91, Am. Philos. Soc., 1970m 81, Denison U. Rsch. Found., 1972, Annenberg/Corp. for Pub. Broadcasting, 1983-84; grantee Ill. Humanities Coun., 1991; fellow Am. Coun. Learned Soc., 1991. Mem. Am. Hist. Assn. (tchg. com. 1990-93), Orgn. Am. Historians (mem. com. on radio, TV, film media 1978-80, Erik Barnouw prize 1985, 87-89), Conf. on Latin Am. History (com. on tchg. materials 1978), Erik Barnouw prize com. 1987-88. Democrat. Jewish. Home Phone: 434-989-3564. Business E-Mail: toplinrb@uncw.edu.

TOPLITT, GLORIA H., music educator, actress, vocalist; b. St. Louis, May 22, 1925; d. Wade Fitzgerald Hamilton and Neyneen Farrell Pires; m. James Parnell, 1942 (div. July 1949); 1 child, Dennis James Parnell; m. Abraham Toplitt, Aug. 19, 1968. Student, Guy Bates Post Acad. Dramatic Arts, LA, 1941-43. Stage performer, NYC, 1944-59; dir. entertainment Holland Am. Lines, 1959-61; tchr. voice North Hollywood Conservatory, Calif., 1965-67; pvt. voice tchr. North Hollywood, 1968-95; music specialist outreach program NASA Space Sci. and Tech., Inc., Springfield, Va., 1997—. Dir. Workshop Theatre Program, North Hollywood, 1968—78; coach for impaired voices, North Hollywood, 1968—. Author, composer: Parade of Planets, 1998, Space Challenge, 1999; actor: (plays, N.Y. stage prodns.) appeared as leading lady Oklahoma, Chocolate Soldier, Lend an Ear, Courtin' Time, Showboat, Take Me Along, Auld Lang Syne, Three Musketeers, Carousel, Oh! Captain, Brigadoon, Guys and Dolls, Hit the Deck, Finian's Rainbow, others; voice rec. Songs of Harriet Ware Meml., Smithsonian Instn. Mem. election bd. Office of Voter Registrar, North Hollywood, 1996—98. Avocations: poetry, travel, theater, elderhostel classes, reading. Home: 4405 Carpenter Ave North Hollywood CA 91607-4110

TOPOL, ERIC JEFFREY, academic administrator, cardiologist, educator; b. NYC, June 26, 1954; s. Erwin and Susan (Lepp) T.; m. Susan Leah Merriman, May 5, 1979; children: Sarah, Evan. BA with highest distinction, U. Va., 1975; MD with honors, U. Rochester, 1979. Med. resident U. Calif., San Francisco, 1979-82; fellow Johns Hopkins U. Med. Ctr., Balt., 1982-85; asst. prof. U. Mich. Sch. Medicine, Ann Arbor, 1985-87, assoc. prof., 1987-90, prof., 1990; dir. cardiac catheterization labs. and interventional cardiology U. Mich. Med. Ctr., Ann Arbor, 1986-91; chmn. dept. cardiovasc. medicine Cleve. Clinic Found., dir. Ctr. for Thrombosis and Arterial Biology, 1991—; founder, provost, chief acad. officer Cleve. Clinic Lerner Coll. Medicine, Case Western Reserve Univ., 2002—05, prof. medicine, 2004—06; prof. genetics Case Western Reserve Univ. Sch. Medicine, 2006—. Editor: Acute Coronary Intervention, 1988, Textbook of Interventional Cardiology, 1990, 4th edit., 2002, Textbook of Cardiovascular Medicine, 1st and 2d edits.; mem. editl. bd. Circulation, Circulation Rsch., Am. Jour. Cardiology, Coronary Art Disease, Jour. Am. Coll. Cardiology, Brit. Heart Jour.; mem. editl. bd. of several med. publs.; contbr. articles to profl. jours. Recipient Clin. Rsch. Innovator award, Doris Duke Charitable Found., 2003, Andres Gruentzig award, European Soc. Cardiology, 2004. Fellow ACP, Am. Coll. Cardiology (editor jour., Simon Dack award, 2005), Am. Soc. Clin. Investigation, Am. Heart Assn. (mem. coun. on clin. cardiology, coun. on circulation and thrombosis), European Soc. Cardiology; mem. Cen. Soc. Clin. Rsch., Am. Fedn. for Clin. Rsch. (councilor), Assn. Am. Physicians, AMA (Dr. William Beaumont award in Medicine 2002), IOM, NAS, John Hopkins Soc. Scholars. being one of the first scientists to raise doubts about the safety of Vioxx, and was a key witness in lawsuits against Merck & Co. Office: Case Western Reserve Univ Sch Medicine 10900 Euclid Ave Cleveland OH 44106 Office Phone: 216-445-9490.

TOPOL, ROBIN APRIL LEVITT, lawyer; b. NYC, Apr. 02; d. Anatole Roy and Phyllis Levitt; m. Clifford Miles Topol, Oct. 23, 1982. Student, Stanford U., Eng., 1974; BA, Barnard Coll., 1976; JD, NYU, 1979; postgrad. exec. mgmt. program, Yale U., 1987. Bar: N.Y. 1980, Fla. 1981. Ptnr. real estate dept., comml. real estate and leasing Kurzman Eisenberg Corbin LLP, White Plains, NY, 1996—. Trustee alumni bd. dirs. Yale U. Sch. Mgmt., 1987-88. Mem. ABA (vice chmn. real property com. 1986-90), N.Y. County Bar Assn. (real estate com. 1986-96), Women's Bar Assn. (chmn. real estate com. 1980-96). Avocations: tennis, golf, running. Office: Kurzman Eisenberg LLP 1 N Broadway White Plains NY 10601-2310 Office Phone: 914-285-9800. Business E-Mail: rtopol@kelaw.com.

TOPPETA, WILLIAM JOHN, insurance company executive, lawyer; b. NYC, Sept. 18, 1948; s. John Francis and Rita Ann (Carretta) Toppeta. BA, Fordham U., 1970; JD, NYU, 1973, ML, 1977. Bar: NY 1974, US Supreme Ct. 1977. Atty. Met. Life, NYC, 1973-79, asst. v.p., 1979-81, asst. gen. counsel, 1981-82, assoc. gen. counsel, 1982-83, v.p., assoc. gen. counsel, 1983-92; pres., CEO MetLife Can. Ops., 1993-95, sr. v.p., 1995—96, exec. v.p. individual bus., 1998—99; sr. exec. v.p., head of client svcs. Met. Life, 1999, pres. (client svcs), chief admin. officer, 1999—2001; pres. (client svcs.), chief administrative officer Met Life Inc., 1999—2001; pres. internat. Met. Life Inc., Met. Life, 2001—. Adj. prof. Pace U. Law Sch., White Plains, NY, 1984—, Bklyn. Law Sch., 1985—. Mem. ABA (vice-chairperson com. on trial techniques 1986—), NY State Bar Assn., Assn. Bar of City of NY. Democrat. Roman Catholic. Office: MetLife Inc 200 Park Ave New York NY 10166 E-mail: btoppeta@metlife.com. *

TOPPING, SEYMOUR, writer; b. NYC, Dec. 11, 1921; s. Joseph and Anna (Seidman) Topolsky; m. Audrey Elaine Ronning, Nov. 10, 1949; children: Susan, Karen, Lesley, Rebecca, Joanna. BJ, U. Mo., 1943; LittD (hon.), Rider Coll., 1983. With I.N.S. (China civil war), 1946-47; with AP, Nanking, 1948—49, corr. Saigon, 1950—51, London, 1952—56, Berlin, 1956—59; mem. staff N.Y. Times, 1959-93, chief corr. Moscow, 1960—63, chief corr. S.E. Asia, 1963-66, fgn. editor, 1966-69, asst. mng. editor, 1969-76, dep. mng. editor, 1976-77, mng. editor, 1977-86; dir. editl. devel. N.Y. Times Regional Newspapers, 1987-93; chmn. New Directions for News, 1990-91; pres. Am. Soc. Newspaper Editors, 1992—93; prof. Grad. Sch. Journalism Columbia U., NYC, 1993—2002, adminstr. Pulitzer Prizes, 1993—2002, Sanpaolo prof. emeritus of internat. journalism, 2002—, pres. emeritus profs., 2004—. Adviser Internat. Ctr. for Journalists, Found. Am. Comm.; juror Pulitzer Prize com.; lectr. in field. Author: Journey Between Two Chinas, 1972, The Peking Letter, A Novel of the Chinese Civil War, 1999, Fatal Crossroads, A Novel of Vietnam 1945, 2005. Spl. advisor to Sec.-Gen. UN to Earth Summit, Rio de Janeiro, 1992; mem. Nat. Com. U.S.-China Rels.; Served with inf. AUS, 1943-46, PTO. Recipient Greenway-Winship award for contbns. to internat. journalism, 2000, Disting. Svc. award, Mo. Sch. of Journalism, 1968, Disting Alumni award, 1993. Mem. Coun. Fgn. Rels., Asia Soc., Am. Soc. Newspaper Editors, Century Assn. Home: 5 Heathcote Rd Scarsdale NY 10583-4413 Personal E-mail: st122@columbia.edu.

TOPSAKAL, ERDEM, science educator; b. Istanbul, Turkey, June 27, 1971; arrived in U.S., 1997; s. Mehmet and Imral Topsakal. PhD, Istanbul Tech. U., 1996. Rsch. scientist U. Mich., Ann Arbor, 2001—03; asst. prof. Miss. State U., 2003—. Recipient Young Scientist award, URSI, 1996, Outstanding Educator award, Miss. State U. Dept. Elec. and Computer Engring., 2005; fellow, NATO, 1997. Mem.: IEEE (sr.), IEEE Antennas and Propagation. Achievements include research in Nanoscale Frequency Selective Surface Design for Near Infrared and Optics; UWB and Multi-band Antennas; Design and Analysis; Fast Computational Electromagnetic Tools; Implantable Antennas for Wireless Data Telemetry. Office Phone: 662-325-3669. Office Fax: 662-325-2298. Business E-Mail: topsakal@ece.msstate.edu.

TORANZO, NILSA CARIDAD, special education services professional; b. Bklyn., Sept. 8, 1958; d. Claide and Aurea Esther Toranzo; m. Kenneth Antoine Cherry, Oct. 10, 1999. BSc, Fordham U., 1980; MA, NY U, 1983. Edn. evaluator St. Francis de Sales Sch. for the Deaf, Bklyn., 1983—. Contbr. articles. Mem.: Internat. Reading Assn. Avocations: exercise, reading, travel. Office: St Francis de Sales Sch for the Deaf 260 Eastern Pkwy Brooklyn NY 11225 Office Phone: 718-636-4573. Business E-Mail: ntoranzo@sfdesales.org.

TORBICA, ZELJKO MARKO, construction executive, educator; arrived in U.S.A., 92; s. Marko and Nadezda Torbica; m. Maria Jovanov, Oct. 30, 1999; children: Talia, Nada, Dara, Djordje. PhD, U. Fla., 1997—97;

diploma, U. of Belgrad, 1986. Cert. quality engr., Am. Soc. Quality; project mgmt. profl. Project Mgmt. Inst. Engr. Energoprojekt, Belgrade, Serbia and Montenegro, 1986—92; asst. prof. Minn. State U., Mankato, 1996—2001; constrn. mgmt. educator Fla. Internat. U., Miami, 2001—04; assoc. prof. Roger Williams U., Bristol, RI, 2004—06; dir. devel. CABI Developers, Aventura, Fla., 2006—.

TORBUSH, DEBORAH NICKELS, psychologist; d. John Harvey and Geraldyne (Cornell) Nickels; m. Douglas Bruce Torbush, June 18, 1977; children: C. Ryan, Katherine M. BA, Emory U., 1974; MEd, Ga. State U., 1977, EdS, 1981. Cert. sch. psychologist Ga. Sch. psychologist Griffin (Ga.) CESA, 1977—78, DeKalb County Sch. Sys., Decatur, Ga., 1978—. Pres. Jr. League DeKalb County, Decatur, 1996—97, Alliance Ga. Dental Assn., 2006—07; trustee DeKalb County Pub. Libr. Bd., Decatur, 2004—; bd. dirs., former chmn. Internat. Women's House, Decatur, 1995—; mem. bd. visitors Grady Hosp., Atlanta, 2000—; mem. spouses' com. Hinman Dental Soc., Ga., 2002—; grad. Leadership DeKalb, 1995—96. Mem.: Nat. Assn. Sch. Psychologists, Ga. Assn. Sch. Psychologists (chmn. profl. stds. 2000—02, publicity chmn. 2002—), Emory U. Alumni Assn. (mem. reunion com.), Smoke Rise Golf and Country Club, Kappa Alpha Theta. Avocations: volunteer work, tennis, travel. Home: 5360 Kanawha Ct Stone Mountain GA 30087 Office: DeKalb Sch Sys EDC Support Svcs 5839 Memorial Dr Stone Mountain GA 30083

TORCHETTI, JOHN, professional hockey coach; b. Boston, 1964; Asst. Greensboro Monarchs, 1992—93; head coach, dir. hockey ops. San Antonio Iguanas, 1994—95, asst. gen. mgr., asst. coach, 1996; coach Komets, 1996—98; asst. coach Tampa Bay Lightning, 1999—2000, 2000—01; gen. mgr. Detroit Vipers, 1998—2002; head coach devel. affiliate Fla. Panthers, San Antonio, 2002—03, asst. coach Sunrise, Fla., 2003—04, interim head coach, 2004, LA Kings, 2006; head coach Moncton Wildcats (Quebec Major Jr. Hockey League), 2006—07; asst. coach Chgo. Blackhawks, 2007—. Asst. scouting dir. Tampa Bay Lightning, 2001—02. Named Coach of Yr., CHL, 1995. Office: Chgo Blackhawks Hockey Team Inc 1901 W Madison St Chicago IL 60612 *

TORELLI, ANTHONY-ALEXANDER, musician, educator, conductor; b. Providence, Sept. 15, 1962; s. Alexander Augustino and Marie Barbara Torelli; m. Adriana Maritza Ramos, June 9, 2001; 1 child, Alexander James. BS, RI Coll., 1986; M, The Hartt Sch. U. Hartford, 1998; D. U. Montreal, 2003; diploma in ARt, The Hartt Sch. U. of Hartford, 2000. Tchg. Cert. RI Dept. of Edn., 2000. Condr. Bel Canto Opera Co., Cranston, RI, 1988—98; assoc. condr. South County Chamber Singers and Orch., Kingston, RI, 1998—; condr. RI Philharm. Youth Orchs., Providence, 2000—05; music dir. and condr. Norton Singers, Mass., 2003—; music dir., condr. German Am. Cultural Soc. Chorus, Pawtucket, RI; music educator North Providence Sch. Dept., North Providence, RI, 2000—. Cons. Pastime Theater Found., Bristol, RI, 2003—. Opera scholar, Bel Canto Opera Scholarship Found., 1993. Mem.: Am. Fedn. of Tchrs. (assoc.), Am. Fedn. of Musicians (assoc.), Conductors Guild (assoc.), Am. Symphony Orch. League (assoc.). Home: 19 Sheridan St Johnston RI 02919 Home Phone: 401-254-1571. Personal E-mail: anthonyatorelli@yahoo.com.

TOREN, MARK, state official, statistician; b. Warsaw, Dec. 7, 1950; s. Jacob Toren and Assia (Hanukayeva) Merson; m. Angela Aleksandrovna, July 12, 1997; children: Alexander Michael, Anna A. Cert., U. Cologne, Fed. Republic Germany, 1974; AA, AAS, SUNY, Suffern, 1972; BA, SUNY, New Paltz, 1975; MA, SUNY, Albany, 1976; MS, Rensselaer Poly. Inst., 1983, PhD, 1992. Sr. statistician Triad Data Scis., Albany, NY, 1980—84; sr. economist NY State Dept. Taxation and Fin., Albany, 1984—85; econometrician NY State Dept. Social Svcs., Albany, 1985—92, NY State Dept. of Health, Albany, 1992—. Faculty bus. mgmt. and econs. SUNY, Empire State Coll., Saratoga Springs, 1994—98; cons. Calay Sys. Inc., Newport Beach, Calif., 1998—2000; rschr. NY State Dept. of Health, Albany, 1999—; part-time faculty Sch. Bus. & Econs. Siena Coll., Loudonville, NY, 2006—. Author: Cost Efficiency in Nursing Homes: A Stochastic Frontier Approach, 1994, Hospital Cost and Efficiency in a Regime of Stringent Regulation, 1996, Economics Macro/Micro, 1996, Economics of Government Regulation and the Market, 1996. With US Army, 1969—71. Mem.: Micro-Computer Users Group, Health Econs. Rsch. Orgn., Am. Statis. Assn., Am. Econ. Assn., Internat. Platform Assn., Omicron Delta Epsilon. Avocations: literature, art, music, photography. Office: NYS Dept of Health Health Care Rsch 433 River St Troy NY 12180 Office Phone: 518-474-2679. Business E-Mail: mxt10@health.state.ny.us.

TORG, JOSEPH STEVEN, orthopaedic surgeon, educator; b. Phila., Oct. 25, 1934; m. Barbara Jane Groenendaal, May 23, 1959; children: Joseph Steven, Elisabeth, Jay Michael. AB, Haverford Coll., 1957; MD, Temple U., 1961. Diplomate: Am. Bd. Orthopaedic Surgeons. Intern San Francisco Gen. Hosp., 1961-62; resident in orthopaedic surgery Temple U. Hosp., Phila., 1964-68, Shriners Hosp. for Crippled Children, Phila., 1966-67; asst. surgeon Episcopal Hosp., Phila., 1968-70; surgeon Shriners Hosp. Crippled Children, 1970-78; mem. staff Temple U. Hosp., 1970-78, instr. orthopaedic surgery, 1968-70, asst. prof., 1970-75, assoc. prof., 1976-78; dir. Center for Sports Medicine and Sci., 1974-78; chief orthopaedic sect. St. Christopher's Hosp. for Children, Phila., 1971-74, mem. staff, 1974—; active staff St. Joseph's Hosp., Phila., 1977—; prof. U. Pa., 1978—, active staff hosp., 1978—; dir. Sports Medicine Center, 1978—; prof. orthopaedic surgery Temple U., 1995. Mem. active staff Children's Hosp., Phila., 1978; med. cons. Pres.'s Coun. on Phys. Fitness and Sports Mem. editl. bd. Sports Medicine, Yearbook of Sports Medicine, Contemporary Orthopaedics, Jour. Clin. Sport Medicine, Am. Jour. Knee Surgery, Orthopaedic Rev.; contbr. articles to profl. jours. Served with M.C. US Army, 1962-64. Recipient Layman Honor award Pa. State Assn. Health, Phys. Edn. and Recreation, 1970, Grad. Honor award, 1975; Commendation of Merit Phila. Public HS Football Coaches, 1974 Fellow Am. Acad. Orthopaedic Surgeons, Am. Coll. Sports Medicine (trustee 1975-78), Phila. Coll. Physicians; mem. AMA, Eastern Orthopaedic Soc., Am. Orthopaedic Soc., Sports Medicine, Phila. County Med. Soc., Phila. Orthopaedic Soc., Pa. State Med. Soc., Pa. State Orthopaedic Soc. Home: 401 Conestoga Rd Wayne PA 19087-4811 Office: Temple U Hospital 6th Floor 3401 N Broad St Philadelphia PA 19140 Office Phone: 215-707-1321. Personal E-mail: torgmd@aol.com. Business E-Mail: torgjs@tuhs.temple.edu.

TORGERSEN, PAUL ERNEST, academic administrator, educator; b. NYC, Oct. 13, 1931; s. Einar and Frances (Hansen) T.; m. Dorothea Hildegarde Zuschlag, Sept. 11, 1954; children: Karen Elizabeth, Janis Elaine, James Einar. BS, Lehigh U., 1953, DEng, 1994; MS, Ohio State U., 1956, PhD, 1959. Grad. tchg. asst. Ohio State U., Columbus, 1957, instr., 1957-59; asst. to assoc. prof. Okla. State U., Stillwater, 1959-66; prof., dept. head, dean Coll. Engring. Va. Tech, Blacksburg, 1967-93, pres., 1993-2000, John W. Hancock chair of engring. Dir. Roanoke (Va.) Electric Steel, 1986-2001, Luna Innovations, 2000—, EDD, 1996—. Author 5 books. Mem. Gov. Mark Warner's Commn. on Bd. of Visitor Appts., Richmond, Va., 2002--; So.State Energy Bd., Richmond, 1986-90. 1st lt. USAF, 1953-55. Fellow Am. Soc. Engring. Edn. (Lamme medal 1994), Inst. Indsl. Engring (Frank and Lillian Gibreth award 2001); mem. Nat. Acad. Engring. (coun. 1999-). Avocation: tennis. Office: Va Tech 201 Durham Hall Blacksburg VA 24061-0118 Business E-Mail: tennis@vt.edu.

TORGERSEN, TORWALD HAROLD, architect, consultant; b. Chgo., Sept. 2, 1929; s. Peder and Hansine Malene (Hansen) T.; m. Dorothy Darlene Peterson, June 22, 1963. BS in Archtl. Engring. with honors, U. Ill., 1951. Lic. architect Ill., D.C., real estate broker, Ill., interior designer, Ill.; registered architect Nat. Coun. Archtl. Registration Bds. Ptnr. Coyle & Torgersen Architects-Engrs., Washington, Chgo. and Joliet, Ill., 1955—56; coord. project Skidmore, Owings & Merrill, Chgo., 1956—60; corp. architect, dir. architecture, constrn. and interiors Container Corp. Am., Chgo., 1960—86; prin. in charge of orgn. and adminstrn. Jack Train Assocs. Inc., Chgo., 1987—88; cons. Torwald H. Torgersen, AIA, FASID, Chgo., 1988—. Guest lectr. U. Wis. Capt. USNR, 1951-82. Recipient Top Ten Design award Factory mag., 1964 Fellow Am. Soc. Interior Designers; mem. AIA, Naval Res. Assn., Ill. Naval Militia, Am. Arbitration Assn., Am. Soc. Mil. Engrs., Paper Industry Mgmt. Assn. (hon.), Sports Car Club Am., Nat. Eagle Scout Assn. Clubs: 20 Fathoms. Home and Office: 3750 N Lake Shore Dr Chicago IL 60613-4238

TORGERSON, LARRY KEITH, lawyer; b. Albert Lea, Minn., Aug. 25, 1935; s. Fritz G. and Lu (Hillman) Torgerson. BA, Drake U., 1958, MA, 1960, LLB, 1963, JD, 1968; MA, Iowa U., 1962; cert., The Hague Acad. Internat. Law, The Netherlands, 1965-69; LLM, U. Minn., 1969, Columbia U., 1971, U. Mo., 1976; PMD, Harvard U., 1973; EdM, 1974. Bar: Minn. 1964, U.S. Dist. Ct. Minn. 1964, Wis. 1970, Iowa 1970, U.S. Dist. Ct. (no. dist.) Iowa 1971, U.S. Tax Ct. 1971, U.S. Supreme Ct. 1972, U.S. Dist. Ct. (ea. dist.) Wis. 1981, U.S. Ct. Appeals (8th cir.) 1981. Asst. corp. counsel 1st Bank Stock Corp. (88 Banks), Mpls., 1963-67, 1st Svc. Corp. (27 ins. agys., computer subs.), Mpls., 1965-67; v.p., trust officer Nat. City Bank, Mpls., 1967-69; sr. mem. Torgerson Law Firm, Northwood, Iowa, 1969-87; trustee, gen. counsel Torgerson Farms, Northwood, 1967—, Redbirch Farms, Kensett, Iowa, 1987—2002, Sunburst Farms, Grafton, Iowa, 1987—, Gold Dust Farms, Bolan, Iowa, 1988—, Torgerson Grain Storage, Bolan, 1988—, Indian Summer Farms, Bolan, 1991—, Sunset Farms, Bolan, 1992—, Sunrise Farms, Grafton, 1994—. CEO, gen. counsel Internat. Investments, Mpls., 1983-96, Transoceanic, Mpls., 1987-96, Torgerson Capital, Northwood, 1996—, Torgerson Investments, Northwood, 1984—, Torgerson Properties, Northwood, 1987—, Torgerson Ranches, Sundance, Wyo., 1998—, Hawaiian Investments Unltd., Maui, Hawaii, 1998—, Internat. Investments Unltd., San Pedro, Belize, 1999—. Recipient All-Am. Journalism award Thomas Arkle Clark Outstanding Achievement award, 1958, Dennis E. Brumfield Outstanding Achievement award, 1958, Johnny B. Guy Outstanding Leadership award, 1958; named to Outstanding Young Men of Am., U.S. Jaycees; Hagen scholar, Honor scholar. Mem. ABA, Am. Judicature Soc., Iowa Bar Assn., Minn. Bar Assn., Wis. Bar Assn., Hennepin County Bar Assn., Mensa, Drake Student-Faculty Coun., Drake Student Alumni Coun. (chmn.), Jaycees, Harvard Bus. Sch. Study (pres., exec. com., univ. editor in chief), Psi Chi, Circle K (pres. local chpt.), Phi Alpha Delta, Omicron Delta Kappa (pres. local chpt.), Pi Kappa Delta (pres. local chpt.), Alpha Tau Omega (pres. local chpt., Silver Bullet Outstanding Leadership award, 1965, 66), Pi Delta Epsilon (founder, chpt. pres.), Alpha Kappa Delta, Alpha Scholastic Hon. (U. editor-in-chief), Harvard Bus. Sch. Exec. Com. (U. editor-in-chief). Lutheran.

TORGERSON, LINDA BELLE, music educator; b. Sioux City, Iowa, Dec. 16, 1951; d. Fredric William and Clara Jeanette Wilson; m. Peter Kinsey Torgerson; children: Christopher, Patricia. Diploma, Ctrl. H.S., 1971; MusB Edn., Morningside Coll., 1976; MEd, City U., 1999. Cert. Iowa tchr., tchr. Mont., Washington. Choral dir. First United Meth. Ch., Sioux City, Iowa, 1974—76, First Presbyn. Ch., Kalispell, Mont., 1976—80; pvt. music instr. Self-employed, Kalispell, Mont., 1976—80; music tchr. St. Matthews Sch., Kalispell, Mont., 1976—77; music dir., coord. Flathead County Rural Schools, Kalispell, Mont., 1979—85; music dir. Clarkston Sch. Dist., Clarkston, Wash., 1985—. Treas. Clarkston Edn. Assn., Clarkston, Wash., 1988—90, v.p., 1990—92, Clarkston, 2001—03, pres., 1991—92; sec. Wash. uniserv polit. action com. Wash. Edn. Assn., Olympia, Wash., 1992—93; bldg. rep. Clarkston Edn. Assn., Clarkston, Wash., 1993—94; jazz band dir. Lincoln Mid. Sch., Clarkston, Wash., 1996—2003; bldg. rep. Clarkston Edn. Assn., Clarkston, Wash., 2000—01, v.p., 2001—03; co-director for asotin county teens against smoking Asotin County Devel. Services, Clarkston, Wash., 2001—02. Singer (composer): (commercial) Flathead County Milk Music Ad for the Radio, 1978; contbr. articles to profl. jours. Mem. U-Pac bd. for SE Wash. Edn. Assn., Kennewick, Wash., 1992—93. Grantee Dist., Clarkston Sch. Dist., 1994, 1995. Mem.: NEA, Clarkston Edn. Assn. (v.p. 2001), Clarkston Edn. Assn. (bldg. rep. 1992—94), Clarkston Edn. Assn. (pres./past pres. 1991—92), Clarkston Edn. Assn. (v.p. 1989—91), Clarkston Edn. Assn. (treas. 1987—89), SE Wash. Music Educators Assn. (pres. 2002—04), Wash. Music Educators Assn., Music Educators Nat. Conf. Home: 1505 8th St Clarkston WA 99403 Office: Lincoln Mid Sch 1945 4th Ave Clarkston WA 99403 Office Phone: 509-758-5506 x5245. Personal E-mail: torgersons@cableone.net. Business E-Mail: torgersonl@csdk12.org.

TORGERSON, WILLIAM T., lawyer, electric power industry executive; b. Annapolis, Md., May 29, 1944; s. Theodore A. and Augusta (Melvin) T.; m. Maureen Glynis Reynolds, Apr. 19, 1994; 1 child, John Theodore. AB, Princeton U., 1966; JD with honors, U. Md., 1973. Atty. Hogan & Hartson, Washington, 1973-82; various Potomac Electric Power Co., Washington, 1982-89, v.p., gen. counsel, 1989-94, sr. v.p., gen. counsel, 1994—; vice chmn., gen. counsel Pepco Holdings Inc. (formerly Potomac Electric Power Co.), Washington, 2003—. Bd. dirs. Leadership Md. Lt. USN, 1966-70, Vietnam. Decorated Bronze Star (2). Office: Potomac Electric Power Co Ste 1100 701 Ninth St NW Washington DC 20068 *

TORGOW, EUGENE N., electrical engineer; b. Bronx, NY, Nov. 26, 1925; s. Frank and Blanche Anita (Revzin) T.; m. Cynthia Silver, Mar. 19, 1950; children: Joan, Martha, Ellen. BSEE, Cooper Union, 1946; MSEE, Poly. Inst. Bklyn., 1949; Engr. in E.E., Poly. Inst. N.Y., 1980; postgrad., UCLA, 1983. Rsch. assoc., sect. leader Microwave Rsch. Inst., Poly. Inst. Bklyn., 1947-51, 53-60, instr., 1954-59; mgr. microwave lab. A.B. Dumont Labs, East Patterson, NJ, 1951-53; chief engr., mgr. microwave products Dorne & Magolin, Inc., Westbury, L.I., NY, 1960-64; chief engr., dir. rsch., dir. mktg. Rantec divsn. Emerson Electric, Calabasas, Calif., 1964-68; with Missle Sys. Group, Hughes Aircraft Co., Canoga Park, Calif., 1968-85, assoc. labs. mgr., 1981-85. Cons. various electronics firms, N.Y.C., 1956-59; cons., 1986—; cons. Exec. Svc. Corps of So. Calif., 1996—; pres. Cons. Adv. Coun., 1999-2000; lectr. Calif. State U., Northridge, 1986-91. Contbr. articles to profl. jours.; patentee in field. Mem. Fair Housing Coun. San Fernando Valley, LA, 1967—, L.A. Co. Mus. Assn., 1976—2001. With USAAC, 1946—47. Recipient Engr. '85 Merit award San Fernando Valley Engrs. Coun., 1985. Fellow IEEE (life), Inst. Advancement of Engring.; mem. WINCON (bd. dirs. 1984-89, chmn. bd. dirs. 1988-89), Microwave Theory and Techniques Soc. of IEEE (pres. 1966, mem. adminstrn. com. 1962-72, Svc. award 1978), Accreditation Bd. Engring. and Tech. (mem. engring. accreditation com. 1994-99), Amiotropic Lateral Sclerosis Assn. (trustee greater L.A. chpt. 1999-2004, adv. trustee 2004-06), Hughes Mgmt. Club (edn. chmn. 1979-80), Sigma Xi. Democrat. Office: 9531 Donna Ave Northridge CA 91324-1816

TORKELSON, ANDREW THOMAS, cardiologist; b. Schenectady, NY, Dec. 11, 1953; MD, U. Rochester Sch. Medicine, NY, 1980. Cert. Internal Medicine, 1983, Cardiovascular Disease, 1985. Resident, internal medicine Dartmouth-Hitchcock Med. Ctr., Hanover, NH, 1980—83, fellow, cardiology, 1983—85, joined, 1985—, dir., cardiac rehabilitation, asst. prof. medicine, staff physician, sect. cardiology. Office: Dartmouth-Hitchcock Med Ctr Cardiology One Medical Ctr Dr Lebanon NH 03756 Office Phone: 603-650-7756, 603-526-5162. Office Fax: 603-650-5267, 603-650-6164. *

TORME, MARGARET ANNE, public relations executive, management consultant; b. Indpls., Apr. 5, 1943; d. Ira G. and Margaret Joy (Wright) Barker; children: Karen Anne, Leah Vanessa. Student, Coll. San Mateo, 1961—65. Pub. rels. mgr. Hoefer, Dieterich & Brown (now Chiat-Day), San Francisco, 1964-73; v.p., co-founder, creative dir. Lowry & Ptnrs., San Francisco, 1975-83; pres., founder Torme and Lauricella Comm., San Francisco, 1983—. Cons. in comm. Mem. Coun. Pub. Rels. Firms, Jr. League (adv. bd.), Pub. Rels. Orgn. Internat. Office: 847 Sansome St San Francisco CA 94111-2908 Office Phone: 415-956-1791. Business E-Mail: margaret@torme.com.

TORMEY, BRIAN B., environmental geomorphologist, aerial mapping consultant; b. S.I., NY, Oct. 8, 1940; s. Bertram M. and Margaret J. Tormey; m. Judith E. Anderson; children: Jennifer E., Brett B., Blair R., Megan A. AAS in Agrl. Scis., SUNY, Morrisville, 1960; BS in Sci. Edn., Western Conn. U., 1964; postgrad., U. Md., 1964—66, Am. U., Washington, DC, 1965—66; DEd in Earth Scis., Pa. State U., 1980. Earth and space scis. tchr. State College Area Schs., Pa., 1968—81; asst. prof. environ. scis. Pa. State U., Altoona, 1981—92, assoc. prof. environ. scis., 1991—. CEO, cons. StoneView Earth Sys. Rsch., Huntingdon, Pa., 2000—; owner, mgr. Hostetler Airport, Jackson Twp., Pa., 2000—; co-owner StoneView Farm, Huntingdon, 2000—; presenter in field. Editor: (textbook) Field Techniques: Atlantic Barrier System, 1984, (guidebook) Central Appalachian Processes, 1990, Iceland - Hot Spot on the Edge of the Arctic, 1994; contbr. more than 100 papers and presentations. Mem., asst. chmn., chmn. Ferguson Twp. Authority, 1989—99; pres., chmn. bd. dirs. Brett B. Tormey Found. Inc., Huntingdon, 1997—; discipline coord. Environ. Earth Sys. Scis.; mem. exec. bd. Juniata Valley coun. Boy Scouts Am., 2005—; mem. Rep. County Com., Huntingdon County, 2003—; bd. dirs. Pa. Earth Scis. Field Sch. Recipient cert. achievement, Pa. Dept. Edn., 1985. Mem.: Geol. Soc. Am. (mem. ednl. initiatives 1992—96, chmn.), Nat. Assn. Geosci. Tchrs. (mem. coun. 1991—94, 2d v.p. 1991—92, 1st v.p. 1992—93, pres. 1993—94, pres. ea. sect. 1993, Outstanding Earth Scis. Tchr. 1980, Disting. Svc. award 2000), Pa. Sci. Tchrs. Assn. (bd. dirs. 1981—96). Roman Catholic. Achievements include research in glacial/periglacial geomorphology. Avocation: breeding and showing Kerry Blue Terriers. Office: Pa State U Altoona Coll Ivyside Dr Altoona PA 16601 Home: 4916 Standing Stone Rd Huntingdon PA 16652 Business E-Mail: stoneview@pennswoods.net.

TORN, RIP (ELMORE RUAL TORN JR.), actor, theater director; b. Temple, Tex., Feb. 6, 1931; s. Elmore and Thelma (Spacek) T.; m. Ann Wedgeworth, Jan. 15, 1955 (div. 1961); 1 child, Danae; m. Geraldine Page, 1963 (div. June 13, 1987); children: Angelica, Anthony, Jonathan; m. Amy Wright. Grad., Tex. A & M U., 1952. Performances include: (stage) Cat on a Hot Tin Roof, 1955, Orpheus Descending, 1958, Chaparral, 1958 (Theatre World award 1959), Sweet Bird of Youth, 1959, on tour, 1960, Daughter of Silence, 1961, Macbeth, 1962, Desire Under the Elms, 1963, Strange Interlude, 1963, Blues for Mr. Charlie, 1964, The Kitchen, 1966, The Country Girl, 1966, The Deer Park, 1967 (Obie award), The Cuban Thing, 1968, The Honest-to-God Schnozzola, 1969, Dream of a Blacklisted Actor, 1969, The Dance of Death, 1970-71, The Marriage Proposal, 1971, Marriage and Money, 1971, Barbary Shore, The Little Foxes, 1974, The Father, 1975, The Glass Menagerie, 1975, Fever for Life, 1975, Creditors, 1977, Night Shift, 1977, Seduced, 1979, Anna Christie, 1992; (motion pictures) Baby Doll, 1956, A Face in the Crowd, 1957, Time Limit, 1957, Pork Chop Hill, 1959, King of Kings, 1961, Hero's Island, 1962, Sweet Bird of Youth, 1962, Critic's Choice, 1963, The Cincinnati Kid, 1965, One Spy Too Many, 1966, Beach Red, 1967, You're a Big Boy Now, 1967, Beyond the Law, 1968, Sol Madrid, 1968, Coming Apart, 1969, Tropic of Cancer, 1970, Slaughter, 1972, Payday, 1973, Crazy Joe, 1974, Birch Interval, 1976, Maidstone, The Man Who Fell to Earth, 1976, Nasty Habits, 1977, Coma, 1978, The Seduction of Joe Tynan, 1979, First Family, 1980, Heartland, 1980, One Trick Pony, 1980, Jinxed, 1982, Airplane II: The Sequel, 1982, The Beastmaster, 1982, A Stranger is Watching, 1982, Cross Creek, 1983, City Heat, 1984, Misunderstood, 1984, Night Shadows, 1984, Song Writer, 1984, Flashpoint, 1984, Summer Rental, 1985, Beer, 1985, Extreme Prejudice, 1987, Defending Your Life, 1991, Beautiful Dreamers, 1992, Hard Promises, 1992, Robocop 3, 1993, Where the Rivers Flow North, 1994, How to Make an American Quilt, 1995, Down Periscope, 1996, Trial and Error, 1997, Men in Black, 1997, Hercules, 1997, The Mouse, 1997, Senseless, 1998, Wonder Boys, 2000, Men in Black Alien Attack, 2000, Men in Black II, 2002, Rolling Kansas, 2003, Welcome to Mooseport, 2004, Dodgeball: A True Underdog Story, 2004, Eulogy, 2004, Forty Shades of Blue, 2005, Yours, Mine and Ours, 2005, Marie Antoinette, 2006, Zoom, 2006; (TV films and miniseries) Two Plays, 1971, The President's Plane Is Missing, 1973, The FBI Versus the Ku Klux Klan, 1975, Song of Myself, 1976, Betrayal, 1976, The Gift of Love, 1978, Blind Ambition, 1979, A Shining Season, 1979, Sophia Loren: Her Own Story, 1980, Rape and Marriage: The Rideout Case, 1980, The Blue and the Gray, 1982, When She Says No, 1984, Dream West, 1986, April Morning, 1988, Sweet Bird of Youth, 1989, By Dawn's Early Light, 1990, Another Pair of Aces: Three of a Kind, 1991, My Son Johnny, 1991, Death Hits the Jackpot, 1991, T-Bone and Weasel, 1992, Dead Ahead: The Exxon Valdez Disaster, 1992, A Mother's Right: The Elizabeth Morgan Story, 1993, The Almost Perfect Bank Robbery, 1996, Seasons of Love, 1998, Passing Glory, 1999, Balloon Farm, 1999, A Vision of Murder: The Story of Donielle, 2000, Maniac Magee, 2003, The Lyon's Denn, 2003; (TV series) The Larry Sanders Show, HBO, 1992-98 (Emmy nominee for best supporting actor 1993, 94, Cable Ace award for best supporting actor 1994), Ghost Stories, 1997 (narrator); dir. plays: The Beard, 1968 (Obie award), Look Away, 1973. Mem. AFTRA, SAG, Actors Equity Assn., Actors' Studio (bd. dirs., prodn. bd., 1st chmn. founding com.), Dirs. Guild Am. *

TORNABENE, RUSSELL C., communications executive; b. Gary, Ind., Sept. 18, 1923; s. Samuel Tornabene and Marion LaVorci Roush; m. Audrey F. Shankey, June 21, 1952; children: Joseph, Leigh, David, Lynn. AA, Gary Jr. Coll., 1941, 46-47; BA, Ind. U., 1949, MA, 1950. Radio, TV newswriter WRC-AM-TV, Washington, 1951-55; network supr. NBC Network News, Washington, 1955-61, network gen. mgr. NYC, 1961-75; v.p. NBC News, NYC, 1975-81; exec. officer Soc. Profl. Journalists, Chgo., 1981-87; Midwest dir. Exec. TV Workshop, Chgo., 1987-96; pres. Russell Communications Cons., 1996—. Bd. dirs. LifeLine Pilots. Contbr. articles on news to mags. and newspapers. Mem. N.Y. Catholic Archdiocese Sch. Bd., N.Y.C., 1972 Recipient Disting. Service award, Sigma Delta Chi, 1949; Ernie Pyle scholar, 1949 Mem. Acad. TV Arts and Scis., Radio TV News Dirs. Assn., Overseas Press Club (former v.p.). Avocation: photography. Office: 626 Sheridan Sq Apt 2 Evanston IL 60202

TORNOW, L. WILLIAM, musician; b. Devils Lake, ND, Feb. 1, 1949; s. E. Edward and Ellen Naomi Tornow. BMus in Pub. Sch. Music, Concordia Coll., Moorhead, Minn., 1971; MA in Music, Trinity U., San Antonio, 1978; DMA in Piano Performance, U. Minn., Mpls., 1983. Artist in residence Cmty. Music Ctr., Fargo, ND, 1978—79; organist Our Saviour's Evang. Luth. Ch., Cannon Falls, Minn., 1984—85, St. George's Episc. Meml. Ch., Bismarck, ND, 1985—86. Composer: Elegy, 1971, Symphony No. 1 for Chamber Orch., 1989, Overture to Spring on Themes of Beethoven for orchestra, 1998, Symphony No. 2 for Piano and Orch., 2002, Symphony No. 3 on Four Hymn Tunes, 2006. Spl. 4 (E-4) US Army, 1971—74, Germany and Tex. Fellow: Nat. Music Tchrs. Assn.; mem.: Am. Guild of Organists. Avocations: fishing, golf. Home and Studio: 1107 W Capitol Ave Apt 62 Bismarck ND 58501

TORNQVIST, ERIK GUSTAV MARKUS, chemical engineer, research scientist, consultant; b. Lund, Sweden, Jan. 13, 1924; came to U.S., 1951; s. Gustav Ivar and Anne Marie (Lassen) T.; m. Linnéa Dagmar Lindborg, June 28, 1969; children: Gunvor, Karin, Carl-Erik. MSChemE, Royal Inst. Tech., Stockholm, 1948; MS in Biochemistry, U. Wis., 1953, PhD in Biochemistry/Organic Chemistry, 1955. Registered engr., Sweden. 1st rsch. asst. divsn. food chemistry Royal Inst. Tech., 1949—51; rsch. asst. dept.

biochemistry U. Wis., Madison, 1951—55; rsch. chemist chem. divsn. Esso Rsch. and Engring. Co., Linden, NJ, 1955—58, rsch. assoc., 1958—66, sr. rsch. assoc., 1966—72, Exxon Chem. Co., Tech., Linden, NJ, 1972—86; internat. cons. Watchung, NJ, 1986—90, 2003—; pres. PolymErik, Inc., Watchung, 1990—2003. Vis prof. Royal Inst. Tech., 1987; invited prin. speaker Scandinavian Day, Chautauqua (N.Y.) Instn., 1983, 87; invited speaker, chmn. numerous nat. and internat. meetings. Co-editor: Polymer Chemistry of Synthetic Elastomers, 2 vols., 1968, 69; patentee in field; contbr. articles to profl. jours., chpts. to books. Treas. United Swedish Socs., N.Y.C., 1972-86, Swedish Sch. Assn. N.J., 1988-91; bd. govs. Am. Swedish Hist. Mus., Phila., 1974-89; trustee New Sweden Co., Bridgeton, N.J., 1986-89, Kalmar Nyckel Found., Wilmington, Del., 1987-96, hon. trustee, 1996; bd. dirs. Watchung Hills Soccer Assn., Watchung/Warren, N.J., 1989-95. Recipient award 1st Nat. Inventors Day, 1973, gold Bicentennial medal King of Sweden, 1980, John Hanson award for excellence in pub. svc. Am.-Swedish Cultural Found., Mpls., 1981, citation Swedish Coun. of Am., 1983, cert. of appreciation Swedish New Sweden '88 Com., 1989; grad. fellow Roos' Found., Stockholm, 1949, 51, Govt. of Sweden, 1948, State Coun. for Technol. Rsch., Stockholm, 1949, Adelsköld fellow Royal Acad. Sci., 1951, 53, Univ. fellow Sweden-Am. Found., Stockholm, 1951. Fellow: Swedish Colonial Soc. (gov. 1977—82, hon. gov. Ad Vitam 1982, gov. 1986—89); mem.: John Ericsson Soc., Internat. Union Pure and Applied Chemistry (affiliate), Swedish Assn. Grad. Engrs., Am. Soc. Swedish Engrs. (life; sec. 1965—68, pres. 1968—72, John Ericsson Gold medal 1984), Swedish Soc. Chem. Engrs., Am. Chem. Soc., NY Acad. Scis., Schlaraffia, Wis. Alumni Assn. (life), Svensk I Varlden (life), Am.-Scandinavian Soc., KTH Alumni, Swedish-Am. C. of C., Swedish Ski Club (pres. 1972—74), Vasa Order Am. (co-cultural leader NJ Dist. 6, 1997, chmn. Lodge Skandia 2000—05), Sigma Xi, Phi Lambda Upsilon. Lutheran. Achievements include invention and development of numerous catalysts for polymerization of olefins and dienes, especially the catalyst for making most of the isotactic polypropylene over a period of more than 20 years (from about 1958) and still in large-scale use, having resulted in production of billions of dollars worth of polymer, also, elucidation of many aspects of the mode of action of these and other catalysts and the preparation of numerous novel polymers. Home and Office: 38 Mareu Dr Watchung NJ 07069-5025 Personal E-mail: erikgmt@yahoo.com.

TORNSTROM, ROBERT ERNEST, lawyer, oil industry executive; b. St. Paul, Jan. 17, 1946; s. Clifford H. and Janet (Hale) T.; m. Betty Jane Hermann, Aug. 5, 1978; children: Carter, Gunnar, Katherine. BA, U. Colo., 1968, JD, 1974; diploma grad. sch. mgmt. exec. program, UCLA, 1990. Bar: Colo. 1974, U.S. Dist. Ct. Colo. 1974, Calif. 1975, U.S. Dist. Ct. (cen. dist.) Calif. 1975. Atty. Union Oil Co. of Calif., LA, 1974-76, counsel internat. div., 1977-78, regional counsel Singapore, 1976-77; sr. atty. Occidental Internat. Exploration and Prodn. Co., Bakersfield, Calif., 1978-81, mng. counsel, 1981-85, v.p., assoc. gen. counsel, 1985-88, v.p., regional ops. mgr., 1988-91; pres. Occidental Argentina, Buenos Aires, 1991-93, Occidental of Russia, Moscow, 1993-94; dir. comml. negotiations Occidental Internat., 1994-96; chmn. of bd. Sullivan Petroleum Co., 1997—. Bd. dir. and chmn. bd. Parmaneft Joint Venture, Vanyogannef JV, Moscow; bd. dir. Calif. Land and Cattle Co., King City, 602 Operating Corp.; legal cons. Island Creek Coal Co., Lexington, Ky. Exec. bd. Cmty. Ho., Bakersfield; pres. Snowbird Assn., Mammoth Lakes. Capt. US Army, 1968—71, Vietnam. Decorated Bronze Star. Mem. Am. Soc. Internat. Law, Am. Corp. Counsel Assn., Soc. Mayflower Descendants, Moscow Country Club, Stockdale Country Club (bd. dirs.). Republican. Episcopalian. Avocations: skiing, tennis, golf, riding, collecting classic automobiles. Home: 310 Mount Lowe Dr Bakersfield CA 93309-2468 Office: 1508 18th St Ste 222 Bakersfield CA 93301 Office Phone: 661-327-5008.

TORO, JORGE R., dermatologist, researcher; b. Mayaguez, PR, Dec. 26, 1966; s. Jorge R. Toro and Carmen N. Rodriguez. Degree, Cornell U., Ithaca, NY, 1988; MD, SUNY, Buffalo, 1992. Diplomate Am. Bd. Dermatology, 1997. Rsch. assoc. Nat. Cancer Inst., Bethesda, Md., 1997—2001; prin. investigator Genetic Epidemiology Br., Nat. Cancer Inst., Rockville, Md., 2001—. Comdr. USPHS, 1997—2006. Recipient Juan Finlay award, USPHS, 2002, Dir.'s award, Nat. Cancer Inst., 2005. Fellow: Am. Acad. Dermatology (licentiate Young Investigator Award 2000). Achievements include invention of. Home: 4706 17th ST NW Washington DC 02011 Office: Nat Cancer Inst 6120 Executive Blvd EPS 7012 Rockville MD 20852 Business E-Mail: toroj@mail.nih.gov.

TORPEY, SCOTT RAYMOND, lawyer; b. Detroit, July 4, 1955; s. Raymond George and Carmela Rose (Aquaro) T. BA in English, Wayne State U., 1978; JD, U. Detroit, 1982. Bar: Mich. 1984, D.C. 1985, N.Y. 1990, Ill. 1990, Calif. 1991, U.S. Dist. Ct. (ea. and we. dist.) Mich., U.S. Dist. Ct. (so., we., no. and ea. dists.) N.Y. 1990, U.S. Dist. Ct. (no., cen. and so. dists.) Ill. 1990, U.S. Dist. Ct. (D.C. dist.) 1989, U.S. Dist. Ct. (cen., so., no. and ea. dists.) Calif., 1991, U.S. Tax Ct., U.S. Ct. Appeals (D.C., fed., 2d, 6th, 7th and 9th cirs.), U.S. Supreme Ct. 1988. Litigation ptnr. Jaffe, Raitt, Heuer and Weiss, PC, Detroit, 2000—; assoc. Long & Levit, San Francisco, 1982-83, Keating, Canham & Wells, Detroit, 1983-85; litigation ptnr. Kohl, Secrest, Wardle, Lynch, Clark & Hampton, Farmington Hills, Mich., 1985-2000. Editor Tax Law Jour., 1981, Corp., Fin. and Bus. Law Jour., 1982. Mem. ABA, Fed. Bar Assn., Lawyer-Pilots Bar Assn., Bar Assn. San Francisco, Mich. State Bar Assn. (chmn. aviation torts com. of aviation law sect. 1992—). Republican. Avocations: sports, music, sports cars. Office: Jaffe Raitt Heuer & Weiss 27777 Franklin Rd 2500 Southfield MI 48034-8214 Office Phone: 248-351-3000.

TORQUATO, SALVATORE, materials scientist, chemistry professor; b. Falerna, Calabria, Italy, Feb. 10, 1954; came to U.S., 1955; s. Vincent and Palma (Vaccaro) T.; m. Kim Tracey Hoberock, Nov. 8, 1975; children: Michelle, Lisa. BSME, Syracuse U., 1975; MSME, SUNY, Stony Brook, 1977, PhD in Mech. Engring., 1980. Rsch. engr. Grumman Aerospace Corp., Bethpage, NY, 1975-78; rsch. asst. dept. mech. engring. SUNY, Stony Brook, 1978-80; asst. prof. dept. mech. engring. GM Inst., Flint, Mich., 1981-82; from asst. to assoc. prof. depts. mech., aerospace & chem. engring. N.C. State U., Raleigh, 1982-90, prof. depts. mech., aerospace & chem. engring., 1991-92; prof. Civil Engring. Princeton (N.J.) U., 1992-99, prof. chemistry, 2000—. Vis. prof. Courant Inst. Math. Scis., N.Y.C., 1990-91; cons. Eastman Kodak, Rochester, N.Y., 1989—; mem. Inst. Advanced Study, 1998-99. Contbr. articles to profl. jours. Grumman Masters fellow, 1975-77; fellow Guggenheim, 1998; recipient Engring. Rsch. Achievement award Alcoa Co., 1987, Disting. Engring. Rsch. award, 1989, Gustus L. Larson Meml. award, 1994. Fellow ASME Am. Phys. Soc.; mem. Am. Inst. Chem. Engrs., Soc. Engring. Sci. (Charles Russ Richards Meml. award, 2002, William Prager medal, 2004), Soc. for Indsl. and Applied Math. Avocations: racquetball, reading, music. Office: Princeton U Princeton Materials Inst Dept Chemistry Princeton NJ 08544-0001

TORRACO, PAMELA LOUISE, psychotherapist; b. Mineola, NY, Feb. 22, 1944; d. Peter and Willamy King Torraco. BA, Wittenberg U., Springfield, Ohio, 1965; MSW, U. Mich., Ann Arbor, 1967. Psychiatric social worker Henry Ford Hosp., Detroit, 1967—69; prin. social caseworker Detroit Health Dept., 1969—72; group & individual psychotherapist Dr. Reuven Bar-Levav & Assoc., PC, Southfield, Mich., 1971—; social worker Kingswood Hosp., Ferndale, Mich., 1972—75. Presenter, panelist in field, 1975—; pres., faculty mem. The Inst. Individual & Group Psychotherapy, Southfield, 1978—; program chair Mich. Group Psychotherapy Soc., Detroit, 1982—84, pres., Southfield, 1984—86. Contbr. articles to profl. jours. Sec. Bar-Levav Family Found., Southfield, 1999—. Mem.: Mich. Group Psychotherapy Soc., Am. Group Psychotherapy Assn., Nat. Assn. Social Workers. Independent. Jewish. Avocations: hiking, music, travel, languages. Office: Dr Reuven Bar-Levav & Assocs PC 29600 Northwestern Hwy Ste 100 Southfield MI 48034 Office Phone: 248-353-0050. Personal E-mail: pamtor@sbcglobal.net.

TORRAS, JOSEPH HILL, pulp and paper company executive; b. Americus, Ga., Nov. 14, 1924; s. Fernando Joseph and Nell Wilson (Hill) T.; m. Mary Ravenel Robertson, Sept. 20, 1952; children: Mary Martin, Fernanda Maria, Joseph Hill. S.B., Yale U., 1948; MBA, Harvard U., 1950; D in Bus. Adminstrn., Piedmont Coll., 1997. Asst. to fin. v.p. Seatrian Lines, Inc., 1950—51; with St. Regis Paper Co., 1951—60, sales mgr. printing papers div., 1956—60; exec. v.p. Brown Co., Boston, 1960—64; pres., chmn. bd. Premoid Corp., West Springfield, Mass., 1964—87; pres. Precon, Inc., Ludlow, 1967—87, Astro Tissue Co., Battleboro, Vt., 1968—72; chmn. bd. Whitman Products, Ltd., West Warwick, RI, 1976—89; pres., CEO, Preco Corp., Amherst, Mass., 1976—98; chmn., CEO Lincoln Pulp & Paper Co., Lincoln, Maine, 1968—2004, Eastern Fine Paper, Inc., Brewer, Maine, 1989—2004. CEO, Shelburne Corp., 1999—; adv. dir. Liberty Mut. Ins. Mem. Mass. Gov.'s Bus. Adv. Coun., 1985—89; devel. bd. Yale U.; bd. govs. Mass. Gen. Hosp., 1985—96; bd. dirs. Mass. Taxpayers Assn., 1976—86; trustee Hist. Deerfield, 1990—2004, Piedmont Coll., Ga., 1991—99; dir. Inst. of World Politics, 1990—. Lt. (j.g.) aviator USNR, 1943—46. Mem. Tissue Paper Mfrs. Assn. (dir. 1963-64), Am. Pulp and Paper Mill Supts. Assn., Salesman's Assn. Paper Industry, NAM (dir. 1981-85), Colony Club, Carolina Yacht Club, Yale Club (NYC). Home: 264 Bardwells Ferry Rd Shelburne Falls MA 01370-9744

TORRE, GARY JEROME, retired lawyer; b. Oakland, Calif., Oct. 14, 1919; s. Giove M. and Jessie (Garibotto) Torre; m. Carol Desaussiere Goodrich, Dec. 25, 1948; children: Michael Durham, Alicia Hayden, Nicholas Goodrich. BA, U. Calif., 1941, JD, 1948. Bar: Calif. Law clerk Justice William Douglas, Wash., DC, 1948—49; ptnr. Litlick, Geary, Wheat, Adams and Charles, San Francisco, 1949—81; ret., 1981. Lt. USAF, 1942—45. Mem.: Sierra Club (pres., dir. legal defense fund 1968—93). Democrat.

TORRE, JOE (JOSEPH PAUL TORRE), professional baseball team manager; b. Bklyn., July 18, 1940; s. Joseph Sr. & Margaret Torre; m. Ali Torre, Aug. 23, 1987; one child, Andrea Rea; children from previous marriages: Michael, Lauren, Tina. HHD (hon.), Rider U., 2006. Profl. baseball player Milw. Braves, 1960-69, St. Louis Cardinals, 1969-74, NY Mets, 1974-77, player-mgr., 1977-82; mgr. Atlanta Braves, 1982-84; TV broadcaster Calif. Angels, 1984-90; mgr. St. Louis Cardinals, 1990-94, NY Yankees, 1995—. Co-founder (with Ali Torre) Joe Torre Safe at Home Found., 2002—. Author: (novels) Chasing the Dream: My Lifelong Journey to the World Series, 1997, Joe Torre's Ground Rules for Winners: 12 Keys to Managing Team Players, Tough Bosses, Setbacks, and Success, 1999; actor: (films) Taking Care of Business, 1990, Analyze That, 2002, (voice) Everyone's Hero, 2006. Named Nat. League's Most Valuable Player, 1971, Player of Yr., Sporting News, 1971, Mgr. of Yr., 1982, 1996, 1998; named to All-Star Team, 1963-67, 70-73, coach 1997, 1999-2002, 2004; recipient Gold Glove award, 1965; hit for cycle, 1973; winner World Series N.Y. Yankees, 1996, 1998, 1999, 2000. over 1,000 career wins, 2006; four world championships. Office: New York Yankees Yankee Stadium E 161 St & River Ave Bronx NY 10451

TORRENCE-THOMPSON, JUANITA LEE, editor, public relations executive; b. Brockton, Mass., Nov. 08; d. James Lee Torrence and Zylpha Odyselle Mapp-Robinson; m. Hugh Warren Thompson, Dec. 19, 1965; 1 child, Derek Rush. BS in Bus. & Comm., Empire State Coll., Old Westbury, NY, 1983; MA in Comm., Fordham U., 1989. Newsletter editor UN Internat. Sch., 1976-77; pub. rels., editl. asst. Nat. Assn. Theatre Owners, 1979-80; asst. acct. exec. Richard Weiner, Inc., 1984; newsletter editor SUNY Empire State Coll., 1985-87; editor Dorf & Stanton Comm., Inc., 1987-88; pub. rels. exec. pvt. practice, 1988—2006; editor, pub., owner Mobius, The Poetry Mag., 2006—. Adj. prof. pub. rels. Coll. New Rochelle, N.Y., 1997. Author: Spanning The Years, Wings Span to Eternity, Celebrating a Tapestry of Life; poetry columnist, 2004—; contbr. articles, poems, short stories, essays to mags., newspapers, newsletters and children's poetry (as Micki Caldwell Nixon, Jr.). Bd. dirs So. Queens Park Assn., Jamaica, N.Y., 1988-91; mem. parent faculty soc. UN Internat. Sch., N.Y.C., 1976-80; pub. rels. cons. UN Coll. Fund, N.Y.C., 1994; mem. Queens Coun. on the Arts. Recipient Feature Article award Writers Digest, 1985, Meritorious Svc. award United Negro Coll. Fund, 1994, Editors Choice award Nashville Newsletter, 1994, 2004, Robins Nest Mag., 1996, First prize NY Pub. Libr. Contest, 1996, Outstanding Achievement award SUNY, Empire State Coll., Old Westbury, Margaret A. Walker Short Story Competition award 1999, 2000, 2d prize in 3 categories Internat. Poetry award Poetry Soc. Mich., HM award in short story competition, award Ky. Poetry Soc. Mem. AAUW, Nat. Assn. Black Journalists, Poetry Soc. Am., Acad. Am. Poets, Black Ams. in Pub., Poets and Writers, Queens Coun. on the Arts, Fresh Meadows Poets. Avocations: travel, theater, films, opera, concerts. Office: PO Box 671058 Flushing NY 11367-1058 E-mail: poetrytown@earthlink.net.

TORRENZANO, RICHARD, public relations executive; BS, NY Inst. Tech., Old Westbury, 1972, LittD (hon.), 1990; postgrad. Exec. Program, Stanford Univ., Calif., 1986. With NY Stock Exch., 1982—90, sr. v.p., mgmt. and exec. com., chief spokesman; sr. v.p., dir. corp. affairs, mgmt. com. SmithKline Beecham, London, 1990—94; chmn., CEO Torrenzano Group, NYC, 1995—. Coord. Pres. Reagan's Bd. Advisors on Pvt. Sector Initiatives, Washington, 1986—89; pvt. sector adv. com. USIA, Washington, 1983—92; coord. program USSR-USA Conf. on Stock Markets, Moscow, 1990, PRC-USA Conf. on Stock Markets, Beijing, 1986; lectr. in field. Contbr. articles to profl. journals. Trustee, mem. exec. com. NY Inst. Tech., 1985—. Decorated knight of Malta, knight comdr. Order of Holy Sepulchre, Order of Sts. Maurice and Lazarus, Royal House of Savoy, knight comdr. jus patronato Sacred Constantinian Order St. George, knight comdr. Constantinian Order of St. George, Royal Order of Francis I, Royal House of Bornone, knight Order of Merit Republic of Italy; recipient Ellis Island Medal of Honor, 1997, Silver anvil, Pub. Rels. Soc. Am. Mem.: Royal Soc. Medicine (London), NY Press Club, Nat. Press Club, Washington, DC. Office: The Torrenzano Group 509 Madison Ave 9th Fl New York NY 10022 Office Phone: 212-681-1700. Office Fax: 212-681-6961. Business E-Mail: richard@torrenzano.com.

TORRES, CYNTHIA ANN, marketing professional; b. Glendale, Calif., Sept. 24, 1958; d. Adolph and Ruth Ann (Smith) T.; m. Michael Victor Gisser, Mar. 11, 1989; children: Spencer Williams Gisser, David Westfall Torres Gisser. AB, Harvard U./Radcliffe Coll., 1980; MBA, Harvard U., 1984. Rsch. assoc. Bain & Co., Boston, 1980-82; assoc. Goldman, Sachs & Co., NYC, 1984-88, v.p., 1988, First Interstate Bancorp, LA, 1989—92; dir. Fidelity Investments Mgmt. Ltd., Hong Kong, 1993-96; pres. Integrity Investments Consultants, Ltd., 1996—99; dir. mktg. Diamond Portfolio Advisors LLC, Santa Monica, Calif., 2000—. Mem. judiciary rev. bd. Bus. Sch. Harvard U., Boston, 1983—84; mem. fin. oversight com. Santa Monica-Malibu Unified Sch. Dist.; chair site governance coun. Franklin Sch. Santa Monica. Rockefeller Found. scholar, 1976; Harvard U. Ctr. for Internat. Affairs fellow, 1979-80; recipient Leadership award Johnson and Johnson, 1980; by Council for Opportunity in Grad. Mgmt. Edn. fellow, 1982-84. Mem.: Fin. Women's Assn. Hong Kong (past pres.), Asia Soc., Acad. Polit. Sci., Harvard Alumni Assn. (chair awards com.), Harvard-Radcliffe Club So. Calif. (pres.). Office: Diamond Portfolio Advisors LLC 10940 Wilshire Blvd Ste 600 Los Angeles CA 90024 Personal E-mail: cynthiatorres@earthlink.net.

TORRES, DALYS E., music educator, consultant; b. Panama, Republic of Panama, Nov. 20, 1948; arrived in U.S., 1970; d. Victor Manuel Torres and Felicidad Bethancourth. Attended, Johnny Colon Sch. Music, 1985—87; studies with Edwina Tyler, 1985—87; BS in Bus. Adminstrn., Boricua Coll., 1986; postgrad. in Bilingual Edn./TESOL (Tchg. English to Students of Other Languages), L.I. U., 1992—94. Eligibility specialist I, translator Spanish/Eng. HRA/Food Stamp Dept. F-14, NYC, 1985—86; eligibility specialist spl. projects HRA/Food Stamp Dept. F-12, NYC, 1986—87; group supr. HRA/Food Stamp Dept. F-16, NYC, 1988—89; classroom bilingual tchr. Bd. Edn. Pub. Sch. 28A Dist. 6, NYC, 1989—92, Bd. Edn. Pub. Sch. 152 Dist. 6, NYC, 1992—95; percussion and creative movement specialist Bd. Edn. Pub. Sch. 27 Dist. 7, Bronx, NY, 1995—98, Bd. Edn. Pub. Sch. 145 Dist. 3, NYC, 2000—; percussion and creative movement instr., cons. and performer, 1992—. Dir. multicultural music activities Pub. Sch. 28A Dist. 6 N.Y.C., 1989—92; percussion specialist N.Y. Pub. Librs., NYC, Bronx, 1993—2000; percussion and creative movement specialist Mich. Internat. Women Music Festival, Grand Rapids, 1998; percussion specialist for HIV Montekiori Hosp./Staten Island Task Force, NYC, Staten Island, 1999; percussion instr. Vision at Selis Manor, NYC, 2002—; marching percussionist Pan-Am. Marching Band, Bklyn., 1999; presenter ann. art edn. conf. Fiorello La Guardia H.S. Arts, 2004. Recipient Cultural Music Contbn. award, UFT/Afro Am. Heritage Com., N.Y.C., 1996, Art Edn. awards, Bravo's 2000 Nat. Awards, N.Y.C., 2000. Roman Catholic. Achievements include design of Percussion and Creative Movement Program for Pub. Sch. at P.S. 27 (Dist. 7); Percussion Program for N.Y. Pub. Libr., 1993-2000; Percussion and Creative Movement for Women, Women with HIV, and Women with Other Diseases, 1999-; Percussion Program for the Blind: Percussion with a Passion at Vision Selis Manor, N.Y.C., 2002-. Avocations: reading, films, rollerskating. Home and Office: 646 9th Ave #5FN New York NY 10036 Office Phone: 212-757-3384. Personal E-mail: panaper81@yahoo.com.

TORRES, DANIEL, literature educator; b. Caguas, PR, Mar. 9, 1961; arrived in U.S., 1984; s. Vicente Torres and Antonia Rodriguez. BA in Comparative Lit., U. P.R., Rio Piedras, 1984; MA in L.Am. Poetry, SUNY, Stony Brook, 1986; PhD in L.Am. Baroque, U. Cin., 1990. Tchg. asst. SUNY, Stony Brook, 1984—86, U. Cin., 1986—88; instr. Ohio State U., Columbus, 1988—90; prof. Ohio U., Athens, 1990—. Author Moriras si da una primavera novels; contbg. editor: Cin. Roman Langs. Rev., 1990—, Chasqui: L.Am. Rev., 2000—, author poetry and criticism. Activitst, bd. mem. United Campus Ministry, Athens, Ohio, 1993—2003. Named Book of Yr., Pen Club, P.R., 1990. Mem.: MLA, Internat. Inst. Iberoamerican Lit., L.Am. Studies Assn. Avocations: reading, dance, travel, music, driving. Office: Ohio U Modern Langs 283 Gordy Hall Athens OH 45701 Office Phone: 740-593-2769. Office Fax: 740-593-0729. Business E-Mail: torres@ohio.edu.

TORRES, DARA, Olympic athlete; b. Beverly Hills, Calif., Apr. 15, 1967; Degree in broadcasting, U. Fla. Intern CNN and NBC Sports; commentator TV sports NBC, ESPN, TNT, Fox News, Fox Sports; ret. swimmer TV reporter: Good Morning America, Inside Edition; host Oxygen Sports. Olympic team capt., 1992; spokesperson Tae Bo workout tapes. Host sci. and tech. show Discovery Channel. Recipient Gold medal (2) 4 x 100-meter freestyle, 4 x 100-meter medley (team), Bronze medal (3) 50 and 100-meter freestyle, 100-meter fly Sydney Olympics, 2000, Gold medal 100-meter freestyle, 4 x 100-meter freestyle, 4 x 100-meter relay (team) Pan Pacific Championships, 1987, Gold medal 4 x 100-meter freestyle relay (team) L.A. Games, 1984, Bronze medal 4 x 100-meter freestyle relay (team), Silver medal 4 x 100-meter medley (team), 1988, Gold medal 4 x 100-meter free relay (team) Barcelona Olympics, 1992; 12-time nat. champion; former world-record holder 50-meter freestyle, Am.-record holder 50-meter freestyle and 100-meter fly, 1991 Summer Nationals Kiphuth award, 1991, Summer Nationals Comeback award Achievements include first American female to swim in four Olympics, five time US Open champion, seven time National A team member, two time All Star team. Office: USA Swimming 1 Olympic Plz Colorado Springs CO 80909-5746

TORRES, ERNEST C., federal judge; b. 1941; AB, Dartmouth Coll., 1963; JD, Duke U., 1968. Assoc. Hinckley, Allen, Salisbury & Parsons, 1968-74; ptnr. Saunders & Torres, 1974-80; assoc. justice RI Superior Ct., 1980-85; asst. v.p. Aetna Life and Casualty, 1985-86; ptnr. Tillinghast, Collins & Graham, 1986-87; judge US Dist. Ct. RI, Providence, 1987—99, chief judge, 1999—. Pres. East Greenwich (R.I.) Town Coun., 1972-74; state rep. R.I. Ho. of Reps., 1975-80, dep. minority leader, 1977-80. Recipient Disting. Svc. award Jaycees, 1974; named Man of Yr., Prince Henry Soc. R.I., 1988, Prince Henry Soc. Mass., 1995; Alfred P. Sloan scholar Dartmouth Coll. Mem. ABA, ATLA, FBA, R.I. Bar Assn., Jaycees (Dist. Svc. award 1974), Prince Henry Soc. of R.I., Prince Henry Soc. of Mass. Office: US Dist Ct One Exchange Terrace Providence RI 02903

TORRES, ESTEBAN EDWARD, former congressman, trade association administrator; b. Miami, Ariz., Jan. 27, 1930; s. Esteban Torres and Rena Baron (Gomez) T.; m. Arcy Sanchez, Jan. 22, 1955; children: Carmen D'Arcy, Rena Denise, Camille Bianca, Selina Andre, Esteban Adrian. Student, East Los Angeles Coll., 1960, Calif. State U., Los Angeles, 1963, U. Md., 1965, Am. U., 1966; PhD (hon.), Nat. U., 1987; DHL (hon.), Whittier Coll., 2001. Chief steward United Auto Workers, local 230, 1954-63, dir. polit. com., 1963; organizer, internat. rep. United Auto Workers (local 230), Washington, 1964; asst. dir. Internat. Affairs Dept., 1975-77; dir. Inter-Am. Bureau for Latin Am., Caribbean, 1965-67; exec. dir. E. Los Angeles Community Union (TELACU), 1967-74; U.S. ambassador to UNESCO, Paris, 1977-79; chmn. Geneva Grp., 1977-78; chmn. U.S. del. Gen. Conf., 1978; spl. asst. to pres. U.S., dir. White House Office Hispanic Affairs, 1979-81; mem. 98th-103rd Congresses from 34th Dist. Calif., 1983-98; mem. appropriations com., subcom. fgn. ops., subcom. transp.; chmn. ho. subcom. coinage; mem. ho. banking com., 1983; mem. ho. small bus. com., 1983. Campaign coord. Jerry Brown for Gov., 1974; Hispanic coord. LA County campaign Jimmy Carter for Pres., 1976; mem. Sec. of State Adv. Group, 1979-81; v.p. Nat. Congress Cmty. Econ. Devel., 1973-74; pres. Congress Mex.-Am. Unity, 1970-71; dir. Nat. Com. on Citizens Broadcasting, 1977; cons. U.S. Congress office of tech. assessment, 1976-77; del to IMF gen. conf., Geneva, 1975, del to U.S. Congress European Parliament meetings, 1984; ofcl. congl. observer Geneva Arms Control Talks; chmn. Congl. Hispanic Caucus, 1987; speaker Wrights Del. to USSR, 1987; Dem. dep. Whip, 1990; chmn. bd. Nat. Latino Media Coun., 1999—. Contbr. numerous articles to profl. jours. Co-chmn. Nat. Hispanic Dems., 1988—; chmn. Japan-Hispanic Inst. Inc.; bd. visitors Sch. Architecture UCLA, 1971-73; bd. dirs. LA County Econ. Devel. Com., 1972-75, Internat. Devel. Conf., 1976-78; chmn. Congrl. Hispanic Caucus, 1985-86; pres. Plaza de la Raza Cultural Ctr., 1972-73, chmn. bd. la Plaza de Cultural Art, 2007—; trustee Am. Coll. Paris, 1977-79; active Calif. Transp. Commn., Sacramento. With AUS, 1949-53, ETO. Recipient Congrl. award Nat. Leadership award 1997; sr. fellow UCLA Sch. Pub. Policy, 2000-05. Mem. Americans for Dem. Action (exec. bd. 1975-77), VFW Post 6315, Pico Rivera, Calif., Am. Legion, Smithsonian Inst. (regent emeritus 1999—), Willy C. Velasqez Inst., Calif. Transp. Commn. Democrat. Home: 1104 Montezuma Way West Covina CA 91791 Personal E-mail: etorres_nlmc@hotmail.com.

TORRES, GERALD, law educator; b. Victorville, Calif., Sept. 29, 1952; s. Frank E. and Mary L. (Lopez) T.; m. Frances Gloria Nash. AB in Polit. Sci., Stanford U., 1974; JD, Yale U., 1977; LLM, U. Mich., 1980. Crew chief Hall's Aboveground Pool Installation, 1973-74; legal intern Ctr. for Advocacy, Rsch. and Planning, NAACP, 1976-77; staff atty. Children's Def. Fund, 1977-78; prof. law U. Pitts. Law Sch., 1980-83, U. Minn.,

1983—93, U. Tex. Sch. Law, Austin, Tex., 1993—. Vis. prof. law Vt. Law Sch., 1986, U. Tex. Law Sch., 1989, Harvard U. Law Sch., 1990-91, Stanford Law Sch.; adj. prof. law Drake Summer Agrl. Law Inst., 1986—; mem. Minn. Atty. Gen.'s Task Force on Agr.; former pres. Assn. Am. Law Sch.; presenter in field. Contbr. articles to profl. jours.; author: (with others) Law Office Without Walls, 1987, (with J. Davidson and L.B. Kurland) Agricultural Law and Policy Institute, 1988, The Miner's Canary: Enlisting Race, Resisting Power, Transforming Democracy, 2002. Appointee U. Mich. Law Sch. Com. of Visitors. Named Law Prof. of Yr. Nat. Hispanic Bar Assn., 1990-91. Mem. DC Bar Assn., Am. Agrl. Law Assn., Am. Law Inst., Rural Am., Rural Coalition, Am. Farmland Trust, Environ. Law Inst., Nat. Petroleum Coun., EPA's Nat. Environ. Justice Adv. Coun. Office: U Tex Sch Law 727 E Dean Keeton St Austin TX 78705 Office Phone: 512-232-1368. Office Fax: 512-471-6988. Business E-Mail: gtorres@law.utexas.edu.

TORRES, JACQUES, food service executive, pastry chef; Master Pastry Chef, Culinary Sch., Cannes, France, 1980—83. Chef Hotel Negresco; corp. pastry chef Ritz-Carlton, Palm Springs, 1988; exec. pastry chef Le Cirque, NYC, 1989—97, Le Cirque 2000, NYC, 1997—; owner, pastry chef Jacques Torres Chocolate, Bklyn., 2000—, Jacques Torres Chocolate Haven, NYC, 2004—. Dean pastry studies French Culinary Inst. N.Y.; cons. Cointreau and Valrhona chocolate; participant Pierre Franey's Birthday Celebrations, Merci Julia for Julia Child; spent culinary weeks, Tokyo, Sydney, Melbourne, Australia, Spain. Guest appearances (TV series) Julia Child's Master Chef, Today Show, NBC, Later Today; author: (cookbooks) Dessert Circus: Extraordinary Desserts You Can Make at Home, 1998, Dessert Circus at Home: Fun, Fanciful, and Easy-to-Make Desserts, 1999 (ICR World Cookbook award, 1999), French Culinary Institute's Salute to Healthy Cooking: From America's Foremost French Chefs, 2001; host (TV series) Dessert Circus with Jacques Torres, 1998, Passion for Pastry with Jacques Torres, Passion for Chocolate with Jacques Torres, Chocolate with Jacques Torres, Food Network. Active God's Love We Deliver, ARC, Meals on Wheels. Named Pastry Chef of Yr., James Beard Found., Am. Pastry Chef of Yr., Chef's of Am.; named one of 10 Best Pastry Chefs, Chocolatier Mag.; recipient award, French Championship of Desserts, 1986, Meilleur Ouvrier de France medal, 1986, Gold medal, Japanese Pastry Chef Assn. Office: Le Cirque 2000 25 Miller Heights Rd Roscoe NY 12776-5413 also: Jacques Torres Chocolate 66 Water St Brooklyn NY 11201 *

TORRES, JOHN D., lawyer; B, U. Notre Dame; law degree, U. Chgo. Pvt. practice atty., Phoenix; comml. law atty. Motorola, 1996; sr. v.p., gen. counsel, sec. Freescale Semiconductor Inc., Austin, Tex. Bd. dirs. Greater Austin C. of C. Office: Freescale Semiconductor Inc 6501 William Cannon Dr W Austin TX 78735 E-mail: john.torres@freescale.com. *

TORRES, MARIBEL, social welfare administrator; b. Lancaster, Pa., Sept. 17, 1975; d. Jose Miguel and Virginia Torres; 1 child, Lissette Adaline Vega. Degree in Internat. Studies, Millersville U., Pa., 1997. Cert. Lancaster Mediation Solution Ctr., 1992. Customer svc. rep. Diversified Data Services Call Centers, Inc., Lancaster, Pa., 1998; adminstrv. asst. Dept. Agr., Harrisburg, Pa., 1998—2001; income maintenance case worker County Assistance Office, Pa. Dept. Pub. Welfare, Harrisburg, 2001—04, human services program specialist third party liability, 2004—. Panelist South East Youth Aid Panel, Lancaster, 1994—94. Dir. Montrose Park Assn., Harrisburg, Pa., 2007—; intercessor Nat. Ch. Coalition Found., Inc., Newark, Del., 2006—07; mem. ministry team Christ Cmty. Ch., Camp Hill, Pa., 2007—. Recipient Appreciation award, Hermandad Latina, 2001. Republican. Avocations: reading, writing. Home: 3926 N 6th St Harrisburg PA 17110 Office: Comm PA DPW BFO TPL DGS Annex Complex Petry Building Harrisburg PA 17110 Home Phone: 717-221-0137; Office Phone: 717-705-8133. Personal E-mail: godsredeamed@yahoo.com. Business E-Mail: mtorres@state.pa.us.

TORRES, RICHARD, literature and language educator; b. Deming, N.Mex., Nov. 17, 1951; s. Esquipula Rascon and Maria Madrid Torres; m. Vicki Lynne Everett, Feb. 16, 1974; children: Victoria Marie, Roxana Michelle. BS in Edn., N.Mex. State U., 1974, MA in Edn. Adminstrn., 1978. Cert. tchr. Tex. Edn. Agy. Tchr., curriculum facilitator Gadsden Ind. Sch. Dist., Anthony, N.Mex., 1974—99; tchr. El Paso Ind. Sch. Dist., 1999—2005. Mid. sch. rep. Dist. Ednl. Improvement Coun., El Paso, 2000—. Named Tchr. of Month, Santa Teresa Jr. H.S. and Mid. Sch., Gadsden, 1992, 1994, 1999, Tchr. of the Day, El Paso Times, 2000, 2004, Unsung Hero award, El Paso Ind. Sch. Dist. Bd., 2002. Mem.: Assn. Supervision and Curriculum Devel., Phi Delta Kappa. Democrat. Roman Catholic. Office: Lincoln Mid Sch 500 Mulberry Ave El Paso TX 79932

TORRES, ROBERT J., JR., judge; b. Guam; m. Mary Camacho Torres; 3 children. BBA in Accounting, U. Notre Dame, South Bend, Ind., 1980; JD, Harvard Law Sch. Bar: Guam 1987, Mass. Tax practitioner Lourie and Cutler, Boston, 1985—89; prtnr. Torres Limtiaco Cruz & Sison, 1989—2004; justice Guam Supreme Ct., 2004—. Former chmn. Guam Ninth Circuit Lawyer Representative Coordinating Com.; former mem. Guam Ninth Circuit Jud. Conference Exec. Com.; mem. Guam Jud. Council, 1990—96; chair U.S. Magistrate Judges Merit Selection Panel for Guam. Player, coach, and match commnr. Federation Internationale de Football Assn., Asian Football Confederation. Mem.: ABA, Guam Bar Assn. (past pres.). Office: Guam Supreme Ct Ste 300 Guam Jud Ctr 120 W OBrien Dr Hagatna GU 96910 *

TORRES, RUDY ARNOLD, artist; b. LA, Dec. 21, 1957; s. Benjamin Tiburcio and Josephine Irene Torres. Student, East Los Angeles Coll., 1981—83, Pacific Inst. Comml. Art, 1984—85, Otis Parsons Sch. Design, 1985—86. Artist, co-owner Echo Park Gallery, LA, 1989—91. Exhibitions include Alpha Contemporary Exhibits, L.A., 1983—86, Mac Houston Art Gallery, Pasadena, Calif., 1986, Brand Libr. Art Gallery, Glendale, Calif., 1987, Design Ctr. L.A., 1987, L.A. Photography Ctr., 1987, 1989, L.A. Mcpl. Gallery, 1989, L.A. Art Assn., 1989, Echo Park Gallery, L.A., 1990—91, Boathouse Gallery, 1992, Weingart Gallery, 1992, Arthur Coons Gallery, 1992, Galeria Las Americas, 1992—94, 1996, Art & Barbee Art Gallery, Hollywood, Calif., 1993, Hilles Libr. at Harvard U., 1995, Olvera St. Gallery, L.A., 1996, Palette Des Artists, Pasadena, 1996, Galeria Otravez, East Los Angeles, Calif., 1996, 2001, Long Beach (Calif.) Gallery, 1998, Calif. State U. Fullerton grand Ctrl. Art Ctr., Santa Ana, 2001, Guggenheim Gallery, Chapman U., Orange, Calif., 2001, Showcase North Gallery, Santa Ana, 2001—02, Huntington Beach (Calif.) Gallery, 2002, City of Brea (Calif.) Gallery, 2002, one-man shows include Minus Zero Gallery, Torrance, Calif., 1990, Mary Norton Clapp Libr., Occidental Coll., L.A., 2000, Galeria Rustica, Pomona, Calif., 2002, Fullerton (Calif.) Branch Libr., 2002, Aliso Viejo (Calif.) Libr., 2002—03, exhibited in group shows at Latino Art Mus., Pomona, Calif., 2002—03, Huntington Beach (Calif.) Art Ctr., 2003, 2005, Eagle Rock Cmty. Cultural Assn., LA, 2003, Self Help Graphics, East LA, 2003, 2004, Latino Art Mus., Claremont, Calif., 2004, The Green Door Gallery, Santa Ana, Calif., 2004. Recipient cert. of appreciation for mural in Herman Dist., 14th Dist. City of L.A., 1986. Avocations: body building, swimming, jogging, camping, fishing. Personal E-mail: rudeart@sbcglobal.net.

TORRESE, DANTE MICHAEL, prosthodontist, educator; b. Yonkers, NY, Feb. 12, 1949; s. Dante Angelo and Matilda (Dal Lago) T.; m. Camille Patricia DiPaola, Aug. 7, 1982. BS in Biology, Manhattan Coll., 1971; DDS, Columbia U., 1975; prosthodontic cert., NYU, 1983. Resident in dentistry Presbyn. Hosp., NYC, 1975-76; clin. instr. dentistry Columbia U., NYC, 1976-78, asst. clin. prof. dentistry, 1978—; pvt. practice dentistry Yonkers, N.Y., 1976—. Attending dentist Presbyn. Hosp., N.Y.C., 1976-86; lectr. in field. Recipient Am. Acad. Oral Pathology Grad. award 1975, Densply Corp. award for removable prosthodontics, 1975, Psi Omega Scholastic Achievement award, 1975. Fellow Am. Coll. of Dentists, Royal Soc. Health; mem. NRA (life), Yonkers Dental Soc., 9th Dist. State Dental Soc., Invested Baker St. Irregular, Sherlock Holmes Wireless Soc., Single Action Shooting Soc. (life), Yonkers Amateur Radio Club, Westchester Astronomy Club, Exch. Club (sec. 1979—), Three Garridebs of Westchester, Priory Scholars of N.Y.C. Club, Montague Street Lodgers of Bklyn. Club, Omicron Kappa Upsilon. Office: 984 N Broadway Ste 503 Yonkers NY 10701-1308 Office Phone: 914-965-4004.

TORRES FILHO, IVO, medical educator; b. Belem, Pará, Brazil, Apr. 17, 1958; s. Ivo Pontes and Vilma Torres; m. Luciana Neves, Aug. 27, 2000;; children: Patricia Torres, Rodrigo Torres, Natasha Torres. MD, State U. of Rio de Janeiro, 1981; MSc, Fed. U. of Rio de Janeiro, 1984, PhD, 1988; postgrad., U. Calif.-San Diego, La Jolla, 1994. Lic. physician State U. of Rio de Janeiro, 1981. Instr. State U. of Rio de Janeiro, 1982—84, asst. prof., 1984—88, assoc. prof., 1988—2003, Va. Commonwealth U., Richmond, 2003—. Dir. Microcirculatory Lab, Va. Commonwealth U., Richmond, Va., 2003—. Contbr. over 100 articles and abstracts to profl. jours. Recipient Innovative Instrumentation award, Microcirculatory Soc., Inc, Travel award, Radiation Rsch. Soc., 1993; fellow Postdoctoral fellow, The PEW Charitable Trusts, Fogarty Internat. Ctr. Mem.: Am. Physiol. Soc. (assoc.), Microcirculatory Soc., Inc (assoc.). Office: Virginia Commonwealth University 1101 East Marshall St Rm B1-012 Richmond VA 23298-0695 Home Phone: 804-755-4960; Office Phone: 804-828-2066. Office Fax: 804-828-6413. E-mail: itorres@vcu.edu.

TORRES-GIL, FERNANDO M., academic administrator; b. Salinas, Calif., June 24, 1948; BA in Polit. Sci., San Jose State U., 1970; MSW, Brandeis U., 1972, PhD in Social Policy, Planning and Rsch., 1976. Spl. asst. to sec. Dept. Health, Edn. and Welfare, Washington, 1978-79, Dept. Health and Human Svcs., Washington, 1979-80; prof. gerontology and pub. adminstrn. U. So. Calif., 1981-91, assoc. dir. Nat. Resource Ctr. on Minority Aging Populations, 1988-92, prof. social welfare, 1991-93; assoc. dean Sch. Pub. Policy and Soc. Rsch. UCLA, 1993—, dir., Ctr. for Policy Rsch. on Aging. Staff dir. Select Com. on Aging, U.S. Ho. of Reps., Washington, 1985-87. Contbr. articles to profl. jours. Bd. dirs. Nat. Steinbeck Ctr., Families USA Found., AARP Andrus Found., Calif. Endowment, 2003—. White House fellow, 1978-79. Mem. Am. Soc. Aging (pres. 1989-92), Nat. Acad. Social Insurance; fellow Gerontological Soc. of Am., 1985, Nat. Acad. Public Administration, 1995. Office: UCLA Sch Pub Plicy & Social Rsch Box 951656 3250 Public Policy Blvd Los Angeles CA 90095-1656

TORREY, BARBARA BOYLE, research council administrator; b. Pensacola, Fla., Nov. 27, 1941; d. Peter F. and Elsie (Hansen) Boyle; m. E. Fuller Torrey, Mar. 23, 1968; children: Michael, Martha. BA, Stanford U., 1963, MS, 1970. Vol. Peace Corps, Tanzania, 1963-65; fiscal economist Office Mgmt. and Budget, Washington, 1970-80; dept. asst. sec. HHS, Washington, 1980-81; dir. Ctr. for Internat. Rsch. Census Bur., Washington, 1984-92; pres. Population Reference Bur., Washington, 1992-93; exec. dir. Commn. on Behavioral and Social Scis. and Edn. NRC, NAS, Washington, 1993—2003; vis. scholar Population Reference Bureau, 2003—. Bd. dirs., Luxembourg Income Study. Co-editor: The Vulnerable, 1987, Population and Land Use, 1992; contbr. articles to profl. jours. Fellow AAAS; mem. Population Assn. Am. (bd. dirs. 1993—). Office: Population Ref Bur 1875 Connecticut Ave NW Ste 520 Washington DC 20009-5728 Office Phone: 202-939-5455.

TORREY, CLAUDIA OLIVIA, lawyer; b. Nashville, June 10, 1958; d. Claude Adolphus and Rubye Mayette (Prigmore) T. BA in Econ., Syracuse U., 1980; JD, N.Y. Law Sch., 1985. Bar: NY 1988. Legal intern Costello, Cooney & Fearon, Syracuse, NY, 1979; legal clk. First Am. Corp., Nashville, 1981; legal asst. James I. Meyerson, NYC, 1982-85; jud. law clk. N.Y. State Supreme Ct., NYC, 1985; interim project supr., legal asst. CUNY Ctrl. Office, 1985-86; legal analyst Rosenman & Colin Law Firm, NYC, 1986-87; asst. counsel N.Y. State Legis., Albany, 1988-90; atty., cons. pvt. practice, Nashville, Cookeville, Tenn., 1991—. Bd. dirs. Children's Corner Day Care Ctr., Albany, 1989-90. Columnist Health Law Jour. NY State Bar Assn., 1996—; co-author Legal Manual for New York Physicians, 2003, 2d edit., 2006. Rep. FOCUS exec. coun. Westminster Presbyn. Ch., Albany, NY, 1990; interim chair COR com. Synod of Living Waters Presbyn. Ch. USA, Nashville, 2002, vice moderator issues, justice and peace Presbyn. Women's Coord. Team, 2007; mem. PDS USN Alumni Bd., Nashville, 2002—; bd. dirs. Nashville Peace and Justice Ctr., 2005—06. Mem. ABA (young lawyers divsn. liaison to ABA forum on health law 1994-96), Internat. Platform Assn., NY State Bar Assn. (chmn., membership sub-com. on non-resident mems. 2004—, chmn. health law sect. study group on health info., privacy and confidentiality 1998-99, mem.-at-large health law section exec. com., 2002-04), Alpha Kappa Alpha (treas., pres., corr. sec. Iota Upsilon chpt. Syracuse U.) Avocations: singing, reading, harp, travel, art. Home and Office: PO Box 150234 Nashville TN 37215-0234 Office Phone: 931-528-4280. E-mail: jewel3@prodigy.net.

TORREY, DAVID LEONARD, investment banker; b. Ottawa, Ont., Can., Oct. 6, 1931; s. Arthur Starratt and Josephine Edith (Leonard) T.; divorced; children: Heather Torrey Murphy, John Winthrop, Diana Bruce (dec.), Arthur Bruce, David Molson. BA in Econs., St. Lawrence U., 1953; diploma, Ivey Sch. Bus., U. Western Ont., 1954. With Pitfield Mackay Ross Ltd., Toronto, Ont., Canada, 1954-84, v.p., 1963-73, sr. v.p., 1973-80, vice chmn., 1980-82, pres., 1982-84, also bd. dirs.; vice chmn. Dominion Securities, Inc., 1984-88, RBC Dominion Securities, Inc., 1988-91. Chmn. Montreal Stock Exch., 1971-73, Phillips Cables Ltd., 1991-96; bd. dirs. Can. Stebbins Engring. and Mfg. Co. Ltd.; mem. coun. Montreal Bd. Trade, 1971-72. Chmn. Montreal Downtown YMCA, 1972-74; trustee St. Lawrence U., 1980-92; bd. dirs. Montreal Gen. Hosp. Found. Mem. Investment Bankers Assn. (gov. 1971-72), Securities Industries Assn. (bd. govs. 1972-73), Multiple Sclerosis Can. (past pres., bd. dirs.), Royal Montreal Golf Club, Mt. Royal (Montreal) Club, Toronto Club, Saifish Club Fla. (Palm Beach), Beta Theta Pi. Home: 389 Carlyle Ave Montreal PQ Canada H3R 1T3 Office: PO Box 6001 1 Pl Ville Marie 2E Montreal PQ Canada H3C 3A9 Home Phone: 514-731-9779; Office Phone: 514-399-9932.

TORREY, RICHARD FRANK, utilities executive; b. Saratoga Springs, NY, Dec. 31, 1926; s. Reginald Frank and Marian (Currey) T.; m. Betty Louise Stetson, July 2, 1949; children: Patricia Ann Torrey Kritsberg, Carol Louise Torrey Kress, Barbara Jean Torrey Friedman. BA cum laude, Syracuse U., 1951. News reporter, Syracuse (NY) Post Standard, 1947-51; pub. rels. account exec. Syracuse, 1951-53; home sec. 35th Congl. Dist., Syracuse, 1952-53; exec. sec. to mayor Syracuse, 1954—57; dir. area devel. Niagara Mohawk Power Corp., Syracuse, 1958-66, comml. v.p. Buffalo, 1966-68, adminstrv. v.p., 1968-72, v.p., gen. mgr., 1972-76, sr. v.p. Syracuse, 1976-88, ret., 1988; pres. Can. Niagara Power Co. Ltd., Niagara Falls, Ont., Canada, 1968-88, dir., 1968-89. Pres., dir. Caragh Investments Ltd., 1981-85; pres. Opinac Investments Ltd., Toronto, 1982-88, bd. dirs., 1982-89; pres. Opinac Energy Ltd., Calgary, Alta., 1983-88, bd. dirs., 1983-89. Pres. Syracuse USO, 1959-61, mem. nat. coun., 1959-62, 68-74; co-chmn. Ctrl. N.Y. Interim Coun. Regional Planning, 1965-66; gen. chmn. Dunbar-Huntington Bldg. Fund, Syracuse, 1963; state campaign chmn. N.Y. Job Devel. Authority, 1961; gen. chmn. United Way of Buffalo and Erie County, 1971; mem. Syracuse U. Corp. Adv. Coun., 1972-76; trustee Elmcrest Children's Ctr., 1962-63, Camp Good Will, Syracuse, 1964-66, Syracuse Area Coun. Chs., 1959-64; bd. dirs. United Way Buffalo and Erie County, 1967-76, Greater Buffalo Devel. Found., Kenmore Mercy Hosp., 1970-76, Crouse Irving Meml. Hosp. Found., 1978-87, Nat. Kidney Found., 1987-89, Bon Secours-Venice (Fla.) Hosp. Found., 1992-98, vice chmn. 1995-96, chmn. 1996-98; bd. dirs. Plantation Cmty. Found., Venice, 1989, pres., 1990-93, pres. emeritus, 1993—; mem. bd. adv. Sisters of St. Joseph, 1967-76; elder Trinity Presbyn. Ch., Venice, 1992-94; assoc. mem. Dewitt Cmty. Ch., Ch. of the Palms, 2006-. Served with Air Corps U.S. Army, 1944-47. Recipient Syracuse Young Man of Yr. award, 1962; Outstanding Citizen award Buffalo Evening News, 1973. Mem. Empire State (v.p., bd. dirs. 1963-80), Buffalo Area (v.p. 1968-72, bd. dirs. 1968-76, pres. 1972-73, chmn. bd. 1973-74, Man of Yr. 1974) C. of C., Associated Industries of N.Y. (bd. dirs. 1978-80), Bus. Coun. N.Y. (bd. dirs. 1980-82), Mfrs. Assn. Cen. N.Y. (bd. dirs. 1977-88), Augusta Villa Assn. (bd. dirs. 1989-92), Buffalo Club (past 2d v.p., dir.), Syracuse Century Club (gov. 1980-83), Onondaga Golf Club, Automobile Club Western N.Y.(bd. dirs. 1971-73, pres. 1973), N.Y.S. Automobile Assn. (dir. 1975-76). Home and Office: 7333 Scotland Way #2303 Sarasota FL 34238 Personal E-mail: dicktorrey@aol.com.

TORREZ, MICHELLE MARIE, artist, educator; b. Denver, Feb. 3, 1956; d. John Thomas and Geri Anne Chestor; children: Gwenevieve Louise, Nicole Michelle. Assocs. Visual Comm. and Advt. Design, Art Inst. Colo., Denver, 1986. Art dir. Mentler and Co., Dallas, 1986—87, Hamilton Sweeney Advt., Denver, 1987—94; owner Studio M, Denver, 1994—98; workshop instr. Art in the Aspens, Colo., 2005—, Taos Painters Workshop, N.Mex., 2005—. Adj. instr. painting Met. State Coll. Denver, 2004—; traveling lectr. U.S. State Dept.-Art in Embassies, Sofia, Bulgaria, 2003; invited participant Coors Invitational We. Art Exhibit, 2002—05. S.W. Art Mag., one-woman shows include Michelle Torrez: One Woman Show, Metaphor - Art in Embassies Calendar, 2003, exhibitions include Colo. Gov.'s Office, 2002—05. Named to Hall of Fame, Art Inst. of Colo., 2004; recipient Colo. ALFIE award for art direction of pub. svc. comml., Denver Advt. Agy., 1991, CLEO award for art direction of pub. svc. TV comml., City of Denver, 1991; Travel grant, Christian Solidarity Internat., 2005. Mem.: Denver Art Students League (assoc.), Denver Art Mus. (assoc.), Nat. Mus. of Women in the Arts (assoc.).

TORRUELLA, JUAN R., federal judge; b. San Juan, June 7, 1933; BS in Bus. and Fin., U. Pa., 1954; LLB, Boston U., 1957; LLM, U. Va., 1984; MPA, U. P.R., 1984; MSt, Oxford U., 2003; LLD (hon.), St. John's U., 1995, Roger Williams U., 1995. Judge US Dist. Ct. PR, San Juan, 1974—82, chief judge, 1982—84; judge US Ct. Appeals (1st cir.), San Juan, 1984—, chief judge, 1994—2001. Former mem. jud. conf. com. Adminstrn. Fed. Magistrate Sys., former mem. jud. conf. exec. com.; former mem. jud. conf. com. Internat. Jud. Rels. Mem.: FBA, ABA, PR Bar Assn., DC Bar Assn., Assn. Labor Rels. Practitioners PR and VI. Office: John J Moakley US Courthouse 1 Courthouse Ste 2500 Boston MA 02210 *

TORTI, FRANK MICHAEL, internist, health facility administrator; BA, MA, Johns Hopkins U., 1969; MPH, Harvard U., 1973, MD, 1974. Diplomate in internal medicine and med. oncology Am. Bd. Internal Medicine. Asst. prof. medicine Stanford (Calif.) U., 1979-84, clin. assoc. prof. medicine, 1984-86, assoc. prof. medicine, 1986-93; prof. medicine Wake Forest U. Sch. Medicine, Winston-Salem, NC, 1993—, dir. Comprehensive Cancer Ctr., 1993—, chmn. dept. cancer biology, 1993—. Chair N.C. Gov.'s Commn. on Cancer Coordination and Control, 1993—2003; mem. study sect. Am. Inst. for Cancer Rsch., Bethesda, Md., 1989—. Mem. Am. Assn. for Cancer Rsch., Am. Soc. Clin. Oncology, Am. Soc. Cell Biology, Internat. Soc. Interferon Rsch., Am. Fedn. for Clin. Rsch., Soc. for Biol. Therapy. Office: Wake Forest U Sch Medicine Medical Center Blvd Winston Salem NC 27157-1082 E-mail: ftorti@wfubmc.edu.

TORTOLANI, ANTHONY JOHN, surgeon, educator; b. Eastchester, NY, Oct. 15, 1943; s. Salvatore Paul and Yolanda (Vecciarelli) Tortolani; m. Beth Callahan, Dec. 15, 1967 (dec. Oct. 1993); children: Julia Sue, Paul Justin; m. Katherine Gormley, Sept. 25, 1999. BS, Fordham U., 1965; MD, George Washington Sch. Medicine, 1969. Diplomate Am. Bd. Surgery, Am. Bd. Thoracic Surgery. Chief divsn. cardiovascular & thoracic surgery North Shore U. Hosp., Manhasset, NY, 1978-90, chmn. dept. surgery, 1988-96, chmn. med. bd., 1994-96, chmn. dept. surgery Glen Cove, NY, 1990-96; John D. Mountain chair surgery North Shore U. Hosp.- Cornell U. Med. Coll., Manhasset, 1989-96, program dir. surg. residency program, 1992-96; prof. surgery Cornell U. Med. Coll., NYC, 1993-97, prof. cardiothoracic surgery, 1997-99; mem. staff N.Y. Hosp., NYC, 1997-99; dir., prof. cardiothoracic surgery Jack D. Weiler Hosp./Montefiore Med. Ctr. Albert Einstein Coll. of Medicine, NYC, 1999-2001; prof. clin. cardiothoracic surgery Weill Med. Coll. Cornell U., 2001—. Vice chmn. N.Y. Presbyn. Cornell Cardiothoracic Surgery Network. Active Columbus Citizens Found., N.Y.C. Maj. USAF, 1974-76. Roman Catholic. Avocation: breeding arabian horses. Office: NY Presbyn Hosp 525 E 68th St Rm M-404 New York NY 10021

TORTOLANI, MICHELLE F., broadcast executive; BS, MSEE, Boston U. Sr. dir., repeater ops. XM Satellite Radio, Inc., Washington. Mem.: IEEE, Soc. Women Engineers (life mem.) (sr.; co-chair Nat. Conf. 2000, pres., treas. Balt.-Washington sect., mem. membership dues task force, leader, joint membership task force, bd. dirs. dir. profl. develop., bd. dirs. v.p. membership intiatives, mem. membershio growth and retention task force, region E dir., bd. dirs. dir. external affairs, pres.-elect 2007, pres. 2007—), Boston U. Engring. Alumni Bd. Office: XM Programming Ctr & Corp Hdqs 1500 Eckington Pl NE Washington DC 20002 *

TORTORELLA, JOHN, professional hockey coach; b. Boston, June 24, 1958; Coach Va. Lancers Atlantic Coast Hockey League, 1986—88; asst. coach Buffalo Sabres, 1989—95; coach Rochester Am. Am. Hockey League, 1995—97; asst. coach Phoenix Coyotes, 1997—99, NY Rangers, 1999—2001; coach Tampa Bay Lightning, 2001—. Named Coach of Yr., Atlantic Coast Hockey League, 1986—87; recipient Jack Adams Award, NHL, 2004. Achievements include coaching Stanley Cup Championship Team, Tampa Bay Lightning, 2004. Office: Tampa Bay Lightning Hockey Club Ice Palace Arena 401 Channelside Dr Tampa FL 33602

TORTORELLO, NICHOLAS JOHN, public opinion and market research company executive; b. Maspeth, NY, Dec. 1, 1948; s. John Anthony and Verla Jean (Odel) T.; m. Joan Elizabeth King, Jan. 13, 1973 (div. July 2006); children: Kerry Ann, Jennifer Joan. BA in Polit. Sci. with highest honors, Williams Coll., 1971; M Religious Studies, St. Joseph's Sem., Yonkers, NY, 1988. V.p. Louis Harris & Assocs., NYC, 1971-73, sr. v.p., 1973-79; exec. v.p. DMT Inc., NYC, 1979-83; pres. Tortorello Corp., Pearl River, N.Y., 1983-85; pres. Tortorello group Market Facts Inc.-N.Y., NYC, 1985-86; v.p. Total Rsch. Corp., Princeton, N.J., 1986-88; chmn. Rsch. and Forecasts Inc., NYC, 1989-93; sr. v.p. Roper Starch Worldwide Inc., NYC, 1993-98; pres. Guideline Consulting, NYC, 1998—2002; v.p., gen. mgr. Lieberman Rsch. Worldwide Inc., 2003—04; v.p. Internat. Comms. Rsch., NYC, 2004—06; sr. v.p. The Mktg. Workshop, Inc., 2006—07, Pert Survey Rsch. Inc., 2007—. Editor, author Tortorello Trendline, 1983-85, Rsch. and Forecasts Trendline, 1989-91. Trustee Riverdale (N.Y.) Country Sch., 1982-90, v.p., 1986-89; trustee Marymount Manhattan Coll., N.Y.C., 1986-88; lectr., tchr. religion St. Anthony's Ch., Nanuet, N.Y., 1984-86; mem. CARA Bd. Georgetown U., Washington, 1992-98, sch. adv. coun., 2000—; mem. Hosp. Chaplaincy Bd., 1991-97; v.p. Class of '71, Williams Coll., 2001. Recipient Am. Legion award for leadership, scholarship, honor and svc., 1967, Disting. Alumnus of Yr. award, Riverdale Country Sch., 1984. Mem. Am. Dirs. Inst. (trustee 1984-87), Coun. Am. Survey Rsch. Orgn. (chmn. bd. dirs. 2001, chmn. publs. com. 1991-94, chmn. pub. rels. com. 1995-97, chmn. mktg. and comms. com. 1997-99, bd. dirs., chmn.

1999 ann. conf., chmn. bd. dirs. 1999, chmn. bd. trustees 2001, chmn. nominating com. 2002), Am. Assn. Pub. Opinion Rsch.(Counselor-AT Large, 2004-05), Williams Club. Democrat. Avocations: collecting Lionel trains, collecting stereo equipment, golf, collecting american coins. Office: Mktg Workshop Inc 60 East 42nd St New York NY 10165 Home Phone: 914-907-7926; Office Phone: 845-215-5921. E-mail: ntortorello@hotmail.com.

TORVALDS, LINUS BENEDICT, application developer; b. Helsinki, Finland, Dec. 28, 1969; s. Nils and Anna Torvalds; m. Tove Torvalds; children: Patricia Miranda, Daniela Yolanda, Celeste Amanda. MS in Computer Sci., Helsinki U., 1996. Developer Transmeta Corp., Santa Clara, Calif., 1997—2003; fellow Open Source Develop. Labs (OSDL), Beaverton, Oreg., 2003—. Co-author (with David Diamond): (autobiography) Just for Fun: The Story of an Accidental Revolutionary, 2001. Named One of the Most Influential People in the World, TIME mag., 2004; recipient Nokia Found. Award, 1997, Lifetime Achievement Award, Uniforum, 1997, Takeda award, 2001. Achievements include invention of Linux operating system. Office: OSDL 12725 SW Millikan Way, Ste 400 Beaverton OR 97005

TOSCAN, RICHARD ERIC, dean, theater educator; b. NYC, July 1, 1941; s. Vincent E. and Stella (Werner) T.; m. Sharon Walker, Dec. 22, 1979. BA, Purdue U., 1963; MA, U. Ill., 1965, PhD, 1970. Postdoctoral teaching resident NEH, 1967-69; dir. Exptl. Coll. Calif. State U., Fresno, 1968-70; asst. chair div. drama U. So. Calif., LA, 1970-76, assoc. dean sch. performing arts, 1976-79, assoc. prof. div. of drama, 1979-86, assoc. dean sch. of cinema, 1986-90, dean sch. of theatre, 1990-92; dean sch. fine and performing arts Portland (Oreg.) State U., 1992—96; dean sch. arts Va. Commonwealth U.: Sch. of Arts, Richmond, Va., 1996—. Adv. bd. Internat. Contemporary Art Fair, L.A., 1989-91, Tygres Heart Shakespeare Co., Portland, 1992—, Portland Ctr. Performing Arts, 1992—, Image Theatre Mask Ensemble, 1994—; mem. theatre panel Cultural Affairs Dept., L.A., 1990-92; mem. selection com. Javits fellows U.S. Dept. Edn., Washington, 1990-2004. Author numerous stage plays, articles to profl. jours.; producer Radio Drama Series, 1981 (nominee Armstrong award 1982). Woodrow Wilson Found. fellow, 1963-64, U. Ill. fellow, 1964. Internat. Coun. Fine Arts Deans (pres. elect). Office: Virginia Commonwealth University School of Arts 325 North Harrison St Richmond VA 23284 E-mail: rtoscan@vcu.edu.

TOSCANO, JAMES VINCENT, medical foundation administrator; b. Passaic, NJ, Aug. 8, 1937; s. William V. and Mary A. (DeNigris) T.; m. Sharon Lee Bowers; children: Shawn Truelson, Lauren Bjorklund, David Brendan, Dania Toscano Miwa. AB summa cum laude, Rutgers U., 1959; MA, Yale U., 1960. Lectr. Wharton Sch., U. Pa., 1961-64; chief opinion analyst Pa. Opinion Poll, 1962-64; mng. dir. World Press Inst., St. Paul, 1964-68, exec. dir., 1968-72; dir. devel. Macalester Coll., St. Paul, 1972-74; v.p. resource devel. and pub. affairs Mpls. Soc. Fine Arts, 1974-79; pres. Minn. Mus. Art, 1979-81; exec. v.p. Park Nicollet Inst., 1981—2006; corp. sec. Park Nicollet Clinic, 1983-86; sr. v.p. Am. Med. Ctrs., Inc., 1985-87; pres. Mpls. (Minn.) Heart Inst. Found., 2006—. Adj. prof. sch. of mgmt. U. St. Thomas, 1989-01; co-chair prin. practices nonprofit excellence com. MCN, 1994-98, 2004—05; lectr. Grad. Sch. Mgmt., Hamline U., 2003—. Author: The Chief Elected Official in the Penjerdel Region, 1964; co-author, co-editor: The Integration of Political Communities, 1964. Bd. dirs., exec. com., sec.-treas. World Press Ins., 1972-2007; bd. dirs., chmn. Southside Newspaper Mpls., 1975-79; chmn. com. to improve student behavior St. Paul Pub. Schs., 1977-79; bd. dirs. Planned Parenthood St. Paul, 1965-72, Mpls. Action Agy., 1976-79; emeritus dir. Help Enable Alcoholics Receive Treatment; mem. St. Paul Heritage Preservation Commn., 1979-82, vice chmn., 1981; mem. Citizens Adv. Com. on Cable Comm.; bd. dirs. Citizens League, 1980, African-Am. Culture Ctr., 1979-82, Am. Composers Forum, 1981-85, St. Paul Chamber Orch., 1976-80, 83-89, United Theol. Sem., 1985-88; dir. emeritus Minn. Citizens for the Arts; mem. exec. com., chmn. Med. Alley Assn., 1986-96, bd. dirs., 1986-96, task force on tech. assessment Med. Alley, 1992-93; mem. health affairs adv. com. Acad. Health Ctr. U. Minn., 1988-95; bd. dirs. Mother Cabrini House, 1985-92, Minn. Civil Justice Coalition, 1987-91, also chmn.; chmn. Gov.'s Task Force on Health Care Promotion, 1985-86, mem. Gov.'s Com. Promotion Health Care Resources, 1986-87; chmn. bd. Minn. Fin. Counseling Svcs., Inc., 1990-93; mem. task force cost effectiveness Med. Alley, 1994-95; bd. dirs. Meml. Blood Bank, 1995-2001, mem. exec. com., 1996-2001; bd. dirs. Bakken Mus., 1997-2003, Stevens Sq. Cmty. Orgn., 1997-99; bd. dirs. Rainbow Rsch., Inc., 2002—, chmn. bd., 2004-07; bd. dirs. Friends of the St. Paul Libr., 2004-07; bd. dirs., treas. Pub. Arts St. Paul, 2004-2007, Minn. Charities Rev. Coun., 2004-07, chmn., 2007—. Woodrow Wilson Nat. fellow, 1960. Mem. Minn. Newspaper Found. (bd. dirs. 1987-92), Minn. Coun. Nonprofits (bd. dirs. 1989-95, 97-2003, bd. mem. Vocal Essence 1993-96, alt. Minn. Healthcare Commn., 1993-95, mem. Minn. Healthcare Commn., 1995-97, chair task force on med. edn. and rsch. costs 1994-96; mem. com. on med. rsch. and edn. costs, 1996-2003, chair 1996-99; liaison health tech. adv. com. 1993-97; pres. 2000-03, bd. dirs. Summit Ave Residential Preservation Assn., 2000-06, co-chair West Summit Neighborhood Adv. Com. 2004-06), Skylight Club, Informal Club, Mpls. Club. Address: 1982 Summit Ave Saint Paul MN 55105-1460 Office: 920 E 28th St Ste 100 Minneapolis MN 55407 Home Phone: 651-699-1765; Office Phone: 612-863-3978. Personal E-mail: jvt2@comcast.net. Business E-Mail: jtoscano@mhif.org.

TOSÉ, MAURICE B., communications executive; b. Ft. Bragg, NC, 1957; married; 6 children. BS in Ops. Analysis, US Naval Acad., 1978. Commd. ensign advanced to lt. USN; damage control asst. USS Bagley; ops. officer USS Mauna Kea; instr. US Naval Acad.; comdr. Naval Reserves; with US Sec. Def.; ret.; dir., dept. def. programs Techmatics, Inc., Silver Spring, Md.; founder, chmn., CEO, pres. Telecomm. Sys. Inc., Indpls., 1987—. Mem. Wireless Data Forum, AT&T Diversity Roundtable, Internat. Engring. Consortium, Intelligent Network Forum. Mem. Annapolis Jaycees, Annapolis Kiwanis; bd. dir. First Night Annapolis, Ginger Cove Retirement Cmty.; treas., v.p., dir. Arudel on the Bay Homeowners Assn.; mem. Budget & Fin. Coun, Antioch Apostolic Ch., Annapolis Neck Small Area Planning Commn.; co-founder, chmn. bd. US Naval Acad. Samuel P. Massie Edn. Endowment. Recipient Granville T. Woods award for Outstanding Achievement, Nat. Assn. of Black Telecommunications Profls., AT&T Spectrum award for Innovators. Office: Telecomm Sys Inc 275 West St Annapolis MD 21401

TOSHACH, CLARICE OVERSBY, real estate developer, retired computer company executive; b. Firbank, Westmoreland, Eng., Nov. 21, 1928; came to U.S., 1955; d. Oliver and Nora (Brown) Oversby; m. Daniel Wilkie Toshach, July 30, 1965 (dec. Aug. 1992); 1 child, Duncan Oversby Toshach; 1 child from previous marriage, Paul Anthony Beard. Textile designer Storeys of Lancaster, Eng., 1949-55; owner, operator Broadway Lane, Saginaw, Mich., 1956-70; pres., owner Clarissa Jane Inc., Saginaw, 1962-70, Over-Tosh Computers, Inc. dba Computerland, Saginaw and Flint, Mich., 1983-95; mgr., ptnr. Mich. Comml. Devel. L.L.C., Saginaw, 1995—. Trustee Saginaw Gen. Hosp., 1977-83, Home for the Aged, 1978-80; bd. dirs. Vis. Nurse Assn., pres., 1981-83; bd. dirs. Hospice of Saginaw, Inc., v.p., 1981-83; mem. long range planning com. United Way of Saginaw, 1982-83; cmty. advisor Jr. League of Saginaw, 1982-83; pres. Saginaw Gen. Hosp. Aux., 1972-82, pres., 1976-77.

TOSKES, PHILLIP PAUL, gastroenterologist, educator, researcher; b. Balt., Jan. 4, 1940; s. John F. and Mary R. (Vonelli) T.; m. Patricia A. Sponsel, June 3, 1961; children: Tammy Lynn Price, Tracey Lynn, Steven D. BA, Johns Hopkins U., 1961; MD, U. Md., 1965. Diplomate Am. Bd. Internal Medicine (bd. dirs.), Am. Bd. Gastroenterology. Intern, resident U. Md. Hosp., Balt., 1965-68; fellow in gastroenterology Hosp. U. Pa., Phila., 1968-70; asst. prof. medicine U. Fla., Gainesville, 1973-75, assoc. prof. medicine, 1975-78, prof. medicine, 1978—, dir. divsn. gastro, hepatology, 1978-97, prof., chmn. dept. medicine, 1997—2002. Chief gastro sect. Gainesville VA Med. Ctr., 1973-92; chmn. Nat. Digestive Disease Adv. Bd., Washington, 1992-94. Author chpts. to books. Maj. U.S. Army, 1970-73. Recipient Disting. Achievement award Can. Gastroenterol. Assn., 1982. Fellow ACP (Meade Johnson scholar 1966-68); mem. Am. Soc. Clin. Investigation, Am. Fedn. Clin. Rsch., Am. Gastroenterol. Assn. (pres. 1997-98). Avocations: travel, swimming, boating. Office: U Fla Box 100214 1600 SW Archer Rd Gainesville FL 32610-3001 Home: 202 NW 114th Way Gainesville FL 32607-1122 Home Phone: 352-332-4429; Office Phone: 352-392-2877. Business E-Mail: toskepp@medicine.ufl.edu.

TOSTE, ANTHONY PAIM, chemistry educator, researcher; b. Mountain View, Calif., June 26, 1948; BS in Chemistry with honors, Santa Clara U., Calif., 1970; PhD in Biochemistry and Chemistry, U. Calif., Berkeley, 1976. Rsch. fellow Cardiovasc. Rsch. Inst., San Francisco, 1977—79; rsch. scientist Battelle Meml. Inst. Pacific N.W. Nat. Lab., Richland, Wash., 1980—88; asst. prof. Mo. State U., Springfield, 1988—94, assoc. prof., 1994—99, prof., 1999—. Cons. Mitsubishi Metal Corp., Tokyo, 1984-87, Dow Chem., Tex., 1994-96; presenter in field. Contbr. articles to jours. in field, cmty. svc. presentations. Bd. dirs. Mid Columbia Arts Coun., Richland, 1987-88, Bot. Soc. S.W. Mo., Springfield, 1997-2002; pres. bd. dirs. Springfield Sister Cities Assn., 1993-96; co-founder, leader Internat. Friendship Dels. to Japan, 1996, 99, 2001, 03, 05, 07. Rsch., equipment grantee NSF, 1990; recipient Diverse Cmty. award Sister Cities Internat., Boston, 1996, STA Rsch. fellow, Japan, 1998 Mem. Am. Chem. Soc. (treas. Ozark sect. 1989-91, chmn.-elect 2000, chmn. 2000-01), Am. Nuc. Soc. (Best Poster award 1987), Assn. Ofcl. Analytical Chemists (program chair 1986, 90), Mo. Acad. Sci. (program chair 1997, 2002). Avocations: picture framing, collecting fine art, woodworking, reading, cinema. Home: 2113 E Woodhaven Pl Springfield MO 65804-6767 Office: Mo State U Dept Chemistry 901 S National Ave Springfield MO 65804 Home Phone: 417-883-1051; Office Phone: 417-836-5150. Business E-Mail: anthonytoste@issouristate.edu.

TOSTESON, DANIEL CHARLES, physiologist, medical school dean emeritus; b. Milw., Feb. 5, 1925; s. Alexis H. and Dilys (Bodycombe) T.; m. Penelope Kinsley, Dec. 17, 1949 (div. 1969); children: Carrie Marias, Heather Tosteson, Tor, Zoe Losada; m. Magdalena Tieffenberg, July 8, 1969; children: Joshua, Ingrid. Student, Harvard U., 1942-44, MD, 1949; DSc (hon.), U. Copenhagen, 1979; Dr. hon. causa, U. Liege, 1983; DSc (hon.), Med. Coll. Wis., 1984, NYU, 1992; DHL (hon.), Johns Hopkins U., 1993; Dr. honoris causa, Cath. U. Louvain, 1996, Duke U., 1996, Emory U., 1996; DMed (hon.), Ludwig Maximilians U., 2002. Fellow physiology Harvard Med. Sch., 1947-48; intern, then asst. resident medicine Presbyn. Hosp., NYC, 1949-51; research fellow medicine Brookhaven Nat. Lab., 1951-53; lab. kidney and electrolyte metabolism Nat. Heart Inst., 1953-55, 57, research fellow biol. isotope research lab. Copenhagen, 1955-56; research fellow Physiol. Lab., Cambridge, Eng., 1956-57; assoc. prof. physiology Washington U. Sch. Medicine, St. Louis, 1958-61; prof., chmn. dept. physiology and pharmacology Duke U. Sch. Medicine, 1961-75, James B. Duke Distinguished prof., 1971-75; dean div. biol. scis., dean Pritzker Sch. Medicine U. Chgo., Lowell T. Coggleshall prof. med. scis., v.p. for Med. Center, 1975-77; dean, Caroline Shields Walker prof. cell biology Harvard Med. Sch., Boston, 1977-97, dean emeritus, Caroline Shields Walker prof., 1997—, pres. Med. Ctr., 1977-97. Mem. molecular biology panel NSF, 1959-62; cons. sci. rev. com. NIH, 1964-67, nat. adv. gen. med. scis. coun., 1982-86; mem. U.S. Office Tech. Assessment, 1976; ethics adv. bd. HEW, 1977-80; nat. adv. gen. med. scis. coun. NIH, 1982—; mem. governing bd. NRC, 1977; mem. sci. com. Found. pour l'Etude du Systeme Nerveux Central et Peripherique, 1982—; nat. adv. com. biomed. scis. PEW Scholars Program, 1984-87. Recipient Harvard medal, 2002. Mem. Inst. Medicine NAS (coun. 1975-78, adv. bd. PEW scholars program 1984-85), AAAS, Acad. Arts and Scis. (pres. 1997-00), Am. Physiol. Soc. (council 1967-75, pres. 1973-74), Soc. Gen. Physiologists (pres. 1968-69), Biophys. Soc. (council 1970-73), Assn. Am. Med. Colls. (chmn. coun. acad. socs. 1969-70, chmn. assembly 1973-74, chmn. physician supply task force 1988-90, Abraham Flexner award 1991), Assn. Am. Physicians, Am. Acad. Arts and Scis. (pres. 1997-2000), Red Cell Club, Soc. Health and Human Values, Danish Royal Soc. (fellow), Alpha Omega Alpha. Achievements include spl. research cellular transport processes, red cell membranes. Office: Harvard Med Sch TMEC Rm 147 260 Longwood Ave Boston MA 02115-5701

TOSTI, ANNETTE BREWER, artist; b. Indpls., June 20, 1958; d. William Marion and Patricia Davis Brewer; m. Donald Thomas Tosti, Dec. 29, 1989; children: Tabitha Szary, Todd, Rene Foppe, Alicia Anderson, Roxanna LaValley, Brett. BA, U. Montevallo, 1979; BS, U. Ala., 1985; MA, U. of Pacific, 1989; MFA, Calif. Coll. Arts, 1992. One-woman shows include San Francisco Art Commission Gallery, Carnegie Art Ctr. Art Commission Gallery, Turlock, Calif., exhibitions include San Diego Mus. Art, Ctr. Visual Arts, Oakland, Calif., Sonoma Valley Mus. Art, SITE, LA, Claudia Chapline Gallery, Stinson Beach, Calif., Carl Cherry Ctr. Arts, Carmel, Calif., Coos Art Mus., Coos Bay, Oreg., Smith Gallery U. Calif., Santa Cruz, Calif. Coll. Arts, Oakland, AXIS Gallery, Sacramento, Calif., Matrix Gallery, Sacramento, California Crafts Mus., San Francisco, Kellogg Gallery Calif. State Poly. U., Pomona, Di Rosa Preserve, Napa, Calif., San Francisco Art Inst., Sebastapol Ctr. Arts, Calif. Recipient Straw Into Gold award, Coll. of Marin, 1991, Discovery award, Art of Calif. Mag., 1992; grantee, Marin Cmty. Found., 1992; Grad. Rsch. scholar, Western Psychol. Soc., 1988, grad. scholar, Calif. Coll. Arts, 1992. Mem.: Coll. Art Assn. Libertarian. Office: Prime Performance 41 Marinita Ave San Rafael CA 94901 Home Phone: 415-456-4947; Office Phone: 415-457-8700. Personal E-mail: annette101@aol.com.

TOSTI, DONALD THOMAS, psychologist, consultant; b. Kansas City, Mo., Dec. 6, 1935; s. Joseph T. Tosti and Elizabeth M. (Parsons) Tosti Addison; m. Carol J. Curless, Jan. 31, 1957 (dec. 1980); children: Rene, Alicia, Roxanna, Brett, Tabitha, Todd Marcus; m. Annette Brewer, Dec. 29, 1989. BSEE, U. N.Mex., 1957, MS in Psychology, 1962, PhD in Psychology, 1967. Chief editor Tchg. Machines, Inc., Albuquerque, 1960-64; divsn. mgr. Westinghouse Learning Corp., Albuquerque, 1964-70; founder, sr. v.p. Ind. Learning Sys., San Raphael, Calif., 1970-74, pres., 1974-76; chmn. bd. Omega Performance, San Francisco, 1976-77; pres. Operants, Inc., San Rafael, 1978-81; v.p. Forum Corp., San Rafael, 1981-83; mng. ptnr. Vanguard Cons. Group, San Francisco, 1983—. Author: Basic Electricity, Advanced Algebra, Fundamentals of Calculus, TMI Programmed Mathematics Series, 1960-63, Behavior Technology, 1970, A Guide to Child Development, Tactics of Communication, 1973; co-author: Learning Is Getting Easier, 1973, Indtroductory Psychology, 1981, Usibility Factors in Hardware and Software Design, 1982, Comparative Usibility, 1983, Performance Based Management, Positive Leadership, 1986, Strategic Alliances, 1990, The Professional Manager, 1995, Power and Governance, 1996, Global Fluency, 1999, Organizational Alignment, 2000, Internal Branding, 2000, Principles of Performance Consulting, 2001. Mem. AAAS, APA, Internat. Soc. for Performance Improvement (v.p. rsch. 1983-85, treas. 1997-99, pres., 2003-, Outstanding Mem. award 1984, Life Membership award 1984, Outstanding product award 1974), Sigma Xi. Home: 41 Marinita Ave San Rafael CA 94901-3443 Office Phone: 415-259-0160. Personal E-mail: change111@aol.com.

TOT, ZVONIMIR, musician, composer, music educator; b. Novi Sad, Serbia-Monteneg, May 26, 1967; s. Milica Čudanov and Ivan Tot. MusB, Franz Liszt Acad. Musical Arts, Budapest, Hungary, 1995, Amsterdam Conservatory, The Netherlands, 1999; MusM, No. Ill. U., 2002. Music theory, aural skills, and guitar instr. Coll. DuPage, Glen Ellyn, Ill., 2001—; vis. prof., music theory and aural skills U. Ill., Chgo., 2002—03, 2004—; founder Groove Art Records, 2007. Guitar instr. McHenry County Coll., Ill.; resident composer-conductor George Soros Found. Jazz Seminars, Serbia and Montenegro, 1995—97. Musician: (compact disk) Travels and Dreams; composer: (concert music classical compositions) Missa Brevis, Ave Maria, Wat Buigt gij u neder, o mijn ziel (psalm 42), numerous jazz compositions, (CD) Blue Quest, 2007. Fellow, No. Ill. U., 2001—02. Mem.: Internat. Assn. Jazz Edn., Am. Composers Forum, ASCAP, Jazz Inst. Chgo., Pi Kappa Lambda. Home: 22S Fernwood Dr Bolingbrook IL 60440 Office Phone: 866-487-6874. Personal E-mail: zt@zt-music.com.

TOTAKURA, SATYANARAYANA RAJU, secondary school educator; b. Andhra Pradesh, India, Apr. 10, 1937; s. Narasimha Raju and Suramma Totakura; m. Sarada Totakura, June 22, 1961; children: Usharani, Srinivasa Raju, Raghurama Raju. BSc, W.G.B. Coll., 1959; BEd, M.R. Coll., 1961; MSc, Banaras Hindu U., 1969; MEd, Andhra U., 1985; PhD, World U., 1987. Vis. prof. of math. Telugu Assn. of North Am., New York, 1993—98; math tchr. Bd. of Edn., Flushing, NY, 1996—; lectr. in math. DNR Coll., 1970—93. Pres. Inst. of Vedic Math., Detroit, 1993—96, Inst. of Vedic Math. Edn. Found., New York, 1997—. Author: (book) Vedic Mathematics, 1995, Fingers Calculator, 1995, Recreational Mathematics, 1995, Vedaganitam, 1980, Mathematical Shortcuts, 1988, Wonders with Numbers, 1989. Recipient Kannadakoota award, Kannadakoota N.Y., 1996, TLC award, Telugu Lit. and Culture Assn., 1996, TTD grant, Tirumal Tirupati Devastanam, 1987, Tana Excellence in Sci. award. Mem.: Indian Sci. Congress. Achievements include invented and re-invented novel techniques that a student of mathematics can follow without any difficulty to not only learn but also master mathematics; disseminated his techniques of learning mathematics through TV programs, radio lectures, lectures, seminars and workshops throughout India and U.S.A. Home: 43-32 Kissena Blvd 10-S Flushing NY 11355 Personal E-mail: srajutotakura@hotmail.com.

TOTARO, MICHAEL WAYNE, information scientist, educator; b. New Orleans, Sept. 3, 1959; s. Peter Salvador and Gloria Ann Totaro; m. Phyllis Ann Judice, Aug. 13, 1982; 1 child, Malorie Marie. BS, U. Southwestern La., Lafayette, 1982, MBA, 1988; MS in Telecom., U. La., Lafayette, 1999. Computer programmer Med. Info. Sys., Inc., Lafayette, 1983—84; computer programmer, anayst Chart Ho., Inc. / Dixiefoods, Inc., Lafayette, 1984—85, MCC Sys., Inc., Lafayette, 1985—86, Lou Ana Foods, Inc., Opelousas, La., 1986—89; dir. info. tech. Aquaculture Techs., Ltd., Lafayette, 1989; dir. computer sys. lab. U. La., Lafayette, 1989—94; instr. theology St. Thomas More Cath. H.S., Lafayette, 1994—96; instr. U. La., 1996—. Dir. info. tech. Broussard, Poche, Lewis, and Breaux, Lafayette, 2001—02. Contbr. articles to profl. jours. Chmn. pastoral coun. St. Peter Roman Cath. Ch., Carencro, La., 1998—2006. Named Outstanding Academic Advisor, U. La., Lafayette, 2005; recipient John T. and Sandra B. Landry Tchg. Excellence award, 2003. Mem.: Assn. Info. Tech. Profls. (Acadiana chpt. 2001—02). Roman Catholic. Avocation: music. Home: 210 La Rue Christ-Roi Carencro LA 70520 Office: Univ La at Lafayette 214 Hebrard Blvd Lafayette LA 70504 Home Phone: 337-896-9632; Office Phone: 337-482-5151. Personal E-mail: mike@mytotaro.com. Business E-Mail: miket@louisiana.edu.

TOTENBERG, NINA, journalist; b. NYC, Jan. 14, 1944; d. Roman and Melanie (Shroder) T.; m. Floyd Haskell, Feb. 3, 1979 (dec.); m. H. David Reines, 2000. Student, Boston U.; LLD (hon.), Georgetown U., Haverford Coll., Mt. Holyoke Coll., Chatham Coll., Gonzaga U., Northeastern U., St. Mary's, SUNY; LHD, Lebanon Valley Coll., Westfield State Coll., Pa. State U., Pine Manor Coll., De Paul U., Simmons Coll. Reporter Boston Record Am., 1965, Peabody Times, 1967, Nat. Observer, 1968-71, New-times, 1973, Nat. Pub. Radio, Washington, 1974—, Inside Washington, 1992—; reporter Nightline ABC, 1993-98. Contbr. articles to N.Y. Times Mag., Harvard Law Rev., NYU Law Rev., Am. U. Law Rev., Christian Sci. Monitor, N.Y. Mag., Parade. Recipient Sidney Hillman award, 1983, Alfred I. Dupont award Columbia U., 1988, 91, George Foster Peabody award, 1991, George Polk award, 1991, Joan Barone award, 1991, Silver Gavel award ABA, 1968-98, Woman of Courage award Women in Film, 1991, Athena award, 1994, Presdl. Commendation, Radcliffe Coll., 1998, Ohio U. Carl van Anda award Outstanding Journalists, 2005; named outstanding broadcast journalist of yr. Nat. Press Found., 1999. Mem. Sigma Delta Chi (award 1991). Office: NPR 635 Massachusetts Ave NW Washington DC 20001-3740

TOTH, BRUCE A., lawyer; b. Toledo, Feb. 14, 1953; s. Louis W. and Marianne (Tschann) T.; m. Christina Maria Schwarz, Aug. 28, 1976. BS, Ga. Inst. Tech., 1976; MBA, JD, Stanford U., 1980. Bar: Ill., 1981. V.p. Prescott, Ball & Turben, Cleve., 1980-82; assoc. Winston & Strawn, Chgo., 1982-87, ptnr., 1987—, mem. exec. com. Republican. Office: Winston & Strawn 35 W Wacker Dr 45th Fl Chicago IL 60601-1695 Office Fax: 312-558-5700. E-mail: btoth@winston.com.

TÓTH, PETER PAUL, physician, researcher; b. Torrington, Conn., May 5, 1959; s. John and Ilona Barbara (Bereczky) T.; m. Karen Faye Ireland, June 3, 1989. AB, Princeton U., 1981; PhD, Mich. State U., 1988; MD, Wayne State U., 1992. Cert. Am. Bd. Family Practice, Am. Bd. of Clin. Lipidology. Resident U. Iowa; dir. preventive cardiology Sterling Rock Falls Clinic, Ltd.; chief of medicine CGH Med. Ctr. Clin. assoc. prof. U. Ill. Coll. Medicine, Peoria, So. Ill. U. Sch. Medicine, Springfield; bd. dirs. Midwest Cardiovascular Rsch. Found. Co-author: (textbooks) Handbook of Family Practice, 1997, Comprehensive Management of High Risk Cardiovascular Patients, 2006, Therapeutic Lipidology, 2007, Current Controversies in Dyslipidemia Management, 2007, Practical Lipid Management, 2007; editor-in-chief: Jour. Applied Rsch. Clin. and Exptl. Therapeutics; co-contbr. articles to Pediatrics Jour., Jour. Pediatrics Surgery, Jour. Biol. Chemistry, Arch. Biochem. Biophysics, Comp. Biochem. Physiol., Methods Enzymol., Nutrition, Circulation, Current Opinion in Cardiology, Am. Jour. Cardiology, Current Opinion in Lipidology, Family Practice Recertification, Clin. Therapeutics; sect. editor: Current Atherosclerosis Reports; mem. editl. bd. Future Lipidology, MosbyGenRx, Jour. Clin. Lipidology. Recipient Searle-Donald F. Richardson Meml. Prize, Am. Coll. Ob-Gyn. Fellow: Am. Coll. Chest Physicians, Am. Coll. Cardiology (mem. coun. cardiovascular disease prevention), Am. Heart Assn. (mem. clin. affairs com.), Internat. Coll. Angiology, Am. Acad. Family Physicians; mem.: AMA, AAAS, Midwest Cardiovascular Rsch. Found. (bd. dirs.), Nat. Lipid Assn. (bd. dirs., bd. dirs. midwest chpt., sec. midwest chpt.), Sigma Xi, Alpha Omega Alpha. Roman Catholic. Achievements include research in mitochondrial respiration, carnitine metabolism, enzymology, spectroscopy, lipidology, heart disease prevention. Home: 17719 Grandview Dr Sterling IL 61081-8564 Office: Sterling Rock Falls Clinic 101 E Miller Rd Sterling IL 61081 Business E-Mail: peter.toth@srfc.com.

TOTH, ROBERT CHARLES, retired journalist; b. Blakely, Pa., Dec. 24, 1928; s. John and Tillie (Szuch) T.; m. Paula Goldberg, Apr. 12, 1954; children: Jessica, Jennifer, John. BS in Chem. Engring., Washington U., St. Louis, 1952; MS in Journalism, Columbia U., 1955; postgrad., Harvard U., 1960-61. Started as engr. in Army Ordnance Dept., 1952—54; reporter Providence Jour., 1955—57; sci. reporter N.Y. Herald Tribune, 1957—62, N.Y. Times, 1962—63; mem. staff Los Angeles Times, 1963—93, bur. chief London, 1965—70, diplomatic corr., 1970—71, White House corr. Washington, 1972—74, bur. chief Moscow, 1974—77, nat. security corr.

Washington bur., 1977—93; ret. Cons. opinion poll in U.S. and abroad by Times Mirror Ctr. (now Pew Rsch. Ctr.) for People and Press, 1990, sr. assoc., 1993-98. Co-author: The Dimishing Divide, Religion's Changing Role in American Politics, 2000. Served with USMC, 1946-48. Recipient Overseas Press Club award, 1977, Sigma Delta Chi award, 1977, George Polk award in Journalism for fgn. reporting L.I. U., 1978, Columbia U. Alumni award, 1978, Wienthal award Fgn. Service Inst., Georgetown U., 1986, Edwin N. Hood award Nat. Press Club, 1986; Pulitzer Travelling scholar, 1955; Nieman fellow Harvard U., 1960-61 Mem. Coun. on Fgn. Rels. Home: 21 Primrose St Chevy Chase MD 20815-4228 E-mail: tothrc@aol.com.

TOTTEN, CHARLES ARTHUR, sales executive; b. Marengo, Ind., Feb. 12, 1942; s. Paul Anthony and Rose Louise (Applegate) Totten; m. Kyong Hui, May 10, 1965; children: Thomas L., Lisa L., Pauline K. Student, Purdue U., Westville, Ind., Valparaiso Inst. Tech., Ind. Cert. supr. Purdue U. North Ctrl. Elec. motor inspector Bethlehem Steel, Burns Harbor Divsn., Chesterton, Ind., 1966—70, foreman, 1970—75, gen. foreman elec. dept., 1975—99, sr. supr. svcs. divsn., 1999—2003, supt. svcs. divsn., 2003—; nat. accts. mgr. Morris Material Handling P&H, Michigan City, Ind., 2003—. Contbr. articles to profl. jours. Sp5 US Army, 1963—66, Korea, Germany, USA. Fellow: Assn. Iron and Steel Tech. (chair mech. working group 1984—2005, Disting. mem., chair 1999—2003); mem.: KC (bd. dirs. 1977, named Grand Knight 1975—77), Am. Soc. Mech. Engrs. Avocations: gardening, carpentry. Office: Morris Material Handling P&H 2712 South 163rd St New Berlin WI 53151 Office Phone: 219-877-8483.

TOTTEN, GEORGE OAKLEY, III, political science professor; b. Washington, July 21, 1922; s. George Oakley Totten Jr. and Vicken (von Post) Börjesson Totten Barrois; m. Astrid Maria Anderson, June 26, 1948 (dec. Apr. 26, 1975); children: Vicken Yuriko, Linnea Catherine; m. Lilia Huiying Li, July 1, 1976 (dec. Nov. 7, 2004); 1 child, Blanche Maluk Lemes. Cert., U. Mich., 1943; AB, Columbia U., 1946, AM, 1949; MA, Yale U., 1950, PhD, 1954; docentur i japanologi, Stockholm U., 1977. Lectr. Columbia U., NYC, 1954-55; rsch. assoc. Fletcher Sch. Law and Diplomacy Harvard U. and Tufts U., Mass., 1956—58; asst. prof. MIT, Cambridge, 1958-59, Boston U., 1959-61; assoc. prof. U. R.I., Kingston, 1961-64, Mich. State U., 1964—65; assoc. prof. polit. sci. U. So. Calif., LA, 1965-68, prof., 1968-92, chmn. dept., 1980-86, prof. emeritus, 1992—96, disting. prof. emeritus, 1996—. Dir., founder Calif. Pvt. Univs. and Colls. Yr.-in-Japan program Weseda U., 1967-73; 1st dir. East Asian Studies Ctr., 1974-77; 1st non-linguistics dir. USC-UCLA Joint East Asian Studies Ctr., 1976-77; sr. affiliated scholar Ctr. for Multiethnic and Transnat. Studies, 1993-98; chair USC Korea Project, 1998—; vis. prof. U. Stockholm, 1977-79, 1st dir. Ctr. Pacific Asia Studies, 1986-89, sr. counselor bd. dirs., 1989—; hon. pres. Huaxiu Pvt. Sch., Anyang City, Henan Province, China, 1999—; vis. prof. Ctr. for Japanese Studies, U. Hawaii, Manoa, 1992-93. Author: The Social Democratic Movement in Prewar Japan, 1966, Chinese edit., 1987, Korean edit., 1997, internet edit., 2005; co-author: Socialist Parties in Postwar Japan, 1966, Japan and the New Ocean Regime, 1984, Japan in the World, the World in Japan, Fifty Years of Japanese Studies at Michigan, 2001; editor: Democracy in Prewar Japan: Groundwork or Facade?, 1965, Helen Foster Snow's Song of Ariran, 1973, Korean edit., 1991, Korean 2d and 3d edits., 2005, Chinese edit., 1993, Kim Dae-jung's A New Beginning, 1996, Lee Hee-ho's (Mrs. KimDae-Jung's) Praying for Tomorrow: Letters to My Husband in Prison, 1999; author, co-editor: Developing Nations: Quest for a Model, 1970, Japanese edit., 1975, The Whaling Issue in U.S.-Japan Relations, 1978, China's Economic Reform: Administering the Introduction of the Market Mechanism, 1992, Community in Crisis: The Korean American Community After the Los Angeles Civil Unrest of April 1992, 1994, Korean edit., 2003, Mini Topical Chinese-English Dictionary, 2005, co-trans.: Ch'ien Mu's Traditional Government in Imperial China, 1982, 1st paperback edit., 2000; contbr. Sources of the Japanese Tradition, 1958, Aspects of Social Change in Modern Japan, 1967, Japan in Crisis: Essays on Taishō Democracy, 1974, The Politics of Divided Nations, 1991, Chinese edit., 1995, Japanese edit., 1997, mem. editl. bd. Acta Koreana, 1997—2003. Mem. coun. China Soc. for People's Friendship Studies, Beijing, 1991—; mem. nat. adv. com. Assn. Korean Polit. Studies in N.Am., 1992—, v.p., 1996—98; advisor Chinese Am. Alliance for China's Peaceful Reunification, 2002—; mem. nat. adv. com. Japan Am. Student Conf., 1984—2005; v.p. Lilia Li's China Seminar, 1985—2004; mem. U.S.-China People's Friendship Assn., Washington, 1974—, Com. on U.S.-China Rels., NYC, 1975—; chmn. L.A.-Pusan Sister City Assn., LA, 1976—77; founding mem. L.A.-Guangzhou Sister City Assn., 1981, bd. dirs., 1990—; mem. World Feds., 1982—2004, Citizens for Global Solutions, 2004—; bd. dirs. Assn. for Study of Korean Culture and Identity, 1999—2000. 1st lt. AUS, 1942—46, PTO. Recipient plaque for program on Korean studies, Consulate Gen. of Republic of Korea, 1974, Philippine Liberation medal, 1994; fellow Social Sci. Rch. Coun., 1952—53; grantee Ford Found., 1955—58, NSF, 1979—81, Korea Found., 1993, Rebuild L.A., 1993. Mem.: U. So. Calif. Faculty Ctr., European Assn. Japanese Studies, Japan-Am. Soc. Calif. (bd. dirs. 1990—94), Japanese Polit. Sci. Assn., Internat. Studies Assn., Internat. Polit. Sci. Assn., Asia Soc., Am. Polit. Sci. Assn., Assn. Asian Studies, Swedish Club of L.A., Phi Beta Delta (founding mem. Beta Kappa chpt. 1993—). Episcopalian. Home: 5129 Village Green Ct 17 Los Angeles CA 90016-5205 Office: USC Korea Project Dept Polit Sci VKC 327 Los Angeles CA 90089-0044 Office Phone: 323-296-3963. Business E-Mail: totten@usc.edu.

TOTTEN, HERMAN LAVON, dean, library and information science educator; BA, Wiley Coll.; MLS, U. Okla., PhD in Ednl. Media/Libr. Sci. Chief libr. Wiley Coll., academic dean Marshall, Tex.; assoc. dean Coll. Libr. and Info. Sci., U. Ky.; prof., dean U. Oreg.; faculty mem. Sch. Libr. and Info. Scis., U. North Tex., Denton, 1977—, Regents prof., 1991—, assoc. dean, dean, 2005—; faculty exec. asst. to pres. U. North Tex., Denton. Commr. US Nat. Commn. on Librs. and Info. Sci., 2004—. Co-editor: Administrative Effects of Education for Librarianship, 1975; co-author: Culturally Diverse Library Collections for Children, 1995, Model Policies for Small and Medium Public Libraries, 1998. Mem.: ALA (life; past pres., Melvil Dewey Award 2001), Am. Records Mgmt. Assn., Tex. Libr. Assn. Office: Sch Libr and Info Sci U North Tex PO Box 311068 Denton TX 76203-1068 E-mail: totten@lis.admin.unt.edu. *

TOTTEN, PATRICIA A., lawyer; b. Cleve., Ohio; BA in Philosophy, Eckerd Coll.; MEd, Kent St. U., Ohio; JD, So. Tex. Coll. Law, 1983. Bar: Tex. Former v.p. mktg. Verizon Wireless; former gen. coun. Houston Data Svc. Co.; dep. gen. counsel Enterprise Products Partners L.P, 2002—06; v.p., gen. coun., corp. sec. TEPPCO Partners, L.P., 2006—. Office: TEPPCO 1100 Louisiana St Houston TX 77002 *

TOTTENHAM, TERRY OLIVER, lawyer; b. Dallas, June 5, 1944; s. Edwin Pier and Ruth Elizabeth (Paris) T.; m. Carolyn Sue Lewis, July 7, 1967; children: Leslie Jo, Dana Elizabeth, Jessica Leigh. Student, Blinn Jr. Coll., 1962-67; BS in Pharmacy with high honors, U. Tex.-Austin, 1967, JD with honors, 1970; LL.M., George Washington U., 1973. Bar: Tex. 1970, U.S. Ct. Mil. Appeals 1971. Assoc. Fulbright, Crooker & Jaworski, Houston, 1970; ptnr. Fulbright & Jaworski LLP, Austin, Tex., 1978—, and head pharmaceutical and med. device litig. group. Mem. faculty South Tex. Coll. Law, U. Houston; vis. prof. med. jurisprudence Baylor U.; vis. prof. health law Tex. Women's U.; adj. prof. law U. Tex. Sch. Law; speaker profl. groups Author: Texas Medical Jurisprudence; editor: Patients Rights Handbook, 1980. Served to capt. USMC, 1971-75. Recipient Gene Cavin award, 1992; named Outstanding Young Lawyer Houston, 1981, Outstanding Young Lawyer Tex., 1981. Fellow Tex. Bar Found. (life, trustee 1986—); mem. Tex. Assn. Def. Counsel, Am. Soc. Law and Medicine, Am. Soc. Pharmacy Law, Tex. Ex-Students Assn. (life), ABA, Nat. Health Lawyers Assn., Am. Acad. Hosp. Attys. (bd. dirs. 1989—), State Bar Tex. (chmn. health law sect., chmn. litigation sect, bd. dirs. 1985-86, chmn. continuing legal edn. com., Cert. of Merit award 1989), Houston Young Lawyers Assn. (dir. 1975-77), Tex. Young Lawyers Assn. (chmn. bd. 1979-80). Democrat. Episcopalian. Office: Fulbright & Jaworski LLP 600 Congress Ave Ste 2400 Austin TX 78701-3271 Office Phone: 512-474-5201. Office Fax: 512-536-4598. Business E-Mail: ttottenham@fulbright.com.

TOTTON, CARL ALLEN, II, psychologist; b. LA, May 10, 1948; s. Carl Allen and Elva T. Student, Calif. State U., 1976, BS in Rehab. Counseling, 1978, MS in Counseling, 1980; PsyD in Clin. Psychology, Pepperdine U., Malibu, Calif., 1998. Cert. sch. psychologist, counselor, Calif.; lic. psychologist, Calif., Diagnostic Ctr. South, 2006; ordained Taoist abbot, 1983. Sch. psychologist Alhambra (Calif.) Sch. Dist., LA, 1990—2006; dir. Taoist Inst., North Hollywood, Calif., 1981—. Faculty mem. Calif. State U., Northridge, 1993-96, SAMRA U. Oriental Medicine, 1996-98; dir., counselor Rehab. Counseling Assocs., North Hollywood, 1981-83; stress mgmt. cons., hypnotherapist; adj. faculty Phillips Grad. Inst. Clin. Psychology, 2005—, adj. faculty sch. psychology, 2006—; bd. advisors Rancho San Antonio Home for Boys, Chatsworth, Calif., 1996—. Author: Comprehensive Guide to Chinese Medicine and Structural Tui Na, Martial Arts Chi Kung, 1997, Pediatric Tui Na, 1998; editor: Tui Na: Chinese Healing and Acupressure Massage, 1984; author, pub., prodr., The Core System for Martial Arts, Health, and Chi Kung, 2005; contbr. articles to mags. Recipient Presdl. Sports award, 1993, 95, 97; elected to US Martial Arts Hall Fame as Grandmaster, 2002. Mem. APA, Calif. Rehab. Counseling Assn. (pres. 1983-84), Assn. Transpersonal Psychology, Nat. Assn. Sch. Psychologists, Calif. Assn. Sch. Psychologists (bd. dirs., 2001-2003, named Outstanding Sch. Psychologist 2000), Calif. Assn. Lic. Ednl. Psychologists (named Lic. Ednl. Psychologist of Yr. 1999), Calif. Assn. Marriage and Family Therapists. Democrat. Office: Taoist Inst 10630 Burbank Blvd North Hollywood CA 91601-2511 Office Phone: 818-760-4219.

TOTTORI, DAICHI, academic and trade association administrator, accountant, lawyer; b. Fukuoka, Japan, Feb. 5, 1980; arrived in US, 2001; s. Takayuki (Stepfather) and Kikuko Tottori (Stepmother), Kazuko Tottori. MBA in Acctg., Americana U., USA, 2002; AS in Fin., Am. Mgmt. and Bus. Adminstrn. Inst. and U., 2003; PhD in Tax Law (hon.), St. Regis U., Liberia, 2003; DBA (hon.), St. Bernard U. Seborga, Italy, 2005; MD, Indian Inst. Alternative Medicine, 2006. CPA Calif.; registered home inspector, Housing Inspection Found., cert. constrn. inspector, Assn. Constrn. Inspectors, constrn. project mgr., Assn. Constrn. Inspectors; registered property mgmt. dir. Japan, lic. real estate broker Japan, cert. property mgr. Japan; adminstrv. atty., Japan, enrolled agt., IRS; ordained minister Universal Ministries; sr. valuer Internat. Real Estate Inst., environ. inspector Environ. Assessment Assn., testing specialist Environ. Assessment Assn., remediation specialist Environ. Assessment Assn., rev. appraiser Nat. Assn. Rev. Appraisers and Mortgage Underwriters, registered tax preparer Calif. Full prof. St. Regis U., Liberia, 2003—05; pres. St. Bernard U. Seborga, Italy, 2004—; trade attache' Seborga Bus. Ctr., Principality of Seborga, Italy, 2004—; full prof. James Monroe U., Liberia, Liberia, 2004—. Rsch. and study Ctrl. Sch. of Plitics of Liberal Dem. Party, Tokyo, Japan, 2004; bishop Universal Ministries, Japan. Sgt. Japan Def. Force, 2006. Recipient Order of Knight, Ethiopian Order of St.Mary Zion, 2004, Insignia for Social and Cultural Achievement, Principality of Seborga, 2004. Mem.: Internat. Real Estate Inst., Housing Inspection Found., Nat. Assn. of Rev. Appraisers and Mortgage Underwrithers, Environ. Assessment Assn., Assn. of Constrn. Insp., Info. Sys. and Contorol Assn., Assn. of Cert. Fraud Examiners, Ethiopian Royal Order of St.Mary Zion, Order of St.Lazaro (Order of Knight 2004), The Imperial Soc. of St. George of Lalibela, Assn. of Frendship for Seborga, Japan. Achievements include Knight Order from Ethipia Royal Family; Insignia from Principality of Seborga. Home Phone: 81-90-1347-3515. Personal E-mail: dtottori@hotmail.com.

TOTTY, TOTTY OKORO, soccer coach; b. Calabar, Cross River, Nigeria, June 26, 1966; arrived in U.S., 1989; s. Joseph Okoro and Rachael Okoro Totty. BS in Bus. Comm., So. NH U., Manchester, 1993, MS in Internat. Bus., 1995. Camp co-dir. John Rootes Soccer Sch., Manchester, 1990—2000; asst. coach women's soccer So. NH U., Manchester, 1995—97; city dir. coaching Amherst Soccer Club, NH, 1996—98; head coach women's soccer Clayton State U., Morrow, Ga., 1998—; state staff coach Ga. Olympics Devel. Program, Atlanta, 2001—. Mem. adv. com. S.E. region NCAA, Hickory, NC, 2001—04; conf. chair Peach Belt Conf. W. Soc. Coaches, Augusta, Ga., 2001—02; mem. Nigerian Nat. Soccer Team. Mem. Global Citizens Cir., 1990—; active Big Brother/Big Sister, Manchester, 1994. Named Rookie of Yr., New Eng. Conf., 1989; named to Hall of Fame, So. NH U., 2000. Mem.: US Soccer Fedn. (youth soccer referee 1998—), Nat. Soccer Coaches Assn. of Am. (All-Am. Soccer Player 1991—93). Independent. Avocations: music, theater, dance, movies, art. Home: 639 Garden Walk Blvd # 336 College Park GA 30349 Office: Clayton State U 2000 Clayton State Blvd Morrow GA 30260 Office Phone: 678-466-4684. Office Fax: 678-466-4699. Business E-Mail: tottytotty@clayton.edu.

TOUBY, KATHLEEN ANITA, lawyer; b. Miami Beach, Feb. 20, 1943; d. Harry and Kathleen Rebecca (Hamper) T.; m. Joseph Thomas Woodward; children: Mark Andrew, Judson David Touby. BS in Nursing, U. Fla., 1965, MRC in Rehab. Counseling, 1967; JD with honors, Nova U., 1977. Bar: Fla. 1978, D.C. 1978. Counselor Jewish Vocat. Svc., Chgo., 1967-68; rehab. counselor Fla. Dept. Vocat. Rehab., Miami, 1968-70; spl. asst., asst. U.S. atty. U.S. Dept. Justice, Miami, 1978-80; assoc. Pyszka & Kessler, P.A., Miami, 1980-83; ptnr. Touby & Smith, P.A., Miami, 1983-89, Touby, Smith, DeMahy & Drake, P.A., Miami, 1989-94, Touby & Woodward, P.A., Miami, 1994—. Chmn. adv. exec. bd. Paralegal Edn. program Barry U., 1986-87; lectr. Food and Drug Law Inst., 1987-89, 91; lectr. environ. law Exec. Enterprises, 1987-88; lectr. trial techniques, Hispanic Nat. Bar Assn., St. Thomas Law Sch.; adj. prof. product liability Can. Govt., U.S. Trade and Mktg. Dept., 1989-95. Co-author: The Environmental Litigation Deskbook, 1989; contbr. chpts. to books, articles to profl. jours. Mem. ABA, Am. Inns of Ct. (pres. 1998-99, pres.-elect St. Thomas Law Sch. chpt. 1997-98, pres. 1998-99), Dade County Bar Assn. (legal aid, pub. svcs. com. 1988), Fed. Bar Assn. (bd. dirs. 1989—, v.p. 1991-92, pres.-elect So. Fla. chpt. 1992-93, pres. 1993-94), Cuban-Am. Bar Assn., Phi Delta Phi (province pres. 1982-85, bd. dirs. 1985-87). Roman Catholic. Home: 4150 Bay Point Rd Miami FL 33137-3352 Office: Touby & Woodward PA 2030 Douglas Rd Ste 217 Coral Gables FL 33134 Office Phone: 305-442-2318.

TOUCHY, DEBORAH K.P., lawyer, accountant; b. Pasadena, Tex., Dec. 9, 1957; d. Donald Carl and Bobbie Jo (Jackson) Putzka; m. Harry Roy Touchy, Jr., Feb. 23, 1980. BBA, Baylor U., 1979; JD, U. Houston, 1988. Bar: Tex. 1989; CPA, Tex.; cert. in estate planning and probate law Tex. Bd. Legal Specialization. Sr. mgr. tax KMPG Peat Marwick, Houston, 1980-86; assoc. Fizer Beck Webster & Bentley, Houston, 1989-90; pvt. practice law Houston, 1990—; chmn. spl. events Jr. League Houston, 1997-98. Editor Houston Law Rev., 1988-89. Chmn. ticket sales incentives Chi Omega, Houston, 1985; active ticket sales Mus. Fine Arts, Houston, 1984; facilities chmn. Woodland Trails West Civic Orgn., Houston, 1982-83; pres. Women Attys. in Tax & Probate, 1994-95, pres., 2004; bd. dirs. Episcopal Ch. Women at St. John the Divine; active St. John's Sch., 1999-, Lower Sch. Scrapbook Chmn. 2001-02; mem. steering com. Girl Scouts of San Jacinto County Capital Campaign, 2003-. Recipient Outsanding Alumni award, Beta Alpha Psi, 1997. Mem. ABA (estate-probate sect. 1989—, vice chmn. commn. property com. 1994—), AICPA (taxation sect., estate and gift tax com. 1992-95, 98-2000), Tex. Soc. CPAs (bd. dirs. 1995—, chmn. tax inst. com. 1996-97, estate planning com. 1990-94, 96—), Houston Chpt. CPAs (chmn. taxpayer edn. 1985-86, chmn. membership com. 1992-93, v.p. 1993-94, 96-97, chmn. tax forums 1994-95, long range planning com. 1995-96, chmn. leadership devel. 1997-98, treas. 1998-99, chmn. ann. charity event 1999-2000, bd. dirs. 1999-2000, 2002-03, pres. 2001-02), Houston Bar Assn. (estate-probate sect. 1989—), State Bar Tex. (estate-probate sect. 1989—, mem. elder law com. 1991-97), Houston Estate and Fin. Forum, Baylor U. Women's Assn. (treas. 1993-94, chmn. fin. com. 1994-95, parliamentarian 1995-96, sec. 1996-97, pres. 1997-98, chmn. audit com. 1999-2000), Chief Justice-Advocates, Tex. Bd. Legal Specializations (cert. estate planning, probate law 1994), Order of Coif, Omicron Delta Kappa, Phi Delta Phi, Beta Alpha Psi (Outstanding Alumni 1997). Office: PO Box 130122 Houston TX 77219-0122 E-mail: deborah@deborahtouchy.com.

TOUFF, MICHAEL, lawyer; b. 1945; AB, Harvard U.; JD, U. Michigan. Officer, law firm Holmes & Starr, Ireland, Stapleton, Pryor & Pascoe, P.C., 1992-94; v.p., gen. counsel MDC Holdings, Inc (Richmond Am. Homes), 1994—99, sr. v.p., gen. counsel, 1999—. Mem.: ABA. Office: MDC Holdings Inc 4350 S Monaco St Denver CO 80237 *

TOUHILL, BLANCHE MARIE, retired academic administrator, historian, educator; b. St. Louis, Mo., July 1, 1931; d. Robert and Margaret (Walsh) Van Dillen; m. Joseph M. Touhill, Aug. 29, 1959. BA in History, St. Louis U., 1953, MA in Geography, 1954, PhD in History, 1962. Prof. history and edn. U. Mo., St. Louis, 1965-73, assoc. dean faculties, 1974-76, assoc. vice chancellor for acad. affairs, 1976-87, vice chancellor, 1987-90, chancellor, 1991—2002, chancellor emeritus, 2002—. Bd. dirs. Peabody Energy, Inc. Author: William Smith O'Brien and His Irish Revolutionary Companions in Penal Exile, 1981, The Emerging University UM-St. Louis, 1963-83, 1985; editor: Readings in American History, 1970, Varieties of Ireland, 1976. Named Outstanding Educator St. Louis chpt. Urban League, 1976; recipient Leadership award St. Louis YWCA, 1986. Mem. Nat. Assn. State Univs. and Land Grant Colls. (exec. com. 1988—), Am. Com. on Irish Studies (pres. 1991—), Phi Kappa Phi, Alpha Sigma Lambda. E-mail: j_touhill@hotmail.com.

TOUHILL, C. JOSEPH, environmental engineer; b. Newark, Aug. 27, 1938; s. Charles J. and Caroline A. T.; m. Helen Elizabeth O'Malley, June 11, 1960; children: Gregory Joseph, Stephen Mark, Christopher Alan, Kathleen Elizabeth. BCE, Rensselaer Poly. Inst., 1960, PhD in Environ. Engring., 1964; SM, MIT, 1961; postgrad., U. Wash., 1970. Diplomate Am. Acad. Environ. Engrs. Mgr. water and land resources dept. Battelle Meml. Inst., Richland, Wash., 1964-71; pres. Baker/TSA Inc., Pitts., 1977-90; group sr. v.p. ICF Kaiser Engrs. Inc., Pitts., 1990-94; exec. v.p. EG&G Environ. Inc., Pitts., 1994-97; pres. Touhill Tech. Mgmt. Corp., Jamison, Pa., 1997-99, 2003—; nat. discipline lead for process and environ. engring. Tetra Tech FW, Inc. (formerly Foster Wheeler Environ. Corp.), Langhorne, Pa., 1999—2003. Co-author: Hazardous Materials Spills Handbook, 1982, Hazardous Waste Management Engineering, 1987; editor: Resource Management in the Great Lakes Basin, 1971; mem. editorial bd. Environ. Progress Jour., 1979-93. Trustee Am. Acad. Environ. Engr., 1971-77, 83-86; bd. dirs. Suburban Gen. Hosp., Pitts., 1986-96; vice chmn. Franklin Park (Pa.) Authority, 1977-96, chmn. adv. com., dept. Environ. and energy Engring., Rensselaer Polytech Inst., 1996-98, mem. adv. bd. dept. civil and environ. engring., 2000-06. Recipient fellow award Rensselaer Alumni Assn., 1994; Kappe lectr. AAEE, 1992. Fellow ASCE (life), AIChE (chmn. environ. engring. div. 1977, Inst. fellow 2000), Am. Chem. Soc. (editl. adv. bd. 1975-77), Am. Water Works Assn. (life), Water Environment Fedn. (life). Office: 2269 Sunrise Way Jamison PA 18929 Home Phone: 215-491-5616; Office Phone: 215-491-5617. Business E-Mail: jtouhill@alum.mit.edu.

TOULANTIS, MARIE J., retail executive; BBA in Mktg., Pace Univ. V.p. The Chase Manhattan Bank, NYC, 1987-96, sr. v.p., 1996-97; exec. v.p. fin. Barnes & Noble Inc., NYC, 1997-99, CFO barnesandnoble.com Inc., 1995—2001, pres., COO, barnesandnoble.com, 2001, now CEO, barnesandnoble.com. Bd. dir. Hershey Foods Corp. Adv. bd. Lubin Sch. Bus., Pace University. Office: Barnes & Noble dot com Barnes & Noble Inc 2nd fl 122 Fifth Ave New York NY 10011

TOULMIN, PRIESTLEY, retired geologist; b. Birmingham, Ala., June 5, 1930; s. Priestley and Catharine Augusta (Carey) T.; m. Martha Jane Slason, Aug. 30, 1952; children: Catharine Bosier (Mrs. Robert G. Gibson), Priestley Chewning. AB, Harvard U., 1951, PhD, 1959; MS, U. Colo., 1953. With U.S. Geol. Survey, Washington, 1953-56, 57-89, staff geologist for exptl. geology, 1966, chief br. exptl. geochemistry, 1966-71, geologist geologic div., 1971-89, Reston, Va., 1974-89, ret., 1989; also leader inorganic chemistry team NASA (Viking Project). Adj. prof. Columbia U., 1966; rsch. asso. in geochemistry Calif. Inst. Tech., 1976-77; vis. lectr. Am. Geol. Inst.; dir. petrogenesis and mineral resources program NSF, 1985; bd. dirs., treas. 28th Internat. Geol. Congress, 1985-86 Mng. sci. editor Geochemistry Internat., 1965-68; assoc. editor Am. Mineralogist, 1974-76; contbr. articles to profl. jours. Mem. adv. com. sch. edn., Alexandria, Va., 1977-80. Recipient Exceptional Service medal NASA, 1977; Meritorious Service award U.S. Dept. Interior, 1978 Fellow Geol. Soc. Am., Mineral Soc. Am. (bd. assoc. editors 1974-76), Soc. Econ. Geologists, Explorers Club; mem. AAAS, Geol. Soc. Washington (2d v.p. 1977, councillor 1973-74, 90-91, 1st v.p. 1981, pres. 1982), Am. Geophys. Union, Soc. Mayflower Descs., Jamestowne Soc., S.R., SAR, Soc. Colonial Wars (DC), Aztec Club of 1847, St. Andrews Soc. (Washington), Cosmos Club (pres. 1993-94, found. trustee 1994—, chmn. 1996-2001), Sigma Xi, Sigma Gamma Epsilon. Home: 418 Summers Dr Alexandria VA 22301-2449 Office: PO Box 183 Alexandria VA 22313-0183

TOUMEY, DONALD JOSEPH, lawyer; BA, Williams Coll., 1978; JD, Yale U., 1981. Bar: N.Y. 1982, D.C. 1985, U.S. Supreme Ct. 1986. Law clk. to judge U.S. Ct Appeals (2d cir.), NYC, 1981-82; spl. asst. to gen. counsel U.S. Dept. Treasury, Washington, 1982-85; assoc. Sullivan & Cromwell, NYC, 1985-90; ptnr., 1990—. Republican. Office: Sullivan & Cromwell LLP 125 Broad St New York NY 10004-2489 Office Phone: 212-558-4077. Business E-Mail: toumeyd@sullcrom.com.

TOUPIN, HAROLD OVID, retired chemical company executive; b. Hibbing, Minn., Jan. 21, 1927; s. Ovid Pascal and Ellen (Holt) T.; m. Edna F. Sallila, Feb. 8, 1948 (div. Feb. 1973); m. Colleen Beverly Lange, Apr. 18, 1981; children: James, Ronald. BS, U. Minn., 1954, MA, 1955, postgrad, 1968; PhD (hon.), Internat. Acad. Color, Las Vegas, Nev., 1982, U. Mont., 1990. Mgr. Firestone Tire Co., East Los Angeles, Calif., 1948-51; dir. vocat. edn. Hopkins (Minn.) Pub. Schs., 1955-75; with research and devel. Power-o-Peat Co., Gilbert, Minn., 1956-67; chief exec. officer, cons. Color Specialties Inc., Mpls., 1976-98; ret., 1999. Pres., founder travel, meeting planners svc. co., 1990; founder internat. office for color specialties, 1994; bd. dirs. Vu-tek Inc., St. Paul, Airport Auto Sales, St. Paul Color Specialties of Nev., Las Vegas, Instant Air Inc., Mpls., Freedom Fin.; cons. Runs Hot Cons. Svc., 1966-75; ptnr. Vermes Jewelry, Mpls., 1956-80. Contbr. articles to profl. jours. Bd. dirs. Hopkins Jaycees, 1958-60. Served with USAAF, 1944-47. Mem. Am. Assn. Mfrs., Internat. Assn. Color, Nat. Ret. Tchrs. Assn., Am. Assn. Self Employeed, Met. Area Dist. Edn. Instrs. Assn. (pres.), Mpls. C. of C. (Super Bowl com. 1992), Am. Legion, VFW, Lions (sec. Hopkins club 1956-76, bd. dirs., 2d v.p. Sun City West Pioneer club 2005—). Democrat. Roman Catholic. Avocations: travel, golf, writing. Personal E-mail: haroldtoupin@peoplepc.com.

TOUR, JAMES M., chemistry educator, researcher; b. NYC, Aug. 18, 1959; s. Eli and Hedi T.; m. Shireen Grace Massey, May 29, 1982; children: Ambreen, Sabrina, Josiah, Benaiah. BS cum laude, Syracuse U., Syracuse, NY, 1981; PhD, Purdue U., West Layafette, Ind., 1986. Asst. prof. dept. chemistry and biochemistry U. S.C., Columbia, 1988—92, assoc. prof. dept. chemistry and biochemistry, 1992—94, prof. dept. chemistry and biochemistry, 1994—96; Disting. faculty assoc. Hanzen Coll. Rice U., Houston, 1999—2000, Chao prof. of chemistry, 1999—, prof. mech. engring. and materials sci., 1999—, prof. computer sci., 1999—; co-founder, v.p. Molecular Electronics Corp., Houston, 1999—; also bd. dirs. Postdoctoral fellow NIH, 1987—88; One week vis. lectr. polymer divsn. IBM, 1988; vis. scholar dept. chemistry Harvard U., 1994; mem. CAREER program adv. com. NSF, 1995, mem. adv. com. Materials Rsch. Ctr., 1996—97; mem. Gov.'s Maths. and Sci. Adv. Bd. S.C., 1996—98, Calif. Molecular Electronics Corp., 1998—99; Weissberger-Williams lectr. Estman Kodak Corp., 1995; Abbott Disting. lectr. Colo. State U., 1997; s. Author: Molecular Electronics: Commercial Insights, Chemistry, Devices, Architecture, and Programming; contbr. articles. Mem. Def. Sci. Study Group, 2003; bible study tchr. Broad River Maximum Security Prison, Columbia, SC, 1989—99. Recipient award, Am. Inst. Chemists, 1981, Exxon Ednl. Found. rsch. and tng. award, Exxon, 1994, NSF Presdl. Young Investigator award in polymer chemistry, NSF, 1991-1996, Office of Naval Rsch. Young Investigator award in polymer chemistry, Office of Naval Rsch., 1989-1992; fellow Celanese Corp. grad. fellowship in chemistry, Celanese Corp., 1981-1982; IBM Corp. full grad. fellowship in polymer chemistry, IBM, 1985-1986. Mem.: AAAS (assoc.), Materials Reserach Soc. (assoc.), Am. Chem. Soc. (assoc.; assoc. dir. polymer divsn. materials rsch. secretariat 1991—95, mem. editl. adv. bd. chem. revs. 1999—2003, Arthur C. Cope Scholar award 2007). Avocations: Bible study, target shooting. Office: Dept Chemistry Rice U 6100 Main St Houston TX 77005 E-mail: tour@rice.edu. *

TOURINO, RALPH GENE, aerospace transportation executive; b. LA, Mar. 11, 1941; s. John Tourino and Zalia Rose (Perez) Chacon; m. Sherry Lane Tisdail, Sept. 5, 1964; children: Christina Marie, Rebecca Kathleen. BS, UCLA, 1964; MPA, Auburn U., 1973; MBA, U. So. Calif., 1975; postgrad. sr. officials in nat. security, Harvard U., 1988. Commd. 2d lt. USAF, 1964, advanced through grades to maj. gen., 1992; student Undergrad. Navigator Tng., James Connally AFB, Tex., 1964-65; C-97 navigator AF Western Test Range, Vanderberg AFB, Calif., 1965-66; navigator HQ 7th AF Flight Ops., Tan Son Nhut AB, Vietnam, 1966-67; mem. KC135 Crew, March AFB, Calif., 1967-70; sect. comdr. Squadron Officer Sch., Maxwell AFB, Ala., 1970-73; program control Space Div., L.A. AF Sta., 1975-78; dir. program control NAVSTAR Global Positioning System, L.A. AF Sta., 1978-80; dir. contracts Space Def. Systems Program Office, L.A. AF Sta., 1980-82; systems program dir. Inertial Upper Stage Program, L.A. AF Sta., 1982-85; asst. dep. cmdr. for Small ICBM Ballistic Missile Office, Norton AFB, Calif., 1985-87; asst. dep. chief of Staff Systems AF Systems Command, Andrews AFB, Md., 1987-88, insp. gen., 1988-89; comdr. Ballistic Missile Orgn., Norton AFB, 1989-91; program dir. B-2 System Program Office, Wright-Patterson AFB, Ohio, 1991—94; retired as maj. gen. USAF, 1994; v.p., space support systems Lockheed Martin, Santa Maria, Calif. Decorated Legion of Merit, Def. Meritorious Svc. medal, Meritorious Svc. medal, Air medal, Air Force Commendation medal; named one of 50 Most Important Hispanics in Tech. & Bus. Hispanic Engr. & Info. Tech. mag., 2005. Mem. Air Force Assn., AIAA. Republican. Avocation: exercising. Office: Lockheed Martin 6801 Rockledge Dr Bethesda MD 20817

TOURKOW, JOSHUA ISAAC, lawyer; b. Fort Wayne, Ind., Mar. 5, 1947; s. Frederick Rhinehold and Leah Sarah (Schwartz) T.; m. Donna Susan Dubin, Aug. 30, 1970; children— Iliana Joy, Lisa Michelle, Benjamin Ahron. Student Bar Ilan U., Israel, 1968; B.S. in Indsl. Mgmt., Purdue U., 1970; JD, Ind. U., Indpls., 1973. Bar: Ind. 1973, U.S. Dist. Cts. (no. and so. dists.) Ind. 1973, U.S. Ct. Appeals (7th cir.) 1973. Asst. dep. prosecutor Marion County, Indpls., 1972-73; ptnr. Tourkow, Crell, Rosenblatt & Johnston, Ft. Wayne, 1973—. Bd. dirs. Housing & Neighborhood Devel. Services, Inc., Ft. Wayne, 1980-84, Ft. Wayne Redevel. Com., 1983; atty. Ft. Wayne Housing Authority, 1983—87; advisor, atty. Parents Without Partners, Ft. Wayne, 1981-85, Fathers United for Equal Rights, Ft. Wayne, 1980—. Mem. ABA, Ind. Bar Assn. (chair of family law, 1992-994), Allen County Bar Assn (chair family law sect. 2000-02). Home: 7022 Winchester Rd Fort Wayne IN 46819-1530 Office: Tourkow Crell Rosenblatt & Johnston 203 E Berry Sts Rm 814 Fort Wayne IN 46802 Office Phone: 260-426-0545. Business E-Mail: jtourkow@tcrjlaw.com.

TOURLITSAS, JOHN CONSTANTINE, radiologist; b. Cavala, Greece, Oct. 4, 1926; came to U.S., 1956; s. Constantine Nacos and Marica Constantine (Athanasiou) T. MD, U. Athens, Greece, 1955. Diplomate Am. Bd. Radiology. Intern Sioux Valley Hosp., Sioux Falls, SD, 1956-57; resident Midway Hosp., Mpls.-St. Paul, 1957-59, New Eng. Deaconess Hosp./Harvard U., Boston, 1959-60, Mass. Meml. Hosps./Boston U., 1960-61, Toronto (Ont., Can.) Western Hosp.-U. Toronto, 1961-62; rsch. fellow in radiology Postgrad. Rsch. Inst. Hosp for Sick Children, U. Toronto, 1962; resident Sunnybrook VA Hosp.-U. Toronto, 1963, Royal Victoria Hosp., McGill U., Montreal, 1963-65; attending radiologist, vis. radiologist Maimonides Med. Ctr., Coney Island Hosp., Bklyn., 1966-68; attending, cons. radiologist Bronx (N.Y.)-Lebanon Hosp. Ctr.-Albert Einstein Coll. Med., 1968-95; ret., 1995. Instr. radiology Albert Einstein Coll. Medicine, 1972-77. Joslin Clinic fellow, Boston, 1959-60. Fellow Am. Coll. Chest Physicians; mem. AMA, Am. Coll. Radiology, Am. Roentgen Ray Soc., Radiol. Soc. N.Am., N.Y. State Med. Soc. Avocations: reading, walking, travel. Home: 372 Fifth Ave Apt 8C New York NY 10018-8109

TOURNILLON, NICHOLAS BRADY, investment company executive; b. New Orleans, Sept. 1, 1933; s. Samuel C. and Anna Mae (Brady) T.; m. Audrey Nicosia, Dec. 15, 1956; children: Brady, Linda, Tracy, Jeffrey, Gregory, Lori. BA, Southeastern La. U., 1958; MBA, La. State U., 1960. Loan officer Export Import Bank U.S., Washington, 1960-66; adminstrv. asst. to exec. officers Atlantic Gulf & Pacific Co. of Manila, 1966-68; asst. treas. GTE Internat., Stamford, Conn., 1968-76, treas., 1976-86, v.p., 1978-86; pres. GTE Fin. Corp., 1984-86; asst. treas. GTE Corp., 1985-86; chmn., chief exec. officer Am. and Internat. Investment Corp., 1986-98; pres., CEO Definco Ltd., 1998—. Bd. dirs. Global Access Corp.; mem. internat. adv. bd. Union Trust Co.; advisor on export fin. to Office of U.S. Pres. (U.S. Trade Rep.). Past chmn. Conn. Dist. Export Council of US Dept. Commerce; mem. monetary com. U.S. Council Internat. Bus.; bd. dirs. Nat. Fgn. Trade Council, Southeastern La. U. Devel. Fund. Served with USNR, 1953-54, Korea. Named Outstanding Alumnus of Yr., Southeastern La. U., 1976 Mem. Soc. Internat. Treasurers, Acad. Internat. Bus., Retired Men's Assn. of Greenwich, Phi Kappa Phi. Home: Midwod Dr Greenwich CT 06831-4400 Office: Definco Ltd 25 Midwood Dr Greenwich CT 06831-4412 *Perseverance is an often mentioned but never overrated quality— the quality that prevents the substitution of expediency for excellence. Throughout life, persevering effort has been responsible for converting ideas and talents into results and recognition.*

TOURTELLOTTE, CHARLES DEE, internist, rheumatologist, educator; b. Kalamazoo, Aug. 28, 1931; s. Dee and Helen May (Lotz) T.; m. Barbara Richwine, June 25, 1955; children: Daniel DeWitt (dec.), Elizabeth Anne, William Charles, Scott David. AB, Johns Hopkins U., 1953; MS in Biochemistry, MD, Temple U., 1957. Diplomate Am. Bd. Internal Medicine. Intern, resident in medicine U. Mich. Hosp., Ann Arbor, 1957-60; fellow in rheumatology Temple U. Hosp., Phila., 1960-61; fellow in biochemistry Rockefeller U., NYC, 1961-63; faculty Sch. Medicine, Temple U., 1963—, prof. medicine, 1972-97, prof. emeritus, 1997—; chief rheumatology Temple U. Hosp., 1994-97, pres. med. staff, bd. govs., 1984-86. Dir. Greater Delaware Valley Arthritis Control Program, 1974-77; pres. Eastern Pa. chpt. Arthritis Found., 1972-74; mem. active/cons. staff 10 area and regional hosps. Contbr. chpts. to textbooks, articles to profl. jours.; mem. editl. bd.: Arthritis and Rheumatism, 1969-77, 19th-24th Rheumatism Revs, 1969-81. Mem. Haddonfield (N.J.) Bd. Edn., 1968-74, pres., 1974; mem. Borough of Haddonfield Environ. Comm., 1975-87, chmn., 1977-85; mem. Haddonfield Civic Assn., 1963—; South N.J. chmn. Johns Hopkins U. Alumni Schs. Com., 1975-90; trustee Bobby Fulton Meml. Fund, 1979—, 1st Presbyn. Ch. of Haddonfield, 1998-2000. With AUS, 1953-61. Helen Hay Whitney Found. fellow, 1962-63; Arthritis Found. fellow, 1963-66 Fellow ACP, Phila. Coll. Physicians, Am. Coll. Rheumatology (founding fellow); mem. Pa. Med. Soc., Phila. County Med. Soc., Babcock Surg. Soc., Phila. Rheumatism Soc. (pres. 1968-69), Pa. Rheumatology Soc. (founding pres. 1985-86), N.J. Soc. of Pa., Nat. Huguenot Soc. (surgeon gen. 2002-04), Huguenot Soc. Pa., Temple U. Med. Alumni Assn. (pres. 1997-99), Tavistock County Club (N.J.), Little Egg Harbor Yacht Club, Med. Club of Phila. (bd. dirs., pres. 1998-99), Sixty-five Club of Haddonfield (dir. 2003—), Interfaith Caregivers (trustee 2004—), Sigma Xi, Alpha Omega Alpha, Delta Upsilon, Phi Chi. Presbyterian. Home: 6 Lane Of Acres Haddonfield NJ 08033-3505 Office: Temple Univ Hosp Dept Rheumatology Philadelphia PA 19140-5192 Office Phone: 215-707-2000. Personal E-mail: cd_tourte@prodigy.net.

TOURTELLOTTE, WALLACE WILLIAM, neurologist, educator; b. Great Falls, Mont., Sept. 13, 1924; B in Philosophy, U. Chgo., 1945, BS, 1945, PhD, 1948, MD, 1951. Instr. pharmacology U. Chgo., 1948—50; intern Strong Meml. Hosp. U. Rochester Sch. Medicine and Dentistry, NY, 1951-52; resident in neurology U. Mich. Med. Ctr., Ann Arbor, 1954-57, asst. prof. neurology, 1957-59, assoc. prof., 1959-66, prof., 1966-71; prof. dept. neurology UCLA, 1971—, vice chmn. dept. neurology, 1971-98, disting. prof., 1992—, emeritus vice chmn. dept. neurology, 1998; chief neurology svcs. VA Wadsworth, West LA, Calif., 1971-99, emeritus dir. neurology tng. program, 1999—, emeritus dir. tng. program, 1999—, staff neurologist, neuroscientist, 1999—. Vis. assoc. prof. Washington U., St. Louis, 1963-64; hon. mem. med. adv. bd. Nat. Multiple Sclerosis Soc., 1968—, 1994—, So. Calif. Multiple Sclerosis Socs., 1972—; dir. Multiple Sclerosis Rsch. and Treatment Ctr., Human Brain and Spinal Fluid Resource Ctr., 1961—; reviewer profl. jours. in field. Co-editor (with Cedric Raines, Henry McFarland): Multiple Sclerosis, Clinical and Pathogenetic Basis, 1997; dedicated The Wallace W. Tourtellotte Clin. and Neurosci. Libr., 1999. Lt. (j.g.) M.C., USNR, 1952-54. Recipient Disting. Alumni Service award U. Chgo., 1982. Fellow Am. Acad. Neurology (S. Weir Mitchell Neurology Reseach award 1959); mem. Am. Neurol. Assn. (counselor 1982—, v.p. 1992), World Fedn. Neurology (founding mem.), Am. Assn. Neuropathologists, Internat. Soc. Neurochemsitry (founding mem.), Am. Soc. Pharmacology and Exptl. Therapeutics, Am. Soc. Neurochemistry (founding mem.), Soc. Neurosci., Confrerie de la Chaine des Rotisseur, Argentier du Baillage de Los Angeles (vice chanceller, comdr.), Pasadena Wine and Food Soc., Physician Wine and Food Soc., Culinary Club French Cuisine LA. Office Phone: 310-268-4638. Fax: 310-454-7650. Business E-Mail: wtourtel@ucla.edu.

TOURTET, CHRISTIANE ANDRÉE, writer, photojournalist, reporter, advocate; b. Grenoble, France, June 18, 1945; came to U.S., 1965; d. André and Maria Tourtet. Cert. completion humanistic psychology, Fla. Jr. Coll., Jacksonville, 1969; AS with high honors, Fla. Jr. Coll., 1973, AA with high honors, 1974; BA with honors, Jacksonville U., 1975. Hostess interpreter-translator Credit Lyonnais, Grenoble, 1963—65; instr. French Albany Acad. for Girls, NY, 1965—66; instr. French, asst. lang. lab. Coll. of St. Rose, Albany, 1966—67; instr. French Bartram Sch., Jacksonville, 1970; instr. French and modeling Fla. Jr. Coll., 1971—74, prodr.-dir., radio personality ednl. French program Sta. WFAM FM radio, Jacksonville, 1977—79; interpreter, translator French Lang. Bank, Jacksonville, 1980—83. Tutor pvt. and small group classes in French; model for publicity ads, brochures in major mags., newspapers; lectr. in field. Author: Fruits of Life; editor, contbr. New Leaf News, Fla. Flambeau, Back to Sch. Mag., editor, pub., contbr. Environ. Med. and Disability Corner, Tallahassee Area Ch. News, FSView, AARP Newsletter, Tallahassee Alliance with Disabilities Newsletter, recs. Flamingo Studios, Tallahassee, 1986—87; Exhibited in group shows at North Fla. Fair, Tallahassee, 2002 (1st, 2d and 3d pl. photography, 2d pl., 2003, 3 second place awards, 2005, 3 certs. pub. Today's Photographer mag, 2004, three 2d place awards, 2005), paintings exhibited in France, Monte Carlo and U.S., photography exhibited in galleries, pub. in mags. including Today's Photographer; guest appearance Phyllis Fouraker Show, Jacksonville, Fla.; actress over 28 TV commls.:; contbr. numerous newspapers and magazines. Pres. Le Cercle Francais, Albany, 1965; founder, pres. Internat. Multiple Chem. Sensitivity Awareness. Named Woman of Yr., Romanian Prince Paltin Sturdza, Princess Cornelia Sturdza and Prince Michael Sturdza, 1995, Internat. Personality of Yr., Ctr. Internat. Biography, 2001; named to Millenium Hall of Fame, Permanent Honor Roll, Internat. Freelance Photographers Orgn., 2004; recipient 1st prize Solfège Artistic Competition, 1957, 1st prize, Accordion Acad. Grenoble, 1958, Bronze medal accordion solo, Cup of France, City of Lyon, 1958, Gold medal Cup of France, 1959, Cup of Europe, 1959, 2d prize in singing, City of Grenoble, 1961, medal of City of Grenoble, 1977, medal of Dauphine County, 1977, medal of Chevalier of Order of Merit, Paris, 1976, medal of Chevalier of French Courtesy, 1977, medal of Nat. Merit, 1976, Silver medal Arts and Scis., 1977, Silver medal honor, Twentieth Century Achievement award, 1993, U.S. flag flown over Capitol in her honor, Washington, 1999—2001, Internat. Woman of Yr., Romanian Prince Paltin Sturdza, Princess Cornelia Sturdza and Prince Michael Sturdza, 1996—97, Lifetime Distinction of Honor for Photographic Achievement, Am. Image Press, 2004, Meritorious Achievement award, Internat. Peace prize, United Cultural Conv. U.S.A., 2005. Mem.: APHA, NAFE, Am. Internat. News Svc. (press), Am. Image Press, Freelance Media Svcs., Nat. Assn. Sci. Writers, Am. Med. Writers Assn., Nat. Ctr. Environ. Strategies, Chem. Injury Info. Network (judge arts and talent contest 1999), Environ. Illness Assn. Tallahassee (founder, pres. 1989—), Am. Acad. Environ. Medicine (assoc.), World Nat. Congress (senator 2003—), H.E.A.L., Share, Care, Prayers, Internat. Platform Assn., India Assn. Tallahassee (publicity officer, fashion show judge), Phi Theta Kappa. Address: PO Box 20517 Tallahassee FL 32316-0517 Personal E-mail: tourtet@yahoo.com.

TOUSLEY, REBECCA PERKINS, retired librarian; b. Columbus, Miss., Mar. 28, 1926; d. Mosey Miles and Virginia Susan (Shelton) Perkins; m. Jasper Clayton Tousley Jr., Aug. 11, 1946; children: Judith Ann, Roger Clayton, Susan Elizabeth. Student, Trevecca Nazarene Coll., 1947-48; BS in Libr. Sci., Miss. Univ. for Women, 1974, MA in English Lit., 1981. Asst. to serials libr. Fant Libr., Miss. Univ. for Women, Columbus, 1966-74, asst. serials libr., govt. publs. libr., 1974-80, govt. publs. libr., 1980-90, ret., 1990. Treas. Miss. Govt. Documents Roundtable, 1978; libr. Ch. of the Nazarene, Columbus, 1975—. Author: History of the Columbus Mississippi Church of the Nazarene, 1978; co-author Libr. Info. Bull., 1983-84. Mem. AAUW (publicity chmn. 1990-91), Miss. Univ. for Women Alumni Assn., Phi Kappa Phi (sec.-treas. 1980-82, 84-86). Avocations: homemaking, gardening, needlecrafts. Home: 415 Highway 373 Columbus MS 39705-9345

TOUSLEY, RUSSELL FREDERICK, lawyer; b. New Haven, Nov. 19, 1938; s. Russell F. and Della (Ermer) T.; m. Sarah Morford, July 23, 1963; children: Ellen Elizabeth, Kenneth Morford. BA cum laude, Yale Coll., 1960; JD, U. Wash., 1967. Bar: Wash. 1967. Assoc. Davis Wright, Seattle, 1967-69; v.p. Safecare Co., Inc., Seattle, 1969-78, Winmar Co., Inc., Seattle, 1977-78; mem. Tousley Brain Stephens PLLC, Seattle, 1978—. Trustee Seattle Opera Assn., 1980—, pres., chmn. bd., 1985-87; trustee Seattle Chamber Music Festival, 1990-93; moderator Plymouth Congl. Ch., Seattle, 1975-77, 83-85, trustee, 1969-93. Lt. (j.g.) USN, 1960-64. Mem. ABA, Wash. State Bar Assn., Seattle-King County Bar Assn., Rainier Club. Avocations: opera, reading, stamp collecting/philately. Office: Tousley Brain Stephens PLLC 1700 Seventh Ave Ste 2200 Seattle WA 98101-1332 Office Phone: 206-682-5600. Business E-Mail: rtousley@tousley.com.

TOUSSAINT, ROGER, labor union administrator; b. Port of Spain, Trinidad, Nov. 7, 1956; m. Donna Toussaint; 4 children. Attended, Brooklyn Coll. Cleaner Met. Transp. Authority (MTA), 1984—85, track maintenance worker, 1985; leader Track Div. Transport Workers Union (TWU) Local 100, NYC, 1994, pres., 2001—. Co-founder On Track newsletter. Office: TWU Local 100 80 West End Ave New York NY 10023 Office Phone: 212-873-6000.

TOUSTER, SAUL, law educator; b. Bklyn., Oct. 12, 1925; s. Ben and Bertha (Landau) T.; m. Helen Davidson, Nov. 23, 1954 (div. 1967); children: Natasha Ann, Jonathan Bach; m. Irene Tayler, Jan. 14, 1978. AB magna cum laude, Harvard U., 1944, JD, 1948. Bar: N.Y. 1949. Practiced in, NYC, 1949-55; prof. law SUNY-Buffalo, 1955-69, asst. to pres., 1966-68, mem. adj. faculty in medicine, edn., psychology, 1964-69; prof. law and social scis. State Coll. at Old Westbury, 1969-71; prof., provost, acad. v.p. CCNY, 1971-73; acting pres. Richmond Coll. City U. N.Y., 1973-74; prof. law CUNY Grad. Sch. also John Jay Coll. of Criminal Justice, 1974-80; prof., dir. legal studies, humanities, professions programs Brandeis U., Waltham, Mass., 1980-93, prof. emeritus, 1993. Legis. cons. N.Y. State Law Rev. Commn., 1956-61; vis. prof. U. Brussels, summer, 1968, Boston Coll. Law Sch., 1994. Author: Still Lives and Other Lives, 1966, Surrealism and the Art of Samuel Bak, in Between Worlds, 2002; editor, author introduction: A Survivors' Haggadah, 1998, Beyond Words: A Holocaust History in Sixteen Woodcuts done in 1945 by Miklos Adler, A Hungarian Survivor, 2001; contbr. articles to legal periodicals. Served to lt. (j.g.) USNR, 1944-46. NEH fellow, 1978; Am. Bar Found. Legal History fellow, 1977-78 Mem. Internat. Inst. Boston (bd. advisors), Phi Beta Kappa. Home: 180 Beacon St Boston MA 02116-1408 E-mail: stouster@mac.com.

TOVI, MURRAY, futurist, research scientist; b. NYC, Mar. 18, 1937; s. Louis Tovi and Jean Cohen; m. Joan H. Granoff, Oct. 30, 1965; 1 child, Rosanna. BBA, CCNY, 1961. Exec v.p. Tovi and Perkins, Inc., NYC, 1969—73; pres. Murray Tovi Designs, Inc., NYC, 1975—78, Concepts in Art and Sci. Inc., Colorado Springs, 1982—89, Transflectors, Inc., Colorado Springs, 1988—90, Theoretical Optics Inc., Colorado Springs, 1988—90, Tovi Scis., Ocala, Fla., 1991—. Cons. Am. Soc. Interior Designers, NYC, 1985—86. Author: Introduction to Neo-Classical Physics, 2001, The Relative Speed of Light Theory, 2003. Achievements include invention of first discreet surveillance system. Office: Tovi Scis PO Box 116 Sparr FL 32192 Home Phone: 352-671-6600; Office Phone: 352-671-6600. Business E-Mail: ToviSciences@aol.com.

TOVISH, HAROLD, sculptor; b. NYC, July 31, 1921; s. Louis Goodman and Anna (Treffman) T.; m. Marianna Pineda (Packard), Jan. 14, 1946 (dec. 1997); children: Margo, Aaron, Nina. Student, WPA Art Project, 1938-40, Columbia U., 1940-43, Ossip Zadkine Sch. Drawing and Sculpture, Paris, France, 1949-50, Acad. De La Grande Chaumiere, Paris, 1950-51. Tchr. sculpture N.Y. State Coll. Ceramics, 1947-49, U. Minn., 1951-54, Sch. of Boston Mus., 1957-66; sculptor in residence Am. Acad. in, Rome, 1966; prof. art Boston U., 1971-85, prof. emeritus, 1986—. Vis. prof. U. Hawaii, 1969-70 Group exhbns. include Met. Mus. of Art, 1943, Toledo Mus. Art, 1948, Galerie 8, 1949, Walker Art Center, 1951, Mpls. Inst. Art, 1953, San Francisco Art Assn., 1953, Whitney Mus. Am. Art, 1954, 58, 60, 64, 80, 28th Venice Biennial, 1956, Mus. Modern Art, 1960, Chgo. Art Inst., 1960, Carnegie Internat, 1960, Am. Fedn. Art, 1964, Decordova Mus., 1964, Internat. Exhbn. of Contemporary Medal, Paris, 1967, Boston Visual Artists Union Gallery, 1975, Boston U., 1975, 78, Colby Coll., 1975, Inst. Contemporary Art, Boston, 1975, 76, Skowhegan Sch., 1975, NYU, 1976, Boston Mus. Fine Arts, 1977, Nat. Mus. Am. Art, 1987, Nat. Acad. Design, 1987, DeCordova Mus., 1987, Howard Yezersky Gallery, 1988; one-man shows include, Walker Art Center, 1953, Swetzoff Gallery, Boston, 1957, 60, 65, Dintenfass Gallery, N.Y.C., 1965, 72, Addison Gallery Am. Art, Andover, Mass., 1965, Alpha Gallery, Boston, 1968, 73, 86, Terry Dintenfass, Inc., N.Y.C., 1980, 85, Boston U., 1980, retrospective exhibit, Wheaton Coll., 1967, Howard Yezerski Gallery, Boston, 1993, 95; survey exhibit, Solomon Guggenheim Meml. Mus., 1968, Fed. Res. Bank, Boston, 1991; retrospective exhbn. Addison Gallery Am. Art, 1988; survey exhibit Muscarelle Mus., Williamsburg, Va., 1990; represented in permanent collections Phila. Mus. Art, Whitney Mus. Am. Art, Walker Art Center, Mpls. Inst. Art, Addison Gallery Am. Art, Chgo. Art Inst., Mus. Modern Art, Boston Mus. Fine Art, Guggenheim Mus., Worcester Mus. Art, Hirshhorn Collection, Sara Roby Found., Colby Coll., Muscarelle Mus. William & Mary Coll., Williamsburg, Va., Nat. Gallery Am. Art, Minn. Gallery Art, Nat. Mus. Am. Art, Boston Pub. Library; (Recipient 1st prize sculpture Boston Arts Festival 1957, 1st prize drawing 1958, award Am. Inst. Arts and Letters 1971, sculpture grantee Am. Inst. Arts and Letters 1960). Guggenheim fellow, 1967; research fellow Center for Advanced Visual Studies, MIT, 1967-68 Mem. NAD (assoc. 1981-90, academician, 1990-)

TOWBIN, A(BRAHAM) ROBERT, investment banker; b. NYC, May 26, 1935; s. Harold Clay and Minna (Berlin) T.; children: Minna Joyce Pinger, Abraham Robert Jr., Zachary Harold. BA, Dartmouth Coll., 1957. With Asiel & Co., NYC, 1958-59; with L.F. Rothschild, Unterberg, Towbin Holdings, Inc. (merged with C.E. Unterberg, Towbin Co. 1977), NYC, 1959-86, vice chmn., 1961-86; mng. dir. Lehman Bros., NY, 1987—94; pres. Russian Am. Enterprise Fund., Moscow and NYC, 1994-95; vice chmn. U.S. Russia Investment Fund, Moscow and NYC, 1995; mng. dir. C.E. Unterberg, Towbin, NYC, 1995—99, co-chmn., 1999—2002; exec. v.p. Stephens, Inc., NYC, 2002—. Bd. dirs. Gerber Sci. Inc., Globecomm Sys. Inc., Intertrust. Hon. mem. N.Y. State Coun. Arts Mem.: Securities Industry Assn., Nat. Golf Links Am., Century Assn., Chelsea Art Club (London), Antigua Yacht Club, N.Y. Yacht Club (fleet capt. 2007—), Bond Club N.Y. Office: Stephens Inc 65 E 55th St New York NY 10022 Office Phone: 212-891-1720. Business E-Mail: rtowbin@stephens.com.

TOWE, THOMAS EDWARD, lawyer; b. Cherokee, Iowa, June 25, 1937; s. Edward and Florence (Tow) T.; m. Ruth James, Aug. 21, 1960; children: James Thomas, Kristofer Edward. Student, U. Paris, 1956; BA, Earlham Coll., 1959; LLB, U. Mont., 1962; LLM, Georgetown U., 1965; student, U. Mich., Ann Arbor, 1965—67. Ptnr. Towe, Ball, Enright, Mackey & Sommerfeld, Billings, Mont., 1967—; legislator Mont. House of Rep., Billings, 1971-75, Mont. State Senate, Billings, 1975-87, 91-94. Com. mem. Mont. Senate, 1975—87, 1991—94. Contbr. articles to law revs. Mem. Alternatives, Inc., Halfway House, Billing, 1977-99, pres., 1985-86; mem. adv. com. Mont. Crime Control Bd., 1973-78, Youth Justice Coun., 1981-83; mem. State Dem. Exec. Com., 1969-73; Dem. candidate for Congress, 1976; bd. dirs. Mont. Consumer Affairs Coun., Regl. Cmty. Svcs. for the Devel. Disabled, 1975-77, Rimrock Guidance Found., 1975-80, Vols. of Am., Billings, 1984-89, Youth Dynamics Inc., 1989-96, Zoo Mont., 1985-2001, Inst. for Peace Studies, 1993—, Mont. State Parks Assn., 1993—. Capt. JAGC US Army, 1962—65. Named as one of 100 Most Influential Montanans in 20th Century, Missoulian newspaper, 1999, one of 12 state officials in US as "Stars of the States," Washington Monthly mag., one of 10 best state and local officials in US, Mother Jones mag. Mem. Mont. Bar Assn., Yellowstone County Bar Assn., Billings C. of C.

Mem. Soc. Of Friends. Avocation: outdoor recreation. Home: 2739 S Gregory Dr Billings MT 59102-0509 Office: Towe Ball Enright Mackey & Sommerfeld 2525 6th Ave N Billings MT 59101 Office Phone: 406-248-7337. Personal E-mail: t.towe@bresnan.net. Business E-Mail: towe@tbems.com.

TOWER, JOAN PEABODY, composer, educator; b. New Rochelle, N.Y., Sept. 6, 1938. B.A., Bennington Coll., 1961; M.A., Columbia U., 1964, D.M.A., 1978. Pianist, Da Capo Chamber Players, 1969-84; compositions include: Sequoia (premiered by Am. Composers Orch.), Silver Ladders, 1985 (premiered by St. Louis Symphony, Grawemeyer award, U. Louisville, 1990), Breakfast Rhythms, Black Topaz, Amazon, Wings (solo clarinet), Fantasy (clarinet and piano), Cello Concerto, Piano Concerto, Clarinet Concerto, Flute Concerto, Violin Concerto, "Music for Cello and Orchestra", "Island Prelude" for oboe and strings by Cleveland, Philadelphia, and Seattle Symphony Orchestras and "Fanfare for the Uncommon Woman" by more than 200 ensembles; works recorded; Compact Discs have been released on Koch International, Delos, and d'Note Records; commns.: Contemporary Music Soc., Jerome Found., Mass. State Arts Council, Schubert Club St. Paul, Richard Stoltzman, St. Louis Symphony, Pitts. Symphony, Houston Symphony, Elmar Oliveira, N.Y. Philharm., Chgo. Symphony, Sharon Isbin, Carol Wincenc, Fromm Found., NEA, Carnegie Hall, Milw. Ballet, Lincoln Ctr. Chamber Soc., Aspen Festival, Cleve. Muir Quartets, L.A. Chamber Orch.; assoc. prof. Bard Coll., Annandale On Hudson, N.Y., from 1972, currently Asher B. Edelman prof. music (composition); composer-in-residence St. Louis Symphony Orchestra, 1985-88, 1999-2002. Recipient N.Y. State Council for Arts award, 1980, Alfred Dupont award for disting. composers and conductors; Guggenheim fellow, 1976, Nat. Endowment Arts fellow, 1974, 75, 80, 84, Koussevitzky Found. grantee, 1982, Meet the Composer Consortium grantee, 1989, 91, 92, Nat. Endowment Rec. grantee, 1993. Fellow Am. Acad. Arts and Sciences; mem. Am. Acad. of Arts and Letters (award in music Am. Acad. and Inst. Arts and Letters, 1983). Office: Bard Coll Conservatory of Music PO Box 5000 Annandale On Hudson NY 12504-5000 Office Phone: 845-758-7196. Business E-Mail: tower@bard.edu.

TOWER, MOLLIE GREGORY, writer, educator, consultant; b. San Antonio, Tex., July 17, 1945; d. Malcolm Russell and Margaret Halm Gregory; children: Debbie Tower Tannert, Sheryl Tower Maklary. MusB, U. Tex., Austin, 1967; MEd, U. Tex., Austin, Tex., 1981. Cert. Texas Music K-12 Tex. Edn. Agy., 1967, Texas Supr. Tex. Edn. Agy., 1981. Elem. music tchr., k - 6 Austin Ind. Sch. Dist., Tex., 1967—78, elem. music coord., 1978—92, coord. of choral and gen. music, k-12, 1992—98; author Glencoe/McGraw-Hill, Woodland Hills, Calif., 1995—, Macmillan/McGraw-Hill Pub. Co., NYC, 1982—96, Silver-Burdett Pub. Co., NYC, 2004—; sr. author arts edn. IDEAS Pub. Co., Norwalk, Conn., 1998—. Cons. Various sch. dist., 1975—2006; pres. Tex. Music Educators Conf., Tex., 1993—96, Tex. Music Admintrs. Conf., Tex., 1996—97, Tex. Coalition for Music Edn., Tex., 1992—93. Author: (ann. elem. curriculum program) Music Memory Bulletin, 1981—2005, (textbook) Music Reading Charts, Grade One & Grade Two, 1988, Songs in Spanish, Primary and Intermediate, 1989, Musica para todas, primary and intermediate, 1995, Choral Connections, 1997, Experiencing Choral Music, 2005. V.p., commr. Austin Arts Commn., Austin, Tex., 1985—89. Mem.: Sigma Alpha Iota, Delta Kappa Gamma. Achievements include Ann. Host of Riverside Symphony Music Memory Contest, Lincoln Ctr., N.Y.C., 1999-2006; Ann. Host of Kansas State Univ. Music Memory Contest, Manhattan, Kan., 2003-2006. Home Phone: 512-476-5574. Personal E-mail: mtower@realtime.net.

TOWERS, JOHN R., manufacturing executive, lawyer; b. NYC, 1941; AB in Econs., Princeton U., 1963; LLB, U. Va., Richmond, 1966. V.p. client adminstrn. State Street Bank, Boston, 1969-81; v.p. product devel. Fidelity Investments, Boston, 1981-89; sr. v.p. mutual funds U.S. Trust Co. of N.Y., 1989-90; sr. v.p. securities Bank of Boston, 1990-94; sr. v.p. State St. Bank & Trust, Boston, 1994-97; exec. v.p., gen. counsel State St. Boston Corp., Boston, 1997-2000, vice chmn., chief adminstrv. officer, 2000—. Mem. ABA, Boston Bar Assn., N.Y. State Bar Assn., Mass. Bar Assn., Am. Soc. Corp. Secs. Office: State Street Corp 225 Franklin St Boston MA 02110-2804

TOWERY, CURTIS KENT, lawyer; b. Hugoton, Kans., Jan. 29, 1954; s. Clyde D. and Jo June (Curtis) Towery. BA, Trinity U., 1976; JD, U. Okla., 1979; LLM in Taxation, Boston U., 1989. Mem. Curtis & Blanton, Pauls Valley, Okla., 1980-81; lawyer land and legal dept. Trigg Drilling Co., Oklahoma City, 1981-82; adminstrv. law judge Okla. Corp. Commn., Oklahoma City, 1982-85; counsel Curtis & Blanton, Pauls Valley, Okla., 1985-88; adminstrv. law judge Okla. Dept. Mines, Oklahoma City, 1985-88, assoc. gen. counsel, 1989-92; contracts and purchasing adminstr., atty. Okla. Turnpike Authority, Oklahoma City, 1992-93; asst. gen. counsel Okla. Corp. Commn., 1993-97; spl. judge City of Oklahoma City, 1997—2000; adminstrv. law judge Okla. Dept. of Labor, 1998, 2002—04; v.p., trust officer Bank One Trust, Oklahoma City, 1998-2000; mgr. Cherokee Capital Holdings, 2000—. Sr. adminstrv. law judge Okla. Corp. Commn., 2003—04; dept. special trustee Office of Special Trustee, dept. interior, 2004—05; asst. gen. counsel Okla. Dept. Labor, 2006—. Assoc. bd. Okla. Mus. Art, 1985—88, Okla. Symphony Orch., 1987—92, Ballet Okla., 1987—92, sec., 1990—91, v.p., 1988—89. Mem.: ABA, Okla. Bar Assn., Tex. Bar Assn., Faculty Ho., Elks, Rotary, Sigma Nu, Phi Alpha Delta. Republican. Presbyterian. Avocations: flying, golf, travel, investment analysis. Home: PO Box 18668 Oklahoma City OK 73154

TOWERY, JAMES E., lawyer; b. Los Alamos, N.Mex., July 12, 1948; s. Lawson E. and Irma (Van Apeldorn) T.; 1 child, Mark J. BA, Princeton U., 1973; JD, Emory U., 1976. Assoc. Morgan Beauzay Hammer, San Jose, Calif., 1977-79; ptnr. Morgan & Towery, San Jose, Calif., 1979-89; assoc. Hoge Fenton Jones & Appel, San Jose, Calif., 1989-90, ptnr., 1990—. Chmn. bd. trustees Alexian Bros. Hosp., San Jose, Calif., 1995-98. Mem. ABA (ho. of dels. 1989-98, standing com. client protection 1996—2000, chair 1998-00), State Bar Calif. (v.p. and chair discipline com. 1994-95, pres. 1995-96, bd. govs. 1992-96, pres. 1995-96, presiding arbitrator, fee arbitration program 1990-92), Santa Clara County Bar Assn. (counsel 1984-85, treas. 1987, pres. 1989). Office: Hoge Fenton Jones 60 S Market St San Jose CA 95113-2351 Home Phone: 408-279-8687; Office Phone: 408-947-2432. Business E-Mail: jet@hogefenton.com.

TOWERY, SARAH CARLISLE, artist, retired educator; b. Alexander City, Ala., Oct. 4, 1911; d. Washington Homer Carlisle and Artimisha Motley; children: Carlisle, Misha Sampson, Sarah Wade. Attended, Huntington Coll., 1930—32, U. Montevallo, 1940—45, Black Mountain Coll., 1944, Pen State U., 1951. Instr. U. Montevallo, Ala., 1945, So. Union Jr. Coll., Wadley, Ala., 1953—56; docent, team leader pvt. studio, Alexander City, 1948—2000; owner, tchr. pvt. kindergarten sch., Alexander City, 1951—53; organizer, session planner World Art Workshop, San Miguel, Mexico, 1972—94. Tchr., mentor Alexander City Pub. Schs., 1959—61; charter mem. World Art Workshop, San Miguel, 1972—94; found., continuing bd. mem. Sarah Carlisle Towery Art Colony-Lake Martin, Alexander City, 1991—. Wall mural, First Meth. Ch., Alexander City, 1952; executor, designer (wall mural) Town History: Racial Segregation, 1978; wall mural, Alexander City Elem. Sch., 1978; contbr. paintings Operation Downtown, Alexander City, 2001, 2002. Recipient Govs. award, Ala. State Coun. Arts, 1999, Artist Select Exhibit award, Comer Mus. Arts Ctr., 1999. Mem.: Ala. Art League, Birmingham Art Assn., Montgomery Art Guild. Republican. Protestant. Avocation: travel. Home: 273 Glenhaven Dr Alexander City AL 35010

TOWEY, ANNE C., lawyer; BA, Coll. St. Catherine, 1996; JD, William Mitchell Coll. Law, 2000. Pvt. practice atty. Anne C. Towey, P.L.L.C., Edina, Minn. Named a Rising Star, Minn. Super Lawyers mag., 2006. Mem.: Minn. Women Lawyers, Hennepin County Bar Assn. (mem. family law sect., mem. juvenile and the law sect.), Minn. State Bar Assn. (mem. professionalism com., mem. family law sect., mem. juvenile and the law sect.), Collaborative Law Inst., Internat. Acad. Collaborative Profls. Office: Anne C Towey PLLC 3300 Edinborough Way Ste 550 Edina MN 55435 Office Phone: 952-405-2030. E-mail: actowey@comcast.net. *

TOWEY, CARROLL FRANCIS, senior education specialist; b. Boston, Jan. 30, 1932; s. Thomas Patrick and Marietta V. (Alcock) T.; m. Marie Elizabeth Linehan, Aug 24, 1957 (dec. Apr., 1992); children Mary Ellen Roth, Michael Carroll, Kevin James; m. Miriam A. Quinlan, Sept. 4, 1993. BS in Edn., Salem State Coll., 1953; MEd, Boston U., 1957, cert. advanced grad. study (adult edn.), 1967; EdD, U. Mass., 1973. Sr. supr. Mass. Dept. Edn., Boston, 1965-67; sr. program advisor U.S. Dept. Edn., Washington, 1967—. Mem. Met. Wash. Assn. for Adult and Continuing Edn., Washington, 1981-85, pres. 1983-84; author: reports to U.S. Dept. Edn. on model programs, evaluation of adult education, and compliance by states to federal regulations; bd. dirs. Northern Va. Chpt. Retired Officers Assn., 1997. Mem. Mass. Soc. Washington, D.C., 1982—, v.p. 1993-95, pres. 1995-96, treas., 1996-97. With U.S. Army, 1955-57, Korea. Recipient Appreciation certs. Nat. Defense U., 1990, Nev. Dept. Edn., 1991, Pima County, Ariz., 1992. Mem. Fed. Vocat. Edn. Assn. (pres. 1993-94), Am. Assn. Adult and Continuing Edn. (founding mem., pres. Met. Washington 1983-84, Appreciation cert. 1988), Ret. Officers Assn. (bd. dirs. Nova Troa 1997, 2d v.p. 1998-99, 1st v.p. 2000), Phi Delta Kappa Boston U. Democrat. Roman Catholic. Avocations: gardening, reading, financial management, sports. Home: 1016 S Wayne St Apt 309 Arlington VA 22204-4435 Office: US Dept Edn 400 Maryland Ave SW # Wdc Washington DC 20202-0001

TOWEY, JIM (H. JAMES TOWEY), academic administrator, former federal official; b. 1956; m. Mary G. Towey; children: James Marion, Joseph Marius, Maximilian Marian, John Mariano, Marie Therese. BS with high honors, Fla. State U., 1978, JD, 1981. Legis. dir., legal counsel to Senator Mark O. Hatfield US Senate, Washington; cons. Fed. Welfare Reform Fla. State U., to Fla. Gov. Lawton Chiles and US Senator Bob Graham, 1995—96; sec. Fla. Dept. of Health and Rehabilitative Svcs., 1993; dep. asst. to Pres. The White House, Washington, 2002—05, asst. to Pres., 2005—06, dir. Office of Faith-Based and Cmty. Initiatives, 2002—06; pres. Saint Vincent Coll., Latrobe, Pa., 2006—. Author: (document) Five Wishes. Legal cons. Missionaries of Charity, Order of Mother Teresa, 1985—97, full-time vol. in home for people with AIDS, 1990; founder Aging with Dignity, 1996, pres., 1996—2002. Named one of Fifty Most Influential Christians in Am., Church World mag., Power and Influence Top Fifty of 2005, Non-Profit Times mag.; recipient Pro Ecclesia et Pontifice Papal Cross, His Holiness John Paul II, Archbishop John Carroll Award, Archdiocese of Miami. Mem.: KC. Roman Catholic. Office: Saint Vincent Coll Office of Pres 300 Fraser Purchase Rd Latrobe PA 15650-2690

TOWLE, ALEXIS CHARLES (LEX TOWLE), education advocate, director; b. Newburyport, Mass., Mar. 23, 1946; s. Sidney Norwood and Nancy Lois (Roberts) Towle; m. Maryellen Foote, Oct. 19, 1991; children: Ian, Devon. BA, Oundle Coll., Northants, Eng., 1964, Yale U., New Haven, 1968. V.p., trust officer Nat. Shawmut Bank, Boston, 1973-78; v.p., fin. cons. Merrill Lynch & Co., Boston, 1979-82, Kidder, Peabody & Co., Boston, 1983-88; v.p., investment banker Boston Bay Capital, Inc., Boston, 1988-93; dir. devel., campaign Boston Renaissance Charter Sch., 1994-95; pres. Apple Tree Inst. Edn. Innovation, Washington, 1995—2005; dir. Apple Tree Inst. Edn., 2004—. Treas., trustee Stoneridge Montessori Sch., Beverly Mass., 1994-2003; co-founder, trustee Cesar Chavez Charter Sch., Washington, 1998-2000, Washington Math Sci. Charter Sch., 1998-2001, Paul Jr. High Charter Sch., Washington, 1999-2001, Apple Early Literacy Presch., Washington, 2001-03; dir. Apple Tree Early Learning Pub. Charter Sch., 2003-. Author (with others) amendments to D.C. School Reform Act of 1995. Lt USMC, 1968—71, Vietnam. Mem.: Nat. Soc. Fundraising Execs. Republican. Episcopalian. Avocations: skiing, ice hockey. Business E-Mail: lex@appletreeinstitute.org.

TOWLE, LELAND HILL, retired federal agency administrator; b. Boston, Mar. 29, 1931; s. Leland and Bertha Mary (Hill) T.; m. Carol Peterson, June 5, 1953; children— Peter Kimball, Gretchen Towle Maynard, Michelle Aurora. BS, U. N.H., 1952; MS, M.I.T., 1953; Cert. in Bus. and Mgmt, U. Calif., Berkeley, 1962. Nuclear chemist Stanford Research Inst., Menlo Park, Calif., 1956-59, community systems economist, economist, nuclear economist, 1959-68, mgr. health scis. research, 1968-74; asst. dir. Nat. Center for Alcohol Edn., Arlington, Va., 1974-75. Cons. Medicine in the Pub. Interest, Washington, 1975, Internat. Ctr. for Alcohol Policies, 1995-98—; vis. scientist Nat. Inst. on Alcohol Abuse and Alcoholism, Rckville, Md., 1975-76, dep. dir. office of program devel. and analysis, 1976-77, assoc. dir. office of program devel. and analysis, 1977-81, dir. internat. and intergovtl. affairs, 1981-95; dir. LHT Assocs., Inc., 1995-98. Contbr. articles to profl. jours. Bd. dirs. Med. Resources Found., Palo Alto, Calif., 1972-73. Served with USAF, 1952-56. Mem. APHA, Sci. Research Soc. Am., Am. Nuclear Soc., Am. Chem. Soc., Colonial Capital Kiwanis Club, Sigma Xi, Phi Kappa Phi.

TOWLER, BRIAN FRANCIS, petroleum engineer, educator; s. Valentine and Nora Towler; m. Shelley Leonard, Nov. 10, 1979; children: Sarah, Renee Clayton, Adam. B in Engring., U. Queensland, Australia, 1972, PhD, 1978. Registered profl. engr., Wyo., 1996. Prof., dept. head U. Wyo., Laramie, 1988—. Author: Fundamental Principles of Reservoir Engineering. Mem.: Soc. Petroleum Engrs. Roman Catholic. Achievements include patents for ultrasonic device to mitigate wax deposition in oil wells. Office: U Wyo 1000 E University Ave Laramie WY 82071 Home Phone: 307-745-9223; Office Phone: 307-766-2500.

TOWLER, EVELYN WHEELER, retired elementary school educator; b. Northport, Mich., June 29, 1924; d. Lennis H. and Caroline Greiner Wheeler; m. Charles F. Towler (dec.); children: Jacquetta Sue, Charles F. Towler Jr. BA in History, BA in English Bible, Bob Jones U., Greenville, SC, 1949; postgrad., U. Fla., 1950—54, Fla. So. Coll., Lakeland, 1966—67, U. S. Fla., 1968, Rollins Coll., Winter Park, Fla., 1970, Fla. Technol. U., 1970—75. Cert. elem. tchr., media specialist Fla. Kindergarten tchr., LaBelle, Fla., 1943—44; primary grades tchr. Spring Lake (Fla.) Elem. Sch., 1950—52; youth dir. Presbyn. Ch., Lakeland, Fla., 1952—54; tchg. prin., co-founder Lakeland Christian Sch., 1954—63; asst. to dean of edn. Fla. So. Coll., Lakeland, 1964—67; tchr., lang. arts coord., media specialist Longwood Elem. Sch., Fla., 1967—85; media specialist, libr. Keswick Christian Sch., St. Petersburg, Fla., 1985—91, ret., 1991. Writer Lifepacs Alpha-Omega Pubs., Tempe, Ariz., 1977. Author: (novels) Under Sheltering Wings, 2001, The Road to Home, 2003, Teach Your Child to Write Creatively, 1985, Chronicles of a Hometown Church, 1993, Visitors Guide to Delightful Dunedin, 1995. Vol. Dunedin Hist. Mus.; mem. Dunedin Hist. Soc., Dunedin Friends of the Libr.; camp counselor Children's Bible Mission; bd. dirs. Dunedine Hist. Soc. Named one of Leaders of Am. Elem. Edn., 1971, Outstanding Elem. Tchrs. of Am., 1973; named to Dunedin Sr. Hall of Fame, 2005; recipient HistoryMaker award, Dunedin Hist. Soc., 2000, Lifetime Vol. Achievement award, 2007. Republican. Avocation: genealogy.

TOWLER, KATHERINE, writer; b. Pontiac, Mich., Sept. 1, 1956; d. Lewis W. Towler and Jane B. Kellogg; m. James A. Sparrell, Sept. 14, 1991. BA in English lit., U. of Mich., Ann Arbor, Michigan, 1974—78; MA in English lit., Middlebury Coll., Middlebury, Vermont, 1980—84; MA in fiction writing, Johns Hopkins U., Baltimore, Maryland, 1981—82. Freelance writer, publications cons., self-employed, Portsmouth, NH, 1987—; mem. faculty MFA Program in Writing, So. NH U., 2006—. Author: (novels) Snow Island, 2002 (Barnes and Noble Discover Great New Writers title, Borders Original Voices title, Booksense selection), Evening Ferry, 2005 (Booksense selection). Fellow George Bennett Fellowship, Phillips Exeter Acad., 1989-1990, Individual Artist Fellowship, NH. State Coun. on the Arts, 2003, Fellowship, Yaddo Artists Colony, 1985, 1983, Va. Ctr. for the Creative Arts, 1987, Working Scholarship, Bread Loaf Writers Conf., 1983. Mem.: Authors Guild, NH Writers Project (assoc.; bd. of trustees 1994—97), PEN New Eng. (assoc.). Avocations: bicycling, gardening, bird watching.

TOWLES, DONALD BLACKBURN, retired publishing executive; b. Lawrenceburg, Ky., Sept. 10, 1927; s. Joseph Sterling and Marjorie (Blackburn) Towles; m. Geraldine Gooch, Dec. 20, 1947 (dec. Nov. 1980); children: Sally Blackburn Towles Clark, Rebecca Neale Towles Brown; m. Julia Mason, Dec. 3, 1981. AB in Journalism, U. Ky., 1948. Asst. dir. publicity, editor In Ky. Mag. Commonwealth of Ky., Frankfort, 1948—55; pub. svc. mgr. Courier-Jour. and Louisville Times Co., Louisville, 1956—66, dir. pub. svc. and promotion, 1966—71, v.p., 1974—92, v.p., dir. circulation, 1971—76, v.p., dir. pub. affairs, 1976—92; ret., 1993. Author: (book) The Press of Kentucky 1787-1994; editor: Newspaper Promotion Handbook, 1983. Chmn. Louisville area chpt. ARC, 1987—89; mem. adv. bd. Salvation Army, 1982—97; elder emeritus Disciples of Christ; chmn. program adv. com. Louisville Devel. Program, 1971—80; bd. dirs. Louisville Med. Ctr., 1982—97; pres. Heritage Corp. Louisville, 1982—85; chmn. Thos. D. Clark Found., 2000—04; adv. bd. Christian Ch. Homes Ky., 1992—96; chmn. Sr. Citizens East, 1996—97. With US Army, 1952—54, Korea. Named Outstanding Chpt. Vol., Louisville area ARC, 1993, Outstanding State Vol., 1994; named to Ky. Journalism Hall of Fame, 1992; recipient Cmty. Svc. award, Louisville Devel. Com., 1980. Mem.: Soc. Profl. Journalists (pres.Louisville chpt. 1991—92), Ky. Press Assn. (pres. 1982, Pres.'s Cup Leadership 1982, Disting. Svc. award 1987), Internat. Newspaper Promotion Area (pres. 1980—82, Silver Shovel 1983), Journalism Alumni Assn. U. Ky. (pres. 1979—94, Outstanding Alumnus award 1976, All-Am. Alumni award 1994). Democrat. Home: 4800 Whitekirk Ct Louisville KY 40222

TOWNE, EDGAR ARTHUR, theologian, educator; b. Albany, NY, Feb. 27, 1928; s. Arthur Bethuel and Margaret (Shug) T.; m. Sara Jean Wright, June 14, 1952 (div. 1961); children: Mary Michal, Jonathan Wright, Nathan Arthur; m. Marian Kleinsasser, Dec. 18, 1961; 1 child, Stephen Edgar. BA, Coll. Wooster, 1949; BD, Pitts. Theol. Sem., 1952; MA, U. Chgo., 1962, PhD, 1967. Ordained to ministry Presbyn. Ch. (USA), 1952. Assoc. prof. systematic theology Winebrenner Theol. Sem., Findlay, Ohio, 1962-67; prof. philosophy and religion Findlay Coll., 1967-70; min. Hyde Park Union Ch., Chgo., 1971-75; prof. theology Christian Theol. Sem., Indpls., 1975-93, prof. theology emeritus, 1993—. Vis. prof. theology Christian Theol. Sem., Indpls., 1970-71; vis. scholar Grad. Theol. Union, Berkeley, Calif., 1981-82, Pitts. Theol. Sem., 1988-89; co-moderator com. on pub. ministry Synod of Lincoln Trails, Ind., Ill., 1986-88. Author: Two Types of New Theism: Knowledge of God in the Thought of Paul Tillich and Charles Hartshorne, 1997. Ethics com. Meth. Hosp. Ind., Indpls., 1985—90. Recipient Robert Risk award, ACLU of Ind., 2002. Mem. Am. Theol. Soc. (pres. Midwest divsn. 1986-87, 2003-04), Am. Acad. Religion, Ctr. Process Studies, Soc. Christian Ethics, Highlands Inst. for Am. Religious and Philos. Thought. Independent. Home: 5129 N Illinois St Indianapolis IN 46208-2613 Business E-Mail: etowne@cts.edu.

TOWNE, GARY SPAULDING, music educator; b. Burlington, Vt., June 12, 1950; s. Raymond Duane and Janet Spaulding Towne; m. Page Maurice Towne (dec.); children: Jonathan, Andrew. AB, Yale U., 1971; PhD, U. Calif., Santa Barbara, 1985. From asst. prof. to assoc. prof. U. N.D., Grand Forks, 1988—2002, prof., 2002—, dept. chair, 1999—2006. Vis. asst. prof. Middlebury (Vt.) Coll., 1985—88; organist, choirmaster St. Paul's Episcopal Ch., Grand Forks, 1995—2003; choirmaster United Luth. Ch., Grand Forks, 1988—91; dir. Collegium Musicum U. N.D., 1989—99. Contbr. articles to profl. publs.; editor: (book) Opera Omnia Gasparis de Albertis, vol. 1, 1999. Recipient Fulbright scholarship, USIA, 1994—95, Gladys Krieble Delmas fellowship, 1982—83, 1993, Stanley Krebs Meml. prize, U. Calif.-Santa Barbara, 1980, 1985. Mem.: Hist. Brass Soc., Coll. Music Soc., Am. Musicol. Soc., Internat. Musicol. Soc., Am. Motorcyclists Assn. Episcopalian. Avocation: motorcycling. Office: U ND Music Dept Box 7125 Grand Forks ND 58202 E-mail: gst1630@gra.midco.net.

TOWNE, JONATHAN BAKER, vascular surgeon; b. Youngstown, Ohio, Jan. 10, 1942; m. Sandra Green Towne, Aug. 24, 1963; children: Timothy, Heidi, Crista. BS, U. Pitts., 1963; MD, U. Rochester, NYC, 1967. Intern in surgery U. Mich., Ann Arbor, 1967-68, resident I, 1968-69; resident II, III, IV U. Nebr., Omaha, 1969-72; chief gen. surgery USAF Hosp., Vandenberg AFB, Calif., 1972-74; asst. prof. surgery Med. Coll. Wis., Milw., 1975-79, assoc. prof., 1979-84, prof., 1984—, chair vascular surgery, 1984—. Editor: (book) Complications Vascular Surgery, 1980, Complications Vascular Surgery, II, 1985, Complications Vascular Surgery, III, 1991. Mem.: Wis. Surg. Soc. (pres. 1991—92), Assn. Program Dirs. Vascular Surgery (pres. 1997—98), Ctrl. Surg. Assn. (recorder 1992—97, pres.-elect 2001), Soc. Vascular Surgery (sec. 1994—98, pres.-elect 1999, pres. 2000). Avocation: photography. Office: Med Coll Wis 9200 W Wisconsin Ave Milwaukee WI 53226-3522 Home Phone: 262-784-0588; Office Phone: 414-805-9160. Business E-Mail: jtowne@mcw.edu.

TOWNE, SARAH PATTON, physician; b. Fountain Hill, Pa., Aug. 28, 1953; d. William Frank and Arline Rose (Patton) T. Degree in Nursing, Geisinger Med. Ctr., Danville, Pa., 1973; BS magna cum laude, Kutztown U. Pa., 1988; DO, Phila. Coll. Osteo. Medicine, 1992, MSc in Family Practice, 1995. Diplomate Nat. Bd. Osteo. Med. Examiners. Psychiatric nurse Allentown State Hosp., Pa., 1973-76, NW Inst. Psychiatry, Ft. Washington, Pa., 1976-78; RN, psychotherapist Boulder County Mental Health Ctr., Colo., 1979-85; intern Phila. Coll. Osteo. Medicine, 1992-93, resident in family practice, 1993-95; physician Troup Family Practice, Tex., 1995-97; pvt. practice Denver, 1997—2003. Physician Harleysville Med. Assn., Pa., 1993-95; asst. dean clin. edn., assoc. prof. primary care Touro U. Coll. Osteo. Medicine, Calif., 2003-. Bd. dirs. Boulder County Rape Crisis Team, 1979-81. Faculty Devel. Fellowship, U. Calif. San Francisco, 2004—05. Mem. Am. Osteo Assn., Am. Coll. Osteo. Family Practitioners (bd. cert.). Avocations: reading, gardening, dogs. Home: 151 Thresher Dr Vallejo CA 94591-7814 Office: Touro U - Calif Coll of Osteo Med 1310 Johnson Ln Mare Island Vallejo CA 94592 Office Phone: 707-638-5200. Business E-Mail: stowne@touro.edu.

TOWNES, BOBBY JOE, travel agency executive; b. Pickens, SC, Aug. 29, 1932; s. James Harold and Coda Lenora (Nations) T.; m. Addie Elise Ray, May 2, 1956; children: John William, Robert Scott. AA, Mars Hill Jr. Coll., NC, 1952; BA, Furman U., Greenville, SC, 1955; diploma, Rutgers U., 1969. V.p. Peoples Nat. Bank, Greenville, 1954-73; exec. v.p. Community Bank, Greenville, 1973-76; pres. Piedmont Travel, Inc., Greenville, 1976-93, chmn., 1993—; mng. ptnr. Long Beach Properties, 1992—, Pawleys Promise, Pawleys Island, SC, 1998—. Chmn. Greenville World of Travel, 1976-80; pres. Piedco Assocs., Greenville, 1973—; mng. ptnr. Cutter Joint Ventures, Hilton Head, S.C., 1972—; pres. Piedco II, 1992—; chmn. Boutique Ltd., 1971-75; mng. ptnr. Townes Properties, Greenville, 2002, Townes Family Partnership, 2002; instr. Am. Inst. Banking, 1964-70, Charter Life Underwriters, Greenville, 1968; mem. adv. com. KLM Dutch

Airlines, Atlanta, 1982, System One Automation, Miami, Fla., 1980, Eastern Airlines, Miami, 1983-87; mem. adv. bd. Mars Plus Data Systems, Miami, 1976-79; bd. dir., Townes Family Charitable Trust Author: Independent Bank Survival, 1968, Townes and Allied Families, 1995. Chmn. United Way, Greenville, 1973; v.p. ARC, Greenville, 1970, Cancer Soc., Greenville, 1966; v.p. Furman U. Alumni Bd., Greenville, 1968-70, Furman U. Paladin Bd., Greenville, 1972-74; mem. Furman U. Com. for Self Study, Greenville, 1976; com. Gov.'s Econ. Coun., Columbia, SC, 1972; v.p., mem. founders com. Cmty. Concerts, Greenville, 1976; pres. YMCA Youth Guides, Greenville, 1970; v.p., organizer Centurian Club, 1978; mem. nat. alumni bd. Mars Hill Coll., 1998, mem. pres.'s bd. advisors, 2003; mng. ptnr. Townes Family Charity Trust, 2001; v.p. Friends of Springwood Found.; chmn. Greenville Little Theatre, 2007—. Recipient Sertoma Internat. Disting. Club Pres. award, 1967, Outstanding Young Mem. of Am. award, 1968, Finalist Ernst & Young Entrepreneur of Yr., 2000. Mem. Am. Inst. Banking (pres. 1964, bd. dirs. 1966), Young Bankers S.C. (bd. dirs. 1965), S.C. Bankers Assn. (bd. dirs. 1969), Greenville Wine Soc. (pres., organzer 1968, 72), S.C. Hist. Soc., Greenville County Hist. Soc., Poinsett Club, Commerce Club, Colonial Club (v.p. 1989, pres. 1991), Sertoma (v.p. 1982, pres. 1968, Gold Honor club 1967), Exec. Sertoma Club (v.p. 1982). Republican. Episcopalian. Avocation: genealogy. Home: 14 Selwyn Dr Greenville SC 29615-1727 Personal E-mail: btownes@bellsouth.net.

TOWNES, CHARLES HARD, physics professor; b. Greenville, SC, July 28, 1915; s. Henry Keith and Ellen Sumter (Hard) Townes; m. Frances H. Brown, May 4, 1941; children: Linda Lewis, Ellen Screven, Carla Keith, Holly Robinson. BA, BS, Furman U., 1935; MA, Duke U., 1937; PhD, Calif. Inst. Tech., 1939. Mem. tech. staff Bell Telephone Lab., 1933—47; assoc. prof. physics Columbia U., 1948—50, prof. physics, 1950—61; exec. dir. Columbia Radiation Lab., 1950—52, chmn. physics dept., 1952—55; provost and prof. physics MIT, 1961—66, inst. prof., 1966—67; v.p., dir. rsch. Inst. Def. Analyses, Washington, 1959—61; univ. prof. physics U. Calif., Berkeley, 1967—86, prof. physics, 1994, prof. physics emeritus, 1986—94, prof. grad. sch., 1994—. Guggenheim fellow, 1955—56; Fulbright lectr. U. Paris, 1955—56, U. Tokyo, 1956; dir. Enrico Fermi Internat. Sch. Physics, 1963; Richtmeyer lectr. Am. Phys. Soc., 1959; Scott lectr. U. Cambridge, 1963; Centennial lectr. U. Toronto, 1967; Lincoln lectr., 1972—73; Halley lectr., 1976; Krishnan lectr., 92; Nishina lectr., 92; Weinberg lectr. Oak Ridge (Tenn.) Nat. Lab., 1997; Rajiv Gandhi lectr., 97; Henry Norris Russell lectr. Am. Astron. Soc., 1998; dir. Gen. Motors Corp., 1973—86; dir. Perkin-Elmer Corp., 1966—69; mem. Pres.'s Sci. Adv. Com., 1966—69, vice chmn., 1967—69; chmn. sci. and tech. adv. com. for manned space flight NASA, 1964—70; mem. Pres.'s Com. on Sci. and Tech., 1976; rschr. on nuc. and molecular structure, quantum electronics, interstellar molecules, radio and infrared astrophysics. Author (with A.L. Schawlow): Microwave Spectroscopy; author: Making Waves, 1996, How the Laser Happened. Adventures of a Scientist, 1999; author, co-editor Quantum Electronics, 1960, Quantum Electronics and Coherent Light, 1964, mem. editl. bd. Rev. Sci. Instruments, 1950—52, Phys. Rev., 1951—53, Jour. Molecular Spectroscopy, 1957—60, Procs. NAS, 1978—84, Can. Jour. Physics, 1995—, contbr. articles to sci. publs. Mem. corp. Woods Hole Oceanographic Instn.; bd. mem. Calif. Inst. Tech., Carnegie Instn. Washington, Ctr. for Theology and Natural Scis., Mount Wilson Inst. Decorated officier Légion d'Honneur (France); named to Nat. Inventors Hall of Fame, 1976, Engring. and Sci. Hall of Fame, 1983; recipient Stuart Ballantine medal, Franklin Inst., 1962, Thomas Young medal and prize, Inst. Physics and Phys. Soc., Eng., 1963, Nobel prize for Physics, 1964, Disting. Pub. Svc. medal, NASA, 1969, Wilhelm Exner award, Austria, 1970, Niels Bohr Internat. Gold medal, 1979, Nat. medal of Sci., 1982, Berkeley citation, U. Calif., 1986, CommonWealth award, 1993, ADION medal, Obs. Nice, 1995, Mendel award, Villanova U., 1999, Frank Annunzio award, Christopher Columbus Fellowship Found., 1999, Rabindranath Tagore Birth Centenary plaque, Asiatic Soc., 1999, Karl Schwarzschild medal, Astronomische Gesellschaft, 2002, Drake award, SETI Inst., 2003, Templeton prize, 2005, Vannevar Bush medal, 2006. Fellow: IEEE (life medal of honor 1967), Calif. Acad. Scis., Indian Nat. Sci. Acad., Optical Soc. Am. (Mees medal 1968), Am. Phys. Soc. (pres. 1967, Plyler prize 1977, Frederick Ives medal 1996); mem.: NAE (founders award 2000), NAS (coun. 1968—72, 1978—81, chmn. space sci. bd. 1970—73, Comstock award 1959, Carty medal 1962), N.Y. Acad. Scis., Max-Planck Inst. Physics and Astrophysics (fgn. mem.), Pontifical Acad. Scis., Russian Acad. Scis. (Lomonosov medal 2000, fgn. mem.), Royal Soc. (fgn. mem.), Am. Acad. Arts and Scis., Am. Astron. Soc., Am. Philos. Soc. Achievements include patents for masers and lasers. Office: U Calif Dept Physics 366 Leconte # 7200 Berkeley CA 94720-0001 Business E-Mail: cht@ssl.berkeley.edu.

TOWNES, PHILIP LEONARD, pediatrician, educator; b. Salem, Mass., Feb. 18, 1927; s. Saul and Lillian (Kravetsky) T.; m. Marjorie Joan Greenstone, Aug. 27, 1956; children: Elizabeth Ann, Susan Jane, David Andrew. AB, Harvard, 1948; PhD, U. Rochester, 1952, MD, 1959. Diplomate Am. Bd. Pediat., Am. Bd. Med. Genetics. Intern Strong Meml. Hosp., Rochester, 1959-60, asst. resident, 1963, chief resident pediatrics, 1965; mem. faculty U. Rochester Sch. Medicine, 1952-79, prof. pediatrics, 1969-79; prof. anatomy (genetics), chmn. div. genetics, dir. Genetic Clinic, 1966-79; prof. pediatrics U. Mass. Sch. Medicine, 1979-95, dir. Genetic Clinic, 1979-95, dir. Cytogenetics Lab., 1981-95, prof. pediatrics/ob-gyn. emeritus, 1995—; pediatrician Strong Meml. Hosp. Cons. attending Newark State Hosp., Genesee Hosp.; hon. research asst. Univ. Coll., London, Eng., 1965-66; mem. adv. com. for genetics services Mass. Dept. Pub. Health, 1979-84, chmn. com., 1982-83; mem. steering com. New Eng. Regional Genetics Group, 1981-82. Contbr. articles to med. jours. Mem. com. qualifications cytogenetics N.Y. State Dept. Health, 1968-74; bd. dirs. Monroe County chpt. Nat. Found., 1965-79, chmn. med. adv. com., 1967-79, hon. bd. dirs., 1979—, also cons.; trustee Seven Hills Found., 1996—. USPHS predoctoral fellow, 1951-52; sr. research fellow, 1960-61; research career devel. award, 1961-66 Mem. Am. Acad. Pediatrics, Am. Assn. Anatomists, Soc. Pediatric Research, Am. Soc. Human Genetics, Am. Pediatric Soc., Teratology Soc., Sigma Xi, Alpha Omega Alpha. Home: 14 Spring Valley Rd Worcester MA 01609-1151 Personal E-mail: pltmdphd@hotmail.com.

TOWNES, SANDRA L., federal judge; BA, Johnson C. Smith, 1966; JD, Syracuse U., 1976. Tchr. English Carver H.S., 1966—67, Dunbar H.S., 1967—70, D.C. Evening Adult Edn. Prog., 1967—70, Corcoran H.S., 1971—73, P.E.A.C.E. Learning Ctr., 1971—73; asst. D.A. County Onondaga, N.Y., 1977—85, sr. asst. D.A., 1983—86, chief asst. D.A., 1986—87; adj. prof. Syracuse U. Coll. Law, 1987—95; judge Syracuse City Ct., 1988—99; adj. prof. Onondaga C.C., 1992—99; justice N.Y. Supreme Ct. (5th jud. dist.), 2000—01; assoc. justice N.Y. Supreme Ct. (Appellate divsn., 2d dept.), 2001—04; judge U.S. Dist. Ct. (ea. dist.) N.Y., 2004—. Mem.: Onondaga County Bar Assn., N.Y. State Women's Bar Assn., N.Y. State Bar Assn. Office: 225 Cadman Plaza E Brooklyn NY 11201 Office Phone: 718-613-2160.

TOWNLEY, HUGH, sculptor, educator; b. West Lafayette, Ind., Feb. 6, 1923; s. Hubert Claude and Marguerite (Ozburn) T.; m. Mary Ross, Oct. 3, 1961; 1 child, Hugh Merlyn Zadkine. Student, U. Wis., 1946-48, London County Council Sch. Arts and Crafts, 1949-50; studied with, Ossip Zadkine, Paris, 1948-49. Tchr. Layton Sch. Art, Milw., 1951-56, Beloit (Wis.) Coll., 1956-57, Boston U., 1957-61; prof. art Brown U., Providence, 1961—. Vis. prof. U. Calif., Berkeley, 1961, U. Calif. at Santa Barbara, 1968; vis. lectr. Harvard, summer 1967; participant symposium on 20th century sculpture Mus. N. Ariz., 1978 One man shows at, Gallerie Appollnaire, London, 1951, Meml. Union Gallery U. Wis., 1955, Milw. Art Inst., 1957, Swetzoff Gallery, Boston, 1958, 59, Pace Gallery, Boston, 1962, 64, 65, N.Y.C., 1964, Tyler Sch. Art, Phila., 1966, Rigelhaupt Gallery, Boston, 1966, Yale, 1966, DeCordova Dana Mus., Lincoln, Mass., 1969, Bradley Galleries, Milw., 1970, Bell Gallery, Brown U., 1972, Tyler Sch. Arts, Phila., 1972, U. Oreg., 1976, Worcester (Mass.) Art Mus., 1980, Gen. Electric Co., 1983, Providence Art Club, 1988, others; 2 man show, Brockton Mus., 1971, U. Oreg., 1975, Dartmouth Coll., 1975, U. N.H. at Keene, 1976, Inst. Contemporary Art, Boston, 1977; exhibited in group shows at, Chgo. Art Inst., 1953, 54, 64, Mus. Modern Art, 1955, 63, Carnegie Inst. Biennial, 1958, Inst. Contemporary Art, Boston, 1960, 61, 62, 65, 66, U. Ill., 1961-63, New Sch. for Social Research, 1962, Wadsworth Atheneum, Hartford, 1963, Decordova Mus., 1964, 65, Flint Inst. Art, 1966, Nat. Inst. Arts and Letters, 1967, Munson-Williams-Proctor Mus., 1970, Monumenta, Newport, R.I., 1974, Portland (Oreg.) Mus. Art, 1976, Keene (N.H.) State U., 1976, others; represented in permanent collections at, San Francisco Art Mus., Whitney Mus., Milw. Art Inst., Munson-Williams- Proctor Inst., Ithaca, N.Y., Addison Gallery, Andover, Mass., Boston Mus. Fine Arts, De Cordova Mus., Fogg Mus., Williams Coll. Mus., Brown U., Wrexham Found., Mead Corp., First Nat. Bank Boston, others. Served with USAAF, 1942-46. Recipient awards Kalamazoo Art Center Lithographic Workshop, 1964, awards Nat. Inst. Arts and Letters, 1967; Award for Arts, Gov. R.I., 1972; Yaddo Found. fellow, 1964; Tamarind Lithography Workshop fellow, 1969 Mem. Soaring Soc. Am. Office: Dept Art Brown U Providence RI 02912-0001

TOWNS, EDOLPHUS, congressman; b. Chadbourn, NC, July 21, 1934; m. Gwendolyn Forbes, 1960; children: Darryl, Deidra. BS in Sociology, NC A&T State U., Greensboro, 1956; MSW, Adelphi U., Garden City, NY, 1973; PhD (hon.), NC A&T State U., Shaw U. Tchr. NYC Pub. Schs., Medgar Evers Coll., Bklyn., Fordham U.; asst. adminstr. Beth Israel Med. Ctr., 1965-71; dep. pres. Borough of Bklyn., 1976-82; mem. US Congress from 11th NY dist., 1983—91, US Congress from 10th NY dist., 1992—, mem. energy and commerce com., mem. govt. reform com., ranking mem. subcommittee on govt. efficiency and fin. mgmt. Mem. adv. council Boy Scouts Am.; active Salvation Army. With US Army, 1956—58. Named Home Care Hero, Nat. Assn. Home Care, Legislator of Yr., Am. Acad. Nurse Practitioners, Am. Acad. Physician Assts., Am. Assn. Cmty. Health Ctrs., Nat. Coalition Poison Control Ctrs., Friend of the Nat. Parks, Nat. Parks and Conservation Assn.; named one of 100 Most Influential Black Americans, Ebony mag., 2006; named to Acad. of Distinction, Adelphi U.; recipient Congl. Leadership award, Am. Coll. Nurse-Midwives, 1999. Mem. NAACP, Nat. Assn. Social Workers, Kiwanis, Phi Beta Sigma. Democrat. Baptist. Office: US House Reps 2232 Rayburn House Office Bldg Washington DC 20515-0001 Office Phone: 202-225-5936. Office Fax: 202-225-1018. *

TOWNS, EVELYN, state government educational administrator; children: David Rodney Beachum, Robert Dale Beachum, James Kevin Beachum. M Ednl. Adminstrn., U. SC, Columbia. Dir. staff devel., testing and tchr. evaluation Allendale County Sch. Dist., Allendale, SC; edn. assoc. SC. Dept. Edn., Columbia, 2002—. Recipient First Pl. School-wide Divsn. award, SC Assn. Curriculum and Devel.; grantee School-wide grantee, SC. Dept. Edn. Mem.: ASCD, Nat. Coun. Staff Devel. Home: 5336 Hwy 321 Gaston SC 29053 Office: SC Dept Edn 1429 Senate St Columbia SC 29201 Home Phone: 803-926-9265. Office Fax: 803-734-0896. Business E-Mail: etowns@ed.sc.gov.

TOWNSEND, ALAIR ANE, publishing executive; b. Rochester, NY, Feb. 15, 1942; d. Harold Eugene and Dorothy (Sharpe) T.; m. Robert Harris, Dec. 31, 1970 (div. 1994). BS, Elmira Coll., 1962; MS, U. Wis., 1964; postgrad., Columbia U., 1970-71; doctorate (hon.), Elmira Coll., NY, Pace U., Coll. New Rochelle, Baruch Coll., Polytechnic U. Assoc. dir. budget priorities Com. on Budget, US House of Reps., Washington, 1975-79, dep. asst. sec. for budget HEW, 1979-80, asst. sec. for mgmt. and budget, 1980-81; dir. Office Mgmt. & Budget NYC, 1981-85; dep. mayor for fin. & econ. devel., 1985-89; pub. Crain's NY Bus., NYC, 1989—2006, v.p., 1993—, pub. dir., 2006, columnist, 2007—. Bd. overseers Tchrs. Ins. and Annuity Assn.-Coll. Retirement Equities Fund; dirs. adv. coun. M & T Bank; former mem. adv. bd. Ford Motor Credit Corp.; former bd. mem. Armor Holdings Inc., Am. Stock Exch., Fay's, Inc. Former vice-chmn., trustee Elmira Coll.; former mem. Coun. Fgn. Rels.; former bd. govs. Am. Stock Exch.; former chmn. Am. Woman's Econ. Devel. Corp.; former chmn. N.Y.C. Sports Commn.; former chmn. Consol. Corp. Fund of Lincoln Ctr.; bd. dirs. Lincoln Ctr.; vice-chmn. Buffalo Fiscal Stability Auth.; bd. dirs., Greater NY Councils-Boy Scouts of Am.; bd. dirs. Levin Inst. SUNY; fmr. mem., Partnership for NYC; fmr. vice chair, Bus. Coun. NY State. Best Bylined Commentary, Alliance of Area Business Publications, 2006; Sara Lee Front Runner Award; Star Award, New York Women's Agenda; Governor's Award for Excellence (Pataki); Directors Emeriti Award, Lincoln Center; Civic Leadership Award, Citizens Union; Elizabeth Cutter Morrow Award, YWCA of New York City; Business Leadership Award, Young Adult Institute; Brotherhood Award, 100 Black Men and Association for a Better New York; Iphigene Ochs Sulzberger Award, Barnard College; Leadership in Business Award, New York Business Group on Health; Franklin Award, Association of Graphic Communications; Women's Achievement Award, Brooklyn Chamber of Commerce; Business Leadership Award, Professional Women in Construction Mem. Women's Forum, Econ. Club NY (bd. dirs.). Office: Crain's NY Bus 711 3d Ave New York NY 10017

TOWNSEND, BRIAN DOUGLAS, paralegal; b. Tokyo, Sept. 22, 1961; s. Thomas and Juanita Evora (Sanford) T.; m. Gloria Ann Wigfall, Aug. 23, 1986; children: Brian D. Jr., Brianna A. BA in Criminology, U. Md., 1983. Legal aide Kirkland & Ellis, Washington, 1984-85; legal asst. to mng. clk. Cadwalader, Wickersham & Taft, Washington, 1985-87; paralegal specialist, Office Chief Counsel US Dept. Transp. Maritime Adminstrn., Washington, 1987-90, US Dept. Treasury, IRS, Washington, 1990-92; litig. support specialist US Dept. Justice, Tax Divsn., Washington, 1992-93; paralegal specialist Resolution Trust Corp., Washington, 1993-95, FDIC, Washington, 1996-98, US Dept. Treasury, OIG, Washington, 1998-99; program specialist FOIA/PA US Dept. Treasury, OFAC, Washington, 1999-2000; mgmt. analyst USDA, Washington, 2000—02; program analyst IRS/OPIP US Dept. Treasury, Washington, 2002—. Avocations: bowling, fishing, swimming, chess, football. Office: US Dept Treasury IRS/OPIP 1111 Constitution Ave NW Washington DC 20224-0002 Personal E-mail: briandouglastownsend@yahoo.com. Business E-Mail: brian.d.townsend@irs.gov.

TOWNSEND, CHARLES H., publishing executive; m. Joanna E. Townsend. Pres., pub. Family Cir. Mag., 1986—90; pres., CEO N.Y. Times Co. Women's Mag. Group, 1990—94; pub., Glamour Mag. Conde Nast Publs. Inc., NYC, 1994—95, exec. v.p., 1995—2000, COO, 2000—04, pres., CEO, 2004—; COO Advance Mag. Group, NYC, 2001—. Office: Conde Nast Publications Inc 4 Times Sq New York NY 10036-6561

TOWNSEND, CHRISTOPHER GORDON, lawyer; b. New Bedford, Mass., June 9, 1947; s. Christopher Gordon and Rita Mary (Fitzgerald) T.; m. Christine P. Davis, June 17, 1972; children: Christopher IV, Jessica C. BA, Providence Coll., 1969; JD, Georgetown U., 1975. Bar: D.C. 1975. Jud. clk. Supreme Ct. Del., Wilmington, 1975-76; atty. U.S. Dept. Justice, Washington, 1976-77, U.S. SEC, Washington, 1977-82; asst. gen. counsel Marriott Corp., Bethesda, Md., 1982-93; dep. gen. counsel Host Marriott Corp., Bethesda, 1993-96, gen. counsel, 1996-01; ptnr. Patton, Boggs LLP, 2001—. Editor: Am. Criminal Law Rev., 1974-75. Lt. USN, 1969-72. Mem. ABA. Office: Patton Boggs LLP 8484 Westpark Dr Mc Lean VA 22102

TOWNSEND, COURTNEY M., surgeon; b. Lubbock, Tex., 1943; MD, U. Tex., Galveston, 1969. Specialty bd. 1 Surgery 1975. Intern U. Tex. Med. Br., 1969—70, resident surgery, 1970—74; fellow surg. oncology U. Calif., LA, 1974—76; staff surgeon, surg. dir. intensive care unit Nat. Naval Med. Ctr., Bethesda, 1976—78; assoc. prof. U. Tex. Med. Br., 1978—83, prof., 1983—95, chair, dept. surgery, 1995—. James IV Surg. Traveller U. Tex. Med. Br., 1986; pres. Am. Pancreatic Assn., 1992—93; mem. Tex. Cancer Coun., 1992—; dir. Am. Bd. Surgery, 2000—. Editor-in-chief: Sabiston Textbook of Surgery: The Biological Basis of Modern Surgical Practice, 16th edit., 17th edit. Recipient Rsch. Career Devel. award, NIH, 1982, Asbel Smith Disting. Alumnus, 1986. Fellow: ACS (exec. com. 1999—2003, chmn. bd. govs. 2004—05, sec. 2006—); mem.: AMA (residency rev. com. 1999—2003), Am. Surg. Assn. (pres. 2007—), Am. Bd. Surgery (chair 2006—), So. Surg. Assn. (sec. 1999—2003, pres. 2003—04). Office: 301 University Blvd Galveston TX 77555-0527

TOWNSEND, CRAIG ARTHUR, chemistry educator; b. Chgo., Aug. 19, 1947; s. Herbert Ward and Thelma Alice (Hayskar) T.; m. S. Darlene Dance, Aug. 7, 1971; children: Reed Lincoln, Andrew Vernon. BA cum laude with honors in Chemistry, Williams Coll., 1969; PhD in Organic Chemistry, Yale U., 1974. Internat. exch. postdoctoral fellow Swiss Fed. Inst. Tech., Zurich, 1974-76; asst. prof. chemistry Johns Hopkins U., Balt., 1976-82, assoc. prof., 1982-85, prof., 1985—, chmn. dept., 1990-94, prof. dept. biology and McCollum-Pratt Inst., 1984—, prof. Thomas C. Jenkins dept. biophysics, 1989—, Alsoph H. Corwin prof. chemistry, 1997—. Vis. prof. chemistry Harvard U., Cambridge, Mass., 1987; disting. lectr. U. Hawaii, 1988; lectr. Robert A. Welch Found., 1989; H. Martin Friedman lectr. Rutgers U., 1990; Boehringer-Ingelheim lectr. Yale U., 1992; also numerous others; cons. Lederle Labs., Pearl River, N.Y., 1984-94, ChekTec Corp., Balt., 1993—, Upjohn Co., Kalamazoo, 1995—; mem. adv. panel Office Tech. Assessment, Washington, 1994-95; organizer, co-founder bio-organic chemistry Gordon Rsch. Conf., Kingston, R.I., 1992; Gomberg lectr. U. Mich., 1997; disting. lectr. Colo. State U., 1999. Mem. editl. adv. bd. Jour. Organic Chemistry, 1987-91; contbr. over 120 articles to sci. jours. Recipient award in chemistry Stuart Pharms., 1986; named Md. Chemist of Yr., 1992; NIH postdoctoral fellow Yale U., 1970-73, rsch. fellow Alfred P. Sloan Found., 1982-86; Camille and Henry Dreyfus tchr.-scholar, 1983-88. Mem. Am. Chem. Soc. (Arthur C. Cope scholar award 1995), Royal Soc. Chemistry, others. Research in biosynthesis of natural products; stereochemical and mechanistic studies of enzyme action; application of spectroscopic techniques to the solution of biological problems; molecular biology of secondary metabolism; activation and mechanism of DNA cleavage by calicheamicin. Office: Johns Hopkins U Dept Chemistry 3400 N Charles St Baltimore MD 21218-2680

TOWNSEND, DAVID W., oceanographer, educator; s. Philip W. and Martha Ferne Townsend; m. Roberta D. Campbell, Aug. 30, 1975; children: Kristy Lynn, Karen Elizabeth. BA, U. Maine, 1974, PhD, 1981; MS, L.I. U., C.W. Post, Greenvale, NY, 1977. Rsch. scientist Bigelow Lab. for Ocean Sci., West Boothbay Harbor, Maine, 1981—93; exec. dir. regional marine rsch. program U. Maine, Orono, 1993—97, assoc. rsch. prof. oceanography, 1993—97, assoc. prof. oceanography, 1997—99, prof. oceanography, 1999—, dir. Sch. Marine Scis., 2001—07. Office: U Maine 5706 Aubert Hall Orono ME 04469 Home Phone: 207-581-4367; Office Phone: 207-581-4367.

TOWNSEND, EARL C., JR., lawyer, writer; b. Indpls., Nov. 9, 1914; s. Earl Cunningham and Besse (Kuhn) T.; m. Emily Macnab, Apr. 3, 1947 (dec. Mar. 1988); children: Starr, Vicki M., Julia E. (Mrs. Edward Goodrich Dunn Jr.), Earl Cunningham III, Clyde G. Student, De Pauw U., 1932-34; AB, U. Mich., 1936, JD, 1939. Bar: Ind. 1939, Mich. 1973, US Supreme Ct. 1973, US Ct. Appeals (4th, 5th, 6th, 7th cirs.), US Dist. Ct. (no. and so. dists.) Ind., US Dist. Ct. (ea. dist.) Va., US Dist. Ct. (ea. dist.) Mich. Sr. ptnr. Townsend & Townsend, Indpls., 1941-64, 1984—, Townsend, Hovde & Townsend, Indpls., 1964-84. Dep. prosecutor, Marion County, Ind., 1942-44; radio-TV announcer WIRE, WFBM, WFBM-TV, Indpls., 1940-53, 1st TV announcer Indpls. 500 mile race, 1949, 50; Big Ten basketball referee, 1940-47; lectr. trial tactics U. Notre Dame, Ind. U., U. Mich., 1968-79; chmn. faculty seminar on personal injury trials Ind. U. Sch. Law, U. Notre Dame Sch. Law, Valparaiso Sch. Law, 1981; mem. Com. to Revise Ind. Supreme Ct. Pattern Jury Instrns., 1975-83; lectr. Trial Lawyers 30 Yrs. Inst., 1986; counsel atty gen., 1988-92. Author: Birdstones of the North American Indian, 1959; editor: Am. Assn. Trial Lawyers Am. Jour., 1964-88; contbr. articles to legal and archeol. jours.; composer (waltz) Moon of Halloween. Trustee Cathedral High Sch., Indpls., Eiteljorg Mus. Am. Indian and Western Art, Cale J. Holder Scholarship Found. Ind. U. Law Sch.; life trustee, bd. dirs., mem. fin. and bldg. coms. Indpls. Mus. Art; life trustee Ind. State Mus.; founder, dir. Meridian St. Found.; mem. dean's coun. Ind. U.; founder, life fellow Roscoe Pound/Am. Trial Lawyers Found., Harvard U.; fellow Meth. Hosp. Found. Recipient Ind. Univ. Writers Conf. award, 1960, Hanson H. Anderson medal of honor Arsenal Tech. Schs., Indpls., 1971, Lifetime Achievement award, 2002; named to Coun. Sagamores of Wabash, 1969; Rector scholar, 1934, Ind. Basketball Hall of Fame, Newcastle, 1981; hon. chief Black River-Swan Creek Saginaw-Chippewa Indian tribe. Fellow: Ind. Bar Found. (life trustee, disting. fellow award), Internat. Soc. Barristers, Internat. Acad. Trial Lawyers; mem.: ATLA (v.p.), ABA (com. on trial techniques 1964—76, aviation and space 1977—), ASCAP, Mich. Trial Lawyers Assn., Bar Assn. 7th Fed. Cir. (bd. govs. 1966—68), 34th Jud. Cir. Bar Assn., Roscommon County Bar Assn., State Bar of Mich. (Champion of Justice award 1989), Am. Judicature Soc., Am. Arbitration Assn. (nat. arbitrators panel), Am. Bd. Trial Advocates (diplomate, pres. Ind. chpt. 1980—86), Ind. Trial Lawyers Assn. (pres. 1965, pres. Coll. Fellows 1984—90), Indpls. Bar Found. (disting. charter 1986), Ind. State Bar Assn. (Golden Career award 1989), Genuine Indian Relic Soc. (founder, pres., chmn. frauds com.), Trowel and Brush Soc. (hon.), Marion County/Indpls. Hist. Soc. (bd. dirs.), Ind. Hist. Soc., Soc. Mayflower Descendants (gov. 1947—49), Columbia Club, U. Mich. Pres. Club, Key Biscayne Yacht Club, The Players Club, U. Mich. Victors Club (founder, charter mem.), Shriners, Masons (33 degree), Scottish Rite, Phi Kappa Phi, Delta Kappa Epsilon. Republican. Methodist. Avocations: art, Indian relics. Home: 5008 N Meridian St Indianapolis IN 46208-2624 E-mail: officeect@aol.com.

TOWNSEND, FRAN (FRANCES FRAGOS TOWNSEND), federal official; b. Mineola, NY, Dec. 28, 1961; m. John M. Townsend; 2 children. BA in Polit. Sci., BS in Psychology, Am. U., 1982; JD, San Diego U., 1984; student, Inst. on Internat. & Comparative Law, London, 1986. Asst. dist. atty., Bklyn., 1985—88; atty., US Atty. Office (so. dist.) NY US Dept. Justice, 1988—91, chief to staff to asst. atty. gen. criminal divsn., 1993—95, dir. internat. affairs criminal divsn., 1995—97, acting dep. asst. atty. gen., 1997—98, counsel Office of Intelligence Policy and Rev., 1998—2001; asst. comdt. for intelligence USCG, US Dept. Homeland Security, 2001—03; dep. asst. to Pres., dep. nat. security adv. for combating terrorism The White House, 2003—04, asst. to Pres for homeland security & counterterrorism, 2004—; chair Homeland Security Coun., 2004—. Office: Eisenhower Exec Office Bldg Rm 313 17th St & Pennsylvania Ave NW Washington DC 20504

TOWNSEND, IRENE FOGLEMAN, accountant, tax specialist; b. Birmingham, Ala., May 29, 1932; d. James Woods and Virginia (Martin) Fogleman; m. Kenneth Ross Townsend, Mar. 18, 1951; children: Marietta Irene, Martha Shapard, Kenneth Ross Jr., Elizabeth Buchanan. BSBA, East Carolina U., 1980. CPA NC, Va. Acct. Norwood P. Whitehurst & Assocs., Greenville, N.C., 1981-86; asst. v.p. Tenet Healthcare Corp., Vienna, Va., 1995—; v.p. NME Psychiatric Hosps., Inc., Vienna, Va., 2001—. Fellow AICPA, N.C. Assn. CPAs, D.C. Inst. CPAs, Va. Soc. CPAs; mem. DAR,

N.C. Soc. Daus. of Colonial Wars, Colonial Dames 17th Century. Democrat. Episcopalian (lay reader, chalice bearer). Avocations: bicycling, genealogy. Home: 2521 Paxton St Woodbridge VA 22192-3414 Office: Tenet Healthcare Corp 501 Church St NE Ste 301 Vienna VA 22180-4734 E-mail: irene_townsend@hotmail.com.

TOWNSEND, JAMES DOUGLAS, controller, accountant; b. Kokomo, Ind., May 20, 1959; s. Lemon Dale and Diamond Sue (Turner) T.; m. Ariane Antonia Atkins, May 7, 1983 (div. July 1992); 1 child, Bradley Alan; m. Mildred Ann Kurtz, Oct. 18, 1992; children: Heather Marie, Tyler Neil. Student, Ind. U., 1977, Ind. State U., 1977—78; BS Acctg. summa cum laude, Ball State U., 1980. CPA, Ind., Colo.; cert. mgmt. acct. Acctg. intern Chevrolet Motor Divsn. GM, Muncie, Ind., 1979; from staff acct. to sr. mgr. Price Waterhouse, Indpls., 1980—89; from contr. to v.p. fin. Raffensperger, Hughes & Co., Inc., Indpls., 1989—95; sr. v.p., chief adminstrv. officer Nat. City Investments, Inc., Indpls., 1995—99; pres. Fin. Mgmt., Inc., Indpls., 1994—2005; sr. v.p. Madison Ave. Capital Group LLC, 1999—2000; CFO Colo.'s Ocean Journey, 2000—01, exec. v.p., COO, 2001, CEO, 2001—05; v.p., contr. Curian Capital LLC, 2004—, Jackson Nat. Life Distbr., Inc., 2004—. Coord. Seek Program Ind. U., Indpls., 1985-86; cons. project bus. Jr. Achievement, Indpls., 1986; treas., asst. sec. Sagamore Funds Trust, 1991-94; treas. Raffensberger Hughes Capitol Corp., 1991-94, RHGP, Inc., 1993-95. Baseball coach Pike Twp. (Ind.) Youth League, 1986-87; cubmaster Pike Twp. Coun. Boy Scouts Am., 1987-88; mem. Pike Twp. Sch. Bd., 1988-92, v.p., 1989-90, pres., 1990-92; bd. dirs. Project I-Star, 1992-94, Crooked Creek Villages Homeowners Assn., 1998-99; fin. com. Highlands Ranch Cmty. Assn., 2000—02. Fellow Life Mgmt. Inst.; mem. AICPA, Inst. Mgmt. Accts., Ind. CPA Soc. (vice chmn. edn. com. 1988-89, chmn. 1989-90, chmn. govt. rels. com. 1999), Colo. Soc. CPAs, Indpls. C. of C. (SKLA exec. coun. 1992-94). Republican. Avocations: boating, guitar, chess, scuba diving, skiing. Address: 10586 Parkington Ln B Highlands Ranch CO 80126

TOWNSEND, JANE KALTENBACH, biologist, educator; b. Chgo., Dec. 21, 1922; BS, Beloit Coll., 1944; MA, U. Wis., 1946; PhD, U. Iowa, 1950. Asst. in zoology U. Wis., 1944-47, asst., project assoc. in pathology, 1950—53; asst., instr. U. Iowa, 1948-50; rsch. fellow Wenner-Grens Inst. Am. Cancer Soc., Stockholm, 1953—56; asst. prof. zoology Northwestern U., 1956-58; asst. prof. to assoc. prof. zoology Mt. Holyoke Coll., South Hadley, Mass., 1958-70, prof., 1970-93, chmn. biol. scis., 1980-86, prof. emeritus, 1993—; summer investigator Marine Biol. Lab., Woods Hole, Mass., 1993—. Contbr. articles to profl. sci. jours. Fellow AAAS (sec. sect. biol. sci. 1974-78); mem. Am. Assn. Anatomists, Am. Inst. Biol. Scis., Soc. Integrated Comparative Biology, Soc. Exptl. Biology and Medicine, Soc. Devel. Biology, Corp. of Marine Biol. Lab., Sigma Xi, Phi Beta Kappa. Achievements include research in amphibian metamorphosis and immune responses in marine sponges. Office: Mount Holyoke Coll Dept Bio Scis South Hadley MA 01075 Office Phone: 413-538-2124. Business E-Mail: jtownsen@mtholyoke.edu.

TOWNSEND, JOHN MICHAEL, lawyer; b. West Point, NY, Mar. 21, 1947; s. John D. and Vera (Nachman) T.; m. Frances M. Fragos, Oct. 8, 1994; children, James E., Patrick M. BA, Yale U., 1968, JD, 1971. Bar: N.Y. 1972, U.S. Dist. Ct. (so. and ea. dists.) N.Y. 1975, U.S. Ct. Appeals (2nd cir.) 1975, U.S. Supreme Ct. 1975, U.S. Ct. Appeals (8th cir.) 1982, U.S. Ct. Appeals (7th and 10th cirs.) 1986, D.C. 1990, U.S. Dist. Ct. D.C. 1990, U.S. Ct. Appeals (D.C. cir.) 1990, U.S. Ct. Appeals (4th cir.) 1991, U.S. Ct. Appeals (fed. cir.) 2000, U.S. Ct. Appeals (11th cir.) 2001, U.S. Ct. Fed. Claims, 2000, U.S. Ct. Appeals (1st cir.) 2003. Assoc. Hughes Hubbard & Reed, LLP, NYC, 1971-73, 75-80, ptnr., 1980—; assoc. Hughes Hubbard & Reed, Paris, 1973-74. Bd. dirs., chair bd. dirs., law com. Am. Arbitration Assn.; trustee US Coun. Internat. Bus. 1st lt. USAR, 1971-75. Mem. ABA, Am. Law Inst., Internat. Bar Assn. (chair mediation com., 2005-06), Assn. Bar City N.Y., Coll. Comml. Arbitrators, Univ. Club, Yale Club (N.Y.C.). Democrat. Episcopalian. Office: Hughes Hubbard & Reed LLP 1775 I St NW Washington DC 20006-2401 Office Phone: 202-721-4600. Office Fax: 202-721-4646. Business E-Mail: townsend@hugheshubbard.com.

TOWNSEND, JOHN WILLIAM, JR., physicist, retired federal agency administrator; b. Washington, Mar. 19, 1924; s. John William and Elenore (Eby) T.; m. Mary Irene Lewis, Feb. 7, 1948; children: Bruce Alan, Nancy Dewitt, John William III, Megan Lewis; m. JoAnn C. Clayton, Sept. 17, 1996. BA, Williams Coll., 1947, MA, 1949, ScD, 1961. With Naval Research Lab., 1949-55, br. head, 1955-58; with NASA, 1958-68, dep. dir. Goddard Space Flight Ctr., 1965-68; dep. adminstrn. Environ. Scis. Svcs. Adminstrn., 1968-70; asso. adminstr. NOAA, 1970-77; pres. Fairchild Space and Electronics Co., 1977-82; v.p. Fairchild Industries, 1979-85; pres. Fairchild Space Co., 1983-85; sr. v.p. Fairchild Industries, 1985-87; chmn. bd. Am. Satellite Co., 1985, sr. v.p., exec. aerospace group, 1987, exec. v.p., 1987; assoc. dep. adminstr. NASA, 1987; dir. NASA Goddard Space Flight Ctr., 1987-90; ret., 1990. Mem. U.S. Rocket, Satellite Rsch. Panel, 1950-60; chmn. space applications bd. NRC, 1985-87; bd. dirs., trustee Telos Corp., 1990-92; mem. adv. bd. Loral Corp., 1990-92; mem. coms. NRC, 1990—; bd. dirs CTA, Inc., 1990-98. Author numerous papers, reports in field. Pres. town council, Forest Heights, Md., 1951-55. Served with USAAF, 1943-46. Recipient Profl. Achievement award Engrs. and Architects Day, 1957; Meritorious Civilian Service award Navy Dept., 1957; Outstanding Leadership medal NASA, 1962; Distinguished Service medal, 1971, 90; recipient Arthur S. Fleming award Fed. Govt., 1963, Edward A. Flinn III award, 1999. Fellow AIAA, AAAS, Am. Meteorol. Soc.; mem. NAE (com. 1990-93), Am. Phys. Soc., Am. Geophys. Union. (fin. com. 1991-98, Edward A. Flinn III award, 1999), Internat. Astronautical Fedn. (mem., tru stee internat., acad. astronautics), Sigma Xi. Home: 6532 79th St Cabin John MD 20818-1201

TOWNSEND, JUSTIN C., lawyer; b. Austin, Tex. BA in English, U. Tex., Austin, 1997; JD, U. Tex. Sch. Law, Austin, 2001. Bar: Tex., US Dist. Ct. (we. dist. Tex.). Software engr. and systems adminstr.; law clk. to assoc. atty. Mithoff & Jacks, L.L.P., Austin, Tex.; solo practice atty. Austin, Tex. Named a Rising Star, Tex. Super Lawyers mag., 2006. Mem.: Austin Young Lawyers Assn., Tex. Young Lawyers Assn., Assn. Trial Lawyers of Am., Capitol Area Trial Lawyers Assn., Tex. Trial Lawyers Assn. Office: Law Office of Justin Townsend 2705 Bee Cave Rd Ste 225 Austin TX 78746 Office Phone: 512-472-3555. E-mail: jt@townsendlaw.com. *

TOWNSEND, KATHLEEN KENNEDY, former lieutenant governor; b. Greenwich, Conn., July 4, 1951; d. Robert F. and Ethel S. Kennedy; m. David L. Townsend; children: Meaghan, Maeve, Kate, Kerry. BA cum laude, Harvard Univ., 1974; JD, U. N.Mex., 1978. Instr. Dundalk Cmty. Coll., 1985-86, Essex Cmty. Coll., 1986-87, U. Pa., 1987-88; exec. dir. Md. Student Svc. Alliance, State dept. of Edn., 1987—93; dep. asst. atty. gen. US Dept. Justice, Washington, 1993-94; lt. gov. State of Md., 1995—2003; pres. Operation Respect, 2003; adj. prof. Georgetown's Sch. of Pub. Policy, 2003. Chair so. region Nat. Conf. Lt. Gov., chair oversight com. Johns Hopkins U., Peabody Inst., 1995-96; nat. adv. bd. Export-Import Bank U.S.; bd. adv. Johns Hopkins U. Sch. Advanced Internat. Studies, Inst. Human Virology U. Md; chair, State House Trust, 1995-2003, Adv. Bd., After-School Opportunity Programs, 1999-, co-chair, Safe Schools Interagency Steering Com., 1999-2003; Delegate, Dem. Party Nat. Conv., 1988, 1996, 2000; chair, Dem. Caucus of Lt. Gov. Editor U. N.Mex. Law Rev.; contbg. articles to profl. jour. and newspapers; author: Failing America's Faithful: How Today's Churches Are Mixing God with Politics and Losing Their Way, 2007 Founder Robert F. Kennedy Human Rights Award; chair Cabinet Coun. Criminal and Juvenile Justice, 1995-2003; chair Cabinet Coun. for Bus. and Econ. Devel.; chair Md. del. Pres. Summit Am. Future, 1997; chair State Sys. Reform Task Force for Children and Youth Reform, 1996, Task Force to study increasing availability of substance abuse programs, 1998-2001, Gov.of the Yr. 2000 Pub. Info.; chair adv. bd. after sch. opportunity programs; co-chair Md. Family Violence Coun.; bd. dir. John F. Kennedy Libr. Found., Nat. Inst. Women's Policy Rsch.; chair external adv. bd. Kennedy Krieger Inst. Early Infant Transition Ctr.; sr. advisor, Appropriations Com., House of Delegates, 1984-85; asst. Atty. Gen., Md., 1985-86; bd. ptnr. Radcliffe Coll. Recipient 4 hon. degrees; Visionary Leadership Award, Healthy Families Am., 2000, Clinton Ctr. Award for Leadership, Dem. Leadership Coun., 2002. Mem., Econ. Devel. Commn., Baltimore County, 1987, Gov. Exec. Coun., Gov. Commn. on Svc. and Volunteerism, 1998-. Democrat. *

TOWNSEND, MARJORIE RHODES, aerospace engineer, engineering executive; b. Washington, Mar. 12, 1930; d. Lewis Boling and Marjorie Olive (Trees) Rhodes; m. Charles Eby Townsend, June 7, 1948; children: Charles Eby Jr., Lewis Rhodes, John Cunningham, Richard Leo. BEE, George Washington U., 1951. Electronic scientist Naval Rsch. Lab., Washington, 1951-59; rsch. engr. to sect. head Goddard Space Flight Ctr.-NASA, Greenbelt, Md., 1959-65, tech. asst. to chief systems divsn., 1965-66, project mgr. small astronomy satellites, 1966-75, project mgr. applications explorer missions, 1975-76, mgr. preliminary systems design group, 1976-80; aerospace and electronics cons. Washington, 1980-83; v.p. systems devel. Space Am., 1983-84; aerospace cons. Washington, 1984-90; dir. space systems engrng. BDM Internat., Inc., Washington, 1990-91; dir. space applications BDM ESC, Washington, 1991-92; sr. prin. staff mem. BDM Fed., Inc., Washington, 1992-93. Aerospace cons., Washington, 1993—. Patentee digital telemetry system. Decorated Knight Italian Republic Order, 1972; recipient Fed. Women's award, 1973, EUR award for Culture, 1974, Engr. Alumni Achievement award George Washington U., 1975, Gen. Alumni Achievement award George Washington U., 1976, Exceptional Svc. medal NASA, 1971, Outstanding Leadership medal NASA, 1980, Eye-of-the-Needle award NASA, 1991. Fellow IEEE (chmn. Washington sect. 1974-75), AIAA (chmn. nat. capitol sect. 1985), AAAS (coun. del. 1985-88), Washington Acad. Sci. (pres. 1980-81); mem. Internat. Acad. Astronautics, Am. Geophys. Union, Soc. Women Engrs., Wing of Aerospace Med. Assn., Inc. (hon.), George Washington U. Hall of Fame (charter mem.), DAR, Daus. Colonial Wars, Mensa, Sigma Kappa, Sigma Delta Epsilon (hon.). Republican. Episcopalian. Home and Office: 3529 Tilden St NW Washington DC 20008-3122 Office Phone: 202-966-2330. E-mail: mrtownsend@aol.com.

TOWNSEND, MILES AVERILL, aerospace and mechanical engineering educator; b. Buffalo, Apr. 16, 1935; s. Francis Devere and Sylvia (Wolpa) T.; children: Kathleen Townsend Hastings, Melissa, Stephen, Joel, Philip. BA, Stanford U., 1955; BS MechE, U. Mich., 1958; advanced cert., U. Ill., 1963, MS in Theoretical and Applied Mechanics, 1967; PhD, U. Wis., 1971. Registered profl. engr., Ill., Wis., Tenn., Ont. Project engr. Sundstrand, Rockford, Ill., 1959-63, Twin Disc Inc., Rockford, 1963-65, 67-68; sr. engr. Westinghouse Electric Corp., Sunnyvale, Calif., 1965-67; instr., fellow U. Wis., Madison, 1968-71; assoc. prof. U. Toronto, Ont., Canada, 1971-74; prof. mech. engring. Vanderbilt U., Nashville, 1974-81; Wilson prof. mech. and aerospace engring. U. Va., Charlottesville, 1981—, chmn. dept., 1981-91. Ptnr., v.p. Endev Ltd., Can. and U.S., 1972—; cons. in field. Contbr. numerous articles on dynamics, design dynamical systems, controls and optimization to profl. jours.; 7 patents in field. Recipient numerous research grants and contracts. Fellow ASME, AAAS; mem. N.Y. Acad. Scis., Sigma Xi, Phi Kappa Phi, Pi Tau Sigma. Avocations: running, reading, music. Home: 212 Alderman Rd Charlottesville VA 22903-1704 Office: U Va Dept Mech and Aerospace Engring Thornton Hall Charlottesville VA 22903-2442 Business E-Mail: mat@virginia.edu.

TOWNSEND, PEGGY (STEPHANIE G.), headmaster; m. J. Michael Townsend III; children: Emily, Charlie. BA in History, U. Conn.; MA in Spanish Language and Lit., Middlebury Coll. Spanish Sch. Tchg. asst. U. Conn.; Spanish tchr. North Mt. Hermon Sch., Taft Sch., Watertown, Conn., dean upper middle class, dir. Modern Languages and Resource Ctr., head Dept. Modern Languages, dir. Summer Sch., dean of faculty, 2001—06; headmaster Pennington Sch., Pennington, NJ, 2007—. Office: The Pennington School 112 W Delaware Ave Pennington NJ 08534 Office Phone: 609-737-1838. *

TOWNSEND, ROBERT I., III, lawyer; b. NYC, Oct. 6, 1965; AB magna cum laude, Harvard Coll., 1987; JD magna cum laude, Harvard Univ., 1990. Bar: NY 1991. Assoc. Cravath Swaine & Moore, NYC, 1990—98, ptnr., corp., 1998—. Exec. editor Harvard Law Rev. Mem.: ABA, NY State Bar Assn. Office: Cravath Swaine & Moore LLP Worldwide Plz 825 Eighth Ave New York NY 10019-7475 Office Phone: 212-474-1964. Office Fax: 212-474-3700. Business E-Mail: rtownsend@cravath.com.

TOWNSEND, ROBERT MORRIS, economics professor, researcher; b. Apr. 23, 1948; BA, Duke U., 1970; PhD, U. Minn., 1975. Rsch. asst. Duke U., Durham, NC, 1970; grad. tchg. asst., microecons. U. Minn., Mpls., 1972—74; asst. prof. econs. Grad Sch. Indsl. Adminstrn. Carnegie-Mellon U., Pitts., 1975—78, assoc. prof. econs., 1978—80, prof. econs., 1980—85, U. Chgo., 1985—94, dir. admissions, 1992—2000, Charles E. Merriam prof., 1994—98, Charles E. Merriam disting. svc. prof. econs., 1997—. Vis. prof. econs. U. Chgo., 1984—86; Sticerd vis. prof. London Sch. Econs., 1996; disting. vis. prof. CEMFI, Madrid, 1997; vis. prof. MIT, Cambridge, Mass., 2001—; mem. exec. bd. Population Rsch. Ctr., NORC, Chgo.; cons. Inter-Am. Devel. Bank, Washington, IMF, 2001—, The World Bank, Fes. Res. Bank Chgo.; mem. econs. panel NSF, Washington, 1989—91. Author: The Medieval Village Economy, Financial Structure and Economic Organization; editor: Jour. Polit. Economy, 1987—89. Recipient Frisch medal, Econometric Soc., 1998; fellow, Woodrow Wilson Found., Fed. Res. Bank Mpls., 1974—75; scholar, Rsch. Dept., Fed. Res. Bank Mpls., 1978—79. Fellow: Econometric Soc., Am. Acad. Arts and Scis.; mem.: Phi Beta Kappa. Office: University of Chicago 1126 E 59th Street Chicago IL 60637 Office Phone: 772-702-7587.

TOWNSEND, ROGER DALE, lawyer; b. Dallas, Aug. 6, 1954; BA with highest honors, U. Tex., Arlington, 1976; JD, Harvard U., 1979. Bar: Tex. 1979, US Dist. Ct. (so. dist.) Tex. 1980, US Ct. Appeals (5th & 11th cir.) 1981, US Supreme Ct. 1984, US Ct. Appeals (2d cir.) 1994, US Ct. Appeals (4th cir.) 1998, US Dist. Ct. (ea. dist.) Tex. 2003. Assoc. Fulbright & Jaworski, Houston, 1979—84, participating assoc., 1984—87, ptnr., head appellate group, 1987-95; ptnr. Hogan Dubose & Townsend, L.L.P., Houston, 1995—2003, Alexander Dubose Jones & Townsend LLP, Houston, 2003—. Adj. prof. appellate adv. U. Houston Law Ctr., 1990. Editor: Texas Allellate Practice Manual, 1993; contbr. articles to publs. Fellow Am. Acad. Appellate Lawyers(dir. 2004-, chair, membership com. 2005-), Am. Bar Found.; life fellow Tex. Bar Found., Houston Bar Found.; mem. ABA (litigation sect., appellate practice com., tort and ins. practice sect., vice chair com. on appellate advocacy 1993-94), Houston Bar Assn. (appellate practice sect. 1990-,. com. on appellate jud. 1989-90), Bar Assn. 5th Fed. Cir, State Bar Tex.,(appellate practice & advocacy sect. 1988-, chair 1989-90, vice-chair 1988-89, com. on administrn. justice 1988-91). Pres. Omicron-Kappa Chpt. Phi Alpha Theta (internat. hon. hist. soc.) 1975-76; adminstrv. counsel, Law Soc. 1975-76; Harvard Civil Rights Civil liberties Review 1977-1979. Office: Alexander Dubose Jones & Townsend LLP 1844 Harvard St Houston TX 77008-4342 Office Phone: 713-523-2358. Office Fax: 713-522-4553. E-mail: rtownsend@adjtlaw.com.

TOWNSEND, TERRY, publishing executive; b. Camden, NJ, Dec. 14, 1920; d. Anthony and Rose DeMarco; m. Paul Brorstrom Townsend, Dec. 8, 1961; 1 child, Kim. BA, Duke U., 1942; LHD (hon.), Dowling Coll., 1991. Dir. pub. rels. North Shore U. Hosp., Manhasset, NY, 1953—68; pres. Theatre Soc., LI, 1967—70, Townsend Comm. Bur., LI, 1970—98; ptnr. L.I. Communicating Svc., Bellport, 1977—. Pub. L.I. Bus. News, 1979-98, pub. emeritus, 1998—; v.p. ParrMeadows Racetrack, Yaphank, N.Y., 1977; mem. Bellport Archtl. Rev. Bd., 1997—. Columnist, writer L.I./Bus., Ronkonkoma, 1970-75. Assoc. trustee North Shore U. Hosp., 1968—; bd. govs. Adelphi U. Friends Fin. Edn., 1978-85; chmn. ann. archtl. awards competition N.Y. Inst. Tech., 1970-83; trustee Dowling Coll., 1984—; trustee L.I. Fine Arts Mus., 1984-85; pub. broadcasting PBS Sta. WLIW TV, Garden City, L.I., N.Y., 1990-93; bd. dirs. Family Svc. Assn. Nassau County, 1982-92; dinner chmn. L.I. 400 Ball, 1987; trustee L.I. Mus. Art, 1994-2003. Recipient Media award 110 Ctr. Bus. and Profl. Women, 1977, Enterprise award Friends of Fin. Edn., 1981, LI Loves Bus. Showcase Salute, 1982, Cmty. Svc. award NY Diabetes Assn., 1983, Disting. Long Islander in Comm. award LI United Epilepsy Assn., 1984, Spl. award Dowling Coll. Spring Tribute, 1989, Disting. Svc. award Episcopal Health Svcs., 1989, Disting. Citizen award Dowling Coll., 1991, Gilbert Tilles award Nat. Assn. Fundraising Execs., 1994, Hadassah Cmty. Svc. award, 1996, Golden rule award Little Village Sch., 1997, Lifetime Achievement award LI Assn., 1998, 2007, Promote LI Achievement award, 1998, Lifetime Achievement award Advancement Commerce & Industry, 1999, Lifetime Achievement award LI Bus. News, 2007; named 1st Lady of LI, LI Pub. Rels. Assn., 1973, LI Woman of Yr. LI Assn. Action Com., 1989; Paul and Terry Townsend Sch. of Bus., Dowling Coll., designated in her honor, 2004. Mem.: Bellport Women's Golf Club (pres. 2003—04), Deepdale Golf Club (assoc.). Office: LI Communicating Svcs PO Box 915 Bellport NY 11713-0915 E-mail: terytowns@aol.com.

TOWNSEND, WILLIAM JACKSON, lawyer; b. Grayson, Ky., June 4, 1932; s. Robert Glenn and Lois Juanita (Jackson) Townsend. BS, Wake Forest U., Winston-Salem, NC, 1954; student, U. Ky., Lexington, 1957, U. Louisville, 1958; JD, U. NC, Chapel Hill, 1960. Bar: NC 1965. Claims adjuster State Farm Ins. Co., 1963; pvt. practice, Fayetteville, NC, 1965—; pub. adminstr. Robeson County, NC, 1966; dir., treas. Colonial Foods, Inc., St. Paul, NC, 1959—; tax atty. City of Lumberton, 1966-67. Served as 1st lt. U.S. Army, 1954-56. Mem.: Cumberland County Bar Assn., NC State Bar, NC Bar Assn., Scabbard and Blade (pres.), Kiwanis (treas. Fayetteville 1973—82), Delta Theta Phi. Presbyterian. Office: PO Box 584 Fayetteville NC 28302 Office Phone: 910-483-4462.

TOWNSHEND, PETE (PETER DENNIS BLANDFORD TOWNSHEND), musician, composer; b. London, May 19, 1945; s. Cliff and Betty Townshend; m. Karen Astley, May 20, 1968 (div. 2000); children: Emma, Aminta, Joseph. Guitarist The Who (formerly The High Numbers, The Detours), 1964—; owner Eel Pie Recording Ltd., 1972—83. Albums (with The Who) The Who Sings My Generation, 1965, Happy Jack, 1966, The Who Sell Out, 1967, The Magic Bus: The Who on Tour, 1968, Tommy, 1969, Live At Leeds, 1970, Meaty Beaty Big & Bouncy, 1971, Who's Next, 1971, Quadrophenia, 1973, Odds & Sods, 1974, The Who By Numbers, 1975, Who Are You, 1978, Face Dances, 1981, Hooligans, 1981, It's Hard, 1982, Who's Greatest Hits, 1983, Who's Last, 1983, Who's Missing, 1985, Two's Missing, 1987, Who's Better, Who's Best, 1988, Join Together, 1990, Thirty Years of Maximum R&B, 1994, Live at the Isle of Wight Festival 1970, 1996, My Generation: The Very Best of The Who, 1996, The BBC Sessions, 1999, The Blues to the Bush, 1999, The Ultimate Colllection, 2002, Live at the Royal Albert Hall, 2003, The Who: Then & Now, 2004, Live from Toronto, 2006, Endless Wire, 2006; (soundtracks) The Kids Are Alright, 1979, Quadrophenia, 1979; (solo albums) Who Came First, 1972, Secret Policeman's Ball, 1980, Empty Glass, 1980, All the Best Cowboys Have Chinese Eyes, 1982, Scoop, 1983, White City: A Novel, 1985, Another Scoop, 1986, Deep End Live, 1987, The Iron Man: A Musical, 1989, Psychoderelict, 1993, The Best of Pete Townsend, 1996, Cool Walking Smooth Talking, 1996, Pete Townshend Live: A Benefit for Maryville Academy, 1998; (with Ronnie Lane) Rough Mix, 1977; performer (films) Monterey Pop, 1968, Woodstock, 1970, Tommy, 1975, The Kids Are Alright, 1979, The Who Rocks America 1982, 1982; musical dir. (film and soundtrack) Tommy, 1975; Broadway musical The Who's Tommy, 1993 (Tony awd.for Best Original Score, 1993, Grammy award for Orginial Cast Recording, 1993, Dora Mayer Moore award, 1994, Olivier award, 1997); author: Horse's Neck, 1985, Pete Townshend: An Autobiography, 1999; co-author (with Des McAnuff) Tommy: The Musical, 1993 Named to The Rock & Roll Hall of Fame (as mem. of The Who), 1990; recipient Ivor Novello award for Contribution to British Music, 1982, Lifetime Achievement award, British Phonographic Industry, 1983, BRIT Lifetime Achievement award, 1983, BRIT award for Contribution to British Music, 1983, Internat. Rock Living Legend award, 1991, Q Lifetime Achievement award, 1997, Ivor Novello Lifetime Achievement award, 2001, BMI Pres. award, 2002, BMI TV Music award, 2004. *

TOWNSLEY, LISA GAIL, mathematics professor; b. Honolulu, June 25, 1960; d. Sidney Joseph and Mary Irmhild (Fuss) Townsley. BS, Santa Clara U., Calif., 1981; MS, Northwestern U., 1983, PhD, 1988. Prof. math. Benedictine U., Lisle, Ill., 1987—. Exam. reader, table leader AP/ETS, Clemson, SC, 1991—2005. Author: The DERIVE Calculus Workbook, 1994, Cohomology Rings of Finite Groups, 2003; contbr. articles to profl. jours. Named to Faculty All Stars, Chgo. Tribune, 1994; grantee, NSF, 1993, 2001. Mem. Math. Assn. Am., Assn. for Women in Math., Am. Math. Soc., Phi Beta Kappa, Kappa Mu Epsilon, Alpha Sigma Nu. Democrat. Office: Benedictine U 5700 College Rd Lisle IL 60532

TOWSNER, CYNTHIA MERLE, academic administrator, educator; b. Washington, Apr. 23, 1939; d. Philip and Edith Towsner; married, 1963; 1 child, Scott David Garrison. BS, U. Md., 1961, postgrad., 1964-65, Am. U., 1987. cert. contracting officer's rep., U.S. Dept. Edn. Tchr. Montgomery County Pub. Schs., Rockville, Md., 1961-66, 72-80; spl. asst. to commr. rehab. svcs. adminstrn. U.S. Dept. Edn., Washington, 1981—85, spl. asst. to the dir. Office Intergovtl. & Interagy. Affairs, 1985—87, acting dir. intergovtl. affairs office, 1987, ednl. program specialist Office Bilingual Edn. & Minority Languages Affairs, 1987—93, edn. program specialist Bilingual Vocat. Tng., 1993—96, nat. coord. health literacy and literacy vols. for adults, 1996—2002, coord lit. vols., 1996—, coord. lit. vols., health literacy, 2005—. Pres. Office Vocat. Adult Edn., U.S. Dept. Edn., Educare Programs, Inc., Chevy Chase, Md., 1988—; cons. R.J. Comer Comm., Inc., Jacksonville, Fla., 1995-97; v.p. Dalmahoy Group Internat., Chevy Chase, 1997-99. Photographer Project Education Reform: Time for Results, vol. 1, 1987. Vol. Holy Cross Hosp., Silver Spring, Md., 1969-74; asst. to pres. for edn. issues, chair nominating com., chair cmty. directory Rock Creek Hills Civic Assn., Kensington, 1968-85; v.p. D.C., Md. and Va. region, chair youth rally, chair radiothon publicity St. Jude's Children's Rsch. Hosp., Aiding Leukemia Stricken Am. Children, Memphis, 1969-81; chair internat. festival Larchmont Elem. Sch. PTA, Montgomery County, MD, 1976-78; bd. dirs., mem., chair Citizens for Edn., Montgomery County, Md., 1977-82; active Renaissance Women, Washington, 1983-87; chair corp. and bus. contbns. Hosp. Relief Fund for the Caribbean, Chevy Chase, 1989-91, annual ball com., 1989-94; vol. tutor Laubach Literacy Action and Literacy Vols. Am., Chevy Chase, 1989-93. Recipient Meritorious Svc. medal Am. Automobile Assn., Washington, Honors award Rock Creek Hills Civic Assn., Kensington, Md., 1979, Pres. award Combined Fed. Campaign, Washington, 1987, Hammer award V.P. of the U.S., Washington, 1996, 1st place ribbon in photography Montgomery County Agrl. Fair, Gaithersburg, Md., 1998, 1st, 2d and 3d place ribbons in photography Montgomery County Agrl. Fair, Gaithersburg, 1999, 1st and 2d place ribbons in photography Md. State Fair, Timonium, 1999, 1st pl. award Md. State Fair, 2000, Achievement in Amateur Photography award, Internat. Libr. Photographs, 2004. Mem. AAUW, Internat. Freelance Photographers Orgn. (life, Master Photographer 2002), Assn. for Career and Tech. Edn., Soc. Govt. Meeting Profls., Nat. Trust for Scotland, Nat. Mus. Women in the Arts (founding mem.), Nat. Women's History Mus. (charter mem.). Avocations: photography, reading, travel. Home: 4620 N Park Ave Apt 1404E Chevy Chase MD 20815-4563 Personal E-mail: cindy.towsner@verizon.net.

TOY, CHARLES DAVID, lawyer, business manager; b. NYC, June 29, 1955; s. Frank H.F. and Louise S.K. (Louie) Toy; m. Sandra Lynn Youla, Mar. 10, 1984; 1 child, Alana May Youla. BA in Social Studies, cum laude, Harvard Coll., Cambridge, Mass., 1977; JD, Harvard Law Sch., Cambridge, Mass., 1980. Bar: NY 1981, DC 2001. Assoc. Milbank, Tweed, Hadley & McCloy, NYC, 1980-84, Kaye, Scholer, Fierman, Hays & Handler, Hong Kong, 1984—88, ptnr., 1989—91, NYC, 1991—93; v.p., gen. counsel Overseas Pvt. Investment Corp., Washington, 1993-2001, v.p. fin., 1995-96, v.p. investment funds, 1998-99; ptnr. Wilmer, Cutler & Pickering, Washington, 2001—02; mem. bd. advisors GMI Capital Corp., Chevy Chase, Md., 2002—04, exec. v.p., corp. sec., 2004; mng. mem., exec. v.p. Pangaea Holdings, LLC, Chevy Chase, 2005—; exec. v.p., corp. sec. Pangaea Trading Corp., 2005—. Spkr. in field; profile subject Internat. Fin. Law Rev., 1996, Ave. Asia, 1996, 97, ABA 1997-99, 2002, Am. Conf. Inst., 1996, 98, Am. Soc. Internat. Law, 1996-97, Assn. Bar City NY, 2000, World Econ. Devel. Conf., 1996, Corp. Legal Times Roundtable, 1996, Com. of 100, 1996, Asian Am. Bar Assn., 1996, Asian Bus. Assn., 1996, Asian Pacific Am. Bar Assn., 1996, Forbes, 1997, Adam Smith Inst., 1998, Jerome Levy Econs. Inst. Bard Coll., 1998, Asian Pacific Am. Inst. Congl. Studies, 1998, Embassy South Africa, 1998, Harvard Inst. Internat. Devel., 1998, 99, Insight Info., 1998, 99, Nat. Asian Pacific Am. Bar Assn., 1998. U. Fla. Levin Coll. Law, 1999, CNA/Schinnerer Conf., 1999, Case We. Res. U. Sch. Law, 1999, Practising Law Inst., 1999, 2000, U. Iowa Tippie Sch. Mgmt., 2000, Met. Corp. Counsel Interview, 2000, Internat. Project Fin. Assn., 2000, Am. Corp. Counsel Assn., 2000, US Inst. Peace, 2001; interview Legal Times, 2001, Bloomberg, 2002. Contbg. editor Taxes and Investment in Asia and the Pacific, 1985-91, Tax News Service, 1986—91, Bull. for Internat. Fiscal Documentation, 1986—91; mem. editl. bd. Strategic Alliance Alert, 1994-95. Bd. trustees Lower East Side Tenement Mus., 1994-98; alumni coun. Philips Acad., 2000-04; mem. strategic planning com. DeLaSalle Acad. Mem. ABA,Internat. Project Fin. Assn., NY State Bar Assn., Assn. Bar City of NY, Nat. Asian Pacific Am. Bar Assn., Asian Pacific Am. Bar Assn., Harvard Law Sch. Assn., Am. Club (Hong Kong), Ladies Recreation Club (Hong Kong), Phi Beta Kappa Democrat. Roman Catholic. Home and Office: Pangaea Holdings LLC 4701 Willard Ave Ste 413 Chevy Chase MD 20815-4610 Home Phone: 301-718-1998.

TOY, HELEN GUERRANT, secondary school educator; d. Edward Owings and Charlotte Tompkins Guerrant (Stepmother); m. Stewart Albert Toy (div.); 1 child, David Edward. BA in English and Honors Humanities, Stanford U., Calif., 1960; MA in TESOL, UCLA, 1983. Grader Harvard U. Sch. Bus. Adminstrn., Boston, 1960—61; HS tchr. Alhambra Sch. Dist., Calif., 1985—89, LA Unified Sch. Dist., 1989—2002, literacy coach, 2002—04, part-time mentor tchr., 2006—; part-time mentor techr. Franklin HS, 1993—98. Part-time ESL tchr. Pasadena CC, Calif., 1983—84, Calif. State U., LA, 1983—84, LA, 1989. Vol. All Sts. Episcopal Ch., Pasadena, 1987—, MoveOn.org, Pasadena, 2004, 2006; bd. dirs. Pasadena Mental Health Assn., 1977—79. Democrat. Avocations: walking, reading, music. Home: 435 Buena Vista St San Marino CA 91108

TOY, STEPHEN J., corporate financial executive; b. Nov. 1972; BS in Bus. Adminstrn., SUNY, 1994. Corp. auditor Kansai Sawayawa; corp. fin. O'Brien Ptnrs., Inc.; mng. dir. WL Ross & Co. LLC, NYC. Office: WL Ross & Co LLC Manhattan Tower 19th Fl 101 East 52d St New York NY 10022

TOY, VIVIAN, journalist; Reporter New York Times. Panelist Covering NYC, 1998, Long Island Land Preservation vs. Sprawl, 2005. Author: (articles) Some Immigrants Begin to Lose Food Stamps Over New Law, 1996, Tough Workfare Rules Used as Way to Cut Welfare Rolls, 1998. Office: The New York Times LI Bur 1325 Franklin Ave Garden City NY 11530 Office Fax: 516-746-0930.

TOYODA, SHOICHIRO, automotive executive; b. Nagoya, Japan, Feb. 27, 1925; s. Kiichiro and Hatako Toyoda; m. Hiroko Mitsui, Nov. 30, 1952; children: Atsuko, Akio. B in Engring., Nagoya U., 1947, D in Engring., 1955. Dir. Toyota (Japan) Motor Co., Ltd., 1952-61, mng. dir., 1961-67, sr. mng. dir., 1967-72, exec. v.p., 1972-81; pres. Toyota Motor Sales Co., Ltd., 1981-82, Toyota Motor Corp., 1982-92, chmn., 1992-99, hon. chmn., 1999—. Bd. dirs. Denso Co., Ltd., Nagoya Broadcasting Network; chmn. bd. dirs. Inst. Internat. Econ. Studies; chmn. Japan Assn. for the 2005 World Exposition, 1997—. Chmn. Keidanren, Tokyo, 1994-98; hon. chmn. KDDI, 2000; consul gen. Honorario de Costa Rica, Nagoya, 1984—. Recipient Medal with Dark-Blue Ribbon, Govt. of Japan, 1972, The Deming Prize, 1980, Medal with Blue Ribbon, Govt. of Japan, 1984, FISITA medal, France, Medal of Isabel la Cath., King of Spain, 2000; decorated knight comdr. Most Noble Order of the Crown (Thailand), gran cruz Order Nacional al Merit, Colombia, knight comdr. Brit. Empire, grand cordon Order of the Sacred Treasure (Japan), Order Francisco de Miranda First Class (Venezuela), Ordem Nat. do Cruzeiro do Sul (Brazil), Order of Merit (Turkey), comdr. Legion of Honor (France), Grande Ufficiale, Govt. of Italy, hon. companion Gen. divsn. Order of Australia, grand decoration of honor in gold with star, Austria, comdr.'s cross Order of Merit (Germany), Grand Cordon of the Order of the Rising Sun (Japan). Office: Toyota Motor Corp 1 Toyota-cho Toyota 471-8571 Japan

TOYOSHIMA, CHIKASHI, structural biologist, educator; b. Honjo, Akita, Japan, July 17, 1954; BS in Physics, U. Tokyo, 1977, PhD in Biophysics, 1982. Prof. supramolecular structure Ctr. for Bioinformatics U. Tokyo, dir. Inst. Molecular and Cellular Biosciences. Named nat. lectr., Biophysics Soc., 2007. Mem.: NAS (fgn. assoc.). Office: Inst Molecular and Cellular Biosciences University Tokyo Bunkyo-ku Tokyo 113-0032 Japan Business E-Mail: ct@iam.u-tokyo.ac.jp.

TOZER, W. JAMES, JR., investment company executive; b. Salt Lake City, Feb. 9, 1941; s. W. James and Virginia (Somerville) T.; m. Elizabeth Farran, July 30, 1965; children: Farran Virginia, Katharine Coppins. BA cum laude, Trinity Coll., 1963; MBA, Harvard U., 1965. Investment officer First Nat. City Overseas Investment Corp., NYC, 1965-70; v.p. corp. devel. Citicorp, NYC, 1970-71; sr. v.p. and head Citicorp Subs. Group, 1971-74; sr. v.p., gen. mgr., head Merchant Banking Group, 1974-75, sr. v.p., gen. mgr. N.Y. banking div., 1975-77; sr. exec. v.p., dir. and head investment banking div. Shearson Hayden Stone, Inc., NYC, 1978-79; sr. exec. v.p. Marine Midland Bank and Marine Midland Banks, Inc., 1979-80, sr. exec. v.p. ops., fin. and strategic staff units, 1980-85, mem. office of chmn., sector exec. corp., instl. and internat. banking, 1985-87; chmn. Mountain West Banking Corp., Denver, 1988-89; pres., chief operating officer Prudential-Bache Securities, Inc., NYC, 1989-90; pres., CEO Lincolnshire Mgmt., Inc., NYC, 1993-94; mng. dir. Vectra Mgmt. Group, 1990—. Bd. dirs. LendingTree, Inc., 1998—2003; dir. Alliance Capital, 1989—90; dir., chmn. exec. com. Draper Bancorp; co-founder, dir. Vectra Bank. Trustee Trinity Coll, 2005—, chmn. bd. fellows; trustee, treas. Community Service Soc., 1976-87; trustee, treas. The Sch. for Field Studies, 1995—; trustee Citizens Budget Commn., 1986—; adv. council Atlanta U. Sch. Bus. Adminstrn., 1985-89; bd., v.p. Episcopal Charities, 1999—. Mem. N.Y. State Bankers Assn. (legis. policy com. 1981-87), Assn. Res. City Bankers (govt. rels. com. 1984-87), Am. Bankers Assn. (govt. rels. coun. 1985-87), Economic Club, University Club, Millbrook Club, Mashomack Club, River Club (N.Y.C.), Alta Club, (S.L.C). Home: 550 Park Ave New York NY 10021-7369 Office: 424 W 33St Ste 540 New York NY 10001-2614 Home Phone: 212-355-2244. Personal E-mail: wjtozer@vectramanagement.com.

TOZER, WILLIAM EVANS, entomologist, educator; b. Binghamton, NY, July 7, 1947; s. William Evans and Gertrude Genevieve (Lewis) T. BS in Natural Sci., Niagara U., 1969; MS in Biology, Ball State U., 1979; PhD in Entomology, U. Calif., Berkeley, 1986. Cert. C.C. biology and zoology tchr. Calif. Jr. H.S. sci. and English tchr. St. Patricks Sch., Corning, NY, 1969-71; tchg. asst. biology Ball State U., Muncie, Ind., 1974-76; pvt. practice biol. environ. cons. Berkeley, Calif., 1976-79, 86-88; rsch. asst. U. Calf., Berkeley, 1979-86; dept. head edn. and tng. USN Disease Vector Ecology and Control Ctr., Poulsbo, Wash., 1988—2004. Mem., acting chmn. San Francisco Bay Area Mosquito Control Coun., Alameda, 1988-96; chmn. Edn. and Tng. com., 1997-06; com. mem. Armed Forces Pest Mgmt. Bd., Washington, 1994—; bd. dirs. EPA Cert. and Tng. Assessment Group, 2001-05. Editor (field handbook) Navy Environmental Health Center, 1994; contbr. articles to profl. jours. With U.S. Army, 1971-73. Mem. Am. Entomol. Soc., Sigma Xi. Achievements include first to publish evidence for underwater behavioral thermoregulation in adult insects. Office: USN Environ Preventive Medicine Unit 5 3235 Albacore Alley San Diego CA 92136 Business E-Mail: william.tozer@med.navy.mil.

TRABITZ, EUGENE LEONARD, aerospace company executive; b. Cleve., Aug. 13, 1937; s. Emanuel and Anna (Berman) T.; m. Caryl Lee Rine, Dec. 22, 1963 (div. Aug. 1981); children: Claire Marie, Honey Caryl; m. Kathryn Lynn Bates, Sept. 24, 1983; 1 stepchild, Paul Francis Rager. BA, Ohio State U., 1965. Enlisted USAF, 1954, advanced through grades to maj.; served as crew comdr. 91st Strategic Missile Divsn., Minot, SD, 1968-70; intelligence officer Fgn. Tech. Divsn., Dayton, Ohio, 1970-73; dir. external affairs Aero. Systems Divsn., Dayton, 1973-75; program mgr. Air Force Armament Divsn., Valparaiso, Fla., 1975-80; dir. ship ops. Air Force Ea. Test Range, Satellite Beach, Fla., 1980-83; dep. program mgr. Air Force Satellite Text Ctr., Sunnyvale, Calif., 1983-84; ret., 1984; sr. staff engr. Ultrasystems Inc., 1984-86; pres. TAWD Systems Inc., Palo Alto, Calif., 1986-92, Am. Telenetics Co., San Mateo, Calif., 1992—; pres., CEO Enterprise Def. Inst., Inc., San Mateo, 2002—. Cons. Space Applications Corp., Sunnyvale, 1986-87, Litton Computer Svcs., Mountain View, Calif., 1987-91, Battelle Meml. Inst. Columbus, 1993—. V.p. Bd. County Mental Health Clinic, Ft. Walton Beach, Fla., 1973-75. Decorated Bronze Star. Mem. DAV (life), ASIS Internat., Nat. Def. Indsl. Assn., Armed Forces Comm. and Electronics Assn., Am. Soc. for Indsl. Security Internat., U.S. Space Found. (charter), Air Force Assn. (life), Nat. Sojourners, Masons (32d degree). Avocations: golf, tennis, racketball, sailing, bridge. Home: 4333 Bareback Ct Sparks NV 89436 Office Phone: 650-533-2730. Personal E-mail: gene@amtelenet.com.

TRABULSI, JUDY, advertising and marketing executive; b. Houston; d. Richard Joseph and Genevieve (Jamail) T. BS in Comm., U. Tex., 1971. Co-founder GSD&M's Idea City (formerly GSD&M Advt.), Austin, Tex., 1971, exec. v.p., exec. media dir., 1971—2007, chairwoman leadership coun., bd. mem., 2007—. Mem. nat. adv. coun. SBA, Washington, 1994-96; adv. coun. U. Tex. Comm. Sch., Austin, 1996—; adv. mem. 21st Century Dems., 1996; mem. hon. com. Jewish Cmty. Assn. Austin. Office: GSD&M's Idea City 828 W 6th St Austin TX 78703-5420 *

TRACEY, DENNIS HENRY, III, lawyer; b. NYC, Nov. 8, 1956; s. Dennis Henry Jr. and Mary Catherine (Lunney) T.; m. Marcia Jean Hamelin, July 20, 1985. BA, Cornell U., 1978; JD, NYU, 1981. Bar: N.Y. 1982, U.S. Dist. Ct. (so. and ea. dists.) N.Y. 1982, U.S. Ct. Appeals (4th cir.) 1982. Assoc. Paul, Weiss, Rifkind, Wharton & Garrison, NYC, 1981-84; litigation counsel CBS Inc., NYC, 1984; assoc. Davis, Markel & Edwards, NYC, 1984—87, ptnr., 1988—2000, Hogan & Hartson LLP, 2000—, mem. exec. com.; mng. ptnr. N.Y. Office. Co-chmn. Lawyers' Com. for Reelection of Robert Abrams, N.Y.C., 1982. Mem. ABA, N.Y. City Bar Assn. Office: Hogan & Hartson LLP 875 Third Ave New York NY 10022 Office Fax: 212-918-3100. Business E-Mail: dhtracey@hhlaw.com.

TRACEY, MATTHEW SEAN, music educator, musician; b. Teaneck, NJ, Feb. 4, 1965; s. Patrick Edward and Kathleen Teresa Tracey; m. Dawn C. Cusimano, Nov. 3, 1990. MusM, Montclair State U., NJ, 1987—89; MusB, William Paterson U., Wayne, NJ, 1983—87. Cert. K-12 tchr. of music NJ, 1987. Musician Ray Sepulveda Orch., New York, 1993—, Tito Nieves Orch., New York; musical dir. Frankie Negron Orch., New York, 1994—96; k-12 music dept. chairperson Ridgefield Pub. Schools, NJ, 1990—; dir. of bands Ridgefield Meml. HS, 1987—. Hon. lifetime mem. Nat. PTA, NJ; mem. Music Educators Nat. Conf., NJ, 1983—, Internat. Assn. of Jazz Educators, NJ, NEA, NJ. Edn. Assn., Music Educators of Bergen County, NJ. Musician: (studio/ recording musician) commericial jingles, Pop, Jazz, Latin recordings; profesional marching drill designer, Drill Designer; composer: (composer/arranger) various works. Recipient World Champion Bushwacker Drum & Bugle Corps, Drum Corps Associates, 1986, 198, 1989, 1990, World Champion-Garfield Cadets, Drum Corps Internat., 1984. Mem.: Nat. PTA (hon. Hon. Lifetime Mem. 2004). Achievements include NJ Governors's Tchr. of the Year. Avocations: music, travel, gastronomy. Office: Ridgefield Memorial High School 555 Walnut street Ridgefield NJ 08657 E-mail: contactus@ridgefieldband.com.

TRACH, SHERRY LYNN, elementary school educator; b. Allentown, Pa., July 16, 1975; d. Lester Raymond Trach, Jr. and Gloria Jean Trach. BS in Elem. Edn., Pa. State U., State Coll., Pa., 1997; cert. in Math. Specialists, Regent U. Cert. nat. trainer Kagan Cooperative Learning, 2005. Tchr. Boeves Elem. Sch., Tulsa, Okla., 1997—99, Young Pk. Elem. Sch., Norfolk, Va., 1999—2000, W.T. Cooke Elem. Sch., Va. Beach, Va., 2000—. Trainer tech. Union Pub. Schs., Tulsa, 1998—99; trainer coop. learning Va. Beach City Pub. Schs., 2003—; presenter in field. Finalist Tchr. of Yr. award, Va. Beach City Pub. Schs., 2005; named Tchr. of Yr., W.T. Cooke Elem. Sch., 2005. Mem.: NEA, Nat. Coun. Tchrs. Math., Va. Soc. Tech. in Edn., Tchr. Forum (mem. leadership coun. 2005—). Home: 1760 Willow Creek Ct Virginia Beach VA 23464 Office: WT Cooke ES 1501 Mediterranean Ave Virginia Beach VA 23451

TRACHSEL, RICHARD KEITH, principal, educator; b. Fairbury, Ill., Mar. 14, 1953; m. Diane Trachsel. PhD, Ill. State, Normal, 1998. Cert. in administrn. ISBE, 1986. Sch. psychologist LCSSU, Pontiac, Ill., 1980—97, program supr., 1998—2004; prin. Flanagan Unit 4, Ill., 2004—. Home Phone: 18159457618.

TRACHSEL, WILLIAM HENRY, corporate lawyer; b. El Paso, Tex., Apr. 20, 1943; BS in Aerospace Engring., U. Fla., 1965; JD, U. Conn., 1971. Bar: Conn. 1971. V.p., counsel Hamilton Standard, Hartford, Conn., 1978; v.p., counsel automotive div. United Tech. Corp., Hartford, Conn., 1979—83, deputy general counsel, 1983—86, v.p., dep. gen. counsel, 1986—93, v.p., sec. and dep. gen. counsel, 1993-98, sr. v.p., sec., 1998—2004, sr. v.p., gen. counsel, 1998—. Mem.: U. Conn. Found. (bd. dir.), Am. Bar Assoc., Conn. Bar Assoc., Conn. Bar Found. (bd. dir.), Hartford Hosp. (bd. dir.), MetroHartford Alliance. Office: United Tech Corp Bldg Hartford CT 06101 Business E-Mail: william.trachsel@utc.com.

TRACHTENBERG, ERIC BERTRAM, foreign service officer, economist; s. William and Nancy Trachtenberg; m. Yeva Krechetova, Sept. 11, 1999. BA in Govt. and Econs., Cornell U., Ithaca, NY, 1986; MS in Agrl. Econs., Mich. State U., East Lansing, 1990; MPA, U. So. Calif., LA, 1993. Stock market analyst Nat. Securities Corp., Taipei, Taiwan, 1990—92; rsch. fellow EPA, Washington, 1993; sys. adminstr. Office Rep. James Bilbray, Washington, 1994; economist Fgn. Agrl. Svc., USDA, Washington, 1995—98, spl. asst. to dep. adminstr., 2005—; agrl. attaché Am. Embassy, Moscow, Moscow, 1998—2001; dep. agrl. sect. chief Am. Inst. in Taiwan, Taipei, 2001—05. Contbr. articles to profl. jours. Recipient Water Resources Bull. Article of Yr., Am. Water Resources Assn., 1994; scholar, U. So. Calif., 1993. Mem.: ASPA, Am. Polit. Sci. Assn., Am. Agrl. Economics Assn., Am. Fgn. Svc. Assn. (mem. scholarship governing bd. 2006—). Democrat. Avocations: photography, travel. Home Phone: 585-354-3132; Office Phone: 202-720-6878.

TRACHTENBERG, MATTHEW J., financial services executive, philanthropist; b. NYC, June 20, 1958; s. Mark Trachtenberg and Joanne Horne. BA magna cum laude, NYU, 1974; JD, Bklyn. Law Sch., 1977; MBA in Fin., Fordham U., 1982. Bar: NY 1979. Mgmt. trainee Mfrs. Hanover Trust Co., NYC, 1977-78, credit analyst, 1978-79, corp. banking rep., 1979-80, asst. sec., 1980-82, asst. v.p., 1982, v.p., 1982-86, v.p., corp. sec., 1987-92; dir. Mfrs. Hanover Found., NYC, 1987-92; v.p., sec. regional bd. Chem. Bank, NYC, 1992-96, v.p., dep. corp. sec., 1992-96, sec. regional bd., 1992-96, v.p., 1992-96, Chem. Banking Corp., NYC, 1992-96; v.p. asst. corp. sec. Chase Manhattan Bank, NYC, 1996—98; sec. Chase Manhattan Regional Bd., NYC, 1996—98; v.p., sr. pvt. banker PNC Bank, NYC, 1999—2000, Fleet Bank, NYC, 2000—02; mng. dir. First Republic Bank, NYC, 2002—04; sr. v.p. US Trust Co., 2004—06. Bd. dirs., chmn., pres., CEO Nat. Orch. Assn.; bd. dirs., past pres. USO Met. NY; bd. dirs., treas., chair fin. com. NY Eye and Ear Infirmary; bd. dirs. Continuum Health Ptnrs. Mem.: NY State Bar Assn., Phi Beta Kappa, Pi Sigma Alpha. Avocations: music, fishing, painting, writing. Office: Nat Orchestral Assn PO Box 7016 New York NY 10150-7016 Office Phone: 212-208-4691. Business E-Mail: mtrachtenberg@nationalorchestral.org.

TRACHTENBERG, STEPHEN JOEL, political science professor, former academic administrator; b. Bklyn., Dec. 14, 1937; s. Oscar M. and Shoshana G. (Weinstock) Trachtenberg; m. Francine Zorn, June 24, 1971; children: Adam Maccabee, Ben-Lev. BA, Columbia U., 1959; JD, Yale U., 1962; M in Pub. Adminstrn., Harvard U., 1966; LHD (hon.), Trinity Coll., 1986, Boston U., 1999, Gratz Coll., 1999; HHD (hon.), U. Hartford, 1989; LLD (hon.), Hanyang U., Seoul, 1990, Richmond Coll., London, 1995, Mount Vernon Coll., 1997, So. Conn. State U., 2001, U. New Haven, 2002, Lyon Coll., Batesville, Ark., 2006, Touro Coll., NYC, 2006; DPA (hon.), Kyonggi U., Seoul, 1994, Sangmyung U., 2004, Dongseo U., Busan, Republic of Korea, 2004; MD (hon.), Odessa State Med. U., Ukraine, 1996. Bar: N.Y. 1964, U.S. Supreme Ct. 1967. Atty. AEC, 1962—65; legis. asst. to Congressman John Brademas of Ind., Washington, 1965; tutor law Harvard Coll.; tchg. fellow edn. and pub. policy John F. Kennedy Sch. Govt., Harvard U., 1965—66; spl. asst. to U.S. edn. commr. Office of Edn., HEW, Washington, 1966—68; assoc. prof. polit. sci. Boston U., 1969—77, assoc. dean, 1969—70, dean, 1970—74, assoc. v.p., co-counsel, 1974—76, v.p. acad. svcs., 1976—77; pres., prof. pub. adminstrn. U. Hartford, Conn., 1977—88, George Washington U., Washington, 1988—2007, pres. emeritus, prof. pub. adminstrn., 2007—; chmn. N.Am. edn. practice Korn/Ferry Internat., 2007—. Mem. joint editl. bd. The Presidency and ACE/Praeger Series on Higher Edn.; mem. Fed. City Coun.; bd. dirs. Consortium of Univs. Washington Met. Area, Riggs Bank, Greater Washington Bd. Trade, Nat. Edn. Telecom. Orgn., Washington Rsch. Libr. Consortium, DC Com. to Promote Washington; exec. adv. coun. SCT Edn. Sys. Contbr. articles to profl. jours. Chmn. nat. svc. task force Am. Jewish Com., 2006; trustee Al-Akhawayn U., Morocco, Com. for Econ. Devel.; active 2001 U.S. Savs. Bonds Vol. Com.; chmn. Md./D.C. Selection Com., 1998—2004, Rhodes Scholarships; mem. Washington Regional Panel for Selection of 2004-05 Class of White House Fellows; chair exec. com. Southeastern Univs. Rsch. Assn.; active D.C. Mayor's Bus. Adv. Coun.; exec. panel Chief Naval Ops.; bd. overseers List Coll. Jewish Theol. Sem. Am.; bd. dirs. D.C. C. of C., Chiang Chen Indsl. Charity Found. Ltd., Hong Kong; chair, pres. council Atlantic 10 Conf.; bd. mem. Bankinter Found. Innovation, 2006. Decorated grand officier du Wissam Al Alaoui King Mohammed VI of Morocco; named Outstanding Young Person, Boston Jr. C. of C., 1970, Alumnus of Yr., James Madison H.S., Bklyn., 1982, Washingtonian of Yr., Washingtonian Mag., 2000; named one of 100 Young Leaders, Acad. Am. Council Learning, 1978, Fifty Outstanding Alumni Problem Solvers, Harvard's John F. Kennedy Sch. Govt., 1987, The 2002 Forty Forward A, Washington Bus. Forward mag., 2002; named to Wall of Distinction, James Madison HS, 2006; recipient Myrtle Wreath award, Hadassah, 1982, Scopus award, Am. Friends of Hebrew U., 1984, Human Rels. award, NCCJ, 1987, NAACP award, 1988, Conn. Bar Assn. citation, 1988, Univ. medal of highest honor, Kyung Hee U., Korea, 1990, Martin Luther King, Jr. Internat. Salute award, 1992, Hannah G. Solomon award, Nat. Coun. Jewish Women, 1992, Father of Yr. award, Washington Urban League, 1993, Univ. Pres. medal, Kyonggi U., Korea, 1993, Merit award, Am. Czech and Slovak Assn., 1993, John Jay award, Columbia U., 1995, Spirit of Democracy award, Am. Jewish Congress, 1995, Newcomen Soc. award, 1995, Disting. Achievement medal, Greenberg Ctr. for Judaic Studies U. Hartford, 1995, Humanitarian award, B'nai B'rith, 1996, Disting. Pub. Svc. award, U.S. Dept. of State Sec.'s Open Forum, 1997, Tree of Life award, Jewish Nat. Fund, 1999, High Twelve Internat. Founders award, 2000, Key of Life award, Egypt's Internat. Econ. Forum, 2001, medal of merit, U.S. Dept. Treasury, 2001, Father Yr. award, Am. Diabetes Assn., 2002, Humanitarian award, The Albert B. Sabin Vaccine Inst., 2003, Madison Freedom award, 2004, Humanitarian Award, Sabin Vaccine Inst., 2006, Award of Excellence, Pigskin Club, 2007; Winston Churchill fellow, Eng., 1969, Hon. Wolcott fellow, 1999, Assoc. fellow, Morse Coll. Yale U. Fellow: Am. Acad. Arts and Scis.; mem.: Bus.-Higher Edn. Forum, Ind. Retail Cattleman's Assn. (adv. coun.), Sr. Soc. Sachems, Coun. Fgn. Rels., Newcomen Soc. U.S. (life; former trustee), Am. Coun. Learned Socs. (assoc.), Internat. Assn. Univ. Pres. (N.Am. coun.), N.Y. Acad. Scis., Am. Assn. Univ. Adminstrs. (pres. 1998—2000, Disting. Svc. award 1996), D.C. C. of C. (named Bus. Leader of Yr. 2005), Am. Coun. for the UN U. (vice chair), Hannibal Club (Ann. award 2004), Nat. Press Club, Cosmos Club, Harvard Club, Tumble Brook Country Club, Univ. Club, George Washington U. Club, Masons (33d degree, Grand Cross pin 2004), Phi Beta Kappa. Office: George Washington U Pres Emeritus 2121 Eye St N W Rm 802 Washington DC 20052-0001 Home Phone: 202-387-4949; Office Phone: 202-994-6500. Business E-Mail: gwupotu@gwu.edu.

TRACHTMAN, JERRY H., lawyer; b. Phila., Aug. 10, 1945; BSEE, Pa. State U., 1967; JD, U. Fla., 1976. Bar: Fla. 1976, U.S. Dist. Ct. (mid. dist.) Fla. 1978, U.S. Supreme Ct. 1980, U.S. Ct. Appeals (11th cir.) 1989; cert. aviation law. Elec. engr. N.Am. Aviation, Columbus, Ohio, 1967-68, Apollo spacecraft systems engr. Kennedy Space Ctr., Fla., 1968-71; Skylab project engr. Martin Marietta, Kennedy Space Ctr., 1971-74; pvt. practice Satellite Beach, Fla., 1976-80; atty., mng. ptnr. Trachtman, Henderson and Futchko, P.A., Melbourne, Fla., 1980—2002; pvt. practice Law Offices of Jerry H. Trachtman P.A., 2002—. Adj. prof. aviation law Fla. Inst. Tech., Melbourne, 1983-90; mem. adv. bd. Kaiser Coll., Melbourne, 1994—. Recipient Apollo achievement award NASA. Mem. ATLA, Fla. Bar Assn. (mem. aviation law com. 1977-, chmn. aviation law com. 1995-96, vice chmn. 1993-95, mem. aviation law cert. com. 2002-, chmn. aviation law cert. com. 2006-07), Lawyer-Pilots Bar Assn., NTSB Bar Assn. (founder 1984—), Acad. Fla. Trial Lawyers, Jewish Fedn. (pres. Brevard County chpt. 2000-2001, 2007, bd. dirs. 1996—). Office: Ste 300 1735 W Hibiscus Blvd Melbourne FL 32901-2616 Office Phone: 321-723-8281. Office Fax: 321-394-4033. Business E-Mail: jtrachtman@trachtman-law.com.

TRACKMAN, PHILIP CHARLES, biochemist, researcher; b. Montclair, NJ, July 15, 1953; s. John C. and Irene (Boveri) T.; m. Susan Kirkpatrick Troxler, Oct. 24, 1979 (div. 2004); children: Louisa, Eric. BA in chem.,

Coll. of Wooster, 1975; PhD, Boston Univ., 1980; post doctoral rsch., Brandeis Univ., 1980-83. Staff scientist Novo Labs., Wilton, Conn., 1983-85, team leader, 1985-86; rsch. asst. prof. Boston U., 1987—92; asst. prof. Boston U. Goldman Sch. Dental Medicine, Boston, 1992—2000, assoc. prof., 2000—04, prof., 2004—. Contbr. articles to profl. jours. Recipient First award Nat. Inst. Health, 1994, fellowship Am. Cancer Soc., 1981. Mem. Am. Chem. Soc. (assoc.), Sigma Xi. Protestant. Achievements include first to demonstrate that non-peptidyl amines are substates for lysyl oxidase and used this to develop a new assay. First to clone lysyl oxidase cDNA; first to study lysyl oxidase regulation by growth factors in osteoblastic cells; and in gingival fibrolasts; first to identify intermediates in a methionine salvage pathway; research in regulation of extracellular matrix biosynthesis in mineralized and non-mineralized tissues in health and disease; discovered mechanism of tumor suppressor function of lysyl oxidase; patentee in field. Office: Boston U Goldman Sch Dental Medicine 700 Albany St # 201 Boston MA 02118-2518 Office Phone: 617-638-4076.

TRACT, MARC MITCHELL, lawyer; b. NYC, Sept. 20, 1959; s. Harold Michael and Natalie Ann (Meyerowitz) T.; m. Sharon Beth Widrow; children: Melissa Hope, Harrison Michael, Sarah Michelle. BA in Biology, Ithaca Coll., 1981; JD, Pepperdine U., 1984. Bar: NY 1985, NJ 1985, DC 1986. Assoc. Kroll & Tract, NYC, 1985—90, ptnr., 1990—94, Rosenman & Colin LLP, NYC, 1994—2002, Katten Muchin Rosenman, LLP, NYC, 2002—. Bd. dirs. Rampart Ins. Co., Navigators Group Inc., NYC, MAPFRE Reins. Corp., Florham Park, NJ, AXA Art Ins. Corp., NYC, Maya Assurance Corp., NYC. Bd. dirs. Italian Acad. Found. Decorated Order of Merit of Savoy. Mem. ABA, Assn. Bar City of NY, NY State Bar Assn., NJ State Bar Assn., NY County Lawyers Assn., Am. Coun. Germany, Old Westbury Golf and Country Club, Met. Club, Econ. Club NY. Republican.

TRACTENBERG, CRAIG R., lawyer; b. Phila., Dec. 5, 1956; s. Jerome and Diane (Epstein) T. BA, La Salle Coll., Phila., 1979; JD, Temple U., 1981. Bar: Pa. 1981, N.J. 1983, U.S. Dist. Ct. (ea. dist.) Pa. 1981, U.S. Dist. Ct. N.J. 1983, U.S. Ct. Appeals (2d cir.) 1983, U.S. Ct. Appeals (3rd cir.) 1990, U.S. Supreme Ct. 1987. Assoc. Abraham, Pressman & Bauer, P.C., Phila., 1981-87, ptnr., 1987-97; shareholder Buchanan Ingersoll, Profl. Corp., Phila., 1998—2003; ptnr. Nixon Peabody LLP, 2003—06. Bd. adv. Rita's Water Ice Franchising, Inc., ALS Assn. and Camp Ramah, 2000-04; judge pro tem Phila. Ct. Common Pleas. Contbg. editor Franchise Law Quar., Franchise Law Digest; articles editor ABA Franchise Law Jour., 2002-04; contbr. articles to law jours. and profl. publs. Trustee Har Zion Temple, Penn Valley, Pa., 1988—2002. Mem. ABA, Pa. Bar Assn. (chmn. com. on franchising), Phila. Bar Assn., N.J. Bar Assn., Internat. Franchise Assn. Home: 249 Ithan Creek Rd Villanova PA 19085-1339 Office: Nixon Peabody LLP 1818 Market St 11th Fl Philadelphia PA 19103 Office Phone: 215-246-3525. Business E-Mail: ctractenberg@nixonpeabody.com.

TRACY, CRAIG ARNOLD, mathematics educator; b. London, Sept. 9, 1945; s. Robert Craig Tracy and Eileen (Arnold) Isenberg; children: Ingrid A., Elizabeth M. BS in Physics, U. Mo., Columbia, 1967; PhD in Physics, SUNY, Stony Brook, 1973. Research assoc. Inst. Fundamental Studies U. Rochester, NY, 1973-75; research assoc. Inst. Theoretical Physics SUNY, Stony Brook, NY, 1975-78; asst. prof. Dept. Math. Dartmouth Coll., 1978—83, assoc. prof., Dept. Math., 1983—84; prof. Dept. Math. U. Calif., Davis, 1984—, chmn. Dept. Math., 1994—98, Disting. prof., 2003, acting dir. Inst. Theoretical Dynamics, 1989, 1992, 2001—02. Visitor Los Alamos Scientific Lab., 1976, Inst. Math. and Its Applications, Univ. Minn., 1982; vis. rsch. scientist Brookhaven Nat. Lab., 1985; rsch. fellow Inst. Scientific Exch., Torino, Italy, 1986; fall rsch. fellow Rsch. Sch. Physical Sciences Australian Nat. U., 1986; rsch. prof. RIMS Kyoto U., 1991; bd. trustees Mathematical Sciences Rsch. Inst., 1998—2002. Mem. editl. bd. Mathematical Physics, Analysis and Geometry, Progress in Mathematical Physics, The Annals of Probability, 2006; contbr. articles to profl. jours. Named Disting. Prof., U. Calif. Davis, 2003; Woodrow Wilson fellowship, 1967—68, Japan Soc. for Promotion Sci. fellowship, 1991. Fellow: Am. Acad. Arts and Sciences; mem.: Am. Math. Soc., Am. Physical Soc., Soc. Indsl. and Applied Math. (George Pólya prize with Harold Widom 2002, and Am. Math. Soc., Norbert Wiener prize in Applied Math. with Harold Widom 2007). Office: Univ of Calif Dept of Math 3146 Math Sciences Bldg One Shields Ave Davis CA 95616-8633 Office Fax: 530-752-6635. Business E-Mail: tracy@math.ucdavis.edu.

TRACY, JAMES DONALD, historian, educator; b. St. Louis, Feb. 14, 1938; s. Leo W. and Marguerite M. (Meehan) T.; m. Nancy Ann McBride, Sept. 6, 1968 (div. 1993); children: Patrick, Samuel, Mary Ann; m. Suzanne K. Swan, May 2, 1997. BA, St. Louis U., 1959; MA, Johns Hopkins U., 1960, Notre Dame U., 1961; PhD, Princeton U., 1967. Instr. U. Mich., 1964-66; instr. to prof. history U. Minn., Mpls., 1966—, dept. chmn., 1988-91, Union Pacific prof. early modern history, 2001—04. Vis. prof. U. Leiden, Netherlands, 1987, U. Paris IV, 2001, U. Amsterdam, 2004. Author: Erasmus: The Growth of a Mind, 1972, The Politics of Erasmus: A Pacifist Intellectual and His Political Milieu, 1979, True Ocean Found.: Paludanus's Letters on Dutch Voyages to the Kara Sea, 1980, A Financial Revolution in the Habsburg Netherlands: Renten and Renteniers in the County of Holland, 1515-1565, 1985, Holland Under Habsburg Rule: The Formation of a Body Politic, 1506-1566, 1990, Erasmus of the Low Countries, 1996, Europe's Reformations, 1450-1650, 1999, 2d edit., 2006, Emperor Charles V, Impresario of War, 2002, The Low Countries in the Sixteenth Century: Erasmus, Religion and Politics, Trade and Finance, 2005; editor: Luther and the Modern State in Germany, 1986, The Rise of Merchant Empires: Long Distance Trade in the Early Modern Era, 1350-1750, 1990, The Political Economy of Merchant Empires: Long Distance Trade and State Power in the Early Modern World, 1991; editor: (with T.A. Brady and H.A. Oberman) Handbook of European History in the Late Middle Ages, Renaissance and Reformation, Vol. 1, 1994, Vol. 2, 1995, City Walls: The Urban Enceinte in Global Perspective, 2000; editor: (with T.A. Brady, K.G. Brady and S. Karant-Nunn) The Work of Heiko A. Oberman, 2003; editor: (with Marguerite Ragnow) Religion and the Early Modern State: Views from China, Russia and the West, 2004; editor: (with K.L. Reyerson and T.G. Stavrov) Pre-Modern Russia and Its World: Essays in Honor of Thomas S. Noonan, 2006; co-editor: Jour. Early Modern History, 1997—2000, editor, 2000—; mem. editl. bd. Sixteenth Century Jour., 1979—2000. Guggenheim fellow, 1972-73; NEH summer grantee, 1977, 85; Fulbright rsch. grantee, Belgium, 1979, Netherlands, 1980; resident fellow Netherlands Inst. for Advanced Studies, 1993-94. Mem. Am. Cath. Hist. Soc. (pres. 1999-00), Soc. Reformation Rsch. (pres. 1995-97), 16th Century Studies Conf. (pres. 1985-86). Republican. Roman Catholic. Home: 757 Osceola Ave # 2 Saint Paul MN 55105-3327 Office: U Minn History 614 Social Sci Bldg Minneapolis MN 55455 Home Phone: 651-227-0466; Office Phone: 612-624-0808. Business E-Mail: tracy001@umn.edu.

TRACY, JAMES FREDERICK, media educator; b. Hornell, NY, Oct. 12, 1965; s. Joseph M. and Ethel M. Tracy; m. Maris L. Hayashi, Nov. 5, 2004; 1 child, Siobhan. BA, San Jose State U., Calif., 1995; MA, U. Ariz., Tucson, 1998; PhD, U. Iowa, Iowa City, 2002. Instr. U. Ariz., Tucson, 1996—98, U. Iowa, Iowa City, 1998—2002; asst. prof. Fla. Atlantic U., Boca Raton, 2002—. Contbr. articles to profl. jours. Scholarly and Creative Arts fellow, Coll. Arts and Letters, Fla. Atlantic U., 2005. Mem.: Union for Dem. Comm. (assoc.; steering com. 2001—). Avocations: gardening, cooking, reading. Office: Fla Atlantic U 777 Glades Rd GCS238 Boca Raton FL 33431 Office Fax: 561-297-2615. Personal E-mail: jftracy@fau.edu.

TRACY, JAMES JARED, JR., retired legal association administrator; b. Cleve., Jan. 17, 1929; s. James Jared and Florence (Comey) T.; m. Elizabeth Jane Bourne, June 30, 1953 (div. 1988); children: Jane Tracy Ahrens, Elizabeth Tracy Jenkins, James Jared IV, Margaret Tracy Rosen; m. Judith Anne Cooper, Feb. 18, 1989. AB, Harvard U., 1950, MBA, 1953. CPA Ohio. Acct., sr. mgr. Price Waterhouse & Co., Cleve., 1953-65; treas., CFO Clevite Corp., Cleve., 1965-69; from asst. treas. to treas. Republic Steel Corp., Cleve., 1969—75; v.p., treas. Johns-Manville Corp., Denver, 1976-81; v.p., treas., CFO Internat. Techs. Corp., LA, 1981—82; exec. dir. Hufstedler, Miller, Carlson & Beardsley, LA, 1983—84, Shank, Irwin & Conant, Dallas, 1984-85, Pachter, Gold & Schaffer, LA, 1985—86; v.p., sr. cons. Right Assocs., LA, 1987—91; dir. adminstrn. Larson & Burnham, Oakland, Calif., 1991-95; adminstrv. dir. Law Offices of Thomas E. Miller, Newport Beach, Calif., 1996-97; human resources adminstr. Baker & McKenzie, San Francisco, 1997-98; dir. adminstrn. Wartnick, Chaber, Harowitz & Tigerman, San Francisco, 1998-2000, Kasdan, Simonds, & Epstein, Irvine, Calif., 2000—03; adj. prof. entreprenurial bus. planning Santa Anna Coll., 2004. Trustee, v.p. Miss Hall's Sch., Pittsfield, Mass., 1970—78; adv. bd. Arkwright-Boston Ins. Co., 1976—81. Trustee, v.p. Cleve. Soc. for Blind, 1965-76; trustee Western Res. Hist. Soc., Cleve., 1972-76; treas. St. Peters by the Sea Presbyn. Ch., Palos Verdes, Calif., 1981-91; trustee, treas. Literacy Coun. Newport Beach (Calif.) Pub. Libr., 2002—; pres. Harvard Club, Cleve., 1958-59, Harvard Bus. Sch. Club, Cleve., 1959-60, Rocky Mountain Harvard Club, Denver, 1978-79; bd. dirs. Met. YMCA, Cleve., 1972-76, Fedn. for Cmty. Planning, Cleve., 1971-76, v.p. Recipient Alumni award, Harvard U., Denver, 1981. Mem. AICPA, Ohio Soc. CPAs, Assn. Legal Adminstrs., Rotary (pres. Piedmont Montclair chpt. 1995-96), Harvard Radcliffe Club So. Calif., Harvard Bus. Sch. Assn. Orange County (treas. 2004—, chair Entrepreneurs Conf. 2007). Avocations: sailing, golf, gardening. Home: 2204 Fortuna Newport Beach CA 92660 E-mail: jimjudytracy@roadrunner.com.

TRACY, JIM (JAMES EDWARD TRACY), professional baseball manager; b. Hamilton, Ohio, Dec. 31, 1955; m. Debra Tracy; children: Brian, Chad, Mark. Attended, Marietta Coll. Bench coach, coord. all on-field activities L.A. Dodgers; mgr. Midwest League Single-A Peoria, Cubs' affiliate, 1987; minor league mgr. Chgo. Cubs, Cin. Reds, Expos, 1987—91, 1993—94; with Reds, 1989—91, minor league field coord., 1992; mgr. Triple-A Ottawa, Montreal's affiliate, 1994; bench coach Felipe Alou, Montreal Expo mgr.; interim mgr. L.A. Dodgers, 2000, mgr., 2000—05, Pitts. Pirates, 2005—. Named The Sporting News' Mgr. of Yr., 1993, Ea. League's Mgr. of Yr., 1993, NCAA Divsn. III All-Am. selection, Marietta Coll., Ohio. Mem.: Marietta Coll. Sports Hall of Fame. Office: Pitts Pirates PNC Pk 115 Federal St Pittsburgh PA 15212

TRACY, LYONEL B., school system administrator; m. Sharlene Tracy. BA, U. Maine, Farmington; MA, U. Maine, Orono; EdD in Ednl. Adminstrn. and Policy Studies, Geroge Washington U., 1997. Tchr., HS English; asst. prin./athletic dir.; supt. of schs. Maine, Vt., Portsmouth Sch. Bd., NH, 2000; commr. edn. State of NH, 2005—. Adj. faculty mem. U. Sys. of NH, Plymouth State U.; mem. Regional Adv. Com. for N.E. Region, US Dept. of Edn., 2004. Mem.: New England Assn. of Sch. Supts. (pres. 2002—), NH PTA (past chair edn. com.), Portsmouth Rotary Club. Office: NH Dept Edn 101 Pleasant St Concord NH 03301-3860 Office Phone: 603-271-3494, 603-271-3144. Office Fax: 603-271-1953. E-mail: ltracy@ed.state.nh.us. *

TRACY, MICHAEL CAMERON, choreographer, educator; b. Florence, Italy, Feb. 1, 1952; s. Stanley B. and Elizabeth Lee (McIntosh) T. BA Magna cum laude, Dartmouth Coll., 1973. Adj. faculty Yale U., New Haven, Conn., 1992—. Artistic dir. Pilobolus Dance Theatre, Washington, Conn., 1974—; choreographer Die Zauberflöte, European prodn. with John Eliot Gardiner's Monteverdi Choir and English Baroque Soloists, 1995, Curiouser and Curiouser Nat. Theatre of Deaf, 1996, Sweet Dreams, 2000, Symbiosis, 2001, The Brass Ring (commissioned by Olympic Arts Festival), 2002, My Brother's Keeper, 2003, Warm Heart, 2004, Aquatica, 2005, Prism, 2005, The Persistence of Memory, 2007; co-choreographer: Ciona, 1974, Monkshood's Farewell, 1975, Untitled, 1976, Day Two, 1980, Pyramid of the Moon, 1996, Aeros, 1996, Elysian Fields, 1997, Apoplexy, 1998, The Hand That Mocked, The Heart That Fed, 1998, A Selection, 1999. Recipient Berlin Critics award, 1975, New Eng. Theatre Conf. prize, 1977, Brandeis award, 1978, Excellence in Arts award Conn. Commn. on the Arts, 1981, Emmy award 1997, Scripps award, 2000; sr. fellow Dartmouth Coll., 1973, Montgomery fellow, Dartmouth Coll., 2007. Mem. Dartmouth Players. Office: PO Box 388 Washington Depot CT 06794-0388 Business E-Mail: michael.tracy@yale.edu.

TRACY, PATRICK F., food products executive; Former CEO Dot Foods, Mt. Sterling, Ill., chmn. bd. dir., 2002—. Office: Dot Foods Inc PO Box 192 1 Dot Way Mount Sterling IL 62353

TRACY, SAUNDRA J., academic administrator; m. Doug Tracy; children: Steve, Elaine. BA in Spanish, Carroll Coll., Waukesha, Wis., 1968; M Ed in Fgn. Lang. Instrn., U. Pitts., 1971; PhD in Edn. Adminstrn., Purdue U., West Lafayette, Ind., 1981. Dir. Greater Cleve. Adminstr. Assessment Ctr., 1968—88; asst. to assoc. prof. edn. Cleve. State U., 1981—88; exec. dir. sch. study coun. Lehigh U., 1989—91, dir. ednl. programs Lee Iacocca Inst., 1990—92, assoc. prof. to prof. edn., 1988—94; dean of coll. of edn. Butler U., 1994—98; v.p. acad. affairs Mt. Union Coll., 1998—2001; pres. Alma Coll., 2001—. Fellow, Am. Coun. of Edn., 1992—93. Office: Alma Coll 614 West Superior St Alma MI 48801-1599 Office Phone: 989-463-7146.

TRACY, THOMAS MILES, international health organization official; b. Great Barrington, Mass., July 8, 1936; s. Thomas Paul and Marion (Miles) T.; m. June Betts, June 17, 1967; children: Miles Christopher, Keir Thomas John. BA, Colgate U., 1958; MA, Stanford U., 1959; MBA, Columbia U., 1973. Fgn. service officer Dept. State, Washington, 1960-84; counselor Am. Embassy, Moscow, 1975-78, Bonn, Germany, 1978-79; asst. sec. Dept. State, Washington, 1979-83; chief adminstrn. Pan Am./WHO, Washington, 1983-98; mgmt. cons. Dept. State, 2003—. V.p. Pan-Am. Health and Edn. Found., treas. Trustee, vice chmn. Chelsea Sch., 1988-2004. With U.S. Army, 1959-60. Recipient Superior Honor award Dept. State, 1978 Mem.: Am. Fgn. Svc. Protective Found. (sec., treas.), Am. Fgn. Svc. Protective Assn. (dir. 1988—, v.p. 1997—2005, pres. 2005—), Am. Fgn. Svc. Assn. (dir. 1970—72). Home: 5902 Devonshire Dr Bethesda MD 20816-3416

TRADER, JOSEPH EDGAR, orthopedic surgeon; b. Milw., Nov. 2, 1946; s. Edgar Joseph and Dorothy Elizabeth (Senzig) T.; m. Janet Louise Burzycki, Sept. 23, 1972 (div. Nov. 1987); children: James, Jonathan, Ann Elizabeth; m. Rhonda Sue Schultz, May 26, 1990. Student, Marquette U., 1964-67; MD, Med. Coll. Wis., 1971. Diplomate Am. Bd. Orthop. Surgery. Physician emergency rm. Columbia, St. Joseph's Hosps., Milw., 1972—76; orthop. surgeon, pres. Orthop. Assn., Manitowoc, Wis., 1979—. Mem. exec. com. Holy Family Meml. Med. Ctr., Manitowoc, 1985-96, chief-of-staff, 1994-96, ethics com., 1995—, chair instnl. rev. com. Former pres., bd. dirs. Holy Innocents Mens Choir; county del. State Med. Soc. Charitable Sci. and Edn. Found.; mem. bd. dirs. (trustee), mem. cobia com. Wis. Maritime Mus. Fellow ACS, Am. Acad. Orthopaedic Surgeons; mem. AMA, Wis. State Med. Soc., Wis. Orthop. Soc., Midwest Orthop. Soc., Milw. Orthop. Soc., Am. Coll. Sports Medicine, Orthop. Assn. Manitowoc (pres.), Crown and Anchor, Wis. Maritime Mus. (cobia com. mem., bd. dirs.), Manitowoc Yacht Club, Phi Delta Epsilon, Psi Chi Roman Catholic. Avocations: singing, tennis, skiing, sailing, golf. Home: 1021 Memorial Dr Manitowoc WI 54220-2242 Office: Orthopaedic Assocs 501 N 10th St Manitowoc WI 54220-4039 Office Phone: 920-682-6376. Personal E-mail: jetrader@lakefield.net.

TRAEGER, CHARLES HENRY, III, lawyer; b. Fountain Hill, Pa., Sept. 30, 1942; s. Charles Henry Jr. and Dorothy Shelly (Weinberger) T.; m. Carole Lynn DeGraff, Feb. 20, 1972; children: Chad, Erin, Seth, Anna, Claire, Ben. AB, Coll. William and Mary, 1964; JD, Stanford U., 1967. Bar: Calif. 1967, N.Y. 1972, Mass. 1976, Ariz. 1980. Assoc. Milbank, Tweed, Hadley & McCloy, NYC, 1967, 71-76; v.p., gen. counsel Shawmut Corp., Boston, 1976-80, Shawmut Bank of Boston, N.A., 1976-80; assoc. Snell & Wilmer, Phoenix, 1980-83, ptnr., 1983-91; v.p., asst. gen. counsel Bank One Ariz. N.A., Phoenix, 1991-95; assoc. gen. counsel Ariz. State U., Tempe, 1996—2007, assoc. dir. alliance constrn. excellence, 2007—. Contbr. Stanford Law Rev. Lt. comdr. USNR, 1968-71. Mem. Phi Beta Kappa. Republican. Mem. Lds Ch. Office Phone: 480-965-1418. Business E-Mail: hanktr@asu.edu.

TRAEGER, NADAV, pediatrician, pulmonologist; MD, Albert Einstein Coll. Medicine, Bronx, 1998. Lic. NY, 1999. Attending physician Maria Fareri Children's Hosp., Westchester Med. Ctr., Valhalla, NY, 2004—. Dir. pediatric sleep medicine Maria Fareri Children's Hosp., Westchester Med. Ctr., 2004—. Fellow, Children's Hosp. Phila., 2001—04. Mem.: Am. Coll. Chest Physicians, Am. Thoracic Soc., Am. Acad. Pediat., Am. Acad. Sleep Medicine. Office: NY Med Coll Munger Pavilion Rm 106 Valhalla NY 10595 Office Phone: 914-493-7585. Office Fax: 914-594-4336. Personal E-mail: ntraeger@gmail.com. E-mail: nadav_traeger@nymc.edu.

TRAFFORD, ABIGAIL, columnist, editor, writer, public speaker; b. NYC, July 14, 1940; d. William Bradford and Abigail (Sard) T.; children: Abigail Brett Miller, Victoria Brett. BA cum laude, Bryn Mawr Coll., 1962. Researcher Nat. Geog. Soc., Washington, 1964-67; tchr. Hermansberg Mission, Northern Ter., Australia, 1967-68; spl. corr. Time mag., The Washington Post, Houston, 1969-74; writer, asst. mng. editor U.S. News & World Report, Washington, 1975-86; health editor The Washington Post, 1986-00, columnist, 2000—. Vis. scholar longevity ctr. Stanford U.; spkr. in field. Author: Crazy Time: Surviving Divorce and Building a New Life, 1982, revised edit., 1992, My Time: Making the Most of the Rest of Your Life, 2004. Journalism fellow Harvard Sch. Pub. Health, 1980, 2000; sr. fellow Civic Ventures. Mem. Washington Press Club Found. (bd. mem. 1989—, pres. 1993-95). Home and Office: 2600 Upton St NW Washington DC 20008-3826 Office Phone: 202-966-3516. Business E-Mail: trafforda@washpost.com.

TRAFICANTI, JOSEPH J., lawyer; b. Cheyenne, Wyo., Feb. 11, 1951; s. Joseph John and Lodema LaVerne (Atwell) T.; m. Kathi McKee, June 7, 1974; 1 child, Nathan. BS, USAF Acad., 1974; JD, Creighton U., 1981. Bar: Nebr. 1981, US Dist. Ct. (dist. Nebr.) 1981, Colo. 1984. Commd. 2nd lt. USAF, 1974, advanced through grades to maj., pilot, 1974-78, prosecuter Omaha, 1981-82, def. atty., 1982-83, trial lawyer civil litig.; chief legal counsel USAF Comiso Air Sta., Sicily, Italy; assoc. prof. law USAF Acad., Colo., 1983; mil. asst. and spl. counsel to USAF Gen. Counsel Pentagon; trial lawyer McGuire Woods, LLP, Richmond, Va.; positions up to v.p., assoc. gen. counsel, asst. corp. sec. Owens & Minor, Richmond, Va., 1996—; sr. v.p., gen. counsel, chief compliance officer, corp. sec. Performance Food Grp., 2004—. Briefer, rschr. mil. investment and estate planning USAF Acad., 1984. Assoc. editor Creighton U. Law Rev., 1979-81. Mem. ABA. Republican. Avocations: golf, hiking. Office: Performance Food Grp 12500 West Creek Pky Richmond VA 23238 *

TRAFIDLO, JAMES FRANCIS, marketing communications executive, commercial photographer; b. Boston, Apr. 16, 1953; s. Edward Joseph and Marian Frances (Hennigar) T.; m. Elizabeth Boyd, May 22, 1982 (div. Mar. 1995); 1 child, Samuel Boyd; m. Sarah Chisholm Lincoln, Oct. 14, 1995; 1 child: Benjamin Lincoln. BA in Psychology, Boston Coll., 1977. Freelance photographer, Boston, 1976—; office mgr., photographers asst. J. Rawle Communications, Bedford, Mass., 1978-80; sr. photographer Liberty Mut. Ins., Boston, 1980-86; owner Trafidlo Communications, Boston, 1986-93; new bus. developmer, project mgr. Boston Photo Imaging, Boston, 1994-2000; dir. new bus. devel., project mgr. Multimedia Comm., Natick, 2000—02; new bus. devel., project mgr. Video Transfer, Boston, 2002—, High Speed Video, Southborough, 2002—. Recipient Award of Achievement Soc. for Tech. Communication, 1984, 85. Mem. Am. Soc. Media Photographers, Assn. Multi-Image, Media Comm. Assn. Internat., Boston Advt. Golf Assn., Weston Golf Club, Longwood Covered Cts., Wellesley Tennis Assn., Natick Raquet Club, The Wellesley Ctr. Avocations: tennis, golf, alpine skiing. Home: 25 Bear Hill Rd Sherborn MA 01770-1135 Office: Video Transfer 580 Harrison Ave Boston MA 02118 also: High Speed Video 150 Cordaville Rd Southborough MA 01772 Office Phone: 617-247-0100. Business E-Mail: jtrafidlo@vtiboston.com.

TRAFIMOW, JORDAN HERMAN, orthopedist; b. Chgo., Nov. 4, 1935; s. Jack and Florence (Silver) Trafimow; m. Alice Emma Lewis, July 11, 1959; children: David, Alan, Janet. BS in Med., U. Ill., 1957, MD, 1958. Orthopedic surgeon Permanente Med. Group, LA, 1966-69, Elmhurst (Ill.) Clin., 1969-86; asst. prof. Rush St. Luke Presbyn. Med. Ctr., Chgo., 1986—; orthopedist Jefferson Pk. Med. Group, 1998—. Contbr. articles to profl. jours. Capt. U.S. Army, 1960-62. Fellow: N.Am. Spine Soc., Am. Acad. Orthopedic Surgeons. Jewish. Avocation: chess. Office: Jefferson Park Med Group PC 5906 N Milwaukee Ave Chicago IL 60646 Office Phone: 773-774-7300.

TRAFTON, LAURENCE MUNRO, astronomer, researcher; b. Boston, July 31, 1938; s. Herbert Meara and Vesta Estelle Trafton. BS, Calif. Inst. Tech., 1960, MS, 1961, PhD, 1965. Assoc. scientist Jet Propulsion Lab., Pasadena, Calif., summers 1961-62; project officer Kirtland AFB, Albuquerque, 1968, project scientist, 1968-69; spl. rsch. assoc. dept. astronomy U. Tex., Austin, 1969-72, rsch. scientist dept. astronomy, 1972-93, sr. rsch. scientist McDonald Obs., 1993—. Mem. editl. bd. Icarus, 1976-79, assoc. editor, 1980—; contbr. over 160 articles to sci. jours. 1st lt. USAF, 1965-68. Fellow AAAS; mem. Am. Astron. Soc. (com. mem. divsn. planetary sci. 1977-80), Internat. Astron. Union. Office: Univ Tex Austin Dept Astronomy Austin TX 78712 Office Phone: 512-471-1476. E-mail: lmt@astro.as.utexas.edu.

TRAGER, D. DAVID, retired pharmacist, consultant; b. Napa, Calif., Oct. 4, 1931; s. Louis D. (dec.) and Frances Amanda (Brose) T. (dec.); m. Ruth (Pacovsky), June 15, 1952 (div. Sept. 1978); children: Louis, Solomon; m. Sarah Ann (Brancato), Dec. 28, 1983 (dec. May 2000); children: Daryl, Randy, Missi Hasnas; m. Phyllis Baldwin (Douglas), Oct. 7, 2001; 1 stepchild, Robert Gordon Douglas. BS in Pharm., U. Calif., San Francisco, 1953; post grad. in Clin. pharmacy, U. So. Calif., 1976, post grad. in Drug action, 1978. Registered pharmacist Calif. Pharmacist multiple locations, Calif., 1953-59; pharmacist, pharmacy mgr. Longs Drugs, West Covina, Calif., 1959-60; pharmacist Bay Pharmacy, Pacific Palisades, Calif., 1960-65; pharmacist, v.p. Palisades Drug Co., Pacific Palisades, 1965—67; pharmacist Bi Rite, Westwood and Santa Monica, Calif., 1967-68; pharmacist, owner Trager, Pacific Palisades, 1968—72; pharmacist Kaiser Found. Hosp. Pharmacy, Panorama City, Calif., 1973—90, Woodland Hills, Calif., 1990-98; ret., 1998. Propr. P-I-E Software, Calif., 1995—; mentor first yr. pharmacy students U. Pacific, Calif., 1998—2001, tech. lit. cons., Calif., 2001—; per diem overnight pharmacist Kaiser Permanente Pharmacy, Woodland Hills, Calif., 2001—03; gen. cons. Mem.: Am. Inst. History of Pharmacy, Calif. Employee Pharmacist Assn., Am. Pharm. Assn.

(life; emeritus), Scottish Rite, Scottish Rite Rsch. Soc. (life), Royal Arch Mason, Masons (life), Shriners, Kappa Psi. Republican. Jewish. Avocations: computers, reading, Masonic research, philosophy.

TRAGER, MICHAEL DAVID, lawyer; b. NYC, Feb. 15, 1959; s. Philip and Ina (Shulkin) T.; m. Mariella Gonzalez, Sept. 12, 1987; children: Nicholas, Alexander. BA, Wesleyan U., Middletown, Conn., 1981; JD, Boston U., 1985. Bar: Mass. 1985, Conn. 1986, Fla. 1988, DC 1989. Staff atty. enforcement divsn. SEC, Washington, 1985-87; assoc. Morgan, Lewis & Bockius, Miami, Fla., 1987-88; participating assoc. Fulbright & Jaworski, Washington, 1989-92, of counsel, 1993-94, ptnr., 1995—2004, co-head securities litig. and enforcement, firm, chair corp. dept.; ptnr. Arnold & Porter LLP, Washington, 2005—, chmn. securities enforcement practice. Bd. dirs. Jewish Nat. Fund-Mid-Atlantic Region, Wash., 1993-97; officer Horace Mann PTA, Washington, 1997-99. Mem. ABA (bus. law sect. fed. regulation securities com. and civil litig. and SEC enforcement matters subcom., litig. sect. securities litig. com. and SEC enforcement subcom., class action and derivative litig. com. and securities litig. subcom., task force on SEC's insider trading and selective disclosure rules), Assn. SEC Alumni, Securities Industry Assn. (legal and compliance divsn.), DC Bar (corp., fin. and securities law sect. corp. counsel and planning group for broker-dealer programs 1992-94, broker-dealer regulation com., task force on SEC's proposed insider trading and selective disclosure rules), Mass. Bar, Fla. Bar., Conn. Bar, Bond Market Assn. (litig. adv. com.), Wesleyan U. Club of Washington (chair 2001-04), Wesleyan U. Alumni Assn. (exec. com. 2001-04), Post-classical Ensemble (adv. bd. 2003-05), Children's Law Ctr. (chair Law Firm Sponsors 2004), Wash. Ballet (bd. dirs. 2004-06). Office: Arnold & Porter LLP 555 12th St NW 1153 Washington DC 20004 Office Phone: 202-942-6976. Office Fax: 202-942-5999. Business E-Mail: michael.trager@aporter.com.

TRAGOS, GEORGE EURIPEDES, lawyer; b. Chgo., July 15, 1949; s. Euripedes G. and Eugene G. (Gatziolis) T.; m. Donna Marie Thalassites, Nov. 18, 1978; children: Louise, Gina, Peter. BA, Fla. State U., 1971, JD, 1974. Bar: Fla., U.S. Dist. Ct. (mid., so. dists.) Fla., U.S. Dist. Ct. (we. dist.) Tenn., U.S. Ct. Appeals (5th, 11th cirs.). Legis. aide Fla. Ho. of Reps., 1972-73; tax analyst tax and fin. com., 1973-74; chief, felony asst. states atty. State of Fla., Clearwater, 1974-78; partner firm Case, Kimpton, Tragos & Burke, P.A., Clearwater Beach, 1978-83; chief criminal div. U.S. Atty.'s Office for Middle Dist. Fla., Tampa, 1983-85; lead trial asst. Pres. Organized Crime Drug Enforcement Task Force, Tampa, 1985; sole practice Clearwater, 1985—. Contbr. articles to profl. jours. and frequent lectr. Mem. Clearwater Bar (pres. 1994), Fla. Bar Assn. (chmn. fed. practice com. 1986, chmn. criminal law sect. 2000, chmn. bar evidence com. 1990), Fla. Assn. Criminal Def. Lawyers (pres. 1991), Fla. State U. Alumni Assn. Law Sch. (bd. dirs.), Tampa Bay Fed. Bar Assn. (v.p. 1989), Clearwater Beach Jaycees (pres. 1979), Fla. U. Gold Key Club (pres. 1972), Ahepa. Mem. Greek Orthodox Ch. Avocations: boating, tennis. Office: 600 Cleveland St Ste 700 Clearwater FL 33755-4158 Office Phone: 727-441-9030. Business E-Mail: greek.law@verizon.net.

TRAIL, MARGARET ANN, retired employee benefits company executive; b. Bryan, Tex., July 17, 1941; d. Louis Milton and Margaret (Stromberg) Thompson; m. Robert A. Rosemier, Aug. 25, 1962 (div. Feb. 1973); 1 child: Gretchen Elisabeth Jolly; m. Newt Shands Trail, Dec. 4, 1989. BSN, U. Iowa, 1963; MS, No. Ill. U., 1971. Cert. master gardener Nat. Soc. DAR. Instr. Cooley Dickinson Hosp., Northampton, Mass., 1964-65; dir. nursing De Kalb (Ill.) Pub. Hosp., Kishwaukee Cmty. Hosp., 1972—76, Terre Haute (Ind.) Regional Hosp., 1976—78; from mgr. clin. systems to dir. spl. projects Hosp. Corp. Am., Nashville, 1978-86; from dir. med. mgmt. to v.p. Equicor, Nashville, 1986-90; divsn. v.p. The Travelers Ins. Co., Hartford, Conn., 1990-93; asst. v.p. health svcs. quality mgmt. Aetna, Hartford, 1993—2003, ret., 2003. Mem. LWV (pres. DeKalb chpt. 1970-72), Nat. Soc. DAR (Sarah Maples chpt.). Avocations: gardening, beekeeping, genealogy.

TRAILLE, JOY MYRA, microbiologist, eldercare service provider; arrived in U.S., 1971; d. Randolph and Leanorah Williams; m. Winston Traille, June 6, 1981; children: Nichola Davis, Kevin. MS, L.I. U., 1981; PhD, Union Inst., Cin., 1991; MBA, Iona, New Rochelle, NY, 2002. Cert. Am. Soc. Clin. Pathologist, 1981. Med. technologist Gouverneur Hosp./NYU, NYC, 1978—83; microbiology clin. scientist Kingsbrook Jewish Med. Ctr., Blkyn., 1983—87; microbiologist Mary Immaculate Hosp., Jamaica, NY, 1987—91; adminstrv. dir. Manhattan Eye Ear & Throat Hosp, NYC, 1991—98; dir. Cryobank for Oncology & Reproduction, Middletown, NY, 1998—; owner/pres. Comfort Keepers, Cortlandt Manor, NY, 2003—. Infectious disease bd. mem. Manhattan Eye Ear & Throat Hosp., NYC, 1991—98; adv. bd. mem. Cryobank for Oncology & Reproduction, Middletown, NY, 1998—. Author, pub.: magazine Caribbean Heritage, 1999—2003; author: (a handbook for caregivers) You Are Not Alone, 1991. Adv. bd. coun. eldercare United Way, Westcherster, NY, 2004—05. Mem.: Soc. For Cert. Sr. Advisors, Am. Soc. Microbiology. Avocations: writing, reading, travel, drama/musicals, dance. Office: Comfort Keepers Ste 104B 2127 Crompond Rd Cortlandt Manor NY 10566 Office Phone: 914-734-2616. Business E-Mail: peekskill@comfortkeepers.com.

TRAIN, HARRY DEPUE, II, retired naval officer; b. Washington, Nov. 5, 1927; s. Harold Cecil and May (Philipps) T.; m. Catharine Peck Kinnear, July 8, 1950; children: Louise Lucas, Catharine Philipps, Elizabeth Langdon, Cecilia Spencer. BS, U.S. Naval Acad., 1949. Commd. ensign U.S. Navy, 1949, advanced through grades to adm., 1978; comdr. Cruiser-Destroyer Flotilla 8, 1971-72; dir. internat. security affairs East Asia and Pacific Region Office Asst. Sec. Def., 1972-73; dir. Systems Analysis Div., Office Chief Naval Ops., 1973-74; dir. joint staff Orgn. Joint Chiefs of Staff, 1974-76; comdr. U.S. 6th Fleet, 1976-78; comdr.-in-chief, supreme allied cmdr., atlantic cmd, atlantic fleet US Navy, 1978-82; ret. US Atlantic Fleet and NATO supreme allied comdr. Atlantic, 1982. Mgr. Hampton Rds. Ops. Sci. Applications Internat. Corp., 1989—2006. Mem. Hart-Rudman Commn. Decorated D.S.M. with 3 gold stars, Def. Disting. Svc. medal, Legion of Merit with 3 gold stars, Meritorious Svc. medal, Joint Svcs. Commendation medal, Navy Commendation medal; comdr. Order Republic of Tunisia; Order Naval Merit Brazil; Pedro Campbell medal Uruguay; Order of Pres. of Republic Chile; decorated Portuguese Mil. Order Christ; Netherlands Order Orange-Nassau; German Order Merit; French Legion of Honor; Colombian Naval Order Admiral Padilla; Mex. Order Spl. Merit; sr. fellow Joint Advanced Warfighting Sch., Joint Forces Staff Coll. Mem. U.S. Naval Inst., Coun. on Fgn. Rels., Columbia Country Club, Town Point Club. Home: 401 College Pl Apt 10 Norfolk VA 23510-1130

TRAIN, JOHN, investment advisor, federal official; b. NYC, May 25, 1928; s. Arthur Cheney and Helen (Coster) T.; m. Maria Teresa Cini di Pianzano, 1961 (div. 1976); children: Helen, Nina, Lisa; m. Frances Cheston, July 23, 1977. BA magna cum laude, Harvard U., 1950, MA, 1951. Founder, mng. editor Paris Rev., 1952-54; staff Asst. Sec. Army, Washington, 1954-56; assoc. de Vegh & Co., 1956-58; chmn. Train, Babcock Advisors (and predecessor firms), NYC, 1958-94, chmn. emeritus, 1995—; co-chmn., then hon. dir. ICAP, S.A., Athens, 1964—; chmn. Montrose Fin. Group, NYC, 1992—; pres. Chateau Malescasse, Lamarque-Margaux, Bordeaux, France, 1970-81; columnist Forbes mag., 1977-83, Harvard mag., 1983-95, Wall St. Jour., 1984—, Worth Mag., Boston, 1991-93, Town and Country mag., 1994-95, Fin. Times, London, 1994—2002, Strategic Rev., 1998—2002, Am. Spectator, 2002—. Bd. dirs. African Devel. Found., Washington, 1988-94; bd. dirs. Bulgarian-Am. Enterprise Fund, Washington, Genesis Funds, London, Internat. Rescue Com., N.Y.C.; chmn. Train Found., 1988—; bd. govs. East-West Ctr., Hawaii, 1993-96. Author: Dance of the Money Bees, 1973, Remarkable Names, 1977, Even More Remarkable Names, 1979, Remarkable Occurrences, 1978, Remarkable Words, 1980, The Money Masters, 1980, Remarkable Relatives, 1971, Preserving Capital and Making it Grow, 1983, Famous Financial Fiascos, 1984, John Train's Most Remarkable Names, 1985, The Midas Touch, 1987, The New Money Masters, 1989, Valsalva's Maneuver, 1989, John Train's Most Remarkable Occurences, 1990, Wit, 1991, Love, 1993, The Craft of Investing, 1994, Crazy Quilt, 1996, Oriental Rug Symbols, 1997, Investing and Managing Trusts under the New Prudent Investor Rule, 1999, Money Masters of Our Time, 2001, The Olive: Tree of Civilization, 2004, The Orange: Golden Joy, 2006; contbr. articles to profl. publs. Chmn. Italian Emergency Relief Com., 1976-77; pres. Afghanistan Relief Com., 1986-95; trustee Harvard Lampoon, Cambridge, Mass., 1974-90, World Monuments Fund, 1988-92; chmn. Free Elections Project, 1990, Brit. Mus. Nat. Hist. Internat. Trust, 1990-95, Northcote Parkinson Fund, 1990—; trustee univ. coun. Am. U. Bulgaria, 1996—; overseer Sch. Govt. and Diplomacy Seton Hall U., South Oroage, NJ. With U.S. Army, 1954-56. Decorated commendatore Ordine del Merito della Repubblica, commendatore Ordine Della Solidarieta, medal Provincia di Udine (Italy); recipient Disting. Grotonian award, 1996, Queen's Birthday honors Order of St. John, 1997. Mem.: Fgn. Policy Assn. (trustee), Internat. Inst. Strategic Studies (London), Coun. on Fgn. Rels., Order Colonial Lords of Manors, Travellers Club (Paris), Beefsteak Club (London), Brook's Club (London), Union Club, Racquet & Tennis Club, Met. Club (Washington), Century Club. Office: 505 Park Ave New York NY 10022

TRAIN, RUSSELL ERROL, environmentalist; b. Jamestown, RI, June 4, 1920; s. Charles R. and Errol C. (Brown) T.; m. Aileen Bowdoin, May 27, 1954; children: Nancy, Emily, Bowdoin, Errol. AB, Princeton U., 1941, LL.D. (hon.), 1970; JD, Columbia U., 1948, LL.D. (hon.), 1970, Bates Coll., 1970, Drexel U., 1970; D.E. (hon.), Worcester Poly. Inst., 1970, U. Md., 1975; Sc.D. (hon.), St. Mary's Coll., 1970, Clarkson Coll. Tech., 1973, Salem Coll., 1975, Southwestern U., 1976, Mich. State U., 1976; D.C.L. (hon.), U. of South, 1973; D public svc., Washington Coll., 1996. Bar: D.C. bar 1949. Atty. staff joint com. on internal revenue taxation U.S. Congress, 1949-53; chief counsel Ways and Means Com., U.S. Ho. of Reps., 1953-54, minority adviser, 1955-56; asst. to sec., head legal adv. staff Treasury Dept., 1956-57; judge U.S. Tax Ct., 1957-65; pres. Conservation Found., 1965-69; also trustee; undersec. Dept. Interior, 1969-70; chmn. Council on Environ. Quality, 1970-73; adminstr. EPA, Washington, 1973-77; sr. assoc. Conservation Found., 1977; pres., chief exec. officer World Wildlife Fund, Washington, 1978-85, chmn. bd., 1985-94, chmn. emeritus, 1994—; chmn. bd. Conservation Found., 1985-90; chmn. Nat. Commn. on the Environment, 1991-93; chmn. Nat. Coun. World Wildlife Fund, Washington, chmn. emeritus. Mem. Washington Nat. Monument Assn., Nat. Water Commn., 1968—69; head U.S. del. UN Conf. Human Environment, 1972; rep. Internat. Whaling Commn., 1972, other internat. confs.; mem. Pres.'s adv. com. on trade and trade negotiations, 1991—93. Author: The Bowdoin Family, 2000, The Train Family, 2000, A Memoir, 2000, Politics, Pollution, and Pandas, 2003. Trustee emeritus African Wildlife Found. Decorated Order of the Golden Ark (The Netherlands); recipient Albert Schweitzer medal, Animal Welfare Inst., 1972, Aldo Leopold medal, Wildlife Soc., 1975, Conservationist of Yr. award, Nat. Wildlife Fedn., 1974, 1986, John and Alice Tyler Ecology award, 1978, Freese award, ASCE, 1978, Pub. Welfare award, Nat. Acad. Scis., 1981, Elizabeth Haub prize in internat. environ. law, 1981, Frances K. Hutchinson medal, Garden Club of Am., 1984, Lindbergh award, 1985, Environ. Law Inst. award, 1986, Presdl. Medal of Freedom, 1991, Heinz Chmns. medal, 2001, Internat. Excellence in Conservation award, Bot. Rsch. Inst., Tex., 2006, Founder's award, St. George's Sch., Newport, RI, 2007. Fellow: AAAS; mem.: Am. Acad. Arts and Scis., Atlantic Coun., Coun. Fgn. Rels. Office: World Wildlife Fund 1250 24th St NW Fl 6 Washington DC 20037-1193

TRAINA, SALVATORE ALBERT, publishing executive; b. Bklyn., Apr. 30, 1927; s. Salvatore and Guilia (LeBarbara) T.; m. Vail Devereux, June 27, 1957; children: Caroline Vail, Robert Brooks. BS, Seton Hall U., 1950; postgrad., Columbia U., 1950-51; MBA, NYU, 1954. Circulation promotion advt. space salesman Fairchild Publs., NYC, 1951-53; Eastern advt. mgr. Modern Bride mag. Ziff-Davis, NYC, 1953-58; advt. mgr. Bride and Home mag. Hearst Mags., NYC, 1958-60, pub. Bride and Home mag., 1960-64; pub. Sports Afield mag., 1964-65, Town and Country mag., 1965-67, Harpers Bazaar mag., 1967-70; pres., chief exec. officer Bartell Media Corp., 1970-74; pres. Ziff-Davis Mag. Network, 1974-76, group v.p., 1976-78; sr. v.p. Ziff-Davis Pub. Co., 1978-81; pres. Ziff-Davis Consumer Mag., 1981-85; exec. v.p. mags. CBS, NYC, 1985; pres. Traina Assocs., NYC, 1985—2000. Mem. Scarsdale Bi-Partisan Com., 1975-78; bd. dirs. Crane Berkeley Assn., 1978-88, pres., 1983-84; mem. nat. bd. dirs., chmn. comms. com., treas. Goodwill Industries of Am., 1979-92, chmn. bd., 1988-92; chmn. bd. trustees Chebeague Island Libr., 1997-2001; pres. bd. dirs. Chebeague Recreation Ctr., 1998-2003; bd. dirs. Chebeague Island Hist. Soc., 2000—. With USNR, 1945-46. NY State War Svc. scholar, Columbia U. and NYU, 1950. Mem. NYU Grad. Sch. Bus. Adminstrn. Alumni Assn., NYU Alumni Fedn. (comms. com. 1970-73), Union League Club (N.Y.C.). Home: 11 Springettes Rd Chebeague Island ME 04017-9723 E-mail: sunsethill@earthlink.net.

TRAINER, KARIN A., librarian; BA in English, Rutgers U., 1970; grad. work in English, Bryn Mawr Coll.; MLIS, Drexel U., 1972; M in liberal studies, NYU, 1983. Descriptive cataloguer Libraries of Princeton U., 1972—74, catalogue maintenance libr., 1974—78; dir. tech. and automated services NYU Libraries, 1978—83; assoc. univ. libr. Yale U., 1983—96, fellow and freshman advisor Ezra Stiles Coll.; univ. libr. Princeton U., 1996—. Trustee Princeton U. Press. Fellow Rockefeller Coll. Office: Princeton U Libr One Washington Rd Princeton NJ 08544 Office Phone: 609-258-3170. Business E-Mail: ktrainer@princeton.edu. *

TRAINES, ROSE WUNDERBAUM, sculptor, educator; b. Monroeville, Ind., Sept. 13, 1928; d. Louis and Leah (Fogel) Wunderbaum; m. Robert Jacob Traines, June 25, 1949; children: Claudia Denise Traines Lang, Monica Rae Traines Martin Student, Ind. State Tchr.'s Coll., 1946—48, Mich. State U., 1948—49; BS, Ctrl. Mich. U., 1951. Lectr. in field. One person shows include Ctrl. Mich. U., Mt. Pleasant, 1964, Alma Artmobile, Mich., 1972, Ctrl. Mich. Homecoming, Mt. Pleasant, 1982, Internat. Inst. Scrap Iron and Steel, Inc., Washington, 1983, Fontainebleau Hotel, Miami Beach, Fla., 1983, Elliott Mus. Art Gallery, Stuart, Fla., 1988, 98, 2006, Walt Kuhn Gallery, Cape Neddick, Maine, 1988, Coll. Club Boston, 1990, Brass Latch Gallery, Montpelier, Ind., 1991, 96, 98, Vero Beach Ctr. Arts, Fla., 1992, Maritime and Yachting Mus., Stuart, 1997, Mid-Mich. Regional Med. Ctr., Healing Arts Gallery, Midland, 1997, Northwood Gallery, Midland, Commerca Bank Art Series, Palm Beach Gardens, 2002, Gallery Five, Tequesta, Fla., 2002, Mich. U. Park Libr. Gallery, 2002, Art Reach Mid. Mich., Mt. Pleasant, 2002, Arthur Glick Jewish Cmty. Ctr., Indpls., 2004, Art Reach Ctr. Mid-Mich., Mt. Pleasant, Elliott Mus. Gallery, Stuart, Fla., 2006, 2007; two-person shows include Gallery One, North Palm Beach, 1973, Midland Ctr. Arts, 1976, Springfield Art Mart, Ohio, 1977, Hillel Student Ctr. Gallery-U. Cin., 1993; exhibited in group shows including Saginaw Mus. Art, Mich., 1965, Grand Rapids Mus., Mich., 1966, Kalamazoo Mus., Mich., 1967, Kellogg/Kresge Art Ctr., Mich. State U., East Lansing, 1967, Art Reach Mid-Mich., 1987, Salmagundi Club, NYC, 1988, 91-92, 96, Copley Soc., Boston, 1990, 95, Allied Artists Am., Inc., NYC, 1995-96, Self Family Arts Ctr., Hilton Head Island, SC, 1996-97, Palm Beach Gardens Fla. City Hall, 2003, Palm Beach Gardens Cmty. Ctr., 2003, Art Reach Mid Mich., 2006, Country Club Orchid Island, Orchid, Fla., 2007; represented in permanent collections at Dow-Corning Corp. Collection, Midland Ctr. Arts, Elliott Mus., Walt Kuhn Gallery, Coll. Club Boston, Pullen Elem. Sch., Isabella Bank and Trust Co., Ctrl. Mich. U., Blake Libr, Stuart, La Belle Mgmt. Corp., Morey Bandit Industries, Mich., Ctrl. Mich. Cmty. Hosp., Northwood U., Vets. Meml. Libr., Mt. Pleasant, Pub. Libr., Clare, Mich., Brass Latch Gallery, Northville (Mich.) Pub. Libr, Norman Cousins, Carl Gerstacker Found., Fannie Traines, Doctor Tom Keating, Olga and Rollie Denison, Claudia and Yaron Lang, Marjorie Fishbain, Kitti Pyne, Donnie Hersee, pvt. collections. Tchr. Jewish Sunday Sch., Mt. Pleasant, 1955-70; officer Child and Youth Study Clubs, Mt. Pleasant, 1963-73; mem. City Recreation Commn., Mt. Pleasant, 1963-73, Area Health Planning Coun., Mt. Pleasant, 1974-80; pres., vol. Hosp. Aux. Med. Care, Red Cross Blood Bank, United Fund Cancer Dr., Mt. Pleasant, 1960-80; storyteller pub. libr., Mt. Pleasant, 1957-79 Recipient Northwood U. Artist award, Midland Ctr. for Arts, Mich., 2002. Mem.: Brass Latch Gallery, Art Reach Mid-Mich., Hilton Head Art League S.C. (Lifetime of Creative Excellence award 1998), Copley Soc. Boston (signature), Allied Artists Am. (Merit award 1996, Raymond H. Brumer Meml. award 1999), Nat. Mus. Women in Arts (charter), Salmagundi Club (Philip Isenberg award 1993, Pamela Singleton award 1997, Elliot Liskin Meml. award 1998, Anonymous award 1998, Peters Sculpture Materials award 2001, Alphaeus P. Cole Meml. award 2001, Meml. award 2003). Jewish. Avocations: lecturing, community work, tennis, presenting humorous programs, drums. Home: 1217 North Dr Mount Pleasant MI 48858-3226 Office Phone: 989-773-3873. Personal E-mail: fundametal2@webtv.net.

TRAINOR, BERNARD EDMUND, retired military officer; b. NYC, Sept. 2, 1928; s. Joseph Patrick and Ann Veronica (Whelan) T.; m. Margaret Ann Hamilton, June 13, 1959; children: Kathleen Marie, Theresa Ann, Eileen Cecile, Claire Hamilton. BS, Coll. of Holy Cross, 1951; MA, U. Colo., 1963, postgrad., 1970-73; student, Air War Coll., Montgomery, Ala., 1969-70. Commd. 2nd lt. USMC, 1951, advanced through grades to lt. gen., 1983, inf. comdr. Korea, 1952, assigned to USS Columbus, 1953-55, mem. staff Marine Corps Hdqrs., 1955-58, with exch. office Royal Marine Commandos, 1958-59, inf. comdr. 1st Marine divsn., 1959-61; asst. prof. naval sci. U. Colo., Boulder, 1961-64; assigned to Marine Corps Command and Staff Coll., 1964-65; adv. Republic of Vietnam, 1965-66; instr. Marine Corps Command and Staff Coll., 1966-69; bn. comdr. Vietnam, 1970-71; staff officer Hdqrs. Marine Corps, Washington, 1970-71; dir. First Marine Corps Dist., NYC, 1974-76; asst. depot comdr. Marine Corps Recruit Depot, Parris Island, SC, 1976-78; dir. Edn. Ctr., Quantico, Va., 1978-81; dep. chief of staff for plans, policies and ops. Hdqrs. Marine Corps, 1981-85; ret., 1985; mil. corr. N.Y. Times, 1986-90; dir. nat. security program Kennedy Sch. Govt. Harvard U., Cambridge, Mass., 1990-96, assoc. Ctr. Sci. and Internat. Affairs, 1996—2005; sr. fellow nat. security Coun. on Fgn. Rels., 1999—. Retired USMC, 1985. Author: History of the U.S. Marine Corps, 1968, The Generals' War, 1995; contbg. author: American Defense Annual, 1990, 2d edit., 1996, Defense Beat, 1991, After the Storm, 1992, The Almanac of Seapower, 1993, Newsmen and National Defense, 1991, Perspectives on Warfighting, 1992; mem. editl. adv. bd. Naval War Coll. Rev.; contbr. articles to profl. jours. Mil. analyst NBC News. Decorated D.S.M., Legion of Merit with Combat V and two stars, Bronze Star with Combat V, Navy Commendation medal with Combat V and two gold stars, others; recipient Anderson Meml. award Air War Coll., 1970. Mem. Naval Inst., Marine Corps Assn., Coun. Fgn. Rels., World Affairs Coun. (bd. dirs.). Roman Catholic. Home: 468741 Grissom St Potomac Falls VA 20165 E-mail: mickt51@adelphia.net.

TRAINOR, JOHN FELIX, retired economics professor; b. Mpls., Dec. 1, 1921; s. James Patrick and Myra Catherine (Pauly) T.; m. Margaret Dolores Pudenz, July 3, 1965 (dec. 1977); children: John Anthony, Patrick James. BA cum laude, Coll. St. Thomas, 1943; MA, U. Minn., 1950; PhD, Wash. State U., Pullman, 1970. Instr. De LaSalle H.S., Mpls., 1946-47, Coll. St. Thomas, 1949-50; v.p. Trainor Candy Co., Mpls., 1949-56; instr., asst. prof. econs. Rockhurst Coll., Kansas City, Mo., 1956-62; instr. Wash. State U., Pullman, 1966-67; asst. prof. Minn. State U., Moorhead, 1967—70, assoc. prof. econs., 1971-87, prof. econ., 1988-89, chmn. dept. econs., 1981-89, prof. emeritus, 1989—. Pres. Minn. Econs. Assn., 1976—77. Author: (with Frank J. Kottke) The Nursing Home Industry in the State of Washington, 1968. Ensign to Lt. (j.g.) USNR, 1943-46, ETO. Roman Catholic. Avocations: reading, crossword puzzles. Home: 1333 4th Ave S Moorhead MN 56560-2971

TRAISMAN, HOWARD SEVIN, retired pediatrician; b. Chgo., Mar. 18, 1923; s. Alfred Stanley and Sara (Sevin) T.; m. Regina Gallagher, Feb. 29, 1956; children: Barry D. Lifschultz, Edward S., Kenneth N. BS in Chemistry, Northwestern U., 1943, MB, 1946, MD, 1947. Intern Cook County Hosp., Chgo., 1946-47; resident in pediat. Children's Meml. Hosp., Chgo., 1949-51, attending physician divsn. endocrinology, 1951—2002; mem. faculty Med. Sch. Northwestern U., Evanston, Ill., 1951—2002, prof. pediat., 1973—2002, pres., 1999—2002; ret., 2002. Author articles in field, chpts. in books. Capt. M.C. AUS, 1943-46, 47-49. Recipient Northwestern U. Alumni Merit award, 1995, Northwestern U. Alumni medal, 2005. Mem. Am. Diabetes Assn. (Disting. Svc. award 1976), Am. Pediatric Soc., Am. Acad. Pediat., Endocrine Soc., Lawson Wilkins Pediatric Endocrine Soc., AMA, Midwest Soc. Pediatric Rsch., Ill. Med. Soc., Chgo. Pediatric Soc., Chgo. Med. Soc., Inst. Medicine Chgo. Democrat. Jewish. Office: 1325 Howard St Evanston IL 60202-3766 Office Phone: 847-869-4330.

TRAKATELLIS, DEMETRIOS See DEMETRIOS

TRALDI, LORENZO, mathematician, educator; b. Rome, May 22, 1955; arrived in U.S., 1955; s. Giuseppe Alberto Traldi, Ila Dawson Little, Charles Little (Stepfather); m. Sharon Richter; children: Arthur, Matthew, Oliver, Rebecca. BA, CUNY, Flushing, NY, 1976; PhD, Yale U., 1980. Asst. prof. Lafayette Coll., Easton, Pa., 1980—86, assoc. prof., 1986—94, prof., 1994—2001, Marshall R. Metzgar prof. math., 2001—. Contbr. articles and revs. to profl. jours. Grantee, Lafayette Coll., 1983, 1987, 1991, 1996, 1997, 2000—07, USAF Office Sci. Rsch., 1991—92, NSF, 1994, 2001, 2003, 2005. Mem.: IEEE, Inst. for Combinatorics and its Applications, Am. Math. Soc. Independent. Home: 725 Coleman St Easton PA 18042 Office: Dept Math Lafayette Coll Easton PA 18042 Office Phone: 610-330-5276. Business E-Mail: traldil@lafayette.edu.

TRAMMEL, KIMBERLY ELISE See ELISE, KIMBERLY

TRAMMELL, ALAN STUART, professional baseball coach, retired professional baseball player; b. Garden Grove, Calif., Feb. 21, 1958; m. Barbara Leverett, Feb. 21, 1978; children: Lance, Kyle, Jade Lynn. Shortstop Detroit Tigers, 1977—96, asst. to baseball ops., 1996—98, mgr., 2003—05; first base coach San Diego Padres, 2000—02; bench coach Chgo. Cubs, 2006—. Named Most Valuable Player, So. League, 1977; winner Gold Glove award, 1980, 81, 83-84; Silver Slugger award, 1987-88, 90; mem. Am. League All-Star Team, 1980, 84, 87, 88, 90, World Series Championship Team, 1984; named Most Valuable Player 1984 World Series. Office: Chgo Cubs Wrigley Field 1060 W Addison St Chicago IL 60613 *

TRAMMELL, BRADLEY ELLIS, lawyer; b. Opelika, Ala., Jan. 11, 1961; s. Herman Bruce and Laura Elizabeth Trammell; m. Katherine Farrell McClintock, Apr. 11, 1992; children: William McClintock, Henry Ellis. BA cum laude, U. of South, Sewanee, Tenn., 1983; JD, U. Ala., Tuscaloosa, 1989. Bar: Tenn. 1989, Ala. 1991. Acct. exec. Travelers Ins. Co., Plantation, Fla., 1983—86; shareholder Baker, Donelson, Bearman,

Caldwell & Berkowitz, Memphis, 1989—, chair Memphis office recruiting com., 2002—06. Campaign chmn. Travelers South Fla. offices United Way, 1984; chmn. ann. ptnrs. campaign Downtown YMCA, Memphis, 1993; jr. warden St. John's Episcopal Ch., Memphis, 2002, vestry mem., 2001—03. Mem.: ABA, Memphis Bar Assn. Young Lawyers (bd. dirs. 1991—93), Memphis Bar Assn., Ala. Bar Assn., Tenn. Bar Assn., Omicron Delta Kappa. Office: Baker Donelson Bearman Caldwell & Berkowitz 165 Madison Ave Ste 2000 Memphis TN 38103 Office Phone: 901-577-2121. Office Fax: 901-557-0781. Business E-Mail: btrammell@bakerdonelson.com.

TRAMMELL, HERBERT EUGENE, retired physicist; b. Laurel, Miss., Apr. 19, 1927; s. Homer Lee and Evie Louisa (Breazeale) T.; m. Jane Walker, Dec. 28, 1948; children— Carmen, Bert, Lisa, Brian. BA in Physics, U. Miss., 1947, MA, 1948. With Nuclear div. Union Carbide, Oak Ridge, 1949-89, mgr. barrier devel. programs, 1967-69, dir. gaseous diffusion devel. div., 1969-77; dir. engring. tech. div. Oak Ridge Nat. Lab., 1977-89, ret., 1989; with Martin Marietta Energy Systems, 1983-89. Bd. dirs. Emory Valley Sch. for Retarded Children, 1962-68, v.p., 1966-68; mem. Tenn. Med. Malpractice Rev. Bd., 1974-80; active PTA. Served with U.S. Navy, 1944-45. Mem.: Rotary (pres. 1980-81). Methodist. Home: 901 Johnson St Key West FL 33040-4745 Personal E-mail: hjtrammell@aol.com.

TRAMONTE, MICHAEL ROBERT, education educator; AB in Sociology, Boston Coll., 1960; EdM, State Coll. Boston, 1963; Cert. Advanced Edn. Specialization, Boston Coll., 1971; Comprehensive Cert. in Paralegal Studies, Bentley Coll., 1982; EdD in Human Devel. and Edn., Boston U., 1986. Lic. psychologist health svc. provider, ednl. psychologist, cert. social worker, cert. tchr. social studies grades 5-9, grades 9-12, moderate spl. needs tchr., sch. psychologist, supr., guidance counselor, supr., dir., secondary sch. prin. Mass., sch. psychologist N.H., Mass., nat. cert. sch. psychologist. Substitute tchr. Medford (Mass.) Pub. Schs., 1960-61, jr. H.S. tchr. social studies, 1961-68; instr. psychology and edn. Anna Maria Coll., 1968-69; adj. instr. psychology Mass. Bay C.C., 1972—77, Middlesex C.C., 1977—; sch. psychologist Lowell (Mass.) Pub. Schs., 1970-98; assoc. prof. edn. Rivier Coll., Nashua, NH, 1998—. Adj. prof. edn. Rivier Coll., 1983, 87-98; spkr. in field. Chmn. Medford chpt. Greater Boston Assn. Retarded Children, 1969-70; vol. spkr. support groups Mass. chpt. Nat. Multiple Sclerosis Soc., 1971-88; mem. ARC Disaster Svcs. Human Resources Sys. Recipient certificate, Medford Mental Health Assn., 1968, Medford chpt. Greater Boston Assn. Retarded Children, 1970, Mass. chpt. Nat. Multiple Sclerosis Soc., 1979, Faculty award for secondary edn., Rivier Coll., 1994, cert. of recognition, ARC of Mass. Bay, 1999, 2000, 2002, 2005. Fellow Am. Acad. Experts in Traumatic Stress. Office Phone: 603-897-8487. E-mail: mtramonte@rivier.edu.

TRAMONTO, RICK, chef; b. Rochester, NY; m. Gale Gand. Grill/saute cook The Scotch & Sirloin; chef Strathallen; garde-mgr. chef Tavern on the Green; chef Gotham Bar & Grill, Aurora, Avanzare, Chgo., The Pump Room, Chgo., Scoozi!, Chgo., Charlie Trotter's, Chgo., Stapleford Park Hotel, London; owner, chef Tru, Chgo., 1999—, Brasserie T, Chgo. Appeared on Oprah TV program. Named one of Am.'s rising Star Chefs, Robert Mondavi, 1995; named to Ten Best New Chefs, Food & Wine, 1994; recipient Outstanding Svc. award, James Beard Found., 2007. *

TRAN, JUDITH THUHA, psychiatrist; arrived in US, 1975; d. Phuong Nguyen and Ailien Huynh; children: Christopher Baoquoc, STephen Anhkhoa. BS in Biology, Tex. U., San Antonio, 1990; MD, Temple U., Phila., 1994. Intern Pa. Hosp., Phila., 1995—96, resident, 1996—99, chief resident, 1998—99; asst. dir. Friends Hosp. Crisis Response Ctr., 1999—2000; med. dir. Friends Hosp., 2000—03, Mercy Hosp. Phila. Crisis Response Ctr., 2003—. Recipient Merit award, Pa. Hosp., 1998—99. Mem.: Phila. Psychiat. Soc. (com. mem. 1999), Am. Psychiat. Assn. Avocations: reading, dance, swimming. Office: Mercy Hosp Phila 501 S 54th St Philadelphia PA 19143

TRAN, KHANH T., insurance company executive; BA in Econ. and Polit. Sci., Whittier Coll.; MBA in Fin. and Mktg., UCLA. With United Calif. Bank, Flying Tiger Line, Inc.; asst. treas. Vons Cos., Inc.; CFO, Pacific Life Ins. Co., Newport Beach, Calif. Mem.: ACLI (CFO Conf.). Office: Pacific Life Ins Co PO Box 9000 Newport Beach CA 92658-9030

TRAN, LONG TRIEU, industrial engineer; b. Saigon, Vietnam, Oct. 10, 1956; arrived in US, 1973; s. Nguyen Dinh and Thiet Thi (Nguyen) Tran; m. Khanh Thi-Hong Phan, Aug. 3, 1988. BSME with honors, U. Kans., 1976; MSME, MIT, 1980; MBA with honors, U. Louisville, 1993. Cert. quality engr., mfg. engr., project mgmt. profl. Tchg. asst. U. Kans., 1975-76, U. Calif., Berkeley, 1977; rsch. asst. Lawrence Berkeley Labs., 1977, MIT, 1977-80; libr. staff Harvard U. Med. Sch. Libr., 1977-78; mem. staff New England Deaconess Hosp., Boston, 1978-80; prodn. programming engr. GE, Cleve., 1980-81, advanced mfg. engr. Louisville, 1981-82, quality sys. engr., 1982-84, quality control engr., 1984-86, sr. quality info. equipment engr., 1986-89, sr. quality indsl. engr., 1990-94, sr. supplier tech. assistance engr., 1995-96, sr. advanced supplier quality engr., 1996-98, program mgr. purchased material quality, 1999, combo blackbelt leader supplier quality, 1999-2000, Six Sigma program mgr., 2000—02, sr. purchased material quality engr., 2003—. Exec. advisor Jr. Achievement, Inc., Louisville, 1983—84; monitor/reader Rec. for Blind, 1994—; fund-raiser Dream Factory Inc., 1994—. Vol. NCCJ, 1994—, Clothe-A-Child, 1993—, Dare-To-Care, 1994—, Ronald McDonald House, 1994—. Mem.: ASME, AAAS, Heritage Found., Am. Assn. Individual Investors, Ctr. for Positive Thinking, Cato Inst., Ctr. Positive Thinking, Indsl. Computing Soc. (founding), N.Y. Acad. Scis., Am. Mgmt. Assn., Robotics Internat. (charter), Robot Inst. Am., Am. Prodn. and Inventory Control Soc., Computer and Automated Sys. Assn. (charter), Am. Soc. Quality Control, Instrument Soc. Am. (sr.), Soc. Mfg. Engrs. (sr.), U.S. Libr. Congress Assocs. (founding), Nat. Pks. Conservation Assn. (founding), Assn. Compassion (life), Internat. Platform Assn., PGA Tour Ptnrs. Club, Handyman Club Am. (life), Sigma Xi, Beta Gamma Sigma, Phi Kappa Phi, Tau Beta Pi, Pi Tau Sigma. Republican. Achievements include research in grinding processes and material surface analysis, mfg. project mgmt., supplier quality mgmt. Home: 3642 Windward Way Louisville KY 40220-1818 Office: Gen Electric Co Appliance Park AP1-162A Louisville KY 40225-0001 Office Phone: 502-452-7082. Business E-Mail: long.tran@ge.com.

TRAN, NAM VAN, secondary school educator; b. Ben Tre, Vietnam, Nov. 18, 1939; s. Ut Van and Thoi Thi Tran; m. Thu Ngoc Nguyen, June 26, 1969; children: Tawny Thuan Tran Huot, Tim, Scott Toai. Degree in pedagogy, U. Saigon, Vietnam, 1967, BA, 1973. H.s. tchr., Vietnam, 1967—81; with Micrographics Inc., Cerritos, Calif., 1985—92, Catalina Inc., Commerce, Calif., 1992—95; printer Lucky and Happy Inc., San Gabriel, Calif., 1995—2002; bookkeeper Todd and Katie Inc., City of Industry, Calif., 2003—07. Author: Trong Dong Cam Thuc Van Hoc Mien Nam-Phan Dinh Thica Hai Ngoai, 2006; contbr. poetry and essays in mag. and newspapers. Home: 755 Rocking Horse Rd Walnut CA 91789

TRAN, NANG TRI, research scientist, electrical engineer; b. Binh Dinh, Vietnam, Jan. 2, 1948; came to the U.S., 1979, naturalized, 1986; s. Cam Tran and Cuu Thi Nguyen; m. Thu-Huong Thi Tong, Oct. 14, 1982; children: Helen, Florence, Irene, Kenneth. BSEE, Kyushu Inst. Tech., Kitakyushu, Japan, 1973, MSEE, 1975; PhD in Materials Sci./Solid State Device, U. Osaka Prefecture, Sakai, Japan, 1979. Rsch. assoc. U. Calif. Irvine, 1979; engr., rsch. scientist Sharp Electronics, Irvine, 1979-80; sr. rsch. scientist Arco Solar Industries, Chatsworth, Calif., 1980-84; sr. rsch. specialist, group leader 3M Co., St. Paul, 1985-96; sr. staff scientist Imation Corp., Oakdale, Minn., 1996—; exec. Khanti Inc. McKnight disting. vis. prof., adj. prof. U. Minn., Mpls.; cons., lectr. Japan industry mgmt.; reviewer NSF; sr. advisor to Vietnamese univs. Author: (poetry) My Journey; contbr. articles to profl. jours. Mem. tech. com. various internat. confs. Recipient R&D awards, Photonic Cir. Excellence award; fellow, Govt. South Vietnam, Japan, USAID, Rotary Internat., 1968—79. Mem. IEEE (sr.), Japan Soc. Applied Physics, N.Y. Acad. Scis. Achievements include invention of direct digital x-rays; transparent conducting zinc oxide doped with group III elements; thin film transistors on flexible substrate; structured phosphors thin film solar cells of selenium-based chalcogenides; patents in field; research in amorphous silicon solar cells; image sensors; solid state memory; photoconductors; CD; high density data storage media; diamond like carbon evaporated lubricant; transparent conducting oxide films. Office: Imation Corp Data Storage and Info Mgmt 1 Imation Pl Discovery 1A-03 Oakdale MN 55128-3414 Office Phone: 651-704-4448. Business E-Mail: nttran@imation.com.

TRAN, QUOC-HUNG, psychiatrist; b. Hue, Vietnam, July 12, 1964; s. Qui-Phiet Tran and Ngan T. Vo; m. Thuy-Linh Nguyen, Apr. 26, 1992; children: Minh, Van. BS Summa Cum Laude, Tex. Luth. U., 1984; MD, U. Tex., Galveston, 1991. Lic. Tex. Med. Bd., 1995, General Psychiatry Am. Bd. Psychiatry and Neurology, 1996, Child and Adolescent Psychiatry Am. Bd. Psychiatry and Neurology, 2000. Ind. cons. Carbomedics, Inc., Austin, Tex., 1984; nat. facilitator Asian Pacific Islander Inst., Ctr. of Substance Abuse Prevention, HHS, Washington, 1994—95; pres. Quoc-Hung Tran MD PA, 2001—, Dallas Psychiat. Assocs., Dallas, 2001—. Pres. MinhVan Found., Houston, 1996—; co-founder, dir. VDV Media Corp., Dallas, 2000—; dir. Asian Am. Family Counseling Ctr., Houston, 1995; founder Vietnamese Am. Youth Orgn., 1990—2000. Organizer Vietnamese New Yr. Festival, Houston, 1991—92. Named America's Top Psychiatrist award, Consumers' Rsch. Coun. Am., 2004—05; recipient Leadership award, AMA, 1995, Physician Recognition award, 2002; Minority Rsch. Tng. Mini fellow, Am. Psychiat. Assn., 1994. Mem.: Am. Acad. of Child and Adolescent Psychiatry. Buddhist. Office: Dallas Psychiat Assocs 17736 Preston Rd Ste 100 Dallas TX 75252 Home Phone: 972-202-0774; Office Phone: 972-248-2299. Office Fax: 972-248-2012. Business E-Mail: ghtranmd@dallaspsychiatry.com.

TRAN, VAN THAI, state legislator; b. Saigon, Vietnam; arrived in US, 1975; m. Cindy Nguyen, 2004. BS in Polit. Sci., U. Calif., Irvine; MS in Public Admin., Hamline U., Saint Paul, Minnesota; JD, Hamline U. Sch. of Law, Saint Paul, Minnesota. Staff aide Congressman Robert K. Dornan, State Sen. Ed Royce; former mng. ptnr. Van Thai Tran & Assoc.; mem. Garden Grove City Council, 2000—02; vice-mayor City of Garden Grove, 2002—03; mem. Calif. State Assembly, 2004—. Mem. Asian-Pacific Congressional Advisory Bd.; mem. bus. and professions com., banking and fin. com., environ. safety and toxic materials com. Calif. State Assembly, mem. select com. on critical issues; mem. Asian Pacific Islander Joint Caucus. Chmn. Vietnamese com. Orange County Republican Party; founder Vietnamese-Am. Voters Coalition, 1990—. Office: Calif Assembly State Capital Rm 4009 Sacramento CA 94249-0068

TRANGSRUD, ROGER H., dean, law educator; BA, Carleton Coll.; JD, U. Chgo. Clerk for Justice Walter Rogosheske Minn. Supreme Ct.; atty. Hogan & Hartson; prof. law George Washington U. Law Sch., 1982—, assoc. dean, 1993—2000, sr. assoc. dean, 2000—04, interim dean, 2004—, Oswald Symister Colclough Rsch. Prof. Law. Contbr. articles to law jours. Office: George Washington U Law Sch 2000 H St NW Washington DC 20052 Office Phone: 202-994-6277. Office Fax: 202-994-5157. E-mail: rtrang@law.gwu.edu.

TRANI, EUGENE PAUL, university president, educator; b. Bklyn., Nov. 2, 1939; s. Frank Joseph and Rose Gertrude (Kelly) T.; m. Lois Elizabeth Quigley, June 2, 1962; children: Anne Chapman, Frank. BA in History with honors, U. Notre Dame, 1961; MA, Ind. U., 1963, PhD, 1966. Instr. history Ohio State U., Columbus, 1965-67; asst. prof. So. Ill. U., Carbondale, 1967-71, assoc. prof., 1971-75, prof., 1975-76; asst. v.p. acad. affairs, prof. U. Nebr., 1976-80; prof., vice chancellor acad. affairs U. Mo. Kansas City, 1980-86; prof., v.p. acad. affairs U. Wis. System, 1986-90; pres. Va. Commonwealth U., 1990—; pres. bd. dirs. Va. Biotech Rsch. Park, 1992-97, chmn., 1997—; pres., chmn. VCU Health Sys., 2000—. Vis. asst. prof. U. Wis., Milw., 1969; bd. dirs. Met. Richmond SunTrust Mid-Atlantic Bank, Universal Corp., LandAm. Fin. Group, Inc.; mem. commn. Internat. Edn. Am. Coun. Ed., 1991—; bd. gov. Ctr. Russian Am. Bus., Washington, 1993-98; adv. coun. on Grad. Studies and Rsch., U. Notre Dame, 1994—, NASULGC, 1980—, chair commn. on internat. affairs, 1993-94; vis. prof. Univ. Coll., Dublin, 2002; bd. advisors Inst. for U.S. Studies, U. London, 1993-99; cons. in field. Author, editor: Concerns of a Conservative Democrat, 1968, The Treaty of Portsmouth: An Adventure in American Diplomacy, 1969; (with Donald E. Davis) The First Cold War, 2002; (with David Wilson) The Secretaries of the Department of the Interior, 1849-69, 1975; The Presidency of Warren G. Harding, 3d edit., 1989; contbr. articles to profl. jours., newspapers; book reviewer. Permanent mem. Coun. Fgn. Rels., N.Y.C., 1979—; bd. dirs. Richmond Ballet, 1991-96, NCCJ, Richmond, 1991-94, Va. Spl. Olympics, 1991-96, YMCA of Greater Richmond, 1992—, Richmond Renaissance, 1992-96, 2001—, chmn., 2001—; bd. dirs. Met. Bus. Found., 1992-98, Va. Tech. Fund Found., 1993--, Met. Bus. League, 1994--; mem. U.S. Savs. Bond Vol. Com., chmn. higher edn. area, 1992-93; adv. bd. Greater Richmond chpt. ARC, 1992—; mem. Gov.'s Commn. Info. Tech. in Va., 1998-2000; bd. dirs. Collegiate Sch., 1998—; adv. bd. Black History Archives Project, 1992-96; bd. dirs. Va. Ctr. for Innovative Tech., 1990-96, Capital Area Assembly, 1990-93, Richmond Symphony, 1991-94, Richmond Symphony Coun., 1995—; mem. coun. advisors Christian Children's Fund, 1992-95; mem. Ctrl. Richmond Assn., 1992-96; bd. trustees Va. Hist. Soc., 1994-96, Theatre Va., 1994-97, Richmond Children's Mus., 1994—, World Affairs Coun. of Greater Richmond, 1999-2003; bd. dirs. Sci. Mus. of Va. Found., 1994—, Va. Tech. Fund Found., 1993—, Met. Bus. Hague, 1994—; mem. Gov.'s Biotech. Initiative Adv. Bd., 2002—; bd. dirs. Qatar Found. for Edn. Sci. Comm. Devel., Va. Tech. Fund Found., 1993—. Fellow Russian and East European Inst., 1964-65, Nat. Hist. Publs. Commn., 1969-70, Woodrow Wilson Internat. Ctr. Scholars, 1972-73, So. Ill. U. Sabbatical Leave, 1975-76, Coun. Internat. Exchange Scholars, 1981, U. Mo. Faculty, 1981; grantee U.S. Dept. Interior Rsch., 1965-66, So. Ill. U. Office Rsch. and Projects, 1967-74, Am. Philos. Soc., 1968, 72, So. Ill U. Summer Rsch. 1970, 72, 75, Lilly Endowment, 1975-76, Sloan Commn. Govt. and Higher Edn., 1978, USIA Am. Participants Program, 1984-86, 88, 90; Inst. for U.S. Studies fellow U. London, 1995, fellow commoner St. John's Coll., Cambridge, 1998; recipient Younger Humanist award NEH, 1972-73, Leadership and Achievement award Ctrl. Richmond Assn., 1992, Biotech. Leadership award Va. Biotech. Assn., 1999; recipient Disting. Leadership award, Nat. Assn. Cmty. Leaders, 1994, Richmond Humanitarian award, NCCJ, 1995, Flame Bearer of Edn. award Ctrl. Fund/UNCF, 1998, Richmond Joint Engrs. Coun. Cmty. Svc. award, 2002; named Style Mag. Richmonder of Yr., 1998, Person of Yr., Fifty Plus Mag., 2004, Crystal Ball Spl. Honoree, Arthritis Found. Ctrl. Va. Chpt., 2005; Hope award, Nat. MS Soc., 2003, others. Mem. Internat. Inst. Strategic Studies, Am. Assn. Advancement Slavic Studies, Orgn. Am. Historians, Soc. Historians Am. Fgn. Rels., Greater Richmond C. of C. (bd. dirs. 1991-96, chmn. 1997-98), Phi Kappa Phi. Roman Catholic. Avocations: reading, travel, basketball, golf. Office: Va Commonwealth U Box 842512 910 W Franklin St Richmond VA 23284-2512 E-mail: etrani@vcu.edu.

TRANI, JOHN M., former consumer products company executive; b. NYC, 1945; B in Aerospace Engring., Bklyn. Poly. Inst., 1966, M in Indsl. Mgmt., Ops. Rsch. With GE, 1978—97; pres., CEO GE Med. Svcs. divsn. GE Co., 1986—97; chmn., CEO Stanley Works, New Britain, Conn., 1997—2003. Home: 30 Stanford Dr Farmington CT 06032 Office Phone: 860-674-3764. E-mail: jmtrani@hotmail.com.

TRANOVICH, MICHAEL A., orthopedist; b. Wheeling, W.Va., July 9, 1949; s. John Tranovich and Margaret Elizabeth (Robotisin) Tranaovich; m. Donna Jean Salisbury; children: Michael J., Matthew A., Meaghan A. BS, Ohio State U., Columbus, 1971, MD, 1974. Resident U. Pitts., 1974—79; surgeon UnMPC Med. Ctr., McKeesport, Pa., 1979—, chief staff, 2000—01, chief surgery, 2000—02, clin. chief surgery, 2003—, chief orthop., 2006—; bd. dirs. Auberle, McKeesport, 2006—. Mem.: Am. Acad. Orth. Surgeon. Roman Catholic. Home: 3018 Grandview Farms Pl Bethel Park PA 15102

TRANQUADA, ROBERT ERNEST, retired internist, educator; b. LA, Aug. 27, 1930; s. Ernest Alvro and Katharine (Jacobus) Tranquada; m. Janet Martin, Aug. 31, 1951; children: John Martin, Katherine Anne, James Robert. BA, Pomona Coll., 1951, DSc (hon.), 2007; MD, Stanford U., 1955; DSc. (hon.), Worcester Poly. Inst., 1985. Diplomate Am. Bd. Internal Medicine. Intern in medicine UCLA Med. Center, 1955—56, resident in medicine, 1956—57; resident Los Angeles VA Hosp., 1957—58; fellow in diabetes and metabolic diseases UCLA, 1958—59; fellow in diabetes U. So. Calif., 1959—60, asst. prof. medicine, 1960—63, assoc. prof., 1964—68, chmn. dept. community medicine, 1967—70; med. dir. Los Angeles County/U. So. Calif. Med. Center, 1969—74; assoc. dean U. So. Calif. Sch. Medicine, 1969—76; regional dir. Central Region, Los Angeles County Dept. Health Services, 1974—76; assoc. dean Sch. Medicine U. Calif., LA, 1976—79; chancellor and dean U. Mass. Med. Sch., 1979—86; dean Sch. Medicine U. So. Calif., 1986—91, prof. medicine LA, 1986—92, Norman Topping/Nat. Med. Enterprises prof. med./pub. policy, 1992—97; prof. emeritus, 1997—. Mem, chair L.A. County Task Force on Health Care Access, 1992—94. Corporator Worcester Art Mus., 1980—86; mem. Ind. Commn. on L.A. Police Dept., 1991—92; governing bd. LA County Local Initiative Health Authority, 1994—, chmn., 2001—05; bd trustees Pomona Coll., 1969—, vice chmn., 1971—79, chmn., 1991—2000, emeritus trustee chmn., 2000—; bd. fellow Claremont U. Ct., 1971—79, 1991—2000; chmn. bd. overseers Claremont U. Consortium, 2000—06, emeritus chmn. bd. overseers, 2006—; vice-chmn., bd. trustees Keck Grad. Inst. Applied Life Scis., 1997—2000, emeritus, 2000—; bd. dirs. Nat. Med. Fellowships, Inc., 1973—2005, chmn., 1980—85; bd. trustees Charles Drew U. Med. and Sci., 1968—79, 1986—95, Orthopaedic Hosp., 1986—91, Barlow Hosp., 1987—89; bd. dirs. Worcester Acad., 1984—86, U. So. Calif. Univ. Hosp., 1988—91, Alliance for Childrens Rights, 1991—95, Cmty. Health Coun., Inc., 1993—, Good Hope Med. Found, 1994—, chmn., 2006—; bd. dirs. Ralph M. Parsons Found., 2000—, Huntington Med. Rsch. Inst., 2006—, Congl. Homes, Inc., Mt. San Antonio Gardens, 2006—; mem. coun. pres. Assn. Governing Bodies Colls. and Univs., 2000—03, chair, 2002—03. Fellow Milbank Found., 1967—72. Fellow: AAAS, Am. Antiquarian Soc.; mem.: Inst. Medicine of Nat. Acad. Scis., Calif. Med. Assn., L.A. Acad. Medicine, L.A. County Med. Assn., AMA, Alpha Omega Alpha, Sigma Xi, Phi Beta Kappa.

TRANSOU, LYNDA LOU, advertising art administrator; b. Atlanta, Dec. 11, 1949; d. Lewis Cole Transou and Ann Lynette (Taylor) Putnam; m. Lue Gregg Loso, Oct. 25, 1991. BFA cum laude, U. Tex., 1971. Art dir. The Pitluk Group, San Antonio, 1971, Campbell, McQuien & Lawson, Dallas, 1973-74, Bozell & Jacobs, Dallas, 1974-75; art dir., ptnr. The Assocs., Dallas, 1975-77; art dir. Belo Broadcasting, Dallas, 1977-80; creative dir., v.p. Allday & Assocs., Dallas, 1980-85; owner Lynda Transou Advt. & Design, 1986—. Recipient Merit award, N.Y. Art Dirs. Show, 1980, Gold award, Dallas Ad League, 1980, Silver award, 1980, 1981, 1982, 2 Merit awards, Houston Art Dirs. Club, 1978, Dallas Ad League, 1986, Merit award, Broadcast Designers Assn., 1980, Merit awards, Dallas Ad League, 1978, 1987, Silver award, Houston Art Dirs. Show, 1982, Gold award, Tex. Pub. Rels. Assn., 1985, N.Y. One Show, 1982, Creativity awrd, Art Direction mag., 1986, Print award, Regional Design Annual, 1988, 2 Gold Adrian awards, 1997, Katy award, Dallas Press Club, 2001. Dallas Soc. Visual Comm. (Bronze award 1980, Merit award 1978-86), Delta Gamma (historian 1969-70).

TRAPA, PETER ENGEL, mathematics professor; BA, Northwestern Univ., 1993; PhD in Math., MIT, 1998. Mem. sch. math. inst. for adv. study Princeton Univ., 1998—2000; NSF postdoctoral fellow Harvard Univ., 2000—03; asst prof., math. Univ. Utah, 2001—05, assoc. prof., 2005—. Achievements include being one of 18 top mathematicians and computer scientists (Atlas of Lie Groups Project) from the US to successfully map E8, one of the largest and most complicated structures in mathematics. Office: Dept Math LCB 118 Univ Utah Salt Lake City UT 84112 Office Phone: 801-585-7671. Office Fax: 801-581-4148. Business E-Mail: ptrapa@math.utah.edu. *

TRAPANE, RUTH, educator, artist; b. Danville, Pa., July 18, 1945; d. Richard L. and Oda M. (Sager) Day; m. Mar. 21, 1965 (div. 1983); children: Michael W., Timothy R.; m. Philip B. Trapane, Aug. 23, 1985; stepchildren: Sean, Philip, Bridget. BS, Bloomsburg U., Pa., 1967, MS, 1975, MA, 1990. Grad. asst. Bloomsburg U., 1989; tchr. Berwick Elem. Sch., Pa., 1967-88, 90—. Speaker 1st European Space Art Symposium & Exhibitor, Montrieux, Switzerland, 1992, tour India 6 wks., 1994; space art exhibitor Spaceweek Internat., 1994, Art on Mir Space Station, First Exhibit in Space, 1995-96, Art to the Stars (Ars Ad Astra) 1996-98, Nova Southeastern U. Author curriculum guides; exhibited in Internat. Encaustic Art Show, Nebr., 1989, Selinsgrove, Pa., 1990 (People's Choice award 1990), Cheney, Wash., 1991, Gagarin Collaboration, Moscow, 1990. Mem. NEA, Pa. Edn. Assn., Internat. Assn. Astron. Artists, Hazelton Art League, Susquehanna Art League, North Mt. Art League. Independent. Avocations: scuba diving, online and mystery games, interior design, video authoring. Home: 511 Hickory Dr Bloomsburg PA 17815-8902

TRAPP, A. C., retired music educator; b. Chase, La., Dec. 4, 1930; parents A. Clayton and Jessie Mae (Stigall) Trapp; m. Beatrice Horn (separated); children: A. Clayton III, Jonathan L. *Mr. Trapp is a descendant of Thomas and Mary Trapp, settlers of Martha's Vineyard in the early 17th century, and of Lt. Thomas Trapp who fought in the Revolutionary War in Connecticut and South Carolina. Mr. Trapp's wife Beatrice is the daughter of Dr. and Mrs. A.E. Horn of Seattle. Mr. Trapp's son A. Clayton III lives in England with his wife Theresa, their three daughters Kasmiri, Alexandra, and Amelia, and their son Myles Vincent. Mr. Trapp's other son Jonathan is on the faculty of Indiana State at Terre Haute.* B in Piano Performance and Vocal Suprervision, Northeast Coll.; M, Northwestern State U., 1961. Music supr. Catahoula Parish, 1957; music tchr. DOD, 1959. Judge Nat. Guild of Piano Tchrs. Exhibitions include Delgado Mus., New Orleans, 1956. Corp. US Army, 1952—54. Named to Hall of Fame, Am. Coll. Musicians, Austin, Tex., 2006. Republican. Episcopalian. Home: 501 S Grand Apt 319 Monroe LA 71201 Personal E-mail: atc124@bellsouth.net.

TRAPP, OLIVER MARCUS, surgeon, consultant; s. Werner and Karin Trapp. Diplomate Bayerische Landesärztekammer, 1996. Asst. surgeon BG Trauma Ctr., Murnau, Bavaria, 1996—2000, 2003—, U. Hosp. LMU Munich, Bavaria, 2000—02, Klinikum Dachau, Dachau, Bavaria, 2002—03. Cons. Stryker Osteosynthesis Corp., Schoenkirchen, Germany, 2004—; course dir. AIOD, Nice, France, 2004—. Contbr. articles to profl.

jours. Paramedic German Red Cross, Kochel, Bavaria, 1978. Avocations: sailing, travel, mountain climbing, mountain biking. Office: BG Trauma Ctr Murnau Prof Kuentscher Str 8 Bavaria Murnau 82418 Germany Business E-Mail: otrapp@bgu-murnau.de.

TRAPP, PETER JARL RUDOLF, portfolio manager, farmer; b. Darlington, Eng., Oct. 5, 1945; arrived in U.S., 1971; s. Jarl Rudolph and Olive Lindsay (Fairley) Trapp; m. Regina Antoinette Thomas, Sept. 6, 1969 (div. Dec. 1986); children: Sophia Antoinette, Alexander Rudolf, Olivia Henrietta Elizabeth. Mi-Lic, Fribourg U., Switzerland, 1971; MBA, Columbia U., 1973. V.p. First Boston Corp., NYC, 1973-78, Goldman Sachs & Co., NYC, 1978-81; mgr. dir. Dean Witter Reynolds Inc., NYC, 1982-84; mgr. dir., exec. officer Marine Midland Bank N.A., NYC, 1985-89; sr. v.p. Gerard Klauer Mattison & Co., NYC, 1990-94; mgr. dir. Needham & Co., NYC, 1994—2003; exec. v.p. Needham Investment Mgmt., NYC, 1998—2003; founding ptnr. Bifrost Ptnrs. LLC and Bifrost Fund LP, NYC, 2003—. Cadet sgt. Swedish Army, 1968—69. Mem.: Coral Beach Club (Bermuda), Annabel's (London), The Leash. Avocations: skiing, fishing, shooting, farming. Home: Bean Creek Farm 341 Tripp Rd Box 948 Pine Plains NY 12567 Office: Bifrost Ptnrs LLC Box 948 Pine Plains NY 12567 Office Phone: 518-398-6810. Business E-Mail: pt@bifrostcapital.com.

TRASK, THOMAS EDWARD, religious organization administrator; b. Brainard, Minn., Mar. 23, 1936; m. Shirley Burkhart; children: Kimberly, Bradley, Todd, Tom. BA, North Ctrl. Bible Coll., 1956, DDiv (hon.), 1994. Ordained min. Assemblies of God, 1958. Pastor First Assembly of God, Hibbing, Minn., 1956-60, pastor Vicksburg, Mich., 1960-64; Mich. dist. youth and Sunday sch. dir. Assembly of God, 1964-68; pastor First Assembly of God, Saginaw, Mich., 1968-73, Brightmoor Tabernacle, Southfield, Mich., 1976-88; supt. Mich. Dist. Coun., Dearborn, 1973-76; gen. treas. The Gen. Coun. Assemblies of God, Springfield, Mo., 1988-93, gen. supt., 1993—. Co-author: Back to the Altar: A Call to Spiritual Awakening, 1994, Back to the Word, A Call to Biblical Authority, 1996, The Battle: Defeating the Enemies of Your Soul, 1997, The Blessing: Experiencing the Power of the Holy Spirit Today, 1998, The Choice: Embracing God's Vision in the New Millennium, 1999, The Fruit of the Spirit, 2000, Ministry for a Lifetime, 2001. Mem. Assemblies Of God Ch. Office: Assemblies of God 1445 N Boonville Ave Springfield MO 65802-1894

TRAUB, J. F. (JOSEPH FREDERICK TRAUB), computer scientist, educator; b. June 24, 1932; m. Pamela Ann McCorduck, Dec. 6, 1969; children: Claudia Renee, Hillary Anne. BS, CCNY, 1954; PhD, Columbia U., NYC, 1959; DSc (hon.), U. Ctrl. Fla., Orlando, 2001. Tech. staff Bell Labs., Murray Hill, NJ, 1959-70; prof. computer sci. and math., head dept. computer sci. Carnegie-Mellon U., Pitts., 1971-79; Edwin Howard Armstrong prof. computer sci., chmn. dept., prof. math. Columbia U., 1979-86; prof. computer sci. Princeton U., NJ, 1986-87; pres. John Von Neumann Nat. Supercomputer Ctr., Consortium for Sci. Computing, Princeton, 1986-87; Edwin Howard Armstrong prof., chmn. dept. computer sci., prof. math. Columbia U., NYC, 1987-89, Edwin Howard Armstrong prof. computer sci., math., 1989—; external prof. Santa Fe Inst., 1995-98, 2004—; fellow Biosgroup, 1998—2003. Dir. N.Y. State Ctr. Computers and Info. Systems, 1982-88; vis. Mackay prof. U. Calif., Berkeley, 1978-79; mem. pres.'s adv. com. computer sci. Stanford U., 1972-75, chmn., 1975-76; adv. com. Fed. Jud. Ctr.; mem. sci. coun. I.R.I.A., Paris, 1976-80; ctrl. steering com. computing sci. and engring. rsch. study NSF, liaison to panel on theoretical computer sci. and panel on numerical comp., 1974-80; adv. com. Carnegie-Mellon Inst. Research, 1978-79; mem. applied math. divsn. rev. com. Argonne Nat. Lab., 1973-75; adv. com. math. and computer sci. NSF, 1978-80, mem. com. visitors, 2005; chmn. computer sci. and tech. bd. NRC, 1986-90, computer sci. and telecomms. bd., 1990-92, Nat. Acads., 2005—; trustee Columbia U. Press, 1983-85; lectr. in field; cons. in field. Author: Iterative Methods for the Solution of Equations, 1964, Russian edit., 1985, (with H. Wozniakowski) A General Theory of Optimal Algorithms, 1980, Russian edit., 1983, (with G. Wasilkowski and H. Wozniakowski) Information, Uncertainty, Complexity, 1983, Information-Based Complexity, 1988, (with A.G. Werschulz) Complexity and Information, 1998, Chelsea, 1998; editor: Complexity of Sequential and Parallel Numerical Algorithms, 1973, Analytic Computational Complexity, 1976, Algorithms and Complexity: New Directions and Recent Results, 1976, Jour. Assn. Computing Machinery, 1970-76, Transactions on Math. Software, 1974-76, Jour. Computer and Sys. Scis., 1973-86, Internat. Jour. on Computers and Math. with Applications, 1974—, Cohabiting With Computers, 1985, Festschrift, 1993, 2004, (with P. Hut and D. Ruelle) Fundamental Sources of Unpredictability, 1997; founding editor Jour. Complexity, 1985—, Ann. Rev. Computer Sci., 1986-92 Festschrift, 1993, 2004; assoc. editor Complexity, 1995—. Sherman Fairchild Disting. scholar Calif. Inst. Tech., 1991, 92; recipient Award for Disting. Svc. to Computing Rsch. Computer Rsch. Assn., 1992, Lezione Lincee Acad. Nat. dei Lincei, 1993, Sr. Scientist award Alexander Von Humboldt Found., 1992-98, City of NY Mayor's award for excellence in sci. and tech., 1999. Fellow AAAS (coun. 1971-74), ACM (chmn. award com. 1974-76), N.Y. Acad. Scis.; mem. IEEE (Emanuel R. Piore Gold medal 1991), NAE (membership com. for computer sci., elec. engring. and control 1986-87, membership com. for computer sci. and engring. 1987-91, presdl. search com. 1993-94), Conf. Bd. Math. Scis. (coun. 1971-74), Soc. Indsl. and Applied Math., Am. Math. Soc., Assn. Computing Machinery (founding chair spl. interest group on numerical math. 1965-71). Office: Columbia U Dept Computer Sci 1214 Amsterdam Ave #MC0401 New York NY 10027-7003 Business E-Mail: traub@cs.columbia.edu.

TRAUB, RICHARD KENNETH, lawyer; b. Lakewood, NJ, Aug. 4, 1950; s. Harold W. and Muriel N. (Zurlin) T.; m. Barbara Lynn Wright, July 9, 1972; children: Russell S., Melissa L. BBA, U. Miami, Coral Gables, Fla., 1972, JD cum laude, 1975. Bar: Fla. 1975, N.Y. 1976, N.J. 1976, U.S. Dist. Ct. N.J. 1976, U.S. Supreme Ct. 1979, U.S. Dist. Ct. (ea. & so. dists.) N.Y. 1981. Ptnr. Wilson, Elser, Moskowitz, Edelman & Dicker, NYC, 1975-95, Traub Eglin Lieberman Straus LLP, Hawthorne, NY, 1996—. Ptnr. Time for Patty Stables, NJ, 1992—; officer, dir. X-Ray Duplications, Inc., NJ; ptnr., founder Fractured Greetings, NJ; mem., lectr., v.p. Fedn. Def. and Corp. Counsel, 1993—, chair tech. com., mem. admissions com., industry cooperation ins. coverage alt. dispute resolution coms. and tech. sect., v.p., dir., 2004—, dean of curriculum, Litigation Mgmt. Coll., 2006-; lectr. Inst. for Internat. Rsch., Washington, 1988, Engring. News Record Constrn. Claims Conf., 1991. Author: Legal and Professional Aspects of Construction Management, 1990, The Year 2000 and Potential Liabilities and Otherwise, 1999, Litigating Year 2000 Cases, Chapter 8, Insurance Coverage, 1999, Practical Environmental Forensics--Process and Case Histories, 2000; contbr. chpt.: Data Security and Privacy Law-Combatting Cyberthreats, The West Group, 2002; contbr. articles to profl. jours. Mem. ABA (forum com. on constrn. industry 1989, tort and ins. practice sect. 1985—), NY State Bar Assn., NJ Bar Assn., Fla. Bar Assn., Fedn. Def. and Corp. Counsel (spkr. The Millennium Bug ins. coverage sect., vice chair tech. and e-commerce sect., chair tech. com., v.p. 2004—), Def. Rsch. Inst., Assn. Def. Trial Atty. Office: 100 Metroplex Dr Ste 203 Edison NJ 08817 Office Phone: 732-985-1000. Personal E-mail: rtraub@tels.com.

TRAUBER, STEPHEN M. (STEVE TAUBER), investment banker; b. Jan. 20, 1962; m. Leticia F. Tauber. BS in Econ., Managerial Studies, Rice U., 1984; MBA, Northwestern U. With Credit Suisse First Boston, 1988—95; mng. dir. energy group Morgan Stanley, Houston, 1995—2003; vice chmn., global head, energy group UBS Investment Bank, Houston, 2003—. Chmn. Houston Econ. Devel. Adv. Com. Pres. Houston Soc. Performing Arts; bd. dir. Theatre Under the Stars, Hobby Center for the Performing Arts, River Oaks Baptist Sch., Greater Houston Partnership; bd. overseers Jones Bus. Sch., Rice Univ. Named a Top Dealmaker, Dealmaker mag., 2006. Office: UBS Energy Investment Banking 1000 Main St Houston TX 77002 Office Phone: 713-655-0075. *

TRAUGER, ALETA ARTHUR, judge; BA in English magna cum laude, Cornell Coll., Iowa, 1968; MAT, Vanderbilt U., 1972, JD, 1976. Tchr., Tenn., Eng., 1970-73; assoc., law clk. Barrett, Brandt & Barrett, P.C., Nashville, 1974-77; asst. U.S. atty., first asst., chief of criminal divsn. Mid. Dist. Tenn., 1977-82, No. Dist. Ill., 1979-80; assoc. Hollins, Wagster & Yarbrough, P.C., Nashville, 1983-84; legal counsel Coll. of Charleston, SC, 1984-85; counsel, ptnr. Wyatt, Tarrant, Combs, Gilbert & Milom, Nashville, 1985-91; judge Tenn. Ct. of the Judiciary, 1987-93; chief of staff Mayor's Office, Nashville, 1991-92; bankruptcy judge U.S. Bankruptcy Ct. (mid. dist.) Tenn., Nashville, 1993-98; dist. judge U.S. Dist. Ct. (mid. dist.) Tenn., Nashville, 1998—. Mem. hearing panel bd. profl. responsibility Tenn. Supreme Ct., 1983-84, mem. adv. com. on rules of civil and appellate procedure, 1989-96; lectr. Vanderbilt U. Sch. Law, 1986-88, mem. Law Sch. alumni bd., 1989-92; master of bench Harry Phillips Am. Inn of Ct., 1990-94; mem. Internat. Women's Forum, 1993—, v.p. Tenn. chpt., 1996-97; mem. Nat. Conf. Bankruptcy Judges, 1994-98, chmn. ethics com., 1994-98; trustee Cornell Coll., 1998-2006. Bd. dirs. Nashville Inst. for Arts, 1992-99, Miriam's Promise (adoption agy.), 1995-98, Renewal House, 1996-98; trustee Cornell Coll, 1998—2006; mem. Vanderbilt Law Sch. Nat. Coun., 2004—. Fellow: Nashville Bar Found., Tenn. Bar Found. (life), Am. Bar Found. (life); mem.: FBA (v.p. 1983—84, 1985—86), ABA, Fed. Judges Assn., Nat. Assn. Women Judges (liaison to ABA commn. on the status of women in the profession 2000—01), Tenn. Lawyers Assn. for Women (v.p. 1988—89, pres. 1989—90, bd. dirs. 1990—91), Lawyers Assn. for Women (pres. 1982—83, bd. dirs. 1983—84, 1986—88), Nashville Bar Assn. (bd. dirs. 1984, 1989—91). Office: 825 US Courthouse 801 Broadway Nashville TN 37203-3816

TRAUGER, DONALD BYRON, nuclear engineer, lab administrator; b. Exeter, Nebr., June 29, 1920; s. Charles C. and Ethel L. (Downey) T.; m. Elaine Causey, Sept. 2, 1945; children: Byron Roscoe, Thomas Charles. AB, Nebr. Wesleyan U., 1942, D.Sc. (hon.), 1974; postgrad., Columbia U., 1942-46, U. Tenn., 1946-49; D.Sc. (hon.), Tenn. Wesleyan Coll., 1977. Supr. test equipment devel. Manhattan Dist. Project, 1942-46; supr. Devel. Lab., Oak Ridge Gaseous Diffusion Plant, 1946-54; with Oak Ridge Nat. Lab., 1954-93, assoc. dir. nuclear and engring. technologies, 1970-84, sr. staff asst. to dir., 1984-93; cons. in energy tech., 1993—. Author: Horse Power to Nuclear Power, 2002; editl. advisor Anns. Nuclear Engring, 1973—; design features editor sect. IV Nuclear Safety Jour., 1989-98. Mem. Oak Ridge Bd. Edn., 1961-67; pres. Oak Ridge PTA Coun., 1969-70, Oak Ridge Parents Adv. Coun., 1958-59; chmn. exec. com., trustee Tenn. Wesleyan Coll., 1976-81, chmn. bd. govs., 1986-90, chmn. bd. trustees, 1990-93. Recipient Alumni Achievement award Nebr. Wesleyan U., 1962 Fellow Am. Nuclear Soc. (chmn. planning com. 1981-83); mem. AAAS, Am. Phys. Soc., Rotary, Sigma Xi (pres. Oak Ridge chpt. 1987-88), Sigma Pi Sigma. Methodist. Office Phone: 865-483-1006. Personal E-mail: dbtrauger@aol.com.

TRAUGOTT, ELIZABETH CLOSS, linguist, educator, researcher; b. Bristol, Eng., Apr. 9, 1939; d. August and Hannah M. M. (Priebsch) Closs; m. John L. Traugott, Sept. 26, 1967; 1 child, Isabel. BA in English, Oxford U., Eng., 1960; PhD in English lang., U. Calif., Berkeley, 1964. Asst. prof. English U. Calif., Berkeley, 1964-70; lectr. U. East Africa, Tanzania, 1965-66, U. York, Eng., 1966-67; lectr., then assoc. prof. linguistics and English Stanford (Calif.) U., 1970-77, prof., 1977—2003, chmn. linguistics dept., 1980-85, vice provost, dean grad. studies, 1985-91, mem. grad. record examinations bd., 1989-93, mem. test of English as a fgn. lang. bd., 1990—92, chmn. test of English as a fgn. lang. bd., 1991—92. Mem. higher edn. funding coun. Eng. Assessment Panel, 1996, 2001. Author: (book) A History of English Syntax, 1972; author: (with Mary Pratt) Linguistics for Students of English Literature, 1980; author: (with Paul Hopper) Grammaticalization, 1993, rev. edit., 2003; author: (with Richard Dasher) Regularity in Semantic Change, 2002; author: (with Laurel J. Brinton) Lexicalization and Language Change, 2005; editor (with ter Meulen, Reilly, Ferguson): (book) On Conditionals, 1986; editor: (with Heine) Approaches to Grammaticalization, 2 vols., 1991; series co-editor: Topics in English Linguistics; contbr. articles to profl. jours. Am. Coun. Learned Socs. fellow, 1975—76, Guggenheim fellow, 1983—84, Ctr. Advanced Study Behavioral Scis. fellow, 1983—84. Fellow: AAAS; mem.: AAUW, AAUP, MLA, Internat. Soc. Linguistis English (pres. 2007—), Internat. Pragmatics Assn. (bd. dirs. 2000—), Internat. Soc. Hist. Linguistic (pres. 1979—81), Linguistic Soc. Am. (pres. 1987, sec.-treas. 1994—98). Office: Stanford Univ Dept Linguistics Bldg 460 Stanford CA 94305-2150 Business E-Mail: traugott@stanford.edu.

TRAUGOTT, PETER, television producer; V.p. Brillstein-Grey TV, 1996—2005, pres., 2005—. Actor: (TV series) Party of Five; (films) Silent Men, 2005; exec. prodr.: (TV series) Numb3rs, Way Downtown, 2002, My Big Greek Fat Life, 2003, The Showbiz Show With David Spade, 2005, Jake in Progress, 2005, Girls on the Bus, 2006, 52 Fights, 2006, Mr. Nice Guy, 2006, Cracking Up, 2006, Sam I Am, 2007, Frangela, 2007, See Jayne Run, 2007. Office: Brillstein-Grey Entertainment 9150 Wilshire Blvd Ste 350 Beverly Hills CA 90212 Office Phone: 310-275-6135. Office Fax: 310-275-6180. *

TRAURIG, ROBERT HENRY, lawyer; b. Waterbury, Conn., June 9, 1925; s. Samuel and Lillian (Rosengarten) T.; m. Jacqueline Block; children: Madeline Traurig Sackel, Wendy Traurig Perlin. Student, U. Fla.; BBA, U. Miami, Fla., 1947, LLB, 1950. Bar: Fla. 1950, U.S. Dist. Ct. Fla. 1950. Co-founder, ptnr., shareholder environ. land devel. Greenberg, Traurig LLP, (formerly Greenberg Traurig, Hoffman, Lipoff, Rosen & Quentel, P.A.), Miami, 1967—. Pres. Greater Miami Opera, 1987-89. Lt. USNR, 1943-46, 51-52. Named one of 100 Most Powerful People in Miami, Miami Bus. mag., 2001; recipient Friend of Israel Humanitarian award, Greater Miami Jewish Fedn., 2003. Mem. Greater Miami C. of C. (chmn.). Democrat. Jewish. Avocation: avid sports spectator. Office: Greenberg Traurig LLP 1221 Brickell Ave Miami FL 33131-3224 Office Phone: 305-579-0500. Office Fax: 305-579-0717. Business E-Mail: traurigr@gtlaw.com.

TRAUTMAN, DONALD W., bishop; b. Buffalo, June 24, 1936; Student, Our Lady Angels Sem., Niagara Falls, NY, Theology Faculty, Innsbruck, Austria, Pontifical Biblical Inst., Rome, Cath. U., St. Thomas Aquinas U., Rome. Ordained priest Roman Cath. Ch., 1962, consecrated bishop Roman Cath. Ch., 1985. Titular bishop of Sassura and aux. bishop Diocese of Buffalo, 1985; bishop, Erie, Pa., 1990—. Past mem. Prolife com. doctrine and migration Nat. Conf. Home: 205 W 9th St Erie PA 16501-1304 Address: 429 E Granview Blvd Erie PA 16514-0397

TRAUTMAN, WILLIAM ELLSWORTH, lawyer; b. San Francisco, Nov. 27, 1940; s. Gerald H. and Doris Joy (Tucker) T.; m. Dorothy (Williamson), June 17, 1962; children: Darcey, Torey. BA, U. Calif., Berkeley, 1962, LLB, 1965. Bar: Calif. 1966, US Supreme Ct., Calif. Dist. Ct., US Ct. Appeals (9th and Fed. Cir.). Assoc. Chickering and Gregory, San Francisco, 1965-71, ptnr., 1972-81, Brobeck, Phleger, and Harrison, San Francisco, 1981—2003, litig. dept. chair, 1984-91, San Francisco mng. ptnr., 1992-96; ptnr. Morgan, Lewis, and Bockius, San Francisco, 2003—05; pvt. practice San Francisco, 2005—. Pres. Oakland, Calif. Mus. Assn., 1981-83; mem. profl. ethics com. State Bar Calif., 1974-77. Fellow: Am. Coll. Trial Lawyers; mem.: Barrister's Club of San Francisco (v.p. 1973), Calif. Barristers (bd. dirs., v.p.), Bar Assn. San Francisco (bd. dirs. 1972—73), Legal Aid Soc. (bd. dirs. 1982—93, pres. 1985—88), U. Calif.-Berkeley Found. (trustee 1998—2000), Boalt Hall Alumni Assn. (bd. dirs. 1993—99, pres. 1997—98). Office: 5283 Broadway Terr Oakland CA 94618 Home Phone: 707-255-5570; Office Phone: 510-547-1555. Business E-Mail: trautman17@sbcglobal.net.

TRAUTMANN, THOMAS ROGER, history professor, anthropology educator; b. Madison, Wis., May 27, 1940; s. Milton and Esther Florence (Trachte) T.; m. Marcella Hauolilani Choy, Sept. 25, 1962; children: Theodore William, Robert Arthur. BA, Beloit Coll., 1962; PhD, U. London, 1968. Lectr. in history Sch. Oriental and African Studies, U. London, 1965-68; asst. prof. history U. Mich., Ann Arbor, 1968-71, assoc. prof., 1971-77, prof., 1977—, Richard Hudson rsch. prof., 1979, prof. history and anthropology, 1984—, chmn. dept. history, 1987-90, Steelcase rsch. prof., 1993-94, dir. Inst. Humanities, Mary Fair Croushore prof. humanities, 1997—2002, Marshall D. Sahlins coll. prof. history and anthropology, 1997—. Author: Kautilya and the Arthasastra, 1971, Dravidian Kinship, 1981, Lewis Henry Morgan and the Invention of Kinship, 1987; author: (with K.S. Kabelac) The Library of Lewis Henry Morgan, 1994; author: (edit. with Diane Owen Hughes) Time: Histories and Ethnologies, 1995, Aryans and British India, 1997; author: (edit. with Maurice Godelier and Franklin Tjon Sie Fat) Transformations of Kinship, 1999, Languages and Nations: The Dravidian Proof in Colonial Madras, 2006; editor: Comparative Studies in Society and History, 1997—2006; contbr. articles on India, kinship and history of anthropology;: The Aryan Debate, 2005. Sr. Humanist fellow NEH, 1984. Mem. Am. Anthrop. Assn., Assn. Asian Studies, Am. Inst. Indian Studies (mem. exec. com. trustee, sr. rsch. fellow in India 1985, 97), Phi Beta Kappa. Office: U Mich Dept History Ann Arbor MI 48109-1003

TRAUTNER, JOHN JAMES, real estate executive; b. Simpson, Minn., Dec. 4, 1935; s. John Sylvester and Oridena Francis (Baker) T.; m. Donna L. Jones, June 1960 (div. Dec. 1969); children: Theresa, Carrie, John; m. Carol Lee Rowberry, July 12, 1974 (div. May 1981); 1 child, Lindsey D.; m. Kathy N. Bucy, July 19, 1992; 1 stepchild, Victor. BA, Anchorage C.C., 1968; BBA, U. Alaska, 1970, MBA, 1998. Masters lic. 100 ton U.S. Coast Guard, lic. comml. pilot. Adminstr., pub. affairs RCA Svc. Co., Anchorage, 1965-70; dir. adminstrn. & pub. rels. Alaska Resort, Inc., Girdwood, 1970-71; mgmt. cons. State of Alaska, 1972-73; exec. dir. City of Lost River (Alaska), 1973-74; v.p., gen. mgr. C. Bruce Ficke Investments, Girdwood, 1974-76; pres., gen. mgr. Gateway, Inc., Girdwood, 1976-85; CEO Alyeska Mgmt. Svcs., Inc., Girdwood, 1985—. Mem. MD49 Coun. Govs., Fairbanks, Alaska, 1996-97, chmn., 1999-2000; marriage commr. 3d Jud. Dist., Anchorage, 1973-93. Patentee in field. Chmn., mem. Girdwood Bd. Suprs., 1992-95; fire chief Girdwood Fire Dept., 1972-75; chmn. Girdwood Cmty. Coun., 1976-78, Jr.-Inter-Fraternity Coun., Seattle, 1957-58. Sgt. U.S. Army, 1953-64. Melvin Jones fellow, chgo., 1993-94. Mem. N.Am. Nature Photographers Assn., Am. Legion, Lions, Disabled VFW, Alaska Airmens Assn., San Francisco Tennis Club. Republican. Roman Catholic. Avocations: photography, music, art, humanitarianism, flying. Office: Alyeska Mgmt Svcs Inc PO Box 909 Girdwood AK 99587-0909 E-mail: outsidermining@msn.com.

TRAVERSE, LYN D., not-for-profit fundraiser, communications executive; b. Kalamazoo, Mich., May 7, 1952; d. Robert Clinton Traverse and Betty Larue Kemp; m. Jonathan G. Tidd (div.); 1 child, Emily. Student, NYU, 1970—74; BA, U. Conn., 1996. Devel. officer NYU, NYC, 1974—80, U. Hartford, Conn., 1980—83; dir. devel. and comms. Forman Sch., Litchfield, Conn., 1983—88, Ethel Walker Sch., Simsbury, Conn., 1988—96, The Nature Conservancy, Middletown, Conn., 1996—2000, Long Wharf Theatre, New Haven, 2000—03, Haskins Labs., New Haven, 2003—06; campaign dir. Friends Sem., NYC, 2006—. Trustee U. Hartford Art, West Hartford, Conn., 1999—; trustee, treas. Endangered Lang. Fund, New Haven, 2004—. Actor: (films) Plainsong, 1983. Mem. patrons bd. New Haven Free Pub. Libr., 2004—; mem. steering com. Simsbury (Conn.) Land Trust, 1999—2002. Mem.: Alpha Sigma Lamda. Office: Friends Seminary 222 E 16th St New York NY 10003

TRAVIS, JAY A., III, lawyer; b. McComb, Miss., June 8, 1940; s. J.A. and Katharine (Brennan) T., Jr.; m. Judith Thompson, Sept. 8, 1965; children: Kathy, John E., William. BBA, U. Miss., 1962, JD, 1965. Bar: Miss. 1965, US Dist. Ct. (so. dist.) Miss. 1967, US Ct. Appeals (5th cir.) 1970. Assoc. Thompson, Alexander & Crews, Jackson, Miss., 1967-69; ptnr. Butler, Snow, O'Mara, Stevens & Cannada, Jackson, 1969—. Chmn. Miss. Law Inst., 1974; pres. Estate Planning Coun. Miss., 1975-76. Mem. vestry, cathedral warden St. Andrew's Episc. Ch., 1983-87. Capt. JAGC, USAR, 1965-73; bd. dirs U. of Miss. Found., 1999—. Fellow Am. Coll. Trust and Estate Counsel (bd. regents, 1994-00, state chmn. 1987-92) Am. Coll. Trust and Estate Counsel Found. (bd. dirs. 2006—), Am. Bar Found.; mem. ABA (fellow young lawyers sect.), Miss. State Bar (pres. young lawyers sect. 1975-76), Miss. Bar Assn. (chmn. estates and trusts sect. 1987-88), Hinds County Bar Assn. (pres. 1988-89), Univ. Club, River Hills Club, Phi Delta Phi. Office: PO Box 22567 Jackson MS 39225-2567 Office Phone: 601-948-5711. Business E-Mail: jay.travis@butlersnow.com.

TRAVIS, JEREMY, academic administrator; b. Worcester, Mass., July 31, 1948; BA in Am. studies cum laude, Yale Coll., 1970; MPA, NYU, 1977, JD cum laude, 1982. Exec. dir. victim/witness assistance project Vera Inst. Justice, 1975—77; exec. dir. NYC Criminal Justice Agy., 1977—79; cons. NYC Bd. Correction, 1979—82; law clk. to Hon. Ruth Bader Ginsburg US Ct. Appeals (DC Cir.), 1982—83; spl. counsel to police commr. NYC Police Dept., 1984—86; spl. counsel to first dep. mayor and asst. dir. law enforcement services, Mayor's Office of Ops. City of NY, 1986, spl. advisor to mayor, 1986—89; chief counsel to subcommittee on criminal justice U.S. Ho. of Reps. Com. on the Judiciary, Washington, 1990; dep. commr. legal matters NYC Police Dept., 1990—94; dir. Nat. Inst. Justice, US Dept. Justice, Washington, 1994—2000; sr. fellow Justice Policy Ctr., The Urban Inst., Washington, 2000—04; pres. John Jay Coll. of Criminal Justice CUNY, 2004—. Vis. lectr. Yale Coll., 1979; adj. prof. Wagner Grad. Sch. Pub. Svc., NYU, 1985-90; adj. assoc. prof., NY Law Sch., 1992-94; vis. prof., George Washington U., 2004; nat. adv. bd., program on State Crime Prevention Initiatives, Nat. Crime Prevention Coun., 2001-, Join Together program, Robert Wood Johnson Found., 2001-, Nat. H.I.R.E. Network, Legal Action Ctr., 2001-, Ctr. for Rsch. on Criminal and Mental Health, Rutgers U., 2002-; nat. adv. com. on Reclaiming Futures, Robert Wood Johnson Found., 2000-; adv. bd., Ctr. for Cmty. Safety, Winston-Salem State U., 2001-; Aspen Inst. Roundtable on Comprehensive Cmty. Initiatives, 1999-. Rockefeller Fellow, Yale Div. Sch., 1970-71; Marden and Marshall Fellow in Criminal Law, NYU Sch. Law, 1983-84; recipient Disting. Alumnus Award, NYU, 1986, Outstanding Pub. Svc. Award, NY County Lawyers Com., 1992, Edmund S. Randolph Award, US Atty. Gen., 2000, August Vollmer Award, Am. Soc. Criminology, 2002, Gerhard O.W. Mueller Award, Internat. Sect., Acad. Criminal Justice Sciences, 2003, Margaret Meade Award, Internat. Cmty. Corrections Assn., 2003. Mem.: NY State Bar. Office: CUNY John Jay Coll Criminal Justice 899 Tenth Ave New York NY 10019

TRAVIS, LAWRENCE ALLAN, accountant; b. Bloomington, Ill., Sept. 17, 1942; s. Willard Burns and Florence May (Harvey) T.; m. Katy Quinones, Apr. 16, 1965 (div. Feb. 1978); children: Lawrence Allan Jr., Matthew B.; m. Kathleen Lucas, May 20, 1995. BS in Bus. Edn., Ill. State U., 1968; MA in Pub. Adminstrn., U. Ill., Springfield, 1976. CPA, Ill. Staff acct. Alexander Grant & Co., Chgo., 1969; internal auditor State Farm Ins., Bloomington, 1969-73; dep. dir. Ill. Dept. Ins., Springfield, 1973-74; audit mgr. Ill. Auditor Gen., Springfield, 1974-81; pres. Lawrence Travis & Co., P.C., CPAs, Virden, Normal, Springfield and Jacksonville, Ill., 1979—, also bd. dirs.; registered rep. Genworth Fin. Securities, 1994—. Pres., bd. dirs.

Travco, Inc., Virden; v.p., bd. dirs. Ka-Lar Enterprises, Inc., Springfield, Miller Comm., Inc. Mem. Ill. Common Cause, Springfield. Mem. AICPA, Assn. Govt. Accts., Ill. CPA Soc., Nat. Space Soc., Smithsonian Assocs., World Future Soc. Democrat. Roman Catholic. Avocation: sports. Home: 2409 Idlewild Dr Springfield IL 62704-5403 Office: Lawrence Travis & Co PC 1700 S 1st St Springfield IL 62704-3902 E-mail: lawrencetraviscpa@insightbb.com.

TRAVIS, NIGEL, food service executive; b. Woodford, Essex, Eng. m. Joanna Travis; 2 children. BA with honors in Bus. Studies, Middlesex U., London. With Kraft, Rolls Royce, Massey Ferguson, Parker Hannifin, Grand Met.; sr. v.p. human resources Burger King, Miami, Fla.; mng. dir. Europe, Mid. East and Africa, 1991; v.p. Europe to sr. v.p. Europe Blockbuster, 1994—97, pres. internat., 1997—98, pres. worldwide stores divsn., 1998—2001, pres., COO, 2001—05; exec. v.p. Papa John's, 2005, pres., CEO, bd. mem., 2005—. Office: Papa John's Internat Inc 2002 Papa Johns Blvd Louisville KY 40299-2334

TRAVIS, RANDY BRUCE, musician; b. Monroe, NC, 1959; married. Musician Country City U.S.A., 1977-82, Nashville Palace, 1982-85; recording artist, 1986—. Rec. artist Warner Bros. Records, 1985-97, DreamWorks Records, 1997-2000, Inspirational Journey Warner Bros. and Atlantic Christian Music Divsn. (Dove award 2001), Word Records 2002-; albums include debut Storms of Life, 1986 (Album of Yr., Acad. Country Music, 1986, Song of Yr. for On the Other Hand, Acad. Country Music, 1986, Single of Yr. for On the Other Hand, Acad. Country Music, 1986, Single of Yr. for On the Other Hand, Music City News 1987, Album of Decade, BBC Radio Two, 1990), Always & Forever, 1987 (Best Country Record of Yr. for Forever and Ever, Amen, AMOA Jukebox, 1987, Single of Yr. for Forever and Ever, Amen, Acad. Country Music, Song of Yr. for Forever and Ever, Amen, Acad. Country Music, 1987, Album of Yr., Country Music Assn. 1987, Single of Yr. for Forever and Ever, Amen, Country Music Assn., 1987, Best Country Male Vocal Performance, Grammy award, 1987, Album of Yr., Country Music Round Up Internat. Awards, 1987, Single of Yr. for Forever and Ever, Amen, Music City News, 1988, Album of Yr., Music City News, 1988, Favorite Country Album, Am. Music Award, 1988, 89, Favorite Country Single for Forever and Ever, Amen, Am. Music Award, 1988, Favorite Country Video for Forever and Ever, Amen, Am. Music Award, 1988, Favorite Album, Nashville Network Viewers' Choice Awards, 1988, Favorite Video for Forever and Ever, Amen, Nashville Network Viewers' Choice Awards, 1988, Favorite Song for Forever and Ever, Amen, Nashville Network Viewers' Choice Awards, 1988, Favorite Country Album, World Music Award, 1988, Favorite Country Single for I Told You So, Am. Music Award, 1989), Old 8x10, 1988 (Best Male Country Vocal Performance, Grammy award, 1988, Favorite album, Nashville Network Viewers' Choice Awards, 1989, Favorite Country Single for Deeper Than the Holler, Am. Music Award, 1990, Favorite Country Album, 1990), No Holdin' Back, 1989 (Best Selling Country Album, NARM, 1989, award, AMPEX Golden Reel Awards, 1990, Country Record of Yr. for It's Just a Matter of Time, AMOA Jukebox, 1990), An Old Time Christmas, 1989, Heroes and Friends, 1990 (award, AMPEX Golden Reel Awards, 1991), High Lonesome, 1991, Greatest Hits Vol. 1, 1992, Greatest Hits Vol. 2, 1992 (#5 Video of Yr. for Look Heart No Hands, CMT Europe, 1993), Wind in the Wire, 1993, This is Me, 1994, Full Circle, 1996, You And Youa Alone, 1998, A Man Ain't Made of Stone, 1999, Inspirational Journey, 2000 (Bluegrass Album of Yr., Dove Award, 2001), Randy Travis Live, 2001 (Country Recorded Song of Yr. for Baptism, Dove Award, 2001), Anthology, 2002, Rise And Shine, 2002 (Country Album of Yr., Dove Award, 2003, Song of Yr. for Three Wooden Crosses, Christian Country Music Assn., 2003, Song of Yr. for Three Wooden Crosses, Country Music Assn., 2003, Best So., Country, Bluegrass, Gospel Album, Grammy award, 2004, Country Recorded Song of Yr. for Three Wooden Crosses, Dove Award, 2004, Song of Yr. for Three Wooden Crosses, Acad. Country Music, 2004), Worship & Faith, 2003 (Country Album of Yr., Dove Award, 2004, Best So., Bluegrass, Gospel Album, Grammy award, 2005), Passing Through, 2004, Glory Train, 2005 (Grammy award, Best Country Gospel Album, 2007); song collaborator (with Alan Jackson) She's Got the Rhythm (And I Got the Blues), (Top Ten Songs of 1993, Music City News Country Songwriters Award, 1993), Same Old Train (Best Country Vocal Collaboration, Grammy award, 1998); film appearances include: Young Guns, 1988, Frank and Jesse, 1995, Wind in the Wire, 1993, 94, A Holiday to Remember, 1995, Outlaws (The Legend of O.B. Taggart), 1995, Edie & Pen, 1996, Boys Will Be Boys, 1996, The Shooter, 1997, Fire Down Below, 1997, Steel Chariots, 1997, The Rainmaker, 1997, Annabelle's Wish, 1997, T-N-T, 1998, Black Dog, 1998, Baby Geniuses, 1999, Boys Will Be Boys, 1998, Major Reno, 1999, Trial Of Old Drum, 2000, Casper's Haunted Christmas, 2000, The Million Dollar Kid, 2000, Texas Rangers, 2002, White River Kid, 2002, John John In The Sky, 2002, The Long Ride Home, 2003(documentary series) Fathers of Our Country, 2000, A&E Biography, 2000; (TV Movie) A Holiday to Remember, 1995;(TV mini-series, video release) Texas, 1995; (TV series) Matlock, 1992, 93, Touched by an Angel, 1994, 95, 97, 2001, 03, Sabrina, 1996, Hey Arnold, 1998, King of the Hill, 2000, Blue's Clues, 2002; (TV movie, video) Dead Man's Revenge, 1994, At Risk, 1993; (TV spl.) Down Home, 1990, Happy Trails, 1990, At Risk, 1993. Named Top New Male Vocalist, Acad. Country Music, 1985, New Country Act of Yr., Performance Mag., 1986, Top Male Vocalist, Acad. Country Music, 1986, Male Vocalist, Acad. Country Music, 1987, Male Artist of Yr., Music City News, 1987, 88, Star of Tomorrow, Music City News, 1987, Male Vocalist of Yr., Country Music Assn., 1987, 88, Most Popular Internat. Male Vocalist, Country Music Round Up Internat. Awards, 1987, 89, Favorite Nat. Artist, NECMA, 1987, Entertainer of Yr., Music City News, 1988, 89, Male Artist of Yr., Music City News, 1988, Favorite Entertainer, Nashville Network Viewers' Choice Awards, 1988, 89, Favorite Male Vocalist, Nashville Network Viewers' Choice Awards, 1988, Favorite Country Male Vocalist, Am. Music Award, 1988, 90, Male Vocalist for Country, Playboy Music Poll, 1988, 89, 90, 91, Artist of Yr., AMOA-Jukebox, 1989, Top Internat. Act, British Country Music Assn., 1989, Favorite Country Male Artist, Am. Music Award, 1989, Favorite Male Musical Performer, People's Choice Award, 1989, Best Country Artist, Rolling Stone Ann. Reader's Poll, 1989, 91, Country Act of Yr., Performance Mag., 1989, Favorite Country Artist, World Music Award, 1990, #1 Country Albums Artist, Billboard Music Award, 1990, #1 Country Artist, Billboard Music Award, 1990, Top Grossing Country Tour, Amusement Bus., 1990, Country Tour of Yr., Performance Mag., 1990, Favorite Country Music Performer, People's Choice Award, 1990, Internat. Artist, Country Music, People Mag. Internat. Awards, 1992, Mainstream Country Artist of Yr., Christian Country Music Assn., 2003; recipient Horizon award Country Music Assn., 1986, For Excellence in Media, Golden Angel Award, 1990, Star on Hollywood Walk of Fame, Hollywood C. of C., 2004. Mem. Grand Ole Opry. E-mail: traviscorp@home.com.

TRAVIS, RICHARD L., lawyer; b. Mobridge, SD, 1954; BA, U. SD, 1976, JD, 1980. Bar: SD 1980, US Dist. Ct. (SD) 1980. Atty. Frieberg Frieberg & Peterson, Beresford, SD, 1980; dep. state atty. Union County, SD; atty. May & Johnson PC, Sioux Falls, SD, 1990—, ptnr. Mem.: SD Def. Lawyers Assn., Def. Rsch. Inst., SD Trial Lawyers Assn. (bd. gov. 1991—93), State Bar SD (pres. young lawyers sect. 1985—86, bar commr. 1989—94, disciplinary bd. mem. 1994—2000, pres.-elect 2006—07), Second Judicial Cir. Bar Assn. Office: May & Johnson PC 4804 S Minnesota Ave Sioux Falls SD 57108 Office Phone: 605-336-2565. Office Fax: 605-336-2604.

TRAVIS, ROBERT M., lawyer; b. Lyons, Ga., Dec. 12, 1945; BA, Univ. NC, Chapel Hill, 1968; JD, Univ. Ga., 1972. Bar: Ga. 1972. Ptnr., chmn. Litig. Dept. Powell Goldstein LLP, Atlanta. Editor (assoc.): Ga. Law Rev. Vice chmn. bd., chmn. devel. com. YMCA, Ga.; mem. Episcopal Diocese Atlanta Registrar, 1988—90. Mem.: ABA, State Bar Ga., Def. Rsch. Inst., Ga. Def. Lawyers Assn. (pres.), Atlanta Bar Assn., Lawyers Club Atlanta, Bleckley Inns of Ct. (Master), Assn. Trial Lawyers Am. (assoc.), U. NC Alumni Assn. (life), YMCA (vice chmn. bd. Ga. chpt., chmn. devel. com.), Phi Delta Phi. Office: Powell Goldstein LLP 1 Atlantic Ctr 14th Fl 1201 W Peachtree St NW Atlanta GA 30309-3488 Home Phone: 404-315-0089; Office Phone: 404-572-6646. Office Fax: 404-572-6999. Business E-Mail: btravis@pogolaw.com.

TRAVIS, SARAH, orchestrator; Trained at City U.; trained at Guildhall Sch. Music and Drama, UK. Orchestrator, musical supervisor Mack & Mabel, Pinafore Swing, Fiddler on the Roof, Gondoliers, Ten Cents a Dance, Piaf and Carmen, Sweeney Todd, 2005 (Tony award, best orchestrations, 2006, Drama Desk award, outstanding orchestrations, 2006); composer: Peter Pan, A Star Danced, The Last Fattybottypuss in the World, Tales My Lover Told Me, A Womb With A View; pianist Fascinating Aida, Drop Dead Divas. Office: Eugene O'Neill Theatre 230 W 49th St New York NY 10036

TRAVIS, TONI-MICHELLE C., political scientist, educator; d. Mark E. and Ada Deans Chapman; m. Theodore W. Travis. BA, Bard Coll., Annandale-on-Hudson, NY, 1969; MA, U. Chgo., 1973, PhD, 1983. Asst. prof., govt. George Mason U., Fairfax, Va., 1984—90, asst. dean, Coll. Arts & Scis., 1993—95, host, prodr., Capital Region Roundtable, 1998—2002, assoc. prof., govt., 1990—2004; vis. prof. Simmons Coll., Boston, 1998—2000. Pres. Women's Caucus, Washington, 1994—95. Co-author: The Meaning of Difference, 1996; author: 4th edit., 2005, Virginia Almanac of Politics, 2006; editor: (book series) Race and Politics, 1995—2002; co-editor: Virginia Almanac of Politics, 2005. Active Higher Edn. Group, Washington, 1997—2003; bd. dirs. Make Women Count, Richmond, Va., 1998—2000; bd. govs. Bard Coll. Alumni Assn., 2004—. Fellow, Rothermere Am. Inst., Oxford U., 2007—; John Bard scholar, Bard Coll., 1968, Ford Found fellow, U. Chgo., 1969—73, Fenwick fellow, George Mason U., 2006—07. Mem.: Com. on Internat. Polit. Sci., Nat. Capital Area Polit. Sci. Assn. (pres. 1994—95), Am. Polit. Sci. Assn. (coun. mem. 1994—96, mem. com. on internat. polit. sci. 2003—), Fairfax Com. of 100. Avocation: walking. Office: Dept Pub and Internat Affairs George Mason Univ MS 3F4 4400 University Dr Fairfax VA 22030 Business E-Mail: ttravis@gmu.edu.

TRAVIS, VANCE KENNETH, petroleum business executive; b. Coriander, Sask., Can., Jan. 30, 1926; s. Roy Hazen and Etta Orilla (Anderson) T.; m. Louise Mary, Nov. 30, 1948 (div. 1979); children: Stuart, Shirley, Gordon, Donald, Marian; m. Mildred Elaine, June 29, 1979; stepchildren: Susan, Nancy, Gordon, Sandra, Karen. Chmn. bd. Turbo Resources Ltd., 1970-83, Challenger Internat., 1977-83, Bankeno Mines Ltd., 1977-83, Queenston Gold Mines Ltd., Toronto, Ont., Canada, 1977-84, Health Risk Mgmt. Inc., Mpls., 1984-86, Triad Internat. Inc., 1985—96; dir. Health Resource Mgmt. Ltd., Edmonton, Alta., Canada, 1990-97. Bd. dirs. Vencap Equities Alta. Ltd., Edmonton, 1981-86, L.K. Resources Ltd., Calgary, 1973-84. Mem. Young. Pres.'s Orgn., Calgary, 1964-76, World Pres. Orgn. Recipient Presdl. pin Jr. Achievement, 1963, Best Pitcher award Petroleum Fastball League, 1955. Mem.: Calgary Petroleum Club. E-mail: kentravis@telus.net.

TRAVOLTA, JOHN, actor; b. Englewood, NJ, Feb. 18, 1954; s. Salvatore and Helen (Burke) T.; m. Kelly Preston Sept. 12, 1991; children: Jett, Ella Bleu. Appeared in TV series Welcome Back Kotter, 1975-77; TV movies: The Boy in the Plastic Bubble, 1976, Chains of Gold, 1991, Eye of an Angel, 1991; films: Carrie, 1976, Saturday Night Fever, 1977 (Best Actor award Nat. Bd. Rev., 1977, Best Actor Acad. award nominee 1977, Best Actor 1st runner up Nat. Soc. Film Critics 1977, Best Actor 2nd runner up N.Y. Film Critics Circle 1977), Grease, 1978 (Golden Globe World Film Favorite 1978), Moment-By-Moment, 1978, Urban Cowboy, 1980, Blow Out, 1981, Staying Alive, 1983 (Male/Box Office Star of Yr., Nat. Assn. Theatre Owners Show East 1983), Two of a Kind, 1983, Perfect, 1985, The Dumb Waiter, 1987, The Experts, 1989, Look Who's Talking, 1989 (Male/Box Office Star of Yr., Nat. Assn. Theatre Owners ShowEast 1989), Look Who's Talking Too, 1990, The Tender, 1991, Shout, 1991, Look Who's Talking Now, 1993, Pulp Fiction, 1994 (Best Actor Acad. award nominee 1994, Best Actor award nominee Brit. Acad. Film and TV Arts 1994, Golden Globe Best Actor award nominee 1994, Best Actor award nominee SAG 1994, Best Actor award nominee Chgo. Film Critics 1994, Best Actor award nominee Comedy awards 1994, Best Actor award L.A. Film Critics 1994, Best Actor award Stockholm Film Festival 1993, Best Actor award London Film Critics Cir. 1994), Get Shorty, 1995, White Man's Burden, 1995, Broken Arrow, 1996, Phenomenon, 1996, Michael, 1996, Face Off, 1997, Mad City, 1997, She's So Lovely (also exec. prodr.), 1997, Primary Colors, 1998 (Golden Globe nominee), A Civil Action, 1998, General's Daughter, 1999, Battlefield Earth, (also prodr.) 2000, Lucky Numbers, 2000, Swordfish, 2001, Domestic Disturbance, 2001, Basic, 2003, The Punisher, 2004, Ladder 49, 2004, Be Cool, 2005, Lonely Hearts, 2006, Wild Hogs, 2007, Hairspray, 2007; author: Staying Fit, 1984, Propeller One Way Night Coach; rec. artist album, 1976, 77; author (books) John Travolta Staying Fit, 1984, Propeller One-Way Night Coach: A Fable for All Ages, 1997. Involved with Fight for Kids. Recipient Best Male Vocalist Billboard award, 1976, Best Male Vocalist award Record World and Music Retail mag., 1976, Best Actor Golden Apple award Cue mag., Juno award Can. Acad. Rec. Arts and Scis., 1978, Golden Apple award 1998, Lifetime Achievement award British Acad. Film and TV Assn., 1998, Chgo. Internat. Film Festival, 1998, Palm Springs Internat. Film Festival, 1999, Alan J. Pakula award U.S. Broadcast Film Critics Assn., 1999,; nominated Best New Male Star Women's Press Club, 1976; named Man of Yr., Hasty Pudding Club, Harvard U., 1981. Office: William Morris Agency 151 El Camino Dr Beverly Hills CA 90212 *

TRAXLER, WILLIAM BYRD, JR., federal judge; b. Greenville, SC, May 1, 1948; s. William Byrd and Bettie (Wooten) Traxler; m. Patricia Alford, Aug. 21, 1972; children: William Byrd III, James McCall. BA, Davidson Coll., 1970; JD, U. SC, 1973. Assoc. William Byrd Traxler, Greenville, 1973—75; asst. solicitor 13th Jud. Ct., Greenville, 1975—78, dep. solicitor, 1978—81, solicitor, 1981—85, resident cir. judge, 1985—92; US Dist. judge Dist. of SC, Greenville, 1992—98; judge US Ct. Appeals (4th cir.), Greenville, 1998—. Recipient Outstanding Svc. award, Solicitors Assn., SC, 1987, Leadership award, Probation, Parole & Pardon Svcs., SC, 1990. Office: Fourth Circuit 300 E Washington St Ste 116 Greenville SC 29601-2431

TRAYLOR, ANGELIKA, stained glass artist; b. Munich, Bavaria, Germany, Aug. 24, 1942; Came to U.S., 1959; d. Walther Artur Ferdinand and Berta Kreszentia (Boeck) Klau; m. Lindsay Montgomery Donaldson, June 10, 1959 (div. 1970); 1 child, Cameron Maria Greta; m. Samuel William Traylor III, June 12, 1970. Student, Pvt. Handelsschule Morawetz Jr. Coll., Munich, 1958. Freelance artist, 1980—. Works featured in profl. jours. including the Daylily Jour., 1987, Design Jour., South Korea, 1989, The Traveler's Guide to American Crafts, 1990, Florida Mag., 1991, Florida Today, 1993, Adventures in Art, vol. 3, 1993, Melbourne Times, 1994, The Orbiter, 1996, The Glass Collector's Digest, 1996, (TV) Focus on History, 1993, Focus, 1998, Space Coast Press, 1999, Weekend Decorating Projects-Women's Day, 1999, Pen Women, 1999, Stained Glass for the First Time, 2000, Creative Stained Glass, 2004, Florida Today, 2006, 2007; represented in permanent collections White House Christmas Ornament Collection, Holmes Regional Med. Ctr., Melbourne, Fla., Williams Childs Hospice House, Palm Bay, Fla., Health First Heart Ctr., Melbourne, Fla., others. Recipient Fragile Art award Glass Art mag., 1982, 1st Yr. Exhibitor award Stained Glass Assn. Am., 1984, 2d pl. Nonfigurative Composition award Vitraux des USA, 1985, Best of Show Stained Glass Assn. Am., 1989, 3d pl., 1989, Merit award George Plimpton All-Star Space Coast Art Open, 1994; named Hist. Woman of Brevard, Brevard Cultural Alliance, 1991, one of 200 Best Am. Craftsmen Early Am. Life mag., 1994-95, 97-98, 2000. Home and Office: 100 Poinciana Dr Indian Harbor Beach FL 32937-4437 Office Phone: 321-773-7640.

TRAYLOR, CHET D., state supreme court justice; b. Columbia, La., Oct. 12, 1945; s. John Hardy and Bernice (Bogan) T.; children: Mary Therese, Leigh Ann, Anna Marie. BA in Govt., N.E. La. State U., 1969; JD, Loyola U. Sch. of Law, 1974. Bar: La. Former La. State Trooper; former investigator La. Dept. of Justice Organized Crime & Racketering Unit; former legal advisor La. State Police Narcotics, Detectives & Intelligence Units; asst. dist. atty. Franklin Parish, 1975—76; judge 5th Jud. Dist. Ct., Franklin, Richland and West Carroll Parishes, La., 1985-97; assoc. justice La. Supreme Ct., 1997—. Founding bd. mem. Winnsboro Econ. Devel. Found.; mem. Rocky Mountain Conservation Fund. Military police investigator US Army. Mem. ABA, La. Bar Assn., La. Dist. Judges Assn., NRA (life), Franklin Parish Mental Health Assn. (past bd. dirs.), Winnsboro Lions Club (past bd. dirs.), Greenwings (founder John Adams chpt.). Methodist. Office: La Supreme Ct 400 Royal St New Orleans LA 70130 *

TRAYNHAM, JAMES GIBSON, chemist, educator; b. Broxton, Ga., Aug. 5, 1925; s. James G. and Eddie Louise (Greer) T.; m. Margaret A. Egert, 1948; children: David F., Peter C.; m. Gresdna A. Doty, 1980. Student, South Ga. Coll., 1942-43; BS, U. N.C., 1946; PhD, Northwestern U., 1950. Instr. Northwestern U., 1949-50; asst. prof. Denison U., 1950-53; mem. faculty La. State U., Baton Rouge, 1953—, prof. chemistry, 1963-88, prof. emeritus, 1988—, chmn. dept. chemistry, 1968-73, vice chancellor for advanced studies and rsch., dean Grad. Sch., 1973-81. Postdoctoral research fellow Ohio State U., 1951-53; oral history cons. Chem. Heritage Found., 1997-2002. Author: Organic Nomenclature: A Programmed Introduction, 1966, 5th edit., 1997; editor: Essays on the History of Organic Chemistry, 1987; contbr. articles to profl. jours. Bd. dirs. Council Grad. Schs. in U.S., 1981. Recipient Petroleum Research Fund-Am. Chem. Soc. Type D award Eidg. Technische Hochschule, Zurich, Switzerland, 1959-60; Charles E. Coates award Baton Rouge sects. Am. Chem. Soc. and Am. Inst. Chem. Engrs., 1965; NATO sr. fellow in sci. Universität des Saarlandes, Saarbrücken, Fed. Republic Germany, 1972 Mem. Am. Chem. Soc. (past councilor, past chmn. Baton Rouge sect., chmn. divsn. history of chemistry 1988), La. Acad. Sci., Internat. Union Pure and Applied Chemistry (former titular mem. commn. on nomenclature of organic chemistry, sec. 1994-99), Phi Beta Kappa, Sigma Xi, Phi Lambda Upsilon, Phi Kappa Phi (past pres. La. State U. chpt.). Home: 122 Highland Trace Dr Baton Rouge LA 70810-5061 Fax: 225-769-7801. Personal E-mail: jimtraynham@msn.com.

TRAYNHAM, LURENE JONES, retired secondary school educator; b. Yazoo City, Miss., July 11, 1925; d. Thomas McKinley and Olivia Purvis Jones; m. Young Robinson (dec.); m. William H. Traynham (dec.); 1 child, Thomas Jefferson Jones. BS, Alcorn State U., Lorman, Miss., 1947; MEd, U. Ill., Urbana, 1958. Tchr. Madison County Tng. Sch., Canton, Miss., 1947—48, pub. schs., West Point, Miss., 1949—57, 1957—69, West Point High, 1969—71, Caldwell HS, Columbus, Miss., 1971—87; ret., 1987. Mem. dist. adv. bd. New Homemakers Am., Columbus, 1952—72; mem. internat. bd. fgn. students Miss. U. for Women, Columbus, 1978—82; mem. adv. bd. Future Homemakers Am., Jackson, Miss., 1972—87. Organizer Columbus Head Start, 1965. Recipient Cmty. Svc. award, Miss. Union Bapt. Ch., Columbus, 1987, Nat. Bapt. Women's Aux. award, So. Regional Conf., Columbus, 2004, cert. of leadership, Nat. Bapt. Conv., Balt., 2006. Mem.: Columbus Ret. Tchrs. Assn., Gamma Gamma Zeta (chaplain 1994—2006, organizer Amicae 1994, Disting. Dove award 2005). Democrat. Avocations: cooking, sewing, singing, travel, piano. Home: 1602 Martin Luther King Dr Columbus MS 39701

TRAYNOR, J. MICHAEL, lawyer; b. Oakland, Calif., Oct. 25, 1934; s. Roger J. and Madeleine (Lackmann) Traynor; m. Shirley Williams, Feb. 11, 1956; children: Kathleen Traynor Millard, Elizabeth Traynor Fowler, Thomas. BA, U. Calif., Berkeley, 1955; JD, Harvard U., 1960; LLD (hon.), U. SC, Columbia, 2007. Bar: Calif. 1961, U.S. Supreme Ct. 1966. Dep. atty. gen. State of Calif., San Francisco, 1961—63; spl. counsel Calif. Senate Com. on Local Govt., Sacramento, 1963; assoc. firm Cooley Godward Kronish, LLP, San Francisco, 1963—69, ptnr., 1969—2004, sr. counsel, 2005—. Adviser 3d Restatement of Unfair Competition, 1988—95, 3d Restatement of Torts, Products Liability, 1992—98, Apportionment, 1994—99, 2d Restatement of Conflict of Laws revs., 1988, 3d Restatement of Restitution and Unjust Enrichment, 1997—; lectr. Boalt Hall Sch. Law U. Calif., 1982—89, 1996—98; chmn. Earthjustice Legal Def. Fund (formerly Sierra Club Legal Def. Fund), 1991—92; trustee EarthJustice Legal Def. Fund (formerly Sierra Club Legal Def. Fund), 1974—96. Mem. bd. overseers Inst. for Civil Justice RAND, 1991—97; bd. dirs. Environ. Law Inst., 1991—97, 1999—2005, Ecojustice Can. (formerly Sierra Legal Def. Fund), Canada, 1990—96. 1st lt. USMC, 1955—57, USMCR, 1957—63. Recipient John P. Frank award, 2004. Fellow: Am. Acad. Appellate Lawyers, Am. Acad. Arts & Scis., Calif. Acad. Appellate Lawyers, Am. Bar Found. (life); mem.: Bar Assn. San Francisco (pres. 1973), Am. Law Inst. (coun. 1985—, pres. 2000—). Home: 3131 Eton Ave Berkeley CA 94705-2713 Office: Cooley Godward Kronish LLP 101 Calif St 5th Fl San Francisco CA 94111-5800 Office Phone: 415-693-2110. Office Fax: 415-693-2222. Business E-Mail: mtraynor@cooley.com.

TREABA, DIANA OLGUTA, physician; b. Ludus, Romania, Nov. 20, 1966; arrived in US, 1999; d. Constantin and Eugenia Treaba; m. Zoltan Szabolcs Szilagyi, June 22, 2004. MD Summa cum laude, U. Medicine and Pharmacy, Targu-Mures, 1987—93. Diplomate Anatomic Pathology and Clin. Pathology Am. Bd. of Pathology, 2003, Hematology Am. Bd. of Pathology, 2004, Specialist in Anatomic Pathology Ministry of Health and Family/Romania, 1998. Intern dr. Clin. County Hosp., Targu-Mures, Romania, 1994—95; resident in anatomic pathology Dept. of Pathology, Clin. County Hosp., Targu-Mures, Romania, 1995—99; resident in anatomic pathology and clin. pathology Dept. of Pathology, Rush Presbyn. St. Luke's Med. Ctr., Chgo., 1999—2003; fellow in hematopathology Northwestern Meml. Hosp., Chgo., 2003—04; fellow in immunohistochemistry PhenoPath Laboratories, Seattle, 2004—. Fellow: US and Can. Acad. of Pathology; mem.: AMA, Am. Assn. of Clin. Pathologists (licentiate), Coll. of Am. Pathologists (licentiate). Christian Orthodox. Office: Miriam Hosp 164 Summit Ave Providence RI 02906 Business E-Mail: dtreaba@lifespan.org.

TREACY, GERALD BERNARD, JR., lawyer; b. Newark, July 29, 1951; s. Gerald B. Sr. and Mabel L. (Nesbitt) T.; m. Joyce M. Biazzo, Apr. 6, 1974. BA summa cum laude, Rider Coll., 1973; JD, UCLA, 1981. Bar: Calif. 1981, Wash. 1982, D.C. 1995. Tchr. English Arthur L. Johnson Regional H.S., Clark, NJ, 1973—77; assoc. Gibson, Dunn & Crutcher, LA, 1981—82; ptnr. Perkins Coie, Bellevue, Wash., 1982—94, McGuire Woods Battle & Boothe, McLean and Bellevue, 1994—96, Egger, Betts, Austin, Treacy, Bellevue, 1996—98; pvt. practice Bellevue and Poulsbo, Wash., 1998—; of counsel Montgomery Purdue Blankinship and Austin, Seattle, 2000—; founder, mgr. Arc Line Cons. LLC, 2006—. Chmn. bd. dirs. estate planning adv. bd. U. Wash., Seattle, 1990-92; presenter TV Seminar, Where There's a Will, PBS affiliate; founder ArcLine Consulting, LLC. Author: Washington Guardianship Law, Administration and Litigation, 1988, supplemented, 1991, 3d edit. supplemented, 2002, Supporting Organizations, 1996, 2d edit., 2002, Community Property, 2005 Endowment fund com. Unitd Way, Seattle, 1987—89; exec. com. Wash. Planned Giving Coun., 1993—94, 1996—98; bd. dirs., adv. bd. ARC, Seattle, 1985—89, Arthritis Gift, 1987—89, Seattle Symphony, 1992, Seattle U., 1996; bd. dirs. Morning Light Found., Flow Chart Found., Eastside Lyric Theatre, Kitsap Opera, 2003—04; founder, prodr. West Sound Lyric Theater, 2003—. Mem. Kitsap County Estate Planning Coun., Eastside King County Estate Planning Coun., Order of Coif. Avocations: photography, hiking, classical music, poetry. Office: PO Box 710 Keyport WA 98345 Office Phone: 360-697-4142. E-mail: gbtreacy@aol.com.

TREACY, SANDRA JOANNE PRATT, retired art educator, illustrator; b. New Haven, Aug. 5, 1934; d. Willis Hadley Jr. and Gladys May (Gell) P.; m. Gillette van Nuyse, Aug. 27, 1955; 1 child, Jonathan Todd. BFA, R.I. Sch. Design, 1956; student, William Paterson Coll., 1973-74. Cert. elem. and secondary tchr., N.J. Tchr. art and music Pkwy. Christian Ch., Ft. Lauderdale, Fla., 1964-66; developer Pequannock Twp. Bd. of Edn., Pompton Plains, NJ, 1970-72, tchr. art, 1972-76; vol. art tchr. Person County Bd. of Edn., Roxboro, NC, 1978-80, tchr. art, 1980-91, So. Jr. High Sch., Roxboro, 1989-91, Woodland Elem. Sch., Roxboro, 1989-93; tchr. Helena Elem. Sch., Timberlake, NC, 1991-93, So. Middle Sch., 1981—2007; ret., 2007. Tchr. elem. art Bethel Hill Sch., Roxboro, 1974-79, vol. art tchr., 1979-80; tchr. basic art, vol. all elem. schs. Person County, Roxboro, 1977-80; tchr. arts and crafts, summers 1981-882; tchr. art home sch. So. Mid. Sch., 1981-2005, Person H.S., 1993-94 Artist, illustrator. Mem. Roxboro EMTs, 1979-81; bd. dirs. Person County Arts Coun., 1980-81, 93-95, pres., 1981-82; piano and organ choir accompanist Concord United Meth. Ch., 1981—; leader Morgan Trotters, 1992-94, asst. dir., 1993-96, bd. dirs.; coach, horseback riding for handicapped. Mem. NEA, Nat. Mus. of Women in the Arts (continuing charter), Smithsonian Assocs., N.C. Assn. Arts Edn., N.C. Assn. Educators, N.C. Art Soc. Mus. of Art, Internat. Platform Assn., Womans Club (tchr. Pompton Plains chpt. 1974-79), Person County Saddle Club (rec. sec. 1981-84), Puddingston Pony Club (dist. sec. 1974-75 Montville Twp. chpt.), Roxboro Garden Club (continuing, commr. 1980-82, pres. 1982-84, 2004—, sec. 1993-94, 97-98, v.p. 1993-95), Roxboro Woman's Club (arts dept.) Republican. Avocations: horseback riding, swimming, sailing, reading, playing piano and organ. Home: 1345 Kelly Brewer Rd Leasburg NC 27291-9622 Personal E-mail: sjptracy@esinc.net.

TREACY, VINCENT EDWARD, lawyer; b. Mass., Jan. 30, 1942; m. Judith Anne Mansfield, May 8, 1999. AB, Boston Coll., 1964; JD with honors, George Washington U., 1971. Bar: Va. 1972, D.C. 1973, Md. 1999; U.S. Supreme Ct. 1976. Atty. Fed. Labor Rels. Coun., Washington, 1971-73; legis. atty. Am. law divsn. Congrl. Rsch. Svc., Libr. Congress, Washington, 1973-98; sole practitioner Washington, 1998—. Cons. Romanian Legal Analysis and Legis. Drafting Conf., Senate and Chamber Duputies Romania, Bucharest, 1996. Mem. law rev. staff George Washington Law Rev., 1970. Mem. George Washington Law Alumni Assn. (pres. Capitol Hill chpt. 1986-87), Order of Coif. Home Phone: 202-966-1497; Office Phone: 202-966-1497. E-mail: vtreacy@msn.com.

TREACY, WILLIAM JOSEPH, electrical and environmental engineer; b. NYC, Jan. 16, 1959; s. William Joseph and Angela Bridget (Keane) T.; 1 child, Denise Marie. BSEE, Manhattan Coll., 1981; M in Aero. Sci., Embry-Riddle U., 1987; MBA, Regis U., 2005. Registered profl. engr., N.Y. Commd. 2d lt. USAF, 1981, advanced through grades to capt., project mgr. Victorville, Calif., 1981—84, dept. chief Netherlands GLCM program office Ramstein, Germany, 1984—88, chief engr. Soesterberg, Netherlands, 1988—91, heavy repair supt. Plattsburgh, NY, 1991—92, CFO, 1992—94, chief environ. engr., 1994—95; bldg. sys. supr. Plattsburgh (N.Y.) Airbase Redevelopment Corp., 1995—2004, Plattsburgh (N.Y.) Mcpl. Lighting Dept., 2004—. Computer technician, Plattsburgh, 1992—. Active Red Cross, Plattsburgh, 1992. Decorated Meritorious Svc. medal, Air Force Commendation medal with one oak leaf cluster, others; USAF ROTC Program Acad. scholar, 1978. Mem. IEEE, ASHRAE, Nat. Fire Protection Assn., Internat. Assn. Elec. Insps., Assn. for Facilities Engring., Aircraft Owners and Pilots Assn., Friends of Ft. Ticonderoga, Am. Legion. Republican. Roman Catholic. Avocations: flying, star trek memorabilia, cross country skiing. Home: 60 Leonard Ave Plattsburgh NY 12901-2565 Office: Plattsburgh Mcpl Lighting Dept 32 Green St Plattsburgh NY 12901 Office Phone: 518-563-2200. Business E-Mail: pmld_wjt@westelcom.com.

TREADWAY, JAMES CRISPIN CURRAN CORBETT, lawyer, brokerage house executive, investor, federal official; b. Anderson, SC, May 21, 1943; s. James C. Treadway and Maxine Hall; m. Susan Pepper Davis, Sept. 6, 1969; children: Elizabeth Pepper Hall, Caroline Worrell Harper Corbett. AB summa cum laude, Rollins Coll., 1964; JD summa cum laude, Washington and Lee U., 1967. Bar: Ga. 1967, Mass. 1968, D.C. 1970. Assoc. Candler, Cox, McClain & Andrews, Atlanta, 1967-68, Gadsby & Hannah, Boston and Washington, 1968-72; ptnr. Dickstein, Shapiro & Morin, Washington, 1972-82; commr. SEC, Washington, 1982-85; ptnr. Baker & Botts, Washington, 1985-87; exec. v.p., chmn. mcht. banking dept., mem. exec. com. Paine Webber Group Inc., NYC, 1987—. Commr. Nat. Study Commn., 1985—87; chmn. Nat. Commn. on Fraudulent Fin. Reporting, 1985—87; chmn. bds. dirs. Washington & Lee U. Sch. Law, 1992—94; dir. U. So. Calif., Sch. of Acctg. and Fin. Disclosure, 1985—93; mem. planning com. Garret Securities Law Inst., Northwestern U., 1985—92; dir. nat. study commn., 1985—87; spl. expert adviser, witness various U.S. congl. coms.; lectr. in field; bd. dirs. Parnounblon, Inc., Matchel Hatchens Asset Mgmt. Inc., Pomawufter, Inc., Gradgne Inc.; bd. dirs. Miran Banking Ctr. Boston (Mass.) U. Editor-in-chief Wash. & Lee U. Law review, 1966-67. Recipient Wildman Medal Am. Acctg. Assn., 1989. Mem. Mass. Bar Assn., Ga. Bar Assn., D.C. Bar Assn., Chevy Chase (Md.) Club, Bedford (N.Y.) Golf and Tennis Club, City Tavern Club (Washington chpt.), Met. Club (Washington chpt.), Verbank Hunting and Fishing Club (Uniondale N.Y.; dir. 1995—), Order of Coif, Phi Beta Kappa, Omicron Delta Kappa, Omicron Delta Epsilon, Kappa Alpha Order Republican. Roman Cath. Office: PaineWebber Group Inc 1285 Ave of Americas New York NY 10019-6028 Home: 1509 Monk Rd Gladwyne PA 19035 Personal E-mail: roundaction@aol.com.

TREADWAY, SANDRA GIOIA, library director; b. Jersey City, Jan. 15, 1950; d. Robert Peter and Essey Grace (Graham) Gioia; m. John David Treadway, Sept. 4, 1976 (div. 2006); 1 child, Robyn Grace. BA in History, Manhattanville Coll., 1971; MA in History, U. Va., 1972, PhD in History, 1978. Instr. history Va. Polytech Inst. & State U., Blacksburg, 1976-78; editor Va. State Libr., Richmond, 1978-91, dir. pubs., 1991-96; deputy dir. Libr. Va., Richmond, 1996—. Author: Women of Mark, 1995; co-author: The Common Wealth: Treasures from the Collections of the Library of Virginia, 1997; co-editor: Dictionary of Virginia Biography, vol. 1, 1999, vol. 2, 2001, vol. 3, 2006. Mdm. bd. St. Mary Sch., Richmond, 1988-96. Mem. Am. Hist. Assn., Orgn. Am. historians, So. Historical Assn., So. Assn. Women Historians (pres. 2002), Va. Hist. Soc., Va. Libr. Assn., Serra Internat. (bd. dirs. 1985—). Roman Catholic. Avocations: reading, travel. Home: 8201 Gaylord Rd Richmond VA 23229-4121 Office: Libr Va 800 E Broad St Richmond VA 23219-8000 Business E-Mail: streadway@lva.lib.va.us.

TREADWAY-DILLMON, LINDA LEE, actress, stuntwoman, dancer, dispatcher, athletic trainer; b. Woodbury, NJ, June 4, 1950; d. Leo Elmer and Ona Lee (Wyckoff) Treadway; m. Randall Kenneth Dillmon, June 19, 1982. BS in Health, Phys. Edn. & Recreation, West Chester State Coll., 1972, MS in Health and Phys. Edn., 1975; postgrad., Ctrl. Mich. U., 1978; Police Officer Stds. Tng. cert. complaint dispatcher, Goldenwest Coll., 1982. Cert. EMT Am. Acad. Orthopaedic Surgeons; in safety edn. West Chester State Coll. Grad. asst., instr., asst. athletic trainer West Chester (Pa.) State Coll., 1972-76; asst. prof., program dir., asst. athletic trainer Ctrl. Mich. U., Mt. Pleasant, 1976-80; police dispatcher City of Westminster, Calif., 1980-89; oncology unit sect. Children's Hosp. Orange County, Calif., 1989-96; control clk. food and beverage Marriott Hotel, Anaheim, 1996—2005. Stuntwoman, actress United Stunt Artists, SAG, L.A., 1982—; dancer Disneyland, Anaheim, Calif., 1988—; contbr. articles to profl. jours. Athletic trainer U.S. Olympic Women's Track and Field Trials, Frederick, Md., 1972, AAU Jr. World Wrestling Championships, Mt. Pleasant, Mich., 1977, Mich. Spl. Olympics, Mt. Pleasant, 1977, 78, 79. Recipient bronze and gold Spirit of Disneyland Resort awards, 1997; named Outstanding Phys. Educator, Delta Psi Kappa, Ctrl. Mich. U., 1980, Outstanding Young Woman of Am., 1984; named to Disneyland Entertainment Hall of Fame, 1995. Mem. SAG, Nat. Athletic Trainers Assn. (sect., women and athletic tng. ad hoc com. 1974-75, placement com. 1974-79, program dirs. coun. 1976-80, ethics com. 1977-80, visitation team 1978-80, 25 Yr. award 1997), U.S. Field Hockey Assn. (player), Pacific S.W. Field Hockey Assn. (player, Nat. Champion 1980, 81, 82), L.A. Field Hockey Assn. (player), Swing Shift Dance Team (dancer). Presbyterian. Avocations: flying, piano, athletics, stitchery, travel. Home: 18073 Scanlan Ct Fountain Valley CA 92708-5865

TREADWELL-RUBIN, PAMELA A., lawyer; b. Arlington, Tex., Dec. 15, 1960; BA in Polit. sci., U. Ariz., 1982, JD, 1985. Bar: Ariz. 1985. Prosecutor, Tucson City, 1985—87; dep. atty. Pima County, 1987—93; atty. Goering, Roberts, Rubin, Brogna, Enos & Treadwell-Rubin, PC, Tucson. Mem. Ariz. Juvenile Justice Adv. Coun., 1993—96. Fellow: Ariz. Bar Found. (bd. dirs. 1991—94, chair victims' rights pro bono panel 1992—93); mem.: Pima County Bar Assn. (bd. dirs. 1989—90, pres. Young Lawyers divsn. 1989—90, bd. dirs. 1996—2005), Ariz. Women Lawyers Assn., State Bar Ariz. (pres. Young Lawyers divns. 1994—95, cert. specialist worker's compensation 1995—, bd. govs. 1996—2005, pres. 2003—04, Outstanding Young Lawyer 1997). Office: Goering Roberts Rubin Brogna Enos & Treadwell-Rubin PC Ste 200 3320 N Campbell Ave Tucson AZ 85719 Office Phone: 520-577-9300.

TREANOR, CHARLES EDWARD, physicist, researcher; b. Buffalo, Oct. 22, 1924; s. William Michael and Margaret Mary (Powers) T.; m. Ruth Ziegelmaier, Jan. 28, 1950; children: Timothy, John, Peter, Michael, Melissa. BA, U. Minn., 1947; PhD, U. Buffalo, 1952-53. Instr. physics U. Buffalo, 1952-53; physicist Cornell Aero Lab., Buffalo, 1954-68, head aerodynamic rsch. dept., 1968-78; v.p. phys. sci. group Calspen Corp., Buffalo, 1978-83, v.p., chief scientist, 1983-90; pres. CTSA, Inc., 1990—2004; ret. Contbr. articles to profl. jours.; patentee in field. Served to lt. U.S. Army, 1943-46. Recipient C.C. Furnas award SUNY, Buffalo, 1989. Fellow Am. Phys. Soc. (div. chmn. 1977), AIAA (com. chmn. 1975-76, 87-89, Fluid and Plasma Dynamics award 1978); mem. NAE. Home: 535 Seabrook Drive Buffalo NY 14221-1919 Personal E-mail: ctreanor@adelphia.net.

TREANOR, MARK C., lawyer, diversified financial services company executive; b. Proctor, Vt., Dec. 2, 1946; BS, U.S. Naval Acad., Annapolis, 1968; JD with honors, U. Md., 1976. Bar: Md. 1976, U.S. Dist. Ct. Md. 1977, U.S. Ct. Appeals (4th cir.) 1979, U.S. Tax Ct. 1980, U.S. Supreme Ct. 1980, Vt. 1997. Ptnr. Miles & Stockbridge, 1982—85, Treanor, Pope & Hughes, 1987—98; sr. exec. v.p., gen. counsel, sec. Wachovia Corp., Charlotte, NC, 1998—. Mem. Md. Law Rev., 1975—76. Bd. visitors U. Md. Sch. Law; bd. advisors U. N.C. Sch. Law Banking Inst., NC. Capt. USMC, 1968—73. Mem.: ABA, Order of Coif, Md. State Bar Assn., Phi Alpha Delta. Office: Wachovia Corp 1 Wachovia Ctr 301 S College St Charlotte NC 28288-0630 *

TREANOR, WILLIAM MICHAEL, dean, law educator; b. Morristown, NJ, Nov. 16, 1957; s. William Joseph and Margaret Treanor; m. Allison Derivaux Ames, Oct. 15, 1994; children: William Paul Ames, Katherine Derivaux. BA summa cum laude, Yale U., 1979, JD, 1985; AM in History, Harvard U., 1982. Spl. asst. to dep. commr. U.S. Office Edn., Washington, 1979-80; speechwriter to sec. U.S. Dept. Edn., Washington, 1980; law clk. to Hon. James L. Oakes U.S. Ct. Appeals, 2d Cir., Brattleboro, Vt., 1985-86; spl. asst. to chmn. Com. on Govt. Integrity, NYC, 1987; spl. asst. U.S. atty. U.S. Atty.'s Office, Washington, 1990; assoc. counsel Office of Ind. Counsel, Washington, 1987-90; assoc. prof. law Fordham U., NYC, 1991-98, prof. law, 2001—, dean, 2002—; dep. asst. atty. gen. office of legal counsel U.S. Dept. Justice, NYC, 1998-2001. Vis. prof. Univ. Paris I, Pantheon-Sorbonne, 1998, 2000. Contbr. articles to profl. jours. Mem.: Phi Beta Kappa. Democrat. Office: Fordham Law Sch Dean Office Rm110 140 W 62nd St New York NY 10023 Office Phone: 212-636-6875. E-mail: wtreanor@fordham.edu.

TREASTER, JOSEPH B(LAND), journalist; s. Ellsworth F. and Anna Katherine (Chalupka) T.; m. Barbara A. Gluck, June 6, 1970 (div. Aug. 1976); m. Barbara J. Dill, Feb. 24, 1990; 1 child, Chloe Qiao Xing. BA, U. Miami, 1965; student, Sorbonne, Paris, 1971, San Francisco de Marroquin, Guatemala, 1988; MS, Columbia U., 1996. Reporter Miami (Fla.) Herald, 1963; staff asst. Saigon bur. N.Y. Times, 1965-67, Vietnam corr., 1968-69, 72-74, reporter NYC, 1969-70, chief Conn. bur., 1970-72, investigative reporter N.J. bur., 1974-75, crime/youth violence writer, 1975-76, rewrite desk and spl. assignments to Washington, L.Am. and Mid. East, 1976-84, chief Caribbean bur., 1984-90, drug policy corr. spl. assignments Latin Am., Mid-East, Europe, Baltic States, 1990-95, fin. writer, 1996—. Freelance corr. Atlantic Monthly, Rolling Stone, The Nation, others; fellow Poynter Inst., St. Petersburg, Fla., 1993, U. Nev. Bus. Journalism, 1995; Knight-Bagehot fellow in econs. and bus. Columbia U., 1995-96; Poynter fellow Yale U., 1975;; tchg. assoc., Ga. State U. Internat. Program, 1997-; adj. prof. Baruch Coll., Univ. NY, 2002. Author: Hurricane Force: In the Patch of America's Deadliest Storms, 2007, Paul Volcker: The Making of a Financial Legend, 2004; co-author: No Hiding Place: Inside Report on the Hostage Crisis (in Iran), 1981; contbg. author: Ency. Brit., Insight Guide to Caribbean, Youth Violence, 1992, Writing About Business, 2000, The New York Times What's Doing Around the World, 2001, The New York Times Almanac, 2006. Served with U.S. Army, 1963-65, Vietnam. Recipient Page One award NY Newspaper Guild, 1977, 79; Tom Wallace award Inter-Am. Press Assn., 1980, citation and awards Overseas Press Club Am., 1977, 80, 85, News Analysis award Soc. of Silurians, 1993, Casey medal for meritorious journalism U. Md., 1995, others. Avocations: skiing, sport fishing, running, bicycling, archaeology. Office: NY Times 620 Eighth Ave New York NY 10018 Office Phone: 212-556-3718. Business E-Mail: treaster@nytimes.com.

TREATMAN, PAUL, retired school system administrator; b. NYC, Nov. 19, 1924; s. Meyer Treatman and Sadie Rosenblum; m. Elaine Cohen (dec.); children: Abbe Jo, Scott. BA, Bkyln. Coll., 1948; MA, NYU, 1949, PhD, 1954. Cert. prin. NY, 1956, supr. schs. NY, 1956, dir. Urban edn. programs NY, 1956, sch. adminstr., supr. NY, 1956, sch. adminstr. NJ, 1990. Tchr. NYC Schs., 1949—56, asst. prin., 1956—62, prin. elem. schs., 1962—71, prin. jr. HS, 1971—73; resident edn. cons. to gov. US VI, 1966—67; adj. assoc. prof. ednl. adminstrn. Pace U., NY, 1973—90, Coll. New Rochelle, NY, 1973—90, St. John U., NY, 1973—90. Author: (book) Back to the Trenches, 1993, Haikus for Punsters, 2006. Mem., commr. Monroe Twp. Cultural Arts Com., 2002—04; pres. Ponds Condominium Assn., Monroe Twp., 2002—04; county committeeman Dem. Orgn., Monroe Twp., NJ, 1996—. Pvt. US Army, 1943—45. Decorated Bronze Star US Army; named NYC Educator Yr., Doctorate Assn. NY Educators, 1979. Mem.: Jewish War Vets., Coun. Suprs. and Adminstrs. (pres. 2002—04), French Legion Honor (chevalier), Disabled Am. Vets., Am. Legion Post 522 (2d vice comdr. 2005—), Am. Mensa (hon.). Democrat. Jewish. Avocations: writing, reading, acting. Home: 219 N Pondview Blvd Monroe Township NJ 08831

TREBEK, ALEX, television game show host; b. Sudbury, Ont., Can., July 22, 1940; came to U.S., 1973; s. George Edward and Lucille (Lagace) T.; m. Elaine Callei (div. 1981); m. Jean Currivan, Apr. 30, 1990; 2 children. BA, U. Ottawa, Ont., 1961, PhB. Staff announcer CBC, Toronto, Ont., 1961-73; game show host Wizard of Odds for NBC, Calif., 1973-74, Stars on Ice for Can. TV, 1974-77, High Rollers for NBC, Calif., 1974-79, $128,000 Question for Global TV, Can., 1976-77, Double Dare for CBS, Calif., 1977-78, Battle Stars for NBC, Calif., 1981-82; producer Jeopardy!, Calif., 1984-87, game show host Calif., 1984—, Classic Concentration, Calif., 1987-90, To Tell the Truth, 1991. Owner Creston Vineyards. Film appearances include: Short Cuts, 1993, Spy Hard, 1996, Ellen's Energy Adventure, 1996, Mafia!, 1998, Random Hearts, 1999, The Male Swagger, 1999. Recipient Star on the Walk of Fame, 1999; named Outstanding Game Show Host for Jeopardy!, Daytime Emmy award, Nat. Acad. TV Arts and Sciences, 2006. Mem. Screen Actors Guild, AFTRA, Assn. Can. TV and Radio Artists. Roman Catholic. Avocations: golf, hockey, tennis. Office: Jeopardy! 1020 W Washington Blvd Culver City CA 90232 *

TREBING, DAVID MARTIN, public policy executive; b. Lincoln, Nebr., June 2, 1961; s. Harry Martin and Joyce Alice (Christie) T. BA in Mktg., Mich. State U., 1984; MBA in Fin., Wake Forest U., 1986. Project mgr. mktg.-sales Gilbarco div. Exxon Corp., Greensboro, NC, 1984-86; cash mgmt. analyst Chrysler Fin. Corp., Troy, Mich., 1986-87; sr. corp. fin. specialist Chrysler Corp., Auburn Hills, Mich., 1987-92, mgr. activity-based costing implementation Detroit, 1993-96, mgr. Asia-Pacific Sales Fin., 1996-98; v.p. fin. and adminstrn. Daimler Chrysler Taiwan Co. Ltd., 1998—2001; sr. corp. mgr. regional govt. affairs Daimler Chrysler Corp., Auburn Hills, Mich., 2001—06; dir. US pub. policy SAS Inst. Inc., Cary, NC, 2006—. Mem. Internat. Armed Forces Coun., Detroit, 1987-92, St. George's Soc. N.Y., N.Y.C.; trustee Detroit Hist. Soc.; mem. Chgo. com. Coun. on Fgn. Rels.; mem. Nat. Com. U.S.-China Rels.; bd. dirs. devel. fund Mich. State U.; trustee Hist. Soc. Mich., bd. dirs. Nat. Flag Found. Lt. (j.g.) USNR, 1987-90. Named to Order of St. John, 2006; Inst. fellow, Inst. Pub. Utilities, 1983. Mem. Econ. Club Detroit, Raleigh Com. on Fgn. Rels., Army and Navy Club, Grosse Pointe Club, Church Club NY, Vet. Corps Arty. State NY, SAR (pres. Detroit chpt. 1987-89), Soc. War 1812, Soc. Colonial Wars (sec. gen.), English-Speaking Union, Am. C. of C. in Taipei (bd. suprs.), Pres. Club Mich. State U., Royal New Zealand Yacht Squadron, Chgo. Yacht Club. Avocations: skiing, tennis, travel, skeet/trap shooting, sailing. Office: SAS Inst Inc SAS Campus Dr Cary NC 27513 Office Phone: 919-531-0073. Business E-Mail: david.trebing@sas.com.

TREBON, THOMAS, academic administrator; m. Scottie Trebon. B magna cum laude, Seattle U.; M, PhD, U. Denver. Tchr., adminstr. Seattle U.; acad. dean Coll. Arts and Scis. Rockhurst Coll., Kansas City; provost, v.p. acad. affairs Sacred Heart U., Trumbull, Conn.; with St. Norbert Coll., 1995—2001; v.p. acad. affairs, dean Carroll coll., Helena, Mont.; pres. Carroll Coll., 2001—. Office Phone: 406-447-4401.

TRECKELO, RICHARD M., lawyer; b. Elkhart, Ind., Oct. 22, 1926; s. Frank J. and Mary T.; m. Anne Kosick, June 25, 1955; children: Marla Treckelo Buck, Mary Treckelo Lucchesi. AB, U. Mich., 1951, JD, 1953. Bar: Ind. 1953, U.S. Dist. Ct. (no. and so. dists.) Ind. Pvt. practice, Elkhart, 1953-70; ptnr. Barnes and Thornburg, Elkhart, South Bend, others, 1971-91, of counsel, 1992—. Sec. Skyline Corp., Elkhart, 1959-94, bd. dirs., 1961-91. Bd. dirs. Elkhart Gen. Hosp. Found., Elkhart Park Found.; co-chmn. Elkhart Constl. Bicentennial Commn. Served with USAF, 1945-46. Mem. ABA, Elkhart City Bar Assn. (pres. 1975), Ind. Bar Assn., Elkhart County Bar Assn., Pres.'s Club (U. Mich.), Christiana Country Club, Michiana Club (chmn., U. Mich. Elbel Scholarship award), Rotary. Republican. Office: Barnes & Thornburg 121 W Franklin St Ste 200 Elkhart IN 46516-3200 Office Phone: 574-293-0681.

TRE COOL, (FRANK EDWIN WRIGHT, III), musician; b. Frankfurt, Germany, Dec. 9, 1972; m. Lisea Lyons, Mar. 1995 (div.); 1 child, Ramona; m. Claudia Tre Cool, 2000 (div. 2003); 1 child, Frankito. Played with the band The Lookouts, 1985—90, Screeching Weasel, Samiam; with the band The Network, 2003—; musician Green Day (formerly Sweet Children), 1990—. Musician, writer (albums) Kerplunk, 1992, musician, writer, singer Dookie, 1994 (Grammy award for Best Alternative Music Performance, 1994); musician: (albums) Insomniac, 1995, Nimrod, 1997, Warning, 2000; musician, writer, singer (albums) American Idiot (Viewers Choice award, MTV Video Music Awards, 2005, Am. Music Awards Favorite Rock Album, 2005); composer: (films) Angus, 1995, Godzilla, 1998, Varsity Blues, 1999, Austin Powers: The Spy Who Shagged Me, 1999; voice (films) Live Freaky Die Freaky, 2003, guest appearances Saturday Night Live, 1994, 2005, Mad TV, 2001, (voice) King of the Hill, 1997, and several others. Recipient Video of Yr., Best Group Video, Best Rock Video, Best Editing in a Video, Best Direction in a Video for Boulevard of Broken Dreams, MTV Video Music Awards, 2005, Pop Group of Yr., Rock Artist of Yr., Modern Rock Artist of Yr., Hot 100 Group of Yr., Billboard 200 Album Group of Yr., Billboard Music Awards, 2005, Rock Song of Yr. for Boulevard of Broken Dreams, 2005, Favorite Group, People's Choice Awards, 2006, Record of Yr. for Boulevard of Broken Dreams, Grammy Awards, 2006.

TREE, MICHAEL, violinist, violist, educator; b. Newark, Feb. 19, 1934; s. Samuel and Sada (Rothman) Applebaum; m. Johanna Kreck, Sept. 8, 1966; children: Konrad Efrem, Anna Louise. Diploma, Curtis Inst. Music, Phila., 1955; DFA (hon.), U. South Fla., 1975, SUNY, Binghamton, 1983. Faculty Harpur Coll., Binghamton, 1965-70, Curtis Inst. Music, 1970—, U. Md., College Park, 1981—, St. Louis Conservatory Music, 1982-88, Rutgers U., 1988—2000, Manhattan Sch. Music, 1993—, Juilliard Sch., NYC, 2002—. Co-artistic dir. Phila. Chamber Orch., 1985-88; Misha Elman chair Manhattan Sch. Music, 1991. Violin recital debut at Carnegie Hall, 1954; soloist with major orchs. and at maj. internat. festivals, 1958—; founding mem. Guarneri String Quartet, 1964—, rec. artist for Philips, RCA, Columbia, Nonesuch, Vanguard, Sony Classics, Arabesque records. Recipient Seal of Recognition City of N.Y., 1982. Avocations: hiking, tennis. Home: PO Box 193 Marlboro VT 05344-0193 Office: care Herbert Barrett Mgmt Inc 1776 Broadway Ste 1610 New York NY 10019-2002

TREECE, JAMES LYLE, retired lawyer; b. Colorado Springs, Feb. 6, 1925; s. Lee Oren and Ruth Ida (Smith) T.; m. Ruth Julie Treece, Aug. 7, 1949 (div. 1984); children: James (dec.), Karen Pelletier, Teryl Wait, Jamilyn Smyser, Carol Crowder. Student, Colo. State U., 1943, Colo. U., 1943, US Naval Acad., 1944—46; BS, Mesa Coll., 1946; JD, U. Colo., 1950; postgrad., U. NC, 1976—77. Bar: Colo. 1952, U.S. Dist. Ct. Colo. 1952, U.S. Ct. Appeals (10th cir.) 1952, U.S. Supreme Ct. 1967. Assoc. Yegge, Hall, Treece & Evans and predecessors, 1951—59, ptnr., 1959—69; U.S. atty. Colo., 1969—77; pres. Treece & Bahr and predecessor firms, Littleton, Colo., 1977—91; mcpl. judge, 1967—68; mem. faculty Nat. Trial Advocacy Inst., 1973—76, Law-Sci. Acad., 1964; ret., 1991. Chmn. Colo. Dept. Pub. Welfare, 1963-68; chmn. Colo. Dept. Social Svcs., 1968-69; active Littleton Bd. Edn., 1977-81. With USNR, 1944-46 Recipient award, Colo. Assn. Sch. Bds., 1981, IRS, 1977, FBI, 1977, DEA, 1977, Fed. Exec. Bd., 1977. Mem. Fed. Bar Assn. (pres. Colo. 1975, award 1975), Colo. Bar Assn. (bd. govs.), Denver Bar Assn. (v.p., trustee). Republican. Episcopalian. Home: 12651 N Pebble Beach Dr Sun City AZ 85351-3327 Home Phone: 623-933-8466. Personal E-mail: jltreece@juno.com.

TREFFERT, DAROLD ALLEN, psychiatrist, writer, hospital administrator; b. Fond du Lac, Wis., Mar. 12, 1933; s. Walter O. and Emma (Leu) T.; m. Dorothy Marie Sorgatz, June 11, 1955; children: Jon, Joni, Jill, Jay. BS, U. Wis., 1955, MD, 1958. Diplomate Am. Bd. Psychiatry and Neurology. Resident in psychiatry U. Wis. Med. Sch., 1959-62, clin. prof. psychiatry, 1965—; chief children's unit Winnebago (Wis.) Mental Health Inst., 1962-64, supt., 1964-79, Ctrl. State Hosp., Waupun, Wis., 1977-78; dir. Dodge County Mental Health Ctr., Juneau, Wis., 1964-74; mem. staff St. Agnes Hosp., Fond du Lac, 1963—; exec. dir. Fond du Lac County Mental Health Ctr., 1979-92. Chmn. Controlled Substances Bd. Wis.; chmn. med. examining bd. State of Wis. Author: Extraordinary People: Understanding Savant Syndrome, 1989, 3d edit., 2006, edits. in U.S., U.K., Italy, Japan, Netherlands, Sweden, Korea, China; autism cons. (movie) Rainman, 1988. Fellow Am. Coll. Psychiatrists; mem. AMA, Wis. Med. Soc. (pres. 1979-80), Wis. Psychiat. Assn. (pres.), Am. Assn. Psychiat. Adminstrs. (pres.), Alpha Omega Alpha. Home: W 4065 Maplewood Ln Fond Du Lac WI 54935-9562 Office: 430 E Division St Fond Du Lac WI 54935-4560 Office Phone: 920-921-9381. Business E-Mail: daroldt@charter.net. *People often spend too much time regretting what they are not and far too little time savoring that which they are.*

TREFNY, JOHN ULRIC, retired college president; b. Jan. 28, 1942; s. Ulric John and Mary Elizabeth (Leech) T.; m. Sharon Livingston, 1992; 1 child from previous marriage, Benjamin Robin. BS, Fordham U., 1963; PhD, Rutgers U., 1968; doctorate (hon.), Colo. Sch. of Mines, 2006. Rsch. assoc. Cornell U., Ithaca, NY, 1967-69; asst. prof. physics Wesleyan U., Middletown, Conn., 1969-77, Colo. Sch. Mines, Golden, 1977-79, assoc. prof., 1979-85, prof., 1985—, assoc. dean rsch., 1988—90, head physics dept., 1990—95, v.p. for acad. affairs, dean faculty, 1995—2000, pres., 2000—06. Dir. Amorphous Materials Ctr. Colo. Sch. Mines, 1986-90; cons. Solar Energy Rsch. Inst., Golden, Energy Conversion Devices, Troy, Mich., others. Contbr. articles to profl. jours. Mem. Golden Civic Found., Lutheran Med. Ctr. Cmty. Found., Red Rocks CC Found.; bd. mem. Denver region Inst. Internat. Edn. Recipient Tchg. award AMOCO Found., 1984, Friend of Sci. Edn. award, 1990. Avocations: golf, travel. Home: 14268 W 1st Ave Golden CO 80401 Personal E-mail: jtrefny@mines.edu.

TREFRY, JOHN H., III, chemical oceanographer, educator; b. Boston, Sept. 2, 1947; s. John H. Trefry, Jr. and Phyllis Nelson Trefry; m. Susan E. Page, July 20, 1969; 1 child, Caroline Page Kempf; 1 child, John H. IV. BA, Syracuse U., 1969; MS in Chem. Oceanography, Tex. A&M U., 1973, PhD in Chem. Oceanography, 1977. Asst. prof. Fla. Inst. Tech., Melbourne, Fla., 1978—82, assoc. prof., 1982—87, prof., 1987—. Vis. scientist MIT, Cambridge, Mass., 1987—88. Editor (assoc.): Marine Chemistry. Grant, NSF, 1990—94, NOAA, 1977—85, 1995—2000, US Dept Interior, 1997—. Mem.: Coastal Soc., Outer Continental Shelf Scientific Com., U.S. Dept. of Interior, Minerals Mgmt. Svc., Fla. Acad. Scis. (pres. 2005—07, medalist 2002), Am. Chem. Soc., Am. Geophys. Union. Achievements include first to co-discover deep-sea hydrothermal vents in the Atlantic Ocean; show positive impact of banning lead in gasoline to the Mississippi River and Gulf of Mexico; extensive global research in environmental studies of offshore oil exploration and production. Office: Florida Inst Tech 150 W Univ Blvd Melbourne FL 32901 Home Phone: 321-728-1730; Office Phone: 321-674-7305. Office Fax: 321-674-7212. Business E-Mail: jtrefry@fit.edu.

TREFRY, ROBERT J., health facility administrator; b. Springfield, Vt., Mar. 29, 1947; married. Bachelors' degree, Ga. Inst. Tech., 1970; Masters' degree, George Washington U., 1974. With Greater Southeast Community Hosp., Washington, 1973, adminstrv. asst., 1973-74, asst. adminstr., 1974-79; sr. v.p. North Kansas City (Mo.) Community Hosp., 1979-83; exec. v.p., chief exec. officer St. Agnes Hosp., White Plains, NY, 1983-88; exec. v.p., chief operating officer Carle Found. Hosp., Urbana, Ill., 1988-91; exec. v.p., chief oper. officer Bridgeport (Conn.) Hosp., 1991-94, pres., CEO, 1994—; exec. v.p. Yale New Haven Health Sys., 1996—. With U.S. mil. 1970-71. Office: Bridgeport Hosp 267 Grant St Bridgeport CT 06610-2870

TREFTS, JOAN LANDENBERGER, retired principal; b. Pitts., Jan. 31, 1930; d. William Henry III and Eleanore (Campbell) Landenberger; m. Albert Sharpe Trefts Sr., June 20, 1952 (dec.); children: Dorothy, Albert Jr., William, Deborah, Elizabeth. AB, Western Coll. for Women, 1952; M, John Carroll U., 1982, M, 1984. Lic. and cert. home economist, cert. prin., N.Y., Ohio, supr., biol. sci., econs., voact. edn., pre-kindergarten edn. Summer sch. prin. John Adams H.S., Collinwood and South High, Cleve., 1972—95; ret., 1995. Cons. Cleve. Partnership Program. Trustee Chautauqua Literacy and Sci. Cir., Presbyn. Assn. Chautauqua, NY. Named Tchr. of Yr., Cleve., 1994. Mem.: DAR (state officer 2000—), Ohio Vocat. Assn. (bd. dirs.), Am. Vocat. Assn. (nat. com.), Am. Home Econs. Assn., Presbyn. Assn. (trustee), Dames of Ct. of Honor (pres. gen. 2001—), Colonial Daus. of 17th Century (nat. officer), Daus. Am. Colonists (state officer), Nat. Officers Colonial Clergy (nat. officer, chancellor), Colonial Dames Am. (pres. chpt. 18, nat. officer ct. honor), U.S. Daus. of 1912, Colonial Dames of XVII Century, New Eng. Soc. of Western Res. (pres.), Clearwater Country Club, Cleve. Skating Club, Union Club. Republican. Presbyterian. Avocations: curling, rug hooking, needlepoint. Home: 20101 Malvern Rd Shaker Heights OH 44122-2825 Address: 219 Park Cir Dunedin FL 34698 also: PO Box 761 Chautauqua NY 14722

TREFZGER, RICHARD CHARLES, surgeon; b. Peoria, Ill., Jan. 27, 1948; s. John Dennis and Marilyn Lestilie (Wilson) Trefzger; m. Nancy Ellen Guy, Dec. 19, 1971; children: Emily Jean, Michael Guy. BS, U. Ill., 1970, MD, 1973. Diplomate Am Bd Surgery. Intern in surgery Med. Coll. Wis., Milw., 1973-74, resident in surgery, 1974-75, Presbyn.-St. Luke's Hosp., Chgo., 1975-78; instr. surgery Rush Med. Coll., Chgo., 1977-78; med. dir. Westminster Village Retirement Ctr., Bloomington, Ill., 1980-84, St. Joseph's Trauma Ctr., Bloomington, 1986-96, BroMenn Regional Trauma Ctr., Normal, Ill., 1994-96; chief surgery Bromenn Regional Med. Ctr., Normal, Ill., 1987-88, 94-96, St. Joseph's Med. Ctr., Bloomington, 1989-91, pres. med. staff, 1991-92. Clin. instr. U. Ill. Coll. Medicine, 1980—2006, clin. asst. prof. surgery, 2006—; chmn. bd. dirs. BroMenn Physician Hosp. Orgn., 1995—96; sec. med. staff BroMenn Regional Med. Ctr., 1998, v.p., 99, bd. dirs., 1999—2002, pres. med. staff, 2000—02. Mem. Ill. State U. Civic Chorale, Normal, 1991—98; bd. dirs. Cmty. Cancer Ctr, Bloomington, 1996—2006, pres., 2000; v.p. ofcl. bd. First Christian Ch., Bloomington, 1981—82, 1999—2002, 2005—06, elder, 1980—; rector Cursillo Christianity, 2001; bd. dirs. Barton Stone Christian Home, Jacksonville, Ill., 1979—82. Fellow: ACS (councilor Ill. chpt. 1986—88, mem. Ill. chpt. com. trauma 1996—2003); mem.: AMA, Ill. Surg. Soc. (gov. 1990—94, v.p. elect 1997, v.p. 1998, pres. elect 1999, pres. 2000, trustee 2001—04), Danvers Cmty. Band-Saxophone, Scottish Rite, Rotary (dir. 1982—85, 1994—99, sec. 1995—96, v.p. 1996—97, pres. 1997—98, band-saxophone, Paul Harris fellow 1989), Masons, Alpha Omega Alpha. Avocations: music, travel. Home: 41 Pendleton Way Bloomington IL 61704-6243 Office: Surg Assocs 1404 Eastland Dr Bloomington IL 61701-3532 Office Phone: 309-663-4351. Personal E-mail: MENDR2@insightbb.com.

TREGEMBA, ROBERT D., telecommunications industry executive; married; 2 children. BS in Civil Engring., U. Kans., Lawrence, 1971. With ops. group Southwestern Bell; several exec. positions including v.p. engring. and planning and v.p. mktg. for local exch. divsn. Sprint Corp.; COO Long Distance US West (now Qwest), 1996; exec. v.p. engring. and ops. Qwest Comm. Internat., Inc., v.p. network svcs., 2004—07, exec. v.p. network ops., 2007—. Office: Qwest Comm Internat Inc 1801 California St Denver CO 80202 Office Phone: 303-992-1400. Office Fax: 303-896-8515. *

TREGENZA, NORMAN HUGHSON, investment banker; b. Morristown, NJ, Feb. 1, 1937; s. Norman J. and Marion Esther (Hughson) T.; m. Alyce Virginia Bruene, Aug. 27, 1966; children: Norman Arthur, Suzanne Carol. BA, St. Lawrence U., 1959; MBA, NYU, 1963. Sr. investment officer Tchrs. Ins. and Annuity Assn., NYC, 1960-71; sr. v.p. Republic Funding Corp., NYC, 1971-82; co-founder Tempo Enterprises, 1975; pres. Convent Capital Corp., 1982—. Bd. dirs. Ameritype Corp., Boulder City, Nev. Chmn. stewardship com. Presbyn. Ch., Morristown, 1978, ruling elder, 1979, pres. bd. trustees, 1982; trustee St. Lawrence U., Canton, N.Y., 1983-95, Gill/St. Bernards Sch. (hon.), 1982-96, The Morris Mus., Morristown, 1983—. Mem. St. Lawrence U. Alumni Assn. N.J. (pres. 1970-72), Nat. Coun. USS Constitution Mus. Clubs: Baltusrol Golf, Park Ave., Indian Mound Golf. Home and Office: PO Box 150 Silver Lake NH 03875-0150 Office Phone: 603-367-8888.

TREGGOR, JOSEF PHILIP, music educator, composer, researcher; b. Hartford, Conn., Dec. 29, 1943; s. Philip Noel and Frances Helen (Hitchcock) Treggor; m. Kumi Sato, Oct. 16, 1993. BM in Music Edn. and Violin/cello, U. Hartford, 1968; MS in Biology, Ctrl. Conn. State U., 1983; postgrad. studies, Columbia Pacific U., Calif., 1996—. Instrumental music tchr. Kellogg Jr. H.S., Newington, Conn., 1968—73; orch. dir. John Wallace Mid. Sch., Newington, 1973—80, Newington H.S., 1973—2002; dir. marine mammal program for gifted and talented Newington, Canton, Bloomfield and East Hartford Schs., Conn., 1978—; prodr., music dir. Newington Musical Prodns., Conn., 1980—2002; string specialist music dept. Ridgefield (Conn.) Pub. Schs., 2003—; sr. scientist Marine Edn. and Rsch. Assocs., Farmington, Conn.; dir. Newington H.S. Marine Program for the Gifted and Talented, Newington, Conn. Contbr. film (NEA award for excellence in broadcasting, 1998); composer: (cantata) Mare Eterna, (cantata for Sept. 11) I Just Called to Say Goodbye (performance in St. Paul's Chapel, NYC, 2002); contbr. articles to profl. jours. Scoutmaster Boy Scouts Am., Newington, 1976—80, mem. eagle bd. rev. Conn., 1979—80; marine mammal stranding responder Mystic Aquarium-NMFS, Conn., 2003; venue designer Woodstock (NY) Internat. Film Festival, 2004; v.p. The Ridge, Farmington, Conn., 1999; chmn. elect Conservation Commn., Farmington, 2003, chmn. Newington, 1978—81; mem. Farmington Land Trust, Farmington, Conn., 2005; coord. Maverick Art Colony Centennial, Woodstock, 2005. Named Outstanding Educator, Sea Grant Univs., 1994, Outstanding Music Educator, Internat. Music Festivals, 1995; recipient Master Class, Mtislav Rostropovich, Hartt Coll., 1969, Tchr. of Yr. award, Newington Bd. Edn., 1993, Enhancement of Edn. Through Film award, NEA, 1996, CEA Salutes award, Conn. Edn. Assn., 1996, reception, White Ho., 1999—2000, Presdl. Performance, Pres. and Mrs. Clinton, White Ho., 2000, Congl. citation, US Congress, 2000, Spl. Recognition, Newington C. of C., 2001, citations and resolutions, Conn. Gen. Assembly, 1985, 1989, 1993, 1999, 2000, 2002; fellow, Marine Biol. Lab., Woods Hole, 1982—83, Ctr. for Coastal Studies, Provincetown, MA, 1984; LI Sound Rsch. grantee, Conn, Dept. Environ. Protection, 1990, 1991, 1993. Mem.: Marine Edn. and Rsch. Assn. (chmn. 1997), Marine Biol. Educators Assn., North Am. Marine Mammal Assn., Conn. Music Educators Assn. (com. chairperson, regional chmn. 1967—98), Nat. Music Educators Assn. (life), Conn. Edn. Assn. (life). Republican. Avocations: hiking, travel, sailing, skiing, bagpipes. Home: 9 Talcott Ridge Rd Farmington CT 06032 Office: Marine Edn and Rsch Assocs 9 Talcott Ridge Rd Farmington CT 06032 Home Phone: 860-677-1201; Office Phone: 860-558-9225. Personal E-mail: jtreggor@snet.ner. E-mail: jtreggor@oceaned.org.

TREGURTHA, PAUL RICHARD, water transportation executive; b. Orange, NJ, 1935; married. BSME, Cornell U., 1958; MBA, Harvard U., 1963. Contr., v.p. Brown & Sharpe Mfg. Co., 1969-71; v.p. fin. Moore McCormack Resources, Inc., Stamford, Conn., 1971-73, exec. v.p. fin., 1973-78, pres., COO, from 1978, pres., CEO, chmn., 1987-88; chmn., CEO, co-owner Mormac Marine Group, Inc., Stamford, 1988—. Vice chmn., co-owner The Interlake Steamship Co., 1988—; chmn., CEO Moran Transp. Co., 1994—; bd. dirs. FPL Group, Inc. Trustee emeritus Cornell U., Ithaca, NY; trustee Tchrs. Ins. and Annuity Assn. 1st lt. USAF, 1958—61. Named Baker Scholar, Harvard U., 1963. Office Phone: 203-977-8950.

TREIBLE, KIRK, retired academic and foundation administrator; b. Newton, NJ, Mar. 29, 1941; s. William Bryan and Grace Almond T.; 1 cons, Todd. BS, W.Va. Wesleyan Coll.; MBA, W.Va. U.; LLD, LaGrange Coll. Bus. mgr. Parkersburg C.C., W.Va., 1969-71; devel. officer W.Va. Wesleyan Coll., 1972-75, acting treas., 1975-77; v.p. fin. Southwestern U., Georgetown, Tex., 1977-88; pres. Andrew Coll., Cuthbert, Ga., 1998—2002, now pres. emeritus; ednl. cons., 2002—; exec. dir. United Meth. Found. for Comm., 2003—. Bd. dirs. Citizen Bank, Geogetown, Tex., 1978-88; bd. dirs. Regions Bank, Cuthbert, Ga., 1989-99; cons. Nebr. Wesleyan U.; cons. So. Assn. Schs. and Colls. Chmn. adminstrv. bd. First United Meth. Ch., 1983-85, univ. senate; mem. W.I.H. and Lula E. Pitts Found., Peed scholarship Trust, United Meth. Ch. Served with USAF, 1966-69. Mem. Assn. Pvt. Colls. and Univs. Ga. (pres. dir.), Nat. Assn. Schs. and Colls. Methodist. E-mail: ktreible@aol.com.

TREICHEL, DIXIE ANN, writer, composer; b. Oshkosh, Wis., Apr. 30, 1956; d. Leona and Carl Treichel. Student, U. Wis., Oshkosh, 1974—76, Vienna Internat. Music Centre, Austria, 1976—77; BMus in Composition, U. Ill., Urbana-Champaign, 1980; postgrad., U. Chgo., 1987—88. Ind. artistic cons., composer, sound designer, theater technician, tchr. Creative Collaborations, 1980—. Co-founder, artistic dir. Diverse Arts Ensemble, Urbana, Ill., Chgo., 1979—86; pres., festival dir. New Music Chgo., Chgo., 1986—87; producing cons., technician, condr. Phoenix Spring Ensemble, San Francisco, 1990—97; founder, dir., composer Unique Sounds Ensemble, Mpls., 2000. Composer (musician): (exploratory music) Portal, Internat. Exptl. Intermedia Festival, 2000, (interdisciplinary performance) Morphos, Internat. Exptl. Intermedia Festival, 2001; composer: (string quartet) Pointed Quarks (Onyx String Quartet Competition Award, 1997); sound designer (theatrical sound design) Street Car Named Desire (Drama-Logue Award, 1996); prodr.: (interdisciplinary performance) Seeds (Producing Grant, 1980); author: We'd Support Tolerance and Acceptance of All People, 2004. Radio host KFAI, Fresh Fruit, Mpls., 1998—. Recipient Logue award, Theatrical Sound Design Drama, 1996, Onyx String Quartet Competition award, 1997; fellow Edn. Fellowship, U. of Chgo., 1987-1988. Mem.: New Music Chgo., Am. Composers Forum, Internat. Assn. Women in Music. Achievements include invention of experimental musical instruments. Avocations: swimming, bicycling, reading, poetry, philosophy. Personal E-mail: dixiet007@yahoo.com.

TREIGER, IRWIN LOUIS, lawyer; b. Seattle, Sept. 10, 1934; s. Sam S. and Rose (Steinberg) T.; m. Betty Lou Friedlander, Aug. 18, 1957; children: Louis H., Karen I., Kenneth B. BA, U. Wash., 1955, JD, 1957; LLM in Taxation, NYU, 1958. Bar: Wash. 1958, D.C. 1982, U.S. Dist. Ct. (we. dist.) Wash., U.S. Ct. Appeals (9th cir.), U.S. Supreme Ct. Assoc. Bogle & Gates, Seattle, 1958—63, ptnr., 1964—99, chmn., 1986—94; ptnr. Dorsey & Whitney LLP, Seattle, 1999—. Trustee Am. Tax Policy Inst., 2004—06. Pres. Jewish Fedn. Greater Seattle, 1993-95; chmn. Mayor's Symphony Panel, 1986, Corp. Coun. for the Arts, 1987-88; pres. Seattle Symphony Found., 1986—; trustee, co-chmn. Cornish Coll. of the Arts, 1990-96, chair elect 2003—; trustee The Seattle Found., 1992—, vice chair, 1999-2003, chair, 2003-05; trustee, sec. Samis Found., 1989—; chmn. King County Baseball Pk. Commn., 1995; chmn. task force tax reform Prosperity Partnership Puget Sound Regional Coun., 2006—. Fellow Am. Coll. Tax Counsel; mem. ABA (chmn. taxation sect. 1988-89, sect. del. 1990-96, bd. govs. 2000-03), Wash. State Bar Assn. (chmn. taxation sect. 1975, co-chmn. nat. conf. lawyers and accts. 1997-2000), Greater Seattle C. of C. (chmn. 1993-94), Seattle Rotary (trustee 1998-2000), Seattle Rotary Svc. Found. (v.p. 1995-96, pres. 1996-97). Jewish. Office: Dorsey & Whitney LLP Ste 3400 1420 5th Ave Seattle WA 98101-4010 Home Phone: 206-328-8404; Office Phone: 206-903-8705. Business E-Mail: treiger.irwin@dorsey.com.

TREISTER, GEORGE MARVIN, lawyer; b. Oxnard, Calif., Sept. 5, 1923; s. Isadore Harry and Augusta Lee (Bloom) T.; m. Jane Goldberg, Jan. 24, 1946; children: Laura, Neil, Adam, Dana. BS, UCLA, 1943; LL.B., Yale U., 1949. Bar: Calif. 1950. Law clk. to chief justice Calif. Supreme Ct., 1949-50; law clk. to Assoc. Justice Hugo L. Black U. S. Supreme Ct., 1950-51; asst. U.S. atty. So. Dist. Calif., 1951-53; dep. atty. gen. Calif., 1953; practiced in Los Angeles, 1953—; mem. Stutman, Treister and Glatt, 1953—; instr. U. So. Calif. Law Sch., 1954-98, Stanford U. Law Sch., 1977-81. Mem., former vice chmn. Nat. Bankruptcy Conf.; former mem. adv. com. on bankruptcy rules Jud. Conf. U.S. Contbr. articles to profl. jours. Served with USNR, 1943-46. Mem. Am. Law Inst. Home: 1201 Neil Creek Rd Ashland OR 97520-9778 Office: 1901 Ave of the Stars 12th fl Los Angeles CA 90067 Home Phone: 541-488-3100; Office Phone: 800-201-3030.

TREITEL, DAVID HENRY, aviation executive; b. Lynn, Mass., Apr. 22, 1954; s. Henry David and Lotte (Elkeses) T.; m. Madelynn Drimmer, Sept. 1982 (div. Oct. 1988); m. Amy Gail Granowitz, Apr. 18, 1990. BA in Econs. with honors, Middlebury Coll., 1976; MBA, Columbia U., 1978. Sr. assoc. Simat Helliesen & Eichner, Inc., NYC, 1980-84, v.p., 1984-88, sr. v.p., 1988-90, exec. v.p., 1990-95; pres. Simat Hellliesen & Eichner, Inc., 1995—, CEO, chmn., 1996—. Bd. dirs. Midwest Airlines, Milw., Aircraft Fin. Trust, Wilmington, Del., Lease Investment Flight Trust, Wilmington, Castle 2003-1 Trust, Wilmington, Castle 2003-2 Trust, Wilmington, ISTAT Found. Contbr. articles to profl. jours. Mem. The Wings Club (bd. dirs.). Republican. Avocations: golf, tennis, tournament bridge, travel. Office: Simat Helliesen & Eichner 90 Park Ave Fl 27 New York NY 10016-1308 Business E-Mail: dtreitel@sh-e.com.

TREJO, JOANN, medical researcher; b. Stockton, Calif., Jan. 23, 1964; BS, U. Calif., Davis, 1986; PhD, U. Calif., San Diego, 1992. Postdoctoral fellow Cardiovasc. Rsch. Inst., U. Calif., San Francisco, 1992—2000; asst. prof. pharmacology U. N.C., 2000—. Undergrad. rsch. asst. Lawrence Berkeley Lab. Divsn. Biology and Medicine, 1983—86; tchg. asst. dept. environ. toxicology U. Calif., Davis, 1986, dept. pharmacology, San Diego, 1988—91, dept. biology, 1989. Contbr. articles to profl. jours. Recipient Nat. Hispanic Scholarship Fund award, 1990—91, Minority Scientist Career Devel. award, Am. Heart Assn., 1995; fellow San Diego and Grad. Opportunity, 1986—88, Dissertation, Nat. Rsch. Coun. Ford Found., 1991—92, Pres.'s Postdoctoral, U. Calif., 1993—95; grantee Tng., NIH/NHLBI Cardiovasc. Rsch. Inst., 1992—93; scholar Katherine Larcara, 1982, Jack O'Keefe, 1982, Kiwanis Club Undergrad., 1982. Mem.: LWV, AAAS, Am. Soc. Cell Biology, Soc. Advancement of Chicanos and Native Americans in Sci. Home: 303 Lorraine St Carrboro NC 27510-1121 Office: UNC-Sch Medicine Dept Pharmacology 1106 Mary Ellen Jones Bldg Chapel Hill NC 27514

TREJOS, CHARLOTTE MARIE, humanities educator, consultant; b. Trout Lake, Mich., July 5, 1920; d. Charles Floyd and Lula May (Force) Draper; m. J. Mario Trejos, Jan. 8, 1961; 1 child, J. Mario Jr. Tchg. credentials, State of Calif., 1989; MA, Hawthorne Coll., 1975; DD, Min. Salvation Ch., 1986. Tchr. English El Colegio Anglo-Am., Cochabamba, Bolivia, 1965-66; tchr. Hawthorne (Calif.) Christian Sch., 1966-75; owner Trejos Literary Cons., Carson, Calif., 1976—. Author: My Carson, Your Carson, 1987, Variegated Verse, 1973, Yesterday Was Sunday, 1994; Artist: Am Legion Post Number 6, Nat. Mus. Women Arts, Mus. Latin Am. Art; contbr. articles to profl. jours. Voter registerer Democrats. With U.S. Army, 1942-43. Named Poet of Yr. Nat. Poetry Pub. Assn., 1974; recipient Golden Poet award World of Poetry, 1993. Mem. Soc. Ibero-Am. Escritores de Los Estados Unidos Am. (pres. 1985—, Cert. Recognition 1986). Avocations: music, tap dancing, art, gardening.

TREJOS, FRANKLIN ANTHONY, retired physician assistant; b. Spokane, Wash., July 6, 1955; s. Frank Trejos and Lloydene Louise (Small) Mielbrecht; children: Cerena, Cebrena, Alyssa. Student, We. Coll., 1978; diploma in physician asst., U. Utah, 1984. Advanced EMT Kootenai County Emergency Med. Rescue Svc., Coeur d'alene, Idaho, 1980—82; physician asst. Franklin Park Minor Emergency Ctr., Spokane, 1984—85; physician asst. family practice Cigna Health Plan, Mesa, Ariz., 1985—95; physician asst. gen. surgery, orthop. surgery, neurosurgery Mayo Clinic Scottsdale, Ariz., 1995—97; faculty physician asst. program, physician asst. Midwestern U., Glendale, Ariz., 1997—2001; physician asst. Pain Mgmt. Specialists, Scottsdale, 2000—, Desert Pain Clinic, Scottsdale, 1997—2001, Desert Pain and Rehab. Specialists, Phoenix, 2002—. Adj. faculty Midwestern U. Coll. Osteo. Medicine, Glendale. Fellow: Am. Acad. Physician Assts. Avocations: water-skiing, mountain biking, astronomy, photography, marine life.

TRELA, RICHARD JOSEPH, conservator, educator; s. Edward Thomas and Marie Catherine Trela; m. Theresa JoAnn Piteo, July 29, 1972; children: Elizabeth Sarah JoAnn, Victoria Marie. BS in Biology, Cleve. State U., 1972—72, BA in Art, 1975; MA of Conservation of Artistic and Hist. Works, SUNY, Oneonta, New York, 1978. Cert. Advanced Study In Conservation of Hist. & Artistics Works SUNY. Pvt. practice, Helena, Mont., 1978—84; conservator Coll. of Fine Arts & Comm. Brigham Young U., Provo, Utah, 1984—93; dir. Conservation Ctr. Panhandle-Plains Hist. Mus. West Tex. A&M U., Canyon, Tex., 1993—. Adj. prof. Coll. of Fine Arts and Humanities West Tex. A&M U., 2004—. Grant, MIT Mus. Loan Network, 1997, Amarillo Area Found., 1993, 1994, 1995. Mem.: Western Assn. for Art Conservation, Am. Inst. for Conservation of Hist. & Artistic Works (assoc.). Achievements include research in Developed Conservation Treatment for World War II Bomber Folk Art. Avocations: painting, skating, skiing, swimming, bicycling. Home: 414 Taylor Ln Canyon TX 79015 Office: Conservation Ctr PPHM WTAMU 2503 Fourth Ave Canyon TX 79016 Home Phone: 806-655-5630; Office Phone: 806-651-2241. Office Fax: 806-651-2250; Home Fax: 806-655-5630. Personal E-mail: rtrela@mail.wtamu.edu.

TRELEASE, ALLEN WILLIAM, historian, educator; b. Boulder, Colo., Jan. 31, 1928; s. William, Jr. and Helen (Waldo) T.; children: William C. (dec. 1990), Mary E., John A. AB, U. Ill., 1950, MA, 1951; PhD, Harvard U., 1955. Mem. faculty Wells Coll., Aurora, NY, 1955-67, prof. history, 1965-67, chmn. dept. history and govt., 1963-67; prof. history U. NC, Greensboro, 1967-94, head dept., 1984-92, prof. emeritus, 1994—. Author: Indian Affairs in Colonial New York: The Seventeenth Century, 1960, White Terror: The Ku Klux Klan Conspiracy and Southern Reconstruction, 1971, Reconstruction: The Great Experiment, 1971, The North Carolina Railroad, 1849-1871, and the Modernization of North Carolina, 1991, Changing Assignments: A Pictorial History of the U. of N.C. at Greensboro, 1991, Making North Carolina Literate: The University of North Carolina at Greensboro, from Normal School to Metropolitan University, 2003. Mem. Am., So. Hist. assns., Orgn. Am. Historians, Hist. Soc. NC (pres. 1986-87), AAUP, Phi Beta Kappa, Phi Kappa Phi, Phi Eta Sigma, Phi Kappa Psi. Personal E-mail: atrelease@triad.rr.com.

TREMAINE, SCOTT DUNCAN, astrophysicist; b. Toronto, May 25, 1950; s. Vincent Joseph and Beatrice Delphine (Sharp) T. BSc, McMaster U., Hamilton, Ont., 1971; PhD, Princeton U., 1975. Postdoctoral fellow Calif. Inst. Tech., Pasadena, 1975-77; rsch. assoc. Inst. Astronomy, Cambridge, England, 1977-78; long-term mem. Inst. for Advanced Study, Princeton, NJ, 1978-81; assoc. prof. MIT, Cambridge, 1981-85; prof., dir. Can. Inst. for Theoretical Astrophysics U. Toronto, 1985-96; dir. program in cosmology and gravity Can. Inst. Advanced Rsch., Toronto, 1996—2002; prof. Princeton U., 1997—, chair dept. astrophys. scis., 1998—. Author: Galactic Dynamics, 1987; contbr. articles to profl. jours. E.W.R. Steacie fellow Natural Scis. and Engring. Rsch. Coun., 1988; recipient H.B. Warner prize Am. Astron. Soc., 1983, Steacie prize, 1989, C.S. Beals award Canadian Astron. Soc., 1990, Rutherford medal Royal Soc. Can., 1990, Heinemann prize for Astrophysics, 1997, Brouwer award, 1997. Fellow Royal Soc. London, Royal Soc. Can.; mem. Am. Acad. Arts and Scis. (fgn. hon.), Nat. Acad. Scis. Office: Princeton U Dept Astrophys Sci Peyton Hall Princeton NJ 08544-1001 E-mail: tremaine@astro.princeteon.edu.

TREMAYNE, ERIC FLORY, lawyer; b. Washington, Nov. 29, 1945; s. Bertram William and Frances (Lewis) Tremayne; m. Barbara Ann Williams, Sept. 18, 1982. BA, Westminster Coll., 1967; JD, Washington U., St. Louis, 1973. Bar: Mo. 1973, U.S. Dist. Ct. (ea. and we. dists.) Mo. 1973, U.S. Tax Ct. 2003. Assoc. Tremayne, Lay, Carr, Bauer, Clayton, Mo., 1973—77, ptnr., 1978—; prosecuting atty. City of Wildwood, Mo., 1996—2000. Dir. Option Computer Corp., St. Louis. Bd. dirs. YMCA of Ozarks; campaign aide Citizens for Kit Bond, St. Louis, 1972. With US Army, 1968—70. Mem.: Bar Assn. Met. St. Louis, St. Louis County Bar Assn. (pres. 1983—84, Outstanding Young Lawyer 1981), Sports Car Club Am. (instr. 1979—), Beta Theta Pi (v.p. 1978—90). Home: 433 Eatherton Valley Rd Wildwood MO 63005-4103 Office: Tremayne Lay & Coleman LLP 7777 Bonhomme Ave Ste 1600 Clayton MO 63105-1911 Home Phone: 636-532-6608; Office Phone: 314-863-4151. Business E-Mail: etremayne@tremayne.org.

TREMBLAY, ANDRÉ-MARIE, physicist; b. Montreal, Que., Can., Jan. 2, 1953; m. Marié à Guylaine Séguin; children: Noémie, Rachel. BSc, U. Montreal, 1974; PhD, MIT, 1978. With Energie Atomique du Can. Limitée, 1973-74, MIT, Boston, 1974-75, Inst. de Recherche de l'Hydro-Que., 1976, Cornell U., Ithaca, NY, 1978-80; prof. physics U. Sherbrooke, Que., 1980—, dir. Rsch. Ctr. Physics of Solids Que., 1991-99. Cons. Cornell U., 1981, Ohio State U., 1982, IBM, 1984; vis. scientist Cornell U., 1986-87, Yale U., 2003; vis. rsch. physicist Inst. for Theoretical Physics, Santa Barbara, Calif., 1989, 96, 2000; vis. scientist Brookhaven (N.Y.) Nat. Lab, 1984; assoc. prof. U. Provence, France, 1982, 83, 97, 99, 2000, 02; Can. Rsch. chair in condensed matter physics, 2000—. Contbr. over 120 articles to profl. publs. Recipient Herzberg medal Can. Assn. Physics, Steacie prize Natural Scis. and Engring. Rsch. Coun., 1987, CAP-CRM prize in Theoretical and Math. Physics, 2001, Urgel-Archaubault prize Assn. francophone pour le savoir, 2003; Killam fellow, 1992-94. Fellow: Royal Soc. Can.; mem.: Can. Inst. Advanced Rsch. Office: Sherbrooke U Dept Physics Sherbrooke PQ Canada J1K 2R1 E-mail: tremblay@physique.usherbrooke.ca.

TREMBLAY, MARC, information technology executive; B in Physics Engrng., Laval U., Can.; M in Computer Sci., D in Computer Sci., UCLA. Co-arch. UltraSPARC I Sun Microsystems, Inc., chief arch. UltraSPARC II, chief arch. MAJC program, arch. picoJava processor core, sr. v.p., chief tech. officer Microelectronics, Sun fellow. Mem.: IEEE, Assn. Computing Machinery. Achievements include patents in field. Office: Sun Microsystems Inc 4150 Network Cir Santa Clara CA 95054 Office Phone: 650-960-1300. *

TREMBLAY, MARC ADÉLARD, anthropologist, educator; b. Les Eboulements, Que., Can., Apr. 24, 1922; s. Willie and Laurette (Tremblay) T.; m. Jacqueline Cyr, Dec. 27, 1949; children: Geneviève, Lorraine, Marc, Colette, Dominique, Suzanne. AB, U. Montreal, 1944, L.S.A., 1948; MA, Laval U., 1950; PhD, Cornell U., 1954; PhD (hon.), Ottawa U., 1982, Guelph U., 1983, U. N. B.C., 1994, Carleton U., 1995, U. Ste. Anne, 1997, McGill U., 1998. Research asso. Cornell U., 1953-56; mem. faculty Laval U., 1956-93, prof. anthropology, 1963-68, 81-93, prof. emeritus, 1994, vice dean social scis., 1968-71, dean Grad. Sch., 1971-79, also mem. univ. council.; pres. Quebec Coun. Social Rsch., 1987-91. Dir. Inuit and Circupolar Study Group Laval U., 1991—93; mem. Nunavik Commn., 1999—2001. Author 25 books and monographs in social scis., about 200 articles. Decorated officer Order of Can., gt. officer Order of Que.; recipient Que. Lit. prize, 1965, Innis-Gerin prize Royal Soc. Can., 1979, Molson prize Can. Coun., 1987, Prix Marcel Vincent ACFAS, 1988, Contbn. exceptionnelle Societé de sociologie et d'anthropolotie, 1990, Esdras Minville award Soc. St.-Jean Baptiste, 1991; named to Internat. Order of Merit, Internat. Biog. Inst., Cambridge, Eng., 1990. Mem. Royal Soc. Can. (pres. 1981-84), Acad. des Scis. Morales et Politiques (sec.), Rsch. Inst. Pub. Policy, Am. Anthrop. Assn. (past fellow), Am. Sociology Soc. (past fellow), Can. Soc. Applied Anthropology, Can. Sociology and Anthropology Assn. (founding pres.), Can. Ethnology Soc. (past pres.), Assn. Can. Univs. for Northern Studies (past pres.), Assn. Internat. Sociology, Societe des savants et sci. Can. (v.p., pres. nat. order Quebec 1998-2000). Home: 835 N Orléans St Sainte-Foy PQ Canada G1X 3J4 Personal E-mail: matremgt@globetrotter.net.

TREMBLAY, RONALD JOSEPH, minister, religious studies educator; b. St. Paul, Mar. 24, 1964; s. Lester Joseph and Mary Jane Trombley; m. Susan Kay Tremblay, Aug. 13, 1994; children: Raegan Marie, Logan Joseph. BA, St. Mary's Coll., Winona, Minn., 1988; MDiv, U. St. Mary, Chgo., 1992. Parish diocesan min. Diocese Winona, Minn., 1992—94; tchr. Bishop Kelley H.S., Tulsa, 1994—95; youth min. Christ The King, Tulsa, 1995—. 1st lt. USAR, 1982—92. Named Eagle Scout, Boy Scouts Am., 1981. Independent. Roman Catholic. Avocations: sailing, boating, skiing, hiking, bicycling. Office: Christ The King Cath Ch 1520 S Rockford Tulsa OK 74120

TREMBLEY, DAVE, professional baseball manager; m. Patti Trembley; 1 child, Kevin. BPE, EdM, SUNY, Brockport; grad. student in Sports Psychology, Pa. State U. Tchr., baseball coach Daniel Murphy HS, LA, 1977—79; head baseball coach Antelope Valley Coll., Calif., 1980—84; LA area scout Chgo. Cubs, minor league instr., coach Wytheville club Appalachian League Va., minor league mgr., 1994—2002; mgr. Kinston team Class A Carolina League, 1986; mgr. Navajoa Mex. Pacific League, 1986—87; third base coach Magallanes Venezuelan Winter League, 1987—89; mgr. AA Harrisburg team Pitts. Pirates, 1987, dir. day-to-day operation minor league complex and spring tng. facility Bradenton, Fla., 1990; mgr. AA Wichita team San Diego Padres; mgr. Class A Daytona team Fla. State League, 1995; mgr. AA West Tenn. team So. League, 1999; mgr. AA Bowie team Balt. Orioles, 2003, mgr. AAA Ottawa team, bullpen coach, bench coach, field coord., 2007, mgr., 2007—. Named Ea. League Mgr. of Yr., 1987, Fla. State League Mgr. of Yr., 1995, So. League Mgr. of Yr., 1999; named one of Minor League Baseball's Top Five Mgrs. of the Previous 20 Yrs., Baseball Am., 2001. Office: Balt Orioles Oriole Park at Camden Yards 333 W Camden St Baltimore MD 21201 *

TREMBLY, CRISTY, television executive; b. Oakland, Md., July 11, 1958; d. Charles Dee and Mary Louise (Cassidy) T.; m. Roman Ziombra. BA in Russian, German and Linguistics cum laude, W.Va. U., 1978, BS in Journalism, 1978, MS in Broadcast Journalism, 1979; advanced cert. travel, West L.A. Coll., 1982; advanced cert. rec. engring., Soundmaster Schs., North Hollywood, Calif., 1985. Engr. videotape Sta. WWVU-TV, Morgantown, W.Va., 1976—80; announcer, engr. Sta. WVVW Radio, Grafton, W.Va., 1979; tech. dir., videotape supr. Sta. KMEX-TV, LA, 1980—85; broadcast supr. Sta. KADY-TV, Oxnard, Calif., 1988—89; dir. news tech. Sta. KVEA-TV, Glendale, Calif., 1985—89; asst. editor, videotape technician CBS TV Network, Hollywood, Calif., 1989—90; supr. videotape Sta. KCBS-TV, Hollywood, 1990—91, mgr. electronic news gathering ops., 1991—92; studio mgr., engr.-in-charge CBS TV Network, Hollywood, 1992—2001, mgr. transmission and satellite, 1994—, mgr. videotape, 2001, mgr. syndication, 2001, mgr. prodn., 2001—. Radio operator KJ6BX Malibu Disaster Comm., 1987—; coun. mem. L.A. World Affairs 2000—. Prodr. (TV show) The Mountain Scene, 1976-78. Vol. Ch. Coun., L.A. Riot Rebldg., Homeless shelter work, VA Hosps., Mus. docent; sponsor 3 overseas foster children; fundraiser La Mision Orphanage Ensenada Libr. Flying Samaritans, 2000—; L.A. Dist. rep. Calif.-Pacific conf.comm. commn. United Meth. Ch., 2002—; chmn. adminstrv. coun. Malibu United Meth. Ch., 1993—, choir, 1995—, comm. commn. rep., 2002—; sec., mem. adv. com. Tamassee (S.C.) Sch., 1992—; sr. orgn. pres. Children of the Am. Revolution, Malibu, Calif., 1992—; mem. internat. vis. coun. Outstanding Program Resource; mem. L.A. World Affairs Coun., 2000—. Named one of Outstanding Young Women of Am., 1988, Internat. Vis. Coun. Outstanding Pvt. Resource, L.A. County, Outstanding Female Broadcast Engr., Soc. Broadcast Engrs., 2006; recipient Asst. editor Emmy award Young and the Restless, 1989-90, Golden Mike award Radio/TV News Assn., 1991, 92, Pub. Svc. commendation, County of L.A., 1999, cert. leadership, USIA, cert. commendation, City of L.A., 1999. Mem.: DAR (state chair motion pictures, radio and TV, Calif. 1988—90, Mex. 1990—, nat. vice-chair units overseas Mex. 1998—, organizing regent Baja Calif. chpt. 1999—, state conf. chair 2001, state sec. 2001—04, 2001—, nat. vice-chair media awards 2001—, nat. vice-chair chpt. devel. 2004—, state conf. chair 2004—, vice regent Mex. 2004—07, state regent 2007—, Nat. Outstanding Jr. 1993), ATAS (judge local and nat. Emmy awards 1991—, exec. com. on electronic prodn. 1992—, membership com. 1994—96, awards com. 1994—, engring. awards com. 1997—, gov. 2000—, daytime awards com. 2000—, awards com. 2000—, chair tech. com. 2001—, activites com. 2002—, theatre stds. com. 2002—, diversity com. 2004—), Acad. Canadian Cinema and TV, Nat. Broadcasting Soc. (conf. spkr. 2001), Women in Comm., Soc. Profl. Journalists, Women in Film Internat. (com. 1999—), Am. Women in Radio and TV (bd. dirs. So. Calif. chpt. 1984—85, 1993—2000, pres. 1996—97, Genii award 2007), Travelers Century Club (life; program chair 1987—), Mensa (life), Travelers Century Club (life), Beta Sigma Phi. Democrat. Methodist. Avocations: singing, cooking, travel, genealogy, languages. Home: 2901 Searidge St Malibu CA 90265-2969 Office: CBS TV City 7800 Beverly Blvd Los Angeles CA 90036-2188

TREMBLY, DENNIS MICHAEL, musician; b. Long Beach, Calif., Apr. 16, 1947; s. Fred Lel and Jewel Fern (Bouldin) T. Student, Juilliard Sch. Music, 1965-68. Adj. asst. prof. U. So. Calif., LA, 1981—. Bass player, 1959—, with Los Angeles Philharmonic Orch., 1970-73, co-prin. bass, 1973—. Recipient 2d pl. Internat. Solo Bass competition, Isle of Man, 1978 Mem. Internat. Soc. Bassists. Office: L A Philharm Orch 151 S Grand Ave Los Angeles CA 90012

TREMERE-PINAUD, LIISA ANNE, neuroscientist, educator; d. Arnold Wesley Tremere and Marcella Shirley Fritz; m. Raphael Ribeiro Pinaud. PhD, Dalhousie U., Halifax, 2000. Asst. prof. U. Rochester, NY, 2007. Contbr. articles to profl. jours., scientific papers. Mem.: Soc. Neruosci. Achievements include research in characterization of role of GABA in neuroplasticity of adult neocortex. Home Phone: 991-681-1681; Office Phone: 919-668-3830.

TREML, VLADIMIR GUY, economist, educator; b. Kharkov, USSR, Mar. 27, 1929; came to U.S., 1950, naturalized, 1953; s. Guy Alexey and Lydia Vladimir (Timofeev) T.; m. Emma Miro, July 12, 1952; children—Irene Treml Cagney, Tatiana, Alexey. BA in Econs, Bklyn. Coll., 1955; MA in Econs, Columbia U., 1956; PhD in Econs, U. N.C., 1963. Dept. supr. Bache & Co., NYC, 1953-58; research asso. Inst. for Social Scis., U. N.C., Chapel Hill, 1958-61; asso. prof. econs. Franklin and Marshall Coll., 1961-66; research asso. Inst. Study USSR, Munich, Germany, 1966-67; prof. econs. Duke U., 1967—; dir. Ctr. for Slavic Studies U.S. Dept. Edn. of Duke U., 1991—. Cons. in field; expert Dept. Commerce, The World Bank, other fed. agys., 1971—; vis. Ford research prof. U. Calif., Berkeley, 1984-85; vis. research prof. U. Hokkaido, Sapporo, Japan, 1985. Author: (with others) Structure of the Soviet Economy, 1972, Input-Output Analysis and the Soviet Economy, 1975, Western Sovietology in the Soviet Union, 1999; contbr. reports to publs. of Joint Econ. Com., U.S. Congress; contbr. articles to profl. publs.; editor: Soviet Economic Statistics, 1972; editor, contbg. author: Studies in Soviet Input-Output Analysis, 1977, Alcohol in the USSR, 1982; contbg. editor: Soviet Economy Jour. Trustee Nat. Council for Soviet and East European Research, Inc., Washington, 1978-84. Served with USMC, 1951-53. Grantee Ford Found., 1972-81, Dept. Def.-Advanced Rsch. Project Agy., 1975-76, Dept. State, 1976-77, Dept. Def., 1985-90, Georgetown U., 1984-86, Olin Found., 1989, Internat. Rsch. and Exch. Bd., 1993-96, Nat. Coun. for Eurasian Rsch., 1996-98; Fulbright fellow Moscow U., 1992. Mem. So. Econ. Assn., Am. Econ. Assn., Assn. Comparative Econ. Studies (exec. com. 1972-74), Am. Assn. Advancement Slavic Studies, So. Conf. on Slavic Studies (pres. 1977-78), Phi Beta Kappa. Democrat. Eastern Orthodox. Home: 603 Longleaf Dr Chapel Hill NC 27517-3039 Office Phone: 919-660-1800. Business E-Mail: treml@econ.duke.edu.

TRENBERTH, KEVIN EDWARD, atmospheric scientist; b. Christchurch, New Zealand, Nov. 8, 1944; came to US, 1977; s. Edward Maurice and Ngaira Ivy (Eyre) T.; m. Gail Neville Thompson, Mar. 21, 1970; children: Annika Gail, Angela Dawn. BSc with honors, U. Canterbury, Christchurch, 1966; ScD, MIT, Cambridge, 1972. Meteorologist New Zealand Meteorol. Service, Wellington, 1966-76, supt. dynamic meteorology, 1976-77; assoc. prof. meteorology U. Ill., Urbana, 1977-82, prof., 1982-84; scientist Nat. Ctr. Atmospheric Research, Boulder, Colo., 1984-86, sr. scientist, 1986—, leader empirical studies group, 1987, head sect. climate analysis, 1987—; dep. dir. climate and global dynamics divsn. Nat. Ctr. Atmospheric Rsch., Boulder, Colo., 1991-95. Joint sci. com. for world climate rsch. programme, com. climate changes and the ocean Tropical Oceans Global Atmosphere Program Sci. Steering Group, 1990-94; mem. Climate Variability and Predictability Sci. Steering Group, 1995—2004, co-chair, 1996-99; joint sci. com. World Climate Rsch. Program, 1999-2006, officer 2002-2006, chair observations and assimilation panel, 2004—, mem. global energy and water cycle experiment, 2007—. Editor: Climate System Modeling, 1992, Earth Interactions, 1996-98; contbr. Intergovernmental Panel on Climate Change, 1990, 92, lead author, 1995, 2001, 07; contbr. articles to profl. jours. Recipient Disting. Achievement award Nat. Ctr. Atmospheric Rsch., 2003; grantee NSF, NOAA, NASA. Fellow Am. Meteorol. Soc. (editor sci. jour. 1981-86, com. chmn. 1985-87, Editor's award 1989, Jule G. Charney award 2000), AAAS (coun. del. sect. atmosphere and hydrosphere sci. 1993-97), Royal Soc. New Zealand (hon.), Am. Geophys. Union; mem. NAS (earth scis. com. 1982-85, tropical oceans global atmosphere adv. panel 1984-87, polar rsch. bd. 1986-90, climate rsch. com. 1987-90, global oceans atmosphere land sys. panel 1994-98, panel on reconciling temperature observations, 1999-2000, com. on global change rsch. 1999-02), Meterol. Soc. New Zealand. Home: 5697 Pennsylvania Pl Boulder CO 80303 Office: Nat Ctr Atmospheric Rsch PO Box 3000 Boulder CO 80307-3000 Home Phone: 303-443-1446; Office Phone: 303-497-1318. Business E-Mail: trenbert@ucar.edu.

TRENNEPOHL, GARY LEE, academic administrator, finance educator; b. Detroit, Dec. 6, 1946; s. Leo Donald and Wilma Mae (Tiesnvold) T.; m. Sandra K. Yeager, June 9, 1968; children: Paige E., Adrienne A. BS, U. Tulsa, 1968; MBA, Utah State U., 1971; PhD, Tex. Tech. U., 1976. Asst. prof. aero. studies Tex. Tech. U., Lubbock, 1972-74; asst./assoc. prof. fin. Ariz. State U., Tempe, 1977—82; prof. U. Mo., Columbia, 1982-86, dir. Sch. Bus., 1984-86; prof., head dept. fin. Tex. A&M U., College Station, 1986-91, assoc. dean Coll. Bus., 1991-93, Peters prof. fin., 1992-95, exec. assoc. dean, 1994-95; dean Coll. Bus. Okla. State U., Stillwater, 1995-99; pres. Okla. State U.-Tulsa, 1999—. Mem. faculty options inst. Chgo. Bd. Options Exch., 1987—; bd. dir. Blue Cross/Blue Shield Okla., Tulsa Econ. Devel. Commn., Tulsa Air and Space Mus., Tulsa Symphony Orch. Author: An Introduction to Financial Management, 1984, Investment Management, 1993; assoc. editor Jour. Fin. Rsch., 1983-96; contr. chpts. Encyclopedia of Investments, Options: Essential Concepts; contbr. articles to profl. jours. Capt. USAF, 1968—74. Decorated Commendation medal with oak leaf cluster, Vietnam Svc. medal. Mem. Fin. Mgmt. Assn. (v.p. program 1993, pres. 1993-94). Lutheran. Office: Okla State U Tulsa 700 N Greenwood Ave Tulsa OK 74106-0702 Home Phone: 918-523-8563; Office Phone: 918-594-8001. Business E-Mail: gary.trennepohl@okstate.edu.

TRENT, B. KEITH, lawyer, energy executive; b. Little Rock, Oct. 16, 1959; m. Lucy Trent; 2 children. BSEE with honors, So. Methodist U., 1981; JD with high honors, U. Tex., 1987. Bar: Tex. 1987, US Ct. Appeals (5th cir.), US Supreme Ct., NC. Reservoir/prodn. engr. Arco Oil & Gas, Houston, 1982; atty. Jackson Walker, Dallas; ptnr. Snell Brannian & Trent, Dallas, 1991—2002; gen. counsel litig. Duke Energy, Charlotte, NC, 2002—05, group v.p., gen. counsel, sec., 2005, group exec., chief devel. officer, 2006, group exec., chief strategy and policy officer Charlotte, NC, 2006—07, group exec., chief strategy, policy and regulatory officer, 2007—. Mem. exec. com. Internat. Inst. Conflict Prevention & Resolution; bd. dirs. NAM. Editor (assoc.): Tex. Law Rev. Bd. visitors Wake Forest U. Babcock Grad. Sch. Mgmt.; mem. Youth Edn. Coun. United Way of Ctrl. Carolinas. Mem.: Mecklenburg County Bar, NC State Bar, ABA, Assn. Corp. Counsel, Tex. State Bar, Dallas Bar Assn., Houston Bar Assn., Dallas Inn of Ct., Order of the Coif, Tau Beta Pi. Office: Duke Energy 526 S Church St Charlotte NC 28202-1904 Office Phone: 704-594-6200. *

TRENT, DARRELL M., ambassador, academic administrator, transportation executive; b. Neosho, Mo., Aug. 2, 1938; s. Clarence Melvin and Edna Ruth T.; children: Darrell Michael, Derek Montgomery, Mercy Ruth. AB, Stanford U., 1961; postgrad., Internat. Law Sch., The Hague, Netherlands, summer 1961, Wharton Grad. Sch. Bus., U. Pa., summer 1962; MBA, Columbia U., 1964. Owner, mgr. Trent Enterprises, Kans. and Mo., 1963-66; pres., CEO N.Am. Carmen, Ltd., Del., 1965-68, Assoc. Stores, Inc., Okla., 1967-69, Plz. Supermarkets, Inc., Kans., 1966-69, Food Svc., Inc., Kans., 1966-69, Supermarkets, Inc., Kans., 1966-69, Acton Devel. Co., Inc., Kans., 1966-81; rsch. writer Nixon for Pres., 1968; staff dir. for pers. Presdl. Transition, 1968-69; commr. Property Mgmt. and Disposal Svc., GSA, 1969; dep. asst. to Pres. U.S., 1969-70; exec. dir. Property Rev. Bd., Exec. Office of Pres., 1969-73; dep. dir. Office Emergency Preparedness, 1970-72, acting dir., 1973; mem. Cost of Living Coun., 1973, Oil Policy Com., 1973; chmn. Joint Bd. Fuel Supply and Fuel Transp., 1973; mem. NSC, 1973; chmn. Pres.'s Adv. Coun. CD, 1973; U.S. mem. NATO Sr. Civil Emergency Planning Com., 1973; sr. rsch. fellow Hoover Inst., Stanford U., 1974-81, 89-94, sr. advisor, 1998—, assoc. dir., 1974-81, bd. overseers, 1985-89; dep. campaign mgr. Citizens for Reagan, 1976; dep. campaign mgr., cons. Reagan for Pres. Com., 1979-80, sr. policy advisor, 1980; dir. Office Policy Coordination, Presdl. Transition, 1980-81; U.S. alt. rep. Nato Com. Challenges of Modern Soc., 1982-83; dep. sec. U.S. Dept. Transp., 1981-82, acting sec., 1982-83; chmn. U.S. del. European Civil Aviation Com., U.S. Amb., 1983-88, chmn. Action Devel. Corp., Inc., 1988—; chmn., CEO Rollins Environ. Svcs., Inc., 1983-88, TEC Systems, Inc., 1990-91, Clean Earth Tech., Inc., 1992-93; amb., sr. adv. Ministry of Transp., Iraq, 2003—04; sr. adv. Sec. Def., 2001—04, Transition on Trans. and Budget, 2000; chmn. Trans Adv. Com., Bush Cheney, 2000. Chmn. Fed. Home Loan Bank Pitts., 1983-91; cons. ACDA, 1974-81, HUD, 1974, Dept. Commerce, 1974-76; bd. advisors Chronicle Info. Svcs., Inc., 1984-87; bd. mem. Continental Materials Corp., 1998—. Author: The U.S. and Transnational Terrorism, 1980, Transportation: Policy, Goals, Accomplishments, 1984; co-author: Terrorism: Threat, Reality, Response, 1979; contbr. articles to profl. publs. Bd. regents Pepperdine U., 1985-92; bd. dirs. Found. Teach Econs., 1988-90; dep. chmn. Ronald Reagan Presdl. Found., 1985-88. Mem. Bohemian Club. Republican. Methodist. Office: 1610 S Broadway St Pittsburg KS 66762-5845 Office Phone: 620-231-8640. Personal E-mail: darrell.trent@att.net. Business E-Mail: darrell@trent.org.

TRENT, DONALD STEPHEN, thermo fluids engineer; b. Cloverdale, Oreg., Mar. 29, 1935; s. James Charles and Emma (Bauer) T.; (div. Jan., 1986); children: Steve, Lynn Trent Wooldridge, Greg; m. Alta Mae Brown, Aug. 20, 1994. BSAE, Oregon State U., 1962, MSME, 1964, PhD in Mech. Engring., 1972. Chief scientist (emeritus) Battelle Meml. Inst., Richland, Wash., 1965-96; retired, 1996; cons., 1996—. Cons. in field, 1996—; courtesy prof. Oreg. State U., Corvallis, 1987—; rsch. affiliate MIT, Cambridge, Mass., 1990—; mem. tchg. staff Wash. State U., Richland, 1991—; vis. U. Md., College Park, 1995—. Sgt. U.S. Army, 1958-61. Recipient Fed. Lab. Consortium award, 1992. Mem. ASME, Phi Kappa Phi, Sigma Xi. Achievements include patent on a heat pipe; 2 copyrights on computational fluid dynamics software. Home: 1225 Country Ridge Dr Richland WA 99352-7763

TRENT, ELTON ROGER, educational assessment administrator, writer; b. Manchester, Ohio, Nov. 18, 1940; s. Wallace V. and Jessie Alise Trent; m. Margaret Vivian Lloyd, Aug. 5, 1978; m. Barbara Wilson, Sept. 12, 1964 (div. Mar. 1975); children: Stephanie Trent Flowers, Stacy Trent Dick. BA in Social Studies, The Ohio State U., 1962, BS in Edn., 1962, MA in Mid. Ea. History, 1964, PhD in Psychology, 1974. Cert. edn. admistrv. specialist Ohio. From cons. test devel. to exec. dir. Ohio Dept. Edn., Columbus, 1963—99, exec. dir. sch. standards and assessment, 1999—2000, exec. dir. emeritus, 2001—; v.p., ops. and devel. Am. Testronics, Iowa City, 1984—86; freelance cons. in field Columbus, 2001—. Vis. lectr., stats. The Ohio State U., Columbus, 1978—78. Author: Ohio Survey Tests, 1977, Ohio Interest Survey, 1983, Career Survey, 1984; co-author (with Nancy Cole and Dena Waddell): 3 R's Achievement Test, 1981; co-author: (with Edward Roeber) Contracting For Testing Services in Handbook of Test Development, 2006. Recipient Governor's Employee award, Gov., State of Ohio, 1991, Disting. Svc. award, Ohio Ho. Reps. and Ohio Senate, 2000, Governor's Employee award, Gov., State of Ohio, 1995, Pioneer in Edn. award, Ohio Dept. Edn., 2001. Mem.: Nat. Coun. Measurement in Edn. (mem. editl. bd. 1998—2000), Am. Edn. Rsch. Assn. Presbyterian. Avocations: travel, reading, sports. Home: 5301 Hollister Street Columbus OH 43235-7603 Personal E-mail: roger-trent@columbus.rr.com.

TRENT, HENRY GIBSON, JR., insurance company executive, educator; b. Knoxville; s. Henry Gibson Trent and Katherine Cooper Brabson; m. Sophie R. Shadow, May 5, 1956; children: Henry Gibson III, William Shadow. BS in Social Sci. summa cum laude, Tenn. Tech., Cookville, 1949; MA in History, So. Meth. U., Dallas, 1950. Tchr. Putnam Co. Schs., Cookville, Tenn., 1950—52, Baylor Sch., Chattagnooga, 1952—53; ins. claims Crawford and Co., 1953—64; regional claims supt. Great Am. Ins. Co., Atlanta, 1964—69; claims mgr. Home Ins. Co., Atlanta, 1969—81, claims officer; claims cons. Alexander and Alexander, Atlanta, 1981—86, Gay and Taylor, Atlanta, 1987—90; ret. Pres. Atlanta Claims Mgr. Council, 1974—80. Pres. Freinds of the Libr., Athens, Tenn., 1992—96; chmn. com.

Athens (Tenn.) Kiwanis Club, 1993—2003; com. mem. United Way, Athens, Tenn., 1992—2006; chmn. Internat. Co-Arbitration Bd., Atlanta, 1969—81; mem. Nat. Auto Theft Bd., Atlanta, 1980—81. Mem.: Sons of the Revolution, Atlanta Claims Assn. (ret. pres.), So. Loss Assn., MENSA, McMinn Heritage Mus. (life; bd. dirs. 1992—2006). Republican. Episcopalian. Avocations: fishing, gardening, reading, ballroom dancing, hunting. Home: 229 Lynwood Dr Athens TN 57303

TRENT, JOYCE MILLER, librarian; b. Dayton, Ohio, Dec. 7, 1946; d. Fielding Leo and Joyce (Henry) Miller; m. Robert Cody Trent, Mar. 17, 1973; children— Michael Frederick Cody, Paul Templeton, Mark Fielding, Harley R. B.A., Stephen F. Austin State U., 1969; M.L.S., U. Tex., Austin, 1975. Pub. service librarian Deer Park Pub. Library, Tex., 1969-73; system interlibrary loan librarian San Antonio Pub. Library, 1975-76; dir. system, county librarian Atascosa County Library System, Jourdanton, Tex., 1976-81; library dir. Leon Valley (Tex.) Pub. Library, 1981—. Pres. parish council St. Brigid's Ch., San Antonio, 1980-81; mem. civic affairs com. Tex. Sesquicentennial Com., Leon Valley, from 1984. Recipient Leon Valley Hometown Hero award; named to San Antonio Women's Hall of Fame. Mem. ALA, Tex. Library Assn. (treas. dist. 10, vice chair-elect, then chair, chair small cmty. librs. roundtable 2006, Libr. of Yr. 2005), Leon Valley Bus. and Profl. Assn., San Antonio Geneal. Hist. Soc. (sec. 1977-78). Democrat. Roman Catholic. Home: 5903 Forest Rim St San Antonio TX 78240-3218 Office: Leon Valley Pub Library 6425 Evers Rd San Antonio TX 78238-1453 E-mail: librarian@leonvalley.lib.tx.us.

TRENT, RICHARD H., protective services official, educator, paramedic; s. Richard and Patricia Trent; m. Lorna B. Tweed, July 28, 2006. Student, Hampton U., Va., 2003—07. Registered paramedic Nat. Registry EMT, 2000. Radio disc jockey Z-104, Virginia Beach, Va., 1994—2001; pharmacy technician Sentara Norfolk Gen., Va., 1997—2001; instr. Tidewater C.C., Virginia Beach, 1999—, adj. faculty ALS field internship coord., 2002—; master firefighter paramedic City of Virginia Beach Fire Dept., 2000—; medic firefighter City of Hampton Fire and Rescue, Va. Named Eagle Scout, Boy Scouts Am., 1986. Mem.: Golden Key, Alpha Kappa Mu. Home Phone: 757-472-3473; Office Phone: 757-385-4228. Personal E-mail: rtrent@tcc.edu.

TRENT, ROBERT HAROLD, retired business educator; b. Norfolk, Va., Aug. 3, 1933; s. Floyd Murton and Myrtle Eugenia (White) T.; m. Joanne Bell, Aug. 17, 1951; 1 child, John Thomas BS, U. Richmond, 1963; PhD, U. N.C., 1968. Asst. prof. U. N.C., Chapel Hill, 1968-69; assoc. prof. commerce McIntire Sch. Commerce U. Va., Charlottesville, 1970-74, prof. commerce, 1975-84, Ralph A. Beeton prof. free enterprise, 1985-91; C. & P. Telephone Co. prof. commerce U. Va., Charlottesville, 1991-98, prof. commerce emeritus, 1998—. Co-author: Marketing Decision Making, 1976, 4th edit., 1988; editor: Developments in Management Information Systems, 1974 Mem.: Omicron Delta Kappa, Beta Gamma Sigma.

TRENTANELLI, JOHN ANTHONY, educational administrator; b. Cleve., Oct. 18, 1939; s. Frank Joseph and Marie Theresa Trentanelli; m. Barbara Kay Trentanelli, Apr. 30, 1977; 1 child, Angela Rose. BS in Edn., S.E. Mo. State U., 1969; postgrad., Cleve. State U., 1980-81; M. Edn. and Adminstrn., Prarie View A&M U., Tex., 1987. Substitute tchr. Parma (Ohio) Pub. Sch. Dist., 1977-78; social studies tchr., Am. Fedn. Tchrs. rep. Cleve. Pub. Schs., 1978-81; social studies tchr., dept. chmn. Houston Ind. Sch. Dist., 1981-87, asst. prin., 1987-99, Yonkers (N.Y.) Pub. Sch. Dist., 1999—. Editor Galveston Bay Power Squadron, Bay Breeze, 1999. Treas. Galveston Bay Power Squadron, Clear Lake, Tex., 1999. Mem. ASCD, Pi Kappa Alpha (pres. Dist. 15, 1972-73). Avocation: power and sail boating. Office: Lincoln HS 375 Kneeland Ave Yonkers NY 10704 Home: 25 Spring Pond Dr Ossining NY 10562-2036 E-mail: jtrentanelli@yonkerspublicschool.org.

TRENTON, PATRICIA JEAN, art historian; m. Norman B. Trenton; children: James Davis, Jeffrey Norman. PhD, U. Calif., 1980. Curator of Am. art Denver Art Mus., 1969—74; Editor Am. Personality Drawing Exhibition Catalog, UCLA, 1976; curator of art Union League Club Chgo., 1981; guest curator Western Am. Art, Palm Spring Desert Mus., 1981—82, Bowers Mus., Santa Ana, Calif., 1984, Southwest Mus., Los Angeles, Calif., 1984, Laguna Art Mus., Laguna Beach, Calif., 1987—91, Autry Mus. Western Heritage, Los Angeles, Calif., 1993—97; art curator Los Angeles Athletic Club, 1982—2001; guest curator San Jose Mus. Art, San Jose, Calif., 2003, Irvine Mus., Irvine, Calif., 2005. Lectr. various profl. conf. Contbr. articles various profl. jours.; Crocker Art Mus., Sacramento, Calif., 1990, Laguna Art Mus., Laguna Beach, Calif., 1990, Dixon Gallery and Gardens, Memphis, Tenn., 1991, Montclair Art Mus., Montclair, NJ, 1991, Gene Autry Western Heritage Mus., 1990, Bowers Mus., 1984, Buffalo Bill Hist. Ctr., Wy., 1983, Palm Springs Desert Mus., 1982. Art adv. bd: Yosemite Exhibition, Autry Mus., 2002—. Recipient Susan Koppleman award, 1995, Caroline Bancroft Hist. prize, Indep. Spirits, 1995, Western Heritage Wrangler award, Nat. Cowboy Hall of Fame and Western Heritage Ctr., 1995, Nat. Am. Publisher's award, U. Okla. Press's Publication, 1983; Rockefeller Fellowship award, UCLA, 1977. Mem.: Mus. Western Art (dir. adv. bd. 1985—87), Am. Mus. Assn., Am. Social Studies, Coll. Art Assn., Los Angeles County Mus. of Art, Am. Art Coun. Steering Com., KCET Women's Coun. Home: 10112 Empyrean Way 303 Los Angeles CA 90067 Personal E-mail: pdtrenton@aol.com.

TREPPER, MYRON, lawyer; b. NYC, Mar. 9, 1943; BA, Hunter Coll., 1965; JD, Bklyn. Law Sch., 1968. Bar: NY 1969; US Dist. Ct. (so., ea. dists.) NY 1971; U.S. Ct. Appeals (2nd, 11th cirs.). Co-chmn. Willkie Farr & Gallagher LLP, NYC. Mem. NY County Lawyers Assn., Assn. of Bar of City of NY Office: Wilkie Farr & Gallagher 787 Seventh Ave New York NY 10019-6018 E-mail: mtrepper@willkie.com.

TREPPLER, IRENE ESTHER, retired state senator; b. St. Louis County, Mo., Oct. 13, 1926; d. Martin H. and Julia C. (Bender) Hagemann; student Meramec Community Coll., 1972; m. Walter J. Treppler, Aug. 18, 1950; children: John M., Steven A., Diane V. Anderson, Walter W. Payroll chief USAF Aero. Chart Plant, 1943-51; enumerator U.S. Census Bur., St. Louis, 1960, crew leader, 1970; mem. Mo. Ho. of Reps., Jefferson City, 1972-84; mem. Mo. Senate, Jefferson City, 1985-96; chmn. minority caucus, 1991-92. Alt. del. Rep. Nat. Conv., 1976, 84. Recipient Spirit of Enterprise award Mo. C. of C., 1992, appreciation award Mo. Med. Assn., Nat. Otto Nuttli Earthquake Hazard Mitigation award, 1993, Disting. Legislator award Cmty. Colls. Mo., 1995; named Concord Twp. Rep. of Yr., 1992. Mem. Nat. Order Women Legislators (rec. sec. 1981-82, pres. 1985), Nat. Fedn. Rep. Women, Tesson Ferry Twp. Rep. Club. Mem. Evangelical Ch. Office Phone: 314-487-4959. Personal E-mail: treppler@att.net.

TRESCOTT, SARA LOU, water resources engineer; b. Frederick, Md., Nov. 17, 1954; d. Norton James and Mabel Elizabeth (Hall) Trescott; m. R. Jeffrey Franklin, Oct. 8, 1983. AA, Catonsville C.C., Balt., 1974; BA in Biol. Sci., U. Md., Balt., 1980. Sanitarian Md. Dept. Health & Mental Hygiene, Greenbelt, 1982; indsl. hygienist Md. Dept. Licensing & Regulation, Balt., 1982-85; from water resources engr. to chief dredging divsn. Md. Dept. Natural Resources, Annapolis, 1985-92, chief navigation divsn. Stevensville, 1992-96, chief ops. & maintenance, 1996, dir. maintenance engring. ops., 1996—. Chair adv. bd. EEO, Annapolis, 1990—92; mem. tech. com. Nat. Mgmt. Info. Sys., Balt., 1983. Contbr. articles to profl. jours. Mem.: ASCE, County Engrs. Assn. Md. Democrat. Achievements include research in beneficial uses of dredged materials; development of technology for hydrographic surveying; design of an improved waterway transportation network for Maryland. Home: PO Box 22 Woodbine MD 21797-0022 Office: DNR 580 Taylor Ave Annapolis MD 21401

TRESNOWSKI, BERNARD RICHARD, retired health insurance company executive; b. Chgo., Oct. 14, 1932; s. Al and Luella (Stewart) T.; m. Beverly Ann Gesmond, Nov. 26, 1955; children: Linda, Judy, Mark, Tom, MaryBeth, David; m. Leanne Patricia Irish, Aug. 1985; 1 child, Megan. BS, U. Mich., 1955; MPH in Hosp. Adminstrn., U. Pitts., 1958; JD, Chgo. Kent Coll. Law, 1998. Bar: Ill. 2000. From 2d asst. adminstr. to asst. adminstr. Albert Einstein Med. Ctr., Phila., 1958-61; rsch. assoc. U. Mich., 1961-62; assoc. adminstr. St. Joseph Mercy Hosp., Pontiac, Mich., 1963-67; sr. v.p. Blue Cross Assn., Chgo., 1967-78, exec. v.p., 1977-78, Blue Cross and Blue Shield Assn., Chgo., 1978-81, pres., 1981-94, ret., 1994. Mem. Health Adminstrs. Study Soc.; staff atty. Legal Assistance Foun. Met. Chgo. Author articles in field. Mem. Am. Hosp. Assn., Am. Coll. Health Care Execs., Am. Pub. Welfare Assn., Health Mgmt. Edn. Assn., Soc. Health Svc. Adminstrs., Internat. Found. Employee Benefit Plans, Internat. Fedn. Vol. Health Svc. Funds. (pres.), Am. Health Planning Assn., Ill. State Bar Assn., Chgo. Bar Assn., The Conf. Bd. Personal E-mail: barneyt650@msn.com.

TRESSEL, GEORGE WALTER, TV producer, science educator, consultant; b. Newport, RI, Jan. 23, 1926; s. Walter Eugene and Mary (Sylvia) T.; m. Suzette Saperston (dec. Feb. 1992); 1 child, Paul S. PhB, U. Chgo., 1943, postgrad. studies, 1943-45. Rsch. asst. Dept. Meteorology U. Chgo., 1945-47; prodn. staff WBKB TV, Chgo., 1947-49; mgr. Tressel Studio, Chgo., 1949-59; supr. motion picture unit GE ANPD, Cin., 1959-61; film, TV producer Argonne Nat. Lab., Chgo., 1961-67; dir. comms. rsch. Batelle Meml. Inst., Columbus, Ohio, 1967-76; dir Materials Devel., Rsch., Informal Sci. Edn. Div. Nat. Sci. Found., Washington, 1976-89; project mgr. Children's TV Workshop, NYC, 1989-92; cons. sci. comms. edn. pvt. practice, Rockville, Md., 1992—. Chmn. adv. com. Fernbank Mus. Nat. History, Atlanta, 1982—; tech. adviser Quality Edn. for Minorities, Washington, 1985—, cons. Smithsonian Instn., Washington, 1988—, New Eng. Aquarium, Boston, Ontario Ednl. TV, Toronto, Can., Bronx Zoo. Author: (book) The Future of Educational Telecommunications; contbr. articles to profl. jours., chpts. to books. Past chmn. film adv. panel Ohio Arts Coun., fed. Interagy. Com. on Mus. Support; former mem. bd. dirs. Chgo. Film Coun., Free the Children Trust. Numerous awards from film festivals including Chgo., Atlanta, Edinburgh, Brussels; named to Centennial Honor Roll Am. Assn. Museums, 2006. Fellow AAAS (hon., past chmn. sect. Y), Assn. Sci. and Tech. Ctrs. (hon.); mem. Nat. Assn. Sci. Writers. Avocations: tango, folk dancing. Home: 11121 Powder Horn Dr Potomac MD 20854-2540

TRESSEL, JIM (JAMES PATRICK TRESSEL), college football coach; b. Mentor, Ohio, Dec. 5, 1952; s. Lee and Eloise Tressel; m. Ellen Watson; children: Zak, Carlee, Eric, Whitney. BS cum laude in Edn., Baldwin-Wallace Coll., Berea, Ohio, 1975; MS in Edn., Akron U., Ohio, 1977. Grad. asst. Akron U., 1975; quarterbacks, receivers & running backs coach U. Akron, 1976—78; quarterbacks & receivers coach Miami U., Ohio, 1979—80; quarterbacks coach Syracuse U., NY, 1981—83; quarterbacks, receivers & running backs coach Ohio St. U., Columbus, 1983—85, head coach, 2001—, Youngstown St., 1986—2000. Named Ohio Valley Conf. Coach of Yr., 1987, Regional Coach of Yr., Am. Football Coaches Assn., 1987, 1993, Nat. Coach of Yr., 1991, 1994, 2002, Chevrolet Nat. Coach of Yr., 1993—94, 1997, Eddie Robinson Nat. Coach of Yr., Football Writers Assn., 1994, 2002; recipient Paul "Bear" Bryant award, Nat. Sportscasters & Sportswriters Assn., 2002. Mem.: Fellowship Christian Athletes, Am. Football Coaches Assn. Achievements include coaching Ohio St. U. to the BCS Nat. Championship, 2002; leading Youngstown U. to Divsn. I-AA Nat. Championship, 1991, 93, 94, 97. Office: Woody Hayes Athletic Ctr 2491 Olentangy River Rd Columbus OH 43210 *

TRESTMAN, FRANK D., distribution company executive, director; b. Mpls., Sept. 3, 1934; s. Saul and Rose (Hyster) T.; m. Carol Lynn Wasserman, Apr. 3, 1960; children— Lisa Ellen, Jill Susan BBA with high distinction, U. Minn., 1955. Exec. v.p., treas. Napco Industries, Inc., Mpls., 1965-74, pres., dir., 1974-84; chmn, CEO Mass Merchandisers, Inc., Hopkins, Minn., 1984-86; pres. Trestman Enterprises, Golden Valley, Minn., 1987—. Bd. dirs. Best Buy Co., Mpls., Western Container Corp., Mpls.; chmn. Avalon Real Estate Group., Mpls., Camir Investment Co., Mpls. Mem. bd. govs. Mt. Sinai Hosp., Mpls., 1978-91, Abbott Northwestern Hosp., 1993-2002; chmn. bd. trustees Mpls. Fedn. Endowment Fund; bd. dirs. Harry Kay Found. With USN, 1957-58. Mem. Oak Ridge Country Club (Hopkins). Office: Trestman Enterprises 5500 Wayzata Blvd Ste 1045 Minneapolis MN 55416-1241 Business E-Mail: frank@trestmanenterprises.com.

TRESTON, SHERRY S., lawyer; BA, Dominican U., 1972; MS, Purdue U., 1973; MBA, U. Chgo., 1979; JD with honors, DePaul U., 1983. Bar: Ill. 1983. With planning dept. Fed. Res. Bank, Chgo., 1973—77; with sys. dept. Sears Bank & Trust Co., Chgo., 1977—78; with trust dept. 1st Nat. Bank Chgo., 1978—83; assoc. Sidley Austin LLP, Chgo., 1983—91, ptnr., 1991—. Trustee Dominican U. Office: Sidley Austin LLP 1 S Dearborn Chicago IL 60603-2000 Fax: 312-853-7036.

TRETHEWEY, NATASHA, poet, literature educator; b. Gulfport, Miss., 1966; BA in English, U. Ga.; MA in English and Creative Writing, Hollins U.; MFA in Poetry, U. Mass. Instr. Auburn U.; poet, assoc. prof. English Emory U., Atlanta, 2001—, now assoc. prof. creative writing. Vis. Lehman Brady Joint Chair Professor of Documentary and American Studies Duke U., Durham, NC, 2005—06. Author: Domestic Work, 2000 (Cave Canem Poetry prize, 1999, Miss. Inst. of Arts and Letters Book prize, 2001, Lillian Smith award for poetry, 2001), Bellocq's Ophelia, Native Guard, 2006 (Pulitzer Prize for Poetry, 2007); contbr. poetry to publs. including Agni, Am. Poetry Review, Callaloo, Gettysburg Review, Kenyon Review, New Engl. Review. Recipient Disting. Young Alumna award, U. Mass., Julia Peterkin award, Converse Coll., Grolier Poetry prize, Grolier Bookstore, Cambridge, Mass., Margaret Walker award for poetry, Poets and Writers mag. and QBR: The Black Book Rev., Jessica Nobel-Maxwell Meml. award for poetry, Am. Poetry Rev.; fellow, John Simon Guggenheim Meml. Found., 2003, Nat. Endowment for the Arts, Ala. State Coun. on the Arts, Money for Women/Barbara Deming Meml. Fund; Bunting fellow, Radcliffe Inst. for Advanced Study, Radcliffe U., 2000—01. Office: Emory Univ Creative Writing Program 537 Kilgo Cir Atlanta GA 30322 Office Phone: 404-727-4683. Office Fax: 404-727-4672. E-mail: ntrethe@emory.edu. *

TRETZ, CHRISTOPHE ROBERT, electrical engineer; b. Strasbourg, France, Mar. 22, 1968; arrived in US, 1991; s. Philippe and Liliane (Gué) T. Diplôme d'Ingénieur, Ecole Nationale Supérieure d'Electronique, d'Electrotechnique, d'Informatique, d'Hydraulique de Toulouse, 1991; MS, Columbia U., NYC, 1992, MPH, 1995, PhD, 1997. Rsch. asst. Columbia U., NYC, 1992—97; adv. engr. IBM Rsch., Yorktown Heights, NY, 1997—2000, mem. rsch. staff, 2000; mem. tech. staff design engr. Advanced Micro Devices, Sunnyvale, Calif., 2000—03; sr. cir. design engr. IBM Engring. and Tech. Svcs., San Jose, Calif., 2003—. Rsch. mentor Semiconductor Rsch. Corp., Durham, NC, 1997—. Mem. IEEE (tech. com. 1996-2001, chair pub. rels. and publicity 2001-02, sr. com. 2001-02, chair short course 2002, exec. com. 2003-06, treas. 2003, chair local arrangement com. 2004, tech. program chair internat. sci. conf., 2005, conf. gen. chair, 2006, mem. adv. com., 2007-). Roman Catholic. Achievements include inventor reduction of hysteresis in soi cmos circuits, method and system to tune integrated circuit, method and system for selecting sizes of components for integrated circuits. Avocations: skiing, golf, wine-tasting, gourmet cooking. Home: 235 Briar Ridge Dr San Jose CA 95123-2667 Office: IBM E&TS San Jose Design Ctr 5600 Cottle Rd Mail Stop F010 San Jose CA 95193 Home Phone: 408-888-3852. Business E-Mail: ctretz@us.ibm.com.

TREU, JESSE ISAIAH, venture capitalist; b. NYC, Apr. 10, 1947; BS, Rensselaer Poly. Inst., 1968; MA, Princeton U., 1971, PhD, 1973. Physicist, liaison sci. components, materials group Gen. Electric Co., Schenectady, N.Y., 1973-77; tech. dir. Technicon Corp., Tarrytown, N.Y., 1977-82; v.p. Channing Weinberg-CW Ventures, NYC, 1982-85; gen. ptnr. Domain Assocs., Princeton, N.J., 1986—. Office: Domain Assocs 1 Palmer Sq Princeton NJ 08542-3718

TREUDEN, TERRY S., music educator, director; b. Milw., Sept. 18, 1947; s. John C. and Alice K. Treuden; m. Dorothy A. Gallert; children: Rachel Boehm, Veronica Wescott, Jesse, Bret Hopf, Peter, Jeremy, Stephanie Lamas, Daniel, Angela Hopf, Rebecca Beckler. BS in Music Edn., U. Wis., Milw., 1965—69. Band dir. Wis. Luth. HS, Milw., 1970—99; dir. instrumental music Wis. Luth. Coll., Milw., 1999—. Choir dir. St. John's Luth. Ch. Mem.: Internat. Jazz Educators Assn., Coll. Band Dirs. Nat. Assn., World Assn. Symphonic Bands & Ensembles, Nat. Band Assn., Wis. Bandmasters Assn. Home: W224 N7557 Wooded Hills Dr Sussex WI 53089 Office: Wis Luth Coll 8800 W Bluemound Rd Milwaukee WI 53226 Home Phone: 262-250-8682. Office Fax: 414-443-8600; Home Fax: 414-443-8600. Personal E-mail: ttreuden@wi.rr.com. Business E-Mail: terry.treuden@wlc.edu.

TREUMANN, WILLIAM BORGEN, university dean; b. Grafton, ND, Feb. 26, 1916; s. William King and Dagny Helen (Borgen) T.; m. Mildred Elizabeth Jenkins, Aug. 14, 1948; children— Richard Roy, Robert Evan, Beverly Kay. BS, U. N.D., 1942; MA, U. Ill., 1944, PhD, 1947. Teaching asst. chemistry U. Ill., 1942-45, teaching asst. math., 1945-46, vis. prof., summers 1948-50; from asst. prof. to prof. chemistry N.D. State U., 1946-55; mem. faculty Minn. State U. Moorhead, 1960—, prof. chemistry, 1962—, asso. dean acad. affairs, 1968-70, dean faculty math. and sci., 1970—. Contbr. to profl. jours. Research Corp. Am. grantee, 1954; Minn. U. Bd. grantee, 1967 Fellow Am. Inst. Chemists; mem. Am. Chem. Soc., Am. Assn. U. Profs., Minn. Acad. Sci., Fedn. Am. Scientists, Phi Beta Kappa, Sigma Xi. Home: 1809 11th Ave S Fargo ND 58103 Office: Math Dept Moorhead State U Moorhead MN 56560

TREUTING, EDNA GANNON, retired nursing administrator, educator; b. New Orleans, Dec. 16, 1925; d. Alphonse Joseph and Clara Josephine (David) Gannon; m. August Raymond Treuting, Sept. 4, 1948 (dec.); children: Keith, Karen Treuting Stein, Madeline Treuting LeBlanc, Jaime Treuting Gonzales, Jay (dec.). Diploma, Charity Hosp. Sch. Nursing, New Orleans, 1946; BS in Nursing Edn., La. State U., 1953; MPH, Tulane U., 1972, DPH, 1978. RN, La.; cert. family nurse practitioner Tulane U. Head nurse premature nursery Charity Hosp., New Orleans, 1946-47, head nurse pediatrics, 1947-49; instr. pediatrics Charity Hosp. Sch. Nursing, New Orleans, 1949-52, 54, instr., LPN, 1953; pvt. duty Touro, Hotel Dieu, New Orleans, 1957-59; instr. maternal and child health La. State U. Sch. Nursing, New Orleans, 1960, 65, 69-71; from instr. to prof., sect. head Tulane Sch. Pub. Health and Tropical Medicine, New Orleans, 1972-83; dean, prof. Our Lady Holy Cross Coll. Nursing Div., New Orleans, 1983-84; chief nurse Dept. Health and Hosp., New Orleans, 1987-94. Region IV nurse practitioner Baylor U., Health Edn. and Welfare, 1974-76; citizen amb. to South Am. People to People, 1979; presentor U. Hawaii Pub. Health and Nursing, 1977; planner, advisor, reviewer continuing edn. U. Tenn., Memphis, 1990-95. Author, editor: Occupation Health Nursing, 1979; sect. head, prin. investigator Practitioner Programs Family and Pediatric, 1973-83; item writer Nurse Practitioners, Community Health and Occupational Nursing, 1974-80; mem. editl. bd. to sci. jours. and Nurse Practitioner Jour., 1974-2005. Pres. Oti-Mrs. Internat., New Orleans, 1955-68; sponsor bd. dirs. Holy Cross H.S. Treuting Scholarship, New Orleans, 1966—; hurricane and disaster nurse ARC, New Orleans, 1966-77; v.p. Pandora Carnival Club, New Orleans, 1968-78; alternate state health dept. Commn. Nursing Supply and Demand by Legislation, 1991-94; planner, presentor La. State Rsch. Day, 1990-92. Named outstanding woman in the mainstream world's fair women of achievement, 1984. Mem. AARP (chpt. 3086 pres. 2000, sr. mem., chpt. pres. 2001—, Mandeville chpt. pres. 2001-, Cmty. Svc. award 2006), New Orleans Dist. Nurses Assn. (First J.B. Hickey Meml. Cmty. award 1985, Great 100 Nurse-First Yr. 1987), La. Pub. Health Assn. (Dr. C.B. White Merritorious Diligent Svc. 1990), La. Nurse Practitioners Assn.(Edna Treuting scholarship named in her honor), Tulane U. Alumni Assn. (past pres.), Tulane Med. Alumni Assn. (past pres.), New Image Club of Mandeville (chmn. 1986-2003), Mandeville Rep. Women, Mandeville Srs., New Image Club (chmn. line dance, co-chmn. trips and travel 1995-2004, Young at Heart, New Image Club (chmn. trips and travel, vice chmn.), Delta Omega (nat. and chpt. past pres.), Sigma Theta Tau Republican. Roman Catholic. Avocations: travel, dance, swimming, photography, reading. Home: 1914 Marlin Dr Mandeville LA 70448-1069

TREVATHAN, JAMES E., waste management executive; Various sales and mktg. positions Stauffer Chem. Co.; regional v.p. indsl. WM Holdings Waste Mgmt., Inc., 1997—98, gen. mgr. environ. remediation, v.p. sales and mktg. So. Group, 1998—2000, sr. v.p. sales and mktg., 2000—04, sr. v.p. Ea. Group, 2004—07, sr. v.p. So. Group, 2007—. Office: Waste Mgmt Inc 2859 Paces Ferry Rd Ste 1600 Atlanta GA 30339 *

TREVENA, JOHN HARRY, lawyer; b. Dunedin, Fla., Dec. 28, 1961; s. Ernest Lewis and Lenora Geraldine (Adelson) T.; m. Susan Lee Corris, Nov. 23, 1988; 1 child, Samuel Alan. BA in criminal justice, Univ. S. Fla., 1982; Fla. Police standards, Pinellas Police Acad., 1982; JD, Stetson Univ., 1985. Bar: Fla., U.S. Dist. Ct. (mid. dist.) Fla. 1986; bd. cert. criminal trial lawyer, Fla. Pvt. practice, Largo, Fla. Mem. editl. bd. Fla. Bar Jour., Fla. Bar News, 1990—93. Named Fla. Super Lawyer, 2006—07. Fellow: Litigation Coun. Am.; mem.: Tampa Bay Cath. Lawyers Guild, Inc., Am. Judicature Soc., Pinellas County Criminal Def. Lawyers Assn., Nat. Assn. Criminal Def. Lawyers (life), Fla. Assn. Criminal Def. Lawyers (life), Pinellas County Trial Lawyers Assn. (pres. 2005), Fla. Bar Assn., Clearwater and Am. Bar Assn. Democrat. Roman Catholic. Home: 423 Buttonwood Ln Largo FL 33770-4060 Office: 801 W Bay Dr Ste 509 Largo FL 33770-3220 Office Phone: 727-581-5813. Personal E-mail: trevenalaw@aol.com.

TREVES, JOHN, neurosurgeon; b. Lincoln, Nebr., July 13, 1964; s. Samuel Blaine and Jane Patricia Treves; m. Nicole Renee Davitt; children: Zachary, Grace, Lydia. BS, U. Nebr., Lincoln, 1987, MS, 1989; MD, U. Nebr., Omaha, 1993. Diplomate Am. Bd. Neurol. Surgery, 2005. Resident in neurology U. Nebr. Med. Ctr., Omaha, 1993—99; neurosurgeon Midwest Neurosurgery PC, Omaha, 1999—; chmn. sect. neurosurgery Nebr. Meth. Hosp., Omaha, 2006—. Contbr. articles to profl. jours. Fellow: ACS; mem.: Congress Neurol. Surgeons, Am. Neurol. Surgeons, Alpha Omega Alpha. Avocations: hunting, exercise. Office: Midwest Neurosurgery PC 8005 Farnam St Ste 305 Omaha NE 68114

TREVES, S. TED, nuclear medicine physician, educator, hospital administrator; BA, Nat. Coll. III, Buenos Aires, 1959; MD, U. Buenos Aires, 1966; MA (hon.), Harvard U., Boston, 1990. Resident in radiology Royal Victoria Hosp., McGill U., Montreal, Canada, 1967—68; clin. fellow in radiology Yale-New Haven Hosp., 1968—70, resident/fellow in nuc. medicine, 1970—71; chief divsn. nuc. medicine Children's Hosp. Boston, 1970—, vice chmn. info. sys., 2000—07; exec. dir. nuc. medicine program, dir. joint program nuc. medicine Brigham & Women's Hosp., Boston, 2003—. From asst. prof. to assoc. prof. radiology Harvard Med. Sch., Boston, 1973—87, prof., 1987—. Author, editor: Pediatric Nuclear Medicine, 1985, 3d edit., 2006. Recipient George V. Taplin award, Soc. Nuc. Medicine, 1987, 7th Ann. Holman-Kaplan Meml. lectureship, New Eng. chpt. Soc. Nuc. Medicine, 2004. Fellow: Am. Coll. Nuc. Physicians (Mentor of Yr. 2006—07). Office: Childrens Hosp Boston 300 Longwood Ave PV2C12 Boston MA 02115

TREVILLIAN, WALLACE DABNEY, retired economics professor, dean; b. Charlottesville, Va., May 1, 1918; s. Robert Carr and Mary Anna (Perry) Trevillian; m. Mary Lou McEachern, Nov. 28, 1963 (dec. Dec. 2001); children: Malcolm McEachern, Edward Dabney. BS, U. Va., Charlottesville, 1940, MA, 1947, PhD, 1954; postgrad., U. Calif., Berkeley, 1950-51. Mem. faculty Clemson U., SC, 1947—, from instr. to assoc. prof., 1947-55, prof., head dept. indsl. mgmt., 1955-63, founding dean bus. edn., 1963-80, prof., dean emeritus, 1983—. Mem. Regional Export Expansion Coun., 1965—77; sec. commn. edn. for bus. professions Nat. Assn. State Univs. and Land-Grant Colls., 1975—77; pres. Nat. Coun. Textile Edn., 1978—80. Master sgt. US Army, 1941—45. Vis. scholar, U. Sussex, Eng., 1980—; Econ. in Action fellow, Case Inst. Tech., 1958. Mem.: Thomas Jefferson Soc. Alumni U. Va., Poinsett Club (Greenville, SC), Piedmont Econs. Club, Newcomen Soc., St. Andrews Soc. Upper SC. Episcopalian. Home: 305 Jones Ave Greenville SC 29605-2862

TREVIÑO, FERNANDO MANUEL, academic administrator, medical educator; b. Brownsville, Tex., Aug. 20, 1949; s. Manuel Emilio and Consuelo Ivern (Galindo) T.; m. Dorothy Dell Bullock, Mar. 1, 1980 (div. Mar.1990); m. Lorene Samora Treviño, Feb. 14, 1992; 1 child, Gabriela Alejandra. BS, U. Houston, 1971; MPH, U. Tex., Houston, 1975; PhD, U. Tex., Galveston, 1979. Sr. scientist AMA, Chgo., 1986-88; assoc. prof. U. Tex. Med. Br., Galveston, 1988-94, dir. Ctr. for Cross-Cultural Rsch., 1989-94; prof. and dean S.W. Tex. State U., San Marcos, 1991-93; exec. dir. APHA, Washington, 1993-96; pres. World Fedn. Pub. Health Assns., Geneva, 1995-97; prof., chmn. dept. pub. health and preventive medicine U. North Tex. Health Sci. Ctr., Fort Worth, 1996, dean Sch. Pub. Health, prof. health mgmt. and policy, 1999—2007, dir. Inst. Pub. Health Rsch., 1999—2007, dir. Tex. Inst. for Hispanic Health, 2002—07; chancellor So. Ill. U., Carbondale, 2007—. Exec. editor Am. Jour. Pub. Health, 1993-96. Mem.Interncultural Cancer Coun., 1995—. Capt. U.S. Army, 1971-79. Recipient Disting. Author award Jour. Allied Health, 1995. Fellow Royal Soc. Health (hon.), Polish Soc. Hygiene; mem. Nat. Medicine/Pub. Health Initiative (co-chair 1994-96). Avocations: photography, motorcycles, camping. Office: So Ill U Carbondale Office of Pres Carbondale IL 62901 *

TREVINO, GUILLERMO PRIETO, stock exchange executive; Chmn., CEO Mexican Stock Exch., 2001—. Office: Mexican Stock Exch Paseo de la Reforma No 255 Col Cuauhtemoc 06500 Mexico City Mexico

TREVINO, JERRY ROSALEZ, retired secondary school principal; b. Bee County, Tex., July 9, 1943; s. Geronimo R. and Hilaria (Rosalez) T.; m. Juanita Escalante, Jan. 1, 1985; 1 child, John-Michael. BA, U. Houston, 1967, MEd, 1974; PhD, Kennedy-Western U., 1988; postgrad., U. Tex., Permian Basin, 1988-92. Cert. tchr., adminstr., supt., Tex. Tchr. N.E. Houston Sch. Dist., 1966-70, pub. rels. officer, 1970-72, asst. prin., 1972-76; tchr. Harris County Dept. Edn., Houston, 1968-72, Austin (Tex.) Ind. Sch. Dist., 1977-87; asst. prin. Tex. Youth Commn., Pyote, 1987-91, prin., 1991-96, ret., 1996. Chair edn. seminar, 24th Internat. Congress, Oxford (Eng.) U., 1997; reader, U.S. Dept. Edn., 1996-97; mentor Austin Ind. Sch. Dist., 1996-98; Title VII project dir. U.S. Dept. Edn., Pyote, 1988-96; instr. Austin C.C., 1980-84, chair, Prin. Coun. for Edn. of Lang. Minority Students, S.W. Ednl. Devel. Lab., Austin, 1994-96; rschr. and ednl. cons. Bentiva Edn. Solutions, 2002—. Editor newsletter The Flyer, 1970-72; contbr. articles to profl. publs. Mem. Cmty. Adv. Coun., Pyote, 1987-96; mem. Tex. Children's Mental Health Plan, Monahans, Tex., 1991-96; mem. planning com. Permian Basin Quality Work Force, Midland, Tex., 1992-96; mem. Supt.'s Coun., Pyote, 1987-96. Named Outstanding Adminstr. of Permian Basin (Golden Apple award) Permian Basin Private Industry Coun., 1994. Mem. ASCD, Nat. Assn. for Bilingual Edn., Order Internat. Ambs., Tex. Assn. Secondary Sch. Prins., Civil Air Patrol, Soc. Leading Intellectuals of the World, Tex. Coun. Humanities, League United L.Am. Citizens, World Acad Letters, Tex. State Hist. Soc. Presbyterian. Avocations: flying, travel, reading, landscaping. Address: PO Box 299 Paige TX 78659-0299 Office Phone: 512-253-0222.

TREVINO, LEE BUCK, professional golfer; b. Dallas, Dec. 1, 1939; s. Joe and Juanita (Barrett) T.; m. Claudia Bove; children: Richard Lee, Lesley Ann, Tony Lee, Troy Liana, Olivia Leigh, Daniel Lee. Student pub. schs. Head profl. Hardy's Driving Range, Dallas, 1961-65; asst. profl. Horizon Hills Country Club, El Paso, Tex., 1966-67; chmn. bd. Lee Trevino Enterprises, Inc., 1967—; joined PGA Tour, 1967, PGA Sr. Tour, 1989. Hon. chmn. Christmas Seal campaign, 1969-72, sports ambassador, 1971; mem. Pres.'s Conf. on Phys. Fitness and Sports; grand marshal Sun Carnival Parade, 1969-70, 71-72; mem. sports com. Nat. Multiple Sclerosis Soc. Mem. Spl. Svcs. Unit USMC, with USMC Res., 1956—60. Recipient Hickok Belt award, 1971; named Golf Rookie of Yr., 1967, PGA Player of Yr., 1971, Tex. Pro Athlete of Yr., 1970, Gold Tee award, 1971, AP Pro Athlete of Yr., 1971, Player of Yr. Golf Mag., 1971, Sportsman of Yr. Sports Illustrated, 1971, PGA Sr. Tour Players of Yr., 1990, 92, 94, Internat. Sports Personality of Yr. Brit. Broadcasting Assn., 1971, Rookie and Player of Yr., Sr. PGA Tour, 1990; mem. Tex. Hall of Fame, Am. Gulf Hall of Fame, World Golf Hall of Fame. Achievements include Tournament winner Tex. Open, 1965, 66, N.Mex. Open, 1966, U.S. Open, 1968, 71, Amana Open, 1968, 69, Hawaiian Open, 1968, Tucson Open, 1969, 70, World Cup, 1969, 71, Nat. Airlines Open, 1970, Brit. Open, 1971, 72, Canadian Open 1971, 77, 79, Can. PGA, 1979, Danny Thomas-Memphis Classic, 1971, 72, 80, Tallahassee Open, 1971, Sahara Invitational, 1971, St. Louis Classic, 1972, Hartford Open, 1972, Jackie Gleason Classic, 1973, Doral-Eastern Open, 1973, Mexican Open, 1973, 75, Chrysler Classic, Australia, 1973, PGA Championship, 1974, 84, World Series Golf, 1974, Greater New Orleans Open, 1974, Fla. Citrus Open, 1975, Colonial Nat. Invitational, 1976, 78, Colgate Mixed Team Matches, 1979, Brit. Masters, 1985, U.S. Sr. Open, 1990; King Hassan Moroccan trophy II, 1977; Lancome trophy Benson & Hedges, 1978, 80; 1st golfer to have scored four sub-par rounds in U.S. Open Competition, 1968; leading Money winner, 1970, 2d pl. money winner 1971, 1972; Vardon trophy winner, 1970 1972, 74, 80; Can. PGA, 1983; PGA Seniors Championship, 1994; capt. Ryder Cup Matches, 1985; first golfer to have scored 4 sub-par rounds in PGA competition. Office: Assured Mgmt Co 1901 W 47th Pl Ste 200 Mission KS 66205-1834

TREVISAN, MAURIZIO, epidemiologist; b. Naples, Italy, Jan. 31, 1952; came to U.S., 1979; s. Ilario and Bianca (Bruni) T.; m. Lisa Monagle, Dec. 22, 1983; children: Simona, Alessia, Stefan. MD magna cum laude, U. Naples, Italy, 1977; MS, SUNY, Buffalo, 1989. Cert. in medicine and surgery, Italy, 1977, diabetes and metabolic disease, Italy, 1980. Resident dept. internal medicine Med. Sch. U. Naples, 1977-79; rsch. fellow dept. community health and preventive medicine Med. Sch. Northwestern U., 1979-82; cons. dept. medicine U. Naples, 1983-85; asst. prof. dept. social and preventive medicine SUNY, Buffalo, 1985-88, clinical asst. prof. dept. family medicine, 1988-89, assoc. prof. dept. social and preventive medicine, 1988-92, clinical assoc. prof. nutrition program, 1989-94, assoc. prof. dept. family medicine, 1989-94, interim chair dept social and preventive medicine, 1991-92, prof. dept. social and preventive medicine, 1993—, prof. dept. family medicine, 1994—, interim dean Sch. Health Related Professions, 2001—03, interim dean Sch. Pub. Health and Health Professions, 2003—04, dean Sch. Pub. Health and Health Professions, 2005—; prin. investigator Women's Health Initiative WNY Vanguard Clin. Ctr., 1993—2003, co-investigator Women's Health Initiative, 2003—; chair dept. social and preventive medicine SUNY, 1992—2003. Vis. physician dept. physiology Harvard Med. Sch., 1982; adj. asst. prof. dept. cmty. health and preventive medicine Northwestern U. Med. Sch., 1987-96; adj. prof. nutrition program SUNY, Buffalo, 1994—, dir., health in housing, SUNY, Buffalo, 1996—; adj. prof. dept. cmty. health and preventive medicine Northwestern U. Med. Sch., 1996—. Fellow Am. Heart Assn. Coun. on Epidemiology. Recipient Rsch. Career Devel. award NIH, 1989-94. Fellow, Am. Coll. of Epidemiology; mem. Am. Epidemiol. Soc. Achievements include research in population-based epidemiological investigation of risk factors for essential hypertension and coronary heart disease. Office: SUNY Buffalo Sch Pub Health and Health Professions 435 Kimball Tower Buffalo NY 14214-3000 Business E-Mail: trevisan@buffalo.edu.

TREVITHICK, RONALD JAMES, underwriter; b. Portland, Oreg., Sept. 13, 1944; s. Clifford Vincent and Amy Lois (Turner) T.; m. Delberta Russell, Sept. 11, 1965; children: Pamela, Carmen, Marla, Sheryl. BBA, U. Wash., 1966. CLU, CPA, ChFC, accredited estate planner. Mem. audit staff Ernst & Ernst, Anchorage, 1966, 68-70; pvt. practice acctg. Fairbanks, Alaska, 1970-73; with Touche Ross & Co., Anchorage, 1973-78, audit ptnr., 1976-78. Exec. v.p., treas., bd. dirs. Veco Internat., Inc., 1978-82; pres., bd. dirs. Petroleum Contractors Ltd., 1980-82; bd. dirs. P.S. Contractors A/S, Norcon, Inc., OFC of Alaska, Inc., V.E. Systems Svcs., Inc., Veco Turbo Svcs., Inc., Veco Drilling Inc., Vemar, Inc., 1978-82; with Coopers & Lybrand, Anchorage, 1982-85; field underwriter, registered rep. New York Life Ins., 1985-2000, Princor, 2000—, Prin. Fin. Group, 2000—; instr. acctg. U. Alaska, 1971-72; lectr. acctg. and taxation The Am. Coll., 1972, 97, instr. adv. sales Life Underwriters Tng. Coun., 1988-89; bd. dirs. Ahtna Devel. Corp., 1985-86. Divsn. chmn. United Way, 1975-76, YMCA, 1979; bd. dirs., fin. chmn. Anchorage Arts Coun., 1975-78, Am. Diabetes Assn., Alaska affiliate, 1985-91, chmn. bd. 1988-89, chmn. hon. bd. 1992-96, Am. Heart Assn., Alaska affiliate, 1986-87, Anchorage dist. com., 1994-96, treas. 1996-98, Alaska State Youth Soccer Assn.; mem. Anchorage Estate Planning Coun., 1996-2000, treas., 1998-99, sec. 1999-2000. With U.S. Army, 1967-68. Mem. Fin. Execs. Inst. (pres. Alaska chpt. 1981-83), Soc. Fin. Svcs. Profs. (v.p. Alaska chpt. 1993-94, pres. 1994-96), Alaska Assn. Life Underwriters (sec., treas. 1987-90), Alaska Goldstrikers Soccer Club (pres. 1992-93, youth coach 1985-95, Ina K tournament dir. 1992-98), Petroleum Club (treas. 1996-2000), Beta Alpha Psi. Home: 4421 Huffman Rd Anchorage AK 99516-2211 Office: 1600 A St Ste 110 Anchorage AK 99501-5146 Office Phone: 907-258-5830. E-mail: ron4berta@aol.com.

TREVOR, ALEXANDER BRUEN, information technology consultant; b. NYC, Apr. 12, 1945; s. John B. Jr. and Evelyn (Bruen) T.; m. Ellen Ruth Armstrong, Sept. 21, 1974; children: Anne Wood Roebel, Alexander Jay Bruen. BS, Yale U., 1967; MS, U. Ariz., 1971. Rsch. asst. U. Ariz., Tucson, 1971; systems analyst CompuServe Inc., Columbus, Ohio, 1971-73, dir. systems, 1973-74, v.p., 1974-81, exec. v.p., chief tech. officer, 1981-96, also bd. dirs., 1985-96; pres. Nuvocom, Inc., Columbus, 1996—. Bd. dirs. State Auto Fin. Corp., Columbus. Author (software program) CB Simulator, 1980. Trustee Aviation Safety Inst., Worthington, Ohio. 1st lt. Signal Corps, U.S. Army, 1968-70, Vietnam. Decorated Bronze Star. Mem. IEEE (sr.), SAR (N.Y.), Union Club (N.Y.). Republican. Episcopalian. Home: 1987 My Tern Ct Sanibel FL 33957

TREXLER, EDGAR RAY, minister, editor; b. Salisbury, NC, Sept. 17, 1937; s. Edgar Ray and Eula Belle (Farmer) T.; m. Emily Louise Rees, Aug. 21, 1960; children: David Ray, Mark Raymond, Karen Emily. AB, Lenoir-Rhyne Coll., 1959, LittD, 1978; MDiv, Luth. Theol. So. Sem., 1962; MA, Syracuse U., 1964; student, Boston U., 1960, Luth. World Fedn. Study Project, Geneva, 1977, Luth. World Fedn. Study Project, 1981; LittD (hon.), Midland Coll., 1990; DD, Wittenberg U., 1994. Ordained to ministry United Luth. Ch. Am., 1962; pastor St. John's Luth. Ch., Lyons, NY, 1962-65; features editor Luth. Mag., Phila., 1965-72, assoc. editor, 1972-78, editor, 1978-87, Chgo., 1988-99. Sec. Commn. Ch. Papers, Luth. Ch. Am., 1971-72, mem. staff team comm., 1972-78; chmn. Interch. Features, 1971-76; chmn. postal affairs com. Assoc. Ch. Press, 1983-90, Work Group on New Ch. Periodical, 1985-86; Evangelical Luth. Ch. Am. Cabinet of Execs., 1988-99. Author: Ways to Wake Up Your Church, 1969, Creative Congregations, 1972, The New Face of Missions, 1973, Mission in a New World, 1977, LWF/6, 1978, Anatomy of a Merger, 1991, High Expectations: Understanding the ELCA's Early Years, 1988-2002, 2003; mem. editl. adv. bd. The New World, Roman Cath. Archdiocese of Chgo., 1994-96. Pres. Lyons Coun. Chs., 1964; trustee Lenoir Rhyne Coll., 1975-84, 97-2006. Luth. Theol. So. Sem., 2003—; vol. Interfaith Assistance Ministries, 2000—. Recipient Disting. Alumnus award Lenoir-Rhyne Coll., 1991, Disting. Svc. award Newberry Coll., 1992, Bachman award for disting. leadership Luth. Theol. So. Sem., 1993, Mauney Leadership Awd., Luth. Theol. So. Seminary (alumni awd.), 1999, award of merit for editls. Assoc. Ch. Press, 1991, 98, award of merit for articles in mission mags. Assoc. Ch. Press, 1974, hon. life mem., Assoc. Ch. Press, 1999. Mem. Nat. Luth. Editors Assn. (pres. 1975-77). Home: 2504 Carriage Falls Ct Hendersonville NC 28791-1816 E-mail: etrexler@bellsouth.net.

TREYZ, JOSEPH HENRY, librarian; b. Binghamton, NY, Nov. 23, 1926; s. Joseph Henry and Edna Belle (Leonard) T. BA, Oberlin Coll., 1950; postgrad., Harvard U., 1951; M.L.S., Columbia U., 1952. Circulation asst. N.Y. Acad. Medicine Library, 1950-51; cataloger Columbia Libraries, NYC, 1951-53, Stevens Inst. Tech., Hoboken, NJ, 1953-54; adminstrv. asst. Yale Library, 1955, asst. head catalogue dept., 1955-61; head new campuses program U. Calif., La Jolla, 1961-65; asst. dir. U. Mich. Library, Ann Arbor, 1965-71; dir. libraries U. Wis., Madison, 1971-83, asst. to chancellor, 1983-85; sec.-treas. L.D. Repos, Inc., 1985-87, pres., 1987—. Univ. rep. Consumer Reaction Project for Catalog Card Reprodn. Study, 1961; condr. survey tech. services Fordham U. Libraries, 1967-69, Brandeis U. Libraries, 1970-71; mem. Wis. Gov.'s Com. on Library Devel., 1973-81, Wis. com. Library Services and Constrn. Act, 1979-81; del. U.S. Mission to China on Libraries, 1979 Author: Books for College Libraries, 1967, also articles. Bd. dirs. Wis. Center for Theatre Research. Served with AUS, 1945-46. Mem. Universal Serials and Book Exchange (v.p. 1976, pres., chmn. bd. dirs. 1977), ALA (councilor 1970-74, 77-81, chmn. various coms. 1967-69, recipient Melvil Dewey medal 1970), Assn. Research Libraries (commn. orgn. materials, dir. 1975-78), Midlnet (v.p. 1978-79, pres. 1979-80), Assn. Coll. and Research Libraries (chmn. editorial bd. Choice 1968-70), Wis. Library Consortium (pres. 1975-76), Wis. Assn. Acad. Libraries (chmn. 1973-74), Council U. Wis. Librarians (chmn. 1975-76, 79-80, 81-83), Wis. Library Assn. (bd. dirs. 1973-74, mem. White House Conf. com. 1977-78), Madison Area Library Council (v.p. 1973-74), Mich. Library Assn. (chmn. tech. services sect. 1968-69), N.Y. Tech. Services Librarians (pres. 1959-60). Methodist. Home: 801 N Venetian Dr Miami FL 33139-1031

TREZZA, ALPHONSE FIORE, librarian, educator; b. Phila., Dec. 27, 1920; s. Vincent and Amalia (Ferrara) T.; m. Mildred Di Pietro, May 19, 1945; children: Carol Ann Trezza Johnston, Alphonse Fiore. BS, U. Pa., 1948, MS, 1950, postgrad.; LHD (hon.), Rosary Coll., 1997. Cert. libr. Drexel Inst., 1949. Page Free Library, Phila., 1940-41, 45-48, library asst., 1948-49; cataloger, asst. reference librarian Villanova U., 1949-50, instr., 1956-60; head circulation dept. U. Pa. Library, 1950-56; lectr. Drexel Inst. Sch. Library Sci., 1956—60; editor Cath. Library world, 1956-60; exec. sec. Cath. Library Assn., 1956-60; assoc. exec. dir. ALA, exec. sec. library adminstrn. div., 1960-67, assoc. dir. adminstrv. services, 1960—69; dir. Ill. State Library, Springfield, 1969-74; lectr. Grad. Sch. Library and Info. Sci., Cath. U., 1975-82; exec. dir. Nat. Commn. on Libraries and Info. Scis., Washington, 1974-80; dir. intergovt. library Cooperation Project Fed. Library Com./Library of Congress, Washington, 1980-82; assoc. prof. Sch. Library and Info. Studies Fla. State U., Tallahassee, 1982-87, prof., 1987-93, emeritus prof., 1993—. Mem. Ill. Library LSCA TITLE I-II Adv. Commn., 1963-69; mem. network devel. com. Library of Congress, 1977-82; bd. visitors Sch. Library and Info. Sci., U. Pitts., 1977-80; cons. Becker & Hayes, Inc., 1980-84, King Research, Inc., 1981-82; mem. planning com and steering com. Fla. Gov.'s Conf. on Library and Info. Svcs., 1988-91. Nat. chmn. Cath. Book Week, 1954—56; pres. Joliet Diocesan Bd. Edn., 1966—68; auditor Borough of Norwood, Pa., 1958—60; mem. patron's bd. Fla. State U. Sch. Theater, 2000—; bd. mem. Lafayette Oaks Home Assn., 2002—; Dem. committeeman Lombard, Ill., 1961—69; extraordinary min. of Eucharistic Blessed Sacrament Cath. Ch., 1984—, mem. pastoral coun., 2000—. 1st lt. USAF, 1942—45. Decorated Air medal with one cluster; recipient Ofcl. commendation White House Conf. on Libr. and Info. Svc., 1979, citation State Libr. Agys., 1994, Silver award Commn. Libr. Info. Sci., 1996. Mem. ALA (coun. 1973-82, 88-92, mem. exec. bd. 1974-79, chmn. stats. coordinating com. 1970-74, mem. pub. com. 1975-78, 81-83, 87-89, chmn. adv. com. interface, 1979-83, chmn. membership com. 1983-84, chmn. nominating com. 1988-89, mem. legis. com. 1989-91, adv. bd. ALA Yearbook 1976-91, Assn. Specialized and Coop. Library Agys. legis. com., 1987-89, ad hoc com. White House Conf. on Libr. and Info. Svcs. 1989-91, chmn. awards com. 1990-92, Exceptional Achievement award 1981, J.B. Lippincott award 1989, hon. mem. award, 2007), Cath. Library Assn. (life, adv. coun. 1960—), Ill. Library Assn. (chmn. legis.-library devel. com. 1964-69, mem. exec. bd., libr's. citation 1974), Fla. Library Assn. (bd. dirs. 1987-93, pres. 1991-92, intellectual freedom com., chmn. com. on Fla. Librs. publ., editor, publ. com., planning com., 1991, site com.), Continuing Libr. Edn. Network and Exchange (pres. 1982-83), Internat. Fedn. Library Assns. and Institutions (statistics standing com. 1976-85, planning com.), Coun. Nat. Library Assns. (chmn. 1959-61), Assn. Coll. and Research Librarians (pres. Phila. chpt. 1953-55), Drexel Inst. Library Sch. Alumni Assn. (pres. 1955-56, exec. bd. 1956-60, chmn. chief officers State Library Agys. 1973-74), Chgo. Library Club (pres. 1969), Assn. Library and Info. Sci. Edn. (govt. relation com. 1985-87), Drexel U. Alumni Assn. (Outstanding Alumnus award 1963), Kappa Phi Kappa (chpt. pres. 1948), Beta Phi Mu (hon.). Lodges: K.C. Personal E-mail: atrezza@mailer.fsu.edu. *You can't do anything alone. You need support and you need opposition. Opposition provides you with challenge. Challenge brings out the best in you. But most of all you need faith in God.*

TRIANDIS, HARRY CHARALAMBOS, psychologist, educator; b. Patras, Greece, Oct. 16, 1926; s. Christos Charalambos and Louise J. (Nikokavouras) T.; m. Pola Fotitch, Dec. 23, 1966; 1 child, Louisa. B.Engring., McGill U., 1951; M.Commerce, U. Toronto, Ont., Can., 1954; PhD, Cornell U., 1958; Doctorate (hon.), U. Athens, Greece, 1987. Asst. prof. U. Ill., Champaign, 1958-61, assoc. prof., 1961-66, prof. psychology, 1966-97; cons. USIA, 1970-75, NSF, 1968-75; prof. emeritus, 1997—. Author: Attitudes and Attitude Change, 1971, The Analysis of Subjective Culture, 1972, Varieties of Black and White Perception of the Social Environment, 1975, Interpersonal Behavior, 1977, Culture and Social Behavior, 1994, Individualism and Collectivism, 1995; editor: Handbook of Cross-Cultural Psychology, Vol. 1-6, 1980-81, Handbook of Industrial and Organizational Psychology, Vol. 4, 1994; editorial cons.; Jour. Personality and Social Psychology, 1963-71, Jour. Applied Psychology, 1970-79, Sociometry, 1971-74, Jour. Cross-Cultural Psychology, 1974—, others. Chmn. fgn. grants com. Am. Psychol. Found., 1968-90. Sr. fellow Ford Found., 1964-65; Guggenheim fellow, 1972-73; grantee USPHS, 1956-60, 62; grantee Office Naval Research, 1960-68, 80-85; grantee Social and Rehab. Service, HEW, 1968-73; grantee Ford Found., 1973-75; recipient award Interam. Soc. Psychology, 1981 Mem. Soc. for Psychol. Study of Social Issues (pres. 1975-76), Internat. Assn. Cross-Cultural Psychology (pres. 1974-76), Interam. Soc. Psychology (pres. 1985-87), Soc. for Exptl. Social Psychology (chmn. 1972-74), Soc. for Personality and Social Psychology (pres. 1976-77), Internat. Assn. Applied Psychology (pres. 1990-94). Office: 603 E Daniel St Champaign IL 61820-6232 Home: 2008 Eagle Ridge Ct Apt A Urbana IL 61802-8695 Business E-Mail: triandis@uiuc.edu.

TRIANTAFYLLOU, MICHAEL STEFANOS, engineering educator; arrived in US, 1974, naturalized, 1985; s. Stefanos M. and Penelopi I. (Koutras) T.; m. Joan L. Kimball, Sept. 22, 1985; children: Stefanos R., Kimon K. MS in Ocean Engring., MIT, 1977, MSME, 1977, ScD, 1979. Rsch. assoc. MIT, Cambridge, Mass., 1978-79, asst. prof., 1979-83, assoc. prof., 1983-86, tenured assoc. prof., 1986-90, prof., dir. ocean engring. testing tank, 1990—; dir. Ctr. Ocean Engring., Cambridge, Mass. Vis. scientist Woods Hole Oceanographic Inst., Mass., 1990—; com. chair MIT/Woods Hole Joint Program in Oceanography. Featured cover Scientific American, Science; contbr. articles to profl. jours. Rsch. grantee, Office Naval Rsch., Office Naval Tech., NSF, Doherty Found. Dept. Commerce, 1979—. Mem. Internat. Soc. Offshore and Polar Engrs. (founding mem.), Soc. Naval Architects and Marine Engrs. (papers com., vice chmn. OC-2 com.), Am. Phys. Soc. Greek Orthodox. Office: MIT 77 Massachusetts Ave Rm 5-323 Cambridge MA 02139-4307 Office Phone: 617-253-9614. Business E-Mail: mistetri@mit.edu.

TRIBBETT, CHARLES, executive recruiter; b. Alexandria, La., Oct. 25, 1955; m. Lisa Tribbett; children: Jillian, Charlie, Jason. BA magna cum laude, Marquette U.; JD, U. Va. Former corp. securities atty. Skadden, Arps, Slate, Meagher & Flom, NYC; ptnr. Abraham & Sons; with Russell Reynolds Assoc., Chgo., 1989—; mng. dir., co-head, CEO/bd. services practice Russel Reynolds Assoc., Chgo., 1994—. Bd. trustees Northwestern J.L. Kellogg Bus. Sch.; bd. dirs. Chgo. Children's Mus., AON Pension and Investment Fund, Chgo. Union League. Office: Russell Reynolds Assoc 200 S Wacker Dr Ste 2900 Chicago IL 60606 Business E-Mail: ctribbett@russellreynolds.com.

TRIBBEY, FERN, mathematics educator; b. Libertyville, Ill., July 7, 1952; d. Bernard and Beatrice Freda (Weinstock) H. BA in Elem. Edn., Nat. Coll. of Edn., 1974, MEd in Ednl. Therapy, 1977; cert. in ednl. leadership, Nat. Louis U., 1991. Cert. elem. edn., secondary math. and spl. edn., learning disabilities tchr., Ill., Iowa. Tchr. Evanston (Ill.) Sch. Dist. 65, 1974-76; resource tchr. Mason City (Iowa) Alternative Sch., 1977-79, Pleasantdale Sch. Dist., LaGrange, Ill., 1979-90, Wilmette (Ill.) Sch. Dist. 39, 1990—98; math. coord. K-12 Indian Prairie Sch. Dist. 207, Naperville/Aurora, Ill., 1998—2000; chair math. dept., tchr. Fenton H.S. Dist. 100, 2000—01; chair math. dept. Highland Park (Ill.) H.S. Dist. 113, 2001—, co-chair new tchr. induction program, chair long-range planning steering com., parent univ. co-chair, 2001—. Dist. math. coord. Pleasantdale Sch. Dist. 107, 1985-90; math. adv. sec. West 40 Edn. Svc. Ctr., Northlake, Ill., 1988-90; presenter in field. Contbr. articles to profl. jours. Mem. Nat. Coun. Tchrs. of Maths., Met. Math. Club, ASCD, Ill. Computer Educators, Ill. Coun. Tchrs. of Maths., Phi Delta Kappa. Avocation: music. Home: 1015 Whitfield Rd Northbrook IL 60062-3944 Office: Highland Park HS 433 Vine Ave Highland Park IL 60035 Office Phone: 224-765-2221. Business E-Mail: ftribbey@dist113.org.

TRIBBLE, HAZEL R., elementary school educator; b. Claiborne County, Tenn., May 16, 1941; d. Garland Azure and Beatrice Anderson Riley; 1 child, Hope C. BA in Edn., U. Ky., Lexington, 1966; MS in Edn., Ind. U., Indpls., 1975. Pub. sch. tchr. cert. and life lic. Ind., 1973. Tchr. Fayette County/Lexington Schs., 1966—68, Indpls. Pub. Schs., 1969—. Recipient

Martha Lea and Bill Armstrong Tchr. Educator award, Ind. U. Sch. Edn., 1997; Christie McAuliffe fellow, Nat. Soc. for Intensified Edn. Mem.: Tchrs. English, Ind. Edn. Assn. (former dist. officer). Avocations: writing, studying, teapot collecting, coin collecting/numismatics. Home: 4574 N Guilford Ave Indianapolis IN 46205 Home Phone: 317-925-6050. Personal E-mail: hazelrtribble@msn.com.

TRIBE, LAURENCE HENRY, law educator; b. Shanghai, Oct. 10, 1941; s. George Israel and Paulina (Diatlovitsky) Tribe; m. Carolyn Ricarda Kreye, June 20, 1964; children: Mark Alexander, Kerry Katrina. AB summa cum laude in Math., Harvard U., 1962, JD magna cum laude, 1966; LLD (hon.), Gonzaga U., 1980, U. Pacific, 1987, Am. U., 1987, Ill. Inst. Tech., 1988, Colgate U., 1997; LHD (hon.), Hebrew U., 1998. Bar: Calif. 1966, Mass. 1978, US Supreme Ct 1978, US Ct. Appeals DC Cir. 1978, US Ct. Appeals 9th Cir. 1979, US Ct. Appeals 1st Cir. 1980, US Ct. Appeals 2nd Cir. 1982, US Ct. Appeals 3rd Cir. 1991, US Ct. Appeals 4th Cir. 1993, US Ct. Appeals Fed. Cir. 1993. Law clk. to Justice Matthew O. Tobriner Calif. Supreme Ct., 1966-67; law clk. to Justice Potter Stewart US Supreme Ct., 1967-68; exec. dir. tech. assessment panel Nat. Acad. Sciences, Washington, 1968-69; asst. prof. law Harvard Law Sch., Cambridge, Mass., 1968—71, prof., 1972-82, Ralph S. Tyler, Jr. prof. constl. law, 1982—2004, Carl M. Loeb univ. prof., 2004—; cons. Akin Gump Strauss Hauer and Feld LLP, Washington, 2007—. Chief appellate counsel Calif. Nuclear Litigation, 1978-83; spl. dep. atty. gen. Hawaii, 1983-84; cons. NSF, Nat. Endowment Humanities, White House, others; cons. Marshall Islands for drafting new constitution, 1978-79; chmn. Marshall Islands Jud. Service Commn.; cons. Akin Gump Strauss Hauer & Feld. Author: Technology: Processes of Assessment and Choice, 1969, Channeling Technology Through Law, 1973, The American Presidency: Its Constitutional Structure, 1974, American Constitutional Law, 1978, 88, 2000, Constitutional Choices, 1985, God Save this Honorable Court, 1985, Abortion: The Clash of Absolutes, 1990; co-author: Environmental Protection, 1971, The Supreme Ct.: Trends and Development, 1979, 80, 82, 83, 84, On Reading the Constitution, 1991; co-editor: When Values Conflict: Essays on Environmental Analysis, Disourse, and Decision, 1976; contbr. articles to profl. jours. Recipient Beale Prize, 1966, Detur prize, 1969, Coif Triennial Book Award, 1980, Scribe Award, 1980; nat. debate champion, 1961; named one of 100 Most Influential Lawyers, Nat. Law Jour., 2006; NSF & Woodrow Wilson Fellow, Harvard U., 1962-63. Fellow Am. Acad. Arts and Sciences; mem. ABA (Silver Gavel Award 1991), ACLU, Phi Beta Kappa. Office: Harvard Law Sch 1563 Massachusetts Ave Cambridge MA 02138 Office Phone: 617-495-4621. Office Fax: 617-495-3383. Business E-Mail: tribe@law.harvard.edu. *

TRIBLE, PAUL SEWARD, JR., former United States senator; b. Balt., Dec. 29, 1946; s. Paul Seward and Katherine (Schilpp) T.; m. Rosemary Dunaway; children: Mary Katherine, Paul Seward III. BA, Hampden-Sydney Coll., 1968; JD, Washington and Lee U., Lexington, Va., 1971. Bar: Va. 1971. Law clk. to U.S. dist. judge Albert V. Bryan, Jr., 1971-72; asst. U.S. atty. Office U.S. Atty. Eastern Dist. Va., 1972-74; commonwealth's atty. Essex County, Va., 1974-76; U.S. Congressman 1st Va. Dist., Washington, 1976-82; U.S. Senator from Va., 1982-89; of counsel Shuttleworth, Ruloff & Giordano, Va., 1989—95, Laxalt, Washington, Washington, 1989—91; pres. Jefferson Group, Washington, 1991-95, Christopher Newport U., Newport News, Va., 1996—. Mem.: Washington and Lee Law Rev. Republican. Episcopalian. Office: Christopher Newport Univ Office of President 1 University Pl Newport News VA 23606-2998

TRIBUS, MYRON, management consultant, educator; b. San Francisco, Oct. 30, 1921; s. Edward and Marie D. (Kramer) T.; m. Sue Davis, Aug. 30, 1945; children: Louanne, Kamala. BS in Chemistry, U. Calif., Berkeley, 1942; PhD in Engring, U. Calif., LA, 1949; DSc (hon.) (hon.), Rockford Coll., Ill., 1965, Oakland U., Mich., 1971. Registered profl. engr., Mass.; cert. trainer Feuerstein's method, 1996. Instr. to prof. engring. U. Calif. at Los Angeles, 1946-61; dir. aircraft icing research U. Mich., 1951-54; dean engring. Thayer Sch. Engring., Dartmouth Coll., 1961-69; asst. sec. sci. and tech. Dept. Commerce, Washington, 1969-70; sr. v.p. tech. and engring. info. tech. group Xerox Corp., Rochester, NY, 1970-74; dir. Center for Advanced Engring. Study, Mass. Inst. Tech., Cambridge, 1974-86; cons. in quality mgmt., 1986—; dir. rsch., co-founder Exergy, Inc., Hayward, Calif., 1987-99. Cons. heat transfer Gen. Electric Co., 1950; cons. Fed. Office Saline Water; tech. adv. bd. Dept. Commerce; adviser to NATO, 1953; mem. Nat. Adv. Com. Oceans and Atmosphere, 1971-72. Author: Thermostatics and Thermodynamics, 1961, Rational Descriptions, Decisions and Designs, 1969; Contbr. articles to profl. jours. Bd. govs. Technion, Haifa, Israel, 1973-84. Served to capt. USAAF, 1942-46. Recipient Thurman H. Bane award Inst. Aero. Scis., 1945, Wright Bros. medal Soc. Automotive Engrs., 1945; Alfred Noble prize Engring. Socs., 1952, Robert Fletcher awrd Thayer Sch. Engring., Dartmouth Coll., 1994; named UCLA Alumnus of Yr., 1972. Mem. ASME, IEEE, NSPE. Office Phone: 850-435-7490. Personal E-mail: mtribus@earthlink.net.

TRICARICO, JOSEPH ARCHANGELO, lawyer; b. NYC, May 6, 1940; s. Nicholas and Frances Tricarico; m. Mildred Grandi, Feb. 12, 1972; 1 child, Nicholas. BS, St. Johns U., 1963, JD, 1967. V.p. trust counsel U.S. Trust Co. N.Y., NYC, 1973—. Author: Generation-Skipping Transfers: A Primer, 1984, Credit Card Rape: Learn How It Is Done; Learn How It Was Undone, 2002. Pro bono arbitrator small claims ct. Civil Ct. of City of N.Y., S.I., 1981—; trustee Eger Health Care Ctr., S.I., 1990—. Mem. ABA (com. bus. law 1990—, vice chair com. generation-skipping transfers 1993—, com. taxation 1984—), Am. Corp. Counsel Assn. (com. securities litigation 1991—, com. environ. law 1992—), N.Y. Bankers Assn. (spl. counsel trust legis. and regulatory com. 1991—), N.Y. Bar Assn., Assn. Bar City N.Y., New York County Lawyers Assn. (com. on legis. 1989—), Am. Judges Assn. (hon. judge 1985—), Am. Inn of Ct. Office: US Trust Co NY 114 W 47th St New York NY 10036-1510 E-mail: jtricarico@ustrust.com.

TRICARO, ROBERT COLLET, biologist, educator, editor, poet; s. Robert and Frances Tricaro. BS cum laude, Adelphi Coll., 1959, MA in Ednl. Philosophy, 1961; MS in Biology, Adelphi U., 1966; Writing Program in Creative Writing, Columbia U., 1998; Writing Program in Poetry, U. Mass., 2001. Asst. prof., then assoc. prof. Miami-Dade C.C., Miami, 1965—80; pres. Med. Data Control, Inc., San Francisco, 1980—95; adj. faculty mem. City Coll. San Francisco, 1981—; co-editor poetry mag. Mother Earth Internat., San Francisco, 2003—; bd. dir. Internat. Poetry Museum Project, 2005—. Cons. in med. mgmt. Author: (book of poetry) Letting Go, 2006; contbr. poetry to lit. jours. Pub. rels. specialist L'Alliance Française, Miami, 1974—78. With US Army, 1954—56. Recipient Svc. award, L'Alliance Française, 1976; biology grantee, NSF, 1963—65. Mem.: Bay Area Poets' Coalition (bd. mem. 2005—, sec. 2005). Independent. Luth. Avocations: opera, sports, poetry. Home: 601 Van Ness Ave Unit 22 San Francisco CA 94102 Office: Internat Poetry Soc 934 Brannan St 2d Fl San Francisco CA 94103

TRICE, DAVID A., oil industry executive; BA managerial sci., Duke Univ.; JD, Columbia Univ. With Roy M. Huffington, Inc., 1980—89; vice-pres., dir., CFO Newfield Exploration Co., 1989—91; CEO, dir. Huffco Group, Inc., 1991—97; chmn, pres., CEO Newfield Exploration Co., Houston, 2000—07, chmn., CEO, 2007—. Mem. bd. dir. Hornbeck Offshore Services, Inc., Grant Prideco, Inc. and NJ Resources. Mem. bd. trustees Houston Museum Natural Sci. Mem.: Independent Petroleum Assn. Am., Domestic Petroleum Coun. Office: Newfield Exploration Co Ste 2020 363 N Sam Houston Pkwy E Houston TX 77060 *

TRICE, WILLIAM HENRY, III, lawyer; b. Vicksburg, Miss., Nov. 19, 1946; s. William Henry and Ethel Preston Trice; m. Judy Martha Trice, July 26, 1976; 1 child, William Carl. BA, U. Ark., 1968, JD, 1971. Bar: Ark. 1974, U.S. Dist. Ct. (ea. and we. dists.) Ark., U.S. Ct. Appeals (8th cir.). Staff atty. Ark. Hwy. Dept., Little Rock, 1974—75; dep. pros. atty. 6th Jur. Dist. Ark., Little Rock, 1975—77; atty. Howell Trice Hope & Files, Little Rock, 1977—2005; of counsel Hope Fugua & Cambell P.A., 2005—. Atty. Ark. State Bd. Dental Examiners, Little Rock, 1981—, Ark. State Med. Bd., Little Rock, 1989—, Ark. State Bd. Optometry, Little Rock, 2000—. Sr. warden vestry St. Margaret's Episcopal Ch., Little Rock, 1999—2001; lobbiest Dist. Judges Assn. Ark., 2000—. Lt. col. ret. Ark. Army Nat. Guard. Mem.: Ark. Criminal Def. Lawyers Assn. (pres.), Ark. Trial Lawyers Assn. (bd. govs.), Scottish Rite Freemasonry (venerable master 1995—2001). Democrat. Episcopalian. Office: Hope Fugua & Campbell PA Ste 400 425 Capital Ave Little Rock AR 72201 Office Phone: 501-372-4144. Business E-Mail: btrice@hfc-law.com.

TRICHOPOULOS, DIMITRIOS VASSILIOS, epidemiologist, educator; b. Volos, Greece, Dec. 9, 1938; s. Vassilios Konstantinou and Alexandra Dimitrios (Kataropoulou) T.; m. Antonia Athanasiou Polychronopoulou, June 17, 1967. MD, Athens U., Greece, 1963, PhD, 1971; MS, Harvard Sch. Pub. Health, 1968; MD honoris causa, Uppsala U., Sweden, 1994. Diplomate Am. Coll. Epidemiology. Lectr. preventive medicine U. Athens Med. Sch., 1965-67, prof., chair preventive medicine, 1972—2005; lectr. epidemiology Harvard Sch. Pub. Health, Boston, 1969-70, prof. cancer prevention and epidemiology, 1989—; prof., dir. Harvard Ctr. Cancer Prevention, Boston, 1994-97. Chmn. health group Coun. European Union, Brussels, 1988; adj. prof. med. epidemiology Karolinska Inst., Sweden, 1998—. Editor: Teaching Epidemiology, 1992, 2001, Textbook of Cancer Epidemiology, 2002; contbr. numerous articles to profl. jours. Decorated officier Ordre Palmes Academiques (France), Commdr. of Honor, Greece. Mem. Acad. of Athens, Royal Acad. Medicine Belgium (corr., fgn.), Nat. Acad. Medicine France (corr., fgn.), Athens Club. Greek Orthodox. Office: Harvard Sch Pub Health 677 Huntington Ave Boston MA 02115-6096 Business E-Mail: dtrichop@hsph.harvard.edu.

TRICOLES, GUS PETER, electrical engineer, physicist, consultant; b. San Francisco, Oct. 18, 1931; s. Constantine Peter and Eugenia (Elias) T.; m. Beverly Mildred Ralsky, Dec. 20, 1953 (dec. Dec. 1974); children: Rosanne, Robin; m. Aileen Irma Arenson, Apr. 1, 1980 (div. June 1980). BA in Physics, UCLA, 1955; MS in Applied Math., San Diego State U., 1958; MS in Applied Physics, U. Calif., San Diego, 1962, PhD in Applied Physics, 1971. Engr. Convair divsn. Gen. Dynamics, San Diego, 1955-59, engr. Electronics divsn., 1962-75, engring. mgr. Electronics divsn., 1975-89, sr. engring. staff specialist, 1989-95, Tracor, 1995-99; engr. Smyth Rsch. Assn., San Diego, 1959-61; rsch. asst. Scripps Instn. Oceanography, La Jolla, Calif., 1961-62; sr. engring. staff specialist G.D.E. Systems, Inc., San Diego, 1992—, BAE Sys., 1999—2000; cons. Sci. Applications Internat. Corp., 2003—04. Engring. staff specialist B&M Sys., 2000-02; cons. Ga. Inst. Tech., Atlanta, 1972, 79-80, Transco Industries, LA, 1973, Aero Geo Industries, San Antonio, 1980-82, Vantage Assocs., San Diego, 1988, Sci. Application Internat. Corp., 2004; rsch. reviewer NRC, NAS, Boulder, Colo., 1986-88. Author: (with others) Radome Engineering Handbook, 1970, Antenna Handbook, 1988; contbr. articles to profl. jours.; 19 patents in field. With USN, 1952-53. Fellow IEEE (antenna standards com. 1980—, advancement com. 1988), Optical Soc. Am. (local sect. v.p. 1966); mem. Am. Geophys. Union. Avocations: woodworking, photography. Home: 4633 Euclid Ave San Diego CA 92115-3226

TRIECE, ANNE GALLAGHER, magazine publisher; b. Bklyn., July 1, 1955; d. Anthony J. and Mary Ann (Clines) Gallagher; m. David Mark Triece, Nov. 3, 1990; 1 child, Elizabeth Renee. BBA cum laude, CUNY, 1978. Media planner Isidore Lefkowitz Elgort, NYC, 1978-80; sr. media supr. Ted Bates Advt., NYC, 1980-83; account mgr. Prevention mag., NYC, 1983-85; N.Y. mgr. Home mag., NYC, 1985-92; assoc. pub. Met. Home mag., NYC, 1992—. Coord. Arts Program for Homeless, N.Y.C., 1994. Recipient advt. excellence award Knapp Comm., 1985. Mem. Advt. Women N.Y. (commendation 1985). Roman Catholic. Avocations: scuba diving, tennis, skiing. Office Phone: 212-767-5516.

TRIER, JERRY STEVEN, gastroenterologist, educator; b. Frankfurt, Germany, Apr. 12, 1933; came to U.S., 1938, naturalized, 1943; s. Kurt J. and Alice L. (Cahn) T.; m. Laurel M. Bryan, June 8, 1957; children: Stanley, Jeryl, Stephen. MD, U. Wash., 1957; MA (hon.), Harvard U., 1973. Diplomate Am. Bd. Internal Medicine. Intern U. Rochester, NY, 1957-58, resident in medicine, 1958-59; clin. asso. Nat. Cancer Inst., Bethesda, Md., 1959-61; trainee in gastroenterology U. Wash., Seattle, 1961-63; asst. prof. medicine U. Wis., Madison, 1963-67; asso. prof. U. N.Mex., Albuquerque, 1967-69, Boston U., 1969-73, Harvard U. Med. Sch., Cambridge, Mass., 1973-76, prof., 1976—. Sr. physician Brigham and Women's Hosp.; cons. Dana Farber Cancer Ctr., Nat. Inst. Diabetes and Digestive and Kidney Disease; adv. coun. NIH, 1986-90. Editor: Internal Medicine; mem. editorial bd.; Anatomical Record, 1969-98, Gastroenterology, assoc. editor, 1971-77, mem. editorial bd., 1967-71, 78-83, 93-98, chmn., 1988-93, Am. Jour. Medicine, 1978-87, Current Opinion in Gastroenterology, 1990—; contbr. articles to profl. jours.; contbr. chpts. to books. Served as surgeon USPHS, 1959-61. Recipient Disting. Med. Alumnus award U. Wash., 2004, NIH Merit award, 1988-94; USPHS/NIH grantee, 1963-94. Mem. Am. Soc. Clin. Investigation, Assn. Am. Physicians, Am. Gastroent. Assn. (pres. 1985-86, Julius Friedenwald medal 1999), Am. Soc. Cell Biology, Am. Fedn. Clin. Research. Office: Brigham and Women's Hosp 75 Francis St Boston MA 02115-6110

TRIGG, JACK WALDEN, JR., retired physician; b. Birmingham, Ala., Apr. 18, 1932; s. Jack Walden Sr. and Florine (Hagood) T.; m. Dorothy Wynne, June 3, 1958; 1 child, James Albert. BS, Va. Mil. Inst., 1953; MD, Med. Coll. of Ala., 1958. Diplomate Am. Bd. Internal Medicine. Intern in medicine Duke U. Hosp., Durham, N.C., 1958-59; resident in medicine Univ. Hosp., Birmingham, 1959-62; physician So. Med. Group, Birmingham, 1964-98. Pres. med. staff St. Vincent's Hosp., 1986. Capt. USAF, 1962-64. Fellow ACP; mem. Birmingham Soc. of Internists, Jefferson County Med. Soc. Republican. Episcopalian. Home: 2006 Garden Pl Birmingham AL 35223-1156 Personal E-mail: jtrig@bellsouth.net.

TRIGGLE, DAVID JOHN, dean, pharmacist, consultant; b. Eng., Apr. 5, 1935; came to U.S., 1962; s. William John and Maud F. (Henderson) T.; m. Ann M. Jones, Sept. 22, 1959; children: Andrew B., Jocelyn A. BSc in Chemistry, U. Southampton, Eng., 1956; PhD, U. Hull, Eng., 1959. Sch. fellow U. Ottawa, Ont., Can., 1959-61; rsch. fellow U. London, 1961-62; asst. prof. SUNY Sch. of Pharmacy, Buffalo, 1962-65, assoc. prof., 1965-69, prof., 1985-95, chmn. dept., 1971-85, dean, 1985-95, Disting. prof., 1987—, vice-provost for grad. edn., 1995-2001, dean Grad. Sch., 1995-2001, provost, 2000-01, univ. prof., 2000—; pres. Ctr. for Inquiry, Inst. Buffalo. Cons. to pharm. industry, 1980—. Author: Chemical Aspects of Autonomic Nervous System, 1965, Neurotransmitter-Receptor Interactions, 1971, Chemical Pharmacology of the Synapse, 1976; editor: Comprehensive Medicinal Chemistry, 2006. Recipient Volwiler Rsch. Achievement award Am. Assn. Colls. Pharmacy, 1988, 89, George Koepf award Biomed. Rsch. Med. Found. Buffalo, 1994. Fellow AAAS; mem. Am. Chem. Soc., Am. Soc. Pharmacology and Therapeutics (Otto Krayer award 1995), Soc. Neurosci., Brit. Pharmacology Soc., Am. Pharm. Assn., Rho Chi (Rho Chi award 1998). Office: SUNY Sch Pharmacy 126 Cooke Buffalo NY 14260-0001 Business E-Mail: triggle@buffalo.edu.

TRIGIANO, LUCIEN LEWIS, physician; b. Easton, Pa., Feb. 9, 1926; s. Nicholas and Angeline (Lewis) T.; children: Lynn Anita, Glenn Larry, Robert Nicholas. Student, Tex. Christian U., 1944-45, Ohio U., 1943-44, 46-47, Milligan Coll., 1944, Northwestern U., 1945, Temple U., 1948-52. Diplomate Am. Bd. Phys. Medicine & Rehab. Intern Meml. Hosp., Johnstown, Pa., 1952-53; resident Lee Hosp., Johnstown, 1953-54; gen. practice Johnstown, 1953-59; med. dir. Pa. Rehab. Ctr., Johnstown, 1959-62, chief phys. medicine & rehab., 1964-70; fellow phys. medicine & rehab. N.Y. Inst. Phys. Medicine & Rehab., 1962—64; dir. rehab. medicine Lee Hosp., 1964-71, Ralph K. Davies Med. Ctr., San Francisco, 1973-75, St. Joseph's Hosp., San Francisco, 1975-78, St. Francis Meml. Hosp., San Francisco, 1978-83, Rehab. Ctr. Nev., Las Vegas, 1998—2000; pvt. practice Las Vegas, 1998—. Asst. prof. phys. medicine and rehab. Temple U. Sch. Medicine; founder Disability Alert; bd. adv. Sch. Medicine Temple U., 2003—, bd. visitors, 2003; adj. prof. Touro U. Sch. Medicine, Las Vegas, 2005—. Served with USNR, 1944-46. Fellow ACP; mem. AMA, Pa. Med. Soc., San Francisco County Med. Soc., Am. Acad. Phys. Medicine and Rehab., Am. Congress Phys. Medicine, Calif. Acad. Phys. Medicine, Nat. Rehab. Assn., Babcock Surg. Soc. Home and Office: 20 Woodside Dr Easton PA 18042 Office Phone: 702-242-8402. Personal E-mail: lltmdmd@aol.com.

TRIGILIO, JOHN PATRICIO, pastor; s. John Trigilio and Elizabeth Lagner. BA, Gannon U., 1983; MDiv, Mary Immaculate Sem., 1988; PhD, LaSalle U., 1998; ThD, Concordia, 2002. Ordained to priesthood Cath. Diocese of Harrisburg, Pa., 1988. Parochial vicar St. Joseph Cath. Ch., Mechanicsburg, Pa., 1988—91, St. John the Bapt. Cath. Ch., New Freedom, 1991—94, St. Joan of Arc Ch., Hershey, 1995—98, Seven Sorrows BVM Ch., Middletown, 1998—2001, Holy Name of Jesus Ch., Harrisburg, 2001—02; sec. to the tribunal Cath. Diocese of Harrisburg, 1994—95; pastor St. Bernadette Parish, Duncannon, 2002, Our Lady of Good Counsel Ch., Marysville, 2002—. Pres. Confraternity Cath. Clergy, Marysville, 2002—. Author: (book) Catholicism for Dummies, The Everything Bible Book, Women in the Bible for Dummies, John Paul II for Dummies, Catholicism Answer Book: 300 Frequently Asked Questions, (weekly television & radio series on EWTN) Web of Faith, Council of Faith, Crash Course in Catholicism; editor: Sapienta Mag., 1992—2006. Mem.: Fellowship Cath. Scholars (life). Conservative. Roman Catholic. Home and Office: Our Lady of Good Counsel Church 121 William St Marysville PA 17053 Home Phone: 717-957-9309; Office Phone: 717-957-2662. Office Fax: 717-957-4247; Home Fax: 717-957-4247. Personal E-mail: fr.trigilio@prodigy.net. Business E-Mail: opus-dei@msn.com.

TRIIPAN, MAIVE, library director; b. Virumaa County, Estonia, Jan. 4, 1942; d. Osvald and Minna (Olesk) Triipan; m. Kalle Dobkevich, Mar. 6, 1971 (div. June 4, 1974); 1 child, Raul. B. of Libr., Tartu U., Tartu, Estonia, 1967. Rsch. mgmt. asst. Libr. of Estonian Acad. Sci., Tallinn, Estonia, 1967-74, asst. dir. rsch. work, 1974-84, dir., 1984—; head PR Astangu Vocat. Rehab. Ctr., Tallinn, 2003. Mem. State Libr. Coun., Tallinn, 1974-87, State Libr. Coun. at Dept. of Culture and Edn., Tallinn, 1989—, Tech. U. Coun., Tallinn, 1993—, Estonian Nat. Libr. Coun., Tallinn, 1994—; fin. mgr. Merelaug, 1998-99; project mgmt. Scis. Dept. Estonian Inst. Pub. Adminstrn.; project mgmr. Style Wear, Tallinn, 2000-01; specialist further edn. Astangu Vocat. Rehab. Ctr., Tallinn, 2000, head dept. IT and staff tng., 2002-, head dept. pub. relationship, 2003. Editl. bd. Estonian Retrospective, 1975; mng. pub. National Bibliography 1525-1940, 1993. Mem. Estonian Librs. Assn. Avocations: literature, music, art. Business E-Mail: maive.triipan@astangu.ee.

TRILLIN, CALVIN, writer, journalist; b. Kansas City, Mo., Dec. 5, 1935; s. Abe and Edyth T.; m. Alice Stewart, Aug. 13, 1965 (dec.); children: Abigail, Sarah Stewart. BA, Yale U., 1957; DLitt (hon.), Beloit Coll., 1987; LHD (hon.), Albertus Magnus Coll., 1990; LHD hon., U. Mo., 2003; DLitt (hon.), SUNY, 1996, U. N.C., 1998, Susquehanna U., 1999; DLitt. (hon.), Long Island U., 2002. Reporter, writer Time mag., 1960-63; staff writer New Yorker mag., 1963—; columnist Nation mag., 1978-85; syndicated columnist, 1986-95; columnist Time mag., 1996-2001. Trustee N.Y. Pub. Libr. Author: An Education in Georgia, 1964, Barnett Frummer is an Unbloomed Flower, 1969, U.S. Journal, 1971, American Fried, 1974, Runestruck, 1977, Alice, Let's Eat, 1978, Floater, 1980, Uncivil Liberties, 1982, Third Helpings, 1983, Killings, 1984, With All Disrespect, 1985, If You Can't Say Something Nice, 1987, Travels With Alice, 1989, Enough's Enough, 1990, American Stories, 1991, Remembering Denny, 1993, Deadline Poet, 1994, Too Soon to Tell, 1995, Messages From My Father, 1996, Family Man, 1998, Tepper Isn't Going Out, 2002, Feeding A Yen, 2003, Obliviously On He Sails, 2004, A Heckuva Job, 2006, About Alice, 2007; author, performer one-man show Calvin Trillin's Uncle Sam, Am. Place Theatre, N.Y.C., 1988, Calvin Trillin's Words, No Music, Am. Place Theatre, 1990. Office: care New Yorker 4 Times Sq New York NY 10036-6522 Home Phone: 212-243-3455; Office Phone: 212-286-5651.

TRILLING, HELEN REGINA, lawyer; b. Boston, May 13, 1950; d. Charles Alexander and A. Lillian Trilling. AB magna cum laude, Radcliffe Coll., 1973; JD, Harvard U., 1976. Bar: Mass. 1977, US Dist. Ct. Mass. 1978, US Supreme Ct. 1980, DC 1984, US Ct. Appeals (10th cir.) 1984, US Ct. Appeals (DC cir.) 1984. Asst. gen. counsel Blue Cross/Blue Shield, Boston, 1976-79; sp. asst. to gen. counsel HHS, Washington, 1979-83; assoc. Hogan & Hartson, Wash., 1979—87, ptnr., 1987—. Spkr. in field. Contbr. articles to profl. jour. Mem. pres.'s coun. Nat. Partnership for Women and Families. Named Outstanding Fraud & Compliance Lawyer, Nightingale's Healthcare News, 2005. Mem. ABA (health law forum com.), Nat. Health Lawyers Assn., Wash. Area Lawyers for Arts (outreach com.), Am. Health Lawyers Assn. Office: Hogan & Hartson 555 13th St NW Washington DC 20004-1161 Office Phone: 202-637-8653, 202-637-5600. Office Fax: 202-637-5910. Business E-Mail: hrtrilling@hhlaw.com.

TRILLING, LEON, aeronautical engineering educator; b. Bialystok, Poland, July 15, 1924; came to U.S., 1940, naturalized, 1946; s. Oswald and Regina (Zakhejm) T.; m. Edna Yuval, Feb. 17, 1946; children: Alex R., Roger S. BS, Calif. Inst. Tech., 1944, MS, 1946, PhD, 1948. Rsch. fellow Calif. Inst. Tech., 1948- 50; Fulbright scholar U. Paris, 1950-51, vis. prof., 1963-64; mem. faculty MIT, Cambridge, 1951—, prof. aerospace and astronautics, 1962-94, prof. emeritus, 1994—, mem. coun. on primary and secondary edn., 1992—. Mem. Program in Sci. Tech. and Soc., Engring. Edn. Mission to Soviet Union, 1958; vis. prof. Delft Tech. U., 1974-75; vis. prof. engring. Carleton Coll., 1987. Pres. Met. Com. Ednl. Opportunity, 1967-70, Coun. for Understanding of Tech. in Human Affairs, 1984—. Guggenheim fellow, 1963-64. Fellow AAAS. Home: 180 Beacon St Boston MA 02116-1408 Office: MIT 77 Massachusetts Ave Cambridge MA 02139-4307 Business E-Mail: trilling@mit.edu.

TRIMBLE, CELIA DENISE, lawyer; b. Clovis, N.Mex., Mar. 3, 1953; d. George Harold and Barbara Ruth (Foster) T.; m. Billy W. Boone, Apr. 21, 1990. BS, Ea. N.Mex. U., 1976, MA, 1977; JD, St. Mary's U., San Antonio, 1982. Bar: Tex. 1982, U.S. Ct. Appeals (5th cir.) 1985, U.S. Supreme Ct. 1986; cert. family law Tex. Bd. Legal Specialization, 1987, Family Law Exam. Commn., 2002. Instr. English Ea. N.Mex. U., Portales, 1977-78; editor Curry County Times, Clovis, 1978-79; assoc. Schultz & Robertson, Abilene, Tex., 1982-85, Scarborough, Black, Tarpley & Scarborough, Abilene, 1985-87; ptnr. Scarborough, Black, Tarpley & Trimble, 1988-90, Scarborough, Black, Tarpley & Boone, 1990-94; of counsel Scarborough, Tarpley, Boone & Fouts, 1994-96; pvt. practice Abilene, 1996—. Instr. legal rsch. and writing St. Mary's Sch. Law, 1981-82; mem. family law exam. com. Tex. Bd. Legal Specialization, 2002—, vice chair, 2005—. Legal adv. bd. to bd. dirs. Abilene Kennel Club, 1983-85; landmarks commn. City of Abilene, 1989-90. Mem. ABA, State Bar Tex. (disciplinary rev. com. 1989-93), Am. Trial Lawyers Assn., Tex. Trial Lawyers Assn., Tex. Criminal Def. Lawyers Assn., Tex. Acad. Family Law Specialists, Abilene Bar Assn. (bd. dirs. 1985-88, sec.-treas. 1985-86),

Abilene Young Lawyers Assn. (bd. dirs. 1985-89, treas. 1985-86, pres.-elect 1987-88, pres. 1988-89). Avocations: needlecrafts, gardening. Office: 104 Pine St Ste 316 Abilene TX 79601 Home Phone: 325-677-0581. E-mail: mail@celia.net.

TRIMBLE, PHILLIP RICHARD, law educator; b. Springfield, Ohio, Nov. 12, 1937; s. Melvin R. and Dorothy T.; m. Stephanie Gardner, July 20, 1963 (div. 1977); children: John, William; m. Valeria Vasilevski, Dec. 21, 2000. BA, Ohio U., 1958; MA, Fletcher U., 1959; JD, Harvard U., 1963. Bar: NY 1964. Legal writing instr. U. Calif., Berkeley, 1963-64; assoc. Cravath, Swaine & Moore, NYC, 1964-70; staff mem. fgn. rels. com. U.S. Senate, Washington, 1971-72; asst. legal adviser Dept. State, Washington, 1973-78; counsel to the mayor NYC, 1978; dep. mayor, 1979; U.S. ambassador Nepal, 1980-81; prof. law UCLA, 1981—2001, vice provost internat. studies, 1999—2000; founding mem. Dalai Lama Found., 2001—. Mem. exec. com. Asia Soc. So. Calif. Ctr., L.A., 1981-94; vis. prof. law Stanford U., 1988-89, U. Mich., 1995-96; U.S. panelist under U.S.-Can. Free Trade Agreement, NAFTA; cons. ACDA, 1989-92. Mem. bd. editors Am. Jour. Internat. Law, 1993-98. Bd. dirs. Milarepa Tibetan Buddhist Ctr., 2001—, Am. Alpine Club, 1978—80, 1982—85. Fellow Explorers Club. Democrat. Avocation: mountain climbing.

TRIMBLE, PRESTON ALBERT, retired judge; b. Salina, Okla., Aug. 27, 1930; s. James Albert and Winnie Louella (Walker) T.; m. Patricia Ann Beadle; children: Todd, Beth, Amy. BA, U. Okla., 1956, LL.B., 1960. Bar: Okla. 1960. Practice law, 1960; asst. county atty. Cleveland County, Okla., 1960-62; county atty., 1962-67; dist. atty., 1967-79; dist. judge, 1979-91. Spl. instr. S.W. Center Law Enforcement Edn.; cons. prosecution mgmt. Mem. Jud. Council Okla.; chmn. Okla. Corrections Workshop; mem. planning com. Nat. Inst. Crime and Delinquency; mem. com. on multi-agy. problems in criminal justice Appellate Judges Conf. Bd. dirs. Okla. U. Crisis Ctr., 1970—, ARC, Lake Murray Conservation Assn.; trustee Nat. Assn. Pretrial Svc. Agys. Resource Ctr., Sarkeys Found., 1994—. With USNR, 1948-52; col. USAFR. Mem. Okla., Cleveland County bar assns., Nat. Dist. Attys. Assn. (past pres.), Okla. Dist. Attys. Assn. (past pres.), Nat. Coll. Dist. Attys. (bd. regents), Am. Legion, Lions, Amateur Field Trial Clubs Am. (trustee 2002—, v.p. 2005—, pres. Okla. chpt.) Democrat. Roman Catholic. Home: 1886 Trailview Dr Norman OK 73072-6655 Office: 231 S Peters Ave Norman OK 73069-6035 Office Phone: 405-321-8272. Personal E-mail: trimble@coxinet.net. *An elected public official must remember that the people own his position and he only holds it in trust for them.*

TRIMBLE, SANDRA ELLINGSON, lawyer; b. Buffalo, Wyo., May 10, 1952; d. Andrew C. and Edna E. Ellingson; children: Samuel James, Stephen Joseph. BA with highest distinction, Colo. State U., 1974; MEd, Sul Ross State U., 1977; JD cum laude, Georgetown U., 1989. Bar: Md. 1989, D.C. 1990. Contract specialist USAF, Pope AFB, N.C., 1979-81; purchasing rep. Damson Oil Corp., Houston, 1982-86; summer assoc. Fried Frank Harris Shriver & Jacobson, Washington, 1988; law clk. Sullivan & Cromwell, Washington, 1988-89; assoc. Cleary Gottlieb Steen & Hamilton, Washington, 1989-97; of counsel Orrick Herrington & Sutcliffe LLP, Washington, 1997—2002; counsel McKee Nelson LLP, 2002—. Assoc. notes editor Georgetown Law Jour., 1988-89. Recipient Disting. Achievement in Advocacy award Internat. Acad. Trial Lawyers, 1989; Nat. Merit scholar, 1970; law fellow Georgetown U. Law Ctr., 1987-88. Mem. ABA, Phi Beta Kappa. Office Phone: 202-327-2110. Business E-Mail: strimble@mckeenelson.com.

TRIMBLE, STANLEY WAYNE, hydrologist; b. Columbia, Tenn., Dec. 8, 1940; s. Stanley Drake and Clara Faye (Smith) T.; m. Alice Erle Gunn, Aug. 16, 1964; children: Alicia Anne, Jennifer Lusanne. BS, U. North Ala., 1964; MA, U. Ga., 1970, PhD, 1973. Asst. prof. hydrology and geography U. Wis., Milw., 1972-75; from asst. prof. to prof. UCLA, 1975—. Vis. asst. prof. U. Chgo., 1978, vis. assoc. prof., 81, vis. prof. environ. geography, 1990—; vis. prof. U. Durham, England, 1998; vis. lectr. U. London, 1985; hydrologist US Geol. Survey, 1974—84; vis. prof. U. Vienna, 1994, 99; Frost lectr. Brit. Geomorphol. Rsch. Group, Durham, 1994; vis. rsch. lectr. Oxford U., 1995; Fulbright scholar in UK, 95; vis. fellow Keble Coll., Oxford U., 1995, Hatfield Coll., U. Durham, 1998. Author: Culturally Accelerated Sedimentation on the Middle Georgia Piedmont, 1971, Man-Induced Erosion on the Southern Piedmont, 1700-1970, 1974, Soil Conservation and the Reduction, 1982, Sediment Characteristics of Tennessee Streams, 1984, (with A Ward) Environmental Hydrology, 2004 (ASAE Blue Ribbon award); joint editor-in-chief: Catena, 1995-2006; editor: Dekker Encyclopedia of Water Science, 2003-; contbr. articles to profl. jours. 1st lt. 101 Airborne Divsn. US Army, 1963—65. Grantee U.S. Geol. Survey, Washington, 1974-79, Wis. Dept. Natural Resources, Madison, 1978, 82, 93, 94, 95, NSF, Washington, 1976, Agrl. Rsch. Svc. of USDA, Washington, 1972, Nat. Geographic Soc., 1993. Mem.: NAS-NRC (Com. on Watershed Mgmt. 1996—98, Com. on Miss. River and Clean Water Act 2005—07), Brit. Geomorphol. Rsch. Group, Soil Conservation Soc. Am., Am. Geophys. Union, Assn. Am. Geographers (Disting. Career award 2006), Sigma Xi. Republican. Avocations: historic houses, documentation and restoration, landscape gardens. Office: UCLA Dept Geography 1255 Bunche Hall Los Angeles CA 90095-1524 Home Phone: 931-363-0457; Office Phone: 310-825-1071. Business E-Mail: trimble@geog.ucla.edu.

TRIMBLE, THOMAS JAMES, retired utilities executive, lawyer; b. Carters Creek, Tenn., Sept. 3, 1931; s. John Elijah and Mittie (Rountree) T.; m. Glenna Kay Jones, Sept. 3, 1957; children: James Jefferson, Julie Kay. BA, David Lipscomb U., 1953; JD, Vanderbilt U., 1956; LLM, NYU, 1959. Bar: Tenn. 1956, Ariz. 1961, U.S. Dist. Ct. Ariz. 1961, U.S. Dist. Ct. D.C. 1963, U.S. Ct. Appeals (10th cir.) 1971, U.S. Supreme Ct. 1972, U.S. Ct. Appeals (9th cir.) 1975. From assoc. to ptnr. Jennings, Strouss & Salmon, Phoenix, 1960-85, mng. ptnr., 1985-87; sr. v.p., gen. counsel, corp. sec. S.W. Gas Corp., Las Vegas, Nev., 1987-96; gen. counsel Primerit Bank, 1987—96, corp. sec., 1990-92; exec. v.p. Energy Ins. (Bermuda) Ltd., 1992-94, bd. dirs., 1992-97, pres., 1994—96. Bd. dirs. Energy Ins. Mut. Ltd., 1988—97, vice chmn., 1992—94, chmn., 1994—96. Mem. editorial bd. Vanderbilt U. Law Rev., 1954-56. Mem. Pepperdine U. Bd. Regents, Malibu, Calif., 1981—, sec., 1982-2000, chmn., 2000-04, mem. exec. com., 1982-89, 95—; bd. visitors Pepperdine Sch. Law, Malibu; trustee Okla. Christian U., Oklahoma City, 1994—; pres. Big Sisters Ariz., Phoenix, 1975, bd. dirs., 1970-76; chmn. Sunnydale Children's Home, Phoenix, 1966-69, bd. dirs., 1965-75; pres. Clearwater Hills Improvement Assn., Phoenix, 1977-79, bd. dirs., 1975-80; trustee Nev. Sch. of Arts, 1988-92, chmn., 1989-90. 1st lt. JAGC, USAF, 1957-60. Fellow Ariz. Bar Found. (editl. bd. Jour. 1975-80), Am. Gas Assn. (legal sect. mng. com. 1987-96), Order of Coif, Southshore Golf Club (Las Vegas), Kiwanis (pres. Phoenix 1972-73), Phi Delta Phi. Republican. Mem. Ch. Christ. Home: 7302 E Berridge Ln Scottsdale AZ 85250 Personal E-mail: ttrimble5@cox.net.

TRIMBLE, VANCE HENRY, retired newspaper editor; b. Harrison, Ark., July 6, 1913; s. Guy L. and Josephine (Crump) T.; m. Elzene Miller, Jan. 9, 1932; 1 dau., Carol Ann. Student pub. schs., Wewoka, Okla. Cub reporter Okemah (Okla.) Daily Leader, 1928; worked various newspapers in Okmulgee, Muskogee, Tulsa and, Okla.; successively reporter, rewrite man, city editor Houston Press, 1939-50, mng. editor, 1950-55; news editor Scripps-Howard Newspaper Alliance, Washington, 1955-63; editor Ky. Post and Times-Star, Covington, 1963-79. Author: The Uncertain Miracle, 1974, Sam M. Walton, 1990, (biography) E.W. Scripps, 1992, Frederick Smith of Federal Express, 1993, An Empire Undone: Rise and Fall of Chris Whittle, 1995, Alice & J.F.B.-The Hundred Year Saga of Two Seminole Chiefs, 2006, Choctaw Kisses Bullets & Blood, 2007; co-author: Happy Chandler Autobiography, 1989; editor: Scripps-Howard Handbook, 1981. Trustee Scripps-Howard Found., 1974-79. Recipient Pulitzer prize for nat. reporting, 1960, Raymond Clapper award, 1960, Sigma Delta Chi award for disting. Washington correspondence, 1960, Frank Luther Mott award for journalism book rsch. U. Mo., 1993; named to Okla. Journalism Hall of Fame, 1974. Mem. Am. Soc. Newspaper Editors, Nat. Press Club (Washington), Press Club (Houston), Wewoka Country Club. Baptist. Home: 25 Oakhurst Rd Wewoka OK 74884-3714 Personal E-mail: vhtrimble@aol.com.

TRIMBLE, WILLIAM CATTELL, JR., retired lawyer; b. Buenos Aires, Feb. 7, 1935; s. William Cattell and Nancy Gordon (Carroll) Trimble; m. Barbara Janney, June 19, 1960; children: William C, Margery M Kennelly. AB, Princeton U., 1958; LLB, U. Md., 1964. Bar: Md 1965. With firm Ober, Grimes & Shriver, Balt., 1965-87, ptnr., 1970-87, mng. ptnr., 1973-77; counsel Semmes, Bowen & Semmes, Balt., 1987—2000; ret., 2000; mem. Gov.'s Commn. to Revise Annotated Code of Md., 1975-83. Hon consul, Netherlands, 1986—2003; pres. bd. trustees Valley Sch., 1968—73; trustee Garrison Forest Sch., 1975—95, Gilman Sch., 1980—84. Lt USNR, 1958—61. Mem.: ABA, Md. Bar Assn., Class of 1958 Princeton U. (pres.), Soc. Cin., Greenspring Valley Hunt Club, Colonial Club (Princeton). Episcopalian. Personal E-mail: williamtrimble@msn.com.

TRIMMIER, CHARLES STEPHEN, JR., lawyer; b. Chgo., June 25, 1943; s. Charles Stephen and Lucille E. (Anderson) T.; m. Rae Wade Trimmier, Aug. 19, 1966; children: Charles Stephen, Hallie Wade. BA, U. Ala., Tuscaloosa, 1965, JD, 1968. Bar: Ala. 1968. From assoc. to ptnr. Rives, Peterson, Pettus and Conway, Birmingham, Ala., 1968-77; pres. TrimmierLaw Firm, Birmingham and Mobile, Ala., Tampa, Fla., 1977—. Gen. counsel Nat. Assn. State Chartered Credit Union Suprs., 1983-2001, Ala. Credit Union League, Fla. Credit Union League, La. Credit Union League; adj. prof. U. Ala. Sch. Law. Editor-in-chief: Ala. Law Rev., 1968. Mem. ABA (bus. and banking law sect., credit union com.), Ala. Bar Assn., Birmingham Bar Assn., Comml. Law League, Ala. Law Inst., Shades Valley Rotary, Shades Valley Jaycees (sec. 1973). Episcopalian. Home: 3819 River View Cir Birmingham AL 35243-4801 Office: Trimmier Law Firm PO Box 1885 Birmingham AL 35201-1885 Home Phone: 205-967-4859; Office Phone: 800-666-3151. Business E-Mail: steve@trimmier.com.

TRIMMIER, ROSCOE, JR., lawyer; b. Charlotte, NC, July 22, 1944; s. Roscoe and Susie Elizabeth (Stitt) T.; divorced; 1 child, Leigh Snowden. AB, Harvard U., 1971, JD, 1974. Bar: Mass. 1974, U.S. Dist. Ct. Mass. 1975, U.S. Ct. Appeals (1st cir.) 1975, U.S. Supreme Ct. 1978, U.S. Claims Ct. 1983, U.S. Ct. Appeals (D.C. cir.) 2002. Assoc. Ropes & Gray, Boston, 1974-83, ptnr., 1983—, chmn. litigation dept. Mem. hearing com. Bd. Bar Overseers, 1983-89; bd. dirs., v.p. Family Counseling & Guidance Ctr., Inc., Boston, 1980-93; gov. Mus. of Sci., 1981-93; mem. exec. com. Jud. Nominating Commn., 1991-96; corp. mem. Mass. Gen. Hosp., 1992—; gov. N.E Med. Ctr. Hosps., 1992—; vice chmn. Mass. Bd. Registration in Medicine, 2001--. 1st lt. U.S. Army, 1965-68. Fellow: Am. Coll. Trial Lawyers, Mass. Bar Found. (life), Am. Bar Found. (life); mem.: ABA (former chair standing com. on fed. judiciary), Am. Law Inst., Boston Bar Assn., Mass. Black Lawyers Assn. (life), Mass. Bar Assn. Home: 1265 Beacon St Brookline MA 02446-5200 Office: Ropes & Gray 1 International Pl Boston MA 02110-2624 Office Fax: 617-951-7050. Business E-Mail: roscoe.trimmier@ropesgray.com.

TRINDAL, WESLEY STEELE, mechanical engineer; b. Superior, Wis., July 21, 1925; s. Glen W. and Mabel Elda Thorp (Steele) T.; m. Mary Elizabeth Steger, Aug. 12, 1949; 1 child, Joseph William. BSME, La. State U., 1956. Test and devel. engr. Ford Motor Co., Chrysler Corp., Detroit, 1956-58; prin. engr. vehicles U.S. Army Mobility Equipment Rsch. & Devel. Command, Ft. Belvoir, Va., 1958-82; mech. engr. Radian, Inc., Alexandria, Va., 1982—94. With US Army, 1943—52, ETO. Mem. Soc. Automotive Engrs., Am. Truck Hist. Soc., Hist. Constrn. Equipment Soc. Avocation: writing. Home: 698 Forest View Rd Edinburg VA 22824-3580 Home Phone: 540-984-8788; Office Phone: 540-984-8788.

TRINDER, RACHEL BANDELE, lawyer; b. Ibadan, Nigeria, Feb. 21, 1955; came to U.S., 1977; d. Victor William John and Margaret (Almond) T. BA with honors, Oxford U., 1977, MA, 1994; LLM, U. Va., 1978. Bar: D.C. 1979, U.S. Dist. Ct. 1979, U.S. Ct. Appeals (D.C. cir.) 1980, U.S. Supreme Ct. 1986. Assoc. Zuckert, Scoutt & Rasenberger, LLP, Washington, 1978-85, ptnr., 1985—. V.p. aviation spl. interest chpt. Transp. Rsch. Forum, 1988-90, exec. v.p., 1990-91, gen. counsel, 1989-91; mem. bd. advisors 3d Ann. Symposium on Law and Outer Space, 1991, program dir., mem. bd. advisors, 4th Ann., 1991-92. Contbr. articles to legal jours. Bd. govs. Internat. Student House, 1986-93, mem. exec. com., asst. treas., 1987-88, mem. bd. advisors, 1993-97. Fellow English Speaking Union, 1977. Mem. FBA (chair space law com. 1990-94, chair internat. law sect. 1994-96), Internat. Inst. Space Law (life), Internat. Aviation Women's Assn. (dir.-at-large 1996-98), Internat. Inst. Air and Space Law (bd. govs., exec. com. 1992-02), Internat. Aviation Club (bd. govs. 1984-86, pres. 1986), Aero Club (bd. govs. 1993-07, pres. 2000), Nat. Aeronautic Assn. (bd. govs. 2000-01). Home: 1266 Dartmouth Ct Alexandria VA 22314-4784 Office: Zuckert Scoutt & Rasenberger LLP 888 17th St NW Washington DC 20006-3939 Home Phone: 703-212-0017; Office Phone: 202-973-7927. E-mail: rbtrinder@zsrlaw.com.

TRINGALE, ANTHONY ROSARIO, insurance executive; b. Syracuse, NY, Apr. 20, 1942; s. Anthony and Susan Marie Tringale; children: Anthony William, Michael Paul, Mark David, Amber Marie. BSFS, Georgetown U., 1967. CLU. Office mgr. trainee N.Y. Life Ins. Co. No. Va., 1965-66, office mgr. Fairfax, Va., 1966, field underwriter, 1966-68; mgmt. asst. home office N.Y. Life Ins. Co., NYC, 1973, gen mgr. Pitts., 1973-76; gen. mgr. Acacia Mut. Life Ins. Co., Annandale, Va., 1976-83, fin. and ins. planner, mgmt. and mktg. cons., 1983-86; from field rep. to mktg. com. Acacia Mut. Life, Annandale, Va., 1983-86; prin. Benefits-By-Design, Fairfax, Va., 1986—; pres. Acacia Prodn. Clubs, 1984, 86. Mem. steering com. Entrepreneurship Forum, Washington, 1980-; founding bd. mem. Commonwealth Va. DECA Found., 2003-; nat. adv. bd. Entrepreurship Inst., Columbus, Ohio, 1985—; mem. supts. bus. and industry adv. coun. Fairfax County Pub. Schs., 1989-2004, mem. mktg edn. adv. bd., 1980-2004, chmn. 1983-84, 90-91; lectr. in field. Contbr. articles in field of personal and bus. fin. strategies to Md. Bus. Observer, Washington Bus. Jour., NALU's Life Assoc. News; radio host Basically Bus. Sta. WGMS-FM, Washington, 1988-91. Trustee SME-1 Accreditation Inst. U. Memphis, 1990—99, Syracuse U., 1995—99; past liaison rep. Am. Soc. CLUs, Bryn Mawr, Pa., 1988—98; arbitrator Fairfax County Dept. Consumer Affairs; pres., bd. dir., exec. com. The Jeane Dixon Children to Children Found., 1980—; chmn. VIP panel DC and No. Va., 1988—92; pres. VIP panel, DC and No. Va., 1992—94, Birch Pond Homeowners Assn., 1998—2000; bd. dir., exec. com., pres. United Cerebral Palsy of D.C. and No. Va., 1985—2006; pres., adv. bd. Fairfax County Corps of Salvation Army, 1996—2004, Front Royal Corps, 2004—07; pres. United Cerebral Palsy of D.C. and No. Va., 2002; dir. at large Nat. Christopher Columbus Quincentary Jubilee Adv. Bd., 1995—; active Nat. Italian-Am. Found. Coun. of 1000, 1989—; mem. Italian Am. Leaders Com. Venture Clinic; founding vice chmn. Fairfax Orgn. Christians/Jews United in Svc.; lector, extraordinary minister Basilica Nat. Shrine Immaculate Conception, 1980—2003; bd. dirs., v.p. exec. com., chmn. grants com. No. Va. Cmty. Found., 1979—2004; bd. dir. Summer Opera Theater Co., 1996—98, Nat. Cath. Cmty. Found., 1996—97; adv. bd., grants com. No. Va. Cmty Found., 2004—; adv. bd. Salvation Army, Fairfax, Va., 1995—2004, Front Royal Waren County Corps., 2004—07; bd. dirs. edn. and conf. ctr. 4-H, Front Royal, Va., 2007—. Recipient 2000 Crystal award No. Va. Cmty. Found. Mem. No. Va. Soc. CLUs (past pres.), Am. Soc. CLUs, No. Va. Assn. Life Underwriters (treas. 1972, nat. com. 1997-99, Pres.' Cup 1991-92), Assn. Advanced Life Underwriting, Sales and Mktg. Execs. Met. Washington (pres. 1979-80, 95-97, treas. 1989-92, bd. dirs. 1990-2000, sr. v.p. profl. devel. 1993-95, Man of Yr. 2000), Nat. Assn. Life Underwriters (Nat. Mgmt. award Gen. Agts. and Mgrs. Conf. 1976-83, exec. com. 1984-85, life qualifying), No. Va. Estate Planning Coun. (exec. com. 1985-92, pres. 1990-91), Internat. Platform Assn. (trustee, bd. govs. 1990-2002), No. Va. Gen. Agts. and Mgrs. Assn. (pres. 1980-81, dir. 1982-83), Greater Washington Area Health Underwriters, Fairfax County C. of C. (dir. small bus. 1989-90, dir. membership 1990-91, exec. com. dir. at large 1991-92, Small Bus. Adv. of Yr. award 1990), Million Dollar Round Table (life), John Carroll Soc. Ins. Club Washington (pres. 1997-98) Office Phone: 540-622-2244. E-mail: icg@hughes.net.

TRINKAUS, ERIK, paleoanthropologist, educator; b. New Haven, Conn., Dec. 24, 1948; s. John Philip Trinkaus, Galina Ivanovna Gorokhoff; m. Kathryn Maurer Maurer; 1 child, Alexander Yuri. BA, U. Wis., 1970; MA, U. Pa., 1973, PhD, 1975. Asst. to assoc. prof., dept. anthropology Harvard U., Cambridge, Mass., 1975—83; asst., assoc. to full prof., dept. anthropology U. N.Mex., Albuquerque, 1983—96, Regents' prof. anthropology, 1996—97; prof. Washington U., St. Louis, 1997—2002, Mary Tileston Hemenway prof. phys. anthropology, 2002—. Author: The Shanidar Neandertals, 1983, The Neandertals: Changing the Image of Mankind, 1993; contbr. articles to peer-reviewed jours., chapters to books. Mem.: NAS (hon.), Am. Anthropological Assn., Am. Assn. Phys. Anthropologists, Société d' Anthropologie de Paris, Anthropological Soc. Nippon, Paleoanthropological Soc., Acad. Sci. St. Louis (hon.). Office: Dept Anthropology Campus Box 1114 Washington Univ Saint Louis MO 63130 Office Phone: 314-935-5207. Office Fax: 314-935-5207. Business E-Mail: trinkaus@artsci.wustl.edu.

TRINKAUS, JOHN WILLIAM, management educator; b. Mt. Vernon, NY, July 17, 1925; s. Bernard and Elsie (Kelly) T.; m. Irene Klimowski, July 31, 1954; children: Joanne Trinkaus Dillon, Robert John, John William. BEE, NYU, 1952, PhD, 1976; MBA, CCNY, 1961. Registered profl. engr., Mass. Engr. Bendix Aviation Corp., Teterboro, NJ, 1947-52, Curtis Wright Corp., Carlstadt, NJ, 1952-53, Sperry Corp., Great Neck, NY, 1953-68; prof. CUNY Baruch Coll., NYC, 1968-81, assoc. dean, 1981-93, prof. emeritus, 1993—. Engring. cons. Electronic Industries Assoc., Washington, 1960-68, USAF, Washington, 1965-68; mgmt. cons. Ford Found., NYC, 1980-82, Interracial Coun. Bus. Opportunity, NYC, 1983-93; vis. disting. prof. St. John's U., NYC, 1993-96. Chmn., rsch. comm. Am. Acad. Profl. Law Enforcement, Mineola, NY, 1978-79; cons. NYC Vol. Urban Con. Group, 1979-84. Sgt. US Army, 1945-46. Recipient 1st prize paper Nat. Fedn. Ind. Bus., Washington, 1992, (Ig)Nobel award, 2003. Mem.: Assn. Pvt. Enterprise Edn., Acad. Mgmt., Inst. Supply Mgmt. Home: 1 Linden St New Hyde Park NY 11040-2311 Office: Baruch Coll CUNY 1 Bernard Baruch Way New York NY 10010-5518 Office Phone: 646-312-3693.

TRINKAUS-RANDALL, GREGOR, librarian, archivist, preservation administrator; b. Balt., Jan. 10, 1946; s. John Phillip and Galina Ivanovna (Gorokhoff) Trinkaus; m. Vickery Edith Trinkaus-Randall, May 22, 1976; children: Jennifer Alison, Christopher Erik. BA, U. Wis., 1968, MA, 1973, MALS, 1980. Archival asst./accessioner State Hist. Soc. Wis., Madison, 1977—81; libr., limnology dept. U. Wis., Madison, 1977—80; conservation/preservation intern Yale U. Libr., New Haven, 1981; asst. curator USS Constitution Mus., Boston, 1981—82; archivist Computer Mus., Marlborough, Mass., 1982; libr./archivist Peabody Mus., Salem, Mass., 1983—88; preservation specialist Mass. Bd. of Libr. Commrs., Boston, 1988—. Mem. adv. com. Northeast Document Conservation Ctr., 1989—; preservation adv. com. NELINET, 1991—2000; mem. preservation com. New England Hist. Geneal. Soc., 1994—2004; chmn. task force theft and mutilation of libr. and archival materials State of Mass., 1989—90, chmn. task force permanent paper, 1989—90; mem. Mass. Emergency Mgmt. Team, 1996—, Cultural Emergency Mgmt. Team, Mass., 2004—; cons. in field. Author: Protecting Your Collections: A Manual of Archival Security, 1995; contbr. articles to profl. jours. Mem. Nat. Ski Patrol, 1966—; active Devil's Head Ski Patrol, Merrimack, Wis., 1976—81, regional tng. advisor, 1978—81, Nashoba Valley Ski Patrol, Westford, Mass., 1981—2007, tng. advisor, 1982—2007, Crotched Mt. Ski Patrol, Bennington, NH, 2007—; instr. outdoor emergency care, 1988—; trainer/evaluator Sr. Outdoor Emergency Care, 1990—, tng. coord., 1999—2002; trainer/evaluator Sr. Ski and Toboggan, 1995—, asst. regional dir. Ea. Mass. and R.I. region, 2005—07; tchr. Royal Scottish Country Dance Soc., Boston, 1976—; instr. first aid, CPR ARC, Ward Hill, Mass.; USSF Grade 7 Referee, USSF D coaching license. Fellow: Soc. Am. Archivists, Soc. Antiquaries of Scotland; mem.: Scottish Dance, Cultural and Edn. Assn. (bd. dirs. 1987—), New England Archivists (pres. 1995—96), Midwest Archives Conf., Soc. Am. Archivists (host com. chair 2003—04, task force on trusted archival preservation repositories 2006—, com. on archival facility guidelines 2006—), Phi Kappa Phi. Office: Massachusetts Board Library Commissioners 98 N Washington St Ste 401 Boston MA 02114-1933 Business E-Mail: gregor.trinkaus-randall@state.ma.us.

TRIO, EDWARD ALAN, lawyer, accountant; b. Newark, N.J., Dec. 29, 1952; s. Edward B. and Dorothy J. (Salvia) T.; m. Patricia Ann Sherwood, June 19, 1982; children: Edward Joseph, Michael John. B.B.A., U. Notre Dame, 1974; J.D., Hamline U., St. Paul, 1977; LL.M. in Taxation with honors, Chgo.-Kent Coll. Law, 1984. Bar: Ill. 1977, U.S. Dist. Ct. (no. dist.) Ill. 1977, U.S. Tax Ct. 1979, U.S. Supreme Ct. 1984. C.P.A. Staff auditor Donald E. Bark, C.P.A., Arlington Heights, Ill., 1972-77; assoc. Graf & Gulbrandsen, Morton Grove, Ill., 1977-80; ptnr. Schneider, Graf & Trio, Morton Grove, 1980-82; tax specialist Deloitte Haskins & Sells, Chgo., 1982-85; assoc. Gould & Ratner, Chgo., 1985-90, ptnr., 1991—. Mem. ABA, AICPA, Ill. State Bar Assn., Chgo. Bar Assn., KC. Roman Catholic. Home: 909 N Derbyshire Ave Arlington Heights IL 60004-5776 Office: Gould & Ratner 222 N La Salle St Ste 800 Chicago IL 60601-1086 Office Phone: 312-236-3003. E-mail: etrio@gouldratner.com.

TRIPATHI, RAM KISHORE, physicist, researcher; b. Rae Bareli, India, Jan. 1, 1942; arrived in U.S., 1966; s. Shiva Kumar and Devi Mani Tripathi; m. Pushpa Shukla Tripathi, May 26, 1966; 1 child, Sanjay. BS, U. Lucknow, 1961, MS, 1963; PhD, U. Kans., 1970. Asst. prof. U. Ky., Lexington, 1970—71, prof., 1986—87; scientist Kern Forschungsanlage, Juelich, Germany, 1971—73; sr. faculty fellow U. Sussex, Brighton, England, 1973—76; fellow Tata Inst. Fundamental Rsch., Bombay, 1975—78; assoc. prof. Dept. Energy/Inst. Physics, Bhubaneswar, India, 1978—85; prof. U. Tuebingen, Germany, 1980—82, U. Liege, Belgium, 1985—86; radiation physicist NASA Langley Rsch. Ctr., Hampton, Va., 1987—. Contbr. numerous articles to profl. jours. Pres. internat. cultural activities U. Kans., Lawrence, 1966-68. Fulbright fellow USIA, Washington, 1966-70, Sr. NRC fellow NAS, Washington, 1999; grantee NASA, Dept. of Def., Dept. of Energy, NSF. Fellow AIAA (assoc.), Am. Phys. Soc. (life), AAAS, Am. Nuc. Soc. (life). Avocations: jogging, travel, anthropology. Home: 13 Natalie Dr Hampton VA 23666-5565 Office: NASA Langley Rsch Ctr Ms 188 B Hampton VA 23681-0001

TRIPATHY, NIRMAL K., retail executive; Grad., Calcutta Univ.; MBA, Tex. Christian Univ. CPA. Fin. analyst Union Carbide Corp., 1982—83; cons. KPMG Peat Marwick, 1983—87; acct. Price Waterhouse, 1987—89;

fin. mgmt. positions Pepsico Inc., 1989—2000; exec. v.p. Macy's Fla., 2002—03, pres., COO, 2003—07; exec. v.p., CFO TJX Companies, Framingham, Mass., 2007—. Office: TJX Companies Inc 770 Cochituate Rd Framingham MA 01701 *

TRIPATHY, SUCHETA, research scientist; d. Gourishankar and Asha Lata Tripathy; m. Pramod Kumar Upadhyaya, Feb. 15, 1967. PhD, Osmania U., Hyderabad, 1997. Sr. scientist DSQ Biotech Ltd., Bangalore, Karnataka, India, 2000—01; scientist Avesthagengraine Technologies Pvt. Ltd., Bangalore, 2001—02; bioinfo. team leader Va. Bioinfo. Inst., Blacksburg, 2002—. Sr. scientist DSQ Biotech Ltd., Bangalore, 2000—01.

TRIPLEHORN, CHARLES A., entomologist, educator; b. Bluffton, Ohio, Oct. 27, 1927; s. Murray E. and Alice Irene (Lora) T.; m. Wanda Elaine Neiswander, June 12, 1949 (dec. Nov. 1985); children: Bradley Alyn, Bruce Wayne; m. Linda Sue Parsons, July 11, 1987. B.Sc., Ohio State U., 1949, MS, 1952; PhD, Cornell U., 1957. Asst. prof. entomology U. Del., Newark, 1952-54; teaching asst. entomology Cornell U., Ithaca, NY, 1954-57; asst. prof. entomology Ohio Agrl. Research and Devel. Ctr., Wooster, Ohio, 1957-61, Ohio State U., Columbus, 1961-62, assoc. prof. entomology, 1962-66, prof. entomology, 1966-92, prof. emeritus, 1992—. Econ. entomologist U.S. AID/Brazil, Piracicaba, Sao Paulo, 1964-66; vis. curator Field Mus. Natural History, Chgo., 1974, Can. Nat. Collection, Ottawa, Ont., 1977, Am. Mus. Natural History, N.Y.C., 1982, U. Mich., 1989, U. Ariz., 1989, Nat. Mus. of Natural History, 1998, Cornell U., 1999, Colo. State U., 2000, Brigham Young U., 2000. Co-author: Introduction to the Study of Insects, 7th edit., 2004. Cubmaster Boy Scouts Am., Wooster, Ohio, 1959-60, scoutmaster, Columbus, 1971-72; football coach Upper Arlington Football Assn., Ohio, 1968-71 Grantee Am. Philos. Soc., 1963, NSF, 1979, 85, 92. Mem. Entomol. Soc. Am. (pres. 1985), Coleopterists Soc. (pres. 1976), Royal Entomol. Soc. London, Entomol. Soc. Washington, Sigma Xi, Gamma Sigma Delta Clubs: Wheaton (pres.). Republican. Methodist. Avocations: sports, music, reading, writing. Home: 3943 Medford Sq Hilliard OH 43026-2219 Office: Mus Biol Diversity Div Insects The Ohio State University 1315 Kinnear Rd Columbus OH 43212-1157 Office Phone: 614-292-6839. Personal E-mail: ctriplhrn@aol.com.

TRIPLETT, E. EUGENE, editor; b. LaJolla, Calif., Mar. 12, 1949; s. Erbin Eugene Triplett and Marjorie Ann (Aldrich) Heath; m. Vannie Carol Crow, July 19, 1968; 1 child, Aaron Eugene. BA in Journalism, Ctrl. State U., 1975. Reporter, columnist The Okla. Jour., Oklahoma City, 1976-80; entertainment editor The Daily Oklahoman, Oklahoma City, 1981-85, asst. city editor, 1985-89, city editor, 1989-99, sr. feature writer, columnist, 1999—. Bd. dirs. Crime Stoppers Oklahoma City; mem. comm. com. Okla. Heart Assn., 1989-92. With U.S. Army, 1969-71, Vietnam. Recipient 1st pl. Feature Writing award Soc. Profl. Journalists, 1987, 97-98, 2d pl., 1999-2000. Mem. AP/Okla. News Exec. (pres.-elect 1994-95, pres. 1995-96, 2nd pl. Feature Writing award 1988, 1st pl. Feature Writing award, 2002, 1st pl. Rev. Writing award 2003). Democrat. Avocations: collecting recorded music, feature films, vintage tv shows. Home: 8116 NW 118th St Oklahoma City OK 73162-1113 Office: The Daily Oklahoman 9000 Broadway Ext Oklahoma City OK 73114-3799 Office Phone: 405-475-4105. E-mail: etriplett@oklahoman.com, geneoat@cox.net.

TRIPODES, JAMES G., nuclear safety and environmental regulatory affairs professional; b. San Francisco, Mar. 12, 1954; s. George J. Tripodes and Daisy Natsoulas Pimentel; m. Nham T. Tripodes, Nov. 5, 1983. BS in Environ. Planning and Mgmt., U. Calif., Davis, 1978. Registered hazardous substances profl. Nat. Environ. Health Assn.; registered environ. assessor Calif. EPA. Envir. health/safety technician, cyclotron health physicist U. Calif., Davis, 1972-79, health physics mgr. Irvine, 1979-89, assoc. dir. envir. health/safety for envir. reg. affairs, 1989-2001, interim dir. environ. health and safety, 2001—02; dep. dept. head environ. protection Lawrence Livermore (Calif.) Nat. Lab., 2002—03, scientist, 2003—. Co-founder, oversight chmn. Internat. Conf. on Incineration and Thermal Treatment Techs., 1980-2000; prin. investigator, project mgr. U.S. Dept. Energy and Calif. Dept. Health Svcs., 1982-95. Editor: (book and CD-ROM) Proceedings of International Conferences on Incineration and Thermal Treatment Technologies, 1985-2000; guest editor spl. issue: Health Physics Jour., 1991. Mem. govt. affairs coun. Irvine C. of C., 1995—2002; patron Heritage Found., Washington, 1995—, Commonwealth Club of Calif., 2003-; commr. Southwestern Low-Level Radioactive Waste Commn., 2004-05. Fellow Acad. Polit. Sci.; mem. AAAS, ASME, Health Physics Soc. (Elda E. Anderson award 1994), Am. Soc. for Quality, Ctr. for Study of the Presidency, N.Y. Acad. Scis. Republican. Avocations: fine art and music appreciation, public affairs. Office: Lawrence Livermore Nat Lab PO Box 808 L-309 Livermore CA 94551 Office Phone: 925-424-2875. Business E-Mail: tripodes2@llnl.gov.

TRIPODI, JOSEPH V., beverage company executive, former insurance company executive; b. Aug. 7, 1955; BA, Harvard Univ., 1977; MS, London Sch. Econ., 1981. Mgmt. positions IBM, 1977—81, Mobil Oil, 1981—88; exec. v.p. glob. mktg. MasterCard Internat., 1989—98; chief mktg. officer Seagram Spirits & Wine, 1999—2002, Bank of NY, 2002—03; sr. v.p., chief mktg. officer Allstate Ins. Co., Northbrook, Ill., 2003—07; sr. v.p., chief mktg. & comml. officer The Coca-Cola Co., Atlanta, 2007—. Bd. mem. Ad Council; past. chmn. Assn. Nat. Advertisers. Trustee Field Mus., Chgo. Office: The Coca Cola Co 1 Coca Cola Pl Atlanta GA 30313 *

TRIPOLI, MASUMI HIROYASU, financial consultant; b. Fukuyama, Japan, Apr. 23, 1956; d. Yoshimi and Suzuko Hiroyasu; 1 child, Mona Lisa Tripoli. BA cum laude, U. Wash., 1978; MA, Sophia U., Tokyo, 1981; postgrad., Sydney U., 1982; MBA, Ecole des Hautes Etudes Comml, Jouy-en-Josas, France, 1983. CFP. Corp. planning mgr. Kowa Corp., Osaka, Japan, 1983-85; internat. bond trader Banque Baribas, Tokyo, 1985-86, Westpac Bank, Tokyo, 1987-88; fin. cons. Masumi Tripoli and Assocs., Irvine, Calif., 1989—; anchor newscaster United TV, LA, 1989-92. Condr. seminars in field. Contbr. articles to profl. jours. CEO Masumi Tripoli and Mona Lisa Tripoli Found. Grantee Sophia U., 1979, H.E.C., 1983. Mem. Internat. Bd. Cert. Fin. Planners. E-mail: masumiusa@hotmail.com.

TRIPP, ALAN H., educational association administrator, consultant; s. Jasper L. and Sarah Y. Tripp. AB in Econ. and Internat. Rels., Stanford U., 1985, MBA, 1989. Editor, reporter Wall St. Jour., European edit., Brussels, 1985—86; cons. Boston Consulting Group, San Francisco, 1989—91; founder, CEO, Score! Ednl. Crs., San Francisco, 1992—99, InsideTrack Learning, Inc., San Francisco, 1999—. Bd. chair GreatSchools.net, San Francisco, 2001—. Mem.: Phi Beta Kappa. Office: InsideTrack Learning Inc 703 Market St 20th Fl San Francisco CA 94114

TRIPP, KAREN BRYANT, lawyer; b. Rocky Mount, NC, Sept. 2, 1955; d. Bryant and Katherine Rebecca (Watkins) Tripp; m. Robert Mark Burleson, June 25, 1977 (div. 1997); 1 child, Hamilton Chase Tripp Barnett. BA, U. NC, 1976; JD, U. Ala., 1981. Bar: Tex. 1981, US Dist. Ct. (so. dist.) Tex. 1982, US Ct. Appeals (fed. cir.) 1983, US Dist. Ct. (ea. dist.) Tex. 1991, US Dist. Ct. (we. dist.), 2005, US Supreme Ct. 1994, US Dist. Ct. (no. dist.) Tex. 1998, US Ct. Appeals (5th and 9th cirs.) 2000, US Ct. Appeals (3d cir.) 2001. Law clk. Tucker, Gray & Espy, Tuscaloosa, Ala., 1978-81; law clk. to presiding justice Ala. Supreme Ct., Montgomery, Ala., summer 1980; atty. Exxon Prodn. Rsch. Co., Houston, 1981-86, coord. tech. transfer, 1986-87; assoc. Arnold, White and Durkee, Houston, 1988-93, shareholder, 1994-98; shareholder, head intellectual property sect. for Houston office Winstead, Sechrest & Minick, Attys. at Law, Houston, 1998; pres. Blake Barnett & Co., 1996—2003; pvt. practice Houston, 1999—. Creator, program planner, master of ceremonies 1st and 2d intellectual property law confs. for women corp. counsels; adj. prof. of intellectual property law Inst. for Advanced Legal Studies, Houston, 2005—. Editor: Intellectual Property Law Rev., 1995—2006; contbr. articles to profl. jour. Chair U. Houston and Houston intellectual Property Law Assoc. Fall CLE Inst. on Intellectual Property, 2000. Mem. ABA (intellectual property law sect., ethics com. 1992-96), Houston Bar Assn. (interprofl. rels. com. 1988-90), Houston Intellectual Property Law Assn. (outstanding inventor com. 1982-84, chmn. 1994-95, sec. 1987-88, treas. 1991-92, bd. dir. 1992-94, 98-2000, nominations com. 1993, 96, chmn. fall CLE Inst. 2000), Houston Bar Found. (fellow), Tex. Bar Assn. (antitrust law com. 1984-85, chmn. internat. law com. intellectual property law sect. 1987-88, internat. transfer tech. com. 1983-84, planning com. continuing legal edn. conf. on intellectual property 2003), planning comm. for 2003 CLE Inst. on Intellectual property Law, Tex. Exec. Women, Women's Fin. Exch., Am. Intellectual Property Lawyers Assn. (patent law com. 1995), Intellectual Property Owners Assn. (copyright com.), Women in Tech. (founder), Lil Eli's Club (founder), Phi Alpha Delta. Republican. Episcopalian. Office: PO Box 1301 Houston TX 77251-1301 Home Phone: 713-658-9323; Office Phone: 713-658-9323. Business E-Mail: ktripp@tripplaw.com.

TRIPP, MICHAEL WINDSOR, accountant; b. Fall River, Mass. s. Frederick and Elizabeth (Azevedo) T.; m. Ella Charlene Middlebrooks, May 24, 1966; children: Sandra Lee, Wendy Ann. Cert. computer programming with honors, Plus Sch. Bus., Providence, 1971; BSBA in Acctg. cum laude, Bryant Coll., 1975. CPA, R.I.; diplomate Am. Bd. Forensic Acctg. Fin. mgr. trainee I.T.T. Aetna Fin., Pawtucket, R.I., 1969-70; computer programmer B.A. Ballou & Co., Inc., East Providence, R.I., 1970-72; adminstrv. asst. Manasett Corp., Providence, 1972-74; profl. staff Peat, Marwick & Mitchell, Providence, 1974-76; ptnr. Turosz, Maccarone, Keenan & Tripp, East Providence, 1976-88; adminstr. Licht & Semonoff, Providence, 1988-89; pvt. practice East Providence, 1989—. Adj. instr. acctg. Roger Williams Coll., 1979-82; dir. A New Leaf, Providence, 1988-96; mem. bd. regents LaSalle Acad., 1999-2005. Vice-chmn., clk. Barrington (R.I.) Sch. Com., 1980-88; active Rep. Town Com., Barrington, 1980—; treas. Hampden Meadows PTA, Barrington, 1976-80, Rhode Islanders for Chafee, Providence, 1976. With USMC, 1965-69, Vietnam. Decorated Purple Heart, Air medal, Navy Commendation medal with combat V. Fellow AICPA; mem. R.I. Soc. CPAs, Manny Moniz Meml. Hockey League (treas. 1992—), Barrington Yacht Club (treas. 1992-93), Narragansett Bay Yachting Assn., Am. Coll. Forensic Examiners, Bryant Coll. Alumni Assn. (exec. dir., treas. 1977-80), La Salle Acad. Alumni Assn. (phonathon chmn. 1992-93), Appalachian Mountain Club, U.S. Sailing Assn., VFW (quartermaster Post 9742, 2002—), Barrington United Vets. Coun. (treas. 2005-), Friends of Pomham Rock Lighthouse (treas. 2006—). Republican. Roman Catholic. Avocations: sailing, hockey, mountain climbing. Home: 40 Lamson Rd Barrington RI 02806-2643 Office: 1481 Wampanoag Trail Ste 2 East Providence RI 02915 E-mail: mtripp@mwt-cpa.coxatwork.com.

TRIPP, SUSAN GERWE, museum director; b. Balt., Dec. 28, 1945; d. Earl Joseph and Maria Elizabeth (Wise) Gerwe; m. David Enders Tripp, June 9, 1977. BS, U. Md., 1967. Home econs. tchr. Balt. County Pub. Sch. Sys., 1967-74; curator of art Johns Hopkins U., Balt., 1974-76, curator of art, archivist, 1976-78, instr. evening coll., 1978-84, dir. univ. collections, 1979-91; supr., instr. art history Goucher Coll., Notre Dame U., Balt., 1977-86; dir. docent tng. Homewood Mus., Balt., 1987-89; exec. dir. Old Westbury Gardens, NY, 1992-96; writer Stuyvesant, NY, 1996—. Dir. Homewood Restoration Adv. Com., 1983-92, Evergreen Restoration Adv. Com., 1988-92, Advancement Basilica Hist. Trust, Inc., 2000-2001; lectr. in field. Co-author: The Garrett Collection of Japanese Art, 1993 (NEA Grant 1980). Contbr. articles to profl. jours. Bd. dirs. Columbia County Hist. Soc., 1996-2002, 2003—, pres. bd. dirs., 1997-2002, chmn. Vanderpoel house restoration, 2002— sec., 2003—, interim exec. dir., 2006-, chmn. curatorial com., 2006—; trustee Regional and Cmty. Hist. Preservation Benefit Plan, 2002; judge Hist. Hudson Preservation Awards, 2000—; trustee Am. Numismatic Soc., 2003—. Recipient Hist. Preservation award Balt. Heritage, Inc., 1988, 91, Rsch. award Am. Soc. Interior Designers, 1991. Fellow Am. Numismatic Soc. (standing com., libr., trustee 2003—); mem. Mus. Art, Furniture History Soc., Columbia County Hist. Soc. (bd. dirs. 2003—, sec. bd. dirs. 2003—), Friends Am. Wing, Omicron Nu. Avocations: architecture, archaeology, chinese ceramics, historical restoration. Office: PO Box G Stuyvesant NY 12173-0009

TRIPP, THOMAS NEAL, lawyer, political scientist; b. June 19, 1942; s. Gerald Frederick and Kathryn Ann (Siebold) T.; m. Ellen Marie Larrimer, Apr. 16, 1966; children: David Larrimer, Bradford Douglas, Corinne Catherine. BA cum laude, Mich. State U., 1964; JD, George Washington U., 1967. Bar: Ohio 1967, U.S. Ct. Mil. Appeals 1968, U.S. Supreme Ct. 1968, Wyo. 1991. Pvt. practice, Columbus, Ohio, 1969—, Wilson, Wyo., 1991—. Real estate developer, Columbus, 1969—; chmn. bd. Black Sheep Enterprises, Columbus, 1969—; polit. cons. David A. Keene & Assocs., Washington, 1986-96; vice chmn. bd. Sun Valley-Elkhorn Assn., Idaho, 1983-85, chmn, 1986-91; vice chmn. Sawtooth Sports, Ketchum, Idaho, 1983-85; legal counsel Wallace F. Ackley Co., Columbus, 1973—; vice chmn. Triathlon LLC, 1996-2003; presiding judge Ohio Mock Trial Competition, 1986-94; chmn. bd. dirs. White House, 1996; mem. small bus. adv. coun. FCC, 1993-95; dep. spl. adviser to pres. N.Am. Free Trade Agreement, 1993; polit. columnist. Trustee Americans for Responsible Govt., Washington, GOPAC; mem. Peace Corps Adv. Coun., 1981-85; mem. U.S. Commn. on Trade Policy and Negotiations, 1985-88; campaign mgr., fin. chmn. Charles Rockwell Saxbe, Ohio Ho. of Reps., 1974, 76, 78, 80; campaign mgr. George Bush for Pres., 1980, nat. dep. field dir., nat. dep. polit. dir., 1980; alumni admissions coun. Mich. State U., 1984-2000, George Washington U., 1988-2000; regional co-chmn. Reagan-Bush, 1984, nat. fin. com., 1984; mem. Victory '84 fin. com.; mem. Victory '88 fin. com. Bush-Quayle; co-chmn. Ohio Lawyers for Bush/Quayle, 1988; Rep. candidate 2d U.S. Congl. Dist., Idaho, 1988; candidate U.S. Senate, Wyo., 1996; transition dir. Ohio Sec. of State, 1990-91; bd. trustees Columbus Acad. Pvt. Co-ed Secondary Sch., 1991-94, Prescott (Ariz.) Coll., 1998-2000; chmn. bd. dirs. T.R.E.E. Coalition, 1991—; vice-chmn. Am. Conservative Union Found., 2002-06, sec., 2006—; chmn. FirstPrinciples.US. Pub. Policy Institute, 2003—. 1st lt. U.S. Army, 1967-69. Fellow Pi Sigma Alpha, Vietnam Vet. Am., Phi Delta Phi. Republican. Home: 5420 Clark State Rd Columbus OH 43230-1956

TRIPP, VICTOR K., electrical engineer, researcher; b. Spring Brook, Wis., Apr. 14, 1947; s. Clovis H. and Mildred M. Tripp; m. Carmen V. Couceyro, Mar. 10, 1948; children: Rebecca S. Ziegler, Rachel L. BA in Physics, U. of Chgo., 1970; MSEE, U. of Ill., Urbanna, 1972. Cert. electromagnetic compatability engr., Nat. Assn. of Radio and Telecom. Engrs., 1990. V.p. Wang-Tripp Corp., Marietta, Ga., 1991—95; prin. rsch. engr. Ga. Tech Rsch. Inst., Atlanta, 1991—. Mem. blue ribbon panel of experts on RF com. U.S. Army CECOM, 1996; editor ElephantJournal.org, Tucker, 2001—; prin. Tripp Tech. Cons., Tucker, Ga., 2002—. Contbr., reviewer: over 50 articles to prof. jours. Elder and deacon various ch. congregations, Tucker, 1979—2000. Recipient Outstanding Performance in Rsch., Ga. Tech Rsch. Inst., ECS Lab, 1988, Commendation for Pioneering New Antenna Technologies, US Air Force, Wright R&D Ctr., Avionics Lab, Electronic Warfare, 1993. Mem.: IEEE (sr.), IEEE Internat. Symposium on Antennas and Propagation (steering com. 1998—98), IEEE Antenna and Propagation Soc. (chmn., atlanta sect. 1987—89), Sigma Xi. Christian. Achievements include 7 patents related to antennas and electromagnetics. Office: Georgia Tech Research Institute 7220 Richardson Rd Smyrna GA 30080 Office Phone: 770-528-7160. Office Fax: 770-528-3187. E-mail: vic.tripp@gtri.gatech.edu.

TRIPPENSEE, GARY ALAN, retired aerospace executive; b. Jefferson City, Mo., May 23, 1940; m. Concha Elvira Perez, Aug. 18, 1981; children: Jena, Darin. BSME, U. Mo., Rolla, 1962; AA in Bus., Antelope Valley Coll., Lancaster, Calif., 1974. Lic. airframe and powerplant mechanic, FAA; single/multi-engine comml. aircraft lic. land & sea, Inst.; cert. flight instr., instrument. Aircraft flight test engr. McDonnell Douglas, St. Louis, 1965-79; project mgr. NASA/Dryden Flight Rsch. Ctr., Edwards, Calif., 1979—2001, project mgr. F14, 1983-84, project mgr. F15, 1984-85, project mgr. X-29, 1985-91, project mgr. X-31, 1991-92, internat. test. orgn. dir. X-31, 1993-95, project mgr. X-33, 1996-2000, project mgr. X-37, 2000-01, ret., 2001. Mem. Grove City Coun., Okla., 2007; capt. U.S. Army C.E., 1962-65, Vietnam. Recipient Laurels award for aeronautics/propulsion Aviation Week & Space Tech., 1990, 93, Outstanding Alumni award U. Mo.-Rolla, 2002. Mem. EAA, Acad. Mech. Engrs. Avocations: flying, fishing, r/c models. Home: 3410 Callie Dr Grove OK 74344 Office Phone: 918-791-1917. Business E-Mail: gfsbtrip@grandsavingsbank.com.

TRIPPLEHORN, JEANNE, actress; b. Tulsa, Okla., June 10, 1963; d. Tommy and Suzanne (Ferguson) T.; m. Leland Orser, Oct. 14, 2000; 1 child August Student, Juilliard Sch. Actress: (theatre off-Broadway) The Big Funk, 1990, 'Tis Pity She's A Whore, 1992; (films) Basic Instinct, 1991, The Firm, 1993, The Night We Never Met, 1993, Reality Bites, 1994, Waterworld, 1995, 'Til There Was You, 1996, Office Killer, 1997, Snitch, 1998, Sliding Doors, 1998, Very Bad Things, 1998, Talk of the Town, 1998, Mickey Blue-Eyes, 1998, Steal This Movie, 2000, Timecode, 2000, Paranoid, 2000, Relative Values, 2000, Dial 9 for Love, 2001, Swept Away, 2002, Word of Honor, 2003, The Moguls, 2005; (TV films) The Perfect Tribute, 1991, Old Man, 1997, My Brother's Keeper, 2002; (TV series) Big Love, 2006-; (TV appearances) The Ben Stiller Show, 1992, Frasier, 2003 Office: c/o William Morris Agency One William Morris Pl Beverly Hills CA 90212 *

TRISCO, ROBERT FREDERICK, church historian, educator; b. Chgo., Nov. 11, 1929; s. Richard E. and Harriet Rose (Hardt) T. BA, St. Mary of Lake Sem., Mundelein, Ill., 1951; STL, Pontifical Gregorian U., Rome, 1955, Hist. Eccl.D., 1962; LHD (hon.), Belmont Abbey Coll., 1992. Ordained priest Roman Catholic Ch., 1954. Faculty Cath. U. Am., Washington, 1959-2000, prof. ch. history, 1975-2000, Kelly-Quinn disting. prof. ch. history, 1999-2000, prof. emeritus ch. history, 2000—. Expert 2d Vatican Coun., 1962-65; pres. Am. subcom. Internat. Commn. Comparative Ch. History, 1978-80, assesseur, 1980—; mem. subcoms. Nat. Conf. Cath. Bishops, 1966-76, 87-92; mem. Pontifical Com. Hist. Scis., 1982—; hon. mem. Accademia di San Carlo (Milan), 1986—; hon. prelate (monsignor), 1992; Protonotary Apostolic Supranumerary, 2005; mem. Internat. Joint Commn. for Theol. Dialogue between Cath. Ch. and Orthodox Ch., 1999-2006; mem. Anglican-Roman Catholic Consultation in U.S., 2002—; mem. adv. com. Assn. Friends of the Archives of Congregation for Doctrine of the Faith (Holy See), 1999—. Author: The Holy See and Nascent Church in the Middle Western U.S., 1826-1850, 1962, Bishops and Their Priests in the United States, 1988; co-author: A Guide to American Catholic History, 2d edit., 1982; editor: Catholics in America, 1976; editor Cath. Hist. Rev., 1963-2005, assoc. editor, 2005-; co-editor, contbr.: Studies in Catholic History in Honor of John Tracy Ellis, 1985; contbr. articles to profl. jours. Decorated knight Equestrian Order of the Holy Sepulchre of Jerusalem, 1993, knight comdr., 1998. Mem. Am. Hist. Assn., Am. Soc. Ch. History (coun. 1980-82), Am. Cath. Hist. Assn. (exec. sec. 1961—, sec., treas. 1983—), Can. Cath. Hist. Assn. Office: Cath U Am Mullen Library Rm 320 Washington DC 20064-0001 Office Phone: 202-319-5079. Business E-Mail: trisco@cua.edu.

TRISTANO, ANTONIO GINO, medical researcher; arrived in U.S., 2003; s. Piero Tristano and Speranza Romano; children: Gianpiero, Fabrizio. MD, Luiz Razetti Sch. Medicine, Caracas, 1991; MS in Biology, Instituto Venezolano de Investigaciones Científicas (IVIC), Caracas, 1997; Specialist in Criminalistics cum laude, U. Inst. Sci. Police, Caracas, 1997; Specialist in Internal Medicine, Luis Razetti Sch. Medicine, Caracas, 2000, Specialist in Rheumatology, 2002. Specialist in Rheumatology Colegio de Medicos del Distrito Metropolitano, 2003, Specialist in Internal Medicine Colegio de Medicos del Distrito Metropolitano, 2001, Medical Assistant Am. Registry of Med. Assistants/Fla., 2004. Rural physician Hosp. de Naiguatá, La Guaira, Vargas, Venezuela; intern Instituto de Clínicas y Urología Tamanaco, Caracas, 1992—93; biology prof. Instituto Universitario de Policía Científica, Caracas, 1996—97; toxicology prof. José María Vargas U., Caracas, 1997—97; internal medicine staff in internal medicine program Hosp. Domingo Luciani (U. Hosp.), Caracas, 2002—04; rsch. assoc. NOVA Southeastern U., Ft. Lauderdale, Fla., 2004—. Chief resident internal medicine Internal Medicine Residency Program Domingo Luciani Hosp. (Univrsity Hosp.), Caracas, 1997—98; chief resident rheumatology U. Hosp. of the City of Caracas, 2001—02; mem. soc. interns and residents Domingo Luciani Hosp., Caracas, 1998—2000; presenter in field. Reviewer: So. Med. Jour.; contbr. articles to profl. jours. Vaccination Ministerio de Sanidad y Asistencia Social, Caracas, 1987—87. Scholar, Fundación Gran Mariscal de Ayacucho, 1995—97. Mem.: Venezuelan Assn. Internal Medicine (Spl. Award by thesis 2000), Internat. Reviewers Panel of the Med. Sci. Monitor, Venezuelan Assn. for Pain Studies, Venezuelan Assn. Rheumatology, Internat. Assn. for the Study of Pain, ACP, Am. Soc. Internal Medicine (Award for 1° prize of best paper Pub. 2003). Roman Catholic. Avocations: travel, classical music. Office: NOVA Southeastern U 3200 S University Dr Fort Lauderdale FL 33328 Office Phone: 954-262-1925. Personal E-mail: mjtristano@cantv.net.

TRITCH, TERESA, editor, writer; b. LA; BA in German, UCLA, 1984; MA in Journalism, Columbia Univ., 2001. Joined Money Mag., 1988, bur. chief Washington, 1993—97, sr. editor NYC, 1997—2000; contributing editor Gallup Mgmt. Jour., 2001—03, Stanford Social Innovation Rev., 2003; editl. bd. mem. NY Times, 2004—. Co-editor: America at War: The Battle for Iraq in Words, 2003. Knight-Bagehot Fellow in Bus. and Econ. Journalism, Columbia Univ., 2000—01. Office: Editl Bd NY Times 229 W 43rd St New York NY 10036 Office Phone: 212-556-1876. Office Fax: 212-556-3815.

TRITLE, LAWRENCE ALAN, history professor; b. Glendale, Calif., Oct. 13, 1946; s. Robert Charles Jr. and Dorothy (Brown) T.; m. Margaret Burlington, Jan. 31, 1970 (dec. Aug. 24, 2000) BA, UCLA, 1968; MA, U. S. Fla., Tampa, 1972; PhD, U. Chgo., 1978. Prof. Loyola Marymount U., LA, 1978—, Marie Chilton chair humanities, 1988. Vis. prof. Loyola U. Chgo., 1981-82, 90-91, UCLA, 1992. Author: Phocion the Good, 1988, From Melos to My Lai. War & Survival, 2000, The Peloponnesian War, 2004; editor: The Greek World in the Fourth Century BC, 1997, Balkan Currents, 1998, Text and Tradition: Studies in Greek History & Historiography, 1999, Crossroads of History Age of Alexander, 2003. Lt. U.S. Army, 1968-71, Vietnam. NEH fellow U. Pa., 1979. Mem. Am. Philol. Assn. (chair com. ancient history 1997-99), Am. Hist. Assn., Assn. Ancient Historians, Soc. Mayflower Descs., Am. Legion. Democrat. Home: 8301 Fordham Rd Los Angeles CA 90045-2559 Office: Loyola Marymount U 1 LMU Dr Los Angeles CA 90045-2699 Office Phone: 310-338-7385. Business E-Mail: ltritle@lmu.edu.

TRITTEN, JAMES JOHN, federal agency administrator, educator; s. James Hanley and Jennie (Szucs) Tritten; m. Kathleen Brattesani (div. 1983); children: Kimberly, James John Jr.; m. Jasmine Clark, Dec. 29,

1990. BA in Internat. Studies, Am. U., 1971; MA in Internat. Affairs, Fla. State U., 1978; AM in Internat. Rels., U. So. Calif., 1982, PhD in Internat. Rels., 1984. Commd. officer USN, 1967, advanced through grades to commdr., 1981; joint strategic plans officer Office Chief Naval Ops., Washington, 1984—85; asst. dir. net assessment Office Sec. Def., Washington, 1985—86; chmn. dept. nat. security affairs Naval Postgrad. Sch., Monterey, Calif., 1986—89; ret. USN, 1989; assoc. prof. nat. security affairs Naval Postgrad. Sch., Monterey, 1989—93; spl. asst. comdr. Naval Doctrine Command, Norfolk, Va., 1993—96; chief policy and plan divsn. US Joint Forces Command, Suffolk, Va., 1996—2001, mem. joint doctrine divsn., 2001—02; chief Def. Threat Reduction U./Def. Threat Reduction Agy., Albuquerque, 2002—; asst. chief staff Def. Threat Reduction Agy., 2002—. Cons. Rand Corp., Santa Monica, Calif., 1982—84; with Nat. Security Rsch., Fairfax, Va., 1992, Amerlnd, Alexandria, Va., 1996. Author: (book) Soviet Naval Forces and Nuclear Warfare, 1986, Our New National Security Strategy, 1992 (George Washington Honor medal, 1991), A Doctrine Reader, 1996; contbr. chapters to books, articles to profl. jours. Mem. Adv. Bd. on Alcohol Related Problems, Monterey, 1987—90; bd. dirs., officer Leadership Monterey Peninsula, 1989—92, Carmel Valley (Calif.) Property Owners Assn., 1989—91; commr. Airport Land Use Commn., Monterey County, 1990—93. Decorated Def. Superior Svc. medal Sec. Def., Washington, DC, Meritorious Svc. medal Sec. Navy, Navy Civilian Supr. Svc. medal; recipient Joint Meritorious Civilian Svc. award, Chmn. Joint Chiefs Staff, 1998, Alfred Thayer Mahan award literary achievement, Navy League US, 1986. Mem.: Mil. Ops. Rsch. Soc. (v.p. 1990—91), U.S. Naval Inst. (Silver and Bronze medals), Naval Order U.S., Pi Gamma Mu, Pi Sigma Alpha. Republican. Presbyterian. Avocations: hiking, writing. Office: Def Threat Reduction Agy-CSU 1680 Texas St SE Kirtland Afb NM 87117 Office Phone: 505-846-8734. Personal E-mail: jtritten121@comcast.net. Business E-Mail: james.tritten@abq.dtra.mil.

TRITTER, RICHARD PAUL, strategic consultant; b. Boston, Sept. 30, 1945; arrived in Israel, 2001, naturalized; s. Herman Louis and Rose (Greenblatt) T.; children: Melissa Rosanne, Matthew Alexander, Rachel Danielle, Adam Levi. AB, Columbia Coll., NYC, 1967; JD, Northeastern U. Law Sch., Boston, 1976. Bar: Mass. 1977, U.S. Supreme Ct. 1980. Mktg. mgr./cons. Digital Equipment Corp., Merrimack, NH, 1979-86; pres. Video/Demo Ctrs., Inc., Burlington, Mass., 1986-88; v.p. bus. devel. Info. Resources, Inc., Boston, 1988-91; dir. facilitation consulting svcs. Arthur Andersen LLP, Boston, Chgo., 1991-96; consulting dir. Computer Assocs., Inc., Andover, Mass., 1998—2001; bus. cons. Israel, 2001—. Panelist MIT Enterprise Forum, Cambridge, 1983-89; ptnr., mng. dir. Horn of Africa Fishing Partnership, 1998. Author: Control Self-Assessment: Experience, Current Thinking and Best Practices, 1996, Control Self Assessment—A Guide to Facilitation-Based Consulting, 2000; creator software application testing svc. in coop. with KPMG Peat Marwick, Compliance Testing and Verification, 1981. UN rep. Jubaland Relief and Rehab. Soc., Somalia; dir. Save Somalia Livestock Campaign, 1993. Recipient Better Govt. award, Pioneer Inst. for Pub. Policy Rsch., 1991, Israel Yoseftal Prize, Min. Labor, 2003. Achievements include facilitating meetings between opposing clans in the Juba region of southern Somalia; initiated lobster export project with cooperation of Gen. Omar Jess, Col. Ahmed Hashi and other Somali leaders. Mailing: Kibbutz Givat Brener 60948 Givat Brener Israel Home Phone: 011-972-5254-00250.

TRITTON, THOMAS RICHARD, former academic administrator, biologist, educator; b. Lakewood, Ohio, Dec. 20, 1947; s. William Frank and Margie Jean (Galbraith) Tritton; m. Louise Meschter Tritton; children: Lara, Christiana. BA, Ohio Wesleyan U., 1969; PhD, Boston U., 1973. Asst. prof. Yale Med. Sch., New Haven, 1975—80; assoc. prof. Yale U., 1980—85; prof. U. Vt., Burlington, 1985—97, vice provost, 1991—97; pres. Haverford Coll., Pa., 1997—2007, Chem. Heritage Found., 2007—. Mem. NIH Exptl. Therapeutics Study Sect., 1988—92; bd. dirs. Fox Chase Cancer Ctr., 1997—. Editor books; mem. editl. bd.: various profl. jours.; contbr. scientific papers to profl. jours. Mem.: Am. Soc. Biol. Chemists, Am. Assn. Cancer Rsch. (com. mem.). Mem. Soc. Of Friends. Avocations: music, tennis. Home: 1 College Circle Haverford PA 19041 Home Phone: 610-896-1021; Office Phone: 215-925-2222. Business E-Mail: ttritton@chemheritage.org.

TRIVELPIECE, ALVIN WILLIAM, physicist, educator, consultant; b. Stockton, Calif., Mar. 15, 1931; s. Alvin Stevens and Mae (Hughes) Trivelpiece; m. Shirley Ann Ross, Mar. 23, 1953; children: Craig Evan, Steve Edward, Keith Eric. BEE, Calif. Poly. Coll., 1953; MEE, Calif. Inst. Tech., Pasadena, 1955, PhD in Elec. Engring. and Physics, 1958. Fulbright scholar Delft U., Netherlands, 1958—59; asst. prof., then assoc. prof. U. Calif. at Berkeley, 1959—66; prof. physics U. Md., 1966—76; on leave as asst. dir. for rsch. divsn. controlled thermonuclear rsch. AEC, Washington, 1973—75; v.p. Maxwell Labs. Inc., San Diego, 1976—78; corp. v.p. Sci. Applications, Inc., La Jolla, Calif., 1978—81; dir. Office of Energy Rsch., US Dept. Energy, Washington, 1981—87; exec. officer AAAS, Washington, 1987—88; dir. Oak Ridge Nat. Lab., Tenn., 1989—2000; v.p. Martin Marietta Energy Systems, 1989—95, Lockheed Martin Energy Systems, 1995; pres. Lockheed Martin Energy Rsch. Corp., 1996—2000; cons. Sandia Nat. Labs., Albuquerque, 2000—. Head del. joint NAS and Soviet Acad. Scis. mtg. and conf. on energy and global ecol. problems USSR, 1989; chmn. math. scis. ednl. bd. NAS, 1990—93; chmn. coordinating coun. for edn. NRC, 1991—93, chmn. com. small innovative firms in Russian nuclear cities, 2001, chmn. com. on Sci. and Tech. in Kazakhstan, 2006—07; mem. Commn. on Phys. Scis., Math. and Applications, 1993—96, com. on tech. issues related to the comprehensive test ban treaty NAS, 2000—02, Tenn. Sci. and Tech. Adv. Commn., 1993—96, chmn., 1996—99, adv. com. Fedn. Networking Coun., 1992—96; chmn. and pres. Tenn. Tech. Devel. Corp., 1998—2000; workshop chmn. NAS and Russian Acad. Scis., Yekaterinburg, Russia, 2004; founding bd. mem., sec., treas. Am. Coun. on Global Nuc. Competitiveness, 2006—; bd. dirs. Environ. Literacy Coun. Author: Slow Wave Propagation in Plasma Wave Guides, 1966, Principles of Plasma Physics, 1973; contbr. articles to profl. jours. Named Disting. Alumnus, Calif. Poly. State U., 1978, Calif. Inst. Tech., Pasadena, 1987; recipient Gold medal for Disting. Svc., US Sec. Energy, 1986, Disting. Assoc. award, 2000, Tenn. Outstanding Svc. commendation, Senate Joint Resolution #530, 2000; fellow Guggenheim, 1966. Fellow: IEEE (Outstanding Engr. award region 3 1995), AAAS, Am. Phys. Soc.; mem.: NAE, AAUP, Am. Assn. Physics Tchrs., Am. Nuc. Soc., Nat. Press Club, Capital Hill Club, Tau Beta Pi, Sigma Xi. Achievements include patents in field. Home and Office: 14 Wade Hampton Trail Henderson NV 89052-6635 Office Phone: 702-492-1602. Personal E-mail: awt511@cox.net.

TRIVERS, ROBERT L., bioscience and anthropology educator, evolutionary biologist, sociobiologist; b. Washington, 1943; PhD in Biology, Harvard U., 1965. Faculty Harvard U., 1973—78; with U. Calif., Santa Cruz, 1978—94; prof. anthropology and biol. sciences, dept. anthropology Rutgers U., New Brunswick, NJ. Sr. scientist The Rutgers Jamaican Symmetry Project, 1996—. Author: Social Evolution, 1985, Natural Selection and Social Theory: Selected Papers of Robert Trivers, 2002; co-author (with Austin Burt): Genes in Conflict: The Biology of Selfish Genetic Elements, 2006; contbr. articles to profl. publications. Named one of 100 Greatest Thinkers and Scientists of the 20th Century, Time mag.; recipient Crafoord prize in Biosciences, Royal Swedish Acad. Sciences, 2007. Achievements include fundamental analysis of social evolution, conflict and cooperation among animals, which laid the foundation for modern sociobiology. Office: Dept Anthropology Rutgers U 131 George St New Brunswick NJ 08901-1414 Office Phone: 732-932-1670, 732-932-1564. Business E-Mail: trivers@rci.rutgers.edu.

TROBERMAN, GAYLE DEBORAH, marketing executive; b. 1966; BS in TV Comm., Ithaca Coll., 1988. Global gen. mgr. Branded Entertainment, dir.; mgr. account services NW Ayer; dir. mktg. several divsn., including eCommerce VNU eMedia Inc.; dir. custom solutions Microsoft Corp., 2004—05; dir. branded entertainment & experiences MSN Search Inc., 2005—06, sr. dir. branded entertainment, 2006—. Named a Woman to Watch, Advt. Age, 2007. Office: Microsoft Corp 1 Microsoft Way Redmond WA 98052 Office Phone: 812-303-2911. *

TROBOUGH, JOHN, communications executive; s. John Michael Trobough and Mary Ellen Buzard; life ptnr. Amy Peters; children: John Derek, Cody David, John Blake. Degree in bus., Wash. State U., Pullman, 1993. Cert. agile devel. process tng., Colo., 2006. CEO Gravitate Inc., South San Francisco, Calif., 1998—2000; v.p. product mgt. Openwave Sys. Inc., Redwood City, Calif., 2001—. Mem. adv. bd. Vocel Inc., San Diego, 2004—; dir. Gravitate Inc., South San Francisco, 1999—2000; bd. observer Webraska Inc., Paris, 2002—05. Vol. Toy for Tots Holiday Dr., Seattle, 2000. Mem.: Assn. Internat. Product Devel. (assoc.), Internat. Bus. Devel. Network (assoc.), Phi Delta Theta (life). Achievements include development of various mobile internet technologies. Home: 676 Nash Ave Menlo Park CA 94025 Office: Openwave Sys 2100 Seaport Blvd Redwood City CA 94063 Home Phone: 650-576-8750; Office Phone: 650-480-4713. Personal E-mail: jtrobough@gmail.com.

TROCANO, RUSSELL PETER, lawyer; b. Hackensack, NJ, Sept. 7, 1963; s. Rosario Mario and Barbara Ann (Costa) T. BA, Seton Hall U., 1984; JD, Fordham U., 1987, LLM, 1992. Bar: N.J. 1987, N.Y. 1988. Law clk. to presiding justice County of Middlesex, New Brunswick, N.J., 1987-88; assoc. Sellar Richardson Law Firm, Newark and Roseland, N.J., 1988, Morgan Melhuish Monaghan Law Firm, Livingston, N.J., 1988-89; prin., owner Russell P. Trocano, Ridgewood, N.J., 1989—. Mem. San Guisseppe Societa de Santa Croce de Camerina, Paterson, N.J., 1989—. Fordham U. scholar, 1987. Mem. ABA, N.J. Bar Assn., N.Y. State Bar Assn., Bergen County Bar Assn., Passaic County Bar Assn., Brehon Law Soc., Arthur T. Vanderbilt Inn of Cts., Phi Alpha Theta. Roman Catholic. Avocations: mineral collecting, travel, reading. Home and Office: 60 S Maple Ave Ridgewood NJ 07450-4542 Office Phone: 201-445-0777. Personal E-mail: russell.trocano@verizon.net.

TROCCOLI, MARIANO, astrophysicist, researcher; b. Bari, Italy, Oct. 13, 1974; s. Vito Troccoli and Anna Tanzella. PhD in Physics, U. Bari, 2001. Post-doctoral mem. tech. staff Bell Labs. Lucent Technologies, Murray Hill, NJ, 2001—03; post doctoral fellow Harvard U., Cambridge, Mass., 2003—. Cons. Agilent Technologies, Palo Alto, Calif., 2004—05. Recipient Premio Civera, 1989, Young Investigator award, European Material Rsch. Soc., 2001. Achievements include patents in field. Office: Harvard University 19 Oxford St Cambridge MA 02138 Home Phone: 973-615-7160; Office Phone: 617-495-1934. Personal E-mail: mtroccoli@gmail.com. Business E-Mail: troccoli@deas.harvard.edu.

TROCKI, LINDA KATHERINE, geoscientist, economist, systems engineer; b. Erie, Pa., Oct. 7, 1952; d. Bernard Joseph and Catherine Frances (Manczka) T. BS in Geology with highest honors, N.Mex. Inst. Mining and Tech., 1976; MS in Geochemistry, Pa. State U., 1983, PhD in Mineral Econs., 1985. Staff mem. Los Alamos (N.Mex.) Nat. Lab., 1976-78, 83-90; geologist Internat. Atomic Energy Agy., Vienna, 1978-80; grad. rsch. asst. Los Alamos (N.Mex.) Nat. Lab., 1981-83, dep. group leader, 1990-92, dep. program dir., 1992-93, program dir., 1993-95; asst. to pres. Chevron Petroleum Tech. Co., Houston, 1995-96; v.p. and mgr. Advanced Technology, Bechtel Nat. Inc., 1996-99; dep. gen. mgr. Bechtel Nevada, Las Vegas, 1999—2000; exec. v.p. Idaho Nat. Engring. & Environ. Lab., 2000—02; prin. v.p. & mgr. Res. & Tech. Bechtel Nat., Inc., 2002—05, project mgr., 2006—. Spl. asst. to dep. sec. U.S. Dept. Energy, 1994-95; com. Global Found., Coral Gables, Fla., 1988-94; mem. Chief of Naval Ops. Task Force on Energy, Alexandria, Va., 1990-91; mem. SRNL and LLNL adv. coms., 2001-; mem. DOE SEAB lab. ops. bd., 2003-; mem. EMS adv. com. Penn State, 2004-; mentorNet Nat. Bd., 2004-. Contbr. to profl. publs. Fellow East West Ctr., Honolulu, 1988. Mem. AAAS, Mineral Econs. and Mgmt. Soc. (pres. 1994-95). Business E-Mail: lktrocki@bechtel.com.

TROCKI-VIDELL, CYLA, psychiatrist, medical association administrator; d. Jack and Mira (Kiejdan) Trocki; m. Jared Steven Videll, Dec. 27, 1969; children: Haviv Elana, Mikhael Alon, Samara Pilar. BA, Temple U., 1968, MA, 1972; postgrad., U. Pa., 1972—74; DO, Phila. Coll. Osteo. Medicine, 1978. Diplomate in med. psychology Am. Bd. Psychol. Spltys., Am. Bd. Forensic Medicine. Pediat. intern Med. Coll. Pa., Phila., 1979—89, resident in psychiatry, 1991—93, fellow in child and adolescent psychiatry, 1993—95; pvt. practice Phila., 1983—91; med. dir., cons. Med-Psych Healthcare Assocs., NJ, 2000—; pvt. practice PR, 1995—. Contbg. author Women's Future World's Future, 2000; contbr. chapters to books. Mem. Nat. Women's History Mus., Washington, 2005, Med. Women's Delegation to Russia, Latvia and Lithuania; mem. USA/China Joint Conf. on Women's Issues, Med. Women's Delegation, mem. World Conf. on Family Values Singapore, mem. NGO Forum-UN 4th World Conf. on Women Beijing; mem. Am. Med. Polit. Action Com., Washington, 1998—. Named to, Am. Biography Polit. Scientists; recipient Nat. Leadership award, Physicians Adv. Bd., Nat. Rep. Congl. Com., Washington, 2000. Mem.: AAUW, AMA, Phila. County Med. Soc., Am. Med. Women's Assn., Pa. Osteopathic Med. Assn., Med. Women's Internat. Assn., Am. Soc. Law, Medicine and Ethics, Am. Acad. Child and Adolescent Psychiatry, Am. Psychiat. Assn., Pa. Med. Soc. Republican. Jewish. Avocations: botany, dance, yoga, politics. Home: 115 S Austin Ave Ventnor City NJ 08406 Office: Med Psych Healthcare Assocs 408 N Exeter Ave Margate City NJ 08402 Office Phone: 609-823-1989. Office Fax: 609-823-1989. Personal E-mail: mixsum@juno.com.

TROFFKIN, HOWARD JULIAN, lawyer; b. Port Chester, NY, Jan. 30, 1937; s. Irving and Frieda Troffkin; m. Rhea Dorothy, May 12, 1963; children: Stephen, Barbara. BS in Chemistry, St. Lawrence U., 1959; postgrad., Columbia U., 1959-60; JD, Georgetown U., 1970. Bar: Va. 1971, D.C. 1972. Rsch. chemist Am. Cyanamid Co., 1961-66, legal trainee, 1966-67, patent agt., 1967-71; assoc. Pennie, Edmonds, Morton, Taylor & Adams, Washington, 1971-77; patent atty. W.R. Grace & Co., Columbia, Md., 1977-86, sr. patent counsel, 1987-98; pvt. practice, 1998—. Patentee in chemistry field. Mem. Willerburn Civic Assn., 1971-75. Served with AUS, 1960-61. Mem. ABA, Va. Bar Assn., D.C. Bar Assn., Washington Patent Lawyers Assn., Md. Patent Law Assn. (pres. 1981-83), Am. Intellectual Property Law Assn., Am. Chem. Soc., Concrete Corrosion Inhibitors Assn. (sec./counsel). Jewish. Avocations: woodcrafting, travel. Home and Office: 7808 Ivymount Ter Potomac MD 20854-3218 Personal E-mail: troffkin@aol.com.

TROGAN, ROLAND BERNARD, composer, educator; b. Saginaw, Mich., Aug. 6, 1933; s. Ricardo Bernardo Trocano and Alicia Archangeli-Trocano; m. Annette Patrice Ellams, Mar. 31, 2001; m. Mona Jane Philpot-Trogan, Feb. 6, 1971 (dec. 2000); m. Barbara Jean Mills-Trogan, July 10, 1955 (div. June 22, 1964); children: Christopher Roland, Timothy Bernard. MusB in Composition, U. Mich., 1954, MusM in Composition, 1955, Dr. of Musical Arts in Composition, 1963. Cert. Am. Fedn. of Musicians Mich., 1948, Broadcast Music Inc. NY, 1966. Performing pianist (live, weekly) WKNX Radio, Saginaw, Mich., 1947—50; assoc. condr., composer-in-residence Saginaw Civic Symphony, 1954—56; fellow English drama U. Mich., Ann Arbor, 1956—59, fellow in music theory, 1956—60; lectr. in music CUNY, 1958—65; dir. music Ecole Francaise, 1967—69, Unitarian Ch., Staten Island, 1967—69; instr. of piano Wagner Coll., Staten Island, NY, 1968; pres. Roland Trogan Inc. dba Dr. Trogan's Music Sch., Staten Island, 1975—, Patrice Editions, L. L. C., Staten Island, 2003—. Pvt. music instr. to internationally-recognized conductors, soloists, diplomats, and stage and film stars. non-affiliated, NYC, 1963—71; prodr. new music concerts performed by Henry Cowell, Wallingford Riegger, Max Polikoff, Paul Jacobs and Walter Trampler, NYC, 1966—69; featured composer Carnegie Recital Hall pvt. concert, introduced by H. Wiley Hitchcock and sponsored by Sybil Burton, Tom Poston and Harold Rome, NYC, 1968. Composer: (cantata) The Seafarer, 1967, (composition for choir and orch.) Hymn to Spring, 1950, (composition) Sextet for Wind Quintet and Piano, 1951, Elegy for String Quartet and Contralto on poems of Elinor Wiley, 1953, Soliloquey for piano, 1955, Divertimenti for two voices on tone rows, 1955, Incidental music to Bertold Brecht's The Good Woman of Szechuan, 1956, Preludes for Piano, 1957 (pub. in Generation mag., 1951), Sonata for solo violin, 1959, Concerto for Violin and Orchestra, 1963, Fantasy for Piano, 1967, Nocturnes for Piano, 1968, Bagatelles for Piano, 1970, Piano Sonata no 1, 1971, Piano Sonata no 2, 1997, Elegy for piano, 1998, Piano Sonata no 3, 1999, Diptych for piano, 2000, Symphony for Chamber Orchestra, 2001, Two Scenes for Orchestra, 2006 (Louisville Orch. award, 1955), Mas ficciones por Juan Luis Borges, for solo violin, 1951, (performance) Preludes for piano, performed by Don Trusdel at University of Michigan, 1951, Septet for Wind Quintet and Piano, performed by the University of Michigan Wind Quintet and Bruce Wise, pianist, 1953, Elegy for String Quartet and Piano, University of Illinois-Urbana, 1954, The Hat Man, performed in Chicago by the After Dinner Opera Co., and at the Interlochen Music Camp, 1956, Incidental music for Bertold Brecht's The Good Woman of Szechuan, University of Michigan Theatre, 1957, (perfomance) Preludes of Piano, premiered by Paul Jacobs in New York City, 1955, (performance) Divertimenti for two voices on tone rows, University of Michigan, 1959, Sonata for solo violin, premiered by Harold Kohon at Town Hall, New York City, 1955, Two Scenes for Orchestra, performed by Louisville Symphony Orchestra, 1971, Piano Sonata no 1, performed by Richard Woitach at Alice Tully Hall, Lincoln Center, New York City, 1967, The Seafarer, performed by Richard Woitach and William Wiederanders, with a dramatic reading of the text by Jean Sullivan at Carnegie Recital Hall, New York City, 1971, Nocturnes for Piano, performed at Alice Tully Hall, Lincoln Center, New York City, 1971, Bagatelles for piano, performed by Richard Woitach, Alice Tully Hall, Lincoln Center, New York City, 1971, (opera) The Hat Man (Broadcast Music Inc. award, 1954). Rep. Staten Island Mus., 1968. Recipient Fulbright scholarship, Dept. of State, US Govt. (rescinded by Ho. Un-American Activities Com. chmn., Eugene McCarthy), 1954, Young Composer award, Broadcast Music Inc., 1954; fellow Music, U. Mich., 1955—56, English, 1955; grantee, AAAL, 1985—87. R-Conservative. Christian. Avocation: travel. Home: 755 Narrows Rd N Apt #914 Staten Island NY 10304-1542 Office: RTrogan Inc /Dr Trogan's Music School 1861 Victory Blvd Staten Island NY 10314-3517 Home Phone: 718-876-7984; Office Phone: 718-981-5418. Office Fax: 718-370-8008; Home Fax: 718-370-8008. Personal E-mail: mymusicfriend@aol.com.

TROGOLO, JEFFREY A., research scientist; b. 1967; m. Julia Saidenberg, Oct. 16, 2004. BA in Materials Engring., Rensselaer Polytechnic Inst., PhD in Materials Sci. Pres. Niche Microstructural Corp., 1993—96; staff scientist and rsch. dir. for orthopedic device applications Spire Corp., 1996—98; chief tech. officer AgION Technologies, 1998—. Author pub. over 10 papers in various jours. including the Jour. of Materials Sci., Jour. of Electronic Materials. Office: AgION Technologies Corporate Offices 60 Audubon Rd Wakefield MA 01880 Office Phone: 781-224-7100. Office Fax: 781-246-3340. E-mail: sales@agion-tech.com.

TROHMAN, JOSEPH MARK, musician; b. Hollywood, Fla., Sept. 1, 1984; Student, DePaul U. Lead guitarist Fall Out Boy, 2001—. Musician: (albums) Fall Out Boy's Evening Out With Your Girl, 2002, Take This to Your Grave, 2003, From Under the Cork Tree, 2005, Infinity on High, 2007, (songs) Sugar, We're Going Down, 2003 (MTV2 award, MTV Video Music Awards, 2005, Viewer's Choice award, MTV Video Music Awards, 2006), Dance, Dance, 2005 (Choice Music Single & Choice Rock Track, Teen Choice Awards, 2006). Recipient Choice Music Rock Group award, Teen Choice Awards, 2006. Office: Fall Out Boy Inc Box 219 1187 Wilmette Ave Wilmette IL 60091

TROIANO, EDWARD, mechanical engineer, researcher; MS, Rensselaer Poly. Inst., Troy, NY, 1989—92. Mech. engr. AEW-E, Watervliet, NY, 1984—92; mech. rsch. engr. AEW-T, 1992—. Office: US ARMY - ARDEC - Benet Labs AEW-T building 115 Watervliet NY 12189 Home Phone: 518-356-5001; Office Phone: 518-266-5112. Business E-Mail: edward.troiano@us.army.mil.

TROJANOWSKI, JOHN Q., medical educator, health facility administrator; b. Bridgeport, Conn., 1946; MD, PhD, Tufts U., 1976. Intern. Mass. Gen. Hosp., Boston, 1977—79, resident, 1977—79, U. Pa. Hosp., Philadelphia, 1979—80; asst. prof. pathology & lab. medicine U. Pa. Sch. Medicine, 1981—90, prof. pathology & lab. medicine, 1990; co-dir. Pa. Ctr. for Neurodegenerative Disease Rsch., 1992—; dir. med. pathology Pa. Inst. on Aging, 1988—2002, interim dir., 2001—02, dir., 2002—; dir. Alzheimer's Disease Ctr. Nat. Inst. Aging, 1991—. Prin. investigator of program project grant on Alzheimers & Parkinson's disease Nat. Inst. Aging, 1990—. Recipient Merit award, NIH, 1986—94, Promising Investigator award for Alzheimer's Disease Rsch., Met. Life Found., 1991, Investigator award, Nat. Alliance for Rsch. on Schizophrenia & Depression, 1994, Pioneer award, Alzheimer's Assn., 1998, Potamkin prize for Rsch. in Pick's, Alzheimer's and Related Diseases, 1998, Stanley N. Cohen Biomed. Rsch. award, 2000. Mem.: Inst. Med., Assn. Am. Physicians, Am. Soc. Clin. Investigation, Am. Assn. Neuropathologists (pres. 1997—98). Office: U Pa Health Sys Dept Pathology and Lab Medicine 3d Fl 36th & Spruce St Philadelphia PA 19104-4283 E-mail: trojanowski@mail.med.upenn.edu.

TROKHAN, PAUL DENNIS, technologist, researcher; With Procter & Gamble Co., 1972—, with paper product devel. area, 1974, technologist upstream tissue/towel tech. devel. Recipient Achievement award, Indsl. Rsch. Inst., 2006. Mem.: Victor Mills Soc. Achievements include over 150 patents in field. Office: Procter & Gamble Co PO Box 599 Cincinnati OH 45201-0599 *

TROLANDER, HARDY WILCOX, engineering executive, consultant; b. Chgo., June 2, 1921; s. Elmer Wilcox and Freda Marie (Zobel) T.; m. Imogen Davenport, July 3, 1946 (dec.); children: Megan, Patricia. BS in Engring., Antioch Coll., 1947. Instr. Antioch Coll., Yellow Springs, Ohio, 1947-48; co-founder, CEO Yellow Springs Instrument Co., Inc., 1948-86. Dir., co-founder Cook Design Ctr., Dartmouth Coll., Hanover, N.H., 1975-88; bd. dirs. Deban Inc., Yellow Springs, Camax Tool co., Arvada, Colo.; mem. evaluation panel Inst. Basic Stds., Nat. Bur. Stds., 1977-79. Contbr. articles to profl. jours.; patentee in field. Co-founder, trustee Yellow Springs Community Found., 1974-83; trustee Antioch Coll., 1968-74, chmn. bd., 1972-74; trustee Engring. and Sci. Found., Dayton, 1982-96, Engrs. Club Dayton Found., 1994-2005, Engring. and Sci. Hall of Fame, 1994-2002; mem. adv. bd. Coll. Engring. and Computer Sci. Wright State U., 1993-2005; bd. dirs. united Way Greater Dayton Area, 1984-92; small bus. innovative rsch. grant panels Nat. Sci. Found., 1988—. 1st lt. USAF, 1943-46. Named Outstanding Engr., Dayton Affiliate Socs., 1967, 89, Fellow Dayton Engrs. Club, Am. Inst. for Med. and Biol. Engring.; mem. ACLU, Nat. Acad. Engring., Am. Inst. Biol. Scis. (bioinstrumentation adv., coun. 1969-75), Internat. Orgn. of Legal Metrology (tech. advisor, sec. 1975-82), Amnesty Internat. Democrat. Achievements include co-development of melting point of gallium which has become recognized as a primary defining point of the International Temperature Scale. Home and Office: 3 Aspen Ct Yellow Springs OH 45387-1326 Office Phone: 937-767-4551.

TROLL, LILLIAN ELLMAN, psychologist, educator; b. Chgo., Sept. 24, 1915; d. Morris C. and Bertha H. (Holland) Ellman; divorced; children: Kathren, Jeanne, Gregory. BS in Psychology, U. Chgo., 1937, MA in Human Devel., 1966, PhD in Human Devel., 1967. Pers. technician U.S. War Dept., Washington, 1941-45; sch. psychologist Newton (Mass.) Pub. Schs., 1957-63; cons. State Calif., San Francisco, 1964-65; sr. rsch. assoc. Merrill-Palmer Inst., Detroit, 1967-70; assoc. prof. psychology Wayne State U., Detroit, 1970-75; prof. Rutgers U., New Brunswick, 1975—87; adj. prof. human devel. and aging, med. anthropology U. Calif., San Francisco, 1986—98; ret. Vis. prof.; lectr. in field 47 convs. and invited talks. Author: Family Issues in Current Gerontology, 1986, Continuations: Development After 20, 1982, Development in Early and Middle Adulthood, 1975, rev. edit., 1985, 32 chpts. in other books; co-author: (with Joan and Kenneth Israel) Looking Ahead: A Woman's Guide to the Problems and Joys of Growing Older, 1977, (with Nancy Schlossberg) Perspectives on Counseling Adults, 1978, (with Sheila Miller and Robert Atchley) Families of Later Life, 1979, (with Barbara Turner) Women Growing Older, 1994; contbr. over 30 articles to profl. jours. Recipient Eminent Women in Psychology award, 1988, Disting. Contbn. Div. Adult Devel. and Aging award APA, 1989, Women's Heritage Inst. award, 1992, Disting. Creative Contbn. to Gerontology award, 1993. Fellow APA (sec.-treas. 1973-76, 84-87, pres. 1986-87), Gerontol. Soc. Am. (sec.-treas. behavioral and soc. scis. sect. 1981-87). Home: 1001 Shoreline Dr Apt 302 Alameda CA 94501-5925 E-mail: l.troll@comcast.net.

TROLLIET, DONNA JEAN, retired elementary school educator; d. Donald Howard and Edna Lucile (Mason) Pope; m. Richard L. Trolliet, June 24, 1967; children: Christen Bell, Todd, Jared. BEd, U. Wis., Whitewater, 1969; MA, U. Iowa, 1989; postgrad. studies, Drake U., U. No. Iowa. Tchr. kindergarten East Aurora Pub. Schs., Aurora, Ind., 1967—69; tchr., curriculum dir. Serendipity Presch. and Day Care Ctr., Aurora, 1974—76; ednl. cons. profl. handscorer Westinghouse Info. Svcs., Iowa City, 1980—82; tchr. third and fourth grades Iowa City Cmty. Sch., 1984—2000. Staff devel. instr. Grant Weed Edn. Agy., Cedar Rapids, Iowa, 1985—86; coord. vis. writer program Shinnek Sch., Iowa City, 1980—82; presenter Educators Confs.; appearances with students Local TV and Radio Shows. Eldercare vol. Bickford Cottage Retirement Residence, Iowa City, 1986—. Named a Tchr. of Excellence, Iowa City Cmty. Sch. Dist., 1989; nominee Excellence in Edn., Thanks to Teachers KCRG, 1992; named Outstanding Tchr. U.S. West, U. Iowa, 1989, Kate Wickham Scholarship honoree, Helen Lemme Elem. Sch. PTA, 2001; recipient Gifted Edn. Recognition, U. Iowa, 1988; grantee Scholarship, Women's Fedn., 1963. Mem.: Iowa Coun. Tchrs. of English Lang. Arts., Iowa State Reading Assn., Iowa Coun. Tchrs. of English, Nat. Coun. Tchrs. of English, Walnut Ridge Book Club, Pi Lambda Theta, Phi Delta Kappa. Republican. Lutheran. Avocations: antiques, gardening, genealogy, reading.

TROMANHAUSER, SCOTT GLENN, orthopaedic surgeon; b. Buffalo, July 8, 1957; MD, Albany Med. Coll., 1986. Diplomate Am. Bd. Orthopaedics, Am. Bd. Surgery. Intern, then resident Albany (N.Y.) Med. Ctr., 1986-91; fellow New Eng. Bapt. Hosp., Boston, 1991-92; mem. staff Exeter (N.H.) Hosp., 1992-94; pvt. practice Boston Spine Group, Boston, 1992—; attending New Eng. Bapt. Hosp., Boston, 1992—, Deaconess Hosp., Boston, 1994—. Co-founder Cortek, Inc. medical devices. Named a Top Doctor, Boston mag., 2006. Fellow Am. Acad. Orthopaedic Surgeons; mem. AMA, N.Am. Spine Soc., Mass. Med. Soc., Mass. Orthopaedic Assn. Office: 70 Parker Hill Ave Boston MA 02120-3224 also: Boston Spine Group 125 Parker Hill Ave Roxbury Crossing MA 02120 Office Phone: 617-754-5782. *

TROMBLEY, EDWARD FRANCIS, III, registrar; b. Oneida, NY, Sept. 24, 1964; s. Edward F., Jr. and Sharonlee (Sterling) Trombley. BA, SUNY, Oswego, 1986, MS, 1996. Cert. secondary English tchr. NY. Adj. instr. Bryant & Stratton Bus. Inst., Liverpool, NY, 1993-96, gen. studies dept. coord., 1996, evening and weekend coll. coord., 1996-98, assoc. dean instrn., 1998-2000, dean adminstrn., 2000—01; homebound student tutor North Syracuse Sch. Dist., NY, 1994-96; registrar DeVry U., Arlington, Va., 2001—06, Ft. Wash., Pa., 2006—07; sr. operational mgr. Walden U., Balt., 2007—. Mem. adv. bd. East Syracuse-Minoa Sch. Dist., 1996—97; sch. bus. partnership Cicero-North Syracuse Sch. Dist., 1997; conf. del. Assn. Proprietary Colls., Copperstown, NY, 1997, Saratoga, NY, 98; media cons. Bryant and Stratton Bus. Inst., Liverpool, 1997. Mem.: Am. Assn. Coll. Registrars and Admissions Officers. Office: Walden Univ Registrar's Office 650 S Exeter St 7th Fl Baltimore MD 21202 Office Phone: 410-528-7624. Office Fax: 410-843-6416. Business E-Mail: ed.trombley@waldenu.edu.

TROMBLEY, MICHAEL JEROME, lawyer; b. Bay City, Mich., Dec. 10, 1933; s. Clare F. and Sarah I. (Ingersol) T.; m. Anna K. Simons (div. 1963); children: Peter, Tad; m. Sandra V. Bybee (dec. 1980); children: Christine, Jacques; m. Sherry V. Cribbs, June 10, 1981. A.A., Menlo Coll., 1953; B.A., Stanford U., 1955; LL.B., U. Mo., 1960. Bar: Mo. 1960, Fla. 1974; bd. cert. elder law. Sole practice, Columbia, Mo., 1960-68; ptnr. Alexander, Wayland, Trombley, Butcher, Columbia, Mo., 1964-68; sole practice, 1969-79; ptnr. Trombley, Matheny & Schommer, Sebring, Fla., 1980-84, Trombley, Lobozzo, Schommer, Disler & Accorsi, Sebring, 1984—; past chmn. Fla. Bar Cert. Com. Charter pres. Estate Planning Coun. of Highlands County, Fla., 1979-80. Served to 1st lt. USMCR, 1955-57. Mem. Am. Judicature Soc., Acad. Fla. Trial Lawyers, Nat. Acad. Elder Law Attys., Acad. Fla. Elder Law Attys. (pres.), Masons, Shriners, Elks. Republican. Episcopalian. Office: 329 S Commerce Ave Sebring FL 33870-3607 Home Phone: 863-385-1428; Office Phone: 863-385-5139. E-mail: miketrombley@aol.com.

TROMETTER, MARY GIONTA, chef, educator; b. Phila., July 25, 1964; d. Joseph and Rosaire Giunta; m. Jeffrey A. Trometter, Mar. 9, 1986; children: Phillip, Vincent. AAS in Food and Hospitality Mgmt., Williamsport Area CC, Pa., 1984; BS in Hotel & Restaurant Mgmt., Widener U., 1989; MS in Edn., Wilkes U., 1999. Sous chef The Inn at Turkey Hill, Bloomsburg, Pa., 1984—86; asst. chef, supr. Pierre's Continental Catering, Trappe, Pa., 1987—89; environ. protection specialist 1 Bucks County Dept. of Health, Quakertown, Pa., 1989—90; asst. prof. Sch. Hospitality Pa. Coll. Tech., Williamsport, 1990—. Adv. bd. St. Boniface Elem. Sch., Williamsport, 2000; active Bishop Neumann H.S., Williamsport, 2004. Mem.: Nat. Environ. Health Assn., Am. Culinary Fedn. Avocations: catering, gardening. Office: Pennsylvania College Technology One College Ave Williamsport PA 17701

TRONGALE, NICHOLAS ALBERT, entrepreneur, researcher; s. Nick and Mary Rose Trongale; m. Mary Kathryn Sullivan, Nov. 30, 1980; children: Daniel Louis, Megan Kathryn. BA, Dominican U., 1978; MA, U.S. Naval Postgraduate Sch., 1986, Stanford U., 1994; EdD, U. San Diego, 2001. Enlisted USN, 1979, advanced through grades to capt., ret., 2001; pres., CEO Pb Solutions, San Diego, 2002—. Author: (research) Changes in Navy Leadership Theory and Practice: Post-Vietnam, China's Defense Moderization, China's Naval Power, Investment Strategy of Information Operations, Implications of Unmaned Air Vehicles for the Future Shape of the Air Force. Decorated Legion of Merit; named E-2C Hawkeye of Yr., Comdr. Fighter/Airborne Early Warning Wing, Pacific, 1988; recipient Nat. Leadership award, Nat. Rep. Congl. Com., 2003; Adm. Arthur S. Moreau scholar, USN, 1992, Fed. Exec. Rsch. fellow, RAND Corp., 1996—97. Mem.: DAV (life), VFW (life), Kappa Delta Pi (life). Office Phone: 630-450-7070. Personal E-mail: trongale@pbsolutions.us.

TRONTELL, MARIE CELESTINE, dean; Diploma, Rutgers State U., 1969, MD, 1976. Diplomate Am. Bd. Internal Medicine (chief proctor exam 1988, 89, 90, 91), Am. Bd. Pulmonary Diseases. Intern in internal medicine, resident in internal medicine Coll. Medicine and Dentistry of N.J.-Rutgers Med. Sch. Hosp., 1976-79, med. chief resident, 1978-79, fellow in pulmonary disease Piscataway, 1979-81; asst. chief medicine for tng. Robert Wood Johnson Univ. Hosp., New Brunswick, 1980-96, dir. resident tng., 1982-96, chief inpatient svcs., 1987-96; asst. prof. medicine UMDNJ-Robert Wood Johnson Med. Sch., New Brunswick, 1981-87, program dir. internal medicine residency, 1983-96, acting chief divsn. gen. internal medicine, 1986-87, assoc. prof. medicine, 1987-96, assoc. chmn. dept. medicine, 1991—, prof. clin. medicine, 1996—, assoc. dean acad. affairs Piscataway, 1996—. Mem. editl. adv. bd. Info Trends: Medicine, Law, and Ethics; contbr. articles to profl. jours.; spkr. in field. Fellow ACP (mem. grad. med. edn. com. N.J., mem. career change task force 1994), Am. Coll. Chest Physicians; mem. Am. Thoracic Soc., Assn. Behavioral Scis. and Med. Edn., Assn. Program Dirs. in Internal Medicine (nat. coun. mem., mem. membership svcs. com., mem. program planning com.), N.J. Thoracic Soc., Soc. Gen. Internal Medicine., Phi Beta Kappa, Alpha Omega Alpha. Home: 1111 S Branch Dr Whitehouse Station NJ 08889-3234 Office: 675 Hoes Ln # R-102 Piscataway NJ 08854-5627 also: UMDNJ Robert Wood Johnson Med Sch Dept Acad Affairs 675 Hoes Ln Piscataway NJ 08854-5627

TROOBOFF, PETER DENNIS, lawyer; b. Balt., June 22, 1942; s. Benjamin M. and Rebecca (Cohen) Trooboff; m. Rhoda Morss, Aug. 10, 1969; children: Hannah, Abigail. BA cum laude, Columbia U., 1964; LLB cum laude, Harvard U., 1967; LLM, London Sch. Econs., 1968; diploma cum laude, Hague Acad. Internat. Law, Netherlands, 1968. Bar: N.Y. 1968, D.C. 1970. Rsch. assoc. Harvard U. Law Sch., Cambridge, Mass., 1968—69; asst. to exec. editor for The Advocates Sta. WGBH-TV, Boston, 1969; assoc. Covington & Burling, Washington, 1969—75, ptnr., 1975—. Lectr., dir. seminars The Hague Acad. Internat. Law, 1972, 82, lectr., 86, mem. curatorium, 1991—; lectr. The Hague Acad. External Program, Beijing, 1987, Harare, 93; lectr. internat. orgns. U. Va. Sch. Law, 1973; head US del. 3d Inter-Am. Specialized Conf. Pvt. Internat. Law, La Paz, Bolivia, 1984; mem. US del. Hague Conf. pvt. internat. law, 1993, 96, 1997—, expert US del., 2003—04; arbitrator Internat. Ctr. Settlement Investment Disputes. Editor: Law and Responsibility in Warfare-The Vietnam Experience, 1975; contbr. chapters to books, columns to jours., articles to profl. publs. Frank Knox Meml. fellow. Mem.: Washington Inst. Fgn. Affairs, Internat. Law Assn., Am. Soc. Internat. Law (bd. editors Am. Jour. Internat. Law 1980—92, pres. 1990—92, bd. editors Am. Jour. Internat. Law 1994—2003, chmn. nominating com. 2006—07), Am. Law Inst., Coun. Fgn. Rels., City Club (Washington), Cosmos Club. Office: Covington & Burling 1201 Pennsylvania Ave NW Washington DC 20004 Office Phone: 202-662-5512. Business E-Mail: ptrooboff@cov.com.

TROOP, PAUL MELVIN, public relations executive, journalist; b. Jersey City, May 13, 1942; s. Bernard Lazarus and Ruth (Weiss) T.; m. Maxine Rubin, Dec. 6, 1970; 1 child, Wendy. BA, U. State of N.Y., 1980. Reporter L.I. Press, Jamaica, NY, 1965-66; political editor Suffolk Sun, Deer Park, NY, 1966-67; asst. news dir. L.I. Network News, Freeport, NY, 1967; asst. editor Am. Sch. & U., NYC, 1967-68; acct. exec. Ruder & Finn, NYC, 1969-70; mng. editor L.I. Comml. Rev., Syosset, NY, 1970; bus. writer Atlanta Jour.-Constn., 1970-78; pres. Fin. Comm. Co., Atlanta, 1978—. Cpl. NJNG, 1965-71. Newspaper Fund scholar, 1961, Banking Sch. of the South fellow, 1975.

TROOSKIN, STANLEY Z., surgeon; b. Linden, NJ, July 24, 1949; s. Martin and Irene Trooskin; m. Estelle Kost Trooskin; children: Stacey, Gerri, Amy. BA, Rutgers U., 1971; MD, U. Pitts., 1975. Diplomate Am. Bd. Surgery, Am. Bd. Surgery, lic. physician Pa., N.J., N.Y. Asst. prof. surgery U. Medicine and Dentistry N.J., Piscataway, 1980—85, assoc. prof. surgery, 1985—89, clin. assoc. prof., 1988—89; prof. surgery SUNY, Bklyn., 1989—92, Med. Coll. Pa., 1993—94, Hahnemann U. Sch. Medicine, 1994, MCP Hahnemann U. Sch. Medicine, 1995—2002, U. Med. and Dentistry NJ-Robert Wood Johnson Med. Sch., New Brunswick, 2002—; chief gen. surgery, chief surgery Robert Wood Johnson U. Hosp., New Brunswick, 2002—. Adj. prof. surgery Drexel U. Sch. Medicine, Phila., 2003—; program dir. gen. surgery residency U. Med. and Dentistry NJ-Robert Wood Johnson Med. Sch., New Brunswick, 2006. Mem. editl. bd.: Trauma Quar., 1989—2002, Trauma Chronicle, 1990—91. Mem.: Ea. Assn. for Surgery of Trauma, Am. Coll. Surgeons. Achievements include patents in field. Office: Robert Wood Johnson Med Sch 1 RWJ Pl CN 19 MEB 443 New Brunswick NJ 08903 Office Phone: 732-235-7920. Business E-Mail: trooskz@umdnj.edu.

TROOST, BRADLEY TODD, neurologist, educator; b. Mankato, Minn., July 5, 1937; s. Henry Bradley and Elizabeth (Todd) T.; m. Elizabeth Gail Godet, Apr. 17, 1976; children: Elizabeth Claire, Laurie Anne. BS with honors in Biophysics, Yale U., 1959; MD, Harvard U., 1963. Diplomate Am. Bd. Psychiatry and Neurology. Intern, Colo. Gen. Hosp., Denver, 1963-64; resident in neurology U. Colo., Denver, 1966-69; NIH fellow in neuro-ophthalmology U. Calif.-San Francisco, 1969-70; asst. prof. U. Miami (Fla.), 1970-76; assoc. prof. U. Pitts., 1976-80; prof. Case Western Res. U., Cleve., 1980-83; prof., chmn. dept. neurology Wake Forest U. Sch. Medicine, Winston-Salem, N.C., 1983—; chief dept. neurology VA med. ctrs., Pitts., Cleve. Bd. dirs. Greater Miami Epilepsy Found., 1973-76. Served to capt. U.S. Army, 1964-66. Fellow Am. Acad. Neurology; mem. Am. Neurol. Assn., Am. Assn. Univ. Profs. Neurology (pres.-elect), Barany Soc. Republican. Episcopalian. Contbr. numerous articles to profl. publs.

TROP, SANDRA, museum director; b. Bklyn. BS, NYU; cert. in arts adminstrn., Harvard U. Dir. Everson Mus. Art, Syracuse, NY, 1995—. Advt. copy writer; adj. prof. Syracuse U. Mem. founding bd. dirs. Lowe Art Ctr., Syracuse U., Salt City Playhouse, Folk Art Gallery, Syracuse Landmark Theatre; mem. Internat. Com. for Museums and Collections of Modern Art; mem. Literacy Vols. Am.; appointed to Mayor's Commn. on Fin. Planning for City of Syracuse. Mem. Am. Arts Alliance, Am. Assn. Museums, N.E. Regional Mus. Conf. Office: Everson Museum Art 401 Harrison St Syracuse NY 13202-3091

TROPE, SORRELL, lawyer; b. June 9, 1927; m. Linda Trope. AB, U. So. Calif., 1947, JD, 1949. Bar: Calif. 1949, US Dist. Ct. (so. dist. Calif.) 1949, US Ct. Appeals (9th cir.) 1952, US Bd. Immigration Appeals 1952, US Supreme Ct. 1954, US Ct. Appeals (7th cir.) 1958, cert.: State Bar Calif. Bd. Legal Specialization (family law). Co-founding ptnr. Trope and Trope, LA, 1949—. Judge pro tem LA Superior Ct., 1970—72; chairperson So. Calif. Com. Family Law Commn. of State Senate Jud. Com., 1983; mem. State Assembly Family Law Adv. Com., 1984. Founder Trope and Trope/Harriett Buhai Family Law Fellowship, 1995. Recipient Spencer Brandeis award, LA County Bar, 1998, Ramsey award, Harriett Buhai Ctr. Family Law 1998. Fellow: Internat. Acad. Matrimonial Lawyers; mem.: ABA, Am. Inns Ct. (bencher emeritus U. So. Calif. Legion Lex chpt. 1985—), Am. Acad. Matrimonial Lawyers, LA County Bar Assn. (mem. exec. com. family law sect. 1980—96, 2000—), Phi Kappa Phi. Office: Trope and Trope 12121 Wilshire Blvd Ste 801 Los Angeles CA 90025 Office Phone: 310-207-8228. Office Fax: 310-870-2726. E-mail: strope@tropeandtrope.com.

TROPEZ-SIMS, SUSANNE, pediatrician, educator; b. New Orleans, Apr. 13, 1949; d. Maxwell Sterling and Ethel (Ross) Tropez; m. James Carnell White, Apr. 10, 1971 (div. 1992); children: Lisa, Janifer, James Carnell; m. Michael Milroy Sims, Feb. 18, 1995. BS, Bennett Coll., 1971; MD, U. N.C., 1975, MPH, 1982. Diplomate Am. Bd. Pediatrics. Resident pediat. N.C. Meml. Hosp., Chapel Hill, 1975—76, 1977—79; pediatrician Darnell Army Hosp., Ft. Hood, Tex., 1976—77; acting dir. pediat. day clinic Wake County Med. Ctr., Raleigh, NC, 1979—82; dir. pediat. day clinic, asst. prof. U. N.C., Chapel Hill, 1982—88; assoc. prof. pediat. La. State U. Med. Ctr., New Orleans, 1988—97; dir. divsn. pediat. emergency rm. La. State U., New Orleans, 1988—89, chief divsn. ambulatory care, 1989—97; chmn. and prof. dept. pediat. Meharry Med. Coll., Nashville, 1997—2005; chair Meharry Med. Svc. Found., Nashville, 2000—02; chair curriculum com. Meharry Med. Coll., Nashville, 2003—, assoc. dean acad. support, 2005—06, assoc. dean clin. svcs., 2006—, Joy McCann prof., 2006—. Clin. dir. maternal and child health units New Orleans Health Dept., 1992-97, chief divsn. cmty. pediat. and adolescent medicine, 1992-97; pediatrician Shelly Child Devel. Ctr., Raleigh, 1981-88, child med. examiner program, 1979-88; chair sch. health com. local chpt. AAP, 1993-96; mem. Nat. Com. Sch. Health, 1992-99; chair health info. network bd. Nat. Edn. Assn., 2000-02. Contbr. articles to profl. jour. Chair adminstrv. bd. Cornerstone U.M.C., 1993-96, chair edn. com., 1991-92; mem. United Meth. Women, Walnut Terr. Child Devel. Ctr., Raleigh, 1981-83, chmn., 1982-83; chmn. pastor parish com. Longview Ch., Raleigh, 1982-84, 87-88, chmn. membership care com.; chair bd. NEA-Health Info. Network, 2000-02; chair bd. trustees Clark Meml. United Meth. Ch., 2002—. Fellow preventive medicine, 1979-82, Faculty Devel. fellow U. NC Sch. Medicine, 1985-87. Fellow Am. Acad. Pediatrics (mem. sch. health com.); mem. N.C. Pediatric Soc. (com. child abuse and neglect, adolescent pregnancy), La. Pediatric Soc., Ambulatory Pediatric Assn., Adolescent Pregnancy Coalition United Way, Bennett Coll. Alumnae Assn. Democrat. Office Phone: 615-327-6925. Business E-Mail: stsims@mmc.edu.

TROPP, LINDA R., psychology professor; b. Gary, Ind., Sept. 24, 1970; d. Henry Samuel and Sheila Ann Tropp. BA in Psychology and Spanish, Wellesley Coll., Mass., 1992; PhD in Social Psychology, U. Calif., Santa Cruz, 2000. Asst. prof. Boston Coll., Chestnut Hill, Mass., 2000—06; assoc. prof. U. Mass., Amherst, 2006—. Mem.: Soc. Tchg. Psychology (McKeachie Early Career Excellence Tchg. award 2000), Soc. Psychol. Study Social Issues (mem. governing coun. 2003—, Gordon Allport Intergroup Rels. prize 2003). Office: Univ Mass Dept Psychology 135 Hicks Way Amherst MA 01003 Office Phone: 413-577-0934. Business E-Mail: tropp@psych.umass.edu.

TROST, BARRY MARTIN, chemist, educator; b. Phila., June 13, 1941; s. Joseph and Esther T.; m. Susan Paula Shapiro, Nov. 25, 1967; children: Aaron David, Carey Daniel. BA cum laude, U. Pa., Phila., 1962; PhD, MIT, Cambridge, 1965; D (hon.), U. Claude Bernard, Lyons, France, 1994, Technion, Israel, 1997. Mem. faculty U. Wis., Madison, 1965—, prof., chemistry, 1969—, Evan P. and Marion Helfaer prof. chemistry, from 1976, Vilas rsch. prof. chemistry; prof. chemistry Stanford U., 1987—, Tamaki prof. humanities and scis., 1990, chmn. dept., 1996—2002; Lord Todd vis. prof. Cambridge U., England, 2002—. Cons. Merck, Sharp & Dohme, E.I. duPont de Nemours.; hon. prof. Shanghai Inst. Organic Chemistry, 2006. Author: Problems in Spectroscopy, 1967, Sulfur Ylides, 1975; editor-in-chief Comprehensive Organic Synthesis, 1991—, ChemTracts/Organic Chemistry, 1993—; editor: Structure and Reactivity Concepts in Organic Chemistry series, 1972—; assoc. editor Jour. Am. Chem. Soc., 1974-80; mem. editl. bd. Organic Reactions Series, 1971—, Chemistry A European Jour., 1995—, Sci. of Synthesis, Houben-Weyl Methods of Molecular Transformations, 1995—; contbr. numerous articles to profl. jours. Named Chem. Pioneer, Am. Inst. Chemists, 1983; recipient Dreyfus Found. Tech.-Scholar award, 1970, 1977, Creative Work in Synthetic Organic Chemistry award, 1981, Baekland medal, 1981, Alexander von Humboldt award, 1984, Guenther award, 1990, Janssen prize, 1990, Roger Adams award, Am. Chem. Soc., 1995, Presdl. Green Univ. Challenge award, 1998, Nicholas medal, 2000, Yamada prize, 2001, Yamada Prize, 2001, ACS Nobel Laureate Signature award, Graduate Ed. Chemistry, 2002, John Scott award, City of Phila., 2004; fellow, NSF, 1963—65, Sloan Found., 1967—69, Am. Swiss Found., 1975—, Zencca, 1997; scholar Cope scholar, 1989. Mem.: NAS, AAAS, Chem. Soc. London, Am. Acad. Arts and Scis., Am. Chem. Soc. (award in pure chemistry 1977, Roger Adams award 1995, Herbert C. Brown award for creative rsch. in synthetic methods 1999, Nobel Laureate Signature award for grad. edn. in chemistry 2002, Arthur C. Cope award 2004, centenary lectr. 1982). Office: Stanford U Dept Chemistry Stanford CA 94305

TROST, CARLISLE ALBERT HERMAN, retired naval officer; b. Valmeyer, Ill., Apr. 24, 1930; s. Elmer Herman and Luella Caroline (Hoffman) T.; m. Pauline Louise Haley, May 1, 1954; children: Carl, Laura Lee, Steven, Kathleen. Student, Washington U., St. Louis, 1948-49; BS, U.S. Naval Acad., 1953; Olmsted scholar, U. Freiburg, W. Ger., 1960-62. Commd. ensign U.S. Navy, 1953, advanced through grades to adm., 1985; exec. officer U.S.S. Scorpion, 1962-63, U.S.S. Von Steuben, 1963-65; mil. asst. to Dep. Sec. Def., 1965-68; comdg. officer U.S.S. Sam Rayburn, 1968-69; staff Comdr. Sub Force Atlantic, 1969-70; exec. asst. to Sec. Navy, 1970-73; comdr. Submarine Group Five, 1973-74; asst. chief Bur. Naval Personnel, 1974-76; dir. systems analysis div. Office Chief Naval Ops., Washington, 1976-78; dep. comdr.-in-chief U.S. Pacific Fleet, 1978-80; comdr. U.S. Seventh Fleet, 1980-81; dir. Navy program planning Office Chief Naval Ops., 1981-85; comdr.-in-chief U.S. Atlantic Fleet, 1985-86, chief naval ops., 1986-90. Bd. dirs. Lockheed Martin Corp., Gen. Pub. Utility Corp., GPU Nuclear Corp., Bird-Johnson Co., Gen. Dynamics Corp., Precision Components Corp.; chmn. Olmsted Fedn. Trustee U.S. Naval Acad. Found. Decorated Def. D.S.M. with cluster, Navy D.S.M. with 2 clusters, Army D.S.M., Air Force D.S.M., Legion of Merit with 2 oak leaf clusters, Navy Achievement medal; named Outstanding Young Man of Am. Nat. Jr. C. of C., 1964 Mem. U.S. Naval Inst., U.S. Naval Acad. Alumni Assn. (chmn.). Episcopalian. Home: 11 Compromise St Annapolis MD 21401-1806

TROST, EILEEN BANNON, lawyer; b. Teaneck, NJ, Jan. 9, 1951; d. William Eugene and Marie Thelma (Finlayson) Bannon; m. Lawrence Peter Trost Jr., Aug. 27, 1977; children: Lawrence Peter III, William Patrick, Timothy Alexander. BA with great distinction, Shimer Coll., 1972; JD cum laude, U. Minn., 1976. Bar: Ill. 1976, U.S. Dist. Ct. (no. dist.) Ill. 1976, Minn. 1978, U.S. Tax Ct. 1978, U.S. Supreme Ct. 1981. Assoc. McDermott, Will & Emery, Chgo., 1976-82, ptnr., 1982-93; v.p. No. Trust Bank Ariz. N.A., Phoenix, 1993-95; ptnr. Sonnenschein Nath & Rosenthal, Chgo., 1995—2006, Bell, Boyd & Lloyd LLP, Chgo., 2006—. Mem. Am. Coll. Trust and Estate Coun., Minn. Bar Assn., Internat. Acad. Estate and Trust Law, Chgo. Estate Planning Coun. Roman Catholic. Office: Bell Boyd & Lloyd LLP 70 W Madison St #3100 Chicago IL 60602 Home Phone: 630-681-8063; Office Phone: 312-807-4411. Business E-Mail: etrost@bellboyd.com.

TROST, FREDERICK RICHARD, retired pastor; b. Ann Arbor, Mich., Dec. 30, 1935; s. Theodore Louis and Mary Ann (McRoberts) Trost; m. Louise Chappel Herrman, Aug. 17, 1957; children: Marianne McRoberts, Margaret Louise, Christine Marie, Paul Gerhardt, Sarah Estelle. BA, U. Mich., Ann Arbor, 1957; BD in Theol. Studies, Yale Divinity Sch., New Haven, Conn., 1962, MDiv, 1962; student in theol. studies, Heidelberg U., Germany, 1960—61; DD (hon.), Elmhurst Coll., Ill., 1969, Northland Coll., Wis., 1984, Lakeland Coll., 1985. Vikar Badische Landeskirche, Germany, 1959—60; asst. pastor St. Pauls United Ch. Christ, Chgo.,

1962—63, assoc. pastor, 1963—64, sr. pastor, 1964—81; pres. Wis. Conf. United Ch. Christ, DeForest, 1981—2001; ret., 2001. Bd. trustees Chgo. Theological Sem., 1965—70, United Theol. Sem., New Brighton, Minn., 1981—90; chmn. United Ch. Christ Theological Edn. Com., NYC, 1970—73. Author: We Know Only In Part (Reflections on a Journey in Faith), 2004; editor: On The Way: The Teaching Church, 2005; co-editor: The Living Theological Heritage: Ancient and Medieval Legacies, 2005; contbr. articles various profl. jours. Official delegate United Ch. of Christ, Synod of the Evang. Ch. of the Union, Berlin, 1980; dir. United Ch. Bd. Homeland Min., NYC, 1965—70, Church Life & Leadership, NYC, 1973—80; editl. bd. The Living Theological Heritage of United Ch. of Christ, Cleve., 1991—2005; official rep. United Ch. of Christ, Worms, Germany, 1984. Mem.: Union Evangelical Ch. (sec. 1981—2001, chair 2002—, ecumenical com. 1976—), Confessing Christ Project (chair 1993—2001), Saint Benedict Ctr. (vice chair 2006—). Independent. Achievements include founder of Biblical-Theological-Liturgical Fellowship; co-founder Mercersburg Society; co-founder Craigville Theological Colloquies; co-founder Confessing Christ project. Avocations: reading, classical music, writing, athletics. Personal E-mail: fredericktrost@yahoo.com. E-mail: frtrost@chorus.net.

TROST, GLENN W., lawyer; b. Boston, Mar. 27, 1956; BS, MIT; JD cum laude, Southwestern Univ., 1984. Bar: Calif. 1984, US Dist. Ct. (no. & ctrl. dist. Calif.), US Ct. Appeals (9th & Fed. cir.), Supreme Ct. Calif., Supreme Ct. Colo., US Supreme Ct. 2000. Ptnr. mng. partner LA office Coudert Bros. LLP, LA. Adj. prof. Southwestern Univ. Sch. Law, 1986—91. Office Phone: 213-229-2900. Office Fax: 213-229-2999. Business E-Mail: gtrost@coudert.com.

TROST, LOUIS FREDERICK, JR., banker, financial planner; b. Kansas City, Mo., Dec. 11, 1926; s. Louis Frederick and Roberta Ford (Broadus) T.; m. Ann Horner Tillma, Mar. 23, 1951 (div. Oct. 1978); children: Louis Frederick III, Scott Tillma; m. Charlotte Granville Graham, Nov. 15, 1984. BBA, U. Okla., 1951; postgrad., Northwestern U., 1960, grad. Bell Sys. Execs. program, 1960; grad., Sch. Banking of South, Baton Rouge, 1968, Coll. Fin. Planning, Denver, 1989. Divsn. mgr. South Western Bell Tel. Co., Oklahoma City, 1951—64; sr. v.p. Liberty Nat. Bank & Trust Co., Oklahoma City, 1964—91; pres., CEO Lincoln Nat. Bank, Oklahoma City, 1991—95, vice chmn., 1995—2003, CEO, 2002—03. Advisor Bapt. Found. Okla., Oklahoma City, 1995-2005, hon. dir. emeritus, 2006—; bd. rep., exec. com. Coun. Fed. Home Loan Banks, Washington, 1998-2001; dir., chmn. housing com. Fed. Home Loan Bank Topeka, 1995-2001; mem. gov.'s Cmty. Devel. Capital Formation Task Force, 1998-2003; cert. fin. planner, 1989-2004; bd. dirs. Great Expectations Found, 2004—; bd.dirs. Educator's Leadership Acad., 2004—05; bd. dirs. Okla. State Capitol Preservation Commn., 2005—. Pres., bd. dirs. Travelers Aid, Oklahoma City, 1962; treas., bd. dirs. Okla. Symphony Orch., 1983—87; pres., bd. dirs. Mental Health Assn., Oklahoma City, 1996; cmty. devel. adv. coun. Fed. Res. Bank Kansas City, 2002—03; dir. exec. com. Omiplex Sci. Mus., 1980—85. Master sgt. US Army, 1945—46, PTO. Named Outstanding Young Man in Oklahoma City, Oklahoma City, 1960; named Ky. Col., Gov. of Ky., 1970; recipient letter of commendation Mental Health Assn., 1996. Mem. Ind. Bankers Assn. Am., Okla. Bankers Assn. (sr. mgmt. com. 1995-2003), Oklahoma City Golf and Country Club (bd. dirs. 1989-91), Petroleum Club Oklahoma City (v.p., treas., bd. dirs. 1979-81), The Assocs. (U. Okla.), Faculty Club (bd. dirs.,1968-1970), Masons, Scottish Rite, Shriners, Kiwanis (past pres. Oklahoma City), Assn. U.S. Army, Phi Gamma Delta (treas., bd. dirs. Ednl. Found. 1989-97, Wall of Fame award 1997, Disting. Fiji award 2004, trustee emeritus 2004). Baptist. Avocations: gardening, reading, travel. Home and Office: 1601 Queenstown Rd Nichols Hills OK 73116-5522 Business E-Mail: ltrost@cox.net.

TROTT, BARRY, librarian; b. 1962; m. Lynn Trott; 1 child. MSLS, Cath. U. Am. Sch. Libr. & Info. Sci., 1997. Sr. adult svcs. dir. Williamsburg (Va.) Regional Libr., reference libr., readers' svcs. libr.; guitarist, mandolinist, & lead singer Runaway String Band, Williamsburg, Va., 1999—. Editl. bd. Reference & User Svcs. Quarterly, RUSQ Online Companion. Co-author: Partnering with Purpose: A Guide to Strategic Development for Libraries & Other Organizations, 2004; editor: Libraries Unlimited: Read On series, 2006—. Named one of the Movers & Shakers, Libr. Jour., 2003; recipient Allie Beth Martin award, Pub. Libr. Assn./Baker & Taylor, 2007. Mem.: ALA, Reference & User Svcs. Assn. (Margaret E. Monroe Libr. Adult Svcs. award 2007). Office: Williamsburg Regional Libr 7770 Croaker Rd Williamsburg VA 23188 Office Phone: 757-259-4053. Office Fax: 757-259-7798. E-mail: btrott@wrl.org.

TROTT, MENA, application developer; b. 1977; m. Ben Trott. Co-founder, pres. Six Apart, Inc., 2004—. Named one of Top 100 Young Innovators, MIT Tech. Review, 2004. Achievements include creator of TypePad and Moveable Type, software tools for publishing weblogs. Office: Six Apart 548 4th St San Francisco CA 94107-1621

TROTT, SABERT SCOTT, II, marketing professional, consultant; b. Concord, NC, Nov. 21, 1941; s. Sabert Scott and Mary Welker (Crooks) T.; m. Brenda Lee Bost, Nov. 27, 1964; children: Sabert Scott III, David Lee BS in Textile Tech., N.C. State U., 1964; MBA, U. N.C., 1969. Mgr. trainee Cannon Mills Co., Kannapolis, NC, 1969-70, mktg. mgr., 1970-75, v.p. mktg., 1975-82, sr. v.p. mktg., 1982-86, dir. telemktg. and premium sales, 1987-89; mgr. spl. markets, mktg. & sales Fieldcrest Cannon Inc., mktg. mgr., telemarketing sales mgr., 1989-92; v.p. mktg. and sales Spencer's Inc., Mt. Airy, NC, 1992-93; v.p. mktg. Carpenter Co., Richmond, Va., 1994—. Chmn. Cabarrus-Rowan Parks and Recreation Commn., N.C., 1982-86; mem. Cabarrus County Parks and Recreation Commn., N.C., 1980-88; Rep. candidate County Commr., Cabarrus County, 1990; bd. dirs. Cabarrus Meml. Hosp., 1992, N.C. Ctr. for Applied Textile Tech.; vestry-man local Episcopal ch., 1988-93. Capt. U.S. Army, 1965-70. Decorated Commendation medal (2) Mem.: Rotary. Republican. Avocations: canoeing, rafting, golf, basketball, racquetball. Office: Carpenter Co 5016 Monument Ave Richmond VA 23230-3620 Home: 1208 Belair Ave Kannapolis NC 28083 Office Phone: 804-897-5557. Personal E-mail: sbtrott@aol.com. Business E-Mail: scott.trott@carpenter.com.

TROTT, STEPHEN SPANGLER, federal judge; b. Glen Ridge, NJ, Dec. 12, 1939; s. David Herman and Virginia (Spangler) Trott; m. Carol C. Trott; children: Christina, Shelley. BA, Wesleyan U., 1962; LLB, Harvard U., 1965; LLD (hon.), Santa Clara U., 1992; LLD (hon.), U. Idaho, 2001. Bar: Calif. 1966, US Dist. Ct. (ctrl. dist.) Calif. 1966, US Ct. Appeals (9th cir.) 1983, US Supreme Ct. 1984. Guitarist, mem. The Highwaymen, 1958—; dep. dist. atty. LA County Dist. Atty.'s Office, LA, 1966—75, chief dep. dist. atty., 1975—79; US dist. atty. Ctrl. Dist. Calif., LA, 1981—83; asst. atty. gen. criminal divsn. US Dept. Justice, Washington, 1983—86; faculty Nat. Coll. Dist. Attys., Houston, 1973—80; chmn. central dist. Calif. Law Enforcement Coord. Com., Houston, 1981—83; coord. LA-Nev. Drug Enforcement Task Force, 1982—83; assoc. atty. gen. US Dept. Justice, Washington, 1986—88; chmn. US Interpol, 1986—88; judge US Ct. Appeals (9th cir.), Boise, Idaho, 1988—2004, sr. judge, 2004—. Trustee Wesleyan U., 1984—87; adv. council Big Brothers, Big Sisters S.W. Idaho, 2001—03; ofcl. photographer World Cup Wrestling Championship, 2003—; bd. dirs., pres. Children's Home Soc., Idaho, 1990—2004. Recipient Gold record as singer-guitarist for Michael Row the Boat Ashore, 1961, Disting. Faculty award, Nat. Coll. Dist. Attys., 1977. Mem.: Am. Coll. Trial Lawyers, Boise (Idaho) Philharm. Assn. (bd. dirs. 1995—, v.p. 1997—99, pre-concert lectr. 1997—, pres. 1999—2003), Idaho Classic Guitar Soc. (founder, pres. 1989—2004), Internat. Brotherhood Magicians, Idaho Racing Pigeon Assn., Magic Castle, Brentwood Racing Pigeon Club (pres. 1977—82), Wilderness Fly Fishers Club (pres. 1975—77). Republican. Office: US Ct Appeals 9th Cir 666 US Courthouse 550 W Fort St Boise ID 83724-0040 *

TROTT, THOMAS G., lawyer; b. Delavan, Wis., Jan. 2, 1946; s. John Jerome and Louise Trott; m. Cynthia Wood, Feb. 13, 1994; children: Owen, Nicholas, Thomas. BA, U. Ill., 1968, MBA, 1977, JD, 1978. Bar: Tex. 1978, U.S. Ct. Appeals (5th cir.) 1978, U.S. Dist. Ct. (so. dist.) Tex. 1978, Pa. 1985; oil, gas and mineral law Bd. Legal Specialization, 1990. Atty. Exxon Co. USA, Houston, 1978—83; v.p. legal Mitchell Energy Corp., The Woodlands, Tex., 1983—2001; assoc. gen. counsel Devon Energy Corp., Houston, 2001—. Mem. dist. adv. group Civil Justice Reform Act, Houston, 1992—93; mem. adv. bd. Ctr. for Am. and Internat. Law, Plano, Tex., 2001—. Mem. allocation com. United Way, Houston, 1985—90; trustee United Way Ctr., Houston, 1985—95. Lt. (j.g.) USN, 1969—74. Office Phone: 713-495-7145. Business E-Mail: tom.trott@dvn.com.

TROTTA, FRANK P., JR., lawyer; BA, JD, LLM, MBA. Bar: NY, US Dist. Ct. (no. and we. dists.) NY, US Ct. Mil. Appeals, US Dist. Ct. (so. and ea. dists.) NY, US Ct. Internat. Trade, US Tax Ct., US Supreme Ct., U.S. Ct. Appeals (DC cir.), US Ct. Customs and Patent Appeals, DC, Conn., Pa. Former assoc. Weil, Gotshal & Manges, NYC; pvt. practice Washington, New Rochelle, NY, Greenwich, Conn. Former mem. bd. govs ABA; former mem. faculty Practicing Law Inst.; former governing mem. Nat. Jud. Coll., Am. Bar Endowment, ABRA Pension Fund; former chmn. bd. advisors Columbia U. Grad. Sch. Bus., Inst. Non-for-Profit Mgmt. Grad. Greenwich (Conn.) Citizens Police Acad., Greenwich, 2003; former bd. dirs. Boys Town of Italy; former mem. Fund for Justice and Edn.; former mem. supervisory com. Members Credit Union; former mem. Greenwich Police Dept., Citizens and Police Partnership; former chmn. New Rochelle Reps.; assoc. mem. Rep. Town Com.; past mem. bd. edn. Greenwich Cath. Sch.; mem. bd. trustees Sch. of Holy Child, Rye, NY; bd. trustees Sch. Holy Child, Rye, NH, 2007—.

TROTTA, RIC CHARLES, aerospace transportation executive, consultant; b. NYC, Mar. 7, 1942; s. Sigmund Robert and Anita Dolores (La Penna) T.; m. Carolyn Carey Bealle Trotta, May 29, 1965; children: Bradley Charles, Ric Charles Jr., Lauren Carey. Student in elec. engring., U. Va., 1959-62; BA in Physics, NYU, 1966; MBA in Mktg., Hofstra U., 1977; postgrad., Carnegie Mellon U., 1987. Engr. Grumman Aerospace Corp., Bethpage, NY, 1966-68, asst. to v.p., 1968-70, advanced programs mgr., 1970-78, mgr. technology planning, 1978-81, asst. dir. advanced systems, 1981-83; dir. corp. ind., rsch. and devel. Grumman Corp., 1983-86, dir. corp. devel. and resources, 1986-94; pres. Trotta Assoc., Cons. to Govt. and Industry, Centerport, 1994—. Sr. player global war games U.S. Naval War Coll., Newport, RI, 1985—; mem. resources working group Fed. Emergency Mgmt. Agy., Washington, 1991—; vice-chair nat. adv. coun. Fed. Lab. Consortium, 1999—, vice chmn., 2000, chmn., 01; mem. nomination and award selection com. L.I. Tech. Hall of Fame, 2003—; bd. dirs. Beachcomber Ltd., Montauk, NY, pres. bd. dirs., 2005. Author: Industry Independent Rsch. and Devel. Study, 1996, Assessing the Impact of Regulatory and Legislative Changes to the DOD Independent Research and Developement Program, 1997, Maritime Industry Definition and Structure- A Workbook for Assessing Organization Capabilities Versus Industry Needs, 1997; Contbg. author: Public Control of Medical Care, 1978, National Security Assessment of the U.S. Maritime Industry Surveys: Building and Repairing of Ships, Boats and other Marine Platforms, Maritime Research Development and Education, 2000, Nat. Security Assesment of Shipbldg. and Repair Ind., 2001, Assessment of Industry Attitudes on Collaborating with U.S. Department of Defense in Research and Development and Technology Sharing, 2003. Mem. com. on sch. utilization Harborfield Sch. Dist., Greenlawn, 1984; bd. dir. Community Sch., Centerport, NY, 1985. Recipient Community Svc. award, Town of Huntington, N.Y., 1985, Merit award, Chief Naval Rsch., 2000, Outstanding Svc. Award, Fed. Lab. Consortium for Tech. Transfer, 2005. Mem. Nat. Security Indsl. Assn., Electronic Industries Assn., Mine Warfare Assn. (bd. dirs. 1997), Assn. Nat. Def. and Emergency Resources, Sigma Nu (historian 1961). Avocations: fishing, tennis, sailing, cooking. Home and Office: 21 Little Bull Ct Centerport NY 11721-1450 Home Phone: 631-424-0494; Office Phone: 631-424-3700. Personal E-mail: RicTrotta@aol.com. Business E-Mail: RTrotta@TrottaAssociates.com.

TROTTER, CHARLIE, chef; Degree in polit. sci., U. Wis., 1982. Owner, chef Charlie Trotter's, Chgo., Trotter's To Go, Lincoln Park, Ill., 2000—, "C", Los Cabos, Mexico, 2004—. Founder Charlie Trotter Culinary Edn. Found., 1999—. Author: Lessons in Excellence, 1999, Kitchen Sessions with Charlie Trotter, 1999, Gourmet Cooking for Dummies, 1999, Great Restaurants of the World: Charlie Trotter's, 2000, Charlie Trotter Cooks at Home, 2000, Charlie Trotter's, 2001, Charlie Trotter's Vegetables, 2001, Charlie Trotter's Seafood, 2001, Charlie Trotter's Desserts, 2001, Charlie Trotter's Meat and Game, 2001, Lessons in Service, 2001, Raw, 2003, Workin' More Kitchen Sessions with Charlie Trotter, 2004, The Cook's Book, 2005, Spa Cuisine; host: (tv series) Kitchen Sessions with Charlie Trotter. Named Best Chef: Midwest, James Beard Found., 1992; named to Who's Who in Food & Beverage in Am., 1996; recipient Grand award, Wine Spectator, 1993—, Humanitarian of Yr. award, Internat. Assn. Culinary Professionals, 2005, Outstanding Chef award, James Beard Found., 1999. Achievements include being one of 5 heroes to be honored by America's Promise. Office: 816 W Armitage Ave Chicago IL 60614

TROTTER, CORTEZ, city official, former fire commissioner; b. Chgo. First dep. fire commr. Chgo. Fire Dept., fire commr., 2001—06; exec. dir. Office of Emergency Mgmt. and Comm. (formerly Office of Emergency Comm.), 2006—. Apptd. to bd. dirs. Emergency Comm. (911) Bd., 1990—. Recipient Martin Luther King Jr. Excellence in Leadership award, Suburban Human Rels. Com. Office: City Hall 121 N La Salle Chicago IL 60602

TROTTER, F(REDERICK) THOMAS, retired academic administrator; b. LA, Apr. 17, 1926; s. Fred B. and Hazel (Thomas) T.; m. Gania Demaree, June 27, 1953; children: Ruth Elizabeth, Paula Anne (dec.), Tania, Mary. AB, Occidental Coll., 1950, DD, 1968; STB, Boston U., 1953, PhD, 1958; LHD, Ill. Wesleyan U., 1974, Cornell Coll., 1985, Westmar Coll., 1987; LLD, U. Pacific, 1978, Wesleyan Coll., 1981; EdD, Columbia Coll., 1984; LittD, Alaska Pacific U., 1987; DD, Emory U., 1989. Exec. sec. Boston U. Student Christian Assn., 1951-54; ordained elder Calif.-Pacific, Methodist Ch., 1953; pastor Montclair (Calif.) Meth. Ch., 1956-59; lectr. Sch. Theology at Claremont, 1959—73; gen. sec. Bd. Higher Edn. and Ministry United Meth. Ch., 1973—87; pres. Alaska Pacific U., Anchorage, 1988-95; ret., 1995. Author: Jesus and the Historian, 1968, Loving God with One's Mind, 1987, God Is with Us, 1997, Politics, Morality, and Higher Education, 1997, weekly column local newspapers; editor-at-large: Christian Century, 1969-84. Trustee Dillard U. Served with USAAF, 1944-46. Kent fellow Soc. for Values in Higher Edn., 1954; Dempster fellow Meth. Ch., 1954 Mem. Rotary Internat. (Anchorage Downtown), Commonwealth North. Home: 900 E Harrison Ave Pomona CA 91767-2075

TROTTER, HERMAN EAGER, JR., (HERMAN TROTTER), retired music critic; b. Providence, Sept. 25, 1925; s. Herman Eager, Sr. and Shelley Fern (Jones) T.; m. Johanne Marguerite Haberstro, Sept. 22, 1956 (div. Apr. 1996); children: Kim Avery. Holly Anne. Joy Caroline; m. Rosa Spillane Whetzle, July 22, 1996. BA, Yale U., 1946. Pub. utility sec. analyst Mass. Mut. Life Ins. Co., Springfield, 1947-51; sales engr., mgr. Buffalo office B-I-F Industries, Providence, 1951-56; asst. sec. Buffalo Batt and Felt Co, Depew, NY, 1956-68; account exec. Harold Warner Advt., Buffalo, 1968-77; freelance music critic Buffalo News, 1968-77, staff music critic, 1977—2001, music critic emeritus, 2002. Contbr. articles to profl. and popular jours., and to New Grove Dictionary of Music. Program annotator Buffalo Philharm., 1964-70. Lt. (j.g.) USN, 1943-46, PTO. Mem.: Music Critics Assn. (v.p. 1988—93, sec. 1999—2003). Avocations: travel, record collecting. Home: 33 Gates Cir Apt 6C Buffalo NY 14209-1197 E-mail: herros72296@aol.com.

TROTTER, JOE WILLIAM, JR., history professor, writer; b. Vallscreek, W.Va., June 18, 1945; s. Joe William and Thelma Odell Trotter; m. H. LaRue Mack, May 19, 1972. AA, Kendall Coll., 1967; BA, Carthage Coll., 1969; MA, U. Minn., 1978, PhD, 1980. Social studies tchr. Tremper Sr. HS, Kenosha, Wis., 1969—75; adult edn. instr. Gateway Tech. Inst., Kenosha, Wis., 1970—73; instr. dept. history U. Minn., 1977—79, vis. prof. dept. history, 1993; asst. prof. dept. history U. Calif.-Davis, 1981—84, assoc. prof. dept. history, 1984—85, Carnegie Mellon U., Pitts., 1985—89, prof. dept. history, 1990—96, Mellon prof. history, 1996—, head dept. history, 2001—; dir. Ctr. for Africanamerican Urban Studies and the Economy, Pitts., 1995—. Editl. bd. mem. Jour. Urban History, Thousand Oaks, Calif., 1997—, Labor History, London, 1991—2003, Jour. Am. Ethnic History, Piscataway, NJ, 1991—, Pa. History, Middletown, 1987—, Labor, Durham, NC, 2003—, Ohio Valley History, 2002—, Jour. of Am. History, Bloomington, Ind., 1992—95, Pa. History, Middletown, Pa., 1987—. Author: (book) Black Milwaukee: The Making of an Industrial Proletariat, 1915-45, 1985, Coal, Class, and Color: Blacks in Southern West Virginia, 1915-32, 1990, African Americans in Depression and War, 1929-1945, 1995, River Jordan: African American Urban Life in the Ohio Valley, 1998, The African American Experience, 2001; editor: (edited volume) The Great Migration in Historical Perspective: New Dimensions of Race, Class, and Gender, 1991; co-editor: Blacks in the Industrial Age: A Documentary History, 1915-1945, 1996, African Americans in Pennsylvania: Shifting Historical Perspectives, 1997, (book) African American Urban Studies: Perspectives From the Colonial Era to the Present, 2004. Spkr. NAACP, Arlington, Va., 1992, 19th dist., Homewood Brushton, Pitts., 1999; keynote spkr. Lemington Elder Care Svcs/, Pitts., 2002; pres. Kenosha Black Caucus, 1972—74; spkr. Friendship Bapt. Ch., Massillon, Ohio, 2001. Recipient Outstanding Svc. award, Pa. chpt. Nat. Assn. Real Estate Brokers, 1991, Gambrinus award, Milw. Hist. Soc., 1985; grantee, U.S. Dept. Edn. Grant, 2002-05, Ford Found., 1997-99, 2001-2002. Mem.: Labor and Working Class History Assn., Am. Studies Assn., So. Hist. Assn., Pa. Hist. Assn., Pitts. Ctr. for Social History, Urban History Assn., Assn. for the Study of Afro-American Life and History, Am. Hist. Assn., Orgn. Am. Historians. Office: Carnegie Mellon Univ Dept of History 5000 Forbes Ave Pittsburgh PA 15213 Office Phone: 412-268-2875. Office Fax: 412-268-1019. Business E-Mail: trotter@andrew.cmu.edu.

TROTTER, LESLIE EARL, operations research specialist, educator; b. Muskogee, Okla., Nov. 17, 1943; s. Leslie Earl and Sylvia Helene (Freeze) T.; m. Jomi Tuggle, July 19, 1968 (div. Dec. 1995); children: Colleen Nicole, Eamonn Scott; m. Jeannine Rouch, July 7, 2000. AB in Math., Princeton U., 1965; MS in Indsl. and Systems Engring., Ga. Inst. Tech., 1971; PhD in Ops. Rsch., Cornell U., 1973. Sci. computer programmer Lockheed-Ga. Co., Marietta, 1965-68; computer applications analyst Control Data Corp., Atlanta, 1968-70; postdoctoral rsch. assoc. Math. Rsch. Ctr., U. Wis., Madison, 1973; asst. prof. Yale U. Sch. Orgn. and Mgmt., New Haven, 1974-75; assoc. prof. Cornell U. Sch. Ops. Rsch. and Indsl. Engring., Ithaca, NY, 1975-84, dir. of Sch., 1983—87, 1998—99, prof., 1984—; dir. Advanced Computational Optimization Lab. Cornell Theory Ctr., 1995—2001. Vis. prof. Bonn (Germany) U., 1977-79, math. dept. E.P.F.L., Lausanne, Switzerland, 1984-85, 91-92, 2000, Math. Inst., Augsburg (Germany) U., 1987-88; ind. eng. lab. E.C.-Paris, 2006—; vis. cons. Bell Labs., Holmdel, N.J., 1981. Editor optimization area Jour. Ops. Rsch., 1982-87; contbr. numerous articles to profl. jours. Recipient tchg. excellence awards Cornell U., 1977, 81, 93, 94, 98, sr. U.S. scientist award Alexander von Humboldt Found., Germany, 1988; numerous rsch. grants NSF, 1974—, including High Performance Computing and Comms. Grand Challenge award, 1995—01. Mem. Inst for Ops Rsch and Mgmt. Sci., Math. Programming Soc. (treas. 1988-94), Soc. for Indsl. and Applied Math. Avocations: exercise, hiking, music. Office: Cornell U Sch Ops Rsch Engring Rhodes Hall Ithaca NY 14853 Office Phone: 607-255-5360. Business E-Mail: ltrotter@cs.cornell.edu.

TROTTER, LLOYD G., manufacturing executive; b. Cleveland, Apr. 9, 1945; m. Teri Trotter; 3 children. BBA, Cleve. State U., 1972, PhD (hon.) in Bus. Adminstrn., 2001. Field svc. engr. GE Lighting, 1970; various positions GE, 1970-90; v.p., gen. mgr. mfg. ED&C, 1990-98; sr. v.p. GE, 1998-99; pres., CEO GE Indsl. Sys., 1999—; CEO, consumer & indsl. divsn. GE, 2004—06; pres., CEO GE Indsl., 2006—; vice chmn. GE, 2006—. Started GE African-Am. forum, 1990; bd. dirs. NAM, Nat. Action Coun. for Minorities in Engring. (NACME). Rep. for GE America's Promise. Named 50 Most Important African-Am. in Tech., USBE&IT and Blackmoney.com, 2004. Avocation: collector of Harlem Renaissance Period art and wine. Office: GE 3135 Easton Tpke Fairfield CT 06431-0002 *

TROTTER, THOMAS ROBERT, lawyer; b. Akron, Ohio, Apr. 11, 1949; s. Fred and Josephine (Daley) Trotter; m. Martha Kaltenbach, 2003. BA, Ohio U., 1971; JD, Tulane U., 1975. Bar: Ohio 1975, D.C. 2000, U.S. Dist. Ct. (no. dist.) Ohio 1975. Assoc. Squire, Sanders & Dempsey, Cleve., 1975-80; shareholder Buckingham, Doolittle & Burroughs, Akron, 1980—2007; of counsel Vorys, Sater, Seymour and Pease LLP, Akron, Ohio, 2007—. Trustee Cascade Capital Corp., Akron, 1983-2000; chair taxation and legis. com. Greater Akron C. of C., 1988-95; trustee Akron-Summit Solid Waste Mgmt. Authority, 1994-97 Trustee Akron Symphony Orch., 1984-93, trustee Weathervane Cmty. Playhouse, 1996-2003, 06—, pres., 1999-2001. Mem. ABA, Ohio Bar Assn. (chair local govt. law com.), Akron Bar Assn., Nat. Assn. Bond Lawyers, Sigma Alpha Epsilon. Democrat. Home: 180 W Fairlawn Blvd Akron OH 44313 Office: Vorys Sater Seymour and Pease LLP 106 S Main St Ste 1100 Akron OH 44308 also: Vorys Sater Seymour and Pease LLP 2100 One Cleveland Ctr 1375 E Ninth St Cleveland OH 44114-1724 Office Phone: 330-208-1126, 216-479-6107. Business E-Mail: trtrotter@vssp.com, trtrotter@vorys.com.

TROTTIER, BRYAN JOHN, professional sports team executive, former professional hockey player and coach; b. Val Marie, Sask., Can., July 17, 1956; s. Eldon J. and Mary (Gardner) Trottier; m. Laura Lynn Theis, July 14, 1976; children: Bryan John, Lindsay Ann. Profl. hockey player NY Islanders, 1975—90, Pitts. Penguins, 1990—92, 1993—94, asst. coach, 1993—97; head coach Portland Pirates (Am. Hockey League), 1997—98; asst. coach Colo. Avalanche, 1998—2002; head coach NY Rangers, 2002—03; exec. dir. player devel. NY Islanders, 2006—. Hockey cons. Right Guard Corp., Phila.; spokesman 1980 Winter Olympics, Lake Placid, NY; former pres. NHL Player's Assn.; owner, operator Bryan Trottier Skating Acad., Port Washington, NY. Recipient Calder Meml. Trophy, 1976, Hart Meml. Trophy, 1979, Art Ross Trophy, 1979, Conn Smythe Trophy, 1980, King Clancy Meml. Trophy, 1989. Achievements include mem. Stanley Cup Champion, NY Islanders, 1980, 1981, 1982, 1983; mem. Stanley Cup Champions, Pitts. Penguins, 1991, 1992; inducted into Hockey Hall of Fame, 1997. Office: NY Islanders Nassau Veterans Meml Coliseum 1255 Hempstead Turnpike Uniondale NY 11553

TROTZ, BARRY, professional hockey coach; Asst. coach U. Manitoba, 1984; head coach, gen. mgr. Dauphin Kings Jr. Hockey Club, 1985-87; head coach U. Manitoba, 1987; chief western scout Washington Capitals, 1988, asst. coach, 1991, head coach, 1992-95, US Team at Am. Hockey

League All Star Game, 1996, Nashville Predators, 1997—. Named NHL Coach of Yr., Sporting News, 2007. Office: Nashville Predators 501 Broadway Nashville TN 37203-3932

TROUILLE, MARY SEIDMAN, foreign language educator; b. Chgo., Feb. 23, 1951; d. Nathaniel and Virginia (Crosley) Seidman; m. Guy Andre Nodot, Apr. 5, 1971 (div. Sept. 1977); 1 child, Jennifer Lynn; m. Bruno Jean-Louis Trouille, Apr. 15, 1978; children: David Alexander, Laura Elizabeth. BA in French, Loyola U., Chgo., 1972; MA in French, Northwestern U., Evanston, Ill., 1974, PhD in French, 1988. Editor Scott, Foresman Publs., Glenview, Ill., 1976-83; grad. teaching asst. Northwestern U., Evanston, Ill., 1983-88, lectr. French, 1988-89; lectr. humanities & French U. Chgo., 1990-93; asst. prof. French Ill. State U., Normal, 1993-96, assoc. prof. French, 1996—2002, prof. French, 2002—. Presenter in field. Author: Sexual Politics in the Enlightenment: Women Writers Read Rousseau, 1997; mem. editl. bd. Studies in 18th-Century Culture, 2000-2003; Translator: The Writing of Melancholy: Modes of Opposition in Early French Modernism, 1993, Les Lieux de Mémoire, vol. 1, 1998; contbr. chpts. to books and articles to profl. jours. Travel grantee Am. Coun. Learned Socs., 1995; Sch. Criticism & Theory fellow, 1985, Internat. Summer Inst. Semiotic and Structural Studies fellow, 1986. Mem. Am. Soc. Eighteenth-Century Studies (co-chair women's caucus 1995-98, mem. editl. bd. Studies in 18th-Century Culture 2000-03, chair tchg. prize selection com. 2002-03), Clifford Prize Com. (chair 2004-2005, mem. exec. bd. 2007-), Internat. Soc. Eighteenth-Century Studies. Office: Ill State U Dept Fgn Langs Lits and Cultures PO Box 4300 Normal IL 61790-0001 Office Phone: 309-438-3604.

TROUNSTINE, PHILIP JOHN, communications consultant, academic administrator; b. Cin., July 30, 1949; s. Henry P. and Amy May (Joseph) Trounstine; children: Jessica, David; m. Deborah Williams, May 1, 1993; children: Amy, Ryan, Patrick Wilkes. Student, U. Vt., 1967-68, Stanford U., 1968-70; BA in Journalism, San Jose State U., 1975. Graphic artist Eric Printing, San Jose, Calif., 1972-75; reporter Indpls. Star, Ind., 1975-78, San Jose Mercury News, Calif., 1978-83, editl. writer Calif., 1983-86, polit. editor Calif., 1986-99; ednl. cons. Teen Recovery Strategies, 1995-99; comms. dir. Gov. Gray Davis, Calif., 1999-2001, comm. cons. Calif., 2001—; dir. Survey and Policy Rsch. Inst. at San Jose State U., 2001—. Co-author: Movers & Shakers: The Study of Community Power, 1981. Creator, writer SPJ Gridiron Show, San Jose, 1981-91. Pulliam fellow, 1975, Duke U., 1991, J.S. Knight fellow Stanford U., 1993-94. Mem. Soc. Profl. Journalists (nat. ethics com. 1993-96), Am. Assn. Pub. Opinion Rsch., Seascape Golf Club. Jewish. Avocations: golf, fishing. Home: 620 Middlefield Dr Aptos CA 95003-3560 Office Phone: 408-924-6993.

TROUP, GORDON A., health products executive; With Am. Hosp. Supply Corp., Cardinal Distbn., 1991—99, exec. v.p. field ops., 1999—2000; pres. pharm. distbn. and splty distbn. bus. Cardinal Health, Inc., 2000—03, exec. v.p., 2003—, pres. nuclear pharmacy svcs., 2003—. Office: Cardinal Health Inc 7000 Cardinal Pl Dublin OH 43017 *

TROUPE, WILLIAM HAROLD, lawyer; b. Quincy, Mass., Aug. 7, 1945; s. George Harold and Elizabeth (Harvey) T.; m. Linda M. Corbett, July 19, 1970; children: Allyson Leigh, Adam Jeremy. BBA, U. Mass., 1967; JD, Suffolk U., 1972. Bar: Mass. 1972, U.S. Dist. Ct. Mass. 1975, U.S. Ct. Appeals (1st cir.) 1975, U.S. Supreme Ct., 1991. New Eng. claims mgr. Greater N.Y. Ins. Co., Boston, 1972-73; ptnr. Lawrence Locke & Assocs., Boston, 1973-84, Wynn & Wynn PC, Boston, 1984-89, Hislop Carney & Troupe, Boston, 1990-98; founding ptnr. Carney & Troupe, Boston, 1999—. Spkr. continuing legal edn. programs. Contbr. numerous articles on worker's compensation to legal jours. Mem. Mass. Bar Assn. (chmn. worker's compensaton com. 1985-87), Boston Bar Assn. Office: Carney & Troupe 5th Fl 10 High St Fl 5 Boston MA 02110-1605 Home Phone: 978-535-4184; Office Phone: 617-426-9797. Personal E-mail: willtrou@aol.com.

TROUSDALE, STEPHEN RICHARD, newspaper editor; b. LA, May 29, 1963; s. Richard Gardner Trousdale and Geraldine Barbara Wisdom. AB, Stanford U., 1985. News editor LA Daily Commerce, 1986—87, edit. page editor, 1987—89, mng. editor, 1989—96; bus. editor Copley LA Newspapers, 1996—97, Contra Costa Times, 2000—07, dep. bus. editor, 1997—2000, San Jose Mercury News, Calif., 2007—. Mem. Soc. Profl. Journalists (past pres. L.A. chpt.), AP Mng. Editors, Calif. Soc. Newspaper Editors, Soc. Am. Bus. Editors and Writers. Avocations: skiing, Karate. Home: 2335 Valley St Berkeley CA 94702-2133 Office: San Jose Mercury News 750 Ridder Park Dr San Jose CA 95190 Office Phone: 408-920-5800. Business E-Mail: strousdale@mercurynews.com.

TROUT, LINDA COPPLE, state supreme court justice; b. Tokyo, Sept. 1, 1951; BA, U. Idaho, 1973, JD, 1977; LLD (hon.), Albertson Coll. Idaho, 1999. Bar: Idaho 1977. Atty. Blake, Feeney & Clark, 1978—83; judge magistrate divsn. Idaho Dist. Ct. (2d jud. divsn.), 1983-90, dist. judge Lewiston, 1991-92, acting trial ct. adminstr., 1987-91; justice Idaho Supreme Ct., 1992—, chief justice, 1997—2004. Instr. coll. law U. Idaho, 1983, 88; chair Idaho State Supreme Ct. Judicial Education Com. Mem. bd. directors Lewiston City Library, Northwest Children's Home, Lewiston YWCA. Mem. Idaho State Bar Assn., Clearwater Bar Assn. (pres. 1980-81). Office: Idaho Supreme Court PO Box 83720 Boise ID 83720-3720 *

TROUT, MAURICE ELMORE, diplomat; b. Clifton Hill, Mo., Sept. 17, 1917; s. David McCamel and Charlotte Temple (Woods) T.; m. Margie Marie Mueller, Aug. 24, 1943; children: Richard Willis, Babette Yvonne. BA, Hillsdale Coll., 1939; MA in Pub. Adminstrn, St. Louis U., 1948, PhD in Polit. Sci, 1950. Joined U.S. Fgn. Service, 1950; assigned Paris, 1950-52, Vienna, 1952-55, London, 1955-59, Vientiane, Laos, 1959-61; with Office Exec. Dir. Bur. Far Eastern Affairs, Dept. State, Washington, 1961-65; Am. consulate gen. Munich, 1965-69; 1st sec., consul Am. embassy, Bangkok, 1969—72; dep. office dir. Bur. Politico-Mil. Affairs, Dept. State, Washington, 1972-75; Dept. State advisor Armed Forces Staff Coll., Norfolk, Va., 1975-77. Bd. dirs. Internat. Sch., Bangkok, 1970-72. Served with USCG, 1939-45; capt. USAFR, 1951-55. Recipient Achievement award, Hillsdale Coll., 1962. Mem. Am. Fgn. Service Assn., Diplomatic and Consular Officers Ret., Delta Tau Delta, Delta Theta Phi, Pi Gamma Mu. Home: 6203 Hardy Dr Mc Lean VA 22101-3114

TROUT, MONROE EUGENE, health facility administrator; b. Harrisburg, Pa., Apr. 5, 1931; s. David Michael and Florence Margaret (Kashner) T.; m. Sandra Louise Lemke, June 11, 1960; children: Monroe Eugene, Timothy William. AB, U. Pa., 1953, MD, 1957; LLB, Dickinson Sch. of Law, 1964, JD, 1969; LLD (hon.), Dickinson Sch. Law, 1996, Bloomfield Coll., 1994, Cumberland Coll., 2003. Intern Great Lakes (Ill.) Naval Hosp., 1957-58; resident in internal medicine Portsmouth (Va.) Naval Hosp., 1959-61; chief med. dept. Harrisburg State Hosp., 1961-64; dir. drug regulatory affairs Pfizer, Inc., NYC, 1964-68; v.p., med. dir. Winthrop Labs., NYC, 1968-70; med. dir. Sterling Drug, Inc., NYC, 1970-74, v.p., dir. med. affairs, 1974-78, sr. v.p., dir. med. affairs, bd. dirs., mem. exec. com., 1978-86; pres., CEO Am. Healthcare Sys., Inc., 1986-95, chmn., 1987-95; also bd. dirs. Am. Healthcare Systems, Inc.; chmn. emeritus Am. Healthcare Sys., Inc., 1995—; interim CEO Cytran Inc., 1996. Chmn. bd. dirs. Cytyc Inc., 1998—2002, Ineed MD, Inc., Am. Excess Ins. Ltd., 1990—95; adj. assoc. prof. Bklyn. Coll. Pharmacy; spl. lectr. legal medicine, trustee Dickinson Sch. Law, 1970—93; trustee Ariz. State U. Sch. Health Adminstrn., 1988—91; mem. rsch. bd. Sterling Winthrop, 1977—86; mem. Joint Commn. Prescription Drug Use, 1976—80; sec. Commn. on Med. Malpractice, HEW, 1971—73, cons., 1974; co-chmn. San Diego County Health Commn., 1992—94. Mem. editl. bd. Hosp. Formulary Mgmt., 1969-79, Forensic Sci., 1971—, Jour. Legal Medicine, 1973-79, Reg. Tox. and Pharmac, 1981-87, Med. Malpractice Prevention, 1985—; editl. reviewer Annals of Internal Medicine; contbr. articles to profl. jours. Exec. com. White House Mini Conf. on Aging, 1980; mem. Nat. Health Adv. Bd. AAA; chmn. bd. Am. Coll. Legal Medicine Found., 1983—87; mem. N.Y. State Commn. Substance Abuse, 1978—80, Town Coun., New Canaan, 1978—86, vice chmn., 1985—86; trustee Cleve. Clinic, 1971—87, Albany Med. Coll., 1977—86, St. Vincent DePaul Ctr. for the Homeless, 1987—90, U. Calif.-San Diego Thornton Hosp. and Med. Ctr., 1990—97, San Diego Mus. Art, 1996—98, Bapt. Health Sys. Found., Knoxville, 1999—; trustee, vice chmn. Morehouse Med. Sch., 1980—89; assoc. trustee U. Pa.; bd. visitors U. Pa. Sch. Nursing, 1988—92; pres. bd. trustees U. Calif. San Diego Found., 1994—97; vice chmn. Med. Commn. for Food and Shelter, Inc.; chmn. Internat. B'nai B'rith Dinner, 1989, 1994; Rep. dist. leader New Canaan, 1966—68; bd. dirs. New Canaan Interchurch Svc. Com., 1965—69, Athletes Kidney Found., Cir. in the Sq. Theatre Inc., 1984—86, Knoxville Symphony Soc., 2001—04, Knoxville Opera Co., 2001—04, East Tenn. Hist. Soc., 2003—04. Recipient Alumni award of merit U. Pa., 1953, Disting. Alumni award Dickinson Sch. Law, 1989, Nat. Healthcare award Internat. B'nai B'rith, 1991, Entrepreneur of Yr. award San Diego, 1994, Horatio Alger award, 1995, Salvation Army Tradition of Caring award, 1996, Civis Universitatus award U. Calif. San Diego, 1997, Gold Medal award, Am. Coll. Legal Medicine, 1999, Bapt. Health Sys. Visionary award, 2002, Knoxville Philanthropist of Yr., 2004, Cumberland Coll. Caring Servant award, 2005; Monroe E. Trout Day named in his honor, Knox County, Tenn., Mar. 13, 2007. Fellow Am. Coll. Legal Medicine (v.p., pres., bd. govs.); mem. AMA (Physician's Recognition awards 1969, 72, 76, 82, 85, 88, 92), Med. Execs. (pres. 1975-76), Delta Tau Delta (Alumni Achievement award 1996, Named to 100 Most Influential Delts of Twentieth Century 2000). Lutheran. Office: 2110 Cove View Way Knoxville TN 37919

TROUTMAN, HOLMES RUSSELL, lawyer; b. Beckley, W.Va., July 27, 1933; s. Holmes Fielding and Florence Lillo (Wallett) T.; m. Patricia Lee Bullion, Nov. 12, 1954; children: Holmes Russell, Richard Byron, Teresa Lee. AB, Marshall U., 1955; postgrad., Stetson Law Sch., 1955-56; LLB, U. Miami, 1958. Bar: Fla. 1958. Assoc., ptnr. firm Akerman, Turnbull, Senterfitt & Eidson, Orlando, Fla., 1958-62; ptnr. firm Fishback, Davis, Dominick & Troutman, Orlando, 1962-69, Troutman, Williams, Irvin, Green, Helms, and Polich, Winter Park, Fla., 1969—. Spl. city prosecutor, City of Winter Park, 1965, city atty., 1968-72, acting county solicitor, 1967-69; spl. counsel Fla. Turnpike Authority, 1968-70, Fla. Pub. Svc. Commn., 1978-79; mem. Fla. Supreme Ct. Nominating Commn., 1978-82, chmn., 1981-82; chmn. bd. trustees Fla. Supreme Ct. Historical Soc., 2000—. Author: Undiscovered Poems; contbr. articles to profl. jours. Host, prodr. Discussion programs Sta. WFTV, 1968-85. Pres. Friends of Orlando Pub. Libr., 1971-73, Fla. Supreme Ct. Hist. Soc., 1997-99; mem. Orange County Charter Study Commn., 1973-74; chmn. Winter Park Charter Study Commn., 1982-83; chmn. bd. advisors Rollins Coll. Hamilton Holt Sch., 1996-98, chmn. emeritus Hamilton Holt Sch. Bd. Rollins Coll.; pres. Fla. Supreme Ct. Hist. Soc., 1997-99; commencement spkr. Rollins Coll., 1999. Recipient Orlando Jr. C. of C. Good Govt. award, 1969, Marshall U. Alumnus Civic Contbrn. award, 1979, Winter Park C. of C. Good Govt. award, 1985. Mem. ABA (mem. ho. of dels. 1978-80), Am. Acad. Trial Lawyers, Fla. Acad. Trial Lawyers, Fla. Bar (mem. bd. govs. 1972-78, pres. 1977-78), Orange County Bar Assn. (mem. exec. coun. 1966-68, pres. 1968-69, driving force and co-founder Legal Aid Soc. 1969), Orlando Tiger Bay Club (pres. 1988-89). Home: 1600 Barcelona Way Winter Park FL 32789-5615 Office: Troutman Williams Irvin Green & Helms PA 311 W Fairbanks Ave Winter Park FL 32789-5094 Home Phone: 407-620-5009; Office Phone: 407-647-2277. Business E-Mail: btroutman@troutmanwilliams.com, rtroutman@troutmanwilliams.com.

TROUTNER, JOANNE JOHNSON, director, consultant, secondary school educator; b. Muncie, Ind., Sept. 9, 1952; d. Donal Russel and Lois Vivian (Hicks) Johnson; m. Lary William Troutner, May 17, 1975. BA in Media and English, Purdue U., 1974, MS in Edn., 1976. Media spls. Lafayette Sch. Corp., Ind., 1974-77, 81-83, computer resource tchr., 1983-84; media splst. Tippecanoe Sch. Corp., Lafayette, 1984-85, ednl. support, 1985-87, coord. instrl. support, 1988-94, dir. tech. and media, 1994—2007; tchr. English Minot Pub. Schs., ND, 1978-79, media specialist, 1979-81; instr. freshman honors seminar Purdue U., Coll. Tech., 2006—. Vis. prof. continuing edn. U. SC, Columbia, 1983, U. ND; instr. Purdue U., West Lafayette; software selector Elem. Sch. Libr. Collection. Author: The Media Specialist, The Microcomputer and the Curriculum, 1983, World Desk-Classroom Internet Guide, 1998, The Internet: A Curriculum Oriented Guide, 1998, 5th edit., 2007, Using the Internet and Technology to Strengthen Learning in English/Language Arts and Social Studies, 1999, Integrating Technology and the Internet into English and Social Studies Classroom, 2002, 2006, Strengthen Your Classroom with Technology, 2004, 2007, Best of the Best Web Sites, 2007; materials rev. columnist: Sch. Libr., Media Quar., computer literacy columnist: Jour. Computers Math. and Sci. Tchg., computer software columnist: Tchr. Libr., 1989—, internet columnist:, 1995—; editor: Ind. Computer Educators newsletter. Active Greater Lafayette Leadership Acad. Alumni Group, 1983—; bd. dirs. Lafayette Family Svc. Agy., 1987—89; treas. Greater Lafayette Mortar Bd. Alumni Group, 2006—; bd. dirs. Tippecanoe County Pub. Libr., trustee, 1990—2000, pres., 1994—95; mem. dean's adv. coun. Sch. Edn. Purdue U., 2003—. Recipient Disting. Alumni award, Purdue U. Sch. Edn., 2003. Mem.: ASCD, ALA, Internat. Soc. Tech. Educators, Ind. Computer Educators (bd. dirs. 1986—92, pres. 1990—91), Internat. Coun. Computers in Edn. (interactive video spl. interest group newsletter editor 1986—87), Am. Assn. Sch. Librs. (sec. 1983—84, 2d v.p. 1985—86), Ind. Assn. Media Educators (chmn. computer divns. 1982—84), Phi Beta Kappa, Phi Delta Kappa (v.p. programs 1987—88, v.p. memberships 1988—89, pres. 1989—90), Kappa Delta Gamma. Home: 4001 Penny Packers Mill Rd Lafayette IN 47909-3557 Office: Tippecanoe Sch Corp 21 Elston Rd Lafayette IN 47909-2899 Office Phone: 765-474-2481, 765-477-7306. Personal E-mail: troutner@mindspring.com.

TROUTT, KENNY, communications executive; b. Mt. Vernon, Ill., Jan. 8, 1948; s. Nadine Adams; m. Lisa Troutt; 3 children. BS, Southern Ill. U. Founder Excel Comm., 1988, CEO, chmn., vice chmn.; co-owner WinStar Farms, Ky.; dir. Mt. Vernon Investments, Inc. Vice chmn. Teleglobe, bd. dirs.; trustee Thoroughbred Owners & Breeders Assn.; bd. dirs. Breeders' Cup. Coach boys' basketball. Named one of Forbes' Richest Americans, 2006. Christian. Mailing: WinStar Farms 3001 Pisgah Pike Versailles KY 40383 Office Phone: 859-873-1717. Office Fax: 859-873-1612.

TROUTT, WILLIAM EARL, academic administrator; b. Bolivar, Tenn., June 13, 1949; s. Jack and Earline (Shearin) Troutt; m. Carole Pearson, Nov. 26, 1970; children: Carole Anne, Jack. BA, Union U., Jackson, Tenn., 1971; MA, U. Louisville, 1972; PhD, Vanderbilt U., 1978. Admissions counselor Union U., 1973—75; asst. dir. Tenn. Higher Edn. Commn., Nashville, 1975—78; sr. assoc. McManis Assocs. Inc., Washington, 1978—80; exec. v.p. Belmont Coll., Nashville, 1981—82, pres., 1982—99, Rhodes Coll., Memphis, 1999—. Chmn. Am. Coun. on Edn. Chmn. Jacob Javits Fellowship Bd., Nat. Assn. Ind. Colls. & Univs., Nat. Commn. Cost Higher Edn. Named one of Nation's Most Effective Coll. Pres., Exxon Found. Study, 1986. Mem.: So. Assn. Colls. and Schs. (commnr. commn. colls. 1986—), Tenn. Ind. Colls. Fund (sec.-treas. 1986—), Tenn. Coun. Pvt. Colls. (chmn.), Nashville Area C. of C. (bd. dirs. 1985—), Rotary. Office: Office of the Pres 2000 N Pkwy Memphis TN 38112-1690 *

TROUTWINE, GAYLE LEONE, lawyer; b. Kansas City, Mo., Feb. 26, 1952; BS, N.W. Mo. U., 1973; JD with honors, U. Mo., 1978, postgrad., 2003—. Bar: Mo. 1978, Oreg. 1983, U.S. Dist. Ct. (we. dist.) Mo., Wash. 1984, U.S. Ct. Appeals (9th cir.), U.S. Dist. Ct. (we. dist.) Wash., U.S. Supreme Ct., Hawaii 1995. Ptnr. Williams & Troutwine, P.C., Portland, Oreg., 1986—99, Troutwine Law Offices, Maui, Columbia, Osage Beach, Mo., 1999—; pres., CEO Hula Moons Farm, Maui, Hawaii, 1999—2002, Apricot Rose, Kahului, Hawaii, 1999—2003; CEO Aloha Enterprises, 2004—. Spkr. in field; mem. Maui Bd. Realtors. Contbr. articles to profl. jours. Mem. Jud. Steering Com., 1994, Made in Hawaii Coun., 2000—02, pres., 2004—; bd. mem. Portland Area Women's Polit. Caucus, 1992—95, Oreg. Women's Polit. Caucus, 1996—99; candidate Columbia City Coun., 2005; steering com. mem. Breast Implant Litig., 1992—, Tobacco Litig. Named Queen of Torts, Wall St. Jour., 1996. Mem.: ATLA (bd. govs.), Cmty. Assn. Inst., Maui Bd. Realtors, Western Trial Lawyers Assn. (bd. govs. 1992—), Greater Kansas City (sec. 1981—82), Women Lawyers Assn., Wash. Trial Lawyers Assn., Hawaii Trial Lawyers Assn., Calif. Trial Lawyers Assn., Oreg. Trial Lawyers Assn. (bd. govs. 1987—91), Wash. State Bar, Oreg. State Bar (exec. bd. litig. sect. 1984—88, chmn. 1987—88, procedure and practice com. 1985—88, bd. govs. 1990—93), Mo. Bar, Hawaii State Bar. Democrat. Office: 1218 Hwy KK Osage Beach MO 65065 Home Phone: 573-634-3848; Office Phone: 573-348-2434. Office Fax: 573-348-4204. Business E-Mail: gtroutwine@troutwinelaw.com.

TROVER, ELLEN LLOYD, lawyer, rancher, art dealer; b. Richmond, Va., Nov. 23, 1947; d. Robert Van Buren and Hazel (Urban) Lloyd; m. Denis William Trover, June 12, 1971; 1 dau., Florence Emma. AB, Vassar Coll., 1969; JD, Coll. William and Mary, 1972. Asst. editor Bancroft-Whitney, San Francisco, 1973-74; owner Ellen Lloyd Trover Atty.-at-Law, Thousand Oaks, Calif., 1974-82; ptnr. Trover & Fisher, Thousand Oaks, Calif., 1982-89; pvt. practice law Thousand Oaks, Calif., 1989-98; mng. ptnr. The Lloyd-Trover Partnership d/b/a Rancho Ellenita & the Gallery at Rancho Ellenita, Calif., 1998—. Editor: Handbooks of State Chronologies, 1972. Trustee Conejo Future Found., Thousand Oaks, 1978—91, trustee emeritus, 1992—, vice chmn., 1982—84, chmn., 1984—88; pres. Zonta Club Conejo Valley Area, 1978—79; trustee Hydro Help for the Handicapped, 1980—85, Atlantis Found., 1994—; pres. Vista Santa Rosa Assn., 2001—; mem. governing bd. Coachella Valley Mountains Conservancy, 2007—; dir. Riverside County Farm Bur., 2005—. Mem. State Bar Calif., Va. State Bar, Phi Alpha Delta. Democrat. Presbyterian. Home: PO Box 297 Coachella CA 92236 Office Phone: 760-398-8326. Personal E-mail: ranchoellenita@gmail.com.

TROWBRIDGE, JOHN PARKS, physician; b. Dinuba, Calif., Mar. 24, 1947; s. John Parks and Claire Dovie (Noroian) Trowbridge; children: Sharla Tyann, Lyndi Kendyll. AB in Biol. Scis., Stanford U., 1970; MD, Case Western Res. U., 1976; postgrad., Fla. Inst. Tech., 1983-85. Diplomate in Preventive Medicine, Am. Bd. Clin. Metal Toxicology (examiner for bd. 1987—, protocol coun. 1996-98), Am. Bd. Biologic Reconstructive Therapy (examiner for bd. 1994-97), Am. Bd. Anti-Aging Medicine, 1998, Nat. Bd. Med. Examiners. Intern in gen. surgery Mt. Zion Hosp. & Med. Ctr., San Francisco, 1976-77; resident in urol. surgery U. Tex. Health Sci. Ctr., Houston, 1977-78; pvt. med. practice (health recovery unit, pain relief unit, life long health unit) Life Celebrating Health Assn., Humble, Tex., 1978—. Chief corp. med. cons. Tex. Internat. Airlines, Houston, 1981-83; immunology rsch. asst. Stanford U. Med. Ctr., Stanford, Calif., 1967-70; night lab. supr. Kaiser Found. Hosp., Redwood City, Calif., 1971-72; advisor to bd. dirs. Am. Inst. Med. Preventics, Laguna Hills, Calif., 1988-90; sr. aviation med. examiner FAA, 1983-96; invited guest lectr. Taipei Med. U., Taiwan, 2005; lectr., cons. in field. Co-author: The Yeast Syndrome, 1986, Chelation Therapy, 1985, 2d edit., 1990, Yeast Related Illnesses, 1987, Do What You Want to Do, 1996, The Rumble in Humble: Heart Surgery and All That Jazz, 1997, Living Well Past 50: Rejuvenate Your Heart and Arteries, 1998; contbr. Challenging Orthodoxy: America's Top Medical Preventives Speak Out, 1991; weekly radio show host (KBME-AM): Feeling Better...Naturally, with Dr. John Trowbridge, Houston, 2003-2004; contbr. articles to profl. jours. Adv. bd. Tex. Chamber Orchestra, Houston, 1979-80; med. dir. Humble unit Am. Cancer Soc., 1980-81; med. cons. personal fitness program Lake Houston YMCA, 1981-83. Nat. Merit scholar, 1965-69, Calif. State scholar, 1967-69; recipient Resolution of Commendation house of dels., 1974 Am. Podiatry Assn., Spl. Profl. Svc. Citation bd. trustees, 1976, Am. Podiatry Students Assn. Fellow: Am. Coll. Advancement in Medicine (v.p. 1987—89, pres.-elect 1989—91), Am. Soc. for Laser Medicine and Surgery; mem.: AMA, Internat. Acad. Biol. Dentistry and Medicine (bd. dir. 2007—), Advanced Med. Edn. and Svcs. Physician Assn., Am. Bd. Clin. Metal Toxicology (bd. dirs. 2006—, sec. bd. dirs. 2007—, sec. 2007—), Neuro Cranial Restructuring Drs. Assn., Neuro Cranial Reconstruction Rsch. Inst. (pres. 2003-) (pres. 2002—03, rsch. inst. pres. 2003—), Am. Soc. Life Ext. Physicians (founding), Am. Assn. Nutritional Cons., Am. Acad. Thermology, Nat. Health Fedn. (chmn. bd. govs. 1989), Am. Soc. Gen. Laser Surgery, Am. Acad. Environ. Medicine, Legal and Edn. Found. Am. Preventive Med. Assn. (bd. dirs. 1996—99, charter), Am. Preventive Medicine Assn. (bd. dirs. 1992—99, charter), Am. Coll. Preventive Medicine, Internat. Coll. Integrative Medicine (editor newsletter 2000—01, bd. dirs. 2000—, sec. 2002—), N.Am. Cervicogenic Headache Soc., Royal Soc. Medicine (London, sect. orthop.), Soc. for Orthomolecular Medicine, Great Lakes Coll. Clin. Medicine (bd. dirs. 1991—95, med. rsch. instnl. rev. bd., v.p. 1993—94, pres. 1994—95, program chair Advanced Tng. Seminar in Heavy Metal Toxicology 1996—98, bd. dirs. 1999—2000), Huxley Inst. for Biosocial Rsch., Inst. Health Freedom (bd. dirs. 1997—2001), Arthritis Trust Am. (med. adv. bd. 1995—), Internat. Acad. Bariatric Medicine, NY Acad. Scis., Aerospace Med. Assn., Houston Acad. Medicine, Harris County Med. Soc., Tex. Med. Assn., Am. Acad. Anti-Aging Medicine, Assn. Am. Physicians and Surgeons. Avocations: private piloting, computer applications. Office: Life Celebrating Health Assn 9816 Memorial Blvd Ste 205 Humble TX 77338-4206 Home Phone: 281-540-2255; Office Phone: 281-540-2329. Personal E-mail: jptlch@earthlink.net. Business E-Mail: info@healthchoicesnow.com.

TROWBRIDGE, THOMAS, JR., mortgage company executive; b. Troy, NY, June 28, 1938; s. of Thomas and Elberta (Wood) T.; m. Delinda Bryan, July 3, 1965; children: Elisabeth Tacy, Wendy Bryan. BA, Yale U., 1960; MBA, Harvard U., 1965. V.p. James W. Rouse & Co., Balt., 1965-66, Washington, 1966-68, San Francisco, 1968-73, 76-78; pres. Rouse Investing Co., Columbia, Md., 1973-76, Trowbridge, Kieselhorst & Co., San Francisco, 1978-97, CEO, chmn., 1997-2000; ret., 2000. Bd. dirs. Columbia Assn., 1975-76; trustee, treas. The Head-Royce Sch., Oakland, Calif., 1980-84; trustee, pres. Gen. Alumni Assn. Phillips Exeter Acad., 1984-90. Lt. USNR, 1960-63. Mem. SAR, Urban Land Inst., Calif. Mortgage Bankers Assn. (bd. dirs. 1991-98, pres. 1996-97), Mortgage Bankers Assn. Am. (bd. govs. 1993-2000), Naval War Coll. Found., 2000-, Olympic Club, Pacific Union Club. Republican. Presbyterian. Avocation: golf. Home: 4 Ridge Ln Orinda CA 94563-1318

TROXELL, LUCY DAVIS, management consultant; b. Cambridge, Mass., Apr. 25, 1932; d. Ellsworth and Mildred (Enneking) Davis; m. Charles DeGroat Bader, June 13, 1952 (div. Aug. 1974); children: Christie P. Walker, Mary Bader Montgomery, Charles D. Bader Jr., David Bradford Bader; m. Victor Daniel Shirer Troxell, Aug. 1974. BA, Smith Coll., Northampton, Mass., 1952; grad., Inst. Paralegal Training, Phila. Cert. employee benefit specialist, assoc. in risk mgmt. Paralegal O'Melveny & Myers, LA, 1976-77; acct. exec. Olanie Hurst & Hemrich, LA, 1977-78; asst. to trustee Oxford Ins. Mgmt., LA, 1978-80; dir. corp. svcs., asst. corp. sec. Consolidated Elec. Distbrs., Inc., Westlake Village, Calif., 1980-93;

pres. MONMAK LDT, Westlake Village, 1993—. Vol. Friends of the Westlake Village Libr., 2000—, ARC; bd.dirs. Friends of the West Lake Village, 2004—, v.p., 2006, pres., 2007; clk. St. Mathew's Parish Vestry, Pacific Palisades, Calif., 1988, sr. warden, 1989—90; lic. lay eucharistic min. Episcopal Ch.; sustaining bd. dirs. Jr. League, Hartford, Conn., 1952—58, LA, 1952—60; bd. dirs. Smith Coll. Club, Hartford, 1952—58, Nat. Charity League, LA, 1964—68, Theatre Palisades, 1960—74; bd. dirs., treas. HOA Lakeshore Cmty. Assn., 1999—2002, v.p., 2005—. Sophia Smith scholar. Fellow: Risk and Ins. Mgmt. Soc. (program chmn. L.A. chpt. 1985—86), Internat. Soc. Cert. Employee Benefit Specialists (bd. dirs., sec., treas. 1988—89, pres. 1989—90, edn. chmn. L.A. chpt. 1986—88). Republican. Avocations: finance, acting, music, art. Home: 450 Puerto Del Mar Pacific Palisades CA 90272-4233 Office: MONMAK LDT 32001 Viewlake Ln Westlake Village CA 91361

TROXLER, WILLIE THOMASENE, retired elementary school educator; b. Raleigh, NC, Sept. 3, 1925; d. Charles Gilmer Cates and Addie Gaye Long; m. Roger Vernon Troxler, Mar. 18, 1950; children: Bonnie Lynn, Teri. BA, St. Mary's Jr. Coll., Raleigh, 1945; BA in Journalism, U. NC, Chapel Hill, 1947; MA in Lang. Arts, U. NC, Charlotte, 1976. Reporter State Advt. Divsn., NC, 1947—48; assoc. editor Carolina Road Builders Trade Mag., NC, 1948—50; tchr. elem. sch. Salisbury City Schs., NC, 1961—78. Exhibited in group shows at Page Walker Arts and History Ctr., Cary, NC, 1999, Rowan Regional Hosp., Salisbury, 1999, Davidson County Mus. Art, Lexington, NC, 1999, one-woman shows include Depot Visual Arts Ctr., Mooresville, NC, 1997, Rowan Pub. Libr., Salisbury, 1982, Chatham County Hosp., Asheboro, NC, 1982, Salisbury Pub. Sch. Supplementary Ctr. Art Gallery, 1982; contbr. poetry to mags. Active Salisbury Symphony Guild; 2d v.p. Rep. Women, Salisbury. Recipient 1st pl. Collage, Rowan County Silver Arts, 2005, 2d pl., Rowan County Art Group, 2005, 1st Pl. Mem. Choice award, Rowan County Art Show, 2005, Gold medal visual divsn., Silver Arts, 2007. Mem.: Stanley County Art Guild, Davidson County Art Guild (Judges Commendation 1986, Pres. Choice Stuffer Myer's Meml. award 1995, Third pl. 1998, First pl. 2002), Mooresville Art Guild, Waterworks Visual Art Works, Watercolor Soc. N.C. (Fifth pl. Fall Show 1997, Merit award Spring Show 1999), Carolina Artist (past pres.). Home: 131 Richmond Rd Salisbury NC 28144-2847 Personal E-mail: ttroxler@salisbury.net.

TROY, ANTHONY FRANCIS, lawyer; b. Hartford, Conn., Apr. 16, 1941; children: Anthony John, Francis Gerard II, Silvio Connor A. BA in Govt., St. Michael's Coll., Vt., 1963; LLB, U. Richmond, Richmond, Va., 1966. Bar: Va. 1966, D.C. 1972, U.S. Dist. Ct. (ea. dist.) Va. 1966, U.S. Dist. Ct. (we. dist.) Va. 1967, U.S. Ct. Appeals (4th cir.) 1967, U.S. Supreme Ct. 1969. Asst. atty. gen. Commonwealth of Va., Richmond, 1966-72, atty. gen., 1977-78; assoc. Colson & Shapiro, Washington, 1972-74; ptnr., govtl. law, spl. investigations Troutman, Sanders LLP, Richmond, 1978—, and mem., exec. com. Conard Mattox Disting. adj. prof. chair law U. Richmond Law Sch. Contbr. articles to profl. jours. Trustee Sci. Mus. Va. Fellow Am. Law Found., Va. Law Found. Office: Troutman Sanders LLP 1001 Haxall Point Richmond VA 23219 Office Phone: 804-697-1318. Office Fax: 804-698-5162. E-mail: tony.troy@troutmansanders.com.

TROY, FREDERIC ARTHUR, II, medical biochemistry professor; b. Evanston, Ill., Feb. 16, 1937; s. Charles McGregor and Virginia Lane (Minto) T.; m. Linda Ann Price, Mar. 23, 1959; children: Karen M., Janet R. BS, Washington U., St. Louis, 1961; PhD, Purdue U., 1966; postdoctoral, Johns Hopkins U., Balt., 1968. Asst. prof. U. Calif. Sch. Medicine, Davis, 1968-74, assoc. prof., 1974-80, prof., 1980—2006, emeritus prof., 2006—, chmn., 1991-94, 2006—; co-founder SialoGen Therapeutics, Inc., Davis, Calif., 2003—, pres., 2003—, CEO, 2003—. Cons. NIH, Bethesda, Md., 1974—, NSF, Washington, 1975—, Damon Runyon Cancer Found., NYC, 1980-81, VA, Washington, 1984-88, US Army Breast Cancer Study Sect., 1999—; vis. prof. Karolinska Inst. Med. Sch., Stockholm, Sweden, 1976-77. Mem. editl. bd. Jour. Biol. Chem., 1988—, Glycobiol., 1990—; contbr. articles to profl. jours. Recipient Research Cancer Devel. award Nat. Cancer Inst., 1975-80; Eleanor Roosevelt Internat. Cancer fellow Am. Cancer Soc., 1976-77. Mem. AAAS, Am. Soc. Biol. Chemistry and Molecular Biology, Am. Assn. Cancer Rsch., Am. Chem. Soc., Am. Soc. Enologists, Biochemistry Soc., Biophysics Soc., Am. Fedn. for Clin. Rsch., NY Acad. Scis., Soc. for Glycobiol. (pres. 1991-92), Am. Med. and Grad. Sch. Dept. Biochem. (pres.-elect 1995—), Sigma Xi. Office: Sch Medicine Dept Biochem and Molecular Medicine U Calif Davis CA 95616 Business E-Mail: fatroy@ucdavis.edu.

TROY, NANCY J., art history educator; BA in Art magna cum laude with honors, Wesleyan U., 1974; MA, Yale U., 1976, PhD, 1979. Gallery asst. Waddington Galleries, London, 1973; rsch. asst. Soc. Anonyme Collection, Yale U., New Haven, 1975, tchg. asst. history of art dept., 1975-76; asst. prof. dept. history of art Johns Hopkins U., Balt., 1979-83; asst. prof. dept. art history Northwestern U., Evanston, Ill., 1983-85, assoc. prof., 1985-92, prof., 1992-93, chmn. dept., 1990-92; vis. prof. UCLA, 1994; vis. prof. art history U. So. Calif., LA, 1994-95, prof., 1995—, chmn. dept., 1997—. Scholar-in-residence Getty Rsch. Inst. for History Art and Humanities, L.A., 1993-96, organizer Work in Progress lecture series, 1993-98; series co-editor Histories, Culturs, Contexts, Reaktion Book, London; curatorial coord., spl. cons. to Ilya Bolotowsky Retrospective, Solomon R. Guggenheim Mus., N.Y.C., summers 1972-74; asst. to curator French paintings Nat. Gallery Art, Washington, summer 1975, bd. advisors Ctr. for Advanced Study in VisualArts, 1999-2002; guest curator Yale U. Art Gallery, 1979; mem. fine arts accessions com. and com. on collections Balt. Mus. Art, 1979-82; cons. De Stijl: 1917-1931, Visions of Utopia exhbn. Walker Art Ctr., Mpls., Washington, The Netherlands, 1982; cons. amplifying art program Art Inst. Chgo., 1984-85; mem. vis. com. Harvard U. Art Mus., Cambridge, Mass., 1992-98; lectr., chmn., moderator numerous symposia, 1980—; numerous invited lectures, 1975—, including U. Brighton, Eng., U. London, Middlexex U., London, Royal Coll. Art, London, U. Toronto, Mt. Holyoke Coll., Barnard Coll., Columbia U., Newcomb Coll., Tulane U., Los Angeles County Mus. Art, Art Inst. Chgo., Terra Mus. Am. Art, Chgo., N.C. Mus. Art, Raleigh, McGill U., Montreal, Vassar Coll.; mus. projects peer rev. panelist NEH, 1991; peer reviewer Woodrow Wilson Ctr., Washington, 1994, 96; external reviewer dept. art history U. Mich., 1987; bd. dirs. Nat. Com. for History Art, 1998—; peer reviewer for promotion and tenure Boston U., Lake Forest Coll., Middlesex U., Occidental Coll., U. Mo., Columbia, U. Va., 1996-98. Author: The De Stijl Environment, 1983, Modernism and the Decorative Arts in France: Art Nouveau to Le Corbusier, 1991, (exhbn. catalog) Mondrian and Neo-Plasticism in America, 1979; editor-in-chief The Art Bull., 1994-97; editor: (with Eve Blau) Architecture and Cubism, 1997; series co-editor Histories, Cultures, Contexts; mem. editl. bd. Art Bull., 1993—, Grey Room, 1998—; contbr. articles and book revs. to profl. jours., including Decorative Arts Soc. Jour., Design Issues, Art Bull., October, Archithese, Arts mag., Portfolio, Design Book Rev., chpts. to books. Mem. Md. Coun. on Arts, 1981-82; trustee Wesleyan U., 1994-97. Recipient Disting. Alumna award Wesleyan U., 1991, postdoctoral tchg. award Lilly Endowment, 1985, Andrew W. Mellon professorship for advanced study in the visual arts Nat. Gallery Art (declined), 2000-02; Fulbright-Hays grantee, The Netherlands, 1977-78, travel grantee Kress Found., summer 1976, spring 1977, grantee Am. Coun. Learned Soc., summers 1981, 91, 98-99; grantee Graham Found. for Advanced Studies in Fine Arts, 1982, publ. grantee, 1989; grantee NEH, 1982-83, Am. Philos. Soc., 1986, Inst. for Advanced Study Sch. Hist. Studies, 1987, Getty Rsch. Inst. for History Art and Humanities, 1989-90, Zumberge Faculty Rsch. and Innovation Fund, U. So. Calif., 1998-99, Guggenheim Found., 1998-99; AT&T rsch. fellow Northwestern U., 1992-93. Mem. Coll. Art Assn. Am. (nominating com. 1990, bd. dirs. 1992-97, ann. meeting local host com. L.A. 1998-99), Soc. Archtl. Historian (sec. Chgo. chpt. 1984-85, peer reviewer Jour. 1996), Nat. Com. for the History of Art (bd. dirs.), Sterling and Francine Clark Art Inst. (mem. fellowship com.). Office: U So Calif Dept Art History University Park 104 Watt MC 0293 Los Angeles CA 90089-0001

TROY, ROBERT SWEENEY, SR., lawyer; b. Quincy, Mass., Aug. 13, 1949; s. Robert F. and Winifred (Sweeney) T.; m. Sabina Greene, Oct. 12, 1985; children: Robert Sweeney Jr., Michael Francis, Matthew Thomas. AB, Georgetown U., 1971; JD, Boston Coll., 1974. Bar: Mass. 1974, Fla. 1976, U.S. Dist. Ct. Mass. 1976, U.S. Ct. Appeals 1977, U.S. Ct. Mil. Appeals 1982, U.S. Supreme Ct. 1990. Asst. dist. atty. Cape and Islands, Mass., 1974-76; counsel Town of Bourne, Mass., 1978—. Counsel Town of Duxbury, Mass., 1986—, Barnstable County, 1992—. Mem. Mass. Bar Assn. (bd. dels. 1977-80), Barnstable County Bar Assn., Plymouth County Bar Assn., Town Counsel Assn. Home: 150 Nichols Rd Cohasset MA 02025 Office: 90 Route 6A Sandwich MA 02563-5301 Office Phone: 508-888-5700.

TROY, TEVI D., federal agency administrator; b. 1967; s. Bernard and Elaine Troy; m. Kami Troy; 4 children. BS Indsl. Design, Labor Rels., Cornell U.; MA Am. Civilization, PhD Am. Civilization, U. of Tex., Austin. Herman Kahn fellow Hudson Inst., Indpls.; rschr. Am. Enterprise Inst., Washington DC; sr. domestic policy adv. Ho. Policy Com., 1996—98, domestic policy dir., 1996—98; policy dir. to Senator John Ashcroft US Senate; dep. asst. sec. for policy US Dept. Labor, dir. Office Faith Based Initiatives; spl. asst. to Pres. The White House, 2003—04, liaison to Jewish Cmty., 2003—04; dep. asst. Pres. Bush, Domestic Policy, 2005—07; dep. sec. US Dept Health & Human Services, Washington, 2007—. Author: (novels) Intellectuals and the Am. Presidency: Philosophers, Jesters, or Technicians, 2002. Office: US Dept Health & Human Services 200 Independence Ave SW Rm 614-G Washington DC 20201 Office Phone: 202-690-6133. Office Fax: 202-690-7755. E-mail: tevi.troy@hhs.gov. *

TROYER, ALVAH FORREST, agricultural products executive, horticulturist; b. LaFontaine, Ind., May 30, 1929; s. Alvah Forrest and Lottie (Waggoner) T.; m. Joyce Ann Wigner, Sept. 22, 1950; children: Anne, Barbara, Catherine, Daniel (dec.). BS, Purdue U., 1954; MS, U. Ill., 1956; PhD, U. Minn., 1964. Rsch. assoc. U. Ill., Urbana, 1955-56; rsch. fellow U. Minn., St. Paul, 1956-58; rsch. sta. mgr. Pioneer Hi-Bred Internat., Inc., Mankato, Minn., 1958-65, rsch. coord., 1965-77; dir. R & D, Pfizer Genetics, St. Louis, 1977-81, v.p. and dir. R & D, 1981-82; v.p. R&D, DEKALB Plant Genetics, 1982-93; cons. Hybrid Seed divsn. Cargill, Mpls., 1993-98; adj. prof. crop sci. dept. U. Ill., 1998—. Rschr. corn breeding, econ. botany, crop physiology, increasing genetic diversity, recent corn evolution. Contbr. articles to numerous publs.; developer of popular corn inbred lines and hybrids. Master sgt. U.S. Army, 1951-53, Korea. Recipient Nat. Coun. Comml. Plant Breeders Genetics and Plant Breeding award, 1992, Outstanding Achievement award U. Minn., 1998, nat. award for agrl. excellence Nat. Agrl. Mktg. Assn., 1999. Fellow AAAS, Am. Soc. Agronomy, Crop Sci. Soc. Am.; mem. Am. Genetic Assn., Genetic Soc. Am., N.Y. Acad. Scis., CAST, VFW, Masons, Sigma Xi, Gamma Sigma Delta (Award of Merit 1996), Alpha Zeta, Lambda Chi Alpha, Gamma Alpha. Methodist. Home: 611 Joanne Ln Dekalb IL 60115 Business E-Mail: atroyer@uiuc.edu.

TROYER, LEROY SETH, architect; b. Middlebury, Ind., Nov. 23, 1937; s. Seth and Nancy (Miller) T.; m. Phyllis Eigsti, May 24, 1958; children: Terry, Ronald, Donald. BArch, U. Notre Dame, 1971. Founder, pres. LeRoy Troyer and Assocs., South Bend, Ind., 1971; chmn. Troyer Group, Inc. (formerly LeRoy Troyer and Assocs.), Mishawaka, Ind., 1988—; pres. Southfield, Inc., 1988—. Pres. Lead Devel., Inc.; founder, sec., treas. Am. Countryside, LLC, Midwest Farmers Market, LLC Author numerous documents; contbr. numerous papers and articles to publs. Past pres., chair Environic Found. Internat., Inc.; bd. dirs. Habitat for Humanity Internat. Americus, Ga., 1987-93, global leadership coun., 2003—; chair The Fuller Ctr. for Housing Ams., Ga., 2006—; bd. dirs. Coun. of Christian Colls. and Univs., 1991-96, Habitat for Humanity St. Joseph County, Ind., 1992-99, 2001-, Bethel Coll. 1988-97, 2001-, bd. chair 2005-, Evangelicals for Social Action, Wynnewood, Pa., 1997-2003, Mishawaka, CONNECT, HHS, South Bend, 1999-2003; bd. dirs., exec. com., trustee Fourth Freedom Forum Internat., 1996—, vice-chmn., 2005—; chmn. Miracle of Nazareth Internat. Found., 2000-03, trustee 2000—; bd. trustee Fuller Ctr. Housing, Americus, Calif., 2005—, chmn. 2006—. Recipient numerous local, state and nat. awards and honors. Fellow AIA (practice mgmt. com., chmn. 1983-84), Ind. Soc. Archs., Mennonite Econ. Devel. Assn. Internat. (chmn. bd., 1987-91). Avocations: photography, travel, reading, art, woodworking. Home: 1442 Deerfield Ct South Bend IN 46614-6429 Office: The Troyer Group Inc 550 Union St Mishawaka IN 46544-2346 Office Phone: 574-259-9976. Business E-Mail: leroy@troyergroup.com.

TROYER, THOMAS ALFRED, lawyer; b. Omaha, Aug. 15, 1933; s. Robert Raymond and Dorothy (Darlow) T.; m. Sally Jean Brown, June 28, 1958; children: Kenneth D., Robert C., Virginia D., Thomas C. BA, Harvard U., 1955; JD, U. Mich., 1958. Bar: Colo. 1958, U.S. Ct. Appeals (D.C. cir.) 1967. Assoc. Holme, Roberts, Moore & Owen, Denver, 1958—61; USAF, Denver, 1961-62; trial atty. U.S. Dept. Justice, Washington, 1962-64; legal staff Asst. Sec. Treasury for Tax Policy, Washington, 1964-66; assoc. tax legis. counsel U.S. Dept. Treasury, Washington, 1966-67; mem. Caplin & Drysdale, Washington, 1967—. Pres. Stern Fund, NYC, 1985—86; bd. dirs. Children's Def. Fund, Washington, 1977—, Mineral Policy Ctr., Washington, 1988—2002; trustee Natural Resources Def. Coun., NYC, 1977—2005, Carnegie Corp., NYC, 1983—91, Cmty. Found. Nat. Capital Region, 1992—2000; chair Ctr. for Lobbying in Pub. Interest, Washington. Contbr. numerous articles to profl. jours. Bd. dirs. Common Cause, Washington, 1980-83; mem. Treasury Adv. Commn. on Pvt. Philanthropy and Pub. Needs, Washington, 1976-77; mem. adv. group to Commr. Internal Rev., Washington, 1978-80; mem. com. of visitors U. Mich. Law Sch., Ann Arbor, 1982—; mem. IRS Commr.'s Exempt Orgn. Adv. Group, Washington, 1987-90. Fellow Am. Bar Found., Am. Coll. Tax Counsel; mem. ABA (vice chmn. govt. rels. tax sect. 1989-91, commn. on homelessness and poverty 1992-94), Coun. for Excellence in Govt., Am. Law Inst. Democrat. Home: 5514 Cedar Pkwy Chevy Chase MD 20815-3444 Office: Caplin & Drysdale Chartered 1 Thomas Cir NW Ste 1100 Washington DC 20005-5894 Office Phone: 202-862-5025. Business E-Mail: tat@capdale.com.

TROZZOLO, ANTHONY MARION, chemistry professor; b. Chgo., Jan. 11, 1930; s. Pasquale and Francesca (Vercillo) T.; m. Doris C. Stoffregen, Oct. 8, 1955; children: Thomas, Susan, Patricia, Michael, Lisa, Laura. BS, Ill. Inst. Tech., 1950; MS, U. Chgo., 1957, PhD, 1960. Asst. chemist Chgo. Midway Labs., 1952-53; assoc. chemist Armour Rsch. Found., Chgo., 1953-56; tech. staff Bell Labs., Murray Hill, NJ, 1959-75; Charles L. Huisking prof. chemistry U. Notre Dame, 1975-92, Charles L. Huisking prof. emeritus, 1992—; asst. dean U. Notre Dame Coll. Sci., 1993-98; P.C. Reilly lectr. U. Notre Dame, 1972, Hesburgh Alumni lectr., 1986, Disting. lectr. sci., 1986. Vis. prof. Columbia U., N.Y.C., 1971, U. Colo., 1981, Katholieke U. Leuven, Belgium, 1983, Max Planck Inst. für Strahlenchemie, Mülheim/Ruhr, Fed. Republic Germany, 1990; vis. lectr. Academia Sinica, 1984, 85; Phillips lectr. U. Okla., 1971; C.L. Brown lectr. Rutgers U., 1975; Sigma Xi lectr. Bowling Green U., 1976, Abbott Labs., 1978; M. Faraday lectr. No. Ill. U., 1976; F.O. Butler lectr. S.D. State U., 1978; Chevron lectr. U. Nev., Reno, 1983; J. Crano lectr. U. Akron, 2000; plenary lectr. various internat. confs.; founder, chmn. Gordon Conf. on Organic Photochemistry, 1964; trustee Gordon Rsch. Confs., 1988-92; cons. in field. Assoc. editor Jour. Am. Chem. Soc., 1975-76; editor Chem. Revs., 1977-84; editorial adv. bd. Accounts of Chem. Rsch., 1977-85; cons. editor Encyclopedia of Science and Technology, 1982-92; contbr. articles to profl. jours.; patentee in field. Fellow AEC, 1951, NSF, 1957-59; named Hon. Citizen of Castrolibero, Italy, 1997; recipient Pietro Bucci prize U. Calabria/Italian Chem. Soc., 1997. Fellow: AAAS (life), Inter-Am. Photochem. Soc., N.Y. Acad. Scis. (chmn. chem. scis. sect. 1969—70, Halpern award in photochemistry 1980), Am. Inst. Chemists (Student award 1950); mem.: Am. Chem. Soc. (lectr., Tex. lectr. 1975, Disting. Svc. award St. Joseph Valley sect. 1979, Coronado lectr. 1980, Pacific Coast lectr. 1981, Coronado lectr. 1993, N.Y. State lectr. 1993, Hoosier lectr. 1995, Ozark lectr. 1995, Rocky Mountain lectr. 1996, Coronado lectr. 1998, Osage lectr. 1998, Rocky Mountain lectr. 2002, SE Tex. lectr. 1996), Sigma Xi. Roman Catholic. Home: 53419 Hansel Ln South Bend IN 46637-5248 Office: U Notre Dame Dept Chemistry-Biochemistry Notre Dame IN 46556-5670 Home Phone: 574-271-7291; Office Phone: 574-631-5768. Business E-Mail: trozzolo.4@nd.edu.

TRPIS, MILAN, vector biologist, educator; b. Mojsova Lucka, Slovakia, Dec. 20, 1930; came to U.S., 1971, naturalized, 1977; s. Gaspar and Anna (Sevcikova) T.; m. Ludmila Tonkovic, Dec. 15, 1956; children: Martin, Peter, Katarina. MS, Comenius U., Bratislava, 1956; PhD, Charles U., Prague, 1960. Research asst. Slovak Acad. Sci., Bratislava, 1953-56, sci. asst., 1956-60, scientist, 1960-62, ind. scientist, 1962-69; ecologist-entomologist East Africa-Aedes Rsch. Unit WHO, Dar es Salaam, Tanzania, 1969-71; asst. faculty fellow dept. biology U. Notre Dame, 1971-73, assoc. faculty fellow, 1973-74; assoc. prof. med. entomology Johns Hopkins U. Sch. Hygiene and Pub. Health, 1974-78, prof., 1978—, dir. labs. med. entomology. Med. entomology, rsch. assoc. U. Ill., Urbana, 1966-67, Can. Dept. Agr., Lethbridge, Alta., 1967-68; dir. Biol. Rsch. Inst. Am., 1971-79; external dir. rsch. Liberiran Inst. Biomed. Rsch., 1981-89; dir. AID project on transmission of river blindness in areas of Liberia, Sierra Leone, and Cote d'Ivoire; dir. WHO rsch. grant; tech. adv. com. AID Vector Biology and Control Project, 1986-91; dir. Johns Hopkins U./Fed. U. Tech. Akure Onchocerciasis Project in Nigeria, 1991-94, Johns Hopkins U./Orgn. Coordination et de Cooperation pour la Lutte les Grandes Endemies-Pierre Richet Inst. Onchocerciasis Project, Bouakè, Ivory Coast, 1993-96; dir. Johns Hopkins U./Pierre Richet Inst./ORSTOM onchocerciasis project in Ivory Coast, 1993-96; prof.,advisor doctoral students, USA, Can., Africa, Asia, Cen. Am., 1979—. Editor: Jour. Biologia, 1956-71, Jour. Entomol. Problems, 1960-72; zool. sect.: Jour. Biol. Works, 1960-71; contbr. articles to profl. jours. Dir. WHO project on prophylactic drugs for river blindness, Liberia, 1985-87. Recipient Slovak Acad. Sci., 1st prize for research project. Mem. AAUP, AAAS, Am. Inst. Biol. Soci., Am. Mosquito Control Assn., Am. Soc. Parasitologists, Helminthol. Soc. Washington, Am. Soc. Tropical Medicine and Hygiene, Entomol. Soc. Am., Am. Genetic Assn., Soc. of Vector Ecology, N.Y. Acad. Scis., Johns Hopkins U. Tropical Medicine Club, Smithsonian Assocs., Royal Soc. Tropical Medicine and Hygiene, Royal Entomol. Soc. of London, Sigma Xi, Delta Omega (Alpha chpt.). Home: 1504 Ivy Hill Rd Cockeysville MD 21030-1418 Office: Johns Hopkins U 615 N Wolfe St Baltimore MD 21205-2103 Business E-Mail: mtrpis@jhsph.edu.

TRUAX, DENNIS DALE, civil engineer, educator, consultant; b. Hagerstown, Md., July 25, 1953; s. Bernard James and Dorothy Hilda Truax; m. Jeanie Ann Knable, Aug. 20, 1977. BSCE, Va. Poly. Inst. and State U., 1976; MS, Miss. State U., 1978, PhD, 1986. Registered profl. engr., Miss.; diplomate Environ. Engring. Asst. dep. constrn. mgr. Fairfax County, Va., 1972-74; design engr. Washington County, Md., 1976; instr. Miss. State U., Starkville, 1980-86, asst. prof. civil and environ. engring., 1986-91, assoc. prof., 1991-96, prof., 1996—2006, James T. White chair, dept. head, prof., 2006—, Bagley Coll. Engring. fellow, 2006—. Prin. corp. pres. ASD, LLC, 1997-2000; prin., v.p. engring. ATi, Inc., 2000—, environ. engring. cons. Mem. editl. bd. ASCE/NSPE Profl. Issues Jour., 1999—. Lay leader Aldersgate United Meth. Ch., Starkville, 1982-85, chmn. pastor/parish rels., 1985-86, chmn. coun. on ministries, 1986-90, chmn. adminstrv. bd., 1990-92, chmn. fin. com., 1992-94, 2001-2003, chmn. bd. trustees, 1996-97; adviser Triangle Fraternity, Starkville, Alumni Bd. Dirs. treas., 1989-96; bd. dirs. Meth. Student Ctr., Miss. State U., 1983-90, chmn. pastor/parish rels., 1984-86, v.p. bd., 1986, pres., 1987-89, treas., 1990-91; del. to ann. conf. Miss. Conf. United Meth. Ch., also vice chmn. com. on higher edn.; active Starkville dist. lay coun. Miss. State Herrin-Hess prof., 1993-94, 94-95, 95-96. Recipient Golden Key Outstanding Faculty award Golden Key Nat. Honor Soc., 1994, Miss. Outstanding Civil Engr. of Yr., ASCE Miss. sect., 1995; named Outstanding Young Man Am., U.S. Jaycees, 1983. Fellow ASCE (chair student svcs. com. 1995-96, vice chair 1996-97, adv. Miss. State student chpt. 1981—, chair career guidance com. 1991-92, sec. 1990-91, Miss. sect. pres. 1991-92, chmn. student svc. com. 1995-96, scholarship com. 1998—, chair scholarship com. 2000-01, No. Miss. br. pres. 2000-01, dist. 14 coun. dir. 2001-04, fin. com., com. on diversity and women in civil engring., Outstanding Faculty Advisor 2001-03, 05-06); mem. NSPE, Am. Water Works Assn. (Ala.-Miss. chpt. scholarship bd. dirs. 1994—, bd. sec.-treas. 1998—), Miss. Engring. Soc. (pres., pres.-elect region 3 v.p., bd. dirs., Tombigbee chpt. pres., chpt. pres.-elect, Engring. educator 1995, Educator of the Yr. award 1995), Water Environ. Fedn. (rsch. com.), Sigma Xi (sec., pres.-elect, pres. Miss. State chpt.), Tau Beta Pi, Chi Epsilon. Democrat. Home: 1054 Southgate Dr Starkville MS 39759-8810 Office: Miss State Univ PO Box 9546 Mississippi State MS 39762-9546 Office Phone: 662-325-7187. Personal E-mail: djcktruax@aol.com, dtruax@aeration101.com. Business E-Mail: truax@cee.msstate.edu.

TRUBECK, WILLIAM LEWIS, air transportation company executive; b. Chgo., July 5, 1946; s. G. William and Priscilla Jeanne (Nelson) T.; m. Judith Carpenter Williams, Aug. 17, 1969; 1 child, William Andrew. BA, Monmouth Coll., Ill., 1968; MBA, U. Conn., 1976. Fin. sales mgr. Ford Motor Credit Co., Walnut Creek, Calif. and Stamford, Conn., 1971—74; v.p. Aetna Bus. Credit (Barclays Am. Corp.), East Hartford, Conn., 1974—81; corp. v.p., treas. Armco Inc., Middletown, Ohio and Parsippany, NJ, 1981—88; exec. v.p. fin. and chief fin. officer Northwest Airlines Inc. and NWA Inc., St. Paul, 1989—91; chief fin. and adminstrv. officer White & Case, NYC, 1991—93; sr. v.p., CFO, Honeywell, Mpls., 1993—94; sr. v.p., CFO SPX Corp., Muskegon, Mich., 1997; sr. v.p., CFO, pres. Latin Am. ops. Internat. Multifoods, Mpls., 1997—2000; exec. v.p., CFO Waste Mgmt., Houston, 2000—04, H&R Block, Kansas City, Mo., 2004—. Bd. dirs. Yellow Roadway, Dynegy, Ceridian Corp. Served to capt. C.E., U.S. Army, 1968-70, Vietnam. Mem. Fin. Execs. Inst., Blue Key, Pi Gamma Mu. Republican. Presbyterian. Avocations: golf, tennis.

TRUBEE, R. ELDON, minister, writer; b. Wauseon, Ohio, Mar. 16, 1944; s. Franklin L. and Viola Harbaugh Trubee; m. Bonnie Mae Cox, June 26, 1971; children: Kenton James, Heather Sue. BA, Coll. of Wooster, Ohio, 1966; MDiv, Pitts. Theol. Seminary, 1969, DDiv, 1994. Ordained pastor Presbyn. Ch., 1969. Pastor First Presbyn. Ch., Hanoverton, Ohio, 1969—75; assoc. pastor John Knox Presbyn. Ch., Canton, Ohio, 1975—77; pastor Columbian-Union Presbyn. Ch., Columbia, Ky., 1977—80; staff mem. Louisville Union Presbyn., 1977—80; pastor Covington (Ohio) Presbyn. Ch., 1980—84, First Presbyn. Ch., Millersburg, Ohio, 1984—, Clark (Ohio) Cmty. Presbyn. Ch., 1984—. Chaplain Jackson Twp. Fire Dept., Canton, Ohio, 1975—78; mem. med. ethics bd. Pomerene Hosp., Millersburg, Ohio, 1999—, Castle Nursing Home, Millersburg, Ohio, 2003—. Author: (book) Like As A Fire, 1986, (newspaper column) Farm & Dairy, 1987—. Mem. Habitat for Humanity, Homes County, Ohio, 1993—, Holmes County Vol. Guardianship Bd., Millersburg, Ohio, 2004—, Holmes Dem. Party, Millersburg, Ohio, 2000—; chaplain Millersburg (Ohio) Police Aux., 1991—; co-founder Assn. of Town and Rural Congregations of the Synod of the Covenant Presbyn. Ch. Mem.:

MENSA, Honorable Order of Ky. Colonels, Royal Arch, Scottish Rite, Freemason, Rotary Internat. (pres. 1992). Democrat. Presbyterian. Avocations: old cars, old radio programs, golf, history. Office: First Presbyn Ch 90 S Clay St Millersburg OH 44654 Home: 263 S Monroe St Millersburg OH 44654 Personal E-mail: mbgpres@valkyrie.net.

TRUBEY, LILLIAN PRISCILLA, retired secondary school educator; b. Hastings, Mich., Jan. 18, 1917; d. Leon George and Ethel Ada (Harlem) Tolhurst; m. Stanley Roger Trubey, Aug. 12, 1940 (dec. May 1965); children: Roger, Cornelia. BA, U. Mich., 1938, MA, 1942; MEd, Fla. Atlantic Univ., 1967; PhD, Fla. State U., 1972. Tchr. River Rouge (Mich.) H.S., 1938-41, South Broward H.S., Hollywood, Fla., 1951-69; tchr., head Eng. dept. Hollywood Hills H.S., 1969-84; tax preparer H&R Block, Ft. Lauderdale, 1985-92. Tchr. Fla. State U., Tallahassee, 1970-71, Miami Dade Jr. Coll., Miami, Fla. 1971-72. Sec. Women's Rep. Club, Broward Co., 1947-49, v.p., 1950-51; sec. Victoria Park Civic Assn., Ft. Lauderdale, 1975-78; vol. VITA, 1993-2005; pres. Fla. Speech Assn., 1968-69; pioneer Broward County Hist. Comm., 2005. Mem. Geneal. Soc. Broward County (sec. 1991-93, pres. 1993-95, 99, editor IMPRINTS 1993-2004), Ret. Educators Broward County (Pioneer of Broward County, 2005), Ft. Lauderdale Hist. Assn, Stranahan House, Ft. Lauderdale Bridge Club (dir. 1995, 97-99), Guild Miniature Artisans, Delta Kappa Gamma. Episcopalian. Avocations: duplicate bridge, miniatures, genealogy. Home: 1415 NE 4th Pl Fort Lauderdale FL 33301-1371

TRUBO, RICHARD M., writer; b. LA, Calif., Apr. 2, 1946; s. William Trubo, Ida Trubo; m. Donna R. Grodin; children: Melissa, Michael. BA, UCLA, 1967, MS, 1968. Co-host ("Confrontation"), writer KOST-FM, LA, 1968—71; bur. chief, contbg. editor Med. World News HEI Pub. / Miller Freeman Pub., San Francisco, 1983—88, Houston; med. editor, writer, cons. Feeling Fine Co., LA, 1989—2000. Cons. documentary film Am. Acad. of Pediat., 2002—03. Author: (book) An Act of Mercy, 1975, From Victim to Victor, 1987, The H.A.R.T. Program, 1992, Flying Through Hollywood by the Seat of My Pants, 1992, The Mental Edge, 1999, Tapping the Healer Within, 2001, Courage, 2001, Stairway to Heaven, 2002, 12 addtional books; prodr.: (Website) WebMD, 2002—06; (films) Children of the State, 1977; contbr. articles to profl. jours. including JAMA. Recipient Journalism award of Excellence, Am. Acad. Facial Plastic and Reconstructive Surgery, 1990, Blakeslee award, Am. Heart Assn., 1991. Mem.: Am. Soc. Journalists & Authors, Nat. Assn. Med. Communicators, Am. Med. Writers Assn., Nat. Assn. Sci. Writers. Office Phone: 949-786-3248.

TRUBY, BETSY KIRBY, artist, illustrator, photographer; b. Winchester, Va., Nov. 8, 1926; d. Thomas Gomery and Nellie Gray Kirby; m. Frank Keeler Truby, Sept. 4, 1948; children: Thomas Lee, Scott R., Susan Alida. Student, Hiram Coll., 1946—48, Cleve. Sch. Art, 1949, N.Mex. Tech., 1951—54, U. N.Mex., 1960. Asst. dir. Yucca Art Gallery, Old Town Albuquerque, 1970—71. One-woman shows include Hiram Coll., 1987, exhibitions include N.Mex. State Mus., 1964—68, Nat. Art Show, Lawton, Okla., 1974, Bardean Gallery, N.Mex., 2004 (2d pl., 2004), commd. by, Congressman Albert G Simms, 1964, Christmas card, Easter Seal Soc., 1969, Cystic Fibrosis Found., N.Mex., 1976—77, PBS TV show, The Creative Process, 1983. Mem.: Pastel Soc. N.Mex. (charter mem.), Nat. League Am. Pen Women (v.p. Yucca br. 1978—79, photographer Nat. Biennal Conv. Washington 1992, photographer Yucca br. 1992—, 1st pl. painting 1974, Best of Show 2003, 1st pl. 2003, 2d pl. in pastel State Show, Socorro, N.Mex. 2005), Yucca Art Gallery (charter mem.). Presbytertian. Avocations: boating, swimming. Home and Office: 6609 Loftus Ave NE Albuquerque NM 87109 Office Phone: 505-884-8459.

TRUCANO, MICHAEL, lawyer; b. Washington, May 28, 1945; s. Peter Joseph and Fern Margaret (Bauer) T.; m. Doreen E. Struck, 1969; children: Michael, David. BA, Carleton Coll., 1967; JD, NYU, 1970. Assoc. Dorsey & Whitney, Mpls., 1970-75, ptnr., 1976—2004, head of office, 2000—03, of counsel, 2005—. Office: Dorsey & Whitney LLP Ste 1500 50 S 6th St Minneapolis MN 55402-1498 Office Phone: 612-340-2673. Business E-Mail: trucano.mike@dorsey.com.

TRUCHARD, JAMES J., engineering executive; BS in Physics, U. Tex., MSEE, PhD, U. Tex. Mng. dir. acoustical measurements divsn. U. Tex. Applied Rsch. Labs., Austin, 1963-76; co-founder, pres., CEO Nat. Instruments Corp., Austin, 1976—, bd. dirs. Mem. Adv. Coun. on Digital Economy. Co-inventor (software) LabVIEW, 1986. Named CEO of Yr., Frost & Sullivan, 2001; named one of 50 Best CEOs in the Country, Worth mag., 1999—2001, 50 Most Influential Industry Innovators, In Tech mag., 2003; named to Engring. Hall of Fame, Electronic Design, 2002. Mem.: Instrumentation, Systems and Automation Soc., Royal Swedish Acad. Engring. Scis., NAE. Office: Nat Instruments Corp 11500 N Mopac Expy Austin TX 78759-3504 *

TRUCKENBRODT, YOLANDA BERNABE, retired air force officer, consultant; b. Manila, June 17, 1952; d. Nestor Leynes Javier and Zenaida Bernabe Javier; m. Edmund Phillip Truckenbrodt, July 27, 1972. BA, Far Ea. U., Manila, 1971; AAS, C.C. of Air Force, 1979; MBA, Angelo State U., 1980; MPA, U. West Fla., 1987; D of Pub. Adminstrn., Nova Southeastern U., 2000; diploma, Air Command and Staff Coll., 1995. Cert. Dept. of Def.'s Acquisition Profl. in Program Mgmt., USAF Software Quality Assurance. Enlisted USAF, 1974, advanced through grades to maj., 1992, ret., 1998; program mgr. KC-135 Reengine Dep. for Airlift and Trainer Sys., Wright-Patterson AFB, Ohio, 1980—84; mgr. electronic warfare program Tactical Sys. Divsn., Eglin AFB, Fla., 1985—89; program mgr. Airborne Warning and Control Sys. Elec. Sys. Ctr., Hanscom AFB, Mass., 1989—92; program analyst ballistic missile def. hdqs. Air Force Materiel Command, Wright-Patterson AFB, 1992—94; congl. liaison staff officer Plans and Programs Divsn., Wright-Patterson AFB, 1995—98. Flight comdr. detachment 847 Res. Officers Tng. Corps, San Angelo, Tex., 1978—80; chairperson Asian-Am. Pacific Islander Heritage Com., Eglin AFB, 1986—87; officer-in-charge Air Force Assn. Nat. Acquisiton Symposium, Wright-Patterson AFB, 1993—94; student-in-residence Def. Sys. Mgmt. Coll., Ft. Belvoir, Va., 1994; staff officer Directorate of Plans and Programs, Wright-Patterson AFB, 1995—98; guest spkr. Nat. Bus. and Profl. Assn., San Angelo, 1993. Contbr. articles to profl. jours. Pres. Filipino-Am. Assn., Fort Walton Beach, Fla., 1987; vol. Air Force Mus., Dayton, Ohio, 1995—96; vol. reading tutor Ohio Reads Program, 2002—; vol. Nightingale Ho., Wright-Patterson AFB, 1996—98; vol. income tax preparer Ret. Officers Assn., Wright-Patterson AFB, 1999—; vol. social worker United Way, Dayton, 1982—84; bd. dirs. Filipino-Am. Assn., Ft. Walton Beach, Fla., 1987, Filipino-Am. Coun. N.W. Fla. Nominee Lt. Robert Sullivan Meml. award, Eglin AFB, 1985; named Airman of the Quarter, Air Weather Svc. Comm. Squadron, 1975, Career Woman of Yr., Gayfers Career Club of Okaloosa County, Fla., 1987, Jr. Officer of the Quarter, Airlift and Trainer Sys., Wright-Patterson AFB, 1983, Airborne Warning and Control Systems, Hanscom AFB, 1991, winner, State of Ohio Summer Biathlon Series Championship Cup, 2002, 2d Pl. Overall winner for half-marathon, 4th Internat. Marathon on Great Wall, China, 1999, winner numerous race awards in track and field and Summer Biathlons; named one of Outstanding Young Women of Am., 1983, 20 Outstanding Filipino-Ams. in U.S. and Can., 2004; recipient Appreciation and Recognition award, Dyess AFB Human Rels. Coun., 1976, 1977, Air Force Res. Tng. Corps (ROTC) Leadership award, 1979, Arnold Air Soc. Outstanding Pledge award, 1979, Drill Commandant of Yr. award, 1978; Robert G. Carr scholar, Detachment 847 ROTC, Angelo State U., 1978, 1980. Mem. Women in Mil. Svc. Am. Meml. (charter), Air Force Women Officers Assoc., Air Force Meml. Found. (charter), Angelo State U. Alumni Assn. (Disting. ROTC Alumnae of Yr. 2002), Air Force Meml. Found. (charter), Ohio River Rd. Runners Club, Sigma Beta Delta. Avocations: travel, arts and music, summer biathlons, marathons, photography.

TRUCKSIS, THERESA A., retired library director; b. Hubbard, Ohio, Sept. 1, 1924; d. Peter and Carmella (DiSilverio) Pagliasotti; m. Robert C. Trucksis, May 29, 1948 (dec. May 1980); children: M. Laura, Anne, Michele, Patricia, David, Robert, Claire, Peter; m. Philip P. Hickey, Oct. 19, 1985 (dec. May 1993). BS in Edn., Youngstown Coll., 1945; postgrad., Youngstown State U., 1968-71; MLS, Kent State U., 1972. Psychometrist Youngstown (Ohio) Coll., 1946-49; instr. ltd. svc. Youngstown State U., 1968-71; libr. Pub. Libr. Youngstown & Mahoning County, Youngstown, 1972-73, asst. dept. head, 1973-74, asst. dir., 1985-89, dir., 1989-97, NOLA Regional Libr. System, Youngstown, 1974-85. Contbr. articles to profl. jours. Mem. bd. Hubbard Sch. Dist., 1980-85. Mem. ALA, Ohio Libr. Assn. (bd. dirs. 1979-81), Pub. Libr. Assn. Address: 133 Viola Ave Hubbard OH 44425-2062

TRUDEAU, GARRETSON BEEKMAN (GARRY TRUDEAU), cartoonist; b. NYC, July 21, 1948; m. Jane Pauley, June 14, 1980; children: Ross and Rachel (twins), Thomas. BA, Yale U., 1970, MFA, 1973, DHL, 1976. Syndicated cartoonist, writer. Creator: comic strip Doonesbury; syndicated nationwide comic strip; author: Still a Few Bugs in the System, 1972, The President is a Lot Smarter Than You Think, 1973, But This War Had Such Promise, 1973, Call Me When You Find America, 1973, Guilty, Guilty, Guilty, 1974, Joanie, 1974, The Doonesbury Chronicles, 1975, What Do We Have for the Witnesses, Johnnie?, 1975, Dare to Be Great, Ms. Caucus, 1975, Wouldn't A Gremlin Have Been More Sensible?, 1975, We'll Take it From Here, Sarge, 1975, Speaking of Inalienable Rights, Amy..., 1976, You're Never Too Old for Nuts and Berries, 1976, An Especially Tricky People, 1977, As the Kid Goes For Broke, 1977, Stalking the Perfect Tan, 1978, Any Grooming Hints for Your Fans, Rollie?, 1978, Doonesbury's Greatest Hits, 1978, But The Pension Fund was Just Sitting There, 1979, We're Not Out of the Woods Yet, 1979, A Tad Overweight, but Violet Eyes to Die For, 1980, And That's My Final Offer!, 1980, The People's Doonesbury, 1981, He's Never Heard of You, Either, 1981, In Search of Reagan's Brain, 1981, Ask for May, Settle for June, 1982, Unfortunately, She Was Also Wired for Sound, 1982, Adjectives Will Cost You Extra, 1982, Gotta Run, My Government is Collapsing, 1982, The Wreck of the Rusty Nail, 1983, You Give Great Meeting, Sid, 1983, Guess Who Fish Face, 1983, It's Supposed to be Yellow Pinhead: Selected Cartoons From Ask For May, Settle For June, Vol. I, 1983, Do All Birders Have Bedrooms, 1983, Farewell to Alms, 1984, Doonesbury Dossier: The Reagan Years, 1984, Doonesbury: A Musical Comedy, 1984, Check Your Egos at the Door, 1985, That's Doctor Sinatra, You Little Bimbo, 1986, Death of a Party Animal, 1986, Doonesbury Deluxe: Selected Glances Askance, 1987, Downtown Doonesbury, 1987, Calling Dr. Whoopee, 1987, The Doonesbury Desk Diary 1988, 1987, Talking Bout My G-G-Generation, 1988, We're Eating More Beets, 1988, Read My Lips, Make My Day, Eat Quiche & Die! A Doonesbury Collection, 1989, Small Collection, 1989, The Doonesbury Stamp Album, 1990, 1990, Recycled Doonesbury: Second Thoughts on a Gilded Age, 1990, You're Smokin' Now, Mr. Butts! A Doonesbury Book, 1990, Welcome to Club Scud: A Doonesbury Book, 1991, Action Figure: The Life and Times of Doonesbury's Uncle Duke, 1992, The Portable Doonesbury, 1993, In Search of Cigarette Holder Man: A Doonesbury Book, 1994, Doonesbury Nation, 1995, Flashbacks: Twenty-five Years of Doonesbury, 1995, The Bundled Doonesbury: A Pre-Millennial Anthology, 1998, Peace Out, Dawg! Tales from Ground Zero, 2002, Got War?, 2003, The Long Road Home: One Step at a Time, 2005; co-author: Tales From the Margaret Mead Taproom, 1979; plays include: Doonesbury, 1983, Rapmaster Ronnie, A Partisan Review (with Elizabeth Swados), 1984 Pulitzer Prize for Editorial Cartooning, 1975, Commander's Award for Pub. Svc., US Dept. Army, 2006.

TRUDEL, MARC J., botanist, educator; PhD, Cornell U. Prof. plant physiology and horticulture Laval U., 1969—2003, prof. emeritus, 2005—, former dean sch. agrl. and food scis., 1983-91, former dir. gen. continuing edn., 1992-97, v.p. devel., 1997—2003. Office: 19 Rue de Liege Saint Jean Sur Richelieu PQ Canada J3B 8N4 E-mail: marc.trudel@plg.ulaval.ca.

TRUDELL, CYNTHIA M., food products executive, former automotive executive; b. St. John, Can., 1953; married; 2 children. Degree in chemistry, U. Wolfville, Can.; D of Phys. Chemistry, U. Windsor, Ont., Can., 1978. Chem. process engr. Ford Motor Co., Windsor, 1979-81; sr. engring. supr., supt. mfg. GM, Windsor, Can., 1981-87, engring. mgr. Willow Run transmission complex Ypsilanti, Mich., 1987-89, ops. mgr., 1989-90; chief engr. process techs. Powertrain Advanced Mfg. Systems, St. Catherines, Ont., Can., 1990-92, mgr. engine & foundry ops., 1992-95; plant mgr. Wilmington (Del.) Assembly Ctr., 1995; pres. Saturn, Spring Hill, Tenn., 1995—2001, chmn., 1997—2001; v.p. GM Corp., 1999—2001; pres. Sea Ray Group, 2001—06; sr. v.p., chief pers. officer PepsiCo, 2007—. Bd. dirs. PepsiCo., 2000—07. Office: PepsiCo 700 Anderson Hill Rd Purchase NY 10577 *

TRUDNAK, STEPHEN JOSEPH, landscape architect; b. Nanticoke, Pa., Feb. 25, 1947; s. Stephen Adam and Marcella (Levulis) T.; m. Arden Batchelder Weill, Sept. 6, 1980. BS in Landscape Arch., Pa. State U., 1970. Jr. landscape arch. Kling Partnership, Phila., 1970-72; mem. landscape arch. firm Keith French Assocs., Washington, 1972-73; head dept. landscape arch. Linganore Ctr. Design, Frederick, Md., 1973-74, Toups and Loiederman, Rockville, Md., 1974-76; project landscape arch. Kaiser Transit Group, So. Calif. Rapid Transit Dist., Dade County Transit Improvement Program, Metro Rail Transit Cons.; v.p. Harry Weese & Assocs., Ltd., Miami, Fla., 1976-84; v.p. landscape arch. Canin Assocs., Orlando, Fla., 1984-87; dir. planning and design Bonita Bay Properties, Inc., Bonita Springs, Fla., 1987-91; prin. Stephen J. Trudnak, P.A. Landscape Arch. and Land Planning, 1991—2006; sr. landscape arch. Johnson Engring., Inc., Ft. Myers, Fla., 2006—. Bd. dirs., v.p. Koreshan State Hist. Site, 1989—94; mem. "not for profit" com. Bonita Springs Cmty. Redevel. Agy., 1994—97; v.p. Bonita Springs Mainstreet Program, 1996, 2000, pres., 1997—98; bd. dirs. Bonita Springs YMCA, 1999—2005, mem. exec. com., 2000—03, chair facilities design task force, 2000—04; del. for Congressman Porter Goss Congl. Small Bus. Summit, 1998, 2000; del. representing Fla. state rep. Carol Green Fla. Small Bus. Summit, 1999. Recipient Alumni Achievement award, Pa. State U., Dept. Landscape Architecture, 2003. Fellow Am. Soc. Landscape Archs. (pres. Fla. chpt. 1983, chpt. adv. bd. 1984-85, elections task force 1986, publs. task force 1987, trustee 1987-89, membership task force, chmn. 1989-90, nat. v.p. chpt. and mem. svcs. 1992-94, non-dues revenue task force 1994-95, ASLA On-Line com. 1997-2005, chair 1999, specifications task force 1998-99), Nat. Xeriscape Coun. (Fla. steering com.), Nat. Speleol. Soc. SCARAB; mem. Bonita Springs C. of C. (chair beautification com. 1991-92, 94-95, chair awards task force 2000, bd. dirs. 1995-2000, v.p. edn. divsn. 1996-98, vice chmn. cmty. devel. divsn. 1998-99, chmn. tech. com. 2003-04, Affiliate of Yr. 1997, Citizen of Yr. 1999, Charter Class Leadership Bonita Grad. 2000). Office: 2158 Johnson St Fort Myers FL 33901 Office Phone: 239-334-0046. E-mail: strudnak@johnsoneng.com.

TRUE, RAYMOND STEPHEN, editor, writer; b. Lowell, Mass., June 29, 1934; s. Sylvester Raymond and Madeline Rose (Farrell) T.; m. Doreen Therese Jambrosek. BA, U. Chgo., 1961, MBA, 1968, postgrad., 1968—69. Commd. 2nd lt. USAF, 1953, advanced through grades to col., 1980; master navigator USAFR, Chgo., 1957—77, dir. ops. Milw., 1977—80, base civil engr., 1980—87, chief planning analyst, 1987—89; regional cons. U.S. Bur. Census, 1970—71; owner Classic Comics Libr., 1990—. Fire marshall Milwaukee County, 1980-87, chmn. membership Res. Officers Assn., Wash. 1975-78. Editor Classics Newsletter, 1971-75; pub. The Platform Rep. Newsmag., 2004—. Precinct committeeman, Libertyville, Ill., 2000—; pres. ROA chpt. 61, 2000-02; chmn. Rep. Assembly Lake County, 2001-; mem. steering com. Ill. Ctr. Rights Coalition, 2004-05, 2007—; mem. Ill. Rep. State Platform Com., 2004; mem. bd. dirs. Project Marriage Initiative. Mem. Air Force Assn., Grad. Sch. Bus. Exec. Coun. U. Chgo. Roman Catholic. Avocations: stamp collecting/philately, antique books, videophile. Address: 839 Terre Dr Libertyville IL 60048-1649 Home Phone: 847-367-5497; Office Phone: 847-367-5231. E-mail: raymon8844@aol.com.

TRUE, ROY JOE, lawyer; b. Shreveport, La., Feb. 20, 1938; s. Collins B. and Lula Mae (Cady) T.; m. Patsy Jean Hudsmith, Aug. 29, 1959; children: Andrea Alane, Alyssa Anne, Ashley Alisbeth. Student, Centenary Coll., 1957; BS, Tex. Christian U., 1961; LLB, So. Meth. U., 1963, postgrad., 1968—69. Bar: Tex. 1963. Pvt. practice, Dallas, 1963—; pres. Invesco Internat. Corp., 1969-70, True & Shackelford and predecessors, 1975—2002; of counsel Shackelford, Melton & McKinley, 2002—. Bus. adviser, counselor Mickey Mantle, 1969-95; dir. The Mickey Mantle Found., 1995-98. Mem. editl. bd. Southwestern Law Jour., 1962-63. With AUS, 1956. Mem. ABA, Dallas Bar Assn., Tex. Assn. Bank Counsel, Phi Alpha Delta. Home: 5837 St Marks Circle Dallas TX 75230 Office: 3333 Lee Pkwy 10th Fl Dallas TX 75219 Home Phone: 214-369-0606; Office Phone: 214-780-1400. Business E-Mail: rtrue@shacklaw.net.

TRUE, WILLIAM L. (BILL TRUE), retired real estate company executive; b. Apr. 1954; s. Cecil True; m. Ruth True. Chmn., CEO Gull Industries, Inc., Seattle. Co-founder Western Bridge Gallery, Seattle; mem. adv. bd. Seattle Arts & Lectures; bd. dirs. Pike Place Market Found., Seattle; mem. Betty Bowen com. Seattle Art Mus., 2004. Named one of Top 200 Collectors, ARTnews mag., 2003—06. Avocation: Collector of Contemporary art. Home: 832 37th Ave E Seattle WA 98112-4326

TRUEB, MARTIN R., toy company executive; Asst. treas. Amway Corp., 1995—97; sr. v.p., treas. Hasbro Inc., 1997—. Adv. bd. The NeuGroup Inc. Office: Hasbro Inc 1027 Newport Ave Pawtucket RI 02862

TRUEBLOOD, HARRY ALBERT, JR., oil industry executive; b. Wichita Falls, Tex., Aug. 28, 1925; s. Harry A. and Marguerite (Barnhart) T.; m. Lucile Bernard, Jan. 22, 1953; children: Katherine T. Astin, John B. Student, Tex. A&M Coll., 1942; BS in Petroleum Engring., U. Tex., 1948. Petroleum engr. Cal. Co., 1948-51; chief engr. McDermott & Barnhart Co., Colo., Tex., 1951-52; cons. petroleum and geol. engr. Denver, 1952-55; pres. Colo. Western Exploration Inc., Denver, 1955-58, Consol. Oil & Gas., Inc., 1958-88, chmn. bd., CEO, 1969-88, Princeville Devel. Corp., 1979-87, pres., 1984-86; chmn. bd., CEO Columbus Energy Corp., 1983-2000; pres., mng. mem. HAT Resources LLC, 2001—. Chmn. bd., CEO, Princeville Airways, Inc., 1979-87; chmn. bd. dirs., pres. CEC Resources, Ltd., 1984-99; bd. dirs. NYTIS Exploration Co. With USNR, 1944-46, ensign, 1949-55. Named to Rocky Mountain Oil and Gas Hall of Fame, 2004. Mem. Soc. Petroleum Engrs., Am. Petroleum Inst., World Pres. Orgn., Chief Execs. Orgn. (bd. dirs.), Ind. Petroleum Assn. Am. (exec. com.; recipient Wildcatter 2006 award for Lifetime Achievement), Natural Gas Supply Assn. (exec. com.), Cherry Hills Country Club, One Hundred Club. Roman Catholic. Home: 2800 S University Blvd Apt 82 Denver CO 80210-6056 Office: 1720 S Bellaire St Ste 912 Denver CO 80222-4334 Office Phone: 303-300-6792. E-mail: hajtrueblood@yahoo.com.

TRUEHILL, MARSHALL, JR., minister; b. New Orleans, Sept. 5, 1948; s. Marshall Truehill and Inez Gray Williams; adopted s. Elizabeth (May) T.; m. Mary Ola Williams, Dec. 20, 1969 (div. 1972); m. Valli Maria Dobard, July 22, 1972 (div. 1999); children: Briana Traci, Marshall III, Jessica, Quentin; m. Miranda Sally Farr, Dec. 28, 1999. B in Music Edn., Xavier U., 1973; BTh, Christian Bible Coll., 1979; MDiv, Orleans Bapt. Theol. Sem., 1986; D Ministry, New Orleans Bapt. Theol. Seminary, 1990; postgrad., U. New Orleans; ThD, A.P. Clay Christian Theol. Coll., 2004. Ordained to ministry Bapt. Ch., 1980; cert. tchr., La. Tchr. Orleans Parish Sch. Bd., New Orleans, 1973-78, Delgado Community Coll., 1975-78; pastor Faith in Action Bapt. Ch., 1982—95; founder, pastor First United Bapt. Ch., 1995—. Founder, dir. Faith in Action Evangel. Team, New Orleans, 1977—; lectr. Nat. Bapt. Conv. on Congl. Evangelism, New Orleans, 1977-79; cons. So. Bapt. Conv. Home Mission Bd., La., 1986-1997; CEO TradeWins Ptnrs. LLC, 2001. Bd. dirs. Project New Orleans, 1983-99, New Orleans Jobs Initiatives, vice chmn., 1997-2002; apptd. by mayor to New Orleans City Planning Commn., 1998-2007. Democrat. Avocations: computers, aquariums, interior decorating, aerobics. Home Phone: 504-488-1178. Personal E-mail: mtruejr@aol.com. *The greatest investment one can make in this life is an investment in the life of another person. That is the only investment with eternal value.*

TRUEMAN, WILLIAM PETER MAIN, broadcaster, columnist; b. Sackville, NB, Can., Dec. 25, 1934; s. Albert William and Jean Alberta (Miller) T.; m. Eleanor Joy Wark, Dec. 22, 1956; children: Anne, Mark, Victoria. Student, U. N.B., 1951-54. UN corr. Montreal Star, 1957-62, Washington corr., 1962-65; parliamentary corr. Toronto Star, Ottawa, Ont., 1965-67; nat. dir. UN Assn. in Can., 1967-68; nat. news writer CBC, Toronto, 1968-69, exec. producer news, head network news, 1969-72; freelance reporter, 1972-73; anchor Global TV News, Don Mills, Canada, 1974—88; free lance broadcaster, 1988-2000; media critic Toronto Star's Starweek mag., 1988-96; Kingston Whig-Std., 1989-96. Host, mng.editor Canadian Discovery Channel TV series Great Canadian Parks, 1995-2000. Decorated officer Order of Can.; recipient Bowater award for journalism, 1962, Sam Ross award, 1983, Queen's Golden Jubilee Medal, 2002; Paul Harris fellow, Rotary, Kingston, 2005. Personal E-mail: peter.trueman@sympatico.ca.

TRUEMPER, JOHN JAMES, JR., retired architect; b. Helena, Ark., June 18, 1924; s. John James and Mary Ann (Jacob) T.; m. Julia Clare Wood, Nov. 21, 1956; children: Zachary Wood, John James III, Ann Truemper Penick. BS in Arch., U. Ill., 1950; DHL (hon.), Lyon Coll., 1995. With archtl. firm Cromwell, Truemper, Levy, Thompson, Woodsmall Inc. (and predecessors), Little Rock, 1950-94, v.p., 1972-74, pres., 1974-81, chmn. bd., 1980-89; ret., 1994. Mem. Ark. Bd. Architects, 1974-82, pres., 1980 Prin. works include Ark. system for edn. and tng. mentally retarded, 1956-78, Winrock Farm, Morrilton, Ark., 1953-58, Ark. State Parks, 1955-75, Ark. Power & Light Co., 1961-89, Lyon Coll., Batesville, 1983-94; author: A Century of Service, 1885-1985, 1985. Pres. Ark. Arts Ctr., 1979, chmn. bd., 1980; mem. Little Rock Bldg. Code Bd. Appeals, 1961-86, chmn., 1971-86; mem. Ark. Hist. Preservtion Rev. Bd., 1987-99; bd. dirs. Little Rock Met. YMCA, 1975-84; pres.Ctrl. YMCA; mem. Friends of Libr. Bd., U. Ark., Little Rock, 1989-99, pres. 1995-97; bd. dirs. Greater Little Rock C. of C., 1986-88. With USAAF, 1943-46. Recipient Winthrop Rockefeller Meml. award Ark. Arts Center, 1980 Fellow: AIA (pres. Ark. chpt. 1968); mem.: Sigma Chi. Roman Catholic. Home: 6502 Cantrell Rd Little Rock AR 72207-4219

TRUESDALE, JOHN CUSHMAN, federal agency administrator, lawyer; b. Grand Rapids, Mich., July 17, 1921; s. John Cushman and Hazel (Christianson) T.; m. Karin A. Nelson, Feb. 10, 1957; children: John Cushman, Charles N., Margaret E., Andrew C. AB, Grinnell Coll., 1942; MS, Cornell U., 1948; JD, Georgetown U., 1972. Bar: Md. bar 1972, D.C. bar 1973. Field examiner NLRB, Buffalo and New Orleans, 1948-52, adminstrv. analyst Washington, 1952-57, assoc. exec. sec., 1963-68, dep. exec. sec., 1968-72, exec. sec., 1972-77, 81-94, mem., 1977-81, 94, 95, chmn., 1998-2001, labor arbitrator, 1996—98, 2001—; mem. Fgn. Svc.

Grievance Bd., 1997—2003. Dir. info., dir. World Data Center/Rockets and Satellites, IGY, Nat. Acad. Scis., Washington, 1957-63 Editor-in-chief: How to Take a Case Before the NLRB, 1997-98, 2002--. With USCG, 1943—46. Recipient Presdl. award Pres. of U.S., 1988. Mem. ABA, Nat. Acad. Arbitrators, D.C. Bar Assn., Assn. Labor Rels. Agys. (pres. 1992-93). Democrat. Congregationalist. Personal E-mail: jctrue@aol.com.

TRUESDELL, TIMOTHY L., private investor; b. Niles, Mich., Oct. 8, 1951; s. Patrick Daniel and LaVonne Marie (Fries) T. BA, U. Notre Dame 1974. Asst. to exec. dir. Notre Dame U. Alumni Assn., 1974-77, asst. dir., 1977-79; alumni editor Notre Dame mag., 1979-83; v.p. Truesdell Real Estate Investment, Sacramento, 1983-85; dir. devel. rsch. U. Notre Dame, 1985-99; portfolio mgr. Kamm Partnership, South Bend, Ind., 1999—2005; pres. Timothy Truesdell Investments, Kalamazoo, 2005—, Marco Island, Fla., 2005—. Devel. cons. Am. Acad. Neurology, 1991-92, Harvest Devel., Ponte Vedra, Fla., 1999-2003, Hospice of St. Joseph County, South Bend, Ind., 1992-93, U. St. Thomas, Mpls., Xavier U., Cin., 1993-94, Niles Comty. Libr., 1993-97, St. Joseph Mishawaka (Ind.) Health Svcs., 1995-96, Berrien County ARC, 1996, Advancement Ptnrs., Inc., Columbus, 1996-2003, Little Flower Cath. Ch., South Bend, Ind., 1997-98, No. Ind. Ctr. for History, South Bend, 1998-2000; bd. dirs. Women's Care Ctr., Mishawaka, Ind., 1999-2000. Councilman City of Niles, 1983-91; pres. St. Mary's Sch Bd. Edn., Niles, 1981-82; chmn. S.W. Mich. Cmty. Ambulance, Niles, 1985-89; active Rep. Nat. Com., Collier County Rep. Exec. Com., 2006—; pres. Fernwood Bot. Garden, Niles, 1997-98. Mem. Am. Assn. Individual Investors, Optimists (sec. 1983-84), Knights of Malta, Notre Dame Club Kalamazoo, Notre Dame Club Greater Naples. Republican. Roman Catholic. Avocations: golf, antiques. Office: 950 N Collier Ste 428 Marco Island FL 34145 Office Phone: 269-353-3800, 239-393-3474. Personal E-mail: timothytruesdell@verizon.net.

TRUETT, HAROLD JOSEPH, III, (TIM), lawyer; b. Alameda, Calif., Feb. 13, 1946; s. Harold Joseph and Lois Lucille (Mellin) T.; 1 child, Harold Joseph IV; m. Anna V. Billante, Oct. 1, 1983 (dec. June 2000); 1 child, James S. Carstensen; m. Patricia Maynord, Mar. 5, 2002. BA, U. San Francisco, 1968, JD, 1975. Bar: Calif. 1975, Hawaii 1987, US Dist. Ct. (ea., so., no., and cen. dists.) Calif. 1976, Hawaii 1987, US Ct. Appeals (9th cir.) 1980, US Supreme Ct. 1988, US Ct. Fed. Claims, 1995. Assoc. Hoberg, Finger et al, San Francisco, 1975-78, Bledsoe, Smith et al, San Francisco, 1979-80, Abramson & Bianco, San Francisco, 1980-83; mem. Ingram & Truett, San Rafael, 1983-90; prin. Winchell & Truett, San Francisco, 1991—. Lectr. in field. Bd. dirs. Shining Star Found. 1991—, pres., 2001-06, Marin County, Calif.; mem. Marin Dem. Coun., San Rafael, 1983-90, 2002. Lt., aviator USN, 1967-74. Mem. ABA, Hawaii Bar Assn., Calif. Bar Assn. (com. for adminstrn. of justice, conf. of dels.), San Francisco Bar Assn., San Francisco Trial Lawyers Assn., Lawyers Pilots Assn. Roman Catholic. Home: 48 Valley Rd San Anselmo CA 94960 Office Phone: 415-989-9001. Business E-Mail: tim@truettlaw.com.

TRUEX, DOROTHY ADINE, retired university administrator; b. Sedalia, Mo., Oct. 6, 1915; d. Chester Morrison and Madge (Nicholson) T AB, William Jewell Coll., 1936; MA, U. Mo., 1937; EdD, Columbia U., 1956. Asst. dean women N.W. Mo. State U., Maryville, 1939-43, dean women, 1943-45, Mercer U., Macon, Ga., 1945-47, U. Okla., Norman, 1947-69, assoc. prof., 1969-72, dir. rsch. and program devel., 1969-74, prof. edn., 1972-74, dir. grad. program in student pers. svcs., 1969-74; vice chancellor for student affairs U. Ark., Little Rock, 1974-83, alumni specialist, 1983-84, acad. adviser, 1984-87. Exec. bd. N. Cen. Assn. Schs. and Colls., 1977—83. Author: Rich Choices, 1994, A Visit to Spitesville, 1999, The 13th Bridesmaid, 1999, Carved in Stone, 2000, Full Circle, 2002, The Twenty Million Dollar Giveaway, 2001, A Left Handed Chord, 2003, Life with Cheryl, 2005. Mem. Nat. Assn. Women Deans, Adminstrs. and Counselors (pres. 1973-74), So. Coll. Pers. Assn. (pres. 1970), Okla. Coll. Pers. Assn. (pres. 1972-73), William Jewell Coll. Alumni Assn. (pres. 1970-73), Woman's City Club (pres. 2000-2001), Pi Beta Phi, Alpha Lambda Delta, Mortar Bd., Sigma Tau Delta, Cardinal Key, Gamma Alpha Chi, Kappa Delta Pi, Pi Lambda Theta, Alpha Psi Omega, Pi Gamma Mu, Delta Kappa Gamma, Phi Delta Kappa, Phi Kappa Phi. (nat. v.p. 1986-89) Avocation: writing. Home: 14300 Chenal Pkwy Apt 7422 Little Rock AR 72211-5819

TRUHLAR, DONALD GENE, chemist, educator; b. Chgo., Feb. 27, 1944; s. John Joseph and Lucille Marie (Vancura) T.; m. Jane Teresa Gust, Aug. 28, 1965; children: Sara Elizabeth, Stephanie Marie. BA in Chemistry summa cum laude, St. Mary's Coll., Winona, Minn., 1965; PhD in Chemistry, Calif. Inst. Tech., 1970. Asst. prof. chemistry and chem. physics U. Minn., Mpls., 1969—72, assoc. prof., 1972—76, prof., 1976—93, Inst. of Tech. prof., 1993—98, Inst. of Tech. disting. prof., 1998—, Lloyd H. Reyerson prof., 2002—. Cons. Los Alamos Sci. Lab.; vis. fellow Joint Inst. for Lab. Astrophysics, 1975-76; sci. dir. Minn. Supercomputer Inst., 1987-88, dir., 1988—. Editor Theoretical Chemistry Accounts (Theoretica Chemica Acta), 1985—2001, Computer Physics Comms., 1986—, Topics Phys. Chemistry, 1992—99, Understanding Chem. Reactivity, 1990—92, mem. editl. bd. Jour. Chem. Physics, 1978—80, Chem. Physics Letters, 1982—, Jour. Phys. Chemistry, 1985—87, Understanding Chem. Reactivity, 1993—, Advances in Chem. Physics, 1993—, Internat. Jour. Modern Physics C., 1994—, IEEE Computational Sci. and Engring., 1994—98, Internat. Jour. Quantum Chemistry, 1996—2000, Computing in Sci. and Engring., 1999—, Jour. Chemical Theory and Computation, 2004—, Chemical Physics, 2005, chief adv. editor Theoretical Chemistry Accounts, 2002—. Recipient Minn. award, 2003, NAS award for Sci. Reviewing, 2004, award for sci. computing, NAS, 2004; fellow, Alfred P. Sloan Found., 1973—77; grantee, NSF, 1971—, NASA, 1987—95, U.S. Dept. Energy, 1979—, NIST, 1995—98, Dept. of Def., 2001—; scholar, Ruhland Walzer Meml. scholar, 1961—62; John Stauffer fellow, 1965—66, NDEA fellow, 1966—68. Fellow AAAS, Am. Phys. Soc.; mem. Am. Chem. Soc. (sec.-treas. theoretical chemistry subdivsn. 1980-89, councilor 1985-87, assoc. editor jour. 1984—, Award for computers in chem. and pharm. rsch. 2000, Peter Debye award in phys. chemistry 2006). Achievements include research, numerous publications in field. Home: 5033 Thomas Ave S Minneapolis MN 55410-2240 Office: U Minn 207 Pleasant St SE Minneapolis MN 55455-0431 Office Phone: 612-624-7555. Business E-Mail: truhlar@umn.edu.

TRUINI PALOMBA, MARIA GIUSEPPINA, supreme court lawyer, judge; b. Borbona, Ri-Latium, Italy, Aug. 25, 1935; d. Costanzo and Ezia (Giorgi) Truini; m. Emilio Palomba, Jan. 11, 1964; children: Francesco Maria, Giovanna Palomba. Degree in Law, State U. Rome, 1960. Tchr. State High Sch., Rieti, Italy, 1955-84; local magistrate Rieti, Italy, 1974-86; judge Fiscal Commn., Rieti, Italy, 1974—, Fiscal Commn. Reg. Rome v.p., 1996—. Author: La Cucina Sabina, 1991; contbr. articles to profl. jours. Mem. drug Prevention Assn., L'Aquila, 1979—; hon. guard Nat. Inst. Royal Tombs of Pantheon, Rome, 1980—. Decorated Cavalier of the Merit of the Italian Rep., 1984, Lady of the Order of Chivalry of the Holy Sepulchre of Jerusalem, Grand Master Cardinal, 1990, Lady of the Sovereign and Military Order of the Temple of Jerusalem, 1998; mem. Italian Red cross, 1986—, patroness, 1978; vol. UNICEF. Mem. Nat. Civil Lawyers Union (dist. pres. Rieti, nat. councillor 1990—), Italian Women Jurists Assn. (dist. pres. Rieti and nat. councillor 1990—), Internat. Assn. of Lawyers, Eurojuris Internat. Geie, Italian Acad. Cooking (nat. cons. 1974, dist. del.), Italian Women's Mgmt. Assn., Italian Women's Nat. Coun., Amnesty Internat. Lawyers, Aeroclub (pres. 1992-93), Rotary (councillor 1994-95, pres., 1996-97, 2006-), v.p. FILDIS-IFUW, Rome, 2000—. Avocations: travel, cinema, theater, cooking, volleyball. Home and Office: A Gherardi 70 02100 Rieti Italy Home Phone: +39-746-274349; Office Phone: +39-746-203077. E-mail: studiolegale@palombatruini.it.

TRUITT, ROBERT RALPH, JR., lawyer; b. Lincoln-Chaves Counties, N.Mex., Jan. 21, 1948; s. Robert Ralph and Dorothy (Butler) T.; m. Susan Donovan, Nov. 28, 1981; children: Patrick Lynn, Maureen Elizabeth. BA, BBA, Southwestern U., 1970; JD, U. Tex., 1973. Bar: Tex. 1973, U.S. Ct. Appeals (5th cir.) 1976, U.S. Dist. Ct. (we. dist.) Tex. 1977, U.S. Dist. Ct. (no. dist.) Tex. 1981. Assoc. Turpin, Smith & Dyer, Midland, Tex., 1973-77; pvt. practice Midland, 1977—. Chmn. planning and zoning com., City of Midland, 1979-80; chmn., dir. and treas. Midland Downtown Lions Fire Prevention and Hist. Found., 1980—; dir. and sec.-treas. Midland Downtown Lions Youth Found., 1992-98, Midland Masonic Hist. Mus. and Libr. Found., 1996-2003; dir. Presdl. Mus., 1998-99; sec. El Paso Scottish Rite Libr. and Hist. Mus. Found., 1999—. Mem.: Midland County Bar Assn., Tex. Bar Assn. Office: 901 W Texas Ave Midland TX 79701-6167

TRUITT, WILLIAM HARVEY, private school educator; b. Alton, Ill., May 27, 1935; s. Howard Earl and Mary Margaret (Haper) T.; m. Janetha Mitchell, Aug. 5, 1961; children: Joy Elizabeth, Janita Ann. BA, Principia Coll., 1957; MA, So. Ill. U., 1964. Headmaster Forman Schs., Litchfield, Conn.; prin. upper and lower sch. The Principia, St. Louis, headmaster; ret., 1998. Musician: The Worlds Greatest Love Songs, Sing Unto the Lord, A New Song. Mem. NASSP, Mo. Assn. Secondary Prins., St. Louis Ind. Sch. Heads, Mo. Ind. Schs. (pres. 1983-84), Am. Coun. for Am. Pvt. Edn. (v.p. 1983-84), North Cen. Accrediting Assn. (exec. bd. dirs. 1988-91). Office: 4002 Radcliffe Place Ct Wildwood MO 63025 Business E-Mail: bill@billtruitt.com.

TRUJILLO, J. ROBERTO, virologist; b. Mexico City, July 14, 1963; s. Maria Guadalupe Martinez and Roberto Trujillo; m. Elaine B. Barbella, Nov. 19, 1988; children: Daniel Robert, Jacquelyn Elizabeth. BS summa cum laude, Inst. Art and Scis., Mex., 1980; MD summa cum laude, U. Autonomous State of Mex., 1988; PhD, Harvard U., Boston, 1995. Lic. surgeon Faculty of Medicine, State of Mex., Mex., 1988. Rsch. fellow Harvard U., Boston, 1989—95, rsch. assoc., 1996—98, rsch. assoc. in neurovirology, 1998—2002; sr. scientist fellow Nat. Inst. of Neurol. Disorders and Stroke, Bethesda, Md., 2002—05; chief lab. of neurovirology Inst. of Human Virology, UMBI, U. Md., Balt., 2005—, asst. prof. Baltimore, 2005—; adj. prof. U. Autonomous of Nuevo Leon, Monterrey, Mexico, 2002—. Pres., founder Pan-Am. Soc. for NeuroVirology, Boston, 2000—; NIH reviewer Nat. Inst. of Allergy and Infectious Diseases, Bethesda, Md., 2005; dir. rsch. virology and neuroscience Inst. of Human Virology, UMBI, U. Md., Baltimore, 2005—; com. mem. of faculty and adminstrs. Harvard Sch. of Pub. Health, Boston, 2003—; instr. Harvard Coll., Cambridge, Mass., 1997—99; supr. Harvard Sch. of Pub. Health, Boston, 1997—2002; sci. advisor U. Autonomous of Nuevo Leon, Monterrey, Mexico, 1998—; prof. advisor biomed. sci. careers program, minority faculty devel. program Harvard Med. Sch., Boston, 2004—; internat. editl. bd. Revista Mexicana de Neurociencia, Mexico City, 2004; reviewer Office of AIDS Rsch., NIH, Bethesda, Md., 2002. Prodr.: (Pan.-Am. symposium programs) Scientific & Graphic Design; contbr. articles to profl. jours. Pres. Pan-Am. Soc. for NeuroVirology, Boston, 2000; mem. Faculty of Medicine, UANL, Monterrey, Nuevo Leon, Mexico, 2000—04; dir. Inst. of Human Virology of Mex., Monterrey, Nuevo Leon, 2005. Recipient A-H Robins of Mex. award, Med. Sch., State of Mex., 1981-83, Outstanding Young Presenter, Govt. of Mex. State, 1987, T32 Tng. award, NIH, 1989-1992, Helena Rubinstein award, Harvard Sch. of Pub. Health, 1996-1999, Key of the City, Acapulco, Mex., 1997, 2000, Group Merit award, Nat. Inst. of Neurol. Disorders and Stroke, 2004, Internat. Prof. award, U. Complutense, Spain, 2005, Key of the City, Chihuahua, Mex., 2005; grantee, NIH, 1999-2002, 2000; Med. scholarship, Med. Sch., State of Mex., 1983-1985, Internat. fellowship, Govt. of Mex. State, 1986-1987. Mem.: AAAS (assoc.), Internat. AIDS Soc., Pan-Am. Soc. Ft. NeuroVirology (pres. 2000), Mexican Acad. of Neurology (assoc.). Achievements include first to Molecular Mimicry in NeuroAIDS; Field of NeuroVirology; research in Mannose Receptor and AIDS Vaccine; design of HIV-1 Neurotropism Movie; development of Latin American Program of Virology; Pan-American Program of NeuroVirology. Avocations: black belt in martial arts, poetry, soccer player. Home: 2308 McCormick Rd Rockville MD 20850 Office: Inst of Human Virology UMBI U Md 725 West Lombard St Baltimore MD 21201 Home Phone: 301-762-7492; Office Phone: 410-706-7443. Office Fax: 410-706-1952; Home Fax: 410-706-7453. Business E-Mail: trujillo@umbi.umd.edu.

TRUJILLO, LORENZO A., lawyer, educator, consultant, director; b. Denver, Aug. 10, 1951; s. Filbert G. and Marie O. Trujillo; m. Ellen Alires; children: Javier Antonio, Lorenzo Feliciano, Kristina Alires. BA, U. Colo., 1972, MA, 1974, postgrad.; EdD, U. San Francisco, 1979; JD, U. Colo., 1993. Bar: Colo. 1994, U.S. Dist. Ct. Colo. 1994, U.S. Ct. Appeals (10th cir.) 1994, U.S. Supreme Ct. 1999; cert. edn. tchr., prin., supt., Colo. Exec. assoc. Inter-Am. Rsch. Assocs., Rosslyn, Va., 1980-82; exec. dir. humanities Jefferson County Pub. Schs., Golden, Colo., 1982-89; pvt. practice edn. cons. Lakewood, Colo., 1989-93; gen. corp. counsel Am. Achievement Schs., Inc., Lakewood, Colo., 1994-96; atty. Frie, Arndt & Trujillo Law Firm, Arvada, Colo., 1994-96, ptnr., 1995-97; dist. hearing officer, dir. of instrn. Adams County Sch. Dist. 14, 1996—97, dir. human resources, 1998-99, dist. attendance officer/legal counsel, prin. H.S., 1999—. Co-chair Mellon fellowships The Coll. Bd., N.Y.C., 1987-93; cons. U.S.I.A. Fulbright Tchr. Exch. Program, Washington, 1987-93; editl. advisor Harcourt, Brace, Jovanovich Pub., Orlando, Fla., 1988-93; mem. Colo. Supreme Ct. Multicultural Commn., 1996-98, 99—; mem. Colo. Supreme Ct. Families in the Cts. Commn., 2001-02; mem. 17th Jud. Dist. Nominating Com., 2002—; adj. prof. law U. Denver Sch. Law, 2002. Contbr. numerous articles to profl. jours. Mem. panel of arbitrators Am. Arbitration Assn., 1994-present; panelist, evaluator Nat. Endowment for the Arts, 1976—. Recipient Legal Aid Clinic Acad. award Colo. Bar Assn., 1993, Pro Bono award, 1993, Loyola U. Acad. award, 1993, Gov.'s award for excellence in the arts State of Colo., 1996, others. Mem. Am. Assn. Tchrs. of Spanish and Portuguese (pres. Colo. chpt. 1985-88), Colo. Hispanic Bar Assn. (bd. dirs. 2001—, pres.-elect 2003, pres. 2004), Am. Immigration Lawyers Assn., Nat. Sch. Bds. Coun. Sch. Attys., Nat. Assn. Judiciary Interpreters and Translators, Colo. Bar Assn. (probate and trust sect., grievance policy com. 1995-97, ethics com. 1995-96), U. San Francisco Alumni Assn. (founder, pres. 1987-90), Phi Delta Kappa (chair internat. edn. com. 1988-89), Phi Alpha Delta. Avocation: violinist. Office: Adams County Sch Dist 14 6500 E 72d Ave Commerce City CO 80022-2380

TRUJILLO, ROBERT, musician; b. Santa Monica, Calif., Oct. 23, 1964; Former band mem. Suicidal Tendencies, Infectious Grooves, Ozzy Osbourne; band mem. Metallica, 2003—. Musician (bassist, also prodr.): (albums) (with Infectious Grooves) Plague That Makes Your Booty Move, 1991, Sarsippius' Ark, 1993; musician: (bassist) Groove Family Cyco, 1994, Mas Borracho, 2000, (with Suicidal Tendencies) Art of Rebellion, 1992, Suicidal for Life, 1994, (with Ozzy Osbourne) Down to Earth, 2001, Live at Budokan, 2002, Ozzman Cometh: Greatest Hits, 2002, (with Metallica) St. Anger, 2003 (Grammy award for Best Metal Performance, 2003), (others) Poder Latino, A.N.I.M.A.L., 1998; musician: (bassist, vocals, prodr., engr., mastering) Twelve Piece Band, Project Tru, 1999; musician: (bassist) Christmas That Almost Wasn't, Various Artists, 2001, Metallic Assault: A Tribute to Metallica, Various Artists, 2001, Problem Child, Cyco Mike, 2001, Revolution, Insolence, 2001, 1919 Eternal, Zakk Wylde's Black Label Society, 2001, Degradation Trip, Jerry Cantrell, Vol. 1 & Vol. 2, 2002, Different Shade of Green: Tribute to Green Day, Various Artists, 2003, Prison Cell, Wirebox, 2003, Immaculate Deception: A Tribute to the Music of Madon, 2004, Stairway to Rock (Not Just) A Led Zepplin Tribute, Various Artists, 2004; performer: (TV soundtrack) Osbourne Family Album, 2002. Office: Elektra Entertainment Group 75 Rockefeller Plaza New York NY 10019-7284

TRULY, RICHARD H., academic and federal agency administrator, retired pilot; b. Fayette, Miss., Nov. 12, 1937; s. James B. Truly; m. Coleen Hanner; children: Richard Michael, Daniel Bennett, Lee Margaret. B in Aero. Engring., Ga. Inst. Tech., 1959; D in Sci. (hon.), Millsaps Coll., Duquesne U.; D in Engring. (hon.), Colo. Sch. Mines, Stevens Inst. Tech. Commd. ensign USN, 1959; advanced through grades to vice adm.; assigned Fighter Squadron 33; served in U.S.S. Intrepid; served in U.S.S. Enterprise; astronaut Manned Orbiting Lab. Program USAF, 1965—69, NASA, 1969—, comdr. Columbia Flight 2, 1981, Challenger Flight 3, 1983; dir. Space Shuttle program, 1986—89; adminstr. NASA, 1989—92; v.p., dir. Georgia Tech Rsch. Inst., Atlanta, 1992—97; dir. Nat. Renewable Energy Lab., Golden, Colo., 1997—2004; ret., 2004. Recipient Robert H. Goddard Astronautics award, AIAA, 1990, Presdl. Citizen's Medal, 1989. Mem.: NAE. Office: Nat Renewable Energy Lab 1617 Cole Blvd Golden CO 80401-3305

TRUMAN, MARGARET, writer; b. Independence, Mo., Feb. 17, 1924; d. Harry S (32nd Pres. U.S.) and Bess (Wallace) T.; m. E. Clifton Daniel Jr., Apr. 21, 1956; children: Clifton T., William, Harrison, Thomas. LHD, Wake Forest U., 1972; HHD, Rockhurst Coll., 1976. Concert singer, 1947-54, actress, broadcaster, author, 1954—; author: Souvenir, 1956, White House Pets, 1969, Harry S. Truman, 1973, Women of Courage, 1976, Murder in the White House, 1980, Murder on Capitol Hill, 1981, Letters from Father, 1981, Murder in the Supreme Court, 1982, Murder in the Smithsonian, 1983, Murder on Embassy Row, 1985, Murder at the FBI, 1985, Murder in Georgetown, 1986, Bess W. Truman, 1986, Murder in the CIA, 1987, Murder at the Kennedy Center, 1989, Murder in the National Cathedral, 1990, Murder at the Pentagon, 1992, Murder on the Potomac, 1994, First Ladies, 1995, Murder in the National Gallery, 1996, Murder in the House, 1997, Murder at the Watergate, 1998, Murder in the Library of Congress, 1999, Murder at Foggy Bottom, 2000, Murder in Havana, 2001, Murder at Ford's Theatre, 2002, The President's House, 2003, Murder at Union Station, 2004, Murder at the Washington Tribune, 2005; editor: Where the Buck Stops: The Personal and Private Writings of Harry S. Truman, 1989. Trustee and v.p. Harry S. Truman Inst.; sec. bd. trustees Harry S. Truman Found.

TRUMBLE, ANGUS A. G., curator, writer; b. Melbourne, Australia, Oct. 6, 1964; arrived in US, 2003; s. Peter Campbell and Helen Borthwick Trumble. BA in Fine Arts and History with honors, U. Melbourne, Australia, 1985, MA, 1992, NYU, NY, 1995. Registered Australian Soc. Indexers, 1993. Aide Office Gov. Victoria, Melbourne, 1987—91; resident tutor fine arts Trinity Coll., Melbourne, 1991—93; assoc. curator European art Art Gallery South Australia, Adelaide, 1996—98, curator European art, 1998—2003; curator paintings and sculpture Yale Ctr. Brit. Art, New Haven, 2003—. Mem. adv. bd. Art and Australia, Sydney, 1998—2002; pres. sr. common rm. Trinity Coll., Melbourne, 1991—92; cons. in field. Author: Bohemian London: Camden Town and Bloomsbury Paintings in Adelaide, 1997, Love and Death: Art in the Age of Queen Victoria, 2001, A Brief History of the Smile, 2004. Recipient Barry Humphries Liberal Arts prize, Melbourne Grammar Sch., 1981, Young Australians award, Queen Elizabeth II Silver Jubilee Trust, 1992; scholar, Fulbright Found., 1994—95. Mem.: Yale Club. Episcopalian. Avocations: art, music, reading, perfume. Office: Yale Ctr British Art 1080 Chapel St New Haven CT 06520 Home Phone: 203-809-4811; Office Phone: 203-432-2844. Office Fax: 203-432-9695. Business E-Mail: angus.trumble@yale.edu.

TRUMBULL, DAVID LEWIS KITCHEN, trade association executive; b. Highland Park, Mich. s. Ben Gordon and Lois Virginia (Wilson) Kitchen; m. Mary N. DiZazzo, Sept. 29, 2003. AB, U. Mich., 1991. Rsch. asst. U. Mass., Boston, 1992-93; programmer Commonwealth of Mass., Boston, 1993-94; dir. mem. svcs. Nat. Textile Assn., Boston, 1994—, exec. dir. Am. Flock Assn., Boston, 1994—2001. Chmn. Cambridge (Mass.) Rep. City Com., 1994-2002; asst. sec. NAACP, Cambridge, 1994-96, v.p., 1996-98; chmn. Ward 3, Boston Rep. Com., 2003—. Mem. Textile Club (exec. com. 1996—, treas. 1998—). Roman Catholic. Home: 130 Bowdoin St # 1110 Boston MA 02108 Office: Nat Textile Assn 6 Beacon St # 1125 Boston MA 02108 E-mail: trumbulld@earthlink.net.

TRUMBULL, STEPHEN MICHAEL, entrepreneur, musician; b. Columbus, Ohio, Sept. 18, 1954; s. Clyde Austin and Patricia Ann (Ranck) T. MusB in Voice Performance and Choral Edn., DePauw U., Greencastle, Ind., 1977; postgrad., Ohio State U., 1982-85; MA in Ch. Music, Trinity Luth. Sem., Columbus, Ohio, 2007. Cert. profl. music educator, Ohio; cert. broker/dealer. Dir. vocal music Columbus City Schs., 1978-87; pres., owner Columbus Music Studios, 1984—; pres. The Trumbull Pub. Co., Washington, 1986—, Stephen M. Trumbull, Inc., Columbus, 1986—, Goldmark Securities Corp., Columbus, 1987-90; exec. v.p. Hamilton Capital Corp., Columbus, 1988-90, also bd. dirs., corp. v.p., sec., bd. dirs., 1987-90; v.p. Hamilton Mktg. Corp., Columbus, 1988-90, Kaiser Enterprises, Columbus, 1988-90; pres. Shelter One Group Corp., Columbus, 1988-90, also bd. dirs.; chmn. bd., chief exec. officer Ascona Communications, Inc., LA, 1990-92; chief exec. officer Recording Industry Sourcebook, LA, 1990-92; mng. ptnr. SRS Pub. Co., 1991-95; pres., CEO Music Bus. Registry, Inc., LA, 1995—. Soloist First Cmty. Ch., Columbus, 1982—90, Bay Shore Cmty. Ch., Long Beach, 1999—2001; dir. music First Bapt. Ch., Granville, Ohio, 2003—; mktg. cons. Beckenhorst Press, Inc., Columbus, 1986—87; exec. prodr. Wake Up and Dream, LA, 1990—92; cons. The Source Group, Toronto, Canada, 1986—, Events Can., Toronto, 1999—. Adviser Lambda Chi Alpha, Ohio State U., chmn. alumni adv. bd., 1982-87; pres. Friends of Neoteric Dance Theatre, Columbus, 1986-88; coord. nat. competition Jr. Achievement Nat. Conf., Bloomington, Ind., 1973-95; bd. dirs. Neoteric Dance Theatre, 1986-88, Susan Van Pelt Dance Ensemble, 1989-92, Reach for the Stars, Inc., L.A., 1990-92, The Awareness Found., L.A., 1992-93; bus.-mktg. com. Jr. Achievement Ctrl. Ohio, Inc., 1987-92; cons. Nat. Hockey League Awards, Toronto, 1990-99; chair Granville (Ohio) Arts Commn., 2004—. Named Outstanding Alumni, Lambda Chi Alpha, 1984. Mem. Columbus Edn. Assn. Lodges: Optimist. Avocations: swimming, travel, sailing. Home: PO Box 411 Granville OH 43023-0411 Office: 7510 W Sunset Blvd # 1041 Los Angeles CA 90046-3400 Home Phone: 740-587-0423; Office Phone: 617-314-6221. E-mail: steve@musicregistry.com.

TRUMKA, RICHARD LOUIS, labor union administrator; b. Nemacolin, Pa., July 24, 1949; s. Frank Richard and Eola Elizabeth (Bertugli) T.; m. Barbara Vidovich, Nov. 27, 1982; 1 child, Richard L. BS, Pa. State U., 1971; JD, Villanova U., 1974. Bar: US Dist. Ct. (DC) 1974, US Ct. Appeals (3d, 4th and DC cirs.) 1975, US Supreme Ct. 1979. Atty. United Mine Workers Am., Washington, 1974-77, 78-79, internat. exec. bd. Dist. 4 Masontown, Pa., 1981-82, internat. pres. Washington, 1982-95; pres. emeritus United Mine Workers Am., 1995—; miner, operator Jones & Laughlin Steel, Nemacolin, Pa., 1977-78, 79-81; sec. treas. AFL-CIO, Washington, 1995—. Bd. dirs. Am. Coal Found.; mem. Nat. Coal Council, 1985. Trustee Pa. State U. Recipient Labor Responsibility Award, Martin Luther King Ctr. for Nonviolent Social Change, 1990; Gompers-Murray-Meany, Massachusetts AFL-CIO; The Jewish Nat. Fund Tree of Life Award; Humanitarian Award, Sons of Italy Found, 2003 Democrat. Roman Catholic. Office: AFL-CIO 815 16th St NW Washington DC 20006-4145 *

TRUMP, DONALD JOHN, real estate developer; b. NYC, 1946; s. Fred C. and Mary Trump; m. Ivana Zelnicek, Apr. 9, 1977 (div. 1991); children: Donald, Jr., Ivanka, Eric; m. Marla Maples, Dec. 30, 1993 (div. June 8, 1999); 1 child, Tiffany Ariana; m. Melania Knauss, Jan. 22, 2005; 1 child, Barron William. BS Economics, U. Pa., Wharton Sch. Fin., 1968. Pres. Trump Orgn., NYC; owner Trump Tower, Trump Parc, Trump Palace, Trump Bldg. at 40 Wall St., NYC, Trump Internat. Hotel and Tower, NYC,

Chgo., Trump Plz. Hotel and Casino, Trump Marina, Trump Taj Mahal, Atlantic City, Trump Casino Riverboat, Buffington Harbor, Ind., Trump 29 Casino, Palm Springs, Calif., W. Side Rail Yards devel. as Trump Pl., NYC, Mansion at Seven Springs, Bedford, NY, Mar-a-Lago Club, Palm Beach, Fla.; ptnr.-owner 610 Park Ave. and Trump World Tower, NYC, Trump Park Ave. (formerly Delmonico Hotel), Trump Grande Ocean Resort and Residences, Miami Beach, Fla., Trump Internat. Hotel and Twr., Chgo.; chmn., pres. Trump Org., NYC; chmn. Trump Entertainment Resorts, Inc., 2005—. Owner Trump Internat. Golf Club, Palm Beach, Trump Nat. Golf Club, Briarcliff Manor, NY, Ocean Trails Golf Course, Palos Verde, Calif., Trump Nat., Bedminster, NJ, Trump Mgmt. Group Modeling/Talent Agy.; pres. Trump Pageants LP, includes Miss Universe, Miss USA and Miss Teen USA.; launched line of men's suits, 2004; launched signature fragrance, Donald Trump The Fragrance, 04; announced launching of Trump University will consist of online courses, CD-ROMS, blogs, consulting services and Learning Annex-type seminars, 05. Author: Trump: The Way to the Top: The Best Real Estate Advice I Ever Received: 100 Top Experts Share Their Strategies, 2004, Trump: The Best Golf Advice I Ever Received, 2005, Think Big and Kick Butt—in Business and Life, 2007; co-author (with Tony Schwartz): Trump: The Art of the Deal, 1987; co-author: (with Charles Leerhsen) Surviving at the Top (renamed Trump: The Art of Survival), 1990; co-author: (with Kate Bohner) Trump: The Art of the Comeback, 1997; co-author: (with Dave Shiflett) The America We Deserve, 2000; co-author: (with Meredith McIver) Think Like a Billionaire: Everything You Need to Know About Success, Real Estate, and Life, 2004; co-author: (with Robert T. Kiyosaki, Sharon Lechter & Meredith McIver) Why We Want You to Be Rich-Two Men-One Message, 2006; host, exec. prodr. (TV series) The Apprentice, 2004—07, launched Trump World mag., 2004, host on syndicated radio program Trumped!, Premiere Radio Networks, 2004. Com. mem., Celebration of Nations Commemorating 50th Anniversary UN and UNICEF; Co-chmn. N.Y. Vietnam Vets. Meml. Fund; founding mem. constrn. com. Cathedral of St. John the Divine; mem. N.Y. Citizens Tax Coun., Fifth Ave Assn., Realty Found. of N.Y., Met. Mus. of Art's Real Estate Coun.; mem. adv. bd. Lenox Hill Hosp., United Cerebral Palsy; spl. advisor to Pres.'s Coun. on Phys. Fitness and Sports; mem. N.Y. Sportsplex Commn.; chmn. N.Y. citizens com. 78th Ann. NAACP Conv., 1987; grand marshall Nation's Parade, 1995; bd. dirs. Police Athletic League; bd. overseers Wharton Sch.; founding mem. adv. bd. Wharton Real Estate Ctr.; bd. dirs. Fred C. Trump Found.; chmn. Donald J. Trump Found. Named Developer of Yr., Constrn. Mgmt. Assn. Am., 1999, Hotel and Real Estate Visionary of the Century, UTA Fedn., 2000; named one of Forbes' Richest Americans, 2006; named to Wharton Hall of Fame, Benefactors bd. dirs., Hist. Soc. Palm Beach County, 2003; recipient Entrepreneur of Yr. award, Wharton Entrepreneurial Club, 1984, Ellis Island Medal of Honor, 1986. Achievements include the three-month rebuilding of Wollman Skating Rink in Central Park. *

TRUMP, ERIC FREDERICK, journalist; b. Ridgewood, NJ, July 22, 1969; s. Christopher Gephardt and Elisabeth Marie Trump; life ptnr. Josephine Johnston. BA in English, U. Toronto, 1992; MS in Journalism, Columbia U., NYC, 1998. Cert. EFL, ESL St. Giles Coll., 1992. Reporter AP, Berlin, 1998—99; prof. lit. and philosophy SUNY, Purchase, 2000—03; editor Hastings Ctr., Garrison, NY, 2003—05; freelance journalist NYC, 1998—; reporter United Press Internat., 2006. Writer NYU, NYC, 2005—, tchr., 2006—. Contbr. articles to profl. jours. Vol. Toronto Gen., Emergency Rm., 1996—97; instr. Harlem Tutorial Program, NYC, 1997—98; writer Thelma Hill Performing Arts Ctr., NYC, 2000—04. Fellow, Fulbright Commn., 1998—99; McCracken fellow, NYU, 2005—, Travel fellow, 2006, Rsch. fellow, NYU Free U., 2007—. Mem.: Nat. Assn. Sci. Writers. Independent. Avocations: hiking, scuba diving, travel, writing, bicycling. Home: 119 Gordon Ave Sleepy Hollow NY 10591 Office: NYU 19 University Pl New York NY 10003 Business E-Mail: eft208@nyu.edu.

TRUMP, STEPHANIE, music educator, choral director; m. Mark Trump; children: Hana, Nicklaus. MusB in Music Edn., Augsburg Coll., 1991, MusB in Voice Performance, 1991; MusM in Edn., U. Hawaii, 2006. Dir. choral Tech. and Lang. Campu, Robbinsdale, Minn., 1992—97, Armstrong H.S., Plymouth, Minn., 1996—. Mem.: Am. Choral Dirs. Assn., Music Educators Nat. Conf. Office: Armstrong High School 10635 36th Ave N Plymouth MN 55441 Home Phone: 763-550-7993; Office Phone: 763-504-8857. Business E-Mail: stephanie_trump@rdale.k12.mn.us.

TRUMPBOUR, JOHN, historian, researcher, director; b. Greensboro, NC, Feb. 23, 1959; s. Robert and Virginia Trumpbour. BA, History, Stanford U., Palo Alto, Calif., 1977—82; PhD, History, Harvard U., Cambridge, Mass., 1982—96. Rsch. dir. Harvard Trade Union Program, 1999—, Labor & Worklife Program at Harvard Law Sch., 2002—. Cons. and rschr. African Am. Labor Leaders' Econ. Summit, Cambridge, Mass., 1997—2005; rschr. and fellowships com. Sci. & Engring. Workforce Project at Nat. Bur. of Econ. Rsch., Cambridge, Mass., 2001—; editl. bd. Labor History, London, 2004—. Author: Selling Hollywood to the World: U.S. and European Struggles for Mastery of the Global Film Industry, 1920-1950, 2002 (Allan Nevins prize for Lit. Excellence.); editor: How Harvard Rules, 1989, The Dividing Rhine: Politics and Society in Contemporary France and Germany, 1989; guest editor: Comparative Labor Law and Policy Jour., 2007. Bd. of directors Boston Moblzn., 1999—2001; co-chair Samia Tenants Orgn., Boston, 1996—2000; fellowships com., Rhodes and Marshall scholarships Leverett Ho., Harvard U., 1987—. Recipient Best Essay prize, NAAA Found., 1987, James Birdsall Weter award, Stanford U., Dept. History, 1982; fellow Sawyer fellow, Mellon Found., 1996-97, Belgian Am. Edn. Found. Fellow, Brussels, Belgium, 1989-1990; grantee, Sloan Found., 2002. Mem.: Labor and Working-Class History Assn., Soc. for Historians of Am. Fgn. Rels. Home: 60 Woodstock Avenue #14 Brighton MA 02135 Office: Harvard Law Sch Labor and Worklife Program 125 Mt Auburn St 3d Fl Cambridge MA 02138 Office Phone: 617-495-9265. Personal E-mail: john_trumpbour@harvard.edu.

TRUNDLE, W(INFIELD) SCOTT, publishing executive newspaper, lawyer; b. Maryville, Tenn., Mar. 24, 1939; s. Winfield Scott and Alice (Smith) T.; m. Elizabeth Latshaw, Oct. 14, 1989; children: Stephen, Allison. BA, Vanderbilt U., 1961, JD, 1967. Bar: Tenn. 1967. Spl. agt. U.S. Secret Service, 1963-66; asso. to partner firm Hunter, Smith, Davis & Norris, Kingsport, Tenn., 1967-72; pub. Kingsport (Tenn.) Times-News, 1972-78; pres. Greensboro (N.C.) Daily News, 1978-80; exec. v.p. Jefferson Pilot Publs., Inc., Greensboro and Clearwater, Fla., 1980-82; v.p., bus. mgr. Tampa Tribune (Fla.), 1982-91; sr. v.p. Hillsborough C.C., 1991-93; publisher Ogden (Utah) Standard Examiner, 1993—2005. Assoc. prof. East Tenn. State U., 1973-77; v.p. spl. projects Sandusky Newspapers, Inc., 2005—; bd. dirs., chmn. Container Recycling Inst., Washington. Trustee Eccles Dinosaur Park and Mus. Found., Ogden, Utah. Mem.: Tenn. Bar Assn. Methodist. Home: 2380 Park Forest Blvd Mount Dora FL 32757 Personal E-mail: scott@thetrundles.com.

TRUNZO, CANDACE, editor-in-chief; Reporter Time; writer & editor Money; features editor Globe, 1994—99, editor-in-chief; exec. editor Star, 1999, editor-in-chief, 2007—; exec. editor Nat. Enquirer, 2006—07. Office: Star Mag 1000 American Way Boca Raton FL 33464-1000 *

TRUOG, WILLIAM EDWARD, III, pediatrician, educator, researcher; b. Kansas City, Mo., Feb. 5, 1947; s. William E. and Virginia (Sylvester) Truog; m. Jill D. Jacobson, July 11, 1992. BA cum laude, Carleton Coll., 1969; MD, U. Chgo., 1973. Intern, resident pediat., chief resident Children's Orthop. Hosp.-U. Wash., Seattle, 1973—76, rsch. fellow neonatology, 1976—78; asst. prof., assoc. prof., prof. pediat. U. Wash., Seattle, 1978—93; prof. pediat. U. Mo. Kansas City Sch. Medicine, 1993—, vice chair faculty devel. dept. pediats., 2007—. Med. dir. infant ICU Children's Orthop. Hosp., Seattle, 1982—91. Author: Critical Care of the Newborn, 1983, 1988; contbr. articles to profl. jours. Named First Physician Scientist, Children's Mercy Hosp., 1993; named to Best Doctors in Am., 2005; recipient Sosland Endowed Chair Neonatal Rsch., 2001; grantee, NIH, 1981, 1984, 1997, 2002. Mem.: Perinatal Rsch. Soc., We. Soc. Pediat. Rsch., Soc. Pediat. Rsch., Am. Pediat. Soc., Am. Thoracic Soc. (grantee 1978). Episcopalian. Office: Children's Mercy Hosp 2401 Gillham Rd Kansas City MO 64108-4619

TRUONG, DOTHANG, information scientist, educator; b. Hanoi, Vietnam, Jan. 22, 1973; arrived in US, 2000; s. Tin Do Truong and Thinh Tiu Le; m. Van T. Nguyen, Oct. 31, 0999; 1 child, My D. BS in Engring. with hons., Hanoi U. Tech., Vietnam, 1994; MBA, Asian Inst. Tech., 1997; PhD in Mfg. Mgmt., U. Toledo, 2004. Instr. Hanoi (Vietnam) U. Tech., 1997—2000; tchg. asst. The U. Toledo, 2000—03; instr. Fayetteville (N.C.) State U., 2003—04, asst. prof., 2004—. Project coord. Vietnam Coal Corp., Hanoi, 1997—98; instr. Vietnam Mgmt. Devel. Program Swiss Asian Inst. Tech., Hanoi, 1998—99. Contbr. articles to profl. jours. Recipient Nguyen Truong To awards, Vietnam Help Orgn., Hanoi U. Tech., 1992—94, Outstanding Tchg. awards, Hanoi (Vietnam) U. Tech., 1998—99, 2004 Student Pacemaker of Yr. award, The U. Toledo, 2004; grantee, Hanoi U. of Tech., 1989—94, Fayetteville State U., 2004; scholar, Swiss-Asian Inst. Tech., Vietnam Mgmt. Devel. Program, 1995—97, 1999, The U. Toledo, 2000—03. Mem.: Mid West Bus. Adminstrn. Assn., Decision Sci. Inst. (Hon. Mention award 2005), Instn. Supply Mgmt. (scholar 2005), Grad. Alumni, Asian Inst. Tech., Info. Sys. Soc. (corr.), Grad. Alumni The U. Toledo, Sigma Iota Epsilon (life). Buddhist. Achievements include research in impacts of radio frequency identification on the supply chain management; e-marketplace usage from the buyer perspective; e-marketplaces and supply chain integration. Office: Fayetteville State University 1200 Murchison Rd Fayetteville NC 28301 Home Phone: 910-486-0147; Office Phone: 910-672-1020.

TRURAN, JAMES WELLINGTON, JR., astrophysicist, educator; b. Brewster, NY, July 12, 1940; s. James Wellington and Suzanne (Foglesong) T.; m. Carol Kay Dell'Acy, June 26, 1965; children— Elaina Michelle, Diana Lee, Anastasia Elizabeth. BA in Physics, Cornell U., Ithaca, NY, 1961; MS in Physics, Yale U., New Haven, Conn., 1963, PhD in Physics, 1966. Postdoctoral rsch. assoc. NAS-NRC Goddard Inst. Space Studies, NASA, NYC, 1965-67; asst. prof. physics Belfer Grad. Sch. Sci., Yeshiva U., 1967-70; rsch. fellow in physics Calif. Inst. Tech., 1968-69; assoc. prof. Belfer Grad. Sch. Sci., Yeshiva U., 1970-72, prof., 1972-73; prof. astronomy U. Ill., Urbana, 1973-91; sr. vis. fellow, Guggenheim Meml. Found. fellow Inst. Astronomy, U. Cambridge, Eng., 1979-80; trustee Aspen Ctr. Physics, 1979-85, 91-93, 96-99, v.p., 1985-88; assoc. U. Ill. Ctr. for Advanced Study, 1979-80, 86-87; prof. astronomy astrophysics U. Chgo., 1991—; sr. physicist Argonne Nat. Lab., 2003—. Alexander von Humboldt-Stiftung sr. scientist Max-Plank Inst., Munich, Germany, 1986-87, 94; Beatrice Tinsley vis. prof. U. Tex., Austin, 1999; Biermann lectr. in astrophysics, Max-Planck Inst., Munich, 2001. Contbr. articles to profl. jours.; co-editor: Nucleosynthesis, 1968, Nucleosynthesis— Challenges and New Developments, 1985, Nuclear Astrophysics, 1987, Type Ia Supernovae: Theory and Cosmology, 2000, Cosmic Chemical Evolution, 2002; editor: Physics Letters B, 1974-80. Co-recipient Yale Sci. and Engring. Assn. annual award for advancement basic or applied sci., 1980 Fellow AAAS, Am. Phys. Soc.; mem. Am. Astron. Soc., Am. Phys. Soc., Internat. Astron. Union. Home: 210 Wysteria Dr Olympia Fields IL 60461-1202 Office: U Chgo Dept Astronomy Astrophysics 5640 S Ellis Ave Chicago IL 60637-1433 Business E-Mail: truran@nova.uchicago.edu.

TRUS, BENES LOUIS, structural chemist; b. Tyler, Tex., May 9, 1946; s. Joseph N. and Ruthie Trus; m. Susan Evans, Apr. 23, 1972; children: Aaron Baram, Anthony Phillip. BS cum laude with honors, Tulane U., 1968; PhD, Calif. Inst. Tech., 1972. Rsch. chemist NIH, Bethesda, Md., 1980—93, chief imaging processing rsch. sect., 1993—2002, chief imaging scis. lab., 2002—, dep. dir. divsn. computational biosci., 2003—07, acting sci. dir. ctr. info. tech., 2007—, acting dir. divsn., 2007—, acting chief computational biosci. and engring. lab., 2007—. Mem. steering com. NIH wide image processing group, 1984— (NIH Dirs. award, 1987, 94, Group Merit award 1998). Contbr. articles to profl. jours., chpt. to books. Mem. NIH Marathon Team, 1986-88, 1st pl. Marine Corps Marathon, Govt. Team Competition, 1986, 3d pl., 1987, 88, 2d pl. Masters Team, 1993. Jane Coffin Childs postdoctoral fellow Calif. Inst. Tech., Pasadena, 1972-75, Rsch. fellow NIH, Bethesda, Md., 1975-77, Sr. Rsch. fellow, 1977-80; Tulane U. scholar and fellow, 1965-68. Mem. Chesapeake Soc. for Microscopy, Microscope Soc. Am., Reston Road Runner Club, Phi Beta Kappa, Sigma Xi. Avocations: music, running, carpentry. Office: NIH Bldg 12A Rm 2033 Bethesda MD 20892-5624

TRUSCOTT, CARL JOSEPH, security firm executive, former federal agency administrator; b. Augusta, Ga., May 21, 1957; married; 1 child. BS in Criminal Justice, U. Del., 1979. Investigator NJ Dept. Law & Pub. Safety, 1980—81; spl. agt. US Secret Svc., US Dept. Treasury, 1981—2004, spl. agt. in charge, Presdl. protective divsn., 2001—03; asst. dir. Office Protective Rsch. US Secret Svc., US Dept. Homeland Security, 2003—04; dir. Bur. Alcohol, Tobacco, Firearms & Explosives US Dept. Justice, Washington, 2004—06; sr. v.p. ASERO Worldwide, 2007—. Recipient Dirs. Life Saving award, 1986, Sr. Exec. Svc. Performance award, 2001, 2002, Spl. award for disting. svc. to the Exec. Office of the Pres., 2002, Presdl. Rank award as Meritorious Exec., 2003. Office: ASERO Worldwide 700 12th St Ste 800 Washington DC 20005 *

TRUSDELL, MARY LOUISE CANTRELL, retired state educational administrator; b. Chandler, Okla., Oct. 24, 1921; d. George Herbert and Lois Elizabeth (Bruce) Cantrell; m. Robert William Trusdell, Jan. 7, 1943; children: Timothy Lee, Laurence Michael. BA, Ga. So. Coll., 1965; MEd, U. Va., 1974. Dir. specific learning disabilities program Savannah Country Day Sch., Ga., 1960-65; learning disabilities tchr. Richmond pub. schs., Va., 1966-73; dir. New Community Sch., Richmond, 1974-75; dir. Fed. Learning Disabilities Project, Dept HEW, Mid. Peninsula, Va., 1975-76; supr. programs for learning disabled Va. Dept. Edn., Richmond, 1976-86; bd. dirs. Learning Disabilities Council, Richmond, Very Spl. Arts- Va., 1986-91; mem. adv. com. Learning Disabilities Research and Devel. Project, Woodrow Wilson Rehab. Ctr., Fisherville, Va., 1983. Co-editor: Understanding Learning Disabilities: A Parent Guide and Workbook, 1989, 3d edit., 2002. Bd. dirs. Savannah Assn. Retarded Children, 1957-60, Meml. Guidance Clinic, Richmond, 1966-69. Named Tchr. of Yr., Learning Disabilities Ctr., Richmond, 1972. Mem. Orton Dyslexia Soc. (pres. capital area br. 1968-70, nat. bd. dirs. 1970-72, Va. br. 1986-91), Alliance for the Mentally Ill. Cen. Va. (pres. 1991-93). Presbyterian. Avocations: travel, theater, reading.

TRUSLOW, DONALD K., bank executive; b. Summit, NJ, May 13, 1958; BA in Commerce, U. Va. Joined Wachovia Corp., 1980, treas., comptr., mgr. middle market corp. banking group, chief credit officer S.C. bank, head loan adminstrn. Piedmont Triad Region, loan adminstrn. mgr. internat. group, loan adminstrn. officer, internat. baking and gen. loan adminstr., sr. exec. v.p. chief risk officer Charlotte, NC, 2001—. Bd. dirs. Risk Mgmt. Assn., Arts and Sci. Coun., Charlotte; bd. visitors Babcock Grad. Sch. Mgmt., Wake Forest U. Mem.: Fin. Svcs. Roundtable. Office: Wachovia Corp Ste 400 301 S College St Charlotte NC 28288 *

TRUSSELL, CHARLES TAIT, columnist; b. Balt., May 9, 1925; s. Charles Prescott and Beatrice (Tait) T.; m. Woodley Grizzard, Dec. 27, 1953 (div. 1990); children: Galen Tait, Thomas Marshall; m. Nancy Rathbun Billington, Dec. 19, 1990. BA in Journalism, Washington and Lee U., Lexington, Va., 1949. Reporter St. Petersburg (Fla.) Times, also; writer Congl. Quar. News Features, 1951-54; reporter Wall St. Jour., 1954-56, Washington Evening Star, 1956; asso. editor Nation's Business mag., 1956-64, mng. editor, 1964-69; sr. editor Congressional Quar., Inc., 1969-70; dir. pub. relations and advt. Investment Co. Inst., Washington, 1970-72; free-lance writer, real estate investor, 1972-74; v.p. Am. Forest Inst., Washington, 1974-79, sr. v.p., 1980-81; v.p. Am. Enterprise Inst., 1981-86; dir. comms. Constitution Bicentennial Commn., 1986-88; freelance writer, columnist, 1988—. Nat. corr. Clear Mountain Comms. Producer: documentary record album The Best of Washington Humor, 1963; author: Beating the Competition, 1992; editor: Successful Management, 1964, (with Paul Hencke) Dear NASA Please Send Me a Rocket, 1964, Timeless Truths for Kids, 2002, Washington Doctor: A Parable on Love & Death. Served with USNR, 1944-46. Recipient Loeb Spl. Achievement award for mags. U. Conn., 1961, Benjamin Fine Journalism award, 1992. Mem. Washington Assembly (exec. com. 1961-65, chmn. 1965), Beta Theta Pi. Home: 2467 Cherry Rd Manistee MI 49660- E-mail: ttrussell@chartermi.net.

TRUSSELL, JAMES, economist, educator, dean; b. Columbus, Ga., Oct. 17, 1949; BS summa cum laude in Maths., Davidson Coll., 1971; BPhil, Oxford U., 1973; PhD in Econs., Princeton U., 1975. From asst. prof. econs. to prof., dean Princeton (N.J.) U., 1975—. Co-author: The Loving Book, 1972, Contraceptive Technology, 18th edit., 2004; contbr. articles to profl. jours. Mem. Am. Statis. Assn., Am. Pub. Health Assn., Population Assn. Am., Australia Population Assn., Phi Beta Kappa., Assn. Reproductive Health Profls., Internat. Union for the Scientific Study of Population. Office: Princeton U Office of Population Rsch Wallace Hall Princeton NJ 08544-2007 Office Phone: 609-258-4946. Business E-Mail: trussell@princeton.edu.

TRUTOR, GENEVIEVE WILLIAMSON, museum director; b. Benson, Vt., Aug. 26, 1923; d. Clayton John and Caroline Aileen (Walker) Williamson; m. John Trutor, May 4, 1946 (dec.); children: Barry, John W., Elizabeth, William C. Diploma, Rutland Bus. Coll., 1942. Sec. War Prodn. Bd., Washington, 1942—45, Soc. Am. Foresters, Washington, 1945—47; adminstrv. asst. Benson Village Sch., Benson, Vt., 1971—89; dir. Benson Lumber Yard Inc., Benson, 1963—2002; founder, curator Benson Mus., Benson, 1980—. Lib. commr. Town of Benson, 1959—61; dir. Lower Champlain Housing Corp., 1977—82; mem. Benson's Cmty. Hall Restoration project, 1975—80; chmn. Nat. Bicentennial Celebration, Benson, Vt., 1976, State Bicentennial Celebration, Vt., 1977, Benson Bicentennial Celebration, 1980; sec., treas. Benson Health Com., 1961—70; trustee Pub. Funds, 1981—87, 1996—, Bertha R. Franke Scholarship Fund, 1971—79. Republican.

TRUTTER, JOHN THOMAS, telecommunications industry executive, educator, writer; b. Springfield, Ill., Apr. 18, 1920; s. Frank Louis and Frances (Mischler) T.; m. Edith English Woods II, June 17, 1950 (dec.); children: Edith English II, Jonathan Woods. BA, U. Ill., 1942; postgrad., Northwestern U., 1947-50, U. Chgo., 1947-50; LHD (hon.), Lincoln Coll., 1986. Various positions Ill. Bell, Chgo., 1946-58, gen. traffic mgr., from asst. v.p. pub. rels. to gen. mgr., 1958-69, v.p. pub. rels., 1969-71, v.p. operator svcs., 1971-80, v.p. community affairs, 1980-85; mem. hdqs. staff AT&T, NYC, 1955-57; pres. John T. Trutter Co., Inc., Chgo., 1985—; pres., CEO Chgo. Conv. and Visitors Bur., 1985-88; pres. Chgo. Tourism Coun., 1988-90; v.p. Profl. Impressions Media Group, Inc., 1998-2000, prof. emeritus, 2001. Mem. adv. bd. The Alford Group, Chgo., 1984—, Bozell-Worldwide, Chgo., 1994-96; chancellor Lincoln Acad. of Ill., 1985-2001. Co-author: Handling Barriers in Communication, 1957, The Governor Takes a Bride, 1977 Past chmn., life trustee Jane Addams Hull House Assn.; chmn. United Cerebral Palsy Assn. Greater Chgo., 1967-95, hon. chmn., 1995—, chmn. Canal Corridor Assn., 1991-99; bd. dirs. Chgo. Crime Commn., Abraham Lincoln Assn., Lyric Opera Chgo.; v.p. English Speaking Union, 1989-91, bd. govs., 1980—; chmn. bd. City Colls. Chgo. Found., 1987-91; past chmn. Children's Home and Aid Soc. Ill.; v.p. City Club Chgo.; treas. Chgo. United, 1970-85; mem. Ill. Econ. Devel. Commn., 1985; past presiding co-chmn. NCCJ; numerous others; bd. govs. Northwestern U. Libr. Coun., 1984—; trustee Lincoln (Ill.) Coll., 1987-90, Mundelein Coll., 1988-91; mem. sch. problems coun. State Ill. Assembly, 1985-91, spl. commn. on adminstrn. of justice in Cook County, 1986-92; founding chmn. adv. coun. Evanston Hist. Soc., 1995-98. Lt. col. U.S. Army, 1945. Decorated Legion of Merit; recipient Laureate award State of Ill., 1980, Outstanding Exec. Leader award Am. Soc. Fundraisers, Humanitarian of Yr. award, Jane Addams award The Hull House Assn., 1991, Nat. Infinitec award for individual leadership in assistive technology for disabled people, 1997, Jack Brickhouse award for outstanding svcs., 2000. Mem. Pub. Rels. Soc. Am., Sangamon County Hist. Soc. (founder, past pres.), Ill. State Hist. Soc. (pres. 1985-87), Coun. on Ill. History (chmn. 1991—), U. Ill. Alumni Assn. (bd. dirs. 1990-94), Tavern Club, Econ. Club, Mid-Am. Club, Alpha Sigma Phi (Nat. Merit Achievement award 1994), Phi Delta Phi. Office Phone: 847-446-4267. Office Fax: 847-441-0582.

TRUWIT, MITCHELL, Internet company executive; b. 1969; BS in Polit. Sci., Vassar College, Poughkeepsie, NY; MBA, Harvard Univ., 1997. Dir. bus. devel. Oxford Health Plans, Conn., 1997; sr. v.p. corp. devel. Priceline.com, COO, exec. v.p. Conn.; pres, CEO Orbitz Worldwide, Travelport, Chgo.; ptnr. Apax Partners, L.P., NYC, 2006—. Spkr. in field; adv. mem. Travelport bd. dirs., 2006—. Bd. mem. Special Olympics, Conn. Named one of 40 Under Forty, Crain's Bus. Chgo., 2005. Avocation: squash. Office: Apax Partners LP 153 E 53rd St 53rd Fl New York NY 10022 Office Phone: 212-753-6300. Office Fax: 312-894-5001, 212-319-6155. *

TRYBAN, ESTHER ELIZABETH, lawyer; b. Chgo., Aug. 14, 1958; d. Chester Joseph and Lottie Elizabeth (Napora) Tryban. AAS with honors, Elgin CC, Ill., 1977, AS with honors, 1982; BS with honors, Roosevelt U., Chgo., 1986; JD, U. Chgo., 1989. Bar: Ill. 1989, U.S. Dist. Ct. (no. dist.) Ill. 1989, U.S. Ct. Appeals (7th cir.) 1990, U.S. Supreme Ct., 1996. Supr. adminstrv. svcs. law dept. Motorola, Inc., Schaumburg, Ill., 1977-86; staff law clk. U.S. Bankruptcy Ct., No. Dist. Ill., Chgo., 1989-90; sr. counsel City of Chgo., 1990—. Mem. ABA, Nat. Lawyers Guild, Assn. Former Bankruptcy Law Clks, Ill. State Bar Assn., Chgo. Bar Assn. (chair govt. svc. com. 1996-97), Advocates Soc. (1st v.p. Chgo. chpt. 2007—), Roman Catholic. Avocations: reading, football, travel. Office: City Chgo Dept Law 30 N Lasalle St Ste 900 Chicago IL 60602-2503 Business E-Mail: lw00026@cityofchicago.org.

TRYGSTAD, LAWRENCE BENSON, lawyer; b. Holton, Mich., Mar. 22, 1937; BA, U. Mich., 1959; JD, U. So. Calif., 1967. Bar: Calif. 1968, U.S. Supreme Ct. 1974. Legal counsel Calif. Tchrs. Assn., United Tchrs. L.A., LA, 1968-71; ptnr. Trygstad & Odell, LA, 1971-80; pres. Trygstad Law Corp., LA, 1980—2004; ptnr. Trygstad, Schwab & Trygstad, LA, 2004—. Instr., tchr. negotiation U. Calif.-Northridge; panelist TV shows Law and the Teacher. Bd. dirs. George Washington Carver Found., L.A. Mem. ABA, Calif. Bar Assn., Consumer Attys. Calif., L.A. County Bar Assn., Calif. Trial Lawyers Assn., Nat. Orgn. Lawyers for Edn. Assns., Am. Trial Lawyers Assn., Consumer Attys. L.A., Phi Alpha Delta. Home: 4209 Aleman Dr Tarzana CA 91356-5405 Office: 1880 Century Park E Ste 1104 Los Angeles CA 90067-1609 Office Phone: 310-552-0500. Business E-Mail: ltrygstad@trygstadlawoffice.com.

TRYON, MARGARET A., director, school psychologist; b. Billings, Mont., July 22, 1950; d. Roy N. and Bunny Morrison; 1 child, Tiffany Nicole. BA, U. Mont., 1972; MS, Ea. Mont. Coll., 1977. Cert. sch.

psychologist. Spl. edn. tchr. Plains Pub. Schs., Mont., 1975—77, Ronan Pub. Schs., Mont., 1977—92; spl. edn. dir., sch. psychologist Miles City Pub. Schs., Mont., 1992—2007; sch. psychologist Yellowstone Boys Girls Ranch, 2007—. Mem.: NASP, Mont. Coun. Adminstrs. Spl. Edn. (Disting. Svc. award 2000), Coun. for Exceptional Children (Spl. Educator award 1999). Home: 2407 Golden Blvd Billings MT 59102 Office Phone: 406-834-3812.

TRYON, PATTI ANN, school psychologist; b. Neptune, NJ, Jan. 17, 1953; d. Boyd Edward Tryon, Jr. and Claudia Ruth (Skidmore) Tryon; 1 child, Shawna Lynn Dunn-Rubio. BS in Home Econs. in Bus., N.Mex State U., Las Cruces, 1974, MS in Home Econs., 1986, EdS in Sch. Psychology, 2004. Cert. sch. psychologist NASP, 2006. Vocat. Edn. for Handicapped food svc./Home Econ. Coop. Edn. tchr. Ysleta Vocat. H.S., El Paso, Tex., 1986—91; living skills/job coaching tchr. N.Mex Sch. for the Visually Handicapped, Alamogordo, 1991—95; ednl. diagnostician Alamogordo Pub. Schs., N.Mex., 1995—2005; sch. psychologist Albuquerque Pub. Sch., 2006—. Fellow Summer Transition Tng. Project, Calif. Sch. for the Blind, San Francisco State U., 1993. Mem.: Phi Kappa Phi (life). Democrat. Methodist. Achievements include research in Asperger's disorder. Avocations: bargain shopping, history, genealogy, antiques, interior decorating. Home: 11616 Terra Bella Ln SE Albuquerque NM 87123 Office: Albuquerque Pub Schs 6400 Uptown Blvd NE Albuquerque NM 87110 Home Phone: 505-280-0292; Office Phone: 505-249-7974. Office Fax: 505-348-8503. Personal E-mail: ptryon@hotmail.com. Business E-Mail: tryon@aps.edu.

TRYTEK, DAVID DOUGLAS, insurance company executive; b. Cleve., Jan. 18, 1955; s. Edmund Trytek and Mary Elaine Salzwedel Blech; m. Lorie Ann Stone, Apr. 10, 1982; children: Dane, Douglas. BS in BA, Bowling Green State U., Ohio, 1977. Claims adjuster Liberty Mus. Ins. Co., Toledo, 1977-80, claims supr. Milw., 1980-85, spl. claims examiner Boston, 1986-89, claims mgr. Green Bay, Wis., 1989-93; tech. svcs. mgr. Liberty Mut. Ins. Co., Milw., 1993-95; regional field investigations mgr. Liberty Mutual Ins. Co., Milw., 1996—, Wausau Ins. Co., Milw., 2001—. Arbitrator Inter-Co. Arbitration Com., Milw., 1984-85. Coach Toledo Optimists Youth Hockey Assn., 1979-80, Wauwatosa (Wis.) Recreation Dept., 1980-85, YMCA Youth Baseball, 1994; alt. Worker's Compensation divsn. Ins. Adv. Com., Madison, Wis., 1994 youth football coach, Sussex, Wis., 1994-99, youth baseball coach, 1994-99, 2002-03. Mem. Exptl. Aircraft Assn., Warbirds of Am., USA Hockey Inc., Internat. Assn. of Spl. Investigation Units, Wis. Street Rod Assn. (bd. dirs. 1999-2002). Avocations: camping, ice hockey, golf, military aircraft. Office: Liberty Mut Ins Co 11800 W Park Pl Milwaukee WI 53224-3009 Business E-Mail: david.trytek@libertymutual.com.

TRYTHALL, HARRY GILBERT, music educator, composer; b. Knoxville, Tenn., Oct. 28, 1930; s. Harry Gilbert and Clara Hannah (Akre) T.; m. Jean Marie Slater, Dec. 28, 1951 (div. 1976); children: Linda Marie, Karen Elizabeth; m. Carol King, Sept. 19, 1985. BA, U. Tenn., 1951; MusM, Northwestern U., 1952; DMA, Cornell U., 1960. Asst. prof. music Knox Coll., Galesburg, Ill., 1960-64; prof. music theory and composition George Peabody Coll. Tchrs., Nashville, 1964-75; dean Creative Arts Ctr., 1975-81; prof. music W.Va. U., Morgantown, 1975-96; ret., 1997. Vis. prof. U. Federal do Espiritu Santo, Vitoria, Brazil, 1999-2000; adj. prof. Brookhaven Coll., Dallas, 2002-. Author: Principles and Practice of Electronic Music, 1974, Eighteenth Century Counterpoint, 1993, Sixteenth Century Counterpoint, 1994; past mem. editorial bd. Music Educators Jour.; composer orchestral music, chamber and electronic music. With USAF, 1953-57. Personal E-mail: htrythal@yahoo.com.

TRYTTEN, DEBORAH ANNE, computer scientist, educator; b. Ann Arbor, Mich., Apr. 14, 1960; d. Richard Wesley and Marilyn McCall Trytten. MS in Applied Math., Mich. State U., 1984, MS in Computer Sci., 1988, PhD in Computer Sci., 1992. Asst. prof. U. Okla., Norman, 1992—98, assoc. prof., 1998—; pres., founder, chief tech. officer Beyond Paper, Inc., Norman, 2001—02. Achievements include patents pending for electronic textbook format. Office: U Okla 200 Felgar Rm 144B Norman OK 73019

TRZASKO, JOSEPH ANTHONY, psychologist, educator; b. Jamaica, NY, June 4, 1946; s. Joseph Anthony and Lottie Marion (Nadraus) T.; m. Ann Elizabeth Kidd, June 26, 1971; 1 son, Joshua Damon. BA cum laude, U. N.H., 1967; MA, U. Vt., 1969, PhD, 1972. Cert. behavioral therapy, 1976, psychologist 1977; fellow Am. Bd. Psychol. Specialties, 1997, Am. Bd. Forensic Examiners, 1998; cert. profl. qualification in psychology Assn. State and Provincial Psychology Bds. Prof. dep. psychology Mercy Coll., Dobbs Ferry, N.Y., 1969—; postdoctoral internship Ridge State Home and Tng. Sch., Colo. Dept. Insts., 1980; staff psychologist St. Dominic's Intermediate Care Facility for Devel. Disabled, Blauvelt, N.Y., 1980—; cons. psychologist Jewish Guild for Blind, NYC, 1983—2002, Orange County A.H.R.C., Newburgh, N.Y., 1985—, Opengate Inc., Somers, NY, 2006—; pvt. practice clin. psychology. Chair ednl. psychology test devel. Ednl. Testing Svc., 2000—04; neuro-forensic psychologist Supervised Life Styles Behavioral Health Clinic, 2002—. Contbg. author: Working with Visually Impaired Young Children: A Curriculum Guide for Birth -3 Year Olds, 1992; contbg. author: Working with Visually Impaired Young Students: A Curriculum Guide for 3 to 5 Year Olds, 1998. NDEA fellow U. Vt., 1967-69; NSF faculty rsch. participation grantee Ednl. Commn. States/Nat. Assessment Ednl. Progress, 1976. Mem. AAUP, APA, Am. Coll. Forensic Examiners. Roman Catholic. Home and Office: 30 Lake Dr Somers NY 10589-2420 Office Phone: 914-277-1743. Personal E-mail: jatphd@optonline.net. Business E-Mail: jtrzasko@mercy.edu.

TRZYNA, CHRIS, physical education educator; b. Chgo. d. Edward and Helen Trzyna. BS, No. Ill. U., 1976, MS, 1983, C.A.S. in Adminstrn. and Supervision, 1991. Cert. tchr. Ill. Tchr., asst. athletic dir. Libertyville HS, 1976—; girls volleyball coach Libertyville HS, 1987—2005. Recipient Volleyball Coach of Yr., Libertyville H.S., 2000, 2005. Mem.: AAHPERD, Ill. Athletic Dirs. Assn., Ill. High Sch. Assn. (soccer adv. com.), Ill. Assn. Health, Phys. Edn. Recreation and Dance, Delta Psi Kappa (v.p. 1975—76). Office: Libertyville High School 708 W Park Ave Libertyville IL 60048-2604 Business E-Mail: chris.trzyna@district128.org.

TSACOUMIS, STEPHANIE, lawyer; b. Aug. 31, 1956; BA magna cum laude, Coll. of William & Mary, 1978; JD, Univ. Va., 1981. Bar: DC 1981, Md. 1982. Of counsel Morrison & Foerster, Washington, 1988—91, ptnr., 1991—96; of counsel, corp. fin. Gibson Dunn & Crutcher LLP, Washington, 1996—2000, ptnr. corp. transactions and securities, 2000—, and co-ptnr.-in-charge DC office. Adj. faculty Georgetown Univ. Law Ctr., 2001—. Sr. editor Va. Jour. of Internat. Law, contributing author Corporate Communications and the Federal Antifraud Rules, 1992, Securities in the Electronic Age, 2001. Mem.: ABA, Md. State Bar Assn., DC Bar, Phi Beta Kappa. Office: Gibson Dunn & Crutcher LLP 1050 Connecticut Ave NW Washington DC 20036 Office Phone: 202-955-8277. Office Fax: 202-530-9613. Business E-Mail: stsacoumis@gibsondunn.com.

TSAI, JAMES C., ophthalmologist, researcher; BA in Neurosci., Amherst Coll., 1985; MD, Stanford U., 1989; MBA, Vanderbilt U., 1998. Diplomate Am. Bd. Ophthalmology, Nat. Bd. Med. Examiners. Intern Cedars-Sinai Med. Ctr., LA, 1989—90; resident in ophthalmology U. So. Calif./Doheny Eye Inst., LA, 1990—93; fellow Bascom Palmer Eye Inst., Miami, Fla., 1993—94, Moorfields Eye Hosp., London, 1994—95; asst. prof. ophthalmology and visual scis. Vanderbilt U. Sch. Medicine, Nashville, 1995—2001; dir. glaucoma divsn., assoc. prof. ophthalmology Harkness Eye Inst., Columbia U. Coll. Physicians and Surgeons, NYC, 2001—06; Robert Young prof., chair dept. opthalmology and visual sci. Yale U. Sch. Medicine, New Haven, 2006—. Homer McK. Rees Glaucoma scholar, Columbia U., 2001—04. Fellow: ACS, Am. Acad. Ophthalmology (Achievement award). Office: Yale Eye Ctr PO Box 208061 New Haven CT 06520-8061 Office Phone: 203-785-2020, 203-785-7233. Office Fax: 203-785-7694. Business E-Mail: james.tsai@yale.edu.

TSAI, JOHN JENGSHYONG, publishing executive; b. Taiwan, Sept. 9, 1942; BS in Physics and Chem., Nat. Taiwan Normal U., 1965; MS in Physics, Coll. of William and Mary, Va., 1970; PhD in Ocean Physics, U. Miami, 1977; MBA, Fla. Internat. U., 1987. Rsch. physicist, ocean acoustics div. Atlantic Oceanographic and Meteorological Lab., 1977—2001; founder, pres. Integrated Tech. Internat., Inc., 1986—90; publisher, chief editor Overseas Chinese News, 1990—. Bd. mem. Atlantic Inst. of Oriental Medicine, Ft. Lauderdale, Fla. Mem. Chinese Federation of Fla., exec. sec., 1994—95, v.p., 1996—97, pres., 1998—99. Mem.: Chinese Am. Press Inst. (pres.), Asian Am. Journalists Assn., Am. Geophysical Union, Acoustical Soc. of Am. Office: Overseas Chinese News 8100 SW 92 Ct Miami FL 33173

TSAI, LI-HUEI, pathologist, researcher; b. Taipei, Taiwan, Mar. 18, 1960; m. Lonarto Liong; 1 child, Jessica Liong. PhD, U. Tex. Southwestern, Dallas, 1990. Asst. prof. pathology Harvard Med. Sch., Cambridge, Mass., 1994—99, assoc. prof., 1999—2002, prof., 2002—06, asst. investigator pathology, 1997—2002; prof. Picower Ctr. Learning and Memory MIT, Cambridge, 2006—, assoc. mem. Broad Inst., 2006—; investigator RIKEN-MIT Neuroscience, Cambridge, 2006—, Howard Hughes Med. Inst., Cambridge, 2006—. Contbr. articles to profl. jours. Mem.: Soc. Neuroscience (assoc.). Office: 77 Massachusetts Ave 46-4235a Cambridge MA 02139 Home Phone: 617-324-1660; Office Phone: 617 324 1660. Office Fax: 617 324 1657; Home Fax: 617-324-1657. Business E-Mail: lhtsai@mit.edu. *

TSAI, MING, chef; b. Dayton, OH; m. Polly Tsai. ME, Yale U.; attended, Le Cordon Bleu cooking school, Paris; M in Hotel Adminstrn. and Hospitality Mktg., Cornell U. Co-owner, exec. chef Blue Ginger, Boston, 1998—. Founding mem. Chefs For Humanity, 2005—; ptnr. Blue Ginger line, Target, 2000—. Host East Meets West, Food Network, 1998 (Emmy award, 1998), Ming's Quest, Fine Living Network, host, exec. prodr. Simply Ming, Pub. TV, celebrity judge Cooking Under Fire, PBS, 2005—; author: Blue Ginger: East Meets West Cooking with Ming Tsai (Named One of 25 Best Cookbooks, Food and Wine Mag., 1999), Simply Ming, 2003, Ming's Master Recipes, 2004. Recipient Chef of Yr., Esquire Mag., 1998, Best Chef Northeast, James Beard Found., 2002, Restaurateur of Yr., Mass. Restaurant Assoc., 2005. Achievements include development of O Water, 2005-. Office: Blue Ginger 583 Wasington St Wellesley MA 02482 *

TSAI, TOM CHUNGHU, chemical engineer; b. Kaohsiung, Taiwan, Oct. 24, 1948; arrived in U.S., 1971, naturalized, 1984; s. Shu and Kwei (Kao) T.; m. Joyce Chionhwa Pai, Dec. 17, 1974; children: Wayne, Jimmy Payne. BS in Chem. Engring., Nat. Taiwan U., Taipei, 1970; MS in Chem. Engring., Purdue U., 1973, PhD in Chem. Engring., 1975. Registered profl. engr., Tex. Sr. process engr. CE-Lummus Co., Bloomfield, NJ, 1975-80; sr. engr. Bechtel Petroleum Inc., Houston, 1980-83; cons. engr. TDS Assocs., Houston, 1983-88; process engring. assoc. Dow Chem. Co., Freeport, Tex., 1988—. Internat. adv. bd. Ency. Chem. Processing and Design, 1995—. Co-author, contbr.: Ethylene-Keystone to the Petrochemical Industry, 1980, Kirk-Othmer Encyclopedia of Chemical Technology, 1980, Pyrolysis: Theory and Industrial Practice, 1983, Refining & Petrochemical Tech Yearbook, 1987, Encyclopedia of Chemical Processing and Design, 1990, 94-96, 2005, 06, Unit Operations Handbook, 1992; contbr. articles to profl. jours. Bd. dirs. H.S. for Performing and Visual Arts PTO, Houston, 1993-95. 2d lt. Republic of China Army, 1970-71. Mem.: AIChE, Assn. Chinese Orgns. (Houston) (pres. 2003), Assn. Chinese Am. Profls. (divsn. chmn. 1988—89, v.p. 2000—01, pres.-elect 2001—02, pres. 2002—03), Taiwan Chorus of Houston (pres. 2005—06). Achievements include patents in field. Office: The Dow Chem Co 400 W Sam Houston Pkwy S Houston TX 77042-1299 Home Phone: 281-870-9256; Office Phone: 713-978-2324. E-mail: tomctsai@dow.com.

TSAI, WEN-YING, sculptor, painter, engineer; b. Xiamen, Fujian, China, Oct. 13, 1928; came to U.S., 1950, naturalized, 1962; s. Chen-Dak and Ching-Miau (Chen) T.; m. Pei-De Chang, Aug. 7, 1968; children: Lun-Yi and Ming Yi (twins). Student, Ta Tung U., 1947-49; BSME, U. Mich., 1953; postgrad., Art Students League N.Y., 1953-57, Faculty Polit. and Social Sci., New Sch., 1956-58. Cons. engr., 1953-63; project mgr. Cosentini Assocs., 1962-63; project engr. Guy B. Panero, Engrs., 1956-60. Creator cybernetic sculpture based on prin. harmonic motion, stroboscopic effects; one-man shows include, Ruth Sherman Gallery, N.Y.C., 1961, Amel Gallery, N.Y.C., 1964, 65, Howard Wise Gallery, N.Y.C., 1968, Kaiser Wilhelm Mus. Haus Lange, Krefeld, Germany, 1970, Hayden Gallery of MIT, Cambridge, Ont. Sci. Centre, Toronto, Can., 1971, Corcoran Gallery Art, 1972, Denise René Gallery, 1972, 73, Musée d'Art Contemporain, Montreal, 1973, Museo de Arte Contemporáneo, Caracas, 1975, Wildenstein Art Center, Houston, 1978, Museo de Bellas Artes, Caracas, 1978, Hong Kong Mus. Art, 1979, Isetan Mus. Art, Tokyo, 1980, Galerie Denise René, Paris, 1983, Nat. Mus. History, Taipei, Taiwan, 1989, Taiwan Mus. of Art, Taichung, 1990, China Nat. Mus. Fine Arts, Beijing, 1997, Centre Georges Pompidou, 2001; one man show: Galerie Denise René, Paris, 2000, Shanghai Art Mus., 2002; represented maj. internat. exhbns., also numerous group exhbns., in permanent collections, Centre Georges Pompidou, Paris; Tate Gallery, London, Albright-Knox Gallery, Buffalo Mus., Addison Gallery Am. Art, Andover, Mass., Museo de Arte Contemporáneo, Caracas, Museo de Bellas Artes, Caracas, Whitney Mus., Chrysler Art Mus., Orlando Sci. Ctr., MIT, Hayden Gallery, Kaiser Wilhelm Mus., Mus. Modern Art, Israel Mus., Jerusalem, Artware, Kunst und Elektronik, Honnover-Messe, Great Exploration-The Hands on Mus., Taiwan Mus. Art, Saibu Gas Mus., Nagoya City Mus., Mus. fü Holographie, Kanagawa Sci. Pk., Hong Kong Sci. Mus., others; commd. works include: fountain at Land Mark, Hong Kong, 1980,, water sculpture at Shell Tower, Singapore, 1982, cybernetic upward falling fountains (2), Paris; creator spatial dynamic hydro-cybernetic systems for 42d Internat. Exhbn. Art-La Biennale di Venezia, 1986, Digital Visions-Computers and Art, Everson Mus. of Art, 1987, Contemporary Arts Ctr. Cin., 1987, IBM Gallery of Sci. and Art, N.Y.C., 1988, Phenomena Art Expo, Fukuoka, Japan, 1989, Wonderland of Sci.-Art Kanagawa Internat. Art Sci. Exhbn., Kawasaki, Japan, 1989, Vienna Messe-Wiener Festwochen, 1989, Kanagawa Internat. Art & Sci. Exhbn., Kawasaki, Japan, 1989, Artec 91, Internat. Biennale in Nagoya, Japan, 1991 (Artec Grand Prix winner), Homage à Denise Rene-Cybernetic Arts, Musée Nat. d'art Modern Ctr. Georges Pompidon, 2001, Shanghai Internat. Biennale for Contemporary Arts, Shanghai Art Mus., 2004; developed concept "5 elements," proposal for new modern sculpture park for Oriental Plz., Beijing, 1996-98; creator first CD-ROM version of cybernetic sculpture, 1995, Info-Art Kwang Ju Internat. Biennale Korea, Osaka Triennale, 1995—, Internet Graphics Gallery, 1995; featured: Art for Tomorrow-The 21st Century, CBS-TV, 1969, Video Variation, WGBH-TV, 1971, Science and Art, Japan TV Man Union, 1982, Art and Sci.-Innovation, Sta. WNET-TV, 1988, The World of Wen-Ying Tsai, Taiwan Pub. TV, 1991. Recipient Soc. Merit award U. Mich., 2001; John Hay Whitney fellow, 1963, MacDowell fellow, 1965, fellow Center Advanced Visual Studies, MIT, 1969, 70. Inventor upward falling fountain, computer mural, multiple light computer array, utilizing environ. feedback control system.

TSAKALIS, KONSTANTINOS, electrical engineer, educator; PhD, U. So. Calif., LA, Calif., 1988. From asst. prof. to rof. Ariz. State U., Tempe, Ariz., 1988—2003, prof., 2003—. Author: Linear Time-Varying Systems: Control and Adaptation; contbr. articles to profl. jours. Mem.: IEEE. Achievements include patents for temperature control system for a thermal reactor and run-to-run controllers for applications in semiconductor manufacturing. Office: Arizona State University PO Box 875706 Tempe AZ 85287-5706 Home Phone: 480-786-6317; Office Phone: 480-965-1467. Personal E-mail: tsakalis@asu.edu. Business E-Mail: tsakalis@asu.eddu.

TSALIKIAN, EVA, physician, educator; b. Piraeus, Greece, June 22, 1949; came to U.S., 1974; d. Vartan and Arousiak (Kasparian) T.; m. Arthur Bonfield, Apr. 8, 2000. MD, U. Athens, 1973. Rsch. fellow U. Calif., San Francisco, 1974-76; resident in pediats. Children's Hosp., Pitts., 1976-78, fellow in endocrinology, 1978-80; rsch. fellow Mayo Clinic, Rochester, Minn., 1980-83; from asst. prof. to prof. dept. pediats. U. Iowa, 1983—2004, dir. pediat. endocrinology hosps. and clinics, 1988—, prof. pediats., 2004—, interim chmn. dept. pediatrics, 2004, vice chmn. clin. affairs Dept. Pediats., 2005—; chief staff hosp. U. Iowa Health Ctr., 2006—. Recipient Young Physician award, AMA, 1977; fellow, Juvenile Diabetes Found., 1978—80, Heinz Nutrition Found., 1980—81. Mem. Am. Diabetes Assn. (bd. dirs. Mid-Am. sect.), Endocrine Soc., Soc. Pediat. Rsch., Am. Pediat. Soc., Lawson Wilkins Soc. for Pediat. Endocrinology, Internat. Soc. Pediat. and Adolescent Diabetes, Midwest Pediat. Endocrino Soc. (pres. 1996-99). Home: 206 Mahaska Dr Iowa City IA 52246-1606 Office: U Iowa Dept Pediatrics 2856 JPP Iowa City IA 52242

TSAO, JENNIE CHING-I, research scientist, educator; d. Jean Huang and James Chih-Ming Tsao; m. Aram Dobalian, June 2, 2002. BA, UCLA, 1981, PhD, 1999; BS, City U., London, Eng., 1994. Cert. clin. psychology Fla. Rsch. asst. City U., London, 1994—94; grad. therapist UCLA Psychology Clinic, 1995—96; project collaborator UCLA Anxiety Disorders Behavioral Program, 1995—97, sr. therapist and assessor, 1996—98, project dir., 1996—99; supr. Cmty. Outreach Prevention and Edn. Svc., UCLA Sch. of Medicine, 1997—98; post-doctoral rsch. coord. UCLA Pediatric Pain Program, Sch. of Medicine, 1999—2000, asst. rsch. psychologist, 2000—01; rsch. asst. prof. NIMH Ctr. for the Study of Emotion and Attention, U. Fla., Gainesville, 2001—03, Nat. Rural Behavioral Health Ctr., U. Fla., Gainesville, 2002—04; rsch. scientist UCLA Pediatric Pain Program, Sch. Medicine, LA, 2004—. Clin. supr. Fanning Springs Primary Care Clinic, Nat. Rural Behavioral Health Program, U. Fla., 2002—04, Nat. Rural Behavioral Health Program, Gainesville, 2002—04, Fear & Anxiety Disorders Clinic, U. Fla., Gainesville, 2001—04; peer reviewer Jour. Abnormal Psychology, 2000—, Health Psychology, 2000—01, Jour. of Pediatric Psychology, 2000—, Psychosomatic Medicine, 2000—, Behavior Rsch. and Therapy, 2000—. Jour. of Pain and Symptom Mgmt., 2000—, Jour. Cons. and Clin. Psychol., 2004—. Sr. sect. editor: Cognitive and Behavioral Practice, 2004—, assoc. editor: Jour. Pediatric Psychology, Spl. Issue: Pain, 2004—; contbr. chapters to books, articles to profl. jours. Recipient Social Sci. prize, KPMG, 1993, Young Investigators Travel award, Am. Pain Soc., 2001, 2003—04; fellow, UCLA Dept. Psychology, 1994—95; grantee, 1995, 1995—97, Nat. Insts. Mental Health, 1996—98, UCLA Dept. Psychology, 1997, Health Resources and Svcs. Adminstrn., 2003—04, Aty. Healthcare Rsch. and Quality, 2003—, Nat. Inst. Drug Abuse, 2004—; Regents scholar, UCLA Coll. Letters and Sci., 1978—81. Mem.: Anxiety Disorders Assn. Am. (Career Devel. Travel award 2003), Am. Pain Soc., Am. Assn. for the Advancement of Behavior Therapy, Phi Beta Kappa. Achievements include Professional Appearance on ABC's 20/20 segment entitled, Don't Panic; Professional Appearance on NBC's Dateline segment entitled, Butterflies are Free; Professional Appearance on Canadian Broadcasting Corporation program The Nature of Things. Office: UCLA Pediatric Pain Rsch Program 10940 Wilshire Blvd Ste 1450 Los Angeles CA 90024 Office Phone: 310-824-7667. Business E-Mail: jtsao@mednet.ucla.edu.

TSAO, VIVIAN J., artist, educator; arrived in US, 1974, naturalized; d. Sheng Fen and Wendy (Hsiung) Tsao; m. Raymond Clyde Coreil, June 5, 1976. BA, Nat. Taiwan Normal U., 1973; MFA Painting, Carnegie Mellon U., Pitts., 1976. Art instr. Nat. Taipei Tchrs. Coll., 1972—74; corr. in US Hsiung Shih Art Monthly, Taiwan, 1980—96; artist Ceres Gallery, NYC, 1984—; artist in residence Asian Am. Arts Ctr., NYC, 1985—86; adj. asst. prof. fine arts Pace U., NYC, 1990—; artist Biddington's Internet Gallery, NYC, 2000—; art commentator in US United Daily News (Chinese), Taiwan, 2003—. Artist presenter on panel China Inst. Gallery, NYC, 1989; program auditor (art reviewer) N. Y. State Coun. Arts, NYC, 1990—96, mem. jury panel, 1996—99. Author: (Chinese) The Mark of Time: Dialogues with Vivian Tsao on Art in New York, 2003, (essays) Boy on the Rocking Horse: An Introduction to the Art and Life of Eugene Speicher, 2005; exhibitions include Pastel Soc. Am., Butler Inst. Am. Art, Ohio, 2003, Nat Arts Club, NYC, 2003, Am. Acad. Arts and Letters, Bklyn. Mus., Butler Inst. Am. Art, Ohio, Ceres Gallery, NYC, 2005, others, paintings pub. in book 100 New York Painters, 2006. Sponsor student presentations Dyson Coll., Soc. Fellows, Pace U., 1994, 1995, 2000; interpreter internat. symposium Met. Mus. Art, NYC, 1985; judge Employees Art Show N.Y. State Supreme Ct., 1995. Scholarship grantee, Carnegie Mellon U., Pitts., 1975, artist in residence grantee, N.Y. State Coun. Arts. Asian Am. Arts Ctr., 1985—86. Fellow: Soc. Fellows Dyson Coll., Pace U.; mem.: Coll. Art Assn. Am., Pastel Soc. Am. (Cert. Merit 1981). Avocations: films, music, seashell collecting. Home: 17 Fuller Pl Brooklyn NY 11215-6006 Office: Pace U Dept Fine Arts 41 Park Row New York NY 10038 Personal E-mail: viviantsao@earthlink.net.

TSCHERNISCH, SERGEI P., academic administrator; BA, San Francisco State U.; MFA in Theatre, Stanford U.; student, San Francisco Actors' Workshop, Stanford Repertory Theatre. Founding mem. Calif. Inst. of Arts, 1969, mem. faculty, assoc. dean Sch. Theatre, dir., 1969-80; prof. dept. theatre U. Md., College Park, 1980-82; dir. divsn. performing and visual arts Northeastern U., Boston, 1982-92; dean Coll. of Comm. and Fine Arts Loyola Marymount U., LA, 1992-94; pres. Cornish Coll. of Arts, Seattle, 1994—. Advisor NEA; mem. com. USIA; cons. to many festivals. Office: Cornish College of the Arts 1000 Lenora St Seattle WA 98121-2718 Office Phone: 206-726-5001. E-mail: stschernisch@cornish.edu. *

TSCHERNY, GEORGE, graphics designer; b. Budapest, Hungary, July 12, 1924; s. Mendel and Bella (Heimann) T.; m. Sonia Katz, July 7, 1950; children: Nadia, Carla Student, Pratt Inst., Bklyn., 1947-50. Staff designer Donald Deskey & Assocs., NYC, 1950-53; designer, assoc. George Nelson & Assocs., NYC, 1953-55; pres. George Tscherny, Inc., NYC, 1955—. Instr. Pratt Inst., Bklyn., 1956, bd. advisors, 1979; instr. Sch. Visual Arts, NYC, 1955-64; curriculum cons. Phila. Coll. Art, 1967; Mellon vis. prof. Cooper Union, NY, 1978 Exhibitions include Visual Art Mus., NYC, 1992, La Galerie Blanche, Briey, France, 2007; exhibited in group shows, Germany, 1962-67, Italy, 1974, US, 1975; represented in permanent collections Mus. Modern Art, NYC, Cooper Hewitt Mus., NYC, Libr. of Congress, Washington, Bibliotheque Nat. France, Paris, Kunstgewerbeschule der Stadt Zurich, Graphic Design Archive at Rochester Inst. Tech.; monograph of work George Tscherny, Minimum Means, Maximum Meaning, 2004; author: Changing Faces, 2004. Contbr. design svcs. to UN Assn., Sta. WNET Pub. TV, Am. Lung Assn., Peace Corps, Cystic Fibrosis Found., L.I. State Park Commn. With U.S. Army, 1943-46, ETO. Recipient numerous awards, Am. Inst. Graphic Arts medal, 1988, Art Dirs. Club N.Y. (hall of fame 1997), N.Y. Type Dirs. Club, Silver medal Warsaw Biennale, 1976; inducted into Art Dirs. Club Hall of Fame, 1997. Mem. Am. Inst. Graphic Arts (pres. 1966-68), Alliance Graphique Internat. Office: 238 E 72nd St New York NY 10021-4503 Office Phone: 212-734-3277. Personal E-mail: gtscherny@aol.com.

TSCHETTER, RONALD ALLEN, federal agency administrator; b. Huron, SD, Oct. 4, 1941; m. Nancy Tschetter; 2 children. BA in Psychology and Social Studies, Bethel Coll. Joined Blyth Eastman Dillon Union Securities, 1970, Dain Rauscher, 1973, pres. pvt. client group, 1991—2001; pres. D.A. Davidson & Co., Great Falls, Mont., 2004—06; dir. Peace Corps, Washington, 2006—. Bd. dirs. D.A. Davidson & Co., 2004—06, Community Bank of Plymouth; mem. Nat. Peace Corps Assn., 1993—99, chmn., 1995—98, hon. mem., 2000—03. Vol. cmty. health worker Peace Corps, India, 1966—68. Avocations: hunting, fishing, woodworking. Office: Peace Corps Paul D Coverdell Peace Corps Headquarter 1111 20th St NW Washington DC 20526 *

TSE, CHARLES YUNG CHANG, pharmaceutical executive, lawyer; b. Shanghai, Mar. 22, 1926; s. Kung Chao and Say Ying (Chen) T.; m. Vivian Chang, Apr. 25, 1955; 1 dau., Roberta. BA in Econs, St. John's U., Shanghai, 1949; MS in Acctg, U. Ill., 1950; JD, N.Y. Law Sch., 1990. Asst. to controller Am. Internat. Group, NYC, 1950-54, asst. mgr. Singapore-Malaysia, 1955-57; with Warner-Lambert Co., Morris Plains, NJ, 1957-86, area mgr. S.E. Asia, 1966-68, regional dir. S.E. Asia, 1968-69, v.p. Australasia, 1970-71, pres. Western Hemisphere Group, 1971-72, pres. Pan Am. Mgmt. Center, 1972-76, pres. European Mgmt. Center, 1976-78, pres. Internat. Group, 1979-86, sr. v.p. corp., 1980-83, exec. v.p. corp., 1984-85, vice chmn., 1985-86. Dir. Foster Wheeler Corp., Livingston, N.J., 1984-98, Superior Telecom., Inc., 1996—, Com. of 100; mem. faculty bus. adminstrn. dept. Fairleigh Dickinson U., 1961-64; pres. Cancer Rsch. Inst., Inc., N.Y.C., 1991-92. Bd. visitors CCNY, 1974-78; trustee Morristown Meml. Hosp. (N.J.), 1982-86; bd. dirs. Bus. Council for Internat. Understanding, 1984-87. Mem. NAM (dir. 1984-86), Assn. of the Bar of the City of N.Y. (mem. Asian affairs com. 1991-2001). Office: 300 Park Ave Fl 17 New York NY 10022-7402

TSE, EDMUND SZE-WING, insurance company executive; b. Hong Kong, Jan. 2, 1938; m. Peggy Pik-Kin Wai, Dec. 18, 1965; children: Ada Koon-Hang, Elaine Koon-Ming. BA in Math., U. Hong Kong, 1960, DSS (hon.), 2002; diploma mktg. mgmt. program, Stanford U., 1980. Dep. gen. mgr. Nan Shan Life Ins. Co., Ltd., Taipei, Taiwan, 1970—74, pres., mng. dir., 1975—, chmn., 1990, hon. chmn., 2003—; various positions Am. Internat. Assurance Co., Ltd., Hong Kong, 1961—70, dir., 1983, chmn., CEO, 2000—; dir. Am. Internat. Group, Inc., 1996—, sr. vice chmn., 2001—. Mng. dir. Nan Shan Life Ins. Co. Ltd., 1975, chmn., 2004; nat. and area chmn. Pacific Ins. Conf. Hong Kong, ', 1985—; dir. Am. Internat. Assurance Co. (Hong Kong), Ltd., 1983, chmn., CEO, 2000; dir. UGC Holdings Ltd., British Virgin Islands, 1994, Shanghai Jin Jiang-Universal Devel. Co. Ltd., China, 1994, Am. Internat. Group, Inc., 1996, sr. vice chmn., 2001; dir. Am. Internat. Assurance Co. (Australia) Ltd., 1985, chmn., 97; dir. AIG Global Investment Corp. (Asia) Ltd., Bermuda, 1996, AIG Global Investment Corp. (Hong Kong) Ltd., 1999, Underwriters Adjustment Co., Inc., Panama, 1997, Project Hope Hong Kong Found. Ltd., 2000—, Am. Internat. Assurance Co. (Bermuda) Ltd., 1983, pres., 92; dir., pres. AIA Found., Hong Kong, 1995—, Tri Star Enterprises Ltd., Bermuda, 2002; dir., chmn. AIA Fin. Svcs. Ltd. (formerly known as Superannuation Co. Ltd.), Australia, 1986—97; dir., chmn. bd. Am. Internat. Assurance Co. (Vietnam) Ltd., 2000; dir., vice-chmn. Philippine Am. Life and Gen. Ins. Co., 1991, Am. Life Ins. Co., Wilmington, Del., United States, 1992; non-exec. dir. PICC Property and Casualty Co. Ltd., China, 2004; pres. Komisaris P.T. Asuransi AIA Indonesia, 1997; chmn. bd. suprs. Dana Pensuin Lembaga Keuangan AIA Indonesia, 1997; v.p. commr. P.T. AIG Life (formerly known as P.T. Asuransi AIG Lippo Life), Indonesia, 1999. Gov.'s advisor Internat. Consultative Conf. on the Future Econ. Devel. of Guandong Province, 2005; chmn. stats. and info. subcom. Ins. Coun. Hong Kong, 1984—88; nat. and area chmn. Hong Kong Pacific Ins. Conf., 1985—; dep. chmn. Gen. Ins. Coun., 1988—89, chmn., 1989—90; mem. Hong Kong Govt.'s Ins. Adv. Com., 1988—96, Working Com. on Reinsurance and Captive Ins., 1996—98, Hong Kong Ins. Industry Coalition, 1996—98, Hong Kong Forum, 1998—, Internat. Consultative Forum Mayor of Tianjin, China, 2006—; mem. election sub-com. Hong Kong Fedn. Insurers, 1990—92, trustee ednl. trust, 1990—93, dep. chmn., 1991—92, chmn., 1992—93; exec. com. mem. Bus. and Profls. Fedn. Hong Kong, Hong Kong, 1994—; mem. bd. dirs. Life Ins. Mktg. and Rsch. Assn. (LIMRA), 1994—97; mem. selection com. election of HKSAR Chief Exec. and Provisional Legislature, 1996; mem. election com. HKSAR Legis. Coun. election, 1998, 2000; mem. adv. bd. Mandatory Provident Fund, 1996—98; mem. adv. bd. BSc in Actuarial Sci. program. Dept. Stats. and Actuarial Sci. U. Hong Kong, 1998—2006, hon. v.p. alumni assn., 2003—06; mem. exec. com. China Overseas Friendship Assn., 1997—; chmn. Asia adv. bd. Project HOPE, USA, 1997—99; mem. Hong Kong com. Pacific Basin Econ. Coun., 1998—; mem. career devel. bd. Chinese U. Hong Kong, 1998—2000, 2000—02, 2002—06; founding mem. Hong Kong chpt. World Presidents' Orgn., 2002—; mem. bd. trustees Fudan U., China, 2003—07, mem. coun. edn. devel. found., 2004; patron Soc. Registered Fin. Planners Ltd., 2003—; mem. adv. coun. Asia Soc. Hong Kong Ctr., 2004; gov.'s econ. advisor Internat. Consultative Conf. Future Econ. Devel. Guangdong Province, 2005. Named to Ins. Hall of Fame, 2003; recipient Disting. Businessman Yr., Taiwan, 1997, Gold Bauhinia Star (GBS), Hong Kong Spl. Adminstrv. Region, 2001; Hon. fellow, U. Hong Kong, 1998. Home: 10C Headland Rd Repulse Bay Hong Kong Office: 35/F AIG Tower 1 Connaught Rd Ctrl Hong Kong Hong Kong Office Fax: 852-2572-4695.

TSE, MARIAN A., lawyer; AB, Vassar Coll., 1976; JD, Columbia U., 1979. Bar: Mass. 1979. Ptnr., chair, ERISA/employment benefits practice Goodwin Procter LLP, Boston, mem., diversity com. Bd. dir. Greater Boston Legal Services. Mem.: ABA, Asian Am. Lawyers Assn. Mass., New England Employee Benefits Coun., Boston Bar Assn. Office: Goodwin Procter LLP Exchange Pl 53 State St Boston MA 02109 Office Phone: 617-570-1169. Office Fax: 617-523-1231. Business E-Mail: mtse@goodwinprocter.com.

TSE, PHILIP KUI, airport engineering maintenance consultant; b. Guangzhou, China, May 15, 1934; arrived in Can., 1994; s. Wai-Woon and Yok-Wun (Leung) T.; m. Helen Chow, Jan. 22, 1960; children: Christina Suyen, Elsie Ba-Sai, Tony Yee-Hin, Vanilla Hung. BSc in Archtl. Engring., Union Coll., 1963; postgrad. cert. in strategic planning and mgmt., Calif. State U., Fresno, 1989; postgrad. cert. in project mgmt., Tongji U., Shanghai, 1994. Registered profl. civil engr., Hong Kong; chartered water and environ. mgr., U.K.; chartered environmentalist, U.K. Various positions Public Works Dept., Hong Kong Govt., 1956-71; foreman engring. draughtsman class I, engr.-in-tng., asst. engr. drainage works, roads and drainage office, roads and hwys. new territories region PWD, Hong Kong, 1971-75, asst. engr. develop. and airport divsn., 1975-83, engr. devel. sect., devel. and airport divsn., 1983-88; project engr. airport maintenance, devel. and airport divsn. Engring. Devel. Dept., Civil Engring. Svcs. Dept., Hong Kong, 1988-93; sr. airport engr. Hong Kong Internat. Airport Civil Engring. Svcs. Dept., Civil Engring. Dept., 1993-95; airport diagnostic engring., environ. mgmt. cons., 1963-68. Lectr. Hong Kong Tech. Coll. (now Hong Kong Poly. U.), 1968—; hon. constrn. and devel. cons., adv. bd. Shun Shin Chee Kit Yin Koon Charity Orgn., Hong Kong, 1968—. Fellow ASCE (life); mem. Hong Kong Instn. Engrs., Instn. Pub. Health Engrs. (U.K.), Chartered Instn. Water and Environ. Mgmt. (U.K.). Avocations: hiking, swimming, calligraphy, reading, drawing. Home: 913-89 Skymark Dr North York ON Canada M2H 3S6 Home Phone: 416-499-8592; Office Phone: 416-499-8592. Office Fax: 416-499-8592.

TSELEV, ALEXANDER, physicist, researcher; s. Yevgeniy Tselev and Ludmila Tseleva. MS in Radiophysics and Electronics, Nizhny Novgorod State U., Russia, 1991; PhD in Materials Sci., U. Tech. Dresden, Germany, 2000. Rsch. assoc. Georgetown U., Washington, 2003—06, Duke U., Durahm, NC, 2006—. Mem.: Am. Physics Soc. Achievements include research in development of crossed-beam pulsed laser deposition; establishment of dielectric properties of Ca-Cu-Ti-oxide thin films; experimental demonstration of the magnetic field induced band gap opening in metallic single-walled carbon nanotubes. Office: Duke U Dept Chemistry Box 90349 Durham NC 27708-0349 Office Phone: 919-660-1590. Business E-Mail: a.tselev@duke.edu.

TSENG, HOWARD SHIH CHANG, business educator, investment company executive, economics professor; b. Tainan, Taiwan, Jan. 14, 1935; came to U.S., 1963; s. Picheng and Chaoliu (Wang) T.; m. Evelina M. Young, Dec. 25, 1965; 1 child, Elaine Evelina. BA, Nat. Taiwan U., Taipei, 1957, MA, 1963; PhD, U. Okla., 1972. Chief economist Cooperative Bank Taiwan, Taipei, 1959-61; dir. tax services Bur. Taxation, Govt. Taiwan, Republic China, Taipei, 1961-63; instr. U. Okla., Norman, 1968; asst. prof. Ga. So. U., Statosboro, 1968-71; prof. bus. and econs. Catawba Coll., Salisbury, 1971—2001; adj. prof. San Francisco State U., 2002—, 2002—. Pres. Am. Prudential Investments, Salisbury, 1981-89; pres. Tsengs Investments, 1990—. Author: Investments, 1982; contbr. articles to profl. jours. Coordinator, supporter study mathematically precocious youth Johns Hopkins U., Balt., 1982—; ptnr. World Vision, Calif., 1986-92. Academic research grantee Academia Sinica, Taipei, 1962; Ford Found. fellow, Taipei, 1963. Mem. AAUP, Ea. Econ. Assn., Am. Econ. Assn., Am. Assn. Individual Investors, Taiwan Investment (organizer 1986—), Taiwanese-Am. Assn. Greater Charlotte (pres. 1994-96), Nat. Travel Club. Avocations: antiques, travel, reading. Office: Catawba Coll W Innes St Salisbury NC 28144 Office Fax: 704-637-5724. Personal E-mail: tsengstrading@yahoo.com.

TSENG, ROSE, academic administrator; BS, Kansas State U.; MS, U. Calif., Berkeley, PhD Nutrition. Registered dietician. Prof., chair, dir., assoc. dean San Jose State U., 1970—86, dean Coll. Applied Scis. and Arts, 1986—93; chancellor, CEO West Valley-Mission C.C., Calif., 1993—98; chancellor U. Hawaii-Hilo, 1998—. Office: U Hawaii-Hilo 200 W Kawili Hilo HI 96720-4091 *

TSIBULSKY, VLADIMIR LVOVICH, psychologist, researcher; b. Moscow, Apr. 19, 1951; arrived in U.S., 1993; s. Lev Nikolaevich Tsibulsky and Anna Sergeevna Subbotovich; m. Svetlana Olegovna Dmitrieva, Feb. 15, 2005; children: Cyril, Veronica, Anastasia, Alice. BS, Moscow State U., 1972, MS, PhD, Moscow State U., 1973. Rsch. scientist Severtsov Inst. Evolutionary Morphology and Ecology Animals, USSR Acad. of Sciences, Moscow, 1973—82; sr. rsch. scientist Lab. Neuropharmacology, Ctrl. Sci. Lab. of USSR Ministry of Health, Moscow, 1982—85, All-Union Sci. Ctr. Narcology USSR Ministry of Health, Moscow, 1985—90; vis. scientist Ctr. Studies Behavioral Neurobiology Concordia U., Montreal, Que., Canada, 1990—92; rsch. asst. prof. U. Cin., 1993—. Grantee, Nat. Inst. Drug Abuse, 2001—05; scholar, Nat. Heart, Lung, and Blood Inst., 1998—2001. Mem.: N.Y. Acad. Scis., Soc. Neuroscience, Pavlovian Physiol. Soc. Orthodox Christian. Achievements include patents for 1 (Silatranyl) Metyl Derivate Lactams possessing Neurotropic activity and the method to produce them. Avocations: travel, reading. Office: U Cin 231 Albert Sabin Way Mail Location 559 Cincinnati OH 45267-0559 Home Phone: 513-435-0869; Office Phone: 513-558-1740. Business E-Mail: vladimir.tsibulsky@uc.edu.

TSIEN, BILLIE, architect; b. Ithaca, NY, 1949; m. Tod Williams; 1 child. BFA, Yale U., New Haven, 1971; MArch, UCLA, 1977. Painter, tchr., 1971—75; tchr. So. Calif. Inst. Architecture, Parsons Sch. Design, NYC, Harvard U. Grad. Sch. Design, U. Tex., Austin; Jane and Bruce Graham co-chair U. Pa., 1998; Louis I. Kahn co-chair Yale U.; prin. Tod Williams Billie Tsien Archs., NYC, 1986—. Bd. mem. Pub. Art Fund, Archtl. League, Am. Acad. Rome. Prin. works include Neurosciences Inst., La Jolla, Calif. (NYC AIA Honor award, 1996, Engring. Excellence Platinum award, NY Assn. Consulting Engrs., 1997, AIA Nat. Honor award, 1997, Time Mag. Best of Design), Cranbrook Natatorium, Mich. (AIA Nat. Honor award, 2001), Am. Folk Art Mus., NYC (AIA Nat. Honor award, 2002, Arup World Architecture award, Best Bldg. in World, 2002, Engring. Excellence award, NY Assn. Consulting Engrs., 2003, NYC AIA Design award, 2003), LI Residence (NYC AIA Design award, 1999, Nat. AIA Honor awards, 2001), exhibitions include Quiet Light. Co-recipient Medal of Honor, NYC AIA, Chrysler award, Design Innovation, Cooper Hewitt Nat. Design award, Architecture, Pres.'s medal, Archtl. League. Fellow: Am. Acad. Arts & Scis.; mem.: Mcpl. Art Soc. (v.p.), AAAL (Brunner award (with Tod Williams) 1996). Office: Tod Williams Billie Tsien Archs 222 Central Park S New York NY 10019 Office Phone: 212-582-2385. E-mail: mail@twbta.com. *

TSIEN, RICHARD WINYU, biology professor; b. Tating, Kweichow, People's Republic China, Mar. 3, 1945; s. Hsue-Chu and Yi-Ying (Li) T.; m. Julia Shiang Aug. 29, 1971; children: Sara Shiang-Ming, Gregory Shiang-An, Alexa Tsien-Shiang. BS, MIT, 1965, MS, 1966; DPhil, Oxford U., Eng., 1970. Rsch. student Eaton Peabody Lab. Auditory, Physiology, Mass. Eye and Ear Infirmary, 1966; asst. prof. dept. physiology, Yale U. Sch. Medicine, New Haven, 1970-74, assoc. prof., 1974-79, prof., 1979-88; George D. Smith prof. molecular and cellular physiology Stanford (Calif.) U., 1988—, chmn. dept., 1988-94. Established investigator Am. Heart Assn., 1974-79. Author: Electric Current Flow in Excitable Cells, 1975. Recipient Otsuka award Internat. Soc. Heart Rsch., 1985; Rhodes Scholar, 1966; Weir Rsch. fellow, 1966-70 Univ. Coll., Oxford, 1966-70, lecturing fellow Balliol Coll., Oxford, 1969-70 Mem. Soc. Gen. Physiologists (pres. 1988), Biophys. Soc. (Kenneth S. Cole award 1985), Soc. for Neurosci. Democrat. Home: 866 Tolman Dr Palo Alto CA 94305-1026 Office: Stanford U Dept Molecular & Cellular Physiology 300 Pasteur Dr Palo Alto CA 94304-2203

TSIEN, ROGER YONCHIEN, chemist, cell biologist; b. NYC, Feb. 1, 1952; s. Hsue Chu and Yi Ying (Li) T.; m. Wendy M. Globe, July 30, 1982. AB in Chemistry and Physics summa cum laude, Harvard Coll., 1972; PhD in Physiology, U. Cambridge, 1977; PhD (hon.), Cath. U., Leuven, Belgium, 1995. Rsch. asst. U. Cambridge, Eng., 1975-78; asst. prof. Dept. Physiology-Anatomy U. Calif., Berkeley, 1981-85, assoc. prof., 1985-87, prof., 1987-89, prof. pharmacology, chemistry and biochemistry San Diego, 1989—; biological investigator Howard Hughes Med. Inst. Rsch. Lab, Calif., 1989—; co-found. Aurora Bioscis. Corp., 1994, Senomyx, Inc., 1998. T.Y. Shen vis. prof. Medicinal Chem., MIT, 1991, Todd vis. prof. Chem., U. Cambridge, 2003. Contbr. chpts. to books, articles to profl. jours. Recipient Herbert Sober Lectureship, Am. Soc. Biochemistry and Molecular Biology, 2000, Pearse Prize, Royal Microscopical Soc., 2000, Am. Chem. Soc. award for Creative Invention, 2002, Anfinsen award, Protein Soc., 2002, Dr. H.P. Heineken Prize for Biochemistry and Biophysics, 2002, Lamport prize NY Acad. Scis., 1986, Javits Neurosci. Investigator award Nat. Inst. Neurol. Disorders and Stroke, 1989, Young Scientist award Passano Found., 1991, W. Alden Spencer Neurobiology award Columbia U., 1991, Bowditch lectureship Am. Physiol. Soc., 1992, Gairdner Found. Internat. award, 1995, Artois-Baillet-Latour Health prize (Belgium), 1995, Basic Rsch. prize Am. Heart Assn., 1995, Faculty Rsch. lectureship U. Calif., San Diego, 1997, Faculty Rsch. Lectureship, Univ. Calif., San Diego, Acad. Senate, 1997, EG&G Wallac award for Innovation in High Throughput Screening Soc. for Biomolecular Screening, 1998, Max Delbrück medal, Max Delbrück Centrum für Molekulare Medizin, Berlin, 2002, Wolf prize in Medicine, Israel, 2004, Keio Med. Sci. Prize, 2004 Keio U., 2004, Assn. Biomolecular Resource Facilities award, 2006; Comyns Berkeley Rsch. fellow Gonville & Caius Coll., 1977-81; Marshall scholar British Govt., 1972-75, Searle scholar, 1983-86; Hugh Davson Disting. Lecturer, Am. Physiological Soc., 2003, Konrad Bloch Lectureship, Harvard U., 2003, Keith Porter Lectureship, Am. Soc. Cell Biology, 2003. Mem. Amer. Acad. Arts & Sciences, NAS, IOM, Phi Beta Kappa. Achievements: development and extensive biological application of molecules to measure and/or manipulate intracellular calcium, sodium, and hydrogen ions, cyclic adenosine-3', 5'-monophosphate, nitric oxide, inositol phosphates, membrane potential, protein trafficking, protein-protein interaction, and gene expression; developed biochemistry and redesign of green fluorescent protein; elucidation fo signal transduction mechanisms in calcium oscillations and synaptic plasticity; inventor new methods for microscopic imaging and pharmaceutical high-throughput screening. Office: Tsien Lab HHMI - UCSD CMM West 310 9500 Gilman Dr La Jolla CA 92093-0647 Office Phone: 858-534-4891. Fax: 858-534-5270. E-mail: rtsien@ucsd.edu.

TSIGELNY, IGOR, research scientist; m. Valentina Kouznetsova. PhD, Inst. Physics and Mechanics, Acad. Sci. Ukraine, 1972—78. Asst. scientist U. Calif., San Diego, 1994—99, assoc. scientist, 2000—07, project scientist, 2007—. Author: Molecular Cybernetics, 1990; editor: Protein Structure Prediction: Bioinformatic Approach, 2002; mng. editor: jour. Analytical Reports in Internat. Edn.; contbr. over 180 articles to profl. jours. Mem.: Biophysical Soc., US Fencing Assn. Achievements include 11 Patents. Business E-Mail: itsigeln@ucsd.edu.

TSIRPANLIS, CONSTANTINE N., theology, philosophy, classics and history educator; b. Kos, Greece, Mar. 18, 1935; arrived in US, 1957; m. Sophia Pappas, July 12, 1975; children: Kallipe-Chrysoula, Nike. BA, STM, lic. in theology magna cum laude, Halke Theol. Sem., Istanbul, Turkey, 1957; ThM, Harvard U., 1962; ThD, Union Theol. Sem., 1963; MA, Columbia U., 1966, PhD, 1970, Fordham U., 1973; DLitt (hon.), World Acad. Arts and Culture, 1993. Instr., organizer Greek-Am. cmtys., 1958-63; founder, chmn., prof. modern Greek studies NYU, 1963-70; prof. world history NY Inst. Tech. NYC and Delaware County Coll., Media, Pa., 1967-75; disting. prof. theology, sociology, history, ecumenism, Greek studies Union Theol. Sem., Barrytown, NY, 1976-97; chmn., prof. scriptures, patristics, Greek lang. St. Sophia Ukraine Orthodox Theol. Sem. Am., Somerset, NJ, 1999—. Chmn., prof. classics Collegiate Sch., NYC, 1967—69; prof. modern Greek lang. and lit. New Sch. Social Rsch., NYC, 1968—70; prof. classical mythology Hunter Coll. CUNY, 1968—70. Author: numerous books, A Short History of the Greek Language, 1966, rev. edit., 1970, rev. augmented edit., 2004, A Modern Greek Reader for Americans, 1967, rev. edit., 1968, A Modern Greek idiom and Phrase Book, 1978, Mark Eugenicus, 1979, N. Cabaslias, 1979, Greek Patristic Theology, 26 vols.; founder, editor: The Patristic and Byzantine Rev., 1981—, pub., editor-in-chief: Hellenism in Am., 38 vols., 1969—; contbr. articles to profl. jours. Decorated medal of Nat. Rebirth 1821 Greece, medals of Byzantine nobility including count, baron, G. Chevalier, Gt. Prior N.Am., medal of Accademia Ferdinandea, medals of Diethnés Hetereia Hellenon Logotechnon. Mem.: Panepistimion Oekoumenikou Ellinismou (pres., founder), Pan-Eureopean Inst. Vvzantinõn Erevnon (pres., founder), Justianum Oikoumenikon R.C. (pres., founder), Am. Inst. Patristic-Byzantine Studies (pres., founder), Am. Soc. Papryologists, Hellenic Philog. Assn., N.Am. Patristic Soc., Am. Philos. Assn., Internat. Assn. Byzantine Studies, Am. Acad. Medieval Studies, Am. Philog. Assn., Am. Hist. Assn., Pan Dodecanisian Fedn. US (founder, pres.), Am. Soc. Neohellenic Studies (founder, v.p.), World Acad. Arts and Culture (hon.), Pan-Eureopan Inst. and U. Ecumenical Hellenism. Home and Office: 12 Minuet Ln Kingston NY 12401-6955 Office Phone: 845-336-8797. Home Fax: 845-336-8797.

TSITSIKLIS, JOHN N., electrical engineering and computer science educator; b. Thessaloniki, Greece, 1958; BS in Math., MIT, 1980, BSEE, 1980, MSEE, 1981, PhD in Elec. Engring., 1984. Acting asst. prof. elec. engring. Stanford U., Calif., 1983—84; positions to prof. dept. elec. engring. and computer sci. MIT, Cambridge, 1984—. Acting co-dir. MIT Lab. Info. and Decision Systems, 1996, 97; co-dir. MIT Ops. Rsch. Ctr., 2002—05; vis. rschr. dept. elec. engring. and computer scis. U. Calif., Berkeley; vis. rsch. Inst. Computer Sci., Iraklion, Greece. Contbr. articles to sci. jours.; co-author: Parallel and Distributed Computation: Numerical Methods, 1989, Neuro-Dynamic Programming, 1996, Intro. to Linear Optimization, 1997, Intro. to Probability, 2002. Recipient IBM Faculty Devel. award, 1983, Presdl. Young Investigator award, 1986, Outstanding Paper award, IEEE Control Systems Soc., Bodossaki Found. prize, 1994, Computer Sci. Tech. Sect. prize, Inst. Ops. Rsch. and Mgmt. Scis., 1997. Fellow: IEEE; mem.: NAE. Achievements include patents in field. Office: Dept Elec Engring and Computer Sci MIT 32-D662 77 Massachusetts Ave Cambridge MA 02139-4307 Office Phone: 617-253-6175. Office Fax: 617-253-4308. Business E-Mail: jnt@mit.edu.

TSITVERBLIT, NAFTALI ANATOL, physicist, fluid mechanics engineer, researcher; b. Kiev, Ukraine, Oct. 29, 1963; arrived in Israel, 1987; s. Isaac Avraham and Zoya (Beletsky) T. MSc, Kiev Poly. Inst., 1981-87; PhD, Tel-Aviv U., 1995. Engr. Scientific Rsch. Inst. Robotics, Kiev, 1985-87; postdoc. fellow Lamont-Doherty Earth Obs. Columbia U., Palisades, NY, 1995-97. Tchg. asst., instr. mech. engring. Tel-Aviv U., 1988-94, vis., 1997—; vis. scientist Cornell U., 1994. Co-author: (chpt.) Nonlinear Instability of Nonparallel Flows, 1994; contbr. papers to profl. jours. Woods Hole Oceanographic Inst. fellow, 1996. Mem. AAAS, N.Y. Acad. Sci., Am. Phys. Soc., Am. Geophys. Union. Achievements include discovery of two new mechanisms for convection in double-component fluid systems, resulting from different boundary conditions; mechanism for three-dimensionality of instability disturbances; finite-amplitude steady flows arising from one such a convective mechanism that are disconnected from the conduction state; research in multiplicity of the equilibrium states in laterally heated stably stratified fluid systems and its role in explaining diversity of previous observations in such systems; clarification of nature of the oscillatory instability in confined vortex flows with vortex breakdown and formulation of general method for identification of nature of complex instability mechanisms; identifying mechanisms and their role in various fluid mechanical configurations. Home: 1 Yanosh Korchak St Apt 6 Netanya 42495 Israel Business E-Mail: naftali@eng.tau.ac.il.

TSIVIDIS, YANNIS P., electrical engineering educator; b. Piraeus, Greece, Dec. 22, 1946; came to U.S., 1970. s. Pelopidas I. and Maria (Filippa) T. BS, U. Minn., 1972; MS, U. Calif., Berkeley, 1973, PhD, 1976. Asst. prof. elec. engring. Columbia U., NYC, 1976-81, assoc. prof., 1981-84, prof., 1984—, Nat. Tech. U., Athens, Greece, 1992-95; Charles Batchelor chair prof. Columbia U., NYC, 1998—. Cons. AT&T Bell Labs., Murray Hill, N.J., 1977-88. Author: Operation and Modeling of the MOS Transistor, 1987, 2d edit., 1999, Mixed Analog-Digital VLSI Devices and Technology, 1996; co-editor: Design of Mos VLSI Circuits for Telecommunications, 1985, Integrated Continuous-Time Filters, 1993, Design of Analog-Digital VLSI Circuits for Telecommunications and Signal Processing, 1994; contbr. over 100 articles to profl. jours.; patentee in field. Recipient best paper award European Solid State Cirs. Conf., 1986, Great Tchr. award Columbia U., 1991, Disting. Faculty Tchg. award Columbia Engring. Sch. Alumni Assn., 1998, Presdl. award for outstanding tchg. Columbia U., 2003. Fellow: IEEE (Baker best paper award 1984, Darlington award 1987, Guillemin-Cauer award 1998, Circuits and Sys. Golden Jubilee 2000, co-recipient L. Winner Outstanding Paper award 2003, Undergrad. Tchg. award 2005, Gustav Robert Kirchhoff award 2007). Office: Columbia Univ Dept Elec Engring New York NY 10027

TS'O, PAUL ON-PONG, biophysical chemist, educator; b. July 17, 1929; BS, Lingnan U., 1949; MS, Mich. State U., 1951; PhD, Calif. Inst. Tech., 1955. Teaching asst. Calif. Inst. Tech., 1952-55, rsch. fellow biology div.,

1955-61, sr. rsch. fellow, 1961-62; assoc. prof. biophys. chemistry dept. radiol. scis. Johns Hopkins U., Balt., 1962-67, prof., 1967-73, prof., dir. div. biophysics Sch. Hygiene and Pub. Health, 1973-90, prof. dept. biochemistry, 1973—2003; chmn., CEO Cell Works, Inc., Balt., 1997—2002, chmn. bd., chief tech. officer, 2002—04; mng. dir. CCC Diagnostics, LLC, Balt., 2004—; mem. bd. scientific counselors NCI, 2005—. Cons. Nat. Cancer Inst., 1972-75; mem. study sect. A on biophysics and biophys. chemistry NIH, 1976-80; mem. Clearinghouse on Environ. Carcinogens, Nat. Cancer Inst., 1976-80; mem. European expert com. on biophysics UNESCO; mem. sci. com. of the consortium Internat. Biomed. Inst., Bari, Italy; mem. bd. sci. counselors, div. intramural rsch. NIEHS, 1995—; mem. bd. sci. counselors, external adv. com. NIH, 1995—. Editor: Basic Principles in Nucleic Acid Chemistry, Vol. I and II, 1974, The Molecular Biology of the Mammalian Genetic Apparatus, Vol. I and II, 1977; co-editor: The Nucleohistones, 1964, Chemical Carcinogenesis, Part A and Part B, 1974, Polycyclic Hydrocarbons and Cancer: Environment, Chemistry and Metabolism; and Molecular and Cell Biology, Vol. 1 and 2, 1978, Vol. 3, 1981, Carcinogenesis: Fundamental Mechanisms and Environmental Effects, 1980, Interrelationship Among Aging, Cancer and Differentiation, 1985, Structure and Function of the Genetic Apparatus, 1986; mem. editorial bd. Molecular Pharmacology, 1964-83, Biophys. Jour, 1969-72, Biochimica et Biophysica Acta, 1971-81, Cancer Rev, 1973-84, Jour. Environ. Health Scis, 1976-81; assoc. editor: Cancer Research, 1975-87; mem. editorial adv. bd. Biochemistry, 1966-74, Biopolymers, 1979-85; contbr. over 350 articles and revs. to profl. jours. Named Md. Chemist of Yr., 1981; named One of 1000 Most Cited Scientists, Citation Index, 1965-78 Fellow AAAS; mem. Biophys. Soc. (chmn. pub. sci. policy com. 1972-76, coun. mem. 1975-78, exec. bd. 1975), Am. Soc. Biol. Chemists, Am. Soc. Microbiology, Am. Soc. Cell Biology, Biology Alliance for Pub. Affairs (chmn. organizing com. 1973-76), Am. Assn. Cancer Rsch., Am. Chem. Soc., Acadmia Sinica (1st dir. inst. molecular biology, chmn. adv. com. 1982-94), European Acad. Arts, Scis. and Humanities, Sigma Xi. Office: CCC Diagnostics, LLC Ste B 3918 Vero Rd Baltimore MD 21227 Home Phone: 410-461-3777; Office Phone: 410-633-4885. E-mail: paul@cccdiag.com.

TSO, TIEN CHIOH, federal agency administrator, researcher, agronomist; b. Hupeh, China, July 25, 1917; came to U.S., 1947, naturalized, 1961; s. Ya Fu and Suhwa (Wang) T.; m. Margaret Lu, Aug. 28, 1949; children: Elizabeth, Paul. BS, Nanking U., China, 1941, MS, 1944; PhD, Pa. State U., 1950; postgrad., Oak Ridge Inst. Nuclear Studies. Supt. exptl. farm Ministry Social Affairs, China, 1944-46; exec. sec. Tobacco Improvement Bur., 1946-47; rsch. chemist Gen. Cigar Rsch. Lab., 1950-51; with USDA, 1952—; prin. plant physiologist crop research div. Agrl. Rsch. Svc./USDA, Beltsville, Md., 1964-66, leader tobacco quality investigations, tobacco and sugar crops research br., 1966-71, chief tobacco lab., 1972-83, sr. exec. service, 1974-83, collaborator, 1984—; exec. dir. Internat. Devel. and Edn. in Agr. and Life Scis., 1984-96, chmn. bd., 1997-2001, hon. chmn. bd., 2001—. Cons. World Bank, Nat. Cancer Inst., Ky. Tobacco Health Rsch. Inst., China Nat. Tobacco Corp., Philippine Tobacco Rsch. Ctr., Philip Morris Tobacco Corp. Author: Physiology and Biochemistry of Tobacco Plants, 1972, Production, Physiology and Biochemistry of Tobacco Plants, 1991, Agriculture in China: 1949-2030, 1998; contbg. author: Ann. Rev. Plant Physiology, Vol. 9, 1958, The Chemistry of Tobacco and Tobacco Smoke, 1972, Toward Less Harmful Cigarettes, 1968, 71, 75, 80; editor: Structural and Functional Aspects of Phytochemistry, 1972, Recent Advances in Tobacco Science, vol. 1, 1975, Agriculture in China: 1949-2030, 1998, Dare to Dream: Vision of 2050 Agriculture in China, 2004, Comfort Ye, My People in My Journey in Science and Life, 2007. Fellow AAAS, Am. Soc. Agronomy (chmn. colloquium on agr. and life scis. in China 1983, 84, 85, 86, 87, 88-89), Am. Inst. Chemists; mem. Am. Chem. Soc., Am. Soc. Plant Physiologists, Phytochem. Soc. N.Am. (pres. 1971, life mem.), Tobacco Chemists Rsch. Conf. (symposium chmn. 1965, 79, chmn. 1975, 83), World Conf. Smoking and Health (sect. chmn. 1967, 71, 75), Tobacco Workers Conf., N.Y. Acad. Scis., Interagy. Smoking and Health Forum (chmn. 1979-83), Nat. Coordinating Com. on Tobacco-Related Rsch., Sigma Xi, Gamma Sigma Delta. Achievements include research in loci of alkaloid formation, biosynthetic pathway, interconversion and fate of alkaloids in tobacco plants, chem. composition as affected by macro and micro elements, homogenized leaf curing, health-related factors including mycotoxins, radioactive elements, air pollutants and phenolics, potential for agricultural self-sufficiency in China in the next century. Home: 3152 Gracefield Rd # 216 Silver Spring MD 20904 Office: Beltsville Agr Rsch Ctr Bldg 005 10300 Baltimore Ave Beltsville MD 20705 Office Phone: 301-504-5422. Business E-Mail: tc.tso@ars.usda.gov. *We are thankful to those fools who dare to dream of something new and seemingly impossible.*

TSODIKOV, ALEXANDER DAVID, biostatistician, educator; b. St. Petersburg, Russia, Dec. 20, 1964; arrived in Germany, 1994; s. David Isac and Vera Semion (Fidelman) Tsodikov; m. Elena Sergei Serbina, Oct. 7, 1999. MS Applied Math., St. Petersburg Tech. U., 1988, PhD Math., 1991; diploma in epidemiology and biostats., Karolinska Inst., Sweden, 1992. Engr. St. Petersburg Tech. U., 1988—90, rsch. fellow, 1990—92, sr. rsch. fellow, 1992—93; postdoctoral fellow Inst. Curie, Paris, 1993—94; rsch. scientist U. Leipzig, Germany, 1995—97; rsch. asst. prof. U. Utah, Salt Lake City, 1997—2002, rsch. assoc. prof., 2002—03; assoc. prof. U. Calif., Davis, 2003—06; prof. U. Mich., Ann Arbor, 2006—. Author: Statistical Models, 1996; contbr. more than 70 articles to profl. jours Grantee Ministry of Sci. France, 1993, Internat. Union Against Cancer Switzerland, 1992, German Rsch. Found., 1995, Nat. Inst. Health, 2002, U.S. Dept. Def., 2002 Achievements include rsch. in cancer models, optimal screening schedules, and statis. methods in cancer. Office Phone: 734-615-6416. Business E-Mail: tsodikov@umich.edu.

TSOI, EDWARD TZE MING, architect, urban planner, interior designer; b. New Orleans, Aug. 7, 1943; s. Edward Mong Yok and Ruby Liu Wei (Hsia) T.; m. Louise Smoyer, June 15, 1968; children: Laura Li Ling, Alison Li Mei. BArch, MIT, 1966; MArch, U. Pa., 1968, M in City Planning, 1968, cert. in urban design, 1969. Registered architect, Mass., La. Assoc. Sert/Jackson & Assocs., Cambridge, Mass., 1969-76; assoc. prin. Skidmore Owings & Merrill, Boston, 1976-83; prin. Tsoi/Kobus & Assocs., Inc., Cambridge, 1983—, pres., 1985-89, 93—. Instr. Sch. Design, Harvard U., Cambridge, 1980-84. Designer Marine Resource Ctr., 1994. Chmn. Arlington (Mass.) Redevel. Bd., 1972—; chmn. 1st parish Unitarian Universalist Ch., Arlington, 1990; pres. bd. dirs. Cambridge Salvation Army, 1990—; mem. Boston Civic Design Commn., 1993—. Recipient Best New Med. Facility award Symposium on Healthcare, 1993, Grand Honor award Assn. Gen. Contractors, 1993, award Lotus Devel. Corp. landscape award Urban Design, 1991, nat. award for renovation Ford Model T plant Urban Land Inst., 1995. Fellow AIA; mem. Boston Soc. Architects (pres. 1993-94). Democrat. Avocations: windsurfing, boating, woodworking, carpentry. Home: 16 Devereaux St Arlington MA 02476-8114 Office: Tsoi/Kobus & Assocs Inc PO Box 9114 Cambridge MA 02238-9114 Office Phone: 617-475-4000. Business E-Mail: etsoi@tka-architects.com.

TSOU, MING-HSIANG, geographer, educator; b. Tao-yuan, Taiwan, Nov. 20, 1969; s. Feng-Shing Tsou and Nancy Lee; m. Chun-Yi Eva Chen, Jan. 8, 1995; children: Shu-An Sophie, Kaiwen, Kailing. BS, Nat. Taiwan U., Taipei, 1991; MA, SUNY, Buffalo, 1996; PhD, U. Colo., Boulder, 2000. Asst. prof. geography dept. San Diego State U., 2000—05, assoc. prof., 2005—. Co-chmn. earth sci. enterprise data sys. working group, std. process group NASA, 2004—; mem. sci. bd. GIS Planet, U.K. GIS Conf., 2005—; mem. web-based geoinfo. and svcs. com. tech. commn. U.K. Soc. Photogrammetry and Remote Sensing, 2005—. Co-author: Internet GIS: Distributed Geographic Information Services for the Internet and Wireless Networks.; website creator: Web-based Mapping Services for San Diego Wildfires, 2003, The Gateway of Geospatial Information Technology. Recipient Outstanding Faculty award, San Diego State U., 2004; grantee, NASA, 2003—, City of San Diego, 2004—06, South Coast Resource Conservation Devel. Coun., 2004—06, NSF, 2005—. Mem.: Am. Assn. Geographers (vice chmn. cartography specialty group 2006—). Achievements include research in advanced web-based cartographic mapping tools; mobile GIS and wireless communication integration; web-based geospatial information technology; web-based GIS education and tool development; web GIS for homeland security and disaster management. Home Phone: 619-741-6543; Office Phone: 619-594-0205. Office Fax: 619-594-4938; Home Fax: 619-594-4938. Business E-Mail: mtsou@mail.sdsu.edu.

TSOU, YU-MIN, science administrator, chemistry researcher; b. Ping-Dong, Taiwan, Aug. 28, 1953; arrived in US, 1979; s. Shung-Chu Tsou and Ping-Wen Chen; m. Yah-Lih Chao, Apr. 26, 1980; children: Amy Meng Shuan, Benjamin Jiann. BS in Chemistry, Nat. Tsing-Hua U., Taiwan, 1975; MS in Chemistry, Nat. Taiwan U., 1979; PhD in Chemistry, Calif. Inst. Tech., Pasadena, 1985. Sci. rsch. assoc. U. of Tex., Austin, 1985—86; sr. rsch. chemist Dow Chem. Co., Freeport, Tex., 1986—88, project leader, 1989—93, rsch. leader, 1994—2000; R&D mgr. E-Tek divsn. De Nora Northamerica, Inc, Somerset, NJ, 2001—04; tech. dir. E-TEK divsn. PEMEAS USA, Somerset, 2005—07; head tech, chief scientist BASF Fuel Cell, Inc., Somerset, 2007—. Chief tech. officer for Dept. of Energy program E-TEK divsn. De Nora Northamerica, Inc., Somerset, 2002—05; leading sceinstist of De Nora for Aqueous Hydrochloric Acid Electrolysis project De Nora NA/Bayer Joint Venture, Somerset, 2001—03; head mfr. and devel. PEMEAS USA, Inc., Somerset, 2006—07. Author: The Key to Understand Lau-Tze Philosophy and Its Practice in Chinese History, (philosophy/history writings) Chinese/Western Philosophy Comparisons; contbr. articles to profl. jours. Fund raiser Calif. Inst. Tech. Alumni Assn., Freeport, 1998. Recipient Electrochem. Soc. New Tech. award, E-TEK, 2005, Dow Chem. Tech. Excellence award, 1990, 1992, 1996. Mem.: Electrochem. Soc. (assoc.). Achievements include development of consistent method to manufacture rhodium catalyst and the rhodium electrode for converting waste hydrochloric acid to chlorine; invention of anode and cathode coating technology; mass production of membrane-cell-assembly with electrode-membrane lamination approach in fuel cell industry; highest performing Pt alloy methanol oxidation anode and Pt oxygen reduction cathode catalysts and supply to customers; poisoning-resistant hydrogen evolution cathode on thin substrates and implemented in zero-gap membrane chlorine cells; novel electrode structure for realizing Pt alloy advantage; first to develop catalysts/gas diffusion electrodes for the pioneering PEMEAS over 160 C high temperature MEA; patents for electrolysis, fuel cells, electro-catalysts, gas diffusion electrodes, porous electrode structure. Home: 533 Mercer Rd Princeton NJ 08540 Office: BASF Fuel Cell Inc 39 Veronica Ave Somerset NJ 08873 Office Phone: 732-545-5100 145. Office Fax: 732-545-5170. Personal E-mail: tsou4507@yahoo.com. E-mail: ym.tsou@etek-inc.com.

TSOUCALAS, NICHOLAS, federal judge; b. NYC, Aug. 24, 1926; s. George Michael and Maria (Monogenis) T.; m. Catherine Aravantinos, Nov. 21, 1954; children: Stephanie, Georgia. BSBA, Kent State U., 1949; LLB, N.Y. Law Sch., 1951. Bar: N.Y. 1953. Sole practice, NYC, 1953-55, 59-68; asst. U.S. atty. (So. dist.) N.Y. US Dept. Justice, 1955-59; judge NYC Criminal Ct., 1968-86; acting judge NY Supreme Ct., NYC, 1975-82; judge U.S. Ct. Internat. Trade, NYC, 1986—96, sr. judge, 1996—. Dist. leader Republican Party N.Y. County, N.Y.C., 1961-68; mem. Rep. Exec. Com., N.Y.C., 1961-68. Served with USN, 1944-46, 51-52. Recipient Proficiency in Constl. Law award N.Y. Law Sch., N.Y.C., 1951, Man of Yr. award St. Paul Soc., N.Y.C., 1971. Mem. ABA, N.Y. County Lawyers Assn., Fed. Bar Assn., Greek Am. Lawyers Assn., Am. Hellenic Ednl. Prog. Assn. Lodges: Parthenon, Masons. Republican. Greek Orthodox. Avocations: basketball, racquetball, stamp collecting/philately, walking, dance. Office: US Ct Internat Trade 1 Federal Plz New York NY 10278-0001 *

TSOUKALAS, LEFTERI H., engineering educator, department chairman; arrived in US, 1975; s. Charalambos Theodore and Elpis Tsoukalas; m. Demetra Evangelou; children: Ellia, Constantine, Arete Trisevgeni, Charie Anatole. BSEE, U. Ill., Champaign-Urbana, 1981, MS, 1983, PhD, 1989. Prof. nuc. engrng. Purdue U., West Lafayette, Ind., 2000—, head Sch. Nuc. Engring., 2001—06. Cons. Internat. Atomic Energy Agy., Vienna, 2004—05. Author: (book) Fuzzy and Neural Approaches in Engineering, 1997 (Keynote Spkr., 1997). Recipient Consortium for the Intelligent Mgmt. of the Electric Power Grid award, Elec. Power Rsch. Inst., 1999—2003, Best Tchr. award, Purdue U. Sch. Engring., 1997. Fellow: Am. Nuc. Soc. (life); mem.: Nuc. Engring. Dept. Heads Orgn. (chmn. 2004—06). Independent. Greek Orthodox. Home Phone: 765-496-9696.

TSOUKAS, MARIA MAGDALENE, dermatologist, educator; arrived in U.S., 1992; d. Ioannis Athanassios and Danai Kalliroi Tsoukas; m. Dimitrios Christos Nikas, June 13, 1999; children: Christos Nikas, Ioannis Nikas, Odysseas Nikas. MD, U. Athens, Greece, 1992, PhD, 2002. Diplomate Am. Bd. Dermatology. Rsch. fellow dermatology Harvard Med. Sch, Boston, 1992—95; intern in medicine Tufts Med. Sch., Boston, 1997; resident in dermatology Roger Williams Med. Ctr., Boston U., Boston, 1998—2000; chief resident in dermatology Dartmouth Med. Sch., Hanover, NH, 2000—01, clin. fellow in cosmetic and surg. dermatology, 2001—02; asst. prof. dermatology U. Chgo., 2005—. Fellow: Am. Acad. Dermatology; mem.: Am. Soc. for Photobiology, Am. Soc. for Laser Medicine and Surgery. E-mail: mtsoukas@med.une.bsd.uchicago.edu.

TSUANG, MING TSO, psychiatrist, educator; b. Tainan, Taiwan, Nov. 16, 1931; came to U.S., 1971; s. Ping Tang and Chhun Kuei (Lin) T.; m. Snow Huei S. Ko; children: John, Debby, Grace. MD, Nat. Taiwan U., Taipei, 1957; PhD in Psychiatry, 1965, PhD (Sino-Brit. Fellowship Trust scholar); certs. in epidemiology and stats., population genetics, psychiat. genetics, U. London, 1965; D.Sc. in Psychiat. Genetics and Epidemiology, Faculty of Sci., U. London, 1981. Intern Nat. Taiwan U. Hosp., 1956-57, resident in psychiatry, 1957-61, assoc. prof. psychiatry, staff psychiatrist, 1968-71; collaborating investigator Internat. Pilot Study of Schizophrenia, WHO, 1966-71; vis. assoc. prof. psychiatry Washington U. Sch. Medicine, St. Louis, 1971-72; assoc. prof., staff psychiatrist U. Iowa Coll. Medicine, Iowa City, 1972-75, prof. psychiatry, 1975-82, prof. psychiat. epidemiology, 1978-82; clin. tchr., lectr. to residents, med. students; cons. psychiatrist VA Hosp., Iowa City, 1972-82; prof., vice chmn. sect. of psychiatry and human behavior Brown U., Providence, 1982-85; assoc. med. dir. Butler Hosp., Providence, 1982-85, dir. psychiat. epidemiology research unit, 1982-85; prof. psychiatry Harvard Inst. Psychiat. Epid. and Genetics Harvard U. Med. Sch. and Harvard Sch. Pub. Health; dir. psychiat. epidemiology and genetics Mass. Mental Health Ctr., Boston; chief psychiatry, chmn. Ctr. for Mental Health Brockton-West Roxbury VA Med. Ctr., 1985-94; head and supt. dept. psychiatry Harvard U. at Mass. Mental Health Ctr., 1992—; Stanley Cobb prof. psychiatry Harvard U., 1993—2003; dir. Harvard Inst. Psychiat. Epedemiology and Genetics, 1994—; behavioral genomics prof. dept. psychiatry, dir. Ctr. Behavioral Genomics U. Calif., San Diego, 2003—, behavioral genomics endowed chair, 2007—. Epidemiol. studies rev. com. NIMH, 1976-79, mem., chmn. rsch. scientist devel. rev. com., 1982-86, chmn. epidemiologic studies rev. com., 1989-90, extramural sci. adv. bd., 1990-93; med. rsch. svc. planning coun. Vets. Health Svcs. and Rsch. Adminstrn., VA Cen. Office, 1990-93; vis. prof. psychiatry (Josiah Macy faculty scholar award) Oxford U., Eng., Warneford Hosp., 1979-80; chmn. mental health policy working group, divsn. health and policy rsch. and edn. Harvard U., 1986-87. Author: (with R. Vandermey) Genes and The Mind: Inheritance of Mental Illness, 1980, Schizophrenia: The Facts, 2d edit., 1997, (with S.V. Faraone) The Genetics of Mood Disorders, 1990; co-editor: Schizoaffective Psychoses, 1986, Handbook of Schizophrenia, vol. 3, 1988, Affective and Schizoaffective Disorders, Similarities and Differences, 1990, (with S.V. Faraone and D. Tsuang) Genetics of Mental Disorders: A Guide for Students, Clinicians and Researchers, 1999, (with M. Tohen) A Textbook on Psychiatric Epidemiology, 2d edit., 2002, (with W.S. Stone and S.V. Faraone) Early Clinical Intervention and Prevention in Schizophrenia, 2004, also monographs.; contbr. chpts. to books, numerous articles to profl. jours. Recipient Clin. Rsch. award Am. Acad. Clin. Psychiatrists, 1983, Rema Lapous award APHA, 1984, Stanley Dean award for rsch. on schizophrenia Am. Coll. Psychiatrists, 1989, Lifetime Achievement award Internat. Soc. Psychiat. Genetics, 1995, Taiwanese-Am. award for Achievement in Sci. and Engring., 1995, Gold Medal award Soc. Biol. Psychiatry, 2000, award for rsch. in psychiatry Am. Psychiat. Assn., 2003. Mem. Am. Psychopathol. Assn. (pres. 2005), Internat. Soc. Psychiat. Genetics (pres. 2005—, Lifetime Achievement award 1995), Inst. of Medicine/NAAS, Academia Sinica Taiwan, Sigma Xi. Office: U Calif San Diego Dept Psychiatry Med Tchg FAcility Rm 453 9500 Gilman Dr Mail Code 0603 La Jolla CA 92093-0603 Office Phone: 858-822-2464. Business E-Mail: mtsuang@ucsd.edu. *My constant goal is to do the best work I can, to eschew anxiety about the result, to learn from failure, and to build upon success, not for personal honor but for the good of mankind, as God's servant within a serving profession. Helping others is not possible without self-discipline, self-sufficience, and self-sacrifice; at the same time, helping others strengthens the self for its tasks.*

TSUBAKI, ANDREW TAKAHISA, theater director, educator; b. Chiyoda-ku, Tokyo, Japan, Nov. 29, 1931; s. Ken and Yasu (Oyama) T.; m. Lilly Yuri, Aug. 3, 1963; children: Arthur Yuichi, Philip Takeshi. BA in English, Tokyo Gakugei U., Tokyo, Japan, 1954; postgrad. in Drama, U. Saskatchewan, Saskatoon, Canada, 1958-59; MFA in Theatre Arts, Tex. Christian U., 1961; PhD in Speech & Drama, U. Ill., 1967. Tchr. Bunkyo-ku 4th Jr. High Sch., Tokyo, 1954—58; instr., scene designer Bowling Green (Ohio) State U., 1964—68; asst. prof. speech & drama U. Kans., Lawrence, 1968—73, assoc. prof., 1973—79; vis. assoc. prof. Carleton Coll., Northfield, Minn., 1974; lectr. Tsuda U., Tokyo, 1975; vis. assoc. prof. theatre Tel-Aviv (Israel) U., 1975—76; vis. prof. theatre Mo. Repertory Theatre, Kansas City, Mo., 1976, Nat. Sch. Drama, New Delhi, 1983; prof. theatre, film, east Asian Languages and Cultures U. Kans., Lawrence, 1979—2000, prof. emeritus, 2000—. Dir. Internat. Theatre Studies Ctr., U. Kans., Lawrence, 1971-2000, Operation Internat. Classical Theatre, 1988—; Benedict disting. vis. prof. Asian studies Carleton Coll., 1993; area editor Asian Theatre Jour., U. Hawaii, Honolulu, 1982-94; chmn. East Asian Langs. and Cultures, U. Kans., Lawrence, 1983-90; mem. editl. bd. Studies in Am. Drama, Oxford, Miss., 1985-88. Dir. plays Kanjincho, 1973, Rashomon, 1976, 96, King Lear, 1985, Fujito and Shimizu, 1985, Hippolytus, 1990, Busu and the Missing Lamb (Japan) 1992, Suehirogari and Sumidagawa, 1992, 93, Tea, 1995; choreographed Antigone (Greece), 1987, Hamlet (Germany), 1989, The Resistible Rise of Arturo Ui, 1991, Man and the Masses (Germany), 1993, The Children of Fate (Hungary), 1994, The Great Theatre of the World (Germany); editor Theatre Companies of the World, 1986; contbg. author to Indian Theatre: Traditions of Performance, 1990; contbr. 7 entries in Japanese Traditional plays to the Internat. Dictionary of Theatre, vol. 1, 1992, vol. 2, 1994. Named to Order of Sacred Treasure, Govt. of Japan, 2006; recipient citation, Min. Fgn. Affairs Japan, 2003, Statement of Appreciation, Chmn. and Bd. Dirs. Hiratsuka Internat. Exch. Assn., 2004; World Univ. Svc. scholar, U. Saskatchewan, 1958—59, University fellow, U. Ill., 1961—62, Rsch. fellow, The Japan Found., 1974—75, 1990, Rsch. Fulbright grantee, 1983. Fellow Coll. Am. Theatre (elected 2002); mem. Am. Theatre Assn., Asian Theatre Program (chair 1976-79), Assn. for Asian Studies, Assn. Kans. Theatres., Assn. Kans. Theatres U/C Div. (chmn. 1980-82), Assn. for Theatre in Higher Edn., Assn. for Asian Performance. Democrat. Buddhist. Avocations: ki-aikido (5th dan), photography, travel. Home: 924 Holiday Dr Lawrence KS 66049-3005

TSUBOUCHI, DAVID H., Canadian provincial official; BA in English, York U., 1972; LLB, Osgoode Hall Law Sch., 1975; LLD (hon.), Assumption U., Windsor, 2006. Ward 5 councillor Town of Markham, 1988-94; sr. ptnr. Tsubouchi & Nichols & Assocs., 1994-95; progressive conservative mem. Legis. Assembly Ont., 1995—2003; Min. Cmty. and Social Svcs. Ont. Progressive Conservative Govt., 1995-99, Min. Consumer & Comml. Affairs Can., 1996—99, chair cabinet legis. and regulations com., 1996, re-elected mem. Provincial Parliament for Markham, 1999; registrar gen. Province of Ont., 1996, solicitor gen., 1999—2001, chair health and social svcs. policy com., chair mgmt. bd. cabinet, 2001—03, min. culture, 2002—03, min. consumer and comml. relations; cons., coun. Fraser Milner Casgrain LLP, Toronto, Canada, 2004—. Chmn. planning and devel. com., econ. alliance com., indsl. and corp. devel. com. Markham Hist. Mus.; bd. dirs. Teranet Inc., Markham Stouffville Hosp.; trustee Teranet Operating Trust. Contbr. articles to Law Gazette. Adv. coun. NYU Sch. Fine Arts; gov. Canadian Internat. Peace Project; campaign chair George Brown Coll. Theatre Arts Sch.; bd. gov., also audit com. York U., 2004—; past dir. Japanese Canadian Cultural Ctr.; bd. dirs. Hitachi Can., Found. Markets Inc. Named Optimist of Yr., 1985-86; recipient Air Can. Heart of Gold award, 1988; granted Coat of Arms, Gov. Gen.'s Office, 1993, award of appreciation, First Nations Chiefs of Police, Ontario Soc. for the Prevention of Cruelty to Animals, Bruce Bryden award for Leadership, York U., 2003, The Queen's Golden Jubilee award, Canadian Horse Racing Industry award of Recognition, Ont. Grape Growers award of Merit, Hon. Patron of the Gardiner Mus. Ceramics, Japanese Cultural Centre award for Leadership; names Invested knight Grand Cross in Holy Order St. Martin de Porres, Invested knight Grand Cross in Holy Military Order St Adrian and St. Sebastian, Invested knight Equestrian Secular and Chapterial Order St Joachim. Mem.: Assumption U. Alumni Assn., Japanese Canadian Cultural Ctr. (hon. chair), Ontario Assn. Former Parliamentarians, Markham Bd. Trade, Sleepy Hollow Golf and Country Club, Albany Club. Office: Fraser Milner Casgrain LLP 1 First Canadian Pl 39th Fl 100 King Street West Toronto ON M5X 1B2 Canada

TSUI, DANIEL C., electrical engineer, physicist; b. Henan, China, 1939; Diploma, Augustana Coll., 1961; PhD in Physics, U. Chgo., 1967. Rsch. assoc. U. Chgo., 1967—68; mem. technical staff Bell Labs., Murray Hill, NJ, 1968—82; Arthur LeGrand Doty prof. dept. elec. engring. Princeton U., NJ, 1982—. Contbr. articles to profl. jours. Recipient Buckley prize for Condensed Matter Physics, 1984, Benjamin Franklin medal in Physics, 1998, Nobel prize in Physics, 1998. Fellow: AAAS; mem.: NAE, NAS, Materials Research Soc., Am. Physical Soc., IEEE, Acad. Sinica. Office: Princeton U Dept Elec Engring Rm B 426 PO Box 5263 Princeton NJ 08544-0001 Fax: 609-258-6279. E-mail: tsui@ee.princeton.edu.

TSUI, FRANK, physicist, educator, researcher; arrived in US, 1980, naturalized; s. Yat K Tsui and Yuching Chen; m. Annie Hsu; 1 child, Albert. BS in Engring. Physics, U. Calif., Berkeley, 1984; ME in Applied and Engring. Physics, Cornell U., 1986; MS in Physics, U. Ill., Urbana-Champaign, 1987, PhD in Physics, 1992. Rsch. fellow U. Mich., Ann Arbor, 1992—95; asst. prof. of physics and materials sci. U. N.C., Chapel Hill, 1995—2001, assoc. prof. physics and materials sci., 2001—06, asst. chair dept. physics and astronomy, 2002—04, prof. physics and materials sci., 2006—. Recipient Career award, NSF, 1997—2001; IBM fellowship, U. of Ill., 1988—91, Sokol fellowship, U. of Mich., 1993—95. Mem.:

Materials Rsch. Soc., Am. Phys. Soc., Tau Beta Bi Engring. Honor Soc., Phi Kappa Phi Nat. Honor Soc. Office: U of NC CB# 3255 Phillips Hall Chapel Hill NC 27599 Business E-Mail: ftsui@physics.unc.edu.

TSUI, LAP-CHEE, academic administrator, molecular genetics educator; b. Shanghai, Dec. 21, 1950; arrived in Can., 1981; s. Jing Lue Hsue and Hui Ching Wang; m. Ellen Lan Fong, Feb. 11, 1977; children: Eugene, Felix. BS, Chinese U. Hong Kong, 1972, MPhil, 1974; PhD, U. Pitts., 1979; DSc (hon.), Chinese U. Hong Kong, 1991; DCL (hon.), U. King's Coll., Halifax, NS, Can., 1991; DSc (hon.), U. N.B., Can., 1991; DLL (hon.), U. St. Francis Xavier, Antigonish, NS, Can., 1994; DSc (hon.), York U., Can., 2001. Postdoctoral investigator Oak Ridge Nat. Lab., Tenn., 1979—80; postdoctoral fellow Hosp. for Sick Children, Toronto, Ont., Canada, 1981—83, geneticist-in-chief, 1996—2002; asst. prof. depts. genetics and med. genetics U. Toronto, Ont., Canada, 1983—88, assoc. prof. Ont., 1988—90, prof. Ont., 1990—, univ. prof. Ont., 1994—; H.E. Sellers chair in cystic fibrosis, 1998—2002; head genetics and genomic biology program, 1998—2002. Chmn. chromosome 7 subcom. Human Gene Mapping Workshop, 1986-97; mem. mammalian genetics study sect. NIH, Bethesda, Md., 1988-93; dir. Cystic Fibrosis Rsch. Ctr., Hosp. for Sick Children Spl. Rsch. Ctr., 1994-2002; scientist Med. Rsch. Coun. Can., 1989-2002; advisor European Jour. Human Genetics, 1992—, Molecular Medicine Today, 1995—; adj. prof. U. New Brunswick, 2000-2002; vice-chancellor U. Hong Kong, 2002—. Editor Cytogenetics and Cell Genetics, 1988-92, Internat. Jour. Genome Rsch., 1990—; assoc. editor Am. Jour. Human Genetics, 1990-93, Genomics, 1994—; mem. editl. bd. Mammalian Genome, 1990, Clin. Genetics, 1991—, Human Molecular Genetics, 1991-99; communicating editor Human Mutation, 1995—, Molec. Medicine Today, sr. editor: Physiological Genomics, 2000-01; internat. adv. The Chinese Jour. of Medical Genetics, 2000—; editor Biochimica et Biophysica Acta, 2002—; contbr. over 300 articles to sci. jours.; co-discoverer cystic fibrosis gene, 1989. Trustee Edn. Found., Fedn. Chinese Canadian Profls., Toronto, 1987—. Recipient Paul di Sant Agnese Disting. Achievement award Cystic Fibrosis Found., 1989, Zellers SR. Scientist award, 2001, Gold medal of honor Pharm. Mfrs. Assn. Can., 1989, award of excellence Genetics Soc. Can., 1990, Gairdner Internat. award 1990, Cresson medal Franklin Inst., 1992, E. Mead Johnson award, 1992, Disting. Scientist award The Canadian Soc. Clin. Investigators, 1992, Canadian Conf. medal 1992, Sarstedt Rsch. prize, 1993, Sanremo Internat. award for Genetic Rsch., 1993, J.P. Lecocq prize Inst. de France, 1994, Henry Friesen award The Canadian Soc. for Clin. Investigation and the Royal Coll. of Physicians and Surgeons of Can., 1995, Can. Med. Assn. award of honour, 1996, Jonas Salk award Ontario March of Dimes, 1997, Initiative Cmty. Svc. award Toronto Biotech., 1998, Disting. Scientist award Med. Rsch. Coun., 2000, Killam prize Can. Coun., 2002; named scholar Can. Cystic Fibrosis Found., 1984-86. Fellow Royal Soc. Can., Royal Soc. London, Academia Sinica, Royal Coll. Physicians U.K. (hon.); mem. Human Genome Orgn., Am. Soc. Human Genetics, NAS (fgn. assoc.). Office: Vice-Chancellor's Office U Hong Kong Pokfulam Rd Hong Kong Hong Kong Office Phone: (852) 2859 2100. Office Fax: (852) 2858 9435.

TSUI, LISA, social scientist, researcher; arrived in US, 1976; BS in Philosophy & Polit. Sci., Amherst Coll., Mass., 1991; MEd, U. Chgo., 1994; PhD, UCLA, 1998. Rsch. analyst Higher Edn. Rsch. Inst., LA, 1995—96; lectr. George Wash. U., DC, 1998, Trinity Coll., DC, 1998—98; rschr. The Urban Inst., DC, 2001—. Rev. panelist US Dept. Edn., DC, 1999—99, NSF, DC, 2007—07. Contbr. articles to profl. jours. Founder, dir. Read With Me Program, LA, 1991—93. Grantee Rsch. grant, NSF, 2006—. Mem.: Assn. Study Higher Edn. Office: Urban Inst 2100 M Street NW Washington DC 20037 Business E-Mail: ltsui@ui.urban.org.

TSUI, STEPHEN ALAN, researcher; b. Houston, Aug. 16, 1980; s. Steve and Annie Lim Tsui. BS in Physics, U. Houston, 2002, MS in Physics, 2004. Undergrad. rsch. asst. Tex. Ctr. Superconductivity, U. Houston, 1999—2000, rsch. asst., 2002—; undergrad. rsch. asst. U. Houston Medium Energy Physics Group, 2000—02; tchg. asst. dept. physics U. Houston, 2002—03. Lit. anthology, Aquilae Stilus: Klein Forest's Literary and Art Anthology; contbr. poetry to anthologies (Internat. Libr. of Poetry Bronze medal, 2000). Ednl. outreach lectr. Tex. Ctr. for Superconductivity, U. of Houston, 2002—06. Recipient merit scholarship, Houston Livestock Show and Rodeo, 1998—2002, 2d Pl. award Student Challenge Undergrad. Divsn., U. of Houston Coll. of Natural Scis. and Math., 2002, 3d Pl. award, Student Challenge Grad. Divsn., 2003, 3d Pl., Tex. Ctr. for Superconductivity and Advanced Materials, 2003, 1st pl., Tex. Ctr. for Superconductivity Student Symposium, 2006. Mem.: Am. Phys. Soc. (pres. chpt. of Soc. Physics Students 2001—02), U. of Houston (pres. 2001—02), U. of Houston Alumni Orgn., Golden Key, Alpha Lambda Delta-Phi Eta Sigma, Sigma Pi Sigma, Nat. Art Honor Soc. (sec. Klein Forest chpt. 1997—98), Phi Kappa Phi (life). Achievements include development of Prototype straw particle tracker for project MECO at the University of Houston; research in Static negative dielectric constant in a nano-colloid; Resistive switching in metal-oxide interfaces. Avocations: jogging, poetry, cooking. Office: U Houston Tex Ctr for Superconductivity Houston TX 77204

TSUJI, FREDERICK ICHIRO, biochemist, molecular biologist; b. Honolulu, Aug. 23, 1923; s. Kijiro Tsuji and Sadako Moriyama; m. Masako Koga, Mar. 31, 1991. BA, Cornell U., Ithaca, NY, 1946, M in Nutritional Sci., 1948, PhD, 1950. Asst. prof. Duquesne U., Pitts., 1950—52; rsch. asst. Princeton (NJ) U., 1952—55; rsch. biochemist, head basic sci. rsch. VA Hosp., Pitts., 1955—72; rsch. prof. U. So. Calif., LA, 1972—76; dir. biochemistry program NSF, Washington, 1976—78; rsch. biochemist, prof. U. Calif., San Diego, La Jolla, 1978—. Head dept. enzymes and metabolism Osaka Bioscience Inst., Japan, 1987—93; vis. prof. dept. protein crystallography Institute for Protein Rsch., Osaka U., 1998—99. Administr. grant applications and awards for rsch. in biochemistry NSF, Washington, 1976—78. Grantee, NSF, 1970—2000. Mem.: ACS, Soc. Gen. Physiologists, Am. Soc. Biochemistry and Molecular Bio., Sigma Xi. Achievements include research in chemistry of light production in animals and plants. Avocations: classical music, history of modern physics, literature, art. Office: University California San Diego 9500 Gilman Dr La Jolla CA 92093-0202 Home Phone: 858-792-8040; Office Phone: 858-534-3197. Office Fax: 858-534-7313. Business E-Mail: ftsuji@ucsd.edu.

TSUJI, TOSHIZO, hospital administrator, educator; b. Kyoto, Jan. 2, 1932; s. Yasujiro and Yuki (Nakamura) T.; m. Yoshiko Taniguchi, Mar. 21, 1977; children: Mari, Toshifumi. MD, Kyoto Prefectural U. Medicine, 1957; DMSc, Kyoto Prefectural U. Medicine, 1964. Intern Kyoto 1st Red Cross Hosp., 1957-58; clin. fellow Kyoto Prefectural U. Medicine, 1959-60, asst. prof., 1971-74, assoc. prof., 1974-97; clin. fellow U. Ala. Med. Ctr., Birmingham, 1964-67, instr. medicine, 1967-68; postdoctoral fellow in molecular biology U. Edinburgh, Scotland, 1968-70; v.p. Kyoto Prefectural Yosanoumi Hosp., Iwataki, 1983—97; pres. Kyoto Prefectural Yosanoumi Blood Ctr., Iwataki, 1974-83; prin. Kyoto Prefectural Nursing Sch., Iwataki, 1988-94; pres., med. juridical person Ohtha Found. Ohta Hosp., Kyoto, 1997—2006; pres., med. juridical person Miyazu Kosei Found., Miyazu Takeda Hosp., Kyoto, 2006—. Mem. WHO, Kyoto, Japan, 1983—. Contbr. articles to profl. jours. Recipient med. diploma Japanese Ministry Health and Welfare, 1958; fellow NIH, 1965, European Molecular Biology Orgn., 1968. Fellow Japanese Soc. Internal Medicine, Japanese Soc. Gastroenterology, Japanese Soc. Hepatology; mem. AAAS, NY Acad. Scis. Avocations: golf, tennis, stamp collecting/philately, gardening, music. Home: 988 Uoya Kyoto 626-0015 Japan Office Phone: 0772-22-2157. Business E-Mail: tsuji7@fine.ocn.ne.jp.

TSUKAMOTO, DANIEL, piano instructor, church organist; b. Encarnación, Itapúa, Paraguay, Apr. 18, 1970; s. Minoru and Yoko Tsukamoto. BA, Asbury Coll., 1994; MusM, U. SD, Vermillion, 1995. Electronic organist Free Meth. Ch., Encarnación, Itapúa, Paraguay, 1982—86; instr. HS orch. Rapid City Ctrl. HS, SD, 1986—88; instr. HS orch. (double bass/cello player) Watertown Sr. HS, SD, 1988—89; instr. coll. orch. (double bass player/cello player) Asbury Coll., Wilmore, Ky., 1989—94; instr. U. orch. (double bass/cello player) U. SD, Vermillion, 1994—95, piano grad. asst., 1994—95; instr. U. orch. (double bass player) SD State U., Brookings, 1996—99; ch. organist Romeo United Meth. Ch., Romeo, Mich., 2000—, piano lesson tchr., 2002—, mem. ch. music com., 2000—, piano accompanist, musical singer (tenor), 2002—03. Double bass player Rapid City Symphony Orch., SD, 1987—88; all-state orch. SD Pub. Schs., Aberdeen, 1988—88, all-state honor's orch., Brookings, 1989—89, all-state band, Huron, 1989—89; double bass player Pit Orch., Wilmore, Ky., 1989—89; ch. organist for weddings, Mich., 2003—. Bell ringer Salvation Army, Watertown, SD; mem. music com. Romeo United Meth. Ch., 2000—. Named to Nat. Honor Soc., Rapid City Ctrl. HS, 1987; recipient Faculty Award, Watertown Sr. High, 1988—89, Nat. HS Orchestra award, 1989. Mem.: Am. Guild Organists (assoc.). Home: 42221 Toddmark Ln Apt 124 Clinton Township MI 48038 Office: Romeo United Methodist Church 280 N Main St Romeo MI 48065 Home Phone: 586-412-9015. Home Fax: 586-412-9015. Personal E-mail: z5aj@sbcglobal.net.

TSUNEOKA, YUTAKA, molecular geneticist; b. Nabari, Mie, Japan, Apr. 15, 1959; s. Tadao and Shuu (Higuchi) T.; m. Yumi Teraoka, Mar. 9, 1986; children: Yu, Ei. BA, Tokyo U. Fgn. Studies, 1984; MD, Kagawa Med. U., 1990, PhD, 1994. Lic. physician, Japan. Rsch. assoc. Nat. Def. Med. Coll., Tokorozawa, Japan, 1994-96, 1998; postdoctoral fellow U. Cin., 1996-98; staff physician Onaga Hosp., Tokorozawa, 1998-99, Kaishindoh Hosp., Tokyo, 1999; postdoctoral fellow U. Cin., 2000—. Mem. AAAS. Avocations: tennis, skiing, baseball, bicycling, basketball. Office: U Cincinnati Dept Environ Health PO Box 670056 Cincinnati OH 45267-0056 Home: 8509 Pondridge Dr Maineville OH 45039-8972 E-mail: yutaka.tsuneoka@uc.edu.

TSUTSUMI, TSUYOSHI, musician, educator; b. Tokyo; arrived in U.S., 1984; s. Kiyoshi and Mineko Tsutsumi; m. Harue Saji, May 14, 1978; children: Seizo, Mie. Diploma, Ind. U., 1965. Artist-in-resident Ind. U., Bloomington, 1966—68, prof. music, 1988—; from artist-in-resident to assoc. prof. U. Western Ont., London, Canada, 1968—84; prof. music U. Ill., Urbana, 1984—88; pres. Toho Gakuen Sch. Music, Tokyo, 2004. Author: My Illinois Diary, 1990, LIfe with the Cello, 2002. Bd. dirs., pres. Suntory Music Found., Tokyo, 1989. Recipient Music prize, Suntory Music Found., 1971, Acad. of Arts prize, Govt. of Japan, 1993, Chevalier du Violon-celle, Ind. U., 2003. Mem.: Japan Cello Soc. (pres.). Avocations: reading, trains. Home: 2715 Bluff Ct Bloomington IN 47401 Office Phone: 812-855-1552. Business E-Mail: tsutsum@indiana.edu.

TSYBAKOV, BORIS SOLOMON, information theory and communication networks researcher, educator; b. Moscow, May 14, 1934; s. Solomon Mark and Evdokia Tikhon (Tsybakova) Pinsker; m. Lidia Sergey Tsybakova, Oct. 14, 1956; 1 child, Alexander. D of Sci. in Engring., Moscow Inst. of Physics/Tech. Jr. rschr. Inst. for Radio and Electronic Engring., Moscow, 1958—63, sr. rschr., 1963—77; head of lab. Inst. for Info. Transmission Problems, Moscow, 1977—2000; prin. engr. Qualcomm, Inc., San Diego, 1999—2006; rsch. scientist U. Calif., San Diego, 2006—. Prof. Moscow Inst. of Physics and Tech., 1965—93; supr. Post-grads. in Info. Theory. Mem. editl. bd. Problems of Info. Transmission Jour., 1965—; editor Wireless Personal Comms., An Internat. Jour., 1992—, Jour. Comms. and Networks, 1999—; mem. internat. adv. com. Advanced Electronic Comm. Rsch. & Edn. Jour.; contbr. articles to profl. publ. and lecture courses on info. theory and commn. sys. Recipient full prof. title diploma, 1979, Prominent Comm. Profl. of Russia award Pres. of Russia, 1996, Paper award INFOCOM'95 on Math. Analysis of the Self-Similar Traffic, 1995. Mem.: IEEE (Info. Theory Soc. paper award on Invention of the Stable Multiple-Access Algorithm 1981), Russian Acad. Sci. Club. Avocation: lawn tennis. Office: U Calif San Diego 9500 Gilman Dr La Jolla CA 92093-0436 Personal E-mail: btsybakov@yahoo.com.

TSYGAN, LEONID IOSIFOVICH, civil engineer, writer; b. Kiev, Ukraine, Dec. 22, 1938; arrived in U.S., 1979; s. Iosif Haim-Garshevech and Bluma Leybovna Tsygan; m. Emmilia Igorevna Shustova, 1971 (div. 1984); 1 child, Russell; m. Zhanna Iosifovna Polonskaya, 1997; 1 child, Joshua 1 stepchild, Lana Polonskaya. BSCE, Kiev Inst. Hwy. Engring., 1968; computer programmer, Syrit Computer Sch. Sys., NYC, 1983. Sr. engr. State Design Inst. Hwys., Kiev, 1968—78; draftsman King and Gavaris Cons. Engrs. Inc., NYC, 1979—81; designer, draftsman Berger, Lehman Assocs. P.C., Rye, NY, 1982—84; bridge designer E. Pavlo Consulting Engr., NYC, 1984—89; engr. Anuman & Whitney Cons. Engr., NYC, 1990—91; asst. civil engr. N.Y.C. Dept. Transp., NYC, 1992—. Contbr. poetry to anthologies. Alt. del. N.Y.C. Dept. Transp. local 375, chpt. 37, DC 37 AFSCME, AFL-CIO, NYC, 2000—. Co-recipient medal for design of Moscow cable-stay bridge, State Design Inst. Hwys., 1976; named to Poetry's Elite: The Best Poets of 2000. Achievements include test track for road pavement and bridge structure with test material in Willowbrook Park, Staten Island.

TU, CHANH M., ophthalmologist; b. Oct. 5, 1967; BS, U. Okla., Norman, 1988; MD, U. Okla., Oklahoma City, 1992. Ptnr. Regional Eye Ctr., Americus, Ga., 1996—. Fellow: ACS, Am. Acad. Ophthalmology. Office: Regional Eye Ctr 1119 E Lamar St Americus GA 31709

TU, JIUFENG J., physics professor; b. Nanjing, Jiangsu Province, China, Nov. 26, 1968; s. Shude Tu and Lizhen Tang; m. Qing R. Fan, Mar. 2, 1971. AB, AM, Harvard U., Cambridge, Mass., 1993; PhD, Cornell U., Ithaca, NY, 2000. Rsch. assoc. Brookhaven Nat. Lab., Upton, NY, 2000—03; prof. of physics CCNY, NYC, 2003—. Exec. prodr.:. Recipient rsch. grants, NSF, 2004—09. Mem.: Am. Phys. Soc. (assoc.). Achievements include patents pending for Room temperature manufacturing of ultra-thin films. Office: CCNY J-330A Dept of Physics 160 Convent Ave New York NY 10031 Home Phone: 212-650-5558; Office Phone: 212-650-5558. Office Fax: 212-650-6940. Business E-Mail: jtu@sci.ccny.cuny.edu.

TU, LAWRENCE P., lawyer, computer company executive; b. NYC, Aug. 23, 1954; AB summa cum laude, Harvard Univ., 1976, JD magna cum laude, 1981; BA, Magdalen Coll., Oxford Univ., 1978. Bar: DC 1983, US Supreme Ct. 1988, Hong Kong 1996. Law clk. Judge Walter R. Mansfield, US Ct. Appeals, 2d cir., 1981—82, Justice Thurgood Marshall, US Supreme Ct., 1982—83; gen. counsel, Asia Pacific Goldman Sachs; spl. asst. to legal adviser U.S. Dept. State, 1985—86; assoc. O'Melveny & Myers LLP, 1986—89, ptnr., 1990—2001, mng. ptnr. Hong Kong office, 1995—2000; exec. v.p., gen. counsel NBC Universal, 2001—04; sr. v.p., gen. counsel Dell Inc., 2004—. Editor (notes): Harvard Law Rev., 1979—81. Rhodes Scholar. Mem.: ABA, Minority Corp. Counsel Assn., DC Bar, Council on Fgn. Rels. Office: Dell Inc 1 Dell Way Round Rock TX 78682-2244 *

TU, YUFENG, business educator; BS in Internat. Bus. Mgmt., U. Md., College Park, 2000, PhD in Mgmt. Sci. and Stats., 2006. Rsch. asst. U. Md.; asst. prof. Tourou U., Cypress, Calif. Contbr. articles to profl. jours. Named one of Top Ten Outstanding Women, Beijing Tech. & Bus. U., 2000; recipient Outstanding Participation award, FAA Ctr. Excellence, 2005; Global Tech. & Mgmt. Consortium fellow, Md., 2005. Mem.: Am. Statis. Assn., Inst. Ops. Rsch. and Mgmt. Scis., Decision Scis. Inst., Nat. Ctr. Excellence Aviation Ops. Rsch.

TUAN, KAILIN, management consultant, educator; b. Hefei, China, Sept. 9, 1925; m. Liau G. Tuan; 1 child, Wayne. BS, Chiao Tung U., Shanghai, 1948; MBA, U. Pa., 1952; PhD, New Sch. for Social Rsch., NYC, 1966. Asst./assoc. prof. Upsala Coll., East Orange, NJ, 1959—74; prof. U. Balt., 1974—77, Temple U., Phila., 1977—93, prof. emeritus, 1993—. Prof., dir. Internat. Ins. Inst., Nankai U., Tianyin, China, 1987—97; hon. prof. various Chinese univs.; lectr. in field; econ. adviser to Taiwan and the Philippines, 1970—73; adviser Ministry of Fin., Taiwan, 1970—90; Far Ea. rep. Internat. Coop. Alliance, 1970; cons. to several maj. U.S. and Brit. ins. and bus. cos., 1970—80. Contbr. articles more than 100 numerous articles to profl. jour. publ. in profl. and academic jour. and bus./ins. mag. USA, UK, Japan, China, Taiwan and other Asian countries; author: Modern Insurance Theory and Edn./Ins. Inst. for Asia and the Pacific, 1972—75, Essays in Risk Management, 1988, The Risk Management Movement, 1999, Studies in the Theory of Risk and Insurance, 1995. Recipient Internat. Friendship award, Chinese Govt., 2000, FLMI Ins. Edn. award, Life Office Mgmt. Assn., 2001, Pres.'s award, Ins. Acctg. and Sys. Assn., 2002. Mem.: U.S. Am.-China C. of C. (founder, bd. dirs.), Am. Risk and Ins. Assn., Internat. Ins. Soc. Avocations: gardening, Go. Office: Temple Univ Dept Risk Mgmt and Ins Philadelphia PA 19122

TUBB, BETTY FREEZE, music educator; b. Oklahoma City, Oct. 6, 1932; d. Eugene Woodrow Freeze and Otha Merle Perkins; m. Boyd Junior Bryce, Aug. 6, 1948 (dec. June 1965); children: Donna Bryce Lacquement, DiAnn Bryce Neff; m. Curtis O'Connor Tubb, Dec. 30, 1969; 1 child, Tara Elizabeth Tubb Foster. BMus in Piano, Oklahoma City U., 1966. Cert. piano tchr. Ala. Pvt. music tchr., Oklahoma City, 1960—70; faculty Tonsmeire Sch. Music, Mobile, Ala., 1970—71, Mobile Christian Sch., 1971—73; pvt. music tchr. Cross City, Fla., 1980—85; faculty Wrights Girls Sch., Mobile, 1986—87; pvt. music tchr., ind. piano tchr. Mobile, 1988—. Adjudicator Nat. Guild Piano Tchrs., 1962—91. Mem.: Music Tchrs. Nat. Assn., Ala. Music Tchrs. Assn., Nat. Guild Piano Tchrs. (adjudicator 1962—99, treas., chair scholarship com.), Mobile Music Tchr. Assn. (pres. 1972—74, treas. 2001—02, scholarship chmn.), Sigma Alpha Iota. Republican. Mem. Church Of Christ. Avocation: heritage. E-mail: bettyt10063@cs.com.

TUBB, JAMES CLARENCE, lawyer; b. Corsicana, Tex. s. Cullen Louis and Sarah Elmore (Chapman) T.; m. Suzanne Alice Smith, Nov. 25, 1954; children: James Richard, Sara Elizabeth, Daniel Chapman. BA, So. Meth. U., 1951, JD, 1954. Bar: Tex. 1954, U.S. Dist. Ct. (no. dist.) Tex. 1955, U.S. Ct. Appeals (5th cir.) 1959, U.S. Supreme Ct. 1978; cert. comml. real estate specialist, 1983; lic. Tex. real estate broker; cert. mediator Dallas Bar Assn. With legal dept. Schlumberger Well Surveying Corp., Houston, 1954-55; claims atty. Franklin Am. Ins. Co., Dallas, 1957-58; ptnr. Vial, Hamilton, Koch, Tubb & Knox and predecessor firm Akin, Vial, Hamilton, Koch & Tubb, Dallas, 1958-84; dir., ptnr. Winstead, McGuire, Sechrest & Minick, Dallas, 1984-90; pvt. practice Dallas, 1990—. Guest lectr. on real estate broker liability Real Estate Ctr., Tex. A&M U., 1987. Mem. bd. deacons Highland Park Presbyn. Ch., Dallas, 1972—78, ruling elder, 1978—84, 1988—91; mem. permanent jud. commn. Grace Presbytery, 1984—90; bd. dirs. Christian Concern Found., 1965—71, Dallas County affiliate Am. Diabetes Assn., 1991—95. With Tex. Air N.G., 1949—51, 1st lt. JAGC, SAC USAF, 1955—57, 1st lt. USAF, ret. Recipient Outstanding Student award Student Bar Assn., 1954. Fellow Tex. Bar Found.; mem. ABA (chmn. comml. law com. gen. practice sect. 1982-84, real estate probate and trust law sect.), Tex. Bus. Law Found., Tex. Bar Assn., Am. Arbitration Assn. (sec. comml. arbitration panelist), Dallas Country Club, Dallas County Rep. Men's Club (sec. 1978-79). Home and Office: 3407 Haynie Ave Dallas TX 75205-1842 Office Phone: 214-232-8964. Personal E-mail: jctubb@sbcglobal.com.

TUBBS, CHRISTOPHER CHARLES, music educator; s. Roger Livingston and Kathryn Jane Tubbs; m. Kelly Jo Brick, July 1, 1995. MusB, U. Wis., Madison, 1994; postgrad., Coll. St. Scholastica, Duluth, Minn., 1998—. Instrument repair U. Wis., Madison, 1989—94; tchr. instrumental music Cassville Sch. Dist., Wis., 1994—. Athletic dir. Cassville Sch. Dist., 2005—. Office: Cassville School District 715 East Amelia St Cassville WI 53806 Home Phone: (608) 725-5389; Office Phone: 608-725-5116. E-mail: ctubbs@cassvillesd.k12.wi.us.

TUBBS, EDWARD LANE, banker; b. Delmar, Iowa, Apr. 17, 1920; s. Clifton Marvin and Mary Ellen (Lane) T.; m. Grace Barbara Dyer, Nov. 27, 1941 (dec.); children: Steven, Alan, William; m. Elaine Marshall, Mar. 11, 2000. BS, Iowa State U., Ames, 1941; postgrad., U. Wis. Grad. Sch. Banking. With Iowa State U. Agrl. Ext. Svc., Newton, 1942; instr. vets. on-farm DeWitt Schs., Iowa, 1957-58; v.p., dir. Jackson State Bank, Maquoketa State Bank, 1959-66, chmn. bd., 1966—. Pres., dir. Ohnward Bancshares, Inc.; chmn., dir. 1st Ctrl. State Bank, DeWitt; dir. Tri-County Bank & Trust; pres., dir. Mabsco Agrl. Svcs., Inc., 1982-87; supt. banking State of Iowa, 1987-89; bd. dirs. Iowa Bus. Growth Corp.; lectr. banking schs.; exeh. del. USSR, 1959, 85; banking indsutry del. Baltic Countries, 1993; state dir. Conf. State Bank Supts., 1988-89. Contbr. articles to profl. jours. Pres. Elwood Sch. Bd., Iowa, 1956-62; treas. City of Maquoketa, 1975-81; mem. People to People; trustee Sharar Found., Clinton Coll., 1983-86; v.p., bd. dirs. Timber City Indsl. Devel. Corp., Jackson County Sr. Ctr.; treas. Maquoketa Cmty. Svcs., 1967-80; trustee Iowa 4-H Found., 1987-91, Hoover Presdl. Libr. Assn. Inc., truatee, 1987—; gov. Iowa State U. Found., 1989—; trustee CCFA Found., 1990-94; coach Little League; elder, moderator United Ch. of Christ; mem. awards com. Pearson Found. With AUS, 1942-43. Recipient 4-H Club Alumni award, 1962, 01, Century Farm award Iowa Dept. Agr., 1976, Disting. Pub. Svcs. award Jackson County, 1990, Gold Clover award Iowa 4-H Club, Heart of Gold award, 1996, Iowa Agrl. Ext. Assn. award, 1982, Floyd Andre award, 1985, Cmty. Svc. award Mt. St. Clare Coll., 2002; named Jaycee Boss of Yr., 1970; named to Iowa Agrl. Hall of Fame, 1985, Clinton Fair Hall of Fame, 1999. Mem. Bank Adminstrn. Inst., Am. Bankers Assn. (dir., coun. 1984-86, Ag Bruning award 2000, award for lifetime contbn. to agrl. banking 2000), Iowa Bankers Assn. (treas. 1978-79, pres. 1980-81, James Leach Lifetime Contribution to Banking award 2002), Am. Legion (60 Yr. award 2006), Iowa State U. Alumni Assn. (dir. 1980-86), Maquoketa C. of C. (dir. 1966-69), Order of Knoll (founders club Iowa State U.), Iowa Friends of Agr. (exec. com. 1987-95, 150 Yr. Family Farm award 2006), Rotary (Paul Harris fellow, Outstanding Svc. award 2006), Gamma Sigma Delta (Alumni Achievement award 1989), Alpha Zeta. Home: 1804 Swagosa Dr Maquoketa IA 52060 Office: 203 N Main St Maquoketa IA 52060-2204

TUBERVILLE, TOMMY, college football coach; b. Sept. 18, 1954; m. Suzanne Fette; children: Thomas Tucker, Troy Allen. BS in Phys. Edn., So. Ark. Univ., 1976. Defensive coach Ark. State, 1980—85, Univ. Miami, 1986—93, defensive coord., 1993, Texas A&M, 1994—95; head football coach Ole Miss, 1995—98, Auburn Univ., 1999—. Office: Auburn Athletics PO Box 351 Auburn AL 36831-0351 *

TUBESING, RICHARD LEE, library director; b. Kansas City, Mo., Nov. 25, 1937; s. Clarence and Letha (Thacker) T. BA, Yale U., 1959; MA, U. Chgo., 1969; MSL, Western Mich. U., 1972. Asst. to dir. U. Louisville, 1972-73; reference libr. Ga. Tech. Libr., Atlanta, 1973-76; head bus. and sci. Atlanta Pub. Libr., 1976-79; libr. dir. Lewis U., Romeoville, Ill., 1979-81; collection devel. coord. U. Toledo Libr., 1981-86; libr. dir. Coll. of the Southwest, Hobbs, N.Mex., 1986-89; libr. dir., dir. libr. sci. program

Glenville (W.Va.) State Coll., 1989-99; ret., 1999. Part-time libr. Gilmer Pub. Libr., Glenville, W.Va. Author: Architectural Preservation, 1978, Architectural Preservation and Urban Renovation, 1982. Program coord. Lea County Archaeol. Soc., Hobbs, 1987-89. Lt. j.g. USNR, 1960-63. Mem. W.Va. Libr. Assn., Lea County Libr. Assn. (v.p. 1987-88, pres. 1988-89). Avocation: collecting primitive and peasant art. Home: 351 E Valley Dr Glenville WV 26351-9416 Personal E-mail: ricktubesing@lycos.com.

TUBMAN, WILLIAM CHARLES, lawyer; b. NYC, Mar. 16, 1932; s. William Thomas and Ellen Veronica Griffin; m. Dorothy Rita Krug, Aug. 15, 1964; children: William Charles Jr., Thomas Davison, Matthew Griffin. BS, Fordham U., 1953, JD, 1960; postdoctoral, NYU Sch. Law, 1960-61. Bar: N.Y. 1960, U.S. Ct. Appeals (2d cir.) 1966, U.S. Supreme Ct. 1967, U.S. Ct. Customs and Patent Appeals 1971. Auditor Peat, Marwick Mitchell & Co., NYC, 1956-60; sr. counsel Kennecott Corp., NYC, 1960-82, Phelps Dodge Corp., NYC, 1982-85, sec., 1985-95, v.p., 1987-95; pres. Phelps Dodge Found., Phoenix, 1988-95. Author: Legal Status of Minerals Beyond the Continental Shelf, 1966. Scholarship adv. U. Ariz., 1990-92; active Big Bros., Inc., N.Y.C., 1963-73; trustee Phoenix Art Mus., 1989-94; bd. dirs. St. Joseph Hosp. Found., 1994-2003, emeritus, 2003—, chmn., 1994-95; bd. dirs. The Phoenix Symphony, 1994-95. Recipient Disting. Svc. cert. Big Brothers Inc., 1968. Mem.: ABA, N.Y. State Bar Assn. Democrat. Roman Catholic. Home: 8008 N 66th St Paradise Valley AZ 85253-2612

TUBMAN-REICHHOFF, DENISE CHRISTINE, music educator; d. Michael Herbert and Christine Elizabeth Tubman; m. Nicholas Frederick Reichhoff, Sept. 9, 2006. MusB, U. Wis., Stevens Point, 2001. Cert. educator Wis. Dept. Edn., 2001. Tchr. Hillsboro Schs., Wis., 2002—05, Jefferson Schs., Wis., 2005—. Home Phone: 608-253-4112; Office Phone: 920-675-1079.

TUBUTIS, TODD J., anthropologist; s. John P. and Barbara J. Tubutis. BA, Beloit Coll., Beloit, Wis., 1988—92; MA, U. B.C., Vancouver, Can., 1996—98. Conversational english tchr. Váci Mihály Gimnázium, Encs, Hungary, 1993—94; pub. programs asst. The Newberry Libr., Chgo., 1994—95; vis. lectr., cultural anthropology U. Miskolc, Hungary, 1998—99; seminars mgr. The Newberry Libr., Chgo., 1999—2001; permanent exhibition mgr. The Field Mus., Chgo., 2001—. Author: (encyclopedia entry) The Encyclopedia of Chgo.; photographer (book) Pepper in Our Eyes: The APEC Affair; contbr. papers to profl. jours. and pubs. Mem. Chgo. Pub. Radio Cmty. Adv. Coun., 2004—. Recipient Departmental Honors, Anthropology, Beloit Coll., 1992; grantee James E. Lockwood Anthropology scholarship, 1991—92, R. Howard Webster fellowship, U. B.C., 1997—98. Mem.: Am. Assn. Museums (Diversity fellowship 2005), Phi Beta Kappa.

TUCCERI, CLIVE KNOWLES, writer, science educator, consultant; b. Bryn Mawr, Pa., Apr. 20, 1953; d. William Henry and Clive Ellis (Knowles) Hulick; m. Eugene Angelo Tucceri, Sept. 1, 1984 (div. Nov. 1991); 1 child, Clive Edna. BA in Geology, Williams Coll., 1975; MS in Coastal Geology, Boston Coll., 1982. Cert. profl. tchr. in Earth and gen. sci. Head sci. dept. Stuart Hall Sch., Staunton, Va., 1975-77; mem. sci. faculty William Penn Charter Sch., Phila., 1977-79, Tower Sch., Marblehead, Mass., 1982-86, Bentley Coll., Waltham, Mass., 1986-88; adminstrv. dir., co-founder Stout Aquatic Libr. Nat. Marine and Aquatic Edn. Resource Ctr., Wakefield, R.I., 1982-89; sci. faculty Mabelle B. Avery Sch., Somers, Conn., 1989—90; faculty, head sci. dept. MacDuffie Sch., Springfield, Mass., 1992—93; sci. faculty East Hampton (Conn.) Middle Sch., 1993—, sci. team leader, 1994—95, sci. chmn. grades K-12, 1995—. Cons. Addison-Wesley Pub. Co., Menlo Park, Calif., 1986—94, Longmeadow (Mass.) Pub. Schs., 1989—94; cons. and freelance writer Prentice-Hall Inc., Needham, 1991; cons. web content devel. Conn. Sci. Ctr., 2005—. Co-head class agt. Williams Coll. Alumni Fund, 2000—, vice chair, 2003—06; admissions rep. Williams Coll., 2001—; vol. The Bushnell Ctr. for Performing Arts, 2001—; mem. search com. Christ Ch., Middle Haddam, Conn., 2000—01, mem. vestry, 2002—05; bd. dir. People Against Rape, Staunton, 1976—77. Mem.: AAUW (bd. dirs., br. pres.-elect 1975—77, v.p. 1985—86, sec. 1986—87), NEA, NSTA, Cousteau Soc., Conn. Edn. Assn., Conn. Sci Tchrs. Assn., Conn. Sci. Suprs. Assn., Mass. Environ. Edn. Soc. (bd. dirs. 1985—88), Mass. Marine Educators (pres. 1987—89, bd. dirs. 1983—91, editor Flotsam and Jetsam MA Marine Educators newsletter 1991—97), Southeastern New Eng. Marine Educators (publs. chair Nat. Conf. com.), Nat. Mid. Level Sci. Tchrs. Assn., Nat. Marine Edn. Assn. (sec. 1986—87, chpt. rep. 1987 1989), Sigma Xi. Episcopalian. Avocations: renovating old homes, sailing, gardening, reading. Home: 12 Birchwood Dr East Hampton CT 06424-1312 Personal E-mail: ctucceri@aol.com.

TUCCI, GERALD FRANK, manufacturing executive; b. NYC, Sept. 9, 1926; s. Frank and Mary (Fattizzi) T.; m. Eva G. Gyllander, May 14, 1968; children: Francis Henrik, Michael Fredrik, Amy Christina. Student, Dartmouth Coll., 1944; BSc in Naval Sci., Brown U., 1946, BSME, 1948; MBA with distinction, Harvard U., 1950. Mfg. trainee Am. Can Co., Jersey City, 1950—51; asst. v.p., plant mgr. Artcraft Hosiery Mills, Inc., Darby, Pa., 1951—53; v.p. Leach & Garner, Co., Attleboro, Mass., 1953-63, Gen. Findings, Inc., Attleboro, 1953-63; chmn. Micro Contacts, Inc., Hicksville, NY, 1963—; pres. Micro Pneumatic Logic, Inc., Ft. Lauderdale, Fla., 1973—. Chmn. Micro Group, 2004—. Lt. (s.g.) USNR, 1944-47. Mem.: ASME, Am. Soc. Mfrs., Harvard Club, Harvard Bus. Sch. Club, North Hempstead Country Club, Met. Club, Beta Theta Pi. Republican. Roman Catholic. Office: 62 Alpha Plz Hicksville NY 11801-2618 Home Phone: 516-767-9692; Office Phone: 516-433-4830. E-mail: gerrytucci@aol.com.

TUCCI, JOSEPH M., information technology executive; b. Bklyn., 1947; m. Maureen Tucci. BA, Manhattan Coll., 1968; MBA, Columbia U., 1984. With RCA Corp., 1970—86; pres. U.S. ops. Unisys Corp., 1986-90; exec. v.p. ops. Wang Labs., Inc., 1990-93, chmn., CEO Lowell, Mass., 1993—99; dep. CEO Getronics NV, 1999; pres., COO EMC Corp., Hopkinton, Mass., 2000—01, pres., CEO, 2001—, chmn., 2006—. Bd. dirs. Paychex, 2000—, EMC Corp., 2001—. Office: EMC Corp 176 South St Hopkinton MA 01748 *

TUCCI, JOSEPH RALPH, endocrinologist, educator; s. Ralph and Brigida Tucci; m. Marjorie Jane Puffer, Sept. 24, 1960; children: Elizabeth Anne, Paula Marie. AB cum laude, Brown U., 1955; MD, Boston U., 1959. Diplomate Nat. Bd. Med. Examiners, lic. R.I., Am. Bd. Internal Medicine. Rotating intern St. Elizabeth's Hosp., Boston, 1959—60, resident in medicine, 1960—62; clin. fellow in nephrology, metabolism, and endocrinology Georgetown Univ. Hosp., Washington, 1962—63, fellow in endocrinology and metabolism, 1963—64; sr. 3d-yr. resident in medicine (endocrinology) VA Hosp., Washington, 1964—65; rsch. fellow in medicine Harvard Med. Sch. and Peter Bent Brigham Hosp., Boston, 1965—67; asst. prof. medicine Brown U., Providence, 1969—74, program dir. fellowship program in endocrinology and metabolism, 1969—84, head subsect. endocrinology, 1974—84, assoc. prof. medicine, 1975—96, prof. medicine, 1997—98, Boston U. Sch. Medicine, 1998—; active med. staff Roger Williams Med. Ctr., Providence, 1969—, dir. endocrinology and metabolism dept. medicine, 1969—, dir. bone and mineral unit, 1984—. Adj. prof. medicine Brown U. Sch. Medicine, Providence, 1998—; cons. in endocrinology; mem. endocrine study sect. NIH, Bethesda, Md., 1968—69; physician, cons. Neighborhood Health Ctr., 1970—99; mem. profl. adv. com. Providence Health Ctrs., 1974—99; cons. diabetes program R.I. Dept. Health, 1978; mem. corp. Blue Cross and Blue Shield of R.I., 1979—, cons., 1984—; chmn. New Eng. Osteoporosis Bd., 2003—06. Assoc. editor: Endo Trends, 2002—, reviewer: profl. jours.; contbr. articles to profl. jours. Comdr. USNR, 1968—69. Fellow: ACP, Am. Coll. Endocrinology; mem.: R.I. Med. Soc., Soc. for Clin. Densitometry, Am. Assn. Clin. Endocrinology, Am. Soc. for Bone and Mineral Rsch., Clin. Diabetes Assn. R.I., Endocrine Soc. Avocations: tennis, swimming, reading. Office: Roger Williams Med Ctr 825 Chalkstone Ave Providence RI 02908

TUCCI, STANLEY, actor; b. Peekskill, NY, Nov. 11, 1960; m. Kate Tucci, 1995; 3 children. BFA, SUNY, Purchase, 1982. Actor (films) Fear Anxiety and Depression, 1990, Billy Bathgate, 1991, Men of Respect, 1991, In The Soup, 1992, Beethoven, 1992, Prelude to A Kiss, 1992, Undercover Blues, 1993, The Pelican Brief, 1993, Somebody to Love, 1994, It Could Happen to You, 1994, Mrs. Parker and the Vicious Circle, 1994, Jury Duty, 1995, Kiss of Death, 1995, A Modern Affair, 1995, Captive, 1995, The Daytrippers, 1996, Montana, 1997, Life During Wartime, 1997, The Eighteenth Angel, 1997, Deconstructing Harry, 1997, A Life Less Ordinary, 1997, The Imposters, 1998, A Midsummer Night's Dream, 1999, Joe Gould's Secret, 1999, In Too Deep, 1999, The Whole Shebang, 2000, Bull, 2000, Sidewalks of New York, 2001, America's Sweethearts, 2001, Big Trouble, 2002, Road to Perdition, 2002, Maid in Manhattan, 2002, The Core, 2003, The Life and Death of Peter Sellers, 2004, The Terminal, 2004, Shall We Dance?, 2004, (voice only) Robots, 2005, Lucky Number Slevin, 2006, Four Las Songs, 2006, The Devil Wears Prada, 2006, The Hoax, 2006; actor, co-dir., co-prodr. (films) Big Night, 1996 (Ind. Spirit award for best 1st screenplay 1996); actor (TV series) Murder One, 1995, 3 Lbs., 2006-, (TV movies) Winchell, 1998 (Emmy award 1998), Conspiracy, 2001 (Golden Globe award 2001) Office: William Morris Agy c/o David Yocum 151 S El Camino Dr Beverly Hills CA 90212-2775 *

TUCHMAN, ALAN, consumer products company executive; V.p. Alliance Entertainment Corp., 1991—96, pres., COO, 2000—05, sr. v.p. strategic planning, 1996—97, pres. AEC One Stop Group, Inc., 1997—2000; exec. v.p., pres. Alliance divsn. Source Interlink Cos., interim co-CEO. Office: Source Interlink Cos 27500 Riverview Center Blvd Bonita Springs FL 34134 Office Phone: 239-949-4450. *

TUCHMAN, AVRAHAM (AVI), physicist, researcher; b. NYC, July 1, 1935; s. Max and Rebecca (Brick) T.; m. Sylvia Crystal, Dec. 26, 1957; children: Davida, Ari, Sima, Pnina. BA, Yeshiva U., NYC, 1956; PhD, MIT, Cambridge, 1963. Scientist, group leader to sect. chief Avco Rsch. and Advanced Devel., Wilmington, Mass., 1963; prin. scientist, staff scientist to prin. staff scientist Avco Systems Div., Wilmington; chief scientist Textron Def. Systems, Wilmington, 1988-93; owner, pres., CEO Added Value Innovations, Brookline, Mass., 1994—. Vis. prof. Weizmann Inst. Sci., Rehovot, Israel, 1974, 78, 82. Contbr. numerous articles to profl. jours. Founder, pres. Kehilla Day Camp of Jewish Community Ctrs., Westwood, Mass., 1975-86; chmn. Brookline Traffic Commn., Mass., 1975-81; pres. Mikvah Rescue Svc., Brighton, Mass., 1969-77; pres. Temple Beth Avraham, Brookline, 1969—. Recipient award for outstanding cantorial artistry Am. Soc. Forktwangers, Detroit, 1970. Fellow AIAA (sr.). Avocations: computers, gardening, homecraft, snowboarding, dowhill racing.

TUCHMAN, PHYLLIS, critic; b. Passaic, NJ, Jan. 4, 1947; d. Jack and Evelyn (Sugarman) T. BA in Fine Arts with distinction, Boston U., 1968; MA, NYU, 1973. Ind. critic, NYC, 1968—. Inst. art hist., Sch. Visual Arts, NY, 1972-75; adj. lectr. art history Hunter Coll., CUNY, NYC, 1976-79; vis. prof. art Williams Coll., Williamstown, Mass., 1981-83; curator Six in Bronze, Williams Coll. Mus. Art and tour, 1985, Big Little Sculpture, Williams Coll. Mus. Art and tour, 1988, Venezuela: The Next Generation, Baruch Col. Gallery, 1990, Drawing Redux, San Jose Mus. Art and tour, 1992, Norte del Sur: Venezuelan Art Today, Philbrook Art Mus., 1997. Author: George Segal, 1983, Venezuela: The Next Generation, 1990; contbr. articles to profl. jours., popular mags. Art Critics grantee NEA, 1978-79; vis. fellow Princeton U., NEH, 1980. Mem. Internat. Assn. Art Critics (Am. sect. pres. 1986-90, v.p. internat. parent body, 89-91), Art Table (bd. dirs. 1984-87, v.p. 1987-88), AICA (v.p. Am. sect. 2004—) Home: 340 E 80th St New York NY 10021-0927

TUCHMANN, ERIC P., lawyer; m. Cheri Fancsali; children: Isabel, Amelia. BS, U. Wis., Madison, 1988; JD, NY Law Sch., 1994. With Am. Arbitration Assn., 1994—, dir. comml. dept. NY, dir. Internat. Ctr. Dispute Resolution, assoc. gen. counsel, gen. counsel, corp. sec. NYC, 2004—. Office: Am Arbitration Assn 1633 Broadway 10th Fl New York NY 10019-6708 Office Phone: 212-716-5800.

TUCHMANN, ROBERT, lawyer; b. NYC, July 7, 1946; s. Frederick C. and Hildegard (Jung) Tuchmann; m. Naomi R. Walfish, June 1, 1969; children: David, Paul. AB, Oberlin Coll., 1967; JD, Harvard U., 1971. Bar: Mass. 1971, U.S. Dist. Ct. Mass. 1971. Assoc. Hale and Dorr, Boston, 1971-76, jr. ptnr., 1976-80, sr. ptnr., 1980—2004, Wilmer, Cutler, Pickering, Hale and Dorr, Boston, 2004—. Lectr. Mass. Continuing Legal Edn., 1976—99. Pres. Project Bread-The Walk for Hunger, Boston, 1990—98; chair Ctrl. Artery Environ. Oversight Com., 1992—; mem. New Fed. Courthouse Task Force, 1993—99; bd. overseers Rogerson Cmtys., 1995—; co-chair Mayor's Ctrl. Artery Completion Task Force, 2001—; mem. com. Oberlin Coll., 1990. Mem.: Real Estate Bar, Boston Soc. Archs. (bd. dirs. 2004—), Downtown Boston Transp. Mgmt. Assn. (chmn. 1996—), Boston Bar Assn. (com. chmn. 1977—81), Island Alliance (trustee 1997—2000), Abstract Club. Office: Wilmer Cutler Pickering Hale and Dorr LLP 60 State St Boston MA 02109-1816 Home Phone: 617-965-2568; Office Phone: 617-526-6920. Business E-Mail: robert.tuchmann@wilmerhale.com.

TUCK, ADRIAN FRANCIS, meteorologist, physical chemist; b. Fakenham, Eng., Nov. 22, 1942; s. Allan Mark and Muriel (Large) T.; m. Diane Marie Gersten, Apr. 27, 1970, Apr. 20, 1989; 1 child, Matthew Hereward. BSc in Chemistry, Manchester U., Eng., 1965; PhD in Phys. Chemistry, Cambridge U., Eng., 1968. Fulbright scholar U. Calif. at San Diego, La Jolla, 1969-71; rsch. fellow Univ Coll., London, 1971-72; rsch. scientist Meterologoical Office, Bracknell, Eng., 1972-86; program chief Nat. Oceanic and Atmospheric Adminstrn., Boulder, Colo., 1986—. Sec. study group on pollution in the atmospere, The Royal Soc., London, 1976-79; chair stratospheric ozone rev. group, UK Dept. of the Environment, London, 1985-86. Contbr. over 80 articles to profl. jours. including, Faraday Transactions, Quarterly Jour. of the Royal Meteorol. Soc., Jour. of Geophys. Rsch., Nature, others. Testified for U.S. Senate Com. on eviron. and pub. works; commerce, science and transport, 1987, 89, U.S. Ho. Reps. com. on space, sci. and tech., 1987. Named Fulbright scholar, 1968-71; recipient Buchan prize Royal Meteorol. Soc., London, 1984, Symons Meml. Lectureship, 1995. Fellow Royal Meteorol. Soc. (councillor 1982-85); mem. Am. Meteorol. Soc., Am. Geophys. Union. Achievements include project scientist in charge of NASA/NOAA Airborne Polar Ozone Missions, 1987, 89, 94. Home: 2285 Grape Ave Boulder CO 80304-2341 Office: Nat Oceanic & Atmospheric Adminstn 325 Broadway St Boulder CO 80305-3337

TUCK, AMY, lieutenant governor; b. Starkville, Miss., July 8, 1963; d. Grady William and Mary (Boykin) Tuck. BA in Polit. Sci., Miss. State U., Starkville, 1985; postgrad., Miss. State U., Miss. State U., Starkville, 1992—; JD, Miss. Coll., 1989. Legal asst. Ben. F. Hilburn Jr., Atty. at Law, Starkville, Miss., 1984-85; grad. asst. dept. polit. sci. Miss. State U., Starkville, 1986-87; law clk. Minor Buchanan, Jackson, Miss., 1987-88, Deposit Guaranty Nat. Bank, Jackson, 1988-89; state senator dist. 15 State of Miss., Jackson, 1990-99, lt. gov., 2000—. Adj. prof. Wood Jr. Coll., Mathiston, Miss., 1990-95. Mem. Oktibbeha County Voter Re-Registration Com., Oktibbeha County Fedn. Dem. Women; bd. dirs. Oktibbeha County Am. Cancer Soc., 1991-92; mem. local rels. com. Children and Family Svcs.; assoc. mem. Nat. Mus. Women in the Arts, 1992-93. Mem. NAFE, Am. Legis. Exch. Com., Am. Soc. Pub. Adminstrs., Nat. Conf. State Legislature, Nat. Order Women Legislators, Miss. State U. Alumni Assn., Starkville Area Bus. and Profl. Women's Club, Oktibbeha County C. of C., Gamma Beta Phi, Pi Sigma Alpha, Omicron Delta Kappa, Phi Delta Phi (vice-magister 1988, historian 1988-89). Democrat. Methodist. Office: Office of the Lt Gov PO Box 1018 Jackson MS 39215-1018 Office Phone: 601-359-3200. Office Fax: 601-359-4054. E-mail: ltgov@mail.senate.state.ms.us.

TUCK, GRAYSON EDWIN, real estate agent, gas industry executive; b. Richmond, Va., May 11, 1927; s. Bernard Okly and Erma (Wiltshire) T.; m. Rosalie Scroggs, June 6, 1947; children— Janice Lorrain, Kenneth Edwin, Carol Lynn. BS, U. Richmond, 1950. Payroll clk., cost clk. Gen. Baking Co., Richmond, 1948-51; jr. accountant Commonwealth Natural Gas Corp., Richmond, 1951-55, sr. accountant, 1956-57, accounting supr., 1957-58, asst. treas., 1959-62, asst. sec., asst. treas., 1963-64, treas., asst. sec., 1965-77; treas. Commonwealth Natural Resources, Inc., 1977-81, CNG Transmission Co. subs., 1977-79; sec.-treas. Air Pollution Control Products, Inc., Richmond, 1970-73; asst. treas., asst. sec. Commonwealth Gas Distbn. Corp., Richmond, 1969-79; mgr. taxes and cash mgmt. Commonwealth Gas Pipeline Corp., subs. Columbia Gas System Inc., 1981-86; investor, realtor Bill Eudailey & Co., 1986—. Active Boy Scouts Am., 1965—69; bd. dirs. Henrico Area Mental Health Retardation Svcs., 1983—85; active Elpis Christian Ch., 2001—; deacon Presbyn. Ch., 1958—86, elder, 1986—2001, treas., 1968—70. With USNR, 1945—46. Mem.: Nat. Assn. Accts. (assoc. dir. 1963—64). Home: 2923 Oakland Ave Richmond VA 23228-5827 Office: 9012 Three Chopt Rd Richmond VA 23229 Office Phone: 804-282-7678. Personal E-mail: realtortuck1@comcast.net.

TUCK, LILY, writer; b. Paris, 1938; Author: Interviewing Matisse; Or the Women Who Died Standing Up, 1991, The Women Who Walked on Water, 1996, Siam; Or the Women Who Shot a Man, 1999 (nominated PEN/Faulkner Award, 2000), The News from Paraguay, 2004 (Nat. Book Award for Fiction, 2004), (collection) Limbo: And Other Places I Have Lived, 2002. Address: c/o Georges Borchardt 136 E 57th St New York NY 10022

TUCK, RUSSELL R., JR., college president emeritus; b. June 9, 1934; m. Marjorie Gay Tuck; children: Russell R. III, Catherine Elizabeth. BS in Chemistry, Union U., 1956; MS in Biology, George Peabody Coll. Vanderbilt U., 1957, PhD in Curriculum and Instrn., 1971; studied, Wash. U., 1960—61. Instr. biology, asst. coordinator Korean Tchr. Edn. Program George Peabody Coll. Vanderbilt U., Nashville, 1957-59; tchr. biology, chmn. sci. dept. University City (Mo.) Sr. High Sch., 1960-63, from asst. prin. to prin., 1963-70; prin. Parkway North Sr. High Sch., St. Louis County, Mo., 1971-78; asst. supt. Parkway Sch. Dist., St. Louis County, 1979-81, assoc. supt., 1981-84; pres. Calif. Bapt. U., Riverside, 1984-94, pres. emeritus, 1994—; assoc. prof. Azusa Pacific U., 1995—2001. Contbr. articles to profl. jours. Bd. dirs. Opera Assn.; pres. Riverside County chpt. ARC, 1989-90; active Bapt. Ch., ch. elder, local hosp. assn. bd., local edn. com.; World Affairs Coun. Mem. Calif. Bapt. Hist. Soc. (bd. dirs.), Calif. Bapt. Devel. Found. (bd. dirs.), Am. Assn. Sch. Adminstrs., Inland Empire Higher Edn. Coun. (pres. 1987-88), Rotary, Kappa Delta Pi, Phi Delta Kappa. Lodges: Rotary. Home: 14000 Chelmsford Dr Gainesville VA 20155

TUCKER, ABIGAIL, journalist; b. Ridgefield, Conn., 1981; BA, Harvard Coll., 2002. Features reporter Post-Star, Glens Falls, NY, 2003—04; feature writer Balt. Sun, 2004—. Recipient Mike Berger award for Human-Interest Reporting, Columbia U. Grad. Sch. Journalism, 2007. Office: Balt Sun Co 501 N Calvert St PO Box 1377 Baltimore MD 21278 Office Phone: 410-332-6000. E-mail: abigail.tucker@baltsun.com. *

TUCKER, ALAN CURTISS, mathematics professor; b. Princeton, NJ, July 6, 1943; s. Albert William and Alice Judson (Curtiss) W.; m. Amanda Almira Zeisler, Aug. 31, 1968 (div. 1997); children: Lisa, Kathryn, Edward, James; m. Ann K. Hong, Feb. 16, 1997. BA, Harvard U., 1965; MS, Stanford U., 1967, PhD, 1969. Asst. prof. applied math. SUNY, Stony Brook, 1970-73, assoc. prof. applied math., 1973-78, prof. applied math., chmn., 1978-89, SUNY Disting. Teaching prof., 1989—. Vis. asst. prof. math. U. Wis., Madison, 1969-70; vis. assoc. prof. computer sci. U. Calif., San Diego, 1976-77; vis. prof. ops. research Stanford U., 1983-84; cons. Sloan Found., 1981-85; acad. cons. 40 colls. and univs. Author: Applied Combinatorics, 1980, Unified Introduction to Linear Algebra, 1987, Linear Algebra, 1993; assoc. editor Math. Monthly, 1996-2001, Applied Maths. Letters, 1986—; contbr. 45 rsch. articles to profl. jours. Ga. U. Consortium Disting. Visitor, 1982; NSF grantee, 1972-86. Mem. Math. Assn. Am. (chmn. publs. 1982-86, editor Studies in Math. series 1979-86, v.p. 1988-90, chmn. ednl. coun. 1990-96, Disting. Tchr. award 1994, Trevor Evans award 1996, Meritorious Svc. award 2005), U.S. Commn. Math. Instrn., Am. Math. Soc., Ops. Rsch. Soc. Am., Soc. Indsl. Applied Maths., Sigma Xi (chpt. pres. 1987—). Home: 19 Crosby Place Cold Spring Harbor NY 11724-2404 Office: SUNY At Stony Brook Dept Of Applied Math Stony Brook NY 11794-3600 Home Phone: 631-367-1841; Office Phone: 631-632-8365. Business E-Mail: atucker@notes.sunysb.edu.

TUCKER, ALAN DAVID, publisher; b. Erie, Pa., Mar. 9, 1936; s. Meredith LaDue and Monica (Klocko) Tucker; m. Kiyoko Iizuka, Feb. 8, 1963; 1 child, Kumi. AB, Princeton U., 1957. Lic. real estate salesperson N.Y. Assoc. editor Hawthorn Books, NYC, 1964-66; editor John Day Co., Inc., NYC, 1966-72; mng. editor David McKay Co., Inc., NYC, 1972-75, v.p., 1975-78, exec. v.p., editl. dir., 1978-84; editl. dir. Fodor's Travel Guides, Inc., NYC, 1978-84; founder, prodr. Penguin Travel Guides and other publs., NYC, 1984-91; gen. editor Berlitz Travellers Guides, NYC, 1991-95; consulting sr. analyst Genesis Group Assocs., Montclair, NJ, 1995—2001; v.p. mktg. strategy Oxygen Advt., Inc., NYC, 1996—; consulting sr. analyst Adis Bus. Intelligence, Langhorne, Pa., 2002. Real estate sales assoc. Halstead Property Co., NYC, 1999—. Author: Capitation and Risk Sharing, 1995, Integrated Health Information Systems, 1997, Provider-Sponsored Managed Care, 1998, Convergence in Coordinated Care, 1998; co-author: The Electronic Superhighway 1997-2010: Opportunities for the Healthcare Industry, 1996, Diabetes Disease Management, 1995, 2d edit., 1998, Asthma Disease Management, 1997, 2d edit., 1999, Hypertension Management, 1999, Management of Congestive Heart Failure, 1999, Intelligence Report: Depression, 1999, Intelligence Report: Lung Cancer, 2000, Strategic Audit: Alzheimer's and Parkinson's Diesease, 2000, Strategic Audit: Stroke and Multiple Sclerosis, 2000, Asthma Forum, 2001, Osteoporosis Forum, 2001, Psoriasis Forum, 2001, Congestive Heart Failure Forum, 2001, Obesity Forum, 2002, Allergic Rhinitis Forum, 2002, Pain Management Forum, 2002, Handbook of Healthcare Marketing, 2003. With USNR, 1957—60. Mem.: Real Estate Bd. N.Y., Am. Coll. Healthcare Execs. (regent's adv. coun. N.Y.C. region), N.Y. Travel Writers Assn. (past pres.), Soc. Am. Travel Writers. Office: 186 Riverside Dr New York NY 10024-1007 also: 34 Still Meadow Rd Sharon CT 06069-2133

TUCKER, ALVIN LEROY, retired government official; b. Bklyn., Sept. 7, 1938; s. Alvin Leroy Jr. and Alveria (Klune) T.; m. Jacqueline Twiggs, Aug. 27, 1966; children: Hazel, Pluma, Jacqueline, Alvin. BS, U. Md., 1965. CPA, Md.; cert. internal auditor; cert. govt. fin. mgr.; cert. def. fin.

mgr. Auditor Dept. Army, Washington, 1965-67; dep. insp. gen. HUD, Washington, 1986-89; auditor Dept. Def., Washington, 1967-72, budget analyst, 1972-79, dir. tng. and edn., 1979-83, dep. asst. insp. gen., 1983-86, dep. comptr., 1989-94, dep. CFO, 1991-97, chmn. concessions com., 1989-97; sr. mgr. Grant Thornton LLP, Alexandra, Va., 1997—2006, dir., 2006—. Mem. steering com. Joint Fin. Mgmt. Improvement Program, 1990-93; mem. CFO's Coun., 1989-97, chmn. fin. sys. com., 1989-97; mem. Fed. Acctg. Stds. Adv. Bd., 1991-97; chmn. Cert. Def. Fin. Mgr. Commn., 2004—. With U.S. Army, 1958-61. Recipient Def. medal for disting. civilian svc. with Bronze Palm, 1997, meritorious sr. exec. medal, 1985, 92. Mem.: AICPA, Md. Assn. CPAs, Inst. Internal Auditors, Assn. Govt. Accts. (nat. exec. com. 1993—94), Am. Soc. Mil. Comptrs., Kiwanis (club pres. 1981—82, 1986—87). Avocation: genealogy. Office: Grant Thornton 333 John Carlyle St Ste 500 Alexandria VA 22314 Office Phone: 703-837-4464.

TUCKER, ANNE WILKES, curator, historian, photographer, critic; b. Baton Rouge, Oct. 18, 1945; BA in Art History, Randolph-Macon Women's Coll., Lynchburg, Va., 1967; AAS in Photographic Illustration, Rochester Inst. Tech., 1968; MFA in Photographic History, SUNY, Buffalo, 1972. Rsch. asst. Internat. Mus. Photography at the George Eastman House, Rochester, NY, 1968—70; rsch. assoc. Gernsheim Collection U. Tex., Austin, 1969, 1970; curatorial intern dept. photography Mus. Modern Art, NYC, 1970—71; photography cons. Creative Artists Pub. Svc. Program, NYC, 1971—72; vis. lectr. New Sch. for Social Rsch., NY, 1973; dir. photography lecture series Cooper Unionn Forum, NYC, 1972—75; lectr. Cooper Union for Advancement of Arts and Sci., NY, 1972—75; vis. lectr. Phila. Coll. Art, 1973—75; affiliate artist U. Houston, 1976—80; curator photography Mus. Fine Arts, Houston, 1976—; Gus and Lyndall Wortham cur., photographic historian and critic, lectr., 1984—. Trustee Visual Studies Workshop, 1980—, Houston Ctr. Photography, 1991—96, Houston Foto Fest, 1988—, art adv. bd., 1987—, bd. dirs., 1990—; visual arts panel The Houston Festival, 1981—83; adv. bd. Randolph-Macon Woman's Coll. Art Gallery, 1982—84; bd. trustees Am. Leadership Forum, 1992—94, co-chair selection com., 1993—94; dir. numerous exhbns. and workshops; lectr. in field; mem. numerous juries and panels. Author: (books and catalogues) Walker Evans: Photographs, 1971, The Woman's Eye, 1973; author: (with Lee Witkin) Rare Books and Photographs, Catalogue 1, The Witkin Gallery, 1973; author: (with William C. Agee) The Target Collection of American Photography, 1977; author: Target II: 5 American Photographers, 1981, Target III: In Sequence, 1982; author: (with Philip Brookman) Robert Frank: New York to Nova Scotia, 1986; author: A Photographic Portrait, Vol. 1: Historic Texas; Vol. II: Contemporary Texas, 1986; author: (with Maggie Olvey) The Sonia and Kaye Marvins Portrait Collection, 1986; author: Photo Notes & Filmfront, 1977; author: (with other curators) The Museum of Fine Arts, Houston: A Guide to the Collection, 1981; author: Unknown Territory: Photography by Ray K. Metzker, 1957-83, 1984, Fifth Annual International Fine Art Photography Exposition, 1984; author: (with Andy Grundberg) American Prospects: The Photographs of Joel Sternfeld, 1987, 2d edit., 1994; author: (with Willie Morris) American Classroom: The Photographs of Catherine Wagner, 1988; author: Five Jerome Artists, 1988; author: (with Pamela Allara) Crosscurrents/Crosscountry, 1988; author: The Art of Photography 1839-1989, 1989, A Permanent Legacy: 150 Masterpieces From the Museum of Fine Arts, Houston, 1989; author: (with other authors) Money Matters: A Critical Look at Bank Architecture, 1990; author: The Blue Man: Photographs by Keith Carter, 1990; author: (with Pete Daniel) Carry Me Home: Photographs by Debbie Fleming Caffery, 1990; author: George Krauze, 1991, Ansel Adams: American Icons, 1992, Tradition and the Unpredictable: The Allan Chasanoff Photographic Collection, 1994, Quest for the Moon and other stories: Three Decades of Astronauts in Space, 1994, Toshio Shibata: Landscape, 1996 (Photo-Eye Best Contemporary Monograph award, 1996), Crimes and Splendors: The Desert Cantos of Richard Misrach, 1996 (Golden Light award, 1996), Charles Schorre, 1997, Myths, Dreams and Realities: Contemporary Argentine Photographs, 1997, Irving Penn, 1999, Mario Carvo Neto, 1999, Amy Blakemore, 1999, Irving Penn Dancer: Photographs of Alexandra Bellar, 2001, Heart and Soul: The Photographs of Ray Carrington III 1993-2002, 2002, Joe Mills: Inner City, 2003, History of Japanese Photography 1853-2000, 2003 (Golden Light award), First Down Houston, Birth of An NFL Franchise, 2003, La Oscura Piel De La Luz; La Obra Fotografica De Mario Cravo Neto, 2003, David Carol: 40 Miles of Bad Road, 2004, Alec Soth: Sleeping by the Mississippi, 2004, Documenting Poetry Contemporary Latin American Photography, 2005, Icons of Photography, 2005, On Assignment, 2005, Mark Cohen: Grim Street, 2005, David Maisel: Terminal Mirage, 2005, (exhbns. and catalogues) A Fotographia Na Arte Contemporanea, 1995;: The Sonia and Kaye Marvins Portrait Collection, 1995, Keith Carter: Reinventing the World, 1995, Illuminations: Women writing on Photography from the 1850's to the present, 1996, Brassai: The Eye of Paris, 1999, Louis Faurer, 2001 (Mus. Pub. Design Competition First prize, 2002), This Was the Photo League: Compassion and the Camera from the Depression to the Cold War, 2001 (Photo-Eye runner-up Best Visual Anthology, 2001), History of Japanese Photography, 2003 (named to Top 12 Photo Books of 2003, Spl. Commendations from Kraszna-Krausz Photography Book Awards, 2005); co-prodr. (video) Fire in the East: The Portrait of Robert Frank, 1986; editor: (books and catalogues) The Anthony G. Cronin Memorial Collection, 1979, (manual) Suzanne Bloom and Ed Hill, 1980, (exhbns. and catalogues) Reframings, New American Feminist Photographies, 1995, The Photo League, 1987, Czech Modernism 1900-1945, 1990, Paul Strand: Essays on His Life and Work, 1990, George Krause, 1992; co-editor: Building a Photographic Library, 2001; singer (photographer): Caught in Act: Lou Stoumen Vintage Photographs, 1995; contbr. articles to numerous profl. jours. and mags., essays to books; subject of numerous interviews and articles. Named Best Curator, TIME Mag., 2001; named to The 100 Most Important People in Photography, American Photo Mag., 2005; recipient Third Ann. Publ. award, Internat. Ctr. Photography, 1987, Bronze Apple award, Am. Film and Video Festival, 1987, John Simon Guggenheim Meml. Alumna Achievement award, Randolph-Macon Woman's Coll., 1993, Alumnae Achievement award, 1993, Lifetime Achievement award, Griffin Mus., 2006; grantee Nat. Endowment Arts grantee, 1976, 1986, 1989; fellowship for mus. profls., Nat. Endowment Arts, 1990, John Simon Guggenheim Meml. Found. fellowship award, 1983—84, Rsch. Support grant, The Getty Ctr. for the History of Art and the Humanities Resource Collections, 1995. Mem.: Houston Ctr. for Photography (adv. bd 1980—90, bd. trustees 1990—93, sec. 1990—93, adv. bd. 1994—95, exhbn. com. pres. 1999—), Art Table, Inc., Coll. Art Assn., Soc. Photographic Edn. (nat. bd. dirs. 1976—80, sec. nat. bd. 1977—79). Office: Mus Fine Arts PO Box 6826 Houston TX 77265 Office Phone: 713-639-7347. Business E-Mail: atucker@mfah.org.

TUCKER, BEVERLY SOWERS, library and information scientist; b. Trenton, NJ, Dec. 1, 1936; d. Eldon Jones and Verbeda Eleanor (Roberts) Sowers; m. Harvey Richard Tucker, Dec. 27, 1958 (div. Nov. 1983); children: Randall Richard, Brian Alan. BS in Chemistry with distinction, Purdue U., 1958; MS in Geology, No. Ill. U., 1985; MA in Library and Info. Sci., Rosary Coll., 1989. Asst. rsch. librarian CPC Internat., Argo, Ill., 1958-62; chem. patent searcher Chgo., 1962-66; info. specialist C. Berger & Co., Wheaton, Ill., 1986, Amoco Corp., Naperville, Ill., 1987-99; faculty Coll. Du Page, Glen Ellyn, Ill., 1989—; libr. cons. Baxter Healthcare, Round Lake, Ill., 1999—2003; libr. Seyfarth and Shaw, Chgo., 2005—. Mem. Spl. Libraries Assn., Ill. Fedn. Women's Club (treas. 5th dist. 1979-81, Outstanding Jr. Clubwoman award 1979-80), Garden Club Council Wheaton (pres. 1981-82), Wheaton Jr. Woman's Club (pres. 1977-78, Single Parent scholar 1984), Gardens Etc. Club (pres. 1978-79), Alpha Lambda Delta, Delta Rho Kappa, Theta Sigma Phi, Alpha Chi Omega (grantee 1985). Republican. Presbyterian. Avocations: bridge, needlecrafts, gourmet cooking. Home: 1507 Paula Ave Wheaton IL 60187-6135

TUCKER, BOWEN HAYWARD, lawyer; b. Providence, Apr. 13, 1938; s. Stuart Hayward and Ardelle Chase (Drabble) T.; m. Jan Louise Brown, Aug. 26, 1961; children: Stefan Kendric Slade, Catherine Kendra Gordon. AB in Math., Brown U., 1959; JD, U. Mich., 1962. Bar: R.I. 1963, Ill. 1967, U.S. Supreme Ct. 1970. Assoc. Hinckley & Allen, Providence, 1962-66; sr. atty. Caterpillar, Inc., Peoria, Ill., 1966-72; counsel FMC Corp., Chgo., 1972-82, sr. litigation counsel, 1982-95, assoc. gen. counsel, 1995-2000; v.p. eLaw Forum, Washington, 2000—01; owner Strategic Litigation Mgmt., Arlington Heights, Ill., 2000—. Chmn. legal process task force Chgo. Residential Sch. Study Com., 1973-74, mem. Commn. on Children, 1983-85, Ill. Com. on Rights of Minors, 1974-77, Com. on Youth and the Law, 1977-79; mem. White House Conf. on Children, ednl. svcs. subcom., 1979-80; chairperson Youth Employment Task Force, 1982-83; mem. citizens com. on Juvenile Ct. (Cook County), 1978-94, chmn. detention subcom., 1982-92; mem. econ. effects adv. com. Rand Inst. Civil Justice, 1990-92; bd. dirs. Voices Ill. Children, 1998—. 1st lt. U.S. Army, 1962-69. Mem. ABA, Am. Law Inst., Ill. State Bar Assn., R.I. Bar Assn., Chgo. (chmn. com. on juvenile law, 1976-77), Chgo. Lincoln Inn of Ct. (sec., treas. 1996-98), Constrn. Industry Mfrs. Assn. (exec. com. of Lawyers' Coun. 1972, 75-79, vice chmn. 1977, chmn. 1978-79), Mfrs. Alliance (products liability coun. 1974-95, vice chmn. 1981-83, chmn. 1983-85), Product Liability Adv. Coun. (bd. dirs. 1986-2000, exec. com. 1990-97, vice chmn. 1991-93, chmn. 1993-95), ACLU (bd. dirs. Ill. divsn. 1970-79, exec. com. 1973-79, sec. 1975-77), Am. Arbitration Assn. (mem. panel of arbitrators 1985-96), Phi Alpha Delta, Brown Univ. of Chgo. Club (Brown alumni schs. com. 1973-85, 2000—, v.p. 1980-81, pres. 1981-86), Lawyers Club of Chgo. Home: 107 W Noyes St Arlington Heights IL 60005-3747 Office Phone: 312-861-5940.

TUCKER, BRENDA BRUNETTE, elementary school educator; b. Corinth, Miss., Nov. 1, 1958; d. Willie Bishop and Maggie Belle Graham; m. Ralph O. Tucker, Dec. 24, 1980; children: Orion, Jonathan, Cameron. BS, Kust Coll., 1980; MEd, We. Ky. U., 1993, cert. in Prin. Supr., 2002. Lic. tchr. Ky. Dept. Profl. Bds. Tchr. spl. edn. Corinth (Miss.) H.S., 1981; instr. Dept. Def., Wurzburg, Germany, 1981—87; tchr. Hardin County Schs., Radcliff, Ky., 1987—98, Ft. Knox (Ky.) Schs., 1998—, guidance counselor, 1999—. Prof. McKendree Coll., Radcliff, 2000—. Chmn. publicity NAACP, Radcliff, 2004. Mem.: Counselors Assn., Optimist Club Radcliff (pres. 1998, chmn. programs 1998—99, named Optimist Educator of Yr.), Delta Sigma Theta (pres. 1995, chaplain 1997—2003). Avocations: reading, g, community service, walking, watching sunrise and sunsets. Office: Kingsolver Elementary Sch 1488 3rd Ave Fort Knox KY 40121-2287

TUCKER, CHRIS, comedian, actor; b. Atlanta, 1973; s. Norris and Mary T.; 1 child, Chris Jr. Appeared in Russell Simmon's Def Comedy Jam, 1993, Arsenio Hall Show; appeared in films, including House Party III, 1994, Friday, 1995, Panther, 1995, Dead Presidents, 1995, The Fifth Element, 1997, Jackie Brown, 1997, Rush Hour, 1998, Rush Hour 2, 2001, Rush Hour 3, 2007; actor, exec. prodr. Money Talks, 1997, Double-O-Soul, 1999. Office: William Morris Agy 151 S El Camino Dr Beverly Hills CA 90212-2775 *

TUCKER, CYNTHIA ANNE, journalist; b. Monroeville, Ala., Mar. 13, 1955; d. John Abney and Mary Louise (Marshall) Tucker; m. Michael Pierce, Dec. 26, 1987 (div. 1989). BA, Auburn U., 1976. Reporter Atlanta Jour., 1976-80, editorial writer, columnist, 1983-86; reporter Phila. Inquirer, 1980-82; assoc. editorial page editor Atlanta Constitution (now Atlanta Journal-Constitution), 1986-91, editorial page editor, 1992—. Bd. dirs. ARC, 1989-93, Families First, 1988—, Internat. Women's Media Found., 1994—. Nieman fellow Harvard U., 1988-89; finalist Pulitzer Prize for commentary, 2004; recipient Pulitzer Prize for commentary, 2007. Mem.: Coun. Fgn. Rels., Nat. Assn. Minority Media Execs., Nat. Assn. Black Journalists, Am. Soc. Newspaper Editors (Disting. Writing award 2000). Mem. United Ch. Christ. Office: Atlanta Journal-Constitution PO Box 4689 Atlanta GA 30302 Office Phone: 404-526-5432. E-mail: cynthia@ajc.com. *

TUCKER, DALE KEITH, church musical director, organist; b. Greenville, SC, Feb. 23, 1952; s. Roderick Hearin and Lillian Murray Tucker. B, MusM, East Carolina U., Greenville, NC, 1976. Music editor Warner Bros. Publs., Miami, Fla., 1983—2001; dir. music, organist 1st Wayne St. United Meth. Ch., Ft. Wayne, Ind., 2001—. Accompanist Ind./Purdue U., Ft. Wayne, 2006—. Mem.: Fellowship of United Methodists in Music and Worship Arts (assoc.), Am. Guild English Handbell Ringers (assoc.), Am. Guild Organists (life; dean 1995—99). Democrat. Methodist. Avocations: tennis, gourmet cooking, travel, reading. Home: 3912 Stone Creek Run Fort Wayne IN 46804 Office: 1st Wayne St United Meth Ch 300 E Wayne St Fort Wayne IN 46802 Home Phone: 260-436-7903; Office Phone: 260-422-4681. Personal E-mail: dalektucker@aol.com.

TUCKER, DON EUGENE, retired lawyer; b. Rockbridge, Ohio, Feb. 3, 1928; s. Beryl Hollis and Ruth (Primmer) T.; m. Elizabeth Jane Parke, Aug. 2, 1950; children: Janet Elizabeth, Kerry Jane, Richard Parke. BA, Aurora Coll., 1951; LL.B., Yale, 1956. Bar: Ohio 1956. Since practiced in, Youngstown, Ohio; asso. Manchester, Bennett, Powers & Ullman, 1956-62, ptnr., 1962-73, of counsel, 1973-87; gen. counsel Comml. Intertech Corp., Youngstown, 1973-75, v.p., gen. counsel, 1975-83, also dir., sr. v.p., gen. counsel, 1983-87, sr. v.p., 1987-93; ret., 1993. Solicitor Village of Poland, Ohio, 1961-63; former chmn. bd., pres., trustee United Cerebral Palsy Assn., Youngstown and Mahoning County; trustee Mahoning County Tb and Health Assn.; former trustee, pres. Indsl. Info. Inst.; former pres., trustee Ea. Ohio Lung Assn.; trustee, former chmn. Cmty. Corp.; trustee, former pres. Butler Inst. Am. Art. With USMCR, 1946-48, 51-53. Mem. Ohio Bar Assn., Mahoning County Bar Assn. (pres. 1972, trustee 1970-73), Youngstown Area C. of C. (chmn. bd. dirs. 1979). Methodist. Home: 6005 Martins Point Rd Kitty Hawk NC 27949-3819

TUCKER, DUANE ERNEST, engineer, military officer; b. Modesto, Calif., Feb. 18, 1933; s. Harland Ed Tucker and Gladys Winefred Gilliam-Tucker; children: Yvonne Miller, Diane Louise. Student, Huntongton U., Ind., 1950—52. Ordained min. United Brethren, Huntington, Ind., 1951. Pastor Christian Ch., Silsbee, Tex., 1993; chaplain Brit. Internat. Sailors, Southhampton, England, 2001; marine surveyor NYC, 1975—86; port engr. Englewood Cliffs, NJ, 1990—92; ret. Author, designer Tucker Spring Moor, 1962. Lt. USN, 1952—74, Korea, Vietnam. Mem.: VFW (life), Am. Legion (life), Navy League (life), Naval Inst. (life).

TUCKER, EDWIN WALLACE, law educator; b. NYC, Feb. 25, 1927; s. Benjamin and May Tucker; m. Gladys Lipschutz, Sept. 14, 1952; children: Sherwin M., Pamela A. BA, NYU, 1948; LLB, Harvard U., Cambridge, Mass., 1951; LLM, NY Law Sch., 1963, JSD, 1964; MA, Trinity Coll., Hartford, Conn., 1967. Bar: NY 1955, US Dist. Ct. (ea. and so. dists.) NY 1958, US Ct. Appeals (2d cir.) 1958, US Supreme Ct. 1960. Pvt. practice, NYC, 1955-63; disting. alumni prof. and prof. emeritus bus. law U. Conn., Storrs, 1963—2002. Author: Adjudication of Social Issues, 1971, 2d edit., 1977, Legal Regulation of the Environment, 1972, Administrative Agencies, Regulation of Enterprise, and Individual Liberties, 1975, CPA Law Review, 1985; co-author: The Legal and Ethical Environment of Business, 1992; book rev. editor Am. Bus. Law Jour., 1964-65, adv. editor, 1974—99; co-editor Am. Bus. Jour., 1965-73; editor Jour. Legal Studies Edn., 1983-85, editor-in-chief, 1985-87, adv. editor, 1987—99; mem. editl. bd. Am. Jour. Small Bus., 1979-86, North Atlantic Regional Bus. Law Rev., 1984—2004. With USAF, 1951-55. Named to, U. Conn. Sch. Bus. Hall of Fame, 2007; recipient medal of excellence, Am. Bus. Law Assn., 1979. Mem. Acad. Legal Studies in Bus., North Atlantic Regional Bus. Law Assn. Home and Office: 11 Eastwood Rd Storrs Mansfield CT 06268-2401

TUCKER, FRANK HAMMOND, history professor; b. Millville, NJ, Dec. 29, 1923; s. Frank Edmund and Evalyn Godfrey Tucker; m. Kathryn Churchill Libby (dec. Dec. 1994), Aug. 23, 1947; children: Elizabeth T. Gould, Sarah T. Owens, Margaret T. Mitchell. BS, Johns Hopkins U., Balt., 1948; MA, Georgetown U., Washington, DC, 1950, PhD, 1954. Bassoonist Balt. Symphony Orch., 1941—43; commd. ensign USN, 1943, advanced through grades to lt. comdr., 1954, ret., 1963; lectr. history extension divsn. U. Md., Yokohama, Japan, 1956-57, lectr. history College Park, 1959-63; prof. history Colo. Coll., Colorado Springs, 1963-89, prof. emeritus, 1989—. Author: The White Conscience, 1969, The Frontier Spirit and Progress, 1979, Knights of the Mountain Trails, 2003; contbr. over 35 articles, 40 revs. to profl. jours. Bassoonist Balt. Symphony Orch., 1941-43; bd. mem., Charter Assn., Colorado Springs, 1964-67; pres. Landmarks Preservation Coun., Pike's Peak Region, 1969-73, mem. exec. bd. ARC, 1965-71, head Pike's Peak region Westerners Internat., 1991-92, gov. Pike Bicentennial com., 2004; mem. curricular com. Pillar Inst., 2006-. Fellow Am. Coun. Learned Socs.; mem. Am. Hist. Assn., Rocky Mountain Social Sci. Assn. (bd. mem. 1966-69), Maine Hist. Soc., Gloucester County Hist. Soc., Cumberland County Hist. Soc., Atlantic County Hist. Soc., Rotary (exec. bd. 1971-73). Episcopalian. Avocation: hiking. Home and Office: 30 E Rio Grande St Colorado Springs CO 80908

TUCKER, GARY JAY, psychiatrist, educator; b. Cleve., Mar. 6, 1934; s. Isadore Martin and Blanche Hanna (Luftig) T.; m. Sharon Ruth Pobby, June 10, 1956; children: Adam, Clare. AB, Oberlin Coll., 1956; MD, Case Western Res. U., 1960; postdoctoral fellow, Yale U., 1961-64; MA (hon.), Dartmouth Coll., 1977. Diplomate Am. Bd. Psychiatry and Neurology. Asst. prof. psychiatry Sch. Medicine Yale U., New Haven, 1967-70, assoc. prof. psychiatry, 1970-71; with Dartmouth Med. Sch., Hanover, N.H., 1971-85, prof. psychiatry, 1974-85, chmn. dept., 1978-85; chmn. psychiatry and behavioral scis. Sch. Med. U. Wash., Seattle, 1985-98; prof. psychiatry U. Wash., Seattle, 1985—99, prof. emeritus, 1999—. Bd. dirs. Am. Bd. Psychiatry and Neurology. Co-author: Rational Hospital Psychiatry, 1974, Behavioral Neurology, 1985; editor: Seminars in Clinical Neuropsychiatry, Jourl. Watch Psychiatry; contbr. articles to profl. jours. Lt. Commdr. USN, 1964-67. Fellow Am. Psychiat. Assn.; mem. W. Coast Coll. Biol. Psychiatry, Sigma Xi, Alpha Omega Alpha. Democrat. Jewish. Avocations: photography, motorcycling.

TUCKER, H. RICHARD, oil industry executive; b. Streator, Ill., Oct. 2, 1936; s. H. L. and Dorothy A. Tucker; m. Cheryl L. Kirk, Jan. 14, 1984; children from previous marriage: Randall R., Brian A. BS in Chem. Engring., Purdue U., 1958; MBA, Northwestern U., 1962. Project engr. crude oil supply Amoco Corp., Chgo., 1958-64, specialist product supply, 1965-66, coord. fgn. crude oil supply, 1967-68; coord. orgn. planning Amoco Internat. Corp., Chgo., 1969-70, Amoco Corp., Chgo., 1970-72, mgr. adminstrv. svcs., 1972-84, mgr. real estate svcs., 1984-86, coord. spl. studies, 1986-89, dir. quality mgmt., 1989-92; mgr. cost mgmt., 1992-94. V.p. Amoco Realty Co., 1984-91, Amoco Devel. Co., 1984-91. Mem. adv. com. Sch. Bd. Wheaton, Ill., 1966; mem. Citizen's Nominating Com., Wheaton, 1972; leader Boy Scouts Am., Wheaton, 1979-82; dir. Oak Brook Colony Condominium Assn., 1992-94. Mem. Westhaven Home Owners Assn. (pres. 1965-67), Phi Eta Sigma, Omega Chi Epsilon, Beta Gamma Sigma, Tau Beta Pi. Avocations: tennis, bridge, hiking.

TUCKER, HELEN WELCH, writer; b. Raleigh, NC, Nov. 1, 1926; d. William Blair and Helen (Welch) Tucker; m. William T. Beckwith, Jan. 9, 1971. BA, Wake Forest Coll., 1946; postgrad., Columbia U., NYC, 1957—58. Reporter Burlington Times-News, NC, 1946—47, Times-News, Twin Falls, Idaho, 1948—49, Idaho Statesman, Boise, 1950—51; copy writer Sta. KDYL, Salt Lake City, 1952—53; copy supr. Sta. WPTF, Raleigh, NC, 1953—55; reporter Raleigh Times, NC, 1955—57; editl. asst. Columbia U. Press, NYC, 1959—60; dir. publicity and publs. N.C. Mus. Art, Raleigh, NC, 1967—70. Author: The Sound of Summer Voices, 1969, The Guilt of August Fielding, 1971, No Need of Glory, 1972, The Virgin of Lontano, 1973, A Strange and Ill-Starred Marriage, 1978, A Reason for Rivalry, 1979, A Mistress to the Regent, 1980, An Infamous Attachment, 1980, The Halverton Scandal, 1980, A Wedding Day Deception, 1981, The Double Dealers, 1982, Season of Dishonor, 1982, Ardent Vows, 1983, Bound by Honor, 1984, The Lady's Fancy, 1991, Bold Impostor, 1991; contbr. (to nat. mags. short stories). Named Artist of Yr., Arts Coun. Frankling Co. (N.C.), 1992; recipient Disting. Alumni Award in Journalism, Wake Forest U., 1971. Anglican. Home: 2930 Hostetler St Raleigh NC 27609-7702

TUCKER, HOWARD MCKELDIN, investment banker, consultant; b. Washington, Apr. 1, 1930; s. Howard Newell and Bessie Draper (McKeldin) T.; m. Julia Spencer Merrell, Feb. 1, 1952 (div. 1975); children: Deborah, Mark, Alexander, H. David; m. Megan Evans, Aug. 17, 1979. BA, U. Va., 1954; postgrad., NYU, 1956. CFA. With J.P. Morgan & Co., 1954—61, Mackall & Coe, Washington, 1962—69, Legg Mason Wood Walker & Co., Washington, 1969—79, Govt. Rsch. Corp./Nat. Jour., 1979—82, Potomac Asset Mgmt., 1982—91; ptnr., mng. dir. Capital Insights Group, Washington, 1992—2001; with Skillsmith, LLC, 2002—05. Mem. task force balance-of-payments U.S.Treasury Dept., 1967-72; cons. County Natwest (Washinton Analysis Corp.), 1985-90; bd. dirs. Monarch Enterprises, Inc., Uniflight, Inc., Sci. Mgmt. Assocs., Inc., Jeffrey Bigelow Assocs. Author: Literature in Medicine, In Memoriam, Michael Halberstam, M.D., 1984; book reviewer Washington Post; contbr. articles to profl. jours. Dir. Washington Area Coun. Chs., 1962-65; vestryman Christ Episcopal Ch., Georgetown, 1962-65; mem. chpt. Washington Nat. Cathedral, 1966-72; del. Va. Republican Conv., 1968; trustee Nat. Cathedral Sch. for Girls, 1972-78; chmn. Missionary Devel. Fund Episcopal Diocese D.C., 1974; co-dir. Andover-Exeter Washington Intern Program, 1976-86; co-organizer U.S.-German Parliamentary Exchange, 1980-82; observer OECD, 1980-82; spl. overseas visitor Australian Govt., 1982; patron West Europe program Woodrow Wilson Ctr., 1985-86; bd. dirs. Am. Hort. Soc., 1998--. With USNR, 1950-56. Mem.: Fin. Analysts Fedn., Washington Soc. Investment Analysts, Nat. Economists Club, Dumplings, Cogswell Soc., Hist. Alexandria Found., Alexandria Seaport Found., Saints and Sinners Club, Naval and Mil. Club London, Nat. Press Club, Georgetown Visitation Tennis Club, Beta Theta Pi. Home: 4 Potomac Ct Alexandria VA 22314-3821 Personal E-mail: hmcktucker@yahoo.com.

TUCKER, J. WALTER, JR., manufacturing executive; Vice chmn. Keystone Consolidated Industries, Inc., Dallas, chmn., 1987—. Office: 3 Lincoln Ctr 5430 LBJ Fwy Ste 1740 Dallas TX 75240-2697 Fax: 972-458-8108.

TUCKER, JAMES L., JR., artist, educator; b. New Eagle, Pa., Mar. 28, 1944; s. James Louis Tucker Sr. and Gueraldine Esther (Johnson) Sawyer. MA, Temple U., 1967, BFA, 1966; postgrad., George Washington U., 1977—79, postgrad., 1982—86. Art instr. continuing edn. Germantown H.S., Phila., 1968—69; chmn. art dept. Woodrow Wilson H.S., Washington, 1969—70; art specialist Gallaudet Coll., Washington, 1970—77; from specialist in the arts to chief arts and humanities program Md. State Dept. Edn., Balt., 1979—2003, coord. fine arts, 2003—. Art instr. Pastorius Elem. Sch., Phila., 1966—69, Emlen Elem. Sch., Phila., 1966—69; steering com.

Art Edn. in Md. Schs. Alliance, 1992—; adj. instr. Md. Inst. Coll. Art, George Washington U.; team leader Brazilian curriculum project Ptnrs. of the Americas, 1984—86; arts assessment standing com. Nat. Assessment Ednl. Progress, 1996—97; cons., presenter in field. Editor: Better Fine Arts Edn., 4 vols., 2004. Co-dir. Kenya-Tanzania project Fulbright-Hays Group Projects Abroad, 1989, co-dir. Ghana-Senegal project, 1993, co-dir.Namibia project, 1995; edn. com. Balt. Symphony Orch., 1995—2004; adv. Ctr. for VSA Arts Md., Balt., 1980—2002, bd. dirs., 2002—, Md. Alliance for Arts Edn., Balt., 1980—2002, exec. sec.-treas., 1980—86; bd. dirs. Md. Artist Equity Found., Balt., 1992—2004, v.p., 2002—04. Named Md. State Adminstr. of Yr., State Employees Assn., 1986; recipient State of Md. Performance award, Md. State Employee's Conf., 1986, Outstanding Svc. award, Md. Coun. for Dance, 2002, Cert. Achievement, Md. State Bd. Edn., 2003. Fellow: Nat. Art Edn. Assn. (review panel Art Edn. 1995—97, chmn. nat. conv. Miami Beach 2002, convention task force 2002, Eastern Region Art Educator of Yr. 1995, J. Eugene Grigsby award 1984, Disting. Svc. award 2003, Nat. Supervision/adminstrn. Art Educator of Yr. 1997, Ea. Supervision/adminstrn. Art Educator of Yr. 1994, Md. Art Educator award 1987); mem.: Music Educators Nat. Conf., Nat. Assn. State Dirs. Art Edn. (pres.), Nat. Coun. State Arts Edn. Cons. (founding mem., pres. 1995—97), Md. Music Educators Assn. (exec. bd. dirs., Corwin Taylor award 1997), Md. Art Edn. Assn. (dept. edn. rep. 1980—82, dir. supervision/adminstrn. divsn. 1982—86, v.p. programs 1986—88, pres.-elect 1990—92, pres. 1992—94, awards coord. 1994—96, parliamentarian 1996—2000, historian 2000—, officer). Avocations: painting, reading, cooking, travel. Office: Md State Dept Edn 200 W Balt St Baltimore MD 21201-2595 Office Phone: 410-767-0352. Business E-Mail: jtucker@msde.state.md.us.

TUCKER, JAMES RAYMOND, primary school educator; b. Pueblo, Colo., Apr. 18, 1944; s. James George and Pauline F. (Sena) T.; m. Kathie Owens; 1 child, Brittany. BA, U. So. Colo., 1966; MA, U. No. Colo., 1990, postgrad., 1991. Tchr. Sinclair Mid. Sch., Englewood, Colo., 1971-93, Denver Pub. Schs., 1993—. Co-dir. Nick Bolleteri Tennis Acad., Boulder, Colo., 1986; head tennis coach Englewood High Sch., 1971—. Sgt. U.S. Army, 1967-70. Finalist Coach of Yr., Nat. H.S. Coaches Assn., 2001, 2004. Mem. NEA, US Profl. Tennis Assn., US Profl. Tennis Registry, Internat. Platform Assn., Colo. Edn. Assn., Meadow Creek Tennis and Fitness, Colo. HS Coaches Assn. (co-founder, Achievement award 1989, 92, Tchr. of Yr. 1973, 78, 86, Coach of Yr. 1986-87, 90, 96-97, Franklin award 1988, 89, Nat. Asst. Coach of Yr., 2002, H.S. Hero of Week). Home: 8801 W Belleview Ave Unit A207 Littleton CO 80123

TUCKER, JOHN, lawyer; b. Oklahoma City, Nov. 2, 1942; s. John Hampton and Elaine Johnston Tucker. BA, U. Okla., Norman, 1964, JD, 1966. Bar: Okla. Ptnr. Rhodes, Heronymus, jones, Tucker & Gayle, Tulsa, Okla., 1966—. Okla. chair US Surpeme Ct. Hist. Soc. Fellow: Okla. Bar Found., Am. Bar Found. Office: Rhodes Hieronymus Jones Tucker & Gayle 100 W 5th St Ste 400 Tulsa OK 74103

TUCKER, JOHN MARK, librarian, educator; s. Paul Marlin and Edith Tucker; m. Barbara Ann Wilson, Mar. 22, 1968. BA, David Lipscomb Coll., 1967; MLS, George Peabody Coll. Tchrs., 1968, specialist in edn., 1972; PhD, U. Ill., 1983. Head libr. Freed-Hardeman Coll., Henderson, Tenn., 1968-71; reference libr. Wabash Coll., Crawfordsville, Ind., 1973-79, Purdue U., West Lafayette, Ind., 1979-82, asst. prof. libr. sci., 1979-85, assoc. prof. libr. sci., 1985-89, sr. reference libr. Humanities, Social Sci. and Edn. Libr., 1982-90, prof. libr. sci., 1989—2003, libr. Humanities, Social Sci. and Edn. Libr., 1990—2003, prof. emeritus library sci., 2003—; dean libr., info. resources Abilene Christian U., 2003—. Mem. grantee com. instl. coop. NEH, 1991—94. Co-editor: Reference Services and Library Education, 1983, User Instruction in Academic Libraries, 1986, American Library History, 1989, Reading for Moral Progress, 1997; editor: Untold Stories: Civil Rights, Libraries and Black Librarianship, 1998; mem. editl. bd. Dictionary of American Library Biography, 2002; mem. editl. bd.: Librs. and Culture: Libr. Issues; contbr. articles to profl. jours. Thomas S. Wilmeth grantee, 1988, Frederick B. Artz Rsch. grantee, Oberlin Coll. Archives, 1991, Rsch. fellow, Coun. Libr. Resources, 1990. Mem.: SCV, ALA (chair libr. history round table 1993—94), Disciples of Christ Hist. Soc., Assn. Coll. and Rsch. Librs., Beta Phi Mu, Phi Kappa Phi. Democrat. Mem. Ch. Of Christ. Home: 1687 Bent Tree Dr Abilene TX 79602 Office: Brown Libr Abilene Christian U Box 29208 Abilene TX 79699-9208 Office Phone: 325-674-2387. Business E-Mail: mark.tucker@acu.edu.

TUCKER, JONATHAN BRIN, political scientist; b. Boston, Aug. 2, 1954; s. Leonard Walter and Deborah Alice (Brin) T.; m. Karen Fern Fifer, Aug. 27, 1980 (div.). BS in Biology, Yale U., New Haven, Conn., 1975; MA in Internat. Rels., U. Pa., 1982; PhD in Polit. Sci., MIT, Cambridge, 1990. Mem. bd. editors Scientific Am. mag., NYC, 1976-79; freelance sci. writer Phila., 1979-83; sr. editor High Tech. mag., Boston, 1983-85; arms control fellow U.S. Dept. of State, Washington, 1989-90; def. policy analyst U.S. Congress Office of Tech. Assessment, Washington, 1990-93; fgn. affairs splst. U.S. Arms Control and Disarmament Agy., Washington, 1993-95; sr. policy analyst Presdl. Adv. Com. on Gulf War Vets. Ilnesses, Washington, 1995; dir. chem., biol weapons nonproliferation program Ctr. for Nonproliferation Studies Monterey Inst. Internat. Studies, Calif., 1996—. Vis. fellow Hoover Instn. Stanford (Calif.) U., 1999-2000, U.S. Inst. Peace, Washington, 2002-03, Am. Acad. in Berlin, 2006. Author: Ellie: A Child's Fight Against Leukemia, 1982; editor: Toxic Terror: Assessing Terrorist Use of Chemical and Biological Weapons, 2000, Scourge: The Once and Future Threat of Smallpox, 2001, War of Nerves: Chemical Warfare from World War I to Al-Qaeda, 2006; govt. reports; contbr. articles to profl. jours. Mem. Arms Control Assn., Coun. Fgn. Rels., Robert Bosch Found. Fellowship Alumni Assn. Democrat. Avocations: ballroom dancing, hiking. Office: Ctr for Nonproliferation Studies/MIIS Fl 12 1111 Nineteenth St NW Washington DC 20036-2623

TUCKER, KEITH A., investment company executive; b. 1945; BBA, U. Tex., 1967, JD, 1970. With KPMG Peat Marwick, Dallas, 1970-85, Stephens, Inc., Little Rock, 1985-87, Trivest Inc., Miami, Fla., 1987-91; dir. Waddell & Reed Inc., Shawnee Mission, Kans., 1989—, vice chmn., 1991—, chmn. Home: 3831 Turtle Creek Blvd Apt 6h Dallas TX 75219-4412

TUCKER, KEVIN W., curator; b. Oct. 20, 1966; BA in History, U. SC, Columbia, 1989, NA in Applied History, Mus. Studies, 1994. Deputy dir., chief curator Columbia Mus. Art, SC, 2002—03; Margot B. Perot curator Dallas Mus. Art, 2003—. Author: (exhibition catalogue) Gustav Stickley and the American Arts and Crafts Movement; editor: Modernism in American Silver: 20th Century Design. Preservation chair Cottontown Nat. Hist. Dist., Columbia, 2000—03. Recipient George Wittenborn Meml. Book award, 2006; Winterthur rsch. fellowship, 2006. Mem.: Am. Assn. Mus., Decorative Arts Trust. Office: Dallas Mus Art 1717 N Harwood Dallas TX 75201

TUCKER, KIMBERLY JOAN, music educator, director; b. Racine, Wis., May 4, 1977; d. Joan Marie and Robert Edward Griswold (Stepfather), Joseph Zoltan and Lilac Kriston (Stepmother); m. Christopher Michael Tucker, Aug. 14, 2004. B in Music Edn., U. North Tex., Denton, 2000; MusM in Instrumental Performance, Tex. A&M U., Commerce, 2007. Asst. band dir. DeSoto West Jr. H.S. and Amber Ter. Intermediate Sch., Tex., 2000—02, head band dir., 2002—05; band tchr. Rockwall ISD, 2005. Sch. rep. DeSoto Dist. Advocacy Com., 2000—02. Recipient Sweepstakes award, U. Interscholastic League Region 20, 2002—04, Beach Within Reach Contest, 2002—04, Sandy Lake Music Festival, 2002—04. Fellow: Alpha Lambda Delta (life); mem.: Tex. Flute Soc., Nat. Flute Assn. (corr.), Internat. Clarinet Assn. (corr.), Music Educators Nat. Conf. (corr.), Tex. Bandmasters Assn. (corr.), Tex. Music Educators Assn. (corr.), Sigma Alpha Iota (life; rec. sec. 1998—2000, Sword of Honor 1999). Roman Catholic. Avocations: practicing instruments, singing, sketching. Home: 684 Danielle Ct Rockwall TX 75087 Office Phone: 972-768-4784. Business E-Mail: ktucker@lonestarwindorchestra.com.

TUCKER, LAUREY DAN, lawyer; s. Floyd A. and Harriet Kathleen (Graves) T.; m. Katherine Washburn, June 21, 1958; children: Laurie Tucker Diaz, Dana Tucker Kleine. BSChemE, U. Okla., Norman, 1959, LLB, 1962. Bar: Okla. 1962, Tex. 1972. Patent atty. Phillps Petroleum Co., Bartlesville, Okla., 1964—67, Monsanto Co., St. Louis, 1967—70, patent mgr. Texas City, Tex., 1970—74; ptnr. Hubbard, Tucker & Harris, Dallas, 1974—94, Harris, Tucker & Hardin, Dallas, 1994—97, Locke Purnell Rain Harrell, Dallas, 1997—98, Locke Liddell & Sapp LLP, Dallas, 1999—2006. Past pres. Dallas-Ft. Worth Patent Assn. Capt. USAR, 1959—69, 1st lt. US Army, 1962—64. Mem.: Internat. Trademark Assn., Dallas Bar Assn., State Bar Tex. (past officer Intellectual Property Law Section), Okla. Bar Assn. Republican. Episcopalian. Avocations: fishing, hunting, travel. Personal E-mail: tucker_dan@sbcglobal.net.

TUCKER, LOUIS LEONARD, retired historical society administrator; b. Rockville, Conn., Dec. 6, 1927; s. Joseph and Dora (Conn) T.; m. Beverley Jones, Mar. 27, 1953; children: Mark T., Lance K.; m. Carolyn woollen, Sept. 14, 1996. BA, U. Wash., 1952, MA, 1954, PhD, 1957. Instr. history U. Calif., Davis, 1958; fellow Inst. Early Am. History and Culture, Williamsburg, Va., 1958-60; instr. history Coll. William and Mary, 1958-60; dir. Cin. Hist. Soc., 1960-66; asst. commr., state historian of NY, N.Y State Edn. Dept., 1966-76; also dir. N.Y. State Bicentennial Commn., 1969-76; dir. Mass. Hist. Soc., Boston, 1977-97. Author: Puritan Protagonist, 1962, Cincinnati During Civil War, 1962, Cincinnati's Citizen Crusaders, 1967, Our Travels, 1968, Cincinnati: Students Guide to Local History, 1969, James Allen, Jr.: From Elkins to Washington, 1969, Connecticut's Seminary of Sedition, Yale College, 1974, Clio's Consort: Jeremy Belknap and the Founding of the Massachusetts Historical Society, 1990, The Massachusetts Historical Society: A Bicentennial History, 1791-1971, 1996, Worthington Chauncey Ford: Scholar and Adventurer, 2001. Dir. Shaker Mus., 1967-74; Am. Heritage Co., 1973-75, Ft. Ticonderoga Assn., 1990-97. Served with AUS, 1946-47. Winston Churchill fellow, 1969 Mem. Am. Assn. State and Local History (pres. 1972-74) Home: 328 Harvard St Cambridge MA 02139-2002

TUCKER, MARC STEPHEN, education policy analyst, author; b. Boston, Nov. 15, 1939; s. David Jones and Natalie (Croman) T.; m. Linda Beth Hepler, Sept 27, 1964 (div. 1973); children: Matthew, Joshua; foster child, Julie Beers. AB, Brown U., 1961; MSS, George Washington U., 1982. Lighting dir., camera Sta. WGBH-TV, Boston, 1962—64, asst. dir. edn. divsn., 1964—66; asst. to pres. Edn. Devel. Ctr., Newton, Mass., 1966—71; asst. dir. NWREL, Portland, Oreg., 1971—72; assoc. dir. Nat. Inst. Edn., Washington, 1972—81; dir. Project on Info. Tech. and Edn., Washington, 1981—84; exec. dir. Carnegie Forum on Edn. and the Economy, Washington, 1985—87; pres., CEO Nat. Ctr. on Edn. and the Economy, Rochester, NY, 1988—; prof. edn. U. Rochester, 1988. Staff dir., prin. author Carnegie report-A Nation Prepared: Tchrs. for the 21st Century, 1986. Contbr. articles to profl. jours.; co-author (with Ray Marshall): Thinking for a Living: Education and the Wealth of Nations; co-author: (with Judy Codding) Standards for Our Schools: How to Set Them, Measure Them and Reach Them; co-editor: The Principal Challenge. Chmn., pres. Brass Chamber Music Soc., Annapolis, Md., 1980-81; mem. bd. advs. Apple Edn. Found., 1984-85, bd. visitors Wake Forest U., 1987, bd. visitors U. Pitts. Sch. Edn., 1987, bd. advs. Bank St. Coll. Edn. Ctr. for Children and Tech., 1987. Democrat. Office: Nat Ctr On Educ And The Economy 555 13th St NW Ste 500 W Washington DC 20004-1109 Office Phone: 202-783-3668. Office Fax: 202-783-3672. *

TUCKER, MARNA S., lawyer; b. Phila., Mar. 5, 1941; BS, U. Tex., 1962; LLB, Georgetown U. Law Ctr., 1965; JD (hon.), U. DC Sch. Law, 1995. Bar: D.C. 1966, Calif. 1969, U.S. Supreme Ct. 1970. Deputy dir. legal svcs. program western region Office Of Econ. Opportunity, 1967-69; spl. asst. to Allard K. Lowenstein, NY congressman, 1969-70; dir. ABA Pro Bono Project, 1971—73; ptnr. Feldesman, Tucker, Leifer, Fidell and Bank (now Feldesman Tucker Leifer Fidell LLP), Washington; sr. ptnr., family law Feldesman Tucker Leifer Fidell LLP, Washington. Adj. prof. of law Georgetown U. Law Ctr., 1972; lectr. of law Cath. U., Columbus Sch. Law, 1972-74. Apptd. Bd. Prof. Responsibility, D.C. Ct. Appeals, 1977-83; mem. U.S. Cir. Ct. Com. on Admissions and Grievances, 1979-89, U.S. Jud. Nominating Com. for D.C., 1977-80; bd. regents Georgetown U., 1986-89; bd. visitors, Georgetown Law Ctr., 1994-2000; trustee Ctr. for Law and Social Policy, 1977-99, Pub. Defender Svc. D.C., 1986-92; founding bd. mem., sec./treas., bd. trustee, Nat. Women's Law Ctr., 1981-2005; mem. exec. com. Washington Lawyers Com. for Civil Rights Under Law, 1973—; chair Mayor's Commn. on Violence Against Women, 1996-2002; commr., U.S. Comm. of Child and Family Welfare, 1994. Named Women Lawyer of Yr. Women's Bar Assn. of D.C., 1985; recipient Annual Alumni Achievement award Georgetown Alumni Club, 1986, Alumni Achievement award, Georgetown Law Ctr., 1998, Exceptional Achievement award NAACP Legal Def. and Ednl. Fund, Inc., Washington Com., 1985; named one of 75 Best Lawyers in Washington, Washingtonian Mag., 2002, (several times) Top Divorce Lawyer. Fellow Am. Bar Found. (chair, 1995), Am. Acad. Matrimonial Lawyers, Am. Coll. Trial Lawyers; mem. ABA (chmn. sect. individual rights and responsibilities 1982-83, chmn. commn. on pub. understanding about law 1979-82, chmn. standing com. profl. discipline 1987-90, house of del. bar del., 1974-80, 1988-, co-chmn. Commn. on Domestic Violence, 1995-97, standing com. fed. judiciary, Margaret Brent Women Lawyers of Achievement award, Robert Drinan Disting. Svc. award), ACLU Nat. Capital Area (bd. dirs. 1973-76), Nat. Legal Aid and Defender Assn. (v.p. 1973-77, Nat. Legal Aid and Defender Assn. Annual award, 1993), D.C. Bar (pres. 1984-85, legal ethics com. 1974-76, del. ABA ho. of dels. 1974-91), Nat. Conf. Bar Pres. (pres.-elect, pres. 1991), Women's Forum Washington; chair Fellows Am. Bar Found., 1995-96; bd. mem. Fed. Jud. Ctr. Found. Bd., 1997-, chair, 2000. Office: Feldesman Tucker Leifer Fidell LLP 2001 L St NW 2nd Fl Washington DC 20036 Office Phone: 202-466-8960. Office Fax: 202-293-8103. Business E-Mail: mtucker@feldesmantucker.com. *

TUCKER, MELVIN JAY, education educator, researcher; s. Earle Homer and Florence Gertrude Tucker; m. N. Evelyn Rapalus, June 27, 1953; children: Ann Evelyn Jobson, Ellen Marie Tucker-Cohen, Michael Jay. BA, U. Mass., Amherst, Mass., 1953, MA, 1954; PhD, Northwestern U., Evanston, Il., 1962. Instr. Colby Coll., Waterville, Maine, 1959—60, MIT, Cambridge, Mass., 1960—63; assoc. prof. U. Buffalo, Buffalo, 1963—. Dir. grad. studies, history Univ. Buffalo, 1979—85; fellow Medieval Ctr., SUNY, Binghampton, 1970—77. Author: The Life of Thoms Howard, Earl of Surrey and Second Duke of Norfolk, 1443-1524; co-author: Centering: A Guide to Inner Growth, 2nd ed.; contbr. chapters to books; contbg. editor: History of Childhood Quarterly, 1973—76, Journal of Psycho History, 1976—84. 1st lt. USAF, 1954—56, Japan. Recipient Fulbright Award, Fulbright Commn., 1958-1959, Cert. of Merit, Buffalo & Erie County Hist. Soc., 1974, Cert. of Recognition, Career Planning, U. Buffalo, 2002. Mem.: Assn. for the Bibliography of History (coun. mem. 1982—92), Am. Hist. Assn., North Am. Conf. of Brit. Studies. Roman Catholic. Avocations: walking, movies. Office: History Dept Univ Buffalo 580 Pk Hall Buffalo NY 14260 Business E-Mail: mjtucker@acsu.buffalo.edu.

TUCKER, RICHARD LEE, civil engineer, educator; b. Wichita Falls, Tex., July 19, 1935; s. Floyd Alfred and Zula Florence (Morris) T.; m. Shirley Sue Tucker, Sept. 1, 1956; children: Bryan Alfred, Karen Leigh. BCE, U. Tex., 1958, MCE, 1960, PhDCE, 1963. Registered profl. engr., Tex. Instr. civil engring. U. Tex., 1960-62, from asst. prof. to prof. Arlington, 1962-74, assoc. dean engring., 1963-74; v.p Luther Hill & Assoc., Inc., Dallas, 1974-76; Joe C. Walter chair in engring. U. Tex., Austin, 1976—, dir. Constrn. Industry Inst., 1983-98, dir. Ctr. Constrn. Industry Studies, 1998—2003. Pres. Tucker and Tucker Cons., Inc., Austin, 1976—. Contbr. numerous articles and papers to profl. jours. Recipient Erwin C. Perry award, Coll. Engring., U. Tex., 1978, Faculty Excellence award, 1986, Joe J. King Profl. Engring. Achievement award, 1990, Hocott Rsch. Award, 2000, Disting. Engring. Grad., 1994; Ronald Reagan award for Individual Initiative, Constrn. Industry Inst., 1991; named Outstanding Young Engr., Tex. Soc. Profl. Engrs., 1965, Outstanding Young Man, City of Arlington, 1967; fellow Inst. for Constructive Capitalism, 1990-91. Fellow ASCE (R.L. Peurifoy award 1986, Thomas Fitch Rowland prize 1987, Tex. sect. award of honor 1990); mem. NSPE (Constrn. Engr. Educator award 1993, Engr. of Yr. 2001), NAE (Engr. of Year, 2003), Soc. Am. Mil. Engrs., The Moles (hon.), Acad. Engring. Sci. Baptist. Office: Univ Tex Coll Engring Constrn Industry Inst ECJ5 2 Austin TX 78712

TUCKER, ROBERT DENNARD, health care products executive; b. Tifton, Ga., July 18, 1933; s. Robert Buck and Ethel Margaret (Dennard) T.; m. Peggy Angelyn Smith, June 23, 1957; children: Robert Barron, Jennifer Lee. BBA, Ga. State U., 1958. With sales and sales mgmt. Johnson & Johnson Inc., New Brunswick, NJ, 1958-68; v.p., gen. mgr. ASR Med. Industries, NYC, 1968-72, Howmedica Suture div. Pfizer Inc., NYC, 1972-75; exec. v.p., chief operating officer R. P. Scherer Corp., Detroit, 1976-79; pres., chief operating officer Scherer Sci. Inc., Atlanta, 1980-95, also bd. dirs; chmn., chief exec. officer Scherer Health Care Inc., Atlanta, 1980-95, also bd. dirs. Bd. dirs., pres., CEO Splty. Surgictrs., Inc., Atlanta, 1997—2002; bd. dirs., chmn., CEO Maximum Benefits Co., Atlanta; chmn., CEO Throwleigh Techs., LLC, 1995—; bd. dirs., mem. exec. com. Horizon Med. Products, 2002—05; bd. dirs., chmn compensation com. Averion Internat. Corp., 2006—. Pub: Tuckers of Devon, 1983; author, pub.: Descendants of William Tucker of Throwleigh, Devon. Chmn. bd. Health Industries Mfrs. Assn. polit. action com., Washington, 1983-85; trustee, past pres. Ga. Horse Found., Atlanta; trustee Brenau Coll., Gainesville, Ga., 1985—. Served with USN, 1951-54, Korea. Decorated Knight of Malta, Imperial Russian Order of St. John; recipient Disting. Service award Brenau Coll., 1987. Mem. Nat. Assn. Mfrs., Health Industries Mfrs. Assn. (bd. dirs. 1979-86, disting. service recognition 1981, 86), Pharm. Mfrs. Assn., Thoroughbred Owners and Breeders Assn. Ky. and Ga. (Man of Yr. 1984). Clubs: Cherokee (Atlanta); Big Canoe (Ga.). Republican. Methodist. Avocations: scuba diving, tennis, genealogy. Home: 405 Townsend Pl NW Atlanta GA 30327-3037 Office: Throwleigh Techs PO Box 220 Ball Ground GA 30107

TUCKER, ROBERT RAND, lawyer; b. Goldsboro, NC, Jan. 1, 1960; s. William Wayne and Myra Boyce (Hollowell) T. BA, U. NC, 1982; JD, U. Mich., 1985. Bar: N.C. 1985. Ptnr. Kilpatrick Stockson LLP, Winston-Salem, NC, 1985—92, 1992—98; v.p., gen. counsel LADD Furniture, Inc., 1999—2001; corp. counsel La-Z-Boy Inc., Greensboro, NC. Mem. ABA, N.C. Bar Assn., Forsyth County Bar Assn. Democrat. Home: 1820 Greenbrier Rd Winston Salem NC 27104-2322 Office: La-Z-Boy 4620 Grandover Pkwy Greensboro NC 27407 Office Phone: 336-315-4093. Office Fax: 336-315-4396. E-mail: rand.tucker@la-z-boy.com.

TUCKER, ROY W., lawyer; b. Buffalo, Aug. 31, 1952; BA in Polit. Sci. & English, with dist. in Polit. Sci., magna cum laude, Kenyon Coll., 1974; JD, SUNY Buffalo, 1979. Bar: NY 1980, Oreg. 1985. Law clk. to Hon. Reid S. Moule Appellate Divsn., NY State Supreme Ct., 1979—80; with Davis Polk & Wardwell, NY, 1980—84; ptnr., mem. mgmt. com. Perkins Coie LLP, Portland, Oreg. Assoc. editor Buffalo Law Rev., 1977—78, sr. editor, 1978—79. Mem.: Phi Beta Kappa. Office: Perkins Coie LLP 1120 NW Couch St Floor 10 Portland OR 97209-4128 Office Phone: 503-727-2044. Office Fax: 503-727-2222. Business E-Mail: rtucker@perkinscoie.com.

TUCKER, SHIRLEY LOIS COTTER, botanist, educator; b. St. Paul, Apr. 4, 1927; d. Ralph U. and Myra C. (Knutson) Cotter; m. Kenneth W. Tucker, Aug. 22, 1953. BA, U. Minn., 1949, MS, 1951; PhD, U. Calif., Davis, 1956. Asst. prof. botany La. State U., Baton Rouge, 1967-71, assoc. prof., 1971-76, prof., 1976-82, Boyd prof., 1982-95, prof. emerita, 1995—. Adj. prof. dept. biology U. Calif., Santa Barbara, 1995—. Co-editor: Aspects of Floral Development, 1988, Advances in Legume Systematics, Vol. 6, 1994; contbr. numerous articles on plant devel. to profl. jours. Recipient, Outstanding Alumni Achievement award U. Minn., 1999; fellow Linnean Soc., London, 1975—, Fulbright fellow Eng., 1952-53; named to Hall of Distinction La. State U., Baton Rouge, 2006. Mem. Bot. Soc. Am. (v.p. 1979, program chmn. 1975-78, pres.-elect 1986-87, pres. 1987-88, Merit award 1989, Centennial award 2006), Am. Bryological and Lichenological Soc., Brit. Lichenological Soc., Am. Inst. Biol. Scis., Am. Soc. Plant Taxonomists (pres.-elect 1994-95, pres. 1995-96), Phi Beta Kappa, Sigma Xi. Home: 3987 Primavera Rd Santa Barbara CA 93110-1467 Office: U Calif Dept Biology EEMB Santa Barbara CA 93106 Home Phone: 805-898-0908. Business E-Mail: tucker@lifesci.ucsb.edu.

TUCKER, STEFAN FRANKLIN, lawyer; b. Detroit, Dec. 31, 1938; Assoc. in Bus., Flint Jr. Community Coll., 1958; BBA, U. Mich., 1960, JD, 1963. Bar: US Dist. Ct. DC 1964, US Ct. Appeals (DC cir.) 1964, US Ct. Claims 1964, US Tax Ct. 1964. Clk. to judge US Tax Ct., Washington, 1963-64; assoc. Arent, Fox, Kintner, Plotkin & Kahn, Washington, 1964-69, ptnr., 1970-74, Tucker, Flyer & Lewis, Washington, 1975—99, Venable LLP, Washington, 2000—. Profl. lectr. law George Washington U. Nat. Law Ctr., 1970—1990; adj. prof. law Georgetown U. Law Ctr., 1990—; adj. profl. lectr. law U. Miami Law Ctr., 1975-78; mem. adv. com. Ann. Inst. Estate Planning, U. Miami, 1978-91; trustee Mass. Sch. Law, Andover, 1989—, chmn. bd. trustees, 1989-95; mem. visitors com. U. Mich. Law Sch., 1989—. Author: Tax Planning for Real Estate Transactions, 1989, semi-ann. supplements; mem. editl. bd. Taxation for Lawyers, 1972—; mem. adv. bd. Bur. Nat. Affairs Housing and Devel. Reporter, 1973-76, Mertens on Federal Income Taxation, 1985-2000, The Tax Times, 1986-87, mem. editl. adv. bd. Real Estate Taxation, 1975—, Practical Real Estate Lawyer, 1984—2001. Mem. nat. com. U. Mich. Law Sch. Fund, 1972-78. Named a Leading Lawyer in Real Estate Law, Legal Times, 2003; named Top Washington Lawyer in Tax Law, Washington Bus. Jour., 2004; named one of Top 100 Attys., Worth mag., 2005—06, Leading Real Estate Lawyers in US, Chambers USA: Am. Leading Lawyers for Bus., 2006; named to Best Lawyers in Am., 1987—2007. Mem. ABA (tax sect., chmn. real estate tax problems com. 1977-79, chmn. continuing legal edn. com. 1984-86, coun. mem. 1987-91, vice chmn. com. ops. 1991-93, chairperson-elect 1997, chair 1998-1999), FBA, D.C. Bar Assn. (taxation divsn., mem. steering com. 1980-82), Nat. Trust Hist. Preservation (mem. com. on legal svcs. 1978-85), Am. Law Inst., Am. Coll. Real Estate Lawyers, 1981-, Am. Coll. Tax Coun., 1995-, Am. Tax Policy Inst. (bd. dirs. 2000-04). Office: Venable LLP 575 7th St NW Washington DC 20004 *I believe that each person has an obligation to share with others, whether through teaching, lecturing or writing, the knowledge and experience gained through his life's work. Such sharing provides a greater reward than monetary gain can ever provide.*

TUCKER, TANYA DENISE, singer; b. Seminole, Tex., Oct. 10, 1958; d. Beau and Juanita Tucker; children: Presley Tanita, Beau Grayson, Layla LaCosta. Singer Tanya Tucker Inc., 1959—. Regular on Lew King Show;

rec. artist formerly with Columbia Records, MCA Records, Capital Records; albums include The Sound of Tanya Tucker, 1972, Tear Me Apart, Chagnes, Delta Dawn, 1972, What's Your Mamma's Name, 1973. Would You Lay With Me (In a Field of Stone), 1974, Girls Like Me, Tanya Tucker's Greatest Hits, 1975, Greatest Hits, 1975, Tanya Tucker, 1975, Greatest Hits Encore, 1976, Here's Some Love, 1976, Lovin' and Learnin', 1976, You Are So Beautiful, 1977, Greatest Hits, 1978, T.N.T., 1978, Ridin' Rainbows, 1979, Tear Me Apart, 1979, Should I Do It, 1981, Dream Lovers, 1981, Live, 1982, The Best of Tanya Tucker, 1982, Changes, 1983, Love Me Like You Used To, 1987, Strong Enough to Bend, 1988, Greatest Hits, 1989, Tennessee Women, 1990, Ridin Rainbows/Here's Some Love, 1990, Lovin' and Learnin'/Tanya Tucker, 1990, Greatest Country Hits, 1991, What Do I Do With Me, 1991, Collection, 1992, The Best of Tanya Tucker, 1992, (with Delbert McClinton) Can't Run From Youself, 1992, Greatest Hits, 1993, Lizzie & the Rain Man, 1993, Greatest Hits (CEMA), 1993, Greatest Hits (Capitol), 1993, Country Queen, 1993, Greatest Hits 1990-1992, 1993, Soon, 1993, Girls Like Me, 1994, Fire to Fire, 1995, (with T. Graham Brown, Delbert McClinton) Tanya, 1995, Christmas with Tanya Tucker and Suzy Bogguss, 1995, The Best of My Love, 1995, Love Songs, 1996, Complicated, 1997, Little Things, 1997, Super Hits, 1998, What's Your Mama's Name/Would You Lay With Me (In a Field of Stone), 1999, Best of My Love, 2000, Sisters: An Anthology, 2000, Country Classics, Vol. 2, 2000, 20 Greatest Hits, 2000, 20th Century Masters-The Millennium Collection: The Best of Tanya Tucker, 2000, The Dresden Dolls, 2001, Tanya Tucker Country Classics, 2001, Tanya, 2002, The Upper 48 Hits 1972-1997, 2002, Country Classics, 2002, Very Best Of, 2004, Country Greatest: EMI Years, 2004, Live at Billy Bob's Texas, 2005; TV appearances include A Country Christmas, 1979, The Georgia Peaches, 1980, The Love Boat, 1982, Delta, 1992; actress: (mini-series) The Rebels, 1979, (film) Jeremiah Johnson, 1972, Amateur Night At the Dixie Bar & Grill, 1978, When I Was A Girl, 2003, (TV series) Tuckerville, 2005-; published (autobiography) Nickel Dreams, 1997; author: 100 Ways to Beat the Blues, 2005. Nat. amb. Nat. Multiple Sclerosis Soc.; philanthropist March of Dimes, St. Jude's Children's Hosp., Doris Kupferle Breast Centers, Coors Literacy Project, Recording Artists Against Drunk Driving, Planet Hope, Boys and Girls Clubs, charitable events for T.J. Martell Found. Named Top New Female Vocalist, Acad. Country Music, 1972, Most Promising Female Artist of Yr., Music City News Country, 1973, Female Vocalist of Yr., Country Music Assn., 1991, Female Video Artist of Yr., Country Music TV, 1993, Showcase Artist of Month, Country Music TV, 1997; recipient Music Video of Yr., Country Music Assn., 1992, Video of Yr. for Two Sparrows in a Hurricane, Acad. Country Music, 1993; nominee for two Grammy awards, 1994. Avocations: avid competitor in cutting horse contests, motorcycling. Office: Tanya Tucker Inc c/o Curtis & Co Plc 109 Westpark Dr Ste 400 Brentwood TN 37027-5032

TUCKER, THOMAS JAMES, retired investment company executive; b. Atlanta, Sept. 5, 1929; s. Thomas Tudor and Carol (Govan) T.; m. Margaret Guerard. BA, U. of the South, 1952. With CIT Corp, NYC, 1957—72; pres., CEO AmSouth Fin. Corp., Birmingham, Ala., 1972—82, chmn. bd., 1982, also dir., 1972—93; exec. v.p. AmSouth Bank N.A., Birmingham, 1982—93, chief credit officer, 1992; prin. Tucker Investments, Birmingham, 1993—2003; ret., 2003. Exec. v.p. AmSouth Bancorp, Birmingham, 1982-93; bd. dirs. Alabanc Properties Corp., Birmingham, chmn., 1991-93; bd. dirs. Birmingham Broadway Series Inc., treas., 1996-97, pres., 1997-99, chmn., 1999-2001; co-founder Garland-Govan Scholarship Fund, Sewanee-U. of the South. Contbr. articles on credit and leasing to trade jours.; photographer gen. interest mags., 1970—. Bd. dirs. Birmingham Cmty. Devel. Corp.; chmn. bd., 1990-93. 1st lt. USAF, 1952-56. Mem. Vulcan Trail Assn., Birmingham Art Mus. Assn., Birmingham Bot. Soc., Friends of Emmt O'Neal Libr., Birmingham Canoe Club (bd. dirs. 1990-96), Photography Guild, Cahaba River Soc. (adv. bd. 1991-92, bd. dirs. 1993-98, v.p. orgnl. devel. 1995-98), Ala. Growth Strategies Task Force, Regional Open Space and Trails Alliance, Manigault Soc., Sewanee Devel. Coun., Order of Purple/Sewanee-U. of the South, Never Failing Succession of Benefactors/Sewanee-U. of the South, Carolynne Scott Writers Group (2d pl. 2006, Hackney award), The Club, Jefferson Club, Silhouettes Club Episcopalian. Avocations: photography, high altitude hiking, white water canoeing. Office: 6 Office Park Cir Ste 308 Birmingham AL 35223 Home: 415 Club Pl Birmingham AL 35223

TUCKER, THOMAS WILLIAM, mathematics professor; b. Princeton, NJ, July 15, 1945; s. Albert William Tucker and Alice Judson (Curtiss) Beckenbach; m. Mollie Dalton; children: Thomas John, Emily McDonnell. AB magna cum laude, Harvard U., 1967; PhD, Dartmouth Coll., 1971. Instr. Princeton U., 1971-73; from asst. prof. to prof. math. Colgate U., Hamilton, NY, 1973-83, prof., 1983—, Charles G. Hetherington prof. math., 1994—, chmn. math. dept., 1982-86, acting dean coll., 1991-92, dir. divsn. nat. sci., 1993-96. Vis. assoc. prof. Dartmouth Coll., Hanover, NH, 1978-79; cons. Ednl. Testing Svc., 1973—, Inst. for Def. Analyses, Princeton, 1974-75, 78-79, 84-85; chmn. advanced placement calculus com. Coll. Bd., NYC, 1983-87; pres. Calculus Consortium for Higher Edn., Inc., 1998-2005. Co-author: Topological Graph Theory, 1987; editor: Priming the Calculus Pump, 1990; contbr. numerous articles to profl. jours. NSF grantee, 1976-77, 80-82, 86-88, 89, 90-97. Mem. Math. Assn. Am. (mem., chmn. many coms., v.p. 1990-92), Am. Math. Soc. Home: 21 Hamilton St Hamilton NY 13346-1329 Office: Colgate U Dept Math Hamilton NY 13346 Business E-Mail: ttucker@mail.colgate.edu.

TUCKER, WATSON BILLOPP, lawyer; b. Dobbs Ferry, NY, Nov. 16, 1940; s. Watson Billopp and Mary (Prema) T.; children: Robin, Craig, Christopher, Alexander, John. BS, Northwestern U., Evanston, Ill., 1962; JD magna cum laude, Northwestern U., 1965. Bar: Ill. 1965, US Dist. Ct. (no. dist.) Ill. 1966, US Supreme Ct. 1971, US Dist. Ct. (no. dist.) NY 1976, US Ct. Appeals (2d, 3d, 5th, 6th, 7th, and 9th cirs.). Ptnr. Mayer, Brown, Rowe & Maw, Chgo., 1972-99, Smith Tucker & Coghlan, Sycamore, Ill., 1999—. Fellow Am. Coll. Trial Lawyers. Office Phone: 815-787-7033. Business E-Mail: wbtucker@smithtucker.com.

TUCKER, WILLIAM EDWARD, academic administrator, minister; b. Charlotte, NC, June 22, 1932; s. Cecil Edward and Ethel Elizabeth (Godley) T.; m. Ruby Jean Jones, Apr. 8, 1955; children: Janet Sue, William Edward, Gordon Vance. BA, Barton Coll., Wilson, NC, 1953, LLD (hon.), 1978; BD, Tex. Christian U., Ft. Worth, 1956; MA, Yale U., New Haven, Conn., 1958, PhD, 1960; LHD (hon.), Chapman U., Orange, Calif., 1981, Ky. Wesleyan Coll., Owensboro, 1989; DH (hon.), Bethany Coll., W.Va., 1982; DD (hon.), Austin Coll., Sherman, Tex., 1985. Ordained to ministry Disciples of Christ Ch., 1956; prof. Barton Coll., 1959-66, chmn. dept. religion and philosophy, 1961-66; mem. faculty Brite Div. Sch., Tex. Christian U., 1966-76, prof. ch. history, 1969-76, dean, 1971-76, chancellor, 1979-98, chancellor emeritus, 1998—. Pres. Bethany (W.Va.) Coll., 1976-79; dir. RadioShack Corp., 1985-2003, Brown and Lupton Found.; mem. gen. bd. Christian Ch. (Disciples of Christ), 1971-74, 75-87, adminstrv. com., 1975-81, chmn. theol. edn. commn., 1972-73, mem. exec. com., chmn. bd. higher edn., 1975-77; dir. Christian Ch. Found., 1980-83; moderator Christian Ch. (Disciples of Christ), 1983-85 Author: J.H. Garrison and Disciples of Christ, 1964, (with others) Journey in Faith: A History of the Christian Church (Disciples of Christ), 1975; also articles. Bd. dirs. Van Cliburn Found., 1981—, Ft. Worth Symphony Orch.; bd. trustee Amon Carter Mus. Mem. Exch. Club, Phi Beta Kappa. Home: 2337 Colonial Pky Fort Worth TX 76109-1030 Office: 777 Taylor St Ste P2-J Fort Worth TX 76102 Office Phone: 817-347-3220. Business E-Mail: w.tucker@tcu.edu.

TUCKER, WILLIAM P., lawyer, writer; b. Kingston, NY, Jan. 26, 1932; s. Philip and Mary (McGowan) T.; m. Dolores F. Beaudoin, June 10, 1961; children: Andrew M., Thomas B., Mary A. BA, Hunter Coll., 1958; JD, St. John's U., 1962. Bar: N.Y. 1962, Fla. 1980, U.S. Dist. Ct. (ea. dist.) N.Y. 1963, U.S. Dist. Ct. (so. dist.) N.Y., 1963, U.S. Cir. Ct. (2d cir.) Ill. Assoc. Mendes & Mount, NYC, 1962-63; ptnr. Cullen and Dykman, Bklyn. and Garden City, NY, Washington, Newark, Hauppauge, 1963-98, Golden, Wexler & Sarnese, Garden City/Purchase/S.I., 1998-2001; pvt. practice, 2001—. Former gen. counsel Broadway Nat. Bank, Wartburg Luth. Svcs., Luth. Ctr. for the Aging, Martin Luther Ter. Apts., Inc., Interfaith Med. Ctr., Roosevelt Savs. Bank, Olympian Bank, GreenPoint Bank, Ridgewood Savs. Bank, Atlantic Liberty Savs., F.A., Bethpage Fed. Credit Union, Mcpl. Credit Union, Lincoln Savs. Bank, Bklyn. Savs. Bank, Met. Savs. Bank, Crossland Savs. Bank, Bushwick Savs. Bank, Anchor Savs. Bank, Episc. Diocese L.I., St. John's Episc. Hosp., Bklyn., Rockaway, Smithtown; former spl. counsel OCI Mortgage Corp., Bklyn C. of C., Downtown Bklyn. Bus. Assn., Bank of N.Y., Chase Manhattan Bank, Fleet Bank, Kraft Credit Union, Apple Bank for Savs., Barclays Bank of N.Y.; chmn. bd. dirs. Broadway Nat. Bank; co-owner Salem Keizer Volcanoes N.W. League baseball team; former owner Norwich Navigators Ea. League baseball beam; former v.p., N.W. Profl. Baseball League; bd. dirs. Bklyn. Sportsplex, Inc.; mem. WWII vets. history com. Libr. of Congress; rschr. U.S. Assassination Archives. Author: DP-or Billy and Jerry in the Promised Land, 1996, Moving Home Plate, 1999, (novels) Excalibur, 2001, With Justice for All, 2003, Kingsway 37, 2004; contbr. articles to profl. jours. Past mem. Selective Svc. Bd. 33; past pres. St. Vincent Ferrer Home Sch. Assn.; del. Diocesan Union Holy Name Socs.; mem. coun. St. John's U.; mem. coun. of regents St. Francis Coll., Bklyn.; bd. dirs. Faith Home Found., St. Joseph's Coll. Served US Army, Korean War. Mem. Am. Coll. Real Estate Lawyers, N.Y. State Bar Assn., Fla. Bar Assn., Savs. Banks Lawyers Assn. Bklyn. (pres.), Suffolk County Bar Assn., Savs. Bank Assn. N.Y. State (law com.), Bklyn. Mcpl. Club (pres.), Knight of Malta. Home: 23 Bunker Hill Dr Huntington NY 11743-5705 Office: 145 East Main St Huntington NY 11743 Office Phone: 631-351-1112. Personal E-mail: wptucker@optonline.net.

TUCK-RICHMOND, DOLETTA SUE, prosecutor; b. Hugo, Okla., June 18, 1966; d. Benny Doyle and Tommie Marie (Cousins) T.; m. Lyle Richmond, Sept. 30, 1995; children: Rachelle Jay Marie, Benjamin Lee. AS, Murray State Coll., Tishomingo, Okla., 1986; BS magna cum laude, S.E. Okla. State U., 1988; JD with highest honors, U. Okla., 1991. Bar: Okla. 1991, U.S. Dist. Ct. (we., ea., and no. dists.), U.S. Ct. Appeals (10th cir.). Summer assoc. Andrews Davis, Oklahoma City, 1989-90; instr. in legal rsch., writing and oral advocacy U. Okla., Norman, 1989-91; assoc. Crowe & Dunlevy, Oklahoma City, 1991-93, Tulsa, 1993-94; pvt. practice Antlers, Okla., 1994; exempt orgn. specialist IRS, Oklahoma City, 1994-95; asst. atty. gen. State of Okla., Oklahoma City, 1995—; asst. U.S. atty. U.S. Atty's. Office (we. dist.) Okla., Oklahoma City, 1999—; chief U.S. Atty's Office, Criminal Appellate Sec., 1999—. Author: Joint Defense Agreements Can It Help Your Client, 1998, King For a Day: An Overview of Federal and State Qui Jam Provisions, 1999, The Fifth Amendment Privilege Against Self-Incrimination: Walking the Tightrope Between Civil and Criminal Law, 2001; contbg. author, editor: Oklahoma Environmental Law Practitioner's Handbook, 1992. Firm com. mem., participant Harvest Food Dr., Oklahoma City, 1991; chairperson Okla. Young Lawyers Rape Victims Assistance Com., 1992-94; bd. dirs. Okla. County Young Lawyers Divsn., 1993; participant, vol. Legal Aide of We. Okla., 1991. Named Miss Murray State Coll., Student Senate Pres., Tishomingo, 1986-86, Order of Coif U. Okla., Norman, 1991, Okla. Law Rev. U. Okla., Norman, 1991. Mem. Fed. Bar Assn., Okla. Bar Assn. (bd. dirs., young lawyers divsn. 1993-95, mock trial com. 1994-95, liaison mental health com. 1994-95), Am. Agrl. Law Assn., Phi Delta Phi, Phi Kappa Phi (Spl. Act award for U.S. Atty. 1996, 97, 98). Democrat. Baptist. Avocations: tennis, reading, writing, knitting, sports events. Home: 1624 SW 128th Pl Oklahoma City OK 73170-5018 Office: US Atty's Office Western Dist of Okla 210 Park Ave Ste 400 Oklahoma City OK 73102-5628

TUCKSON, REED V., physician, health insurance company executive; Grad., Howard U.; MD, Georgetown U. Residency & fellowship in internal med. Hosp. Univ. Pa.; commr. pub. health Washington, 1986—90; sr v.p. progs. March of Dimes Birth Defects Found., 1990—91; pres. Charles R. Drew U., LA, 1991—97; sr. v.p. profl. stds. AMA, Chgo., 1998—2000; sr. v.p. consumer health and med. care advancement UnitedHealth Group, Mpls., 2000—06, exec. v.p., head med. affairs, 2006—. Office: UnitedHealth Grp PO Box 1459 Minneapolis MN 55440 *

TUDMAN, CATHI GRAVES, elementary school educator; b. Fresno, Calif., June 24, 1953; d. Robert Eugene and Bettyelou (Seagraves) Graves; divorced; children: Colleen Melissa, Andrew James. BA in Music cum laude, Calif. State U., Fresno, 1978, MA in Communication, 1991. Gen. elem., English, music and gen. sci. teaching credentials, Calif. Founder, coord. Lake Sequoia Symphonic Music Camp, Miramonte, Calif., 1985—; asst. lectr. communications speech dept. Calif. State U., 1988-91, instr. reading ednl. opportunity program summer bridge, 1990, instr. writing ednl. opportunity program summer bridge, 1991, coach, judge Peach Blossom Festival, 1988-91; band dir. Yosemite Mid. Sch., 1991—2004, Mayfair Elem. Sch., 1991—2000, Hidalgo Elem. Sch., 1991-92, 94-96, Balderas Elem., 1992-93, Turner Elem., 1993-96, Burroughs Annex Elem. Sch., 1993-95; art dir. Yosemite Mid. Sch., 2000—04, Ft. Miller Med. Careers Magnet Sch., SC, 2004—; physical sci. instr. Ft. Miller Med. Careers Ctr., 2004—. Instr. comms. dynamics Phillips Coll., Fresno, 1989-90; rsch. assoc. Renshaw Assocs., Fresno, 1989-91; flutist, piccoloist Fresno Philharm. Orch., 1981—, libr., 1985, pers. mgr., 1984-85; flute clinician Selmer Corp., Ind., 1988-93; festivals chmn. cen. sect. Calif. Music Educators, 1972-82, publicity chmn., 1992-93; pvt. tutor in math., music and social studies; chmn. Fresno Unified Showcase Mid. Sch. Massed Band, 1991, 93. Flute clinician Fresno County Schs., 1980—; founder San Joaquin Valley Instrument Fund, 1984; bd. dirs. Community Concert Series, Fresno County, 1986-88; liaison com. bd. dirs. Fresno Philharm. Orch., 1992-94, mem. bd., 2002-04, edn. com., 2003-05; asst. chair FMCMEA Hon. Band, 1992-93; bd. dirs. Cen. Valley YMCA, 1994-95; music chair Fresno Met. Mus., 1996-97; mem. Yosemite Mid. Sch. Site Coun. 2000-2003, pres., sec., by-laws chair Fresno Arts Coun., bd. dirs. 2002-04, Tree Fresno-Rails to Trails Project, 2000; Great TV auction vol. Valley Pub. TV, 2005. Rsch. grantee Calif. State U., 1991, Cmty. Enrichment grant, 1999-2002; recipient Outstanding Teaching award Internat. Communication Assn., 1991. Mem. Western States Communication Assn., Fresno-Madera Music Educators Assn., Fresno Tchrs. Assn. (dir.-at-large, 2002-05), Calif. Tchrs. Assn. (rep. coun. 2000-2005), Fresno Mus. Club (social chmn. 1992-95) Calif. Music Educators (festival chmn. cen. sect. 1972-82), Sci. & Math. Educators Consortium, Calif. State U.-Fresno Alumnae Assn. (sec. 1982-83, nat. friendship chmn. 1979-81), Blue Key (Tokalon alumni 1978), Phi Kappa Phi, Mu Phi Epsilon (pres., v.p. Phi Chi chpt.). Avocations: quilting, kite making, church musician. Home: 5467 E Saginaw Way Fresno CA 93727-7536 Office: Fort Miller Mid Sch 1302 E Dakota Fresno CA 93704 Office Phone: 559-248-7100. E-mail: cgtudman@att.net.

TUDOR, HELEN E. A., materials engineer, consultant; b. Bucharest, Romania, Sept. 16, 1958; m. Colin C. Harris. PhD in Materials Sci. and Mineral Engring., Columbia U., NYC, 2001. Analysis engr. Grumman Aerospace Corp., Bethpage, 1977—88; tchg. and rsch. asst. MIT, Cambridge, Mass., 1980—83; vis. scientist Matsushita Electric Co., Osaka, Japan, 1983—84; materials engr. Intel Corp., Santa Clara, Calif., 1984—86; rsch. asst. Columbia U., NYC, 1994—2002; rsch. scientist Hosp. Spl. Surgery, NYC, 2002—06; pvt. cons. and advisor, 2006—. Cons. and advisor environ. issues and water decontamination methodologies, 1995—; dir. r&d ShellGen Water Purification Corp., NYC, 1996—2002. Contbr. articles to profl. jours. Sustaining mem. Rockefeller U. Concert Series, NYC, 2002—06. Recipient Presdl. Recognition award, Columbia U., 1997; grantee, MIT and Matsushita Ctrl. Rsch. Labs, Osaka, Japan, 1983—84; STAR fellow, US EPA, 1996—99. Mem.: AAAS, NY Acad. Sci., Am. Chem. Soc., MIT Alumni Assn., Penn Club. Achievements include patents for method for treating contaminated liquids using waste shells; using waste shells; complexed acidic phospholipid-collagen composites for bone induction; patents pending for. Avocations: seashore preservation, classical music, architectural conservation, Japanese art and architecture, wildlife protection. Home: 110 E 57th St New York NY 10022 Business E-Mail: tudorh@alum.mit.edu.

TUELL, JACK MARVIN, retired bishop; b. Tacoma, Nov. 14, 1923; s. Frank Harry and Anne Helen (Bertelson) T.; m. Marjorie Ida Beadles, June 17, 1946; children: Jacqueline, Cynthia, James. BS, U. Wash., 1947, JD, 1948; MDiv, Boston U., 1955; MA, U. Puget Sound, 1961, DHS, 1990; D.D., Pacific Sch. Religion, 1966; LLD, Alaska Pacific U., 1980. Bar: Wash. 1948; ordained to ministry Meth. Ch., 1955. Practice law with firm Holte & Tuell, Edmonds, Wash., 1948-50; pastor Grace Meth. Ch., Everett, Wash., 1950-52, South Tewksbury Meth. Ch., Tewksbury, Mass., 1952-55, Lakewood Meth. Ch., Tacoma, 1955-61; dist. supt. Puget Sound dist. Meth. Ch., Everett, 1961-67; pastor 1st United Meth. Ch., Vancouver, Wash., 1967-72; bishop United Meth. Ch., Portland, Oreg., 1972-80, Calif.-Pacific Conf., United Meth. Ch., LA, 1980-92, ret., 1992; interim sr. pastor First United Meth. Ch., Boise, Idaho, 1995; interim supt. Seattle Tacoma Dist., 2004—05. Mem. gen. conf. United Meth. Ch., 1964, 66, 68, 70, 72; pres. coun. of Bishops United Meth. Ch., 1989-90. Author: The Organization of the United Methodist Church, 1970, 10th edit. 2005, (autobiography) From Law to Grace, 2004. Pres. Tacoma U.S.O., 1959-61, Vancouver YMCA, 1968; v.p. Ft. Vancouver Seamens Cnt., 1969-72; vice chmn. Vancouver Human Rels. Commn., 1970-72; pres. Oreg. Coun. Alcohol Problems, 1972-76; trustee U. Puget Sound, 1961-73, Vancouver Meml. Hosp., 1967-72, Alaska Meth. U., Anchorage, 1972-80, Willamette U., Salem, Oreg., 1972-80, Willamette View Manor, Portland, 1972-80, Rogue Valley Manor, Medford, Oreg., 1972-76, Sch. Theology at Claremont, Calif., 1980-92, Methodist Hosp., Arcadia, Calif., 1983-92; pres. nat. div. bd. global ministries United Meth. Ch., 1972-76, pres. ecumenical and interreligious concerns div., 1976-80, Commn. on Christian Unity and intereligious concerns, 1980-84, Gen. Bd. of Pensions,1984-92, Calif. Coun. Alcohol Problems, 1985-88. Jacob Sleeper fellow, 1955. Methodist. Home and Office: 816 S 216th St 637 Des Moines WA 98198-6331

TUERK, WILLIAM F., federal agency administrator, lawyer; AB, U. Notre Dame, 1971; JD, George Washington U., 1978. Bar: D.C. 1978. Legis. analyst US Dept. Treasury, 1974—76; atty. pvt. practice, 1978—86, US Dept. Vet. Affairs, 1986—91, under sec. memorial affairs Washington, 2005—; minority gen. counsel Com. Vet. Affairs, U.S. Senate, 1991—95, gen counsel, 1995—99, chief counsel & staff dir., 1999—2005. Mil. policeman US Army, 1971—73. Office: US Dept Vets Affairs 810 Vermont Ave NW Rm 400 Washington DC 20420

TUETING, SARAH, professional hockey player; b. Winnetka, Ill., Apr. 26, 1976; Student, Dartmouth Coll., 1994—96. Goaltender U.S. Nat. Women's Hockey Team, 1996—. Recipient ice hockey Gold medal Olympic Games, Nagano, Japan, 1998. Avocations: soccer, tennis, playing piano and cello. Office: c/o USA Hockey 1775 Bob Johnson Dr Colorado Springs CO 80906

TUFANO, PAUL J., computer company executive; Degree in Econs., St. John's U.; MBA in Fin., Acctg., Internat. Bus., Columbia U. With IBM, 1984—2001; CFO Maxtor Corp., 1996—2001, exec. v.p., COO, 2001—03, pres., CEO, 2003—04; CFO Solectron Corp., Milpitas, Calif., 2006—, interim CEO, 2007—. Bd. dir. Terradyne Corp. Office: Solectron Corp 847 Gibraltar Dr Milpitas CA 95035-6332 *

TUFT, MARY ANN, executive search firm executive; b. Easton, Pa., Oct. 11, 1934; d. Ben and Elizabeth (Reibman) T. BS, West Chester State Coll., Pa., 1956; MA, Lehigh U., 1960. Cert. assn. exec. Nat. trainer Girl Scouts U.S.A., NYC, 1965-68; cons. Nat. League for Nursing, NYC, 1968-69; exec. dir. Nat. Student Nurses Assn., NYC, 1970-85; mem. Commn. on Dietetic Registration, Am. Dietetic Assn., 1981-85; pres. Specialized Cons. Ltd., 1983-85; exec. dir. Radiol. Soc. N.Am., Oak Brook, Ill., 1985-88; pres. Tuft & Assocs., Inc., 1989—. Trustee, Found. of the Nat. Student Nurses Assn., 2001—; adv. bd. Cognitive Neurology and Alzheimer's Disease Ctr. of Northwestern Univ./Feinberg Sch. of Medicine, 2002-; mem. pres.'s adv. coun. Sch. Nursing, Saint Xavier U., 2006—. Bd. dirs. Nurses House, Inc., 1981-85, Chgo. chpt. Am. Friends of Hebrew U., 2000-, nat. bd. Am. Friends of Hebrew U., 2006-06; mem. exec. com. Chgo. Sinai Cong., 1987-91, v.p., 1988. Recipient Disting. Alumnus award West Chester State Coll., 1979; Mary Ann Tuft Scholarship Fund named in her honor Found. Nat. Student Nurses Assn.; Kepner-Tregoe scholar, 1966. Mem.: ALA (pub. mem. com. on accreditation 1993—95), Am. Dietetic Assn. (pub. mem. commn. on accreditation for dietetics edn. 2005—), Specialized Cons. in Nursing (faculty), Continuing Care Accreditation Assn. (bd. dirs. 1983—85), NY Soc. Assn. Execs. (bd. dirs. 1975—78, pres. 1978—79, 1st Outstanding Exec. award 1982), Am. Soc. Assn. Execs. (bd. dirs. 1980—83, trustee for cert. 1980—83, vice chmn. 1983—84), Sigma Theta Tau (hon.). Home Phone: 312-642-7490; Office Phone: 312-642-8889. Business E-Mail: matuft@tuftassoc.com.

TUFTE, EDWARD ROLF, statistician, educator; b. Kansas City, Mo., Mar. 14, 1942; s. Edward E. and Virginia (James) T.; m. Inge Druckrey BS, Stanford U., 1963, MS, 1964; PhD, Yale U., 1968; HHD (hon.), Cooper Union, 1992, Conn. Coll., 1995, St. Joseph's Coll., 1997, Md. Art Inst., 1999, Mpls. Coll. Art, 2000, Williams Coll., 2000; HHD hon., Univ. of the Arts, 2003. Asst. prof. pub. policy Princeton U., 1967-71, assoc. prof., 1971-74, prof., 1974-77; prof. polit. sci., stats., computer sci. Yale U., New Haven, 1977-99; pres. Graphics Press, Cheshire, 1983—. Author: Quantitative Analysis of Social Problems, 1970, Size and Democracy, 1973, Data Analysis, 1974, Political Control of the Economy, 1978 (Kammerer award 1979, Citation Classic 1989), The Visual Display of Quantitative Information, 1983 (Citation Classic 1992), 2d edit., 2001, Envisioning Information, 1990, Visual Explanations, 1997, Beautiful Evidence, 2006 Pres. Cheshire Neighborhood Assn., 1984-87. Recipient Best Graphic Design award Internat. Design, 1990, Wittenborn award, 1991, Best Book Design award Assn. Ind. Publs., Computer Press Assn. award, 1991, Sci. award Phi Beta Kappa, 1991, AIGA book show, 1998, book award AIA, 1998, book award STC, 1998, book award Internat. Design, 1998, book award Am. Ctr. for Design, 1998; Ctr. for Advanced Study in Behavioral Scis. fellow, 1973-74; Guggenheim fellow, 1977. Fellow Am. Acad. Arts and Scis., Am. Statis. Assn. Office: Graphics Press PO Box 430 Cheshire CT 06410

TUGGLE, FRANCIS DOUGLAS, entrepreneur, consultant, management educator, scientist; b. Portsmouth, Va., Jan. 19, 1943; s. Francis Joyner and Florence Eleanor (Dahlgren) T.; m. Mary Ann Tredway, June 3, 1967; children: Wendy Elizabeth, Laura Michelle. SB, MIT, 1964; MS, Carnegie-Mellon U., 1967, PhD, 1971. Prof. bus. adminstrn. and computer sci. U. Kans., Lawrence, 1968-78; Jesse H. Jones prof. mgmt. Rice U., Houston, 1978-90; dean Kogod Coll. Bus. Adminstrn., Am. U., Washington, 1990-96, prof. info. systems and strategic planning, 1996—2002; Robert J. & Carolyn A. Waltos Jr. dean Argyros Sch. Bus. Econs. Chapman U., Orange, Calif., 2002—06, prof., 2006—; founder Family Health Info. Svcs., Inc., Yorba-Linda, Calif., 2006—, Anderson & Tuggle Inc., 2002—; ptnr. Insight Cons., 2006—. Bd. dirs. Equus II, Inc., Houston, Internat. Expert

Sys. Inc., Houston, v.p. mktg. devel.; dir.-at-large Inst. for Ops. Rsch. and Mgmt. Scis., 1995; cons. in field. Author: How to Program a Computer, 1975, Organizational Processes, 1978. Com. chmn. United Way Tex. Gulf Coast, Houston, 1985-88. Fellow, Ford Found., 1966. Mem. Inst. for Ops. Rsch. and Mgmt. Scis. (bd. dirs. 1995, v.p. 1992-94), Am. Assn. Artificial Intelligence, Assn. for Computing Machinery, Acad. of Mgmt., Sigma Xi, Beta Gamma Sigma, Alpha Kappa Psi. Episcopalian. Avocations: golf, bicycling, jogging, painting, drawing. Home: 20465 Via Torralba Yorba Linda CA 92887 Office: Argyros Sch Bus Econs Chapman U 1 University Dr Orange CA 92866 Office Phone: 714-997-6537. Business E-Mail: tuggle@chapman.edu.

TUITE, GERALD FRANCIS, lawyer, commercial real estate manager; b. Rockford, Ill., Nov. 15, 1928; s. John Christopher and Mildred Tuite; m. Francine Lynn Williams, Aug. 2, 1980; children: Gregory, Gerald F., Michael, Tracy. Degree, Georgetown U., 1955; JD, Chgo. Kent Coll. Law, 1958. Bar: Ill. 1958. Sr. ptnr. Gerald Tuite & Assocs. Law Firm, Rockford, Ill., 1958—; asst. atty. gen. Ill., 1961—68. Spkr. in field. Vice chmn. Dem. Party, Ill., 1961—64, precinct committeeman; candidate State Atty., 1960. Cpl. US Army, 1950—52, Korea. Recipient Svc. to Youth award, City and County Officials Rockford, Ill., 1960, Svc. award, Am. Legion, 1961, AFL-CIO Unions, 1980, 1986. Mem.: ATLA, ABA, Ill. Trial Assn., Ill. Bar Assn. Democrat. Roman Catholic. Avocations: travel, boating, swimming, golf, tennis. Office: Greg Tuite & Assocs 119 North Church St Rockford IL 61101 Home: Embassy Club #604 1717 Gulf Shore Blvd N Naples FL 34102

TUITELE, LUI, retired school system administrator; b. Leone Village; BS in Biology, Truman State U., Mo.; MEd in Secondary Edn., Brigham Young U., EdD in Ednl. Leadership. Classroom tchr., Am. Samoa; high school principal Am. Samoa; asst. dir. edn. Am. Samoa Dept. Edn., dir. edn., 2003—06. Program dir. Goals 2000, Teacher Cert.; dep. dir. Instrnl. Services. Mem.: Am. Samoa Humanities Coun. (chmn.), Bd. Higher Edn., Territorial Planning Commn., Coun. Chief State Sch. Officers.

TUKE, ROBERT DUDLEY, lawyer, educator; b. Rochester, NY, Dec. 5, 1947; s. Theodore Robert and Doris Jean (Smith) T.; m. Susan Devereux Cummins, June 21, 1969; children: Andrew, Sarah. BA with distinction, U. Va., 1969; JD, Vanderbilt U., 1976. Bar: Tenn. 1976, U.S. Dist. Ct. (mid. dist.) Tenn. 1976, U.S. Ct. Appeals (6th cir.) 1976, U.S. Ct. Appeals (4th cir.) 1978, U.S. Ct. Appeals (fed. cir.) 1993, U.S. Supreme Ct. 1986, U.S. Ct. Internat. Trade 1993. Assoc. Farris, Warfield & Kanaday, Nashville, 1976—79, ptnr., 1980—94, Tuke Yopp & Sweeney, Nashville, 1994—99, Trauger, Ney & Tuke, Nashville, 2000—05, Trauger & Tuke, Nashville, 2006—. Adj. prof. law Vanderbilt U. Law Sch., Nashville; faculty PLI, 1995—. Author: (with others) Tennessee Practice, 1992—; editor-in-chief Vanderbilt Law Rev.; contbr. articles to profl. jours. Mem. Tenn. Adoption Law Study Commn., 1993-96, Metro CATV Com.; chmn. Tenn. Dem. Party, 2005-07. Capt. USMC, 1969-73. Decorated Cross of Gallantry; Patrick Wilson Merit scholar. Mem. ABA, Am. Health Law Assn., Nat. Assn. Bond Lawyers, Am. Acad. Adoption Attys. (past pres.), Tenn. Bar Assn., Nashville Bar Assn., Order of Coif. Democrat. Episcopalian. Avocations: rowing, running, bicycling, hiking, travel. Office: 222 4th Ave N Nashville TN 37219-2115 Home Phone: 615-385-2786; Office Phone: 615-256-8585. Business E-Mail: rtuke@tntlaw.net.

TULAFONO, TOGIOLA T.A., governor; b. Aunu'u Island, American Samoa, Feb. 28, 1947; s. Aitu and Silika (Vaatu'itu'i) T.; m. Maryann Taufaasau Mauga, Sept. 17, 1984; children: Puataunofo, Olita, Cherianne, Emema, Timoteo, Rosie. Grad., Honolulu Police Acad., 1967; BA, Chadron State Coll., 1970; JD, Washburn U., 1975. Bar: Kans., Am. Samoa. Police instr. Am. Samoa Police Dept., Pago Pago, 1967; adminstrv. asst. Sec. of Samoan Affairs, Pago Pago, 1970-71; legal asst. Atty. Gen., Pago Pago, 1971-72; assoc. Law Offices of George A. Wray, Pago Pago, 1975-77; v.p. South Pacific Island Airways, Pago Pago, 1977-79; judge Dist. Ct. of Am. Samoa, Pago Pago, 1979-80; chmn. bd. dirs. Am. Samoa Power Authority, Pago Pago, 1978-80; mem. Am. Samoa Senate, Pago Pago, 1981-85, 89—; pres. Nayram Samoa, Ltd., Pago Pago, 1985-88; lt. gov. Am. Samoa Pago Pago, 1997—2003; gov. Am. Samoa, 2003—. Chmn. Senate Investigation Com., 1993—. Chmn. Bd. Higher Edn., Am. Samoa, 1993—; bd. dirs. Am. Samoa Jr. Golfers' Assn.; deacon Sailele Congrl. Ch. Mem. ATLA, Am. Samoa Bar Assn., Kans. Bar Assn., Samoa Profl. Golfer's Assn. (pres. 1985-87), Am. Samoa Golf Assn. (pres.). Democrat. Congregationalist. Office: Office of the Gov Ter of American Samoa Pago Pago AS 96799 Office Phone: 684-633-4116. Office Fax: 684-633-2269. *

TULCHIN, DAVID BRUCE, lawyer; b. NYC, Dec. 2, 1947; s. Philip Tulchin and Mary (Weiner) Black; m. Nora Barrett, Aug. 20, 1972; children: Rachel, Daniel, Laura. BA, U. Rochester, 1970; JD, Harvard U., 1973. Bar: N.Y. 1974, U.S. Dist. Ct. (so. & ea. dists.) N.Y. 1975, U.S. Ct. Appeals (2d cir.) 1975, U.S. Supreme Ct. 1977, U.S. Ct. Appeals (5th cir.) 1978, U.S. Ct. Appeals (1st & 6th cirs.) 1984, U.S. Dist. Ct. (no. dist.) Ohio 1984, U.S. Ct. Appeals (3d, 4th & Fed. cirs.) 1988, U.S. Ct. Appeals (7th cir.) 1991, U.S. Dist. Ct. (we. dist.) N.Y., 1996. Law clk. to Judge Frederick V.P. Bryan U.S. Dist. Ct. So. Dist. N.Y., NYC, 1973-75; assoc. Sullivan & Cromwell, NYC, 1975-82, ptnr., 1982—. Fellow Am. Coll. Trial Lawyers; mem. ABA, Assn. Bar City N.Y., Fed. Bar Coun., N.Y. State Bar Assn., Fed. Cir. Bar Assn. Office: Sullivan & Cromwell 125 Broad St Fl 28 New York NY 10004-2489

TULEKO, JAMES STANLEY, engineering educator, nuclear engineer; s. John Truman and Anna Bagdus Tulenko; m. Lois Wagner aWagner, May 1, 1965; children: Mark Wagner Tulenko, Christina Lee Tulenko, Katherine Ann Tulenko. BA cum Laude, Harvard Coll., Cambridge, Mass, 1958; MA, Harvard U., Cambridge, Mass., 1960; MS, Mass. Inst. Tech., Cambridge, 1963; M in Engring. Adminstr., Geo. Washington, Washington, 1980. Mgr. nuc. devel. United Nuc., White Plains, NY, 1963—70; mgr. nuc. fuel engring. Babcock and Wilcox, Lynchburg, Va., 1970—86; chmn., prof. U. Fla., Gainesville, 1986—2001, prof., dir., 2001—. Cons. Los Alamos Nat. Lab., Afghanistan, 2002—. Author: (handbook) Nuclear Fuel Cycle, 1997. Commr. Applied Sci. Accreditation Comm., Balt., 2004—; bd. dirs. Nat. Nuc. Accrediting bd., Atlanta, 1998—2004; commr. Engring. Accreditation Comm., Balt., 1996—2002. 1st lt. US Army, 1960. Named Glenn Murphy Outstanding Nuc. Educator, Am. Soc. Engring. Educators, 1997. Fellow: Am. Nuc. Soc. (hon.; pres. 2002—04, Mishima award for Material rsch. 1997, Arthur Holly Compton award 2000). Achievements include patents for water hole in Boiling Water Reactors assemblies. Office: Univ Fla 202 Nuclear Sci Ctr Gainesville FL 32611-8300 Home Phone: 352-377-7028; Office Phone: 352-392-1401. Personal E-mail: jmtulenko@mail.com.

TULL, THERESA ANNE, retired diplomat; b. Runnemede, NJ, Oct. 2, 1936; d. John James and Anna Cecelia (Paull) T. BA, U. Md., 1972; MA, U. Mich., 1973; postgrad., Nat. War Coll., Washington, 1980. Fgn. svc. officer Dept. State, Washington, 1963, Brussels, 1965-67, Saigon, 1968-70; dep. prin. officer Am. Consulate General, Danang, Vietnam, 1973-75; prin. officer Cebu, Philippines, 1977-79; dir. office human rights, 1980-83; charge d'affaires Am. Embassy, Vientiane, Laos, 1983-86; Dept. State Senior Seminar, 1986-87; ambassador to Guyana, 1987-90; diplomat-in-residence Lincoln U., Pa., 1990-91; dir. office regional affairs, bur. East Asian & Pacific affairs Dept. State, Washington, 1991-93; amb. to Brunei Bandar Seri Begawan, 1993-96. Recipient Civilian Service award Dept. of State, 1970, Superior Honor award, 1977 Mem. Am. Fgn. Svc. Assn., Women's Civic Club. Address: 3500 Boardwalk Apt 726N Sea Isle City NJ 08243

TULL, WILLIS CLAYTON, JR., retired librarian; b. Crisfield, Md., Feb. 22, 1931; s. Willis Clayton and Agnes Virginia (Milbourne) T.; m. Taeko Itoi, Dec. 18, 1952. Student, U. Balt., 1948, Johns Hopkins U., 1956; BS, Towson State Coll., Md., 1957; MLS, Rutgers U., 1962; postgrad., Miami U., Oxford, Ohio, 1979. Editl. clk. 500th Mil. Intelligence Svc. Group, 1952-53; tchr. Hereford Jr.-Sr. H.S., Parkton, Md., 1957-59; aide Enoch Pratt Free Libr., Balt., 1959-61, profl. asst., 1962-64; coord. adult svcs. Washington County Free Libr., Hagerstown, Md., 1964-67; asst. regional libr. Eastern Shore Regional Libr., Salisbury, Md., 1967; br. libr. Balt. County Pub. Libr., Pikesville, Md., 1968-71, asst. area br. libr. Essex, Md., 1971-72, sr. info. specialist Catonsville, Md., 1972-87, on-line supr. Towson, Md., 1988-89, sr. info. specialist Reisterstown, Md., 1989-90; exec. dir. Milbourne and Tull Rsch. Ctr., 1991—2002; ret. Contbr. to profl. and geneal. jours. Mem. Rep. Ctrl. Com. Baltimore County, 1971-72. With U.S. Army, 1949-52. Fellow Nat. Congress Patriotic Orgns.; mem. Freedom To Read Found., Md. Libr. Assn. (chmn. intellectual freedom com. 1969-70), Friends Johns Hopkins U. Librs., Md. Assn. for Adult Edn. (coord. Western Md. region 1965-67), Am. Coun. Trustees and Alumni, Am. Acad. Religion, Ctr. for Theology and the Natural Scis., Metaphys. Soc. Am., Nat. Assn. Scholars, Woodrow Wilson Internat. Ctr. for Scholars, Assn. for Asian Studies, World Future Soc., Freedom House, Internat. Rescue Com., Nature Conservancy, Unitarian Universalist Hist. Soc, Unitarian and Universalist Geneal. Soc. (founder, bd. dirs. 1971-87), Md. Geneal. Soc., Royal Soc. St. George, Jamestowne Soc., Sons and Daus. Pilgrims, Descs. Early Quakers, SAR, Soc. War of 1812, Ancient and Hon. Mech. Co. Balt., Rutgers Club, Kappa Delta Pi. Home: 800 Southerly Rd Apt 414 Towson MD 21286-8407 E-mail: wctulljr@bcpl.net.

TULLER, JOEY DAVID, manufacturing engineer; b. Ottumwa, Iowa, July 11, 1981; s. Michael Dee and Linda Sue Tuller. AA, Indian Hills CC, Ottumwa, 2001; BSME, Iowa State U., Ames, 2004. Design engr. Vermeer Mfg., Pella, Iowa, 2004—05; mfg. engr. John Deere Ottumwa Works, 2005—. Baptist. Avocations: building cars and trucks, farming, golf, hunting, fishing. Home: 10858 Angle Rd Ottumwa IA 52501 Office: John Deere Ottumwa Works 928 E Vine St Ottumwa IA 52501

TULLIS, EDWARD LEWIS, retired bishop; b. Cin., Mar. 9, 1917; s. Ashar Spence and Priscilla (Daugherty) T.; m. Mary Jane Talley, Sept. 25, 1937; children: Frank Loyd, Jane Allen (Mrs. William Nelson Offutt IV); m. Katharine Crum Irwin, Sept. 4, 1997. AB, Ky. Wesleyan Coll., 1939, LHD, 1975; BD, Louisville Presbyn. Theol. Sem., 1947; DD, Union Coll., Barbourville, Ky., 1954, Wofford Coll., 1976; LHD, Claflin Coll., 1976, Lambuth Coll., 1984. Ordained to ministry Methodist Ch., 1941; service in chs. Frenchburg, Ky., 1937-39, Lawrenceburg, Ky., 1939-44; asso. pastor 4th Ave. Meth. Ch., Louisville, 1944-47, Irvine, Ky., 1947-49; asso. sec. ch. extension sect. Bd. Missions, Meth. Ch., Louisville, 1949-52; pastor First Meth. Ch., Frankfort, Ky., 1952-61, Ashland, Ky., 1961-72; resident bishop United Meth. Ch., Columbia, SC, 1972-80, Nashville area, 1980-84, ret., 1984. Instr. Bible Ky. Wesleyan Coll., 1947-48; instr. Louisville Presbyn. Theol. Sem., 1949-52; mem. Meth. Gen. Conf., 1956, 60, 64, 66, 68, 70, 72, Southeastern Jurisdictional Conf., 1952, 56, 60, 64, 68, 72, bd. mgrs. Bd. Missions, 1962-72, mem. bd. discipleship, 1972-80, v.p. Gen. Coun. on Fin. and Adminstrn., 1980-84; Chaplain Ky. Gen. Assembly, 1952-61; chmn. Frankfort Com. Human Rights, 1956-61, Mayor's Adv. Com. Human Rels., Ashland, 1968-72. Author: Shaping the Church from the Mind of Christ, 1984, The Birth of the Book: A Study in the Origin and Growth of the Bible, 1998. Contbr. articles to religious jours. Sec., bd. dirs. Magee Christian Edn. Found.; trustee Emory U., 1973-80, Alaska Meth. U., 1965-70, Ky. Wesleyan Coll., Martin Coll., Lambuth Coll., McKendree Manor, Meth. Hosps., Memphis, Lake Junaluska Assembly, 1966-88; chair adv. bd. Found. for Evangelism, United Meth. Ch., 1991—. Recipient Outstanding Citizen award Frankfort VFW, 1961, Mayor's award for outstanding svc. Ashland, 1971, Heroes, Sts. and Legends award, Wesley Meth. Village Ky., 1997, Chief Junaluska award Lake Junaluska Assembly, 1998, Outstanding Alumnus award Ky. Wesleyan Coll., 2000, Disting. Alumnus award Louisville Presbyn. Sem., 2002; named to Ky. Wesleyan Coll. Hall of Fame, 2004. Mem.: Kiwanis. Methodist. Home: 510 Crum Dr Lake Junaluska NC 28745 E-mail: etullis1@mindspring.com.

TULLIS, GREGORY EARL, research scientist; PhD, U. Mo., Columbia, 1992. Postdoctoral fellow Princeton U., NJ, 1993—99; rsch. scientist Avigen, Inc, Alameda, Calif., 1999—2000; rsch. asst. prof. U. Mo., 2001—06; assoc. prof. Boston U. Med. Sch., 2006—. Mem. editl. bd. Biomarkers Insights, 2006—. Contbr. articles to profl. jours., chapters to books. Jane Coffin-Childs Rsch. fellow, Jane Coffin-Childs Meml. Fund Med. Rsch., 1993—96. Mem.: AAAS, Internat. Soc. Stem Cell Rsch., Am. Soc. Virology, Am. Soc. Microbiology, Assn. Rsch. Vision and Ophthalmology, Am. Soc. Gene Therapy. Office: Boston U Med Sch 715 Albany St L905 Boston MA 02118 Office Phone: 617-638-5071. Business E-Mail: tullisg@bu.edu.

TULLMAN, GLEN, management consultant; BA in Economics and Psychology, Bucknell U., 1981; Masters in Social Anthrop., Oxford U., Eng. With CCC Info. Svcs. Group, 1983—94; CEO Enterprise Sys., Inc., 1994—97, Allscripts Healthcare Solutions Inc., Libertyville, Ill., 1997—, chmn., 2001—. Capital campaign chmn. Juvenile Diabetes Rsch. Found. Ill. Chap. Office: Allscripts Healthcare Solutions Inc 2401 Commerce Ave Libertyville IL 60048

TULLY, CATHERINE T., lawyer; b. NY, Aug. 22, 1953; d. Charles S. and Julia T. Tully; m. Jack Dierks, June 21, 1975; children: Erin Tully Dierks, Stephen Tully Dierks, Caitlin Tully Dierks. BA, Valparaiso U., Valparaiso, Ind., 1975; JD, Marquette U. Law Sch., Milw., Wis., 1978. Atty. Riordan, Crivello & Carlson, Milw., 1978—83; atty./shareholder Habush Habush & Rottier, Milw., 1983—. Sch. coun. Elm Creative Arts Sch., Milw., 1991—97, Roosevelt Mid. Sch. for the Arts, Milw., 1996—2000; jr. class parents/parents assoc/athletic assoc/fine arts assoc Divine Savior Holy Angels HS, Milw., 1997—2006; parents assoc Marquette U. HS, Milw., 2000—04; mgr. Milw. Kickers Soccer, Milw., 1991—99, Little League, Milw., 1995—2000; trinity booster club Trinity Acad. of Irish Dance, Milw., 1996—2005; core team coord. Milw. Inner City Congregations Allied for Hope, Milw., 1986—93; social concerns com. Holy Angels Congreation, Milw., 1985—93, All Saints Congregation, Milw., 1993—2006. Mem.: ABA, Am. Assn. of Trial Lawyers, Wis. Assoc of Trial Lawyers, Milw. Bar Assn., Wis. Bar Assn. Avocation: quilting. Office: Habush Habush & Rottier SC 777 E Wis Ave Ste 2300 Milwaukee WI 53202 Home Phone: 414-964-2924; Office Phone: 414-271-0900. Business E-Mail: ctully@habush.com.

TULLY, DARROW, newspaper publisher; b. Charleston, W.Va., Feb. 27, 1932; s. William Albert and Dora (McCann) T.; m. Victoria Lynn Werner; children: Bonnie Tully Paul, Michael Andrew. Student, Purdue U., 1951; BA in Journalism, St. Joseph's Coll., 1972; PhD in Journalism (hon.), Calumet Coll., Ind., 1975. V.p., gen. mgr. Stas. WDSM-AM-FM and WDSM-TV, Duluth, Minn., 1956-59; bus. mgr. Duluth Herald & News Tribune, 1960-62; gen. mgr. St. Paul Dispatch & Pioneer Press, 1962-66; pub. Gary (Ind.) Post-Tribune, 1966-73; v.p., pub. Wichita (Kans.) Eagle & Beacon, 1973-75; pres. San Francisco Newspaper Agy., 1975-78; exec. v.p., pub. Ariz. Republic & Phoenix Gazette, 1978-85; editor., pub., chief exec. officer Ojai (Calif.) Valley News, 1987-90; pres., pub., CEO Beacon Comms., Acton, Mass., 1990-92; asst. to pres. newspaper divsn. Chronicle Pub. Co., 1992-94. Author: Minority Representation in the Media, 1968. Trustee Calumet Coll. Recipient Disting. Achievement award Ariz. State U., 1982, Disting. Journalist award No. Ariz. U./AP, 1983, 1st Pl. Editorial Writing award Ariz. Planned Parenthood, 1983. Mem. Am. Soc. Newspaper Editors, Soc. Profl. Journalists. Office: 9862 Bridgeton Dr Tampa FL 33626-1802 Office Phone: 813-926-9709. Personal E-mail: dtully1@tampabay.rr.com.

TULLY, HERBERT BULLARD, chemical manufacturing executive; b. Glen Ridge, NJ, Sept. 3, 1943; s. Richard Golfe and Marie Foster (Towne) T.; m. Nancy Dee Zook, Dec. 22, 1967; children: Kimberly, Christine, Gregory. BS, U. Calif., Berkeley, 1967. Mem. fin. mgmt. staff Gen. Electric Co., San Jose, Calif., 1967-70, mem. corp. audit staff Schenectady, N.J., 1970-73, mgr. acct. dept. San Leandro, Calif., 1973-75; mgr. audit dept. Am. Express Co., Fireman's Fund, San Francisco, 1975-77; asst. controller Fireman's Fund Ins. Co., San Francisco, 1977-81; controller Wilbur-Ellis Co., San Francisco, 1981-86, asst. treas., 1986-89, vp treas., 1989—2000, CEO, pres., 2000—. Bd. dirs. Overseas Cos., San Francisco. Office: Wilbur Ellis 345 California Street Flr 27 San Francisco CA 94104

TULLY, JOHN CHARLES, research chemical physicist; b. NYC, May 17, 1942; s. Harry V. and Pauline (Fischer) T.; m. Mary Ellen Thomsen, Jan. 23, 1971; children: John Thomsen, Elizabeth Anne, Stephen Thomsen. BS, Yale U., 1964; PhD, U. Chgo., 1968. NSF postdoctoral fellow U. Colo. and Yale U., 1968-70; mem. tech. staff AT&T Bell Labs., Murray Hill, NJ, 1970-82, disting. mem. tech. staff, 1982-85, head phys. chemistry rsch. dept., 1985-90, head materials chem. rsch. dept., 1990-96; Kemp prof. dept. chemistry, physics and applied physics Yale U., New Haven, 1996—. Vis. prof. Princeton (N.J.) U., 1981-82, Harvard U., Cambridge, Mass., 1991. Contbr. articles to sci. jours.; author, prodr. movie Dynamics of Gas-Surface Interactions, 1979. NSF predoctoral fellow, 1965-68. Fellow AAAS, Am. Phys. Soc. (chem. physics exec. com. 1983-86), Am. Acad. Arts & Scis.; mem. Am. Chem. Soc. (chmn. theoretical chemistry subdiv. 1991-92, phys. chemistry divsn. 1993-94, Peter Debye award 1995, Madison Marshall award 1999, Theoretical Chemistry award 2004), NAS, Internat. Acad. Quantum Molecular Scis., Conn. Acad. Sci. and Engring., Sigma Xi. Achievements include patent on Method and Apparatus for Surface Characterization Utilizing Radiation from Desorbed Particles; fundamental theoretical contributions towards atomic level understanding of chemical reaction dynamics. Office: Yale Univ Dept Chemistry PO Box 208107 New Haven CT 06520-8107

TULLY, MAC, publishing executive; m. Cindy Tully. BA, U. Kans. Pres. & pub. Bradenton (Fla.) Herald; v.p. advt., pub. Arlington (Tex.) Star-Telegram; corp. v.p. ops. Knight Ridder, 2004; pub. Kansas City (Mo.) Star, 2005—. Recipient John S. Knight Gold medal, Knight Ridder. Office: Kansas City Star 1729 Grand Blvd Kansas City MO 64108 Office Phone: 816-234-4490. E-mail: mtully@kcstar.com. *

TULLY, MARY JEAN, travel company executive; m. Brad Tully. Chmn., CEO Cruise Profls. Ltd., 1987—. Bd. mem. Crystal Cruises, Holland Am., Silversea, Condé Nast Traveler. Named an World's Most Amazing Travel Specialists, Condé Nast Traveler, 2004; named one of 128 Top Travel Specialists, 2006. Office: Cruise Profls Ltd 130 Dundas St E Mississauga ON L5A 3V8 Canada Office Phone: 905-275-3030.

TULLY, MATHEW B., lawyer; s. Kevin Timothy and Alice Tully; m. Kimberly Jill Tully. JD, Bklyn Law Sch., Brooklyn, NY, 1998—2002; BA, Hofstra U., Hempstead, NY, 1993—95; AA, Nassau C.C., Garden City, NY, 1991—93. Attorney: NY State 2002, DC 1993. Atty. Law Office of Mathew B Tully, Hunter, NY, 2002—; peace officer/investigator Columbia-Greene SPCA, Hudson, NY, 1991—; army officer US Army Paratrooper, Seoul, Korea (South), 1995—98; n.g. officer NY Army N.G., Latham, NY; litig. mgr. Morgan Stanley, New York City, NY, 2000—02; fed. law enforcement officer US Dept. of Justice, New York City, NY, 1995—2000. Mem. NY State Juvenile Justice Adv. Group, Albany, NY, 2000—, Nassau County Cultural Devel. Commn., Mineola, NY, 1992—2000; sec./mem. of the bd. Scribner Hollow Homeowners Assoc., Hunter, NY, 1998—. Capt. US Army, 1995—98, Fort Sill. Mem.: VFW (life). Office: Tully Rinckey & Assocs PLLC Attys & Counselors at Law 3 Wembly Ct Albany NY 12205 Personal E-mail: mtully@tullylegal.com. E-mail: info@tullylegal.com.

TULLY, ROBERT GERARD, lawyer; b. Dubuque, Iowa, Sept. 7, 1955; s. Thomas Alois and Marjorie May (Fosselman) T. BA, U. Notre Dame, 1977; postgrad., U. Notre Dame, London, summer 1979; JD, Drake U., 1981. Bar: Iowa 1981, U.S. Dist. Ct (no. and so. dists.) Iowa 1981, U.S. Ct. Appeals (8th cir.) 1981, U.S. Supreme Ct. 1986. Assoc. Verne Lawyer & Assocs., Des Moines, 1981-93, Michael J. Galligan Law Firm; ptnr. Galligan, Tully, Doyle & Reid P.C., 1993, Anderson & Tully, Des Moines, 2003—. Bd. dirs. Dubuque Lumber Co., sec., treas., 1984-87; lectr. Nat. Collegiate Mock Trial Drake U., Des Moines, 1984-93, atty., coach, 1985-93; bd. counselors Drake U. Law Sch., 1986-92, 2005—, chmn. alumni rels. com. Contbr. articles to profl. jours. Com. mem. Dubuque County Dem. party, 1976-78, Polk County Dem. party, 1982-83, 87-89, 92—, del. state convs., 1988, chmn. IA Dem. Party, 1999-2007; bd. dirs. nat. Coun. Alcoholism and Other Drug Dependencies for Des Moines Area, pres. 1985-92; mem. nat. commn. on future of Drake U.; Dem. candidate for U.S. Congress 2d Dist., 1998. Fellow Iowa Acad. Trial Lawyers (compiler various profl. publs.); mem. ABA, ATLA (state del. 1991—, bd. govs. 1993-2003, key peron com.), Iowa Bar Assn. (Uniform Jury Instructions rules com., young lawyers sect., com. legal svcs. for elderly chmn. fed. practice com., law related edn. com.), Assn. Trial Lawyers Iowa (pres. 1992-93, pres.-elect 1991-92, v.p. legis. 1988-91, bd. govs. 1985—, Outstanding Key Person 1983-84, 91-92, chmn. key person com. 1985-88), Polk County Bar Assn. (bd. dirs. 1993—, grievance com.), Iowa Citizens Action Network (bd. dirs. 1989-98), Blackstone Inn of Ct., Notre Dame Club of Des Moines (pres. 1981-83), Drake Student Bar Assn. (pres. 1980-81), Phi Alpha Delta. Roman Catholic. Home: 4315 Greenwood Dr Des Moines IA 50312 Office: Anderson and Tully 700 W Towers 1200 Valley West Dr West Des Moines IA 50266-1908 E-mail: tully@andersontullylaw.com.

TULLY, THOMAS ALOIS, building materials executive, consultant, educator; b. Dubuque, Iowa, Nov. 11, 1940; s. Thomas Aloysius and Marjorie Mae (Fosselman) T.; m. Joan Vonnetta Dubay, Nov. 30, 1963; children: Thomas Paul, Maureen Elizabeth. BA, Loras Coll., 1962; postgrad., Georgetown U., 1963-66; MPA, Harvard U., 1968. Mgmt. trainee Office of Sec. Def., Washington, 1962-63, fgn. affairs officer, 1963-70; v.p. Dubuque Lumber Co., 1970-84, pres., 1984-91, Tully's, 1991-92, LBM Mktg. Assocs., Inc., 1992—; gen. mgr. Kane How Appraisor Svcs., 2006—. Adj. instr. Divine Word Coll., 1971, Loras Coll., 1972; adj. instr. Clarke Coll., 1987-89, instr., 1989-91, asst. prof., 1992-97, chmn. dept. acctg. and bus., 1993-97, dir. small bus. inst., 1994-97; dir. MBA program U. Dubuque, 1997-2000; founder, exec. dir. Dubuque Area Com. on Fgn. Rels., 2001—, pres., 2002—; pres. Hills and Dales Child Devel. Ctr., Inc., 1992-96; trustee Alverno Apts., 1995-2001, pres., 1999-2001. Mem. Dubuque Human Rights Commn., 1974—75, chmn., 1975, Iowa State Com. for Employer Support of Guard and Res. Forces, 1988—, area chmn., 2000—05, Iowa state coord., 2004—06, state vice chair, 2006—; city councilman Dubuque, 1975—79; bd. dirs. League Iowa Municipalities, 1977—79; mayor City of Dubuque, 1978; vice chmn. Iowa Temporary State Land Preservation Policy Com., 1978—79; pres. N.E. Iowa Regional Coordinating Coun., 1985—93, East Ctrl. Intergovtl. Assn. Bus. Growth, Inc., 1987—2002, chmn., 1993—2002; bd. dirs. Pvt. Industry Coun. of Dubuque and Delaware Counties, Inc., 1983—86; trustee Divine Word Coll., 1989—97; pres. Barn Cmty. Theatre, 1988—89; chmn. bd. trustees United Way Svcs. of Dubuque, 1990, campaign chmn., 1991, bd. mem., 1980—94; trustee Carnegie-Stout Pub. Libr., 2001—05, pres., 2003—04; Iowa state chair Nat. Security Network, 2006—. Recipient Meritorious Civilian Svc. award Sec. of Def., 1970, Gov.'s Vol. award, 1989. Mem. Nat. Lumber and Bldg. Material Dealers Assn. (exec. com. 1988-90), Iowa Lumbermen's Assn. (pres. 1984, chmn. legis. com. 1985-90), Northwestern Lumbermen Assn. (bd. dirs. 1984-87, 2d v.p. 1988, 1st v.p. 1989-90, pres. 1990-91). Democrat. Roman Catholic. Home: 838 Stone Ridge Pl Dubuque IA 52001-1362 Office: LBM Mktg Assocs 838 Stone Ridge Pl Dubuque IA 52001 Home Phone: 563-556-1904; Office Phone: 563-590-6565. E-mail: tully.thomas@alumni.ksg.harvard.edu.

TUMA, STANISLAV JOSEF, radiologist; b. Mělník, Czech Republic, Mar. 30, 1934; s. Josef and Marta (Panochová) T.; m. Vanda Langrová, May 10, 1954 (div. 1966); children: Zuzana, Ondřej, Magdalena; m. Jitka Fabichová, Nov. 2, 1990. MD, Charles U., Prague, Czech Republic, 1958, cert. pediat. I, 1962, cert. radiology I, 1964, CSc, 1970, cert. radiology II, 1971. Med. registrar Dist. Hosp., Šumperk, Czech Republic, 1958-60, Clinic of Pediat., Prague, 1960-64, X-Ray Dept., Prague, 1964-70; rsch.fellow Pediat. Cardiocenter, Prague, 1970-90; head Clinic Imaging Methods, Prague, 1990-99; head dept. rsch. and edn. Ministry Health Czech Republic, 2000—02. Prof. South Bohemian U., Ceske Budejovice, 2003. Editor: Congenital Anomalies, 1995, Dextrocardia, 1999; contbr. articles to profl. jours. Office: Clinic Imaging Methods U Hosp Motol V Uvalu 84 CZ 150 06 Prague 5 Czech Republic Office Phone: 420-22-443-8101. Business E-Mail: sttuma@volny.cz.

TUMAS, MICHAEL B., lawyer; b. South Bend, Ind., Apr. 25, 1959; BA in Econs., SUNY, Binghamton, 1981; JD, U. Pa., 1984. With Potter Anderson & Corroon LLP, Wilmington, Del., 1984—, mem. firm, 1992—, chmn. corp. group, 2006—. Office: Potter Anderson & Corroon LLP 1313 N Market St Wilmington DE 19801 Office Phone: 302-984-6029. Office Fax: 302-778-6029. E-mail: mtumas@potteranderson.com.

TUMAY, MEHMET TANER, geotechnical engineering educator, researcher, consultant; b. Feb. 2, 1937; arrived in US, 1959; s. Bedrettin and Muhterem (Uybadin) T.; m. Karen Nuttycombe, June 15, 1962; children: Peri, Suna. BSCE, Robert Coll. Sch. Engring., Istanbul, Turkey, 1959; MSCE, U. Va., 1961; postgrad., UCLA, 1963—64; PhD, Tech. U. Istanbul, 1971. Lic. civil engr., La., Ga., SC, Turkish Chamber of Civil Engring. Instr. civil engring. U. Va., Charlottesville, 1961-62; asst. prof. civil engring. U. Louisville, 1962-63; tchg. fellow UCLA, 1963-64; asst. prof. civil engring. Robert Coll. Sch. Engring., Istanbul, 1966-71; assoc. prof. dept. civil engring. Bogazici U., Istanbul, 1971-75; Fugro-Cesco postdoctoral rsch. fellow U. Fla., Gainesville, 1975-76; Ga. Gulf disting. prof. La. State U., Baton Rouge, 1976—2005, prof. emeritus, 2005—. Adv. prof. U. Vicosa, Minas Gerais, Brazil, 1991—, Tongji U., Shanghai, 1991—; dir. geomechanics program NSF, Washington, 1990-94; dir. rsch. La. Transp. Rsch. Ctr., Baton Rouge, 1994-97; assoc. dean rsch. and grad. studies Coll. Engring., La. State U., 1997-2004; maitre de conferences Ecole Nationale des Ponts et Chaussees, Paris, 1980-94; geotech. cons. Sauti, Spa, Cons. Engrs., Italy, 1969-72, SOFRETU-RATP, Paris, 1972-73, D.E.A., Cons. Engrs., Istanbul, 1974-75, BOTEK, Ltd., Istanbul, 1975—, Senler-Campbell Assocs., Louisville, 1979-90, Fugro Gulf-Geogulf, Houston, 1980-83; cons. in field. Contbr. articles to profl. jours. AID scholar, 1975-76, French Ministry External Rels. scholar, 1982. Fellow: ASCE; mem.: ASTM, Transp. Rsch. Bd. of the Nat. Acads (emeritus), Internat. Soc. Soil Mechanics and Found. Engring., Turkish Chamber Civil Engrs., Turkish Soil Mechanics Group, La. Engring. Soc., Am. Soc. Engring. Edn., Tau Beta Pi, Chi Epsilon, Sigma Xi. Home: 2217 Dove Hollow Dr Baton Rouge LA 70809-1275 Office: La State U Coll Engring Baton Rouge LA 70803-0001 Home Phone: 225-927-7719; Office Phone: 225-578-9165. Business E-Mail: mtumay@eng.lsu.edu.

TUMBARELLO, PHILLIP A., lawyer; b. Bklyn., May 22, 1952; BA cum laude, SUNY, New Paltz, 1974; JD cum laude, St. John's U., 1979. Bar: NY 1980, US Dist. Ct. So., Ea., No. & We. Districts NY. Ptnr. Wilson, Elser, Moskowitz, Edelman & Dicker LLP, White Plains, NYC. Mem.: Indsl. Truck Assn. (lawyers com.), NY State Bar Assn. (com. on ins. negligence & compensation law). Office: Wilson Elser Moskowitz Edelman & Dicker LLP 3 Gannett Dr White Plains NY 10604 Office Phone: 914-323-7000 ext. 4343. Office Fax: 914-323-7001. Business E-Mail: tumbarellop@wemed.com.

TUMPOSKY, DANIEL L., education assessment specialist; s. Lawrence A. Tumposky and Shirley I. Samuels; life ptnr. Patricia A. Byrne; 1 child, Jessica E. BA, MA, Syracuse U., NY, 1967. Instr. English as a fgn. lang. Food and Agrl. Orgn., UN, Rome, 1977—80; prof. English China People's U., Beijing, 1980—82; Fulbright lectr. English as a fgn. lang. Somali Nat. U., Mogadishu, Somalia, 1984—87; assessment specialist Ednl. Testing Svc., Princeton, NJ, 1992—2002, assessment dir., 2002—. Mem.: TESOL. Liberal. Avocations: travel, reading. Home: 389 Dutch Neck Rd East Windsor NJ 08520 Office: Educational Testing Service Rosedale Rd Princeton NJ 08541 Home Phone: 609-490-0535; Office Phone: 609-683-2520. Business E-Mail: dtumposky@ets.org.

TUNE, BRUCE MALCOLM, pediatrics educator, renal toxicologist; b. NYC, Aug. 26, 1939; s. Buford M. and Sylvia Tune; m. Nancy Carter Doolittle, Sept. 13, 1969; children: Sara E., Steven M. AB, Stanford U., 1963, MD, 1965. Diplomate Am. Bd. Pediat., Am. Bd. Pediatric Nephrology, Nat. Bd. Med. Examiners. Intern in medicine and pediatrics Strong Meml. Hosp., Rochester, NY, 1965—66; rsch. assoc. Lab. Kidney and Electrolyte Metabolism, Nat. Heart Inst., NIH, Bethesda, Md., 1967—69, clin. assoc., 1968—69; resident in pediat. Stanford (Calif.) U. Sch. Medicine, 1966—67, chief resident, 1969—70, fellow in pediatric renal and metabolic disease, 1970—71, asst. prof. pediat., 1971—77, assoc. prof., 1977—83, prof., 1983—, acting chmn. dept., 1991—93, dir. pediatric nephrology, 1971—97, prof. pediat. divsn. pediatric nephrology, 1998—, now emeritus prof. pediat. divsn. pediatric nephrology. Attending physician, chief pediatric renal svcs. Stanford U. Hosp., Palo Alto, Calif., 1971—76, Children's Hosp. at Stanford, Palo Alto, 1971—91; cons. physician Santa Clara Valley Med. Ctr., San Jose, Calif., 1973—; attending physician, chief pediatric renal svcs. Lucile Salter Packard Children's Hosp. at Stanford, 1991—98, acting chief pediatric medicine, 1991—93, attending physician, 1997; mem. rev. panel internat. study kidney diseases in children N.Y.C. NIH, 1973—74; polycystic kidney disease study group, Albuquerque, 1984; mem. spl. study sect. on genetics and kidney maturation, Bethesda, Md., 92; cons. Lilly Rsch. Labs., Indpls., 1980, Merck Sharp and Dohme Labs., Rahway, NJ, 1980, Bristol Labs., Syracuse, NY, 1982, ICI Pharms., Cheshire, England, 1992, Gilead Scis., Foster City, Calif., 1993, Zeneca Pharms., Mereside, England, 1994—; organizing mem., chmn. session on antibiotics NIH and EPA Conf. on Nephrotoxicity of Drugs and Environ. Toxicants, Pinehurst, NC, 1981; co-dir. Coop. Study Therapy of Steroid-Resistant Focal Glomerulosclerosis in Children, 1988—; mem. rsch. grant rev. panel Ont. (Can.) Ministry Health, 1992—, Wellcome Trust, London, 1994—; reviewer bd. environ. studies and toxicology NRC, 1994. Editl. bd. Am. Jour. Kidney Diseases, 1981—94, guest editor Contemporary Issues in Nephrology, 1984, Jour. Am. Soc. Nephrology, 1991; contbr. articles to med. jours. Grantee NIH, 1974—77, 1979—83, 1985—89, 1990—95. Mem.: Am. Soc. Pharmacology and Exptl. Therapeutics, Am. Heart Assn. (coun. on kidney diseases, grantee 1985—88, 1989—92), Western Soc. for Pediatric Rsch., Internat. Pediatric Nephrology Assn., Am. Soc. Pediatric Nephrology (coun. 1978—82, rsch. subcom. 1993—), Internat. Soc. Nephrology, Am. Soc. Nephrology, Alpha Omega Alpha, Phi Beta Kappa. Office: Stanford U Sch Medicine Dept Pediatrics 300 Pasteur Dr Rm G306 Palo Alto CA 94304-2203

TUNE, JAMES FULCHER, lawyer; b. Danville, Va., May 13, 1942; s. William Orrin and Susan Agnes (Fulcher) T.; m. Katherine Del Mickey, Aug. 2, 1969; children: Katherine Winslow, Jeffrey Bricker. BA, U. Va., 1964; MA, Stanford U., 1970, JD, 1974. Bar: Wash. 1974, U.S. Dist. Ct. (we. dist.) Wash. 1974. Assoc. Bogle & Gates, Seattle, 1974-79, ptnr., 1980-99, head comml./banking dept., 1985-93, mng. ptnr., 1986-93, chmn., 1994-99; ptnr. Dorsey & Whitney LLP, Seattle, 1999-2001, Stoel Rives LLP, Seattle, 2001—05, Seattle mng. ptnr., 2002—05; pres., CEO Arts-Fund, Seattle, 2006—. Bd. dirs. Keynetics Inc., Boise, Idaho, Click Sales Inc., Boise, Coloc8 Inc., Boise, Pay-Track Inc., Boise, Puget Sound Bank, Bellevue, Wash.; chmn. Seattle-King City Econ. Devel. Coun., 1992. Chmn. Seattle Repertory Theatre, 1995, Corp. Coun. for the Arts, 2001—02, United Way King County, 2004. Lt. USN, 1964—69, Vietnam. Woodrow Wilson fellow, 1964, Danforth Found. fellow, 1964. Mem. ABA, Wash. State Bar Assn. (lectr. CLE 1976, 78, 84, 99, 02), Seattle C. of C. (vice chmn. City Budget Task Force 1980-82), Greater Seattle C. of C. (trustee 2006—), Ranier Club (trustee 2006—), Seattle Tennis Club, Phi Beta Kappa. Presbyterian. Office: ArtsFund PO Box 19780 10 Harrison St Ste 200 Seattle WA 98109 Home Phone: 206-329-0372; Office Phone: 206-281-9050. Business E-Mail: jimtune@artsfund.org. E-mail: jftune@stoel.com.

TUNG, KO-YUNG, lawyer; b. Peking, China, Feb. 20, 1947; came to U.S., 1964; s. Hung-Fang T. and Koichiro Tanaka; m. Alison Heydt, Feb. 2, 1975; children: Vanessa, Adrian, Cameron, Gregory. BA, Harvard U., 1970; JD, U. Tokyo, 1972. Bar: NY, 1972. Assoc. Debevoise & Plimpton, NYC, 1973—76; ptnr. Tung, Drabkin & Boynton, NYC, 1976—84, O'Melveny & Myers, NYC, 1985—99; v.p., gen. counsel The World Bank, Washington, 1999—2003; sec.-gen. Internat. Ctr. Settlement Investment Disputes, Washington, 2000—03; sr. counsellor Morrison & Foerster, NYC, 2003—. Adj. assoc. prof. sch. law NYU, 1974—88; vis. lectr. Yale Law Sch., 2003—. Mem. Coun. on Fgn. Rels., N.Y.C., 1986—, The Brookings Inst., 1999, Overseas Devel. Coun., Washington, 1999, The Japan Soc., 1990, Asia Soc., 1994-99, Presl. Commn. U.S. Pacific Trade Investment Policy, 1996-97, Trilateral Commn., N.Y.C., 1990-97; bd. govs. East West Ctr., Honolulu, 1990-99, 2003—, chmn., 1997-99; U.S. Nat. Commn. for Pacific Econ. Cooperation, 1991—; bd. dirs. Asian Am. Legal Def. and Edn. Fund, 1990-99, 2003—; vice chmn. adv. coun. Human Rights Watch/Asia, 1997-99, Am. Law Inst., 1997—. Fellow Harvard Law Sch., 1973. Mem. Am. Law Inst., Am. Arbitration Assn., Internat. Panel Arbitrators, Phi Beta Kappa. Office: Morrison & Foerster 1290 Avenue of the Americas New York NY 10104 Office Phone: 212-468-8055. Business E-Mail: Ktung@mofo.com.

TUNG, PRABHAS, plastic surgeon; b. Ubol, Thailand, Apr. 3, 1944; s. Sathee and Seng (Ngium) T.; m. Patarin C. Sinjin; children: Tony, Tommy. MD, Mahidol U., Bangkok, 1968. Diplomate Am. Bd. Plastic Surgery. Plastic surgeon pvt. practice, Flint, Mich., 1980-82, Sacramento, Calif., 1982—. Office: 2801 K St Ste 200 Sacramento CA 95816-5118

TUNG, YE, engineering educator; s. Chi-Wei and Shuhui Tung; m. Yu Xia; 1 child, Brandon. PhD, Pa. State U., University Park, 2001. Tchg. asst. Pa. State U., University Park, 1996—2001. Recipient Engring. award, Mace, Mobile, Ala., 2006, 2007. Mem.: IEEE (corr.). Home Phone: 251-635-1169; Office Phone: 251-461-1378.

TUNHEIM, JERALD ARDEN, academic administrator, physicist, educator; b. Claremont, SD, Sept. 3, 1940; s. Johannes and Annie Tunheim; children: Jon, Angie, Alec. BS in Engring. Physics, S.D. State U., 1962, MS in Physics, 1964; PhD in Physics, Okla. State U., 1968. Vis. scientist Sandia Corp., Albuquerque, 1970-71, Ames (Iowa) AEC Labs., 1972; asst. prof. S.D. State U., Brookings, 1968-73, assoc. prof., 1973-78, prof., 1978-80, prof., head physics dept., 1980-85; dean Ea. Wash. U., Cheney, 1985-87; pres. Dakota State U., Madison, S.D., 1987—. Bd. dirs. Nat. Skill Stds. Bd., 1998—. Co-author: Elementary Particles and Unitary Symmetry, 1966, Quantum Field Theory, 1966; contbr. articles to profl.jours. Bd. dirs. Lake Area Improvement Corp. Grantee USDA, 1987-88, S.D. Govt. Office Edn. Devel., 1988-89, U.S. Dept. Edn., Eisenhower Program, 1985-86, 87-90, 92-93, 95-96, U.S. Dept. Edn. Math. and Sci. Program, 1989-92; named Tchr. of Yr. S.D. State U., 1972. Mem. NSPE, Am. Phys. Soc., Am. Assn. Physics Tchrs., Madison C. of C. (bd. dirs. 1990—), Rotary. Republican. Lutheran. E-mail: Jerald.Tunheim@dsu.edu.

TUNNEY, JOHN VARICK, lawyer, former senator; b. NYC, June 26, 1934; s. Gene and Mary (Lauder) T.; m. Kathinka Osborne, April 1977; children: Edward Eugene, Mark Andrew, Arianne Sprengers, Tara Theodora. BA in Anthropology, Yale, 1956; JD, U. Va., 1959; student, Acad. Internat. Law, The Hague, Netherlands, 1957. Bar: N.Y. 1959, Calif. 1963, Va. 1963. With firm Cahill, Gordon, Reindel & Ohl, NYC, 1959-60; tchr. bus. law U. Calif., Riverside, 1961-62; practice law Riverside, 1963—; mem. 89th-91st Congresses from Calif. 38th Dist., U.S. Senate from Calif., 1971-77; mem. firm Manatt, Phelps, Rothenberg & Tunney, Los Angeles, 1977-86; chmn. bd. Cloverleaf Group, Inc., Los Angeles, 1986—; gen. ptnr. Sun Valley Ventures, 1994—; pres. JVT Consulting, Inc., 1997—. Chmn. bd. Enterprise Plan, Inc., chmn. bd. Trusted Brands Inc.; bd. dirs. Prospect Group Inc., Garnet Resources Corp., Ill. Central Railroad, The Forschner Group, Inc., Foamex Internat.; bd. dir. Proscpect Group Inc. Polit. commentator Station KABC-TV. Trustee Westminster Sch., St. Matthews Sch.; bd. visitors Loyola Law Sch.; vice chmn. Limited Incomes Housing Corp.; mem. Lawyers Adv. Council. Constl. Rights Found., Citizens Rsch. Found., Commn. on Soviet Jewry. Served to capt. USAF, 1960-63. Chubb fellow Yale U., 1967 Mem. Am. Bar Assn. Democrat. Episcopalian. Office: 1819 Ocean Ave Santa Monica CA 90401-3223 *

TUNNICLIFF, DAVID GEORGE, retired civil engineer; b. Ord, Nebr., Sept. 18, 1931; s. George Thomas and Ada Ellen (Ward) Tunnicliff; m. Elaine Jean Interrante, Oct. 17, 1959 (div.); children: Martha Allison Tunnicliff Loeb, Vivian Jean; m. Joan Elizabeth Duchesneau, Oct. 25, 1975. BS, U. Nebr., Lincoln, 1954; MS, Cornell U., Ithaca, NY, 1958; PhD, U. Mich., Ann Arbor, 1972. Registered profl. engr., Nebr., Mass. Engr. Nebr. Dept. Rds., Lincoln, 1954-60; from asst. prof. to assoc. prof. Wayne State U., Detroit, 1960-67; chief tech. svcs. Warren Bros. Co., Cambridge, Mass., 1967-79; prin., cons. engr. D.G. Tunnicliff, Cons. Engr., Omaha, 1979—2007; ret. Contbr. articles to profl. jours. Rep. precinct del., Detroit, 1965—66. With US Army, 1955—56. Mem.: ASCE, ASTM, Transp. Rsch. Bd. (com. chair 1983—89), Assn. Asphalt Paving Tech. (bd. dirs. 1976—78). Mem. Evangel. Convenant Ch. Home and Office: DG Tunnicliff Cons Engr 9624 Larimore Ave Omaha NE 68134-3038 Office Phone: 402-572-8955. Personal E-mail: dgtnnclff@aol.com.

TUNSTALL, GRAYDON ALLEN, history professor, professional society administrator; b. Laurel, Md., May 29, 1941; s. Graydon Allen and Valance Townsend Tunstall; m. Wendy Marie Tunstall-Werner; 1 child, Graydon Allen III. AB, Dickinson Coll., Carlisle, Pa., 1963; MA, Rutgers U., New Brunswick, NJ, 1967, PhD, 1973. V.p. for advancement St. Johns, The Gt. Book Coll., Santa Fe, 1987—88; vis. prof. European history U. Cin., 1988—90; post-graduate seminar in mil. history US Mil. Acad., West Point, NY, 1991—93; assoc. prof. European history Cedar Crest Coll., Allentown, Pa., 1993—2000; lectr. U. South Fla., Tampa, 2000—. Vis. prof. European history Lafayette Coll., Easton, 1990—93; exec. dir. Phi Alpha Theta History Honor Soc., Tampa, 1994—. Author: Planning for War Against Russia and Serbia: Austro-Hungarian and German Military Strategies, 1871-1914, Blood in the Snow: The Carpathian Winter War 1915; contbr. book, articles to profl. jours. Exec. dir. Usher Lifelong Learning Inst., U. South Fla., Tampa, 2006—07. 1st lt. US Army, 1963—65. Recipient Superior Tchr. award in the Social Sciences, Lafayette Coll., 1991, 1993. Mem.: Assn. Coll. Honor Socs., The Gt. War Soc., Soc. for Mil. History, Soc. for the Advancement of Habsburg Studies, Orgn. Am. Historians, Am. Hist. Assn., The Hist. Soc. (bd. mem. 2006—07), Western Front Assn. (bd. mem. 2003—07), Assn. for the Study of Hungarian History (bd. mem. 1998—2002), Am. Assn. for the Advancement of Slavic Studies. Office: Univ South Florida 4202 E Fowler Ave SOC 107 Tampa FL 33620-8100 Home Phone: 813-994-8642; Office Phone: 813-974-8212. Office Fax: 813-974-8215. Personal E-mail: graydontunstall@yahoo.com. Business E-Mail: tunstall@cas.usf.edu.

TUOHEY, CONRAD GRAVIER, lawyer; b. Bklyn., Dec. 27, 1933; s. James L. and Rose Gravier Tuohey; m. Judith Octavia Jeeves, July 7, 1956; children: Octavia Jeeves, Heather Gravier, Meighan Judith, Caragh Rose. BA, George Washington U., 1957; JD, U. Mich., 1960. Bar: Calif. 1962, N.Y. 1980, D.C. 1980. Dir. Fed. Home Loan Bank, San Francisco, 1980—83; legal cons., counsel Calif. State Senate, 1981—87; counsel Senate Select com. Pacific Rim, 1986—87. Mem. Citizens adv. bd. Orange County Transit com., 1966—68; pres. Friends of Calif. State U., Fullerton, 1969—71, Calif. Alliance Ptnrs. Progress, 1969—72; mem. InterAm. bd. Ptnrs. Alliance Progress, 1969—72; mem. nat. bd. dirs., 1970—72. Contbr. articles to profl. jours. With US Army, 1951—54, leader rifle squad. Decorated Combat Infantryman's badge, Korean Svc. medal with 3 battle stars. Mem.: D.C. Bar Assn., State Bar Calif., Phi Sigma Kappa, Phi Delta Phi. Home and Office: 23391 Rockrose Mission Viejo CA 92692-1686 E-mail: tuohey@lawyer.com.

TUOHEY, MARK HENRY, III, lawyer; b. Rochester, NY, Sept. 27, 1946; s. Mark Henry Tuohey; m. Martha Tuohey; children: Brendan, Sean, Devin. BA in History, St. Bonaventure U., 1968; JD, Fordham U., 1973. Bar: D.C. 1973, U.S. Supreme Ct. 1980, U.S. Ct. Appeals (D.C. cir.) 1974, U.S. Dist. Ct. D.C. 1974, N.Y. 1984. Asst. U.S. atty. U.S. Atty.'s Office, Washington, 1973-77; spl. trial counsel U.S. Dept. Justice, Washington, 1977-79; spl. counsel to U.S. Atty. Gen. Washington, 1979; co-adminstrv. ptnr. Washington office Vinson & Elkins, Washington; dep. ind. counsel Whitewater Investigation, 1994-95; spl. counsel D.C. City Coun. Investigation of Met. Police Dept., 1998. Trustee Cath. U. Am., 2002—, Washington Jesuit Acad., 1999—, Gonzaga Coll. H.S., 1993—2003. Served to 1st lt. US Army, 1970—71. Named Washingtonian of Yr., Washingtonian Mag., 2006. Master: Wm. Bryant Inn. of Ct.; fellow: Am. Bar Found. (bd. dirs. 1980—85), Am. Law Inst., Am. Coll. Trial Lawyers; mem.: ABA (chair standing com. on continuing edn. bar 1980—85, litig. sect. coun. 1980—90, mem. Am. Law Inst./ABA com. continuing profl. edn. 1983—), Bar Assn. D.C. (Lawyer of the Yr. 2001), Jud. Conf. US Ct. Appeals (DC cir.), DC Bar Found. (chair 1998—), DC Bar (bd. govs. 1988—94, pres. 1993—94), DC Sports and Entertainment Commission (chair 2003—). Home: 1655 Kalmia Rd NW Washington DC 20012-1125 Office: Vinson & Elkins The Willard Office Bldg 1455 Pennsylvania Ave NW Fl 7 Washington DC 20004-1013 Office Phone: 202-639-6660. Business E-Mail: mtuohey@velaw.com.

TUPPER, LEON F., manufacturing executive; BS in Indsl. Psychology, Wayne State U.; MS in Indsl. Psychology, U. Mich.; postgrad., Dartmouth U. Tng. mgr. Am. Motors Corp., Detroit, 1972-77, buyer/procurement specialist, 1977-83, sr. buyer interior trim group, 1983-86, purchasing mgr. interior trim group, 1986-88; sales mgr. steering divsn. Sheller-Globe Corp., Toledo, Ohio, 1984-88; dir. sales and engring. Gilreath Mfg., Inc., Howell, Mich., 1988-91, pres., CEO, owner, 1991—. Trustee Cleary Coll., Ypsilanti, Mich.; treas., trustee High/Scope Edn. Rsch. Found.; bd. trustees Rehab. Inst. of Mich., Detroit Med. Ctr.; bus. sch. bd. exec. advisors Wayne State U.; mem. friends of the Detroit Area Pre-Coll. Engring. Program, Nat. Conf. for Cmty. Justice, 100 Black Men of Detroit. Address: PO Box 408 Howell MI 48844-0408 Fax: 248-728-1753.

TUPPER, RON, public health service officer, finance educator; b. Natick, Mass., Aug. 25, 1945; s. Ralph and Madeline (Boyde) Moore-Tupper; m. Malinda McGilvray, July 28, 1987; children: Michelle, Melissa, Madeline Marie. BA in Psychology, U. Nebr., 1969; MSc in Health Mgmt./Health Edn., S.W. Tex. State U., 1975. Asst. dir.-unit mgmt. Bexar County Hosp., San Antonio, Tex., 1971-72; assoc. dir. adminstrv. svcs. Robert B. Green Hosp., San Antonio, 1972-74; hosp. adminstr. Maverick County (Tex.) Hosp., 1975-78, Hosp. Affiliates, Internat., Nashville, Tenn., 1978-82; divsn. mgr. Mgmt. Recruiters Internat., Irving, Tex., 1983-88; v.p. adminstrn. Stores, Inc., McAllen, Tex., 1990—; exec. dir. Area Health Edn. Ctr., Weslaco, Tex., 1995-99; dir. South Tex. Ctr. for Rural Pub. Health Tex. A&M U. Sys. Health Sci. Ctr., McAllen, 1999—; prof., dir. Sch. Rural Pub. Health Tex. A&M U. System Health Sci. Ctr., College Station, 2001—; faculty prof., dir. McAllen br. campus Tex. A&M U. Sys. Health Sci. Ctr. Sch. Rural Pub. Health, College Station. Founder, bd. chair Cmty. Health Mgmt. Corp.-El Milagro Indigent Clinic, McAllen, 1996—, U. Tex. Med. Br. at Galveston Indigent Cancer Clinic. Chair, health and health edn. adv. com. State of Tex. Senator Appt., Tex./Mex., 1996, mem. South Tex. health adv. com., Lower Rio Grande Valley, 1996; mem. steering com. Tex. A&M U. Sch. of Rural Public Health, Rio Grande Valley rep., 1997—; mem. Tex. Dept. of Health U. Tex. Mobile Health Van com., 1996—. Staff sgt. USAF, 1964-70. Decorated Vietnam Svc. medal, Air Force conduct medal. Mem. Tex./Mex. Border Assn., Midwest Migrant Health Com. Avocations: writing, carpentry, community development. Office: South Tex Ctr for Rural Pub Health Tex A&M Uni Sys Hlth Sci 3700 N 10th St Ste 210 Mcallen TX 78501-1775 E-mail: Tupper@medicine.tamu.edu.

TURANO, DAVID A., lawyer; b. Ashtabula, Ohio, Sept. 9, 1946; s. Egidio A. and Mary Agnes (Bartko) T.; m. Karen J. Emmel, Aug. 29, 1970; children: Aaron, Thad, Bethen, Kyle. BS, Kent State U., 1968; JD, Ohio State U., 1971. Bar: Ohio 1971. Staff atty. The Pub. Utilities Commn. Ohio, Columbus, 1971-72; assoc., then ptnr. George, Greek, King, McMahon and McConnaughey, Columbus, 1972-79; ptnr. Baker & Hostetler, Columbus, 1979-96, Harris, Carter, Mahota, Turano & Mazza, Columbus, 1996-97, Harris, Turano & Mazza, Columbus, 1997—2003; of counsel Shoemaker, Howarth & Taylor, LLP, Columbus, 2003—. Mem. ABA, Ohio State Bar Assn., Columbus Bar Assn., Transp. Lawyers Assn. Roman Catholic. Office: Shoemaker Howarth & Taylor LLP 471 E Broad St Ste 2001 Columbus OH 43215 Home Phone: 614-888-4686; Office Phone: 614-232-0426. Business E-Mail: dturano@midohiolaw.com.

TURBIDY, JOHN BERRY, investor, management consultant; b. Rome, Ga., Oct. 18, 1928; s. Joseph Leo and Louyse (Berry) T.; m. Joan Marsales, Dec. 19, 1958 (dec.); children: John Berry, Trevor Martin; m. Jaquelin Lamond Schulter, June 8, 1996 Grad., Darlington Sch., 1945; BA, Duke U., 1950; postgrad., NYU, 1952, Emory U., 1954-56. Various positions Lockheed Aircraft, Marietta, Ga., 1951-56; gen. mgmt. cons. McKinsey & Co., NYC and London, 1956—62; v.p. adminstrn. ITT Europe, Inc., Brussels, 1963, v.p., group exec. European consumer products, 1963—65, v.p., group exec. for No. Europe, 1965-67; corp. v.p. adminstrn. Celanese Corp., NYC, 1967-68; pres., mng. dir. SIACE, SP.A. subs., Milan, 1968-69; chmn. bd., pres. Vecta Group, Kalamazoo, 1970-74; sr. v.p. corp. devel. IU Internat. Corp., Phila., 1974-78, exec. v.p., 1978-83; pres., chief exec. officer Pitcairn Fin. Mgmt. Group, Jenkintown, Pa., 1984-90; chmn. Office John Turbidy, 1990-95; mng. dir. Friedman, Turbidy & Co., Inc., NYC, 1995—2000. Bd. dirs. Statute of Liberty Ellis Island Found., chmn. 2004-07. Served with USNR, 1952 Mem. Sea Island Club, Sea Bright Beach Club. Address: 113 Biltmore Saint Simons Island GA 31522 Personal E-mail: jbturb@hotmail.com.

TURBIN, RICHARD, lawyer; b. NYC, Dec. 25, 1944; s. William and Ruth (Fiedler) T.; m. Rai Saint Chu-Turbin, June 12, 1976; children: Laurel Mei, Derek Andrew. BA magna cum laude, Cornell U., 1966; JD, Harvard U., 1969. Bar: Hawaii 1971, U.S. Dist. Ct. Hawaii 1971. Asst. atty. gen., Western Samoa, Apia, 1969-70; dep. pub. defender Pub. Defender's Office,

Honolulu, 1970-74; dir. Legal Aid Soc. Hawaii, Kaneohe, 1974-75; sr. atty., pres. Law Offices Richard Turbin, Honolulu, 1975—. Legal counsel Hawaii Crime Commn., 1980-81. Co-author: Pacific; author: Medical Malpractice, Handling Emergency Medical Cases, 1991; editor Harvard Civil Rights-Civil Liberties Law Rev., 1969. Legal counsel Dem. Party, Honolulu County, 1981-82; elected Neighborhood Bd., 1985, elected chair, 1990-97; bd. dirs. Hawaii chpt. ACLU, 1974-78, East-West Ctr. grantee, 1971, 72; commn. State of Hawaii Civil Rights com., 2002-05. Recipient Traphagen Disting. Alumnus award, Harvard Law Sch. Mem. ATLA, ABA (chair internat. torts and ins. practice section 1999-2000., governing coun., chair tort and ins. practice sect. 1999-2000), Hawaii Bar Assn. (pres. 2005), Hawaii Trial Lawyers Assn. (pres. 2002), Hawaii Jaycees (legal counsel 1981-82), Chinese Jaycees Honolulu (legal counsel 1980-81), Honolulu Tennis League (undefeated player 1983), Hawaii Harlequin Rugby Club (sec., legal counsel 1978-82), Pacific Club, Outrigger Canoe Club.' Jewish. Home: 4817 Kahala Ave Honolulu HI 96816-5231 Office Phone: 808-528-4000. Personal E-mail: richturbin@aol.com.

TURCO, ALFRED, JR., language educator; b. Providence, 1940; s. Alfred and Delia Maria Turco; m. Elizabeth Nora Davis, 1969 (div. 1981); children: Ellen, Jeffrey AB, Brown U., 1962; A.M., Harvard U., 1963, PhD, 1969; MA ad eundem gradum (hon.), Wesleyan U., 1981. Instr. English Wesleyan U., Middletown, Conn., 1967-69, asst. prof., 1969-74, assoc. prof., 1974-80, prof., 1980—; vis. assoc. prof. Cornell U., Ithaca, N.Y., 1980. Cons. Cornell U. Press, U. Toronto Press, Hartford Stage Co., Hackett Pub. Co.; mem. adv. coun. Internat. Shaw Soc., 2003—. Author: Shaw's Moral Vision, 1976; guest editor: Shaw's Neglected Plays (Shaw: Vol. 7), 1987; contbr. articles on Scandinavian lit. to profl. jours.; mem. editorial bd. Ann. of Bernard Shaw Studies, 1985—. Danforth Found. fellow, 1963-67; Woodrow Wilson Found. hon. fellow, 1963 Mem. Phi Beta Kappa Avocation: gourmet cooking. Home: 58 Prospect St Portland CT 06480-1131 Office: Wesleyan U Middletown CT 06459 Office Phone: 860-685-3599. E-mail: aturco@wesleyan.edu.

TURCO, LEWIS PUTNAM, language educator; b. Buffalo, May 2, 1934; s. Luigi and May Laura (Putnam) T.; m. Jean Cate Houdlette, May 29, 1934; children: Melora Ann, Christopher Cameron. BA, U. Conn., Storrs, 1959; MA, U. Iowa, Iowa City, 1962; LHD (hon.), Ashland U., Ohio, 2000. Instr. Cleve. State U., 1960-64; asst. prof. Hillsdale Coll., Mich., 1964-65; asst. prof. to full prof. SUNY, Oswego, 1965-96, poet-in-residence, 1995, prof. emeritus, 1996. Grad. asst. English, U. Conn., 1959; editl. asst. Writer's Workshop, U. Iowa, 1959-60; vis. prof. SUNY, Potsdam, 1968-69; Bingham Poet in Residence, U. Louisville, 1982; Writer in Residence, Ashland U., 1991; founding dir. Cleve. State U. Poetry Ctr., 1962, program in writing arts, SUNY Oswego, 1968. Author: First Poems, 1960, Awaken, Bells Falling: Poems 1959-67, 1968, numerous other poetry books including The Shifting Web: New and Selected Poems, 1989, The Collected Lyrics of Lewis Turco/Wesli Court, 2004; author numerous non-fiction books including The Book of Forms: A Handbook of Poetics, 1968, 3d edit., 2000, Visions and Revisions of American Poetry, 1986, Emily Dickinson, Woman of Letters, 1993, The Book of Literary Terms, 1999, The Book of Dialogue, 2004, A Sheaf of Leaves: Literary Memoirs, 2004, Fantaseers, A Book of Memories, 2005, Fearful Pleasures, The Complete Poem, 2007, others; editor: The Life and Poetry of Manoah Bodman, 1999; contbr. articles to profl. jours. Sec. City of Oswego Charter Revision Commn., 1990-91; active Oswego Opera Theater Chorus, Oswego Festival Chorus, 1986—. With USN, 1952-56. Recipient scholarship Meriden Record-Jour. Pub. Co., U. Conn., 1957-58, 58-59, Disting. Alumnus award, 1992, Melville Cane award Poetry Soc. Am., 1986, Bordighera Bilingual Poetry prize Sonia Raiziss-Giop Charitable Found., 1997, John Ciardi award for lifetime achievement in poetry Italian-Am., Found., 1999, others; resident fellowships Yaddo Found., 1959, 77, Faculty fellowships Rsch. Found. of SUNY, 1966-67, 69, 71, 73, 78; grant-in-aid, 1969; inducted into Meriden Hall of Fame, 1993. Home: PO Box 161 Dresden ME 04342-0161 Office Phone: 207-737-4512.

TURCOT, MARGUERITE HOGAN, medical researcher; b. White Plains, NY, May 19, 1934; d. Joseph William (dec.) and Marguerite Alice (dec.) Barrett) Hogan; children: Michael J., Susan A. Turcot, William R. Student, Syracuse U., 1951-54; BSN, U. Bridgeport, 1968. RN, Conn., N.C. Nurse Park City Hosp., Bridgeport, Conn., 1968-69, Meml. Mission Hosp., Asheville, N.C., 1969-70; instr. St. Joseph's Hosp., Asheville, 1970-71, oper. rm. nurse, 1973-77, charge nurse urology-cystoscopy, 1977-85; tchr. Asheville-Buncombe Tech. Coll., Asheville, 1971-72, Buncombe County Child Devel., Asheville, 1972-73; rschr. VA Med. Ctr., Asheville, 1988—; owner Reed House Bed & Breakfast, Asheville, 1985—2001. Bd. dirs. RiverLink, Quality Foreward. Charter mem. French Broad River Planning Com., Asheville, 1987—, Biltmore Village Hist. Mus.; mem. Asheville Bicentennial Commn., 1990-93; exec. dir. Preservation Soc. Asheville and Buncombe County. Recipient Griffin award, 1994, Friend of the River award, Land of Sky Regional Coun., 1995, Sondley award, Hist. Resources Commn. Asheville and Buncombe County, 1996, Vol. of Yr. award, RiverLink, 2001, Critical Link award, 2003; grantee U. Bridgeport, 1967—68; scholar Syracuse U. Faculty, 1951—54. Mem. Am. Urology Assn. (presenter VA urology workshop Asheville chpt. 1981, nat. meeting allied), Am. Bd. Urologic Allied Health Profls., Nat. Trust for Hist. Preservation, Preservation Found. N.C., Blue Ridge Pkwy. Assn., Preservation Soc. Asheville and Buncombe County (bd. dirs., past pres.), Asheville Newcomers Club (founder, 1st pres.), Earthwatch, Friends of Blue Ridge Pkwy. Inc. Republican. Roman Catholic. Avocations: preservation, history, architecture, sewing, hiking. Office: Preservation Soc Asheville & Buncombe County PO Box 2806 Asheville NC 28802

TURCOTTE, DONALD LAWSON, geophysical sciences educator; b. Bellingham, Wash., Apr. 22, 1932; s. Lawson Phillip and Eva (Pearson) Turcotte; m. Joan Meredith Luecke, May 17, 1957; children: Phillip Lawson, Stephen Bradford. BS, Calif. Inst. Tech., 1954, PhD, 1958; M in Aero. Engring., Cornell U., 1955; PhD (hon.), U. Paris, 2005. Asst. prof. aero. engring. U.S. Naval Postgrad. Sch., Monterey, Calif., 1958-59; asst. prof. aero. engring. Cornell U., Ithaca, NY, 1959-63, assoc. prof., 1963-67, prof., 1967-73, prof. geol. scis., 1973-85, Maxwell Upson prof., 1985—2002, chmn., 1981-90; disting. prof. geology U. Calif. Davis, 2003—. Author (with others): Statistical Thermodynamics, 1963, Space Propulsion, 1965, Geodynamics, 1982, Fractals and Chaos in Geology and Geophysics, 1992, Mantle Convection, 2001. Trustee U. Space Rsch. Assn., 1975—79. Recipient Wegener medal, European Union Geosci., 1991, Disting. Alumni award, Calif. Inst. Tech., 1999; sr. postdoctoral rsch. fellow, NSF, 1965—66, Guggenheim fellow, 1972—73. Mem.: NAS, Am. Acad. Arts and Scis., Seismol. Soc. Am., Geol. Soc. Am. (Day medal 1982), Am. Geophys. Union (Charles A. Whitten medal 1995, William Bowie Medal 2003), El Macero Country Club. Home: 27104 Middle Golf Dr El Macero CA 95618 Office: Univ Calif Dept Geology Davis CA 95616 Office Phone: 530-572-6808. Business E-Mail: turcotte@geology.ucdavis.edu.

TURCOTTE, JEAN-CLAUDE CARDINAL, archbishop; b. Montreal, Que., Can., June 26, 1936; s. Paul-Émile and Rita (Gravel) Turcotte. Student, U. Cath., Lille, France; DD (hon.), McGill U.; lic. theology, Grand Seminaire Montreal. Ordained priest Roman Catholic Ch., 1959, consecrated bishop. Aux. bishop Diocese of Montreal, Que., Canada, 1982—90, archbishop, 1990—. Mem.: Coun. of Social Commn., Congregation of Causes of Saints. Roman Catholic. Office: 2000 Sherbrooke Ouest Montreal PQ Canada H3H 1G4

TURCOTTE, JOHN ARTHUR, JR., lawyer; b. Lowell, Mass., Mar. 27, 1950; s. John A. and Dorothy J. (Gillette) Turcotte; m. Mary Catherine Willett, Nov. 12, 1976; 1 child, Sarah Hamilton. BS, Boston Coll., 1972; JD, St. Louis U., 1976. Bar: Mo. 1977, U.S. Dist. Ct. (ea. dist.) Mo. 1979, U.S. Ct. Appeals (8th cir.) 1981. Law clk. to presiding justice Mo. Ct. Appeals (ea. dist.), St. Louis, 1976—78; assoc. Lashly, Caruthers, Baer & Hamel, 1978—81, ptnr., 1981—83, Hammond, Shiners, Turcotte & Larrew, 1983—. Fellow: Am. Acad. Matrimonial Lawyers; mem.: ABA, Bar Assn. Met. St. Louis (chmn. com. on cts., Merit award 1983), Mo. Assn. Trial Attys., Assn. Trial Lawyers Am. Democrat. Roman Catholic. Home: 139 Wildwood Ln Saint Louis MO 63122-5135 Office: Hammond Shinners Turcotte & Larrew 7730 Carondelet Ave Ste 200 Saint Louis MO 63105-3326 Office Phone: 314-727-1015. Business E-Mail: jturcotte@hstl.com.

TURCOTTE, MARGARET JANE, retired nurse; b. Stow, Ohio, May 17, 1927; d. Edward Carlton and Florence Margaret (Hanson) McCauley; m. Rene George Joseph, Nov. 24, 1961 (div. June 1967); 1 child, Michael Lawrence. Degree, St. Thomas Hosp. Sch. Nursing, Akron, Ohio, 1949. cert. RN Ohio, 1950. Nurse St. Thomas Hosp., 1949-50; pvt. duty nurse, 1950-57; polio nurse Akron Children's Hosp., 1953-54; mem. nursing staff Robinson Meml. Hosp., Ravenna, Ohio, 1958-67, head ctrl. svc., 1963-67; supr. ctrl. svc. Brentwood Hosp., Warrensville Heights, Ohio, 1967-93, infections control nurse, 1982-91; emergency med. technician. Mem. aux. Robinson Meml. Hosp.; vol. Portage County Vis. Nurse Svc. and Hospice; active RSVP, Cozy Christian Quilters. Mem.: St. Thomas Hosp. Alumni Assn., Cozy Christian Quilters. Democrat. Mem. Christian Ch. (Disciples Of Christ). Home: 714 Woodgate Blvd Apt 201 Ravenna OH 44266-2548

TUREK, PAUL JOHN, III, construction executive; b. Columbia, SC, Feb. 10, 1964; s. Paul John Jr. and Patricia Veronica (Saluta) T.; m. Emma Lactao, Dec. 24, 1995; children: Samantha Claire, Paul John, Isabella. BS in Civil Engring., Northwestern U., 1986. Registered civil engr., Calif. Constrn. mgr. Brown & Root Inc., Houston, 1990-94; sr. project mgr. Shorenstein Co., San Francisco, 1994-98; v.p. Thompson Brooks, Inc., San Francisco, 1998-2000; pres. Summa III, Inc., San Francisco, 2000—04; sr. assoc. Marx Okubo, San Francisco, 2004—05, asst. v.p. constrn. mgmt., 2006—. Active Walnut Creek Masters Swim Team. 1st lt. USMC, 1986-90. Avocations: fly fishing, swimming. Home: 2121 Carrol Rd Walnut Creek CA 94596-5714 Office: Marx Okubo 444 Spear St # 205 San Francisco CA 94105 Office Phone: 415-957-9240. E-mail: turekpe@sbcglobal.net.

TUREK, SONIA FAY, journalist; b. NYC, Aug. 2, 1949; d. Louis and Julia (Liebson) Turek; m. Gilbert Curtis, June 18, 1995. BA in English, CCNY, 1970; MSLS, Drexel U., 1972; MS in Journalism, Boston U., 1979. Children's libr. Wissahickon Valley Pub. Libr., Ambler, Pa., 1973; supr. children's svcs. Somerville Pub. Libr., Somerville, Mass., 1973-78; stringer The Watertown (Mass.) Sun, 1979, The Bedford (Mass.) Minuteman, 1979; reporter The Middlesex News, Framingham, Mass., 1979-83, The Boston Herald, 1983, asst. city editor, city editor, 1983-86, asst. mng. editor features, 1986-89, asst. mng. editor Sunday, 1989-93, dep. mng. editor, arts and features, 1993-99, wine columnist, 1984—. Tchr. Cambridge (Mass.) Ctr. for Adult Edn., 1982, 83; adj. prof. Boston U., 1986; travel writer The Boston Herald, 1984-2003. Avocations: wine and food, travel, sailing. Personal E-mail: sfturek@aol.com.

TURETSKY, AARON, lawyer; b. Bklyn., Mar. 23, 1951; s. Victor and Edith (Levine) T.; m. Edna M. Real, July 21, 1990; children: Persephone Fatima, Aaron Jr. BA summa cum laude, Hunter Coll., NYC, 1979; JD magna cum laude, N.Y. Law Sch., 1986. Bar: N.J. 1986, U.S. Dist. Ct. N.J. 1986, N.Y. 1987, U.S. Dist. Ct. (so. and ea. dist.) N.Y. 1987, U.S. Dist. Ct. (no. dist.) N.Y. 1988. Appellate law rsch. asst. appellate div. 2d dept. Supreme Ct. State of N.Y., 1986-87; atty. North Country Legal Svcs., Inc., Plattsburgh, N.Y., 1987-89; assoc. Holcombe & Bruno, Plattsburgh, 1989-90; pvt. practice, Keeseville, N.Y., 1990—. Law guardian Essex County Family Ct., 1990—; impartial hearing officer for children with disabilites, 1996—. Chmn. Essex County, NY Conservative Com., 1990-06; NY St. Conservative Party N.E. regional vice. chmn., 1992—; eucharistic min. Cath. Cmty., Keeseville, NY. Mem. N.Y. State Bar Assn., Clinton County Bar Assn., Essex County Bar Assn., Elks, KC, Phi Beta Kappa. Roman Catholic. Office: PO Box 367 Keeseville NY 12944-0367

TURGEON, MARK, men's college basketball coach; b. Topeka, Feb. 5, 1965; m. Ann Fowler; children: William Harris, Ella, Leo. BS in Pers. Adminstrn., U. Kans., Lawrence, 1987; MS in Edn., U. Okla., 1987. Asst. coach U. Kans., 1987—92, head jr. varsity coach, 1988—92; asst. coach U. Oreg., Eugene, 1992—97, Phila. 76ers, 1997—98; head coach Jacksonville State U., Ala., 1998—2000, Wichita State U., Kans., 2000—07, Tex. A&M U., College Station, 2007—. Named Mo. Valley Conf. Coach of Yr., 2006. Office: Tex A&M U Mens Basketball Athletic Dept PO Box 30017 College Station TX 77842-3017 *

TURILLI, M. LOUISE, lawyer; Grad., Oberlin Coll., Ohio; M, U. Cin.; law degree, U. Conn. Sch. Law. Ptnr. east coast law firm; law v.p., asst. sec. NCR Corp.; v.p., assoc. gen. counsel Bellsouth Corp., Atlanta; v.p., dep. gen. counsel Qwest Comm. Internat. Inc., Denver; v.p., gen. counsel Ryerson Inc., Chgo., 2007—. Office: Ryerson Inc 2621 W 15th Pl Chicago IL 60608-1712 *

TURINO, GERARD MICHAEL, internist, educator; b. NYC, May 16, 1924; s. Michael and Lucy (Arciero) T.; m. Dorothy Estes, Aug. 25, 1951; children: Peter, Phillip, James. AB, Princeton U., 1945; MD, Columbia U., 1948. Diplomate: Am. Bd. Internal Medicine. Intern Columbia U., Bellevue Hosp., 1948-49, asst. resident in medicine, 1949-50; resident in medicine New Haven Hosp., 1950-51; chief resident in medicine Columbia U. div. Bellevue Hosp., 1953-54; sr. fellow N.Y. Heart Assn., 1956-60; career investigator Health Research Council City of N.Y., 1961-71; asst. prof. medicine Columbia U., 1960-67, assoc. prof., 1967-72, prof. medicine, 1973-83, John H. Keating prof. medicine, 1983—; mem. staff Presbyn. Hosp., NYC, 1960—, attending physician, 1983—; dir. med. svcs. St. Lukes-Roosevelt Hosp., NYC, 1983-92; dir. St. Lukes-Roosevelt Hosp. James P. Mara Ctr, 1997. Cons. on sci. affairs Am. Thoracic Soc., 1992—; mem. sci. adv. com. Nat. Heart, Lung, and Blood Inst., Am. Lung Assn., Am. Heart Assn., N.Y. Lung Assn., N.Y. Heart Assn., Alpha, Antitrypsin Found.; mem. staff divsn. med. sci. Nat. Rsch. Coun., Washington; cons. VA Hosp., East Orange, N.J., 1962-67; cons. in medicine Englewood (N.J.) Hosp., Hackensack (N.J.) Hosp.; pres.-elect Am. Bur. Med. Advancement in China, 1994, pres., 1994-2001, chmn., 2001-; chmn. bd. dirs. Chronic Obstructive Pulmonary Disease Found., 2004 Contbr. articles to med. jours. Mem. Bd. Edn., Alpine, N.J., 1960-67; chmn. Chronic Obstructive Pulmonary Disease Found., 2004. Served to capt. USAF, 1951-53. Recipient Joseph Mather Smith prize Columbia U., 1965, Alumni medal, 1983, Silver medal Alumni Assn. Coll. Physicians and Surgeons Columbia U., 1979, gold medal, 1986, Edward Livingston Trudeau medal Am. Lung Assn., 2003, Fellow AAAS; mem. Assn. Am. Physicians, Am. Soc. Clin. Investigation, Harvey Soc., Am. Thoracic Soc. (pres. 1987-88, Edward Livingston Trudeau prize 2003), Am. Fedn. Clin. Rsch., Am. Physiol. Soc. (chmn. steering com. respiration sect.), Am. Heart Assn. (award of merit 1980, Disting. Achievement award 1989, bd. dirs.), N.Y. Heart Assn. (pres. 1981-83, dir.), N.Y. Lung Assn. (dir.), N.Y. Med.-Surg. Soc. (pres. 1995), N.Y. Clin. Soc., Princeton Club (N.Y.C.), Maidstone Club, Devon Yacht Club, Century Assn. Club. Home: 66 E 79th St New York NY 10021-0244 Office: St Lukes Roosevelt Hosp 1000 10th Ave New York NY 10019-1192 Business E-Mail: GMT1@Columbia.edu.

TURINSKY, PAUL JOSEF, nuclear engineer, educator; b. Hoboken, NJ, Oct. 20, 1944; s. Paul J. and Wilma A. (Budig) T.; m. Karen Ann DeLuca, Aug. 29, 1966; children: Grant Dean, Beth Noelle. BS, U. R.I., 1966; MSE, U. Mich., 1967, PhD, 1970; MBA, U. Pitts., 1979. Asst. prof. Rensselaer Poly. Inst., Troy, NY, 1971-73; engr., mgr. nuc. design Westinghouse Elec. Corp., Pitts., 1973—78, mgr. core devel., 1978-80; head dept. nuc. engring. NC State U., Raleigh, 1980—88, 1999—2006, prof., 1980—, dir. Electric Power Rsch. Ctr., 1989—; pres. Nuclear Fuel Mgmt. Assocs., 1994—. Bd. dir. Quantum Rsch. Svcs.; cons. Electric Power Rsch. Inst., Palo Alto, Calif., 1980-98, Sci. Applications Internat. Corp., 1990-92, US Dept. Energy, 1993; tech. specialist Internat. Atomic Energy Agy., Vienna, Austria, 1982—; mem. nuc. safety rev. bd. Duke Power Co., Charlotte, NC, 1986-2001; cons. Can. Nuc. Safety Commn., 2000-, Western Svcs. Corp., 2006-; mem. nuc. sci. advisory bd. Commissariat l'Energie Atomique, France, 2006-. Author: (with others) CRC Handbook of Nuclear Reactor Calculations, 1986; contbr. more than 100 articles to tech. jours. Recipient Outstanding Tchr. award, N.C. State U., 1985, Supercomputer award, IBM, 1991, Alcoa Disting. Rschr. award, 1993, E.O. Lawrence award in nuc. tech., U.S. Dept. Energy, 2002, Merit award, Alumni Soc. U. Mich., 2003. Fellow: Am. Nuc. Soc. (chmn. reactor physics divsn. 1987—88, chmn. math. and computer divsn. 1995—96, bd. dirs. 1990—93, Mark Mills award 1971, Eugene E. Wigner Reactor Physics award 2003, Arthur Holly Compton award 2004); mem.: AAAS (math. com.), Soc. Indsl. and Applied Math., Edison Electric Inst. (Power Engring. Educator award 1992), Am. Soc. Engring. Educators (chmn. nuc. engring. divsn. 1984—85, Glenn Murphy award 1990). Office: NC State U Dept Nuclear Engring PO Box 7909 Raleigh NC 27695-7909 Office Phone: 919-515-5098. Business E-Mail: turinsky@ncsu.edu.

TURITS, RICHARD LEE, history professor; b. Passaic, NJ, Oct. 11, 1960; s. Philip Daniel Turits and Nancy Barnett Morse; m. Hannah Rosen, July 22, 1963. BA, Brown U., 1983; MA, Yale U., 1986; PhD, U. Chgo., 1997. Asst. prof. history Princeton U., NJ, 1997—2003; assoc. prof. history and Afro-Am. and African studies U. Mich., Ann Arbor, 2003—. Author: Foundations of Despotism: Peasants, the Trujillo Regime, and Modernity in Dominican History, 2003. Recipient Outstanding Acad. Book award, Choice Mag., 2003, James Alexander Robertson Meml. prize, Conf. Latin Am. History, 2003, Bolton-Johnson prize, 2005, John Edwin Fagg prize, Am. Hist. Assn., 2004; scholar, Harvard Acad. Internat. and Area Studies, 1996—97, 1998—99. Home: 702 N 5th Ave Ann Arbor MI 48104-1058 Office: Univ Mich Dept History 1029 Tisch Ann Arbor MI 48109-1003 Home Phone: 734-222-7032; Office Phone: 734-647-4873.

TURITZIN, JOHN N., entertainment company executive, lawyer; b. Manhasset, NY, Sept. 5, 1955; m. Barbara Turitzin; children: Allison, David, Emily. Grad., Earlham Coll., 1976; M in Pub. Affairs, Princeton U., 1981; JD, NYU, 1981. Assoc. Cahill Gordon & Reindel, NY, 1981—84; ptnr. Battle Fowler LLP, Stamford, Conn., 1985—2000, Paul, Hastings, Janofsky & Walker LLP, 2000—04; exec. v.p., gen. counsel Marvel Entertainment Inc., NYC, 2004—06, exec. v.p., Office Chief Exec., 2006—. Office: Marvel Entertainment Inc 417 Fifth Ave 11th Fl New York NY 10016 Office Phone: 212-576-4000. Office Fax: 212-576-8517.

TURK, AUSTIN THEODORE, social studies educator; b. Gainesville, Ga., May 28, 1934; s. Hollis Theodore and Ruth (Vandiver) T.; m. Janet Stuart Irving, Oct. 4, 1957 (div. 1977); children: Catherine, Jennifer; m. Ruth-Ellen Marie Grimes, July 27, 1985. BA cum laude, U. Ga., 1956; MA, U. Ky., 1959; PhD, U. Wis., 1962. Acting instr. sociology U. Wis., Madison, 1961-62; from instr. to prof. sociology Ind. U., Bloomington, 1962-74; prof. U. Toronto, Can., 1974-88, U. Calif., Riverside, 1988—, chmn. dept. sociology, 1989-94; interim dir. Robert B. Presley Ctr. for Crime and Justice Studies, 1994-95. Author: Criminality and Legal Order, 1969, Political Criminality, 1982; gen. editor crime and justice series SUNY Press, Albany, 1990—; contbr. articles to jours. in field. Mem. Calif. Mus. Photography, 1988—, Citizens Univ. Com., 1990—. Recipient Paul Tappan award Western Soc. Criminology, 1989. Fellow Am. Soc. Criminology (pres. 1984-85); mem. Am. Sociol. Assn. (chair criminology sect. 1975-76), Law and Soc. Assn. (trustee 1982-85), Acad. Criminal Justice Scis. Democrat. Avocations: gardening, reading, swimming, tennis. Office: Dept Sociology U Calif Riverside Riverside CA 92521-0001 E-mail: austin.turk@ucr.edu.

TURK, ELIZABETH ANN, music educator; b. NYC, July 10, 1957; d. William Robert Turk, Elizabeth Ann Brittingham. BA in Music and History, Dowling Coll.; MA in German Lang. and Lit., Hofstra U.; MA in European History, SUNY Stony Brook; MA in Music Libr. Sci., Columbia U. Tchg. asst SUNY, Stony Brook, 1986—88; lectr. music Dowling Coll., Oakdale, NY, 1988—91; choral tchr. music Amityville (NY) Pub. Schs., 1991—; dir. theater arts, dir. choral music Miller Pl. HS; theater dir. Amityville HS; music dir. theater prodns. Commack HS South, Carriage House Players, Kids for Kids Theater, Inc.; music dir. theater Syosset Mid. Sch., Conn., Jericho H.S. Tchr. vocal music Miller Place Middle Sch., Miller Place, NY, Hewlett Woodmere HS, NY; pvt. tchr. and vocal coach, Massapequa, NY. Singer (soloist): (lead rolls) Rome Opera Festival, 1989, 1990; performer: Tchaikovsky Competition, 1978, 1982, 1986, Minn. Opera, 1979, 1980, 1981, L.I. Youth Orch. Summer Tours; dir.: Sleeping Beauty, Sound of Music, Fiddler on the Roof, Little Shop of Horrors, Cinderella, Oliver, numerous others; choreographer Fiddler on the Roof, Sound of Music, Little Shop of Horrors, Oliver, Grease; dir.: 42nd Street, West Side Story, Guys & Dolls, Mikado, HMS Pinafore & Pirates of Penzance, King and I, Best of Broadway. Recipient award for further study, Met. Opera, 1981—90, Herald award for choreography and music dir. Mem.: Suffolk County Music Educators Assn., Music Educators Nat. Assn., Suffolk County Wrestling Assn. (tournament dir. league V 1974—, numerous awards), White Star Triangle (Beloved Queen 1973—74), Order Ea. Star (various offices, assoc. condr.). Home: 90 Clock Blvd Massapequa NY 11758

TURK, JAMES CLINTON, federal judge; b. Roanoke, Va., May 3, 1923; s. James Alexander and Geneva (Richardson) T.; m. Barbara Duncan, Aug. 21, 1954; children: Ramona Leah, James Clinton, Robert Malcolm Duncan, Mary Elizabeth, David Michael. AB, Roanoke Coll., 1949; L.L.B., Washington and Lee U., 1952. Bar: Va. 1952. Assoc. Dalton & Poff, Radford, Va., 1952-53; ptnr. Dalton, Poff & Turk, Radford, 1953-72; state senator from Va., 1959-72; judge U.S. Dist. Ct. (we. dist.) Va., Roanoke, 1972-73, chief judge, 1973—. Dir. 1st & Mchts. Nat. Bank of Radford Mem. Va. Senate, from 1959, minority leader.; Trustee Radford Community Hosp., 1959—. Served with AUS, 1943-46. Mem.: Order of Coif, Omicron Delta Kappa, Phi Beta Kappa. Baptist (deacon). Home: 1002 Walker Dr Radford VA 24141-3018 Office: US Dist Ct 246 Franklin Rd SW # 220 Roanoke VA 24011-2214 Office Phone: 540-857-5122. Office Fax: 540-857-5123. Business E-Mail: jamest@vawd.uscourts.gov.

TURK, JAMES CLINTON, JR., lawyer; b. Radford, Va., Oct. 27, 1956; s. James Clinton and Barbara (Duncan) T.; m. Allison Blanding, Oct. 16, 1993; children: Lindsey Leigh, Katherine Alexandra, Alana Rae. BA in Econs., Roanoke Coll., 1979; JD, Samford U., 1984. Bar: Va. 1984, US Dist. Ct. (ea. and we. dists.) Va. 1984, US Bankruptcy Ct. 1985, US Ct. Appeals (4th cir.) 1985, US Supreme Ct. 1988; cert. specialist in civil and criminal trial advocacy Nat. Bd. Trial Advocacy; cert. players agt. Nat. Basketball Players Assn.; cert. players agt./contract advisor NFL. Ptnr. Harrison & Turk, Radford, 1985—. Adj. prof. criminal justice dept. Radford U.; bd. dirs. New River brs. SunTrust Bank, Va. Tech. Found., Intrexon Transcriptional Therapeutics Corp., Intrexon Corp. Sec. Radford Rep. Com., 1984—; fundraising chmn. Am. Heart Assn., Radford, 1986—; bd. dir. New River Valley Workshop, Inc., v.p., 1990-92, pres., 1992-93; bd.

dirs. new River CC Ednl. Found.; apptd. chmn. and dir. Va. Student Assistance Authorities by Gov. George Allen, 1994—; escheator City of Radford and Pulaski County; rep. western dist. CJA Panel Atty., Va.; mem. 4th Cir. Jud. Conf., 2000-01; bd. dirs. Va. Tech. Athletic Found. Named a Va. Super Lawyer, 2006—07, 2007; recipient Bill Geimer Capital Defender award, Va. Capital Case Clearinghouse, 2000—01. Mem. ATLA (sustaining, fellow Coll. of Advocacy), Ted Dalton Am. Inn Courts (barrister), ABA, Am. Bd. Trial Adv., Am. Coll. Barristers, Va. Bar Assn. (civil litig. sect. coun. 1991—, criminal litig. sect. coun. 1994—), Nat. Assn. Criminal Def. Lawyers (life; death penalty com. and indigent def. com.), Va. Trial Lawyers Assn., Inn of Cts., Jaycees, Am. Inn of Ct., Rotary. Republican. Roman Catholic. Avocations: weightlifting, golf, travel, flying, scuba diving. Home: 460 Quailwood Dr Blacksburg VA 24060-6724 Office: Stone Harrison Turk PC PO Box 2968 Radford VA 24143-2968 Office Phone: 540-639-9056. Personal E-mail: jimturk@aol.com.

TURK, JOHN COBB, retired architect, educator; b. Buffalo, Oct. 16, 1930; s. Roswell Lester and Alice Knoche (Cobb) Turk; m. Joanna D. Paulat, 1959 (dec. Apr. 1966); 1 child, Christine Paulat; m. Sandra Miriam Baruch, Mar. 18, 1967 (dec. June 1986); m. Mary Jean Raftery, June 25, 1988. BA, Colgate U., 1952. Registered arch., S.C., 1979. Apprentice Frank Lloyd Wright's Taliesin Fellowship, Spring Green, Wis., Scottsdale, Ariz., 1955—57; archtl. draftsman various archs., Buffalo, 1959-72; instr. archtl. engring. tech. Midlands Tech. Coll., Columbia, SC, 1972-77, head dept. archtl. engring. tech., 1977-79, head constrn. tech. dept., 1979-84; arch. Carlisle Assocs., Columbia, 1984-87; arch., dir. engring. and housing Ft. Jackson, Columbia, 1987-88; arch., head design and estimating dept. Facilities Mgmt. Office U. S.C., Columbia, 1988-2000, arch., 2001—04, arch. emeritus, 2004; owner Architecture Light, Columbia, 2004—07. Dir. Lake Murray Assn., 2001—02. With C.E. US Army, 1953—55. Mem.: Constrn. Specifications Inst. (bd. dirs. Columbia chpt. 1996—98, v.p. 1998—99, pres.-elect 1999—2000, pres. 2000—01, dir. 2001—06, constrn. documents technician), Intertel, Mensa (v.p. Ctrl. SC chpt. 1978, sec. 1998—2001, v.p. 2005—07, pres. 2007—). Unitarian Universalist. Avocation: boating. Home: 112 Schooner Ln Columbia SC 29212-8032 Personal E-mail: johncturk@att.net.

TURK, RICHARD ERRINGTON, retired psychiatrist; b. Staten Island, NY, Oct. 6, 1925; s. Richard Jason and Marian (Errington) T.; m. Dec. 30, 1948 (widowed Dec. 23, 1978); children: Stephanie, Jeffrey, Alan. BA, Dartmouth Coll., 1945; MD, Johns Hopkins Med. Sch., 1948. Diplomate Am. Bd. Psychiatry. Intern Highland-Alameda County Hosp., Oakland, Calif., 1948-49; resident Herrick Meml. Hosp., Berkeley, Calif., 1949-50; fellow psychiatry Med. Sch. Harvard U., Boston, 1950-51, 53-54; clin. instr. Med. Sch. U. Calif., San Francisco, 1954—70; pvt. practice psychiatry Berkeley, 1954-85. Pvt. practice, Walnut Creek, Calif., 1972-88; staff Herrick Meml. Hosp., 1954-85, Walnut Creek Hosp., 1972-88, John Muir Meml. Hosp., Walnut Creek, 1972-88. Capt. USAF Res., 1951—53, Korea. Mem. AMA, Am. Psychiat. Assn., No. Calif. Psychiat. Assn., Calif. Med. Assn., Alameda-Contra Costa County Med. Assn. Avocations: travel, bicycling, boating, car camping.

TURK, THOMAS LIEBIG, arts consultant; b. Indpls., July 4, 1936; s. Laurel Herbert and Esther Lucille (Liebig) T.; m. Judith Ann Prochnow, July 26, 1969; children: Martisha Emily, Benjamin Edward. AB, DePauw U., 1958; MA, Mich. State U., 1960; cert., Harvard U., 1973. Promotion and publicity dir. Sta. WMSB-TV Mich. State U., East Lansing, 1961, asst. editor news bur., 1962-63, fine arts assoc. producer Sta. WKAR-TV, 1963-68, fine arts producer Sta. WKAR-TV, 1969-81; acting dir. publicity DePauw U., Greencastle, Ind., 1961-62; exec. dir. Cultural Activities Ctr., Temple, Tex., 1981-91, Met. Nashville Arts Commn., 1993—2003, Tennesseans for the Arts, 2003—06; mng. dir. Texarkana (Tex.) Regional Arts & Humanities Coun., 1991-93. Pres. Met. Lansing (Mich.) Fine Arts Coun., 1975-77, Mich. Assn. Comm. Arts Agys., East Lansing, 1979-81; Gov. apptd. mem. Mich. Coun. for Arts, 1979-81; chmn. Mich. Arts Forum, 1980-81; pres. U.S. Urban Arts Fedn., 1999-00; mem. State Arts Action Network Coun., 2005-06. Producer, co-producer: 400 programs for local, nat. and internat. distbn. on pub. TV, 1963-81. Bd. dir. Alias Chamber Music Ensemble, 2006—, Univ. Club Nashville, 2006—. With USAF, 1960. Mem.: Tennesseans for Arts (bd. dirs. 2000—03), Nat. Assembly Local Arts Agys. (bd. dirs. 1979—85), Rotary, Sigma Chi. Episcopalian. Home and Office: 643 Harpeth Trace Dr Nashville TN 37221-3147 Personal E-mail: turktj@comcast.net.

TURKEL, STANLEY, hotel executive, management consultant; s. Nathan and Mollie (Kurtzman) Turkeltaub; m. Barbara Bell (div. Apr. 1971); children: Marc Alexander, Allison Lee; m. Rima Sokoloff; stepchildren: Joshua Bernard Forrest, Benay Debra Forrest. BS, NYU, 1957. Laundry cons. Victor Kramer Co. Inc., NYC, 1957—62; with spl. hotel svcs. Loews Hotel Corp., NYC, 1962-63; res. mgr. Americana Hotel, NYC, 1963-64; gen. mgr. Drake Hotel, NYC, 1964-66, Summit Hotel, NYC, 1966-67; product line mgr. hotels ITT, NYC, 1968—75; owner Stanley Turkel Co., Hotel Cons., Kew Gardens Hills, NY, 1976—. Bd. advisors NYU Ctr. Hospitality, Tourism and Sports Mgmt. Author: Heroes of the American Reconstruction, 2005; contbr. articles to NY Times, Cornell Quar., Lodging Hospitality, The Bottomline, Hotel Interactive, Hotel Online. Mem.: ACLU, Internat. Soc. Hospitality Cons. (cert.), Am. Hotel and Lodging Assn. (MHS cert.), City Club NY (trustee 1964—97, chmn. 1977—88). Avocations: Reconstruction period of America, autograph collecting, tennis. Office Phone: 917-628-8549. Personal E-mail: stanturkel@aol.com. *As a lifelong civic activist, I cherish the godless constitution and especially the first amendment which provides protection for unpopular speech and creates a wall of separation between church and state.*

TURKOVÁ, HELGA, librarian; b. Prague, Czech, Apr. 20, 1942; d. Johann Turek and Anna (Kusbachová) Turková. Grad., Charles U., Prague, Czech, 1964, PhD, 1969. Diploma in librarianship. Libr. Czechoslovak Acad. of Scis., Prague, 1964—65, Prague Info. Svc., 1965—65; ind. specialist. libr. Nat. Mus. Libr., Prague, 1967—90, dir., 1990—2005; dir. dept. hist. Castles Libr., Prague, 2005—. Co-author: (book) Rilke and Kraus and Vrchotovy J., 1985, (catalogue) Catalog incunabula in Castle Libraries, 1992, 2001; editor: Sborník Národního muzea-rada C-literární historie, 1990—. Mem coun Friends Old Prague, 1963—, Soc R M Rilke, 1992—. Mem.: Literary Sci Soc Sci Acad Czech Republic, Spolecnost Národního muzea, Asn Librarians. Roman Catholic. Avocations: history of Prague, art. Office: Knihovna Národni muzeum Václavské náměsti 68 115 79 Prague 1 Czech Republic Home Phone: 00420 251512010; Office Phone: 00420 224497368. Business E-Mail: helga_turkova@nm.cz.

TURKUS, ALBERT H., lawyer; b. Newark, 1945; BS cum laude, U. Pa., 1967; JD, Harvard U., 1971. Bar: D.C. 1971, Md. 1978. Asst. U.S. atty. U.S. Attys. Office, Washington, 1972-78; ptnr. Dow, Lohnes & Albertson, Washington; mem. Skadden, Arps, Slate, Meagher & Flom LLP, Wash., DC, 1994, ptnr. Named one of Wash. DC's top 10 lawyers, by Washingtonian mag., 1992, Am. Leading Lawyers Bus., by Chambers USA, 2006; recipient US Atty. Gen's. Spl. Achievement award, 1975. Mem.: fellow Am. Coll. Trial Lawyers 1995-. Office: Skadden Arps Slate Meagher & Flom LLP 1440 NY Ave NW Washington DC 20005 Office Phone: 202-371-7360. Office Fax: 202-371-7891. Business E-Mail: aturkus@skadden.com.

TURLEY, J. WILLIAM, lawyer; b. Van Nuys, Calif., Jan. 11, 1948; s. Billy Brown and Kathryn Ann Turley; children: Timothy Jay, Damon Andrew, William Ross. BA, U. Mo., 1970, JD, 1974. Bar: Mo. 1974, U.S. Dist. Ct. (we. dist.) Mo. 1974. Stockholder Wesner, Turley & Kempton, Inc., Sedalia, Mo., 1975-84; ptnr. Carnahan, Carnahan & Turley, Rolla, Mo., 1984-87, ptnr. Williams, Robinson, Turley, & White, 1987-96; sr. counsel Shelter Ins. Cos., 1996—. Author: Trial Handbook for Missouri Lawyers, 1984; contbr. articles to profl. jours.; v.p. Mo. Lawyer's Trust Acct. Found., 1990. Mem. Mo. Bar Assn. (bd. govs. 1986-96, exec. com. 1989-90), Assn. Trial Lawyers Am. (bd. govs. 1985-89), Mo. Assn. Trial Attys. (pres. 1985). Home: 2626 Huntleigh Pl Jefferson City MO 65109 Office: Shelter Ins Cos 1817 W Broadway Columbia MO 65218 Home Phone: 573-761-0673; Office Phone: 573-214-4110. Personal E-mail: jwturley@hotmail.com. Business E-Mail: bturley@shelterinsurance.com.

TURLEY, JAMES S., corporate financial executive; m. Lynn Turley; 1 child, Jay. BS in Economics and Managerial Studies, Rice U., 1977, MS in Acctg., 1978. With Ernst & Young, Houston, 1977—79, St. Louis, 1979—87, US nat. dir. client services and bus. devel. NYC, 1987—90, coord. ptnr. St. Louis, 1991—93, area dir. entrepreneurial svcs., 1993—94, mng. ptnr. upper midwest area, 1994—98, met. NY area mng. ptnr. NYC, 1998—2000; dep. global chair Ernst & Young Internat., NYC, 2000—01, global chair, 2001—, global CEO, 2003—. Mem. Bus. Roundtable, Com. to Encourage Corp. Philanthropy, Transatlantic Bus. Dialog; co-chmn. adv. council Russia Fgn. Investment. Bd. dirs. Boy Scouts of Am., Catalyst; v.p. bd. dirs. Nat. Corp. Theater Fund; mem. nat. leadership coun. Character Edn. Partnership. Avocations: golf, tennis. Office: Ernst & Young 5 Times Sq New York NY 10036 *

TURLEY, LINDA, lawyer; b. Altus, Okla., July 16, 1958; d. Windle and Shirley (Lacey) Turley; 1 child, Lacey. BS, Georgetown U., 1980; JD with honors, U. Tex., 1983. Bar: Tex. 1983; bd. cert. in personal injury trial law. Atty., head product liability dept. Law Offices of Windle Turley, P.C., Dallas, 1986-95; personal injury trial lawyer Turley Law Firm, 2001—05; ptnr. Turley & Stutz, P.C., Dallas, 1997—2001; with Turley Law Firm, 2006—. Mem. task force on Tex. rules of civil procedure Tex. Supreme Ct., 1992-93. Mem. ATLA (bd. govs. 1993-96, chair women trial lawyers' caucus 1989-90, chair product liability sect. 1996-97), Am. Bd. Trial Advocates, Tex. Trial Lawyers Assn. (bd. dirs. 1989—). Office: 1000 Turley Law Ctr 6440 N Central Expy Dallas TX 75206 Office Phone: 214-691-4025. Business E-Mail: lindat@wturley.com.

TURLEY, MICHAEL ROY, lawyer; b. St. Louis, Mar. 7, 1945; s. W. Richard and Mary Jeanne (Ogle) T.; m. Patricia Ederle, Aug. 21, 1968; children: James, Alisyn. AB, Princeton U., 1967; JD, Mo. U., 1970. Bar: Mo. 1970, U.S. Dist. Ct. (ea. dist.) Mo. 1975. Assoc. Lewis, Rice & Fingersh (formerly Lewis & Rice), St. Louis, 1970-71, 74-80, ptnr., 1980—. Mem. Jefferson County Planning and Zoning Commn., 1987—2000; chmn., sec.-treas. Ctr. for Emerging Techs. Mem. ABA, Mo. Bar Assn., St. Louis Met. Bar Assn., Princeton Club. Episcopalian. Office: Lewis Rice & Fingersh 500 N Broadway Ste 2000 Saint Louis MO 63102-2147 E-mail: mturley@lewisrice.com.

TURLEY, ROBERT JOE, lawyer; b. Mt. Sterling, Ky., Dec. 6, 1926; s. R. Joe and Mavis Clare (Sternberg) T.; m. Mary Lynn Sanders, Dec. 17, 1948 (dv.); children: Leighton Turley Isaacs, Lynn Turley McComas, R. Joe, Mavis Lee Turley Scully. Student, Berea Coll., 1944-45, St. Mary's Coll., Calif., 1945-46; LLB, U. Ky., 1949. Bar: Ky. 1949, U.S. Dist. Ct. (ea. dist.) Ky. 1950, U.S. Supreme Ct. 1959. Ptnr. Mooney & Turley and successor firms, Lexington, Ky., 1949-84, Turley & Moore, Lexington, 1984-89, of counsel, 1989-93, Savage, Elliott, Houlihan, Moore, Mullins & Skidmore, Lexington, 2004—. Chmn. Fed. Jud. Selection Commn. Ky., 1985-89; gen counsel Shriners Hosps. for Children, 1976-77, trustee, 1981-90, emeritus trustee, 1990—; mem. exec. coun. and character first! edn. program team Character Coun. Ctrl. Ky., 2002—; mem. devel. team Lexington Leadership Found., 2001—. Author: The Choices Are Yours, 1997, The Bridge of Faith, 2000; contbr. articles to legal jours. Active duty USN, 1944-46, USNR, 1946-59. Diplomate Nat. Bd. Trial Advocacy, 1980. Fellow Am. Coll. Trial Lawyers, Ky. Bar Found. (life); mem. Ky. Bar Assn. (sr. counselor, ethics com. 1998—, Outstanding Lawyer award 2001), Christian Legal Soc., The Federalist Soc., St. Ives Jour. Club, Masons, Shriners. Home: 217 Fontaine Cir Lexington KY 40502

TURLEY, STEWART, retired retail company executive; b. Mt. Sterling, Ky., July 20, 1934; s. R. Joe and Mavis S. Turley; children from previous marriage: Carol Cohen, Karen Shockley; m. Linda A. Mulholland; stepchildren: Kathleen Smiley, Kristine Johnson. Student, Rollins Coll., 1952-53, U. Ky., 1953-55. Plant mgr. Crown Cork & Seal Co., Orlando (Fla.), Phila., 1955-66; mgr. non-drug ops., dir. corporate employee rels. and spl. svcs. Eckerd Corp. (formerly Jack Eckerd Corp.), Clearwater, Fla., 1966-68; v.p. Eckerd Corp., Clearwater, Fla., 1968-71, sr. v.p., 1971-74, dir., 1971-97, pres., chief exec. officer, 1974-96, chmn. bd., 1975-97. Bd. dirs. WCI Cmtys., Inc. Past chmn. U.S. Ski Team Found.; bd. dirs. Vilar Ctr. Found., Vail Valley Found., Steadman-Hawkins Sports Medicine Found., Eckerd Youth Alternatives, Inc. Mem. Nat. Assn. Chain Drug Stores (bd. dirs., chmn. bd. 1978-79, 88-89), Fla. Coun. 100 (past chmn.), Chief Execs. Orgn., Carlouel Yacht Club, Belleair Country Club, Eagle Springs Golf Club, Kappa Alpha. Office: 1465 S Fort Harrison Ave Clearwater FL 33756-2505

TURLEY, SUSAN LYNN WELKER, military officer; b. Dudley Struan and Marilyn Post Welker; m. Ernest Carl Turley, Aug. 24, 1984; children: Jared Carl, Robert Carl, Cody Carl. AA in Journalism, Ea. Ariz. Coll., Thatcher, 1980; BA in Journalism, U. Ariz., Tucson, 1983; JD, U. Tex. Sch. of Law, 1995; LLM, Judge Adv. General's Sch. of the Army, 2002. Admitted to Practice: US Supreme Ct. 2002, US Ct. of Appeals for the Armed Forces 1995, Supreme Ct. of Tex. 1995. Missile launch officer 351st Strategic Missile Wing, Whiteman AFB, Mo., 1988—92; polit. reporter, bus. editor Cox Ariz. Publs., Mesa, Ariz., 1983—85; nat. editor Latter-Day Sentinel, Phoenix, 1985—87; chief civil law and adverse actions 30th Space Wing Staff Judge Adv.'s Office, Vandenberg AFB, Calif., 1995—97; area def. counsel Air Force Legal Svcs. Agy., Western Circuit, Vandenberg AFB, 1997—99; dep. staff judge adv. 36th Air Base Wing Staff Judge Adv.'s Office, Andersen AFB, 1999—2001; acquisition atty. Air Force Materiel Command Law Office, Wright-Patterson AFB, Ohio, 2002—03; staff judge adv. Hdqs. Ops. and Sustainment Sys. Group, Maxwell-Gunter AFB, Ala., 2004—06; dep. staff judge adv. Hdqs. Air U., Maxwell AFB, Ala., 2006—. Acting pub. affairs officer Hdqs. Ops. and Sustainment Systems Group, Maxwell-Gunter Air Force Base, Ala., 2004—05. Author: (book review) Military Law Review; associate editor (journal) Texas Law Review. Merit badge advisor, instr. Boy Scouts of Am., Montgomery, Ala., 2004—06; media rels. asst. Ch. of Jesus Christ of Latter-day Saints, Montgomery, Ala., 2005—06, edn. counselor, women's group Prattville, Ala., 2005—06. Lt. col. USAF, 1987—2006. Decorated Crew Mem. Excellence award Eighth Air Force, Disting. Grad. U.S. Air Force Officer Tng. Sch.; recipient Outstanding Career Armed Services Atty. award, Judge Advocates Assn., 2005, Disting. Honor Grad., Judge Adv. General's Sch. of the Army, 2002, Award for Profl. Merit, ABA, 2002, Achievement award, Bus. Associations, Real Estate Transactions, U. of Tex. Sch. of Law, 1994. Mem.: FBA, Jr. Mgmt. Assn. (chair, bd. of sr. adv. 2004—06), Montgomery Chpt. (exec. com. mem. 2004—). Mem. Lds Ch. Home: 5351 Jane Rd Millbrook AL 36054 Office: Maxwell AFB 50 LeMay Plz Montgomery AL 36112

TURNAGE, FRED DOUGLAS, retired lawyer; b. Ayden, NC, Sept. 24, 1920; s. Fred C. and Lou (Johnson) T.; m. Margaret Futrell, Aug. 21, 1943 (div. Nov. 1980); children: Betty Lou Griffith, Douglas C.; m. Elizabeth Louisa Turnage, Jan. 23, 1981. Grad. Naval Sch. on Far Eastern Civil Affairs, Princeton U., 1945; LLB, Wake Forest U., 1948, LLD, 1970. Bar: N.C. 1948, U.S. Supreme Ct. 1953, U.S. Dist. Ct. D.C. 1965, U.S. Ct. Appeals (D.C. cir.) 1967, U.S. Ct. Appeals (4th and 7th cirs.) 1979. Trial atty. antitrust div. U.S. Dept. Justice, Kansas City, Mo., 1948-51, sr. trial atty. antitrust div. Washington, 1951-65, spl. asst. to atty. gen., 1965; sr. ptnr. Cleary, Gottlieb, Steen & Hamilton, Washington, 1968—, counsel, 1990—2004, ret., 2004. Lectr. continuing legal edn. courses, 1973-77. Contbr. articles to profl. jours. Bd. Visitors Wake Forest U. Sch. Law, Winston-Salem, N.C., 1980—. Served to 1st lt. AUS, 1942-46. Recipient Disting. Service in Law citation Wake Forest U., 1979. Mem. ABA (antitrust and litigation sects.), Fed. Bar Assn., Adv. Bd. Antitrust Bulletin, Wake Forest U. Alumni Assn. (pres. 1977), Nat. Lawyers Clubs. Methodist. Avocations: fishing, golf, writing.

TURNAGE, JEAN ALLEN, retired state supreme court chief justice; b. St. Ignatius, Mont., Mar. 10, 1926; JD, Mont. State U., 1951; D of Laws and Letters (hon.), U. Mont., 1995. Bar: Mont. 1951, US Supreme Ct. 1963. Former ptnr. Turnage, McNeil & Mercer, Polson, Mont.; former Mont. State senator from 13th Dist.; pres. Mont. State Senate, 1981—85; chief justice Supreme Ct. Mont., 1985-2001. Mem. Mont. State Bar Assn., Nat. Conf. Chief Justices (past pres.), Nat. Ctr. State Courts (past chair). Office: Turnage & Mercer PO Box 460 Polson MT 59860 Home Phone: 406-883-9329; Office Phone: 406-883-5367. Personal E-mail: jeanturnage@centurytel.net.

TURNAGE, MARTHA ALLEN, academic administrator; b. Wake County, NC, May 23, 1922; d. Charles Nicholas and Lona (Williams) Allen; widowed; children: Sherrod, Barbara, Russell, Charles. BA, Wake Forest U., Winston-Salem, NC, 1944; MA, Coll. William and Mary, Williamsburg, Va., 1970; EdD, Va. Inst. Tech., 1978. Dir. learning resources Va. Highlands C.C., Abingdon, 1970—71; dean students and cmty. svc. Mountain Empire C.C., Big Stone Gap, Va., 1971-73; dean cmty. devel. J. Sargeant Reynolds CC, Richmond, Va., 1974-76; exec. asst. to pres. Bluefield State Coll., W.Va., 1976-77; lifelong learning project dir. Am. Assn. Cmty. & Jr. Colls., Washington, 1978; v.p. external affairs and govt. rels. George Mason U., Fairfax, Va., 1978-84; v.p. for univ. rels. Ohio U., Athens, 1984-92; ret., 1992. Author: Company Town Shutdown, 1994. Founder Job Preparedness Ctr., Saltville, Va., 1970—71; vol. Colonial Nat. Pk., Yorktown, Va., 2003—; mem. Northwest Ordinance Bicentennial Commn., Ohio, 1987. Mem. Phi Beta Kappa, Phi Kappa Phi. Democrat. Methodist. Home: 3800 Treyburn Dr Apt B122 Williamsburg VA 23185-6410

TURNAU, VIVIAN WILLIAMSON, retired literature and language educator; b. NYC, Apr. 16, 1957; d. Albin Creo and Elizabeth Chaffers Williamson; m. Roger William Turnau, Apr. 1 (dec.); children: Theodore Arthur III, Roger Williamson. BA in French Edn., Russell Sage Coll., Troy, NY, 1958; cert. French studies, U. Lausanne, Switzerland, 1959; MA in Spanish, State U. Pa., Millersville, 1995; postgrad., U. N.C., Greensboro, 2003. Adminstrv. asst. United Way Berks County, Reading, Pa., 1988—90; tchr. Spanish and ESL Reading Area C.C., 1991—93; tchr. French and Spanish Wyomissing Sch. Dist., Pa., 1990—94, Bishop Wood H.S., Warminster, Pa., 1994; tchr. Spanish Salem Acad., Winston-Salem, NC, 1995—96; ret., 1997; tutor YMCA, Winston-Salem, 1999—2006; substitute tchr. Summit Sch., Winston-Salem, 2004—05. Exch. fellow, Inst. Internat. Edn., 1958—59. Personal E-mail: vturnau@triad.rr.com.

TURNBAUGH, CHARLES W., state agency administrator; BA, Western Md. Coll.; JD, U. Md. Sch. Law. Legal and managerial positions Comml. Credit. Co.; dir. govt. affairs Citibank, v.p., gen. counsel Md.; sr. v.p., gen. counsel Loyola Fed. Savings Bank; first v.p., counsel MBNA Am. Bank, N.A.; commr. Md. Divsn. Fin. Regulation, 2003—. Office: Dept Labor Licensing and Regulation Commr Fin Regulation 500 N Calvert St Ste 402 Baltimore MD 21202 Office Phone: 410-230-6100. Office Fax: 410-333-3866.

TURNBAUGH, WILLIAM ARTHUR, archaeologist, educator; b. Williamsport, Pa., June 1, 1948; s. William Hugh and Louise Elizabeth (Muller) Turnbaugh; m. Sarah Ropes Peabody, Oct. 12, 1974. BA in History summa cum laude, Lycoming Coll., 1970, LHD (hon.), 2006; PhD in Anthropology, Harvard U., 1973. Accredited mem. Register Profl. Archaeologists. Curator of archaeology Lycoming County Mus., Williamsport, 1968-70; tchg. fellow, dept. anthropology Harvard U., Cambridge, Mass., 1971-72, asst. to dir. Peabody Mus., 1973-74; asst. prof. anthropology U. R.I., Kingston, 1974-78, assoc. prof. anthropology, 1978-83, prof. anthropology, 1983—2006, prof. emeritus, 2006—. Ind. contracting archaeologist ea. U.S. and Can., 1968—74; dir. U. R.I. Mus., 1975—77; adv. bd. Inst. Conservation Archaeology, Cambridge, 1976—83. Author: Man, Land and Time, 1975, Material Culture of RI-1000, 1984; co-author: Indian Baskets, 1986, rev. edit., 2004, R.F.D. Country!, 1988, Indian Jewelry of the American Southwest, 1988, rev. edit., 2006, Basket Tales of the Grandmothers, 1999, Understanding Physical Anthropology & Archaeology, 1981, 8th edit., 2002; assoc. editor: Historical Archaeology, 1986—; contbr. articles to profl. jours., chapters to books. V.p., acting pres. Lycoming County Hist. Soc., Williamsport, 1968—70; designed ofcl. flag Lycoming County, Pa., 1970. Recipient Archie award, Soc. Pa. Archaeology, 1967, J. Alden Mason award, 1988; fellow NSF, 1970—73, Woodrow Wilson Found., 1970—71. Fellow: Explorers Club; mem.: Soc. Hist. Archaeology, Soc. Am. Archaeology, Sigma Xi, Phi Alpha Theta, Phi Kappa Phi. Unitarian Universalist. Avocations: travel, geology, American history. Office: Univ RI Dept Sociol and Anthropol Kingston RI 02881 Business E-Mail: wtu4496u@postoffice.uri.edu.

TURNBULL, ANN PATTERSON, special education educator, consultant, research director; b. Tuscaloosa, Ala., Oct. 19, 1947; d. H. F. and Mary (Boone) Patterson; m. H. Rutherford Turnbull III, Mar. 23, 1974; children: Jay, Amy, Kate. BS in Edn., U. Ga., 1968; MEd, Auburn U., 1971; EdD, U. Ala., 1972. Asst. prof. U. N.C., Chapel Hill, 1972-80; disting. prof., co-dir. Beach Ctr. U. Kans., Lawrence, 1980—. Author: Free Appropriate Public Education, 2000, Exceptional Lives: Special Education in Today's Schools, 2004, Families, Professionals and Exceptionality, 2006. Recipient Rose Kennedy Internat. Leadership award, Kennedy Found., 1990, 20th Century award in Mental Retardation, 1999; Joseph P. Kennedy Jr. Found. fellow, 1987-88. Mem.: The Arc-U.S. (named Educator of Yr. 1982), Am. Assn. on Mental Retardation (bd. dirs. 1986—88, v.p. 2001, pres.-elect 2002, pres. 2003—04, Rsch. award 2004). Democrat. Avocations: travel, exercise. Office: Univ Kans Beach Ctr 3136 1200 Sunnyside Dr Lawrence KS 66045-7534 Home: 730 New Hampshire St Ste 3K Lawrence KS 66044 Home Phone: 785-843-9500; Office Phone: 785-864-7608. E-mail: turnbull@ku.edu.

TURNBULL, CHARLES WESLEY, former governor; b. St. Thomas, V.I., Feb. 5, 1935; BS, Hampton U., 1958, MS, 1959; PhD, U. Minn., 1976. Elem., sec. sch. tchr.; prin. Charlotte Amalie H.S.; from asst. commr. to commr. V.I. Dept. Edn.; prof. history U. V.I.; gov. U.S. V.I., Charlotte Amalie, 1999—2007. Chair V.I. Bd. Edn.; bd. dirs. U. V.I., Roy Lester Schneider Hosp.; chmn., Public Fin. Authority. Democrat. Methodist. Office: PO Box 302265 St Thomas VI 00803

TURNBULL, H. RUTHERFORD, III, lawyer, educator; b. NYC, Sept. 22, 1937; s. Henry R. and Ruth (White) T.; m. Mary M. Slingluff, Apr. 4, 1964 (div. 1972); m. Ann Patterson, Mar. 23, 1974; children: Jay, Amy, Katherine. Grad., Kent (Conn.) Sch., 1955; BA, Johns Hopkins U., 1959; LLB with honors, U. Md., 1964; LLM, Harvard U., 1969. Bar: Md., N.C. Law clk. to Hon. Emory H. Niles Supreme Bench Balt. City, 1959-60; law clk. to Hon. Roszel C. Thomsen U.S. Dist. Ct. Md., 1962-63; assoc. Piper & Marbury (now LDA Piper), Balt., 1964-67; prof. Sch. Govt. U. N.C., Chapel Hill, 1969—80, U. Kans., Lawrence, 1980—. Disting. prof. spl.

edn., courtesy prof. law U. Kans. Editor-in-chief Md. Law Rev. Cons., author, lectr., co-founder, co-dir. Beach Ctr. on Disability, U. Kans.; pres. Full Citizenship Inc., Lawrence, 1987-93; spl. staff-fellow U.S. Senate subcom. on disability policy, Washington, 1987-88; bd. dirs. Camphill Assn. N.Am., Inc., 1985-87; trustee Judge David L. Bazelon Ctr. Mental Health Law, 1993-2007, chmn., 2000-05. With US Army, 1960-65. Recipient Nat. Leadership award Nat. Assn. Pvt. Residential Resources, 1988, Internat. Coun. for Exceptional Children, 1996, Am. Assn. on Mental Retardation, 1997, Century award Nat. Trust for Hist. Preservation in Mental Retardation, 1999, Nat. Adv. award Am. Music Therapy Assn., 2002, Leadership award Camphill Assn. N.Am., 2004, Leadership award The Arc of the US, 2004, U. Kans. Gene A. Budig Disting. Tchg. Professorship award, 2005, Nat. award advocacy positive supports Assn. Persons with Severe Handicaps, 2005, Kans.U. Sch. of Edn. Disting. Leadership award, 2005, Burton Blatt award Coun. Exceptional Children, 2006; named Nat. Educator of Yr., The Arc of the U.S., 1982; Pub. Policy fellow Joseph P. Kennedy, Jr. Found., 1987-88. Fellow Am. Assn. on Mental Retardation (pres. 1985-86, bd. dirs. 1980-86); mem. ABA (chmn. disability law commn. 1991-95), U.S.A. Assn. for Retarded Citizens (sec. and dir. 1981-83), Assn. for Persons with Severe Handicaps (treas. 1988, bd. dirs. 1987-90), Nat. Assn. Rehab. Rsch. and Tng. Ctrs. (chair govt. affairs com. 1990-93), Internat. Assn. Sci. Study of Mental Deficiency, Internat. League of Assns. for Persons with Mental Handicaps, Johns Hopkins U. Alumni Assn. (pres. N.C. chpt. 1977-79). Democrat. Episcopalian. Office: U Kans 3111 Haworth Hall 1200 Sunnyside Ave Lawrence KS 66045-7534 Office Phone: 785-864-7600. Business E-Mail: Rud@ku.edu.

TURNBULL, JOHN CAMERON, retired pharmacist, consultant; b. Regina, Sask., Can., Sept. 5, 1923; s. Cameron Joseph and Lillian Irene (Pentz) T.; m. Hazel Evelyn Rockwell, July 31, 1948; children: Lillian Elizabeth, John Rockwell, Jocelyn Hazel. BS in Pharmacy, U. Sask., 1949. Pharmacist with village and city pharmacies, 1945-50; supr. pharm. services Dept. Pub. Health, Sask., Regina, 1950-52; ops. mgr. Nat. Drugs, Ltd., Winnipeg, and Saskatoon, 1953; exec. dir. Can. Pharm. Assn., Toronto, Ont., 1953-78; ret. Sec.-treas., mng. dir. Canadian Pharm. Realty Co. Ltd.; mem. provisional bd. Pharmacare Ltd.; registrar-treas. Pharmacy Examining Bd. of Can., 1963-68, mem. bd., 1963-78; pharmacy cons., dir. drug service Ministry of Health, Barbados, 1979-84; staff assoc. Mgmt. Scis. for Health, Boston, 1984-85; cons. logistics and pharms. USAID, East Caribbean, PanAm. Health Orgn./WHO (Belize, Cen. Am.), 1985—. Chmn. Govt.'s Spl. Com. on Acetylsalicylic Poisonings, 1967; mem. Emergency Health Svcs. Adv. Com.; gen. chmn. Allied Air Forces Reunion, 1995, 96. Served to squadron leader RCAF, 1941-45. Decorated D.F.C., 1944, Order of Can., 1975; recipient Can. Centennial medal, 1967, Queen's Jubilee medal, 1977, Can. 125th Anniversary medal, 1992, John C. Turnbull rsch. ann. award in socio-econs. pharmacy established in his honor Can. Pharm. Assn., 1990. Mem. Fedn. Internationale Pharmaceutique (v.p.), Inst. of Assn. Execs. (hon. life), Conf. of Pharmacy Registrars of Can. (sec.), Commonwealth Pharm. Assn. (coun. 1969-78); hon. mem. Am., Canadian, Saskatchewan, B.C., Alta., Ont., Man., N.S. Pharm. Assns., Sask. Pharm. Assn., Ont. Pharmacists Assn., Canadian Soc. Hosp. Pharmacists, Rho Pi Phi. Mem. United Ch. of Canada. Club: Bayview Country (past dir.). Office: John and Hazel Turnbull 303-15 Barberry Pl Toronto ON Ontario Canada M2K 1G9 Office Phone: 416-222-4086.

TURNBULL, LOWELL D., lawyer; b. Albany, NY, Sept. 16, 1947; s. David and Carol May (Cornell) T.; m. Randi Jay Greenwald, Feb. 15, 1981; children: Ian David, Derek Jay. BA magna cum laude, Harvard U., 1969, JD magna cum laude, 1972. Bar: DC 1973, Commonwealth Va. 2001. Assoc. Leva, Hawes, Symington, Martin & Oppenheimer, Washington, 1972-79, ptnr., 1980-83, Leva, Hawes, Symington & Martin, Washington, 1983-85, Leva, Hawes, Mason & Martin, Washington, 1985-90, Robins, Kaplan, Miller & Ciresi, Washington, 1990-93; mng. dir. Ackerson & Bishop, Washington, 1993, Simon, Turnbull & Martin, Chartered, Wash., 1994; owner Garvey Schubert Barer, Wash., DC. Mem. DC, Va., ABA, Internat. Club, Harvard Law Sch. Assn. Wash. (pres. 1988-89), Phi Beta Kappa. Avocations: biking, hiking, travel. Office: Garvey Schubert Barer 1000 Potomac St NW 5th Fl Flour Mill Bldg Washington DC 20007 Office Phone: 202-298-2531. Office Fax: 202-965-1729. Business E-Mail: lturnbull@gsblaw.com.

TURNBULL, THOMAS LEIGH, social studies educator, secondary school educator; b. Bronxville, NY, Mar. 2, 1951; s. Kenneth Hamilton and Carolyn Mays Turnbull; 1 child, Sarah McCurrach. BA, U. Calif., Berkeley, Calif., 1983; MA, San Francisco State U., Calif., 1987. Tchr. San Ramon Valley H.S., Danville, Calif., 1986—87, Ygnacio Valley H.S., Concord, Calif., 1993—94, Acalanes H.S., Lafayette, Calif., 1994—95, Clayton Valley H.S., Concord, 1996—. Home: 10 Park Ave Walnut Creek CA 94595 Office: Clayton Valley High Sch 1101 Alberta Way Concord CA 94521-3799 Office Phone: 925-682-7474.

TURNBULL, VERNONA HARMSEN, retired education educator, counseling administrator; b. Teeds Grove, Iowa, Dec. 6, 1916; d. Henry Ferdinand and Ida Amelia (Dohrmann) Harmsen; m. Alexander Turnbull, Oct. 12, 1961. BA, Cornell Coll., Mt. Vernon, Iowa, 1939; MEd, U. Colo., Boulder, 1947, profl. cert. edn., 1955. Cert. secondary and h.s. tchr. Tchr. English, Latin and phys. edn. Winslow H.S., Ill., 1939-45; dir. women's activities, instr. Trinidad State Jr. Coll., Colo., 1947-53; counselor women, assoc. prof. edn. Western State Coll., Gunnison, Colo., 1953-54; instr., residence counselor Stephens Coll., Columbia, Mo., 1955-61; ret., 1961. Active Salvation Army Aux. Mem. AAUW, AARP (corr. sec. 1986-87), Kena Kampers Camping Club. Avocations: photography, camping, art, dance, baking.

TURNDORF, HERMAN, anesthesiologist, educator; b. Paterson, NJ, Dec. 22, 1930; s. Charles R. and Ruth (Blumberg) T.; m. Sietske Huisman, Nov. 24, 1957; children: David, Michael Pieter. AB, Oberlin Coll., 1952; MD, U. Pa., 1956. Diplomate Am. Bd. Anesthesiology. Instr. anesthesiology U. Pa. Hosp., 1957-59; asst. anesthetist med. sch. Harvard U., Mass. Gen. Hosp., Boston, 1961-63; assoc. attending anesthesiologist, asst. dir. dept. anesthesiology Mt. Sinai Hosp., NYC, 1963-70, clin. prof. anesthesiology, 1966-70; prof., chmn. dept. anesthesiology W.Va. U. Sch. Medicine and Med. Ctr., Morgantown, 1970-74, NYU Sch. Medicine, 1974—2000; dir. anesthesiology NYU Tisch Hosp., Bellevue Hosp. Ctr., 1974—2000; pres. med. bd., med. dir. Bellevue Hosp. Med. Ctr., 1990—91, 1997; ret., 2000. Co-author: Anesthesia and Neurosurgery, 2nd edit., 1986, Trauma, Anesthesia and Intensive Care, 1990; contbr. over 200 articles to profl. jours. Lt. M.C., USNR, 1959-61. Fellow Am. Coll. Chest Physicians, Am. Coll. Anesthesiologists (mem. bd. govs. 1977-85, chmn. bd. govs. 1984), N.Y. Acad. Medicine; mem. AMA, Am. Soc. Anesthesiologists, Assn. Univ. Anesthetists, Internat. Soc. Study of Pain, Soc. Acad. Anesthesia Chairmen, Soc. Critical Care Medicine, Soc. Neurosurg. Anesthesia and Neurologic Supportive Care, N.Y. Acad. Scis., N.Y. State Soc. Anesthesiologists. Personal E-mail: hermanturndorf@bellsouth.net.

TURNDORF, JAMIE, psychotherapist; b. Boston, July 12, 1958; d. Gary Owen and Sharon (Sandow) Turndorf; m. Emile Jean Pin, Jan. 2, 1988. AB in Am. Culture, Vassar Coll., Poughkeepsie, NY, 1980; MSW, Adelphi U., Garden City, NY, 1983; PhD, Calif. Coast U., 1994. Lic. clin. social worker N.Y. Pvt. practice psychotherapy, NYC and Millbrook, NY, 1981—. Lead creative movement and psychodrama program Lincoln Farms Work Camp, Roscoe, NY, 1976; with Astor Child Guidance Clinic, Poughkeepsie, NY, 1982—83; leader various groups Craig House Hosp., Beacon, NY, 1982—87, developer, dir. eating disorders program, 1984—86; founder, dir. INC.TIMACY, 1990—, J. T. Developers, Inc., Poughkeepsie, 1983—91; dir. Hudson Valley br. Ctr. Advancement Group Studies, Ctr. Emotional Comm., Millbrook, NY, 1990—. Author (with Emile Jean Pin): The Pleasure of Your Company: A Socio-Psychological Analysis of Modern Sociability, 1985; author: Till Death Do Us Part (Unless I Kill You First): A Step-by-Step Guide to Resolving Relationship Conflict, 2007; columnist: Dr. Love various newspapers and web-site (award); host Ask Dr. Love, Sta. WEVD, N.Y.C., 1992, creator, inventor LoveQuest: The Game of Finding Mr. Right, 1990 (One of the Best New Games award Fun and Games mag., 1991). Mem.: NASW. Avocations: house restoration, opera singing, antiques. Home and Office: PO Box 475 Millbrook NY 12545-0475 Office Phone: 845-677-3450. Personal E-mail: drlove@askdrlove.com.

TURNER, ALICE KENNEDY, editor; b. Mukden, Manchuria; d. William Taylor and Florence Bell (Green) T. BA, Bryn Mawr Coll., 1962. Sr. editor Holiday mag., NYC, 1969-70; assoc. editor Publishers Weekly, NYC, 1972-74; sr. editor Ballantine Books, NYC, 1974-76, New York mag., NYC, 1976-80; fiction editor Playboy mag., Chgo., NYC, 1980—2001. Author: Yoga for Beginners, 1973, The History of Hell, 1993; co-author: The New York Woman's Guide, 1975; editor: Playboy Stories, 1993, The Playboy Book of Science Fiction, 1996; contbg. editor: Playboy Mag., 2001—; co-editor: Snake's-hands: The Fiction of John Crowley, 2002. Home: 2 Charlton St New York NY 10014-4909 Personal E-mail: aktnyc@gmail.com.

TURNER, ALMON RICHARD, retired art historian, educator; b. New Bedford, Mass., July 28, 1932; s. Louis Alexander and Margaret (Mather) T.; m. Jane Beebe; children: Louis Hamilton, David Alexander. AB, Princeton U., 1955, MFA, 1958, PhD, 1959. Instr. in fine arts U. Mich., Ann Arbor, Mich., 1959-60; from instr. to prof. art and archaeology Princeton U., NJ, 1960-68; prof. fine arts Middlebury Coll., Vt., 1968-74, dean faculty Vt., 1970-74; prof. fine arts, pres. Grinnell Coll., Iowa, 1975-79; prof., dir. Inst. Fine Arts NYU, NYC, 1979-82, dean faculty arts and scis., 1982-85, prof. dept. fine arts, 1985-2000, dir. N.Y. Inst. Humanities, 1986-93, Paulette Goddard prof. in arts and humanities, 1994—2000, prof. emeritus, 2000—. Sec. Princeton Project 55, 2002—. Author: Vision of Landscape in Renaissance Italy, 1966, 73, (With G. Andres and J. Hunisak) Art of Florence (L'Art de Florence), 1988 (prix 1989), Inventing Leonardo, 1993, Renaissance Florence: The Invention of a New Art, 1997, La Pietra: Florence, a Family, and a Villa, 2002 Bd. dirs. Pinelands Preservation Alliance, 2007—. Mem. Coll. Art Assn., Century Assn., NJ Audubon Soc. (1st v.p. 1990-93, pres. 1993-96), Phi Beta Kappa. Democrat. Unitarian Universalist. Avocations: birding, photography. Home: PO Box 2322 Cape May NJ 08204-7322

TURNER, AMY, music educator; s. Michael Dawes and Emmie Manning Turner. BMusEd, Wheaton Coll. Conservatory of Music, Ill., 2002; MusM, Ohio State U., Columbus, 2004. Chorus dir. and camp counselor Blue Lake Fine Arts Camp, Twin Lakes, Mich., 2002; children's choir dir. and organist Winnetka Bible Ch., Ill., 2002—03; chorus and music tchr. Abbott Mid. Sch., Waukegan, 2003; choir dir. Meadowcreek H.S., Norcross, Ga., 2004—. Honors condr. Wheaton Coll. Concert Choir, Ill., 2001—02; pvt. piano tchr., 2003—; mem. Atlanta Sacred Chorale, 2004—; reader Coll. Bd. AP music theory, 2005—06; accompanist Ohio State U. Women's Glee Club, Ohio State U. Chorale, Ohio State U. Mastersingers, Ga. Music Educators Assn. Dist. 13 Honors Chorus. Mem. choir Peachtree Corners Bapt. Ch., Norcross, Ga., 2004—06. Named to Wheaton Coll. Honor Soc., 2003; fellow, Ohio State U. Grad. Sch., 2003—04. Mem.: Music Educators Nat. Conf., Am. Choral Dir. Assn., Phi Kappa Lambda. Avocations: hiking, reading, photography.

TURNER, BEAU (REED BEAUREGARD TURNER), professional sports team owner, philanthropist; s. Ted and Jane Smith Turner; m. Elizabeth Gannon Hunt, Dec. 11, 1999. Grad., The Citadel. Investor Atlanta Spirit, LLC (parent co. of NBA Atlanta Hawks and NHL Atlanta Thrashers). Chmn. bd. trustees Turner Endangered Species Fund; fish and wildlife mgr. Turner Enterprises, Inc.; trustee Turner Found.; bd. dirs. Tall Timbers, Wetlands Am. Trust, Peregrine Fund, Land Trust Alliance, Wildlife Conservation Soc. Mailing: Turner Found Inc 2nd Fl 133 Luckie St NW Atlanta GA 30303 *

TURNER, E. DEANE, lawyer; b. Auburn, NY, Aug. 4, 1928; s. Alfred Edward and Bertha (Deane) T. AB summa cum laude, Princeton U., 1950; LLB cum laude, Harvard U., 1953. Bar: NY 1953. Assoc. Dewey Ballantine LLP and predecessor firms, NYC, 1953-63, ptnr., 1963—, of counsel, 1991—. Treas. Harvard Law Sch. Assn., N.Y.C., 1964-83; elder, trustee Brick Presbyn. Ch., N.Y.C., 1976—, pres. bd. trustees, 1988-90; trustee Presbytery N.Y.C., 1993-98, pres. bd. trustees, 1995-98; com. to adminstr. James N. Jarvie Endowment, 1993-2000. Fellow Am. Coll. Investment Counsel (emeritus); mem. Soc. Mayflower Descendants, Soc. Colonial Wars, Union Club, John's Island Club, Phi Beta Kappa. Republican. Home: 1120 5th Ave New York NY 10128-0144 also: 381 Llwyds Ln Johns Island Vero Beach FL 32963 Office: Dewey Ballantine LLP 1301 Avenue Of The Americas New York NY 10019-6022

TURNER, ELAINE S., allergist, immunologist; b. Glen Cove, NY, 1947; MD, Med. Coll. Pa., 1974. Diplomate Am. Bd. Allergy & Immunology, Am. Bd. Internal Medicine. Intern Michael Reese Hosp., Chgo., 1974-75; resident in internal medicine Cleve. Clinic, 1976-78; fellow in allergy & immunology Northwestern U., Chgo., 1978-80; with St. Mary's Hosp., Va., Henrico Drs. Hosp., Va. Mem. ACP, Am. Acad. Allergy, Asthma and Immunology, Va. Allergy Soc., Richmond Acad. Medicine. Office: Va Adult & Pediat Allergy & Allergy Ste 103 7605 Forest Ave Richmond VA 23229-4936

TURNER, ELIZABETH ADAMS NOBLE (BETTY TURNER), real estate company executive, writer; b. Yonkers, NY, May 18, 1931; d. James Kendrick and Orrel (Baldwin) Noble; m. Jack Rice Turner, July 11, 1953; children: Jay Kendrick, Randall Ray. BA, Vassar Coll., 1953; MA, Tex. A&I U., 1964. Ednl. cons., Tex. sales mgr. Noble & Noble Pub. Co., NYC, 1956-67; psychometrist Corpus Christi Guidance Ctr., 1967-70; psychologist Corpus Christi State Sch., 1970-72, dir. programs, asst. supt., 1972, dir. devel. and vol. svc., 1972-76, dir. rsch. and tng., 1977-79; psychologist Tex. Mental Health and Mental Retardation, 1970-79, program cons., 1979-85; pres. Turner Co., 1975-82; mayor pro tem Corpus Christi, 1981-85; mayor, 1987-91; CEO, pres. Corpus Christi C. of C., 1991-94; pres. Betty Turner Real Estate, 1999—. V.p. bus. and govt. rels. ctrl. and south Tex. divsns. Columbia Healthcare Corp., 1994—99; family co-founder Barnes and Noble, NYC. Author: The Noble Legacy. Bd. dirs. Nat. AARP, 2002—04; coord. vols. Summer Head Start Program, Corpus Christi, 1967; chmn. spl. gifts com. United Way, Corpus Christi, 1970; founder Com. 100, Goals for Corpus Christ, Bay Area Sports Assn., Assn. Coastal Bend Mayor's Alliance, Mayor's Commn. on Disabled, Mayor's Task Force on Homeless; pres. USO; bd. dirs. Coastal Bend Coun. Govts., Corpus Christi Mus., Harbor Playhouse, Cmtys. in Schs., YWCA, Y-Teen Sponsor, Del Mar Coll. Found., 1998—2005, Tex. A&M at Corpus Christi Pres. Coun., Hispanic C. of C., TAMACC Corp. Ptnrs., Salvation Army, Jr. League, Coun. Deaf Silent Found., 2001—, Am. Heart Assn., 1999—2000, Bethune Day Care Nursery, 1999—2004, Jr. League Cmty. Adv. Coun., 1999—2000, 21st Century Charter Sch., 2001—02, Boys and Girls Club Corpus Christi, 2002—05, Food Bank, pres., 2004—05; dir. vols. Adm. Tex. Navy; mem. Gov.'s Commn. Women, 1984—85, Leadership Tex. Class I, Corpus Christi, Class II; fundraising chair Port Aransas Cmty. Theatre; libr. bd. Chartes Rev. Commn.; mem. Corpus Christi City Coun., 1979—91; elder Cmty. Presbyn. Ch., 2004—06; dir. alumni Corpus Christi State U., 1976—77; bd. dirs. Southside Cmty. Hosp., 1987—93; mem. strategic planning com. Meml. Hosp., 1992, Tex. Capital Network Bd., 1992—95, Humana Hosp., Physician Relocation and Condo Sales, Rehab. Hosp.; bd. dirs. St. David's/Austin and Medth. Healthcare Sys., San Antonio, 1997—99; active adv. coun. Sch. Nursing U. Tex., 1998—99; bd. dirs. Pacific Southwest Bank, 1997—2000. Named Corpus Christi News-maker of Yr., 1987; recipient Love award, YWCA, 1970, Y's Women and Men in Careers award, 1988, Recognition award, Rotary, 1991, Comdr.'s award for pub. svc., U.S. Army, Scroll of Honor award, Navy League, award, Tex. Hwy Dept., Road Hand award, Tex. Hwy. Commn., Women of Distinction award, Girl Scouts Tex. Mem.: NAACP (life), Tex. Assn. Realtors, Tex. Bookman's Assn., Tex. Mcpl. League (bd. dirs.), Psychol. Assn. (pres., founder), Tex. Psychol. Assn. (pres., mem. exec. bd.), Jr. League Corpus Christi, Jr. Cotillion Club, Corpus Christi Yacht Club, Corpus Christi Town Club, Kappa Kappa Gamma, Delta Kappa Gamma (hon.). Home: 403 Blue Heron Dr Port Aransas TX 78373 Office Phone: 361-749-5712. Business E-Mail: bettyturner@centurytel.net.

TURNER, ELVIN L., retired school system administrator; b. Springfield, Ohio, Jan. 9, 1938; s. Willie and Jinada (Lawson) T.; 1 child, Anthony; m. Carrie Johnson, Aug. 3, 1972; 1 child, Brenetta Bell. BS in Biology and Chemistry, Knoxville Coll., Tenn., 1962; MEd, U. Cin., 1968; postgrad., Nova U., Ft. Lauderdale, Fla., 1973, Kensington U., Glendale, Calif., 1993—. Cert. secondary prin., tchr., Ohio. Spl. edn. tchr. Cin. Pub. Schs., 1965-69, coord. spl. edn., 1969-72, asst. prin., 1972-78, prin., 1978-90, asst. prin., 1990-93. Part-time adj. prof. Mt. St. Joseph Coll., Ohio, 1987—88; mem. adv. com. Millcreek Psychiat. Ctr. for Children, Cin., 1988—89; bus driver Bristol Village Retirement Cmty., 1997—99; ombudsman Pro-Srs., Cin., 1993—96, Waverly, Ohio, 1997—2005; vol. ombudsman rep. Area Agy. on Aging Dist. Seven, Inc., Portsmouth, Ohio; sec. Bristol Village Residents Assn., 1997. Author: numerous poems. Vol. Ohio Dept Aging, Columbus, 2002—; asst. feeding program Visiting The Sick Ministries; master of ceremonies Black History Month Soul Food Luncheon; elected sec. exec. adv. coun. Bristol Village Nat. Ch. Residencies, Waverly, 1997; bd. deacons New Hope Bapt. Ch., Hamilton, Ohio, 1993; Sunday sch. tchr. Bethel AME Ch., Lebanon, Ohio, 1996; chmn. sick com. Usher Bd.; Bible study course instr. Asbury North United Meth. Ch., Columbus, 2000—01, instr. Vacation Bible Sch., 2000; bd. dirs. Big Bros./Big Sisters, Cin., 1973. Recipient plaque for statewide outstanding sr. vol. radio, TV and newspaper coverage, Independence, Ohio, 2001; named Outstanding Young Man, Montgomery C. of C., 1966. Mem. Nat. Assn. for Secondary Sch. Prins., Ohio Assn. Secondary Sch. Adminstrs., So. Law Poverty Ctr. (named to Wall of Tolerance 2004), Knoxville Coll. Alumni Assn., Phi Delta Kappa (pres. U. Cin. chpt. 1970), Alpha Phi Alpha. Avocations: bowling, golf, reading, travel, writing. Home: PO Box 13617 Columbus OH 43213-0617

TURNER, EUGENE ANDREW, manufacturing executive; b. Bridgeton, NJ, Aug. 7, 1928; s. Benjamin Homer and Pearl Irene (Wolbert) T.; m. Paula Ann Webb, 1987; children: Mary Ann, John-Reed. BA, Rutgers U., 1956; student, Columbia U., 1980. With Owens Ill., 1950-73, regional mgr. West Coast, 1970-73; v.p. adminstrn. Midland Glass Co., Cliffwood, NJ, 1973-76, pres., chief operating officer, 1981-82, also bd. dirs.; v.p., gen. mgr. Anchor Hocking Corp., Lancaster, Ohio, 1976-81; dir. ops. Theo Chem. Labs., Tampa, Fla., 1988-90, Profit Counselors Inc, Sarasota, Fla., 1990-94; pres. Profit Sys. Inc., Oklahoma City, 1994—. Mng. cons. 1987-88; trustee Glass Packaging Inst. Mem. Harbor Island Club, Seaview Country Club, Navesink Country Club. Home: 1103 Tedford Way Oklahoma City OK 73116-6006 Office Phone: 405-209-1103. Personal E-mail: gene227@juno.com. *Take time to learn the chosen business then develop credibility by doing what you say you will do.*

TURNER, FLORENCE FRANCES, ceramist; b. Detroit, Mar. 9, 1926; d. Paul Pokrywka and Catherine Gagal; m. Dwight Robert Turner, Oct. 23, 1948; children: Thomas Michael, Nancy Louise, Richard Scott, Garry Robert. Student, Oakland C.C., Royal Oak, Mich., 1975-85, U. Ariz., Yuma, 1985, U. Las Vegas, 1989—. Pres., founder Nev. Clay Guild, Henderson, 1990-94, mem. adv. bd., 1994-2000, v.p., 2000—02. Workshop leader Greenfield Village, Dearborn, Mich., 1977-78, Plymouth Hist. Soc., Mich., 1979, Las Vegas Sch. System, 1989-90, Detroit Met. area, 1977-85. Bd. dirs. Las Vegas Art Mus., 1987-91; corr. sec. So. Nev. Creative Art Ctr., Las Vegas, 1990-94. Mem.: Nev. Camera Club, Las Vegas Gem Club, Phi Kappa Phi. Avocations: photography, collecting gems, travel.

TURNER, FRANK MILLER, historian, educator; b. Springfield, Ohio, Oct. 31, 1944; s. Ronald O. and Mary Elizabeth (Miller) T.; m. Margaret Good, Aug. 26, 1967 (div. 1981); m. Nancy Rash, July 29, 1984 (dec. Mar. 1995); m. Ellen L. Tillotson, Aug. 7, 1999. BA, Coll. of William and Mary, 1966; MPhil, Yale U., 1970, PhD, 1971; LHD (hon.), Coll. William and Mary, 1991. Asst. prof. Yale U., New Haven, 1972-77, assoc. prof., 1977-82, prof., 1982—, provost, 1988-92, John Hay Whitney prof. history, 1992—, dir., Beinecke Rare Book and Manuscript Libr. Author: Between Science and Religion, 1974, The Greek Heritage in Victorian Britain, 1981, Contesting Cultural Authority: Essays in Victorial Intellectual Life, 1993, Reflections on the Revolution in France, 2003; co-author: The Western Heritage, 1979, 83, 87, 91, 94, 97, 2000, 2003, Heritage of World Civilizations, 1985, 90, 93, 96, 99; editor: John Henry Newman, The Idea of a University, 1996.; contbr. articles to profl. jours. Trustee Conn. Coll., New London, 1996—. Guggenheim fellowship, 1983; recipient Brit. Coun. prize Conf. on Brit. Studies, 1982, Yale Press Gov.'s award, 1983. Office: Yale U History Dept PO Box 208324 New Haven CT 06520-8324 Office Phone: 203-432-1367. E-mail: frank.turner@yale.edu.

TURNER, GEORGE MASON, lawyer; b. Butte, Mont., Sept. 2, 1935; s. William Dale and Bernice (Ownby) T.; m. Angela Gloria Aparicio, Oct. 14, 1995; children: Esther, Lesley, Allyson, Aarin, Alexander. BS in Polit. Sci., Brigham Young U., Provo, Utah, 1959, MS in Polit. Sci., 1960; JD, UCLA, 1968. Bar: Calif. 1969, U.S. Dist. Ct. Calif. 1969, U.S. Supreme Ct. 1976, U.S. Ct. Claims 1981, U.S. Tax Ct. 1981. Assoc. Munns & Kofford, Pasadena, Calif., 1969-72; ptnr. Turner & Smart, Pasadena, 1972-85, The Law Offices of George M. Turner, Pasadena, 1985—; pvt. practice, 1972—. Instr. estate tax law Am. Coll. Bryn Mawr, Pa., 1976; monitor Continuing Edn. of Bar, Calif., 1985. Author: Revocable Trusts, 5th edit., 2003, Irrevocable Trusts, 3d edit., 1997, Revocable Trusts-The Centerpiece of Estate Planning, 2d edit., 2005, Practical Approaches to Estate Planning, 2005. V.p. San Gabriel Valley Boy Scouts Am., Pasadena, 1976-78; pres. San Gabriel Valley Estate Planning Co., Pasadena, 1979-80; bd. dirs., chmn. bd. Calif. Family Study Ctr., North Hollywood, 1975-92, Ettie Lee Homes, Los Angeles, 1984-90. Recipient Silver Beaver award Boy Scout Am., 1979. Mem. ABA, Calif. Bar Assn., Los Angeles Bar Assn., Pi Sigma Alpha. Republican. Mem. Lds Ch. Avocation: photography. Office Phone: 626-795-8491. Personal E-mail: gmt9235@yahoo.com.

TURNER, GINGER L., management science and engineering scholar; b. Tex. d. Jimmy A. T. BA in English, Stanford Univ., 2005, MS in Mgmt. Sci., Engring., 2005; MPhil. student in Internat. Rels, Oxford Univ., 2007—. Analyst, indsl. policy environment on African firms in off. of chief economist World Bank, Washington, 2005—07. Asia Tech. Initiative fellow in India, 2004, Rhodes Scholar. Achievements include co-founding first HIV/AIDS hotline in Kazakhstan; served as a Haas Public Svc. fellow in S. Africa, researching the feasibility of solar-powered LED lighting in rural areas, 2004; first American to swim from Robben Island to Cape Town, S. Africa. Avocations: ballet, swimming. *

TURNER, HARRY SPENCER, preventive medicine physician, educator; b. Dayton, Ohio, July 25, 1938; s. Eli and Daphne (Cunagin) T.; m. Jan (Fairley) T.; children: Michael, Mary, Daniel. BA, Manchester Coll., North

Manchester, Ind., 1960; MD summa cum laude, Ohio State U., 1963, MS in Preventive Medicine, 1968. Diplomate Am. Bd. Preventive Medicine. Resident in preventive (aerospace) medicine Ohio State U., Columbus, 1966-69, chief resident, 1968-69, clin. asst. prof. dept. preventive medicine, 1969-80, dir. Univ. Health Svc., 1970-80; pvt. practice Dayton, 1980-90; dir. Univ. Health Svc., head team physician U. Ky., Lexington, 1991—2003, prof. preventive medicine and environ. health, 1991—2003, prof. emeritus, 2003, dir. emeritus, 2003; med. dir. Sutton Pl. Behavioral Health, 2003—. Editor: (textbook) History and Practice of College Health, 2002; contbr. articles and papers to profl. jours. and meetings. Bd. dirs. Blue Shield, 1981-86; mem. Cin. Internat. Chorale, 1989-94; mem. Lexington Singers, 1992—2003, Inland Chamber Singers, 2005-. Capt. U.S. Army, 1964-66. Fellow Am. Coll. Preventive Medicine, Am. Coll. Health Assn. (pres. 1980, Ruth Boynton award 1982, Edw. Hitchcock award 1996, Lifetime Achievement award 2003), Alpha Omega Alpha Avocation: music. E-mail: hsturner904@comcast.net.

TURNER, HARRY WOODRUFF, lawyer; b. Blairsville, Pa., May 2, 1939; s. James McKinnie and Dorothy Elizabeth (Tittle) Turner; m. Mary Elizabeth Phelan, Dec. 30, 1972; children: James William, David Woodruff. AB, U. Pitts., 1961; JD, Harvard U., 1964. Bar: Pa. 1965, U.S. Supreme Ct. 1979. Assoc. Kirkpatrick & Lockhart, Gates LLP, Pitts., 1964-71, ptnr., 1971—. Bd. vis. Coll. Arts & Scis. U. Pitts., 1988—2003, chmn. bd. vis. Sch. Info. Scis., 1994—2002, trustee, 1995—2003, bd. visitors Med. Sch., 1995—2002; mem. Fed. Jud. Selection Commn., Pa., 1995—, chmn., 1997—; dir. Foxwall Emergency Med. Svcs., 2007—. Trustee Pitts. Opera, 1993—, pres., 2001—04; trustee, v.p. Torrance (Pa.) State Hosp., 1969—73; chair distbn. com. William L. Benz Found., 1985—; bd. dirs. Am. Heart Assn., Pitts., 1993—2002; mem. Fox Chapel Vol. Fire Dept.; alt. del. Rep. Nat. Conv., Miami, 1968, Houston, 1992, Phila., 2000, Rep. State Com., 1994—; trustee U. Pitts., 1995—2003, Wilson Coll., Chambersburg, Pa., 1978—89, Pitts. Cultural Trust, 2002—04, Foxwall Emergency Med. Svc., 2007—. Mem.: SAR (pres. 1995—96), ABA, Supreme Ct. Hist. Soc., Bar Assn. of Third Cir., Allegheny County Acad. Trial Lawyers, Allegheny County Bar Assn., Internat. Acad. Trial Lawyers, Am. Law Inst., Pa. Bar Assn., Hist. Soc. Western Pa. (trustee 1993—2006, vice chmn. 1999—2003), U. Pitts. Alumni Assn. (pres. 1991—92), Duquesne Club, Fox Chapel Golf Club. Presbyterian. Office: Kirkpatrick & Lockhart Henry W Oliver Bldg 535 Smithfield St Ste 535 Pittsburgh PA 15222 Office Phone: 412-355-6478. Business E-Mail: woodruff.turner@klgates.com.

TURNER, HENRY BROWN, finance company executive, director; b. NYC, Sept. 3, 1936; s. Henry Brown III and Gertrude (Adams) T.; m. Sarah Jean Thomas, June 7, 1958 (div.); children: Laura Eleanor, Steven Bristow, Nancy Carolyn. AB, Duke U., 1958; MBA, Harvard U., 1962. Controller Fin. Corp. of Ariz., Phoenix, 1962-64; treas., dir. corporate planning Star-Kist Foods, Terminal Island, Calif., 1964-67; dir., 1st v.p. Mitchum, Jones & Templeton, Los Angeles, 1967-73; asst. sec. Dept. Commerce, Washington, 1973-74; v.p. fin. N-Ren Corp., Cin., 1975-76; v.p. Oppenheimer & Co., NYC, 1976-78; exec. v.p., mng. dir. corporate fin. Shearson Hayden Stone Inc., NYC, 1978-79; sr. mng. dir. Ardshiel Inc., 1980-81, pres., 1981-93, chmn. emeritus, 1994—. Vis. lectr. U. Va. Sch. of Bus.; bd. dirs. MacDonald & Co., Pembrook Mgmt., Inc., Golden State Vitners, Inc., Cellu-Tissue Corp., Wrangler Four Peaks Ranch, Rio Verde, Ariz. Sponsor Jr. Achievement, 1964-67. Served to lt. USNR, 1958-60. Coll. Men's Club scholar Westfield, N.J., 1954-55 Mem. Fed. Govt. Accountants Assn. (hon.), Duke Washington Club, Omicron Delta Kappa.

TURNER, HUGH JOSEPH, JR., lawyer; b. Paterson, NJ, Oct. 5, 1945; s. Hugh Joseph and Louise (Sullivan) T.; m. Charlene Chiappetta, Feb. 11, 1983. BS, Boston U., 1967; JD, U. Miami, Coral Gables, Fla., 1975. Bar: Fla. 1975, U.S. Dist. Ct. (so., no. and mid. dists.) Fla. 1975, U.S. Ct. Appeals (11th cir.) 1981, U.S. Supreme Ct. 1984. Tchr. Browne & Nichols, Cambridge, Mass., 1968-72; ptnr. Smathers & Thompson, Miami, Fla., 1981-87, Kelley Drye & Warren, Miami, 1987-93, English, McCaughan & O'Bryan, Ft. Lauderdale, 1993—2001, Redgrave & Turner LLP, Boca Raton, Fla., 2001—03, Akerman Senterfitt, Ft. Lauderdale, 2003—. Chmn. Fla. Bar internat. law sect., 1988-89. Contbg. author book on internat. dispute resolution Fla. Bar, 1989; contbr. articles to profl. jours. Bd. dirs. Japan Soc. South Fla., Miami, 1989-97; mem. Sea Ranch Lakes Village Coun., 1997-2000; mayor Sea Ranch Lakes, 2000-02. Mem.: ABA, Def. Rsch. Inst. Avocation: running. Office: Akerman Senterfitt Ste 1600 350 E Las Olas Blvd Fort Lauderdale FL 33301-2229 Home Phone: 954-942-8073; Office Phone: 954-463-2700. Business E-Mail: hugh.turner@akerman.com.

TURNER, JACKSON PARKS, financial company executive; b. Oct. 28, 1924; Pres. Cabin Crafts, Inc., Dalton, Ga., 1946-70; chmn. bd. First Nat. Bank, Dalton, 1970-80, Ga. Ports Authority, Savannah, 1976-86, CC Fin., Inc., Dalton, 1975—, Alliance Nat. Bank, Dalton, 1999—. Office: 210-214 W Morris St PO Box 607 Dalton GA 30722-0607

TURNER, JAMES BENJAMIN, science educator; s. Rod and Carol Turner; m. Carina Eizmendi, Apr. 3, 1999; 1 child, Leilani. BS, Iowa State U. Sci. & Tech., Ames, 1992—95; MS, Purdue U., W.Lafayette, Ind., 1995—99. Rsch. internship NASA, Houston, 1995; tchg. asst. Purdue U., 1995—99; biology instr. Waubonsee CC, Sugar Grove, Ill., 2003—. Recipient Eagle Scout award, Boy Scouts Am., 1987. Mem.: Am. Mensa. Home Phone: 630-897-2062.

TURNER, JAMES HILTON, JR., lawyer; b. Chattanooga, Oct. 31, 1946; s. J. Hilton and Helen Cornelia (Herbert) T.; m. Betty Pei-Cheng Lee, Aug. 21, 1971; 1 child, Justin Lee. B.S., Westminster Coll., 1968; M.Div., Yale U., 1972; J.D., Georgetown U., 1975. Bar: D.C. 1979, Pa. 1975. Dir. legal writing program Georgetown U., Washington, 1974-75; counsel, legis. asst. to Rep. Gary Myers, Washington, 1975-77; Republican energy counsel Com. on Sci. and Tech., U.S. Ho. of Reps., 1977-81; dir. govt. relations Internat. Coal Refining Co., Washington, 1981-84; counsel sci. research and tech. subcom., U.S. Ho. of Reps., 1984, chief counsel, 2007-. Elder, treas. N.Y. Ave. Presbyn. Ch., 1984; chmn. edn. com. Haycock Sch. PTA, Falls Church, 1984-86; basketball coach McLean Youth Inc., 1985. Law fellow Georgetown U., 1973-74. Awards William T. Cavanaugh Meml. award, 2000. Mem. D.C. Bar Assn., Pa. Bar Assn. Clubs: Washington Coal, Georgetown, Tuckahoe Swim, Yale. Office: Committee on Science 2320 Rayburn HOB Washington DC 20515

TURNER, JAMES LEE, energy executive; b. Muncie, Ind., Aug. 20, 1959; s. Jack Edwin and Nancy Kathleen (Marvin) T.; m. Leah Wakeland, Dec. 26, 1981; 3 children. BS, Ball State U., Muncie, 1981; JD cum laude, Ind. U., Indpls., 1984. Bar: Ind. 1984, US Dist. Ct. (so. dist. Ind.) 1984. Assoc. Bingham, Summers, Welsh & Spilman, Indpls., 1984—90, ptnr., 1990—91; Utility Consumer Counselor State of Ind., 1991—93; prin. Lewis & Kappes, Indpls., 1993—95; with Cinergy Corp., Cin., 1995, v.p. customer svc., 1999—2000, pres. energy delivery bus. unit, 2000—01, CEO regulated bus. unit, 2001—04, exec. v.p., CFO, 2004—05, pres., 2005; group exec., pres. US Franchised Electric and Gas Duke Energy, group exec., pres. and COO US Franchised Electric and Gas, 2007—. Mem. exec. com. Nat. Assn. State Utility Consumer Advs., 1992; bd. dirs. NAM, Electric Power Rsch. Inst. Mem. Ohio State Bd. of Edn., 1999—2004; bd. mem. Cin. Mus. Ctr., Boys & Girls Clubs Greater Cin., Charlotte C. of C., NC, Charlotte Ctr. City Ptnrs. Mem. ABA, (environ. law com., Tort & Ins. Practice Sect.), Ind. State Bar Assn., Indpls. Bar Assn. Def. Rsch. Inst. Clubs: Sierra (Hoosier chpt. Indpls.). Democrat. Office: Duke Energy 526 S Church St Charlotte NC 28202-1904 Office Phone: 704-594-6200. *

TURNER, JANA L., real estate company executive; b. 1955; BSBA in Mktg., No. Ariz. U., 1977. Cert. property mgr. Inst. Real Estate Mgmt. Leasing receptionist R&B Comml. Mgmt., LA; pres. Pacific S.W. Region Koll Real Estate Svcs., Newport Beach, Calif., 1990—97; exec. v.p., mgr. western divsn. CB Comml., 1997—98; pres. asset svcs. CB Richard Ellis, 1998—. Bd. dirs. SiteStuff, Inc. Office: CB Richard Ellis 3501 Jamboree Rd Ste 100 Newport Beach CA 92660 Office Phone: 949-809-4057. E-mail: jana.turner@cbre.com. *

TURNER, JANET SULLIVAN, painter, sculptor; b. Gardiner, Maine, Nov. 15, 1935; d. Clayton Jefferson and Frances (Leighton) Sullivan; m. Terry Turner, Oct. 6, 1956; children: Lisa Turner Reid, Michael Ross, Jonathan Brett. BA cum laude, Mich. State U., East Lansing, 1956. Rep. Am. Women in Art, UN World Conf. on Women, Nairobi, Kenya, 1985. One-woman shows include San Diego Art Inst., 1971, St. Joseph U., Phila., 1981, Villanova U. Gallery, 1982, Pa. State U., Middletown, 1985, Temple U., 1986, Widener U. Art Mus., Chester, Pa., 1987, 94, Rosemont Coll., Pa., 1995, Sande Webster Gallery, Phila., 1998, 2000, 50 Yr. Retrospective Widener U. Art Gallery, 2005; exhibited in group shows at Del. Art Mus., Wilmington, 1978, Woodmere Art Mus., Phila., 1980, 2000, Port of History Mus., Phila., 1984, Allentown Art Mus., 1984, Trenton City Mus. Ellarslie Open VIII, NJ, 1989, Ammo Gallery, Bklyn., 1989, Pa. State Mus., Harrisburg, 1990-94, Galeria Mesa, Ariz., 1991, Del. Ctr. for Contemporary Arts, Wilmington, 1992, Holter Mus., Helena, Mont., 1992, S.W. Tex. State U., San Marcos, 1993, Fla. State U. Mus., Tallahassee, 1993, Newark Mus., 1993, U. Del., 1994, 1st St. Gallery, NYC, 1994, Noyes Mus., NJ, 1995, Sande Webster Gallery, Phila. 1995-2006, Phila. Art Mus., 1997, Krasdale Gallery, White Plains, NY, 2001, Moore Coll. of Art, Phila. Sculptors, Phila. Pa., 2002, Philips Mus, Franklin Marshall Coll., 2004, Sumner Sch. Art Mus., Washington, Art Trust Gallery, West Chester, Pa., 2006, others; represented in permanent collections Nat. Mus. Women in Arts, American Album, Wash., Kresge Art Mus., East Lansing, Mich, ARA Svc. Inc., Phila., Blue Cross/Blue Shield, Phila., Am. Nat. Bank and Trust Co., Rockford, Ill., Burroughs Corp., Lisle, Ill., State Mus. Pa., Harrisburg, Bryn Mawr (Pa.) Coll., Rosemont Coll., Villanova (Pa.) Coll., LaSalle U. Art Mus., Phila., Noyes Mus., NJ, Nat. Liberty Mus., Phila., Kimmel Ctr., Phila. Bd. dirs. Rittenhouse Sq. Fine Arts Ann., Phila., 1984—86. Recipient 2d pl. award San Diego Art Inst. 19th Ann. Exhbn., 1971, award of merit Pavilion Gallery, Mt. Holly, NJ, 1991, 3d pl. Katonah Mus. of Art, NY, 1992, Purchase award State Mus. Pa., Harrisburg, 1992. Mem. Artists Equity (pres. 1987-88), Nat. League of Am. Pen Woman, Phila. Watercolor Club, Delta Phi Delta. Republican. Roman Catholic. Home: 88 Cambridge Dr Glen Mills PA 19342-1545 Office Phone: 610-358-2094. Personal E-mail: jsullivanturner@comcast.net.

TURNER, JIM (JAMES W.), lawyer, former congressman; b. Ft. Lewis, Wash., Feb. 6, 1946; m. Ginny wARD, oCT. 3, 1970; 2 children. BBA, U. Tex., 1968, MBA, JD, U. Tex., 1971. Bar: Tex. 1971, DC 2005. Lawyer, 1971—; mayor City of Crockett, Tex., 1989—91; mem. Tex. House Reps., 1981—84, Tex. State Senate, 1991—96, 105-108th Congresses from 2nd Tex. dist., 1997—2005; mem. govt. oversight com.; former mem. nat. security com.; ranking mem. House Select Com. on Homeland Security. Mem. Econ. Growth, Natural Resources, and Regulatory Affairs subcom., Nat. Security, Internat. Affairs, and Criminal Justice subcom. House Govt. Reform and Oversight Com., Mil. Rsch. and Devel. subcom., Mil. Procurement subcom., ranking mem. Terrorism subcom., House Nat. Security Com.; ptnr. Arnold & Porter LLP, 2005-. Served in US Army, 1970—78. Democrat. Baptist. Office: Arnold & Porter LLP 555 Twelfth St NW Washington DC 20004

TURNER, JOHN ANDREW, economist; b. Chgo., July 9, 1949; s. Henry Andrew and Mary Margaret (Tilton) T.; m. Kathleen King Peery, June 21, 1975; 1 child, Sarah. BA, Pomona Coll., Claremont, Calif., 1971; MA, Stanford U., Calif., 1972; PhD, U. Chgo., 1977. Rsch. econ. SSA, Washington, 1976-80, ILO, Geneva, 1996-98, US Dept. Labor, Washington, 1980-96, rsch. econ. Office of Sec., 1999-2000, Pub. Policy Inst., AARP, 2000—06, pension policy cons., 2006—. Cons. OECD, Paris, 1989, IMF, 1995, AFL-CIO, 1996; chmn. Internat. Pension Conf., US Dept. Labor, Washington, 1990; adj. prof. George Washington U., 1994-96. Author: Pension Policy for a Mobile Labor Force, 1993, Individual Accounts for Social Security Reform, 2006; editor: Trends in Pensions, 1989 (transl. into Japanese 1991), Pension Policy: An International Perspective, 1991, Trends in Health Benefits, 1993, Private Pension Policies in Industrialized Countries, 1995, Securing Employer-Based Pensions, 1996, Social Security: Development and Reform, 2000. Fulbright scholar Institut de Recherches Economiques et Sociales, France, 1994. Mem. Am. Econ. Assn., Nat. Acad. Social Ins. Methodist. Avocation: tennis. Home: 3713 Chesapeake St NW Washington DC 20016-1813 Personal E-mail: turnerjilo@aol.com, jturner47@verizon.net.

TURNER, JOHN FREELAND, former federal agency administrator, retired state legislator; b. Jackson, Wyo., Mar. 3, 1942; s. John Charles and Mary Louise (Mapes) T.; m. Mary Kay Brady, 1969; children: John Francis, Kathy Mapes, Mark Freeland. BS in Biology, U. Notre Dame, 1964; postgrad., U. Innsbruck, 1964-65, U. Utah, 1965-66; MS in Ecology, U. Mich., 1968. Rancher, outfitter Triangle X Ranch, Moose, Wyo.; chmn. bd. dirs. Bank of Jackson Hole, 1985-89; photo-journalist; mem. Wyo. Ho. of Reps., 1970-74, Wyo. Senate, 1974-89, pres., 1987-89; dir. Fish and Wildlife Svc. US Dept. Interior, Washington, 1989-93; pres. Conservation Fund, Arlington, Va., 1993—2001; asst. sec. for oceans, internat. environ., & scientific affairs US Dept. State, Washington, 2001—05. Exec. adv. Hancock Timber Resource Group, 1993—2001; chmn. rev. com. Argonne Nat. Lab.-West, U. Chgo., 1999—2001; bd. dirs. Land Trust Alliance, 1994—2000, N.E. Utilities, 1995—2001, Internat. Paper Co., Stamford, Conn., 2005—, Ashland Inc., 2006—; chmn. bd. dirs. Inst. Environ. and Natural Resources, U. Wyo., Laramie, 2001—; mem. Nat. Coal Coun., 1995—, Teton Sci. Sch. Bd., Nat. Wetland Forum, 1983, 87; mem. exec. com. Coun. of State Govts.; chmn. Pride in Jackson Hole Campaign, 1986; chmn. steering com. UN Conv. on Wetlands of Internat. Importance, 1990—93; head U.S. delegation Conv. on Internat. Trade Endangered Species. Author: The Magnificent Bald Eagle: Our National Bird, 1971. Named Citizen of Yr. County of Teton, 1984; recipient Nat. Conservation Achievement award Nat. Wildlife Fedn., 1984, Sheldon Coleman Great Outdoors award, 1990, Pres.'s Pub. Svc. award The Nature Conservatory, 1990, Stewardship award Audubon Soc., 1992, Nat. Wetland Achievement award Ducks Unlimited, 1993, Chevron/Times-Mirror Nat. Conservation Leadership award, 1995. Mem. Nat. Wildlife Refuge Assn. (bd. dirs.), Boone and Crocket Club (profl. mem.). Republican. Roman Catholic.

TURNER, JOHN GOSNEY, insurance company executive, director; b. Springfield, Mass., Oct. 3, 1939; s. John William and Clarence Oma (Gosney) T.; m. Leslie Corrigan, June 23, 1962; children: John Fredric, Mary Leslie, James Gosney, Andrew William. BA, Amherst Coll., 1961; student, Advanced Mgmt. Program, Harvard U., 1980. Assoc. actuary Monarch Life Ins. Co., Springfield, Mass., 1961-67; group actuary Northwestern Nat. Life Ins. Co., Mpls., 1967-75, sr. v.p. group, 1975-79, sr. v.p., chief actuary, 1979-81, exec. v.p., chief actuary, 1981-83, pres., chief operating officer, 1983—; chmn., CEO Northwestern Nat. Life Ins. Co. (now ReliaStar Fin. Corp.), Mpls., 1993—. Dir. NWNL Reins. Co., NWNL Gen. No. Life, North Atlantic Life Ins. Co. N.Y. Trustee Abbott-Northwestern Hosps., Evans Sch. Found.; chmn. Minn. Trustees of the Evans Scholars Found. Fellow Soc. Actuaries; mem. Am. Acad. Actuaries, Western Golf Assn. (dir.), Minn. Golf Assn. Clubs: Minikahda (Mpls.). Home: 301 Kenwood Pkwy Apt 502 Minneapolis MN 55403-1165

TURNER, JOHN SIDNEY, JR., retired otolaryngologist, educator; b. Bainbridge, Ga., July 25, 1930; s. John Sidney and Rose Lee (Rogers) T.; m. Betty Jane Tigner, June 5, 1955 (dec.); children: Elizabeth, Rebecca, Jan Marie; m. Nina Jones, June 16, 1999. BS, Emory U., 1952, MD, 1955. Diplomate Am. Bd. Otolaryngology. Intern U. Va. Hosp., 1955-56; resident in otolaryngology Duke U. Med. Ctr., 1958-61; prof. otolaryngology Emory U., Atlanta, 1961-95, chmn. divsn., 1961—95; ret. Ear specialist, chief otolaryngology Emory Clinic, 1961-95; area cons. in field U.S. 3d Army, 1962-69; assoc. dir. heart disease control program Fla. Bd. Health, 1956-58; Ga. state chmn. Deafness Rsch. Found., 1968-95; v.p. Clifton Casualty Ins. Co., Atlanta, 1975-95. Mem. internat. editl. bd. Drugs Jour., 1982-2004, Ethicals in Med. Progress, 1982—, Dialogue Jour., 1988-95; mem. editl. bd. Otolaryngolog—Head and Neck Surgery, 1991; contbr. chpts. to books, articles to profl. jours. With USPHS, 1956-58. Recipient Appreciation award Children of Fulton County and Fulton County Health Dept., 1975, Citation for Disting. Svc., Fla. divsn. Am. Cancer Soc., 1957, Lester A. Brown award Ga. Soc. Otolaryngology*Head and Neck Surgery, 1995. Mem. AMA, So. Med. Assn. (chmn. otolaryngology sect. 1974, cert. of appreciation 1974), Am. Acad. Otolaryngology--Head and Neck Surgery (Honor award 1994), Triological Soc. (v.p., chmn. so. sect. 1991—), Am. Acad. Otolaryngic Allergy, Ga. Soc. Otolaryngology (pres. 1973), Med. Assn. Ga., Med. Assn. Atlanta, Assn. Acad. Depts. Otolaryngology, Optimists (pres. Atlanta 1975), Alpha Omega Alpha. Democrat. Methodist.

TURNER, JONATHAN SHIELDS, computer science educator, researcher; b. Boston, Nov. 13, 1953; m. Helen Gaddy; 1 child, Gregory. AB, Oberlin Coll., 1977; BS in Computer Sci., Washington U., St. Louis, 1977, BSEE, 1977; MS in Computer Sci., Northwestern U., 1979, PhD in Computer Sci., 1982. Mem. tech. staff Bell Labs., Naperville, Ill., 1977-83; sr. to assoc. prof. computer sci. Washington U., St. Louis, 1983-90, prof., 1990—, chmn. computer sci. dept., 1992-97, Henry Edwin Sever prof. engring., 1994—2006, Barbara J. and Jerome R. Cox Jr. prof. computer sci., 2006—. Adv. NSF, 1990; co-founder Growth Networks. Editl. bd. IEEE/Assn. Computing Machinery Transactions on Networking, 1993; contbr. numerous articles to profl. jours.; patentee in field. Recipient Tech. Devel. award St. Louis, Econ. Coun., 1995. Fellow IEEE (Koji Kobayashi Computers and Comm. award 1994), Assn. Computing Machinery; mem. NAE. Avocations: music, tennis, reading. Office: Computer Sci and Engring Dept Washington U Campus Box 1045 Saint Louis MO 63130-4899 Office Phone: 314-935-8552. Office Fax: 314-935-7302. E-mail: jon.turner@wustl.edu. *

TURNER, KATHLEEN, actress; b. Springfield, Mo., June 19, 1954; m. David Guc, 1977 (div. 1982); m. Jay Weiss, 1984; 1 child, Rachel Ann. Student, Cen. Sch. of Speech and Drama, London, Southwest Mo. State U.; BFA, U. Md., 1977. Various theater roles, Broadway debut: Gemini, 1978, Cat on a Hot Tin Roof, 1990, Indiscretions, 1995, Who's Afraid of Virginia Woolf?, 2005 (Evening Standard Best Actress award, 2006); appeared in TV series The Doctors, 1977, Style and Substance, 1996; TV movies inlcude Friends At Last, 1995, Moonlight and Valentino, 1995; films include Body Heat, 1981, A Breed Apart, 1982, The Man With Two Brains, 1983, Crimes of Passion, 1984, Romancing the Stone, 1984, Prizzi's Honor (Golden Globe award for best actress), 1985, The Jewel of the Nile, 1985, Peggy Sue Got Married, (D.W. Griffith award for best actress, Oscar nomination for best actress) 1986, Julia and Julia, 1988, Switching Channels, 1988, Who Framed Roger Rabbit, 1988, Accidental Tourist, 1988, The War of the Roses, 1989. V.I. Warshawski, 1991, Undercover Blues, 1993, House of Cards, 1993, Serial Mom, 1994, Naked in New York, 1994, A Simple Wish, 1997, The Real Blonde, 1998, Baby Geniuses, 1999, The Virgin Suicides, 1999, Prince of Central Park, 2000, Beautiful, 2000, Without Love, 2004, (voice) Monster House, 2006, (TV films) Love in the Ancient World, 1997, Legalese, 1998, Cinderella, 2000; dir. (Showtime cable movie) Leslie's Folly, 1994; also performed in radio shows with the BBC, 1992, 93; voice: Bad Baby, 1997, Beautiful, 2000. Office: ICM care Chris Andrews 8942 Wilshire Blvd Beverly Hills CA 90211-1934 *

TURNER, KATHY ANN, special education services professional, director; b. Cinn., May 16, 1962; d. James Robert and Alice Louise Taylor; m. Michael Arcia Turner, Jr., June 1, 1985; children: Joseph Paul, Christopher James, Sarah Alyse 1 stepchild, Talinthea Virginia. AA, Riverside C.C., 1998; BS in Edn., Lewis Clark State Coll., 2002. Spl. edn. asst. Corona-Norco Unified Sch. Dist., Norco, Calif., 1996—98; direct care provider devel. disabilities Inclusion North, Inc., Grangeville, Idaho, 1998—2000; tech. for tchrs. asst. Lewis Clark State Coll., Lewiston, Idaho, 2000—01; sub. tchr. Prairie Sch., Idaho, 2001—03; specialist devel. disabilities Opportunities Unltd., Inc., 2003—05; psycho social rehab provider Camas Profl. Counseling, 2005—06; spl. edn. tchr. lower Kuskokwim sch. dist. Bethel Regional High Sch., Ark., 2006—07; devel. disabilities dir. Yukon Kuskokwim Health Corp., 2007—. Psychol. social rehab. provider Frontier Journeys, Grangeville, Idaho, 2002—05; counselor Hope Pregnancy Ctr., Grangeville, 2003—06. Portrait, Liz (2nd pl. award Idaho County Art Competition, 1998). Daffodil days chmn. Am. Cancer Soc., Corona, Calif., 1995—98; com. mem. Relay for Life, 2005. Named Life Woman of the Yr., Norco C. of C., 1995. Mem.: Coun. for Exceptional Children, Grangeville Elks, Kappa Delta Pi (pres. 2001—03). Republican. Avocations: baking, fishing, sewing, card playing, ballroom dancing. Home: PO Box 1901 Bethel AK 99559 Office Phone: 907-543-1786. Personal E-mail: imspcl2002@yahoo.com.

TURNER, KATHY RAE, councilman, former mayor, retired real estate agent; d. Edward A. and Frances A. Osina; m. Gary James Turner, Dec. 6, 1982; 1 child, Angelic Victoria Little-Turner. Cert. mcpl. leadership Assn. Wash. Cities, 2002, Leadership Achievement Bronze Nat. League Cities, 2003. Real estate profl. Prudential Contact Corp., Puyallup, Wash., 1984—2001; councilmember City of Puyallup, 1993—, mayor, 2002—06, city councilmember, 2006—. Cmty. contbn. com. mem. Puyallup Tribe, Tacoma, 1998—; pub. safety policy com. Nat. League Cities, Washington, 2000—; mem. Meml. and Vets. Day com. VFW, Puyallup, 2002—; farmers market adv. com. Main St., Puyallup, 2004—; bd. mem. Puyallup Libr., 2006—. Chair planning commn. City of Puyallup. Named to Citizen Hall of Fame, Ft. Lewis, 2006; recipient Cmty. Svc. Realtor award, Pierce County Realtor Assn., 1997, Wash. State Realtors Assn., 1998, Cmty. Svc. award, C. of C., 2000, Congl. Recognition for Outstanding Cmty. Svc. award, US Congress, 2002, Outstanding Svc. award, Puyallup Police Dept., 2004. Home Phone: 253-848-2507; Office Phone: 253-840-6673.

TURNER, KEVIN (B. KEVIN TURNER), information technology executive; m. Shelly Turner; 3 children. BS, E. Ctrl. U., 1987. Cashier Wal-Mart Stores, Inc., Ada, Okla., 1985—88, with internal audit dept., 1988—89, bus. analyst info. sys. div., strategy mgr. info. sys. div., dir. info. sys. div., v.p and asst. chief info. officer info. sys. div., chief info. officer info. sys. div., 2000—03, exec. v.p., 2000, pres. and CEO Sam's Club div., 2002—05; COO Microsoft Corp., Redmond, Wash., 2005—. Office: Microsoft Corp 1 Microsoft Way Redmond WA 98052-6399 *

TURNER, LAURA LOUISE, webmaster; b. Flint, Mich., Sept. 10, 1962; 1 child, Leonardo Turner Crisostomo. Diploma, Endicott Coll., Beverly, Mass., Plymouth State U., NH, Montserrat Coll. Art, Beverly, Mass. Webdesigner Dartmouth Coll., 2001—04, webmaster, 2005—; owner, designer Turner Design Group, Hanover, NH, 2004—. Mem.: Internat. Soc. Philos. Enquiry (webmaster 1999—), Mensa. Avocations: art, tennis, skiing, sailing, travel. Personal E-mail: turner146@yahoo.com.

TURNER, LEE IRWIN, lawyer; b. Cleve., May 2, 1944; s. Louis and Harriet (Keizer) T.; married; children: Brooke, Brett, Brittany, Breanne,

Brenna. B.S., Ohio State U., 1966, J.D. cum laude, 1969. Bar: Mich. 1969, Ohio, 1969, U.S. Dist. Ct. (no. dist.) Ohio 1971, U.S. Dist. (ea. dist.) Mich. 1971, U.S. Ct. Appeals (6th cir.) 1984. Assoc., Sommer, Schwartz, Silver, Schwartz, Detroit, 1969-73; ptnr. Turner & Turner, P.C., Southfield, Mich., 1973—. Mem. Assn. Trial Lawyers Am., Mich. Trial Lawyers, Detroit Bar Assn., Southfield Bar Assn., Oakland County Bar Assn. Democrat. Jewish. Office: 26000 W 12 Mile Rd Southfield MI 48034-1783

TURNER, LESTER NATHAN, lawyer, international trade consultant; b. Colmar, Ky., July 11, 1933; s. Clifford G. and Minnie G. (Ensor) T.; m. Sandra B. Ward, July 3, 1976; children: Kimberly L., Michele M., Renee S., Mark L., Jeffrey S., Derek Kyle. BS, Lincoln Meml. U., 1955; JD, U. Mich., 1959. Bar: Mich. 1960, US Dist. Ct. (ea. and we. dist.) Mich., US Ct. Appeals (6th cir.), US Supreme Ct. 1982. Law clk. to presiding justice, research atty. Mich. Supreme Ct., Lansing, 1960-62; ptnr. Sinas, Dramis, Brake & Turner, Lansing, 1960-78; sole law practice, bus. law, internat. cons. primarily in Mid. East Countries with emphasis on Palestine Nat. Authority, Lansing, Mich., 1978—, Harbor Springs, 1978—; prin., CEO Palestinian Tourism Co. Ltd., Palestinian Co. Transp. Ltd., North Bay Ltd. Std. jury instrn. com. Mich. Supreme Ct., Lansing, 1963-73; cons. higher commn. investment and fin. Palestinian Pres., 1997-98. Mem. Mich. State Bar Assn., Mich. Trial Lawyers Assn. (bd. dirs. 1963-74, v.p. 1974). Methodist. Office: PO Box 499 Harbor Springs MI 49740-0499 Office Phone: 231-526-1103. Business E-Mail: lntlaw@chartermi.net.

TURNER, LETITIA RHODES, artist; b. Media, Pa., Aug. 17, 1923; d. Samuel Noblit and Letitia (Eves) Rhodes; m. Ellwood Jackson Turner Jr., Aug. 1, 1942; children: Rue Baronsky, Letitia Mayo, Elizabeth Rorke. Diploma, Cowanova Sch. Dancing, 1941. Dance instr. Cowanova Sch. Dancing, 1939—41; sec., treas. Rose Tree Realty Inc., Media, Pa., 1961-81. Dance tchr., 1939, 40, 41. Portrait painter (Portrait of Mary 3d pl. 1990, Portrait of Brett 2d pl. 1987); painter portrait commns., 1977-95. Mem. Optimisses 1956-1958, pres Am. Legion Aux., Media, 1991-2002, photographer, 1992, sec., 1993—; sec. Del. County Am. Legion Aux., 1994, historian, 1995; 1st v.p. Woman's Aux. Media Presbyn. Ch., Media, 1963; mem. D.A.R.E., Media, 1983-91, 92, 93—. Mem. Artist Guild Delaware County, Art League Delaware County, Artist Guild of Riddle Village, Am. Legion Aux. (sec. Del. County 1993, historian 1994). Republican. Avocation: needlepoint. Home and Office: Riddle Village L-302 Media PA 19063

TURNER, LINDA JEANNETTE CHAPMAN, artist, historian; b. Camp Gordon, Ga., July 22, 1945; d. Lawrence Moore and Dale White Chapman; m. Joseph Michael Turner, Aug. 19, 1967; 1 child, Jennifer Lin Turner Abbott. AB in Edn., Glenville State Coll., W.Va., 1968. Dir. art Braxton County Schs., Sutton, W.Va., 1968—71, tchr. spl. program art, basic skills, sci., 1972—75; artist Laurelwood Art Studio, 1976—; tchr. various art orgns., 1977—; historian W. Va., Am. Civil War, 1983—. Exhibitions include W.Va. Watercolor Soc., 1985—2007, So. Watercolor Soc., 1999, 2001, 2003, Midwest Watercolor Soc., 1999, W.Va. Juried Biennial Exhbn., 1999, New England Watercolor Soc. Biennial N. Am. Open, 2000, Am. Watercolor Soc. Internat., 2001, La. Watercolor Soc., 2005, Nat. Watercolor Soc. Mem.: So. Watercolor Soc., W.Va. Watercolor Soc. (co-founder, pres. 2000—02), Transparent Watercolor Soc. Am., Nat. Watercolor Soc. Baptist. Avocations: gardening, hiking, wildflower study. Studio: 327 High St Jane Lew WV 26378

TURNER, LISA PHILLIPS, human resources executive; b. Waltham, Mass., Apr. 10, 1951; d. James Sinclair and Virginia Turner. BA in Edn. and Philosophy magna cum laude, Washington Coll., Chestertown, Md., 1974; AS in Electronics Tech., AA in Engring., Palm Beach Jr. Coll., 1982; MBA, Nova U., 1986, DSc, 1989; PhD, Kennedy Western U., 1990. Cert. sr. profl. in human resources; cert. quality engr.; lic. USCG capt.; lic. pvt. pilot FAA, IFAA lic. airframe and powerplant mechanic, 2004; cert. Black Belt, 2006. Founder, pres. Turner's Bicycle Svc., Inc., Delray Beach, Fla., 1975-80; electronics engr., quality engr. Audio Engring. and Video Arts, Boca Raton, Fla., 1980-81; tech. writing instr. Palm Beach Jr. Coll., Lake Worth, Fla., 1981-82; adminstr. tng. and devel. Mitel Inc., Boca Raton, 1982-88; mgr. comm. and employee rels. Modular Computer Systems, Inc., Ft. Lauderdale, Fla., 1988-89; U.S. mktg. project mgr. Mitel, Inc., Boca Raton, 1990-91; v.p. human resources Connectronics, Inc., Ft. Lauderdale, 1991-93; sr. mgr. human resources Sensormatic Electronics Corp., Boca Raton, 1993-98, dir. human resources, 1998—2001; chief tng. officer and dir. human resources Tyco Fire and Security Svcs., Inc., Boca Raton, 2001—05, Six Sigma black belt, 2005—06; pres. Turner Bus. Svcs., Inc., Boynton Beach, Fla., 2006—. Contbg. author Kitplanes Mag. With USCG Aux. Recipient Human Resources Profl. Excellence award, Soc. Human Resource Mgmt., 1999. Mem. Soc. for Human Resource Mgmt., Internat. Assn. Quality Cirs., Am. Soc. Quality Control, Fla. Employment Mgmt. Assn., Am. Acad. Mgmt., Employment Assn. Fla., Am. Capts. Assn., Citizens Police Acad., Aircraft Owners and Pilot's Assn., Exptl. Aircraft Assn., Fla. Aero. Club. Achievements include being the first female to construct, complete and fly a pulsar XP aircraft. Home: 1358 Fairfax Cir E Boynton Beach FL 33436-8612 Office: Turner Bus Svcs 1358 Fairfax Cir E Boynton Beach FL 33436-8612 Home Phone: 561-964-5656; Office Phone: 561-642-0402. Personal E-mail: lisaturner@prodigy.net. Business E-Mail: lisaturner@lisaturner.com.

TURNER, LOUISE (LEE) KREHER, retired dance educator; b. New Orleans, July 30, 1914; d. Charles William Kreher and Hazel Hilliary Brennan; m. Frank Allen Turner, Sept. 5, 1954. BA, Southwestern La. Inst., 1933; MA, La. State U., 1936; MS, La State U., 1937; PhD, NYU, 1970; Assoc. Prof. Emerita (hon.), Auburn U., 1975. Dance instr. La. State Normal Coll., Natchitoches, 1934; tchg. fellow La. State U., Baton Rouge, 1935—37; dance instr. Stuart Hall, Staunton, Va., 1937; assoc. prof. Auburn U., Ala., 1938—76. Playground and teenage ctr. dir. City of St. Petersburg, Fla., 1948—49; recreation dir. City of Opelika, Ala., 1950; recreation broadcaster Sta. WJHO, Auburn, 1952; in-sch. ednl. telecaster PBS Channel 7, Auburn, 1953; dir./coord. Forest Ecology Preserve, Sch. of Forestry, Auburn U., 1997—2000. (choreography) Choreography; author: (genealogy/historical novel) Margaretha's Trunk. Recipient Assoc. Health, Phys. Edn. and Recreation award, State of Ala., 1956, Auburn Citizen of Yr., Auburn Civitan Club, 1954, 2000, Outstanding Alumnus, U. of SW La., 1979, W. Kelly Mosley Environ. award, Auburn U., 2000, Martha Wayles Jefferson Cmty. Svc. award, DAR, 2004, Environ. Awareness award, 2004. Mem.: Am. Assn. Health Phys. Edn. Recreation and Dance, Delta Zeta, Delta Kappa Gamma. Achievements include donated land and established Forest Ecology Preserve, Auburn University, 1993; established F. Allen and Louise K. Turner Charitable Foundation, 2000; development of cultural exchange program with Guatemala, Partners in America with Auburn, 1974; historic preservation of Pre-Civil War dwelling, 1980-1985. Home: P O Box 1407 Auburn AL 36831 Home Phone: 334-887-6297. Personal E-mail: turnelo@mindspring.com.

TURNER, MARGUERITE ROSE COWLES, retired library director; b. June 21, 1941; d. John Clinton and Marguerite Eileen (Slaybaugh) Cowles; 1 son, Jeffrey Jason. BA, U. New Orleans, 1963; MLS, La. State U., 1966; MA in History, U. So. Miss., 1970. Reference libr. U. So. Miss., 1966—70, Pascagoula Jr. H.S., Miss., 1970-71, Irwin County HS, Ocilla, Ga., 1971-72; dir. Fitzgerald Carnegie Libr., Ga., 1974-80, Jacob S. Mauney Meml. Libr., Kings Mountain, NC, 1983—2004; adminstrv. libr. Assumption Parish Libr., Napoleonville, La., 1980-83; ret., 2004. Author poems, short stories; writer weekly column Kings Mountain Herald, Shelby Star: contbr. articles to profl. jours. Sunday sch. tchr., First Baptist Ch., libr., 1975—, Fitzgerald, 1978-80, Napoleonville, 1980-83. Mem. ALA, NC Libr. Assn., Broad River Libr. Assn. Republican. Avocations: gardening, sewing, quilting, reading, writing.

TURNER, MARY ALICE, curriculum specialist; b. Birmingham, Ala., Aug. 8, 1946; d. Henry and Elzona (Griffin) Johnson; m. Raymond Carver Turner, July 6, 1968; 1 child, Taunya Nicole. BS in Edn., Ala. A&M U., 1968, MEd, 1992. Cert. tchr. home econs. edn., elem. edn., early childhood edn., adminstrn. and supervision 1994. Title I curriculum specialist Huntsville City Schs., Ala., 1969—. Mem. Parent/Sch./Tchr. adv. bd. Ridgecrest Elem. Sch., Huntsville, 1978; tchr. rep. PTA, Rolling Hills Elem. Sch., Huntsville, 1988-93. Recipient Award for Dedicated Svc. Rolling Hills PTA, 1988. Mem. ASCD, NEA, Ala. Edn. Assn., Huntsville Edn. Assn. (sch. rep. 1969-96, mem. budget com., rule and regulations com. review), Ala. Reading Assn., Alpha Kappa Alpha. Democrat. Baptist. Avocations: needlepoint, sewing, reading, public speaking. Home: 213 Lake Carmel Ct Huntsville AL 35811-8005 Office: Terry Heights Elem Sch 2820 Barbara Dr Huntsville AL 35816 Business E-Mail: mturner@hsv.k12.al.us.

TURNER, MICHAEL R., congressman; b. Dayton, Ohio, Jan. 11, 1960; s. Ray and Vivian Turner; m. Lori Turner; 2 children. BS in Polit. Sci., Ohio No. U., Ada, 1982; JD, Case Western Res. U. Sch. Law, 1985; MBA, U. Dayton, Ohio, 1992. Bar: Ohio 1985. Corp. counsel Modern Technologies Corp., Dayton, Ohio; pres. JMD Devel.; mayor Ohio, 1994—2002; mem. US Congress from 3rd Ohio dist., 2003—. Mem. armed svcs. com. US Congress, 2003—, mem. govt. reform com., 2003—, chmn. federalism and the census subcommittee, 2005—, mem. vets. affairs com., 2005—. Recipient Nat. Legis. Leadership award, US Conf. Mayors, 2005, Restore Am. Hero award, Nat. Trust Hist. Preservation and HGTV, 2005. Mem.: Am. Corp. Counsel Assn., Ohio Bar Assn., Dayton Bar Assn., ABA. Republican. Office: US House Reps 1740 Longworth House Office Bldg Washington DC 20515 Office Phone: 202-225-6465. Office Fax: 202-225-6754. *

TURNER, MICHAEL STANLEY, astrophysics professor, researcher; b. LA, July 29, 1949; s. Paul Joseph and Janet Mary (Lindholm) Turner; m. Terri Lee Shields, Aug. 1978 (div. Sept. 1980); m. Barbara Lynn Ahlberg, Sept. 10, 1988; children: Rachel Mary, Joseph Lucien. BS in Physics, Calif. Inst. Tech., Pasadena, 1971; MS in Physics, Stanford U., Calif., 1973, PhD in Physics, 1978; DSc (hon.), Mich. State U., East Lansing, 2005. Enrico Fermi fellow U. Chgo., 1978-80, from asst. to assoc. prof. physics and astronomy and astrophysics, 1980-85, prof., 1985—, chmn. dept. astronomy and astrophysics, 1997—2003, Bruce V. and Diana M. Rauner Disting. Svc. prof., 1998—; scientist Fermi Nat. Accelerator Lab., Batavia, Ill., 1983—2003, 2006—; asst. dir. US NSF, 2003—06; chief scientist Argonne Nat. Lab., 2007—. Trustee Aspen Ctr. Physics, Colo., 1984—97, pres., 1989—93, hon. trustee, 2002—; Halley lectr. Oxford U., 1994; Klopsteg lectr. Am. Assn. Physics Tchrs., 1999; Neils Bohr lectr. Copenhagen U., 2001; Marker lectr. Pa. State U., 2002; W. Paul fellow Bonn U., 2000; Houston lectr. Rice U., 2003; Herzfield lectr. Cath. U., 2004; Buhl lectr. Carnegie Mellon U., 2004; Heinrich Hertz lectr. DESY-Germany, 2004; Kaczmarczk lectr. Dexel U., 2004; Buhl lectr. Carnegie Mellon, 2004; Fisher lectr. Brandeis U., 2005; Centennial lectr. Purdue U., 2005; Shaw lectr. So. Ill. U., 2005; Mohler Prize lectr. U. Mich., 2007. Author: (with E.W. Kolb) The Early Universe, 1990; contbr. over 200 articles to profl. jours. Trustee Ill. Math. Sci. Acad., 1998-2003, Project Exploration, Ill., 2002-03, Fermi Rsch. Alliance, 2006-. Sloan fellow A.P. Sloan Found., 1983-88; recipient Disting. Alumni award Caltech, 2006. Fellow AAAS (chair physics sect. 2003), Am. Acad. Arts and Scis., Am. Phys. Soc. (mem. exec. bd. 1992-94, chmn. publ. oversight com. 1993-94, chmn. nominating com. 1999-2000, Lilienfeld prize 1997, Primakoff lectr., 2003, chair-elect, dir. astrophysics, 2007), Phi Beta Kappa (nat. lectr. 2002-2003); mem. NAS (NRC astronomy astrophysics survey com. 1998-2000, chair NRC com. Physics of Universe, 2000-02, chair physics sect. 2007-, bd. on physics and astronomy), Am. Astron. Soc. (Helen B. Warner prize 1984), Internat. Astron. Union, Sigma Xi. Office: U Chgo Astron & Astrophysics Ctr 5640 S Ellis Ave Chicago IL 60637-1433 Office Phone: 630-252-3575. Business E-Mail: mturner@uchicago.edu.

TURNER, MONICA GOIGEL, ecologist; b. NYC, Dec. 9, 1958; d. Peter Joseph and Dorothy Ann (Burger) Goigel; m. Michael G. Turner, Aug. 28, 1982. BS in biology summa cum laude, Fordham U., 1980; PhD in ecology, U. Ga., 1985. Environ. specialist US Nat. Park Svc., Washington, 1981; grad. non-teaching asst. U. Ga., Athens, 1980-83, rsch. asst. Inst. Ecology, 1983-85, postdoctoral rsch. assoc. Inst. Ecology, 1985-87; Hollaender fellow Oak Ridge Nat. Lab., Tenn., 1987-89, rsch. staff scientist environ. scis. divsn., 1989—94; asst. prof. zoology U. Wis., 1994—95, assoc. prof. zoology, 1995—99, prof. zoology, 1999—. Adj. asst. prof. ecology U. Tenn., 1990—94. Editor: Landscape Heterogeneity and Disturbance, 1987; co-editor-in-chief: Ecosystems; mem. editl. bd.: BioScience, Conservation Ecology, Ecological Applications. Mem. Internat. Assn. Ecology, Internat. Assn. Landscape Ecology (program chair U.S. chpt. 1986—), AAAS, Am. Inst. Biol. Scis., Ecol. Soc. Am., NAS, Phi Beta Kappa, Phi Kappa Phi. Roman Catholic. Office: Univ Wis Dept Zoology 432 Birge Hall 430 Lincoln Dr Madison WI 53706 Office Phone: 608-262-2592. E-mail: turnermg@wisc.edu.

TURNER, NATALIE A., retired consultant; b. Vancouver, BC, Can. d. Walter P. and Jenny (Ferley) Koohtow; m. George M. Turner, Jr. BS, McGill U., 1949. Rsch. asst. in neurophysiology Allen Meml. Inst., Montreal, 1949—51; rsch. asst. Harvard Med. Sch., Boston, 1951—54; chem. program mgr. in r&d, tech. svc. mgr. to Internat. Ops., clearance officer for Latin-Am. and Asia-Pacific comapnies Gillette Co., Boston, 1954—88; ret., 1989. Technician Red Cross Blood Transfusion Svc., Montreal, 1949; tech. cons. Damon Biotech, Boston, 1988-89, rsch. asst., Harvard Sch. of Pub. Health Co-author rsch. publs. in field. Bd. dirs. Children's Mus. in Easton, Mass., 1989—. Mem. NAFE, Internat. Congress Physiology, Am. Chem. Soc., Soc. Cosmetic Chemists (life, pres. New Eng. chpt., dir. US Nat. Bd., US rep. to Internat. Fedn. Exec. Bd.), New Eng. Women Bus. Owners, Kappa Alpha Theta (life). Avocations: sewing, golf, portraits in fabric and oils.

TURNER, NORV(AL) (EUGENE), professional football coach; b. LeJeune, NC, May 17, 1952; m. Nancy Turner; children: Scott, Stephanie, Drew. Asst. coach U. So. Calif. Trojans, 1976—84; receivers coach LA Rams, 1985—90; offensive coord. Dallas Cowboys, 1991—93, San Diego Chargers, 2001, Miami Dolphins, 2002—03, San Francisco 49ers, 2006—07; head coach Washington Redskins, 1994—2000, Oakland Raiders, 2004—06, San Diego Chargers, 2007—. Office: c/o San Diego Chargers PO Box 609609 San Diego CA 92160 *

TURNER, PATRICK NOEL WADDINGTON, portfolio manager; b. Burnham, Eng., Mar. 31, 1960; came to U.S., 1981; s. Noel Walter and Shirley (Vaughn) T.; m. Hilary Jennifer Cosell, Sept. 18, 1982 (div. Dec. 1989); 1 child, Payton; m. Amber Lea Bohmfalk, Feb. 2, 1991; children: Benton, Lily. BA with honours, Oxford U., Eng., 1981, MA with honours, 1982; MBA in Fin., NYU, 1988. Asst. treas. Bankers Trust Co., NYC, 1981-84; v.p. Marine Midland Bank, NYC, 1984-89; dir. Barclays Bank PLC, NYC, 1989-95; mng. ptnr. Canterbury Mezzanine Capital LP, NYC, 1995—; mng. dir. TCW/Crescent Mezzanine, NYC, 2005—. Trustee Manhattan Sch. Music, NYC, 1998-. Mem. Racquet and Tennis Club, Creek Club, Field Club. Episcopalian. Avocations: music, golf, skiing, tennis, charities. Office: TCW/Mezzanine Crescent 200 Park Ave Ste 2200 New York NY 10166 E-mail: patrick.turner@tcw.com.

TURNER, PHILIP MICHAEL, academic administrator, writer; b. West Acton, Mass., Nov. 26, 1948; s. William Albert and Evelyn Olena (Peterson) T.; m. Lis Jane VanderBeke, Aug. 16, 1969; children: Gabrielle, Adrienne. BS in Edn., Boston State Coll., 1970; MS, U. Wis. at La Crosse, 1972; MSLS, EdD, East Tex. State U., 1977. Tchr. math. Edgewood Jr. High Sch., Merritt Island, Fla., 1969-71; ptnr. Video Guide Prodn. Co., Denver, 1973; libr. media specialist Edison Jr. High Sch., Green Bay, Wis., 1973-76; prof. libr. sci. U. Ala., Tuscaloosa, 1977-88; dean Sch. Libr. and Info. Studies U. North Tex., Denton, 1996—2004; asst. vice chancellor acad. affairs U. Ala. System, 1991-96; assoc. v.p. for acad. affairs for distance edn. U. North Tex., Denton, 1996—2004, vice provost learning enhancement, 2004—. Chair distance edn. adv. com. Tex. Higher Edn. Coordinating Bd., 2004—. Author: Handbook for In-School Media Personnel, 1980, Helping Teachers Teach, 1985, 3d edit., 2003. Vol. Meals on Wheels, Tuscaloosa, 1987-96. Recipient Outstanding Commitment To Teaching award U. Ala. Alumni Assn., 1979, Outstanding Svc. award Ala. Libr. and Media Prodrs., 1987, publ. award Div. Sch. Libr. Media Specialist, 1987, award for mng. info. tech., 1994, Ala. Libr. Assn. Disting. Svc. award, 1996; named Libr. of Yr., Beta Phi Mu, 1991. Mem. ALA (mem. accreditation com. 2000—04), Assn. Sch. Librs. (chair rsch. com. 1987-90, bd. dirs. 1990-94). Unitarian Universalist. Office: U North Tex PO Box 310889 Denton TX 76203-0889 Home Phone: 940-484-8214; Office Phone: 940-565-4462. Business E-Mail: pturner@unt.edu.

TURNER, RALPH HERBERT, sociologist, educator; b. Effingham, Ill., Dec. 15, 1919; s. Herbert Turner and Hilda Pearl (Bohn) T.; m. Christine Elizabeth Hanks, Nov. 2, 1943; children: Lowell Ralph, Cheryl Christine. BA, U So. Calif., 1941, MA, 1942; postgrad., U. Wis., 1942-43; PhD, U. Chgo., 1948. Rsch. assoc. Am. Coun. Race Relations, 1947-48; faculty UCLA, 1948—, prof. sociology and anthropology, 1959-90, prof. emeritus, 1990—, chmn. dept. sociology, 1963-68; chmn. Acad. Senate U. Calif. System, 1983-84. Vis. summer prof. U. Wash., 1960, U. Hawaii, 1962; vis. scholar Australian Nat. U., 1972; vis. prof. U. Ga., 1975, Ben Gurion U., Israel, 1983; vis. fellow Nuffield Coll. Oxford U., 1980; disting. vis. prof. Am. U., Cairo, Egypt, 1983; adj. prof. China Acad. Social Scis., Beijing, People's Republic China, 1986. Author: (with L. Killian) Collective Behavior, 1957, 2d edit., 1972, 3d edit., 1987, The Social Context of Ambition, 1964, Robert Park on Social Control and Collective Behavior, 1967, Family Interaction, 1970, Earthquake Prediction and Public Policy, 1975, (with J. Nigg, D. Paz, B. Young) Community Response to Earthquake Threat in So. Calif., 1980, (with J. Nigg and D. Paz) Waiting for Disaster, 1986; editl. cons., 1959-62; editor: Sociometry, 1962-64; acting editor: Ann. Rev. of Sociology, 1977-78; assoc. editor, 1978-79, editor, 1980-86; adv. editor: Am. Jour. Sociology, 1954-56, Sociology and Social Rsch., 1961-74; editl. staff: Am. Sociol. Rev., 1955-56; assoc. editor: Social Problems, 1959-62, 67-69; cons. editor: Sociol. Inquiry, 1968-73, Western Sociol. Rev., 1975-79; mem. editl. bd. Mass Emergencies, 1975-79, Internat. Jour. Crit. Sociology, 1974-76, Symbolic Interaction, 1977-90, 95—, Mobilization, 1996—. Mem. behavioral scis. study sect. NIH, 1961-66, chmn., 1963-64; dir.-at-large Social Sci. Rsch. Coun., 1965-66; chmn. panel on pub. policy implications of earthquake predictions Nat. Acad. Scis., 1974-75, also mem. earthquake study del. to Peoples Republic of China, 1976; mem. policy adv. bd. So. Calif. Earthquake Preparedness program, 1987-92, mem. com. social edn. and action L.A. Presbytery, 1954-56. Served to lt. (j.g.) USNR, 1943-46. Recipient Faculty prize Coll. Letters and Scis. UCLA, 1985; Faculty Rsch. fellow Social Sci. Rsch. Coun., 1953-56; Sr. Fulbright scholar U.K., 1956-57; Guggenheim fellow, U.K., 1964-65; Faculty Rsch. lectr. UCLA, 1987, UCLA Emeritus of Yr., 1997. Mem. AAAS (exch. del. to China 1988), AAUP, Am. Sociol. Assn. (coun. 1959-64, chmn. social psychology sect. 1960-61, pres. 1968-69, chmn. sect. theoretical sociology 1973-74, chmn. collective behavior and social movements sect. 1983-84, Cooley-Mead award 1987), Pacific Sociol. Assn. (pres. 1957), Internat. Sociol. Assn. (coun. 1974-82, v.p. 1978-82), Soc. Study Social Problems (exec. com. 1962-63), Soc. for Study Symbolic Interaction (pres. 1982-83, Charles Horton Cooley award 1978, George Herbert Mead award 1990), Sociol. Rsch. Assn. (pres. 1989-90), Am. Coun. of Learned Soc. (exec. com. of coun. 1990-93), UCLA Emeriti Assn. (coun., pres. 1992-93), U. of Calif. Emeriti Assns. (chair-elect 1996-97, chair 1997-98, Panunzio award 2002, Lifetime Svc. award 2007). Home: 1126 Chautauqua Blvd Pacific Palisades CA 90272-3808 Office: UCLA 405 Hilgard Ave Los Angeles CA 90095-9000

TURNER, REGINALD MAURICE, JR., lawyer; b. Detroit, Feb. 25, 1960; s. Reginald and Anne Laura (Mims) T.; m. Marcia Holland, June 10, 1989. BS in Indsl. Psychology, Wayne State U., 1982; JD, U. Mich., 1987. Bar: Mich. With UPS, Livonia, Mich., 1977-83, Profl. Pers. Svc. div. B.P.A. Enterprises, Detroit, 1983-84; summer assoc. Office of the Gen. Counsel GM Corp., Detroit, 1985, 86; law clk. Sachs, Nunn, Kates, Kadushin, O'Hare, Helveston & Waldman, Detroit, 1987; jud. law clk. to Hon. Dennis W. Archer Mich. Supreme Ct., Detroit, 1987-89; ptnr. Sachs, Waldman PC, Detroit, 1989—2000; atty. Clark Hill PLC, Detroit, 2000—. Vice chair Detroit Police Found.; active Mich. State Bd. Edn., 2003—, Detroit Bd. edn., 2000-2003. White House fellow, 1996-97; recipient Irving Stenn Jr. award U. Mich. Law Sch., 1987; named Barrister of the Yr., Outstanding Young Lawyer State Bar Mich., 1999; named one of the Best Lawyers in Am., 2002-; named to Super Lawyers, 2006-; named one of Most Influential Black Americans, Ebony mag., 2006. Mem. ABA, ACLU, NAACP, Fed. Bar Assn., Nat. Bar Assn. (pres. 2005—), State Bar Mich. (commn., pres. 2002-03), Wolverine Bar Assn. (pres. 1994-95, Damon J. Keith award 2004), Detroit Bar Assn., Alpha Phi Alpha. Office: Clark Hill PLC 500 Woodward Ave Ste 3500 Detroit MI 48226-3435 E-mail: rturner@clarkhill.com.

TURNER, ROBERT COMRIE, composer; b. Montreal, Que., Can., June 6, 1920; s. William Thomson and Myrtle Wellsteed (Snowdon) T.; m. Sara Nan Scott, June 30, 1949; children: Alden, Martin, Carolyn. BM, McGill U., 1943, MusD, 1953; postgrad., Royal Coll. Music, London, 1947—48; MusM, Vanderbilt U., 1950. Sr. music producer Canadian Broadcasting Corp., Vancouver, B.C., 1952—68; lectr. music U. B.C., Vancouver, 1955—57; prof. composition U. Manitoba, Winnipeg, 1969—85, prof. emeritus, 1985—. Composer-in-residence MacDowell Colony, Peterborough, N.H., 1987. Composer: Opening Night: A Theatre Overture, 1955, The Third Day (Easter Cantata), 1962, Symphony for Strings, 1960, Capriccio Concertante, 1975, 3 String Quartet, 1944, 1954, 1975, opera The Brideship, 1967, Trio (transition) for Violin Cello and Piano, 1969, The Phoenix and the Turtle, 1964, Concerto for Two Pianos and Orchestra, 1971, Johann's Gift to Christmas, 1972, Eidolons, 1972, Variations on The Prairie Settler's Song, 1974, From a Different Country, 1976, Lament for Linos, 1978, Amoroso Canto, 1978, Shadow Pieces (after Joseph Cornell), 1981, opera Vile Shadows, 1983, Symphony in One Movement, 1983, Encounters I-IX, 1984, Time for Three, 1985, Playhouse Music, 1986, Concerto for Viola and Orchestra, 1987, Shades of Autumn, 1987, Manitoba Memoir, 1989, Third Symphony, 1990, a Group of Seven, 1991, The River of Time, 1994, House of Shadows, 1994, Four "Last Songs", 1995, Festival Dance, 1997, Diverti-Memento for Chamber Orch., 1997, Premiere of House of Shadows by Winnipeg Symphony, 2006; All-Turner concert, 1989, Canada House, London, All-Turner concert, Victoria, 2003, All Turner concert, Winnipeg, 2005; composer (recordings): Portrait, Robert Turner, 2005, Ovation IV, Robert Turner, 2005; adjudicator Met. and San Francisco Opera auditions; Bramwell Tovey and The Winnipeg Symphony Orch. premiered The River of Time for SATB chorus and orch. in celebration of Robert Turner's 75th yr., 1996. Bd. dirs. Vancouver Internat. Festival. Recipient Commemorative medal for 125th Anniversary of Confedn. Can., 1993, Queen's Golden Jubilee medal, 2003, Order of Can., 2003, Outstanding Classical Composition award Western Can. Music

Alliance, 2004; nominee Juno award Can. Acad. Recording Arts and Scis., 2004. Mem.: Can. League Composers, Authors and Music Pubrs. of Can., Soc. Composers, Can. Music Ctr. Home: One Evergreen Pl #2602 Winnipeg MB Canada R3L 0E9

TURNER, ROBERT FOSTER, law educator, writer; b. Atlanta, Feb. 14, 1944; s. Edwin Witcher and Martha Frances (Williams) T. AB, Ind. U., Bloomington, 1968; postgrad., Stanford U., 1972-73; JD, U. Va., 1981, SJD, 1996. Bar: Va. 1982, U.S. Supreme Ct. 1986. Rsch. assoc., pub. affairs fellow Hoover Instn. on War, Revolution and Peace, Stanford U., 1971-74; spl. asst., legis. asst. U.S. Sen. Robert P. Griffin, 1974-79; co-founder, assoc. dir. Ctr. for Nat. Security Law U. Va., Charlottesville, 1981, 87—; sr. fellow, 1985-86; spl. asst. undersec. for policy Dept. Def., 1981-82; counsel Pres.'s Intelligence Oversight Bd., White House, 1982-84; prin. dep. asst. sec. for legis. and intergovtl. affairs Dept. State, 1984, acting. asst. sec., 1984—85; pres. U.S. Inst. Peace, Washington, 1986-87; lectr. in law and in govt. and fgn. affairs U. Va., Charlottesville, 1988-93, assoc. prof., 1993-97, prof., 1997—; Charles H. Stockton prof. internat. law Naval War Coll., 1994-95. Disting. lectr. U.S. Mil. Acad., West Point, 1995. Author: Myths of the Vietnam War: The Pentagon Papers Reconsidered, 1972, Vietnamese Communism: Its Origins and Development, 1975, The War Powers Resolution: Its Implementation in Theory and Practice, 1983, Nicaragua v. United States: A Look at the Facts, 1987, Repealing the War Powers Resolution: Restoring the Rule of Law in U.S. Foreign Policy, 1991, The ABM Treaty and the Senate: Issues of International and Constitutional Law, 1999, The Real Lessons of the Vietnam War, 2002, (with John Norton Moore) The Legal Structure of Defense Organization, 1986, International Law and the Brezhnev Doctrine, 1987, Readings on International Law, 1995, National Security Law, 2d edit., 2005, (with John Norton Moore and Guy B. Roberts) National Security Law Documents, 1995, 2d edit., 2006, (with John Norton Moore and Ross A. Fisher) To Oppose Any Foe, 2006; contbr. articles to profl. jours. and newspapers. Pres. Endowment of U.S. Inst. Peace, 1986-87; trustee Intercollegiate Studies Inst., 1986-92; bd. dirs. Thomas Jefferson Inst. for Pub. Policy, 1997—; chmn. scholars commn. on Jefferson-Hemings matter Thomas Jefferson Heritage Soc., 2000-01. Grantee Hoover Press, 1972, Earhart Found., 1980, 1989-90, Inst. Ednl. Affairs, 1980, Carthage Found., 1980. Mem. ABA (chmn. com. on exec.-congl. rels., sec. internat. law and practice 1983-86, adv. com. on law and nat. security 1984-86, standing com. on law and nat. security 1986-92, chmn. 1989-92, editor ABA Nat. Security Law Report 1992-99), Federalist Soc. (chmn. subcom. on nat. security law 1998—), Com. on the Present Danger, 2005-, Bd. Rsch. Cons., Inst. Fgn. Policy Analysis, Mensa, Am. Soc. Internat. Law, Nat. Eagle Scout Assn., Coun. on Fgn. Rels., Acad. of Polit. Sci. Office: Univ Va Sch of Law Ctr for Nat Security Law 580 Massie Rd Charlottesville VA 22903-1738 Home Phone: 434-978-7838; Office Phone: 434-924-4083. Business E-Mail: bobturner@virginia.edu.

TURNER, R(OBERT) GERALD, academic administrator; b. Atlanta, Tex., Nov. 25, 1945; s. Robert B. and Oreta Lois (Porter) T.; m. Gail Oliver, Dec. 21, 1968; children: Angela Jan, Jessica Diane AA, Lubbock Christian Coll., 1966, LLD (hon.), 1985, Pepperdine U., 1989; BS, Abilene Christian U., 1968; MA, U. Tex., 1970, PhD, 1975. Tchr. Weatherford High Sch., Tex., 1968-69; tchr. Lanier High Sch., Austin, Tex., 1969-70; instr. psychology San Antonio Coll., 1970-72; instr. Prairie View A & M U., Tex., 1973-75; asst. prof. psychology Pepperdine U., Malibu, Calif., 1975-78, assoc. prof. psychology, 1978-79, dir. testing, 1975-76, chmn. social sci. div., 1976-78, assoc. v.p. univ. affairs, 1979; assoc. prof. psychology U. Okla., Norman, 1979-84, exec. asst. to pres., 1979-81, acting provost, 1982, v.p. exec. affairs, 1981-84; chancellor U. Miss., University, 1984-95; pres. So. Meth. U., Dallas, 1995—. Pres. Southeastern Conf., 1985-87; trustee Pepperdine U., 1994-95; mem. Pres.'s Commn., NCAA, 1989-92, chmn., 1991-92; mem. Knight Commn. on Intercollegiate Athletics, 1991—; chmn. pres. coun. Miss. Assn. Colls., 1985-86; mem. def. adv. com. Svc. Acad. Athletic Programs, 1992—; bd. dirs. J.C. Penney, Am. Beacon Funds. Author: (with L. Willerman) Readings About Individual and Group Differences, 1979. Contbr. articles to profl. jours. Recipient Outstanding Alumni award Abilene Christian U., 1989; named to New Boston HS Athletic Hall of Fame, 1993. Mem. Young Pres. Orgn., Sigma Xi, Beta Alpha Psi, Phi Theta Kappa, Alpha Chi, Phi Kappa Phi. Mem. Ch. of Christ. Avocations: reading, tennis, golf, travel. Office: So Meth Univ Office Of The Pres Dallas TX 75275-0001

TURNER, ROBERT LLOYD, state legislator; b. Columbus, Miss., Sept. 14, 1947; s. Roosevelt and Beatrice (Hargrove) T.; m. Gloria Harrell; children: Roosevelt, Robert, Ryan. BS, U. Wis., Racine, 1976. Mgr. French Quarter Restaurant, Racine, 1989; legislator Wis. State Assembly, Madison, 1990—, mem. transp. com. bldg. commn., mem. ways and means com., labor com., fin. institutions com., minority vice chmn. caucus, highway com., chmn. Dem. Caucus. Br. sales mgr. ETG Temporaries, Inc., Racine, 1989—; pub. Communicator News, Racine, 1989—; v.p. Racine Raider Football Team. State chmn. Dem. Black Polit. Caucus, Madison; pres. Bd. Health, Racine; chmn. Wis. State Elections Bd., Madison, 1990; alderman Racine City Coun., 1976—; chair Econ. Devel. Com., Racine; regional dir. Badger State Games, Racine; active Pvt. Industry Coun. Southeastern Wis., 1988-89, bd. dirs. Racine County Youth Sports Assn.; active Racine Juneteenth Day Com., bd. advisors Big Bros./Big Sisters. Sgt. USAF, 1967-71, Vietnam. Decorated Commendation medal; named Man of Yr. 2d Missionary Bapt. Ch., 1983. Mem. Dem. Caucus (chmn. 2003, 05), Urban League (pres. bd. dirs.), NAACP (2d v.p.), VFW, Vietnam Vets. Am. (life mem.), Am. Legion, Masons (supreme coun. 33rd degree), Shriners. Democrat. Home: 36 Mckinley Ave Racine WI 53404-3414 Office: Wis Assembly PO Box 8953 Madison WI 53708-8953

TURNER, ROBERT W., rail transportation executive; married; 2 children. Grad. in Econs., Hiram Coll., Ohio. V.p. pub. affairs Champion Internat. Corp.; sr. v.p. corp. rels. Union Pacific Corp., Omaha, 2000—. Pres. Union Pacific Found.; head Union Pacific RR Mus.; vice chair Omaha Sister Cities Assn.; trustee Nebr. chpt. Nature Conservancy; bd. dirs. US Bank Adv. Bd., Omaha C. of C., Durham Western Heritage Mus. Office: Union Pacific Corp 1400 Douglas St Omaha NE 68179 Office Phone: 402-544-5000. *

TURNER, ROGER D., lawyer; b. Madison, Ind., Feb. 3, 1952; BS with highest honors, Purdue Univ., 1973; JD, Univ. Chgo., 1976. Bar: NY 1977. Assoc. Cravath Swaine & Moore LLP, NYC, 1976—83, ptnr., 1983—, head corp. real estate. Mem. Chgo. Law Rev. Mem.: Assn. Bar City NY. Office: Cravath Swaine & Moore LLP Worldwide Plz 825 Eighth Ave New York NY 10019-7475 Office Phone: 212-474-1668. Office Fax: 212-474-3700. Business E-Mail: rturner@cravath.com.

TURNER, RONALD L., information services executive; BS in Aerospace Engring., U. Tenn.; MS in Engring., U. Fla.; MS in Mgmt., MIT. Sys. command USAF, 1968—73; sys. mgr. through v.p. Martin Marietta, 1973—87; pres., CEO GEC Marconi Electronic Sys., 1987—93; pres., CEO computing devices internat. Ceridian Corp., Mpls., 1993—97, exec. v.p. ops., 1997—98, pres., COO, 1998—2000, chmn., pres., CEO, 2000—06, pres., CEO, 2006. Bd. dir. Ceridian Corp., Brink's Co.; mem. bd. gov. Electronic Industries Alliance. Bd. dir. Danny Thompson Meml.; Minn. Bus. Partnership; mem. Bus. Roundtable. Office: Ceridian Corp 3311 E Old Shakopee Rd Minneapolis MN 55425-1640

TURNER, SCOTT MACNEELY, lawyer; b. Clinton, NY, Nov. 8, 1948; s. Frederick George and Ruth Alys (Thomas) T.; children: Katherine, Benjamin, Robert; m. Mary A. Worboys, June 15, 2002. AB with honors, Colgate U., 1970; JD magna cum laude, Washington and Lee U., 1973. Bar: N.Y. 1974, D.C. 1996, U.S. Dist. Ct. (we. dist.) N.Y. 1974, U.S. Ct. Appeals (2d cir.) N.Y. 1987, (3d cir.) N.Y. 1988, (7th cir.), 2007. Assoc. Nixon Hargrave Devans & Doyle, Rochester, NY, 1973-80; ptnr. Nixon Peabody LLP (formerly Nixon Hargrave Devans & Doyle), Rochester, NY, 1981—; chmn. eviron. practice group Nixon Hargrave Devans & Doyle, 1984-97, Rochester mng. ptnr., 2006—. Chmn. legis. regulatory affairs com. Internat. Gas Turbine Inst. Atlanta, 1993-95; chair coll. coun. SUNY Coll. at Brockport, 2004—. Editor: N.Y. Environmental Law Handbook, 1999. Bd. dirs. Unity Health Sys., Rochester, N.Y., 1992—, Park Ridge Found., Rochester, 1987-92, Rochester Hist. Soc., 2004—; town leader Ogden Rep. Party, Spencerport, N.Y., 1981-86. Capt. USAR, 1972-73. Mem. Air and Waste Mgmt. Assn. (chmn. legal com. 1984-88), N.Y. State Bar Assn. (environ. sect., co-chmn. solid and hazardous waste com. 1982-94), Genesee Valley Club, Order of Coif. Republican. Home: 408 Dewey St Churchville NY 14428-9103 Office: Nixon Peabody LLP Clinton Sq PO Box 31051 Ste 1300 Rochester NY 14603-1051 E-mail: sturner@nixonpeabody.com.

TURNER, SHARON P., dean, dentist, educator; b. Charleston, W.Va., Aug. 8, 1950; d. George Brock and Anna Hopkins Pullen; m. Aubrey Williams Turner, Jr., Feb. 26, 1972; children: Brock Leslie Turner, Martin Gresham Turner, Karen Anna Turner. BA in Biology, Winthrop U., 1971; DDS, U. N.C., 1979; JD, N.C. Ctrl U., 1995. Bar: NC; lic. dentist NC, Oreg., Ky., diplomate Am. Acad. Pain Mgmt. Pvt. dental practitioner Dengler & Turner, Raleigh, NC, 1985-86; asst. prof. of diagnostic scis. U. N.C. Sch. of Dentistry, Chapel Hill, 1986-94, assoc. prof. of diagnostic scis., 1994-98, dir. patient admissions and emergency svcs., 1986-94, dir. dental faculty practice, 1989-98, assoc. dean for adminstrn. planning, 1994-98; dean, prof. dentistry Oreg. Health and Sci. U. Sch. Dentistry, Portland, 1998—2003; dean U. Ky. Coll. Dentistry, Lexington, 2003—. Cons. VA Hosp., Durham, N.C., 1999. Contbg. author: Oral Surgery, 1999. Youth group leader Eno River Unitarian Universalist, Durham, 1996-97, Sunday Sch. tchr., 1997-98; girl scout leader Pines of Carolina Coun., Girl Scouts U.S., Durham, N.C., 1990-94. Named one of Top 25 Visionary Leaders in Dentistry, Am. Student Dental Assn., 1999. Fellow Internat. Coll. Dentists, Am. Coll. Dentists, Am. Coll. Legal Medicine, Piere Fourchard Acad.; mem. ADA, Am. Dental Edn. Assn., Am. Acad. Pain Mgmt., Internat. Assn. Dental Rsch., Intenat. Assn. for Study of Pain, Soc. for Exec. Leadership in Academic Medicine (v.p. 1999-2000, pres. 2000-01, Excellence award 2004), Acad. General Dentistry, Rotary Club Lexington. Avocations: swimming, hiking, singing, reading. Office: U Ky Coll Dentistry Chandler Med Ctr D136 800 Rose St Lexington KY 40536-9707 Business E-Mail: turnersp@uky.edu.

TURNER, STANSFIELD, former CIA director, retired military officer; b. Chgo., Dec. 1, 1923; s. Oliver Stansfield and Wilhelmina Josephine (Wagner) T.; m. Eli Karin Gilbert, Mar. 16. 1985 (dec. Jan. 2000); m. Marion Weiss Turner, Sept., 2003. Student, Amherst Coll., 1941-43, DCL, 1975; BS, U.S. Naval Acad., 1946; MA (Rhodes scholar), Oxford U., 1950; LHD, Sierra Nev. Coll., 1984; HumD, Roger Williams Coll., 1975; DSc in Edn, Bryant Coll., 1977; LLD, Salve Regina Coll., 1977, The Citadel, 1980, Pace U., 1980. Ensign USN, 1946, advanced through grades to adm., 1975, ret., 1979; served primarily in destroyers; commd. U.S.S. Horne, guided missile cruiser, 1967-68; aide to Sec. Navy; comdr. carrier task group 6th Fleet, 1970-71; dir. systems analysis div. Office Chief Naval Ops., Navy Dept., Washington, 1971-72; pres. Naval War Coll., Newport, RI, 1972-74; comdr. U.S. Second Fleet, 1974-75; comdr.-in-chief Allied Forces So. Europe, NATO, 1975-77; dir. CIA, Washington, 1977-81; John M. Olin Disting. prof. nat. security U.S. Mil. Acad., West Point, 1989-90; prof. U. Md. Grad. Sch. Pub. Policy, College Park, 1991—2007; Raymond H. Spruance Disting. Fellow Naval War Coll., Newport, RI, 2000—01. Sr. rsch. fellow Norwegian Nobel Inst., Oslo, Norway, 1995-96; bd. dirs., Chase Investment Counsel Corp.; bd. visitors U.S. Naval Acad., 1996-2000. Author: Secrecy and Democracy, 1985, Terrorism and Democracy, 1991, Caging the Nuclear Genie: An American Challenge to Global Security, 1997, Caging the Genies: A Workable Plan for Chemical, Biological and Nuclear Weapons, 1999, Burn Before Reading: Presidents, CIA Directors, and Secret Intelligence, 2005. Decorated Legion of Merit, Bronze Star; Recipient Nat. Security medal, 1981, Fgn. Policy Assn. medal, 1998, Office: 488 River Bend Rd Great Falls VA 22066 Office Phone: 703-438-8408. Personal E-mail: admturner@aol.com.

TURNER, STEPHEN PARK, philosopher, sociologist, educator; b. Chgo., Mar. 1, 1951; s. Lawrence Lynn and Natalie (Stephens) Turner; m. Kimberly Anne Wills, Apr. 21, 1990; children: Evan Wills, Douglas Carrera. AB, U. Mo., Columbia, 1971, AM in Sociology, 1971, AM in Philosophy, 1972, PhD in Sociology, 1975. Asst. prof. U. South Fla., 1975—80, assoc. prof., 1980—84, prof., dept. sociology, 1984—87, grad. rsch. prof., dept. of sociology, 1987—89; vis. prof. Boston U., 1987; grad. rsch. prof. dept. philosophy U. South Fla., Tampa, Fla., 1989—; dir. Ctr. Social and Polit. Thought, 1994—. Simon hon. prof. U. Manchester, 1996—97; vis. prof. Va. Poly. Inst. and State U., Blacksburg, 1982, U. Notre Dame, 1985. Author: (book) Sociological Explanation as Translation, 1980, The Search for a Methodology of Social Science: Durkheim, Weber, and the 19th Century Problem of Cause, Probability, and Action, 1986, Brains/Practices/Relativism: Social Theory after Cognitive Science, 2002, Liberal Democracy 3.0: Civil Society in an Age of Experts, 2003, The Social Theory of Practices: Tradition, Tacit Knowledge, and Presuppositions, 1994; co-author (with F. Weed): Conflict in Organizations, 1983; co-author: (with R. Factor) Max Weber and the Dispute Over Reason and Value: A Study in Philosophy, Ethics, and Politics, 1984; co-author: (with Jonathan Turner) The Impossible Science: An Institutional Analysis of American Sociology, 1990; co-author: (with Regis A. Factor) Max Weber: The Lawyer as Social Thinker, 1994; editor: The Cambridge Companion to Weber; editor: (with Dirk Käsler) Sociology Responds to Fascism, 1992; editor: Emile Durkheim: Sociologist and Moralist, 1993; co-editor (with M. Wardell): Sociological Theory in Transition, 1986; co-editor: (with Alan Sica) The Disobedient Generation: Social Theorists in the Sixties, 2005; co-editor: (with Mark Risjord) Philosophy of Anthropology and Sociology, 2007; collaborating editor: jour. Social Studies of Science, 1986—; contbr. articles to profl. jours., NEH fellow, 1991-1992, Swedish Collegium for Advanced Study in Social Scis. fellow, 1992, 1998. Mem.: Soc. Social Studies Sci., Am. Sociol. Assn., Am. Philos. Assn., St. Petersburg Yacht Club. Home: 103 2nd Ave Saint Petersburg Beach FL 33706-4303 Office: U South Fla Dept Philosophy Tampa FL 33620 Office Phone: 813-974-5549. E-mail: turner@shell.cas.usf.edu.

TURNER, (CLYDE) TAB (CLYDE TAB TURNER), lawyer; b. 1959; JD with high honors, U. Ark., 1984. Bar: Ark. 1985, Ark. Supreme Ct., US Dist. Ct. (we. and ea. dists. Ark., ea. dist. Okla., no. and we. dists. Tex., ea. dist. Mo.), US Ct. Appeals (5th and 8th cirs.), US Supreme Ct. Prin. Turner & Assocs., P.A., North Little Rock, Ark. Named one of 40 Under 40, Ark. Bus. mag.; recipient Trial Lawyer of Yr. award, Trial Lawyers for Pub. Justice Found., 2001. Mem.: Tex. Trial Lawyers Assn., Orange County Trial Lawyers Assn., So. Trial Lawyers Assn., Western Trial Lawyers Assn., Million Dollar Advs. Forum, Trial Lawyers for Pub. Justice, Pub. Citizen, ATLA, Ark. Trial Lawyers Assn., Pulaski County Bar Assn., ABA, Ark. Bar Assn. Achievements include winning the highest monetary jury verdict ($20.2 million) in the history of Arkansas. Office: Turner & Assocs PA 4705 Somers Ave Ste 100 North Little Rock AR 72116 Office Phone: 501-791-2277. Office Fax: 501-791-1251. E-mail: tab@tturner.com. *

TURNER, TED (ROBERT EDWARD TURNER), retired broadcast company executive, philanthropist; b. Cin., Nov. 19, 1938; s. Robert Edward and Florence (Rooney) Turner; m. Judy Nye (div.); children: Laura Lee, Robert Edward IV; m. Jane Shirley Smith, June 1965 (div. 1988); children: Beau, Rhett, Jennie; m. Jane Fonda, Dec. 21, 1991 (div. 2001). Grad. in classics, Brown U.; DSc in Commerce (hon.), Drexel U., 1982; LLD (hon.), Samford U., 1982, Atlanta U., 1984; D Entrepreneurial Sci. (hon.), Cen. New Eng. Coll. Tech., 1983; D in Pub. Adminstrn. (hon.), Mass. Maritime Acad., 1984; D in Bus. Adminstrn. (hon.), U. Charleston, 1985. Account exec. Turner Advt. Co., Atlanta, 1961—63, pres., COO, 1963—70; pres., chmn. bd. Turner Broadcasting Sys., Inc. (TBS), Atlanta, 1970—96; vice chmn. Time Warner Inc. (merger Turner Broadcasting Sys.), 1996—2000; vice chmn., sr. advisor AOL Time Warner (merger of Time Warner Inc. and AOL, Inc.), 2001—03; chmn. Turner Enterprises, Inc., 2003—; owner Atlanta Braves, 1976—. Bd. dirs. Time Warner, 1996—2001, Time Warner Inc. (formerly AOL/Time Warner), 2001—06. Co-founder, co-chair Nuclear Threat Initiative, Washington, 2001—; bd. dirs. Martin Luther King Ctr., Atlanta; donations to a number of non-profit foundations, including Turner Found., Inc., Endangered Species Fund, UN Found. and the Nuclear Threat Initiative. Named Yachtsman of Yr. 4 times; named one of 50 Most Generous Philanthropists, Fortune Mag., 2005, Forbes Richest Americans, 2006; named to Hall of Fame, Promotion and Mktg. Assn., 1980, Nat. Assn. for Sport and Phys. Edn. Hall of Fame, 1986; recipient Outstanding Entrepreneur of Yr. award, Sales Mktg. and Mgmt. Mag., 1979, Salesman of Yr. award, Sales and Mktg. Execs., 1980, Pvt. Enterprise Exemplar medal, Freedoms Found. at Valley Forge, 1980, Communicator of Yr. award, Pub. Rels. Soc. Am., 1981, N.Y. Broadcasters, 1981, Internat. Communicator of Yr. award, Sales and Mktg. Execs., 1981, Nat. News Media award, VFW, 1981, Disting. Svc. in Telecomm. award, Ohio U. Coll. Communication, 1982, Carr Van Anda award, Ohio Sch. Journalism, 1982, Spl. award, Edinburgh Internat. TV Festival, Scotland, 1982, Media Awareness award, United Vietnam Vets. Orgn., 1983, Bd. Govs. award, Atlanta chpt. NATAS, 1982, Spl. Olympics award, Spl. Olympics Com., 1983, Dinner of Champions award, Ga. chpt. Multiple Sclerosis Soc., 1983, Praca Spl. Merit award, N.Y. Puerto Rican Assn. for Cmty. Affairs, 1983, World Telecomm. Pioneer award, N.Y. State Broadcasters Assn., 1984, Golden Plate award, Am. Acad. Achievement, 1984, Outstanding Supporter Boy Scouting award, Nat. Boy Scout Coun., 1984, Silver Satellite award, Am. Women in Radio and TV, Lifetime Achievement award, N.Y. Internat. Film and TV Festival, 1984, Corp. Star of Yr. award, Nat. Leukemia Soc., 1985, Disting. Achievement award, U. Ga., 1985, Tree of Life award, Jewish Nat. Fund, 1985, Bus. Exec. of Yr. award, Ga. Security Dealers Assn., 1985, Life Achievement award, Popular Culture Assn., 1986, George Washington Disting. Patriot award, SAR, 1986, Mo. Honor medal, Sch. Journalism, U. Mo., 1987, Golden Ace award, Nat. Cable TV Acad., 1987, Sol Taishoff award, Nat. Press Found., 1988, Citizen Diplomat award, Ctr. for Soviet-Am. Dialogue, 1988, Chmn.'s award, Cable Advt. Bur., 1988, Directorate award, NATAS, 1989, Paul White award, Radio and TV News Dirs. Assn., 1989, Bus. Marketer of Yr. award, Am. Mktg. Assn., 1989, Disting. Svc. award, Simon Wiesenthal Ctr., 1990, Glasnost award, Vols. Am. and Soviet Life mag., 1990, Time Mag. Man of the Year, 1991, Cable & Broadcasting's Man of the Century, 1999, Carnegie Medal of Philanthropy, 2001, Bower award for Bus. Leadership, Franklin Inst., 2006, numerous others; won America's Cup in his yacht Courageous, 1977. Mem.: NAACP (life; bd. dirs. Atlanta chpt.), Nat. Cable TV Assn. (Pres.'s award 1979, 1989, Regional Employer of Yr. award 1976), Cousteau Soc., Nat. Audubon Soc., Bay Area Cable Club (hon.). Avocations: sailing, fishing. Office: Nuclear Threat Initiative 1747 Pennsylvania Ave NW 7th Flr Washington DC 20006

TURNER, TINA (ANNA MAE BULLOCK), singer; b. Brownsville, Tenn., Nov. 26, 1939; m. Ike Turner, 1956 (div. 1978); children: Craig, Ike Jr., Michael, Ronald. Singer (with): Ike Turner Kings of Rhythm, and Ike and Tina Turner Revue; appeared in (films) Gimme Shelter, 1970, Soul to Soul, 1971, Tommy, 1975, Sgt. Pepper's Lonely Hearts Club Band, 1978, Mad Max Beyond Thunderdome, 1985, Break Every Rule, 1986, Last Action Hero, 1993, concert tours of Europe, 1966, Japan and Africa, 1971, Showtime TV concert Wildest Dreams, albums with Ike Turner Hunter, 1970, Ike and Tina Show II, Ike and Tina Show, 1966, Ike and Tina Turner, Bad Dreams, 1973, Ike and Tina Turner Greatest Hits, vol. 1.2 and 3, 1989, Greatest Hits, 1990, Proud Mary, 1991, The Ike and Tina Turner Collection, 1993, solo albums Let Me Touch Your Mind, 1972, Tina Turns the Country On, 1974, Acid Queen, 1975, Love Explosion, 1977, Rough, 1978, Airwaves, 1979, Private Dancer, 1984, Break Every Rule, 1986, Tina Live In Europe, 1988, Foreign Affair, 1989, Simply the Best, 1991, What's Love Got to Do With It? (soundtrack), 1993, All the Best, 2005, recordings Sixties to Nineties, with others, 1994, Wildest Dreams, 1996, Twenty Four Seven, 2000; performer (with USA): for Africa on song We are The World, 1985; author: (autobiography) I, Tina, 1985; (film of autobiography) What's Love Got To Do With It?, 1993. Nominee Grammy (Best Pop Female Vocal) for "I Don't Wanna Fight", 1994; named to Rock and Roll Hall of Fame, 1991; recipient Grammy award, 1972, 1985, 1986, Kennedy Ctr. Honor, John F. Kennedy Ctr. for Performing Arts, 2005.

TURNER, VICKY JO, music educator; b. Kansas City, Mo., Mar. 17, 1968; d. James Phillip and Virginia Joan Turner. BS in Music Edn., N.W. Mo. State U., 1992. Lic. tchr. Mo., 1993. Music tchr. Linn County Sch. Dist., Purdin, Mo., 1994—96, McDonald County Sch. Dist., Jane and Rocky Comfort, Mo., 1999—2002, Kennett Sch. Dist., Mo., 2002—06, Adrian R-III Sch. Dist., 2006—. Mem. first bapt. choir First Bapt. Ch., Kennett, 2002, Sunday sch. sec. 1st and 2d grade students, 2003. Recipient Cert. of Appreciation, Am. Legion, 1999. Mem.: Mo. Band Dir.'s Assn. (licentiate), Am. Choral Dir.'s Assn. (licentiate), Music Educator's Nat. Conf. (licentiate), Mo. State Tchr.'s Assn. (licentiate). Baptist. Avocations: exercise, singing, birdwatching, hiking, music. Office: Adrian R III Sch Dist Butler MO 64730 Office Phone: 816-287-2158. Office Fax: 816-297-2980. E-mail: vjturner@netection.net.

TURNER, WARREN AUSTIN, state legislator; b. Berkeley, Calif., Dec. 21, 1926; s. Warren Mortimer and Rebecca Oline (Noer) T.; m. Beverly Daune Mackay, Mar. 29, 1952; children: Daune Scott, Warren Adair, Alan Corey. BA, U. Calif., Berkeley, 1950, BS, 1952, MPH, 1958. Pub. acct. Price Waterhouse, San Francisco, 1951-52, AW Blackman, Las Vegas, Nev., 1952-56; asst. adminstr. Marin Gen. Hosp., San Rafael, Calif., 1958-60; assoc. dir. UCLA Hosp., 1960-68; founding adminstr. Walter O. Boswell Meml. Hosp., Sun City, Ariz., 1968-81; pres. Sun Health Corp., 1981-89; mem. Ariz. Senate, Phoenix, 1993-97, chmn. rules com., vice chair health com., mem. appropriations, family svcs. and transp. com., 1995-97. Chmn. appropriation subcom., K-12, C.C.'s and natural resources. With USN, 1944—46. Mem.: Ariz. Acad. Republican. Avocations: breeding and showing siamese cats, fishing, mining. Home: 18432 W Glendale Ave Waddell AZ 85355-9737

TURNER, WELD W(INSTON), industrial psychologist; b. St. Paul, July 25, 1931; s. Frank and Hazel Thirza (Weld) Prevratil; m. Helen Theo Kralicek, June 12, 1953 (div. 1969); children; Jean Ann, Alan Weld. BS in Commerce, Okla. A&M Coll. (now Okla. State U.), 1954; MS, Purdue U., 1955, PhD in Indsl. Psychology, 1959. Pers. evaluation assoc. GM Inst., Flint., 1955-60; supr. pers. rsch. B.F. goodrich Co., Akron, 1960-67; sr. manpower adv. Mobil Oil Corp., NYC, 1967—. Lectr. adult edn. divsn. U. Akron, part-time. With U.S. Army, 1951-52. Mem. APA, Am. Psychol. Soc., Sigma Xi, Phi Kappa Phi, Pi Gamma Mu.

TURNER, WESLEY R., publishing executive; m. Shirley Turner; children: Sara, Leslie. Grad., U. Tex. With Ft. Worth Press, 1973-75; from advt. sales rep. to v.p. advt. Ft. Worth Star-Telegram, 1975-86, pres. & pub., 1997—; exec. v.p., gen. mgr. Kansas City Star, 1990-97; pres. Sutton Industries, 1987-90. Bd. visitors Coll. Mass Communication Middle Tenn. State U. Recipient John S. Knight Gold Medal, 2002. Mem.: Tex. Daily Newspaper Assn. (Pat Taggart award for Tex. Newspaper Leader of Yr.

2005), Southern Newspaper Publishers Assn. Office: Fort Worth Star-Telegram 400 W 7th St Fort Worth TX 76102-4701 Office Phone: 817-390-7454. E-mail: wturner@star-telegram.com. *

TURNER, WILLARD CRAIG, academic administrator; b. Mobile, Ala., Jan. 7, 1947; s. A. C. and Sybil Willard Turner; m. Annette Louise Enloe, Dec. 20, 1969; children: Scott Craig, Shannon Leigh Hays. BA, Baylor U., 1969, MA, 1971; PhD, Tulane U., 1977. Asst., assoc. prof. English Tex. A&M U., Coll. Station, Tex., 1976—85; prof., chair English Miss. Coll., Clinton, 1985—92; exec. v.p., chief academic officer Hardin-Simmons U., Abilene, Tex., 1996—2001, pres., 2001—. Mem., distance edn. adv. com. Tex. Higher Edn. Coordinating Bd., Austin, Tex., 1999—2001; bd. dirs. Ind. Coll., Univ. Tex., 2001—, Assn. Tex. Coll., Univ., 2004—. Editor: Critical Essays on Eudora Welty, Critical Essays on American Humor, The Poet Robert Browning and His Kinsfolk, by His Cousin, Cyrus Mason. Bd. dirs. Abilene (Tex.) C. of C., 2001, United Way of Abilene, 2000—05, Serenity Found. of Tex., Abilene, 2003, Consortium for Global Edn., Atlanta, 2005; bd. govs. Abilene Philharm., 2002—05. Avocations: fishing, reading, motion pictures. Office: Hardin-Simmons U Box 16000 Abilene TX 79698 Home Phone: 325-672-9381; Office Phone: 325-670-1227. Business E-Mail: cturner@hsutx.edu.

TURNER-RICHARD, LANA R., musician, director, composer; b. Wood River, Ill., Oct. 14, 1952; d. George A. and Grace E. (Brake) Turner; m. Robert Richard, Oct. 27, 1984. MusB in Edn. and Piano Performance, So. Ill. Univ., Edwardsville, Ill., 1974, M in Piano, 1977; doctoral studies in piano, Washington Univ., 1984. Instr. various C.C., St. Louis, 1985—95; accompanist St. Louis (Mo.) Children's Choir; music dir. Summer Playhouse Prodns., Crestwood, 1989—, St. Lucas U.C.C., St. Louis, 1996—. Chmn. auditions Piano Guild, Ill., Mo., 1974—90; judge variuos music festivals U.S., 1971—. Worker habitat for Humanity, St. Louis., 2006. Mem.: U.S. humane Soc., Pi Kappa Lambda. Office: St Lucas UCC 11735 Denny Rd Saint Louis MO 63126

TURNER THORNE, CHARLI, women's college basketball coach; d. Jim Turner; m. Will Thorne, May 14, 1994; children: Conor, Liam, Quinn. BA in Psych., Stanford U., 1988; MEd, U. Wash., 1990. Grad. asst. U. Wash., 1988-90; asst. coach, recruiting coord. Santa Clara U., Calif., 1990-93; head coach No. Ariz. U., Flagstaff, 1993—96, Ariz. State U., Tempe, 1996—. Named Dist. VIII Coach of Yr., Women's Basketball Coaches Assn., 2006. Office: Ariz State U Womens Basketball Carson Ctr PO Box 872505 Tempe AZ 85287-2505 Office Phone: 480-965-6086. E-mail: ASUHoop@asu.edu. *

TURNER VANLYDEGRAF, CLAUDIA BETH, writer, researcher; b. Salinas, Calif., Mar. 19, 1945; d. Prentiss Dixon Hill and Barbara Clayborne, Leonard Francis Balch (Stepfather); m. Robert Michael Turner, May 21, 1966 (div. Aug. 14, 1972); m. Jay Frank VanLydegraf, 1980; children: David Michael Reinhardt, Jeffrey Warren Gregory, Amber Beth Turner. Student, El Camino Coll., 1969—72. Cert. Nev. State Ins. Bd., 1999; Nev. Real Estate Divsn., 1979, notary public load signing agent. Cost, manpower budget analyst Hughes Aircraft Co., Culver City, Calif., 1972—77; auditor No. Nev. Health & Welfare & Pension Plans Adminstrv. Office, Reno, 1980—81; co-owner TV Signal Corp, Cold Springs, Nev., 1981—86; flagger, laborer Laborers Local 169, Reno, 1989—94; jewelry sales assoc. SuperPawn/Camco, Reno, 1994—96; sales, loan assoc. Pioneer Jewelry and Loan, Reno, 1996—97; owner document rsch. firm Coyote Svcs., Cold Springs, 1998—; pub./owner Coyote News, Cold Springs, 1998—2002. Author: Notes from Nobody, 2001. Citizens adv. bd. Washoe County Commn., Cold Springs, 1999—2001; adv. - reporter Cold Springs Cmty. Assoc, 1998—2003; lobbyist Nev. Mem.: UnNamed Writers Group, Ea. Star. Independent. Avocations: genealogy, gemology, antiques, history, art. Home: 17890 Fantail Circle Cold Springs NV 89506 Office: Coyote Services 17890 Fantail Circle Cold Springs NV 89506 Office Phone: 775-972-6530. E-mail: cltvcoyote@aol.com.

TURNER-WRIGHT, MARIE ANNETTA, retired librarian; d. Clarence and W. Marie Turner; 1 child, Milicent Anne Wright. AB, Ind. U., Bloomington, 1957, MLS, 1971. Specialist in libr. info. sci. Ind. U., 1986. Adminstrv. asst. childrens svcs. Indpls.-Marion County Pub. Libr., 1971—74, br. libr., 1974—79; assoc. faculty Ind. U. Sch. Libr. and Info. Sci., Bloomington, 1974—84; assoc. libr. Ind. U.-Purdue U. Indpls., U. Libr., Indpls., 1985—2001; adj. faculty dept. English Ind. U.-Purdue U. Indpls., Sch. Liberal Arts, Indpls., 1989—2002; adj. faculty. Martin U., Indpls., 2006—. Vis. asst. libr. Ind. U. -Purdue U. Indpls., U. Libr., Indpls., 1981—82. Author: (bibliography) African-American Archaeology and African Diaspora Archaeology Resources, 2000. Recipient Glenn W. Irwin, Jr., MD Experience Excellence Recognition award, Ind. Purdue U., Indpls., 1995, Herbert S. and Va. White Profl. Devel. award, Ind. U. Libraries, 1999, Outstanding Contbn. award, Ind. Purdue U. Black Faculty and Staff Coun., Indpls., 2002; grantee, NEH, 1996, 1998, 2000, Clowes Fund, Inc., 1996, Ind. Humanities Coun., 1996, 1998, Nissan Motors, 2000, Lila Wallace Readers' Digest Fund, 2000—01, Indpls. Found. Libr. Fund and Associated Writing Programs, Cooper Canyon Press, Pubs. of MLA, 2001, Nat. Endowment Arts, 2001. Mem.: ALA (elected coun. mem. 2001—04), Assn. for the Study of African Am. Life and History, Freedom to Read Found., Am. Hort. Soc. Episcopalian. Avocations: African American folklife, gardening, birdwatching. Home: 328 N East St Indianapolis IN 46202 Personal E-mail: mtwright@iupui.edu.

TURNEY, RICHARD KENNETH, display designer, artist; s. Marcellus Reuter Turney and Jennie Elvira Erickson; m. Dorothy Smith, Jan. 1, 1940; children: Pamela A., Marda Jan. Attended, Carnegie Inst., Pitts., 1929, U. Pitts., 1933. Display dir. C. Livingston & Sons, Youngstown, Ohio, 1950—75, G.M. Mckelvey Co., Youngstown, Ohio, 1976—77; owner Ken T. Sailboats, Boardman, Ohio, 1973—79; artist Fort Meyers, Fla., 1970—. Set designer Amateur Theatricals, Greensburg, Pa.; fashion shows set designer, Youngstown, Ohio. One-man shows include Fort Myers Beach Art Assn., 1986, 1987, 1988, 1989, 1990, 2007, Lee County Alliance of Arts, 1987, exhibitions include Cape Coral Art Studio, 1985, Merrick Free Art Gallery, New Brighton, Pa., 1988. Pres. Art Coun. S.W. Fla., 1983—84. With Destroyer Escort #51 USN, 1943—45. Mem.: Fla. Watercolor Soc., B.I.G. Arts, Lee County Alliance of Arts, Naples Art Assn., Sanibel-Captiva Art League, Fort Myers Beach Art Assn. (treas. 1982—83, bd. mem. 1982—84, dir.). Democrat. Avocation: sailing. Office Phone: 239-466-1247.

TURNEY, SHAREN JESTER, apparel executive, cosmetics executive; b. 1956; BA in Bus. Edn., U. Okla. With Foley's, 1979, Byer Calif. Federated Dept. Stores; exec. v.p. merchandising, creative prodn., advt., pub. rels. Neiman Marcus; sr. v.p., gen. merchandise mgr. Neiman Marcus stores; pres., CEO Neiman Marcus Direct, 1999—2000, Victoria's Secret Direct, 2000—06, Victoria's Secret Megabrand and Intimate Apparel, 2006—. Campaign chmn. United Way, Dallas; hon. co-chair Children's Hunger Alliance, Ohio, 2006; bd. dirs. Winston Sch., Addison Theater, Columbus Coalition Against Family Violence, Jay H. Retailing Initiative Adv. bd., Wharton Sch., U. Pa. Named to Hall of Fame Bus. Edn., U. Okla., 2005; recipient Fashion Medal Hon. for Fashion Retailing, 1997, Dr. Catherine White Achievement award, HeartShare Human Services, 2005. Office: Victoria's Secret PO Box 16589 Columbus OH 43216-6589 *

TURNEY, SHARON JESTER, retail executive; b. 1958; BA in Bus. Edn., U. Okla. With Foley's, 1979—88, Neiman Marcus, 1989—2000, sr. v.p. gen., mgr. gen. merchandise, 1997—98, exec. v.p. merchandising, creative prodn., advt. and pub. rels., 1998; pres., CEO Neiman Marcus Direct, 1999—2000; CEO, pres. Victoria's Secret Catalogue Limited Brands, Inc., Columbus, Ohio, 2000—06, pres., CEO Victoria's Secret megabrand & intimate apparel, 2006—. Office: Limited Brands Inc 3 Limited Pkwy Columbus OH 43230 *

TURNG, LIH-SHENG, education educator; b. Taiwan, Sept. 21, 1959; MS, Cornell U., Ithaca, NY, 1987, PhD, 1990. Task leader C-MOLD, Ithaca, 1990—2000; prof. U. Wis., Madison, Wis., 2000—; hon. prof. Zheng Zhou U., China, 2006—. Co-dir. Polymer Engring. Ctr., Madison, Wis., 2001—. Dir., prin. investigator (engring. rsch.) Microcellular Nanocomposites (3M Non-Tenured awards, 2002, 2003). Bd. mem., chair edn. com. Soc.Plastics Engrs., Injection Molding Divsn., Brookfield, Conn., 2002—. Grantee, NSF, 2001—. Mem.: ASME. Achievements include research in computer simulation optimization and nanocomposites for injection molding and lightweight, high-performance polymer composites. Office: Univ Wis 1513 University Ave Madison WI 53706 Home Phone: 608-826-0412; Office Phone: 608-262-0586. Business E-Mail: turng@engr.wisc.edu.

TURNIPSEED, BARNWELL RHETT, III, journalist, public relations consultant; b. Apr. 6, 1929; s. Barnwell Rhett and L. (Rogers) T.; m. Jane Whitley, June 12, 1982. BA in Journalism, U. Ga., 1950, MA in Journalism, 1960. With Sta. WGGA, Gainesville, Ga., 1943-46; prodn. mgr. Sta WGGA, Gainesville, Ga., 1958-60; with Sta. WRFC, Athens, Ga., 1947-50; program dir. Sta. WKYW, Louisville, 1953, Sta. WGBA, Columbus, Ga., 1953-55; broadcasting cons., 1955—60; sr. corr., sci. editor Voice of Am. Worldwide English, 1960-72; coord. radio-TV pub. affairs HEW, 1972-73; mem. staff Ga. Congressman Phil Landrum, 1974-75; dir. solar energy tech. info. Dept. Energy, Washington, 1975-77, spl. asst., 1977-81; pvt. practice, 1981-88, 94—; instr. West Ga. Coll., Carrollton, 1988-89, 90-94; asst. prof. Brenau Coll., Gainesville, Ga., 1989-90; mgr. WBCX-FM, Gainsville, Ga., 1989—90, WWGC-FM, Carrollton, Ga., 1990-94. Dir. Ga. Broadcasters Annual Awards, 1998—2005. Author: History of Georgia Broadcasting, 1972; prin. corr. Voice of Am. (Peabody award winning space exploration broadcasts, 1969). Symphony Guild rep. Louisville, Columbus, Ga. Jaycees; active symphony and arts devel. Sgt. U.S. Army, 1950-52. Named to Ga. Broadcasters Hall of Fame, 2003; recipient Two Meritorious Svc. awards, USIA. Mem. Nat. Assn. Sci. Writers (life), Aircraft Owners and Pilots Assn., Sigma Delta Chi, Kappa Sigma. Democrat. Methodist. Home and Office: 295 Greenfield Cir Fayetteville GA 30215-2622

TURNLEY, DAVID CARL, photojournalist; b. Ft. Wayne, Ind., June 22, 1955; s. William Loyd and Elizabeth Ann (Protsman) Turnley; m. Karin Nicolette, Apr. 15, 1989. BA in French, U. Mich., 1977; student, Sorbonne, Paris, 1975; DMus (hon.), Keele U., Eng., 1991. Staff photogapher Sliger Home Newspapers, Northville, Mich., 1978—80, Detroit Free Press, 1980—99; European based photographic corr. Detroit Free Press/Black Star Paris, 1988—99; Neiman fellow Harvard U., Boston, 1997—98; internat. exec. prodr. Corbis Sygma, NYC, 1999—. Author: Why Are They Weeping? South Africans under Aparthied, 1988, Beijing Spring, 1989, Moments of Revolution: Eastern Europe, 1990; London Decca Records. Recipient Canon essay award for S. African coverage, 1985, World Press Picture of Yr. award for Earthquake in Armenia, 1988, Robert Capa Gold medal for China, Romania coverage, 1990, Pulitizer Prize for China, E. Europe coverage, 1990.

TURNOVSKY, STEPHEN JOHN, economics professor; b. Wellington, New Zealand, Apr. 5, 1941; came to U.S., 1981; s. Frederick and Liselotte Felicitas (Wodak) T.; m. Michelle Henriette Louise Roos, Jan. 21, 1967; children: Geoffrey George, Jacqueline Liselotte. BA, Victoria U., Wellington, 1962, MA with honors, 1963; PhD, Harvard U., 1968. Asst. prof. econs. U. Pa., Phila., 1968-71; assoc. prof. U. Toronto, Ont., Canada, 1971-72; prof. Australian Nat. U., Canberra, 1972-82; IBE disting. prof. econs. U. Ill., Champaign, 1982-87; prof. econs. U. Wash., Seattle, 1987—, chmn. dept., 1990-95; Castor prof., 1993—. Rsch. assoc. Nat. Bur. Econ. Rsch., Cambridge, Mass., 1983-93. Author: Macroeconomic Analysis and Stabilization Policy, 1977, International Macroeconomic Stabilization Policy, 1990, Methods of Macroeconomic Dynamics, 1995, 2d edit., 2000, International Macroeconomic Dynamics, 1997; mem. editl. bd. several jours.; contbr. articles to profl. jours. Fellow Econometric Soc., Acad. Social Scis. in Australia; mem. Soc. Econ. Dynamics and Control (pres. 1982-84, editor Jour. Econ. Dynamics and Control 1981-87, 95-2001), Soc. Computational Econs. (pres. 2004-05). Avocations: skiing, hiking, music. Home: 6053 NE Kelden Pl Seattle WA 98105-2045 Office: Dept Econs U Wash Box 353330 Seattle WA 98195-3330 Office Phone: 206-685-8028. E-mail: sturn@u.washington.edu.

TURNQUIST, JERRY L., communications educator, journalist; b. Elgin, Ill., Mar. 5, 1949; s. Ralph C. and Frances B. T.; m. Kathleen A. Turnquist, Dec. 29, 1984; adopted children: Dennis, Eric. AA, Elgin C.C., 1969; BS, No. Ill. U., 1971, MS, 1979. Tchr. history and sci. Sch. Dist. U - 46, Elgin, Ill., 1972—; tax preparer H&R Block Premium, Elgin, 1977—. Columnist Daily Herald, Elgin, 1995—; co-host: (local radio show) Elgin 100 Years Ago, Sta. WRMN, 1995—. Trustee Gail Borden Pub. Libr., Elgin, 1999-2005; bd. dirs. Ill. State Hist. Soc., Elgin, Springfield, 1998-2000; chmn. Elgin Heritage Commn., 1986-91, others. Named Disting. Alumnus Elgin C.C., 1989, Keyman of the Yr., Elgin Jaycees, 1981; recipient Outstanding Svc. award Elgin Heritage Commn., 1995. Mem. Elgin Area Hist. Soc. (bd. dirs. 1986-98). Home: 619 Canyon Ln Elgin IL 60123-2523 Personal E-mail: ibemrt@aol.com.

TURO, JOANN K., psychoanalyst, psychotherapist, consultant; b. Westerly, RI, Feb. 13, 1938; d. Angelo and Anna Josephine (Drew) T. BS in Biology and Chemistry, U. R.I., 1959; MA in Human Rels. and Psychology, Ohio U., 1964; postgrad., NYU, 1966-71, N.Y. Freudian Inst., NYC, 1977-85, Mental Health Inst., 1977-80. Rsch. asst. biochemistry studies on schizophrenia Harvard U. Med. Sch., Boston, 1959-60; indsl. psychology asst. studies on managerial success N.Y. Telephone Co., NYC, 1964-66; staff psychologist Testing and Advisement Ctr. NYU, 1966-70; psychology intern Kings County Hosp., Bklyn., 1970-71; staff psychologist M.D.C. Psychol. Svcs., NYC, 1971-72; clin. dir. Greenwich House Substance Abuse Clinic, NYC, 1973-76; cons. psychotherapist Mental Health Consultation Ctr., NYC, 1977-82; pvt. practice NYC, 1981—. Mental health cons. Bklyn. Ctr. for Psychotherapy, 1976-78; with Psychoanalytic Consultation Svcs., 1994—; presenter in field. Mem. Internat. Psychoanalytic Assn. (cert., panel discussant 2007), Soc. for Personality Assessment (cert.), N.Y. Freudian Soc. (cert., co-chmn. grad. com. 1985-86, mem. continuing edn. com. 1986—, pub. rels. com. 1992-93, psychoanalytic consult svc. 1994—, tng. and supr. psychoanalyst 1995—, ethics com. 1999—, tng. analyst panel 2000—, chair 2002-03, presenter 2002, bd. dirs. 2003-06, v.p. 2005-2006), N.Y. Coun. Psychoanalytic Psychotherapists (cert.), Met. Assn. for Coll. Mental Health Practitoners (cert.). Office: 175 W 12th St Apt 15A New York NY 10011-8211 Office Phone: 212-691-2041.

TURO, RON, lawyer; b. Ft. Wayne, Ind., Apr. 2, 1955; s. John B. and Joan L. (Gluntz) T.; m. Claire Teresa Fetterman T., May 24, 1980; children: Andrew Jacob, Patricia Erin, Dominic Earl. BA in History with honors, Pa. State U., 1978; JD, Dickinson Sch. Law, 1981. Bar: Pa. 1981, U.S. Dist. (mid. dist.) Pa. 1982, U.S. Supreme Ct. 1987, U.S. Ct. Appeals (3d cir.) 1989; pvt. pilot, 2004. Ast. pub. defender Cumberland County, Carlisle, Pa., 1981-84; ptnr. Griffie & Turo, Carlisle, 1984-89; pvt. practice Carlisle, 1989—. Lectr. Dickinson Sch. Law, 1996—, Widener U. Sch. Law, 2000, adj. prof., trial advocacy program faculty, 2001—06. Founder Cumberland County Police Recognition Dinner, Carlisle, Pa., 1985—; active Nat. Cath. Com. on Scouting, 1988—; chmn. Region III, Pa., NJ, 1993—95, parliamentarian and legal counsel, 1991—2002, advisor religious act, 1998—2000, chair by-laws com., 2004—; bd. dirs. AHEDD, Inc., 1993—, vice chmn., 1994—95, chmn., 1995—2002; trustee David E. Baker Scholarship Trust, 1997—; bd. dirs. Safe Harbour, 2006—, Pa. Assn. for the Blind, 1998—, exec. search com., 1999—2000; dist. chmn. Boy Scouts Am., 2005—06. Recipient St. George Emblem, Boy Scouts Am., 1983, Eagle Scout, 1969, Golden AAD emblem, 1989. Mem.: Pa. Pub. Defender Assn. (chair juvenile law com. 2003—), Cumberland County Bar Assn. (social chmn. 1985—2006, pub. rels. com. 1998—2006, bench-bar com. 1998—, membership chmn. 2000—06), Pa. Assn. Criminal Def. Lawyers, Pa. Bar Assn., Nat. Assn. Criminal Def. Lawyers, Mensa (local sec. 1990—92, editor 1992—95, ombudsman 2000—), St. Thomas More Soc. (v.p. 1996—98, treas. 1998—2004), Carlisle Cigar Club (founder 2006), KC (grand knight 1985—87, pres. Capital area chpt. 1989, grand knight 1993—95, fin. sec. 1996—2002, dist. dep. 1998—2002, Knight of Yr. 1981). Republican. Roman Catholic. Avocations: scuba diving, travel, flying. Office: 28 S Pitt St Carlisle PA 17013-3211 Office Phone: 717-245-9688. Business E-Mail: ronturo@turolaw.com.

TUROCK, BETTY JANE, library and information science professor; b. Scranton, Pa., June 12; d. David and Ruth Carolyn (Sweetser) Argust; m. Frank M. Turock, June 16, 1956; children: David L., B. Drew. BA magna cum laude (Charles Weston scholar), Syracuse U., 1955; postgrad. (scholar), U. Pa., 1956; MLS, Rutgers U., 1970, PhD, 1981. Library and materials coordinator Holmdel (N.J.) Public Schs., 1963—65; story-teller Wheaton (Ill.) Public Library, 1965—67; ednl. media specialist Alhambra Public Sch., Phoenix, 1967—70; br. librarian, area librarian, head extension service Forsyth County Public Library System, Winston-Salem, NC, 1970—73; asst. dir., dir. Montclair (N.J.) Public Library, 1973—76; asst. dir. Monroe County Library System, Rochester, NY, 1978—81; asst. prof. Rutgers U. Sch. Comm., Info. and Libr. Studies, 1981—87, assoc. prof., 1987—93, prof., 1994—, dept. chair, 1989—95, 2002—03, dir. MLS program, 1990—95, 2002—03, assoc. dean, 2002—04, 2004—06, prof. emerita, assoc. dean emerita; pres. Rock Info. Assocs., 2004—. Vis. prof. Rutgers U. Grad. Sch. Library and Info. Studies, 1980-81; adviser U.S. Dept. Edn. Office of Libr. Programs, 1988-89. Author: Serving Older Adults, 1983, Creating a Financial Plan, 1992; editor: The Bottom Line, 1984-90; contbr. articles to profl. jours. Trustee Raritan Twp. (N.J.) Pub. Libr., 1961—62, Keystone Coll., 1991—, Freedom to Read Found., 1994—97, Librs. for the Future, 1994—97, Fund for Am.'s Librs., 1995, Trejo Found., 1995—, Bd. Am. Libr., Paris, 1999—; mem. Bd. Edn. Raritan Twp., 1962—66; ALA coord. Task Force on Women, 1978—80; mem. action coun.; treas. Social Responsibilities Round Table, 1978—82; mem. bd. visitors Johns Hopkins Sch. Medicine, 2005—. Recipient NJ Libr. Leadership award, 1994; named Woman of Yr., Raritan-Holmdel Woman's Club, 1975; Charles Weston scholar Syracuse U., 1955. Mem. AAUP, Am. Soc. Info. Sci., Assn. Libr. and Info. Sci Edn., ALA (pres. 1995-96, pres.-elect 1994-95, exec. bd. 1991-97, coun. 1988-97, Equality award 1998, Lippincott award 2006), Rutgers U. Grad. Sch. Library and Info. Studies Alumni Assn. (pres. 1977-78, Disting. Alumni award 1994), Phi Theta Kappa, Psi Chi, Beta Phi Mu, Pi Beta Phi. Unitarian Universalist. Office: Rutgers Univ 4 Huntington St New Brunswick NJ 08901-1071 Office Phone: 732-742-6579. Business E-Mail: bturock@scils.rutgers.edu.

TUROK, PAUL HARRIS, composer, commentator, music critic; b. NYC, Dec. 3, 1929; s. Joseph and Esther (Pashman) T.; m. Susan Kay Frucht, Mar. 24, 1967. BA, Queens Coll., NYC, 1950; MA, U. Calif., Berkeley, 1951; MS, Baruch Coll., 1986. Music dir. Sta. KPFA, Berkeley, 1955-56; lectr. CCNY, 1959-63; vis. prof. Williams Coll., Williamstown, Mass., 1963-64; music critic New York Herald-Tribune, 1964-65; critic, columnist Music Jour., New York, 1964-79, Ovation mag., New York, 1980—, critic, contbr. New York Times, 1984—, Sta. WQXR, First Hearing, New York, 1985—. Pub. Turok's Choice, 1990—. Composer musical compositions, premiered Indpls. Symphony, 1971, Louisville Orch., 1973, Cleve. Orch., 1973, Phila Orch., 1976; opera Richard III, 1975, Sousa Overture, 1976, Lanier Songs, 1978, English Horn Quintet, 1982, Cello Sonata, 1984, Organ Toccata, 1984, Tourist Music, 1985, String Quartet No. 4, 1986, Rhapsody for Band, 1987, Piano Dance, 1988, Violin Sonata, 1989, From Sholem Aleichem, 1990, Abac for trumpet and organ, 1990, Partita for three winds, 1991, Concerto for two violins and orchestra, 1991, Piano Trio, 1992, C.C. 6 for bassoon and orchestra, 1992, Fantasy for 4 flutes and piano, 4 hands, 1994, Clap, Cluck, Count: Three Interactive Proverbs for Chidren and Orchestra, 1995, Sonata No. 2 for Cello and Piano, 1996, Concerto for Piano and Orch., 1997, Canzone Concertante No. 7 for viola, percussion and strings, 1998, Reeling in the Y2K, 1999, Flute Sonata, 2000, Behold, Thou Art Fair, 2001, Sextet for piano and winds, Partita No.3 for English horn, 2002, Variations on a theme by Grieg for 8 trombones, Elegy in Memory of Nathan Schwartz, 2002, C.C. No. 8 for Violin and Orch., String Quartet No. 5, 2003, C.C. No. 9 for Trumpet and Strings, 2003, C.C. No. 10 for Piano and Strings, 2006, Caprice d'Octobre for 3 violins, 2004, Brass Quintet No. 2, 2004, Fanfare for Brass Ensemble, 2005, Sonata for Piano, 2006, Barbershop Variations for Five Horns, 2006. Served with U.S. Army, 1953-55. Hertz travelling scholar, U. Calif., 1956-58; Grammy nominee 1992, 93. Jewish. Avocations: world travel, computing. Personal E-mail: paulhtk@verizon.net.

TUROVER, BENJAMIN PHILIP, account executive; b. San Francisco, Oct. 26, 1973; s. Philip Vincent Aelfwald and Nancy Susan Turover; m. Lindsey Marie Cameron, June 3, 2001; 1 child, Shiloh Jacob. BA, George Washington U., DC, 1995. Lottery mktg. rep. Sci. Games Internat., Dover, Del., 2005—07; account exec. New Castle County C. of C., Wilmington, Del., 2007—. Media and pub. rels. dir. Wilmington Jaycees, 2005—07. Mem.: Phi Alpha Theta. Democrat. Jewish. Avocations: hiking, gardening, travel. Home: 1201 New St Wilmington DE 19808 Office: New Castle County Chamber of Commerce PO Box 11247 Wilmington DE 19850 Home Phone: 302-998-3038; Office Phone: 302-737-4345. Personal E-mail: benturover@yahoo.com.

TUROW, SCOTT F., writer, lawyer; b. Chgo., Apr. 12, 1949; s. David D. and Rita (Pastron) Turow; m. Annette Weisberg, Apr. 4, 1971; 3 children. BA magna cum laude, Amherst Coll., 1970; MA, Stanford U., 1974; JD cum laude, Harvard U., 1978. Bar: Ill. 1978, U.S. Dist. Ct. (no. dist.) Ill. 1978, U.S. Ct. Appeals (7th cir.) 1979. Asst. U.S. atty. US Dept. Justice (no. dist.) Ill., Chgo., 1978—86; ptnr. Sonnenschein Nath & Rosenthal LLP, Chgo., 1986—. E.H. Jones lectr. Stanford U., 1972—75; pres. Author's Guild, 1997—98. Author: (novels) Presumed Innocent, 1987, The Burden of Proof, 1990, Pleading Guilty, 1993, The Laws of Our Fathers, 1996, Personal Injuries, 1999, Reversible Errors, 2002, Ordinary Heroes, 2005, Limitations, 2006, (non-fiction) One L.: An Inside Account of Life in the First Year at Harvard Law School, 1977, Ultimate Punishment: A Lawyer's Reflections on Dealing With the Death Penalty, 2003 (Robert F. Kennedy Book award, 2004); contbr. articles to profl. jours. Mem.: Chgo. Coun. Lawyers, Chgo. Bar Assn. Office: Sonnenschein Nath Rosenthal 233 S Wacker Dr Ste 8000 Chicago IL 60606-6491 E-mail: sturow@sonnenscheim.com. *

TURPENING, PATRICIA EILEEN KELLER, retired law librarian; b. Columbus, Ohio, Mar. 1, 1952; d. William Waite and Eileen Catherine (Miller) Keller; m. Richard Whitley Denham, Oct. 10, 1981 (div. Mar. 1986); 1 child, Michael Richard; m. Glen Thomas Turpening, Apr. 16, 1997. BS, Findlay Coll., 1974; MSLS, U. Ky., 1978. Cert. in preservation mgmt. Sch. Communication, Info. and Libr. Studies, Rutgers U., 1999. Acquisitions libr. Supreme Ct. Ohio Law Libr., Columbus, 1974-76, Robert S. Marx Law Libr., U. Cin., 1978-88, head preservation and archives, 1988—2006, sr. libr., 2003—06; ret., 2006. Libr. Rendigs, Fry, Kiely &

Dennis, Cin., 1979-85. Editor Tech. Svcs. Law Libr., 1990-94, The Abbey Newsletter: Preservation of Library and Archival Materials, 2003; contbr. articles to profl. jours. Mem. ALA, LWV, AAUW, NOW, Am. Assn. Law Librs. (travel grantee 1984, preservation cons., coord. of library programs, Renee D. Chapman Meml. award for Outstanding Contbns. in Tech. Svcs. Law Librarianship 2004), Ohio Preservation Coun., Ohio Regional Assn. Law Librs. Episcopalian. E-mail: bookloverconsulting@yahoo.com.

TURPIN, DAVID HOWARD, biologist, educator, academic administrator; b. Duncan, BC, Can., July 14, 1956; s. George Howard and Marilyn Elizabeth (Jones) T.; children: Chantal, Joshua. BSc in Biology, U. BC, 1977, PhD in Botany and Oceanography, 1980. Postdoctoral rsch. fellow Natural Scis. Engring. Rsch. Coun., 1980—81; rsch. assoc. Simon Fraser U., 1980; v.p. Sigma Resource Cons., Vancouver, BC, 1980—81; from asst. prof. to assoc. prof. Queen's U., Kingston, Ont., Canada, 1981—90, prof. biology, 1990—91, dean arts and sci., 1993—95, vice prin. acad., 1995—2000; prof., head botany U. BC, 1991—93; pres., vice-chancellor U. Victoria, BC, 2000—. Invited spkr. profl. meetings univs. worldwide. Co-editor: Plant Physiology, Biochemistry and Molecular Biology, 1990, 2d edit., 1996; mem. editl. bd. Jour. Phycology, 1992-96, Plant Physiology, 1988-92, Plant Cell and Environ., 1994-96, Jour. Exptl. Botany, 1995-98; contbr. chpts. in books; author numerous articles, conf. procs. V.p. Great Lakes Tomorrow, 1986-90; mem. program com. Great Lakes Course-Ont. Sci. Ctr., 1988; Kingston City rep. Cataraqui Regional Conservation Authority, 1984-86; hon. adv. mem. Soong Ching Ling Found. Ltd., 2001-. Recipient Excellence in Tchg. Alumni award Queen's U., 1989, Outstanding Alumni award U. B.C., 1990, Darbaker prize in phycology Am. Bot. Assn., 1991; Natural Scis. and Engring. Rsch. Coun. E.W.R. Stacie Meml. fellow, 1989-90, Royal Soc. Can. fellow, 1998-; Capt. T.S. Byrne Meml. scholar U. B.C., 1980; postgrad. scholar Natural Scis. and Engring. Rsch. Coun., 1979-81, Edith Ashton Meml. scholar U. B.C., 1979, NRC scholar, 1978-79; Natural Scis. and Engring. Rsch. Coun. grantee, 1982—. Mem. Phycological Soc. Am., Am. Soc. Limnology and Oceanography, Can. Soc. Plant Physiologists (C.D. Nelson award 1989), Am. Soc. Plant Physiologists (cert. recognition 1992), Minister Nat. Defence Edn. Adv. Bd., Discovery Found. Bd., Assn. Univs. and Colls. Can. (mem. bd. dirs. 2002-). Office: Office of the Pres U Victoria Bus and Econ Bldg Rm 454 Victoria BC Canada V8W 2Y2 Business E-Mail: pres@uvic.ca.

TURQUETTE, ATWELL RUFUS, logician; b. Texarkana, Tex., July 14, 1914; s. Rufus Watson and Dale Cook (Warmack) Turquette; m. Lucille Case Le Roy, June 2, 1937 (dec. Feb. 1956); m. Maxine Harriot Kennedy, Apr. 2, 1958 (dec. Aug. 1992); m. Frances D. Bond, Dec. 27, 1998. BA, U. Ark., 1936; MA, Duke U., 1937; PhD, Cornell U., 1943. Asst. prof. Fla. So. Coll., Lakeland, 1937-38; fellow U. Chgo., 1938-39; assoc. prof. Fla. So. Coll., Lakeland, 1939-40; assistantship, fellow Cornell U., Ithaca, N.Y., 1940-43, instr., 1943-45; asst. prof. U. Ill., Champaign-Urbana, 1945-48, assoc. prof., 1948-52, prof., 1952-75, prof. emeritus, 1975—. Co-author: Many-valued Logics, 1952; contbg. author: Les 265 communications, Congrès International des Mathématiciens, Nice, 1970; editor: Jour. of Symbolic Logic, 1950-68; patentee in field. Duke U. scholar, 1936; U. Chgo. fellow, 1938; grantee NSF, 1968-70, Rockefeller Gen. Edn. Bd., 1954. Mem. Am. Math. Soc., Soc. Indsl. and Appl. Math., Symbolic Logic Assn., London Math. Soc., Calcutta Math. Soc., AAAS, N.Y. Acad. Scis., Am Phil. Assn. Achievements include design for multi-valued circuits, functional completeness and incompleteness results for many-valued logics; minimal axiomatizations for many-valued logics; relating Pascal triangles to Post sets; deciphering Peirce's triadic logic; discovery of quasistrokes and their application to networks. Home: 914 W Clark St Champaign IL 61821-3328 Personal E-mail: turquette@sbcglobal.net.

TURQUETTE, FRANCES BOND, editor; b. Atlanta, Sept. 25, 1931; d. Sewell Hinton and Lavonia DeLay Dixon; m. Charles Eugene Bond, Sept. 12, 1952 (div. Jan. 1969); children: Turner D., Laura S., L. Irene, Cynthia D., Nelson K.; m. Atwell Rufus Turquette, Dec. 27, 1998. Student, Wesleyan Coll., 1948—50; BA in Journalism, U. Ga., 1952; MA in Art History, U. Ill., 1971. Editl. asst. Meth. Pub. Ho., Nashville, 1952-53, Rsch. Press, Champaign, Ill., 1972-73; editing supr. McGraw-Hill Book Co., NYC, 1974-80; publs. editor pub. affairs U. Ill., Urbana, 1974, 80-88; editor Nat. Ctr. for Supercomputing Applications, Champaign, 1988-96. Vis. faculty, editor Coll. of Commerce, U. Ill. Urbana, 1972-74; ref. com., Editorial and Composition Standards McGraw Hill Book Co., N.Y.C., 1975-77; editor, writer access, 1988-96. Mem. program chair, liaison, bd. govs. Channing Murray Found., Urbana, 1982-92; mem. adv. bd. to freeze nuclear weapons 15th Congrl. Dist., 1982-87; co-pres. SANE/Freeze, Champaign County, 1992-94. Mem. Art Inst. Chgo., Lyric Opera Chgo., Oriental Inst., U. Chgo., Channing-Murray Found., Am. Assn. U. Women, Theta Sigma Phi. Unitarian Universalist. Avocations: travel, writing, gardening, photography. Home: 914 W Clark St Champaign IL 61821-3328 Personal E-mail: turquette@sbcglobal.net.

TURRELL, JAMES ARCHIE, sculptor; b. Los Angeles, May 6, 1943; s. Archibald Milton and Margaret (Hodges) T.; children: Shana Sequoia, Jennifer Lynn, Anya Regina. BA, Pomona Coll., Claremont, Calif., 1965; MA in Art, Claremont Grad. Sch., 1974; ArtsD, Chgo. Art Inst., 1999; Doctorate (hon.), Clarenont Grad. Sch., 2001, Royal Acad. Art, London, Eng., 2002. Vis. artist, Pomona Coll., 1971-73, Claremont Grad. Sch., 1972-73; artist-in-residence Mus. No. Ariz., Flagstaff, 1979—; exhbns. include, Pasadena (Calif.) Art Mus., 1967, Main and Hill Studio, Santa Monica, Calif., 1968-70, Stedelijk Mus., Amsterdam, Netherlands, 1976, ARCO Center Visual Arts, Los Angeles, 1976, Whitney Mus., N.Y.C., 1980, Castelli Gallery, 1980, Ctr. Contemporary Art, Seattle, 1982, Israel Mus., Jerusalem, 1983, Flow Ace Gallery, Los Angeles, 1983, Hayden Gallery, MIT, Boston, 1983, Portside Gallery, Yokohama, Japan, 1995, Whitney Mus. of Am. Art, NY, 1999 & 2000, Angles Gallery, Santa Monica, Calif., 2000, Scottsdale Mus. of Contemporary Art, Scottsdale, Ariz., 2001, Mus. Modern Art, N.Y., 2001, National Gallery of Art, Washington D.C., 2002, Galerie Henry Art, Seattle, Wash., 2003, Pace Wildenstein Gallery, N.Y., 2004 and several others; commns. include, Villa Panza, Varese, Italy, 1974, Villa Schiebler, Milan, Italy, 1979, Roden Crater (Ariz.) project, 1975—. Conscientious objector 1966. Recipient Lumen award, 1981, Bessie award, 1985, Chevalier des Arts et des Lettres, France, 1991, Freidrich Prize, Frankfurt, Germany, 1992, Skowhegan Award for Sculpture, 1997 Governor's Arts Award, Artist of the Year, Ariz., 1994, Wolf prize in arts (sculpture), Wolf Found., Israel, 1998, Grande Médailles d'argent, Arts Plastiques, Fondation Académie d'Architecture, Paris, France 2000, Jefferson medal in Architecture, U. Va., 2002, Distinguished Alumnus award, Claremont Grad. U., Calif., 2003; named Artist of the Year, Scottsdale Cultural Arts Coun., 2000; grantee Nat. Endowment Arts, 1968, 75, 80; Dia Art Found., 1975-79; Guggenfellow fellow, 1974, Katherine T. and John D. MacArthur Found. Fellowship, 1984; Ariz. Commn. for the Arts and Humanities, visual arts fellowship, 1980 Fellow: Am. Acad. Arts and Sciences.

TURRELL, RICHARD HORTON, SR., banker; b. Kingston, Pa., Apr. 9, 1925; s. George Henry and Margaret (Clark) T.; m. Sally Wolfe, May 28, 1955; children: Richard H. Jr., David C., Douglas W. (dec.). Student, Cornell U., 1943; BS in Commerce, Washington and Lee U., 1949. Rep. sales Del. Lackawanna and Western Coal Co., Phila., 1949-51; asst. to pres. NYC, 1951-58; broker Auchincloss Parker & Redpath, NYC, 1958-61; mgr. investments Fiduciary Trust Co. Internat., NYC, 1961-94, v.p., 1965-94, sr. v.p., 1968-94, sec., 1971-84. Asst. sec. Blue Coal Corp., N.Y.C., 1953-58; v.p., bd. dirs. Pine Raleigh (N.C.) Corp., 1966-93. Trustee, overseer Simon's Rock of Bard Coll., Gt. Barrington, Mass., 1968-93; trustee Monmouth U., West Long Branch, NJ, 1980—, chmn. bd. trustees, 1989-92; chmn. Millburn-Short Hills Rep. Com., NJ, 1973-78; trustee Children's Specialized Hosp. Found., Mountainside, NJ, 1989-95; bd. dirs. ARC Martin County, Fla., 2000. With Signal Corps, U.S. Army, 1943-46, PTO. Named Disting. Alumnus, Washington and Lee U., 1986. Mem. Baltusrol Golf Club (Springfield, N.J., gov. 1977), Capitol Hill Club (Washington), Turtle Creek Club (Tequesta, Fla.), Masons, Irem Temple Aaonms, Phi Beta Kappa, Phi Eta Sigma, Alpha Kappa Psi, Omicron Delta Kappa (hon.), Beta Gamma Sigma, Phi Delta Theta. Presbyterian. Avocations: golf, history, education. Home: 114 Turtle Creek Dr Tequesta FL 33469-1547

TURRENTINE, HOWARD BOYD, federal judge; b. Escondido, Calif., Jan. 22, 1914; s. Howard and Veda Lillian (Maxfield) T.; children: Howard Robert, Terry Beverly; m. Marlene Lipsey, Nov. 1, 1991. AB, San Diego State Coll., 1936; LLB, U. So. Calif., 1939. Bar: Calif. 1939. Practiced in, San Diego, 1939-68; judge Superior Ct. County of San Diego, 1968-70, U.S. Dist. Ct. (so. dist.) Calif., Calif., sr. judge San Diego, 1970—. Served with USNR, 1941-45. Mem. ABA, Fed. Bar Assn., Am. Judicature Soc. Office: US Dist Ct 940 Front St San Diego CA 92101-8994 Office Phone: 619-557-6630.

TURRI, JOSEPH A., lawyer; b. Seneca Falls, NY, July 24, 1943; s. Louis Arthur and Assunta (Faiola) T.; m. Susan Ruth Testa, Dec. 29, 1975 (dec.); 1 child, Michael James. BA, SUNY, Buffalo, 1965; JD, Cornell U., 1970. Bar: N.Y. 1971, U.S. Dist Ct. (we. dist.) N.Y. 1971, U.S. Supreme Ct. 1974, U.S. Dist. Ct. (so. dist.) N.Y. 1996, U.S. Ct. Appeals (2d cir.) 1996. Mem. Harris Beach PLLC, Rochester, NY, 1970—, chmn. constrn. law dept., 1992-98, 2002—, 1994-96, pres., 1999—2002. Bd. dirs. Thousand Island Park Corp., N.Y., O'Connell Electric Co.; v.p. Castle Bay Ltd., Rochester, N.Y.; arbitrator Am. Arbitration Assn., Syracuse, 1985—. Bd. dirs. Rochester Downtown Devel. Corp., 1992-97. Named to Best Lawyers in Am. in constrn. law, 2006. Mem. N.Y. State Bar Assn., Monroe County Bar Assn., Assn. Gen. Contractors, Met. Forum (trustee). Avocations: horseback riding, antique wooden boats. Home: 21 Evergreen Ln Rochester NY 14618-4719 Office: Harris Beach PLLC 99 Garnsey Rd Pittsford NY 14534 Office Phone: 585-419-8644.

TURRO, NICHOLAS JOHN, chemistry professor; b. Middletown, Conn., May 18, 1938; m. Sandra Jean Misenti, Aug. 6, 1960; children: Cynthia, Claire. BA, Wesleyan U., 1960, DSc (hon.), 1984; PhD, Calif. Inst. Tech., 1963; doctorate (hon.), U. Fribourg, Switzerland, 2004. Instr. chemistry Columbia U., NYC, 1964-65, asst. prof., 1965-67, assoc. prof., 1967-69, prof. chemistry, 1969—, William P. Schweitzer prof. chemistry, 1982—, chmn. chemistry dept., 1981-84, co-chmn. dept. chem. engring. and applied chemistry, 1997-2000, prof. earth and environ. engring., 1998—. Author: Molecular Photochemistry, 1965; author: (with A.A. Lamola) Energy Transfer and Organic Photochemistry, 1971; author: Modern Molecular Photochemistry, 1978; mem. editl. bd.: Jour. Reactive Intermediates, Langmuir and Proceedings of Nat. Acad. Scis., 2004. Recipient Eastman Kodak award for excellence in grad. rsch. pure chemistry, 1973, award, E.O. Lawrence U.S. Dept. Energy, 1983, Porter medal, European Photochem. Soc., Inter-Am. Photochem. Soc., 1994, Havinga medal, Leiden, The Netherlands, 1994, Disting. Alumnus award, Calif. Inst. Tech., 1996, Strahlenchemie preis, Max-Planck-Inst., Mülheim, Germany, 1998, Dir's. award for Tchr.-Scholar, NSF, 2002, Mayor's award excellence in sci. and tech., NYC, 2004; fellow NSF, Alfred P. Sloan Found., Guggenheim fellow, Oxford U., 1985. Mem.: AAAS, NAS (editl. bd. Procs. NAS 2002—), European Photo-Chem. Assn. (Porter medal), Inter-Am. Photochemistry Soc. (award 1991, 1994), N.Y. Acad. Scis. (Freda and Gregory Halpern award in photochemistry 1977), Am. Chem. Soc. (mem. editl. bd. jour. 1984—87, Fresenius award 1973, award for pure chemistry 1974, Harrison Howe award Rochester, N.Y. sect. 1986, Arthur C. Cope award 1986, James Flack Norris award 1987, award in colloid and surface chemistry 1999, Gibbs medal award Chgo. sect. 2000, George C. Pimentel award 2004, Nichols Medal award 2007), Sigma Xi, Phi Beta Kappa. Office: Columbia U 3000 Broadway New York NY 10027-6941 Business E-Mail: njt3@columbia.edu.

TURSO, VITO ANTHONY, government agency administrator, public information officer; b. NYC, Jan. 3, 1948; s. Vito Anthony and Helen (Smanko) T.; m. MaryAnn Ponzo, July 12, 1980; children: Lisa Lynn, Laura Mae, Nicole Vita. Student, Queens Coll., Flushing, NY, 1965-69. Reporter L.I. Press, Jamaica, N.Y., 1966-77; asst. Metro editor The Trib, NYC, 1977-78; dir. pub. affairs N.Y.C. Dept. Sanitation, 1978-90; dep. commr. for pub. affairs N.Y.C. Dept. Correction, 1990-94; dep. commr. for pub. affairs and community svcs. N.Y.C. Dept. of Environ. Protection, 1994-95; exec. v.p. Dan Klores Comms. Pub. Rels., 1995—2002; dep. commr. pub. info and cmty. affairs N.Y.C. Dept. Sanitation, 2002—. Guest lectr. New Sch. for Social Rsch., NYC, 1988, Pace U., 1990, NYU, 1998, St. John's U., 2004-05. Host pub. affairs shows on TV and radio, 1981, 88, 2004, 2005; contbr. articles to pop. mags. Bd. dirs. Ozone Tudor Civic Assn., Ozone Park, N.Y., 1982-90. Recipient Bronze medal Internat. Film and TV Festival N.Y., 1985, Page One award N.Y. Newspaper Guild, 1976. Mem. Pub. Rels. Officers Soc. N.Y. (pres. 1983-85), Pub. Rels. Soc. Am. (bd. dirs. 1987-88), Am. Diabetes Assn. (bd. dirs. N.Y. chpt. 1989-91), Bklyn. Tech. H.S. Alumni Assn. (bd. dirs. 1984—90), N.Y. Press Club, Inc. (bd. dirs. 1978, journalism award judge 1996-). Roman Catholic. Avocations: golf, music. Home: 133-33 84th St Ozone Park NY 11417-1919 Office: 125 Worth St New York NY 10013 Office Phone: 646-885-5020. E-mail: vturso@dsny.nyc.gov.

TURTELL, NEAL TIMOTHY, librarian; b. NYC, Nov. 1, 1949; s. Richard Roland and Ann Grace (Glover) T. AB, Fordham U., 1971; MLS, Pratt Inst., 1975. Cataloger-libr. Ford Found., NYC, 1972-75, U.S. Dept. Transp., Washington, 1975-77; spl. projects libr. Smithsonian Instn., Washington, 1977-81, chief catalogue records, 1981-82; asst. dir. tech. svcs. U. Wis., Oshkosh, 1982-83, asst. prof. libr. sci., 1982-83; asst. chief libr. Nat. Gallery of Art, Washington, 1983-87, exec. libr., 1987—. Contbr. to book revs. Libr. Jour., 1972-75, exhbn. catalogue. Bd. trustees Pyramid Atlantic Ctr. for Printmaking and the Art of the Book, Riverdale, Md., 1988—, v.p. bd. trustees, 1991—. Mem. Art Librs. Soc. N.Am., Rsch. Librs. Group (steering com. for art and architecture 1988-89), Assn. Internat. de Bibliophilie, Grolier Club. Office: Nat Gallery of Art 4th & Constitution Ave NW Washington DC 20565-0001

TURTIL, LAWRENCE CHARLES, psychiatrist; b. NYC, Dec. 30, 1951; s. Joseph Fredric and Estelle Rebecca Turtil. BA cum laude, U. Pa., 1972; MD, Georgetown U., 1977. Diplomate Am. Bd. Psychiatry and Neurology, Am. Bd. Internal Medicine, Am. Bd. Adolscent Psychiatry. Resident in internal medicine Lenox Hill Hosp., NYC, 1977-80, attending physician emergency svc., 1980-81, attending physician dept. psychiatry, 1989-90, asst. chief inpatient psychiatry unit, 1990-94; resident in psychiatry Cornell, N.Y. Hosp., White Plains, 1981-84; attending physician N.Y. Hosp., Westchester div., 1984-85; med. dir. Four Winds Hosp., Katonah, N.Y., 1985-89; pvt. practice NYC & Katonah, N.Y.; attending psychiatrist Manhattan Psychiatric Ctr., NYC, 1994; med. dir. Four Winds Hosp., Katonah, N.Y., 1994-97; med. dir. Psych Sys. Manhattan partial hospitalization Gracie Square Hosp., NYC, 1997—2001; psychiatric cons. Counseling Ctr. Student Health Svcs. Fashion Inst. Tech., 1999—2001, Children's Aid Soc. PINS Diversion Program, 2001—04. Mem. Am. Psychiat. Assn. Office: 40 E 83d St Ste 1E New York NY 10028 Office Phone: 212-734-5482.

TURTLETAUB, MARC, film producer; Grad., U. Pa. Wharton Sch., NYU Sch. Law. Bar: Calif. Founder, pres., CEO The Money Store, Calif.; co-founder Deep River Prodns., 2000—, Big Beach Films, NYC, 2004—. Duane Hopwood, 2005, The Honeymooners, 2005, Everything is Illuminated, 2005, SherryBaby, 2006; prodr., prodr.: (films) Little Miss Sunshine, 2004 (Darryl F. Zanuck Prodr. of Yr. award in Theatrical Motion Pictures, Prodrs. Guild of Am., 2007); actor, actor: (films) Little Miss Sunshine, 2004. Office: Big Beach Films 5th Fl 41 Great Jones New York NY 10012 *

TURTURRO, JOHN, actor; b. Brooklyn, Feb. 28, 1957; s. Nicholas and Katherine Turturro; m. Katherine Borowitz, 1985; children: Amedeo, Diego. Grad., SUNY, 1978; student, Yale Drama Sch. Worked in regional theater and off-Broadway prodns.: Danny and the Deep Blue Sea; Men Without Dates; Tooth of the Crime; La Puta Vida; Chaos and Hard Times; The Bald Soprano; Of Mice and Men; The Resistable Rise of Arturo Ui, 1991; Waiting for Godot; appeared in Broadway prodn.: Death of a Salesman, 1984; appeared in films: Raging Bull, 1980; The Flamingo Kid, 1984; To Live and Die in L.A., 1985; Desperately Seeking Susan, 1985; Hannah and Her Sisters, 1986; Gung Ho, 1986; Offbeat, 1986; The Color of Money, 1986; The Sicilian, 1987; Five Corners, 1988; Do the Right Thing, 1989; Miller's Crossing, 1990; Men of Respect; Mo Better Blues, 1990; Jungle Fever, 1991; Barton Fink, 1991; Backtrack, 1991; Brain Donors, 1992; Fearless, 1993; Festival, 1991; Being Human, 1994; Quiz Show, 1994; Grace of My Heart, 1996; Search and Destroy, 1995; Unstrung Heroes, 1995; Clockers, 1995; Box of Moonlight, 1996; Girl 6, 1996; The Big Lebowski, 1997; Animals, 1997; The Truce, 1998; Lesser Prophets, 1998; Rounders, 1998; He Got Game, 1998; The Source, 1999; The Cradle Will Rock, 1999; Company Man, 1999; Two Thousand and None, 1999; Oh Brother, Where Art Thou?, 1999; The Man Who Cried, 1999; The Luzhin Defense, 1999; Anger Management, 2003; appeared in films Collateral Damage, 2000, Mr. Deeds, 2002, Secret Passage, 2002, Secret Window, 2004, 2BPerfectly Honest, 2004, She Hate Me, 2004, A Few Days in September, 2006, The Good Shepherd, 2006; actor: (TV films) Monday Night Mayhem, 2002; dir.: (films, debut) Mac; (films) Illuminata, 1998, Thirteen Conversations About One Thing, 2000; actor, dir.: Romance & Cigarettes, 2005; dir.: (plays) A Spanish Play, 2007. also: 16 N Oak St 2 A Ventura CA 93001-5620 *

TURTURRO, NICHOLAS, actor; b. Queens, NY, Jan. 29, 1962; m. Jamie Biunno, 1984 (div. 1985) 1 child; m. Lissa Espinosa, 1986; 1 child. Actor films including: Mo' Better Blues, 1990, Men of Respect, 1991, Jungle Fever, 1991, Mac, 1992, Malcolm X, 1992, Men Lie, 1994, Cosmic Slop, 1994, Federal Hill, 1995, The Search for One-eye Jimmy, 1996, Shadow Conspiracy, 1997, Excess Baggage, 1997, Recess: School's Out, 2001, The Shipment, 2001, Purgatory Flats, 2002, The Biz, 2002, The Hollow, 2004, The Hillside Strangler, 2004, The Longest Yard, 2005, (TV series) NYPD Blue, 1993-2000, (TV movies) Dead and Alive: The Race for Gus Farace, 1991, Cosmic Slop, 1994, In the Line of Duty: Hunt for Justice, 1995, Falling from the Sky: Flight 174, 1995, Mercenary II: Thick & Thin, 1997, Witness to the Mob, 1998, Monday Night Mayhem, 2002, Big Shot: Confessions of a Campus Bookie, 2002; TV guest appearances include: Law & Order, 1992, L.A. Law, 1993, Drew Carey Show, 1997, The District, 2001, Touched by an Angel, 2002, The Twilight Zone, 2002, Third Watch, 2003, 04. Office: United Talent Agy 9560 Wilshire Blvd Ste 500 Beverly Hills CA 90212-2427

TUSCHMAN, JAMES MARSHALL, lawyer; b. Nov. 28, 1941; s. Chester and Harriet (Harris) T.; m. Ina S. Cheloff, Sept. 2, 1967; children: Chad Michael, Jon Stephen, Sari Anne. BS in Bus., Miami U., Oxford, Ohio, 1963; JD, Ohio State U., 1966. Bar: Ohio 1966, U.S. Ct. Appeals (6th and 7th cirs.), U.S. Supreme Ct. Assoc. Shumaker, Loop & Kendrick, Toledo, 1966—84, ptnr., 1970—84; co-founder, chmn. ops. com. Jacobson Maynard Tuschman & Kalur, Toledo, 1985—97; COO Ohio Ferrous Group Omnisource Corp., Toledo, 1998—99, dir. bus. devel. No. Ohio group, 1999—2001; of counsel Barkan & Robon Ltd., Maumee, Ohio, 2002—. Chmn. bd., sec. Tuschman Steel Co., Toledo, 1969-76, Toledo Steel Supply Co., 1969-86; vice-chmn. bd. Kripke Tuschman Industries, Inc., 1977-85; ptnr. Starr Ave. Co., Toledo, 1969-86. Past trustee, chmn. bd. trustees U. Toledo; past trustee, chmn. fin. com., past treas. Maumee Valley Country Day Sch.; past trustee, v.p., treas. Temple B'nai Israel, 1984-88; mem. nat. alumni coun. Ohio State U. Coll. Law; mem., co-chmn. subcom. on structure, governance and fin. Gov.'s Commn. on Higher Edn. and Economy; mem Ohio Bd. Regents. Fellow Internat. Soc. Barristers; mem. ATLA, Am. Bd. Trial Advocates, Ohio Bar Assn., Toledo Bar Assn., Ohio Trial Lawyers Assn., Million Dollar Advocates Forum, Inverness Country Club, Zeta Beta Tau, Phi Delta Phi. Home: 2579 Olde Brookside Rd Toledo OH 43615-2233 Office: Barkan & Robon Ltd 1701 Woodlands Dr Maumee OH 43537-4092 Home Phone: 419-536-2557; Office Phone: 419-897-6500. Business E-Mail: jmt.bar-rob@buckeye-express.com.

TUSIANI, JOSEPH, foreign language educator, author; b. Foggia, Italy, Jan. 14, 1924; came to U.S., 1947, naturalized, 1956; s. Michael and Maria (Pisone) T. Dottore in Lettere summa cum laude, U. Naples, 1947, LittD, 1971; Dottore (hon.), U. Foggia, 2004. Lectr. in Italian lit. Hunter Coll., 1950-62; chmn. Italian dept. Coll. Mt. St. Vincent, 1948-71. Vis. assoc. prof. NYU, 1956-64, CUNY, 1971-83; prof. Herbert H. Lehman Coll., 1971-83; NDEA vis. prof. Italian Conn. State Coll., 1962. Author: Dante in Licenza, 1952, Two Critical Essays on Emily Dickinson, 1952, Poesia Missionaria in Inghilterra ed America, 1953, Sonettisti Americani, 1954, Melos Cordis: Poems in Latin, 1955, Lo Speco Celeste, 1956, Odi Sacre; poems, 1958, The Complete Poems of Michelangelo, 1960, Rind and All, 1962, Lust and Liberty (The Poems of Machiavelli), 1963, The Fifth Season, 1963, (novels) Envoy from Heaven, 1965, Tasso's Jerusalem Delivered, 1970, Boccaccio's Nymphs of Fiesole, 1971, Gente Mia and Other Poems, 1978, (poems in Latin) In Exilio Rerum, 1985, (autobiography) La Parola Difficile, vol. I, 1988, (poems in Latin) Confinia Lucis et Umbrae: La Parola Nuova, vol. II, 1991, La Parola Antica, vol. III, 1992, (poems in Italian) Il Ritorno, 1992, Bronx America, 1992, Annemale Parlante, 1994, Carmina Latina, 1994, La Poceide, 1996, Carmina Latina, vol. 11, 1998, Li Quatte Staggione, 1998, Lu Deddú, 1999, Maste Peppe Cantarine, 2000, Lu Ponte de Sóla, 2001, In Quattro Lingue, 2001, Dante's Divine Comedy (As told for young people), 2001, L'ore de Gesu Bambine (a Christmas play in verse), 2001, La Prima Cumpagnia, 2002, (in Apulian dialect) La Tomba de Patre Pí, 2003, (plays) (in verse) La Cunte de Pasqua, 2003, La Padula (in Apulian dialect, 2004, Lu Scazzamuredde, 2005, Storie dal Gargano, 1955-2005, 2006; translator: Pulci's Morgante, 1998. Recipient Greenwood prize for poetry in England, 1956, Outstanding Tchr. award, 1969, cavaliere ufficiale Italian Republic, 1973, Leonardo Covello's educator award, 1980, Leone di San Marco award, 1982, Avis award, 1983, Joseph Tusiani scholarship fund established in his honor at Lehman Coll., 1983, Congl. medal merit, 1984, Progresso medal liberty, 1986, Gold plaque City Hall San Marco, 1986, Outstanding tchr. award Am. Assn. Tchrs. Italian, 1986, Renoir literary award, 1988, Joseph Tusiani, Poet, Translator, Humanist (An Internat. Homage), 1995, Enrico Fermi award, 1995, Fiorello La Guardia award, 1998; Melvin Jones fellow, 1995, Gov.'s award for excellence, 1999, Apulia prize of Regione Puglia, 1999, Gold medal at Rome's Capitol, 2004, Gold medal Gov. of Regione Puglia, 2004, prize Italiani nel Mondo, 2004; Joseph Tusiani Found. established at U. Lecce, 1998, NEH, 1998. Mem. Poetry Soc. Am. (v.p.), Cath. Poetry Soc. Am. (dir. 1958, Spirit gold medal 1968) Home: 308 E 72nd St New York NY 10021-4727 *Strange how this continually re-edited Who's Who forces one to work and achieve.*

TUSK, CLAUDE M., lawyer; b. NYC, Nov. 11, 1954; AB magna cum laude, Harvard U., 1974, JD magna cum laude, 1977. Bar: NY 1978, US Dist. Ct. (so. and ea. dists.) NY 1978, US Ct. Appeals (2d cir.) 1980, US Ct. Appeals (11th cir.), US Supreme Ct. 1981. Law clk. to Hon. J. Edward Lumbard U.S. Ct. Appeals (2d cir.), 1977-78; atty. Graham & James, NYC; ptnr. Dechert LLP, NYC. Contbr. articles to profl. jour. Mem. ABA, Assn.

of Bar NYC, Fed. Bar Coun., Phi Beta Kappa. Editor Harvard Law Review. Office: Dechert LLP 30 Rockefeller Plz New York NY 10112 Office Phone: 212-698-3612, 212-698-3599. Business E-Mail: claude.tusk@dechert.com.

TUSKA, JON, writer, publishing executive; b. South Milwaukee, Wis., Apr. 30, 1942; s. Andrew and Florence Catherine (Tommet) T.; m. Vicki Piekarski, May 24, 1980; 1 child, Jennifer Lee. BA, Marquette U., 1965. Owner Pers. Cons., Milw., 1969-74; editor, pub. Views & Revs. mag., 1969-75; freelance writer, 1975--91; co-owner, agt. Golden West Literary Agy., Portland, Oreg., 1992—. Adj. faculty MA and tchg. program and undergrads. Lewis and Clark Coll., 1979-88' staff music critic Ovation mag., 1987-89, Fanfare mag., 1989-95; spl. film. cons. Images of Indians, PBS, 1980, Images of Appalachia, PBS, 1984, Mommy, Who's Winning Now? The Cold War in America, Turner, 1986, Say It with Music: Irving Berlin's America, PBS, 1986, Broadway's Eternal Romantics: Lerner and Loewe, PBS, 1988, John Wayne: Standing Tall, PBS, 1989, Big Guns Talk, Turner, 1997; prodr. classical music programs, art and news features and interviews with musicians and motion picture personalities, and film revs. for radio stas. Oreg. Pub. Broadcasting. Author: Philo Vance: The Life and Times of S.S. Van Dine, 1973, The Films of Mae West, 1973, The Filming of the West, 1976, The Detective in Hollywood, 1978, The Vanishing Legion: A History of Mascot Pictures 1927-35, 1982, 2d edit., 1986, Billy the Kid: A Bio/Bibliography, 1983, Dark Cinema: American Film Noir in Cultural Perspective, 1984, The American West in Film: Critical Approaches to the Western, 1985, In Manors and Alleys: A Case-Book on the American Detective Film, 1988, A Variable Harvest: Essays and Reviews in Literature and Film, 1989, Encounters with Filmmakers: Eight Career Studies, 1991, The Complete Films of Mae West, 1992, Billy the Kid: His Life and Legend, 1994, (with Vicki Piekarski) The Frontier Experience: A Reader's Guide to the Life and Literature of the American West, 1984; editor-in-chief (with Piekarski) Ency. of Frontier and Western Fiction, 1983; editor: The Western Story: A Chronological Treasury 1894-1994, 1994, Shadow of the Lariat, 1995, Star Western: Twenty-Two Western Stories from the Golden Age, 1995, The Big Book of Western Action Stories, 1995, (with Piekarski) The Morrow Anthology of Great Western Short Stories, 1997, The First Five Star Western Corral, 2000, Five Star Westerns, 2000, Stories of the Golden West, Book One, 2000, Book Two, 2001, Book Three, 2002, Book Four, 2003, Book Five, 2004, Book Six, 2005, Odyssey to the North: Northwestern Stories, 2003, Stories of the Golden West: Book Seven, 2006. Avocations: reading, classical music, film history, book collecting. Home and Office: 2327 SE Salmon St Portland OR 97214-3943 Office Phone: 503-232-0238. Personal E-mail: jtuska@qwest.net.

TUSKEY, LAURA JEANNE, music educator, pharmacologist; b. Virginia Beach, Va., May 7, 1966; d. Cromer Lee Ishmael and Annabell E. Eschbach; m. John Phillip Tuskey, June 26, 1998. Student, Old Dominion U., Norfolk, Va., 1984—86. Cert. pharmacy technician Pharmacy Technician Certification Bd., 2003. Pianist Cath. Ch. of St. Mark, Virginia Beach, Va., 1991—; office mgr. CompuGeek, L.L.C., Chesapeake, Va., 2002—03; pharmacy technician Farm Fresh, Inc., Virginia Beach, Va., 2002—, Phar Mor, Inc., Norfolk and Virginia Beach, Va., 1991—98; music therapist Our Lady of Perpetual Health, Virginia Beach, Va., 1999—2000. Aromatherapy educator, Hampton Roads, Va., 2000—. Contbr. articles to profl. jours. Mem.: Alzheimer's Assn. (chmn. memory walk com. 2001), Nat. Pastoral Musicians Assn. R-Liberal. Roman Catholic. Avocations: aromatherapy, musical events, reading, travel. Office: Catholic Church of St Mark 1505 Kempsville Rd Virginia Beach VA 23464

TUSSING, MARILEE APPLEBY, music educator; b. Decatur, Ill., Feb. 6, 1953; d. Robert William and Dorothymaie (Mallory) Appleby; m. Donald Tussing, April 17, 1976; 1 child, Torrance Ashley. B in Music Edn., Ill. State U., 1975; M in Music Edn., U. Okla., 1985. Nat. bd. cert. early and mid. childhood music 2004. Music tchr. Shannon Elem., Shannon, Ill., 1976-80, Thompson Schs., Thompson, Ill., 1980-82; Kodaly music specialist Southgate Elem., Moore, Okla., 1982—. Riding instr. Shenandoah Riding Ctr., Galena, Ill. 1977-81, freelance Norman, Okla., 1982—; creator Sooner Pony Club Worksheet Program; founder Southgate String Players; clinician Orgn. Am. Kodaly Educators Conf., Chgo., 2002, Charlotte, NC, 2006. Musician: (band) Traditions, 1999—. Dist. Commr. Sooner Pony Club, 1985—; judge Okla. Kids Talent Search, 1993-96; mem. Moore Assn. Classroom Tchrs. 1982—; pres. Moore Elem. Music Orgn., 1990-91; founder Southgate Entertainer's Club; dir. Am. Kids Celebrity Chorus, 1996-97; mem. Irish Arts Project, 2002—; mem. Comhaltas Ceoltiori Eirhann, 2004—. Recipient Equestrian Event Silver medal Sooner State Games, Okla., 1989; grantee Okla. Found. for excellence in edn., 2006. Mem. Midwest Kodaly Music Educators (bd. dirs. 1983-85), US Pony Club (knowdown judge, 1990-98, tech. del.), US Combined Tng. Assn. (cert. of achievement, 1985, 89, area V adult team mem. award, 1993), Nat. Edn. Assn., Okla. Edn. Assn., Am. Quarter Horse Assn., Orgn. Am. Kodaly Educators, Okla. City Traditional Music Assn., Am. Connemera Pony Soc Republican. Mem. Christian Ch. (Disciples Of Christ). Avocations: skiing, needlepoint, violin, guitar, collecting and reading horse books. Home: 11850 E Rock Creek Rd Norman OK 73026-8155 Personal E-mail: mrstussing@aol.com.

TUTASHINDA, KWELI (BRIAN P. ALTHEIMER), chiropractic physician, educator; b. Wynne, Ark., May 14, 1956; s. Joe Porché and Lura Ella (Darden) Altheimer; divorced; 1 child, Chinyere R.; m. Leonor Quiñonez, June 13, 1987; children Xihuanel, Rukiya, Jomoké. BA in Philosophy summa cum laude, U. Ark., 1978; D of Chiropractic cum laude, Life Chiropractic Coll. West, San Lorenzo, Calif., 1989. Tchr. English Oakland (Calif.) Pub. Schs., 1984-86; instr. phys. diagnosis and chiropractic tech. Life Chiropractic Coll. West, Haywood, Calif., 1989—99; pvt. practice Berkeley, 1989—; owner Imhotep Chiropractic & Wellness Clinic; dir. Imhotep Wellness Workshops & Seminars. Tchr. spl. programs U. Calif., Berkeley, Calif., 1984—92, 1994—95, 1998—2000, 2005; faculty advisor, lectr. Sch. Humanities, New Coll., San Francisco, 2007—; lectr. in field. Editor, pub. Foresight Mag., 1982-84; author, pub. Toward a Holistic Worldview, 1985, Therapeutic Exercises for the Spine, 1999, Nature, Holism and African-American Struggle, 2004, It's Our Time: Ella Baker, Participatory Democracy and Oakland, California, 2007; contbr. articles to Chiropractic History. Recipient 1st degree Black Belt Tae Kwon Do, 1976. Mem. Sufi Order of the West, Naqshbandi Sufi Order. Islam. Avocations: yoga, martial arts, writing, reading, walking. Office: 3358 Adeline St Berkeley CA 94703-2737 Business E-Mail: tutateam@sbcglobal.net.

TUTELA, ROCCO, plastic surgeon; BA, U. Notre Dame; MD, Bolognia U. Bd. cert. plastic surgery Am. Bd. Plastic Surgery. Plastic surgeon, 1982—. Named Man of Yr., Fedn. Italian Am. Socs., 2001; recipient Upjohn Achievement award for excellence in medicine - Intern of Yr., 1971, UNICO Achievement award, 1992, Christopher Columbus Heritage award, 1999. Office: 405 Northfield Ave Ste 100 West Orange NJ 07052

TUTHILL, JAY DEAN, II, investment executive; b. Wilmington, Del., Dec. 10, 1953; s. Jay Dean Tuthill and Annabelle (Carney) Kressman; m. Laura Ann Behr, Nov. 23, 1972 (div. May 1981); 1 child, Elizabeth; m. Assunta Sera, Oct. 10, 1991; children: Lori, Michael, Mark. BSChemE, U. Del., 1981; MBA with honors, U. Mich., 1988. Engr. Exxon, Detroit, 1981-86; mgr. bus. planning Am. Cyanamid, Wayne, NJ, 1988-94; portfolio mgr. Am. Express, Paramus, NJ, 1994-95; pres. Buckingham Fin., Ridgewood, NJ, 1995—; CFO Prismatic Corp., Newburgh, NY, 1997—; mng. dir. Tuthill & Merker LLC, Ridgewood, NJ, 1999—. Mem. Assn. Investment Mgmt. and Rsch., N.Y. Soc. Security Analysts (vice chair comms. and mktg. com. 1994—, Vol. of Yr. award 1995), Inst. Chartered Fin. Analysts (chartered CFA), Ridgewood C. of C. (profl. com. 1996), Beta Gamma Sigma, Tau Beta Pi. Republican. Roman Catholic. Avocations: golf, piano. Home: 530 Valley Rd Apt 3T Montclair NJ 07043-2714 Office: Tuthill & Merker LLC 999 Riverview Dr Ste 304 Totowa NJ 07512-1165

TUTHILL, OLIVER W., JR., psychologist, consultant, independent film producer, director; b. Orange, NJ, Aug. 8, 1945; s. Oliver W. and Virginia Tuthill. BA in Sociology, Olivet Coll., 1968, BA in Psychology, 1968; MA in Psychology, Antioch U., 2002. Singer, songwriter, Chgo., 1955—72; actor Hollywood, Calif., 1972—84, Universal, Hollywood, 1973—84; pres., profl. spkr. Autumn Tree Prodns., Seattle, 1999—2005; pres. Blue Pony Trail Music, Seattle, 2005—. Pres. 140th St Promotions, Seattle, 1986—88, Blue Wood Films LLC, Seattle, 2003—05; cons. Jr. Achievement, Seattle, 1996—2000; advisor, com. mem. Gov. Blue Ribbon Commn., Seattle, 2000—02. Dir.: (films) Understanding 6 Forms of Emotional, 1999 (Bronze Telly award, 2000, 2003), Dysphoria, 2001 (Best Feature Film, 2001), Children's Rights: Why America Says No, 2004 (4 Bronze Telly awards, 2004); prodr.: (albums) Acoustic Concerto, 2005; prodr.(dir.): (films) Willatuk: The Legend of Seattle's Sea Serpent, featuring Graham Greene, 2006; prodr. (dir.): (films) Child Abuse; prodr.(dir.): (films) Wounded Heart: Pine Ridge Run and The Sioux Featuring Russell Means, 2005 (Bronze Telly award, 2005, Grand Goldie Film award, 2005); dir.: (documentary) Questions for Crazy Horse. Recipient Media award, Gov. Wash. State, 2002, Horace Mann award, Antioch U., 2003, Silver Plaque, Music Intercom Video Competition, 2001, Silver Telly award for Complex: Life Inside a Section 8 Apt., 2006. Mem.: APA (assoc.), Am. Screenwriters Assn., Internat. Documentary Assn., Screen Actors Guild, Broadcast Music Inc. Avocations: sports, swimming, singing, reading, politics. Office: Blue Wood Films 17171 Bothell Way NE PMB 108 Seattle WA 98155 Home: 20044 Bagley Dr N Y304 Seattle WA 98133 Office Phone: 206-364-9202. Personal E-mail: owtuthi@earthlink.net.

TUTHILL, WALTER WARREN, accountant, management consultant; b. Madison, NJ, Nov. 28, 1941; s. Walter Warren and Elizabeth Emma (Kniskern) T.; m. Barbara Ann Stephens, Apr. 22, 1967. BSBA, U. NC, Chapel Hill, 1964. CPA NY, NJ, NC; cert. info. systems auditor. Sr. mgr. Price Waterhouse, NYC, 1964-77; dir. internal audit Carter Hawley Hale Stores Inc., LA, 1977-82, gen. auditor, 1982-85, v.p., 1985-93; sr. v.p. retail control Broadway Stores, Inc., LA, 1993-96; v.p. retail control Federated Dept. Stores, Inc., LA, 1996-97; COO Gelfand, Rennert & Feldman divsn. PricewaterhouseCoopers LLP, LA, 1997-2001; dir. comprehensive bus. svcs. WongHolland LLP, CPAs, Woodland Hills, Calif., 2001—. Lectr. in field. Contbr. articles to profl. jours. Mem. AICPA, NY Soc. CPAs, Am. Acctg. Assn., Nat. Retail Fedn. (chmn. bd. internal audit group 1982-84, bd. dirs.), Info. Sys. Audit and Control Assn. Avocations: international travel, computers, classical music, photography, philanthropy. Office: WongHolland LLP CPAs and Cons 4919 Topanga Canyon Blvd Woodland Hills CA 91364-3113 Home Phone: 818-609-8099; Office Phone: 818-999-5273. Office Fax: 818-999-5274. Personal E-mail: wwtuthill@earthlink.net. Business E-Mail: wtuthill@wongholland.com. *Life is what happens when we're planning something else.*

TUTOR, RONALD N., construction executive; b. Oct. 13, 1940; BS in Fin., U. So. Calif., LA, 1963. Pres., CEO Tutor-Saliba Corp., Calif.; bd. dirs. Perini Corp., 1997—, COO, 1997—2000, vice chmn., 1998—99, chmn., 1999—, CEO, 2000—. Bd. dirs. Southdown Corp.; mem. adv. com. U. So. Calif. Sch. Engring. Recipient LA Conservancy Preservation award, 1994, Greater LA African-Am. C. of C. Contractor of Yr. award, 1994, US Army C.E. LA Dist. Contractor of Yr. award, 1994, NCCJ Real Estate and Constrn. Industry Humanitarian award, 1992. Mem. Am. Concrete Inst. Office: Tutor-Saliba 15901 Olden St Sylmar CA 91342-1093 also: Perini Corp 73 Mt Wayte Ave Framingham MA 01701 *

TUTTLE, JEREMY BALLOU, neuroscientist; s. John Bauman and Charlotte Marion (Root) T.; m. Sara Jane Stasko, Mar. 23, 1971. AB, U. Rochester, 1969; PhD, Johns Hopkins U., 1977. Postdoctoral fellow U. Conn., Storrs, 1976-79, vis. asst. prof., 1980, asst. prof. in residence, 1981-84; asst. prof. physiology U. Va., Charlottesville, 1984-87, asst. prof. neuroscience, 1987-90, rsch. asst. prof., 1990-93, assoc. prof. urology neuroscience, 1993-98, prof., 1998—. Contbr. articles to Devel. Biology, Science, Jour. Neuroscience, others; mem. editl. bd. Investigative Urology, Jour. Urology, Jour. Hypertension. Chmn. mem. Common Area Planning Commn., 1984-87; pres. bd. Earlysville Forest Homeowner's Assn., 1986-89, Earlysville, Va.; chmn. urology spl. emphasis panel NIH, 1996-2001; chmn. spl. emphasis panel on female pelvic floor disorders Nat. Inst. Child Health and Human Devel., 1999; mem. promotion and tenure com. U. Va., 2004—. U. Rochester Hon. scholar, 1965-69, Regent's scholar for Medicine, 1969, NIH predoctoral fellow, 1971-75, Nat. Rsch. Svc. fellow, 1976-79, Nat. Spinal Cord Injury Found. rsch. fellow, 1979-80; recipient Rsch. Career Devel. award Nat. Inst. Neurol. Disease/NIH, Muscular Dystrophy Assn. Rsch. award, 1990—; Am. Heart Assn. grantee, 1987-89, 90—, fellowship, Fogarty Internat. Ctr. for Rsch. NIH, Japan, 1997. Mem.: AAAS, Am. Soc. Cell Biology, Biophys. Soc., Soc. Neuroscience, Sigma Xi. Achievements include research on NGF dynamics in hypertrophic disease, carbon dioxide transport and chemosensitivity, molecular mechanisms of quantal synaptic transmission, nerve growth factor synthesis by vascular smooth muscle, trophic regulation of motor neurons, neurodegenerative diseases. Office: U Va Med Sch PO Box 801392 Charlottesville VA 22908-1392 Office Phone: 434-924-5634. Business E-Mail: tuttle@virginia.edu.

TUTTLE, KENNETH LEWIS, retired engineering educator, consultant, researcher; b. Toledo, Oreg., Apr. 4, 1944; s. Martin Lewis and Norma Corinne (Nichols) Tuttle; m. Susanna Anna Maria Woodworth, June 24, 1967; children: Stephanie, Meghan, Lewis. BS, US Naval Acad., 1967; MS, Oreg. State U., Corvallis, 1974, PhD, 1978. Registered profl. engr., Oreg. (environ. branch added in 1995). Commd. ensign USN, 1967, advanced through grades to lt., 1971, shipboard line officer Norfolk, Va., 1967-69, intelligence officer Tan An, Vietnam, 1970-71; grad. asst. Oreg. State U., Corvallis, 1972-76; rsch. engr. Weyerhaeuser Co., Tacoma, 1977-81; pvt. practice Federal Way, Wash., 1982-83; assoc. prof. mech. engring. US Naval Acad., Annapolis, Md., 1983—2004, dir. marine propulsion labs., 1984—90, ret., 2004; rschr. and cons. solid fuel rsch. Tuttle Engring., 2004—. Dir. Ocean and Marine Engring. Divsn., Am. Soc. for Engring. Edn., Washington, 1989-91; mem. com. on shipboard pollution control, Nat. Rsch. Coun., Washington, 1994-96; chmn. environ. panel Soc. Naval Arch. and Marine Engrs., Jersey City, 1993-2000; prin. cons. Solid Fuel Rsch., Annapolis, 1984—. Author: Combustion Mechanisms in Wood Fired Boilers, 1978, Review of Biomass Gasification in Progress in Biomass Conversion, 1984, Thermodynamics: A Computer-Based Approach, 2001, 2003; contbr. articles to profl. jours. Mem. Combustion Inst., George C. Marshall Inst. Achievements include development of a prototype for new high compression-ratio vane-in-rotor compressor; pulverized-wood burner and fixed-bed wood gasifier; discovery of the effect of underfire air on particulate emissions; patents in field. Avocations: travel, fishing. Home and Office: 25609 Dog Creek Rd John Day OR 97845 also: 405 Widgeon Way Chester MD 21619 Office Phone: 410-490-9534. Personal E-mail: kentuttle@1967.usna.com, tklewis66@peoplepc.com. Business E-Mail: tklewis@my180.net.

TUTTLE, RICHARD, artist; b. Rahway, NJ, 1941; BA, Trinity Coll., 1963. One-man shows at Betty Parsons Gallery, N.Y.C., 1965, 67, 68, 70, 72, 74, 78, 82, Galerie Schmela, Dusseldorf, Fed. Republic Germany, 1968, 78, 84, 85, Nicholas Wilder Gallery, N.Y.C., 1969, Albright-Knox Gallery, Buffalo, 1970, Dallas Mus. Fine Arts, 1971, The Helman Gallery, St. Louis, 1971, Mus. Modern Art, N.Y.C., 1972, Galerie Rudolf Zwirner, Cologne, Fed. Republic Germany, 1972, Galerie Yvon Lambert, Paris, 1972, 74, 76, 78, 81, 84, 85, 87, The Clocktower Inst. for Art and Urban Resources, N.Y.C., 1973, Kunstraum Munchen, Munich, 1973, 77, Daniel Weinberg Gallery, San Francisco, 1973, 78, Los Angeles, 1984, Francoise Lambert, Milan, 1973, 78, Galerie Heiner Friedrich, Munich, 1973, 77, Galleria Toselli, Milan, 1974, 85, Galleria Marilena Bonomo, Bari, Italy, 1974, 79, 85, Annemarie Verna Galerie, Zurich, 1974, 79, 81, 84, 87, Barbra Cusack Gallery, Houston, 1974, 75, Nigel Greenwood Inc. Ltd., London, 1974, 77, 82, Wadsworth Atheneum, Hartford, Conn., 1975, Whitney Mus. Am. Art, N.Y.C., 1975, Parsons-Truman Gallery, N.Y.C., 1975, Brooke Alexander Inc., N.Y.C., 1976, Fine Arts Bldg. Gallery, N.Y.C., 1976, Graeme Murray Gallery, Edinburgh, 1976, McIntosh Gallery U. Western Ont., London, Can., 1976, Galleria Ugo Ferranti, Rome, 1977, 78, 79, 81, 82, 83, 84, Kunsthalle Basel, 1977, Young Hoffman Gallery, Chgo., 1978, Bell Gallery Brown U., Providence, 1978, Mus. van Hedendaagse Kunst, Gent, Belgium, 1978, Stedelijk Mus., Amsterdam, 1979, Truman Gallery, N.Y.C., 1979, Centre d'Arts Plastiques Contemporains de Bordeaux, 1979, Centre d'Art Contemporain, Geneva, 1980, Ga. State U. Art Gallery, Atlanta, 1980, Baxter Art Gallery Calif. Inst. Tech., Pasadena, 1980, Baronian-Lambert, Gent, 1981, Mus. de Calais, 1982, Taidemaalariliiton Galleria 4, Helsinki, 1983, Blum Helman Gallery, N.Y.C., 1983, 84, 86, Galerie Hubert Winter, Vienna, 1983, 87, Studio La Citta, Verona, 1984, Galleriet, Lund, Sweden, 1984, Portland (Oreg.) Ctr. for Visual Arts, 1984, Stadtisches Mus. Abteiberg, 1985, Inst. Contemporary Arts, London, 1985, Victoria Miro Gallery, London, 1986, Reinhard Onnasch Galerie, Berlin, 1986, CAPC Mus. d'Art Contemporain, Bordeaux, 1986, Neue Galerie Am Landesmuseum Joanneum, Graz, Austria, 1987, Galerie des Arènes, Nîmes, France, 1987, Anders Tornberg Gallery, Lund, 1987, various others; exhibited in group shows at San Francisco Mus. Art, 1965, 73, Byron Gallery, N.Y.C., 1965, Ralph Wilson Gallery Lehigh U., Bethlehem, Pa., 1965, 66, Penthouse Gallery Mus. Modern Art, N.Y.C., 1966, 70, 74, 76, 80, Bykert Gallery, N.Y.C., 1968, 71, Austin Art Ctr. Trinity Coll., Hartford, 1968, 70, Pitts. Plan for Art, 1968, 80, Brainerd Art Gallery SUNY at Potsdam, 1968, 82, Corcoran Gallery Art, Washington, 1969, Whitney Mus. Am. Art, N.Y.C. and Fairfield, Conn., 1969, 73, 77, 78, 81, 83, 84, 85, Detroit Inst. Arts, 1969, 76, 79, Paula Cooper Gallery, N.Y.C., 1971, U. N.C., Greensboro, 1969, 75, Galerie Schmela, Dusseldorf, 1972, 82, 85, Galerie Yvon Lambert, 1970, 72, Yale U. Art Gallery, New Haven, 1973, 75, 82, Art Inst. Chgo., 1975, 82, Stedelijk Mus., Amsterdam, 1978, 82, 84, Brooke Alexander Inc., N.Y.C., 1974, 78, 80, 85, Betty Parsons Gallery, N.Y.C., 1979, 83, Centre Nat. d'Art et de Culture Georges Pompidou, Paris, 1981, Daniel Weinberg Gallery, Los Angeles, 1983, N.Y.C., 1984, Kent Gallery, N.Y.C., 1987, Blum Helman Gallery, 1982, 84, 86, 87, Kunsthalle, Bielefeld, Fed. Republic Germany, 1987, Galerie Harald Behm, Hamburg, Fed. Republic Germany, 1987, Holly Solomon Gallery, N.Y.C., 1987, Damon Brandt Gallery, N.Y.C., 1986, 87, Galería Juana de Aizpuru, Madrid, Spain, 1986, 87, Genovese Graphics, Boston, 1987, Madison Art Ctr., Wis., 1987, numerous others; represented in permanent collections Fogg Art Mus., Cambridge, Mass., Kaiser Wilhelm Mus., Kreefeld, Fed. Republic Germany, Kunsthaus, Zurich, La. Mus. Modern Art, Humleback, Denmark, Ludwig Mus., Cologne, Fed. Republic Germany, Met. Mus. Art, N.Y.C., Mus. Nat. d'Arte Moderne, Paris, Staatliche Kunstsammlungen, Kassel, Fed. Republic Germany, Stedelijk Mus., Whitney Mus. Am. Art; subject of retrospective tour The Art of Richard Tuttle, San Francisco Mus. Modern Art, Whitney Mus., etc. Mailing: c/o Sperone Westwater 415 W 13th St #2 New York NY 10014-1104

TUTTLE, ROBERT BRUCE, mechanical engineer, educator; b. State College, Pa., Feb. 7, 1979; s. B. Lee and Carol Ann Tuttle; m. Jennie Lynne Heger, July 19, 2003. BSME, Worcester Poly. Inst., Mass., 2001; PhD in Metall. Engring., U. Mo., Rolla, 2004. Intern GM Powertrain, Saginaw, Mich., 1998—2000; tchg. asst. U. Mo., 2001—04, rsch. asst., 2001—04; asst. prof. mech. engring. Saginaw Valley State U., University Center, Mich., 2004—. Dir. ctr. rapid prototyping and innovaction Saginaw Valley State U., 2004—, investigator ind. testing lab., 2004—; trustee Saginaw Valley Amateur Radio Club, 2007—. Mem.: ASM (assoc.), Am. Soc. Mech. Engring. (assoc.), Am. Soc. Engring. Edn. (assoc.), Am. Foundry Soc. (assoc.; mem. steel divsn. exec. com. 2005—, mem. program and papers com. steel divsn. 2005—, mem. program com. Saginaw Valley chpt. 2006—), Am. Radio Relay League (assoc.), Saginaw Valley Amateur Radio Assn. (assoc.). Lutheran. Avocations: ice skating, camping, amateur radio. Office: Saginaw Valley State U 7400 Bay Rd University Center MI 48710 Office Phone: 989-964-4676. E-mail: rtuttle@svsu.edu.

TUTTLE, ROBERT HOLMES, ambassador, former federal official; b. Calif., 1944; m. Maria Hummer; children: Tiffany, Alexandra. BA, Stanford U., Calif., 1965; MBA, U. So. Calif., 1968. Asst. to US Pres. Office Presdl. Pers., Washington, 1982-85, dir., 1985—89; bd. dirs. Woodrow Wilson Internat. Ctr. Scholars, Washington, 1989—93; mng. ptnr. Tuttle-Click Automotive Grp., Irvine, Calif.; US amb. to UK US Dept. State, London, 2005—. Mem. bd. Ronald Reagan Presdl. Libr., U. So. Calif. Sch. Comm., LA Mus. Contemporary Art, chmn. bd., 2001—04. Co-chmn. Calif. Rep. Presdl. Campaign, 1980. Office: American Embassy London England UK PSC 801 Box 3 FPO AE 09498-4040 also: DOS Amb 8400 London Pl Washington DC 20521-8400 *

TUTTLE, WILLIAM MCCULLOUGH, JR., history professor; b. Detroit, Oct. 7, 1937; s. William McCullough and Geneva (Duvall) T.; m. Linda Lee Stumpp, Dec. 12, 1959 (div.); children: William McCullough III, Catharine T., Andrew S.; m. Kathryn Nemeth, May 6, 1995. BA, Denison U., 1959; MA, U. Wis., 1964, PhD, 1967. From mem. faculty to prof. history U. Kans., Lawrence, 1967—2000, prof. Am. studies, 2000—, John Adams disting. Fulbright chair in Am. history, 2007. Vis. scholar Radcliffe Coll., 1993—94; Charles Warren fellow Harvard U., Cambridge, Mass., 1972—73; sr. fellow Johns Hopkins U., 1969—70; vis. prof. U. S.C., Columbia, 1980; fellow Humanities Ctr. Stanford U., 1983—84; rsch. assoc. U. Calif., Berkeley, Calif., 1986—88. Author: Race Riot: Chicago in the Red Summer of 1919, 1970, 2d edit., 1996, W.E.B. Du Bois, 1973, (with David M. Katzman) Plain Folk, 1982, (with others) A People and A Nation, 1982, 7th edit., 2005, Daddy's Gone to War: The Second World War in the Lives of America's Children, 1993, (with others) World War II and the American Home Front, 2004; contbr. chpts. to books, articles to profl. jours. Dem. precinct committeeman, Lawrence, 1980-90. Lt. USAF, 1959-62. Recipient Merit award Am. Assn. for State and Local History, 1972, Balfour S. Jeffrey Rsch. Achievement award Humanities and Social Scis., 2004, Chancellors Club Career Tchg. award, 2004, Steeples Svc. to Kans. award, 2006; Younger Humanist fellow NEH, 1972-73, Guggenheim fellow, 1975-76, NEH fellow, 1983-84, rsch. fellow Hall Ctr., 1990, Kemper fellow for tchg. excellence, 1998; Evans grantee, 1975-76, Beveridge grantee, 1982; NEH grantee, 1986-89. Mem. Soc. Am. Historians (elected), Am. Hist. Assn., Orgn. Am. Historians, Am. Studies Assn., Assn. for Study of African Am. Life and History, Lawrence Trout Club, Golden Key (hon.), Omicron Delta Kappa, Phi Beta Delta, Phi Gamma Delta. Home: 713 Louisiana St Lawrence KS 66044-2339 Office: U Kans Dept Am Studies Lawrence KS 66045-0001 Office Phone: 785-864-9476. Business E-Mail: tuttle@ku.edu.

TUTU, DESMOND MPILO, retired archbishop; b. Klerksdorp, Republic of South Africa, Oct. 7, 1931; m. Leah Nomalizo Shenxane; children: Trevor Thamsanqa, Theresa Thandeka, Naomi Nontombi, Mpho Andrea. Diploma in teaching, Pretoria Bantu Normal Coll., South Africa, 1953; BA, U. South Africa, 1954; licentiate in theology, St. Peter's Theol. Coll., South Africa, 1960; postgrad, King's Coll., U. London; DD (hon.), Gen. Theol. Sem., NY, 1978, Aberdeen U., Scotland, 1984, Trinity Luth. Sem., 1985, Trinity Coll., Hartford, Conn., 1986, Chgo. Theol. Sem., 1986, U. West

Indies, Trinidad and Tobago, 1986, Oberlin Coll., 1986, U. South, 1988, Emory U., 1988, Wesleyan U., 1990, Lincoln U., Pa., 1990, Oxford U., Eng., 1990; DCL (hon.), Kent U., Eng., 1978; LLD (hon.), Harvard U., 1979, Claremont Grad. Sch., 1984, Temple U., 1985-86, Mt. Allison U., Can., 1988, Northeastern U., 1988; ThD (hon.), Ruhr U., 1981; STD (hon.), Columbia U., 1982, Dickinson Coll., 1984; LHD (hon.), St. Paul's Coll., 1984, Howard U., 1984, Morehouse Coll., 1986, Cen. U., 1986, CUNY, 1986; HHD (hon.), Wilberforce U., 1985; PhD (hon.), U. Rio, Rio de Janiero, 1986; doctorate (hon.), U. Strasbourg, France, 1988, Wesleyan U., 1990, Lincoln U., 1990, U. Mo., 1990, U. New Rochelle, 1990, 1990, Brown U., 1990, Seton Hall U., 1990, U. PR, 1990. Ordained priest Anglican Ch., 1961. Schoolmaster, 1954-57; parish priest, 1960—; lectr. Fed. Theol. Sem., 1967-69, UBLS Roma, Lesotho, 1970-72; assoc. dir. theol. edn. fund World Coun. Chs., Bromley, Kent, England, 1972-75; dean of Johannesburg South Africa, 1975-76; bishop of Lesotho, 1976-78; bishop of Johannesburg, 1985-86; archbishop of Cape Town South Africa, 1986-96; archbishop emeritus City of Capetown, 1996—; chairperson Truth and Reconciliation Commn., 1996—; vis. prof. The Episcopal Div. Sch., Cambridge, 2002. Sec.-gen. South African Council Chs., 1978-85; vis. prof. Anglican Studies, N.Y. Gen. Theol. Sem., 1984; pres. All Africa Conf. of Chs., 1987-97; chancellor U. Western Cape, Republic of South Africa, 1988—. Author: (collections of sermons and addresses) Crying in the Wilderness, 1982, Hope and Suffering, 1983, The Rainbow People of God: The Making of a Peaceful Revolution, 1994, An African Prayer Book, 1995, No Future Without Forgiveness, 1999, God has a Dream, 2004. Vice chmn. Internat. Alert, 1986; mem. disbursements adv. com. Fund for Edn. in South Africa, N.Y.C., 1988; mem. com. of honor for meml. to Imre Nagy and companions Hungarian Human Rights League, 1988; mem. hon. com. Spl. Fund for Health in Africa, 1990. Recipient Prix d'Athene Onassis Found., 1980, Family of Man gold medallion, 1983, Martin Luther King Jr. Humanitarian award Ann. Black Am. Hero and Heroines Day, 1984; Nobel prize for peace, 1984, Martin Luther King Jr. Peace award, 1986, Internat. Integrity award John-Roger Found., 1986, Pres. award Glassboro State Coll., 1986, World Pub. Forum award City of San Rafael, Calif., 1986, Order of So. Cross Govt. of Brazil, 1987, Order of Merit Govt. of Brazil, 1987, Pacem in Terris award Quad Cities, 1987, Albert Schweitzer Humanitarian award Emmanuel Coll., 1988, Freedom of the City Florence, Italy, 1985, Methyr Tydfil, U.K., 1986, Durham, Eng., 1987, Hull, Eng., 1988, Disting. Peace Leadership award Nuclear Age Peace Found., 1990, Pres.'s medal Claremont Grad. Sch., U.S., 1990, Freedom of the Borough of Lewisham, U.K., 1990, Freedom of the City of Kinshasa, 1990, Grand Officier de la Légion d'Honneur, Pres. Chirac of France, 1998, Lifetime Achievement award CARE USA, 1999, Vision 2000 award Cath. Charities USA, 1999, award Ho. of Commons, Can., 1999, The Wilberforce medallion Lord Mayor and City Coun. Kingston upon Hull, 1999, Pres. meda. Georgetown U., Washington, 2001, Humanitarian award N.Y.C. Office Comptr., 2002; co-recipient Third World prize, 1989; King's Coll. fellow, 1978. Mem. NAACP (life), World Council Global Co-operation. Anglican. Office: PO Box 1092 Milnerton 7435 Cape Town South Africa

TUUL, JOHANNES, physics professor, researcher; b. Tarvastu, Viljandi, Estonia, May 23, 1922; came to US, 1956, naturalized, 1962; s. Johan and Emilie (Tulf) T.; m. Marjatta Murtoniemi, July 14, 1957 (div. Aug. 1971); children: Melinda, Melissa; m. Sonia Esmeralda Manosalva, Sept. 15, 1976; 1 child, Johannes. Elem. Tchg. Credential, Tartu Normal Sch., Estonia, 1941; diploma in Elec. Engring., Stockholm Tech. Inst., 1947; BS, U. Stockholm, 1955, MA, 1956; ScM, Brown U., 1957, PhD, 1960. Tchr. Valuste Elem. Sch., 1941-43; escaped to Finland December, 1943; after Finland surrendered to Russia escaped to Sweden, 1944; instr. Stockholm Tech. Inst., 1947-49; lab. engr. Electrical Prospecting Co., Stockholm, 1949-53; elec. engr. LM Ericsson Telephone Co., Stockholm, 1954-55; rsch. physicist Am. Cyanamid Co., Stamford, Conn., 1960-62; sr. rsch. physicist Bell & Howell Rsch. Ctr., Pasadena, Calif., 1962-65; from asst. to assoc. prof. Calif. State Poly. U., Pomona, 1965-68, chmn. physics and earth scis. dept., 1971-75, prof. physics, 1975-91; prof. emeritus, 1992—. Vis. prof. Pahlavi U., Shiraz, Iran, 1968-70; cons. Bell & Howell Rsch. Ctr., Pasadena, Calif., 1965, Teledyne Co., Pasadena, Calif., 1968; guest researcher Naval Weapons Ctr., China Lake, Calif., 1967, 72; resident dir. Calif. State U. Internat. Programs in Sweden and Denmark, 1977-78. Author: Physics Made Easy, 1974; contbr. articles to profl. jours. Pres. Group Against Smoking Pollution, Pomona Valley, Calif., 1976; foster parent Foster Parents Plan, Inc., Warwick, RI, 1964-2003; block capt. Neighborhood Watch, West Covina, Calif., 1982-84; citizen amb. People to People Internat., 1990—; mem. Physics Edn. Del. to Peoples Rep. China, 1990, 30th Anniversary Caravan to Soviet Union, 1991, Baltic Assist Delegation, 1992, Industry and Sci. Initiative 1 Delegation to Cuba, 2000, Mission in Understanding to Iceland and Greenland, 2002, Global Peace Initiative to Egypt, 2003. Fellow Brown U., 1957-58; rsch. grantee U. Namur (Belgium), 1978, Ctr. Nat. Recherche Scientifique, France, 1979; recipient Humanitarian Fellowship award Save the Children Fedn., 1968, spl. award Travelers' Century Club, 1998. Mem. AAAS (life), NY Acad. Scis., Am. Phys. Soc. Republican. Roman Catholic. Achievements include research in energy conservation and new energy technologies. Personal E-mail: tuuljohannes@hotmail.com.

TUZEL, SUZANNE L., psychiatrist; b. Jacksonville, Fla., Aug. 12, 1960; children: Haldun, Kenan. MD, U. Istanbul Med. Sch., 1986. Diplomate bd. cert. in psychiatry and neurology 1992. Chief resident Creedmoor Psychiatric Ctr., Queens Village, NY, 1992—95, chief psychiatrist, 1995—96; chief of psychiatry Pilgrim Psychiatric Ctr., Brentwood, 1997—99, acting clin. dir., 1999—2000, asst. clin. dir., 2000—02; pvt. practice North Shore Psychiatric Cons., Smithtown, 2002—; attending psychiatrist St. Catherine of Siena Med. Ctr., 2002—; med. dir. Huntington Drug and Alcohol Project, 2006—. Addiction fellow North Shore U. Hosp., Manhasset, 2000. Mem.: Am. Psychiatric Assn. Office: 222 Mid Country Rd Smithtown NY 11787 Office Phone: 631-265-6868.

TUZLA, KEMAL, mechanical engineer, researcher; b. Adapazari, Sakarya, Turkey, Feb. 23, 1943; came to U.S., 1974; s. Hayrettin and Muberra (Horozlu) T.; m. Asuman Fatma Cokmez. MME, Istanbul Tech. U., Turkey, 1966, PhD in Mech. Engring., 1972. Instr. Istanbul Tech. U., 1966-72, asst. prof., 1974, assoc. prof., 1978-81; instr. Air Force Coll., Istanbul, 1973-74; rsch. asst. prof. U. Wash., Seattle, 1974-78; sr. rsch. scientist Lehigh U., Bethlehem, Pa., 1981—2002, assoc. chair, dept. chem. engring., 2003. Mem. organizing com. 2d Thermal Sci. Conf., Istanbul; 1979, 3d Conf., Trabzon, Turkey, 1981; cons. Goodyear Tire & Rubber Co., Akron, Ohio, 1984-86, Exxon Nuclear, Richland, Wash., 1985-88. Editor Proc. 2d Thermal Sci. Conf., 1979; contbr. articles in area of thermal scis. to profl. jours. Co-founder Turkish Am. Cultural Assn., Seattle, 1977. Grantee rsch. grantee, Los Alamos (N.Mex.) Nat. Lab, 1989—91, Ben Franklin Tech. Ctr., Bethlehem, 1989—2001, Gas Rsch. Inst., 1987—91, Elec. Power Rsch. Inst., 1991—94;, Goodyear Tire & Rubber Co., 1985—86. Mem. ASHRAE, AIChE, Sigma Xi. Achievements include research in heat transfer in two-phase flows, boiling, fluidized beds, electronic components and nuclear safety. Office: Lehigh U Chem Engring Iacocca Hall 111 Research Dr Bethlehem PA 18015-4732 Home: 968 N 33rd St Allentown PA 18104-3404

TVILDIANI, DIMITRY, cardiologist; b. Tbilisi, Georgia, June 30, 1956; s. David Tvildiani and Juliana Zubiashvili; m. Khatuna Chkheidze; children: Tamar, Gegi, Michael. MD, State Med. U., Tbilisi, 1978; PhD, State Inst. Transplantology, Moscow, 1980. Chief cardiologist diagnostic dept. State Inst. Cardiology, Tbilisi, 1980—89; dean AIETI Med. Sch., Tbilisi, 1989—99; gen. mgr. Dimas Radiology, NYC, 1999. Achievements include patents for noninvasive index of cardiac contractility; noninvasive method of renal blood flow assesmnet. Office: Image Pro LLC 101-18 Queens Blvd Forest Hills NY 11375 Personal E-mail: tvildianid@aol.com.

TWAGILIMANA, AIMABLE, language educator, writer; b. Muyira, Butare, Rwanda, Dec. 4, 1961; arrived in U.S., 1992; s. Louis Mudugu and Belancila Nyiragakinga; m. Marie-Rose Nkundimfura, Dec. 26, 1987; children: Leandre Munyana, Raissa Umwari. BA in English, Nat. U. of Rwanda, Butare, 1984, MA in English, 1986; MA in Applied Linguistics, U. of Reading, Berkshire, Eng., 1989; PhD in English, SUNY, Buffalo, 1995. Cert. tchr. h.s. Nat. U. of Rwanda. Lectr. Nat. U. of Rwanda, Ruhengeri, 1986—92; asst. prof. SUNY, Buffalo, 1995—2000, assoc. prof. English, 2000—04, prof., 2004—. Dir. of studies faculty of letters Nat. U. of Rwanda, Ruhengeri, 1991—92. Author: (novel) Manifold Annihilation, 1996, (book) Race and Gender in the Making of an African American Literary Tradition, 1997, In Their Own Voices: Rwandan Refugees Speak Out, 1997, Hutu and Tutsi (The Heritage Library of African People series), 1998, The Debris of Ham: Ethnicity, Regionalism and the 1994 Rwandan Genocide, 2003. Fellow, NEH, 1999, 2003; scholar, Fulbright Found., 1992—95, Brit. Coun., 1988—89. Mem.: MLA, Assn. of Am. Transls., Nat. Coun. of Tchrs. of English, Nat. Assn. of Lit. Critics. Roman Catholic. Home: 68 Fairchild Pl Buffalo NY 14216 Office: SUNY 1300 Elmwood Avenue Buffalo NY 14222 Office Phone: 716-878-5407. Personal E-mail: twagila12@hotmail.com. E-mail: twagila@bscmail.buffalostate.edu.

TWAIN, SHANIA (EILLEEN REGINA EDWARDS), musician; b. Windsor, Ontario, Can., Aug. 28, 1965; d. Sharon and Jerry Twain (Stepfather), Clarence Edwards; m. Robert John Lange, Dec. 28, 1993; 1 child, Eja. Recs. Beginnings, 1989—90, 1999, Shania Twain, 1993, The Woman in Me, 1995 (Acad. Country Music Assn. Award for Album of Yr., 1995, ABC Radio Networks Country Music Award for Female Video Artist of Yr., 1995, Billboard Music Award for Country Album of Yr., 1996, Grammy award for Best Country Album, 1996), These Blues are Mine, 1996, Come on Over, 1997, Star Profile, 1999, Maximum Shania, 2000, Complete Limelight Sessions, 2001, Up!, 2002 (Can. Country Music Assn. Award for Album of Yr., 2003, Billboard Music Award for Country Album of Yr., 2003), Greatest Hits, 2004. Recipient Country Music TV (Europe) Rising Star award, 1993, Am. Music Award for Favorite New Country Artist, 1995, Can. Country Music Assn. Award for female vocalist of yr., 1995, Acad. of Country Music Award for Top New Female Vocalist, 1995, Best Country Album Grammy award, 1995, Blockbuster Entertainment Award for Favorite New Country Artist, 1996, Country Music TV (Europe) award for Female Artist of Yr., 1996, Juno Award for Country Female Vocalist of Yr., 1996, Juno Award for Entertainer of Yr., 1996, World Music Award for World's Best Selling Country Artist, 1996, Favorite New Artist award, Am. Music Awards, 1996, Am. Music Award for Best Female Country Artist, 1997, Juno Award for Country Female Vocalist of Yr., 1997, Juno Award for Internat. Achievement, 1997, Am. Music Award for Favorite Female Country Artist, 1998, Billboard Music Award for Female Artist of Yr., 1998, Country Music Assn. Award for Entertainer of Yr., 1999, Acad. Country Music Award for Entertainer of Yr., 1999, Am. Music Award for Favorite Female Country Artist, 1999, Am. Music Award for Favorite Female Pop/Rock Artist, 1999, Blockbuster Entertainment Award for Favorite Overall Single, 1999, Juno Award for Country Female Vocalist of Yr., 1999, Grammy Award for Best Female Country Vocal Performance (You're Still The One), 1999, Grammy Award for Best Country Song (You're Still The One), 1999, Juno Award for Best Songwriter, 2000, Juno Award for Best Country Female Artist, 2000, Grammy Award for Best Female Vocal Country Performance (Man!I Feel Like A Woman), 2000, Grammy Award for Best Country Song (Come On Over), 2000, Acad. Country Music Award for Entertainer of Yr., 2000, Billboard Music Award for Top County Artist of Yr., 2003, Billboard Music Award for Country Album Artist of Yr., 2003, Juno Fan Choice Award, 2003, Juno Award for Artist of Yr., 2003, Juno Award for Country Rec. Yr. (I'm Gonna Getcha Good), 2003, Can. Country Music Assn. Award for Video of Yr. (I'm Gonna Getcha Good), 2003, Can. Country Music Assn. Award for Female Artist of Yr., 2003, Order of Canada, 2005. Office: Mercury Records 66 Music Sq W Nashville TN 37203-4315 Address: Shore Fire Media c/o Georgette Pascale 32 Court St Fl 16 Brooklyn NY 11201-4404 Office: c/o Q Prime 131 S 11th St Nashville TN 37206

TWARDY, STANLEY ALBERT, JR., lawyer; b. Trenton, NJ, Sept. 13, 1951; s. Stanley Albert Twardy and Dorothy M. Stonaker. BS with honors, Trinity Coll., 1973; JD, U. Va., 1976; LLM, Georgetown U., 1980. Bar: Conn. 1976, DC 1978, US Supreme Ct. 1979, US Ct. Appeals (2d cir.) 1984. Assoc. Whitman & Ransom, Greenwich, Conn., 1976-77; counsel com. on small bus. US Senate, 1977-79, counsel to Senator Lowell Weicker Jr., 1979-80; ptnr. Silver, Golub & Sandak, Stamford, Conn., 1980-85; US atty. Dist. of Conn., 1985-91; chief of staff Office of Gov. Lowell Weicker, Conn., 1991-93; ptnr. Day Pitney LLP, Stamford, Conn., 1993—. Pres. LCD, 2007—; chmn.police chief selection panel City of Stamford, 1993—94; mem. nat. alumni exec. com. Trinity Coll., 1985—90, mem. athletic adv. com., 1992—97; chmn. program com. Drugs Don't Work!, 1989—91, bd. dirs., 1989—93, 1994—2000; mem. area adv. com. U. Conn., Stamford, 1993—96, mem. strategic planning mgmt. com., 1993—95; bd. dirs. Rehab. Ctr., 1995—2002, Stamford Health Found., 1995—, Trinity Coll., 1996—2002, Nat. Conf. Cmty. and Justice Fairfield County Region, 1996—2004. Mem.: ABA, Conn. Bar Assn., Phi Beta Kappa. Office Phone: 203-977-7300. E-mail: satwardy@dbh.com.

TWEARDY, DAVID JOHN, physician, educator; b. Monessen, Pa., Feb. 12, 1952; s. John Tweardy Sr. and Helen Kotch Tweardy; m. Ruth Falik, Jan. 21, 1982; children: Samuel David, Benjamin John, Daniel James. AB in Chemistry, Princeton U., 1974; MD, Harvard U., 1978. Diplomate Am. Bd. Internal Medicine, 1983, Am. Bd. Infectious Diseases, 1984. Asst. prof. medicine U. Pitts. Sch. Medicine, 1987—93, assoc. prof. medicine, 1993—99; prof. medicine Baylor Coll. Medicine, Houston, 1999—, chief sect. infectious diseases, 1999—. Grantee, NIH, 1997—2005, 2002—, 2004—. Mem.: Am. Clin. and Climatalogical Assn., Assn. Am. Physicians. Home: 3769 Nottingham St Houston TX 77005 Office Phone: 713-798-8918. E-mail: dtweardy@bcm.edu.

TWEED, LORNA BARBARA, protective services official, paramedic; d. John and Thelma Tweed; m. Richard Trent, July 28, 2006. BS in Emergency Med. Systems Mgmt., Hampton U., Va., 2007. Registered paramedic Nat. Registry Emergency Med. Technicians, 2002. EMT, paramedic Virginia Beach Vol. Rescue Squad, 1999—2003; firefighter paramedic City of Virginia Beach Fire Dept., 2003—. Instr. Tidewater C.C. Mem.: Golden Key, Alpha Kappa Mu. Home Phone: 757-217-5095; Office Phone: 757-385-4228.

TWEEN, DOUGLAS M., lawyer, former prosecutor; b. 1962; BA, Columbia Univ., 1984; JD cum laude, Northwestern Univ., 1989. Bar: NY, Conn. Law clk. Judge William Timbers, US Ct. Appeals 2d Cir.; trial atty. Antitrust Div., U.S. Dept. Justice, 1990—2005; ptnr., Global Antitrust & Global Litigation practices Baker & McKenzie LLP, NYC, 2005—. Moderator Prog. on Cartel Enforcement So. African Competition Com., 2004. Recipient Antitrust Div. Award of Distinction, U.S. Dept. Justice, 2000, Attorney Gen. Disting. Svc. award, 2003. Mem.: Bar of City of N.Y., NY State Bar Assn., ABA. Office: Baker & McKenzie LLP 1114 Ave of the Americas New York NY 10036 Office Phone: 212-626-4355. Office Fax: 212-310-1655. Business E-Mail: douglas.tween@bakenet.com.

TWERSKY, LAURA HARRIET, biologist, educator; b. NYC, June 17, 1952; d. Jacob and Esther Twersky; m. Benjamin Stempel; 1 child, Rachel. BA in Biology, Barnard Coll., NYC, 1974; MS in Biology, NYU, 1977, PhD in Biology, 1981. Asst. prof. biology Wagner Coll., Staten Island, NY, 1982—84; substitute asst. prof. biology and natural sci. CUNY, 1985—90; fellow in immunology Meml. Sloan-Kettering Inst. Cancer Rsch., NYC, 1990—91; adj. asst. prof. biology Lehman Coll. (CUNY), Bronx, 1995—96; asst. prof. biology St. Peter's Coll., Jersey City, 1996—2000, assoc. prof. biology, 2000—. Summer rschr. Marine Biol. Lab., Woods Hole, Mass., 1986, 90, 97, 98, 99; faculty advisor Rho Nu chpt. Tri Beta Biol. Honor Soc., Jersey City, 1998—2006, supr. cmty. svc. activities, 1998—, co-organizer NE Dist. II Rsch. Conv., 2004; grant supr. TriBeta Rsch. Found., 1998—; St. Peter's Coll. rep. NJ Marine Sci. Consortium Bd. Dirs.; St. Peter's Coll. faculty liaison NJ Higher Edn. Partnership for Sustainability; faculty advisor Environ. Club St. Peter's Coll. Contbr. articles to profl. jours. Initiator, organizer, St. Peter's Coll. March of Dimes Healthy Baby Awareness Day; exec. bd. PS 24 Parents Assn., Bronx, 2002—05. Recipient PSC-CUNY Rsch. award, 1986—87, Schuch Rsch. Mentor award, St. Peter's Coll., 2004. Mem.: AAAS, NJ Acad. Sci., NY Soc. Exptl. Microscopists, Soc. Devel. Biology, Sigma Xi. Avocations: photography, hiking, music. Office: St Peter's Coll Biology Dept 2641 Kennedy Blvd Jersey City NJ 07306

TWICHELL, CHASE, poet; b. New Haven, Conn., Aug. 20, 1950; d. Charles P. and Ann (Chase) T. BA, Trinity Coll., Hartford, 1973; MFA, U. Iowa, 1976. Editor Pennyroyal Pr., W. Hatfield, Mass., 1976-84; assoc. prof. English U. Ala., 1984-88; mem. MFA Program in Creative Writing, Warren Wilson Coll., 1999—; editor Ausable Press, 1999—. Asst. prof. Hampshire Coll., 1983-84; co-editor Alabama Poetry Series, 1984-88; lectr. Princeton U., 1990-98; faculty MFA program in creative writing Goddard Coll., 1997-99. Author: (poetry) Northern Spy, 1981, The Odds, 1986, Perdido, 1991, The Ghost of Eden, 1995, (book) Dog Language, 2005; editor: The Practice of Poetry, 1992, The Snow Watcher, 1998, Ausable Press, 1999—; translator The Lover of God, 2003. Recipient Acad. award in lit. Am. Acad. Arts and Letters, 1994; Nat. Endowment for Arts fellow, 1987, 93, Guggenheim fellow, 1990. Office Phone: 518-576-9273. Business E-Mail: editor@ausablepress.org.

TWIETMEYER, DON HENRY, lawyer; b. Rochester, NY, June 4, 1954; s. Frederick Herman and Norma Frances (Porter) T.; m. Victoria Lynne Engleman, July 1, 1989; children: Laura Elizabeth, Jill Ann Magoon, Anthony R. Cafarelli. BA in Polit. Sci., Econs. with honors, SUNY, Buffalo, 1976; JD, Union U., Jackson, Tenn., 1979; LLM in Taxation, U. Miami, 1980; MBA in Acctg., Rochester Inst. Tech., 1983. Bar: NY 1980, Fla. 1980, US Dist. Ct. (we. dist.) NY 1980, US Dist. Ct. (so. dist.) Fla. 1980, US Tax Ct. 1980, US Ct. Appeals (5th and 11th cirs.) 1981, US Supreme Ct. 1994, US Bankruptcy Ct. 1994; CPA, NY. Tax acct. Davie, Kaplan & Braverman, Rochester, 1980-82; assoc. DeHond-Stowe Law Office, Rochester, 1982-84, Lacy, Katzen, Ryen & Mittleman, Rochester, 1984-87; mng. atty. DeHond Law Office, Rochester, 1987-91, prin., 1991-92; assoc. Fix, Spindelman, Brovitz, Turk, Himelein & Shukoff, Rochester, 1992-98; of counsel Hiscock & Barclay, LLP, Rochester, 1998—. Lectr. estate and gift taxes Found. Acctg. Edn., 1987—96. Author: Review and Update for Experienced Practitioners: Fiduciary, Estate and Gift Taxation, 1987-96. V.p. coun. Hope Luth. Ch., 1989-91, meml. fund com., 1990-91, chmn. bldg. use com., 1990-91; chmn. missions and social concerns com. Bethlehem Luth. Ch., 1992-2000, ch. coun., 1993-95, pres. ch. coun., 1994-95, deacon, 1994-95; orgn. com. Luth. Charities Rochester Region, 1993-95, pres., dir., 1995-2000, adv. bd. dirs., 2000-04; dir. Prevention Ptnrs., Inc., 1997-2003, pres., 2000-03, fin. com., 1997-2003; planned and deferred giving com. Genesee Hosp. Found., 1998-2000; bd. dirs. Rochester Gen. Hosp. Found., 2003—, planned giving com., 2001—, com. chair, 2003—, prospect rev. com., 2004—, exec. com., 2004—, first vice chair 2006-07, chair, 2007-. Named one of Best Lawyers in Am., 2007, NY Super Lawyers, 2007. Fellow Am. Bar Found.; mem. ABA (tax sect., entertainment and sports industries forum) Fla. Bar Assn. (tax sect., out of state practitioners divsn., real property, probate and trust sect.), NY State Bar Assn. (tax sect., entertainment and sports law sect, trusts and estates sect.), Monroe County Bar Assn. (trusts and estates sect., exec. coun. 1996-2003, sec. 2000-01, chair 2001-02, elder law com., intellectual property law com., chair tax sect. 2004—), NY State Soc. CPAs (rels. with the legal cmty. com. 2003—), Am. Assn. Atty.-CPAs, Estate Planning Coun. Rochester (exec. coun. 2000-03), Found. Monroe County Bar (bd. dirs. 2004—, investment com. 2004—, sec. 2006—, mem. by-laws com. 2006—, chmn. 2006—), Rotary (internat. svc. com. 1994-2002, Rotary Internat. Found. com. 1994-2002, chair com. 1996-2002, Rochester Rotary Golf Tournament com. 1995-2000, planned giving com. 1997—, mem. World Cmty. Svc. com. 2002-, co-chair 2003—, dist. conf. com. 2002-03, treas. 2007—), Phi Beta Kappa, Phi Alpha Delta, Omicron Delta Epsilon, Phi Eta Sigma. Republican. Lutheran. Avocations: golf, tennis, skiing, stamp collecting/philately. Office: 2000 HSBC Plz 100 Chestnut St Rochester NY 14604 Office Phone: 585-325-7570. Business E-Mail: dtwietmeyer@hiscockbarclay.com.

TWIGG-SMITH, THURSTON, newspaper publisher; b. Honolulu, Aug. 17, 1921; s. William and Margaret Carter (Thurston) Twigg-S.; m. Bessie Bell, June 9, 1942 (div. Feb. 1983); children: Elizabeth, Thurston, William, Margaret, Evelyn; m. Laila Roster, Feb. 22, 1983 (div. Dec. 1994); m. Sharon Smith, Feb. 28, 1996. B.Engring., Yale U., 1942. With Honolulu Advertiser, 1946-2000, mng. editor, 1954-60, asst. bus. mgr., 1960-61, pub., 1961-86; pres., dir., chief exec. officer Honolulu Advertiser, Inc., 1962-93, chmn., 1993-2000. Chmn., dir., CEO Persis Corp., 1962-2002, chmn. Twigg-Smith Group LLC, 2002—. Trustee Honolulu Acad. Arts, The Contemporary Mus., Hawaii, The Skowhegan Sch., Maine, Yale Art Gallery, New Haven. Maj. AUS, 1942-46. Mem. Waialae Country Club, Pacific Club, Oahu Country Club, Outrigger Canoe Club. Office Phone: 808-735-3883. Personal E-mail: ttwiggsmith@aol.com.

TWINAME, JOHN DEAN, minister, human services administrator; b. Mt. Kisco, NY, Dec. 27, 1931; s. C. G. and Constance Jean (Ulmer) Twiname; m. Carolyn Anderson, Aug. 6, 1955; children: Karen, Jeanne, Julia. AB, Cornell U., 1953; MBA, Harvard U., 1957; MDiv, Union Theol. Sem., 1983. Ordained to ministry Presbyn. Ch., 1983. Sales rep. Am. Hosp. Supply Corp., Evanston, Ill., 1957-60, dir. product research, 1961, sales mgr., 1962, asst. to div. pres., 1963, product mgr., 1964, mktg. mgr., 1965-67, mktg. v.p., 1968-69; dep. adminstr. Social and Rehab. Svc., HEW, Washington, 1969-70, adminstr., 1970-73; adminstr. Office Health Cost of Living Coun., 1973-74; pvt. cons. Mott-McDonald Assocs., Inc., Washington, 1974-76, pres., 1976-78; exec. v.p. Am. Health Found., NYC, 1978-81; co-pres. HealthCare Chaplaincy, Inc., NYC, 1983-93, co-chair exec. com., 1993-94, life trustee, 1995—, exec. v.p., 1999—2000. Cons. exec. Coll. Chaplains, 1997; acting sr. min. Green's Farms Congl. Ch., Westport, Conn., 2001—03, pastoral assoc., 2003—. Treas. U.S. com. Internat. Coun. Social Welfare, 1977—80; mem. pres. coun. United Hosp. Fund, 1991—99; voting mem. Empire Blue Cross/Blue Shield, 1994; chmn. bd. dirs. Bauman Bible Telecasts, Inc., 1976—80; sec. bd. dirs. U.S. Coun. Internat. Yr. of Disabled Persons, 1979—81; founding bd. dirs. Am. Paralysis Assn. (formerly Paralysis Cure Rsch.), 1976—83; bd. dirs. Epilepsy Found. Am., 1978—85; chmn. bd. dirs. Chgo. Bus.-Indsl. Project, 1967—68, People to People Com. for Handicapped, 1976—78; bd. dirs. N.Y. Regional Transplant Program, 1988—92, Beck Mack & Oliver Ptnrs. Fund, 2000—05. 1st lt. AUS, 1953—55. Recipient Disting. Svc. award, Coll. Chaplains, 1992, Wholeness of Life award, The Health Care Chaplaincy, Inc., 2003, Disting. Alumnus award, Union Theol. Sem., 2004; Baker scholar, Bus. Sch. Harvard U. Home: 60 East End Ave New York NY 10028 Office: 163 Harbor Rd Southport CT 06890 Office Phone: 203-254-1506.

TWISDALE, HAROLD WINFRED, dentist; b. Roanoke Rapids, NC, Apr. 28, 1933; s. James Robert and Elma (Smith) T.; m. Barbara Ann Edmonds, Aug. 2, 1958 (div. Apr. 1974); children: Harold Winfred, Leigh Ann.; m. Frances Jean Winstead, July 1983. BS in Dentistry, U. N.C., 1955, D.D.S., 1958. Individual practice dentistry, Charlotte, NC, 1961—; head, dept. dental prosthetics Meml. Hosp., 1964-66; lectr. dental subjects.; pres., gen. mgr. WCTU-TV, Charlotte Telecasters, Inc., 1967-69, WATU-TV, Augusta, Ga., Augusta Telecasters, Inc., 1968-69, Television Presentations, Inc., Charlotte, 1967-69; partner Twisdale and Steel Assos., Charlotte, 1965-70; propr. Twisdale Enterprises, Charlotte, 1965-70. Pres. Memphis Telecasters, Inc., 1966-76, Va. Telecasters, Inc., Richmond, 1966—, Durham-Raleigh Telecasters, Inc., Durham, N.C., 1966-70, Gentil Elite, Inc., 1979— Transp. chmn. Miss N.C. Pageant, 1965; v.p. N.C. Jaycees, 1963-64; Trustee Boys Home, Lake Waccomaw, N.C., 1966-67. Served to capt. USAF, 1958-60. Recipient various awards Charlotte Jaycees, 1962-66. Fellow Acad. Dentistry Internat.; mem. ADA, N.C. Dental Found., N.C. Dental Soc., Charlotte Dental Soc. (chmn. various coms. 1961—), Am. Analgesia Soc., Internat. Analgesic Soc. (dir. 1980-85), N.C. Dental Soc. Anesthesiology (v.p. 1983-84), Charlotte Analgesia Study Club (co-founder 1970), N.C. 2d Dist. Dental Soc., Metrolina Dental Soc. (founder 1994, pres. 1994-95), U. N.C. Dental Alumni Assn., Southeastern Analgesia Soc. (founder 1972, pres. 1972-74), Lambda Chi Alpha, Delta Sigma Delta. Republican. Methodist. Home: 2221 Streatley Ln Matthews NC 28105-6648 Office: 3104 Weddington Rd Ste 200 Matthews NC 28105 Office Phone: 704-849-2595. *I must give the full credit for any achievement I might have accomplished in life to my mother and father. They not only provided me the means and direction one needs to make even the slightest accomplishment in our mortal life, but most of all, they gave me love, understanding, and a sense of values. These values have never deserted me, nor have they been compromised, even in the darkest hours of depression or during the brightest times of accomplishment. They have been my steady companions.*

TWITCHELL, E(RVIN) EUGENE, retired lawyer; b. Salt Lake City, Mar. 4, 1932; s. Irvin A. and E. Alberta (Davis) Twitchell; m. Joyce A. Newey, Aug. 9, 1957 (div. May 1989); children: Robert R., Lauren E., David J., Michael S.; m. Linda Sue Wilson, 1991; children: Bonnie Wilson, Jimmy Wilson, Benjamin Wilson, Stefanie Wilson. Student, Brigham Young U., Provo, Utah, 1954-55; BA, Calif. State U., Long Beach, 1959; JD, UCLA, 1966. Bar: Mich. 1977, US Dist. Ct. (ea. dist.) Mich., US Supreme Ct. 1987. Contract adminstr. Rockwell No. Am. Aviation, Seal Beach, Calif., 1966-68; sr. contracts adminstr. McDonnell Douglas Corp., Long Beach, Calif., 1968-73; in-house counsel Albert C. Martin & Assocs., LA, 1973-77; instr. bus. law Golden West Coll., Huntington Beach, 1973-74; corp. counsel, corp. sec. Barton Malow Co., Southfield, Mich., 1977-97, ret., 1997; freelance cartoonist. Mem. Detroit EEO Forum, 1983—97; arbitrating and cons., 1997—. Editl. cartoonist: Eufaula Tribune, 2001—; host (local TV series) Who's Who in Eufaula, 2002—; author: Slices from Life, 2004, of poems. Pres. Corona Musical Theater, Calif., 1975—76; dist. chmn. Boy Scouts Am.-North Trails, Oakland County, Mich., 1978—80; vol. art tchr., storyteller Explorers Day Care Ctrs., 2006—; treas. Barton Malow PAC, Southfield, 1983—97; vol. missionary dept. history LDS Ch., 2006—. Sgt. USAF, 1950—52. Mem.: ABA, Am. Corp. Counsel Assn. (v.p., dir. 1983—97), Am. Arbitration Assn. (arbitrator Detroit, Ala., Ga., and Fla. areas 1985—97, arbitrator Ala.-Ga. area 1997—), Mich. Bar Assn. Republican. Mem. Lds Ch. Avocations: cartooning, painting, Karate, music, theater, writing. Home and Office: 303 Nashua St Murray UT 84107 Office Phone: 334-695-1817. Personal E-mail: etwitchell2005@msn.com.

TWITCHELL, THEODORE GRANT, music educator, composer; b. Melrose, Kans., Jan. 26, 1928; s. Curtis and Sarah Frances (Lane) T.; m. Rebecca Janis Goldsmith, Nov. 18, 1989; stepchildren: Ralph Norman, Russell Norman, Dawn Jiricek. AA in Music, L.A. City Coll., 1949; BA in Social Studies, Calif. State U., LA, 1951, MA in Secondary Edn., 1955; EdD in Secondary and Higher Edn., U. So. Calif., LA, 1964. Tchr. Barstow (Calif.) Union High Sch., 1952, Burbank (Calif.) Unified Sch. Dist., 1954-66; dean instrn., dir. evening divsn., dir. summer sessions, 1966-69; pres. Palo Verde Coll., Blythe, Calif., 1969-70; adult tchr. L.A. Unified Sch. Dist., 1977-78; faculty Columbia West U., LA, 1993—. Pvt. English tutor, 1979—. Composer: The Gettysburg Address, Tidewater, The Pride of Monticello, Labor Day March, Valley Forge, Normandy Prayer, Christmas in L.A., L.A., Overture to Tidewater, The Lord Is My Shepherd, The Joy of Snow, Walt Whitman and Friends, over 90 others; contbr. articles to profl. jours.; author: Dear Mr. President, 1982, Courage, Conflict and Love, 1988, The Magnificent Odyssey of Michael Young, 1992; author of poems. With U.S. Army, 1952-53. Recipient Coll. Faculty Senate Award for Achievements for the coll., Palo Verde Coll., Student Body award. Mem. Internat. Poetry Hall Fame, Cmty. Coll. Pres.'s Assn., Am. Assn. Composers, Authors and Pubs., Calif. PTA (hon. life mem.), Rho Delta Chi. Republican. Methodist. Avocations: music, writing, travel, hiking, photography.

TWITTY, SUSAN KAY, music educator; b. Peoria, Ill., Sept. 9, 1950; d. William Paul Evans and Alberta Eugenie Gebhardt; m. Lillard Bates Twitty, Jr., Aug. 22, 1970; children: Regina Lynne Leffers, Anne Elizabeth Degenhart. AA, Ill. Ctrl. Coll., 1970. Cert. piano tchr. Pvt. practice piano tchr., Peoria, 1982—; tchr. music Montessori Children's Ho., Peoria, 1991—2002. Editor (columnist): Pamta Notes, 1999—. Mem.: Nat. Guild Piano Tchrs., Ill. State Music Tchrs. Assn., Music Tchrs. Nat. Assn., Peoria Area Music Tchrs. Assn. (sec. 1990—92, v.p. 1996—98, pres. 2001—03, Mem. of Yr. 2001). Independent. Roman Catholic. Avocations: reading, gardening, swimming. Home: 604 Fondulac Dr East Peoria IL 61611

TWOMBLY, STEPHEN DOANE, magazine publisher; b. Summit, NJ, July 26, 1953; s. Doane and Betty (Bowers) T.; m. Jean Sawyer. BA summa cum laude, Drew U., 1976. Dist. mgr. McGraw-Hill Publs. Co., NYC, 1978-83; dir. advt. IDG Communications, Peterborough, NH, 1983—84, pub. RUN, 1984—87, pub. AmigaWorld, 1985—88, v.p., 1988-89, exec. v.p., 1989—90, exec. v.p., pub. dir. PCResource, 1989—90; pub. dir. PC Resource, 1988—90, Weider Pubs. Natural Health mag., 2001—03; group pub. Consumer/Home Mag., Special Products, 1987-88, Advanstar Comm. Sensors & Frontline Solutions, 2003—04; exec. v.p., pub. dir. PCResource Cahners Pubs. Co., Newton, Mass., 1990—97; nat. sales mgr. Datamation, 1990—92, assoc. pub., 1993—94; pub. Digital News & Rev., 1994—95, Reseller Mgmt., 1995—97, Boston Globe Media Design New Eng., 2006—; v.p. sales IDG Channel Svcs. Corp., Framingham, Mass., 1997—98; v.p., pub. New Age Jour. & Body & Soul, 1998—2001; pub. CMO mag. Internat. Data Group, 2004—06. Spkr. in field. Mem. Sigma Phi. Avocations: composing, painting, outdoor sports. Home: PO Box 1365 New London NH 03257 Office: Boston Globe Media Design New England 320 Congress St Boston MA 02210 Office Phone: 617-929-2706.

TWOMEY, KEVIN, retail executive; BA in Econs. and Acctg., St. John's U. Various positions Deloitte & Touche, 1972—89, Fleming Cos., Inc., 1989—2000, dir. planning and analysis to ops. contr. to v.p., contr., 1995—99, sr. v.p. fin., contr., 1999—2000; sr. v.p., chief acctg. officer Rite Aid Corp., 2000—05, exec. v.p., CFO, 2005—. Office: Rite Aid Corp 30 Hunter Lane Camp Hill PA 17011 Office Phone: 717-761-2633. *

TWOMEY, TERESA MARIE, lawyer; b. Albany, NY, Sept. 25, 1965; d. Daniel Francis and Rosemarie Twomey; m. Drew L. Harris; children: Ariana, Elizabeth, Katherine. BS in Journalism, W.Va. U., Morgantown, 1988, JD, 1993. Bar: Pa. 1993, NJ 1994, US Fed. Dist. Ct. 1994. Pvt. practice law, Madison and Teaneck, NJ, 1993—94, Scranton, Pa., 1994—97; pvt. practice profl. mediator Teaneck, 1996—98; postpartum support internat. coord. for Va. Postpartum Support Internat., Farmville, Va., 2001—06. Adj. prof. Longwood U., Farmville, 2004—06; cons. in field; pub. reviewer NIMH, Washington, 2005—; mediator EEOC, NYC, 1997—98; appeared on Paul Zahn Show CNN, 2006. Author, editor: website www.postpartumexperience.com, 2005—. Mem. com., founder Farmer's Market, Teaneck, 1997—98; chmn. First Night Teaneck, 1999—2000; coord. Katrina relief project Families for Farmville, 2005—06. Scholar, W.Va. U., 1989—93; featured on An Am. Family, GoodLife TV. Avocations: dance, studying religion, women's issues. Home: 670 Cornwall Ave Cheshire CT 06410

TWOMEY, THOMAS A., JR., lawyer, educator; b. NYC, Dec. 8, 1945; s. Thomas A. and Mary (Maloney) T.; m. Judith Hope Twomey, Dec. 15, 1979; stepchildren: Erling Hope, Nisse Hope. BA, Manhattan Coll., 1967; postgrad., U.Va., 1967-68; JD, Columbia U., 1970. Bar: N.Y. 1972, U.S. Tax Ct. 1974. Asst. town atty. Town of Southampton N.Y., 1973-74; spl. asst. dist. atty. Suffolk County, NY, 1973-74; pvt. practice law Riverhead, NY, 1974-75; ptnr. Hubbard & Twomey, Riverhead, 1976-79, Twomey, Latham, Shea & Kelley, Riverhead, 1980—. Chair N.Y. State East End Econ. and Environ. Task Force, 1993; mem. deans coun. Stonybrook Sch. Medicine, 1991—; adj. prof. environ. law Southampton Coll., 1977-78. Bd. dirs. East End Arts Coun., Riverhead, 1983, Guild Hall East Hampton, 1993—; bd. dirs. East Hampton Libr., 1994—, pres., 1998—; trustee L.I. Power Authority, 1989-94; town historian, Town of East Hampton, 1999, vice chair East Hampton Town 350th Anniversary com., 1998, editor East Hampton Histor. Collection; historian N.Y. State Dem. Com., 2000-01; chair East Hampton 350th lecture series, 1998. Recipient Environ. award, U.S. EPA, 1980, Citizen of Yr. award L.I. Farm Bur., 2002. Mem. ABA, Suffolk County Bar Assn., State Energy Coun., N.Y. State Fresh Water Wetlands Appeals Bd. Democrat. Home: #9 Two Holes of Water Rd East Hampton NY 11937 Office Phone: 631-727-2180.

TWOMEY, TIMOTHY, architect; Grad., U. So. Calif.; MArch, Harvard U.; JD, UCLA. Prin. Shelpley Bulfinch Richardson & Abbott, Boston, 1993, prin. chief adminstrv. officer, in-house counsel, 1993—. Past mem. bldg. design and constrn. faculty Northeastern U.; lectr. in field; constrn. dispute mediator, arbitrator, ct. apptd. master. Contbr. articles to profl. jours. Chair local cmty. planning commn. and sch. com. Mem.: AIA, Boston Soc. Archs.

TYACK, THOMAS MICHAEL, lawyer; b. Columbus, Ohio, June 20, 1940; s. George E. and E. Naomi (Ballard) T.; m. Patricia J. Clark, Sept. 7, 1969; children: Jonathan, Jeffrey, James, Justin. BA cum laude, Ohio State U., Columbus, 1962, Jd, 1965. Bar: Ohio 1965, U.S. Ct. Appeals (6th cir.) 1970, U.S. Supreme Ct. 1970, U.S. Dist. Ct. (so. dist.) Ohio 1972. Ptnr. Tyack, Scott & Colley, Columbus, 1965-79, Tyack Scott & Wiseman, Columbus, 1979-81; prin. Thomas M. Tyack Assocs. Co., L.P.A., Columbus, 1981-90; ptnr. Tyack & Blackmore Co., L.P.A., Columbus, 1991-94; pres. Tyack, Blackmore & Liston Co. LPA, Columbus, 1994—. Bar examiner Ohio Supreme Ct., 1975-80; lectr., legal asst. program Capital U., Ohio, 1977-90. Fellow Am. Coll. Trial Lawyers; mem. ABA, Ohio Bar Assn., Columbus Bar Assn., Franklin Ct. and Trial Lawyers, Assn. Trial Lawyers Am., Ohio Acad. Trial Lawyers, Ohio Acad. Trial Lawyers, Ohio Acad. Criminal Def. Lawyers, NDCDL. Republican. Methodist. Office: 536 S High St Columbus OH 43215-5605 Office Phone: 614-221-1341.

TYAVNAGIMATT, SHANTHAKUMAR R., research scientist, pharmacist; b. Shimoga, Karnataka, India, Feb. 14, 1968; s. Rudraiah and Dakshayani Tyavanagimatt; m. Sujatha S. Km, July 2, 1999; children: Parinita S. Tyavanagimatt, Devesh S. Tyavanagimatt. B Pharm, Govt. Coll. Pharmacy, Bangalore, India, 1991; M Pharm, Coll. Pharm. Scis., Manipal, India, 1993; PhD in Pharm. Tech., B.V. Patel PERD Ctr., India, 1997. Cert. pharmacist Karnataka, 2005. Sr. scientist Ranbaxy Laboratories Ltd., New Delhi; assoc. dir. Dr. Reddy's Labs. Ltd., Hyderabad, India, 2002—04; postdoctoral fellow U. Utah, Salt Lake City, 2004—05; sr. scientist Lipocine Inc., Salt Lake City, 2005—06; dir. CMC and formulation SIGA Technologies, Corvallis, Oreg., 2007—. Fellow, BV Patel PERD ctr. Achievements include development of drugs for disease caused due to bioterroris, with main focus to treat smallpox and anthrax; patents pending for fast acting analgesic medications; composition for immunosuppressant; controlled release medication to treat cough; research in patient friendly and safer drug delivery technologies for migraine, cardiovascular diseases and cancer. Office: SIGA Technologies 4575 SW Research Way Ste 230 Corvallis OR 97333 Home Phone: 541-766-3744; Office Phone: 541-753-2000. Home Fax: 541-753-9999.

TYBOUT, RICHARD ALTON, economics professor; b. Phila., Sept. 28, 1920; s. Richard Raymond and Lillian (Alton) T.; m. Rita Holloway, Sept. 7, 1946; children: Alice Marie, James Richard, Robert Maxwell. BChemE, U. Del., 1943; MSChemE, U. Mich., 1946, MA in Econs., 1947, PhD in Econs., 1952. Instr. U. Mich., Ann Arbor, 1952-54; asst. prof. Ohio State U., Columbus, 1954-57, assoc. prof., 1957-62, prof., 1962-88, prof. emeritus, 1988—. Editor: Economics of Research and Development, 1965, Environmental Quality and Society, 1975; author: Government Contracting in Atomic Energy, 1956, The Reactor Supply Industry, 1960, Atomic Power and Energy Resource Planning, 1958; co-author: The Columbus Area Economy, 1966. Named Ford Faculty Study Fellow, Ford Foun., 1959-60, Phoenix Predoctoral Fellow, U. Mich., 1949-51. Mem. Am. Econ. Assn., Sierra Club (chmn. econs. com. 1975-85), Toastmasters Internat. (pres. Worthington chpt., 2002-03), Tau Beta Pi, Phi Kappa Phi, Beta Gamma Sigma. Avocations: construction, swimming, sailing. Home: 324 Pingree Dr Columbus OH 43085-3158 Office: Ohio State U Dept Econs 1945 N High St Columbus OH 43210-1120

TYBURSKI, CHARLES J., lawyer; b. New Kensington, Pa., Feb. 25, 1934; s. Steven John and Estella Ann Tyburski; m. Nancy Cara Brown, July 20, 1963. BA, Ohio Wesleyan U., Deleware, 1956; JD, The Ohio State U., Columbus, 1964. Bar: 1964, ct. cert. specialist in trust and estate law: 2003. Atty., ptnr. Black, McCuskey, Souers & Arbaugh, Canton, Ohio, 1964—. Dir. Hilscher-Clarke Electric Co., Canton, 1980—2006, Gregory Industries, Canton, 1985—2006; dir. regional bd. KeyBank, N.A., Canton, Ohio, 1990—2002. Nat. coun. The Moritz Coll. Law, Columbus, 1984—; trustee Walsh U., North Canton, Ohio, 1992—2004. Lt. col. USAF, 1956—84. Fellow: Ohio Bar Found. (life). Democrat. Roman Catholic. Avocations: fishing, hunting, gardening, travel, reading. Home: 130 Brookview Cir North Canton OH 44709 Office: Black McCuskey Souers & Arbaugh Ste 1000 220 Market Ave Canton OH 44702

TYBURSKI, JAMES GERARD, surgeon; s. Chester and Elizabeth Tyburski; m. Julie Fleming, May 5, 1990. BS, SUNY, Binghamton, 1983; MD, Upstate Med. Ctr., Syracuse, NY, 1987. Cert. Am. Bd. Surgery, 1993, critical care Am. Bd. Surgery, 1993. Resident surgery Wayne State U. Detroit Med. Ctr., 1987—92, trauma fellow, 1992—94; asst. prof. surgery Wayne State U. Sch. Medicine, Detroit, 1994—2001, assoc. prof. surgery, 2001—07, prof. surgery, 2007—; program dir. Wayne State Dept. Surgery, Detroit, 1997—; chief surgery Detroit Receiving Hosp., 2004—. Recipient Wayne State Faculty Tchg. award, Wayne State U. Sch. Medicine, 2003, 2005. Mem.: Western Surg. Assn., Midwest Surg. Assn., Eastern Assn. for the Surgery of Trauma, Am. Assn. for the Surgery of Trauma, ACS, Alpha Omega Alpha Honor Med. Soc. (life). Office: Detroit Receiving Hosp 4201 St Antoine Ste 4S-13 Detroit MI 48201 Office Phone: 313-745-3487.

TYCKOSON, DAVE, library director, library association executive; BS in Physics, U. Ill., Urbana-Champaign, MLS. Sci. libr. Miami U., Ohio; reference libr. Iowa State U.; head reference libr. SUNY Albany; head pub. services Henry Madden Libr., Calif. State U., Fresno, 1997—. Mem.: Calif. Libr. Assn., Fresno Area Libr. Coun., Reference and User Services Assn. (pres.-elect 2006—07, chair reference services sect., director-at-large, pres. 2007—, Isadore Gilbert Mudge-R.R. Bowker award 2005), ALA. Office: Henry Madden Libr Calif State U - Fresno 5200 N Barton Ave MS ML34 Fresno CA 93740-5014 Office Phone: 559-278-5678. Business E-Mail: davety@csufresno.edu. *

TYDINGCO-GATEWOOD, FRANCES MARIE, federal judge; b. Oahu, Hawaii, Jan. 21, 1958; d. Daniel J. and Francesca S. Tydingco; m. Robert Gatewood; children: Daniel Gatewood, Michael Gatewood, Stephen Gatewood. BA in Polit. Sci., Marquette U., 1980; JD, U. Mo., Kansas City, 1983. Law clk. to Hon. Forest W. Hanna Jackson County Cir. Ct., Kansas City, 1983—84; asst. atty. gen. Govt. of Guam, 1984—88, chief prosecutor, 1990—94; asst. prosecutor Jackson County Prosecutor's Office, Mo., 1988—90; trial judge Superior Ct. Guam, 1994—2002; assoc. judge Supreme Ct. Guam, 2002—06; chief judge Dist. Ct. Guam, 2006—. Profl. Tech. scholar, Govt. of Guam. Home: 222 Chalan Santo Papa Ste 222 Hagatna GU 96910 Office: US Courthouse 4th Fl 520 W Soledad Ave Hagatna GU 96910 Business E-Mail: ftgate@guamsupremecourt.com. *

TYER, TRAVIS EARL, librarian, consultant; b. Lorenzo, Tex., Oct. 23, 1930; s. Charlie Earl and Juanita (Travis) T.; m. Alma Lois Davis, Nov. 6, 1951; children: Alan Ross, Juanita Linn. BS, Abilene Christian U., 1952; BLS, U. North Tex., 1959; AdM in LS, Fla. State U., 1969, postgrad., 1969-71. Librarian, tchr. pub. schs., Gail, Lubbock, and Seminole, Tex., 1952-61; with Dallas Pub. Library, 1961-66, coordinator young adult services, 1962-66; library dir. Lubbock Pub. Library, 1966, Lubbock City-County Libraries, 1967-68; grad. library sch. faculty-state personnel coordinator Emporia (Kans.) State U., 1971-72; sr. cons. profl. devel. Ill. State Library, Springfield, 1972-80; exec. dir. Great River Libr. Sys., Quincy, Ill., 1980-94; cons. pub. rels. and comm. Alliance Libr. Sys., Quincy, 1994-97; ind. libr. cons., 1997—. Lectr. summer workshops Tex. Woman's U., U. Okla., U. Utah, Fla. State U., U. North Tex.; adj. faculty U. Mo., 1986-89; cons. in field; mem. adv. com. Ill. State Libr., 1984-87, 93-96; pres. Resource Sharing Alliance West Ctrl. Ill., Inc., 1981-94, sec., 1994-97; pres. Ill. Libr. System Dirs. Orgn., 1992-94. Contbr. articles to library jours. Inductee U. North Tex. Libr. and Info. Sci. Hall of Fame, 1990. Mem. ALA, Ill. Libr. Assn., Ill. Ctr. for the Book, Friends of Librs. U.S.A., U. North Tex. Sch. Libr. and Info. Sci. (life), Friends Lubbock City-County Librs. (life), Ill. Sch. Libr. MEdia Assn. Democrat. Mem. Ch. of Christ. Home and Office: 2008 S Arrowood Ct Quincy IL 62305-8961 Office Phone: 217-223-5024.

TYGRETT, HOWARD VOLNEY, JR., judge, lawyer; b. Lake Charles, La., Jan. 12, 1940; s. Howard Volney and Hazel (Wheeler) T.; m. Linda Lee; children: Carroll Diane, Howard V. III. BA, Williams Coll., 1961; LLB, So. Methodist U., 1964. Bar: Tex. 1964. Gen. atty. SEC, 1964-65; law clk. to chief judge U.S. Dist. Ct. No. Dist. Tex., 1965-67; ptnr. Tygrett & Walker and predecessors, Dallas, 1968-98; state dist. judge, 86th dist. Kaufman County, Tex., 2003—. Bd. dirs. Routh St. Ctr., 1976-83, Theatre Three, 1974-75, Shakespeare Festival, 1978-81, Suicide and Crisis Ctr., 1983-88, Kaufman County Civic Theatre, 2005—, Terrell Christian Acad., 2006—; bd. dirs. Dallas Ctr. for Developmentally Disabled, pres., 2006—; chmn. Terrell Hist. Preservation Commn., 2000-03. Mem. Tex. Bar Assn., Civitan (lt. gov. Tex. dist. 1976-77, gov. 1979-80), Terrell Heritage Soc. (v.p. 1999—), Delta Phi, Delta Theta Phi. Episcopalian. Home: 505 Pacific Ave Terrell TX 75160-2073 Office: Kaufman County Courthouse 100 W Mulberry Kaufman TX 75142

TYKESON, DONALD ERWIN, broadcast executive; b. Portland, Oreg., Apr. 11, 1927; s. O. Ansel and Hillie Martha (Haveman) T.; m. Rilda Margaret Steigleder, July 1, 1950; children: Ellen, Amy, Eric. BS, U. Oreg., 1951. V.p., dir. Liberty Comm., Inc., Eugene, Oreg., 1963-67, pres., CEO, dir., 1967-83; mng. ptnr. Tykeson/Assocs. Enterprises, 1983—; chmn. bd. Bend Cable Comm., LLC, 1983—2002, vice chmn., 2002—; chmn. bd. Ctrl. Oreg. Cable Advt., LLC, 1992—. Mem. coun. pub. reps. NIH, 2002-05, NIH Pub. Access Working Group Bd of Regents Nat. Libr. Medicine, 2005-; trustee. Tykeson Family Charitable Trust, 1995—; mem. Hoover Instn. bd. overseers Stanford U., 2002-. Vice-chmn. we. area Nat. Multiple Sclerosis Soc., 1983—2002, bd. dirs., 1987—2003, life bd. dirs., 2004—; bd. dirs. Nat. Coalition Rsch. in Neurol. and Communicative Disorders, 1984—89, Sacred Heart Med. Ctr. Found., 1995—2004; chmn. pub. and gov. info. com. Nat. Coaltion in Rsch., C-SPAN, 1980—89; trustee U. Oreg. Found., 1996—2006, Eugene Art Found., 1980—85, Oreg. Health Scis. U. Found., 1988—91; trustee emeritus Sacred Heart Med. Ctr. Found., 2004—; mem. bus. adv. coun. U. Oreg. Coll. Bus. Adminstrn., 1973—, mem. steering com., 1997—2001, dean search com., 1998; mem. Oreg. Investment Coun. State of Oreg., vice chmn., 1988—92. Recipient 1st Citizen honoree, Eugene C. of C., 2006. Mem. Nat. Assn. Broadcasters, Nat. Cable TV Assn. (dir. 1976-83), Chief Execs. Orgn., Vintage Club (bd. dirs. 1996-99, chmn. fin. com., treas. 1996-99, pres. Custom Lot Assn. 1992-97), Country Club Eugene (dir. 1975-77, sec. 1976, v.p. 1977), Multnomah Athletic Club, Arlington Club, Rotary, Alexis de Tocqueville Soc., Confrérie Chevaliers du Tastevin Sous Commanderie de Coachella Valley. Home: 447 Spyglass Dr Eugene OR 97401-2091 Office: Tykeson Assocs Enterprises PO Box 70006 Eugene OR 97401-0101 Office Phone: 541-683-4511.

TYL, NOEL JAN, retired vocalist, astrologer, writer; b. West Chester, Pa., Dec. 31, 1936; BA, Harvard U., 1958. Bus. mgr. Houston Grand Opera Assn., 1958-60; account exec. Ruder and Finn Pub. Rels., NYC, 1960-62; profl. astrologer, 1970—; editor Astrology Now mag., 1974-79. Pres. Tyl Assocs., Inc. pub. rels. and advt., 1980-89; media spokesman; internat. lectr., locations including U.S., Moscow, London, Oslo, Copenhagen, Berlin, Amsterdam, The Netherlands, Toronto, Ont., Tel Aviv, Bologna. Winner Am. Opera Auditions, 1964; opera singer U.S. and Europe, 1964-80; Wagner specialist; appearances include Vienna State Opera, Düsseldorf, Rome, Milan, Barcelona, N.Y.C. Opera, also throughout U.S.; author: Principles and Practice of Astrology, 12 vols., 1973-75, Teaching and Study Guide, 1976, The Horoscope as Identity, 1974, Holistic Astrology, 1980, Prediction in Astrology, 1991, Synthesis and Counseling in Astrology, 1994, Astrology of the Famed, 1995, Predictions for a New Millennium, 1996, Astrological Timing of Critical Illness, 1998, Creative Astrologer, 1999, Solar Arcs, 2001, Intimacy, Sexuality, and Relationship, 2002, Vocations, 2005. Mem. Astrology's World Orgn./AFAN (presiding officer 1982-98). Home: 15634 N Cholola Dr Fountain Hills AZ 85268-1225 Home Phone: 480-816-0000; Office Phone: 480-816-0000. E-mail: noeltyl@cox.net.

TYLE, CRAIG S., lawyer, investment company executive; b. Syracuse, NY, 1960; BA with high honors, Swarthmore Coll., 1982; JD magna cum laude, Harvard Univ., 1985. Bar: NY 1988, DC 2004. Assoc. Sullivan & Cromwell, NYC, 1982—88; atty. Investment Company Inst., Washington, 1988—97, gen. counsel, 1997—2004; prin., asset mgmt. group Shearman & Sterling LLP, Washington, 2004—05; exec. v.p. & gen. counsel Franklin Resources Inc. (Franklin Templeton Investments), San Mateo, Calif., 2005—. Mem. NASDAQ Quality of Markets com., 1997—2003, co-chmn., 2003. Contbr. articles to profl. jours. Mem.: ABA, Assn. Bar City of NY. Office: Franklin Resources Inc 1 Franklin Pkwy San Mateo CA 94403-1906 Office Phone: 202-508-8016. Office Fax: 202-508-8100. Business E-Mail: craig.tyle@shearman.com. *

TYLER, ANNE (MRS. TAGHI M. MODARRESSI), writer; b. Mpls., Oct. 25, 1941; d. Lloyd Parry and Phyllis (Mahon) T.; m. Taghi M. Modarressi, May 3, 1963 (dec. Apr. 1997); children: Tezh, Mitra. BA,

Duke U., 1961; postgrad., Columbia U., 1962. Author: If Morning Ever Comes, 1964, The Tin Can Tree, 1965, A Slipping-Down Life, 1970, The Clock Winder, 1972, Celestial Navigation, 1974, Searching for Caleb, 1976, Earthly Possessions, 1977, Morgan's Passing, 1980, Dinner at the Homesick Restaurant, 1982, The Accidental Tourist, 1985 (Nat. Book Critics Cir. award 1986), Breathing Lessons, 1988 (Pulitzer Prize for fiction 1989), Saint Maybe, 1991, (juvenile) Tumble Tower, 1993, Ladder of Years, 1995, A Patchwork Planet, 1998, Back When We Were Grownups, 2001, The Amateur Marriage, 2004, (juvenile) Timothy Tugbohom Says No, 2005, Digging to America, 2006; contbr. short stories to nat. mags. Home: 222 Tunbridge Rd Baltimore MD 21212-3422 *

TYLER, CLIFFORD ERNEST, school superintendent; b. San Francisco, Feb. 12, 1944; s. Steve Allen and Helen Ernestine (Shores) T.; m. Anne Clare Davis, June 13, 1971. B.S., Oreg. State U., 1966; M.Ed., U. Oreg., 1968; postgrad. San Jose State U., 1970-71; Ed.D., U. Pacific, 1981. Tchr., Palo Alto Unified Sch. Dist., Calif., 1968-72; prin. Fern Ridge Sch. Dist., Elmira, Oreg., 1973-74, Modesto City Schs., Calif., 1974-78; supt., prin. Falls City Sch. Dist., Oreg., 1978-79, Aumsville Sch. Dist., Oreg., 1979-81; dist. supt. Cutler-Orosi Unified Sch. Dist., Calif., 1981-86, Amador County Unified Sch. Dist., Jackson, Calif., 1986—. Contbr. articles to profl. jours. Bd. dirs. Muir Trail council Girl Scouts U.S.A., Modesto, Calif., 1977. Oreg. State U. scholar, 1966. Mem. Assn. Calif. Sch. Adminstrs. (dir.), Confedn. Oreg. Sch. Adminstrs., Assn. Supervision and Curriculum Devel., Am. Assn. Sch. Adminstrs., C. of C., Phi Delta Kappa. Democrat. Methodist. Lodges: Lions, Kiwanis. Clubs: Sportsmen of Stanislaus, Visalia Racquet. Office: Amador County Unified Sch Dist 217 Rex Ave Jackson CA 95642-2020

TYLER, DAVID EARL, retired veterinary medical educator; b. Carlisle, Iowa, July 12, 1928; s. Guy Earl and Beatrice Virginia (Slack) T.; m. Alice LaVon Smith, Sept. 6, 1952; children: John William, Anne Elizabeth. BS, Iowa State U., 1953, D.V.M., 1957, PhD, 1963; MS, Purdue U., 1960. Instr. dept. vet. sci. Purdue U., 1957-60; asst. prof. dept. pathology Coll. Vet. Medicine, Iowa State U., 1960-63, asso. prof., 1963-66; prof., head dept. pathology and parasitology Coll. Vet. Medicine, U. Ga., 1966-71, head dept. pathology, 1971-79, prof., 1971-91, prof. emeritus, 1991—; ret., 1991. Co-founder internat. vet. pathology slide bank, 1984, co-dir., 1984-98; apptd. discussant Charles L. Davis Found. for Advancement Vet. Pathology, 1977-91. Cub Scout master, 1967-69, scout com. chmn., 1970-72; elder Disciples of Christ Ch., 1968—, chmn. ch. bd., 1973-74, 92-94; mem. citizens com. to County Bd. Edn., 1968-70; bd. dirs. Christian Coll., Ga., 1974-77. With AUS, 1946-48. Recipient Borden award Gail Borden Co., 1956, Norden Disting. Teaching award Norden Labs., 1964, 69, 81, 85, 91, Prof. of Yr. award Coll. Vet. Medicine, Iowa State U., 1965, Outstanding Prof. award Coll. Vet. Medicine, U. Ga., 1970, 76, 80-81, 83, 86, 87-88, 90, Joshia Meigs Teaching award, 1985, Stange award Coll. Vet. Med., Iowa State U., 1987, Phi Zeta Teaching award, 1985, N.Am. Outstanding Tchr. award, 1991, Omicron Delta Kappa Outstanding Prof. award U. Ga., 1981, Harold W. Casey award C.L. Davis Found., 1995. Mem. AVMA, Farm House, Am. Coll. Vet. Pathologists (mem. council 1975-77, exam. com. 1982-85), Am. Assn. Vet. Med. Colls. (chmn. com. teaching-learning materials 1975-77), Nat. Program for Instructional Devel. in Vet. Pathology (adv. com. 1976-77), Aghon, Sigma Xi, Phi Eta Sigma, Alpha Zeta, Gamma Sigma Delta, Phi Kappa Phi, Phi Zeta (chpt. sec.-treas. 1982-84), Omega Tau Sigma. Home: 160 Sunny Brook Dr Athens GA 30605-3348

TYLER, H. RICHARD, physician; b. Bklyn., Oct. 16, 1927; s. Max M. and Beatrice F. T.; m. Joyce Colby, June 17, 1951; children: Kenneth, Karen, Douglas, Lori. AB, Syracuse U., 1947; BS in Medicine, Washington U., 1951, MD, 1951; MA (hon.), Harvard U., 1989. Diplomate Am. Bd. Neurology and Psychiatry. Intern Peter Bent Brigham Hosp., Boston, 1951-52; resident in neurology Boston City Hosp., 1952-54; public health fellow Neurol. Inst., Queen's Sq., London, Salpêtrière, Paris, 1954-55; asst. in pediatrics and neurology Johns Hopkins Hosp., Balt., 1955-56; neurologist Peter Bent Brigham Hosp., Boston, 1956-74; asst. in neurology Harvard Med. Sch., Boston, 1956-59, assoc. in neurology, 1959-61, from instr. to prof., 1961—98, prof. emeritus, 1998—; ret., 1999. Sr. physician Brigham and Women's Hosp., Boston, 1974—, dir. neurol. svc., 1979-88. Co-editor: Current Neurology I and II, 1979, 80; mem. editorial bd.: Jour. Neurology, 1979-84, Classics on Neurology and Neurosurgery Libr., 1983—; contbr. articles to profl. jours. Trustee Brookline Pub. Libr., 1970-2001, chmn. bd. trustees, 1985-86, 90-91. Served with U.S. Army, 1946-47. Mem. Am. Neurol. Assn., Am. Acad. Neurology (hon.), Mass. Med. Soc. Office: 1 Brookline Pl Ste 503 Brookline MA 02445-7224 Personal E-mail: HTyler1798@aol.com.

TYLER, JOHN DUKE, psychologist, educator; b. Nashville, Nov. 30, 1943; s. John Duke and Eleanora (Hammond) Tyler; m. Shirley Kay Montgomery; 1 child, Wade McLeod. BA, Vanderbilt U., 1965; PhD, U. Tex., Austin, 1970. Bd. cert. diplomate Am. Bd. Profl. Psychology. Prof. psychology U. ND, Grand Forks, 1970—2006; dir. Family Inst., Grand Forks, 1980—2006; prof. emeritus psychology, 2006—. Dir., Psychol. Svcs. Ctr. U. ND, Grand Forks, 1979—98. Contbr. articles to profl. jours. Fellow: Acad. Clin. Psychology; mem.: APA, N.D. Psychol. Assn. (pres. 1982—83). Personal E-mail: jdtyl@mfire.com.

TYLER, JOHN EDWARD, III, lawyer; b. Kansas City, Mo. BA, U. Notre Dame, 1986, JD, 1989. Bar: Mo. 1989, Kans. 1990. From assoc. to ptnr. Lathrop & Gage L.C., Kansas City, 1989-99; gen. counsel, sec. Ewing Marion Kauffman Found., Kansas City, 1999—, chief ethics officer, 1999—. Adj. prof. Rockhurst U., Kansas City, 2000—; bd. advisors Nat. Ctr. Philanthropy and Law, NYU, 2003-06; bd. dirs. Kauffman Scholars, Inc., Kansas City, sec., 2003—; bd. dirs. UEP Gulf Coast, Inc., Kansas City, sec., 2006—; bd. dirs. Urban Entrepeneur Partnership, Inc., sec., 2006—; bd. dirs. Kauffman Innovation Network, Inc., Kansas City, 2005—, chair, 2006—. Contbr. articles to profl. jours. Pres. Genesis Sch., Kansas City, 1995-97; pres. Archbishop O'Hara H.S., Kansas City, 1994-97, bd. dirs.; pres. Sch. Bd. Diocese of Kansas City-St. Joseph, 2002-2004; chmn. tax increment fin. commn. city of Raytown, Mo., 1997-99; bd. dirs. Ctr. for Mgmt. Assistance, Kansas City, pres., 1999-2001. Recipient Bernie Hoffman award Cmty. Svc. Awards Found., 1997; named Man of Yr. Leukemia Soc., Kansas City, 1998, Best of the Bar, Kansas City Bus. Jour., 2004. Mem. ABA, Mo. Bar Assn. (Thomas D. Cochran award for cmty. svc. 1995), Kans. Bar Assn., Kansas City Met. Bar Assn. (Young Lawyer of Yr. 1998). Home: 2420 SW Wintercreek Ct Lees Summit MO 64081-4085 Office: Ewing Marion Kauffman Found 4801 Rockhill Rd Kansas City MO 64110-2046 Office Phone: 816-932-1293.

TYLER, LIV, actress; b. Portland, Maine, Jan. 7, 1977; d. Steven Tyler (lead singer: Aerosmith) and Bebe Buell; m. Royston Langdon, Mar. 25, 2003; 1 child. Motion picture actress and print model. Actress (films): Silent Fall, 1994, Heavy, 1995, Empire Records, 1995, Stealing Beauty, 1996, That Thing You Do!, 1996, Inventing the Abbotts, 1997, U-Turn, 1997, Armageddon, 1998, Onegin, 1999, The Little Black Book, 1999, Cookie's Fortune, 1999, Plunkett & MaCleane, 1999, Dr. T & the Women, 2001, One Night at McCool's, 2001, Lord of the Rings: The Fellowship of the Ring, 2001, The Lord of the Rings: The Two Towers, 2002, The Lord of the Rings: The Return of the King, 2003, Jersey Girl, 2004, Lonesome Jim, 2005, Reign Over Me, 2007; appeared in Aerosmith's music video, Crazy, 1994. Office: c/o Creative Artists Agy 9830 Wilshire Blvd Beverly Hills CA 90212-1804 *

TYLER, LLOYD JOHN, retired lawyer; b. Aurora, Ill., May 28, 1924; s. Lloyd J. and Dorothy M. (Curtis) T.; m. Inez Chappell Busener, Feb. 25, 1970; children by previous marriage: Barbara Tyler Miller, John R., Benjamin C., Robert B., Amy C. Tomas. BA, Beloit Coll., 1948; JD, U. Mich., 1951. Bar: Ill. 1951, Mich. 1951. Mem. firm Sears, Streit, Tyler and Dreyer and predecessors, Aurora, 1951-62, Tyler and Hughes P.A., Aurora, 1962-99; ret. Lectr., spkr. on profl. subjects, 1964—. Contbr. chpts. to profl. books, articles to profl. jours. Democratic precinct committeeman, 1954-59; mem. Batavia (Ill.) Sch. Bd., 1959-62. Served with USAAF, 1943-46. Fellow Am. Bar Found.; mem. ABA (ho. of dels. 1975-79), Ill. Bar Assn. (gov. 1970-78, pres. 1978-79, chmn. legis. com. 1980, task force on alternative forms of legal service 1981-82, long range planning com. 1982-88, fed. judiciary appointment com. 1984-90, spl. com. on merit selection 1987—), Ill. Bar Found. (pres. 1972-75), Ill. Inst. Continuing Legal Edn. (dir. 1971-75, 77-79), Ill. Lawyers Polit. Action Com. (trustee 1982—, chmn. 1987-88), Soc. Trial Lawyers Ill., Appellate Lawyers Assn., Phi Beta Kappa, Omicron Delta Kappa. Presbyterian. Home and Office: 701 Fargo Blvd Geneva IL 60134-3227 Office Phone: 630-232-8575.

TYLER, MICHAEL ROBERT, lawyer; b. Hollywood, Calif., May 20, 1956; m. Christine D. von Wrangel. BA in history, UCLA, 1979, MA in history, 1980; JD, Loyola Law Sch., LA, 1983; LLM in comparative law, Fitzwilliam Coll., Cambridge U., 1986. Bar: Calif. 1984. Law clk. to the Hon. Arthur Alcaron US Ct. Appeals (9th Cir.), San Francisco, 1987—88; assoc. Heller Ehrman White & McAuliffe, LA, 1991—95; sr. corp. counsel internat. Northrop Grumman Corp., LA, 1995—2000; v.p., group counsel for Europe, Middle East, and Africa ops. Gateway Inc., London, 2000—02, v.p. law for procurement activities Irvine, Calif., 2002—03, v.p., asst. gen. counsel, 2003—04, sr. v.p., gen. counsel, sec., 2004—05, sr. v.p., chief legal & adminstrv. officer, 2005—. Mem.: State Bar Calif. (chair internat. law sect. 1999), ABA (editor-in-chief European Law Bulletin 1989—91, chair European law com. of internat. law and practice sect. 1998). Office: Gateway Inc 7565 Irvine Ctr Dr Irvine CA 92618 *

TYLER, PEGGY LYNNE BAILEY, retired lawyer; b. Seattle, Oct. 15, 1948; d. John Thomas and Doris Mae (Lindgren) Bailey; m. Tom Kenneth Newton, May 25, 1975 (div. 1980); m. Allan Gregory Lambert, Aug. 3, 1980 (div. May 1996); m. Charles Kevin Tyler, Sept. 12, 1997; children: Eli Raven, Joshua Alec. BA in Psychology, Beloit Coll., 1970; MS in Counseling Psychology, Ill. Inst. Tech., 1973; JD, Syracuse U., NY, 1978. Bar: D.C. 1983. Mental health specialist Ill. Dept. Mental Health, Chgo., 1971-72; mem. rsch. faculty Cornell U., Ithaca, N.Y., 1973-75; assoc. O'Connor, Sovocool, Pfann and Greenburg, Ithaca, 1978, Dacy, Richin & Meyers, Silver Springs, Md., 1979-81; ins. adminstr. Nat. Assn. Broadcasters, Washington, 1981-86, dir. ins. programs, 1986-90; assoc. gen. counsel Architect of the Capitol, Washington, 1990—2006, ret., 2006. Co-author, editor: Broadcaster's Property and Liability Insurance Buying Guide, 1989. Bd. dirs. Hartford-Thayer Condominium Assn., 1994-2006, pres., 1995-96, sec., 1996-2000, treas., 2000-05. Mem. D.C. Bar Assn. (mem. steering com. of arts entertainment, sports law sect. 1989-90, sect. editor newsletter 1989-90). Independent. Jewish. Avocations: antiques, gourmet cooking, ballet. Home Phone: 616-607-9217; Office Phone: 202-225-1210, 240-216-8287. Business E-Mail: ptyler@aoc.gov, pctyler@charter.net.

TYLER, RALPH SARGENT, III, lawyer; b. Cleve., Feb. 7, 1947; s. Ralph Sargent Jr. and Marion (Clark) T. BA, U. Ill., 1969; JD, Case Western Res. U., 1972; LLM, Harvard U., 1977. Bar: Mass. 1972, Mich. 1973, Ohio 1978, D.C. 1981, Md. 1982, U.S. Dist. Ct. Mass. 1973, U.S. Dist. Ct. (we. dist.) Mich. 1973, U.S. Dist. Ct. (no. dist.) Ohio 1978, U.S. Dist. Ct. D.C. 1981, U.S. Dist. Ct. Md. 1982, U.S. Ct. Appeals (1st, 4th, 6th and D.C. cirs.) 1982, U.S. Supreme Ct. 1981. Atty. Greater Boston Legal Services, 1973-76, Mass. Law Reform Inst., Boston, 1977-78; asst. prof. law Cleve. State U., 1978-80; lectr. law Nat. U. Singapore, 1980-81; asst. atty. gen. State of Md., Balt., 1982-91, chief of litigation, 1986-91, dep. atty. gen., 1991-96; ptnr. Hogan L. Hartson, LLP, Balt., 1996—2004; city atty. Law Dept., Balt., 2004—06. Mem. Balt. City Pub. Sch. Bd., 2003—04. Mem. ABA, Md. Bar Assn. Home: 205 Gittings Ave Baltimore MD 21212-2504 Office Phone: 410-396-8393. Office Fax: 410-659-4077. E-mail: ralph.tyler@baltimorecity.gov.

TYLER, RICHARD, fashion designer; b. Sunshine, Australia, Sept. 22, 1950; m. Doris Taylor (div.); 1 child, Sheridan; m. Lisa Trafficante, 1989; 1 child, Edward Charles. Prin. Zippity-doo-dah, Melbourne, Australia, 1968-80, Tyler-Trafficante, LA, 1988—; design dir. Anne Klein Collection, NYC, 1993-94, 99; fashion dir. owner Tyler Trafficante, Inc., 1999—. Designer Richard Tyler Couture introduced for Women, 1989, Richard Tyler Collection debut for Men, April 1997, Richard Tyler Shoes for Women, 1996, Richard Tyler Collection for Women, 1997, Richard Tyler Shoes for Men, 1997. Recipient New Fashion Talent Perry Ellis award Coun. Fashion Designers Am., 1993, Womenswear Designer of Yr. award, 1994, Perry Ellis award for new fashion talent in menswear, 1995.

TYLER, RICHARD JAMES, personal and professional development educator; b. Warwick, RI, June 16, 1957; s. Virginia (Campanella) Tyler. Gen. mgr. Gem Exch., Charlotte, NC, 1977; mgr. nat. sales So. Merchandising, Charlotte, 1978; pres. Direct Import Distributing, New Orleans, 1981; dir. nat. territory TV Fanfare Pub., 1982; v.p. ARC Pub., New Orleans, 1983; exec. v.p., gen. mgr. Superior Bedrooms, Inc., 1984; CEO Richard Tyler Internat., Inc., Houston, Internat. Bus. Inst., Inc., Houston, Tyler Internat. Rsch. Inst., Inc., Houston, Shopportunities, Houston, Richard Tyler Investments Ltd., 2000. Mem. adv. bd. Sales and Mktg. Mag., N.Y.C., 1991—; founder Leadership of Tomorrow program; profl. speaker, cons. in field. Author: Creating Excellence in Quality and Service, 1991, The Science and Art of Excellent Selling, 1993, Richard Tyler's Guide to Entrepreneurial Excellence, 1993, Richard Tyler's Smart Business Strategies: The Guide to Small Business Marketing Excellence, 1996, The Power of Professional Selling Program, 2002; co-author: Conversations on Faith, 2004, Conversations on Customer Service and Sales, 2005, Conversations on Health and Wellness, 2004, Conversations on Success, 2004, Marketing Magic, 2005, Real World Service Strategies That Work, 2004, Real World Teambuilding Strategies That Work, 2004, Real World Human Resource Strategies That Work, 2004, Leadership Defined, 2005; pub.: (newsletter) Richard Tyler's Excellence Edge, 1992, Entrepreneur Cover Story, 1999; contbr. articles to profl. publs. Mem. Rep.-Senatorial Inner Cir., Washington, 1991, presdl. victory team Rep. Nat. Com., 2002, Tex. rep. press club, 2002, Be An Angel Fund Charity. Mem. ASTD, Soc. Human Resource Mgmt., Nat. Speakers Assn., Internat. Platform Assn., Internat. Assn. Entrepreneurs. Avocations: sports, theater, deep sea fishing, amateur wrestling. E-mail: richardtyler@richardtyler.com.

TYLER, RONALD LEE, religious studies educator; b. St Joseph, Mo., Apr. 30, 1938; s. June Laveta Tyler; m. Carolyn Ann Bradley, Aug. 26, 1963; 1 child, Paul Bradley. MA in Sociology, Geography, and Religion, Eastern N.Mex. U., 1960, MA in Religion, 1963; PhD, Baylor U., Waco, Tex., 1973. Instr. bibl. studies Kilgore Coll., Tex., 1962—68; prof. religion Pepperdine U., Malibu, Calif., 1972—. Mem. task forces and seminars Cath. Bibl. Assn. Am., Washington. Min. Ch. of Christ, Clifton, Tex., 1968—72, mem. Camarillo, Calif., 1975—. Sgt. first class US Army, 1956—62. Home: 1468 Wolverton Ave Camarillo CA 93010-3735 Office: Pepperdine Univ 24255 Pacific Coast Hwy Malibu CA 90263 Office Fax: 310-506-4352. Business E-Mail: ronald.tyler@pepperdine.edu.

TYLER, RONNIE CURTIS, museum director, art historian; b. Temple, Tex., Dec. 29, 1941; s. Jasper J. and Melba Curtis (James) T.; m. Paula Eyrich, Aug. 24, 1974. BSE, Abilene Christian Coll., TEx., 1964; MA, Tex. Christian U., 1966, PhD (Univ. fellow), 1968; DHL, Austin Coll., 1986. Instr. history Austin Coll., Sherman, Tex., 1967-68, asst. prof., 1968-69; curator history Amon Carter Mus., Ft. Worth, 1969, dir. publications, asst. dir. history and publications, asst. dir. collections and programs, 1984—86, dir., 2006—; prof. history U. Tex., Austin, 1986—2006. Adj. prof. history Tex. Christian U., 1971-72; dir. Tex. State Hist. Assn., 1986-2005; cons. visual materials Western. Am. art. Author: Santiago Vidaurri and the Confederacy, 1973, The Big Bend: The Last Texas Frontier, 1975, The Image of America in Caricature and Cartoon, 1975, The Cowboy, 1975, The Mexican War: A Lithographic Record, 1974, The Rodeo Photographs of John Addison Stryker, 1978, Visions of America: Pioneer Artists in a New Land, 1983, Views of Texas: The Watercolors of Sarah Ann Hardinge, 1852-56, 1988, Nature's Classics: John James Audubon's Birds and Animals, 1992, Audubon's Great National Work: The Royal Octavo Edition of the Birds of America, 1993, Prints of the West, 1994, Alfred Jacob Miller: Artist as Explorer, 1999; (with Paula Eyrich Tyler) Texas Museums: A Guidebook, 1983; editor: (with Lawrence R. Murphy) The Slave Narratives of Texas, 1974, Posada's Mexico, 1979, Alfred Jacob Miller: Artist on the Oregon Trail, 1982, Wanderings in the Southwest in 1855 (J.D.B. Stillman), 1990, Prints and Printmakers of Texas, 1997. Pres. Tarrant County (Tex.) Hist. Soc., 1975-77; dir. Tex. State Hist. Soc., 1986-2005. Good Neighbor Commn. scholar Instituto Tecnologico Monterrey, Mex., 1967; Am. Philos. Soc. grantee, 1970-71; recipient H. Bailey Carroll award, 1974; Coral H. Tullis award, 1976, Alonso de León medal Sociedad Nuevoleonsa História Geografía y Estadistica, 2002. Mem. Am. Antiquarian Soc., Tex. Inst. Letters (Friends of Dallas Pub. Libr. award), Philos. Soc. Tex. (sec. 1990), Phi Beta Kappa. Office: Amon Carter Museum 3501 Camp Bowie Blvd Fort Worth TX 76107-2695 Home Phone: 817-377-1297; Office Phone: 817-989-5095. Business E-Mail: ron.tyler@cartermuseum.org.

TYLER, W(ILLIAM) ED, finance company executive; b. Cleve., Nov. 3, 1952; s. Ralph Tyler and Edith (Green) Kauer; m. Vickie Sue Boggs, Feb. 7, 1976; children: Stacia Leigh, Adam William. BSEE, Ind. Inst. Tech., 1974; MBA, Ind. U., 1977; postgrad., Harvard U., 1981, Baruch U., 1988. From electronic engr. to exec. v.p. R.R. Donnelley & Sons Co., Warsaw, Ind., 1974—95, exec. v.p. & chief tech. officer, 1995—98; CEO, pres. Moore Corp. Ltd., 1998—2001, Willoughby Capitol, Lake Forest, Ill., 2001; CEO Ideapoint Ventures, 2002—. Home: 1000 N Lake Shore Plz Ste 45A Chicago IL 60611 Office Phone: 847-567-7111.

TYLER, WILLIAM HOWARD, JR., advertising executive, educator; b. Elizabethton, Tenn., May 21, 1932; s. William Howard and Ethel Margaret (Schueler) T.; m. Margery Moss, Aug. 31, 1957; children: William James, Daniel Moss. Student, Iowa State U., 1950-52, U. Iowa, 1952; AB in Lit., BJ in Advt., U. Mo., 1958, MA in Journalism, 1966. Advt. mgr. Rolla (Mo.) Daily News, 1958-59; instr. sch. journalism U. Mo., Columbia, 1959-61; copy writer, then v.p. copy dir. D'Arcy Advt. Agy., St. Louis, 1961-67; writer, producer, creative supr. Gardner Advt. Co., St. Louis, 1967-69; sr. v.p., creative dir. D'Arcy, McManus, Masius, St. Louis, 1969-77; exec. v.p., creative dir. Larson Bateman Advt. Agy., Santa Barbara, Calif., 1977-80; v.p. advt. Pizza Hut, Inc., Wichita, Kans., 1980-82; v.p., creative dir. Frye-Sills/Y&R, Denver, 1980; exec. v.p., creative dir. Gardner Advt. Co., St. Louis, 1982-88; exec. v.p., ptnr., creative dir. Parker Group, St. Louis, 1988-91; pres. Tylertoo Prodns., St. Louis, 1991—. Assoc. prof. St. Louis U., 1993-2003, prof., 2003—. Mng. editor St. Louis Advt. Mag., 1992-95. Trustee Blackburn Coll., Carlinville, Ill., 1983—84; bd. advisors U. Mo. Journalism Sch., 1986—91. 1st lt. USMC, 1952—55, Japan, Korea. Named AAF 9th Dist. Educator of Yr., 1998, 2007; recipient Faculty and Excellence Award, 2001, 2002, Outstanding Advisor awards, 1999, 2007. Mem. U. Mo. Alumni Assn. (bd. dirs. 1969-70), Advt. Club Greater St. Louis, Golden Key (hon.), Mensa, Kappa Tau Alpha (hon.). Episcopalian. Office: Saint Louis U Dept Comm Xavier 300 3733 W Pine Blvd Saint Louis MO 63108-3305 Office Phone: 314-977-3190. Business E-Mail: tylerwh@slu.edu.

TYLEVICH, ALEXANDER V., sculptor, architect; b. Minsk, Belarus, Sept. 12, 1947; arrived in U.S., 1989; s. Wulf Tylevich and Asia Klebanova; m. Poline M. Dvorkin, Jan. 22, 1981; children: Alexei, Katherine. BA in Arch., Minsk Archtl. Inst., 1965; MA in Arch., Byelorussian Poly. Inst., Minsk, 1971. Prin., sr. arch. Minskprojekt, 1971-84; artist, arch. Fine Arts Found., Minsk, 1984-89; sculptor-arch. Tylevich Studio Inc., St. Paul, 1989—. Prin. works include Vincentian Letter, DePaul U., Chgo., Letterdance, Minn. State U., Mankato, River of Memory, La. State Mus., Baton Rouge, Midtown Exchange Sculpture, Mpls., Inver Hills C.C., Inver Grove Heights, Minn., St. Francis de Sales, Morgantown, W.Va., Thomas More Chapel, U. St. Thomas, Mpls., Suspended Cross, Church of St. Peter, Mendota, Minn., St. Victoria Ch., Victoria, Minn., Processional Cross, Cathedral of Christ the King, Superior, Wis., Blue Springs.Net, Blue Springs, Mo., Letters of Creation, Wayzata, Minn., Montessori's Vision: Through the Eyes of a Child, Lake Country Sch., Mpls., Tree of Life, U. Minn., Mpls., Sculpture Anoka Ramsey C.C., Coon Rapids, Minn., Resurrection, Ch. of St. Stephen, Anoka, Minn., Madonna and Child, The Ch. of St. Mary, Alexandria, Minn., Gateway to Belief/Point of Belief, St. Mary's U., Winona, Minn., Thomas Becket, Cath. Cmty. of Thomas Becket, Eagan, Minn., Tribute to Erich Mendelsohn, FORECAST Pub. Artwork, St. Paul, Zenon Possis, North Meml. Hosp., Mpls., Winona Tech. Coll. Aviation Facility, North Shore Synagogue, Syosset, N.Y., Mt. Zion Temple, St. Paul, St. Paul Sem., St. Joseph Abbey, St. Benedict, La., Mepkin Abbey, S.C., Immaculate Conception Cath. Ch., Durham, N.C., Ctr. of Minsk, Minsk City Govt. Bldg., Subway Sta., pvt. collections, exhibited in group shows at Monumental Art of Byelorussia, Minsk, 1989, Nat. Jewish Mus., Washington, 1993, Harvard U. Grad. Sch. Design New Eng., 1993, St. John's U., Collegeville, Minn. Recipient Internat. Design Honor award IFRAA, 2006, Henry Hering Meml. medal, 2007;grantee Minn. Met. Regional Arts Coun., 1991, Howard B. Brin Arts Endowment, 1991, FORECAST Pub. Artworks, 1993. Fellow Archtl. Assn. USSR. Home: 1937 Highland Pkwy Saint Paul MN 55116-1350 Personal E-mail: tyleart@aol.com.

TYLKA, GREGORY L., plant pathologist, educator; BS in Biology, California U. Pa., 1983, MS in Biology, 1985; PhD in Plant Pathology, U. Ga., 1990. Asst. prof. dept. plant pathology Iowa State U., Ames, 1990-95, assoc. prof. dept. plant pathology, 1995—. Recipient Prodn. Rsch. award United Soybean Bd., 1998. Mem. Agronomy Soc. Am., Am. Phytopathol. Soc. (Excellence in Ext. award 1999), Am. Soybean Assn., Iowa Soybean Assn., Helminthological Soc. Washington, Soc. Nematologists, Soil Sci. Soc. Am., Sigma Xi, Beta Beta Beta (Outstanding Alumnus award 1992), Gamma Sigma Delta. Achievements include research on the effects of cultural practices and soybean resistance and tolerance on soybean cyst nematode population densities and soybean yields. Office: Iowa State U Dept Plant Pathology 321 Bessey Hall Ames IA 50011 Fax: 515-294-3851. E-mail: gltylka@iastate.edu.

TYLLIA, FRANK MICHAEL, academic administrator, educator; b. Rossland, BC, Can., Dec. 1, 1942; arrived in US, 1942; s. Alex J. and Lenora M. (Janni) T.; m. Kathryn A. McWalter, Mar. 21, 1970. BBA, Gonzaga U., Spokane, Wash., 1965, BA in Edn., 1967; MA in Edn., Seattle U., 1972. Tchr. pub. schs., Seattle, 1967-72, prin., 1972-78, Edmonds Sch. Dist., Lynnwood, Wash., 1978-97; field supr. M Tchg. City U., Bellevue, Wash., 1997—, field supr. edn. leadership, 1999—. Adj. prof. Seattle Pacific U., 1990—, Mont. State U., 1999—. Active alumni mentoring program Gonzaga U., Seattle, 1993—; mem. Kirkland Cmty. Accountability Bd.; active King County Juvenile Justice, 1997—; mem. King County Diversion Adv. Bd., 1998—. Mem. ASCD, Assn. Wash. Sch. Prins. (various coms.), Washington Athletic Club, Phi Delta Kappa. Home and Office: 4527 103d Ln NE Kirkland WA 98033-7639

TYMKOVICH, TIMOTHY MICHAEL, federal judge; b. Denver, Nov. 2, 1956; married; 2 children. BA, Co. Coll., 1979; JD, U. Colo. Sch. Law, 1982. Clk. Co. Supreme Ct., 1982—83; assoc. Davis, Graham, & Stubbs, 1983—89; of counsel Bradley Campbel Carney & Madsen, 1990—91; solicitor gen. Office of Co. Atty. Gen., 1991—96; ptnr. Hale Hackstaff Tymkovich & ErkenBrack, 1996—2003; judge US Ct. of Appeals (10th cir), 2003—. Mem.: ABA, Internat. Soc. Barristers, Colo. Bar Found., Am. Law Inst. Office: Byron White US Courthouse 1823 Stout St Denver CO 80257 *

TYMOCZKO, DMITRI, music educator, composer; b. Cambridge, Mass., Dec. 16, 1969; s. Andrew Thomas Tymoczko and Marie Anne Fleming; m. Elisabeth Maura Camp, July 6, 2002. AB, Harvard U., 1992; student, Oxford U., 1992—94; MA in Music Composition, U. Calif., 1999, PhD in Music Composition, 2002. Asst. prof. Princeton (N.J.) U., 2002—. Spkr. in field; lectr. in field. Contbr. articles to profl. jours. and mags.; composer: (albums) The Agony of Modern Music, 2002, (songs) Five Cummings Songs, 1992 (Hugh F. MacColl prize), Forgotten Showtunes, 1998 (DeLorenzo prize), This Picture Seems to Move, 1998 (DeLorenzo prize), A Network of Stoppages, 1999, His Heart an Aviary, 1999, I Will Not, 2000, Collidascope I, 2001, The Agony of Modern Music, 2002, Echo Code, 2003, Piano Games, 2002 (Eisner prize), Fools and Angels, 2004, Estudios Technocraticos, 2004, Cathedral, 2004. Recipient Reuben A. Brower Excellence in Humanities prize, 1994, others; fellow, Radcliffe Inst. Advanced Study, 2005—; Rhodes scholar, 1992—94, Leonard Bernstein fellow, Tanglewood Music Ctr., 2003. Mem.: Phi Beta Kappa. Office: Princeton Univ 310 Woolworth Ctr Princeton NJ 08544

TYMOCZKO, JULIANNA SOPHIA, mathematics professor; b. Northampton, Mass., Aug. 10, 1975; d. Thomas and Maria Tymoczko. BA, Harvard U., Cambridge, Mass., 1998; PhD, Princeton U., NJ, 2003. Hildebrandt asst. prof. U. Mich., Ann Arbor, 2003—. Contbr. articles to profl. jours. Nat. Def. Sci. and Engring. grad. fellow, Dept. of Def., 1999—2002, Postdoctoral Rsch. fellow, NSF, 2004—.

TYNDALL, JAY MARK, lawyer; b. Indpls., Feb. 29, 1964; s. William Mark and Jewetta Corine (Main) T.; m. Yuko Shigetomi, Feb. 14, 1991; children: Saige Mark, Hanna. BA, Earlham Coll., 1986; JD, U. Dayton, 1991. Bar: Wash. 1992, DC 2002. Fgn. law advisor Kitahama Law Office, Osaka, Japan, 1994-96; U.S. law cons. Adachi, Henderson, Miyatake & Fujita, Tokyo, 1996—98; contract atty. Puget Sound Area, Wash., 1999—2001; prin. Trans-Jur-Lex, Seattle and Bellevue, 2002—. Presenter of continuing legal edn. in field. Mem.: D.C. Bar Assn., Wash. State Bar Assn. (mem. rules of profl. conduct com. 2000—04).

TYNER, LEE REICHELDERFER, lawyer; b. Annapolis, Md., Mar. 12, 1946; d. Thomas Elmer and Eleanor Frances (Leland) Reichelderfer; m. Carl Frederick Tyner, Aug. 31, 1968; children: Michael Frederick, Rachel Christine, Elizabeth Frances. BA, St. John's Coll., 1968; MS, U. Wash., 1970; JD, George Washington U., 1975. Bar: DC, US Dist. Ct. (DC), US Ct. Appeals (4th cir., 1st cir., 9th cir., DC cir., 5th cir., 8th cir., 11th cir., 10th cir.), US Ct. Claims, US Supreme Ct. Profl. staff US Senate Commerce Com., Washington, 1970-72; trial atty. Land and Natural Resources div. US Dept. Justice, Washington, 1975-85; atty. Office of Gen. Counsel US EPA, Washington, 1985—. Bd. dirs. Grace Episcopal Day Sch., Silver Spring, Md., 1987-89, vestry Grace Episcopal Ch., 1997-2003, 2004—, sec., 2004-; den leader, cubmaster Boy Scouts Am., Silver Spring, 1987-91. Recipient Bronze medals, US EPA, 1988, 1992, 2002, 2003, 2006. Mem.: Order of the Coif. Episcopalian. Home: 1401 Geranium St NW Washington DC 20012 Office: US EPA 2366A 1200 Pennsylvania Ave NW Washington DC 20460 Personal E-mail: skildpadde@aol.com. Business E-Mail: tyner.lee@epa.gov.

TYNER, NEAL EDWARD, retired insurance company executive; b. Grand Island, Nebr., Jan. 30, 1930; s. Edward Raymond and Lydia Dorothea (Kruse) T.; children: Karen Tyner Redrow, Morgan. BBA, U. Nebr., 1956. Jr. analyst Bankers Life Nebr., Lincoln, 1956-62, asst. v.p. securities, 1962-67, v.p. securities, treas., 1967-69, fin. v.p., treas., 1970-72, sr. v.p. fin., treas., 1972-83, pres., chief exec. officer, 1983-87, chmn., pres., chief exec. officer, 1987-88; chmn., CEO Ameritas Life Ins., Lincoln, 1988—95; pres. Net Cons., Paradise Valley, Ariz., 1995—. Bd. dirs. Union Bank & Trust Co. Trustee U. Nebr. Found., Lincoln Found. Capt. USMC, 1950-54, Korea. Fellow: CFAs. Lutheran. Avocations: tennis, computers. Office: 8225 N Golf Dr Paradise Valley AZ 85253-2716

TYNER, WALLACE EDWARD, agricultural economics educator; b. Orange, Tex., Mar. 21, 1945; s. Richard D. and Jeanne (Gullahorn) T.; m. Jean M. Young, May 2, 1970; children: Davis, Jeffrey. BS in Chemistry, Tex. Christian U., 1966; MA in Econs., U. Md., 1972, PhD in Econs., 1977. Vol. Peace Corps., India, 1966-68, math, sci., ednl. skill desk chief Washington, 1968-70; grad. teacher asst. U. Md., Balt., 1971-73; assoc. scientist Earth Satellite Corp., Washington, 1973-74; rsch. assoc. Cornell U., Ithaca, NY, 1974-77; asst. prof., assoc. prof. natural resource econs. and internat. devel. policy Purdue U., West Lafayette, Ind., 1977-84, prof., asst. dept. head, 1983-88, dept. head, 1989—2002. Cons. UN Food and Agrl. Orgn., Rome, Office Tech. Assessment, Washington, U.S. Dept. Interior, Washington, OECD, Paris, World Bank, Washington, USDA, Washington. Author: Energy Resources and Economic Development in India, 1978, A Perspective on U.S. Farm Problems and Agricultural Policy, 1987. Recipient Disting. Policy Contbn. award, AAEA, 2005. Mem. Am. Assn. Agrl. Economists, Am. Econs. Assn., Internat. Assn. Agrl. Economist, Sigma Xi, Gamma Sigma Delta. Home: 116 Arrowhead Dr West Lafayette IN 47906-2105 Office: Purdue U Krannert Bldg West Lafayette IN 47907-1145 Office Phone: 765-494-0199. Business E-Mail: wtyner@purdue.edu.

TYNES, ROBERT DICK, artist, educator; b. Chgo., Jan. 7, 1953; s. Marion F. and Faye Tynes Dick; m. Bette L. Bates, June 13, 1981; children: Alison Hayley, Robin Elizabeth. BA with hons. in Art, Rhodes Coll., Memphis, Tenn., 1975; MFA in Painting, East Carolina U., Greenville, NC, 1981. Lectr. art East Carolina U., 1981—82, Humboldt State U., Arcata, Calif., 1982—84; vis. asst. prof. art U. Hawaii Manoa, Honolulu, 1986—87; artist-in-residence U. NC, Asheville, 1987—91, from asst. prof. to prof. art, 1991—2004, prof. art, 2004—. Dir. S. Tucker Cooke Gallery U. NC, 1994—. Over 20 solo exhbns., over 100 group shows, one-man shows include Fay Gold Gallery, Atlanta, Ga., 2001, Lee Hansley Gallery, Raleigh, NC, 2004, Weizenblatt Gallery, Mars Hill Coll., 2005, Blue Spiral, Asheville, NC, 2006, Represented in permanent collections Charlotte Pub. Arts Commn., IBM Corp., Field Engring. Ctr., Atlanta, Ga. Chair Black Mountain Coll. Mus. and Art Ctr., Asheville, NC, 1993—95; dir. Asheville Area Arts Coun., 1994—2002, sec., 2000—02; dir. Black Mountain Ctr. Arts, NC, 2003—04, sec., 2004. Recipient We. NC Regional Juried Exhbn. 1st prize, Asheville Art Mus., 1993; fellow, Roswell Mus. and Art Ctr., Roswell, N.Mex., 1985, 1991, Ucross Found. Residency Program, Wyo., 1986. Democrat. Unitarian Universalist. Achievements include development of original style of painting juxtaposing abstract brush marks with hyperrealistic trompe l'oeil illusionism; original style of cutout paintings. Avocations: hiking, tennis. Office: Dept of Art Univ of NC Asheville One University Heights Asheville NC 28804 Home Phone: 828-669-9202; Office Phone: 828-251-6880. Business E-Mail: rtynes@unca.edu.

TYNG, ANNE GRISWOLD, architect; b. Kuling, Kiangsi, China, July 14, 1920; d. Walworth and Ethel Atkinson (Arens) T.; 1 child, Alexandra Stevens. AB, Radcliffe Coll., 1942; M of Architecture, Harvard U., 1944; PhD, U. Pa., 1975. Assoc. Stonorov & Kahn, Architects, 1945-47; assoc. Louis I. Kahn Architect, 1947-73; pvt. practice architecture Phila., 1973—; adj. assoc. prof. architecture U. Pa. Grad. Sch. Fine Arts, 1968-96. Assoc. cons. architect Phila. Planning Commn. and Phila. Redevel. Plan, 1954; vis. disting. prof. Pratt Inst., 1979-81, vis. critic architecture, 1969; vis. critic architecture Rensselaer Poly. Inst., 1969, 78, Carnegie Mellon U., 1970, Drexel U., 1972-73, Cooper Union, 1974-75, U. Tex., Austin, 1976; lectr. Archtl. Assn., London, Xian U., China, Bath U., Eng., Mexico City, Hong Kong U., 1989, Baltic Summer Sch., Architecture and Planning, Tallinn, Estonia, Parnu, Estonia, 1993, Alicante U., Spain, 1997, Barcelona U., Spain, 1997; panel spkr. Nat. Conv. Am. Inst. Architects, N.Y.C., 1988, also univs. throughout U.S. and Can.; asst. leader People to People Archtl. del. to China, 1983; vis. artist Am. Acad., Rome, 1995; spkr. in field. Subject of films Anne G. Tyng at Parsons Sch. of Design, 1972, Anne G. Tyng at U. of Minn., 1974, Connecting, 1976, Forming the Future, 1977; interview by Robert Kirkbride, Form is Number and Number is Form, 2005; work included in Smithsonian Travelling Exhbn., 1979-81, 82, Louis I. Kahn: In the Realm of Architecture, 1990-94, Mus. Contemporary Art Travelling Exhbn., L.A., 1998—; author, editor: Louis Kahn to Anne Tyng, The Rome Letters 1953-1954, 1997; contbr. articles to profl. publs.; prin. works include Walworth Tyng Farmhouse (Hon. mention award Phila. chpt. AIA 1953); builder (with G. Yanchenko) Probability Pyramid, 1984. Fellow, Graham Found. for Advanced Study in Fine Arts, 1965, 1979—81. Fellow AIA (Brunner grantee N.Y. chpt. 1964, 83, dir., mem. exec. bd. dirs. Phila. chpt. 1976-78, John Harbeson Disting. Svc. award Phila. chpt. 1991); mem. Nat. Acad. Design (nat. academician), C.G. Jung Ctr. Phila. (planning com. 1979-97), Form Forum (co-founder, planning com. 1978-85). Democrat. Episcopalian. Home and Office: 501 Via Casitas Apt 907 Greenbrae CA 94904-1936

TYRANGIEL, JOSH, editor; MA in Am. Studies, Yale U. News prodr. MTV; with Rolling Stone, Vibe; music critic Time mag., NYC, 2001—06; editor Time.com, NYC, 2006—. Office: Time & Life Bldg Rockefeller Ctr 1271 Ave of the Americas New York NY 10020-1393 Office Phone: 212-522-9883. Office Fax: 212-522-0003. E-mail: josh_tyrangiel@timemagazine.com.

TYREE, ALAN DEAN, clergyman; b. Kansas City, Mo., Dec. 14, 1929; s. Clarence Tillman and Avis Ora (Gross) T.; m. Gladys Louise Omohundro, Nov. 23, 1951; children: Lawrence Wayne, Jonathan Tama, Sharon Avis. BA, U. Iowa, 1950; postgrad., U. Mo.-Columbia, 1956-58, U. Mo.-Kansas City, 1961-62. Ordained to ministry Cmty. of Christ, 1947. Appointee min., Lawrence, Kans., 1950-52; mission adminstr. (Mission Sanito), French Polynesia, 1953-64; regional adminstr. Denver, 1964-66; mem. Council Twelve Apostles, Independence, Mo., 1966-82, sec., 1980-82, mem. First Presidency, 1982-92; ret. First Presidency, 1992; pastor East 39th Street Congregation Cmty. of Christ, Independence, 2000—02. Mem. Joint Coun. and Bd. Appropriations, 1966-92; originator music appreciation broadcasts Radio Tahiti, 1962-64, Mission Sanito Radio Ministry, 1960-64; instr. Music/Arts Inst., 1992-2005, Met. C.C.'s, 1994-2005. Editor: Cantiques des Saints French-Tahitian hymnal, 1965, Exploring the Faith: A Study of Basic Christian Beliefs, 1987; mem. editing com.: Hymns of the Saints, 1981; author: The Gospel Graced by a People: A Biography of Persons in Tahiti, 1993, Evan Fry: Proclaimer of Good News, 1995, Priesthood: For Other's Sake, 1996, God: Getting to Know the Unknown, 1998. Bd. dirs. Outreach Internat. Found., 1979-82, mem. corp. body, 1982-92; mem. corp. body Independence Regional Health Ctr., 1982-92, v.p., 1983-92, bd. dirs., 1984-93; mem. bd. publs. Herald House, 1984-92; mem. corp. body Restoration Trail Found., 1982-92; chmn. Temple Art Com., 1988-94; bd. dirs. Independence Symphony Orch., 1992-96, pres., 1995-96; mem. human rels. commn. city of Independence, 1995-97, chmn., 1996-97. Recipient Elbert A. Smith Meml. award for publ. articles, 1968, 72 Mem. Phi Beta Kappa, Phi Eta Sigma. Home and Office: 3408 S Trail Ridge Dr Independence MO 64055 Office Phone: 816-373-8151. E-mail: adtyree@gmail.com.

TYREE, JAMES C., insurance company executive; b. 1957; m. Eve Tyree; 3 children. BS in Finance, Ill. State U., 1978, MBA, 1980. With Mesirow Ins. Svcs. Inc., Chgo., 1980—, chmn., CEO, 1994—. Mem. Juv. Diabetes Rsch. Found. Internat.; bd trustee Roosevelt Univ.; bd. dirs. Illinois State U. Found., Saint Xavier U., Marist High Sch.; chmn. bd. City Colleges of Chgo. Named Person of the Year, Juv. Diabetes Rsch. Found., 2004; recipient E. Burton Mercier Service award, Illinois State U., 2000, Coll. of Business Alumni Hall of Fame, 2003, Disting. Alumni award, 2005. Mem.: Exec. Club, Econ. Club. Office: Mesirow Ins Svcs Inc 350 N Clark St Chicago IL 60610-4712

TYRL, PAUL, mathematics professor, researcher; b. Prague, Czech Rep., Dec. 24, 1951; came to U.S., 1970, naturalized, 1978; s. Vladimir Tyrl and Marta Kocian. BA with honors, N.J. City U., 1977, MA, 1980; EdD, Rutgers U., 1987. Cert. tchr. secondary edn., higher edn. N.J. quality contr. Agfa-Perutz, Munich, 1969—70; technician AT&T, Kearny, NJ, 1970—73; acquisition libr. N.J. City U., 1973—74, supr. post office, 1974—76, dir. math. lab., instr. math., 1976—80; instr. math. Hudson County C.C., NJ, 1980—82, assoc. prof., coord. math., 1982—84; prof., chmn. math., acad. coord., curriculum dir. Sch. New Resources-New Rochelle Coll., NYC, 1984—. Rschr. Rutgers U., New Brunswick, N.J., 1980—; cons. Jersey City Bd. Edn., N.J., 1982—. Contbr. articles to profl. jours. Recipient Commemorative medal of honor, 1986. Mem. AAAS, ASCD, Nat. Coun. Tchrs. Math. (reviewer and referee), N.Y. Acad. Scis., Am. Ednl. Rsch. Assn., Math. Assn. Am., Am. Math. Assn. 2-Yr. Colls., Am. Math. Soc., Am. Mus. Natural History, Nat. Geog. Soc., Nat. Wildlife Fedn., Smithsonian Instn. Roman Catholic. Achievements include research in math. anxiety and math. problem solving.

TYRRELL, COLE BROOKS, music educator; BA, MA, Mich. State U., East Lansing, 1974. Choir dir. Benton Harbor Pub. Sch., Mich., 1969—78, Whitehall Pub. Schs., Mich., 1978—89, South Haven Pub. Schs., Mich., 1989—. Mem. adj. faculty Lake Mich. Coll., Benton Harbor, 1976—78; dir. White Lake Madrigals, Whitehall, 1982—89, Lakeland Choral Soc., St. Joseph, Mich., 1990—2000. Author: (music text) Rhythmic Sight Reading Made Easy, 2000, (music text) Sight Reading: The Fixed Do Method, 2001. Named Regional Coach of Yr., Mich. HS Athletic Assn., 1995, Wal-Mart Tchr. of Yr., S.W. Mich. Wal-Mart, 2000; recipient Carolyn Leep scholarship, Mich. Sch. Vocal Music Assn., 1994. Mem.: Nat. Assn. Tchrs. Singing, Music Educator's Nat. Conf., Am. Choral Dir.'s Assn. (life). Office: South Haven HS 600 Elkenburg St South Haven MI 49090-1999

TYRRELL, D. LORNE J., university dean; Dean U. Alberta Faculty Medicine and Dentistry, Edmonton, Canada, 1994—; dir. Glaxo Heritage Research Institute. Officer of the Order of Canada Govt. of Canada, 2002. Recipient ASTech award for innovation and science, Kaplan award for excellence in research, Prix Galien Canada medal for research, Gold medal, The Canadian Liver Foundation, 2000, Alberta Order of Excellence, Province of Alberta, 2000. Office: Dept Medical Microbiology & Immunology Univ Alberta 606 Heritage Medical Rsch Ctr Edmonton AB T6G 2S2 Canada

TYRRELL, GERALD GETTYS, banker; b. Canton, China, Dec. 27, 1938; came to U.S., 1940. s. Gerald Fraser and Virginia Lee (Gettys) T.; m. Jane Haldeman, June 1961 (div. Aug. 1975); children: Gerald F., Jane N., Robert M.; m. Elizabeth Ann Drautman, Mar. 31, 1978. BA, Yale U., 1960; MA, Rutgers U., 1971. Cert. real estate financier. With 1st Nat. Bank of Louisville, 1961—89, sr. v.p., 1975—81, exec. v.p., 1981—89; pres., chmn. Churchill Mortgage Corp., 1975—77; chief fin. cons. City of Louisville Office of Downtown Devel., 1989—2000; exec. v.p. Univ. Group, Consultants for Bus., Prospect, 2000—06, assoc., 2006—. Vice chmn. bd. dirs. Porcelain Metals Corp., 2001—06; assoc. Venture Resource Bus. Brokers, 2006—; adv. bd. Skyway LLC, 2007—. Author: A Positive Approach to Financing Black Business, 1972 Trustee, treas. Patton Mus., Ft. Knox, Ky., 1970—96; mem. exec. bd. Boy Scouts Am., 1983—; bd. dirs. The Louisville Orch., 1984—90, Crane Ho., The Asia Inst., 1988—, pres., 1995—97; bd. dirs., chmn. fin. com. Glassworks Found., Inc., 2001—03; bd. dirs. Thomas Merton Found., 2003—05. Served to capt. US Army, 1960—68. Recipient Disting. Service Ribbon Ky. Nat. Guard, 1966 Mem. Robert Morris Assocs., Nat. Soc. Real Estate Fin. (bd. govs), Soc. Colonial Wars Commonwealth Ky. (treas. 1970-89, sec. 1996-99, gov. 2000-05), Gen. Soc. Colonial Wars (treas. gen. 2004-07, lt. gov. gen. 2007—), Louisville Country Club, Pendennis Club. Democrat. Avocations: fine wines, tennis. Office Phone: 502-458-2661. Personal E-mail: betsyandgerald@aol.com.

TYRRELL, JOSEPH MORTEN, retired history professor; b. Kirkland Lake, Ontario, Can., Sept. 19, 1927; s. George Carey and Dora Madeline Joslin Tyrrell; m. Margaret Bell Smith, Dec. 17, 1955; children: Anne Katherine Mary Tyrell, Joseph Douglas George Tyrell, Diana J.B. Tyrell Suchla. BA, U. Toronto, Can., 1950; diplome in French, U. Rennes, France, 1951; MA, U. Toronto, Can., 1955; PhD, Emory U., Atlanta, 1961. Acting asst. prof. Coll. Charleston, SC, 1958—59; asst. prof. Old Dominion U., Norfolk, Va., 1959—79, prof. emeritus of history, 1984—. Author: A History of the Estates of Poitou, 1968, Louis XI (#82 in Twayne World Leaders Series), 1980; contbr. articles to encys., to profl. jours. Mem.: Mediaeval Acad. of Am., Am. Hist. Assn. Episcopalian.

TYRRELL, ROBERT EMMETT, JR., editor-in-chief, writer; b. Chgo., Dec. 14, 1943; s. R. Emmett and Patricia (Rogers) T.; m. Judy Mathews Tyrrell, Feb. 12, 1972 (div. Dec. 1989); children: Patrick, Kathryn, Anne; m. Jeanne Hauch Tyrrell, May 23, 1998. BA, Ind. U., 1965, MA, 1967. Founder, editor-in-chief The Am. Spectator, Arlington, Va., 1967—. Chmn. Am. Alternative Found., Inc., Arlington, Va., 1967—; adj. fellow Hudson Inst. Author: Public Nuisances, 1979, The Liberal Crack-Up, 1984, The Conservative Crack-up, 1992, Boy Clinton: The Political Biography, 1996, (with anonymous author) The Impeachment of William Jefferson Clinton, 1997, Madame Hillary: The Dark Road to the White House, 2004; The Clinton Crack-Up: The Boy President's Life After the White House, 2007; editor: Network News Treatment of the 1972 Democratic Presidential Candidates, 1972, The Future That Doesn't Work, 1977, Orthodoxy, 1987; writer nationally syndicated polit. column; contbg. editor: The New York Sun. Recipient Am. Eagle award Invest in Am. Coun., 1977; named Greatest Pub. Svc. Performed by an American 35 Years or Under award Am. Inst. for Pub. Svc., 1977, Ten Most Outstanding Young Men in Am., Jaycees, 1978. Roman Catholic. Avocations: handball, fishing, listening to classical music, reading. Office: The American Spectator 1611 N Kent St Arlington VA 22201

TYSOE, RONALD W., investment banker, former retail executive; b. Vancouver, British Columbia; married; 4 children. Degree in commerce, U. of British Columbia1, 1976; degree in law, University of British Columbia, 1978. Sr. dir. of adminstrn. to sr. dir. corp. adminstrn. to sr. dir. of fin. to v.p. corp. develop., 1981—86; v.p., treas., prin. fin. officer Allied Stores Corp., 1986—88; exec. v.p. of corp. develop. Campeau Corp., 1987—90; pres. Campeau U.S., 1988—90; CFO Federated Dept. Stores, 1990—97, vice chair, fin. and real estate, 1990—2006; adv. Perella Weinberg Partners LP, NYC, 2006—. Bd. dirs. Federated Dept. Stores, 1988—2005, E.W. Scripps Co., 1996—, Gt. Am. Fin. Resources, Inc. Office: Perella Weinberg Partners LP 767 Fifth Ave New York NY 10153 *

TYSON, CYNTHIA HALDENBY, academic administrator; b. Scunthorpe, Lincolnshire, Eng., July 2, 1937; came to U.S., 1959; d. Frederick and Florence Edna (Stacey) Haldenby; children: Marcus James, Alexandra Elizabeth. BA, U. Leeds, Eng., 1958, MA, 1959, PhD, 1971; DHL (hon.), Mary Baldwin Coll., 2003, Queens U., Charlotte, 2006. Lectr. Brit. Council, Leeds, 1959; faculty U. Tenn., Knoxville, 1959-60, Seton Hall U., South Orange, NJ, 1963-69; faculty, v.p. Queens Coll., Charlotte, NC, 1969-85; pres. Mary Baldwin Coll., Staunton, Va., 1985—2003, pres. emerita, 2003—; pres. Robert Haywood Morrison Found., 2002—. Pres. adv. cir. Queens U., Charlotte, NC, 2005—; WDAV radio adv. bd. Davidson (NC) Coll., 2005—. Contbr. articles to profl. jours. Mem. Va. Internat. Trade Commn., Richmond, 1987; trustee Am. Frontier Culture Mus., Va.; mem. Va. Lottery Bd., 1987-94; chair selection com. State of Va. Rhodes Scholarship Competition, 1993-97; bd. dirs. Cmty. Found. Staunton, Augusta County and Waynesboro, 1993-98; mem. adv. bd. WDAV Radio of Davidson Coll., 2005—; mem. pres.'s adv. cir. Queens U. of Charlotte, NC, 2005—. Fulbright scholar, 1959; Ford Found. grantee Harvard U., 1981; Shell Oil scholar Harvard U., 1982. Mem.: Assn. Presbyn. Colls. and Univs. (bd. dirs. 1998), So. Assn. Colls. and Schs. (vice chair 1998, pres.-elect 2001, pres. 2002), Assn. Va. Colls. and Univs. (pres. 1997—98), So. Assn. Colls. for Women (pres. 1980—81), Mary Baldwin Coll. (hon.), Phi Beta Kappa. Republican. Office: Robert Haywood Morrison Found 1373 East Morehead St Ste 2 Charlotte NC 28204-2979

TYSON, H. MICHAEL, retired bank executive; b. Houston, Aug. 16, 1938; s. Howard Ellis and Myrle (Daunoy) T.; m. Judith O. Gilbert, June 24, 1960; children: H. Michael II, Michelle Lee. BBA cum laude, U. Tex., 1962; postgrad., Rutgers U., 1974. Personnel mgr. Foods div. Anderson Clayton Co., Dallas, 1962-70; exec. v.p. adminstrn. Tex. Commerce Bancshares, Houston, 1970-79; v.p. fin. and adminstrn., chief fin. officer, dir. Houston Chronicle Pub. Co., 1979-87; vice chmn., dir. Tex. Commerce Bank-Houston; exec. v.p., exec. trust officer Tex. Commerce Bancshares, 1987-95. Dir. Paranet Inc., Assoc. Bldg. Svcs., MCG/Dulworth Inc., Kanaly Trust Co. Bd. dirs. Sam Houston coun. Boy Scouts Am., Houston Livestock Show & Rodeo, Houston Festival Found.; trustee McCullough Found., W.A. Smith Found.; chmn. The Houston Parks Bd. Served with USMCR, 1961-67. Mem. Houston C. of C. (com. chmn.), Pers. Round Table, Am. Newspaper Pub. Assn., Houston Indsl. Rels. Group, Fin. Execs. Inst. (bd. dirs.), Internat. Newspaper Fin. Execs., Houston Club (dir., pres.), River Oaks Country Club (dir.), Houston Yacht Club (dir.). Methodist. E-mail: hmtyson@sbcglobal.net.

TYSON, JOHN H., food products executive; b. Springdale, Ark., Sept. 5, 1953; s. Don and Jean Tyson; m. Kimberly McCoy; children: John Randal, Olivia Laine. BBA, So. Meth. U., 1975. Complex mgr. N.C. area Tyson Foods, Inc., Springdale, Ark., v.p. mktg. corp. accounts, purchasing mgr., retail sales mgr. N.E. states, pres. beef and pork divsn.; pres., chmn. Tyson Foods Inc., Springdale, 1998-00, pres., chmn., CEO, 2000—01, chmn., CEO, 2001—06, chmn., 2006—. Polit. liaison to Washington and Little Rock Tyson Foods, Inc. Bd. dirs. Area United Way; supporter Farm Aid; vol. activities for well-being and edn. of Ark. children. Named Man of Yr., Ark. Poultry Industry, 1994. Mem.: Ark. Poultry Fedn. (past pres.), Am. Meat Inst., Nat. Assn. Mfrs. Avocations: deep sea fishing, music, golf. Office: Tyson Foods Inc 2210 W Oaklawn Dr Springdale AR 72762-6999 *

TYSON, JOSEPH B., JR., lawyer; b. Roanoke Rapids, NC, Feb. 19, 1949; AB, U. N.C., 1971; JD, U. Va., 1977. Bar: N.Y. 1978, Wis. 1979. Ptnr. Foley & Lardner LLP, Milw., chmn. bus. law dept. Mem. ABA, State Bar Wis., Phi Beta Kappa, U. Club (officer & dir.). Office: Foley & Lardner LLP Firstar Ctr 777 E Wisconsin Ave Ste 3800 Milwaukee WI 53202-5367 Office Phone: 414-297-5631. Office Fax: 414-297-4900. Business E-Mail: jtyson@foley.com.

TYSON, KATHLEEN HAYHURST, educational association administrator; b. Oakland, Calif., Mar. 6, 1947; d. Amos Ira and Marie Gertrude (Sanchez) Hayhurst; 1 child, Kathryn Elena. BA, San Jose State U., Calif., 1971; MA, St. Mary's Coll., Moraga, Calif., 1995. Cert. tchr. Calif., tchr. learning handicapped Calif., resource specialist Calif., in addiction studies. Tchr. elem. Richmond Sch. Dist., Calif., 1972—79; tchr. learning handicapped Richmond Elem. Sch. Dist., Calif., 1979—81; resource specialist West Contra Costa Sch. Dist., Pinole and Hercules, Calif., 1992—. Software designer Beck Tech., Berkeley, Calif., 1991—92; coord. At Risk Program Dept. Drug and Alcohol, Hercules, Calif., 1994—97; dir. Reading Intervention Program Elem. Schs., Hercules; instr. lang. arts Calif. State U., Hayward San Pablo; ednl. cons., intervention tutor, Orinda; supr. student tchrs. San Francisco State U., Hercules, 2005. Author: (Intervention Program) Star Trak, 1989—92, (Reading Intervention program) Firebear, 1995—2003; editor: (book) Habitats, 1998. Organizer, fund raiser Tsunami Toy Drive Orinda Sch., Hercules, 2005; facilitator, instr. Parent Workshop for At Risk Students, Hercules, 1996—97; literacy trainer staff training workshops Hercules, 1998—99; min. Unity Ch., 1999—, spiritual mentor, 1997—99; amb. People to People, Spokane, Wash., 2000. Recipient You Make a Difference award, Contra Costa County, 1991, Cert. Excellence in Svc., Contra Cost. County, 1992. Mem.: Nat. Alliance Mental Health, Calif. Reading Assn., Coun. Exceptional Children, Calif. Tchrs. Assn. Avocations: gardening, reading, travel, tennis. Office: West Contra Costa Sch Dist 1616 Pheasant Dr Hercules CA 94563

TYSON, KENNETH ROBERT THOMAS, surgeon, educator; b. Houston, July 30, 1936; s. Howard Ellis and Myrle Henrietta (Daunoy) T.; m. Sue Ann Delahoussaye, Nov. 20, 1971; children: Deborah, Kenneth, Michael, Jill. BA, U. Tex., 1956; MD, U. Tex. Med. Br., 1960. Diplomate: Am. Bd. Surgery, Am. Bd. Thoracic Surgery. Intern Ind. U. Med. Ctr., Indpls., 1960-61; resident in gen. and thoracic surgery Ind. U. Med. Center, 1961-66; resident in pediatric surgery Children's Hosp. Med. Center, Boston, 1966-67; chief pediatric gen., thoracic surgery U. Tex. Med. Br., Galveston, 1967-80, asst. prof. surgery, 1967-71, asso. prof., 1971-75, prof., 1975-80; surgeon-in-chief Child Health Center, 1974-80; clin. prof. surgery U. Calif., Davis, 1980-91, U. Tex. Med. Br., Galveston, 1991—. Contbr. articles to profl. jours. Fellow A.C.S., Am. Acad. Pediatrics, Am. Coll. Cardiology; mem. Am. Assn. Thoracic Surgery, Soc. Surgery Alimentary Tract, So. Thoracic Surg. Assn., Am. Pediatric Surg. Assn., Soc. Univ. Surgeons, So. Surg. Assn., Pacific Coast Surg. Assn., Sigma Xi, Alpha Omega Alpha, Delta Kappa Epsilon, Alpha Kappa Kappa. Episcopalian. Office: U Tex Med Br Dept Pediatric Surgery Galveston TX 77550 Home: 5717 Louise Ln Austin TX 78757-4418

TYSON, KIRK W. M., management consultant; b. Jackson, Mich., July 2, 1952; s. George Carlton and Wilma Marion (Barnes) Tyson; m. Terri Lynn Long, Mar. 25, 2000; 1 child, Gabriel 1 stepchild, Robert. BBA, Western Mich. U., 1974; MBA, DePaul U., Chgo., 1982. CPA, Ill.; cert. mgmt. cons. Bus. cons. Arthur Andersen & Co., Chgo., 1974-84; v.p. cons. First Chgo. Corp., 1984; chmn. Kirk Tyson Internat., 1984-2000; pres. The Perpetual Strategist, Chgo., 2001—. Adj. prof. coll. bus. Write State U., 2007—. Author: Business Planning, 1982, Business Intelligence: Putting It All Together, 1986, Competitor Intelligence: Manual and Guide, 1990, Competition in the 21st Century, 1996, The Complete Guide to Competitive Intelligence, 1998, 4th rev. edit. 2006. Pres., Chgo. Jr. Assn. Commerce and Industry Found., 1977-79; active Easter Seals Soc., 1977, Am. Blind Skiing Found., 1977-78, Jr. Achievement, 1976-77, United Way Met. Chgo., 1979-80, Urban Gateways, 1975; Rep. precinct committeeman Downers Grove Twp., 1985-88; treas. St. Charles H.S. Football Booster club, 1994-95. Fellow Soc. Competitive Intelligence Profls. (Meritorious award, 2005); mem. Rotary Club of Springboro (asst. dist. gov., 2005-), Alpha Kappa Psi (Disting. Alumni Svc. award 1974-86, named Alumnus of Yr. 2003). Office: The Perpetual Strategist 30 S Wacker Dr Ste 2200 Chicago IL 60606-7456 Office Phone: 312-466-5733. Business E-Mail: kirk.tyson@perpetualstrategist.com.

TYSON, LAURA D'ANDREA, economics professor, former dean, federal official; b. Bayonne, NJ, June 28, 1947; BA, Smith Coll., 1969; PhD, MIT, 1974. Asst. prof. econ. Princeton U., 1974—77; prof. econ. U. Calif., Berkeley, 1977—2001; prof. econ. & bus. adminstrn. Haas Sch. Bus., U. Calif., Berkeley, 1990—2001, 2007—, dean, 1998—2001; chmn. Coun. Econ. Advisors Exec. Office of the Pres., Washington, 1993-95; nat. econ. adv. to Pres. Nat. Econ. Coun., Washington, 1995-96; dean London Sch. Bus., 2002—06; dir. LECG, LLC, Emeryville, Calif., 2007—. Bd. dirs. Eastman Kodak Co., 1997—, Morgan Stanley, 1997—, 24/7 Customer, 2007, Coun. Fgn. Rels., 1997; bd. trustees Brookings Instn., 2003—; econ. viewpoint columnist Business Week mag., 1997—2006. Editor: (with John Zysman) American Industry in International Competition, 1983, (with Ellen Comisso) Power, Purpose and Collective Choice: Economic Strategy in Socialist States, 1986, (with William Dickens and John Zysman) The Dynamics of Trade and Employment, 1988, (with Chalmers Johnson and John Zysman) Politics and Productivity: The Real Story of How Japan Works, 1989, Who's Bashing Whom? Trade Conflict in High Technology Industries, 1992 Mem. Nat. Bipartisan Commn. Future Medicare, 1997—99. Office: Haas Sch Bus U Calif Berkeley 545 Student Services Bldg #1900 Berkeley CA 94720 also: LECG LLC 2000 Powell St Ste 600 Emeryville CA 94608 Business E-Mail: tyson@haas.berkeley.edu.

TYSON, MIKE G., boxer; b. NYC, June 30, 1966; s. John Kilpatrick and Lorna Tyson; m. Robin Givens, Feb. 7, 1988 (div. Feb. 14, 1989); m. Monica Turner Apr. 19, 1997 (div. Jan. 13, 2003); 2 children. Defeated Trevor Berbick to win World Boxing Coun. Heavyweight Title, Nov. 1986; defeated James Smith to win World Boxing Assn. Heavyweight Title, 1987; defeated Tony Tucker to win Internat. Boxing Fedn. Heavyweight Title, Aug. 1987; defeated Michael Spinks to win Internat. Boxing Fedn. Heavyweight Title, June 1988; undisputed heavyweight champion 1988-90 (defeated by James "Buster" Douglas); defeated Frank Bruno to win WBC Heavyweight Title, 1996; defeated by Evander Holyfield, 1996; won over Frans Botha, 1998. Commentator for Showtime. Film appearances: Crocodile Dundee in Los Angeles, 2001; Rocky Balboa, 2006. Hon. sports chmn. Cystic Fibrosis Assn. N.Y., 1987—, Young Adult Inst., N.Y.C., 1987—. Achievements include being the youngest heavyweight champion in history. *

TYSON, NEIL DEGRASSE, astrophysicist, museum director; b. NYC; married; 2 children. BA in Physics, Harvard U., 1980; MA in Astronomy, U. Tex., Austin, 1983; PhD in Astrophysics, Columbia U., 1991; DS (hon.), CUNY, 1997, Ramapo Coll., 2000, Dominican Coll., 2000, U. Richmond, 2001, Bloomfield Coll., 2002. Postdoctoral rsch. assoc. dept. astrophysics Princeton U., 1991—94; staff scientist Am. Mus.-Hayden Planetarium, NYC, 1994—95, acting dir., 1995—96; chair dept. astrophysics Am. Mus. Natural Hist., NYC, 1997—99, Frederick P. Rose dir. Hayden Planetarium, 1996—, rsch. assoc., 2003. Contbr. articles to profl. jours., chapters to books; author: Merlin's Tour of the Universe, 1989, Universe Down to Earth, 1994, Just Vis. This Planet, 1998, The Sky is Not the Limit: Adventures of an Urban Astrophysicist, 2000, Death by Black Hole: And Other Cosmic Quandaries, 2007; co-author: One Universe: At Home in the Cosmos, 2000 (Sci. Writing award, Am. Inst. Physics, 2001), Origins: Fourteen Billion Years of Cosmic Hist., 2004; co-editor: Cosmic Frontiers: Astronomy at the Cutting Edge, 2001. Named Sexiest Astrophysicist Alive, People Mag., 2000; named one of 40 under 40, Craines Mag., 1996, The World's Most Influential People, TIME Mag., 2007; named to The Ebony Power 150, Ebony mag., 2007; recipient Medal of Honor, Columbia U., 2001, Disting. Pub. Svc. medal, NASA. Fellow: NY Acad. Scis.; mem.: Nat. Soc. Black Physicists, Internat. Planetarium Soc., Astron. Soc. Pacific, Am. Phys. Soc., Am. Astron. Soc. Office: Dept Astrophysics American Museum Natural History Central Park W at 79th St New York NY 10024 E-mail: tyson@amnh.org. *

TYSON, PETER, editor-in-chief; b. Bryn Mawr, Pa., May 25, 1960; s. Noel Jon Tyson and Patricia McCurdy; m. Melissa Banta (div.); children: Olivia, Nicholas 1 stepchild, Christopher Legare. BA in English, Trinity Coll., Hartford, Conn., 1982. Asst. editor Omni Mag., NYC, 1983—86; sr. staff writer Interleaf, Inc., Boston, 1988—89; mng. editor Earthwatch Mag., Watertown, Mass., 1989—96, sr. editor, 1996—98; contbg. editor Tech. Rev. Mag., Cambridge, Mass., 1993—97; editor-in-chief Nova Online, Boston, 1998—. Author: Acid Rain, 1992, Groucho Marx, 1995, Vincent Van Gogh, 1996, The Eighth Continent: Life, Death and Discovery in the Lost World of Madagascar, 2000, 2001; contbr. articles to mags., newspapers. Mem.: New Eng. Sci. Writers, Nat. Assn. Sci. Writers. Avocations: travel, mountaineering, fly fishing, rowing, tennis. Home: 45A Fayerweather St Cambridge MA 02138 Office: WGBH Ednl Found 1 Guest St Boston MA 02135 Office Phone: 617-300-4371. Office Fax: 617-300-1003. Business E-Mail: peter_tyson@wgbh.org.

TYSON LI, LAURA, journalist; d. Kenneth W. and Roberta D. Tyson; m. Richard W. Li, 2000; children: Sienna Li, Isabella Li. BA, Dartmouth Coll., Hanover. Taipei corr. Financial Times, Taipei, Taiwan, 1994—98; bureau chief Knight-Ridder Fin. News, Taipei, Taiwan, 1993—94; reporter South Asia Morning Post, Hong Kong, 1992—93. Author: Madame Chiang Kai-shek: China's External First Lady, 2006. Fundraising com. mem. Shudrig Wen Sch., N.Y.C. Mem.: Overseas Press Club, Asia Soc., Am. Hist. Assn.

TYTELL, JOHN, literature educator, writer; b. Antwerp, Belgium, May 17, 1939; arrived in U.S., 1941; s. Charles and Lena (Gano) T.; m. Mellon Gregori, May 28, 1967. BA, CCNY, 1961; MA, NYU, 1963, PhD, 1968. Grad. reader NYU, 1963-67; lectr. Queens Coll., NYC, 1963-68, assoc. prof., 1968-73, 1973-76, prof. English, 1977—; exec. editor Am. Book Rev., 1979—; vis. prof. Rutgers U., 1980, U. Paris, 1983; cons. Nat. Humanities Faculty, Ga., 1978—. Author: The American Experience, 1970, Naked Angels, 1976, 3d edit., 2006, Ezra Pound: The Solitary Volcano, 1987, 2d edit., 2004, Passionate Lives, 1991, The Living Theatre: Art, Exile and Outrage, 1995, Paradise Outlaws: Remembering the Beats, 1999, Reading New York,, 2003; contbr. articles to mags. including Am. Scholar, Partisan Rev., Vanity Fair, Fame. Fellow, NEH, 1974. Home: 69 Perry St New York NY 10014-3297 Office: Queens Coll Flushing NY 11367

TYTLER, LINDA JEAN, emergency manager, retired state legislator; b. Rochester, NY, Aug. 31, 1947; d. Frederick Easton and Marian Elizabeth (Allen) Tytler; m. George Stephen Dragnich, May 2, 1970 (div. July 1976); m. James Douglas Fisher, Oct. 7, 1994. AS, So. Va. Coll., Buena Vista, Va., 1967. Spl. asst. to Congressman John Buchanan, Washington, 1971-75; legis. analyst US Senator Robert Griffin, Washington, 1975-77; ops. supr. Pres. Ford Com., Washington, 1976; office mgr. US Senator Pete Domenici Re-election, Albuquerque, 1977; pub. info. officer S.W. Cmty. Health Svc., Albuquerque, 1978-83; cons. pub. rels. and mktg. Albuquerque, 1983-84; account exec. Rick Johnson & Co., Inc., Albuquerque, 1983-84; dir. mktg. and comm. St. Joseph Healthcare Corp., 1984-88; mktg. and bus. devel. cons., 1987-90; dir. comm. and pub. affairs Def. Avionics Systems Honeywell Inc., 1990-2000, dir. comms., 2000—01; dep. dir. pub. affairs Los Alamos Nat. Lab., 2001—05, group leader emergency response instl. svcs., 2006—. Capt. N.Mex. Mounted Patrol, 1998—2002; bd. dirs. Jobs for N.Mex., N.Mex chpt. ARC, Albuquerque, 1984; chmn. legis. campaign com. Rep. Com.; co-chair del. to China Am. Coun. Young Polit. Leaders, 1988; mem. N.Mex. Ho. of Reps., Santa Fe, 1983—95, vice chmn. appropriations and fin. com., 1985—86, chmn. Rep. Caucus, 1985—88. Recipient award, N.Mex. Advt. Fedn., Albuquerque, 1981, 1982, 1985, 1986, 1987, Honeywell Cmty. Svc. award, 1997. Mem.: N.Mex. Assn. Commerce and Industry (bd. dirs., exec. com. 1996—2002), Am. Mktg. Assn., Soc. Hosp. Planning and Mktg., Nat. Advt. Fedn., Am. Soc. Hosp. Pub. Rels. (cert.). Republican.

TYURIN, MIKHAIL, cosmonaut; b. Kolomna, Russia, Mar. 2, 1960; m. Tatiana Anatoleyvna; 1 child, Alexandra. Grad. with a degree in engring. and specialization in creating math. models related to mechanical flight, Moscow Aviation Inst., 1984. Engr. Energia Corp.; began cosmonaut tng., 1993; started tng. as flight engr. for Expedition-3 crew, 1998. Served as back-up crew mem. for the first Internat. Space Station (ISS) mission STS-105 Discovery, 2001; Soyuz comdr., flight engr. on the Expedition-14 mission to the Internat. Space Station, 06; performed spacewalk to repair antenna on Russian cargo ship, 07. first person to strike a lightweight golf ball from outside international space station in a promotional stunt for golf club manufacturer E21 Golf on November 22, 2006. *

TYUS, GORDON, graphics designer, educator; b. Salinas, Calif., Dec. 9, 1966; s. Bobby and Joan Tyus; life ptnr. Jamie Aronson. BA in Graphic Comm. magna cum laude, Ea. Wash. U., Cheney, 1989, BS in Design Tech., 1989, MS in Comm., 1993. Instr. tech. graphics Ea. Wash. U., 1990—94; graphic designer City of Spokane, 1991—93; instr. computer aided drafting and design ITT Tech. Inst., Spokane, 1993—96; instr. graphic and interior design Spokane Falls C.C., 1996—97; graphic design specialist Maricopa Assn. Govts., Phoenix, 1997—. Testing coord., cert. proctor Greater Phoenix Mensa, 2005—. Graphic designer (publication) MAG Annual Budget and Work Program (GFOA Disting. Budget Presentation award, 2006), Regional Report: A Resource for Policy Makers in the Maricopa Region (Ariz. Planning Association's Best Regional Plan award, 2005), graphic design and web support (transportation plan public outreach) MAG Regional Transportation Plan (Fed. Hwy. Adminstrn. Leadership award for Regional Transp., 2005), graphic designer (newsletter) MAGAZine (Pub. Rels. Soc. Am. Copper Anvil award Merit, 2001), graphic and web support (domestic violence prevention) Domestic Violence Council Web Site and Safety Plan (Desert Peaks award Public-Private Partnership, 2001), graphic designer (logo, brochure and program) Arizona Alternatives, Clean Fuel for Clean Cities Forum (Valley Forward Environ. Excellence award, 2000), (logo) Safety First. Scholar, Dale Wilson Scholarship Fund, 1985. Mem.: ACLU, Chronic Fatigue Immune Dysfunction Syndrome Assn. Am., Am. Mensa. Avocations: running, video editing, video games, reading. Office: Maricopa Association of Governments 302 N 1st Avenue Suite 300 Phoenix AZ 85003 Home: 4326 E Everett Dr Phoenix AZ 85032 Office Phone: 602-452-5035. Personal E-mail: gtyus@hotmail.com.

TZEKOVA, KRASSIMIRA KRUSTEVA, resident director; d. Svetlinka Tzekova and Tzeko Tzekov. BA in Polit. Sci., U. NH, Durham, 2001; MBA, Franklin Pierce Coll., Rindge, NH, 2005. Legal asst. Swartz and Swartz Law Office, Portland, Maine, 1995—2000; asst. resident dir. U. NH, Durham, 2000—01; resident dir. Colby-Sawyer Coll., New London, NH, 2001—, office of citizenship edn., 2001—06; asst. dir. residence life U. Maine, Farmington, 2006—. Advisor coll. jud. hearing bd. Colby-Sawyer Coll., 2001—. Named Advisor of Yr., Colby-Sawyer Coll., 2005; recipient Maine's Leadership Award, 1997, New Hampshire's Movers and Shakers, U. NH, 2000. Mem.: Student Affairs Adminstr. Higher Edn., Assn. for Student Jud. Affairs, N.E. Assn. Coll. and Univ. Housing Officers, Am. Coll. Pers. Assn., N.E. Assn. Colls., Residence Life Assn. of the Granite State (assoc.; plannnig bd. 2004—05).

TZIMAS, NICHOLAS ACHILLES, orthopedic surgeon, educator; b. Greece, Apr. 18, 1928; arrived in U.S.A., 1955, naturalized, 1960. s. Archilles Nicholas and Evanthia B. (Exarchou) T.; m. Helen J. (Papastylopoulos), Apr. 22, 1958; children: Yvonne and Christina. MD, U. Athens, Greece, 1952. Intern St. Mary's Hosp., Hoboken, NJ, 1955—86; resident in gen. surgery Miscricordia Hosp., NYC; resident in orthopedic surgery Bellevue Hosp., NYC, 1957—60; instr. orthopedic surgery N.Y. U. Sch. Medicine, 1961—63, asst. clin. prof., 1963—65, asso. clin. prof., 1965—71, clin. prof., 1971—. Staff Univ. and Bellevue Hosp.; chief children's orthopedics, 1966; orthopedic cons. Inst. Rehab. Medicine, NYU, 1966, St. Agnes Hosp., White Plains, NY, 1972; advisory com. Bur. Handicapped Children, NYC, 1975; spl. invitations for tchg., Osaka, Japan, 1970, Jerusalem, 1974, São Paolo, Brazil, 1976, Taranto, Italy, 1977, Bari, Italy, 1978, Barquisimeto, Venezuela, 1979, Bogotá, Colombia, 1983, Buenos Aires, Argentina, 1983. Author of articles on spina bifida child mgmt. Served with M.C. Greek Army, 1952-55. Named Ofcl. Knight of Italian Republic, 1979 Fellow Am., Internat. Coll. Surgeons; mem. N.Y. Acad. Medicine, N.Y. State, N.Y. County Med. Soc., Am. Acad. Orthopedic Surgeons, Am. Congress Rehab. Medicine, Am. Acad. Cerebral Palsy. Mem. Greek Orthodox Ch.; Archon of the Ecumenical Patriarchate of Constantinople. Home: 33 Edgewood St Tenafly NJ 07670-2909 Office: 530 1st Ave New York NY 10016-6402 Office Phone: 212-263-7278. Personal E-mail: ntzimas@aol.com. Business E-Mail: nicholasotzimas@med.nyu.edu.

TZITSIKAS, HELENE, retired literature educator; b. Athens, Greece, Apr. 2, 1926; arrived in US, 1944; d. Christos Jean and Evangelia (Chouases) T. BA, Lake Forest Coll., Ill., 1952, MA, Northwestern U., 1954, PhD, 1963. Instr. Rockford (Ill.) Coll., 1962-63, asst. prof., 1963-65; assoc. prof. Hispanic lit. Mich. State U., East Lansing, 1965-71, prof., 1971-91, prof. emerita, 1991—. Author: Santiago Ramón y Cajal-Obra Literaria, 1965, El Pensamiento Español 1898-1899, 1967, Fernando Santiván - Humanista y Literato, 1971, 2d edit., 1985, Dos Revistas Chilenas: Los Diez y Artes y Letras, 1973, El sentimiento ecológico, 1977, La supervivencia existencial de la mujer, 1982, El Quijotismo y la raza en la Generacion de 1898, 1988, Los exiliados argentinos en Montevideo durante la época de Rosas, 1991. Recipient Diana award YWCA, Lansing, Mich., 1988, cert. of employee recognition, 1988. Mem. MLA, AAUP, MLA Am., Am. Assn. Tchrs. Spanish and Portuguese, Univ. Club Mich. State U., Daus. Penelope. Greek Orthodox. Avocations: theater, music, painting, gardening. Office: Mich State U Dept Romance and Classical Langs East Lansing MI 48824 Office Phone: 517-355-8350.

UBBEN, DONALD THOMAS, lawyer; b. Pekin, Ill., May 9, 1946; s. Wilbert Donald and Verna Lanelle (Ducker) U. BA, Furman U., 1968; MA, Baylor U., 1972; JD, U. Va., 1982. Bar: SC 1983, DC Ct. Appeals 1983, US Dist. Ct. DC 1984, US Dist. Ct. SC 1984, US Ct. Appeals (DC, 4th and fed. cirs.) 1984, US Claims Ct. 1984, US Tax. Ct. 1984, Va. 1991. Asst. to sec. for spl. programs HEW, Washington, 1973-75; legis. asst. U.S. Senate, Washington, 1975-77, 81-82; dir. exec. br. liaison U.S. C. of C., Washington, 1977-79. With Legal Svcs. Corp., acting dir. N.Y. regional office, 1984, acting dir. bar rels., 1985; atty. U.S. Dept. of Interior, 1988-91. Del. to county and state Rep. convs., S.C. and Va., 1968-94; alt. delt. Rep. Nat. Conv., 1972, 84, del., 1976; mem. Albemarle County (Va.) Rep. Ctrl. Com., 1981-88, 91—; precinct capt., 1992-93; bd. dirs. Opera Americana, 1990-92, Va. Ctr. Creative Arts, 2006-; bd. dirs. Alexandria Symphony, 1987-90, mem. exec. com., 1988-89, chmn. nominating com., 1988-89, chmn. govt. liaison com., 1989-90, mem. long range planning com., 1988-90. Mem. Nat. Rep. Lawyers Assn., Conservative Network (counsel 1986-87), English Speaking Union (bd. dirs. 1992-98, chmn. membership com. 1992-94, chmn. program com. 1994-96, pres. 1996-98), Albemarle County Geneal. Assn., Greencroft Club (bd. dirs. 1992-94, sec. 1993-94). Republican. Home: PO Box 171 Ivy VA 22945-0171

UBELL, ROBERT NEIL, editor, educator, publishing executive, consultant; b. Bklyn., Sept. 14, 1938; s. Charles and Hilda (Kramer) U.; m. Rosalyn Deutsche, Sept. 24, 1976; children: Jennifer Hayslett, Elizabeth Miller. BA, Bklyn. Coll., 1961; postgrad., Acad. Fine Arts, Rome, Italy, 1959-60, CUNY, 1961-62, Pratt Graphic Arts Workshop, NYC, 1972-73. Assoc. editor Nuclear Industry, Atomic Indsl. Forum, 1962-64; from editor to sr. editor Plenum Pub. Corp., NYC, 1965-70, v.p., editor in chief, 1970-76; editor The Sciences, N.Y. Acad. Scis., NYC, 1976-79; Am. pub. Nature, NYC, 1979-83; founding pub. Nature Biotechnology, 1983; pres., CEO Robert Ubell Assocs., NYC, 1983—97; pres. BioMedNet, Ltd., 1996-97; exec. v.p. Marcel Dekker, Inc., NYC, 1997-99; dir. web-based distance learning Stevens Inst. Tech., Hoboken, NJ, 1999—2001, dean online learning, 2001—03, dean sch. profl. edn., 2004—07; exec. dir. Inst. for the Advancement of Online Learning and Profl. Edn., 2007—. Instr. MIT, 1987, Columbia U. Coll. Physicians and Surgeons, 1987; mem. editl. com. The Scientist, 1987—90; mem. Book Industry Study Group, Inc., 1992; mem. vis. com. Nat. Acad. Press, NRC, NAS, 1986; mem. books subcom. Am. Inst. Physics, 1985—91; mem. awards com. Am. Inst. Physics-US Steel Sci. Writing Awards, 1982—83, Corp. Univ. Xchange, 2006—; mem. publs. com. Am. Inst. Biol. Scis., 1994, NY Acad. Scis., 1976—97; cons. Lotus Devel. Corp., 1987—89, Coalition for Networked Info., 1995—98, Am. Soc. Addiction Medicine, 2003—04; mem. pub. info. com. NAE, 1989—2002; mem. program com. Soc. Scholarly Pub., 1989—91; mem. rev. panel NSF, 2000, 03, Nat. Sci., Math. and Tech. Edn. Digital Libr., 2000, Internat. Opportunities Scientists and Engrs., 2003, Reform Undergrad. Engring. Edn., 2003; distance learning observer Mid. States Commn. on Higher Edn., 2000—04; chair Sloan Found. Greater NYC ALN Conf., 2002; mem. planning com. Breakthrough Thinking in Online Bus. Edn., 2002—03; mem. adv. panel Nat. Rsch. Inst. on Wireless Tech. in Edn. and Industry, 2002; mem. adv. coun. Alliance Expanded Tchr. Preparation CCs; co-host Stevens Views Radio, 2002—06; mem. adv. bd. comm. industry network NJ Tech. Coun., 2002—, Sloan Found. Corp. e-Learning, 2003—04, Sloan Found. Program Com., Sloan C-Conf., 2005—; prin. invesetigator Sloan Greater NYC Online Learning Ctr., 2003—05; co-chair Sloan Workshop Corp.-Acad. Online Learning, 2004; mem. adv. task force Nat. Hwy. Inst. Distance Learning Program; cons. in field; mem. adv. bd. Sci. Learning Through Cyber Resources. Author: (with Marvin Leiner) Children Are the Revolution, 1974; (with Mark Tesoriero) Negotiating Networked Licensing Agreements, 1995, Cost Centers and Measures in the Networked Information Value Chain, 1997, The R&D Economics in the Digital Environment, 1998; editor Nature Directory of Biologicals, 1981, Physics Today Buyer's Guide, 1984-89; exec. editor: Linguistics: The Cambridge Survey, 1987-88, Pre-Med Handbook, 1986, International Encyclopedia of the Social Sciences, Vol. 19, 1991, Encyclopedia of Astronomy and Astrophysics, 1991, Sci. Am. Triumph of Discovery, 1995, Oxford Encyclopedia of Climate and Weather, 1996; cons. editor ISI Press, 1985-87, Am. Inst. of Physics Book Program, 1986-96; Am. Chem. Soc. Book Program, 1989; cons. pub. Computers in Physics, 1987-91; series editor Masters of Modern Physics, 1991-96, Creators of Modern Chemistry, 1994-95, Sci. Am. Focus, 1995-96; mem. editl. bd. ISI Press, 1986-90, Grants Mag., 1981-85, Nonprofit Mgmt. and Fin., 1980-85; editl. dir. Nutrition Advisor, 1998-99; mem. editl. bd. Innovations in End of Life Care, 1999-2003; editl. advisor Cancer Practice, Am. Cancer Soc., 1997-98; contbr. articles to profl. jours. V.p. bd. dirs. Stevens Ctr. Sci. Writings; chmn. bd. Woodword Sch., 1971—74; mem. adv. com. Children's TV Workshop, 1980, Interpool, Inc., 2006; mem. Stevens Ctr. for Sci. Writings, 2006—; v.p. bd. dirs. Parkinson's Walk Found., 2001—, Hekate, 2003—04, Lianyungang Universal Vehicle Mfg. Co., Ltd., 2006—. Mem. AAAS, ASTD, NY Acad. Scis. (mem. publs. com. 1976-97). Office: Stevens Inst Tech Castle Point Hudson Hoboken NJ 07030

UBERALL, HERBERT MICHAEL STEFAN, physicist, researcher; b. Neunkirchen, Austria, Oct. 14, 1931; arrived in U.S., 1953, naturalized, 1963; s. Michael and Stefanie U.; m. Reyna Tosta, 1981; children by previous marriage: Bernadette Chauvallon, Bertrand. PhD, U. Vienna, Austria, 1953, Cornell U., 1956; PhD (honoris causa), U. Le Havre, France, 1987. Staff mem. Signal Corps Labs., Ft. Monmouth, NJ, 1953-54; research asst. Cornell U., 1954-56; research fellow Nuclear Physics Research Lab., U. Liverpool, Eng., 1956-57; Ford Found. fellow CERN, Geneva, 1957-58; research physicist Carnegie Inst. Tech., Pitts., 1958-60; asst. prof. U. Mich., Ann Arbor, 1960-64; assoc. prof. Cath. U. Am., Washington, 1964-65, prof. physics, 1965-94, prof. emeritus, 1994—. Vis. prof. U. Paris VII Jussieu, 1984-85, U. Le Havre, 1990, 92, 94, 96, U. Bordeaux, 1993, 95, U. Aix-Marseille II and Lab. Mech. Acoustics, 1995, Ecole Centrale de Lille, 1997, Tech. U. Denmark, 1998; cons. Naval Rsch. Lab., Washington, 1966-92. Author: Electron Scattering from Complex Nuclei, 1971; co-author: Giant Resonance Phenomena, 1980, Nuclear Pion Photoproduction, 1991; editor: Acoustic Resonance Scattering, 1992; co-editor: Long Distance Neutrino Detection, 1979, Classical and Quantum Dynamics, 1991, Coherent Radiation Sources, 1985, Coherent Radiation Processes in Strong Fields, 1991, Radar Target Imaging, 1994; contbr. 300 articles to profl. jours. Recipient Fgn. medal French Soc. Acoustics, 1996. Fellow (life) IEEE, (life) Am. Phys. Soc., Acoustical Soc. Am., Washington Acad. Scis. (Achievement award 1984); mem. AAUP, Am. Acad. Mech., Electromagnetics Acad., Internat. Union Radio Sci. Office: Catholic U Dept Physics Washington DC 20064-0001 Personal E-mail: uberallh@msn.com.

UBEROI, MAHINDER SINGH, aerospace engineer, researcher; b. Delhi, India, Mar. 13, 1924; arrived in U.S., 1945, naturalized, 1960; s. Kirpal Singh and Sulaksha (Kochar) Uberoi. BS, Punjab U., Lahore, India, 1944; MS, Calif. Inst. Tech., 1946; DEng, Johns Hopkins U., 1952. Registered profl. engr. Mem. faculty U. Mich., Ann Arbor, 1953-63, prof. aerospace engring., 1959-63, vis. prof., 1963—64; prof. U. Colo., Boulder, 1963—2000, chmn. dept. aerospace engring., 1963-75; fellow F. Joint Inst. Lab. Astrophysics, Boulder, 1963-74; rschr., 2004—. Exch. scientist Soviet Acad. Scis., 1966, U.S. Nat. Acad. Scis.; invited prof. U. Que., Canada, 1972—74; vis. scientist Max Planck Inst. Astrophysics, Munich, 1974; hon. rsch. fellow Harvard U., 1975—76. Contbr. articles to profl. jours.; editor: Cosmic Gas Dynamics, 1974. Coun. mem. Ednl. TV Channel 6, Inc., Denver, 1963—66. Guggenheim fellow, Royal Inst. Tech., Sweden, 1958. Mem.: Am. Phys. Soc., Tau Beta Pi. Home: 819 6th St Boulder CO 80302-7418

UBINAS, LUIS A., management consultant; b. 1962; m. Deborah L. Tolman. BA in Govt., Harvard Coll., 1989; MBA, Harvard Bus. Sch. Reporter LA Times, The Wall St. Jour.; asst. to the CEO Honduran beer and soft drink (Coca-Cola) monopoly; mktg. and strategy assignments Booz, Allen, and Hamilton; with McKinsey & Co., San Francisco, 1989—; pres.-elect The Ford Found., NYC, 2007—. Mem. bd. dirs. Digital Coast Roundtable, LA, SteppingStone Found., Boston. Office: McKinsey & Co 55 E Grand St 21st Fl New York NY 10022 Office Phone: 212-446-7000. Office Fax: 212-446-8575. *

UBINGER, JOHN WALTER, JR., lawyer; b. Pitts., Jan. 31, 1949; m. Linda S. Gehrke, Apr. 24, 1982; children: Megan, Timothy. BBA cum laude, Ohio U., 1970; JD, U. Notre Dame, 1973. Bar: Pa. 1973. Ptnr. Jones Day, Pitts. Instr. environ. dispute resolution Duquesne U. Bd. dirs. Pa. Environ. Coun., 1990-07, chair policy com., 2007; pres., chmn. bd. Allegheny Land Trust, 2006-07; adv. com. Allegheny County Dept. Air Pollution Control, 1992-95, Allegheny County Contaminated Sites Redevel. Study, 1994-95; adv. com. Western Pa. Brownfield Ctr., Carnegie Mellon U., 2007. Named one of Am. Leading Lawyers for Bus., Chambers Publishing, 2003—07, Pa. Superlawyers, Law and Politics Publishing, 2004—07, Best Lawyers in Am., Woodward/Whyte Inc., 2006—07. Fellow: Air and Waste Mgmt. Assn., Allegheny County Bar Found.; mem.: ABA (mem. environ., energy and resources sect., chair alternative dispute resolution com., dispute resolution sect.), Allegheny County Bar Assn. (chmn. environ. law sect. 1991), Environ. Law Inst. (assoc.), Pa. Bar Assn. (chmn. environ., mineral and nat. resources law sect. 1990—91), Assn. Conflict Resolution. Office: Jones Day 1 Mellon Ctr 500 Grant St Pittsburgh PA 15219-2502 Home Phone: 412-487-3145; Office Phone: 412-394-7908. Business E-Mail: jwubinger@jonesday.com.

UBOGU, EROBOGHENE EKAMERENO, physician; s. Roland and Rebecca Ubogu; m. Anisa Seana Namirimo Ssengoba, Aug. 10, 2002; children: Orezimena Nanyanzi children: Oghenekome Kaddu. MBBS with honors, Imperial Coll. Sch. Medicine, U. London, 1998. Diplomate in neurology and in clin. neurophysiology Am. Bd. Psychiatry and Neurology, bd. cert. Am. Bd. Electrodiagnostic Medicine. Adult neurology resident, chief resident Case Western Res. U., Univ. Hosps. of Cleve., 2000—03; clin. neurophysiology fellow Emory U. Sch. Medicine, Atlanta, 2003—04; asst. prof. neurology Case Western Res. U. Sch. Medicine, Cleve., 2004—; staff neurologist Louis Stokes Cleve. Vets. Affairs Med. Ctr., Cleve., 2004—. Fellow: Am Assn. for Neuromuscular and Electrodiagnostic Medicine; mem.: NY Acad. Scis., Am. Acad. Neurology. Achievements include research in role of chemokines in neuroinflammation, electrodiagnostic criteria for carpal tunnel syndrome in axonal polyneuropathies; asymptomatic middle cerebral artery stenosis diagnosed by magnetic resonance angiography; the preferential involvement of extraocular muscles in myasthenia gravis; acute motor sensory axonal neuropathy associated with systemic lupus erythematosus; amaurosis fugax and phencyclidine inhalation; vertebrobasilar dolichoectasia diagnosed by magnetic resonance angiography and risk of stroke and death; transverse myelitis associated with acinetobacter baumanii intrathecal pump catheter-related infection; mirtazapine-induced serotonin syndrome; ketamine in refractory status epilepticus and neurotoxicity; rectus sheath hematoma complicating percutaneous endoscopic gastrostomy; recurrent transient ischemic attacks and type A aortic dissections; otalgia as the sole presenting manifestation of subdural hematoma; cervicomedullary junction compression and vertebral artery dolichoectasia. Office: Neurology Svc Louis Stokes Cleve Vets Affairs Med Ctr 10701 E Blvd Cleveland OH 44106 Office Phone: 216-421-3040, 216-791-3800 x 5230. Business E-Mail: Eroboghene.Ubogu@med.va.gov. E-mail: eroboghene.ubogu@case.edu.

UBUKA, TOSHIHIKO, biochemist, educator, academic administrator; b. Kagaminocho, Okayama, Japan, Jan. 31, 1934; s. Yoshio and Shigeko (Hashimoto) U.; m. Satoko Iwamiya, Oct. 18, 1960; children: Takayoshi, Hiromi, Atsue. MD, Okayama U., 1959, PhD, 1964. Rsch. assoc. Med. Coll. Cornell U., NYC, 1968—71; with Okayama U., Japan, 1964-73, asst. prof., 1973-80, assoc. prof. Med. Sch., 1980-81, prof. Med. Sch., 1981-99, dean Med. Sch., 1997-99, prof. emeritus, 1999—; prof., dean Kawasaki U. of Med. Welfare, 1999—2001, prof., v.p., 2001—05, prof., dean, v.p., 2005—07, prof., v.p., 2007—. Co-author: Methods in Enzymology, vol. 143, 1987; editor Acta Med. Okayama, 1980-99, Physiol. Chem. Phys. and Med. NMR, 1982—, Amino Acids, 1991—; chief editor Acta Med. Okayama, 1987-90. Fellow Japanese Biochem. Soc., Japanese Soc. Nutrition and Food Sci.; mem. AAAS, Am. Chem. Soc., NY Acad. Scis., Internat. Soc. Amino Acid Rsch., Soc. Study Inborn Errors Metabolism, The Protein Soc. Achievements include research in sulfur biochemistry, sulfur nutrition, cysteine metabolism in mammals, protein modification with mixed disulfides; inborn errors of cysteine metabolism, analysis of sulfur compounds. Avocation: Kendo (Japanese fencing). Home: 527-1 Nishikarakawa Okayama 701-1213 Japan Office: Kawasaki U Med Welfare De Clin Nutrition 288 Matsushima Kurashiki Okayama 701-0193 Japan

UCHIBORI, CHIHIRO J., materials scientist, researcher; b. Kyoto, June 23, 1967; arrived in US, 2002; m. Mizuho Michelle Tanabe. BA, Kyoto U., 1991, MA in Material Sci., 1993, PhD in Engring., 1997. Tchg. asst. Kyoto U., 1993—96; rschr. Fujitsu Laboratories Ltd., Atsugi, Kanagawa, Japan, 1996—2004; vis. scientist U. Tex., Austin, 2002—03; rsch. staff mem. Fujitsu Laboratories Am., Inc., Sunnyvale, Calif., 2004—. Mem. com. 9th Internat. Workshop on Stress-Induced Phenomena in Metallization, 2006—07. Contbr. articles to profl. jours., conf. procs. in field. Recipient Fujitsu Infinity award, Fujitsu Ltd., 2002. Mem.: IEEE (mem. interconnect com. internat. reliability physics symposium 2004—05). Achievements include patents in field. Office: Fujitsu Labs Am Inc 1240 E Arques Ave MS345 Sunnyvale CA 94085 Office Phone: +1-408-530-4672. Business E-Mail: chihiro.uchibori@us.fujitsu.com.

UCHIDA, MITSUKO, pianist; b. Dec. 20, 1948; d. Fujio and Yasuko Uchida. Student, Hochschule für Musik, Vienna, Austria. Performer: performs with Berlin Philharm., Vienna Philharm., Cleve. Orch., LA Philharm., Chgo. Symphony Orch., London Symphony, NY Philharm., others, recs. include complete piano sonatas and concertos of Mozart, Beethoven's piano concertos, Debussy's Etudes, Schubert Sonatas and Impromptus, Schoenberg Piano Concerto, Carnegie Hall recital series Mitsuko Uchida: Vienna Revisited, 2002—; artist-in-residence Cleve. Orch., 2001—07. Recipient Gramophone award, 2001, Instrumental Award, Royal Philharm. Soc., 2004. Mem. Am. Acad. Arts & Scis. (hon. fgn.). Avocation: music. Address: Victoria Rowsell Artist Mgmt Ltd 34 Addington Sq London SE5 7LB England E-mail: management@victoriarowsell.co.uk.

UCHIDA, RICHARD Y., lawyer; b. Mars, Pa., Sept. 18, 1957; s. Henry S. and Sachiko (Sakaguchi) U. BA, Colby Coll., 1979; JD, Franklin Pierce Law Ctr., 1984. Bar: N.H. 1984, U.S. Dist. Ct. N.H. 1984. Reporter, editor Lake Charles (La.) Am. Press., 1979-81; assoc. Rinden Profl. Assn., Concord, NH, 1984-86, Law Offices Raymond P. D'Amante, Concord, 1986—92; ptnr. Hebert & Uchida, Concord, NH, 1992—. Lectr. Franklin Pierce Law Ctr., Concord, 1985—96, N.H. Liquor Commn., Concord, 1986—92. Overseer Colby Coll., 1997-05, trustee, 2005-. Mem. Assn. Trial Lawyers Am., NH Trial Lawyers, NH Bar Assn. (chmn. pub. info. com. 1987-90, CLE com. 1990, ethics com. 1990, bar news com. 1996-, fin. com. 2003-, pres. 2005), NH Bar Found. (treas. 1999-02, dir. 2003-). Republican. Avocations: golf, hiking. Address: Hebert and Uchida PLLC 2 Pillsbury St Ste 502 Concord NH 03301-3549 Office Phone: 603-224-5004.

UCHIN, ROBERT ALLEN, dean, endodontist; b. Phila., Apr. 19, 1933; s. Harry and Doris (Goodman) U.; m. Marlene Florence Neiman; children: Andrew, Richard, Carol. Student, Franklin and Marshall Coll., 1951-53; DDS, Temple U., 1957. Diplomate Am. Bd. Endodontics. Fellow research teaching. dept. endodontics Temple U., Phila., 1959-60, instr. Sch. of Dentistry, 1960-69; co-chmn. endodontic sect. Dade County (Fla.) Dental Research Clinic, 1961-75; founding v.p., chmn. Endodontic sect. Broward County (Fla.) Dental Research Clinic, 1974-79; clin. assoc. Sch. of Dentistry U. Fla., Gainsville, 1970; practice dentistry specializing in endodontics Ft. Lauderdale, Fla., 1960—2000; assoc. dean, dir. extramural programs Coll. Dental Medicine, Nova Southeastern U., Ft. Lauderdale, Fla., 1996—2000, dean, 2000—. Chmn. Endodontic sect. Atlantic Coast Research Clinic, 1971-75; vis. lectr. Emory U., 1965, U.N.C., 1970, 72, U. Wash., 1972, U. Pitts., 1974, U. Pa., 1973-89; cons. VA Hosp., Miami, 1968-86, Cen. Office, 1972-84, dir. endodontic residency, 1972-79; bd. dirs., founding chmn. Gold Coast Savs. and Loan Assn. of Fla., 1984-90, Commonwealth Savs. and Loan of Fla., Ft. Lauderdale, 1979-84; adv. dir. Landmark First Nat. Bank, Ft. Lauderdale, 1974-81; vice chmn. Fla. Dental Assn. Services, Inc. Assoc. editor Jour. Endodontics and Traumatology, 1981-89; contbr. numerous articles to profl. jours. Pres., Temple Emanu-El Reform Congregation, Ft. Lauderdale, 1967-69; trustee, Vanguard Sch., Haverford, Pa., 1971-77; bd. dirs., Vanguard Sch., Ft. Lauderdale, 1970-73, Performing Arts Found., Broward County, Fla., 1986-90. Served to capt. USAF, 1957-59. Fellow: Am. Assn. Endodontists (pres. 1976), Internat. Coll. of Dentists, Am. Coll. of Dentists; mem.: Broward County Dental Assn. (pres. 1982), Fla. Dental Assn. (past pres.), Am. Dental Assn. Holding Co. (past pres.), Fla. Assoc. of Endodontics, So. Endodontic Study Group, Am. Dental Assn., Rotary (pres. Ft. Lauderdale 1969—70). Republican. Jewish. Avocations: fly fishing, stamp collecting/philately, orchids. Office: Coll Dental Medicine Nova Southeastern U 3200 S Univ Dr Fort Lauderdale FL 33328 Office Phone: 954-262-7312. Office Fax: 954-262-1782. Business E-Mail: ruchin@nova.edu.

UCHITELLE, LOUIS, journalist; b. NYC, Mar. 21, 1932; s. Abraham and Alice Lee (Cronbach) Uchitelle; m. Joan Eva Shapiro, Oct. 7, 1966; children: Isabel Anne, Jennifer Emily. BA, U. Mich., 1954. Reporter Mt. Vernon Daily Argus, 1955-57; with AP, 1957-80, fgn. corr. and bur. chief San Juan, 1964-67, Buenos Aires, 1967-73; supervising editor AP Newsfeatures, NYC, 1974-76; bus. news editor AP, 1977-80; asst. bus. and fin. editor NY Times, 1980-87, economics reporter, 1987—. Instr. journalism Sch. Gen. Studies Columbia U., 1976—89. Author: The Disposable American: Layoffs and Their Consequences, 2006. Office: NY Times 229 W 43rd St New York NY 10036-3959 Home Phone: 914-723-0372; Office Phone: 212-556-1705. Office Fax: 212-556-8762. Business E-Mail: louisu@nytimes.com.

UCHIYAMA, CRAIG LYONS, neuropsychologist; s. John Keyomara Uchiyama and Mary Louise Lyons. BA in Psychology, U. Minn., Mpls., 1986; PhD, U. Minn., 1990; postgrad., UCLA, 1993. Cert. clin. neuropsychology Am. Bd. Profl. Psychology. Asst. clin. prof. U. Calif., San Francisco, 1993—95; neuropsychologist Tolwin Psychiat. Med. Group, LA, 1995—2001, LA County Dept. Mental Health, LA, 2001—. Asst. clin. prof. UCLA, 1997—2001. Contbr. articles to profl. jours. Mem.: APA, Am. Acad. Clin. Neuropsychology, Psi Chi. Achievements include co-development of the Color Trails Test. Business E-Mail: cuchiyama@dmh.lacounty.gov.

UCHRIN, CHRISTOPHER GEORGE, environmental engineer and scientist; b. South Amboy, NJ, Oct. 27, 1950; s. George Christopher and Annette Rose Marie (Skokan) U.; m. Lisa C. Ferguson, July 31, 1998; 1 child, George Henry. B in Civil Engring., Manhattan Coll., 1972, M. in Environ. Engring., 1974; PhD in Environ. Engring., U. Mich., 1980. Registered profl. engring. N.Y. Environ. engr. U.S. EPA, NYC, 1972-77; Rackham fellow U. Mich., Ann Arbor, Mich., 1977-78, rsch. asst., 1978-80; asst. prof. Rutgers U., New Brunswick, NJ, 1980-86, assoc. prof., 1986-90, prof. environ. sci., 1990—. Chair dept. environ. sci. Rutgers U., New Brunswick, 1991-94, dir. grad. program in environ. sci., 1986-91; co-dir., co-founder Joint PhD Program in Exposure Assessment, Rutgers U. & UMDNJ/Robert Wood Johnson Med. Sch., 1991—, dir. undergrad. curriculum in bioenvironmental engring., 1999—. Mem. Lebanon Borough (N.J.) Planning Bd., 2003—. Recipient Excellence in Tchg. award, Cook Coll./N.J. Agrl. Experiment Sta., 2005. Mem. ASCE, Am. Chem. Soc., Water Environment Fedn., Am. Soc. for Materials, Soc. Environ. Toxicology and Chemistry, N.J. Acad. Sci. (pres. 1991-92). Personal E-mail: cuchrin@rci.rutgers.edu.

UCHUPI, ELAZAR, geologist, researcher; b. NYC, Oct. 31, 1928; parents Alfonso and Carmen (Urbizu) U. BS, CCNY, 1952; MS, U. So. Calif., 1954, PhD, 1962. Rsch. asst. U. So. Calif., LA, 1955-62, Woods Hole (Mass.) Oceanographic Inst., 1962-64, assoc. scientist, 1964-79; sr. scientist Woods Hole (Mass.) Oceanog. Inst., 1979-93, sr. scientist emeritus, 1993—, J. Seward Johnson chmn. oceanography, 1989-93. Mem. Gulf of Mexico panel Joint Oceanog. Instns. Deep Earth Sampling, 1972-74; sci. com. Oceanic Rsch. Working Group 41, 1973-74; steering com. U.S. Oceanog. Office Relief Map Worlds' Oceans; site survey panel Joint Oceanog. Instns., 1978-85; compiler geol. maps on ocean margin drilling; adj. rschr. Inst. Exploration, Mystic, Conn., 1997—. Mem. editl. staff Offshore Mag., 1972-74, Marine Geology, 1971-75; co-author 4 books North Atlantic, geology of Atlantic Ocean, and morphology of rocky mems. of Solar Sys. Recipient cert. of recognition Nat. Assn. Geology Tchrs., Inc., and its Crustal evolution Edn. project, 1979, medal editl. adv. bd. Offshore Mag., 1974, Frances P. Shepard award, 1991. Mem. Am. Geophys. Union, Archeol. Inst. Am., Sociedad Geologica de España. Achievements include research in seismic reflection, magnetic and gravity profiles of the eastern Atlantic continental margin and adjacent deep seafloor, Caribbean, Bahamas, Iberian Margins, New England margin, Branefield Trough, South Scotia Ridge, Canary Islands, Red Sea, Persian Gulf, Gulf of Oman, Black Sea, Egyptian Margin, Western Mediterranean, East Pacific Rise, Mohns Ridge, suspended matter and other properities of surface waters of the northeastern Atlantic Ocean, the continental margin off western Africa: Angola to Sierra Leone, Senegal to Portugal, sediments of 3 bays of Baja, Calif.: Sebastian Viscaino, San Cristobal and Todos Santos, characteristics of sediments of the mainland shelf of southern Calif., submarine geology of the Santa Rosa-Cortes Ridge, sediments on the continental margin off eastern U.S., the continental slope between San Francisco and Cedrow Island, Mex., sediments of the Palos Verdes shelf, sediments and topography of Kane Basin, statistical parameters of Cape Cod Beach and eolian sands, basins of Gulf of Mex., structure of Georges Bank, and the continental margin of the Atlantic coast of the U.S. and off west Africa, topography and structure of Northeast Channel, Gulf of Mex., and Cashes Ledge, Gulf of Maine, distribution and geologic structure of Triassic rocks in the Bay of Fundy and the northeastern part of the Gulf of Maine, microrelief of the continental margin south of Cape Lookout, N.C., shallow structure of the Straits of Fla., sub-surface morphology of L.I., Block Island, Rhode Island sounds, and Buzzards Bay, bathymetry of the Gulf of Mex., slumping on the continental margin southeast of L.I., N.Y., woody debris on the mainland shelf off Ventura, southern Calif., the continental margin south of Cape Hatteras, N.C., the Atlantic continental shelf and slope of the U.S., geological structure of the continental margin off Gulf Coast of the U.S., continental margin of West Africa, the Caribbean Canary Islands, margin off northwest Spain. Office: Woods Hole Oceanographic Inst Dept Geology Geophysic Woods Hole MA 02543

UCKO, BARBARA CLARK, writer; b. Cambridge, Mass., Mar. 27, 1945; d. Hugh Kidder and Marie (Folsom) Clark; m. David Alan Ucko, Aug. 13, 1972; 1 child, Aaron Mark. BA in Art History, Oberlin Coll., 1967; MA in English, U. Mo., Kansas City, 1992. Copywriter Bantam Books, NYC, 1974—76; promotion dir. Pocket Books, NYC, 1976—77, Antioch Bookplate, Yellow Springs, Ohio, 1977; instr. composition Sch. of Chgo. Art Inst., Chgo., 1986; mgr. corp. comm. Sprint, Westwood, Kans., 1992—98; pvt. piano tchr. Kansas City, Mo., 1998—2001. Author: (novels) Family Trappings, 1985, Scarlett Greene, 1987, (short stories) Laurel Review, Nit and Wit, Open, Artful Dodge and Chatelaine. Various libr. bds., sch. vol. and hosp. bds. Calif., Mo., Washington D.C. Recipient 1st pl. award, Barbara Storck Short Fiction Competion, U. Mo., 1991, 2d pl., 1992. Mem.: Soc. Midland Authors. Democrat. Avocations: crafts, crossword puzzles, piano, walking, reading. E-mail: Barbara.Ucko@verizon.net.

UCKO, DAVID ALAN, science foundation official; b. NYC, July 9, 1948; s. Lawrence L. and Helen H. Ucko; m. Barbara Alice Clark, Aug. 13, 1972; 1 child, Aaron. BA, Columbia Coll., NYC, 1969; PhD, MIT, 1972. Asst. prof. chemistry Hostos C.C., CUNY, Bronx, 1972-76, Antioch Coll., Yellow Springs, Ohio, 1976-79, assoc. prof. chemistry, 1979; rsch. coord. Mus. Sci. and Industry, Chgo., 1979-80, dir. sci., 1981-87, v.p., 1986-87, dep. dir. Calif. Mus. Sci. and Industry, LA, 1987-90; pres. Kansas City (Mo.) Mus., 1990-2000, Sci. City at Union Sta., 1999-2000; exec. dir. Koshland Sci. Mus. and Sci. Outreach, NAS, Washington, 2001—02; pres. Mus. + More LLC, 2002—, head sci literacy section, 2004—, dep. dir. divsn. rsch. learning in formal and informal settings, 2007—; program dir. Informal Sci. Edn. NSF, 2003—; guest faculty mus. mgmt. program U. Colo., Boulder, Colo., 2001. Rsch. assoc. and assoc. prof. dept. edn. U. Chgo., 1982—87; adj. staff scientist C. F. Kettering Rsch. Lab., Yellow Springs, Ohio, 1977—79; mem. pub. engagement working group, nanoscale sci. edn. and tech. subcom. Nat. Sci. and Tech. Coun., 2005—. Author: (book) Basics for Chemistry, 1982, Living Chemistry, 2d edit., 1986; contbr. articles to profl. jours.; host, prodr. (radio program) Science Alive!, 1983—87, developer numerous mus. exhibits. Apptd. Nat. Mus. Svcs. Bd., 1996—2003; trustee Mus. Without Walls, 1996—2000, Sci. Pioneers, 2000. Recipient Up and Comers award, Jr. Achievement Mid.-Am., 1992; fellow Woodrow Wilson, 1969, NIH postdoctoral, 1972; grantee, NSF, NEH, U.S. Dept. Edn., Ill. Humanities Coun., 1976—88. Fellow: AAAS (at large sect. Y 1987—93); mem.: Am. Assn. Museums (mus. assessment program adv. com. 2000—03), Assn. Sci. Tech. Ctrs. (publs. com. 1984—94, chmn. 1988—94, ethics com. 1994—95, legis. com., chmn. 1996—2000), Phi Lambda Upsilon, Sigma Xi, Alpha Sigma Nu (hon.). Home: 2528 Queen Anne's Ln NW Washington DC 20037-2148 Office Phone: 703-292-5126. Personal E-mail: d.ucko@verizon.net.

UDALL, MARK, congressman; b. Tucson, July 18, 1950; m. Maggie Fox; children: Jed, Tess. B.Am. Civilization, Williams Coll., 1972. Course dir., educator Colo. Outward Bound Sch., 1975-85, exec. dir., 1985-95; mem. dist. 13 Colo. Ho. of Reps., 1997-99; mem. U.S. Congress from 2d Colo. dist., Washington, 1999—; Dem. dep. regional whip for western U.S.; mem. armed svcs. com., resources com., sci. com. Democrat. Avocation: mountain climbing. Office: US Ho Reps 240 Cannon Ho Office Bldg Washington DC 20515-0602 also: Ste 206 8601 Turnpike Dr Westminster CO 80031-7044 *

UDALL, THOMAS S. (TOM), congressman; b. Tucson, May 18, 1948; s. Stewart and Lee Udall; m. Jill Z. Cooper; 1 child, Amanda Cooper. BA in Govt. and Polit. Sci., Prescott Coll., Ariz., 1970; LLB in Internat. Law, Cambridge U., Eng., 1975; JD, U. N.Mex. Sch. Law, 1977. Bar: N.Mex. 1978. Legis. asst. Staff of US Senator Joseph R. Biden of Del., 1973; law clk. to Chief Justice Oliver Seth US 10th Cir. Ct. Appeals, Santa Fe, 1977-78; asst. US atty. criminal divsn. US Atty.'s Office, 1978-81; atty. pvt. practice, Santa Fe, 1981-83; chief counsel N.Mex. Health and Environ. Dept., 1983-84; atty. to ptnr. Miller, Stratvert, Togerson and Schlenker, P.A., Albuquerque, 1985-90; atty. gen., 1991—99; mem. US Congress from 3rd N.Mex. dist., 1999—, mem. appropriations com., co-vice chair Native Am. caucus, mem. Bipartisan Rural Caucus. Pres. Rio Chama Preservation Trust; mem. N.Mex. Environ. Improvement Bd., 1986—87; bd. dirs. La Compania de Teatro de Albuquerque, Santa Fe Chamber Music Festival, Law Fund, 1991—98. Recipient Leadership award, Nat. Commn. Against Drunk Driving, Legal Impact award, N.Mex. Bar Prosecution Sect., Pub. Svc. award, Nat. Highway Traffic Safety Adminstrn. Mem. Nat. Assn. Attys. Gen. (pres. 1996), Kiwanis. Democrat. Office: US House Reps 1410 Longworth House Office Bldg Washington DC 20515 Office Phone: 202-225-6190. Office Fax: 202-226-1331. *

UDALL, VESTA HAMMOND, special education educator; b. Jacksonville, Fla., Dec. 8, 1942; d. Vesta Shields and Gladys Wilcox Hammond; m. John Scriven Udall, July 18, 1964 (div. Feb. 27, 1973); children: Adrien Evelyn, Peter John. BA, Winthrop U., 1964; MEd, U. Phoenix, 1997; postgrad., U. Fla., No. Ariz. U., Ariz. State U. Cert. tchr. Ariz. Various elem. and H.S. tchg. positions Duval County Schs., Jacksonville, 1964—68; tchr. Flagstaff (Ariz.) Jr. H.S., 1974—76, Fickett Jr. H.S., Tucson, 1976—78, Devereux Sch., Scottsdale, Ariz., 1978—80, East Valley H.S., Maricopa County Regional Sch. Dist., Phoenix, 1989—97,

Madison Jail and Maricopa County Sheriff's Office, Phoenix, 1997—2000; prof. Phoenix Coll., 1998—; spl. edn. tchr. Westwood H.S., Mesa (Ariz.) Sch. Dist., 2000—. Presenter in field; developer spl. edn. programs. Precinct committeeman Rep. Party, Mesa, 1985—. Named Educator of Yr., Phoenix Sun, 1995. Mem.: Nat. Edn. Assn., Mesa Edn. Assn. Ariz. Republican. Mem. Lds Ch. Avocations: hiking, river running, birdwatching, biking. Home: 2264 E Fairfield St Mesa AZ 85213 Office: Phoenix Coll 1100 W Thomas Rd Phoenix AZ 85013 Personal E-mail: vhudall@aol.com.

UDASHEN, ROBERT NATHAN, lawyer; b. Amarillo, Tex., June 10, 1953; s. Leo Joe and Esther K. (Klugsberg) U. BA with high honors, U. Tex., 1974, JD, 1977. Bar: Tex. 1977, U.S. Ct. Appeals (5th cir.) 1978, U.S. Dist. Ct. (no. and so. dists.) Tex. 1978, U.S. Ct. Appeals (11th cir.) 1981, U.S. Supreme Ct. 1981, U.S. Dist. Ct. (ea. dist.) Tex. 1989, U.S. Dist. Ct. (we. dist.) Tex. 1991, U.S. Dist. Ct. (ea. and we. dists.) Ark. 2000, U.S. Ct. Appeals (8th cir.) 2002. Staff atty. Staff Counsel for Inmates, Huntsville, Tex., 1977-79; assoc., ptnr. Crowder, Mattox & Udashen, Dallas, 1979-85; ptnr. Udashen & Goldstucker, Dallas, 1985-87; pvt. practice, 1987-94; ptnr. Milner, Lobel, Goranson, Sorrels, Udashen & Wells, Dallas, 1995-2000, Milner, Goranson, Sorrels, Udashen & Wells, Dallas, 2000—02, Sorrels & Udashen, Dallas, 2002—06, Sorrels, Udashen & Anton, 2006—. Bd. dirs. Open, Inc., Dallas; instr. trial advocacy Sch. Law So. Meth. U., 1993-95; adj. prof. criminal procedure Sch. Law So. Meth. U., 1998-99, 2001—. Contbr. articles to profl. jours. Adv. bd. Coalition for Safer Dallas, 1994. Mem. State Bar Tex. (penal code com. 1992-93), Nat. Assn. Criminal Def. Lawyers, Tex. Criminal Def. Lawyers Assn., Dallas Criminal Def. Lawyers Assn. (pres. 2007). Office: Sorrels Udashen & Anton 2301 Cedar Springs Rd Ste 400 Dallas TX 75201 Home: 1999 McKinney Ave 1203 Dallas TX 75201 Home Phone: 214-468-8142; Office Phone: 214-468-8100. Business E-Mail: rnu@sualaw.com.

UDELL, RICHARD, lawyer; b. Bklyn., Dec. 27, 1932; s. Alvin and Gertrude (Langsam) U.; m. Marguerite Hartshorne, July 3, 1955; m. children: Benjamin Alan, Edward H. BA, Reed Coll., 1955; LLB, U. Pa., 1958. Bar: N.Y. 1958, Fla. 1984. Pvt. practice, NYC, 1959-65; counsel RCA Records, NYC, 1965-69; assoc. firm Machat & Kronfeld, NYC, 1969-71; counsel Famous Music Corp., NYC, 1971-72, Random House, Inc. subs. RCA, NYC, 1972-75; gen. counsel Simon & Schuster, Inc. subs. Gulf & Western Industries, Inc., NYC, 1975-77; adminstrv. v.p., chief counsel Harcourt Brace Jovanovich, Inc., NYC, 1977-92; v.p., gen. counsel The McGraw Hill Sch. Pub. Co. unit McGraw-Hill Cos., Inc., 1992—. Mem. Bar Assn. City N.Y., Orange County Bar Assn., Fla. Bar Assn. Jewish. Office: McGraw-Hill Sch Pub Co 2 Penn Plz New York NY 10121-0101

UDEVITZ, NORMAN, publishing executive; b. Cheyenne, Wyo., Jan. 22, 1929; s. Jay and Edith (Stienberg) U.; m. Marsha Rae Dinner, Dec. 17, 1960; children: Jane, Kathryn, Andrew. Student, U. Colo., 1946-49. With Cheyenne Newspapers Inc. Cheyenne, 1949-54; editor-pub. Wyo. Buffalo, Cheyenne, 1954-63; account supr. Tilds & Cantz Advt. Agy., LA, 1963-66; exec. v.p. Fitzgerald, Maahs & Miller, LA, 1966-71; staff writer The Denver Post, 1971-88; dir. pubs. Am. Water Works Assn., Denver, 1988-97; ret., 1997. Sgt. USNG, 1950-53. Named Colo.'s Outstanding Journalist, U. Colo., 1977; recipient Pulitzer Prize Gold medal Columbia U., 1986. Mem. Investigative Reporters and Editors Inc., (bd. dirs. 1978-80, 81-83), The Newspaper Guild (McWilliams award 1976, 77). Jewish. Home: 4677 E Euclid Ave Littleton CO 80121-3224

UDLER, RUBIN YAKOVLEVICH, linguist; b. Braila, Muntenia, Romania, Sept. 27, 1925; came to U.S., 1992; s. Yakov Aronovich and Dina Vladimirovna (Gleizer) U.; m. Malka Il'inichna Alexenberg, July 8, 1956; children: Arthur, Angela. B in Philol. Sci., U. Chernovtsy, Ukraine, 1951; M in Philol. Sci., USSR Acad. Scis., Moscow, 1961; D in Philol. Sci., USSR Acad. Scis., Leningrad, 1974. Dep. chmn. fgn. langs. dept. Chernovtsy State Pedagogical Inst., 1951-56; jr. sci. rschr. dialectology sect. Moldavian br. USSR Acad. Scis., Kishinev, Moldova, 1956-61; chief dialectology and exptl. phonetics sect. Moldavian Acad. Scis., 1961-80, chief dialectology and history of lang. sect., 1980-86, chief dialectology and linguistic geography dept., 1986-92, dep. of academician-sec. of social studies dept., 1989-92; ctr. assoc. U. Ctr. for Internat. Studies U. Pitts., 1994—. Translator Soviet Bucovina newspaper, Chernovtsy, 1951-52; sr. sci. rschr. All-Union Cert. Com., Moscow, 1963; presenter in field. Author: Moldavian Dialects of the Chernovtsy Area Consonantism, 1964, Dialectological Division of the Moldavian Language, Parts 1 and 2, 1976, The Cursed Years, 2003, Russian edit., 2005, English edit., 2006, Romanian edit.; co-author: The Moldavian Linguistic Atlas, 4 parts, 1968-73, Dialectological Dictionary, 5 vols., 1985-86, Dialectological Texts, 6 parts, 1969-87, The Historical Grammar of the Moldavian Language, 1964, Notes on Modern Moldavian Literary Language, 1967, Moldavian Dialectology, 1976, The Carpathian Dialectological Atlas, 7 vols., 1987-2005, The Romanian Linguistic Atlas by Regions, 4 vols., 1993-2003; mem. editl. bd. Moldavian Lang. and Lit., 1961-91, Jour. Linguistics and Study of Lit., 1991-92; contbr. articles to profl. jours., chpts. to books. Corr. mem. Moldavian Acad. Scis. Presidium of Moldavian Acad. Scis.; mem. Holocaust Ctr. United Jewish Fedn. Greater Pitts. Jewish. Avocations: collecting old books, coin collecting/numismatics, travel. Home: 1535 Shady Ave Pittsburgh PA 15217-1455 Office: Univ Ctr Internat Studies U Pitts 41 G40 Forbes Quadrangle Pittsburgh PA 15260 Personal E-mail: rubin.udler@gmail.com.

UDOFF, ERIC JOEL, diagnostic radiologist; b. Balt., Oct. 8, 1948; s. Melvin Jerome and Esther (Fisher) U.; m. Ronni Ann Chapin, June 7, 1980; children: Brian Evan, Jonathan Andrew. AB, Washington U., 1969; MD, U. Rochester, 1973. Intern, resident in diagnostic radiology U. Chgo., 1973-77; instr. in cardiovasc. radiology Johns Hopkins U., Balt., 1977-79; radiologist Sinai Hosp., Balt., 1979-86, Mt. Sinai Med. Ctr., Milw., 1986-88, Sinai Hosp., Balt., 1988-90; asst. prof. radiology Johns Hopkins U. Hosp., 1990-91; radiologist North Fulton Regional Hosp., Roswell, Ga., 1991-97; instr. thoracoabdominal imaging U. Va., 1997-98. Radiologist, Diagnostic Imaging Specialists, Atlanta, 1998—. Mem. AMA, Am. Roentgen Ray Soc., Am. Coll. Radiology, Radiol. Soc. N.Am., Ga. Radiol. Soc., Phi Beta Kappa. Avocations: reading, tennis. Office: 6000 Lake Forrest Dr Ste 475 Atlanta GA 30328 Office Phone: 404-459-8440. Personal E-mail: ejurad@yahoo.com.

UDOLF, BRUCE LEE, lawyer; s. Roy Joseph and Marcelle Udolf; m. Sheryl Singer Udolf, Oct. 24, 1992; 1 child, Hayley. BA, Hofstra U., 1973; JD, Emory U. Sch. Law, 1979. Bar: Ga. 1979, US Dist. Ct. (no. dist.) Ga. 1979, US Ct. Appeals (11th cir.) 1982, Fla. 1991, US Dist. Ct. (so. dist.) Fla. 1998, US Dist. Ct. (mid. dist.) Fla. 1999. Atty. Mishan, Sloto, Greenberg, Hellinger & Udolf, P.A., Miami, Fla., 1998—2000, Eckert, Seamans, Cherin and Mellott, LLC, Ft. Lauderdale, 2000—01, Ruden McClosky, P.A., 2001—06, Berger Singerman, Ft. Lauderdale, 2006—; law clerk to Hon. Arthur W. Fudger Tallapoosa Jud. Cir. Ga., 1979—80; asst. dist. atty. Northeastern Jud. Cir. Ga., 1980—83, dist. atty., 1983—87; asst. US atty. US Atty.'s Office, So. Dist. Fla., 1987—98, appellate divsn., 1987; major crimes sect. US Dept. Justice, 1987—88, narcotics sect., 1988, pub. corruption sect., 1988—97, chief pub. corruption sect., 1992—97, assoc. ind. counsel Office Ind. Counsel Washington, 1997—98. Lectr. Law Edn. Inst., 2002, US Dept. Treasury, Office Tech. Assistance, US Dept. Justice, Office Profl. Devel. and Tng. Corruption and Organized Crime Symposium, St. Petersburg, Russia, Fla. Internat. U., Ctr. Adminstrn. Justice Pub. Corruption Seminars in La Paz, Bolivia; Caracas, Venezuela; Tegucigalpa, Honduras, Atty. Gen.'s Advocacy Inst., Washington, Nat. Inst. Trial Advocacy, Trial Techs. Program, Emory U. Sch. Law, Atlanta, Fla. Bar CLE, Professionalism and Ethics Symposium, U. Miami Sch. Law; mem. Fla. Bar Atty. Client Privilege Task Force; mem. adv. com. on rules on procedures US Dist. Ct., So. Dist. Fla. Recipient commendation, Bur. Alcohol, Tobacco and Firearms, 1989, Dirs., FBI, 1991, 1994, Drug Enforcement Adminstrn., Office Profl. Responsibility, 1994, US Customs Svc., Office Internal Affairs, 1997, Outstanding Achievement award, US Dept. Justice, 1990, 1991, 1994. Mem.: Fla. Bar (criminal law sect. edn., ethics subcom.), Fla. Bar Criminal Procedure Rules com. (chair subcom. I, fast track subcom., chair joint appellate, civil, criminal rules subcom.), Palm Beach County Bar Assn., Broward County Bar Assn., Dade County Bar Assn. (chair meetings com., vice chair fed. practice com.), ABA (mem. criminal justice sect., white collar crime com.), Fla. Assn. Criminal Def. Lawyers, Nat. Assn. Criminal Def. Attys., Eugene Spellman Am. Inns of Ct., Fed. Bar Assn. (past pres., v.p., dir. Broward County chpt., asst.), US Atty.'s Assn. (past pres.). Office: Berger Singerman 350 E Las Olas Blvd Ste 1000 Fort Lauderdale FL 33301 Business E-Mail: bruce.udolf@ruden.com.

UDRYS, ALMIS GERARDAS, health policy consultant; s. Arunas Teodoras Udrys and Virginia Ruta Ruzgas; m. Claudia Orsi, Feb. 28, 2002; 1 child, Sofia Aurora. BA in Internat. Bus., Hillsdale Coll., 1999; M Pub. Policy, Pepperdine U., 2001. Auditor evaluator Bur. State Audits, Sacramento, 2001—03, sr. auditor evaluator, 2003—05; policy cons. Calif. Assembly Rep. Caucus, Sacramento, 2005—. Named Rookie of Yr., Bur. State Audits, 2002. Republican. Roman Catholic. Avocations: travel, reading, basketball, hiking.

UDVAR-HAZY, STEVEN F., leasing company financial executive; b. Budapest, Hungary, Feb. 23, 1946; came to U.S., 1958. m. Christine L. Henneman, June 7, 1980; 4 children. BA, UCLA, 1968; HHD (hon.), U. Utah, 1990; D (hon.), Emory Riddle Aero. U., 2000. Cert. airline transp. jet pilot. Chmn., CEO Internat. Lease Fin. Corp., Beverly Hills, Calif., 1973—. Bd. dirs. Sky West Inc., St. George, Utah; chmn. bd. dirs. Ocean Equities, Inc. Active Smothsonian's Udvar-Hazy Nat. Air & Spave Mus. Named one of Forbes' Richest Americans, 2000—, World's Richest People, Forbes mag., 2001—. Mem. Wings Club (Achievement to Aviation award 1989). Office: Internat Lease Fin Corp 10250 Constellation Blvd 35th Fl Los Angeles CA 90067 Office Phone: 310-788-1999.

UDWADIA, FIRDAUS ERACH, engineering educator, consultant; b. Bombay, Aug. 28, 1947; arrived in US, 1968; s. Erach Rustam and Perin P. (Lentin) Udwadia; m. Farida Gagrat, Jan. 6, 1977; children: Shanaira, Zubin. BS, Indian Inst. Tech., Bombay, 1968; MS, Calif. Inst. Tech., 1969, PhD, 1972; MBA, U. So. Calif., 1985. Mem. faculty Calif. Inst. Tech., Pasadena, 1972-74; asst. prof. engring. U. So. Calif., LA, 1974-77, assoc. prof. mech., civil, and aerospace engring. and bus. adminstrn., 1977-83, prof., 1983-86, bd. dirs. Structural Identification Computing Facility, prof. engring, bus. adminstrn., maths., 1986—2005, prof. civil engring., aerospace mech. engring., math., info. ops., mgmt., and sys. architecture engring., 2005—. Cons. Jet Propulsion Lab., Pasadena, 1978—, Argonne Nat. Lab., 1982—83, Air Force Rocket Lab., Edwards AFB, Calif., 1984—, Air Force Rsch. Lab., 1990—; vis. prof. applied mechanics and mech. engring. Calif. Inst. Tech., Pasadena, 1993. Author: Analytical Dynamics, A New Approach, 1996; assoc. editor: Applied Math. and Computation, Discrete Dynamics Nature and Soc., Jour. Optimization Theory and Applications, Jour. Franklin Inst., Jour. Differential Equations and Dynamical Sys., Nonlinear Studies, Jour. Math. Analysis and Applications, Jour. Math. Problems in Engring.; editor: Jour. Aerospace Engring., Advances in Dynamics and Control, 2000; co-editor: Dynamics and Control, 1999; chief editor Dynamical Systems and Control, 2004; hon. editor: Jour. Math. Control and its Applications; mem. adv. bd. Jour. Tech. Forecasting and Social Change; contbr. articles to profl. jours. Bd. dirs. Crisis Mgmt. Ctr. U. So. Calif., LA. Recipient Golden Poet award, 1990; NSF grantee, 1976—. Fellow: ASME, AIAA; mem.: ASCE (Outstanding Tech. Contributions award 2006), Seismol. Soc. Am., Soc. Indsl. and Applied Math., Am. Acad. Mechanics, Sigma Xi (mem. Earthquake Engring. Rsch. Inst. 1971, 1974, 1984). Achievements include patents in field; patents for control of nonlinear systems, 2002. Avocations: poetry, piano, chess. Home: 2100 S Santa Anita Ave Arcadia CA 91006-4611 Office: U So Calif 430K Olin Hall University Park Los Angeles CA 90007 Office Phone: 213-740-0495. Business E-Mail: fudwadia@usc.edu.

UDY, RAE, columnist, writer; b. Ogden, Utah, Mar. 24, 1950; d. Verl Nish Udy and Elizabeth Jones White; m. Steven James Weese, Apr. 9, 1971; children: Nation Verl Weese, Luke Ray Weese. Student, Weber State U., 1968. Columnist Longview News-Jour., Longview, Tex., 1989—; lifestyle editor Marshall News Messenger, Marshall, Tex., 1999—2000. Mem. and past v.p. East Tex. Writers Assn., 1987—; former contbr. Idaho Enterprise, Harleton Happenings. Author: (book) Countdown Cooking, 1993. Mem.: Ladies Aux. of Frat. of Eagles. Democrat. Christian. Avocations: gardening, travel, camping. Office: PO Box 5965 Longview TX 75608 Office Phone: 903-777-2723. Personal E-mail: raeudy@gmail.com.

UEBERROTH, HEIDI J., sports association executive; d. Peter Ueberroth. With NBA, NYC, 1994—, head global TV and media distbn. divsn., 1996—, exec. v.p. global media properties and mktg. partnerships, 2000—06, pres. global mktg. partnerships and internat. bus. ops., 2006—. Bd. dirs. Quiksilver, Inc., 2006—. Dir. Ueberroth Family Charitable Found., 1990—; bd. trustees Cancer Rsch. Inst., 2003—; bd. mem. Advt. Coun. Named one of 40 Under 40, Sports Bus. Jour., 2000, 2001, 2002, 20 Most Influential Women in Sports Bus., 2005; named to Advt. Hall of Achievement, Am. Advt. Fedn., 2005. Office: NBA Olympic Tower 645 5th Ave Fl 10 New York NY 10022-5986 *

UEBERROTH, LINDSEY, hotel executive; d. John Ueberroth. BA, Wake Forest Univ., Winston-Salem, NC. Change mgmt. cons. Anderson Consulting; with Ambassadors Internat., mng. dir. Golf divsn.; joined Preferred Hotel Group, Newport Beach, Calif., 2004—; pres. Preferred Boutique (subs. Preferred Hotel Group), Newport Beach, Calif., 2005—. Named one of America 's Top Women in Bus.-Game Changers, Pink mag. & Forté Found., 2007. Office: Preferred Boutique HQ Ste 150 26 Corporate Plz Newport Beach CA 92660 Office Phone: 949-719-3300. Office Fax: 949-719-3301. *

UEBERROTH, PETER VICTOR, former baseball commissioner; b. Evanston, Ill., Sept. 2, 1937; s. Victor and Laura (Larson) U.; m. Virginia Nicolaus, Sept. 1959; children: Vicky, Heidi, Keri, Joe BS in Bus., San Jose State Coll., 1959. Ops. mgr. then v.p. Trans Internat., 1959-62; founder, chmn. Transp. Cons. Internat., 1963-79; pres., mng. dir. Los Angeles Olympic Organizing Com., 1979-84; commr., chief exec. officer of major league baseball NYC, 1984-89; mng. dir. Contrarian Group, 1990—; co-chmn. Doubletree Hotels Corp., Phoenix, 1993—; co-owner, co-chmn. Pebble Beach Co., 1999—; chmn. U.S. Olympic Comm., 2004—; dir. McLeodUSA, 2001—. Former chmn. Ask Mr. Foster Travel Service; chmn. Colony Hotels, Intercontinental Tours, Inc., First Travel Corp; mem. bd. dirs. California Angels. Ambassadors Internat., Coca-Cola Co., Hilton Hotels Corp. Author: Made in America, 1985 Named Man of Yr., Time Mag. and Sporting News, 1984; recipient Scopus award Am. Friends of Hebrew U., Jerusalem, 1985 Fellow: Am. Acad. Arts and Scis. Office: Ambassadors Intl Inc 110 S Ferrall St Spokane WA 99202

UECKER, BOB, actor, radio announcer, former baseball player, television personality; b. Milw., Jan. 26, 1935; m. Judy Uecker, 1976 (div. 2001); 4 children. Major league baseball player Milw. Braves, Nat. League, 1962, 63; major league baseball player St. Louis Cardinals, 1964, 65, Phila. Phillies, 1966-67, Atlanta Braves, 1967; commentator ABC Monday Night Baseball, 1976-82; commentator playoff and world series NBC Baseball, 1994-98; radio-TV baseball announcer Milw. Brewers, 1971—. Host War of the Start, Bob Ueckers Wacky World of Sports, Saturday Night Live; guest Tim Conway show, Who's the Boss, Peter Marshall Show; appeared in Fatal Instinct. Co-star TV series Mr. Belvedere, ABC-TV, 1985-1990; guest TV appearances include Late Night with David Letterman, The Tonight Show, Midnight Special, LateLine, 1998; also numerous commls.; author: Catcher in the Wry, 1985; films include: Major League, 1989, Major League 2, 1994, (voice over) Homeward Bound II: Lost in San Francisco, 1996, Major League: Back to the Minors, 1998, Andre the Giant: Larger Than Life, 1999. Recipient Big B.A.T. award Baseball Assistance Team, 1995; inducted Wis. Performing Artists Hall of Fame, 1993, Wis. Broadcasters Assn. Hall of Fame, 1994, Wis. Sports Hall of Fame, 1998. Office: Milw Brewers Baseball Club Milw County Stadium 1 Brewers Way Milwaukee WI 53214-3651

UEDA, REED TAKASHI, historian, educator; b. Honolulu, Sept. 14, 1949; s. Goro and Mildred (Yoshimoto) Ueda; m. Peggy Lynn Rubin; children: Andrea, Alyona. BA, UCLA, 1970; MA, U. Chgo., 1973, Harvard U., 1976, PhD, 1981. Rsch. editor Harvard Ency. Am. Ethnic Groups, Cambridge, Mass., 1977-79; instr. Harvard U., Cambridge, 1980-81, assoc. Ctr. Am. Polit. Studies, 2001—; prof. Tufts U., Medford, Mass., 1981—. Vis. prof. Brandeis U., Waltham, Mass., 1986, Harvard U., 1987—89, 1996; co-chair com. on internat. migration MIT, 2007—; assoc. New Global History Initiative. Author: Avenues to Adulthood, 1987, Postwar Immigrant America, 1994; editor: The Companion to Immigration, 2006; adv. editor: New Dictionary of the History of Ideas, 2005; co-editor: Faces of Community, 2003, The New Americans, 2007; assoc. editor: Jour. Interdisciplinary History, 1996—; mem. editl. bd. Harvard Ednl. Rev., 1977—78, Am. Quar., 1993, Mass. Hist. Rev., 2000—. Mem. Gov.'s Edn. Reform Rev. Commn., 1994—2002; mem. coun. fgn. rels. Boston Working Group Nat. Interest, 1995; mem. coun. for basic edn. Review Panel for Nat. Standards in History, 1995; mem. US Dept. Edn. Nat. Assessment of Ednl. Progress, 1991—92, Nat. Adv. Planning Com. for U.S. Hist. Framework, 1992—94, Nat. Standards in Civics and Govt., 1994—95, Nat. Standards in Profl. Tchg. Fellow, Am. Coun. Learned Soc., Woodrow Wilson Internat. Ctr., NEH, Charles Warren Ctr. Fellow: Mass. Hist. Soc. (mem. rsch. com. and planning com. immigration and urban history sem. 1999—); mem.: Immigration and Ethnic Hist. Soc. (exec. bd. 2001—04). Office: Tufts U Dept History Medford MA 02155 Office Phone: 617-627-3520. Business E-Mail: reed.ueda@tufts.edu.

UEHLEIN, EDWARD CARL, JR., lawyer; b. Boston, May 7, 1941; s. Edward Carl and Elizabeth (Thatcher) U.; m. Judith Taylor, June 16, 1962; children: Christine, Sara. Student, Bowdoin Coll., Brunswick, Maine, 1958-59; BA, Swarthmore Coll., 1962; LLB, Boston Coll., 1965. Bar: Mass. 1965, D.C. 1968. Atty. Nat. Labor Relations Bd., Atlanta, 1965-68; assoc. Morgan, Lewis & Bockius, Washington, 1968-71; exec. asst. to sec. U.S. Dept. Labor, Washington, 1971-73; ptnr. Morgan Lewis & Bockius, Washington, 1973—2001, counsel, 2001—. Sec.-treas. Carlou Corp., Wilmington, Del., 1969-71. Fellow, Ford Found., 1961. Mem. ABA, FBA, D.C. Bar Assn., Belle Haven Country Club, Ballybunion Golf Club, Royal Dornoch Golf Club. Avocations: travel, golf, reading. Office: Morgan Lewis & Bockius 1111 Pennsylvania Ave Washington DC 20004 Office Phone: 202-739-5075. Business E-Mail: ecuehlein@morganlewis.com.

UEHLING, BARBARA STANER, academic administrator; b. Wichita, Kans., June 12, 1932; d. Roy W. and Mary Elizabeth (Hilt) Staner; children: Jeffrey Steven, David Edward. BA, U. Wichita, 1954; MA, Northwestern U., 1956, PhD, 1958; degree (hon.), Drury Coll., 1978; LLD (hon.), Ohio State U., 1980. Mem. psychology faculty Oglethorpe U., Atlanta, 1959-64, Emory U., Atlanta, 1966-69; adj. prof. U. R.I., Kingston, 1970-72; dean Roger Williams Coll., Bristol, RI, 1972-74; dean arts scis. Ill. State U., Normal, 1974-76; provost U. Okla., Norman, 1976-78; chancellor U. Mo.-Columbia, 1978-86, U. Calif., Santa Barbara, 1987-94; mem. Pacific Rim Pub. U. Pres. Conf., 1990-92; exec. dir. Bus. and Higher Edn. Forum, Washington, 1995-97. Cons. North Ctr. Accreditation Assn., 1974-86; mem. nat. educator adv. com. to Comptr. Gen. of U.S., 1978-79; mem. Commn. on Mil.-Higher Edn. Rels., 1978-79, Am. Coun. on Edn., bd. dirs. 1979-83, treas., 1982-83, mem. Bus.-Higher Edn. Forum, 1980-94, exec. com. 1991-94; sr. vis. fellow Am. Coun. Edn., 1987; mem. Commn. on Internat. Edn., 1992-94, vice chair 1993; bd. dirs. Coun. of Postsecondary Edn., 1986-87, 90-93, Meredith Corp., 1980-99; mem. Transatlantic Dialogue, PEW Found., 1991-93; mem. West Coast adv. bd. Inst. Internat. Edn., 2004—. Author: Women in Academe: Steps to Greater Equality, 1979; mem. editl. bd. Jour. Higher Edn. Mgmt., 1986-95; contbr. articles to profl. jours. Bd. dirs., chmn. Nat. Ctr. Higher Edn. Mgmt. Sys., 1977-80; trustee Carnegie Found. for Advancement of Tchg., 1980-86, Santa Barbara Med. Found. Clinic, 1989-94; bd. dirs. Resources for the Future, 1985-94; mem. select com. on athletics NCAA, 1983-84, also mem. presdl. commn.; mem. Nat. Coun. on Edn. Rsch., 1980-82. Social Sci. Rsch. Coun. fellow, 1954-55; NSF fellow, 1956-57; NIMH postdoctoral rsch. fellow, 1964-67; named one of 100 Young Leaders of Acad. Change Mag. and ACE, 1978; recipient Alumni Achievement award Wichita State U., 1978, Alumnae award Northwestern U., 1985, Excellence in Edn. award Pi Lambda Theta, 1989. Mem. Am. Assn. Higher Edn. (bd. dirs. 1974-77, pres. 1977-78), Western Coll. Assn. (pres.-elect 1988-89, pres. 1990-92), West Coast Adv. Bd., Inst. Internat. Edn., Golden Key, Sigma Xi. Personal E-mail: buc2193@mac.com.

UEHLING, GORDON ALEXANDER, JR., investment company executive; b. Providence, Sept. 1, 1939; s. Gordon Alexander and Alice Bishop (Tomb) U.; m. Victoria M. Eckert, Dec. 30, 1967 (div. Oct. 1975); 1 child, Gordon A. III; m. Mary Elizabeth Shields, Sept. 15, 2002. BS, U.S. Naval Acad., 1961; postgrad., Columbia U., 1968. Mktg. mgr. Communitype Corp., NYC, 1968-70; asst. treas. Mfrs. Hanover Trust Co., NYC, 1970-73; v.p. The Manhattan Savs. Bank, NYC, 1973-87; pres. Turnstone, Inc., Cresskill, NJ, 1988—2000; gen. ptnr. Palisades Ptnrs., L.P., Cresskill, 1988—. Lt. USN, 1961-67, Vietnam; mem. US Naval War Coll. Found. Recipient Air medal (14 awards), USN, 1967. Mem. Naval Inst., Naval Acad. Alumni Assn., Army Navy Country Club, Gipsy Trail Club. Republican. Avocations: flying, playing tennis, skiing. Home: 222 Ruckman Rd Closter NJ 07624 Office: Palisades Ptnrs LP 100 Union Ave Cresskill NJ 07626-2137 Office Phone: 201-871-2200. E-mail: duehling@alpineassociates.com.

UEJO, COLLEEN MISAYE, elementary school educator; b. Honolulu, Oct. 18, 1953; d. Masaichi and Esther Itoyo Uejo. EdB, U. Hawaii, Manoa, 1976, M in Spl. Edn., 1983. Tchr. Liholiho Elem., Honolulu, 1979, Tenrikiyo Preschool, Honolulu, 1976—84, Queen Emma Preschool, Honolulu, 1984—88, Kaimuki Mid. Sch., Honolulu, 1988—99, Linapuni Elem., Honolulu, 1999—. After sch. care staff Waiolani Judd Sch., Honolulu, 1971—76; big sister Big Bros./Big Sisters Hawaii, Honolulu, 1984—88; coach Spl. Olympics, Honolulu, 1988—99. Yonashiro Chojin Kai v.p. Hawaii United Okinawan Assn., Honolulu, 1994. Named Uchinanchu of Yr., Hawaii United Okinawan Assn., 1998, Honolulu Dist. Tchr. of Yr., State Hawaii Dept. Edn., 2006. Mem.: ASCD, Nat. Coun. Tchrs. for Math., Nat. Assn. for the Edn. Young Children, Coun. for Exceptional Children, Phi Delta Kappa Internat. Office: Linapuni Elementary School 1434 Linapuni St Honolulu HI 96819 Home Phone: 808-537-9163; Office Phone: 808-832-3303.

UELTSCHI, ALBERT LEE, air transportation executive; b. Ky., May 15, 1917; s. Robert and Lena Ueltschi; m. Eileen Ueltschi (dec.); 4 children. Pilot Pan Am, 1941—68; founder FlightSafety Internat., Flushing, NY,

1951, pres., 1951—2003, now chmn. Chmn. Orbis Internat. Named one of Forbes' Richest Americans, 2006; named to Nat. Aviation Hall of Fame, 2001; recipient Nat. Bus. Aircraft Assn. Award, 1991, Award for Extraordinary Svc., FAA, 1991, Disting. Achievement Award, The Wings Club, 2006. Office: Teterboro Airport 100 Moonachie Ave Moonachie NJ 07074

UFBERG, MURRAY, lawyer; b. Danville, Pa., July 30, 1943; s. Alfred Eugene and Leah (Abrams) U.; m. Margery Ann Fishman, June 29, 1969; children: Aaron, Joshua, Rachel. BA, Bucknell U., 1964; JD, Duquesne U., 1968. Bar: Pa. 1968, U.s. Dist. Ct. (mid. dist.) Pa. Assoc. Rosenn, Jenkins & Greenwald, Wilkes-Barre, Pa., 1969—74; ptnr. Rosenn, Jenkins & Greenwald, L.L.P., Wilkes-Barre, 1974—. Chair bd. dirs. Greater Wilkes-Barre Partnership, Inc., 2000—02; bd. dirs. WVIA TV/FM/HDTV, 2000—, F.M. Kirby Ctr. Performing Arts, 2007—; mem. Commonwealth of Pa. Ind. Regulatory Rev. Commn., 2003—06; mem. exec. com., Transition Team Gov.-elect Edward G. Rendell, 2002—03. Chmn. United Way Wyoming Valley Gen. Campaign, Wilkes-Barre, 1990, bd. dirs., 1992—94; mem. Luzerne County adv. com. Pa. Economy League; mem. pres. adv. coun. Keystone Coll.; past pres. Ohav Zedek Synagogue, Wilkes-Barre, 1986—88, Jewish Cmty. Ctr. Wyoming Valley, 1982—83, Seligman J. Strauss lodge B'nai B'rith, Wilkes-Barre, 1970—74; pres. Jewish Fedn. Greater Wilkes-Barre; trustee United Hebrew Inst.; chmn. Jewish Cmty. Rels. Coun., 1993—97, 2000; trustee Coll. Misericordia. Recipient Disting. Svc. award Wilkes-Barre Jaycees, 1979, Cmty. Svc. award, Seligman J. Strauss Lodge No. 139 of B'nai B'rith, 2003. Mem. ABA, Pa. Bar Assn., Luzerne County Bar Assn. (chmn. cmty. rels. com. 1997—), Duquesne U. Law Alumni Assn. (bd. govs.). Jewish. Avocations: sports, recreational reading. Home: 644 Charles Ave Kingston PA 18704 Office: Rosenn Jenkins & Greenwald LLP 15 S Franklin St Wilkes Barre PA 18711-0075 also: 120 E Broad St Hazleton PA 18201 also: 120 Wyoming Ave Scranton PA 18503 also: 221 Broad St Milford PA 18337 Office Phone: 570-826-5638. E-mail: mufberg@rjglaw.com.

UFFELMAN, MALCOLM RUCJ, electronics executive; b. Clarksville, Tenn., Oct. 22, 1935; s. Malcolm C. and Margaret Lillian (Davidson) U.; m. Sarah White Barksdale, June 11, 1957; children: Malcolm Rucj Jr., Katharina White, Davidson Barksdale, Jefferson Churchill. BS, Vanderbilt U., 1957; MS, George Washington U., 1963. Engr. Melpar, Inc., Falls Church, Va., 1957-60; v.p. Scope, Inc., Reston, Va., 1960-73; sr. cons. MRI, Inc., McLean, Va., 1973-78; v.p. Racal Communications Inc., Rockville, Md., 1978-80; sr. cons. MRJ, Inc., Fairfax, Va., 1980-82; v.p., gen. mgr., Ctr. Advanced Planning and Analysis E-Systems Inc., Fairfax, 1982-96; v.p. Constellation Comm., Inc., Fairfax, 1996-99; patent agt., 1999—2000; exec. v.p. Contact Corp., 2000—. Contbr. numerous articles to profl. jours.; holder 7 patents in field. Scoutmaster Troop 183 Boy Scouts Am., Oakton, Va., 1973-79; bd. dirs. Camco Fund, 2002—. Capt. USAR, 1957-69. Fellow IEEE; mem. Cosmos Club (Washington), Internat. Brotherhood Magicians. Episcopalian. Avocations: sailing, reading, travel, magic, fly fishing. Personal E-mail: rucj@ieee.org.

UFFNER, MICHAEL S., automotive executive; b. Phila., July 18, 1945; s. Ray and Shirley A. (Block) Uffner; m. Marilyn A. Ursomarso; 1 child, Lauren R. BA, MA, U. Pa., Phila., 1971. V.p. Union Park Pontiac, BMW, Honda, Wilmington, Del., 1972-82; pres. Del. Motor Sales Inc., Auto Team Del., Wilmington, 1982—. Mem. manpower tng. adv. com. GM, pres. dealer adv. coun., 1985, mem. dealer policy bd., 1990—91; trustee Christiana Health Care Sys., 2002—. Mem. Wilmington Police Bus. Adv. Coun., 1991—, New Castle County Small Bus. Commn., 1993—; trustee Golden-Beacom Coll., 2007—; bd. dirs., mem. exec. com. BBB Del., 1992—2007, chmn., 1998—2000. Recipient Quality Dealer award, Time Mag., 1997, numerous other awards. Mem.: Del. Automobile and Truck Dealers Assn. (bd. dirs., v.p. 1992—93, pres. 1994—95), Am. Econ. Assn., Cadillac Motor Car Divsn. Nat. Dealers Coun. (vice chmn. 1989—90, chmn. 1990—91, chmn. DeVille brand com. 1995—97), Tavistock Civic Assn. (pres. 1976—77), US C. of C. (bd. dirs. 1998—2004, chmn. pub. affairs com. 2001—04), Del. C. of C. (chmn. small bus. com. 1991—95, bd. dirs. 1993—, chmn. small bus. alliance 1995—96, mem. exec. com. 1995—, vice chmn. bd. dirs. 1996—99, chmn. bd. dirs. 2000—02), Am. Heart Assn. (bd. dirs. Del. chpt. 1981—98, pres. 1985—86, chmn. 1986—87, v.p., bd. dirs. Nat. Ctr. 1987—90), U. Pa. Alumni Assn. (v.p. Del. chpt. 1978—80, pres. 1980—81), Univ. Whist Club, Ocean City Yacht Club, Hidden Creek Golf Club, Fieldstone Golf Club. Office: 1606 Pennsylvania Ave Wilmington DE 19806-4018

UFFORD, CHARLES WILBUR, JR., lawyer; b. Princeton, NJ, July 8, 1931; m. Isabel Letitia Wheeler, May 20, 1961; children: Eleanor Morris Ufford Léger, Catherine Latourette Ufford-Chase, Alison Wistar Ufford Salem. BA cum laude (Francis H. Burr scholar), Harvard U., Cambridge, Mass., 1953, LLB, 1959; postgrad. (Lionel de Jersey Harvard studentship), Cambridge U., Eng., 1953-54. Bar: NY 1961, US Tax Ct. 1963. Assoc. Riggs, Ferris & Geer, NYC, 1959-61; from assoc. to ptnr. Jackson, Nash, Brophy, Barringer & Brooks, 1961-78; ptnr. Skadden, Arps, Slate, Meagher & Flom, NYC, 1978-92, of counsel, 1993-96. Contbr. articles to legal jours. Trustee Nat. Squash Racquets Ednl. Found., NYC, 1972-81; mem. Princeton Monthly Meeting, Soc. of Friends, clk., 1986-88, 99; mem. exec. com. Friends Com. on Nat. Legislation, 1997-98; bd. dirs. Pennswood Village, 1998-2007, Friends Fiduciary Corp., 1999-. Nat. Intercollegiate Squash Racquets champion, 1952-53; mem. NCAA All-Am. Soccer lst team, 1952. Fellow Am. Coll. Trust and Estate Counsel (transfer tax study com. 1990-93); mem. ABA, NY Bar Assn. (chmn. trusts and estates law sect. 1984), Assn. Bar City NY, NY State Office of Ct. Adminstrn. (Surrogates Ct. Adv. Com., 1994-96), US Squash Racquets Assn. (hon. life; trustee endowment fund 1984-96), Internat. Lawn Tennis Club U.S.A. (dir. 1982-2005). Office: 150 Mercer St Princeton NJ 08540-6827 Office Phone: 609-921-8085. Personal E-mail: cuffordl@aol.com. *Integrity, perseverance, compassion and humor are all very well--but the key is to be blessed by a Divine Improvidence.*

UFIMTSEV, PYOTR YAKOVLEVICH, physicist, electrical engineer, educator; b. Ust'-Charyshskaya Pristan', Altai Region, Russia, July 8, 1931; s. Yakov Fedorovich and Vasilisa Vasil'evna (Toropchina) U.; m. Tatiana Vladimirovna Sinelschikova; children: Galina, Ivan, Vladimir. Grad., Odessa State U., Ukraine, 1954; PhD, Ctrl. Rsch. Inst. Radio Industry, 1959; DSc, St. Petersburg State U., Russia, 1970. Engr., sr. engr., sr. scientist Ctrl. Rsch. Inst. of Radio Industry, Moscow, 1954-73; sr. scientist, head scientist Inst. Radio Engring. & Electronics Acad. Scis., Moscow, 1973-90; prin. engr. Northrop Grumman Corp., 1995—2000; prof. U. Calif., Irvine, 2003—04. Vis. prof., adj. prof. UCLA, 1990—2003; mem. sci. bd. radio waves Acad. Scis., Moscow, 1960—90. Author: Method of Edge Waves in the Physical Theory of Diffraction, 1962, Theory of Edge Diffraction in Electromagnetics, 2003, Fundamentals of the Physical Theory of Diffraction, 2007; contbr. articles to profl. jours. Recipient USSR State Prize, Moscow, 1990, Leroy Randle Grumman medal for outstanding sci. achievement, N.Y.C., 1991, 20th Century Achievement medal, Cambridge, 1996, Hall of Fame medal, Cambridge, 1996. Fellow IEEE; assoc. fellow AIAA; mem. Electromagnetics Acad. (U.S.), A.S. Popov Sci. Tech. Soc. Radio Engring., Electronics & Telecommunication (Russia). Achievements include origination of the Physical Theory of Diffraction, used for design of American stealth aircrafts and ships; for radar-cross-section calculation, and antenna design.

UGGAMS, LESLIE, entertainer; b. NYC, May 25, 1943; d. Harolde Coyden and Juanita Ernestine (Smith) Uggams; m. Grahame John Kelvin-Pratt, Oct. 16, 1965; children: Danielle Nicole Pratt, Justice Harolde John Kelvin-Pratt. Student, Juillard Sch. Music, 1961-63; degree (hon.), Jarvis Coll., Tyler, Tex., Wilberforce U., Ohio. Appeared on (TV series) Beulah, 1949, featured on Sing Along with Mitch, 1961—64, starred in (Broadway plays) Hallelujah Baby, 1967 (Tony award, 1968), Her First Roman Broadway Musical, 1968, On Golden Pond, 2005 (nominated Helen Hayes award for best actress, 2005), star of (weekly TV variety show) The Leslie Uggams Show, 1969, appearances in nightclubs top TV mus. variety shows, appeared in films Two Weeks in Another Town, Black Girl, 1962, Skyjacked, 1972, Poor Pretty Eddie, 1973, appeared in (TV miniseries) Roots, ABC-TV, 1977 (Critics Choice award as best supporting actress, 1977), (TV films) Sizzle, 1981, Harlem, 1993, star (Broadway musicals) Blues in the Night, 1982, (Broadway musical) Jerry's Girls, 1985, Anything Goes, 1987, (off-Broadway) The Old Settler, 1999 (Audelco award as best actress), (dramatic play), 1999; apeared in: Thoroughly Modern Millie, 2004; star (musical play) King Hedley II, 2001 (nominated Tony award best actress, 2001), Thunder Knocking on the Door, 2002 (Audelco award best actress, 2002), (TV miniseries) Backstairs at the White House, 1979, co-host (TV series) Fantasy TV, 1982—83 (Emmy award 1983, 1983); author: The Leslie Uggams Beauty Book, 1966. Founding mem. BRAVO chpt. City of Hope, Los Angeles, 1969, treas., 1969—79. Named best singer on TV, 1962—63; recipient Drama Critics award, Newspaper and TV critics, 1968, Tony award, 1968, Emmy award, 1993. Mem.: SAG, NARAS, AFTRA, Actors' Equity Assn. Democrat. Presbyterian. Avocations: needlepoint, knitting, tennis, squash, exercising. Business E-Mail: leslie@leslieuggams.com.

UGHETTA, JAMES C., lawyer; BA, Denison U., 1977; JD, St. John's U., 1981. Bar: NY 1982, NJ 1982, US Dist. Ct. Dist. NJ, US Dist. Ct. Ea. Dist. NY, US Dist. Ct. So. Dist. NY, US Dist. Ct. No. Dist. NY, US Supreme Ct. Ptnr. Wilson, Elser, Moskowitz, Edelman & Dicker LLP, White Plains, NYC, Littleton Joyce Ughetta, Park and Kelly, LLP, NYC. Mem.: Soc. Automotive Engineers (product liability adv. coun.), Assn. for the Advancement of Automotive Medicine, Def. Rsch. Inst. Office: LIttleton Joyce Ughetta Park and Kelly LLP ONe Manhattanville Rd Purchase NY 10577

UGHETTA, WILLIAM CASPER, lawyer, manufacturing executive, director; b. NYC, Feb. 8, 1933; s. Casper and Frieda (Bohland) U.; m. Mary L. Lusk, Aug. 10, 1957; children: William C., Robert L., Edward F., Mark R. AB, Princeton U, 1954; LLB, Harvard U., 1959. Bar: N.Y. 1959. Assoc. Shearman & Sterling, NYC, 1959-67; asst. sec. Corning Glass Works, NY, 1968-70, sec., counsel NY, 1971-72, v.p., gen. counsel NY, 1972-82, sr. v.p., gen. counsel NY, 1983-98. Bd. dirs. Covance Inc. Bd. dirs. Steuben Area coun. Boy Scouts Am. Lt. (j.g.) USN, 1954-56. Mem. Assn. of Bar of City of N.Y., ABA, N.Y. State Bar Assn., Am. Corp. Counsel Assn. (trustee 1982-85), Princeton Club (N.Y.C.), Univ. Club (N.Y.C.), Corning Country Club. Home: 10519 North Rd Corning NY 14830-3235

UGOROWSKI, PHILIP BRIEN, nuclear scientist, researcher; s. Felix Joseph and Mary Margaret (Van Tiem) Ugorowski. BA in Physics, Kalamazoo Coll., Mich., 1983, BA in Math, 1983; MS in Rsch. Physics, Mich. State U., East Lansing, 1987; PhD in Exptl. Nuc. Physics, Western Mich. U., Kalamazoo, 2002. Grad. asst. temp. faculty Western Mich. U., 1995—99; vis. faculty mem. Kalamazoo Coll., 1999—2000; postdoctoral rschr. Youngstown State U., Ohio, 2003—05; nuc. rschr., educator Glen Oaks CC, Centreville, Mich. Recipient Tchg. Awards, Western Mich. U., 1995, 1996, 1999. Mem.: Am. Phys. Soc., Am. Mensa. Achievements include research in hafnium controversy using nuclear calorimetry. Avocations: swimming, hiking. Home: 22115 Shady LN Saint Clair Shores MI 48080 Home Phone: 269-383-4357; Office Phone: 269-467-9945. Personal E-mail: phil.ugorowski@juno.com.

UHDE, THOMAS WHITLEY, psychopharmacology, psychiatrist; s. George Irwin and Maurine U.; m. Marlene Ann Kraus, Oct. 22, 1977; children: Miles August, Katherine Kraus. BS, Duke U., 1971; MD, U. Louisville, 1975. Diplomate Am. Bd. Psychiatry and Neurology. Postdoctoral fellow Yale U., New Haven, 1975-79, chief resident clin. rsch. unit, 1979; rsch. fellow NIMH, 1979-81; pvt. practice in psychiatry Bethesda, Md., 1979-93; clin. adminstr. sect. psychobiology BPB, NIMH, ADAMHA, Bethesda, Md., 1979-80, chief unit on anxiety and affective disorders, 1982-89, chief 3-West clin. rsch. unit, 1980-90, chief sect. on anxiety and affective disorders, 1989-93; asst. clin. prof. Uniformed Svcs. U. Health Scis., Bethesda, Md., 1982-85, assoc. clin. prof. uniformed svcs., 1985-91; attending staff Clin. Ctr. NIH, Bethesda, Md., 1982-93; chmn. dept. psychiatry Detroit Receiving Hosp. and Harper Hosp., 1994-98; psychiatrist in chief Detroit Med. Ctr., 1993—2001; clin. prof. Uniformed Svcs. U. Health Scis. Sch. Medicine, Bethesda, 1991—; chmn. dept. psychiatry and behavorial neuroscis. Wayne State U. Sch. Medicine, Detroit, 1993—2001; prof. dept. pharmacology Wayne State U. Sch. of Medicine, Detroit, 1993—2003, 1999—2001; prof., chair dept. psychiatry Penn State Coll., Hershey, Pa., 2004—, dir. ctrl. Pa. Psychiatric Inst., 2004—, dir. neurosci. rsch. inst., 2004—06. Prof., psychiatry and behavioral neuroscis. dept., Wayne State U. Sch. Medicine, 1993-2003, assoc. dean rsch. and grad. programs, 1999-2001; asst. dean neuroscis., 2001-03; mem. sci. adv. com. Bethesda, Md., 1990; cons. Rsch. Scientist Devel. Rev. Com., HHS, ADAMHA, 1983, Career Devel. Program Awards Com., VA, Washington, 1986, Primary Care Rsch. Program, ADAMHA, 1988; exec. bd. Anxiety Disorders Assn. Am., 1991-93, 99-, chair sci. adv. bd., Rockville, Md., 1991-93; biomed. instr. review bd. Penn State U., 2004-; mem. sci. adv. bd. VA VISN4 MIREXX, 2005-. Editor-in-chief (jour.) Anxiety 1993-1996; Co-editor-in-chief (jour.) Depression and Anxiety 1996-2002; Editor-in-chief (jour.) Depression and Anxiety 2002--; mem. editl. bd. Actualities Medicales Internationales en Psychiatrie, 1983, Jour. Affective Disorders, 1986, Jour. Anxiety Disorders, 1987-95, Biol. Psychiatry, 1998—2001; contbr. more than 300 sci. articles to profl. jours. Sr. asst. surgeon US Pub. Health Svc., 1979—80, surgeon US Pub. Health Svc., 1980—84, sr. surgeon US Pub. Health Svc., 1984—91, med. dir. US Pub. Health Svc., 1991—93. Recipient Ackerly award, Nat. Rsch. Svc. award, A.E. Bennet Neuropsychiat. Rsch. Found. award, Brain, Body & Mind award Uniformed Svc. Univ. Health Sci., Recognition award ADAA; Am. Coll. Neuropsychopharmacology travel fellow; Commendation medal, US Public Health Svc.; Meritous Svc. medal; named disting. lectr., U. Va., Heninger Lectr., Yale, Highly Cited Scientist in Psychology/Psychiatry, ISI. Fellow Am. Psychiatric Assn. (disting.); mem. Am. Coll. Neuropsychopharmacolgoy, Am. Coll. Psychiatry, Am. Soc. of Clin. Psychopharmacology, Internat. Brain Rsch. Orgn., Sleep Rsch. Soc., Biol. Psych. Soc., Am Psych Assoc., Penn Psych. Soc., Anx. Dis. Assoc. Am., Anx. Assoc. Argentina (hon), Am. Assoc. Chair Dept. Psych., Int. Soc. Psychoneurology. Independent. Unitarian Universalist. Avocations: art, piano, hiking, boating. Office: Penn State Coll Medicine Dept Psychiatry PO Box 850 500 University Dr Hershey PA 17033-0850 Office Phone: 717-531-8516. Office Fax: 717-531-6491. Business E-Mail: tuhde@psu.edu.

UHI, JUDD R., lawyer; b. Sept. 18, 1973; m. Leslee Uhi. BA in Hist., Miami U., Ohio, 1995, BA in Polit. Sci., 1995; JD, U. Akron, 1999. Bar: Ohio 1999, US Dist. Ct. Northern Dist. Ohio 1999, US Dist. Ct. Southern Dist. Ohio 1999, Ky. 2003. Adj. prof., Trial Advocacy Ohio State U., 2000—01; assoc. Freund, Freeze & Arnold, Cin. Named one of Ohio's Rising Stars, Super Lawyers, 2006. Mem.: Ohio Assn. Civil Trial Attorneys, Ohio State Bar Assn., Ky. Bar Assn., Northern Ky. Bar Assn., Cin. Bar Assn. Avocations: indoor soccer, travel, horseracing, softball. Office: Freund Freeze & Arnold Fourth and Walnut Ctr 105 E Fourth St Ste 1400 Cincinnati OH 45202 Office Phone: 513-665-3500. Office Fax: 513-665-3503.

UHL, CHRISTOPHER MARTIN, lawyer; b. Balt., Feb. 21, 1958; s. Robert Henry and Marie Antoinette (Carosella) U.; m. Gael Anna Evangelista, Feb. 16, 1991; children: Christopher Martin Uhl, Grace Molinari Uhl. BS in Acctg., Northeastern U., Boston, 1989, MBA, 1991; JD, New Eng. Sch. Law, 1992. Bar: Mass. 1993, NY 1993, Md. 2004, US Dist. Ct. Mass. 1993, DC 1994, Maine 1994, US Dist. Ct. DC 1994, US Dist. Maine 1994, Conn. 1995, US Supreme Ct., 1998, US Dist. Ct. (ea. and so. dists.) NY 1999, US Dist. Ct. Conn. 1999, US Ct. Appeals (1st cir.) 2000. Fingerprint technician FBI, Washington, 1976-79; project mgr. various constrn. cos., Balt., 1979-87, Admiral Constrn. Co., Boston, 1987-91; asst. dist. atty. Worcester Dist. Atty.'s Office, Mass., 1992-96; prin. Christopher Uhl, Attorney at Law, Worcester, 1997—. Prof. Becker Coll., Worcester, 1993-97. Bd. dirs. Am. Cancer Soc., Boston, 1990-96; ward coord. Reelect Dist. Atty. Campaign, Worcester, 1994; elected mem. Southborough Rep. Town Com., Southborough Housing Authority, Northborough/Southborough Regional Sch. Com. Named Hon. Mem. Rep. State Com. Republican. Roman Catholic. Roman Catholic. Office: 5 State St Worcester MA 01609-2893 Office Phone: 508-797-9000. Office Fax: 508-797-4210. Business E-Mail: chris@uhllaw.com.

UHL, KATHLEEN, federal agency administrator; b. May 12, 1962; BA in Chemistry, Temple U.; MD, Med. Coll. Pa. Intern, resident Fort Benning, Ga.; fellow Uniformed Svcs. U. Health Scis.; physician Walter Reed Army Med. Ctr., Washington; with FDA, Rockville, Md., 1998—, reviewer office clin. pharmacology and biopharmaceutics, dep. divsn. dir. office post-mktg. drug risk assesment, acting divsn. dir., supervisory med. officer ctr. drug eval. and rsch., dir. Office Women's Health, 2005—. Capt. USPHS. Contbr. articles to profl. jours. Recipient Meritorious Svc. Medal. Office: FDA 5600 Fishers Ln Rockville MD 20857

UHL, PHILIP EDWARD, artist, photographer, cinematographer; b. Toledo, Aug. 19, 1949; s. Philip Edward and Betty Jean U. Student, Dayton Art Inst., 1967-68, Art Students League, 1974. Creative dir. Ctr. for Civic Initiative, Milw., 1969-71; VISTA vol. Office Econ. Opportunity, 1969-71; artist, photographer Assn. Honolulu Artists, 1974-77; pres. Uhl Enterprises div. Makai Photography, Honolulu, 1977—, Videoscapes div. Channel Sea TV, Honolulu, 1977—. Cons. Pan Am. Airways, N.Y.C., Honolulu, 1979-84, ITTC Travel Ctr., Honolulu, 1982-83, Royal Hawaiian Ocean Racing Club, Honolulu, 1984—, Sail Am.-Am's Cup Challenge, Honolulu, 1985-86, Am. 3 Found., Am. Cup Def., San Diego, 1991-92, Am. 3 Found. Womens Team, 1994-95, UHL Studios, Hawaii, 2000—. Co-prodr. video documentary White on Water, 1984 (Emmy 1984), Racing the Winds of Paradise (Golden Monitor award Internat. TV Assn. 1989); prodr.: Joy of Life (Golden Monitor award Internat. TV Assn. 1988), Sailors on the Sea, 1990, Teamwork, Talent, Technology (Tele award 1993); cameraman, prodr.: Pan Am. Clipper Cup 1980, 82, 84, Kenwood Cup, 1986, 88, 90, 92, 94, 96, 98, 2000 (2 Tele awards 1994), ESPN Kenwood Cup, 1990, 92, 94, ESPN Am.'s Cup, 1991-92, 94-95, Transpac, 1991, 93, 95, 97, 99, 2001, 05, (video documentary) Rocking the Boat, 1994-95, Dateline NBC Setting Sail 1994-95, numerous spls., reports on ABC-TV, NBC-TV, CBS-TV, PBS, NHK, BBC, TFI, F1, TVNZ and numerous other major worldwide broadcast networks; prodr. At the Helm, America' Cup 2000 TVNZ; coord. prodr. Disney feature film documentary Morning Light; photographer, dir. graphic design/photography (video documentary) Transpac 100 years across the Pacific, 2001: (book) Nautical Quar. (Soc. Pub. Designer award 1984); contbr. numerous articles, photos to yachting publs., numerous exhbns. fine/digital art; exhibited in group shows in Honolulu, Washington, DC (Smithsonian), Tokyo, Hong Kong, Syndey, Paris, Boston, Palm Beach, Isle of Wight, Las Vegas, San Diego, San Francisco, L.A., N.Y.C., Osterville, Mass.; represented in permanent collections City and County of Honolulu, Hawaii Maritime Mus., UCLA Med. Ctr., others. Mem. Am. Print Alliance, Am. Soc. Marine Artists, Soc. Internat. Nautical Scribes, Internat. Yacht Restoration Sch., Honolulu Printmakers, Digital Art Soc. Hawaii, Assn. Hawaii Artists, U.S. Sailing Assn., Royal Hawaiian Ocean Racing Club, Tutukaka South Pacific Yacht Club, Waikiki Yacht Club. Office: UHL Enterprises 1750 Kalakaua Ave Ste 3-757 Honolulu HI 96826-3766 E-mail: uhl@aol.com.

UHL, SCOTT MARK, state agency administrator; b. Balt., July 6, 1950; s. Edward George and Maurine Barbara (Keleher) Uhl; m. Charlene Hughins, Feb. 29, 1988. BA, Lehigh U., 1972. Cmty. systems developer Md. Mental Hygiene Adminstrn., Balt., 1979-82, chief, housing and cmty. support, 1982-89; adminstr., cmty. programs, dep. secretariat pub. health Md. Health and Mental Hygiene, Balt., 1989-95; dep. dir. Md. Devel. Disabilities Adminstrn., Balt., 1995—2007, acting dir., 2007; cons., 2007—. Pres. Waterfields Press, Inc., 1994—2004; mem. CARE adv. bd. Md. Dept. Human Resources, Balt., 1987—94; prin. staff Md. Gov.'s Task Force Long Term Fin. Planning for Individuals with Disabilities, 1991—92; cons. Mem. State Adv. Coun. Adminstrv. Hearings, 1993—97. Recipient Gov's Citation, 1992, 2007. Republican. Home: 2004 Sleepy Hollow Dr Woodbine MD 21797

UHLENBECK, KAREN KESKULLA, mathematician, educator; b. Cleve., Aug. 24, 1942; d. Arnold Edward and Carolyn Elizabeth (Windeler) Keskulla; m. Olke Cornelis, June 12, 1965 (div.) BS in Math., U. Mich., 1964; PhD in Math., Brandeis U., 1968. Instr. math. MIT, Cambridge, 1968-69; lectr. U. Calif., Berkeley, 1969-71; asst. prof., then assoc. prof. U. Ill., Urbana, 1971-76, assoc. prof., then prof. Chgo., 1977-83; prof. U. Chgo., 1983-88; Sid W. Richardson Found. Regents' Chair in Math. U. Tex., Austin, 1988—. Spkr. plenary address Internat. Conress Maths., 1990; mem. com. women on sci. and engring. NRC, 1992-94; co-founder, mem. steering com., dir. mentoring program for women Inst. for Advanced Study/Park City Math. Inst.; co-founder, Women and Math. in Princeton. Author: Instantons and Four Manifolds, 1984. Contbr. articles to profl. jours. Recipient Common Wealth award for Sci. and Technology, PNC Bank, 1995, Presdl. Medal of Sci., 2000; NSF grad. fellow, 1964-68, Sloan Found. fellow, 1974-76, MacArthur Found. fellow, 1983-88. Fellow AAAS, NAS; mem. Alumni Assn. U. Mich. (Alumnae of Yr. 1984), Am. Math. Soc.(Leroy P. Steele for Seminal Contribution to Rsch., 2007), Assn. Women in Math., Phi Beta Kappa. Avocations: gardening, canoeing, hiking. Office: U Tex Dept Math Austin TX 78712 *

UHLENHUTH, EBERHARD HENRY, psychiatrist, educator; b. Balt., Sept. 15, 1927; s. Eduard Carl Adolph and Elisabeth (Baier) Uhlenhuth; m. Helen Virginia Lyman, June 20, 1952; children: Kim Lyman, Karen Jane, Eric Rolf. BS in Chemistry, Yale U., 1947; MD, Johns Hopkins U., 1951. Intern Harborview Hosp., Seattle, 1951-52; resident in psychiatry Johns Hopkins Hosp., Balt., 1952-56, asst. psychiatrist in charge outpatient dept., 1956-61, psychiatrist in charge, 1961-62; chief adult psychiatry clinic U. Chgo. Hosps. Clinics, 1968-76; instr. psychiatry Johns Hopkins U., 1956-59, asst. prof., 1959-67, assoc. prof., 1967-68, U. Chgo., 1968-73, prof., 1973-85, acting chmn., 1983-85; prof. psychiatry U. N.Mex., Albuquerque, 1985-97, prof. emeritus, 1997—, Disting. Univ. prof., 2005—, vice chmn. for edn., 1991-94. Cons. in field; clin. psychopharmacology rsch. rev. com. NIMH, 1968-72, mem. treatment devel. and assessment rsch. rev. com., 1987-88; mem. psychopharmacology adv. com. FDA, 1974-78; adv. group to Treatment of Depression Collaborative Rsch. Program, NIMH, 1978-92; study rev. com. Xanax discontinuation program Upjohn Co., 1988-92, Nat. Adv. Coun. on Drug Abuse, NIDA, 1989-92, Coop. Studies Evaluation Com., VA, 1989-92. Mem. editl. bd. Jour. Affective Disorders, 1978—, Psychiatry Rsch., 1979-96, Behavioral Medicine, 1982—, Neuropsychopharmacology, 1992-95, Exptl. and Clin. Psychopharmacology, 1992-99, Depression and Anxiety, 1992—; contbr. articles to profl. jours. Recipient Rsch. Career Devel. award USPHS, 1962-68, Rsch. Scientist award, 1976-81. Fellow: Collegium Internat. Neuro-Psychopharmacologicum, Am. Psychopath. Assn., Am. Psychiat.

Assn., Am. Coll. Neuropsychopharmacology (pres. 1986); mem.: Psychiat. Rsch. Soc., Balt.-Washington Soc. Psychoanalysis. Office: U NMex Dept Psychiatry MSC09 5030 1 Univ New Mex Albuquerque NM 87131-0001 Home Phone: 505-265-0663; Office Phone: 505-272-8876. Business E-Mail: uhli@unm.edu.

UHLER, WALTER CHARLES, government official, writer; b. Lebanon, Pa., Feb. 23, 1948; s. Victor Cornelius and Barbara Jean (Malin) U.; m. Judy Ann Sherk, Aug. 7, 1967 (div. 1984); children: Terry Allen, Matthew David. Life partner: Carol A. DePrisco. BA in Polit. Sci. cum laude, Pa. State U., 1973, BA in Russian cum laude, 1973, cert. Russian area, 1973, MPA, 1992. Tchg. asst. Pa. State U., University Park, 1975-76; procurement agt. Naval Aviation Supply Office, Phila., 1976-80; contracts adminstr. GSA, Phila., 1980-81; contracting officer Def. Logistics Agy., Phila., 1981-86, corp. contracting officer, 1986-94; chief fin. svcs., 1993—2001; chief of ops. Def. Contract Mgmt. Agy., Lockheed Martin Delaware Valley, 2001—; dir. Def. Contract Mgmt. Agy., Valley Forge, 2006—; regional cons. Def. Logistics Agy., LA, 1985-86, nat. cons. Cameron Station, Va., 1989-90, leader Testing Labs. Privatization Assessment Team Ft. Belvoir, Va., 1997-98. Participant Air Force Intelligence Conf. on Soviet Affairs, Arlington, Va., 1988, Venona Conf., Washington, 1996, Ballistic Missile Def. Conf., Washington, 1998, AP/Harriman Inst. Conf., N.Y.C., 1999, State of the World Forum, N.Y.C., 2000; testified against nat. missile def., Vt. Ho. of Reps., 2002; gave radio interviews on nat. missile def., Vt., Calif., Wis., Radio Free Europe/Radio Liberty, 2002; presenter, 11th ann. Russia-Am. Conf., St. Petersburg, Russia, 2002; spkr. on contracts DOD Conf., Cleve., 1988, on restructuring costs, Memphis, 1994; chmn. Ann. Nat. Conf. Contracting Officers and Auditors, 1987-93; mem. Citizen Amb. Archivists' Del. to Russia and Poland, 1995, Citizen Amb. Del. to China, 1996, Russia and Finland, 1998; prodr., interviewer (with George Enteen) Sergei Vasilievich Utechin's Oral Reminiscences, 1997—; pres, Russian-American Internat. Studies Assn, 2004-. Contbr. articles to profl. publications. Baseball coach Valley Athletic Assn., Bensalem, Pa., 1979-88, basketball coach, 1980-85, coord., 1981; tutor Ctr. for Literacy, Phila., 1991-93, Project GIVE, Phila., 1995-98. Recipient Comdrs. Excellence award Defense Contract Mgmt. Area Ops., 1993. Mem. Am. Assn. for Advancement Slavic Studies, Soc. for Mil. History, Nat. Book Critics Cir., Russian Am. Internat. Studies Assn., Penn State Nittany Lion Club Democrat. Avocations: history, literature, Pennsylvania State University football. Personal E-mail: waltuhler@aol.com.

UHLIR, ARTHUR, JR., electrical engineer, academic administrator; b. Chgo., Feb. 2, 1926; s. Arthur and Helene (Houghteling) U.; m. Ingeborg Williams, July 24, 1954; children: Steven, Donald, David. BS, Ill. Inst. Tech., 1945, MSChemE, 1948; SM in Physics, U. Chgo., 1950, PhD in Physics, 1952. Process analyst Douglas Aircraft, Chgo., 1945; asst. engr. Armour Rsch. Found., Chgo., 1945-48; tech. staff Bell Telephone Labs., Murray Hill, NJ, 1951-58; dir. semi- condr. research and devel., mgr. semicondr. div., group v.p. engring. Microwave Assos., Inc., Burlington, Mass., 1958-69; dir. rsch. Computer Metrics, Rochelle Park, NJ, 1969-73; prof. elec. engring. Tufts U., Medford, Mass., 1970-94, chmn. dept. elec. engring., 1970-75, dean of engring., 1973-80. Fellow, AEC, 1949—51. Fellow: AAAS, IEEE; mem.: Am. Phys. Soc., Sigma Xi. Home: 45 Kendal Common Rd Weston MA 02493-2159 Office: Tufts Univ Dept Elec & Computer Engring Medford MA 02155 Personal E-mail: auhlir@mailaps.org.

UHLMANN, FREDERICK GODFREY, securities trader; b. Chgo, Dec. 31, 1929; s. Richard F. and Rosamond G. (Goldman) U.; m. Virginia Lee Strauss, July 24, 1951; children: Richard, Thomas, Virginia, Karen, Elizabeth. BA, Washington and Lee U., 1951. Ptnr. Uhlmann Grain Co., Chgo., 1951-61; v.p. Uhlmann & Co., Inc., Chgo., 1961-65; sr. v.p. H. Hentz & Co., Chgo., 1965-73, Drexel Burnham Lambert Inc., Chgo., 1973-84; exec. v.p., dir. bus. futures Dean Witter Reynolds Inc., Chgo., 1984-85; sr. v.p., mgr. commodity dept. Bear, Stearns & Co., Inc., Chgo., 1985-88; exec. v.p. Rodman & Renshaw, Inc., 1988-95; sr. v.p. LIT-Divsn. of First Options Inc., Chgo., 1995-98; chmn. Chgo Bd. Trade, Ill., 1973-74; sr. v.p., exec. dir. MAN Financial, 1998—. Ptnr. Uhlmann Price Securities LLC. Bd. dir. Dist. 113 H.S. Found., 1990—, Mt. Sanai Hosp. Inst., Chgo., 1999—. Mem. Nat. Futures Assoc. (dir. 1981-2000, vice chair 1998-2000), Futures Industry Assn. (bd. dir., chmn. 1975-76), Futures Industry Inst. (bd. dir.). Home: 783 Whiteoaks Ln Highland Park IL 60035-3656 Office Phone: 847-444-1104. E-mail: fgu73@aol.com.

UHRIG, ROBERT EUGENE, nuclear engineer, educator; b. Raymond, Ill., Aug. 6, 1928; s. John Matthew and Anna LaDonna (Fireman) U.; m. Paula Margaret Schnepf, Nov. 27, 1954; children: Robert John, Joseph Charles, Mary Catherine, Charles William, Jean Marie, Thomas Paul, Fredrick James. BS with honors, U. Ill., 1948; MS, Iowa State U., Ames, 1950, PhD, 1954; grad. Advanced Mgmt. Program, Harvard U., Cambridge, Mass., 1976. Registered profl. engr., Iowa, Fla. Instr. engring. mechanics Iowa State U., 1948-51; assoc. engr., rsch. asst. Inst. Atomic Rsch. (at univ.), 1951-54, assoc. prof. engring. mechanics and nuc. engring., also group leader, 1956-60; prof. nuc. engring., chmn. dept. U. Fla., Gainesville, 1960-68, on leave, 1967-68, dean Coll. Engring., 1968-73, dean emeritus, 1989—; dep. asst. dir. rsch. Dept. Def., Washington, 1967-68; dir. nuc. affairs Fla. Power & Light Co., Miami, 1973-74, v.p. for nuc. affairs, 1974-75, v.p. nuc. and gen. engring., 1976-78, v.p. advanced systems and tech., 1978-86; disting. prof. engring. U. Tenn., Knoxville, 1986—2002, disting. prof. engring. emeritus, 2003—; disting. scientist Oak Ridge Nat. Lab., 1986—2002, disting. scientist emeritus, 2003—. Instr. engring. mechanics US Mil. Acad., 1954-56; rep. Dept. Def. to com. on acad. sci. and engring. Fed. Coun. Sci. and Tech., 1967; chmn. engring. adv. com. NSF, 1972-73; bd. dirs. Engring. Coun. Profl. Devel., 1968-72; mem. commn. edn. for engring. profession Nat. Assn. State Univs. and Land Grant Colls., 1969-72; apptd. mem. adv. com. on reactor safeguards US Nuc. Regulatory Commn., 1997-2001. Author: Random Noise Techniques in Nuclear Reactor Systems, 1970, trans. into Russian, 1974; co-author: (with Lefteri H. Tsoukalas) Fuzzy and Neural Approaches in Engineering, 1997—. Served to 1st lt. USAF. Recipient Sec. of Def. Civilian Svc. award, 1968, Outstanding Alumni award U. Ill. Coll. Engring., 1970, Alumni Profl. Achievement award Iowa State U., 1972, President's medallion U. Fla., 1973; Disting. Achievement citation Iowa State U. Alumni Assn., 1980, Glenn Murphy award Am. Soc. for Engring. Edn., 1992; Named to Hall Disting. Alumni, Aerospace Dept., Iowa State U., 2005. Fellow ASME (life, Richards Meml. award 1969, ASME medal, 2005), AAAS, Am. Nuc. Soc. life, chmn. edn. com. 1962-64, chmn. tech. group for edn. 1964-66, bd. dirs. 1965-68, exec. com. bd. 1966-68); mem. Am. Soc. Engring. Edn. (pres. S.E. sect. 1972-73, chmn. nuc. engring. divsn. 1966-67, 88-89, rsch. award S.E. sect. 1962), John Henry Newman Honor Soc., Sigma Xi, Tau Beta Pi, Phi Mu Epsilon, Pi Tau Sigma, Phi Kappa Phi (Disting. Mem. award 1997). Home: 5221 NW 44th Pl Gainesville FL 32606-4328 Office: U Tenn Pasqua Nuc Engring Bldg Knoxville TN 37996-2300 Business E-Mail: ruhrig@utk.edu.

UICKER, JOSEPH BERNARD, retired engineering company executive; b. Mar. 29, 1940; s. John Joseph and Elizabeth Josephine (Flint) U.; m. Mary Catherine Howze, June 5, 1965 (div. Oct. 1971); children: Patricia, Suzzane; m. Janet Ann Ballman, Sept. 22, 1973. BSME, U. Detroit, 1963, MS, 1965. Registered profl. engr., Mich. Engr. Smith Hinchman & Grylls, Detroit, 1964-72, chief mech. engr. health facilities, 1972-73, asst. dir. health facilities, 1973-75, v.p., dir. mech. engring., 1975-82, v.p., dir. profl. staff, 1983-2000; also bd. dirs.; ret., 2000. Dir. Smith Group, Detroit, 1984-2000. Capt. US Army, 1966—67. Mem. NSPE, ASME, ASHRAE, Soc. Am. Mil. Engrs., Engring. Soc., Athletic Club. Avocations: golf, photography, gardening. Home: 15250 Knolson St Livonia MI 48154-4736 E-mail: juicker@ameritech.net.

UILKEMA, JOHN K., lawyer; BSE in Mech. Engring., U. Mich., 1957; JD, George Washington U., 1961. Bar: D.C. 1962, Calif. 1963, U.S. Patent and Trademark Office, U.S. Dist. Ct. (all dists.) Calif., U.S. Ct. Appeals (Calif.), U.S. Dist. Ct. (all dists.) D.C., U.S. Ct. Appeals (D.C.), U.S. Ct. Appeals (fed. cir.), U.S. Supreme Ct. Ptnr. Thelen Reid Brown Raysman & Steiner LLP, San Francisco. Mem.: ABA (region patent law sect. 1987—88, ho. dels. 1992—, bd. govs. sect. intellectual property 2002—05). Office: Thelen Reid Brown Raysman & Steiner Ste 1800 101 Second St San Francisco CA 94105 Office Phone: 415-369-7960. Business E-Mail: juilkema@thelen.com.

UKPOLO, VICTOR, economics educator; b. Lagos, Nigeria, Mar. 23, 1950; came to U.S., 1972; s. Samuel Obuje and Gladys (Arugbo (Olotewo) U.; m. Pamela Davies, June 19, 1977 (div.); 1 child, Victor; m. Fawn Teresa Coffey, Dec. 30, 1989; children: Mercy, Oghenekewe. BA in Econs., U. Md., 1975; MA in Econs., Am. U., 1977, PhD in Econs., 1985. Asst. prof. Ahmadu Bello U., Zana, Nigeria, 1986-87, Austin Peay State U., Clarksville, Tenn., 1988-92, assoc. prof.; interim assoc. vice chancellor academic affairs, spl. asst. to chancellor for academic rsch. Tenn. Bd. Regents; assoc. v.p. academic affairs Calif. State U., LA; sys. v.p. academic and student affairs So. U. New Orleans (SUNO), 2003—05, chancellor, 2005—06, pres., 2006—. Adj. lectr. Am. U., Washington, 1984-85, U. Washington, 1985-86; adj. assoc. prof. Lagos (Nigeria) State U., 1993—. Contbr. articles to profl. pubs. Bd. dirs. United Meth. Urban Ministry, Clarksville, 1991—. Mem. Rotary (sec. 1992-93), Phi Kappa Phi, Omicron Delta Kappa. Avocations: tennis, running. Office: So Univ at New Orleans 6801 Press Dr New Orleans LA 70126

UKROPINA, JAMES R., lawyer; b. Fresno, Calif., Sept. 10, 1937; s. Robert J. and Persida (Angelich) Ukropina. AB, Stanford U., 1959, MBA, 1961; LL.B., U. So. Calif., 1965. Bar: Calif. 1966. Assoc. firm O'Melveny & Myers, Los Angeles, 1965-72, ptnr., 1972—80, 1992—2000, of counsel Los Angeles, 2001—; exec. v.p., gen. counsel Santa Fe Internat. Corp., Alhambra, Calif., 1980-84, dir., 1981-86; exec. v.p., gen. counsel Pacific Enterprises, Los Angeles, 1984-86, pres. and dir., 1986-89, chmn. bd. and chief exec. officer, 1989-91; chmn., CEO Directions, LLC, 2002—. Bd. dir. Lockheed Martin Corp., Pacific Life Ins. Co., Trust Co. of West Group, Inc., Ctrl. Natural Resources, Keck Found., Internet Brands. Editor in chief So. Calif. Law Rev, 1964-65. Trustee Stanford U., 1991-2000 Mem. ABA, Calif. Bar Assn., Los Angeles County Bar Assn., Annandale Golf Club, Calif. Club, Beta Theta Pi. Office: O'Melveny & Myers 400 S Hope St Los Angeles CA 90071-2899

ULABY, FAWWAZ TAYSSIR, engineering educator, director, science administrator; b. Damascus, Syria, Feb. 4, 1943; came to US, 1964; s. Tayssir Kamel and Makram (Ard) Ulaby; children: Neda, Aziza, Laith. BS in Physics, Am. U. Beirut, 1964; MSEE, U. Tex., Austin, 1966, PhD in Elec. Engring., 1968. With Boeing Co., 1966; asst. prof. elec. and computer engring. U. Kans., Lawrence, 1968-71, assoc. prof., 1971-76, prof., 1976-84; prof. elec. engring. and computer sci. U. Mich., Ann Arbor, 1984—, dir. NASA Ctr. for Space Terahertz Tech., 1988, R. Jamison and Betty Williams Disting. prof. elec. engring. and computer sci., 1993—, v.p. for rsch., 1999—2005. Author: Microwave Remote Sensing, Vol. 1, 1981, Vol. 2, 1982, Vol. 3, 1986, Radar Polarimetry, 1990. Recipient Kuwait prize in applied scis. Govt. of Kuwait, 1987, NASA Grp. Achievement award, 1990. Fellow IEEE (gen. chmn. internat. symposium 1981, Disting. Achievement award 1983, Centennial medal 1984, Edison medal 2006, Geoscience and Remote Sensing Soc. Edn. award 2006); mem. IEEE Geoscience and Remote Sensing Soc. (exec. editor jour., pres. 1979-81), Internat. Union Radio Sci., NAE. Avocations: flying kites, racketball. Office: U Mich 3228 Elec Engring and Computer Sci 1301 Beal Ave Ann Arbor MI 48109-2122 E-mail: ulaby@eecs.umich.edu. *

ULANOFF, LANCE, editor-in-chief; Positions up to sr. assoc. editor PC Mag., 1991—96, with, 2000—, editor revs., editor-in-chief, v.p. content, 2007—; online editor HomePC mag., 1996—98; sr. editor online Windows Mag., 1998—99; prodr. computing and consumer electronics channels to sr. dir. content Deja.com, 1999—2000. Office: PC Mag Ziff Davis Media Inc 28 E 28th St New York NY 10016 E-mail: Lance_Ulanoff@ziffdavis.com. *

ULANOFF, STANLEY M., communications executive; b. Bklyn., May 30, 1922; s. Samuel H. and Minnie (Druss) U.; m. Bernice Mayer, June 15, 1947; children: Roger, Amy Ulanoff Christie, Lisa M. Ulanoff, Dory Ulanoff Kennedy. BA in Journalism, U. Iowa, 1943; MBA in Mktg., Hofstra U., 1955; PhD in Comm., NYU, 1968. Copywriter promotions dept. N.Y. Times, 1946—49; asst. to pres. SUNY, Stony Brook, 1962—64; prof. mktg., head advt., sales promotion & pub. rels. divsn. Baruch Coll. (CUNY), NY, 1964—86; pres. Viewmark Prodns. Inc. d.b.a. Advisions, 1986—. Cons. U.S. Dept. Def., Grosset & Dunlap pubs., Siebel/Mohr, U.S. Postal Svc.; cons, asst. to pres. Compton Advt.; arbitrator N.Y. Stock Exch., Nat. Assn. Securities Dealers; cons. Hasbro Toys. Author or editor 34 books including Handbook of Sales Promotion, also mags., newspaper articles, rsch. papers; prodr. over 200 video documentaries. From pvt. E-1 to brig. gen. U.S. Army, 1942-84. Decorated chevalier Ordre des Palmes Academique, Republic of France, Legion of Merit, Meritorious Svc. medal, Army Commendation medal, Army Achievement medal, U.S. Army, Silver Conspicuous Svc. Cross, Merit medal State of N.Y., 1st prize award Am. Assn. Advt. Agys.; named VIP (Very Important Prof.) Splty. Adv. Assn. Internat. (2); Am. Assn. Advt. Agys. fellow, Eastman-Kodak fellow in film prodn.; Lewis Kleid Direct Mail Advt. scholar. Mem. Mil. Intelligence Res. Soc. (pres.), Res. Officers Assn. (pres.); disting. alumnus, Hofstra Univ. Office: 17 The Serpentine Roslyn NY 11576-1736 Office Phone: 516-621-1603. Fax: 516-801-2501.

ULE, GUY MAXWELL, JR., stockbroker; b. Chgo., Jan. 2, 1940; s. Guy Maxwell and Margaret (Karahuta) U.; m. Angela Joanne Genelli, Nov. 17, 1975. BA, Harvard U., Cambridge, Mass., 1961, MBA, 1967. Analyst, phys. distbn. specialist TWA, NYC and Phila., 1967—69, supr. comml. passenger sales NYC, 1969—71; pvt. practice cons. NYC, 1971—72; mgr. sales mktg. Source Equities, NYC, 1972; ptnr., N.Y.C. office mgr. Daley, Coolidge & Co., 1973—77; v.p., divsn. mgr. Rosenkrantz, Ehrenkrantz, Lyon & Ross Inc., 1977—85, Ingham Becker & Co., Inc., 1985—87; v.p., asst. sec. Meyers, Pollock, Robbins Inc., 1987—89; v.p., Max Ule divsn. Herzog Heine Geduld Inc., 1989—2000; v.p. investments Shields & Co., Inc., 2000—. Pres. Max Ule & Co., Inc., N.Y.C., 1977-2004, Max Ule Advt. & Mktg., Inc., N.Y.C., 1980—; brokerage info. cons. Internet World Wide Web, 1995 Creator first discount brokerage sys. on computer, 1980. Chmn., pres. Assn. in Manhattan for Autistic Children, 1985-86. Lt. USN, 1962-65 Mem.: Racquet Club Phila., Knickerbocker Club, Racquet and Tennis Club. Republican. Episcopalian. Avocations: photography, tennis, travel. Home: 8 Gramercy Park S Apt 5B New York NY 10003-1721 Office: Shields and Co 140 Broadway 44th Fl New York NY 10005 Office Phone: 800-809-1160. Business E-Mail: max.ule@shieldsandco.com.

ULER, ROBIN, hotel executive; Corp. food, beverage dir. to v.p. food, beverage, spa, retail svcs. Marriott Internat., Washington, sr. v.p., ops., planning, support. Named one of America's Top Women in Bus.-Game Changers, Pink mag. & Forté Found., 2007. Office: Marriott Internat Marriott Dr Washington DC 20058 Office Phone: 301-380-3000. *

ULEVICH, NEAL HIRSH, photojournalist; b. Milw., June 18, 1946; s. Ben and Lea Jean (Klitsner) U.; m. Maureen Ann Vaughan, Sept. 25, 1974; children: Jacob Vaughan, Sarah Beatrice. BA in Journalism, U. Wis., 1968. Reporter A.P., 1968-69, photographer, photo editor, 1971-78, Asia photo editor, 1978-83. Freelance writer, Vietnam, Hong Kong, 1969-71; fellow in journalism U. Wis.-Madison, 1971-72 Recipient Pulitzer prize for news photography, 1977. Jewish.

ULIN, DAVID LAWRENCE, writer, editor, educator; b. NYC, Aug. 21, 1961; s. Richard Irwin and Susan Dana (Borkow) U.; m. Rae Dubow, Aug. 27, 1988; children: Noah Dubow, Sophie Dubow. BA, U. Pa., 1984. Contbr. LA Times, 1991—; book editor LA Reader, 1993-96; instr. UCLA Extension, 1993—; contbr. Newsday, Melville, NY, 1994—, LA Weekly, 1996—, Chgo. Tribune, 1997—; editor LA Times Book Rev., 2005—. Author: Cape Cod Blues, 1992, Myth of Solid Ground, 2004 (Best Book of 2004, Chgo. Tribune and San Francisco Chronicle), Clash's London Calling (33 1/3), 2005; (editor) Another City: Writing from Los Angeles, 2001, Writing Los Angeles: A Literary Anthology, 2002. Trustee Beyond Baroque Literary Arts Ctr., Venice, Calif., 1995. Mem. PEN West (treas. 1995—), Nat. Book Critics Cir. (bd. dirs. 1994-2002).

ULIN, RICHARD IRWIN, pediatric orthopedist, educator; b. NYC, May 26, 1936; s. Albert Jay and Ruth Charlotte (Newman) Ulin; m. Susan Dana Borkow; children: David, John. BS, Franklin and Marshall Coll., 1958; MD, Columbia U., 1962. Diplomate Am. Bd. Orthopedic Surgery. Chief pediatric orthopedics Mt. Sinai Med. Ctr., NYC, 1975—2005, acting chair dept orthopedics, 1994—96, clin. prof. orthopedics, 1995—. Oral examiner Am. Bd. Orthopedic Surgeons, 1975—. Cpt. U.S. Coast Guard, 1964—70. Fellow: Am. Acad. Orthopedic Surgeons, Scoliosis Rsch. Soc., Pediat. Orthopedic Soc. Am., Am. Orhtopedic Assn. Avocations: photography, reading, writing. Office: 1095 Pk Ave New York NY 10128

ULLBERG, KENT JEAN, sculptor; b. Gothenburg, Sweden, July 15, 1945; arrived in US, 1974; s. Jean Wilgot and Kerstin Aina (Axelson) U.; m. Veerle Rufina Vermeir, May 5, 1978; children: Robert, Gerald. Diploma in scuplture, Swedish State Sch. Art, 1966. Cert. conservator German Assn. Museology. Curator Nat. Mus. and Art Gallery, Botswana, Africa, 1971-74; curator III Mus. Natural History, Denver, 1974-75. Prin. works include Lincoln Ctr. Eagle, Dallas, 1981, Wind in the Sails, Corpus Christi, Tex., 1983, Genesee Eagle, Mumford, N.Y., 1984, Deinonychus Dinosaurs, Phila., 1987, Whooping Cranes Fountain, Washington, 1989, Swordfish Monument, IGFA Hdqs., Dania, Fla., 1999, Broward Conv. Ctr., Fountain, Ft. Lauderdale, Fla., Rudor Monument, Stockholm, 1991, Monumental Triptych Art Mus. South Tex., 1993, Bird Mountain Telecom. Hdqs., Stockholm, 1994, Christ Monument, Corpus Christi, 1995, Grizzly Bear Monument, Nat. Mus. Wildlife Art, Jackson, Wyo., 1994, King Penguin Monument, Mystic Marine Life Aquarium, Conn., 1997, R.T. Peterson Meml., Cougar Monument San Antonio Zoo, 1998, Otters Monument St. Louis Zoo, 1998, Tex. State Aquarium, 1998, Swordfish Monument, Dania Beach, Fla., 1998, Spanish Bull Monument, Johnson C. Smith U., Charlotte, N.C., 1999, Ram Monum, U. N.C., Chapel Hill, 2001, First Nat. Bank Omaha Can. Geese Monument, 2002, Eagle Monument, Fed. Res. Bank, Houston, 2005, Danzamar, Performing Arts Ctr., Tex. A&M, Corpus Christi, 2005, Chub Cay Marlin Monument, Bahamas, 2006. Recipient Gold medal Tex. Rangers Hall of Fame, 1980, Rungius award Nat. Mus. Wildlife Art, 1996, Prix de West award Nat. Cowboy Hall of Fame, 1998, award for wildlife Autry Nat. Ctr., 2004; named Master Wildlife Artist, 1987. Fellow: NAD (academician 1990, Barnett prize 1995, Speyer prize 1995), Am. Soc. Marine Artists, Nat. Acad. Western Art (gold medal 1981, 1982, 1988, 1995, 1999), Nat. Sculpture Soc. (Percival Dietsch award 1979, gold medal 1983, Hering award 1993, Silver medal and John Cavanaugh Meml. prize 2002); mem.: Soc. for Wildlife Art of Nations, Allied Artists of Am. (N.Y. Silver medal 1989), Soc. Animal Artists (medal merit 1979, 1980, 1982, 1987, 1996, 2001, E. Haller award 2001, Sponsor award 2002), Explorers Club N.Y.C. Office Phone: 361-851-1600. Personal E-mail: ullberg@sbcglobal.net.

ULLESTAD, MERWIN ALLAN, tax specialist, director; b. Hampton, Iowa, June 29, 1949; s. Allan L. and Georgia E. (Simms) Ullestad; m. Crystal R. Kleppinger, Sept. 17, 1977. BS, Iowa State U., 1971. CPA; PFS Iowa, Tenn., lic. capt. inland waters USCG. Ptnr. Coopers and Lybrand, Des Moines, 1971-83; ptnr. in charge, tax svcs. Touche Ross and Co., Nashville, 1983-89; ptnr. tax svcs. Deloitte & Touche, LLP, Nashville, 1989—2002; mem.-in-charge tax svcs., mgmt. com. Kraft CPAs LLC, Nashville, 2002—. Adj. tax prof. Simpson Coll., 1981—82; sprk. prof. acct. seminar Lipscomb U., 1990—2004. Editor: Abingdon Clergy Income Tax Guide, 1989—98. Sustaining membership capt. Mid. Tenn. coun. Boy Scouts Am., 1985—88; ednl. adv. com. Nashville Health Care Coun., 1998—2002; bd. dirs., exec. com., treas. United Way Mid. Tenn., 1990—96, mem. allocations panel, 1983—89; bd. dirs., mem. exec. com. Am. Cancer Soc., Des Moines, 1977—83, Nashville City Ballet, 1983—85; bd. dirs., chmn. fin. com. Watkins Coll. Art and Design, 1996—2001; bd. dirs. Gilda's Club, Nashville, treas., 1996—2002; trustee, program chmn., sec., pres. Tenn. Fed. Tax Inst., 2001—; bd. dirs., treas. Tenn. chpt. Arthritis Found., 2003—. Mem.: AICPA (cert. pers. fin. specialist), Nashville Songwriters Assn. Internat. (fin. cons. to bd. dirs. 1990—97), Nashville Estate Planning Coun. (pres. 1996—97, bd. dirs.), Internat. Assn. Fin. Planning (pres., bd. dirs. Nashville chpt. 1987—90), Iowa Soc. CPAs, Tenn. Soc. CPAs, Nashville C. of C. (mem. econ. devel. com. 1988—90, mem. employment coun. 1999—2002, editor HR notes 2000—01, mem. small bus. coun. 2006—), Seven Seas Cruising Assn., Nashville Tax Club (founding mem.), Nlue Yacht Club, Commonwealth Yacht Club, Nashville City Club, Old Hickory Country Club. Avocations: sailing, hiking, music. Office: 555 Great Circle Rd #200 Nashville TN 37228-1310 Office Phone: 615-782-4281. Business E-Mail: mullestad@kraftcpas.com.

ULLMAN, EDWIN FISHER, biotechnologist, consultant; b. Chgo., July 19, 1930; s. Harold P. and Jane F. Ullman; m. Elizabeth J. Finlay, June 26, 1954; children: Becky L., Linda J. BA, Reed Coll., 1952; MA, Harvard U., 1954, PhD, 1956. Rsch. chemist Lederle Labs., Am. Cyanamid, Pearl River, NY, 1955-60; group leader ctrl. rsch. divsn. Am. Cyanamid, Stamford, Conn., 1960-66; sci. dir. Synvar Rsch. Inst., Palo Alto, Calif., 1966-70; v.p., dir. rsch. Syva Co., Palo Alto, 1970-95, Behring Diagnostics Inc., San Jose, Calif., 1995-97; sci. cons., 1997—; chief sci. officer Thau MDx, LLC, Santa Barbara, Calif., 2001—02, Adv. DiscoverRx, Corp., Fremont, Calif., 2002—. Mem. various sci. adv. bds.; mem. adv. bd. San Francisco State U. Coll. of Sci. and Engring., 1994-96. Mem. editl. bd. Jour. Organic Chemistry, 1969-74, Jour. Immunoassay, 1979—, Jour. Clin. Lab., Analysis, 1986-87, Jour. Clin. Ligand Assay Soc., 1999-2000; contbr. articles to sci. jours.; patentee in field. NSF predoctoral fellow, 1952-53; U.S. Rubber Co. fellow, 1954-55. Recipient Clin. Ligand Assay Soc. Mallinckrodt award, 1981, Can. Soc. Clin. Chemists Health Group award, 1982, Inventor of Yr. award Peninsula Patent Law Assn., 1987. Fellow AAAS; mem. Am. Chem. Soc., Am. Assn. Clin. Chemistry (Van Slyke award N.Y. sect. 1984, No. Calif. sect. award 1991, Outstanding Contbns. to Clin. Chemistry in Selected Area of Rsch. award 1997, Ann. Edwin F. Ullman award established 1998), Phi Beta Kappa.

ULLMAN, GERALD LEE, transportation engineer; b. Grand Junction, Colo., Feb. 15, 1961; s. Sylvester Lawrence and Bernice Maxine Ullman; m. Brooke Rae Durkop, Nov. 3, 2001; children: Brandon Lee, Nicholas John. BS, U. Nebr., 1983, MS, 1984; PhD, Tex. A&M U., 1995. Registered profl. engr., Tex., 1989. From engring. rsch. assoc. to rsch. engr. Tex. Transp. Inst., College Station, 1985—2007, sr. rsch. engr., 2007—. Contbr. articles to profl. jours. Tchr. religious edn. St. Joseph's Cath. Ch., Bryan,

Tex., 1993—2006. Recipient TTI/Trinity Rschr. award, Tex. Transp. Inst., 1999. Mem.: Transp. Rsch. Bd. (mem. work zone traffic control tech. com., Fred Burggraff award 1994), Inst. Transp. Engrs. Roman Catholic. Avocations: scuba diving, golf. Office: Texas Transportation Institute 3135 Tamu College Station TX 77843-3135 Office Phone: 979-845-9908. Office Fax: 979-845-6006. Business E-Mail: g-ullman@tamu.edu.

ULLMAN, JEFFREY DAVID, computer scientist, educator; b. NYC, Nov. 22, 1942; s. Seymour and Nedra L. (Hart) Ullman; m. Holly E. Ullman, Nov. 19, 1967; children: Peter, Scott, Jonathan. BS, Columbia U., 1963; PhD, Princeton U., 1966; PhD (hon.), U. Brussels, 1975, U. Paris-Dauphine, 1992. Mem. tech. staff Bell Labs., Murray Hill, NJ, 1966-69, cons., 1969-89; prof. elec. engring., computer sci. Princeton (N.J.) U., 1969-79; prof. computer sci. Stanford (Calif.) U., 1979—2003, prof. emeritus, 2003—; CEO Gradiance Corp., 2003—. Mem. computer sci. adv. panel NSF, 1974—77, mem. info., robotics and intelligent sys. adv. panel, 1986—88; mem. exam. com. computer sci. grad. record exam. Endl. Testing Svc., 1978—86; chmn. doctoral rating com. computer sci. N.Y. State Regents, 1989—93, 1998—99; mem. tech. adv. bd. Google, 1998—, Viquity, 1999—2002, Surromed, 1999—, Whizbang Labs, 1999—2002, Quiq, 1999—2002; adv. bd. World Wide Web Consortium, 1998—99; bd. dirs. Junglee, 1996—98, Kirusa, 2001—03, Enosys software, 2000—01, 2002—03; mem. internat. sci. advisory group Nat. Info. & Comms. Tech., Australia, 2003—. Author: (book) Principles of Database and Knowledge-Base Systems, 1988, 1989; author: (with A. V. Aho and J. E. Hopcroft) Data Structures and Algorithms, 1983; author: (with A. V. Aho and R. Sethi) Compilers: Principles, Techniques and Tools, 1986; author: (with A. V. Aho) Foundations of Computer Science, 1992, Elements of ML Programming, 1994, 1998; author: (with J. Widom) A First Course in Database Systems, 1997, 2002; author: (with H. Garcia-Molina and J. Widom) The Complete Book of Database Systems, 2002; author: (with J. E. Hopcroft and R. Motwani) Intro. to Automata, Languages, and Computation, 2006. Guggenheim fellow, 1989. Fellow: Assn. Computing Machinery (coun. 1978—80, Spl. Interest Group Mgmt. Data Contbns. award 1996, Outstanding Educator award 1998, Knuth prize 2000, Spl. Interest Group Mgmt. Data E.F. Codd Innovations award 2006); mem.: NAE, Spl. Interest Group Mgmt. Data (vice chmn. 1983—95), Computing Rsch. Assn. (bd. dirs. 1994—2001), Spl. Interest Group Automata and Computability Theory (sec.-treas. 1973—75). Home: 1023 Cathcart Way Palo Alto CA 94305-1048 Office: Stanford U Dept Computer Sci 433 Gates Hall 4A-Wing Stanford CA 94305-9040 E-mail: ullman@gmail.com.

ULLMAN, LEO SOLOMON, lawyer; b. Amsterdam, The Netherlands, July 14, 1939; s. Frank Leo and Emily (Konijn) U.; m. Katharine Laura Marbut, Aug. 27, 1960; chldren: Laura, Susan, Valerie, Frank. AB, Harvard U., 1961; JD, MBA, Columbia U., 1964. Bar: N.Y. 1966, U.S. Ct. Claims 1966, U.S. Tax Ct. 1969, U.S. Customs Ct. 1970. Assoc. Sullivan & Cromwell, NYC, 1965-68; pres., mem. Ullman, Miller & Wrubel and predecessors, NYC, 1970-81; mem. Reid & Priest, 1984-91, of counsel, 1991-92, Schnader, Harrison, Segal & Lewis, NYC, 1993-99; chmn., CEO Cedar Shopping Ctrs., Inc. (NYSE), 1998—. Adj. prof. internat. bus. NYU, 1972-77; lectr., panelist profl. organs. programs. Co-author: Investeringen in Onroerend Goed in de Verenigde Staten, 1982; editor: European Taxation, Internat. Bur. Documentation, Amsterdan, 1964-65; founding editor: Taxation of Private Investment Income in Europe; contbr. articles to profl. publs. Mem. Port Washington (N.Y.) Bd. Edn., 1970-73, pres., 1972-73; bd. dirs. Found. for Jewish Hist. Mus. in Amsterdam, Inc.; bd. dirs. Anne Frank Ctr., U.S.A., chmn., 1994-00; bd. dirs. Cmty. Chest of Port Washington. Served with USMCR, 1959-65; nat. judge Ernst & Young Entrepreneur of Yr. Awards, 2006, 07. Co-recipient Cmty. Svc. award, Port Washington, 1981, Citizen of Yr. award, Cmty. Chest, Port Washington, 2005, Entrepreneur of Yr. award in Greater NY area Ernst & Young, 2005, 06; Harlan Fiske Stone scholar Columbia Law Sch., 1963. Mem. ABA (tax sect. com. U.S. taxation of fgn. persons), N.Y. State Bar Assn. (tax sect. com. internat. trade and investment), Harvard Club, Netherlands Club. Home: Seacoast Ln Sands Point NY 11050-1230 Office: 44 S Bayles Ave Port Washington NY 11050 E-mail: leoullman@aol.com.

ULLMAN, MYRON EDWARD, III, (MIKE ULLMAN), retail executive; b. Youngstown, Ohio, Nov. 26, 1946; s. Myron Edward Jr. and June (Cunningham) U.; m. Cathy Emmons, June 20, 1969; children: Myron Cayce, Denver Tryan, Peter Brynt, Benjamin Kyrk, Kathryn Kwynn, Madylin Ming Yan. BS in Indsl. Mgmt., U. Cin., 1969; postgrad. Inst. Ednl. Mgmt., Harvard U., 1977. Internat. account mgr. IBM Corp., Cin., 1969-76; v.p. bus. affairs U. Cin., 1976-81; White House fellow The White House, Washington, 1981-82; exec. v.p. Sanger Harris div. Federated Stores, Dallas, 1982-86; mgr. dir., chief oper. officer Wharf Holdings Ltd., Hong Kong, 1986-88; chmn., CEO, dir. R.H. Macy & Co. Inc., NYC, 1988-95; dir., deputy chmn. Federated Dept. Stores, Inc.; chmn., CEO DFS Group Ltd., San Francisco, 1995-98, group chmn., 1999-2000; also bd. dirs.; dir. gen., group mng. dir. LVMH, Louis Vuitton Moet Hennessy, Paris, 1999—2002; chmn. DeBeers-LV, 2000—02; dir., chmn., CEO J.C. Penney Co. Inc., 2004—. Mng. dir. Lane Crawford Ltd., Hong Kong, 1986-88; bd. advisors Gt. Traditions Corp., Cin.; chmn. Omni Hotels, Hampton, N.H., 1988; co-chmn. Global Crossing, Ltd., 2002-04; chmn. bd. dirs. Mercy Ships Internat., 1992-; bd. dirs. Starbuck's Coffee Co., Polo Ralph Lauren, Taubman Ctrs., 2002-04, Kendall Jackson Wine Estates, 2001-04, Lucille Packard Found. Children's Health, 2001-04, Segway LLC, 2003-05. Internat. v.p. U. Cin. Alumni Assn., 1980—; bd. dirs. Nat. Multiple Sclerosis Soc., NYC; bd. dirs. Brunswick Sch., Greenwich, Conn., U. Cin. Found., Lincoln Ctr. Devel., Deafness Rsch. Found., 1997-01, Stanford U. Children's Med. Ctr., 2004-04; chmn. exec. coun. U. Calif. Med. Ctr. Found., San Francisco, 2002-, bd. dirs., 1998—. Mem. White House Fellow Alumni Assn., Econ. Club N.Y.C. (bd. dirs., exec. com.), Nat. Retail Fedn. (vice chmn., bd. dirs., exec. com. 1993—). Republican. Office: c/o Jackson Hole Group Ste 935 100 Spear St San Francisco CA 94105 also: JC Penney Corp Inc 6501 Legacy Dr Plano TX 75024-3698 Business E-Mail: mike@meullman.com.

ULLMAN, PIERRE LIONI, retired Spanish educator; b. Nice, France, 1929; (parents Am. citizens); s. Eugene Paul and Suzanne (Lioni) U.; m. Mary Meade McDowell, June 9, 1956; children: Katherine Meade Turner, Susan Randolph Johnson. BA, Yale U., 1952; AM, Columbia U., 1956; PhD, Princeton U., NJ, 1962. Instr. Rutgers U., New Brunswick, NJ, 1961-63; asst. prof. U. Calif., Davis, 1963-65; assoc. prof. U. Wis., Milw., 1965-69, prof., 1969-94, prof. emeritus, 1994—. Vis. prof. U. Minn., Mpls., 1970-71, U. Mich., Ann Arbor, 1975. Author: Mariano Jose de Larra and Spanish Political Rhetoric, 1971, A Contrapuntal Method for Analyzing Spanish Literature, 1988; translator: The Friend from Kananam: Adventures in the New Guinea Jungle, by Kenneth G. Linton, 2002; contbr. articles to profl. jours. Past pres. U. Wis. Milw. Retired Faculty Assn., 2000-2002. With U.S. Army, 1952-54. Mem. MLA (emeritus), U. Esperanto Assn. (2d prize for drama 1981), Esperanto League for N.Am., Sigma Delta Pi. Address: 1840 N Prospect Ave Milwaukee WI 53202 Personal E-mail: ullmanpl@uwm.edu.

ULLMAN, TRACEY, actress, singer; b. Slough, Eng., Dec. 30, 1959; m. Allan McKeown, 1983; children: Mabel Ellen, John Albert Victor. Student, Itaia Conti Stage Sch., London. Appeared in plays Gigi, Elvis, Grease, The Rocky Horror Show, Four in a Million, 1981 (London Theatre Critics award), The Taming of the Shrew, 1990, The Big Love, (one-woman stage show) 1991; films include Give My Regards to Broad Street, 1984, Plenty, 1985, Jumpin' Jack Flash, 1986, I Love You To Death, 1990, Household Saints, 1993, Robin Hood: Men in Tights, 1993, I'll Do Anything, 1994, Bullets over Broadway, 1994, Ready to Wear (Prêt-à-Porter), 1994, Everybody Says I Love You, 1996, Panic, 2000, Small Time Crooks, 2000, A Dirty Shame, 2004, (voice) Corpse Bride, 2005, (TV films) Women of the Night IV, 1995, Once Upon a Mattress, 2004; Brit. TV shows include Three of a Kind, A Kick Up the Eighties, Girls on Top; actress TV series: The Tracey Ullman Show, from 1987-90 (Emmy award Best Performance, Outstanding Writing, 1990, Golden Globe award Best Actress, 1987), Tracey Takes On, 1996—99 (four Emmys including Outstanding Music, Comedy and Variety Show 1997, Cable Ace award for best comedy variety series 1996), Visible Panty Lines, 2001-; albums You Broke My Heart in Seventeen Places (Gold album), You Caught Me Out, 1984, Takes on the Hits, 2002. Recipient Brit. Acad. award, 1983, Am. Comedy award, 1988, 90, 91, Emmy award for Best Performance in a Variety/Music Series for "Tracey Ullman Takes on New York", 1994. Office: IFA Talent Agy 8730 W Sunset Blvd Ste 490 Los Angeles CA 90069-2248

ULLRICH, ROBERT ALBERT, academic administrator; b. Port Jefferson, NY, Mar. 25, 1939; s. Albert Herman and Marie Kathryn (Miller) U.; m. Portia M. Little; children: Karl Albert, Eleanor Marie. BS, U.S. Mcht. Marine Acad., 1960; MBA, Tulane U., 1964; D in Bus. Adminstrn., Washington U., 1968. Marine engr. Lykes Bros. Steamship Co., New Orleans, 1960-62; trainee IBM Corp., New Orleans, 1964-65; sr. rsch. officer London Sch. Econs., 1968-69; prof. Vanderbilt U., Nashville, 1969-88; dean Clark U., Worcester, Mass., 1988-96, prof., 1996-98; dean Ithaca (N.Y.) Coll., 1998—2004. Author: Motivation Methods, 1981, Robotics Primer, 1983; co-author: Organization Theory and Design, 1980; editor: The American Work Force, 1984. Lt. j.g. USNR, 1960-66. Mem. Beta Gamma Sigma. Office: 33 Friendship St Jamestown RI 02835 Home Phone: 401-423-0259. E-mail: rullrich1@msn.com.

ULMER, EVONNE GAIL, health science association administrator; b. Bagley, Minn., Sept. 12, 1947; d. John Ferdinand and Elsie Mabel (McCollum) Lundmark; m. G. Bryan Ulmer, Jan. 11, 1969; 1 child, G. Bryan. Diploma, St. Luke's Hosp., Duluth, Minn., 1968; BS, St. Joseph's Coll., N. Windam, Maine, 1981; MHA, U. Minn., 1984; JD, T.M. Cooley Law Sch., Lansing, Mich., 1997. Bar: Mich. 1997. Staff nurse Baton Rouge Gen., 1969—70, St. Luke's Hosp., Duluth, Minn., 1968—69, 1971—72; asst. adminstr. Hickory Heights Care Ctr., Metarie, La., 1972—73; asst. head nurse Eisenhower Hosp., Colorado Springs, Colo., 1973—74; dir. patient care svcs. St. Vincent's Gen. Hosp., Leadville, Colo., 1974—78; dir. insvc., quality assurance Watsatch Hosp., Heber City, Utah, 1979; adminstr. Prospect Park Living Ctr., Estes Park, Colo., 1982—84; asst. adminstr. Estes Park Med. Ctr., 1979—84; CEO Weston County Hosp. and Manor, Newcastle, Wyo., 1984—92, Ionia County Meml. Hosp., Mich., 1992—; pres. Ionia County Health Sys., 1995—, Ulmer Law Firm Evonne G. Ulmer, PLC, 2006—. Mem. Am. Hosp. Assn. Chgo. (trustee 1998-01, past tech. small and rural governing coun., past del. region and policy bd., past chair small and rural governing com., leadership com.), Am. Soc. Healthcare Risk Mgmt. (editl. adv. bd.), Medicare Geog. Reclassification Rev. Bd., Mich. Health and Hosp. Assn. (past bd. dirs., vice-chair smaller hops. coun.). Republican. Lutheran. Home: 536 Skyview Dr Ionia MI 48846-9776 Home Phone: 616-527-6627; Office Phone: 616-523-1000. Personal E-mail: evonneulmer@hotmail.com. Business E-Mail: eulmer@ioniahospital.org.

ULMER, FRANCES ANN, academic administrator, retired state official; b. Madison, Wis., Feb. 1, 1947; m. Bill Council; children: Amy, Louis. BA in Econs. and Polit. Sci., U. Wis.; JD with honors, Wis. Sch. Law. Polit. advisor Gov. Jay Hammond, Alaska, 1975-81; former mayor City of Juneau, Alaska; mem. Alaska Ho. of Reps., 1986-94, minority leader, 1992-94; lt. gov. State of Alaska, 1995—2002; U.S. rep. to North Pacific Anadramous Fish Commn., 1994—; disting. prof. U. Alaska, Anchorage, 2003—, dir. Inst. Social and Econ. Rsch., 2004—, interim chancellor, 2007—. Office: U Alaska Anchorage Office of Chancellor 3211 Providence Dr, ADM 216 Anchorage AK 99508 Office Phone: 907-786-7710. E-mail: fran.ulmer@uaa.alaska.edu. *

ULMER, GREGORY C., lawyer; b. Houston, Dec. 18, 1969; BA, U. Pa., 1992; JD, U. Houston Law Ctr., 1995. Bar: Tex. 1995, US Dist. Ct. (ea., no. and so. dists. Tex.) 1996, US Ct. Appeals (5th cir.) 1996. Briefing clk. to Justice Jack Hightower Tex. Supreme Ct.; ptnr. Baker Hostetler, Houston, 2000—. Editor: Tex. Assn. Def. Coun. Comml. Litig. Newsletter; contbg. author:. Named a Rising Star, Tex. Super Lawyers mag., 2006. Mem.: Houston Lawyers Assn. (mem. exec. bd.), Tex. Bar Assn., ABA, Houston Young Lawyers Assn., Houston Bar Assn. (bd. dirs. 1998—), Am. Inns of Ct. Office: Baker Hostetler 1000 Louisiana Ste 2000 Houston TX 77002 Office Phone: 713-646-1363. E-mail: gulmer@bakerlaw.com. *

ULMER, MELVILLE PAUL, physics and astronomy educator; b. Washington, Mar. 12, 1943; s. Melville Jack and Naomi Louise (Zinkin) U.; m. Patricia Elifson, Dec. 28, 1968; children: Andrew Todd, Jeremy John, Rachel Ann. BA, Johns Hopkins U., 1965; PhD, U. Wis., 1970. Asst. research U. Calif., San Diego, 1970-74; astrophysicist Harvard Smithsonian Ctr. for Astrophysics, Cambridge, Mass., 1974-76; dir. Lindheimer and Dearborn Obs. Northwestern U., 1982—; asst. prof. Dept. Physics and Astoronomy, Northwestern U., Evanston, Ill., 1976-82, assoc. prof., 1982-87, dir. astrophysics program, 1982—, prof., 1987—, chmn. Co-investigator on Gamma Ray Ob. experiment and Orbiting Solar Ob. 7. Contbr. articles to profl. jours. Fellow Am. Phys. Soc.; mem. Am. Astron. Soc., Soc. Photo-optical Instrumentation Engrs., Internat. Astron. Union. Office: Northwestern U Dearborn Obs 2131 Tech Dr Evanston IL 60208-2900 Office Fax: 847-491-3135. E-mail: m-ulmer2@northwestern.edu.

ULMER, WILLIAM H., SR., dentist; b. Wilmington, Del., Sept. 20, 1946; s. Horace Hiate Ulmer and Lillian Palmer Queripel; m. Patricia Ann Kokoszka, July 10, 2004; m. Loreta Harriet Pasquine, June 6, 1970 (div. Oct. 15, 2001); children: Robert John II, William H. Jr., Alison Theresa Kristunas. BS in Biology, Pa. Mil. Coll., 1967; DDS, Fairleigh Dickenson U., Teaneck, NJ, 1971. Cert. forensic dentistry Armed Forces Inst. Pathology, 1990, forensic odontology Northwestern U., 1990. Intern gen. dentistry Del. State Hosp., 1972; dentist Dental Assocs. Del., Hockessin, 1972—. Forensic dentist Office of the Med. Examiner, State Del., Wilmington, 1989—; forensic facial recontruction sculptor Office of the Med. Examiner, State of Del., Wilmington, Del., 1992—; forensic dentist Pa. Dental Identification Team, Harrisburg, 1990—, Dept. Health Dimort Team, 1994—2001; cert. police instr. Del. State Police, Wilmington. Dental surgeon Team Health Care, Towaco, NJ, 2002—03, Jamaica. Recipient Gold medal Weight Lifting, Sr. Olympics, 2006. Master: TaeKwonDo Internat. (4th Degree Black Belt 2006); fellow: Acad. Dentistry Internat., Acad. Forensic Sciences, Acad. Gen. Dentistry; mem.: Surfers Med. Assn., Am. Dental Soc., Del. State Dental Soc. (chmn. emergency response team 1990—2007). Avocations: trumpet, guitar. Office: Dental Associates of Delaware 7197 Lancaster Pike Hockessin DE 19707 Home Phone: 302-530-8709; Office Phone: 302-239-5917. Office Fax: 302-239-3657; Home Fax: 302-239-3657.

ULRICH, BRIAN, photographer, educator; b. Northport, NY, Jan. 25, 1971; s. Hans Juergen Ulrich and Anja Wilson. BFA in Photography, U. Akron, Ohio, 1996; MFA in Photography, Columbia Coll., Chgo., 2004. Adj. faculty Columbia Coll., Chgo., 2004—, Sch. of Art Inst. Chgo., 2006—. Author, photographer: book MP3, Midwest Photographers Project, Copia; exhibitions include Mus. Contemporary Art, San Diego, Mus. Contemporary Photography, Art Inst. Chgo., Rhona Hoffman Gallery, Robert Koch Gallery, Shoppers. Follett fellow, Columbia Coll. Chgo., 2001, 2002. Home Phone: 312-829-6360.

ULRICH, CORNELIA (NELI), research scientist; b. Stuttgart Bad-Cannstatt, Germany, Oct. 1967; d. Raimund and Helga Ulrich; m. Bruce Edgar; children: Nicolas, Noah. Vordiplom in Nutritional Sci., U. Hohenheim, 1990; MS in Nutrition, Oreg. State U., 1993; PhD in Epidemiology, U. Wash., 1998. Rsch. asst. prof. U. Wash., Sch. Pub. Health and Cmty. Medicine, Epidemiology, Seattle, 2000—04, assoc. prof., 2004—; asst. mem., pub. health scis., cancer prevention rsch. Fred Hutchinson Cancer Rsch. Ctr., Seattle, 1999—2004, assoc. mem., pub. health scis., cancer prevention rsch., 2004—. Core faculty, nutritional scis., grad. sch. U. Wash., Seattle; adj. rsch. assoc. prof. U. Wash., Sch. Pub. Healh and Cmty. Medicine, Health Svcs. Contbr. articles to profl. jours. Recipient Pre and Post-doctoral award, Assn. Health Svcs. Rsch., 15th Ann. Mtg., 1998; Fulbright scholarship, 1991—92, German Academic Exchange Svc. (DAAD) scholarship, Spl. Program for Epidemiology, Deutscher Akademischer Austauschdienst, 1993—95. Mem.: Women in Cancer Rsch., Internat. Soc. of Exercise Immunology, Am. Soc. Preventative Oncology, Am. Coll. Epidemiology (Student Prize Paper 1999), Am. Assn. for Cancer Rsch. (Am. Assn. for Cancer Rsch.-Bristol-Myers Squibb Young Investigator award 1998). Office: Fred Hutchinson Cancer Rsch Ctr 1100 Fairview Ave N M4-B402 Seattle WA 98109-1024 Office Phone: 206-667-7617. Office Fax: 206-667-7850. E-mail: nulrich@fhcrc.org. *

ULRICH, LARS, musician; b. Gentofte, Denmark, Dec. 26, 1963; m. Skylar Satenstein, 1997 (div. 2004); children: Myles, Layne; (one child with Connie Nielsen) Bryce Thadeus Drummer, co-founder Metallica, 1981—. Drummer (albums with Metallica) Kill 'em All, 1983, Ride the Lightning, 1984, Master of Puppets, 1986, The $5.98 E.P.: Garage Days Re-Revisited, 1987, ...And Justice for All, 1988, Metallica (The Black Album), 1991, Live Sh*t: Binge and Purge, 1993, Kill 'Em All, 1995, Load, 1996, Reload, 1997, Garage Inc., 1998 (Grammy award), S & M, 1999, St. Anger, 2003 (Grammy award best metal performance, 2003); played on compilation albums including Metal Massacre, 1982, The Good, The Bad and The Live, 1990, Rubaiyant: Elektra's 30th Anniversary, 1990, For Those About To Rock: Moscow, 1992, Woodstock '94, 1994, Spawn: The Album, 1997, Woodstock '99, 2000, WCW: Mayhem The Music, 1999, M:I-2, 2000, NASCAR: Full Throttle, 2001, Swizz Beatz Presents G.H.E.T.T.O. Stories, 2002, Biker Boyz Soundtrack, 2003, We're A Happy Family: Tribute to the Ramones, 2003, I've Always Been Crazy: Tribute to Waylon Jennings, 2003. Office: care Metallica Elektra Records 75 Rockefeller Plz New York NY 10019-6908 *

ULRICH, PAUL GRAHAM, lawyer, writer, editor; b. Spokane, Wash., Nov. 29, 1938; s. Donald Gunn and Kathryn (Vandercook) U.; m. Kathleen Nelson Smith, July 30, 1982; children: Kathleen Elizabeth Pennington, Marilee Rae Timbrooks, Michael Graham Ulrich. BA with high honors, U. Mont., 1961; JD, Stanford U., 1964. Bar: Calif. 1965, Ariz. 1966, U.S. Ct. Appeals (9th cir.) 1965, U.S. Supreme Ct. 1969. Law clk. judge U.S. Ct. Appeals, 9th Circuit, San Francisco, 1964-65; assoc. Lewis and Roca, Phoenix, 1965-70, ptnr., 1970-85; pres. Paul G. Ulrich P.C., Phoenix, 1985-92, Ulrich, Thompson & Kessler, P.C., Phoenix, 1992-94, Ulrich & Kessler, P.C., Phoenix, 1994-95, Ulrich, Kessler & Anger, P.C., Phoenix, 1995-2000, Ulrich & Anger, P.C., Phoenix, 2000—03, Paul G. Ulrich P.C., 2003—; owner Pathway Enterprises, 1985-91. Judge pro tem divsn. 1, Ariz. Ct. Appeals, Phoenix, 1986; instr. Thunderbird Grad. Sch. Internat. Mgmt., 1968-69, Ariz. State U. Coll. Law, 1970-73, 78, Scottsdale CC, 1975-77, also continuing legal edn. seminars. Author and pub.: Applying Management and Motivation Concepts to Law Offices, 1985; co-editor: Arizona Appellate Handbook, 1978-2000, Working With Legal Assistants, 1980, 81; editor, co-author Future Directions for Law Office Management, 1982, People in the Law Office, 1985-86; co-author, pub.: Arizona Healthcare Professional Liability Handbook, 1992, supplement, 1994, Arizona Healthcare Professional Liability Defense Manual, 1995, Arizona Healthcare Professional Liability Update Newsletter, 1992-99; co-author, editor: Federal Appellate Practice: Ninth Circuit, 1994, 2d edit., 1999, supplement, 2007; contbg. editor Law Office Econs. and Mgmt., 1984-97, Life, Law and the Pursuit of Balance, 1996, 2d edit., 1997; co-author Ariz. Appellate Handbook, 1978-. Mem. Ariz. Supreme Ct. Task Force on Ct. Orgn. and Adminstrn., 1988-89; mem. com. on appellate cts. Ariz. Supreme Ct., 1990-91; bd. visitors Stanford U. Law Sch., 1974-77; adv. com. legal assisting program Phoenix Coll., 1985-95; atty. rep. 9th Cir. Jud. Conf., 1997-2000. With U.S. Army, 1956. Recipient continuing legal edn. award State Bar Ariz., 1978, 86, 90, Harrison Tweed spl. merit award Am. Law Inst./ABA, 1987. Fellow Ariz. Bar Found. (founding 1985—); mem. ABA (chmn. selection and utilization of staff pers. com., econs. of law sect. 1979-81, mem. standing com. legal assts. 1982-86, co-chmn. joint project on appellate handbooks 1983-85, co-chmn. fed. appellate handbook project 1985-88, chmn. com. on liaison with non-lawyers orgns. Econs. of Law Practice sect. 1985-86), Am. Acad. Appellate Lawyers, Am. Law Inst. (life), Am. Judicature Soc. (Spl. Merit citation 1987), Ariz. Bar Assn. (chmn. econs. of law practice com. 1980-81, co-chmn. lower ct. improvement com. 1982-85, co-chmn. Ariz. appellate handbook project 1976-2000), Coll. Law Practice Mgmt., Maricopa County Bar Assn. (bd. dirs. 1994-96), Calif. Bar Assn., Phi Kappa Phi, Phi Alpha Delta, Sigma Phi Epsilon. Democrat. Home and Office: 131 E El Caminito Dr Phoenix AZ 85020-3503 Office Phone: 602-248-9465. Personal E-mail: ulrichpc@aol.com.

ULRICH, PETER HENRY, banker; b. Munich, Nov. 24, 1922; s. Hans George and Hella (Muschweck) U.; m. Carol A. Peek, Oct. 21, 1944; children: Carol Jean Hewes, Patricia Diane (Mrs. Damon Eberhart), Peter James. Student, Northwestern U., 0194—1942, U. Iowa, 1943, Sch. Mortgage Banking, 1954—56. Lic. real estate broker, cert. mortgage banker; cert. rev. appraiser; cert. mortgage underwriter. Escrow officer Security Title Ins. Co., Riverside, Calif., 1946-53; asst. cashier Citizens Nat. Trust & Savs., Riverside, 1953-57; v.p. Security First Nat. Bank, Riverside, 1957-63; sr. v.p. Bank of Calif. (N.A.), LA, 1963-72; pres. Ban Cal Mortgage Co., 1972-74, Ban Cal Tri-State Mortgage Co., 1974-75; cons., 1975-76; pres., dir. Beneficial Std. Mortgage Co., 1976-88; real estate cons., 1988—. Instr. real estate and bus. San Bernardino Valley Coll., Riverside City Coll., Pasadena City Coll. Pres. Residential Rsch. Com. So. Calif., 1965, Riverside Opera Assn., 1956—59, Riverside Symphony Soc., 1959—61; trustee Idyllwild Arts Found., 1957—, pres., 1970—73, sec., 1986—87; mem. adv. bd. Salvation Army, 1959—, vice chmn., 1971—74, chmn., 1975, Harbor Light Com., 1965—68, 2002—; convocator Calif. Luth. U., 1976—80, 1981—83, regent, 1981—90; v.p. Guild Opera Co., 1991—99; bd. dirs. Lark Ellen Lions Charities, 1994—, pres., 1994—; treas. Opera Buffs, 1983—; mem. Arcadia Beautiful Commn., 1989—95, vice chair, 1991—92, chmn., 1992—93; trustee Calif. Luth. Edn. Found., 1989—2001; v.p. Arcadia Tournament Roses Assn., 1997; mem. Arcadia City Coun., 1995—96; trustee Arcadia Pub. Libr., 1997—2005, chair, 1999, 2005; vol. Arcadia Police Dept., 2002—; v.p. ch. coun. Ch. of the Cross, 2003—04, 2006—; bd. dirs. Arcadia Tournament Roses Assn., Guild Opera Co., Am. Heart Assn. Foothill divsn. chair, 1997—99, South Pasadena-Arcadia Adult Reading Ctrs., 1998—2002, pres., 2002; bd. dirs. Arcadia Coordinating Coun., 2005, 2006; v.p. Arcadia Libr. Found., 2005—. With AUS USAR, 1943—46. Recipient Resolution of Commendation Riverside City Coun., 1963; Resolution of Appreciation LA City Coun., 1968, 1973; named Arcadia Vol. of Yr., 1997. Mem.: Arcadia Human Resources Commn., Arcadia C. of C. (dir. 2004—, chmn. legis. affairs com. 2005—), Assn. Corp. Real Estate Execs. (sec. 1967—71, pres. 1974—75), Inland Empire Mortgage Bankers Assn. (pres. 1962, hon. dir.), So. Calif. Mortgage Bankers Assn. (dir. 1975, 1980—81, v.p. 1982, pres. 1983), Calif. Mortgage Bankers Assn. (sec. 1965, dir. 1972—75, Disting. Svc. award 1997), Nat. Mortgage Bankers Assn. (chmn. Life Ins. Co. com. 1986—87), Lambda Alpha Internat. (historian, dir. 2004—05). Lutheran. Home: 618 Fairview Ave 232 Arcadia CA 91007-6784 Office: 37 E

Huntington Dr Arcadia CA 91006-3210 Office Phone: 626-294-1058. Business E-Mail: pulrich@sprintmail.com. *Being of foreign birth, I particularly appreciate and cherish the American way of life. I am grateful for the opportunities which it has afforded me. I also feel strongly that we who have had the benefit of these opportunities owe something in return to our communities and to our country. I have tried to the best of my abilities to conduct myself and my business affairs in an honorable and forthright manner, thus helping to preserve what I feel is still the best life style in the world.*

ULRICH, ROBERT J., retail executive; b. 1944; Grad., U. Minn., 1967, Stanford U., 1978. Chmn., chief exec. officer, dir. Dayton Hudson Corp.; with Dayton Hudson Corp. (now Target Corp.), Mpls., 1967—, exec. v.p. dept. stores divsn., 1981-84, pres. dept. stores divsn., 1984-87, chmn., CEO Target stores divsn., 1987-93, dir., 1993—; chmn, CEO Target Corp. (formerly Dayton Hudson Corp.), Mpls., 1994—. Bd. dirs. Yum Brands!, Inc. Office: Target Corp 1000 Nicollet Mall Minneapolis MN 55403-2467 *

ULRICH, THEODORE ALBERT, lawyer; b. Spokane, Wash., Jan. 1, 1943; s. Herbert Roy and Martha (Hoffman) Ulrich; m. Nancy Allison, May 30, 1966; children: Donald Wayne, Frederick Albert. BS cum laude, U.S. Mcht. Marine Acad., 1965; JD cum laude, Fordham U., 1970; LLM, NYU, 1974. Bar: NY 1971, U.S. Ct. Appeals (2d cir.) 1971, U.S. Supreme Ct. 1974, U.S. Ct. Claims 1977, U.S. Customs Ct. 1978, U.S. Ct. Internat. Trade 1981, U.S. Ct. Appeals (5th cir.) 1988, U.S. Ct. Appeals (DC cir.) 1992, Colo. 1993, U.S. Ct. Appeals (10th cir.) 1994. Mng. clk. U.S. Dept. Justice, NYC, 1968-69, law clk. to fed. dist. judge, 1969-70; assoc. Cadwalader, Wickersham & Taft, NYC, 1970—94, ptnr., 1980-94, Popham, Haik, Schnobrich & Kaufman, Ltd., Denver, 1994-96; pvt. practice law Denver, 1996—. Author: Arbitration of Construction Contracts, V, 1991; co-author: Encyclopedia of International Commercial Litigation, 1991; contbg. author: Marine Engineering Economics and Cost Analysis, 1995; author, editor Fordham Law Rev., 1969. Leader Boy Scouts Am., Nassau County, NY, 1984-94, Denver, 1994—. Capt. USCGR, 1965-86. Mem. ABA, Colo. Bar, Denver Bar, Maritime Law Assn., Am. Soc. Internat. Law, Soc. Naval Archs. and Marine Engrs., U.S. Naval Inst., Am. Arbitration Assn. Home and Office: 4300 E 6th Ave Denver CO 80220-4940 E-mail: tnulrich@verizon.net.

ULRICH, WERNER, b. Munich, Mar. 12, 1931; came to U.S., 1940, naturalized, 1945; s. Karl Justus and Grete (Rosenthal) U.; m. Ursula Wolff, June 28, 1959; children: Gerta, Kenneth. BS, Columbia U., 1952, MS (NSF fellow 1952-53), 1953, Dr.Engring. Sci., 1957; MBA, U. Chgo., 1975; JD, Loyola U., Chgo, 1985. Bar: Ill. 1985. With AT&T Bell Labs, Naperville, Ill., 1953-95; head electronic switching dept. AT&T Bell Labs., Naperville, Ill., 1964-68; dir. Advanced Switching Tech., Naperville, 1968-77, head maintenance architecture dept., 1977-81; sr. atty. Intellectual Property Law Orgn., Naperville, 1981-95; pvt. practice Glen Ellyn, Ill., 1995—2007. Vis. lectr. U. Calif., Berkeley, 1966-67 Inventor of over 20 telecommunications inventions; patentee electronic switching systems. Fellow IEEE; mem. ABA, Ill. State Bar Assn., Am. Intellectual Property Law Assn., Tau Beta Pi, Beta Gamma Sigma.

ULSENHEIMER, DEAN, language educator; b. Cleve., Dec. 20, 1941; s. Lon Sherwood and Mary Dorothy (Kupstas) U.; m. Sharon Lee Williams, Dec. 27, 1963 (div. June 1980); children: Cathi, Chris, Shelley, Scott.; m. Monica Joan Rigo, Aug. 10, 1984. BS in Edn., Ohio U., Athens, 1964; postgrad., John Carroll U., 1969—70, postgrad., 2006, Kent State U., 1979. Cert. secondary sch. tchr. Tchr. English South Amherst (Ohio) Schs., 1964-66; project engr. Otto Konigslow Mfg. Co., Cleve., 1966-67; tchr. English Cardinal Schs., Middlefield, Ohio, 1967-80, Shaw High Sch., East Cleveland, Ohio, 1980-92; instr. English Cuyahoga C.C., Cleve., 1980—, Lakeland C.C., Mentor, Ohio, 1984—; owner, cons. DU Power Reading, 2000—. Owner, cons. Power Writing; spkr. Lakeland C.C. Spkrs. Bur., Mentor, 1988—; hon. poetry intern NEH, Hiram Coll., 1977; cons. in field. Author: Easy Writing, 1977, Sentence Analysis, 1977, Communication Problems, 1978, Short Story Starters, 1980. Mem. NEA, Am. Cons. League, Ohio Edn. Assn., Greater Cleve. Growth Assn., Coun. Smaller Bus. Ent. Roman Catholic. Avocations: tennis, golf, phys. fitness. Home and Office: 6691 Morley Rd Concord OH 44077-5924

ULSH, GORDON A., battery manufacturing company executive; BA, Butler Univ. With Ford Motor Corp., 1968—84; v.p. Cooper Industries, 1984—97, exec. v.p., 1997—98; exec. v.p. worldwide aftermarket div. Federal-Mogul Corp., 1998, pres., COO, 1999; ptnr. Ripplewood Equity Partners, 1999—2001; chmn., pres., CEO Fleetpride Inc., 2001—05; pres., CEO, dir. Exide Technologies, Lawrenceville, NJ, 2005—. Mem.: Soc. Mfg. Engineers, Soc. Automotive Engineers. *

ULSOY, ALI GALIP, engineering educator; b. Kozlu, Zonguldak, Turkey, Aug. 17, 1950; s. Muzaffer and Fatma Emel (Tugsal) U.; m. Susan Kathleen Glowski, Apr. 17, 1975; 1 child, Jessie Elif. BS, Swarthmore Coll., 1973; MS, Cornell U., 1975; PhD, U. Calif., Berkeley, 1979. Teaching and rsch. asst. Cornell U., Ithaca, N.Y., 1973-74, U. Calif., Berkeley, 1975-79, postdoctoral fellow, 1979-80; asst. prof. U. Mich., Ann Arbor, 1980-86; assoc. prof. engring. Bogazici U., Istanbul, Turkey, 1986-87, U. Mich., Ann Arbor, 1986-92, prof., 1992-96, chmn. grad. program, 1987-89, assoc. chair dept. mech. engring., 1992-93, chair program in mfg., 1992-98, William Clay Ford prof. mfg., 1996—, chair dept. mech. engring., 1998—. Vis. rschr. Ford Motor Co. Rsch. Labs., Dearborn, Mich., summer 1989; dir. NSF Mfg. Ctr., Ann Arbor, 1992—. Author (book) Microcomputer Applications in Manufacturing, 1989; contbr. articles to profl. jours.; tech. editor ASME Jour. of Dynamic Systems Measurement and Control, 1999—. Recipient Rsch. Incentive award Exxon Found., 1984-85, Wood award Forest Products Rsch. Soc., 1979, O. Hugo Schuck Best Paper award, 1994, Southwest Mechs. Lectr., 1995. Fellow ASME; mem. IEEE, NAE, Soc. Mfg. Engrs. (Outstanding Young Mfg. Engr. award 1986), Am. Soc. Engring. Edn., U. Mich. Rsch. Club, Sigma Xi. Avocations: reading, poetry, soccer, bicycling, canoeing, fishing. Office: U Mich Dept Mech Engring Ann Arbor MI 48109-2125

ULSTROM, ROBERT A., retired pediatrician; b. Mpls., Feb. 23, 1923; m. Mary Janet McGrath, 1946 (dec. 1981); 3 children; m. Betty Bernard, 1982 (div. 1985). BS, U. Minn., 1944, MD, 1946; postgrad., Strong Meml. Hosp. Lic. physician, Minn., Calif.; diplomate Am. Bd. Pediatrics with subsplty. in endocrinology (bd. dirs. 1980-86, v.p. 1985, chmn. rsch. and devel. com. 1980-86, tech. adv. com. for devel. of computerized exams. 1983-86), Am. Bd. Emergency Medicine (bd. dirs. 1982-86). Intern, resident in pediats. U. Rochester, 1946-48; instr., asst. prof. U. Minn., Mpls., 1950-53, assoc. prof., 1956-61, prof. pediatrics, 1961-64, 66-90, prof. emeritus, 1990—, mem. Ctr. for German and European Studies, Inst. for Global Studies, 2004—, acting head dept. pediats., 1961—62, assoc. dean Coll. Med. Scis., 1967-70; asst. prof. UCLA, 1953-56, prof., 1964-67, chmn. dept. pediatrics, 1964-67; vis. prof. medicine U. So. Calif., 1982-83, ret. Chief pediats. 97th Gen. Hosp., 1949-50; cons. in pediats. Harbor Gen. Hosp., L.A., 1953-56, 64-67, Mpls. Gen. Hosp., 1956-64, Hennepin County Gen. Hosp., 1967-90, hon. staff, 1990—; Well Child Clinic cons. City of L.A., 1953-56; track physician Donneybrooke Racetrack, Brainerd, Minn., 1968-73; dir. Reg. Ctr. for Metabolic Defects, 1975-79; cons. Ellwood & Assocs., 1986-87; med. legal cons. various plantiffs, 1985-95; mem. med. adv. bd. Group Health, Inc., 1967-90, Diabetes Detection and Edn. Ctr., 1969-71; mem. grants review com. Human Growth Inc., 1974-78; mem. tech. adv. com. on human genetics Minn. State Bd. Health, 1976-90; mem. pers. selection com. NIH, 1979, mem. gen. medicine study sect. NIH, 1964-68; mem. divsn. med. scis. NRC, 1961-64; oral examiner Am. Bd. Pediats., 1970-89; expert witness for prosecution U.S. Fed. Dist. Ct., Mpls., 1994-95; instr. computer course for beginners Elder Learning Inst., Coll. Continuing Edn., U. Minn., 1995—, bd. dirs., 1996-2000, webmaster, author, 1997-2002, v.p., 1998-99, mentor undergrad. students Coll. Liberal Arts, 1992—2004. Mem. editl. bd. Jour. Pediats., 1962-65; contbr. articles to profl. jours. Sec.-treas. Minn. Med. Found., 1967-68. With M.C., U.S. Army, 1948-50. Markle scholar in med. scis., 1954-59; Pew Found. fellow, 1985-86; recipient Wyeth award for med. rsch., 1963. Mem. AAAS, Am. Pediat. Soc., Am. Soc. Clin. Investigation, Ctrl. Soc. for Clin. Rsch., Endocrine Soc., Lawson-Wilkins Pediat. Endocrine Soc. (founding mem., membership com. 1971-75, chmn. 1975), Midwestern Pediat. rsch. Soc. (coun. 1961-64), Soc. for Pediat. Rsch. (NRC rep. 1961-64), Western Soc. for Clin. rsch., Western Soc. for Pediat. Rsch., Ctr. for German and European Studies at U. Minn., Alpha Omega Alpha, Phi Rho Sigma. Home: 4616 Sunset Rdg Minneapolis MN 55416-3335 Personal E-mail: ulstr001@tc.umn.edu.

ULTAN, LLOYD, historian, educator; b. Bronx, NY, Feb. 16, 1938; s. Louis and Sophie U. BA cum laude, Hunter Coll., 1959; MA, Columbia U., 1960. Assoc. Edward Williams Coll., Fairleigh Dickinson U., Hackensack, NJ, 1964-74, asst. prof. history, 1974-75, assoc. prof., 1975-83, prof., 1983—. Adj. prof. history H. Lehman Coll. CUNY, 2004-; cons. in field. Editor Bronx County Hist. Soc. Jour., 1964—, Bronx County Hist. Soc. Press, 1981—; author: The Beautiful Bronx, 1920-50, 1979, Legacy of the Revolution: The Valentine-Varian House, 1983, The Bronx in the Innocent Years, 1890-1925, 1985, The Presidents of the United States, 1989, The Bronx in the Frontier Era: From the Beginning to 1696, 1993, The Bronx: It Was Only Yesterday, 1935-65, 1993, Roots of the Republic, Vol. VI, 1996, The Bronx Cookbook, 1997, Bronx Accent: A Literary and Pictorial History of the Borough, 2000, The Birth of The Bronx, 1609-1900, 2000; contbr. Ency. NY City, 1995. Gen. sec. Bronx Civic League, 1964—67; v.p. bd. trustees Bronx County Hist. Soc., 1965—67, 1977—84, curator, 1968—71, pres., 1971—76, historian, 1986—; founding mem., bd. dirs. Bronx Coun. on Arts, 1968—71; chmn. Bronx County Bicentennial Commn., 1973—76, Bronx Borough Pres.'s Bicentennial Adv. Com., 1974—76; vice chmn. Commn. Celebrating 350 Yrs. of the Bronx, 1989; mem. program guidelines com. N.Y.C. Dept. Cultural Affairs, 1976—77; mem. N.Y.C. Com. on Cultural Concerns, 1982—88, N.Y.C. Mayor's Task Force on Spontaneous Memls., 2002; bd. sponsors Historic Preservation com. St. Ann's Ch. Morrisania, 1987—; ofcl. historian Bronx Borough, NY, 1996—; bd. dirs. Nat. Shrine Bill of Rights, Mt. Vernon, NY, 1983—, 91 Van Cortlandt Owners Corp., 1986—. Recipient Fairleigh Dickinson U. 15-Yr. award, 1979, 20-Yr. award, 1984, 25-Yr. award, 1989, 30-Yr. award, 1994, 35-Yr. award, 1999, Outstanding Tchr. of Yr. award, 1994, 40-Yr. award, 2004; named NYC Centennial Historian, 1999, NYC Book award for borough history NY Soc. Libr., 2001; named to Hunter Coll. Alumni Hall of Fame, 1974; NY State Regents Coll. tchg. fellow, 1959. Mem.: AAUP (v.p. Teaneck chpt. 1992—93, sec. coun. of FDU chpts. 1992—93), NY Hist. Soc., Am. Hist. Assn., Sigma Lambda, Alpha Chi Alpha, Phi Alpha Theta. Home and Office: 91 Van Cortlandt Ave W Bronx NY 10463-2712 *Transmitting the heritage of the past to the youth and to the mature adult, either through the spoken or written word, not only ensures that the civilization we inherited will be passed on, it will also warn people about earlier mistakes that should now be shunned and will, hopefully, inspire them to add their own positive contribution. I believe I am continuing to perform this service.*

UM, KI SUNG, research scientist; b. Gongju, Choongnam, Republic of Korea, Apr. 13, 1961; s. Dong Seop Um and Kyung Sook Lee; m. Soon Yi Yang, Apr. 16, 1988; children: Jung Yong, Se Yong. MPH, Yonsei Grad. Sch. Health Sci. and Mgmt., Seoul, 1989; PhD, Kyungpook Nat. U., Daegu, Republic of Korea, 2004. Cert. info. process engr. Human Resources Devel. Svc. Korea. Rschr. Ctr. Bioinformatics Nat. Cancer Inst./NIH, Rockville, Md., 2005—. Maj. Republic of Korea Air Force, 1985—2001. Recipient Sci. award for best paper of yr., Korean Soc. Med. Informatics, 2003; Postdoctoral fellow, Korea Rsch. Found., 2004—05. Mem.: Health Level Seven Inc. (cert. specialist). Achievements include patents for linear streaming algorithm as an HL7 parsing method. Office: Nat Cancer Inst NIH Ctr Bioinformatics 2115 E Jefferson St Ste 5000 Rockville MD 20852 Office Phone: 301-451-6364. Office Fax: 301-480-4222. Business E-Mail: umkis@mail.nih.gov.

UMANS, ALVIN ROBERT, manufacturing executive; b. NYC, Mar. 11, 1927; s. Louis and Ethel (Banner) U.; m. Nancy Jo Zadek, June 28, 1953 (div.); children: Kathi Lee Umans Lind, Craig Joseph; m. Madeleine Sayer, Sept. 21, 1985; 1 child, Valentine Brett. Student, U. Rochester, NY, 1944—45. Sales mgr. Textile Mills Co., Chgo., 1954-56; regional sales mgr. Reflector Hardware Corp., Melrose Park, Ill., 1956-58, nat. sales mgr., 1959-62, v.p., 1962-65, pres., treas., dir., 1965-92; pres., CEO RHC/Spacemaster Corp., Melrose Park, 1992-97, chmn., CEO, 1997—2003, Commerce Nat. Group, Chgo., 2004—. Past chmn., bd. dirs. Goer Mfg. Co., Inc., Charleston, SC, Morgan Marshall Industries, Inc., Ill., Capitol Hardware, Inc., Ill., Spartan Showcase Inc., Mo.; v.p., dir. Adams Comm., Chgo.; bd. dirs. Monroe Comm., Chgo.; trustee Driehaus Mut. Funds, 1996—, chmn. bd., 2005—; mem. adv. bd. Capsonic Group, Elgin, Ill. Trustee Mt. Sinai Hosp. Med. Ctr., Chgo., 1970—, chmn. bd., 1987-89; trustee Schwab Rehab. Hosp., Chgo., 1987—, chmn. bd., 1987-89; trustee Sinai Health Sys., Chgo., 1993—, chmn., 1995-97; mem. Cook County Bur. Adv. Com., 1994—; bd. dirs. Milton & Rose Zadek Fund, 1965-78; governing bd. mem. Cinema/Chgo., 1988-89. Served with US Army, 1945-46. Mem. Nat. Assn. Store Fixture Mfrs. (dir. 1969-70), World Pres.'s Orgn., Chgo. Pres.'s Orgn. Clubs: Standard (Chgo.). Home: 132 E Delaware Pl Chicago IL 60611-1445 Office: Commerce Nat Group 194 E Delaware Pl Ste 501 Chicago IL 60611 Office Phone: 312-654-9150. Office Fax: 312-654-9180. Business E-Mail: arumans@gmail.com.

UMANSKY, DIANE, editor-in-chief; B in Journalism, U. RI. Corr. Bergen Record; writer various teen publs. including Scholastic; mng. editor Nickelodeon; sr. editor First for Women; editor-in-chief MediZine Guidebook, 1995—. Freelance writer First for Women, SELF, Family Circle, American, Harper's Bazaar, Working Mother, Good Housekeeping, Weight Watchers. Office: MediZine 500 Fifth Ave Ste 1900 New York NY 10110 Office Phone: 212-695-2223.

UMANSKY, EDITH SIMON, retired school librarian, retired elementary school educator; b. NYC, Feb. 9, 1924; d. Abraham and Mary Mednick Simon; m. Harlan Lieberman Umansky, June 26, 1948 (dec.); children: Carol Raphael, Deborah, Diane. BA, Hunter Coll., NYC, 1944. From counselor to asst. head counselor Cejwin Camps, Port Jervis, NY, 1943—63; tchr. NYC Bd. Edn., 1944—49; ednl. media specialist Emerson HS, Union City, NJ, 1965—89; media specialist, co-founder Ednl. Media Assn., 1989—. Co-founder Media Assn. of Hudson County, NJ, 1965—89, pres., 1975—77. Bd. dirs. Hadassah, Cliffside Pk., 1950—; scout leader Temple Israel of Cliffside Pk., NJ, 1959—63, sec., bd. dirs., 1980—2002, pres. bd. edn., 1984—86; bd. dirs. Jewish Women Internat., 1996—. Avocations: singing, clay building, opera, theater, ballet. Home: 2150 Center Ave Apt 22B Fort Lee NJ 07024

UMBAYEMAKE, LINDA, library branch manager, rehabilitation services professional; b. Cleve., Feb. 19, 1953; d. Charles Morgan and Helen Loretta (Ballard) McDonald; m. Thomas L. Hayes; children: Manu, Kumar, Bari, Mayi, Thurayya, GlennChinua. AA, Cuyahoga C.C., Cleve., 1980; BA, Kent State U., Ohio, 1984; MLS, Tex. Woman's U., 1989; MRC, U. Ky., Lexington, 1998. Dir. African Am. Ctr. Toledo-Lucas County Pub. Libr., Toledo, 1989; libr. young adult, correctional and homebound Cuyahoga County Pub. Libr., Warrensville, Ohio, 1989-90; libr. supr. Western N.Mex. Correctional Facility, Grants, 1990; instr. and libr. supr. Santa Fe C.C., 1990; libr. supr. Ga. Dept. Corrections, Buford, 1991; instr. Ky. State U., Frankfort, Ky., 1992—96, head circulation, 1992—93, inter libr. loan and reference libr., 1993—96; pub. svcs. asst. libr. Owensboro C.C., 1996; substitute tchr. Franklin County Pub. Schs., Frankfort, 1997—98; offender rehab. counselor, substance abuse program Luther Luckett Correctional Ctr., 1998—99; collection devel. specialist Book Wholesalers Inc., 1999-2000; STAR program coord. U. Akron, Ohio, 2001—02; br. mgr. East Cleve. Pub. Libr. Caledonia Br., 2001—. Founder Lumbay6, 1996—, Lumbay 6 Intervention Journeys, Inc., 2004—; mem. Kent Ohio Cable Commn., 2003—. Apptd. to Ky. Foster Care Rev. Bd., 1999—2000; child support, visitation com. Franklin County Family Ct., Ohio, 1999—2000; mem. Bd. Elections Franklin County. Mem.: NAMI, Nat. Rehab. Assn., Black Caucus of ALA (chair new mem. orientation com. 1994—96, membership com. 1989—96, ALA Shirley Olofson com. 1993—96, mem. minority recruitment com. 1993—96), Chi Sigma Iota. Address: 798 Ellis Ave Orangeburg SC 29115 Personal E-mail: lumbay2000@yahoo.com.

UMBDENSTOCK, RICHARD J., medical association administrator; b. 1950; BA in Politics, Fairfield U., Conn., 1972; MSc in Health Services Adminstrn., SUNY, Stony Brook, 1974; LLD (hon.), Gonzaga U., Spokane, Washington, 2003. Diplomate Am. Coll. Healthcare Executives. Independent cons. for voluntary hosp. governing boards in the US and Can.; pres., CEO Providence Services, Spokane, Wash., 1993—2006; chmn. Premier, Inc., Charlotte, NC, 2006; exec. v.p. Providence Health & Services (merger of Providence Services and Providence Health System), 2006; spl. asst. to pres. Am. Hosp. Assn., Inc., Chgo., trustee, 2000—04, chmn.-elect, 2005, chmn., 2006, COO, 2006, pres.-elect, 2006, pres., 2006—. Mem. nat. bd. advisors Ctr. for Healthcare Governance. Author: of several books and articles for the hosp. bd. audiences, nat. survey reports for Am. Hosp. Assn., Health Rsch. Ednl. Trust, and Am. Coll. Healthcare Executives. Office: Am Hosp Assn One North Franklin St Chicago IL 60606-3421 Office Phone: 312-422-3000. Office Fax: 312-422-4796. *

UMBEL, TAMMIE, cosmetics executive; b. Atlanta, Aug. 12, 1972; d. Christine Brooks and Floyd Umbel; m. Syed N Ishaq, June 10, 1960. Founder Shea Terra Organics, Fairfax, Va., 2004—06. Office: Shea Terra Organics 8400-C Hiltop Rd Fairfax VA 22031 Office Phone: 703-846-9881.

UMBERG, THOMAS JOHN, lawyer; b. Cin., Sept. 25, 1955; s. John H. and Joan (Jansen) U.; m. Robin Bailey; children: Erin, Brett, Tommy. BA cum laude, UCLA, 1977; JD, U. Calif., San Francisco, 1980. Bar: Calif. 1980, U.S. Dist. Ct. (ctr. dist.) Calif. 1981, U.S. Dist. Ct. (so. dist.) Calif. 1986, U.S. Ct. Appeals (9th cir.) 1988. Asst. U.S. atty. Ctrl. Dist. Calif., criminal div., LA, 1987—90; mem. Calif. Assembly, Sacramento, 1990—94, 2004—; ptnr. Morrison & Foerster LLP, Irvine, Calif., 1995—97; dep. dir. White House Office Nat. Drug Control Policy, 1997—2000; mng. ptnr.-Orange County Office Morrison & Foerster LLP, Irvine, Calif., 2000—. Adj. prof. law Southwestern U., 1995—97. Military Prosecutor, U.S. Army, Korea, Italy 1980-1985; col. USAR. Mem.: Calif. Coun. Criminal Justice (mem. 1991—95). Roman Catholic. Office: Morrison & Foerster LLP 19900 MacArthur Blvd Irvine CA 92612-2445 Office Phone: 949-251-7500. Office Fax: 949-251-0900. Business E-Mail: tumberg@mofo.com.

UMBREIT, WAYNE WILLIAM, bacteriologist, educator; b. Markesan, Wis., May 1, 1913; s. William Traugott and Augusta (Abendroth) U.; m. Doris McQuade, July 31, 1937; children: Dorayne Loreda, Jay Nicholas, Thomas Hayden. BA, U. Wis., 1934, MS, 1936, PhD, 1939. Instr. soil microbiology Rutgers U., 1937-38; faculty U. Wis., Madison, 1938-44, asst. prof. bacteriology and chemistry, 1941-44; faculty Cornell U., 1944-47, prof. bacteriology, 1946-47; head dept. enzyme chemistry Merck Inst., Rahway, NJ, 1947-58; asso. dir., 1958; chmn. dept. bacteriology Rutgers U., New Brunswick, NJ, 1958-75, prof. microbiology, dir. grad. programs, 1969-83, prof. emeritus microbiology, 1983—; dir. labs. So. Br. Watershed Assn., 1983-89. Author: (with Burris, Stauffer) Manometric Techniques, 1945, 5th edit., 1972, (with Oginsky) An Introduction to Bacterial Physiology, 1954, Metabolic Maps, 1960, Modern Microbiology, 1962, Essentials of Bacterial Physiology, 1976; Editor: Advances in Applied Microbiology, vols. 1-10, 1959-68; Contbr. articles to profl. jours. Recipient Biochem. Congress Symposium medal Paris, France, 1952 Fellow Am. Acad. Microbiology, NY Acad. Sci., AAAS; mem. Am. Soc. for Microbiology (Eli Lilly award 1947, Carski Found. award 1968), Soc. Biol. Chemists, Am. Chem. Soc., Theobald Smith Soc. (Waksman award 1957, past pres.), AAUP, Sigma Xi. Home: c/o TH Umbreit PO Box 5352 Rockville MD 20848

UMEBAYASHI, CLYDE SATORU, lawyer; b. Honolulu, Sept. 2, 1947; s. Robert S. and Dorothy C. Umebayashi; m. Cheryl J. Much, June 27, 1975. BBA in Travel Industry Mgmt., U. Hawaii, 1969, JD, 1980. Spl. dept. atty. gen. Labor and Indsl. Rels. Appeals Bd., Honolulu, 1980-81; atty., dir., shareholder Kessner, Duca, Umebayashi, Bain & Matsunaga, Honolulu, 1981—. Commr. Hawaii Criminal Justice Commn. Bd. dirs. Wesley Found., Honolulu, 1993-97. Mem. Hawaii State Bar Assn. Office: Kessner Duca Umebayashi Bain & Matsunaga 220 S King St Fl 19 Honolulu HI 96813-4526

UMENYIORA, OSI, professional football player; b. Nov. 16, 1980; Graduate, Troy State U. Defensive end NY Giants, 2003—. Named to NFC Pro-Bowl Team, 2005, NFL All-Pro Team, 2005. Office: New York Football Giants Giants Stadium East Rutherford NJ 07073

UMHOEFER, AURAL M., retired dean, educational consultant; b. Wausau, Wis., May 11, 1942; d. Mark John Vladick, Alice Marion Vladick; m. Paul Anthony Umhoefer. MS, U. Wis., Madison, 1965; BA in French, Rosary Coll., River Forest, Ill., 1964—64; AA (hon.), U. Wis., Baraboo, 2006. Head libr. Green Bay ctr. U. Wis., 1965—68, dir. learning resource ctr. Baraboo, 1968—80, dean, campus exec. officer Baraboo/Sauk county campus, 1980—2002, ret., 2002; cons. U. Wis. Sys., 2003—05. Bd. dirs. Wells Fargo, Baraboo; bd. dirs. Hist. Sites Found. Circus World Mus., Baraboo, 1984—90. Bd. dirs. Al Ringling Theatre, Friends of Campus, Inc., Boy Scouts Am., Madison, Wis., 1985—97; devel. coun. St. Clare Hosp., Baraboo, 1993—97. Named Outstanding Young Women of Am., 1975, Aural M. Umhoefer bldg. in her honor, U. Wis., Baraboo, 2002; recipient Outstanding Alumni award, Newman H.S. - Wausau, Wis., 1992, Citation from Senate, State of Wis., 1991, 2002, Pub. Svc. award, Fed. Bur. Prisons, 1991, 2002, Appreciation award, Circus World Mus., 1986, Citation from Govt., State of Wis., 2002. Mem.: AAUW (corp. rep. 1985—97, Wis. Women Leaders in Edn. award 1986, 1989), Wis. Correctional Edn. Assn. (v.p., pres. 1994—98), U. Wis. Alumni Assn. (pres. 1984—86, Spark Plug award 1992), Rotary Internat. (vocat. chair, bd-.dirs.). Avocations: cooking, reading, travel, gardening. Home: 700 Effinger Rd Baraboo WI 53913 Office: University of Wisconsin 1006 Connie Rd Baraboo WI 53913 Personal E-mail: pauralum@julmet.com. Business E-Mail: aumhoefe@uwc.edu.

UMHOLTZ, CLYDE ALLAN, financial analyst; b. Du Quoin, Ill., Dec. 20, 1947; s. Frederick Louis and Opal Kathleen (Beard) U. BS, U. Ill., 1969; MS, U. Miss., 1972; MBA, Memphis State U., 1983, PhD, 1986; Dr of Higher Learning (hon.), London Sch. Econs., 2002. CFA; cert. systems profl., tax practitioner; registered profl. engr.; cert. data processor. Supr. quality control Champion Internat. Corp., Oxford, Miss., 1971-72; mgr. divsn. quality control Cook Industries, Memphis, 1973; engring. planner

Northwest Industries and subs., Memphis, 1974-75; long range planning and analysis W.R. Grace and Co. and subs., Memphis, 1975-78; mgr. planning and analysis Ctr. Nuc. Studies Memphis State U., 1979-83; data processing mgr. Shelby County (Tenn.) Govt., 1983-87, dep. adminstr., 1987—2005, spl. asst. to county exec., 1989—2005, vice chancellor higher edn. commn., 2005—. Adj. prof. U. Tenn., Memphis, 1985—; ptnr. Custom Data Systems Inc., Memphis, 1987—, Western Techs. Inc., Memphis, 1988—; bd. dir. Am. Tech. Inst., Memphis, Am. Info. Cons., Atlanta, Eastgate Corp., Anaheim, Calif., CIPCO Corp., Chgo., Sanford Cons. Group, London, Paris; bd. underwriters Lloyd's of London; diplomate editl. adv. bd. Brent's Peerage, London, Memphis-Amsterdam Gateway Com., Holland, 1997; Goodwill Amb. Am. Ukrainian Trade Alliance, Kiev, 1997—, Asian Econ. Recovery Coun., Tokyo, 1998—; elected to U.S. China Bd. of Trade, 2002; adv. bd. Fed. Res. Bank, Memphis, 1998—; mem. Am.-Japanese Tire Safety Adv. Bd., 2000, Tenn. Commn. on Homeland Security, 2002—; diplomate Multi-Country Healthcare Exch., 2003, Medicare Nat. Study Com., 2003; oversight com. Internat. Energy Prodn. Alliance, 2003, 06; adv. com. OPEC Price Stblzn. Coop., 2004, 06; mem. Internat. Symposium Strategic Energy Resources, 2005, 06, Congressional Com. Social Security Reform, 2005, 06, Citizens' Congl. Ethics Coun., 2006, Emergency Mgmt. Comms. Coordinating Com., 2006, Accreditation Com., Internat. Baccalaureate Edn. Program, 2006, Mid-East Stabilization Planning Conf., 2006; mem. Govt. Ethics Reform Task Force, 2007; internat. bus. cons. McKinsey Co., 2007; cons. in field. Author: Prototyping of Computerized Financial Systems, 3d edit., 1997, Context Analysis in System Design, 2d edit., 1999, The Family Partnership-An Estate Planning Model, 3d edit., 2000, The Use of Chemical Molecules as Computer Switches, 2002, The Science of Plastics, 2007; contbr. articles to profl. jours.; inventor angle trisector. Active presdl. election campaigns, 1968-72, 80-2004; del. Rep. Nat. Conv., 1996-2004; mem. Rep. Nat. Com., 2002—; active mayoral campaign, Memphis, 1975, 83, 87, 91, Shelby County, 1990, 94, sheriff's campaign Shelby County, 1990, 94, Mid-South Billy Graham Crusade, 1978; del. So. Govs.' Conf., 1992-93; gov. staff State of Tenn., 1993-94; mem. Mayor's Adv. Com., Memphis, 1991; steering com. Future Memphis, 1992, Arena Football League, Memphis, 1994; active Houston Oilers Relocation Com., 1996; adv. coun. Kordes' Gardens, Hamburg, Germany; study com. Nat. Electoral Coll., 2001; co-chmn. 27th Ann. Pres.'s Dinner, 2002; oversight com. Fin. Acctg. Stds. Bd., 2002—; bd. dirs. West Tenn. Cmty. Found., 2006—, Memphis Biomed. Rsch. Found., 2007—, Resources for the Future, Washington, 2007—. Recipient Oratorical award Optimist Club, 1963, Leadership and Human Rels. award Dale Carnegie Inst., 1977, Disting. Svc. award State of Tenn., 1991; NSF fellow, 1970-72. Fellow NAS, Australian Acad. Scis., NY Acad. Scis., Am. Acad. Info. Tech., Internat. Enterprise Inst. (hon.); mem. AAAS, AIChE, Am. Mgmt. Assn., Fin. Execs. Inst., Am. Chem. Soc., Assn. MBA Execs., Data Processing Mgmt. Assn., Planning Execs. Inst., Am. Assn. Investment Advisors, U. Ill. Alumni Assn., U. Miss. Alumni Assn., Memphis State U. Alumni Assn., Am. Rose Soc. (accredited life rose judge 1990), Am. Iris Soc., Am. Hemerocallis Soc., Elvis Presley Meml. Soc., Am. Hort. Soc., Internat. Platform Assn., Gt. Am. Pyramid Boosters Memphis, Mensa, Admirals Club, Oxford Club, London Club, Exec. Club Memphis, Petroleum Club Memphis, Olympic Soc. Atlanta, Order of De Molay, Phi Beta Kappa. Baptist. Achievements include patent on fiber optic router. Home: 3580 Hanna Dr Memphis TN 38128-3451 Office: 100 N Main St Memphis TN 38103-5011 Office Phone: 901-388-3997. Business E-Mail: cau@memphis.gov. E-mail: cau@hannamem.gov.

UMLAUF, KARL ALLEN, artist; b. Chgo., May 16, 1939; s. Charles Julius and Angeline McMoran (Allen) U.; m. Shirley Ann Franks, Jan. 25, 1961; children: Stuart, Kurt. BFA, U. Tex., 1961; MFA, Cornell U., 1963. Teaching asst. Cornell U., Ithaca, N.Y., 1961-63; instr. U. Pa., Phila., 1963-66; asst. prof. U. No. Iowa, Cedar Falls, 1966-67, East Tex. State U., Commerce, 1967—; vis. prof. art Ind. U., Bloomington, 1974-75, 1980; vis. artist Baylor U., Waco, Tex., 1978, 80, Austin Coll., Sherman, Tex., 1974, So. Colo. State U., Pueblo, 1973; vis. lectr. Longview Mus., 1983, Joslyn Mus., Omaha, 1975. Represented in permanent collections Everson Mus., Okla. Art Ctr., Silvermine Guild, Masur Mus., Dallas Mus., Joslyn Mus., Ark Arts Ctr., Cornell U., New Orleans Mus. Art, IBM Corp., N.Y.C. Recipient purchase award Joslyn Mus. 1974, New Orleans Mus. Art 1973, Evansville Mus. Art 1975, Ark. Art Ctr. 1981; East Tex. State U. grantee 1969, 72, 73, 78, 82; Grand Prize winner Tex. Arts Celebration, Houston, 1986. Mem. Coll. Art Assn., Tex. Assn. Coll. Tchrs., Tex. Assn. Schs. Art, Tex. Fine Arts Assn.

UMMER, JAMES WALTER, lawyer; b. Pitts., July 16, 1945; s. Walter B. and Rose P. (Gerhardt) U.; m. Janet Sue Young, Dec. 21, 1968; children: James Bradley, Benjamin F. BA, Thiel Coll., 1967; JD, Duke U., 1972. Bar: Pa. 1972. Trust officer Pitts. Nat. Bank, 1972-75; tax atty., shareholder Buchanan Ingersoll P.C., Pitts., 1975-92; prin. Hirtle, Callaghan & Co., Pitts., 1992-93; shareholder Babst, Calland, Clements and Zomnir, Pitts., 1993-99; ptnr. Reed, Smith, Shaw & McClay, Pitts., 2000—03, Rothman Gordon, P.C., Pitts., 2003—. Golf course cons., Orlando, Fla. Trustee Thiel Coll., Greenville, Pa., 1984—, The Childrens' Inst., Pitts., 1984—; mem. bd. visitors Duke U. Div. Sch., 1999—. Fellow Am. Coll. Probate Counsel, Am. Coll. Trust and Estate Counsel; mem. Estate Planning Coun. Western Pa. (pres. 1986-87), Tax Club (Pitts.), Duquesne Club, Rolling Rock Club, Oakmont Country Club. Republican. Presbyterian. Home: 200 Woodland Farms Rd Pittsburgh PA 15238-2024 Office: Rothman Gordon PC 3d Fl Grant Bldg 310 Grant St Pittsburgh PA 15219 Office Phone: 412-338-1105. E-mail: jwummer@rothmangordon.com.

UMMINGER, BRUCE LYNN, government agency administrator, research scientist, educator, consultant; b. Dayton, Ohio, Apr. 10, 1941; s. Frederick William and Elnora Mae Umminger; m. Judith Lackey Bryant, Dec. 17, 1966; children: Alison Grace, April Lynn. BS in Biology magna cum laude with honors, Yale U., 1963, MS, 1966, MPhil, 1968, PhD, 1969; postgrad., U. Calif., Berkeley, 1963—64; cert. univ. adminstrv./mgmt. tng. program, U. Cin., 1975; cert., Fed. Exec. Inst., 1984. Asst. prof. dept. biol. scis. U. Cin., 1969-73, assoc. prof. dept. biol. scis., 1973-75, acting head dept. biol. scis., 1973-75, prof. dept. biol. scis., 1975-81, dir. grad. affairs, 1978-79; program dir. regulatory biology program NSF, Washington, 1979-84, dept. dir. cellular bioscis. divsn., 1984-89, mem. sr. exec. svc., 1984—2006, acting divsn. dir., 1985-87, 88-89, divsn. dir. cellular bioscis. divsn., 1989-91, divsn. dir. integrative biology and neurosci., 1991—99, sr. scientist office integrative activities, office of dir., 1999—2006, cons., 2006—; sr. advisor on health policy Office of Internat. Health Policy Dept. State, Washington, 1988; sr. advisor on biodiversity Smithsonian Instn., Washington, 1993-94. Exec. sec. Nat. Sci. Bd. Com. on Ctrs. and Individual Investigator Awards, 1986-88; rev. panel exptl. program to stimulate competitive rsch. NSF, 1989, Rsch. Improvement in Minority Instns., 1986-87, US-India Coop. Rsch. Program, 1981-82, U.S.-India Exch. of Scholars Program, 1979-81; vice chmn. biotech. rsch. subcom. Fed. Coord. Coun. on Sci. Engring. and Tech., Office Sci. and Tech. Policy, 1991-94; exec. sec. subcom. biodiversity and ecosystem dynamics, com. on environment and natural resources Nat. Sci. and Tech. Coun., 1994, interag. working group on rsch. misconduct policy implementation, 2000-06; group nat. experts on safety in biotech. OECD, 1988-89; sr. exec. panel Exec. Potential Program, Office Pers. Mgmt., 1988-89; space shuttle proposal rev. panel in life scis. NASA, 1978, rsch. assocs. in space biology award com., 1985-91, chmn. cell and devel. biology discipline working group, space biology program, 1990-91, chmn. gravitational biology panel, NASA Specialized Ctrs. Rsch. and Tng., 1990, chmn. specialized ctrs. rsch. and tng. peer rev. panel NASA, 1995, exec. steering com. in life scis., 1991, gravitational biology facility sci. working group, 1992-95, space sta. biol. rsch. project sci. working group, 1995-96, neurolab. steering com., 1993; panel study biol. diversity, Bd. Sci. and Tech. Internat. Devel. NRC, 1989; exec. sec. adv. planning bd. Nat. Biodiversity Info. Ctr., Smithsonian Instn., 1993-94; adv. screening com. in life scis. Coun. for Internat. Exch. of Scholars, 1978-81; liaison rep. nat. heart, lung and blood adv. coun. NIH, 1979-87, nat. adv. child health and human devel. coun., 1990-99; recombinant DNA adv. com., 1988; liaison rep. agrl. biotech. Rsch. Adv. com., USDA, 1989-94; animal com. Interag. Rsch., 1984-88; Interag. working group on Internat. Biotech., 1988-94; chmn. proposal panel in biology Sci. Found. Ireland, 2002, Human Proteomics Site Visit, 2003; cons. Implementation Group, DC, 2006-, Rsch. Torrain, 2007—. Author book chpts. and contbr. articles to profl. jours.; assoc. editor Jour. Exptl. Zoology, 1977-79; editl. adv. bd. Gen. and Comparative Endocrinology, 1982. World mission com. Ch. of the Redeemer, New Haven, 1967-68; Sunday Sch. steering com. Calvary Episcopal Ch., Cin., 1972-73, sr. acolyte, 1972-77, adult edn. com., 1975-76; deacon Faith Presbyn. Ch., Springfield, Va., 1996-99; adv. com. Wakefield H.S., 1991-92, PTA exec. bd., 1991-92; sci. adv. com. Arlington Pub. Schs., 1987-92, adv. coun. on instrn., 1991-92; adv. bd. Campbell Comml. Coll., Cin., 1977-79. Recipient George Rieveschl, Jr. Rsch. award U. Cin., 1973, Presdl. Rank Meritorious Exec. award NSF, 1992; U. Cin. Grad. Sch. fellow 1977—, NSF fellow 1964; Rsch. grant NSF 1971-79. Fellow AAAS (coun. 1980-83, 89-90, program com. for 1989 ann. meeting 1988, chmn.-elect sect. G-Biol. Scis. 1987-88, chair 1988-89, ret. 1989-90); mem. Assn. of Yale Alumni (del. 1990-93), Mory's Assn., Sigma Xi (Disting. Rsch. award U. Cin. chpt. 1973, pres. U. Cin. chpt. 1977-79), Mensa. Home: 205 Helmsdale Dr Chapel Hill NC 27517 Personal E-mail: bruce.u@hotmail.com.

UNAKAR, NALIN JAYANTILAL, biological sciences educator; b. Karachi, Sindh, Pakistan, Mar. 26, 1935; came to U.S., 1961; s. Jayantilal Virshankar and Malati Jaswantrai (Buch) U.; m. Nita Shantilal Mankad; children: Rita, Rupa. BS, Gujerat U., Bhavnagar, India, 1955; MSc, Bombay U., 1961; PhD, Brown U., 1965. Research asst. Indian Cancer Research Ctr., Bombay, 1955-61; USPHS trainee in biology Brown U., Providence, 1961-65; research assoc. in pathology U. Toronto, Ont., Canada, 1965-66; asst. prof. biology Oakland U., Rochester, Mich., 1966-69, assoc. prof., 1969-74, prof., chmn. biology dept., 1974-87, prof., 1974-2000, prof. emeritus, 2000—, adj. prof. biomed. scis., 1984—. Mem. coop. cataract research group Nat. Eye Inst., Bethesda, Md., 1977—; mem. visual scis. study sect. NIH, Bethesda, 1982-86, mem. cataract panel, 1980—. Mem. vis. bd. Lehigh U., Bethlehem, Pa., 1986-89. Grantee Nat. Cancer Inst., NIH, 1967-70, Nat. Eye Inst., NIH, 1976-97. Mem. AAAS, Am. Soc. Cell Biology, Assn. Rsch. in Vision and Ophthalmology, Sigma Xi. Home: 2822 Rhineberry Rd Rochester Hills MI 48309-1912

UNAN, GEORGE VINCENT, adult education educator; b. Bell Island, Newfoundland, Can., July 19, 1920; arrived in U.S., 1958; s. Samuel S. Unan and Ellen A. Kennedy-Unan; m. Myra Lanza Unan, Apr. 3, 1948 (div. July 1974); children: Veronica Gonzalez, Vivien Irving, Valerie Kitto, Venessa Mangione, Vernon A.; m. Gahyle Rich Unan, July 26, 1975; 1 child, Diane Baer. BS, Calif. State U., Long Beach, 1965, MBA, 1967. Cost estimator Hydro Electric Power Commn., Toronto, Ont., Canada, 1950—58; chief acct. Darco Industries, El Segundo, Calif., 1959—62; contr., sec./dir. State Industries, LA, Calif., 1962—68; contr. Direct Image Corp., Monterey Park, Calif., 1968—70, Harrington Indsl. Plastics, LA, 1970—83; CFO Long Beach Conv. Ctr., 1984—86; educator Anaheim (Calif.) Adult H.S. Dist., 1997—. Seminar instr. in field; educator, exploratory seminars U. Sydney, Australia, 1987—96, Nat. U. Buenos Aires, Argentina, 1993, Charles U., Prague, Czech Republic, 1996. Author: Anecdotes and Quintessences From The Holy Bible, 1999. Adv. bd. Orange County, Santa Ana, Calif., 1984—97; mem. oversight com. Orange County Transp. Authority, Santa Ana, 1997—99; chmn., mem. Citizens Adv. Commn., Cypress, Calif., 1985—96. Home: 6424 Anguilla Ave Cypress CA 90630-5308 Office: Anaheim Adult High Sch Dist 1800 Ball Rd Anaheim CA 92804 Office Phone: 714-999-5616.

UNDAR, AKIF, research scientist, biomedical engineer, educator; b. Istanbul, Turkey, Aug. 3, 1963; arrived in U.S., 1987; s. Fikret and H. Neriman Undar; m. F. Pinar Albayrak; children: Damla, Akifcan. BS, Yildiz U., Istanbul, 1986; MS, S.W. Tex. State U., 1992; MSE, U. Tex., 1994, PhD, 1996. Asst. instr., dir. surg. rsch. U. Tex. Health Sci. Ctr., San Antonio, 1996—97; instr. Baylor Coll. Medicine, Houston, 1997—99, asst. prof. surgery, 1999—2002, assoc. prof., 2002—03; assoc. prof. pediat., surgery and bioengring. Pa. State Coll. Medicine, Hershey, 2003—. Tchg. asst. U. Tex., Austin, 1994—96; dir. perfusion rsch. Tex. Children's Hosp., Houston, 1997—2001, dir. rsch., 2001—03; presenter, lectr. in field. Mem. editl. bd. Artificial Organ, 2003—, ASAIO Jour., 2004—; contbr. articles to profl. jours. Rsch. grantee, AHA Tex. affiliate, 1998-2000, Tanox, Inc., 1999-2001, NIH, 2000, NHLBI, 2005—, Pa. Health Dept., 2004—. Mem.: ASAIO, AHA (cert. 2000), Internat. Soc. Rotary Blood Pumps, Biomedical Engring. Soc., Internat. Soc. Artificial Organs. Office: Pa State Milton S Hershey Med Ctr Pa State Children's Hosp Dept Pediat 500 University Dr P Box 850 Hershey PA 17033 Office Phone: 717-531-6706. Business E-Mail: aundar@psu.edu.

UNDE, MADHAVJI ANANT (MARK UNDE), engineering executive; b. Pune, India, June 28, 1934; came to U.S., 1974; s. Anant Narasinh Unde and Laxmibal A. Unde; m. Dhanawanti B. Joshi, June 11, 1982 (div. Oct. 1983); 1 son, Abhijeet, 2 adopted daughters: Swati, Bhagyashree. M.I.E., Instn. Engrs., Calcutta, India, 1973; M.I.Prod.E., Instn. Prodn. Engrs., London, 1972; MS in Welding Engring., Ohio State U., 1978. Chartered engr., U.K. Divsn. welding engr. Fruehauf Corp.; tool engr. Danly Machine/Ingersoll Milling Machines, Inc.; mech. engr. Sacramento Army Depot; pres. Calif. Consulting Engrs., Sacramento. Recipient Presdl. award Advanced Rsch. Project Agy., 1994. Achievements include invention of metal working tech. including In Process Stress Relief Tech. for Welds; patents for processes on Thermal Fork, Equivalent Heat Sink Process; covered trailing edge of weld process; processes on the physical fork. Office: Calif Consulting Engrs 1980 Watt Ave Sacramento CA 95825-2151 Office Phone: 916-978-9438. Business E-Mail: ccemimde@jps.net.

UNDERBERG, MARK ALAN, lawyer; b. Niagara Falls, NY, July 9, 1955; s. Alan Jack and Joyce Love (Wisbaum) U.; m. Diane Englander, Mar. 22, 1986; children: Andrew Englander, James Englander. BA, Cornell U., 1977, JD, 1981. Bar: N.Y. 1981. Law clk. to chief judge U.S. Ct. Appeals (3d cir.), Wilmington, Del., 1981-82; assoc. Debevoise & Plimpton, NYC, 1982-87; mng. dir., dep. gen. counsel Henley Group, Inc., NYC, 1987-90, mng. dir., gen. counsel, 1990-92; v.p., gen. counsel Abex Inc., Hampton, NH, 1992-95; counsel Paul, Weiss, Rifkind, Wharton & Garrison, NYC, 1998—99, ptnr., 2000—. V.p., gen. counsel Fisher Sci. Internat. Inc., Hampton, N.H., 1991-97, cons. 1997-98. Editor-in-chief Cornell Law Rev., 1980-81. Bd. dirs. Catalog for Giving of NYC. Mem. ABA, Assn. Bar of City of N.Y., Genesee Valley Club, University Club. Office: Paul Weiss Rifkind Wharton & Garrison 1285 Avenue Of The Americas New York NY 10019-6065 Office Phone: 212-373-3368. Business E-Mail: munderberg@paulweiss.com.

UNDERDAL, OLAV M., engineering executive; b. Hoersholm, Denmark, Feb. 21, 1966; s. B. Underdal Olav and Edith Underdal; m. Li Qin Underdal, June 29, 1994; 1 child, Olav Loon Qin. MS, Manchester U., Eng., 1991; MS in Software Engring., Tech. U. Denmark, Lyngby, 1991. Mgr. Accenture, Copenhagen, 1992—2000; v.p. engring. LogicTree Corp., College Park, Md., 2000—03; dir. engring. SPX Corp., Portage, Mich., 2003—. Mem.: Assn. for Computing Machinery. Achievements include 8 US patents pending. Office: SPX Service Solutions 8001 Angling Rd Portage MI 49024 Home Phone: 269-353-5795; Office Phone: 269-329-7600. Business E-Mail: olav.underdal@servicesolutions.spx.com.

UNDERDOWN, DAVID EDWARD, historian, educator; b. Wells, Eng., Aug. 19, 1925; s. John Percival and Ethel Mary (Gell) U. BA, U. Oxford, 1950, MA, 1951, Yale U., 1952; B.Litt., U. Oxford, 1953; D.Litt. hon., U. of South, 1981. Asst. prof. U. of South, Sewanee, Tenn., 1953-58, assoc. prof., 1958-62; then assoc. prof. U. Va., Charlottesville, 1962-68; prof. Brown U., Providence, 1968-85, Munro-Goodwin Wilkinson prof., 1978-85; vis. prof. Yale U., New Haven, 1979, prof., 1986-94, George Burton Adams prof., 1994-96, emeritus, 1996—. Dir. Yale Ctr. Parliamentary History, 1985-96; vis. Mellon prof. Inst. for Advanced Study, 1988-89; vis. fellow All Souls Coll., Oxford, 1992; Ford's lectr. Oxford U., 1992. Author: Royalist Conspiracy in England, 1960, Pride's Purge, 1971, Somerset in the Civil War and Interregnum, 1973, Revel, Riot and Rebellion, 1985, Fire from Heaven, 1992, A Freeborn People, 1996, Start of Play, 2000. Guggenheim fellow, 1964-65, 91-92, fellow Am. Coun. Learned Socs., 1973-74, NEH fellow, 1980-81. Fellow Royal Hist. Soc., Brit. Acad. (corrs.); mem. Am. Hist. Assn. (award for scholarly distinction 2005), Conf. Brit. Studies. Office: Yale U Dept History New Haven CT 06520 Business E-Mail: david.underdown@yale.edu.

UNDERHILL, JACOB BERRY, III, retired insurance company executive; b. NYC, Oct. 25, 1926; s. Jacob Berry, Jr. and Dorothy Louise (Quinn) U.; m. Cynthia Jane Lovejoy, Sept. 9, 1950 (div. Sept. 1962); children: David Lovejoy, Kate Howell Underhill Kerwin, Benedict Quinn; m. Lois Beachy, Nov. 2, 1963 (div. July 1987); m. Betsy F. Ashton, Oct. 17, 1987 (div. Apr. 2007); m. Nancy McDonnell Maloney, June 5, 2007. Grad., Phillips Exeter Acad., 1944; AB, Princeton U., 1950. Editor Courier & Freeman, Potsdam, NY, 1950-53; reporter Democrat & Chronicle, Rochester, NY, 1953-56; chief editorial writer St. Petersburg (Fla.) Times, 1956-59; asso. editor McGraw Hill Publ. Co., NYC, 1959-61, Newsweek, NYC, 1961-63; asst. press sec. to Gov. N.Y., 1963-67; dep. supt., 1st dep. supt. State N.Y. Ins. Dept., 1967-72; v.p., sr. v.p., exec. v.p., dir., vice chmn. bd., pres. N.Y. Life Ins. Co., NYC, 1972-86. Hon. chmn. bd. dirs. Manhattan Eye, Ear and Throat Hosp.; trustee emeritus Nat. Trust for Hist. Preservation. With USNR, 1944-46. Mem. Players Club, Links Club, Piping Rock Club (Locust Valley, N.Y.).

UNDERWEISER, IRWIN PHILIP, mining executive, lawyer; b. NYC, Jan. 3, 1929; s. Harry and Edith (Gladstein) U.; m. Beatrice J. Kortchmar, Aug. 17, 1959; children: Rosanne, Marian, Jeffrey. BA, CCNY, 1950; LL.D., Fordham U., 1954; LL.M., NYU, 1961. Bar: N.Y. 1954. With firm Scribner & Miller, NYC, 1951-54, 56-62; partner firm Feuerstein & Underweiser, 1962-73, Underweiser & Fuchs, 1973-77, Underweiser & Underweiser, 1977—. V.p., sec. Sunshine Mining Co., Kellogg, Idaho, 1965-70, chmn. bd., 1970-78, pres., 1971-74, 77, v.p., 1977-83; vice chmn., dir. Underwriters Bank and Trust Co., N.Y.C., 1969-73; sec., dir. Bus. Consortium Fund, 1994—, Triad Capital Corp. N.Y., 1994—; dir. Anchor Post Products, Inc. Bd. dirs. Silver Inst. Inc., vice chmn., 1998-2001; bd. dirs. Bronx Mus. of the Arts, 1993-2001, Sheltering the Homeless is Our Responsibility, 1993-2001, 02—; gen. counsel, mem. bus. council Friends City Center Music and Drama, N.Y.C., 1966-67; pres. W. Quaker Ridge Assn., 1969-70; treas. Scarsdale Neighborhood Assn. Presidents, 1970-71. Served with AUS, 1954-56. Mem. Am., N.Y. State bar assns., Bar Assn. City N.Y., Phi Beta Kappa, Phi Alpha Theta. Home: 7 Rural Dr Scarsdale NY 10583-7701 Office: 1 Water St White Plains NY 10601

UNDERWOOD, BLAIR, actor, television producer; b. Tacoma, Aug. 25, 1964; s. Frank and Marilyn Underwood; m. Desiree Da Costa, Sept. 17, 1994; 3 children. Student, Carnegie-Mellon U. TV debut The Cosby Show, 1985; actor, prodr.: (films) Straight Out of Compton 2, 2005; actor (films) Krush Groove, 1985, The Second Coming, 1992, Posse, 1993, Just Cause, 1995, Set it Off, 1996, Gattaca, 1997, Deep Impact, 1998, Asunder, 1998, The Wishing Tree, 1999, Rules of Engagement, 2000 (NAACP Image award for sup. actor, 2001), G, 2002, Full Frontal, 2002, Malibu's Most Wanted, 2003, Fronterz, 2004, How Did it Feel, 2004, Do Geese See God?, 2004, Something New, 2006, Madea's Family Reunion, 2006; (TV series) One Life to Live, 1985-86, Downtown, 1986, LA Law, 1987-94, High Incident, 1996, City of Angels, 2000 (NAACP Image award for lead actor, 2001), Fatherhood, 2004-, LAX, 2004-05, (TV movies) The Cover Girl and the Cop, 1989, Murder in Mississippi, 1990, Heat Wave, 1990, Father and Son: Dangerous Relations, 1993, Soul of the Game, 1996, Mistrial, 1996, Mama Flora's Family, 1998; theater credits include Measure for Measure, 1993, El Negro en Peru, The Game of Love and Chance, and Love Letters, Purlie, 2005. Co-founder Artists for a New South Africa, 1989. Named Artist of the Year, Harvard Found., Harvard U., 2002; recipient Humanitarian Award, Muscular Dystrophy Assoc., LA, 1993. Office: William Morris Agency 151 El Camino Dr Beverly Hills CA 90212

UNDERWOOD, CARRIE MARIE, singer; b. Muskogee, Okla., Mar. 10, 1983; d. Stephen and Carol Underwood. BA magna cum laude, Northeastern State U., 2006. Recording artist RCA Music Group, NYC, 2005—. Singer: (albums) Some Hearts, 2005, Carnival Ride, 2007, (songs) Inside Your Heaven, 2005 (Billboard Hot 100 Song of Yr., 2005), Jesus, Take the Wheel, 2005 (Single Record of Yr., Acad. Country Music, Female Video of Yr. & Breakthrough Video of Yr., Country Music TV, 2006, Best Female Country Vocal Performance & Best Country Song, Grammy Awards, 2007), Some Hearts, 2005 (Billboard Album of Yr. & Country Album of Yr., 2006, Album of Yr., Acad. Country Music, 2007), Before He Cheats, 2006 (Favorite Country Song, People's Choice awards, 2007, Video of Yr., Female Video & Best Video Dir., County Music TV awards, 2007, Video of Yr., Acad. Country Music, 2007). Named Favorite Female Singer, People's Choice Awards, 2007, Best New Artist, Grammy Awards, 2007; recipient Top-Selling Country Single of Yr., Billboard Music Awards, 2005, Country Single Sales Artist of Yr., 2005, New Country Artist of Yr., 2006, Female Country Artist of Yr., 2006, Female Billboard 200 Album Artist of Yr., 2006, New Female Vocalist award, Acad. Country Music, 2006, Top Female Vocalist award, 2007, Horizon award, Country Music Assn., 2006, Female Vocalist of Yr. award, 2006, Favorite New Breakthrough Artist, Am. Music Awards, 2006. Baptist. Achievements include winning the fourth season of American Idol on May 25, 2005. Avocations: guitar, piano. Office: c/o Jeff Frasco Creative Artists Agy 2000 Ave of the Stars Los Angeles CA 90067 *

UNDERWOOD, CECIL HARLAND, retired governor, diversified financial services company executive; b. Josephs Mills, W.Va., Nov. 5, 1922; s. Silas and Della (Forrester) U.; m. Hovah Hall, July 25, 1948 (dec.); children: Cecilia A., Craig Hall, Sharon. AB, Salem Coll., W.Va., 1943; AM, W.Va. U., 1952; rsch. fellow, Amelia Earhart Found., Ann Arbor, Mich., 1954-56; LLD (hon.), Marietta Coll., Ohio, 1957, Bethany Coll., 1957, W.Va. U., 1957, W.Va. Inst. Tech., 1957; doctorate of Humanics (hon.), Salem Coll., 1957; degree in pub. adminstrn. (hon.), W.Va. Wesleyan Coll., 1958; LLD (hon.), Concord Coll., 1960, W.Va. State Coll., 1961; LHD (hon.), Shepherd Coll., 1964; LittD (hon.), Western New Eng. Coll., 1969; LHD (hon.), Marshall U., 1997; degree in pub. svc. (hon.), Alderson Broaddus Coll., 1997; DSc (hon.), W. Va. Sch. Osteopathic Med., 1998; degree (hon.), Davis and Elkins Coll., 1998, Fairmont State Coll., 1999. Tchr. high sch., 1943-46; staff Marietta Coll., 1946-50; v.p. Salem Coll., 1950-56; gov. State of W.Va., 1957—61, 1997—2001; v.p. Island Creek Coal Co., 1961-64; dir. civic affairs Monsanto Co., 1965-67, v.p., 1967; pres. Cecil H. Underwood Assocs., 1965-80, Franswood Corp., 1968-75, Bethany (W.Va.) Coll., 1972-75, Princess Coals, Inc., Huntington, 1978-81, Morgantown (W.Va.) Indsl. Park, Inc., 1983-96, Software Valley, 1989-92, Mon View Heights of W.Va., 1993-96; field underwriter N.Y. Life Ins. Co., 1976-78; chmn. bd. Princess Coals, Inc., Huntington, 1981-83. Sec. bd. dirs. Huntington Fed. Savs. and Loan Assn., 1961-96; pres. Huntington Found. Mem. W.Va. Ho. Dels., 1944-56, minority floor leader,

1949, 51, 53, 55; Mem. exec. com. Gov.'s Conf., 1959; chmn. So. Regional Edn. Bd., 1959-60, 1999-2000; Pres. Young Republican League of W.Va., 1946-50; parliamentarian Young Rep. Nat. Conv., Boston, 1951; del.-at-large Rep. Nat. Conv., 1960, 64, 72, 76, 80, 84, 88, 2000, temporary chmn., 1960; Chmn. bd. dirs. W.Va. Found. Ind. Colls., Appalachian Regional Hosps.; chmn. bd. dirs. W.Va. div. Am. Cancer Soc., nat. bd. dirs., chmn. nat. crusade com., 1976-77, chmn. com. on legacies and planned giving, 1979; chmn. bd. dirs. Salem Coll., 1978-89, Salem Internat. U., 1989—; bd. dirs. Higher Edn. Loan Program of W.Va., 1980-94; chair W.Va. Coun. on Vocat. Edn., 1982-96, W.Va. State Coll. System, 1991, Nat. Edn. Goals Panel, 1998-99; regional vice chmn. Boy Scouts Am., 1961-67; dir. Fed. Home Loan Bank of Pitts. Mem. Nat. Assn. State Coun. Vocat. Edn. (pres. 1994-96), Masons, Shriners, Elks, Rotary, Sigma Phi Epsilon, Pi Kappa Delta. Republican. Methodist. Personal E-mail: underwood@marshall.edu.

UNDERWOOD, DEANNA KAY, librarian; b. Medicine Lodge, Kans., Oct. 2, 1962; d. Kenneth Edward and Janet Sue (Hammond) Winters; m. Roger Alan Underwood, Aug. 2, 1986; children: Lane Alan, Lindsey Kay. BS in Elem. Edn., Sterling Coll., Kans., 1984. Tchr. 4th grade White Rock Elem. Sch., Burr Oak, Kans., 1984-86, tchr. kindergarten Esbon, Kans., 1986-87; libr. aide mid. and high schs. White Rock Schs., Esbon and Burr Oak, 1987-91, K-12 libr., 1992—2006, Rock Hills Schs., Mankato and Burr Oak, Kans., 2006—. Chmn. adminstrv. coun. United Meth. Ch., Esbon, 1989—, trustee coun., 1993—. Mem.: Kans. Assn. Sch. Librs. Republican. Avocations: reading, cooking, cross-stitch. Home: 701 Kansas Ave Esbon KS 66941-9703 Office: Rock Hills Elem 303 N West St Mankato KS 66956 Business E-Mail: dunderwood@usd.107.org.

UNDERWOOD, EARL FREDERICK, JR., clergyman; b. Ft. Smith, Ark., Aug. 31, 1943; s. Earl Fredrick and Pearl Lucille (Kukuk) U.; m. Laura Ruth Anderson, July 23, 1967; 1 child, Ray Charles. B.A., Huron Coll., 1968; M.Div., Louisville Presbyterian Sem., 1971. Ordained to ministry Presbyn. Ch., 1971. Pastor, Faith Pres. Ch., Brandon, S.D., 1971-76, Riverside Presbyn. Ch., Sioux Falls, S.D., 1971-76, Akron Plymouth Presbyn. Ch., Iowa, 1976-79, Meml. Presbyn. Ch., Marysville, Kans., 1979—. Author (booklets) Family Budgeting, 1984, Your Money: Make It Do More, 1985, Marshall County Kans.: 1540-1880, 1986, 125 Years of Presbyterianism in Marysville, Kansas, 1988; (genealogy) From Vilson Germany to Linn Kansas, 1980; editor (geneology) Reedy Family Assn., 1980-84. Treas. Pride Marysville Kans., 1982-84. Mem. Iowa Genealogy Soc. (Outstanding Genealogist award 1975), Blue Valley Genealogy Soc. (pres. 1980-82, v.p. 1983-84). Avocation: Bridge; geneology. Office: Meml Presbyn Ch 200 N 10th St Marysville KS 66508-1604

UNDERWOOD, JANE HAINLINE HAMMONS, anthropologist, educator; b. Ft. Bliss, Tex., Oct. 30, 1931; d. Frank and Lydia (Williams) Hammons; m. Van K. Hainline, Oct. 20, 1947 (div. 1966); children: Michael K., Susan J.; m. John W. Underwood, July 4, 1968; 1 dau., Anne K. AA, Imperial Valley Coll., 1957; BA, U. Calif., Riverside, 1960; MA, UCLA, 1962, PhD, 1964. Asst. prof. U. Calif., Riverside, 1963-68; research anthropology Yap Islands, 1964, 65-66; prof. anthropology U. Ariz., Tucson, 1968-99, prof. emeritus, 1999—, assoc. dean Grad. Coll., 1979-80, asst. provost for grad. studies, 1980-82, acting dir. Sch. Health Related Professions, 1980-82, asst. v.p. research, assoc. dean Grad. Coll., 1982-87; assoc. Micronesian Area Rsch. Ctr., 1987—. Contbr. articles to profl. jours. Woodrow Wilson fellow, 1960-61; UCR Jr. Faculty fellow, 1968 Fellow AAAS; mem. Am. Assn. Phys. Anthropologists (v.p. 1980-82), Assn. Study Human Biology, Pacific Sci. Assn. (life), Assn. Study Social Biology (bd. dir. 1996-99), Sigma Xi (pres. U. Ariz. chpt. 1991-92). Home: 2228 E 4th St Tucson AZ 85719-5118 E-mail: kammagar@prodigy.net.

UNDERWOOD, JOSEPH WARREN, athletic trainer, educator; b. Indpls., Jan. 18, 1953; s. Warren E. Underwood and Kay A. Craft; m. Nancy Nelson, Nov. 16, 1984; 1 child, Jolene. B in speech, theatre, Tenn. Technol. U., Cookeville, 1975; M in sports sci., US Sports Acad., Daphne, Ala., 1987; EdD in Ednl. Leadership, Nova Southeastern U., 2006. Cert. real estate agt. Fla., 1982, athletic trainer Nat. Athletic Trainers Assn., 1990, tchr. Fla., 2003, lic. athletic trainer Fla., 2000. Tchr. earth sci. Miami HS, Fla., 1984—85, tchr. English to Spanish spkrs., 1985—86, tchr. drama, 1986—88, leading learner ARTEC, 1988—; instr. H.S. football rules clinic Greater Miami Athletic Conf., 1995—. Mem. Black history month com. Miami HS, 1994—, chair grant com., 2000—05; state bd. athletic tng. Fla. Dept. of Health, Tallahassee, 2002—; pres. Greater Miami Athletic Conf. Football Ofcls. Assn., Greater Miami Athletic Conf., 2003—; football ofcls. adv. com. Fla. H.S. Athletic Assn., Gainesville, 2005—; state H.S. football championship com. Greater Miami Conv. and Visitors Bur., 2005. Actor(referee #4): (film) Any Given Sunday - Oliver Stone, Dir., (instructional video series) Wally Word's Word of the Day, (the wise prof.) (ednl. video series) Words of Wisdom from the Wise Professor (Grant award, 2003), (basketball referee) (national print ad) Cingular Wireless March Madness; author (writer and voice over): (ednl. video) Miami High Centennial Video; prodr.(videographer and editor): (ednl. video) Galapagos Adventures; author (editor): (inspirational tchr.book) Today I Made A Difference: A Collection of Inspirational Stories from America's Top Teachers; actor, prodr.: Miami Undercover; actor(football referee): (Super Bowl comml.) Budweiser Select, (presdl. candidate) (feature length documentary) Dear Mr. President, (various roles) (TV), (TV series) Miami Vice; dir.(tech. advisor for football ofcls.): (TV comml.) Mountain Dew - Spike Lee, Dir.; actor(Billy Joe Bob): (instrl. video series) Billy Joe Bob's FCAT Tips. Student coord. for casted audience MTV Video Music Awards, Miami, 2004—05; vol. Orange Bowl Com. Youth Football Championships, Miami, 1990—2007; prodr. Martin Luther King parade video Dr. Robert Ingram, Sch. Bd. Mem., Miami, 2005; video team Miami Schs. Emergency Response Ops. Drill, 2006; campaign vol. Barrera for Sch. Bd., Miami, 2004—06; nat. selection com. Disney Tchr. Awards, Anaheim, Calif., 2006; football ofcl. Greater Miami Athletic Conf., 1990—2007; ext. com. Pi Lambda Theta Ednl. Assn. Finalist Tchr. of Yr. award, Miami-Dade County Pub. Schs., 2002, Nat. Teachers Hall of Fame, 2006; named to Nat. Tchrs. Hall of Fame, 2007; recipient State HS Basketball Championship ring as team's athletic trainer, Miami High Boys Basketball, 1987, 1989—91, 1993, 1996—97, 1998, 2005, Key to City of Miami, Miami Mayor Xavier Suarez, 1987, Four Way Test - Tchr. Fellowship award, Miami Rotary Club, 2002, Tchr. of Yr. award, Miami HS, 2003, 2005, Cert. of Honor, City of Miami, Miami Mayor Manny Diaz, 2004, Disney Tchr. Awards Honoree, Walt Disney Co., 2004, Cert. of Appreciation, Miami City Commn., Commr. Joe Sanchez, 2004, Spl. Recognition Ana Logan Sch. Bd., Miami-Dade County Pub. Schs., 2005, Cancer Rsch. Marathon Honoree, Run for Leukemia/Lymphoma Rsch., 2005, All-Star Tchr. Team award, USA Today Newspaper, 2005, State HS Basketball Championship ring as team's athletic trainer, Miami High Girls Basketball, 2005, Proclamation for Effective and Creative Tchg., City of Miami City Commn., 2006, Internat. Tchrs. Program to Galapagos, Toyota Motor Co., 2006; numerous grants, various granting bodies, 1996—, Industry Focus grant, One Cmty. One Goal, 1999, Doctoral scholarship, Nova Southeastern U., 2005, grant, Best Buy, 2005. Mem.: ASCD, Vocat.-Tech. Edn. Consortium of States (pilot site sch. coord. 1999—2002), U. Fla. Alliance, Nat. Coun. Tchrs. of English, Nat. Bd. Cert. Tchrs., Athletic Trainers Assn. Fla. (various positions including newsletter editor 1985—, H.S. Athletic Trainer of Yr. 1995), SE Athletic Trainers Assn., Nat. Athletic Trainers Assn. (various coms. 1986—), Am. Coll. of Sports Medicine, Fla. Film Educators, So. States Football League Ofcls. Assn. (So. rep. 2004—07, Referee of Yr. 2003), South Fla. Football Ofcls. Assn. (various coms. 1985—), Fla. Inst. for Film Edn., Am. Youth Football League (game ofcl. 1999—2006), Nat. Assn. Sports Ofcls., Greater Miami Athletic Conf. Football Ofcls. Assn. (various positions including pres. 1985—), Pi Lambda Theta (ext. com. 2005, music scholarship 2005), Nat. Scholars Honor Soc. Roman Catholic. Avocations: football officiating, travel, writing. Office: Miami HS 2450 SW 1 St Miami FL 33135 Home Phone: 954-252-0875; Office Phone: 305-649-9800. Business E-Mail: underwoodj@dadeschools.net.

UNDERWOOD, LORAINNE BALLARD, literature and language educator; b. Opelousas, La., Feb. 6, 1940; d. Lawrence James and Vertna Estelle Ballard; m. Albert McThomas Underwood, Jan. 7, 1976 (dec. Aug. 12, 2004); children: Kirk Albert, Antonio McVhea; m. Charles James Taylor (dec.); children: Christopher Charles, Jennifer Vertna. BA in Polit. Sci., So. U., Baton Rouge, 1963; MEd, U. La., 1987. Cert. tchr. Chgo. State U., 1966. Sec. Kraft Foods Divsn., Nat. Dairy Products Corp., Chgo., 1964—65; tchr. Chgo. Bd. Edn., 1965—80, St. Landry Parish Sch. Bd., Opelousas, 1980—2000, Lafayette Parish Sch. Sys., La., 2002—. Fellow mem. The Nature Conservancy, Arlington, Va., 2002—, So. Poverty Law Ctr., 2004—, Nat. Com. to Preserve Social Security, Washington, 2004—, NAACP, Balt., 2004—; organizer, coord. com. to erect a commemorative marker for St. Landry Parish Tng. Sch., 2004—; fellow mem. Dem. Nat. Com., Washington, 2004—; recording sec. Seventh Dist. Bapt. Assn. Women's Aux. and Missionary Soc.; deaconess Little Zion Bapt. Ch. Mem.: La. Fedn. Tchrs./AFT Profl. Educators Group (membership chair 1989—95), La. Ret. Tchrs. Assn. (life). Democrat. Baptist. Avocations: sewing, Bible reading, singing. Home: 1508 Laurent St Opelousas LA 70570

UNDERWOOD, MARK FOREST, lawyer; b. Ft. Campbell, Ky., Feb. 14, 1964; s. Harry Wayne and Alicia Elkins Underwood; m. Cynthia Jean Walker, Sept. 13, 2003. BBA, Marshall U., 1986; JD, Pepperdine U., 1989; grad., Nat. Trial Advocacy, 1992, Am. Trial Lawyers Ultimate Advocacy Coll., 2002; diplomate, Gerry Spence Trial Lawyers Coll., 2002. Bar: Calif. 89, W.Va. 96, D.C. 97, U.S. Ct. Appeals (4th cir.) 99. Assoc. Hagenbaugh & Murphy, LA, 1989—92, Crosby, Healey, Roach & May, LA, 1992—94; ptnr. Fredeking & Fredeking, Huntington, W.Va., 1994—96; pvt. practice Underwood Law Offices, Huntington, 1997—. Mem. W.Va. State Legis., 1997—98. Recipient Frasure Singleton Legis. fellowship, W.Va. Legislature, 1985. Mem.: ATLA, Nat. Coll. DUI Defense. Democrat. Presbyterian. Home Phone: 304-522-0508; Office Phone: 304-522-0508. Business E-Mail: markunderwood@markunderwood.com.

UNDERWOOD, PAUL BENJAMIN, gynecologist, oncologist, educator; b. Greer, SC, Aug. 8, 1934; s. Paul Benjamin and Gladys (Guest) Underwood; m. Peggy Joyce Outen, July 7, 1957; children: Paul Benjamin III, Mary Barton. MD, Med. U. S.C., 1959. Diplomate Am. Bd. Ob-gyn., Am. Bd. Gynecol. Oncology. Intern Med. U. S.C., Charleston, 1959—60, resident, 1960—64; fellow M.D. Anderson Hosp. and Tumor Inst., Houston, 1966—67; asst. prof. U. S.C., Charleston, 1967—70, assoc. prof., 1970—74, prof., 1974—99, staff, dir. gynecology, assoc. dean admissions Med. Sch., 1999—, dir. divsn. gynecol. oncology, 2002; chmn. dept. ob-gyn. U. Va. Sch. Medicine, Charlottesville, 1979-99. Contbr. articles to profl. jours. With USN, 1964—66. Recipient Alumni of Yr. award, Med. U. S.C., 1989. Mem.: Thegos Soc., S.C. Ob-Gyn. Soc., Charlottesville Med. Soc., So. Med. Soc., Felix Rutledge Soc. (pres. 1977), Am. Assn. Ob-Gyn. (sec. 1992—95, pres. 1999—), Soc. Gynecol. Oncologists (mem. coun. 1972—75, v.p. 1977—78, pres. 1983), Am. Coll. Ob-Gyn., Am. Gynecol. Club (pres. 1996), Alpha Omega Alpha. Office: 171 Ashley Ave Charleston SC 29425-0001 Office Phone: 843-792-4026. Business E-Mail: underwp@musc.edu.

UNDERWOOD, PAUL LESTER, cardiologist; b. Knoxville, Tenn., Mar. 23, 1960; MD, Mayo Med. Sch., 1984. Diplomate Am. Bd. Cardiovascular Disease. Intern Henry Ford Hosp., Detroit, 1984-85; resident internal medicine Mayo Grad. Sch. Medicine, Rochester, Minn., 1985-87; fellow in cardiology Cleve. Clinic, 1990-93; fellow in interventional cardiology Iowa Heart Ctr., Des Moines, 1993; dir. emergency medicine, dir. ICU St. Croix Hosp., U.S. V.I., 1987-90; staff N. Phoenix Heart Ctr., Ariz., 2001—07; dir. rsch. Sonoran Health Specialists, 2007—. Mem. AMA, Nat. Med. Assn., Assn. Black Cardiologists (former pres.), Am. Coll. Cardiology (councilor), Am. Heart Assn. (bd. dirs. Ariz. affiliate), Soc. for Cardiac Angiography and Interventions. Home: 4727 E Berneil Dr Phoenix AZ 85028-5506 Office: Sonoran Health Specialists 8414 E Shea Bld Ste 103 Scottsdale AZ 85260 Office Phone: 480-767-3877. Business E-Mail: punderwood@sonoranhealth.com.

UNDERWOOD, RICHARD ALLAN, English language educator; b. Plymouth, Mich., Mar. 28, 1933; s. Harold Raymond and Yvonne Clara (Foster) U.; m. Sandra Jane Hayes, Nov. 17, 1962; 1 child, Eric Michael. BA, U. Mich., 1955, MA, 1967, PhD, 1970. Asst. prof. Clemson U., SC, 1970-77, assoc. prof., 1977-84, prof. English SC, 1984—. Author: A Little Bit of Love, 1963, Shakespeare's The Phoenix and Turtle: A Survey of Scholarship, 1974, Shakespeare on Love: The Poems and the Plays, 1985, The Two Noble Kinsmen and Its Beginnings, 1993; translator: En Smula Karlek, 1969, 81; editor: Phoenix with a Bayonet: A Journalist's Interim Report on the Greek Revolution (by Bayard Stockton), 1971. 1st lt. U.S. Army, 1955-57. Fellow Bread Loaf Writers Conf., 1963; vis. scholar Rackham Sch. Grad. Studies, U. Mich., 1983-85, 90-91, 91-92, 92-93, 93-94. Avocation: piano music. Home: 111 Lakeview Cir Clemson SC 29631-1019

UNDERWOOD, ROBERT LEIGH, venture capitalist; b. Paducah, Ky., Dec. 31, 1944; s. Robert Humphreys and Nancy Wells (Jessup) Underwood; m. Susan Lynn Doscher, May 22, 1976; children: Elizabeth Leigh, Dana Whitney, George Gregory. BS with great distinction, Stanford U., 1965, MS, 1966, PhD, 1968; MBA, Santa Clara U., 1970. Rsch. scientist, project leader Lockheed Missiles & Space Co., Sunnyvale, Calif., 1967—71; spl. asst. for engring. scis. Office Sec., Dept. Transp., Washington, 1971—73; sr. mgmt. assoc. Office Mgmt. and Budget, Exec. Office Pres., 1973; with TRW Inc., LA, 1973—79, dir. retail nat. accts., 1977—78, dir. product planning and devel., 1978—79; pres., CEO OMEX, Santa Clara, Calif., 1980—82; v.p. Heizer Corp., Chgo., 1979—85; pres. No. Capital Corp., Chgo., 1985—86; mng. ptnr. ISSS Ventures, 1986—88; founding ptnr. N.Am. Bus. Devel. Co., Chgo., 1988—; pres., CEO Polymer Corp., Rockland, Mass., 2003—. Trustee Burridge Mut. Funds, 1996—98. Contbr. articles to profl. jours. Sch. bd. Avoca Dist. 37, 1990—99, v.p., 1996—99; adv. bd. Leavy Sch. Bus. and Adminstrn. Santa Clara U., 1995—; adv. com. on indsl. innovation NSF, 1982—96; trustee Kenilworth Union Ch., 2003—; elder Presbyn. Ch., 1978—79. Fellow, NASA, NSF; scholar, Alcoa. Mem.: IEEE, Farmington Country Club (Charlottesville, Va.), Indian Hill Club (Winnetka, Ill.), Union League Chgo., Chgo. Club, Beta Gamma Sigma, Tau Beta Pi, Phi Beta Kappa, Sigma Xi. Home: 59 Woodley Rd Winnetka IL 60093-3748 Office: 135 S La Salle St Chicago IL 60603-4159

UNDERWOOD, STEVEN CLARK, finance company executive; b. Arlington Heights, Ill., Dec. 1, 1960; s. Donald William and Mary Frances (Clark) U.; m. Gloria Jean Dec, Sept. 8, 1999. BBA, U. Tex., 1982, MBA, 1987; JD, So. Meth. U., 1985. Bar: Tex. 1985; cert. fin. mgr. Inst. Cert. Mgmt. Accts., 2006, managerial acct. Inst. Cert. Mgmt. Accts., 2006. Sr. fin. analyst CBS, Inc., NYC, 1987—89; assoc. bus. mgr. Supplementary Edn. Group Simon & Schuster, Englewood Cliffs, NJ, 1989—90, bus. mgr. Fearon/Janus/Quercus divsn. Belmont, Calif., 1990—91, pres. Fearon/Janus/Quercus divsn., 1991—92, pres. Globe Fearon divsn. Upper Saddle River, NJ, 1993—96, v.p. bus. devel. NYC, 1997—98; v.p. dir. bus. devel. Secondary Edn. Group, Upper Saddle River, NJ, 1996—97; v.p. sch. markets Troll Comms., Mahwah, NJ, 1998—2001; v.p., contr. Current Med. Directions Divsn., WWP Group, NYC, 2002—06; CFO Bronson & Migliaccio, LLP, Ft. Lee, NJ, 2006—. Mem. ABA, Am. Mgmt. Assn. (pres.'s assn.), Assn. Am. Pubs., Inst. Cert. Mgmt. Accts. (cert.), Nat. Eagle Scout Assn., Coll. Bus. Adminstrn. Found., Tex. Bar Assn., Tex. Alumni Assn., U. Tex. Century Club, Alpha Phi Omega, Beta Gamma Sigma, Phi Kappa Phi, Phi Eta Sigma, Golden Key. Republican. Methodist. Avocations: sailing, camping. Home: 902 Somerset Ct Ramsey NJ 07446-2919 Office: 2200 Fletcher Ave Fort Lee NJ 07024

UNGAR, ERIC EDWARD, mechanical engineer; b. Vienna, Nov. 12, 1926; arrived in U.S., 1939; s. Irwin Isidor and Sabina (Schlesinger) U.; m. Goldie Edna Becker, July 1, 1951; children: Judith Fishman, Susan Green, Ellen Borgenicht, Sharon Ungar Lane. BSME, Washington U., St. Louis, 1951; MS, U. N.Mex., 1954; D.Eng.Sc., NYU, 1957. Aero-ordnance engr. Sandia Corp., Albuquerque, 1951-53; rsch. scientist, asst. prof. NYU, 1953-58; chief cons. engr. Bolt Beranek & Newman, Inc., Cambridge, Mass., 1958-96. Chief engring. scientist Acentech Inc., Cambridge, 1993—. Co-author: Structure-Borne Sound, 1973, 2nd edit. 1988; contbr. articles to profl. jours., chpts. to books. 1st lt. US Army, 1945—48, ETO. Recipient Lifetime Achievement award, Shock and Vibration Info. Analysis Ctr., 2004. Fellow ASME (life; chmn. design engring. divsn. 1978-80, Centennial medallion 1981, Per Bruel Gold medal for noise control and acoustics 1994), AIAA (assoc.), Acoustical Soc. Am. (pres. 1991-92, Trent-Crede Silver medal 1983); mem. Inst. for Noise Control and Engring. (bd. cert., pres. 1985, Disting. Noise Control Engr. award 2004). Home: 15 Considine Rd Newton MA 02459-3603 Office: Acentech Inc 33 Moulton St Cambridge MA 02138-1118 Home Phone: 617-244-2096; Office Phone: 617-499-8022. E-mail: eungar@acentech.com.

UNGARETTI, RICHARD ANTHONY, lawyer; b. Chgo., May 25, 1942; s. Dino Carl and Antoinette (Calvetti) U.; children: Joy A., Paul R. BS, DePaul U., 1964, JD, 1970. Bar: Ill. 1970, U.S. Dist. Ct. (no. dist.) Ill. 1970, U.S. Supreme Ct. 1980. Assoc. Kirkland & Ellis, Chgo., 1970-74; ptnr. Ungaretti & Harris, Chgo., 1974—. Mem. adv. coun. DePaul Coll. Law, Chgo., 1988. Mem. ABA, Chgo. Bar Assn., Ill. State Bar Assn., Internat. Coun. Shopping Ctrs., Am. Coll. Real Estate Lawyers, Justinian Soc., Urban Land Inst. (assoc.), Lamda Alpha Avocations: golf, fishing, hunting. Office: Ungaretti & Harris 3500 Three First Nat Plz Chicago IL 60602 Office Phone: 312-977-4430. Business E-Mail: raungaretti@uhlaw.com.

UNGARO, MARIO, pathologist, educator; s. Fabricio Ungaro and Enriquetta Zevallos. MB, Nat. U. San Marcos, Peru, 1954, MD. Diplomate in pathology. Intern Marymount Hosp., Cleve., 1954-55; resident St. Vincent Charity Hosp., Cleve., 1955-57; resident in pathology New Britain Gen. Hosp., 1958-59, Roswell Park Meml. Inst., Buffalo, 1959-60; fellow forensic pathology Frank E. Bunts Ed. Inst., Cleve., 1957-58; asst. pathologist Mercy Hosp., Buffalo, 1960-61; prof. pathology Nat. U. Trujillo, Peru, 1961—87; chmn. pathology Hosp. Regional Tchg. Hosp., Trujillo, Peru, 1980—87; prof. emeritus Nat. U. Trujillo, 1992. Mem. Peruvian Assn. Pathology, Peruvian Med. Assn., Nat. Club, Golf Country Club. Avocation: swimming. Office: Hosp Regional Tchg Hosp Trujillo Peru

UNGARO, SUSAN KELLIHER, foundation administrator, former magazine editor; married; 3 children. BA, MA, William Patterson Coll., Wayne, NJ. From editl. asst. to editor-in-chief Family Circle mag., NYC, 1976—94, editor-in-chief, 1994—2005; pres. James Beard Found., NYC, 2006—. Bd. dirs. Brazelton Found., Nat. Marrow Found., H.E.L.P. (Housing Enterprise for the Less Privileged). Named named Top Businessperson of Yr., Irish America magazine; recipient President's Award, New Jersey Press Women's Assn., 1995, William Paterson University Legacy Award, 1998, Muriel Fox communications award for professional excellence and commitment to advocacy journalism, NOW Legal Defense Fund, 1998. Mem.: Am. Soc. Mag. Editors (bd. dir. 1998—, pres. 2003—). Office: James Beard Foundation 167 West 12th St New York NY 10011 Office Phone: 212-499-1986, 212-675-4984.

UNGARO-BENAGES, URSULA MANCUSI, federal judge; b. Miami Beach, Fla., Jan. 29, 1951; d. Ludivico Mancusi-Ungaro and Ursula Berliner; m. Michael A. Benages, Mar., 1988. Student, Smith Coll., 1968-70; BA in English Lit., U. Miami, 1973; JD, U. Fla., 1975. Bar: Fla. 1975. Assoc. Frates, Floyd, Pearson et al, Miami, 1976-78, Blackwell, Walker, Gray et al, Miami, 1978-80, Finley, Kumble, Heine et al, Miami, 1980-85, Sparber, Shevin, Shapo et al, Miami, 1985-87; cir. judge State of Fla., Miami, 1987-92; U.S. dist. judge U.S. Dist. Ct., Miami, 1992—. Mem. Fla. Supreme Ct. Race & Ethnic & Racial Bias Study Commn., Fla., 1989-92, St. Thomas U. Inns of Ct., Miami, 1991-92; mem. Jud. Resources Com. Jud. Conf. U.S.; chmn. Ct. Svcs. Com. So. Dist. Fla., chmn. Magistrate Judge Com.; mem. personnel com. 11th Cir. Jud. Coun. U.S. Bd. dirs. United Family & Children's Svcs., Miami, 1981-82; mem. City of Miami Task Force, 1991-92. Mem. ABA, Fed. Judges Assn., Fla. Assn. Women Lawyers, Dade County Bar Assn., Eugene Spellman Inns of Ct. U. Miami. Office: US Dist Ct 301 N Miami Ave Fl 11 Miami FL 33128-7702 Office Phone: 305-523-5550.

UNGER, BARBARA, poet, writer, retired literature and language professor; b. NYC, Oct. 2, 1932; d. David and Florence (Schuchalter) Frankel; m. Bernard Unger, 1954 (div. 1976); m. Theodore Sakano, 1987; children: Deborah, Suzanne. BA, CCNY, 1955, MA, 1957; advanced cert., NYU, 1970. Grad. asst. Yeshiva U., 1962-63; edn. editor County Citizen, Rockland County, NY, 1960-63; tchr. English N.Y.C. Pub. Schs., 1955-58, Nyack (N.Y.) H.S., 1963-67; guidance counselor Ardsley (N.Y.) H.S., 1967-69; prof. English Rockland C.C., Suffern, NY, 1969—95, ret., 1995. Adj. prof. Rockland C.C., 1995-2003, Rockland Sr. Citizen Program, 2001-2003; poetry fellow Squaw Valley Cmty. of Writers, 1980; writer-in-residence Rockland Ctr. for Arts, 1986. Author: (poetry) Basement, 1975, Learning to Fox Trot, 1989, The Man Who Burned Money, 1980, Inside the Wind, 1986, Blue Depression Glass in Troika One, 1991, (fiction) Dying for Uncle Ray, 1990; co-author (with Lloyd Ultan): (non-fiction) Bronx Accent: A Literary and Pictorial History of the Borough, 2001 (N.Y. Soc. Libr. Book award, 2001, J.M. Kaplan Furthermore grantee, Hermalyn Family Urban History award, 05); contbr. Anthology Mag. Verse, Yearbook Am. Poetry, 1984, Anthology Mag. Verse, Yearbook Am. Poetry, 1989, poetry and fiction to more than 75 lit. mags. Ragdale Found. fellow, 1985, 86, 89, SUNY Creative Writing fellow, 1981-82, Edna St. Vincent Millay Colony fellow, 1984, Djerassi Found. fellow, 1991, Hambidge Ctr. for Creative Arts and Scis. fellow, 1988, Dorset Colony fellow, 2005; NEH grantee, 1975; recipient Goodman Poetry award, 1989, Anna Davidson Rosenberg award Judah Magnes Mus., 1989, Roberts Writing award, 1990, New Letters Lit. awards, 1990; finalist Am. Fiction Competition, 1992, John Williams Narrative Poetry Competition, 1992; honorable mention Chester Jones Nat. Poetry Contest. Mem.: PEN, Assn. Writers and Writing Programs, Poets and Writers.

UNGER, DAVID C., journalist; b. Bklyn. AB, Cornell U., 1967; postgrad., U. Wis., Madison, 1967—68; PhD, U. Tex., Austin, 1979. Elem. sch. tchr., Staten Island, Bklyn.; joined NY Times, 1977, now sr. editl. writer, fgn. affairs, mem. editl. bd. Office: Editl Bd NY Times 229 W 43rd St New York NY 10036 Office Phone: 212-556-7159. Office Fax: 212-556-3815. Business E-Mail: editorial@nytimes.com.

UNGER, GERE NATHAN, emergency physician, lawyer; b. Monticello, NY, May 15, 1949; s. Jessie Aaron and Shirley (Rosenstein) Unger; m. Alice J. McGowan, July 21, 1990; children: Elijah, Breena, Ari, Sasha, Arlen. JD, Bernadean U., 1979; MD, Inst. Polytecnico, Mexico City, 1986;

D Phys. Medicine, Met. U., Mexico City, 1987; postgrad., Boston U., 1993, Harvard Law Sch., 1994-96; LLM in Med. Law, U. Glasgow, 2001. Diplomate Am. Bd. Forensic Examiners, Am. Bd. Med. Legal Analysis Medicine and Surgery, Am. Bd. Forensic Medicine, Am. Bd. Risk Mgmt., Am. Bd. Disability Analysts. Med. dir. Vietnam Vets. Post-Traumatic Stress Disorder Program, 1988-90; emergency rm. physician, cons. in medicaid fraud Bronx (N.Y.)-Lebanon Hosp., 1990—; clin. legal medicine Paladin Profl. Group, P.A., Palm Beach, Fla., 1992-98; pres. Albany Law Jour. Co., Inc., 1998—; jurisconsult Office of Gere Unger, M.D., J.D., 1999—. Mem. surg. critical care com. Am. Soc. Critical Care Medicine, 1992; mem. peer rev. com. Nat. Inst. Disability and Rehab. Rsch., Office Spl. Edn., U.S. Dept. Edn., 1993; mediator, arbitrator, negotiator World Intellectual Property Orgn., 1994; mem. clin. ethics com. Inst. Medecine Legale et de Medecine Sociale, Strasbourg, France, 1994; mediator, arbitrator World Bank, 2000—. Mem. editl. bd. Am. Bd. Forensic Examiners, 1993, Jour. Neurol. and Orthopaedic Medicine and Surgery, 1993. Comdt. Broward County Marine Corps League, 1995—. With USMC, 1968—72. Fellow: The Cognitive Sci. Soc., Exec. Practice Mgmt., Am. Coll. Forensic Examiners, Internat. Coll. Surgeons (mem. ethics com. 1994, mem. emergency response program eastern region 1994), Am. Acad. Neurol. and Orthopedic Surgeons, Am. Coll. Legal Medicine; mem.: FBA (mem. health com., rep. ABA 1994, chmn. med. malpractice/tort com., liaison to AMA), ATLA (N.Y. state capt. 1992), ABA, N.Y. State Defenders Assn., Nat. Am. Indian Ct. Judges Assn., N.W. Indian Bar Assn., Internat. Assn. Prosecutors, Am. Soc. Investigative Pathology, Internat. Criminal Law Network (The Hague), Internat. Assn. Prosecutors, Internat. Royal Soc. Medicine (London), Nat. Assn. Forensic Econs., Am. Soc. Laser Medicine and Surgery, Kennedy Inst. Ethics, Am. Coll. Physician Execs. (chair forum law and med. mgmt. 1995), Internat. Bar Assn., Nat. Coll. Advocacy. Avocations: flying, boating. Business E-Mail: rumpole@justice.com.

UNGER, IRWIN, historian, educator; b. Bklyn., May 2, 1927; s. Elias C. and Mary (Roth) U.; m. Bernate Myra Spaet, Feb. 1956 (div.); children: Brooke David, Miles Jeremy, Paul Joshua; m. Debi Irene Weisstein, May 11, 1970; stepchildren: Anthony Allen, Elizabeth Sarah. B in Social Scis., CCNY, 1948; MA, Columbia U., 1949, PhD, 1958; student, U. Wash., 1949—51. Instr. Columbia U., 1956-58; asst. prof. Long Beach (Calif.) State Coll., 1959-62; assoc. prof. U. Calif., Davis, 1962-66; prof. history NYU, NYC, 1966—2000, prof. emeritus, 2000—. Vis. lectr. U. PR, 1958—59. Author: The Greenback Era: A Social and Political History of American Finance: 1865-1879, 1964 (Pulitzer prize for History, 1965), The Movement: A History of the American New Left 1959-1972, 1974, These United States: Questions of Our Past, 1978, The Best of Intentions: The Triumph and Failure of the Great Society Under Kennedy, Johnson and Nixon, 1996; (with Debi Unger) The Vulnerable Years: The United States, 1896-1917, 1978, Turning Point: 1968, 1988, LBJ: A Life, 1999, The Guggenheims: A Family History, 2005. Served with AUS, 1952-54. Guggenheim fellow, 1972-73, 1987-88; Rockefeller humanities fellow, 1980-81. Home: 507 Evergreen Ave Bradley Beach NJ 07720 Home Phone: 732-775-8136. Personal E-mail: ungerclio@aol.com.

UNGER, LAURA SIMONE, lawyer, commissioner; b. NYC, Jan. 8, 1961; d. Raymond and Susan Marie (Vopata) Simone; m. Peter Van Buren Unger, June 29, 1991. BA in Rhetoric, U. Calif., Berkeley, 1983; JD, N.Y. Law Sch., 1987. Bar: Conn. 1987, N.Y. 1988. Staff atty. divsn. enforcement SEC, 1988-90; legis. counsel to Sen. Alfonse M. D'Amato, 1990-91; minority counsel Senate com. banking, housing and urban affairs, 1991-95, counsel, 1995-97; commr. U.S. SEC, Washington, 1997—, acting chmn., 2001. Bd. dirs. MBNA Corp., 2004—. Recipient Performance award SEC, N.Y., 1988, D.C., 1989. Mem. ABA (subcom. on civil litigation and SEC enforcement matters and subcom. on SEC adminstrn., budget and legislation of the ABA bus. law sect. com. on federal regulation of securities), Fed. Bar Assn., Jr. League Washington, Decade Soc., Women in Housing and Fin. Roman Catholic. Avocations: tennis, jogging, movies, concerts, music. Office: US SEC 450 5th St NW Ms 6/8 Washington DC 20549-0001

UNGER, PAUL WALTER, retired soil scientist; b. Winchester, Tex., Sept. 10, 1931; s. Edwin Herman and Elsie Anna U.; m. Barbara Charlene Dutton Steelman, Sept. 13, 1960; children: Gary Robert, Paula Dianne. BS, Tex. A&M U., 1961; MS, Colo. State U., 1963, PhD, 1966. Soil scientist USDA Agrl. Rsch. Svc., Bushland, Tex., 1965-81, soil scientist/rsch. leader, 1981-87, supervisory soil scientist/rsch. leader, 1987-93, soil scientist, 1993-2000; ret., 2000. Cons. Food and Agrl. Orgn. UN, Rome, 1986. Author and co-author bulls. and articles; co-editor conf. proc.; editor Managing Agricultural Residues; author Soil and Water Conservation Handbook-Policies, Pratices, Conditions, and Terms. With U.S. Army, 1952-55. Recipient Disting. Svc. award Great Plains Agrl. Coun., 1984; named Scientist of Yr., USDA-Agrl. Rsch. Svc., So. Plains Area, 1987. Fellow Am. Soc. Agronomy (emeritus, selection com. 1988-89), Soil Sci. Soc. Am. (emeritus, assoc. editor 1977-82, divsn. chmn. 1986, mem. selection com. 1994-95, Applied Rsch. award 1991), Soil and Water Conservation Soc. (various local and state offices, photography awards 1990-92); mem. Internat. Soil Tillage Rsch. Orgn., World Assn. Soil and Water Conservation. Lutheran. Avocations: woodworking, gardening, photography. Personal E-mail: pwunger@suddenlink.net.

UNGER, PETER KENNETH, philosophy educator; b. N.Y.C., Apr. 25, 1942; s. Sidney and Naomi (Fein) U.; m. Susan Gill, June 2, 1977; 1 child, Andrew. BA, Swarthmore Coll., 1962 DPhil, Oxford U., Eng., 1966. Instr. U. Wis., Madison, 1965-66, asst. prof., 1966-70, assoc. prof., 1970-72; assoc. prof. NYU, N.Y.C., 1972-75, prof., 1975—. Author: Ignorance, 1975, 2d edit., 2002, Philosophical Relativity, 1984, 2d edition, 2002, Identity, Consciousness and Value, 1990, Living High and Letting Die, 1996, All the Power in the World, 2006, Philosophical Papers, Vols. 1 and 2, 2006; contbr. articles to profl. jours. Guggenheim fellow, 1974, NEH fellow, 1993. Mem. Am. Philos. Assn. Democrat. Home: 100 Bleecker St New York NY 10012-2202 Office: Dept Philosophy NYU 5 Washington Pl New York NY 10003 Office Phone: 212-998-8321. E-mail: peter.unger@nyu.edu.

UNGER, PETER VAN BUREN, lawyer; b. Cin., Nov. 15, 1957; s. Sherman Edward and Polly Van Buren (Taylor) U.; m. Laura Meth Simone, June 29, 1991; children: Simone Taylor, Natalie Van Buren. BA in History, Polit. Sci., Miami U., Oxford, Ohio, 1980; JD, U. Cin., 1983; LLM in Securities, Georgetown U., 1987. Bar: Ohio 1984, D.C. 1985, U.S. Supreme Ct. 1991. Law clk. chief judge U.S. Dist. Ct. (so. dist.) Fla., Ft. Lauderdale, 1983-85; atty. enforcement divsn. SEC, NYC, 1986-88; assoc. Fulbright & Jaworski, Washington, 1988-89, participating assoc., 1990-94, ptnr., 1995—2003, Howrey LLP, Washington, 2004—. Mem. ABA (bus. law sect., com. fed. regulation of securities, sub-com. on civil litigation and SEC enforcement matters 1989—, litigation sect. com. on securities litigation sub-com. on SEC enforcement practice 1990—), Securities Industry Assn. (compliance and legal divsn.), D.C. Bar Assn. (corp., fin. and securities law sect.). Home: 3308 N St NW Washington DC 20007-2807 Office: Howrey LLP 1299 Pennsylvania Ave NW Washington DC 20004-2402 Office Phone: 202-383-6830. Business E-Mail: ungerp@howrey.com.

UNGER, RICHARD JONATHAN, medical educator, anesthesiologist; b. Richmond, June 30, 1955; s. Allan M. and Jane Ruth Unger; married; children: Sarah P., Julia R., Jesse M. MD, Med. Coll. Va., Richmond, 1981. Bd. Cert. Anesthesiology and Internal Medicine ABIM, AB Anesthesiology, 1986. Asst. prof. U. Calif., San Diego, 1984—86; staff anesthesiologist ASMG, La Jolla, Calif., 1988—2006; vice chair dept. anesthesiology Scripps Meml. Hosp., La Jolla, 2004—. Med. spkr., San Diego. Mem.: Am. Bd. Anesthesiology (assoc.), Am. Bd. Internal Medicine (life). Office: Anesthesia Svc Med Group 3626 Ruffin Rd San Diego CA 92138 Home Phone: 619-501-8856; Office Phone: 858-565-9666. Personal E-mail: richard.unger@gmail.com.

UNGER, RICHARD WATSON, history professor; b. Huntington, W.Va., Dec. 23, 1942; s. Abraham I. and Marion Patterson U.; 1 child, Emily Patterson. BA, Haverford Coll., Pa., 1963; AM, U. Chgo., 1965; MA, Yale U., 1967, MPhil, 1969, PhD, 1971. Prof. dept. history U. B.C., Vancouver, Canada, 1969—. Author: Dutch Shipbuilding Before 1800, 1978, The Ship in the Medieval Economy, 600-1600, 1980, The Art of Medieval Technology: The Image of Noah the Shipbuilder, 1991, Ships and Shipping in the North Sea and Atlantic, 1400-1600, 1997, A History of Brewing in Holland, 900-1900, Economy, Technology and the State, 2001, Beer in the Middle Ages and the Renaissance, 2004; editor: Cogs, Caravels and Galleons, 1994; co-editor: War at Sea in the Middle Ages and the Renaissance, 2003, Studies in Medieval and Renaissance History, 1978-95; contbr. articles to profl. jours. Trustee Vancouver Maritime Mus., 1979-83, 97-98. Mem. Medieval Assn. Pacific (pres. 1994-96), Econ. History Soc., Soc. Nautical Rsch. Office: U BC Dept History 1297-1873 East Mall Vancouver BC Canada V6T 1Z1 Business E-Mail: richard.unger@ubc.ca.

UNGER, ROGER HAROLD, physician, research scientist; b. NYC, Mar. 7, 1924; s. Lester and Beatrice (Raphael) Unger. BS, Yale U., 1944; MD, Columbia U., 1947; MD (hon.), U. Geneva, 1976, U. Liège, Belgium, 1980. Diplomate Am. Bd. Internal Medicine. Asst. prof. internal medicine U. Tex. Med. Sch., Dallas, 1959—64, assoc. prof., 1964—69, prof., 1969—; dir. Ctr. for Diabetes Rsch., U. Tex. Health Sci. Ctr., Dallas, 1985—2007, Touchstone/West Disting. chair diabetes rsch., 1989—. Sr. med. investigator VA Med. Ctr., Dallas, 1979—99; mem. Nat. Diabetes Adv. Bd., Bethesda, Md., 1985—; mem. adv. coun. Nat. Inst. Diabetes, Digestive and Kidney Diseases, 1990—94. Editor: Glucagon, 1972, Glucagon Physiology etc., 1981; assoc. editor Diabetes, 1979—84, mem. editl. bd., 1975—79, Endocrinology, 1976—81; contbr. articles to profl. jours., chapters to books. With US Army, 1946—48, with USPHS, 1950—52. Recipient Lilly award, Am. Diabetes Assn., 1964, Banting medal, 1975, David Rumbough award, Juvenile Diabetes Assn., 1975, Joslin medal, Harvard U., 1979, Claude Bernard award, European Assn. for Study of Diabetes, 1979, Fred Conrad Koch award, Endocrine Soc., 1983, Maurice Derot prize, Jour. Diabetique, Paris. Mem.: Am. Soc. for Clin. Investigation (emeritus), Assn. Am. Physicians, Am. Acad. Arts and Scis., NAS. Office Phone: 214-648-6742. E-mail: roger.unger@utsouthwestern.edu.

UNGER, SUSAN J., automotive executive; b. Detroit, Apr. 8, 1950; BA in Economics, Mich. State U., 1972; MBA in Fin., Wayne State U., 1976. Fin. analyst, sales and mktg. DaimlerChrysler AG, 1972, various financial positions, fin. dir. product devel. and Jeep/Truck Ops., exec. dir. mgmt. info. sys., 1993, sr. v.p., 1998—, chief info. officer, 1998—. Mem., past pres., Eli Broad Bd., Coll. Bus. Mich. State U.; bd. dir. Cyberstate.org; nat. adv. com. Coll. of Engring. U. Mich.; adv. tech. bd. Oakland U. Named 100 Leading Women in N.Am. Auto Industry, Automotive News, 2002, CIO of Yr., Automation Alley, 2002, Salomon Smith Barney, 2002, Disting. Alumnus of Yr., Wayne State U. Sch. Bus. Adminstrn., 2002; named one of Detroit's Most Influential Women, Crain's Detroit Bus., 2002; recipient Top Am. Woman award, Assn. Woman in Computing, 2003, Pioneer award, Phoenix Hill Women's Mus., 2004, Disting. Svc. Citation, Automotive Hall of Fame, 2006. Mem.: Automotive Womens Alliance, Kleiner Perkins CIO Strategy Exch. Forum. Office: Daimler-Chrysler Corp 1000 Chrysler Dr Auburn Hills MI 48326-2766

UNGER, SYDNEY ELLIOTT, lawyer; b. 1947; BA, U. Chgo., 1968; MBA with distinction, NYU, 1970, JD cum laude, 1974, LLM in Taxation, 1979. Bar: NY 1975, US Tax Ct. 1975, US Ct. Claims 1975, US Dist. Ct. (so. and ea. dists.) NY 1975, US Ct. Appeals (2d cir.) 1975, US Ct. Appeals (fed. cir.) 1982, US Supreme Ct. 1995. Ptnr., chair Tax Dept. Kaye, Scholer LLP, NYC; adj. prof. NY Law Sch., 2005—. Lectr. in field. Editor, bus. mgr. Ann. Survey Am. Law, 1973-74; articles editor The Tax Lawyer, 1981-84, mng. editor, 1984-87; contbr. articles to profl. jours. Mem. ABA (publications com., chmn. Tax Lawyer subcom., sect. on taxation 1984-87), NY State Bar Assn., Assn. of Bar of City of NY (tax com. 1988-89, taxation of corporations com. 1990-99). Office: Kaye Scholer LLP 425 Park Ave New York NY 10022-3506 E-mail: sunger@kayescholer.com.

UNGLESBY, LEWIS O., lawyer; b. New Orleans, July 6, 1949; s. Lewis Huber and Mary Jane (Holloway) U.; m. Gail Hoy, Aug. 15, 1970; children: Lewis, Lance, Blake. BS, U. Miss., 1971; JD, La. State U., 1974. Bar: La. 1974, U.S. Dist. Ct. (ea., mid., and we dists.) La. 1974, U.S. Ct. Appeals (5th cir.) 1974, U.S. Supreme Ct. 1980; bd. cert. criminal and civil trial adv. Nat. Bd. Trial Advocacy. With Unglesby & Marionneaux Law Firm; mem. judge's benchbook com. La. Supreme Ct., 1982—. Spl. counsel La. State Senate, 1991-98, Gov. La., 1996-98; lectr. La. Assn. Criminal Def. Lawyers, 1987-91. Editor criminal law sect. La. Trial Lawyers Brief, 1988—. Fellow Am. Bd. Criminal Lawyers; mem. ABA, La. Bar Assn. (ho. of dels. 1979-87, lectr.), NACDL, ATLA (criminal law com. 1989-90, Best Lawyer Am. 1987-2006), La. Trial Lawyers Assn. (chmn. criminal law sect. 1983-85, bd. govs. 1983-94, exec. com. 1991-2005, lectr.). Home: 14415 Highland Rd Baton Rouge LA 70810-5312 Office: 246 Napoleon St Baton Rouge LA 70802-5937 Office Phone: 509-387-0120. Business E-Mail: lwestmoland@bellsouth.net.

UNHJEM, MICHAEL BRUCE, lawyer; b. Fargo, ND, Aug. 22, 1953; s. Kalmer Joseph and Lorelei Mae (Myhra) U.; m. Mary Ruth Burges, June 19, 1976; children: Kaia Mary, David Burges, Kirsten Elizabeth. BA magna cum laude, Jamestown Coll., 1975; JD with distinction, U. N.D., 1978. Bar: N.D. 1978. Pvt. practice, Jamestown, ND, 1978-86; compliance officer Norwest Bank, Jamestown, ND, 1981-84; planned giving officer Jamestown Coll., Anne Carlsen Sch., Jamestown, 1984-86; asst. to pres., gen. counsel Blue Cross Blue Shield of N.D., Fargo, 1986-91, pres., chief exec. officer, 1991—, Pioneer Mutual Life Ins. Co., Fargo, 1997—99. Chmn. bd. dirs. Lincoln Mut. Life & Casualty Ins. Co., Fargo, Noridian Adminstr. Svc., LLC, Fargo, Noridian Ins. Svc., Inc., Fargo; chmn. TriWest HC All,; bd. dirs. Prime Ther, Western Conf. Prepaid Health Plans, Jamestown Coll., Cass Clay United Way, Blue Cross Blue Shield Assn. State rep. N.D. Legis. Assembly, Bismarck, 1974-86; mem. Nat. Conf. Commrs. on Uniform State Laws, Chgo., 1981—, chmn., Bismarck, 1982-86; co-chmn. Bush for Pres. Com., 1980, 88, 92; presdl. appointee Nat. Coun. on Disability, Washington, 1990. Named Outstanding Young North Dakotan, N.D. Jaycees, 1983; recipient Nat. Excellence in Leadership award State of N.D., 1988, Disting. Leadership award N.D. Psychol. Assn., 1988, Spl. Presdl. Commendation award Am. Psychiatric Assn., 1989, Toastmaster Internat. Comm. and Leadership award, 1992. Mem. ABA, N.D. Bar Assn., Cass County Bar Assn., Kiwanis, Elks, Masons, Shriners. Republican. Lutheran. Office: Blue Cross Blue Shield 4510 13th Ave S Fargo ND 58121-0002

UNIKEL, EVA TAYLOR, interior designer; b. Hungary; arrived in Can., 1956; came to U.S., 1967; d. Istvan Domolky and Lea Maria (Koszegi) Coan; m. Alan L. Unikel; 1 child, Renee Christine; m. June 26, 1993. BS, So. Ill. U., 1972. Dir. mktg. Lococo Design, St. Louis, 1982-83; project mgr., nat. dir. mktg. hosp. div. Hotel Restaurant Planners div. Profl. Interiors, St. Louis, 1983-87; founder Interior Solutions Inc., Hinsdale, Ill., 1987—. Mem. AIA (assoc.), Nat. Assn. Women Bus. Owners, Am. Soc. Interior Design (chairperson 1984-86), Interior Design Assn. Roman Catholic. Office: 500 E Ravine Rd Hinsdale IL 60521-2449 Home Phone: 630-986-4464; Office Phone: 630-464-9696.

UNIS, RICHARD L., judge; b. Portland, Oreg., June 11, 1928; BS, JD, U. Oreg. Bar: Oreg. 1954, U.S. Dist. Ct. Oreg. 1957, U.S. Ct. Appeals (9th cir.) 1960, U.S. Supreme Ct. 1965. Judge Portland Mcpl. Ct., 1968-71, Multnomah County Dist. Ct., 1972-76, presiding judge, 1972-74; former judge Oreg. Cir. Ct. 4th Judicial Dist., 1977-90; former sr. dep. city atty. City of Portland; assoc. justice Oreg. Supreme Ct., Portland, 1990-96; spl. master US Dist. Ct. House, Portland, 1996—2005. Adj. prof. of local govt. law and evidence Lewis & Clark Coll. Northwestern Sch. Law, 1969-76, 77-96; spl. master supr. La.-Pacific Inner-Seal Siding nationwide class action litig.; faculty mem. The Nat. Judicial Coll., 1971-2000; former faculty mem. Am. Acad. Judicial Edn. Author: Procedure and Instructions in Traffic Court Cases, 1970, 101 Questions and Answers on Preliminary Hearings, 1974. Bd. dirs. Oreg. Free from Drug Abuse; mem. Oreg. Adv. Com. on Evidence Law Revision, chmn. subcom., 1974-79. Maj. USAFR, JAGC, ret. Recipient Meritorius Svc. award U. Oregon sch. Law, 1988; named Legal Citizen of Yr. Oreg. Law Related Edn., 1987; inducted into The Nat. Judicial Coll. Hall of Honor, 1988. Mem. Am. Judicature Soc. (bd. dirs. 1975, Herbert Harley Nat. award 1999), Am. Judges Assn., Multnomah Bar Found., Oregon Judicial Conf. (chmn. Oreg. Judicial Coll. 1973-80, legis. com. 1976—, exec. com. of judicial edn. com., judicial conduct com.), N.Am. Judges Assn. (tenure, selection and compensation judges com.), Dist. Ct. Judges of Oreg. (v.p., chmn. edn. com.), Nat. Conf. Spl. Ct. Judges (exec. com.), Oreg. State Bar (judicial adminstrn. com., sec. local govt. com., com. on continuing certification, uniform jury instrn. com., exec. com. criminal law sect., trial practice sect. standards and certification com., past chmn., among others), Oreg. Trial Lawyers Assn. (named Judge of Yr. 1984). Office: 28338 Hist Colum Riv Hwy Troutdale OR 97060-9372 Home Phone: 503-665-9459; Office Phone: 503-669-7286. Personal E-mail: rlugg@comcast.net.

UNITHAN, DOLLY, visual artist; b. Kelantan, Malaysia; arrived in US, 1976; Postgrad., Brit. Coun. Fine Arts Exch., 1974, Ecole Nationale des Beaux Arts de Nancy, France, 1974; BFA, Hornsey Coll. Art, 1975; MFA, Pratt Inst., 1978. Summer intern Guggenheim Mus, NYC, 1976; panelist, artist in residence Asian Am. Arts Ctr., 1993; lectr. in field. One-woman shows include Internat. Art Ctr., London, 1975, Am. Assn. State Colls., Univ., Orlando, Fla., 1977, Sloan Gallery, Lock Haven State Coll., Pa., 1978, Permanent Mission Malaysia, UN, NYC, 1987, Kerr Gallery, 1987, Lyman Allyn Art Mus., New London, Conn., 1990, UN Secretariat, NYC, 1991, Gracie Mansion, 1994, Angel Orensanz Found., 1995, Cathedral of St. John the Divine, St. Boniface Chapel Gallery, 1996, exhibited in group shows at Palace of Westminster, Hos. of Parliament, London, 1978, City Mus. Art Gallery, Gloucester, Eng., 1978, Contemporary Gallery, Warsaw, Poland, 1978, BWA Gallery, Wroclaw, Poland, 1978, Szczecin, Poland, 1978, Arts Coun. Gallery, Belfast, No. Ireland, 1978, Parrish Art Mus., Southampton, NY, 1979, Modern Art Ctr., Guadalajara, Mex., 1979, Alternative Mus., NYC, 1981, Nat. Mus. Fine Arts, Havana, Cuba, 1986, Hillwood Art Mus., Brookville, NY, 1988, PS 1 Mus., NYC, 1990, Nat. Art Gallery, Kuala Lumpur, 1991—92, League of Nations Archives, Palais des Nations, Geneva, 1993, Jewish Mus., Vienna, Austria, 1993, Peace Mus., Remagen, Germany, Westbeth Galleries, NYC, Tweed Courthouse Gallery, 1994, China Art Mus., Beijing, 1995, Raiffeisenkasse, Ulrich bei Steyr, Peace parish, Austria, 1996, Ctrl. Children's & Youth Arts Palace, Samarkand, Uzbekistan, 1997, Palais des Nations, UN Office, Geneva, 1998, Firehouse, NYC, 1999, Cathedral of St. John the Divine Synod Hall, 2002, Asian Am. Arts Ctr., 2002, Represented in permanent collections Lock Haven State Coll., Pa., Am. Assn. State Colls., Univ., Washington, Permanent Mission of Malaysia to UN, Wilfredo Lam Ctr., Havana, Malaysian Embassy, Washington, Spirit Found., NYC, Asian Am. Arts Ctr., World Bank, Washington, Lib. Congress, artwork included in jours., Multicultural Edn., 1994, Artspiral, 1994, books, Imagine Strawberry Fields, Sculpture, Technique, Form, Content. Named grad. scholar, Mara, Malaysia, 1976—78, Archives of Contemporary Arts, Venice Biennale, 1990; recipient Artist award, Rainbow Art Found., NYC, 1985, Art award ArtQuest '88, Internat. Art Competition, Calif., 1988; grantee, Lee Found., Singapore, 1972, 1976, Pollock-Krasner Found., 1991—92. Avocation: collecting antiques. Office Phone: 212-583-1946. Personal E-mail: dollyunithan@yahoo.com.

UNKOVIC, JOHN CLARK, lawyer; b. Pitts., Oct. 2, 1943; s. Nicholas and Mary (Clark) Unkovic; m. Mary L. Marks, Mar. 15, 1980; 1 child, Rachel. BA in history, Harvard U., 1965; diploma in economics, St. Edmund Hall, Oxford, Eng., 1966; JD, U. Mich., 1970. Bar: Pa., 1971, US Supreme Ct., US Ct. Appeals 3rd Cir., 1973, US Ct. Appeals 5th Cir., 1981, US Ct. Appeals 11th Cir., 1981, US Ct. Appeals 6th Cir., 1986, US Ct. Appeals Fed. Cir., 1984, US Ct. Appeals 7th Cir., 1989. Atty. Reed Smith LLP (formerly Reed Smith Shaw & McClay), Pitts., 1971—, now ptnr., gen. counsel. Adj. prof. law Duquesne U., Pitts., 1978-89; bd. mem. Mine Safety Appliances Co., 2002-. Contbr. articles to profl. journals. Chair Pitts. Pub. Schools Found.; bd. mem. Manchester Bidwell Corp. Fulbright Fellow, 1970-71. Mem. ABA, Pa. Bar Assn., Allegheny County Bar Assn., Acad. Trial Lawyers Allegheny County, Am. Law Inst. Office: Reed Smith LLP 435 Sixth Ave Pittsburgh PA 15219 Office Phone: 412-288-3294. Office Fax: 412-288-3063. Business E-Mail: junkovic@reedsmith.com.

UNKOVIC, NICHOLAS C., lawyer; b. Pitts., 1951; AB magna cum laude, Harvard U., 1973; JD with honors, U. Mich., 1976. Bar: Calif. 1976. Mng. ptnr.-Palo Alto Office Squire, Sanders & Dempsey LLP, mem. mgmt. com. Dir. British Am. Coun. No. Calif., Redem Corp. Named a No. Calif. Super Lawyers, Law & Politics Mag., 2004; named one of Silicon Valley's top corp. lawyers, San Jose Mag. Mem.: ABA (Bus. Law Sect.), State Bar Calif. Fluent in French. Office: Squire Sanders & Dempsey LLP 600 Hansen Way Palo Alto CA 94304-1043 Office Phone: 650-843-3238. Office Fax: 650-843-8777. Business E-Mail: nunkovic@ssd.com.

UNPINGCO, JOHN WALTER SABLAN, federal judge; b. 1950; BA, St. Louis U., 1972; MBA, JD, NYU, 1976; LLM, Georgetown U., 1983. Bar: Guam 1977, D.C. 1983, Calif. 1992. Atty. Ferenz, Bramhall, Williams & Gruskin, Guam, 1976-77; atty. Office Staff Judge Advocate USAF, 1977-85, civilian atty., Office Staff Judge Advocate, 1985-87; counsel US Naval Air Warfare Ctr., China Lake, Calif., 1987-92; judge US Dist. Ct. (Guam dist.), 1992—, now chief judge. Part-time instr. U. Md. Far East divsn., Yokota Air Base, Tokyo, 1983-87, European divsn., RAF Mildenhall, Suffolk, U.K., 1979-82, U. Guam, 1994-99. Pres. Guam Swim League, 2000; pres. parish coun. Our Lady of Hope Parish, 2000-. Mem. ABA, State Bar Calif., Guam Bar Assn., Internat. Legal Soc. Japan, D.C. Bar Assn., NWC Community Fed. Credit Union (bd. dirs. 1991-92). Office: US Dist Ct 4th Fl US Courthouse 520 W Soledad Ave Hagatna GU 96910

UNRUH, GARY LEE, retired music educator; b. Reedley, Calif., July 7, 1941; 1 child, Holly Elizabeth. MusD, U. Ill., 1973. Prof. emeritus Calif. State U., Fresno, Calif., 1999—. Dir. performance tours Kingsway Internat., Colo. Springs, Colo., 1997—2003; condr. internat. choral performance tours; v.p. Santa Barbara Vocal Jazz Found., 2005. Named Educator of Yr., Fresno Arts Coun., 1976; recipient, 1979, 1984, 2001, award, Calif. State Senate Resolutions, 1998. Mem.: Am. Choral Dirs. Assn. (life; pres. we. divsn. 1989—91).

UNRUH, HOWARD K., JR., military officer, university administrator; b. Balt. m. Diane R. Caslow; three children: Meredith, Allison, H. Kirk III. AB, Princeton U., 1970; MEd, Harvard U.; MA in Am. Studies, U. Hawaii. Commd. ensign USN, 1970, advanced through ranks to rear adm.; various assignments to Dep. Comdr. Naval Surface Force, U.S. Atlantic Fleet, 1995—; comdr. Readiness Command Midwest. Dir. devel. rels., rec. sec. Princeton U.; trustee or bd. dirs. several civic orgns. Decorated Legion of Merit (2), Meritorious Svc. medal (2), Navy Commendation medal (4),

Nat. Def. medal with Bronze Star, Republic of Vietnam Svc. medal with Bronze Star, others. Mem. Naval Res. Assn., Surface Navy Assn., Univ. Cottage Club, Princeton Club N.Y.C. Office: Princeton Univ Recording Sec 330 Alexander St Princeton NJ 08540-7123

UNRUH, JAMES ARLEN, bank executive; b. Goodrich, ND, Mar. 22, 1941; m. Candice Leigh Voight, Apr. 28, 1984. BSBA, Jamestown Coll., 1963; MBA, U. Denver, 1964. Dir. corp. planning and analysis Fairchild Camera & Instrument, Calif., 1974-76, v.p. treasury and corp. devel. Calif., 1976-79, v.p. fin. Calif., 1979-80, Memorex Corp., Santa Clara, Calif., 1980-82, Burroughs Corp. (now known as Unisys Corp.), Detroit, 1982-84, sr. v.p. fin., 1984-86, exec. v.p. fin., 1986, exec. v.p., 1986-89, pres., COO, 1989-90, pres., CEO, 1990-91, chmn. bd. dirs., CEO, 1991-97; founding prin. Alerion Capital Group L.L.C., Scottsdale, Ariz., 1998—. Bd. dirs. Prudential Fin. Corp., Qwest Comm. Internat. Inc., Tenet Healthcare Corp., CSG Sys. Internat., Inc., LumenIQ Corp., BioVigilant Corp., Steton Tech. Group, Inc., Worldlink, Inc. Trustee Jamestown Coll., N.D. Home: 5426 E Morrison Ln Paradise Valley AZ 85253 Office Phone: 480-367-0900. E-mail: jimunruh@alerion.com.

UNSAL-TUNAY, NURAN, geological engineer, researcher; b. Igdir, Turkey, Dec. 26, 1956; came to U.S., 1995; d. Kamil and Feride (Gunay) Tunay; m. Ilhan Unsal, Oct. 28, 1979; 1 child, Volkan. Diploma in Geol. Engring., Earth Sci. Geol. Engring. Turkey, 1982; cert. in Civil Engring., Min. Pub. Works Turkey, 1985. Geol. engr. Gen. Directorate of Bank of Provinces, Konya-Ankara, Turkey, 1982—84, Gen. Directorate of Hwy., Kayseri-Ankara, Turkey, 1984—89, Adminstrn. Pub. Works, Manisa, Turkey, 1989—95. Cons. Pub. Works, Manisa, Turkey, 1989-95; adv. bds. Pub. Works, Municipality, Civil Cts., Manisa, Turkey, 1992-95. Inventor: Adaptation of Stabilized Hydrated Lime, Publication of the Chamber of Geol. Engring. of Turkey, 1993. Recipient of presentations 46th Congress of Geology of Turkey, Ankara, 1993. Fellow Geol. Assn. Can.; mem. Geol. Soc. Am., Chamber of Geol. Engrs. of Turkey. Achievements include the soil improvement with hydrated lime stabilization; applied in the area of Manisa Teachers House Buildings, was one of the first applications in Turkey. Home: 23-13 28th Ave Apt 2F Astoria NY 11102 Personal E-mail: nuranunsal@gmail.com.

UNSWORTH, JOHN M., dean, library and information science educator; BA magna cum laude, Amherst Coll., 1981; MA in English, Boston U., 1982; PhD in English, U. Va., 1988. Instr. Dept. English U. Va., 1985—87, lectr., 1988—89, dir. Inst. Advanced Tech. in Humanities, 1993—2003, assoc. prof., 1993—2003; assoc. faculty mem. Multi-Disciplinary Studies Program NC State U., 1992—93, asst. prof., 1989—93; dean, prof. Grad. Sch. Libr. and Info. Sci., U. Ill., Urbana-Champaign, 2003—. Spkr. in field. Editl. com. mem. Literary and Linguistic Computing, 2004—, editl. bd. mem. Digital Humanities Quarterly, 2006—; co-editor: Library Trends, 2006—; contbr. articles to profl. jours. Recipient Richard W. Lyman Award, 2005; Vodafone Fellow, Kings Coll., Univ. Coll. London, 2005. Mem.: ALA, Assn. Computers and Humanities, Modern Language Assn., Am. Soc. Info. Sci. and Tech., Assn. Libr. and Info. Sci. Edn., Ill. Libr. Assn. Office: Grad Sch Libr and Info Sci U Ill Urbana-Champaign 501 E Daniel St Champaign IL 61820 Office Phone: 217-333-3281. Office Fax: 217-244-3302. E-mail: unsworth@uiuc.edu. *

UNSWORTH, RICHARD PRESTON, minister, educator, director; b. Vineland, NJ, Feb. 7, 1927; s. Joseph Lewis and Laura (MacMillan) U.; m. Joy Merritt, Aug. 20, 1949; children: Sarah, John, Mary, Lucy. BA, Princeton U., 1948; BD, Yale U., 1954; ThM, Harvard U., 1963; STD, Dickinson Coll., 1971; LHD, Washington and Jefferson Coll., 1971; LLD, Smith Coll., 1992. Ordained to ministry Presbyn. Ch., 1953. Tchr. Bible and English Mt. Hermon Sch., 1948-50; asst. chaplain Yale U., New Haven, 1950-54; chaplain, assoc. prof. Smith Coll., Northampton, Mass., 1954-64, chaplain, prof. religion, 1967-80; dean William Jewett Tucker Found. and prof. religion Dartmouth (N.H.) Coll., 1963-67; headmaster Northfield (Mass.) Mt. Hermon Sch., 1980-88, pres., 1989-91, headmaster emeritus, 1991—; headmaster Berkshire Sch., Sheffield, Mass., 1991-96; dean of the chapel Smith Coll., 1996-98, lectr. religion, 1996—99, sr. fellow Kahn Inst., 1998—. Pres. Critical Langs. and Area Studies Consortium, 1987-97; cons. Ednl. Assocs., Inc., 1967-69, U.S. Office Edn., 1969-77. Author: Sexuality and the Human Community, 1970, Dignity and Exploitation: Christian Reflections on Images of Sex in the 1970s, 1974, A Century of Religion at Smith College, 1975; (with Arnold Kenseth) Prayers for Worship Leaders, 1978; editor: Rethinking Childhood, 2004; contbg author: The Dispossessed, 2005; contbr. chpts. to books. Leader Operation Crossroads Africa unit, Nigeria, 1961, mem. adv. bd., 1961-66; mem. adminstrv. com. Student Christian Movement New Eng., 1964; mem. Mass. unit So. Christian Leadership conf., 1968; trustee Conf. on Religion in Ind. Schs., 1961-63; pres. Am. Friends of Coll. Cevenol, France, 1957-63, 90-94, Am. rep., 1958-82; trustee Mt. Holyoke Coll., 1982-89, chair, 1984-89, chmn. emeritus, 1989—, Am. Sch. Tangier, Morocco, 1982-87, Eaglebrook Sch., 1992-98, Acad. Music, Northampton, 1998-99, Mus. Sci., Boston, 1993-95; bd. dirs. Family Planning Coun. Western Mass., 1972-81; bd. dirs. Ind. Schs. Assn. Mass., 1992-96. Mem. AAUP, Nat. Assn. Coll. and Univ. Chaplains, Am. Acad. Religion, Assn. Ind. Schs. New Eng. (pres. 1993-96), Headmasters Assn., Nat. Commn. on Asia in Schs., Asia Soc. N.Y.C., U. Club.

UNTERBERGER, BETTY MILLER, retired history professor; b. Glasgow, Scotland, Dec. 27, 1922; d. Joseph C. and Leah Miller; m. Robert Ruppe, July 29, 1944; children: Glen, Gail, Gregg. BA, Syracuse U., NYC, 1943; MA, Harvard U., 1946; PhD, Duke U., 1950. Asst. prof. E. Carolina U., Greenville, 1948-50; assoc. prof., dir. liberal arts ctr. Whittier Coll., Calif., 1954-61; assoc. prof. Calif. State U.-Fullerton, 1961-65, prof., chmn. grad. studies, 1965-68; prof. history Tex. A&M U., College Station, 1968—2004, ret. Regents prof. emerita, 2004. Vis. prof. U. Hawaii, Honolulu, 1967, Peking U., Beijing, 1988; vis. disting. prof. U. Calif., Irvine, 1987—, Patricia and Bookman Peters prof. history, 1991-2005; vis. prof. Charles U., Prague, Czechoslovakia, 1992, Regents prof., 2000—; adv. com. fgn. rels. U.S. Dept. State, 1977-81, chair, 1981; hist. adv. com. U.S. Dept. Army, 1980-82, USN, 1991—; mem. Nat. Hist. Publs. and Records Commn., 1980-84; history rev. panel to Dir. of CIA, 1999—. Author: America's Siberian Expedition 1918-1920: A Study of National Policy, 1956, 69 (Pacific Coast award Am. Hist. Assn. 1956); editor: American Intervention in the Russian Civil War, 1969, Intervention Against Communism: Did the U.S. Try to Overthrow the Soviet Government, 1918-20, 1986, The United States, Revolutionary Russia and the Rise of Czechoslovakia, 1989, paperback edit. with a 2000 yr. perspective, 2000; contbr.: Woodrow Wilson and Revolutionary World, 1982, The Liberal Persuasion, 1997, The United States and the Russian Civil War, microfilm edit., 25 reels, 2001; mem. editl. adv. bd. The Papers of Woodrow Wilson, Princeton U., 1982-92, Internt. History, 1999—; bd. editors: Diplomatic History, 1981-84, Red River Valley Hist. Rev., 1975-84. Trustee Am. Inst. Pakistan Studies, Villanova U., Pa., 1981—, sec., 1989-92; mem. League of Women Voters. Woodrow Wilson Found. fellow, 1979; recipient Disting. Univ. Tchr. award State of Calif. Legislature, 1966; Betty Miller Unterberger dissertation prize, Soc. Historians Am. Fgn. Rels., 2004. Mem. LWV, NOW, AAUW, Am. Hist. Assn. (chair 1982-83, nominating com. 1980-83), Orgn. Am. Historians (govt. relations com.), Soc. Historians of Am. Fgn. Relations (exec. council 1978-81, 86-89, govt. relations com. 1982-84, v.p. 1985, pres. 1986, co-winner Myrna F. Bernath prize 1991), Am. Soc. for Advancement Slavic Studies, Coordinating Com. on Women in Hist. Profession, Rocky Mountain Assn. Slavic Studies (program chair 1973, v.p. 1973-74), So. Hist. Assn., Asian Studies Assn., Assn. Third World Studies, Czechoslovak Soc. Arts and Scis., Czechoslovak History Conf., Women in Nat. Security, Women's Fgn. Policy Coun., Beyond War, Peace History Soc., Sierra Club, Phi Beta Kappa, Phi Beta Delta.

UNTERMAN, EUGENE REX, aviation sales and consulting company executive; b. Mpls., Sept. 3, 1953; s. Melvin and Nancy (Wolfson) U.; m. Melanie Wells Munson, July 12, 1980 (div., Mar. 1997); children: H. Aaron, Jeffery Wells, Julie Ann; m. Patricia Joan Bishop, Oct. 11, 1998. Student, Loyola U., Chgo., 1971-73, Northwestern U., 1973-75. Trader Chgo. Mercantile Exchange, 1975-76; pres. Mid-West Aircraft Co., Sandwich, Ill., 1976-89, Heartland Aircraft Group Ltd., Geneva, Ill., 1990-96, Unterman Aviation Cons., Batavia, Ill., 1996—. Computer cons. Chgo. Rawhide Corp., Elgin, Ill., 1983. Author: How to Buy A Used Aircraft Without Taking a Dive, 1989. Airport adv. bd. City of Geneva, Ill., 1983; alderman 2d ward City of Geneva, 1988-89. Mem. Jaycees (Jaycee of Yr. 1988, 89, 90, pres. 1988-89, 94-95, 2001-03), St. Charles (Ill.) Sportsman Club (treas. 1985-86, pres. 1987-88, 90—, bd. dirs. 1988-89). Jewish. Avocations: golf, coaching youth hockey, refereeing hockey. Office: Unterman Aviation Cons 75965 Armour Way Palm Desert CA 92211-8958 Office Phone: 760-346-3399. E-mail: gene@unterman-aviation.com.

UNTERMAN, THOMAS, venture capitalist, lawyer; b. Newport, RI, Oct. 23, 1944; s. Martin D. and Ruth (Marcus) U.; m. Janet M. Mead, Sept. 27, 1980; children: Rebecca, Amy. AB, Princeton U., 1966; JD, U. Chgo., 1969. Bar: Calif. 1970. Assoc. Orrick, Herrington & Sutcliffe, San Francisco, 1969-75, ptnr., 1975-86, Morrison & Foerster, San Francisco, 1986-92; sr. v.p., gen. counsel The Times Mirror Co., LA, 1992-95, sr. v.p., CFO, 1995—, exec. v.p., CFO, 1998-99; mng. ptnr. Rustic Canyon Ventures, Santa Monica, Calif., 2000—. Democrat. Jewish. Office: Rustic Canyon Ventures 2425 Olympic Blvd Ste 6050W Santa Monica CA 90404-4030

UNTERMEYER, CHARLES GRAVES (CHASE UNTERMEYER), ambassador, diplomat; b. Long Branch, NJ, Mar. 7, 1946; s. Dewitt Edward and Marguerite Alonza (Graves) U.; m. Diana Cumming Kendrick, Oct. 6, 1990; 1 child, Ellyson Chase. AB, Harvard Coll., 1968. Polit. reporter Houston Chronicle, 1971-74; exec. asst. County Judge of Harris County, Houston, 1974-76; state rep. Tex. Ho. of Reps., Austin, 1977-81; exec. asst. V.P. George H.W. Bush, Washington, 1981-83; dep. asst. sec. installations & facilities Navy Dept., Washington, 1983—84, asst. sec. manpower & reserve affairs, 1984—88; asst. to the pres. White House, Washington, 1989-91; dir. Voice of Am., Washington, 1991-93; dir. govt. affairs Compaq Computer Corp., Houston, 1993—2002; v.p. prof. pub. policy U. Tex. Health Sci. Ctr., Houston, 2002—04; U.S. amb. to Qatar US Dept. State, 2004—. Bd. visitors U.S. Naval Acad., Annapolis, Md., 1993-96, chmn., 1995; mem. Tex. State Bd. Edn., 1999-2003, chmn., 1999-2001. Author: Houston Survival Handbook, 1980. Commnr. Port of Houston, 1995-98; bd. dirs. Nat. Pub. Radio, 1996-98. Lt. USNR, 1968-70. Inst. Politics fellow Harvard U., 1980; recipient George Washington Honor medal Freedoms Found., 1969. Republican. Episcopalian. Home and Office: Am Embassy Arcent-QA Box 520 APO AE 09898 Office Phone: 974-488-4101 ext. 6055. E-mail: untermeyercg@state.gov.

UNUSAN, CAGATAY, finance educator; b. Konya, Turkey, June 20, 1961; s. Teoman and Fahamet Unusan; m. Nurhan Ilbiz, Nov. 1, 1986; 1 child, Teomanhan. BA in Bus. Adminstrn., 1988; PhD, Nottingham U., 1992. 1987-1988 rsch. asst. Selcuk University, Konya, Turkey, 1987—88; studies for ph.d. in nottingham u. Nottingham U., UK, Nottingham, UK, United Kingdom, 1988—92. Asst. prof. of mktg. Selcuk U., Konya, Turkey, 1993—95, assoc. prof. of mktg., 1995—2000, prof. of mktg., 2001—; bd. mem. Turkish Mktg. Assn., 2007. Contbr. articles to profl. jours. Achievements include development of Honarary member of Turkish Franchising Association. Home: Meram Yeni Yol Caddesi No 282 Meram Konya 42090 Turkey Office Phone: 90 332 2233093. Office Fax: 90 332 3252132; Home Fax: 90 332 3252132. Personal E-mail: cagatayunusan@gmail.com. Business E-Mail: cagatayunusan@selcuk.edu.tr.

UNWIN, STEPHEN FORMAN, advertising executive, educator; b. Higham, Leicestershire, Eng., Aug. 7, 1927; s. Philip Henry and Decima (Forman) Unwin; m. Pamela Susan Brett, June 6, 1953; children: Philip, Tessa, Sam. BA with honors, Oxford U., 1952, MA, 1968. Account exec. London Press Exch., 1951-66; dir. London Press Exch. Orgn. Ltd., 1966-67; assoc. dir. LPE Ltd., London, 1967-69; vis. lectr. U. Ill., Urbana, 1969-70, asst. prof., 1970-74; assoc. prof. U. Ala., Tuscaloosa, 1974-79, Wash. State U., Pullman, 1979-81, U. Oreg., Eugene, 1981-85; pres. Bus. Dynamics, Kingwood, Tex., 1985—. Cons. advt. Ill. Bell, Chgo., 1974—75, J. Walter Thompson, San Francisco, 1983; dir. Forest Industries Comm. Inst., Atlanta, 1975—76; publicist Brit. Tourist Authority, London, 1978—81; vis. prof. Am. Assn. Advt. Agys., Chgo., 1971, Am. Ad Fedn., San Francisco, 1983; instr. Lifelong Learning, Kingwood, 2005—. Author: How Nations Grow Rich, 1992; co-author: The Future of Advertising, 2003; contbr. articles to profl. jours. Mem. Nat. Com. Advt. Edn., NYC, 1983—84; bicentennial judge Advt. Age mag., Chgo., 1976; mem. Future Journalism Edn., Eugene, Oreg., 1982—84, Internat. Advt. Edn. Com., Chgo., 1982, Wheelwright Mus., Santa Fe, Worcester Coll., Oxford U. 2d lt. Brit. Army, 1946—48. Libr. fellow, Mass. Hist. Soc., 1990—95. Mem.: Am. Sci. Affiliation, Am. Acad. Advt., Brotherhood St. Andrew. Episcopalian. Avocations: travel, genealogy.

UPADHIAYA, UMESH CHANDRA, engineer, consultant; b. Dabha, India, July 11, 1927; arrived in US, 1977; s. Bhagwati Prashad and Shri Devi Upadhiaya; m. Susila Devi, Nov. 7, 1954; children: Anita, Amit. Diploma in Elec. and Mech. Engring., Tech. Coll., Dayalbagh, India, 1948; MSME, Fla. Internat. U., 1991. Registered profl. engr., Fla. Asst. engr. Hindusthan Sugar, Gola, India, 1954—60; mech. engr. Bagpat Sugar, India, 1960—61; erection engr. Dhampur Sugar, India, 1961—62; cons. Mehta Group, Uganda, 1962—73; project mgr. KCP Ltd., Madras, India, 1973—74; design engr. Joint Sugar Project Unit, Surabaya, Indonesia, 1974—77; cons. engr. Tate & Lyle Enterprises Inc., Miami, Fla., 1977—85, ATV Projects, Bombay, 1990—93; ind. cons. Davie, Fla., 1993—. Contbr. articles to profl. jours. Home and Office: 6510 Sedgewyck Cir W Davie FL 33331-3455 Office Phone: 954-434-5265. Personal E-mail: ravay2k@bellsouth.net.

UPADHYAY, YOGENDRA NATH, physician, educator; b. Gorakhpur, India, Dec. 21, 1938; arrived in U.S., 1963; s. Murlidhar and Vansraji (Pande) U.; m. Cecile R. Yonish; children: Asha, Sameer, Sanjay. MB, BS, All India Inst. Med. Scis., New Delhi, 1962. Diplomate Am. Bd. Psychiatry and Neurology, Am. Bd. Psychiatry and Child and Adolescent Psychiatry. Instr. in pediatrics Johns Hopkins U. Sch. Medicine, Balt., 1969-71; fellow in child psychiatry Johns Hopkins Hosp./Johns Hopkins U., Balt., 1971-72; resident, then sr. resident in psychiatry Albert Einstein Coll. Medicine/Bronx Mcpl. Hosp. Ctr., 1972-74, fellow in child psychiatry, 1974-75; chief, partial hosp. program for children, dept. psychiatry Brookdale Hosp., Bklyn., 1976-77; med. dir. West Nassau Mental Health Ctr., Franklin Sq., NY, 1977-80; asst. prof. clin. psychiatry SUNY, Stony Brook, 1978-92; dir. child and adolescent psychiatry Nassau County Med. Ctr., East Meadow, NY, 1980-92; sr. psychiatrist South Oaks Hosp., Amityville, NY, 1992—, pres. med. staff, 1995-97, svc. med. dir. child and adolescent psychiatry, 1995-97, med. dir., 1997—; sr. v.p., Medical Affairs South Oak Hosp. and Broadlawn Nursing Home, 2001—. Sr. v.p. med. affairs LI Home, Amityville, NY, 2001—. Fellow Am. Psychiat. Assn. (cons. task force treatments psychiat. disorders 1989—), Am. Acad. Child and Adolescent Psychiatry, Allmsonians of Am. (founding pres. 1982-86). Office: S Oaks Hosp 400 Sunrise Hwy Amityville NY 11701-2508 Office Phone: 631-608-5227. Business E-Mail: yupadhyay@south-oaks.org.

UPATNIEKS, JURIS, retired optical engineer; b. Riga, Latvia, May 7, 1936; arrived in U.S., 1951; s. Karlis and Eleonora (Jegers) Upatnieks; m. Ilze Induss, July 13, 1968; children: Ivars, Ansis. BSEE, U. Akron, Ohio, 1960; MSEE, U. Mich., 1965. Rsch. asst., then rsch. assoc. Willow Run Labs. U. Mich., Ann Arbor, 1960-69; rsch. engr. Inst. Sci. and Tech., U. Mich., Ann Arbor, 1969-72, Environ. Rsch. Inst. Mich., Ann Arbor, 1973-93; sr. engr. Applied Optics, Ann Arbor, 1993—2001; ret., 2001. Lectr. elec. engring. dept. U. Mich., 1971—73, adj. assoc. prof. elec. engring. and computer sci. dept., 1974—2001, adj. rsch. scientist dept. mech. engring. and applied mechanics, 1996—2001. Contbr. articles to profl. jours. 2d lt. US Army, 1961—62. Recipient Holley medal, ASME, 1976, Inventor of the Yr. award, Assn. Advancement Invention and Innovation, 1976. Fellow: Latvian Acad. Sci. (Grand medal 1999), Acad. Soc. Austrums, Soc. Photographic Instrumentation Engrs. (Robert Gordon award 1965), Optical Soc. Am. (R. W. Wood prize 1975), Am. Latvian Assn. Achievements include patents in field. Avocations: camping, gardening, hiking. Personal E-mail: upatnks@netrek.net.

UPBIN, HAL J., consumer products company executive; b. Bronx, NY, Jan. 15, 1939; s. David and Evelyn (Sloan) U.; m. Shari Kiesler, May 29, 1960; children: Edward, Elyse, Danielle. BBA, Pace Coll., 1961. CPA, NY. Tax sr. Peat, Marwick, Mitchell & Co., NYC, 1961-65; tax mgr. Price Waterhouse & Co., NYC, 1965-71; dir. taxes Wheelabrator-Frye Inc., NYC, 1971-72, treas., 1972-74; pres. Wheelabrator Fin. Corp., NYC, 1974-75; v.p., chief fin. officer Chase Manhattan Mortgage and Realty Trust (became Triton Group Ltd. 1980), NYC, 1975-76, pres., 1976-78, pres., chmn., 1978-83, also dir.; chmn., pres., dir. Isomedics, 1983-85; chmn., pres. Fifth Ave. Cards, Inc., Fifth Retail Corp., Ashley's Stores, Ashley's Outlet Stores, 1984-88; bd. dirs. Stacy Industries, 1984-88; vice chmn. Am. Recreation Products, St. Louis, 1985-88, vice chmn., pres., 1988—, chmn., 1992—; v.p. corp. devel., chmn. acquistion com. Kellwood Co., Chesterfield, Mo., 1990—, exec. v.p. corp. devel., chmn. acquistion com., 1992—, pres., COO, 1994—, pres., COO, dir., 1995-97, pres., CEO, 1997—2005, chmn., 1999—2006, chmn. emeritus, 2006—, also bd. dirs. Bd. dirs. First Banks, Inc., Regional Bus. Coun., Coun. Nat. Trustees, Nat. Jewish Med. and Rsch. Ctr., Nat. Coun. Wash. U. Olin Sch. Bus., Brown Shoe Co.; trustee Pace U. Past pres. Jewish Temple. Mem. AICPA, NY State Soc. CPA's, Franklin Jaycees (v.p.). Home: 3740 S Ocean Blvd Apt 801 Highland Beach FL 33487-3403 Office Phone: 314-576-3100. Business E-Mail: HJU@kellwood.com.

UPBIN, SHARI, agent; b. NYC; children: Edward, Elyse, Danielle. Master tap instr. Talent mgr. Goldstar Talent Mgmt., Inc., NYC, 1989-91. Faculty Nat. Shakespeare Conservatory, N.Y. Asst. dir.: (plays, 1st Black-Hispanic Shakespeare prodn.) Julius Ceasar, 1979; dir.(choreographer): (plays) Matter of Opinion, 1980, Side by Side, 1981; prodr.(dir.): Vincent, The Passions of Van Gogh, 1981,: (Broadway plays) Bojangles, The Life of Bill Robinson, 1984; dir.: Captain America, 1996; dir., choreographer (plays) Fiddler of the Roof, Cabaret, Life with Father, Roar of the Grease Paint, 1979—82; dir.: (plays) Feminist Movements, 1997, Danny Kaye and Sylvia, 2005; co-prodr.: One Mo' Time; prodr., dir.: Flypaper, 1991—92; Women on Their Own, Things My Mother Never Told Me; How Could Cupid Be So Stupid!, 1999; Timeless Divas, 2003, 2005; prodr., dir. (plays) Divas in Divaland, 2007; prodr.: (plays) Vintage 2001, Timeless Divas! Salute to Women in Cabaret, Broadway Over 40, Timeless Divas! Musical Stars of The Silver Screen, 2004, Dames in Divaland, 2007, Timeless Divas. Founder Queens Playhouse, N.Y., Children's Theatre, Flushing, N.Y.; mem. Willy Mays' Found. Drug Abused Children. Recipient Jaycees Svc. award Jr. Miss Pageants Franklin Twp., N.J., 1976. Mem. League Profl. Theatre Women (past pres.), Soc. Stage Dirs. and Choreographers, Coalition of Women in Arts & Media (bd. dirs.), Actors Equity Assn., Villagers Barn Theatre (1st woman pres.), N.Y. Womens Agenda (bd. dirs.). Personal E-mail: shariupbin@aol.com.

UPCHURCH, LESLIE PURCELL, music educator; b. Pitts., Sept. 22, 1953; d. John (Jack) Edward and Jeanne Jolliffe Purcell; 1 child, Alicia Nicole. BFA, Carnegie Mellon U., 1976; MusM, U. Wis., Madison, 1980. Elem. cert. in Dalcroze Eurhythmics Carnegie-Mellon U./Jaques-Dalcroze Inst., 1976, cert. in Dalcroze Eurhythmics Ithaca Coll./Jaques-Dalcroze Inst., 1981, lic. Carnegie-Mellon U./Jaques-Dalcroze Inst., 1982. Tchr. Muskingum Coll., New Concord, Ohio, 1981—83, Horace Mann Sch. Nursery Years, NYC, 1989—92, Sonatina Sch. Music and Sonatina Internat. Piano Camp, Bennington, Vt., 1992—97, Maple St. Sch., 1998—2005, music dept. dir., 1998—2005; tchr. Carnegie Mellon U., Pittsburgh, Pa., 2003—, Mustard Seed Sch., Hoboken, NJ, 2005—06, dir. chorus, 2005—06; tchr. Blue Rock Sch., W. Nyack, NY, 2006—; vocal accompanist Muskingum Coll., Ohio; tchr. trainer Westchester Conservatory Music, White Plains, NY, 1987—89; organist and choir dir. St. James Episcopal Ch., Arlington, Vt., 1994—99; dir. dalcroze eurhythmics program Thurnauer Sch. Music, Tenafly, NJ, 2004—. Adv. bd. mem. Manchester Music Festival, Manchester, Vt., 1998—2001; bd. dirs. Vt. MIDI Project, Essex Junction, 2003—, sec., 2003—05. Prodr., host (TV series) Music and The Young Child, 1994—96, asst. music dir., musician Arlington Lions Variety Shows, 1999—2005; musician, choir master children's chorus: opera Hansel and Gretel with Opera Theater of Weston, 2001, Help! Help! The Globolinks!, 2003; musician, music dir. Dorset Players holiday prodns., 2002, 2004. Vol. Manchester Sch. Fund, 1999—2000; bd. dirs. GNAT-TV, Manchester, Vt., 1994—96. Grantee, Mockingbird Found., 2005. Mem.: Dalcroze Soc. Am. (treas. tri-state chpt. 1983—85, treas. nat. assn. 1984—88, tri-state Chpt., Elsa Findlay scholar 1991). Achievements include invention of double adjusting piano seat that adjusts for seat and feet. Avocations: cross country skiing, hiking, gardening, travel. Home Phone: 201-776-4037. Personal E-mail: upchurch_leslie@yahoo.com.

UPDIKE, HELEN HILL, financial advisor; b. NYC, Mar. 27, 1941; d. Benjamin Harvey and Helen (Gray) Hill; m. Charles Bruce Updike, Sept. 7, 1963 (div. 1989); m. Asa Rountree, Oct. 10, 1998. BA, Hood Coll., 1962; PhD, SUNY, Stony Brook, 1978; postgrad., Harvard U., 1986. Lectr. SUNY, Stony Brook, 1969-75; asst. prof. U. Mass., Boston, 1975-77, Hofstra U., Hempstead, NY, 1978-85, assoc. prof., 1985-90, chmn. dept. econs. and geography, 1981-84, assoc. dean Hofstra Coll., 1984-87; pres. Interfid Capital Corp., 1987—2001; prin. Bridgewater Advisors, NYC, 2001—. Cons. econ. policy, 1973—; vis. asst. prof. SUNY, Stony Brook, 1977—78; commentator WNYC Radio, 1997—; bd. dirs. Faberge, McCrory Corp. Author: (book) The National Banks and American Economic Development, 1870-1900, 1985. Trustee Madeira Sch., Greenway, Va., 1984—88, Literacy, Inc., 1998—2001; mem. nat. adv. bd. Outward Bound, 1986—92; trustee, v.p. L.I. Forum Tech., 1979—85; trustee NY Outward Bound, 1988—97. Mem.: AAAS. Office: Bridgewater Advisors 489 Fifth Ave New York NY 10017

UPDIKE, JOHN HOYER, writer; b. Shillington, Pa., Mar. 18, 1932; s. Wesley R. and Linda G. (Hoyer) U.; m. Mary E. Pennington, June 26, 1953 (div. 1976); children: Elizabeth, David, Michael, Miranda; m. Martha Bernhard, Sept. 30, 1977. AB, Harvard U., 1954; student, Ruskin Sch. Drawing and Fine Art, 1954-55. With New Yorker mag., NYC, 1955-57. Author: (novels) The Poorhouse Fair, 1959 (Richard and Hinda Rosenthal Found. award Am. Acad. and Nat. Inst. Arts and Letters 1960), The Same Door, 1959, Rabbit, Run, 1960, Pigeon Feathers, 1962, The Centaur, 1963 (Nat. Book award for fiction 1963, Prix Medicis Etranger 1966), Olinger Stories, 1964, Of the Farm, 1965, The Music School, 1966, Couples, 1968,

Bech: A Book, 1970, Rabbit Redux, 1971, Museums and Women, 1972, Warm Wine, 1973, A Month of Sundays, 1975, Marry Me, 1976, Couples, 1976, The Coup, 1978, From the Journal of a Leper, 1978, Problems, 1979, Too Far to Go: The Maples Stories, 1979 (Am. Book award nomination 1980), Three Illuminations in the Life of an American Author, 1979, Your Lover Just Called: Stories of Joan and Richard Maple, 1980, The Chaste Planet, 1980, Rabbit Is Rich, 1981 (Pulitzer prize for fiction 1982, Nat. Book Critics Circle award 1982, Am. Book award 1982), Invasion of the Book Envelopes, 1981, Bech Is Back, 1982, The Beloved, 1982, The Witches of Eastwick, 1984, Confessions of a Wild Bore, 1984, Roger's Version, 1986 (Nat. Book Critics Circle award nomination 1986), Trust Me, 1987, More Stately Mansions, 1987, S., 1988, Rabbit at Rest, 1990 (Pulitzer prize for fiction 1991, Nat. Book Critics Circle award 1991), Memories of the Ford Administration, 1992, Brazil, 1994, The Afterlife, 1994, In the Beauty of the Lilies, 1996, Toward the End of Time, 1997, Bech at Bay, 1998, Gertrude and Claudius, 2000, Licks of Love: Short Stories and a Sequel, Rabbit Remembered, 2000, The Complete Henry Bech, 2001, Seek My Face, 2002, The Early Stories 1953-75, 2003 (PEN/Faulkner award 2004), Villages, 2004, Terrorist, 2006; (non-fiction) Assorted Prose, 1965, On Meeting Authors, 1968, A Good Place, 1973, Picked-Up Pieces, 1975, Hub Fans Bid Kid Adieu, 1977, Talk from the Fifties, 1979, Ego and Art in Walt Whitman, 1980, Hawthorne's Creed, 1981, Hugging the Shore, 1983 (Nat. Book Critics Circle award 1984), Emersonianism, 1984, Just Looking, 1989, Self-Consciousness, 1989, Odd Jobs, 1991, Golf Dreams, 1996, More Matter, 1999, On Literary Biography, 1999, Still Looking: Essays on American Art, 2005, Due Considerations, 2007; (poetry) The Carpentered Hen and Other Tame Creatures, 1958, Telephone Poles, 1963, A Child's Calendar, 1965, The Angels, 1968, Bath after Sailing, 1968, Midpoint, 1969, Seventy Poems, 1972, Six Poems, 1973, Tossing and Turning, 1977, Sixteen Sonnets, 1979, Five Poems, 1980, Spring Trio, 1982, Jester's Dozen, 1984, Facing Nature, 1985, Collected Poems 1953-1993, 1993, A Helpful Alphabet of Friendly Objects, 1995, In the Cemetery High Above Shillington, 1996, Radiators, 1998, Americana, 2001, Not Cancelled Yet, 2003; adapter: (librettos) The Magic Flute, 1962, The Ring, 1964; (plays) Bottom's Dream, 1969, Three Texts from Early Ipswich, 1968, Buchanan Dying, 1974; author words and music: (with Gunther Schuller) The Fisherman and His Wife, 1970; editor: Pens and Needles, 1970, (with S. Ravenel) The Best American Short Stories 1984, 1984, A Century of Arts and Letters, 1998, (with K. Kenison) The Best Am. Short Stories of the Century, 1999, Karl Shapiro: Selected Poems, 2003. Recipient O. Henry First Short Story award, 1966, 91, MacDowell medal for literature, 1981, Medal of Honor for literature Nat. Arts Club, 1984, PEN/Malamud Meml. prize PEN/Faulker award Found., 1988, Nat. Medal of Arts, 1989, Harvard Arts medal, 1998, Nat. Book Found. award Lifetime Achievement, 1998, Nat. Humanities medal, 2003, Golden Plate award, Acad. Achievement, 2004, Rea award for the short story, 2006, Gold Medal Fiction, 2007; Guggenheim fellow, 1959. Mem. AAAL, Am. Acad. Arts. and Scis. Democrat. Episcopalian.

UPFAL, ELIEZER (ELI UPFAL), computer scientist, educator; b. Haifa, Israel, July 29, 1954; s. Moshe and Miriam Upfal; m. Liane L. Live, Sept. 3, 1994; children: Tamara L., Ilan M.L. BSc in Math. and Stats., Hebrew U., Jerusalem, 1980; MSc in Computer Sci., Weizmann Inst. Sci., Rehovot, Israel, 1980; PhD, Hebrew U., Jerusalem, 1983. Rsch. staff mem. and project mgr. IBM Rsch. Divsn., San Jose, Calif., 1985—97; prof. computer sci. Brown U., Providence, 1998—, chair computer sci., 2002—. Author: Probability and Computing, 2005. Recipient Outstanding Innovation Award, IBM, 1993, Levinson Prize in Math. Scis., The Weizmann Inst., 1994, IBM Rsch. Divsn. award, IBM, 1997. Fellow: IEEE (hon.), Assn. for Computing Machinery (hon.). Achievements include patents in field. Office: Brown University Dept Computer Sci 115 Waterman St Providence RI 02906 Office Phone: 401-863-7645. Office Fax: 401-863-7657. Business E-Mail: eli@cs.brown.edu.

UPGREN, ARTHUR REINHOLD, JR., astronomer, educator, writer; b. Mpls., Feb. 21, 1933; s. Arthur Reinhold and Marion (Andrews) U.; m. Joan Koswoski, Jan. 7, 1967; 1 child, Amy Joan. BA, U. Minn., 1955; MS, U. Mich., 1958; PhD, Case Western Res. U., 1961. Research assoc. Swarthmore Coll., Pa., 1961-63; astronomer U.S. Naval Obs., Washington, 1963-66; asst. prof. Wesleyan U., Middletown, Conn., 1966-73, assoc. prof., 1973-81, dir. Van Vleck Obs., 1973-93, John Monroe Van Vleck prof., 1981—, chmn. dept. astronomy, 1968-86, 90-93; v.p. Fund Astrophys. Research, NYC, 1973—, chmn. grants com., 1985—2005. Vis. lectr. U. Md., 1964-66, George Washington U., 1965-66, Thames Sci. Ctr., New London, Conn., 1990, 92; vis. prof. Yale U., 1979-80, sr. rsch. scientist, 1997—; adj. prof. U. Fla., 1984-99; outdoor lighting cons. Wesleyan U., 1991—, Vt. State Agy. Natural Resources, 1993-94; reviewer books in astronomy, meteorology, classical music and urban demographics. Author: Night Has a Thousand Eyes: A Naked-Eye Guide to the Sky, its Science and Lore, 1998; co-author (with Jurgen Stock): Weather: How it Works and Why It Matters, 2000, The Turtle and The Stars: Observations of an Earthbound Astronomer, 2002, Many Skies: Alternative Histories of the Sun, Moon, Planets, and Stars, 2004; editor: The Nearby Stars and the Stellar Luminosity Function, 1983, Mapping the Sky-Past Heritage and Future Directions, 1988, Star Catalogues: A Centennial Tribute to A.N. Vyssotsky, 1989, Fundamentals of Astronomy, 1990, Precision Photometry: Astrophysics of the Galaxy, 1991, Objective Prism and Other Surveys, 1991, Databases for Galactic Structure, 1993, Hot Stars in the Halo, 1994, New Developments in Array Technology and Applications, 1995, Anni Mirables: A Symposium Celebrating the 90th Birthday of Dorrit Hoffleit, 1997. Conn. state chair New Eng. Light Pollution Adv. Group, 1994—. Grantee NSF, 1967-99; fellow Wesleyan Ctr. for Humanities, 1996. Fellow Royal Astron. Soc.; mem. Internat. Astron. Union (commn. v.p. 1982-85, pres. commn. 24 1985-88), Am. Astron. Soc. (Harlow Shapley lectr. 1977—, vice-chmn. dynamical astronomy div. 1988-89, chmn. 1989-90, chmn. AAS com. on light pollution 2000-04), Astron. Soc. Pacific, Internat. Dark Sky Assn. (bd. dirs. 1997—).

UPHAM, STEADMAN, academic administrator, anthropologist, educator; b. Denver, Apr. 4, 1949; s. Albert Tyler and Jane Catherine (Steadman) U; m. Margaret Anne Cooper, Aug. 21, 1971; children: Erin Cooper, Nathan Steadman. BA in English Lit and Spanish, U. Redlands, Calif., 1971; MA in Anthropology, Ariz. State U., 1977, PhD in Anthropology, 1980. Dist. sales mgr. Ind. News Co. Inc., Los Angeles, 1971-72; regional sales mgr. Petersen Pub. Co, Los Angeles, 1972-74; archeologist, researcher Bur. Land Mgmt., Phoenix, 1979; research asst. Ariz. State U., Tempe, 1979-80; chief archeologist Soil Sytems Inc., Phoenix, 1980-81, N.Mex. State U., Las Cruces, N.Mex., 1981-85, asst. prof. to assoc. prof., 1982-87, assoc. dean, 1987-90; prof. anthropology, vice provost for rsch., grad. dean U. Oreg., Eugene, 1990—98; pres. Claremont Graduate Univ., Calif., 1998—2004, U. Tulsa, Okla., 2004—. Interim dir. Cultural Resources Mgmt. divsn. N.Mex. State U., Las Cruces, 1988; mem. exec. com. Assn. Grad. Schs., 1994—2004; bd. dirs. Coun. Grad. Schs., 1995—2004. Author: Polities and Power, 1982, A Hopi Social History, 1992; editor: Computer Graphics in Archaeology, 1979, Mogollon Variability, 1986, The Sociopolitical Structure of Prehistoric Southwest Societies, 1989, The Evolution of Political Systems, 1990; also articles. Advanced seminar grantee Sch. of Am. Rsch., 1987, research grantee NSF, 1979, 1984-85, Hist. Preservation grantee State of N.Mex., 1982-84, 1991, 92, Ford Found. 1991-92, U.S. Dept. Edn. 1991-93. Fellow Am. Anthropol. Assn.; mem. Nat. Phys. Sci. Consortium (pres. 1992-95), We. Assn. Grad. Schs. (pres. 1994-95), Assn. Grad. Schs. (exec. com. 1995—), Coun. Grad. Schs. (bd. dirs. 1995—). Office: Off of Pres Univ of Tulsa 600 S College Ave Tulsa OK 74104 Office Phone: 918-631-2305. E-mail: steadman-upham@utulsa.edu. *

UPMACIS, RITA KARINA, chemist; d. Janis and Herta Paulina Upmacis; m. Gerard Parkin, July 30, 1993; children: Lia Aleksandra Parkin, Catherine Emma Parkin. BS in Chemistry, U. Nottingham, England, 1983, PhD in Inorganic Chemistry, 1986. Postdoctoral fellow Calif. Inst. Tech., 1986—88; sr. rsch. chemist Rohm and Haas Co., Spring House, Pa., 1988—94; rsch. assoc. biochemistry Weill Med. Coll. Cornell U., NYC, 1994—97, instr. biochemistry, 1997—99, asst. prof. pathology and lab. medicine, 1999—2006, assoc. rsch. prof. pathology and lab. medicine, 2006—. Contbr. articles to profl. jours. Named Gertrude Cropper scholar, U. Nottingham, 1985; recipient Coop. award Sci. and Engring., ICI New Sci. Group, 1983—86, Sam Tallucci Quality award, Rohm and Haas Chem. Co., 1994; fellow, Weill Med. Coll. Cornell U., 1996—98, Calif. Inst. Tech., Pasadena, 1986—88; grantee Scientist Devel. award, Am. Heart Assn., 1997—2000, The Atorvastatin award, Parke-Davis and Pfizer, 1999—2001, External Rsch. Program award, Philip Morris USA Inc. and Philip Morris Internat., 2005—; Postdoctoral Fellowship award, Norman and Rosita Winston Found. Mem.: Am. Soc. Investigative Pathology, North Am. Vascular Biology Orgn., Am. Chem. Soc., Royal Soc. Chemistry. Achievements include patents for processes for the preparation, purification and stabilization of acrylic acid. Office: Weill Medical College of Cornell Univ 1300 York Avenue New York NY 10021 Home Phone: 212-932-2183; Office Phone: 212-746-6469. Business E-Mail: rupmacis@med.cornell.edu.

UPPOT, RAUL N., radiologist, researcher; s. Janardanan Ondan and Vijay Uppot; m. Darshana D. Dhananjayan, June 18, 2003. MD, La. State U., Shreveport, 1995. Diplomate Am. Bd. Radiology, 2003. Clin. and rsch. fellow Mass. Gen. Hosp., Boston, 2003—05, asst. radiologist, 2005—. Dir. abdominal imaging fellowship program Mass. Gen. Hosp., Boston, 2006—; asst. radiology clerkship dir. Harvard Med. Sch., Boston, 2006—. Achievements include research in impact of obesity on medical imaging. Office Phone: 617-726-2000.

UPRIGHT, DIANE WARNER, art dealer; b. Cleve. d. Rodney Upright and Shirley (Warner) Lavine. Student, Wellesley Coll., 1965-67; BA, U. Pitts., 1969; MA, U. Mich., 1973, PhD, 1976. Asst. prof. U. Va., Charlottesville, 1976-78; assoc. prof. Harvard U., Cambridge, Mass., 1978-83; sr. curator Ft. Worth Art Mus., 1984-86; dir. Jan Krugier Gallery, NYC, 1986-90; sr. v.p., head contemporary art dept. Christie's, NYC, 1990-95; pres. Diane Upright Fine Arts, NYC, 1995—. Author: Morris Louis: The Complete Paintings, 1979, Ellsworth Kelly: Works on Paper, 1987, various exhbn. catalogues; contbr. articles to art jours. Mem.: Art Table, Inc. Office: Diane Upright Fine Arts 188 E 76th St New York NY 10021-2826

UPRIGHT, KIRBY GRANT, lawyer; b. South Canaan, Pa., Sept. 12, 1946; s. Lyle Lee and Ellen May (Kirby) U.; m. Joyce Ann Keyasko, Oct. 4, 1975; children: Chad, Scott. BS, Pa. State U., 1970; JD, U. Akron, 1973; LLM in Taxation, Temple U., 1977. Bar: Pa. 1973, U.S. Dist. Ct. (mid. dist.) Pa. 1978, U.S. Ct. Appeals (3d cir.) 1981, U.S. Tax Ct. 1979; CPA, Pa. Staff acct. Peat, Marwick, Mitchell, Phila., 1973-77; assoc. Henkleman, Kreder, O'Connell & Brooks, Scranton, Pa., 1977-82; ptnr. Young, Upright, Catina & Parker, Stroudsburg, Pa., 1982—2003; mem. King, Spry, Herman, Freund & Faul, LLC, Bethleham, Pa., 2004—. With U.S. Army, 1964-67, Vietnam. Fellow Am. Coll. Trust and Estate Counsel; mem. Pa. Bar Assn. (chmn. Real Property, Probate, and trust sect.), Pa. State U. Alumni Assn., Pocono Mountain Club (Stroudsburg, pres. 1982-85), Masons, Rotary (pres. 2005-), Penn State Planned Giving Adv. Coun. Home: 53 Wyndham Hills Cresco PA 18326-0053 also: 47 S Courtland St East Stroudsburg PA 18301-2826 Office Phone: 610-332-0390. Business E-Mail: kupright@kingspry.com.

UPSHAW, ANTHONY N., lawyer; b. Washington, July 3, 1960; BS, US Coast Guard Acad., 1982; JD, Univ. Miami, 1990. Bar: Fla. 1990, US Dist. Ct. (so., mid. dists.) Fla. 1991, US Dist. Ct. (ea. dist.) Wis., US Ct. Appeals, 11th cir. Ptnr., admiralty, maritime law, products liability def., litig. Adorno & Yoss, Miami, Fla. Former bd. dirs. Univ. Miami Sch. Law Alumni Assn. Lt. USCG, 1982—87. Mem.: Fla. Bar Assn., Dade County Bar Assn. (pres., young lawyers sect. 1995—96), ABA (bd. govs. 2006—). Office: Adorno & Yoss Ste 400 2525 Ponce de Leon Blvd Miami FL 33134 Office Phone: 305-460-1052. Office Fax: 305-460-1422. Business E-Mail: anu@adorno.com.

UPSHAW, GENE (EUGENE UPSHAW), sports association executive; b. Robstown, Tex., Aug. 15, 1945; s. Eugene and Cora (Riley) U.; 1 son, Eugene; m. Teresa Buich, 1986; children: Justin, Daniel. BS, Tex. A&I U., 1968; postgrad., Calif. State U., 1969, Golden Gate U., 1980. Player Oakland Raiders, 1967-82; player rep.-alt. NFL Players Assn., Oakland, Calif., 1970-76, mem. exec. com., 1976-80, pres., 1980-83, exec. dir., 1983—; ptnr. Gene Upshaw & Assocs., Mgmt. Cons. Firm, Oakland, Calif., 1970-78. Chmn. bd. NFL Players Inc., or Players Inc. Mem. Calif. Gov.'s Council Wellness and Phys. Fitness; mem. Calif. Bd. Govs. for Community Colls.; former planning commr. Alameda County, Calif., coordinator voter registration and fund raising. Served with U.S. Army, 1967-73. Named Offensive Lineman of Yr., Am. Football Conf., 1973, 74, 77, Lineman of Yr., NFL, 1977, Pro Bowl selection 6 times, All Pro selection Sporting News, 1967-77, All Pro selection UPI, 1967-77, All Pro selection AP, 1967-77, All Pro selection TV Guide, 1967-77, All Pro selection Profl. Football Writers, 1967-77; mem. NFL Championship Team, 1976, 1980; recipient Byron (Whizzer) White Humanitarian award NFL Players Assn., 1980, A. Philip Randolph A. Philip Randolph Inst., 1982; listed 13th in Top 100 Most Powerful People in Sports, Sporting News, 1993; Named one of Most Influential Black Americans, Ebony mag., 2006. Mem. Alpha Phi Alpha Democrat. Baptist. Office: NFL Players Assn 2021 L St NW Fl 6 Washington DC 20036-4909

UPSHAW, HARRY STEPHAN, psychologist, educator; b. Birmingham, Ala., July 10, 1926; s. N.H. and Florence (Arnold) U.; m. Paula Binyon, June 18, 1950; children: Alan Binyon, Phyllis, David Arnold, Stephan Lipner. Student, U. Ala., 1946-47; AB, U. Chgo., 1949; MA, Northwestern U., 1951; PhD, U. N.C., 1956. Asst prof. psychology U. Ala., 1954-57; spl. instr. psychology Simmons Coll., Boston, 1957-58; research asso. Ednl. Research Corp., Cambridge, Mass., 1957-58; asst. prof., then assoc. prof. pub. health U. N.C., 1958-61, lectr., assoc. prof. psychology, 1958-64, rsch. prof. psychology, 1991-97; assoc. prof. Bryn Mawr (Pa.) Coll., 1964-65; assoc. prof., then prof. emeritus psychology U. Ill., Chgo., 1965-91, prof. emeritus, 1991—, dept. head, 1968-72; assoc. dir. Office of Social Sci. Rsch., 1981-87. Guest prof. U. Mannheim, Germany, 1975, Fulbright scholar Technische U., Berlin, 1978-79; vis. scholar Inst. for Rsch. in Social Sci., U. NC, 1991-92; del. to South Africa, People to People Amb. Program, 2004. Editorial cons., Jour. Exptl. Social Psychology, Research in Personality, Jour. Applied Social Psychology, Jour. Personality Social Psychology; Contbr. articles to profl. jours. Served with AUS, 1944-46. Fellow Am. Psychol. Assn., Soc. Exptl. Social Psychol. Home: 155 N Harbor Dr Apt 1303 Chicago IL 60601-7397 Home Phone: 312-819-0408; Office Phone: 312-819-0408. Personal E-mail: hupshaw@uic.edu.

UPSON, DONALD V., retired corporate financial executive; b. Hutchinson, Kans., Feb. 8, 1934; s. William Ernest and Luella Beatrice (Hutchison) U.; m. Janis Carol Anderson, Sept. 16, 1956; children: Mark Steven, Brent William. BS, Kans. State U., 1956. C.P.A. With Peat, Marwick, Mitchell & Co., 1956, 60-81, ptnr., 1974-81; exec. v.p., dir. internal audit Del E. Webb Corp., Phoenix, 1981-85; mgr. info. systems Tiernay Turbines Inc., Phoenix, 1986; chief fin. officer Schomac Corp., Tucson, 1986-88; adminstr. U. Ariz., Tucson, 1988-90; pres., chief exec. officer Ariz. Commerce Bank, Tucson, 1990-91; chief fin. officer O'Connor, Cavanagh, Anderson, Westover, Killingsworth & Beshears, P.A., Phoenix, 1991-94; fin. cons., 1995-97; ret., 1997. Pres. Community Orgn. for Drug Abuse, Alcohol and Mental Health Services, Inc., 1977-78; bd. dis. Phoenix council Boy Scouts Am., elder Presbyterian Ch. Served to lt. USAF, 1956-59. Mem. Am. Inst. C.P.A.s, Ariz. Soc. C.P.A.s, Beta Theta Pi (pres. 1955-56) Republican. Home and Office: 1313 E Sheena Dr Phoenix AZ 85022-4485 Personal E-mail: dupson2@cox.net.

UPSON, STUART BARNARD, advertising agency executive; b. Cin., Apr. 14, 1925; s. Mark and Alice (Barnard) U.; m. Barbara Jussen, Nov. 2, 1946; children: Marguerite Nichols, Anne Marcus, Stuart Barnard. BS, Yale U., 1945. With Dancer, Fitzgerald, Sample, Inc., NYC, 1946-86, sr. v.p., 1963-66, exec. v.p., 1966-67, pres., 1967-74, chmn., 1974-86, DFS-Dorland, NYC, 1986-87; dir. Saatchi & Saatchi Inc., NYC, 1987—. Bd. dirs. Fresh Air Fund, N.Y., Advt. Coun. With USNR, 1943-46. Mem. St. Elmo Soc. Clubs: Wee Burn Country (Darien); Sky (N.Y.C.); Blind Brook, Pine Valley Golf, Ocean Forest Golf. Home: 16 Wrenfield Ln Darien CT 06820-2201 Office: Saatchi & Saatchi Inc 375 Hudson St New York NY 10014-3658

UPSON, THOMAS FISHER, judge, retired state senator, lawyer; b. Waterbury, Conn., Sept. 30, 1941; s. J. Warren and Grace (Fisher) U.; m. Barbara Secor (div. Jan. 1979); children: Secor, Chauncey Julius; m. Katherine Wolff, June 1, 1996. BA in History, Washington and Jefferson Coll., 1963; LLB, U. Conn., 1968; postgrad., Trinity Coll., 1969—72, Georgetown U., 1971—72. Bar: Conn., 1969, U.S. Dist. Ct. (2d dist.) 1969, U.S. Supreme Ct. 1973. Lawyer Upson & Secor, Waterbury, 1969—70, 1974—76; lawyer, spl. asst. U.S. Dept. Commerce, Washington, 1970—72; lawyer, spl. asst. to adminstr. GSA, Washington, 1973—74; dir. admissions St. Margaret's McTernan Sch., Waterbury, 1977—78; with divsn. spl. revenue State of Conn., Hartford, 1978—82; assoc. Moynahan & Ruskin, Waterbury, 1979—81; ptnr. Upson & Daly, Waterbury, 1981—2001; mem. Conn. Senate, Hartford, 1985—2001, chmn. gen. law com., vice-chmn. jud. com., majority whip, 1985—86, asst. minority leader, 1987-88, 89-90, minority leader protempore, 1991-92, dep. minority leader, 1993-94, dep. majority leader, chmn. jud. com., 1995-96, dep., then asst. minority leader, ranking mem. jud. com., 1997-2000; judge Superior Ct. State of Conn., Hartford, 2001—. Moderator 1st Congl. Ch., Waterbury, 1986-91; bd. dirs. Easter Seals-United Way, Waterbury, 1984-88; Rep. candidate for Congress, 6th Dist. Conn., 1976; mem. Conn. Rep. Ctrl. com., 1983-91; mem. Waterbury Rep. Town Com., 1980-85; dir. Mattatuck Mus., 1993-2003; former dir. Waterbury Symphony Orch.; former sec. and dir. First Ch. Housing, Inc.; pres. Naugatuck Valley Devel. Corp., 1975-76. Mem. ABA, Conn. Bar Assn., Waterbury Bar Assn., SAR, Soc. Colonial Wars, Soc. of the Founders of the Hartford, Phi Gamma Delta, Univ. Club (Waterbury). Lodges: Kiwanis (former pres., lt. gov. SW New Eng. dist.), Elks. Republican. Congregationalist. Avocations: hiking, music, history. Home: 210 Southwest Rd Waterbury CT 06708-3214 Office: Waterbury Jud Dist 300 Grand St Waterbury CT 06702

UPTON, ARTHUR CANFIELD, experimental pathologist, educator; b. Ann Arbor, Mich., Feb. 27, 1923; s. Herbert Hawkes and Ellen (Canfield) Upton; m. Elizabeth Bache Perry, Mar. 1, 1946; children: Rebecca A., Melissa P., Bradley C. Grad., Phillips Acad., Andover, Mass., 1941; BA, U. Mich., 1944, MD, 1946. Intern Univ. Hosp., Ann Arbor, 1947, resident, 1948—49; instr. pathology U. Mich. Med. Sch., 1950—51; pathologist Oak Ridge (Tenn.) Nat. Lab., 1951—54, chief pathology-physiology sect., 1954—69; prof. pathology SUNY Med. Sch. at Stony Brook, 1969—77, chmn. dept. pathology, 1969—70, dean Sch. Basic Health Scis., 1970—75; dir. Nat. Cancer Inst., Bethesda, Md., 1977—79; prof., chmn. dept. environ. medicine NYU Med. Sch., NYC, 1980—92, prof. emeritus, 1993—; clin. prof. radiology U. N.Mex. Sch. Medicine, 1993—95, clin. prof. pathology, 1992—95; clin. prof. environ. and cmty. medicine U. Medicine and Dentistry N.J.-Robert Wood Johnson Med. Sch., 1995—. Attending pathologist Brookhaven Nat. Lab., 1969—77; dir. Inst. Environ. Medicine, Med. Sch., NYU, 1980—92; mem. various coms. nat. and internat. orgns.; lectr. in field; mem. adv. bd. GM Cancer Rsch. Found. Assoc. editor Cancer Rsch., mem. editl. bd. Internat. Union Against Cancer. With US Army, 1943—46. Named nat. lectr., Sigma Xi, 1989—91; recipient Ernest Orlando Lawrence award for atomic field, 1965, Claude M. Fuess award, 1980, Sarah L. Poilley award for pub. health, 1983, CHUMS Physician of Yr. award, 1985, Basic Cell Rsch. in Cytology Lectureship award, 1985, Fred W. Stewart award, 1986, Ramazzini award, 1986, Lovelace Med. Found. award, 1993. Fellow: N.Y. Acad. Sci., Soc. Risk Analysis (Outstanding Achievement award 1997); mem.: AAAS, Ramazzini Inst. (pres. 1992—2003), Assn. Univ. Environ. Health Sci. Ctrs. (pres. 1982—90), Internat. Assn. Radiation Rsch., N.Y. State Health Rsch. Coun. (chmn. 1982—90), Soc. Exptl. Biology and Medicine, Sci. Rsch. Soc. Am., Gerontol. Soc., Peruvian Oncology Soc. (hon.), Japan Cancer Assn. (hon.), Am. Soc. Exptl. Pathology (pres. 1967—68), Am. Assn. Cancer Rsch. (pres. 1963—64), Internat. Assn. Radiation Rsch. (pres. 1983—87, 1983—87), Radiation Rsch. Soc. (councilor 1963—64, pres. 1965—66), Inst. Medicine of NAS (Comfort-Crookshank award for cancer rsch. 1979), Internat. Acad. Pathology, Am. Assn. Pathologists and Bacteriologists, Sigma Xi, Nu Sigma Nu, Alpha Omega Alpha, Phi Gamma Delta, Phi Beta Kappa. Achievements include research in on pathology of radiation injury and endocrine glands, on cancer, on carcinogenesis, on experimental leukemia on aging. Home (Winter): 250 E Alameda Apt 636 Santa Fe NM 87501 Home (Summer): 780 West End Ave Apt 20 New York NY 10025 Office: 303 George St Ste 110 New Brunswick NJ 08901 Office Phone: 732-235-3460. Business E-Mail: acupton@cresp.org.

UPTON, B.J. (MELVIN EMANUEL UPTON), professional baseball player; b. Norfolk, Va., Aug. 21, 1984; d. Manny and Yvonne Upton. Shortstop Tampa Bay Devil Rays, 2004—05, third baseman, 2006—07, second baseman, ctr. fielder, 2007—. Named #1 Prospect, Baseball Am., 2004. Achievements include being the youngest player in the major leagues in 2004; becoming the youngest Devil Ray in franchise history. Mailing: Tropicana Field One Tropicana Dr Saint Petersburg FL 33705 Office Phone: 727-825-3137. *

UPTON, FREDERICK STEPHEN, congressman; b. St. Joseph, Mich., Apr. 23, 1953; s. Stephen E. and Elizabeth Brooks (Vial) U.; m. Amey Richmond Rulon-Miller, Nov. 5, 1983; 2 children. BA in Journalism, U. Mich., 1975. Staff asst. to Congressman David A. Stockman, Washington, 1976-81; legis. asst. Office Mgmt. and Budget, Washington, 1981-83, dep. dir. legis. affairs, 1983-84, dir. legis. affairs, 1984-85; mem. US Congress from 6th Mich. dist., Washington, 1987—; mem. energy and commerce com. Field mgr. Stockman for Congress, St. Joseph, 1975; campaign mgr. Globensky for Congress, St. Joseph, 1981. Recipient Spirit Enterprise award, US C. of C., 1988—93, Legis. of Yr., Am. Ambulance Assn., 2000. Mem.: Emil Verban Soc. Republican. Congregationalist. Office: US House of Reps 2183 Rayburn House Office Bldg Washington DC 20515-2206 also: District Office 157 S Kalamazoo Mall Ste 180 Kalamazoo MI 49006 also: District Office Ste 106 800 Ship Street Saint Joseph MI 49085-2182 Office Phone: 202-225-3761, 269-385-0039, 269-982-1986. Office Fax: 269-982-0237, 202-225-4986. *

UPTON, HOWARD B., JR., writer, lawyer; b. Tahlequah, Okla., May 17, 1922; s. Howard B. and Marjorie (Ross) U.; m. Jean Devereaux, June 14, 1945; children— Pamela, Barbara, Martha, Brian BA, U. Okla., 1943, LLB, 1948. Cert. assn. exec. Dir. indsl. relations Western Petroleum Refiners Assn., Tulsa, 1948-51; exec. v.p. Petroleum Equipment Inst., Tulsa, 1951-87; dir. Telex Corp., Tulsa, 1972-88; mgmt. columnist Inflight Mag. of Southwest Airlines, 1988-93. Lectr. dept. engring. profl. devel. U. Wis., 1988-97, U. Alaska, Fairbanks, 1991-93. Frequent contbr. to Wall St.

Jour.; columnist Petroleum Equipment and Tech. Mag.; book rev. Tulsa World, 1999--. Dir. Tulsa Zoo Friends, Inc., 1993-97. Mem. Am. Soc. Assn. Execs. (bd. dirs. 1964-68, Gold Circle award 1977, 82), Okla. Bar Assn. Home: 5133 E 25th Ct Tulsa OK 74114-3749

UPTON, RICHARD THOMAS, artist; b. Hartford, Conn., May 27, 1931; s. Ray Granville and Helen Marie (Colla) U.; 1 son, Richard Thomas, II. BFA, U. Conn., 1960; MFA, Ind. U., 1963. Artist-in-residence Artists for the Environ., Del. Water Gap, 1972, UGA Program Abroad, Cortona, Italy, 1982-85. Numerous exhibns. including most recently, exhibitions include Condeso/Lawler Gallery, N.Y.C., 1995, Nat. Acad. of Design, 1996, The Language of Landscape, 1997, Sordoni Art Gallery, 1997, The Drawings of Richard Upton: Ireland & Italy, List Art Gallery, Swarthmore, Ben Shahn Art Galleries, 1998, Landscape and Memory: The Paintings and Drawings of Richard Upton, 1982-1999, Houghton Gallery, The Cooper Union for the Advancement of Sci. and Art, N.Y.C., 1999, Selby Gallery, 2006, Represented in permanent collections Zimmerli Art Mus., Nat. Mus. of Am. Art, Smithsonian Instn., Mus. Modern Art, N.Y.C., Victoria and Albert Mus., London, Bibliot Nat., Paris, Montreal Mus. Fine Arts, Rose Art Mus. Brandeis, Mus. Fine Art, Houston, Nat. Acad. Design, N.Y.C., Met. Mus. Art, The Tang Tchg. Mus. and Art Gallery, Skidmore Coll.; artist (commns. include) Eros Thanatos Suite (German poem and woodcuts), Interlaken Corp., Providence, 1967, Salamovka Poster, Okla. Art Ctr., 1974, artist (with poems by Stanley Kunitz) River Road Suite, 1976, suite of drawing Robert Lowell at 66, 1977, suite of drawings Salmagundi mag. for humanities, The Anxious Landscape, paintings, drawings Bellarmine Coll., Louisville, 1989; one-man shows include 20th Anniv. Exhbt., Selby Gallery, 2007. With USNR, 1950-54. Recipient designer award Interlaken Corp., 1967; subject of monographs: Richard Upton and the Rhetoric of Landscape, Paul Hayes Tucker, U. Mass., U. Wash. Press, 1991, The Tuscan Landscapes of Richard Upton, Stanley C. Grand, Sordoni Art Gallery & Fred Licht, curator, Collezione Peggy Guggenheim, Venice, Wilkes U., 1997, The Drawings of Richard Upton, David Shapiro, Salmagundi, Skidmore Coll., 1997, Landscape & Memory: The Paintings & Drawings of Richard Upton, 1982-98, The Irwin S. Chanin Sch. Architecture of Cooper Union, 1999, A Table of Green Fields: Richard Upton's Cortona Landscapes, Richard Howard, 1999, List Gallery, Ben Shahn Galleries About Painting; Tang Teaching Mus. Art Gallery, 2004; fellow Fulbright Found., 1964, Ballinglen Arts Found., Ireland, 1994; grantee Nat. Endowment for Arts/Artists for Environ., 1972, Richard Florsheim Fund, 1992; elected to Nat. Acad. of Design, 1995, Tang Teaching Mus. and Art Gallery, 2004. Home: 1 North Ln Saratoga Springs NY 12866-4369

UPTON, WADE, energy executive; Mem. staff to sr. v.p. transp. svcs. Valero Energy Corp., San Antonio, 1984—. State fuel coord., Tex. Bd. dirs. Waterways Coun., Inc. Office: Valero Energy Corpn 1 Valero Way San Antonio TX 78292-0500 Office Phone: 210-345-2555. E-mail: wade.upton@valero.com.

URABE, TOHSUKE, mathematics professor, researcher; b. Tokyo, Aug. 3, 1953; s. Syun-ichi and Mariko (Namikawa) U.; m. Yasuko Ichikawa, May 25, 1986; 1 child, Mika. BA, Kyoto U., Japan, 1978, MA, 1980, PhD in Math., 1984. Sci. worker Max-Planck Inst. for Math., Bonn, Germany, 1987-89, 98-99; assoc. prof. math. Tokyo Met. U., 1981-87, 89-98; prof. math. Ibaraki (Japan) U., 1999—. Author: (with Heisuke Hironaka) Introduction to Analytic Spaces, 1981; Dynkin Graphs and Quadrilateral Singularities, 1993. Avocations: mountain climbing, personal computers. Office: Ibaraki U Dept Math Scis Mito Ibaraki 310-8512 Japan

URAM, GERALD ROBERT, lawyer; b. Newark, July 11, 1941; s. Arthur George and Mildred (Stein) U.; m. Melissa Gordon, May 27, 1995; children: Michael, Alison, Carolyn Gordon Lewis. BA, Dartmouth Coll., 1963; LLB, Yale U., 1967. Bar: NY 1967. Assoc. Paul, Weiss, Rifkind, Wharton & Garrison, NYC, 1967-74; v.p., corp. counsel Prudential Bldg. Maintenance Corp., NYC, 1974; ptnr. Davis & Gilbert, NYC, 1974—. Lectr. NY Law Sch. Contbr. to profl. pubs. Bd. dirs. St. Francis Friends of Poor, Inc. Mem. ABA, NY State Bar Assn., Assn. Bar City of NY. Office: 1740 Broadway Fl 3 New York NY 10019-4315 Home Phone: 212-794-3914; Office Phone: 212-468-4815. Business E-Mail: guram@dglaw.com.

URAZGHILDIIEV, ILDAR R., mathematician; b. Belushye, Arkhangelsk Reg., Russia, Sept. 22, 1967; s. Ravil I. Urazgildiyev and Iraida F. Urazgildiyeva; m. Tetiana V. Bruenko, Aug. 21, 2002; 1 child, Renat I. Urazgildiiev. MS (hon.), Inst. Radioelectronics, Zhitomir, Ukraine, 1989; PhD, 1996. Rsch. assoc. Gen. Staff Rsch. Ctr. Armed Forces, Ukraine, 1989—94; scientist Gen. Stat. Rsch. Ctr. Armed Forces, Ukraine, 1994—97; leading scientist Nat. Rsch. Ctr. Def. Tech. and Mil. Security, Ukraine, 1997—2001; asst. prof. Nat. Tech. U. Ukraine, Kiev, 1999—2003; rsch. assoc. Cornell Lab Ornithology, Ithaca, NY, 2004—. Contbr. scientific papers to profl. jours. Recipient Young Scientist award Best Conf. Paper, MMET2000 Conf., 2000, Young Scientist award, URSI, 2002; fellow, Sensys Traffic AB, Sweden., 2001—02, Carl Trygger Found., Sweden, 2003—04, Uppsala U., Signals and Systems Group, Sweden, 2003—04. Mem.: IEEE. Home: 606 Winston CT apt 2 Ithaca NY 14850 Office: Cornell Lab of Ornithology BRP 159 Sapsucker Woods Rd Ithaca NY 14850 Office Phone: 607-254-2126. E-mail: iru2@cornell.edu.

URBACH, ADAM ROBERT, chemistry professor; s. Michael Urbach and Rose Marie Mauzy; m. Dana Michelle Norwood, June 11, 2000; 1 child, Sebastian River. BS in Chemistry, U. Tex., Austin, 1996; PhD in Chemistry, Calif. Inst. Tech., Pasadena, 2002. Postdoctoral rsch. fellow Harvard U., Cambridge, Mass., 2002—04. Faculty adviser Am. Chem. Soc. Student Affiliates, Trinity U., San Antonio, 2004—; asst. prof. chemistry Trinity U., San Antonio, San Antonio, 2006—. Contbr. articles to sci. jours. Judge Jr. Acad. of Sci., San Antonio, 2006. Recipient Dean's Honored Grad. award, Coll. Natural Sci., U. Tex., Austin, 1996, Nat. Rsch. Svc. award, NIH, 2003—04, Cottrell Coll. Sci. award, Rsch. Corp., 2006—08, Disting. Jr. Faculty award, Trinity U., 2007; Summer Undergrad. Fellowship, Pfizer Inc., 1995, grad. fellowship, NSF, 1996—99, Type G grant, Am. Chem. Soc. Petroleum Rsch. Fund, 2005—07. Mem.: Project Kaleidoscope, Coun. on Undergrad. Rsch., Am. Chem. Soc. (Outstanding Sr. award cen. Tex. divsn. 1996, student affiliate scholarship 1995), Phi Beta Kappa. Achievements include research in bioorganic chemistry and molecular recognition; artificial receptors and sensors for proteins. Avocations: snowboarding, skiing, skateboarding, rock climbing. Office: Trinity Univ Dept Chemistry One Trinity Pl San Antonio TX 78212 Home Phone: 210-999-7660; Office Phone: 210-999-7660. Business E-Mail: adam.urbach@trinity.edu.

URBAN, AMANDA (BINKY URBAN), literary agent; m. Ken Auletta, 1977; 1 child. BA in English, Wheaton Coll., Mass. Gen. mgr. N.Y. mag.; editl. mgr. Esquire mag.; literary agent Internat. Creative Mgmt., NYC, v.p., co-dir. lit. dept., 1988—98, co-head, 1999—2006, exec. v.p., 2007—. Named one of 100 Most Powerful Women in Entertainment, Hollywood Reporter, 2006. Office: Internat Creative Mgmt 825 8th Ave New York NY 10019 E-mail: aurban@icmtalent.com. *

URBAN, DIANE, psychologist, educator; b. Queens, NY, June 27, 1954; d. Jerome and Carmela Chiappise; m. Walter Urban, Dec. 29, 1979; children: Nicholas, Amanda. BA, Queens Coll., 1976; MA, St. John's U., Queens, NY, 1979; PhD, New Sch. U., NYC, 1987. Lic. psychologist N.Y. Asst. prof. Westchester C.C., Valhalla, NY, 1980—; instr. Manhattan Coll., Riverdale, NY, 2004—. Active Westchester Emergency Vol. Res., Med. Res. Corps. Mem.: APA. Home: 106 Eastview Dr Valhalla NY 10595 Home Phone: 914-769-0109.

URBAN, DONALD WAYNE, lawyer; b. Belleville, Ill., Oct. 9, 1953; s. Andrew Anthony and Eileen Marie (Tibbitt) U.; m. Mary Beth Evans, June 9, 1979 (div. Oct. 1994); m. Georgianna Dowling, Feb. 2, 1995; 1 child, Andrew Jared. BA, So. Ill. U., 1976; JD, Washington U., 1979. Assoc. Sprague & Sprague, Belleville, 1979-96; ptnr. Sprague & Urban, Belleville, 1996—. Author, lectr. Ill. Inst. for CLE, Springfield. Author: Blasting & Subsidence Illinois Institute for Continuing Legal Education Handbook, 1983, vol. 2, 1986, vol. 3, 1989. Pres. Looking Glass Playhouse, Lebanon, Ill., 1988-90, 95-97, 99-01, 04-05; spokesman St. Clair County Bicentennial, Belleville, 1989. Mem. Gamma Theta Upsilon. Democrat. Avocation: community theatre. Home: 815 Belleville St Lebanon IL 62254-1312 Office: Sprague & Urban 26 E Washington St Belleville IL 62220-2101 Home Phone: 618-537-2544; Office Phone: 618-233-8383.

URBAN, HENRY ZELLER, publishing executive; b. Buffalo, July 11, 1920; s. George Pennock and Florence Lenhard (Zeller) U.; m. Ruth deMoss Wickwire, Apr. 28, 1948; children: Ruth Robinson Urban Smith, Florence de Moss Urban Hunn, Henry Zeller, Ward Wickwire. Grad., Hotchkiss Sch., 1939; BS, Yale U., 1943. Treas. George Urban Milling Co., 1946-53; with Buffalo Eve. News, 1953—, asst. bus. mgr., 1957-62, bus. mgr., 1962-71, treas., dir., 1971-74, pres., pub., 1974-83. Bd. dirs. Travelers Aid Soc., 1953-59, Buffalo Fine Arts Acad., 1960-63, 73-76, 82-89, YMCA, 1955-68; trustee Elmwood-Franklin Sch., 1967-70; trustee Canisius Coll., 1977-83, bd. regents, 1972-78; adv. bd. Medaille Coll., 1968-83; chmn. parents council Hamilton Coll., 1977. Lt. USNR, 1942-46. Mem. Buffalo C. of C., N.Y. State Pubs. Assn. (dir. 1970-73, 76-79) Clubs: Mid-day (Buffalo), Tennis and Squash (Buffalo), Buffalo (Buffalo), Buffalo Country (Buffalo), Saturn (Buffalo), Pack (Buffalo); Sankaty Head (Nantucket); Nantucket Yacht. Home: 57 Tudor Pl Buffalo NY 14222-1615 Office: 1 News Plz Buffalo NY 14203-2930

URBAN, JOSEPH JAROSLAV, engineer, consultant; b. Chocen, Czechoslovakia, Mar. 11, 1922; came to U.S., 1955; s. Josef and Ludmila (Moravcova) U.; children: H.U. Heinicke, R. Bruce. Diploma in engring., U. Prague, Czechoslovakia, 1948; postgrad., U. Toronto, 1952-55. Registered profl. engr. Mgr. Urban Mfg., Chocen, 1942-48; prof. Masaryk U., Ludwigsburg, Germany, 1950; designer C.A. Meadows Cons. Engrs., Toronto, 1952-55, Rondo Devel. Corp., Stamford, Conn., 1955-58; designer, chief engr., v.p. Huck Co. Inc. Engrs., Montvale, NJ, 1958-72, also bd. dirs.; pvt. practive cons. engr. Pleasantville, NY, 1972—. Exec. cons. Crown Cork and Seal Co. Inc., Phila., 1972=94. Designer various types of machines for U.S. govt. and U.S. industries-printing presses, book binding and can mfg. equipment, pinsetter, computers, glass machines; writer tech. books; patentee in field. Recipient World War II decoration Field Marshall Alexander, 1945., Outstanding Person 20th Century Internat. Biographical Ctr., Eng, named one of top 100 scientists, 2005. Mem. Acad. Art and Sci., Moose, K.C. (worthy sir knight). Roman Catholic. Avocations: naturalist, painting, classical music, fine art collector. Home and Office: 71 Bacon Hill Rd Pleasantville NY 10570-3501

URBAN, KEITH, country singer, songwriter; b. New Zealand, Oct. 26, 1967; m. Nicole Kidman, June 25, 2006. Former band mem. (with Peter Clarke) The Ranch, Nashville, 1997; signed record deal with Capital Nashville, 1997; signed mgmt. contract with I.R.S., Tenn., 1997. Singer: (albums) Keith Urban "1991", 1997, Ranch, 1997, Keith Urban, 1999, Golden Road, 2002, In the Ranch, 2004, Be Here, 2004 (Album of Yr., Acad. Country Music Awards, 2005), Days Go By, 2005, (singles) Raining on Sunday, 2003; singer, prodr.: singles "Somebody Like You", How To Lose A Guy In 10 Days (Original Soundtrack), 2003; singer: (songs) Days Go By (Video of Yr., Country Music Television Music award, 2005), You'll Think of Me (Grammy award, Best Male Country Vocal Performance, 2006). Named Top New Male Vocalist, Acad. Country Music, 2001, 2005, Top Male Vocalist, 2006, Male Vocalist of Yr., Country Music Assn., 2004—06, Entertainer of Yr., 2005, Country Artist Yr., Radio Music Awards, 2005, Best-Selling Australian Artist, World Music Awards, 2007; recipient Grammy award nomination for best country instrumental performance for "Rollercoaster", ARIA award for outstanding achievement, Australian Record Industry Assn., 2001, Horizon award, Country Music Assn., 2001, Video of Yr for Better Life, CMT award (Country Music TV), 2006. Mailing: Capital Records 3322 W End Ave Nashville TN 37203 Office Phone: 615-269-2000. *

URBAN, RICHARD J., library and information scientist; BA in History with honors, Pa. State U., 1993; MA in History, U. Del., 1997; MS in Libr. and Info. Sci., U. Ill., Urbana-Champaign, 2006, student. Grad. tchg. asst. Dept. Hist. U. Del., 1995—96; adj. faculty Coll. Edn., Libr. and Info. Sci. Prog. U. Denver, 2005—; jr. fellow Manuscripts Divsn. Libr. of Congress, Washington, 1993; libr. tech. Smithsonian Inst. Libraries, Washington, 1993—95; asst. cur. Hist. Soc. Del., Wilmington, Del., 1997—2000; web site coord. Hist. Soc. Pa., Phila., 2000—02; instr. Collaborative Digitization Prog. Workshops, 2002—06, ops. coord., 2002—05; grad. rsch. asst. ECHO Depository Project U. Ill., Urbana-Champaign, 2005—06, metadata ecologist WILL Radio/TV, 2006; grad. asst. Ill. Digitization Inst. U. Ill. Libr., 2005—06, project coord. Metadata for You & Me: Tng. Prog. for Shareable Metadata, 2006—. Cons. Friends of Margaret Rose Henry, Sokola For Senate; cons. Preservation Del., Inc. Save Outdoor Sculpture Inventory; cons. Christiana Sch. Dist.; cons. Southern NY Libr. Resources Consortium Hudson River Valley Heritage. Author: The City That Launched a Thousand Ships: Shipbuilding in Wilmington 1644-1997, 1999, Reflections of Dravo: The Dravo Oral History Project, 2001. Recipient Jane B. and Robert B. Downs Profl. Promise award, 2006; Rare Books and Manuscripts Preconference Scholarship, 2006. Mem.: Visual Resources Assn., Mus. Computer Network (chmn. digital media 2003—05, chmn. conf. publicity 2004—06, chmn. conf. workshop 2005, mem. joint blog com. 2006—07, mem. website com. 2006—, chmn. membership com. 2007, bd. mem. 2004—), Am. Soc. Info. Sci. and Tech., Am. Assn. Museums. Office: Grad Sch Libr and Info Sci Univ Ill 501 E Daniel St MC 493 Champaign IL 61820 Office Phone: 217-333-3280. Office Fax: 217-244-3302. E-mail: rjurban@uiuc.edu.

URBAN, THEODORE W., lawyer, brokerage house executive; b. 1950; BSEE, Cornell Univ.; JD, Catholic Univ. Bar: Md. 1974. Asst. dir. SEC Div. Market Regulation; dep. dir. CFTC Div. Trading & Markets; exec. v.p., gen. counsel Ferris Baker Watts, Balt., 1984—. Mem. NASD Nat. Adjudicatory Council; chmn. Trust Corp. Am. Dir. Tonley Found. Office: Ferris Baker Watts 100 Light St Baltimore MD 21202 Office Phone: 410-468-2720.

URBANETTI, JOHN SUTHERLAND, internist, consultant; b. Mineola, NY, Aug. 14, 1943; s. Anthony Joseph and Mildred S. U.; children: Andrew, Alexis. AB, Johns Hopkins U., 1964, MD, 1967. Diplomate Am. Bd. Internal Medicine and Pulmonary Diseases. Internal medicine intern Johns Hopkins Hosp., Balt., 1967-68, internal medicine resident, 1968-69; fellow in pulmonary cardiology McGill U., Montreal, Can., 1971-74; asst. prof. medicine and dir. pulmonary lab. Tufts New Eng. Med. Ctr. Hosp., Boston, 1974-80; asst. prof. clin. medicine and pulmonary diseases Yale U., New Haven, Conn., 1980—. Cons. toxic inhalation US Surgeon Gen., U.S. Army, USN, USAF, 1974—; cons. biochem. terrorism Dept. of Def., Dept. Justice, 1974—, Dept. State, 1999—. Author: Carbon Monoxide Poisoning, 1980, Pulmonary Management of Surgical Patients, 1982, Battlefield Chemical Inhalation, 1988, Chemical and Biological Warfare, 1997; contbr. articles to profl. jours. Capt. USAF, 1969-71. Recipient Commdr's award for pub. svc. U.S. Army, 1990. Fellow Royal Coll. Physicians and Surgeons (Can.), Am. Coll. Physicians, Am. Coll. Chest Physicians; mem. Am. Thoracic Soc., Aerospace Medicine Soc. Avocation: swimming. Office: Southeastern Pulmonary Assocs 155 Montauk Ave New London CT 06320-4842 Office Phone: 860-444-2223. Business E-Mail: jsu@jhu.edu.

URBANIK, THOMAS, II, civil engineering educator, researcher; b. Oceanside, NY, Feb. 15, 1946; s. John George and Helen Rita (Waterhouse) U.; m. Cynthia Ellen Myers, Feb. 23, 1948; children: Michael T., Steven J. BS, N.Y. State Coll. Forestry, 1968; BSCE, Syracuse U., 1969; MSCE, Purdue U., 1971; PhD, Tex. A&M U., 1982. Registered profl. engr., Mich., Tex., Tenn. Traffic engr. City of Ann Arbor (Mich.), 1971-76; rsch. engr. Tex. A&M U., College Station, 1977—2001; prof., Goodrich chair of excellence in transp. U. Tenn., Knoxville, 2001—. Cons. Battelle Pacific N.W. Labs., Richland, Wash., Fed. Hwy. Adminstrn., Washington, Kittelson and Assocs., Portland, Oreg., Entergy, Buchanan, NY. Mem. ASCE, Inst. Transp. Engrs., Transp. Rsch. Bd. (assoc.). Republican. Lutheran. Office Phone: 865-974-7709. Business E-Mail: turbanik@utk.edu.

URBANO, JUAN ANTONIO, broadcast executive, television producer, television director; b. Havana, Cuba, Jan. 5, 1968; s. Antonio and Nereyda (Perez) Urbano; m. Veronica Delgado; children: Christian Michael children: John Anthony. AS in Film Prodn., Miami Dade C.C. Creative svcs. editor WSVN Channel 7, Miami Beach, Fla., 1988—94; prodr., editor Visionline, Inc., Miami, Fla., 1994—2005; sr. prodr., sr. editor MGM Networks L.Am. LLC, Miami, Fla., 1999—, promotions mgr., 2002—03, promotions and opers. mgr., 2003—04; prodr., editor MTV Networks Latin Am., 2004—. Recipient Suncoast Regional Emmy, NATAS, 1997, 1998. Mem.: Nat. Acad. of Arts and Scis. Roman Catholic. Avocations: scuba diving, camping, travel. Office Phone: 308-934-2740. Personal E-mail: urbanob@bellsouth.net. E-mail: juanurbano@bellsouth.net.

URBANOWICZ, E(UGENE) PETER, (JR.), lawyer; b. NYC, Jan. 26, 1964; BA in English and Polit. Sci., Tulane U., 1985, JD, 1989. Bar: La. 1989, US Dist. Ct. (ea, mid. and we. dists. La.) 1989, US Supreme Ct. 2003. Ptnr. Monroe & Lemann, New Orleans, 1987—98, Liskow & Lewis, New Orleans, 1998—2000, Locke, Liddell & Sapp, New Orleans, 2000—01; dep. gen. counsel US Health and Human Svcs., 2001—03; gen. counsel Tenet Healthcare Corp., Dallas, 2003—. Mem. ABA, Am. Law Inst., La. Bar Assn., Am. Health Lawyers Assn., Supreme Ct. Hist. Soc., Delta Tau Delta, Omicron Delta Kappa. Republican. Episcopalian. Office: Tenet Healthcare 13737 Noel Rd Ste 100 Dallas TX 75240 *

URBANOWSKI, JOHN RICHARD, lighting systems company official; b. Jamaica, NY, May 31, 1947; s. John Casimir and Alfreda (Dabrowski) U.; m. Linda Holmes, Dec. 17, 1967 (div. June 1973); 1 child, Richard. BA, U. South Fla., 1968. Cert. lighting profl. Nat. Coun. Qualifications for Lighting Professions. Ptnr. Freeman Assocs., Ft. Lauderdale, Fla., 1972-76; sales engr. Holophane Lighting Co., Portland, Oreg., 1977—. Author computer program Microlux, 1984. With USN, 1969-72. Mem. Illuminating Engring. Soc. (bd. dirs. 1981-86, 96-98, pres. 1983-84, Cert. Tech. Knowledge 1996, lighting cert. 1998), Holophane Lighting Co. Dir.'s Club, Founder's Club, Quarter Century Club. Unitarian Universalist. Avocations: writing, aviation. Office: Holophane Lighting Co 3015 NE Couch St Portland OR 97232 Personal E-mail: jurbanowski@comcast.net.

URBANOWSKI, MELENA HASKOVEC, elementary school educator; b. Waukon, Iowa, May 10, 1976; d. Melvin William and Edna Lena Haskovec; m. Jesse J. Urbanowski, June 10, 2006. BA in Elem. and Early Childhood Edn., U. No. Iowa, 1998, MS in Literacy Edn., 2003. Lic. tchr. Iowa, 1998, cert. Nat. Bd. Profl. Tchg. Stds., 2006. Tchr. Gladbrook Elem. Sch., Gladbrook, Iowa, 1998—2004, Van Buren Elem. Sch., Cedar Rapids, Iowa, 2004—. Asst. camp dir. Girl Scouts, Dorchester, Iowa, 2002. Girl scout trainer Conestoga Coun. of Girl Scouts, Waterloo, Iowa, 1997—2006. Grantee, McElroy Excellence in Edn. Enrichment grantee, 2002—03; scholar Purple and Gold Merit scholar, U. of No. Iowa, 1998. Mem.: Internat. Reading Assn. Avocations: camping, hiking, travel, canoeing, crafts. Office: Van Buren Elementary 2525 29th St Cedar Rapids IA 52404 Home Phone: 319-390-0407; Office Phone: 319-558-3799. Business E-Mail: murbanowski@cr.k12.ia.us.

URBANSKI, JANE F., retired microbiologist; b. Buffalo, Aug. 21, 1943; d. Francis C. and Jane J. Urbanski. BS in Med. Tech. cum laude, Rosary Hill Coll., 1965. Registered med. tech. Am. Soc. Clin. Pathology. Med. tech. Millard Fillmore Hosp., Buffalo, 1965—68, microbiology supr., 1968—72; lab. supr. Physician's Diagnostic Lab., Buffalo, 1972—73; microbiology supr. Sister's of Charity Hosp., Buffalo, 1973—74; chief bacteriologist Erie County Pub. Health Lab. Health Dept., Buffalo, 1974—2002; ret., 2002. Clin. instr. SUNY, Buffalo, 1975—2002. Vol. Haven House, Buffalo, 1985, City Mission, Buffalo, 2004. Mem.: Am. Soc. for Clin. Lab. Sci. (ret.), Empire State Assn. for Med. Tech. (ret.), Am. Soc. Clin. Pathologists (ret.), English First, Am. Immigration Control, Second Amendment Found., Mensa. Conservative. Roman Catholic. Avocations: travel, growing orchids, reading, logic puzzles. Home: 185 Bridle Path Orchard Park NY 14127

URBANSKI, JOSEPH V., mathematics educator; b. Balt., Feb. 14, 1942; s. Barney Joseph and Lottie (Chiborowski) U.; m. Mary Margaret Lewis, Nov. 4, 1967 (div. Oct. 1996); children: Deborah, Christopher, Mary Kathrine. BS in Phys. Sci. Edn., Bloomsburg U., Pa., 1963; MMath., U. S.C., 1969; PhD in Math. Edn., N.C. State U., 1981. Cert. secondary phys. sci. and math. tchr., Pa. Tchr. math. Annapolis (Md.) High Sch., 1963-68; asst. prof. edn. West Tex. State U., Canyon, 1981-82; instr., adj. asst. prof. Pa. State U., State College, 1983-89; asst. prof. math. W.Va. Inst. Tech., Montgomery, 1969-80, assoc. prof., 1990—2001, chmn. dept. math., 1992—2001, prof. math., 2001—. U. S.C. scholar, 1968-69; W.Va. Inst. Tech. grantee, 1977. Mem. Math. Assn. Am., Nat. Coun. Tchrs. Math., Phi Delta Kappa. Office Phone: 304-442-3273.

URBIK, JEROME ANTHONY, financial consultant; b. Chgo., Oct. 30, 1929; s. Anthony Frank and Sophie Elizabeth Urbik; m. Barbara Jean Chamernik, Sept. 1956; children: Laura M. Kern, Michael A., Anthony J., Mary King Gil, John T., Maria T. BA in Philosophy, St. Mary's Coll., Techny, Ill., 1953; CLU degree, Am. Coll., 1970, ChFC degree, 1979. Chartered fin. cons. Field underwriter MONY Fin. Svcs., Chgo., 1955-59, merchandising specialist NYC, 1959; pvt. practice brokerage cons. Northfield, Ill., 1960-64; CEO Hinsdale (Ill.) Assocs. Fin. Svcs. Corp., 1964-90, CEO emeritus, 1990—. V.p. Interstate Coll. Personology, San Diego, 1982-87; pres. Gen. Agts. Mgrs. Conf., 1967-68. Mem. publ. com. Crisis mag., Washington, 1989—; contbr. articles on industry to profl. jours.; mem. editl. bd. Leaders mag., 1981-90. Mem. adv. coun. Congressman Henry Hyde, Nat. Rep. Com., Washington; mem. Small Bus. Devel. Ctr. exec. bd. advisors Lewis U., Lockport, Ill., 1987-90; exec. coord. Legatus of Chgo., 1990-91 (Cath. CEO); bd. dirs. United Rep. Fund, 1987-92; bd. advisors Am. Life League, Washington, 1990-98, Cath. Ciizens Ill., 1997—; bd. dirs. Nat. Rep. Coalition for Life, 1990—. Named Small Bus. Acct. of Yr. for State of Ill. SBA, 1987. Mem. Am. Soc. CLUs, Chgo. Orchestral Assn., Chgo. Lyric Opera, Latin Liturgy Assn. (v.p. Chgo. chpt. 1997—). Roman Catholic. Avocations: reading, writing, power boating, classical music. Home: 474 South St Elmhurst IL 60126-4120 Office: Hinsdale Assoc Fin Svc Corp 15 Spinning Wheel Rd Ste 308 Hinsdale IL 60521-2987 Office Phone: 630-325-4545. E-mail: jaurbik@comcast.net.

URBINA, MANUEL, II, legal research historian, history professor; b. Rodriguez, Nuevo Leon, Mex., Sept. 23, 1939; came to U.S., 1947; s. Manuel and Irene (Salce) de Urbina. BA, Howard Payne Coll., 1962; postgrad., Nat. Autonoma U. Mex., Mexico City, 1963-64; MA, U. Tex.,

1967, PhD, 1976; postgrad., Cambridge U., Eng., 1982; JD, U. Houston, 1983. Prof. Latin Am. history Coll. of the Mainland, Texas City, Tex., 1967—. Founder, curator Urbina Mus. History of Mex., Houston, 1990—; chmn., legal counsel Urbina Found., Houston, 1985—; chmn., CEO Urbina Pub. Co. Inc., Houston and Mexico City, 1985—. Author: (TV Series) The Mexican Side of the Texas Revolution, 1985, The Mexican Side of the Mexican War, 1985, The Battle of San Jacinto-A Mexican Viewpoint, 1985, The Battle of the Alamo-A Mexican Viewpoint, 1986, Relations Between the United States and Mexico, 1987, General Emiliano Zapata in North American Historiography, 1989, The Mexican War in International Law, 1995, The Mexican War in United States Constitutional Law, 1996, Efectos De La Independencia De Texas Sobre El Gobierno, La Política, Y La Sociedad De México, 1996, Bilingual Dollars of the Bank of Texas (1835) in the Context of the Separation of Texas From Mexico, 1998, General Pancho Villa in International Law, 1999; editor, interviewer history videos, oral history interviews with participants in the Mexican Revolution; contbr. articles to newspapers and mags. including Houston Chronicle, Mexico City Novedades, San Antonio Light, Boletin Del Archivo General Del Estado de Nuevo León, Boletin de la Sociedad Numismatica de Mexico. Founder Cinco de Mayo Assn., Galveston County, Tex., 1976; founder, faculty sponsor Mex. Am. Student Assn., Coll. of Mainlan, 1974—. Named Hispanic of Yr. Galveston County League of United Latin Am. Citizens, 1982; NEH grantee, 1971-72; U.S. Dept. State scholar diplomat, 1979. Mem. League of United Latin Am. Citizens, Tex. State Hist. Assn., Howard Payne U. Alumni Assn., U. Houston Law Alumni Assn., U. Tex. Alumni Assn., Interam. C. of C., Soc. Numismatica Mex. Democrat. Baptist. Avocations: reading, research, travel, trumpet playing, volunteer work. Home: 887 Old Genoa Red Bluff Rd Houston TX 77034-4010 Home Phone: 281-478-5554; Office Phone: 409-938-1211 x307. Personal E-mail: murbina@com.edu.

URBOM, WARREN KEITH, federal judge; b. Atlanta, Nebr., Dec. 17, 1925; s. Clarence Andrew and Anna Myrl (Irelan) U.; m. Joyce Marie Crawford, Aug. 19, 1951; children: Kim Marie, Randall Crawford, Allison Lee, Joy Renee. AB with highest distinction, Nebr. Wesleyan U., 1950, LLD (hon.), 1984; JD with distinction, U. Mich., 1953. Bar: Nebr. 1953. Mem. firm Baylor, Evnen, Baylor, Urbom, & Curtiss, Lincoln, Nebr., 1953—70; judge U.S. Dist. Ct. Nebr., 1970—; chief judge U.S. Dist. Ct. Dist. Nebr., 1972—86, sr. judge, 1991—. Mem. com. on practice and procedure Nebr. Supreme Ct., 1965-95; mem. subcom. on fed. jurisdiction Jud. Conf. U.S., 1975-83; adj. instr. trial advocacy U. Nebr. Coll. Law, 1979-90; bd. dirs. Fed. Jud. Ctr., 1982-86; chmn. com. on orientation newly apptd. dist. judges Fed. Jud. Ctr., 1986-89; mem. 8th Cir. Com. on Model Criminal and Civil Jury Instrns., 1983—; mem. adv. com. on alternative sentences U.S. Sentencing Com., 1989-91. Contbr. articles to profl. jours. Trustee St. Paul Sch. Theology, Kansas City, Mo., 1986-89; active United Methodist Ch. (bd. mgrs., bd. global ministries 1972-76, gen. com. on status and role of women, 1988-96, gen. conf. 1972, 76, 80, 88, 92, 96, 2000); pres. Lincoln YMCA, 1965-67; bd. govs. Nebr. Wesleyan U., chmn. 1975-80. With AUS, 1944-46. Recipient Medal of Honor, Nebr. Wesleyan U. Alumni Assn., 1983. Fellow Am. Coll. Trial Lawyers; mem. ABA, Nebr. Bar Assn. (ho. of dels. 1966-70, Outstanding Legal Educator award 1990, Pres.'s award for Professionalism 2006), Lincoln Bar Assn. (Liberty Bell award 1993, pres. 1968-69), Kiwanis (Disting. Svc. award 1993), Masons (33 deg., Grand Master's Humanitarian award 2003), Am. Inns of Ct. (Lewis F. Powell Jr. award for Professionalism and Ethics 1995), Robert Van Pelt Am. Inn of Ct. (Lifetime Mentor award, 2002). Methodist. Home: 4421 Ridgeview Dr Lincoln NE 68516-1516 Office: US Dist Ct 586 Fed Bldg 100 Centennial Mall N Lincoln NE 68508-3859 Office Phone: 402-437-5231. Personal E-mail: urbom1@neb.rr.com. Business E-Mail: warren_urbom@ned.uscourts.gov.

URCIOLO, JOHN RAPHAEL, II, finance and real estate educator, developer; b. Washington, June 29, 1947; s. Joseph John and Phillie Marie (Petrone) U.; m. Jean Marie Manning, Jan. 2, 1972 (dec. Jan. 1990); m. Andrea Zedalis, Mar. 9, 2002. BBA, Am. U., 1969, MS in real estate, 1971. Cert. real estate broker, appraiser. Rschr. Homer Hoyt Inst., Washington, 1967-69; econ. Nat. Assn. Home Builders, Washington, 1971-75; lectr., assoc. prof. Montgomery Coll., Rockville, Md., 1971-72; assoc. prof. U. Md., College Park, 1972-79; property mgr. Urciolo Realty Co., Washington, 1976-79; comml. broker Urciolo & Urciolo, Washington, 1980-82; real estate developer Urciolo Properties, LLC, Takoma Park, Md., 1982—. Cons. Nat. Ski Area Assn., Hartford, 1978-79, Montgomery County Govt., Rockville, 1980-81; adj. prof. Am. U., Washington, 1980-91; court expert Superior Ct. for D.C., Civil and Criminal divsns.; lectr. to various orgns. Author: Real Estate Manual, 1976; co-author: The White Book of Ski Areas (U.S. and Can.), 1977-79, Industry Edition-The White Book, 1978, The Housing Fact Book, 1976, Housing Component Costs, 1975, 2d edit., 1976, Material Usage in Housing, 1970; co-editor: Labor Wage Rate Bulletin, 1976. Co-chair bd. dirs. Liz Lerman Dance Exch., Takoma Park, Md., 1997—; chmn. facade adv. bd. and Econ. Devel. Com., City of Takoma Park; chmn. bd. Lido Civic Club of Washington. Fellow Urban Mass Transp. Assn., 1969, Am. U., 1970; Soc. Real Estate Appraisers scholar, 1968. Mem. Cert. Real Estate Appraisers, Am. Planning Assn., Am. Univ. Real Estate Assn. (charter, v.p. edn., v.p. award 1983), Rho Epsilon (editor newsletter 1969). Republican. Roman Catholic. Avocations: skiing, golf. Office: Urciolo Properties LLC 6935 Laurel Ave Ste 100 Takoma Park MD 20912-4413 Office Phone: 301-270-4442. Personal E-mail: jurciolo@comcast.net.

URCIUOLI, J. ARTHUR, brokerage house executive; b. Syracuse, NY, Nov. 13, 1937; s. Joseph R. and Nicoletta Anne (Phillips) U.; m. Margaret Jane Forelli, Aug. 13, 1966; children: Caryn Sloan Jacoby, Christian J.A. BS, St. Lawrence U., 1959; JD, Georgetown U., 1966; grad. Advanced Mgmt. Program, Harvard Bus. Sch., 1982. Bar: N.Y. 1966. Atty. Brown, Wood, Fuller, Caldwell & Ivey, NYC, 1966-69; internat. investment banker, dir. internat. fin. Merrill Lynch, NYC, Paris, 1970-78; pres. Merrill Lynch Internat., 1978-82; chmn. Merrill Lynch Internat. Bank, London; dir. banking div. Merrill Lynch Capital Markets, 1980-84; dir. Merrill Lynch Bus. Fin. Services, Merrill Lynch Co., 1984-93; dir. mktg. group Merrill Lynch Pvt. Client, 1993-97, chmn. Internat. Pvt. Client Group NYC, 1997-99, ret., 1999; chmn. Archer Group, 1999—. Bd. dirs. Kroll Inc., 1999—2004, Family Capital Growth Ptnrs., L.P. Contbr. articles to profl. jours. Trustee St. Lawrence U., 1976-89, Bruce Mus., Greenwich, Conn., 1990-94; bd. dirs. United Way, Greenwich, 1978-81. Capt. USMC, 1959-65. Mem. Securities Assn. (chmn. sales and mktg. com. 1987-89), Forum Investor Advice (chmn. 1996-98), River Club (NYC), Riverside (Conn.) Yacht Club, The Oaks Club (Sarasota, Fla.). Republican. Congregationalist. Office Phone: 941-966-4941. E-mail: archie22@comcast.net.

URDAN, TIMOTHY CAMERON, psychology professor, consultant; BA in Psychology, U. Calif., Berkeley, 1986; MEd, Harvard U., Cambridge, Mass., 1988; PhD in Psychology and Edn., U. Mich., Ann Arbor, 1994. Asst. prof. Emory U., Atlanta, 1994—96; prof. psychology Santa Clara U., Calif., 1996—. Cons. in field. Editor: International Perspectives on Adolescents and Education, 2003, Educating Adolescents: Challenges and Strategies, 2004; author: Statistics in Plain English, 2005. Grantee, W. T. Grant Found., 1998—2001. Mem.: Am. Edn. Rsch. Assn. Office: Santa Clara U 500 El Camino Real Santa Clara CA 95053 Office Phone: 408-554-4495. Business E-Mail: turdan@scu.edu.

URDANG, LAURENCE, editor, publishing executive; b. NYC, Mar. 21, 1927; s. Harry Rudman and Annabel (Schafran) U.; m. Irena B. Ehrlich vel Sluszny, May 23, 1952 (div.); children: Nicole Severyn, Alexandra Stefanie. BS, Columbia U., 1954, postgrad., 1954-58. Lectr. gen. linguistics NYU, 1956-61; assoc. editor dictionary dept. Funk & Wagnalls, Inc., NYC, 1957; reference editor Random House, Inc., NYC, 1957-61, dir. reference dept., 1962-69; pres. Laurence Urdang, Inc., Old Lyme, Conn. and Aylesbury, Eng., 1969—; chmn. bd. Laurence Urdang Assocs., Ltd., Aylesbury, 1969-78; editor Verbatim Books, Old Lyme and Aylesbury, 1974—. Compiler, editor, author numerous books; mng. editor: Random House Unabridged Dictionary, 1966; editor in chief: Random House College Dictionary, 1968, Random House Dictionary of Synonyms and Antonyms, 1960, N.Y. Times Everyday Reader's Dictionary of Misunderstood, Misused, Mispronounced Words, 1972, 2d edit., 1985, Editor, Verbatim, The Language Quar., 1974-97, Dictionary of Advertising Terms, 1977, Official Associated Press Almanac, 1976, Hammond Almanac, 1977, Picturesque Expressions, 1980, 2d edit., 1985, Illustrated Children's Dictionary, 1979, Basic Dictionary of Synonyms and Antonyms, 1979, 2d edit., 1986, The Synonym Finder, 1979, Collins English Dictionary, 1979, Verbatim: Vols. I, II, 1978, Vols. III, IV, V, VI and Index, 1981, -Ologies & -Isms, 1978, 81, 86, Twentieth Century American Nicknames, 1979, A Treasury of Biblical Quotations, 1980, The Timetables of American History, 1981, 3d edit., 2001, Mosby's Medical and Nursing Dictionary, 1983, Allusions, 1982, 86, Modifiers, 1982, Suffixes, 1982, Prefixes, 1984, Holidays and Anniversaries, 1985, Slogans, 1985, Mottoes, 1986, Numerical Allusions, 1986, Names and Nicknames of Places and Things, 1987, Loanwords Dictionary, 1987, The Whole Ball of Wax, 1988, The Dictionary of Confusable Words, 1988, A Fine Kettle of Fish, 1990, The Oxford Thesaurus, 1992, 2nd edit., 1997, The Oxford Desk Dictionary, 1995, The Oxford Desk Thesaurus, 1995, The New Century Dictionary, 1996, The New Century Thesaurus, 1996, The Compact Oxford Thesaurus, 1997. Served with USNR, 1944-45. Fellow Dictionary Soc. N.Am. (hon.), Soc. Indexers (hon.), Euralex (hon.); mem. Linguistic Soc. Am. (hon.), Soc. Nautical Rsch., Nat. Maritime Mus. (bd. dir.), N.B. White Libr., Mystic Mus., Am. Name Soc., Am. Dialect Soc. Office Phone: 860-434-2104. Personal E-mail: urdang@sbcglobal.net.

URE, COLIN, research scientist; Scientist Procter & Gamble Co., Cin. Co-recipient Nat. Inventor of Yr. award, Intellectual Property Owners Edn. Found., 2006. Achievements include development of PuR Purifier of Water Sachets, which can purify 10 liters of non-drinkable water by pulling out contaminants; patents in field. Office: Health Scis Inst Procter & Gamble Co 1 P&G Plaza Cincinnati OH 45202

UREMOVICH, MICHAEL ELLIOT, transportation company executive; b. Phila., Apr. 23, 1943; s. A. M. and Edythe (Fidcca) U.; m. Carrea S. Cotlow, Aug. 27, 1966. BA, U. Ariz., 1966; MBA, CCNY, 1972; MA, St. Johns Coll. Sr. v.p. mktg. Lee Way Motor Freight, Oklahoma City, 1976-79; prin. Booz, Allen & Hamilton, NYC, 1972-76, 1979-82; v.p. through sr. v.p. mktg. Am. Pres. Lines, Oakland, Calif.; v.p. mktg. So. Pacific Transp.; pres. TSSI; prin. Manalytics Internat., San Francisco; vice-chmn. Pacer Internat., Concord, Calif., 2003—06, chmn., CEO, 2006—. Served with USN, 1961-66. Office: Pacer Internat Ste 1200 2300 Clayton Rd Concord CA 94520 *

UREÑA, ALEX, chef; Garde mgr., dishwasher River Café, Brooklyn; chef Bouley, NYC; apprentice chef El Bulli, Spain; chef Restaurant Martin Berasategui, Jo Jo, NYC, Le Cote Basque, NYC, La Caravelle, NYC; chef de cuisine, co-owner Blue Hill, NYC, 2000—01; exec. chef Marseille, NYC, 2001—03; consulting chef Suba, NYC, 2004—; owner, chef Ureña, NYC, 2006—. Named one of NYC's Rising Stars, StarChefs.com, 2006. Office: Urena 37 E 28th St New York NY 10016 Office Phone: 212-213-2328.

URGAS, SANDRA S., emergency physician; arrived in US, 1979; d. Edip and Susan Sermin Ugras. D of Osteopathy, U. Medicine & Dentistry NJ, Stratford, 2001. Emergency physician Newark Beth Israel Med. Ctr., 2006—. Mem.: Am. Coll. Osteo. Physicians, Am. Coll. Emergency Physicians, Am. Osteo. Assn. Home: 537 Roosevelt St Northvale NJ 07647

URI, GEORGE WOLFSOHN, accountant; b. San Francisco, Dec. 8, 1920; s. George Washington and Ruby Uri; m. Pamela O'Keefe, May 15, 1961. AB, Stanford U., 1941, IA, 1943, MBA, 1946; postgrad., U. Leeds, Eng., 1945. CPA, Calif.; CFP. CMA, ChFC; Accredited Estate Planner. Mem. acctg., econs. and stats. depts. Shell Oil Co., Inc., San Francisco, 1946—48; ptnr., ret. Irelan, Uri, Mayer & Sheppie; pres. F. Uri & Co., Inc. Instr. acctg. and econs. Golden Gate U., 1949-50. Contbr. articles to profl. jours. Chmn. San Rafael Redevel. Adv. Com., 1977-78, mem., 1978-91, mem. emeritus, 1991—; bd. dirs. San Francisco Planning and Urban Renewal Assn., 1958-60. Served with AUS, 1942-46, to col. Aus. (ret.). Recipient Meritorious Service medal, Sec. of Army, 1978. Mem. AICPA (hon., personal fin. specialist), Calif. Soc. CPA (hon.; sec.-treas. San Francisco chpt. 1956-57, dir. 1961-63, state dir. 1964-66, Forbes medal com. 1968-69, chmn. 1969-71), San Francisco Estate Planning Coun. (dir. 1965-68, Am. Soc. Mil. Comptr., Execs. Assn. San Francisco (pres. 1965-66), Soc. Fin. Profls., Fin. Planning Assn., Commonwealth Club (quar. chmn. 1971), Stanford Alumni Assn. (San Francisco; dir. 1990-99), Army and Navy Club Washington. Office: 1209 Tennessee St San Francisco CA 94107 Personal E-mail: georgeuri@aol.com.

URIARTE, CHRIS J., information technology executive; Student, Rutgers Univ., NJ. Positions in music industry, NYC area, 1996—2000; dir. tech. svcs. IDT Corp.; chief tech. officer, chief architect, sr. ptnr. AdPro Tech. Group, NJ; dir., chief tech. officer Retail Decisions, Hazlet, NJ, 1999—. Dir. Dynamic Vision Distributions, Miami. Named one of Hot 30 Under 30, InfoWeek mag., 1998, Top 25 Chief Tech. Officers, InfoWorld mag., 2007. Office: Retail Decisions 100 Village Ct Ste 102 Hazlet NJ 07730 Office Phone: 732-888-0088. Business E-Mail: curiarte@red.usa.

URIE, ALAN T., bank executive; b. Ogden, Utah, Sept. 25, 1957; s. Hurschell G. and E. Mary (Petersen) Urie; m. M. Mae Christensen, July 26, 1980; children: Marcus Timothy, Kristi Mae Harvey, Scott Alan, Catherine Elizabeth, Teresa Janette, Mary Elizabeth. BS, Brigham Young U., 1982; MBA, U. Utah, 1984. National Compliance School Graduate Am. Bankers Assn., 1991. Officer First Security Bank of Utah, N.A., Salt Lake City, 1983—91, asst. v.p., 1991—94, v.p., sr. compliance officer, 1994—2000; v.p. First Security Corp., Salt Lake City, 1996—2000; sr. v.p. Wells Fargo Bank NW, N.A., 2000—, Wells Fargo Bank, N.A., 2004—, Wells Fargo Cmty. Devel. Corp., 2007—. Unit com. mem., leader Boys Scouts Am., South Salt Lake, 1985—; budget adv. bd. Ogden City, Utah, 1986—88; commr., chair South Salt Lake Planning Commn., 1985—86, 1988—95; chmn. Cmty. Affairs Com., South Salt Lake, 1988—90, Gen. Plan Com., South Salt Lake, 1992—96, City Housing Rehab. Loan Com., South Salt Lake, Utah, 2002—; bishop Ch. of Jesus Christ of Latter-day Saints, South Salt Lake, 2003—04, stake presidency mem., 2004—; exec., governance com. Girl Scouts of Utah, 2002—; exec. com. Utah Microenterprise Loan Fund, Inc., 2000—; bd. mem., incorporator South Salt Lake Works, Inc., 2004—; com. mem. Utah Bankers Assn., 1990—2007. Lds Ch. Office: Wells Fargo 299 South Main St Salt Lake City UT 84111-2263 Home Phone: 801-467-8234.

URKOWITZ, MICHAEL, banker; b. Bronx, NY, June 18, 1943; s. David and Esther (Levy) U.; m. Eleanor Naomi Dreazen, July 2, 1966; children—Brian, Denise. B.Engring., CCNY, 1965, M.M.E., 1967. Project engr. Lunar Module program Grumman Corp., Bethpage, NY, 1964-72; asst. to dep. commr. for housing code compliance, project mgr. City of N.Y., 1972-74; 2d v.p. Chase Manhattan Bank, NYC, 1974-77, v.p. group exec. ops. dept., 1977-80, sr. v.p., 1980-85, exec. v.p., corp. ops. and sys. exec., 1985-87; sector exec. Chase InfoServ Internat., NYC, 1987-95, exec. consumer products integration and tech., 1995-96, Chase credit card bus. exec., 1996-2000, ret., 2000; sr. adv. Deloitte Cons., NYC; prin. Michael Urkowitz, LLC, 2005—. Bd. dirs. Bank Leumi, U.S.; lectr. CCNY, 1967—68. Contbg. author: Thermal Control and Radiation, 1972. Mem. adv. bd. NYC chpt. Salvation Army, 1989—2001. Mem. Tau Beta Pi, Pi Tau Sigma. Home Phone: 212-879-6123. Personal E-mail: murkowitz@aol.com. *Working against my own standards as opposed to the standards set by others, provides the greater challenge but yields greater satisfaction.*

URLACHER, BRIAN KEITH, professional football player; b. Pasco, Wash., May 25, 1978; s. Brad and Lavoyda Urlacher; m. Laure Urlacher (div.); 1 child, Pamela; 1 child, Riley. BA, U. N.Mex., Albuquerque, 2000. Linebacker Chgo. Bears, 2000—. Vol. United Way. Vol. Spl. Olympics, Ill., N.Mex. Named NFL Defensive Rookie of Yr., AP, 2000, NFL Defensive Player of Yr., 2005; named to Nat. Football Conf. Pro Bowl Team, 2002—07, NFL All-Pro Team, 2005—06. Office: Chgo Bears Halas Hall 1000 Football Dr Lake Forest IL 60045 *

URMY, NORMAN B., hospital administrator; b. Ft. Smith, Ark., June 26, 1944; married. BA, Williams Coll., 1966; MA, U. Chgo., 1969. Various positions Mass. Gen. Hosp., Boston, 1966-67; adminstrv. resident NYU Med. Ctr., 1968, adminstrv. asst., 1969-70; asst. adminstr. U. Hosp., NYU Med. Ctr., 1970—76, assoc. adminstr., 1976—79, adminstr., v.p. ops., 1979—82, 1982—86; exec. dir. Vanderbilt Univ. Hosp. & Clinic, Nashville, 1985-98; exec. v.p. clin. affairs Vanderbilt Univ. Med. Ctr., Nashville, 1998—; exec. dir. and CEO Vanderbilt U. Hosp. and Clinic, 2002—05. Mem. ACHE. Office: D-3300 MCN Vanderbilt U 1161 21st Ave Nashville TN 37232-2104

UROWSKY, RICHARD J., lawyer; b. NYC, June 28, 1946; s. Jacob and Anne (Granick) Urowsky. BA, Yale U., 1967, JD, 1972; BPhil, Oxford U., Eng., 1970. Bar: N.Y. 1973, U.S. Dist. Ct. (so. dist.) N.Y. 1973, U.S. Ct. Appeals (2d cir.) 1973, U.S. Supreme Ct. 1977. Law clk. to Justice Reed U.S. Supreme Ct., Washington, 1972—73; assoc. Sullivan & Cromwell LLP, NYC, 1973—80, ptnr., 1980—. Mem. ABA, NYC Bar Assn., Fed. Bar Coun., N.Y. County Lawyers Assn., Yale Club, Links Club, India House Club, Lyford Cay Club. Office: Sullivan & Cromwell LLP 125 Broad St New York NY 10004-2498 Business E-Mail: urowskyr@sullcrom.com.

URQUHART, JOHN, medical researcher, educator; b. Pitts., Apr. 24, 1934; s. John and Wilma Nelda (Martin) U.; m. Joan Cooley, Dec. 28, 1957; children: Elizabeth Urquhart Vdovjak, John Christopher (dec. 1965), Robert Malcolm, Thomas Jubal. BA with honors, Rice U., 1955; MD with honors, Harvard U., 1959; D honoris causa, U. Utrecht, 1997. Lic. physician, Calif. Walter B. Cannon fellow in physiology Harvard Med. Sch., Boston, 1956, Josiah Macy, Jr. fellow, 1956-58, 59-61; intern in surgery Mass. Gen. Hosp., 1959-60, asst. resident, 1960-61; investigator Nat. Heart Inst., NIH, Bethesda, Md., 1961-63; asst. prof. physiology U. Pitts. Sch. Medicine, 1963-66, assoc. prof., 1966-68, prof., 1968-70; prof. biomed. engring. U. So. Calif., LA, 1970-71; prin. scientist ALZA Corp., Palo Alto, Calif., 1970-86, dir. biol. scis., 1971-74, pres. rsch. divsn., 1974-78, dir., 1976-78, chief scientist, 1978-82, sr. v.p., 1978-85. Co-founder APREX Corp., Fremont, Calif., pres., 1986-88, dir., 1986-95, chmn., 1988-91, chief scientist, 1988-95; co-founder, chief scientist AARDEX Ltd., Zug, Switzerland, 1995-; vis. prof. pharmacology U. Limburg Sch. Medicine (now Maastricht U.), Maastricht, Netherlands, 1984-85, vis. prof. pharmacoepidemiology, 1986-91, prof. pharmacoepidemiology, 1991-2004, prof. emeritus, 2004—; adj. prof. biopharm. scis. U. Calif., San Francisco, 1984-; dir.'s adv. com. NIH, 1986-88; Boerhaave lectr. U. Leiden, Netherlands, 1991, 94-95, 97; bd. dirs. HBM BioVentures Ltd., Cayman Islands. Co-author: Risk Watch, 1984; contbr. articles to profl. jours.; patentee therapeutic systems for controlled drug delivery and regimen compliance monitoring. Trustee Kettering U. (formerly GMI Engring. and Mgmt. Inst.), Flint, Mich., 1983—. Served with USPHS, 1961-63. Recipient Disting. Alumni award, Rice U., 2002; NIH grantee, 1963-70. Fellow AAAS, Royal Coll. Physicians of Edinburgh, Royal Soc. Edinburgh (corr.), Internat. Soc. for Pharmacoepidemiology, Biomed. Engring. Soc. (pres. 1976, Disting. Svc. award 2005), Internat. Soc. Pharmaco-epidemiology; mem. Boyleston Med. Soc., Am. Soc. Clin. Pharmacology and Therapeutics, Soc. for Clin. Trials, Endocrine Soc., Saturday Morning Club Palo Alto, Am. Physiol. Soc. (Bowditch lectr. 1969), Soc. Risk Analysis, Calif. Acad. Medicine, Illuminati Edinburgh. Home and Office: 975 Hamilton Ave Palo Alto CA 94301-2213 E-mail: urquhart@ix.netcom.com.

URQUHART, TONY, artist, educator; b. Niagara Falls, Ont., Can., Apr. 9, 1934; s. Archer Marsh and Maryon Louise (Morse) U.; m. Madeline Mary Jennings, July 1958 (div. 1976); children: Allyson, Robin, Marsh, Aidan; m. Mary Jane Carter Keele, May 1976; 1 dau., Emily. At, Yale U., New Haven, 1955; diploma, Albright Art Sch. Buffalo Fine Arts Acad., 1956; BFA, U. Buffalo, 1958. Artist-in-residence U. Western Ont., London, 1960-63, 64-65, asst. prof. fine arts, 1967-70, assoc. prof., 1970-72; lectr. McMaster U., Hamilton, Ont., 1966—67; prof. fine art U. Waterloo, Ont., 1972—79, chmn. dept. Ont., 1977-79, 82-85, Ont., 94-96, ret. Ont., 1999. One-man shows Winnipeg Art Gallery, 1959, Walker Art Gallery, Mpls., 1960, Richard Demarco Gallery, Edinburgh, Scotland, 1975, Power of Invention: Drawings from seven decades, Nat. Gallery Can., 2003; group shows, Pitts. Biennial, 1958, Guggenheim Internat., N.Y.C., 1958, Art of the Ams. and Spain, Madrid, Barcelona, Rome, Paris, 1964, Nat. Gallery Can., Toronto, 1972, Mus. Modern Art, Paris, 1976, Mus. Modern Art, N.Y.C., 2006; represented permanent collections, Nat. Gallery Can., Art Gallery, Ont., Fed. Art Bank of Ottawa, Montreal Mus., Vancouver Art Gallery, Mus. Modern Art, Victoria and Albert Mus., London, Museo Civico, Lugano, Switzerland, Hirshhorn Mus., Washington, Bibliotec Nat., Paris; chmn., Jack Chambers Meml. Found., 1978-85, 2004—; artist in residence Kitchener-Waterloo Art Gallery, Kitchener, Ont., 1981-83, City of Kitchener, 2005; illustrator: (by Michael Ondaatje) The Broken Ark: A Book of Beasts, 1969, I Am Walking in the Garden of His Imaginary Palace by Jane Urquhart, 1982, False Shuffles by Jane Urquhart, 1982, (50 drawings) Cells of Ourselves (text G.M. Dault), 1989, Memories of a Governor General's Daughter, 1990, Warbrain: poems by Stuart MacKinnon, 1994, (by Anne McPherson) Walking to the Saints, 2000 (by Rohinton Mistry) The Scream, 2006. Artist in residence City of Kitchener, 2005. Decorated Order of Can.; recipient Edits, I Arts Coun., Ont., 1974, Kilchener Waterloo Visual Arts award, 1994; winner Nat. Outdoor Sculpture Competition MacDonald Stewart Art Ctr., 1987, Outdoor Sculpture competition, Rim Park, Waterloo, 2002; grantee Can. Coun. award, 1963, 79, travel grantee, 1967, 69, 70, 74, 75, 76, 88, 91, project cost grantee, 1981, 82, short-term grantee, 1991, All Can. Coun. Mem. Can. Artists Representation (1 of 3 founding mem.'s, sec. 1968-71, life 1999), Nat. Gallery of Can. (life), Art Gallery of Ont. (life), London Reginal Art Gallery (life), MacDonald Stewart Art Centre Gallery Stratford (life). Office: Dept Fine Arts U Waterloo Waterloo ON Canada N2L 3G1 Personal E-mail: urk.art@hotmail.com.

URSANO, ROBERT JOSEPH, psychiatrist; b. Heidelberg, Ger., May 26, 1947; s. James Joseph and Neoma Faye (Summers) U.; m. Diane T. Ursano; children: Amy, Anna. BS magna cum laude, U. Notre Dame, 1969; MD, Yale U., 1973; grad., Washington Psychoanalytic Ins, 1986. Diplomate Nat. Bd. Med. Examiners, Am. Bd. Psychiatry and Neurology; lic. physician N.Y., Tex., Md. Resident in psychiatry Wilford Hall USAF Med. Ctr., 1973-75; postdoctoral fellow in psychiatry Yale U./Yale Psychiat. Inst., 1975-77; staff psychiatrist USAF Sch. Aerospace Medicine, Brooks AFB, Tex., 1977-79; clin. asst. prof. U. Tex. Health Sci. Ctr., San Antonio, 1977-79; asst. prof. and dir. third yr. clerkships dept. psychiatry Uniformed

Svcs. U. Health Scis., Bethesda, Md., 1979-81, assoc prof. and dir. 3rd yr. clerkships, 1981-83, assoc. prof. and assoc. chmn. dept. psychiatry, 1983-86, prof. and assoc. chmn. dept. psychiatry, 1987-92, prof., chair dept. psychiatry, dir.Ctr. for the Study of Traumatic Stress Bethesda, Md., 1987—. Examiner Am. Bd. Psychiatry and Neurology, 1984-1995; asst. prof. Nat. Naval Med. Ctr Dept. Psychiatry, Georgetown U. Sch. Medicine, Washington, 1980-84, assoc. prof., 1984-88, prof., 1988—; mem. grant rev. study sect. for trauma and disaster, NIMH, 1990—, chmn. various study sects. Author: Concise Guide to Psychodynamic Psychotherapy, 1990, Concise Guide to Principles and Practice of Psychodynamic Psychotherapy in the Era of Managed Care, 1998; editor: Individual and Community Responses to Trauma and Disaster: The Structure of Human Chaos, 1994, Emotional Aftermath of The Persian Gulf War: Veterans, Families, Communities and Nations, 1996, Acute and Chronic PTSD, 1997, Trauma and Disaster: Responses and Management, 2003, Terrorism and Disaster: Individual and Community Mental Health Interventions, 2004, Bioterrorism: Indivduals and the Public's Health, 2004, Principles of Psychodynamics Psychotherapy: Brief, Intermittent and Long-Term, 2004, Textbook of Disaster Psychiatry, 2007; reviewer Am. Jour. Psychiatry, Jour. Nervous and Mental Disease, Psychosomatics, Psychiatry, Jour. Applied Social Psychology, Archives of Gen. Psychiatry, Hosp. and Community Psychiatry, all 1986—, Jour. Neuropsychiatry and Clin. Neurosci., 1988—, Jour. Traumatic Stress, 1989—; editor-in-chief Psychiatry, 1999—; mem. editl. bd. Mil. Medicine; contbr. articles to profl. jours., chpts. to books. Decorated Air Force Commendation medal; recipient Dept. Def. Humanitarian Svc. medal, Dept. Def. Superior Svc. award, William C. Porter award Assn. Mil. Surgeons of U.S.; recipient Disting. Tchg. award Am. Soc. Psychoanalyst Physicians, Life Time Achievement award Internat. Soc. Traumatic Stress Studies. Fellow Am. Psychiat. Assn. (disting.), Am. Coll. Psychiatrists, Am. Coll. Psychoanalysts; mem. Am. Psychoanalytic Assn., Psychosomatic Soc., Washington Psychiat. Soc., Washington Psychoanalytic Soc., Acad. Medicine Washington DC, Soc. USAF Psychiatrists (v.p. 1981-82), Assn. for Acad. Psychiatry, Washington DC Academy Medicine, Alpha Epsilon Delta, Phi Beta Kappa. Home: 3900 Cleveland St Kensington MD 20895-3804 Office: Uniformed Svcs U Health Sci 4301 Jones Bridge Rd Bethesda MD 20814-4712

URSERY, FREDERICK STANLEY, lawyer; b. Pine Bluff, Ark., Mar. 5, 1942; s. William Stanley and Mary Charles (Lee) U.; m. Sharon Lee Davidson, Jan. 30, 1971; children: Stephen, Catherine. BA, Vanderbilt U., 1964; LLB, Columbia U., 1967. Bar: Ark. 1967, US Dist. Ct. (ea. and we. dists.) Ark. 1970, US Ct. Appeals (8th cir.) 1970. Atty. Friday, Eldredge & Clark, Little Rock, 1969—. Chmn. Pulaski County Red Cross, Little Rock, 1989-90; bd. dirs. Ouachita Girl Scout Coun., Little Rock, 1987-93. With U.S. Army, 1967-69, Vietnam. Fellow Am. Coll. Trial Lawyers, Am. Bar Found.; mem. State Bd. Law Examiners 1979-82, Am. Bd. Trial Advocates, Ark. Bar Assn. (exec. coun. chmn. 1989-90, pres. 2004, Outstanding Lawyer award 1996), Pulaski County Bar Assn. (pres. 1987-88), Downtown Kiwanis Club (pres. 1991-92), William R. Overton Inn of Ct. (pres. 1990-91). Democrat. Methodist. Home: 2804 N Taylor St Little Rock AR 72207-2837 Office: Friday Eldredge & Clark 2000 Regions Ctr 400 W Capitol Ave Little Rock AR 72201-3436 Office Phone: 501-370-1555. Business E-Mail: ursery@fec.net.

URSO, IDA, psychologist; arrived in U.S., 1954; BA, Kent State U., 1969; MA, UCLA, 1974, PhD, 1983; cert., N.Y. Open Ctr., 1997. Sr. staff assoc. Ctr. for Human Interdependence, Orange, Calif., 1986—90; lectr. Chapman Coll., Orange, 1988—90; dir. World Goodwill, NYC, 1990—96; integrative spiritual psychologist Chaitanya, Hoboken, NJ, 1997—; pres., founder Aquarian Age Cmty., Jersey City, 1998—. Elem. sch. cons. St. Pedro St. Sch., LA, 1976—77; bd. mem. Calif. Coun. for UN U., LA, 1982—84; lectr. Immaculate Heart Coll. Ctr., LA, 1985, LA, 98; organizer, presenter seminars on consciousness and spirituality of UN, 1999—. Writer, editor: newsletter Diamond Light, 1997—; contbr. chapters to books. Bd. mem. Orange County chpt. UN Assn./USA, 1988—90; edn. chairperson UN Assn., Orange County, 1989—90; UN Dept. Publ. Info., Non Govtl. Orgn. World Goodwill, NYC, 1990—96, Children of Earth Lifebridge, NYC, 1998—2000, Aquarian Age Cmty., NYC, 2003—. Mem.: Assn. Humanistic Psychology, Nicholas Roerich Mus., Am. Mus. Natural History. Avocations: community service, reading, music, meditation. Office: Aquarian Age Cmty 233 Bay St #206 Jersey City NJ 07302 Office Phone: 201-659-3060 ext. 45. Business E-Mail: un@aquaac.org.

URSTADT, CHARLES J., real estate company officer; b. Oct. 27, 1928; s. Charles G. and Claire (Jordan) U.; m. Elinor McClure Funk, Mar. 23, 1957; children: Charles Deane, Catherine Urstadt Biddle. BA, Dartmouth Coll., 1949, MBA, 1951; LLB, Cornell U., 1953; LLD with honors, Pace U., 1990. Bar: N.Y. Assoc. Nevius Brett & Kellogg, NYC, 1953-58; asst. sec. Webb & Knapp, Inc., NYC, 1958-63; v.p., sec., counsel Alcoa Residences, Inc., NYC, 1963-67; commr. N.Y. State Divsn. Housing and comty. Renewal, NYC, 1967-73; chmn. Battery Park City Authority, NYC, 1968-78, Urstadt Property Co. Inc., 1979—. Chmn. Urstadt Biddle Properties, 1986—; trustee Tchrs. Ins. and Annuity Corp., 1985-97; N.Y.; mem. NY Stock Exch., 2004—06. Trustee Pace U., 1973— Hist. Hudson Valley, 1997—; mem. fin. com. N.Y. Rep. State Com., 1981—, del. Rep. Nat. Conv., 1988; mem. Gov.'s Task Force on N.Y. Housing, 1988-90; bd. dirs. N.Y.C. Partnership, Inc., 1984-93; chmn. Realty Found. of N.Y., 1989—. N.Y. State Statue of Liberty Celebration Found., 1983-84, N.Y. State Housing Fin. Agy., 1969, Tri-State Regional Planning Commn., 1969-70; vice-chmn. Battery Park City Authority, 1997—; mem. Pres.'s Commn. on Housing, 1981-82, others. Lt. USNR, 1954-56. Office: Urstadt Biddle Properties 321 Railroad Ave Greenwich CT 06830-6306

URWITZ, JAY P., lawyer; b. 1949; BA cum laude, Harpur Coll., SUNY, Binghampton, 1970; MPP, Harvard Univ., 1974, JD cum laude, 1974. Bar: DC 1976. Law clk. Judge Irving L. Goldberg, US Ct. Appeals (5th cir.), 1974—75; former legis. asst. for domestic policy U.S. Senator Edward M. Kennedy, Washington; ptnr. Wilmer Cutler Pickering Hale & Dorr, Washington, 1985—, co-chmn. Def., Nat. Security & Govt. Contracts dept. Mem. & chmn. Software Com. Govt.-Industry Technical Data Com.; mem. Presdl. Rank Rev. Bd., Washington, 1995. Editor (sr.): Harvard Law Rev.; contbr. articles to newspapers & profl. jours. Office: Wilmer Cutler Pickering Hale & Dorr 1801 Pennsylvania Ave NW Washington DC 20006 Mailing: Wilmer Cutler Pickering Hale & Dorr Willard Office Bldg 1455 Pennsylvania Ave NW Washington DC 20004 Office Phone: 202-663-6880. Office Fax: 202-663-6363. Business E-Mail: jay.urwitz@wilmerhale.com.

URY, FREDERIC STEPHEN, lawyer; b. Zanesville, Ohio, Sept. 11, 1952; s. Perry S. and Lorraine (Greenstein) U.; m. Debby Hagopian, June 6, 1976; children: Jennifer, Robert. BS, Babson Coll., 1974; JD, Suffolk U., 1977. Bar: Conn. 1977, U.S. Dist. Ct. Conn. 1978, U.S. Supreme Ct. 1982. Assoc., ptnr. Sherwood, Garlick & Cowell, Westport, Conn., 1977-84; ptnr. Rubenstein & Ury, Westport, Conn., 1984; mng. ptnr. Ury & Moskow LLC, Fairfield, Conn. Instr. Fairfield (Conn.) U., 1979-86; mem. exec. coun. Nat. Conf. Bar Pres., 2005. Pres. Cmty. Coun., Westport, 1983-85; bd. dirs. Westport-Weston United Way, 1985—, exec. v.p., 1988—; corp. mem., trustee Babson Coll., Wellesley, Mass., 1974-84, pres. Congregation For Humanistic Judaism 1997-2000; founder Charity Treks, Inc. Mem. ABA, Conn. Bar Assn. (exec. com. civil justice, pres. 2005), Assn. Trial Lawyers Am., Westport Bar Assn., Kiwanis. Democrat. Jewish. Avocations: hiking, skiing, long distance cycling. Office: Ury & Moskow LLC 883 Black Rock Tpk Fairfield CT 06825 Office Phone: 203-610-6393. Office Fax: 203-610-6399. Business E-Mail: fred@urymoskow.com.

USCHUPLICH, VEDRAN, pathologist; s. Midhat and Emilija Uscuplic. MD, U. Sarajevo, Bosnia and Herzegovina, 1992. Resident anatomic and clin. pathology U. Tenn. Grad. Sch. Medicine, Knoxville, 2002—06; surg. pathology fellow U. Mass. Meml. Med. Ctr., Worcester, 2006—. Rsch. assoc. Baylor Coll. Medicine, Houston, 2000—02. Home: 501 Plantation St 3520 Worcester MA 01605 Home Phone: 508-756-4042. Personal E-mail: gradskodete@hotmail.com.

USCINSKI, RONALD HENRY, medical educator; b. NYC, Apr. 3, 1943; s. Henry John and Marie Antionette Uscinski; m. Donna Lyn Cutsail, May 25, 1975; children: Benjamin Joseph, David Michael, Daniel Eric, Jessica Lyn. BS, Fordham U., NYC, 1964; MD, Georgetown U., Washington, 1968. Clin. prof. neurol. surgery & pediat. Georgetown U., Washington, 1980—; clin. prof. neurol. surgery George Wash. U., 1995—. Lt. USN, 1969—71. Scholar, Potomac Inst. Policy Studies, Arlington, Va., 2004—. Fellow: ACS (life); mem.: Congress Neurosurgeons (licentiate), Am. Assn. Neurol. Surgeons (licentiate), Polish Acad. Neurosurg. (corr.), Potomac Boat Club. Roman Catholic. Avocations: rowing, music, writing. Office: 18111 Prince Philip Dr Olney MD 20832 Home Phone: 703-438-1920; Office Phone: 301-260-0535. Business E-Mail: ruscinski@potomacinstitute.org.

USELTON, BILL W., secondary school educator; b. Oklahoma City, Dec. 14, 1959; s. Jerry Max and Minnie Jewel Uselton; m. Cathy Sue Uselton, Oct. 16, 1982; children: Kelly Irene, Jennifer Elaine. A in Fine Arts, Oscar Rose Jr. Coll., Midwest City, Okla., 1980; BFA, Ctrl. State U., Edmund, Okla., 1982. Cert. secondary sch. tchr. Constract substitute Choctaw (Okla.) Pub. Schs., 1982-84; tchr. Choctaw Jr. H.S., 1984-86, Choctaw H.S., 1986—. Author: Triad of Evil, 1993. Mem. World Jewish Congress; tour guide S.W. Radio Ch., Oklahoma City, 1982; chmn. Confederate Meml., Choctaw, 1996—. Republican. Baptist. Home: 1024 S Anderson Rd Choctaw OK 73020 Office Phone: 405-390-8899. Business E-Mail: buselton@cnpschools.org.

USERA, VINCENT L., state agency administrator; b. Buenos Aires, 1942; BS, Coll. Holy Cross, 1964; BA in Philosophy, cum laude, George Washington U., 1978; JD, Catholic U., 1981. Bar: Alaska 1985, admitted to practice: US Fed. Ct. 1985, US Ct. Appeals (9th Cir.) 1985, US Dist. Ct. (Alaska) 1986. Asst. atty. gen. Alaska Dept. Law, Comml. Sec., 1991—99; acting dir. Dept. Cmty. and Econ. Devel., 1999—. Office: Dimond Courthouse PO Box 110300 123 4th St Juneau AK 99811-0300 Office Phone: 907-562-0440. Office Fax: 907-465-2520.

USHAKOV, YURY VIKTOROVICH, ambassador; b. Moscow, Mar. 13, 1947; married; 1 daughter. Grad., Moscow State Inst. Internat. Rels., 1970; PhD in Hist., Diplomatic Acad. With Soviet Embassy in Denmark Ministry Fgn. Affairs of the USSR, 1970-75, with, 1975-86; dep. chief mission, min.-counsellor Embassy of the USSR/Russian Fedn., Denmark, 1986-92; dir. Dept. of All-European Coop. Ministry Fgn. Affairs Russian Fedn., 1992—96; amb., permanent rep. Russian Fedn. to the Orgn. Security and Coop. Europe, Vienna, 1996-98; dep. min. fgn. affairs Govt. Russian Fedn., 1998-99, amb. to the US Washington, 1999—. Office: Embassy of the Russian Fedn 2650 Wisconsin Ave NW Washington DC 20007-4600 Office Phone: 202-298-5757. Fax: 202-298-5749. E-mail: russianembassy@mindspring.com.

USHER, THOMAS JAMES, metal products executive; b. Reading, Pa., Sept. 11, 1942; s. Paul T. and Mary (Leonard) Usher; m. Sandra L. Mort, Aug. 14, 1965; children: Leanne, Jimmy, Lauren. BS in Indsl. Engring., U. Pitts., 1964, MS in Ops. and Rsch., 1965, PhD in Systems Engring., 1971. Indsl. engr. U. S. Steel Corp., Pitts., 1966—76, asst. gen. supt., 1975—78, asst. div. supt. Gary, Ind., 1978—81, asst. to pres., mng. dir. facility planning and engring. Pitts., 1982—83, v.p. engring., 1982—83, pres., 1991, U.S. Steel Mining Co., Inc., Pitts., 1983—84, v.p. engring. steel, 1984—, sr. v.p. steel ops., 1984—, exec. v.p. heavy products steel divsn., 1986—89, pres. steel divsn., 1990; pres., COO USX Corp., Pitts., 1994—95, chmn., CEO, 1995—2001; chmn. US Steel Corp., Pitts., 2001—06. Bd. dir. PNC Fin. Svcs.; bd. dirs. PPG Industries, H.J. Heinz Co.; bd. dir., non-exec. chmn. Marathon Oil Corp., 2007—. Mem. Leadership Pitts., 1984; trustee Multiple Sclerosis, Pitts., 1985; chmn. Allegheny Trails coun. Boy Scouts Am., Pitts, 1985, United Way, Pitts., 1985, U.S.-Korea Bus. Coun., 1993—; U.S.-Japan Bus. Coun.; trustee U. Pitts., 1994—, The Bus. Roundtable Nat. Found., 1995; vice chmn. Internat. Iron and Steel Inst. Bus. Coun., 1997. Mem.: Am. Iron and Steel Engrs. (bd. dirs. 1984—85), Dinamo/Ovia (bd. dirs. 1985), Am. Iron and Steel Inst., The Club at Nevillewood, Augusta Nat. Golf Club, Burning Tree Club, Oakmont Club, Dougle Eagle Club, Laurel Valley Club, Duquesne Club, Rolling Rock Club. Avocations: golf, tennis, racquetball, scuba diving, swimming. Mailing: Marathon Oil Corp Bd Directors 5555 San Felipe Rd Houston TX 77056-2723 *

USHER, See RAYMOND, USHER IV

USISKIN, ZALMAN PHILIP, mathematics educator; b. Chgo., Jan. 1, 1943; s. Nathan and Esther (Chukerman) U.; m. Karen Hesse, Sept. 2, 1979; children: Robert, Laura. BS in Math., U. Ill., 1963, BS in Edn., 1963; MA in Teaching of Math., Harvard U., 1964; PhD in Edn., U. Mich., 1969. Tchr. math. Niles Twp. High Sch.-West, Skokie, Ill., 1964-66; asst. prof. U. Chgo., 1969-74, assoc. prof., 1974-82, prof. edn., 1982—. Vis. prof. U. Ga., Athens, 1980; mem. nat. adv. bd. Children's TV Workshop, Square One TV, N.Y.C., 1986-92; dir. U. Chgo. Sch. Math. Project, 1987—; mem. math. scis. edn. bd. NRC, Washington, 1988-91; mem. U.S. Nat. Commn. on Math. Instrn., 1995-97, chmn., 1998—2001. Co-author: Geometry-A Transformation Approach, 1971, UCSMP Geometry, 1990, 2nd edit., 1996; author: Advanced Algebra with Transformations and Applications, 1975, Algebra Through Applications, 1976, UCSMP Transition Mathematics, 1989, 2nd edit., 1995, Mathematics for High School Teachers, 2003; mem. editl. bd. Am. Jour. Edn., 1983—2003; contbr. articles to profl. jours. Recipient Max Beberman award Ill. Coun. Tchrs. Math., 1981, Glenn Gilbert award Nat. Coun. Suprs. Math., 1994; named Disting. speaker ASCD, 1991; grantee. Mem. Nat. Assessment Ednl. Progress (mem. math. adv. com. 1995—2005), Nat. Coun. Tchrs. Math. (bd. dirs. 1995-98, Lifetime Achievement award 2001), Math. Assn. Am., Nat. Coun. Suprs. Math. (1st v.p. 1982-83), Met. Math. Club Chgo. (bd. dirs. 1970-73), Phi Beta Kappa, Phi Delta Kappa. Office: U Chgo 6030 S Ellis Chicago IL 60637

USLAY, CAN, finance educator; s. Yuksel and Nezihe Uslay. MBA, Ga. Inst. Tech., Atlanta, 2000, PhD, 2005. Area sales mgr. Vestel Fgn. Trade, Manisa, Turkey, 1997—98; asst. prof. mktg. Chapman U., Orange, Calif., 2005—. Internal advisor State of Ga.; advisor City of Orange Econ. Devel. Agy. Contbr. articles to profl. jours. 1st lt. Turkish Army, 1996—97. Fellow, Ga. Inst. Tech., 1999—2004. Mem.: Acad. Mktg. Sci., Am. Mktg. Assn. Office: Chapman Univ One University Dr Orange CA 92866 Office Phone: 714-628-2658.

USSERY, TERDEMA L., II, professional sports team executive; b. Watts, Calif. B in Pub. and Internat. Affairs, Princeton U., 1981; M in Govt., Harvard U., 1984; degree in law, U. Calif., Berkeley, 1987. Bus. and entertainment atty. Morrison & Foerster, LA; dep. commr., gen. counsel Continental Basketball Assn., 1990—91, commr., 1991—93; pres. Nike Sports Mgmt., 1993—97; pres., CEO Dallas Mavericks, 1997—; CEO HDNet, 2001—. Bd. dirs. Timberland Co., 2005—, TreeHouse Food, Inc., 2005—; alt. gov. NBA. Bd. trustees Princeton U., 2004—, Presbyn. Healthcare Found. Named Corp. Exec. of Yr., Black Enterprise mag., 2003; named one of Top 100 Most Powerful People in Sports, Sporting News, Top 101 Most Influential Minorities in Sports, Sports Illus. Office: Dallas Mavericks The Pavilion 2909 Taylor St Dallas TX 75226-1909 E-mail: terdema.ussery@dallasmavs.com. *

USTIAN, DANIEL C., trucking executive; With Navistar Internat. Corp., 1973—, group v.p., gen. mgr. engine group, 1990—99, pres., 1999—, COO, 2002—03, CEO, 2003—, chmn., 2004—. Office: Navistar International Corp PO Box 1488 4201 Winfield Rd Warrenville IL 60555 Office Phone: 630-753-5000.

USUI, LESLIE RAYMOND, apparel executive; b. Wahiawa, Hawaii, Feb. 2, 1946; s. Raymond Isao and Joyce Mitsuyo (Muramoto) U.; m. Annie On Nor Hom, Oct. 23, 1980; 1 child, Atisha. BA in Zool., U. Hawaii, 1969, MA in Edn., 1972. Cert. tchr. Hawaii. Flight steward United Airlines, Honolulu, 1970; spl. tutor Dept. Edn., 1971-73; v.p. Satyuga, Inc., Honolulu, 1974-80, pres., 1980-97; also bd. dir.; pres. Masktique LLC, 2006—. Cons. Hawaii Fashion Guild, 1978-79. Composer: Song to Chenrayzee, Song to Karmapa: author: The Early History of Tibetan Buddhism in Hawaii, 2005. Co-founder, Kagyu Thegchen Ling Meditation Ctr., 1974-03; bd. dir. Maitreya Inst., 1983-86, Palpung Found., 1984-2006; mem. US Senatorial Bus. Adv. Bd., Wash., 1988; charter mem. Citizens Against Govt. Waste, 1988—, Citizens for Sound Economy, 1987-91, Nat. Tax Limitation Com., 1988-89. Mem. Am. Biog. Inst. (life, bd. govs. 1990), Internat. Biog. Centre (life), World Inst. Achievement (life), Cousteau Soc., Nature Conservancy, Waikiki Aquarium. Republican. Buddhist. Avocations: oriental gardening, music. Home: PO Box 161257 Honolulu HI 96816-0926 Office: Satyuga Inc PO Box 161257 Honolulu HI 96816-0926

UTAS, CENGIZ, nephrologist; b. Kayseri, Turkey, May 23, 1959; s. Emin and Sevim Utas; 1 child, Alper. Grad., Ankara U., Turkey, 1984. Diplomate Ankara U., 1984. Asst. prof. Erciyes U., Kayseri, Turkey, 1991—94, assoc. prof., 1994, prof., 2000; dir. hematology unit Erciyes U. Hosp., 1991—, tng. coord., 1995—96, head nephrology dept., 1996—; vice dean Erciyes U. Sch. Medicine, 1996—2000, dean, 2000—01, rector, 2004—. Editor: (books) Manual For Hemattialysis Nurses, 2000, Daily Drug Use In Nephrology and Kidney Failure, 2005, Nephrology Manuel. Recipient Internat. Socrates award, Europe Bus. Assembly, Oxford, Eng., 2006. Mem.: Turkish Soc. Nephrology, European Dialysis and Transplant Assn.

UTECHT, ANDREA E., lawyer; b. Olean, NY, Nov. 30, 1948; BA magna cum laude, Elmira Coll., 1970; MS, U. Pa., 1972, MBA, JD, U. Pa., 1975. Bar: Pa. 1975, NY 1976. Assoc. corp. counsel Colonial Penn Group, Inc., 1975—81; sr. v.p., gen. counsel, sec. AtoFina Chemicals, Inc., 1996—2001; v.p., gen. counsel, sec. FMC Corp., Chgo., 2001—. Mem.: Am. Corp. Counsel Assn., Phila. Bar Assn., Assn. Corp. Counsel (bd. mem.), Am. Arbitration Assn. (bd. mem.), Phi Beta Kappa. Fluent in French. Office: FMC Corp 200 E Randolph Dr Chicago IL 60601 Office Phone: 312-861-6000. Office Fax: 312-861-7127.

UTGOFF, KATHLEEN PLATT, federal agency administrator; b. Trenton, NJ, Feb. 5, 1948; d. Francis J. and Helen Platt; m. Victor Utgoff; children: Anna, Margaret. Student, Rutgers U., 1966-68; BA in Econs., Calif. State U., Northridge, 1971; PhD in Econs., UCLA, 1978. Employment counselor Dept. Human Resources, Van Nuys, Calif., 1971-72; economist Ctr. for Naval Analysis, Alexandria, Va., 1974-83; sr. staff economist Coun. Econ. Advisors, Exec. Office of the Pres., Washington, 1983-85; exec. dir. Pension Benefit Guaranty Corp., US Dept. Labor, Washington, 1985—89; ptnr., chief economist Groom & Nordberg, Washington, 1989—95; v.p., dir. Ctr. for Naval Analysis, Alexandria, Va., 1995—99; commr. Bur. Labor Statistics, US Dept. Labor, Washington, 2002—. Mem. Women in Govt. Relations, Am. Econ. Assn., Women in Employee Benefits. Republican. Office: Bur Labor Statistics Postal Sq Bldg 2 Massachusetts Ave NW Washington DC 20212 *

UTHMAN, BASIM MOHAMMAD, neurologist, epileptologist, consultant; b. Tripoli, Lebanon, Sept. 25, 1958; came to the U.S., 1984; s. Mohammad Assa'ad and Mariam Mohammad (Moukalled) U. BSc, Am. U. Beirut, 1978, MD, 1984. Diplomate Am. Bd. Clin. Neurophysiology, Am. Bd. Psychiatry and Neurology (adult neurology), Am. Bd. Psychiatry and Neurology with spl. qualifications in clin. neurophysiology. Intern Am. Univ. Beirut Med Ctr., Lebanon, 1983-84; resident in neurologyDept. Neurology U. Cin., 1984-87, clin. fellow in neurophysiology, epilepsy, preceptor, 1987-88; clin. rsch. fellow in epilepsy, neurophysiology and neuropharmacology U. Fla., Gainesville, 1988-90, clin. instr., 1990-91, vis. asst. prof. dept. neurology, 1991—92, asst. prof. dept. neurology, 1992—96, assoc. prof. dept. neurology, 1996—; assoc. prof. dept. neurosci. U. Fla. Brain Inst., 1997—; staff neurologist VA Med. Ctr., Gainesville, 1990—, asst. chief neurology svc., 1992—, dir. status epilepticus team, 1990-95, contracting officers tech. rep., 1990-92, acting chief neurology svc., 1993, dir. clin. neurophysiology lab. EEG/EP, 1991—, dir. vagus nerve stimulation therapy, 1991—; champion dementia clin. practice guidelines Southeast Dept. Vets. Affairs Med. Ctrs., 1997—99. Chmn. med. record rev. com. VA, 1995-99; chmn. adminstrv. bd. investigation VA Med. Ctr., Gainesville, 1993; attending epileptologist Shands Hosp., 1993-98; mem. instnl. rev. bd. U. Fla. Health Sci. Ctr., 1994-96; mem. subcom. for clin. investigations Malcom Randall VA Med. Ctr., 1996-2002; mem. pharmacy benefit mgmt./med. adv. panel VA Med. Ctrs. Sys., 1998—. Ad hoc referee U.S. Pharmacopeial Conv., 1988-89, Drug Evaluations, 1990, Epilepsia, 1990, Jour. Neuroimaging, 1990, Drugs, 1993-2001; contbr. articles to profl. jours., chpts. to books. Active emergency blood donation campaign, Beirut, 1982-83, worker war disaster plan, 1982-83; vol. Lebanese Red Cross, Beirut, 1982-83; organizer children's med. ednl. presentations, 1984; profl. adv. bd. Epilspsy Found. Fla., 1992-93, chmn., 1993. A.S. Khalidi scholar Am. U. Beirut, 1978, Azeez B. Ajloini scholar, 1979, Tamari-Saab scholar, 1979, Dr. Haddad, 1980; fellow Bowman Gray Med. Sch., Winston-Salem, N.C., 1987; grantee Epilepsy Rsch. Found. Fla., 1988-90, Cyberonics, 1989-98, Marion Merryl Dow and Hoechot, Marion, Roussel, Inc., 1994-98, VA Coop. Studies Program Coordinating Ctr., 1990-95, 97-2003, VA Affairs Med. Ctr. Allotment, 1991-92, Abbott Labs., 1991--, U. Fla., 1991-92, Ceiba-Geigy, 1991-94, U. Fla. Brain Inst., 1992, Parke-Davis 1993-2000, Novartis, 1998—, Pfizer, 2000--, Elan, 2000-01, Schwarz, 2001-, Ivax, 2001--, Nat. Brain Injury Fund for Treatment and Tchg., 2001-; recipient J. Kiffin Penry Eagle award, 1998. Mem. AMA, Am. Acad. Neurology, Am. Epilepsy Soc., Am. Sleep Disorders Assn., Am. Electroencephalographic Soc., Am. Soc. Neurophysiological Monitoring, Am. Coll. Internat. Physicians, Nat. Stroke Assn., So. Clin. Neurol. Soc., So. Electroencephalographic Soc., Fla. Med. Assn., Alachua County Med. Soc., Nat. and Internat. Spkrs. Bur. (Pfizer, Glaxo-Wellcome Novartis, UCB Pharma, Ortho-McNeil, Elan, Abbott Labs., Cyberonics 1993—), Internat. Neuromodulation Soc. (bd. dirs. 1996—), Epilepsy Found. Am. (mem. adv. bd. 2003-). Muslim. Avocations: tennis, cooking, travel, jogging, music. Office: VA Med Ctr-Neurology Svc 127 1601 SW Archer Rd Gainesville FL 32608-1135 Office Phone: 352-374-6058. Personal E-mail: basim.uthman@gmail.com. Business E-Mail: basim.uthman@va.gov.

UTHMANN, RICHARD W., retired music educator; b. Chanute, Kans., Mar. 18, 1938; s. Walter Henry and Susie Elizabeth Uthmann; m. Edith L. Uthmann, June 29, 1963; 1 child, James Richard. BA in Music Edn., Wash. State U., 1960; MA in Music Edn., Wash. Music Edn., 1971. Tchr. band Garfield Pub. Schs., Wash., 1961—63, Mukilteo Pub. Schs., 1963—67; tchr. music Granger Pub. Schs., 1967—68, Billings Pub. Schs., 1971—73; tchr. band Kelso Pub. Schs., Wash., 1973—88, Wahkiakum Pub. Schs., Cathlamet, 1988—97, Cornerstone Christian Sch., Kelso, 1997—2006;

with Principally Winds Woodwind Quintet, 2004—. Dir. theatre orch. Performing Arts Ctr., Longview, Wash., 1976—; bd. dirs. Mt. Solo Homeowners Assn., 1997—. Capt. US Army, 1968—69, Vietnam. Mem.: Wash. Music Educators Assn. (Hall of Fame 2002), Southwest Wash. Symphony (bd. dirs. 1980—. Pres. Vol. Svc. award 2007), Southwest Wash. Youth Symphony (bd. dirs. 2006—07). Methodist. Avocations: gardening, woodworking, music. Home: 120 Ridgecrest Ln Longview WA 98632 Office Phone: 360-430-7283. Personal E-mail: duthmann@peoplepc.com.

UTKU, SENOL, civil engineer, computer science educator; b. Suruc, Turkey, Nov. 23, 1931; s. Sukru and Sukufe (Gumus) U.; m. Bisulay Bereket, May 9, 1964; children: Ayda, Sinan. Diploma in engring., Istanbul Tech. U., 1954; MS, MIT, 1959, ScD, 1960. Civil engr., Istanbul, Turkey. Rsch. engr. IBM, 1959-60; asst. prof. structural engring MIT, 1960-62; assoc. prof. Middle East Tech U., Ankara, Turkey, 1962-63; exec. dir., head of founding com. Computation Ctr., Istanbul Tech. U., 1963-65; tech. staff Jet Propulsion Lab., Pasadena, Calif., 1965-70, tech. cons., 1975—91; assoc. prof. civil engring Duke U., Durham, N.C., 1970-72, prof., 1972-79, prof. civil engring., prof. computer sci., 1979—2001, dir. undergrad. studies, 1980-87, dir. grad. studies, 1987-89, prof. emeritus civil engring. and computer sci., 2002—; prof. emetirus engring. scis. Istanbul Tech. U., 1994—. Sr. Fulbright lectr., Turkey, 1998. Author: ELAS Software, 1968, Elementary Structural Analysis, 4th edit., 1991, Linear Analysis of Discrete Structures, 1991, Theory of Adaptive Structures, 1998; co-author: Dynamics of Offshore Structures, 1984, Finite Element Handbook, 1987, Parallel Processing in Computational Mechanics, 1992, Intelligent Structural Systems, 1992; contbr. articles to profl. jours. Fulbright scholar, Turkey, 1957, Fulbright lectr., Turkey, 1998; recipient Pres.'s Fund award Calif. Inst. Tech., 1981, NASA award, 1969, 71, 77, 84, 86-87, Internat. Joint Rsch. award NSF, 1991-92. Fellow ASCE; mem. AAUP, Am. Acad. Mechanics, Fulbright Assn., Am. Soc. for Engring. Edn., Structural Engring. Inst. (charter), Sigma Xi, Chi Epsilon. Office: Duke U 121 Hudson Hall Durham NC 27708-0287 E-mail: bsutku@ttnet.net.tr, senol.utku@duke.edu.

UTLEY, CHASE CAMERON, professional baseball player; b. Pasadena, Calif., Dec. 17, 1978; m. Jennifer Cooper, Jan. 20, 2007. Grad., UCLA. Draft pick Phila. Phillies, 2000, second baseman, 2003—. Mem. US Team World Baseball Classic, 2006. Named to Nat. League All-Star Team, Maj. League Baseball, 2006—07, Postseason Nat. League All-Star squad, The Sporting News, 2006; recipient Mike Schmidt MVP award, Baseball Writers' Assn. of Am., Phila. chpt., 2005, Silver Slugger award, 2006. Achievements include leading the Nat. League in runs scored (131), 2006. Avocations: golf, fishing. Mailing: Phila Phillies Citizens Bank Park One Citizens Bank Way Philadelphia PA 19148 *

UTLEY, F. KNOWLTON, library director, educator; b. Northampton, Mass., May 4, 1935; s. Frederick K. and Florence E. (Moore) Utley; m. Faith E. Green, July 2, 1960; children: Richard F., Stephen R., David E. BS, Castleton State Coll., 1960; MA, U. Conn., 1967; EdD, Boston U., 1979; MLS, U. Ala., 1983. Tchr. indsl. arts Montpelier HS, Vt., 1960-61, Southwick HS, Mass., 1961-63; tchr., drafting instr. Putnam HS, Conn., 1963-68; media specialist Ctrl. Conn. State U., New Britain, 1968-69, dir. media svcs., 1969-72; doctoral tchg. fellow Boston U., 1972-73; dir. libr., media svcs. Manchester Pub. Schs., Mass., 1973-79; assoc. prof. libr. scis. U. Maine, Farmington, 1979—80; dir. grad. program libr. media Livingston U., Ala., 1980—83; dir. libr. media svcs. Am. Internat. Coll., Springfield, Mass., 1983—2007, dean learning resources, 2007—. Pres. C/W Mars-Ctrl. and We. Mass. Auto Res., 1987—88; chmn. bd. dirs. Cooperating Librs. of Great Springfield, 1988—89, We. Mass. Media Coun., 1991—93; founder, headmaster Hampshire Christian Acad., South Hadley, Mass., 1996—2002. Active Belchertown Housing Authority, Mass., 2000—, Belchertown Hist. Commn., 2004—; trustee Clapp Meml. Libr., Belchertown, 2003—. Mem.: ALA, Mass. Libr. Assn., New Eng. Libr. Assn., Phi Delta Kappa. Home: 11 Canal Dr Belchertown MA 01007-9224 Office: Am Internat Coll 1000 State St Springfield MA 01109-3151 Office Phone: 413-205-3225. Business E-Mail: f_knowlton.utley@aic.edu.

UTLEY, JON BASIL, think-tank executive, journalist; b. Moscow, Mar. 10, 1934; came to U.S., 1939, naturalized, 1952; s. Arcadi and Freda (Utley) Berdichevsky; m. Ana Maria Hijar, 1968. Student, U. Munich, 1952, Alliance Française, Paris, 1956; BS, Georgetown U., 1956. Mgr. Am. Internat. Underwriters, Cali, Colombia, 1959-60; editor, pub. Bogotá Bull., 1960-61; v.p. Universal Investors Svcs., Nassau, 1962-67; real estate developer Washington, 1968—; mng. gen. ptnr. Kimwill Oil Assocs., Warren, Pa., 1978-86; pres. Ocean McLean Corp., 1989-97, Needle in a Haystack, Washington, 1990-98, Needle Express, 1993-98; fgn. corr. Jour. Commerce, Internat. Reports, S. Am., 1969-74; columnist Times of the Ams., 1974-92, assoc. editor, 1981-92; columnist Washington Inquirer, 1981-90, Washington Times, 1981-82; contbg. editor Conservative Digest, 1984-89; mem. editl. adv. bd. Internat. Reports, 1981-91. Lectr. Accuracy in Media, treas., Ukraine, 1997, Cyprus, 99, Freedoms Found. Valley Forge; commentator Voice of Am., 1985—2003; Jamestown Found. observer Russian elections, 2000. Assoc. pub. The Am. Conservative, 2005—; contbr. articles to Washington Post, Harvard Bus. Rev., Nat. Rev., Human Events, Miami Herald, Lincoln Rev., NYC Tribune, Am. Legion mag., El Salvador Gazette, The World and I, Antiwar.com, Lima Times, others. Observer Guatemalan elections Georgetown U. Ctr. Strategic Studies, 1985, Romanian elections, 1990; trustee Ctr. Internat. Rels., adv. com. Solidarity Endowment; co-founder Com. to Avert a Mideast Holocaust, 1990-94; pres. Freda Utley Found., 2002—. Assoc. scholar Competitive Enterprise Inst., 1995-98; Robert A. Taft fellow Ludwig Von Mises Inst., 1998—. Fellow: Atlas Econ. Rsch. Found. (sr.; dir. Russian projects 2000—); mem.: Coun. Nat. Policy, Ams. Against Bombing/Ams. Against World Empire (chmn. 1998—), Hispanic Am. Ctr. Econ. Rsch. (bd. dirs. 1997—), World English Lang. Newspaper Assn. (pres. 1996), United Srs. Assn. (bd. dirs. 1993—2001, v.p. Amcham Cuba 2003—), Coun. Inter-Am. Security (bd. dirs. 1988—93), Phila. Soc., Nat. Press Club. Office: 910 17th St NW Ste 422 Washington DC 20006-2605

UTLEY, NANCY, film company executive; Exec. v.p. mktg., media, and rsch. 20th Century Fox, Beverly Hills, Calif.; pres. mktg. Fox Searchlight Pictures. Named one of 100 Most Powerful Women in Entertainment, Hollywood Reporter, 2006. Office: 20th Century Fox PO Box 900 Beverly Hills CA 90213-0900 *

UTT, GLENN S., JR., retired medical products executive; b. Neodesha, Kans., Aug. 7, 1926; s. Glenn S. and Reba Pauline (White) U.; m. Mary Lou Ford, Aug. 8, 1948; 1 child, Jan A. BSEE, BSBA, Kans. State U., 1949; MBA, Harvard U., 1951. Salesman Drexel Furniture Co., NC, 1951-55; v.p. Booz Allen & Hamilton, Chgo. and Zurich, Switzerland, 1955-62; exec. v.p. Abbott Labs., North Chicago, Ill., 1962-83, also dir., ret., 1983. Chmn. bd. U.P. Hotel Group Inc., Houghton, Mich.; ret. dir. Synergen, Selectide and Sugen biotech cos. Co-author: Lalique Perfume Bottles, 1990. Alderman City of Lake Forest, Ill., 1972-76, chmn. recreational bd., 1975-78; mem. exec. com. Lake County Republican Fedn., Waukegan, Ill., 1974-83. With USN, 1944-46, USAF (res.), 1948-53. Mem.: Beta Theta Pi. Avocations: antiques, objects of art. Home: PO Box 810 Houghton MI 49931 Personal E-mail: mlbud@webtv.net.

UTT, WILLIAM P. (BILL UTT), construction executive; B in Mech. Engring., U. Va., 1979, M in Mech. Engring., 1980, MBA, 1984. With CRS Sirrine Engrs., Inc., 1984; various sr. mgmt. and exec. positions CRSS, Inc.; pres., CEO North Am. Energy businesses Tractebel, 1995—2000; pres., CEO SUEZ Energy N.Am., 2000—06, KBR, 2006—, chmn., 2007—. Chmn. Electric Power Supply Assn.; mem. Nat. Petroleum Coun. Trustee Sch. Engring. and Applied Sci. U. Va.; trustee Episcopal HS, Houston. Office: KBR 601 Jefferson St Houston TX 77002 Office Phone: 713-753-2000. *

UTTAL, LYNET, education educator; b. Mount Kisco, NY, Feb. 27, 1959; d. William Reichenstein and Michiye Uttal; m. Daniel Laban Veroff, Aug. 4, 1985; children: David Misaku Uttal-Veroff, Eli Michio Uttal-Veroff, Benjamin Teruo Uttal-Veroff. BA, U. Mich., Ann Arbor, 1980; PhD, U. Calif., Santa Cruz, 1993. Asst. prof. Ctr. Rsch. Women, U. Memphis, 1993—97, U. Wis., Madison, 1997—2002, assoc. prof., 2002—. Author: (academic book) Making Care Work: Employed Mothers in the New Childcare Economy. Co-director Formando Lazos: Bicultural Parenting and Bldg. Stronger Latino Cmty., Madison, 2000—07. Grantee, Oscar and Elsa M. Mayer Family Found., 2003, 2006. Democrat. Office: Human Development and Family Studies 1430 Linden Dr # 202 Madison WI 53706 Home Phone: 608-240-9594; Office Phone: 608-263-4026. Business E-Mail: luttal@wisc.edu.

UTTAL, SUSAN, legal administrator; b. NYC, Oct. 8, 1954; d. Sheldon and Jane Louise (Kaufmann) Uttal. BA, Clark U., 1976; cert. paralegal, Inst. Paralegal Tng., Phila., 1978. Legal asst. Winthrop, Stimson, Putnam & Roberts, NYC, 1978-80; legal coord. Schroder Real Estate Corp., NYC, 1980-83; legal asst. supr. real estate svcs. dept. Cravath, Swaine & Moore, NYC, 1983-89; sr. legal asst. real estate dept. Rackemann, Sawyer & Brewster, Boston, 1989-90; sr. legal asst. leasing and real estate depts. Goulston & Storrs, Boston, 1990-97; contracts adminstr. Cabletron Systems, Inc., Rochester, NH, 1997-99; v.p. ops. Nonpareil Software, New Durham, NH, 1999—2003; mgr. legal lease mgmt. The Stop & Shop Supermarket Co. LLC, Quincy, Mass., 2005—. Mem. Clark U. N.Y. Young Alumni Assn. (steering com.). Democrat. Jewish. Avocations: pottery, piano, photography, bicycling, gourmet cooking. Personal E-mail: susan@panaceapottery.com.

UTTAL, WILLIAM R(EICHENSTEIN), psychology and engineering educator, research scientist; b. Mineola, NY, Mar. 24, 1931; s. Joseph and Claire (Reichenstein) U.; m. Michiye Nishimura, Dec. 20, 1954; children: Taneil, Lynet, Lisa. Student, Miami U. Oxford, Ohio, 1947-48; BS in Physics, U. Cin., 1951; PhD in Exptl. Psychology and Biophysics, Ohio State U., 1957. Staff Psychologist, mgr. behavioral sci. group IBM Rsch. Ctr., Yorktown Heights, NY, 1957-63; assoc. prof. U. Mich., Ann Arbor, 1963-68, prof. psychology, 1968-86, rsch. scientist, 1963-86, prof. emeritus, 1986—; grad. affiliate faculty dept. psychology U. Hawaii, 1986-88; rsch. scientist Naval Ocean Systems Ctr.-Hawaii Lab., Kailua, 1985-88; prof., chmn. dept. psychology Ariz. State U., Tempe, 1988—90, prof. dept. indsl. engring., 1992—99, affiliated prof., Dept. of Computer Sci. and Engring., 1993-98, prof. emeritus, 1999—. Vis. prof. Kyoto (Japan) Prefectural Med. U., 1965-66, Sensory Sci. Lab., U. Hawaii, 1968, 73, 2003-07, U. Western Australia, 1970-71, U. Hawaii, 1978-79, 80-81, U. Auckland, 1996, U. Freiburg, 1997, U. Sydney, 1999; pres. Nat. Conf. on On-Line Uses Computers in Psychology, 1974. Author: Real Time Computers: Techniques and Applications in the Psychological Sciences, 1968, Generative Computer Assisted Instruction in Analytic Geometry, 1972, The Psychobiology of Sensory Coding, 1973, Cellular Neurophysiology and Integration: An Interpretive Introduction, 1975, An Autocorrelation Theory of Visual Form Detection, 1975, The Psychobiology of Mind, 1978, A Taxonomy of Visual Processes, 1981, Visual Form Detection in Three Dimensional Space, 1983, Principles of Psychobiology, 1983, The Detection of Nonplanar Surfaces in Visual Space, 1985, The Perception of Dotted Forms, 1987, On Seeing Forms, 1988, The Swimmer: A Computational Model of a Perceptual Motor System, 1992, Toward a New Behaviorism: The Case Against Perceptual Reductionism, 1998, A Computational Model of Vision: The Role of Combination, 1999, The War Between Mentalism and Behaviorism, 2000, The New Phrenology: Limits on the Localization of Cognitive Processes in the Brain, 2001, A Behaviorist Looks at Form Recognition, 2002, Psychomythics, 2003, Dualism, 2004, Neural Theories of Mind, 2005, Human Factors in the Courtroom, 2006, The Immeasurable Mind, 2007; editor: Readings in Sensory Coding, 1972; assoc. editor Behavioral Rsch. Method and Instrn., 1968—90, Computing: Archives for Electronic Computing, 1963—75, Jour. Exptl. Psychology, Perception and Performance, 1974—79, cons. editor Jour. Exptl. Psychology: Applied, 1994—97; contbr. articles to profl. jours. Served to 2d lt. USAF, 1951-53. USPHS spl. postdoctoral fellow, 1965-66; NIMH research scientist award, 1971-76 Fellow AAAS, APA, Am. Psychol. Soc. (charter), Soc. Exptl. Psychologists (chmn. 1994-95), Ariz. Acad. Sci., Arts & Tech. (founding fellow). Achievements include patents in field. Office: Ariz State U Dept Indsl Engring Tempe AZ 85287-1104 Business E-Mail: aowru@asu.edu.

UTTER, ROBERT FRENCH, dean, retired judge; b. Seattle, June 19, 1930; s. John and Besse (French) Utter; m. Elizabeth J. Stevenson, Dec. 28, 1953; children: Kimberly, Kirk, John. BS, U. Wash., 1952; LLB, 1954. Bar: Wash. 1954. Pros. atty., King County, Wash., 1955-57; individual practice law Seattle, 1957-59; ct. commr. King County Superior Ct., 1959-64, judge, 1964-69, Wash. State Ct. Appeals, 1969-71, Wash. State Supreme Ct., 1971-95, chief justice, 1979-81; ret., 1995; dean of faculty Ctrl. and Eastern European Legal Inst., Prague, Czech Republic, 2001—04, faculty, 2005—. Adj. prof. constl. law U. Puget Sound, 1987—94; cons. CEELI, 1991, 1993—, USIA, 1992; vis. scholar Kyrgyzstan Judiciary, Kazakhstan, 1993—96, Mongolia, 1997; commentator on Moldovan constitution, 2003; leader comparative law tours; participant internat. confs.; lectr. in field. Editor: books on real property and appellate practice; author: books on state consl. law. Pres., founder Big Brother Assn., Seattle, 1955—67, Job Therapy Inc., 1963—71; mem. exec. com. Conf. Chief Justices, 1979—80, 1981—86; pres. Thurston County Big Bros./Big Sisters, 1984; lectr Soviet Acad. Moscow, 1991; USIA visitor to comment on jud. sys. Latvia, 1992, Kazakhstan, 1993—94; trustee Linfield Coll. Named Alumnus of the Yr., Linfield Coll., 1973, Judge of the Yr., Wash. State Trial Lawyers, 1989, Outstanding Judge, Wash. State Bar Assn., 1990, Seattle-King County Bar Assn., 1992, Outstanding Jurist, 2005, Conder-Faulkner lectr., U. Wash. Sch. Law, 1995, Disting. Alumnus, Sch. Law U. Wash., 1995; recipient Henry Jackson Disting. Pub. Svc. award, Nat. Wash. Sch. Law, 2000, Warren E. Burger award, Nat. Ctr. for State Cts., 2003, Vol. award, ABA-CEELI Program, 2003; Disting. Jud. scholar, U. Ind., 1987. Fellow: Chartered Inst. Arbitrators; mem.: ABA (commentator on proposed consts. of Albania, Bulgaria, Romania, Russia, Lithuania, Azerbaijan, Uzbekistan, Byelarus, Kazakhstan, and Ukraine), Am. Judicature Soc. (sec. 1987—, chmn. bd. dirs., mem. exec. com., Herbert Harley award 1983, Justice award 1998), Order of Coif. Baptist. Personal E-mail: rutter4804@aol.com.

UTZ, SARAH WINIFRED, nursing educator; b. San Diego; d. Frederick R. and Margaret M. (Gibbons) U.; BS, U. Portland, 1943, EdM, 1958; MS, UCLA, 1970; PhD, U. So. Calif., 1979. Clin. instr. Providence Sch. Nursing, Portland, Oreg., 1946-50, edn. dir., 1950-62; edn. dir. Sacred Heart Sch. Nursing, Eugene, Oreg., 1963-67; asst. prof. nursing Calif. State U., L.A., 1969-74, assoc. prof., 1974-81, prof., 1981—, assoc. chmn. dept. nursing, 1982—; cons. in nursing curriculum, 1978—; healthcare cons., 1991—; past chmn. ednl. adminstrs., cons., tchrs. sect. Oreg. Nurses Assn., past pres. Oreg. State Bd. Nursing; mem. rsch. program Western Interstate Commn. on Higher Edn. in Nursing; chmn. liaison com. nursing edn. Articulation Coun. Calif. Author articles and lab manuals. Served with Nurse Corps, USN, 1944-46. HEW grantee, 1970-74, Kellogg Found. grantee, 1974-76, USDHHS grantee, 1987—; R.N., Calif., Oreg. Mem. Am. Nurses Assn., Calif. Nurses Assn. (edn. commr. region 6 1987—, chair edn. interest group region 6, 1987—), Am. Ednl. Rsch. Assn., AAUP, Phi Delta Kappa, Sigma Theta Tau. Formerly editor Oreg. Nurse; reviewer Western Jour. Nursing Rsch. Office: 5151 State University Dr Los Angeles CA 90032-4226

UVA, JOE, broadcast executive; b. 1956; BA, SUNY Albany. Account exec. for CNN Turner Broadcasting Sales, Inc., 1984, v.p. & sales mgr., 1985—90, exec. v.p. sales for CNN/Headline News, 1990—95, pres., Turner Entertainment Group Sales & Mktg., 1996—2001; pres. & CEO OMD Worldwide, NYC, 2002—07; CEO Univision Comm. Inc., 2007—. Bd. dirs. TiVo, Inc., 2004—. Office: Univision Communications Inc Ste 3050 1999 Ave of the Stars Los Angeles CA 90067 Office Phone: 310-556-7665. *

UVENA, FRANK JOHN, retired printing company executive, lawyer; b. Ernest, Pa., Feb. 2, 1934; AB, Ohio U., Athens, 1959; LLB, Ohio State U., Columbus, 1963. Bar: Ill. 1963. Assoc. firm McDermott, Will & Emery, Chgo., 1963-68; atty. R.R. Donnelley & Sons, Chgo., 1968-75, v.p., gen. counsel, 1975-84, sr. v.p. law and corp. staffs, 1984-95. Bd. dirs. Am. Liver Found., Ill., 1996, national, 2001, Parents/Friends Elizabeth Ludeman Devel. Ctr., 1986. With AUS, 1954-56. Mem.: Chgo. Bar Assn., Ill. Bar Assn.

UYEHARA, OTTO ARTHUR, mechanical engineering educator emeritus, consultant; b. Hanford, Calif., Sept. 9, 1916; s. Rikichi and Umi (Nakayama) U.; m. Chisako Suda, Aug. 12, 1945; children: Otto Kenneth, Susan Joy Uyehara Schultheiss, Emi Ryu Uyehara-Stewart. BS, U. Wis., 1942, MS, 1943, PhD, 1946. Postdoctoral fellow U. Wis., Madison, 1945-46, rsch. assoc., 1946-47, asst. prof., then assoc. prof., 1949-57, prof., 1957-82, prof. emeritus, 1982—; pvt. practice cons. Anaheim, Calif., 1985—. Mem. sci. adv. com. Echlin Corp., Branford, Conn., 1980—. Recipient Sci. Achievement award Japan Soc. Automotive Engrs, Internal Combustion Engine award ASME, 1994. FEllow Soc. Automotive Engrs.; mem. ASME (internal combustion divsn., Internal Combustion award 1994), Japan Soc. Mech. Engrs. (hon.). Home: 824 Ashbury St San Francisco CA 94117-4464

U-YEN, KONGPOP, electrical engineer; s. Kalyanuwat and Kannika U-Yen; m. Manisa Pipattanasomporn, May 23, 2005. BS in Engring. (hon.), Chulalongkorn U., Bangkok, Thailand, 1999; MS in Engring., Ga. Inst. Tech., Atlanta, 2002, PhD in Engring., 2006. Rschr. Chulalongkorn U., 1999; engr. CT Rsch., Bangkok, 1999, L3 Comm., Sylmar, Calif., 2000; rsch. assistance Ga. Inst. Tech., 2000—02; grad. co-op Tex. Instruments, Dallas, 2001; sr. engr. NASA Goddard Space Flight Ctr., Greenbelt, Md., 2004—. Contbr. articles to prof. jours., procs. in field. Fellow, Tex. Instruments, 2000—02. Mem.: IEEE. Achievements include research in planar microwave filters with wide stopband; low loss and broadband microwave hybrids; low loss slotline structures; ultrawide-band bias filters. Office: NASA Goddard Space Flight Ctr Code 555 Greenbelt Rd Greenbelt MD 20771 Business E-Mail: kongpop.u-yen-1@nasa.gov.

UYS, JURGEN PETER BRINKER, securities analyst; came to U.S., 1955; s. Johannes Marthinus and Reinette McKay (Weidemann) U. BS, U. Pa., 1974; MBA, Columbia U., 1977. CFA. Securities analyst Equibank, N.A., Pitts., 1974-76; fin. analyst Amax Inc., Greenwich, Conn., 1978-80; v.p. Equitable Investment Mgmt., NYC, 1980-85; securities analyst Swiss Am. Securities, NYC, 1986-91; gen. ptnr. Peter Uys Partnership, Ltd., Atlanta, 1991—; mng. mem. J.P. Brinker Uys & Co. LLC. Mem.: CFA Inst., Huguenot Soc. Am. (treas. 1991—92), Commerce Club. Episcopalian. E-mail: jpbu@msn.com.

UZMAN, BETTY BEN GEREN, retired pathologist; b. Ft. Smith, Ark., Nov. 17, 1922; d. Benton Asbury and Myra Estelle (Petty) Geren; m. L. Lahut Uzman, Dec. 17, 1955 (dec.); 1 dau., Betty Tuba. Student, Ft. Smith Jr. Coll., 1939—40; BS, U. Ark., 1942; MD, Washington U., 1945; postgrad., MIT, 1948—50; MA (hon.), Harvard U., 1968. Intern Childrens Hosp., Boston, 1945—46; resident pathology Barnes Hosp., St. Louis, 1946—48; Am. Cancer Soc. rsrch. fellow MIT, Cambridge, 1948—50; chief biol. ultra structure and exptl. pathology Children's Cancer Rsch. Found., Boston, 1950—71; instr. Harvard Med. Sch., Boston, 1949—53, assoc., 1953—56, rsch. assoc., 1956—67, assoc. prof., 1967—71, prof., 1971-72; head rsch. dept. Sparks Regional Med. Ctr., Ft. Smith, 1972—74; prof. pathology La. State U., Shreveport, 1974—77, U. Tenn., Memphis, 1978—89, ret., 1989. Assoc. chief staff rsch. VA, Shreveport, 1974-77; staff pathologist VA, Memphis, 1978-89, chief lab. svc., 1986-87; chief field ops., spl. asst. to dir. VA Ctrl. Office, Washington, 1978-79, dir. med. rsch. svcs., 1979-80; chmn. pathology A Study sect. NIH, 1973-76; cons. to sci. dir. Children's Cancer Rsch. Found., Boston, 1971-73; mem. adv. com. on prevention, diagnosis and treatment Am. Cancer Soc., 1970-73, 77-80; mem. adv. bd. Office Regeneration Rsch., VA, 1985-89; disting. vis. investigator Inst. Venezolano Investigation Cientificas, Caracas, 1972-74 Decorated Order Andres Bello 1st class Venezuela; recipient Weinstein award United Cerebral Palsy, 1964 Mem. AAAS, Am. Soc. Cell Biology (emerita), Microscopy Soc. Am. (emerita, Diatome poster award 1985), Internat. Acad. Pathology (emerita), Am. Assn. Neuropathology (emerita, assoc.), Soc. Neurosci. (emerita), Am. Assn. Cancer Rsch. (emerita). Home and Office: Geren Farm 16048 E State Hwy 197 Scranton AR 72863-0048 Personal E-mail: bettyguzman@wildblue.net, bguzman@aol.com.

UZODINMA, MINTA LAVERNE SMITH, retired nursing administrator, nurse midwife; b. Des Moines, Mar. 29, 1935; d. Gerald Stanley and Dorothy LaVerne (Miles) Smith; m. John E. Uzodinma, Aug. 8, 1957 (dec. June 1994); children: Chinwe Uzodinma Thomas, Chika Uzodinma Hunter, Eze A., Amechi J. BSN, U. Iowa, 1957; cert nurse-midwifery, U. Miss., Jackson, 1970, MSN, 1975. Staff-head nurse pediatrics unit, supr. insvc. edn. Univ. Hosp., Iowa City, 1957-58, 61-64; clin. instr. med.-surg. nursing Iowa Meth. Sch. Nursing, Des Moines, 1958-59, 60; staff nurse, instr., assoc. dept. ob-gyn-dir. midwifery svc. U. Miss. Med. Ctr., Jackson, 1966-74, instr. nurse-midwifery edn., 1974-77, asst. prof., 1979-85, module coord. nurse-midwifery edn., 1977-81; staff nurse VA Med. Ctr., Jackson, 1985-87; nurse-midwife Coastal Family Health Ctr., Gulfport, Miss., 1987-89; asst. dir. nursing Miss. Dept. Health, Jackson, 1989-95, chief nurse cons., 1995—2001; clin. instr. nursing U. Miss. Med. Ctr., Jackson, 1992—2005, ret., 2001. Acting dir. nursing area Rust Coll., Holly Springs, Miss., 1975; mem. Miss. Bd. Nursing, 1979-84, treas., 1980-82, pres., 1983-84. Asst. editor region 3 Jour. Nurse-Midwifery, 1986-94; contbr. article to nursing jour. Bd. dirs. Hinds County unit Am. Cancer Soc., 1976-83; v.p. Poindexter Elem. Sch. PTA, 1966, pres., 1974-75. Recipient Alton B. Cobb Lifetime Achievement award Miss. Pub. Health Assn., 1996, Thelma Worksman award LWV Miss., 1998, Nursing Alumni of Decade award U. Miss., 1998; U. Iowa scholar, 1953-56; named Maternal-Child Health Cmty. Nurse of Yr., Miss. March of Dimes, 1995,98. Fellow Am. Coll. Nurse-Midwives (chpt. sec.-treas. 1985-86, treas. 1978-80, proctor divsn. examiners 1975-85, nat. chmn. nominating com. 1978-79, mem. task force on refresher programs 1984-88, chpt. chair 1991-94, bd. rev. 1987-90, sec. region III chpt. 4 1984-86, bd. govs. regional gov. 1997—, award for excellence 1997); mem. ANA, Miss. Nurses Assn. (chmn. affirmative action com. 1977-78, continuing edn. approval unit 1990-95, nurse practitioner spl. interest group 1984—, dir. edn. 1995-97, Pub./Cmty. Health Nurse of Yr. 1998, named Nurse of Yr. 2001), Eliza Pillars RN Assn., AAUW, U. Miss. Alumni Assn. (Nursing Alumni of Decade award 1971-80, 1998), Sigma Theta Tau. Home: 2832 Gretna Green St Jackson MS 39209-6907 Personal E-mail: muzocnm@aol.com.

UZZELL-BAGGETT, KARON LYNETTE, career officer; b. Goldsboro, NC, Apr. 28, 1964; d. Jesse Lee and Ernestine Smith Uzzell; m. Ronald Walter Baggett, July 26, 1990; 1 child, Kathleen; stepchildren: Christina, Brian, Adam. BS, U. N.C., Chapel Hill, 1986; postgrad., U. Md., College Park, 1993—96. Commd. 2nd lt. USAF, 1986, advanced through grades to lt. col., 1990, exec. officer 6ACCS Langley AFB, Va., 1986—88, ops. tng. officer 7393MUNSS Murted AFD, Turkey, 1988—89, command and control officer 52FW Spangdahlem AB, Germany, 1989—92, SENEX mission dir. 89AW Andrews AFB, Md., 1995—95, dep. chief classified control Office Sec. Def., 1995—97, chief classified control Office Sec. Def., 1998—99, flight comdr., dir. ops. 82TRSS Sheppard AFB, Tex., 1999—2001; detachment comdr. USAFE MSS, Vicenza, Italy, 2001—02; comdr. 78MSS, Robins AFB, Ga., 2002—04, 416EMSS, Karshi-Khanabad, Uzbekistan, 2003—04; dir. pers. OSC-A, Kabul, Afghanistan, 2005, plans officer, 2005; dir. pers. Air U., Maxwell AFB, Ala., 2004—. Emergency med. technician Orange County Rescue Squad, Hillsborough, N.C., 1985-86; treas. Melwood PTA, Upper Marlboro, Md., 1994-97; meml. vol. Women in Mil. Svc., Washington, 1993—; entitlements vol. Whitman Walker Clinic, Washington, 1993-98. Mem. So. Poverty Law Ctr. Democrat. Baptist. Avocations: running, weightlifting, sewing, cross stitching, gardening. Home: 2319 Walbash Dr Montgomery AL 36116

VACANO, JOST, cinematographer; Cinematographer Skouras Agy., Santa Monica, Calif., 1977—. Cinematographer: (films) Soldier of Orange, 1977, Spetters, 1980, Das Boot, 1981, The Neverending Story, 1984, 52 Pick-up, 1986, Robocop, 1987, Rocket Gibraltar, 1988, Total Recall, 1990, Untamed Heart, 1993, Showgirls, 1995, Starship Troopers, 1997, The Hollow Man, 1999.

VACANTI, JOSEPH PHILIP, pediatric and transplant surgeon; b. Omaha, Oct. 31, 1948; BS summa cum laude, Creighton U., 1970; MD with high distinction, U. Nebr., 1974. Diplomate in gen. surgery and pediatric surgery Am. Bd. Surgery. Clin. fellow in surgery Harvard Med. Sch., Boston, 1979-83; asst. in surgery Children's Hosp., Boston, 1983-90, sr. assoc. in surgery, 1990-98, dir. organ transplant, 1990-98, dir. lab. for transplant and tissue engring., 1990—; asst. prof. surgery Harvard Med. Sch., Boston, 1983-90, assoc. prof., 1990-97, prof., 1997—; John Homans prof. surgery Harvard Med. Sch./Mass. Gen. Hosp., 1998—; dir. Lab. Tissue Engring. and Organ Fabrication Mass. Gen. Hosp., 1998—, dir. Pediat. Transplant, 1998—, chief Dept. Pediat. Surgery, 2003—; surgeon-in-chief Mass. Gen. Hosp. Children, 2003—. Rsch. affiliate MIT, Cambridge, 1988—. Author some 30 book chpts. and more than 150 sci. articles; co-founder, sr. editor Tissue Engring.; mem. editl. bd. Cell Transplantation; mem. editl. adv. bd. Tissue Engring. Intelligence Unit, R.G. Landes. Recipient Sidney Farber award Children's Hosp., 1983, Spl. Recognition award Am. Liver Found., 1987. Fellow ACS; mem. Tissue Engring. Soc. (co-founder, pres.), Am. Soc. Transplant Surgeons, Transplantation Soc., Am. Pediat. Surg. Assn., Soc. Univ. Surgeons, Inst. Medicine. Office: Mass Gen Hosp 55 Fruit St Boston MA 02114-2696 Office Phone: 617-724-1725. Business E-Mail: jvacanti@parthners.org.

VACCARIELLO, LIZ, editor-in-chief; b. 1968; m. Steve Vaccariello; 2 children. BA, U. Mich. Editor-in-chief, v.p. editorial Cleve. mag.; articles editor, dep. editor Fitness mag., 1999, exec. editor, 2000—06; editor-in-chief Prevention mag., 2006—. Office: Rodale Inc 33 E Minor St Emmaus PA 18098-0099 Office Phone: 610-967-5171. Office Fax: 610-967-7726.

VACCARO, BRENDA, actress; b. Bklyn., Nov. 18, 1939; d. Mario and Christine (Pavia) V. Student, Neighborhood Playhouse, 1958-60. Appeared in Broadway plays: Everybody Loves Opal, 1961, The Affair, 1962, Tunnel of Love, 1962, Children from Their Games, 1963, Cactus Flower, 1965 (Tony award best supporting actress), The Natural Look, 1967, How Now Dow Jones, 1968 (Tony nomination best actress in mus. comedy), The Goodbye People, 1968 (Tony nomination for best actress in drama), Father's Day, 1971, California Suite with Neil Simon, The Odd Couple, 1985 with Sally Struthers, Jake's Women, 1992 with Alan Alda-A Neil Simon Play, Full Gallop (one woman show), 1998; motion pictures include: House by the Lake, 1977, Midnite Cowboy, 1969, Where It's At, 1969, I Love My Wife, 1970, Summer Tree, 1971, Going Home, 1971, Once Is Not Enough, 1975, Airport '77, 1977, Fast Charlie, 1977, Capricorn One, 1978, First Deadly Sin, 1980, Zorro, The Gay Blade, Supergirl, 1984, Water, 1986, Heart of Midnight, 1988, Cookie, 1988, Ten Little Indians, 1988, Masque of the Red Death, 1989, Love Affair, 1994, The Mirror Has Two Faces, 1996, Sonny, 2002, The Boyton Beach Bereavement Club, 2005; TV appearances in The Greatest Show on Earth, 1963, Fugitive, 1963, Defenders, 1965, Doctors and Nurses, 1965, Coronet Blue, 1967, Naked City, The FBI, 1969, The Psychiatrist, 1971, Name of the Game, 1971, Marcus Welby, M.D, 1972, Banacek, 1972, McCloud, 1972, McCoy, Streets of San Francisco, Sara, 1976 (Emmy nomination for best dramatic actress), Paper Dolls, Dear Detective, 1979, The Pride of Jesse Hallam, 1980, A Long Way Home, 1981, Star Maker, 1981, The Love Boat, 1984, Deceptions, 1985, St. Elsewhere, Murder She Wrote, 1990, Trials of Rosie O'Neil, 1991, Civil Wars, 1991, Flesh and Blood, 1991, Friends, 1995, The King of Queens, 1998, Ally McBeal, 1998, Becker, 2001, American Dad!, 2005, The War at Home, 2006; TV movie appearances in Travis Logan, D.A, 1971, What's A Nice Girl Like You, 1971, Honor Thy Father, 1973, Sunshine, 1973, The Big Ripoff, 1975, Julius and Ethel Rosenberg, 1978, Guyana Tragedy: The Story of Jim Jones, 1980, Paper Dolls, Dear Detective, 1989, Stolen: One Husband, Columbo, 1990, Once Is Not Enough (Academy award, Golden Globe award, People's Choice award), The Shape of Things (Emmy award for supporting actress), Golden Girls Ebbs Tide Revenge (Emmy award 1991), Red Shoe Diaries, 1991, Following Her Heart, 1994, Sing Me the Blues Lena, 1995, Touched by an Angel, 1996, Stolen One Husband, 1997, Johnny Bravo Show (voice over series animation), 1993-2000, When Husbands Cheat, 1998, Fat Girl (voice over series animation), 2001, Just A Walk in the Park, 2002, Just Desserts, 2004; TV Series (voice) Spawn, 1997. Recipient Theatre World award, 1961-62, 3 Tony nominations, 2 Hollywood Fgn. Press Assn. nominations.

VACCARO, JEROME VINCENT, psychiatrist, educator, healthcare executive; b. Bklyn., Apr. 17, 1955; BS, CUNY, 1977; MD, Albert Einstein U., 1981. Diplomate Am. Bd. Psychiatry. Chief resident Albert Einstein U., Bronx, NY, 1984-85; assoc. prof. U. Hawaii, Honolulu, 1985-89, UCLA, 1989—. Med. dir. PacifiCare Behavioral Health, 1996-2001, pres., CEO, 2001–; pres., CEO PacifiCare Dental/Vision, 2001-. Editor: Community Psychiatry, 1995; contbr. articles to med. jours. including Hosp. and Comty. Psychiatry, Comty. Mental Health Jour. Mem. Am. Psychiat. Assn., Am. Assn. Comty. Psychiatrists (editor jour. 1984-93). Office: Pacificare Behavioral Health PO Box 25186 Santa Ana CA 92799-5186

VACCARO, JOHN J., neurologist; m. Annette Vaccaro; children: Alexandra K., Michael Seaver, Matthew John. MD, Ea. Va., Norfolk, 1988—92. Diplomate Am. Bd. Psychiatry & Neurology, 1998, Am. Bd. Electrodiagnostic Medicine, 2000. Intern, 1992—93; resident, 1993—96; neurologist Neurol. Cons., Glen Ridge, NJ, 1997—2006. Fellow, Wake Forest, Winston-Salem, NC, 1996—97. Mem.: AMA, Am. Acad. Neurology. Office: Neurolog Cons 230 Sherman Ave Glen Ridge NJ 07044 Office Phone: 973-743-9555. Office Fax: 973-743-7663.

VACCHELLI, ROBERT FRANCIS, judge; b. Hartford, Conn., Jan. 29, 1951; s. Frank P. and Helen (DeRobertis) V.; m. Cathy Kinnane; 1 child. AB, Coll. of the Holy Cross, Worcester, Mass., 1973; JD, Suffolk U., 1977. Bar: Conn. 1977, U.S. Dist. Ct. Conn. 1978, U.S. Ct. Appeals 1979, U.S. Supreme Ct. 1981, Calif. 1983. Assoc. Stoner, Gross & Chorches, Hartford, 1977-78; asst. atty. gen. Conn. Atty. Gen.'s Office, Hartford, 1978—2007; judge Conn. Superior Ct., 2007—. Tutor Sch. Law U. Conn., 1997-98; contbr. seminar U.S. Bur. Alcohol, Tobacco & Firearms, 1984; spkr. various seminars, 1986—; argued before U.S. Supreme Ct., 1989; advisor Conn. Gen. Assembly Law Revision Commn., 1992; state coord. Internat. Extraditions, 1998—. Author: Liquor Licensing in Connecticut, 1987. Mem. Glastonbury, Conn. Pub. Bldg. Commn., 1986, Glastonbury Wetlands Authority, 1987; mem. Dem. Town Com., Glastonbury, 1986-91; vice chmn. bd. dirs. Glastonbury ABC, 1989-94; elected mem. Glastonbury Conn. Bd. Assessment Appeals, 2003-07. Recipient Am. Jurisprudence Book prize Lawyer's Co-op. Publ. Co., 1976, proclamation Glastonbury Conservation Commn., 1988, Merit award State of Conn., 1986, 91, 92, 95, 97, 98, 2004, 06. Mem. ABA (mem. adv. panel 2006-07), Conn. Bar Assn. (chmn. adminstrv. law exec. com., specialization cert. subcom. 1982-89, mcpl. law com. 1982-87), Wadsworth Atheneum.

VACCO, DENNIS C., lawyer, former state attorney general; b. Buffalo, Aug. 16, 1952; s. Carmen A. and Mildred V.; m. Kelly McIlroy; children: Alex, Connor. BA, Colgate U., 1974; JD, SUNY, Buffalo, 1978. Bar: N.Y. 1978, Fed. Ct. 1978, 82. Asst. dist. atty. Office of Erie County Dist. Atty., Buffalo, 1978-82, chief G.J. bureau, 1982-88; U.S. Atty. We. Dist. N.Y. Buffalo, 1988-93; atty. gen. State of New York, Albany, 1993-98; v.p. for govtl. affairs Waste Mgmt. Inc., 1998-99; pres. Waste Mgmt. N.Y. LLC, 1999—2003; pvt. practice atty. Boston, 2003—; ptnr. Carne & Vacco LLC, 2004—. Chmn. Atty. Gen.'s Environ. Subcom., Atty. Gen.'s Subcom. on Organized Crime and Violent Crime; mem. Nat. Environ. Enforcement Coun. Co-chair Erie County Community Commn. on Alcohol and Substance Abuse; bd. dirs. United Way of Erie County. Recipient Environ. Enforcement Leadership award Atty. Gen. Dept. of Justice, Washington, 1991. Mem. N.Y. State Bar Assn., Erie County Bar Assn., Nat. Dist. Attys. Assn., N.Y. State Dist. Attys. Assn., NCCJ, Hamburg Devel. Corp., 100 Club of Buffalo, U. Buffalo Law Alumni Assn. (bd. dirs.). Republican. Roman Catholic. Avocations: travel, sports.

VACEK, JAMES, cardiologist; b. Omaha, July 13, 1951; BS in Math., Creighton U., Omaha, 1977, MD, 1977. Cons. cardiology Mid Am. Cardiology, Kansas City, Mo., 1989—2001, U. Kans. Hosp., Kansas City, 2001—, dir. rsch. Contbr. articles to profl. jours. Maj. United State Air Force USAF, 1982—86. Named a Kans. City Super Doctor, Kans. City mag., 2007. Achievements include patents for catheter design. Office: Mid Am Cardiology KU Hosp 3901 Rainbow Blvd Ste G600 Kansas City KS 66061 Office Phone: 913-588-9600. E-mail: jlvacek@mac.md. *

VACHON, REGINALD IRENEE, mechanical engineer; b. Norfolk, Va., Jan. 29, 1937; s. Rene Albert Vachon and Regina (Galvin) Radcliffe; m. Mary Eleanor Grigg, Jan. 16, 1960; children: Reginald Irenee, Eleanor Marie. Student, U.S. Naval Acad., 1954-55; BME, Auburn U., 1958, MS, 1960; PhD, Okla. State U., 1963; LLB, Jones Law Sch., 1969. Registered profl. engr., Ala., Ga., Miss., La., Wis., Tex., chartered engr., U.K., cert. d'Iugenieur Mecanicien, France, lic. engr., European Fedn. Nat. Engring. Assns.; bar: Ala. 1971. Engr. Hayes Internat., 1958; instr., rsch. asst. Auburn U., 1958-60, rsch. assoc., 1961, assoc., prof., 1963-78; R&D engr. E.I. DuPont, 1960; aerospace engr., technologist NASA Marshall Space Flight Ctr., summers, 1964, 65; pres. Vachon Nix & Assoc., 1977—, VNA Sys. Inc., 1982—. COO Thacker Constrn. Co., Thacker Orgn., Inc., 1981—90, United Info. Techs., Inc., Global Interated Techs. Inc.; pres., CEO Compris Tech., Inc., 1991—92; chmn. Global Risk Mgr., Inc., 1992—, Direct Measurements, Inc., 2002—; prin. Gipco Holdings Internat., Ltd., 1994—; mem. sci. tech. adv. com. U.S. Dept. Homeland Security. Contbr. articles to profl. jours. With US Army, 1960—61. Fellow: ASCE, AIAA (assoc.), Singapore Instn. Engrs., Hong Kong Instn. Engrs., Instn. Mech. Engrs. U.K.; mem.: NSPE, ABA, ASME (hon.; pres. 2003—04), Soc. Frances des Mecaniciens, Ala. Bar Assn., Pan Am. Acad. Engring., Phoenix Soc. Atlanta, Peachtree Racket Club, N.Y. Yacht Club, Cosmos Club. Roman Catholic. Achievements include patents in field. Home: 1414 Epping Forest Dr NE Atlanta GA 30319-2539 Office: PO Box 190093 Atlanta GA 31119-0093 Office Phone: 404-388-6588. Business E-Mail: vachonr@asme.org.

VACHSS, ANDREW HENRY, lawyer, writer, juvenile justice and child abuse consultant; b. NYC, Oct. 19, 1942; s. Bernard and Geraldine (Mattus) V. BA, Case Western Res. U., 1965; JD magna cum laude, New Engl. Sch. Law, 1975; LLD (hon.), Case Western Res. U., 2004. Bar: N.Y. 1976, U.S. Dist. Ct. (so. and ea. dists.) N.Y. 1976. Program rep. USPHS, Ohio, 1965-66; unit supr N.Y.C. Dept. Social Svcs., 1966-69; urban coord. Community Devel. Found., Norwalk, Conn., 1969-70; dir. Uptown Community Orgn., Chgo., 1970-71; dep. dir. Medfield (Mass.)-Norfolk Prison Project, 1971-72; dir. intensive treatment unit ANDROS II, Roslindale, Mass., 1972-73; project dir. Mass. Dept. Youth Svcs., Boston, 1972-73; dir. Juvenile Justice Planning Project, NYC, 1975-85; pvt. practice NYC, 1976—. Organizer, coord. Calumet (Ind.) Cmty. Congress, 1970; bd. dirs. Libra Inc., Cambridge, Mass., Advocacy Assocs., N.Y. and N.J.; adj. prof. Coll. New Resources, N.Y.C., 1980-81; lectr. trainer, spkr. to numerous orgns.; cons. on juvenile justice and child abuse to numerous orgns., 1971—. Author: The Life-Style Violent Juvenile: The Secure Treatment Approach, 1979, (novels) Flood, 1985, Strega, 1987, Blue Belle, 1988, Hard Candy, 1989, Blossom, 1990, Sacrifice, 1991, Shella, 1993, Down in the Zero, 1994, Another Chance to Get it Right, 1995, 2003, Footsteps of the Hawk, 1995, Batman: The Ultimate Evil, 1995, False Allegations, 1996, Safe House, 1998, Choice of Evil, 1999, Dead and Gone, 2000, Pain Management, 2001, Only Child, 2002, The Getaway Man, 2003, Down Here, 2004, Two Trains Running, 2005, Mask Market, 2006, Terminal, 2007, (graphic novels) Predator: Race War, 1995, Hard Looks, 2002, (audiobook) Proving It, 2001, (short stories) Born Bad, 1994, Everybody Pays, 1999; editor-in-chief: New Eng. Law Rev., 1974—75; contbg. editor: Parade; contbr. articles. Mem. bd. counselors Childtrauma Acad., Baylor Coll. Medicine; mem. bd. advisors Protect PAC; mem. expert adv. panel on catastrophic child abuse N.Y. State Office of Mental Health. Recipient Grand Prix de Lit. Policiére, 1988, Falcon award Maltese Falcon Soc. Japan, 1988, Deutschen Krimi Preis, Die Jury des Bochumer Krimi Archivs, 1989, Raymond Chandler award Giurìa a Noir Festival, 2000, 1st Annual Harvey R. Houck award Justice for Children, 2003, 1st Annual Illuminations award St. Vincent's Ctrs. Nat. Child Sexual Abuse Prevention Program, 2003; Indsl. Area Found. Tng. Inst. fellow, 1970-71, John Hay Whitney Found. fellow, 1976-77. Mem. PEN, Writers Guild Am. Office Phone: 212-581-8121.

VACKETTA, CARL LEE, lawyer, educator; b. Danville, Ill., Aug. 3, 1941; s. Peter G. and Julia M. (Columbus) V. BS with honors, U. Ill., Urbana-Champaign, 1963, JD, 1965. Bar: Ill. 1965, DC 1968, US Dist. Ct. DC 1968, US Ct. Fed. Claims 1968, US Supreme Ct. 1970. Tax lawyer GM, Detroit, 1965; ptnr. Sellers, Conner & Cuneo, Washington, 1968—74, Pettit & Martin, 1974—95, Piper & Marbury, 1995—99, Piper Rudnick LLP, 1999—2004; ptnr., former chmn. Govt. Contracts practice group DLA Piper Rudnick Gray Cary, Washington, 2005—06, DLA Piper LLP, 2006—. Adj. prof. law Georgetown U., 1971—. Co-author: Government Contract Default Termination, 1991, 93, 95, 97, 99; co-editor Extraordinary Contractual Relief Reporter, 1974-2002; editor in chief, pub. contract law sect., Pub. Contract Law Jour., 1994-2006; mem. adv. bd. The Government Contractor. Past pres. Bd. vis., U. Ill. Coll. Law Capt. Judge Advocate Corps US Army, 1966—68. Fellow ABA (sec. pub. contract law sect. 1978-79, coun. 1979-82, Nat. Contract Mgmt. Assn.; mem. Fed. Bar Assn., DC Bar Assn., Ill. State bar Assn., Nat. Assn. Purchasing Mgrs., University Club (Washington). Roman Catholic. Office: DLA Piper LLP 1200 19th St NW Washington DC 20036-2412 Office Phone: 202-861-6460. Office Fax: 202-223-2085. Business E-Mail: carl.vacketta@dlapiper.com.

VADDI, KRISHNA, pharmaceutical executive; s. Subba Rao Venkata and Swarajya Lakshmi Vaddi; m. Lakshmi Ayalasomayajula, Dec. 4, 1994; children: Tej, Neel. B in Vet. Sci. and Animal Husbandy, Andhra Pradesh Agrl. U., Tirupati, India, 1986; PhD, U. Fla., Gainesville, 1992. Postdoctoral fellow DuPont Merck Pharm. Co., Wilmington, Del., 1992—94; sr. scientist ProScript, Inc, Cambridge, Mass., 1994—95; sr. rsch. scientist Genzyme Corp., Framingham, Mass., 1995—98; dir. inflammatory diseases rsch. DuPont Pharmaceuticals Co., Wilmington, 1998—2001; v.p. preclinical biology Incyte Corp., Wilmington, 2002—. Author: (book) Chemokine Facts Book; contbr. articles to profl. jours. Bd. dirs. Sci., Math and Tech. Alliance, Wilmington, 1999—2002. Doctoral fellow, U. Fla., 1989—92. Mem.: AAAS, Soc. for Leukocyte Biology, Am. Assn. Immunology, Am. Assn. Cancer Rsch. Achievements include patents for method to monitor proteasome activity following Velcade administration in multiple myeloma; discovery of molecules that inhibit a key mediator of inflammation; molecules that inhibit a receptor on inflammatory cells; role of a chemokine receptor in mediating insulin resistance; patents for use of sheddase inhibitors to treat cancer. Home: 108 Forest Dr Kennett Square PA 19348 Office: Incyte Corporation Henry Clay Rd Wilmington DE 19880 Home Phone: 610-925-3244; Office Phone: 302-498-6733. Business E-Mail: kvaddi@incyte.com.

VADLAMUDI, RATNA K., healthcare educator; s. Venkateswara Rao and Koteswaramma Vadlamudi; m. Kumari Vadlamudi; 1 child, Chaitanya. PhD, U. Wyo., 1994. Postdoctoral rschr. Harvard Med. Sch., Boston, 1995—97; asst. prof. UT MD Anderson Cancer Ctr., Houston, 1998—2004; assoc. prof. LSU Health Scis. Ctr., New Orleans, 2004—05, UT Health Scis. Ctr., San Antonio, 2006—. Mem.: AACR. Achievements include patents for estrogen receptor modulators and uses. Office: UT Health Scis Ctr 7703 Floyd Curl Dr San Antonio TX 78229 Business E-Mail: vadlamudi@uthscsa.edu.

VADUS, GLORIA A., scientific document examiner; b. Forrestville, Pa. Diploma, Cole Sch. Graphology, Calif., 1978; BA in Psychology Counseling, Columbia Pacific U., 1981, MA in Psychology, 1982; diploma handwriting expert, Edith Eisenberg, Bethesda, Md., 1991. Diplomate Am. Bd. Forensic Examiners (founding mem.); cert. Am. Acad. Graphology, Washington, 1978, ct. qualified sci. document examiner, registered graphologist 1978, cert. behavioral profiling and cert. questioned documents Am. Bd. Forensic Examiners, CHS I Am. Bd. Homeland Security, 2004, cert. Am. Handwriting Analysis Found. Pres., owner Graphinc, Inc., 1985—. Accredited instr. graphology Montgomery County Schs., Md., 1978—79; instr. Psychogram Centre, 1978—85, Coun. Graphol. Socs., 1980; developed Trilogy base for rsch. Am. Handwriting Analysis Found.; lectr, cons. in field; founding mem. Am. Bd. Forensic Examiners. Contbr. articles to profl. jours. Chmn. Letter of Hope for POWs; vol. Montgomery County, 1985—87; bd. dirs. East Gate I Civic Assn., Potomac, Md., 1985—87, cmty. affairs chair, 1985—87; sovereign amb. Order Am. Ambs. USA, 2006. Named Global fellow, World Forum Fedn., 2007, Disting. Symposium Lectr., 2007; named to Amb. USA, 2007; recipient Spl. award, US, Japan Marine Facilities Panel Valuable Contbr. Japanese Panel UJNR, MFP, 1978—94, Gold Nib Analyst of Yr. award, Am. Handwriting Analysis Found., 1982, Dancing Fan award, Marine Tech. Soc., Tokyo chpt., 1991, Profound Contbr. to Soc. to the Yr., 2000, Am. Bronze Medal of Hon., 2001, Internat. Peace prize, United Cultural Conv. of USA, 2003, Legion of Honor Gold medal, United Cultural Conf., 2005, Lifetime Achievement award, World Congress of Arts, Scis. and Comm., 2005, World Freedom medal, United Cultural Ctr., 2006, Excellence medal, World Congress Arts, Scis., and Comm., 2006, Svcs. and Achievement Gold medal, ABI, 2006. Fellow: Am. Coll. Forensic Examiners Internat. (life; awards chair 1993—94, Meritorious award 1994, Outstanding Contbn. cert.); mem.: Coun. Graphical Socs. (bd. dirs. 1982—84), Soc. Francaise de Graphologie for Am. Handwriting Analysis Found., Nat. Assn Document Examiners (bd. dirs. 1985—92, ethics hearing bd. 1986, chmn. nominations com. 1987—88, elections chmn. 1988, parliamentarian 1988—92), Nat. Forensic Ctr., Am. Handwriting Analysis Found. (life; chmn. rsch. com., chmn. adv. bd. 1981—87, bd. dirs. 1981—91, pres. 1982—84, chmn. nominations com. 1985—86, officiator 1986, policy planning and ethics com. 1986—91, ethics chmn. 1989—91, chmn., past pres. adv. bd. 1989—91, hon. profl. women's adv. bd. 1999, cert.), Nature Conservancy, Charles F. Menninger Soc., IEEE-Distaff (internat. chmn. bd. dirs. 1969—72, fashion show chair 1969—72), Internat. Platform Assn., Nat. Wildlife Fedn., Nat. Capitol Jaguar Owners Club (judge 1975—78), Sierra Club, Henry Hicks Garden Club of the Westburys, NY (v.p., pres. elect, judge, chair flower shows, bd. dirs. 1967—71), Soroptimist Internat. (internat. chair, regional del., v.p. chpt., bd. dirs. 1987—92, regional dir. 1987—92), Nat. Writers Club. Home: 8500 Timber Hill Ln Potomac MD 20854-4237 Office Phone: 301-299-5477. Personal E-mail: j.vadus@ieee.org.

VAFIADIS, JON, recording industry executive; b. NYC, Mar. 11, 1980; s. Saavas Vafiadis and Stella Kostopoulos. BS, NYU, 2002. Pres. Whoa Oh Recs., Astoria, NY, 1998—2006, Are You Listening Recs., Astoria, 2006—. Dir. bus. devel. Rock 'n Roll Fantasy Camp, NYC, 2006—. Bd. mem. Stern Alumni Assn., NYC, 2006—. Mem.: Mensa (corr.). Home Phone: 646-772-1157. Personal E-mail: jvafiadis@gmail.com. Business E-Mail: whoaoh@gmail.com.

VAGT, ROBERT F., former academic administrator; m. Ruth Anne Vagt, 1968; children: Ashley, Lindsey. BA in Psychology, Davidson Coll., 1969; MDiv, Duke U. Ordained to ministry Presbyn. Ch. Dir. clin. programs N.W. Ala. Mental Health Ctr.; exec. dir. Mcpl. Assistance Corp., NYC, 1979—80; chmn., pres., COO Seagull Energy Corp.; pres. Davidson Coll., 1997—2007. Bd. dirs. Cornell Cos., Inc., El Paso Corp., Houston, 2005—. Bd. vis. Davidson Coll., 1992—, mem. Ultra Soc., nat. leader Ann. Fund, 1993—95. Recipient Alumni Svc. award, Davidson Coll., 1996. *

VAGTS, DETLEV FREDERICK, law educator; b. Washington, Feb. 13, 1929; s. Alfred and Miriam (Beard) Vagts; m. Dorothy Larkin, Dec. 11, 1954; children: Karen, Lydia. Grad., Taft Sch., 1945; AB, Harvard U., 1948, LLB, 1951. Bar: Mass. 1961. Assoc. Cahill, Gordon, Reindel & Ohl, NYC, 1951-53, 56-59; asst. prof. law Harvard U. Law Sch., Cambridge, Mass., 1959-62, prof., 1962—, Eli Goldston prof., 1981-84, Bemis prof. internat. law, 1984—2005, prof. emeritus, 2005—, dir. internat. tax program, 1998-2000. Counselor internat. law dept. of State, 1976—77. Author (with others): Transnational Legal Problems, 1968, 4th edit., 1994, Basic Corporation Law, 1973, 3d edit., 1989, Transnational Business Problems, 3d edit., 2003; editor: Secured Transactions Under the Uniform Commercial Code, 1963—64; assoc. reporter (with others): Restatement of Foreign Relations Law, book rev. editor: Am. Jour. Internat. Law, 1986—93, co-editor-in-chief:, 1993—98. 1st lt. USAF, 1953—56. Recipient Max Planck Rsch. award, 1991. Mem.: ABA, Coun. Fgn. Rels., Am. Soc. Internat. Law, Phi Beta Kappa. Home: 29 Follen St Cambridge MA 02138-3502 Office: Sch Law Harvard U Cambridge MA 02138 Business E-Mail: vagts@law.harvard.edu.

VAHAVIOLOS, SOTIRIOS JOHN, electrical engineer, researcher, engineering executive; b. Mistra, Greece, Apr. 16, 1946; s. John Apostolos and Athanasia (Pavlakos) Vahaviolos; m. Aspasia Felice Nessas, June 1, 1969; children: Athanasia, Athena, Kristy. BSEE, Fairleigh Dickinson U., 1970; MSEE, Columbia U., 1972, M in Philosophy, 1975, PhDEE, 1976. Mem. tech. staff Bell Tel. Labs., Princeton, NJ, 1970-75, supr., 1975-76, dept. head, 1976-78; founder, pres., CEO Phys. Acoustics Corp., Princeton, 1978—, MISTRAS Group Inc., Princeton, 1984—94, chmn. quality svcs. labs., 2000—. Adviser Greece Ministry Def., Athens, 1986—88; bd. dirs. Orthosonics, Inc., NYC; chmn. policy com., life fellow Internat. Com.

Nondestructive Testing, life mem. bd. dirs., 2004—. Contbr. scientific papers to profl. publs. Chmn. Princeton sect. United Fund, 1976—78; adv. bd. Trenton State Coll., 1983—; chmn. Greek Independence Parade, NYC, 2002—03; v.p. Fedn. Greek Soc. in Greater N.Y.; bd. dirs. Holy Cross Greek Orthodox Sch. Theology, Boston, 1989—; pres. bd. trustees St. George Greek Orthodox Cmty., Trenton, NJ; elector archon Order of St. Andrew the Apostle of the Holy Ecumenical Patriarchate of Constantinople, 2004. Recipient Spartan Merit award, Spartan World Soc., 1987, Entrepreneur of the Yr. award, Arthur Young/Inc. Mag., 1989. Fellow: IEEE (Centennial Medal award 1984, Mittleman Achievement award 1993), Acoustic Emission Working Group (Gold medal 2005), Am. Soc. Nondestructive Testing (bus. and fin. com. 1984—87, 1988—, bd. dirs. 1985, sec. 1989, treas. 1990, v.p. 1991, pres. 1992, chmn. bd. 1993, chmn. internat. com. nondestructive testing 1994—, editor handbook on acoustic emission 1988, Lester Honor award 1998, Gold medal 2001); mem.: ASTM, Fairleigh Dickinson U., Coll. of Sci. and Math. Adv. Coun., Montclair State U., Internat. Fund Advancement Nondestructive Testing (v.p.), N.Y. Acad. Scis., IEEE Indsl. Electronics Soc. (sr. mem. adminstv. com. 1988, founder, v.p. conf. 1974—78, editor Trans. on Indsl. Electronics 1976—82, 2d prize Student Paper Constest 1970, Outstanding Young Engr. award 1984). Greek Orthodox. Achievements include patents in field. Avocations: bird hunting, soccer, technical writing, gardening. Home: 7 Ridgeview Rd Princeton NJ 08540-7601 Office: Mistras Holdings Group 195 Clarksville Rd Princeton Junction NJ 08550 Personal E-mail: sotirios@pacnett.com.

VAIDHYANATHAN, SIVA, journalist, educator; b. Buffalo, June 16, 1966; s. Vishnampet S. and Virginia Ann (Evans) V. BA, U. Tex., 1992, PhD in Am. Studies, 1999. Reporter Dallas Morning News, 1988, Austin Am. Statesman, Tex., 1989-91, Ft. Worth Star-Telegram, Tex., 1992; freelance journalist, 1992—; history lectr. Concordia U., Austin, 1996; instr. Am. studies U. Tex., 1997, Wesleyan U., U. Wis., Madison; asst. prof. culture and comm. NYU, 1999—2007; assoc. prof. media studies and law U. Va., Charlottesville, 2007—. Author: Copyrights and Copywrongs: The Rise of Intellectual Property and How It Threatens Creativity, 2001, The Anarchist in the Library: How the Clash Between Freedom and Control is Hacking the Real World and Crashing the System, 2004. Election judge Travis County, Tex., 1984. Mem. MLA (exec. com. 1996), Am. Studies Assn. of Tex. (students com. 1995-97). Hindu. Office: U Va 401 Cabell Hall PO Box 400866, Cabell Dr Charlottesville VA 22904-4866 Office Phone: 212-992-9494. Office Fax: 212-995-4046. E-mail: sv24@nyu.edu. *

VAIDYANATHAN, BALACHANDRAN, operations research specialist, industrial engineer; b. New Delhi, Nov. 26, 1980; s. S. Vaidyanathan and V. Bharathi; m. Sirisha Govindaraju, June 8, 2006. B in Tech., Naval Arch. and Ocean Engring., Indian Inst. Tech. Madras, Chennai, India, 2002; student in Indsl. and Systems Engring., U. Fla., Gainesville, 2003—. Software engr. Infosys Techs. Ltd., Chennai, India, 2002—03; asst. rsch. and tchg. U. Fla., Gainesville, 2003—. Contbr. chapters to books, articles to profl. jours. Recipient Best Thesis award, Indian Inst. Tech. Dept. Ocean Engring., 2002, Best Paper award, Transp. Rsch. Forum, 2007. Mem.: Rail Applications Spl. Interest Group, Inst. Ops. Rsch. and Mgmt. Sci. (Student Paper hon. mention 2004, nominee colloquium 2006, Student Paper hon. mention 2006). Office: Univ Florida 303 Weil Hall Gainesville FL 32611 Home Phone: 352-665-2821; Office Phone: 352-392-1464. Business E-Mail: vbala@ufl.edu.

VAIDYANATHAN, VIJAY V., engineering educator; arrived in US, 1988; s. P.B. and Radha Vaidyanathan; m. Sheela Vijay; children: Rohan, Rohit. BSc, U. Bombay, India, 1985, BSc in Tech., 1988; MS, Tex. A&M U., Coll. Sta., Tex., 1991, PhD, 1998. Registered profl. engr., Tex., 1992. R&D engr. Perkins Electronics Co., 1998—2000; cons. edn. svcs. i2 Techs., Irving, Tex., 2000—02; asst. prof. dept. engring. tech. U. North Tex., Denton, Tex., 2002—, dir. electronics engring. tech. program, 2002—. Contbr. articles to profl. jours. Grantee, NSF, 2002, 2006, Industry, 2003—07. Mem.: IEEE, Internat. Soc. for Optical Engring., Am. Soc. Elec. Engring., Soc. Photo-Optical Instrumentation Engrs., Tau Alpha Pi (advisor 2007). Achievements include research in biomedical optics and non-invasive detection of oral cancer. Office Phone: 940-369-8996. Office Fax: 940-565-2666. Business E-Mail: vvaidyan@unt.edu.

VAIL, CHARLES DANIEL, veterinarian, consultant; b. Denver, June 11, 1936; s. Allan Paden and Katherine Marie (Phillips) V.; m. Jean Williams Ebsen, June 15, 1963; children: Ellen Marie, David Elston. BS, Colorado A&M, 1958; DVM, Colo. State. U., 1960. Asst. veterinarian Colo. Racing Commn., Littleton, 1958-60; equine practitioner Littleton Large Animal Clinic, 1960—; track veterinarian Centennial Race Track, Littleton, 1962-63. Editor in chief Equine Practice, 1986-2000; contbr. articles to profl. jours. Mem. selection com. Outstanding Biology Tchr. award Colo., 1978-80, 88—, Arapahoe Fair Assn., Littleton, 1965-84, gallery disting. grads. Colo. State U. Coll. Vet. Medicine, 1989; chmn. Littleton Rotary Western Heritage Art Fair; bd. dirs. Animal Assistance Found. Denver, 1991-2004, v.p., 1995-96, pres., 1996-97, Western Vet. Conf., 1997-2000, v.p., 2001, pres. elect, 2002, pres., 2003, Friends Littleton Pub. Libr./Mus., 2000-04, Rocky Mountain Stroke Assn., Araphoe C.C. Found., 2004—; mem. devel. coun. Colo. State U., 2002—; ednl. commn. fgn. vet. grads. Recipient Honor Alumni award Coll. Vet. Medicine, Colo. State U., 1991. Mem. AVMA (publs. com. 1981-87, examination faculty 2005—), Am. Assn. Equine Practitioners (pres. 1985, dist. life mem.), Colo. Vet. Medicine Assn. (pres. 1980, Veterinarian of Yr. award 1987), Denver Area Vet. Medicine Soc. (pres. 1975), Arapahoe Town and Gown Soc. (v.p. 1999, pres. 2000), Colo. State U. Alumni Assn. (pres. 2001-02), Nottingham Club, Rotary (pres. Littleton 1992-93), Sigma Alpha Epsilon, Omicron Delta Kappa. Home: 5921 S Cherrywood Cir Littleton CO 80121-2465 Office: Littleton Large Animal Clinic 8025 S Santa Fe Dr Littleton CO 80120-4305 Office Phone: 303-794-6359. Office Fax: 303-794-9466. Personal E-mail: cdvm1@yahoo.com.

VAIL, IRIS JENNINGS, civic worker; b. NYC, July 2, 1928; d. Lawrence K. and Beatrice (Black) Jennings; grad. Miss Porters Sch., Farmington, Conn.; m. Thomas V.H. Vail, Sept. 15, 1951; children: Siri J., Thomas V.H. Jr., Lawrence J.W. Mem. exec. com. Garden Club Cleve., 1962—83; mem. women's coun. Western Res. Hist. Soc., 1960—, Cleve. Mus. Art, 1953—. Chmn. Childrens Garden Fair, 1966-75, Public Square Dinner, 1975; bd. dirs. Garden Center Greater Cleve., 1963-77; trustee Cleve. Zool. Soc., 1971-98, life trustee 1998—; mem. Ohio Arts Coun., 1974-76, pub. sq. com. Greater Cleve. Growth Assn., 1976-93, pub. sq. preservation and maintenance com. Cleve. Found., 1989-93, chmn. pub. sq. planting com., 1993. Hon. trustee Cleve. Bot. Garden, 2001. Recipient Amy Angell Collier Montague medal Garden Club Am., 1976, Ohio Gov.'s award, 1977. Mem. Chagrin Valley Hunt Club, Cypress Point Club, Kirtland Country Club, Colony Club, Women's City of Cleve. Club (Margaret A. Ireland award). Home: 14950 County Line Rd Chagrin Falls OH 44022-6800 Office Phone: 216-360-0505.

VAIL, NANCY L. SCOTT, retired elementary school educator, artist; d. Mitchell Clark and Mollie Lee (Turner) Savage; m. Jackie C. Scott (dec. 1999); 1 child, Jeff Michael Scott; m. Joseph L. Vail, Sr., Nov. 4, 2000; stepchildren: Joseph L. Vail, Jr., Chris, Jennifer Allison. BE with summa cum laude, Abilene Christian Coll., Tex., 1962, MEd with summa cum laude, 1965. Cert. in Tchg. Tex., 1962, Tex., 1985. Tchr. Jane Long Elem., Abilene, Tex., 1962—65, Canyon Creek Elem., Richardson, Tex., 1965—71, Prestonwood Elem., Richardson, 1971—78, Rountree Elem., Allen, Tex., 1978—89, Vaughan Elem., Allen, 1989—98; ret., 1998. Display, Anthurium Gallery, McKinney, Tex. Nominee Tchr. of Yr., Allen Ind. Sch. Dist., 1988, 1989. Mem.: DAR, Rountree Retirees Assn., Women's Mus. Art, Scarlet O'Hatters, Richardson Civic Art (Ribbon award 2000, 2001), Allen Ret. Educators Assn. (officer, com. chmn. 2001—, Outstanding Vol. of Yr. 2003, 2004, 2006), Alpha Delta Kappa (pres., v.p., historian, corresponding sec., Silver Sister award 2003). Republican. Ch. Of Christ. Achievements include starting the Epsilon Lambda Chpt. of Alpha Delta Kappa in Allen, Texas. Avocations: piano, reading, exercise, travel, painting.

VAIL, THOMAS LEIGHTON, military officer; b. Millinocket, Maine, Apr. 23, 1970; s. William Jackson and Sue Louise Vail; m. Melissa Ruth Williams, July 3, 1998; children: Audrey Elise, Thomas William. BS in Criminal Justice, St. Joseph's, Standish, Maine, 2006. 2d class petty officer US Navy, Charleston, SC, 1988—96; police officer Richland County Sheriff's Dept., Columbia, SC, 1996—2002, Biddeford Police Dept., Maine, 2002—04; army officer US Army, Ft. Walton Beach, Fla., 2006—. Instr. Naval Res. Security unit Naval Res. Ctr., Columbia, 1999—2002. Mem. SAR, Augusta, Maine, 1992—2007. Lt. US Army, 2006—07, Ft. Walton Beach. Decorated Surface Warfare Specialist US Navy, Meritorious Svc. medal, Navy Achievement medal, Vol. Svc. medal, Res. Forces Moblzn. medal US Dept. Def.; recipient Commendation letter, US Dept. Justice, 1999, Dep. of Yr. award, Richland County Sheriff's Dept., 2000, Age Grp. award, Various road racing bodies, 2000—07, Exemplary Pub. Svc. award, SC Dept. Pub. Safety, 2001, Citizenship medal, SAR, 2002, Disting. Mil. Grad. award, US Army ROTC Command, 2004—06, Leadership Excellence award, George C. Marshall Found., 2005—06, Disting. Honor Grad. award, US Army Ordnance Ctr., 2006, Ky. Col. award, Govt. Ky., 2006, Decius Wadsworth award, Army Ordinance Ctr. Schs., 2006, Exemplary Leadership award, Nat. Def. Indsl. Assn., 2006, Nebr. Adm. award, Govt. Nebr., 2007, Gold award, Pres. Coun. Phys. Fitness, 2005. Mem.: Assn. US Army (assoc.), Am. Legion (assoc.), Mensa (corr.). Conservative. Achievements include development of and implementation of a uniformed police drug unit model still in use. Avocation: running. Office: Naval Sch Explosive Ordnance Disposal Officer Detachment 304 N McCarthy Ave Eglin Afb FL 32542-5649 Business E-Mail: thomas.l.vail@us.army.mil.

VAIL, THOMAS PARKER, orthopaedic surgeon; m. Lisa Ann Giannetto. MD, Loyola U., 1985. Diplomate Am. Bd. Orthopaedic Surgery. Prof. orthop. surgery Duke U. Med. Ctr., Durham, NC, 1992—2007; prof. and dept. chmn. orthop. surgery U. Calif., San Francisco, 2007—. Dir. adult reconstructive surgery Duke U. Med. Ctr., Durham. Office: Univ Calif San Francisco MU 326W 500 Parnassus Ave San Francisco CA 94143-0728 Office Phone: 415-502-5183.

VAIL, THOMAS VAN HUSEN, retired publishing executive; b. Cleve., June 23, 1926; s. Herman Lansing and Delia (White) V.; m. Iris W. Jennings, Sept. 15, 1951; children: Siri Jennings Burki, Thomas Van Husen, Jr. AB in Politics cum laude, Princeton U., 1948; HHD (hon.), Wilberforce U., 1964; LHD, Kenyon Coll., 1969, Cleve. State U., 1973. Reporter Cleve. News, 1949-53, polit. editor, 1953-57; with Cleve. Plain Dealer, 1957-91, v.p., 1961-63, pub., editor, 1963-91, pres., 1970-91; dir. AP, 1968-74; ret., 1991. Bd. dirs. Greater Cleve. Growth Assn.; bd. dirs., past pres. Cleve. Conv. and Visitors Bur.; mem. Nat. Adv. Commn. on Health Manpower; presdl. apptd. to U.S. Adv. Commn. on Info., Pres.'s Commn. for Observance 25th Anniversary UN; trustee No. Ohio region NCCJ, Nat. Brotherhood Week chmn., 1969; trustee Cleve. Coun. World Affairs; fellow Cleve. Clinic Found.; former mem. Downtown Cleve. Corp.; former mem. distbn. com. Cleve. Found.; chmn., founder New Cleve. Campaign; trustee, founder Cleve. Tomorrow; former trustee Com. Econ. Devel.; former mem. Pres.'s Adv. Coun. on Pvt. Sector Initiatives. With USNR, 1944-46, lt. (j.g.), 1950. Recipient Nat. Human Rels. award, 1970. Cleve. Man of Year award Sales and Mktg. Execs. Cleve., 1976, Ohio Gov.'s award, 1982, Downtown Bus. Coun. recognition award Greater Cleve. Growth Assn., 1983, award NCCJ, 1970, award Mt. Vernon Adv. Com., 1994. Mem. Nat. Assn. Profl. Journalists (Lifetime Hall of Fame), Am. Newspaper Pubs. Assn., Am. Soc. Newspaper Editors, Soc. Profl. Journalists, Kirtland Country Club (Willoughby, Ohio), Sand Ridge Golf Club (Chardon, Ohio), Cypress Point Club (Pebble Beach, Calif.), Bohemian Club (San Francisco), Chagrin Valley Hunt Club (Gates Mills, Ohio), Links Club (NYC). Episcopalian. Home: L'Ecurie 14950 County Line Rd Hunting Valley Chagrin Falls OH 44022 Office: 29225 Chagrin Blvd Ste 200 Pepper Pike OH 44122-4632

VAIL, VAN HORN, German language educator; b. Buffalo, Dec. 23, 1934; s. Curtis Churchill and Faith Newbrook (Ely) V.; m. Michele Juliette Edelstein, May 5, 1969; 1 son, Mark Curtis. BA, U. Wash., 1956; MA, Princeton U., 1961, PhD, 1964. Instr. Princeton U., 1962-65, asst. prof., 1965-66; asst. prof. German Middlebury (Vt.) Coll., 1966-69, assoc. prof., 1969-75, prof., 1975—; chmn. dept. Middlebury Coll., Vt., 1970-73, 87-88, dir. studies Middlebury Sch. in Germany, 1967-68, 70-71, 74-75, 85-86, 88-89, 92-93, 95-96. Mem. nat. screening com. Fulbright Scholarships, 1979-81. Author: German in Review, 1967, 4th edit., 2004, Der Weg zum Lesen, 1967, 3d edit., 1986, Modern German, 1971, 3d edit., 1992, Tonio Kröger als Weg zur Literatur, 1974, Workbook for Modern German, 1992, Student Manual for 3d edit. of German in Review, 2000, Classroom Manual for 4th Edit. of German in Review, 2004. Served to 1st lt. M.I., U.S. Army, 1956-58. Fulbright scholar U. Heidelberg, 1958-59 Mem. MLA Home: 352 Cider Mill Rd Middlebury VT 05753-9407 Office: Middlebury Coll Middlebury VT 05753 E-mail: vail@middlebury.edu.

VAILAS, ARTHUR C., biomechanics educator; m. Laura Vailas. BS in Exercise Physiology, U. N.H., 1973; PhD in Exercise Physiology, U. Iowa, 1979, postgrad. in Biochem., 1979-82. Asst. prof. dept. kinesiology UCLA, 1982-88, assoc. prof., 1988, U. Wis., Madison, 1988-91, prof., 1991-95, dir. biodynamics lab., 1988-95; vice provost for rsch. and grad. studies U. Houston, 1995, prof., disting. chair biology and biochemistry, 1995, v.p., chancellor, rsch. and intellectual property mgmt., 1998—, prof., mech. engring., Coll. Engring, 2002—, prof., biology and biochemistry, Coll. Natural Sciences and Math., 2002—; vice chancellor U. Houston System; pres. Idaho State U., Pocatello, Idaho, 2006—. Session chair Gordon Rsch. Conf.; mem. life sci. adv. com. NASA, life sci. del. to COSMOS 1887, 2044 Missions; com. chair Musculoskeletal Implementation Group EDO and Countermeasure Sci. Plan; SLS-1 scientist. Contbr. 60 articles to profl. jours. Recipient Rsch. Svc. award NIH, Outstanding Sci. award USSR-NASA; named Disting. Scientist, CSU. Mem. Nat. Rsch. Coun. (mem. NASA com.). Office: Idaho State University Adminstrn Bldg 921 S 8th Ave STOP 8310 Pocatello ID 83209 Office Phone: 208-282-3440. Office Fax: 208-282-4487. *

VAILLANCOURT, JEAN-GUY, sociology educator, researcher; b. Chelmsford, Ont., Can., May 24, 1937; s. Royal A. and Marie (Lavallée) V.; m. Pauline Hansen, June 6, 1966 (div. 1983); 1 child, Véronique. BA magna cum laude, Laurentian U., Sudbury, Ont., 1957; licenciate in Philosophy, Faculté des Jésuites, Montreal, Que., Can., 1961; licentiate in Sociology, Gregorian U., Rome, 1964; PhD in Sociology, U. Calif., Berkeley, 1975. Lectr. St. Boniface (Man.) Coll., Canada, 1964-65; asst. prof. U. Montréal, Que., Canada, 1969-76, assoc. prof., 1976-83, prof. sociology, 1983—, chmn. dept., 1984-87. Adminstr., 1998; mem. consultative com. Can. amb. for disarmament, Ottawa, Ont., 1984-91, consultative com. on environ. Hydro-Que., 1984-90. Author: Papal Power, 1980, Essais d'écosociologie, 1982; co-editor: Le processus électoral au Québec, 1976, Roots of Peace, 1986, Environnement et développement Problèmes socio-politiques, 1991, Gestion de l'environnement, éthique et société, 1992, Instituer le développement durable, 1994, Aspects sociaux des précipitations acides au Québec, 1994, La recherche sociale en environnement, Nouveaux paradigmes, 1996, L'énergie au Québec, Quels sont nos choix? Montréal, Ecosocieté, 1998, Les sciences sociales de l'environnement, 1999, La gestion écologique des déchets, 2000, Développement durable et participation publique, 2003, Mouvements Sociaux et Changements Institutionnels, 2005; editor-in-chief Sociologie et Sociétés, 1978-87. Mem. coun. City of Dunham, Que., 1976-80; bd. dirs. Oxfam-Que., 1976-79, Can. Inst. Internat. Peace and Security, Ottawa, Ont., 1986-89, European Univ. Ctr. for Peace Studies, Burg Schlaining, Burgenland, Austria, 1989-93, Groupement forestier du Haut-Yamaska, 1993—, Club 2/3, 1995-2005. Grantee Conseil de Recherche en sci. sociale du Canada, 1982, FCAR, 1989-95, 96—, Social Sci. Rsch. Coun., 1983-86, 90—, Can. Inst. Internat. Peace and Security, 1985, 91; fellow Can. Coun., 1965-68. Mem. Internat. Sociol. Assn., Assn. Can. des sociologues et anthropologues de langue française, Sci. for Peace, Pugwash, Group 78. Roman Catholic. Avocations: tree farming, travel. Home: 953 Cherrier Apt 3 Montreal PQ Canada H2L 1J2 Office: U Montréal Dept Sociology Montreal PQ Canada H3C 3J7 Office Phone: 514-343-5959. Business E-Mail: jean.guy.vaillancourt@umontreal.ca.

VAIRA, PETER FRANCIS, lawyer; b. McKeesport, Pa., Mar. 5, 1937; s. Peter Francis and Mary Louise (Bedogne) V.; m. Mary Hohler, 1981. BA, Duquesne U., 1959, JD, 1962. Bar: Pa. 1963, D.C. 1968, Ill. 1984, U.S. Dist. Ct. (no. dist.) Ill., U.S. Dist. Ct. (ea. dist.) Pa., Ill. Supreme Ct. 1984. Atty. Chgo. Strike Force, Justice Dept., 1968-72; atty. in charge Phila. Strike Force, 1972-73, Chgo. Strike Force on Organized Crime, 1973-78; U.S. atty. Ea. Dist. Pa., Phila., 1978—83; ptnr. Lord Bissel & Brook, Chgo., 1983-86, Fox, Rothschild, O'Brien & Frankel, Phila., 1986-90, Buchanan Ingersoll, Phila., 1990-92, Vaira & Assocs., Phila., 1992-93, Vaira & Riley, Phila., 1993—. Exec. dir. Pres.'s Commn. on Organized Crime, 1983; ind. hearing officer Laborers Internat. Union N.Am., 1995—; panelist, seminar, controlling internat. organized crime, Rome, Sorrento, Italy, June 1994; panelist, Internat. Conf. on Trial by Jury, Buenos Aires, Oct. 1996. Author: Eastern District Practice Rules Annotated, 2006, Corporate Responses to Grand Jury Investigations, 2004; contbr. articles to profl. jours. Mem. Mayor's Search Com. Police Commr., Phila., 1992; corruption task force Phila. Police, 1997; press officer women's amateur championship U.S. Golf Assn., 2003. Lt. USNR, 1963-68. Recipient Spl. Commendation award Justice Dept., 1976, Disting. Alumni award Duquesne U. Law Sch., 2005; named a Pa. Super Lawyer, Phila. Mag., 2006. Fellow Am. Coll. Trial Lawyers (chmn. criminal procedure com. 1995-98, comms. com.), Chartered Inst. Arbitrators; mem. ABA (criminal justice coun. 1986), Am. Law Inst. (mem. editl. bd. Legal Intelligencer, Phila. Lawyer), Union League (Chgo.), Phila. Country Club, Com. of 70. Office: Vaira & Riley 1600 Market St Ste 2650 Philadelphia PA 19103-7226 Home Phone: 610-353-7488; Office Phone: 215-751-2700. Personal E-mail: p.vaira@vairariley.com.

VAIRO, ROBERT JOHN, insurance company executive; b. Bklyn., Sept. 27, 1930; s. John and Antonietta (DeRose) V.; m. Carol P. Andross, Apr. 8, 1951 (div. Feb. 1979); children: Robert J., Gregory J.; m. Inge R. Buhlbecker, Feb. 20, 1979. Student, Coll. Ins., NYC, 1953-62; Exec. Program in Bus. Adminstrn., Columbia U., 1973. CPCU. Under asst. mgr. Atlantic Cos., NYC, 1952-62; underwriter mgr., v.p. Fireman's Fund Ins. Co., NYC, 1962-75; v.p., sr. v.p. underwriting C & F Ins. Cos., Morristown, NJ, 1975-79; exec. v.p., pres. U.S. Ins. Group, Morristown, NJ, 1979-82; chmn., chief exec. officer C & F Underwriters Group and The North River Ins. Co., Morristown, NJ, 1982-86; pres., chief oper. officer Crum and Forster, Inc., Morristown, 1987-88, pres., chief exec. officer, 1988-90, chmn., pres., chief exec. officer, 1990-92, also bd. dirs. Chmn. Ins. Services Office, N.Y.C., 1983, Am. Ins. Assn., Washington, 1990. Pres. Lincoln Park City Council, N.J., 1971-76. Served with USMC, 1951-53. Mem. Soc. CPCUs, Am. Inst. for Chartered Property Casualty Underwriters (dir., chmn. 1991-92), Desert Highlands Golf Club (pres. 1997-99), Coalition Pinnacle Peak, Inc. (pres. 1998—). Roman Catholic. Home: # 451 10040 E Happy Valley Rd Scottsdale AZ 85255-2388 E-mail: sonoran@aol.com.

VAISEY, DAVID GEORGE, librarian, archivist; b. Tetbury, Eng., Mar. 15, 1935; s. William Thomas and Minnie (Payne) V.; m. Maureen Anne Mansell, Aug. 7, 1965; children: Katharine, Elizabeth. BA, Oxford U., Eng., 1959, MA, 1962. Archivist Staffordshire County Council, Stafford, Eng., 1960-63; from asst. librarian to sr. asst. librarian Bodleian Library, Oxford, Eng., 1963-75, keeper of western manuscripts, 1975-86, Bodley's librarian, 1986-96, Bodley's librarian emeritus, 1997—. Dep. keeper Oxford U. Archives, 1966-75, keeper, 1995-2000; vis. prof. dept. library studies UCLA, 1985; commr. Royal Commn. Hist. Manuscripts, 1987-98; founding chmn. Nat. Coun. Archives, 1988-91. Served to 2d lt. Brit. Army, 1954-56. Decorated encomienda Order of Isabel la Catolica (Spain), comdr. Order Brit. Empire; fellow Exeter Coll., Oxford, 1975, emeritus fellow, 2000; hon. rsch. fellow, Univ. Coll., London, 1987, hon. fellow Kellogg Coll., Oxford, 1996. Fellow: Soc. Antiquaries, Royal Hist. Soc.; mem.: Soc. Archivists (pres. 1999—2002), Brit. Records Assn. (v.p. 1998—2006). Office: Bodleian Libr Broad St Oxford OX1 3BG England E-mail: david.vaisey@bodley.ox.ac.uk.

VAITUKAITIS, JUDITH LOUISE, medical researcher; b. Hartford, Conn., Aug. 29, 1940; d. Albert George and Julia Joan (Vaznikaitis) V. BS, Tufts U., 1962; MD, Boston U., 1966. Investigator, med. officer reproductive rsch. Nat. Inst. Child Health and Human Devel., NIH, Bethesda, Md., 1971-74; assoc. dir. clin. rsch. Nat. Ctr. Rsch. Resources NIH, 1986-91, dir. gen. clin. rsch. ctr., 1986-91, dep. dir. extramural rsch., 1991, acting dir., 1991-92, dir., 1993—2005; sr. advisor on sci. infrastructure and resources to dir. of NIH, 2005—; from assoc. prof. to prof. medicine Sch. Medicine Boston U., 1974-86, assoc. prof. physiology, 1975-80, assoc. prof. ob-gyn., 1977-80, program. dir. gen. clin. rsch. ctr., 1977-86, prof. physiology, 1980-86; head sect. endocrinology and metabolism Boston City Hosp., 1974-86. Mem. internat. sci. adv. bd. Wellcome Trust-UIC. Author: Clinical Reproductive Neuroendocrinology, 1982; mem. editl. bd. Jour. Clin. Endocrin. and Metabolism, 1973-80, Proc. Soc. Exptl. Biol. and Medicine, 1978-87, Endocrine Rsch., 1984-88; contbr. articles to profl. jours. Chair rev. com. Nat. Space Biomedical Rsch. Inst. Strategic Rsch. Plan Office of Biol. and Phys. Rsch., NASA, Washington, 2002; mem. NIH Stem Cell Task Force, 2002; bd. trustees Tufts U., 1998—. Recipient Disting. Alumna award Sch. Medicine, Boston U., 1983, Mallincrodt award for Inv. Rsch. Clin. Radiossay Soc., 1980, Alumni award Boston U., 2003; named to Nat. Inst. for Child Health and Human Devel. Hall of Honor, 2003. Mem. Am. Fedn. Clin. Rsch., Endocrine Soc., Am. Soc. Clin. Rsch., Inst. Medicine-NAS. Office: Sr Advisor Sci Infrastructure & Resources NIH Dir Elias A Zerhouni MD Bldg 1 Rm 25 1 Center Dr MSC 0162 Bethesda MD 20892-0162 Office Phone: 301-435-6721, 301-435-6721. Personal E-mail: vaitukai@verizon.net. Business E-Mail: vaitukai@mail.nih.gov.

VAJDA, JUDITH PARSONS, psychology educator; b. Norfolk, Va., July 16, 1945; d. Harry Vernon Parsons and Carrie Elizabeth Petty; m. Frank Stephen Vajda, June 7, 1983. AS, No. Va. C.C., Annandale, 1986; BA in Psychology, George Washington U., 1990, MA in Applied Social Psychology, 1995. Adj. instr. Mt. Vernon Coll. for Women, Washington, 1995—98, No. Va. C.C., Annandale, 1995—; instr. police sci. program George Washington U., Washington, 1998—. Vol. Neighborhood Watch, Annandale, 1989—2006. Mem.: APA, Va. Psychol. Assn., Am. Psychol. Soc. Achievements include research in psychology of violent criminal offenders. Office: George Washington University 2125 G Street NW Washington DC 20052 Home Phone: 703-641-9380; Office Phone: 202-994-6323. Business E-Mail: jvajda@gwu.edu.

VAJK, HUGO, manufacturing executive; b. Ljubljana, Slovenia, Mar. 26, 1928; emigrated to Can., 1947, naturalized, 1953; s. Hugo and Magda (Slatnar) V.; m. Barbara Lois Hallin, June 13, 1953; children: Tanja Astrid, Hugo Anthony, Madeleine Louise, Anita Marie, Nicolette Cecile, Moira Suzanne. Student, Inst. Poly., Grenoble, France, 1947; B.Eng. with honors, McGill U., Montreal, Que., Can., 1951; MS, Carnegie Mellon U., 1953. With Standard Iron and Steel Works Ltd., Toronto, Canada, 1953—56; product mgr. Joy Mfg. Co., Buffalo, 1957-59, dir. gen. Paris, 1960-63; pres. Massey-Ferguson, SA, Paris, 1966—69; v.p. logistics Massey-Ferguson Ltd., Toronto, Canada, 1970—72, exec. v.p., 1973—78; dir. GEC Inc., subs. Gen. Electric Co., Eng., 1979; chmn. English Electric Corp., Elmsford, N.Y., 1979; with Garrett Corp. divsn. Signal Cos., 1980-84; v.p. Garrett Automotive Products; pres. Garrett Automotive Group, Allied-Signal, Inc., 1985—90; chmn. Inovatek Advisors, Inc., New Port Richey, Fla., 1988—; pres. ATM Communications Internat., Inc., Wilmington, Del., 1991—. Mem.: ASME, Assn. Profls. Engrs. Ont., Yacht Club de France (Paris), Royal Can. Yacht Club (Toronto), Univ. Club of Toronto. Home and Office: PO Box 1115 New Port Richey FL 34656-1115

VAJTAY, STEPHEN MICHAEL, JR., lawyer; b. New Brunswick, NJ, Mar. 18, 1958; s. Stephen Michael and Veronica Gizella (Fehèr) V.; m. Gabriella Katherine Soltèsz, Aug. 5, 1989; children: Stephen, Andrew, Gregory, Daniel. BA, Rutgers U., 1980; JD, Georgetown U., 1983; LLM, NYU, 1989. Bar: N.J. 1984, U.S. Tax Ct. 1985. Assoc. McCarter and English LLP, Newark, N.J., 1983-91, ptnr., 1991—. Trustee Hungarian Scout Assn. in Exteris, Garfield, N.J., 1985—; trustee Partnership for a Drug-Free N.J., Inc., Montclair, 1993—; adj. prof. law Seton Hall U. Sch. Law, Newark, 1995—; spkr. at lectrs. and seminars, 1992—. Contbr. articles to profl. jours. Mem. Bd. of Adjustment, New Brunswick, N.J., 1993-98. Mem. ABA, N.J. Bar Assn. (chmn. tax sect. 2001-02), Essex County Bar Assn., Phi Beta Kappa. Roman Catholic. Office: McCarter and English LLP Four Gateway Ctr 100 Mulberry St Newark NJ 07102 Office Phone: 973-639-2004. Business E-Mail: SVAJTAY@mccarter.com.

VAKERICS, THOMAS VINCENT, lawyer; b. Lorain, Ohio, Mar. 26, 1944; s. Paul Peter and Margaret Theresa (Dobos) V.; m. Kathryn Ida Rogers, Aug. 7,1965; children: Meredith Vakerics Ehler, Mitchell Thomas. BA, Bowling Green State U., 1965; JD with honors, George Washington U., 1968. Bar: U.S. Dist. Ct. D.C. 1968, U.S. Ct. Appeals (D.C. cir.) 1969, U.S. Supreme Ct. 1974, U.S. Ct. Internat. Trade 1982, U.S. Ct. Appeals (Fed. cir.) 1982. Antitrust trial atty. FTC, Washington, 1969—73; assoc. Gore, Cladouhos & Brashares, Washington, 1973—75; ptnr. O'Connor & Hannan, Washington, 1975—84, Bayh, Tabbert & Capehart, Washington, 1984—86, Morgan, Lewis & Bockius, Washington, 1986—88, Winthrop, Stimson, Putnam & Roberts, Washington, 1988—94, Perkins Coie, 1994—2004, Sandler, Travis & Rosenberg, P.A., Washington, 2004—. Vis. prof. Nihon U., Tokyo, 1981-88. Author: Antitrust Basics, 1985, Antidumping, Countervailing Duty and Other Trade Actions, 1987; contbr. articles to profl. jours. Mem. ABA (vice chmn. internat. antitrust law com. sect. internat. law and practice 1992-95), Internat. Bar Assn., D.C. Bar Assn., Solar Energy Rsch. Inst. (editl. adv. bd. Solar Energy Law Reporter 1979-82), Order of Coif, Phi Delta Phi, Pi Sigma Alpha, Phi Alpha Delta, Sigma Chi. Democrat. Roman Catholic. Office: Sandler Travis & Rosenberg PA 1300 Pennsylvania Ave NW Ste 400 Washington DC 20004 Home Phone: 703-620-9163; Office Phone: 202-216-9307. Office Fax: 202-842-2247. Business E-Mail: tvakerics@strtade.com.

VAKHSHOORI, DARYOOSH, chemicals executive; BS, U. California, Irvine; PhD in Quantum Electronics, U. California, Berkeley. Rsch. scientist Bell Laboratories; co-founder CoreTek, Inc.; founder, v.p. bus. devel., v.p. engring., chief tech. officer, CEO Ahura Inc. Achievements include patents for 28 filed or pending. Office: Ahura Corp 46 Jonspin Rd Wilmington MA 01887 Office Phone: +1 978 657 5555. Office Fax: +1 978 657 5921. E-mail: info@ahuracorp.com.

VAKILI, BAHMAN FAKHIMI, urologist; b. Soossangard, Khoozes, Iran, Jan. 22, 1936; arrived in U.S., 1962; s. Mehdi Fakhimi Vakili and Noah Jalali; m. Sarah Ann Lovejoy, June 4, 1967 (div. 2002); children: Susan Elizabeth Vakili Ballenwag, David Andrew, Daniel Edward. MD, Tehran U., Iran, 1962. Diplomate Am. Bd. Urology, 1974. Intern Worcester City Hosp., Mass., 1962—63; resident gen. surgery Beth Israel Hosp., NYC, 1963—64; resident Urology Boston U. Med. Ctr., 1964—67; fellow Urology and Nuc. Medicine Roger Williams Gen. Hosp., Providence, 1967—68; urologist VA, Newington, Conn., 1968—69; fellow Pediat. Urology Babies Hosp. Columbia-Presbyn. Med. Ctr., NYC, 1971—72; urologist A.O. Fox Meml. Hosp., Oneonta, NY, 1972—86, VA Hosp., Beckly, W.Va., 1986—87, Bath, NY, 1987—89, Lebanon, Pa., 1990—2000; ret., 2000. Assoc. clin. prof. Urology Pa. State Med. Sch., Hershey, 1990—98; cons. Urology Margarettvill Meml. Hosp., NY, 1972—86, Stamford Cmty. Hosp., NY, 1974—86. Contbr. articles to profl. jours. Maj. Med. Corps US Army, 1969—71. Fellow: ACS; mem.: AMA, Am. Urol. Assn. Republican. Unitarian Universalists. Avocations: carpentry, gardening, bicycling, writing, poetry.

VAKULENKO, SERGEI BORISOVICH, medical researcher, educator; b. Stavropol, Russia, Oct. 31, 1952; s. Boris Vladimirovich and Valentina Michailovna Vakulenko; m. Marta Toth. MD, Sch. Medicine, St. Petersburg, Russia, 1976; PhD, Nat. Ctr. for Antibiotics, Moscow, 1981, DSc, 1991. Rsch. assoc. Nat. Ctr. for Antibiotics, Moscow, 1981—86, asst. prof., 1986—91, assoc. prof., 1991—93; rsch. assoc. Sch. Medicine Wayne State U., Detroit, 1993—98, rsch. asst. prof. Sch. Medicine, 1998—2003; rsch. asst. prof. dept. chemistry and biochemistry U. Notre Dame, Ind., 2003—06, rsch. assoc. prof., 2006—. Mem.: Am. Soc. for Microbiology. Office: Univ Notre Dame 417 Nieuwland Sci Hall Notre Dame IN 46556-5670 Office Phone: 574-631-2935. E-mail: svakulen@nd.edu.

VALACHOVIC, RICHARD W., medical association administrator; Former assoc. prof. oral medicine Harvard U., former chief of dentistry, Health Svcs.; exec. dir. Am. Assn. Dental Schs., Washington, 1997; now exec. dir. Am. Dental Edn. Assn., Washington. Fellow: Am. Coll. Dentists, Am. Acad. Pediat. Dentistry. Office: Am Dental Edn Assn Ste 1100 1400 K St NW Washington DC 20005 Office Phone: 202-289-7201. Business E-Mail: ValachovicR@adea.org.

VALADE, ALAN MICHAEL, lawyer; b. Berwyn, Ill., Jan. 26, 1952; s. Merle F. and Vera M. Valade; m. June 17, 1978. Attended, Oakland C.C., 1970—72; BA, U. Mich., 1974; JD, Wayne State U., 1977; LLM in Taxation, NYU, 1978. Bar: Mich. 1978, Fla. 1987. Assoc. Kemp, Klein, Endelman & Beer, Southfield, Mich., 1978-79; shareholder Valade, MacKinnon & Higgins, P.C., Detroit, 1979-84, Schwendener & Valade, P.C., Mason, Mich., 1985-91; ptnr. Honigman Miller Schwartz and Cohn LLP, Detroit, 1991—, chmn. tax. dept., 2002—06. Co-author: The Michigan Single Business Tax, 1991; contbr. articles to profl. jours. Fellow Mich. State Bar Found.; mem. ABA, State Bar Mich. (chmn. state and local tax com. 1991, tax. coun. 1989-92), State Bar Fla. Office: Honigman Miller Schwartz and Cohn LLP 2290 First National Bldg 660 Woodward Ave Detroit MI 48226-3506 Office Phone: 313-465-7636. Business E-Mail: avalade@honigman.com.

VALANCE, MARSHA JEANNE, library director, storyteller; b. Evanston, Ill., Aug. 2, 1946; Children's libr. trainee N.Y. Pub. Libr., NYC, 1968-69; ref. libr. Acton (Mass.) Meml. Pub. Libr., 1969-70; mgr. The Footnote, Cedar Rapids, Iowa, 1976-78; assoc. editor William C. Brown, Dubuque, Iowa, 1978-79; dir. Dubuque County Libr., 1979-81, G.B. Dedrick Pub. Libr., Geneseo, Ill., 1981-84, Grand Rapids (Minn.) pub. Libr., 1984-89; mgmt. libr. Wis. Regional Libr. for Blind and Physically Handicapped, 1989—. Workshop coord., participant, sect. chmn. profl. confs.; LSCA grant reviewer Dept. Edn., 1989-95. Author: (with others) Mystery, Value and Awareness, 1979, Pluralism, Similarities and Contrast, 1979; contbr. articles and book revs. to pubs. Troop leader Miss. Valley Coun. Girl Scouts USA, Cedar Rapids, 1976-78; mem. liturgy com. St. Malachy's Roman Cath. Ch., Geneseo, 1983; com. judging clinic 4-H, Moline, Ill., 1984; trustee KAXE No. Cmty. Radio, 1986-89, ICTV, 1988-90; sec. Grand Rapids Cmty. Svcs. Coun., 1986; coach Itasca County 4-H Horse Bowl Team, 1987; dir. Grand Rapids Storyfest, 1987-89; program chmn. Spotlight on Books Conf., 1989; bd. dirs., trustee Vols. in Svc. to the Visually Handicapped, 1989—; audio describer Artreach, Milw., 1991-98. Recipient Weavers award, Tel. Pioneers, 1992, Outstanding Svc. award, Badger Assn., 1999; grantee, Iowa Humanities Bd., 1981, Minn. Libr. Found., 1985, 1986, 1987, Blandin Found., 1986, Arrowhead Regional Arts Coun., 1987, 1989, Ms. Soc., 1989, Sunrise Found., 2000, LSTA, 2007; Nat. Merit scholar, 1964—68. Mem. ALA, Wis. Libr. Assn., Iowa Librs. Medium Size (sec. 1981), Northlands Storytelling Network (bd. dirs. 1988-94, v.p. 1989, pres. 1990, editor Grapevine 1991-94), Nat. Storytelling Assn., Alliance Info. and Referral Svcs., DAR (constn. chmn. 1983-84), Miss. Valley Morgan Horse Club, Wis. Morgan Horse Club (newsletter editor 1994-95, sec. 1995), Western Working Family Morgan Horse Club, Am. Morgan Horse Assn., Geneseo Jr. Women's Club (internat. chmn. 1983-84), UCLA Club Wis. (pres. 1990-91), Alpha Gamma Delta. Home: 343 N 62d St Milwaukee WI 53213-4130 Office: Wis Regional Libr Blind & Physically Handicapped 813 W Wells St Milwaukee WI 53233-1436 Home Phone: 414-607-0288; Office Phone: 414-286-3010.

VALASQUEZ, JOSEPH LOUIS, industrial engineer; b. Balt., Apr. 15, 1955; s. Jose Louis and Edith Rosabel (Saunders) V.; m. Nicole Diane Feldser, Sept. 4, 1983; children: Alexandra Nicole, Joseph Jr. AA, Essex Coll., 1977; BS in Indsl. Engring., U. Ariz., 1982; MBA in Fin., So. Ill. U., 1985. Registered profl. engr., Fla.; cert. quality engr.; cert. quality auditor; cert. quality mgr.; cert. project mgmt. profl.; cert. integrated resource mgmt.; pvt. pilots license. Machinist Bausch & Lomb, Balt., 1974-77; indsl. engr. IBM Corp., Tucson, 1980-81; sr. indsl. engr. Gen. Dynamics, San Diego, 1981-83; supr. engring. Avco Corp., Nashville, 1983-84; mgr. engring. Burroughs Corp., Coral Springs, Fla., 1984-85; dir. total quality mgmt. Lambda Novatronics, Inc., Pompano Beach, Fla., 1984-94; champoint of continuous improvement Allied Signal, 1994-97, Sensormatic Corp., 1997-98; v.p. corp. quality Sunbeam Corp., Delray Beach, Fla., 1998-2001; quality/productivity exec. Bank Am., Charlotte, NC, 2001—. Computer cons., Margate, Fla., 1987; founder, owner E.P.I. Cons., Pompano Beach. Mem. Am. Inst. Indsl. Engrs., Fla. Engring. Soc. Republican. Roman Catholic. Avocations: real estate management, computer programming, mountain climbing, canoeing, private pilot. Home: PO Box 49616 Charlotte NC 28277-0082 Personal E-mail: jlvalasquez@yahoo.com. Business E-Mail: joe.l.valasquez@bankofamerica.com.

VALBONESI, LUCIA, systems engineer; d. Franco Valbonesi and Maria Ricci; m. Roberto Battaglia, June 28, 2003. MSEE in Computer Sci., U. Ill., Chgo., 2001, PhD in Elec. Engring., 2005. Lic. profl. engr., Italy, 2003. Sr. sys. engr. Motorola, Schaumburg, Ill., 2005—. Contbr. chapters to books, articles to profl. jours. Recipient Marisa Bellisario award, Marisa Bellisario Assn., 2003; fellow, U. Ill., 2001—02; scholar, Politecnico Milano, Italy, 1996—2000, Collegio Ingegneri Ferroviari Italiani, 1997—98. Mem.: IEEE. Office Phone: 847-305-3305.

VALBUENA-BRIONES, ANGEL JULIAN, retired language educator, author; b. Madrid, Jan. 11, 1928; naturalized, 1963; s. Angel Valbuena-Prat and Francisca Briones; m. Barbara Northrup Hobart, Nov. 9, 1957; children: Teresa, Vivian. Licenciado summa cum laude, Murcia U., Spain, 1949; PhD with honors, Madrid U., 1952. Prof. Ayudante Murcia U., 1949-51; lectr. Oxford (Eng.) U., 1953-55; prof. Ayudante Madrid U., 1955-56; vis. lectr. U. Wis., 1956-58; asst. prof. Yale U., 1958-60; Elias Ahuja prof. Spanish lit. U. Del., 1960-2000, Elias Ahuja prof. emeritus, 1999—. Lecture tour, S.Am., 1957; vis. prof. NYU, 1960, 61, U. Madrid, 1970-71, 1965, 77, U. Mex. at Aragon, 1979, Inst. Caro y Cuervo, Bogota, Colombia, 1980; mem. Fulbright-Hays nat. screening com., 1981-83, 89-90; mem. editl. com. for CD-ROM edit. Spanish Golden Age Theatre, Chadwyck-Healey/Spain, 1995-98; bd. dirs. publs. U. Barcelona, Spain, Bull. Comediantes, U. Calif., Riverside, Hispanic Jour., Pa., Juan de la Cuesta Edits., Del.; profl. cons. NEH. Author: Nueva Poesia de Puerto Rico, 1952, Comedias de Capa y Espada de Calderon, 1954, Dramas de Honor de Calderon, 2 vols., 1956, Obras Completas de Calderon, vol. I, 1959, 3d reprinting, 1991, vol. II, 1956, 6th edit. 2 vols., 1988, Literatura Hispanoamericana, 1962, revised and enlarged, 1969, Perspectiva critica de los dramas de Calderon, 1965, Ideas y Palabras, 1968, El alcalde de Zalamea de Calderon, 1971, rev. 13th edit., 1995, Primera Parte de Comedias de Pedro Calderon de la Barca, Vol. 1, 1974, Vol. 2, 1981, La Dama Duende de Calderon, 1976, 8th printing, 1986, Calderon y la comedia nueva, 1977, La vida es sueno. Antes que todo es mi dama. Pedro Calderon de la Barca, 1988, El mayor monstruo del mundo. de Calderon, 1995; author: (cd-rom) Teatro Espanol de Siglo de oro, 1998, Historia y Creación Literaria en Don Pedro Calderón de la Barca, 2002. Founder, pres. Valbuena Inst. Spanish Lit., Inc., 1986-99. Consejo Superior de Investigaciones Cientificas fellw, 1951, 70-71, Instituto de Cultura Hispánica fellow, 1951-52; recipient Excellence in Teaching award U. Del., 1988, Outstanding Scholar award U. Del. Coll. Arts and Sci., 1996. Mem. MLA, AAUP, Am. Assn. Tchrs. Spanish and Portuguese, Inst. Iberoam. Lit., Internat. Fedn. Modern Langs. and Lits., Assn. Lit. Scholars and Critics, Internat. Assn. Hispanists, Am. Comparative Lit. Assn., Assn. for Hispanic Classic Theatre, Old Bohemia Hist. Soc., Sigma Delta Pi (hon., Order of Don Quijote, 1999), Phi Kappa Phi. Home: 726 Loveville Rd Cottage 6 Hockessin DE 19707-1504

VALDES, ANNMARIE, history professor, researcher; b. Chgo., July 25, 1969; d. Charles Paul Kuss and Margaret Ester Valdes; m. Michael Keith Mcknight, June 28, 1997; children: Isabella Valdes Mcknight, Michael Valdes Mcknight. BA in History, Loyola U., Chgo., 1992; MA in History, DePaul U., Chgo., 2002. Cert. tchr. Ill., 1992. Asst. archivist DePaul U. Libr., Chgo., 1993—94; history tchr. Chgo. Pub. Sch. Kenwood Acad., 1994—98; adj. prof. Triton CC, Riversgrove, Ill., 2003—, Oakton CC, Desplaines, Ill., 2006—. Rschr., presenter Great Lakes History Conf., Grand Rapids, Mich., 2006; asst. coach, Chgo., 2004—05, NYC, 2004—05. Vol., organizer Operation Warm Hug, Chgo., 2005—06, Operation Read-A-Book, Chgo., 2006; vol. St. Paul of Cross, Park Ridge, Ill., 2002—. Recipient Oustanding Adj., Triton CC, River Grove, 2006. Mem.: U. Chgo. Katz Ctr. Mex. Studies, U. Chgo. Ctr. Latin Am. Studies. Democrat. Roman Catholic. Avocations: travel, reading, running. Office: Oakton CC 1600 E Golf Rd Des Plaines IL 60016 Business E-Mail: avaldes@oakton.edu.

VALDÉS-PÉREZ, RAUL E., computer scientist, researcher; b. Havana, Cuba, Oct. 13, 1956; came to U.S., 1961; s. Thomas Valdes and Hilda (Perez) Booth; m. Carmen B. Arenas, Apr. 9, 1988; children: Tomas, Daniela. BSE, U. Ill., Chgo., 1980, MS, 1982; PhD, Carnegie Mellon U., Pitts., 1991. Engr. Itaú Tecnologia, São Paulo, Brazil, 1982-84; rsch. scientist MIT AI Lab., Cambridge, Mass., 1984-86; adj. rsch. computer scientist Carnegie Mellon U., Pitts., 1991—; co-founder, pres., chmn. Vivisimo Inc., Pitts., 2000—. Vis. lectr. Hefei Poly. U., China, 1987, Nat. U. Cordoba, Argentina, 1994. Contbr. articles to profl. jours. including Artificial Intelligence, Machine Learning, Catalysis Letters, Jour. Computational Chemistry, Jour. Phys. Chemistry, Jour. Theoretical Biology, Computer Physics Comms. USAF grad. fellow, 1987-91; named one of 50 Most Important Hispanics in Tech. & Bus. Hispanic Engr. & Info. Tech. mag., 2005. Mem. AAAS, ACM, Am. Assn. Artificial Intelligence. Achievements include various machine discoveries in natural science. Office: Vivisimo Inc Ste 300 1710 Murray Ave Pittsburgh PA 15217 Office Phone: 415-422-2499. Office Fax: 415-422-2495.

VALDEZ, JEFF, broadcast executive, television producer; b. Pueblo, Colo., 1956; married; 2 children. Mobile home maker, janitor, drill bit factory worker, Colo. Springs; owner, stand-up comedian Comedy Corner, Colo. Springs; stand-up comedian, TV writer LA; exec. position Tri-Star TV; founder, chmn. Sí TV, LA, 2004—. Creator Latino Laugh Festival, San Antonio, 1996; apptd. by Pres. Clinton to adv. com. arts John F. Kennedy Ctr. Performing Arts; bd. trustees Am. Mus. Moving Image, 2000. Musician (drummer): Wildfire; prodr.: (TV series) Comedy Compadres, 1993—94, (TV Special) Latino Laugh Festival, 1997; prodr., writer: (TV series) Cafe Ole' with Giselle Fernandez, 1997; Funny is Funny, 1997; exec. prodr.: The Brothers Garcia, 2000, Urban Jungle, 2004, Latino Laugh Festival: The Show, 2004, The Rub, 2004, The Drop, 2004, Across the Hall, 2004, Breakfast, Lunch and Dinner, 2004, Urban Jungle 2: South Ctrl., 2005. Named one of 100 Most Influential Hispanics, Hispanic Bus., 36 Faces to Watch, LA Times, 1997, 50 Who Matter Now, CNNMoney-.com Bus. 2.0, 2006; recipient Am. Latino Media Arts award, 1998, Hispanic Achievement award, Hispanic Mag., 1998, Vision award, Latino Entertainment Media Inst., 2000. Office: Sí TV 3030 Andrita St Bldg D Los Angeles CA 90065 *

VALDEZ, JOSH, health insurance company executive; A, CC AF; BS, Nat. U. Sacramento; MBA, Golden State U.; D in Bus. Adminstrn., So. Calif. U. V.p. managed care AltaMed Health Svcs., Calif.; CFO, exec. dir. West Covina Med. Clinic, Eastland Med. Group, Combined Mgmt. Svcs.; regional dir. Fed. Dept. Health and Human Svcs., 2001—04; sr. v.p. Blue Cross Blue Shield, 2004—. Health care adminstr. USAF. Named Man of Yr., Hollenbeck Youth Ctr./Inner-City Games LA, 2005; named one of Top 10 Latinos in Healthcare, LatinoLeaders mag., 2004. Office: Blue Cross Calif 1 WellPoint Way Thousand Oaks CA 91362-5035

VALDIVIA ARENAS, MARTIN A., pulmonary and critical care physician; s. Martin T. Valdivia Duenas and Luisa Hilda Arenas de Valdivia; m. Liliana A. Concha, May 26, 2001; 1 child, Alejandro M. Valdivia. MD, Nat. U. San Agustin, Arequipa, 1997. Lic. physician and surgeon Nat. U. San Agustin. Internal medicine resident U. Miami, 2001—04; pulmonary and critical care fellow Ohio State U., Columbus, 2004—. Contbr. articles to med. jours. Mem.: Am. Coll. of Chest Physicians, Am. Thoracic Soc. Office: Davis Heart and Lung Rsch Inst 473 W 12th Ave Columbus OH 43210 Home Phone: 614-486-2238; Office Phone: 614-247-7707. Business E-Mail: martin.valdivia-arenas@osumc.edu.

VALE, PATRICE J., musician, consultant; d. Maurice Bob and June Gwendolyn (Olsen) Mizzell; m. L. Kenneth Vale, June 29, 1968; 1 child, Michelle Patrice Baggett. BS, Tex. Woman's U., 1962; MA in Sociology, U. Mo., 1998. Cert. cons. in workplace mediation Mediation Tng. Inst. Internat., Mo., 2003, ABE tchr. ABE State of Mo., 2000, paralegal diploma Paralegal Studies, Mo., 1983. Music therapist State Hosp., Fulton, Mo., 1962—64; music and dance therapist DePaul Hosp., New Orleans, 1964—66; exec. dir. lions eye tissue bank U. Mo., Columbia, 1967—73; harpist self-employed, Columbia, Mo., 1982—; paralegal and legal sec. Petri, Shurtleff, Froeschner & Smith Law Firm, Columbia, 1982—84; tchg. asst. U. oMo., Columbia, 1996—98; staff devel. trainer Mo. AEL Resource Ctr., Moberly and Fulton, 1998—2000; libr. cons. for continuing edn. Mo. State Libr., Jefferson City, 2000—04. Contbr. textbook. Recipient Nat. Honor, Nat. Music Fedn. Festivals, Tex., 1952, gold certificate for yrs. of superior rating in piano, Nat. Fedn. Music Clubs, 1952, winner piano contest judged by Liberace, Las Vegas, Nev. Mem.: TOPS, INTERTEL, Mensa, Alpha Kappa Delta. Home and Office: 908 Lynnwood Court Columbia MO 65203 Home Phone: 573-441-2305. Personal E-mail: patrice.vale@mchsi.com.

VALENCIA, MARGARITA, Spanish language educator; b. Bogotá, Colombia, Nov. 28, 1952; arrived in U.S., 1973; BA, U. Calif., Santa Barbara, MA in Polit. Sci. Profl. clear single subject tchg. credential in Spanish; cert. eligibility for Calif. prelim. adminstrv. svcs. credential. Tchr. Spanish Manual Arts H.S. L.A. Unified Sch. Dist., 1994—. Mem.: Acad. Polit. Sci. N.Y., L.A. World Affairs Coun., Sierra Club. Home Phone: 562-692-3778; Office Phone: 562-692-3778. Personal E-mail: mvalenciab@aol.com.

VALENCIA LAVAO, JESUS M., electrical engineer, consultant; b. Bogota, Distrito Capital, Colombia, Sept. 19, 1965; s. Jesus Maria Valencia Tapiero and Maria Elena Lavao de Valencia; m. Zoraya Ines Contecha Carrillo, Jan. 6, 1996 (div. May 15, 2002); m. Isabel Cristina Patino Devia, Feb. 20, 2005; children: Angel Gabriel Valencia Patino children: Nicolas Andres Valencia Contecha, Daniela Valencia Contecha. Degree in mgmt., Servicio Nacional De Aprendizaje, Bogota, 1988; degree in electrical engring., Distrital U., Bogota, 1994; MSEE, Los Andes U., Bogota, 2004. Lic. Consejo Nacional de Ingenierias, 1998. Radiofrequency engr. SKYTEL, Bogota, 1994—97; sr. engr. Avantel Motorola, Bogota, 1997—2001, Galaxy Engring. Svcs., Alpharetta, Ga., 2001—03, Incode Wireless, St. Louis, 2003—06, Verisign, Milw., 2006—. Math and physics tchr. Grancolombiano H.S., Bogota, 1992—93; info. tech. and computer engr. cons. Microlink, Bogota, 1993—94; internat. telecom. cons. Skytel Mobile Telecomm. Techs. Corp., Bogota, 1995—97; assoc. prof. San Buenaventura U., Bogota, 1998—2001. Author: (drama) Once in the heavens; composer: (song) While the Sun Rises. Mem.: Profl. Assn. Diving Instrs. Diving Soc. (assoc.), IEEE (assoc.), Consejo Profesional Nacional de Ingenieria (life; electronic engr. 1998—). Achievements include invention of electronic circuit to generate chaotic signals for use in broadband telecommunications. Avocations: scuba diving, snowboarding, mountain biking, travel. Office: 7055 Samuel Morse Dr Columbia MD 21046 Office Phone: 410-953-7591. Business E-Mail: jesus.valencia@sprint.com.

VALENTE, GIORGIO, finance educator; b. Rome, Oct. 9, 1973; s. Antonio Valente and Rita Leonino; m. Vicky Poon, July 10, 2002. Laurea in Economics, La Sapienza U. Rome, 1998; MA in Econ. and Econometrics, Centre for Econ. Rsch., U. Tilburg, The Netherlands, 2000; PhD in Fin., Warwick Bus. Sch., U. Warwick, Coventry, UK, 2003. Assoc. prof. fin. U. Warwick, Coventry, England, 2003—05, Chinese U. of Hong Kong, 2005—07; prof. fin. U. Leicester, England, 2007—. Recipient Oddone Fantini award, Inst. Credit and Banking Studies, Rome, 1998, Angelo Costa award, Rivista di Politica Economica, Rome, 1998; grantee, ESRC, London, UK, 2000, 2003. Office: U Leicester Dept Econs Leicester LE1 7RH England Office Phone: (852) 2609 7443. Business E-Mail: giorgio.valente@cuhk.edu.hk.

VALENTE, LOUIS PATRICK (DAN VALENTE), financial planner, director; b. Somerville, Mass., July 26, 1930; s. Luigi and Mary Constance (Fedele) V.; m. Jeanne Barbara Peters, Oct. 3, 1992; children: Louis, Marianne, Steven, Diane, Richard, Carol, Susan. CPA, Bentley Coll., Boston, 1955. Cost acct. Cambridge Corp., Lowell, Mass., 1953-55; sr. acct. Flaherty, Bliss & Co., CPAs, Boston, 1956-61; fin. analyst Sanders Assocs., Nashua, NH, 1961-62; contract audit adminstr. Dept. Def. Audit Agy., Boston, 1962-66, DOE, Las Vegas, 1966-68; asst. controller EG&G, Inc., Wellesley, Mass., 1968-71, asst. v.p., treas., 1971-74, dir. fin., 1974-79, officer, corp. treas., 1979-83, v.p. bus. devel., 1985-91, sr. v.p. mergers, acquisitons and investments, 1991-95; bus. and fin. cons., 1995-97; chmn., CEO Palomar Med. Tech., Inc., Burlington, Mass.,

1997—. Bd. dirs. Meditech Inc., Westwood, Mass., MKS Instruments, Inc., Andover, Mass., Palomar Med. Tech. Inc., Burlington, SurgiLight, Inc., Orlando, Fla. Selectman Town of Burlington, 1970-73, 76-79, chmn., 1972-79; trustee, mem. fin. com. Choate-Symmes Hosp., Woburn, Mass., 1972-80; pres.'s adv. coun. Bentley Coll. With USAF, 1951-53. Mem. AICPA, Fin. Execs. Inst., Mass. Soc. CPAs, Bentley Coll. Alumni Assn., New Eng. Coun., KC Lodge. Roman Catholic. Home: 44 Concord Rd Weston MA 02493-1223 Business E-Mail: dvalente@palmed.com.

VALENTE, PETER CHARLES, lawyer; b. NYC, July 3, 1940; s. Francis Louis and Aurelia Emily (Cella) V.; m. Judith Kay Nemeroff, Feb. 19, 1966; children: Susan Lynn, David Marc. BA, Bowdoin Coll., 1962; LLB, Columbia U., 1966; LLM, NYU, 1971. Bar: N.Y. 1967. Assoc. Blank Rome LLP (formerly Tenzer Greenblatt LLP), NYC, 1967-73, ptnr., 1973—, practice group leader pvt. client practice group, 2002—06. Co-author column on wills, estates and surrogates's practice N.Y. Law Jour. Fellow Am. Coll. Trust and Estate Counsel; mem. ABA, N.Y. State Bar Assn. (lectr. on wills, trusts and estates), Assn. of Bar of City of N.Y., N.Y. County Lawyers' Assn. (former bd. dirs. and chmn. com. on surrogates' ct., lectr. on wills, trusts and estates), Phi Beta Kappa. Office: Blank Rome 405 Lexington Ave New York NY 10174-0002 Office Phone: 212-885-5320. Office Fax: 917-332-3717. Business E-Mail: pvalente@blankrome.com.

VALENTI, MANUELA SAMANTHA, artist; b. Caracas, Venezuela, Apr. 14, 1968; d. Azzurrino Valenti and Luciana Saviozzi; m. Miguel Angel Ruiz, Dec. 22, 1990; children: Carlos Alfredo Ruiz, Daniela Cristina Ruiz, Gabriel Alexander Ruiz. Degree in spl. edn., Coll. Univ. Moneñor de Talavera, Venezuela, 1989. Artist Manuela Valenti Studio & Art Gallery, Macomb, Mich., 1999—. Recipient hon. mention best landscapes small format, 2004, Artists' Choice award/2d pl. best landscape small format, 2005, Artists' Choice award/2nd pl. best cityscape large format, 2006. Home Phone: 586-202-9429. Personal E-mail: mvstudioartgallery@gmail.com.

VALENTI, THOMAS PETER, painter; b. NYC, May 16, 1953; s. Sebastian Valenti and Yolanda Deprima-Valenti; m. Noha F. Khalil-Valenti, June 19, 2000; 1 child, Dana. BFA, Newark Sch. Fine and Indsl. Art, 1974. Lectr. in field. Recipient Traveling Exhibit award, Am. Watercolor Soc., NYC, 2004. Mem.: NJ Watercolor Soc. (Forbes Mag. award 2004), Allied Artists Am. (pres. 2007—), Salmagundi Club (hon.). Avocation: reading. Home: 345 Howard St Township Of Washington NJ 07676

VALENTINE, APRIL SUE, elementary school educator, department chairman; d. Frederick E. Krenz; m. Mark S. Valentine, June 29, 1985; 1 child, Rebecca M. B, U. Md. Balt. County, Catonsville, 1978—82; M, Loyola Coll., Balt., 1982—84. Gen. educator Anne Arundel County Pub. Sch., Annapolis, 1983—. Dept. chairperson (sci.) Anne Arundel Co Pub. Sch., 2000—; interdisciplinary leader Anne Arundel Co Pub. Schools, 1987—. Mem.: Nat. Sci. Assn. Office: Brooklyn Park Mid Sch 200 Hammonds Ln Baltimore MD 21225 Home Phone: 410-461-9694; Office Phone: 410-636-2967. Office Fax: 410-636-1774. Personal E-mail: avalentine@aacps.org.

VALENTINE, BOBBY (ROBERT JOHN VALENTINE), professional baseball manager; b. Stamford, CT, May 13, 1950; m. Mary Branca, Jan. 8, 1977; 1 child, Robert John Jr. Student, U. Southern California, Arizona State U. Player Pioneer League, Ogdon, 1968, Pacific Coast League, Spokane, Wash., 1969-71, Los Angeles Dodgers, Los Angeles, Calif., 1971-72, California Angels, Calif., 1973-75, International League, Charleston, W.Va., 1975, Pacific Coast League, Salt Lake City, 1975, Hawaii, Hawaii, 1976, San Diego Padres, San Diego, 1975-77, New York Mets, NY, 1977-78, Seattle Mariners, Seattle, W.Va., 1979; scout, infield instr. San Diego Padres, San Diego, 1981; minor league infield instr. New York Mets, 1982, third base coach, 1983-85; mgr. Texas Rangers, Arlington, Tex., 1985-96, N.Y. Mets, 1996—2002, Chiba Lotte Marines, Japan, 2004—; commentator, Baseball Tonight ESPN, 2003. Owner Bobby Valentine's Sports Gallery Cafe, Conn., Tex., and R.I. Named Am. League Mgr. of Yr. UPI, 1986; recipient William A. Shea Disting. Little League Grad. award, 1987; inductee Italian Am. Sports Hall Fame, 1990. mgr., Japan Series Champions, 2005. Office: Bobby Valentine's Sports Gallery Cafe 225 Main St Stamford CT 06903

VALENTINE, BRIAN, information technology executive; BS in Computer Sci., Ea. Washington U. Software engr. Intel Corp.; with Microsoft Corp., Redmond, Wash., 1987—, gen. mgr., server application div., 1998, v.p., Windows group, 1998—99, v.p., bus. and enterprise, 1999, sr. v.p. Windows core operating systems divsn., 1999—.

VALENTINE, DEAN, film producer; AB, U. Chicago, 1976. Pres. Walt Disney TV/Touchstone TV; pres., CEO United Paramount Network, Los Angeles, 1997—2002; with Europlay Capital Advisors, LLC, 2002—03; pres. First Family Entertainment, Beverly Hills, 2004. Named one of Top 200 Collectors, ARTnews Mag., 2004, 2006. Avocation: Collector of Contemporary Art. Office: Dean Valentine First Family Entertainm 11601 Wilshire Blvd Ste 750 Los Angeles CA 90025-1743

VALENTINE, DEBRA A., lawyer; b. Cleve., Apr. 16, 1953; AB magna cum laude in History, Princeton U., 1976; JD, Yale U. Law Sch., 1980. Bar: D.C., U.S. Dist. Ct. D.C., U.S. Ct. Appeals (D.C. Cir., 3d Cir., 11th Cir.), U.S. Supreme Ct. Law clk. Judge Arlin M. Adams, U.S. Ct. Appeals, 3d Cir., Phila., 1980-81; atty./advisor Office of Legal Counsel, Dept. of Justice, Washington, 1981-85; assoc. O'Melveny & Myers, Washington, 1985-91, ptnr., 1991-95; dep. dir. policy planning FTC, Washington, 1995-96, asst. dir. for internat. antitrust, 1996-97, gen. counsel, 1997-2001; ptnr., co-chair antitrust practice group O'Melveny & Myers, Washington, 2001—04; v.p., dep. gen. counsel, sec. United Technologies Corp., 2004—. Cons. Sec. of State's Adv. Com. South Africa. Bd. editors BNA Antitrust & Trade Regulation Reporter; contbr. articles to profl. jours. Bd. dirs. The Hartford Symphony, The Hartford Stage Co.; bd. electors Wadsworth Athenaeum. Fulbright scholar, 1976-77. Mem. ABA, Internat. Bar Assn., Am. Law Inst., D.C. Bar, Coun. on Fgn. Rels., Phi Beta Kappa. Office: United Technologies Corp United Technologies Bldg Hartford CT 06101

VALENTINE, FOY DAN, clergyman; b. Edgewood, Tex., July 3, 1923; s. John Hardy and Josie (Johnson) V.; m. Mary Louise Valentine, May 6, 1947; children: Mary Jean, Carol Elizabeth, Susan Foy. BA, Baylor U., 1944, LLD (hon.), 1979; ThM, Southwestern Baptist Theol. Sem., 1947, ThD, 1949; DD, William Jewell Coll., 1966, Louisiana Coll., 1989. Ordained to ministry Bapt. Ch., 1942. Dir. Bapt. student activities colls. in Houston, 1949-50; pastor First Bapt. Ch., Gonzales, Tex., 1950-53; dir. Christian life commn. Bapt. Gen. Conv. Tex., 1953-60; exec. dir., treas. Christian life commn. So. Bapt. Conv., 1960-87, exec. officer for devel., 1987-88; chmn. So. Bapt. inter-agy. council, 1965-67. Willson lectr. applied Christianity Wayland Bapt. Coll., 1963; Christian ethics lectr. Bapt. Theol. Sem., Ruschlikon-Zurich, Switzerland, 1966; Layne lectr. New Orleans Bapt. Theol. Sem., 1974; Jones lectr. Union U., 1976; Staley Disting. Christian scholar/lectr. La. Coll., 1981; Simpson lectr. Acadia Divinity Coll., Nova Scotia, 1982; H.I. Hester lectr. on preaching Midwestern Bapt. Theol. Sem., 1984; Belote lectr. Christian ethics Hong Kong Bapt. Theol. Sem., 1990; co-chmn. commn. religious liberty and human rights Bapt. World Alliance, 1966-75, chmn. commn. Christian ethics, 1976-80, mem. gen. coun., 1976-80; mem. Nashville Met. Human Rels. Commn., 1966-78, Pres.'s Commn. for Nat. Agenda for the Eighties, 1980; guest columnist USA Today; lectr. on Christian ethics Bible Inst. for Evangelism and Missions, St. Petersburg, USSR, 1991; co-chmn. Baylor U. Heritage Club, 2000-01. Author: Believe and Behave, 1964, Citizenship for Christians, 1965, The Cross in the Marketplace, 1966, Where the Action Is, 1969, A Historical Study of Southern Baptists and Race Relations 1917-1947, 1980, What Do You Do After You Say Amen?, 1980, Hebrews, James, 1 and 2 Peter: Layman's Bible Book Commentary, 1981, Whatsoever Things Are Lovely, 2004; editor: Christian Faith in Action, 1956, Peace, Peace, 1967, Christian Ethics Today, 1995-2000; contbr. to numerous anthologies, articles to profl. jours. Pres. Ctr. for Christian Ethics, 1990-2000; trustee Interfaith Alliance, 1994—, Ams. United for Separation of Ch. and State, 1960-93, pres., 1989-93; bd. dirs. Bapt. Joint Com. Pub. Affairs, 1960-87, Chs. Ctr. Theology and Pub. Policy, 1976-87, T.B. Maston Found., Texans Against Gambling; mem. bd. fellows Interpreter's House, 1967-78, Ctr. for Dialogue and Devel., 1987-96. Recipient Disting. Alumnus award Southwestern Bapt. Theol. Sem., 1970, Brooks Hays Meml. Christian Citizenship award, 1983, Disting. Alumni award Baylor U., 1987. Mem. Am. Soc. Christian Ethics. Democrat. Home and Office: 12527 Matisse Ln Dallas TX 75230-1741

VALENTINE, GENE C., securities dealer; b. Washington, Pa., June 19, 1950; s. John N. and Jane S. Valentine. BS in Psychology, Bethany Coll., 1972; student, U. Vienna, Austria, 1971-72. Commd. ensign USN, 1972, advanced through grades to lt., 1987, hon. discharged, 1978; owner Horizon Realty, San Francisco, 1978-82; dir. land acquisitions Windfarms Ltd. subs. Chevron, U.S.A., San Francisco, 1980-82; v.p. mktg. Christopher Weil & Co., Sherman Oaks, Calif., 1982-85; chmn., CEO Pacific Asset Group Inc. (name now Fin. West Group, Inc.), Westlake Village, Calif., 1985—. Bd. dirs. Fin. West Group, Inc., Paradox Holdings; founder, chmn., dir. Second Byte Found.; founder, chmn. Peace Point Farms Equestrian Facility, LLC and Found., Bethany, W.Va. Mem. Rep. Party, L.A. Mem. NASD, Internat. Assn. Fin. Planning (bd. dirs. L.A. chpt. 1982-87). Episcopalian. Avocations: equestrian, sailing, tennis, golf, running. Home Phone: 304-829-9099; Office Phone: 304-829-4800. Personal E-mail: qcvalentine@yahoo.com.

VALENTINE, H. JEFFREY, legal association executive; b. Phila., Sept. 28, 1945; s. Joshua Morton and Olga W. (Wilson) V.; 1 child, Karyn. BS, St. Louis U., 1964, postgrad., 1966-68. Programmer, systems analyst Honeywell Electronic Data Processing, Wellesley Hills, Mass., 1964-66; account exec. Semiconductor div. Tex. Instruments, New Eng., 1966-68; New Eng. sales exec., Mid-Atlantic regional mgr. Electronic Instrumentation Co., 1968-70; pres. Nat. Free Lance Photographers Assn., Doylestown, Pa., 1970-89; pres., dir. Towne Print & Copy Ctrs. Inc.; v.p., exec. dir. Nat. Paralegal Assn., 1982—; pres. Paralegal Assocs., Inc., 1982—; chief operating officer Doylestown Parking Corp., 1977-88. Bd. dirs. Law Enforcement Supply Co., Solebury, Valtronics Supply Co., Towne Print & Copy Centers Inc., Solebury, Doylestown Stationery and Office Supply, Energy Mktg. Assocs., Inc., Solebury, Paralegal Placement Network; pres. Paralegal Pub. Corp., 1983-90; pub. Paralegal Jour.; pres. Valco Enterprises Inc., 1986—, Paralegal Employment Sys., Inc., 1988, Solebury Press, Inc., 1989—; ptnr. J&S Gen. Contractors, 1993—, J&S Landscaping Tree Svc., 1993—, J&S Estate and Property Mgmt., 2001--; owner Specialized Computer Consulting, 1992—. Author: Photographers Bookkeeping System, 1973, rev. edit., 1978, Photographers Pricing Guides, 1971, 72, 74, 75, Available Markets Director's - 4 Vols., 1973-77, National Model Sources Directory, Nat. Paralegal Salary and Employment Survey, 1985-86, 88, 90-92, 93-94; also articles, bulls. and pamphlets. Exec. sec. Doylestown Bus. Assn., 1972-78, pres., 1979, 83, v.p., 1981. Recipient Internat. Men of Achievement award, 1988; named Personalities of the Am., 1988. Mem. London Coll. Applied Scis., Nat. Fedn. Paralegal Assns., Photog. Industry Coun., Nat. Assn. Legal Assts., Am. Soc Assn. Execs., Soc. Assn. Mgrs., Nat. Fedn. Ind. Business (mem. action coun. com.), Nat. Parking Assn., Nat. Office Products Assn., Graphic Arts Assn. Delaware Valley, Nat. Assn. Federally Licensed Firearms Dealers, Nat. Compostition Assn., Internat. Platform Assn. Office: PO Box 406 Solebury PA 18963-0406

VALENTINE, JAMES BURGON, musician; b. Lincoln, Nebr., Oct. 5, 1978; Guitarist Maroon 5, LA, 2001—. Musician: (albums) Songs About Jane, 2002, 1.22.03.Acoustic, 2004, Live Friday the 13th, 2005, It Won't Be Soon Before Long, 2007, (songs) Harder to Breathe, 2003, This Love, 2004 (MTV Video Music award for Best New Group, 2004, Grammy award for Best Group Pop Performance, 2006), She Will Be Loved, 2004, Shiver, 2005, contbr. to Spider-Man 2 soundtrack, 2004. Recipient World Music award for Best New Group, 2004, MTV Europe award for Best New Act, 2004, Grammy award for Best New Artist (with Maroon 5), 2005. Address: Maroon 5 PO Box 884564 San Francisco CA 94188 Office: Octone Records Rm 500 560 Broadway New York NY 10012 Office Phone: 646-613-0200. E-mail: maroon5@maroon5.com.

VALENTINE, JAMES WILLIAM, paleontologist, educator, writer; b. LA, Nov. 10, 1926; s. Adelbert Cuthbert and Isabel (Davis) V.; m. Grace Evelyn Whysner, Dec. 21, 1957 (div. 1972); children: Anita, Ian; m. Cathryn Alice Campbell, Sept. 10, 1978 (div. 1986); 1 child, Geoffrey; m. Diane Mondragon, Mar. 16, 1987. BA, Phillips U., 1951; MA, UCLA, 1954, PhD, 1958. From asst. prof. to assoc. prof. U. Mo., Columbia, 1958-64; from assoc. prof. to prof. U. Calif., Davis, 1964-77, prof. geol. scis. Santa Barbara, 1977-90, prof. integrative biology Berkeley, 1990-93, prof. emeritus, 1993—. Author: Evolutionary Paleoecology of the Marine Biosphere, 1973, On the Origin of Phyla, 2004; editor: Phanerozoic Diversity, 1985; co-author: Evolution, 1977, Evolving, 1979; contbr. articles to profl. jours. Served with USNR, 1944-46, PTO. Recipient Lapworth medal Palaeontological Assn., 2004; Fulbright rsch. scholar, Australia, 1962-63; Guggenheim fellow Yale U., Oxford U., Eng., 1968-69; Rockefeller Found. scholar in residence, Bellagio, Italy, summer 1974; grantee NSF, NASA. Fellow: AAAS, Geol. Soc. Am., Am. Acad. Arts and Scis.; mem.: NAS, Paleontol. Soc. (medal 1996). Avocation: collecting works of Charles Darwin. Home: 1351 Glendale Ave Berkeley CA 94708-2025 Office: U Calif Dept Integrative Biology Berkeley CA 94720-0001 Office Phone: 510-643-5791. Business E-Mail: jwvsossi@socrates.berkeley.edu.

VALENTINE, JEAN, poet, educator, writer; b. Chgo., 1934; BA, Radcliffe Coll. Poetry workshop tchr. Swarthmore Coll., 1968—70, Hunter Coll., 1970—75, Sarah Lawrence Coll., NYU, Grad. Writing Prog., Columbia U., 92nd St Y, New York, NY. Author: Dream Barker, 1965, Pilgrims, 1969, Ordinary Things, 1974, The Messenger, 1979, Home Deep Blue: New and Selected Poems, 1989, The River at Wolf, 1992, The Under Voice: Selected Poems, 1995, Growing Darkness, Growing Light, 1997, The Cradle of the Real Life, 2000, Door in the Mountain: New and Collected Poems 1965-2003, 2004 (Nat. Book Award for Poetry, 2004). Recipient awards, NEA, Bunting Inst., Rockefeller Found., NY Coun. for Arts, NY Found. for Arts, Maurice English Prize, Teasdale Poetry Prize, Shelley Mem. Prize, Poetry Soc. Am., 2000; grantee Guggenheim Fellowship.

VALENTINE, JOHN LESTER, state legislator, lawyer; b. Fullerton, Calif., Apr. 26, 1949; s. Robert Lester and Pauline C. V.; m. Karen Marie Thorpe, June 1, 1972; children: John Robert, Jeremy Reid, Staci Marie, Jeffrey Mark., David Emerson, Patricia Ann. BS in Acctg. and Econs., Brigham Young U., 1973, JD, 1976. Bar: Utah 1976, U.S. Dist. Ct. Utah, U.S. Ct. Appeals (10th cir.), U.S. Tax Ct., U.S. Supreme Ct. 2002; CPA. Atty. Howard, Lewis & Petersen, Provo, Utah, 1976—; mem. Utah Ho. Reps., 1988-98, Utah Senate, Dist. 14, Salt Lake City, 1999—, pres. of Senate, 2004—. Instr. probate and estates Utah Valley State Coll.; instr. fin. planning., adj. prof. law Brigham Young U.; chmn. revenue and taxation com. Utah Senate, 1999-2000, vice chmn. exec. appropriations com., judiciary com., pub. edn. subcom., majority whip 2001—; mem. exec offices, cts., corrections and legis. appropriations subcom., Utah Ho. of Reps., 1988-90, capital facilities subcom., 1988-90, retirement com., 1988-90, judiciary com., 1988-92, strategic planning steering com., 1988-90, interim appropriations com., 1988-94, tax. review commn., 1989-98, ethics com., 1990-92, human svcs. and health appropriations subcom., 1990-92, revenue and taxation com., 1988-98, vice chmn. 1990-92; vice chmn. exec. appropriations., 1990-92; chmn. exec. appropriations com., 1992-94, chmn. rules com., 1994-96, higher edn. appropriations com. 1994-96, asst. majority whip, 1996-98; apptd. to state senate, 1998, elected, 2000, majority whip, 2000-04, pres., 2004—. Mem. adv. bd. Internat. Sr. Games, 1988—; active Blue Ribbon Task Force on Local Govt. Funding, Utah League Cities and Towns, 1990-94, Criminal Sentencing Guidelines Task Force, Utah Judicial Coun., 1990-92, Access to Health Care Task Force, 1990-92, Utah County Sheriff Search and Rescue, Orem Met. Water Bd., Alpine Sch. Dist. Boundary Line Com., 1986-90, Boy Scouts Am.; bd. regents Legis. Adv. Com. UVCC.; mem. exec. bd. Utah Nat. Parks Coun.; mem. adv. coun. Orchard Elem. Sch., Mountainlands Com. an Aging; bd. trustees Utah Opera Co.; judge nat. and local competitions Moot Ct.; voting dist. chmn.; state, county del.; lt. incident command sys. Utah County Sheriff. Recipient Silver Beaver award Boy Scouts Am., Taxpayer Advocate award Utah Taxpayer Assn. Mem. ABA (tax sect.), Utah State Bar, CPA Com., Tax Sect. Specialization Com., Bicentennial Com. Republican. Mem. Lds Ch. Avocation: mountain climbing. Office: Howard Lewis & Petersen 120 E 300 N Provo UT 84606-2907

VALENTINE, LONA J., lawyer; b. Ashland, Ky., Nov. 17, 1972; BS in Math./Actuarial Sci., Bellarmine U., 1994; MBA, U. Ky., 1995, JD, 2000. Bar: Ohio 2000, Ky. 2006; cert. Arbitrator Coun. Better Bus. Bureaus. Assoc. Peck, Shaffer & Williams LLP, Cin. Named one of Ohio's Rising Stars, Super Lawyers, 2005, 2006; recipient J. Oexmann Criminal Law award, 1999. Mem.: Cin. Bar Assn., Ohio State Bar Assn., ABA, Nat. Assn. Bond Lawyers. Office: Peck Shaffer & Williams LLP 201 E 5th St Ste 900 Cincinnati OH 45202 Office Phone: 513-639-9238. Office Fax: 513-621-3813.

VALENTINE, MARK CONRAD, dermatologist; b. Parkersburg, W.Va., Sept. 26, 1948; s. Sestel and Margaret Elaine (Sabolo) V.; m. Elizabeth Michelle Monezis, Apr. 21, 1975; children: Perry Martin, Owen Mark. BA, W.Va. U., 1970; MD, Johns Hopkins U., 1974. Intern, resident U. Hosps. Cleve., 1974-76, resident, 1976-79; dermatologist pvt. practice, Everett, Wash., 1979—. Clin. prof. U. Wash., Seattle, 1979—; active med. staff Providence Everett Gen. Med. Ctr., 1979—. Editl. bd. Jour. of Am. Acad. Dermatology, 1998—2005. Bd. dirs., sec. City Libr. Bd., Mukilteo, Wash., 1994-99; bd. dirs., v.p. Everett Symphony Bd., 1982-85, 2001—2006; bd. dirs. Book Arts Guild, Seattle, 1988-90. Nat. Merit scholar, 1966. Mem. AMA, Am. Acad. Dermatology (adv. coun. 1983-86), Wash. State Dermatol. Assn. (pres.-elect 1996, pres. 1996-97), Seattle Dermatology Soc. (pres. 1985-86), Snohomish County Med. Soc. (bd. dirs. 2001—, pres. 2006), Rotary (Everett), Phi Beta Kappa. Avocations: book collecting, book binding, guitar, piano. Office: 3327 Colby Ave Everett WA 98201-6403 Home Phone: 425-348-6256; Office Phone: 425-258-6767. Personal E-mail: mark1105@aol.com.

VALENTINE, PHYLLIS LOUISE, counseling administrator; d. Harold Gray and Velma Eura Long; m. Samuel L. Valentine, Dec. 30, 1995. BA, St. Augustine's Coll., 1970; MEd, Bowie State U., 1992; student, Trinity Coll., 1974—77, Georgetown U., 1989, U. D.C., 1974—88. Cert. sch. counselor K-12, reading tchr. K-12. Evening reading reacher Loton Reformatory Youth Ctr. II PSI Assocs., Washington, 1984—86; chpt. 1 reading/math. lab tchr. D.C. Pub. Schs., 1986—92, chpt. 1 resource asst., 1992—93; chpt. 1 CAI lab tchr./team coord. C.W. Harris Elem. Sch., Washington, 1992—95; sch. counselor J.C. Nalle Elem. Sch., Washington, 1995—. Mem. tchr. adv. bd. Ctr. for Artistry in Tchg., Washington, 1999—; dir., presenter J.C. Nalle Sch. Extended Day, 1998. V.p. Brandywine Sta. Townhouse Assn., Upper Marlboro, Md., 1990—97. Recipient Letter of Commendation, Exec. Dir. Chpt. 1 program, 1987, AIMs Pilot, Bryan Elem. Sch., 1984, HOST Corp., 1994, DCPS Parent Ctr. Incentive, 1997. Mem.: D.C. Sch. Counseling Assn. (newsletter editor 2004—05, corr. sec.), Am. Sch. Counseling Assn., Am. Counseling Assn., Tots & Teens Inc. (pres. 1985—93, corr. sec. 1985—93, youth leader 1987—91, D.C. chpt., award 1990—91), D.C. Counseling Assn. (pres.-elect 2001—02, pres. 2002, dedicated svc. plaque 1993), Phi Delta Kappa (mem. Beta chpt., grammateus 2003—), Nat. Sorority Phi Delta Kappa (Beta chpt.), Sigma Gamma Rho (recording sec., anti-basilus 1971—78). Avocations: gardening, listening to jazz music, dance. Business E-Mail: phyllis.valentine@k12.us.

VALENTINE, RALPH SCHUYLER, chemical engineer, director; b. Seattle, Nov. 3, 1932; s. John Campbell and Elizabeth Florence (Patterson) V.; m. Jeanne Marie Belanger, June 15, 1957; children: Susan Diana, Jacqueline Leigh, John Campbell. BSChemE, U. Wash., 1955, PhDChemE, 1963; MSChemE, U. Ill., 1956. Registered profl. engr., Calif., Va., Wash. Rsch. engr. Chevron Rsch. Corp., Richmond, Calif., 1956-61; instr. U. Wash., Seattle, 1961-63; mgr. fluid dynamics Aerojet-Gen., Sacramento, 1963-69; mgr. chem. tech. Atlantic Rsch. Corp., Alexandria, Va., 1969-79; mgr. rsch. United Techs. Chem. Systems, San Jose, Calif., 1979-91; gen. mgr. Greater Pocatello Sr. Citizens, Inc., 2001—. Lectr. U.S. Naval Postgrad. Sch., Monterey, Calif., 1968, UCLA Modern Devels. in Propulsion, L.A., 1967-68, USAF Astronautics Labs., Lancaster, Calif., 1967, U.S. Army R & D Unit, Sacramento, 1966. Contbr. 23 tech. articles to profl. jours.; patentee in field. Recipient NASA commendation for Apollo work, Houston, 1969, 1st prize Ceramographic Exhbn. Am. Ceramics Soc., 1974, Andrus award AARP, 2005. Mem. AIChE (life). Republican. Home: 1515 Satterfield Dr Pocatello ID 83201-8002 Personal E-mail: ralph_s_valentine@yahoo.com.

VALENTINE, STEVEN RICHARDS, lawyer; b. Memphis, Jan. 30, 1956; s. William Robert and Lenita Joanne (Nelms) V.; m. Susan Marie Burke, Jan. 14, 1984; children: Christina Michele, William Robert II, Steven Richards Jr., Thomas Burke, Diana Elizabeth. Grad., Capitol Page Sch., Washington, 1974; student, Earlham Coll., 1974-77; B of Gen. Studies with distinction, Ind. U., 1979, JD, 1982. Bar: Ill. 1983, D.C. 1985, U.S. Ct. Appeals (D.C. cir.) 1986, U.S. Supreme Ct. 1986, U.S. Ct. Appeals (9th cir.) 1989. Chief investigator consumer protection divsn. Office Atty. Gen., State of Ind., 1980-82; exec. dir. Ams. United for Life Legal Def. Fund, Chgo., 1982-83; chief counsel subcom. on separation of powers U.S. Senate, Washington, 1983-85, chief counsel subcom. on cts., 1985; adminstrv. asst. U.S. Senator John P. East, Washington, 1985-86; dir. Office of Policy Devel. and Comm. Legal Svcs. Corp., Washington, 1986-87; counselor to asst. atty. gen. civil divsn. U.S. Dept. Justice, Washington, 1987-88; dep. asst. atty. gen. civil divsn. U.S. Justice Dept., Washington, 1988-93, gen. counsel to U.S. Senator Robert C. Smith, 1993-99; legis. dir. to U.S. Senator Robert C. Smith, 1996-99; of counsel Preston Gates Ellis & Rouvelas Meeds LLP, Washington, 1999—2002; ptnr. Kirkpatrick & Lockhart, Preston, Gates Ellis LLP, Washington, 2002—. Mem. exec. com., bd. dirs. Deluxe West, Inc.; sr. fellow John C. Stennis Ctr. for Pub. Svc.; bd. visitors Ind. U. Sch. Law, Indpls.; presdl. rank review bd. US Office Personnel Mgmt., 2006. Author: Each Time A Man, 1978, All Shall Live, 1980; co-author: Abortion and the Constitution, 1987, Principle Over Politics, 2004; contbr. articles to profl. jours. Recipient spl. commendation U.S. Atty. Gen., 1993; John C. Stennis Congl. staff fellow, 1995-96. Mem.: SAR, Rep. Nat. Lawyers Assn., Federalist Soc., Capitol Hill Club. Republican. Roman Catholic. Avocations: history, baseball. Home: 6487

Warwick Cir Alexandria VA 22315-5045 Office: Kirkpatrick et al 1601 K St NW Washington DC 20006 Home Phone: 703-924-3554; Office Phone: 202-661-3802. Personal E-mail: rick.valentine@cox.net.

VALENTINE, WILLIAM NEWTON, retired physician, educator; b. Kansas City, Mo., Sept. 29, 1917; s. Herbert S. and Mabel W. Valentine; m. Martha Hickman Winfree; children: William, James, Edward. Student, U. Mich., 1934—36, U. Mo., Columbia, 1936—37; MD, Tulane U., 1942. Diplomate Am. Bd. Internal Medicine. Intern Strong Meml. Hosp., Rochester, NY, 1942—43, asst. resident in medicine, 1943, chief resident in medicine, 1943—44; specialist, attending physician in internal medicine Wadsworth Hosp., LA, 1949—88, VA Ctr., LA, 1949—88; specialist, attending physician in internal medicine Ctr. Health Scis. UCLA, 1949—, prof. medicine, 1957—88, chmn. dept., 1963—71, prof. emeritus medicine, 1988—. Contbr. articles to profl. jours. Capt. MC AUS, 1944—47. Recipient Mayo Soley award for excellence in rsch., Western Soc. Clin. Rsch., 1978, 53d Annual UCLA faculty rsch. lectr., 1978. Master: ACP (John Phillips Meml. award for disting. achievements in internal medicine 1979); fellow: Am. Soc. Hematology (Henry Stratton lectr. 1978), Internat. Soc. Hematology (v.p. U.S. 1976—80); mem.: NAS, Am. Acad. Arts and Scis., We. Soc. Clin. Rsch., We. Assn. Physicians (pres. 1969—70), Assn. Am. Physicians, Am. Soc. Clin. Investigation (v.p. 1962), Am. Bd. Internal Medicine. Republican.

VALENTINE-SIBERT, KIMBERLY A., lawyer; b. Lakewood, Calif., Aug. 13, 1967; BA, Golden West Coll.; JD, Western State Univ., 1997. Bar: Calif. 1998, Ariz. Ptnr., elder abuse & malpractice litigation Barbaro & Valentine, Santa Ana, Calif. Named a Rising Star, So. Calif. Super Lawyers, 2006. Mem.: Assn. Trial Lawyers Am., Orange County Trial Lawyers Assn., Consumer Attorneys Calif. Office: Barbaro & Valentine 2d Fl 200 N Main St Santa Ana CA 92701 Office Phone: 714-835-2122. Office Fax: 714-973-4892.

VALENTINO, (VALENTINO GARAVANI), fashion designer; b. Voghera, Italy, May 11, 1932; Student, Academia Dell'Arte, Paris, Ecole des Beaux-Arts. Asst. designer Fashion Ho. of Jean Dessès, 1950-55, Fashion Ho. of Guy Laroche, 1956-58; opened House of Valentino, Rome, 1959, began partnership with Giancarlo Giammetti, 1960; internat. debut Florence, Italy, 1962; launched women's & men's ready-to-wear collections, 1972; opened boutiques in Rome and Milan, 1972; developer Valentino Più, 1973; launched Valentino perfume in Paris, 1978; established boutiques in US & Japan, 1980. Designer Italian athletes' uniforms Olympic Games, Los Angeles, Calif., 1984. Exhibited at Victoria and Albert Mus., London, 1971, La Jolla Mus. Art, Calif., 1982; costume designer (films) Wild and Wonderful, 1964, Hello-Goodbye, 1970; designer and prodr. exhibition: Atelier of Illusion, 1985, Accademia, 1991. Founder (with Giancarlo Giamcarlo) L.I.F.E., 1990—. Recipient Neiman-Marcus award, 1967, Grand'Ufficiale dell'Ordine al Merito, Italian Ministry of Industry, 1985, Lifetime Achievement award, American Designer awards, NY, 2000; named Cavaliere di gran Croce, Italy, 1986, Cavaliere del Lavoro, 1996. Office: Piazza Mignanelli 22 00187 Rome Italy also: 11 W 42nd St New York NY 10036

VALENZUELA, HERALDO MUÑOZ See **MUÑOZ, HERALDO**

VALENZUELA, JULIO SAMUEL, sociologist, educator; b. Concepción, Chile, Mar. 30, 1948; came to U.S., 1970; s. Raimundo Arms and Dorothy Dueul (Bowie) V.; m. Erika Fresia Maza, Mar. 22, 1969. Licenciatura, U. Concepción, Chile, 1970; PhD, Columbia U., NYC, 1979. Asst. prof. Yale U., New Haven, 1977-80, Harvard U., Cambridge, Mass., 1980-85, assoc. prof., 1985, U. Notre Dame, Ind., 1986—89, prof. Ind., 1989—, dept. chairperson Ind., 1989—92, fellow Kellogg Inst. Ind., 1986—. Sr. assoc. fellow St. Antony's Coll., Oxford U., 1992-93, 96—; campaign adv. presidl. election, Chile, 1999; cons. labor policy Chilean Govt., 2000, 01; advisor, Chilean Govt. Pension Reform Commn., 2006. Author: Democratización vía Reforma, 1986; co-author: Chile, A Country Study, 1994; co-editor: Chile: Politics And Society, 1976, Military Rule In Chile, 1986, Issues In Democratic Consolidation, 1992, El Eslabón Perdido: Familia, Modernización y Bienestar en Chile, 2006; contbr. chpts. to books, articles to profl. jours. Pres. New Eng. Coun. of Latin Am. Studies, 1984—85. Fellow NEH ind. scholarship rsch. 1983-84, conf. grant 1987; John Simon Guggenheim fellow, 1996. Mem. Am. Sociol. Assn., Internat. Sociol. Assn. (v.p. rsch. com. #44 1990-94), Latin Am. Studies Assn. (nominating com. 1987-88), Am. Polit. Sci. Assn., Soc. for the Advancement of Socio-econs., Chilean Polit. Sci. Assn. Methodist. Office: U Notre Dame Kellogg Inst Notre Dame IN 46556 Office Phone: 574-631-6410. Business E-Mail: valenzuela.1@nd.edu.

VALENZUELA, MANUEL ANTHONY, JR., lawyer; b. LA, Dec. 4, 1955; s. Manuel and Artimesa B. (Ruiz) V.; m. Guadalupe Roa, Nov. 8, 1980; children: Manuel Anthony III, Nancy Christine. BA in Polit. Sci., UCLA, 1978; MPA, U. So. Calif., 1982; JD, Southwestern U., LA, 1987. Bar: Calif. 1987, U.S. Dist. Ct. (ctrl. dist.) Calif. 1987, U.S. Ct. Appeals (9th cir.) 1988, U.S. Supreme Ct. 1991. Legis. analyst L.A. City Coun., 1981-88; legal extern ACLU, LA, 1985; assoc. county counsel County of L.A., 1988-89, sr. assoc county counsel, 1989-90, dep. county counsel, 1990-94, sr. dep. county counsel, 1994-98, prin. dep. county counsel, 1998—. Contbr. articles to profl. jours. Mem.: Constnl. Rights Found. (mock trial competition 1997—99, 2001, 2003), UCLA Latino Alumni Assn. (founder, bd. dirs. 1989—90, scholarship com. 1995—99), L.A. County Counsel Assn. (bd. dirs. 1989—99), Mexican Am. Bar Assn. (bd. dirs. 1990, 1991), L.A. County Bar Assn. (exec. com. govtl. law sect. 1990—91, sec. govtl. law sect. 1991—92, 2d vice chair govtl. law sect. 1992—93, 1st vice chair govtl. law sect. 1993—94, chair govtl. law sect. 1994—95, exec. com. govtl. law sect. 1995—96, bd. trustees 1995—96, exec. com. govtl. law sect. 1996—97). Democrat. Roman Catholic. Avocations: tennis, backpacking, photography. Home: 9647 Val St Temple City CA 91780-1438 Office: Office of County Counsel 648 Hall of Adminstrn 500 W Temple St Los Angeles CA 90012-2713 Office Phone: 213-974-1926. Business E-Mail: mvalenzuela@counsel.co.la.ca.us.

VALERI, TONY, Canadian government official, small business owner; m. Terri Boswell; 2 children. Degree in econs., McMaster U. M.P. for Hamilton East-Stoney Creek House of Commons, 1993—, parliamentary sec. to Min. Fin. Paul Martin, 1997—99, mem. standing com. on fin., vice chair standing com. on industry, chair standing com. on govt. ops., leader govt. Parliament Hill, 2004—06; min. transport Govt. of Canada, Ottawa, 2003—04; exec. in fesidence DeGroote Sch. Bus., McMaster U., 2006—; cons. for profit and not for profit orgns. in area of strategic advocacy programs, 2006—. Chair Nat. Liberal Caucus Task Force on Jobs and Small Bus.

VALERIANI, NICHOLAS J., health products executive; b. Newark; married; 2 children. BS in Indsl. Engring., Rutgers U., MBA. With engring. divsn. Ethicon, Inc. Johnson & Johnson, 1978, v.p. profl. edn. Ethicon Endo-Surgery, Inc., 1991, mem. mgmt. bd. Ethicon Endo-Surgery, Inc., 1991, gen. mgr. Indigo Med., Inc., 1996—97, pres. Ethicon Endo-Surgery, Inc., 1997, co. grp. chmn., 2001, worldwide chmn. DePuy, 2002, corp. v.p. human resources, mem. exec. com., 2003, worldwide chmn. diagnostics, 2004—05, worldwide chmn. cardiovasc. devices and diagnostics grp., mem. exec. com., 2005—. Bd. dirs. Action for Healthy Kids; bd. visitors U. NC Kenan-Flagler Bus. Sch. Office: Johnson & Johnson 1 Johnson & Johnson Plz New Brunswick NJ 08933

VALERIO, MATTHEW F., lawyer; b. Lawrence, Mass., Sept. 28, 1963; s. Fred Ernest Jr. Valerio and Carole Elaine (Closson) Mimeault; m. Joanne F. Stockton, Aug. 6, 1988. BA, St. Michael's Coll., 1985; JD, Western New Eng. Coll., 1988. Bar: Mass. 1989, Vt. 1989, U.S. Dist. Ct. Mass. 1989, U.S. Dist. Ct. Vt. 1989, U.S. Ct. Appeals (2d cir.) 1998. Pvt. practice, Springfield, Mass., 1989; assoc. Abatiell & Wysolmerski, Rutland, Vt., 1989-94; ptnr. Abatiell & Valerio, Rutland, Vt., 1994—2001; defender gen. State of Vt., 2001—. Adj. prof. Coll. St. Joseph, Rutland, 1993-99. Fin. chmn. Rutland County Rep. Com., 1991-93. Mem. ABA (young lawyers divsn. dist. rep. Vt., Maine 1994-96, Vt. state membership chair 1995—), New Eng. Bar Assn. (bd. dirs. 1997—, pres. 1999-2000, 05-06), Vt. Trial Lawyers Assn., Vt. Bar Assn. (treas., exec. com. young lawyers sect. 1990-92, chmn. exec. com. 1993-94, bd. bar mgr. 1992-2003, pres. 2001-02, bd. bar mgrs. 2005—, treas. 2005—), Vt. Criminal Def. Lawyers Assn. (bd. dirs. 1993-96), Assn. Trial Lawyers Am., Kiwanis (bd. dirs. Rutland chpt. 1990-96, v.p. 1991-92, pres. 1993-94, pres. Rutland area mentor program 1994-96, disting. svc. award 1989-92, N.E. dis disting. pres. award 1993-94). Avocations: baseball, wrestling, blues. Office: Office Defender Gen 14-16 Baldwin St Montpelier VT 05633-3301 Office Phone: 802-828-3168.

VALERIO, MICHAEL ANTHONY, diversified financial services company executive; b. Detroit, Sept. 20, 1953; s. Anthony Rudolph and Victoria (Popoff) V.; m. Barbara Ann Nabozny, Oct. 8, 1983. BA, U. Mich., Dearborn, 1975. CPA, Mich. Jr. acct. Carabell, Bocknek CPA's, Southfield, Mich., 1975-76; sr. acct. Purdy, Donovan & Beal, CPA's, Detroit, 1976-77; mgr. Buctynck & Co., CPA's, Southfield, 1978-79; contr. Transcontinental Travel, Harper Woods, Mich., 1979—80; exec. v.p. Holland Cons., Inc., Detroit, 1980-85; contr., CFO SLC Recycling Industries, Inc., Warren, Mich., 1985—98; owner Pinnacle Fin. Consulting, PLLC, Livonia, Mich., 1994—. Rep. Wealth and Wisdom, Inc.; fin. cons. Am. Group Retirement Strategy Ctrs.; owner Michael Valerio, CPA/PFS, LLC, 2006—. Mem. AICPA, Mich. Soc. CPAs. Roman Catholic. Office: Pinnacle Fin Consulting PLLC 33300 Five Mile Rd Ste 102 Livonia MI 48154-3074

VALERO, MARIA TERESA, photographer, art educator; b. Venezuela; BFA in Graphic Design, Art History, U. Kans., M in Art History. Dir. Sch. Art, U. Tulsa, prof., Gallery Dir., Alexandre Hogue Gallery; founder & dir. Third Floor Designs (a student run design studio). Exhibitions include, Kans., Mo., Okla., Ariz., Tex., Ark., Venezuela, Beauty of the Levant (Images of Lebanon & Syria Through Western Eyes), Syria. Recipient Graphex Award, Tulsa Addy, Creativity Today Award. Office: University of Tulsa Phillips Hall 104 600 South College Ave Tulsa OK 74104 Office Phone: 918-631-2740. Office Fax: 918-631-3423. E-mail: maria-valero@utulsa.com.

VALERO, RENÉ ARNOLD, clergyman; b. N.Y.C., Aug. 15, 1930; s. Caesar J. and Maria Luisa (Cordova) Valero; B.A. in Liberal Arts, Immaculate Conception-Cathedral Coll., 1952; M.S.W., Fordham U., 1962. Ordained to ministry Roman Cath. Ch., 1956; asso. pastor St. Michael-St. Edward, Bklyn., 1956-57, St. Agatha, Bklyn., 1957-60; dir. Bklyn. Cath. Charities Family Service, 1960-69; dir. Bklyn. Diocesan Office for Aging, 1969-74; coordinator Bklyn. Diocesan Hispanic Apostolate, 1974-79; pastor Blessed Sacrament, Jackson Heights, N.Y., 1979-82; aux. bishop Diocese of Bklyn., 1980—; vicar for immigrants and refugees Diocese of Bklyn., 1983-90; regional bishop Queens, 1990-94, Queens North, 1994—. Home: 34-43 93rd St Jackson Heights NY 11372-3743 Office: Immaculate Conception Ctr 7200 Douglaston Pky Douglaston NY 11362-1941 Office Phone: 718-229-8001 x710.

VALERO-LOPEZ, ARI YAKOV, electrical engineer; b. Mexico City, Oct. 26, 1972; arrived in US, 1999; s. Mario Alberto Valero Huerta and Elizabeth Lopez Sotelo; m. Marcia Gisela Mendez, Aug. 31, 1996; 1 child, Nadia Elizabeth Valero-Mendez; 1 child, Aimee Carolina Valero-Mendez. BSEE, U. Guanajuato, Mexico, 1995; MSEE, Inst. Nat. de Astrofiscia, Optica y Electronica, Puebla, Mexico, 1998; PhD, Tex. A&M U., College Station, 2004. Rsch. asst. Tex. A&M U., 1999—2004; analog integrated cir. design engr. Agere Systems, Allentown, Pa., 2004—. Scholar, Conacyt Mex., 1995—2000. Achievements include design of GHz analog to digital converter; high speed phase interpolator. Office: Agere Sys 1110 American Pkwy NE Allentown PA 18109 Home Phone: 610-965-5190; Office Phone: 610-712-2459. Personal E-mail: ari.valero@gmail.com.

VALETTE, JEAN PAUL, writer; b. Paris, Oct. 21, 1937; s. Jean and Monique (Lavie) V.; m. Rebecca M. Valette, Aug. 6, 1959; children: Jean-Michel, Nathalie, Pierre. Baccalaureat, U. Poitiers, France, 1954; Diplome, Hautes Etudes Commls. de Paris, 1959; PhD, U. Colo., 1962. Acct. Arthur Andersen, 1964-66; rsch. economist Charles River Assocs., 1966-69. Author: Lisons, 1968, The Role of Transportation in Regional Economic Development, 1971, France, A Cultural Review Grammar, 1973, C'est comme ça, 1978, 1986, Spanish for Mastery, 1980, 1984, 1988, 1996, French for Mastery, 1975, 1981, 1986, 1989, 1990, Contacts: langue et culture françaises, 1976, 1982, 1985, 1989, 1994, 1997, 2001, French for Fluency, 1985, Rencontres, 1985, Situaciones, 1988, 1994, Discovering French Nouveau, 1993, 5th edit., 2000, Discover French, 2004, 2007, Discovering French Interactive, 1994, A votre tour, 1995, Ventanas, 1998, Europak, 2000, Weaving the Dance, Navajo Yeibichai Textiles (1910-1950), 2000. Decorated officer Palmes Académiques (France). Mem. Am. Assn. Tchrs. French, Am. Coun. on Tchg. of Langs. Address: 16 Mount Alvernia Rd Chestnut Hill MA 02467-1019

VALETTE, REBECCA MARIANNE, Romance languages educator; b. NYC, Dec. 21, 1938; d. Gerhard and Ruth Adelgunde (Bischoff) Loose; m. Jean-Paul Valette, Aug. 6, 1959; children: Jean-Michel, Nathalie, Pierre. BA, Mt. Holyoke Coll., 1959, LHD (hon.), 1974; PhD, U. Colo., 1963. Instr., examiner in French and German U. So. Fla., 1961-63; instr. NATO Def. Coll., Paris, 1963-64, Wellesley Coll., 1964-65; asst. prof. Romance Langs. Boston Coll., 1965-68, assoc., 1968-73, prof., 1973—2003, prof. emeritus, 2003—. Lectr., cons. fgn. lang. pedagogy; Fulbright sr. lectr., Germany, 1974; Am. Coun. on Edn. fellow in acad. adminstrn., 1976-77. Author: Modern Language Testing, 1967, rev. edit., 1977, French for Mastery, 1975, rev. edit., 1988, Contacts, 1976, rev. edit., 1993, 97, 2001, C'est Comme Ça, 1978, rev. edit., 1986, Spanish for Mastery, 1980, rev. edit., 1989, 94, Album: Cuentos del Mundo Hispanico, 1984, 3d edit., 2005, French for Fluency, 1985, Situaciones, 1988, rev. edit., 1994, Discovering French, 1994, 97, 2001, A votre tour, 1995, 2nd edit., 2007, Ventanas Uno, 1998, Images 1, 2, 3, 1999, Reflections on the Connolly Book of Hours, 1999, Weaving the Dance, 2000, Discovering French Nouveau, 2004, 2d edit., 2007, Federation of Alliances Francaises USA Edn. Handbook, 2005; contbr. articles to fgn. lang. pedagogy and Native Am. art publs. Decorated comdr. Palmes Académiques, chevalier Ordre Nat. du Mérite (France). Mem. MLA (chmn. divsn. on tchg. of lang. 1980-81), Am. Coun. on Tchg. Fgn. Langs., Am. Assn. Tchrs. French (v.p. 1980-86, pres. 1992-94), Alliance Francaise of Boston and Cambridge (pres. 2002—), Fedn. Alliances Francaises USA (v.p. 2003—06), Phi Beta Kappa, Alpha Sigma Nu, Pi Delta Phi. Home: 16 Mount Alvernia Rd Chestnut Hill MA 02467-1019 Office: Boston Coll Lyons 304 Chestnut Hill MA 02467-3804 Business E-Mail: valette@bc.edu.

VALGEMAE, MARDI, language educator; b. Viljandi, Estonia, Nov. 10, 1935; came to U.S., 1949; s. Parfeni and Ella (Peterson) V.; m. Mare M. Kivijarv, Dec. 28, 1957; children: Monika L., Sven M. BA, Rutgers U., 1957; PhD, UCLA, 1964. Asst. prof. English UCLA, LA, 1964-68; assoc. prof. English Lehman Coll., CUNY, Bronx, 1968-74; prof. English Lehman Coll. CUNY, Bronx, 1975—; dir. city and humanities program Lehman Coll., CUNY, 1984-88, chmn. English dept., 1988-97. Vis. asst. profl. lectr., George Washington U., Washington, 1968. Author: Accelerated Grimace, 1972, Ikka Teatrist Moteldes, 1990, Linn ja Teater, 1995, Kaugekone, 1999, Eelarvamusi, 2003; co-editor: Baltic Literature and Linguistics, 1973. 1st lt. U.S. Army. 1958-60. ACLS European Travel grantee, 1970, 81; Woodrow Wilson fellow, 1960. Mem. Modern Lang. Assn. Am., Assn. Advancement Baltic Studies, PEN. Office: CUNY Lehman Coll Dept English Bronx NY 10468 Office Phone: 718-960-8372. Personal E-mail: mardival@mindspring.com.

VALIANT, LESLIE GABRIEL, computer scientist, educator; b. Mar. 28, 1949; s. Leslie and Eva Julia (Ujlaki) V.; m. Gayle Lynne Dyckoff, 1977; children: Paul A., Gregory J. BA, Kings Coll., Cambridge, UK, 1970; DIC, Imperial Coll., London, 1973; PhD, U. Warwick, UK, 1974. Vis. asst. prof. Carnegie-Mellon U., Pitts., 1973-74; lectr. U. Leeds, Eng., 1974-76; lectr., reader U. Edinburgh, Scotland, 1977-82; vis. prof. Harvard U., 1982, Gordon McKay prof. computer sci. and applied math., 1982-2001, T. Jefferson Coolidge prof. computer sci. and applied math., 2001—. Guggenheim fellow, 1985-86; recipient Nevanlinna prize Internat. Math. Union, 1986, Knuth prize, 1997. Fellow Royal Soc., Am. Assn. for Artificial Intelligence; mem. NAS. Office: Harvard U 33 Oxford St Cambridge MA 02138-1903

VALIANTI, DEBORAH L., playwright; b. Marlboro, Mass., May 10, 1952; d. Frank J. and Kathlyn V. Valianti; m. Henry J. Klim; children: Genevieve Marie Klim, Delia Goodness Klim. MAET, Lesley Coll., Cambridge, Mass., 1992; MA, Boston U., 1987; BA, Goddard Coll., Plainfield, Vt., 1977. Dir. Mission-in-Action Players, Mission Hill, Mass., 2000—04, All-bad Teen Theater Co., Brighton, Mass., 1993—98; educator expressive therapies Lesley Coll., Cambridge, Mass., 1992—98; dir. City Hall Smoking Cessation Project, Boston Against Drugs, Boston, 1995; dir. and co-founder Uppity Productions, Boston Playwright Theater, Boston, 1985—90; tchg. fellow Creative Writing Program, Boston U., Boston, 1985—87; Celtic cantor All Saints Parish, Brookline, Mass., 2003—. Lectr. in field. Author: (plays) 39 Witherbees St., 1977, Starcrossed, 1987, The Friendship of Her Thighs, 1992, Too Many Willies, 2002, Thou Shalt Break Them, 2005, Choir Stalls, 2007, (screenplays) Europe, 1988, Build to Suit, 2002, (book) First and Foremost A Playwright: the Dramatist's Tools as Applied to the Practice of Expressive Therapy, 1991, numerous poems. Mem.: Internat. Ctr. Women Playwrights. Democrat. Roman Catholic. Avocations: singing, tap dance, liturgical dance, travel, skiing. Home: 8 Oak Square Avenue Brighton MA 02135-2517

VALINSKY, MARK STEVEN, podiatrist; b. Chgo., May 24, 1951; m. Michelle Susan Morgan; children: Cara Linda, Erin Abra, Noah Allen, Hannah Rae, Arielle Lauren. Student in biology and pre-medicine, Ohio State U., 1969-71, SUNY, Buffalo, 1971-72; BS, D in Podiatric Medicine, Ill. Coll. Podiatric Medicine, 1976; MD (hon.), Inst. Orthopaedics & Traumatology China Acad. Traditonal Chinese Medicine, Beijing, 1989. Lic. podiatrist, Ill., Calif., N.Y.; diplomate Am. Bd. Podiatric Examiners, Am. Bd. Ambulatory Foot Surgery, Am. Bd. Podiatric Surgery ambulatory divsn.; cert. Am. Inst. Foot Medicine, 1987, Am. Assn. Cert. Podatric Physicians and Surgeons, 1988, ambulatory foot surgery. With Podiatry Assocs. Ltd., Des Plaines, Ill., 1975, Children's Foot Clinic, Mont., Okla., 1975; pvt. practice podiatric surgery Oak Park, Ill., 1977—; founder, dir. The Foot Care Ctr., P.C., Oak Park; intern at colls. Franklin Blvd. Comty., Downey Vets. Hosp., Forkosh Meml. Hosp., Ill., 1975, 76. Mem. 1st foot surg. team to China, 1983, also 1987; instr. minimal incision foot surgery to orthopaedic surgeons in China; lectr. 1st Sino N.Am. Treatise of Foot Disorders, Beijing, 1987, vis. prof., 1989; pres., founder Biol. Scis. Rsch. Inst., Inc.; lectr. and del. on minimal incision and radiowave foot surgery in Australia and throughout U.S., 1986; internat. lectr. and tchr. on health care of feet, also radio and TV appearances; student asst. instrnl. media dept. Ill. Coll. Podiatric Medicine, 1975; mem. Nat. Assn. Ednl. Broadcasters, 1975-79, Ill. Audio-visual Assn., 1975-79; orthop. technician Evanston Hosp., 1974-75; instr. in field; mem. cons. staff Riveredge Hosp., Forest Park, Ill., 1987—, Westside Vets. Adminstrn. Hosp., Chgo., 1981-84, Applewood Manor, Bloomingdale, Ill., 1977-87; med. del. People's Republic China, 1983, lectr. 1st Sino-North Am. Treatise foot Surgery, 1987; comty spkr. in field; vis. prof. orthops. Inst. Orthopaedics and Traumatology-China Acad. Traditional Chinese Medicine, 1989; cameraman, editing tech., med. photographer Ill. Coll. Podiatric Medicine, 1975, pub. rels. photographer, 1975; mem. Ill. Assn. Bio-Communicators, 1975-79; class co-chmn. seminar on infections, 1975; with Northlake Comty. Hosp., Northlake, Ill., 1979-82, Hugar Surg. Ctr., Elmwood Park, Ill., 1978-79; cons. staff Riveredge Hosp., Forest Park, Ill., 1987—, Westside Vets. Adminstrn. Hosp., Chgo., 1981-84, Applewood Manor, Bloomingdale, Ill., 1977-87; med. del. People's Repub. China, 1983; comty. spkr. in field. Columnist: Focus on the Foot; contbr. articles to profl. and popular publs., author video tapes in field; contbr. numerous videotape programs Ill. Coll. Podiatric Medicine; contbr. photography Ill. Coll. Podiatric Medicine, 1975 Nat. Podiatry Conv.; contbr. media instrnl. programs; author: (with David F. Hettinger DPM) The Uses of Trental in Elective Foot Surgery, 1991, (with David F. Hettinger DPM, Julie K. Mortvedt BA) The Hallux Interphalangeal Joint Sesamoidectomy Utilizing Minimal Incision Technique, 1989, (with David F. Hettinger DPM) A Corrective Bunion Procedure for Hallux Abducto Valgus Utilizing Minimal Incision Technique, 1990, (with David F. Hettinger DPM and Parker M. Gennett, BS) Treatment of Verrucae Via Radiowave Surgery, 1990, (with David F. Hettinger, DPM, Gina Nuccio BS, Robert Lim BS) Nail Matrixectomies Using Radiowave Technique, 1991, (with David F. hettinger DPM, Parker M. Gennett BS) Subungual Exostosis Removal using a Minimal Incision Technique, 1991, The Advances in Therapy, 1991, The Valinsky Tibial Sesamoid Planing Procedure Utilizing Mi-Tech tm) Minimal Incision Technology (with David F. Hettinger), 1992, others; book review editor: Current Podiatry, 1982-83; bd. dirs. Wednesday Jour., 1982-86; guest numerous TV and radio shows regarding minimal incision foot surgery. Former mem. Chgo. Mayor's Coun. for Sr. Citizens and Handicapped, Nat. Assn. Human Devel., Oak Park River C. of C., bd. dirs., 1984-89, Biol. Photographer Assn., Smithsonian Inst., others, Am. Karate Assn.; bd. dirs. Wednesday Jour., 1982-86. Recipient Cert. Svc. to Podiatric Edn. award, 1976. Mem. Am. Inst. Foot Medicine (cert.), Nat. Bd. Podiatric Examiners (diplomate 1978), Podiatric Soc. (sec. Zone I, 1980-82, zone pres. 1981-82, del. to bd. dirs. 1980-82), Ill. Podiatric Med. Assn. (Continuing Edn. award 1980), Ill. Podiatry Soc. (pres. Zone 1 1981, sec. Zone 1 1980-81, bd. dirs. 1980-82), Am. Podiatric Med. Assn., Am. Podiatric Soc., Podiatric Med. Assn., Am. Acad. Ambulatory Foot Surgeons (pres. midwest V & VI region 1986-87 to regional dir. 1986-87, area coord. midwest and ctrl. areas 1988, del. minimal incision foot surgery 1986), Oak Park-River Forest C. of C. (bd. dirs. 1984-89), Am. Karate Assn., Am. Analgesia Soc., Biol. Scis. Rsch. Inst. (founder, dir. 1978), Aaron Podiatry Assocs. (founder, dir. 1979), Inc. (founder, dir. 1980), Aaron Podiatry Assocs. A Profl. Corp. (founder, dir.), Am. Analgesia Soc., ALP Bus. Assn., others. Personal E-mail: president@valcommedia.com.

VALLABHAN, GIRISH C., urologist; b. Bombay, Sept. 25, 1963; arrived in US, 1965; s. C.V.G. and Shakuntala Vallabhan; m. Monique Vallabhan (div.); children: Tara, Sonia. BA in Chemistry, Tex. Tech. U., San Antonio, 1984; MD, U. Tex., San Antonio, 1988. Cert. Am. Bd. Urology, 1996. Intern then resident U. N.Mex., Albuquerque, 1988—93; pvt. practice Lubbock, Tex., 1994—2006. Fellow then staff robotics program Henry Ford Hosp., Detroit, 2006. Contbr. articles to profl. jours. Bd. mem. Internat. Cultural Ctr., Lubbock, Tex., 2006. Fellow: ACS; mem.: AMA, Am. Urological Assn. Avocations: racquetball, reading, music.

VALLADARES-BARBUSH, LISETTE MARIE, mathematics educator; d. Jorge Luis Valladares, Jr. and Violeta Gutierrez Valladares; m. J. Otto Barbush; children: Alec, Noah. BS in Math., UCLA, 1992, MA in Math., 1994; secondary tchg. credential, Nat. U., LA, 2004. Computer programmer Hughes Aircraft Co., LA, 1994—96; math. tchr., math. dept. chair Archer Sch. for Girls, LA, Calif., 1996—2001; math. tchr. Milken Cmty. H.S., LA, 2001—. Mem.: Nat. Coun. Tchr. Math. Home: 5325 Royer Ave Woodland Hills CA 91367 Office: 15800 Zeldins Way Los Angeles CA 90049

VALLAS, PAUL G., school system administrator; b. June 10, 1953; m. Sharon Vallas; children: Paul, Gus, Mark. BA in Polit. Sci. & History, We. Ill. U., 1976, MA in Polit. Sci., 1980. Policy adv. to Elementary & Secondary Edn. & Appropriations Com. Ill. State Senate; exec. dir. Ill. Econ. Fiscal Com., 1985—90; revenue dir. City of Chgo., 1990—93, budget dir., 1993—95; CEO Chgo. Pub. Schools Sys., 1995—2001, Phila. Pub. Schools Sys., 2002—07; supt. Recovery Sch. Dist., New Orleans, 2007—. Office: La Dept Edn Recovery Sch Dist PO Box 94064 Baton Rouge LA 70804

VALLBONA, CARLOS, physician; b. Granollers, Barcelona, Spain, July 29, 1927; came to U.S., 1953, naturalized, 1967; s. José and Dolores (Calbó) V.; m. Rima Gretel Rothe, Dec. 26, 1956; children: Rima Nuria, Carlos Fernando, María Teresa, Marisa. BA, BS, U. de Barcelona, 1944, MD, 1950. Diplomate Am. Bd. Pediatrics. Child health physician Escuela de Puericultura, Barcelona, 1952, Stagier Etranger Hôpital des Enfants Malades, Paris, 1952-53; intern, resident U. Louisville, 1953-55; resident Baylor Coll. Medicine, Houston, 1955-56, prof. rehab. medicine, 1967—, assoc. prof. physiology and pediatrics, 1962-69, prof., chmn. dept. community medicine, 1969-95, prof. family medicine, 1980-95, Disting. Svc. prof. family and cmty. medicine, 1995—. Adj. prof. U. Tex. Sch. Pub. Health, U. Tex. Health Sci. Ctr., Houston; chief community medicine service Harris County Hosp. Dist.; staff gen. med. service Tex. Children's Hosp.; staff The Inst. Rehab. and Research; staff St. Luke's Episcopal Hosp., con. staff VA Med. Ctr., Houston; Fulbright vis. prof., 1967; cons. WHO, NIH, Nat. Center Health Stats. Pan Am. Health Orgn., Nat. Center Health Service Research; advisor Conseller Sanitat, Catalunya. Author numerous articles in field; editorial bd. several Sci. jours. French Ministry of Edn. fellow, 1952; Children's Internat. Center fellow, 1953; co-recipient Gold medal 6th Internat. Congress Phys. Medicine, 1972; Public Citizen of Yr. San Jacinto chpt. Nat. Assn. Social Workers, 1974; Outstanding Tchr. award Baylor Coll. Medicine Class of 1980, 83, 85, 87, 88; decorated officer Order of Civil Merit (Spain), Medalla Narcis Monturiol (Catalunya). Mem. Am. Acad. Family Physicians, Am. Coll. Med. Informatics (founding mem. 1984), Nat. Acad. Practice (disting. practitioner 1984), Soc. Pediatric Research (emeritus), AMA, Tex. Med. Assn., Am. Coll. Chest Physicians, Am. Pub. Health Assn. (chmn. elect med. care sect. 1989-90), Am. Coll. Preventive Medicine, U.S.-Mex. Border Health Assn., AAAS, Am. Congress Rehab. Medicine, Catalan Soc. Pediatrics (hon.), Argentinian Soc. Internal Medicine (hon. 1986), Argentinian Med. Soc. (hon. 1986), Spanish Acad. Pediatrics (ambulatory pediatrics sect. hon. 1987), Assn. Tchrs. Preventive Medicine, Spanish Profls. Am. (pres. 1988), Soc. Catalana Hipertensio (hon. pres.), Sigma Xi, Alpha Omega Alpha. Roman Catholic. Home: 2001 Holcombe Blvd Houston TX 77030-4222 Office: Baylor Coll Medicine One Baylor Plz Rm 650E Houston TX 77030-3404

VALLBONA, RIMA-GRETEL ROTHE, retired foreign language educator, writer; b. San Jose, Costa Rica, Mar. 15, 1931; arrived in U.S., 1956, naturalized, 1997; d. Ferdinand Hermann and Emilia (Strassburger) Rothe; m. Carlos Vallbona, Dec. 26, 1956; children: Rima-Nuri, Carlos-Fernando, Maria-Teresa, Maria-Luisa. BA/BS, Colegio Superior de Senoritas, San Jose, Costa Rica, 1948; diploma, U. Paris, 1953, diploma in Spanish Philology, U. Salamanca, Spain, 1954; MA, U. Costa Rica, 1962; D in Modern Langs., Middlebury Coll., 1981. Tchr. Liceo J.J. Vargas Calvo, Costa Rica, 1955—56; faculty U. St. Thomas, Houston, 1964—95, prof. Spanish, 1978—95, Cullen Found. prof. Spanish, 1989, head Spanish dept., 1966—71, chmn. dept. modern fgn. lang., 1978—80, prof. emeritus, 1995—. Vis. prof. U. Houston, 1975—76, Rice U., 1974, 1980—83, 1995, U. St. Thomas, Argentina, 1972, U. St. Thomas, Merida program, 1987—95. Author: Noche en Vela, 1968, Yolanda Oreamuno, 1972, La Obra en Prosa de Eunice Odio, 1981, Baraja de Soledades, Las Sombras que Perseguimos, 1983, Polvo del Camino, 1972, La Salamandra Rosada, 1979, Mujeres y Agonias, 1982, Cosecha de Pecadores, 1988, El arcangel del perdon, 1990, Mundo, demonio y mujer, 1991, Los infiernos de la mujer y algo mas, 1992, (crit. edit.) Vida i sucesos de la Monja Alferez, 1992, Flowering Inferno-Tales of Sinking Hearts, 1994, La narrativa de Yolanda Oreamuno, 1996, Tormy, la Prodigiosa Gata de Donaldito, 1997, Tejedoras de sueños versus realidad, 2003; mem. (editl. bd.) Letras Femeninas, 1984—98, Alba de America, U.S., sec. (culture) Inst. Literario y Cultural Hispanico; co-dir.: Foro Literario, 1987—89; contbg. editor: The Americas Rev., 1989—95; contbr. numerous articles and short stories to lit. mags. Mem. scholarship com. Inst. Hispanic Culture, 1978, 1979, 1988, 1991, chmn., 1979, bd. dirs., 1974—76, 1988—89, 1991—92, chmn. cultural activities, 1979, 1980, 1985, 1988—89; bd. dirs. Houston Pub. Libr., 1984—86, Cultural Arts Coun. Houston, 1991—92. Recipient Aquileo J. Echeverria Novel prize, 1968, Jorge Luis Borges Short Story prize, Argentina, 1977, Agripina Montes del Valle Novel prize, 1978, Constantin Found. grant for rsch., U. St. Thomas, 1981, Lit. award, S.W. Conf. Latin Am. Studies, 1982, Ancora Lit. award, Costa Rica, 1984, Civil Merit award, King Juan Carlos I of Spain, 1989, Children's Book award, Bay Area Writers League, 2003. Mem.: Soc. Children's Book Writers and Illustrators, Nat. Writers Assn., Inst. Lit. y Cultural Hispanico, Casa Argentina de Houston, Inst. Hispanic Culture Houston, Latin Am. Writers Assn. Costa Rica, Inst. Internat. de Lit. Iberoam., Latin Am. Studies Assn., Academia Norteamericana de la Lengua Espanola (elected), S.W. Conf. Orgn. Latin Am Studies, South Ctrl. MLA, Houston Area Tchrs. Fgn. Lang., Houston Area Tchrs. Spanish and Portuguese, Am. Assn. Tchrs. Spanish and Portuguese, Sigma Delta Pi, Phi Sigma Iota. Roman Catholic. Home: 3706 Lake St Houston TX 77098-5522 Personal E-mail: rvallbona@aol.com.

VALLEE, JACQUES FABRICE, venture capitalist; b. Pontoise, France, Sept. 24, 1939; arrived in US, 1962; s. Gabriel and Madeleine (Passavant) V.; m. Janine M. Saley, Oct. 19, 1960; children: Olivier, Catherine. BS in Math., U. Paris Sorbonne, 1959; MS in Astrophysics, U. Lille, France, 1961; PhD in Computer Sci., Northwestern U., Evanston, Ill., 1967. Sr. software specialist RCA Corp., Cherry Hill, NJ, 1969-70; mgr. infosystems Stanford U., Palo Alto, Calif., 1970-71; rsch. engr. SRI Internat., Menlo Park, Calif., 1971-72; sr. rsch. fellow Inst. for Future, Menlo Park, 1972-76; chmn. Infomedia Corp., Palo Alto, 1976-81; v.p. Sofinnova, Inc., San Francisco, 1982-86; gen. ptnr. Euro-Am. Ventures, 1987—, Sigefi, Burnette & Vallee, LLP, 2000—, Red Planet Capital, 2006—. Bd. dirs. Triformix, Inc., Santa Rosa, Calif., Alter-G, Menlo Park. Author: Computer Message Systems, 1984, Dimensions, 1988, Confrontations, 1990, Revelations, 1991, Forbidden Science, 1992, FastWalker, 1996, The Four Elements of Financial Alchemy, 2000, The Heart of the Internet, 2003, Stratagème, 2006. Vice chmn. Inst. for the Future, Menlo Park. Recipient Jules Verne prize, Paris, 1961. Business E-Mail: jacques@RedPlanetCapital.com.

VALLEE, JUDITH DELANEY, environmentalist, writer, not-for-profit fundraiser; b. NYC, Mar. 14, 1948; d. Victor and Sally Hammer; m. John Delaney, Apr. 9, 1974 (div. 1978); m. Henry Richard Vallee, May 15, 1987. BA, CUNY, 1976. Exec. dir. Save the Manatee Club, Maitland, Fla., 1985—. Apptd. U.S. Manatee Recovery Plan Team, Jacksonville, Fla., 1988-97, Fla. Manatee Tech. Adv. Coun., Tallahassee, 1989-2002, Save the Manatee Com., Orlando, Fla., 1985-92, World Conservation Union/Sirenia Specialist Group, Switzerland, 1996; advisor Save the Wildlife Inc., Chuluota, Fla., 1992-93; bd. dirs. Environ. Fund for Fla. Lobbyist Save the Manatee Club, 1989; vol. Broward County Audubon Soc., Ft. Lauderdale, 1983-84, Wild Bird Care Ctr., Ft. Lauderdale, 1984. Recipient Refuge Support award Chassahowitzka Nat. Wildlife Refuge, 1989. Democrat. Avocations: creative writing, antiques, wildlife observation, canoeing. Office: Save the Manatee Club Inc 500 N Maitland Ave Ste 210 Maitland FL 32751-4458 Office Phone: 407-539-0990. E-mail: jvallee100@aol.com.

VALLEE, MICHELLE LINDA, pre-school educator; b. Passaic, NJ, Dec. 18, 1973; d. Rudolph Herman Vallee Jr. and Linda Marguerite Lombardi. Cert. in Child-Related Careers, Morris County Sch. of Tech., Denville, NJ, 1991—93; AS, County Coll. of Morris, Randolph, NJ, 2002. Cert. child devel. assoc. Washington, 1999. Presch. tchr. Page Sch., Morris Plains, NJ, 1999—2003, PACE Presch., Lake Hiawatha, NJ, 2003—05; dance tchr. Mary Lou Hale's Sch. of Dance, Lake Hiawatha, NJ, 1998—; presch. tchr. Sunnyfields, Whippany, NJ, 2005—. 3rd grade ccd tchr. St. Peter the Apostle Ch., Parsippany, NJ, 1999—. (dance solo) Dinner Party Tap Solo. 3rd grade CCD tchr. St. Peter the Apostle Ch., Parsippany, NJ, 1999—2006. Mem.: MCSSA (assoc.). Independent. Roman Catholic. Avocations: bowling, soccer, volleyball, softball, travel. Home: 4 Oak Ln Lake Hiawatha NJ 07034 Office: Sunnyfields Learning Center 494 Rte 10 W Whippany NJ 07981 Home Phone: 973-263-9028; Office Phone: 973-887-8522. Personal E-mail: wrightgrl05@aol.com.

VALLEE, ROY A., electronics executive; b. Southbridge, Mass. married; 2 children. AS in Electronics Tech., Don Bosco Tech. Inst., 1971. Electronics tech. radio products Don Bosco Tech. Inst., 1971—77; field sales rep. Avnet, Inc., Great Neck, NY, 1977, systems bus. mgr. to gen. sales mgr. to gen. mgr. to regional dir. to v.p., pres. Hamilton/Avnet Computer, 1989—90, sr. v.p., dir. worldwide electronics ops., 1990—92, bd. dirs. Phoenix, 1991—, pres., COO, 1992—98, chmn., CEO Phoenix, 1998—. Bd. dirs. Teradyne, Synopsys, Inc.; mem. exec. com. Global Tech. Distbn. Coun. Mem. Govs. Coun. of Innovation and Tech. Named one of Hot 25 Execs., Electronic Buyer's News, 1997, 1999, 2000; named to CRN Industry Hall of Fame, 2007. Office: Avnet Inc 2211 S 47th St Phoenix AZ 85034-6403 Office Phone: 480-643-2000. *

VALLERAND, PHILIPPE GEORGES, sales executive; b. Montreal, Que., Can., June 12, 1954; arrived in U.S., 1982; m. Laura Jean Frombach, Sept. 25, 1979. Cert. mktg. and sales Internat. Orgn. for Standardization, 2002. Dir. resort Club Mediterranee Inc., Bahamas, Switzerland, Africa, Guadaloupe, West Indies, 1978—80; v.p. Franglo/Sunsaver Inc., London and Hyeres, France, 1980-82; v.p. sales Source Northwest, Inc., Woodinville, Wash., 1982—93; pres., CEO The PGV Group, Inc. Sr. comdr. Royal Rangers Boys Club, Monroe, Wash., 1988-96; bd. dirs. Christian Faith Ctr., Monroe, 1988-94; mem. Rep. Nat. Com.; co-chmn. Rep. Bus. Adv. Coun.; bd. dirs. Northwest U., 2005; pres. leadership coun., Trinity Western U.; bd. dirs. Northwest U. Recipient Disting. Sales & Mktg. Exec. award Internat. Orgn. Sales & Mktg. Execs., 1993, 96. Avocations: skiing, travel. Personal E-mail: phil.vallerand@verizon.net.

VALLES, JAMES M., JR., physics professor; BA magna cum laude in Physics, Dartmouth Coll., 1981; PhD in Physics, U. Mass., 1988. Tchg. asst. U. Mass., 1981—82, rsch. asst., 1982—87; postdoctoral assoc. AT&T Bell Labs., 1987—89; asst. prof. physics U. Oreg., 1989—92; asst. prof. Brown U., 1992—96, assoc. prof., 1996—2002, prof., 2002—. Exec. officer dept. physics Brown U., 1999—2002. Contbr. articles to profl. jours. Grantee Alfred P. Sloan Found. fellowship, 1990—92. Mem.: Am. Phys. Soc., Sigma Xi. Office: Dept Physics Brown U Box 1843 Providence RI 02912 E-mail: valles@physics.brown.edu.

VALLETTA, AMBER, actress, model; b. Phoenix, Feb. 9, 1974; m. Herve Le Bhihan, 1994 (div. 1996); m. Christian McCaw, Sept. 2003; 1 child, Auden. With Boss Models, NYC; Elite Models, NYC, 1996—. Exec. prodr.: (films) Ticks, 1999; actor: Drop Back Ten, 2000, What Lies Beneath, 2000, The Family Man, 2000, Perfume, 2001, Max Keeble's Big Move, 2001, Duplex, 2003, Raising Helen, 2004, Hitch, 2005, Transporter 2, 2005, Man About Town, 2006, The Last Time, 2006, Premonition, 2007, Dead Silence, 2007; (TV films) Hysteria: The Def Leppard Story, 2001. Office: Fl 2 300 Park Ave S New York NY 10010-5313 *

VALLIANT, JAMES STEVENS, lawyer; b. Glendale, Calif., Sept. 29, 1963; s. William Warren and Carol Dee (Heath) V.; m. Holly Lynne White. BA, NYU, 1984; JD, U. San Diego, 1989. Bar: Calif. 1989. Law instr. U. San Diego, 1988-89; dep. dist. atty. Dist. Atty.'s Office, San Diego, 1989—. Host talk show WJM Prodns., Hollywood, Calif., 1996; polit. and legal commentator Sta. KUSI and other TV news programs. Author, The Passion of Ayn Rand's Critics, Durban House, 2005; contbr. articles in objectivism and early Christianity. Recipient Citation of Appreciation, MADD, 1993. Office: Dist Attys Office 330 W Broadway San Diego CA 92101-3825

VALLIÈRES, ERIC, thoracic surgeon; b. Detroit, Apr. 28, 1959; s. André Vallières and Huguette Poulin; life ptnr. Christine Ann Lee; children: Frédérique Paule, Charles-Antoine, Thomas Eric. MD, U. Laval, Quebec, Can., 1982. Asst. prof. surgery U. Alta., Edmonton, Canada, 1991—94, U. Ottawa, Ontario, Canada, 1994—96; assoc. prof. surgery U. Wash. Med. Sch., Seattle, 1996—2004; surg. dir. lung cancer program Swedish Cancer Inst., Seattle, 2004—. Chair S.W. Oncology Group Thoracic Surg. Com., 1998—. Recipient John K. Stevenson awardfor Tchg. Excellence, U. Wash., 1996-7, Outstanding Faculty in Continuing Med. Edn. award, U. Wash. Sch. of Medicine, 1999. Fellow: Royal Coll. of Surgeons Can. (Walter C. Mackenzie-Ethicon fellowship 1991). Office: Swedish Cancer Inst 1221 Madison Ste 400 Seattle WA 98104 Office Phone: 206-215-6800. Office Fax: 206-215-6801.

VALOIS, ROBERT ARTHUR, lawyer; b. NYC, May 13, 1938; s. Frank Jacob and Harriet Frances (LaCroix) V.; m. Ruth Emilie Skacil, Dec. 23, 1961; children: Marguerite Jeannette, Robert Arthur Jr. BBA, U. Miami, 1962; JD, Wake Forest U., 1972. Bar: N.C. 1972, Fla. 1972, U.S. Ct. Appeals (4th cir.) 1973, U.S. Dist. Ct. (ea. and mid. dists.) 1974, U.S. Supreme Ct. 1975, U.S. Ct. Appeals (6th cir.) 1986. Field examiner NLRB, Winston-Salem, NC, 1962-70; from assoc. to ptnr. Maupin, Taylor & Ellis, P.A., Raleigh, NC, 1972—, chmn. labor and employment sect., 1972-97, chmn. bd. dirs., pres., 1997—2002. Vice chmn. Legal Svcs. Corp., Washington, 1984-90, bd. dirs. Served with USN, 1956-59. Mem. Greater Raleigh C. of C. (chmn. fed. govt. com. 1991—). Democrat. Presbyterian. Home: 3952 Bentley Bridge Rd Raleigh NC 27612 Office Phone: 919-981-4000. E-mail: rvalois@maupintaylor.com.

VALONE, KEITH EMERSON, psychologist, psychoanalyst; b. Austin, Tex., Aug. 3, 1953; s. James Floyd and Elizabeth Niles (Emerson) V.; m. Leona Marie Lagace, July 22, 1978; children: Kyle Stephen James, Christienne Marie. BA, U. So. Calif., 1975; MA, U. Ill., 1979, PhD, 1981; PsyD, Inst. Contemporary Psychoanaly, LA, 1995. Lic. psychologist, Calif. Pvt. practice, Pasadena, Calif., 1983—; chief psychology svc. Las Encinas Hosp., Pasadena, 1988; dir. psychology Ingleside Hosp., Rosemead, Calif., 1990-92; candidate Inst. of Contemporary Psychoanalysis, LA, 1991-95; clin. dir. Las Encinas Residential Treatment Ctr., Pasadena, 2006—. Clin. asst. prof. dept. psychology Fuller Theol. Sem., Pasadena, Calif., 1984—85; asst. clin. prof. dept. psychology UCLA, 1984—87; clin. asst. prof. psychiatry and behavioral scis. U. So. Calif. Kock Sch. Medicine, LA, 2006—. Contbr. articles to profl. jours. Mem. APA, Calif. State Psychol. Assn., Phi Beta Kappa. Episcopalian. Office: Ste 321 One W California Blvd Pasadena CA 91105 Office Phone: 626-405-9066. Personal E-mail: kev@valone.com.

VALUKAS, ANTON RONALD, lawyer, former prosecutor; b. Chgo., June 21, 1943; s. Anton J. and Mary Ann (Giusto) Valukas; m. Janice C. Valukas (div.); children: Amy Paige, Beth Catherine; m. Maria Finitzo; children: Catherine Sara, Paul Alexander. BA in Polit. Sci., Art History, Lawrence U., 1965; JD, Northwestern U., 1968. Bar: Ill. 1968, U.S. Dist. Ct. (no. dist.) Ill. 1968, U.S. Ct. Appeals (7th cir.) 1969, U.S. Ct. Appeals (10th cir.) 1977, U.S. Ct. Appeals (3d cir.) 1982. Asst. dir. Nat. Defender Project, Chgo., 1968-70; asst. U.S. atty. (No. dist.) Ill. US Dept. Justice, Chgo., 1970—74, chief spl. prosecutions divsn. (No. dist.) Ill., 1974, first asst. US atty (No. dist.) Ill., 1975—76, U.S. atty. (No. dist.) Ill. Chgo., 1985-89; ptnr. Jenner & Block LLP, Chgo., 1976—85, 1989—. Instr. John Marshal Law Sch., 1972—76; adj. prof. law Northwester U. Sch. Law, 1980—82; dir., treas. Met. Fair and Exposition Authority, Chgo., 1985; spl. counsel to investigate report health care sys. City of Chgo., 1991. Bd. dirs. Boys Scouts Am., Bus. and Profl. People for Pub. Interest, 1998—, Smithsonian Inst. Librs., 2004—, mem. judicial conf. adv. com. on civil rules, 2006—; chmn. Ill. Task Force Crime and Corrections, 1992—93; mem. vis. com. Northwestern U. Sch. Law, 1992—95. Named one of Ten Outstanding Young Citizens of Chgo., Jr. C. of C., 1976; recipient Spl. Commendation award, U.S. Dept. Justice, Chgo., 1975, Disting. Grad. award, Palatine HS, Ill., 1984, Freedom award, John Marshall Sch. Law, 1985, Citizen of the Yr. award, Constn. Rights Found., 1987, Civillian of the Yr. award, Armed Forces Coun. Chgo., 1988, Man of the Yr. award, WBBM Radio, 1988, Disting. Pub. Svc. award, Anti-Defamation League B'nai B'rith, 1990, Disting. Achievement award, Lawrence U., 1990, Disting. Svc. award, Chgo. C. of C. and Industry, 1990, Alumni Merit award, Northwestern U. Alumni Assn., 1995, Richard N. Rovner award, Epilepsy Found. Greater Chgo., 2004, Judge Learned Hand award, 2005. Fellow: Am. Coll. Trial Lawyers; mem.: ABA, Chgo. Inn Ct. (pres. 2000—01), Ill. State Bar Assn., Chgo. Bar Assn., Chicagoland C. of C. (bd. dirs. 1999—), Law of Chgo. Club, Exec. Club Chgo. (bd. dirs. 1996—), Econ. Club. Chgo. (bd. dirs. 1990—). Office: Jenner & Block LLP 330 N Wabash Ave Chicago IL 60611-7603 Office Phone: 312-923-2903. Business E-Mail: avalukas@jenner.com.

VALVERDE, JOSE RAFAEL, professional baseball player; b. San Pedro de Macoris, Dominican Republic, July 24, 1979; m. Luisa Valverde. Pitcher Ariz. Diamondbacks, 2003—. Named to Nat. League All-Star Team, Maj. League Baseball, 2007. Mailing: Ariz Diamondbacks PO Box 2095 Phoenix AZ 85001 *

VALVERDE, PALOMA, biochemist, educator; b. Murcia, Murcia, Spain, Jan. 15, 1968; d. Gregorio Valverde and Paz de los Angeles Hernandez; m. David Irwin Sherris, Nov. 2, 1997; children: Gregory Alexander Sherris children: Michael Gregory Sherris. BSc, U. Murcia, Spain, 1990, MSc, 1991, PhD, 1994. Scientist Human Nutrition Rsch. Ctr. of Aging, Tufts U., Boston, 2002—04; asst. prof. Sch. Dental Medicine, Tufts U., Boston, 2004—. Contbr. articles to profl. jours. John W. Hein Rsch. fellow, Forsyth Inst., Boston, 1999—2002. Mem.: Internat. Assn. for Biomed. Rsch. (v.p. 2004—). Achievements include discovery of first mutations in human melanocortin receptor 1; gene called WW45 or Salvador; first to use of scorpion venom to treat periodontal disease; development of first antibody to recognize WW45/Salvador gene; discovery of axl receptor tyrosine kinase is ubiquitinated by its ligand Gas6; RANKL and BSP induce bone loss synergistically. Avocations: painting, writing. Home: 37 Neillian Crescent Jamaica Plain MA 02130 Office: Tufts Univ DHS Bldg Gavel Ctr Rm 833 One Kneeland St Boston MA 02111 Home Phone: 617-522-7681, Office Phone: 617-259-7699. Business E-Mail: paloma.valverde@tufts.edu.

VALVO, BARBARA-ANN, lawyer, surgeon; b. Elizabeth, NJ, June 7, 1949; d. Robert Richad and Vera (Kovach) V. BA in Biology, Hofsta U., 1971; MD, Pa. State U., 1975; JD, Loyola Sch. Law, 1993. Bar: La. 1993; diplomate Am. Bd. Surgery. Surg. intern Nassau County Med. Ctr., East Meadow, NY, 1975-76; resident gen. surgery Allentown-Sacred Heart Med. Ctr., Pa., 1976-80; asst. chief surgery USPHS, New Orleans, 1980-81; pvt. practice gen. surgery New Orleans, 1981-89; pvt. practice med. malpractice law, 1995—. Upjohn scholar, 1975. Fellow ACS; mem. ABA, Fed. Bar Assn., La. Bar Assn., La. Trial Lawyers Assn. Republican. Avocations: computers, raising animals. Office: 41 Harley Pl Willow Spring NC 27592 Personal E-mail: bavalvo@nc.rr.com.

VALYI-NAGY, TIBOR G., neuropathologist, virologist; b. Debrecen, Hungary, Jan. 7, 1958; arrived in U.S., 1988; s. Tibor Valyi-Nagy and Ilona Gonczol; m. Klara Peto, Sept. 11, 1982; children: Tibor, Zsofia. MD, Debrecen U., 1982; PhD, Hungarian Acad. Scis., Budapest, 1994. Cert. anatomic and neuropathology Am. Bd. Pathology, 2003, med. microbiology Hungarian Bd. Med. Microbiology, 1988. Rsch. assoc. Nat. Inst. Dermatology, Budapest, 1982—88; rsch. fellow U. Tex. Med. Br., Galveston, 1984—86; rsch. assoc. Wistar Inst., Phila., 1988—95; resident physician in anatomic and neuropathology Vanderbilt U. Med. Ctr., Nashville, 1995—2000; instr. and attending neuropathologist Vanderbilt U. Sch. Medicine, Nashville, 2000—02; dir. neuropathology, asst. prof. U. Ill., Chgo., 2002—07, dir. neuropathology, assoc. prof., 2007—. Home: 597 Glen Ellyn Pl Glen Ellyn IL 60137 Office: U Ill at Chgo 840 S Wood St Rm 130 Chicago IL 60612-4325 Office Phone: 312-996-1772. Personal E-mail: valyint@aol.com. E-mail: tiborv@uic.edu.

VAMOS, FLORENCE M., lawyer; b. NYC, Apr. 09; d. Joseph Calabro and Louise Marie Horvath; m. Joseph S. Vamos. BA magna cum laude, U.Minn., 1974; JD, William Mitchell Coll. Law, St. Paul, 1978. Bar: Ind. 1978, Mich. 1982, U.S. Dist. Ct. (so. dist.) Ind. 1978, U.S. Dist. Ct. (no. dist.) Ind. 1979, U.S. Dist. Ct. (so. dist.) Mich. 1981, U.S. Dist. Ct (ea. dist.) Mich. 1982. Pvt. practice, South Bend, Ind., 1978-90, Mishawaka, Ind., 1990-2000, Edwardsburg, Mich., 2001—. Mem. Ind. State Bar Assn., Mich. State Bar Assn., Cass County (Mich.) Bar Assn., St. Joseph County (Ind.) Bar Assn., Nat. Inst. Trial Advocacy. Address: 3230 SW 3rd Ln Cape Coral FL 33991-1011 Personal E-mail: fvamos8229@aol.com.

VAN, FRITZ See VAN DUYSE, FRANCIS

VANAGAS, RIMANTAS (RAY) ANDRIUS (RAY VANAGAS), entrepreneur, real estate developer, real estate company executive; b. Chgo., Jan. 10, 1958; s. Liudas and Birute A. (Bielskis) Vanagas. Student, Northwestern U., 1980-81; BA in Physics, Econs. and Polit. Sci., Lake Forest Coll., Ill., 1982. Prof. basketball player European divsn., Munich, 1982; ski instr., capt. race team Breckenridge (Colo.) Ski Sch., 1979-80; chmn. bd. dirs. Vancher Corp., Wheeling, Ill., 1980-84; sales exec. Chgo. HMO, 1984-85; exec. dir. Physique, Inc., Highland Park, Ill., 1985; pres., CEO Sports Life, Inc., Highland Park, 1985-88; sr. v.p. JPC Consulting, Chgo., 1988-91; pres., CEO Printing Advisors, Inc., Naperville, Ill., 1990-94, Cafe Alexander, Naperville, 1995—2002; sr. exec. George S. May Internat. Consulting Co., Park Ridge, Ill., 1994-95; pres. Movie Magic Workshops, 2002—; founder, real estate investor and devel. RBML Real Estate Inc., 2002—; pres. and CEO Pinemeadow Corp. DBA Park Shore Marina, 2004—, Vanagas Investment Group, LLC, 2005—. Cons. Nautilus Exercise Ctrs., Inc., Wheeling, 1979—83, G. Ross Comm., Lake Bluff, Ill., 1986; mng. dir. Ford Model Mgmt., Chgo., 2000—; pres., CEO Alexander Talent Mgmt., 2001—. Actor:, 1981—; (films) Shut-Eye, 2001; prodr.:, 1981—, numerous music videos, commls., inds. and corp. films. Leader Lithuanian Air

Scouts, 1976—80; campaign asst. Ronald Reagan Re-Election Campaign, Ill., 1983; active Baltic Nations Athletic Olympiad; vol. coach basketball, baseball, 1984—87. Mem.: Mensa. Roman Catholic. Avocations: collecting coins and stamps, travel, skiing, golf, tennis. Home: 1684 Greene Ridge Dr Naperville IL 60565-6753 Office Phone: 269-445-3100. E-mail: rayvanagas@aol.com.

VAN AKEN, JOHN HENRY, retired marine engineer; b. Haarlem, Netherlands, Sept. 26, 1922; arrived in U.S., 1952; s. Antony and Maria Petronella (Renzen) van Aken; m. Hendrika A. Bonneur, Sept. 25, 1947 (div. Feb. 1960); 1 child, Antony Laurens; m. Helen Jemison Waterman, July 17, 1962 (dec. Feb. 1978); m. Marilyn McDaniel, July 13, 1980 (dec. Sept. 2001). Marine Engr., Acad. Tech. Sci. and Arts of Design, 1940. Asst. mgr. repair dept. Wilton-Feyenoord Dockyards, Schiedam, Netherlands, 1945—52; supt. machinery Ala. Dry Dock & Shipbldg. Co., Mobile, 1958—60; mgr. project Kerr-McGee Oil Industries, Oklahoma City, 1954—58, 1960—63; insp. George Sharp Co., Naval Architects, Newport News, Va., 1960; pres. John H. van Aken Co. Inc., Marine Surveyors and Cons. Inc., Mobile, 1963—99; ret., 2002. Non-exclusive surveyor Panama Bur. Shipping, Internat. Cargo Gear Bur., Registr. Italiano Navale, Lloyd's Register of Shipping; v.p. Westminister Village Found., Inc. Decorated comdr. Order Good Hope, South Africa; Paul Harris fellow Rotary. Mem. Soc. Naval Architects and Marine Engrs., Nat. Assn. Marine Surveyors, Netherlands Soc. Marine Technologists, Rotary Home: 500 Spanish Ft Blvd #52 Spanish Fort AL 36527-5004 Personal E-mail: jhvanaken@wvsf.org.

VAN AKEN, NORMAN, chef; Chef, owner Norman's Restaurant, Coral Gables, Fla., Orlando, Fla., LA. Chef's coun. Chefs for Humanity. Author: Feast of Sunlight, 1988, The Exotic Fruit Book, 1995, Norman Van Aken's New World Cuisine, 1997, New World Kitchen, 2003. Named Best Chef in the Southeast, James Beard Found.; recipient Robert Mondavi Culinary Award of Excellence, Food Arts Silver Spoon Lifetime Achievement award.

VAN ALFEN, NEAL K., plant pathologist; b. Ogden, Utah, July 17, 1943; s. Gerrit Johan and Marguerite (Noorda) Van A. BS, Brigham Young U., 1968, MS, 1969; PhD, U. Calif., Davis, 1972. Asst. plant pathologist Conn. Agr. Exp. Sta., New Haven, Conn., 1972-75; asst. prof. biology Utah State U., Logan, 1975-78, extension plant pathologist, 1975-78, assoc. prof. of biology, 1978-82, prof. of biology and molecular biology/biochem., 1982-90; prof. and head/dept. of plant pathology/microbiology Tex. A&M U., College Station, Tex., 1990-99; dean agrl. and environ. scis. U. Calif., Davis, 1999—. Fellow AAAS, Am. Phytopathol. Soc.; mem. Am. Phytopathol. Soc. (councilor-at-large 1994-97, v.p., pres. 1997-2000), Am. Soc. for Microbiology. Office: U Calif-Davis Coll Agrl and Environ Scis 1 Shields Ave Davis CA 95616-5270 Home Phone: 530-661-2298; Office Phone: 530-752-1605, 530-661-2298. Business E-Mail: nkvanalfen@ucdavis.edu.

VAN ALLEN, VERONICA ELAINE, marketing and public relations professional; b. Jamaica, NY, May 6, 1936; d. William James and Florence Veronica (Lester) Van Allen; children: Veronica E. Davis, Valerie E. Boyd; m. Ian Helsby, July 4, 1998. BEd, U. Miami, 1963. Cert. tchr. Fla. English, phys. edn. tchr. Dade County Sch. Sys., Miami, Fla., 1963-67; founder, coach girls' track team Acad. of the Holy Names, Tampa, Fla., 1972—74; exec. dir. Royal Palm Festival Inc., West Palm Beach, Fla., 1978-82; exec. v.p. No. Palm Beaches C. of C., Palm Beach Gardens, Fla., 1982-88; dir. mktg., pub. rels. Operation Explore, Palm Beach Gardens, Fla., 1993—. Exec. dir. World Trade Coun., 1983-86. Editor (newspaper supplement) Royal Palm Festival, 1978-82 (Advt. Club aw ard 1980), video pub., 1981 (Internat. Festival Assn. award 1981); editor (ann. chamber mag.) Guide to No. Palm Beaches, 1984-88, Air Show mag., 1987. Vice chmn. Tourist Devel. Coun. Palm Beach County, 1987, mem., 1983—88; vice chmn. Leadership Palm Beach County, 1985—86, bd. dirs., 1984—89; mem. mil. acad. screening com. Congressman Tom Lewis, Palm Beach Gardens, 1986—94; bd. dirs. Sun Fest, 1982—84; mem. Internat. Coun. Air Shows, 1981—86, Alumni Assn.LPBC, 1987—; coord. religious instrn. St. Paul of the Cross, North Palm Beach, Fla., 1977—80. Mem. U. Miami Alumni Assn., Internat. Festival Assn., Am. C. of C. Execs. Republican. Roman Catholic. Avocations: reading, yoga, theater, tennis, dance. Home: 170 Esperanza Way Palm Beach Gardens FL 33418 Personal E-mail: ronnieandian@adelphia.net.

VAN ALLEN, WILLIAM KENT, lawyer; b. Albion, NY, July 30, 1914; s. Everett Kent and Georgia (Roberts) Van A.; m. Sally Schall, Nov. 11, 1944; children: William Kent, Jr., George Humphrey, Peter Cushing. AB, Hamilton Coll., 1935; LL.B., Harvard U., 1938. Bar: N.Y. 1938, D.C. 1939, N.C. 1951, U.S. Dist. Ct. (we. dist.) N.C. 1951, U.S. Dist. Ct. (mid. dist.) N.C. 1953, U.S. Ct. Appeals (4th cir.) 1951, U.S. Ct. Claims 1946, U.S. Tax Ct. 1940, FCC 1939, ICC 1940, U.S. Supreme Ct. 1946. With Hanson, Lovett & Dale, Washington, 1938-41, 46-50; ptnr. Lassiter, Moore and Van Allen and Moore and Van Allen, Charlotte, NC, 1951-87; of counsel Moore & Van Allen, Charlotte, 1988—. Permanent mem. Jud. Conf. 4th Jud. Circuit. Vestryman Episc. Ch., 1957-60, 66-69; mem. Mecklenburg County Bd. Public Welfare, 1954-59, chmn. 1957-59; bd. dirs. N.C. Found. Commerce and Industry, 1965-73, Found. U. N.C. at Charlotte, 1979-89, Charlotte Symphony Orch., 1981-82, Mercy Health Svcs., 1983-88; chmn. Charlotte Area adv. coun. Am. Arbitration Assn., 1967-76; bd. dirs. United Community Svcs., 1972-77, v.p., 1972; bd. mgrs. Charlotte Country Day Sch., 1956-61, chmn., 1959-61, bd. visitors, 1978-2004, chmn., 1987-88; bd. advisers U. N.C.-Charlotte, 1983-84; trustee Spastics Hosp., 1951-60, Mint Mus. Art, 1976-79, Surtman Found., 1955-90, Mercy Hosp. Found., 1979-84; bd. visitors Johnson C. Smith U., 1978-89; pres. Charlotte Symphony League, 1980-81, Friends of U. N.C. at Charlotte, 1990-91. Served with USNR, 1941-45, commdg. officer destroyer escort ATO and PTO; released to inactive duty as lt. comdr. Mem. ABA, Charlotte C. of C. (bd. dirs. 1971-75, v.p. 1972-75). Mil. Order of Carabao, Holland Soc. N.Y., Charlotte Country Club, Charlotte City Club, Chevy Chase Club (Md.), Mullett Lake Country Club (Mich.), Mill Reef Club, Phi Beta Kappa, Chi Psi. Office: Moore & Van Allen Ste 4700 100 N Tryon St Charlotte NC 28202-4003 Office Phone: 704-331-1021.

VAN ALLSBURG, CHRIS, writer, artist; b. Grand Rapids, Mich., June 18, 1949; s. Richard Allen and Doris Marie (Christiansen) Van A.; m. Lisa Carol Morrison, Aug. 17, 1976. BFA, U. Mich., 1972; MFA, R.I. Sch. Design, 1975. Tchr. R.I. Sch. Design, Providence. Author, illustrator: The Garden of Abdul Gasazi, 1979 (Caldecott Honor Book 1980, Irma Simonton Black award Bank St. Coll. Edn. 1980, Boston Globe/Horn Book award 1980), Jumanji, 1981 (Caldecott medal 1982, Boston Globe/Horn Book award 1982, Children's Choice award Internat. Reading Assn. 1982, Am. Book award, 1982, Ky. Bluegrass award No. Ky. U. 1983, Buckeye Children's Book award Ohio State Libr. 1983, Wash. Children's Choice Picture Book award Wash. Libr. Media Assn. 1984, W. Va. Children's Book award 1985), Ben's Dream, 1982 (Parents Choice award for illustration Parents' Choice Found. 1982), Wreck of the Zephyr, 1983 (Silver medal Soc. Illustrators 1983), The Mysteries of Harris Burdick, 1984 (Parents Choice award for illustration Parents' Choice Found. 1984, Irma Simonton Black award Bank St. Coll. Edn. 1985, Boston Globe/Horn Book award 1985, World Fantasy award 1985), The Polar Express, 1985 (Parents Choice award for illustration Parents' Choice Found. 1985, Caldecott medal 1986, Boston Globe/Horn Book award 1986, Ky. Bluegrass award No. Ky. U. 1987), The Stranger, 1986 (Parents Choice award for illustration Parents' Choice Found. 1986), The Z Was Zapped: A Play in Twenty-Six Acts, 1987, Two Bad Ants, 1988, Just A Dream, 1990, The Wretched Stone, 1991, The Widow's Broom, 1992, The Sweetest Fig, 1993, The Two Figs, 1993, Bad Day at River Bend, 1995, Zathura, 2002; illustrator: Swan Lake, 1989; exhibited works at Whitney Mus. Art, N.Y.C., Mus. Modern Art, N.Y.C., Alan Stone Gallery, N.Y.C., Grand Rapids (Mich.) Art Mus., Port Washington (N.Y.) Pub. Libr.; permanent collections include Kerlan Collection at U. Minn. Recipient Hans Christian Andersen award nomination, 1985. Jewish. Office: Houghton Mifflin Co 222 Berkeley St Boston MA 02116-3748

VAN ALSTYNE, VANCE BROWNELL, management consultant; b. Rochester, NY, Feb. 3, 1924; s. Guy and Jessie Van Alstyne; m. Jane Van Alstyne, Aug. 12, 1950; children: Cary B., Stacey E. BA, U. Rochester, 1948; LLB, Blackstone Coll. Law, 1964. Rsch. asst. indsl. rels. Gilbert Assoc, Inc., NYC, 1950-56; corp. sec., v.p., dir. R.C. Simpson & Staff Inc., Newark and Ridgewood, NJ, 1956-74; pres., dir. R.C. Simpson, Inc., Ridgewood, NJ, 1975—91, Charlotte, NC, 1991—. 2d lt., navigator 12th Air Force USAF, 1942—45. Mem.: Indsl. Rels. Rsch. Assn., Am. Arbitration Assn., Atlantic Salmon Fedn. Republican. Office: RC Simpson Inc 5950 Fairview Rd Ste 604 Charlotte NC 28210-3178 Office Phone: 704-553-0716. E-mail: van.fsh@att.net.

VAN ALSTYNE, W. SCOTT, JR., lawyer, educator; b. East Syracuse, NY, Sept. 21, 1922; s. Walter Scott and Cecil Edna (Folmsbee) Van A.; m. Margaret Reed Hudson, June 23, 1949 (div.); children: Gretchen Anne, Hunter Scott; m. Marion Graham Walker, May 3, 1980. BA, U. Buffalo, 1948; MA, U. Wis., 1950, LL.B., 1953, S.JD, 1954. Bar: Wis. 1953. Assoc. Shea & Hoyt, Milw., 1954-56; asst. prof. law U. Nebr., 1956-58; pvt. practice Madison, Wis., 1958-72; prof. law U. Fla., 1973-90, prof. emeritus, 1990—; lectr. law U. Wis., 1958-72; lectr. Cambridge-Warsaw Trade Program Cambridge U., England, 1976. Vis. prof. law Cornell U., 1977, U. Leiden, The Netherlands, 1988, 91; spl. lectr. U. Utrecht, The Netherlands, 1991; vis. prof. Wake Forest U., 1997; spl. counsel Gov. of Wis., 1966-70; bd. dirs. non-resident divsn. State Bar Wis., 1981-96, pres., 1988-90, bd. govs. 1988-90. Prin. author: Goals and Missions of Law Schools, 1990; contbr. articles to profl. jours. Mem. Gov.'s Commn. on Edn., Wis., 1969-71; cons. Wis. Commn. on Legal Edn., 1995-96. Served with AUS, 1942-45, 61-62; col. Res., ret. Decorated Legion of Merit. Fellow: Wis. Bar Found. (life); mem.: Holland Soc., S.R. (NY), Netherland Club (NYC), Madison Club (Wis.), Ft. Rensselaer Club (NY), Phi Beta Kappa, Order of Coif, Phi Delta Phi, Omicron Delta Kappa. Republican. Presbyterian. Office: U Fla Holland Law Ctr Gainesville FL 32611

VAN ANDEL, STEVE ALAN, consumer products company executive; b. Ada, Mich., Oct. 9, 1955; BLS in Econs. and Bus., Hillsdale Coll., 1978; MBA in MKtg., Miami U., Oxford, Ohio, 1979. V.p. mktg. Amway Corp., Worldwide, chmn. exec. com. policy bd. Ada; vice chmn. Amway Japan Ltd.; chmn. Amway Asia Pacific Ltd., Amway Corp., 1995—, CEO, 1995—. Dir. Met. Found., Operation Enterprise-AMA; bd. dirs. Met. Hosp. Found., Mich. Nat. Bank Corp., Ctr. for Internat. Pvt. Enterprises, Gerald Ford Found., Std. Fed. Bank, Grand Rapids John Ball Zoo Soc., Borgess Metro Health Alliance, Met. Health Corp.; mem. dean's adv. bd. Seidman Sch. of Bus.; co-CEO, Alticor Inc. Bd. dirs. Grand Rapids John Ball Soc., Amway Environmental Found. Mem. U.S. C. of C. (chmn. 2002). Office: Amway Corp 7575 Fulton St E Ada MI 49355-0001

VAN ANTWERP, ROBERT L., JR., career military officer; m. Paula Eberly; children: Jeff, Luke, Rob, Julia, Kathryn. BS, US Mil. Acad., 1972; MME, U. Mich.; MBA, LI U. Registered Profl. Engr., Va. Commd. 2d. lt. US Army, 1972, advanced through grades to lt. gen., 2007, platoon leader, 76th Engr. Battalion Fort Meade, Md., 1973—74; exec. officer 65th Engr. Battalion, 25th Infantry Div. Schofield Barracks, Hawaii, 1975—76, asst. div. engr. Hawaii, 1976—79, exec. officer 84th Engr. Battalion, 45th Gen. Support Group Hawaii, 1985—87; chief mil. construction US Army Western Command, Fort Shafter, Hawaii, 1987—88; exec. officer Office of Chief of Engrs. US Army, Washington, 1988—89; comdr. 326th Engr. Battalion, 101st Airborne Div., Fort Campbell, Ky., 1989—91; dist. comdr. LA Dist. US Army CE, LA, 1992—94, chief of staff Washington, 1994—95, comdr. South Atlantic Div. Atlanta, 1996—98; exec. asst. to vice chmn. Joint Chiefs of Staff US Dept. Def., Washington, 1995—96; dir. Office of Competitive Sourcing, Office of Asst. Sec. of Army US Army, Washington, 1998—99, asst. chief staff installation mgmt., 1999—2002; comdr. US Army Maneuver Support Ctr., 2002—04; chief US Army Accessions Command, Fort Knox, Ky., 2004—07; chief engrs., commdg. gen. US Army CE, Washington, 2007—. Instr., mech. engring. US Mil. Acad., West Point, NY, 1981—82, asst. prof., exec. officer, 1982—84; commdg. gen. US Army Engr. Sch., Fort Leonard Wood, Mo. Pres. Officers' Christian Fellowship. Decorated Defense Superior Svc. Medal, Legion of Merit, Bronze Star Medal, Meritorious Svc. Medal. Office: US Army Corps of Engineers 441 G St, NW Washington DC 20314-1000 Office Phone: 703-428-6572. *

VAN ANTWERPEN, FRANKLIN STUART, federal judge; s. Franklin John and Dorothy Van Antwerpen; m. Kathleen Veronica O'Brien, Sept. 12, 1970; children: Joy, Franklin W., Virginia. BS in Engring. Physics, U. Maine, 1964; JD, Temple U., 1967; postgrad., Nat. Jud. Coll., 1980. Bar: Pa. 1969, U.S. Dist. Ct. (ea. dist.) Pa. 1971, U.S. Ct. Appeals (3d cir.) 1971, U.S. Supreme Ct. 1972. Corp. counsel Hazeltine, Corp., NYC, 1967-70; chief counsel Northampton County Legal Aid Soc., Easton, Pa., 1970-71; assoc. Hemstreet & Smith, Easton, 1971-73; ptnr. Hemstreet & VanAntwerpen, Easton, 1973-79; judge Ct. Common Pleas of Northampton County, Pa., 1979-87, US Dist. Ct. (ea. dist.) Pa., Phila., 1987—2004, US Ct. Appeals (3rd. cir.), 2004—. Apptd. to US Sentencing Commn. Jud. Working Group, 1992-93; apptd. to US Jud. Conf. Com. on Defender Svcs., 1997, chmn. subcom. on fed. defender funding, 2000-01; trial judge US vs. Scarfo, 1988-89; adj. prof. Northampton County Area CC, 1976-81; solicitor Palmer Twp., 1971-79; gen. counsel Fairview Savs. and Loan Assn., Easton, 1973-79; lectr. on law of evidence Pa. Bar Inst., 1985-92. Contbr. articles to Cardozo Law Rev., 1967. Recipient Booster award Bus. Indsl. and Profl. Assn., 1979, George Palmer award Palmer Twp., 1980, Citizen of Yr. award, 1981, Law Enforcement Commendation medal Nat. Soc. SAR, 1990, Disting. Alumni Achievement award Newark Acad., 2001, Law Day award Temple Law Sch. Alumni Assn., 2004; named an Alumnus Who Has Made a Difference in the World, U. Maine, 1991. Mem. ABA (com. on jud. edn.), Fed. Bar Assn. (hon.), Fed. Cir. Bar Assn., Pa. Bar Assn., Northampton County Bar Assn., Am. Judicature Soc., Fed. Judges Assn., Pomfret Club, Union League Club, Pa. Soc. Club, Sigma Pi Sigma. Office: 4th Fl Holmes Bldg 101 Larry HOlmes Dr Easton PA 18042-7722

VAN ARSDALEN, KEITH NORMAN, urologist; b. Plainfield, NJ, Sept. 26, 1951; s. Norman Charles and Thelma Marie Svendsen Van Arsdalen; children: Bryce, Leigh, Jill, Kyle. BS, Muhlenberg Coll., 1973; MMS, CMDNJ, 1975; MD, Med. Coll. Va., 1977. Intern, resident U.Md., Balt., 1977-79; resident Med. Coll. Va., Richmond, 1979-82; asst. prof. surgery, urology U. Pa., Phila., 1983-89, asst. prof. surgery, urology, radiology, 1989-97, prof. surgery, urology, radiology, 1997—. Dir. male fertility sect. U. Pa. Sch. Medicine Divsn. Urology, 1983—, dir. shock wave lithotripsy svcs., 1985—; attending urologist Children's Hosp. Phila., 1989—; chief urology sect. Phila. V.A. Med. Ctr., 1990—2001; expert adv. panel U.S. Pharm. Conv., Rockville, Md., 1990—95; mem. scientific bd. Nat. Kidney Found., NYC, 1992—98. Asst. editor Jour. Endourology, 1987-2003; contbr. articles to profl. jours., chpts. to books. Recipient Paul Rodin Leberman Teaching award Urology Residents, Phila, 1993, 98, Alumni Star award Va. Commonwealth U., 1993, John Morgan Soc. award, 1998; U. Pa. NKF-AUA rsch. fellow, 1982-83. Fellow: ACS (program com. 1992); mem.: AAAS, Urodynamics Soc., Soc. Univ. Urologists, Soc. Study Male Reproduction, Soc. Study Impotence, Soc. Reproductive Surgeons, Soc. Minimally Invasive Therapy, Soc. Laparoendoscopic Surgeons, Soc. Basic Urologic Rsch., Internat. Soc. Urology, Phila. Urol. Soc. (sec.-treas. 1992—98, pres.-elect 1998—99, pres. 1999—2000), Urol. Assn. Pa., Assn. Acad. Surgery, Am. Soc. Reproductive Medicine, Am. Soc. Andrology, Am. Assn. Clin. Urologists, Am. Urol. Assn., Coll. Physicians Phila. (mid-Atlantic sect. edn. com. 1989—90, rsch. com. rep. 1990—94, local arrangements com. 1991—94, chmn. 1992—93, program com. 1996—97, rsch. com. rep. 1999—2002). Avocations: fishing, skiing, swimming, reading, house restoration. Office: Urology 9 Penn Tower 3400 Spruce St Philadelphia PA 19104-4206 Home Phone: 856-428-1273; Office Phone: 215-662-6790.

VAN ARSDALL, ROBERT ARMES, engineer, retired military officer; b. Omaha, Oct. 5, 1925; s. Samuel Peter and Althea (Armes) Van A.; m. Margaret Cooper Kiersted, June 9, 1948; children— Robert Armes, Janet Althea, Susan DeBaun, Kathryn Ann. BS, U.S. Mil. Acad., 1948; postgrad., U. Colo., spring 1961; MS, George Washington U., 1968. Commd. 2d lt. USAF, 1948, advanced through grades to col., 1968; grad. Randolph AFB, Tex., 1949; assigned 5th Air Rescue Group, Westover AFB, Mass., 1949-51; student USAF Squadron Officer Sch., Maxwell AFB, Ala., 1950; pilot, ops. officer 9th Air Rescue Group, Burton-Wood, Manston and Bushy Park, England, 1951-55; ops. officer Hdqrs. Air Rescue Service, Orlando AFB, Fla., 1955-57; plans officer Hdqrs. Air R & D Command, Balt., also Andrews AFB, Md., 1957-60; grad. USAF jet qualification course, Randolph AFB, 1959; tng.-with-industry Air Force Inst. Tech., Martin Co., Denver, 1960-61; chief plans div. Hdqrs. Space Systems Div., LA, 1961-63; exec. officer Office Space Systems, Office Sec. Air Force, 1963-67; assoc. Air War Coll. program, Washington, 1964-66; student Naval War Coll., 1967-68; dep. dir. Dept. Def. Manned Space Flight Support Office, Patrick AFB, Fla., 1968-69; dir. range engring., 1969-70; dir. range ops. Air Force Eastern Test Range, 1970-72; comdr. USAF Satellite Test Ctr., Sunnyvale, Calif., 1972-73; vice comdr. USAF Satellite Control Facility, LA, 1973-74, comdr., 1974-76; staff engr. Pan Am. World Airways, Cocoa Beach, Fla., 1976-78, project dir., 1978-79, program mgr., 1980-85, dir. internat. projects, 1985-88; program dir. Diego Garcia, 1989, ret., 1989. Decorated Air Force Commendation medal with two oak leaf clusters, Legion of Merit with oak leaf cluster. Life mem. Assn. Grads. U.S. Mil. Acad.; charter mem. Nat. Soujourners, USAF Acad. Athletic Assn. Clubs: Mason, Burtonwood Air Force (gov.), Bushy Park Air Force (gov.), Orlando Air Force (gov.), Andrews Air Force (gov.), Space Systems Division Air Force (gov.). Republican. Methodist. Home: 660 Cinnamon Ct Satellite Beach FL 32937-4301 Personal E-mail: ravanarsdall@earthlink.net.

VANARSDALL, ROBERT LEE, JR., orthodontist, educator; b. Crewe, Va., Feb. 7, 1940; s. Robert Lee Sr. and Margie Mae (Jenkins) V.; m. Sandra E. Hoffman, Aug. 11, 1962; children: Robert Lee III, Lesley, Ashley. BA in Econs., Coll. William and Mary, 1962; DDS, Med. Coll. Va., 1970; cert. Orthodontics and Periodontics, U. Pa., 1973. Diplomate Am. Acad. Periodontology, Am. Bd. Orthodontics. Staff Children's Hosp., Phila., 1973—; prof. orthodontics, chmn. dept. orthodontics U. Pa., Phila., 1981—; prof. dentistry, chmn. Med. Coll. Pa., Phila., 1989—. K.G. prof. orthodontics U. Sydney, Australia, 2001; bd. dir. Nat. Dental Ins. Co., Denver. Editor: Internat. Jour. Adult Orthodontics and Orthognathic Surgery, 1986-2003, Orthodontics: Current Principles and Techniques, 2d edit., 1994, 4th edit., 2005, Applications of Orthodontic Mini-Implants, 2007; editl. bd. profl. jours.; contbr. articles to profl. jours. Bd. dirs. Phila. Soc. William and Mary Alumni Assn. Lt. USNR, 1962-65. Fellow Coll. Physicians of Phila. 1978, Am. Coll. Dentistry 1980. Mem. ADA, Am. Assn. Orthodontists, Stomatological Club Phila., Angle Soc. Orthodontists (v.p. ea. component, pres. 2004-2005), Phila. Soc. Orthodontists (pres. 1989, chmn. sci. affairs coun. 1990—), Internat. Coll. of Dentists. Roman Catholic. Avocations: antiques, architecture. Home: 208 Ashwood Rd Villanova PA 19085-1504 Office: Penn Dental 34th and Market St Philadelphia PA 19104 Office Phone: 215-898-5910. Office Fax: 215-898-0998. Business E-Mail: rlv@pobox.upenn.edu.

VANARSDEL, ROSEMARY THORSTENSON, retired English studies educator; b. Seattle, Sept. 1, 1926; d. Odin and Helen Catherine (McGregor) Thorstenson; m. Paul P. VanArsdel Jr., July 7, 1950 (dec. Jan. 1994); children: Mary M., Andrew P. BA, U. Wash., 1947, MA, 1948; PhD, Columbia U., 1961. Grad. tchg. asst. Columbia U., NYC, 1948—50; acting instr. U. Wash., Seattle, 1961—63; asst. prof. U. Puget Sound, Tacoma, 1967—69, assoc. prof., 1970—77, chair dept. English, 1970—75, prof. English, 1977—87, dir. Writing Inst., 1976—86, dir. semester abroad, 1977, dir. Legal English program Sch. Law, 1973—77, disting. prof. emeritus, 1987—. Vis. prof. Gonzaga U., Pacific Luth. U., Whitman Coll., Willamette U., 1977. Author: Victorian Periodicals: A Guide to Research, Vol. I, 1978, Vol. II, 1989, George Eliot: A Centenary Tribute, 1982, Victorian Periodicals and Victorian Society, 1994, Periodicals of Queen Victoria's Empire, An Exploration, 1996, Florence Fenwick Miller: Victorian Feminist, Journalist, Educator, 2001, Victorian Periodicals, Aids to Research: A Selected Bibliography on the Internet, 8th edit., 2007; mem. editl. bd. Wellesley Index to Victorian Periodicals, 1824-1900, 1968-88, A Union List of Victorian Serials, 1979-85, Victorian Rev., 1990—; contbr. articles to encys. and profl. jours. Recipient Doris Bronson Morrill award Kappa Kappa Gamma, 1982, Disting. Alumnae award Broadway H.S., Seattle, 1991. Fellow Royal Soc. Lit.; mem. MLA, Oxford Bibliog. Soc., Nat. Coun. Tchrs. English (Achievement awards, dir. 1974-77), Rsch. Soc. for Victorian Periodicals (pres. 1981-83).

VANATTA, BOB, athletic administrator; b. Columbia, Mo., July 7, 1918; s. Claude W. and Viola (Toler) V.; m. Lois A. Williams; children: Robert, Thomas, Timothy. BA, Ctrl. Meth. Coll., 1942; MEd, U. Mo., 1949. Tchr., coach Boonville (Mo.) High Sch., 1942-43, Kemper Mil. Sch., Boonville, 1943-44, Springfield (Mo.) High Sch., 1944-47; tchr., dir. athletics, coach Ctrl. Meth. Coll., Fayette, Mo., 1947-50, S.W. Mo. State U., Springfield, 1950-53; coach U.S. Mil. Acad., West Point, NY, 1953-54; dir. athletics, coach Bardley U., Peoria, Ill., 1954-56; tchr., coach Memphis State U., 1956-62, U. Mo., Columbia, 1962-68; bank mktg. officer Empire Bank, Springfield, 1968-71; profl. basketball exec. dir. Memphis Pros, 1971-72; tchr., coach Delta State U., Cleve., 1972-73; dir. athletics Oral Roberts U., Tulsa, 1973-77; commr. Ohio Valley Athletic Conf., Nashville, 1977-80, Trans Am. Athletic Conf., Shreveport, La., 1980-83; dir. athletics La. Tech. U., Rustin, 1983-86; commr. Sunshine State Athletic Conf., Jupiter, Fla., 1986-94. Assoc. dir athletics Fla. Atlantic U. Author: Coaching Pattern Play Basketball, 1959; contbr. articles to profl. jours. Chpt. mem. Nat. Football Found. Hall of Fame. Named to Ctrl. Meth. Coll. Hall of Fame, S.W. Mo. State U. Hall of Fame, Nat. Athletic Intercollegiate Assn. Hall of Fame, Greater Springfield Hall of Fame, John Q. Hammons Mo. Sports Hall of Fame, U. Memphis Hall of Fame, Nat. Assn. Collegiate Dir. of Athletics, Nat. Assn. Collegiate Dir. of Athletics Hall of Fame, 1997, Helms Hall of Fame, Palm Beach Athletes Hall of Fame, 2007; recipient Lifetime Achievement award in football All-Am. Football Found., 1997, NCAA Divsn. II Commrs. award Merit, 1999, Champions of Character award NAIA, 2002, numerous others. Mem. Nat. Assn. Basketball Coaches, Am. Football Coaches Assn., Nat. Assn. Collegiate Dirs. Athletics, All Am. Football Found. (Bud Dudley Outstanding Exec. award in Football, 2000, Asa Bushnell Commr. award 2001). Office: Apt 103 301 Ocean Bluffs Blvd Jupiter FL 33477-7329

VANATTA, CHESTER B., management consultant, educator; b. Bartlesville, Okla., Sept. 3, 1935; s. Benjamin Franklin and Iona Ruth (Hayes) V.; m. Patsy Lou (Straub), May 29, 1958; children: Tracy Ann, Christopher B., John Scott BS in Mktg., U. Kans., Lawrence, 1959, MS in Acctg., 1962; Advanced Mgmt. Program, Harvard U., Cambridge, Mass., 1972; MA in

Theology, Fuller Theol. Sem., Pasadena, Calif., 2006. Mem. staff Arthur Young and Co., Kansas City, Mo., 1962—69, regional dir, Dallas, 1969—72, ptnr., 1969—85, mng. ptnr. Chgo., 1972—76, dir., 1973—85, mng. ptnr., vice chmn. ops. NYC, 1976—81, mng. ptnr., vice chmn. S.W. Region Dallas, 1981—85; exec. in residence, Paul J. Adam Disting. lectr. U. Kans. Sch. Bus., Lawrence, 1985—90; pres. Exec. Cons. Group, Lawrence, 1985—96. Bd. dir. Atlantis Plastics, Inc., Atlanta. Trustee Kans. U. Endowment Fund, 1983-2005; bd. dir. Kans. Alumni Assn., 1984-91, pres., 1986-87; staff minister First United Meth. Ch., Grove, Okla., 2003—. Mem. AICPA, Shangri La Country Club. Democrat. Avocations: golf, travel, auctioneering, photography. Home: 29990 S 567 Rd Monkey Island OK 74331-8180 Personal E-mail: chet@aboutvanatta.com.

VAN BAALEN, DONNA GALE, artist, retired pharmacist; b. Sterling, Colo., Jan. 29, 1930; d. Felix Thomas and Edna (Burgess) Ems; m. Chase Van Baalen, June 20, 1954 (dec. Jan. 1986); children: Patricia, Aaron, Julie. BS in Pharmacy, U. Tex., Austin, 1954. Mem.: South Tex. Miniature Art Soc., Corpus Christi Art Guild, Art Ctr. Corpus Christi, World Fedn. Miniaturists, Hilliard Soc. Miniaturists, Miniature Art Soc. Fla., Miniature Artists Am. Home: 116 N 11 PO Box 417 Port Aransas TX 78373 Personal E-mail: cen52303@centurytel.net.

VAN BEEM, JANNY, geneticist, researcher; d. Gilbert van Beem and Graciela Sanchez de van Beem; m. Fred Harwood, Jan. 4, 1999; children: Maya Harwood, Alani Harwood. PhD, Cornell U., NY, 1990—95. Scientist CIMMYT, Internat., Mexico City, 1996—2002. Contbr. articles to profl. jours. Rsch. grant for wheat breeding program, German Govt., 1998—2002. Home: 5007 Riverside Oaks Dr Kingwood TX 77345 Home Phone: 281-358-2982. Personal E-mail: jvanbeem@kingwoodcable.net.

VANBEMMELEN, PAUL S., surgeon, educator; b. The Hague, Netherlands, Sept. 13, 1956; s. Anthonius M. and Estera StruickvanBemmelen; m. Daphne G. Geiringer, June 10, 1979; children: Lauren Rebecca, Jeremy Daniel, Joel Noah, Jonah Gabriel. MD, Rijksuniversiteit Leiden, 1972, PhD, 1978. Cert. Surgeon European Cmty., 1988, Vascular Surgeon Netherlands Bd. of Surgeons, 1991. Assoc. prof. surgery SUNY, Stony Brook, 1998—2003; chief vascular surgery VA Med. Ctr., Northport, NY, 1998—2003; assoc. prof. surgery Temple U., Phila., 2004—07, prof. surgery, 2007—. Author: (jours. vascular surgery/tech.) Venous valve incompetence (Young Investigator Award -Soc. Vascular Tech., 1990). Lt. Royal Dutch Navy, 1980—81. Fellow: Soc. Vascular Surgery (disting.). Achievements include patents for Arterial Assist Device: ArtAssist. Avocation: classic sportscars. Office: Temple Univ Dept Surgery 3401 N Broad St Philadelphia PA 19140 Office Phone: 215-707-6143.

VANBIESBROUCK, JOHN, hockey analyst, retired professional hockey player; b. Detroit, Sept. 4, 1963; m. Rosalinde V. Vanbiesbrouck. Goaltender NY Rangers, 1981—83, Vancouver Canucks, Canada, 1993, Florida Panthers, 1993—97, Phila. Flyers, 1998—2000, NY Islanders, 2000—01, NJ Devils, 2001—02; head coach Sault Ste. Marie Greyhounds, 2002—03; analyst NHL on Versus. Mem. NHL All-Star Team, 1985—86; player NHL All-Star Game, 1994. Named NHL All-Star, 1985—86, Sporting News NHL All-Star, 1985—86, 1993—94; recipient Vezina Trophy, 1986, Terry Sawchuk Trophy, 1983—89, Tommy Ivan Trophy, 1983—84. Achievements include holding the all time record for most wins by American born goaltender with 374. *

VAN BOKKELEN, JOSEPH SCOTT, federal judge, former prosecutor; b. Chgo., June 7, 1943; s. Robert W. and W. Louise (Reynolds) Van B.; m. Sally Wardall Huey, Aug. 14, 1971; children— Brian, Kate. B.A., U. Ind., 1966, J.D., 1969. Bar: Ind. 1969, US Dist. Ct. (so. dist.) Ind. 1969, US Dist. Ct. (no. dist.) Ind. 1973, US Ct. Appeals (7th cir.) 1973, US Supreme Ct. 1973. Dep. atty. gen. State of Ind., Indpls., 1969-71, asst. atty. gen., 1971-72; asst. US atty. (no. dist.) Ind., Hammond, 1972-75; ptnr. Goldsmith, Goodman, Ball & Van Bokkelen, Highland, Ind., 1975—78, Goodman, Ball, Van Bokkelen & Leonard, 1978-2001, US atty. (no. dist.) Ind., 2001-07, judge, US Dist. Ct. (no. dist.) Ind., 2007- Recipient Outstanding Asst. US Atty. award US Dept. Justice, 1974. Mem. ABA, Fed. Bar Assn., Ind. Bar Assn., Criminal Def. Lawyers Assn. Office: US Dist Ct 5400 Fed Plz Ste 4200 Hammond IN 46320 *

VAN BOSSE, HAROLD J.P., orthopedic surgeon; MD, U. Ill., 1984—89. Cert. Orthopedic Surgery, 1997. Residence orthopedics U. Ill., Chgo.; fellow Hosp. for Sick Children, Toronto, 1994—95; surgeon Schneider Children's Hosp. Long Island Jewish Med. Ctr.; pediatric orthopedic surgeon NYU Hosp. for Joint Diseases, 1998—; asst. prof. orthopaedic surgery NYU Med. Ctr. Founder A Leg to Stand On, India, 2003; vol. surgeon Silver Service Children's program, Colombia. Named one of Medical Marvels, New York Mag., 2006. Mailing: NYU Hosp for Joint Diseases 301 East 17 St New York NY 10003 Office: 4 Weber Ave Malverne NY 11565 also: 240 E. 18th S 1st Fl New York NY 10003 Office Phone: 212-598-2310, 516-596-2514. Office Fax: 212-598-2311. *

VAN BRUGGEN, COOSJE, artist, writer; b. Groningen, The Netherlands, June 6, 1942; came to U.S., 1978, naturalized, 1993; d. J.A.R. Van Bruggen and A.M. Andriessen; m. Claes Oldenburg, July 22, 1977. DRS in Art History, Rijks U. Groningen, 1967; DFA (hon.), Calif. Coll. Art and Craft, 1996, Nova Scotia Coll. Art and Design, Halifax, 2005, Coll. Creative Studies, Detroit, 2005; DLitt (hon.), U. Teesside, Middlesbrough, Eng., 1999. Asst. curator Stedelijk Mus., Amsterdam, The Netherlands, 1967-71; prof. Acad. Fine Arts, Enschede, The Netherlands, 1971-76; sr. critic landscape arch. Harvard U., Cambridge, Mass., 1993; sr. critic dept. sculpture Yale U., New Haven, 1996-97. Co-editor Catalogue Sonsbeek, 1971; mem. selection com. Documenta 7, Kassel, Germany, 1982; curator (with Dieter Koepplin) Bruce Nauman: Drawings, 1965-1986, Basel, Switzerland, 1986-88. Author: Bruce Nauman, 1989, John Baldessari, 1990, Frank O. Gehry: Guggenheim Museum Bilbao, 1997; co-author (with Claes Oldenburg): Claes Oldenburg: Sketches and Blottings Toward the European Desk Top, 1990, Large-Scale Projects, 1994, Claes Oldenburg Coosje van Bruggen, 1999, Down Liquidambar Lane: Sculpture in the Park, 2001; co-author: (with Claes Oldenburg and Frank O. Gehry) Il Corso del Coltello, 1985; two-person shows (with Claus Oldenburg), No. Ctr. Contemporary Art, Sunderland, 1988, Leeds City Art Gallery, 1988, Palais des Beaux-Arts, Brussels, 1988, IVAM Ctr. Julio González, Valencia, 1988, Galleria Christian Stein, Milan, 1990, Leo Castelli Gallery, NYC, 1990, Pace Gallery, 1994, Museo Correr, Venice, 1999, Museu Serralves, Porto, 2001, Met. Mus. Art, NYC, 2002, PaceWildenstein, 2002, Frederik Meijer Gardens and Sculpture Park, Grand Rapids, Mich., 2002, Paula Cooper Gallery, 2004, Pace Wildenstein Gallery, 2005, Konrad Fischer Galerie, Düsseldorf, 2005, group shows with Claes Oldenburg, Guggenheim Mus., NYC, 1993, Venice Biennale, 1997, Nat. Gallery, London, 2000, others; contbr. Artforum, 1983—88; numerous pub. sculptures including, Nollen Plz., Civic Ctr., Des Moines, Mpls. Sculpture Garden, Walker Art Ctr., Mpls., Parc de la Villette, Paris, Ctrl. Gardens, Middlesborough, Eng., Guggenheim Found., Neumarkt Galerie, Cologne, Cheonguyeon Stream, Seoul, Korea, and many others. Co-recipient (with Claes Oldenburg) Distinction in Sculpture, Sculpture Ctr., N.Y.C., 1984, (with Claes Oldenburg) Nathaniel S. Saltonstall award, ICA, Boston, 1996, (with Claes Oldenburg) Ptnrs. in Edn. award, Guggenheim, N.Y., 2002, (with Claes Oldenburg) Nat. Medal award, Sch. Mus. Fine Arts, Boston, 2004.

VAN BRUNT, EDMUND EWING, physician; b. Oakland, Calif., Apr. 28, 1926; s. Adrian W. and Kathryn Anne (Shattuck) Van B.; m. Claire Monod, Feb. 28, 1949; children: Karin, Deryk, Jahn. BA in Biophysics, U. Calif., Berkeley, 1952; MD, U. Calif., San Francisco, 1959; ScD (hon.), U. Toulouse, France, 1978. Postdoctoral fellow NIH, 1961-63; rsch. assoc. U. Calif., San Francisco, 1963-67; staff physician Kaiser Permanente Med. Ctr., San Francisco, 1964-91; dir. div. rsch. Kaiser Permanente Med. Program, Oakland, Calif., 1979-91; assoc. dir. Kaiser Found. Rsch. Inst., Oakland, 1985-91, sr. cons., 1991—; Kaiser Permanente Med. Program No. Calif. region. Adj. prof. U. Calif., San Francisco, 1975-92; chmn. instnl. rev. bd. Kaiser Permanente No. Calif. region, 1986-. Contbr. articles to profl. books and jours. Mem. bd. dirs Alameda County Meals on Wheels, 2004—; pres. bd. trustees French Found. Med. Res. & Edn., San Francisco, 1994-98. With US Army, 1944—46. Fellow ACP, Am. Coll. Med. Informatics; mem. Calif. Med. Assn., U. Calif. San Francisco Emeritus Faculty Assn. Avocations: flying, photography, swimming. Office Phone: 510-625-3140. Personal E-mail: e.vanbrunt@comcast.net.

VAN BRUNT, GARY T., tire dealer company executive; Asst mgr. to mgr., 2d Phoenix store Discount Tire Co. Inc., Scottsdale, Ariz., 1970—77, asst. v.p. Ariz. region, 1977—80, v.p. purchasing, We. region, 1980—85, sr. v.p. purchasing, all regions, 1985—97, exec. v.p. co. ops., 1997—99, CEO, 1999—2004, vice chmn., 2004—. Office: Discount Tire Co Inc 20225 N Scottsdale Rd Scottsdale AZ 85255

VAN BRUNT, WILLIAM A., lawyer; m. Gail Van Brunt; 3 children. BS with honors, Pa. State U.; MS, MIT; JD, Boston U. Sch. Law; LLM, Harvard Sch. Law. Rschr. AVCO Rsch. and Develop.; with Kenway and Jenny, Boston, McNee, Wallace, and Nurick, Harrisburg, Pa., Hershey Foods Corp., General Mills; sr. v.p., gen. counsel Carlson Companies, Inc, Minnetonka, Minn., 2000—. Office: Carlson Companies Inc PO Box 59159 Minneapolis MN 55459 E-mail: bvanbrunt@carlson.com. *

VAN BULCK, HENDRIKUS EUGENIUS, accountant; b. Beek en Donk, The Netherlands, Dec. 13, 1950; came to US, 1972; s. Marcellus Maria and Josephina Theodora (Koelman) Van B.; m. Margaret West, Aug. 7, 1976; children: Marcel Allen, Sydney Josette. Grad., Nijenrode, The Netherlands, 1972; MBA, U. Ga., Athens, 1974, PhD in Bus. Adminstrn., 1979. CPA, SC. Instr. U. SC, Sumter, 1975-77; asst. prof. Clemson U., SC, 1977-80; chmn. dept., assoc. prof. St. Andrew's Presbyn. Coll., Laurinburg, NC, 1980-83; staff acct. L. Allen West, CPA, Sumter, 1983-84; ptnr. West & Van Bulck, CPAs, Sumter, 1984-88, Van Bulck & Co., Sumter, 1989—. Instr. U. SC, Sumter, 1983—85, asst. prof., 2006—; cons. in field. Contbr. articles to profl. jours. Chmn. Make-a-Wish Found., Midlands, SC, 1983-90; asst. scoutmaster, dist. com. chmn. Boy Scouts Am.; treas. YMCA, Sumter; exec. com., fin. com. Pee Dee Area Coun. Recipient Mktg. award Netherlands Ctr. of Dirs., 1972. Mem. AICPA (accredited in bus. valuation 1999), SC Assn. CPAs, Ga. Soc. CPAs, Physicians Viewpoint Network, Kiwanis (pres. Sumter chpt. 1996-97), Med. Group Mgmt. Assn., Beta Gamma Sigma. Presbyterian. Avocations: sailing, photography. Home: 234 Haynsworth PO Box 1327 Sumter SC 29151-1327 Office: Van Bulck & Co CPAs 15 Broad St Sumter SC 29150-4224 Office Phone: 803-775-3000. Business E-Mail: hennie@vanbulckCPAs.com.

VAN BUREN, ABIGAIL (JEANNE PHILLIPS), columnist, educator; b. Mpls., Apr. 10, 1942; d. Morton and Pauline (Friedman) Phillips, (the founder of the Dear Abby advice column in 1956). Student, U. Colo., 1960—62. Writer Dear Abby Radio Show, CBS, 1965—71; columnist Dear Abby, 1987—. Bd. mem. Planned Parenthood of Los Angeles, 1989—90; life-time cons. Group for Advancement of Psychiatry, 1995—; bd. adv. Alzheimers Assn. of Los Angeles, 1996—; bd. mem. Rose and Jay Phillips Found., 1991—, ACLU of So. Calif. Found., 1998—; adv. bd. L.A. Internat. Women's Media Found. Courage in Journalism, 2000—; bd. adv. UCLA Med. Ctr., Ctr. for Rsch. and Training in Humane and Ethical Med. Care (CHEC), 2000—. Bd. advs. Planned Parenthood Fedn. Am., 2004; bd. judges Talbot's Charitable Found. Women's Scholarship Fund, 2006—; mem. White House Commn. Rememberance; bd. dirs. Planned Parenthood of LA, 1989—90, MADD, 2003—, Children's Rights Coun., 2003—; mem. Leadership Coun. Aids Project, LA, 2004; bd. dirs. Nat. Kidney Found., 2004. Recipient Generations of Choice award, Planned Parenthood of L.A., 1999, Minority Organ/Tissue Transplant Edn. Program (MOTTEP) Key of Life award, Howard U., Wash. DC, 2000, award of appreciation, US Gen. Svcs. Adminstrn. Fed. Consumer Info. Ctr., 2000, Star on Hollywood Walk of Fame for Dear Abby Radio Show, 2001, Recognition by the Office of Nat. Drug Control Policy (ONDCP), award from the White House and Substance Abuse and Mental Health Svcs. Adminstrn. for help in launching Nat. Inhalants and Poisons Awareness Week, 2001, Erasing the Stigma Leadership award, Didi Hirsch Mental Health Ctr., 2001, MOTTEP Award of Excellence, 2001, Commendation for Operation Dear Abby and OperationDearAbby.net, Dept. Navy and USMC, 2002, Appreciation for support of the military svc. mems. of the U.S. for Operation Dear Abby and OperationDearAbby.net, Space and Naval Warfare Sys. Ctr. (SPAWAR), 2002, Alzheimer's Assn. Maureen Reagan Advocacy Award, 2003, Appreciation award, Overeaters Anonymous, 2003, Advocacy award, Alzheimer's Assn. L.A., 2003, award of appreciation, US GSA Fed. Citizen Info. Ctr., 2004. Mem.: Nat. Adv. Coun. of Alzheimers Assn. Syndicated in the US, Brazil, Mex., Japan, Philippines, Fed. Republic Germany, India, Holland, Denmark, Can., Korea, Thailand, Italy, Hong Kong, Taiwan, Ireland, Saudi Arabia, Greece, France, Dominican Republic, P.R., Costa Rica, US Virgin Islands, Bermuda, China, Kuwait and Guam; published on the Internet at DearAbby.com and OperationDearAbby.net for messages to the military. Office: Phillips-Van Buren Inc 1880 Century Park E Ste 1400 Los Angeles CA 90067

VANBUREN, CAROLYN JEAN, special education educator; d. Joseph A. and Hannah Caroline Meyers; m. Robert Mathew Simons, Sept. 1, 2001; children: Garrick Rhett, Kari Jane. BS magna cum laude, Bemidji State U., 1972; MS with honors in Edn., U. Wis., 1987. Cert. mentally retarded tchr. Wis. Dept. Pub. Instrn., 1978, early childhood-exceptional needs tchr. Wis. Dept. Pub. Instrn., 1978, 1st-8th grade tchr. Wis. Dept. Pub. Instrn., 1978. Spl. edn. tchr. Anoka Sch. Dist., Minn., 1972—74, Rice Lake Sch. Dist., Wis., 1980—; spl. edn. cons. Coop. Ednl. Svc. Agy., Cumberland, 1975—76; exceptional edn. early childhood tchr. Turtle Lake Sch. Dist., 1976—78. Ednl. cons. Countryway Group Home, Cameron, Wis., 1984—87; home health care worker Gemini, Richfield, Wis., 2004, Indianhead, Barron, Wis., 2000—00; group home house parent Ag-Ri-Cove, Cameron, 2000—01. Vol. Spl. Olympics, Barron County, 2000—01; pub. rels. rep. First Luth. Ch., Barron, 2001—05. Mem.: NEA (assoc.), Wis. Edn. Assn. (assoc.). Democrat-Npl. Lutheran. Avocations: travel, interior design, walking, yoga, gardening. Home Phone: 715-458-2062. Personal E-mail: carolyn@rmsimons.com.

VANBUREN, DENISE DORING, corporate communications executive; b. Troy, NY, May 15, 1961; d. James L. and Eunice A. (Myers) Doring; m. Steven Paul VanBuren, Apr. 1, 1989; children: Schuyler Paul, Troy James Doring, Brett Steven VanBuren. BA in Mass Comm. magna cum laude, St. Bonaventure U., 1983; MBA, Mount St. Mary Coll., 1997. Reporter, news anchor Sta. WGNY-AM-FM, Newburgh, NY, 1984; news dir., anchor NewsCtr. 6, Dutchess County, NY, 1985-90; dir. media rels. Ctrl. Hudson Gas & Electric, Poughkeepsie, NY, 1993—, mgr. corp. comms., 1998-99, asst. v.p. corp. comm., 1999-2000, v.p. corp. comm. and cmty. rels., 2000—. Adj. prof. Marist Coll., Poughkeepsie, NY. Co-author: Historic Beacon, 1998, Beacon Revisited, 2003. Councilwoman City of Beacon, 1992-93, chmn. 85th anniversary celebration; pres. Beacon Hist. Soc., 1989-94; bd. dirs. Locust Grove Hist. Site, Stony Kill Found., Inc.; chmn. Dutchess County United Way Campaign, 2005. Recipient Salute to Women in Bus. & Industry award D.C. YWCA, 1990, 97, Outstanding Chpt. Regent award N.Y. State orgn. DAR, 1999, Dutchess award, Dutchess County Hist. Soc., 2005; named Vol. of Yr. award, City of Beacon, 1999. Mem.: DAR (vice regent Melzingah chpt. 1990—98, regent 1998—2001, chmn. state historian com. NY state 1998—2001, nat. chmn. PR 1999—2004, editor-in-chief, Am. Spirit mag.), Greater So. Dutchess C. of C. (bd. dirs.), Nat. Soc. Daus. of Union Vets. of the Civil War, Exch. Club of So. Dutchess (bd. dirs.). Republican. Roman Catholic. Avocations: genealogy, needlecrafts. Office: CH Energy Group Inc 284 South Ave Poughkeepsie NY 12601-4838

VAN BUREN, WILLIAM RALPH, III, lawyer; b. Newport News, Va., May 28, 1956; s. William Ralph Jr. and Anna Lee (Hite) Van B.; m. Kathryn Ann Moore, Dec. 31, 1983; children: Kathryn Meagan, Kaitlin Marie, William R. IV. BBA, Coll. William and Mary, 1978; JD, U. Va., 1981. Bar: Va. 1981. Ptnr. Kaufman & Canoles, Norfolk, Va., 1981—. Asst. sec., bd. dirs. Daily Press, Inc., Newport News, 1983-86; mem. Peninsula adv. bd. Investors Savs. Bank, 1988-91. Vice chmn. United Way Campaign, Norfolk, 1990; bd. dirs., Va. Opera, Norfolk, 1986-95, mem. exec. com., 1986-95; pres. Norfolk Planning Coun., 1987-98, mem. exec. com., 1987-98; trustee Chrysler Mus., Norfolk, 1995-2003, Shenandoah U., 1992-98; trustee, capital campaign chair Norfolk Acad., 1998-; chmn. bd. Va. Coll. Fund, Richmond, 1987-91; pres. Norfolk Forum, 1999-2000, bd. dirs., 1989-2000; bd. dirs. Peninsula Fine Arts Ctr., 1990-93; bd. visitors Ea. Va. Med. Sch., 1996-2002. Mem. ABA (comml. bus. and banking sect.), Va. Bar Assn. (chmn. young lawyers sect. 1991, pres. 2006), Va. Law Found. (pres. 2006), Am. Health Lawyers Assn., Norfolk-Portsmouth Bar Assn. (chmn. young lawyers sect. 1988-89, Newcomen Soc., Norfolk Yacht and Country Club, James River Country Club. Episcopalian. Avocations: golf, skiing, sailing. Home: 1552 Blanford Cir Norfolk VA 23505-1707 Office: Kaufman & Canoles PO Box 3037 150 W Main St Norfolk VA 23514-3037 Office Phone: 757-624-3220. Business E-Mail: wrvanburen@kaufcan.com.

VAN BUSKIRK, RONALD E., lawyer; b. Santa Fe, N. Mex., Oct. 19, 1946; BA, Stanford Univ., 1968; JD, Univ. Mich., 1974. Bar: Calif. 1975, US Dist. Ct. (ea., no., ctrl., so. dist. Calif.), US Ct. Claims, US Ct. Appeals (9th cir.). Assoc. to ptnr. Pillsbury Winthrop Shaw Pittman, San Francisco, 1975—, gen. counsel, chmn. Profl. Responsibility com. Founding mem. Law Firm Gen. Counsel Roundtable; bd. dir. Pacific Legal Found., 1994—, MPC Insurance Ltd., 1995—. Served US Army, 1968—71. Office: Pillsbury Winthrop Shaw Pittman 50 Fremont St San Francisco CA 94105 Office Phone: 415-983-1496. Office Fax: 415-983-1200. Business E-Mail: ronald.vanbuskirk@pillsburylaw.com.

VANBUTSEL, MICHAEL R., real estate broker, construction executive; b. Alma, Nebr., Dec. 7, 1952; s. Julius and Margaret (McCorkle) VanB.; m. Susan Parsons; children: Jamie, Krysta, Alexis. BArch, U. Nebr., 1975. Lic. real estate broker Fla. V.p. devel. J.C. Nichols Co. Real Estate, St. Petersburg, Fla., 1987-96; pres. North Star Devel., St. Petersburg, 1996—; real estate mgr., designated broker Danka Office Imaging, 1998-99; v.p., project exec. Beers Skanska USA Bldg. Co., Tampa, Fla., 1999—2004; project mgr. Tower divsn. Taylor Woodrow Cmtys., 2004—06; v.p. The Beach Residences Condominiums The Ritz Carlton Beach Club, 2004—06; sr. project mgr. tower divsn. WCI Cmtys. Inc., Palm Beach Gardens, Fla., 2006—. Chair Environ. Devel. Commn., St. Petersburg, 2003-04; chair cmty. advancement coun. U. So. Fla., St. Petersburg, 1998—2004. Housing commr. City of Phoenix; mem. Paradise Valley Planning Com.; bd. dirs. Am. Stage Theater, Cmty. Water Leadership Program; chmn. facilities and strategic planning com. U. South Fla., St. Petersburg, 1999—2002, chmn. acad. planning com.; bd. dirs. Pinellas Econ. Devel. Coun.; vice-chair environ. adv. com. S.W. Fla. Water Mgmt. Dist., 2002—; Pinellas adv. bd. ARC; allocations com. United Way, 1998—2000; mem. Real Estate Investment Coun., St. Petersburg USA and Russia Birthday Commemoration, 2002—03, Pinellas County Transp. Task Force, Pinellas Redevel. Task Force; mem. CEO search com. U. South Fla., St. Petersburg; chair legis. affairs com. devel. coun. All Children's Hosp.; pres. Mariners for Sen. John McCain, Ariz.; surrogate spkr. for Congressman Eldon Rudd; mem. Senate roundtable Sen. Connie Mack, Fla.; Westside campaign chair Rick Baker for Mayor, 2001; mem. Ivory Club Pinellas County Rep. Party, 2001—05, Pinellas County Assembly, 2002; bd. dirs. Gran Prix St. Petersburg 2003 Found. Mem. Fla. Gulfcoast Comml. Assn. Realtors, Pinellas Leadership (mem. selection com. 2003), Leadership Tampa Bay, St. Petersburg C. of C. (chair environ. com., chair transp. com.), Valley Leadership (Phoenix). Republican. Avocations: gourmet cooking, geo-political books, tai chi. Office: WCI Cmtys Inc 11601 Kew Gardens Ave Palm Beach Gardens FL 33410 Home Phone: 941-776-9648; Office Phone: 727-563-9882, 561-340-1100. Personal E-mail: michaelvb4@yahoo.com. Business E-Mail: michael.vanbutsel@us.taylorwoodrow.com, michaelvanbutsel@wcicommunities.com.

VAN CAMP, BRIAN RALPH, judge; b. Halstead, Kans., Aug. 23, 1940; s. Ralph A. and Mary Margaret (Bragg) Van C.; m. Diane D. Miller, 1992; children: M. Megan, Laurie E. AB, U. Calif., Berkeley, 1962, LLB, 1965. Bar: Calif. 1966. Dep. atty. gen., Calif., 1965-67; agy. atty. Redevel. Agy., City of Sacramento, 1967-70; asst./acting sec. Bus. and Trans. Agy., State of Calif., 1970-71; commr. of corps. State of Calif., Sacramento, 1971-74; partner firm Diepenbrock, Wulff, Plant & Hannegan, Sacramento, 1975-77, Van Camp & Johnson, Sacramento, 1978-90; sr. ptnr. Downey, Brand, Seymour & Rohwer, 1990-97; judge Superior Ct. Calif., Sacramento County, 1997—. Lectr. Calif. Continuing Edn. Bar, Practicing Law Inst., Calif. CPA Soc., Calif. Ctr. for Jud. Edn. and Rsch.; mem. jud. adv. bd. Am. Enterprise Inst./Brookings Jud. Edn. Program, 2007—. Contbr. articles to profl. jours. Mem. Rep. State Ctrl. Com. Calif., 1974-78; mem. electoral coll. Presdl. Elector for State of Calif., 1976; mem. Calif. Health Facilities Fin. Authority, 1985-89; mem. Capital Area Devel. Authority, 1989-97, chmn., 1990-97; mem. Calif. Jud. Coun. Task Force on Quality of Justice, 1998-99, Jud. Coun. Adv. Com. on Civil and Small Claims Law, 2002—, chair subcom. uniform rules, 2004-; bd. dirs. Sacramento Symphony Assn., 1973-85, Sacramento Symphony Found., 1993-2003, Sacramento Area Commerce and Trade Orgn., pres. 1986-87, Sacramento Valley Venture Capital Forum, 1986-90, League to Save Lake Tahoe, 1988-95, Valley Vision, Inc., 1993-97; elder Fremont Presbyn. Ch., 1967-. Recipient Sumner-Mering Meml. award Sacramento U. Calif. Alumni Assn., 1962, Thos. Jefferson award Am. Inst. Pub. Svc., 1994, Excellence in Achievement award Calif. Alumni Assn., 1997; named Outstanding Young Man of Yr., Sacramento Jaycees, 1970, Internat. Young Man of Yr., Active 20-30 Club Internat., 1973, Judge of Yr., Capitol City Trial Lawyers Assn., 2003. Mem. Am. Coll. Bus. Ct. Judges (charter), Boalt Hall Alumni Assn. (bd. dirs. 1991-94), Lincoln Club Sacramento Valley (bd. dirs. 1975-90, pres. 1984-86), U. Calif Men's Club (pres. 1968), Sutter Club, Kanadhar Ski Club, Rotary Club Sacramento (pres. 1993-94, Paul Harris Fellow award 1995), Comstock Club (pres. 1976-77). Republican. Presbyterian. Office: 720 9th St Sacramento CA 95814-1302 Office Phone: 916-874-8030. Business E-Mail: vancamp@saccourt.com.

VAN CAMPEN, STEPHEN BERNARD, executive recruiter, consultant; b. East Stroudsburg, Pa., Oct. 1, 1941; s. Bernard Allen and Marion (Van Whye) Van C.; m. Ellen Baars, July 22, 1989; children: Brendon, Regan, Meghan, Taylor, Hannah. BS in Sci. and Pre-Veterinary Med., Pa. State U., 1959-64; postgrad. in indsl. rels., George Washington U. Grad. Sch., 1965-68; law student, U. Balt., 1966-68. With FDA, Balt., Washington, 1964-66; indsl. rels. officer Joseph E. Seagrams & Sons, Balt., NYC, San Francisco, 1966-72; worldwide dir. exec. staffing RCA/Hertz Corp., NYC, 1972-74; dir. internat. indsl. rels. Revlon Internat., NYC, 1974; pres., owner, cons. Gilbert & Van Campen Exec. Search, Internat. (subs.: J.B. Gilbert Assocs., Inc., Amtrade Assocs., Internat., GVC Fin. Svcs.), NYC, 1974—; past owner, pres. Lillagaard Hotel Corp., Ocean Grove, NJ,

1992—; owner N.J. Profl. Meeting Planners Group; chmn. No. Shore Region Convention and Vis. Bur., Encore Svcs., Hackettstown, NJ, 1999—; pres. spl. investigations and verificatiuons divsn. Van Campen Assoc. Internat., 2003—. Appointed to N.J. Gov.'s Commn. on Internat. Trade, 1992; Bush White House nominee to Nat. Parks Adv. Commn., Dept. Interior; chmn. internat. trade subcom. ad hoc N.J. Assembly Small Bus. Adv. Coun.; bd. dirs. N.J. SBDC, N.J. Shore Region Tourism Coun.; named to Commerce and Econ. Devel. Transition Team for Gov.-elect Christine Todd Whitman; chmn. Econ. Devel. Task Force, Warren County, N.J., 1994; participant in meetings. with Pres. Castro 1st U.S.-Cuba Bus. Summit, Havanna, 1998. Rep. fundraiser; active N.J. Rep. Gov.'s Club, N.J. State Fin. Com.; appointed to Congressman Zimmer's Warren County N.J. Fed. Adv. Com., Warren County Econ. Adv. Coun., N.J. Gov.'s appointee 1988— and chmn. fed. enacted Del. Water Gap Nat. Recreation Area citizens adv. com., Gov.-elect Christie Todd Whitman Transition Team-Commerce and Econ. Devel. and Tourism; elected to Warren County Rep. Com.; chmn. adv. bd. Warren Presdl. Correctional Facility; chmn. Calno Cemetery Assn.; chmn. Warner County Econ. Devel. Blue Ribbon Task Force; vice chmn. bd. trustees Warren County C.C., 1983—, chmn. found. bd., presdl. search com. 2003, ops. com. 2003, ambassador N.Y. Coun. Cmty. Colls.; exec. bd. Tri-County Washington coun. and George Washington coun. Boy Scouts Am.; bd. dirs. N.J. Shore Regional Tourism Coun., N.Y. dir. SBDC, N.J. Juvenile Justice Adv. Bd.; mem. 1st N.J. Trade Del. Soviet Union; mem. commerce and econ. devel. transition team Gov.-elect Christie Whitman, N.J., 1994; chmn. N.J. assembly bus. retention Com. of Task Force for Bus. Rentention, Attraction, Expansion and Internat. Trade; chmn. N.J. Gov.'s Conf. Travel and Tourism, Atlantic City, 1994; chmn. N.J. No. Shore Region CUB Allaire Airport Conv. Ctr.; pres.-elect Warren County Econ. Partnership. Recipient Medal of Honor, Ellis Island, 1994, Disting. Citizen award Boy Scouts Am., 1992. Mem. ASTD, Am. Mgmt. Assns., Am. Coun. on Germany, U.S. C. of C., Nat. Fgn. Trade Coun., World Trade Inst., U.S.-USSR Trade and Econ. Coun., N.Y. C. of C. and Industry, N.J. C. of C., Commerce and Industry Assn. N.J., Am. C. of C.s and U.S. Bus. Couns. Abroad, Soc. Human Resource Mgmt., Nat. Assn. Corp. and Profl. Recruiters, Employment Mgmt. Assn., N.J. Hotel/Motel Assn. (bd. dirs., mem. exec. bd.), N.J. Travel Industry Assn. (bd. dirs., v.p. exec. bd.), N.Y. Pers. Mgmt. Assn., Soc. Plastics Engrs., Soc. Cosmetic Chemists, Small Bus. Adv. Coun., Ocean Grove C. of C. (vice chmn.). Republican. Methodist. Home: 37 Petersburg Rd Hackettstown NJ 07840-4903 Personal E-mail: stevevancampen@goes.com.

VANCASTLE, ROBIN, bank executive; b. Dec. 18, 1953; BS in Acctg., No. Ill. U., 1977. CPA. Pub. acct., 1979—90; dir. internal audit Cole Taylor Bank, 1990—93; grp. sr. v.p. fin. mgmt. Taylor Capital Group, Inc., 1993—2006, exec. v.p., 2004, chief acctg. officer, 2006—07, CFO, 2007—. Office: Taylor Capital Grp Inc 9550 West Higgins Rd Des Plaines IL 60018 Office Phone: 847-653-7978. *

VANCE, DAVID A., information systems educator; b. Anchorage, 1948; s. Alvin V. and Mary Vance; m. Nancy Niemann; children: John, Emily, Ryan. AA, Grossmont Coll., 1976; BBA, Nat. U., 1982, MBA, 1984, postgrad., 1985; PhD, So. Ill. U., 2000; postgrad., Trinity Sem., Ind., 2004—. Ordained to ministry United Christian Faith Ministries, 2002. Tech. supr. USN, San Diego, 1970-74; engr., project mgr. Wavetek Data Communications, San Diego, 1975-79; v.p. ops. Specialized Systems, Inc., San Diego, 1979-81; prin. Sunhill R&D, San Diego, 1981-84; exec. dir. Brunswick Inst. Tech., San Diego, 1985; tech. staff mem. Veda, Inc., Orlando, Fla. and San Diego, 1985-88; tng. analyst Eagle Tech., Inc., Winter Park, Fla., 1988-89; prof. mgmt. Fla. So. Coll., Orlando, 1988-94; tchr., student mgmt. doctoral program So. Ill. U., Carbondale, 1994-99; asst. prof. Miss. State U., 1999—2006. Prin. DA Vance & Assocs., Winter Park, 1986-94; adj. prof. mgmt. Webster U., 1991-94, Fla. So. Coll., 1988-94; vis. asst. prof. So. Ill. U., 1991-94; lectr. in field. Rep. precinct committeeman, Orange County, Fla., 1988, del. state conv., 1988; chmn. svc. com. CSO, Inc., 1991. Recipient Achievement award ACCESS, San Diego, 1980; Worthy scholar Woodrow Wilson Found., 1966, Leadership scholar Nat. U., San Diego, 1984. Mem.: Info. Resources Mgmt. Assn., Computer Profls. for Social Responsibility, Am. MENSA, Ltd. Avocations: outdoor sports, music. Office: Miss State U Dept Mgmt and IS PO Box 9581 Mississippi State MS 39762-9581

VANCE, DIANNE SANCHEZ, mathematician, educator; d. Thomas Clarence and Jean Rose Sanchez; 1 child, Jeney Michelle Sanchez. BA, Calif. State U., Fullerton, 1977; MEd, U. Utah, Salt Lake City, 1993. Tchr. Tahoe Truckee Sch. Dist., Calif., 1971—76, Wasatch Sch. Dist., Heber City, Utah, 1980—90; tennis coach Park City High Sch., 1993—98, tchr., 1990—2002; tchr., coord. English as 2d lang. Phillips Acad., Andover, Mass., 1991—2003; tchr. math. TED Kolej, Ankara, Turkey, 2002—03, Fulbright Exch. Park City Sch. Dist., 2003—. Vol. Sundance, Park City, 1995—2006; gate judge Olympics, 2002. Mem.: ASCD, Park City Edn. Assn. Avocations: travel, skiing, tennis, golf. Office: Park City Sch Dist 2700 Kearns Blvd Park City UT 84060 Business E-mail: dvance@pcshools.us.

VANCE, KIM, lawyer; BA with highest honors, U. Ctrl. Ark.; JD with honors, U. Ark. Ptnr., supr. employment discrimination law sect. King & Ballow, Nashville; gen. counsel, corp. sec. Tractor Supply Co., Brentwood, Tenn., 2003—. Spkr. in field. Bd. dirs. Ctr. Nonprofit Mgmt. Mem.: ABA (mem. labor sect., employment law sect.), Lawyers' Assn. for Women. Office: Tractor Supply Co 200 Powell Pl Brentwood TN 37027 Office Phone: 615-366-4600.

VANCE, MARY LEE, academic administrator; b. Seoul, Korea, Nov. 16, 1957; d. Irwin F. and Mae Hoeft; m. Eric J. Vance. BA, U. Wis., 1979, MA, 1983; PhD, Mich. State U., 1993. From advisor to coord, Mich. State U., East Lansing, 1984-93; coord. Holmes Scholars Holmes Group, East Lansing, 1993-94; dir. edn. student svcs. Iowa State U., Ames, 1994-97; dir. acad. support and advising svcs. George Mason U., Fairfax, Va., 1997—2001; dir. career, disability and advisement svcs. U. Wis. Superior, 2002—. Adj. asst. prof. Iowa State U., 1994-97; cons. Southeastern Assn. Edn. Opportunity Program Personnel, Memphis, 1993-94. Author: Disabled Faculty and Staff in a Disabling Society: Multiple Perspectives in Higher Education, 2007; mem. editl. bd. Nat. Acad. Advising Assn. Jour., 2002, Jour. Postsecondary Edn. and Disability, 2007—; contbr. articles to jours. Mem. strategic planning steering com. Ames Cmty. Sch. Dist., 1995-96; mem. Leadership Ames, 1995; bd. dirs. YWCA, Ames, 1996; mem. Make A Wish, 1998—. Recipient Outstanding Asian Pacific Am. Faculty/Staff awards, 1985-93, All U. Diversity Photo award, 1992, Outstanding Grad. Woman Spl. Merit award, 1992, Appreciation, Southeastern Assn. Ednl. Opportunity Program Pers., 1992, 93, 94, Office Supportive Svcs., 1993, Holmes Scholars, 1994, Holmes Group, 1994, Cert. of Achievement, Leadership Ames, 1995, Cert. Recognition, Univ. Disability Group, 2000, Cert. Appreciation, Korean Quar., 2003, Woman of Color, UW Superior, 2003, Multicultural Alumni award, U. Wis., 2007; named to AHEAD Leadership Inst. Universal Design, 2005, Ann. Citizen's Police Acad., 2006. Mem. Nat. Orgn. Acad. Advising Assn. (cons. 2006—, mem. jour. editl. bd., 2002—), Assn. Higher Edn. and Disability (bd. dirs., 2007—, Nat. Orientation Dirs. Assn., Asian Pacific Am. Women's Leadership Inst., Acad, Affairs Adminstrs., Nat. Assn. Colls. and Employers (chair acad. staff senate). Bapt. Avocations: reading, gourmet cooking, movies, writing book reviews. Office: Wis Pub Liberal Arts Coll Univ Wis PO Box 2000 134 Old Main Belknap & Catlin Superior WI 54880-4500 Office Phone: 715-394-8580. Business E-mail: mvance@uwsuper.edu.

VANCE, MICHAEL C., lawyer; b. Marshalltown, Iowa, May 31, 1951; s. Randall S. and Irma Vance; m. Bonnie K. Becker, Jan. 1, 1995; children: Thomas R., Patrick M. BA in Polit. Sci. and Econs., U. Iowa, 1973, JD with distinction, 1976. Bar: Iowa 1976, U.S. Dist. Ct. (so. dist.) Iowa 1976, U.S. Tax Ct. 1991. Sole practice, Mt. Pleasant, Iowa, 1976—. Atty. City of Wayland, Iowa, 1976—; instr. bus. law Iowa Wesleyan Coll., Mt. Pleasant, 1977-78; asst. county atty. Henry County, Mt. Pleasant, 1979-97, jud. magistrate, 1997—. Bd. dirs. Cmty. Mental Health of Henry, Louisa and Jefferson Counties, Mt. Pleasant, 1977-82; chairperson Henry County Dems., Mt. Pleasant, 1978-83; pres. Mt. Pleasant Sesquicentennial Assn., 1984-86; mem. St. Alphonsus Ch. Parish Coun. pres., 1983-85; trustee Mt. Pleasant, 1985-2006, Fin. Coun., 1985—. Mem. ABA, Iowa Bar Assn. (bd. govs. 1996-2002, jud. adminstrn. com. 2002, scope and correlations 2003-05, chmn. 2004-05, adminstrv. coun. 2004-05), Henry County Bar Assn. (sec.-treas. 1977-78, v.p. 1978-79, pres. 1979-80, 88-91), Iowa Trial Lawyers Assn., Iowa Conf. Bar Assn. Presidents (bd. dirs. 1979-81), Iowa Assn. Jud. Magistrates (bd. dirs. 1998-2002, 04—), Mt. Pleasant C. of C. (bd. dirs. 1991-93, named Citizen of Yr. 1985), Mt. Pleasant Jaycees (bd. dirs. 1978-83), Rotary, KC, Omicron Delta Kappa, Omicron Delta Epsilon. Roman Catholic. Home: 2005 Bittersweet Cir Mount Pleasant IA 52641-8301 Office: PO Box 469 101 N Jefferson St Mount Pleasant IA 52641-0469

VANCE, PATRICIA H., state senator; b. Williamsport, Pa., Mar. 19, 1936; RN, Harrisburg Hosp. Sch. Nursing, 1957. Former mem. Pa. Ho. of Reps., Harrisburg, 1990—2004; mem. Pa. Senate, Harrisburg, 2004—. Home: 3806 Market St Camp Hill PA 17011-4327 Office: Pa Senate Rm 187 Main Capitol PO Box 203031 Harrisburg PA 17120-3031

VANCE, ROBERT PATRICK, lawyer; b. Feb. 12, 1948; s. James Robert and Lucy Juanita (McMath) V.; m. Sarah Elizabeth Savoia, June 11, 1971; 1 child, Robert Patrick, Jr. BA with honors, La. State U., 1970, JD, 1975. Bar: La. 1975, U.S. Dist. Ct. (ea. dist.) La. 1975, U.S. Dist. Ct. (mid. dist.) La. 1978, U.S. Dist. Ct. (we. dist.) La. 1979, U.S. Ct. Appeals (5th cir.) 1975, U.S. Ct. Appeals (11th cir.) 1981, U.S. Supreme Ct. 1981. Assoc. Jones, Walker, Waechter, Poitevent, Carrere & Denegre, New Orleans, 1975-80, ptnr., 1980—, exec. com., 1991—95, 1997—2002, 2004—05, mng. ptnr., 1994—95, 1999—2000, 2004, chmn. litigation, 2003—. Contbr. articles to profl. jours. Fellow Am. Coll. Bankruptcy, Nat. Bankruptcy Conf. (mem. exec. com.); mem. ABA (past chair bankruptcy litigation com.), Am. Law Inst., La. State Bar Assn. (past chair consumer and bankruptcy law sect., chmn. continuing legal edn. com.), New Orleans Bar Assn., La. Bankers Assn. (chmn. bank counsel com. 1992-93), Pi Sigma Alpha, Phi Beta Kappa (Faculty Group award), Phi Kappa Phi. Democrat. Roman Catholic. Office: Jones Walker Waechter Poitevent Carrere & Denegre 201 Saint Charles Ave Ste 5200 New Orleans LA 70170-5100 Office Phone: 504-582-8194. Business E-Mail: pvance@joneswalker.com.

VANCE, RODNEY, film producer, writer; s. Clifford and Bonnie Vance; life ptnr. Mary Elizabeth Bland; 1 child, Chelsea. MA, Andrews U., Berrien Springs, Mich., 1981; MFA, Cath. U. Am., Washington, 1988. Pres. Singular Entertainment, Pasadena, Calif., 2007—. Head writer: (TV series) The Evidence (Best New Religion/Ethics Show and Best New Pilot, 2001); Lifestyle Magazine (Telly award, 2001); prodr.: (screenplays) Operation Babylift, Conspiracy Cafe; prodr.: (TV series) Discovery; author: (films) Angel in Chains (Best in Category Sonscreen Film and Video Festival, 2004), In the Shadow of Bin Laden, (plays) Token (Judge's Choice award Edward Albee Internat. Playwrighting Competition, 1999), The Man, the Woman, the Indian. Mem.: Acad. TV Arts and Sciences, Writer's Guild of Am. West, Dramatist's Guild (assoc.), Mensa. Office: Singular Entertainment 275 S Marengo Ave Ste 30 Pasadena CA 91101 Office Phone: 310-492-5571. Office Fax: 310-492-5563. Business E-Mail: rod@singularent.com.

VANCE, SUE ANN, musician, educator; b. Medicine Lodge, Kans., Aug. 16, 1937; d. Trice Hubert and Catherine O. (Stone) Newsom; m. Jerry Wayne Vance, Aug. 15, 1962 (dec.); children: Todd, Kayla Vance Ginnings. B Music Edn., Wichita State U., Kans., 1959, M Music Edn., 1962. Piano instr. Labette County Cmty. HS, Altamont, Kans., 1959—61; accompanist U. La., Monroe, 1967—88; K-12 music instr. Deer Pub. Sch. Dist., Ark., 1991—2002; adj. piano instr., accompanist Ark. Tech. U., Russellville, 2002—. Part-time instr. piano U. La., Monroe, 1978—86; organist various chs., Monroe, 1976—88; organist 1st Presbyn. Ch., Harrison, Ark., 1993—2003; piano adjudicator Federated Music Clubs, Monroe, 1970—88; mem. Vance-White Duo piano team, Monroe, 1978—90. Pres. NW Ark. Concert Assn., Harrison, 1995—99. Recipient Naftzager Judges award, Wichita Symphony, 1958. Mem.: Am. Choir Dirs. Assn., Music Educators Nat. Conf., Nat. Guild Piano Tchrs. (piano adjudicator 1999—). Avocations: knitting, reading, sewing, crossword puzzles. Home: HC31 Box 393 Deer AR 72628 Office: Ark Tech U Music Dept Q St Russellville AR 72802

VANCE, VANESSA L., lawyer; b. Beaumont, Tex., Aug. 21, 1968; BA in Biology, Tex. A&M U., Coll. Sta., 1989; JD, South Tex. Coll. Law, Houston, 1994. Bar: Tex. 1994, US Dist. Ct. (all dists. Tex.). Atty. Connelly, Baker, Maston, Wotring & Jackson, L.L.P., Houston. Bd. dirs. Vance-Sandovel Enterprises, L.L.P., 1998—, Slaney Designs, 2003—. Named a Rising Star, Tex. Super Lawyers mag., 2006. Fellow: Houston Bar Found.; mem.: Tex. Assn. Def. Counsel, Houston Bar Assn. *

VANCE, VERNE WIDNEY, JR., retired lawyer; b. Omaha, Mar. 10, 1932; s. Verne Widney and June Caroline (Henckler) V.; m. Anita Paine, June 27, 1970; children: Lisa J. Castleton, Charles Hebard Paine, Virginia Caroline. AB, Harvard U., 1954, JD, 1957. Bar: D.C. 1957, Mass. 1964. Law clk. U.S. Dist. Judge, Mass., 1957-58; assoc. Covington & Burling, Washington, 1958-60; atty. adv. Devel. Loan Fund, Washington, 1960-61; legal counsel US AID, Washington, 1961-63; assoc. Foley, Hoag & Eliot LLP, Boston, 1963-67, ptnr., 1967-2000; ret., 2001. Lectr. law Boston U., 1964-66; corp. clk. S.S. Pierce Co., 1971-72. Pres. UN Assn. Greater Boston, 1964-66, 77-78, treas., 1974-77; mem. Mass. Adv. Council on Edn., 1969-75, chmn., 1975; mem. Dem. City Com., Newton, Mass., 1972—, Gov.'s Local Govt. Adv. Commn., 1986-90; alderman City of Newton, 1982-91, 2004—; pres. Newton Bd. of Aldermen, 1988-91; mem. Newton Sch. Com., 1994-2001, chair 2000-01; trustee Judge Baker Children's Ctr., 1994—, clk., 2002--; trustee Mass. Bay C.C., 1987-98, vice chmn., 1989-91, chmn. 1991-97; pres. Mass. C.C. Assn., 1996-97. Contbr. articles to profl. jours. Bd. dirs. Newton-Needham C. of C., Boston Archtl. Ctr. Recipient Disting. Cmty. Svc. award, Mass. Bay CC, 1997. Democrat. Unitarian Universalist. Avocations: politics, art, reading, cooking, travel. Home: 101 Old Orchard Rd Chestnut Hill MA 02467-1202 Home (Summer): 185 Colony Rd Arkville NY 12406 Personal E-mail: vvance@rcn.com.

VAN CLEAVE, MICHELLE KIM, former federal official; b. 1953; BA, MA, JD, U. So. Calif. Assoc. Horvitz and Greines, LA; asst. for def. and foreign policy to Congressman Jack Kemp, 1981—87; nat. security asst. Ho. Rep. Conf., 1981—87; staff mem. Ho. Appropriations subcom. on Fgn. Ops., 1981—87; gen. counsel, asst. dir. nat. security affairs White House Office of Sci. and Tech. Policy, 1987—93; minority counsel to com. on sci., space, and tech., 1989; of counsel Feith & Zell, P.C., 1993—97; co-founder, pres. Nat. Security Concepts, Inc., 1997—2001; spl. asst. to under sec. for policy, sr. advisor for homeland def. US Dept. Def., Washington, 2001—03; nat. counterintelligence exec. Office Nat. Counterintelligence Exec., Washington, 2003—06. Mem.: DC Bar Assn., Calif. Bar Assn.

VAN CLEVE, LIBBY (ELIZABETH W. VAN CLEVE), music educator, writer; b. Alexandria, Va., Aug. 22, 1958; d. Harry Rae Jr. and Ruth Gill Van Cleve; m. Jack M. Vees, June 29, 1985; 1 child, Nola Vees. BA magna cum laude, Bowdoin Coll., Brunswick, Maine, 1980; MFA, Calif. Inst. Arts, Valencia, 1984; MA, Yale U. Sch. Music, New Haven, 1987, MusMA, 1988, DMA, 1992. Adminstrv. asst. New Music Festival, LA, 1985, Meet the Composer, LA, 1985—86; coord. Area Innovators and Local Circuits Concert Series, Real Art Ways, Hartford, Conn., 1990—92; mgr. Chez Vees, 1990—93; asst. dir. oral history, Am. music Yale U., New Haven, 1993—2000, assoc. dir. oral history, Am. music, 2000—. Radio broadcast rev. com. Minn. Composers Forum, 1981—82; adj. prof. oboe Conn. Coll., New London, Wesleyan U., Middletown, 1990—; cons. Common Sense Composers Collective, 1993; panelist, spkr. New England Found. Arts, Providence, 1993; performer, interviewee WNYC- NPR, NYC, 1997, performer, 98; recording performer. Author: Oboe Unbound, 2004; co-author: (book and CD) Composer's Voices from Ives to Ellington, 2005 (Deems Taylor award, ASCAP, 2006, Ind. Book Pub. award, 2006); performer: Anthony Braxton Festival, NYC, 1995. Recipient Sue Winchell Burnett Music prize, Bowdoin Coll., 1980, Alumni Assn. prize, Yale U. Sch. Music, 1988; fellow, Bach Aria Group Festival and Inst., 1991; grantee, Jerome Found, 1986, North West Area Found., 1986, Minn. Composers Forum, 1986, summer residency, Banff Ctr., 1989, Mary Flagler Cary Charitable Trust, 1991, chamber music residency, Cervantino Music Festival, Mex., 1994, Wesleyan U., 1997; Ellen Battel Stoeckel scholar, Yale U., 1985, 1987, commission, Digital Media Ctr., 1999. Mem.: Internat. Double Reed Soc. (columnist Drastic Measures). Avocation: gardening. Home: Apt 1W 8 Hughes Pl New Haven CT 06511-4910 Office: OHAM Yale Univ 310 Prospect St New Haven CT 06521 Office Phone: 203-432-1988.

VAN CLEVE, ROBERT BALDWIN, cardiologist; b. St. Louis, Dec. 1, 1931; s. William T. and Catherine Cornelia (Moore) Van C.; m. Sarah Agnes Towers, July 9, 1955; children: Sarah Elizabeth Weldon, Catherine Moore Bauman, Mary Agnes Miller, Robert B. Jr. AB, Princeton U., 1954; MD, Columbia U., 1958. Diplomate Am. Bd. Internal Medicine, Am. Bd. Cardiovasc. Disease. Intern, resident U. of Va. Hosp., Charlottesville, 1958-61; ward resident Barnes Hosp., St. Louis, 1962; Harvard Med. Sch. fellow Mass. Gen. Hosp., 1965; cardiologist Riverside Clinic, Jacksonville, Fla., 1965-98, Jacksonville Cardiology Clinic, 1998—2004, Diagnostic Cardiology, 2004—. Cardiology cons. USN Hosp., Jacksonville, 1965-72; clin. prof. medicine U. Fla., 1977-88; chief of staff Riverside Hosp., Jacksonville, 1983-84, chief cardiology, 1985-90; chmn. hosp. authority U. Hosp.; v.p. attending staff Found. Duval County Interns and Residents. Contbr. articles to profl. jours., including Circulation, Jour. Am. Med Assn., Jour. Fla. Med. Assn. Chmn. recreation adv. bd. City of Jacksonville; elder 1st Presbyn. Ch.; bd. dirs. Salvation Army, Jacksonville. Lt. comdr. USN, 1962—64. Fellow: ACP, Am. Coll. Cardiology. Republican. Avocations: tennis, scuba diving, golf, gardening. Home: 3500 Richmond St Jacksonville FL 32205-9422 Office: 1824 King St Ste 300 Jacksonville FL 32205 Office Phone: 904-388-1820.

VAN CLEVE, RUTH GILL, retired lawyer; b. Mpls., July 28, 1925; d. Raymond S. and Ruth (Sevon) Gill; m. Harry R. Van Cleve, Jr., May 16, 1952 (dec. Oct. 2001); children: John Gill, Elizabeth Webster, David Hamilton Livingston. Student, U. Minn., 1943; AB magna cum laude, Mt. Holyoke Coll., 1946, LLD, 1976; LLB, Yale U., 1950. Bar: DC 1950, Minn. 1950. Intern Nat. Inst. Pub. Affairs, 1946-47; atty. Dept. Interior, 1950-54, asst. solicitor, 1954-64; dir. Office Territorial Affairs, 1964-69, 1977-80, dep. asst. sec., 1980-81, acting asst. sec., 1993; atty. Solicitor's Office, 1981-93, FPC, 1969-75, asst. gen. counsel, 1975-77. Author: The Office of Territorial Affairs, 1974, The Application of Federal Laws to the Territories, 1993. Mem. Guam War Claims Rev. Commn., 2003—04. Recipient Fed. Woman's award, 1966, Disting. Svc. award Dept. Interior, 1968, Presdl. Rank award, Pres. U.S., 1989. Mem.: Phi Beta Kappa. Unitarian. Home: 3440 S Jefferson St Apt 1015 Falls Church VA 22041

VANCO, JOHN L., art museum director; b. Erie, Pa., Aug. 21, 1945; s. John Jr. and Alice (Crozier) V.; m. Kathleen Merski, 1971; children: John H., Jesse L. BA, Allegheny Coll., 1967. Dir. Erie (Pa.) Art Mus., 1968—. Mem. adv. panels Pa. Coun. on the Arts, Harrisburg, 1974—, Mid Atlantic Arts Found., Balt., 1992, 2002, Nat. Endowment for Arts, 2000; curator Contemporary Music Series, 1982—, Erie Art Mus. Blues and Jazz Festival, 1992—. Photographer miscellaneous exhbns.; curator miscellaneous exhbns. including A Peculiar Vision: The Work of George Ohr, Eva Zeisel: The Shape of Life, The Mad Potter of Biloxi, From Mickey to the Grinch: Art of the Animated Film, Poems in Clay: Arthur Osborne's Plastic Sketches for the Low Art Tile Works, Teco: Art Pottery of the Prairie Sch., In Harmony with the Earth; author: A Roycroft Desktop: Musings on Elbert Hubbard and the Roycroft Shops, 1994, Loud & Clear: Resonator Guitars and the Dopyera Brothers' Legacy to American Music, 1998, Structured Color: Kiyokatsu Matsumiya, 2003. Chief adminstrv. officer Discovery Square, Erie, 1991-92; bd. dirs. Pa. Humanities Coun., 2001—, Pa. Fedn. Mus. and Hist. Orgns. Office: Erie Art Mus 411 State St Erie PA 16501-1106 Office Phone: 814-459-5477. Business E-Mail: jvanco@erieartmuseum.com.

VAN CURA, JOYCE BENNETT, librarian; b. Madison, Wis., Mar. 25, 1944; d. Ralph Eugene and Florence Marie (Cramer) Bennett; m. E. Jay Van Cura, July 5, 1986. BA in Liberal Arts (scholar), Bradley U., Peoria, Ill., 1966; MLS, U. Ill., Champaign-Urbana, 1971. Libr. asst. Rsch. Libr. Caterpillar Tractor Co., Peoria, Ill., 1966-67; ref. libr., instr. libr. tech. Ill. Ctrl. Coll., East Peoria, Ill., 1967-73; asst. prof. Sangamon State U. (U. Ill.-Springfield), Springfield, Ill., 1973-80, assoc. prof., 1980-86; head libr. ref. and info. svcs. dept. Ill. Inst. Tech., 1987-90; dir. Learning Resources Ctr. Morton Coll., 1990—2003. Reviewer Libr. Jour., Am. Ref. Books Ann.; convenor Coun. II, Ill. Clearinghouse for Acad. Libr. Instrn., 1978; presentor 7th Ann. Conf. Acad. Libr. Instrn., 1977, Nat. Women's Studies Assn., 1983, others; participant Gt. Lakes Women's Studies Summer Inst., 1981, Nat. Inst. Leadership Devel. seminar, 1995. Contbr. articles to profl. jours. Pres. Springfield chpt. NOW, 1978—79; invited Susan B. Anthony luncheon, 1978, 1979; mem. adv. bd. Suburban Libr. Sys., 1992—94, Nat. Commn. Learning Resources; v.p. membership Riverside chpt. Lyric Opera Chgo., 1994—96, 1999—, mem. chpts. exec. bd., 2006—; active Riverside Arts Ctr.; Dem. precinct Committeewoman, 1982—85; vice-moderator Fourth Presbyn. Women, 1989—90; elder Riverside (Ill.) Presbyn. Ch., 1992—, mem. session, 1993—96, 2000—01, mem. adminstrn. com., 1993—2003, chmn. adminstrn. com., 1993—96, 1999, 2000—01, mem. endowment com., 1996—98, treas. bd. trustees, 2004—, bd. trustees, 2005—, sec. bd. trustees, 2005—; bd. dirs. Berwyn-Cicero Coun. on Aging, 2000—03. Ill. state scholar, 1962-66; recipient Citizenship award Am. Legion, 1962, Cert. of Recognition Ill. Bicentennial Commn., 1974. Mem.: AAUW (bd. dirs. Riverside br. 1992—94, 1997—99, chmn. standing com. on women Springfield br., com. on women Ill. state divsn.), ALA, Ill. Libr. Assn. (presenter 1984), Nat. Assn. Women in C.C., Springfield Art Assn., No. Ill. Learning Resources Consortium (del. 1990—2003, steering com. West Suburban postsecondary consortium 1996—2000), Nat. Women's Studies Assn. (presenter 1983, 1984, 1995), Women in Mgmt., Am. Mgmt. Assn., No. Ill. Learning Resources Consortium Bd. (del. 2006—), Spl. Librs. Assn., Ill. Assn. Coll. and Rsch. Librs. (bibliog. instrn. com.), Libr. Info. and Tech. Assn., Libr. Adminstr. and Mgmt. Assn. (ref. and adult svcs. divsn.), Assn. Coll. and Rsch. Librs., Riverside Presbyn. Ch. Women, Nat. Trust Hist. Preservation, Am. Opera Soc., Riverside Dancing Club, Riverside Garden Club, Musicians Club of Women Chgo., Beta Phi Mu. Home: 181 Scottswood Rd Riverside IL 60546-2221

VANDAELE, BART, chef; Chef de cuisine Piet Huyentruyt, 1990—96; sous chef de cuisine Restaurant Scholteshof, 1996—97; exec. chef residence of Head Del. European Comm. to US, 1997—2000, Dutch Amb. to US, 2000—03, Belga Café, Washington. Contbr. The new generation: young chefs from Belgium, Original restaurants: Jan Maesen, Piet Huysentruyt: Eigentijds & Eigenzinng. Named one of Washington DC's Rising Stars, StarChefs.com, 2006. Office: Belga Cafe 514 8th St SE Washington DC 20003 Office Phone: 202-544-0100. Office Fax: 202-522-0204. *

VAN DAM, HEIMAN, psychoanalyst; b. Leiden, Netherlands; s. Machiel and Rika van D.; m. Barbara C. Strona, Oct. 6, 1945; children: Machiel, Claire Ilena, Rika Rosemary. AB, U. So. Calif., 1942, MD, 1945. Fellow in child psychiatry Pasadena (Calif.) Child Guidance Clinic, 1950; gen. practice psychiatry and psychoanalysis LA, 1951—2006; instr. L.A. Psychoanalytic Inst., LA, 1959—2000, co-chmn. com. on child psychoanalysis, 1960-67, tng. and supervising psychoanalyst, 1972—; supr. child and adolescent psychoanalysis So. Calif. Psychoanalytic Inst., 1986—. Cons. Reiss Davis Child Study Center, 1955-76, Neighborhood Youth Assn., LA, 1964-69; assoc. clin. prof. psychiatry and pediats. UCLA Sch. Medicine, 1960-96, clin. prof. psychiatry and pediats., 1996—; vis. supr. child psychoanalysis San Francisco Psychoanalytic Inst., 1969-79, 2002—, Denver Psychoanalytic Inst., 1972-74; adv. bd. Western State U. Coll. Law, Fullerton, Calif., 1965-83. Corr. editor Arbeits Hefte Kinderanalyse, 1985—2005; contbr. articles to profl. jours. Trustee, edn. com. Center for Early Edn., 1964-92, v.p., 1978-79; bd. dirs. Child Devel. and Psychotherapy Tng. Program, LA, 1975-80, pres., 1975-77; bd. dirs. LA Child Devel. Center, 1977-86, treas., 1978-80; mem. cult clinic Jewish Family Service, L.A., 1978-86; bd. dirs. Lake Arrowhead Crest Estates, 1990-99. Capt. M.C. AUS, 1946-48. Mem. Am. Psychoanalytic Assn. (com. on ethics 1977-80), Assn. Child Psychoanalysis (councillor 1966-69, sec. 1972-74, nominating com. 1978-84, membership com. 1988—2005, Marianne Kris lectr. 1995), Internat. Assn. Infant Psychiatry (co-chmn. program com. 1980-83), Internat. Soc. Adolescent Psychiatry (sci. adv. com. 1988-2004), Phi Beta Kappa. Office: 2864 McConnell Dr Los Angeles CA 90064-4658 Office Phone: 310-839-3232.

VANDAME, JEAN-MARIE RICHARD, diversified financial services company executive; b. Gien, France, Oct. 30, 1960; s. Marc and Antoinette (Dumouchel de Premare) V.; m. Chantal Marie de Blocquel de Croix de Wismes, Sept. 3, 1983; children: Thomas, Camille, Clemence, Alix. MS, Inst. Super. Electronique, Paris, 1982; MBA, Inst. Adminstrn. Entreprises, Paris, 1984. Product mktg. engr. Tex Instruments, Paris, 1983-84, field sales engr. Rennes, France, 1984-86; sr. mgr. Ernst & Young, Paris, 1986—92, assoc. ptnr., 1995—96, internat. ptnr., 1996—2000; pres. KnowledgeWare, Brussels, 1992—95; v.p. CG Ernst & Young, Chgo., 2000—03; ptnr. Ernst & Young, Paris, 2004—. Home: 24 Avenue Theophile Gautier 75016 Paris France Home Phone: +33 145 24 23 93; Office Phone: +33 146 93 44 03. E-mail: jean-marie.vandame@fr.ey.com.

VANDAMENT, WILLIAM EUGENE, retired academic administrator; b. Hannibal, Mo., Sept. 6, 1931; s. Alva E. and Ruth Alice (Mahood) V.; m. Margery Vandament, Feb. 2, 1952; children: Jane Louise, Lisa Ann. BA, Quincy Coll., 1952; MS, So. Ill. U., 1953; MS in Psychology, U. Mass., 1963, PhD, 1964; LittD, No. Mich. U., 1997. Psychologist Bacon Clinic, Racine, Wis., 1954-61; NDEA fellow U. Mass., Amherst, 1961-64; asst. prof. SUNY, Binghamton, 1964-69, univ. examiner and dir. instl. research, 1969-73, asst. v.p. planning, instl. research, 1972-76; exec. asst. to pres., dir. budget and resources Ohio State U., Columbus, 1976-79, v.p. fin. and planning, 1979-81; sr. v.p. adminstrn. NYU, NYC, 1981-83; provost, vice chancellor acad. affairs Calif. State U. System, Long Beach, 1983-87; Trustees prof. Calif. State U., Fullerton, 1987-92; pres. No. Mich. U., 1991-97, ret., 1997. Contbr. articles to psychol. jours. and books on higher edn. Office: 2662 E 20th St Apt 310 Signal Hill CA 90755 E-mail: vandament@aol.com.

VAN DE BOGART, DEBRA SCHERWERTS, medical/surgical nurse, researcher; b. Claremont, NH, Aug. 6, 1954; d. William Earl and Barbara Louise (Hadley White) Scherwerts. RN, Sacred Heart Sch. Nursing, Manchester, NH, 1975; student, Cypress Coll., Calif., 1976, U. Calif., Riverside, 1978. RN Calif., 1975, cert. home health nurse, Calif., 1997. Charge nurse, med.-surg. pediat. West Anaheim Cmty. Hosp., Anaheim, Calif., 1975—84; charge nurse, med.-surg. geriat. Humana West Anaheim, Anaheim, Calif., 1984—87; home health nurse, obstet. Physician's Care, Brea, Calif., 1988—90, Am. Home Health, Santa Ana, Calif., 1988—92; staff nurse, rsch. clin. studies ctr. Harbor-UCLA Med. Ctr., Torrance, Calif., 1993—94; nurse rschr. various profit and non-profit orgns., Anaheim, Calif., 1994—, RN coord., cons., 1994—. Contbr. workshop Focus on Health, 1982; mem. citizens adv. com., health Calif. State Assembly, 1982—; cons., home care for MD's Am. Home Health We. Med. Ctr., Santa Ana, 1991—; RN clin. advisor, staff devel. Cmty. Svcs. Projects, Orange and LA Counties, 2000—. Recipient cert. of recognition, Calif. State Legis., 1982. Mem.: ANA, Assn. Am. Acad. Bereavement, Sigma Theta Tau. Democrat. Roman Catholic. Avocations: violin, travel.

VAN DE BOVENKAMP, SUE ERPF, charitable organization executive; b. N.Y.C.; d. George Norton and Bettina Lions (Hearst) Mortimore; student Gardner Sch., Art Students League, Cooper Union; m. Armand Grover Erpf, 1965 (dec.); children: Cornelia Aurelia, Armand Bartholomew; m. Gerrit Pieter Van de Bovenkamp, Aug. 11, 1973 (div.). Pres. Armand G. Erpf Fund, N.Y.C., 1971—; founder, hon. chmn. Erpf Catskill Cultural Ctr., 1972—. Bd. advisors, founder N.Y. Zool. Soc., 1971—, 1001 Nature Trust, 1973, William Beebe fellow, 1983—; fellow in perpetuity Met. Mus. Art, 1977; life fellow Pierpont Morgan Libr., 1974—; mem. coun.of friends Whitney Mus. Am. Art, 1971-77; mem. Whitney Circle, 1978-93; bd. dirs. Catskill Ctr. for Conservation and Devel., 1983-86; mem. adv. coun., dept. art history and archaeology Columbia U., 1972—, established univ. seminar on uses of oceans, 1977, mem. adv. coun. Translation Ctr., 1986; life conservator N.Y. Pub. Libr., 1980; fellow Frick Collection; 1971—, Whitney fellow, 2994—; mem. coun. Agribus. Coun., Inc., 1979-87; founder, life mem. World Wildlife Fund, 1973—, bd. dirs., 1984-89; mem. pres.'s coun. Columbia U., 1973-78; life mem. Mus. City N.Y., 1972—, mem. pres.'s coun., 1971—. Mem. N.Y. Acad. Scis., The Planetary Soc., Mus. Natural History (life), Asia Soc. (pres.'s coun.), Wildlife Fedn. (adv.), African Wildlife Found. (pres.'s cir.). mem. Mus. of Natural Hist. pres., coun. of the Asia Soc. Office: The Armand G Erpf Fund 640 Park Ave New York NY 10021-6126

VANDEBROEK, SOPHIE VERDONCKT, printing company executive; b. Leuven, Belgium, Feb. 17, 1962; came to U.S., 1986; d. Norbert and Jeanine (Ringoir) V.; m. Bart Vandebroek, Aug. 2, 1986 (dec. Aug. 1996); children: Elena, Arno, Jonas. B in Engring. magna cum laude, Katholieke U., 1982, MS in Electro-Mech. Engring. magna cum laude, 1985; PhDEE in Microelectronics, Cornell U., 1990. Devel. staff mem. IBM T.J. Watson Rsch. Ctr., Yorktown Heights, NY, 1990-92; competency leader J.C. Wilson Ctr. for Rsch. and Tech., Xerox, Webster, NY, 1992-95, lab. mgr., 1995-96; platform mgr. Ink-Jet Supplies Bus. Unit Xerox Corp., Webster, 1996-97, mgr. document systems coherence program, 1997-98, tech. advisor Office of the Chmn., 1998-99, chief engineer Stamford, Conn., 2002—06, chief tech. officer, 2006—, corp. v.p., 2006—; v.p. Xerox Rsch. Ctr. Can., 1999—2000, Xerox Engring. Ctr., 2002—06; pres. Xerox Innovation Group, 2006—; chief tech. officer Carrier Corp., 2000—02. Contbr. articles to profl. jours. Fulbright fellow, 1986; hon. grad. fellowship Belgian-Am. Ednl. Found., 1986; internat. travel grant Belgium Nat. Sci. Found., 1986-87; recipient Monsanto award 1986, Kieckhefer Adirondack award 1986. Fellow IEEE; mem. IEEE Electron Devices Soc. (adminstrv. com. 1995-97, internat. electron device meeting 1994-98, tech. program com. 1994-95, chair solid state devices com. 1996, publicity chair 1998, chair Rochester chpt. IEEE/EDS 1994, disting. lectr. 1994). Avocations: reading, skiing, kayaking, rollerblading. Office: Xerox Corp 800 Long Ridge Rd Stamford CT 06904 *

VANDEHEI, JIM W. (JAMES W. VANDEHEI), political executive editor; b. 1971; m. Autumn Hanna VandeHei; children: Sophie, James. Grad. in journalism & polit. sci., U. Wis., Oshkosh, 1995. Journalist Brillion News, Wis., 1993; sports reporter Oshkosh Northwestern; intern Sen. Herb Kohl, 1994; with Inside Washington Publishers, 1995—96, Inside the New Congress, 1996—97, Roll Call, 1997—2000; White House and Congress reporter The Wall Street Journal, 1998—2002; nat. polit. reporter, White House corr. The Washington Post, 2002—06; co-founder, exec. editor The Politico, Arlington, Va., 2006—; exec. editor Politico.com, Arlington, Va., 2007—. Contbr. works to Capital Style and The New Republic. Guest appearances Face the Nation, CNN-Inside Politics, Hardball, analyst of politics Washington Post Radio, biweekly chats about politics Washingtonpost.com. Hoover Institution Media Fellow, 2005, 2006. Avocations: fishing, football. Office: The Politico 1000 Wilson Blvd Ste 601 Arlington VA 22209 *

VANDE HEY, JAMES MICHAEL, retired air force officer; b. Maribel, Wis., Mar. 15, 1916; s. William Henry and Anna (Zimmerman) VandeH.; m. Jean Margretta Schilleman, June 23, 1944; children: James Todd, Dale Michael, Dean Clark. Student, U. Wis., 1947-49; BA, U. Philippines, 1955; postgrad., Air War Coll., Maxwell AFB, Montgomery, Ala., 1956-57. Commd. 2d lt. USAAF, 1941; advanced through grades to brig. gen. USAF, 1967; fighter pilot PTO, 1941-45; including Hawaii, Dec. 7, 1941; duty in command and USAF level including duty in Europe (NATO) and Philippines, 1945-69; dep. chief of staff Hdqrs. USMACV, Saigon, Vietnam, 1969-71; assigned Hdqrs. Tactical Air Command, 1971—; mem. faculty Air War Coll., 1957-59, dep. for acads., dean of faculty, 1959-61; ret., 1971; pres. Vanson Inc., 1971—, Vande Hey Inc., 1976—. Decorated D.S.M., Legion of Merit with two oak leaf clusters, D.F.C. with two oak leaf clusters, Bronze Star, Air medal with 7 oak leaf clusters, decorations from Philippine, Vietnamese and Korean govts. Mem. USAF Hist. Found., Air Force Assn., Pearl Harbor Survivors Assn., Iwo Jima Survivors Assn. Roman Catholic. Home: 3374 S El Dorado Austin TX 78734-5232

VAN DE KAMP, JOHN KALAR, lawyer; b. Pasadena, Calif., Feb. 7, 1936; s. Harry and Georgie (Kalar) Van de K.; m. Andrea Fisher, Mar. 11, 1978; 1 child, Diana. BA, Dartmouth Coll., 1956; JD, Stanford U., 1959. Bar: Calif. 1960. Asst. US atty., LA, 1960—66; US atty., 1966—67; dep. dir. Exec. Office for US Attys., Washington, 1967—68, dir., 1968—69; spl. asst. Pres.'s Commn. on Campus Unrest, 1970; fed. pub. defender LA, 1971—75; dist. atty. LA County, 1975—83; atty. gen. State of Calif., 1983—91; ptnr. Dewey Ballantine, LA, 1991—96, of counsel, 1996—; pres. Thoroughbred Owners, Calif., 1996—2004. Mem. Calif. Dist. Attys. Assn. (pres. 1975-83), Nat. Dist. Attys. Assn. (v.p. 1975-83), Peace Officers Assn. LA County (past pres.), Nat. Assn. Attys. Gen. (exec. com. 1983-91), Conf. Western Attys. Gen. (pres. 1986), State Bar Calif. (bd. govs. 2001-04, pres. 2004-05), Calif. Commn. Fair Adminstrn. of Justice (chair 2006-). Office: Dewey Ballantine LLP 333 So Grand Ave Ste 2600 Los Angeles CA 90071-1530 Office Phone: 213-621-6511. Business E-Mail: jvandekamp@deweyballantine.com.

VANDE KOPPLE, WILLIAM JOHN, literature and language professor; b. Grand Rapids, Mich., Dec. 16, 1949; s. Roger James and Wilma Jane Vande Kopple; m. Wanda Beth Vande Kopple, July 25, 1980; children: Jonathan, Joel, Jason. BA, Calvin Coll., Grand Rapids, 1972; MA, U. Chgo., 1973, PhD, 1980. English tchr. Illiana Christian H.S., Lansing, Ill., 1973—80; English prof. Calvin Coll., Grand Rapids, Mich., 1980—. Author: Clear and Coherent Prose, 1986, The Catch, 2004; co-author (with Gary Schmidt): Communities of Discourse, 1993. Mem.: Conf. on Coll. Composition and Comm., Nat. Coun. Tchrs. English. Avocations: fishing, hiking, photography. Office: Calvin College English Dept 3201 Burton St SE Grand Rapids MI 49507

VANDELL, KERRY DEAN, real estate consultant, educator, director, finance educator; b. Biloxi, Miss., Jan. 8, 1947; s. Benedict Sandy and Eleanor Ruby (Lenhart) V.; m. Deborah Ann Lowe, May 16, 1970; children: Colin Buckner, Ashley Elizabeth. BA, MME, Rice U., 1970; M City Planning, Harvard U., 1973; PhD, MIT, 1977. Assoc. engr. Exxon Co., USA, Houston, 1970-71; asst. prof. So. Meth. U., Dallas, 1976-80, assoc. prof., 1980-86, prof., chmn. dept., 1986-89; prof. real estate and urban land econs., chm. dept. U. Wis., Madison, 1989-93, dir. Ctr. for Urban Land Econs. Rsch., 1991—2004, Tiefenthaler chair holder, 1996—2006; exec. dir. Bolz Ctr. Arts Adminstrn., Madison, 2000—05; prof. fin., dir. Ctr. Real Estate Paul Merage Sch. Bus. U. Calif.-Irvine, 2006—. Vis. assoc. prof. Harvard U., Cambridge, Mass., 1985-86; vis. prof. U. Calif., Berkeley, 1988-89, U. Hong Kong, 1997. Mem. editl. bd. Jour. Real Estate Fin. and Econs., 1989—, Land Econs., 1989—, Jour. Property Rsch., 1989-94, Real Estate Econs., 1980—, Internat. Real Estate Rev., 2002—; contbr. numerous articles on mortgage default risk, real estate liquidity, housing market behavior, econs. of architecture, and appraisal theory to profl. jours. Fellow Homer Hoyt Advanced Studies Inst. (faculty 1989—); mem. Urban Land Inst., Am. Real Estate and Urban Econs. Assn. (2nd v.p. 1989, 1st v.p. 1990, pres. 1991, co-editor jour. 1991-96), Asian Real Estate Soc. (bd. dirs. 2002—), Am. Real Estate Soc. Episcopalian. Office: U Calif Irvine Paul Merage Sch Bus Irvine CA 92697 Home: 2658 Victoria Dr Laguna Beach CA 92651 Office Phone: 949-824-1985. Business E-Mail: kvandell@bus.wisc.edu, kvandell@uci.edu.

VANDEMARK, MICHELLE VOLIN, critical care, neuroscience nurse; b. Sioux Falls, SD, Feb. 14, 1962; d. Verlynne V. and Suzanne (Cronin) Volin; m. Richard E. VanDemark, June 5, 1982; children: Andrew Porter, Hannah Elizabeth. BA in Biology, Lake Forest Coll., Ill., 1984; BSN, Northwestern U., Chgo., 1986; MS in Nursing, Loyola U., Chgo., 1990. RN, Ill., SD; cert. in neuroscience nursing, CNRN, MSCN. Staff nurse neurosci. unit Evanston Hosp., Ill., 1986-90, staff nurse intensive care unit Ill., 1990-93; neuroscience clin. nurse specialist Sioux Valley Hosp. (now named Sanford USD Med. Ctr.), Sioux Falls, 1995—. Mem. Am. Assn. Neurosci. Nurses (pres. Gt. Plains chpt. 1995-96, bd. dirs. 2000-03), Sigma Theta Tau, Alpha Sigma Nu. Home: 321 E 27th St Sioux Falls SD 57105-3032

VANDEMARK, ROBERT GOODYEAR, retired retail executive; b. Youngstown, Ohio, Sept. 1, 1921; s. Arthur Glenn and Lola (Goodyear) V.; m. Jean Chapman, Sept. 19, 1943; children: Ann (Mrs. William K. Butler), Peggy Lynn (Mrs. Michael Murray). BSc, Ohio U., 1943. Dept. mgr. F. & R. Lazarus, Columbus, Ohio, 1947-54; asst. controller Boston Store, Milw., 1954-57; v.p., treas. Cleland Simpson Co., Scranton, Pa., 1957-65; asst. to exec. v.p. Bergdorf Goodman, NYC, 1965-68; treas. Garfinckel, Brooks Bros., Miller & Rhoads, Inc., Washington, 1968-69, v.p., 1969-73, exec. v.p., 1973-79, vice chmn., 1979-83; chmn., chief exec. officer Garfinckel's, 1983-87. Head dept. and specialty stores div. United Fund, Scranton, Pa., 1960-65; bd. dirs. Goodwill Industries, 1964-65; treas. Washington Nat. Cathedral. Served to 1st lt. AUS, 1943-46; col. Res. Decorated Bronze Star with V and cluster, Mil. Order of Wilheim. Mem. Fin. Execs. Inst., Nat. Retail Mchts. Assn. (sec., treas., 1st v.p., pres., dir., mem. exec. com. fin. exec. divsn.), Delta Tau Delta, City Club Washington, Washington Golf and Country Club, Army-Navy Club, Burning Tree Golf Club, Laurel Oak Country Club (Fla.), Masons (32d degree), Kiwanis (Fla.), Tower Club. Home: 933 Woburn Ct Mc Lean VA 22102-2132 also: 3362 Charles MacDonald Dr Sarasota FL 34240

VAN DEMARK, RUTH ELAINE, lawyer; b. Santa Fe, May 16, 1944; d. Robert Eugene and Bertha Marie (Thompson) Van D.; m. Leland Wilkinson, June 23, 1967; children: Anne Marie, Caroline Cook. AB, Vassar Coll., 1966; MTS, Harvard U., 1969; JD with honors, U. Conn., 1976; MDiv, Luth. Sch. Theology, Chgo., 1999. Bar: Conn. 1976, Ill. 1977, U.S. Dist. Ct. Conn. 1976, U.S. Dist. Ct. (no. dist.) Ill., U.S. Ct. Appeals (7th cir.) 1984, U.S. Supreme Ct. 1983; ordained to ministry, Luth Ch., 1999. Instr. legal rsch. and writing Loyola U. Sch. Law, Chgo., 1976-79; assoc. Wildman, Harrold, Allen & Dixon, Chgo., 1977-84, ptnr., 1985-94; prin. Law Offices of Ruth E. Van Demark, Chgo., 1995—2003; pastor Wicker Park Luth. Ch., Chgo., 1999—. Mem. rules com. Ill. Supreme Ct., 1999-2002, chair appellate rules subcom., 1996-2002; mem. dist. ct. fund adv. com. U.S. Dist. Ct. (no. dist.) Ill., 1997—. Assoc. editor Conn. Law Rev., 1975-76. Bd. dirs. Lutheran Soc. Svcs. Ill., 1998—, sec., 2000—02, chmn., 2002-; mem. adv. bd. Horizon Hospice, Chgo., 1978—, YWCA Battered Women's Shelter, Evanston, Ill., 1982-86; del.-at-large White House Conf. on Families, L.A., 1980; mem. alumni coun. Harvard Divinity Sch., 1988-91; vol. atty. Pro Bono Advs. Chgo., 1982-92, bd. dirs., 1993-99, chair devel. com., 1993; bd. dirs. Friends of Pro Bono Advs. Orgn., 1987-89, New Voice Prodns., 1984-86, Byrne Piven Theater Workshop, 1987-90, Luth. Social Svcs. Ill. (sec., 2000—), 1998—; founder, bd. dirs. Friends of Battered Women and Their Children, 1986-87; chair 175th Reunion Fund Harvard U. Div. Sch., 1992; dean Ctrl. Conf. Met. Chgo. Synod ELCA. Mem. ABA, Ill. Bar Assn., Conn. Bar Assn., Chgo. Bar Assn., Appellate Lawyers Assn. Ill. (bd. dirs. 1985-87, treas. 1989-90, sec. 1990-91, v.p. 1991-92, pres. 1992-93), Women's Bar Assn. Ill., Jr. League Evanston (chair State Pub. Affairs Com. 1987-88, Vol. of Yr. 1983-84), Chgo. Vassar Club (pres. 1979-81), Cosmopolitan Club (N.Y.C.). Home: 2046 W Pierce Ave Chicago IL 60622-1946 E-mail: revwplc@earthlink.net.

VANDENBERG, BYRON F., cardiologist; b. Sacramento, Aug. 15, 1953; s. John Byron and Jeannette Vandenberg; m. Anne Carroll. BA, Occidental Coll., 1975; MD, Georgetown U., 1980. Diplomate cert. Bd. of Nuc. Cardiology. Intern, resident Parkland Hosp., Dallas, 1980-83; mem. faculty U. Iowa Coll. Medicine, Iowa City, 1985-97; cardiologist Prairie Cardiovascular Cons., Springfield, Ill., 1997—2003, Northern Calif. Cardiology Assoc., Sacramento, 2003—. Med. dir. adult echocardiography lab. Prairie Heart Inst., Springfield, 1997-2003; mem. editl. bd. Am. Jour. Cardiology, Dallas, 1997-2006. Contbr. articles to profl. jours. Named Best Drs. in Am., Woodward/White, 1998, 99, 2000, 02, 05. Fellow ACP, Am. Coll. Cardiology, Am. Heart Assn., Am. Soc. Echocardiography. Office: No Calif Cardiology Assocs 1004 Fowler Way Placerville CA 95667 *

VAN DEN BERG, SARA JANE, language educator; b. St. Paul, May 19, 1942; d. Henry John and Edith Ann (Hutchins) Streich; m. Kent Talbot van den Berg, June 11, 1976; 1 child, David Talbot. BA summa cum laude, U. Minn., 1964; MA, Yale U., 1965, PhD, 1969. Instr. Fordham U., NYC, 1968-70; asst. prof. Fairfield (Conn.) U., 1970-73, Occidental Coll., LA, 1973-76, Ohio State U., Columbus, 1976-80, U. Wash., Seattle, 1980-87, assoc. prof. English, 1987—2000, chmn. curricular policy bd., 1996-98; prof. English St. Louis U., 2000—, chmn. English dept., 2000—, Dorothy McBride Orthwein prof., 2004—05; dir. Walter J. Ong. S Ctr. Lang. and Culture, St. Louis, 2007—. Mem. editl. bd. Modern Lang. Quar., 1995-2000, Ben Jonson Jour., 1995—, Psyart: The Jour., 1997—, Conversations, 2004-07, Explorations in Media Ecology, 2005—; author: The Action of Ben Jonson's Poetry, 1987. Huntington Libr. fellow, 1987, NEH fellow, 1987, 2003. Mem. MLA (divsn. lit. and psychology 1990-94, chmn. 1992-93), Renaissance Soc. Am., Milton Soc. Am., Pacific Ancient and Modern Lang. Assn. (exec. com. 1997-99). Office: St Louis U Dept English 3800 Lindell Blvd Saint Louis MO 63108 Home Phone: 314-776-2016; Office Phone: 314-977-3010. Business E-Mail: vandens@slu.edu.

VANDENBERG, THOMAS E., lawyer, transportation services executive; BA in Bus. Adminstrn. and Fin., U. Notre Dame; JD, U. Wis., Madison. Bar: Wis. 1979. Atty. Schneider Nat., Inc., Green Bay, 1979, assoc. gen. counsel, gen. counsel. Mem.: Wis. Motor Carriers Assn. (dir.), Nat. Lawyers Assn., Transport Lawyers Assn. Office: Schneider Nat Inc PO Box 2545 3101 S Packerland Dr Green Bay WI 54306-2545 Office Phone: 920-592-3895. Office Fax: 920-592-3891. Business E-Mail: vandenbergt@schneider.com.

VAN DEN BERGH, SIDNEY, astronomer; b. Wassenaar, Netherlands, May 20, 1929; emigrated to U.S., 1948; s. Sidney J. and Mieke (van den Berg) vandenB.; m. Paulette Brown; children by previous marriage: Peter, Mieke, Sabine. Student, Leiden U., The Netherlands, 1947-48; AB, Princeton U., 1950; M.Sc., Ohio State U., 1952; Dr. rer. nat., Goettingen U., 1956, DSc (honoris causa), 1995, DSc (honoris causa), 2001. Asst. prof. Perkins Obs., Ohio State U., Columbus, 1956-58; research assoc. Mt. Wilson Obs., Palomar Obs., Pasadena, Calif., 1968-69; prof. astronomy David Dunlap Obs., U. Toronto, Ont., Canada, 1958-77; dir. Dominion Astrophys. Obs., Victoria, B.C., 1977-86; prin. rsch. officer NRC Can., 1977-98, rschr. emeritus, 1998—. Adj. prof. U. Victoria, 1977—. Decorated officer Order of Can. Fellow Royal Soc. London; mem. Am., Royal Astron. Soc. (assoc.), Canadian Astronomy Soc. (sr. v.p. 1988-90, pres. 1990-92). Home: 418 Lands End Rd Sidney BC Canada V8L 5L9 Home Phone: 250-656-6020; Office Phone: 250-363-0006. Business E-Mail: sidney.vandenbergh@nrl.com.

VANDENBERGHE, JAMES H., manufacturing executive; BBA, Western Mich. U., Kalamazoo; MBA, Wayne State U., Detroit. Fin. analyst Lear Siegler, Inc., 1973, v.p. fin. plastics divsn., v.p. ops. gen. seating divsn.; sr. v.p. fin., CFO, sec. Lear Corp., 1988-93, exec. v.p. fin., CFO, 1993-97, pres., COO N.Am. ops., 1997-98, vice-chmn., CFO Southfield, Mich., 1998—. Bd. dirs. DTE Energy. Bd. trustees Coll. Creative Studies; bd. visitors Wayne State U. Sch. Bus.; bd. dirs. United Way Southeastern Mich. Office: Lear Corp 21557 Telegraph Rd Southfield MI 48034-4248 *

VAN DEN BERGHE, PIERRE LOUIS, sociologist; b. Lubumbashi, Congo, Jan. 30, 1933; s. Louis and Denise (Caullery) van den B.; m. Irmgard C. Niehuis, Jan. 21, 1956; children: Eric, Oliver, Marc. BA, Stanford U., 1952, MA, 1953; PhD, Harvard U., 1960. Asst. prof. sociology Wesleyan U., Middletown, Conn., 1962-63; asso. prof. sociology SUNY, Buffalo, 1963-65; prof. sociology and anthropology U. Wash., Seattle, 1965-98, prof. emeritus, 1998—. Vis. prof. U. Natal, South Africa, 1960-61, Sorbonne, Paris, 1962, U. Nairobi, Kenya, 1967-68, U. Ibadan, Nigeria, 1968-69, U. Haifa, Israel, 1976, U. New South Wales, Australia, 1982, U. Strasbourg, France, 1985, U. Tuebingen, Germany, 1986, Tel Aviv U., 1988, U. Cape Town, South Africa, 1989, U. Ljubljana, Slovenia, 2005; fellow Advanced Study in Behavioral Scis., Stanford, Calif., 1984-85. Author: 22 books including South Africa, A Study in Conflict, 1965, Race and Racism, 1967, Academic Gamesmanship, 1970, Man in Society, 1978, Human Family Systems, 1979, The Ethnic Phenomenon, 1981, Stranger in Their Midst, 1989, State Violence and Ethnicity, 1990, The Quest for the Other, 1994. Served with M.C. U.S. Army, 1954-56. Mem. Am. Sociol. Assn., Am. Anthrop. Assn., Sociol. Rsch. Assn., Human Behavior and Evolution Soc. Home: 2006 19th Ave E Seattle WA 98112-2902 Office: U Wash Dept Sociology 353340 Seattle WA 98195-3340 Office Phone: 206-543-2051. Business E-Mail: plvdb@u.washington.edu.

VAN DEN BOSCH, MARGARETA, apparel company executive; Grad., Beckman's Sch. Design; educated as a profl. tailor, St. Göran's Sch., Stockholm. Designer, Italy, 1976—88; head of design H&M Hennes & Mauritz AB, 1988—. Head of design complete off-stage wardrobe for

Team Madonna on Confessions World Tour, 2006. Named one of 25 Masters of Innovation, BusinessWeek. Office: H&M Hennes & Mauritz AB Regeringsgatan 48 SE-106 38 Stockholm Sweden

VANDEN BOUT, PAUL ADRIAN, astronomer, physicist, educator; b. Grand Rapids, Mich., June 16, 1939; s. Adrian and Cornelia (Peterson) Vanden B.; m. Rachel Ann Eggebeen, Sept. 1, 1961; children: Thomas Adrian, David Anton AB, Calvin Coll., 1961; PhD, U. Calif.-Berkeley, 1966. Postdoctoral fellow U. Calif., Berkeley, 1966-67, Columbia U., NYC, 1967-68, instr., 1968-69, asst. prof., 1969-70, U. Tex., Austin, 1970-74, assoc. prof., 1974-79, prof., 1979-84; dir. Nat. Radio Astronomy Obs., Charlottesville, Va., 1985—2002, sr. sci., 2003—; dir. Atacama Large Millimeter Array, Charlottesville, Va., 2002—03. Cons. NSF, NASA, NRC. Fellow Fulbright Found., Heidelberg, Fed. Republic Germany, 1961-62, Leiden, Netherlands, 1977 Fellow AAAS, Am. Phys. Soc.; mem. Am. Astron. Soc., Internat. Astron. Union, Internat. Radio Sci. Union. Office: Nat Radio Astronomy Obs 520 Edgemont Rd Charlottesville VA 22903-2454 Office Phone: 434-296-0231. Business E-Mail: pvandenb@nrao.edu.

VAN DEN BRANDE, RENE ALBERT, retired accountant; b. Antwerp, Belgium, Aug. 14, 1916; arrived in Can., 1925; s. Henry Van den Brande and Maria Josephine Christ; m. Lily Pearson, July 7, 1947 (dec.). Cert. in pub. adminstrn., Queen's U., Ont., Can., 1963. Chartered acct., Can. Instr. Leamington Bus. Coll., Ont., 1938—40; asst. dept. head Dept. Nat. Revenue, Toronto, 1948—51; pvt. practice acct. Oakville, Ont., 1951—54; office mgr. Erb Lumber Co., Royal Oak, Mich., 1954—57; mgr. Sullivan Homes Inc., Dunedin, Fla., 1957—60; county adminstr. County of Essex, Ont., 1960—81; cons. Fed. Bank Can., Windsor, Ont., 1981—83; town adminstr. Town of South Palm Beach, Fla., 1983—88; ret. Flying officer Royal Can. Air Force, 1940—45, Camp Borden. Avocations: woodworking, reading. Address: 1792 Trappers Ave N8P1T1 Windsor Canada Personal E-mail: van814@email.com.

VANDEN EYKEL, IKE, lawyer; b. Slayton, Minn., Mar. 25, 1949; s. Martin D. and Wilma J. V.; m. Cathy A., Aug. 5, 1978; children: Eric, Lindsey, Steven. BS, Drake U., 1971; JD, Baylor U., 1973. Bar: Tex. 1973, US Dist. Ct. (no. dist. Tex.) 1973, US Supreme Ct. 1976. Assoc. Stroud & Smith, Dallas, 1973-78; ptnr. Secugson, Doiuglass, Falooner & Vanden Eykel, Dallas, 1978-90, Koons, Fuller & Vanden Eykel, Dallas, 1990-95; mng. ptnr. Koons, Fuller, Vanden Eykel and Robertson, P.C., Dallas, 1995—. Author: Successful Lone Star Divorce, 1998. Bd. dir. Collin County Children's Advocacy Ctr., Tex. Named one of Top 10 Divorce Lawyers, Town & Country mag., top lawyers for Dallas women, Vogue mag., 2003, Best Lawyers in Dallas, D Mag., 2001, 2003, 2005. Fellow: Intern. Acad. Matrimonial Lawyers, Am. Acad. Matrimonial Lawyers; mem.: Tex. Trial Lawyers Assn., Dallas Bar Assn. (bd. dir. 2000—), ABA, Am. Coll. Family Trial Lawyers. Republican. Methodist. Avocations: golf, tennis. Office: Koons Fuller Vanden Eykel & Robertson 2311 Cedar Springs Rd Ste 300 Dallas TX 75201-1899 Office Phone: 214-871-2727. Office Fax: 214-871-0196. E-mail: Ike@koonsfuller.com. *

VAN DEN HENDE, FRED J(OSEPH), human resources executive; b. Chgo., Sept. 28, 1953; s. Maurice Everett and Alice Helen (Davey) Van Den H.; m. Sharon Joyce Kucharski, Oct. 4, 1975; children: John Michael, Karen Michelle. BA in Secondary Edn. and Social Sci., DePaul U., Chgo., 1975; grad., U. Wash. Sch. Exec. Dev., Seattle, 1981; MS in Human Resource Mgmt. and Devel., Nat. Louis U., Evanston, Ill., 1998. Cert. sr. profl. human resources. Asst. v.p. human resources Land of Lincoln Savs. and Loan, Berwyn, Ill., 1977-84; v.p. human resources Uptown Fed. Bank FSB, Niles, Ill., 1984-88; dir. human resources Archdiocese of Chgo., 1988—. Mem. Savs. Assn. Pers. Adminstrn., Berwyn, 1977-84; part-time instr. Inst. Fin. Edn., Chgo., 1984-90, Moraine Valley C.C., Palos Hills, Ill., 1984-90; adj. prof. Coll. Mgmt. and Bus., nat. Louis U., 1998-, Coll. Commerce, Dept. Mgmt., Kellstadt Graduate Sch. Bus., De Paul U., 2006-; cons. in field 1990- Sch. bd. treas. St. Rene Sch., Chgo., 1981; sch. bd. mem. St. Daniel the Prophet Sch., Chgo., 1986-88, 93-95, sch. bd. chmn., 1988-89; boy scout leader St. Daniel Parish, Chgo., 1987-94; coach, track, St. Rene Sch., 1979-81, Vittum Park boys' baseball, 1989-92, boys' basketball, St. Daniel the Prophet Sch., 1991-95, basketball coord., 1995-96; meet official Conf. USA Indor Track and Field Championships, 2000, Conf. USA Cross-Country Championship, 2004. Recipient Outstanding Achievement in the Field of Athletics award St. Rita H.S. Alumni Assn., Chgo., 1991; Athletic scholar DePaul U., Chgo., 1971-75. Mem. Nat. Assn. Ch. Pers. Adminstrs., Soc. for Human Resource Mgmt. (mem. sch.-to-work com. 1998-2000), Ill. State C. of C. (human resources com. 1979-2003, healthcare com. 1998-2003), Inst. Internat. Human Resources, Am. Mgmt. Assn. (Chicago Area Tng. Coun. 2001—), Soc. for Human Resource Profls. (edn. adv. com. 2002—), KC (4th degree). Roman Catholic. Avocations: camping, fishing, coaching youth sports teams, horseback riding. Home: 5130 S Mulligan Ave Chicago IL 60638-1316 Office: Archdiocese of Chgo 155 E Superior St Chicago IL 60611-2911 Office Phone: 312-751-5352. Business E-Mail: fvandenhende@archchicago.org.

VANDEN HEUVEL, KATHLEEN, law librarian; BA, U. Calif., Berkeley, 1981, MLIS, JD, U. Calif., Berkeley, 1986. Libr. Boalt Hall Sch. Law, U. Calif., Berkeley, 1986—, dep. dir. to dir. Law Libr., 1992—. Libr. fellow Townsend Ctr. for Humanities, 1995—96. Office: Law Libr U Calif Berkeley Boalt Hall Sch Law Berkeley CA 94720-7200

VANDEN HEUVEL, KATRINA, publishing executive; b. NYC, Oct. 7, 1959; d. William Jacobus and Jean Babette (Stein) Vanden H.; m. Stephen F. Cohen, Dec. 4, 1988; 1 child, Nicola Anna. BA summa cum laude in Politics, Princeton U., 1982. Prodn. assoc. ABC Closeup Documentaries, 1982-83; asst. editor The Nation, NYC, 1984-89, editor-at-large, 1989-93, acting editor-in-chief, 1994-95, editor-in-chief, 1995—, and pub., gen. ptnr., 2005—. Vis. journalist Moscow News, 1989; Moscow coord. Conf. Investigative Journalism After the Cold War, 1992; co-founder, co-editor Vyi i Myi, 1990—. Editor: The Nation, 1865-1990; The Best of the Nation, 1990-2000: Selections from the Independent Magazine of Politics and Culture, 2001, A Just Response: The Nation on Terrorism, Democracy and September 11, 2001, 2002, The Dictionary of Republicanisms, 2005; co-editor: Voices of Glasnost: Interviews with Gorbachev's Reformers, 1989, Taking Back America-And Taking Down the Radical Right, 2004; mem. nat. adv. bd. Facing South mag.; mem. editl. bd. The Progressive Book Club; contbr. articles to newspapers. Recipient Maggie award Planned Parenthood Fedn. Am., 1994, Nat. Mag. award for Reviews & Criticism, Am. Soc. Mag. Editors, 2007. Mem. Correctional Assn. N.Y. (dir.), Inst. for Women's Policy Rsch. (bd. dirs.), Coun. Fgn. Rels., Inst. Policy Studies (trustee), Network of East-West Women (bd. advisors), Franklin and Eleanor Roosevelt Inst. (trustee), Moscow Ctr. for Gender Studies (mem. adv. com.), Century Assn. Office: The Nation 33 Irving Pl Fl 8 New York NY 10003-2332 Office Phone: 212-209-5412. Personal E-mail: kat@thenation.com.

VAN DEN HOOGEN, INGRID, information technology executive; BA in Math. and Computer Sci., San Jose State U., Calif. Various software devel. positions GTE Govt. Systems, United Techs., Megatek; with Sun Microsystems, Inc., Santa Clara, Calif., 1987—, head software strategic mktg., sr. v.p. brand, global comm. & integrated mktg. Office: Sun Microsystems Inc 4150 Network Cir Santa Clara CA 95054 Office Phone: 650-960-1300. *

VANDENHOUTEN, PETER G., lawyer; BA, Marquette U.; JD, U. Wis., Madison. Atty. Wis. State Legis., Quarles & Brady LLP, Madison, Wis.; sr. corp. counsel, asst. sec. Shopko LLC, Green Bay, Wis., 1999—2003, asst. gen. counsel, corp. sec., 2003—06, v.p., gen. counsel, 2006—. Office: Shopko LLC PO Box 19060 Green Bay WI 54307-9060

VANDEPUTTE, DIXIE DIANNE, psychologist, educator; b. Little River, Kans., Oct. 16, 1942; d. William Dean and Charlotte Juanita Wright; m. Gregory Charles Vandeputte, Aug. 21, 1959; children: Holly Ann Bell, Gregory Jr., Kerry Lynn Doll. BA summa cum laude in English and Psychology, U. Colo., 1990, MA in Psychology, 1992; PhD in Clin. Psychology, U. Kans., 1997. Lic. clin. psychologist Colo. Program mgr., lead clinician Pikes Peak Mental Health, Colo. Springs, Colo., 1997—2002; dir. Rocky Mountain Brain Injury Rehabilitation Day Clinic, Colo. Springs, 2002—03; dir. Counseling and Testing Ctr. U. Colo., Colo. Springs, 2003—. Mem. first del. to Vietnam and Cambodia APA, 2006; instr. U. Colo., 2003—; presenter in field. Contbr. articles to profl. jours. Sec. bd. dirs. Suicide Prevention Partnership, Colo. Springs, 2001—; sec. bd. Nat. Alliance for the Mentally Ill-CS, Colo. Springs, 2002—; mem. steering com. KP Women's Endowment, Colo. Springs, 2003—; bd. dirs. Suicide Prevention Edn. and Advocacy Coalition, Colo. Springs, 2004—. Recipient Outstanding Undergrad. Social Sci. award, U. Colo., 1990. Republican. Avocations: reading, hunting, crafts. Office: Univ Colo Colo Springs 1420 Austin Bluffs Pky Colorado Springs CO 80918 Office Phone: 719-262-3257. Business E-Mail: dvandepu@uccs.edu.

VANDER ARK, TOM, foundation administrator; s. Gary; m. Karen Vander Ark. B in mineral engring., Colo. Sch. Mines; MBA, U. Denver. Sr. exec. Pace Membership Warehouse, Inc.; dir. mktg. devel. Cap Gemini Am.; supt. Fed. Way Pub. Schools, Seattle, 1994—99; exec. dir. for edn. Bill & Melinda Gates Found., Seattle, 1999—2006, sr. fellow, 2007—. Office: Bill & Melinda Gates Found PO Box 2350 Seattle WA 98102 Office Phone: 206-709-3100.

VANDERBEEK, JEFFREY, professional sports team executive; b. July 19, 1957; m. Deborah Vanderbeek; children: Rem, McKenna, Rhiannon. BS, Bloomfield Coll. With Donaldson Lufkin & Jenrette; mng. dir., COO fixed income ctrl. funding dept. Lehman Brothers Holdings Inc., 1984—93, COO fixed income govt. dept., 1993—96, COO fixed income derivative dept., 1993—96, head global fixed income divsn., 1996—2000, head capital markets divsn., 2000—02, head global risk mgmt., pvt. equity and strategy, 2002—04; prin. owner, chmn., mng. ptnr. NJ Devils, 2004—. Pres. Devils Renaissance Devel., LLC. Vice chmn., bd. mem. Dorothy Rodbell Cohen Found. for Cancer Rsch.; chmn. Greater Newark Holiday Fund, 2006; bd. mem. Newark Alliance, Boys & Girls Clubs of Greater Newark; mem. exec. com. Boston Coll. Wall St. Coun. Office: Nat Newark Bldg 33 Fl 744 Broad St Newark NJ 07102 *

VANDERBEKE, PATRICIA K., architect; b. Detroit, Apr. 3, 1963; d. B. H. and Dolores I. VanderBeke. BS in Architecture, U. Mich., 1985, MArch, 1987. Registered arch., Ill. Archtl. intern Hobbs & Black, Assocs., Ann Arbor, Mich., 1984-86, Fry Assocs., Ann Arbor, 1988; arch. Decker & Kemp Architecture/Urban Design, Chgo., 1989-92; prin., founder P. K. VanderBeke, Arch., Chgo., 1992—. Mem. adv. com. dept. arch., Triton Coll. Contbr. photographs and articles to Inland Arch. mag.; contbr. photographs to AIA calendar. Chair recycling com. Lake Point Tower Condo. Assn., Chgo., 1990-05, chair. ops. com., 1993; mem. benefit com. The Renaissance Soc., U. Chgo., Redmoon Theater, Chgo. George S. Booth travelling fellow, 1992. Mem. AIA (participant 1st ann. leadership inst. 1997, 1st place nat. photog. contest award 1992, hon. mention 1994, Chgo. chpt. membership com., bd. dirs. 2006—), Chgo. Archl. Club, hon. mention 2000 Burnham Prize Competition, The Cliff Dwellers (mem. arts com.). Office: 155 W Burton Pl Apt 16 Chicago IL 60610-1326

VANDERBILT, ARTHUR T., II, lawyer; b. Summit, NJ, Feb. 20, 1950; s. William Runyon and Jean (White) V. BA, Wesleyan U., Middletown, Conn., 1972; JD, U. Va., 1975. Bar: N.J. 1975, U.S. Dist. Ct. N.J. 1975, U.S. Supreme Ct. 1978. Jud. clk. to presiding justice N.J. Superior Ct., 1975-76, dep. atty. gen., 1976-78, asst. counsel to gov., 1978-79; ptnr. Carella, Byrne, Bain & Gilfillan, Roseland, NJ, 1979—. Chmn. Supreme Ct. Ethics Com.; mem. Supreme Ct. Adv. Com. Profl. Ethics. Author: Changing Law, 1976, Jersey Justice, 1978, Law School, 1981, Treasure Wreck, 1986, Fortune's Children, 1989 (Book of the Month Club, Readers Digest and fgn. edits.), New Jersey's Judicial Revolution, 1997, Golden Days, 1998 (fgn. edits.), Jersey Jurists, 1998, The Making of a Bestseller, 1999, Gardening in Eden, 2003. Trustee Elizabeth Presbytery, Summit Free Pub. Libr., Manley-Winser Found., Land of PureGold Found., Greenwood Gardens. Named to N.J. Literary Hall of Fame. Fellow: ABA Found.; mem.: ABA (Scribes award 1976), Nat. Writers Union, The Authors Guild, Inc., Nat. Assn. Bond Lawyers, Am. Judicature Soc., N.J. Bar Assn., Eastwood House Country Club, Baltusrol Golf Club, Capitol Hill Club, Hyannis Yacht Club. Republican. Presbyterian. Avocation: writing. Office: Carella Byrne Bain & Gilfillan 5 Becker Farm Rd Roseland NJ 07068-1735 Office Phone: 973-994-1700. Business E-Mail: avanderbilt@carellabyrne.com.

VANDERBILT, DAVID, physics professor; BA in Physics, Swarthmore Coll., 1976; PhD in Physics, MIT, 1981. Miller postdoctoral fellow U. Calif. Berkeley, 1981—84; asst. to assoc. prof., physics dept. Harvard U., 1984—91; prof. dept. physics and astronomy Rutgers U., Piscataway, NJ, 1991—. Spkr. in field. Contbr. articles to profl. jours. Recipient Aneesur Rahman Prize for Computational Physics, Am. Phys. Soc., 2006. Fellow: Am. Phys. Soc. (Aneesur Rahman prize 2006). Office: Dept Physics & Astronomy Office Serin E275 Rutgers State Univ NJ Busch Campus 136 Frelinghuysen Rd Piscataway NJ 08854-8019 Office Phone: 732-445-2514. Office Fax: 732-445-4400. Business E-Mail: dhv@physics.rutgers.edu.

VANDERBILT, KERMIT, language educator; b. Decorah, Iowa, Sept. 1, 1925; s. Lester and Ella (Qualley) V.; m. Vivian Osmundson, Nov. 15, 1947; 1 dau., Karen Paige. BA, Luther Coll., Decorah, 1947, Litt. D. (hon.), 1977; MA, U. Minn., 1949, PhD, 1956. Instr. English U. Minn., 1954-57; instr. U. Wash., 1958-60, asst. prof. English, 1960-62; asst. prof. San Diego State U., 1962-65, assoc. prof., 1965-68, prof., 1968-90, prof. emeritus, 1990—. Vis. prof. Am. lit. U. B.C., Can., Vancouver, summer 1963; vis. prof. U. Oreg., summer 1968 Author: Charles Eliot Norton: Apostle of Culture in a Democracy, 1959, The Achievement of William Dean Howells: A Reinterpretation, 1968, Kurt Vonnegut in The Utopian Vision, 1983, American Literature and the Academy: The Roots, Growth and Maturity of a Profession, 1986 (Choice award for outstanding acad. books), Theodore Roethke in A Literary History of the American West, 1987; editor: (with others) American Social Thought, 1972, April Hopes (W.D. Howells), 1975, The Rise of Silas Lapham, 1983, spl. issue Am. Literary Realism, winter 1989, La Litterature Americaine, 1991, 3d edit., 1997, The Beautiful and Damned (F. Scott Fitzgerald), 1998; mem. edit. bd. U. Wash. Press, 1960-62, Twentieth Century Lit., 1969-2002; contbr. numerous articles to profl. jours. Served with USNR, 1943-46. Outstanding Prof. San Diego State U., 1976; Guggenheim fellow, 1978-79; Huntington Library fellow, 1980; Am. Philos. Soc. grantee, 1964, Am. Council Learned Socs. grantee, 1972, Nat. Endowment for Humanities grantee, 1986. Mem. Am. Studies Assn. (exec. council 1968-69), So. Calif. Am. Studies Assn. (pres. 1968-69), Philol. Assn. Pacific Coast (chmn. sect. Am. lit. 1968), MLA, Internat. Mark Twain Soc. (hon.), United Profs. of Calif. (Disting. prof. 1978) Home: 6937 Coleshill Dr San Diego CA 92119-1920

VANDERBURG, PAUL STACEY, insurance executive, consultant; b. Detroit, Apr. 13, 1941; s. Harold Stacey and Alice Bertha (Lyle) V. Cert. in plastics tech., Oakland U., 1966; AS in Bus., C.S. Mott C.C., 1971; Casualty Claims Law Assoc., Am. Ednl. Inst., 1986; BA in Bus. Adminstrn. and Mgmt., Columbia Pacific U., 1990; cert. in human resource devel., U. South Fla., 1992; fraud claims law assoc., Am. Ednl. Inst., 1995; grad., FBI Citizens Acad., Tampa, 2003. Lic. ins. adjuster Mich., Fla.; cert. cir. civil mediator U. South Fla. Mediation Inst., 2001, cert. county court mediator State Fla. Supreme Ct., 2002. Ins. field claims adjuster Underwriters Adjusting Co., Pontiac, Mich., 1972-76; pres., CEO Sun Cycle, Inc., Drayton Plains, Mich., 1975-77; sr. ins. claims adjuster Kemper Ins. Group, Tampa, Fla., 1979-80; ins. field claims adjuster Auto-Owners Ins. Co., Lakeland, Fla., 1981-82; sr. recovery specialist CIGNA Corp., Tampa, 1984-85; ins. field claims adjuster Seaboard Adjustment Bur., Lakeland, 1985-87; sr. field claims ins. adjuster Hallmark Ins. Adjusters, Clearwater, Fla., 1987-88; pvt. practice Tampa, 1988—. Author: Insurance Subrogation Management, 1991. Apptd. law enforcement rep. Hillsborough County (Fla.) Human Rels. Bd., 1999-2007. Staff sgt. U.S. Army, 1963-69. Mem.: Assn. Property and Casualty Claims Profls., Soc. of Claims Law Assocs., Assn. of Workers' Compensation Claims Profls., Fla. Acad. Profl. Mediators, Ctr. for Internat. Security Studies, Fla. Sheriffs Assn., Am. Security Coun. (nat. adv. bd.), FBI Citizens Acad. Alumni Assn. (bd. dirs.), Am. Legion. Republican. Avocations: boating, fishing, photography. Home and Office: 5448 Circle Dr (WWG) Spring Hill FL 34607-1407 Office Phone: 813-886-9669. Office Fax: 352-592-2191. Personal E-mail: A_Van0123@bellsouth.net.

VANDERGRIFF, KENNETH LYNN, religious studies educator; b. Knoxville, Tenn., Nov. 12, 1954; s. Kenneth Charles and Dorothy Jean Vandergriff; m. Beth Foster, Aug. 6, 1976; children: Kenny, Jeananne. BS in English Edn., Fla. State U., 1976; MDiv, Southwestern Bapt. Seminary, Ft. Worth, 1981, PhD in Old Testament, 1988. Tchg. fellow Southwestern Bapt. Theol. Sem., 1984-87, adj. instr., 1989; min. of edn. Northwest Hills Bapt. Ch., San Antonio, 1989-95. Instr. Inst. Christian Studies, Ft Worth, Tex., 1983, Ft Worth, 86, Wayland Bapt U., San Antonio, 1988—95, Campbell U., NC, 1996—; participant Oxford Round Table, 2005. Recipient Stella Rossa award, Southwestern Bapt. Theol. Sem., 1981. Mem.: Christians Bibl. Equality, Am. Acad. Religion, Soc. Bibl. Lit. Democrat. Home: 212 Forest Brook Dr Cary NC 27519-5863 Office Phone: 919-274-3467. *Integrity in relationships and the pursuit of excellence in endeavors—these I have found yield a life of satisfaction and joy.*

VAN DER HARST, JOHN JAY, environmentalist; b. Detroit, May 15, 1955; s. Juan and Marylyn Wilda van der Harst. Student in Landscape Architecture, Mich. State U., East Lansing, 1973—75, Calif. State Poly. U., Pomona, 1976; BA in Humanities (History of Art and English), Mich. State U., Ann Arbor, 1977; AS in Sci., Schoolcraft Coll., Livonia, Mich., AS in Sci., 1979; postgrad. in Civil Engring., U. Mich., Ann Arbor, 1979—81. Draftsman, delineator Grables, Mills and Young Inc., Lansing, Mich., 1975; designer, draftsman Leisure and Recreation Concepts, Inc., Dallas, 1976; project asst. Wehrman Chapman Assocs., Inc., Mpls., 1978; draftsman Cook Wandrey Peterman Design Group, John R. Cook Assocs., Ltd., Bartlett, Ill., 1980; designer, illustrator Ronald Sias and Assocs., Nashville, 1982; designer Cumberland Tectonics, Inc., Nashville, 1982—83; designer, draftsman Barge, Waggoner, Sumner and Cannon, Inc., Nashville, 1983—84; designer, technician Wamble and Assocs., Nashville, 1985; draftsman, delineator, designer Hastings Architecture Assocs., Nashville, 1986; contract draftsman IDI Corp., Milw.; assigned to Kroger Co., Nashville, 1988—89, Marquette U., Milw., 1990; contract draftsman, cons., illustrator various orgns., 1975—. Cons. in field; presenter in field. Contbr. articles to profl. jours.; radio and television guest (to various stations in Tenn. and Nebr.). Vol. Navajo Gospel Mission, Oraibi, Ariz., 1978, Recycle! Nashville, Methodology Com., 1988—89, Bring Urban Recycling to Nashville Today, 1989—92. Mem.: Grass Roots Alliance for Solid Waste Solutions, EPA (rev. team 1991—92), Citizen's Clearinghouse Hazardous Wastes, Inc., Green Party Mid. Tenn., Cumberland Green Bioregional Coun., Recycling Advocates Mid. Tenn., Tenn. Environ. Coun. (life). Avocations: gardening, cartooning, triathlons.

VANDERHOEF, LARRY NEIL, academic administrator; b. Perham, Minn., Mar. 20, 1941; s. Wilmar James and Ida Lucille (Wothe) Vanderhoef; m. Rosalie Suzanne Slifka, Aug. 31, 1963; children: Susan Marie, Jonathan Lee. BS, U. Wis., Milw., 1964, MS, 1965; PhD, Purdue U., 1969, Doctorate (hon.), 2000, Inje U. Korea, 2002. Postdoctorate U. Wis., Madison, 1969—70; asst. prof. biology U. Ill., Urbana, 1970-74, assoc. prof., 1974—77, prof., 1977—80, head dept. plant biology, 1977—80; provost Agrl. and Life Scis., U. Md., College Park, 1980—84; exec. vice chancellor U. Calif., Davis, 1984—91, exec. vice chancellor, provost, 1991—94, chancellor, 1994—. Rsch. assoc. U. Wis., 1970—72; vis. investigator Carnegie Inst., 1976—77, Edinburgh (Scotland) U., 1978; cons. in field. Fellow, NRC, 1969—70, Eisenhower fellow, 1987; grantee Dimond Travel grantee, 1975, NSF, 1972, 1974, 1976—79, NATO, 1980. Mem.: AAAS, Nat. Assn. State Univ. and Land Grant Colls. (exec. com. 2000—), Am. Soc. Plant Physiology (bd. editors 1977—82, trustee, exec. com., treas. 1982—88, chmn. bd. trustees 1994—97). Home: 16 College Park Davis CA 95616-3607 Office: U Calif Davis Office Chancellor Davis CA 95616

VAN DER HOEK, SHERRY A., counselor; b. Chgo., July 20, 1956; d. John Albert and Stella Rose (dec.) Troike; m. Herman Vanderhoek (dec.); stepchildren: Michiel, Martin. AAS, Prairie State Coll., 1992; BA, Govs. State U., 1994, MA, 1997. Lic. profl. counselor, Ill.; cert. counselor Nat. Bd. Cert. Counselors. Counselor South Suburban Coun. on Alcoholism, East Hazel Crest, Ill., 1990-93, South Suburban Family Shelter, Hazel Crest, Ill., 1996-97; facilitator Aunt Martha's Youth Svcs. Ctr., Inc., Park Forest, Ill., 1991-92; grad. asst. Govs. State U., University Park, Ill., 1995-97; pvt. practice counselor Matteson, Ill., 1998—. Mem.: ACA, Aunt Martha's Youth Svcs. Ctr. (founding mem. 1972), Ill. Alcoholism and Drug Dependence Assn., Assn. Counselor Edn. and Supervision (Outstanding Grad. Student Scholarship award 1997), Internat. Assn. Addiction and Offender Counselors, Ill. Counselor Educators and Suprs. (Outstanding Grad. Student award 1996), Ill. Alcohol and Other Drug Profl. Cert. Assn., Ill. Counseling Assn. (founder Govs. State Chpt., pres. 1996, regional gov. 1997—2000), Chi Sigma Iota (chpt. sec. 1995), Psi Chi (chpt. founder, pres. 1997). Avocations: stained glass, cross-stitch, cooking. Home and Office: 3761 W 216th Pl Matteson IL 60443

VAN DER HORST, BRIAN CHRISTOPHER, communications consultant, author, educator; b. NYC, Sept. 11, 1944; s. Louis Ferdinand von Pritzelwitz Van der Horst and Emilia (Jennewein) Triggs; children: Nicholas Christopher, Lorelei Eloise. Student, Duke U., 1960-62, New Sch. for Social Rsch., 1962-64, NLP Ctr. for Advanced Studies, Larkspur, Calif., 1981-83. Promotion mgr. Loew's Theatres, NYC, 1965-66; publicist Metro-Goldwyn-Mayer, NYC, 1966-67; publicity mgr. 20th Century-Fox, NYC, 1967-70; v.p. Cannon Group, NYC, 1970-71; dir. publicity and advt. Atlantic Recording Corp., NYC, 1971-73; dir. Neuro-Linguistic Programming Ctr. for Advanced Studies, 1986—90, Repere: Centre Internat. des Etudes Advancees NLP, Paris, 1985—2003, Dirigeants et Partenaires, Paris. Chief facilitator Integral Inst. Europe, Paris, 2000—; columnist, staff writer Village Voice, N.Y.C., 1973-77; columnist Playboy mag., N.Y.C., 1975-77; editor J.P. Tarcher, Inc., San Francisco, 1979-82; cons. SRI Internat., Menlo Park, Calif., 1980-81. Author: Folk Music in America, 1970, Rock Music, 1971, The Outcome Strategy, 2006; author more than 1000 articles on sci., music, and psychology; contbr. articles to Playboy, Omni, Practical Psychology, Penthouse, Cosmopolitan, others. Recipient 5 Motion Picture Advertising of Yr. awards, 1970; named Toastmaster of Yr., Paris Toastmasters, 1989. Fellow Nat. Assn. NLP, Internat. Coaching

Confederation (founder), Internat. Coaching Fedn.; mem. Assn. for Humanistic Psychology, Toastmasters Am., French Assn. NLP (founding fellow). Avocations: guitar, skin diving, painting, skiing, gardening, cooking. Personal E-mail: brianvdh@gmail.com.

VANDERHORST, MONICA S., physical education educator; b. Bluffton, Ohio, July 4, 1966; d. John Leslie and Judith Kay Badertscher; m. Gerald Keith VanderHorst, Dec. 19, 1987; 1 child, Ryan John. BA, Bluffton Coll., Ohio, 1988; M, Wright State U., Fairborn, Ohio, 1998. Instr. health and phys. edn. Hardin Houston Schs., Ohio, 1989—96, St. Marys City Schs., 1996—. Recipient Martha Harding Jennings award, 2001. Mem.: NEA, Ohio H.S. Volleyball Coaches Assn. Home: 10305 State Rte 66 Saint Marys OH 45885 Office: Meml HS 101 W South St Saint Marys OH 45885-2599 Office Phone: 419-394-4011.

VANDER LAAN, MARK ALAN, lawyer; b. Akron, Ohio, Sept. 14, 1948; s. Robert H. and Isabel R. (Bishop) Vander L.; m. Barbara Ann Ryzenga, Aug. 25, 1970; children: Aaron, Matthew. AB, Hope Coll., Holland, Mich., 1970; JD, U. Mich., Ann Arbor, 1972. Bar: Ohio 1973, U.S. Dist. Ct. (so. dist.) Ohio 1973, U.S. Ct. Appeals (6th cir.) 1978, U.S. Supreme Ct. 1981. Assoc. Dinsmore, Shohl, Coates & Deupree, Cin., 1972-79; ptnr. Dinsmore & Shohl, Cin., 1979—. Chair litig. dept., 2001—, spl. counsel Ohio Atty. Gen.'s Office, 1983—; spl. prosecutor State of Ohio, 1985-94; city solicitor City of Blue Ash, Ohio, 1987—, City of Silverton, Ohio, 1999-2005; trustee Cin. So. Railway, 1994—, pres., 1999—. Mem. Cin. Human Rels. Commn., 1980-86; mem. Leadership Cin. Class XIII, 1989-90; trustee Legal Aid Soc. of Cin., 1981-94, pres., 1988-90; trustee Volunteer Lawyers for the Poor Found., pres., 2003-06. Mem. ABA, Ohio Bar Assn., Cin. Bar Assn. (ethics com. 1983—), Sixth Cir. Jud. Conf. (life), Potter Stewart Am. Inn of Ct. (master), Queen City Club. Office: Dinsmore & Shohl 1900 Chemed Ct 255 E 5th St Cincinnati OH 45202-4700 Home Phone: 513-861-8818; Office Phone: 513-977-8000. Business E-Mail: mark.vanderlaan@dinslaw.com.

VANDERLINDE, DAISY, consumer products company executive; BA, Ohio State U., Columbus. Head human resources Broadway Stores, Marshalls Inc., Tractor Supply Co.; sr. v.p. human resources and loss prevention, mem. exec. com. AutoZone; exec. v.p. human resources Office Depot, Inc., 2005—. Office: Office Depot Inc 2200 Old Germantown Rd Delray Beach FL 33445 *

VANDERLINDEN, CAMILLA DENICE DUNN, telecommunications industry executive; b. Dayton, July 21, 1950; d. Joseph Stanley and Virginia Danley (Martin) Dunn; m. David Henry VanderLinden; Oct. 10, 1980; 1 child, Michael Christopher. Student, U. de Valencia, Spain, 1969; BA in Spanish and Secondary Edn. cum laude, U. Utah, 1972, MS in Human Resource Econs., 1985. Asst. dir. Davis County Community Action Program, Farmington, Utah, 1973-76; dir. South County Community Action, Midvale, Utah, 1976-79; supr. customer service Ideal Nat. Life Ins. Co., Salt Lake City, 1979-80; mgr. customer service Utah Farm Bur. Mutual Ins., Salt Lake City, 1980-82; quality assurance analyst Am. Express Co., Salt Lake City, 1983-86, quality assurance and human resource specialist, 1986-88, mgr. quality assurance and engring. Denver, 1988-91; mgr. customer svc. Tel. Express Co., Colorado Springs, Colo., 1991-97; dir. Call Ctr. United Membership Mktg. Group, Lakewood, Colo., 1997-98; telesvcs. industry mgr. Piton Found., Denver, 1998—; customer care and tng. dir. SafeRent, 2000—; dir. quality assurance Tele-Servicing Innovations, 2000—02; ops. mgr. Bayaud Industries, 2002—05. Adj. faculty Westminster Coll., Salt Lake City, 1987-88. adj. faculty, quality adv. bd. Red Rocks C.C., 1990-91; cons. in field. Vol. translator Latin Am. community; vol. naturalist Roxborough State Park; internat. exch. coord. EF Fgn. Exch. Program. Mem. Internat. Customer Svc. Orgn. (officer call ctr. chpt.), Colo. Springs Customer Svc. Assn. (officer). Christian. Avocation: swimming. Home: 44 Lake Lea Rd Rochester NY 14617 Personal E-mail: camillavan@usa.net.

VAN DER LINDEN, FRANK MORRIS, historian; b. Hendersonville, NC, Mar. 8, 1919; s. William Harrison and Floride Bowden (Morris) van der L.; m. Georgia Kathlyn Huddle, Feb. 11, 1951; children: Frank Robert, Margaret Lyn, Anne Morris. AB, Lenoir-Rhyne Coll., 1939. Reporter, editl. writer Hickory N.C. Daily Record, 1939-42; mng. editor Hickory Daily Record, 1942-45; reporter Cottrell News Bur., Washington, 1945-52; Washington bur. chief Nashville Tenn. Banner, 1952-86; White House corr. Sacramento Calif. Union, 1979-89; columnist United Feature Syndicate, N.Y., 1971-76. Guest panelist NBC-TV Meet the Press, 1956-75. Author: Dark Horse, 1944, The Turning Point: Jefferson's Battle for the Presidency, 1962, Nixon's Quest for Peace, 1972, The Real Reagan, 1981, Lincoln: The Road to War, 1998, The Dark Intrigue, 2007. Mem. The Lincoln Commn., Washington, 1989-98. Mem. U.S. Capitol Hist. Soc. (oral history program dir. 1976-94), The Cosmos Club (editl. bd. 1988—). Presbyterian. Avocation: historical research. Home and Office: 5301 Westbard Cir Apt 247 Bethesda MD 20816-1430

VANDERLIP, ELIN BREKKE, professional society administrator, volunteer; b. Oslo, June 7, 1919; came to the U.S., 1934; m. Kelvin Cox, Nov., 1946 (dec. 1956); children: Kelvin Jr., Narcissa, Henrik and Katrina (twins). With Norwegian Embassy, Washington, Norwegian Fgn. Ministry, London, 1941-44, Red Cross, Calcutta, India; pres. Friends of French Art, Portuguese Bend, Calif. Sponsor of charity art conservation fundraising events Friends of French Art; tour leader Ile de France, Anjou, Bordelais, Provence-Cote d'Azur, Alsace, Dordogne, Lyonnais-Isere, Brittany, Burgundy, Normandy, Languedoc, Loire, Gascony, Le Nord, Charente, Champagne, Eure et Loir, 1978-96, Route de Berry, Auvergne and Toulouse. Decorated Comdr. Order of Arts and Letters (France) Chevalier of the Legion of Honor. Home and Office: Villa Narcissa 100 Vanderlip Dr Rancho Palos Verdes CA 90275-5920 Fax: (310) 377-4584. E-mail: VillaCissa@aol.com.

VAN DER MARCK, JAN, art historian; b. Roermond, The Netherlands, Aug. 19, 1929; arrived in U.S., 1957; s. Everard and Anny (Finken) van der Marck; m. Ingeborg Lachmann, Apr. 27, 1961 (dec. 1988); m. Sheila Stamell, May 24, 1990. BA, U. Nijmegen, The Netherlands, 1952, MA, 1954, PhD in Art History, 1956; postgrad., U. Utrecht, The Netherlands, 1956-57, Columbia U., NYC, 1957-59. Curator Gemeentemuseum, Arnhem, Netherlands, 1959-61; asst. dir. fine arts Seattle World's Fair, 1961-62; curator Walker Art Ctr., Mpls., 1963-67; dir. Mus. Contemporary Art, Chgo., 1967-70; assoc. prof. art history U. Wash., Seattle, 1972-74; dir. Dartmouth Coll. Mus. and Galleries, 1974-80, Ctr. for Fine Arts, Miami, 1980-85; curator 20th century art, chief curator Detroit Inst. Arts, 1986-95. Author: (book) Romantische Boekillustratie in Belgie, 1956, Enrico Baj, 1969, Lucio Fontana, 1974, George Segal, 1975, Arman, 1984, Bernar Venet, 1988, The Art of Contemporary Bookbinding, 1997, Art and the American Experience, 1998, Lucio Pozzi, 2001, Jef Bourgeau: A User's Manual, 2007; contbr. articles to art jours., essays to catalogues. Decorated officer Order Arts and Letters, knight Order of Orange Nassau; fellow Netherlands Orgn. Pure Rsch., 1954—55, Rockefeller Found., 1957—59, Aspen Inst., 1974, 1994, Ctr. Advanced Study in Visual Arts, Nat. Gallery, Washington, 1986. Fellow: Pierpont Morgan Libr.; mem.: Les Amis de la Reliure Originale, Internat. Art Critics Assn.

VANDERMEER, JOHN H., ecologist, educator; Sloan Found. postdoctoral fellow U. Chgo., 1969; coord., mem. full-time faculty, vis. scientist Orgn. Tropical Studies, 1969—99; asst. prof. biology SUNY, Stony Brook, 1969—70; asst. prof. zoology U. Mich., 1970—74, assoc. prof. biology, 1974—81, prof., 1981—, Margaret Davis Collegiate prof. ecology and evolutionary biology, 2002—. Vis. scholar Princeton U., 1969; vis. scientist Nat. Inst. Rsch. Amazon, Manaus, Brazil, 1974; vis. lectr. Superior Sch. Tropical Agr., Tabasco, Mexico, 1978; vis. prof. Autonomous U. Nicaragua, 1984, Southeastern Ctr. Ecol. Investigations, Chiapas, Mexico, 1991, U. C.Am., Managua, Nicaragua, 1994, Fed. U. Minas Gerais, Belo Horizonte, Brazil, 2004; chair dept. ecology and evolutionary biology U. Mich., 1985—86, faculty assoc. prog. in Latin Am. and Caribbean Studies, 1993—, faculty assoc. prog. in Am. culture, 1994—, Alfred Thurnau Disting. prof., 1994—97, Sokal scholar, 1996—97, faculty assoc. Ctr. Study of Complex Systems, 2000—, faculty assoc. Mich. Consortium on Theoretical Physics, 2001—; vis. prof. agroecology Superior Inst. Farming Scis., 1986—87, Fulbright scholar, Nicaragua, 1986—87; Fulbright scholar dept. ecol. agr. Wageningen Agrl. U., Netherlands, 1996—97. Contbr. articles to sci. jours., chapters to books; co-editor: Biology as a Social Weapon, 1977, Nicaraguan Reader: Documents of a Revolution Under Fire, 1983, Nicaragua: Unfinished Revolution, 1986, Agroecology, 1990; author: Elem. Math. Ecology, 1981, The Ecology of Intercropping Systems, 1989, Reconstructing Biology: Genetics and Ecology in the New World Order, 1996; co-author: A Breakfast of Biodiversity: The True Causes of Rain Forest Destruction, 1995, Population Ecology: First Principles, 2003, Elem. Population Ecology, 2003; editor: Tropical Agroecosystems, 2002. Office: Dept Ecology and Evolutionary Biology U Mich Ann Arbor MI 48109 E-mail: jvander@umich.edu.

VANDERMEER, ROBERT D., orthopedic surgeon; b. Toronto, Canada, Feb. 1, 1933; MD, U. Tex. Southwestern Med. Sch., Dallas, Tex., 1958. Cert. Am. Bd. Orthop. Surgeons. Intern, orthop. surgery Parkland Meml. Hosp., Dallas, 1958—59, resident, orthop. surgery, 1961, Baylor U. Hosp., Dallas, 1960, 1963; resident Tex. Scottish Rite Hosp., Dallas, 1962; hosp. appointment, orthop., mem. tchg. staff Baylor U. Med. Ctr., Dallas; chief Mary Shiels Hosp., Dallas; clin. assoc. prof., orthop. surgery U. Tex. Health Sci. Ctr., Dallas; with Carrell Clinic, Dallas, 1963—. Orthop. cons. So. Methodist U. Athletics Dept., 1982—; asst. team orthop. surgeon Dallas Stars Hockey Team; team physician, knee injuries Dallas Cowboys Football Club, 1994—; presenter in field. Contbr. articles to profl. jours. Mem. exec. bd. Southwestern Diabetic Found. Mem.: Nat. Football League Team Physicians Soc., Am. Orthop. Soc. for Sports Medicine, Internat. Arthroscopy Assn., Arthroscopy Assn. N.Am. (charter mem.), Am. Acad. Orthop. Surgeons, Nat. Athletic Trainers' Assn. (hon.), Alpha Omega Alpha. Avocations: fishing, hunting, travel. Office: Carrell Clinic 9301 N Central Expy Ste 400 Dallas TX 75231 Office Phone: 214-220-2468. Office Fax: 214-397-1560. *

VAN DER MEULEN, JOSEPH PIERRE, neurologist; b. Boston, Aug. 22, 1929; s. Edward Lawrence and Sarah Jane (Robertson) Van Der Meulen; m. Ann Irene Yadeno, June 18, 1960; children: Elisabeth, Suzanne, Janet. AB, Boston Coll., 1950; MD, Boston U., 1954. Diplomate Am. Bd. Psychiatry and Neurology. Intern Cornell Med. div. Bellevue Hosp., NYC, 1954-55, resident, 1955-56, Harvard U., Boston City Hosp., 1958-60, instr., fellow, 1962-66; assoc. Case Western Res. U., Cleve., 1966-67, asst. prof., 1967-69, assoc. prof. neurology and biomed. engring., 1969-71; prof. neurology U. So. Calif., LA, 1971—2006, prof. emeritus, 2006—, chmn. dept., 1971—78, v.p. health affairs, 1977—2005, v.p. health affairs emeritus, 2006—, dean Sch. Medicine, 1985—86, 1995—97, vice dean med. affairs, 1995—97; dir. Ind. Health Professions, LA, 1991—2005. Dir. dept. neurology LA County/U. So. Calif. Med. Ctr., 1971—2006; vis. prof. Autonomous U., Guadalajara, Mexico, 1974; pres. Norris Cancer Hosp. and Rsch. Inst., 1983—98, chmn., 2004; pres. Scott Newman Ctr., 1987—89; dir. Ind. Health Professions, LA, 1991—2005. Contbr. articles to profl. jours. Mem. med. adv. bd. Calif. chpt. Myasthenia Gravis Found., 1971—75, chmn., 1974—75, 1977—78; mem. adv. bd. Amyotrophic Lateral Sclerosis Found., Calif., 1973—75, chmn. Calif., 1974—75; mem. Com. to Combat Huntington's Disease, 1973—; bd. dirs. Calif. Hosp. Med. Ctr., Good Hope Med. Found., LA Hosp. Good Samaritan, Barlow Respiratory Hosp., U. So. Calif. Univ. Hosp., chmn., 1991—2004; bd. dirs. Assn. Acad. Health Ctrs., chmn.; bd. dirs. Children's Hosp. LA, Eisenhower Med. Ctr. Served to lt. M.C. USN, 1956—58. Nobel Inst. fellow, Karolinska Inst., Stockholm, 1960—62, NIH grantee, 1968—71. Mem.: AMA, LA Acad. Medicine, Calif. Med. Soc., LA Med. Assn., LA Soc. Neurology and Psychiatry (pres. 1977—78), Am. Acad. Neurology, Am. Neurol. Assn., Phi Kappa Phi, Alpha Omega Alpha (councillor 1992—). Roman Catholic. Home: 39 Club View Ln Palos Verdes Peninsula CA 90274-4208

VAN DER PAARDT, TAMARA ANN, music educator; d. Glenn Elmer and Darlene Margaret Schultz; m. Peter van der Paardt, June 27, 1987; children: Nicole Marie, Melissa Krystine, Andrew Scott. BA in Music Edn., Calif. State U., Fresno, 1985. Cert. clear credential music edn. Calif., 1987. Profl. musician Fresno Philharm. Orch., Calif., 1979—; music tchr. Clovis Unified Sch. Dist., 1987—. Dir. Winter Drumline Ensemble, Jazz Ensemble. Named Outstanding Jazz Ensemble, Downbeat Internat. Music Awards, 1995, Class A World Champions, WGI Drumline Competition, 2003. Mem.: CBDA (assoc.), FMCMEA (assoc.), IAJE (assoc.), Internat. Assn. Jazz Educators, Calif. Band Dirs. Assn., Fresno-Madera (Calif.) County Music Educators Assn., Music Educators Nat. Conf. (assoc.), Calif. Music Edn. Assn. (assoc.; pres. ctrl. Calif. sect. 2003—), Winter Guard Internat. Avocations: travel, gardening, softball. Home: 1692 Richert Ave Clovis CA 93611 Office: Reyburn Intermediate Sch 4300 N DeWolf Clovis CA 93611 Home Phone: 559-348-1031; Office Phone: 559-327-4731.

VANDERPAN, NORMA, retired elementary school educator; b. Starkweather, ND; m. Leslie Vanderpan; 7 children. BA, Concordia Coll.; MA, U. S.D. Mem. negotiation team West Lyon Tchr. Assn., Inwood, Iowa, 1967—69, Brookings Edn. Assn., 1973—74; organizer, rep. Ea. S.D. Uniserv, Sioux Falls, SD, 1974—75. Named Brookings Tchr. of Yr., Brookings Pub. Schs., 1976; Nat. Def. Edn. grant, U. S.D., 1965. Mem.: PEO (chaplain Chpt. P 2004—05), BARTA, Saturday Literary Club (pres. 2005—), Phi Delta Kappa, Alpha Delta Kappa (Eta chpt. sec., Eta chpt. treas., state treas. 1976—78, state chaplain 1990—92, Fidelis Gamma chpt. pres. 1992—94, Fidelis Gamma chpt. chaplain 1995—2005). Republican. Lutheran. Avocations: reading, writing, quilting, antiques, needlepoint. Home: 2009 Derdall Dr Brookings SD 57006

VANDERPLOEG, HENRY A., ecologist, researcher; b. Chgo., Aug. 23, 1944; m. Barbara Howland Abramson, July 6, 1968. BS in Biol. Scis., Mich. Technol. U., Houghton, 1966; MS in Zoology, U. Wis., Madison, 1968; PhD in Oceangraphy, Oreg. State U., Corvalis, 1973. Aquatic ecologist environ. sci. divsn. Oak Ridge Nat. Lab, Tenn., 1972—74; rsch. ecologist Gt. Lakes environ. rsch. lab. Nat. Oceanic and Atmospheric Adminstrn., Ann Arbor, Mich., 1974—. Contbr. over 60 articles to profl. jours. Mem.: Internat. Assn. Gt. Lakes Rsch., Amer. Soc. Limnology and Oceanogrpahy. Office: Great Lakes Environ Res Lab NOAA 2205 Commonwealth Blvd Ann Arbor MI 48105 Office Phone: 734-741-2284.

VANDERPLOEG, JAMES M., preventive medicine physician; b. Upland, Calif., Nov. 22, 1950; BA, U. Iowa, 1975. Cert. Aerospace Medicine and Occupational Medicine. Intern U. Hosp./U. Calif., San Diego, 1975-76; resident in otolaryngoloty U. Iowa Hosps., Iowa City, 1978-79; resident in occupational medicine U. Tex. Sch. Pub. Health, Houston, 1980-82, assoc. prof. occupational health; mem. staff St. John Hosp., Nassau Bay, Tex.; pres., partner Ctr. Aerospace & Occupl. Medicine, Houston. Bd. mem. Am. Bd. Preventive Medicine, Schiller Park, Ill., 1993—98, exec. dir., 1998—. Mem. Am. Coll. Occupational Medicine, ACPrM-AerosMA. Office: Ctr for Aerospace & Occupl Medicine 700 Gemini St Ste 110 Houston TX 77058-2735

VANDERRYN, JACK, environmental services administrator; b. Groningen, The Netherlands, Apr. 14, 1930; came to U.S., 1939; s. Herman Gabriel and Henrietta S.E. (Hartog) V.; m. Margrit Wolfes, Mar. 18, 1956; children: David, Judith, Amy, Daniel. BA, Lehigh U., 1951, MS, 1952, PhD, 1955. Rsch. and grad. teaching asst. Lehigh U., Bethlehem, Pa., 1952-55; asst. prof. chemistry Va. Poly. Inst., Blacksburg, 1955-58; rsch. participant Oak Ridge (Tenn.) Nat. Lab., 1957; chemist AEC, Oak Ridge, 1958-62, tech. adviser to asst. gen. mgr. R & D, Washington, 1962-67, asst. to gen. mgr., 1971-72, tech. asst. to dir. div. applied tech., 1972-73, chief energy tech. br., div. applied tech., 1973-75; acting dir. div. energy storage Energy Rsch. and Devel. Adminstrn., Washington, 1975, dir. Office Internat. R & D Programs, 1975-77; dir. Office Internat. Programs Dept. Energy, Washington, 1977-82; dir. energy and natural resources AID, Washington, 1982-91; program dir. environment Moriah Fund, Washington, 1991—2003; sr. fellow, environ. and devel. Moriah Fund, 2003—06. Sr. sci. adviser U.S. Mission to Internat. Atomic Energy Agy., Dept. State, Vienna, Austria, 1967-71; lectr. Brookings Instn., 1965-66. Mem., dep. pres., exec. bd. Am. Internat. Sch., Vienna, 1968-71; v.p. Oak Ridge Civic Music Assn., 1959-60; pres. Washington Print Club, 1986-91; pres. Consultative Group on Biodiversity, 1997-2000; bd. dirs. Ctr. for Internat. Environ. Law, 2004—, Forest Stewardship Coun. U.S., 2004—, Inst. for Conservation Leadership, 2003—, Endangered Species Coalition, 2003—. Home: 207 Park Ave San Carlos CA 94070 Personal E-mail: jackvanderryn@msn.com.

VANDERSLICE, ELLEN, architect, composer; b. Ann Arbor, Mich., 1953; d. Ralph L. Vanderslice, Carolyn G. Vanderslice; married. BS, U. Mich., Ann Arbor, 1981, MArch, 1983. Lic. Architect, Oreg., 1996. Project mgr. Office of Transp., City of Portland, 1994—99, 2003—; project designer David Giulietti and Assocs., Portland, 1990—94; pres. America Walks, Portland, Oreg., 1996—2003. Pres. Willamette Pedestrian Coalition, Portland, 2001—03; mem. com. on pedestrians Transp. Rsch. Bd., Washington, 2001—04; mem. adv. com. Pub. Rights-of-Way Access, Washington, 1999—; co-treas. Portland chpt. Women's Transp. Seminar, 1997—98; prin. Ellen Vanderslice AIA, Portland, 1999—2003; bd. dirs. Internat. Fedn. Pedestrians, 2007—. Composer (CD): Once in a Blue Moon, 2000, The Standard Vanderslice, 2001, Don't Look Before You Sing, 2003. Sec. Northwest Dist. Assn., Portland, 1986—88. Recipient Pl. Planning award for Portland Pedestrian Master Plan and Pedestrian Design Guide, Environ. Design and Rsch. Assn., 2000, Exemplary Svc. to Pedestrian Transp. Program and Unwavering Commitment to Advocacy of Walking award, Portland Office of Transp. Engring. and Devel., 1999, Outstanding Project award for Portland Pedestrian Design Guide, Inst. Transp. Engrs. Oreg. Sect., 1999, Reclaiming Our Streets All-Star award, City Commr. Earl Blumenauer, 1991, Northwest Traffic Circulation Project Leadership award, Neighbor Newspaper, 1987, 1st prize jazz, USA Songwriting Competition, 2002, Golden Sole award, Willamette Pedestrian Coalition, 2005. Mem.: AIA (sec. Portland chpt. 1998—99, Nehemiah Housing Project award of excellence Portland chpt. 1993), Assn. Pedestrian and Bicycle Profls., Women's Transp. Seminar (co-treas. Portland chpt. 1997, Woman of Yr. Portland chpt. 2000), Nat. Assn. Watch and Clock Collectors, Jazz Soc. Oreg., Portland Songwriters Assn. (1st pl. Blues/Jazz/R&B Category 1999, 2000, 2001, 2003). Office: 1120 SW 5th Ave Rm 800 Portland OR 97204 Office Phone: 503-823-4638. Business E-Mail: ellen.vanderslice@pdxtrans.org.

VANDERSLICE, MARA, religious organization executive; BA, Earlham Coll., Richmond, IN. Worked Sojourners, Call to Renewal, Jubilee 2000 campaign for debt-relief, Howard Dean Campaign, Cmty. and Faith Outreach, 2004; dir. Religious Outreach for the Kerry-Edwards 2004 campaign, 2004; founder, sr. ptnr. Common Good Strategies. Office: Common Good Strategies 949 North Pitt St Alexandria VA 22314 Office Phone: 202-213-7425. E-mail: mara@cg-strategies.com. *

VANDERSLICE, THOMAS AQUINAS, electronics executive; b. Phila., Jan. 8, 1932; s. Joseph R. and Mae (Daly) V.; m. Margaret Hurley, June 9, 1956; children: Thomas Aquinas, Paul Thomas Aquinas, John Thomas Aquinas, Peter Thomas Aquinas. BS in Chemistry and Philosophy, Boston Coll., 1953; PhD in Chemistry and Physics, Cath. U. Am., 1956. With GE, Fairfield, Conn., from 1956, gen. mgr. electronic components bus. div., 1970-72, v.p., 1970, group exec. spl. systems and products group, 1972-77, sr. v.p., sector exec. Power System Sector, 1977-79, exec. v.p., sector exec. Power System Sector, 1979-84; pres., chief oper. officer, dir. Gen. Tel. & Electronics Corp., Stamford, Conn., 1979-83; chmn., CEO, Apollo Computer, Inc., Chelmsford, Mass., 1984-89, M/A COM, Inc., Lowell, Mass., 1989-95. Bd. dirs. Texaco, Inc. Patentee low pressure gas measurements and analysis, gas surface interactions and elec. discharges; co-author: Ultra High Vacuum and Its Applications, 1963; reviser: Scientific Foundations of Vacuum Technique, 1960; contbr. to profl. jours. Trustee Boston Coll., past chmn., past trustee Comm. Econ. Devel. Recipient Bicentennial medal Boston Coll., 1976; Fulbright scholar, 1953-56. Mem. NAE, ASTM, Am. Vacuum Soc., Am. Chem. Soc., Am. Inst. Physics, Royal Poinciana Golf Club (Naples, Fla.), Oyster Harbors Club, Sigma Xi, Tau Beta Pi, Alpha Sigma Nu, Sigma Pi Sigma. Office: LeRivage Unit 10N 4351 Gulf Shore Blvd N Naples FL 34103-2697

VANDERVEER, TARA, women's college basketball coach; b. Niagara Falls, NY, June 26, 1953; Grad., Ind. U., 1975. Head coach U. Idaho, 1978—80, Ohio State U., 1980—85, Stanford U., 1985—. Head coach US Olympic Women's Basketball Team (gold medal), 1996. Author: Shooting From The Outside, 1997. Named Big Ten Coach of Yr., 1984, 1985, Nat. Coach of Yr., 1988, 1989, 1990, Dist. Coach of Yr., 1988, 1989, 1990, Coach of Yr., Pacific-10 Conf., 1989, 1990, 1995, 1997, 2002, 2003, 2004, 2005, 2006, No. Calif. Women's Intercollegiate Coach of Yr., 1988, 1989, 1990, 1992, 1993, USA Basketball Nat. Coach of Yr., 1996, US Olympic Com. Elite Basketball Coach of Yr., 1996; named to Ind. U. Hall of Fame, 1995, Women's Basketball Hall of Fame, 2002, Women's Sports Found. Hall of Fame, Greater Buffalo Hall of Fame. Achievements include champions NCAA Divsn. 1 A, 1990, 92. Office: Stanford U Womens Basketball Dept Athletics Arrillaga Family Sports Ctr Stanford CA 94305-6150 Office Phone: 650-723-0284. E-mail: tarahoop@stanford.edu. *

VANDERVELD, JOHN, JR., diversified financial services company executive; b. Chgo., Oct. 24, 1926; s. John J. and Rose (Renkema) V. Pres. Nat. Disposal Contractors, Barrington, Ill., 1952-71; sr. v.p., dir. Browning Ferris Industries, Houston, 1971-78; pres. Pioneer Equities, Inc., 1975-90, C.J.V. Corp., Dallas, 1990-92; sr. corp. advisor Vector Environmental Techs., Inc., 1993-96. Dir. Am. Far East, Inc., Dallas and Tokyo; adv. bd. Southwestern Legal Found., 1975-1998. Bd. dirs. Internat. Bible Soc., mem. exec.com., 1982-98; bd. dirs. Global Action; chmn. Brookshire Capital Corp., 2000—. Mem. Nat. Solid Waste Mgmt. Assn. (former chmn. govt. industry coordinating council, mem. environ. research com.) Home: 7031 Brookshire Dr Dallas TX 75230-4248 Office Phone: 214-692-8995. E-mail: jv-brookshire@sbcglobal.net.

VANDER VELDE, WALLACE EARL, aeronautical and astronautical engineering educator; b. Jamestown, Mich., June 4, 1929; s. Peter Nelson and Janet (Keizer) Vander V.; m. Winifred Helen Bunai, Aug. 29, 1954; children: Susan Jane, Peter Russell. BS in Aero Engring, Purdue U., 1951; Sc.D., Mass. Inst. Tech., 1956. Dir. applications engring. GPS Instrument Co., Inc., Newton, Mass., 1956-57; faculty MIT, Cambridge, 1957—2004, prof. aero. and astronautics, 1965—2004, prof. emeritus, 2004—. Cons. to industry, 1958— Author: Flight Vehicle Control Systems, Part VII of Space Navigation, Guidance and Control, 1966, (with Arthur Gelb) Multiple-Input Describing Functions, 1968; also papers. Served to 1st lt. USAF,

1951-53. Recipient Edn. award Am. Automatic Control Coun., 1988. Fellow AIAA; mem. IEEE. Home: 50 High St Winchester MA 01890-3314 Office: MIT Rm 9-335 Dept Aero and Astronautics Cambridge MA 02139

VANDERVER, TIMOTHY ARTHUR, JR., lawyer; b. Birmingham, Ala., Jan. 25, 1944; s. Timothy Arthur and Jeanette (Grimes) V.; m. Virginia Cassandra Nye, Oct. 1, 1966 (dec. July 2001); m. Susan Elliotte McVay, Mar. 20, 2003; children: Timothy A. III, Glenn Bruce, Benjamin Richard. BA, Washington and Lee U., 1965; BA in Law, Oxford U., Eng., 1967, MA, 1983; JD, Harvard U., 1969. Bar: D.C., U.S. Ct. Appeals (D.C. cir.) 1969, U.S. Ct. Appeals (5th cir.) 1984, U.S. Ct. Appeals (3d and 11th cirs.) 1989, U.S. Supreme Ct. 1978. Assoc. Covington & Burling, Washington, 1969—72, Dept. of Interior, Washington, 1972—73, Dept. Housing and Urban Devel., Washington, 1973—76; ptnr. Patton Boggs L.L.P., Washington, 1976—. Editor: Clean Air Law and Regulation, 1992, Environmental Law Handbook, 1994. Capt. U.S. Army, 1970-71. Presbyterian. Home: 9000 Congressional Ct Potomac MD 20854-4608 Office: Patton Boggs LLP 2550 M St NW Ste 500 Washington DC 20037-1350 Office Phone: 202-457-6074. Business E-Mail: tvanderver@pattonboggs.com.

VAN DER VOO, ROB, geophysicist; b. Zeist, The Netherlands, Aug. 4, 1940; arrived in U.S., 1970; s. Maximiliaan and Johanna Hendrika (Baggerman) Van der V.; m. Tatiana M. C. Graafland, Mar. 26, 1966; children: Serge Nicolas, Bjorn Alexander. BS, U. Utrecht, Netherlands, 1961, MS, 1965, PhD, 1969. Rsch. asst. U. Utrecht, 1964-65, rsch. assoc., 1965-69, sr. rsch. assoc., 1969-70; vis. asst. prof. U. Mich., Ann Arbor, 1970-72, asst. prof., 1972-75, assoc. prof., 1975-79, prof. geophysics, 1979—, chmn., 1981-88, 91-95, Arthur F. Thurnau prof., 1994-97, dir. honors program Coll. Lit., Sci. and the Arts, 1998—2003. Guest prof. ETH, Zurich, Switzerland, 1978, Kuwait U., 1979, Utrecht U. and Delft U. Tech., 1997-98. Author: Paleomagnetism of the Atlantic, Tethys and Iapetus Oceans, 1993; contbr. articles to profl. jours. Recipient Russell award, U. Mich., 1976, Disting. Faculty Achievement award, 1990, Benjamin Franklin medal in Earth Scis., 2001. Mem. Geol. Soc. Am. (pres. 2004), Am. Geophys. Union, Geologische Vereinigung (Germany), Royal Acad. Scis. (Netherlands), Royal Norwegian Soc. Scis. and Letters, Sigma Xi, Phi Kappa Phi. Home: 2305 Devonshire Rd Ann Arbor MI 48104-2703 Office: U Mich 4534 CC Little Bldg Ann Arbor MI 48109-1005 Office Phone: 734-764-8322. Business E-Mail: voo@umich.edu.

VANDERWAGEN, W. CRAIG (WILLIAM CRAIG VANDERWAGEN), federal agency administrator, physician; b. Grand Rapids, Mich., 1949; m. Suzanne M. Vanderwagen; 3 children. Bachelor's degree, Calvin Coll. and Seminary; MD, Mich. State U., 1978. Advanced through ranks to rear adm. upper half US Pub. Health Svc. Corps., 2006; chief pub. health Coalition Provisional Authority, Iraqi Ministry of Health; dir., Office Clin. & Preventative Services, acting chief med. officer, Zuni Indian Hosp. Indian Health Svc., Albuquerque; spl. asst. to the dep. sec. for preparedness US Dept. Health & Human Services, Washington, asst. sec. for pub. health emergency preparedness, 2006, dep. asst. sec. for preparedness & response, chief preparedness officer, 2006—07, asst. sec. for preparedness & response, 2007—. Decorated Meritorious Svc. medal; named Alumni of Yr., Mich. State U. Coll. Human Medicine, 2005; recipient Disting. Svc. award for leading fed. disaster response to Hurricanes Katrina and Rita, AMA, 2006. Office: US Dept Health & Human Services OPHEP 200 Independence Ave SW Rm 638G Washington DC 20201 E-mail: craig.vanderwagen@hhs.gov. *

VANDER WEG, PHILLIP DALE, art educator, academic administrator, sculptor; b. Benton Harbor, Mich., Aug. 16, 1943; s. Sam Dirk and Trena (Poort) Vander W.; m. Judith Greville, Dec. 15, 1966; 1 child, Kara Sue. BS in Design, U. Mich., 1965, MFA, 1968. Art instr., prof. art Mid. Tenn. State U., Murfreesboro, 1968-89, acting head Mufreesboro, 1983-85, 88-89; chair dept. art, prof. art We. Mich. U., Kalamazoo, 1989-97, 00—, prof. art, 1998—, dir. sch. art, 1999—. Cons., editl. reviewer Prentice-Hall Pubs., Englewood Cliffs, N.J., 1978-90; mem. region 5 adv. panel Mich. Artist Program, Detroit Inst. Art, 1990-92; mem. rev. panel Tenn. Art Commn. Visual Arts, Nashville, 1986-89. Prin. works include Columbia State U., 1979, Vanderbilt U., Nashville, 1987, Tenn. Arts Commn., 1988. Mem. Kalamazoo Pub. Art Commn., 1992—. Mem. Nat. Assn. Schs. of Art and Design, Nat. Coun. Art Adminstrs., Founds. in Art Theory and Edn. (founder, bd. dirs. 1976-84). Home: 6791 Penny Ln Kalamazoo MI 49009-8539 Office: Western Mich U Dept Art Oliver St Kalamazoo MI 49008 Home Phone: 269-372-3469; Office Phone: 616-387-2436. Business E-Mail: vanderweg@wmich.edu.

VANDER WEIDE, BOB, professional sports team executive; m. Cheri Vander Weide; 5 children. V.p. basketball ops. Orlando Magic, Fla., 1992—94, pres., CEO, 1994—; CEO RDV Sports, 1994—; pres., CEO Internat. Hockey League Orlando Solar Bears, 1995—2001; chmn. investment com. RDV Corp., bd. dirs. Mem. bd. govs. NBA, mem. planning com.; mem. Fla. Olympics and Pan Am. Games Task Force. Chmn. Orlando Magic Youth Found. Named Orlandoan of Yr., Orlando Mag., 1997. Office: Orlando Magic 8701 Maitland Summit Blvd Orlando FL 32810-5915 *

VANDE STEEG, NICKOLAS W., manufacturing executive; m. Jeanne Vande Steeg; 3 children. BS, Univ. Calif., Irvine, 1968; MBA, Pepperdine Univ., 1985. With Parker Hannifin Corp., Cleve., 1971—, pres. seal group, 1987—2002, v.p., 1995—2002, corp. v.p., 2002, sr. v.p., 2002—03, exec. v.p., COO, 2003—04, pres., COO, bd. dir., 2004—. Bd. dir. Trimble Navigation Ltd. Bd. dir. Azusa Pacific Univ. Office: Parker Hannifin Corp 6035 Parkland Blvd Cleveland OH 44124-4141

VAN DEVENDER, J. PACE, research scientist, science administrator; b. Jackson, Miss., Sept. 12, 1947; m. Nancy Jane Manning, 1971; 3 children. BA in Physics, Vanderbilt U., 1969; MA in Physics, Dartmouth Coll., 1971; PhD in Physics, U. London, 1974. Physicist diagnostics devel. Lawrence Livermore Lab., 1969; mem. tech. staff pulsed power rsch. and devel. Sandia Nat. Labs., Albuquerque, 1974-78, divsn. supr. pulsed power rsch. divsn., 1978-82, dept. mgr. fusion rsch., 1982-84, dir. pulsed power scis., 1984-93, dir. corp. comm., 1993, dir. Nat. Indsl. Alliances Ctr., 1993-95; pres. Prosperity Inst., 1995-98; dir. strategic scis. ctr. Sandia Nat. Labs., Albuquerque, 1998—, chief info. officer, 1998—2002, dir. exec. staff, 2002—03, v.p. sci., tech. and partnerships, chief tech. officer, 2003—. Mem. bd. trust Vanderbilt U., 1969-73. With U.S. Army, 1969-71. Recipient Ernest Orlando Lawrence Meml. award US Dept. Energy, 1991; named one of 100 Most Promising Scientists Under 40, Sci. Digest, 1984; Marshal scholar U. London, 1971-74. Fellow Am. Phys. Soc.; Phi Beta Kappa, Omicron Delta Kappa, Sigma Xi. Office: Sandia Nat Labs MS 0103 PO Box 5800 Albuquerque NM 87185-0103 Office Phone: 505-844-5148. E-mail: jpvande@sandia.gov.

VANDEVER, WILLIAM DIRK, lawyer; b. Chgo., Aug. 1, 1949; s. Lester J. and Elizabeth J. V.; m. Kathi J. Zellmer, Aug. 26, 1983; children: Barton Dirk, Brooke Shelby. BS, U. Mo., Kansas City, 1971, JD with distinction, 1974. Bar: Mo. 1975, Kans. 2005, U.S. Dist. Ct. Mo. 1975. Dir. Popham Law Firm, Kansas City, Mo., 1975—. Lectr. in field, Kansas City Mo., 1979—. Issue editor U. Mo.-Kansas City Law Rev., 1974. Bd. govs. IOLTA, 1989—91. Fellow Am. Bd. Trial Advs. (treas. 2004-05, pres. 2007); mem. ABA, ATLA, Mo. Assn. Trial Attys., Kansas City Met. Bar Assn. (treas., sec., pres., elected to 16th Jud. Commn. 1988-94), Kanssas City Bar Found. (treas. 1992, sec. 1994, pres. 1996-98, pres. award domestic violence 1999), Kansas City Mem. Svcs. (pres. 1988—), U. Mo. Kansas City Found. (fin. com. 1998), Phi Delta Phi, Beta Theta Pi. Avocations: tennis, skiing, running, reading. Home: 11380 W 121st Ter Shawnee Mission KS 66213-1978 Office Phone: 816-221-2288.

VAN DE VOORT, EVERATT, educational association administrator, psychology educator, consultant; b. Pella, Iowa, Sept. 8, 1920; s. Gerrit and Cornelia (Willemsen) Van De Voort; m. Vera Cannaday Van De Voort (dec.); children: Jerry, Deborah, David, Paul, Nancy, Gregory. BA, Ctrl. Coll., Pella, 1943; MS, Drake U., Des Moines, 1951; DEd, Ill. State U., Normal, 1974. Advanced state cert. U. Iowa, Iowa City, 1950. Social studies tchr. Pella H.S., 1945—49; supt. Cotter Cons. Schs., Iowa, 1949—51, Brighton Pub. Schs., Iowa, 1951—55, Riverside Pub. Schs., Iowa, 1955—59, Mid Prairie Pub. Schs., Wellman, Iowa, 1959—63, Dwight Pub. Schs., Ill., 1963—68; sr. adminstr. No. Ill. U., DeKalb, 1977—87; dean Joliet Coll., Ill., 1970—77, sr. adminstr., 1987—92. Pres. Local Tchrs. Orgn., Della, 1946—49; pres. curriculum coords. State Ill., 1972—78. Sgt. USAF, 1942—45, Europe. Mem.: NEA, Am. Legion, Lions Club, Rotary Club, Phi Delta Kappa. Independent. Methodist. Avocations: woodworking, gardening, fishing, softball, hunting.

VANDEWALKER, RICHARD EDWARD, music educator; b. Ada, Okla., Oct. 20, 1965; MusB in Edn., East Ctrl. U., Ada, 1989; MusM, U. Tex., Arlington, 2003. Dir. choirs Amon Carter-Riverside HS, Ft. Worth, 1994—2000; dir. choral and vocal studies Northwestern Okla. State U., 2006—. Music min. United Meml. Christian Ch., Euless, Tex., 2002—06; dir. music 1st Presbyn. Ch., Alva, 2006—. Mem.: Phi Mu Alpha Sinfonia Frat. (alumni sec. 2005—06). Office: Northwestern Okla State U 709 Oklahoma Blvd Alva OK 73717 Home Phone: 817-521-8667; Office Phone: 580-327-8692. Business E-Mail: revandewalker@nwosu.edu.

VANDEWALLE, GERALD WAYNE, chief justice; b. Noonan, ND, Aug. 15, 1933; s. Jules C. and Blanche Marie (Gits) VandeW. BSc, U. N.D., 1955, JD, 1958. Bar: N.D., U.S. Dist. Ct. N.D. 1959. Spl. asst. atty. gen. State of ND, Bismarck, 1958-75, 1st asst. atty. gen., 1975-78; justice ND Supreme Ct., 1978-92, chief justice, 1993—. Mem. faculty Bismarck Jr. Coll., 1972-76; mem. Nat. Ctr. for State Cts. Rsch. adv. coun.; mem. fed.-state jurisdiction com. Jud. Conf. of the U.S. Editor-in-chief N.D. Law Rev, 1957-58. Active Bismarck Meals on Wheels Recipient Sioux award U. N.D., 1992, Ednl. Law award N.D. Coun. Sch. Attys., 1987, Love Without Fear award Abused Adult Resource Ctr., 1995, N. Dakota State Bar Assoc. Dist. Service award, 1998. Mem. ABA (co-chmn. bar admissions com. 1991-99, mem. coun. sect. legal edn. and admissions, chmn. coun. sect. legal edn. and admissions), State Bar Assn. N.D., Burleigh County Bar Assn., Conf. of Chief Justices (past pres., bd. dirs. 1996-98, chmn. fed.-state tribal rels. com.), Am. Contract Bridge League, Order of Coif, N.D. Jud. Conf. (exec. com.), Elks, KC, Phi Eta Sigma, Beta Alpha Psi (Outstanding Alumnus award Zeta chpt. 1995), Beta Gamma Sigma, Phi Alpha Delta. Roman Catholic. Office: ND Supreme Ct State Capitol 600 E Boulevard Ave Bismarck ND 58505-0530 Office Phone: 701-328-2221. Business E-Mail: gvandewalle@ndcourts.gov.

VAN DE WATER, READ, federal official; b. Charlotte, NC; m. Mark Van de Water; 3 children. Degree, U. South, 1986; M, George Washington U.; JD, Georgetown U. Appropriations assoc., legis. asst. Congressman Tom DeLay, Tex., 1987—91; legis. coun., dir. govt. affairs Northwest Airlines, 1991—97; legis. coun. internat. trade and investment Bus. Roundtable, 1997—99; founder Carson King Cons., 2000; asst. sec. aviation & internat. affairs U.S. Dept. Transp., Washington, 2001—03. Mem. Nat. Mediation Bd., Washington, 2003—, chmn., 2005—. Republican. Office: Nat Mediation Bd 1301 K St NW Ste 250 E Washington DC 20005-7011 E-mail: vandewater@nmb.gov.

VAN DE WORKEEN, PRISCILLA TOWNSEND, small business owner and executive; b. Denver, July 9, 1946; d. Reginald and Ruth (Poor) Townsend; m. Melvin Charles Van de Workeen, Oct. 27, 1973. BA in Chinese History, Wheaton Coll., Norton, Mass., 1968; postgrad., Cornell U., 1965. Asst. dir. Nat. Info. Bur., NYC, 1969-73; dep. dir. Harkness Fellowships, NYC and London, 1973-83; owner, mgr. Vernalwood Enterprises, Splty. and Custom Crafts, Dudley, Mass., 1984-93; co-owner, mgr. Vernalwood Bed & Breakfast, Dudley, 1989-93, Folkstone Bed & Breakfast Reservation Svc., Dudley, 1989-94; co-founder, chairperson Vernalwood Conceptual Enhancements, Dudley, 1991-95. Tchr. quilting and needlework Chester Corbin Libr., Webster, Mass.; bd. dirs. Hubbard Regional Hosp. Guild, Webster, 1986-91, Internat. Ctr., Worcester, Mass., 1989-90; chair bd. trustees Pearle L. Crawford Libr., Town of Dudley, 1993-97; coord. Nat. Coun. Internat. Visitors, Washington, 1989-90; founder, chmn. The Concordia Found., Dudley, 1992—. Mem.: Garden Club Fedn. Mass. (exec. bd. 1997—2005, dir. south ctrl. dist. 1999—2001), The Tuesday Club (pres. 1994—95, sec. 1997—2005), Webster Dudley Garden Club (bd. dirs., pres. 1997—2005). Democrat. Avocations: sewing and needlework, reading, cooking, gardening, travel. Home and Office: Vernalwood Darling Rd Dudley MA 01571

VAN DINE, ALAN CHARLES, advertising agency executive, writer; b. Ford City, Pa., Jan. 12, 1933; s. Albert and Helen (Remaley) Van D.; m. Joan Anne Hodges, Jan. 29, 1955 (div. Jan. 1971); children: Lynn, Mark, Barbara, Michael; m. Holly Long Shefler, Apr. 23, 1977. BA, Duquesne U., 1955; postgrad., U. Pitts., 1968—71. Editor Mt. Lebanon News, Pa., 1956-58; editorial dir. Pitts. Suburban Newspapers, 1958-61; writer and assoc. creative dir. Batten, Barton, Durstine & Osborne, Pitts., 1961-70; pres., creative dir. Van Dine, Horton, McNamara, Manges, Inc., Pitts., 1970-89; chmn. Van Dine, Humphrey, Inc., Pitts., 1989-95; cons. in field, 1996—. Mem. adv. coun. Internat. Poetry Forum, Pitts., 1969-80. Author: Can You Imagine?, 1967, Unconventional Builders, 1977, revised edit., 2001, (humor) The Encyclopedia of Advertising, 1987, Clyde Hare's Pittsburgh, 1994, Light Verse for a Heavy Universe, 2005; columnist Pitts. mag., 1977-78, Pa. Illustrated, 1979-81; contbr. articles, essays, short stories, and poems to mags. 1st lt. USAF, 1956. Recipient numerous awards Art Dirs. Club NY, 1964—, Bus. and Profl. Advt. Assn., 1964—, Am. Advt. Fedn., 1999. Mem.: Chartiers Country Club. Avocations: golf, tennis, darkroom photography, cartooning, computer programming. E-mail: AVDZZZ@bellatlantic.net.

VAN DINE, HAROLD FORSTER, JR., architect, artist; b. New Haven, Aug. 28, 1930; s. Harold Forster and Marguerite Anna (Eichstedt) Van D.; m. Maureen Kallick, Mar. 1, 1983; children by previous marriage: Rebecca Van Dine, Stephanie Van Dine Natale, Gretchen Van Dine Natale. BA, Yale Coll., 1952; MArch, Yale Sch. Arch., 1958. Registered architect. Designer Minoru Yamasaki & Assocs., Detroit, 1958-60; chief designer Gunnar Birkerts & Assocs., Detroit, 1960-67; prin. Straub, Van Dine & Assocs., Troy, Mich., 1967-80; chief architecture and design officer Harley Ellis, Southfield, Mich., 1980-95; archtl. cons. Birmingham, Mich., 1995—, San Miguel de Allende, Mexico, 1995—. V.p. Fields, Devereaux, HEPY, L.A., 1984-95. Prin. works include Mcpl. Libr., Troy, Mich., campuses for Oakland CC, Mich., North Hills Ch., Troy, First Ctr. Office Plaza, chemistry bldgs at. U. Mich. and Ind. U,, G.M.F. Robotics Hdqrs., Flint Ink Rsch. and Devel. Ctr., Comerica Bank Ops. Ctr., Christ the King Mausoleum, Chgo., Resurrection Mausoleum, Staten Island, Mich. Biotech Inst., Ford Sci. Rsch. Labs, Fetzer Inst. Hdqrs. and Retreat Ctr., Cen. Mich. U. Music Sch., Oakland U. Sci. Techs. Bldg., Corning Credit Union, NY. Bd. dirs. Cultural Coun. Birmingham/Bloomfield, 1990-99. Served to lt. (j.g.) USN, 1952-55 Recipient Book award AIA, 1958, Excellence in Architecture Silver medal AIA, 1958, Gold medal Detroit chpt. AIA, 1987, Mich. Soc. of Architects gold medal, 1991, over 50 major design awards; William Wirt Winchester travelling fellowship Yale U. Sch. Architecture, 1958; elect. to AIA Coll. Fellows, 1979. Mem.: Pewabic Soc. (bd. dirs. 1983—2002). Home Phone: 248-246-5814; Office Phone: 248-246-5814. Personal E-mail: mvandhv@aol.com. E-mail: artwork@harryvandine.com.

VAN DINE, VANCE, investment banker; b. San Francisco, July 2, 1925; s. Melvin Everett and Grace Winifred (Harris) Van D.; m. Isabel Erskine Brewster, Sept. 8, 1956 (dec.); 1 dau., Rose M. (dec.). BA, Yale U., 1949; LLB, NYU, 1955. Assoc. Morgan Stanley & Co., NYC, 1953-59, 61-63, ptnr., 1963-75; mng. dir. Morgan Stanley & Co., Inc., NYC, 1970-83; adv. dir. Morgan Stanley & Co., NYC, 1983—. Cons. Internat. Bank for Reconstn. and Devel., 1959-61. Author: The Role of the Investment Banker in International Transactions, 1970, The US Market After Controls, 1974. Bd. dirs. Yale U. Alumni Fund, Combined Health Appeal of Greater NY, Rec. for Blind, Inc., NYC, 1979-89; trustee Cancer Rsch. Inst., NYC, Nassau County Art Mus., LI U., 1979-91; gov. dir. Fgn. Policy Assn., 1980-89. With USN, 1943-46. Recipient Yale Class of 1949 Disting. Service award, 1983. Mem. The Pilgrims of the US, Union Club, Piping Rock Club, NY Yacht Club, Seawanhaka Corinthian Yacht Club, Church Club, Yale Club (NYC), Met. Opera Club. Republican. Episcopalian. Home: 525 E 72nd St Apt 251 New York NY 10021-9608 Office Phone: 212-634-1220. Personal E-mail: vanvan515@aol.com.

VANDIVER, SARA ELIZABETH SHARP RANKIN, retired postmaster; d. James Earl and Celeste Heskett Sharp; m. William Doyle Vandiver, Aug. 18, 1978 (dec. Feb. 27, 1997); m. James Dorothy Rankin, Sr., Aug. 25, 1934 (dec. Aug. 3, 1971); children: James Dorothy Rankin Jr., William Earl Rankin, Carolyn Vandiver Pollan. Postmaster US Postal Svc., Driver, Ark., 1954—80; ret. Sec. St. Louis Region Postmaster Tng. Conf., 1962—73; v.p. Ark. Chpt., Nat. Assn. Postmasters, 1976—78; columnist Ark. Postmaster. Charter mem. Nat. Mus. Women in the Arts, Washington, 1990—2006; contbg. mem. Smithsonian Instn., Washington, 2000—06; pres. Wilson PTA, Ark., 1950—52, Wilson Co-Operative Club, 1952—54, Gen. Fedn. of Women's Clubs Prog. Club, Osceola, 1985—90; organizer Adopt-a-Teacher Program, Osceola Pub. Schs., 1985, Kids and Kindness Program, Osceola Pub. Schs., 1985, Gt. Am. Family Recognition and Awards Program, Osceola, Ark., 1987; pres., state advisor Gen. Fedn. Women's Clubs, Dist. II, Ark., 1990—92, state chmn. cmty. improvement program, 1994—96; mem. Miss. County Geneal. and Hist. Soc., 1993—2006; bd. mem. Interfaith Neighbors, Osceola, 1996—2006; leader Miss. County Explorers Bible Study, Ark., 1983—96; pres. Wilson Women's Missionary Union, 1953—55; Sunday sch. tchr., 1963—. Mem.: Riverlawn Country Club.

VANDIVER, THOMAS K., lawyer; b. Leonard, Mo., Mar. 1, 1951; BA cum laude, DePauw U., 1973; JD, Wash. U., 1977. Bar: Mo. 1977, Ill. 1978, DC 1983. Named ptnr. Armstrong, Teasdale, Kramer & Vaughan, St. Louis, 1984; now ptnr. Sonnenschein Nath & Rosenthal LLP, St. Louis. Mem.: ABA, Am. Health Lawyers Assn., Nat. Assn. Bond Attorneys, DC Bar Assn., Ill. Bar Assn., Mo. Bar Assn. Office: Sonnenschein Nath & Rosenthal LLP Ste 3000 One Met Sq Saint Louis MO 63102 Office Phone: 314-259-5829. Office Fax: 314-259-5959. Business E-Mail: tvandiver@sonnenschein.com.

VANDIVIER, BLAIR ROBERT, lawyer; b. Rapid City, SD, Dec. 24, 1955; s. Robert Eugene and Barbara Jean (Kidd) V.; m. Elizabeth Louise Watson, July 26, 1980; children: Jessica Elizabeth, Jennifer Louise. BS magna cum laude, Butler U., 1978; JD cum laude, Ind. U., 1981. Bar: Ind. 1981, U.S. Dist. Ct. (so. dist.) Ind. 1981, U.S. Tax Ct. 1985. Assoc. Henderson, Daily, Withrow, Johnson & Gross, Indpls., 1981-83; assoc., ptnr. Johnson, Gross, Densborn & Wright, Indpls., 1983-85, of counsel, 1985-87; v.p., sec. Benchmark Products, Inc. (formerly Benchmark Chem. Corp.), Indpls., 1985-91, pres., 1991—2006, also bd. dirs.; ptnr. Gross & Vandivier, Indpls., 1987-89; of counsel Riley, Bennett & Egloff, Indpls., 1990—; mgmt. rep. Pro Com, L.L.C., 1991—2007. V.p. Seleco Inc., Indpls., 1988-93, pres., 1993—. Mem. com. Conner Prairie Settlement Fund Dr., Indpls., 1983-85, Riley Run, 1987—; mem. regulatory study com. City of Indpls., 1993-98. Named to First Top 50 Alumni under 50, Butler U., 2004. Mem. ABA, Ind. Bar Assn., Indpls. Bar Assn (bd. dirs. young lawyers divsn. 1982-85), Am. Electroplaters and Surface Finishers Soc. (chmn. nat. law com. 1986-97, pres. Indpls. br. 1989, bd. mgrs. 1997-2005, tech. conf. bd. 1991-97, chmn. surface finishers ann. tech. conf. and exhbn. 1994, chmn. surface finishers focus group 1994—, Tech. Conf. Bd. Recognition award 1996), Nat. Assn. Surface Finishers (chmn. SUR/FIN 2006), Nat. Assn. Metal Finishers (bd. dirs. 1998-2005, 06—, exec. com. 1998—04, sec./treas. 2000-2001, v.p. 2001-02, pres. 2002-03, past pres. 2003-2004), Metal Finishing Suppliers Assn. (spl. projects svcs. com., 1988-93, chmn. 1993—, chmn. hazardous materials br. 1991-93, trustee 1992-95, v.p. 1995-97, pres. 1997-99, Award of Merit 1997, August P. Munning Commemorative award of merit 2001), Crooked Stick Golf Club (house com. 2003—), Highland Country Club (chmn. ins. com. 1989-94, golf. com. 1992-94, bd. dirs. 1995-97, chmn. fin. com. 1996-97), Surface Finishing Industry Coun. (bd. dirs., sec. 1997-98, pres. 1999, chmn. SUR/FIN 2005, 06, events com. 2006), Econ. Club Indpls., Metal Finishing Found. (pres. 1999), Delta Tau Delta (chmn. 1987-97, bd. dirs. Beta Zeta Found. 1986, Outstanding Alumnus Beta Zeta chpt. 1986). Republican. Episcopalian. Avocations: reading, golf, aviation. Home: 8927 Woodacre Ln Indianapolis IN 46234-2848 Office: Benchmark Products Inc PO Box 68809 Indianapolis IN 46268-0809

VAN DOKKUM, JAN, electric power industry executive; m. Lynn van Dokkum; 3 children. B of Elec. Engring., M of Elec. Engring., Inst. Tech. Albertus Magnus, Netherlands. Regional v.p. sales Seimens Transmission and Distbn.; pres., COO Seimans Power Transmission & Distbn., Inc., 1997—2002; pres. UTC Power United Technologies, South Windsor, Conn., 2002—. Office: United Techs Corp UTC Power 195 Govs Hwy South Windsor CT 06074 *

VAN DRESER, MERTON LAWRENCE, ceramics engineer; b. Des Moines, June 5, 1929; s. Joseph Jerome and Victoria (Love) Van D.; m. Evelyn Lenore Manny, July 12, 1952; children: Peter, Jennifer Sue. BS in Ceramic Engring., Iowa State U., 1951. Tech. supt. Owens-Corning Fiberglas Corp., Kansas City, Mo., 1954-57; rsch. engr. Kaiser Aluminum & Chem. Corp., Milpitas, Calif., 1957-60, rsch. sect. head, 1960-63, lab. mgr., 1963-65, assoc. dir. rsch., 1965-69, dir. refractories rsch. Pleasanton, Calif., 1969-72, dir. non-metallic materials rsch., 1972-83, v.p., dir. rsch. Indsl. Chem. div. and Harshaw/Filtrol Partnership Cleve., 1983-85, dir. bus. devel. Pleasanton, 1985-88, cons., 1988—2003. Mem. adv. bd. dept. ceramic engring. U. Ill., 1974-78; chmn. tech. adv. com. Refractories Inst., 1980-84; mem. nat. materials adv. bd. Nat. Acad. Sci.; mem. Indsl. Rsch. Inst. Contbr. articles to sci. jours.; patentee in field. Sustaining membership chmn. local dist. Boy Scouts Am., 1980; pres. PTA, 1967-68; vol. exec. Pakistan Internat. Exec. Svc. Corps, 1990-91. Aviator C.E., U.S. Army, 1951-54. Recipient Profl. Achievement citation Iowa State U., 1978; named to Lambda Chi Alpha hall of fame, 1996. Fellow: Am. Ceramic Soc. (v.p. 1973—74); mem.: AIME, ASTM (hon.), Metall. Soc., Nat. Inst. Ceramic Engrs., Brit. Ceramic Soc., Masons, Rotary (pres. Pleasanton Club 2002—03, pres. Club Found. 2003—04, Paul Harris fellow), Keramos (pres. 1976—78, herald 1980—84, Greaves Walker Roll of Honor award). Avocation: flying. Home and Office: 40 Castledown Rd Pleasanton CA 94566-9749

VAN DUSEN, ALBERT CLARENCE, academic administrator; b. Tampa, Fla., Aug. 30, 1915; s. Charles H. and Maude E. (Green) Van D.; m. Margaret Davis, Jan. 3, 1943; children: Margaret Van Dusen Pysh, Jane Katherine, Sara Elizabeth (Mrs. Frank J. Matyskiela). BS, U. Fla., 1937, AM, 1938; PhD, Northwestern, 1942; LittD, U. Tampa, 1959; L.H.D., Duquesne U., 1967. Instr., asst. prof. dept. psychology U. Fla., 1938-41;

asso. prof. psychology Northwestern U., 1946, dir. summer session, 1948-52, v.p. pub. relations, 1952-56; prof. psychology, bus. adminstrn. and edn. U. Pitts., 1956-85, asst. chancellor for planning and devel., 1956-59, vice chancellor the professions, 1959-67, vice chancellor program devel. and pub. affairs, 1967-71, vice chancellor, sec. univ., 1971-80, vice chancellor emeritus, spl. asst. for pub. affairs, 1980-85, vice chancellor emeritus, prof. emeritus psychology, bus. adminstrn. and edn., 1985—, ctr. assoc. univ. ctr. for internat. studies, 1986—. Editor: Proc. Am. Coll. Personnel Assn; contbr. articles to profl. jours. Bd. govs. Pinchot Inst. Conservation Studies; vice chmn., bd. dirs. The Buhl Found., World Affairs Coun. Pitts., vice chmn. bd. dirs. Duquesne U., acting chmn., 1987-88; bd. dirs. Pitts. YMCA, ACTION Housing, Inc., Assn. Am.'s Pub. TV Stas., QED Communications Inc., chmn. 1981-88; bd. dirs. Japan-Am. Soc. Pa.; mem. Pa. Pub. TV Network Commn.; chmn., bd. trustees Pitts. History and Landmarks Found.; pres. bd. trustees H.C. Frick Ednl. Commn., United Way Pa.; dir. South Hills Child Guidance Ctr.; chmn. selfcare study Health Edn. Ctr., Pitts., 1979-80; mem. Walter Reed Hovey Fellowship com. Pitts. Found. Lt. USNR, 1942-46. Fulbright sr. scholar Australian-Am. Ednl. Found., 1980 Fellow Am. Psychol. Assn., Am. Psychol. Soc., Pa. Psychol. Assn., Internat. Found. Social Econ. Deve.; mem. Internat. Assn. Schs. Insts. Adminstrn., C. of C. (dir. 1953-55), Am. Coll. Pub. Rels. Assn. (v.p. 1956-58), Assn. Deans and Dirs. Summer Sessions (sec. 1950-51), Profl. Schs. and World Affairs Com. (chmn. edn. and world affairs 1965-67), Am. Pers. and Guidance Assn., Midwest Psychol. Assn., Ea. Psychol. Assn., Pitts. Psychol. Assn., Internat. Assn. Applied Psychology, Western Pa. Coun. Econ. Edn., Internat. Assn. Schs. and Insts. Adminstrn., Friends of Art for Pitts. Schs. (charter mem.), Phi Beta Kappa, Sigma Xi, Beta Theta Pi, Beta Gamma Sigma. Clubs: Univ. (Pitts.), Duquesne (Pitts.). Home: 1290 Boyce Rd Apt C333 Pittsburgh PA 15241-3958

VAN DUYNE, RICHARD PALMER, analytical chemistry educator, chemical physics educator; b. Orange, NJ, Oct. 28, 1945; s. John Palmer and Lorraine Montgomery (Stoller) Van D.; m. Jerilyn Elise Miripol BA, Rensselear Poly. Inst., 1967; PhD, U. N.C., 1971. Asst. prof. analytical chemistry and chem. physics Northwestern U., Evanston, Ill., 1971-76, assoc. prof., 1976-79, prof., 1979-87, Charles E. and Emma H. Morrison prof. chemistry, 1987—. Cons. Beckman Instrument Co., Fullerton, Calif., 1982-90, Eastman Kodak Co., Rochester, N.Y., 1978-91; disting. vis. prof. U. Tex., Austin, 1979; chmn. Vibrational Spectroscopy Gordon Conf., 1982; Camille and Henry Dreyfus lectr. U. Colo., Boulder, 1981; Kilpatrick lectr. Ill. Inst. Tech., 1982; O.K. Rice lectr. U. N.C., 1984; Henry Werner lectr. U. Kans., 1986; Arthur A. Vernon lectr. Northeastern U., 1992. Mem. adv. bd. Jour. Phys. Chemistry, 1983-88; contbr. chpts. to books, articles to profl. jours. Recipient Coblentz award, 1980, Fresenius award, 1981, Excellence in Surface Sci. award, 1996, Pitts. Spectroscopy award, 1991. Fellow AAAS, Am. Phys. Soc. (recipient Earle K. Plyler prize, 2004), Am. Acad. Arts & Sci.; mem. Am. Chem. Soc. Home: 1520 Washington Ave Wilmette IL 60091-2417 Office: Northwestern Univ 2145 Sheridan Rd Evanston IL 60208-0834

VAN DUYSE, FRANCIS DONALD (FRITZ VAN), publisher; b. Sturgeon Bay, Wis., May 2, 1926; s. Francis Lewis and Gertrude (Simon) Van D.; m. Dorothy Marie Walden, May 15, 1953 (div. Feb. 1978); children: Susan, Rebecca, Francis Roy, Sarah. BBA, Spencerian Coll., 1949. Baseball announcer Albany Cardinals, Ga., 1953—54, Waycross Bears, Ga., 1955, Valdosta Tigers, Ga., 1956; pub., editor Wis. All-Sports, Green Bay, 1958—68, Wis. Playground, Green Bay, 1958—68, Pro Football Exclusive, 1969—72; dir. sports WLUK-TV, Channel 11, Green Bay, 1962—63; CEO, announcer Gemini Broadcasting Co., Appleton, Wis., 1980—82; pres., CEO MegaPrint Internat., Sturgeon Bay, Wis., 1986—2000; pub., editor Fritz Van Newsletter, 2002—05, Pro Mag., 2005—; pub. Mega Press Internat., Wis., 2004—. Freelance sports announcer, 2003—. Author: History of the Green Bay Packers, 1965; pub., editor (yearbooks) Salute to the Packers 1961-68. With USN, 1944—46. Avocations: chess, writing. Home: 1811 Michigan St Apt 9C Sturgeon Bay WI 54235-3704

VAN DYCK, PETER CUYLER, federal agency administrator; b. Dec. 9, 1939; married; 3 children. BA in Physiology, U. Ill., 1962; MS in Physiology, U. Ill., Chgo., 1966, MD, 1966; MPH in Maternal and Child Health, U. Calif., Berkeley, 1973. Diplomate Nat. Bd. Med. Examiners. Intern then resident in pediatrics Children's Meml. Hosp., Chgo., 1966-68, chief resident, 1968-89; instr. Med. Sch. Northwestern U., Chgo., 1968-89; chief pediatrics Health Clinic U.S. Army, Frankfurt, Germany, 1969-71, primary nursery physician 97th Gen. Hosp., 1971-72; pediatric cons. Internat. Red Cross, Amman, Jordan, 1973; dir. maternal and child health Utah State Divsn. Health, Salt Lake City, 1973-74, dir. divsn. family health services, 1974-92, acting exec. dir., 1984-85, acting dir. divsn. health care financing (Medicaid), 1986-87; asst. prof. Med. Ctr. U. Utah, Salt Lake City, 1976-82, prof. Med. Ctr.; sr. med. advisor to the directors of Maternal and Child Health Bur. and Health Resources and Services Adminstrn., HHS, 1992—95; dir. Office of State and Cmty. Health Maternal and Child Health Bur., Health Resources and Services Adminstrn., US HHS, 1995—98, acting assoc. adminstr., 1998—99, assoc. adminstr., 1999—. Adj. assoc. prof. health Univ. Utah, Salt Lake City, 1975—, adj. asst. prof. Coll. Nursing, 1976—; mem. adv. com. U. Utah Coll. Nursing, 1976-80, Albert Einstein Coll. Medicine, Ctr. for Disease Control, 1983-86, John F. Kennedy Child Devel. Ctr., Denver, 1979-82; faculty coord. Crippled Children's Svcs. Advanced Inst., Children's Hosp., Columbus, Ohio, 1983—; mem. maternal and child health/Medicaid tech. assistance group Health Care Financing Adminstrn., 1987-93; mem. planning com., faculty Surgeon Gens. Conf., 1987; mem. various coms. and task forces; presenter, cons., reviewer in field; cons. Interagy. Efforts Children Spl. Health Needs Federated States Micronesia, 1991, Third Pacific Basin Interagy Conf. Individuals Spl. Health Care Needs No. Marianas Islands, 1992; faculty mem. Med. Ctr. Georgetown U., Washington, 1993; chief party U.S. Del. Third Regional Follow-up Meeting World Summit Children, Antigua, Guatemala, 1995. Contbr. articles to profl. jours. Co-chmn. sch. health com. Utah State Bd. Edn., Utah Dept. Health, 1974-92, statewide immunization action com. Awareness Com., 1977-78; project dir. Sudden Infant Death Syndrome Regional Ctr., Utah, 1975-80; chmn. Govs. Adv. Coun. for Developmentally Disabled Children, 1976-78; mem. task force on svcs. to presch. handicapped children Utah State Legis., 1984, tech. adv. coun. Utah Children, 1985-88, adv. bd. Jr. League, 1985-88; bd. dirs. Exceptional Child Ctr., Utah, 1975-80. Recipient Nat. Leadership award Dept. Health and Human Svcs., 1989, Nat. Achievement award Healthy Mothers, Healthy Babies, 1991; named one of 500 Most Influential Healty Policy-makers Health Care 500, 1992; grantee U.S. Dept. Health and Human Svcs., Ctrs. for Disease Control., Devel. Diabetes Coun., Bur. Edn. for the Handicapped, Bur. Community Health Svcs.; WHO fellow, 1995. Mem. APHA (mem. various coms., chmn. maternal and child health sect. 1988—, Ross award 1977), Nat. Acad. for State Health Policy (mem. steering com. 1987-95), Nat. Found. March of Dimes (chmn. med. adv. bd. 1975-93, Plaque for Outstanding Svc. 1977-78), Nat. Early Childhood Tech. Assistance System (mem. nat. adv. com. 1988-90), Am. Acad. Pediatrics (mem. various coms.), Nat. Assn. of State Bds. Edn. (mem. task force on adolescent pregnancy 1979-80), Nat. Assn. State and Territorial Maternal and Child Health and Crippled Children Dirs. (pres. 1978-80), March of Dimes Birth Defect Found. (mem. nat. chpt. grants rev. com. 1988-92), Intermountain Pediatrics Soc. (mem. legis. and child abuse coms. 1974-76), Utah Pub. Health Assn. (mem. various coms., pres. 1984-86, mem. editorial bd. 1976-77, Beaty award 1985). Office: Maternal & Child Health Bur Parklawn Bldg Rm 18-05 5600 Fishers Ln Rockville MD 20857 Office Phone: 301-443-2170.

VAN DYCK, WENDY, dancer; b. Tokyo; Student, San Francisco Ballet Sch.; BA in Performing Arts, St. Mary's Coll., 2003. With San Francisco Ballet, 1979—96, prin. dancer, 1987—96, instr., tchr., 1996; co-dir. Lawrence Pech Dance, San Francisco, 1996—. Performances include Forgotten Land, The Sons of Horus, The Wanderer Fantasy, Romeo and Juliet, The Sleeping Beauty, Swan Lake, Concerto in d: Poulenc, Handel-a Celebration, Menuetto, Intimate Voices, Hamlet and Ophelia pas de deux, Connotations, Sunset, Rodin, In the Night, The Dream: pas de deux, La Sylphide, Beauty and the Beast, Variations de Ballet, Nutcracker, The Comfort Zone, Dreams of Harmony, Rodeo, Duo Concertant, Who Cares; performed at Reykjavik Arts Festival, Iceland, 1990, The 88th Conf. of the Internat. Olympic Com., LA, 1984, with Kozlov and Co. Concord Pavilion; guest artist performing role Swan Lake (Act II), San Antonio Ballet, 1985, Giselle, Shreveport (La.) Met. Ballet, 1994; featured in the TV broadcast of Suite by Smuin. Mailing: PO Box 29190 San Francisco CA 94129 Office Phone: 415-308-5881. E-mail: wvandyck@comcast.net.

VAN DYK, FREDERICK THEODORE, political scientist, writer; b. Bellingham, Wash., Oct. 6, 1934; s. Ted and June Ellen (Williams) Van Dyk; m. Julia Jean Covacevich, Nov. 22, 1957 (dec. 1996); children: Theodore, Robert, Terry Jean, Sue Ellen. BA, U. Wash., Seattle, 1955; MS, Columbia U., NYC, 1956. Reporter, editor Seattle Times, 1956-57; advt. public relations exec. Boston and NYC, 1958-62; acting dir. European Community Info. Service, Washington, 1962-64; asst. to Hubert Humphrey, Vice Pres. of U.S., 1964-68; v.p. Columbia U., NYC, 1968-69; pres. Van Dyk Assocs., Washington, 1969-76; asst. adminstr. AID, Washington, 1977; v.p. Weyerhaeuser Co., Tacoma, 1978—80; pres. Center for Nat. Policy, Washington, 1981-85, Van Dyk Assocs., 1985-98; exec. v.p. Milken Inst., Santa Monica, Calif., 1998-99; vis. scholar Claremont (Calif.) Grad. U., 1999-2000; sr. fellow UCLA Sch. Pub. Policy and Social Rsch., 1999-2000; columnist Seattle Post-Intelligencer, 2001—. Author: Heroes, Hacks and Fools, Memoirs, 2007; contbr. articles to newspapers incl. the Wall St. Jour., NY Times, Wash. Post, L.A. Times. Mem. Coun. Fgn. Rels., Presdl. Commn. Fgn. Assistance, Pacific Coun. Internat. Policy; bd. dirs. Com. Study Am. Electorate, Franklin and Eleanor Roosevelt Inst., Jean Monnet Coun., Humphrey Inst. With M.I. US Army, 1957, with M.I. US Army, 1961—62. Mem.: Rainier Club (Seattle), Delta Upsilon. Personal E-mail: t_van_dyk@hotmail.com.

VAN DYKE, CRAIG, psychiatrist, director; b. Detroit, Oct. 4, 1941; married; two children. BS, U. Wash., 1963, MD, 1967. Asst. prof. psychiatry Yale U., New Haven, Conn., 1974-78; from assoc. to prof. psychiatry U. Calif., San Francisco, 1979-86, prof., chmn. dept. psychiatry, 1994—. Mem. Am. Psychosom. Soc., Internat. Coll. Psychosom. Medicine, Soc. Neurosci., Internat. Neuropsychol. Soc. Office: U Cal San Francisco Langley Porter Psychiatric Inst 401 Parnassus Ave San Francisco CA 94143-0984 E-mail: cvd@lppi.ucsf.edu.

VAN DYKE, DANIEL L., geneticist; b. Paterson, NJ, Mar. 1, 1947; PhD, Ind. U., 1976. Cert. med. genetics and clin. cytogenetics Am. Bd. Med. Genetics. Divsn. head genetics labs. Henry Ford Hosp., Detroit, 1975—; faculty U. Mich. Med. Sch., Detroit, 1978-94, Case Western Res. U., Cleve., 1994—. Mem.: Am. Bd. Med. Genetics (pres. 1998—2000, chair dept. med. genetics 1999—). Office: Mayo Clinic 200 1st St SW Rochester MN 55902 Office Phone: 507-284-6776.

VAN DYKE, DICK, actor, comedian; b. West Plains, Mo., Dec. 13, 1925; m. Marjorie Willett, Feb. 12, 1948 (div. May 1984); children: Christian, Barry, Stacey, Carrie Beth. With Wayne Williams, founded advt. agy., Danville, Ill., 1946. Chmn. Nick at Nite, 1992—. Appeared with Philip Erickson in pantomine act The Merry Mutes, Eric and Van, 1947-53; TV master ceremonies The Music Shop, Atlanta, Morning Show, CBS, 1955, Cartoon Show, 1956; TV variety show Dick Van Dyke Show, New Orleans; guest appearances TV shows, 1958, Golden Girls, 1985 (Emmy nominee), Jake and the Fatman, 1987, Coach, 1989, Sabrina the Teenage Witch, 1996, Becker, 1998; TV host Flair, ABC, 1960; Broadway debut in The Girls Against the Boys, 1959, Van Dyke and Company, 1976, The Van Dyke Show, CBS, 1988; performed in Broadway musical Bye Bye Birdie, 1960-61 (also motion picture version); (TV) Dick Van Dyke Show, CBS, 1961-66, New Dick Van Dyke Show, 1971-74; performer weekly comedy program Carol Burnett Show; (TV series) Diagnosis Murder, 1993-2002; (TV movies) Daughters of Privilege, 1991, The House on Sycamore Street, 1992, Diagnosis of Murder, 1992, A Twist of the Knife, 1993, The Dick Van Dyke Show Remembered, 1994; star, exec. prodr. Without Warning, 2002, A Town Without Pity, 2002, Murder 101, 2006; performed in motion pictures including What a Way To Go, 1964, Mary Poppins, 1965, Divorce American Style, 1967, Chitty, Chitty, Bang, Bang, 1968, The Comic, 1969, Some Kind of Nut, 1969, Cold Turkey, 1971, The Morning After, 1974, The Runner Stumbles, 1979, Drop-Out Father, 1982, Found Money, 1983, Dick Tracy, 1990, Buitenspel, 2005, (voice) Curious George, 2006; Author: Faith, Hope, and Hilarity, 1970. With USAAC, World War II. Recipient Theater World award 1960, Antoinette Perry award for best mus. comedy actor 1961, Emmy award for comedy NATAS, 1962, 64, 65, 77, Life Career award Acad. Sci. Fiction, Fantasy and Horror Films, 2000, Lifetime Achievement award in comedy, 1994. Office: William Morris Agy Inc care Sol Leon 151 S El Camino Dr Beverly Hills CA 90212-2775

VAN DYKE, GENE, oil industry executive; b. Normal, Ill, Nov. 5, 1926; BS in Geol. Engring., U. Okla., 1950. Geologist Kerr-McGee, Oklahoma City, 1950; chief geologist S.D. Johnson Co., Wichita Falls, Tex., 1950-51; ind. geologist, oil operator, 1951-58; ptnr. Van Dyke and Mejlaender, Houston, 1958-62; founder, owner, chmn. Van Dyke Oil Co. (now Vanco Energy Co.), Houston, 1962—, also bd. dir. Bd. dirs. Van Dyke Netherlands, Inc. Compiler index of geol. articles to South La. With AC US Army, 1945. Named Living Legend in Wildcatting, Houston Geol. Soc., 2000; named to Hall of Fame, Dutch Am. Heritage Soc., 2001. Mem.: Am. Assn. Petroleum Geologists, Ind. Petroleum Assn., Houstonian Club, Houston Petroleum Club, Houston Club (pres.). Republican. Episcopalian. Vanco Energy Company is active in deepwater west Africa and is currently the largest license holder with over 15 million acres in depths between 1,000 and 10,000 feet; Vanco has been awarded the Prykerchenska Block in southeast Ukraine Black Sea, being 3.2 million acres and its water depth ranges from 150 meters to 2,200 meters. Office: Vanco Energy Corp 3 Greenway Plz 12th Fl Houston TX 77046 Home Phone: 713-629-0713; Office Phone: 713-877-8544. Office Fax: 713-877-8476. Business E-Mail: info@vancoenergy.com, gvandyke@vancoenergy.com.

VAN DYKE, MILTON DENMAN, aeronautical engineering educator; b. Chgo., Aug. 1, 1922; s. James Richard and Ruth (Barr) Van D.; m. Sylvia Jean Agard Adams, June 16, 1962; children: Russell B., Eric J., Nina A., Brooke A. and Byron J. and Christopher M. (triplets). BS, Harvard U., 1943; MS, Calif. Inst. Tech., 1947, PhD, 1949. Research engr. NACA, 1943-46, 50-54, 55-58; vis. prof. U. Paris, France, 1958- 59; prof. aero. Stanford, 1959—; prof. emeritus, 1992—. Pres. Parabolic Press. Author: Perturbation Methods in Fluid Mechanics, 1964, An Album of Fluid Motion, 1982; editor: Ann. Rev. Fluid Mechanics, 1969-99. Trustee Soc. For Promotion of Sci. and Scholarship, Inc. Served with USNR, 1944-46. Guggenheim and Fulbright fellow, 1954-55 Mem. Am. Acad. Arts and Scis., Nat. Acad. Engring., Am. Phys. Soc., Phi Beta Kappa, Sigma Xi, Sierra Club. Office: Stanford U Div Mechs & Computation Stanford CA 94305-4040

VAN DYKE, THOMAS WESLEY, lawyer; b. Kansas City, Mo., May 12, 1938; s. Harold Thomas and Elizabeth Louise (Barritt) Van D.; m. Sharon Edgar, Jan. 30, 1960; children: Jennifer Van Dyke Winters, Jeffrey. BA, U. Kans., 1960; JD, U. Mich., 1963. Bar: Mo. 1963, Kans. 1983. Atty. SEC, Washington, 1963-64; legal asst. to commr. Hamer E. Budge, Washington, 1964-65; from assoc. to ptnr. Linde Thomson Langworthy Kohn & Van Dyke, P.C., Overland Park, Kans., 1965-91. Co-chmn. ALI-ABA Tax and Bus. Planning Seminar, 1987-96, 2005, 07; securities adv. panel Sec. of State of Mo., 1984-89. Mem. ABA (fed. regulation securities com. bus. law sect. 1982-2007, negotiated acquisitions com. 1989-2007), Kans. Bar Assn., Mo. Bar Assn. (corp. banking and bus. law com., chmn. full com. 1983-84, past chmn. securities law subcom.), Carriage Club (bd. dirs. 1986-89). Republican. Avocations: tennis, golf, reading. Office: Bryan Cave LLP 3500 One Kansas City Pl 1200 Main St Kansas City MO 64105 Home Phone: 913-469-8638; Office Phone: 816-374-3201. Business E-Mail: twvandyke@bryancave.com.

VAN DYKE, WILLIAM GRANT, manufacturing executive; b. Mpls., June 30, 1945; s. Russell Lawrence and Carolyn (Grant) Van D.; m. Karin Van Dyke; children: Carolyn Julie, Colin Grant, Alexander Grant, Stephanie Joyce. BA in Econs., U. Minn., 1967, MBA, 1972. V.p., CFO Northland Aluminum Co., Mpls., 1977-78; controller Donaldson Co., Inc., Mpls., 1978-80, v.p. controller, 1980-82, v.p., CFO, 1982-84, v.p., gen. mgr. indsl. group, 1984-94, pres., COO, 1994-96, pres., CEO, 1996—2004, chmn., 1996—, also bd. dirs. Bd. dirs. Graco Inc., Alliant Techsystems. Lt. U.S. Army, 1968-70, Vietnam. Mem. Kappa Sigma Alumni Assn. Avocations: running, bicycling. Office: Donaldson Co Inc 1400 W 94th St Minneapolis MN 55431-2370

VANE, SYLVIA BRAKKE, anthropologist, writer; b. Fillmore County, Minn., Feb. 28, 1918; d. John T. and Hulda Christina Brakke.; m. Arthur Bayard Vane, May 17, 1942; children: Ronald Arthur, Linda, Laura Vane Ames. AA, Rochester Jr. Coll., 1937; BS with distinction, U. Minn., Mpls., 1939; postgrad, Radcliffe Coll., Cambridge, Mass., 1944; MA, Calif. State U., Hayward, 1975. Med. technologist Dr. Frost and Hodapp, Willmar, Minn., 1939-41; head labs. Corvallis Gen. Hosp., Oreg., 1941-42; dir. lab. Cambridge Gen. Hosp., 1942-43; staff Peninsula Clinic, Redwood City, Calif., 1947-49; v.p. Cultural Systems Rsch. Inc., Menlo Park, Calif., 1978—; pres. Ballena Press, 1981—2005. Cons. cultural resource mgmt. So. Calif. Edison Co., Rosemead, 1978-81, San Diego Gas and Elec. Co., 1980-83, Pacific Gas and Elec. Co., San Francisco, 1982-83, Wender, Murase & White, Washington, 1983-87, Yosemite Indians, Mariposa, Calif., 1982-91, San Luis Rey Band of Mission Indians, Escondido, Calif., 1986-89, US Ecology, Newport Beach, Calif., 1986-89, Riverside County Flood Control and Water Conservation Dist., 1985-95, Infotec, Inc., 1989-91, Alexander & Karshmer, Berkeley, Calif., 1989-92, Desert Water Agy., Palm Springs, Calif., 1989-90, Met. Water Dist., 1992-2001, Nat. Park Svc., 1992-2001, Applied Earthworks, Inc., 1997-2001, NW Econ. Assocs., 2002-2004, County of Riverside, 2002-03, Aqua Caliente Cultural Mus., 2005—; bd. dirs. XEl Scientific. Author: (with L.J. Bean), California Indians, Primary Resources, 1977, rev. edit., 1990, The Cahuilla and the Santa Rosa Mountains, 1981, The Cahuilla Landscape, 1991, Ethnology of the Alta California Indians, vol. I Pre Contact, vol. II Post Contact, 1992, Spanish Borderlands Sourcebooks, vols. 3, 4; contbr. chpts. to books. Bd. dir. Sequoia Area coun. Girl Scouts US, 1954-61; bd. dirs., v.p., pres. LWV, South San Mateo County, Calif., 1960-65. Recipient Lifetime Achievement award, Calif. Indian Conf., 2005. Fellow Soc. Applied Anthropology, Am. Anthropology Assn.; mem. Southwestern Anthropology Assn. (prog. chmn. 1976-78, newsletter editor 1976-79), Soc. for Am. Archaeology, Soc. Calif. Archaeology (Martin A. Baumhoff Spl. Achievement award 1998). Mem. United Ch. of Christ. Office: 823 Valparaiso Ave Menlo Park CA 94025-4206 Office Phone: 650-323-9261.

VANE, TERENCE G., JR., finance company executive, lawyer; b. Elgin, Ill., Jan. 17, 1942; s. Terence Gregory and Velma Mary (Mersman) V.; m. Patricia Bryant, Aug. 29, 1964; children: Terence Gregory III, Lourdene DeLynne, Christopher Theodore. BA, Ind. U., 1964, JD, 1967. Bar: Ind. 1967, Tex. 1977, N.C. 1992, Fla. 2002. Staff atty. Assocs. Discount Corp., South Bend, Ind., 1967-69; asst. gen. counsel Assocs. Mgmt. Corp., South Bend, 1969-74, Assocs. Comml. Corp., South Bend, 1974-76, Assocs. Ins. Group, Inc., Dallas, 1976-77; gen. counsel, v.p. ins. ops. Assocs. Corp. N.Am., Dallas, 1977-80, gen. counsel, sr. v.p. ins. ops., 1981-82, gen. counsel, sr. v.p. consumer fin. and ins. ops., 1982-86, gen. counsel, sr. v.p. diversified consumer fin. svcs. and credit card ops., 1986-88; exec. v.p., gen. counsel, sec., dir. Barclays Am. Corp., Charlotte, NC, 1988-91; pres. Vector Fin. Svcs., Inc., Charlotte, 1991-95, bd. dirs.; sr. v.p., assoc. gen. counsel EquiCredit Corp., Jacksonville, Fla., 1996-97; sr. v.p., gen. counsel, sec. First Street Mortgage Corp., Jacksonville, 1997-98, Home Alliance Mortgage Co., Jacksonville, 1998-2000, Alliance Capital Ptnrs. Group, Jacksonville, 2000—02, Slott & Barker, Jacksonville, 2002—04; pvt. practice Jacksonville, 2005—. Chmn. bd. dirs., sec. Youth Concert Found. for Promotion Creative Arts, 1981—; bd. dirs. N.C. Bus. Com. Edn., 1988-91. Mem. ABA (com. on consumer fin. svcs. law), Fla. Bar Assn., Ind. Bar Assn., Tex. Bar Assn., N.C. Bar Assn., Nat. Assn. Ind. Insurers (laws com. 1978-86), Consumer Credit Ins. Assn. (chmn. property ins. legis. com. 1979-85), Am. Fin. Svcs. Assn. (law com., chmn. environ. law subcom.), Conf. Consumer Fin. Law (governing com.), Nat. Home Equity Mortgage Assn., Lawyers Round Table, Safari Club Internat. (pres., dir. North Fla. chpt.). Conservative. Episcopalian. Office: Terence G Vane Jr PA 233 E Bay St Ste 620 Jacksonville FL 32202-3447

VAN EECKHOUDT, MARC VICTOR CELESTIN, oil industry executive; b. Pamel, Belgium, July 24, 1950; s. Alfons and Alma (Staels) Van Eeckhoudt; m. Beatrix J. F. Ruttens, Dec. 21, 1973; children: Karlien, Bastlaan, Pepljn, Stoffel. Lic., Vlekho, Brussels, 1972; grad., Cath. U. Leuven, Belgium, 1972, MBA, 1978, PhD, 1980. Analyst Essochem Belgium, Brussels, 1977-79, acctg. mgr., 1982-84; acctg. supr. Essochem Plastics, Meerhout, Belgium, 1980-81; coord. Exxon Chem. Co., Darien, Conn., 1984-87; contr. Esso Benelux, Breda, Netherlands, 1988-92, Exxon Chem. Europe, Brussels, 1992-95; mgr. purchasing and contracting Esso Internat., Brussels, 1995-99; dep. mgr. procurement Exxon Mobil, Fairfax, Va., 2000—02, gen. mgr. Bus. Support Ctrs., 2002—. Home: 2715 Newman St Houston TX 77002 Office: Exxon Mobil 800 Bell St Rm 3497M Houston TX 77052 E-mail: vaneeckhoudt@yahoo.com.

VANEK, JAROSLAV, economist, educator; b. Prague, Czechoslovakia, Apr. 20, 1930; came to U.S., 1955, naturalized, 1960; s. Josef and Jaroslava (Tucek) V.; m. Wilda M. Marraffino, Dec. 26, 1959; children: Joseph, Francis, Rosemarie, Steven, Teresa. Degree in stats., Sorbonne, Paris, 1951; license in econ., U. Geneva, 1954; PhD, MIT, 1957. Instr., then asst. prof. Harvard U., 1957-63; adviser AID, 1964; mem. faculty Cornell U., 1964-96, prof. econs., 1966-96, Carl Marks prof. internat. studies, 1969-96, dir. program comparative econ. devel., 1968-73, dir. program participation and labor-managed systems, 1969-96, prof. emeritus, 1996—. Mem. nat. adv. bd. econs. NSF, 1969-70; founder, pres. S.T.E.V.E.N. Found. (Solar Tech. and Energy for Vital Econ. Needs), 1985—. Author: International Trade: Theory and Economic Policy, 1962, The Balance of Payments, Level of Economic Activity and the Value of Currency, 1962, The Natural Resource Content of United States Foreign Trade, 1870-1955, 1963, General Equilibrium of International Discrimination, 1965, Estimating Foreign Resource Needs for Economic Development, 1966, Maximal Economic Growth, 1968, The General Theory of Labor-Managed Market Economies, 1970, The Participatory Economy, 1971, Self-Management: Economic Liberation of Man, 1975, The Labor-Managed Economy, 1977, Crisis and Reform: East and West: Essays in Social Economy, 1989, Toward Full Democracy, Political and Economic, In Russia, 1993, Unified Theory of Social Systems: A Radical Christian Analysis, 2000; also manuscripts on solar tech., contbr. to Advances in the Economic Analysis of Participatory and Labor-Managed Firms, Vol. 2, 1987, Vol. 7, 2003, Destructive International Trade from Justice for Labour to Global Strategy,

1998, inventor several solar tech. designs, including solar steam engines, pumps, refrigerators, cookers, holder 1 patent. Roman Catholic. Home: 414 Triphammer Rd Ithaca NY 14850-2521 Business E-Mail: jv19@cornell.edu.

VAN EMBURGH, JOANNE, lawyer; b. Palmyra, NJ, Nov. 18, 1953; d. Earl Henry and Clare (Kemmerle) Van E.; m. Samuel Michael Surloff, July 6, 1993. BA summa cum laude, Catholic U., 1975; JD cum laude, Harvard Law Sch., 1978. Bar: Calif. 1978. Assoc. atty. Agnew Miller & Carlson, LA, 1978-82; ptnr. Sachs & Phelps, LA, 1982-91, Heller, Ehrman, White & McAuliffe, LA, 1991-93; mng. council Toyota Motor Sales, USA, Inc., Torrance, 1993—, asst. gen. coun., 2000—. Mem. ABA. Avocations: reading, cooking, sports. Office: Toyota Motor Sales USA Inc 19001 S Western Ave Mail Stop A107 Torrance CA 90501-1106 Office Phone: 310-468-4700. Office Fax: 310-468-4052.

VAN ETTEN, PETER WALBRIDGE, foundation executive; b. Boston, May 10, 1946; s. Royal Cornelius Van Etten and Peggy June (Walbridge) Hutchins; m. Mary Peters French, Sept. 5, 1968; children: Molly, Clarissa, Ellen. BA, Columbia U., 1968; MBA, Harvard U., 1973. Br. mgr. BayBanks, Brookline, Mass., 1968-71; loan officer Bank of Boston, 1973-76; CFO Univ. Hosp., Boston, 1976-79; exec. v.p., CFO New Eng. Med. Ctr., Boston, 1979-89; pres., CEO Transition Systems, Boston, 1986-89; dep. chancellor U. Mass. Med. Ctr., Worcester, 1989-91; CFO Stanford U., Calif., 1991-94; pres., CEO Stanford Univ. Hosp., 1994-97; CEO UCSF Stanford Health Care, 1997-99; exec. com. U. Healthsystem Consortium, 1997-99, vice chmn., 1998-99; dir. Calif. Healthcare Assn., 1998-99, IDX Sys., Inc., 1999-2001; pres., CEO Juvenile Diabetes Found. Internat., NYC, 2000—06. Dir. Transition Sys., Inc., 1996—98, Duke U. Health Sys., 2003—, Rsch. Am., 2005—06. Chair campaign United Way San Francisco, 1998. Business E-Mail: pvanetten1@yahoo.com.

VAN EXEL, NICKEY MAXWELL, professional basketball player; b. Kenosha, Wis., Nov. 27, 1971; s. Nickey Maxwell and Joyce Van Exel; 1 child, Nickey Maxwell III. Attended, Trinity Valley C.C., 1989-91; BA in Sociology, U. Cin., 1993. Guard L.A. Lakers, 1993-98, Denver Nuggets, 1998—2002, Dallas Mavericks, 2002—03, Golden State Warriors, 2003—04, Portland Trailblazers, 2004—. With Nat. Benevolent Assn., Christian Ch. Named to NBA All-Rookie Team, 1994, NBA All-Star Game, 1998; recipient Victor Award for Comeback Player of the Yr., 1998, Chopper Travaglini award. Avocation: collecting baseball cards, hats, books. Office: c/o Portland Trailblazers 1 Cneter Court ste 200 Portland OR 97227

VAN FAASEN, WILLIAM C., health insurance company executive; Past sr. v.p. operational svcs. Blue Cross/Blue Shield Mich.; exec. v.p., COO Blue Cross/Blue Shield Mass., Boston, 1990-92, pres., CEO, 1992—2002, chmn., pres., CEO, 2002—04, chmn., CEO, 2004—05, chmn., 2005—. Bd. dirs. IMS Health, Inc., Liberty Mut. Group, NSTAR, PolyMedica Corp. Office: Blue Cross/Blue Shield MA Landmark Ctr 401 Park Dr Boston MA 02215-5000

VAN FLEET, CONNIE JEAN, library and information scientist, educator; b. New Orleans, La., Oct. 3, 1950; d. Cornelius and Elizabeth Fisher Van Fleet; m. Danny Paul Wallace; children: Robyn Solomon, Elizabeth Wallace. BA, U. of Okla., 1972; M of Libr. Info. Sci., La. State U., 1987; PhD, Ind. U., 1990. Libr. assoc. New Orleans Pub. Libr., 1982—85; instr. La. State U., Baton Rouge, 1989—90, asst. prof., 1990—94, assoc. prof., 1994—96; adj. assoc. prof. Kent (Ohio) State U., 1996—98, assoc. prof., 1998—2000, U. of Okla., Norman, 2000—. Panelist, proposal evaluator NEH, Washington, 1999; participant forum on libr. and info. svcs. policy Nat. Ctr. for Edn. Stats. and U.S. Nat. Commn. on Librs. and Info. Sci., Washington, 1996; panelist White House conf. on aging mini-conf. on the arts, the humanities, and older adults NEH/ Nat. Coun. on the Aging, Washington, 1995; co-investigator on grant project Okla. Dept. of Librs./U. of Okla., Oklahoma City, 2001—02, Inst. for Mus. and Libr. Svcs., USDE, Washington, 1999—2001; project cons. Ohio Libr. Coun. and State Libr. of Ohio, Columbus, 1998—99; co-investigator on grant Libr. Edn. and Human Resource Devel. Program, USDE, Washington, 1997—98; project cons. Ohio Libr. Coun., Columbus, 1996—98; inst. co-organizer Libr. Career Tng. and Devel. Program Inst. Awards, USDE, Washington, 1995—96, Libr. Career Tng. Program, USDE, Washington, 1994—95; project supr., grant adminstr. Libr. Career Tng. Program Fellowship Awards, USDE, Washington, 1992—94; project cons. Nat. Coun. on the Aging, Inc., Washington, 1990—91; guest instr. Mo. State Libr., Jefferson City, 1999. Editor: (jour.) Reference & User Svcs. Quar., 2000; co-editor: RQ, 1997, (book) Library Evaluation: A Casebook for Managers, 2001; co-author: Preparing Staff to Serve People with Disabilities, 1995; co-editor: A Service Profession, a Service Commitment: A Festschrift in Honor of Charles D. Patterson, 1992; co-author: (book chpt.) The Readers' Advisor's Companion, 2001, Research Issues in Public Librarianship: Trends for the Future, 1994; author: Adult Services: An Enduring Focus for Public Libraries, 1990, (procs.) Public Libraries and Community-Based Education for Lifelong Learning, 1995; co-author: Proceedings of Philosophical, Ethical and Practical Aspects of Refereed Science Journals; contbr. articles to profl. jours. Pres. Patrons of the Pub. Libr., East Baton Rouge Parish, Baton Rouge, 1994—96. Recipient John Edwards fellowship, Ind. U., 1988—89, grant Seminar: Ohio Libr. Evaluation, Libr. Edn. & Human Resource Devel. Program, U.S. Dept of Edn., 1997—98, grant for Rural Econ. Devel. Inst., Libr. Career Tng. and Devel. Program, U.S. Dept. of Edn., 1995—96, grant La. Pub. Librs. Electronic Access Seminar, 1994—95, scholarship support for interest in svcs. to people with disabilities, Libr. Career Tng. Program, U.S. Dept of Edn., 1993—94, 1992—93. Mem.: ALA (steering com., conf. on profl. edn. 1988—99, chair rsch. com. 1989—91, editl. adv. bd. co-chair Reference and Adult Svcs. Divsn. 1991—96, mem. (ex officio) bd. dirs. Reference and Adult Svcs. Divsn. 1991—97, Resolution of Appreciation Reference & User Services Assn. 1997, mem. task force on fgn. credentialing 1997—2000, chair, com. on edn. 1998—99, steering com. Congress on Profl. Edn. 1998—99, councilor at large 1998—2002, mem. (ex officio) bd. dirs. Reference and Users Svcs. Assn. 2000—03, reference & user svcs. quar. editl. adv. bd. co-chair 2000—03, planning and budget assembly 2001—02, Pub. Libr. Assn., Assn. Specialized and Coop. Libr. Agys., Intellectual Freedom Round Table, Margaret E. Monroe Libr. Adult Svcs. award Reference and Adult Services Divsn. 1996), Assn. Libr. & Info. Sci. Edn. (pres.), La. Libr. Assn. (mem. com. on paraprofl. continuing edn. 1989—91, co-founder/mem. minority recruitment and profl. concerns group 1989—92, mem. scholarship com. 1989—92, mem. pub. libr. stds.com. 1993—95), Okla. Libr. Assn. (intellectual freedom com. 2001—04), Beta Phi Mu (chpt. advisor 1992—94, Rho chpt. advisor 1998—2000). Democrat. Avocations: reading, watercolor, needlecrafts. Office: U Oklahoma SLIS Rm 120 401 W Brooks Norman OK 73019-6032 Business E-Mail: cvanfleet@ou.edu.

VAN FLEET, DAVID DOMINIC, management educator; b. Binghamton, NY, Nov. 27, 1940; s. Walter Anthony Van Fleet, Sr. and Katherine Elizabeth Van Fleet; m. Ella Webb, Aug. 27, 1966; children: Marijke, Dirk. BS, U. Tenn., 1962, PhD, 1969. Instr. U. Tenn., Knoxville, 1963—67, Kingsport Grad. Study Program, Kingsport, Tenn., 1967—70; asst. prof. U. Akron, Akron, 1970—73; from asst. prof. to prof. Tex. A&M U., College Station, 1973—89; prof. Ariz. State U., Phoenix, 1989—, MBA dir., 1999—2004. Prin. lectr. A. Frank Smith Jr. Lectureship series Southwestern U., 2000. Author: (book) Military Leadership: An Organizational Behavior Perspective, 1986, Organizational Behavior: A Managerial Viewpoint, 1983, Contemporary Management (3rd. edition), 1994, Contemporary Management (2nd edition), 1991, Contemporary Management (1st edition), 1991, Behavior in Organizations, 1991; contbr. numerous articles to profl. jours., chpts. to books; editor: N-File Newsletter, 1976—78, Acad. of Mgmt. Newsletter, 1979—82, Jour. of Mgmt., 1987—89, Jour. Behavioral and Applied Mgmt. Recipient Faculty Achievement award in Rsch., Scholarship, and Creative Activity, Ariz. State U. West Campus, 2001, Faculty Achievement award in Svc., 2005, Outstanding Svc. award, Coll. Bus. Adminstrn., Tex. A&M U., 1985. Fellow: Acad. Mgmt. (chmn. mgmt. history divsn. 1980—81, dep. dean 1996—99), So. Mgmt. Assn. (pres. 1995, Sustained Outstanding Svc. award 2005); mem.: Southwestern Fedn. of Adminstrv. Disciplines (bd. dirs. 1985—87), Allied So. Bus. Assn. (pres. 1995), S.W. Acad. of Mgmt. (pres. 1986—87). Home: 4849 E Altadena Ave Scottsdale AZ 85254 Office: Arizona State University PO Box 37100 Phoenix AZ 85069-7100 Office Phone: 602-543-6104. Personal E-mail: ddvf@asu.edu.

VAN FLEET, GEORGE ALLAN, lawyer; b. Monterey, Calif., Jan. 20, 1953; s. George Lawson and Wilma Ruth (Williams) Van F.; m. Laurie Elise Koch, July 20, 1975; children: Katia Elaine, Alexander Lawson. BA summa cum laude, Rice U., 1976; JD summa cum laude, Columbia U., 1977. Bar: Tex. 1978, US Dist. Ct. (so. dist.) Tex. 1978, US Dist. Ct. (we. dist.) Tex. 1987, US Dist. Ct. (no. dist.) Tex, 1988, US Dist. Ct. (ea. dist.) Tex. 1991, US Tax Ct., 1984, US Ct. Appeals (5th cir.) 1978, US Ct. Appeals (11th cir.) 1981, US Ct. Appeals (DC cir.) 1982, US Ct. Appeals (fed. cir.) 1993, US Supreme Ct. 1981. Law clk. U.S. Ct. Appeals (2d cir.), NYC, 1977; assoc. Vinson & Elkins, Houston, 1977-84, ptnr., 1984—2006; shareholder Greenberg Traurig, LLP, 2006—. Co-author: Federal Civil Procedure Before Trial--Firth Circuit, 1997, The Competition Laws of NAFTA, Canada, Mexico and the United States, 1997, Business and Commercial Litigation in Federal Courts, 1998, supplement, 2005; editor: Annual Review of Antitrust Law Developments, 2000; co-author: Am. Legal Ethics Libr., 2002, Doing Business in Texas, 2003, Spanish edit., 2007, State Antitrust Practice and Statutes, 2004, Inside the Minds: Leading Lawyers on Unfair Competition, Trade Regulation and Litig., 2003; contbr. articles to profl. jour. Mem. bd. visitors Columbia U., 1992—; mem. City of Houston Ethics Com., 1992—98, chmn., 1995—98; bd. dirs. Nat. Appleseed Found., 2002—, Tex. Appleseed Ctr., 1998—, vice chmn., 1999—2002, chmn., 2002—04. Recipient Ordroneaux prize Columbia U., 1977, W. Frank Newton award for outstanding contbns. in provision of access to legal svcs. to the poor State Bar Tex., 2002; James Kent scholar Columbia U., 1974-77. Fellow: Am. Bar Found., Tex. Bar Found.; mem.: ABA (com. chmn. 1987—95, coun. 1996—99, com. chmn. 2000—02, sect. officer 2002, ho. dels. 2002—05, nominating com. 2003—05), Latin Am. Law Initiative (coun. 2005—), Tex.-Mex. Bar Assn. (pres. 1998—2000), Houston Bar Assn. (sect. chair 1991—93), Tex. Commn. on Access to Justice, State Bar Tex. (coun. 2000—04, dir. 2005—), Phi Beta Kappa. Democrat. Jewish. Home: 3430 S Parkwood Dr Houston TX 77021-1238 Office: Greenberg Traurig LLP 1000 Louisiana Ste 1800 Houston TX 77002 Home Phone: 713-748-6344; Office Phone: 713-374-3555. Business E-Mail: vanfleetg@gtlaw.com.

VAN FLEET, LISA A., lawyer; BSW, Valparaiso U., 1982, JD, 1985. Bar: Ind. 1985, US Tax Ct. 1987, US Claims Ct. 1988, Mo. 1989, Ill. 1990. Ptnr., practice leader Employee Benefits and Exec. Compensation Bryan Cave LLP, St. Louis. Office: Bryan Cave LLP One Metropolitan Square 211 N Broadway, Ste 3600 Saint Louis MO 63102 Office Phone: 314-259-2326. Business E-Mail: lavanfleet@bryancave.com.

VANFOSSEN, PHILLIP J., academic administrator; b. East Lansing, Mich., Jan. 18, 1964; s. Gerald James VanFossen, Jr. and Margaret Joyce VanFossen; m. Bethany Hutchings, June 27, 1987; children: Madsion Tayler, Liliana Grace. BS in Ed., Miami U., Oxford, Ohio, 1986, MEd, 1990; PhD, Ohio State U., Columbus, 1993. Dir. Ackerman Ctr. for Dem. Citizenship Purdue U., West Lafayette, Ind., 2000—, James F. Ackerman prof. of social studies edn. Coll. Edn., 2004—. Assoc. dir. Purdue U. Ctr. for Econ. Edn., West Lafayette, 1997—. Author: (textbook) Using Internet Primary Sources to Teach Critical Thinking Skills in Government, Economics, and Contemporary World Problems, Focus: Institutions and Markets, Learning, Earning and Investing, Focus: Globalization. Mem. Purdue U. Ctr. for Econ. Edn., West Lafayette, 1997—2006. Named Outstanding U. Prof., Kappa Delta Pi, 2002, 2000; recipient univ. scholarship, Purdue U., 2002—07, Outstanding Tchg. award, Coll. of Edn., Purdue U., 2001. Mem.: Nat. Coun. for the Social Studies, Nat. Coun. on Econ. Edn. (chair tech. com. 2002—05). United Methodist. Avocations: golf, home repair, weightlifting, reading. Office: Ackerman Ctr for Dem Citizensh Purdue Univ 100 N University St West Lafayette IN 47907-2098 Home Phone: 765-463-5143; Office Phone: 765-494-2367. Business E-Mail: vanfoss@purdue.edu.

VAN GALDER, VALERIE, marketing executive; b. Chgo. Grad., UCLA. Asst. Rogers & Cowen, 1985—90; v.p. mktg. & publicity Hard Rock Am., 1990—94; head mktg. Fox Searchlight Pictures, 1994—99; exec. v.p. mktg. Sony Screen Gems, 1999—2004; pres. TriStar Pictures, 2004—05; pres. domestic mktg. Columbia TriStar Motion Picture Group, 2005—. Internat. adv. bd. Bermuda Internat. Film Festival, 2005—. Named one of 100 Most Powerful Women in Entertainment, Hollywood Reporter, 2006. Mailing: Sony Pres TriStar Pictures 9050 West Washington Blvd Culver City CA 90232 *

VANGATES, DESS, retired military officer; b. Monticello, Fla., June 1, 1942; s. Fred and Rachel Etta Vangates. Contbr. articles to profl. jours. Sgt. US Army, 1975—81, Korea. Mem.: Vet. Foreign Wars of U.S. (life). Democrat. Achievements include research in global warming; the cause and effect of hydrogen part five, nitrogen part one-Avian bird flu influenza; 1N1HiV fussion recognizing germ 1N1 as base germ. Avocations: poker, reading, singing. Home: 2145 NW 152nd Ter Miami Gardens FL 33054 Office Phone: 305-687-9671.

VAN GEEN, ALEXANDER, geochemist, researcher; BS in Oceanography, U. Wash., Seattle, 1982, BS cum laude in Chemistry, 1982; PhD in Oceanography, MIT/Woods Hole Oceanog. Instn., Cambridge, Mass., 1989. Watch officer rsch. vessel Tydeman Dutch Navy, 1982—84; rsch. asst. dept. earth, atmospheric and planetary scis. MIT, 1984—89; postdoctoral fellow dept. civil and environ. engring. Stanford U., Calif., 1989—90; post-doctoral investigator water resources divsn. US Geol. Survey, Menlo Pk., Calif., 1990—93; adj. rsch. scientist Lamont-Doherty Earth Obs., Palisades, NY, 1993, assoc. rsch. scientist, 1994—97, rsch. scientist, 1997—2000, sr. rsch. scientist, 2000—. Invited prof. Université d'Aix-Marseille III, France, 1997, 2002. Contbr. articles to profl. jours. Office: Lamont-Doherty Earth Obs Columbia U Rt 9W Palisades NY 10964 Office Phone: 845-365-8644. Office Fax: 845-365-8154. E-mail: avangeen@ldeo.columbia.edu. *

VANGELDER, KIM E., information technology executive; BS, Rochester Inst. Tech. With Eastman Kodak Co., Rochester, NY, 1984—, dir. global ERP competency ctr., 1996—2000, dir. info. tech. for R&D org., 2000—03, dir. info. tech. digital & film imaging systems, 2003, v.p. chief info. officer, 2004—. Mem. dean's council Golisano Coll. Computing & Info. Office: Eastman Kodak Co 343 State St Rochester NY 14650 *

VANGER, MILTON ISADORE, historian, educator; b. NYC, Apr. 11, 1925; s. Max Manuel and Rose (Rothstein) V.; m. Elsa M. Oribe, Sept. 10, 1956; children: John, Mark, Rachel. AB, Princeton U., 1948; MA, Harvard U., 1950, PhD, 1958. Teaching fellow history Harvard U., 1952-56; instr. Okla. State U., 1956-58; asst. prof. history Sacramento State Coll., 1958-62; mem. faculty Brandeis U., Waltham, Mass., 1962—, prof. history, 1973-84, prof. emeritus, 1984—. Chmn. com. Latin Am. studies, 1971-81; invited lectr. 50th anniversary conf. commemorating death of Batlle y Ordoñez of Uruguay, 1979; invitee to inauguration of pres. Sanguinetti, Uruguay, 1985; Barnette Miller vis. prof. history, Wellesley Coll., 1990. Author: José Batlle y Ordoñez of Uruguay: The Creator of His Times, 1902-1907, 1963, 2d edit., 1980, Spanish transl., 1968, 2d edit., 1992, The Model Country: José Batlle y Ordoñez of Uruguay, 1907-1915, 1980, Spanish transl., 1983, 2d edit., 1991, Reforma o Revolución La Polémica Batlle-Mibelli, 1917, 1989; outside reviewer NEH, Radcliffe Inst.; contbr. articles to profl. jours. Juror for Lindahl Prize, Inst. Latin Am. Studies, Stockholm. With AUS, 1943-45. Doherty Found. fellow, 1950-52; grantee Am. Philos. Soc., 1966; recipient Hermes prize for best history pub. in Uruguay, 1983. Mem. New Eng. Council Latin Am. Studies (sec.-treas. 1970-72), Am. Hist. Assn., Conf. on Latin Am. History, Amnesty Internat., Phi Beta Kappa. Democrat. Jewish. Address: 931 Massachusetts Ave Ste 503 Cambridge MA 02139

VAN GESTEL, ALLAN, judge; b. Boston, Dec. 3, 1935; BA, Colby Coll., 1957; LLB, Boston U., 1961; MA (hon.), Colby Coll., 1999. Bar: Mass. 1961, U.S. Dist. Ct. Mass. 1963, U.S. Ct. Appeals (1st cir.) 1969, U.S. Supreme Ct. 1972, U.S. Ct. Claims 1979, U.S. Ct. Appeals (2d cir.) 1980, U.S. Dist. Ct. (no. dist.) N.Y. 1980, U.S. Dist. Ct. (we. dist.) N.Y. 1993, U.S. Ct. Appeals (3d cir.) 1993, U.S. Ct. Appeals (5th cir.) 1995. Assoc. firm Goodwin, Procter & Hoar, Boston, 1961-70, ptnr., 1970-96; assoc. justice Superior Ct. Mass., 1996—2005, recalled, 2006—; presiding justice Superior Ct. Bus. Litigation Session, 2000—. Spl. counsel Boston Fin. Commn., 1974; spl. counsel to Mass. Commn. on Jud. Conduct, 1986; mem. Scituate (Mass.) Bd. Zoning Appeals, 1970, Scituate Planning Bd., 1972; spl. counsel Gov. of N.Y. on Indian Land Claims, 1985-96; spl. counsel to Gov. and Atty. Gen. of Vt. on Indian Claims, 1987-90; chmn. standing adv. com. Mass. Rules Civil Procedure, 1986-93; overseer Colby Coll., 1990-99, trustee, 1999—2005. Contbr. numerous articles on Eastern Indian land claims, ct. adminstrn., capital punishment to profl. jours. Recipient Haskell Cohn Disting. Jud. Svc. award, 2006. Fellow Am. Coll. Trial Lawyers; mem. ABA, Mass. Bar Assn., Boston Bar Assn. (chmn., task force on drugs and the cts.), Supreme Jud. Ct. Hist. Soc. (chmn. bd. overseers 1993-96), Mass. Hist. Soc.

VAN GILDER, JOHN CORLEY, neurosurgeon, educator; b. Huntington, W.Va., Aug. 14, 1935; s. John Ray and Sarah Pool (Corley) Van G.; m. Kerstin Margarita Olesson, Mar., 1965; children: Sarah, John, Rachel, David. BA, W.Va. U., 1957, BS, 1959; MD, U. Pitts., 1961. Diplomate Am. Bd. Neurol. Surgery (examiner 1976, 79, 84). Intern Pa. Hosp., Phila., 1961, asst. resident in surgery, 1964-65, Wilkes-Barre Hosp., Pa., 1962; asst. resident neurosurgery Barnes Hosp., St. Louis, 1966-68, sr. resident, 1968-69; instr. neurosurgery Yale U. Sch. Medicine, New Haven, 1970, asst. prof., 1970-73, assoc. prof., 1973-76; prof. neurosurgery U. Iowa, Iowa City, 1976—, chmn. divsn. neurosurgery, 1976—, exec. com. dept. surgery, 1978-81. Fellow neurosurgery Washington U. Sch. Medicine, St. Louis, 1965 -66, instr., 1966; attending neurosurgeon VA Hosp., New Haven, 1970-73, cons. 1973-76; assoc. to attending neurosurgeon Yale-New Haven Med. Ctr., 1970-76; cons. VA Hosp., Iowa City, 1976—; neurol. surg. cons. Vets. Affairs Hdqrs., Washington; mem. clin. coordinating com. U. Iowa Cancer Ctr., 1979—; vis. prof. U. Tenn., 1984, Tufts U. Med. Ctr., Boston, 1986, U. Tex., San Antonio, 1987, U. Mich., Ann Arbor, 1988, People's Republic China at Hunan Med. Coll., Beijing Neurol. Inst., Tianjin Med. Coll. Hosp., Tiantan Xili, Xian Gen. Hosp., 2d Mil. Coll., Shanghai, Suzhou Med. Coll. Shanghai, 1985, USSR at Burdenk Inst., Kiev Neurol. Inst., Leningrad Neurol. Soc., 1989, Western Res. U., Cleve., 1993, Yale U., 1994, U. Wash., Seattle, 1997, Mayo Clinic, 1998, U. Calif., San Francisco, 1998, Ind. U., 1999; mem. ad. hoc rev. bd. Surg. Neurology, 2001—, Spine, 2000—, Army-Navy, Bethesda-Walter Reed, 2005; presenter in field. Author: (with others): Principles of Surgery, 2d edit., 1973, Brief Textbook of Surgery, 1976, Aneurysmal Subarachnoid Hemorrhage, 1981, Operative Neurosurgical Techniques, Indications, Methods, and Results, 1982, Sports Medicine, 1982, Neurosurgery, 1982, Clinical Neurosurgery, 1982, Operative Neurosurgical Technique, Vol. II, 1982, 88, Vol. III, 1995, Current Therapy in Neurosurgical Surgery, 1985, 2d edit., 1987, Craniovertebral Junction Abnormalities, 1987, Decision Making in Neurological Surgery, 1987, Neurological Surgery, 3d edit., 1988, Anterior Cervical Spine Surgery, 1993, Brain Surgery: Complication Avoidance and Management, 1993, Neurosurgical Emergencies, 1994, Techniques of Spinal Fusion and Instrumation, 1995, Somatic Gene Therapy, 1995, Infections in Neurological Surgery, 1999; contbr. numerous articles and abstracts to profl. jours.; co-author teaching films; mem. editorial bd. Neurosurgery jour., 1978-84. Capt. USAF, 1962-64. Grantee NIH, 1973-78, Nat. Cancer Inst., 1980-88. Fellow: ACS (membership com. Iowa dist. #1 1983—); mem.: AMA, Am. Bd. Neurol. Surgery (dir. 1992—98, chmn. 1997—98, residency rev. com.-neurol. surgery 1995—2001, neurosurgery chmn. 1999—2001), Am. Acad. Neurol. Surgery (v.p. 1995—), Midwest Surg. Assn., Soc. Neurol. Surgeons (chmn. membership com. 1986—87, treas. 1991—, pres 1997—98, treas. 1991—96, pres. 1997, Disting. Svc. award 2004), Iowa-Midwest Neurosurg. Soc. (pres. 1978—79), Johnson County Med. Soc. (program com. 1984—88, chmn. 1985—86), Iowa Med. Soc., Neurol. Soc. Am. (long range planning com. 1984—, v.p. 1985, pres. 1998—99), Rsch. Soc. Neurol. Surgeons, Am. Assn. Neurol. Surgeons (awards com. 1986—87, bd. dirs. 1986—90, chmn. 1987—88, Disting. Svc. award 2005), Congress Neurol. Surgeons (resident placement com. 1970), Am. Physiol. Soc., Ga. Neurosurg. Soc. (hon.), Sigma Xi. Home: 330 S Summit St Iowa City IA 52240-3220 Office: U Iowa Hosps & Clinics Dept Neurosurgery 200 Hawkins Dr Iowa City IA 52242-1009 Home Phone: 319-338-9805; Office Phone: 319-356-2772. Business E-Mail: johnvangilder@uiowa.edu.

VAN GINKEL, BLANCHE LEMCO, architect, educator; b. London, 1923; d. Myer and Claire Lemco; m. H. P. Daniel van Ginkel, 1956; children: Brenda, Marc. B.Arch., McGill U., 1945; M.C.P., Harvard U., 1950; Doctorate (hon.), U. Aix-Marseille, France, 2005. Tech. asst. Nat. Film Bd. Can., 1943-44; mgr. City Planning Office, Regina, Sask., Canada, 1946; architect Atelier Le Corbusier, Paris, 1948; asst. prof. architecture U. Pa., 1951-57; ptnr. van Ginkel Assocs., Montreal, Que., Canada, also Toronto, Ont., Canada, 1957—; prof. architecture U. Toronto, 1977—92, dir. Sch. Architecture, 1977-80, dean faculty architecture and landscape architecture, 1980-82. Vis. critic Harvard U., 1958, 70; adj. prof. U. Montreal, McGill U., others; curator exhbns. RCA, U. Toronto, others. Contbr. articles to profl. jours. Mem. Nat. Capital Planning Com., Ottawa, Art Adv. Com., Ottawa; mem. adv. com. Nat. Mus.'s Corp.; mem. Que. Provincial Planning Commn.; founder, v.p. Corp. of Urbanists of Que., 1963-65; bd. dirs. Montreal Internat. Film Festival, 1961-66. Decorated Order of Can., 2000; recipient Internat. Fedn. Housing and Planning Grand Prix award, 1956, Massey medal for arch., 1962, Mademoiselle Mag. award, 1957, Queen's Silver Jubilee medal, 1977, Citizenship citation Can. Govt., 1991, Queen's Golden Jubilee medal, 2002, award Order of Urbanists of Que., 2003. Fellow AIA (hon.), Royal Archtl. Inst. Can. (exec. com. 1971-74), Toronto Soc. Arch.; mem. Can. Inst. Planners (bd. dirs. 1961-64), Assn. Collegiate Schs. Architecture (bd. dirs. 1981-84, v.p. 1985-86, pres. 1986-87, Disting. Prof. award 1989), Royal Can. Acad. Art (bd. dirs. 1992—2000), Internat. Archive of Women Architects (bd. dirs. 1985-2001), Ont. Assn. Arch. (life), Order of Can. Office: 38 Summerhill Gardens Toronto ON Canada M4T 1B4

VAN GOOR, ANTHONY JAY, retired military officer, medical executive; b. Yankton, SD, Feb. 16, 1953; s. Marjorie L Van Goor; m. Marilyn Judy Staehli, Oct. 27, 1990; children: Brittany Marie, Michael Joseph. MD, U. of SD, 1978—82; M in med. mgmt., Tulane U., 2004—05. Board Certification in Internal Medicine Am. Bd. of Internal Medicine, 1990, Board Certification in Medical Management Certifying Commn. in Med.

Mgmt., 2004. Advanced through grades to col. USAF, commd. officer, 1978; chief med. staff 21st Med. Group, Peterson Air Force Base, Colo., 1994—97; comdr. 77th Med. Ops. Squadron, McClellan/Mather Air Force Base, Calif., 1997—2000, 347th Med. Group, Moody Air Force Base, Ga., 2000—02, 42nd Med. Group, Maxwell Air Force Base, Ala., 2002—04; assoc. chief, med. staff Keesler Med. Ctr., Keesler Air Force Base, Miss., 2004—06; exec. v.p., med. dir. Sutter Delta Med. Group, Antioch, Calif., 2006—; ret. USAF, 2006. Pres. parish coun. Maxwell/Gunter Cath. Parish, Maxwell Air Force Base, Ala., 2002—03. Decorated Legion of Merit USAF, 5 Meritorious Svc. medals, Air Force Commendation Medal. Mem.: AMA, ACP, Am. Coll. Healthcare Execs., Am. Coll. Physician Execs. Catholic. Avocations: vocal performance, travel, physical conditioning, skiing.

VAN GORDER, JAN REID, lawyer, insurance company executive; b. Endicott, NY, Dec. 28, 1947; s. George Austin and Elizabeth Anne Van G.; m. Linda Susan Massarelli, July 31, 1976; children: Austin Reid, Lewis Evan, Thomas Drew, Elizabeth Marie. BA, U. Pa., 1970; JD, Temple U., 1975. Assoc. gen. counsel Phila. Life Ins. Co., 1975-78, Harleysville Ins. Co., Pa., 1978-81; v.p., sec., gen. counsel Erie Ins. Group, Pa., 1981-82, sr. v.p., sec., gen. counsel Pa., 1983-90, exec. v.p., sec., gen. counsel Pa., 1990—. Bd. dirs. Pa. Assigned Claims Plan, Ins. Fedn. Pa., Pa. Profl. Liability Joint Underwriting Assn. Bd. dirs. Pennsylvanians for Effective Govt. Mem. ABA, Pa. Bar Assn., Erie County Bar Assn., Nat. Assn. Ind. Insurers (legis. com.), Newcomen Soc. U.S., Kahkwa Club, Erie Club. Republican. Episcopalian. Avocations: hunting, fishing, skiing, golf. Office: Erie Ins Group 100 Erie Insurance Pl Erie PA 16530-0001 *

VAN GORDER, JOHN FREDERIC, lawyer; b. Jacksonville, Fla., Mar. 22, 1943; s. Harold Burton and Charlotte Louise Van G.; m. Sandra Joan Hagen, June 4, 1977 (div. June 1995); children: Alyssa Jane, Kathryn Ann; m. Ann Michele Brancato, Oct. 7, 1995. Grad., Dover Coll., Eng., 1961; AB, Dartmouth Coll., 1965; postgrad., Air Force Inst. Tech., 1967-68; MS in Adminstrn., George Washington U., 1973; postgrad., U. Va., Coll. William and Mary, Cath. U. Am., Northeastern U., Babson Coll., U. South; JD, Fordham U., 1981. Bar: N.J. 1981, U.S. Dist. Ct. N.J. 1981, N.Y. 1983, U.S. Supreme Ct. 1989. Commd. 2d lt. USAF, 1965, advanced through grades to capt., 1968; weapons contr. Aerospace Def. Commd., Ft. Lee, Va., 1965-67; buyer electronics sys. divsn. Air Force Sys. Commd., Bedford, Mass., 1968-69; project mgr. rsch. and devel. Hdqrs. USAF, Washington, 1969-73, br. chief pers., 1973-74; presdl. social aide The White House, Washington, 1971-74; assoc. Louis C. Kramp & Assocs., Washington, 1975; program officer J.M. Found., NYC, 1975-81; assoc. Winne, Banta & Rizzi Esqs., Hackensack, N.J., 1981-83; asst. sec., program adminstr. Glenmede Trust Co., Phila., 1983—86; exec. dir., asst. sec. Leon Lowenstein Found., 1986—. Atty. Rent Leveling Bd., Borough of Bergenfield, N.J., 1983; pres. Vanguard Corp., Massapequa, N.Y., 1996-2001; adj. prof. Grad. Sch. Edn., Fordham U., N.Y.C., 1997—, mem. adv. com. N.Y.C. Pub. Schs. Supts.' Network, 1998—2007, judge Nat. Sch. Change awards, 2001—, mem. program devel. adv. com. Grad. Sch. Edn., 2000—07. Chmn. NYC steering com. Nat. Congress on Volunteerism and Citizenship, 1976; mem. exec. com. Mayor's Vol. Action Coun., 1977-78; bd. govs. NY Jaycees Found., 1978-79; bd. govs., 4th v.p. First Assembly Dist. Rep. Club, 1977-82; vestryman All Saints Episc. Ch., Bergenfeld, 1982-83; mem. Tabernacle Twp. Planning Bd., 1985-88, Tabernacle Bd. Edn., 1988-91, Tabernacle Rep. Club, 1983-93; jr. warden, 1987-88, sr. warden, 1989-90, vestryman, lay reader St. Peter's Episc. Ch., Medford, N.J., 1985-93; program adv. com. Toshiba Am. Found., 1993-99; trustee, dir. Support Ctr. of NY, 1995-97, Robert A. Taft Inst. Govt., NYC, 1994-97; bd. dirs. NYC Pub./Pvt. Initiatives, Inc., 1996-2000, NY Regional Assn. Grantmakers, 1998-2006; bd. trustees Calvin K. Kazanjian Econs. Found., 2002—; mem. adv. com. Ctr. for Advancement of Children's Mental Health, Columbia U., NYC, 2003-05; serving brother Priory in USA, Order of St. John, 2003-, bd. dirs. USO Met. NY, 2005-06. Col. USAFR, ret. Named Outstanding Young Man of VA., 1975, USAF Res. Officer of Yr., 1985. Mem. Internat. (senator; v.p. 1975; rep. to UN 1976), U.S. (nat. v.p. 1973-74), D.C. (pres. 1972-73), N.Y.C. (bd. govs. 1978-79) Jaycees, SAR, Soc. Mayflower Descs., ABA, N.Y. Bar Assn., Student Bar Assn. (class pres. 1978-81), Toastmasters (local pres. 1969-70, area gov. 1970-71), Lions (pres. Medford Twp. club 1985-86, co-chmn. Charity Ball 1987), Masons, Alpha Delta Phi. Republican. Episcopalian. Office Phone: 212-319-0670.

VAN GORP, GARY WAYNE, minister; b. Reasnor, Iowa, July 16, 1953; s. Laverne Leroy, Sr. and Emma Jean (Meyers) Van Gorp; m. Marietta Louise Burns, Dec. 29, 1972; children: Caleb Aaron Van Gorp, Kari Beth Van Gorp, Micah Alan Van Gorp, Faith Elise Van Gorp, Melinda Amy Van Gorp, Joy Annette Van Gorp, Kristina Nicole Van Gorp. Diploma in Pastoral Studies, Bible and Doctrine, Berean Coll., 1975; BS in Pastoral Studies, Religious Edn., North Cen. U., Mpls., 1978; Diploma in profl. office mgmt., Alexandria Tech. Coll., Minn., 1984; various positions, ADIA Employment, 1993. Ordained to ministry Assembly of God Ch., 1981. Pastor Verndale (Minn.) Assembly of God Ch., 1979—82; asst. mgr., caretaker Lake Geneva Bible Camp, Alexandria, 1982—83; Christian edn. and outreach pastor Alexandria Assembly of God Ch., 1983—84; pastor, adminstrv. asst. Allison Park (Pa.) Assembly God Ch., 1984—90; interim pastor Assembly God Ch., Bklyn. Ctr. and Winona, Minn., 1991; mem. maintenance pers. staff South Ridge Mall, 1991—92; farmhand J&V Van Gorp, Inc., 1992; developer ministry program Berean Assembly of God Ch., Des Moines, 1992; founder, owner GW Enterprize, 1993—; with ADIA The Employment People, Temp. Svc., 1992—94; pastor Lighthouse Assembly of God, Glencoe, Minn., 1994—99; security officer Roland Security, 1995—99; office mgr. Spruce Ridge Resource Mgmt., 1999—2000; adminstrv. asst. Koobi LLC, 2000—06; sr. pastor Two Rivers Fellowship, Greeley, Colo., 2001—. Vice prin. Faith Acad. Christian Sch., 1980—82; mgr. book store Gospel Supply Ctr., Minn., 1981—82; pastor Elbow Lake Assembly of God, Minn., 1983—84; chmn. Glencoe Ministerium, 1995—96. Bd. dirs., treas., mem. adv. bd. DoorWay, Inc., Pitts., 1988—92; mem. adv. bd. Glory Home Sch. Corp., Des Moines, 1994; coach Rocky Mountain Dist. Coun., 2002—; chmn. Faith Cmty. Svc. Fund, Greeley, Colo., 2005—; mem. Bldg. Stronger Marriages Weld County, Colo., 2005—, Housing Emergency Svcs. Network, United Way Weld County, 2005—06; vol. night chaplain, sec., mem. pastoral care adv. com. No. Colo. Med. Ctr., 2006—; coord. W. League Jr. Bible Quiz State of Minn., 1995—2001; mem. Weld County Faith Based Adv. Bd., 2005—; mem. adv. com. Weld Assn. Evang. Chs., 2006—. Named to, Outstanding Young Men Am. Mem.: Nat. Assn. Ch. Bus. Adminstrs. (pres. Pitts. chpt. 1987—90). Home: 3915 W 21st St Greeley CO 80634 Office Phone: 970-351-6622. Personal E-mail: vangorp53@msn.com.

VAN GORP, JON D., lawyer; b. Denver, Colo., June 12, 1969; BA, Calvin Coll., 1991; JD cum laude, So. Methodist Univ., 1994. Bar: Tex. 1994, Ill. 1998, NY 2004. Assoc. Thompson & Knight, Dallas, 1994—97; atty. Mayer Brown Rowe & Maw, Chgo., 1997—2003, ptnr., fin. & securitization, 2003—. Spkr. in field on fin. and securitization topics. Editor (staff): The Internat. Lawyer; contbr. articles to profl. jours. Greater Chgo. Leadership fellow, 2005. Office: Mayer Brown Rowe Maw Llp 71 S Wacker Dr Chicago IL 60606-4637 Office Phone: 312-701-7091. Office Fax: 312-706-8362. Business E-Mail: jvangorp@mayerbrownrowe.com.

VAN GRACK, STEVEN, lawyer; b. Memphis, Oct. 6, 1948; s. Irving and Edna (Schwartz) Van Grack; m. Gail Beverly Lang, Nov. 18, 1972 (div.); children: Adam, Ryan, Brandon, Allison; m. Susan M Freeland, May 21, 1993. BA, U. Md., 1970, JD, 1974. Bar: 1974 (Md), DC 1976, US Dist Ct Md 1976, US Dist Ct DC 1976, US Ct Appeals (4th cir) 1977, US Supreme Ct 1978. Law clk. to presiding justice Montgomery County Cir. Ct., Rockville, Md., 1974-75; assoc. Joseph Roesser Law Offices, Silver Springs, Md., 1975-78; ptnr. Ebert & Bowytz, Washington, 1978-80; mng. ptnr. Van Grack, Axelson & Williamowsky, Rockville, 1980—. Instr, lectr Montgomery Col, Germantown, Md., 1983—85. Cubmaster packs 1343 and 1449 Boy Scouts of Am.; coach Rockville Baseball Assn.; trustee Shady Grove Adventist Hosp. Found.; co-chmn. Montgomery County March of Dimes WalkAmerica Com., 1998—2003; pres. Md. Inst. for Countinuing Profl. Edn. of Lawyers, 2003—; chmn. Md. Real Estate Commn., 2001—; gen. counsel Montgomery County Dem. Ctrl. Com., Kensington, Md., 1978—82; campaign mgr. Com. to Elect the Sitting Judges, Rockville, Md., 1982; mayor City of Rockville, Md., 1985—87; Dem. candidate 8th Congl. Dist. Md., 1994; bd. dirs. Washington Met. Coun. Govts. With USAR, 1970—71. Named one of Oustanding Young Men Am, Jaycees, 1978, 1981; recipient Fifth Ann Pro Bono Serv Award, Montgomery County Bar Found, 1998, Extraordinary Commitment to the Delivery of Legal Servs Award, 1999, Nancy Dworkin Award, Montgomery County Comn Children and Youth, 2001, Pro Bono Svc. award, Women's Bar Assn. Md., 2003, The Daily Record Leadership in Law award, 2004. Fellow: Md Bar Found (Profl. Legal Excellence award 2002); mem.: ATLA, ABA, Rockville CofC (bd dirs), Montgomery County Bar Asn (Outstanding Comt Chair of the Yr Award 2001), Md Trial Lawyers Asn, Md Bar Asn. Jewish. Avocations: running, swimming, exercising, coin collecting/numismatics, political button collecting. Home: 808 Fordham St Rockville MD 20850-1018 Office: Van Grack Axelson & Williamowsky 401 N Washington St Rockville MD 20850-2223 Office Phone: 301-738-7671. E-mail: sug@vawlaw.com.

VAN GUNDY, GREGORY FRANK, retired lawyer; b. Columbus, Ohio, Oct. 24, 1945; s. Paul Arden and Edna Marie (Sanders) Van G.; m. Lisa Tamara Langer. BA, Ohio State U., Columbus, 1966, JD, 1969. Bar: N.Y. 1971. Assoc. atty. firm Willkie Farr & Gallagher, NYC, 1970-74; v.p. legal, sec. Marsh & McLennan Cos., Inc., NYC, 1974-79, v.p., sec., gen. counsel, 1979-2000, sec., 2000—03, retired, 2003. Mem. Phi Beta Kappa. Roman Catholic. Home: 232 Fox Meadow Rd Scarsdale NY 10583-1640 Personal E-mail: vgfam@aol.com.

VAN GUNDY, JEFF, former professional basketball coach; b. Hemet, Calif., Jan. 19, 1962; married. Grad. cum laude, Nazareth Coll., Rochester, NY. Head coach McQuaid Jesuit HS, Rochester, 1985-86; grad. asst. Providence Coll., 1986—87, 1987—88; asst. coach Rutgers U., NJ, 1988-89, NY Knicks, NYC, 1989-96, head coach, 1996—2001, Houston Rockets, 2003—07; NBA analyst Turner Sports, 2002—03. Head coach NBA Ea. Conf. All-Star Team, 2000. Named to Nazareth Coll. Sports Hall of Fame, 1996. *

VAN GUNDY, SEYMOUR DEAN, plant pathologist, educator; b. Feb. 24, 1931; s. Robert C. and Margaret (Holloway) Van G.; m. Wilma C. Fanning, June 12, 1954; children: Sue Ann, Richard L. BA, Bowling Green State U., 1953; PhD, U. Wis., 1957. Asst. nematologist U. Calif., Riverside, 1957-63, assoc. prof., 1963-68, prof. nematology and plant pathology, 1968-73, assoc. dean rsch., 1968-70, vice chancellor rsch., 1970-72, chmn. dept. nematology, 1972-84; prof. nematology and plant pathology, assoc. dean rsch. Coll. Natural and Agrl. Scis., 1985-88, acting dean, 1986, interim dean, 1988-90, dean, 1990-93, emeritus dean, prof., 1993—. Former mem. editl. bd. Rev. de Nematologie, Jour. Nematology and Plant Disease; contbr. numerous articles to profl. jours. Grantee, Rockefeller Found., Cancer Rsch., NSF, USDA; NSF fellow, Australia, 1965—66. Fellow AAAS, Am. Phytopathol. Soc., Soc. Nematologists (editor-in-chef 1968-72, v.p. 1972-73, pres. 1973-74, hon. mem. 1997); mem. (hon.) Acad. Scis. Moldova. Home: 1188 Pastern Rd Riverside CA 92506-5619 Office: U Calif Dept Nematology Riverside CA 92521-0001 Personal E-mail: vangundy@hotmail.com.

VAN GUNDY, STAN, professional basketball coach; b. Indio, Calif., Aug. 26, 1959; s. Bill Van Gundy; m. Kim Van Gundy; children: Shannon, Michael, Alison, Kelly. BA in English, SUNY, Brockport, 1981, BS in Phys. Edn., 1981. Asst. coach U. Vt., 1981—83, Canisius Coll., 1987, Fordham U., 1988; head coach Castleton State Coll., Vt., U. Mass., Lowell, 1988—92; asst. coach to head coach U. Wis.; asst. coach Miami Heat, 1995—97, asst. head coach, 1997—2003, head coach, 2003—05, cons.; head coach Orlando Magic, Fla., 2007—. Office: Orlando Magic 8701 Maitland Summit Blvd Orlando FL 32810 *

VAN HALEN, ALEX, musician; b. Amsterdam, May 8, 1953; m. Kelly Van Halen (div.); 1 child; m. Stine Van Halen, 2000; 1 child. Founding mem., drummer Mammoth, 1972—74, Van Halen, 1974—. Musician: (albums) Van Halen, 1978, Van Halen II, 1979, Women & Children First, 1980, Fair Warning, 1981, Diver Down, 1982, 1984, 1984, 5150, 1986, OU812, 1988, For Unlawful Carnal Knowledge, 1991 (Grammy award, Best Hard Rock Performance, 1992, Am. Music award, Favorite Hard Rock Album, 1992), Live: Right Here, Right Now, 1993, Balance, 1995, Van Halen III, 1998, Best of Both Worlds, 2004, Twister film soundtrack, 1996, (songs) Jump, 1984 (MTV Video Music award, 1984), Right Now, 1992 (3 MTV Video Music awards, 1992), Respect the Wind, 1996. Named to Rock & Roll Hall of Fame, with Van Halen, 2007. Office: Warner Bros Records 75 Rockefeller Plz New York NY 10019 *

VAN HALEN, EDDIE (EDWARD LODEWIJK VAN HALEN), musician; b. Nijmegan, The Netherlands, Jan. 26, 1957; arrived in U.S., 1967; s. Jan and Eugenia Van Halen; m. Valerie Bertinelli, Apr. 11, 1981 (separated); 1 child, Wolfgang William. Student, Pasadena City Coll.; studied piano. Formed group with brother Alex: Broken Combs (name changed later to Mammoth); founder, lead guitarist Van Halen, 1974—; musician: (albums) Van Halen, 1978, Van Halen II, 1979, Women and Children First, 1980, Fair Warning, 1981, Diver Down, 1982, Nineteen Eighty-Four, 1984, 5150, 1986, OU812, 1988, For Unlawful Carnal Knowledge, 1991 (Am. Music Awards Favorite Hard Rock Album, 1992), Van Halen Live: Right Here Right Now, 1993, Balance, 1995, Best of Van Halen, Vol. 1, 1996, Van Halen III, 1998, The Best of Both Worlds, 2004, (songs) Runnin' With the Devil, 1978, Jump, 1984, Hot for Teacher, 1984, Right Now, 1991 (3 MTV Video Music awards, 1992). Named one of Greatest Artists of Rock & Roll, VH1, 1998, 100 Greatest Artists of Hard Rock, 2000; named to Rock & Roll Hall of Fame, with Van Halen, 2007; recipient Grammy Award, Best Hard Rock Performance, 1992. Office: Warner Bros Records 75 Rockefeller Plz New York NY 10019-6908

VAN HAMEL, MANETTE C., artist, writer; b. Deventer, The Netherlands, Aug. 4, 1913; d. Hendrik Cramer and Maria Christina Heyligers; m. Diederik A. van Hamel, Feb. 6, 1940; children: Alfred, Jan Willem, Martine. Student, Conservatory Music, Holland; studied art with Rolph Scarlett. Profl. violinist. One-woman shows of sculpture to wear include Stedelijk Mus., Amsterdam, 1971, Rosenthal Studio Haus, N.Y.C., 1968; exhibited in group show at Cooper Hewitt Mus., N.Y.C., 1978, Jewelry Mus., Phorzheim, Germany, 1973; represented in permanent collections including Metropolitan Mus. Art, Stedelyk Mus.; author: The Flamboyent Tree, numerous short stories. Recipient 1st prize CNE Toronto, 1965, 1st prize Craftsmen N.Y., 1970. Avocation: chamber music. Home: 10 Lower Byrdcliffe Rd Woodstock NY 12498-1214 Personal E-mail: mvanhamel@hvc.rr.com.

VAN HANDEL, MICHAEL J., employment services executive; BS magna cum laude in Acctg., Marquette U., Milw.; MBA in Fin., U. Wis. Audit mgr. Arthur Andersen & Co.; dir. internal audit Manpower, Inc., Milw., 1989—93, v.p. internat. acctg., 1993—95, chief acctg. officer, treas., 1995—98, sr. v.p., 1998—2002, CFO, 1998—, exec. v.p., 2002—. Bd. dirs., mem. audit and risk oversight coms. Harris Bank. Bd. dirs., chmn. audit com. Milw. Pub. Mus. Named one of Best CFOs in Am., Instl. Investor, 2006. Office: Manpower Inc 5301 N Ironwood Rd Milwaukee WI 53217 Office Phone: 414-906-6305. E-mail: michael.vanhandel@manpower.com. *

VAN HAREN, W(ILLIAM) MICHAEL, lawyer; b. Grand Rapids, Mich., Feb. 15, 1948; s. Adrian William and Donna Bell (Burkett) Van H.; m. Kathryn Mary Desmet, Aug. 7, 1971; children: Ryan C., Amy K., Andrew M., Megan E. BS, U. Mich., 1970; JD magna cum laude, U. Detroit, 1975. Bar: Mich. 1975, U.S. Dist. Ct. (we. dist.) Mich. 1975. Assoc. Warner, Norcross & Judd, Grand Rapids, 1975-81, ptnr., 1981—. Adj. prof. taxation Seidman Sch. Bus., Grand Valley State U., Grand Rapids, 1983-85. Assoc. editor U. Detroit Sch. Law Jour. Urban Law, 1974-75; co-editor (handbook) Probate Practice in Decedents Estates, 1985. Co-chmn. profl. divsn. Kent County United Way, Grand Rapids, 1983, 84; pres. Garfield Pk. Nature Ctr., Grand Rapids, 1977, Garfield Pk. Neighborhod Assn., Grand Rapids, 1979; bd. dirs. Western Mich. Estate Planning Coun., 1986-89, Cath. Social Svcs., 1997-2002, Goodwill Found., 2002—; mem. fin. com. St. Robert's Ch., Ada, Mich., 1997-2002. Fellow Am. Coll. Trust and Estate Coun.; mem. Mich. Bar Assn. (probate and estate planning coun. 1981-93, treas. 1987-88, sec. 1989-90, vice chmn. 1990-91, chair 1992-93, exec. officer 1993—), Mich. Bar Found., Univ. Club. Republican. Roman Catholic. Avocations: squash, golf, hunting. Home: 3790 Bridgehampton Dr Grand Rapids MI 49546 Office: Warner Norcross & Judd 900 Fifth Third Ctr 111 Lyon St NW Ste 900 Grand Rapids MI 49503-2487 Office Phone: 616-752-2125.

VAN HEERTUM, RONALD LANNY, physician; b. Englewood, NJ, Nov. 23, 1940; s. Arnold and Irene Gladys (Ostheimer) V.; children: Richard Jonathan, Beth Jennifer, Jonathan Jason, Kristin Ashley; m. Elyse Ann Murphy, Apr. 3, 2004. BA, Gettysburg Coll., 1962; MD, N.J. Med. Sch., 1966. Diplomate Nat. Bd. Med. Examiners, 1967, Am. Bd. Radiology, 1971, Am. Bd. Nuclear Medicine, 1973. Intern Hackensack Hosp., NJ, 1966-67; resident in radiology St. Vincent's Hosp. & Med. Ctr. NY, 1967—70, fellow in radiology and nuclear medicine, 1970-71, clin. asst. dept radiology, 1971, asst. chief nuclear medicine sect., asst. attending radiologist, 1975-76, chief nuclear medicine sect., 1977-91, assoc. attending physician depts. radiology and medicine, 1977-78, attending physician depts. radiology and medicine, 1978-91, dir. Nuclear Radiology Residency Tng. Program, 1980-88, 80-91, asst. dir. dept. radiology, 1981-91, med. dir. Sch. Nuclear Medicine Tech., 1982-91; asst. chief nuclear medicine svc. Tripler Army Med. Ctr., Honolulu, 1972, chief nuclear medicine svc., 1972-74; adj. prof. Sch. Pharmacy U. Pacific, Stockton, Calif., 1973-74; fellow in nuclear medicine SUNY, 1974-75; clin. asst. prof. of radiology Sch. Medicine NYU, 1977-83; assoc. prof. clin. radiology NY Med. Coll., Valhalla, 1983-88, prof. clin. radiology, 1988-91; dir. mini-fellowship program St. Vincent's Hosp. Cerebral SPECT Learning Ctr., 1991—2001; prof. clin. radiology Coll. Physicians & Surgeons of Columbia U., NY, 1991—2001; attending physician dept. radiology Columbia-Prsbyn. Med. Ctr., 1991—, dir. nuclear medicine residency tng. program, 1980—88, 1991—; attending physician dept brain imaging NY Psychiatric Inst., 1993—, attending physician Dept. Neurosci., 1996—; vice chmn. dept. radiology Coll. Physicians and Surgeons Columbia U., 1993—, prof. radiology, 2002—. Cons. nuclear medicine Catholic Med. Ctr. of Bklyn. and Queens, 1979-88, The Long Island Coll. Hosp., 1980-88, dept. radiology St. Vincent's Hosp. and Med. Ctr. of NY, 1991-92, biol. studies unit NY Psychiat. Inst., 1993—, The Oxford Project to Investigate Memory and Aging, The John Radcliffe Infirmary and Dept. of Clin. Pharmacology Oxford U., 1993—; alt. del. Am. Coll. Nuclear Physics, 1980-82; core mem. DOE Sponsored Consensus Panel Brain SPECT Perfusion Imaging: Optimizing Image Aquisition and Processing, 1991; vis. prof. Brooke Army Med. Ctr., San Antonio, 1978, Howard U. Med. Coll., Washington, 1980, South Hills Health Systems, Pitts., 1981, St. Barnabas Med. Ctr., Livingston, NJ, 1989, Eastern Va. Med. Sch. Norfolk Gen. Hosp., 1990, U. PR Med. Ctr., VA Med. Ctr., 1993, U. Wash. Med. Ctr., Seattle, 1994, Washington U., St. Louis, 1998, Robert Wood Johnson Med. Sch., 1999, Stonybrook HSC, 2005, U. Puerto Rico, 2005; mem. Am. Bd. Nuc. Medicine, 1995—, vice chair, 1999-2000, chair, 2000-02; dir. Columbia Kreitchman PET Ctr., 1993-. Contbr. articles to profl. jours. Major USAR, 1971-74. Recipient Physician Recognition award AMA, 1974-93; numerous rsch. grants in field. Fellow Am. Coll. Radiology (commn. on nuc. medicine 1994-2000, chmn. nuc. medicine accreditation com. 2000-06, chair accreditation program chiefs com., 2002-06, vice chmn., 2002-06), NY Acad. Medicine (sec. nuclear medicine sect. 1993—); mem. Am. Roentgen Ray Soc., Radiological Soc. N. Am., NY Roentgen Soc., Soc. Nuclear Medicine (mem. bd. govs. greater NY chpt. 1982-84, 86-89, mem. acad. coun. 1988, mem. brain imaging coun. 1988—, sub-chmn. gastroenterology sci. program com. 1989-90, pres. elect brain imaging coun. 1990-92, pres. 1992-94, sub.-chmn. psychiatry-clin. sci. program com. 1993-94), Soc. Thoracic Radiology (sr. mem.). Presbyterian. Business E-Mail: rvhs@columbia.edu.

VAN HELDEN, PETE, food products executive; Sr. v.p. of oper., Jewel-Osco (subs. of Albertson's Inc.), Melrose Park, Ill.; pres., Midwest Div. Albertson's Inc., Melrose Park, Ill., 1999—, pres. & CEO, Calif. Food Div., 2004—. Office: Albertsons Inc 250 Parkcenter Blvd Boise ID 83706 Office Phone: 208-395-6200. Office Fax: 208-395-6349.

VAN HOESEN, BETH MARIE, artist, printmaker; b. Boise, Idaho, June 27, 1926; d. Enderse G. and Freda Marie (Soulen) Van H.; m. Mark Adams, Sept. 12, 1953. Student, Escuela Esmaralda, Mexico City, 1945, San Francisco Art Inst., 1946, 47, 51, 52, Fontainbleau Ecole Arts, France, Acad. Julian and Acad., 5Grande Chaumier, Paris, 1948-51; BA, Stanford U., 1948; postgrad., San Francisco State U., 1957-58. One-Woman shows include, De Young Mus., San Francisco, 1959, Achenbach Found., Calif. Palace Legion of Honor, San Francisco, 1961, 74, Santa Barbara (Calif.) Mus., 1963, 74, 76, Oakland (Calif.) Mus., 1980, John Berggruen Gallery, San Francisco, 1981, 83, 85, 88, 91; traveling exhibit Am. Mus. Assn., 1983-85; group shows include, Calif. State Fair, Sacramento, 1951 (award), Library of Congress, Washington, 1956, 57, San Francisco Mus. Modern Art, 70 (award), Boston Mus. Fine Arts, 1959, 60, 62, Pa. Acad. Fine Arts, Phila., 1959, 61, 63, 65, Achenbach Found., 1961 (award), Bklyn. Mus., 1962, 66, 68, 77, Continuing Am. Graphics, Osaka, Japan, 1970, Hawaii Nat. Print. Exhbn., Honolulu, 1980 (award), Oakland Mus., 1975 (award); represented in permanent collections, including, Achenbach Found., San Francisco, Fine Arts Mus., Bklyn. Mus., Mus. Modern Art, N.Y.C., Oakland Mus., San Francisco Mus. Modern Art, Victoria and Albert Mus., (London), Chgo. Art Inst., Cin. Mus., Portland (Oreg.) Art Mus. (Recipient award of Honor, San Francisco Art Commn. 1981); author: Collection of Wonderful Things, 1972, Beth Van Hoesen Creatures, 1987, Beth Van Hoesen: Works on Paper, 1995, Beth Van Hoesen Teddy Bears, 2000. Mem. Calif. Soc. Printmakers (award 1993), San Francisco Women Artists. Office: c/o John Berggruen 228 Grant Ave Fl 3D San Francisco CA 94108-4612

VAN HOFTEN, JAMES DOUGAL ADRIANUS, retired astronaut, retired transportation executive; b. Fresno, Calif., June 11, 1944; s. Adriaan and Beverly (McCurdy) van H.; m. Vallarie Davis, May 31, 1975; children: Jennifer Lyn, Jamie Juliana, Victoria Jane. BS, U. Calif.-Berkeley, 1966; MS, Colo. State U., 1968, PhD, 1976. Asst. prof. U. Houston, 1976-78; astronaut NASA, Houston, 1978-86; sr. v.p., mgr. advanced systems line Bechtel Nat., Inc., San Francisco, 1986-93; project mgr. Hong Kong New Airport projects, 1993-96; sr. v.p., mgr. N.E. Asia, gen. mgr. Bechtel Civil Co., Hong Kong, 1996-98; sr. v.p., mgr. N.Am. projects Bechtel Infrastructure, San Francisco, 1998-99; program mgr. New Scottish Air Traffic

Control Ctr., London, 1999-2000; dir. programmes Nat. Air Traffic Svcs., 2000—02; mng. dir. aviation Bechtel Corp., 2002—06; ret., 2006—. Mem. bd. trustees, U. Calif. Berkley; Served with USN, 1969-74; lt. col. Air N.G. 1984-88. Recipient Disting. Service award Colo. State U., 1984; Disting. Citizen award Fresno Council Boy Scouts Am., 1984; Disting. Achievement award Pi Kappa Alpha, 1984 Fellow AIAA; mem. ASCE (Aerospace Sci. and Tech. Application award 1984). Republican.

VAN HOLDE, KENSAL EDWARD, biochemistry educator; b. Eau Claire, Wis., May 14, 1928; s. Leonard John and Nettie (Hart) Van Holde; m. Barbara Jean Watson, Apr. 11, 1950; children: Patricia, Mary, Stephen, David. BS, U. Wis., 1949, PhD, 1952. Rsch. chemist E.I. du Pont de Nemours & Co., 1952-55; rsch. assoc. U. Wis., 1955-56, asst. prof. Milw., 1956-57; mem. faculty U. Ill., Urbana, 1957-67; prof. dept. biochemistry and biophysics Oreg. State U., Corvallis, 1967, Am. Cancer Soc. rsch. prof., 1977-93, disting. prof., 1988-93, disting. prof. emeritus, 1993—; instr.-in-charge physiology course Marine Biol. Lab., Woods Hole, Mass., 1977-80; mem. research staff Centre des Recherches sur les Macromolecules, Strasbourg, France, 1964-65; mem. study sect. USPHS, 1966-69, 91—; staff Weizmann Inst., Israel, 1981, Lab. Léon Brillouin, Saclay, France, 1989-90. Author: Physical Biochemistry, 1971, Chromatin, 1988; author: (with C. Mathews) Biochemistry, 1989, 3d edit., 2000; author: Principles of Physical Biochemistry, 1998, 2d edit., 2006; editor: Biochmica Biophysica Acta, 1966—68; mem. editl. bd. jours. Biol. Chemistry, 1968—75, 1981—87, 1991—92, assoc. editor, 1992—; assoc. editor: Biochemistry, 1973—76, 1982—89; contbr. articles to profl. jours. Trustee Marine Biol. Lab., Woods Hole, 1979—82, 1984—92. NSF sr. postdoctoral fellow, 1964—65, Guggenheim fellow, 1973—74, European Molecular Biology Orgn. fellow, 1975, Humboldt fellow, 2000—01. Fellow: AAAS; mem.: NAS, Am. Acad. Arts and Scis., Biophys. Soc., Am. Soc. Biochemistry and Molecular Biology. Home: 229 NW 32nd St Corvallis OR 97330-5020 Office: Oreg State U Dept Biochemistry Corvallis OR 97331 Home Phone: 541-752-5203.

VAN HOLLEN, CHRISTOPHER, JR., congressman; b. Karachi, Pakistan, Jan. 10, 1959; s. Christopher and Eliza (Farnsworth) Van H.; m. Katherine A. Wilkens; children: Anna, Nicholas, Alexander. BA, Swarthmore Coll., 1982; MPP, Harvard U., 1985; JD cum laude, Georgetown U., 1989. Legis. asst. for def. and fgn. policy Office of Senator Charles McC. Mathias, Md., 1985-87; profl. staff mem. US Senate Fgn. Rels. Com., Washington, 1987-89; sr. legis. advisor Washington office Md. Gov. William D. Schaefer, 1989-91; assoc. Arent, Fox, Kintner, Plotkin & Kahn, Washington, 1991—; mem. Md. Ho. Dels., Annapolis, 1991-94; mem. dist. 18 Md. Senate, Annapolis, 1995—2001; mem. US Congress from 7th Md. dist. (formerly 8th), Washington, 2003—. Mem. Ho. Judiciary com., chair Health./Human Svcs. subcom., 2000—. Councillor Atlantic Coun. US; mem. Kensington Citizens Assn. Recipient Resolution of Excellence, US Senate Fgn. Rels. Com. Democrat. Office: US Ho Reps 2235 Rayburn HoOffice Bldg Washington DC 20515-2007 *

VAN HOLLEN, J(OHN) B(YRON), state attorney general, former prosecutor; b. Rice Lake, Wis., Feb. 19, 1966; s. John C. and Rosella Van Hollen; m. Lynne Pliner; children: Byron, Madelyn. BA in Polit. Sci. and Econs., St. Olaf Coll., Northfield, Minn., 1988; JD, U. Wis., Madison, 1990. Bar: Wis. 1990, US Dist. Ct. (we. dist. Wis.) 1990. Asst. state pub. defender, Spooner, Wis., 1990—91; dist. atty. Ashland County, Wis., 1993—99, Bayfield County, Wis., 1999—2002; asst. US atty. (we. dist.) Wis. US Dept. Justice, 1991—93, US atty., 2002—05; atty. Dewitt, Ross & Stevens, S.C., Madison, Wis., 2005—07; atty. gen. State of Wis., Madison, 2007—. Mem.: ABA, Dane County Bar Assn. Republican. Office: Office of Atty Gen State Capitol Ste 114E PO Box 7857 Madison WI 53707-7857 *

VANHOOK, TRACIE LYNNETTE, small business owner; b. Oakland, Calif., May 17, 1965; d. Herman Curtis Gray and Ritchie Lee Ross; children: Titus Alexander, Lawrence Emanuel. Assoc. in Sci., Merritt Coll., 1999; BS, San Francisco State U., 2002; MS, Calif. U. Pa., 2005. Cert. health and fitness instr. Am. Coll. Sports Medicine, performance enhancement specialist, personal trainer Nat. Acad. Sports Medicine, in enhanced sports nutrition HK Academic Online Edn. Ctr. Cons., presenter E.C. Reems Women's Internat. Ministries Nat. Conf., Oakland, 1997—2000; fitness supr. Sports Club LA-San Francisco, 2002—05; therapy and rehab asst. Body Focus Health Ctr., San Francisco, 2003—04; fitness mgr./master trainer Axis Performance Ctr., Menlo Park, Calif., 2005—06; owner Fit to the Core Personal Tng., Menlo Park, 2006—. Dancer/actor (play) Navigators. Avocations: youth dance choreography, hiking. Office: Axis Performance Ctr 550 Ravenswood Ave Menlo Park CA 94025 Office Phone: 650-463-1920. Office Fax: 650-463-1926. Business E-Mail: tracie@fittothecorept.com.

VAN HOOMISSEN, GEORGE ALBERT, state supreme court justice; b. Portland, Oreg., Mar. 7, 1930; s. Fred J. and Helen F. (Flanagan) Van H.; m. Ruth Madeleine Niedermeyer, June 4, 1960; children: Geroge T., Ruth Anne, Madeleine, Matthew. BBA, U. Portland, 1951; JD, Georgetown U., 1955, LLM in Labor Law, 1957; LLM in Jud. Adminstrn., U. Va., 1986. Bar: D.C. 1955, Oreg. 1956, Tex. 1971, U.S. Dist. Ct. Oreg. 1956, U.S. Ct. Mil. Appeals 1955, U.S. Ct. Customs and Patent Appeals 1955, U.S. Ct. Claims 1955, U.S. Ct. Appeals (9th cir.) 1956, U.S. Ct. Appeals (D.C. cir.) 1955, U.S. Supreme Ct. 1960. Law clk. for Chief Justice Harold J. Warner Oreg. Supreme Ct., 1955-56; Keigwin teaching fellow Georgetown Law Sch., 1956-57; dep. dist. atty. Multnomah County, Portland, 1957-59; pvt. practice Portland, 1959-62; dist. atty. Multnomah County, 1962-71; dean nat. coll. dist. attys., prof. law U. Houston, 1971-73; judge Cir. Ct., Portland, 1973-81, Oreg. Ct. Appeals, Salem, 1981-88; justice Oreg. Supreme Ct., Salem, 1988—2001. Adj. prof. Northwestern Sch. Law, Portland, Willamette U. Sch. Law, Portland State U.; mem. faculty Am. Acad. Judicial Edn., Nat. Judicial Coll.; Keigwin Teaching fellow Georgetown U. Law Sch. Mem. Oreg. Ho. of Reps., Salem, 1959-62, chmn. house jud. com. Ret. col. USMCR. Recipient Disting. Alumnus award U. Portland, 1972. Master Owen M. Panner Am. Inn of Ct.; mem. ABA, Oreg. State Bar, Tex. Bar Assn., Oreg. Law Inst. (bd. dirs.), Arlington Club, Multnomah Athletic Club, Univ. Club. Roman Catholic. Office: Oreg Supreme Ct 2105 SW Elm St Portland OR 97201 Office Phone: 503-228-2202. Personal E-mail: gavanhoomissen@msn.com.

VANHORN, BRADLEY KENT, musician; b. Mason City, Iowa, Sept. 26, 1970; s. Myron John and Lyla Pearl VanHorn; m. Brenda Diane Baily, July 9, 1994; children: Melanie, Jonah. BA in Music Edn., Ctrl. Coll., Pella, Iowa, 1993. Vocal instr., band instr. Spring Grove (Minn.) Pub. Schs., 1993—96; 7-12 grade vocal instr. Hampton (Iowa)-Dumont Pub. Schs., 1996—99; music dir., organist Trinity Luth. Ch., Mason City, Iowa, 1999—. Recipient Thirty Under Forty award, Globe Gazette, Mason City, 2005. Avocations: singing, golf, farming. Home: 2110 Hwy 65 Sheffield IA 50475

VAN HORN, CHARLES E., lawyer; b. Phila., Jan. 30, 1942; BSChemE, Lehigh U., 1963; JD, Am. U., 1968; MBA, George Washington U., 1973. Bar: Va. 1968, DC 1998, US Patent & Trademark Office. Ptnr. Finnegan, Henderson, Farabow, Garrett & Dunner LLP, Washington, mem. mgmt. com., leader, Prosecution Sect. Mem.: Patent & Trademark Soc., Intellectual Property Owners Assn., Am. Intellectual Property Law Assn. Office: Finnegan Henderson Farabow Garrett & Dunner LLP 901 New York Ave NW Washington DC 20001-3315 Office Phone: 202-408-4000. Office Fax: 202-408-4400. Business E-Mail: charles.vanhorn@finnegan.com.

VAN HORN, HUGH M., physicist, astronomer, educator; b. Williamsport, Pa., Mar. 5, 1938; s. Robert Dix and Virginia Elizabeth (Moody) Van H.; m. Mary Susan Boon, Sept. 17, 1960; children: Kathleen Susan, Mary Margaret, Michael Hugh George. BSc, Case Inst. Tech., 1960; PhD, Cornell U., 1965. NASA predoctoral trainee Cornell U., Ithaca, 1963-65; rsch. assoc. U. Rochester, 1965-67, asst. prof., 1967-73, assoc. prof., 1973-77, prof., 1977-96, chmn. dept. physics and astronomy, 1980-86, acting assoc. dean Coll. Arts and Scis., 1987-89, acting chmn. dept. physics and astronomy, 1992-93, adj. prof., 1996—2005, prof. emeritus, 2005—; Shapley lectr. Am. Astron. Soc., 1981-95; dir. divsn. astron. sci. NSF, Arlington, Va., 1993-2000, sr. sci. advisor Directorate Math. Phys. Sci., 2000—02, dir. nat. facilities divsn. materials rsch., 2002—04. Vis. fellow Joint Inst. Lab. Astrophysics, 1973—74; sr. scientist Lab. Laser Energetics, 1985—96; vis. prof. U. Tex., 1987; vis. investigator dept. terr. magnetism Carnegie Inst. Washington, 2000—02; prin. investigator NASA and NSF grants. Editor: (with V. Weidemann) White Dwarfs and Variable Degenerate Stars, 1979, (with S. Ichimaru) Strongly Coupled Plasma Physics, 1993; contbr. articles on white dwarfs, neutron stars and dense matter to profl. jours. Fellow AAAS; mem. Internat. Astron. Union. E-mail: vanhorns@frontiernet.net.

VAN HORN, KEITH, professional basketball player; b. Oct. 23, 1975; m. Amy Van Horn; children: Sabrina, Nicholas. Grad., U. Utah, 1997. Basketball player N.J. Nets, East Rutherford, NJ, 1997—2001, Phila. 76ers, 2002—03, New York Knicks, 2003—04, Milwaukee Bucks, 2004—05, Dallas Mavericks, 2005—06. Named first team All-Am., U. Utah, 1997. Achievements include being the top scorer U. Utah and Western Athletic conf. hist; 3 time Western Athletic Conf. Player of Yr. 1995-97. *

VAN HORN, O. FRANK, retired counselor, consultant; b. Grand Junction, Colo., Apr. 16, 1926; s. Oertel F. and Alta Maude (Lynch) Van H.; m. Dixie Jeanne MacGregor, Feb. 1, 1947 (dec. Nov. 1994); m. Evelyn Anne Carroll, Mar. 22,1998; children: Evelyn (dec.), Dorothy. AA, Mesa Coll., 1961; BA, Western State Colo., 1963; MEd, Oreg. State U., 1969. Counselor, mgr. State of Oreg.-Employment, Portland and St. Helens, 1964-88; pvt. practice counselor and cons. St. Helens, 1988-96. Chair Task Force on Aging, Columbia County, 1977-79; advisor Western Interstate Commn. on Higher Edn., Portland, 1971, Concentrated Employment and Tng., St. Helens, 1977, County Planning Bd., Columbia County, Oreg., 1977-80, City Planning Bd., St. Helens, 1978, Youth Employment Coun., St. Helens, 1978, Task Force on Disadvantaged Youth, St. Helens, 1980; counselor Career Mgmt. Specialists Internat.; instr. Portland C.C. Mem. ACA, Oreg. Counseling Assn., Internat. Assn. Pers. in Employment Svc. (Outstanding Achievement award 1975), Nat. Employment Counselors Assn. Democrat. Home: 464 Leelo Ct Florence OR 97439-8909 Personal E-mail: frannke@msn.com.

VAN HORN, RICHARD LINLEY, academic administrator; b. Chgo., Nov. 2, 1932; s. Richard Linley and Mildred Dorothy (Wright) Van H.; m. Susan Householder, May 29, 1954 (dec.); children: Susan Elizabeth, Patricia Suzanne, Lynda Sue; m. Betty Pfefferbaum, May 29, 1988. BS with highest honors, Yale U., 1954; MS, MIT, 1956; PhD, Carnegie-Mellon U., 1976; D of Bus. (hon.), Reitsumeikan U., Kyoto, Japan, 1991. Asst. dir. Army EDP Project, MIT, Cambridge, 1956-57; research staff Rand Corp., Santa Monica, Calif., 1957-60, head mgmt. systems group, 1960-67; dir., prof. mgmt. systems European Inst. Advanced Studies in Mgmt., Brussels, 1971-73; asso. dean Grad. Sch. Indsl. Adminstrn., Carnegie-Mellon U., Pitts., 1967-71, dir. budget and planning, 1973-74, v.p. for bus. affairs, 1974-77, v.p. for mgmt., 1977-80, provost and prof. mgmt., 1980-83; chancellor U. Houston, 1983-86, pres., 1986-89, U. Okla., 1989-94; pres. emeritus and regent's prof. Coll. of Bus. U. Okla., Norman, 1994—; Clarence E. Page prof. aviation U. Okla., Norman, 1995—; dir. mgmt. info. sys. divsn. Coll. Bus. U Okla., 1997—2000. Author: (with Robert H. Gregory) Automatic Data Processing Systems, 1960, 2nd edit. 1963, (with R.H. Gregory) Business Data Processing and Programming, 1963, (with C.H. Kriebel and J.T. Heames) Management Information Systems: Progress and Perspectives, 1971, (with A. Schwarzkopf and R. Leou Price) Information System Solutions: a Project Approach, 2006; contbr. articles to profl. jours.; asso. editor: Jour. Inst. Mgmt. Scis, 1964-78 Mem. Inst. Mgmt. Sci. (nat. council mem. 1963-65, sec.-treas. 1964), Assn. for Computing Machinery (nat. lectr. 1969-70), Council on Govt. Relations (bd. dirs. 1981-83) Avocation: commercial pilot. Office: U Okla Coll Of Bus Norman OK 73019-0001 Home: 3900 N Harvey Pkwy Oklahoma City OK 73118 Office Phone: 405-325-0900. E-mail: rvanhorn@ou.edu.

VAN HORNE, JAMES CARTER, economist, educator; b. South Bend, Ind., Aug. 6, 1935; s. Ralph and Helen (McCarter) Van H.; m. Mary A. Roth, Aug. 27, 1960; children: Drew, Stuart, Stephen. AB, De Pauw U., 1957, DSc (hon.), 1986; MBA, Northwestern U., 1961, PhD, 1964. Comml. lending rep. Continental Ill. Nat. Bank, Chgo., 1958-62; prof. fin. Stanford U. Grad. Sch. Bus., 1965-75, A.P. Giannini prof. fin., 1976—, assoc. dean, 1973-75, 76-80; dep. asst. sec. Dept. Treasury, 1975-76. Bd. dirs. Montgomery St. Income Securities, 2d Synnex Corp.; commr. workers compensation Rate Making Study Commn., State of Calif., 1990-92. Author: Function and Analysis of Capital Market Rates, 1970, Financial Market Rates and Flows, 2001, Financial Management and Policy, 2002; co-author: Fundamentals of Financial Management, 2005; assoc. editor Jour. Fin. and Quantitative Analysis, 1969—85, Jour. Fin., 1971—73, Jour. Fixed Income, 1990—. Mem. bd. trustees DePauw U., 1989-96. With AUS, 1957. Mem. Am. Fin. Assn. (past pres., dir.), Western Fin. Assn. (past pres., dir.), Fin. Mgmt. Assn. Home: 2000 Webster St Palo Alto CA 94301-4049 Office: Stanford U Grad Sch Bus Stanford CA 94305

VAN HORNE, JON W., lawyer; b. Chgo., Apr. 6, 1945; BA, Andrews U. (formerly Emmanuel Missionary Coll.), 1967; JD, Harvard U., 1971; MPA, Kennedy Sch. Govt., 1971. Bar: Ohio 1971, Pa. 1979, D.C. 1988. Ptnr. McDermott, Will & Emery, Washington; founder VHT Law PLLC, Wash., DC, 2005—. Chmn. Bus. Coun. Reduction of Paperwork, 1990—. Mem. D.C. Bar. Office: VHT Law PLLC 1725 I St NW Ste 300 Washington DC 20006 Office Phone: 202-465-3285. Office Fax: 202-474-2921. Business E-Mail: jvanhorne@vhtlaw.com.

VAN HOUSE, ROBERT ARTHUR, small business owner, contractor; b. Evanston, Ill., Sept. 12, 1945; s. Eldon Russell and Lorraine Ellen Huff; m. Sharon Lynn Leonard, Apr. 10, 1999; children: Michael, Jackie. Commd. USN, 1962, advanced through grades to radioman chief petty officer, ret., 1986; comms. sys. analyst Validity Corp., Clinton, Md., 1989—96; with Arlington Annex Comms. Ctr. HQ Marine Corps, Washington, 1989—90; with Naval Electromagnetic Spectrum Ctr. USN, Alexandria, Va., 1990—97; with Integrated Sys. Control., Inc., San Diego, 1997—99; with Space and Missile Sys. Ctr. Spectrum Mgmt. Office, LA, 1999—2001; coord. naval frequency We. U.S. Dept. Def., Magu, Calif., 2001—04, ret, 2004. Recipient Outstanding Svc. award, USN, 1986. Mem.: IEEE (sr.), Nat. Defense Internat. Assn. Democrat. Lutheran. Avocations: history, classical music, reading. Home and Office: Van House RF Spectrum Consulting 1456 Barca St Camarillo CA 93010 Office Phone: 805-484-5145.

VAN HOUSEN, THOMAS CORWIN, III, architect; b. Oak Park, Ill., Jan. 2, 1927; s. Thomas Corwin and Dorothea (Saunders) Van H.; children: Deborah, Victoria, Constance. BA, Lawrence U., 1951; BArch, U. Minn., Mpls., 1954; MArch in Urban Design, Harvard U., 1962. Registered architect, Minn., Wis. With Ellerbe Assocs., Inc., St. Paul, 1951-61; architect, prin. Progressive Design Assocs., Inc., St. Paul, 1961-71; architect, developer, v.p. Landmark Devel. Corp./Appletree Enterprises, Inc., Bloomington, Minn., 1971-85; architect, developer Mortenson Devel. Co., Mpls., 1985-88; architect, design, bldg. dir. D&B Collaborative, Inc., Mpls., 1989—99; mktg. cons. Horty, Elving & Assoc., Mpls., 1999—. Bldg. official City of North Oaks, Minn., 1964-78; mem. Minn. League of Municipalities-Metro, St. Paul, 1970-72, Gov.'s Open Space Adv. Com., St. Paul, 1972-74. With U.S. Air Force, 1945-47, ETO. Recipient Outstanding House award St. Paul Jaycees, 1958, 62; named finalist (team mem.) Archtl. competition Boston City Hall, 1962. Fellow AIA (nat. bd. dirs. 1985-88, v.p., pres.-elect Minn. chpt. 1994-95, pres. 1995, spl. award 1981, Presdl. citation 1988, 90, 2000); mem. N.W. YMCA. Republican. Lutheran. Avocations: tennis, swimming, music, reading. Office Phone: 612-332-4422.

VAN HOUTEN, FRANKLYN BOSWORTH, geologist, educator; b. NYC, July 14, 1914; s. Charles Nicholas and Hessie Osborne (Bosworth) Van H.; m. Jean Oliver Sholes, Feb. 18, 1943 (dec. Sept. 23, 1997); children: Jean S., F. Bosworth, David Gordon. BS, Rutgers U., 1936; PhD, Princeton U., 1941. Instr. dept. geology Williams Coll., 1939-42; asst. prof. Princeton U., 1946-51, assoc. prof., 1951-55, prof., 1955-85, prof. emeritus, 1985—; vis. prof. geology UCLA, 1964, State U. N.Y. at Binghamton, 1971; geologist U.S. Geol. Survey, 1948-67. Temporary geologist Geol. Survey Can., 1953, Yukon Expdn., geol. expdns. to Morocco, Tunisia, Libya, Egypt, Madagascar Author reports and articles on geology. Served as lt. USN, 1942-46. Fellow Geol. Soc. Am.; mem. Am. Assn. Petroleum Geologists, Soc. Econ. Paleontologists and Mineralogists (hon. mem., Twenhofel medal), Internat. Assn. Sedimentologists, Colombia Geol. Soc. (hon.), Delta Upsilon. Home: 168 Fitzrandolph Rd Princeton NJ 08540-7224

VAN HOUTEN, G. DAVID, JR., beverage company executive; b. Waco, Tex. m. Carol Van Houten; children: Tara, Brant, Blaine. Mgmt. degree, Tex. A&M U. Various positions Coca-Cola Bottling Bus., 1972—86; pres., gen. mgr. Coca-Cola Bottling Co. of N. Tex., 1986—96; sr. v.p., pres., Ctrl. N.Am. Group Coca-Cola Enterprises Inc., Atlanta, 1996—2000, sr. v.p., pres., Western N.Am. Group, 2000—01, pres. N.Am. Group, 2001—05, exec. v.p., 2001—05, COO, 2004—05.

VAN HOUTEN, JAMES FORESTER, former insurance company chief executive, educator, consultant; b. Fullerton, Calif., Jan. 13, 1942; s. James Forester and Lois Evangeline (Trout) V.H.; m. Mary Ann Nelson; children: Kimberly Evangeline, Lori Lynn. BA in English Lit., St. Mary's U.; MBA, Ill. State U. CPCU, CLU. Sales mgr. for Can. Motors Ins. Corp. divsn. GM, Detroit, 1963-74; v.p. sales Volkswagen Group, St. Louis, 1974-78; v.p. personal lines mktg. Wausau Ins. Cos., St. Louis, 1978-80, v.p., chief mktg. officer life and health, 1980-84; v.p., chief mktg. and strategic planning officer Country Cos., Bloomington, Ill., 1984-89; pres., CEO Mut. Svc. Ins. Cos., St. Paul, 1989—2002. Prof. strategic mgmt. Carlson Sch. Mgmt. and Humphrey Inst., U. Minn., 1990—, Metro State U., 2002-2004; bd. dirs. Strategic Mgmt. Rsch. Ctr., U. Minn., EMPO Corp., J.J. Hill Bus. Ref. Libr; pres. Minn. Assn. of Scholars, Tocquelville Ctr.; vis. prof. Vienna U. Econs., 2006. Program leader Youth Black Achievers, St. Paul; exec. bd. Arrowhead coun. Boy Scouts Am.; lead planning cons. Sisseton Wahpeton Sioux Tribe, 2004 active Minn. Acad. Stds. Com., Minn. Acad. Excellence Found-Friends; trustee Minn. State Coll. and Univ. Sys. Mem. Assn. State Coll. Assn. (dir.), Ins. Fedn. Minn. (past chmn. bd.), Minn. Assn. Mutual Ins. Cos. (past pres.), Nat. Coop. Bus. Assn. (bd. dirs. and exec. com., chair fin. com.), Minn. Bus. Partnership (bd. dirs., Minn. K-12 edn. com.), Minn. Assn. Scholars (pres., chair), Ctr. Am. Experiment Think Tank (bd. dirs., ex com., chair fin. and audit com.), Milestone Growth Fund (chair devel. com.). Office Phone: 612-836-0120. Personal E-mail: jvanhouten01@msn.com.

VAN HOY, PHILIP MARSHALL, lawyer; b. Washington, Nov. 8, 1947; s. Joe Milton and Helen Virginia (Spangler) V.; m. Sylvia Kathryn Smith, Dec. 30, 1972; children: Marshall, Travis. AB, Duke U., Durham, NC, 1970; JD, U. NC, 1973. Bar: NC 1973, US Dist. Ct. (ea., we. and mid. dists.) NC 1974, US Ct. Appeals (4th cir.) 1974, US Supreme Ct. 1978. Labor counsel Duke Power Co., Charlotte, NC, 1973—80; assoc. Siegel, O'Connor & Kainen, Charlotte, 1980—83; ptnr. Mullins & Van Hoy, Charlotte, 1983—89, Van Hoy, Rentlinger, Adams & Dunn, Charlotte, 1989—. Mem. NC OSHA Rev. Bd., 1985-92, Mecklenburg County, NC Personnel Commn., 1985-92, NC Leadership Coun. Co-state chmn. Gardner for Lt. Gov., 1988, alt. del. Rep. Nat. Conv., Detroit, 1980; chmn. Mecklenburg County Young Rep. Com., 1979, vice chmn., 1980-83; Duke U. Athletics Coun., 1999-02. 1st lt. US Army, 1973-81. Named Top Employment Lawyer NC, Bus. NC mag., 2002; named to Best Lawyers in Am., 2001—, Outstanding Lawyers of Am., 2003; recipient Salute to Am.'s Best Lawyers, Forbes mag. and Am. Airlines Sky Radio, 2005. Mem. NC Bar Assn. (councillor labor and employment law sect. 1985-88, chmn. EEOC com. 1983-92), NC State Bar, 4th Cir. Jud. Conf., Rotary, Charlotte Cotillion Club (pres. 1979-80), City Club, Myers Park Country Club (dir. 1994-96, 2000-03). Republican. Methodist. Office: Van Hoy Reutlinger Adams & Dunn 737 East Blvd Charlotte NC 28203-5113 Home: 16631 Harbor View Rd Charlotte NC 28278 Office Phone: 704-375-6022.

VANIER, JACQUES, physicist; s. Henri and Emma Vanier; m. Lucie Beaudet, 1961; children: Lyne, Pierre. BA, U. Montreal, 1955, BSc, 1958; MSc, McGill U., 1960, PhD, 1963. Lectr. U. Montreal, 1961-63, McGill U., 1960-63; physicist Varian Assocs., Beverly, Mass., 1963-67, Hewlett Packard Co., Beverly, 1967; prof. elec. engring. U. Laval, Que., 1967-83; physicist Nat. Rsch. Coun., Ottawa, 1983-94, head elec. and time standards, 1984-86, dir. Lab. Basic Standards, 1986-90, dir. gen. Inst. for Nat. Measurement Standards, 1990-93; prof. physics U. de Montreal, 1995—. Gov.'s Bd. Symposium on Frequency Standards and Metrology, 1971-; cons. Comm. Components Corp., Costa Mesa, Calif., 1974-76, EGG Co., Salem, Mass., 1979-82, Kernco, Danvers, Mass., 1995—; chmn. com. A URSI, 1990-93; chmn. exec. com. CPEM, 1990-94; mem. Internat. Com. Weights and Measures, 1992-96; guest worker IEN, Torino, Italy, 1996-97; adv. bd. Precision Time and Time Interval Com., 2006—. Author: Basic Theory of Lasers and Masers, 1971, (with C. Audoin) The Quantum Physics of Atomic Frequency Standards, 1989; contbr. articles to profl. jours.; patentee (4) in field. Recipient Disting. Precision Time & Time Interval Svc. award PTTI Organizing Com., 1998. Fellow IEEE (Centennial medal 1984, I.I. Rabi award 1994, Instrument & Measurement Soc. award 1999), Royal Soc. Can., Am. Phys. Soc. Business E-Mail: jac.vanier@sympatico.ca.

VAN INWAGEN, PETER JAN, philosophy educator; b. Rochester, NY, Sept. 21, 1942; s. George Butler and Mildred Gloria (Knudson) van I; m. Margery Bedford Naylor, Mar. 31, 1967 (div. Apr. 1988); 1 child, Elizabeth Core; m. Elisabeth Marie Bolduc, June 3, 1989. BS, Rensselaer Poly. Inst., 1965; PhD, U. Rochester, 1969. Vis. asst. prof. U. Rochester, NY, 1971-72; asst. prof. Syracuse U., NY, 1972-74, assoc. prof. NY, 1974-80, prof. philosophy NY, 1980-95; John Cardinal O'Hara prof. of philosophy U. Notre Dame, South Bend, Ind., 1995—. Vis. prof. U. Ariz., Tucson, 1981; lectr. U. of St. Andrews, 2003, Oxford U., 2000, U. London, 1998. Author: An Essay on Free Will, 1983, Material Beings, 1990, Metaphysics, 1993, God, Knowledge and Mystery, 1995, The Possibility of Resurrection, 1997, Ontology, Identity, and Modality, 2001, The Problem of Evil, 2006; editor: Time and Cause, 1980, Alvin Plantinga, 1985, Metaphysics: The Big Questions, 1998, Christian Faith and The Problem of Evil, 2004, Persons: Human and Divine, 2007; mem. editl. bd. Jour. Faith and Philosophy, Philos. Perspectives, Nous, Philos. Studies, Jour. of Ethics, Philosophy and Phenomenological Rsch.; contbr. articles to profl. jours. Served to capt. U.S. Army, 1969-71 NEH grantee, 1983-84, 89-90. Mem. Am. Acad. Arts and Scis., Am. Philos. Assn., Soc. Christian Philosophers. Democrat.

Episcopalian. Home: 52145 Farmington Square Rd Granger IN 46530-6403 Office: U Notre Dame Dept Philosophy South Bend IN 46556-4619 Office Phone: 574-631-5910. E-mail: peter.vaninwagen.1@nd.edu.

VAN KERREBROOK, MARY ALICE, lawyer; b. Houston, Aug. 21, 1961; d. Richard Rene and Phyllis Law (Banks) Van K. BA in Econs., Northwestern U., 1983; JD, So. Meth. U., 1986. Bar: Tex. 1986, U.S. Dist. Ct. (so. dist.) Tex. 1987, U.S. Ct. Appeals (5th cir.) 1988, U.S. Dist. Ct. (ea. dist.) Tex. 1989, U.S. Supreme Ct. 2000. Assoc. Wilson, Cribbs, Goren & Flaum, P.C., Houston, 1986-94, shareholder, 1994—2003; prin. Van Kerrebrook & Assocs. P.C., Houston, 2003—. Trustee Tex. Com. on Natural Resources, Dallas, 1988—; mem. exec. com. Galveston Bay Found., Webster, Tex., 1991-93; pres. Katy Prairie Conservancy, Houston, 1995—. Office: 1125 Lyric Centre 440 Louisiana Houston TX 77002 Office Phone: 713-425-7152. Business E-Mail: mary@vkalawyers.com.

VAN KIRK, JOHN ELLSWORTH, retired cardiologist; b. Dayton, Ohio, Jan. 13, 1942; s. Herman Corwin and Dorothy Louise (Shafer) Van K.; m. Patricia L. Davis, June 19, 1966 (div. Dec. 1982); 1 child, Linnea Gray. BA cum laude, DePauw U., Greencastle, Ind., 1963; BS, Northwestern U., Chgo., 1964, MD with distinction, 1967. Diplomate Am. Bd. Internal Medicine, Am. Bd. Internal Medicine subspecialty in cardiovasc. disease; cert. Nat. Bd. Med. Examiners. Intern Evanston (Ill.) Hosp., 1967-68; staff assoc. Nat. Inst. of Allergy & Infectious Diseases., Bethesda, Md., 1968-70; resident internal medicine U. Mich. Med. Ctr., Ann Arbor, 1970-72, fellow in cardiology, 1972-74, instr. internal medicine, 1973-74; staff cardiologist Mills Meml. Hosp., San Mateo, Calif., 1974—2001, vice-chief medicine, 1977-78, dir. critical care, 1978-96, critical care utilizaton rev., 1988-99, dir. pacemaker clinic, 1976-99; staff cardiologist Mills-Peninsula Hosp., Burlingame, Calif., 1996-99; ret., 1999. Dir. transitional care, 1996—99; mem. courtesy staff Sequoia Hosp., 1984—2001, ret., 1999. Contbr. rsch. articles to profl. jours. Recipient 1st prize in landscaping Residential Estates, State of Calif., 1977. Fellow Am. Coll. Cardiology; mem. AMA (Physician's Recognition award 1968, 72, 75, 77, 80, 82, 85, 87, 89, 93, 97, 2000), Calif. Med. Assn., San Mateo County Med. Soc., Am. Heart Assn., San Mateo County Heart Assn. (bd. dirs. 1975-78, mem. Bay area rsch. com. 1975-76, mem. edn. com. 1975-77, pres.-elect 1976-77, pres. 1977-79), Alpha Omega Alpha. Republican. Mem. United Brethren Ch. Avocations: gardening, computer science, tennis, woodworking, electronics, amateur radio. Home: 235 Amherst Ave San Mateo CA 94402-2201 Personal E-mail: John_VanKirk@msn.com.

VAN KIRK, ROBERT JOHN, nursing case manager, educator; b. Jersey City, Sept. 18, 1944; s. Robert and Doris Van Kirk; m. Marjorie Ann Carroll, Mar. 23, 1968 (div. Nov. 1993); children: Walter, Michael, Robert Jr., Peggy; m. Nancy A. Fix, Aug. 31, 1996. BA cum laude, U. Conn., Storrs, 1974; MEd, Kent State U., Ohio, 1983; D of Nursing, Case Western Res. U., Cleve., 1986. RN Ohio, cert. diabetes educator (CDE). Sales mgr. Nutmeg Home Protection, Middlebury, Conn., 1972-74; theater mgr. SBC Mgmt. Corp., Boston, 1974; dist. supr. Selected Theatres Mgmt. Corp., Lyndhurst, Ohio, 1974-86; nat. sales mgr. ZBS Video, Inc., Lyndhurst, 1981-82; staff nurse Cleve. Clinic Found., 1986-87, clin. instr., 1987-88, head nurse, 1988-93, case mgr., 1993—, diabetes educator, 2002—; asst. clin. prof. Case Western Res. U., Frances Payne Bolton Sch. Nursing, Cleve., 1990—; case mgr. Cleve. Clin. Home Care, 1993—2002; CEO Lifelong Learning, Inc., Chagrin Falls, Ohio, 2002—. Health officer Lake County (Ohio) Bd. Alcohol, Drug Addiction and Mental Health Svcs., 1991—; co-chmn. United Way, Cleve., 1991-93. Staff sgt. US Army, 1964—71, Vietnam. Recipient Achievement award, Greater Cleve. Nurses Assn., 1986, Carol Udycz Nursing Excellence award, Cleve. Clinic, 2007. Mem. AACN, Am. Assn. Tchrs. German, Am. Assn. Tchrs. Portuguese and Spanish, Assn. Specialists in Aging, Frances Payne Bolton Sch. Nursing Alumni Assn. (pres. 1992-93), Kappa Delta Pi, Sigma Theta Tau. Avocations: pocket billards, furniture making. Home: 495 Bell Rd Chagrin Falls OH 44022-4160 Office: Cleve Clinic Found 6801 Brecksville Rd Ste 10 Independence OH 44131 also: Lifelong Learning Inc 495 Bell Rd Chagrin Falls OH 44022 Home Phone: 440-247-0953. E-mail: drbobvankirk@adelphia.net.

VAN KIRK, THOMAS L., lawyer; b. Pa., June 25, 1945; s. Theodore and Mary Jane (Young) Van K.; children: Thomas Jr., Christopher. BA, Bucknell U., 1967; JD cum laude, Dickinson U., 1970. Bar: Pa., U.S. Dist. Ct. (we. and ea. dists.) Pa. 1971, U.S. Ct. Appeals (3d cir.) 1972, U.S. Supreme Ct. 1976. Clk. Pa. Superior Ct., 1970-71; assoc. Buchanan Ingersoll PC, Pitts., 1971-77, ptnr., 1978—, COO, 1985—2003; CEO, chmn. Buchanan Ingersoll & Rooney PC, Pitts., 2006—. Bd. dirs. Buchanan Ingersoll P.C.; exec. com. bd. mem. State Pa. Economy League; bd. dirs. Western Pa. Economy League, chair. Chmn. emeritus Pitts. Downtown Partnership; bd. dirs., exec. com. mem. Pitts. Cultural Trust, Catalyst Connection, U. Pitts. Cancer Inst., Doyle Ctr. for Mfg. Tech., Allegheny Conf., PEG. Mem.: ABA, Allegheny County Bar Assn., The Club at Nevillewood, Rivers Club, Duquesne Club. Democrat. Lutheran. Home: 1010 Osage Rd Pittsburgh PA 15243-1014 Office: Buchanan Ingersoll Rooney One Oxford Ctr 301 Grant St Fl 20 Pittsburgh PA 15219-1410 Office Phone: 412-562-8875. Business E-Mail: vankirktl@bipc.com.

VANLANDINGHAM, MARK REED, materials engineer; b. Radford, Va., Oct. 16, 1968; s. Hugh Foch and Patricia Maureen VanLandingham; m. Jennifer Sorensen; 1 child, Luke George. PhD, U. Del., Newark, 1993—97. Nrc postdoctoral fellow Nat. Inst. Standards & Tech., Gaithersburg, Md., 1997—99, materials rsch. engr., 1999—2002; materials engr. US Army Rsch. Lab., Aberdeen Proving Ground, Md., 2002—05, chief multi-functional materials br., 2005—. Contbr. tech. papers in field. Mem.: Am. Chem. Soc., Materials Rsch. Soc. Achievements include patents for humidity chamber for scanning stylus atomic force microscope with cantilever tracking. Office: US Army Rsch Lab 4600 Deer Creek Loop Aberdeen Proving Ground MD 21005-5069 Home Phone: 410-398-2632. Office Fax: 410-306-0676. Business E-Mail: mark.vanlandingham@us.army.mil.

VAN LARE, WENDELL JOHN, lawyer, director; b. Newark, NY, Mar. 1, 1945; s. Julian J. and Doris Elizabeth (Lacknor) Van L.; m. Sheila Gilbert, Aug. 20, 1967 (div. Apr. 1987); children: Jonathan S., Allison R.; m. L. Karen Stack, May 7, 1987. BS, SUNY, New Paltz, 1967; JD, Union U., 1972. Bar: N.Y. 1973, U.S. Supreme Ct., 1980; cert. corp. counsel VA, 2004. Assoc. Harter, Secrest & Emery, Rochester, NY, 1972-77; asst. dir. labor rels. Gannett Co., Inc., Rochester, 1977-80, dir. labor rels. Rochester and Arlington, NY, 1980-93, v.p., labor counsel Arlington, 1993-94, v.p., sr. labor counsel, 1994—2006, sr. v.p. labor rels., 2006—. Comments editor Albany Law Rev., 1971-72. Pres. Opera Theatre of Rochester, N.Y., 1983-85; trustee SUNY New Paltz Found. Lt. (j.g.) USNR, 1968-70. Mem. ABA, N.Y. Bar Assn., Va. Bar Assn., River Bend Golf and Country Club. Avocation: genealogy. Office: Gannett Co Inc 7950 Jones Branch Dr Mc Lean VA 22102

VAN LEEUWEN, DIRK JACOB, hepatology educator; b. Emmen, The Netherlands, Nov. 9, 1951; s. Hendrik J. and Gerarda C. Creutzberg. MD, U. Amsterdam, 1979, PhD, 1988. Internist, gastroenterologist Dutch Splst. Registration Com. Med. dir. hepatobiliary unit Acad. Med. Ctr. U. Amsterdam, 1987-92; med. dir. hepatology and liver transplantation U. Ala., Birmingham, 1992-95, prof., medicine, pub. health, hepatologist, 1992—2002; dir. hepatology Dartmouth-Hitchcock Med. Ctr., Lebanon, NH, 2002—. Prof. medicine Dartmouth Med. Sch. Editor: Imaging in Hepatobiliary and Pancreatic Disease, 2000. Mem. Am. Assn. Study of Liver, Am. Gastroenterology Assn., Internat. Liver Pathology Study Group (Elves), European Assn. Study of Liver. Office: Dartmouth-Hitchcock Med Ctr 1 Medical Center Dr Lebanon NH 03755 Office Phone: 603-650-6678. Business E-Mail: dirk.van.leeuwen@hitchcock.org.

VAN LEEUWEN, JEAN See GAVRIL, JEAN

VAN LEUVEN, ROBERT JOSEPH, lawyer; b. Detroit, Apr. 17, 1931; s. Joseph Francis and Olive (Stowell) Van Leuven; m. Merri Lee Van Leuven; children: Joseph Michael, Douglas Robert, Julie Margaret. Attended, Albion Coll., 1949-51; BA, Wayne State U., 1953; JD, U. Mich., 1957. Bar: Mich. 1957. Practice in law, Muskegon, Mich.; ptnr. Hathaway, Latimer, Clink,and Robb, Mich., 1957-68, McCroskey, Libner, and Van Leuven, Mich., 1968-81, Libner and Van Leuven, Mich., 1982—99; ret. Mich., 1999. Mem. coun. negligence law sect. State Bar Mich. Bd. dir., Muskegon Children's Home, 1965—75. With Aus., 1953—55. Fellow: Am. Coll. Trial Lawyers, Mich. Bar Found.; mem.: Delta Sigma Phi. Home: 8545 Gatewood Ct Englewood FL 34224

VAN LIEU, THOMAS JERRY, school system administrator; b. Indpls., Feb. 5, 1955; s. Thomas Edward and Rosemary Jackson Van Lieu; m. Sandra L. Van Lieu, June 9, 1979; children: Chuck, Katie, Becca. BA, Franklin Coll., Ind., 1977; MA, Ind. U.-Purdue U. Ind., Indpls., 1982. 6th grade tchr. Indpls. Pub. Schs., 1977—79, MSD Lawrence Twp. Schs., 1979—99; asst. prin. Belzer Mid. Sch., 1999—2001, athletic dir., 2002—. Mem.: NIAAA, IIAAA, NEA. Avocations: reading, golf, travel. Office: Belzer Mid Sch 7555 E 56th St Indianapolis IN 46226

VAN LINT, VICTOR ANTON JACOBUS, physicist; b. Samarinda, Indonesia, May 10, 1928; came to U.S., 1937; s. Victor J. and Margaret (DeJager) Van L.; m. M. June Woolhouse, June 10, 1950; children: Lawrence, Kenneth, Linda, Karen. BS, Calif. Inst. Tech., Pasadena, 1950, PhD, 1954. Instr. Princeton (N.J.) U., 1954-55; staff mem. Gen. Atomic, San Diego, 1957-74; physics cons. San Diego, 1974-75; staff mem. Mission Research Corp., San Diego, 1975-82, 83-91; cons., 1991—; spl. asst. to dep. dir. sci. and tech. Def. Nuclear Agy., Washington, 1982-83. Author, editor: Radiation Effects in Electronic Materials, 1976; contbr. articles to profl. jours. Served with U.S. Army, 1955-57. Recipient Pub. Service award NASA, 1981. Fellow IEEE. Republican. Mem. United Ch. of Christ. Home and Office: 1032 Skylark Dr La Jolla CA 92037-7733 Home Phone: 858-454-5978.

VAN LOUCKS, MARK LOUIS, venture capitalist, financial planner; b. Tampa, Fla., June 19, 1946; s. Charles Perry and Lenn (Bragg) Van L.; children: Brandon, Charlie; m. Lee Ann Strubel, Oct. 1, 1998. BA in Comm. and Pub. Policy, U. Calif., Berkeley, 1969. Sr. v.p. mktg., programming and corp. devel. United Cable TV Corp., Denver, 1970-81, advisor, 1983-89; sr. v.p., office of chmn. Rockefeller Ctr. TV Corp., NYC, 1981-83; advisor United Artists Commun. Corp., Englewood, 1989-91; investor, business advisor in pvt. practice Englewood, 1983—; founder, prin. owner Glory Hole Saloon & Gaming Hall, Central City, Colo., 1990—, The Canyon Casino, Black Hawk, Colo., 1990—; chmn., CEO Bask Internat., Englewood, 1990—. Bd. dirs. Wild West Devel. Corp., Denver; sr. v.p., bd. dirs. GSI Cable TV Assocs., Inc., San Francisco, 1984-90; guest lectr. on cable TV bus., 1985-91; cons. Telecommunications, Inc., Denver, 1989-93. Producer HBO spl. Green Chili Showdown, 1985; producer TV spl. 3 Days for Earth, 1987; producer, commd. artist nuclear war armament pieces; contbr. articles to profl. jours. Chmn. Cops in Crisis, Denver, 1990—; bd. dirs. The NOAH Found., Denver, 1976—; founding dir. Project for Responsible Advt., Denver, 1991-92; chmn. mayor's mktg. adv. bd., Central City, Colo. Named hon. capt. Denver Police Dept., 1991—, fin. advisor L. Rose Co., 1995—. Mem. Casino Owners Assn. (founding dir. 1989—), Colo. Gaming Assn. (dir. 1990—), recipient S'nnaeel Evol award, 1995), Glenmoor Country Club, The Village Club. Republican. Jewish. Avocations: music, woodworking, philanthropy, classic cars. Office: MLVL Inc 1515 E Tufts Ave Cherry Hills Village CO 80113 Office Phone: 303-781-0827. E-mail: mvanloucks@msn.com.

VANMARCKE, ERIK HECTOR, civil engineer, educator; b. Menen, Belgium, Aug. 6, 1941; arrived in U.S., 1965, naturalized, 1976; s. Louis Eugene and Rachel Louisa (van Hollebeke) Vanmarcke; m. Margaret Marie Delesie, May 25, 1965 (div. Feb. 22, 1999); children: Lieven Vanmarcke, Ann Vanmarcke Forzani, Kristien Vanmarcke Webber; m. Marilyn Durkee, July 14, 2001. BS, U. Leuven, Belgium, 1965; MS, U. Del., 1967; PhD in Civil Engring, MIT, 1970. From instr. to prof. civil engring. MIT, Cambridge, 1969—85, Gilbert W. Winslow Career Devel. prof., 1974—77, dir. civil engring. sys. group, 1976—80; prof. civil engring. and ops. rsch. Princeton U., 1985—, affiliated faculty mem. Bendheim Ctr. Fin., 1998—, dir. grad. studies civil engring. and ops. rsch., 1990—94. Cons. Office Sci. and Tech. Policy, 1978—80, Nat. Inst. Stds. and Tech., 2003, various govt. agys. and engring. firms; vis. scholar in engring. Harvard U., 1984—85; Shimizu Corp. vis. prof. Stanford U., 1991; mem. exec. com. Princeton Materials Inst., 1991—93; mem. Princeton Environ. Inst., 1996—; mem. com. vulnerability critical infrastructure Nat. Res. Coun., 1999—2001; mem. com. program on robotics and intelligent sys. Princeton U., 1999—. Author: Random Fields: Analysis and Synthesis, 1983, revised and expanded edit., 2005, Quantum Origins of Cosmic Structure, 1997; editor: Internat. Jour. Structural Safety, 1981—91. Named Disting. Probabilistic Methods Educator, Soc. Automotive Engrs., 2002; recipient Sr. Scientist award, Japan Soc. Promotion Sci., 1991, Disting. Engring. Alumnus award, U. Del., 1994. Mem.: ASME (mem. earthquake engring. rsch. inst.), ASCE (chair com. risk assessment and mgmt. Geo-Inst. 1996—2000, chair com. risk and vulnerability Coun. Natural Disaster Reduction 1998—2003, chair exec. com. coun. disaster risk mgmt. 2003—06, chair internat. roundtable disaster risk mgmt. 2005, Raymond C. Reese Rsch. award 1975, Walter L. Huber Rsch. prize 1984), Royal Acad. Arts and Scis. Belgium (fgn.), Internat. Soc. Soil Mechanics and Geotech. Engring. (chair com. TC32 risk assessment and mgmt. 1998—2001), Am. Geophys. Union. Home: 148 Springdale Rd Princeton NJ 08544 Office Phone: 609-258-5896. Business E-Mail: evm@princeton.edu.

VANMEER, MARY ANN, publishing executive, writer, webmaster; b. Mt. Clemens, Mich., Nov. 22, 1947; d. Leo Harold and Rose Emma (Gulden) VanM. Student, Micha. State U., 1965-66, 67-68, U. Sorbonne, Paris, summer 1968; BA in Edn., U. Fla., 1968-70. Pres. VanMeer Tutoring and Translating, NYC, 1970-72; freelance writer, 1973-79; pres. VanMeer Publs., Inc., Clearwater, Fla., 1980-88, VanMeer Media Advt., Inc., Clearwater, 1987-88; exec. dir., founder Nat. Ctrs. for Health and Med. Info., Inc., Palm Beach, Fla., 1990-93; pres., CEO ThriftyTraveling.com, Inc. (formerly Traveling Free Pubs.,), 1993—. Author: Traveling with Your Dog, U.S.A., 1976, How to Set Up a Home Typing Business, 1978, Freelance Photographer's Handbook, 1979, See America Free, 1981, Free Campgrounds, U.S.A., 1982, Free Attractions, U.S.A., 1982, VanMeer's Guide to Free Attractions U.S.A., 1984, VanMeer's Guide to Free Campgrounds, 1984, The How to Get Publicity for Your Business Handbook, 1987, Asthma: The Ultimate Treatment Guide, 1991, Allergies: The Ultimate Treatment Guide, 1992, Thrifty Traveling, 1995, 2d edit., 1996; pub. Nat. Health and Med. Trends Mag., 1986-88, ThriftyTraveling.com Newsletter and website, 1993—, online and hard-copy edits., 1999—, Over 50 Thrifty Traveler Newsletter, 1997-98, Net News for the Thrifty Traveler Newsletter, 1997-98, LuxuryTraveling.com newsletter and website, 2001—; webmaster ThriftyTraveling.com, ThriftyTravelPortal.com, 2003—, LuxuryTraveling.com and VanMeer.com websites. Pub. info. chairperson, bd. dirs. Pinellas County chpt. Am. Cancer Soc., Clearwater, 1983-84, 86-88; mem. fin. devel. com. ARC, Palm Beach County, 1990-92. Mem. Am. Booksellers Assn., Soc. Am. Travel Writers. Office: ThriftyTraveling.com Inc PO Box 8168 Clearwater FL 33758-8168 Office Phone: 800-532-5731. Personal E-mail: thriftytravel@aol.com.

VAN METER, ABRAM DEBOIS, lawyer, retired banker; b. Springfield, Ill., May 16, 1922; s. A.D. and Edith (Graham) Van M.; m. Margaret Schlipf, Dec. 1, 1956; children: Andy, Alice, Ann. BS, Kings Point Coll., 1946; JD, Northwestern U., 1948. Bar: Ill. 1949. Ptnr. Van Meter, Oxtoby & Funk, Springfield, 1949—2001; adminstrv. asst. to treas. State of Ill., Springfield, 1963; v.p. Ill. Nat. Bank, Springfield, 1964-65, pres., 1965-88, chmn. bd. dirs., 1988-90, also bd. dirs.; chmn. bd. dirs. Nat. City, Springfield, 1990-93, dir. emeritus, 1993—. Chmn. bd. dirs. Ill. Housing Devel. Authority, 1977-2003; chmn. bd. trustees So. Ill. U., 1989-2001; past bd. dirs., exec. com. Meml. Med. Ctr. Mem. ABA, Ill. Bar Assn., Sangamon Bar Assn., Chgo. Club, Chgo. Athletic Club, Sangamo Club, Island Bay Yacht Club, Cariton Club. Home: 6 Fair Oaks St Springfield IL 62704-3222 Office: Nat City 1 N Old State Capitol Plz Springfield IL 62701-1323 Personal E-mail: omvideo@aol.com.

VANMETER, VANDELIA L., retired library director; b. Seibert, Colo., July 17, 1934; d. G.W. and A. Pearl Klockenteger; m. Victor M. VanMeter, Jan. 21, 1954; children: Allison C., Kristopher C. BA, Kansas Wesleyan U., 1957; MLS, Emporia State U., 1970; PhD, Tex. Woman's U., 1986. Cert. libr. media specialist. Tchr. Ottawa County Rural Sch., Kans., 1954-55; social scis. tchr. McClave (Colo.) High Sch., 1957-58, Ellsworth (Kans.) Jr. High Sch., 1959-68; libr., media specialist Ellsworth (Kans.) High Sch., 1968-84; asst. prof. libr. sci. U. So. Miss., Hattiesburg, 1986-90; chair dept. libr./info. sci. Spalding U., Louisville, 1990-96, libr. dir., 1991-99, prof., 1991—99. Cons. to sch., pub. and spl. librs., Kans., Miss., Ky., 1970-99; mem. Ky. NCATE Bd. Examiners. Author: American History for Children and Young Adults, 1990, World History for Children and Young Adults, 1992, America in Historical Fiction, 1997; editor: Mississippi Library Media Specialist Staff Development Modules, 1988, Library Lane Newsletter, 1991-99; contbr. chpts. to books; contbr. articles to profl. jours. Active City Coun., Ellsworth, Kans., 1975-79, Park Bd., Ellsworth, 1975-79; bd. dirs. Robbins Meml. Libr., 1977-79. Grantee Kans. Demonstration Sch. Libr., 1970-72, Miss. Power Found., 1989, Project Technology Enhances Curriculur Instrn., 1996-97; named Women of Yr. Bus. and Profl. Women of Ellsworth, Kans., 1976. Mem. ALA, Assn. Coll. and Rsch. Librs., Ky. Libr. Assn., Assn. for Libr. and Info. Sci. Educators.

VAN METRE, MARGARET CHERYL, performing company executive, dancer, educator; b. Maryville, Tenn., Nov. 24, 1938; d. Robert Fillers and Margaret Elizabeth (Goddard) Raulston; m. Mitchell Robert Van Metre II, Aug. 25, 1956; 1 child, Mitchell Robert. Elem., intermediate and advanced tchg. certs. Dir. Van Metre Sch. of Dance, Maryville, 1958-96; artistic dir. Appalachian Ballet Co., Maryville Coll., 1972-96; founding dir. Appalachian Ballet Co., 1972; dir. Van Metre Arts Mgmt., SC, 1996—. Chmn. dance panel Tenn. Arts Commn., 1973-74; chmn. Bicentennial Ballet Project, Tenn., 1975-76; mem. Nat. Bd. Regional Dance Am., 1997—; owner Van Metre Arts Mgmt., Edisto Island, S.C., 1996—. Choreographer ballets: Delusion, 1965, Hill Heritage Suite, 1972, Dancing Princesses, 1983. Mem. Tenn. Assn. of Dance (pres. 1972), Southeast Regional Ballet Assn. (pres. 1996, 97, 98, 99, 2003—). Democrat. Episcopalian. Home: 2103 Myrtle St Edisto Island SC 29438-3437

VAN MIDDLESWORTH, LESTER, physiology, biophysics and medicine educator, internist; b. Washington, Jan. 13, 1919; s. Lester and Hazel Lucile (Brandt) VanM.; m. Nellie Rue Franklin, June 29, 1948; children: Linda V. Anderson, Jane V. Norman, Frank L., Paul E. BS in Chemistry, U. Va., 1940, MS in Chemistry, 1942, MS in Physiology, 1944; PhD in Physiology, U. Calif., Berkeley, 1946; MD, U. Tenn., 1951. Teaching asst. dept. physiology U. Va., 1944, U. Calif., Berkeley, 1944—45; instr. U. Tenn. Med. Units, Memphis, 1946—52, instr. in medicine, 1953—57, asst. prof. physiology, 1952—54, assoc. prof., 1954—59, prof., 1959—89, prof. emeritus physiology and biophysics, 1989—, asst. prof. medicine, 1957—61, assoc. prof., 1961—72, prof. medicine, 1972—89, prof. medicine emeritus, 1989, Disting. prof. physiology and medicine, 1986—. Rotating intern City of Memphis Hosps., 1951-52; cons. chief chemist Piedmont Apple Products Corp., Charlottesville, Va., 1940-46, Crocker Radiation Lab., U. Calif., Berkeley, 1946-47, Oak Ridge Inst. Nuclear Studies, 1950-54; guest co-investigator Endocrine Labs. Tufts Med. Coll., Boston, summers 1954, 55, 56, 59, 61, 64, 66, 69, Scripps Clinic and Rsch. Found., La Jolla, Calif., 1957; guest investigator in endocrinology Harbor Gen. Hosp., UCLA, 1971, Frederick Joliot Hosp., Orsay, France, 1972, Lawrence Livermore Radiation Lab. U. Calif., 1970; staff mem. clinic for med. thyroid disease patients, City of Memphis and U., Tenn., 1951—; mem. internat. com., 1990-2002. Author 145 publs. in profl. jours., 186 abstracts and oral presentations; work on permanent display Smithsonian Nat. Mus. Am. History, Washington, D.C. Recipient Disting. Svc. award, 1985, Disting. Alumnus award, U. Tenn. Coll. Medicine, 1989, USPHS career rsch. grantee, 1962-89. Mem. Am. Chem. Soc., Am. Physiol. Soc., AAAS, Soc. Exptl. Biology and Medicine, Am. Soc. Clin. Investigation, So. Soc. Clin. Investigation, Health Physics Soc., Endocrine Soc., Am. Thyroid Assn. (Disting. Svc. award 1988), Sigma Xi (rsch. award 1944, 86, nat. lectr. 1989-91), Alpha Chi Sigma. Achievements include research in audiogenic siezures and worldwide radioiodine fallout, and radium in normal human thyroid glands. Home: 1950 Lyndale Ave Memphis TN 38107-5109 Office: U Tenn Health Sci Ctr 894 Union Ave Memphis TN 38163-3514 Office Phone: 901-448-5837. Business E-Mail: lvanmid@physio1.utmem.edu.

VAN MOL, LOUIS JOHN, JR., public relations executive; b. Knoxville, Tenn., Oct. 7, 1943; s. Louis John and Evelyn (Ramsay) Van M.; m. Deborah Ruth Boyd, Nov. 1, 1969; children: Derek, Millicent. BS, U. Tenn., 1966. Staff writer, editor AP, Knoxville and Nashville, 1963-66, 69; account exec. to exec. v.p. Holder, Kennedy & Co., Nashville, 1970-74, exec. v.p., 1978-79; dir. info. TVA, Knoxville, 1974-78; co-founder, ptnr. Dye, Van Mol & Lawrence, Nashville, 1980—. Bd. dirs. East Tenn. Children's Hosp., Knoxville, 1977-78, Martha O'Bryan Ctr., Nashville, 1985-87, United Way Comm. Com., 1987-91, Am. Heart Assn. Mid. Tenn., Nashville, 1991-92, Leadership Nashville, 1992-93, Crime Stoppers Nashville, 1986-92, Alcohol and Drug Coun. Mid. Tenn., Nashville, 1991-93, Martha O'Bryan Found., 1998-2000, Pencil Found., 2003—, Nashville Songwriters Found., 2004—, vice chmn., 2006-07, Tenn. Chamber Commerce and Industry, 2005—; chmn. bd. dirs. Nashville Downtown Partnership, 1999-2000, bd. dirs., 2006—; bd. govs., exec. com. Nashville C. of C., 1999-2000; chmn. Goodwill Industries Mid. Tenn., 1996-97, mem. exec. com., 1996-. Lt. U.S. Army, 1966-68. Decorated Bronze Star. Mem. Richland Country Club (bd. dirs. 1997-99, pres. 1999), Soc. Profl. Journalists. Presbyterian. Home: 2836 Wellesley Trace Nashville TN 37215-1049 Office: Dye Van Mol & Lawrence Pub Rels 209 7th Ave N Nashville TN 37219-1802

VANN, ESTHER MARTINEZ, science educator; d. Gabriel Narvaez and Cecilia Wolfe Martinez; m. Raymundo Vann, June 10, 1973; children: Raymundo Jr., Joseph Noel, Michael Steven, Daniel Christopher. BA, St. Mary's U., San Antonio, Tex., 1975; MA, U. Tex., San Antonio, 1990. Sci. dept. head Wrenn Jr. H.S.-Edgewood Ind. Sch. Dist., San Antonio, 1978—83, Jordan Mid. Sch.-Northside Ind. Sch. Dist., San Antonio, 1992—93, Somerset Jr. H.S.-Somerset Ind. Sch. Dist., Tex., 1998—2004, Terrell Wells Mid. Sch.-Harlandale Ind. Sch. Dist., San Antonio, 2004—. Adminstrv. asst. Nurses At Home - Home Health Agy., San Antonio, 1993—98. Named one of Outstanding Young Women of Am., 1987; recipient Trinity Prize for Tchg. Excellence award, Trinity U., 2002, Tchr.

of the Month award, Somerset Jr. H.S.-Somerset Ind. Sch. Dist., 2003, 2004; Tex. Aerospace scholar, NASA Johnson Space Ctr., 2002. Home Phone: 210-623-4712; Office Phone: 210-921-4774.

VANN, JOHN DANIEL, III, library consultant, historian; b. Raleigh, NC, June 14, 1935; s. John Daniel Jr. and Sybil Dean (Wilson) V.; m. Ellen Jane Rogers, June 21, 1969; children: John Daniel IV, Justin Fitz Patrick. BA with honors, U. N.C., 1957; MA, Yale U., 1959, PhD, 1965; M in Librarianship, Emory U., 1971; postgrad., Columbia U., 1962-63, Stanford U., 1977-78. Ordained deacon, elder Presbyn. Ch., commd. temporary supply preacher Northumberland Presbytery. Assoc. prof. history Campbell Coll., Buie's Creek, N.C., 1961-63; bibliographer European history and lit. Newberry Libr., Chgo., 1963-65, asst. reference librarian, 1963-65; prof. history Calif. Bapt. Coll., Riverside, 1965-66; dir. libr., prof. history Bapt. Coll. at Charleston, S.C., 1966-69; libr. Keuka Coll., Keuka Park, N.Y., 1969-71; chief libr., prof. libr., chmn. libr. dept. S.I. Community Coll. CUNY, 1971-76; prof. libr. Coll. S.I. CUNY, 1976-79; head libr. Lockwood Libr./SUNY, Buffalo, 1979-80; asst. dir. for planning, univ. librs. SUNY, Buffalo, 1980-81; exec. dir. librs. and learning resources, prof. U. Wis., Oshkosh, 1981-87; dir. libr. svcs. Bloomsburg U. Pa., 1987-89, dean libr. svcs., 1989-98; spl. asst. to vice chancellor for info. technology Pa. State Sys. Higher Edn., 1999; prin. J. Daniel Vann Consulting, 2000—. Interim dir., vis. prof. bibliography Union Theol. Sem. and Presbyn. Sch. Christian Edn., 2003-04; resident planner, cons. on libr. bldgs. and collection devel.; sec.-treas. Susquehanna Libr. Coop., 1993-95. Mem. internat. editl. bd. Libr. Times Internat., 1984—; contbr. chpts. to books, articles to profl. jours. Trustee Maplewood (N.J.) Meml. Libr., 1977-79, v.p., 1979; bd. dir. Coun. Wis. Librs., 1983-86, Midwest Rotary Multi-Dist. Short Term Internat. Youth Exch., 1987, Oshkosh (Wis.) Symphony Assn., 1986-87, Protestant campus ministry Bloomsburg U., 1999—2002, United Cerebral Palsy of Winnebagoland, Oshkosh, 1986-87; active coms. Winnebago Presbytery, Presbyn. Ch., 1984-87; com. on min. Northumberland Presbytery, Presbyn. Ch., 1992-96, com. on preparation for ministry, 1996—2002, coun., 1999—2002; commr. Synod of Trinity Presbyn. Ch. (USA), 1999—2003, exec. com., 2002—2003. Paul Harris fellow Rotary Internat.; Acad. Libr. Mgmt. intern Coun. on Libr. Resources Stanford U., 1977-78. Mem. ALA (com. mem.), Am. Hist. Assn., Archons of Colophon, Assn. for Libr. Collections and Tech. Svcs., Assn. Coll. and Rsch. Librs. (com. chmn., sec. chmn. 1977-78, editl. bd., bd. dirs. 1976-78), Bibliog. Soc. Am., Libr. Adminstrn. and Mgmt. Assn. (com. mem.), Libr. and Info. Tech. Assn., Reference and User Svcs. Assn., Medieval Acad. Am., Beta Phi Mu, Phi Alpha Theta. Republican. Home: 1216 Rennie Ave Richmond VA 23227-4723 Home and Studio: 1 Clear Vista Dr Asheville NC 28805 Personal E-mail: vann@aya.yale.edu.

VAN NAGELL, JOHN RENSSELAER, oncologist, gynecologist; b. NYC, Sept. 16, 1939; s. John Rensselaer and Rosamond Musgrave Van Nagell; m. Elizabeth Gay, June 10, 1977; children: John R Van Nagell III, Elizabeth Knox Pfister, Lucy Tepper. MD, U. Pa., 1967. Diplomate Am. Bd. Ob/Gyn. Prof., dir. divsn. gynecol. oncology U. Ky. Med. Ctr., Lexington, 1973—, Am. Cancer Soc prof. clin. oncology. Cons. NCI - PLCO Trial, Bethesda, Md., 1992—. Author: Modern Concepts of Gynecologic Oncology. Lt. USN, 1971—77. Named one of Top Doctors for Women, Ladies Home Jour., 2001—06, Ams. Top Doctors, Castle Connolly, 2002—06. Mem.: Masters of Foxhounds Assn. (bd.dirs. 2005), Soc. Gynecol. Oncologists (pres. 1994—95). Avocations: horseback riding, fox hunting. Office Phone: 859-323-5553. Business E-Mail: jrvann2@email.uky.edu.

VAN NATTA, BRUCE WAYNE, plastic surgeon; b. Shelbyville, Ind., Apr. 12, 1955; BA, DePauw U., Greencastle, 1977; MD, Ind. U., 1981. Cert. Am. Bd. Plastic Surgery. Resident gen. surgery Ind. U. Hosps., Indpls., 1981—86, resident plastic surgery, 1986—88; with Perkins Van Natta Ctr. for Cosmetic Surgery and Med. Skincare, 2002—. Hand surgery fellowship U. Louisville Hosps., 1986; clin. asst. prof. plastic surgery Ind. U. Med. Ctr.; mem. med. adv. panel Inamed Med. Corp.; with St. Vincent Hosp., Indpls., Women's Hosp., Indpls., Cmty. Hosp., Indpls., Major Hosp., Shelbyville; presenter in field. Fellow: Am. Coll. Surgeons; mem.: AMA, Ohio Valley Soc. Plastic and Reconstructive Surgery, Am. Burn Assn., Indpls. Med. Soc., Ind. State Med. Assn., Am. Soc. Aesthetic Plastic Surgery, Am. Soc. Plastic Surgeons. Office: 170 W 106th St Indianapolis IN 46290 Office Phone: 317-575-0330, 800-345-1962. *

VAN NESS, JAMES EDWARD, electrical engineering educator; b. Omaha, June 24, 1926; s. Hubert James and Jean (Woodruff) Van N.; m. Mary Ellen Dolvin, Dec. 28, 1948; children: Rebecca Ellen, Barbara Jean, Margaret Ann, Julie Lynn. BS, Iowa State U., 1949; MS, Northwestern U., 1951, PhD, 1954. Faculty elec. engring. dept. Northwestern U., 1952—, prof. emeritus, chmn. dept., 1969-72; dir. Computer Center, 1962-65; vis. assoc. prof. U. Calif., Berkeley, 1958-59. Vis. prof. MIT, 1973-74, Ariz. State U., winter 1984 Contbr. articles to profl. jours. Served with USNR, 1944-46. Fellow: IEEE; mem.: NAE (elected). Home: 17 Calvin Cir Evanston IL 60201 Personal E-mail: vanness@northwestern.edu.

VAN NESS, ROSS HOWARD, education educator; b. Constantine, Mich., Oct. 12, 1932; s. George Phillip and Doris Gwen (Miller) Van N.; m. Harlean Gwen Bond, July 23, 1955; children: Connie, Lynne, Paul. MusB cum laude, Western Mich. U., Kalamazoo, 1955; MusM, U. Mich., Ann Arbor, 1960, EdD, 1970. Cert. tchr., Mich. Tchr. Mendon Schs., Mich., 1956-58, Quincy Schs., Mich., 1958-61; dir. music Marshall Schs., Mich., 1961-68; asst. prin. Marshall H.S., 1968-69; fellow C.S. Mott Found., U. Mich., Flint, 1969-70; asst. prof. community edn. Ball State U., Muncie, Ind., 1970-72, assoc. dir. Inst. for Community Edn. Devel., 1973-81, program dir., 1981-86, dir. program devel., prof. continuing edn., 1986-92, prof. emeritus, 1992—. Bd. dirs. Rehab. Plus, Inc., Muncie, 1990-92; pres. Growth and Effective Mgmt. Assocs., Muncie, 1985—; spkr. in field; presenter over 1,200 presentations on mgmt. and edn. in 42 states and 13 countries, 1970-2006. Author: I Win You Win, 1981, Eliminating Procrastination Without Putting It Off, 1988, Raising Self-Esteem of Learners, 1995; editor mgmt. div. Home Health Executive Report, 1986-88; contbr. articles to profl. jours. Choir dir. St. Andrew Presbyn. Ch., Muncie, 1971-88, bd. dirs., 1973-75, 85-87, 2000-04; chmn. bd. dirs. United Ministries of Ball State, 1989-91; chmn. bd. dirs. Acad. Cmty. Leadership Del. County, 1998-2007, Muncie Civic Theatre, 1993-95, United Way Delaware County, 1993-95, Christian Ministries Del. County, 1995—, pres. 2005, Masterworks Chorale, 1992-99, 2002-06, pres., 1997-99, East Ctrl. Ind. Cmty. Orch., 2004—. Lt. US Army, 1956. Mem. Mich. Sch. Band and Orch. Assn. (v.p. 1968, Orch. Dir. of Yr. 1968), Very Important Vol. award Del. County 2003), Ind. Cmty. Edn. Assn. (pres. 1982-83, bd. dirs. 1978-84), Ind. Assn. Adult and Continuing Edn. (bd. dirs. 1982-88, pres. 1986-87). Avocations: music, fishing, reading, cooking. Home and Office: 1405 N Briar Rd Muncie IN 47304-3049 Personal E-mail: vanness32@gmail.com.

VAN NESTE, KAREN LANE, librarian, editor; b. Washington, Oct. 18, 1951; d. Wilbur Lane and Phyllis Worthington Van Neste; m. Howard Wayne Owen, Aug. 18, 1973. BA, U. Va., Charlottesville, 1973; MS in Libr. Sci., U. NC, Chapel Hill, 1976. Libr. divsn. disorders devel. and learning U. N.C., Chapel Hill, 1976—77; libr. Fla. State U., Tallahassee, 1977—78; libr., rschr. Media Gen., Inc., Richmond, Va., 1979—88; libr. Richmond Times-Dispatch, Va., 1988—98, restaurant critic, 2003—04, libr., 2004—; pub. Van Neste Books, Midlothian, Va., 1996—2001. Copy editor Richmond Times-Dispatch, 1999—2002; freelance editor, Richmond, 2001—. Author: The Question Finder, 1986; editor: Littlejohn, 1992, Fat Lightning, 1994, Answers to Lucky, 1996, The Measured Man, 1997, Styll in Love, 1998, One August Day, 1998, The Edge of Things, 1999, Floating in a Most Peculiar Way, 1999, Lumen, 1999, Survivors, 2000, A Better Man, 2000, Steal My Heart, 2000 (Peace Corps Fiction award, 2001), Harry and Ruth, 2000, Divisible by One, 2001, Liar Moon, 2001, The Rail, 2002, Turn Signal, 2004, Rock of Ages, 2006. Mem. Edgehill Condominium Assn., Richmond, Va., 1981—83; contbr. James River Writers Festival, Richmond, 2002—06; editor, writer newsletter The Prestwould Condominium Assn., Richmond, 2001—07. Mem.: Am. Biographical Inst., Va. Mus. Fine Arts, Spl. Libraries Assn., Profl. Women's Adv. Bd., U. Va. Alumni Assn. (life), 2300 Club (house rules com. 2006, mem. house rules com.). D-Liberal. Avocations: travel, interior decorating, cooking. Office: Richmond Times-Dispatch 300 E Franklin St Richmond VA 23219 Home: 900 Cadmus Dr Fredericksburg VA 22401 also: PO Box 25 Fredericksburg VA 22404 Home Phone: 804-343-3433; Office Phone: 804-649-6074. Business E-Mail: kowen@timesdispatch.com.

VANNICE, M. ALBERT, chemical engineering professor, researcher; b. Broken Bow, Nebr., Jan. 11, 1943; s. Duane M. and Eugenia R. (Farmer) Vannice; m. Bette Ann Clark, Jan. 2, 1971. BSChemE, Mich. State Univ., 1964; MS, Stanford Univ., 1966, PhD, 1970. Engr. Dow Chem. Co., Midland, Mich., 1966, Sun Oil Co., Marcus Hook, Pa., 1970; sr. rsch. engr. Esso Rsch. & Engr. Co., Linden, NJ, 1971—76; assoc. prof. Pa. State Univ., State College, 1976—80, prof., 1980—, disting. prof., 1991—2002, M.R. Fenske prof. chem. engring., 1996—2002, W.H. Joyce chair in chem. engring., 2002—05, emeritus, 2005—. Cons. Eastman Chem. Co., Kingsport, Tenn., 1980—2000; mem. adv. bd. Absorption Sci. and Tech., 1982—95. Mem. editl. bd. Jour. of Catalysis, 1988—94, assoc. editor, 1994—2001; contbr. articles to profl. jours. Recipient award, N.Y. Catalysis Soc., 1985, P.H. Emmett award, 1987, award, Pa.-Cleve. Catalysis Soc., 1988, Humboldt Rsch. award, 1990, Fulbright award, 1996. Mem.: AIChE (profl. Progress award 1986), N.Am. Catalysis Soc. (pres. 1997—2001), Am. Chem. Soc. Achievements include patents in field; research in effects of strong metal-support interactions on catalytic behavior; studies of CO hydrogenation; studies NOx reduction; catalyst characterization. Office: Pa State Univ 107 Fenske Lab University Park PA 16802-4400 Home Phone: 814-466-6115; Office Phone: 814-863-4803. Business E-Mail: mavche@engr.psu.edu.

VANNIEUWENHOVEN, VICKI, professional sports team executive; b. 1966; Team acct. Green Bay Packer, 1995—99, dir. finance, 1999—2007, v.p. finance, 2007—. Achievements include bring first female v.p. in Green Bay Packers team history. Office: Green Bay Packers 1265 Lombardi Ave Green Bay WI 54304 Fax: 920-569-7301.

VAN NOORD, DIANE C., artist, educator; b. Muskegon, Mich., Dec. 12, 1950; d. Ernest Raymond and Judith Ann Olsen; m. Calvin G. Van Noord, Sept. 26, 1981; children: Tawn Star, Brian Calvin, Timothy John. BA, Hope Coll., 1991; MA, We. Mich. U., 1994. Artist, Holland, Mich.; tchr. pvt. and group art, 2000—. Guest lectr. Counterpart Assn., Grand Haven, Mich., 1997, Lakeland Painters, Grand Haven, 1997, Traverse City (Mich.) Art Assn., 1997, Holland Christian Schs., 1998, 99, 2000. Exhbns. include Neville Pub. Mus., Green Bay, Wis., 1994, Carillon Gallery, Ft. Worth, 1995, 97, Sedona Arts Ctr., Ariz., 1995-96, 99, Holland Area Arts Coun., 1995, Pitts. Ctr. for the Arts, 1995, Miss. Mus. Art, Jackson, 1995, Unitarian Universalist Ch., Phoenix, 1996, Lakeland Painters, Grand Haven, Mich., 1996, Sun Cities Mus. Art, Sun City, Ariz., 1997, Art Inst. Phoenix, 1998, Hill Country Arts Found., Ingram, Tex., 1998, Mus. Tex. Tech. U., Lubbock, 1998, Dunton Gallery, Arlington Heights, Ill., 2000, Internat. Mus. Art, El Paso, 2000; one-woman shows include Gallery Upstairs, Grand Haven, 1996, Moynihan Gallery, Holland, 1997, Trinity Presbyn. Ch., Denton, 1997, Show Sabbatical, 1998-99, Freedom Village, Holland, 2000, Acad. Artists Assn., Springfield, Mass., 2001, Hilton Head Art League, 2001, Oil Painters Am., Chgo., 2002, Audubon Artists NY, 2002, Magnum Opus XIV, Sacramento, 2002, Am. Artists Profl. League, NYC, 2002, Celebration of Western Art, San Francisco, 2002, Hilton Head Art League, 2003, 2004, Oil Painters Am., Taos, N.Mex., 2003, Scottsdale Artists Sch, 2004, Nat. Watercolor Soc., 2004, Rocky Mountain Plein Air Painters, 2004, Allied Artists, Inc., NYC, Biennale Internat. Dell'Arte Contemporanea, Florence, Italy, 2005—, Catharine Lorillard Wolfe Art Club, NY, 2006; exhibited in group shows at Gallery Uptown, 2006, El Presido Gallery, Ariz., 2006, Karin Newby Gallery, Ariz., 2006; permanent collections in Fla., Ariz., Mich., Nebr., Ind.; contbng. author: How Did You Paint That? 100 Ways to Paint the Landscape, 2004, How Did You Paint That? 100 Ways to Paint Flowers and Gardens, 2004, Art Still on the Easel, Am. Art Collector Mag., 2006; contbr. articles to profl. jours. Recipient Mcht.'s award Lakeland Painters, 1996, No. Ariz. Watercolor Soc., Sedona Arts Ctr., 1999, Diane Parssinen Meml. award No. Ariz. Watercolor Soc., 2001, 2d prize Internat. Artist Mag., 2002, Honorable Mention, Artists Mag., 2002, 2004. Mem. Ariz. Watercolor Assn., No. Ariz. Watercolor Assn., Oil Painters Am. (assoc.), Nat. Watercolor Soc. (assoc.), Allied Artists (assoc.), Tucson Plein Air Painters Soc., Great Lakes Plein Air Painters. Republican. Home: 6418 Oakridge Dr Holland MI 49423-8999 Personal E-mail: dvn@dianevannoord.com.

VAN NOSTRAND, RICHARD CHARLES, lawyer; b. Johnstown, NY, Sept. 20, 1955; s. Charles F. and Delores M. (Trajlinek) Van N.; m. Deborah A. Genovese, Aug. 6, 1977; children: Emily Kate, Kelsey Lynn. BA in History, Binghamton U., Binghamton, 1977; JD, Duke U., 1980. Bar: Mass. 1980, U.S. Dist. Ct. Mass. 1981, U.S. Ct. Appeals (1st cir.) 1983, U.S. Ct. Claims 1983, U.S. Supreme Ct. 2003. Assoc. Bloom and Schwartz, Westborough, Mass., 1980-83, Bloom and Van Nostrand, Westborough, 1983-84; pvt. practice Westborough, 1984; assoc. Mirick, O'Connell, DeMallie and Lougee, Worcester, Mass., 1984-87, ptnr., 1988—. Legal counsel Mass. Jaycees, 1985—86; bd. dirs. Legal Assistance Corp. of Cen. Mass., treas., 1996—99; chmn. Northborough Pers. Bd., 1994—97; trustee Mass. Legal Assistance Corp., 2001—; mem. Joint Bar on Judicial Appointments, 2001—, chair, 2001—02. Bd. dirs. United Way of Cen. Mass., 1991—99, chmn. allocations divsn., 1991—93. Named Outstanding Young Leader of Worcester, 1995. Mem.: ABA (nat. conf. bar pres. 1995—96, del. 2003—04), New Eng. Bar Assn. (v.p. 2003—04, pres. 2004—05), Mass. CLE, Inc. (trustee 1997—2004), Worcester County Bar Assn. (chmn. trial practice sect. 1988—90, chmn. Superior Ct. com. 1990—91, exec. com. 1991—97, pres. 1995—96, Pres. award 1990, 1995, 1997), Mass. Bar Assn. (bd. dels. 1995—96, budget and fin. com. 1997—2004, v.p. 2001—02, pres.-elect 2002—03, pres. 2003—04, bd. dels. 2000—06), Worcester County Bar Found. (life; pres. 1996—97), Worcester Jaycees (pres. 1984—85). Democrat. Lutheran. Home: 109 Madison Rd Northborough MA 01532-2280 Office: Mirick OConnell 100 Front St Worcester MA 01608-1477 Home Phone: 508-393-5563; Office Phone: 508-791-8500. Business E-Mail: rvannostrand@modl.com.

VAN NOY, TERRY WILLARD, health care executive; b. Alhambra, Calif., Aug. 31, 1947; s. Barney Willard and Cora Ellen (Simms) V.; m. Betsy Helen Pothen, Dec. 27, 1968; children: Bryan, Mark. BS in Bus. Mgmt., Calif. State Poly. U., 1970; MBA, Pepperdine U., 1991. CLU. Group sales rep. Mutual of Omaha, Atlanta, 1970-74, dist. mgr., 1974-77, regional mgr. Dallas, 1977-82, nat. sales mgr. Omaha, Neb., 1982-83, v.p. group mktg., 1983-87, div. dir. Orange, Calif., 1987-95; pres., CEO, Amil Internat., Las Vegas, 1995-98; prin. Van Noy Consulting Group, Henderson, Nev., 1998—. Vice-chmn. State Nev. Reinsurance Bd., mem. divsn. ins. health adv. com.; presenter in field. Vice-chmn. Morning Star Luth. Ch., Omaha, 1987; adv. bd. Chapman U. Sch. Bus.; exc. com. ABL Orgn.; chmn. bd. trustees Desert Rsch. Inst. Found. Mem. Am. Soc. CLU, Orange County Employee Benefit Coun., We. Pension and Benefits Conf., Las Vegas Valley Soaring Assn. (v.p.), Great Basin Soaring Inc. (pres.), Internat. Found. Employee Benefit Plans. Republican. Avocations: skiing, scuba diving, soaring. Home and Office: 2312 Prometheus Ct Henderson NV 89074-5324 Office Phone: 702-433-9677. Personal E-mail: tvannoy@earthlink.net.

VAN OEVEREN, EDWARD LANIER, lawyer, biologist, physician; b. Washington, Apr. 12, 1954; BA with high distinction, U. Va., 1976; MD, Med. Coll. Va., 1995; JD, U. Va., 1981; BS with distinction, George Mason U., 1983; MPH, Johns Hopkins U., 1998. Bar: Va. 1981, U.S. Dist. Ct. (ea. dist.) Va. 1988, U.S. Temporary Emergency Ct. Appeals 1989; lic. physician, Va.; bd. cert. pub. health & preventive medicine. Pvt. practice legal cons., Falls Church, Va., 1984-85; pvt. practice law, 1986-89; pvt. practice law and biology, 1989-95; intern Med. Coll. Va., 1996-97; resident in preventive medicine Johns Hopkins U., Balt., 1997-99; pvt. practice law, medicine and biology Falls Church, 1997—2003; dir. W. Piedmont Health Dist. Va. Dept. Health, 2003—. Editor: Federal Special Court Litigation, 1982; contbr. articles to profl. jours. Election officer Fairfax County (Va.) Electoral Bd., 1989-90, 1994-2002. Capt. Va. Army NG, 1996-97; 1st lt. USAR, 1995-96, capt., 1997-2003, maj., 2003-. Mem.: George Mason U. Alumni Assn. (scholarship, awards, rules and policies coms. 1989—91), Va. State Bar Assn., Alpha Chi. Avocation: photography. Home: 1511 Whittle Rd Martinsville VA 24112-5532

VANORA, JEROME PATRICK, lawyer; b. Dec. 18, 1941; s. Jerome Anthony and Mary (Fitzpatrick) V.; m. Marianne Elizabeth Hartmann, Oct. 12, 1968; children: Judith, Kimberly. BA, Queens Coll., 1963; JD, St. John's U., 1966. Bar: N.Y. 1967. Atty. N.Y. Dept. of State Corp. Bur., Albany, 1967-70; sr. atty. divsn. human rights NYC, 1970-81; assoc. atty. divsn. housing cmty. renewal, 1981—2002. Dir. hearings unit (chief adminstrv. law judge) office of rent adminstrn., divsn. housing and cmty. renewal, NYC, 1984—99; asst. counsel Nassau County Rent Guidelines Bd., 1982—86; lectr. (twice yearly) L.I. U., Greenvale, NY, 1984—85; per diem adminstrv. law judge N.Y. State Divsn. Human Rights, 2002—07. Contbr. articles to profl. jours. Mem.: N.Y. State Bar Assn., Nat. Assn. Adminstrv. Law Judges, Phi Beta Kappa. Republican. Roman Catholic. Home: 1100 Delmar Ave Franklin Square NY 11010-2703

VAN ORDEN, PHYLLIS JEANNE, librarian, educator; b. Adrian, Mich., July 7, 1932; d. Warren Philip and Mabel A. Nancy (Russell) Van O. BS, Ea. Mich. U., 1954; AMLS, U. Mich., 1958; EdD, Wayne State U., 1970. Sch. librarian East Detroit (Mich.) Pub. Schs., 1954-57; librarian San Diego Pub. Library, 1958-60; media specialist Royal Oak (Mich.) Pub. Schs., 1960-64; librarian Oakland U., Rochester, Mich., 1964-66; instr. Wayne State U., Detroit, 1966-70; asst. prof. Rutgers U., New Brunswick, NJ, 1970-76; prof. library science Fla. State U., Tallahassee, 1977-91, assoc. dean for instrn., 1988-91; prof. libr. sci. program Wayne State U., Detroit, 1991-93; dir. Grad. Sch. of Libr. and Info. Sci. U. Wash., Seattle, 1993-96; cons. in field, 1996—. Author: Collection Program in Schools, 2001, Library Service to Children, 2005, Selecting Books for the Elementary School Library Media Center, 2000, A Practical Guide to Selection, 2007; editor: Elementary School Library Collection, 1974—77. Fla. State Libr. grantee, 1984, 86, 88; Lillian Bradshaw scholar Tex. Woman's U., 1993. Mem.: ALA (libr. resources and tech. svcs. divsn., Blackwell/N.Am. scholarship award 1983), Assn. for Libr. and Info. Sci. Edn. (pres. 1990, Svc. award 1997), Assn. Libr. Svc. to Children (past pres., Dist. Svc. award 2002), Pi Lambda Theta. Avocations: music, knitting, physical fitness, cooking, travel. Personal E-mail: vanordp@u.washington.edu.

VAN OTTEREN, JULIET, photographer; d. Wilbur van Otteren. Student, Santa Monica City Coll., Calif., 1968—69, UCLA, 1968, student, 1970. Photography book, Heart of the Horse, Represented in permanent collections Bibliothèque Nat., Paris, Mus. City of N.Y., N.Y.C., Nat. Portrait Gallery, London, Santa Barbara Mus. Art, Calif., Nat. Arts Club, N.Y.C., Nat. Portrait Gallery, Canberra, Australia, Nat. Mus. Women in Arts, Washington, Bklyn. Mus. Art, High Mus. Art, Atlanta, Internat. Ctr. Photography, N.Y.C., Musée d'Art Moderne et d'Art Contemporain, Nice, France, Internat. Mus. Horse, Lexington, Ky. Mailing: PO Box 29282 Austin TX 78755 Home Phone: 512-491-8297. Personal E-mail: juliet@jvop.com. Business E-Mail: mail@jvop.com.

VAN OTTERLOO, JANICE HELENE, musician, educator; b. Sioux Center, Iowa, Aug. 28, 1954; d. Melvin John Van Otterloo and Lucille Marie Warntjes; m. Ray J. Humphreys, Jan. 7, 1982. B in Ch. Music summa cum laude, Drake U., Des Moines, 1976; MusM summa cum laude, So. Meth. U., Dallas, 1979. Organist First Bapt. Ch. Ft. Myers, Fla., 1987—96; organist, dir. music Redeemer Luth. Ch., Ft. Myers, 1996—99; organist St. Hilary's Episcopal Ch., Ft. Myers, 1999—2006, Faith Luth. Ch., Prairie Village, Kans., 2006—07, Raymore Christian Ch., Mo., 2007—; staff organist Cmty. Christ World HQ, Independence, Mo., 2007—. Pvt. organ, harpsichord and piano tchr., Ft. Myers, 1987—2006; pvt. organ, harpsichord and piano instr., Raymore, Mo., 2006—; adj. prof. organ Edison C.C., Ft. Myers, 1999—2006. Grad. assistantship in organ and harpsichord, So. Meth. U., 1977—79. Mem.: Nat. Fedn. Music Clubs, Music Tchrs. Nat. Assn., Am. Guild Organists (dean SW Fla. chpt. 1992—94). Avocations: reading, walking my three dogs, cooking. Home Phone: 816-322-4942; Office Phone: 816-322-0561.

VAN OVERBEKE, DEBBIE ANN, education educator; m. Gary Van Overbeke; children: Troy, Jeffrey, Brittany. BS in Elem. Edn., S.W. Minn. State U., Marshall, 1989, MS in Ednl. Leadership, 2000; EdD in Adult and Higher Edn., U. S.D., 2003. Tchr. 4th grade Canby (Minn.) Parochial Sch., 1989—94; tchr. 6th grade Holy Redeemer Sch., Marshall, Minn., 1994—98, tchr. mid. sch., 1998—2003; assoc. prof. undergrad. and grad. edn. S.W. Minn. State U., Marshall, 2003—07. Bd. dirs. ARC, Lincoln/Lyon County, 2003—05. Mem.: ASCD, Internat. Reading Assn., Minn. Coun. Tchrs. Math., Nat. Coun. Tchrs. Math. Home: 2582 State Hwy 19 Ivanhoe MN 56142 Office: SW Minn State U 1510 State St Marshall MN 56258 Home Phone: 507-694-1890; Office Phone: 507-537-7120. E-mail: vanoverbeke@southwestmsu.edu.

VAN PATTEN, JAMES JEFFERS, education educator; b. North Rose, NY, Sept. 8, 1925; s. Earl F. and Dorothy (Jeffers) Van P.; married. BA, Syracuse U., 1949; ME, Tex. Western Coll., 1959; PhD, U. Tex., Austin, 1962. Asst. prof. philosophy and edn. Central Mo. State U., Warrensburg, 1962-64, assoc. prof., 1964-69; assoc. prof. fis. overseas U. Okla., Norman, 1969-71; prof. edn. U. Ark., Fayetteville, 1971-99, prof. emeritus, 1999—. Visiting scholar, U. Mich., 1981, UCLA, 1987, U. Tex., Austin, 1987; vis. prof./scholar U. Fla., Gainesville, 1994; adj. Fla. Atlantic U., 2000-07. Editor: Conflict, Permanency and Change in Education, 1976, Philosophy, Social Science and Education, 1989, College Teaching and Higher Education Leadership, 1990, Social-Cultural Foundations of Educational Policy in the U.S., 1991, Watersheds in Higher Education, 1997, Challenges and Opportunities For a New Millennium, 1998, Challenges and Opportunities for Education in the 21st Century, 1999, Higher Education Culture, Case Studies For A New Century, 2000, A New Century In Retrospect and Prospect, 2000; Author: Academic Profiles in Higher Education, 1992, The Many Faces of the Culture of Higher Education, 1993, The Culture of Higher Education: A Case Study Approach, 1996, What's Really Happening in Education: A Case Study Approach, 1997; Co-author: (with G. Chen and George C. Stone) Individual and Collective Contributions to Humaneness In Our Time, 1997, (with John Pulliam) History of Education in America, 9th edit., 2007, (with Timothy J. Bergen) A Case Study Approach to a Multi-Cultural Mosaic for Education, 2003; contbr. articles to profl. jours. including Futures Rsch. Quar.; founder Jour. of Thought, Educational Systems for the 21st Century, Futures Rsch. Quarterly, summer 2000. Served with inf. U.S. Army, 1944-45. Decorated Purple Heart, Bronze Star.

Mem. Am. Ednl. Studies Assn., Southern Future Soc., World Future Soc., Am. Philosophy Assn., Southwestern Philosophy of Edn. Soc. (pres. 1970), Am. Ednl. Rsch. Assn., Edn. Law Assn., Nat. Assn. Legal Assts., Kiwanis, Phi Delta Kappa (pres. chpt. U. Ark. 1976-77). E-mail: jvanpatt@aol.com.

VAN PELT, ROBERT IRVING, retired firefighter; b. Chgo., May 4, 1931; s. Irving Henry and Lillian Christene (Balder) Van P.; m. Donna Arlene Bengtson, Feb. 3, 1962; children: Robert Scott, Barbara Gail, James Arthur. Grad. H.S., Chgo. Fire dept. capt. Chgo. Fire Dept., 1954—89; ret., 1989. Dir. Edgebrook Cmty. Assn., Chgo., 1974-95, U. Ill. Dad's Assn., 1981-92; dist. vice-chmn. programs Chgo. Area coun. Boy Scouts Am., 1985-93; scouting coord. Edgebrook Luth. Ch., Chgo., 1971—; active PTA Edgebrook Sch., Taft HS. With U.S. Naval Air Res., 1949-65. Decorated Combat Air Crew Wings, 1951, Armed Svcs. medal; recipient Merit award Boy Scouts Am., 1982, Silver Beaver award, 1987, Svc. award VFW, 1987, Lamb award Luth. Ch., 2000; named to Chgo. Sr. Citizen Hall of Fame, 2000; PTA scholar, 1956. Mem. Naval Air Mus. (founding life), Exptl. Aviation Assn., War Birds Am., E.A.A. War Bird Squadron 4, Am. Legion, Order of Arrow, Liberator (San Diego), U.S. Navy Meml. Washington (plank), Patrol Bomber Y Consolidated MFG (PBY) Catalina Assn. (life). Avocations: photography, woodworking, model making. Home: 6317 N Hiawatha Ave Chicago IL 60646-4219

VAN PILSUM, JOHN FRANKLIN, biochemist, educator; b. Prairie City, Iowa, Jan. 28, 1922; s. John Peter and Vera Elisabeth (Moore) Van Pilsum; m. Shirley Elaine Newsom, Oct. 14, 1958; children: John Robert, Patricia Mona, Barbara Joyce, Mary Ann, Elizabeth Joan, William Franklin. BS, State U. Iowa, 1943, PhD, 1949. Instr. L.I. Coll. Medicine, Bklyn., 1949-51; asst. prof. coll. medicine U. Utah, Salt Lake City, 1951-54; asst. prof. biochemistry U. Minn., Mpls., 1954-63, assoc. prof. biochemistry, 1963-71, prof. biochemistry, 1971—92, prof. biochemistry emeritus, 1992—. Contbr. articles to profl. jours. Lt. USN, 1944-46. Recipient numerous grants NIH. Mem. Am. Soc. Biochemistry and Molecular Biology, Am. Inst. Nutrition, Histochem. Soc. Achievements include work with Guanidinium compound metabolism. Home: 4356 Leander Ln Columbia Heights MN 55421-3067 Office: U Minn Dept Biochem Molecular Biolog & Biophysics 1395 Gortner Ave Saint Paul MN 55108 Office Phone: 612-624-1542.

VAN PRAAG, HERMAN MEIR, psychiatrist, educator, researcher; b. Schiedam, The Netherlands, Oct. 17, 1929; s. Marinus Maurits and Charlotte Frederique (Leverpoll) V.P.; m. Cornelia Eikens; children: Marinus, Gido, Charlotte, Bart. MD, Leiden U., The Netherlands, 1956; PhD in Neurobiology, U. Utrecht, The Netherlands, 1962. Chief of staff dept. psychiatry Dijkzigt Hosp., Rotterdam, The Netherlands, 1963-66; founder, prof., head dept. biol. psychiatry Psychiat. Univ. Clinic State U., Groningen, Netherlands, 1966-77; prof., head dept. psychiatry Acad. Hosp. State U., Utrecht, 1977-82, Albert Einstein Coll. Medicine, Bronx, NY, 1982—92; prof., head dept. psychiatry and neuropsychology Acad. Hosp. U. Maastricht, Netherlands, 1992—99, sci. advisor dept. psychiarty and neuropsychology, 1999—. Emeritus prof. Albert Einstein Coll. Medicine, 1992—; psychiatrist-in-chief Montefiore Med. Ctr., Bronx, 1982—92; Lady Davis vis. prof. Hebrew U. Hadassah U. Hosp., Jerusalem, 1976—77; head WHO Nat. Ref. Ctr. for Study of Psychotropic Drugs, 1969, WHO Collaborating Ctr. for Rsch. and Tng. in Biol. Psychiatry, 1974; founder Interdisciplinary Soc. Biol. Psychiatry, 1966, Found. for Psychiatry and Religion, 1998; guest lectr. numerous univs. around the world. Editor: Psychiatria Neurologia Neurochirurgia, 1968-70, Advances in Biological Psychiatry, 1978—; editor-in-chief Psychiatria Neurologia Neurochirurgia, 1971-74, Biology of Behavior, 1975-82, Handbook of Biological Psychiatry, 1975-81, Einstein Monograph Series in Experimental and Clinical Psychiatry, 1988—; European chief-editor Progress in Neuro-Psychopharmacology, 1993—; mem. editl. bd. numerous publs. in field; reviewer Am. Jour. Psychiatry, Archives of Gen. Psychiatry, Jour. Nervous and Mental Disease; mem. internat. scientific commn. Jour. Brazilian Psychiat. Assn. Decorated knight Order of the Dutch Lion, Queen Beatrix of The Netherlands; recipient numerous awards and honors. Fellow Am. Coll. Neuropsychopharmacology, Am. Psychiat. Assn.; mem. Royal Acad. Scis. of The Netherlands, Soc. Biol. Psychiatry, Collegium Internationale Neuro-Psychopharmacologicum, Assn. for Advancement of Psychotherapy, Internat. Group for Study of Affective Disorders, Internat. Soc. Psychoneuroendocrinology, European Brain and Behavior Soc., Internat. Assn. for Suicide Prevention, Brit. Pharmacol. Soc., European Soc. for Clin. Investigation, Bataafsch Genootschap der Proefondervindelijke Wijsbegeerte, Am. Coll. Neuropharmacology, Deutsche Gesellschaft fur Psychiatrie und Nervenheilkunde, Israel Med. Assn., Psychiat. Rsch. Soc., NY Acad. Medicine, Am. Psychopathol. Assn., Internat. Coll. Neurobiology, Biol. Psychiatry and Psychopharmacology, Serotonin Club, Internat. Soc. for Rsch. on Emotion, Internat. Soc. Psychoneuroendocrinology, Arbeitsgemeinschaft fur Neuropsychpharmakologie und Pharmakopsychiatrie, World Psychiat. Assn. (chmn. religion, spirituality and psychiatry sect.). Office: Acad Hosp Maastricht PO Box 5800 6202 AZ Maastricht Netherlands Office Phone: 31-55-5760795. Personal E-mail: h.m.van.praag@vanpraag.com.

VAN RHYN, JACQUELINE J., curator; b. Greenwich, Conn., May 29, 1970; d. Richard and Stephanie van Rhyn; m. James J. Hoisington, July 30, 2005. Bachelor, NYU, 1992; Masters, Williams Coll., 1997. Asst. curator Mass MoCA, North Adams, Mass., 1996—97; Werner and Maren Otto curatorial intern Busch-Reisinger Mus., Cambridge, Mass., 1997—98; curatorial asst. Fogg Art Mus., Cambridge, 1998—2000; curator prints and photographs The Print Ctr., Phila., 2000—07. Chair exhbns. and adv. com. Art in City Hall Adv. Coun., Phila., 2002—06; guest curator Allentown (Pa.) Art Mus., 2003; mem. programming com. Philagrafika, Phila. Print Collaborative, 2004—. Author: (exhibition catalogs) IMPRINT: A Public Art Project, Taken with Time: A Camera Obscure Project. Mem.: Am. Assn. Museums, Coll. Art Assn. Office: The Print Ctr 1614 Latimer St Philadelphia PA 19103 Home Phone: 267-259-3401; Office Phone: 215-735-6090. Office Fax: 215-735-5511. Business E-Mail: jvanrhyn@printcenter.org.

VAN RIPER, PAUL PRITCHARD, political science professor; b. Laporte, Ind., July 29, 1916; s. Paul and Margaret (Pritchard) Van R.; m. Dorothy Ann Dodd Samuelson, May 11, 1964; 1 child, Michael Scott Samuelson. AB, DePauw U., 1938; PhD, U. Chgo., 1947. Instr. Northwestern U., 1947-49, asst. prof. polit. sci., 1949-51; mgmt. analyst Office Comptroller Dept. Army, 1951-52; mem. faculty Cornell U., 1952-70, prof., 1957-70; chmn. gov. bd., exec. com. Cornell Social Sci. Research Center, 1956-58; prof., head dept. polit. sci. Tex. A&M U., 1970-77, prof., 1977-81, prof. emeritus, 1981—, coordinator M.P.A. program, 1979-81, named prof. Bush Sch. Govt. and Pub. Svc., 1997—. Vis. prof. U. Chgo., 1958, Ind. U., 1961, U. Strathclyde, Scotland, 1964, U. Mich., 1965, U. Okla., 1969-97, U. Utah, 1979. Author: History of the United States Civil Service, 1958, Some Educational and Social Aspects of Fraternity Life, 1961, (with others) The American Federal Executive, 1963, Handbook of Practical Politics, 3d edit., 1967; editor and co-author: the Wilson Influence on Public Administration, 1990. Exec. com. Civil Svc. Reform Assn., NY, 1960-64, hist. adv. com. NASA, 1964-66; bd. dir. Brazos Valley Cmty. Action Agy., 1975-79, Brazos County Hist. Commn., 1976-2006; charter mem. Brazos Heritage Soc., pres. 1977-79. Maj. AUS, 1942-46; lt. col. USAR ret. Decorated Croix de Guerre (France). Mem. Am. Polit. Sci. Assn., So. Polit. Sci. Assn., S.W. Polit. Sci. Assn. (exec.com. 1975-77), Am. Soc. Pub. Adminstrn. (nat adv. com. 1957-60, Dimock award 1984, Waldo award 1990, Van Riper award created in his honor 2002), Internat. Personnel Mgmt. Assn., Rotary (pres. Bryan club 1991-92), Phi Beta Kappa, Beta Theta Pi (v.p. 1962, gen. sec. 1963-65), Pi Alpha Alpha, Pi Sigma Alpha, Phi Kappa Phi, Sigma Delta Chi. Republican. Baptist. Home: 713 E 30th St Bryan TX 77803-4789 Office: Tex A and M Univ Dept Polit Sci College Station TX 77843-4348 Office Phone: 979-845-2511.

VAN RIPER, ROBERT AUSTIN, writer, retired public relations executive; b. Mt. Vernon, NY, June 18, 1921; s. Austin Millard and Gladys Brownell Van R.; m. Barbara Jean Jacobs, Dec. 2, 1944; children: Alexandra, Tracy. BA, Oberlin Coll., 1943. Acct. exec. Edward L. Bernays Pub. Rels., NYC, 1946-50, N.W. Ayer & Son, Inc., NYC, 1950-54, acct. supr. Phila., 1954-61, v.p. NYC, 1961-67, sr. v.p., 1967-73; pub. rels. counsel Fin. Acctg. Standards Bd., Norwalk, Conn., 1973-91, ret., 1991. Author: (novels) A Really Sincere Guy, 1958, The Governor, 1970, (nonfiction) Setting Standards for Financial Reporting: FASB and the Struggle for Control of a Critical Process, 1994, A Life Divided: George Peabody, Pivotal Figure in Anglo-American Finance, Philanthropy and Diplomacy, 2000; contbr. articles to profl. jours. Bd. dir., exec. com. United Fund, Phila., 1956-61; trustee Lawrence Hosp., Westchester County, 1966-73, v.p., 1971-73. Lt. (j.g.) USN, 1943-46. Mem. Pub. Rels. Soc. Am. (pres. Phila. chpt. 1960-61), Fairfield County Pub. Rels. Assn. (bd. dir. 1987-89), Holland Soc., Bronxville Field Club (N.Y.). Presbyterian. Avocations: tennis, music. Home: 4100 N Charles St Apt 810 Baltimore MD 21218

VAN ROEKEL, DENNIS, educational association administrator; b. LeMars, Iowa; m. Julie Van Roekel; children: Brian, Chad. BA, U. Iowa; MA, No. Ariz. U. Pres. Paradise Valley Edn. Assn., Ariz. Edn. Assn.; sec., treas. NEA, Washington, DC, 1997—2002, v.p., 2002—, chair Interactive and Adv. Com. on Membership. Mem. Nat. Commn. on Math. and Sci. Tchg. for 21st Century, 1999; math tchr. Paradise Valley HS, Phoenix. Office: NEA 1201 16th St, NW Washington DC 20036-3290 Office Phone: 202-833-4000. Office Fax: 202-822-7974.

VAN SAMBEEK, JEROME WILLIAM, plant physiologist, educator; b. Milbank, SD, Aug. 1, 1947; s. Henry Lambert and Janet Marie Van Sambeek; m. Carol Marie Crandall, Dec. 30, 1972; children: Rachel Virginia, Jeffrey Crandall, Melissa Janet Van Sambeek Ambler, William Glenn, Lindsey Marie. BS, S.D. State U., 1969; PhD, Washington U., St. Louis, 1975. Postdoctoral rsch. fellow U. Mo., Columbia, 1975; rsch. plant physiologist biochemist USDA Forest Svc., So. Forest Experiment Sta., Pineville, La., 1976—79; rsch. plant physiologist USDA Forest Svc., No. Ctrl. Forest Experiment Sta., Carbondale, Ill., 1980—88, project leader, physiologist, 1989—97; rsch. plant physiologist USDA Forest Svc., No. Rsch. Sta., Columbia, Mo., 1998—. Editor: (procs.) Knowledge for the Future of Black Walnut (Black Walnut Achievement award, 1989); contbr. articles to profl. jours. and conf. procs. Recipient Gen. Motors Acad. scholarship, S.D. State U., 1966—69, Sta. Tech. Transfer award, USDA Forest Svc., North Cen. Res. Stn., 2000. Mem.: Soc. Am. Foresters, No. Nut Growers Assn., Walnut Coun. Internat. (bd. dirs. 1981—). Achievements include research in procedures for white ash micropropagation and vegetation management in hardwood plantings. Avocation: gardening. Office: USDA Forest Svc Northern Res Stn 202 Natural Resource Building UMC Columbia MO 65211-7260 Home Phone: 573-256-2424; Office Phone: 573-875-5341 233. Office Fax: 573-882-1977. E-mail: jvansambeek@fs.fed.us.

VANSANT, FRANKLIN STEVEN, mathematician, educator; s. Ruth Mary Vansant; m. Lois Kay Messick, July 10, 1985; children: Krista Leyan Wolhever, Michel Peter. BA in Edn., U. Del., Newark, 1975; MS in Human Resource Mgmt., Wilmington Coll., Del., 1991. Tchr. math. Lake Forest Sch. Dist., Felton, Del., 1976—. Mem. Shawnee Country Club, Milford, Del., 2003—06. Grantee, Lake Forest, 2006. Mem.: Del. Coun. Tchrs. Math. (bd. dirs. 2003—), Nat. Coun. Tchrs. Math, Methodist. Avocation: golf. Office: Lake Forest School District 5407 Killens Pond Rd Felton DE 19943 Home Phone: 302-422-4899; Office Phone: 302-284-9291. Business E-Mail: fsvansant@lf.k12.de.us.

VAN SAUN, BRUCE W., bank executive; married; 3 children. BS in Bus. Adminstrn., Bucknell U., 1979; MBA in Fin. and Gen. Mgmt., U. NC, 1983. Various sr. positions including corp. contr. and sr. v.p. internat. bus. devel. Kidder Peabody & Co., Inc.; COO, CFO, Wasserstein Perella Group, Inc., 1990-94; mng. dir. Deutsche Bank N.Am., 1994—97; mgmt. positions with The Bank of NY Co., Inc., NYC, 1997—99, sr. exec. v.p., CFO, 1999—2005, vice-chmn., CFO, 2005—06, vice-chmn., market-related bus., 2006—. Bd. dirs. Stride Rite Corp., Bowater Inc., 2005—. Mem. Bucknell U. Bus. Adv. Coun. Office: The Bank of NY Co Inc 1 Wall St New York NY 10286 *

VAN SCHILFGAARDE, JAN, retired agricultural engineer, federal agency administrator; b. The Hague, Netherlands, Feb. 7, 1929; came to US, 1946, naturalized, 1957; married; 3 children. BS, Iowa State Coll., 1949, MS, 1950, PhD in Agrl. Engring. and Soil Physics, 1954. Instr., assoc. agrl. engr. Iowa State Coll., 1949-54; asst. prof. agrl. engring. NC State Coll., 1954-57, assoc. prof., 1957-62, prof., 1962-64; drainage engr. Agrl. Rsch. Svc. USDA, Raleigh, NC, 1954-64, from chief water mgmt. engr. soil/water conservation rsch. divsn. to dir. Beltsville, Md., 1964—72, dir. Salinity Lab. Riverside, Calif., 1972-84, dir. Mountain States Area Agrl. Rsch. Svc. Ft. Collins, Colo., 1984-86, assoc. dir. no. plains area Agrl. Rsch. Svc., 1986-91, assoc. dep. adminstr. for natural resources Agrl. Rsch. Svc. Beltsville, Md., 1991-96, dir. Pacific West area, 1996-97; ret., 1997. Vis. prof. Ohio State U., 1962 Mem. ASCE, NAE, Am. Soc. Agrl. Engrs., Soil Sci. Soc., Soil Conservation Soc. Am. E-mail: j.-r.vanschilfgaarde@worldnet.att.net, jj_rvs@msn.com.

VAN SCHOONENBERG, ROBERT G., lawyer, consumer products company executive; b. Madison, Wis., Aug. 18, 1946; s. John W. and Ione (Henning) Schoonenberg. BA, Marquette U., 1968; MBA, U. Wis., 1972; JD, U. Mich., 1974. Bar: Calif. 1975, Fla. 1976. Atty. Gulf Oil Corp., Pitts., 1974-81; v.p., gen. counsel to sr. v.p., gen. counsel, sec. Avery Dennison Corp., Pasadena, Calif., 1981—2004, exec. v.p., gen. counsel, sec., 2004—07, exec. v.p., chief legal officer, sec., 2007—. Judge pro tem Pasadena Mcpl. Ct., 1987-89. Dir., v.p. fin. adminstrn. Am. Cancer Soc., San Gabriel Vally Unit, 1987—; v.p., treas., dir., v.p. investments Pasadena Symphony Assn.; bd. dirs. Pasadena Recreation and Parks Found., 1983-84; mem. Pasadena Citizens Task Force on Crime Control, 1983-84; dir. Boy Scouts, San Gabriel Valley Coun., dir. pub. coun.; bd. dirs. Verugo Hills Hosp. Found.; trustee Southwestern U. Sch. Law. Mem.: Am. Soc. Corp. Secs. (pres., so. Calif. chpt.), Am. Corp. Counsel Assn. (dir.), L.A. County Bar Assn. (past chmn., corp. law dept. sect.). Office: Avery Dennison Corp 150 N Orange Grove Blvd Pasadena CA 91103-3534 Office Phone: 626-304-2000. Office Fax: 626-792-7312. E-mail: rgvs@averydennison.com. *

VAN SCOTER, JOHN C., electronics executive; BS in Engring., U. Vt., 1983. Tech. sales engr. Tex. Instruments, Inc., Boston, 1983, dep. fab mgr. Miho5 wafer fabrication facility Japan, mgr. worldwide ASIC product devel. & engring., v.p., sr. v.p., gen. mgr. DLP Products, 2000—. Mem.: IEEE, Soc. Motion Pictures and TV Engrs., Consumer Electronics Assn. Office: Tex Instruments Inc PO Box 660199 Dallas TX 75266-0199 Office Phone: 972-995-2011. Office Fax: 972-995-4360. *

VANSELOW, NEAL ARTHUR, retired academic administrator, internist; b. Milw., Mar. 18, 1932; s. Arthur Frederick and Mildred (Hoffmann) Vanselow; m. Mary Ellen McKenzie, June 20, 1958; children: Julie Ann, Richard Arthur. AB, U. Mich., 1954, MD, 1958, MS, 1963. Diplomate Am. Bd. Internal Medicine, Am. Bd. Allergy and Immunology. Intern Mpls. Gen. Hosp., 1958—59; resident Univ. Hosp., Ann Arbor, Mich., 1959—63; instr. medicine U. Mich., 1963—64, asst. prof., 1964—68, assoc. prof., 1968—72, prof., chmn. dept. postgrad. medicine and health professions edn., 1972—74; dean Coll. Medicine U. Ariz., Tucson, 1974—77; chancellor med. ctr. U. Nebr., Omaha, 1977—82, v.p., 1977—82; v.p. health scis. U. Minn., 1982—89, prof. internal medicine, 1982—89; chancellor Tulane U. Med. Ctr., New Orleans, 1989—94, chancellor emeritus, 1997—; prof. internal medicine Tulane U., New Orleans, 1989—97, prof. internal medicine emeritus, 1997—. Adj. prof. health sys. mgmt. Tulane U., New Orleans, 1993—99, prof. emeritus, 1999—; chmn. Joint Bd. Osteo. and Med. Examiners Ariz., 1974—77; chmn. coun. on Grad. Med. Edn. Dept. Health and Human Svcs., 1986—91; mem. com. on educating dentists for future Inst. Medicine NAS, 1993—95, chairperson com. on future of primary care, 1994—96, co-chairperson com. on U.S. physician supply, 1995—96, scholar in residence, 1994—95, mem. com. to assess occupl. health and safety tng. needs, 1999—2000, chmn. com. on introducing social and behavioral sci. into med. sch. curriculum, 2002—04; chairperson continuing eval. panel Am. Internat. Health Alliance, 2000—01; mem. adv. com. Medschool.com, 2000—01; adj. prof. Sch. Health Adminstrn. and Policy Ariz. State U., 2000—05; mem. spl. emphasis panel NIH, 2005. Panel on interdisciplinary health prof. edn. Nat. League Nursing, 1996—97; exec. com. United Way Midlands, 1980—82, vice-chmn. 1981 campaign; mem. Commn. on Health Professions Pew Charitable Trusts, 1990—92, 1997—99, Commn. on the Future of Med. Edn. U. Calif, 1996—97; mktg. mgmt. governing coun. U. Hosp. Consortium, 1993—95; trustee Meharry Med. Coll., 1996—, chair presdl. search com., 2006; pres., chmn. bd. Am. Friends London Sch. Hygiene and Tropical Medicine, 1998—2002; com. on relationships between medicine and nursing Josiah Macy Jr. Found., 1999—2000; mem. Gov.'s Pan Am. Commn., La., 1991—92; bd. dirs. Devel. Authority for Tucson's Economy, 1975—77, Minn. High Tech. Coun., 1983—86, Minn. Coalition for Health Care Costs, 1983—87, La. Health Care Authority, 1989—90, United Way Greater New Orleans Area, 1992—97; bd. dirs., exec. com. Health Planning Coun. Midlands, Omaha, 1978—82, v.p., 1981—82. Recipient Disting. Alumnus award, U. Mich. Med. Ctr. Alumni Soc., 2007. Fellow: ACP (workgroup on physician workforce and financing med. edn. 1996), Ariz. Acad. Arts, Sci. and Tech. (bd. govs. 2005—, 2005—, founding mem.), Am. Coll. Physician Execs., Am. Acad. Allergy; mem.: Inst. Med. NAS, Soc. Med. Adminstrs., Assn. Acad. Health Ctrs. (bd. dirs. 1983—89, chmn. bd. dirs. 1988), Rio Verde (Ariz.) Cmty. Assn. (bd. dirs. 2000—04), Phi Beta Kappa, Nu Sigma Nu, Beta Theta Pi, Alpha Omega Alpha, Sigma Xi. Office: 18942 E Mountainaire Dr Rio Verde AZ 85263-7093

VAN SETERS, JOHN, retired biblical literature educator; b. Hamilton, Ont., Can., May 2, 1935; s. Hugo and Anne (Hubert) Van S.; m. Elizabeth Marie Malmberg, June 11, 1960; children: Peter John, Deborah Elizabeth. BA, U. Toronto, 1958; MA, Yale U., 1959, PhD, 1965; BD, Princeton Theol. Sem., 1962; ThD (hon.), U. Lausanne, Switzerland, 1999. Asst. prof. dept. Near Eastern studies Waterloo Luth. U., 1965-67; assoc. prof. Old Testament Andover Newton Theol. Sch., 1967-70; assoc. prof. dept. Near Eastern studies U. Toronto, 1970-76, prof., 1976-77; James A. Gray prof. Bibl. lit., dept. religion U. N.C., Chapel Hill, 1977-2000, chmn. dept. religious studies, 1980-88, 93-95, prof. emeritus, 2000—. Adj. prof. dept. religion and culture Wilfrid Laurier U., 2000—. Author: The Hyksos: A New Investigation, 1966, Abraham in History and Tradition, 1975, In Search of History, 1983, Der Jahwist als Historiker, 1987, Prologue to History, 1992, The Life of Moses, 1994, The Pentateuch, 1999, A Law Book for the Diaspora, 2003, The Edited Bible, 2006. Recipient James Henry Breasted prize Am. Hist. Assn., 1985, Book award Am. Acad. Religion, 1986, R.B.Y. Scott Book award Can. Soc. Bibl. Studies, 2004; Woodrow Wilson fellow, 1958, J.J. Obermann fellow, 1962-64; Guggenheim fellow, 1979-80; NEH fellow, 1985-86, Am. Coun. Learned Socs. fellow, 1991-92, sr. rsch. fellow Cath. U. Leuven, Belgium, 1998, Fgn. Rsch. fellow Nat. Rsch. Fund S.Africa, 2002. Mem. Soc. Bibl. Lit., Am. Schs. Oriental Rsch., Soc. Study of Egyptian Antiquities, Am. Oriental Soc., Cath. Bibl. Assn., Can. Soc. Bibl. Studies (pres. 1999-2000), Old Testament Soc. South Africa (hon.). Home: 70-139 Father David Bauer Dr Waterloo ON Canada N2L 6L1 E-mail: john.vanseters@sympatico.ca.

VAN SICE, JAMES, career military officer, academic administrator; b. Wilmington, Del. m. Clarke Hutchinson; 2 children. BS, USCG Academy, 1974; MS in Engring., Purdue Univ.; MA in Bus., Webster Coll. Commd. ensign USCG, 1974, advanced through grades to rear adm.; comdr. Coast Guard Air Station, Borinquen, PR; chief of ops. & chief of staff Eighth Coast Guard Dist., New Orleans; dep. dir. U.S. No. Command, Peterson AFB, Colo.; dir. reserve & training USCG, 2004—05; supt. USCG Academy, New London, Conn., 2005—. Decorated Def. Superior Svc medal, Meritorious Svc medal (3 awards), Coast Guard Commendation medal, Coast Guard Achievement medal, Commandant's Letter of Commendation Ribbon with disting. device. Office: US Coast Guard Academy 31 Mohegan Ave New London CT 06320-8103

VAN SICKLE, FREDERICK L., federal judge; b. 1943; m. Jane Bloomquist. BS, U. Wis., 1965; JD, U. Wash., 1968. Ptnr. Clark & Van Sickle, 1970-75; prosecuting atty. Douglas County, Waterville, Wash., 1971-75; judge State of Wash. Superior Ct., Grant and Douglas counties, 1975-79, Cheland and Douglas Counties, Wash., 1979-91, US Dist. Ct. (ea. dist.) Wash., Spokane, 1991—, chief judge, 2000—. Co-chair rural ct. com. Nat. Conf. State Trial Judges, 1987-91. 1st lt. U.S. Army, 1968-70. Mem. Am. Adjudicature Soc., Wash. State Bar Assn., Masons (pres. Badger mountain lodge 1982-83), Scottish Rite, Spokane Rotary, Shriners. Office: US Dist Cts US Courthouse 920 W Riverside Ave Rm 840 PO Box 2209 Spokane WA 99201

VANSKA, OSMO, music director; m. Pirkko Vanska. D (hon.), U. Glasgow. Prin. chair Turku Philharm., 1971—76; co-prin. chair Helsinki Philharm., 1977—82; music dir. Lahti Symphony Orch., 1988—96; chief condr. BBC Scottish Symphony Orch. of Glasgow, 1996—2002; music dir. Minn. Orch., 2002—. Guest condr. Boston Symphony Orch., 2002. Condr. numerous recordings with the Lahti Symphony Orch. (Gramophone award, 1996, Cannes Classical award, 2002), (recording) The Tempest (1993 Prix Academie Charles Cros.). Nominee Grammy award for Best Orchestral Performance for a recording with the BBC Scottish Symphony; named Conductor of Yr., Musical Am. Internat. Dir. Performing Arts, 2005; recipient First prize, Besancon Internat. Young Conductor's Competition, Royal Philharm. Soc. award, 2002. Achievements include led Lahti Ensemble on US tour, includign performance at Avery Fisher Hall, NYC. Avocations: sports, motorcycling. Office: Minnesota Orchestra Orchestra Hall 1111 Nicollet mall Minneapolis MN 55403 *

VAN SLAMBROUCK, JOHN G., lawyer; b. Toledo, Sept. 27, 1955; BA summa cum laude in Polit. Sci., Western Mich. U., 1977; JD cum laude, Thomas M. Cooley Law Sch., 1981. Bar: Mich. 1981, US Dist. Ct. (we. dist. Mich.) 1981, US Dist. Ct. (ea. dist. Mich.) 1983. Legis. aide Mich. Ho. Reps., 1978—79; law clk. State of Mich., 1979—81, asst. atty. gen., 1981—85; pvt. practice atty. The Navigators, Inc., 1985—93; shareholder Ford, Krikard, Domeny & Byrne, P.C., 1994; sr. atty. Miller, Canfield, Paddock & Stone, PLC, Kalamazoo, 1994—97, prin., 1998—, dep. leader personal svcs. grp., 2004—. Bd. dirs. Western Mich. U., 2002—. Named one of Top 100 Attys., Worth mag., 2005. Mem.: West Mich. Estate Planning Coun., Western Mich. Planned Giving Grp., Nat. Acad. Elder Law Attys., State Bar Mich. (mem. probate and estate planning sect. 1991—), ABA (real property, probate and trust law sect.), Kalamazoo County Bar Assn. (chmn. probate practice com., chmn. profl. responsibility com.).

Office: Miller Canfield Paddock & Stone PLLC 444 W Michigan Ave Kalamazoo MI 49007-3751 Office Phone: 269-383-5829. Office Fax: 269-382-0244. E-mail: vanslambrouck@millercanfield.com.

VAN SLOOTEN, RONALD HENRY JOSEPH, dentist; b. Paterson, NJ, July 12, 1937; s. Henry and Edythe (De Marco) Van S.; m. Joyce Elenor Mandel, 1962 (div. 1969); children: Ronald Henry Jr., Timothy Jay, Lauren; m. Barbara Rose Durante, July 1, 1979; children: Jonathan Henry, Brian Joseph. DDS, Fairleigh Dickinson U., Teaneck, NJ, 1962. Dentist pvt. practice, Paterson, 1965-76, Ridgewood, NJ, 1969-78, Ho Ho Kus, NJ, 1978—; staff mem. Bainert Meml. Hosp., Paterson, 1966-75, Ridgewood Valley Hosp., 1975—2004; assoc. prof. Fairleigh Dickinson Dental Sch., Hackensack, NJ, 1973-90; pres. Van Slooten Harbour Marina Inc., Port Henry, NY, 1989—. Cons. NJ Mfrs. Ins. Co., Trenton, 1966-2003. Pres. Fairleigh Dickinson Sch. Dentistry Alumni Assn., 1976-77. Lt. comdr. USN, 1962-65. Fellow Acad. Gen. Dentistry, Acad. Dentistry Internat.; mem. ADA, Internat. Dental Health Found., NJ Dental Soc., Bergen County Dental Soc. (chmn. Nat. Dental Health Week citation 1970), Moriah C. of C., Ho-Ho-Kus C. of C. Republican. Roman Catholic. Avocations: racquetball, fishing, boating. Office: Ho Ho Kus Profl Bldg 110 Warren Ave Ho Ho Kus NJ 07423-1561 Office Phone: 201-447-1116.

VAN SLYKE, ROSEMARY, tax specialist; b. Albany, NY, June 23, 1939; d. William and Edna Elizabeth (Lawler) Van Slyke; children: Rosemary Van Vorse, Christopher Van Vorse, Elizabeth Hudson. Assoc. Bus. Adminstrn., Albany Bus. Coll., NY, 1969; cert. med. asst., Mildred Elley Coll., Colonie, NY, 1993. With NY Staet Dept. Labor, Albany, 1969—96, Albany County Mental Health, Albany, 1997—2001, NY State Tax Dept., Albany, 2002—04, GE Corp. Tax, Albany, 2005—. Mem.: ACLU, NOW, CSEA (sec. 1981—88). Democrat. Roman Catholic. Avocations: exercise, reading, internet. Home: 2 Oceanspray Blvd Clifton Park NY 12065

VAN STEENWYK, JOHN JOSEPH, healthcare plan consultant; b. Mpls., July 25, 1931; s. Elmer Arnold and Marion Ione (Thompson) van S.; m. Janice Kevin Sharp, July 11, 1959; children: Jennifer Lee, Edward Arnold, Julie Anne AB, Oberlin Coll., 1953; MBA, U. Pa., 1955. V.p., cons. The Segal Co., NYC, 1957—81; pres. Health Econs., Inc., Spring House, Pa., 1982—. Clin. asst. prof. cmty. and preventive medicine N.Y. Med. Coll., Valhalla, NY, 1980—2002. With USN, 1955-57. Sr. scholar, Dept. Health Policy, Jefferson U., 2005—. Mem.: APHA, Am. Health Ins. Plans, Acad. Health (formerly Assn. Health Svs. Rsch.). Episcopalian. Avocation: gardening. Home: 921 Tennis Ave Ambler PA 19002-2312 Office: Health Economics Inc 768 N Bethlehem Pike PO Box 710 Spring House PA 19477 Office Phone: 215-628-3838.

VANSTONE, CATHERINE, library and information scientist; d. Dan and Mary Lou Ponder; m. Daaron Vanstone. BA in History and Art Hist. cum laude, Agnes Scott Coll., Ga., 2003; MLS, Ind. U., 2005. Asst. dir. tech., tng. and develop. Southwest Ga. Regional Libr., Bainbridge, Ga. Named one of the Movers & Shakers, Libr. Jour., 2007. Mem.: Beta Phi Mu. Office: Southwest Ga Regional Lirary 301 South Monroe St Bainbridge GA 39819

VAN STONE, WILLIAM WEBB, psychiatrist; b. Denver, Mar. 14, 1929; s. Wilfred Douglas and Cora Coleman (Kampf) Van S.; m. Joan Kay Kinnear, Nov. 27, 1958 (dec. Dec. 2004); children: Lisa Kay, Kathryn Louise, David William. BA, Swarthmore Coll., 1951; MD, Cornell U., 1955. Intern Mary Hitchcock Meml. Hosp., Hanover, N.H., 1955-56; resident Menninger Sch. Psychiatry, Topeka, 1958-61; unit chief Topeka VA Hosp., 1963-67; asst. chief of staff Palo Alto (Calif.) VA Med. Ctr., 1967-89, chief treatment svcs., 1989-2000; assoc. chief for psychiatry VA Central Office, Washington, 2001—. Clin. assoc. prof. psychiatry emeritus Stanford (Calif.) U. Med. Sch., 1968—; mem. faculty Menninger Sch. Psychiatry, 1963-67. Contbr. 30 articles to profl. jours., chpts. to books. Chmn. bd. Miramonte Mental Health Assn., Palo Alto, 1976; pres. No. Calif. Psychiat. Soc., San Francisco, 1986-87, bd. dirs. Cmty. Sch. Music and Arts, Mountain View, Calif., 1969-75, Parents Family and Friends of Lesbians and Gays, 1996-2003. Capt. USNR, 1956-79. Postdoctoral fellow C.F. Menninger Meml. Hosp., 1961-63. Fellow Am. Psychiat. Assn. (disting. life); mem. Washington Psychiat. Assn. E-mail: wvsdc@aol.com.

VAN SUSTEREN, GRETA CONWAY, newscaster, lawyer; b. Appleton, Wis., June 11, 1954; d. Urban Peter and Margery (Conway) Van Susteren; m. John Purcell Coale, Oct. 12, 1987. BA in Econs (with distinction), U. Wis., 1976; JD, Georgetown U., 1979, LLM, 1982; LLD (hon.), Stetson Law Sch. Bar: D.C. 1979, U.S. Supreme Ct. 1982, Md. 1985, Wis. 1987, U.S. Ct. Appeals (D.C., 2d and 4th cirs.). Ptnr. Milliken, VanSusteren & Canan, Washington, 1982—; with CNN, 1991—2002, host The Point with Greta Van Susteren, co-host Burden of Proof, legal cons. The World Today; host On the Record With Greta Van Susteren Fox News Channel, 2002—. Adj. prof. Georgetown Law Ctr., Washington, 1984—99; lectr., panelist Jud. Conf., Washington, 1986. Co-author: My Turn at the Bullypulpit: Straight Talk About the Things That Drive Me Nuts. Bd. dirs. Stuart Stiller Found., Washington, 1982—. Named one of 100 Most Powerful Women, Forbes; recipient Sandra Day O'Conner Medal of Honor, Seton Hall Univ., 2000—01, 1st Place, "Attack on America", Nat. Headliners award, 2002; Stiller fellow, Georgetown Law Ctr., 1980. Mem.: ATLA (lectr. conf. 1986—), ABA (Presdl. award for Excellence in Journalism 2001), D.C. Bar Assn. Office: FOX News Channel 1211 Avenue of the Americas New York NY 10036

VAN TASSEL, JAMES HENRY, retired electronics executive; b. LaCrosse, Wis., Feb. 15, 1929; s. John Henry and Agnes Cecilia (Anderson) Van T.; m. Mary Louise Carman, Dec. 23, 1961; children: John Peter, James George. BS, U. Wis.-LaCrosse, 1951; MS, Tex. Tech. Coll., 1957, PhD, 1959. Postdoctoral fellow Princeton U., NJ, 1959-60; mem. tech. staff, mgr. Tex. Instruments Co., Dallas, 1960-80; v.p. microelectronics div. NCR Corp., Dayton, Ohio, 1980-91; ret., 1991. Cons. in field; mem. adv. group on electron devices DOD, 1992-97. Contbr. articles to profl. jours.; patentee in field; co-inventor of hand-held caculator Bd. dirs. Dayton Philharm. Orch., 1983-89, Miamisburg (Ohio) Mound Cmty. Improvement Corp., 1993—. Recipient Florilege d'Or Am Ecia, Paris, 1976, Disting. Alumnus award U. Wis.-LaCrosse, 1979, Holley medal ASME, 1989. Episcopalian.

VAN TASSEL, LOWELL THOMAS, mathematics professor; b. Mpls., Jan. 31, 1932; s. Evan Thomas Van Tassel and Sophia Anna Huebner; m. Diane Laura Diedrich, June 14, 1953; children: Thomas, Laurie, Karin. BS, U. Minn., 1952, MA, 1962. Cert. secondary tchr. Calif. Rsch. asst. U. Minn., Mpls., 1954-56; math. tchr. San Diego Unified Sch. Dist., 1956-65; prof. math. San Diego C.C. Dist., 1965-92, prof. emeritus of math., 1992—. Dept. chmn. math. dept. San Diego City Coll., 1971-72, 74-75; math/physics instr. Naval Tgn. Ctr., San Diego, 1962-66; proctor profl. engring. exams State of Calif. License Bd., Sacramento, 1957-65. Contbr. articles to profl. jours. V.p. Am. Fedn. of Tchrs., San Diego, 1971-72; faculty advisor Ind. Dems. for Action San Diego City Coll., 1967-71; mem. Clairemont Dem. Club, San Diego, 1966-76; juror, criminal trial Superior Ct., San Diego, 1990; elder Holy Cross Luth. Ch., San Diego, 1972-74, 92-94. With USMC, 1951-54; USMCR, 1954-71, maj., 1966-71. Mem. Math. Assn. Am., Calif. Retired Tchrs. Assn., Marine Corps Mus., U. Minn. Alumni Assn. (life.), Nat. Coun. of Tchrs. of Math., Am. Fedn. of Tchrs. (retiree mem.), Phi Delta Kappa, Psi Chi. Lutheran. Avocations: travel, reading, word puzzles, games, bridge. Home: 5550 Lodi St San Diego CA 92117-1138 Personal E-mail: lowellv@webtv.net.

VAN TASSEL, MICHAEL L., music educator; b. Grand Forks, ND, Jan. 31, 1962; MusB, U. Mich., 1985, MusM, 1986. Cert. tchr. State of Mich. Dir. of bands and coord. of instrumental music Van Buren Pub. Schs., Belleville, Mich., chair dept. music and tchr. mentor. Named Dist. 12 Tchr. of Yr., mich. Sch. Band and orch. Assn., 2005; recipient Citation of Excellence, Nat. Band Assn., 1999, 2002, Exemplary Svc. award, Van Buren Pub. Schs., 1992, Golden Apple award, Wayne County RESA, 1992. Mem.: Music Educators Nat. Conf., Mich. Sch. Band and Orch. Assn. (v.p., dist. 12 1991—94), Pi Kappa Lambda (life). Home: 2709 Lillian Ann Arbor MI 48104 Office: Belleville High School 501 West Columbia Belleville MI 48111 Home Phone: 734-677-6668; Office Phone: 734-697-9133. Personal E-mail: mvantass@vanburenschools.net.

VAN TASSEL-BASKA, JOYCE LENORE, education educator; b. Toledo, July 28, 1944; d. Robert Rae and Eleanor Jane (Kenyon) Sloan; m. Thomas Harold Van Tassel, May 21, 1964 (div. 1975); m. Leland Karl Baska, July 25, 1980; 1 child, Ariel Sloan. BEd cum laude, U. Toledo, 1966, MA, MEd, 1969, EdD, 1981. Tchr. Toledo Pub. Schs., 1965-72, coord. gifted programs, 1973-76; dir. Ill. gifted program Ill. State Bd. Edn., Springfield, 1976-79; dir., area svc. ctr. Matteson (Ill.) Sch. Dist., 1979-82; dir. Ctr. for Talent Devel. Northwestern U., Evanston, Ill., 1982-87; Smith prof. edn. Coll. William and Mary, Williamsburg, Va., 1987—, dir. Ctr. for Gifted Edn., 1988—2002, exec. dir. Ctr. for Gifted Edn., 2002—. Mem. Va. Adv. Bd. on Gifted and Talented, 1988-2000; mem. State Ohio Adv. Bd. Gifted and Talented, 1975-76; mem. edn. coun. Nat. Bus. Consortium, 1981-84. Mem. editorial bd. Roeper Rev., 1980-82; pub. Talent Devel. Quar., 1983-87; manuscript rev. editor Jour. Edn. of Gifted, 1981—; mem. editorial adv. bd. Critical Issues in Gifted Edn. series; mem. editorial bd. Gifted Child Quar., 1984-97, Jour. Advanced Devel.; column editor Understanding the Gifted Newsletter, 1984-90: editor Gifted and Talented Internat., 1997—; book review ed., Gifted Child Quarterly, author 16 books; contbr. chpts. and over 300 articles to profl. jours. Bd. trustees Lourdes High Sch., Chgo., 1985-86. Recipient Outstanding Faculty award State Coun. Higher Edn. Va., 1993, 97; grantee U.S. Office Edn., 1977-78, 78-79, Ill. State Bd. Edn., 1979-82, 84-91, Richardson Found., 1986, 89, Fry Found., 1987-90, Va. State Coun. Higher Edn., 1987-89, 90-91, 93-95, Bur. Indian Affairs, 1989, Hughes Found., 1989-94, Va. State Libr., 1989-90, Va. State Dept. Edn., 1990-93, 93-95, Funding Agy. U.S. Dept. Edn., 1989, 90-93, 93-95, 96-99, 2000-02, 02—, 04—; eminent scholar Coll. William and Mary, 1987—, Nat. Ednl. policy fellow U.S. Office Edn., 1979-80, Paul Witty fellow in gifted edn., 1979, Outstanding Rsch. Paper award Mensa, 1995, Phi Beta Kappa Fac. Awd., 1995. Mem. ASCD, Nat. Assn. Gifted Children (bd. dirs. 1984-90, Disting. Scholar award 1997), Coun. Exceptional Children, Assn. for Gifted (pres. 1980-81), World Coun. on Gifted, Am. Ednl. Rsch. Assn., Phi Beta Kappa, Phi Delta Kappa (pres. Northwestern chpt. 1986-87). Avocations: photography, tennis, writing. Home: 128 Harvest Cir Williamsburg VA 23185-3183 Office: Coll William and Mary Jones Hall Williamsburg VA 23185 Business E-Mail: jlvant@wm.edu.

VAN TATENHOVE, GREGORY F., federal judge, former prosecutor; JD, U. Ky. Aide to Senator Mitch McConnell US Senate, Ky.; law clerk US Dist. Ct., Ky.; trial atty. US Dept. Justice, DC, U.S. atty. (ea. dist.) Ky, 2001—06; chief of staff, legal counsel to Congressman Ron Lewis US Congress; judge US District Ct. (ea. dist.) Ky, 2006—. Office: US Dist Ct 110 Main St Ste 210 -H Pikeville KY 41501

VAN TINE, KIRK KELSO, lawyer, former federal agency administrator; b. Syracuse, NY, Aug. 30, 1948; s. George Kelso and Hariot (Van Alst) V.; m. Barbara Ann Byers, Aug. 14, 1971; children: Lindsay, Meredith. BS in Fgn. Affairs, U.S. Naval Acad., 1970; JD, U. Va., 1978. Bar: D.C. 1978, U.S. Ct. Appeals (D.C. crct.) 1979, U.S. Ct. Appeals (5th crct.) 1980, U.S. Ct. Appeals (8th crct.) 1992, U.S. Ct. Appeals (9th crct.) 1992, U.S. Ct. Appeals (10th crct.) 1993, U.S. Supreme Ct., 1982, U.S. Dist. Ct. D.C. 1979. Commd. ensign USN, 1970, advanced through grades to lt., 1974, resigned, 1975; assoc. Baker & Botts LLP, Washington, 1978-86, ptnr., 1986—2001, sr. ptnr., 2005—; gen. counsel U.S. Dept. Transp., Washington, 2001—03, acting dep. sec., 2003—04, dep. sec., 2004. Mem.: Order of the Coif, DC Bar Assn. (former co-chair litig. and law practice mgmt. sect., chair election bd.). Office: Baker Botts LLP 1299 Pennsylvania Ave NW Washington DC 20004 Office Phone: 202-639-7741.

VAN TINE, MATTHEW ERIC, lawyer; b. Tomahawk, Wis., June 21, 1958; s. Kenneth G. and Louise Van T.; m. Rena Marie David, Apr. 30, 1988; 1 child, Kristen. AB cum laude, Harvard Coll., 1980; JD magna cum laude, Boston U., 1983. Bar: Ill. 1983, Mass. 1983, U.S. Dist. Ct. Mass. 1984, U.S. Dist. Ct. (no. dist.) Ill. 1986, Seventh Cir., 2001, U.S. Supreme Ct. 2005. Law clk. to Hon. Raymond J. Pettine U.S. Dist. Ct. R.I., Providence, 1983-84; assoc. Palmer & Dodge, Boston, 1984-85, Schiff, Hardin & Waite, Chgo., 1985-88; asst. corp. counsel City of Chgo., 1988-92; assoc. to ptnr. Saunders & Monroe, Chgo., 1993-99; of counsel Miller Faucher and Cafferty, Chgo., 2000—06; with Miller Law LLC, Chgo., 2007—. Exec. editor: Boston University Law Rev., 1982-83. Mem. ABA, Chgo. Bar Assn., Inns of Ct. (pres. Abraham Lincoln Marovitz Inn of Ct. 2004-06). Office: Miller Law LLC 101 N Wacker Dr Ste 2010 Chicago IL 60606 Business E-Mail: mvantine@millerlawllc.com.

VAN TREECK, JENNIFER LYNN, music educator; b. Milw., Feb. 18, 1981; d. Joseph Robert and Sandra Marie Van Treek. BA in Instrumental Music Edn., Cardinal Stritch U., Milw., 2003. Cert. pre-K-12 music tchr. Wis., 2003. Woodwind specialist, instr. Brass Bell Music Store, Glendale, Wis., 1999—, lesson dir. Milw., 2001—03; band dir. CYO Band, Racine, Kenosha, Wis., 2003—04; spl. edn. paraprofl. Lake Shore Mid. Sch., Mequon, Wis., 2004—05; band dir. St. Monica Sch., Whitefish Bay, Wis., 2005—, Holy Angels Sch., West Bend, Wis., 2005—, St. Frances Cabrini Sch., West Bend, 2005—. Founder La Berceuse Quartet, Milw., 2005—. Author: (book) Scale Syllabus, 2005. Mem.: Milw. Local 8 Musician's Union, Nat. Cath. Band Assn., Music Educators Nat. Conf. Democrat. Avocations: cooking, photography. Office: Holy Angels Sch Star Band 230 N 8th Ave West Bend WI 53095

VAN TYNE, ARTHUR MORRIS, geologist; b. Syracuse, NY, Aug. 12, 1925; s. Roy Hanford and Isabelle Marguerite (Hoag) Van T.; m. Patricia Wilson Boyd, July 13, 1946; children: Judith, Cynthia, Mark, Peter. AB, Syracuse U., 1951, MS, 1958. Cert. petroleum geologist; lic. geologist, Pa., 1994. Field asst. Syracuse U. Rsch. Inst., 1951-53; geologist Shell Oil Co., Rockies, Gulf Coast, 1953-57; sr. geologist-in-charge NY State Geol. Survey-Oil and Gas Rsch. Office, Wellsville and Alfred, NY, 1958-81; geol. cons. Van Tyne Cons., Wellsville, NY, 1981—. Gov. appointee mem. NY State Oil, Gas, and Solution Mining Adv. Bd., 1996. Contbr. articles to profl. jours. Dep. mayor Village of Wellsville, 1992—2004; mem. Allegany County Econ. Devel. Com.; committeeman Rep. Party, 1962—77, 1998—2000; bd. dir. Jones Meml. Hosp., Wellsville, 1973—2001, bd. chmn., 1986—95; bd. dir. Wellsville United Way, 1968—80, pres., 1974—75; bd. mem. Drake Well Found. Recipient Cert. of Appreciation Am. Petroleum Inst., 1975, 80, Award of Merit Internat. Oil Scouts Assn. and Appalachian Sect., 1961, 66, 88. Mem.: Syracuse U. Geol. Devel. Coun., Geol. Soc. Am., No. Appalachian Geol. Soc. (pres. 1966—68), Ind. Oil and gas Assn. NY (pres. 1985—88), N.Y. State Oil Prodrs. Assn. (exec. com. 1980—, dir., Svc. award 1981, Oilman of Yr. award 2001), Russian Assn. Oil and Gas Geologists, Am. Assn. Petroleum Geologists (sec., dir. 1989—91, nat. and ea. sect. hon. mem., Nat. and Ea. Disting. Svc. award 1987, 1994, John T. Galey Meml. award ea. sect. 1997, Ho. of Dels. long svc. award 2001), N.Y. Acad. Sci., Rotary (pres. Wellsville 1979—80, Paul Harris fellow). Achievements include discovery of gas production from Queenston formation in NY; Bass Islands thrust structure, a major oil and gas producer in N.Y. and Pa.; contributed for N.Y. State to Appalachian Gas Atlas. Home: 24 Oak St Wellsville NY 14895-1026 Office: Van Tyne Cons PO Box 326 159 1/2 N Main St Wellsville NY 14895-0326 Home Phone: 585-593-4352; Office Phone: 585-593-6650. Personal E-mail: avantyne@yahoo.com.

VAN UMMERSEN, CLAIRE A., academic administrator, biologist, educator; b. Chelsea, Mass., July 28, 1935; d. George and Catherine (Courtovich) m. Frank Van Ummersen, June 7, 1958; children: Lynn, Scott. BS, Tufts U., 1957, MS, 1960, PhD, 1963; DSc (hon.), U. Mass., 1988, U. Maine, 1991; LHD (hon.), U. New Eng., 2005. Rsch. asst. Tufts U., 1957-60, 60-67, grad. asst. in embryology, 1962, postdoctoral tchg. asst., 1963-66, lectr. in biology, 1967-68; asst. prof. biology U. Mass., Boston, 1968-74, assoc. prof., 1974—86, assoc. dean acad. affairs, 1975-76, assoc. vice chancellor acad. affairs, 1976-78, chancellor, 1978-79, dir. Environ. Sci. Ctr., 1980-82; assoc. vice chancellor acad. affairs Mass. Bd. Regents for Higher Edn., 1982-85, vice chancellor for mgmt. systems and telecom., 1985-86; chancellor Univ. System NH, Durham, 1986-92; sr. fellow New Eng. Bd. Higher Edn., 1992-93; sr. fellow New Eng. Resource Ctr. Higher Edn. U. Mass., 1992-93; pres. Cleve. State U., 1993—2001, pres. emerita, 2001—; v.p., dir. Office of Women Am. Coun. Edn., Wash., DC, 2001—05, v.p. Ctr. for Effective Leadership, 2005—. Cons. Mass. Bd. Regents, 1981-82, AGB, 1992—, Kuwait U., 1992-93; asst. Lancaster Course in Ophthalmology, Mass. Eye. and Ear Infirmary, 1962-69, lectr., 1970-93, also coord.; reviewer HEW; mem. rsch. team which established safety stds. for exposure to microwave radiation, 1958-65; participant Leadership Am. program, 1992-93; bd. dirs. Nat. Coun. Sci. Environment, 1998—, mem. subcom. for future and fin. Active NH Ct. Systems Rev. Task Force, 1989-90, Leadership Cleve. Class '95, Ohio Gov.'s Coun. on Sci. and Tech., 1996-98, Strategy Coun. Cleve. Pub. Schs., 1996-98, Cleve. Sports Commn., 1999-2001, Cleve. Mcpl. Sch. Dist. Bd., 1999-2001; New Eng. Bd. Higher Edn., 1986-92, exec. com., 1989-92, NH adv. coun., 1990-92; chair Rhodes Scholarship Selection Com., 1986-91; bd. dirs. NH Bus. and Industry Assn., 1987-93; governing bd. NH Math. Coalition, 1991-92; exec. com. 21st Century Learning Cmty., 1992-93; state panelist NH Women in Higher Edn., 1986-93; bd. dirs. Urban League Greater Cleve., 1993-2001, strategic planning com., chair edn. com., 1996-99, sec., exec. com., 1997-99; bd. dirs. Great Lakes Sci. and Tech. Ctr., 1993-2001, edn. com., 1995-2001; bd. dirs. Greater Cleve. Growth Assn., 1994-2001, Civic Vision 2000 and Beyond, Cleve., 1997-98; bd. dirs., exec. com. Sci. and Tech. Coun. Cleve. Tomorrow, 1998-99; rep. NE Ohio Tech. Coalition, 1999-2001; trustee Ohio Aerospace Inst., 1993-2001, exec. com., 1996-2001; strategic planning com. United Way, 1996-2000, chair environ. scan subcom. 1996-2001; leadership devel. com. ACE, 1995-98, women's commn., 1999-2001; bd. dirs. United Way, 1995-2001; co-chair Pub. Sector Campaign, 1997-98; bd. dirs. NCAA, divsn. 1, exec. com., 1999-2001; mem. AGB Ctr. for Pub. Higher Edn. Trusteeship and Goverance, 2001-03, Assn. Liaison Officers Adv. Com., 1998-2001. Recipient Disting. Svc. medal U. Mass., 1979, Woman of the Yr. Achievement award YWCA, 1998; Am. Cancer Soc. grantee Tufts U., 1960. Mem. Am. Coun. on Edn. (com. on self-regulation 1987-91), Nat. Conf. Cmty. and Justice (program com. 1996-2001), Nat. Coun. for Sci. and the Environment (bd. dirs. 1999-, fin. and futures coms.), State Higher Edn. Exec. Officers (fed. rels. com., 1986-92, cost accountability task force, exec. com. 1990-92), ACE (com. leadership devel.), Nat. Assn. Sys. Heads (exec. com. 1990-92), Nat. Ctr. for Edn. Stats. (network adv. com. 1989-92), New Eng. Assn. Schs. and Colls. (commn. on higher edn. 1990-93), North Ctrl. Assn. Schs. and Colls. (evaluator 1993-2001, chair accreditation teams 1986-90), Greater Cleve. Round Table (bd. dirs. 1993-2001, exec. com. 1995-2001), Cleve. Playhouse (trustee 1994-2001), Nat. Assn. State Univs. and Land Grant Colls. (exec. com. on urban agenda, mem. commn. tech. transfer), Am. Assn. State Colls. and Univs. (state rep. 1994-96, commn. on urban agenda 1996-2001, bd. dirs. 1996-99, mem. emerging issues task force 1996-98), Phi Beta Kappa, Sigma Xi. Office: American Coun on Edn One DuPont Cir NW Washington DC 20036-1193 Home Phone: 202-965-3072; Office Phone: 202-939-9376. Business E-Mail: claire_van_ummersen@ace.nche.edu.

VAN VALER, JOE NED, lawyer, real estate developer; b. Gas City, Ind., Mar. 13, 1935; s. Richard Carl and Wilma Amy (Kelly) Van V.; m. Constance Joy Richardson, June 25, 1960; children: Kimberly Joy, Kelli June, Lynn Louise, Joseph Jeffrey. AB, Franklin Coll., 1959; LLB, Ind. U., 1963. Bar: Ind. 1963, U.S. Dist. Ct. (so. dist.) Ind. 1963. Assoc. Van Valer Law Firm and predecessor firms, 1963-65, ptnr., 1965-75, sr. ptnr., 1975—. Pres. Home Owners Warranty Corp. of Central Ind., Indpls., 1984-91, chmn. bd. dirs. 1991-95; cons. bd. Nat. City Bank Greenwood; chmn. adv. group Home Owners Warranty Corp., Washington, 1988-90, 92-94 also bd. dirs.; pros. atty. 8th Jud. Dist., Franklin, Ind., 1967-74; chmn. Johnson County, Ind., Contractors' Listing Bd.; chmn. bd. Bldg. Industry Svc. Corp., 1995-2000. With AUS, 1957-58. Recipient Alumnus Citation award Franklin Coll., 1996. Mem. ABA, Indpls. Bar Assn., 8th Jud. Cir. Bar Assn., Nat. Assn. Home Builders (bd. dirs.), Ind. Home Builders Assn. (pres. 1981), Builders Assn. Greater Indpls. (dir., pres. 1981, parliamentarian emeritus 2007), Indpls. Soc. Republican. Methodist. Office: 299 W Main St Greenwood IN 46142-3129 Office Phone: 317-881-7575. Business E-Mail: joe@vanvalerlaw.com.

VAN VALKENBURG, EDGAR WALTER, lawyer; b. Seattle, Jan. 8, 1953; s. Edgar Walter and Margaret Catherine (McKenna) Van V.; m. Turid L. Owren, Sept. 29, 1990; children: Ingrid Catherine, Andrew Owren. BA, U. Wash., 1975; JD summa cum laude, Willamette Coll. of Law, 1978; LLM, Columbia U., 1984. Bar: Oreg. 1978, U.S. Dist. Ct. Oreg. 1979, U.S. Ct. Appeals (9th cir.) 1980. Law clk. to assoc. justice Oreg. Supreme Ct., Salem, 1978-79; assoc. Stoel, Rives, Boley, Fraser & Wyse, Portland, Oreg., 1979-82, 84-86; ptnr. Stoel Rives LLP, Portland, Oreg., 1986—; instr. Columbia U., NYC, 1982-84. Bd. dirs. Oreg. Sports Authority; chair Oreg. Econ. and Cmty. Devel. Commn., 2003—. Editor-in-chief: Willamette Law Jour. 1977-78. Bd. dirs., chmn. Multnomah County Legal Aid, 1997-98; bd. dirs. Portland Ctr. Stage, 2004—. Mem. ACLU (pres. Oreg. chpt. 1991-93), Oreg. State Bar (chmn. antitrust sect. 1989-90, mem. Ho. of Dels. 1996-98). Office: Stoel Rives LLP 900 SW 5th Ave Ste 2300 Portland OR 97204-1229 E-mail: wvanvalkenburg@stoel.com.

VAN VALKENBURGH, HOLLY VIOLA, librarian, consultant; b. NYC, Nov. 22, 1936; d. Horace Bulle III and Viola (Gerfe) Van V.; children: Leland V. Lammert, Jeni L. Muniz, Gary F. Ohm. BA, U. Colo., 1957; MA, U. Denver, 1965; MEd, Lesley Coll., Cambridge, Mass., 1988. Elem. sch. tchr., Tenn., 1958-60, Colo., 1961-62; sch. librarian Colo., 1962-66, Wyo., 1984-88; coll. librarian Sheridan (Wyo.) Coll., 1966-74, Morrison Coll., Reno, Nev., 1989-92; owner, operator Nanny Placement Agy., Reno, 1991-96, Word Pro, Carson City, Nev., 1996—. Cons. Nev. State Libr., Carson City, 1993—; adminstr. weatherization assistance project Dept. of Energy, Sheridan, 1975-84. Bd. dirs. Grassroots Lobby, Carson City, 1995-99; chmn. Nev. Women's History Project, Reno, 2000-02, treas., 2004—, Letters from Nev. Daughters., 2000—; treas., mem. Sheridan County Recreation Bd., 1972-78. Josephine Halverson Morris scholar U. Denver, 1965. Mem.: AAUW (pres. local chpts. 1972—73, 1996—98, newsletter editor), Nev. Libr. Assn. (newsletter editor 1997—2002, pres. 2003), Red Hat Soc., Nat. Assn. Van Valkenburgh Family (newsletter editor 1991—, bd. dirs. 1998—2004). Avocations: white water rafting, reading.

VAN VLEET, WILLIAM BENJAMIN, lawyer, retired insurance company executive; b. Milw., Dec. 4, 1924; s. William Benjamin and Irene (Peppey) Van V.; m. Marilyn Nilles, Dec. 26, 1946; children: Terese Van Vleet Svetich, Susan Van Vleet Waldo, William Benjamin III, Monica Van Vleet McCarthy, Mark. Student, Marquette U., 1942-43, Lawrence Coll.,

Appleton, Wis., 1943-44; LLB, JD, Marquette U., 1948. Bar: Wis. 1948, Ill. 1950. Gen. counsel George Rogers Clark Mut. Casualty Co., Rockford, Ill., 1948-59, Pioneer Life Ins. Co. Ill., Rockford, 1950-68, 81-94, v.p., 1959-91, gen. counsel, 1968-91, exec. v.p., 1981-95, also bd. dirs.; exec. v.p., gen. counsel Pioneer Fin. Svcs., Inc., Rockford, 1985-95, gen. counsel emeritus, dir., 1995-97; pres. Nat. Group Life Ins. Co., Rockford, 1992-93, exec. v.p., gen. counsel, 1993-94, also bd. dirs. Pres. Western Life Ins. Co. Am., Rockford, 1981-82, Health & Life Ins. Co. Am., Rockford, 1984-92, exec. v.p., gen. counsel, 1993-94; pres. Manhattan Nat. Life Ins. Co., Cin., 1990-92, exec. v.p., gen. counsel, 1993-94, also bd. dirs.; exec. v.p., gen. counsel Continental Life and Accident Co., Boise, Idano, 1993-94, also bd. dirs.; bd. dirs. Nat. Health Svcs. Milw. Mem. adminstrn. Boylan Ctrl. Cath. H.S., Rockford, 1965-72; pres. Diocesan Bd. Edn., Rockford, 1970-78; v.p., pres. Nat. Assn. Bds. Edn., 1972-78; mem. bd. advisors Marion Coll., 1976-79; mem. adv. bd. St. Anthony's Hosp., Rockford, 1978-91; bd. dirs. Crimestoppers, Rockford, 1982-90; co-chmn. United Cerebral Palsy Telethon, Rockford, 1985-95. Mem. Ill. Bar Assn., Winnebago County Bar Assn.

VAN VLIET, CAROLYN MARINA, physicist, researcher; b. Dordrecht, Netherlands, Dec. 27, 1929; arrived in U.S., 1960, naturalized, 1967; d. Marinus and Jacoba (de Lange) Van V.; m. A.J. Cappon, Dec. 29, 1953 (div. 1983); children: Elsa Marianne, Mark Edward, Cynthia Joyce, Renata Annette Carolina. BS, Free U. Amsterdam, Netherlands, 1949, MA, 1953, PhD in Physics, 1956. Rsch. fellow Free U. Amsterdam, 1950-54, rsch. assoc., 1954-56, asst. dir., 1958-60; postdoctoral fellow U. Minn., Mpls., 1956-57, faculty, 1957-58, 60-70, prof. elec. engrng. and physics, 1965-70; prof. theoretical physics U. Montreal, Que., Can., 1969-95, sr. rschr. math. rsch. ctr. Que., 1969-2000, prof. emerita, 1998—. Vis. prof. U. Fla., 1974, 78-88; prof. elec. and computer engring. Fla. Internat. U., 1992-2000; adj. prof. physics U. Miami, 2001—. Contbg. author: Fluctuation Phenomena in Solids, 1965; contbr. articles to profl. jours. Rsch. grantee, NSF, Air Force OSR, Wright Patterson AFB, Nat. Sci. and Engring. Rsch. Coun., Ottawa. Fellow IEEE (life); mem. Am. Phys. Soc., NY Acad. Scis. Office: U Miami James L Knight Physics Bldg 1320 Campo Sano Dr Coral Gables FL 33146 Home Phone: 305-232-7576; Office Phone: 305-284-2325. Business E-Mail: vanvliet@physics.miami.edu. *The purpose of life is to honor God and to serve mankind.*

VAN VLIET, CLAIRE, artist; b. Ottawa, Ont., Can., Aug. 9, 1933; d. Wilbur Dennison and Audrey Ilene (Wallace) Van Vliet. AB, San Diego State Coll., 1952; MFA, Claremont Grad. Sch., 1954; DFA (hon.), U. of the Arts, Phila., 1993, San Diego State U., 2002. Instr. printmaking Phila. Coll. Art, 1959-65; owner The Janus Press, 1954—; vis. lectr. printmaking U. Wis.-Madison, 1965-66. Mem. bd. advisors Hand Papermaking. One-man exhbns. include Print Club Phila., 1963, 66, 73, 77, Wiggin Gallery, Boston Pub. Libr., 1977, Rutgers U. Art Gallery, 1978, AAA Gallery, Phila., 1980, Dolan/Maxwell Gallery, Phila., 1984, 91, Mary Ryan Gallery, NYC, 1986, Mills Coll., 1986, U. of the Arts, Phila., 1989, Victoria and Albert Mus., London, 1994, Ottawa Sch. of Art Gallery, Can., 1994, Bates Coll. Mus. of Art, Lewiston, Maine, 1994, 99, ND Mus. Art, 1999, Rosenwald Wolf Gallery U. Arts. Phila, 2001, La. State U. Libr., 2005, Grolier Club, NY, 2006, Nat. Gallery Art Libr., 2006, Humanities Gallery, Scripps Coll., 2006, Boston Pub. Libr., 2006, Wellesley Coll. Libr., 2006, U. Va. Libr., 2007; group exhbns. include Bklyn. Nat., Phila. Arts Festival, Kunst zu Kafka, Germany, Paper as Medium, Smithsonian Instn., Washington, Paper Now, Cleve. Mus. Art, 1986, Boyle Arts Festival, Ireland, 1993, Libr. Congress, 1997—, ND Mus. Art, 1999; represented in permanent collections Nat. Gallery Art, Phila. Mus. Art, Boston Pub. Libr., Libr. of Congress, Cleve. Mus. Art, Montreal Mus. Fine Arts, Victoria and Albert Mus. London, Tate Gallery, London, US Dept. State, Nat. Libr. Can., British Libr. Grantee, Ingram-Merrill Found., 1989; NEA grantee, 1976—80, MacArthur fellow, 1989—94. Mem.: Nat. Acad., Soc. Printers Boston, Vt. Arts and Scis. Home and Office: 101 Schoolhouse Rd West Burke VT 05871-9773

VAN VOORST, CAROL, ambassador; BA, Hope Coll.; MA, Nat. War Coll., 1998; MA, PhD, Princeton U. Tchr. City U. NY; spl. asst. to dep. sec. US Dept. State, 1984—85, Norway/Denmark desk officer, 1989—91, spl. asst. to under sec. polit. affairs, 1991—92, assigned to Panama, 1992—95, dir. Office Nordic & Baltic Affairs, 1995—97, chief polit. dept. to dep. high rep. office of high rep. Sarajevo, 1998—99; dep. chief of mission Am. Embassy, Helsinki, 1999—2002; dir. Austrian, German, Swiss affairs, Bur. European and Eurasian Affairs US Dept. State, 2002—04, US. amb. to Iceland Reykjavik, 2005—. Office: Am Embassy 5640 Reykjavik Pl Washington DC 20521

VAN VOORST, ROBERT E., theology educator, minister; b. Holland, Mich, June 5, 1952; s. Robert Eugene and Donna Mae (Boeve) Van V.; m. Mary Lind Bos, June 15, 1974; children: Richard William, Nicholas John. BA, Hope Coll., 1974; MDiv, Western Sem., 1977; PhD, Union Sem., NYC, 1988. Ordained to ministry Classis of Holland Reformed Ch. in Am., 1977. Pastor Rochester Reformed Ch., Accord, NY, 1977-89; prof. religion Lycoming Coll., Williamsport, Pa., 1989-99, dept. chair, 1997-99; prof. New Testament Western Theol. Sem., Holland, Mich., 1999—. Adj. prof. Susquehanna U., Selinsgrove, Pa., 1991, Bucknell U., Lewisburg, Pa., 1993; vis. prof. Westminster Coll., Oxford, England, 1997; New Testament seminar lectr. Oxford U., 2000; interim pastor Lycoming Presbyn. Ch., Williamsport, 1997—99; mem. Ch. Herald editl. coun., 2007—. Author: Ascents of James, 1989, Building New Testament Vocabulary, 1990, 3d edit., 2001, Anthology of World Scriptures, 1994, 5th edit., 2005, Readings in Christianity, 1996, 2d edit., 2000, Anthology of Asian Scriptures, 1999, Jesus Outside the New Testament, 2000, Italian edit., 2004, Reading the New Testament Today, 2004, Anthology of World Scriptures: Eastern Religions, 2006, Anthology of World Scriptures: Western Religions, 2006; co-author: Death of Jesus in Early Christianity, 1998, Pastor's Bible Study, vol. 3, 2006; editor Reformed Rev., 2000-07; mem. editl. coun. Ch. Herald, 2007—; contbr. articles Eerdmans Dictionary of the Bible, 2001, Ency. of Jesus in History, Culture and Thought, 2003, Eerdmans Bible Commentary, 2003, New Interpreters Dictionary of the Bible, 2006-07; contbr. articles to profl. jours. Mem. Phi Beta Kappa, Phi Kappa Phi, Eta Sigma Phi, Phi Sigma Iota. Avocations: golf, cooking. Home: 1114 Post Ave Holland MI 49424-2550 Office: Western Theol Sem 101 E 13th St Holland MI 49423-3622 Home Phone: 616-786-2272. Business E-Mail: bob.vanvoorst@westernsem.edu.

VAN VUGT, ERIC J., lawyer; b. Grand Rapids, Mich., Sept. 17, 1951; s. Ernest and Phyllis N. (Van Someren) Van Vugt; m. Wendy S. Yonker, June 3, 1972; children: Erin L., Heather J., Timothy D. BA, Calvin Coll., 1973; JD, Marquette Univ., 1976. Bar: Wis. 1976, U.S. Dist. Ct. (ea. and we. dist. Wis., ea. & we. dist. Mich., Ariz., no. dist. Ill.), Fed. Trial Bar, U.S. Ct. Appeals (3d, 6th, 7th, 9th, Fed. cir.), U.S. Supreme Ct. 1994. Assoc. Kluwin, Dunphy & Hankin, Milw., 1976-80; ptnr. Kluwin, Dunphy, Hankin & McNulty, Milw., 1980-85, Minahan & Peterson, Milw., 1985-91; ptnr., litig. practice Quarles & Brady, Milw., 1991—. Fellow Am. Coll. Trial Lawyers; mem. ABA, State Bar Wis., Milw. Bar Assn. Avocations: aviation, golf. Office: Quarles & Brady Ste 2040 411 E Wisconsin Ave Milwaukee WI 53202-4497 Office Phone: 414-277-5625. Office Fax: 414-978-8625. Business E-Mail: ejv@quarles.com.

VAN WACHEM, LODEWIJK CHRISTIAAN, petroleum company executive; b. Pangkalan Brandan, Indonesia, July 31, 1931; m. Elisabeth G. Cristofoli, June 10, 1958; 3 children. Degree Mech. Engring., Delft U., Delft, The Netherlands., 1953. With Bataafsche Petroleum Maatschappij, The Hague, Netherlands, 1953; pres. Royal Dutch Petroleum Co., The Hague, The Netherlands, 1982-92; chmn. com., mng. dir. Royal Dutch/Shell Group, The Hague, Netherlands, 1985—92; chmn. supr. bd. Royal Dutch Petroleum Co., The Hague, Netherlands, 1992—2002; with Maersk Holding B.U., Rotterdam, Netherlands, 2002—. Chmn. bd. dirs. Zurich Fin. Svcs., 2002—05, Global Crossing Ltd.; supervisory bd. De Nederlandsche Bank N.V., 1987—92, AKZO Nobel n.v., Arnhem, 1992—2002, BMW A.G., Munich, 1994—2002, Bayer A.G., Leverkusen, 1997—2002; non. exec. dir. IBM Corp., Armonk, 1992—2002, AAB Area Brown Boveri Ltd, Zurich, 1996—99; chmn. supervisory bd. Philips Electronics n.v., Amsterdam, 1993—2005; bd. dirs. Atco Ltd., Calgary. Decorated comdr. Brit. Empire, knight Brit. Empire (Eng.), comdr. Order of Oranje Nassau, knight Order Netherlands Lion (Netherlands). Office: Maersk Holding BU PO Box 487 NL-3000 AL Rotterdam Netherlands Office Phone: 31104006810.

VAN WAGENEN, PAUL G., gas industry executive; BA, Brigham Young Univ., 1970; JD, Univ. Washington, 1973. With Exxon Corp.; mgmt. positions with Pogo Producing, 1979—90, pres., 1990—91, chmn., pres., CEO, 1991—. Dir. Domestic Petroleum Council; mem. exec. com. U.S. Oil & Gas Assn. Mem. Greater Houston Round Table, Greater Houston Partnership; mem. exec. com. Greater Houston YMCA. Mem.: Ctr. Strategic and Internat. Studies-Houston Roundtable, Royalty Owners Assn., Texas Independent Producers, Nat. Ocean Industries Assn. (exec. com., bd. dir.), Nat. Petroleum Coun., All-American Wildcatters. Office: Po Box 2504 Ste 2700 5 Greenway Plz Houston TX 77252-2504 Office Phone: 713-297-5000. *

VAN WIE, PAUL DAVID, secondary school educator, historian; b. Manhasset, NY, Sept. 29, 1956; s. Joseph Paul and Florence Elizabeth (Wagner) van W.; m. Ellen Mary van Wie, June 25, 1983; children: Mary Ellen, Elisabeth, Paul David, Joseph. BA, C.W. Post Coll., 1978, MA, 1987; PhD, CUNY, 1989. Cert. secondary edn. Tchr. Spackenkill High Sch., Poughkeepsie, N.Y., 1981-82, Schreiber High Sch., Port Washington, N.Y., 1982-84, Wheatley Sch., Old Westbury, NY, 1984—2006; adj. prof. N.Y. Inst. Tech., Old Westbury, 1987—92, Hofstra U., Hempstead, 1992—; curriculum advisor East Williston Schs., 2006—. Mem. dean's adv. com. LI U., Old Brookville, NY, 1992—96; adj. prof. NY Inst. Tech., Old Westbury, 1984—2006, Hofstra U., Hempstead, 1992—. Author: The Way it Was, 1994, Image, History and Politics, 1998, The German Settlements of 19th Century Long Island, 2005. Historian Village of Franklin Square, N.Y., 1979—, libr. trustee, 1989—; landmarks commr. Town of Hempstead, 1989—; pres. Franklin Square Hist. Soc.; v.p. Franklin Square Cmty. League, 1990-96. Nat. Humanities fellow U.S. Govt., 1988, Fulbright scholar U.S. Govt., 1990, Coun. Basic Edn. fellow, 1996; recipient Leadership award Nat. Soc. Daughters of Am. Revolution, 1982, N.Y. State Tchr. of Yr. award N.Y. Dept. Edn., 1992. Mem. Am. Hist. Assn., L.I. Coun. Social Studies, Franklin Square Hist. Soc. (pres.). Office: The Wheatley Sch 11 Bacon Rd Old Westbury NY 11568-1502

VAN WINKLE, EDGAR WALLING, retired electrical engineer; b. Rutherford, NJ, Oct. 12, 1913; s. Winant and Jessie Walcott (Mucklow) Van W.; m. Jessie Stetler, Apr. 23, 1938 (dec. July 1992); children: Barbara Van Winkle Clifton (dec. Mar. 2000), Catrina Van Winkle Poindexter, Cornelia Van Winkle Schloss; m. Martha Polyé, May 22, 1993. BEE, Rutgers U., 1936; MS in Indsl. Engring., Columbia U., 1943, PE in Indsl. Engring., 1966. Registered profl. engr., N.J. Elec. engr. A.B. Dumont Labs., Passaic, NJ, 1943-48; chief engr. Facsimile Electronics, 1948-52; cons. Bur. Ships, Washington, 1952; asst. sr. staff scientist Bendix Corp., Teterboro, NJ, 1952-67; sr. staff scientist Conrac Corp., West Caldwell, 1967-78; pres. Empac, Inc., Rutherford, 1979-2001; ret., 2001. Contbr. articles to profl. jours.; patentee in field. Ruling elder Presbyterian Ch., Rutherford, 1984-91, chmn. endowment com., 1984—. Mem. IEEE (life, treas. artificial intelligence sect. North N.J. Chpt. 1982-84), Bendix Mgmt. Club (life), North N.J. Automatic Control Group (chmn. 1967-68), Met. Engring. Mgmt. (chmn. 1966-67), Mensa, Holland Soc., Green Pond Yacht Club (past commodore), Upper Montclair Country Club, Delta Phi. Republican. Achievements include research in artificial intelligence, mathematical software. Home (Summer): 154 Lake End Rd Newfoundland NJ 07435-1207 Personal E-mail: empacem@aol.com.

VANWOERKOM, JACK A., lawyer, consumer products company executive; b. 1953; m. Barbara L. Moore; 1 child, Carolyn. BS, MIT, 1975; JD cum laude, Boston U., 1978. Atty. Hale & Door, LLP, Boston, 1978—85; with Winthrop Fin. Assocs., Boston, 1985—94, gen. counsel, COO, vice chmn., mng. dir. Asian ops., 1993—94; chief legal counsel, v.p. devel., mng. dir. Europe A.W. Chesterton Co., 1994—97; gen. counsel Teradyne, Inc., 1998—99; sr. v.p., gen. counsel, sec. Staples, Inc., Framingham, Mass., 1999—2003, exec. v.p., gen. counsel, sec., 2003—07; exec. v.p., gen. counsel, corp. sec. The Home Depot, Inc., Atlanta, 2007—. Office: The Home Depot Inc 2455 Paces Ferry Rd Atlanta GA 30339 *

VAN WYCK, GEORGE RICHARD, insurance company executive; b. Wilmington, Vt., Feb. 6, 1928; s. Harold Wait Van Wyck and Ruth Anna Learnard; m. Jeanne Mildred Anderson, Apr. 17, 1948; children: Diana Lee Van Wyck Jenkins, Beryl Jeanne. BS in Math. cum laude, St. Lawrence U., 1953. Actuarial clk. Aetna Life Ins. Co., Hartford, Conn., 1953-55; with Am. Bankers Ins. Group, Miami, Fla., 1955-91, sec., bd. dirs., 1983-89, ret., 1991. Bd. dirs. Jr. Achievement of Greater Miami, 1966-83, pres., 1975-76; bd. dirs. Epworth Village Retirement Complex, Miami, 1966-2000, v.p., 1998-99, chmn. investment com. 1995-99; founding dir., pres. Brickel Children's Ctr., Miami, 1980-82; mem. pers. adv. bd., vice chmn. Dade County, Miami, 1987-89. With USAF, 1946-49. Fellow Life Office Mgmt. Inst.; mem. 1st United Meth. Ch. So. Miami, Phi Beta Kappa. Democrat. Methodist. Avocations: photography, golf, bridge, writing. Home: 8455 SW 44th St Miami FL 33155-4126 Personal E-mail: gvanwyck@cs.com.

VAN WYLEN, GORDON JOHN, former college president; b. Grant, Mich., Feb. 6, 1920; s. John and Effa (Bierema) Van W.; m. Margaret E. DeWitt, Dec. 29, 1951; children: Elizabeth Ann Van Wylen Rudenga, Stephen John, Ruth Margaret Van Wylen Jasperse, David Gordon, Emily Jane Van Wylen Overway. AB, Calvin Coll., 1942; BSE., U. Mich., 1942, MS, 1947; Sc.D., MIT, 1951. Indsl. engr. duPont Co., 1942-43; instr. mech. engring. Pa. State U., 1946-48; asst. prof. mech. engring. U. Mich., 1951-55, assoc. prof., 1955-57, prof., 1957-72, chmn. dept., 1958-65, dean Coll. Engring., 1965-72; pres. Hope Coll., Holland, Mich., 1972-87, pres. emeritus, 1987—. Author: Thermodynamics, 1959; author: (with R.E. Sonntag) Fundamentals of Classical Thermodynamics, 1965; author: 6th edit., 2003, Fundamentals of Statistical Thermodynamics, 1966, Introduction to Thermodynamics, 1971, 3d edit., 1991, Encounter at Sea, 1994; contbr. articles to profl. jours. Trustee Van Andel Edn. Inst. Lt. USNR, 1943-46. Fellow ASME, AAAS; mem. Phi Beta Kappa (hon.), Sigma Xi, Tau Beta Pi, Phi Kappa Phi. Mem. Reform Ch. Am. Home: Apt 600 145 Columbia Ave Holland MI 49423-2980

VANYO, BRUCE GORDON, lawyer; b. Cleve., Dec. 4, 1945; BS summa cum laude, Miami U., 1967; JD, Columbia U., 1972. Bar: Calif. 1974. Law clk. to Hon. William Timbers US Ct. Appeals (2nd cir.), 1972-73; ptnr. McCutcheon, Doyle, Brown & Enersen, 1979—84, Wilson, Sonsini, Goodrich & Rosati, Palo Alto, Calif., 1984—2006, co-chair litigation group, 1984—96; ptnr. Kirkland & Ellis LLP, LA, 2006, Katten Muchin Rosenman LLP, LA, 2006—, co-chair securities litig. practice. Prof. securities regulation Hastings Coll. Law, 1983-86; chmn. recent devels. in securities litigation, PLI, 1984-85; chmn. securities litigation prosecution and def. strategies, PLI, 1985, 86, 87; panelist ALI-ABA patent litigation avoidance and successful resolution, 1986. Mng. editor Columbia Law Rev., 1971-72. Named one of 500 Leading Lawyers in Am., Lawdragon, 2005, 100 Most Influential Lawyers, Nat. Law Jour., 2006. Mem. ABA (litigation sect., securities litigation com., corp. counsel com. 1981—), State Bar Calif. (chair administrn. of justice com. 1985-86), Bar Assn. San Francisco, Order of Coif. Office: Katten Muchin Rosenman LLP 2029 Century Pk E Ste 2600 Los Angeles CA 90067 E-mail: bruce.vanyo@kattenlaw.com. *

VAN ZANDT, DAVID E., dean, law educator; b. Princeton, NJ, Feb. 17, 1953; m. Lisa A. Huestis; children: Caroline, Nicholas. AB summa cum laude, Princeton U., 1975; JD, Yale U., 1981; PhD in Sociology, U. London, 1985. Bar: Ill. Lectr. New England Coll., Arundel, England, 1977, U. London, England, 1977—78; clk. to Hon. Pierre N. Leval U.S. Dist. Ct. (so. dist.) N.Y., 1981-82; clk. to Hon. Harry A. Blackmun U.S. Supreme Ct., Washington, 1982-83; atty. Davis, Polk & Wardwell, 1984-85; spl. U.S. legal counsel Artal Grp. S.A., 1985—; asst. prof Northwestern U. Law Sch., Chgo., 1985—88, assoc. prof, 1988—91, prof., 1991—95, dean, 1995—. Mem. planning com. Northwestern U. Corporate Counsel Inst., Northwestern U. Corp. Counsel Ctr. Author: Living in the Children of God, 1991; mng. editor Yale Law Jour., 1980-81; contbr. articles to profl. jours. Recipient Isidore Brown Thesis Prize, Princeton U., 1975. Mem.: Am. Law Dean's Assn. (dir. 1998—), AMR Rsch., Inc. (dir. 1998, audit com. 2000—, compensation com. 2000—), Am. Bar Assn. (dir. 1995—, exec. com. 1998—, treas. 2000—), Phi Beta Kappa. Office: Northwestern U Sch Law Office of Dean 357 E Chicago Ave Chicago IL 60611-3059 Office Phone: 312-503-8460. Office Fax: 801-650-6873. Business E-Mail: d-van2@law.northwestern.edu. *

VAN ZANDT, STEVEN, actor, musician, radio personality; b. Winthrop, Mass., Nov. 22, 1950; m. Maureen Santoro. Guitarist E-Street Band, 1975—84, 1999—; host/D.J. Little Steven's Underground Garage, Syndicated Radio, 2002—. Actor: (TV series) The Sopranos, 1999—2007; musician: (albums) Men Without Women, 1982, Voices of America, 1984, Sun City, 1985, Freedom - No Compromise, 1987, Revolution, 1989, Born Again Savage, 1999. Office: c/o The Endeavor Agy 10th Fl 9601 Wilshire Blvd Beverly Hills CA 90212

VAN ZANTEN, DAVID THEODORE, humanities educator; b. Aug. 31, 1943; BA, Princeton U., 1965; MA, Harvard U., 1966, PhD, 1970. Asst. prof. McGill U., Montreal, 1970-71; from asst. to assoc. prof. U. Pa., Phila., 1971-79; from assoc. prof. to prof. Northwestern U., Evanston, Ill., 1979—. Office: Northwestern Univ 3-400 Kresge Hall Evanston IL 60208-2208 Office Phone: 847-491-8024. Business E-Mail: d-van@northwestern.edu.

VAN ZANTEN, FRANK VELDHUYZEN, library director; b. Heemstede, The Netherlands, Oct. 21, 1932; came to U.S., 1946, naturalized, 1953; s. Adrian V. and Cornelia (Van Eesteren) Van Z.; m. Lois Ruth Holkeboer, June 17, 1961; children: Kiki Maria, Lili Roxanne, Amy Suzanne. AB, Calvin Coll., Mich., 1959; postgrad., U. Wash., 1960; MA in L.S, U. Mich., 1961. Cataloger, extension project asst. Mich. State Library, Lansing, 1961-62; dir. Dickinson County (Mich.) Library, 1962-65, Mid-Peninsula Library Fedn., Iron Mountain, Mich., 1963-65, St. Clair County (Mich.) Library, 1965-68, Tucson Pub. Library, 1968-73; library cons. Ill. State Library, Springfield, 1973-75, asso. dir. for library devel., 1975-78; dir. Mid-Hudson Library System, Poughkeepsie, NY, 1978-95; ret., 1996. Served with AUS, 1953-55. Mem. ALA, N.Y. Libr. Assn. Home: 138 Wilbur Blvd Poughkeepsie NY 12603-4635 Personal E-mail: fvzcolors@aol.com.

VAN ZELST, THEODORE WILLIAM, civil engineer, engineering company executive; b. Chgo., May 11, 1923; s. Theodore Walter and Wilhelmina (Oomens) Van Z.; m. Louann Hurter, Dec. 29, 1951; children: Anne, Jean, David. BS, U. Calif., Berkeley, 1944; BS in Naval Sci., Northwestern U., 1944, BAS., 1945, MS in Civil Engring., 1948. Registered profl. engr., Ill. Pres., Soil Testing Services, Inc., Chgo., 1948-52; pres. Soiltest, Inc., Chgo., 1948-78, chmn. bd., 1978-80; sec., dir. Exploration Data Cons., Inc., 1980-82; exec. v.p. Cenco Inc., Chgo., 1962-77, vice chmn., 1975-77, also dir., 1962-77. Bd. dirs. Minann, Inc., Testing Sci., Inc., Van Zelst, Inc.; chmn. bd. dirs. Envirotech Svcs., Inc., 1983-85; sec., bd. dirs. Van Zelst, Inc. Wadsworth, Ill., 1983—; pres. Geneva-Pacific Corp., 1969-83, Geneva Resources, Inc., 1983-91. Treas. Internat. Road Fedn., 1961-64, sec., 1964-79, dir., 1973-88, vice chmn., 1980-87; pres. Internat. Road Edn. Found., 1978-80, 87-88, hon. life bd. dirs., 1988—; bd. dirs. Chgo. Acad. Scis., 1983-86, v.p., 1985-86, hon. dir., 1986-2007; bd. dirs. Pres.'s Assn., Chgo., 1985-86, Friends of Mitchell Mus., 2003-2004; Asian art coun. Art Inst. Chgo., 2004—. Lt. j.g. USNR, 1944—46. Recipient Service award Northwestern U., 1970, Merit award, 1974, Alumni medal, 1989, Svc. award U. Wis., 1971, La Sallian award, 1975; named Disting. Engring. Alumnus, U. Calif., Berkeley, 2002. Mem. ASCE (Chgo. Civil Engr. of Yr., 1988), Nat. Soc. Profl. Engrs., Western Soc. Engrs., Evanston C. of C. (v.p. 1969-73), Ovid Esbach Soc. (pres. 1968-80), Northwestern U. Alumni Assn., Tau Beta Pi, Sigma Xi. Clubs: Economic, North Shore. Achievements include invention of engring. testing equipment for soil, rock, concrete and asphalt; co-invention of Swing-wing for supersonic aircraft. Home: 1213 Wagner Rd Glenview IL 60025-3297 Office: PO Box 582 Glenview IL 60025-0582 Home Phone: 847-724-3244. Personal E-mail: tvz@earthlink.net.

VAN ZILE, PHILIP TAYLOR, III, lawyer, educator; b. Detroit, Feb. 17, 1945; s. Philip Taylor II and Ruth (Butzel) Van Z.; m. Susan Jones, Sept. 12, 1981; children: Caroline Sage, Philip Taylor IV. BA, Oberlin Coll., 1968; MDiv, Union Theol. Sem., 1971; JD, Mich. State U., 1975. Bar: Mich. 1976, D.C. 1976, U.S. Dist. Ct. (ea. dist.) Mich. 1976, U.S. Ct. Appeals (6th cir.) 1976, U.S. Supreme Ct. 1977, Pa. 1981. Law clk. Mich. Ct. Appeals, Detroit, 1976-78, Mich. Supreme Ct., Detroit and Lansing, Mich., 1978-80; asst. corp. counsel Office of Corp. Counsel, Washington, 1980-87; assoc. Killian & Gephart, Harrisburg, Pa., 1987-89; prin. Law Office of Philip T. Van Zile, Harrisburg, 1989-91; assoc. coun. Office Chief Coun. Pa. Dept. Conservation and Natural Resources, Harrisburg, 1991—; assoc. realtor M.C. Walker Realty, Mechanicsburg, Pa., 1997—. Teaching fellow Detroit Coll. Law, 1976-80; teaching asst. Detroit Gen. Hosp., 1978-80; teaching assoc. Acad. Med. Arts and Bus., Harrisburg, 1990-91. Contbr. articles to profl. jours. Ordained elder Mechanicsburg Presbyn. Ch., 1995—, chmn. vol. ministries, 1995, chmn. peacemaking, 1996, chmn. staff, 1997—. Mem. ABA, Kenwood Club (Chevy Chase, Md.). Office: Pa Dept Conservation/Natural Resources Office Chief Counsel 400 Market St Harrisburg PA 17101-2301

VANZURA, LIZ (ELIZABETH K. VANZURA), automotive executive; b. May 1964; m. Rick Vanzura; children: Danielle, Jacqueline. BS, GMI Engring. and Mgmt. Inst.; MBA, Harvard U. With GM Corp., 1984—96, global dir. mktg. Hummer, 2001—06, mktg. dir. Cadillac, 2006—; dir. mktg. Volkswagen of Am., 1996—2000. Exec. bd. mem. Internat. Automotive Advt. Awards. Named Marketer of Yr., Advertising Age, 1998; named one of Top 100 Mktg. Profls., 1999, 50 Women to Watch, Wall St. Jour., 2006; recipient Top Women to Watch Award, Advertising Age, 2001, All Star award, Automotive News, 1999, 2000. Office Phone: 313-556-5000. Office Fax: 313-556-5108. *

VAN ZWEDEN, JAAP, conductor; b. Amsterdam, Dec. 1960; m. Aaltje van Zweden; 4 children. Student, Julliard Sch., NYC. Concertmaster Royal Concertgebouw Orch., violinist, part-time condr., 1994; chief condr. Netherlands Symphony Orch., 1996—2003; music dir. Residentie Orch. The Hague, 2000—05, Netherlands Radio Philharm. Orch. and Kamer Filharmonie, 2005—; music dir. designate Dallas Symphony Orch.,

2007—; prin. condr. Royal Flemish Philharm. Orch. Belgium. Guest condr. St. Louis Symphony Orch., 1996, Dallas Symphony Orch., 2006, Royal Concertgebouw and Orchestre National de France, Munich Philharm., Rotterdam Philharm., Oslo Philharm., St. Petersburg Philharm., Tokyo Philharm., Hong Kong Philharm., London Philharm., Acad. of St. Martin-in-the-Fields and City of Birmingham Symphony Orch., West German Radio Symphony Orch. of Cologne, Danish Radio Orch. Co-founder Papageno Found., Netherlands. Office: Dallas Symphony Orch 2301 Flora St Dallas TX 75201 Office Phone: 214-871-4000. *

VAPNIK, VLADIMIR N., mathematician, researcher, educator; MA in Math., Uzbek State U., 1958; PhD in Statistics, Inst. Control Sci., 1964. Prof. to head Computer Sci. Dept. Inst. Control Scis., 1961—91; cons. AT&T Bell Labs., Holmdel, NJ; fellow NEC Labs. Am. Inc., Princeton, NJ, 2001—. Prof. computer scis. Royal Holloway, U. London, 1995—. Recipient Humboldt Research Award, 2003. Mem.: NAE. Office: NEC Labs 4 Independence Way Princeton NJ 08540

VARADARAJAN, SRINIDHI, computer scientist; PhD in Computer Sci., SUNY, Stony Brook, 2000. Dir. Terascale Computing Facility Va. Polytechnic Inst. and State U., asst. prof. computer sci. Named one of Top 100 Young Innovators, MIT Tech. Review, 2004. Achievements include architect of System X, the third fastest supercomputer in the world. Office: Terascale Computing Facility Va Polytechnic Inst and State U Blacksburg VA 24061 Business E-Mail: srinidhi@cd.vt.edu.

VARADHAN, SRINIVASA S.R., mathematics educator; b. Madras, India, Jan. 2, 1940; came to U.S., 1963; s. Ranga and Janaki Ayyangar; m. Vasundara Narayanan, June 5, 1964; children: Gopalakrishnan, Ashok BSc with honors in Statistics, Madras U., India, 1959, MA in Statistics, 1959; PhD in Statistics, Indian Statis. Inst., Calcutta, 1963. Instr. Indian Statis. Inst., Calcutta, 1962-63; vis. mem. Courant Inst. Math. Sciences, NYU, NYC, 1963-66, asst. prof. math., 1966-68, assoc. prof. math., 1968-72, prof. math., 1972—, Frank J. Gould Professorship in Sci., 1999—; dir. Courant Inst. Math. Scis., NYU, NYC, 1980-84, 92-94. Co-author, Multidimensional Diffusion Processes, 1979; author Diffusion Problems and Partial Differential Equations, 1980, Large Deviations and Applications, 1984; contbr. articles to profl. jours. Alfred P. Sloan fellow, 1969-71, Guggenheim fellow, 1984-85; recipient Abel prize, Norwegian Acad. Sci. & Letters, 2007. Fellow Royal Soc., Inst. Math. Statistics, Indian Acad. Sciences; mem. NAS, Am. Acad. Arts and Scis., Am. Math. Soc. (George David Birkhoff Prize in applied math. 1994 (& SIAM), Leroy P. Steele prize for fundamental contribution to rsch., 1996), Soc. Indsl. and Applied Math. (SIAM), Third World Acad. Scis. Office: Courant Inst Math Scis 251 Mercer St New York NY 10012 Office Phone: 212-998-3334. Office Fax: 212-995-4121. Business E-Mail: varadhan@cims.nyu.edu. *

VARAIYA, PRAVIN P., electrical engineer; Mem. tech. staff Bell Labs., 1962-63; instr. MIT, Fed. U. Rio de Janeiro; prof. econ. U. Calif., Berkeley, 1975-92, James Fife prof. elec. engrng. and computer scis., Nortel Networks disting. prof. elec. engrng./computer sci. Dir. Calif. PATH. Mem. editl. bd. Transp. Rsch. Part C, Discrete Event Dynamical Sys: Theory and Applications, Jour. Econ. Dynamics and Control, (Birkhauser series) Progress in Sys. and Control Theory; contbr. numerous articles to profl. jours. Guggenheim fellow; Miller Rsch. prof. Fellow IEEE, Am. Acad. Arts & Sciences; mem. NAE Office: Dept Elec Engring U Calif 271M Cory Hall Berkeley CA 94720 Office Phone: 510-642-5270. Office Fax: 510-642-7815. Business E-Mail: varaiya@eecs.berkeley.edu.

VARANASI, KRIPA KIRAN, research scientist; b. Bhimavaram, Andhra Pradesh, India, Jan. 2, 1977; s. Jagan Mohan Rao Varanasi and Suryakantham Kompella; m. Manasa Kambhampati, Dec. 13, 2004. B in Tech., Indian Inst. Tech., Madras, Chennai, India, 1998; MS in Mech. Engring., MIT, Cambridge, 2002, MS in Elec. Engring. and Computer Sci., 2002, PhD in Mech. Engring., 2004. Grad. rschr. MIT, Cambridge, 1998—2004; rsch. scientist Gen. Electric Global Rsch. Ctr., Nanotechnology Advanced Tech. Program, Energy and Propulsion Technologies, Niskayuna, NY, 2004—. Summer intern Bajaj Auto Ltd., Pune, Maharastra, India, 1996—96; student rschr. Machine Dynamics Lab, Indian Inst. Tech., Madras, Chennai, 1997—98, Thermodynamics Lab, Indian Inst. Tech., Madras, Chennai, 1997—98, Machine Elements Lab, Indian Inst. Tech., Madras, Chennai, 1997—98; cons. Indian Space Rsch. Orgn., 1997; cons. Precision Engring. Rsch. Group MIT, Cambridge, 1998—2004, cons. Rapid Autonomous Machining Lab, 2002; cons. New Way Air Bearings, Aston, Pa., 1999, Optikos Inc., Cambridge, 2000, Laser Interferometer Gravity Wave Obs. (LIGO), MIT/Caltech, Cambridge, 2003—04; vis. rschr., cons. Silicon Valley Group Inc., Ridgefield, Conn., 2000—01. Contbr. articles to profl. jours. Vol., blood donor Red Cross, 1994—98. Named Best Tech. Project of Yr., GE Rsch. Ctr., 2005; recipient Best Sci. Project award, Dept. Edn., A.P., India, 1988—92, Math. Olympiad award, Assn. Math. Tchrs., India, 1993, Inventor award, GE, 2005, GE Mgmt. award for rsch. in nanotechnology, GE Rsch. Ctr., 2005; scholar, Eveready Welfare Svcs., 1994—98, H.E.H. Nizam Trust, India, 1998; Merit scholar, Dept. Telecom., India, 1989—94, Govt. Andhra Pradesh, India, 1989—94, Nat. Merit scholar, Govt. India, 1994—98, Excel scholar, Excel Industries India, Ltd., 1998. Mem.: ASME (mem. nanomanufacturing com. Nanotechnology Inst.), Internat. Soc. for Optical Engring., Am. Soc. Precision Engring., Materials Rsch. Soc., Sigma Xi. Achievements include patents pending for method and apparatus for damping vibrations using low-wave-speed media; area of nanotechnology; area of energy at GE Research; research in Low-Wave-Speed Materials at MIT; nanotextured superhydrophobic and superhydrophilic surfaces at GE Research. Avocations: music, reading, sports, documentaries, movies, cooking. Home: 27 Squire Ln Clifton Park NY 12065 Office: General Electric Global Research Center One Research Circle Niskayuna NY 12309 Home Phone: 518-371-7315; Office Phone: 518-387-6732. Office Fax: 518-387-7292. Personal E-mail: kripa@alum.mit.edu. Business E-Mail: varanasi@research.ge.com.

VARAT, JONATHAN D., law educator, dean; b. 1945; BA, U. Pa., Phila., 1967, JD, 1972. Law clk. to judge Walter Mansfield U.S. Ct. Appeals (2d cir.), NYC, 1972-73; law clk. to justice Byron White U.S. Supreme Ct., Washington, 1973-74; assoc. O'Melveny & Myers, Los Angeles, 1974-76; acting prof. UCLA Sch. Law, 1976-81, prof., 1981—, assoc. dean, 1982-83, 91-92, dean, 1998—2003. Co-author: Constitutional Law: Cases and Materials, 2005. Office: UCLA Sch Law PO Box 951476 Los Angeles CA 90095-1476

VARCHMIN, THOMAS EDWARD, public health service officer; b. Chgo., Dec. 5, 1947; s. Arthur William and Laurie Eileen (Allen) V.; m. Beth Virginia Plank, Dec. 16, 1972; children: Jeffrey Thomas, Brian Arthur, Jennifer Beth, Matthew James. BA, St. Mary's Coll., Winona, Minn., 1969; MS, Western Ill. U., Macomb, 1977. Registered sanitarian Wis., lic. envirin. health practitioner Ill. Virologist, microbiologist Chgo. Dept. Health, 1974-78; environ. health and safety mgr. Great Atlantic & Pacific Tea Co., Chgo., 1978-79; adminstr. occupational safety and environ. health Nat. Safety Council, Chgo., 1979-80; mgr. environ. health Lake County Health Dept., Waukegan, Ill., 1980-84, mgr. environ. health and pub. relations, 1984-87; mgr. environ. health Cook County Dept. Pub. Health, Oak Park, Ill., 1987-89, asst. dir. environ. health, mgr. intergovtl. rels., 1989-98, dir. environ. health, 1998—. Co-chmn. West Nile Virus Com. Cook County, Ill., 2001—03; environ. health cons. Author: Final Report of West Nile Virus Committee for Cook County, 2002—03; editor: Food and Beverage Newsletter, Hospital and Health Care Newsletter, Trades and Services Newsletter, 1979—80; contbr. articles to profl. jours. NSF grantee, 1968-69 Mem.: Am. Soc. Microbiology, Nat. Safety Coun., Ill. Environ. Health Assn., Nat. Environ. Health Assn., Delta Epsilon Sigma, Phi Mu Alpha. Achievements include research on autumn food habits of game fish, behavioral and phys. devel. of barred owl nestlings in Ill. Office: Cook County Dept Pub Health 1010 Lake St Ste 300 Oak Park IL 60301-1133

VARDALOS, NIA, actress, screenwriter; b. Winnipeg, Can., Sept. 24, 1962; d. Constantine and Doreen Vardalos; m. Ian Gomez, 1993. Attended, Ryerson U. Actor: (films) No Experience Necessary, 1996, Men Seeking Women, 1997, Short Cinema, 1998, Meet Prince Charming, 1999, (also writer) My Big Fat Greek Wedding, 2002, (also writer, exec. prodr.) Connie and Carla, 2004, (voice): (TV series) Team Knight Rider, 1997, (guest appearance): High Incident, 1996, Common Law, 1996, The Drew Carey Show, 1997, Boy Meets World, 1998, It's Like, You Know, 1999, Two Guys, a Girl, and a Pizza Place, 1999, Curb Your Enthusiasm, 2000. Office: c/o Brillstein Grey Mgmt 9150 Wilshire Blvd Ste 350 Beverly Hills CA 90212

VARDAMIS, ALEX A., foundation administrator, retired military officer; b. Bangor, Maine, Sept. 10, 1934; s. Alex and Pauline Vardamis; m. Frances Diem, June 29, 1957; children: Sharon, Daniel. BS, US Mil. Acad., West Point, 1957; MA, Columbia U., NYC, 1967, PhD, 1970. Commd. 2d lt. US Army, 1957, advanced through grades to col., 1979, ret., 1986; from asst. to assoc. prof. Dickinson State U., ND, 1986—88; adj. prof. English U. Vt., Burlington, 1988—98; pres., CEO, trustee Robinson Jeffers Tor House Found., Carmel, Calif., 2000—. Author: (non-fiction) The Critical Reputation of Robinson Jeffers, 1972, (novels) Dingus Dreaming, 2003, The Canine Condition, 2006; contbr. articles to newspapers and periodicals. Fellow, Ctr. Sci. and Internat. Affairs, Harvard U., Cambridge, Mass., 1978; Fulbright fellow, Norway, 1996. Home: PO Box 5323 Carmel CA 93921 Office: Robinson Jeffers Tor House Found PO Box 2713 Carmel CA 93921

VARDAVAS, STEPHANIE J., lawyer; b. Balt., Aug. 3, 1956; d. John and Elaine V. BA, Yale U., 1979; JD, Fordham U., 1985. Bar: NY 1986. Exec. trainee Maj. League Baseball Office of Commr., NYC, 1979-80, asst. counsel, 1986—89; mgr. waivers and player records Am. League of Profl. Baseball Clubs, NYC, 1980-85; v.p. legal and bus. affairs ProServ, Inc. (SFX Sports), 1989—97; atty. endorsement and league affairs Nike, Inc., NYC, 1997—. Vol. D'Amours for U.S. Senate, N.H., 1984, Kanjorski for U.S. Ho. of Reps., Pa., 1986, Mark Green for U.S. Senate, N.Y., 1986, Dukakis for Pres., N.Y., 1988, Clinton-Gore, 1992-96, Gore-Lieberman, 2000, Howard Dean for Pres., 2004; pres. Friends of the Multnomah County Libr. Mem.: ABA (forum com. on the entertainment and sports law industries), Sports Lawyers Assn. (bd. dirs. and co-chair tech. com.). Democrat. Greek Orthodox. Avocations: reading, writing, photography, travel. Office: Nike World Headquarters One Bowerman Dr Beaverton OR 97005-6453

VARDELL, JAMES C., III, lawyer; b. Columbia, SC, Dec. 18, 1954; BA, Washington & Lee Univ., 1977; JD, Yale Univ., 1980. Bar: NY 1981. Assoc. Cravath Swaine & Moore LLP, NYC, 1980—87, ptnr., corp. dept., 1987—. Office: Cravath Swaine & Moore LLP Worldwide Plz 825 Eighth Ave New York NY 10019-7475 Office Phone: 212-474-1900. Office Fax: 212-474-3700. Business E-Mail: jvardell@cravath.com.

VARELA, ALAN MARK, state agency administrator, lawyer; b. Santa Fe, NMex, 1962; BA in Philosophy and Psychology, Univ. NMex., JD, 1987; graduate Leadership for 21st Century, Harvard JFK Sch. Govt. Prin. Varela Law Office, Albuquerque; engring. dept. Qwest Comm.; policy, law dept. US West Comm.; now exec. dir. State Workers' Compensation Adminstrn., Albuquerque, 2004—. Mem.: NMex Hispanic Bar Assn. (past pres.), Hispanic Nat. Bar Assn. (pres. 2004—05, regional pres., NMex, Utah, v.p., pres.-elect). Office: Workers' Compensation Adminstrn 2410 Centre Ave SE PO Box 27198 Albuquerque NM 87106 Office Phone: 505-841-6007. Office Fax: 505-841-6009. Business E-Mail: a.varela@state.nm.us.

VARELLA, HAZEL L., historian, educator; b. Beverly, Mass., Dec. 17, 1932; d. John Luke and Olivia McDonald Luke; m. M David Varella, June 24, 1961; children: John David, James Robert. BS, Bridgewater State Coll., 1954, MEd, 1956; MA, Boston U., 1962. Chmn. social studies Easton (Mass.) Sch. Sys., 1956—97; adj. faculty Bridgewater State Coll., Mass., 1998—; sr. lectr. Curry Coll., Milton, Mass., 1988—. Adv. placement cons. Coll. Bd., Princeton, 1988—. Author: (book) History of Easton V II, 1972, (pamphlets) Growing Up at Sheep Pasture, 1976. Trustee North Easton Savings Bank, 1996—; dir. Ames Free Libr., Easton, 1989—. Recipient Hon. Grand Marshall, Town of Easton, Mass., 2000, Ind. Study Scholar, NEH, Washington, DC, 1984, Outstanding Svc. award, Easton Lions Club, 1997, Disting. Svc. award, Curry Coll., 2004. Mem.: Easton Hist. Soc. (sec., pres. 1969—71, 1990—94). Episcopalian. Avocations: reading, travel. Home: 121 Center St North Easton MA 02356 Personal E-mail: mdhvarella@comcast.net.

VARELLAS, SANDRA MOTTE, judge; b. Anderson, SC, Oct. 17, 1946; d. James E. and Helen Lucille (Gilliam) Motte; m. James John Varellas, July 3, 1971; children: James John III, David Todd. BA, Winthrop U., 1968; MA, U. Ky., 1970, JD, 1975. Bar: Ky. 1975, Fla. 1976, U.S. Dist. Ct. (ea. dist.) Ky. 1975, U.S. Ct. Appeals (6th cir.) 1976, U.S. Supreme Ct. 1978. Instr. Midway Coll., Ky., 1970-72; adj. prof. U. Ky. Coll. Law, Lexington, 1976-78; instr. dept. bus. adminstrn. U. Ky., Lexington, 1976-78; ptnr. Varellas, Pratt & Cooley, Lexington, 1975-93, Varellas & Pratt, Lexington, 1993-97, Varellas & Varellas, Lexington, 1998—. Fayette County judge exec., Ky., 1980—; hearing officer Ky. Natural Resources and Environ. Protection Cabinet, Frankfort, 1984-88; bd. trustees Lexington Network 1994-98, 2002-2004, sec., 1994-98. Committeewoman Ky. Young Dems., Frankfort, 1977-80; pres. Fayette County Young Dems., Lexington, 1977; bd. dirs. Ky. Dem. Women's Club, Frankfort, 1980-84, bd. dirs., Bluegrass Estate Planning Coun., 1995-98; grad. Leadership Lexington, 1981; chairwoman Profl. Women's Forum, Lexington, Ky., 1985-86, bd. dirs., 1984-87, Aequum award com., 1989-92; mem. devel. com. Midway Coll., 1990-92; co-chair Gift Club Com., 1992; mem. pub. svc. sector com. United Way of Bluegrass, 2004. Named Outstanding Young Dem. Woman, Ky. Young Dems., Frankfort, 1977, Outstanding Former Young Dem., Ky. Young Dems., 1983. Mem. Ky. Bar Assn. (treas. young lawyers divsn. 1978-79, long range planning com. 1988-89), Fla. Bar, Fayette County Bar Assn. (treas. 1977-78, bd. govs. 1978-80), LWV (nominating com. 1984-85), Greater Lexington C. of C. (legis. affairs com. 1994-95, bd.d irs. coun. smaller enterprises 1992-95), The Lexington Forum (bd. dirs. 1996-99), Lexington Philharm. Guild (bd. dirs. 1979-81, 86-2006), Nat. Assn. Women Bus. Owners (chmn. cmty. liaison/govtl. affairs com. 1992-93). Office: Varellas & Varellas 167 W Main St Ste 1310 Lexington KY 40507-1398 Office Phone: 859-252-4473.

VARESE, FEDERICO, sociology professor; b. Italy, Nov. 12, 1965; m. Galia Kravtchenko. Laurea, Bologna U., Italy, 1990; PhM, Cambridge U., Eng., 1991; PhD, Oxford U., Eng., 1997. Rsch. fellow Oxford U., 1996-2000; William H. Orrick asst. vis. prof. Yale U., New Haven, 2000—02; asst. prof. Williams Coll., Williamstown, 2002—03; sr. lectr. in criminology Ctr. for Criminological Rsch. U. Oxford, England, 2003—06, prof. criminology Law Faculty, 2006—. Author: The Russian Mafia, 2001. Cpl. maj. paratrooper Italian armed forces, 1992-93. Grantee Internat. Consortium for Polit. and Social Rsch., 1997; Nuffield Coll. studentship, 1991; Lester B. Pearson scholar Ministry of Fgn. Affairs, 1982; receipient Ed. A. Hewett Book Prize, Am. Assoc. for the Advancement of Slavic Studies, in conj. with Nat. Coun. for Eurasian and East European Rsch., 2002. Mem. Am. Polit. Sci. Assn., Am. Sociol. Assn. Office: Linacre Coll Univ Oxford St Cross Rd Oxford OX1 3JA England Office Phone: 44-1865-281150. Business E-Mail: federico.varese@linacre.ox.ac.uk.

VARET, MICHAEL A., lawyer; b. NYC, Mar. 9, 1942; s. Guster V. and Frances B. (Goldberg) V.; m. Elizabeth R. Varet, June 3, 1973; 3 children. BS in Econs., U. Pa., 1962; LLB, Yale U., 1965. Bar: N.Y. 1966, U.S. Supreme Ct. 1975, U.S. Dist. Ct. (ea. and so. dists.) N.Y. 1975, U.S. Tax Ct. 1975, U.S. Claims Ct. 1975, U.S. Ct. Appeals (2d cir.) 1975. Mem., chmn. Varet & Fink PC (formerly Milgrim Thomajan & Lee PC), NYC, 1982—95; mem. DLA Piper US LLP (and predecessor firms), NYC, 1995—. Bd. dir., exec. com., chmn. audit com., compensation com., Salisbury Bank and Trust Co., Lakeville, Conn., Salisbury Bancorp, Inc., Lakeville. Trustee Montefiore Med. Ctr., Bronx, NY, 1980-92, mem. exec. com., 1985-92; bd. dirs. Sem. Libr. Corp. Jewish Theol. Sem., NYC, 1983-87, United Jewish Appeal-Fedn. Jewish Philanthropies of Greater NY, Inc., 1979-86, coun. of overseers, 1986-95, bd. overseers, 2005—; bd. dirs. Mosholu Preservation Corp., Bronx, 1982-88, Yale Law Sch. Fund, 2000—; bd. overseers Jewish Theol. Sem., 1982-90, Jewish Publ. Soc. Am., 1986-96, exec. com., 1989-96; exec. com. Yale Law Sch. Assn., 1990-93; bd. dirs. B. de Rothschild Found. for Advancement Sci. in Israel, 1986—, Piatigorsky Found., 1990—, Scenic Hudson, Inc., 2003-06; v.p., sec., bd. dirs. Am. Found. for Basic Rsch. in Israel, 1990—; dir. Plz. Jewish Cmty. Chapel, 2001—; bd. dirs. Am. and Internat. Friends of Victoria and Albert Mus., Inc., 1997-99, treas., 1997-99. Mem. ABA, N.Y. State Bar Assn., Assn. of Bar of City of N.Y. (bd. dirs., exec. com. 1971-75), Internat. Fiscal Assn., Internat. Tax Planning Assn., Yale Club of N.Y.C., Lotos Club. Democrat. Office: DLA Piper US LLP 1251 Ave of Americas New York NY 10020-1104 Office Phone: 212-335-4650. Business E-Mail: mavaret@varet.com, michael.varet@dlapiper.com.

VARGA, PAUL C., beverage products executive; b. Louisville, 1964; m. Melissa Varga; 2 children. BA business administration, finance, U Ky.; MBA, Purdue U. Various marketing positions Brown-Forman Corp., 1987—96, sr. v.p., 1996—2003; CEO, bd. dir. Brown-Forman Beverages Co., 2003—; pres., CEO Brown-Forman Corp., 2005—07, chmn., pres., CEO, 2007—. Office: c/o Brown-Forman PO Box 1080 Louisville KY 40201 *

VARGA, RICHARD STEVEN, retired mathematics professor; b. Cleve., Oct. 9, 1928; s. Steven and Ella (Krejcs) V.; m. Esther Marie Pfister, Sept. 22, 1951; 1 dau., Gretchen Marie. BS, Case Inst. Tech., Cleve., 1950; AM, Harvard U., Cambridge, Mass., 1951, PhD, 1954; doctorate (hon.), U. Karlsruhe, Germany, 1991, U. Lille, 1993. With Bettis Atomic Power Lab., Westinghouse Electric Co., 1954-60, adv. mathematician, 1959-60; prof. math. Case Inst. Tech. (now Case We. Res. U.), Cleve., 1960—69; univ. prof. math. Kent State U., Ohio, 1969—2006, dir. rsch. Inst. for Computational Math., 1980—; ret., 2006. Cons. to govt. and industry. Author: Matrix Iterative Analysis, 1962, Functional Analysis and Approximation Theory in Numerical Analysis, 1971, Topics in Polynomial and Rational Interpolation and Approximation, 1982, Zeros of Sections of Power Series, 1983, Scientific Computation on Mathematical Problems and Conjectures, 1990, Matrix Iterative Analysis, 2d revised and expanded edit., 2000, Gersgorin and his Circles, 2004; editor: Numerical Solution of Field Problems in Continuum Physics, 1970, Padé and Rational Approximations: Theory and Applications, 1977, Rational Approximations and Interpolation, 1984, Computational Methods and Function Theory, 1990, Numerical Linear Algebra, 1993; editor-in-chief. Numerische Math., 1988-2002, Electronic Transactions Numerical Analysis; mem. editl. bd. Linear Algebra and Applications, Constructive Approximation, Computational Mathematics (China), Numerical Algorithms, Analysis, Electronic Jour. Linear Algebra, Comms. in Applied Analysis. Recipient Rsch. award Sigma Xi, 1965, von Humboldt prize, 1982, Pres.' medal Kent State U., 1981, Hans Schneider prize, 2005; Guggenheim fellow, 1963; Fairchild scholar, 1974. Home: 7065 Arcadia Dr Cleveland OH 44129-6065 Office: Kent State U Inst Computational Mat Kent OH 44242-0001 Business E-Mail: varga@math.kent.edu.

VARGAS, ELIZABETH, newscaster; b. Paterson, NJ, Sept. 6, 1962; m. Marc Cohn, July 20, 2002; children: Zachary Raphael, Samuel Wyatt; 2 stepchildren. BA in Journalism, U. Mo., Columbia. Reporter/anchor KOMU-TV, Columbia, Mo.; reporter KTVN-TV, Reno; lead reporter KTVK-TV, Phoenix, 1986—89; reporter/anchor WBBM-TV, Chgo., 1989—93; corr./anchor NBC News, NYC, 1993—97; corr. Dateline, NBC, NYC, 1993—96; news anchor, substitute co-host Good Morning Am., NBC, NYC, 1996—97; corr. ABC News, NYC, 1997—2005, co-anchor, 20/20 newsmagazine, 2004—; interim anchor ABC World News Tonight, NYC, 2005, co-anchor, 2006. Recipient Emmy award for Outstanding Instant Coverage of News Story (Elian Gonzales case), 2000. Office: ABC News Press Rels Fl 2 47 W 66th St New York NY 10023-6201

VARGAS, TRACI JUNELLE, special education educator; b. Wichita, Kans., Mar. 30, 1964; d. Judith Ann and James Dwayne Hilliard (Stepfather); children from previous marriage: Steven Dwayne, Christopher Jordan. BS, Northeastern State U., Tahlequah, Okla., 1997, BEd, 2005. Emotional disturbance Okla. State Dept. Edn., learning disability Okla. State Dept. Edn., other health impairment Okla. State Dept. Edn., autism Okla. State Dept. Edn. Spl. educator Claremore Pub. Schs., Okla., 1997—2006, Cherry Tree Elem. Sch. Carmel-Clay Sch. Dist., Carmel, Ind., 2006—07, Westside Elem. Claremore Pub. Schs., Okla., 2007—. Trainer Crisis Prevention and Intervention, Claremore, 2000—06; presenter Diffusing Volatile Situations in Classrooms Okla. Edn. Assn. Conv.; candidate Nat. Bd. Profl. Tchg. Stds., 2005. Named Tchr. of Yr., 1998, 2004. Mem.: NEA (corr.), Okla. Edn. Assn. (corr.), Coun. Exceptional Children (corr.). Democrat. Avocations: gardening, reading. Office: Westside Elem 2600 S Holly Rd Claremore OK 74017 Personal E-mail: nanatraci@cox.net. Business E-Mail: tvargas@claremore.k12.ok.us.

VARGAS LEGASPI, JUAN, manufacturing executive; b. Aguascalientes, Mex., Feb. 25, 1953; s. Juan Medina and Maria Legaspi De La Luz; m. Martha Perez Carreño; children: Juan, Abraham, Christopher. Bookkeeper, UNAM, Mexico City, 1974-78; diploma in taxes and fin., Inst. of Specialization, Mexico City, 1987; diploma human resources, U. Iberoam., Mexico City, 1979; diploma in fin. analysis, Dun & Bradstreet Inc., 1980; diploma in Econs., Inst. Integration Ibero Am., Mexico City; MBA in Mgmt., Grad. Coll., Mexico City, 1992. Dir. Guantes Vargas, S.Am., 1977—. Chmn. bd. Colegio de Graduados en Alta Direccion, 1995-2000, Centro de Investigaciones sobre la Libre Empresa, A.C., 1990-2000; CEO Grupo Banacci, 1996-2000; fin. cons. in field. Contbr. articles to profl. publs. Cesar Gaviria's bus. assessor Am. States Orgn., 1994-98. Roman Catholic. Avocations: writing, speaking, Karate, soccer. Home: Col Indsl Calz de Guadalupe 392 07800 Mexico City Mexico Office: Guantes Vargas SAm Calzada de Guadalupe 392 Col Industrial 07800 Mexico City Mexico

VARGHA, REBECCA B., university librarian, library association executive; BA, U. NC, Chapel Hill, 1979; MLS, NC Ctrl. U., 1980. Libr. asst. Nat. Humanities Ctr., Rsch. Triangle Park, NC, 1979—80, asst. libr., 1980—87, assoc. libr., 1987—94; info. analyst SAS Inst. Inc., Cary, NC, 1994; sr. rsch. specialist Nortel Networks; adj. faculty U. NC, Chapel Hill, 1996—98; libr. U. NC Sch. Info. & Libr. Sci., Chapel Hill, 2001—. Mem.: ALA, Spl. Librs. Assn. (chair conf. com. 1993, chair elect & chair divsn. cabinet 1996—98, pres. 2006—07, NC ch. archivist, chair networking com., chair scholarships com., chair student & academic rels. com., NC ch. Meritorious Achievement award 1994), Beta Phi Mu. Office: U NC Manning Hall CB #3360 Chapel Hill NC 27599-3360 Office Phone: 919-962-8361. Office Fax: 919-962-8071. E-mail: vargha@ils.unc.edu.

VARGHESE, OOMMAN KULATHINTHEKKETHIL, materials scientist, researcher; s. Varghese Kochumman Geevarghese and Marykutty Varghese; m. Maggie Paulose, Jan. 19, 1998; children: Grishma Miriam Oomman children: Tushar Varghese Oomman. BSc, Mahatma Gandhi U., Kerala, India., 1989; MSc, Mahatma Gandhi U., 1991; PhD, Indian Inst. of Tech., Delhi, 2001. Rsch. fellow Mahatma Gandhi U., Kottayam, Kerala, India, 1992—94, Indian Inst. of Tech., New Delhi, 1994—98, project scientist, 1998—2000; postdoctoral fellow U. of Ky., Lexington, 2000—01; postdoctoral scholar Pa. State U., University Park, 2001—06, rsch. assoc., 2006—. Mem. editl. bd.: Sensor Letters, 2003—, mem. internat. adv. bd.: Ency. of Sensors, 2004—, peer reviewer: IEEE Electron Device Letters, 2004—, Jour. Applied Physics, 2004—, Nanotech. Jour., 2005—, Jour. Phys. Chemistry, 2005—, Semiconductor Sci. and Tech., Advanced Functional Materials, 2006—, Jour. Physics D.: Applied Physics, 2007—; contbr. more than 60 articles to profl. jours. Fellow Jr. Rsch. fellow, Indian Inst. of Tech., Delhi, India, 1994—97, Sr. Rsch. fellow, Coun. of Sci. and Indsl. Rsch. (CSIR), India., 1997—98. Mem.: Am. Phys. Soc., Materials Rsch. Soc. Christian. Achievements include patents in field; development of multi-wall carbon nanotube based gas sensors; nanocrystalline tin oxide based high sensitivity ethanol sensors; rare earth metal hydride thin films based optical switching devices; plasma polymerized Furan thin films; invention of methods for growing low to high aspect ratio titanium dioxide (titania) nanotube arrays on titanium foils; method to fabricate transparent nanotube array thin films; first to methods for fabricating various nanostructures like copper-oxide nano-belts, aluminum-silicon nanowires, gold-silicon composite nanowires and nanoporous oxides of iron, tin and tungsten; invention of titania nanotube array based ultra-high sensitivity hydrogen gas sensors; development of titania nanotube array photoanodes for highly efficient hydrogen production through water splitting; titania nanotube array dye sensitized solar cells; nanoporous alumina based Surface Acoustic Wave (SAW) ammonia sensors; nanoporous alumina based resistive humidity sensors. Avocations: music, reading, travel, basketball. Home: 10 Vairo Blvd Apt # 239C State College PA 16803 Office: The Pennsylvania State University 212 Materials Research Laboratory University Park PA 16802 Home Phone: 814-237-7782; Office Phone: 814-865-6780. Office Fax: 814-865-6780. Personal E-mail: mag_oom@yahoo.com. E-mail: dkv3@psu.edu.

VARGO, LOUISE ANN, landscape artist, music educator; b. LaGrange, Ill., Oct. 30, 1974; d. Charles Patrick and Loretta Ann Vargo. BA, Benedictine U., Lisle, Ill., 1997. Irrigation designer Century Rain Aid, Downers Grove, Ill., 1996—99; piano tchr. Louise Vargo Studio, Plainfield, Ill., 1997—; irrigation designer John Deere Landscapes, Downers Grove, 2002—05, irrigation design mgr., 2006—. Sales cons. Mary Kay Cosmetics, Plainfield, 2003—. Mem.: Music Educators Nat. Conf. Avocations: gardening, cooking. Home: 13605 Golden Meadow Dr Plainfield IL 60544 Personal E-mail: louisevargo@hotmail.com.

VARGO, RONALD PAUL, information technology executive; b. Painesville, Ohio, Mar. 26, 1954; s. Anton M. and Ingrid E. (Olson) V.; m. Kathleen M. Martell, Nov. 20, 1976; children: Mary Christine, Kevin Matthew. BA in Econs., Dartmouth Coll., 1976; MBA, Stanford U., 1981. Various fin. positions GE, Stamford, Conn., 1976-79, Standard Oil Co., Cleve., 1981-87, dir. corp. fin., 1986-87; comml. mgr. BP Exploration, Houston, 1987-89; gen. mgr. crude oil trading BP Oil Supply Co., 1989—91; joined TRW, 1991, v.p. bus. devel. automotive electronics, v.p., treas., corp. treas., v.p. investor relations, 2001—04; v.p., treas. Electronic Data Systems Corp., 2004, co-interim CFO, 2006, exec. v.p., CFO, 2006—. Office: EDS Corp 5400 Legacy Dr Plano TX 75024 *

VARI, SANDOR GEORGE, physician, research scientist; b. Turkeve, Hungary; came to the U.S., 1988; s. George Peter and Rozalia Roza (Balpataki) V.; m. Julianna Irma Gaal, Dec. 23, 1982; 1 child, Judith. MD, Semmelweis Med. U., Budapest, Hungary, 1978; Surgeon, Postgrad. Sch. Medicine, Budapest, Hungary, 1985. Resident Semmelweis Med. U., Budapest, Hungary, 1978-85, asst. prof. surgery, 1985-90; rsch. fellow Cedars-Sinai Med. Ctr., LA, 1988-89, rsch. scientist, 1990—. Vis. scientist Found. Rsch. Tech., Hellas, Heraklion, Greece, 1994, Laser-und Medizin Tech., Berlin, 1995, 96, 97, 98; spkr. USA Fulbright Assn., Washington, 1993-94; invited ind. expert European Commn., 1996. Contbr. articles to profl. jours. Founder Hungoptika Hungarian chpt. Internat. Soc. Optical Engrng., 1989-90, Hungarian Fulbright Assn. Fulbright scholar Cedars-Sinai Med. Ctr., 1989-90; small bus. innovation rsch. grant NIH and Dept. of Def., 1991, 93-97; recipient numerous grants NIH, Dept Defense, European Union Cmty. R & D. Mem. Am. Fedn. Clin. Rsch., Am. Soc. Laser Medicine Surgery (chair conf. 1991-93), Internat. Soc. Optical Engrng. (chair conf. 1989), Internat. Biomed. Optical Soc. (chair conf. 1989, 93, 96-99), Internat. Soc. Laser Surgery Med. (chair conf. 1991, 95), European Laser Assn. (chair conf. 1989), Hungarian Coll. Surgeons. Achievements include patent for fluorescence based biopsy needle, 1994, for biodistribution of fluorescence substances, 1995, for spectroscopy of blood perfusion, 1995, for fiber-optic endodontic apparatus, 1996, for spectroscopic burn injury evalutaion, 1997; research and applications of optics and photonics; research in spectral characterization of cervical cancer, multi dimensional spectroscopy in pathology, spectral topography microscope for histopathology evaluation; research and technology development in health telematics; development of optical imaging and integrated telematics applications for healthcare. Office: Cedars-Sinai Med Ctr Laser Rsch and Tech Devel Ctr 650 S San Vicente Blvd Los Angeles CA 90048-4620 Address: PO Box 17623 Encino CA 91416-7623 E-mail: vari@cshs.org.

VARIAN, HAL RONALD, economics professor; b. Wooster, Ohio, Mar. 18, 1947; s. Max Ronald and Elaine Catherine (Shultzman) V.; m. Carol Johnston, Nov. 1986. S.B., MIT, 1969; MA, U. Calif.-Berkeley, 1973, PhD (NSF fellow), 1973. Asst. prof. econs. MIT, 1973-77; prof. U. Mich., 1977-95, prof. fin., 1983-95, Reuben Kempf prof. econs., 1984-95; prof. sch. bus., dean sch. info. mgmt. and sys. U. Calif., Berkeley, 1995—, Class of 1944 prof., 1996—. Siena chair in econs., U. Siena, Italy, 1990. Author: Microeconomic Analysis, 1978, Intermediate Microeconomics, 1987, Information Rules, 1998; co-editor Am. Econ. Rev., 1987-90. Guggenheim fellow, 1979-80; Fulbright scholar, 1990 Fellow AAAS, Econometric Soc.; mem. Am. Econ. Soc. Home: 1198 Estates Dr Lafayette CA 94549-2749 Office: U Calif Sims 102 South Hl Berkeley CA 94720-0001

VARILEK, JULIE, music educator; b. Fort Dodge, Iowa, Mar. 14, 1956; d. Earl and Mavis Freeman; m. Charles Varilek, Aug. 5, 1978; children: Jennifer Marie, Audra Ann. BFA, U. SD, Vermillion, 1974—78. Music tchr. Bon Homme Sch. Dist., Tyndall, SD, 1980—85, Centerville Pub. Sch. Dist., SD, 1985—89, Thompson Sch. Dist., Loveland, Colo., 1990—95, Pk. Sch. Dist., Estes Park, Colo., 1995—. Ch. choir dir. Our Lady Mountains Cath. Ch., Estes Park, 1995—2006; mem. Fine Arts Guild Rockies, Estes Park, 2003—06. Recipient Outstanding Women Educator of Yr., AAUW, 2000. Mem.: Delta Kappa Gamma (mem. tchrs. orgn. 1993—2003, v.p. 1995—97), Rotary (hon.). Home: 1010 Acacia Dr Estes Park CO 80517 Office: Estes Park Intermediate Sch 1505 Brodie Ave Estes Park CO 80517 Home Phone: 970-586-8776.

VARIN, ROGER ROBERT, textile executive; b. Bern, Switzerland, Feb. 15, 1925; came to U.S., 1951; s. Robert Francois and Anna (Martz) V.; m. Annemarie Louis, May 24, 1951; children: Roger R.R., Edward C.H., Viviane A.H. BBA, Mcpl. Coll., Bern, 1944; PhD in Chemistry, U. Bern, 1951. Rsch. fellow Harvard U., Cambridge, Mass., 1951-52; rsch. assoc. E.I. DuPont De Nemours, Wilmington, Del., 1952-62; dir. rsch. Riegel Textile Corp., Ware Shoals, S.C., 1962-71; founder, chief exec. officer Varinit Corp., Greenville, S.C., 1971—. Pres. Greenville Sister City Internat., 1993; bd. dirs. Greenville Symphony Assn., 1997-2000; trustee Brevard Music Ctr., 2000-06. Mem. Am. Chem. Soc., Fiber Soc., Soc. Advanced Materials and Process Engrng., Rotary (pres. Greenville chpt. 1979-80), Sigma Xi. Office: Varinit Corp PO Box 6602 Greenville SC 29606-6602

VARIS, AGNES, pharmaceutical executive; b. Lowell, Mass., 1930; d. Dionysis and Demetroula Koulovaris; m. Karl Leichtman. B in English and Chemistry, Brooklyn Coll.; D of Public Service (hon.), Tufts U., 2003. From entry-level chemist to exec. v.p. Fine Organics Inc., 1950—70; founder Agvar Chemicals, 1970—; co-founder Marsam Pharmaceuticals, 1985—; founder, pres. Aegis Pharmaceuticals, 1992—. Mem. consolidated corp. fund Lincoln Ctr.; pres., trustee MAKK Found.; bd. overseers Tufts Sch. Veterinary Medicine; bd. dirs. Nat. Org. Rare Disorders (NORD), Eleanor Roosevelt Legacy Com.; mng. dir. Met. Opera; bd. trustees Tufts U., 2004. Recipient Industry Leadership award, Nat. Org. Rare Disorders (NORD), 1999. Mem.: Sales Assn. Chemical Industry, Drug Chemical Allied Trade Assn., Chemist Club. Office: Agvar Chemicals 58 Rte 15 Little Falls NJ 07424

VARITEK, JASON, professional baseball player; b. Apr. 11, 1972; Attended, Ga. Tech. Catcher Boston Red Sox, 1997—. Mem. Team USA, World Baseball Classic, 2006. Named to Am. league All-Star Team, 2005; recipient Silver Slugger award, MLB, 2005, A.L. Gold Glove, 2005. Office: Boston Red Sox Fenway Park 4 Yawkey Way Boston MA 02215

VARLEY, HERBERT PAUL, Japanese language and cultural history educator; b. Paterson, NJ, Feb. 8, 1931; s. Herbert Paul and Katharine L. (Norcross) V.; m. Betty Jane Geiskopf, Dec. 24, 1960 BS, Lehigh U., 1952; MA, Columbia U., 1961, PhD, 1964; DHL (hon.), Lehigh U., 1988. Asst. prof. U. Hawaii, Honolulu, 1964-65; asst. prof. dept. East Asian Langs. and Cultures Columbia U., NYC, 1965-69, assoc. prof., 1969-75, prof., 1975-94, prof. emeritus Japanese history, 1994—, chmn. dept. East Asian Langs. and Cultures, 1983-89. Sen Soshitsu XV prof. Japanese cultural history U. Hawaii, spring 1991-93, 94—2004, prof. emeritus, 2004—. Author: The Onin War, 1967, The Samurai, 1970, Imperial Restoration in Medieval Japan, 1971, Japanese Culture, 1973, 4th edit., 2000, A Chronicle of Gods and Sovereigns, 1980, Tea in Japan: Essays on the History of Chanoyu, 1989, Warriors of Japan, As Portrayed in the War Tales, 1994; co-editor Sources of Japanese Tradition, Vol. 1, 2d edit., 2001. Bd. govs. Japanese Cultural Ctr. of Hawaii. Served with U.S. Army, 1952-54, Japan. Recipient Imperial Decoration Govt. Japan, Order of Rising Sun, Gold Rays With Rosette. Mem. Assn. Asian Studies, Japan Soc., Soc. Am. Magicians (pres. local chpt. 1983-84). Avocations: magic, piano. Home: 38 S Judd St Apt 15B Honolulu HI 96817-2609 Office: U Hawaii History Dept Sakamaki Hall A 203 2530 Dole St Honolulu HI 96822-2303 Business E-Mail: pvarley@hawaii.edu.

VARMA, ANUJAN, computer engineer, educator; PhD, U. So. Calif., LA, 1982—86. Rsch. staff IBM Rsch., Yorktown Hts., NY, 1986—91; prof. U. Calif., Santa Cruz, 1991—. Contbr. articles to profl. jours. Recipient Darlington award, IEEE, 1991, Young Investigator award, NSF, 1992. Achievements include patents in field. Office: Univ Calif 1156 High St Santa Cruz CA 95064

VARMA, ARVIND, chemical engineering educator, researcher; b. Ferozabad, India, Oct. 13, 1947; s. Hans Raj and Vijay L. (Jhanjhee) V.; m. Karen K. Guse, Aug. 7, 1971; children: Anita, Sophia. BS ChemE, Panjab U., 1966; MS ChemE, U. N.B., Fredericton, Can., 1968; PhD ChemE, U. Minn., 1972. Asst. prof. U. Minn., Mpls., 1972-73; sr. research engr. Union Carbide Corp., Tarrytown, NY, 1973-75; asst. prof. chem. engring. U. Notre Dame, Ind., 1975-77, assoc. prof., 1977-80, prof., 1980-88, Arthur J. Schmitt prof., 1988—2003, chmn. dept., 1983-88; dir. Ctr. for Molecularly Engineered Materials, 2000—03; R. Games Slayter Disting. prof., head Purdue U. Sch. Chem. Engrng., 2004—. Vis. prof. U. Wis., Madison, 1981; Chevron vis. prof. Calif. Inst. Tech., Pasadena, 1982; vis. prof. Ind. Inst. Tech.-Kanpur, 1989, U. Cagliari, Italy, 1989, 92; vis. fellow Princeton U., 1996; Piercy vis. prof. U. Minn., 2001; Kane vis. prof. U. Mumbai, 2007. Co-author: Mathematical Methods in Chemical Engineering, 1997, Parametric Sensitivity in Chemical Systems, 1999, Catalyst Design, 2001; editor: (with others) The Mathematical Understanding of Chemical Engineering Systems, 1980, Chemical Reaction and Reactor Engineering, 1987; series editor: Cambridge Series in Chemical Engineering, 1996—; contbr. numerous articles to profl. jours. Recipient Tchr. of Yr. award Coll. Engrng. U. Notre Dame, 1991, Spl. Presdl. award 1992, R.H. Wilhelm award AIChE, 1993, Burns Grad. Sch. award 1997, E.W. Thiele award AIChE, 1998, Chem. Engrng. Lectureship award, ASEE, 2000, Rsch. Achievement award U. Notre Dame, 2001, Techs. of Yr. award Industry Week, 2005; Fulbright scholar; Indo-Am. fellow, 1988-89. Office: Purdue U Sch Chem Engring West Lafayette IN 47907 Office Phone: 765-494-4075. Business E-Mail: avarma@purdue.edu.

VARMA, DATLA G.K., radiologist, researcher; b. Bobbili, Andhra, India, June 2, 1951; came to U.S., 1976; now naturalized; s. Datla V. Raju and Datla Satyavathi; m. Siva Kumari, Dec. 20, 1980; children: Datla Kirti, Datla Vivek. MBBS, Andhra Med. Coll., 1975. Diplomate Am. Bd. Radiology, Am. Bd. Nuclear Medicine. Intern King George Hosp., Visakha Patnam, India, 1974-75; resident in anat. pathology Good Samaritan Hosp., Cin., 1977-78; resident in nuclear medicine Univ. Hosp., Cin., 1978-80, resident in radiology, 1980-83; asst. prof. radiology Tulane U., New Orleans, 1983-88, med. dir. diagnostic svcs./radiology dept., 1987-89, assoc. prof. radiology, 1988-89, sect. chief body CT, 1983-89, sect. chief body MRI, 1988-89; assoc. prof. radiology U. Tex./M.D. Anderson Cancer Ctr., Houston, 1989-99, acting sect. chief MRI, 1991-99, prof. radiology, 1999—. Contbr. articles to profl. jours., chpts. to books. Avocations: sports, travel, reading. Home: 3915 Marlowe St Houston TX 77005-2045 Office: Md Anderson Cancer Ctr PO Box 57 Houston TX 77001-0057 E-mail: dvarma@di.mdacc.tmc.edu.

VARMUS, HAROLD ELIOT, health science administrator, educator, science researcher; b. Oceanside, NY, Dec. 18, 1939; s. Frank and Beatrice (Barasch) V.; m. Constance Louise Casey, Oct. 25, 1969; children: Jacob Carey, Christopher Isaac. BA in English, Amherst Coll., 1961; MA in Lit., Harvard U., 1962; MD, Columbia U. Med. Sch., 1966. Intern, resident Presbyn. Hosp., NYC, 1966-68; lectr. dept. microbiology U. Calif., San Francisco, 1970-72, asst. prof., 1972-74, assoc. prof., 1974-79, prof. depts. microbiology and immunology, biochemistry and biophysics, 1979—93, Am. Cancer Soc. research prof., 1984—93; clin. assoc. NIH, Bethesda, Md., 1968-70, dir., 1993—99; pres., CEO Meml. Sloan-Kettering Cancer Ctr., NYC, 2000—. Chmn. bd. on biology NRC, 1991—93; served on WHO Commn on Macroeconomics and Health; co-founder, chmn. bd. dirs. Pub. Libr. Sci. (PLoS), 2003—; sci. bd. Grand Challenges in Global Health. Co-recipient Scientist of Yr. award, Calif. Acad. Sci., 1982, Lasker Found. award, 1982, Passano Found. award, 1983, Armand Hammer Cancer prize, GM Alfred Sloan award, Shubitz Cancer prize, 1984, Internat. award, Gardner Found., 1984, Nobel Prize in Physiology or Medicine, 1989; recipient Nat. Medal of Sci., 2002, Vannevar Bush award, NSF, 2001. Fellow World Tech. Network (World Tech. Network award Media and Journalism, 2005); mem. NAS, Inst. Medicine, Am. Soc. Virology, Am. Soc. Microbiology, Am. Soc. Cell Biology, Am. Acad. Arts and Scis., Am. Soc. for Biochemistry and Molecular Biology. Democrat. Achievements include rsch. (with J. Michael Bishop) on the the cellular origin of retroviral oncogenes. Office: Meml Sloan-Kettering Cancer Ctr 1275 York Ave New York NY 10021-6094 also: PLoS 185 Berry St St 3100 San Francisco CA 94107 Business E-Mail: varmus@mskcc.org. *

VARNER, ARTHUR E., allergist, researcher; b. Xenia, Ohio, Mar. 18, 1966; s. Kenneth H. and Virginia L. Varner; m. Heidi Harris, Aug. 8, 1992; children: Madeleine L., Grant H., Gretchen L. BA, Miami U., Oxford, Ohio, 1988; MD, Ohio State U., 1992. Intern and resident in internal medicine Riverside Meth. Hosp., Columbus, Ohio, 1992—95; allergy fellow U. Wis., Madison, 1995—97; allergist Allergy Diagnostic, Beachwood, Ohio, 1997—. Pollen counter, 2005—. Achievements include first to relate acetaminophen use with asthma; research in decreased use of pediatric aspirin has contributed to the increasing prevalence of childhood asthma. Home: 4103 Meadowbrook Blvd University Heights OH 44118 Office: Allergy Diagnostic 23250 Mercantile Rd Beachwood OH 44122 Home Phone: 216-321-5997. Personal E-mail: wiscart@aol.com.

VARNER, CARLTON A., lawyer; b. Creston, Iowa, July 14, 1947; BA, U. Iowa, 1969; JD magna cum laude, U. Minn., 1972. Bar: Calif. 1972, DC 1979. Mng. ptnr. Sheppard Mullin Richter & Hampton LLP, LA, 1991—, chmn. exec. com., 1991—98. Spkr. in field. Author: California Antitrust & Unfair Competition Law, 2nd edit., 2001, Old Wine in New Bottles: The Competitor Collaboration Guidelines, 2000. Vice-chair Constitutional Rights Found., 2000—03. Mem.: ABA (chair exemptions & immunities com., antitrust sect. 2002—05), State Bar of Calif. (chair, antitrust sect. 2004), Constl. Rights Found. (v.p.), LA County Bar Assn. (chmn. antitrust sect. 1993—94), Chancery Club of LA. Office: Sheppard Mullin Richter & Hampton LLP 333 S Hope St Fl 48 Los Angeles CA 90071-1406 Office Phone: 213-620-1398.

VARNER, CHARLEEN LAVERNE MCCLANAHAN, nutritionist, educator, administrator, dietitian; b. Alba, Mo., Aug. 28, 1931; d. Roy Calvin and Lela Ruhama (Smith) McClanahan; student Joplin (Mo.) Jr. Coll., 1949-51; BS in Edn., Kans. State Coll. Pittsburg, 1953; MS, U. Ark., 1958; PhD, Tex. Woman's U. 1966; postgrad. Mich. State U., 1955, U. Mo., 1962; m. Robert Bernard Varner, July 4, 1953. Apprentice county home agt. U. Mo., 1952; tchr. Ferry Pass Sch., Escambia County, Fla., 1953-54; tchr. biology, home econs. Joplin Sr. H.S., 1954-59; instr. home econs. Kans. State Coll., Pittsburg, 1959-63; lectr. foods, nutrition Coll. Household Arts and Scis., Tex. Woman's U., 1963-64, rsch. asst. NASA grant, 1964-66; assoc. prof. home econs. Central Mo. State U., Warrensburg, 1966-70, adviser to Colhecon, 1966-70, adviser to Alpha Sigma Alpha, 1967-70, 72, bd. adv. Honors Group, 1967-70; prof., head dept. home econs. Kans. State Tchrs. Coll., Emporia, 1970-73; prof., chmn. dept. home econs. Benedictine Coll., Atchison, Kans., 1973-74; prof., chmn. dept. home econs. Baker U., Baldwin City, Kans., 1974-75; owner, operator Diet-Con Dietary Cons. Enterprises, cons. dietitian, 1973—, Home-Con Cons. Enterprises; adj. prof. Highland (Kans.) CC, 2004—. Active Joplin Little Theater, 1956-60. Mem. NEA, AAUW, AAUP, Mo. State Tchr. Assn., Kans. State Tchr. Assn., Am. Dietetic Assn., Mo. Dietetic Assn., Kans. Dietetic Assn., Am. Home Econs. Assn., Mo. Home Econs. Assn., Kans. Home Econs. Assn., Mo. Acad. Scis., U. Ark. Alumni Assn., Alumni Assn. Kans. State Coll. of Pittsburg, Am. Vocat. Assn., Assn. Edn. Young Children, Sigma Xi, Beta Sigma Phi, Beta Beta Beta, Alpha Sigma Alpha, Delta Kappa Gamma, Kappa Kappa Iota, Phi Upsilon Omicron, Theta Alpha Pi, Kappa Phi. Methodist (organist). Home: PO Box 1009 Topeka KS 66601-1009

VARNER, CHILTON DAVIS, lawyer; b. Opelika, Ala., Mar. 12, 1943; d. William Cole and Frances (Thornton) Davis; m. K. Morgan Varner, III, June 19, 1965; 1 child, Ashley Elizabeth Davis. AB with distinction, Smith Coll., 1965; JD with distinction, Emory U., 1976. Assoc. King & Spalding, Atlanta, 1976-83, ptnr., 1983—, mem. mgmt. com., 1995—, gen. counsel. Bd. dirs. Wesley Woods Healthcare, 11th Cir. Ct. Appeals Hist. Soc.; trustee Emory U., Atlanta, 1995—, Product Liability Adv. Coun. Found., 1996—2004; mem. Adv. Com. Fed. Civil Rules, 2004—. Author: Appellate Handbook for Georgia Lawyers, 1995. Mem. Leadership Atlanta, 1984—85; mem. exec. com. Atlanta Arts Alliance, 1981—85; mem. Atlanta Symphony Chorus, 1970—74; asst. clk., elder, bd. elders Trinity Presbyn. Ch., Atlanta, 1975—88. Named one of Top 10 Women Litigators, Nat. Law Jour., 2001; recipient Disting. Alumna award, Emory U. Law Sch., 1998. Fellow: Am. Coll. Trial Lawyers; mem.: ABA (mem. adv. com. fed. civil rules 2004—), Atlanta Bar Assn., Ga. Bar Assn., Phi Beta Kappa, Order of Coif. Office: King & Spalding 1180 Peachtree St NE 37th Fl Atlanta GA 30309-3521 Office Phone: 404-572-4789, 404-572-4789. Office Fax: 404-572-5100. E-mail: cvarner@kslaw.com.

VARNER, DAVID EUGENE, lawyer; b. Dallas, Oct. 9, 1937; s. E.C. and D. Evelyn (Bauguss) V.; m. Joan Paula Oransky, Aug. 13, 1962; children: Michael A., Kevin E., Cheryl L. BA, So. Meth. U., Dallas, 1958, JD, 1961. Bar: Tex. 1961, Fla. 1974, Okla., 1977, U.S. Supreme Ct. 1978. Assoc. Eldridge, Goggans, Davidson & Silverberg, Dallas, 1962-65; atty., asst. sec. Redman Industries, Inc., Dallas, 1965-66; assoc. gen. atty. Tex. Instruments, Inc., Dallas, 1966-73; sr. atty., asst. sec. Fla. Gas Co., Winter Park, 1973-76; v.p., gen. counsel, sec. Facet Enterprises, Inc., Tulsa, 1976-78, Summa Corp., Las Vegas, Nev., 1978-82; sr. v.p., gen. counsel, sec. Transco Energy Co., Houston, 1982-95; pres. The MKC Group, Houston, 1995—. Mem. royalty mgmt. adv. com. U.S. Minerals Mgmt. Svc., 1985—87. Mng. editor Southwestern Law Jour., 1960-61 Mem.: Fla. Bar Assn., Tex. Bar Assn. Office: PO Box 79571 Houston TX 77279-9571

VARNER, JOYCE EHRHARDT, retired librarian; b. Quincy, Ill., Sept. 13, 1938; d. Wilbur John and Florence Elizabeth (Mast) Ehrhardt; m. Donald Giles Varner, Sept. 12, 1959; children: Amy, Janice, Christian, Matthew, Nadine. BA, Northeastern Okla. State U., 1980; MLS, U. Okla., 1984. Lab. analyst Gardner Denver Co., Quincy, 1956-60; sales rep. Morrisonville, Ill., 1963-69; libr. clk. U. Ill., Urbana, 1973-75; libr. tech. asst. Northeastern Okla. State U., Tahlequah, 1976-86; asst. reference libr. Muskogee (Okla.) Pub. Libr., 1986-90; libr. Jess Dunn Correctional Ctr., Taft, Okla., 1990-98; ret., 1998; field office supr. Census 2000 Dept. of Commerce, Welling, Okla., 1998. Editor Indian Nations Audubon Nature Notes, 1977-81, 96-2007; contbr. articles to newspaper. Vol. Lake-Wood coun. Girl Scouts U.S.A., 1975-98, bd. dirs. 1992-98, pres., 1995-96; sec.-treas. Cherokee County Rural Water Dist. 7, 1987—; edn. chmn. Indian Nations chpt. Nat. Audubon Soc., 1989-2000, pres., 2000-04; project dir. Tahlequah Friends of the Libr., 2002-04, pres. 2004—. Recipient Thanks Badge, Lake-Wood coun. Girl Scouts U.S.A., 1990. Mem. AAUW (chair diversity com. 2000), Okla. Libr. Assn. (nominating com. 1989), Okla. Acad. Sci., Okla. Ornithol. Soc. (chmn. libr. com. 1978-88, Award of Merit 1990, pres.-elect 1994, pres. 1995-96), Alpha Chi, Beta Beta Beta, Phi Delta Kappa (Found. rep. 1984-86, historian 1992-2006). Avocations: nature study, needlecrafts, square dancing, genealogy.

VARNER, VANCE SIEBER, principal; b. Lewistown, Pa., Aug. 8, 1967; s. George Thomas and Kay (Sieber) V. BS, Pa. State U., 1991, MEd. Earth sci., geosci. and environ. tchr. Upper Dauphin Area High Sch., Elizabethville, Pa., 1991—. Varsity soccer coach Upper Dauphin High Sch., 1991—, asst. varsity wrestling coach, 1991—. Recipient Nat. Sallie Mae Tchr. award Student Loan Mktg. Assn., 1992. Avocations: fly fishing, hunting. Home: RR 3 Box 255 Mifflintown PA 17059-9803 Office: 2 Manor Dr Lewistown PA 17044 Business E-Mail: vsv55@mcsdk12.org.

VARNEY, CARLETON BATES, JR., interior designer, columnist, educator; b. Lynn, Mass., Jan. 23, 1937; s. Carleton Bates and Julia (Raczkowskos) V.; divorced; children: Nicholas, Seamus, Sebastian. BA, Oberlin Coll., 1958; student, U. Madrid, 1957; MA, NYU, 1969; LHD (hon.), U. Charleston, 1987. Sch. tchr., 1958-59; asst. to pres. Dorothy Draper & Co., Inc., 1959-63, exec. v.p., 1963-66, pres., 1966—; dean Carleton Varney Sch. of Art & Design, U. Charleston, W.Va. Designer: Varney and Sons Furniture Collection Kindel Furniture Co., Carleton

Varney by-the-yard decorative fabrics, dinnerware and china, crystal glassware, table and bed linen, lamps and light fixtures, ready to wear resort collection Cruzanwear, 1987, mens' wear furnishings for Rawlinson & Marking, London, 1987; Ready to wear resort coll., "A Perfect Day in Paradise", 1998, Colours Resort Collection, 2000; interior designer: Dromoland Castle, Ireland, 1963, 88, Westbury Hotel, Belgium, 1964, NY World's Fair, 1965, Clare Inn, Ireland, 1968, Greenbrier Hotel, White Sulphur Springs, W.Va., 1968-, Westbury Hotel, San Francisco, 1973, Copley Plaza Hotel, Boston, 1976, 96, Amway Grand Plaza Hotel, Grand Rapids, Mich., 1980, The Grand Hotel, Mackinac Island, Mich., 1978-, Equinox House, Manchester, Vt., 1984, Brazilian Ct. Hotel, Palm Beach, Fla., 1985, Waldorf Towers, NYC, 1985, Dawn Beach Hotel, St. Maarten, 1985, Christian Broadcasting Conv. Ctr., 1986, Met. Opera House boutique, NYC, 1985, (cruise ship) World Discoverer, 1984, Arrowwood Conv. Ctr., Purchase, NY, 1987, Boca Raton Hotel and Club, Fla., 1987, Speedway Club, Charlotte, NC, 1987, Coccoloba Plantation, Anguilla, Brit. Virgin Islands, 1987, Villa Madeleine, St. Croix, VI, 1987, Ashford Castle, Ireland, 1988, Adare Manor, Ireland, 1988, The Breakers, Palm Beach, Fla., 1989, Jackson Lake Lodge, Wyo., 1989, V.P.'s Residence, Washington, 1989, Cormorant Cove, St. Croix, VI, 1990, The Buccaneer Hotel, St. Croix, 1991, Dromoland Castle, Internat. Ctr., Ireland, 1991, West Village Golf Resort, Tokyo, 1993, Half Moon Bay Club, Jamaica, The Plaza, NY, 1997, The Hibiscus Restaurant, Palm Beach, Fla., 1999, North Shore Country Club, LI, NY, 2002, Mount Wash. Hotel and Resort, N.H., 2003, Lago Mar Resort and Club, Ft. Lauderdale, Fla., 2003-04, McJukin Corp., W.Va., 2005, Harder Hall Resort and Spa, Sebring, Fla., 2005, Stoneleigh Hotel Penthouse Suites, Dallas, 2007; numerous pvt. residences; designer: White House party for celebration Israel-Egypt Peace Treaty, 1979; Palm Beach Cares fashion benefit for Am. Found. for AIDS Research, 1988, log home for Pres. and Mrs. Carter, Ellijay, Ga., 1983; color cons. Carter Presdl. Library, 1986; trustee and curator: former presdl. yacht U.S.S. Sequoia, 1982; author: numerous books including You and Your Apartment, 1960, The Family Decorates a Home, 1962 Carleton Varney Decorates Windows, 1975, Be Your Own Decorator, 1979, There's No Place Like Home, 1980, Down Home, 1981, Carleton Varney's ABC's of Decorating, 1983, Staying in Shape: An Insider's Guide to the Great Spas, 1983, Room by Room Decorating, 1984, Color Magic, 1985, The Draper Touch, 1988, Kiss the Hibiscus Goodnight, 1992, The Decorator, 1999, In the Pink--Dorothy Draper, America's Most Fabulous Decorator, 2006; syndicated columnist: Your Family Decorator, 1968—; decorating column Familyclick.com, 2000, Inside Design column N.Y. Post, 2001; contbg. editor Good Housekeeping Mag., 1993-95; contbg. design editor Social and Personal Mag. (Ireland) 1996-; style editor Men's Style mag.; editor-at-large Hamptons Mag., 2000—. Recipient Shelby Williams award for design achievement, 1967, Tommy design award for Covington's Heraldry collection, 1989, Interior Design Hall of Fame award, 1990; named as one of 30 Deans of Am. Design, Archtl. Digest, 2005. Mem. Indsl. Designers Soc. Am., NY State Bd. for Interior Design, NY Athletic Club, Shannon Rowing Club (Ireland), Millbrook Golf and Tennis Club (NY). Office: Dorothy Draper & Co Inc 60 E 56th St New York NY 10022-3204 Office Phone: 212-758-2810. Business E-Mail: cvarney@dorothydraper.com. *My success, I believe, is due to an ability to understand and use vibrant color appropriately, and to strive for perfection of detail in all my designs as details separate the excellent from the ordinary.*

VARNEY, CHRISTINE A., federal official; Degree in Politics, Philosophy and Econs. (hon.), Trinity Coll., Dublin, Ireland, 1975; BA in Polit. Sci. and History magna cum laude, SUNY, Albany, 1977; MPA in Policy Analysis, Legislation and Rsch. magna cum laude, Syracuse U., 1978; JD cum laude, Georgetown U., 1986. Legis. asst. N.Y. Senate, Albany, 1977; econ. analyst GAO, Washington, 1978; econ. devel. dir. El Centro, Calif., 1979; dir. Neighborhood Outreach Program, San Diego, 1980-82; assoc. Surry & Morse, Washington, 1984-86, Pierson, Semmes & Finley, Washington, 1986-88; counsel Hogan & Hartson, Washington, 1990-92; chief counsel Clinton for Pres. Primary Campaign, 1992, Clinton-Gore Campaign, 1992; gen. counsel Dem. Nat. Com., 1992, Presdl. Inauguration Com., 1993; dep. asst. to President U.S., sec. to Cabinet The White House, Washington, 1993-94; commissioner FTC, Washington, 1994—97; ptnr. Hogan & Hartson LLP, Washington, 1997—, mem. exec. com. Active Women's Legal Def. Fund. Mem. D.C. Bar Assn., N.Y. State Bar Assn., Nat. Lawyer's Coun. Office: Hogan & Hartson Columbia Sq 555 Thirteenth St NW Washington DC 20004-1109 Office Phone: 202-637-6823. Office Fax: 202-637-5910. Business E-Mail: cavarney@hhlaw.com.

VARNEY, RICHARD ALAN, health facility administrator; b. Concord, NH, July 8, 1950; s. John Berry and Hattie Elizabeth (Harrington) V.; m. Suzanne Glaab, Dec. 31, 1983; stepchildren: Alysen Suzanne Bidle, Craig Judson Bidle. BS in Phys. Edn., U. N.H., 1972; MHA in Healthcare Adminstrn., Baylor U., 1984; diploma, Command and Gen. Staff Coll., 1986. Commd. 2d lt. U.S. Army, 1973, advanced through grades to lt. col., 1991; dep. asst. CEO Cutler Army Hosp., Ft. Devens, Mass., 1973—76; field med. asst. 38th ADA Bde., Osan Air Base, Republic of Korea, 1977—78; dep. asst. CEO 15th Med. Battalion, Ft. Hood, Tex., 1979—81; adminstrv. resident Ireland Army Hosp., Ft. Knox, Ky., 1982—83; COO, exec. officer U.S. Army Dental Activity, Ft. Knox, 1983—86; grad. instr. Army-Baylor Healthcare Program, San Antonio, 1986—90; project mgr. Office of the Army Surgeon Gen., Washington, 1990—93; ret. U.S. Army, 1993; office mgr. Aebi, Ginty, Romaker & Sprouse MD's, Inc., Lancaster, Ohio, 1993—2000; dir. gen. internal medicine program The Ohio State U. Med. Ctr., Columbus, 2000—04; dir. ops. Fairfield Dept. Health, Lancaster, 2005—. Mem. Source Selection Evaluation Bd.-Champus Reform, Arlington, Va., 1987; mem. adv. com. for assoc. degree program in med. assisting Ohio U., Lancaster, 1998-2000. Adult leader Boy Scouts Am., Tex., Va. and Ohio, 1988-97, 2003—; mem. Lancaster City Bd. of Health, 1996-2001, pres. pro tem, 1999-2001; mem. Fairfield County Combined Gen. Health Dist. Bd., 2002-04. Officer US Army Med. Svc. Corps, 1973—93. Decorated Legion of Merit, Order of Mil. Med. Merit award, Expert Field Med. badge; named to Hon. Order Ky. Cols., 1989, Outstanding Young Man of Am., 1982. Fellow Am. Coll. Healthcare Execs.; mem. Ctrl. Ohio Health Adminstrs. Assn., Ohio Med. Group Mgmt. Assn., Mid-Ohio Med. Mgmt. Assn., Profl. Assn. Med. Mgrs., Am. Assn. Procedural Coders, Lancaster Area Soc. for Human Resource Mrmt. (legis. rep. 1998-99, membership chair 1999—), Am. Hosp. Assn., Nat. Eagle Scout Assn., The Ret. Officers Assn., Am. Legion, Fraternal Order of Eagles, Alpha Phi Omega. Avocations: home improvement, music. Home: 1025 E 5th Ave Lancaster OH 43130-3276 Home Phone: 740-681-5665; Office Phone: 740-653-4489 x155. Personal E-mail: richvarneyosu@yahoo.com. Business E-Mail: rvarney@co.fairfield.oh.us.

VARNEY, ROBERT NATHAN, retired physicist, researcher; b. San Francisco, Nov. 7, 1910; s. Frank Hastings Sr. and Emily Patricia (Rhine) V.; m. Astrid Margareta Riffolt, June 19, 1948; children: Nils Roberts, Natalie Rhine. AB in Physics with highest honors, U. Calif., Berkeley, 1931, MA, 1932, PhD, 1935; DSc (hon.), Leopold Franzens U., Innsbruck, Austria, 1983. Instr. NYU, 1936-38; asst. prof., assoc. prof., prof. Washington U., St. Louis, 1938-64; mem. rsch. lab. Bell Labs., Murray Hill, NJ, 1951-52; sr. mem. rsch. lab., sr. sci. cons. Lockheed Missiles & Space Co., Palo Alto, Calif., 1964-75; ret., 1975. Mem. Mo. Gov.'s Sci. Adv. Com., St. Louis, 1960-64; guest prof. Leopold Franzens U., 1977-78. Author: Engineering Physics, 1948; (with others) Methods of Experimental Physics, 1968, Introduction to...Atmospheric Pollution, 1972, Brain Injury without Head Injury, 1999; contbg. author textbook; contbr. over 80 articles to scholarly and profl. jours. Comdr. USNR, 1931-57. Fulbright fellow Leopold Franzens U., Innsbruck, 1971-72, 76-77, NSF sr. postdoctoral fellow Inst. Tech., Stockholm, 1958-59, NRC sr. postdoctoral fellow U.S. Army Ballistic Rsch. Lab., Aberdeen, Md., 1975-76; recipient Cross of Honor 1st Class Austrian Govt., 1981. Fellow Am. Phys. Soc.; mem. Am. Assn. Physics Tchrs., Phi Beta Kappa, Sigma Xi, Tau Beta Pi, Omicron Delta Kappa. Episcopalian. Achievements include research in electron swarms and atmospheric pollutants; studies of closed head brain injuries. Home: 4156 Maybell Way Palo Alto CA 94306-3820 Personal E-mail: riffolt@batnet.com.

VARNHOLT, HEIKE, pathologist; d. Manfred and Else Varnholt. MD, Hannover Med. Sch., Germany, 2000. Pathologist-in-tng. Mass. Gen. Hosp., Harvard Med. Sch., Boston, 2000—03; chief resident in pathology Baystate Med. Ctr./Tufts U. Sch. of Medicine, Springfield, Mass., 2003—. Contbr. articles to profl. jours. Mem.: Am. Soc. for Clin. Pathology, Rodger C. Haggitt Gastrointestinal Pathology Soc. (Travel award 2003), Assn. Pathology Informatics, Coll. Am. Pathologists (Informatics award 2004), U.S. Acad. Pathology. Home Phone: 413-218-9647.

VARPAHOVSKY, ANDREY, computer scientist, educator; b. Moscow, July 26, 1936; s. Solomon Milikovsky and Irina Varpahovsky; m. Lina Feldman, Jan. 22, 1960; children: Fred, Katherine Bella. M, Moscow Inst. Energy, 1959; diploma, Inst. Math. Machines, Erevan, Armenia, 1971. Group leader Inst. Control Systems, Moscow, 1972—78; engr. Control Data Corp., Lexington, Mass., 1979—85; group leader Digital Equipment Corp., Marlborough, 1986—92; adv. engr. IBM, Rochester, Minn.; tchr. computer sci. Worcester State Coll., Mass., 2000—. Achievements include patents in field. Office: Worcester State Coll 486 Chandler St Worcester MA 01602 Home Phone: 508-620-2593; Office Phone: 508-929-8560. Office Fax: 508-929-8146. Personal E-mail: avarpah@yahoo.com. E-mail: avarpahovsky@worcester.edu.

VARRO, BARBARA JOAN, retired editor; b. East Chicago, Ind., Jan. 25, 1938; d. Alexander R. and Lottie R. (Bess) V. BA, Duquesne U., 1959. Feature reporter, asst. fashion editor Chgo. Sun-Times, 1959-64, fashion editor, 1964-76, feature writer, 1976-84; v.p. pub. rels. Daniel J. Edelman Inc., Chgo., 1984-85; v.p. PRB/Needham Porter Novelli, Chgo., 1985-86; editor Am. Hosp. Assn. News, Chgo., 1987-94; editor spl. sects. Chgo. Tribune, 1995-2000; ret. Recipient awards for feature writing Ill. AP, 1978, 79, 80 Mem.: PEO. Home: 219 Autumn Trail N Michigan City IN 46360

VARSHAVSKY, ALEXANDER JACOB, molecular biologist; b. Moscow, Nov. 8, 1946; came to U.S., 1977; s. Jacob M. and Mary B. (Zeitlin) V.; m. Vera Bingham, Aug. 30, 1990; children: Roman, Anna, Victoria. BS in Chemistry, Moscow State U., 1970; PhD in Biochemistry, Inst. of Molecular Biology, Moscow, 1973. Rsch. fellow Inst. Molecular Biology, Moscow, 1973—76; asst. prof. dept. biology MIT, Cambridge, 1977-80, assoc. prof. dept. biology, 1980-86, prof. dept. biology, 1986-92; Howard and Gwen Laurie Smits prof. cell biology, divsn. biology Calif. Inst. Tech., Pasadena, 1992—. Vis. fellow Internat. Inst. for Advanced Studies, Kyoto; mem. molecular cytology study sect. NIH. Author more than 150 articles in the field of genetics and biochemistry; holder 14 patents. Recipient Novartis-Drew award, Novartis, 1998, Merit award, NIH, 1998, Gairdner Internat. award (Can.), 1999, Alfred P. Sloan Jr. prize, GM Cancer Rsch. Found., 2000, Lasker award in basic med. rsch., Albert and Mary Lasker Found., 2000, Hoppe-Seyler award, Soc. for Biochemistry and Molecular Biology, Germany, 2000, Merck award, Am. Soc. Biochemistry and Molecular Biology, 2001, Pasarow award in cancer rsch., Pasarow Found., 2001, Wolf prize in medicine, Wolf Found., Israel, 2001, Massry prize, Massry Found., 2001, Max Planck Rsch. prize, Germany, 2001, Horwitz prize, Columbia U., 2001, Wilson medal, Am. Soc. Cell Biology, 2002, Stein & Moore award, Protein Soc., 2005, March of Dimes prize devel. biology, March of Dimes Found., 2006, Gagna and Van Heck prize, Belgium, 2006, Griffuel Cancer Rsch. prize, France, 2006, Schleiden medal, Germany, 2007. Fellow AAAS, Am. Acad. Microbiology, Am. Acad. Arts and Scis.; mem. NAS, Am. Philos. Soc., European Molecular Biology Orgn. (fgn., academia Europaea). Achievements include discoveries in the fields of DNA replication, chromosome structure, ubiquitin system, and intracellular protein turnover. Office: Calif Inst Tech Divsn Biology 1200 East California Blvd Pasadena CA 91125-0001 Office Fax: 626-440-9821. Business E-Mail: avarsh@caltech.edu.

VARTANIAN, THOMAS P., lawyer; b. Forest Hills, NY, Nov. 16, 1949; BA cum laude, Cathedral Coll., 1971; JD cum laude, Bklyn. Law Sch., 1976. Bar: N.Y. 1977, D.C. 1979, U.S. Supreme Ct. 1983. Special asst. to chief counsel and sr. trial atty. Office of Comptroller of the Currency, US Dept. Treasury, 1976-81; gen. counsel Fed. Home Loan Bank Bd. and Fed. Savings & Loan Ins. Corp., 1981-83; ptnr. Fried, Frank, Harris, Shriver & Jacobson LLP, Washington, 1983—, mng. dir. DC office, chair corp. dept., 1986—99. Bd. contbrs. Nat. Bank Law Report, 1984; bd. advisors Banking Law Rev.; mem. U.S. League Attys. Com., 1987. Edtl. bd. Banking Policy Reporter, 1988. Mem. ABA (sect. bus. law, chmn. com. on cyberspace law, 1998-2002), Fed. Bar Assn., D.C. Bar Assn. Office: Fried Frank Harris Shriver & Jacobson LLP 1001 Pennsylvania Ave NW Washington DC 20004-2505 E-mail: Thomas.Vartanian@friedfrank.com. *

VARVAK, MARK, mathematician, researcher; b. Kiev, Russia, Feb. 13, 1939; came to U.S., 1987; s. Shlyoma and Anna (Berimskaya) V.; m. Nellie Albert, Feb. 1, 1973 (div. Oct. 1983); 1 child, Alexander; m. Lidiya Zolotarenko, Aug. 30, 2002. MS in Applied Math., Ukraine U., 1969; candidate of sci., Rsch. Inst. of Structures, Kiev, 1970. Sr. rschr. Rsch. Inst. of Structures, Kiev, 1963-79; sr. engr. Constrn. Authority, Kiev, 1979-86; programmer Consulting Engrng. Co., NYC, 1988-91; scientist Sci. Application Internat. Corp., 1997—99, Navair Tng. Sys. Divsn., Orlando, Fla., 2002—. Contbr. more than 40 articles to profl. jours. Mem. Am. Math. Soc. Office: Training Sys Divsn 12350 Rsch Park Orlando FL 32826 Personal E-mail: varvakm@bellsouth.net.

VARZEGAR, MINOO, literature educator, reading specialist; b. Kerman, Iran; d. Abdolrahim and Amjad (Vali) Varzegar; m. Saeid Fatemi, May 8; children: Delaram, Arezou. BA in English summa cum laude, U. Tehran, 1966, MA in Psychology, 1969; MA in Tchg. English, U. Tchr. Edn., 1967; MA in Tchg. ESL, U. Ill., 1971, PhD in Tchg. ESL, 1975, postgrad., 1994. Cert. tchr. English, cert. high acad. adminstrn. Asst. prof. U. Tehran, 1979—84, assoc. prof., 1984—94, prof. dept. English, 1984—97, head dept. English of Evening Classes, 1975—83, dir. Lang. Lab., 1975—80, dir. lang. ctr., 1981—83, head dept. English, 1983—97. Vis. prof. U. Ill., Champaign-Urbana, 1997-99, rsch. scholar, 1997-99; assoc. faculty Columbia U., N.Y.C., 1999-2001, exec dir PCF, 2004—; faculty English dept. Rutgers U., Newark, 1999—, William Paterson U., Wayne, NJ, 1999-2001; dir. Ctr. Testing and Psychometrics, Min. of Culture and Higher Edn., Tehran, 1975-77; mem. mng. editl. bd. and adv. bd. PCF Who's Who in The Iranian-Am. Cmty. Author: Children's English series, 1990-95, Reading Through Reading (Best Acad. Book), 1992, Testing and Measurement (Best Acad. Book), 1993, A Comprehensive Grammar of English, 1996, Testing TEFL, 1997; author/editor: Issues in Teaching English as a Second Language, 1990, English for the Students of Medicine, 1989; co-author: English for Medical Students, 1974; editor: English for the Students of Medicine (II), 1993, Novin English-Persian Dictionary, vols. I and II, 1993; co-editor: Yadvareh Persian-English Dictionary, vols. I, II, III, 1991, Yadvareh English-Persian Dictionary, vols. I and II, 1991, Yadvareh Unabridged English-Persian Dictionary, 1993, others; contbr. numerous articles to profl. jours. Mem. com. Ctr. Studying and Compiling Univ Books in Humanities Min. Culture and Higher Edn., 1984—97, mem. com. curriculum devel., 1984—97, com. for testing, 1977—79; mem. com. lang. testing Lang. Ctr., 1979—81. Recipient award for creating an Innovative Model of Reading Comprehension, U. Ill., 1975, Cert. of Appreciation for best adminstrn. U. Mich., 1998, award for extraordinary ability INS, 1998, Disting. Prof. award, 2000, Disting. Rschr. award, 2000, Woman of Achievement award BBC, 2002; U. Ill. grantee, 1975; Fulbright scholar, 1970-75, Profl. Devel. scholar TESOL, 1999; fellow in rsch. U. Ill., 1973-75. Mem. TESOL, U. Ill. Alumni Assn., Am. Assn. for Applied Linguistics, Nat. Coun. Tchrs. English, Internat. Reading Assn. Avocations: reading, painting, tennis, swimming. Home: 290 Anderson St # 6K Hackensack NJ 07601 Office: Rutgers Univ Dept English 156 Conklin Hall 175 Univ Ave Newark NJ 07102 Personal E-mail: varzegar@gmail.com.

VASANA, SUSAN (CHUN-YE), engineering educator; d. De-Jun and Yi-Hua Ye; m. William Vasana, Feb. 14, 2001; children: Danica Hill Chang, Anna Ye Vasana. BS, Shanghai Jiaotong U., 1983; MS, Tongji U., 1986; PhD, Queen's U., Can., 1994. Lectr. Tongji U., Shanghai, 1986—89; scientist Nat. Inst. Sci. Rsch., Montreal, Que., Canada, 1994; sr. staff engr. Motorola Inc., Boynton Beach, Fla., 1994—2002; adj. prof. Fla. Atlantic U., Boca Raton, Fla., 2000—01; prof. U. North Fla., Jacksonville, 2002—. Recipient Silver Quills award, Motorola Inc., 2000. Mem.: IEEE, Internat. Assn. Sci. and Tech. for Devel. Achievements include patents for communication device having antenna switch diversity and method therefor; method and apparatus for demodulating a frequency shift keyed signal; method and apparatus for decoding a 2-level radio signal; method in a selective call receiver for synchronizing to a multi-level radio signal; method and apparatus for baud detection in a communication device; method and apparatus for accurate synchronization using symbol decision feedback; method and apparatus for correlation detection of multi-level signals with non-standard deviations; method and apparatus for automatic simulcast correlation for a correlation detector; method and apparatus for gain normalization of a correlation demodulator. Office: U North Fla 4567 St Johns Bluff Rd S Jacksonville FL 32224

VASCONEZ, LUIS OSWALDO, plastic surgeon, educator; b. Ambato, Ecuador, July 17, 1937; s. Luis Fernando and Lida Maria Vasconez; m. Diane Arlene Drury, Sept. 12, 1964; children: Cristina Vasconez-Herrera, Nessa Vasconez-Richards, Rachel. MD, Washington U., St. Louis, 1962. Diplomate Am. Bd. Surgery, Am. Bd. Plastic Surgery. Intern Rochester-Strong Meml. Hosp., 1962—63, resident, 1963—70, U. Fla., Gainesville, Fla., 1966—69; chief divsn. plastic surgeru U. Calif., San Francisco, 1978—85; prof., surg., chief divsn. plastic surgery U. Ala., Birmingham, 1985—. Bd. dirs. Am. Bd. Plastic Surgery, 1998—. Co-author: Post Mastectomy Reconstruction, 1981, Grabb's Encyclopedia of Flaps, 1998. Capt. USAF, 1964—66. Conservative. Roman Catholic. Avocations: travel, reading. Office: U Ala Divsn Plastic Surgery Faculty Office Tower Ste 1102 510 20th St S Birmingham AL 35294-3411 Personal E-mail: luis.vasconez@ccc.uab.edu. E-mail: luis.vascoez@ccc.uab.edu. *

VASEY, ANN L., pre-school administrator, counselor; b. Cleve., May 3, 1949; d. Albert and Norma (Miller) Ringler; m. Graham C. Vasey, Feb. 20, 1972; children: Rachel Nora Vasey, Corinne Elisabeth Vasey. BS in Elem. Edn. and Early Childhood, Boston U., 1972; MEd in Counseling Psychology, Northeastern U., Boston, 1974. Lic. mental health counselor State of Mass., marriage and family therapist State of Mass., cert. clin. mental health counselor Nat. Bd. Cert. Counselors; supr. and dir. K-12 Mass. Dept. Edn., prin. pre-K-6 Mass. Dept. Edn., registered tchr. Yoga Yoga Alliance, cert. Parent Child Home Program, Parent Leadership Tng., EMDR. Adolescent and family therapist SHARE, Lowell, Mass., 1974-76; instr. Framingham (Mass.) State Coll., 1976; instr. psychol. Quinsigamond C.C., Worcester, 1978—92; founding head The Learning Experience Elem. Sch., Marlborough, 1981—88; early childhood coord. Southbridge Pub. Schs., Mass., 1993—2006; psychotherapist YOU, Inc. Family Svcs., 1995—; founding supr. Family Ctr., 2000—06; pvt. practice, 2006—. Psychol. cons. Childcare Lab. Sch., Worcester, Mass., 1989—91; founding chair Family Literacy Coalition, Southbridge, 1998—2006; presenter Assn. Early Childhood Dirs., Oxford, 2002; ednl. and psychol. cons. HMEA Children's Svc., Hudson, 2003; team mem. comprehensive rev. and site visits Mass. Dept. Edn., 2004, 05; trainer psychological cons. Together for Kids, 2007—. Co-author: (tchrs. guide) Some Psychological Issues Concerning Adolescent Debvelopment, 1987. Mem. Mass. Cmty. Partnerships Children, Northboro; bd. mem. Ashland Cultural Coun., Ashland, Mass., 1992—98; pres. bd. dir. Early Childhood Coun., 1993—2006; steering com. Cmty. Connections, Southbridge, Mass., 1998—. Grantee, Mass. Dept. Edn., 1993—2006. Mem.: Nat. Assn. Edn. Young Children (validator), Mass. Mental Health Counselors Assn., Delta Kappa Gamma. Avocations: yoga, travel. Home: 83 Woodland Rd Ashland MA 01721-1411 Office: Southbridge Pub Sch 156 West St Southbridge MA 01550 Office Phone: 978-562-3823.

VASHOLZ, LOTHAR ALFRED, retired insurance company executive; b. Milw., Feb. 20, 1930; s. Alfred and Charlotte Vasholz; m. Marji Cartwright, Dec. 26, 1954; children: Julie, Ann, Eric. BS, U. Colo., 1952; M of Pub. Svc. (hon.), U. Rio Grande. ChFC. Sr. cons. Life Ins. Mktg. & Rsch., Hartford, Conn., 1966—70; v.p. N.Am. Life, Chgo., 1970—73; sr. v.p. Bankers Mut., Freeport, Ill., 1973—75; dir. sales Security Life Denver, 1975—81; v.p. Union Ctrl. Life Ins. Co., Cin., 1981—85, sr. v.p., 1985—86, mgr. Columbus, Ohio, 1986—87, sr. v.p., chief mktg. officer Cin., 1987—91, exec. v.p., corp. mktg. officer, 1991—95; chmn. Carillon Investments, 1991—95; cons. mktg. and sales to life ins. industry, 1995—. Emeritus trustee U. Rio Grande, Ohio; co-chair adv. com. Salvation Army, Coachella Valley, Calif., 2006—. Fellow Life Mgmt. Inst.; mem. Phi Delta Theta (past internat. pres., past pres. ednl. found.) Republican. Office Phone: 760-345-5052.

VASILYEVA, ANNA, artist, writer; b. Kiev, Ukraine, Nov. 24, 1977; d. Tamara Balenko and Vladimir Vasylyev. Fine Art Degree, T.G. Shevchenko State Art Sch., 1997; BA in Art, Calif. State U., Northridge, 2005. Tchr. asst. KidsArt, Tarzana, Calif., 1999; designer, illustrator Pub. House KM Academia, Kiev, 1996, All Electronics Corp., Van Nuys, Calif., 2002—; tchr. art Marina's Sch. Music and Art, Northridge, Calif., 2001; tchg. assoc. Calif. State U., Northridge, 2004—05; graphic designer Big Screen Network Prodns., Westlake Village, Calif., 2005—06; web designer Dinair Airbrush Makeup Inst., Van Nuys, Calif., 2006—; art dir., owner Digital Saddle Prodns., Tarzana, Calif., 2006—. Exhibitions include State Fall Exhbn. Art, 1993, First Internat. Exhbn. -Presentation of Periodical Publs. about Pets, 1995, Art Gallery of U. Kiev-Mogila Acad., 1996, Art Acad. L.A., 1999, Svitozor Gallery, 1999—2001, L.A. Valley Coll., 2000, L.A. Mission Coll., 2002, Limner Gallery, 2003, Pacific Design Ctr., LA, 2004, 2006, Art Assn. Harrisburg's 76th Ann. Juried Exhbn., 2004, Palos Verde Art Ctr., Calif., 2007; film editor, designer: Streetlight Cinema, 2004—; contbr. articles to mags. Recipient Biography Pub., The Nat. Dean's List, 2002—03; State U. Fee grant, Calif. State U., Northridge, 2003—, Campus Fee grant, 2003—. Avocations: reading, travel, horseback riding. Office: All Electronics Corp 14928 Oxnard St Van Nuys CA 91411 Office Phone: 818-481-0169. Personal E-mail: anya@artistanya.com.

VASKEVITCH, DAVID, information technology executive; 3 children. BS in Math., Computer Sci., Philosophy, U. Toronto, M in Computer Sci. With Standard Software; owner PlanDesign, Toronto, Canada; with 3Com Corp., Microsoft Corp., Redmond, Wash., 1986—, dir. U.S. mktg., 1986, gen. mgr. enterprise computing, 1993, v.p., distributed applications platform, chief architect, 1998—99, sr. v.p., developer, 1999—2000, sr. v.p. Bus. Applications Divsn., 2000—01, sr. v.p., chief tech. officer Bus. Platform, 2001—. Mem. adv. bd., Live Labs (Rsch. partnership between MSN and Microsoft Rsch.) Microsoft Corp., 2006—. Author: Client/Server Strategies: A Survival Guide for Corporate Re-engineers, 1993. While at the U. Toronto in the 1970's, he invented a typewriter-terminal-based communications messaging network that predated PC-based e-mail systems. Office: Microsoft Corp One Microsoft Way Redmond WA 98052-6399

VASKO, FRANCIS JOSEPH, mathematics professor; b. Bethlehem, Pa., Mar. 23, 1952; s. Frank and Ann Vasko; m. Nancy Louise Rosenberger, July 1, 1978; 1 child, Lisa Elizabeth. MS in Math., Lehigh U., Bethlehem, Pa., 1976; MS in Indsl. Engring., Lehigh U., 1978, PhD, 1983. Math. prof. Kutztown U., Pa., 1986—. Applied math. cons. Dr.Francis Vasko, Cons., Hellertown, Pa., 1986—. Contbr. over 48 articles to profl. jours. Bd. of trustees Hellertown Libr., Pa., 1995—98. Recipient Big Brother of the yr., Big Bros./Big Sisters of the Lehigh Valley, 1994. Mem.: Sigma XI (full mem.). Achievements include research in new mathematical solution procedures for steel industry production planning and scheduling problems. Home: 510 Ellen St Hellertown PA 18055 Office: Kutztown University 170 Lytle Hall Kutztown PA 19530 Home Phone: 610-838-7590; Office Phone: 610-683-4417. Business E-Mail: vasko@kutztown.edu.

VASKO, PETER THEODORE FREDERICK, priest; b. Bklyn., Nov. 28, 1943; s. Theodore Frederick and Catherine (Buday) V. BA in Philosophy, Cath. U. Am., 1966, BD in Theology, 1969; postgrad., Duke U., 1972-73, Franciscan Studium Biblicum, Jerusalem, 1985-86. Ordained priest Roman Cath. Ch., 1987. Pub. rels. asst. Holiday Inn/Oak Grove, Durham, N.C., 1972-74; dir. devel. NAA, Charlotte, N.C., 1974-76; dir. CETA, New Orleans, 1976-78; v.p. sales Peachtree Corners Corp. Travel, Atlanta, 1978-81; bd. dirs. Franciscan Custody, Jerusalem, 1992—2001; pres. Franciscan Found. for The Holy Land, Jerusalem, 1994—. Editor photo essay See the Holy Land, 1993, Our Visit to The Holy Land, 2004; editor The Holy Land Mag., 1993-95; writer, narrator video On the Road of Christ, 1994; narrator video The Life of Jesus: Scriptural Journey, 1997; guest Mother Angelica Live, 1996-98, 02-03, Pat Robertson 700 Club, 1996, EWTN's World Over Show, 2004-06, others; co-prodr.: (documentary) Crisis in the Holy Land, 1994; (TV series) The Holy Land with Fr. Peter Vasko, 2006. Bd. dirs. St. Ives Soc., Jerusalem, 1992-94; guide White House Via U.S. Embassy, Jerusalem, 1992—; chaplain U.S. Marines/U.S. Consulate, Jerusalem, 1988—. Decorated mem. Equestrial Order of the Holy Sepulchre, 1992, order of merit Sovereign Mil. Order of The Knights Templar, 2005, order of the Holy Spirit Knights Templar, 2007; recipient Achievement in Pub. Rels. award Pub. Rels. Soc., Raleigh, 1975, Marine Security Guard Bn. Co. B Cert. of Appreciation, 1995, 99, U.S. Marine Security Detachment Comdr. Commendation award, 1999, State of Tex. Commn.: Theodore Peter F. Vasko commd. as Hon. Texan by Gov. R. Perry, 2002, Cert. of Flag Presentation of USS Ariz. by Rear Adm. Robert T. Conway, Jr., USN, Comdr., Navy Region, Hawaii, 2002, Cert. of Appreciation for Good Conduct, 2002-03, UNMC-MSG Detachment of Jerusalem, Cert. of Appreciation, MSG Det. for Outstanding Svc. as Det. Chaplain, 2003; named Jaycee of Yr., NC chpt., 1973, Top Ten People in Cath. Ch. Inside the Vatican mag., 2006. Mem.: Marine Embassy Guard Assn. (mem. 2003).

VASQUEZ, GADDI H., ambassador, former federal agency administrator; b. Carrizo Springs, Tex., Jan. 22, 1955; m. Elaine Vasquez; 1 child, Jason. AA in Criminal Justice, Rancho Santiago C.C., 1972; BA in Pub. Svc. Mgmt., U. Redlands, 1980; DHL (hon.), U. LaVerne, 2003. Police officer City of Orange, Calif., 1975-79; coord. community rels., mgr.'s office City of Riverside, Calif., 1979-81; exec. asst. Orange County Bd. Suprs., 3d Dist., Calif., 1981-85, mem. Calif., 1987—95; area mgr. So. Calif. Edison Co., 1985; hispanic liaison Office of Gov. George Deukmejian, Calif., 1985, from dep. appointments sec. to chief dep. appointments sec. Calif., 1985-87; dir. Peace Corps, Washington, 2002—06; US rep. to UN agencies for food & agrl. US Dept. State, 2006—. Mem. Transp. Corridor Agys. Bd., 1987—, chmn. 1990-91; local agy. formation commn., 1988-93, chmn. 1990-91; mem. Calif. Film Commn., 1988-91, Calif. Coun. Criminal Justice, 1989—; founder, co-chair, Orange County Health Care Task Force, 1990—; with White House Fellowships Commn., 1990-91; co-chmn. Orange County Congestion Mgmt. Policy Task Force, 1990—; bd. dirs. Orange County Transp. Authority, 1991—, exec. com. 1992—, vice chmn. 1993—; regional advisory and planning coun., 1991—, vice chmn. 1992, chmn. 1993; official observer Armenian Independence elections, 1991. Bd. dirs. Future Leaders Am., Southwest Voter Rsch. Inst., calif. First Amendment Coalition, Orange County Boy Scout Coun., So. Area Foster Care Effort, Orange County Performing Arts Ctr., Opera Pacific; trustee Am. Coun. Young Polit. Leaders; adv. bd. Pediatric Cancer Rsch. Found, Orange County Juvenile Connection Project, Calif. Office Traffic Safety, The Salvation Army Orange County, Project AERO, Constitutional Rights Found. Orange County; community coun. Prentice Day Sch.; hon. adv. bd. Adam Walsh Ctr.; hon. bd. govs. Bower Mus.; leadership coun. Orange County Points Light. Named Officer of Yr., Am. Legion, 1977. Outstanding Young Man of Am. U.S. C.of C., 1985, One of 100 Most Influential Hispanics in U.S. Hispanic Bus. Mag., 1986-87, 88-89, 91-92, 92-93, 2002-03, Govt. Hispanic Bus. Advocate of Yr. U.S. Hispanic Champer Region I, 1991; recipient Alumni Achievement award Santa Ana Coll., 1988, Alumni of Yr.award U. Redlands, 1989, Humanitarian award NCCJ, 1989, award State Child Devel. Adv. Com., 1990, Tree of Life award Jewish Nat. Fund, 1991, Ralph E. Hudson Open Space award Landscape Architects Found., 1992, Disting. Alumni award Coun. Young Polit. Leaders, 2002, Outstanding Alumni award Am. Assn. C.C.s, 2003.

VASQUEZ, HORACIO, mechanical engineer, educator; s. Horacio Vasquez and Teresa Cespedes; m. Brooke M. Dacy, July 8, 1995; children: Baylee, Avery. PhD in Mech. Engring., U. Ala., Tuscaloosa, 2003. Assoc. prof. U. Costa Rica, San Pedro de Montes de Oca, 1994—2000; asst. prof. U. Tex. Pan Am., Edinburg, 2003—. Cons. U. Costa Rica, San Pedro de Montes de Oca, 1995—2000. Scholar, AID, 1989—91. Mem.: ASME (student sect. advisor 2004—07). Achievements include development of simplified mathematical model for a 6/4 switched reluctance motor (SRM). Avocation: mountain biking. Office: U Tex Pan American 1201 W University Dr Edinburg TX 78539 Home Phone: 956-292-7419; Office Phone: 956-292-7419. Business E-Mail: vasqu002@utpa.edu.

VASQUEZ, JO ANNE, retired science educator; BS in Biology, No. Ariz. U., 1965, MA in Early Childhood Edn., 1968; PhD in Curriculum and Instrn., Kennedy-Western U., 1999. Assoc. prof. sci. and edn. Ariz. State U.; lead curriculum developer, sci. specialist Mesa Pub. Schs.; profl. devel. cons. Macmillan/McGraw Hill, 2000—. Writer MacMillan/McGraw-Hill K-6 Sci., 1998—; bd. dirs. Nat. Sci. bd., 2002—; chair elem. sci. tchg. and assessment standards Nat. Bd. Profl. Tchg. Standards; mem. exec. bd. Nat. Acad. Sci. Ctr. for Sci., Math., and Engring. Edn.; former com. chair, reviewer Nat. Sci. Found.; cons. in field. Past pres. adv. bd. Sally Ride's TOYChallenge. Named Tchr. Yr., Nat. Environ. Assn.; recipient honoree, Nat. Assn. Latino Elected and Apptd. Officials, 2004, Gustave Oahus Elem. Sci. Tchg. award, Robert H. Carleton award, Nat. Sci. Teachers Assn., 2006. Mem.: Nat. Coun. Elem. Sci. Educators (past pres.), Internat. Coun. Sci. Edn. Orgn. (past pres.), Ariz. Sci. Tchrs. Assn. (past pres.), Nat. Sci. Edn. Leadership Assn. (pres.-elect), Nat. Sci. Tchrs. Assn. (past mem. nat. bd. dirs., elected first Hispanic pres., Disting. Svc. to Sci. Edn. award Search for Excellence in Elem. Sci. Edn. and Supervision). Achievements include first K-12 tchr. apptd. to bd. dirs. NSF Nat. Sci. Bd.

VASQUEZ, JUAN FLORES, federal judge; b. San Antonio, June 24, 1948; s. Jose and Amelia (Flores) V.; m. Mary Theresa Schultz, Aug. 22, 1970; children: Juan Jr., Jaime. BA, U. Tex., 1972; JD, U. Houston, 1977; LLM in Taxation, NYU, 1978. Bar: Tex. 1977, US Dist. Ct. (so. dist. Tex.) 1982, US Dist. Ct. (we. dist.) Tex. 1985, US Ct. Appeals (5th cir.) 1982, US Supreme Ct. 1996, US Tax Ct. 1978. Acct. Coopers & Lybrand, LA, 1972-74; tax atty. Office of Chief Coun. IRS, Houston, 1978-82, Leighton, Hood & Vasquez, San Antonio, 1987; pvt. practice San Antonio, 1987-95; judge US Tax Ct., Washington, 1995—. Mem. ABA, Mex.-Am. Bar Assn. Tex. and San Antonio, Nat. Hispanic Bar Assn., Nat. Jud. Coll., Hispanic Bar Assn. DC, Coll. State Coll. Tex., Tex. State Bar Assn., San Antonio Bar Assn. Office: US Tax Ct 400 2nd St NW Washington DC 20217-0002

VASQUEZ, PAUL I., director; b. Chgo., Oct. 16, 1958; s. Rudolph J. and Mildred F. Vasquez; m. Coy M. Vasquez, Sept. 18, 1981; children: Sabrina F., Logan O. AAS in Computers, Clackamas C.C., Oregon City, Oreg., 1999; BA in Psychology, Concordia U., Portland, 2003; MEd, Concordia U., Portland, 2005. Dir. cmty. English as 2d lang. programs Western Pacific Coll., Portland; v.p. Cojco Enterprises, Inc., Portland. Pres. AM. Chinese Cultural Exch., Oregon City, 2001—. With USN, 1977—80. Mem.: TESOL, Optimist Club (bd. dirs.), Am. Legion. Avocations: hiking, photography. Home and Office: 330 Morton Rd Oregon City OR 97045

VASQUEZ, RAMON FRANCISCO, music educator; b. Del Rio, Tex., Mar. 7, 1972; s. Ramon Vasquez and Maria Carolina Torres. MusB, Northwestern State U. La., 1994; MusM, U. N. Tex., 1997. Asst. prof. music Auburn U., Ala. Adjudicator Nat. Trumpet Competition, Fairfax, 1999—, McKnight Artist Fellowships for Performing Musicians, Mpls., 2003. Assoc. mem. Chgo. Civic Orch., 1997. Recipient Masters Divsn. Winner, Nat. Trumpet Competition, 1997. Mem.: Internat. Trumpet Guild. Avocations: music, drum corps. Office: Auburn U Dept Music 101 Goodwin Hall Auburn AL 36849-5420 Personal E-mail: trptjock@aol.com.

VASQUEZ, WILLIAM LEROY, business educator, consultant; b. Austin, Tex., Mar. 9, 1944; s. Eliseo M. and Janie (Garcia) V. BS with distinction, Nova Southeastern U., 1983, MBA, 1985, DBA, 1992. Cert. Inst. Cert. Profl. Mgrs., 1990, Inst. Cert. Computing Profls., 1993. Svc. mgr. Data Gen. Corp., various, Latin Am., 1972-80; product mgr. Gould, Inc., Ft. Lauderdale, Fla., 1980—84, Tektronix Inc., Portland, Oreg., 1984—86, Racal-Milgo, Ft. Lauderdale, 1988—90, Citibank Internat., Ft. Lauderdale, 1991—2001; ret., 2001. Instr. City U., Portland campus, 1987-88; Maryhurst Coll., 1985-88, Nova Southeastern U. (domestic and internat.), 1988—, pres. internat. alumni assn.; instr. St. Thomas U., 1989—, Fla. Atlantic U., 1993—. Mem. VFW, Nat. Bus. Edn. Assn., U.S. Submarine Vets., Inc., Mensa. Republican. Avocations: guitar, model trains, fine arts. Home: 9788 NW 18th St Coral Springs FL 33071-5824 Office: Keiser Coll Online Divsn 1900 W Commercial Blvd Fort Lauderdale FL 33309 Office Phone: 954-351-4040. E-mail: wvasquez@earthlink.net.

VASSALLO, EDWARD E., lawyer; b. NYC, Aug. 12, 1943; BS, Columbia U., 1965, MS, 1967; JD cum laude, Fordham U., 1973. Bar: N.Y. 1974. Ptnr. Fitzpatrick, Cella, Harper & Scinto, NYC. Mem.: ABA, N.Y.C. Bar Assn., N.Y. Intellectual Property Law Assn. (pres.), Fed. Cir. Bar Assn., Internat. Trademark Assn., Am. Intellectual Property Law Assn. Office: Fitzpatrick Cella Harper & Scinto 30 Rockefeller Plz Fl 38 New York NY 10112-3800 Office Phone: 212-218-2241. Business E-Mail: evassallo@fchs.com.

VASSALLO, JOHN A., lawyer; b. NYC, Aug. 19, 1937; s. John and Gilda (Di Desidero) Vassallo; children: John C., Elena L., Edward F. AB, Columbia U., 1959, JD, 1962. Bar: N.Y. 1963, U.S. Dist. Ct. (so. and ea. dists.) N.Y. 1964, U.S. Ct. Appeals (2d cir.) 1965. Assoc. Saxe, Bacon & O'Shea, NYC, 1962-68; ptnr. Barovick & Konecky, NYC, 1968-70, Kurtz & Vassallo, NYC, 1970-78, Franklin, Weinrib, Rudell & Vassallo, NYC, 1978—. Fellow: Am. Coll. Family Trail Lawyers (diplomate), Am. Acad. Matrimonial Attys.; mem.: Friars Club. Office: Franklin Weinrib Rudell & Vassallo 488 Madison Ave New York NY 10022-5702 Office Phone: 212-935-5500. Business E-Mail: jvassallo@fwrv.com.

VASSALLUZZO, JOSEPH S., retail company executive; BA, Pa. State U.; MBA, Temple U. Exec. v.p. growth and support svcs. Staples, Inc., Framingham, Mass., 1993, exec. v.p. growth and devel., 1993—96, pres. realty and devel. divsn., 1997—99, vice chmn., 1999—. Worked in real estate Mobil Oil Amerada Hess Corp., Am. Stores Co. Office: Staples Inc PO Box 9265 Framingham MA 01701-9265

VASSAR, CLAUDIA SUE GEE, lawyer; b. Houston, Dec. 16, 1976; d. Harry and Antje Gee; m. David Keith Vassar, June 21, 2003. BA in Sociology, Rice U., Houston, 1999; JD, U. Va., Charlottesville, 2004. Bar: Tex. 2004. Assoc. Gardere Wynne Sewell, Houston, 2004—05, Cochran & Baker, LLP, Houston, 2005—. Co-chair Thomas Tang Moot Ct. Competition, Houston, 2005. Sec. Small World Books, Houston, 2004—07; vol. Star of Hope, Houston, 2004—07; elder Grace Presbyn. Ch., Houston, 2006—07; bd. mem. Houston Children's Chorus, Houston, 2005—07. Mem.: Gee Family Assn. (pres. 2006—07). Office: Cochran & Baker LLP 1177 W Loop S Ste 1600 Houston TX 77027 Office Fax: 713-888-3550. Business E-Mail: claudia@cochranbaker.com.

VASSELL, GREGORY S., electric utility consultant; b. Moscow, Dec. 24, 1921; came to U.S., 1951, naturalized, 1957; s. Gregory M. and Eugenia M. Wasiljeff; m. Martha Elizabeth Williams, Apr. 26, 1957; children: Laura Kay, Thomas Gregory. Dipl. Ing. in Elec. Engring, Tech. U. Berlin, 1951; MBA in Corp. Fin., NYU, 1954. With Am. Electric Power Svc. Corp., Columbus, Ohio, 1951-88, v.p. system planning, 1973-76, dir., 1973-88, sr. v.p. system planning, 1976-88; electric utility cons. Upper Arlington, Ohio, 1988—. Bd. dirs. Columbus & Southern Ohio Electric Co., 1981-88, Cardinal Operating Co.; mem. tech. adv. com. transmission FPC, 1968-70, FERC Task Force on Power Pooling, 1980-81; mem. U.S. com. World Energy Coun. Contbr. articles to profl. jours. Fellow IEEE (life); mem. NAE, Athletic Club Columbus Home and Office: 6000 Riverside Dr Dublin OH 43017

VASSER, ALBERT GLENN, lawyer; b. Pine Bluff, Ark., July 20, 1947; s. Albert P. Vasser and Bobbie Ann (Nipper) Hogan; m. Judith Jackson, Aug. 16, 1969; 1 child, Vicki Suzanne. BS in Bus. Adminstrn. with honors, U. Ark., 1969, JD, 1972. Bar: Ark., U.S. Dist. Ct. Ark., U.S. Ct. Appeals (8th cir.), U.S. Supreme Ct. From assoc. to ptnr. McKenzie, Graves, McRae, Vasser and Baler, Prescott, Ark., 1972—. Pres. Prescott (Ark.) Sch. Bd., 1985; mcpl. judge City of Prescott, Ark.; bd. dirs. S.W. Ark. Regional Health Ctr., El Dorado; bd. trustees, adminstr. Bd. First United Meth. Ch. 1st lt. U.S. Army. Recipient Spl. Justice award Ark. Supreme Ct., 1991. Fellow Am. Coll. Mortgage Attys., Ark. Bar Found. (bd. mem., pres.); mem. Ark. Bar Assn. (del. and com. chmn., pres.-elect 2004, Golden Gavel award 1984), Nevada County Bar Assn. (pres., com. mem.). Avocations: tennis, golf. Office: McKenzie McRae & Vasser 122 E 2nd St PO Box 599 Prescott AR 71857-0599

VASSEUR, DOMINIQUE HENRI, curator; BA, Oberlin Coll., Ohio, 1973; MA, U. Chgo., 1976. Curator European art, sr. curator Dayton Art Inst., Ohio, 1979—99; dep. dir., mus. curator Springfield Mus. Art, Ohio, 2000—04; curator European art Columbus Mus. Art, Ohio, 2005—. Author: (exhbn. catalogue) Edna Boies Hopkins Color Woodblock Prints, The Soul Unbound: The Photographs of Jane Reece, Edgar Degas: The Many Dimensions of a Master French Impressionist, The Lithographs of Pierre-Nolasque Bergeret. Office: Columbus Museum Art 480 E Broad St Columbus OH 43215 Home Phone: 614-457-6645; Office Phone: 614-629-0374. Business E-Mail: dominique.vasseur@cmaohio.org.

VASSIL, JOHN CHARLES, lawyer; b. Youngstown, Ohio, Mar. 3, 1930; s. Callias and Anastasia (Kyriakides) V.; m. Anita Devlin, Nov. 28, 1965; 1 son, Russell. BS in Chem. Engring., Carnegie Inst. Tech., Pitts., 1952; JD, George Wash. U., Washington, 1958. Bar: NY 1960, US Dist. Cts. (so. and ea. dists.) NY 1961, US Ct. Appeals (2d cir.) 1965, US Ct. Appeals (fed. cir.) 1982, US Supreme Ct. 1961. Patent examiner U.S. Patent Office, 1955-58; ptnr. Morgan & Finnegan, LLP, NYC, 1961—2001, counsel, 2002—. Lectr. in field. Served with C.E., US Army, 1953-55. Mem. ABA, Assn. Bar City NY, NY Patent Law Assn., Am. Patent Law Assn., Am. Arbitration Assn. Office: 21st Fl 3 World Financial Ctr New York NY 10281-2101 Home: 138 Sherman Rd Greene NY 13778 Office Phone: 212-465-8700. Business E-Mail: jcvassil@morganfinnegan.com.

VASSILOPOULOU-SELLIN, RENA, researcher; b. Dec. 29, 1949; MD, Albert Einstein Coll. Medicine, 1974. Resident Montefiore Hosp., Bronx, 1974-77; fellow Northwestern U., Chgo., 1977-80; prof. Univ. Tex., Houston, 1980—. Fellow ACP, Am. Assn. Clin. Endocrinol.; mem. AAAS, AMA, Am. Soc. Bone and Mineral Rsch., Am. Diabetes Assn., Am. Soc. Clin. Oncology, Endo Soc. Office: Anderson Cancer Ctr 1515 Holcombe Blvd # 15 Houston TX 77030-4009

VASSILYADI, MICHAEL, pediatric neurosurgeon; b. Istanbul, Turkey, Nov. 25, 1961; s. Irakli and Cristal Vassilyadi; m. Anastasia Lyras, Aug. 23, 1986; children: Frank Photios, Christal, Anthony Irakli. BSc, McGill U., 1980—83, MSc, 1984—86, MD, CM, 1986—90. Diplomate Am. Bd. Pedait. Neurol. Surgery, Am. Bd. Neurol. Surgery. Med. staff Children's Hosp. of Ea. Ont., Ottawa, Canada, 1996—. Asst. prof. surgery U. of Ottawa, 1996—2003; assoc. prof. surgery and pediat. U. Ottawa, 2003—; investigator Children's Hosp. Ea. Ont. Rsch. Inst., Canada. Contbr. articles to profl. jours.; mem. editl. bd. Pediat. Neurosurgery. Ottawa chpt. dir. Think First Can. Recipient Matching Travel award, Children's Hosp. of Ea. Ont. Rsch. Inst., 1998, 2003—05, Best sci. posters, Neurol. Sciences of Que., 1995, Tchg. Skills Attainment award, Faculty of Medicine, U. Ottawa, 2007; Farquharson Rsch. scholarship, Med. Rsch. of Can., 1987, Dr. James Douglas Rsch. fellowship in Pathology, McGill U., 1985. Fellow: ACS, Am. Acad. Pediat., Royal Coll. Physicians and Surgeons Can.; mem.: Can. Neurol. Scis. Fedn., Can. Pediat. Neurosurgery Group, Am. Bd. Neurol. Surgery, Am. Bd. of Pediat. Neurol. Surgery, Can. Neurosurg. Soc., Am. Soc. Pediatric Neurosurgeons, Coll. Physicians and Surgeons Ont., Coll. des Medecins du Que., Can. Med. Assn., Am. Epilepsy Soc., Am. Assn. Neurol. Surgeons (pediat. neurol. surgery sect.), Ont. Med. Assn., Internat. Soc. Pediatric Neurosurgery, Congress Neurol. Surgeons (pediat. neurol. surgery sect.). Greek Orthodox. Achievements include research in pediatric neurosurgery. Office: Children's Hosp of Eastern Ontario 401 Smyth Rd Ottawa ON Canada K1H 8L1 Office Phone: 613-738-3985. Business E-Mail: vassilyadi@cheo.on.ca.

VASUDEV, BRAHM SARUP, nephrologist; b. New Delhi, Apr. 12, 1971; MBBS, U. Pune, India, 1994. Resident Brookdale Hosp. Med. Ctr., Bklyn., 2001, chief resident in internal medicine, 2001; fellow critical care medicine Albert Einstein Coll. Medicine, NYC, 2002—03; fellow nephrology Med. Coll. of Wis. Affiliated Hosps., Milw., 2004, fellow transplant nephrology, 2004—. Evaluator kidney transplantation Froedtert Meml. Luth. Hosp., Milw., 2004—; clin. rschr. Med. Coll. Wis., 2002—, investigator clin. trials, 2004—; instr. Med. Coll. of Wis. Affiliated Hosps., 2002—; cons. Shire Pharmaceuticals, Milw., 2003—04. Recipient Excellence award, American Transplant Congress, 2004, Young Investigator award, 2005. Mem.: Am. Soc. Nephrology (assoc.), Renal Physician Assn. (assoc.), Delhi Med. Assn. (assoc.), Indian Med. Assn. (assoc.), Am. Soc. Transplantation (assoc.). Home Phone: 262-786-8335; Office Phone: 414-805-9073.

VASUDEVAN, SRIRAM, risk management consultant, energy executive; b. Bombay, June 7, 1970; arrived in U.S., 1991; s. R. and Rama Vasudevan; m. Archana Ramaswamy, Feb. 2, 1998. BTech in Mech. Engring., Indian Inst. Tech., 1991; MS in Mech. Engring., U. Calif., Santa Barbara, 1992; PhD in Aerospace Engring., Ga. Inst. Tech., 1998. Chartered, Chartered Fin. Analyst Inst., 2004. Air resources engr. Calif. Air Resources Bd., El Monte, 1992-93; grad. rschr. Computational Modelling Ctr. Ga. Inst. Tech., Atlanta, 1993-97; devel. engr. Schlumberger Tech. Corp., Sugarland, Tex., 1997—2001; mgr. quantitative analysis Sempra Energy Solutions, San Diego, 2002—04, dir. strategic risk mgmt., 2004—05, dir. corp. devel., 2005—. Panelist Symposium, 2003; lectr. in field; spkr. in field. Contbr. articles to profl. jours. Vol., organizer South Asian task force Nat. Marrow Donor Program, LA and Atlanta, 1993—. Recipient Best Student Presentation award AIAA, 1997. Mem. ASME (assoc.), Soc. Petroleum Engrs., Sigma Xi. Hindu. Achievements include co-invention of post closure anlaysis in hyudraulic fracturing; development of systematic risk management strategies for end-users of gas and power. Office: 101 Ash St HQ 09 San Diego CA 92108 Business E-Mail: svasudevan@sempraglobal.com.

VATANDOOST, NOSSI MALEK, art school administrator; b. May 22, 1935; d. Adullah Goodar and Mahtaban (Goodar) Malek; m. Ira Varandoost, May 30, 1964; children: Debbie, Cyrus. BA, Western Ky. U., 1970. Art tchr. Met.-Davidson County Sch. Sys., Nashville, 1970-71; dir., owner Nossi Coll. Art, Goodlettsville, Tenn., 1973—. Pres. Crimson Corp.; dir. EXCEL Edn. Corp., 1980-86; vis. lectr., cons. EXCEL Bus. Inst., 1980-86. Active mem. Nat. Trust for Hist. Preservation. Mem.: NAFE, Internat. Coun. Design Schs. (pres. 1997—98), Art Inst. Nashville (founder, CEO), Art Resources of Tenn. (pres. 2000—01), Nat. Assn. of Schs. of Art and Design, Nat. Mus. Women in the Arts (charter), Hendersonville Art Guild, Hendersonville Art Coun. (com. chmn.). Club: Soroptimists (Upper Cumberland Valley, Tenn.). Home: 104 Whirlaway Ct Hendersonville TN 37075 Office: 907 Rivergate Pkwy # E6 Goodlettsville TN 37072 Home Phone: 615-826-0238; Office Phone: 615-851-1088. E-mail: nossi@nossi.com.

VATER, CHARLES J., lawyer; b. Pitts., Feb. 8, 1950; s. Joseph A. and Helen M. (Genellie) V.; m. Diane E. Vater, June 10, 1972; children: Allison D., Elizabeth A. BA, U. Notre Dame, 1971; JD, U. Pitts., 1975. Bar: Pa. 1975, U.S. Dist. Ct. (we. dist.) Pa. 1975, U.S. Ct. Appeals (3d cir.) 1979. Assoc. Tucker Arensberg, P.C., Pitts., 1975-80, ptnr., shareholder, 1980—. Contbr. articles to profl. jours. Mem.: Estate Planning Coun. Pitts. (bd. dirs. 1988—90, 1995—97, past pres.), Allegheny County Bar Assn. (probate coun. 1988—98, 1999—2000, chair 2006—), Phi Beta Kappa, Order of Coif. Home: 1615 Trolist Dr Pittsburgh PA 15241-2650 Office: Tucker Arensberg 1 Ppg Pl Ste 1500 Pittsburgh PA 15222-5413 Office Phone: 412-594-5556. Business E-Mail: cvater@tuckerlaw.com.

VATER, YOURI L., medical educator; b. Riga, Latvia, Apr. 14, 1954; s. Eva Lazar Vater; m. Hanna Bernstein; children: Roman, Maxim (Max). MD, Riga Univ. Sch. of Medicine, Riga Latvia, 1977; PhD, U. Tartu, Estonia, 1988. Cert. sr. bd. anesthesia Israel, 1997. Rsch. fellow Riga Med. Sch., 1980—87, sr. rsch. fellow, 1987—90; dir. cardioanesthesiology dept. Heart Surgery Ctr. Sch. of Medicine Republic of Latvia, Riga, Latvia, 1980—90; residency anesthesia U. Tel Aviv Sackler Med. Ctr., Ichilov, 1990—97; assoc. prof., attending anesthesiologist U. Wash. Sch. of Medicine, Seattle, 1999—. Contbr. articles various profl. jours. Active participant Doctors for Democracy, Tel Aviv, Israel, 1995. Lt. Israeli Mil. Forces., 1995—2004, Israel. Mem.: Am. Soc. Transplantaion Anesthesiologists, Latvian Soc. Anesthesiologists, Am. Soc. Anesthesiologists, Israeli Soc. Anesthesiologists. Achievements include Art Show Promotions. Avocations: travel, journalism, research in anesthesiology, art show promotion. Home: 11623- 24 th Ave NE Seattle WA 98125 Office: U Wash 1959 Pacific St POB 356540 Seattle WA 98105-6540 Office Phone: 206-598-4260. Personal E-mail: yvater@yahoo.com.

VATNER, STEPHEN F., physiologist, researcher, research scientist; m. Dorothy E. Vatner, Aug. 22, 1944; children: Jonathan, Daniel, Ralph. BA, Grinnell Coll., Grinnell, Iowa, 1957—61; MD, NYU, New York, NY, 1961—65; Intern,Residence, U of Va., Charlottesville,VA, 1966—67; Postdoctoral fellow, U of WA, Seattle, WA, 1969. Cardiology. Asst. rsch. physiologist U of CA, San Diego, 1969—70, asst. prof. of medicine, 1971—72, Harvard Med. Sch., Boston, 1972—74; assoc. prof. of medicine Peter Bent Brigham Hosp.-Harvard Med. Schoolm, Boston, 1974—90; prof. of medicine Harvard Med. Sch., Boston, 1990—97; George J. Magovern prof. and dir., cardiovasc. and pulmonary rsch. inst. Allegheny U. of the Health Sciences, Pitts., 1997—99; dir. Weis Ctr. for Rsch., Henry Hood Rsch. Program, Charles B. Degenstein Prof., Penn State Coll. of Medicine, Danville, Pa., 1999—2000; u. prof. of medicine and dir. Cardiovasc. Rsch. Inst., U. of Medicine and Dentistry-New Jersey Med. Sch., Newark, 2000—01; chair, dept. of cell biology and molecular medicine UMDNJ-New Jersey Med. Sch., Newark, 2001—. Editor: (editor-in-chief) Circulation Rsch.; author (contributing author): (manuscript publications) Sci. articles in peer-reviewed jour. Recipient Established Investigatorship, AHA, 1974 -1979, Thomas L. O'Donohue Meml. Lecture in Neuropharmacology, Washington,D.C., 1997, Invited Lecture in Honor of Emeritus Prof. Andre Charlier, Unit of Cardiovasc. Physiology, Universite Catholique De Louvain, Brussels,Belgium, 1997, Hon. Prof., The fourth Mil. Med. U., Xian, China, 1998, George E. Brown Lecture, AHA, 1986, Hawthorne Lecture, Howard U., 1990, Hon. MD Degree, Kagawa Med. Sch., Kagawa,Japan, 1992, Welcome Vis. Prof., U of Nebr., 1993, Wiggers Award, Am. Physiology Soc., 1995, Foaud A. Bashour Disting. physiologist Lectr., U. of TX, S.W. Med. Ctr., 1996, Konrad Witzig Meml. Lectr., The Cardiovasc. Sys. Dynamics Soc., 1996, J.R. Neely Lectr., Geisinger Clinic, Danville, PA, 1997; fellow Fellowship, The Internat. Soc. for Heart Rsch.; grantee Myocardial Hypertrophy and Heart Failure (Program Project)-Project 1 Cardiac Control in gsAlpha and 403 Mice, Nih/nhlbi (Po1 Hl59139-01), 09/15/97 - 08/31/02, Myocardial Hypertrophy and Heart Failure (Program Project) - Core A Adminstrn. of PPG, 09/15/97 - 08/31/02, Myocardial Hypertrophy and Heart Failure (Program Project) - Core B Transgenic Mouse Models for PPG, 09/15/97 - 08/31/02, Effects of Aging on Cardiovasc. Function in Primates, NIH/Aging (7RO1 AG14121-01), 08/01/97 - 07/31/02, Mechanisms of Myocardial Ischemia and Reperfusion (Program Project) - Project 2, Nih/nhlbi (1 Po1 Hl69020-01), 09/30/01 - 08/31/06, (PENDING) Integrative Mechanism in Cardiovasc. Disease (Instl. Tng. Grant), Nhi/nhlbi (1T32 Hl69752-01), 07/01/02 - 06-30-07. Mem.: AHA (executive,credentials,program and nominating committees 1968), Jour. of Molecular and Cellular Cardiology (consulting editor 2000), Circulation Rsch. (consulting editor 1999), Circulation (editl. bd. mem. 1999), Circulation Rsch. (editor-in-chief 1991—99), Am. Jour. of Physiology: Heart and Circulatory Sect. (bd. of med. editors 1998), Hypertension (editl. bd. mem. 1983—89), Procs. of The Soc. for Exptl. Biology and Medicine (editl. bd. mem. 1981—87), Circulation Rsch. (editl. bd. mem. 1981—87), Am. Jour. of Physiology (editl. bd. mem. 1985—90), Am. Jour. of Physiology (editl. bd. mem. 1979—81), AHA (mem. 1968), Am. Assn. of Physicians (assoc.), AHA, Keystone, CO (assoc.; co-director, sci. sessions of councils on sci. and circ. 1986), AHA, Keystone, CO (assoc.; co-director, sci. sessions of councils on sci. and circ.), Coun. on Circulation, AHA (assoc.; chmn., program com. 1982—85), Am. Soc. for Pharmacology and Exptl. Therapeutics (assoc.), Am. Soc. for Clin. Investigation (assoc.), Am. Physiol. Soc. (assoc.), Am. Fedn. for Clin. Rsch. (assoc.), Biophysical Soc. (assoc.), AHA (assoc.; bd. of directors, allegheny county 1997), AHA (assoc.; chmn., nominating com., coun. on circulation 1997—99), Am. Assn. for Accreditation of Lab. Animal Care Bd. of Trustees (assoc.), AHA, Mass. Affiliate (assoc.; v.p. 1990—92), AHA (assoc.; chmn., coun. on circulation 1990—92), AHA (assoc.; vice chmn., coun. on circulation 1988—90). Achievements include research in American Heart Association Research Achievement Award; American Heart Association, Scientific Councils Distinguished Achievment Award; National Institute of Health Merit Award. Office: UMDNJ-NJ Medical School 185 So Orange Ave - Ste G609 PO Box 1709 Newark NJ 07101-1709 Personal E-mail: vatnersf@umdnj.edu.

VATSIA, SHEEL KUMAR, cardiothoracic surgeon; b. Washington, Sept. 25, 1961; MBBS, U. Mysore, India, 1985; MD. Cert. Am. Bd. Thoracic Surgery, 1996, Am. Bd. Surgery. Intern SUNY Stony Brook Univ. Hosp., 1986—89, resident gen. surgery, 1991—93; clin. assoc. cardiac surgery br. NIH, 1989—91; resident cardiothoracic surgery NYU Med. Ctr., NYC, 1993—95; fellow pediatric and congenital heart surgery, as well as heart transplantation Denver Children's Hosp., 1995—96; with cardiovasc. and thoracic surgery dept. North Shore Univ. Hosp., Manhasset, NY, 1996—; pediatric and neonatal cardiac surgeon Schneider Children's Hosp. at North Shore, Manhasset. Contbr. articles to profl. jours. Fellow: ACS, Soc. Thoracic Surgeons, Am. Coll. Cardiology. Office: North Shore Univ Hosp 300 Community Dr Manhasset NY 11030 Office Phone: 516-562-4970. Office Fax: 516-562-3787. E-mail: svatsia@nshs.edu. *

VAUDRY, J. WILLIAM, JR., lawyer; b. Jacksonsville, Fla., Jan. 18, 1941; BBA, Tulane U., 1962, LLB, 1967. Bar: La. 1967. Of cousel Lemle & Kelleher, LLP, New Orleans. Bd. editors Tulane Law Rev., 1965-67. Lt. (j.g.) USN, 1962-64. Mem. ABA, La. State Bar Assn., Order of Coif, Phi Delta Phi. Address: Lemle & Kelleher LLP Pan Am Life Ctr 21st flr 601 Poydras St New Orleans LA 70130-6029 Office Phone: 504-584-9408.

VAUGHAN, ALDEN TRUE, history professor; b. Providence, Jan. 23, 1929; s. Dana Prescott and Muriel Louise (True) V.; m. Lauraine A. Freethy, June 1, 1956 (div. 1981); children: Jeffrey Alden, Lynn Elizabeth; m. Virginia Mason Carr, July 16, 1983. BA, Amherst Coll., 1950; MEd, Columbia U., 1956, MA in History, 1958, PhD, 1964. Tchr. Hackley Sch., Tarrytown, NY, 1950-51, A.B. Davis High Sch., Mt. Vernon, NY, 1956-60; From history instr. to prof. Columbia U., NYC, 1961—, prof. emeritus, 1994. Editor Polit. Sci. Quar., NY, 1970-71; vis. adj. prof. CUNY, Lehman Coll., NYC, 1971; vis. prof. Clark U., Worcester, Mass., 1987. Author: New England Frontier, 1965, 3d edit., 1995, American Genesis, 1975, Shakespeare's Caliban, 1991, Roots of American Racism, 1995, Transatlantic Encounters, 2006, others; co-editor: Arden Shakespeare's The Tempest, 1999; gen. editor Early Am. Indian Documents, 20 vols., 1977-2004; mem. editl. bd. Ency. of the N.Am. Colonies, 1993; contbr. articles to profl. jours. including Am. Heritage, Am. Hist. Rev., New Eng. Quar. Lt. (j.g.) USNR, 1951-55. Guggenheim Found. fellow, 1973, Sr. fellow Folger Shakespeare Libr., 1977, 89, Sr. fellow Am. Antiquarian Soc., 1983. Mem. Am. Antiquarian Soc., Am. Soc. for Ethnohistory, Shakespeare Assn. Am., Soc. Am. Historians (exec. sec., treas. 1965-70), Orgn. Am. Historians (program chmn. 1976), Inst. Early Am. History and Culture (coun. mem. 1985-87), Colonial Soc. Mass., Mass. Hist. Soc. Home: 50 Howland Ter Worcester MA 01602-2631

VAUGHAN, BRIAN K., writer, scriptwriter; b. Cleve., 1976; married. BA in Film and Dramatic Writing, NYU, 1994—98. Writer Marvel Comics, NYC, 1996—; writer Vertigo, Wildstorm, DCU DC Comics, NYC, 1998—; screenwriter New Line Cinema, LA, 2005—; exec. story editor, writer LOST ABC/Touchstone Television, Burbank, Calif., 2006—. Named Comic's Best Writer, Wizard mag., 2006; recipient Eisner award best writer, 2005, Rave award, Wired mag., 2007. E-mail: BrianKVaughan@aol.com. *

VAUGHAN, C. PORTER, III, lawyer; b. Denver, Aug. 26, 1945; BA, Yale U., 1967; JD, U. Va., 1970. Bar: Va. 1970. Ptnr., co-head, bus. practice group Hunton & Williams LLP, Richmond, Va. Mem. editorial bd. Va. Law Rev., 1968-70. Mem.: ABA, Va. State Bar Assn. Office: Hunton & Williams Riverfront Plz E Tower PO Box 1535 Richmond VA 23218-1535 Office Phone: 804-788-8285. Office Fax: 804-788-8218. Business E-Mail: pvaughan@hunton.com.

VAUGHAN, DAVID JOHN, corporate financial executive; b. Detroit, July 17, 1924; s. David Evans and Erma Mildred V.; divorced; children; David John, Melissa Ann, Julia Crawford McLaughlin; m. Anne McKeown Miles, Aug. 21, 1975. AB, U. Ill., 1950. Chemist Midland Electric Colleries, Galesburg, Ill., 1950-52; pres. Varrco Distbg. Co., Peoria, 1953—, David Vaughan Investments, Inc., Peoria, 1970—. Adv. bd. Charles Schwab Inc. Trustee Eureka Coll., chmn. bd. trustees; trustee Opera Ill. Lt. USAAF, 1942-46, USAF, 1951-52, Korea. Mem. Peoria Country Club, Northport Point Club (Mich.), Peoria Skeet Club, Racquet Club, Naples Club (Fla.), Naples Bath & Tennis Club, Royal Poinciana Country Club (Naples), Masons, Shriners, Alpha Tau Omega, Phi Eta Sigma, Phi Alpha Delta. Republican. Presbyterian. Office: 5823 N Forest Park Dr Peoria IL 61614-3559 also: 824 N Birchwood Dr Northport MI 49670-9761 also: Office Comstock Bldg Winter Park FL 32789 Home: 4413 Grandview Dr Peoria IL 61614 also: 5823 N Forest Park Dr Ste 1 Peoria IL 61614-3568 Home Phone: 309-699-6966; Office Phone: 309-685-0033. Business E-Mail: dvaughan@dviequity.com.

VAUGHAN, EDWARD GIBSON, lawyer; b. Dallas, Nov. 22, 1948; s. S.J. III and Martha (Gibson) V. BBA, U. Tex., 1971; cert., City of London Coll., 1970; JD, St. Mary's U., 1975. Bar: Tex. 1975. Assoc. Johnson & Jones, Austin, 1975-76; ptnr. Harris & Vaughan, Uvalde, Tex., 1976-79, Kessler, Kessler & Vaughan, Uvalde, 1979-94. Dir. First State Bank Uvalde, Security State Bank of Persall. Mem. ABA, Tex. and Southwestern Cattle Raisers (bd. dirs.), Uvalde C. of C. (bd. dirs. 1979-83), Tex. State C. of C. (bd. dirs. 1982-85), Tex. Lyceum Assn. (bd. dirs. 1980-85), Tex. Assn. Bank Counsel (bd. dirs. 1984-87), Southwestern Legal Found., State Bar Tex., Uvalde County Bar Assn. (pres. 1979-80), Kendall County Bar Assn., Tex. Water Found. (bd. dirs. 1998—). Office: 1580 S Main St Ste 200 Boerne TX 78006-2300

VAUGHAN, EDWIN DARRACOTT, JR., urologist, surgeon; b. Richmond, Va., May 13, 1939; s. Edwin Darracott and Blanche V. (Bashaw) V.; m. Virginia Anne Lloyd, June 30, 1962; children: Edwin Darracott III, Barbara Anderson. BS, Washington and Lee U., 1961, DSc, 1982; MD, U. Va., 1965, MS, 1969. Diplomate Am. Bd. Urology (trustee, v.p. 1988, pres. 1989). Intern Vanderbilt U., 1965—66, asst. resident, 1966—67; chief resident in urology U. Va., 1970—71, asst. prof. urology, 1973—75, assoc. prof., 1975—78, prof., 1978; clin. rsch. fellow Columbia U., 1971—72, rsch. assoc. dept. medicine, 1972—73; James J. Colt prof. urology, chmn. dept. urology Cornell U. Med. Coll., NYC; attending urologist-in-chief NY Hosp., NYC, 1978—; sr. assoc. dean clin. affairs Cornell U. Med. Coll., NYC, 1993—2001, chmn. dept. urology, 1993—2001, exec. vice dean sr. assoc. dean clin affairs, 2005. Chief med. officer Cornell Physician Orgn., 1997-2005; sci. adv. bd. Nat. Kidney Found., 1977-81; sec.-treas. Urology Coun., 1977-80, chmn., 1980-81; med. adv. bd. Coun. High Blood Pressure, 1977; acting co-chief exec. officer Columbia-Cornell Care, L.L.C., 1997; adv. coun. Nat. Diabetes and Digestive and Kidney Diseases, 2002-06; bd. visitors U. Va. Editor: Seminars in Urology, 1983-95, Timely Topics in Urology, 2007; assoc. editor Investigative Urology, 1977-78, mem. editl. bd., 1978-94, assoc. editor, 2004; mem. editl. bd. Brit. Jour. Urology, 2004; editor Campbell's Urology; assoc. editor Brit. Jour. Urology, 2004, asst. editor, 2004—; editor-in-chief Timely Topics in Urology, 2007; contbr. articles to profl. jours. Mem. adv. coun. Nat. Diabetes and Digestive and Kidney Diseases, 2002—; bd. visitors U. Va., 2002. Recipient Rsch. Career Devel. award NIH, 1976-78, Russell and Mary Hugh Scott award Am. Found. Urol. Disease, 1998, J.K. Latimer award NY-NJ Kidney Found., 1999, Valentine medal NY Acad. Medicine, 2000, Maurice R. Greenberg Disting. Svc. award, 2002, Good Scout award, BSA, 2002, Presdl. award Soc. Basic Sci. Rsch., 2004, Walter Reed award U. Va. Med. Sch., 2005; NIH tng. grantee, 1967-68; USPHS grantee, 1971-77; Am. Heart Assn. grantee, 1976-79 Mem. ACS, AAAS, Internat. Soc. Urology, NY Acad. Scis., Soc. Univ. Urologists, Am. Urol. Assn. (hon., chmn. rsch. com. 1980-91, treas. NY sect. 1985, v.p. NY sect. 1986, pres. NY sect. 1987, bd. dirs. 1992-97, pres.-elect 2000, pres. 2001, immediate past pres. 2002, Golden Cystoscope award 1981, Disting. Contbn. award 1992, Hugh Hampton Young award 2000), Urol. Soc. Australasia (hon.), Soc. Exptl. Biology and Medicine, Soc. Univ. Surgeons, Soc. Internat. Urology (chmn. bd. 1997—), Am. Found. Urol. Disease (pres. 1987-92, Presdl. Founder award 2004), NY Med. Surgical Soc. (pres. 2005), Soc. Basic Urol. Rsch. (Pres. award 2004), Nat. Kidney and Urol. Disease Adv. Bd. (dep. chmn.), Intersoc. for Kidney and Urol. Disease Rsch. (chmn. 1987), Am. Assn. Genito-Urinary Surgeons (Barringer medal 1993), Am. Surg. Assn., Brit. Assn. Urol. Surgeons (hon., St. Paul's medal), Japanese Urol. Soc. (hon.), Clin. Soc. Genitourinary Surgeons (pres. 2006), Sigma Chi (Significant Sig award 2000), Alpha Omega Alpha (award 1976), Omicron Delta Kappa (award 1981). Home: 1165 Park Ave Apt 6A New York NY 10128-1210 Office: 525 E 68th St New York NY 10021-4870 Office Phone: 212-746-5480. Business E-Mail: evaughan@med.cornell.edu.

VAUGHAN, ELIZABETH JEAN, education educator; d. Richard Curtis and Ida Martell Vaughan. BSEd, Stephen F. Austin State U., 1974, MEd, 1977; PhD, U. South Fla., 1984. Assoc. prof. Stephen F. Austin State U., Nacogdoches, Tex., 1983—92; prof. Shippensburg (Pa.) U., 1992—. Author: (book) Learning Centers for Child-Centered Classrooms, 1992, Teaching Numeracy, Language and Literacy with Blocks, 2006. Mem. Success by 6 Leadership Coun., Carlisle, Pa., 2001—06; bd. dirs. Montessori Acad. of Chambersburg, Pa., 2006—. Mem.: Pa. Assn. for Edn. of Young Children (pres. 2005—07), Mid-Atlantic Assn. for Edn. of Young Children (pres. 2001—03), Assn. Childhood Edn. Internat., Nat. Assn. for Edn. of Young Children. Home: 8 Lynn Ave Newburg PA 17240 Office: Shippensburg U 1871 Old Main Dr Shippensburg PA 17257 Home Phone: 717-423-5147; Office Phone: 717-477-1379.

VAUGHAN, EUGENE H., investment company executive; b. Brownsville, Tenn., Oct. 5, 1933; s. Eugene H. Sr. and Margaret (Musgrave) V.; m. Susan Bolinger Westbrook, May 11, 1963; children: Margaret Corbin, Richard Bolinger. BA, Vanderbilt U., 1955; MBA, Harvard U., 1961. CFA, 1967. Security analyst Putnam Mgmt. Co., Boston, 1961-64; dir., dir. rsch. Underwood, Neuhaus & Co., Inc., Houston, 1964-70; pres., chief exec. officer Vaughan, Nelson & Boston, Inc., Houston, 1970-77, Vaughan, Nelson, Scarborough & McCullough, L.P., Houston, 1970—. Chmn. bd. dirs. Dreyfus Founders Asset Mgmt. Co., Denver, 1970—. Chair Fin. Analyst Fedn., N.Y.C., 1973-74, bd. dirs., 1969-76; dir. U. Tex. Health Sci. Ctr., Houston, 2002—; pres. Houston Soc. Fin. Analysts, 1967-68; trustee exec. com. Vanderbilt U., Nashville, 1972—, St. John's Sch., Houston, 1980-85, Goodwill Industries, Houston, 1978—, United Way of Tex. Gulf Coast, 1994—; elder First Presbyn. Ch., 1976—; founding chmn., trustee Presbyn. Sch., Houston, 1986-90. Lt. USN, 1955-58. Recipient Disting. Svc. award Fin. Analyst Fedn., 1978, Humanitarian award Am. Jewish Com., 1993, Bus. Leader of Yr. award U. St. Thomas, 1996. Mem. Inst. Chartered Fin. Analysts (trustee 1986-93, chmn. 1989), Assn. for Investment Mgmt. and Rsch. (founding chmn. 1990-91, gov. 1990-93), Greater Houston Partnership (bd. dirs. 1990—, exec. com. 1993—, chair Ctr. Houston's Future 1999—), Houston Club (pres. 1983-84, bd. dirs. 1979-85, chair centennial celebration, 1992-94), Houston Country Club, Coronado Club (Houston), Houston Forum (pres. 1991-92, chmn. 1992-93), Harvard U. Bus. Sch. Club Houston (pres. 1968-69, bd. dirs. 1966-71, 86-90), Vanderbilt Club Houston (chmn. 1984—, pres. 1966-68, Disting. Svc. award 1994), Conferie des Chevaliers du Tastevin, Belle Meade Country Club (Nashville). Republican. Avocations: travel, sailing. Home: 3465 Inwood Dr Houston TX 77019-3129 Office: Vaughan Nelson Scarborough & McCullough 600 Travis Ste 6300 Houston TX 77002

VAUGHAN, GREGORY V., financial planner; Mng. dir. private wealth mgmt. group Morgan Stanley, Menlo Park, Calif. Mem. adv. bd. Leavey Sch. Bus. Santa Clara Univ.; bd. dir. NativityMiguel Network of Schools. Named one of Top 100 Fin. Advisors, Barron's Mag. Office: Morgan Stanley 2725 Sand Hill Rd Menlo Park CA 94025 *

VAUGHAN, HERBERT WILEY, retired lawyer; b. Brookline, Mass., June 1, 1920; s. David D. and Elzie G. (Wiley) Vaughan; m. Ann Graustein, June 28, 1941 (dec. June 2002). BS cum laude, Harvard U., 1941, LLB, 1948. Bar: Mass. 1948. Assoc. Hale and Dorr, Boston, 1948-54, jr. ptnr., 1954-56, sr. ptnr., 1956-89, co-mng. ptnr., 1976-80, ret. ptnr., 1990—2004, Wilmer Cutler Pickering Hale and Dorr, LLP, 2004—. Bd. dirs. fin. com. Boston and Maine RR, 1961—64; vis. fellow New Coll., Oxford U., 1985. Mem. standing com. Trustees of Reservations, 1986—98, chmn., 1988—92, sec., 1992—98, asst. sec., mem. adv. coun., 1998—2006, life trustee, 2004—; mem. adv. coun. James Madison Program in Am. Ideals and Instns., Princeton U. Fellow: Mass. Hist. Soc., Am. Bar Found. (life); mem.: ABA, Am. Coun. Trustees and Alumni (mem. alumni leadership coun.), Am. Coll. Real Estate Lawyers (charter mem.), Am. Law Inst., Boston Bar Assn., Mass. Bar Assn., Boston Econ. Club, Union Club (Boston), Badminton and Tennis Club. Office: Wilmer Cutler Pickering Hale and Dorr LLP 60 State St Boston MA 02109-1816 Office Phone: 617-526-6718. Business E-Mail: herbert.vaughan@wilmerhale.com.

VAUGHAN, JACK M., lawyer; b. Austin, Tex., Aug. 27, 1947; BBA in Acctg., U. Tex., 1969; JD, U. Houston, 1974. Bar: Tex. 1974, CPA. Tax ptnr. Deloitte Haskins & Sells acctg.; ptnr. Fulbright & Jaworski LLP, Houston, now adminstrv. ptnr. Fellow: Coll. of Law Practice Mgmt., Texas Bar Found., Houston Bar Found. Mem. ABA, State Bar of Tex., Houston Bar Assn., Am. Inst. CPA, Tex. Soc. CPA, Assn. Legal Adminstr. Meth. Office: Fulbright & Jaworski LLP Ste 5100 1301 McKinney St Houston TX 77010-3031 Office Phone: 713-651-5151. Office Fax: 713-651-5246. Business E-Mail: jvaughan@fulbright.com.

VAUGHAN, JAMES JOSEPH MICHAEL, lawyer; b. Mar. 19, 1942; s. James M. and Elizabeth (McDonnell) Vaughan; m. Jeanette Rae Gerber, Aug. 5, 1967; children: Karen, Adrianne, Jennifer. BS, U. Scranton, 1963; JD, Cath. U., 1966. Bar: U.S. Dist. Ct. Md. 1979, U.S. Ct. Appeals (D.C. cir.) 1972, U.S. Ct. Claims 1973, U.S. Supreme Ct. 1977. Assoc. Dukes, Troese, et al, Chevy Chase, Md., 1969—72; atty. Assn. Am. Law Schs., Washington, 1972—76, 2001—; mem. firm Giordano, Villareale & Vaughan, Upper Marlboro, Md., 1976—2001; pvt. practice, 2001—. Mem.: Prince George's County Bar Assn., Md. Bar Assn., D.C. Bar Assn., Bar Assn. D.C., Assn. Trial Lawyers Am. Democrat. Roman Catholic. Office: Giordano Villareale and Vaughan 9300 Livingston Rd 106 Fort Washington MD 20744-4905

VAUGHAN, JAMES M., historic trust administrator; Dir. Historic Strawbery Branke, NH, Hagley Mus. and Libr., Del., San Diego Historical Soc., Calif.; exec. dir. The Hermitage, the Home of Pres. Andrew Jackson; v.p. stewardship of historic sites Nat. Trust for Historic Preservation, Washington, 2000—. Named to Centennial Honor Roll, Am. Assn. Museums, 2006. Office: National Trust for Historic Preservation 1785 Massachusetts Ave NW Washington DC 20036 *

VAUGHAN, JOSEPH LEE, JR., education educator, consultant, director, academic administrator; b. Charlottesville, Va., Dec. 31, 1942; s. Joseph Lee and Ann (Doner) Vaughan; m. Mary Linda De Silva; children: Leigh Ann, Kelley, Stephen, Kathleen. BA, U. Va., 1964, MEd, 1968, EdD, 1974. Tchr. Madison (Va.) High Sch., 1965-67, Darlington Sch., Rome, Ga., 1967-69, Woodberry Forest (Va.) Sch., 1969-74; asst. prof. edn. U. Ariz., Tucson, 1974-80; prof. Tex. A&M U.-Commerce, Mesquite, 1980—2006, dir. programs in reading edn., 1980-86, 91-92. Dir. Tex. Ctr. Learning Styles, 1989—95; exec. dir. Children's Inst. Literacy Devel., Inc., 1995—2004, The Ctr. Acad. Progress, Inc., 2004—05; cons. faculty in humanities St. Alban's Episcopal Sch., 2000—; pres. Learning and Literary Sys. Co-author: Reading and Learning in Content Classrooms, 1978, 2d rev. edit., 1985, Reading and Reasoning Beyond The Primary Grades, 1986. Bd. govs. Sancta Sophia Sem., 1991-98. Mem. ASCD, Nat. Reading Conf., Internat. Reading Assn., Soc. Effective Affective Learning. Avocations: golf, travel, reading, antiques. Home: 447 Ridgemont Dr Heathridge TX 75126 Office: Tex A&M U-Commerce 2600 Motley Dr Mesquite TX 75150-3840 Personal E-mail: learningcaps@aol.com.

VAUGHAN, KAREN LYNN, soil scientist; b. Warwick, RI, Nov. 9, 1979; d. Richard Lee and Carol Sus Castenson; m. Robert Edward Vaughan, July 29, 2006. BS, U. Del., Newark, 2001; MS, U. Md., College Park, 2004. Grad. rsch. asst. U. Md., College Park, 2001—04; grad. fellow U. Idaho, Moscow, 2004—. Fellow, Idaho Nat. Lab., 2006—07; grantee, Natural Resources Conservation Svc. and Nat. Pk. Svc., 2005—06. Mem.: Assn. Women Soil Scientists, Soc. Wetland Scientists, Soil Sci. Soc. Am., Sigma Xi. Home: 915 E 6th St Moscow ID 83843 Office: U Idaho PO Box 442339 Moscow ID 83844-2339 Home Phone: 208-892-1402; Office Phone: 208-885-7505. Personal E-mail: karen.vaughan@vandals.uidaho.edu.

VAUGHAN, KEITH W., lawyer; b. Bluefield, W.Va., Oct. 1, 1950; BA cum laude, Wake Forest U., 1972; JD cum laude, U. Ga., 1975. Bar: Ga. 1975, NC 1975, US Dist. Ct. (Eastern, Middle & Western Dists. NC), NC Supreme Ct., US Ct. Appeals (4th Cir.), US Supreme Ct. Ptnr. litigation practice group leader, mem. firm mgmt. com. Womble Carlyle Sandridge & Rice PLLC, Winston-Salem, NC, chmn. mgmt. com., mng. mem. Bd. dir. NC Assn. Def. Attys., 1985—88. Editor-in-chief Ga. Law Rev., 1974-75. Named to Bus. North Carolina's Legal Elite (Litigation). Mem. ABA, NC Bar Assn., Forsyth County Bar Assn., Ga. Bar Assn., Forsyth County Young Lawyers Assn. (pres., 1981),, Am. Inns of Ct. (Master of the Bench), Omicron Delta Kappa, Delta Sigma Rho, Tau Kappa Alpha; Fellow, Am. Coll. of Trial Lawyers Office: Womble Carlyle Sandridge & Rice PLLC One W 4th St Winston Salem NC 27101 Office Phone: 336-721-3600. Office Fax: 336-733-8417. Business E-Mail: kvaughan@wcsr.com.

VAUGHAN, MARTHA, biochemist, educator; b. Dodgeville, Wis., Aug. 4, 1926; d. John Anthony and Luciel (Ellingen) V.; m. Jack Orloff, Aug. 4, 1951 (dec. Dec. 1988); children: Jonathan Michael, David Geoffrey, Gregory Joshua. Ph.B., U. Chgo., Ill., 1944; MD, Yale U., New Haven, Conn., 1949. Intern New Haven Hosp., Conn., 1950-51; research fellow U. Pa., Phila., 1951-52, Nat. Heart Inst., Bethesda, Md., 1952-54, mem. research staff, 1954-68; head metabolism sect. Nat. Heart and Lung Inst., Bethesda, 1968-74; acting chief molecular disease br. Nat. Heart, Lung and Blood Inst., Bethesda, 1974-76, chief cell metabolism lab., 1974-94; dep. chief pulmonary and critical care medicine br. Nat. Heart, Lung, and Blood Inst., Bethesda, 1994—. Mem. metabolism study sect. NIH, 1965-68; mem. bd. sci. counselors Nat. Inst. Alcohol Abuse and Alcoholism, 1988-91. Mem. editl. bd. Jour. Biol. Chemistry, 1971-76, 80-83, 88-90, assoc. editor, 1992—; editl. adv. bd. Molecular Pharmacology, 1972-80, Biochemistry, 1989-94; editor: Biochemistry and Biophysics Rsch. Comms., 1990-91; contbr. articles to profl. jours., chpts. to books. Bd. dirs. Found. Advanced Edn. in Scis., Inc., Bethesda, 1979-92, exec. com., 1980-92, treas., 1984-86, v.p., 1986-88, pres., 1988-90; mem. Yale U. Coun. com. med. affairs, New Haven, 1974-80. Recipient Meritorious Svc. medal HEW, 1974, Disting. Svc. medal HEW, 1979, Commd. Officer award USPHS, 1982, Superior Svc. award USPHS, 1993. Mem. NAS, Am.

Acad. Arts and Scis., Am. Soc. Biol. Chemists (chmn. pub. com. 1984-86), Assn. Am. Physicians, Am. Soc. Clin. Investigation. Home: 11608 W Hill Dr Rockville MD 20852-3751 Office: Nat Heart Lung & Blood Inst Nih Bldg 10 Rm 5N 307 Bethesda MD 20892-0001 Business E-Mail: vaughanm@nih.gov.

VAUGHAN, MICHAEL RICHARD, lawyer; b. Chgo., Aug. 27, 1936; s. Michael Ambrose and Loretta M. (Parks) Vaughan; m. Therese Marie Perri, Aug. 6, 1960; children: Charles Thomas, Susan Enger. Student, U. Ill., 1954-59; LLB, U. Wis., 1962. Bar: Wis. 1962. Chief atty. bill drafting sect. Wis. Legislature, Madison, 1962-68, dir. legis. attys., 1968-72; assoc. Murphy Desmond, and predecessor, Madison, 1972-73, ptnr., 1974—. Mem. Commn. Uniform State Laws, 1966—72; cons. Nat. Commn. Marijuana and Drug Abuse, 1971—73; lectr. CLE seminars. Contbr. articles to profl. jours. Warden, vestryman St. Dunstan's Episcopal Ch., 1973—78, 1980—87; mem. Wis. Episcopal Conf., 1972—76. Mem.: ABA, Dane County Bar Assn., State Bar Wis. (dir. govtl. and adminstrv. law sect. 1971—78, mem. interprofl. and bus. rels. com. 1976—89), The Club at Olde Cypress (Naples, Fla.), Nakoma Golf Club, Madison Club, U. Wis. Law Sch. Bencher Soc., Delta Kappa Epsilon. Office: 2 E Mifflin St Ste 800 Madison WI 53701-2038 Office Phone: 608-257-7181.

VAUGHAN, PATRICK J., lawyer; b. Port Arthur, Tex., Sept. 15, 1943; m. Julia Smith; 3 children. BS in Commerce, U. Va., 1965, LLB, 1968; LLM in Taxation, Georgetown U., 1976. Bar: Va. 1968, US Tax Ct. 1972, US Supreme Ct. 1972, Md. 1999, DC 1999; CPA, Va.; ChFC. Assoc. Adams, Porter & Radigan, Ltd., McLean, Va., 1970-74, prin., 1974—2003, Vaughan, Fincher & Sotelo, P.C., Vienna, Va., 2003—. 1st lt. US Army, 1968-70. Named one of Top 100 Attys., Worth mag., 2005. Fellow Am. Coll. Trust and Estate Counsel; mem. ABA, Va. Bar Assn., Fairfax Bar Assn., Va. Soc. CPA, No. Va. Estate Planning Coun. (pres. 1994-95). Avocations: hiking, biking, swimming, reading, attending professional baseball and football games. Office: Vaughan Fincher & Sotelo PC 8619 Westwood Center Dr Ste 400 Vienna VA 22182-2220 Office Phone: 703-506-1810. Office Fax: 703-506-1850. E-mail: pvaughan@vfspc.com.

VAUGHAN, ROBERT OREN, lawyer; b. Elko, Nev., Mar. 19, 1925; m. Barbara Schreiner, 1950 (dec. June 1996); children: Meg, Brad; m. Betty Kelly Pearson, 1997. BA, U. Nev., Reno, 1950; JD cum laude, U. Denver, 1952; Assoc. degree (hon.), Gt. Basin Coll., 1996. Bar: Nev. 1952, U.S. Dist. Nev. 1955, U.S. Supreme Ct. 1961, U.S. Ct. Appeals (9th cir.) 1973. Ptnr. Vaughan & Hull, Ltd. and predecessor firms, Elko, 1953—; mem. Nev. State Assembly, 1955-58, minority floor leader, 1958. City atty. City of Wells, Nev., 1957-75; dep. city atty. City of Elko, 1962-82; gen. counsel Wells Rural Electric Co., 1958—, Mt. Wheeler Power, Inc., 1963-92, Nev. Rural Electric Assn., 1974; mem. Nev. Jud. Selection Commn., 1960-66; ptnr. AAA Self Storage, Western Enterprises; owner Vaughan Ranch, Ruby Valley, Nev., 1958-95. Bd. editors U. Denver Law Rev., 1952. Trustee Elko County Libr. Bd., 1959-63; bd. dirs. Elko Knife and Fork Club, 1962; dir. Heart Fund, 1957-85; active youth sports; trustee Gt. Basin Coll. Found., 1983-2002, mem. exec. com., planned giving com., 1991—, chmn. spkrs. bur., 1989-90, chmn. major gifts com., 1991-98; deacon, ruling elder 1st Presbyn. Ch. of Elko. 1st lt. USAF, 1943-47; with Nev. N.A.G., 1948-50. Mem. ABA, Nev. State Bar Assn. (adminstrv. com. 1956-66, probate and property practice com., unauthorized practice of law com., fee dispute com.), Elko County Bar Assn. (pres. 1963-64), Elko C. of C. (past bd. dirs., treas.), Rotary (pres. 1964-65), Masons, Royal and Select Masters, Royal Arch, K.T., Shriners, Ea. Star. Republican. Home: PO Box 281859 Lamoille NV 89828-1859 Office: Vaughan & Hull Ltd 530 Idaho St PO Box 1420 Elko NV 89803-1420 Home Phone: 775-777-0977; Office Phone: 775-738-4031. Business E-Mail: rvaughan@frontiernet.net.

VAUGHAN, SAMUEL SNELL, editor, writer, publishing executive; b. Phila., Aug. 3, 1928; s. Joseph and Anna Catherine (Alexander) Vaughan; m. Jo LoBiondo Vaughan, Oct. 22, 1949; children: Jeffrey Marc, Leslie Jane, Dana Alexander, David Samuel. BA, Pa. State U., 1951. Deskman, King Features Syndicate, NYC, 1951; asst. mgr. Doubleday Syndicate, 1952—54; advt. mgr. Doubleday, NYC, 1954—56; sales mgr., 1956—58; sr. editor, 1958—68; exec. editor Doubleday, 1969—70; pub., pres. pub. div. Doubleday & Co., Inc., 1970—82, v.p. parent co., 1970—86, editor in chief, 1982—86; sr. v.p. and editor Random House, Inc., 1986—90, editor-at-large, 1990—2004. Mem. faculty, Columbia U., 1978-88; bd. dirs. Ch. Pub. Co.-Seabury Press; lectr. in field. Author: (juveniles) Whoever Heard of Kangaroo Eggs? 1957, New Shoes, 1961, The Two-Thirty Bird, 1965, (history) The Little Church, 1969, Medium Rare: A Look at the Book and Its People, 1977, (humor) Little Red Hood, 1979, The Accidental Profession, 1979, The Community of the Book, 1983, The State of the Heart, 1985; editor: Buckley: The Right Word, 1996; contbr. to N.Y. Times, Sunday Times of London, Daedalus, Am. Heritage, others. Served with USMC, 1946-48. Named Disting. Alumnus, Pa. State U., 1977, Alumni fellow, 1979. Mem. Tenafly Tennis Club, Quantuck Beach Club (Westhampton, N.Y.), Century Assn. Episcopalian.

VAUGHAN, THERESE MICHELE, insurance educator; b. Blair, Nebr., June 12, 1956; d. Emmett John and Lonne Kay (Smith) V.; m. Robert Allen Carber, Aug. 15, 1993; children: Kevin Leo Vaughan-Carber, Thomas S. Vaughan-Carber. BBA, U. Iowa, 1979; PhD, U. Pa., 1985. CPCU. Asst. prof. Baruch Coll., CUNY, 1986-87; cons. Tillinghast, NYC, 1987-88; dir. ins. ctr. Drake U., Des Moines, 1988-94; ins. commr. State of Iowa, Des Moines, 1994—2004; Robb B. Kelley Disting. prof. ins. and actuarial sci. Drake U., 2005—. Bd. dirs. Endurance Splty. Holdings, Prin. Fin. Group, Nat. Coun Comp. Ins. Co-editor Jour. Ins. Regulation Bd., 2005—; co-author: Fundamentals of Risk and Insurance, 1996, 99, 2003, Essentials of Insurance: A Risk Management Approach, 1995, 2001; contbr. articles to profl. jours. S.S. Huebner fellow U. Pa., 1979-82; recipient Outstanding Young Alumnus award U. Iowa, 1996; named to Iowa Ins. Hall of Fame, 2003. Mem. Nat. Assn. Ins. Commrs. (pres. 2002), Ins. Marketplace Stds. Assn. (bd. dirs. 2004—), Am. Risk and Ins. Assn. (v.p. 2006—), Beta Gamma Sigma, Omicron Delta Epsilon. Avocations: hiking, biking, reading. Home: 4632 Elm St West Des Moines IA 50265-2993 Office: Drake Univ 2507 University Ave Des Moines IA 50311 Business E-Mail: terri.vaughan@drake.edu.

VAUGHAN, THOMAS JAMES GREGORY, historian, writer; b. Seattle, Oct. 13, 1924; s. Daniel George and Kathryn Genevieve (Browne) V.; m. Elizabeth Ann Perpetua Crownhart, June 16, 1951; children: Meagan, Margot, Stephen, Cameron. BA, Yale U., 1948; MS, U. Wis., 1950, doctoral residence, 1951-53; LittD, Pacific U., 1969; LLD, Reed Coll., 1975. Exec. dir. Oreg. Hist. Soc., Portland, 1954-90; editor in chief Oreg. Hist. Quar., 1954-89; adj. prof. Portland State U., 1968—. Chmn. bd. Salar Enterprises, Ltd.; bd. dir. Am. Heritage Pub. Co., 1976-85; film producer, 1958-99; historian laureate State of Oreg., 1989—. Author: A Century of Portland Architecture, 1967, Captain Cook, R.N, The Resolute Mariner: An International Record of Oceanic Discovery, 1974, Portland, A Historical Sketch and Guide, 1976, 2d edit., 1983, Voyage of Enlightenment: Malaspina on the Northwest Coast, 1977; editor: Space, Style and Structure: Building in Northwest America, 2 vols., 1974, The Western Shore, 1975, Ascent of the Athabasca Pass, 1978, Wheels of Fortune, High and Mighty, 1981, Soft Gold, 1982, 2d edit., 1990, To Siberia and Russian America, Vols. I, II and III, Frances Fuller Victor, 2002, others; co-editor: Siberica, 1989; mem. adv. bd. Am. Heritage Mag., 1977-90; prodr. film The Crimean War, 1994, Wellington's Last Parade, 1997, George Dewey: A Monarch of the Seas, 2003, George Catlin: the American Indians' Painter, 2006, The Russo-Japanese War 1904-05 A Study in Extremes, 2007, Incredible Lies: Stories of Old Fashioned Golf, 2007. 1st chmn. Oreg. State Com. for Humanities, NEH, 1969—; 1st chmn. Gov.'s Adv. Com. on Historic Preservation Oreg., 1970-77; sec. Oreg. Geog. Names Bd., 1958-89; adviser 1000 Friends of Oreg., 1972—; lay mem. Oreg. State Bar Disciplinary Rev. Bd., 1975-82; vice chmn. adv. panel Nat. Endowment Arts, 1975—; mem. Nat. Hist. Publs. and Records Commn. Matrix, 1975-76; historian laureate State of Oreg., 1989. With USMC, 1942-45. Decorated comdr. Order Brit. Empire; recipient Aubrey Watzek award Lewis and Clark Coll., 1975;, Edith Knight Hill award, 1977, Disting. Svc. award U. Oreg.; grantee English Speaking Union, 1961; Columbia Maritime Mus. 1st rsch. fellow, 1992, Thomas Jefferson medal, 2002. Fellow Royal Geog. Soc.; mem. Am. Assn. State and Local History (bd. dir. 1955-74, pres. 1976-78), Am. Assn. Mus. (coun., exec. com.), Nat. Trust Hist. Preservation (adv. coun.), Ctr. for Study Russian Am., Russian Acad. Scis., City Club (Portland, bd. govs.), Univ. Club (Portland, bd. govs.), The Arts Club (London). Home: 2135 SW Laurel St Portland OR 97201-2367 Personal E-mail: goldengrove@spiretech.net.

VAUGHAN, WILLIAM WALTON, atmospheric scientist; b. Clearwater, Fla., Sept. 7, 1930; s. William Walton and Ella Vermelle (Warr) Vaughan; m. Wilma Geraldine Stapleton, Dec. 23, 1951; children: Stephen W., David A., William D., Robert T. BS with honors, U. Fla., 1951; grad. cert., USAF Inst. Tech./Fla. State U., 1952; PhD, U. Tenn., 1976. Cert. cons. meteorologist. Sci. asst. Air Force Armament Ctr., Eglin AFB, Fla., 1955-58, Army Ballistic Missile Agy., Huntsville, Ala., 1958-60; chief aerospace environ. div. Marshall Space Flight Center, NASA, Huntsville, 1960-76, chief atmospheric scis. div., 1976-86; rsch. prof. atmospheric sci. U. Ala., Huntsville, 1986—, dir. Rsch. Inst., 1986-94; ret., 1994. Cons. atmospheric sci. and tech. stds.; mem. adv. com. NASA. Contbr. articles to profl. jours. Served to capt. USAF, 1951—55. Recipient Exceptional Svc. medal, NASA, 1971. Fellow: AIAA (standard exec. coun., Losey Atmospheric Scis. award 1980, Excellence in Aerospace Stds. award 2003, Sustained Svc. award 2007), Am. Meteorol. Soc.; mem.: AAAS, Am. Geophys. Union, Stds. Engring. Soc., Sigma Xi. Office: Univ Ala Atmospheric Sci Dept Huntsville AL 35899-0001 Business E-Mail: vaughan@nsstc.uah.edu. *

VAUGHAN, WORTH EDWARD, retired chemistry professor; b. NYC, Feb. 1, 1936; s. Royal Worth and Sylvia Marie (Fernholz) V.; m. Diane Marilyn Mayer, Aug. 9, 1969; 1 child, Wayne John BA, Oberlin Coll., 1957; MA, Princeton U., 1959, PhD, 1960. Asst. prof. chemistry U. Wis.-Madison, 1961-66, assoc. prof., 1967-76, prof., 1977—2002, prof. emeritus, 2002—. Mem. bd. advisors Am. Exchange Bank West Br., Madison, 1983-87. Author: Dielectric Properties and Molecular Behavior, 1969; editor: Digest of Literature on Dielectrics, 1974; translation editor: Dipole Moments of Organic Compounds, 1970; contbr. articles to profl. jours. Mem. Am. Chem. Soc. (pres. Wis. sect. 1968, 1998), Phi Beta Kappa Avocations: canoeing, contract bridge. Home: 501 Ozark Trl Madison WI 53705-2538 Office: Univ Wis 1101 University Ave Madison WI 53706-1322 Office Phone: 608-262-7924. Business E-Mail: vaughan@chem.wisc.edu.

VAUGHN, CARY EDWARD, minister, director; b. Memphis, May 16, 1971; s. Brenda Jane Vaughn; m. Lalania Star Goodman, June 26, 1992; children: Logan Star, Colton Edward. BA, Lambuth U., 1993; MSc in Orgnl. Leadership, Breyer State U., 2004. Cert. in Christian Leadership Belmont U., Tenn., 2004, in Advanced Skilltrack Christian Leadership Belmont U., Tenn., 2004, in Bivocational Ministry Leadership Belmont U., Tenn., 2005; Payroll Adminstr. HRCertification.com., Ga., 2005, ROI bd. devel. cert. YMCA. Min. lay leadership Bellevue Bapt. Ch., Cordova, Tenn., 2002—, dir. lay ministry, 2002—, dir. men's ministry, 2003—, dir. new mems., 2004—, dir. career svcs., 2004—, program adminstr. spl. events, 2005—, dir. guest svcs., 2005—; pres. Convenant Staffing Solutions LLC, 2006—. Co-chmn. capital campaign Tipton-Rosemark Acad., 2007. Mem. Rotary Internat., Millington, Tenn., 2005—06; bd. dirs. Am. Families Assn. Discipleship Ministry, 2006; chmn. Tipton-Rosemark Acad., Millington, 2000—; ex-officio mem. Lambuth U., Jackson, Tenn., 2003—04; chmn. fundraising com. YMCA, Millington, Tenn., 2005—; chmn. bd. dirs. Millington Family YMCA, 2007; bd. dirs. Metro YMCA, 2007—, Chrosscheck Athletic Assn., 2006; chmn. bd. dir. Millington Family YMCA, 2007. Recipient John G. Tower Disting. Alumni award, Kappa Sigma Nat. Frat., 1999, First Yr. Outstanding Vol. award, Kappa Sigma Nat. Fraternity, Leadership award, Comforce, Inc., 1998, Alumnus of Yr., Lambuth U., 2000; grantee Leadership scholarship, Kappa Sigma Nat. Frat., 1992. Mem.: Christian Educators Assn. Internat. (dir. pub. rels. Lower Miss. Valley region 2006), Assn. Christian Schs. Internat., Christian Mgmt. Assn., Harvard U. Prin. Ctr., Rotary Internat. (chmn. Taste of Millington 2007). R-Conservative. Baptist. Avocations: reading, exercise, hunting. Home: 8880 Gragg Rd Millington TN 38053-4945 Office: Covenant Staffing Solution LLC 6465 Quail Hollow Ste 102 Memphis TN 38120 Home Phone: 901-829-2292. Home Fax: 901-829-2994. Personal E-mail: caryvaughn@peoplepc.com. Business E-Mail: cary@covenantstaffingsolutions.net.

VAUGHN, CARYN CARPENTER, zoologist, educator; b. Oklahoma City, Nov. 15, 1955; d. Charles C. and Mary P. Carpenter; m. Joe T. Vaughn, Aug. 4, 1979; children: Andrew Thomas, Katherine Mary. BS, U. Okla., Norman, 1977, MS, 1979, PhD, 1984. Dir. Okla. Biol. Survey, Norman, 1999—; presdl. prof. Zoology, U. Okla., Norman, 2005—. Contbr. articles to profl. jours. Commr. Norman Greenbelt Commn., 2004—. Grantee Rsch. Grants, NSF, 1993—. Mem.: Ecol. Soc. Am., North Am. Benthological Soc. (assoc. editor 2005—). Office: Univ Okla 111 E Chesapeake St Norman OK 73019 Office Phone: 405-325-4034.

VAUGHN, CLYDE A., career military officer; BS, S.E. Mo. State Coll., 1968; grad., U.S. Army Command and Gen. Staff Coll., 1989, U.S. Army War Coll., 1994; MPA, Shippensburg U., 1994. Advanced through grades to lt. gen. Army N.G., 2005—, numerous assignments including platoon leader, 1221st Transp. Co. Dexter, Mo., 1974—76, platoon leader Detachment 1, A Co. 1140th Engr. Battalion Charleston, Mo., 1976—78, engring. officer 1140th Engr. Battalion Sikeston, Mo., 1980—83, ops. officer 135th Engr. Group Cape Girardeau, Mo., 1984—85; comdr. Task Force 354 U.S. Army South, Panama, 1990—91; plans sect. chief N.G. bur. Army N.G., Arlingotn, Va., 1991—92, chief ops. and exercise br. N.G. bur., 1992—93, chief ops. divsn. Arlington, Va., 1997—2000, dep. dir., 2002—03; comdr. exercise support command, dep. chief staff reserve affairs N.G. U.S. Army South, Panama, 1995—97; dep. dir. ops., readiness and mobilization, office G3/G5 U.S. Army, Washington, 2000—02; asst. to chmn. of joint chiefs of staff nat. guard matters The Pentagon, Washington, 2003—05; pres., dir., N.G. bur. Army N.G., Arlington, Va., 2005—. Office: US Army NG 111 S George Mason Dr Arlington VA 22204

VAUGHN, GLADYS GARY, federal agency administrator, researcher, not-for-profit executive; m. Joseph B. Vaughn (dec. 2000). BS, Fla. A&M U., 1964; MS in Clothing and Textiles, Iowa State U., 1968; PhD in Home Econs. Edn. and Adminstrn., U. MD.-College Park, 1974; LHD (hon.), Fontbonne U., 2006. Nat. program leader for human scis. rsch. Families, 4-H and Nutrition Unit Cooperative State Rsch., Edn. and Extension Svcs., US Dept. of Agr., Washington. Named one of Most Influential Black Americans, Ebony mag., 2006. Mem.: The Links, Inc. (pres. 2002—), Black Women's Agenda, Nat. Coalition of Black Devel. in Home Econs., Delta Sigma Theta Sorority. Office: The Links, Inc 1200 Massachusetts Ave, NW Washington DC 20005

VAUGHN, ISSAC J., lawyer; b. San Francisco, Dec. 12, 1962; BS, Santa Clara U., 1984; attended, Hastings Coll. Law, 1988—89; JD, U. Mich. Law Sch., 1991. Bar: Calif. 1991. Ptnr. Wilson Sonsini Goodrich & Rosati, Palo Alto, Calif. Mem. bd. regents Santa Clara U., 1992—. Named one of Top 20 Lawyers Under 40, Calif. Law Bus., 2001, Am. Top Black Lawyers, Black Enterprise Mag., 2003. Office: Wilson Sonsini Goodrich & Rosati 650 Page Mill Rd Palo Alto CA 94304-1050 Office Phone: 650-493-9300. Business E-Mail: ivaughn@wsgr.com.

VAUGHN, JOHN ROLLAND, auditor; b. Iola, Kans., Aug. 4, 1938; s. Ralph H. and Alice (Dille) V.; m. Doris K. Black, Sept. 4, 1960; children: Lisa Ann, Brian Douglas. BS in Bus., Emporia State U., 1960. Sr. auditor Arthur Andersen & Co., Kansas City, Mo., 1961-66; gen. auditor First Nat. Bank Kansas City, 1966-69, Commerce Bancshares, Inc., 1969-73; sr. v.p. adminstrv. svcs. divsn. Peoples Trust Bank, Ft. Wayne, Ind., 1973-77; dep. gen. auditor, v.p. Crocker Nat. Bank, San Francisco, 1978-79; v.p., gen. auditor S.W. Bancshares, Houston, 1980-83; sr. v.p., gen. auditor MCorp., Houston, 1984-87, mng. dir., 1988-89; audit dir. Banc One Corp., Dallas, 1990-92; v.p., gen. auditor St. Paul Cos., St. Paul, 1992-97; dir. internal audit Conseco Fin., St. Paul, 1998—2001; v.p., chief audit officer Calif. State Automobile Assn., 2001—02, v.p., chief risk officer, 2002—07. Treas. Overland Park (Kans.) Jr. C. of C., 1965—66; outside dir. Overland Park Credit Union; contr. Ft. Wayne Bicentennial Commn., 1974—77; mem. chmns. cabinet Indianhead coun. Boy Scouts Am., 2000—01. Mem. Inst. Internal Auditors (1st v.p. Kansas City 1969-70, pres. 1970-71, midwest regional v.p. 1971-72, Twin Cities chpt. gov. 1993-97, pres. 1994-95, internat. profl. conf. com. 1995-98, internat. ednl. products com. 1999-2002, San Francisco chpt. gov. 2004—07), Fin. Execs. Inst. (dir. Ft. Wayne 1976-77), Risk and Ins. Mgmt. Soc., Hartsmen, Voices in Harmony Chorus, Vocal Majority Chorus, Barbershop Harmony Soc., Gt. No. Union Chorus, Sigma Tau Gamma. Home: 5 Henry Ranch Dr San Ramon CA 94583

VAUGHN, LINDA MARIE, municipal official; b. Moline, Ill., Aug. 6, 1947; d. Merwin Perry and Margaret Anne Baker; m. Jeffery M. Vaughn, Aug. 16, 1969; children: Jason P., Eric M. Student, Moline Inst. Commerce, 1965. Clk. data entry Eagle Warehouse, Milan, Ill., 1966—69, Lennox Heating/AC, Marshalltown, Iowa, 1970—73, Farmall (Internat. Harvester), Rock Island, Ill., 1973—75, Ingersoll, Rockford, 1975—87; trustee Village of Machesney Park, Ill., 1987—89, clk., 1989—2001, mayor, village pres., 2001—. Guest columnist Parks Jour., 1997—; charter mem. Parks Chamber Women's Network, Loves Park, Ill., 1995; 8 gal. mem. Rock River Valley Blood Ctr. Mem. Northwestern Ill. Mcpl. Clks. Assn. (sec. 1990-92, treas. 1997-99), C. of C. (ambassador 1987—). Democrat. Roman Catholic. Avocations: writing, fishing, reading, walking. Home: 9519 Shore Dr Machesney Park IL 61115-2058 Office: Village Machesney Park 300 Machesney Rd Machesney Park IL 61115-2495

VAUGHN, LISA MICHELLE, assistant principal; b. Aug. 23, 1971; BS in Edn., Athens State U., Ala., 1994; MS in Edn., U. South Fla., Tampa, 2003. Cert. tchr. Ga., specific learning disabilities Ga., ednl. leadership Ga. Tchr. Polk County Schs., Bartow, Fla., 1994—2003, exceptional student facilitator Lakeland, 2003—04; asst. prin. Oconee County Schs., Watkinsville, Ga., 2004—. Mem.: Ga. Assn. Ednl. Leaders, Nat. Mid. Sch. Assn. Office: Oconee County Mid Sch 1101 Mars Hill Rd Watkinsville GA 30677-4829 Home: 1050 Windsor Dr Watkinsville GA 30677 Office Phone: 706-769-3575.

VAUGHN, MICHAEL S., law educator; s. Harley (Bud) Dewitt and Judith Ann Vaughn; m. Tzu-Hsiu Nancy Vaughn, Dec. 2, 1989; 1 child, Rachel. PhD in Criminal Justice, Sam Houston State U., Huntsville, Tex., 1990—93. Prof. Ga. State U., Atlanta, 1993—2006, chmn. dept. criminal justice, 2002—05; prof. Sam Houston State U., Huntsville, Tex., 2006—; co-dir. Inst. Legal Studies Criminal Justice, 2006—. Editor: Internat. Criminal Justice Rev., Criminal Justice Rev., Ga. State U., 2001-05;book rev. editor Jour. Criminal Justice Edn. Acad. Criminal Justice Scis., Greenbelt, Md., 1993—1996, editor, police forum police sect., Md., 1996—2001; contbr. correctional health care report Civic Rsch. Inst., NYC, 1999—2007, articles to profl. jours. and publs. Named Outstanding Alumnus, Coll. of Criminal Justice, Sam Houston State U., 2002; recipient Outstanding Service award, Police Section, Acad. of Criminal Justice Sciences, 1998, Outstanding Paper, Acad. of Criminal Justice Scis., 1996, Outstanding Faculty Achievement award, Ga. State U., 2004. Mem.: Am. Assn. Univ. Profs., Am. Judicature Soc., Am. Psychology-Law Soc., Am. Soc. Criminology, Acad. Criminal Justice Scis. Democrat. Methodist. Avocation: reading. Office: Sam Houston State Univ Criminal Justice PO Box 2296 Huntsville TX 77341-2296 Office Phone: 936-294-1349. Business E-Mail: mvaughn@shsu.edu.

VAUGHN, MO (MAURICE SAMUEL VAUGHN), real estate company executive, retired professional baseball player; b. Norwalk, Conn., Dec. 15, 1967; Student, Seton Hall U., 1987—89. First baseman Boston Red Sox, 1991—98, Anaheim Angels, Calif., 1999—2001, NY Mets, NYC, 2002—03; co founder, ptnr. Omni New York LLC, NYC, 2004—. Active cmty. svc. Youth Groups, Boston. Named Am. League MVP, Baseball Writers' Assn. Am., 1995—96; named to Silver Slugger team, Sporting News, 1995, Am. League All-Star Team, 1995—96, 1998; recipient Thomas A. Yawkey award, 1993—96, A. Bartlett Giamatti award, 1995. *

VAUGHN, NOEL WYANDT, lawyer; b. Chgo., Dec. 15, 1937; d. Owen Heaton and Harriet Christy (Smith) Wyandt; m. David Victor Koch, July 18, 1959 (div.); 1 child, John David; m. Charles George Vaughn, July 9, 1971. BA, DePauw U., 1959; MA, So. Ill. U., 1963; JD, U. Dayton, 1979. Bar: Ohio 1979, U.S. Dist. Ct. (so. dist.) Ohio 1979, U.S. Cir. Ct. (6th cir.) 1987. Lectr. Wright State U., Dayton, 1965-67; communications specialist Charles F. Kettering Found., Dayton, 1968-71; tchr. English Miami Valley Sch., Dayton, 1971-76; law clk. to judge Dayton Mcpl. Ct., 1978-79; coordinator Montgomery County Fair Housing Ctr., Dayton, 1979-81, 85-89; atty. Henley Vaughn Becker & Wald, Dayton, 1981-90; pvt. practice Noel W. Vaughn Law Offices, Dayton, 1990—. Chmn. Dayton Playhouse, Inc., 1981—92; pres. Freedom of Choice Miami Valley, 1980—83, 1986—87; com. mem. Battered Woman Project-YWCA, 1983—84; pres. Legal Aid Soc., 1983—84; chmn. Artemis House, Inc., 1985—88, bd. dirs., 1988—97, ACLU, 1982—86, Miami Valley Arts Coun., 1985—86, AIDS Found., 1988—90, Miami Valley Fair Housing Ctr., Inc., 1992—94, Human Race Theatre Co., Inc., 1995—2000, Housing Justice Fund, 1979—, Dayton Sister City Com., 2001—02. Recipient Order of Barristers award U. Dayton, 1979. Mem.: ABA, Ohio State Bar Assn., Ohio Fair Plan Underwriting Assn. (bd. govs. 1986—92), Dayton Bar Assn. (chmn. delivery legal svcs. com. 1983—84, family law com. 1991—, chmn. juvenile law com. 2001—03). Office: 1205 Talbott Tower 131 N Ludlow St Dayton OH 45402-1110 Office Phone: 937-222-6635.

VAUGHN, ROBERT CANDLER, JR., lawyer; b. Winston Salem, NC, Sept. 6, 1931; s. Robert Candler and Douglas Arthur V.; m. Carolyn (Hartford), May 2, 1959; children: Patricia Anne, Robert Candler III. BS in Bus. Adminstrn., U. N.C., 1953, JD, 1955. Bar: N.C., 1955, U.S. Dist. Ct. (mid. dist.), 1959, U.S. Tax Ct., 1981. Assoc. Petree, Stockton, Robinson, and predecessor firms, Winston Salem, 1959-65, ptnr., 1965-2000. Bd. dirs. Forsyth Bank & Trust Co., Winston-Salem. Pres. United Way Forsyth County, Winston Salem, 1970-71, Forsyth County Bar Assn.; chmn. Winston Salem Coliseum and Conv. Ctr. Commn., 1974-78; bd. adv.U. NC Tax Inst., Chapel Hill; bd. dirs. Leadership Winston Salem; chmn. Winston Salem Found., 2003, Forsyth Med. Ctr. Found., 1999-01; chmn. Forsyth Tech. Coll. Found., 2006-. Lt. USN, 1955-58. Fellow Am. Bar Found., Am. Coll. Trusts and Estates Counsel (N.C.chmn. 1990-1995); mem. N.C. Bar Assn. (pres. 1985-86, bd. dirs.), U. N.C. Law Alumni Assn. (pres. 1974-75), Am. Coll. Tax Counsel, Old Town Club, Piedmont Club, Rotary. Republican. Methodist. Home: 2575 Club Park Rd Winston Salem NC 27104-2009 Office: Vaughn Perkinson Ehlinger Moxley & Stogner PO Box

25715 Winston Salem NC 27114 Home Phone: 336-722-8068; Office Phone: 336-794-6001. E-mail: bob.vaughn@vpems.com.

VAUGHN, ROSALYN MAE, academic administrator; d. Emmet and Rosie Mae Smith; children: Sherolyn Yvonne Spencer, Sonja Annette King, Rosa Leoma. BS in Elem. Edn., So. Ill. U., 1968; MA in Ednl. Leadership, Western Mich. U., 1974; PhD in Workforce Edn. Devel. and Adminstrn., So. Ill. U., 1996. Educator St. Clair County Pub. Schs., Caseyville, Ill., 1968—69, University City (Mo.) Pub. Schs., 1970—71, Calhoun County Pub. Schs., Battle Creek, Mich., 1971—72; pers. rep., trainer Ralston-Purina Co., Battle Creek, Mich., 1972—74; pub. affairs specialist Kellogg Co., Battle Creek, Mich., 1974—76; MIOSHA dir. Mich. Dept. Labor, Lansing, 1976—80; educator Escambia County Pub. Schools, Pensacola, 1980—83; mgr. Combined Ins. Co. Am., New Orleans, 1983—87; instr., rschr. Pensacola (Fla.) Jr. Coll., 1990—91; grad. internist La. Dept. Labor, Metarie, La., 1993—93; assoc. dean Jones Coll., Jacksonville, Fla., 1996—97; human resources mgr. Dynamic Ednl. Sys., Inc., Jacksonville, Fla., 1997—99; asst. prof. Barry U., Miami Shores, Fla., 1999—, adminstr. human resources devel. and adminstrn. Orlando, Fla., 2000—03; site adminstr. higher edn. leadership doctoral program Nova Southeastern U., Orlando, 2004—. Rev. panelist Family Transition Program, Fla. Dept. Health and Rehab. Svcs., Jacksonville, 1997—99; adminstrv. vol. Polk County Adult Edn. Program, Davenport, Fla., 2002—03; chairperson Mich. Commn. Employment Handicap Persons, Lansing, Mich., 1976—80; steering com., exec. bd. Ctrl. Fla. Higher Edn. Alliance, Orlando, 1999—; mem. Fla. Hosp. Diabetes Ctr., Orlando, 2000—. Recipient Diana award, Mich. Safety Conf., 1978; fellow Ill. Consortium Ednl. Opportunity Program fellow, State Ill. Dept. Edn., 1994—96; scholar State Tchrs.' scholar, 1964—68. Mem.: Ctrl. Fla. Higher Edn. Alliance (mem.-at-large 2001—), Assn. Career Tech. Educators (exec. bd. 2001—), Fla. Exec. Women (assoc.). Achievements include development of Employment Law Certification Program. Home: 6166 Stevenson Dr 205 Orlando FL 32835 Personal E-mail: rvmshrda@aol.com.

VAUGHN, THOMAS JOSEPH, earth science educator, administrator; b. Lawrence, Mass., Dec. 23, 1944; s. Thomas Wilbur and Dorothy Agnes (Mallon) V.; m. Priscilla Margaret Bastian, June 30, 1973; children: Matthew Thomas, Judith Diane. BA in History/Geography, Mt. Carmel Coll., Niagara Falls, Ont., Can., 1968; AM in Geography, Boston U., 1972; MEd in Secondary Ednl. Adminstrn., U. Lowell, Mass., 1977; CAGS in Computers in Edn., Lesley U., Cambridge, Mass., 1985. Cert. tchr. earth sci., geography, history, cert. gen. supr., jr.-sr. h.s. prin., Mass. Tchr. earth sci. DeSales H.S., Louisville, 1968-69; tchg. fellow Boston U., 1969-71; liberal arts prof. Bryant-McIntosh Jr. Coll., Lawrence, 1971-72; earth sci. tchr., lead sci. tchr. Arlington H.S., 1972—2004; adult edn. instr. Arlington (Mass.) Pub. Schs., 1985-90; asst. dir. project ESTEEM Harvard-Smithsonian, Cambridge, Mass., 1993; instr. earth sci. Northeastern U., Boston, 1997—; prof. environ. studies Middlesex C.C., 2004—; prof. sci. edn. U. Mass, Darmouth, 2005—. Telecom. moderator Harvard U. Sci. Tchr. Network, Cambridge, 1986-89; chair study groups for sci. edn. reform Mass. Dept. Edn., Malden, 1995—, sci. tchr. leader, 1998. Co-author: Integrating Computers in Your Classroom: Middle and Secondary Science, 1994, Harvard Smithsonian Project IMAGE, 1997; presenter in field. Lector St. Theresa's Ch., Billerica, Mass., 1975—; trustee Billerica Pub. Libr., 1993—; mem. Billerica Friends of the Libr., 1995—; bd. dirs. Tchr. Leadership Acad. Mass. Recipient Pathfinder award in tech. Mass. Dept. Edn., 1991, Sci. Educator of Yr. award for Middlesex County, Mass. Assn. Sci. Tchrs., 1998, Presdl. award for excellence in tchg. math. and sci. NSF, 2000; Disting. Alumni award U. Mass., Lowell, 2000, Boston U., 2002, Lesley U., 2005, Sally K. Lenhardt Profl. Leadership award, Lesley U., Cambridge, 2005; Tandy Tech. scholar, 1996; inducted into Mass. Sci. Educators Hall of Fame, 1992 Fellow Tchr. Leadership Acad. Mass. (bd. dirs.); mem. NSTA, Nat. Assn. Geosci. Tchrs. (pres. New Eng. sect. 2005-06), Nat. Geog. Soc., Mass. Assn. Scis. Tchrs. (award sect., Educator Yr. 2006), Mass. Assn. Sci. Suprs. (pres. 2004-05, Mass. Sci. Educator Yr. award 2006), Ind. U. Alumni Assn. at Lowell (bd. dirs. 2005—), Alpha Omega Alpha, Gamma Theta Upsilon (local pres.). Democrat. Roman Catholic. Avocations: computers, telecommunications and internet, reading, walking. Office: Middlesex Cmty Coll Sci Dept Springs Rd Bedford MA 01730 Office Phone: 781-280-3200 3842. Personal E-mail: tomvaughn@aol.com. Business E-Mail: vaught@middesex.mass.edu.

VAUGHN, VINCE, actor; b. Mpls., Mar. 28, 1970; s. Vernon and Sharon Vaughn. Actor: (films) For the Boys, 1991, Rudy, 1993, At Risk, 1994, Swingers, 1996, Just Your Luck, 1996, The Lost World: Jurassic Park, 1997, The Locusts, 1997, A Cool, Dry Place, 1998, Return to Paradise, 1998, Clay Pigeons, 1998, Psycho, 1998, South of Heaven, West of Hell, 2000, The Cell, 2000, The Prime Gig, 2000, Zoolander, 2001, Domestic Disturbance, 2001; prodr.: Made, 2001; actor: Dust: An Extraordinary Correspondence, 2002, Old School, 2003, I Love Your Work, 2003, Blackball, 2003, Starsky & Hutch, 2004, Dodgeball: A True Underdog Story, 2004, Anchorman: The Legend of Ron Burgundy, 2004, The Sky Is Green, 2004, Thumbsuckers, 2005, Be Cool, 2005, Mr. & Mrs. Smith, 2005, Wedding Crashers, 2005, The Break-Up, 2006 (with Jennifer Aniston Movies-Choice Chemistry, Teen Choice Awards, 2006), Other Side of Simple, 2006; (TV films) Lies of the Heart, 1991, Sex and the Matrix, 2000, (guest appearance): (TV series) China Beach, 1989, 21 Jump Street, 1989, Hercules, 1998, Mr. Show with Bob and David, 1998, Sex and the City, 2000, Dinner for Five, 2001; guest appearance (TV series) Getaway, 2005. Named Favorite On-Screen Match-Up (with Owen Wilson), People's Choice Awards, 2006, Favorite Leading Man, 2007; named one of 50 Most Powerful People in Hollywood, Premiere mag., 2006, 100 Most Powerful Celebrities, Forbes.com, 2007; recipient Best On-Screen Team (with Owen Wilson), MTV Movie awards, 2006. Address: United Talent Agy Ste 500 9560 Wilshire Blvd Beverly Hills CA 90212 *

VAUGHN, WILLIAM PRESTON, retired historian, educator; b. East Chgo., Ind., May 28, 1933; s. James Carl and Georgiana (Preston) V.; m. Virginia Lee Meyer, June 10, 1961 (dec. 2006); 1 child, Rhonda Louise Horton. AB, U. Mo., Columbia, 1955; MA, Ohio State U., 1956, PhD, 1961. Instr. in history U. So. Calif., 1961-62; asst. prof. history U. N. Tex., Denton, 1962-65, assoc. prof., 1965-69, prof., 1969-91; ret., 1991. Instr. Tex. Project, Malaysia, 1986, 88. Author: Schools for All: The Blacks and Public Education in the South, 1865-77, 1974, The Antimasonic Party in the United States, 1826-43, 1983, Masonic Home and School of Texas, 2002; editor Transactions Tex. Lodge of Rsch., 1988—; contbr. articles to profl. jours. With arty. U.S. Army, 1956-57 Mem. SAR, SCV, So. Hist. Assn. (life), Historians Early Am. Republic, Blue Friars, Masons, Phi Beta Kappa, Phi Alpha Theta (manuscript competition winner 1972). Republican. Disciples Of Christ. Home: 22 CR 1602 Mount Pleasant TX 75455-8450

VAUGHN, WILLIAM WEAVER, retired lawyer; b. LA, Aug. 29, 1930; s. William Weaver and Josephine (Sweigert) V.; m. Claire Louise M'Closkey, June 2, 1962; children: Robert, Gregory, Elizabeth, Anthony, Christina, James. BA, Stanford U., 1952; LLB, UCLA, 1955. Bar: Calif. 1956. With O'Melveny & Myers, LA, 1955-56, 57—, ptnr., 1964-96, of counsel, 1996—2002; ret., 2002. Served with U.S. Army, 1956-57. Recipient Learned Hand award Am. Jewish Com., 1991, Joseph A. Ball award for outstanding advocacy Brennan Ctr. for Justice, 1998. Fellow Am. Coll. Trial Lawyers (bd. regents 1992-95); mem. L.A. County Bar Assn. (trustee 1976-78, 80-82), L.A. County Bar Found. (bd. dirs. 1991-95), Assn. Bus. Trial Lawyers (bd. govs. 1980-82), Order of Coif, Calif. Club, Chancery Club I(pres. 1997-98). Office: O'Melveny & Myers 400 S Hope St Los Angeles CA 90071-2899

VAUPEL, JAMES W., demographer; b. NYC, May 2, 1945; MPP in Demographics, Harvard U., 1971, PhD in Demographics, 1978. Prof. public affairs and planning U. Minn., 1985—91; prof. demographics & epidemiology Odense U. Medical Sch., Germany, 1991—2002; sr. rsch. scientist Duke U., 1992—, Terry Sanford Inst. Public Policy, 1992—; dir. Max Planck Inst. for Demographic Rsch., 1996—; hon. prof. U. Rostock, Germany, 2003—. Recipient Irene B. Tauber prize, 2001, Ipsen Found. Longevity prize, 2003. Mem.: NAS. Office: Max Planck Inst für Demografische Forschung Konrad Zuse Strasse 1 D-18057 Rostock Germany

VAUSE, EDWIN HAMILTON, research foundation administrator; b. Chgo., Mar. 30, 1923; s. Harry Russell and Sylvia Clair (Webster) V.; m. Harriet Evelyn Oestmann, June 30, 1951; children— Karen L., Russell E., Kurt H., Dirk C., Luke E. BS, U. Ill., 1947, MS, 1948; MBA, U. Chgo., 1952; D.Sc. (hon.), U. Evansville, 1977. Registered profl. engr., Ill., Ind. Engr., research dept. Standard Oil Co., Ind., 1948-52, asst. gen. foreman mfg. dept., 1952-57; dir. research adminstrn. Mead Johnson & Co., Evansville, Ind., 1957-60; v.p. Charles F. Kettering Found., Dayton, Ohio, 1960-66, v.p., adminstrn. dir., 1966-67, exec. v.p., 1967-71, v.p. for sci. and tech., 1971-88. Trustee The Found. Center, 1967-73; mem. adv. com. Acad. Forum, Nat. Acad. Scis. Vice-pres. Washington Twp. Bd. Edn., 1963-67; mem. Centerville-Washington Twp. Joint Planning Commn., 1967-68; mem. adv. bd. Center for Students Rights, Dayton, 1966-70; active Boy Scouts Am. Mem. Am. Inst. Chem. Engrs. (past chmn. Chgo. sect.), N.Y. Acad. Scis., Agrl. Research Inst., Nat. Industry State Agrl. Research Council. Clubs: Elks, Kiwanis (past pres.), Masons. Republican. Lutheran. Home: 11834 Calle Parral San Diego CA 92128-4534

VAUX, HENRY JAMES, JR., economics professor; b. Portland, Oreg., Feb. 2, 1940; s. Henry James and Jean (Macduff) V.; m. Prindle Anders, June 19, 1964; children: Robert, Katherine. BA, U. Calif., Davis, 1962; MA, U. Mich., 1964, MS, 1968, PhD, 1973. Examiner U.S. Office Mgmt. and Budget, Washington, 1964-67; economist U.S. Nat. Water Commn., Arlington, Va., 1969-70; prof. econs. U. Calif., Riverside, 1970—, dir. water resources, 1986-93, assoc. v.p., 1992—. Pres. Nat. Inst. Water Resources, Washington, 1986-93; pres. bd. dirs. Water Edn. Found., Sacramento, 1990—; mem., chair water sci. and tech. bd. Nat. Rsch. Coun., 1994-2001; co-chair adv. bd. Rosenberg Internat. Forum, Oakland, 1996—. Recipient Nat. Leadership award Univ. Coun. Water Resource Rsch., 1994. Mem. Cosmos Club.

VAVALA, DOMENIC ANTHONY, medical research scientist, educator, retired military officer; b. Providence, Feb. 1, 1925; s. Salvatore and Maria (Grenci) V BA, Brown U., Providence, 1947; MS, U. RI, Kingston, 1950; MA, Trinity U., San Antonio, 1954; PhD Physiology, Accademia di Studi Superiori "Minerva", Italy, 1957; MEd, U. Houston, 1958; LittD, Univ. Internazionale Sveva "Frederick II", Bergamo, Italy, 1979; DSc (hon.), Nobile Accademia di Santa Teodora Imperatrice, Rome, 1966, DMS (hon.), 1970; DPH (hon.), Nobile Accademia di Santa Teodora Imperatrice, 1983; D Pedagogy (hon.), Studiorum Universitas Constantiniana of Sovrano Ordine Constantiniano di San Giorgio, Rome, 1966; EdD (hon.), Imperiale Accademia di San Cirillo, Pomezia, Italy, 1977; D Health Scis. (hon.), Johnson & Wales U., 1993; LLD (hon.), Fridericus II U., Capua, Italy, 1997; MD (hon.), Frederick II U., Providence, 1999. Cert. Yale U. Army Specialized Tng. Program, 1944. Asst. tumor rsch. U. R.I., also asst. entomol. rsch., 1950; rsch. asst. pharmacology Boston U. Sch. Medicine, 1950—51; commd. 2d lt. med. svc. USAF, 1951, advanced through grades to lt. col., 1968; rsch. team physiologist cold injury Army Med. Rsch. Lab., Osaka Army Hosp., Osaka, Japan, 1951—52; rschr. aviation physiologist USAF Sch. Aviation Medicine, Randolph AFB, Tex., 1952—54, 3605th USAF Hosp., Ellington AFB, Tex., 1955—57, chief physiol. tng., 1957; cons. aviation physiology, film prodn. dept. U. Houston, 1956; rschr. aviation physiologist, head acad. sect. dept. physiol. tng. USAF Hosp., Lackland AFB, Tex., 1957—58; vis. prof. physiology Incarnate Word Coll., San Antonio, 1958; rschr. aviation physiologist, chief physiol. tng. comdr. 832d Physiol. Tng. Flight, 832d Tactical Hosp., Cannon AFB, N.Mex., 1958—64; adj. faculty mem. Ea. N.Mex. U., Portales, 1959—64; instr. adult edn. divsn. Clovis Mcpl. Schs., N.Mex., 1960; rschr. aviation physiologist, comdr. 15th Physiol. Tng. Flight, 824th USAF Dispensary, Kadena Air Base, Okinawa, 1965—66; rsch. scientist, directorate fgn. tech., aerospace med. divsn. Brooks AFB, Tex., 1966—68; chief R & D support and interface divsn., dep. dir. for fgn. tech., 1969—70; adj. instr. Johnson & Wales U., Providence, 1973—74; instr. humanities Johnson and Wales U., Providence, 1974—75, asst. prof. humanities, 1975—77, prof. health scis. and nutrition, 1977—93, prof. emeritus, 1993—, coord. biomed. and behavioral scis. Day Coll. divsn., 1973—75, psychology coord. vets. divsn. Coll. Continuing Edn., 1974—76, assoc. dean adj. faculty, 1975, dean faculty, 1975—77, coord. acad. devel., 1977—78, dir. mus. series, 1990—, curator Chapel Empress St. Theodora, 1992—. Pres. corp., chmn. bd. dir. Sovereign Constantinian Order of St. George, Inc., R.I., 1986—; pres. corp., chmn. bd. dir. The Noble Acad. of Empress St. Theodora of R.I., Inc., 1988—; instr. anatomy, physiology and med. terminology R.I. Hosp., Providence, 1987-90 Writer, prodr.: (TV Series) Your Body in Flight, Sta. KUHT, Houston, 1956; (TV series) Highway to Health, Okinawa, 1965; compiled and edited: Fifty Years of Progress of Soviet Medicine, 1917-67; abstractor, translator in medicine Chem. Abstracts Svc., Am. Chem. Soc., Ohio State U., 1963-74; editor: (Cath. parish newspaper) The Logos, Kadena Air Base, Okinawa, 1965-66 (1st pl. 5th Air Force chapel printed news contest); contbr. articles to profl. jours Trustee, Gov. Ctr. Sch., Providence, 1979-85; mem. scholarship com. St. Sahag and, St. Mesrob Armenian Apostolic Ch., Providence; choir master, music dir. Cannon AFB, Cath. Parish, 1958-65; received in pvt. audience Pope John Paul II, 1997. Served with AUS, 1943-44 Recipient Disting. Svc. award Clovis Jaycees, 1959, Acad. Palms Gold medal Accademia Studi Superiori "Minerva", 1960, citation, chief chaplains USAF, 1970, commendation medal USAF, 1970, chief biomed. scientist insignia, biomed. scis. corps USAF Med. Svc., 1970, spl. faculty citation Johnson and Wales U., 1981, contbn. awd. doctoral program ednl. leadership Alan Feinstein Grad. Sch., Johnson and Wales U., Providence, 1999, academician divsn. scis. Accademia di Studi Superiori "Minerva", 1960; Min. Plenipotentiary for U.S. of Nobile Accademia di Santa Teodora Imperatrice, Rome, 1967, rector pro tempore, France, 1980, Achievement cert. Dept. Army Headquarters, US Army Ryukyu Islands, APO San Francisco, 1966; decorated knight grand officer Merit Class, Sovereign Constantinian Order St. George, Rome, 1969, Knight of Grand Cross with Constantinian neckchain, Justice Class, Sovereign Constantinian Order St. George, 1969, Knight of Grand Cross Justice Class, Order St. John of Jerusalem, Knights of Malta, Bari, Italy, 1984, Knight of Grand Cross Justice Class, Order St. John of Jerusalem, Knights of Cyprus, Rhodes and Malta, Bari, 1984, Knight of Grand Cordon Justice Class, Order Teutonic Knights, Sao Paulo, 1986, Knight of Grand Cross Justice Class, Mil. Order St. Gereon, Sao Paulo, 1986, Knight of Grand Cross Justice Class, Mil. and Hospitalier Order St Jean d'Acre and St. Thomas, Capua, Italy, 1987, Knight of Grand Cross Justice Class, Mil. and Hospitalier Order St. Mary of Bethlehem, Capua, 1987; recipient Ednl. Professionalism award Domei Toastmasters Internat., 1965; named Magnificent Rector and Pres., The Constantinian U. (Studiorum Universitas Constantiniana), Italy, 1970, Marquis of Royal Throne of Swabia of Hohenstaufen Dynasty, Prince Jean von Schwaben, Bergamo, Italy, 1984, Duke of the New Rome, Constantinople, of Imperial Dynasty of Amorium by His Imperial Highness Prince Don Francesco Amoroso d'Aragona, Capua, 2000, Citizens Citation, Hon. Vincent A. Cianci Jr., Mayor City Providence, 1995, Spl. Citation, Johnson & Wales U., Alan Shawn Feinstein Grad. Sch., Sch. Edn., 2007. Fellow AAAS (emeritus, life), Tex. Acad. Sci., Royal Soc. Health (London; emeritus), Am. Inst. Chemists (emeritus); mem. Assn. Mil. Surgeons US (life), Nat. Assn. Doctors US (founder 1958, sec.-treas. 1958-85, editor-in-chief The NADUS Jour. 1963-68), Accademia di San Cirillo Italy (hon.), NY Acad. Scis., Phi Sigma, Kappa Delta Pi, Phi Kappa Phi, Alpha Beta Kappa (charter, pres. RI Alpha chpt. Johnson and Wales U. 1984-92), Acad. Europea for Econ. Cultural Rels. (acad. senate, medallion 2004), 1916 Soc. RI Found., Providence.

VAWTER, MARQUIS PHILIP, psychologist, researcher; s. Marquis Glen Miller and Geraldine Mae Ryken; m. Karen Lee Harvey, May 5, 1989. BA, U. Calif., Santa Cruz, 1973; MA, Calif. State U., Long Beach, 1978; MS in Edn., U. So. Calif., LA, 1986; PhD in Psychology, Calif. Coast U., 1992. Cert. marriage and family therapist Bd. of Behavioral Sci., Calif., 1990, rehabilitation counselor Commn. Rehab. Certification, 1986; psychologist Bd. Psychology, Calif., 2000. Rsch. biochemist Beckman I; rsch. technician Long Beach Veterans Adminstrn., 1973—75; rsch. biochemist Beckman Instruments, Fullerton, Calif., 1975—80; rehab. counselor Underwriters Adjusting Co., Newport Beach, 1980—85; rehab. dir. counseling, assessment Rehab. Experts, Inc., Orange, Calif., 1986—94; postdoctoral fellow NIH, Bethesda, Md., 1994—2000; asst. prof. Dept. Psychiatry U. Calif., Irvine, Calif., 2001—. Marriage and family counselor internship various mental health agencies, Orange County, 1985—90; predoctoral fellowship Rijksuniversiteit, Utrecht, Netherlands, 1985—86; psychol. asst. Nat. Inst. Mental Health, Washington, 1994—96. Contbr. over 50 articles to profl. jours. Fellow, U. So. Calif., 1984—85, Rijksuniversiteit, 1985; scholar, Calif. State Scholar Bd., 1969—73. Mem.: Soc. Biol. Psychiatry, Am. Assoc. Advance Sci., APA (assoc.), Am. Coll. Neuropsychopharmacology (assoc.). Achievements include patents pending for treatment and diagnosis of mental disorders; NCAM and schizophrenia. Avocations: gardening, reading, travel. Office Phone: 949-824-9014.

VAWTER, TONI VALENTINE, artist; b. Des Moines, Feb. 14, 1968; Artist Art Buyers, Des Moines, 1984—. Home: 9708 Candleridge Cir Johnston IA 50131 Home Phone: 515-555-1234.

VAYALAKKARA, JYOTHI, neuropsychologist, director, educator; b. Kannur, Kerala, India, July 20, 1968; d. Gangadharan Nambiar and Jayalakshmi Vayalakkara; m. Karamdas Velluva Puthiya, Apr. 23, 1990; 1 child, Jyotsna Vayalakkara Karamdas. BS in Chemistry, Calicut U., India, 1989, MA in English Lit., 1991; MS in Clin. Psychology, Nova Southeastern U., Ft. Lauderdale, Fla., 1996, PsyD, 2000; diploma in journalism, Bharatiya Vidya Bhavan, India, 1991. Cert. clin. psychologist Conn., 2004. Postdoctoral fellowship in neuropsychology New Eng. Med. Ctr., Boston, 2001—03; clin. neuropsychology fellow Tufts Med. Sch., New Eng. Med. Ctr., Boston, 2001—03; program dir., neuropsychologist Conn. Valley Hosp., Middletown, Conn., 2004—. Program dir. Conn. Valley Hosp., Middletown, 2004—; adj. psychology faculty U. Hartford, Conn., 2005—. Contbr. articles to profl. jours., chapters to books. Mem. Psychologists for Peace (PsySR), Washington, 2006—; com. mem. South Asian Womens' Network (SNEHA), Hartford, 2006—. Ann. Scholarship award, Broward Internat. Womens' Club, Fla., 1994—99. Mem.: APA (assoc.), Conn. Psychol. Assn. (assoc.), Bharatiya Vidya Bhavan (life), Asia-Pacific Coalition, Phi Theta Kappa (hon.). Avocations: writing, volunteering. Home Phone: 860-638-4638; Office Phone: 860-262-6049. Personal E-mail: kjjy@earthlink.net.

VAYO, DAVID JOSEPH, composer, music educator; b. New Haven, Mar. 28, 1957; s. Harold Edward and Joan Virginia (Cassidy) V.; m. Marie-Susanne Langille, 2002; children: Rebecca Lynn, Gordon Francis. MusB, Ind. U., 1980, MusM, 1982; D of Musical Arts, U. Mich., 1990. Prof. Nat. U., Heredia, Costa Rica, 1982-84, Nat. Symphony Youth Sch., San Jose, Costa Rica, 1982-84; asst. prof. music Conn. Coll., New London, 1988-91, Ill. Wesleyan U. Sch. Music, Bloomington, 1991-95, assoc. prof., 1995-2000, prof., 2000—. Resident artist Banff Ctr. for Arts, 1992, 94, Va. Ctr. for Creative Arts, 1994, Centrum, Port Townsend, Wash., 1996; participating composer Internat. Soc. Contemporary Music-World Music Days, Yokohama, 2001, Mexico City, 1993, Internat. Double Reed Festival, Rotterdam, The Netherlands, 1995, Internat. Trombone Festival, 1997, Grand Teton Music Festival, 2006. Composer chamber composition Signals, 1997 (commd. by Koussevitzky Music Found. and Orkest de Volharding), Symphony: Blossoms and Awakenings, 1990 (performer St. Louis Symphony, Leonard Slatkin condr. 1993), Mosaics and Webs, 2003 (commd. by Nat. Assn. Coll. Wind and Percussion Instrs.), Eight Poems of William Carlos Williams for solo trombonist, 1994 (commd. by St. Louis Symphony), piano trio Awakening of the Heart (commd. Barlow Endowment for Music Composition), 1998; works pub. by Internat. Trombone Assn. Press, Berben/Italia Guitar Soc. Series and A.M. Percussion Publs. John Simon Guggenheim Meml. Found. fellow, 2001; Ill. Arts Coun. fellow, 2000. Mem. ASCAP (awards 1988—), Am. Music Ctr. (copying assistance grantee 1992), Coll. Music Soc. (presenter nat. confs.), Soc. for Electro-Acoustic Music in U.S. (presenter nat. conf.), Soc. Composers (membership chmn. 1990-2000, presenter at nat. confs.), Am. Composers Forum. Avocations: athletics, popular music, travel, reading, cooking. Office: Ill Wesleyan U Sch Music PO Box 2900 Bloomington IL 61702-2900 Home Phone: 309-828-3192; Office Phone: 309-556-3068. E-mail: dvayo@iwu.edu.

VAZ, KATHERINE ANNE, writer; b. Castro Valley, Calif., Aug. 26, 1955; d. August Mark and Elizabeth (Sullivan) Vaz; m. Michael Trudeau, May 1, 1994. BA, U. Calif., Santa Barbara, 1977; MFA, U. Calif., Irvine, 1991. Assoc. prof. English U. Calif., Davis, 1995-99; lectr. Harvard U. Briggs-Copeland, 2003—. Keynote spkr. Libr. of Congress, 1997; keynote spkr. lit. confs. U. Ariz., Ariz., U. Calif., Berkeley, U. Mass., Dartmouth U., Rutgers U.; mem. U.S. Presdl. del. to Expo 98/World's Fair, Lisbon, Portugal; Briggs-Copeland lectr. Harvard U., Cambridge, Mass., 2003. Author: (novels) Saudade, 1994, Mariana, 1997, (short stories) Fado & Other Stories, 1997 (Drue Heinz Lit. prize, 1997). Fellow, Radcliffe Inst. for Advanced Study, 2006—07; grantee, Nat. Endowment Arts, 1993, Davis Humanities Inst., U. Calif., Davis, 1998—99. Mem.: PEN, Portuguese-Am. Leadership Coun. U.S., Authors Guild. Democrat. Roman Catholic. Personal E-mail: katherineavaz@hotmail.com. Business E-Mail: kvaz@fas.harvard.edu.

VAZACOPOULOS, ALKIS, application developer, educator; b. Athens, Greece, Mar. 18, 1965; s. Panagiotis and Dominique Vazacopoulos; m. Lora Pilalis; children: Dominique, Theodora, Anastasia. BBA, U. Piraeus, Greece, 1986; MSc, Fla. Internat. U., Miami, Fla., 1988; MSc in Ops. Rsch., Carnegie Mellon U., Pitts., Pa., 1990, PhD in Indsl. Adminstrn., 1994. Asst. prof. Fairleigh Dickinson U., Hackensack, NJ, 1994—99, assoc. prof., 2000—02; dir. Dash Optimization, Inc., Englewood Cliffs, NJ, 1998—2006, mng. dir., 2007—. Vis. scientist Faw U., Ulm, Germany, 1997; adj. assoc. prof. Fairleigh Dickinson U., 2002—; panelist, reviewer NSF, Washington, 2004—07; faculty ctr. applied optimization U. Fla., Gainesville, 2005—. Author: (book) Data mining in Biomedicine; contbr. articles to profl. jours. Recipient Rsch. award, Fairleigh Dickinson U., 2000; fellow, Nat. Found. Fellowships, Greece, 1986; William Larimer fellow, Carnegie Mellon U., 1988—91. Office: Dash Optimization 560 Sylvan Ave Englewood Cliffs NJ 07632 Home Phone: 201-750-7388; Office Phone: 201-567-9445. Office Fax: 201-567-9443. Business E-Mail: av@dashoptimization.com.

VAZIRI, NOSRATOLA DABIR, internist, nephrologist, educator; came to U.S., 1969, naturalized, 1977; s. Abbas and Tahera Vaziri. MD, Tehran U., Iran, 1966. Diplomate Am. Bd. Internal Medicine, Am. Bd. Nephrology; cert. hypertension specialist Am. Soc. Hypertension. Intern Cook County Hosp., Chgo., 1969-70; resident Berkshire Med. Ctr., Pittsfield, Mass., 1970-71, Wadsworth VA Med. Ctr., LA, 1971-72, UCLA Med. Ctr.,

1972-74; prof. medicine U. Calif.-Irvine, 1979—, prof. physiology and biophysics, 2001—, prof. biol. scis., 2006—, chief nephrology and hypertension divsn., 1977—, dir. hemodialysis unit, 1977-94, vice chmn. dept. medicine, 1982-94, chmn. dept. medicine, 1994-98, chair faculty Coll. Medicine, 2000—02. Sr. assoc. editor: Jour. Spinal Cord Medicine, 1991-2005; mem. editl. bd. Kidney Internat., Am. Jour. Nephrology, 1999-02, Nephron, 1999-02, Advancements in Renal Replacement Therapies, 1999-04, Internat. Jour. Artificial Organs, Spinal Cord Medicine, Jour. Renal Nutrition; contbr. articles to profl. jours. Mem. sci. adv. coun. Nat. Kidney Found., 1977—. Recipient Golden Apple award, U. Calif. Irvine Coll. Medicine, 1977, Lauds and Laurels award, U. Calif. Irvine Alumni Assn., 1999, Spirit Nephrology award, Nat. Kidney Found., 2002, Athalie Clarke's Outstanding Health Sci. Rschr. award, 2003, Presdl. Lectureship award, Can. Hypertension Soc., Disting. Svc. award, Western Assn. Physicians, 2007. Master: ACP; fellow: Am. Heart Assn. (fellow coun. high blood pressure rsch.); mem.: Am. Soc. Hypertension, Internat. Soc. Nephrology, Assn. Profs. Medicine, Western Assn. Physicians (councilor 2003—05, pres. 2006—07), Am. Paraplegia Soc. (pres. 1992—94, Donald Munro award 2002), Am. Physiol. Soc., Am. Soc. Nephrology, Alpha Omega Alpha. Avocation: gardening. Home: 66 Balboa Cv Newport Beach CA 92663-3226 Office: U Calif Irvine Med Ctr Div Nephrology Dept Medicine 101 The City Dr Orange CA 92868-3201 Business E-Mail: ndvaziri@uci.edu.

VÁZQUEZ, MARTHA ALICIA, federal judge; b. Santa Barbara, Calif., Feb. 21, 1953; d. Remigio and Consuelo Medina Vazquez. BA in Govt., U. Notre Dame, 1975, JD, 1978. Bar: N.Mex. 1979, admitted to practice: US Dist. Ct. (Dist. N.Mex.) 1979. Atty. Pub. Defender's Office, Santa Fe, 1979-81; ptnr. Jones, Snead, Wertheim, Rodriguez & Wentworth, Santa Fe, 1981-93; chief judge U.S. Dist. Ct. N.Mex., Santa Fe, 1993—. Democrat. Roman Catholic. Office: US Courthouse PO Box 2710 Santa Fe NM 87504-2710 Home Phone: 505-231-3810; Office Phone: 505-988-6330. Business E-Mail: vazquezchambers@nmcourt.fed.us.

VAZQUEZ-AZPIRI, A. JAMES, lawyer; b. Madrid, May 3, 1962; s. Hector Tomas and Iris Belinda Mary Vazquez-Azpiri; m. Yanira E. Molina, July 22, 2002; 1 child, Virginia M. MA, U. St. Andrews, Scotland, 1985, Princeton U., 1987; JD, NYU, 1992; LLM, Harvard U., 1995. Bar: Calif. 1992. Adj. atty. U.S. Commn. on Immigration Reform, Washington, 1996—97; atty. Morrison & Foerster, San Francisco, 1992—97; ptnr. Cooley Godward LLP, San Francisco, 1997—2004, Morgan, Lewis & Bockius, San Francisco, 2005—. Contbr. articles to profl. jours. Recipient C. Arthur Friedrich award, Internat. Human Rights Law Group, 1993, Wiley M. Manuel award, State Bar of Calif., 1998, Armstrong prize, Princeton U., 1997. Mem.: MLA, Royal Overseas League, Hispanic Bar Assn., Bar Assn. San Francisco, Am. Immigration Lawyers Assn., Princeton Alumni Assn., Princeton Club of No. Calif., Harvard Club, Sigma Delta Pi, Phi Eta Sigma, Phi Delta Theta. Avocations: hiking, scuba diving, travel, literature. Home: 672 Sky Hy Cir Lafayette CA 94549 Office: Morgan Lewis & Bockius Spear St Tower One Market San Francisco CA 94105 E-mail: ajvazquez@morganlewis.com.

VAZQUEZ RIVERA, ORNELA AMLIV, psychologist; b. Malaga, Spain, Feb. 23, 1978; d. Sigfredo Vazquez Calderon and Vilma Celenia Rivera Merced. BA in Soc. Work magna cum laude, U. PR, 2001; MA, CAS in Sch. Psychology, Alfred U., NY, 2004. Lic. Sch. Psychologist NC, 2004. Intern, bilingual sch. psychologist Buffalo Pub. Schs., Buffalo, 2003—04; student svc. specialist Albemarle Rd. Elem., Charlotte, NC, 2004—. Leader Girl Scouts, Caguas, PR, 1999—2001, Charlotte, NC, 2004—. Recipient Gold Medal award, Girl Scouts, 1996. Mem.: NC Assn. of Educators, Nat. Assn. of Sch. Psychologist. Office: Charlotte Mecklenburg Schs Charlotte NC Home Phone: 704-968-1614.

VAZZANO, FRANK PAUL, historian, educator; b. Lorain, Ohio, July 31, 1941; s. Anthony Joseph and Dorothy Marie Vazzano; m. Charlotte Louise Schmidt, Aug. 17, 1963; children: Frank Jr., Kristen, Ann-Marie. BS, Bowling Green State U., Ohio, 1964, MA, 1965; PhD, Kent State U., Ohio, 1972. Prof. Walsh U., North Canton, Ohio, 1971—. Adj. prof. Kent State U., Stark Campus, Canton, Ohio, 1990—2001. Contbr. articles to profl. jours. Recipient Tchg. Excellence award, Ohio Coun. Higher Edn.; scholar, Walsh U. Mem.: Am. Italian Hist. Assn., Ohio Acad. History, Orgn. Am. Historians. Roman Catholic. Avocations: writing, gardening, sports. Home: 1043 Liberty Ln NW North Canton OH 44720 Office Phone: 330-490-7057. Business E-Mail: fvazzano@walsh.edu.

VEACH, ROBERT RAYMOND, JR., lawyer; b. Charleston, SC, Nov. 28, 1950; s. Robert Raymond and Evelyn; m. Lori Sue Erickson, May 27, 1989. Student, St. Olaf Coll., 1968-70; BS in Acctg., Ariz. State U., 1972; JD, So. Meth. U., 1975. Bar: Tex. 1975, Nebr. 1975, U.S. Dist. Ct. Nebr. 1975, U.S. Dist. Ct. (no. dist.) Tex. 1975, Temporary Emergency Ct. Appeals 1975. Acctg. instr. Sch. Bus. So. Meth. U., Dallas, 1973-74; law clk. to Hon. Joe E. Estes U.S. Dist. Ct. No. Dist. Tex.-Temp. Emergency Ct. Appeals, Dallas, 1975-76; assoc. Locke Purnell Boren Laney & Neely, Dallas, 1976-80; v.p. The Lomas & Nettleton Co., Dallas, 1980-83, Rauscher Pierce Refsnes, Inc., Dallas, 1983-87; pres. RPR Mortgage Fin. Corp., Dallas, 1985-87; sr. shareholder Locke Purnell Rain Harrell, Dallas, 1987-97; exec. v.p. Precision Imaging Solutions, Inc., Dallas, 1998—; pvt. practice Dallas, 1998—. Allied mem. N.Y. Stock Exch., 1985-87; lectr. securities and banking confs.; bd. dirs. pvt. corps.; trustee CentraCore Properties Trust (NYSE-CPV), chmn. audit and fin. com., 1998-2002, 05—, chmn. bd., 2002—, chmn. corp. gov. and nominating com., 2003—. Author legal articles. Dir. North Tex. affiliate Am. Diabetes Assn., Dallas, 1978-81; mem. Gov.'s Task Force Wash. State Housing Commn., 1982-83. Fellow Nebr. State Bar Found.; mem. ABA, State Bar of Tex., Nebr. State Bar Assn., Fed. Bar Assn., Dallas Bar Assn. Republican. Methodist. Avocation: golf. Home: 4223 Brookview Dr Dallas TX 75220-3801 Office: 2911 Turtle Creek Blvd Ste 1240 Dallas TX 75219-6277 Home Phone: 214-352-4289; Office Phone: 214-520-7544. Business E-Mail: bob@veachlaw.com.

VEACO, KRISTINA, lawyer; b. Sacramento, Mar. 4, 1948; d. Robert Glenn and Lelia (McCain) V.; 1 child, Nina Katherine. BA, U. Calif., Davis, 1978; JD, Hastings Coll. Law, 1981. Legal adv. to commr. William T. Bagley Calif. Pub. Utilities Commn., San Francisco, 1981-86; sr. counsel Pacific Telesis Group, San Francisco, 1986-94; sr. counsel corp. and securities and pol. law AirTouch Comms., San Francisco, 1994-98; asst. gen. counsel, asst. sec. McKesson Corp., San Francisco, 1999—2006; corp. governance advisor Veaco Group, 2006—. Mem.: NACD, ABA, Soc. Corp. Secs. and Governance Profls. (pres. San Francisco chpt. 2001—02, nat. bd. dirs. 2002—07, mem. adv. com. San Francisco chpt.), San Francisco Bar Assn., Phi Beta Kappa. Office: 2470 16th Ave San Francisco CA 94116 Office Phone: 415-731-3111. Personal E-mail: kveaco@veacogroup.com.

VEAL, REX R., lawyer; b. Lafayette, Ga., May 2, 1956; s. Boyd Herman and Barbara Ann (Sharp) V.; m. Vicky Elizabeth Wilkins, Dec. 13, 1980; children: Matthew Aaron and Richard Andrew (twins). BA, U. Tenn., 1978, JD, 1980. Bar: Tenn. 1981, U.S. Dist. Ct. (ea. dist.) Tenn. 1981, U.S. Ct. Appeals (10th cir.) 1981, U.S. Ct. Appeals (6th cir.) 1984, U.S. Ct. Appeals (4th cir.) 1987, Ga. 1991, U.S. Dist. Ct. (no. dist.) Ga. 1991, U.S. Ct. Appeals (11th cir.) 1991, D.C. 1993, U.S. Dist. Ct. D.C. 1993, U.S. Ct. Appeals (D.C. and fed. cir.) 1993. Assoc. Finkelstein, Kern, Steinberg & Cunningham, Knoxville, Tenn., 1980-83; atty. FDIC, Knoxville, 1983-84, sr. atty., 1984-88, counsel liquidation Washington, 1988-89, assoc. gen. counsel, 1989-90; spl. counsel Resolution Trust Corp., Washington, 1989-90; ptnr. Powell, Goldstein, Frazer & Murphy, Atlanta and Washington, 1990-99, Kilpatrick Stockton LLP, Atlanta, 1999—. Lectr. in field. Contbr. articles to profl. jours. Mem. ABA, Tenn. Bar Assn., Ga. Bar Assn., Atlanta Bar Assn. Avocations: hiking, golf, collecting books. Home: 6201 Blackberry Hl Norcross GA 30092-1375 Office: Kilpatrick Stockton 1100 Peachtree St NE Ste 2800 Atlanta GA 30309-4501 Office Phone: 404-815-6240. E-mail: rveal@kilpatrickstockton.com.

VEALE, SCOTT, editor, columnist; Editor Week in Review NY Times, columnist Book Review, daily book review editor Culture Desk. Office: NY Times 229 W 43rd St New York NY 10036 Office Phone: 212-556-7872. Office Fax: 212-556-1516.

VEALE, TINKHAM, II, retired chemicals executive, engineer; b. Topeka, Dec. 26, 1914; s. George W. and Grace Elizabeth (Walworth) V.; m. Harriett Alice Ernst, Sept. 6, 1941; children: Harriett Elizabeth Veale Leedy, Tinkham III, Helen Ernst Veale Gelbach. BS in Mech. Engring., Case Inst. Tech., 1937; LLD, Kenyon Coll., 1981. Registered profl. engr. With Gen. Motors Corp., 1937-38, Avery Engring. Co., 1939, Reliance Electric Co., 1940-41; asst. to pres. Ohio Crankshaft Co., 1942-46; gen. mgr. Tocco Co., 1947-51; pres. Ric Wil Corp., 1952-53, Alco Chem. Corp., 1954-56, dir., 1954-86. Spl. ptnr. Ball Burge & Kraus, investment bankers, 1957-60; chmn. bd. V. and V. Cos., Inc. and subs., Cleve., 1960-65, Alco Standard Corp. and subs., Valley Forge, Pa., 1965-86, Horsehead Industries, Inc. and subs., N.Y.C., 1981—2001, HTV Industries Inc. and subs., Cleve., 1978—; ptnr. Fair Elm Farm, 1948-2000, Kennedy Veale Stable, 1954-2000. Trustee Veale Charitable Found., 1966—. Recipient Silver Bowl award Case Inst. Tech., 1980; recipient Gold Medal Case Inst. Tech., 1982, Univ. medal Case We. Res. U., 2003. Mem. Cleve. Engring. Soc., Nat. Soc. Registered Profl. Engrs., Newcomen Soc., Phi Kappa Psi. Home: PO Box 39 Gates Mills OH 44040-0039 Office Phone: 440-423-4144.

VEATCH, JULIAN LAMAR, JR., library director; b. Atlanta, Apr. 9, 1949; AA, Young Harris Coll., 1969; BA, U. Ga., 1971; MLS, Emory U., 1973; Advanced MLS, Fla. State U., 1977, PhD in Library Sci., 1979. Acting dir. Jefferson County Libr., Louisville, Ga., 1971-72; libr. The Ga. Conservancy, Atlanta, 1972-73; asst. dir. Ohoopee Regional Libr., Vidalia, Ga., 1973, dir., 1974-76; libr. Fla. subdist. office U.S. Geol. Survey, Tallahassee, 1977-79; dir. High Plains Regional Libr. System, Greeley, Colo., 1979-82, Irving (Tex.) Pub. Libr. System, 1982—98, Ala. Pub. Libr. Svc., Montgomery, 1998—2001; state libr. Ga. Pub. Libr. Svc., Atlanta, 2001—. Mem. library adv. com. Tex. Woman's U., 1988—; bd. dirs. Southeastern Libr. Network (SOLINET), 2001-04. Mem. ALA (standards com. on libr. edn. 1984-85, local arrangements com. 1983-84), Pub. Libr. Assn. of ALA (goals, guidelines, and standards com. 1979-83), Tex. Libr. Assn. (conf. program planning com. 1988-89), Libr. Adminstrn. and Mgmt. Assn. (exec. com. bldg. and equipment sect. 1980-82, architecture for pub. librs. com. 1985-87, chair exec. com. 1989-90, chair publs. com. 1991—), Intellectual Freedom Round Table (chmn. Eli M. Oboler Meml. award com. 1984-86), Chief Officers of State Libr. Agencies, Beta Phi Mu. Office: Ga Pub Libr Svc Ste 150 1800 Century Pl Atlanta GA 30345-4304 Office Phone: 404-235-7120. Office Fax: 404-235-7201. E-mail: lveatch@georgialibraries.org.

VEATCH, ROBERT MARLIN, philosopher, researcher; b. Utica, NY, Jan. 22, 1939; s. Cecil Ross and Regina V.; m. Laurelyn Kay Lovett, June 17, 1961 (div. Oct. 1986); children: Paul Martin, Carlton Elliot; m. Ann Bender Pastore, May 23, 1987. BS, Purdue U., 1961; MS, U. Calif. at San Francisco, 1962; BD, Harvard U., 1964, MA, 1970, PhD, 1971; DHL (hon.), Creighton U., 1999, Union U., 2004. Teaching fellow Harvard U., 1968-70; research assoc. in medicine Coll. Physicians and Surgeons, Columbia U., 1971-72; assoc. for med. ethics Inst. of Society, Ethics and Life Scis., Hastings-on-Hudson, NY, 1970-75, sr. assoc., 1975-79; prof. med. ethics Kennedy Inst. Ethics Georgetown U., 1979—, prof. philosophy, 1981—, dir., 1989-96; adj. prof. depts. community and family medicine and ob/gyn, 1984—. Mem. vis. faculty various colls. and univs.; mem. gov. bd. Washington Regional Transplant Consortium, 1988—; bd. dirs. Hospice Care D.C., 1989-96, 97-99, pres., 1993-95; active United Network Organ Sharing Ethics Com., 1989-95. Author: Value-Freedom in Science and Technology, 1976, Death, Dying and the Biological Revolution, 1976, rev. edit., 1989, Case Studies in Medical Ethics, 1977, A Theory of Medical Ethics, 1981, The Foundations of Justice, 1987, The Patient as Partner, 1987; (with Sarah T. Fry) Case Studies in Nursing Ethics, 1987, 3d edit., 2006, The Patient-Physician Relationship: The Patient as Partner, Part 2, 1991; (with James T. Rule) Ethical Questions in Dentistry, 1993, 2nd edit., 2004, (with Harley Flack) Case Studies in Allied Health Ethics, 1997, (with Paul DeVries and Lisa Newton) Ethics Applied, 2d. edit., 1999, (with Amy Haddad) Case Studies in Pharmacy Ethics, 1999, The Basics of Bioethics, 2000, 2d edit., 2003, Transplantation Ethics, 2000, Disrupted Dialogue, 2005; editor or co-editor: Bibliography of Society, Ethics and the Life Sciences, 1973, rev. edit., 1978, The Teaching of Medical Ethics, 1973, Death Inside Out, 1975, Ethics and Health Policy, 1976, Teaching of Bioethics, 1976, Population Policy and Ethics, 1977, Life Span: Values and Life Extending Technologies, 1979, Cases in Bioethics From the Hastings Center Report, 1982, Medical Ethics, 1989, 2d edit., 1997, Cross Cultural Perspectives in Medical Ethics, 1989, rev. edit., 2000; (with Edmund D. Pellegrino and John P. Langan) Ethics, Trust, and the Professions, 1991; (with Tom L. Beauchamp) Ethical Issues in Death and Dying, 1996, (with Hans-Martin Sass and Rihito Kimura) Advance Directives and Surrogate Decision Making in Health Care: United States, Germany, and Japan, 1998, (with Albert R. Jonsen and LeRoy Walters) Source Book in Bioethics: A Documentary History, 1998; assoc. editor Encyclopedia of Bioethics, 1998; editl. bd. Jour. AMA, 1976-86, Jour. Medicine and Philosophy, 1980—, Harvard Theol. Rev., 1975—, Jour. Religious Ethics, 1981—; editl. adv. bd. Forum on Medicine, 1977-81; contbg. editor Hosp. Physician, 1975-85, Am. Jour. Hosp. Pharmacy, 1989-99; sr. editor Kennedy Inst. Ethics Jour., 1991—; contbr. articles to profl. jours. Bd. dir. Washington Reg. Transplant Consortium, 1988-, Hospice Care of DC, 1989-1998, pres. bd., 1993-96; mem. United Network for Organ Sharing Ethics Com., 1989-95, Ad Hoc Living Donor Com., 2002-06. Recipient Disting. Svc. award, United Meth. Assn., Career Achievement award, Georgetown U., 2005. Office: Georgetown U Kennedy Inst Of Ethics Washington DC 20057-0001 Office Phone: 202-687-6771. Business E-Mail: veatchr@georgetown.edu.

VEBLEN, THOMAS CLAYTON, management consultant; b. Hallock, Minn., Dec. 17, 1929; s. Edgar R. and Hattie (Lundgren) V.; m. Susan Alma Beaver, Sept. 1, 1950 (div. 1971); children: Kari Kristen, Erik Rodli, Mark Andrew, Sara Catherine; m. Linda Joyce Eaton, Aug. 30, 1975; 1 child, Kristen Kirby. Student, U. Calif., Santa Barbara, 1950—51; BS, Calif. Poly. U., 1953; MS, Oreg. State U., 1955. Corp. v.p. Cargill, Inc., Wayzata, Minn., 1955-75; spl. asst. Sec. Interior, Washington, 1965; dir. food and agr. SRI Internat., Menlo Park, Calif., 1975-80; pres. Food Sys. Assocs., Inc., Washington, 1980-94; also bd. dirs. Food System Assocs., Inc., Washington; chmn. Enterprise Cons. and Devel., Inc., Mpls., 1990—; dir. Georgetown Cons., Inc., 1993-95; convener The Superior Bus. Firm Roundtable, 1993—; chmn. Kirby Ventures LLC, Mpls., 1997—, Wyatt Ventures, LLC, Mpls., 1999—, Northshore, LLC, Mpls., 2000—. Mem. CMC Inst. Mgmt. Cons., 1988—97, pres. Washington chpt., 1991—93. Co-author: (with M. Nichols) The U.S. Food System, 1978; (with M. Abel) Creating a Superior National Food System, 1992; author: The Way of Business: An Inquiry Into Meaning and Superiority, 2006; editor Food System Update, 1986-95. Treas., bd. dirs. White House Fellows Assn., Washington, 1985; trustee Freedom from Hunger Found., Davis, Calif., 1980-99, chmn., 1986-89; bd. dirs. Patterson Sch., U. Ky., Lexington, 1976-99, Am. Near East Refugee Aid, 1994-2006. Recipient Presdl. Appointment White House Fellows Program, Washington, 1965. Mem.: Coun. on Fgn. Rels., Cato Inst., Cosmos Club. Episcopalian. Avocations: canoeing, gardening, writing. Office: Enterprise Cons and Devel Inc 2817 Lyndale Ave South Minneapolis MN 55409 Office Phone: 202-342-7640. Personal E-mail: superbizrt@aol.com.

VECCHIO, ROBERT PETER, business management educator; b. Chgo., June 29, 1950; m. Betty Ann Vecchio, Aug. 21, 1974; children: Julie, Mark. BS summa cum laude, DePaul U., 1972; MA, U. Ill., 1974, PhD, 1976. Instr. U. Ill., Urbana, 1973-76; mem. faculty dept. mgmt. U. Notre Dame, 1976—, dept. chmn., 1983-90, Franklin D. Schurz Prof. Mgmt., 1986—. Editor: Jour. of Mgmt., 1995—2000. Fellow: APA, Am. Psychol. Soc., Soc. for Indsl. and Orgnl. Psychology; mem.: Midwest Psychol. Assn., Midwest Acad. Mgmt., Acad. of Mgmt., Phi Eta Sigma, Delta Epsilon Sigma, Phi Kappa Phi. Home: 16856 Hampton Dr Granger IN 46530-6907 Office: U Notre Dame Dept Mgmt Notre Dame IN 46556

VECCHIONE, KENNETH A., corporate financial executive; Grad., SUNY Albany. CFO Citicorp Credit Card; CFO, group pres. First Data Corp.; CFO AT&T Universal Card Svcs.; div. head fin. MBNA Corp., Wilmington, Del., 1998—2000; CFO MBNA Am. Bank, Wilmington, Del., 2000—; vice chmn., CFO MBNA Corp., Wilmington, Del., 2004—. Mem. Fin. Exec. Inst. Bd. dir. Del. Jewish Cmty. Ctr. Office: MBNA Corp 1100 N King St Wilmington DE 19884

VECCHIOTTI, ROBERT ANTHONY, management and organizational consultant; b. NYC, May 21, 1941; s. R. Lucien and Louise Victoria V.; m. Dorothea Irene Hoban, Oct. 12, 1963; children: John Robert, Rachel Irene, Sara Christine. BS, St. Peter's Coll., 1962; MA, Fordham U., 1964; PhD, St. Louis U., 1973. Lic. psychologist, Mo. Psychologist Testing and Advisement Ctr., NYU, Washington Sq. campus, 1964-65; group psychologist McDonnell Douglas, St. Louis, 1967-76, sr. bus. analyst, 1976-77, mgr. bus. planning, 1977-79; pres. Orgnl. Cons. Svcs., Inc., St. Louis, 1980—. Adj. assoc. prof. mgmt. Maryville Coll., St. Louis, 1975-81. Bd. dirs. Cath. Charities St. Louis, 1981-86, Cath. Family Svc., 1986-00, Mental Health Assn. St. Louis, 1989-05, Sta. KWMU-FM, 1989-94; trustee St. Patrick;s Ctr., 2001-. With US Army, 1965-67. Fellow Soc. Indsl. and Orgnl. Psychologists; mem. APA, Rotary (past pres.). Office: Organizational Consulting Svcs Inc 230 S Bemiston Ave Ste 1107 Clayton MO 63105-1907 Home Phone: 314-991-4323; Office Phone: 314-863-1200.

VECCHIOTTI, TONY V., insurance agent; b. Rochester, NY, Mar. 16, 1960; s. Anthony V. and Julia D. Vecchiotti; m. Leslie E. Elliott, Feb. 16, 1985; children: Julianna C., Anthony E., Carly S. B of Mgmt. Sci., Nazareth Coll. Rochester, NY, 1981. Lic. agt. NY, 1982. Sales mgr. Prudential Fin. Svcs., Fairport, NY, 1982—92; comml. account exec. Barker, Heslip, Bradshaw Agy., Rochester, 1992—97; personal lines mgr. Riedman Ins./Brown and Brown of NY, Rochester, 1997—2003; pres. Northcoast NY, Geneva, 2004—06; v.p. The Northwoods Corp, Williamsville, NY, 2006—. Cont. edn. instr. ins. Ctr. Profl. Advancement, Rochester, 1992—98. Chmn. Genesee Valley/FingerLakes chpt. March of Dimes, Rochester, 1995—99, chmn. pub. affairs com. NY state chpt. NYC, 2003—07. Named Vol. of Yr. Genesee Valley FingerLakes chpt., March of Dimes, 1996, 2006, Citizen of Yr., Monroe County Fire Chiefs Assn., 2002, Rochester Ins. Profl. of Yr., Ind Ins Agents and Rochester CPCU Soc., 2006. Mem.: Ind. Ins. Agents Monroe (dir. 2003—), Ind. Ins. Agents NY (pres. 1999—2000, dir. 2000—01), Am. MENSA. Roman Catholic. Avocations: golf, bicycling, boating. Office: The Northwoods Corp 742 A Pre Emption Rd Geneva NY 14456 Home Phone: 315-986-8648; Office Phone: 315-789-7227. Office Fax: 315-789-0474. Personal E-mail: tonyvinsurance@aol.com. Business E-Mail: tvecchiotti@thenorthwoodscorp.com.

VECELLIO, LEO ARTHUR, JR., construction company executive; b. Beckley, W.Va., Oct. 26, 1946; s. Leo Arthur and Evelyn (Pais) V.; m. Kathryn Grace Cottrill, Nov. 29, 1975; children: Christopher Scott, Michael Andrew. BCE, Va. Poly. Inst. and State U., 1968; MCE, Ga. Inst. Tech., 1969; LLD, Northwood U., 1992. Sr. v.p. Vecellio & Grogan, Inc., West Palm Beach, Fla., 1973-96, pres., CEO, chmn. bd. dirs., 1996—; mng. ptnr. Vecellio Realty Co., Palm Beach, Fla., 1990—; pres. Vecellio Realty Inc., Palm Beach, Fla., 1997—; mng. ptnr. Orlando Property Assn. Ltd., 1997—, WRQ Property Assn. Ltd., 1997—; chmn., pres., CEO The Vecellio Group-Holding Co., West Palm Beach, Fla., 2002—. Pres. Vecellio Contracting Corp. and subs. (Ranger Constrn. Industries, West Palm Beach, dba Ranger Const., South, Deerfield Beach, White Rock Quarries, Miami 1990—), Fla., 1982—; founder, past dir. Gulf Nat. Bank, Sophia, W.Va., Nat. Bankers Trust, Beckley; bank dir. Raleigh County Nat. Bank (now United Nat. Bank), W.Va., 1975-87, mem. adv. bd. Sun Trust Banks; bd. dirs. Natural Resource Ptnrs. Chmn. bd. dir. Econ. Coun. Palm Beach County, Fla., 1985—, chmn.-elect, 1987, chmn., 1989; gov. Northwood U., West Palm Beach, 1985—; organizer, trustee Beckley Area Found., 1985; v.p., trustee Vecellio Family Found., Beckley, 1972-96, pres., trustee, 1996—; active Mini-Grace Commn., Fla. Coun. 100, 1989—2004, vice-chmn., 1991—; commn. dir., v.p. Criminal Justice Commn.; chmn. Budget Rev. Task Force, Budget Oversight Task Force; bd. dir. Palm Beach County Cultural Coun. and Art Sch. Task Force, Fla. Coun. 100, Floridians for Better Transp., exec. com.; corporator Schepens Eye Rsch. Inst., Harvard U., 1993—; mem. engring. coun. 100 Va. Tech.; mem. pres.'s adv. bd. Ga. Inst. Tech., 2000-06; trustee, chair investment com. Va. Tech. Found., 2001, exec. com., 2004-05. Capt. USAF, 1969—73. Recipient Free Enterprise medal, Palm Beach Atlantic U., 1988, Disting. Engring. Alumni award, Ga. Tech., 2002, Disting. Civil Engring. award, Va. Tech. U., 2006. Mem. Am. Rd. and Transp. Builders Assn. (dir. 2000, regional vice chmn. 2002-05, 1st v.p. 2007), Flexible Pavements Assn. (found, bd. dir. 1979—), Contractors Assn. W. (bd. dir. 1975—), Mayacoo Lakes Country Club (West Palm Beach), Adios Golf Club (Coconut Creek, Fla.), Jupiter Hills Club (Fla.), Everglades Club, Club Colette, Greenbrier Sporting Club, Glade Springs Club. Republican. Roman Catholic. Avocations: golf, boating, skiing. Home: 210 Via Del Mar Palm Beach FL 33480 Office: Vecellio Group Inc PO Box 15065 West Palm Beach FL 33416-5065 Office Phone: 561-793-2102.

VECOLI, RUDOLPH JOHN, retired history educator, director; b. Wallingford, Conn., Mar. 2, 1927; s. Giovanni Battista and Settima Maria (Palmerini) V.; m. Jill Cherrington, June 27, 1959; children: Christopher, Lisa, Jeremy. BA, U. Conn., 1950; MA, U. Pa., 1951; PhD, U. Wis., 1963. Fgn. affairs officer Dept. State, 1951-54; instr. history Ohio State U., 1957-59, Pa. State U., 1960-61; asst. prof. Rutgers U., 1961-65; assoc. prof. U. Ill., Champaign, 1965-67; prof. history, dir. Immigration History Rsch. Ctr., U. Minn., Mpls., 1967—2005; ret., 2005. Vis. prof. U. Uppsala, Sweden, 1970, U. Amsterdam, The Netherlands, 1988, Maria Curie-Sklodowsk U., Lublin, Poland, 1992. Author: The People of New Jersey, 1965, Foreword to Marie Hall Ets, Rosa: The Story of an Italian Immigrant, 1970, (with J. Lintelman) A Century of American Immigration, 1884-1984, (with others) The Invention of Ethnicity, 1990; contbg. author: Gil italiani fuori d'Italia, 1983, They Chose Minnesota: A Survey of the State's Ethnic Groups, 1981, Pane e Lavoro: The Italian American Working Class, 1980, Perspectives in Italian Immigration and Ethnicity, 1977, Immigrants and Religion in Urban America, 1977, The State of American History, 1970, The Reinterpretation of American History and Culture, 1973, Failure of a Dream, Essays in the History of American Socialism, 1984, Italian Americans: New Perspectives, 1985, May Day Celebration, 1988, In the Shadow of the Statue of Liberty, 1988, From Melting Pot to Multiculturalism, 1990, Studi Sull' Emigrazione, 1991, The Lebanese in the World, 1992, Swedes in America: New Perspectives, 1993, The Statue of Liberty Revisited, 1994, La Riscoperta delle Americhe, 1994, The Encyclopedia of Twentieth Century America, 1996, The Cambridge Survey of World Migration, 1995, Print Culture in a Diverse America, 1998; editor, contbg.

author: The Other Catholics, 1978, Italian Immigrants in Rural and Small Town America, 1987, The Gale Encyclopedia of Multicultural Am., 1994, Beyond the Godfather, 1997, The Lost World of Italian American Radicalism, 2003; mem. editl. bd. Jour. Am. Ethnic History, Studi Emigrazione, America: History and Life Mid-Am., Estudios Migratorios Latino Americanos, Altreitalle; co-editor (with S. Sinke) A Century of European Migrations, 1830-1930, 1991; contbr. articles to jours. Chair history com. Statue of Liberty-Ellis Island Centennial Commn. & Found., 1983-98. With USNR, 1945-46. Decorated Knight Officer, Order of Merit (Italy), 1992; recipient Campus Major honor City of Camaiore, Italy, 1996; Newberry Libr. fellow, 1964, Am.-Scandinavian Found. fellow, 1970, NEH fellow, 1985-86; Am. Philos. Soc. grantee, 1970, Fulbright-Hays sr. rsch. scholar Italy, 1973-74; Am. Coun. Learned Soc. grantee, 1974, 86, U.S. Dept. State Travel grantee, 1977, Acad. Specialist, U.S. Info. Agy., Brazil, 1993; endowed Rudolph J. Vecoli professorship Am. immigration history, 2005. Mem. Am. Italian Hist. Assn. (pres., mem. exec. coun.), Am. Hist. Assn., Orgn. Am. Historians, AAUP, Immigration History Soc. (pres., exec. coun.) Home: 2338 Chilcombe Ave Saint Paul MN 55108-1626 Business E-Mail: vecol001@tc.umn.edu.

VECSEY, GEORGE SPENCER, sports columnist; b. Jamaica, NY, July 4, 1939; s. George Stephen and May (Spencer) V.; m. Marianne Graham; children: Laura, Corinna, David. BA in English, Hofstra Coll., 1960; LHD (hon.), Hofstra U., 1991. Sports reporter Newsday, Garden City, NY, 1960-68, NY Times, NYC, 1968-70, nat. corr., 1970-73, met., religion reporter, 1973-80, sports reporter, 1980-82, sports columnist, 1982—. Author: (with others) Naked Came the Stranger, 1969, Joy in Mudville: Being a Complete Account of the Unparalleled History of the New York Mets, 1970, One Sunset a Week: The Story of a Coal Miner, 1974, (with Loretta Lynn) Coal Miner's Daughter, 1976, (with Jacques Lowe) Kentucky: A Celebration of American Life, 1979, (with George C. Dade) Getting Off the Ground: The Pioneers of Aviation Speak for Themselves, 1978, (with Leonore Fleischer) Sweet Dreams, 1985, (with Martina Navratilova) Martina, 1985, (with Bob Welch) Five O'Clock Comes Early: A Young Man's Battle with Alcoholism, 1982, A Year in the Sun, 1989, (with Barbara Mandrell) Get to the Heart, 1991, (with Harry Wu) Troublemaker: One Man's Crusade Against China's Cruelty, 1996, (with Lorrie Morgan) Forever Yours, Faithfully, 1997, Macguire and Sosa: Baseball's Greatest Homerun Story, 1998, Subway 2000: The Dramatic Story of the First Subway Series Since 1956, 2001, Baseball, 2006; author 8 children's books; editor: The Way It Was: Great Sports Events from the Past, 1974. Recipient Disting. Writing award Am. Soc. Newspaper Editors, 1995; named NY State Sportswriter of Yr. Nat. Sportscasters and Sportswriters Assn., 1985-97. Mem. Kentuckians (bd. dirs. 1988—). Avocations: running, swimming, music, travel, languages. Office: NY Times 229 W 43rd St New York NY 10036-3959

VEDDER, JAMES J., lawyer; b. Menominee, Wis., Oct. 1, 1973; BA, U. Minn., 1995; JD, Hamline U. Sch. Law, St. Paul, 1999. Bar: Minn. 1999. Clk. Hennepin County Dist. Ct.; atty. M. Sue Wilson Law Offices; assoc. Moss & Barnett, P.A., Mpls. Contbr. articles to profl. publs. Named a Rising Star, Minn. Super Lawyers mag., 2006. Mem.: Minn. State Bar Assn., Hennepin County Bar Assn. Office: Moss & Barnett PA 4800 Wells Fargo Ctr 90 S 7th St Minneapolis MN 55402-4129 Office Phone: 612-877-5294. E-mail: vedderj@moss-barnett.com. *

VEDDER, RICHARD KENT, economics professor; b. Urbana, Ill., Nov. 5, 1940; s. Byron C. and Kathleen (Fry) V.; m. Karen Pirosko, June 18, 1968; children: Virin, Vanette. BA, Northwestern U., Evanston, Ill., 1962; MA, U. Ill., 1963, PhD, 1965. Asst. prof. econs. Ohio U., Athens, 1965-69, assoc. prof. econs., 1969-74, prof. econs., 1974-85; economist Joint Econ. Com. of Congress, Washington, 1981-82; Dist. Prof. of econs. Ohio U., Athens, 1985—. Vis. prof. Claremont McKenna Coll., Calif., 1979-80, Econs. Inst. U. Colo., Boulder, 1979, 80, Washington U., St. Louis, 1995, 96; adj. scholar Am. Enterprise Inst., 2003-; dir. Ctr. for Coll. Affordability and Productivitiy, 2006; mem. Sec. of Edn.'s Commn. on Future of Edn., 2005. Author: American Economy in Historical Perspective, 1976, Can Teachers Own Their Own Schools?, 2000, Going Broke by Degree: Why College Costs Too Much, 2005; co-author: Out of Work: Unemployment and Government in Twentieth-Century America, 1993, rev. edit., 1997, The Wal-Mart Revolution. 2006. Mem. Athens Bd. Edn., 1987-91; bd. dirs. Athens Cmty. Music Sch., 1987-92, Ohio Valley Summer Theater, 2002—. Recipient rsch. grants Earhart Found., 1970, 90, Rockefeller Found., 1974, Nat. Chamber Found., 1990, fellowship Inst. for Humane Studies, Palo Alto, Calif., 1983. Mem. Am. Econ. Assn., Econ. History Assn., Rotary, U. Club. Republican. Presbyterian. Home: 7464 Ridgeview Cir Athens OH 45701-9005 Office: Ohio Univ Dept Econs Bentley Hall Annex 316 Athens OH 45701 Home Phone: 740-593-0813. Business E-Mail: vedder@ohio.edu.

VEDERNIKOV, YURI P., pharmacologist, educator; b. Tomsk, Russia, Aug. 3, 1937; arrived in U.S., 1991; s. Pavel D. Vedernikov and Tatjana P. Vedernikova; m. Valentina G. Budkina, Mar. 2, 1960 (dec.); 1 child, Alexander Y. Veder. MD, PhD, Sverdlovsk Med. Inst., Russia, 1963. Cert. medicine pharmacology Med. Inst., Sverdlovsk. Asst. prof. dept. pharmacology Med. Inst., Sverdlovsk, 1963—69; rschr. Inst. Plant and Animal Ecology Ural's Sci. Ctr., USSR Acad. Scis., Sverdlovsk, 1969—73; sr. rschr. All-Union Inst. Med. Info. USSR Health Ministry, Moscow, 1973—74; sr. rschr. Brain Rsch. Inst. Acad. Med. Scis., Moscow, 1974—78, sr. rschr. Cardiology Rsch. Ctr., 1978—91; rsch. instr. dept. medicine Coll. Medicine Baylor U., Houston, 1991—93, asst. prof. dept. anesthesiology and ob-gyn., 1993—95; asst. prof. U. Tex. Med. Br., Galveston, 1995—2000, assoc. prof., 2000—. Contbr. scientific papers to profl. jours. Mem.: Nitric Oxide Soc., Acad. Problems Hypoxy (academician). Achievements include patents for device for the study of mechanical properties of the vessels. Home: 21 Back Bay Cir Galveston TX 77551 Office: U Tex Med Br 301 University Blvd Galveston TX 77555-1062 Business E-Mail: yvederni@utmb.edu.

VEDROS, NEYLAN ANTHONY, microbiologist, educator; b. New Orleans, Oct. 6, 1929; s. Phillip John and Solange Agnes (Melancon) V.; m. Elizabeth Corbett, Apr. 9, 1955; children: Sally Ann, Philippa Jane. BS in Chemistry, La. State U., 1951, MS in Microbiology, 1957; PhD, U. Colo., 1960. Postdoctoral fellow Nat. Inst. Allergy and Infectious Diseases, U. Oreg., Portland, 1960-62; microbiologist Naval Med. Research Inst., Bethesda, Md., 1962-66; research microbiologist Naval Biosci. Lab., Oakland, Calif., 1966-67; assoc. prof. med. microbiology and immunology U. Calif., Berkeley, 1967-72, prof., 1972-91, prof. emeritus, 1991—. Dir. Naval Biosci. Lab., 1968-81; mem. expert panel on bacteriology WHO, 1972-91. Bd. trustees Alameda (Calif.) Library, 1973-78. Served to comdr. M.S.C. USNR, 1952-55, 62-67. Mem.: Internat. Assn. Aquatic Animal Medicine, Internat. Assn. Microbiol. Sci., Am. Soc. Microbiology. Home: 209 Almond Way Healdsburg CA 95448 E-mail: nvedros@earthlink.net.

VEECH, LYNDA ANNE, musician, educator; b. Montclair, NJ, July 19, 1969; d. Robert Gerald, Sr. and Josephine Veech. B in Music Edn., Rutgers U., New Brunswick, 1991, MA in Music History, 1995; MusM in Piano Performance and Pedagogy, Westminster Choir Coll., Princeton, NJ, 1998. Cert. tchr. N.J. Faculty mem. Westminster Conservatory, Princeton, 1995—2000; pvt. studio dir. Studio of Lynda A. Veech, Verona, NJ, 1995—; faculty mem. Essex County Coll., Woodbridge, NJ, 1996—98, Caldwell (N.J.) Coll., 2000—01; choral dir. Caldwell and West Caldwell Pub. Schs., 2000—02; music tchr. Bartle Elem. Sch., Highland Park, NJ, 2002—03, Morris Cath. HS, Denville, NJ, 2003—, chmn. Dept. Performing Arts, 2005—. Cons. freelance work, Verona, NJ, 1995—; participant Hands Across the Water Internat. Tchr. Exch. Program, Australia, 2002. Performer Ameropa Internat. Music Festival, Prague, Czech Republic, 2001, Montclair Music Festival, 2005. Bd. dirs. Music and More Booster Club, Caldwell, NJ, 2001—02; vocalist Canticle AIDS Benefit Ensemble, NJ, 1999—2000; ch. musician 1st Bapt. Ch., Montclair, 2000—01; organist, choir dir. Calvary Luth. Ch., Verona, NJ, 2003—04; organist St. Luke's and All Saints Ch., Union, NJ, 2001—, St. Anne's Ch., Hoboken, NJ, 2005—. Grantee, Rutgers U., 1991—95, Westminster Choir Coll., 1995—97. Mem.: Music Edn. Assn. (co-founder 2000—), Nat. Conf. Piano Pedagogy, Piano Tchrs. Guild, N.J. Edn. Assn., Am. Choral Dir.'s Assn., Music Educator's Nat. Conf. (treas. 1987, v.p. 1991). Roman Catholic. Avocations: reading, swimming, ballet, poetry, music. Home: 124 Sunset Ave Verona NJ 07044 Office: Morris Cath High Sch 200 Morris Ave Denville NJ 07834-1360 Personal E-mail: notenut@comcast.net.

VEECH, WILLIAM AUSTIN, mathematics professor; b. Detroit, Dec. 24, 1938; s. Max Lincoln and Muriel Thayer Veech; m. Kathryn Lunceford, Dec. 29, 1965; children: Kathryn Muriel, Maude Elizabeth. BA, Dartmouth Coll., Hanover, NH, 1960; PhD, Princeton U., NJ, 1963. H. B. Fine instr., Higgins lectr. Princeton U., 1963—66; asst. prof. U. Calif., Berkeley, 1966—69; from assoc. prof. to prof. Rice U., Houston, 1969—88, Milton Brockett Porter prof., 1988—2003, Edgar Odell Lovett prof., 2003—. Mem. Inst. Advanced Study, Princeton, 1968—69, Princeton, 1972, Princeton, 1976—77, Princeton, 1983—84; mem. adv. com. math. and computer sciences NSF, Washington, 1979—82; professeur associe Universite d'Aix-Marseille 2, Luminy, France, 1982, Luminy, 95, Universite de Rennes, Rennes, France, 1977; trustee Math. Scis. Rsch. Inst., Berkeley, Calif., 1989—94; vis. mem. Inst. Hautes Etudes Sci., France, 1989; disting. vis. prof. Nat. U. Singapore, Singapore, 1999. Author: A Second Course in Complex Analysis; contbr. articles to profl. jours.; mem. editl. bd. Ergodic Theory and Dynamics Sys., 1981—90, Caribbean Jour. Math., 1982, Annals of Mathematics, 1985—90. Fellow, NSF, 1960—63; Alfred P. Sloan Found. fellow, 1971—73, Woodrow Wilson Found. fellow, 1960—61, Rsch. grantee, NSF, 1969—2002. Mem.: Am. Math. Soc. (life; rep. Joint Policy Bd. Math. 1989—90, chmn. long range planning com. 1988—89, mem. exec. com. 1986—90). Republican. Episcopalian. Achievements include research in Structure Theorems in Topological Dynamics for Almost automorphic, point-distal and minimal flows; unique ergodicity in interval exchange transformations (Kronecker-Weyl Theorem Mod 2 and proof of Keane Conjecture); existence of free actions of locally compact topological groups; Ergodic theory of the Teichmuller geodesic flow and calculation of its metric entropy; first to introduce objects in dynamics now called Veech surfaces, Veech groups, Veech dichotomy and Siegel-Veech constants; introduce zippered rectangles in construction of Gauss measures on the space of interval exchange transformations. Office: Rice U Mathematics MS136 6100 S Main Houston TX 77005 Home Phone: 713-526-6158; Office Phone: 713-348-4881. Office Fax: 713-348-5231. Business E-Mail: veech@rice.edu.

VEEDER, PETER GREIG, lawyer; b. Pitts., Aug. 13, 1941; AB, Princeton U., 1963; JD, U. Pitts., 1966. Bar: Pa. 1966, D.C. 1976. Lawyer Thorp Reed & Armstrong, Pitts., 1970-99; of counsel Thorp, Reed & Armstrong LLP, Pitts., 1999—. Office: Thorp Reed & Armstrong LLP 1 Oxford Ctr 301 Grant St Fl 14 Pittsburgh PA 15219-1425 Office Phone: 412-394-7793.

VEENEMA, RALPH JAMES, retired urologist; b. Paterson, NJ, Dec. 13, 1921; s. Ralph Veenema and Sadie Van Dyke; m. Henriette E. Van DerMolen, Sept. 19, 1944; children: Shirley, Lois, Ralph J. Jr., Kenneth. AB, Calvin Coll., Grand Rapids, Mich., 1942; MD, Jefferson Med. Coll., Phila., 1945. Diplomate Am. Bd. Urology. Intern Paterson Gen. Hosp., NJ, 1945—46; resident in surgery U.S. Army Hosps., Alexandri La. and Jackson, Miss., 1946—48; fellow in surg. pathology Columbia Presbyn. Med. Ctr., 1948, resident in urology, 1949—52; attending urologist Presbyn. Hosp., 1957—87; chief urology Francis Delafield Hosp., 1960—72; prof. urology Columbia U. Coll. Physicians and Surgeons, NYC, 1949—87, prof. emeritus, 1987—. Contbr. articles to profl. jours. Capt. Med. Corps US Army, WWII. Fellow: ACS, NY Acad. Medicine (former pres. urology sect.); mem.: Am. Urol. Assn. (former pres. NY sect., awards for work in bladder cancer and prostate cancer). Avocation: beef cattle farming. Home: 40 Nelson Ave Cooperstown NY 13326

VEERAMACHANENI, RAVINDRA, pathologist; b. Bangalore, Karnataka, India, Jan. 8, 1971; s. Gangadhara Rao and Ratna Kumari Veeramachaneni; m. Sarada Gummadi, July 2, 1999. B in Medicine and Surgery, Mysore Med. Coll., India, 1994. Physician Postgrad. Inst., Chandigarh, India, 1994—96, La. State U. Health Sci. Ctr., Shreveport, 1997—. Author: Diagnostic Cytopathology. Fellow: U.S. Can. Acad. Pathologist; mem.: AMA, Soc. Ultrastructural Pathology (Meritorious Achievement award 2002), Coll. Am. Pathologists (jr.), Am. Soc. Clin. Pathologists, Renal Pathology Soc., Am. Soc. Cytopathologists (jr.). Office: La State U HSC 1501 Kings Hwy Shreveport LA 71130 Home: 4404 Santa Fabiola Mission TX 78572-0521 Home Phone: 318-798-3896. Personal E-mail: rveeram@hotmail.com. Business E-Mail: rveera@lsuhsc.edu.

VEGA, CAROLYN JANE, elementary educator, consultant, writer; b. Loma Linda, Calif., June 29, 1949; d. Ora Harrison Miller and Magil Muriel Rhodes; children: Matthew Harrison, Sarah Christine. AA, Orange Coast Coll., Costa Mesa, Calf., 1970; BA in Fine Arts and Humanities, San Diego State U., 1972; MA in Ednl. Tech., US Internat. U., San Diego, 1987. Std. elem. tchg. credential Calif., specially designed academic instrn. in English and lang. devel. Calif., cert. gifted and talented edn. Calif. Classroom tchr. San Diego Unified Sch. Dist., 1973—, edn. tech. resource tchr., 1988—95. Lectr. U. Calif. San Diego, La Jolla, 1989—95; cons. AAAS, Washington, 1994—2000; project 2061 team contb. Benchmarks for Sci. Literacy, 1993. Author: (textbooks) SRA Real Science, SRA Science Math and You. Del. NEA, Washington, 2000—; bd. dirs. San Diego Educators Assn., San Diego, 2004—06. Mem.: NEA (del. 2000—), San Diego Educators Assn. (elem. seat 2004—), San Diego Edn. Assn. (bd. dirs. 2004—), Calif. Tchrs. Assn. (svc. ctr. coun. 2001—06, We Honor Ours award 2005), Delta Kappa Gamma. Democrat. Achievements include research in implementing technology in the curriculum. Home: 6218 Winona Ave San Diego CA 92120 Office: San Diego Unified Sch Dist 4100 Normal St San Diego CA 92103 Home Phone: 619-287-3074. Personal E-mail: cjvega@cox.net.

VEGA, FRANK J., newspaper publishing executive; With Gannett Co. Inc., 1978—; asst. to pub., circulation dir. Oakland Tribune; mem. task force to launch USA Today, 1980—82, v.p. circulation, 1982—83; asst. to pres. Mid-Atlantic Regional Newspaper Group, 1983—84; gen. mgr. El Diario-La Prensa, NYC, 1983—84; pub., CEO Cape Publications, Brevard County, Fla., 1984—91; pres. South Regional Newspaper Group, 1985—91; pres., CEO Detroit Newspaper Agy., 1991—2004; pres., pub. San Francisco Chronicle, 2005—. Office: San Francisco Chronicle 901 Mission St San Francisco CA 94103 Office Phone: 415-777-1111. *

VEGA, J. DAVID, thoracic surgeon; BA, Wake Forest U., Winston-Salem, NC, 1982; MD, U. Mich., Ann Arbor, MI, 1986. Cert. Am. Bd. Surgery, Am. Bd. Thoracic Surgery. Intern, gen. surgery U. Tex. Health Sci. Ctr., Houston, 1986—87, resident, general surgery, 1987—88, 1990—92, chief resident, general surgery, 1992—93; Boerhinger Ingelheim Cardiovascular Surgical Rsch. Fellow Tex. Heart Inst., Houston, 1988—90, resident, thoracic and cardiovascular surgery, 1993—95; fellow, cardiopulmonary transplantation U. Pitts. Med. Ctr., 1995—96; chief, cardiothoracic surgery VA Med. Ctr., Decatur, Ga., 1997—; assoc. dir., adult heart and lung transplant program Emory U. Hosp., Atlanta, 1996—97, dir., lung transplant program, 1997—2004, dir., heart transplant program, 1997—; asst. prof., dept. surgery, divsn. cardiothoracic surgery Emory U. Sch. Medicine, Atlanta, 1996—2001, assoc. prof., dept. surgery, divsn. cardiothoracic surgery, 1997—. Mem. solid organ transplant com. Emory U. Hosp., 1996—; mem., CEO adv. com. Emory Clinic, 2003—, mem., clin. claims review working group, 2005—; mem. adv. com. on organ transplantation to the Sect. Dept. HHS, 2005—; mem. adv. com. on organ transplantation Health Resources & Services Adminstrn., 2005—. Contbr. chapters to books, articles to publications; manuscript reviewer Jour. Heart & Lung Transplantation, 2004—. Bd. governor LifeLink Found., 2003—; mem. Organ Procurement & Transplantation Network/United Network for Organ Sharing (OPTN/UNOS) thoracic organ transplantation com. United Network for Organ Sharing, 2002—04, vice-chmn., Organ Procurement & Transplantation Network/United Network for Organ Sharing (OPTN/UNOS) thoracic organ transplantation com., 2004—06, mem., membership & profl. standards com., 2002—05, mem., Organ Procurement & Transplantation Network/United Network for Organ Sharing (OPTN/UNOS) policy oversight com., 2005—06, chmn., Organ Procurement & Transplantation Network/United Network for Organ Sharing (OPTN/UNOS) thoracic organ transplantation com., 2006—08. Fellow: Am. Coll. Surgeons; mem.: Am. Assn. for Thoracic Surgery, Soc. Thoracic Surgeons (mem. ad hoc com. on circulatory support & thoracic transplantation 2001—02, mem. clin. edn. resource group 2002—, workforce on surgical treatment of end-stage cardiopulmonary disease 2004—05), Internat. Soc. for Heart & Lung Transplantation, Denton A. Cooley Cardiovascular Surgical Soc. (mem. exec. com. 2004—), Am. Soc. Transplant Surgeons, Am. Soc. for Artificial Internal Organs (manuscript reviewer 1999—), Am. Coll. Chest Physicians. Office: Emory Clinic A-2216 1365 Clifton Rd NE Atlanta GA 30322 Office Phone: 404-778-5289. Office Fax: 404-778-4346. *

VEGA, MATIAS ALFONSO, lawyer; b. Paris, Feb. 2, 1952; s. Matias Guillermo and Colette (Lafosse) V.; m. Carmella Margarita Kurczewski, Nov. 20, 1982; 1 child, Alexandra Lafosse. AB, Yale U., 1974; JD, Harvard U., 1977. Bar: N.Y. 1978, U.S. Dist. Ct. (so. and ea. dists.) N.Y. 1979, U.S. Supreme Ct. 1984, U.S. Ct. Appeals (6th and 9th cirs.) 1985, U.S. Dist. Ct. (no. dist.) Calif. 1985. Assoc. Curtis, Mallet-Prevost, Colt & Mosle, NYC, 1977-85, ptnr., 1986—. Contbr. articles to profl. jours. Mem. ABA, Am. Soc. Internat. Law, N.Y. State Bar Assn. (chmn. com. Latin Am. law, internat. law and practice sect. 1987-90), Yale Club. Republican. Roman Catholic. Home: 8 Cerf Ln Mount Kisco NY 10549 Office: Curtis Mallet-Prevost Colt 101 Park Ave Fl 34 New York NY 10178-0061 Home Phone: 914-244-0954; Office Phone: 212-696-6929. Personal E-mail: matvega@optonline.net. Business E-Mail: mvega@cm-p.com.

VEGA, REINALDO, research scientist; b. Manhattan, NY, Aug. 13, 1981; s. Juan Vega and Dawn Brocco. BS in Microelectronic Engring., Rochester Inst. Tech., NY, 1999—2004, MS in Microelectronic Engring., 2004—06. Co-op student, microelectronics divsn. Integrated Nano-Technologies, LLC, Rochester, NY, 2001; co-op pre-profl. engr., emerging products & sige passives integration Internat. Bus. Machines, 2002, co-op pre-profl. engr., silicon-on-insulator device characterization, internat. bus. machines, 2003; NSF rsch. experience for undergraduates Rochester Inst. Tech., Rochester, 2004, grad. rsch. asst., tchg. asst., 2004—06. Engring. cons. Biophan Technologies, Inc., Rochester, 2005—06. Mem.: IEEE, U. Calif. Berkeley Elec. Engring. Grad. Student Assn. (outreach coord. 2006—), IEEE Electron Devices Soc., RIT Microelectronic Engring. Student Assn. (process design mgr., mem. gear project 2003, grad. student advisor 2004—06, sr. design award com. mem., sr. judge 2005—06, exec. committe mem. 2005—06), RIT IEEE Student Chpt. (exec. com. mem. 2005—06). Achievements include patents pending for multi-valued logic/memory and circuits and methods thereof; metallic source/drain CMOS circuits and methods thereof. Avocations: running, golf, bicycling. Office: Univ Ca 373 Cory Hall Berkeley CA 94720 Home Phone: 585-313-5654. Personal E-mail: beeps_and_buzzes@yahoo.com.

VEGA, STEVE, poet, protective services official; b. NYC, Nov. 13, 1949; s. Exio Ocasio Vega; children: Katherine, James-Paul Christian, Diamond Zhane. Cert. in Bus. Mgmt., Marion Bus. Coll., 1973; cert., John Marshall Law Sch., 1977; cert. in corrections and probations svcs., Chgo. Loop Coll., 1986; BA, Coll. of Comml. Sci., 1995, M in Comml. Svc., 1996, postgrad., 1997; PhD, Lord Baden-Powell Coll., Lake Geneva, Wis., 1998, fellow of Scouting degree, 2003; wilderness survival course, with APO wardogs, 1988; winter camping survival course, OKPIK, Woodstock, Ill., 1996; sea badge course, Great Lakes Navy Base, 1998. Cert. diploma pvt. investigator course US Acad. Pvt. Investigation, 2004. Adult probation officer Cook County, Ill., 1979-93; pub. safety officer, police-fireman aide Morton Grove Emergency Svcs. and Disaster Agy., Ill., 1998—, police aide, fire rescue mem. Homeland Security; CEO pvt. practice, 2002—. Union chief steward Cook County Adult Probation Dept., AFSCME, 1989—91; 1st v.p. AFSCME local 3486 APD officers, Chgo., 1991—92; cons. Chgo. Police Dept., FBI, U.S. Secret Svc.; dep. dir. Internat. Biog. Ctr., Cambridge, England, 2000. Author: numerous poems; actor: (films) Music Box, Only the Lonely, Gladiator, Hero, Mo Money, Hoffa, Natural Born Killers, Mad Dog and Glory, Eye for and Eye (The Shadow of a Killer), Curly Sue, others; composer, rec. artist: The President Is Crying-September 11, 2001, 2001. Asst. coun. commn. Boy Scouts Am., Chgo., 1997, mem. ctrl. region com. Sea Scouting, 1998; vol., mem. com. City of Chgo. Health Sys. Agy., 1981—85. With USAF, 1970, with mil. aircraft command, mil. honor guard. Decorated Commendation medal USAF, 443d Svs. Squadron and Honor Guard USAF Mil. Aircraft Command, knight comdr. European Order Knighthood Italy; named World Poet, 1987—, Living Legend, Internat. Biog. Ctr., 2005, State of Ill. Father of the Yr., Ill. Gov., 2006, Disting. Eagle Scout, Boy Scouts Am., 2000; named one of World's Great Living Poets, 1991, The Greatest Chicagoans of the 20th Century, Chgo. Sun-Times, 1999; named to Hall of Fame, Lord Baden-Powell U., 2001; recipient Presdl. Sports award, Pres. Gerald Ford, 1975, Presdl. commendation, Pres. Ronald Reagan, 1987, 1988, Pres. George Bush, 1990, Arrowhead award, Boy Scouts Am., 1994, Nat. Fire Acad. Emergency Response to Terrorism cert., 2001. Mem.: ASCAP (composer, writer), Fraternal Order Police (officer 1988, sgt.-at-arms), Sovereign Mil. and Hospitaller Order St. George in Karinthia (titular head). Roman Catholic. Avocations: singing, composing, guitar, motorcycling, chess. Home: PO Box 221 Morton Grove IL 60053-0221 Personal E-mail: steve_vega_records@yahoo.com.

VEGA, SUZANNE, singer, songwriter; b. Santa Monica, Calif., July 11, 1959; m. Paul Mills, Feb. 11, 2006. Grad., Barnard Coll., 1982. Singer, songwriter, concert performer, 1975—. Began performing in Greenwich Village coffeehouses, NYC, 1975; albums include Suzanne Vega, 1985, Solitude Standing, 1987, Days of Open Hand, 1990, 99.9 F, 1992, Nine Objects of Desire, 1996, Songs in Red and Gray, 2001, Beauty & Crime, 2007; songs include Cracking, Marlene on the Wall, Tom's Diner, Luka, Solitude Standing, (song for Pretty in Pink soundtrack) Left of Center; concert tours of US, Can., Europe and Far East, 1987. Buddhist. Office: c/o Michael Hausman 511 Ave of the Americas #197 New York NY 10011 *

VEILLE, JEAN-CLAUDE, obstetrician, educator; b. France; came to U.S., 1982; m. Ann Veille; children: Olivier, Xavier, Patrique, Robert. BS, McGill U., 1971; MD, U. Montpellier, France, 1977. Fellow in maternal-fetal medicine Oreg. Health Scis., Portland, 1982-84; from asst. prof. to assoc. prof. Case Western Res. U., Cleve., 1984-90; chief maternal, fetal medicine Case Western Reserve U., Cleve., 1989-90; assoc. prof., dir. maternal-fetal med. fellowship program Wake Forest U. Sch. Medicine, Winston-Salem, NC, 1990-95, prof., 1995—, chief maternal-fetal medicine sect., 1997—2002; chmn. dept. ob-gyn. Albany (N.Y.) Med. Ctr., 2002—. Contbr. articles to profl. jours. Grantee NIH, 1991-2002. Office: 47 New Scotland Ave Albany NY Office Phone: 518-262-5013. E-mail: veillej@mail.amc.edu.

VEINOTT, ARTHUR FALES, JR., university educator; b. Boston, Oct. 12, 1934; m. 1960; children: Elisabeth, Michael; m. 1988. BS, BA, Lehigh U., 1956; D Eng Sc, Columbia U., 1960. From asst. prof. to assoc. prof. indusl. engring. Stanford (Calif.) U., 1962-67, prof. ops. rsch., 1967—, chmn. dept. indsl. engring., 1975-85, prof. mgmt. sci. engring., 1999—. Cons. Rand Corp., 1965, IBM Rsch. Ctr., 1968-69, 89-90; vis. prof. Yale U., 1972-73. Editor Jour. Math. Ops. Rsch., 1974-80. 1st lt. USAF, 1960-62 Guggenheim fellow 1978-79. Fellow Inst. Math. Stats.; mem. Nat. Acad. Engring., Inst. Mgmt. Sci., Ops. Rsch. Soc. Am. Achievements include development of lattice programming, qualitative theory of optimization for predicting the direction of change of optimal decisions resulting from alteration of problem parameters; structure and computation of optimal policies for supply chains and dynamic programs. Office: Stanford U Dept Mgmt Sci Engring Terman 415 Stanford CA 94305-4026

VEITCH, BOYER LEWIS, printing company executive; b. Phila., Oct. 20, 1930; s. Samuel Lewis and Agnes Mae (Bell) V.; m. Emmeline Barbara Smith, Nov. 22, 1952 (dec. Dec. 1994); children: William S., Nancy B., Thomas C.; m. Mary Chisholm Kiehn, Feb. 21, 1998. AB, Lafayette Coll., 1953; postgrad. Wharton Evening Sch., Acctg. and Fin., U. Pa., 1957-59. Advt. dir. Ware Bros. Co., Phila., 1956-62, v.p., 1962-69; salesman Zabel Bros. Co., Phila., 1969-75; chmn. Veitch Printing Corp., Lancaster, Pa., 1975—. Trustee Printers Disability Trust. Trustee Lafayette Coll., Easton, Pa., 1981-86, 87—, vice chmn. coll. rels. com., chmn. ann. fund, 1982-86, mem. fin. com., 1987-92, chmn. athletics and student affairs comn., 1992-97, mem. emeritus exec. com., 1997; mem. gen. adv. com. Lancaster County Career and Tech. Sch. System, 1996—; bd. dirs. Boys and Girls Club, Lancaster, 1980—, pres., 1990-92; dir. Boy's Club Lancaster Found., 1989—, pres., 1992—, elected to Boys and Girls Hall of Fame, 1999; dir. Gt. Valley Civic Assn., 1969-79; trustee Fulton Opera House Found., 1985-91, treas., 1987-89; bd. dirs. North Mus., 1992-94, Lancaster Airport Authority, 1994—, treas., 1994—; trustee PIA Disability Trust, 1994—; chmn. citizens for Schulze Com., Pa. 5th Congressional Dist., 1972-78; vestryman, sr. warden St. Peter's Ch. of Gt. Valley, 1972-78. Served with CIC, U.S. Army, 1954-56. Recipient Bronze Hope Chest award Nat. Multiple Sclerosis Soc., 1982, Nat. Svc. to Youth award Boys and Girls Clubs Am., 1992; named Small Bus. Person of Yr. Lancaster Co., 1991; named to Boys and Girls Club of Lancaster Alumni Hall of Fame, 1999, Graphic Arts Assn. Person of Yr., 2001; named Graphic Arts Assn. Person of Yr, 2001. Mem. SAR, Printing Industries Am. (dir. 1993-98), Graphic Arts Assn. (dir. 1980-98, chmn. 1990-92, Man of Yr. 2001), Lancaster C. of C. and Industry (dir. 1990-93), Lafayette Coll. Alumni Assn. (dir. 1974-78, pres. 1978-80), Pa. Economy League, Nat. Fedn. Ind. Bus., Phi Kappa Psi (past pres. and dir. chpt. alumni assn.), Ash Khan Soc. (hon.). Clubs: Hamilton (bd. dirs. 1995—), Wash Day, Lancaster Country, Avalon Yacht, Lancaster Aero., Lancaster Pirates (first mate 2001-2003, chief 2003-), Susquehanna Litho (dir. 1976-80, pres. 1979-80). Lodges: Rotary (Paul Harris fellow). Republican. Episcopalian. Home: 1044 Sylvan Rd Lancaster PA 17601-1933 Office: Veitch Printing Corp 1740 Hempstead Rd Lancaster PA 17601-5889 Personal E-mail: boygin@msn.com.

VEITH, FRANK J., vascular surgeon, researcher, educator; Cert. in gen. sugery 1961, in thoracic surgery 1968, in vascular surgery 1983. William J. von Liebig chmn. for vascular surgery Montefiore Med. Ctr., Bronx, NY, vice-chmn., prof. surgery, Albert Einstein Coll. Medicine, Bronx, NY Ann host VEITHsymposium. Contbr. more than 1,000 articles and chapters in profl. med. jours. and books.; serves on editl. bds. for four major vascular jours., editor-in-chief Vascular. Recipient Julius H. Jacobson, II, MD award for Physician Excellence, Vascular Disease Found., 2004. Mem.: Internat. Soc. for Vascular Surgery (founding sec.), Eastern Vascular Soc. (past pres.), Soc. for Vascular Surgery (past pres.). Considered role model in the field of vascular surgery; heading effort to have vascular surgery as a specialty board under the umbrella of the American Board of Specialties. Office: Montefiore Medical Ctr Med Arts Pavilion 3400 Bainbridge Ave 4th Fl Bronx NY 10467 Office Phone: 718-920-4108. Office Fax: 718-231-9811.

VEITH, G. JOHN, lawyer; b. Washburn, Wis., Nov. 6, 1967; BA, SUNY, Potsdam, 1989; JD, William Mitchell Coll. Law, 1993. Bar: Minn. 1993, US Dist. Ct. (dist. Minn.) 1994, US Dist. Ct. (ctrl. dist. Ill.) 1999, US Ct. Appeals (8th cir.) 2004. Asst. city atty., St. Paul, 1992; law clk. Medicaid-Fraud Unit Minn. Atty. Gen., St. Paul, 1993; pvt. practice atty., 1993—96; atty. complex bus., probate and civil litig. Westrick & McDowall-Nix, P.L.L.P., 1996—2001; assoc. Brown & Carlson, P.A., Mpls., 2001—. Named a Rising Star, Minn. Super Lawyers mag., 2006. Mem.: Minn. Def. Lawyers Assn., ABA, Ramsey County Bar Assn., Minn. State Bar Assn., Hennepin County Bar Assn. Office: Brown & Carlson PA 5411 Circle Down Ave Ste 100 Minneapolis MN 55416 Office Phone: 763-591-9950. E-mail: jveith@brownandcarlson.com. *

VEIZER, JÁN, geology educator; b. Pobedim, Slovakia, June 22, 1941; arrived in Can., 1973; s. Viktor and Brigita (Brandstetter) Veizer; m. Elena Ondrus, July 30, 1966; children: Robert, Andrew Douglas. Prom. Geol., Comenius U., Bratislava, Slovakia, 1964; RNDr, Comenius U., Bratislava, Slovak Republic, 1968; CSc, Slovak Acad. Sci., Bratislava, Slovakia, 1968; PhD, Australian Nat. U., Canberra, 1971. Asst. lectr. Comenius U., 1963-66; research scientist Slovak Acad. Sci., 1966-71; vis. asst. prof. UCLA, 1972; vis. rsch. scientist U. Göttingen, Fed. Republic Germany, 1972-73; rsch. scientist U. Tübingen, Fed. Republic Germany, 1973; from asst. prof. to full prof. U. Ottawa, Ont., Canada, 1973—2004, rsch. chair NSERC/Noranda/Can. Inst. Advanced Rsch. Ont., 1997—2006; prof. Ruhr U., Bochum, Germany, 1988—2004; Disting. Univ. prof. U. Ottawa, 2001—, prof. emeritus, 2004—. Cons. NASA, Houston, 1983—86; vis. prof., scholar Northwestern U., Evanston, Ill., 1983—87; vis. fellow Australian Nat. U., 1979; vis. prof. U. Tübingen, 1974; Lady Davis professorship Hebrew U., Jerusalem, 1987. Contbr. articles to profl. jours., chapters to books. Served to jr. lt. Med., 1965—66. Named Rsch. Prof. of Yr., 1987; recipient W. Leibniz prize, German Rsch. Found., 1992, gold medal, Slovak Geol. Survey, 2000; fellow Humboldt, 1980, 2006, Killam Rsch., Can. Coun., 1986—88. Fellow: US Geochemical Soc., European Assn. Geochemistry (elected geochemistry fellow 1998), Geol. Soc. Am., Geol. Assn. Can. (Logan medal 1995, past pres. medal 1987), Royal Soc. Can. (W.G. Miller medal 1991, Bancroft medal 2000), Slovak Geol. Soc. (hon.); mem.: Ski Club. Roman Catholic. Avocations: reading, hiking, skiing, history. Office: Dept Earth Scis U Ottawa Ottawa ON Canada K1N 6N5 Home Phone: 613-747-9801; Office Phone: 613-562-5800 6461. Business E-Mail: jveizer@uottawa.ca.

VEKLEROV, EUGENE, mathematician, computer scientist; b. Kamen, Altay Territory, Russia, Nov. 17, 1942; arrived in US, 1976; s. Benish Veksler and Serafima Fridland; children: Mark Wexler, Jessica, Kimberly. BS, Moscow U., Russia, 1965; PhD, Inst. for Info. Transmission Problems, Moscow, 1972. Rsch. scientist Inst. for Control Problems, Moscow, 1969—75, Lawrence Berkeley Nat. Lab., Berkeley, Calif., 1977—. Editor, translator: book Political Anti-Semitism in Post-Soviet Russia, author 2 computer science textbooks; editor: Computer Science, Electrical Engineering Dictionaries; contbr. articles to profl. jours. Home: 555 Pierce St Apt 628 Albany CA 94706 Office: Lawrence Berkeley Lab 1 Cyclotron Rd Berkeley CA 94720 Personal E-mail: veklerov@sbcglobal.net.

VELARDE, RACHEL DAY, voice educator, vocalist, educator, small business owner; b. Bloomington, Ind., June 11, 1973; d. Mark Tyler and Dorothy Lynn Autenrieth Day; m. Arturo Velarde, June 8, 1996; children: Alessandra Tyler, Angelynn Michelle. AB, Smith Coll., Northampton, Mass., 1994; MusM in Vocal Performance, MusM in Vocal Pedagogy, Ariz. State U., 1997. Owner, instr. Velarde Voice Studio, Scottsdale, Ariz., 1993—; chorister Ariz. Opera, Phoenix, 1997—. Sec. chorus payroll Ariz. Opera, Tucson, 2002—. Singer: (oratorio alto soloist with Musica Nova) Bach/Pergolesi Psalm 51/Stabat Mater; singer: (Lady with Hat Box, Foreign Singer) (Opera in the Ozarks) Postcard from Morocco by Dominick Argento; singer: (Mother and Witch) (Ariz. Opera Outreach) Hansel & Gretel; singer: (Second Witch) (opera, Catalina Chamber Orch.) Dido & Aeneas by Henry Purcell; singer: (Tisbe) (Ariz. Opera Outreach) Cenerentola by Gioacchino Rossini; singer: (Zita) (Lyric Opera Theater of Ariz. State U.) Gianni Schicchi by Puccini. Recipient tchg. assistantship, Ariz. State U., 1994—96. Mem.: Am. Guild Mus. Artists (sec./treas. Ariz. chpt. 1998—99, 2006—), Nat. Assn. Tchrs. Singing (sec. no. chpt. 2005—), Pi Kappa Lambda Zeta (Omega chpt.). Independent. Roman Catholic. Avocations: singing, reading, Tae Kwon Do. Office Phone: 480-221-7390. Personal E-mail: rachelvelarde@cox.net.

VELASQUEZ-GARCIA, LUIS FERNANDO, research scientist, consultant; s. Hector Velasquez-Gutierrez and Flor Nicolasa Garcia de Velasquez. Degree in mech. engring. magna cum laude, Los Andes U., Bogota, 1998, degree in civil engring. magna cum laude, 1999; MS in Aeroanutics and Astronautics, MIT, Cambridge, Mass., 2001, PhD in Space Propulsion, 2004. Postdoctoral assoc. MIT, Cambridge, 2004—05, rsch. scientist, 2006—. Cons. Busek, Co., Natick, Mass., 2004—. Contbr. scientific papers to profl. jours. Sponsor Boston Ballet, 2005—06. Recipient Ramon de Zubiria award, Los Andes U., 1997, 1998, 1999. Mem.: Sigma Xi. Roman Catholic. Achievements include development of highly packed electrospray emitter MEMS technology, intended for space propulsion applications, in both open and closed architectures, for doped solvents and ionic liquids as propellant; world's first MEMS Singlet Oxygen Generator for an Oxygen-Iodine Chemical Laser; high aspect ratio, re-assemblable MEMS Quadrupoles for portable, low power, fast gas analyzer technology; Carbon Nano Tube (CNT)-based field ionization / Field Emission MEMS technology for gas analyzer technology and space propulsion; micro-fabricated ionized species sensor techology using micro balances and vibrating Reed Electrometers; high current MEMS/NEMS field emitter arrays that use ungated transistors for ballasting; patents pending for.

VELAYUTHAM, MURUGESAN, research scientist; b. Sattur, Virudhunagar, India, June 5, 1967; s. Thillaiyambalam Murugesan and Murugesan Kaleeswari; m. Jeyanthi Senthur, Mar. 17, 2004. PhD in Phys. Chemistry, Indian Inst. Madras, Chennai, Tamil Nadu, India, 1998. Scientific Researcher The Ohio State U., 2006. Vis. postdoctoral fellow NC State U., Raleigh, 1998—99; postdoctoral fellow Fla. State U., Tallahassee, 1999, Johns Hopkins U., Balt., 1999—2002; postdoctoral rschr. Ohio State U., Columbus, 2002—06, rsch. scientist, 2006—. Recipient Langmuir award, Indian Inst. Tech. Madras, 1998. Mem.: Soc. Free Radical Biology and Medicine (hon.), Internat. Electron Paramagnetic Resonance Soc. (hon.), Asia-Pacific Electron Paramagnetic Resonance Soc. (life; founding mem.). Achievements include first to solve the important molecular structure of a vanadium dimer complex; proposed a novel mechanism of cancer chemoprevention involving reactive oxygen specific R05. Home: 5039 Dierker Rd Columbus OH 43220 Office: Ohio State Univ 420 W 12th Ave Columbus OH 43210 Office Fax: 614-292-8454. Personal E-mail: mvelayutha@yahoo.com. Business E-Mail: velayutham.1@osu.edu.

VELÁZQUEZ, NYDIA MARGARITA, congresswoman; b. Yabucoa, PR, Mar. 28, 1953; BA magna cum laude in Polit. Sci., U. PR, Rio Piedras, 1974; MA in Polit. Sci., NYU, 1976. Mem. faculty U. PR, Humacao, 1976—81; adj. prof. Puerto Rican studies CUNY Hunter Coll., 1981—83; spl. asst. Staff of US Rep. Edolphus Towns from NY, 1983; mem. City Coun., NYC, 1984—86; dir. Migration Divsn. Office Puerto Rico Dept. Labor and Human Resources, 1986—89; dir. Dept. Puerto Rican Cmty. Affairs in the US for the Commonwealth of PR, 1989—92; mem. US Congress from 12th NY dist., 1993—. Chairwoman small bus. com. US Congress, mem. fin. svcs. com. Named Woman of Yr., Hispanic Bus. Mag., 2003; recipient Small Bus. Beacon award, Nat. Small Bus. United, 2000, HerMANA award, MANA, 2002, Champion of Small Bus. Devel. award, Assn. Small Bus. Devel. Ctr., 2005. Democrat. Achievements include being the first Puerto Rican woman elected to the US Congress. Office: 266 Broadway Ste 201 Brooklyn NY 11211 Office Phone: 202-225-2361, 718-599-3658. *

VELAZQUEZ, OMAIDA CARIDAD, vascular surgeon, researcher; b. Pinar del Rio, Cuba, Oct. 25, 1966; d. Telesforo and Andrea Velazquez; m. Romulo Cuy, 1991; 1 child, Peter James Cuy. MD, U. Medicine and Dentistry N.J., 1991. Lic. physician N.J. Instr. gen. surgery U. Pa. Med. Sch., Phila., asst. instr. gen. surgery, 1992—96; attending surgeon Hosp. U. Pa., Phila., 1999—. Clin. faculty gen. and vascular surgery U. Pa. Med. Sch., Phila., 1999—; adj. asst. prof. Wistar Inst., Phila., 2001—, vis. scientist, 1999—2001; attending surgeon Presbyn. Med. Ctr., Phila., 1999—, Phila. VA Med. Ctr., 2001—03, Children's Hosp. Phila., 2001—; asst. prof. surgery U. Pa. Med. Sch., 1999—, ednl. coord. vascular divsn., 2002—. Contbr. articles to sci. rsch. jours. (Joel J. Roslyn award Assn.for Acad. Surgery, 2003); external reviewer: med. jours. Recipient Scholarship for the Advancement of Med. Edn., William F. Grupe Found., Inc., 1988, 1990, Krans-Henle Meml. Fund Scholarship, Krans-Henle Meml. Fund, 1989, von Liebig Found. Award for Excellence in Vascular Surg. Rsch., von Liebig Found., 2001, Residents Rsch. award, Phila. Acad. of Surgery, 1996, Young Careerist award, N.J. Bus. and Profl. Women, 1995, Surg. Student Rsch. award, Assn. for Academic Surgery, 1991, Dr. Gertrude Ash Meml. award, N.J. Med. Women's Assn., 1991, Merck Manual award for highest grade in internal medicine, 1990; grantee, NIH, 2003—. Fellow: ACS; mem.: AMA, AAAS, John Morgan Soc., Internat. Acad. Clin. and Applied Thrombosis/Hemostasis, Pa. Med. Soc., Am. Soc. Angiology, Soc. U. Surgeons, Phila. Acad. Surgery, Internat. Soc. Vascular Surgery, Bus. and Profl. Women, Assn. Women Surgeons, Assn. for Acad. Surgery, Am. Surg. Assn. Found., Am. Assn. Vascular Surgery, Soc. Clin. Vascular Surgery, N.Y. Acad. Sci., N.J. Med. Sch. Alumni Assn., Sigma Xi, Alpha Omega Alpha. Office: Hosp of Univ of Pa 3400 Spruce St 4 Silverstein Philadelphia PA 19104 Office Phone: 215-662-6451.

VELCULESCU, VICTOR E., oncologist, educator; MD in Medicine, Johns Hopkins U., Balt., PhD in Human Genetics and Molecular Biology. Postdoctoral fellow Sidney Kimmel Comprehensive Cancer Ctr. at Johns Hopkins, Balt.; assoc. prof. oncology, dir. cancer genetics Ludwig Cancer Ctr. at Johns Hopkins, Balt. Contbr. articles to profl. jours. Named one of Brilliant 10, Popular Sci. mag., 2003. Office: 1650 Orleans St Rm 5M05 Baltimore MD 21231 Office Phone: 410-955-8878. E-mail: velculescu@jhmi.edu.

VELENTINE, RALPH BURNET, music educator, department chairman; b. NYC, June 16, 1944; s. Burnet and Volina Cline Valentine; m. Carole Lynne Kirk, Dec. 28, 1969; children: Christopher Kirk, Wende Burnet. BA, Harvard U., Cambridge, Mass., 1966; MusM, Union Theol. Seminary, NY, 1968. Head music Convent Sacred Heart, Noroton, Conn., 1968—69, Choate Rosemary Hall, Wallingford, Conn., 1971—. Tchg. fellow St. Andrew's U., Scotland, 1985. Organist St. Andrew's Ch., Stamford, Conn., 1966—71, choirmaster, 1966—71, organist Meriden, Conn., 1971—76, choirmaster, 1971—76; organist St. John's Ch., West Hartford, Conn., 1976—, choirmaster, 1976—; bd. dir. Law Enforcement Assistance Found., NYC, 1968—; bd. dirs. Midstate Med. Ctr., Meriden, Conn., 1980—. Mem.: Organ Hist. Soc., Assn. Anglican Musicians, Am. Guild Organists (dean New Haven chpt. 1968—70). Avocations: model railroading, car restoration, pipe organ repair, hiking. Home: 747 Old Durham Rd Wallingford CT 06492 Office: Choate Rosemary Hall 333 Christian St Wallingford CT 06492

VELEV, MIROSLAV N., electrical and computer engineer, educator; arrived in US, 1991; BSEE, Yale U., New Haven, Conn., 1994, BS in Econs., 1994, MSEE, 1994; PhD in Elec. and Computer Engring., Carnegie Mellon U., Pitts., 2004. Tech. assoc. info. svcs. Credit Suisse First Boston Corp., NYC, 1994—95; rsch. asst. Carnegie Mellon U., Pitts., 1995—2001; instr. dept. elec. and computer engring. Ga. Inst. Tech., Atlanta; pvt. practice rschr. and cons., 2003—; founder, pres., CEO, Aries Design Automation, LLC, 2005—, Self-Actualizer, LLC, 2006—. Adj. lectr. Dept. Elec. and Computer Engring. U. Ill., Chgo., 2006—; mem. program coms. over 98 internat. computer sci. and computer engring. confs.; instr. dept. elec. and computer sci. Ga. Inst. Tech., Atlanta, 2002—03. Mem. editl. bd.: Jour. Universal Computer Sci., 2001—, Jour. on Satisfiability, Boolean Modeling and Computation, 2003—; contbr. articles and papers to confs. and jours. Recipient Franz Tuteur Meml. prize, Yale U., 1994, EDAA Outstanding Dissertation award, 2005. Mem.: IEEE, Am. Assn. for Artificial Intelligence, Am. Soc. for Engring. Edn., Assn. for Computing Machinery. Achievements include development of over 1,100 formulas used in research in the computer science field of Boolean satisfiability (SAT).

VELEZ, INES, oral pathologist, educator; b. Bogota, Colombia, Apr. 15, 1946; arrived in US, 1999; d. Jose and Emilia (Marulanda) Velez; m. Eduardo Tamara (div.); children: Luis Tamara, Clara Lucia Tamara; m. Guillermo Torres, Mar. 30, 1992. DDS, Colombian Coll. Odontology, 1979; postgrad., U. Fla., 1982—84; MEd, U. Los Andes, 1989; M in Laser Dentistry, Acad. Laser Dentistry, 1997. Cert. tchr. Fla. Chair., prof. pathology Colombian Coll. Odontology, 1984—92, pres. asst., 1989—92, dir. biopsy svc., 1984—95; chair, prof., dir. biopsy svc. Columbian Sch. Medicine, 1991—98, dir. bioclinical area, 1997—98; asst. prof. to assoc. prof., dir. oral and maxillofacial pathology, dir. biopsy svc. Nova Southeastern U., Ft. Lauderdale, Fla., 2000—. Lectr. in field. Contbr. articles to profl. jours. Recipient Best Student award, Coll. Sans Facon, 1963, Colombian Coll. Odontology, 1979, Educator award, Fla. Dental Assn., 2003, Golden Apple award, Nova Southeastern U., 2003, Ctr. of Excellence award, 2004. Mem.: ADA, Broward County Dental Assn., Fla. Dental Assn., Pierre Fouchard Acad., Acad. Laser Dentistry, Columbian Acad. Oral Pathology (founder), Am. Acad. Oral and Maxillofacial Pathology, Omicron Kappa Upsilon. Home: 3524 Parkside Dr Davie FL 33328 Office: Nova Southeastern U 3200 S University Dr Fort Lauderdale FL 33328 Home Phone: 954-262-7382; Office Phone: 954-472-7810. Business E-Mail: ivelez@nova.edu.

VELEZ, WILLIAM, education educator; b. Ponce, PR, Apr. 9, 1951; s. William Velez and Alicia Rodriguez; m. Barbara Jean Eckl, Dec. 12, 2003; children: Alfredo Joel, Marilka Rebeca. BA, U. P.R., San Juan, 1973; PhD, Yale U., 1983. Prof. U. Wis., Milw., 1981—. Author: Race and Ethnicity in the United States: An Institutional Approach, 1998, Foundations of American Higher Education, 1999. Bd. mem. Puerto Rican Found. Wis., Milw., 2001—07. Recipient Nat. Rsch. Svc. award, U. Wis.-Madison, Ctr. for Demography & Ecology, 1985—86; fellow, Ford Found., 1977—79; postdoctoral fellow, 1989—90. Mem.: Am. Sociol. Assn. (chair Latino sociology sect. 2001—02, Minority fellow 1974—77). Avocations: travel, golf. Home: 1820 N Oakland Ave Milwaukee WI 53202 Office: Univ Wis-Milwaukee 3210 N Maryland Ave Milwaukee WI 53211 Home Phone: 414-223-4494; Office Phone: 414-229-4388. Office Fax: 414-229-4266. Business E-Mail: velez@uwm.edu.

VELICER, JANET SCHAFBUCH, retired elementary school educator; b. Cedar Rapids, Iowa, Aug. 27, 1941; d. Allan J. and Geraldine Frances (Stuart) Schafbuch; m. Leland Frank Velicer, Aug. 17, 1963 (dec. Dec. 2000); children: Mark Allan, Gregory Jon, Daniel James. BS, Iowa State U., 1963, MS, 1966; cert. Elem. Edn., Mich. State U., 1976. Tchr. chemistry Prendergast High Sch., Upper Darby, Pa., 1964-65; tchr. home econs. Cardinal O'Hara High Sch., Springfield, Pa., 1965-66; substitute tchr. Pa., Mich., 1967-76; elem. tchr. Winans Elem. Sch., Waverly, Mich., 1976-78, Wardcliff Elem. Sch., Okemos, Mich., 1978-94; tchr. gifted and talented alternative program grades 4 and 5 Hiawatha Elem. Sch., Okemos, 1994-95; tchr. grade 4 Wardcliff Elem. Sch., 1995-2001; ret., 2001. Computer coord., Great Books coord.; dist. com. mem. math, computer, substance abuse, cable TV, evaluation revision Okemos Pub. Schs., Instrnl. Coun.; del. Mich. Edn. Exch. Opportunity Program, Germany, 1999. Author: (video) Wardcliff School Documentary, 1982, The Integrated Arts Program of the Okemos Elementary Schools, 1983. Citizens adv. com. to develop a five-yr. plan, 1982-83, bldg. utilization adv. com., 1983-84, cmty. use of schs. adv. com., 1984-85, strategic planning steering com., 1989-90, taking our schs. into tomorrow com., 1990-91, bonding election steering com., 1991; chmn. wellness com. Okemos Pub. Schs., 1993-95; bd. dirs. Okemos Music Patrons, 1981-86, pres., 1984-86; faculty rep. PTO; leadership coun. Nat. Inst. Clin. Application Behavioral Medicine, 1998-2004; chaperone Okemos HS German Club Exch., 1987, Benton Cmty. HS Spanish Club Exch., Mex., 1995, Costa Rica, 1999, Spain, 2001, 03. Recipient Classrooms of Tomorrow Tchr. award, Mich. Dept. Edn., 1990. Mem. NEA, NAFE, AARP, Nat. Ret. Tchrs. Assn., Mich. Edn. Assn., Okemos Edn. Assn. (exec. coun.), Mich. Coun. Tchrs. Math., Lansing Woman's Club (social com. 2003-04, program com. 2005-06), Mich. Athletic Club, Phi Kappa Phi, Omicron Nu, Iota Sigma Pi. Democrat. Avocations: swimming, reading, hiking, travel, cultural events. Home: 12880 Bradshaw St Overland Park KS 66213 Business E-Mail: jvelicer@msu.edu.

VELICK, SIDNEY FREDERICK, research biochemist, educator; b. Detroit, May 3, 1913; s. Harry Alexander and Ella (Stocker) V.; m. Bernadette Stemler, Sept. 5, 1941; children: William Frederick, Martha Elizabeth. BS, Wayne State U., 1935; PhD, U. Mich., 1938. Rsch. fellow parasitology Johns Hopkins U., Balt., 1939-40; rsch. assoc. chemistry Yale U., New Haven, 1941-45; mem. biol. chemistry dept. Washington U. Sch. Medicine, St. Louis, 1946-63, prof. biol. chemistry, 1958-64; prof., head dept. biol. chemistry U. Utah Coll. Medicine, 1964-79, prof. emeritus, 1988—. Mem. biochemistry study sect. NIH. Assoc. editor: Archives Biochemistry and Biophysics; editl. bd.: Jour. Biol. Chemistry; contbr. papers on enzyme chemistry to tech. lit. Co-founder, pres. Alliance for the Mentally Ill Utah, 1980-85. Mem. NAS, AAAS, Am. Soc. Biol. Chemists, Am. Chem. Soc., Sigma Xi. Home: 2514 S Elizabeth St # 6 Salt Lake City UT 84106

VELISAVLJEVIC, NENAD, physicist; b. Cuprija, Serbia, Serbia-Monteneg, Aug. 8, 1975; s. Filip and Snezana Velisavljevic. BS in Physics, Kutztown U., Pa., 1996—2000; MS in Physics, U. Ala., Birmingham, 2000—04, PhD in Physics, 2004—05. Grad. tchg. asst. dept. physics, U. Ala., 2000—01, rsch. asst., 2001—05, preparing future faculty intern, 2003—05; postdoctoral rsch. assoc. Los Alamos Nat. Lab., N.Mex., 2006—. Contbr. articles to profl. jours. Recipient Outstanding Grad. Tchg. Asst. award, Assn. Physics Tchrs., 2002, Cert. Excellence award, U. Ala., 2004; Space Grant Consortium NASA Space grant, Ala. NASA, 2003—04. Mem.: Am. Phys. Soc., Los Alamos Postdoctoral Assn.

VELLA, RUTH ANN, real estate executive; b. West Chester, Pa., Aug. 18, 1942; d. Eric and Carmella Tanberg; children: Michele Francette Vella, Nicole Renae Vella. Grad., Realtor's Inst. Real estate sales assoc. Reeve

Realty, Wilmington, Del., 1966-72; owner Realtor Heritage Realty, Wilmington, 1972—92; instr. sales Wilmington Coll., 1978-85; mem. faculty Del. State Coll., 1979—; prin., owner Omega Real Estate Sch., Newark, Del., 1989—; mgr. Weichert Realtors, 1996—2002; profl. devel. coord. Prudential Fox & Roach Realtors, 2002—. Instr. Realtor's Inst., dean, 1983, asst. dean, 1983—; owner, pres. Corporate Fitness of Del., 1991—; mem. edn. com. Del. Real Estate Commn., 2003-07; spkr. in field. Edn. com. Real Estate Commn., 2002—06, Del. Real Estate Commn.; dir. Del. Assn. Realtors, 2004—06. Named Educator of Yr., New Castle County, 1996. Mem. Del. Assn. Realtors (dir. 2005-07), New Castle County Bd. Realtors (dir. 1983-86, edn. com.), Womens Coun. Realtors (past state pres., gov.), Nat. Assn. Realtors (nat. speaker, energy conservation instr., Cert. Real Estate Broker instr.), Leading Edge Soc. Roman Catholic. Avocation: aerobics instr. and personal trainer. Office Phone: 302-999-9999. Business E-Mail: omega@realestateschool.com.

VELLACOTT, MAURICE, legislator; b. Wadena, Can., Sept. 29, 1955; married; 4 children. B, Briercrest Sch.; M, Can. Theol. Sem.; D, Trinity Internat. U. Elected mem. Saskatoon Dist. Health Bd.; mem. House of Commons, Ottawa, Canada, 1997—, vice chair standing com. human resources develop. Can., dep. critic com. human resources develop. Can., mem. sub. com. status of persons with disabilities, dep. critic health, dep. critic aboriginal affairs, vice-chair com. aboriginal affairs and natural resources, co-chair all-party pro-life caucus. Mem. Can. Alliance Family Caucus, ofcl. langs. com., environment com. Mem.: Sask. Landlord Assn., Sask. Taxpayers Assn., Saskatoon C. of C., Toastmasters, Can. Club Saskatoon. Conservative Party Can. Office: House of Commons Justice Bldg Ste 610 Ottawa ON Canada K1A 0A6 Address: Unit 3-844 51st St Saskatoon SK S7K 5C7 Canada E-mail: vellacott.m@parl.gc.ca.

VELLENGA, KATHLEEN OSBORNE, retired state legislator; b. Alliance, Nebr., Aug. 5, 1938; d. Howard Benson and Marjorie (Menke) Osborne; m. James Alan Vellenga, Aug. 9, 1959; children: Thomas, Charlotte Vellenga Landreau, Carolyn Vellenga Berman. BA, Macalester Coll., 1959. Tchr. St. Paul Pub. Schs., 1959-60, Children's Ctr. Montessori, St. Paul, 1973-74, Children's Ho. Montessori, St. Paul, 1974-79; mem. Minn. Ho. of Reps., St. Paul, 1980-94, mem. tax. com. and rules com., 1991—94, chmn. St. Paul del., 1987—90, chmn. criminal justice div., 1987—90, mem. Dem. steering com., 1981—94, chmn. judiciary, 1991, 92, chmn. edn. fin., 1993—94. Mem. St. Paul Family Svcs. Bd., 1994-95; exec. dir. St. Paul/Ramsey County Children's Initiative, 1994-2000. Chmn. Healthstart, St. Paul, 1987-91; mem. Children, Youth and Families Consortium, 1995-99, Macalester Coll. Bd. Alumni, 1995-2001; chair Minn. Higher Edn. Svcs. Coun., 2000—05, mem. 1995—; mem. Citizens League Bd., Minn., 1999-2002, State Commn. Cmty. Svc., 2000-04; bd. dirs. Sexual Violence Ctr., 2004-06; mem. U. Minn. Out of School Time Commn., 2004; mem. H.B. Fuller Found. Bd., 2005—. Mem. LWV (v.p. St. Paul chpt. 1979), Minn. Women Elected Ofcls. (vice chair 1994). Democrat. Presbyterian.

VELTMAN, MARTINUS J.G., retired physics educator; b. Waalwijk, The Netherlands, June 27, 1931; m. Anneke Veltman; children: Helene, Hugo, Martijn. BS in math and physics, U. Utrecht, The Netherlands, 1953, MS in theoretical physics, 1956, PhD in theoretical physics, 1963. Mem. FOM, Utrecht, Netherlands, 1959—61; fellow CERN, Geneva, 1961—63, staff mem., 1963—66, cons., 1966—72, sci. assoc., 1972—73, mem. sci. policy com., 1976—81, sci. assoc., 1996—97; prof. U. Utrecht, Netherlands, 1966—81; vis. prof. U. Mich., Ann Arbor, 1980, John D. McArthur prof. of physics, 1981—97, emeritus John D. McArthur prof. of physics, 1997—; prof. U. Autonoma de Madrid, 1988—96; Lorentz prof. of physics U. Leiden, Netherlands, 1989; Humboldt scientist Max Planck Inst., Munich, 1989—90, DESY, Hamburg, Germany, 1989—90. Postdoctoral SLAC, Stanford, Calif., 1963—64, Brookhaven Nat. Lab., LI, NY, 1966; vis. prof. U. Paris, Orsay, France, 1968—69. Recipient High Energy and Particle Physics prize, European Physics Soc., 1993, P.A.M. Dirac Medal and Prize, Internat. Ctr. for Theoretical Physics, 1996, Nobel prize in Physics, 1999. Office: U Mich Dept Physics Randall Lab 500 E University Ave Ann Arbor MI 48109-1120

VELUCHAMY, PETHINAIDU, marketing executive; m. Parameswari Veluchamy; children: Arun, Anu. BS in Chem., U. Madras, India; BS in Chem. Engring., Oreg. State U.; PhD in Chem. Engring., U. Ill. Founder Univ. Subscription Svc., 1974; owner, chmn., CEO Creative Automation Co., 1969—. Office: Veluchamy Cos 1213 Butterfield Rd Downers Grove IL 60515

VELURY, UMA, finance educator, researcher; arrived in U.S., 1988; d. RameshChandra Banerjee and Jagadeeswari Banerjee Kolachina; 1 child, Rajiv. BCom, Osmania U., 1986; PhD, U. SC, Columbia, 1999. Asst. prof. U. Del., Newark, 1999—2005, assoc. prof., 2005—. Mem. editl. bd.: Rsch. in Acctg. Regulation, 2006—; contbr. articles to profl. jours. Recipient Les Chadwick Excellence in Tchg. award, Beta Alpha Psi, 2003; grantee, U. Del., 2001, Coll. Bus. and Econs., 2004, 2006. Mem.: Am. Acctg. Assn. Office: University of Delaware 223 Purnell Hall Newark DE 19716 Home Phone: 302-454-7947; Office Phone: 302-831-1764.

VELZ, JOHN WILLIAM, retired literature educator; b. Englewood, NJ, Aug. 5, 1930; s. Clarence Joseph and Harriet Josephine (O'Brien) Velz; m. Judith M. Palmer, Jan. 22, 1953 (div. Aug. 1967); m. Sarah Elizabeth Campbell, Oct. 18, 1967 (div. Apr. 2001); children: Sue Marie, Gwendolyn Anne, Jennifer Germaine. BA in English with high distinction and honors, U. Mich., 1953, MA in English and French, 1954; PhD in English and Classical Tradition, U. Minn., 1963. Instr. Coll. St. Thomas, St. Paul, 1958-60; asst. prof. English Rice U., Houston, 1963-69; prof. U. Tex., Austin, 1969-96, prof. emeritus, 1996—. Vis. prof. U. Paul Valery, Montpelier, France, 1977-78, Julius Maximillians U., Wuerzburg, Germany, 1981-82, 85-86; asst. dir., lit. adv. Odessa Shakespeare Festival, 1977; faculty mem. Oreg. Shakespeare Festival, 1979; lectr. tour Cen. and Ea. Europe univs., 1993; dir. acad. prodns. of Shakespeare and medieval drama; mem. Acad. Adv. Coun. Globe Theatre Ctr., 1981—; mem. U.S. Com. for Shakespeare's Globe, 1990—; presenter over 100 papers and lectures to learned socs.; reviewer over 50 books and theatrical prodns. Author: Shakespeare and the Classical Tradition, 1968, electronic edit., 2000 (ALA citation, Assn. Coll. and Rsch. Librs. citation); editor: Julius Caesar in MLA's New Variorum Shakespeare, 1966-95, (N.Am.) Cahiers Elisabethains, 1979-81; Shakespeare's English Histories: A Quest for Form and Genre, 1996; co-editor: Collected Papers of James G. McManaway, 1969, One Touch of Shakespeare: Letters of Joseph Crosby to Joseph Parker Norris 1875-1878, 1986, Pegasus Bibliography of Shakespeare's Roman Works, 2003; contbr. over 60 scholarly, interpretive articles, mainly on Shakespeare and on medieval drama, to profl. jours.; mem. editl. bd. Shakespeare Quar., 1975-98, Classical and Modern Lit., 1981-85, Tex. Studies in Lit. and Lang., 1969-92, Shakespeare and the Classroom, 1993—; mem. editl. adv. bd. Complete Works of Shakespeare, 3d edit., 1980, 4th edit., 1992, 5th edit., 1997, 6th edit., 2003; cons. editor South Ctrl. Rev., 1989-92; mem. cons. com. Internat. Studies in Shakespeare and His Contemporaries, 1990—. Recipient Fulbright award, 1977-78, 81-82; recipient Oreon E. Scott award U. Mich., 1953; NEH fellow, 1967-68; Folger Library fellow, 1968 Mem. MLA (life), Assn. Lit. Scholars and Critics, Internat. Shakespeare Assn. (charter), Shakespeare Assn. Am., Malone Soc., Renaissance English Text Soc., Medieval and Renaissance Drama Soc., Marlowe Soc. of Am., H.W. Fowler Soc. (charter), Internat. Soc. Classical Tradition, Phi Beta Kappa, Phi Kappa Phi, Phi Eta Sigma. Home: 809 W 32d St Austin TX 78705-2115 Business E-Mail: jvelz@ccwf.cc.utexas.edu. *Academic life is predicated on the obligation to teach as generously as we have been taught, to serve others as we have been served. This sense of mutuality has been a rationale for my professional life, though it would be impossible to pay all I owe.*

VELZY, CHARLES O., mechanical engineer; b. Oak Park, Ill., Mar. 17, 1930; s. Charles R and Ethel B. V.; m. Marilyn A. Gilman, Aug. 17, 1957; children: Charles Mark, Barbara Helen, Patricia Ethel. BSM.E., U. Ill., 1953, BS in Civil Engring., 1960, MS in San. Engring., 1959. Registered profl. engr., Pa., 8 other states. Design engr., project engr. Nussbaumer, Clarke & Velzy, NYC, 1959-66; sec.-treas., dir. Charles R Velzy Assos., Inc., Armonk, N.Y., 1966-76; pres. Charles R. Velzy Assoc., Inc., 1976-92; v.p. Roy F. Weston Inc., 1987-92; pres. Charles O. Velzy, P.E., White Haven, Pa., 1992—. Contbr. articles to profl. jours. Mem. White Plains (N.Y.) Bldg. Code Appeals Bd., 1970-92; mem. Kidder Township Planning Bd., 2006—. With U.S. Army, 1954-56. Recipient Disting. Alumnus award U. Ill., 1989. Fellow ASME (hon.; chmn. solid waste processing divsn 1973-74, mem. bd. rsch. and tech. dev. 1974-78, 2000—, bd. govs. 1983-84, pres. 1989-90, Centennial medal 1980, medal of achievement 1981, Dedicated Svc. award 1986), Am. Cons. Engrs. Coun.; mem. ASCE (life), NSPE (Engr. of the Yr. 1980), Am. Acad. Environ. Engrs. (trustee 1984-87, treas. 1993-97, Stanley E. Kappe award 1998), Am. Water Works Assn. (life), Water Environ. Fedn., Air Waste Mgmt. Assn. Methodist. *After deciding on what is needed in a specific situation, based on the facts, establish your objectives and goals and persist to a successful conclusion.*

VEMPATI, RAJAN K., research scientist, educator; arrived in US, 1984, naturalized; s. Venkateswarlu and Saraswati Vempati; m. Padmavathy Patla Vempati; 1 child, Krishna. BS, Punjab Agrl. U., India, 1976—80, MS, 1980—83; PhD, Tex. A&M U., Coll. Station, 1984—88. NRC jr. postdoctoral canditate NASA-Johnson Space Ctr., Houston, 1990—92; vis. prof. Lamar U., Beaumont, Tex., 1992—95; pres. ChK Grp., Inc., Plano, Tex., 1998—. Vis. postdoctoral candidate U. Ill., Urbana, 1988—89; adj. prof. U. Arlington, Tex., 2000—06, So. Meth. U., Dallas, 2000—. Contbr. articles to profl. jours. Mem. RMI Found., Dallas, 2004—06; advisor Paul Quinn Coll., Dallas, 2006—. Grantee Jr. NRC Postdoctoral Fellow award, NAS, 2000—02; Rsch. grant to convert off-white rice hulls to ZSM 5 (Zeolite), NSF, 1998, Rsch. grant for zeolite coated nanophase Fe oxide for arsenic removal, USDA, 2000, 2002, Rsch. grant to convert rice hulls to off-white rice hull ash, NSF, 2006. Mem.: Am. Water & Wastewater Assn. Achievements include patents for off-white rice hull ash for high performance cement; ZSM 5 zeolite from rice hull ash; zeolite coated nanophase Fe oxide for arsenic removal; innovative methods to stabilize Mn(III)- and Mn(VII)-oxides; manufacturing of zeolite coated nanophase Fe oxide; patents pending for methods to degrade chemical warfare agents; complete plant growth medium to save excess use of fertilizer and water. Home: 2045 Belgium Dr Plano TX 75025 Office: ChK Group Inc 2045 Belgium Dr Plano TX 75025 Office Phone: 214-768-1278. Office Fax: 214-768-4089; Home Fax: 214-768-4089. Personal E-mail: chkgroup@worldnet.att.net. Business E-Mail: chkgroup@smu.edu.

VENABLE, ANDREW A., JR., library director; BBA, Va. State U., 1967; MLS, Case Western Res. U. Rschr. Std. Oil Co. Ohio; asst. dir. pers. to head fin. and adminstrv. svcs. Cleve. Pub. Libr., 1970—83, bus. mgr.- treas., head cmty. svcs., dep. dir., 1997—99, dir., 1999—, East Cleve. Pub. Libr., 1983—89, Gary Pub. Libr. Sys., Ind.; dir. libr. svcs. Vocat. Tech. Coll.; dep. dir. DC Pub. Libr. Sys., 1994—97. Mem. Ohio Libr. Coun. Named Libr. of Yr., OLC, 2001. Mem.: ALA, Alpha Phi Alpha. Office: Cleve Pub Libr 325 Superior Ave NE Cleveland OH 44114 Office Phone: 216-623-2827. Business E-Mail: andrew.venable@cpl.org. *

VENABLE, DIANE DAILEY, retired elementary school educator; b. Sedro Woolley, Wash., June 11, 1939; d. Howard A. and LaVerne L. Dailey; m. Thomas C. Venable, June 28, 1974; 1 child, Erin Dailey. B, Simpson Coll., 1962; B of Elem. Edn., Seattle Pacific U., 1966. Tchr. elem. sch. Kent Schs., Calif., 1966—69, Seattle Schs., 1969—76, Calif. Schs., Simi Valley, 1996—98; ret., 1998. Chair 37th Dem. Assembly Dist., 1993—94; missions elder Emmanuel Presbyn. Ch., Thousand Oaks, Calif., 2000—03. Mem.: Red Hat Soc. Avocations: scrapbooks, reading, travel, golf. Home: 1024 Via Palermo Thousand Oaks CA 91320 E-mail: ddvenable@adelphia.net.

VENAYAGAMOORTHY, GANESH KUMAR, electrical engineer, computer engineer, educator; b. Jaffna, Sri Lanka, Feb. 25, 1972; s. Sinnathamby Nagalingam Venayagamoorthy and Neelambigai Kathiravetpillai. B of Engring. with honors, Abubakar Tafawa Balewa U., Bauchi, Nigeria, 1994; MS of Engring., U. Natal, Durban, South Africa, 1999, PhD, 2003. Grad. asst. Abubakar Tafawa Balewa U., Bauchi, Nigeria, 1994—94; computer engr. Sq. One Comnet, Maseru, Lesotho, 1994—95; sr. lectr. Durban Inst. Tech., Durban, Kwazulu Natal, South Africa, 1996—2002; asst. prof. U. Mo., Rolla, 2002—06, assoc. prof., 2006—. Dir. Real-Time Power and Intelligent Systems Lab., U. Mo., Rolla, 2004—. Contbr. articles to profl. jours. Recipient Young Investigator award, ONR, 2002, Internat. Neural Network Soc., 2003, Outstanding Young Engr. award, IEEE St. Louis Sect., 2004, Outstanding Sect. Mem. award, 2006, Faculty Excellence award, U. Mo., Rolla, 2005, Tchg. Excellence award, 2006, Outstanding Young Mem. award, IEEE Industry Applications Soc., 2005, Young Achievers award, South Inst. Elec. Engrs., 2005, Walter Fee Outstanding Young Engr. award, IEEE Power Engring. Soc., 2006; grantee, NSF, 2004, NSF Career award, 2004. Mem.: IEEE (sr.; chair St. Louis chpt. 2004—06, Outstanding Sect. Mem. 2006), Inst. of Engring. and Tech. U.K., Inst. Elec. Engrs., Am. Soc. Engring. Edn., Internat. Neural Network Soc., South African Inst. Elec. Engrs. (sr.). Office: Univ Mo 132 Emerson Electric Co Hall Rolla MO 65409 Office Phone: 573-341-6641. Office Fax: 573-341-4532. E-mail: gkumar@ieee.org.

VENCLOVA, TOMAS A., literature and language professor, writer; b. Klaipeda, Lithuania, Sept. 11, 1937; US; s. Antanas Venclova and Eliza Rackauskaite; m. Tanya L. Milovidova, Mar. 18, 1990; children: Andrius, Maria. Degree, U. Vilnius, Lithuania, 1960; PhD, Yale U., 1985; D (hon.), U. Lublin, Poland, 1991, Jagallonien U., Krakow, Poland, 2000, U. Torun, Poland, 2005. Lectr. U. Vilnius, 1966—73; jr. fellow Acad. Sci., Lithuania, 1974—76; regents prof. U. Calif., Berkeley, 1977; lectr. UCLA, 1977—80; lectr. to assoc. prof. Yale U., New Haven, 1980—93, prof., 1993—. Author: Sign of Speech, 1972, Winter Dialogue, 1991, Aleksander Wat: Life and Art of an con-dost, 1996 (Waclaw Ledwicki prize, 96, Urechinich prize, 97), Forms of Hope, 1999. Founding mem. Lithuanian Helsinki Group, 1976. Recipient Internat. Lit. prize, Vilenica, Slovenia, 1990, Lithuanian Nat. prize, 0, New Culture of New Europe award, Poland, 2005. Mem.: ATSEEL, AAASS, Assn. for Advancement of Pub. Studies (pres. 1989—91), Pen in Exile, Pen (mem. exec. bd. 1981—). Achievements include exiled from USSR due to activity with Lithuanian Helsinki Group. Avocation: travel. Home: 100 York St Apt 12-5 New Haven CT 06511 Office: Yale Univ Slovic Dept New Haven CT 06520

VENDER, ROBERT LOUIS, medical educator; b. Scranton, Pa., Dec. 26, 1952; s. Louis and Martha Vender; m. Lucina Marie DeRoner, Oct. 2, 1982; children: Stephanie Rose, Jonathan Robert, Robert John. BA in Math., Franklin Marshall Coll., Lancaster, Pa., 1974; MD, Hahnemann U., Phila., 1979. Resident Med. Coll. Va., Richmond, 1979—82; fellow pulmonary and critical care medicine U. NC, Chapel Hill, 1982—86; asst. prof. medicine Med. Coll. Pa., Phila., 1986—94; assoc. med. dir. DuPont-Merck/DuPont Pharm. Co., Wilmington, Del., 1994—99; assoc. prof. medicine Pa. State Milton S. Hershey Med. Ctr., 2001—, dir. adult Cystic Fibrosis program, 2001—. Home: 740 Zermatt Dr Hummelstown PA 17036 Office: Pa State Milton S Hershey Med Ctr 500 University Dr Hershey PA 17033

VENDITTI, CLELIA ROSE See PALMER, CHRISTINE

VENDLER, HELEN HENNESSY, literature educator, poetry critic; b. Boston, Apr. 30, 1933; d. George and Helen (Conway) Hennessy; 1 son, David. AB, Emmanuel Coll., 1954; PhD, Harvard U., 1960; PhD (hon.), U. Oslo, 1981; DLitt (hon.), Smith Coll., 1980, Kenyon Coll., 1982, U. Hartford, 1985, Union Coll., 1986, Columbia U., 1987, Washington U., 1991, Marlboro Coll., 1989, Yale U., 2000; DHL (hon.), Fitchburg State U., 1990, Dartmouth Coll., 1992, U. Mass., 1992, Bates Coll., 1992, U. Toronto, Ont., Can., 1992, Trinity Coll., Dublin, Ireland, 1993, U. Cambridge, 1997, Nat. U., Ireland, 1998, Wabash Coll., 1998, U. Mass, Dartmouth, 2000, Yale U., 2000, U. Aberdeen, 2000, Tufts U., 2001, Amherst Coll., 2002, Colby Coll., 2003; DHL, Bard Coll., 2005. Instr. Cornell U., Ithaca, NY, 1960-63; lectr. Swarthmore (Pa.) Coll. and Haverford (Pa.) Coll., 1963-64; asst. prof. Smith Coll., Northampton, Mass., 1964-66; assoc. prof. Boston U., 1966-68, prof., 1968-85. Fulbright lectr. U. Bordeaux, France, 1968-69; vis. prof. Harvard U., 1981-85, Kenan prof., 1985—, Porter U. prof., 1990—, assoc. acad. dean, 1987-92, sr. fellow Harvard Soc. Fellows, 1981-93; poetry critic New Yorker, 1978-99; mem. ednl. adv. bd. Guggenheim Found., 1991-01, Pulitzer Prize Bd., 1991-99; Mellon lectr. Nat. Gallery, 2006. Author: Yeats's Vision and the Later Plays, 1963, On Extended Wings: Wallace Stevens' Longer Poems, 1969, The Poetry of George Herbert, 1975, Part of Nature, Part of Us, 1980, The Odes of John Keats, 1983, Wallace Stevens: Words Chosen Out of Desire, 1984; editor: Harvard Book of Contemporary American Poetry, 1985, Voices and Visions: The Poet in America, 1987, The Music of What Happens, 1988, Soul Says, 1995, The Given and the Made, 1995, The Breaking of Style, 1995, Poems, Poets, Poetry, 1995, The Art of Shakespeare's Sonnets, 1997, Seamus Heaney, 1998, Coming of Age as a Poet, 2003, Poets Thinking, 2004, Invisible Listeners, 2005, Our Secret Discipline, 2007. Bd. dirs. Nat. Humanities Ctr., 1989—93. Recipient Lowell prize, 1969, Explicator prize, 1969, award Nat. Inst. Arts and Letters, 1975, Radcliffe Grad. Soc. medal, 1978, Nat. Book Critics award, 1980, Keats-Shelley Assn. award, 1994, Truman Capote award, 1996; Fulbright fellow, 1954, Guggenheim fellow, 1971-72, Am. Coun. Learned Socs. fellow, 1971-72, NEH fellow, 1980, 85, 94, 04, 05, fellow Churchill Coll., Cambridge, 1980, Charles Stewart Parnell fellow Magdalene Coll., Cambridge, 1996, hon. fellow, 1996—; NEH Jefferson Lectr. scholar US Fed. Govt., 2004-05. Mem. MLA (exec. coun. 1972-75, pres. 1980), AAAL, English Inst. (trustee 1977-85), Am. Acad. Arts and Scis. (v.p. 1992-95), Norwegian Acad. Letters and Sci., Am. Philos. Soc. (Jefferson medal 2000), Phi Beta Kappa. Home: 54 Trowbridge St 2 Cambridge MA 02138-4113 Office: Harvard U Dept English Barker Center Cambridge MA 02138-3929 Office Phone: 617-496-6028.

VENEGAS, ARTURO, JR., protective services official; b. San Nicolas de Ibarra, Jalisco, Mexico, Dec. 22, 1948; m. Anna Marie Venegas; children: Angela, Adriana, Anthony, Andrew. BA, U. San Francisco, 1978; MS in Mgmt., Calif. Poly., Pomona, 1991. Police officer Fresno (Calif.) Police Dept., 1970-75, police specialist, 1975-79, sgt., field supr., 1979, 80-85, lt., 1985-90, lt., acting divsn. comdr. adminstrv. svcs., 1990-92, dep. chief police investigations divsn., 1992-93; chief program devel., program mgr. State Office Criminal Justice Planning, Sacramento, 1979-80; chief of police Sacramento Police Dept., 1993—2006; police super session exec. Camden (NJ) Police Dept., 2006—. Mem. Calif. Atty. Gen.'s Policy Coun. on Violence Prevention; bd. dirs. Safety Ctr.; mem. exec. bd. Sacramento Safe Sts.; mem. adv. bd. Cath. Social Svcs. With U.S. Army, 1966-68. Mem. Internat. Assn. Chiefs of Police, Calif. Assn. Chiefs of Police, Calif. Peace Officers Assn. (chair law and legis. com.), Police Exec. Rsch. Forum, Ctrl. Sierra Police Chiefs Assn., FBI Nat. Acad. Assocs., Latino Peace Officers Assn., Hispanic-Am. Command Officers Assn., Am. Legion, Footprinters Internat., KC. Office: Camden Police Dept Police Adminstrn Bldg 8th & Fed St One Police Plz Camden NJ 08103

VENEMAN, ANN MARGARET, international organization official, former secretary of agriculture; b. Modesto, Calif., June 29, 1949; d. John G. and Nita D. (Bomberger) V.; div. BA in polit. sci., U. Calif., Davis, 1970; MA in pub. policy, U. Calif., Berkeley, 1971; JD, Hastings Coll. Law, 1976. Bar: Calif. 1976, U.S. Supreme Ct. 1981. Atty. San Francisco Bay Area Rapid Transit Dist., 1976-78; dep. pub. defender Stanislaus County., Calif., 1978-80; ptnr. Damrell, Damrell & Nelson, Modesto, 1980-86; asst. to adminstr., Fgn. Agrl. Svc. USDA, Washington, 1986-87, assoc. adminstr., Fgn. Agrl. Svc., 1987-89, dep. under sec. Internat. Affairs and Commodity Programs, 1989-91, dep. sec., 1991-93, sec. of agr., 2001—05; atty. Patton, Boggs & Blow LLP, Washington, 1993—95; sec. Calif. Dept. Food and Agr., 1995—99; ptnr. Nossaman, Guthner, Knox & Elliott LLP, Sacramento, 1999—2000; exec. dir. UNICEF, 2005—. Bd. dir. Close Up Found. Office: UNICEF 3 United Nations Plz New York NY 10017 *

VENERABLE, GRANT DELBERT, II, chemist, educator, systems scientist; b. LA, Aug. 31, 1942; s. Grant Delbert and Thelma L. (Scott) Venerable. BS Chemistry, UCLA, 1965; MS Chemistry, U. Chgo., 1967, PhD Physical Chemistry, 1970; postdoctoral studies, UCLA Lab. Nuclear Medicine, 1971. Assoc. prof. chemistry Calif. Polytech. State U., San Luis Obispo, 1972—78; Sloan lectr. chemistry U. Calif., Santa Cruz, 1978—80; cons. software Motorola and other Cos., Cupertino, 1981—89; lectr. Coll. Ethnic Studies San Francisco State U., 1989—96; assoc. provost, assoc. v.p., prof. chemistry Chgo. (Ill.) State U., 1996—98; provo and v.p. acad. affairs Morris Brown Coll., Atlanta, 1998—2002; v.p. acad. affairs Lincoln U., Pa., 2002. Sec. State Bd. Calif. Alliance for Arts Edn., 1985—91. Author: (Book) The Discovery of Calculus of Transformations in Chemistry, 1974, The Paradox of the Silicon Savior, 1988, Managing in a Five Dimension Economy, 1999. Bd. dirs. City Quest, Chgo., 1998—2000. Recipient Achievement award, Calif. Alliance for Art Edn., 1990, Urban Edn. Achievement award, JGT Found., San Francisco, 1996. Mem.: AAAS, Am. Chem Soc., Nat. Orgn. for Profl. Advancement of Black Chemists and Chem. Engrs., Alpha Chi Sigma. Avocations: organist, painting, swimming. Office: Office Acad Affairs Lincoln U Box 179 Lincoln University PA 19352 Home: 300 Gaelic Way Tyrone GA 30290 Office Phone: 484-365-7436. Office Fax: 484-365-8101. Personal E-mail: ventwo@aol.com.

VENERABLE, SHIRLEY MARIE, retired gifted and talented educator; b. Washington, Nov. 12, 1931; d. John Henry and Jessie Josephine (Young) Washington; m. Wendell Grant Venerable, Feb. 15, 1959; children: Angela Elizabeth Maria Venerable-Joyner, Wendell Mark. PhB, Northwestern U., 1963; MA, Roosevelt U., 1976, postgrad., 1985; student in Life Long Studies, Triton C.C., River Grove, Ill., 2002. Cert. in diagnostic and prescriptive reading, gifted edn., finger math., fine arts, Ill. Tchr. Lewis Champlin Sch., 1963-74, John Hay Acad., Chgo., 1975-87, Leslie Lewis Elem. Sch., Chgo., 1988-99, Robert Emmet Sch., Chgo., 1999—; self employed tutorial programs, 1999—2003; ret., 2003. Sponsor Reading Marathon Club, Chgo., 1991—; co-creator Project SMART-Stimulating Math. and Reading Techniques John Hay Acad., Chgo., 1987-90, curriculum coord., 1985-87; creative dance student, tchr. Kathryn Duham Sch., N.Y.C., 1955-56; creative dance tchr. Doris Patterson Dance Sch., Washington, 1953-55; recorder evening divsn. Northwestern U., Chgo., 1956-62; exch. student tchr. Conservatory Dance Movements, Chgo., 1958-59; art cons. Chgo. Pub. Sch., 1967. Author primary activities Let's Act and Chat, 1991-94, Teaching Black History Through Classroom Tours, 1989-90. Solicitor, vol. United Negro Coll. Fund, Chgo., 1994; sponsor 37th Ward Reading Assn. Marathon, Chgo., 1991-94, 99; active St. Giles Coun. Cath. Women, 1985-96; vol. REAC Ctr. Programs Books, Info., Literacy and Learning, 1997-98. Recipient Meritorious award United Negro Coll. Fund, 1990, 94, Recognition award Alderman Percy Giles, Chgo., 1993,

Hall of Fame award Nat. Women in Achievement, Inc., 2005. Mem.: ASCD (assoc. Recognition of Svcs. award 1989), Internat. Reading Assn., Nat. Women of Achievement Assn. (Chgo. chpt.), Nat. Women's History Mus., Phi Delta Kappa (charter), Sigma Gamma Rho (Delta Sigma grad. chpt. 1963—93, Sigma chpt. 1992, Eta Xi Sigma chpt.), Eta Xi Sigma (Pearl award for excellence in edn. 1997). Roman Catholic. Home: 1108 N Euclid Ave Oak Park IL 60302-1219

VENETSANOPOULOS, ANASTASIOS NICOLAOS, electrical engineer, educator; b. Athens, Greece, June 19, 1941; arrived in Can., 1968; s. Nicolaos Anastasios and Elli (Papacondilis) Venetsanopoulos. Diploma, Athens Coll., 1960; B in Elec. and Mech. Engring., Nat. Tech. U., Athens, 1965; MS, Yale U., 1966, MPhil, 1968, PhD, 1969; doctorate (hon.), Nat. Tech. U., Athens, 1994. Registered profl. engr., Greece, Ont. Asst. in instrn. engring. and applied sci. Yale U., 1966-68, research asst., 1968-69; lectr. U. Toronto, Ont., Can., 1968-69, asst. prof. elec. engring., 1970-73, assoc. prof., 1973-81, prof., 1981—, chmn. communications group dept. elec. engring., 1974-78, 81-86, assoc. chmn. elec. and computer engring., 1978—79, 1997—, acting chmn. elec. and computer engring., 1998—99, dean applied sci. and engring., 2001—06; v.p. rsch.-innovation Ryerson U., Toronto, 2006—. Acad. visitor Imperial Coll. Arts and Tech. U. London, 1979—80; vis. prof. Nat. Tech. U. Athens, 1979—80, Fed. U. Tech. Lausanne, Switzerland, 1986—87, Switzerland, 1993—94, U. Florence, Italy, 1987; cons. elec. engring. Consociates Ltd.; chmn. multimedia Bell-Can., 1999—. Editor: Can. Elec. Engring. Jour., 1981—83; contbr. articles to profl. jours., chapters to books. Mem. allocations and agy. rels. com. United Cmty. Fund, Toronto, 1971—74; pres. Hellenic-Can. Cultural Soc., 1972—75; sec. gen. Greek Cmty. Met. Toronto, 1973—75. Recipient Excellence in Innovation award, Info. Tech. Rsch. Ctr., 1996; grantee Fulbright Travel, US, 1965, Def. Rsch. Bd. Can., 1972—75, UN, NSF, J. P. Bickell Found., Natural Scis. and Engring. Rsch. Coun. Can. Fellow: IEEE (fin. chmn. internat. symposium on circuit theroy 1973, tech. program chmn. internat. conf. comm. 1978, 1986, vice-chmn. Toronto sect. 1976—77, chmn. 1977—79, assoc. editor Transactions on circuits and sys. 1985—87, guest editor spl. 1987, tech. prgram chmn. internat. conf. on acoustics speech and signal proc 1991, Millenium medal 2001—), Can. Acad. Engring., Engring. Inst. Can.; mem.: Intercultural Coun. (chmn. ednl. com. 1971—80, sr. v.p. 1977—80), Am.-Hellenic Ednl. Progress Assn. (v.p. Toronto sect. 1973—75, pres. 1975—77), N.Y. Acad. Scis., Yale Sci. and Engring. Assn., Can. Soc. Elec. Engring. (chmn. Toronto sect. 1975—77, nat. dir. 1976—88, pres. 1983—86), Assn. Profl. Mech. Engrs. Greece, Assn. Profl. Elec. Engrs. Greece, Assn. Profl. Engrs. Ont., Tech. Chamber Greece, Sigma Xi. Office: Ryerson U 350 Victoria St Toronto ON Canada M5B 2K3 Office Phone: 416-979-5283. Business E-Mail: tasvenet@ryerson.ca.

VENEZIA, WILLIAM THOMAS, school system administrator, counseling consultant; b. Jersey City, Mar. 20, 1952; s. Thomas Michael and Carmela (Crocarno) Venezia; m. Josephine DePaul. BA in History, St. Peter's Coll., 1974, postgrad., 1978-79, MA in Adminstrn./Supervision, 1984; postgrad., Jersey City State Coll., 1988-90. Cert. tchr., prin., supt., N.J.; cert. in student personnel svcs., N.J. Tchr. various schs. Jersey City Bd. Edn., 1976-92; guidance counselor P.S. # 27/Dickinson High Sch., Jersey City, 1990-92; counselor Montclair (N.J.) State Coll., 1991-92; asst. prin. Frelinghuysen Sch., Morristown, NJ, 1992-97; prin. Alexander Hamilton Sch., Morristown, 1997—2001; dir. guidance Morris Sch. Dist., 2001—02; prin. Thomas Jefferson Sch., Morristown, 2002—; interim prin. Frelinghuysen Mid. Sch., 2003. Asst. football coach various schs., 1975-89; instr., adminstr. G.E.D. and A.B.E. programs Jersey City Bd. Edn., 1977-82; interim bd. sec., bus. adminstr. Weehawken Bd. Edn., 1984; mem. adv. bd. Cornerstone Sch., Jersey City, 1988-91; pre-coll. counselor UPWARD Bound project Montclair State Coll., 1991; cons. N.J. Devils hockey team, East Rutherford, 1992, D.A.R.E. program Hudson County Prosecutor, Jersey City, 1992.h Vol. counselor Giant Steps adolescent substance abuse treatment facility; active Jersey City, 1993, Jersey City Parents' Coun. Mem. ASCD, NEA, Am. Football Coaches Assn., N.J. Edn. Assn., Assn. Adult Edn. in N.J., N.J. Assn. Sch. Bus. Officials, Hudson County Personnel and Guidance Assn., Morris Sch. Dist.Adminstrv. Assn. (pres. 2004—), Iron Bound Execs. Assn., Hoboken Elks. Avocations: basketball, travel, antiques. Home: 1 Hickory St Clark NJ 07066-1924 Office: Thomas Jefferson Sch 101 James St Morristown NJ 07960 Office Phone: 973-292-2089. Personal E-mail: vendpl@comcast.net. Business E-Mail: bill.venezia@msdk12.net.

VENINGA, JAMES FRANK, humanities educator, editor, writer; b. Milw., Aug. 26, 1944; s. Frank and Otila Ann (Mauch) V.; m. Catherine M. Williams, Apr. 5, 1969; 1 child, Jennifer Elisa. BA, Baylor U., 1966; MTheol Studies, Harvard U., 1968; MA, Rice U., 1973, PhD, 1974. Instr. U. St. Thomas, Houston, 1971-73, asst. prof., 1974; asst. dir. Tex. Coun. for Humanities, Austin, 1975, exec. dir., 1976-97; pres., dir. Inst. for the Humanities at Salado, 1997—2000; CEO, campus dean U. Wis.-Marathon County, Wausau, 2000—07, assoc. prof. religious studies, 2000—. Dir. Nat. Fedn. State Humanities Couns., Washington, 1980-83; trustee Inst. for Humanities at Salado, Tex., 1980-85; vis. prof. Am. studies U. Tex., Austin, 1984, sr. lectr. Am. studies, 1986; vis. prof. Am. studies Baylor U., 1999. Author: The Humanities and Civic Imagination, 1999; editor: The Biographer's Gift, 1983, Vietnam in Remission, 1985, Standing with the Public, 1997; editor-in-chief Tex. Jour. Ideas, History and Culture, 1982-97. Recipient Baylor Man of Merit award Baylor U., 1985. Office: U Wis 518 S 7th Ave Wausau WI 54401-5362 Home: 11074 N Loon Bay Ln Hayward WI 54843 Office Phone: 715-261-6223. Business E-Mail: james.veninga@uwc.edu.

VENKATA, SUBRAHMANYAM SARASWATI, engineering educator, researcher; b. Nellore, Andhra Pradesh, India, June 28, 1942; came to U.S., 1968; s. Ramiah Saraswati and Lakshmi (Alladi) V.; m. Padma Subrahmanyam Mahadevan, Sept. 3, 1971; children: Sridevi Ramakumar, Harish Saraswati. BSEE, Andhra U., Waltair, India, 1963; MSEE, Indian Inst. Tech., Madras, 1965; PhD, U. S.C., 1971. Registered profl. engr., W.Va., Wash. Lectr. in elec. engring. Coimbatore (India) Inst. Tech., 1965-66; planning engr. S.C. Elec. & Gas Co., Columbia, 1969-70; postdoctoral fellow U. S.C., Columbia, 1971; instr. elec. engring. U. Mass., Lowell, 1971-72; asst. prof. W.Va. U., Morgantown, 1972-75, assoc. prof., 1975-79; prof. U. Wash., Seattle, 1979-96; prof., chmn. dept. elec. and computer engring. Iowa State U., Ames, 1996—2002, Palmer chair prof. dept. elec. and computer engring., 2003—; dean, disting. univ. prof. Wallace H. Coulter Sch. Engring., Clarkson U., Potsdam, NY, 2004—05; v.p., exec. cons. KEMA, 2005—. Cons. Puget Sound Energy Co., Bellevue, Wash., 1980-93, GEC/Alsthom, NYC, 1991-92; series editor, bd. dirs. PWS Pub. Co., 1991-98; affiliate prof. U. Wash., Seattle, 1997-00. Author: Introduction of Electrical Energy Devices, 1987; editor, IEEE Transactions on Power Systems, 1998-00, IEEE/PES Rev. Letters, 1999-03, Internat. Jour. Sys.; mem. editl. bd. IEEE/PES/Power and Energy Mag., 2003-; patentee adaptive var compensators, adaptive power quality conditioner, distribution reliability based design software. Advisor Explorers Club, Morgantown, 1976-78; sec. Hindu Temple and Cultural Ctr. Pacific N.W., Seattle, 1990, chmn., 1991, 95; founding chmn. Hindu Temple and Cultural Ctr., Ames, Iowa, 1999—. Recipient W.Va. U. Assocs. award W.Va. U. Found., 1974, 78. Fellow IEEE (editor IEEE Trans. Power Sys. 1998-00, IEEE/PES Rev. Letters 1999-03, Internat. Jour. Sys., mem. editl. bd. IEEE/PES/Power and Energy Mag., 2003-, v.p. publs., Best Paper award 1985, 88, 91, 2005, mem. Conf. Internat. des Grands Reseaux Electriques, IEEE Press for Power Series, 1998—, Outstanding Power Engring. Educator award 1996, chmn. power engring. edn. com. 2000—, Millenneum medal 2000, Power Edn.Com. Disting. Svc. award 2005), Power Engring. Soc. IEEE (v.p. 2004—), Sigma Xi, Tau Beta Pi, Eta Kappa Nu, Rotary. Democrat. Avocations: photography, tennis, ping pong/table tennis. Home and Office: 13224 N Risky Dr Tucson AZ 85755 Office Phone: 520-797-1161. Personal E-mail: psvenkata@comcast.net. Business E-Mail: ss.venkata@kema.com.

VENKATESH, VISWANATH, information systems professional, educator, consultant; s. Viswanath Hariharan and Subhalakshmi Viswanath. BE, Bharathiar U., Coimbatore, India, 1991; post grad., Temple U., Phila., 1993; PhD, U. Minn., Mpls., 1997. Cert. bus. process mgr. and practitioner del. Bus. Process Mgmt. Group, 2006. Asst. prof. and Tyser fellow U. Md., College Park, 1997—2002, assoc. prof. and Tyser fellow, 2002—04; prof. and George and Boyce Billingsley chair info. sys. Walton Coll. Bus. U. Ark., Fayetteville, 2004—. Dir. MBA consulting U. of Md., College Park, 2002—04; doctoral program dir. info. sys. U. Ark., Fayetteville, 2004—; assoc. editor Mgmt. Sci., Jour. Assn. of Info. Sys., Info. Sys. Rsch., MIS Quar.; invited spkr. at univs. Contbr. scientific papers to refereed profl. jours., articles. Vol. tax preparation for underprivileged, College Park, Md., 1997—2003, Fayetteville, Ark., 2004—05; donor and social supporter Lions Orgn., Chennai, Tamil Nadu, India, 1995—2006. Named Reviewer of the Yr., MIS Quar., 1999, 4th most cited article 1970-2005, Decision Scis. Jour., 2005; recipient Tchg. Innovation award, U. Md., 1998, 2001, Gen. Tchg. Excellence award, 2000, 2003, Celebrating Teachers award, 2002; grantee, NSF, Microsoft, U.S. Dept. Transportation, Veterans Health Admnstrn. Mem.: Assn. Info. Sys., Inst. Ops. Rsch. and the Mgmt. Scis. Achievements include research in technology acceptance; design of 10 different courses at the PhD, MBA, and undergraduate levels. Avocations: travel, badminton, racquetball, swimming, stamp collecting/philately. Office: Univ Ark Walton Coll of Bus Fayetteville AR 72701 Home Phone: 240-353-6666; Office Phone: 479 573 869. Business E-Mail: vvenkatesh@vvenkatesh.us.

VENKATESWAR, SHYAMA, international relief organization executive; b. Calcutta, India, 1967; 2 children. Attended, Smith Coll. Dir. social isssues program Asia Soc., NYC; exec. dir. World Hunger Action Ctr., Mercy Corps, NYC, 2007—. Former program officer for studies Carnegie Coun. for Ethics in Internat. Affairs, NYC; assoc. editor India Rev.; former mem. Allocations Com., Women's Found., NYC, Grants Rev. Com. U.S. Inst. Peace. *

VENKAYYA, RAJEEV V., federal agency administrator, biomedical researcher, educator; b. Dayton, Ohio, Mar. 6, 1967; BS, U. Akron; MD, Northeastern Ohio U., 1991. Resident Internal Medicine U. Mich., chief med. resident, 1994—95; fellow Pulmonary and Critical Care Medicine U. Calif., San Francisco, asst. prof. medicine; dir. High Risk Asthma Clinic San Francisco Gen. Hosp., co-dir. Med. Intensive Care Unit; founder, dir. Neomedicus, LLC, 2000—, Sapient Medical Group, Inc.; White House fellow US Dept. Energy, Washington, 2002—03; dir. Biodefense and Health White House Homeland Security Coun., 2003—, spl. asst. to Pres. for Biological Defense Policy. Advisor San Francisco Asthma Task Force Steering Com. Contbr. articles to profl. jours. Grantee Rsch. Grant, Am. Lung Assn., 1999, NIH, 1999. Mem.: Am. Lung Assn. San Francisco, Alpha Omega Alpha. Office: White House Homeland Security Coun 1600 Pennsylvania Ave NW Washington DC 20500 *

VENNAT, MICHEL, former bank executive, lawyer; b. Sept. 17, 1941; m. Marie-Anne Tawil; children: Catherine, Charles-Alexandre, Frédéric-André, Michèle-Anne, Philippe-Olivier. BA magna cum laude, Coll. Jean-de-Brébeuf, Montreal, Que., Can., 1960; LL.L., U. Montreal, 1963; MA in Econs., Oxford U., Eng., 1965. Bar: Que. 1966, Paris 1995; apptd. Queen's Counsel 1983, Officer of the Order of Can., 1995. Fgn. affairs officer Dept. External Affairs, Ottawa, Ont., Canada, 1965; spl. asst. to Min. Fin., 1966-68; spl. asst. to Hon. Pierre E. Trudeau, Prime Min. of Can., 1968-70, spl. counsel, 1977; chmn. Can. Film Devel. Corp., Montreal, 1976-81, sr. ptnr. Stikeman, Elliott, Montreal, 1970-90; pres. Dumez Investments Inc., 1986-87, Westburne Internat. Industries Ltd., 1987; vice chmn. United Westburne Inc., 1990, vice chmn., CEO, 1991-93, chmn., CEO, 1993-94, also bd. dirs.; pres. Bastos du Canada Limitée, 1987—2000, also bd. dirs.; sr. ptnr. Stikeman Elliot, Montreal, 1994-2000; pres., CEO bus. devel. Bank Canada, 2000—04. Chmn. bd. dirs. Bus. Devel. Bank of Can.; lectrt. in constl. law U. Montreal, 1970. Rhodes scholar, 1963-65. Mem. Barreau du Que., Barreau de Paris, Mt. Bruno Country Club, Hillside Tennis Club, Mt. Royal Club, Knowlton Golf Club, St. John Salmon Club, Montreal Badminton and Squash Club. Avocations: golf, tennis, skiing, fishing, hunting. Home Phone: 514-483-8888; Office Phone: 514-849-8000. Business E-Mail: mvennat@iron-hill.com.

VENNING, ROBERT STANLEY, lawyer; b. Boise, Idaho, July 24, 1943; s. William Lucas and Corey Elizabeth (Brown) V.; m. Sandra Macdonald, May 9, 1966 (div. 1976); 1 child, Rachel Elizabeth; m. Laura Siegel, Mar. 24, 1979; 1 child, Daniel Rockhill Siegel. AB, Harvard U., 1965; MA, U. Chgo., 1966; LLB, Yale U., 1970. Bar: Calif., U.S. Dist. Ct. (no. dist.) Calif., 1971, U.S. Dist. Ct. (cen. dist.) Calif. 1973, U.S. Ct. Appeals (9th cir.) 1977, U.S. Supreme Ct. 1977, U.S. Ct. Appeals (fed. cir.) 1986, U.S. Ct. Appeals (D.C. cir.) 1987, U.S. Ct. Fed. Claims 1996. Assoc. Heller Ehrman White & McAuliffe (now known as Heller Ehrman LLP), San Francisco, 1970-73, 73-76, ptnr., 1977—, mem. exec. com., 1991-94. Vis. lectr. U. Wash., Seattle, 1973, Boalt Hall Sch. Law, U. Calif., Berkeley, 1982-85, 89, Sch. Bus., Stanford U., 1986-87. Editor Yale Law Jour., 1969-70. Early neutral evaluator U.S. Dist. Ct. (no. dist.) Calif. Alternative Dispute Resolution Program, 1987—, mediator, 2000-. Fellow Am. Bar Found. (life); mem. ABA, San Francisco Bar Assn. (past chair judiciary com.), CPR Inst. for Dispute Resolution, Olympic Club. Office: Heller Ehrman LLP 333 Bush St San Francisco CA 94104-2878 Office Phone: 415-772-6158.

VENTANTONIO, JAMES BARTHOLOMEW, lawyer; b. Orange, NJ, Jan. 5, 1940; s. Benjamin B. and Grace (D'Onofrio) V.; m. Anita L. Winkler, July 7, 1962; children: Peter, Lisa. BS, Seton Hall U., 1961, JD, 1964. Bar: NJ 1965, US Dist. Ct. NJ 1965, US Ct. Mil. Appeals 1965, US Supreme Ct. 1969, NY 1981. Dir. Somerset Sussex Legal Services Corp., NJ, 1969-74; assoc. prof. law Seton Hall U., Newark, 1974-78; atty. Bell Labs., Murray Hill, NJ, 1978-83; gen. atty. NJ Bell Co., Newark, 1983-91; counsel Bell Atlantic, 1991-93; mcpl. prosecutor Bridgewater, NJ, 1996—2000, Manville, 2004—; mcpl. judge Bridgewater, 2000—03; city solicitor Plainfield, NJ, 2005—; prosecutor South Bound Brook, NJ, 2007—. Pres. Somerset-Sussex Legal Services Corp., 1978-85. Chmn. govs. adv. com. Legal Services, Trenton, NJ, 1979-83; pres. Community Health Law Project, East Orange, NJ, 1980-81; vice chmn. Somerset Alliance For The Future, 1991-94, mem. bd. visitors, Seton Hall Law Sch., 2004-, sec. bd. trustees, Raritan Valley C.C. Served to maj. US Army, 1965-69. Mem. ABA, NJ Bar Assn. (chmn. standing com. on legal services 1979-80), Somerset County C. of C. (chair 1995). Home: 747 Foothill Rd W Bridgewater NJ 08807-1804 Office: Ventantonio & Wildenhain 95 Mount Bethel Rd Warren NJ 07059-5126 Home Phone: 908-725-7816; Office Phone: 908-757-3900. Business E-Mail: jventantonio@vwlaw.com.

VENTER, J. CRAIG (JOHN CRAIG VENTER, CRAIG VENTER), science foundation director, geneticist; b. Salt Lake City, Oct. 14, 1946; m. Claire Fraser. BS in Biochemistry, U. Calif., San Diego, 1972, PhD in Physiology and Pharmacology, 1975; D (hon.), Ariz. State U., 2007. Prof. SUNY, Buffalo; with Roswell Pk. Meml. Inst.; sect. and lab chief Nat. Inst. Neurol. Disorders and Stroke NIH, Bethesda, Md., 1984—92; co-founder, chair, chief scientist The Inst. for Genomic Rsch., 1992—98; co-founder, CEO, pres., chief sci. officer Celera Genomics Corp., Rockville, Md., 1998—2002; chmn. sci. adv. bd. Applera Corp., Norwalk, Conn.; chmn., co-founder, pres. The J. Craig Venter Sci. Found. Joint Tech. Ctr., 2003—, J. Craig Vetner Inst.; co-founder, pres. Ctr. for the Advancement Genomics, 2003—, Inst. for Biol. Energy Alternatives, 2003—. Bd. dirs. High Tech. Coun. Md.; mem. sci. adv. bd. ValiGene; chmn., bd. trustees The Inst. for Genomic Rsch. Contbr. more than 160 articles to profl. jours. Served in US Army, 1967—68. Named one of the World's Most Influential People, TIME Mag., 2007; recipient Beckman award, 1999, Chiron Corp. Biotech. Rsch. award, 1999, King Faisal Internat. award for Sci., 2000, Taylor Internat. prize in Medicine, Robarts Rsch. Inst., 2001, Gairdner award, 2002, Award for Indsl. Application of Sci., NAS, 2002. Fellow: AAAS, Am. Acad. Microbiology. Achievements include research in functional and comparative analysis of genome and gene products in viruses, eubacteria, pathogenic bacteria, archea and eukaryotes, both in plants and animals including humans; first to use automated gene sequencers; development of expressed sequence tags (ESTs); discovery of more than half of all human genes. Office: The Inst for Genomic Rsch 9712 Medical Ctr Dr Rockville MD 20850 also: J Craig Venture Sci Found 5 Research Pl Rockville MD 20850 *

VENTERS, HARLEY EUGENE, lawyer; b. Okla., Nov. 12, 1922; s. Albert Harley Venters and Margaret Emily Tate; m. Anne Matilda Liccione, Oct. 4, 1946; children: Anne Eleanor, Christopher William, Harley Eugene Jr., Wanda Jean, Shelly Laura. BS, US Mil. Acad., West Point, 1946; LLB, Okla. U., Norman, 1953. Bar: US Supreme Ct. 1971. Air cadet US Army Air Corps, San Antonio, 1942—43; cadet West Point Corps Cadets, NY, 1943—46; lt. US Army, 1946—50; county judge Carter County, Ardmore, Okla., 1953—54, state counsel, 1957—58; state rep. Okla. State Legis., Oklahoma City, 1955—56; presiding judge Okla. State Indsl. Ct., Oklahoma City, 1960—61; sr. ptnr. Venters & Venters, Oklahoma City, 1961—. Bd. dirs. UN Assn.-USA, Oklahoma City. Founder Okla. Interfaith Alliance, Oklahoma City. Mem.: ACLU, Sierra Club, Phi Alpha Delta. Democrat. Congregationalist. Office Phone: 405-478-1177.

VENTIMIGLIA, VINCENT J., JR., federal agency administrator; married; 5 children. BA magna cum laude, Yale U.; JD, Georgetown U. Legis. asst. to Senator Gordon Humphrey US Senate Com. on Health Issues, Washington, 1985—88; dir. Capitol Hill Improvement Partnership, 1988—90; staff atty. US Sentencing Commn., 1990—94; counsel to Senator Dan Coats US Senate Labor and Human Resources Com., 1995—98; dir. Govt. Affairs Office Medtronic, Inc., 1998—2001; health policy dir. Health Policy Team Senate Health Edn. Labor and Pensions Com., 2001—05; policy dir. Senate Budget Com., 2005—06; asst. sec. for legis. US Dept. Health & Human Services, 2006—. Office: HHS 200 Independence Ave SW Washington DC 20201 Office Phone: 202-690-7627. Office Fax: 202-690-7380.

VENTO, M. THÉRÈSE, lawyer; b. NYC, June 30, 1951; d. Anthony Joseph and Margaret (Stechert) V.; m. Peter Michael MacNamara, Dec. 23, 1977; children: David Miles, Elyse Anne. BS, U. Fla., 1974, JD, 1976. Bar: Fla. 1977, U.S. Dist. Ct. (so. and mid. dists.) Fla. 1982, U.S. Ct. Appeals (5th and 11th cirs.) 1981, U.S. Supreme Ct. 1985. Clk. to presiding justice U.S. Dist. Ct. (so. dist.) Fla., Miami, 1976-78; assoc. Mahoney, Hadlow & Adams, 1978-79, Shutts & Bowen LLP, 1979-84, ptnr., 1985-95; founding ptnr. Gallwey Gillman Curtis & Vento, P.A., 1995—2004; ptnr. Shutts & Bowen, LLP, 2004—. Trustee Miami Art Mus., 1988—, v.p., 1999—; trustee The Beacon Coun., 1995-97, Law Sch. Alumni Coun., U. Fla., 1994-2004. Fellow Am. Bar Found.; mem. Dade County Bar Assn. (dir. young lawyers sect. 1978-83, editor newsletter 1981-83), Fla. Assn. for Women Lawyers, Fla. Bar Assn. (bd. govs., young lawyers div. 1983-85, civil procedure rules com. 1983-90, exec. coun. trial lawyers sect. 1996-2004), The Miami Forum (v.p. 1987-88, bd. dirs. 1989-91, co-pres. 2001-2002). Home: 3908 Main Hwy Miami FL 33133-6513 Office: Shutts & Bowen LLP 201 S Biscayne Blvd Ste1500 Miami FL 33131 Office Phone: 305-347-7318. Business E-Mail: TVento@shutts.com.

VENTO, SERGIO, ambassador; b. May 30, 1938; m. Maria Magdalena Zelent; 2 children. M Polit. Sci., U. Rome. Cabinet sec. State Fgn. Affairs, Italy, 1963—67; 2nd sec. then 1st sec. Italian Embassy, The Hague, Netherlands, 1967—70; Italian consul Buenos Aires, 1970—72; counsellor Italian Embassy, Ankara, 1972—75; with Italian Fgn. Min., 1975—79; 1st counsellor permanent Italian del. Orgn. Cooperation and Devel. Europe, 1979—85; min. plenipotentiary 2nd class, 1985—87; min., fin. min., 1987—89; diplomatic counsel Italy's Prime Min., 1988; chief of mission Italian Embassy, Serbia and Montenegro, 1989—92; diplomatic counsellor Prime Min. Italy, 1992—95; amb. to France, 1995—99; permanent rep. UN, NYC, 1999—2003; Italian amb. to US, 2003—. Italian rep. Halifax and Lyon Summits Grp. of Seven. Office: Embassy of Italy 3000 Whitehaven St NW Washington DC 20008

VENTRELLI, ANITA MARIE, lawyer; b. Berwyn, Ill., Apr. 20, 1964; d. Jose M. and Anita Marie (Loycano) Bolaños. AB, U. Mich., 1986; JD, DePaul U., 1989. Bar: Ill. 1990. Ptnr. Schiller DuCanto & Fleck, Chgo., 1997—. Fellow: Am. Acad. Matrimonial Lawyers; mem.: ABA, Cook and Lake County Justinian Socs., Hispanic Lawyers Assn. Ill., Ill. Bar Assn. Roman Catholic. Avocations: running, piano. Office: Schiller DuCanto & Fleck 200 N La Salle St Ste 2700 Chicago IL 60601-1098 Office Phone: 312-609-5509. Business E-Mail: aventrelli@sdflaw.com.

VENTURA, HECTOR OSVALDO, cardiologist; b. Buenos Aires, Mar. 21, 1951; came to U.S., 1981; s. Osvaldo Domingo and Nelida (Scocozza) V.; m. Laurie Anne Zeringue, Apr. 21, 1990; children: Austin Alejandro, Leighton Leandro, Kendra Mariel. BS, Nat. No. 10 Coll., Buenos Aires, 1968; MD, U. Buenos Aires, 1974. Diplomate Am. Bd. Internal Medicine with subspecialty in cardiovascular diseases. Resident in internal medicine Mil. Hosp., Argentina, 1975-78; rsch. fellow hypertension Ochsner Found., New Orleans, 1981-84; internal medicine resident Oschsner Found. Hosp., New Orleans, 1984-86, cardiology fellow, 1986-88; heart failure/heart transplant fellow Loyola U., Chgo., 1989; co-dir. heart failure heart transplant Oshsner Med. Inst., New Orleans, 1989-97, transplant adv. bd., 1992-97, ethics com., 1995-97; assoc. prof. medicine La. State U. Sch. Medicine, New Orleans; co-dir. advanced heart failure/cardiac transplant Tulane U. Med. Ctr., New Orleans, 1998-2000; prof. medicine Tulane U. Sch. Medicine, New Orleans, 2000—. Dir. cardiovasc. disease tng. program and edn. Ochsner Clinic Found., New Orleans, 2000—; chmn. Grad. Med. End. Com., Ochsner Clin. Found., 2004-; jour. manuscript reviewer. Mem. editl. bd. Jour. Heart & Lung Transplantation, 1994; contbr. articles to profl. jours. 1st lt. Argentine Army, 1974-80. Ochsner Found. fellow, 1985-86. Fellow Am. Coll. Cardiology; mem. Am. Soc. Transplant (organ thoracic com. 1993—), Am. Heart Assn. Roman Catholic. Avocations: tennis, aerobic exercise. Home: 3746 Rue Chardonnay Metairie LA 70002-1500 Office: Ochsner Clinic Found 1514 Jefferson Hwy New Orleans LA 70121 Office Phone: 504-842-6281. Business E-Mail: hventura@ochsner.org.

VENTURA, JESSE (JAMES JANOS), former governor; b. Mpls., July 15, 1951; s. George and Bernice Janos; m. Terry Ventura; children: Tyrel, Jade. Student, North Hennepin C.C. Profl. wrestler, 1973-84; ret.; gov. State of Minn., St. Paul, 1998—2003; host The Jesse Ventura Show, 2003—. Actor starring in several films including Predator; radio talk show host. Mayor City of Brooklyn Park, Minn., 1990-95; bd. advisors Make a Wish of Minn.; vol. football coach Champlin Park H.S. Served with USN, USNR. Mem. Am. Fedn. of TV and radio Announcers, Screen Actors Guild. Independent.

VENTURI, ROBERT, architect; b. Phila., June 25, 1925; s. Robert C. and Vanna (Lanzetta) Venturi; m. Denise Lakofski, July 23, 1967; 1 child, James Charles. Grad., Episcopal Acad., 1944; AB summa cum laude,

Princeton U., 1947, MFA, 1950, DFA (hon.), 1983, Oberlin Coll., 1977, Yale U., 1979, U. Pa., 1980; Laurea Honoris Causa in Architecture, U. Rome "La Sapienza", 1994. Designer firms of Oskar Stonorov, Eero Saarinen and Assos., Louis I. Kahn, 1950—58; ptnr. firm Venturi, Cope & Lippincott, Phila., 1958—61, Venturi and Short, Phila., 1961—64, Venturi and Rauch, Phila., 1964—80, Venturi, Rauch & Scott Brown, Phila., 1980—89, Venturi, Scott Brown and Assocs., Inc., 1989—; from asst. to assoc. prof. architecture U. Pa., 1957—65; Charlotte Shepherd Davenport prof. architecture Yale, 1966—70. Author: Complexity and Contradiction in Architecture, 1966, Iconography and Electronics upon a Generic Architecture, 1996; co-author (with Denise Scott Brown and Steven Izenour): Learning from Las Vegas, 1972;; 2d edit., 1977;; co-author: (with Denise Scott Brown) A View from the Campidoglio, Selected Essays, 1953-84, Architecture as Signs and Systems for a Mannerist Time, 2004; contbr. articles to profl. jours.; prin. works include Vanna Venturi House, Phila., 1961, Guild House, 1961, Humanities Bldg., SUNY, 1972, Franklin Ct., Phila., 1972, addition to Allen Meml. Art Mus., Oberlin Coll., 1973, Inst. for Sci. Info. Corp. Hdqs., Phila., 1978, Gordon Wu Hall, Princeton U., 1980, Seattle Art Mus., 1984, The Nat. Gallery, Sainsbury Wing, London, 1986, Fisher and Bendheim Halls, Princeton U., 1986, Gordon and Virginia MacDonald Med. Rsch. Labs. (with Payette Assocs.), UCLA, 1986, Charles P. Stevenson Jr. Libr., Bard Coll., 1989, Roy and Diana Vagelos Labs. IAST (with Payette Assocs.), U. Pa., 1990, Regional Govt. Bldg., Toulouse, France, 1992, Kirifuri Resort Facilities, Nikko, Japan, 1992, Trabant U. Ctr., U. Del., Newark, 1992, Meml. Hall Restoration and Addition, Harvard U., 1992, The Barnes Found. Restoration and Renovation, Merion, Pa., 1993, Disney Celebration (Fla.) Bank, 1993, Gonda (Goldschmied) Neuroscience and Genetics Rsch. Ctr. (with Lee, Burkhart, Liu Inc.), UCLA, 1993, Princeton Campus Ctr., Princeton U., 1996, Anlyan Ctr. for Med. Rsch. and Edn., Yale U. Sch. Medicine, 1998, (with Payette Assocs.) Master Plan and Buildings for U. Mich., 1997—, Baker/Berry Libr., Dartmouth Coll., 1996, Woodmere Art Mus. addition, 2000, Biomed. Rsch. Bldg., U. Ky., 2000, Dumbarton Oaks Libr. Expansion, Washington, D.C., 2001, Stuart Country Day School Theater/Auditorium/Sanctuary, Princeton, N.J., 2001, Lehigh Valley Hosp.-Muhlenberg, Allentown, Pa., 2002. Trustee Am. Acad. Rome, 1966—71. Decorated comdr. Order Arts and Letters (France); recipient Nat. Medal of Arts, 1992, Pritzker Architecture prize, 1991, Benjamin Franklin medal, The Royal Soc. for Encouragement of Arts, Mfrs. and Commerce, 1993, Vincent J. Scully prize, 2002; fellow Rome Prize Am. Acad., Rome, 1954—56. Fellow: AIA (award 1974, 1977, 1978), Accademia Nazionale di San Luca, Am. Acad. Arts and Scis., Am. Acad. of Arts and Letters, Royal Inc. Architects of Scotland (hon.), Royal Inst. Brit. Architects (hon.), Am. Acad. in Rome; mem.: European Acad. Scis. and Arts, Phi Beta Kappa. Office: Venturi Scott Brown & Assocs Inc 4236 Main St Philadelphia PA 19127-1603 Office Phone: 215-487-0400. Business E-Mail: venturi@vsba.com.

VENTURINI, JUDITH ANNE, education educator; b. Oakland, Calif. d. Arthur Francis Venturini and Germaine Junet. BS, Calif. State U., Hayward, 1969, MS in Phys. Edn., 1985, MS in Edn. Leadership, 1991; MS in Edn., Nat. U., San Jose, Calif., 1999. Practitioner of science of mind RScP. Tchr., adminstrv. intern Redwood City (Calif.) Elem. Sch. Dist., 1970—91; ednl. cons., exec. dir. Kids-at-Heart, Fremint, Calif., 1991—94; D.A.T.E. coord. Hayward Unified Sch. Dist., 1994; regional dir. Sonoma County Office of Edn., Santa Rosa, Calif., 1994—95; prin. tchr. San Jose Unified Sch. Dist., 1995—2000; spl. edn. tchr. for autistic students Santa Clara County Office of Edn., San Jose, 2001—02; adj. prof. Calif. State U., Hayward, 2000—, Nat. U., San Jose, 2000—, Nat. Hispanic U., San Jose, 2000—. Facilities chair Bay Area Career Women, San Francisco, 1987—90; chair Sonoma County Phys. Edn. Com., Santa Rosa, Calif., 1994—95; dir. Sonoma County Office of Edn. Gang Prevention Network Task Force, Santa Rosa, 1994—95. Contbr. poetry to anthologies. Bd. dirs. Ardenwood Homeowners, Fremont, Calif., 1987—88; practitioner, divinity student Ctr. of Positive Living, 2000—. Recipient multiple honors in athletics, Playmates award, Calif. Dept. Edn., 1994, Healthy Start award, 1994, 1996, award for inspirational programs for children, Housing Authority of Santa Clara County, 2000. Mem.: NEA, Calif. Tchrs. Assn. Avocations: dancesport, poetry, art, golf, writing songs. Home: 5206 Tacoma Ln Fremont CA 94555 Office: Kids-at-Heart 5206 Tacoma Ln Fremont CA 94555 Personal E-mail: junu@earthlink.net, jav123@earthlink.net.

VENTURINI, TISHA LEA, professional soccer player; b. Modesto, Calif., Mar. 3, 1973; Degree in phys. edn., U. N.C. Mem. U.S. Women's Nat. Soccer Team. Mem. championship team CONCACAF, Montreal, 1994. Named Player of Yr., Mo. Athletic Club, 1994; recipient Gold medal, Centennial Olympic Games, 1996, Silver medal, World Univ. Games, 1993, Hermann trophy, 1994. Achievements include 1999 World Cup Champion. Office: c/o US Soccer Fedn 1801 S Prairie Ave # 1811 Chicago IL 60616-1319

VENUGOPAL, THAYANITHY, biologist, geneticist, researcher; s. Thayanithy and Vijayalakshmi Maniagar; m. Madhumathi Venugopal, Dec. 11, 2003; 1 child, Neya. BSc, Madura Coll., India, 1992; MSc, Madurai Kamaraj U., India, 1994, PhD, 2002. Jr. rsch. fellow Madurai Kamaraj U., 1995—97, sr. rsch. fellow, 1997—2000, rsch. assoc., 2000—02; postdoctoral rschr. U. Mass. Med. Sch., Worcester, 2002—. Author (book chapter) Fish Genetics and Aquaculture; contbr. chapters to books. Student voluntary worker Nat. Svc. Scheme, Madurai, 1989—92. Recipient Srinivasan Endowment award for Academic Excellence, Madura Coll., 1991—92; Jr. Rsch. fellow, U. Grants Commn., India, 1995—97, Sr. Rsch. fellow, 1997—2000, Rsch. Assoc. fellow, Indian Coun. Agr. Rsch., 2000—02, Post-Doctoral Rsch. fellow, U. Mass. Med. Sch., 2002—. Mem.: AAAS (assoc.), Index Copernicus, Comparative Biochemistry and Physiology (hon.; referee, peer reviewer Marine Biotech. and Med. Sci. Monitor jour. 2006), Internat. Brain Rsch. Orgn. (assoc.), Soc. Biol. Chemists India (life), V. O. Chidambaram Hostel Rsch. Scholars (hon.; gen. sec. 1999—2000). Achievements include research in isolated and characterized growth hormone genes of economically important Asian fish species; generated transgenic technology for the Indian major carps; generated fast growing auto-transgenic Indian major carp Labeo rohita by gene manipulation and transgenesis; isolated and studied the transposable elements from economically important Indian fishes. Home: 65 Frank St 139 Worcester MA 01604 Office: Univ Mass Medical Sch Dept Biochemistry and Molec Pharmacology 364 Plantation St Worcester MA 01605 Office Fax: 508-856-2003. Business E-Mail: thayanithy.venugopal@gmail.com.

VENUGOPAL, VEERAKUMAR, materials scientist, physicist, researcher; b. Tiruchirappalli, India, Feb. 18, 1974; arrived in US, 2005; s. Venugaopal Subramaniapillai and Devasena Natesan; m. Vasumathi Nallusamy, Aug. 21, 2002; 1 child, Ekaanth Sravan Subramaniapillai Veerakumar. BS in Physics, Bharathidasan U., Tiruchirappolli, India, 1991; MS, Bharathidasan U., Tiruchirappalli, India, 1996; M in Engring., Nat. Inst. Tech., Tiruchirappalli, India, 1998; PhD in Nonlinear Dynamics, Bharathidasan U., Tiruchirappalli, India, 2002. Asst. prof. Manipal U., India, 2003—04, Asian Inst. Medicine, Sci. and Tech., Sungai Petani, Malaysia, 2004—05; sr. rsch. assoc. ctr. magnetism and magnetic nanostructures U. Colo., Colo. Springs, 2005—. Contbr. articles to profl. jours. Fellow, Govt. India, 1998, Abdus Salam Internat. Ctr. Theoretical Physics, Italy, 2001, 2005. Achievements include design of modeling and design of novel microwave filters. Office: Univ Colo 1420 Austin Bluffs Pkwy Colorado Springs CO 80918 Office Phone: 719-262-3420. Personal E-mail: venuveera@rediffmail.com. Business E-Mail: vveeraku@uccs.edu.

VENZAGO, MARIO, conductor, music director; b. Zurich, Switzerland, 1948; m. Marianne Venzago; children: Mario, Gabriel. Studied with, Hans Swarowsky, Vienna, 1973. Music dir. Basel Symphony Orch., 1995—2003, Heidelberg Opera, 1986—89, Deutsche Kammerphilharmonie, 1989—92, Graz Opera Ho., 1990—95, Euskadi Nat. Opera, Spain, 1998—2001, Indpls. Symphony Orch., 2002—, Swedish Nat. Orch., 2003—. Guest condr. Berlin Philharmonic, BBC, London, Leipzig Gewandhaus Orchester, London Philharmonic, City of Birmingham Symphony, Orchestre de la Suisse Romande, Phila. Orch., Tonhalle Orchestra Zurich, Tokyo's NHK Symphony, Berlin's Komische Oper, Salzburg Festival, Hannover Radio-Philharmonie, invited by Kurt Masur, Leipzig; guest condr.: Boston Symphony, Helsinki Philharmonic, Helsinki Radio; Am. debut Hollywood Bowl, 1988, appeared N.J. Symphony, Ind. Symphony, Fla. Philharmonic, 1988; dir.: Balt. Symphony, 1995 (named artistic dir. symphony's summer festival, 2000); prin. conductor Winterthur City Orch., Lucerne Opera Ho., Orchestre de la Suisse Romande. Recipient award, Diapason d'or, awards, Grand Prix du Disque, Edison prize. Office: Ind Symphony Orch 32 E Washington St Ste 600 Indianapolis IN 46204-2919 Business E-Mail: mvenvago@IndianapolisSymphony.org.

VÉR, ISTVÁN LÁSZLÓ, acoustical engineer, consultant; b. Tápiószecsö, Hungary, Dec. 22, 1934; came to U.S., 1965; s. István and Erzsebet G. V.; 1 child, Kristina M. BSEE, Tech. U., Budapest, 1956; MSEE, Tech. U., Aachen, Germany, 1960; PhD in Acoustics, Tech. U., Munich, 1963. R&D engr. Rohde and Schwarz, Munich, 1960-65; prin. cons. BBN Techs., Cambridge, Mass., 1965—2000; ind. cons. acoustics, noise and vibration control, 2000—. Vis. scientist Indian Inst. Sci., Bangalore, India, 2005. Author, editor: Noise & Vibration Control Engineering, 1992, 2005; holder patents. Recipient U.S. Sr. Scientist award Alexander von Humboldt Found., Germany, 1978, Best Paper award Am. Soc. Heating and Refrigeration Engring., 1979. Fellow Acoustical Soc. Am.; mem. Inst. Noise Control Engring. USA (dir. 1976-77), European Acoustics Assn. Avocations: literature, philosophy, travel, tennis. Office Phone: 978-568-0556.

VERANO, ANTHONY FRANK, retired banker; b. West Harrison, NY, Jan. 4, 1931; s. Frank and Rose (Viscomi) Verano; m. Clara Cosentino, July 8, 1951; children: Rosemarie, Diana Lynn. Student, Am. Inst. Banking, 1956-60, Bank Adminstrn. Inst., U. Wis., 1962-64, RCA Programmers Sch., 1965, Burroughs Programmers Sch., 1965, N.J. Bankers Data Processing Sch., 1966-68. With County Trust Co., White Plains, NY, 1949-61, sr. auditor, 1960-61; with State Nat. Bank Conn., Bridgeport, 1961—, auditor, 1962-79, exec. auditor, 1979—, Conn. Bank & Trust Co., 1983—; from v.p., auditor to sr. v.p., auditor Gateway Bank, Newtown, Conn., 1987-94, ret., 1996. Tchr. bank auditing Am. Inst. Banking, 1976-78. Mem. adv. bd. Norwalk Community Coll., 1968—. Served with USN, 1951-52. Mem. Bank Adminstrn. Inst. (dir. Stamford chpt. 1967-68, sec. Western Conn. chpt. 1968-69, treas. 1969-70, v.p. 1970-71, pres. 1971-72), Am. Acctg. Assn., Inst. Internal Auditors (cert. bank auditor, cert. bank compliance officer, cert. fin. svcs. auditor). Home: 224 Columbus Ave West Harrison NY 10604-2614 *It is difficult to define the elements of success. There are those who say success is achieved through drive and ambition only. However, those who have achieved their goals in life using only these two principles have probably destroyed more than they have created. Success, I feel, is achieved when drive and ambition are tempered with honesty, fairness, and respect for others. An individual must have a sense of dedication not only to his work and for those with whom he works but, most importantly, for those who work for him. This has been my philosophy in achieving my success.*

VERANT, WILLIAM J., state agency administrator; b. Washington, Dec. 19, 1941; m. Donna M. Verant; children: Bill Jr., Sharon. BSBA, Am. U., Washington, DC. V.p. Fed. Home Mortgage Corp., Calif.; recruited by the Fed. Home Loan Bank Bd. to manage various savings & loan instns. during savings & loan crisis in 1980s; dept. head comml. and multi-family real estate loans/assets Resolution Trust Corp., Newport Beach, Calif.; dir. fin. instns. divsn. N.Mex. Regulation and Licensing Dept., Santa Fe, 1995—, acting dir. securities divsn. Avocation: restoring old cars. Office: NMex Fin Instns Divsn PO Box 25101 Santa Fe NM 87504 Office Phone: 505-476-4885. Office Fax: 505-476-4670. E-mail: william.verant@state.nm.us.

VERBA, SIDNEY, political science professor, retired library director; b. Bklyn., May 26, 1932; s. Morris Harold and Recci (Salman) Verba; m. E. Cynthia Winston, June 17, 1955; children: Margaret Lynn, Ericka Kim, Martina Claire. BA, Harvard U., 1953; MA, Princeton U., 1955, PhD, 1959. Asst. prof. polit. sci. Princeton U., 1960-63, assoc. prof., 1963-64; prof. Stanford U., 1964-68, U. Chgo., 1968-72; prof. govt. Harvard U., 1972—, chmn. dept. govt., 1976-80, Carl H. Pforzheimer U. Prof., assoc. dean Faculty Arts and Sciences, 1981—84; dir. Harvard U. Libr., 1984—2007. Chmn. bd. dirs. Harvard U. Press, 1991-2005; chmn. policy com. Social Sci. Rsch. Coun., 1980-86; mem. Commn. on Behavioral and Social Sciences, NRC, 1986-91; Commn. on Preservation and Access, chair com. on internat. conflict and cooperation, NRC, 1991-93; vis. com. MIT Polit. Sci. Dept.; bd. dirs. Social Sci. Rsch. Coun.; Tanner Lectr., Oxford, 1998. Author: Small Groups and Political Behavior, 1961, The Civic Culture, 1963, Caste, Race and Politics, 1969, Participation in America, 1972 (Gladys Kammerer Award, Am. Polit. Sci. Assn., 1972), Vietnam and the Silent Majority, 1972, The Changing American Voter, 1976 (Woodrow Wilson Found. Award, Am. Polit. Sci. Found., 1976), Participation and Political Equality, 1978, Injury to Insult, 1979, Introduction to American Government, 1983, Equality in America, 1985, Elites and the Idea of Equality, 1987, Designing Social Inquiry, 1994, Voice and Equality, 1995, The Private Roots of Public Action, 2001. Recipient Johan Skytte Prize in Polit. Sci., Skytte Found., 2002; Guggenheim Fellow, 1980-81. Fellow: Am. Acad. Arts and Sciences; mem.: NAS (chair social and polit. sci. sect. 2002-), Am. Philos. Soc., Am. Polit. Sci. Assn. (exec. coun. 1971-74, v.p. 1979-81, pres.-elect 1993-94, pres. 1994-95, James Madison Award 1993, Warren Miller Award 2000), Internat. Studies Assn. (v.p. 1971-72, John Skytte prize 2002). Jewish. Office: Harvard U Libr Office Dir Wadsworth House 1340 Massachusetts Ave Cambridge MA 02138 also: Polit Sci Dept Harvard Univ 1737 Cambridge St Cambridge MA 02138 Office Phone: 617-495-4421. Business E-Mail: sverba@harvard.edu. *

VERBEKE, JOHAN C., ambassador; b. 1951; married; 3 children. Student in Law and Philosophy, Ghent U., Belgium; LLM, Yale U., New Haven. Asst. prof. European law; diplomat Govt. Belgium, Beirut, 1982, Amman, Jordan, 1984, Bujumbura, Burundi, 1985, Santiago, Chile, 1988, spokesman Ministry Fgn. Affairs, 1990, diplomat Mission to European Union, 1993, dep. chief of mission Washington, 1994, dep. dir. gen. polit. affairs Ministry Fgn. Affairs, 1998, chef de cabinet of min. fgn. affairs, 2000, permanent rep. to UN NYC, 2004—. Office: Belgium Mission to UN One Dag Hammarskjold Plz 885 Second Ave 41st Fl New York NY 10017 Office Phone: 212-378-6300. Office Fax: 212-681-7618. E-mail: newyorkUN@diplobel.be.

VERBIN, JEFFREY HAROLD, lawyer; b. Chgo., July 28, 1948; s. Marvin Verbin and Eleanor (Chernoff) Cohen; m. Jacqueline Rochelle Lewis, Aug. 23, 1970; children: Matt, Dana, Alexis. BS, U. Ill., 1971; JD, Washington U., St. Louis, 1974. Bar: Ill. 1974, Calif. 1979, Ariz. 1981. With firm Altheimer & Gray, Chgo., 1974-79, Kaufman & Waring, San Diego, 1979-80, O'Connor Cavanagh Anderson Westover Killingsworth & Beshears, Phoenix, 1981—, sr. ptnr.; now mng. shareholder Greenberg Traurig LLP, Phoenix. Co-chair dinner Multiple Sclerosis Soc., Phoenix, 1992; vice chair 39th ann. testimonial dinner NCCJ, Phoenix, 1992; mem. legal and fin. com. Temple Chai, Phoenix, 1991-92. Mem. ABA (comml. fin. svcs., consumer fin. svcs., banking law and savs. instns. coms. of bus. law sect.) Ill. State Bar Assn., State Bar Ariz. chair spl. subcom. of bus. law sect., mem. legis. subcom. of bus. law sect., chair bus. law sect. 1988-89), State Bar Calif., Maricopa County Bar Assn., Order of Coif. Jewish. Avocation: sports. Office: Greenberg Traurig LLP Ste 700 2375 E Camelback Rd Phoenix AZ 85016-9000 Office Phone: 602-445-8202. Office Fax: 602-445-8100. Business E-Mail: verbinj@gtlaw.com.

VERBINSKI, GORE, film director; b. NYC, Mar. 16, 1964; Grad., UCLA Film Sch., 1987. Former punk band guitarist; worked on various advertising campaigns; creator of the Budweiser frogs. Dir., writer: (films) The Ritual, 1996; dir.: Mousehunt, 1997, The Mexican, 2001, The Ring, 2002, Pirates of the Caribbean: The Curse of the Black Pearl, 2003, The Weather Man, 2005, Pirates of the Caribbean: Dead Man's Chest, 2006 (Best Movie, MTV Movie Awards, 2007), Pirates of the Caribbean: At World's End, 2007. Recipient 4 Clio awards. *

VERBOV, LEV FALKOVICH, metallurgical engineer, freelance/self-employed translator, writer; b. Leningrad, Russia, Jan. 10, 1937; came to U.S., 1977; s. Falka Shevelevich and Elka Abramovna Verbova; m. Larisa Ivanovna Fedkushova, Nov. 26, 1990; 1 child, Kristina Kulbe. MS in Metall. Engring., State Polytechnic U., St. Petersburg, Russia, 1962. Sr. engr. All-Union Inst. Aluminum, Magnesium and Electrode Industry, St. Petersburg, 1962-77; engr.-scientist Aluminum Co. of Am., New Kensington, Pa., 1979-82; asst. editor Chem. Abstracts Svcs., Columbus, Ohio, 1985-87; cons. R&D scientist ECC Am., Inc., Sandersville, Ga., 1988-90; clk., team mem. Local Census Ctr., Bklyn., 1999-2000; freelance writer Bklyn., 1966—; freelance translator, 1982—. Author: (books) Commercial Star, 1999, Swan Song of Ugly Duckling, 2000; composer: Solemn Melody, 1999; patentee in field. E-mail: lverbov@aol.com.

VERBURG, EDWIN ARNOLD, management consultant; b. Lakehurst, NJ, Oct. 6, 1945; s. Edwin Donald Verburg and Dorothy (Orrell) Hoodless; m. Joyce Elaine Majack, Sept. 14, 1968; children: Adelle Kristine, Wendi Elizabeth. BS, Calif. Poly. U., 1968; M in City Planning, U. Calif., Berkeley, 1970; D in Pub. Adminstrn., George Washington U., 1975. Asst. planner City of Inglewood, Calif., 1970-71; planner City of Glendale, Calif., 1971-72; grad. assoc. U.S. Army Corps Engrs., Washington, 1974-75; mgr. fiscal analysis Met. Washington Coun. Govt., 1975-77; sr. program analyst U.S. Fish and Wildlife Svc., Washington, 1977-79, asst. divsn. chief, 1979-80, divsn. chief, 1980-82, asst. dir. planning and budget, 1982-86, dep. asst. dir. policy budget and adminstrn., 1986-87; dir. office of fin. U.S. Dept. Treas., Washington, 1987-88, dir. fin. svc. directorate, 1988-91, dir. fin. svc. directorate, dep. CFO, 1991-95; assoc. adminstr. adminstrn. FAA, 1995-98; prin. ptnr. Avant Mgmt. Group, Inc., 1998-99; prin., fedn. govt. svc. Kelly, Anderson & Assocs., 1999—2002, v.p., 2003—, trustee, bd. dirs., 2005—. Author: Local State and Federal Fiscal Flows, 5 Vols., 1976; contbr. articles to profl. jours. Recipient Disting. Pub. Svc. award George Washington U., Sch. Bus. and Pub. Mgmt., 1994, Sec. of Treasury Disting Svc. award, 1995, Fin. Mgmt. Svc. Commr. award, 1996. Mem. Am. Inst. Cert. Planners, Am. Planning Assn. (cert. govt. fin. mgr., Merit award Calif. chpt. 1973, First award Nat. Capital area chpt. 1980, Peer award for pub. svc. Dept. of Treasury 1990, sec. of treas. cert. appreciation 1991, Pres.'s Meritorious Svc. award 1991, Commr. Citation Fin. Mgmt. Svc. 1996, Pres. award Combined Fed. Campaign 1997), Kiwanis (Arlington chpt. bd. dirs. 1999-2001, v.p. 2001-02, pres.-elect 2002-03, disting. pres. 2003-04, Capitol dist. disting. lt. gov. 20th divsn. capitol dist. Kiwanis Internat. 2005-06, Hixson award 2004) Home: 538 N Oakland St Arlington VA 22203-2219 Office: Kelly Andersen & Assocs Inc 424 N Washington St Alexandria VA 22314-2312 Business E-Mail: everburg@kellyandersen.com.

VERCAMMEN, KENNETH ALBERT, lawyer, prosecutor; b. Edison, NJ, Aug. 7, 1959; BS, U. Scranton, 1981; JD, Univ. Del. Law Sch., 1985. Bar: N.J., Pa. 1985, N.Y. 1986, D.C. 1987; cert. mediator N.J. Superior Ct., 1997-. Mng. atty., Cranbury, NJ, 1990—; prosecutor Township of Cranbury, Middlesex County, NJ, 1991—99; spl. acting prosecutor Delaware County, Pa. District Office, Middlesex County Probation Dept., Scranton Dist. Magistrate Office, Woodbridge, East Brunswick, Metuchen, South Brunswick, Clark, Berkeley; acting assoc. prosecutor Carteret Mcpl. Ct., Middlesex County, NJ, 2000. Adj. prof. Middlesex County Coll., Edison, 1990-91, 2001; instr. criminal law and procedure and bus. law; mem. com. mcpl. ct. edn. N.J. Supreme Ct., 1990-97; spkr. litig. engagements, wills, elder law and probate. Author 132 separate law rev. and legal periodicals articles to profl. jours. including N.J. Law Jour., ABA Barrister, N.J. Lawyer, ABA Law Practice Mgmt., Dictum; editor N.J. Municipal Ct. Law Review, 1993-; author, DWI & Drug Cases, 2005. Winner of NJ State Bar Gen. Practitioner of Yr. award, 2002, Atty. of Yr. award NJ Bar Assn. Mcpl. Ct., 2006. Mem.: N.J. State Bar Assn. (chair mcpl. ct. sect.), Middlesex Mcpl. Prosecutor's Assn. (co-chmn. mcpl. ct. practice com. 1997—, mem. bd. trustees 2000—). Avocations: cross-country running, soccer. Office: 2053 Woodbridge Ave Edison NJ 08817

VERCAUTEREN, RICHARD FRANK, career officer; b. Manchester, Feb. 9, 1945; s. Louis P. and Janet (Beliveau) V.; m. Gail Anne Settoon, June 3, 1972. BA in Sociology, Providence Coll., 1967; MA in Bus. Mgmt., George Washington U., 1980; MA in Internat. Studies, Georgetown U., 1996. Commd. 2d lt. USMC, 1967, advanced through grades to brig. gen., 1993; platoon comdr. 2d bn., 9th Marines, Vietnam, 1968; comdg. officer Rifle Co., Hawaii, 1971-73; mil. observer UN, Egypt, Israel, Lebanon, 1976-78; comdg. officer Spl. Task Force, S.Am., 1982; aide de camp Marine Forces Atlantic, Norfolk, Va., 1982-84; bn. comdr. 3d bn., 2nd Marines, Camp Lejeune, N.C., 1985-87; regional comdr. Embassy Guards SubSahara Africa, Nairobi, Africa, 1987-90; dep. dir. plans Hdqs., USMC, Washington, 1990-92, dir. plans, 1990-92; comdg. officer 2nd Marine Regiment, Camp Lejeune, 1992-93; comdg. gen. 1st Marine Exped Brigade, Honolulu, 1993-95; dir. stragety and plans Hdqr. USMC, 1995—. Mem. exec. bd. Capitol dist. Boy Scouts Am., Washington, 1991-92; sr. counselor Seminar XXII, MIT, Washington, 1995-96; bd. dirs. Girl Scouts U.S. Decorated Silver Star medal, Legion of Merit, Distinguished Svc. Medal; recipient Holland M. Smith award Navy League, 1982; MIT Ctr. Internat. Tech. Studies fellow in fgn. politics, 1991, fellow in nat. security studies Harvard U., 1995. Mem. Navy League (bd. dirs.), Army-Navy Club (Washington), Oahu Country Club (Honolulu), Plaza Club, Rotary. Avocations: running, golf, skiing, history, travel. Home: PO Box 222 Occoquan VA 22125-0222

VERCELLOTTI, JOHN RAYMOND, chemist, researcher; b. Joliet, Ill., May 2, 1933; s. Joseph Francis and Mary Teresa (Walowski) V.; m. Sharon Cecile Vergez, Sept. 3, 1966; children: Ellen Theresa, Paul Auguste. BA, St. Bonaventure U., 1955; MS, Marquette U., 1960; PhD, Ohio State U., 1963. Lectr., rsch. assoc. Ohio State U., Columbus, 1963-64; asst. prof. Marquette U., Milw., 1964-67; assoc. prof. U. Tenn., Knoxville, 1967-70; prof. Va. Poly. Inst. & State U., Blacksburg, 1970-79; vis. prof. Inst. G. Ronzoni, Milan, 1977-78; sr. scientist Gulf South Res. Inst., New Orleans, 1980-85; rsch. chemist, rsch. leader So. Regional Rsch. Ctr. USDA, New Orleans, 1985-96, collaborator, 1999—. V.p. and sr. chemist V-Labs Inc., Covington, La., 1980-85, 96—; sr. rsch. advisor Sugar Processing Rsch. Inst., Inc., New Orleans, 1996-99, 2001--; adj. prof. chemistry and physics S.E. La. U., Hammond, 1986—. Contbr. articles to profl. jours., chapters to books. U. Tenn. minority colls. grantee, 1968-70, NSF grantee, 1964—. Fellow Sigma Xi; mem. Am. Chem. Soc. (sec. 1968-90, Melville L. Wolfrom award 1994), Inst. Food Technologists. Democrat. Roman Catholic. Achievements include research on food flavor quality and agricultural commodity utilization, origin of flavor from carbohydrates, lipid oxidation products, and peptides. Home: 113 E 25th Ave Covington LA 70433-2819 Office: V-Labs Inc 423 N Theard St Covington LA 70433-2837 Office Phone: 985-893-0533. Business E-Mail: v-labs@v-labs.com.

VERDE, MICHAEL I., lawyer; b. NYC, Jan. 26, 1959; BA cum laude, Columbia Coll., 1980; JD magna cum laude, NY Law Sch., 1988. Bar: NY 1989, Maine 1992, US Dist. Ct., So. and Ea. Dist. NY 1989. Ptnr. Katten Muchin Zavis Rosenman, NYC. Mem.: ABA. Office: Katten Muchin Zavis Rosenman 575 Madison Ave New York NY 10022 Office Phone: 212-940-8541. Office Fax: 212-940-8776. E-mail: michael.verde@kmzr.com.

VERDERY, DAVID NORWOOD, broadcast programming executive; b. Waco, Tex., Dec. 12, 1943; s. David Paul and Ruthe (McCawley) V.; m. Randy Lee Mahan, June 6, 1968 (div. 1970); 1 child, David Roderick. Student, Baylor U., 1961-64. Announcer KEFC, Waco, 1962-64; announcer, producer KHFI, Austin, Tex., 1964-65; announcer, prodn. dir. KIXL, Dallas, 1965-66; program dir. KVIL, Dallas, 1967, KABL, San Francisco, 1968-69; nat. program coord. The McLendon Co., Dallas, 1969-73; v.p. programming TM Programming, Dallas, 1973-80, Bonneville Broadcasting Sys., Northbrook, Ill., 1980-86; music dir. KBIG, LA, 1985-95, asst. program dir., music dir., 1996-97, program dir., 1997; ret., 1998. Mem. Project Angel Food, L.A., 1992-94; mem. Permanent Charities Com., L.A., 1995-97, mem. Reading for the Blind, L.A., 1996-97; bd. dirs. Waco Civic Theatre, 1999-2001, v.p., 2000-01; bd. dirs. Met. Cmty. Ch., 2001-04; emperor X Royal Sovereign and Imperial Ct. of Ctrl. Tex. Empire, 2003-04. Named Adult Contemporary Music Dir. of Yr., The Gavin Report, 1992, 93. Avocations: gourmet cooking, theater, travel, musical composition, magic. Personal E-mail: wacodave@hot.rr.com.

VERDI, ROBERT, jewelry designer, fashion expert, television personality; b. Maplewood, NJ, Aug. 28, 1968; Grad., Fashion Inst. of Tech. Designed jewelry, pieces sold at Barneys, Bendels, Bloomingdales and Bergdorf Goodman; style correspondent Gay Entertainment Television, 1994; prodr. Cynthia Rowley Fall'97 fashion show; host Full Frontal Fashion; personal designer to Sandra Bernhard, Richard Kind, Marishka Hargitay, Bobby Flay, Jolie Fisher, Hugh Jackman and Eva Longoria; co-host Suprise by Design Discovery Channel, 2002—04; host Fashion Police, 2004. Host: (fashion events and specials) E!, Style, Discovery Channel and Women's Entertainment; appeared in two episodes: (TV series) Hope and Faith, 2004; judge: Miss America Pageant, 2006; appeared in: (films) The Devil Wears Prada, 2006; appeared as interior design and fashion expert on: Regis and Kelly; The View; The Today Show; The Fabulous Life of... Office: E! Networks 5750 Wilshire Blvd Los Angeles CA 90036 *

VERDIER, DAVID D'OOGE, ophthalmologist, educator; b. Grand Rapids, Mich., Jan. 22, 1949; s. Leonard D'Ooge and Anita Beatrice (Carvalho) V.; m. Beverly Deane Johnson; children: Renée Leigh, Travis D'Ooge, Eric Leonard, Nora Claire. BA in Polit. Sci., U. Mich., 1971; MD, U. Mich. Med. Sch., 1977. Resident in family practice Med. U. S.C., Charleston, 1977-80; resident in ophthalmology Pitts. Eye and Ear, U. Pitts., 1980-83; corneal and external eye fellowship U. Iowa, Iowa City, 1983-84; pvt. practice med. and surg. ophthalmology Verdier Eye Ctr. P.L.C., Grand Rapids, Mich., 1984—; clin. prof. Mich. State U. Coll. Medicine, East Lansing, 1986—. Med. dir. Mich. Tissue Bank, Lansing, Mich., 1995-98; mem. med. adv. bd. Eye Bank Assn. Am., 2003—; bd. dirs. SEECOM, 1995—, Cape Elethra Found., 2004—. Contbr. articles to profl. jours. and textbook chpts. Bd. dirs. East Grand Rapids (Mich.) Sch. Found., 1992-2000, Macatawa Bay Yacht Club, Holland, Mich., 1988-90, 94-95, Grand Rapids Art Mus., 1995-2001; bd. dirs. Macatawa Park Cottagers Assn., Holland, 1993-99, pres., 1993-98. Named to Galens Hon. Med. Soc., 1975-77. Mem. Mich. Ophthalmologic Soc. (bd. dirs. 1994-2000), Mich. State Med. Soc. (del. 1993-2000, Eye Bank Assn. Am. (med adv bd. 2003—). Home: 3043 Mary St SE Grand Rapids MI 49506-3150 Office: Verdier Eye Center PLC 1000 E Paris Ave SE Ste 130 Grand Rapids MI 49546-3680

VERDILE, VINCENT PAUL, dean, emergency physician; b. Troy, NY, Aug. 13, 1955; s. Raphael Mario and Frances (Marinucci) V.; m. Louise Ann Wickware, Aug. 30, 1985. BS, Union U., 1977, MS, 1980; MD, Albany Med. Coll., 1984. Intern U. Pitts., 1984-85, resident in emergency medicine, 1985-87; assoc. med. dir. dept. pub. safety City of Pitts., 1985—93; flight physician Ctr. for Emergency Medicine, Pitts., 1988—93; chair. dept. of emergency med. Albany Med. Coll., 1993—2000, interim dean, 2000, dean, 2001—. Mem. adj. staff dept. emergency medicine Mercy Hosp., Pitts, 1987—93; med. dir., emergency med. technician Community Coll. Allegheny Coll., 1987—93; attending physician emergency dept. Presbyn.-Univ. Hosp., 1987—93; assoc. program dir. residency in emergency medicine Univ. of Pitts., 1987—93, asst. prof. medicine, 1987—93. Contbr. numerous articles to profl. jours. Mem. Soc. Acad. Emergency Medicine, Nat. Assn. Emergency Med. Svcs. Physicians (chmn. membership com. 1988—), Am. Coll. Emergency Physicians, Pa. chpt. Am. Coll. Emergency Physicians, Pa. State Med. Soc., Allegheny County Med. Soc., Am. Assn. Poison Control Ctrs. Roman Catholic. Office: Albany Med Coll Office of Dean 43 New Scotland Ave Albany NY 12208

VERDONI, SHAWN MARIE, not-for-profit fundraiser; b. South Sioux City, Iowa, Apr. 12, 1968; d. Mark Francis Hanrahan and Kristine Jane Engaas; m. Richard J. Verdoni; children: Erin, Jonah. BE, U. Wis., Whitewater, 1990. Adminstrv. asst. Med. Coll. Wis., Wauwatosa, 1992—95, sr. adminstrv. asst., 1995—99, database analyst, 1999—2001; philanthropy assoc. Aurora Vis. Nurse Assn. Wis., Milw., 2001—06, sr. philanthropy officer, 2006, philanthropy officer, 2006—. Cabinet mem. Aurora Partnership campaign Aurora Healthcare, Milw., 2004—05; mentor Aurora Leadership Acad., Milw. Team capt. AIDS walk AIDS Resource Ctr. Wis., Milw., 2000—06; vol. Mukwonago Libr. Expansion, Wis.; lectr. St. James Cath. Ch., Mukwonago. Recipient Aurora Star, Aurora Healthcare, 2002, 2004. Mem.: Assn. Healthcare Profls., Assn. Fundraising Profls. Avocations: camping, gardening, sewing. Office: Aurora Vis Nurse Assn Wis 1155 Honey Creek Pky Wauwatosa WI 53213

VERDU, SERGIO, engineering educator; b. Barcelona, Aug. 16, 1958; arrived in U.S., 1980; s. Tomas Verdu and Visitacion Lucas; m. Mercedes Paratje, Jan. 19, 1982; 1 child, Ariana. Diploma in Telecom. Engring., Poly. U. Barcelona, 1980; MS, U. Ill., Urbana-Champaign, 1982, PhD, 1984; DHL (hon.), Polytechnic U., Catalonia, 2005. Asst. prof. dept. elec. engring. Princeton U., NJ, 1984-89, assoc. prof., 1989-92, prof., 1993—. Prin. investigator US Office Naval Rsch., NJ Dept. Higher Edn., US Army Rsch. Office, NJ Commn. Sci. and Tech., NSF, US-Israel Binational Sci. Found.; vis. prof. U. Calif., Berkeley, 1998; vis. rsch. prof. Math. Sci. Rsch. Inst., 2002. Author: Multiuser Detection, 1998, Information Theory: Fifty Years of Discovery, 1999; mem. editl. bd. Transactions on Info. Theory, 1990-94;; editor-in-chief Foundations and Trends in Comm. and Info. Theory, 2003—; contbr. numerous articles to profl. jours, chpts. to books. Recipient Nat. U. prize Ministry Edn., Spain, 1982, Presdl. Young Investigator award NSF, 1988, Frederick E. Terman award Am. Soc. Engring. Edn., 2000, Joint IEEE Comm. Info. Theory Paper award, 2007, Claude E. Shannon award, 2007. Fellow: IEEE (Outstanding Paper award 1998, Millennium medal 2000, Comm./Info. Theory Paper award 2006); mem.: NAE, Info. Theory Soc. (bd. govs. 1989—99, v.p. 1995, pres. 1997, Golden Jubilee Paper award 1998, Leonard G. Abraham Paper award 2002). Office: Dept Elec Engring Princeton U B-308 Engring Quadrangle Princeton NJ 08544 Office Phone: 609-258-5315. Office Fax: 609-258-3745. E-mail: verdu@princeton.edu. *

VER DUIN, D'ARLENE K., sociologist, researcher; b. Grand Rapids, Mich., Sept. 19, 1952; m. O. Lynn Sims, Mar. 15, 1996. BA in Sociology, U. North Tex., Denton, 1995, MPA, 1998. Rsch. scientist U. North Tex., 1999—. Author: (plays) Not Even a Goodbye, 1983. Mem. Ft. Worth Civic Orch. (pres. 1985-87), Pi Alpha Alpha. Democrat. Christian. Avocations: genealogy, needle arts, viola. Office: Univ North Tex Survey Rsch Ctr PO Box 310637 Denton TX 76203 Office Phone: 940-565-4939. Business E-Mail: dverduin@pacs.unt.edu.

VEREB, TERESA B., psychiatrist; b. Poland; d. Joseph and Henryka Biskup; m. Bartholomew Vereb, Aug. 3, 1968; children: Bartholomew Jr., Teresa Tilden. MD, Acad. Medicine, Warsaw, 1966. Cert. stress mgmt. Am. Acad. Experts in Traumatic Stress, 2005. Resident psychiatry Hosp. Wolsky, Warsaw, 1966—68, Med. Sch. Safarik U., Kosice, Czech Republic, 1968—70, staff psychiatry, 1971—72; resident psychiatry SUNY, Buffalo, 1977—78; clin. instr. psychiatry Meyer Meml. Hosp., Buffalo, 1977—78; resident psychiatry U. Fla., Gainesville, 1978—80; pvt. practice gen. psychiatry Bradenton, Fla., 1980—; staff psychiatrist Blake Hosp., Bradenton, 1980—, Manatee Meml. Hosp., Bradenton, 1980—, chief psychiatry, sectional chief psychiatry, 1981—85, 1987—91, chairperson psychiat. sect., 2000. Active Sacred Heart Cath. Ch., Bradenton, 1980—. Named Am. Top Psychiatrist, Consumer's Rsch. Coun. Am., 2006; recipient Disting. Physician award, Fla. Med. Assn., 2005. Mem.: AMA (Physician Recognition award 1995—2002, 2005—06), Am. Acad. Experts in Traumatic Stress, Manatee County Med. Soc., Fla. Psychiat. Assn., Fla. Med. Assn. (Physician Recognition award 1995—2005, Rogeriem Pfizer Re-Commn. 1999, Am. Top Rate Physician 1999, Top Psychiatrist 2004—05, Boar Cert. for stress mgmt. 2005), Am. Psychiat. Assn. Achievements include successfully climbed Mount Kilimanjaro, 1997. Avocations: water-skiing, skiing, swimming, hiking, mountain climbing. Office: Vereb and Vereb MDs PA 5015 Manatee Ave West Bradenton FL 34209

VEREBEY, KARL GEZA, toxicologist, pharmacologist, educator; b. Budapest, Hungary, Mar. 12, 1938; came to U.S., 1956; s. Karoly and Etelka (Szabo) V.; m. Debra Adler, Feb. 22, 1962; children: Rita, Todd, Marc. AA, Eotvos J. Gimnazium, Budapest, Hungary, 1956; BA, Hunter Coll., 1965; MA, CUNY, 1968; PhD, Cornell U. Med. Coll., 1972. Diplomate Am. Bd. Forensic Toxicology; cert. clin. lab. dir. Am. Bd. Bioanalysis; lic. clin. lab. dir., N.Y., N.J., Ill., Md., Vt. Dir. clin. pharmacology State of N.Y., NYC, 1973-88; dir. clin. lab. Psychiat. Diagnostic Lab. Am., South Plainfield, N.J., 1982-89; chief toxicologist City of N.Y., 1989-92; dir. toxicology N.Y. State Inst. Basic Rsch., SI, 1992-95; pres., dir. Leadtech Corp., North Bergen, NJ, 1992—2001; dir. Ammon Analytical Lab., 1999—. Assoc. prof. SUNY Health Sci. Ctr., 1978; mem. exec. com. Drug Abuse Adv. Bd., N.Y. State Dept. Health, 1985; advisor subcom. on trace metals analysis to Nat. Com. on Clin. Lab. Stds., 1992; insp. Nat. Lab. Cert. Program dept. Health and Human Svcs., 1989. Mem. editl. bd. Jour. Addictive Diseases, 1981; contbr. over 100 articles to sci. jours., chpts. to books. With U.S. Army, 1961-63. Rsch. fellow USPHS, 1968-73; grantee Cornell U. Med. Coll., 1974-77, Narcotic and Drug Rsch., Inc., 1974-76, 79-81, DuPont Pharm., 1985; inductee Hunter Coll. Hall of Fame, 1989; named Water Polo Champion, NY Athletic Club, 1959, 60, 61. Fellow Am. Acad. Forensic Sci.; mem. N.Y. Acad. Sci., Am. Soc. Pharmacology and Exptl. Therapeutics, Soc. Forensic Toxicologists. Avocations: water polo, soccer, tennis, photography. Home: 638 Debchar Ct River Vale NJ 07675-6409 Home Phone: 201-391-0015; Office Phone: 908-862-4404. Personal E-mail: k.verebey@att.net.

VEREEN, BEN, actor, singer, dancer; b. Miami, Fla., Oct. 10, 1946; m. Nancy Vereen; children: Benjamin, Malakia, Naja, Kabara, Karon. Student, High Sch. of Performing Arts; LHD (hon.), Emerson Coll., 1977. Debut off-Broadway in The Prodigal Son, 1965; played Brother Ben in Sweet Charity, N.Y.C., Las Vegas, San Francisco, 1966, Daddy Brubeck in Can. tour, 1968, in Los Angeles co. of Hair, 1968, joined Broadway cast, 1969; played role of Judas in Jesus Christ Superstar, 1971 (Theatre World award); leading role in Pippin', 1972 (Tony award, Drama Desk award); appeared in Grind, 1985, Jelly's Last Jam, 1993, Wicked, 2005; numerous theatrical appearances, including I'm Not Rappaport, San Francisco, 1989, A Christmas Carol, 1995, 96; appeared in TV films Louis Armstrong-Chicago Style, 1976, Uptown: A Tribute to the Apollo Theatre, 1980, Pippin: His Life and Times, 1981, Breakin' Through, 1984, The Jesse Owens Story, 1984, Lost in London, 1985, The Saint in Manhattan, 1987, Jenny's Song, 1988, The Kid Who Loved Christmas, 1990, Intruders, 1992, Fosse, 2001, Feast of All Saints, 2001; created role of Chicken George in TV miniseries Roots, 1977 (TV Critics award); other TV miniseries include Ellis Island, 1984, A.D., 1985, Silk Stalkings, 1991; appeared in TV spl. Ben Vereen-His Roots, 1978, Uptown-A Tribute to the Apollo Theatre; film appearances: Funny Lady, 1975, All That Jazz, 1979, Buy and Cell, 1989, Once Upon a Forrest, 1993 (voice only), Why Do Fools Fall in Love, 1998, I'll Take You There, 1999, The Painting, 2001, Idlewild, 2006; TV appearances: Touched by an Angel, 1997; TV series include: Tenspeed and Brown Shoe, 1980, Webster, J.J. Starbuck, 1988, Promised Land, 1996, The Jamie Foxx Show, 1996, (narrator) Vaudeville: An American Masters Special, 1997; also nightclub appearances. Chmn. Dance for Heart campaign Am. Heart Assn.; internat. chmn. Sudden Infant Death Syndrome; established Naja Vereen Meml. Scholarship Fund, 1988; founder, pres. Celebrities for a Drug-Free Am. Recipient George M. Cohan award Am. Guild Variety Artists, 1976, Image award NAACP, 1978, 79, Israel's Cultural award, 1978, Israel's Humanitarian award, 1979, Eleanor Roosevelt Humanitarian award, 1983. Mem. Actor's Equity Assn., Am. Guild Variety Artists, AFTRA, SAG. Office: care Pamela Cooper 2968 Corral Canyon Rd Malibu CA 90265-2915 *I am like the turtle--determined and will stick my neck out; turtles also teach me patience.*

VEREEN, ROBERT CHARLES, retired trade association administrator; b. Stillwater, Minn., Sept. 8, 1924; s. George and Leona Lucille (Made) Wihren; m. Rose Catherine Blair, Nov. 5, 1945; children: Robin, Stacy, Kim. Grad. high sch. Mng. editor Comml. West Mag., Mpls., 1946-50, Bruce Pub. Co., St. Paul, 1950-53, Nat. Retail Hardware Assn., Indpls., 1953-59; mng. dir. Liberty Distbrs., Phila., 1959-63; editor Hardware Retailing, Indpls., 1963-80; assoc. pub., dir. communications Nat. Retail Hardware Assn., 1980-84, sr. v.p., 1984-87; Vereen & Assocs., Mgmt., Mktg. Cons., 1987—. Lectr. mgmt. insts.; guest lectr. on distbn. pub.; co-founder U.S.A. Direct; co-founder, ptnr. Eurotrade Mktg., 1988—; ptnr. Hardlines Pers. Finders, 1987—. Author: (with Paul M. Doane) Hunting for Profit, 1965, The Computer Age in Merchandising, 1968, Perpetuating the Family-Owned Business, 1970, The How-To of Merchandising, 1975, The How-To of Store Operations, 1976, A Guide to Financial Management, 1976, Productivity: A Crisis for Management, 1978, Hardlines Rep Report Newsletter, 1984-94, Guidelines to Improve the Rep/Factory Relationships, 1992; contbr. articles to profl. jours. and mags. Served with AUS, 1943-46. Mem. Am. Soc. Bus. Press Editors (dir., v.p. 1966-70), Soc. Nat. Assn. Publs. (dir., pres. 1970-75, chmn. journalism edn. liaison com. 1976-79), Toastmasters (v.p., treas., sec. 1955-59), Am. Hardware Mfrs. Assn. (co-founder, sec.-treas. Young Execs. Club 1958-.59, 63-65), Hardware-Housewares Packaging Expn. (founder 1960, chmn. com. packaging 1960-62, chmn. judging com. Hardware-Packaging Expn. 1975-78), Packaging Inst., Household Consumer Products Export Coun. (chmn. 1981-83), World-Wide DIY Coun. (exec. sec. 1981-99, dir. emeritus 1999—). Home and Office: 10769 Oriole Ct Indianapolis IN 46231-1006 Home Phone: 317-838-7632; Office Phone: 317-838-7632.

VEREEN, WILLIAM JEROME, uniform manufacturing company executive; s. William Coachman and Mary Elizabeth V.; m. Lula Evelyn King; children: Elizabeth King, William Coachman. BS in Indsl. Mgmt, Ga. Inst. Tech., 1963. With Riverside Mfg. Co., Moultrie, 1967—, from v.p. to exec. v.p., 1970-77, pres., 1977-84, pres., treas., CEO, 1984—; v.p., dir. Moultrie Cotton Mills, 1969—; exec. v.p. Riverside Industries, Inc., Moultrie, 1973-77, pres., 1977-84, CEO, 1984—, also dir. V.p. Riverside Uniform Rentals, Inc., Moultrie, 1971-80, pres., 1980-84, CEO, bd. dirs.; pres. Riverside Mfg. Co. (Ireland) Ltd., 1977—, Right Image Corp., Riverside Mfg. Co. GmbH, Germany, 1979—, also CEO, dir., 1984; pres., treas., CEO G.A. Rivers Corp., Riverside Mfg. Co. (U.K.) Ltd.; pres., treas. CEO, bd. dirs. Textile Clothing Tech. Corp.; chairholder Tyner eminent scholars, prof. coll. human scis. Fla. State U., 1993-94, mem. coll. human scis. devel. bd.; bd. dirs. Ga. Power Co., Gerber Sci., Inc., Blue Cross/Blue Shield Ga., Cerulean Cos., Inc., Trade and Tourism, Ga. Rsch. Alliance, Ga. Corp. Indsl. Devel.; mem. trilateral commn. apparel labeling NAFTA; so. regional adv. dir. Bank of Am. (GA) (formerly Nations Bank, N.A.; advisor textile and apparel tariffs and quotas U.S. Dept. State Bd.; mem. World Econ. Forum, Davos, Switzerland. Bd. dirs. Moultrie-Colquitt County (Ga.) Devel. Authority, 1973-77, Moultrie-Colquitt County United Givers, 1968-75, Moultrie YMCA, 1968-75, Colquitt County Cancer Soc., 1969-73; trustee Cmty. Welfare Assn. Moultrie, 1970—, Pineland Sch., Moultrie, 1971-75, Leadership Ga., 1972—, Ga. Coun. Econ. Edn.; trustee Am. Apparel Edn. Found.; adv. bd. Ga. Tech. sch. of textile and fiber engring.; elder 1st Presbyterian Ch. Capt. USMCR, 1963-67. Decorated Bronze Star with combat V, Purple Heart. Mem. Internat. Apparel Fedn. (2d v.p., 1st v.p., bd. dirs., exec. com., chmn. 1991-92), Am. Apparel Mfrs. Assn. (bd. dirs., exec. com., edn. found. com., 2d vice chmn., chmn. 1990-91), Nat. Assn. Uniform Mfrs. and Distbrs. (bd. dirs. 1988-91), Am. Apparel Edn. Found. (v.p., trustee), Capital City Club (Atlanta), Commerce Club (Atlanta), World Econ. Forum, Sunset Country Club, Ga. C. of C., Elks, Kiwanis, Sigma Alpha Epsilon. Office: PO Box 460 Moultrie GA 31776-0460

VERGANO, LYNN (MARILYNN BETTE VERGANO), artist; b. NYC, Nov. 14; d. George and Sis (Helaine Haas) Anagnostis; children: Scott, Stephen, Sandy, Sefton. Student, Pratt Inst.; BA, MA, NYU. Lectr. art Morris County Coll., 1982. Lectr. various museums and art assns., 1979—. Author, illustrator: Paintings by Lynn Vergano, 1980, Paintings by Lynn Vergano, 1998; one-woman shows include Paper Mill Playhouse, NJ, 1976, 79, 83, Fairleigh Dickinson U., NJ, 1977, Drew U., NJ, 1977, Rutgers U., NJ, 1978-79, Hong Kong Arts Ctr., 1980, Am. Univ. Alumni, Bangkok, Thailand, 1980, Caldwell Coll., NJ, 1980, União Cultural Brasil-Estados Unidos, São Paulo, Brazil, 1982, Galleria Fenice, Venice, Italy, 1985, St. Sophia Mus., Istanbul, Turkey, 1988, Nat. Arts Club, NYC, 1989, Centreplace, Hamilton, New Zealand, 1990, Coll. Club White Plains, NY, 1996, UN Pan Pacific and SE Women's Assn., 2001, 06, Chang Gung Meml. Hosp., Kaohsiung, Taiwan, 2002, Puebla, Mex., 2003, El Paso, Tex., 2006, UN, 2006, Morris Mus., 2006, Hudson River Mus., 2006, Macculloch Hall Mus., 2006; exhibited in group shows at Monmouth Mus., Lincroft, NJ, 1976-77, 82, Morris Mus., Morristown, NJ, 1977-78, 88, 2003, NJ State Capital Mus., Trenton, 1979, Nat. Audubon Artists, NYC, 1981, Salmagundi Club, NYC, 1981, World Trade Ctr., NYC, 1981, Nat. Arts Club, NYC, 1981—, Bergen Mus., Paramus, NJ, 1983, Macculloch Hall Hist. Mus., NJ, Morristown, 1984, 87, 89, 92, 96, Lincoln Ctr., NYC, 1987, 2002, Montclair State Coll., 1986, Bklyn. Botanic Gardens, NY, 1987, Seton Hall U., South Orange, NJ, 1998, Johnson & Johnson, New Brunswick, NJ, 2000, 7th Annual Internat. Artisans' Ball, NY Acad. Scis., 2004, 06, AAUW, New Providence, NJ, 2006, others; exhbn. UN Pan Pacific and SE Asia Women's Assn.-NY chpt. NY Acad. Sci., 1998, 2001, Nabisco World Hdqrs., Hanover, NJ, 1982, 99. Recipient UN 25th Anniversary Creative Writing award, 1970, John H. Miller award Morris County Coll., 1979, Audubon award Messiah Coll., Pa., 1980, State Competition award, AAUW, 1981, Painting award, AAUW Douglass Coll., 1981, Grumbacher Gold medallion, 1984, Torch award NYU, 1993, Heydenryk Painting award Nat. Arts Club, 2007; Winston scholar 2005-07. Mem. Nat. Arts Club (exhibiting, Heydenryk award 108th Ann. Exhibiting Artist Members' exhibition 2007), Nat. Soc. Arts and Letters (exec. bd. NJ chpt. 1979—, judge 1980, 82, 83, 2005-07), Federated Art Assns. NJ (trustee 1982—, pres., chmn. bd. dirs. 1982-88, Heritage plaque 1989), Am. Soc. Geolinguistics (bd. dirs. 2003, 04), Shanghai-Tiffin Club (hon., Disting. Svc. award 1998), Welcome Wagon Club (hon., pres., chpt. charter mem., 1969-70), Hudson River Mus. (hon.), Morris Mus. Friends (hon.), Delta Kappa Gamma (hon.).

VERGARA, CAMILO JOSÉ, photographer; BA in Sociology, U. Notre Dame, 1968; MA in Sociology, Columbia U., 1977, postgrad. Co-author: Silent Cities: The Evolution of the American Cemetery, 1989; author: The New American Ghetto, 1995 (Robert E. Park award Am. Sociol. Assn., 1997), American Ruins, 1999, Unexpected Chicagoland, 2001, Twin Towers Remembered, 2001; contbr. art, Loud Paper Mag. Fellow Revson fellow, Columbia U., 1986—87, MacArthur Found. fellow, 2002.

VERGE, PIERRE, legal educator; b. Quebec City, Can., Jan. 9, 1936; s. Francis and Regina (Roy) V.; m. Colette Habel, June 29, 1963; children—Marc, Caroline, Louis. BA, Laval U., 1956, LL.L., 1959, LL.D., 1971; MA, McGill U., 1962, Cambridge U., 1977; LL.M., U. Toronto, 1968; 1971. Bar: Que. 1961, Queen's Counsel 1976. Pvt. practice law, Quebec City, Can., 1961-66; mem. faculty Laval U. Faculty of Law, 1966—, dean, 1973-77, prof. emeritus, 2003—. Commonwealth fellow St. John's Coll., Cambridge U., 1977-78 Mem. Assn. Can. Law Tchrs. (pres. 1972-73, chmn. conf. law deans 1975-76), Que. Bar, Canadian Bar, Royal Soc. Can. Home: 2542 avenue de Parc-Falaise Sillery PQ Canada G1T 1W3 Office: Cite Universitaire Universite Laval Quebec City PQ Canada

VERGHESE, MOHAN, urologist, surgeon; b. Tiruvalla, India, Oct. 12, 1952; arrived in US, 1978; s. S. K. V. and P. Abraham; m. Susan Thomas Verghese, Oct. 26, 1978; children: Ajit A., Ashok T. MBBS, U. Delhi, India. Surg. resident Bay State Med. Ctr., 1979—80; urology resident Washington Hosp. Ctr., 1980—84, dir. sect. urologic surgery, chmn. dept. urology; fellow urol. oncology Roswell Park Cancer Inst., 1991—92. Mem.: Internat. Coll. Surgeons, Am. Coll. Surgeons. Avocations: scuba diving, kayaking, travel. Office: Washington Hosp Ctr 100 Irving St NW Washington DC 20010

VERGNAUD, JEAN-MAURICE, science educator, researcher; b. Audincourt, Doubs, France, Dec. 3, 1932; s. Joseph and Marie-Louise (Buthod-Ruffier) V.; m. Michele Trouin, Dec. 20, 1979. MS, U. Lyon, France, 1956, PhD in Chromatography, 1965; PhD in Catalysis, U. Dijon, France, 1960. Engr. CEA, Paris, 1959, Progil, Lyon, 1960-68; prof. U. Algiers, Algeria, 1968-71, U. St. Etienne, France, 1972—. Spkr. in field. Author: Drying of Polymeric and Solid Materials, 1992, Cure of Thermosetting Resins, 1992, Dosage Forms for Controlled Release with Polymers, 1993, Liquid Transport Processes in Polymeric Materials, 1994, Assessing Bioavailability of Drug Delivery Systems, 2005, Assessing Food Safety with Polymer Packaging, 2006, In the Light of Gabe, Birth of an Engineer, 2006; mem. editl. adv. bd. Polymer Testing, Rubber Plastics and Composites, Polymer and Polymer Composites, Jour. Polymer Engring., Jour. Drying Tech.; referee Am. Assn. Pharm. Sci., 7 jours. on polymers and 2 jours. on pharmacy; contbr. over 500 articles to internat. jours. Pres. French Chem. Soc. of Lyon, 1963-68; v.p. U. St. Etienne, 1972-75. Recipient French Indsl. Soc. award, Paris, 1965, French Acad. Scis. award, Paris, 1977. Mem. Am. Chem. Soc. (George S. Whitby award 1998). Avocations: skiing, tennis, piano. Home: Rte de Chavanne Chemin de Grange Bruyas 42400 Saint Chamond France Office: Univ St Etienne 23 Dr P Michelon 42023 Saint Etienne France Home Phone: 33(0) 4 77 31 86 73. Personal E-mail: vergnaud.jean-maurice@wanadoo.fr.

VERHEYEN, PETER DAVID, librarian, conservator; b. Princeton, NJ, Jan. 14, 1963; s. Egon Verheyen and Hanne Schulten; m. Hope Elizabeth Kuniholm, June 4, 1994; 1 child, Sofia Klara. BA in German Lit., Johns Hopkins U., 1985; MLS, Syracuse U. Sch. Info. Studies, 1997. Hand bookbinding apprentice Chamber of Trades, Munster, Germany, 1987; asst. conservator William Minter Bookbinding and Conservation, Chgo., 1988—91, Yale U. Libr., New Haven, 1991—92; rare book conservator Cornell U. Libr., Ithaca, NY, 1993—95; conservation libr. Syracuse U. Libr., NY, 1995—98; archival product mgr. Gaylord Bros., 1998—99; preservation and access libr. Syracuse U. Libr. Spl. Collections Rsch. Ctr., NY, 1999—. Exhbns. chair Guild Book Workers, NYC, 1990—96, 2004—06, publicity chair, 1998—2002. Exhibitions include Reliures du Monde: Les Amis de la Reliure d'Art, 2nd Nat. Book and Paper Arts Biennial, Guild Book Workers, Columbia Coll. Ctr. for Book and Paper Arts, Chgo., 2000, Soc. Bookbinders Bookbinding Competition, 2003 (Harmatan Leather award, 2003); author: Springback Ledger Bindings in German Tradition, 2003; contbr. articles to profl. jours. Mem.: ALA, Can. Bookbinders and Book Artists Guild, Designer Bookbinders, Soc. Am. Archivists, Am. Inst. Conservation (cipp web, list mgr. 2002—04). Achievements include design of Tube storage unit for architectural and other oversized archival materials; development of and coordination of special collections digitization projects; Bonefolder: an e-journal for the bookbinder and book artist, 2004-; Book Arts Web, 1994-. Office: Peter Verheyen Spl Collections Rsch Ctr Syracuse Univ Libr Syracuse NY 13244 Home Phone: 315-446-4336; Office Phone: 315-443-9756. Office Fax: 315-443-2671. Personal E-mail: verheyen@philobiblon.com. Business E-Mail: pdverhey@syr.edu.

VERHOEK, SUSAN ELIZABETH, botany educator; b. Columbus, Ohio, 1942; m. S.E. Williams; 1 child. Student, Carleton Coll., 1960-62; BA, Ohio Wesleyan U., 1964; MA, Ind. U., 1966; PhD, Cornell U., 1975. Herbarium supr. Mo. Bot. Garden, St. Louis, 1966-70; asst. prof. Lebanon Valley Coll., Annville, Pa., 1974-82, assoc. prof., 1982-85, prof., 1985—. Vis. researcher Cornell U., Ithaca, N.Y., 1982-83; content cons. Merrill Pub. Co., 1987-89; vis. profl. Chgo. Bot. Garden, 1991. Author: How to Know the Spring Flowers, 1982; contbr. articles to profl. jours., newspapers, and bulls. Trustee Lebanon Valley Coll., Annville, 1979-82, 84-90, 92-98; dir. Lebanon Valley Coll. Arboretum, 1996—. Mem. Soc. for Econ. Botany (pres. 1985-86), Bot. Soc. Am., Am. Pub. Gardens Assn. Office: Lebanon Valley Coll Dept Biology Annville PA 17003-0501 Office Phone: 717-867-6178. Business E-Mail: verhoek@lvc.edu.

VERHOEVEN, CHARLES K., lawyer; b. 1963; BBA with distinction, U. Iowa, 1985, JD with high distinction, 1988. Assoc. Cravath, Swaine & Moore, NYC, 1988—93; ptnr., head No. Calif. offices Quinn Emanuel et al, Redwood Shores, Calif., 1993—. Mem.: Iowa Law Rev., 1986—87, articles editor:, 1987—88. Named one of Top 20 Lawyers in Calif. Under 40 Yrs. Ol, Calif. Law Bus., Top 30 IP Lawyers, Calif. Daily Jour., 2005, Litigation's Rising Stars, The Am. Lawyer, 2007. Mem.: ABA, Assn. Bar City of New York, State Bar N.Y., State Bar Calif. Office: Quinn Emauel et al 555 Twin Dolphin Dr Ste 560 Redwood City CA 94065 Business E-Mail: charlesverhoeven@quinnemanuel.com. *

VERHOFF, GLEN CHARLES, reading educator, choir director; b. Lima, Ohio, Nov. 10, 1961; s. Virgil Hubert and Anita Abnus Verhoff. AA, Ohio State U., 1982; MusB, Ohio No. U., 1985; M in Tchg., Bowling Green State U., 2004. Tchr. music Port Clinton Schs., Ohio, 1986—90, tchr. 2d grade, 1994—2004, tchr. reading, 2004—; tchr. 1st grade Parochial Schs., 1991—94; choir dir. Immaculate Conception Ch., Port Clinton, Ohio, 1990—. Mem. Playmakers Theatre, Port Clinton, Ohio. Mem.: Nat. Assn. Pastoral Musicians, Nat. Reading Assn. Roman Catholic. Avocation: collecting daylilies and hostas.

VERHOFF, JULIE, international relations scholar; BA in Internat. Rels., Stanford Univ., 2007; MPhil student Devel. Studies, Oxford Univ., 2007—. Rhodes Scholar. Achievements include interning at State Dept; doing vol. work on behalf of women's and refugees' rights in Nicaragua, Ghana, and Zambia through a UN partner organization (FORGE) focused on refugee empowerment. Avocation: flute. *

VERING, JOHN ALBERT, lawyer; b. Marysville, Kans., Feb. 6, 1951; s. John Albert and Bernadine E. (Kieffer) V.; m. Ann E. Arman, June 28, 1980; children: Julia Ann, Catherine Ann, Mary Ann. BA summa cum laude, Harvard U., 1973; JD, U. Va., 1976. Bar: Mo. 1976, U.S. Dist. Ct. (we. dist.) Mo. 1976, U.S. Ct. Appeals (8th cir.), 1977, U.S. Ct. Appeals (10th cir.), 1980, U.S. Ct. Appeals (4th cir.) 1987, Kans. 1990, U.S. Dist. Ct. Kans. 1990; arbitrator, mediator. Assoc. Dietrich, Davis, Dicus, Rowlands, Schmitt & Gorman, Kansas City, Mo., 1976-81, ptnr., 1982—88, Armstrong Teasdale LLP, Kansas City, 1989—. Editor: U. Va. Law Rev., 1974—76. Bd. dirs. Greater Kansas City YMCA Southwest Dist., 1987. Named one of Am.'s Leading Lawyers for Bus., Chambers USA, 2007, Super Lawyers, Mo., 2007, Kans., 2007. Mem.: Kansas City Metro Bar Assn. (chmn. fed. cts. com. 2007, chmn. labor and employment law com. 2003), Harvard Club (adv. bd. schs. com. Kansas City 1977—2007, v.p. 1981—82, 1992—93, pres. 1994—96). Home: 1210 W 68th Ter Kansas City MO 64113-1904 Office: Armstrong Teasdale LLP 2345 Grand Blvd Ste 2000 Kansas City MO 64108-2617 Office Phone: 816-221-3420. Business E-Mail: jvering@armstrongteasdale.com.

VERINK, ELLIS DANIEL, JR., metallurgical engineering educator, consultant; b. Peking, China, Feb. 9, 1920; s. Ellis Daniel and Phoebe Elizabeth (Smith) V.; m. Martha Eulala Owens, July 4, 1942; children: Barbara Ann, Wendy Susan. BS, Purdue U., 1941; MS, Ohio State U., 1963, PhD, 1965. Registered profl. engr., Fla., Pa., Calif. Mgr. chem. sect., sales devel. divsn. Alcoa, New Kensington, Pa., 1946-59, mgr. chem. and petroleum indsl. sales Pitts., 1965—68; prof. materials sci. and engring. U. Fla., Gainesville, 1968—, disting. svc. prof., 1984-91, prof. emeritus, 1991—; pres. Materials Cons., Inc., 1970—. Cons. Aluminum Assn., Washington, 1966-84; mem. U.S. nuclear waste tech. rev. bd., 1989-97. Author: Corrosion Testing Made Easy, The Basics, 1993; editor: Methods of Materials Selections, 1968, Material Stability and Environmental Degradation, 1988; contbr. articles to profl. jours. Pres. Gainesville YMCA, 1977. Recipient Sam Tour award ASTM, 1979, Donald E. Marlowe award Am. Soc. Engring. Edn., 1991; recipient Disting. Alumnus award Ohio State U., 1982, Disting. Faculty award Fla. Blue Key, 1983; named Tchr.-Scholar of Year U. Fla., 1979 Fellow Metall. Soc. of AIME (pres. 1984, Educator of Yr. award 1988), Am. Soc. Materials Internat., Nat. Assn. Corrosion Engrs. Internat. (bd. dirs. 1984-87, Willis Rodney Whitney award; mem. Masons, Shriners, Kiwanis, Sigma Xi, Tau Beta Pi. Republican. Presbyterian. Office: U Fla Dept Materials Sci Eng Gainesville FL 32611 Home: Apt M224 7805 NW 28th Pl Gainesville FL 32606-8659

VERKHOVSKY, BORIS, computer scientist, educator; PhD, USSR Acad. Scis. Wallace J. Eckert scientist IBM TJW Rsch. Ctr.; assoc. prof. Princeton U.; mem. tech. staff Bell Labs; Charles A. Dana Endowed chair professorship; prof. computer sci. NJIT, Newark. Recipient USSR Ministry of Radio-Electronics award, USSR award, Acad. Scis., Alvin Johnson award, Millennium award and Medal of Excellence. Fellow: European Acad. Scis. (v.p., bd. govs. 2004—, gov. 2002, v.p. 2003, mem. nominating com. for Nobel Prize, Blaise Pascal medal in Computer Sci. 2003). Office: NJIT Computer Sci Dept GITC 4407 University Heights Newark NJ 07102 Office Phone: 973-596-3393. Office Fax: 973-596-5777. Business E-Mail: verkhovsky@homer.njit.edu, verb@cs.njit.edu.

VER KUILEN, MARION JANE, retired instructional aide; b. Junction City, Wis., July 22, 1928; d. Fred A. and Mary Swanson; m. Theodore William Ver Kuilen, Feb. 8, 1947 (dec. Oct. 24, 1990); children: Victor Vernon, Van Vardon, Valerie Victoria, Venetta Venise Parrish(dec.), Vincent Vaughn. Student, Mt. San Antonio Coll., Walnut, Calif., 1977—78. Asst. mgr. Plz. Stationers and Book Store, West Covina, Calif., 1971—77; instrnl. aid elem. and ESL adult edn. Hacienda La Puente Unified Sch. Dist., La Puente, Calif., 1985—2005; ret., 2005. Photographer Reflections from the Past: Desert Twilight, America at the Millennium- The Best Photos of the 20th Century. Sec. Sunset Wesleyan Ch., La Puente, 1985—86; pres. Am Vets Auxillary, La Puente, 1958—61; den mother Cub Scouts, Rockford, Ill., 1954—57, San Pedro, Calif., 1958—59, La Puente, 1969—71. Named Outstanding Salesperson of Yr., West Covina C. of C., 1977, Outstanding Classified Employee of the Yr., Hacienda-La Puente Unified Sch. Dist., 1997; recipient In Svc. of Our Youth award, Mayor of Rockford, 1956, Best Photos of 2003 award, Editors Choice award, Internat. Libr. Photography, 1998—99. Mem.: DAV (assoc.), Nat. Geog. Soc. (corr.), Mt. Vernon Assn. (corr.), Colonial Williamsburg Assoc. (assoc.), WWII Veterans Meml. (life Charter Mem.), History (assoc.), WWII Mus. (assoc.), Sierra Club (corr.). Avocations: photography, reading, gardening. Home: 16105 Harvest Moon St La Puente CA 91744-1337

VERLANDER, JUSTIN BROOKS, professional baseball player; b. Manakin Sabot, Va., Feb. 20, 1983; s. Richard Verlander. Student, Vanderbilt U., Nashville. Pitcher Detroit Tigers, 2006—. Named Am. League Rookie of Yr., Maj. League Baseball Writers Assn., 2006, Am. League Outstanding Rookie, Players Choice Awards, 2006; named to Am. League All-Star Team, 2007. Achievements include pitching in World Series during rookie season, 2006; pitched a no-hitter against the Milwaukee Brewers, June 12, 2007. Office: Detroit Tigers Comerica Park 2100 Woodward Ave Detroit MI 48201 *

VERLICH, JEAN ELAINE, writer, public relations executive, consultant; b. McKeesport, Pa., July 5, 1950; d. Matthew Louis and Irene (Tomko) Verlich; m. S(tanley) Wayne Wright, Sept. 29, 1979 (div. June 1988). Student, Bucknell U., 1968-69; BA, U. Pitts., 1971. Pres. sec. Com. to Re-elect Pres., S.W. Pa., 1972; adminstrv. asst. Pa. Rep. James B. Kelly III, 1972-73; reporter Beaver (Pa.) County Times, 1973-74; proofreader Ketchum, MacLeod & Grove, Pitts., 1975-76; cmty. rels. specialist PPG Industries, Pitts., 1976-77; editor PPG News, 1977-79, sr. staff writer, 1979-84, comm. coord., 1984-85; pub. rels. assoc. Glass Group, 1986-87; mgr. pub. rels. Glass Group PPG Industries, 1987-92; account mgr. Maddigan Comm., Pitts., 1992-93; owner JV Comm., Pitts., 1993—; news editor Clovis News Jour., 2006—. Mem.: Automotive Pub. Rels. Coun., Travelers Aid Soc. Pitts. (bd. dirs. 1992—95, v.p. 1994—95), Internat. Assn. Bus. Communicators (bd. dirs. Pitts. chpt. 1981, v.p. pub. rels. Pitts. chpt. 1982, v.p. programs Pitts. chpt. 1985, pres. Pitts. chpt. 1986), Phi Beta Kappa, Delta Zeta. Business E-Mail: jverlich@jvcommunications.com.

VERLIN, JONATHAN R., secondary school educator; b. Phila., Jan. 3, 1966; s. Jerome Robert Vrelin and Eileen Lois Verlin. BA, Ursinus Coll., Colperville, Pa., 1988; MA, Duquesne U., Pitts., 1996; MEd, Arcadia U., Glenside, Pa., 1992; MS, Drexel U., Phila., 1999. Cert. instrnl. tchr. I Pa., 1988, instrnl. tchr. II Pa., 2007. Specialist microcumputer support W.B. Saunders Co., Phila., 1996—2000; programmer Jerome Software, Inc., Elkins Pk., Pa., 2000—02; tchr. Hope Charter Sch., Phila., 2002—03, career edn. dept. head, 2003—04, info. tech. dir., 2003—04; tchr. Sch. Dist. Phila., 2004—. Co-author: Sanctity of Reason: Science, Religion and the State in Samuel Clarke Boyle's Lectures: 1704-1705, 1996, By No Means Run in Debt: Richard Price's Life Expectancy Analysis and England's National Debt, 1997. Treas. Ogontz Vol. Fire Co., Elkins Park, 2002—03; sec. Ogontz Vol. Fire Co. Relief Orgn., Elkins Park, 2007—. Recipient Citation Valor award, Cheltenham Twp., Elkins Park, Pa., 1998. Avocations: amateur radio, bicycling, computers. Office: South Phila HS 21015 Broad St Philadelphia PA 19148

VERMA, ANILA, epidemiologist; d. Bishamber Nath and Bimla Mehta; m. Mukesh K Verma, May 16, 1991; children: Kshitij Varma, Rajat Varma. MBBS, Delhi U., New Delhi, India, 1976; MSc, U. Alta., Edmonton, Can., 1994, PhD, 1998. Lic. physician Delhi Bd., 1978. Faculty, investigator Cmty. Health Dept., Brown U., Providence, 1998—2003; med. epidemiology expert Novartis Pharm., East Hanover, NJ, 2003—. Sci. reviewer Internat. Soc. of Pharmacoepidemiologists. Contbr. numerous articles to profl. jours. Recipient Marie Imrie Travel award, U. Alta., 1994, LCDC Travel award, Internat. Soc. Epidemiologists and Biostatisticians, 1997; scholar Perinatal Rsch. scholar, Periantal Rsch. Ctr., U. Alta., 1993—94, 1996—97; Study grantee, Alta. Heritage Found. for Med. Rsch., 1998—2000, Hosp. for Sick Children Found., Toronto, Can., 1996. Mem.: Drug Info. Assn. (assoc.), Internat. Soc. Pharmacoepidemiologists (assoc.). Achievements include design of an outcome measure of newborn morbidity; research in performance criteria of Morbidity Assessment Index for Newborns; risk management planning for drugs. Office: Novartis Pharmaceuticals One Health Plz East Hanover NJ 07936 Home Phone: 650-863-2244; Office Phone: 650-244-3619. Personal E-mail: thayer2710@yahoo.com. Business E-Mail: averma@amger.com.

VERMA, ARUN K., mathematician, educator; b. Dibrugarh, India, June 1955; 3 children. MSc, Dibrugarh U., India, 1977; Diploma, PhD, Indian Inst. of Tech., Kharagpur, 1984. Lectr. in math. Regional Engring. Coll., Silchar, Assam, India, 1984—89; rsch. assoc. Hampton U., Hampton, Va., 1989—89, vis. lectr. in math., 1989—92, asst. prof. of math., 1992—93, assoc. prof. of math., 1993—2001, prof. of math., 2001—. Reader for AP calculus Ednl. Testing Svcs., Princeton, NJ, 1998—2004; ASEE summer faculty fellow NASA Langley Rsch. Ctr., Hampton, Va., 2000; US EdD project cons. Ala. State U., Montgomery, Ala., 2002—03; Schev project cons. Norfolk State U., Norfolk, Va., 2002—03; faculty summer rsch. participant Oak Ridge Inst. for Sci. and Rsch., Oak Ridge, Tenn., 1993—93; lead tchr. Thompson Learning Brooks Coll., Inc., 2004—; coord. Math. Counts Peninsula Chpt., Va., 2005—; project dir. various grants. Treas. Yorktown 4th July Committe, Yorktown, Va., 2003—; elected com. mem. Internat. Baccalaureate Adv. Coun., Yorktown, Va., 2000—04; nominated com. mem. New Horizon Governors Sci. & Tech. Adv. Com., Hampton, Va., 2000—; v.p. Hindu Temple of Hampton Roads, Chesapeake, Va., 2000—. Named Leader in Edn., Hewlett-Packard Inc., 2000; recipient William C. Lowry Outstanding Math. Tchr. award, coll. level, Va. Coun. of Teachers of Math., 2001, 2002 QEM (Quality Edn. for Minorities) Excellence in Math. and/or Sci. Tchg. award, 2002. Mem.: Va. Acad. Sci. (treas. 2006—), Nat. Tech. Assn., Va. Coun. of Teachers of Math., Math. Assn. of Am., Sigma Xi. Office: Hampton U E Queen St Hampton VA 23668 Office Phone: 757-728-6983. Business E-Mail: arun.verma@hamptonu.edu.

VERMA, INDER M., biochemist; b. Sangrur, Punjab, India, Nov. 28, 1947; MSc in Biochemistry, Lucknow U., India, 1966; PhD in Biochemistry, Weizmann Inst. Sci., Rehovot, Israel, 1971. From asst. prof. to assoc. prof. Salk Inst., 1974-83; sr. mem. Molecular Biology & Virology Lab, 1983-85; prof. Molecular Biology, 1985-95; prof. Lab. Genetics Salk Inst. for Biol. Sciences, 1995—, Am. Cancer Soc. prof. Molecular Biology. Fellow Jane Coffin Childs Meml. Fund, 1970-73; Reverend Soloman B. Caulker Meml. fellow, 1967-70; adj. assoc. prof. U. Calif. San Diego, 1979-83, adj. prof. Biology, 1983—; March of Dimes Birth Defects Found. Franklin D. Roosevelt Investigator, 1997; mem. Virology Study Sec., 1981-85, elected mem., Inst. of Medicine, 1999. Recipient medal Outstanding Scientist N. Am. Scientists of Indian Origin, 1985-86; merit award NIH, 1987, outstanding investigator award, 1988; bd. trustees Salk Inst., 1989-91 & 94—; mem. acad. coun., 1989—; vchmn. Fac. and Acad. coun., 1989-90 & 94-95; chmn., 1991-92 & 96-97; prof. Molecular Biology, Am. Cancer Soc., 1990; lectr. Purdue U., 1991, Sch. Med. Vanderbilt U., 1992, TATA Meml. Hosp., Bombay, India, 1992, U. Chgo., 1992, Queenstown, New Zealand, 1993, N.Y.U., 1993, Bar-Ilan U., Ramat Gan, Israel, and others. Mem. NAS (councilor, 2006-), Am. Cancer Soc., Third World Acad. Sciences, IOM, Am. Soc. for Gene Therapy (pres. 2000-2001). Office: Salk Inst Biol Studies PO Box 85800 10010 N Torrey Pines Rd San Diego CA 92186-5800 Office Phone: 619-453-4100. Business E-Mail: verma@salk.edu.

VERMA, SURJIT KUMAR, retired school system administrator; b. India, May 17, 1940; arrived in Canada 1966; s. Sohara Lal and Gian Devi V.; m. Raj Verma; 1 child, Soania. MEd, St. Francis Xavier U., NS, 1975; postgrad., Dalhousie U., NS, U. Ottawa, Ont., Can, 1979. Cert. tchr. Nova Scotia. Sci. dept. head Halifax County Bedford Dist. Sch. Bd., N.S., Canada, 1968-88, curriculum supr. N.S., 1988-94; ret., 1995. Served on C.T.F. Project Overseas Can. Teams, W.I., Nigeria, 1976, 77; mem. provincial sci. task force, biology rev. com., elem. sci. Nova Scotia Dept. Edn.; mem. Internat. Sci. Symposium, 1979; mem. selection panel PromoSci. Program. Natural Scis. and Engring. Rsch. Coun. of Can.; mem. exec. coun. N.S. Inst. Sci.; worksop presenter numerous sci. workshops. Contbr. to profl. jours. Chmn. First Metro Halifax Dartmouth Reg Sci. Fair, 1975; co-chmn. Canada Wide Sci Fair, 1984. Recipient Sci. Tchg. Achievement Recognition award, U.S. Nat. Sci. Tchrs. Assn. and Am. Gas Assn., 1993, Profl. Devel. award, N.S. Tchrs. Union, Tchg. Excellence in Sci., Tech. and Math. award, Prime Min. Can., 1993, 1994, Sci. on Display award, NASCO, 1993—94, Outstanding Achievement in Sci. Edn. award, Halifax County Sch. Bd., 1993, Surjit Verma award for tchg. excellence created in his honor, Halifax County Bedrod Dist. Sch. Bd., 1994, Michael Smith award, Industry Can., 1996, Maritimer of the Week award, Atlantic TV and Can. TV Network, 2003, Maritimer of Week award, Atlantic T.V. and Can. T.V. Network, 2003; fellow, U. Ottawa, 1979; scholar, N.S. Tchrs. Union, 1979; grad. fellow, Dalhousie U., 1980, Math. Sci. Tech. Edn. fellow, Royal Bank Queen's U., 1994, rsch. devel. grantee, Dalhousie U., 1979, Can./N.S. Tech. Devel. grantee, 1995. Mem. Nova Scotia Inst. Sci. (coun. mem.), Natural Sci. and Engring. Rsch. Coun. (mem. selection panel promosci. project). Avocations: jogging, yoga. Personal E-mail: rsverma49@yahoo.ca.

VERMEER, MAUREEN DOROTHY, sales executive; b. Bronxville, NY, Mar. 21, 1945; d. Albert Casey and Helen (Valentine Casey) Vermeer; m. John R. Fassnacht, Feb. 11, 1966 (div. 1975); m. George M. Dallas Peltz IV, Oct. 26, 1985. Grad., NYU Real Estate Inst., 1976. Lic. real estate broker NY. With Douglas Elliman, NYC, 1965-74, mgmt. supr., 1974-78, v.p., 1978-83; real estate broker Rachmani Corp., NYC, 1983-84; v.p. sales and mktg. Carol Mgmt. Corp., NYC, 1984-90; v.p. mktg. The Sunshine Group, NYC, 1990; v.p., sec., bd. dirs. H.J. Kalikow & Co., NYC, 1991—. Named one of 100 Women in Real Estate, Real Estate Weekly. Mem. Real Estate Bd. N.Y. (bd. dirs., residential mgmt. com.), Assn. Real Estate Women (bd. dirs.officer, chmn. charitable fund, co-chair Man of Yr. Award event, Founders award). Republican. Presbyterian. Avocations: skiing, scuba diving. Home: 111 Broadway Norwood NJ 07648-1412 Office: H J Kalikow & Co 101 Park Ave Fl 25 New York NY 10178-0002

VERMEIL, DICK (RICHARD ALBERT VERMEIL), retired professional football coach; b. Calistoga, Calif., Oct. 30, 1936; m. Carolyn Drake; 3 children. Head coach UCLA, 1974—75, Phila. Eagles, 1976—82, St. Louis Rams, 1997-2000, Kans. City Chiefs, 2001—05; pub. spkr. Nationwide Spkrs. Bur., Beverly Hills, Calif., 2000—01. Tv analyst with CBS, ABC. Named NFL Coach of the Yr. 1980, 1999; Man of the Yr., Walter Camp Football Found., 2006 Career highlights include:first fulltime spl. teams coach in NFL history, L.A. Rams, 1969; head coach Super Bowl XXXIV champion St. Louis Rams, 2000, becoming the oldest coach in NFL history to win a Super Bowl; only coach in history to win both the Super Bowl and the Rose bowl; only 4th coach in history to lead two different teams to Super Bowl (Phil., St. Louis). Home Phone: 816-931-4199; Office Phone: 816-920-4255.

VERMETTE, RAYMOND EDWARD, retired health facility administrator; b. Lewiston, Maine, June 30, 1942; m. Ernestine Pero, Dec. 29, 1963; children: Tamara, Gregory. BS in Bacteriology, U. Maine, 1964; MS in Biochemistry, U. Wis., 1966; MBA, Temple U., 1973; master tchr.'s cert., Cath. Diocese Boston, 1981. Cert. in pers. mgmt., Va. Supr. animal toxicology Hazleton Labs., Vienna, Va., 1967-71; pers. mgr. Damon Clin. Lab., Phila., 1971-73, ops. mgr., 1973-75, gen. mgr. Needham Heights, Mass., 1975-90; v.p. ops. Damon Corp., Needham Heights, 1983-87, corp. v.p., 1987-89, sr. v.p., 1990—93; sr. v.p., gen. mgr. Corning/MetPath, Westwood, Mass., 1994-95; ret., 1995. Vis. lectr. fin. mgmt. and bus. adminstrn. Framingham State Coll., 1978—84; instr. mgmt. Newbury Jr. Coll., Boston, 1976—79; health care mgmt. cons., 2001—. Author: (with B. Kliman and E. Kolowrat) What You Should Know About Medical Lab Tests, 1979. V.p. fin. com., Framingham, Mass., 1982—84; mem. capital budget com. Town of Framingham, 1987; mem-elect Framingham Town Meeting, 1987—90, Govt. Study Com., 1995—97, mem. fin. com., 1997—2001; chmn. bd. religious edn. Cath. Ch., Framingham, 1981—84, co-chmn. pre-marriage preparation coun., 1981—99, organist, 1979—. Republican. Home: 2 Old Town Hwy Unit 16 East Haven CT 06512-4530

VERMEULE, CORNELIUS CLARKSON, III, museum curator; b. Orange, NJ, Aug. 10, 1925; s. Cornelius Clarkson, Jr. and Catherine Sayre (Comstock) V.; m. Emily Dickinson Townsend, Feb. 2, 1957 (dec. Feb. 6, 2001); children: Emily D. Blake, Cornelius Adrian Comstock. Grad., Pomfret Sch., 1943; AB, Harvard, 1949, MA, 1951; PhD, U. London, Eng., 1953; DHL (hon.), Boston Coll., 1995. Instr. fine arts, then asst. prof. U. Mich., 1953-55; asst. prof. classical archaeology Bryn Mawr (Pa.) Coll., 1955-57; curator classical art Mus. Fine Arts, Boston, 1956-96, curator emeritus, 1996—, acting dir., 1972-73, hon. visitor ancient art, 2002—; assoc. curator coins Mass. Hist. Soc., 1965-71, curator, 1971—86. Lectr. fine arts Smith Coll., 1960-64, Boston U., Harvard, Wellesley Coll.; vis. prof. Yale, 1969-70, 72-73; Thomas Spencer Jerome lectr. U. Mich., 1975-76; vis. prof. Boston Coll., 1978-97; vis. prof. U. Aberdeen, Scotland, 1993; pres. Internat. Com. to Save Jewish Catacombs of Italy, 1980-84, chmn., 1984-98, dir. 1998-2000; cons. classical art Worcester Art Mus., 1998-2001. Author: (with N. Jacobs) Japanese Coinage, 1948, 2d edit., 1972, Bibliography of Applied Numismatics, 1956, The Goddess Roma, 1959, 2d edit., 1974, Dal Pozzo-Albani Drawings, 1960, European Art and the Classical Past, 1964, Drawings at Windsor Castle, 1966, Roman Imperial Art in Greece and Asia Minor, 1968, Polykleitos, 1969, Numismatic Art in America, 1971, 2d edit., 2007; (with M. Comstock) Greek Etruscan and Roman Bronzes, 1972; (with N. Neuerburg) Catalogue of the Ancient Art in the J. Paul Getty Museum, 1973, Greek and Roman Sculpture in Gold and Silver, 1974, Greek and Roman Cyprus, 1976, (with M. Comstock) Sculpture in Stone, 1976, Greek Sculpture and Roman Taste, 1977, Roman Art: Early Republic to Late Empire, 1978; (with A Herrmann) The Ernest Brummer Collections, Vol. II, 1979, Greek Art: Socrates to Sulla, 1980, The Jewish Experience in Roman Art, 1981, Masterpieces of Greek and Roman Sculpture in America, 1982, Greek Art: Prehistoric to Perikles, 1982, Numismatic Studies, 1983, Alexander the Great Conquers Rome, 1985, The Cult Images of Imperial Rome, 1986, Numismatic Art of the Greek Imperial World, 1987, Philatelic Art in America, 1987; (with M. Comstock) Sculpture in Stone and Bronze, 1988; (with A. Brauer) Stone Sculptures, The Greek, Roman and Etruscan Collections of the Harvard University Art Museums, 1990; (with others) Le Sport dans la Grèce Antique, 1992, Du Jeu à la Compétition, 1992, El Deporte en la Grecia Antigua, La génesis del olimpismo, 1992-93, Vase-Painting in Italy, 1993, (with others) Eye of the Beholder, Masterpieces from the Isabella Stewart Gardner Museum, 2003, Art and Archaeology of Antiquity, Vols. I-IV, 2001-04, (with others) J.D. Beazeley, The Lewes House Gems, 2002-05; mem. editl. bd. Minerva, 2002—. Trustee Cardinal Spellman Philatelic Mus., 1980-93. Served to 1st lt. AUS, 1943-47. Recipient Bicentennial medal Boston Coll., 1976; Fulbright fellow, 1951-53; Guggenheim fellow, 1968 Fellow AAAS, Am. Numis. Soc. (life), Royal Numis. Soc., Soc. Antiquaries; mem. Coll. Art Assn. (life), Archaeol. Inst. Am. (life) German Archaeol. Inst., Holland Soc. N.Y., Colonial Lords of Manors in Am., Mass. Hist. Soc. (hon. curator); Tavern Club (medalist 1986, Boston). Home: 47 Coolidge Hill Rd Cambridge MA 02138-5509 Office: Mus Fine Arts 465 Huntington Ave Boston MA 02115-5597 *To teach, collect and record the past, as exemplar for the present, as prologue to the future, can there be any better use of a historian's and archaeologist's professional life?.*

VERMEULEN, KEVIN J., publishing executive; BA, Brockport State Univ. Regional sales mgr. Miller Freeman & Gordon Pub.; dir. advertising New York Law Journal, Nat. Law Journal; assoc. publisher Law Tech. Product News; v.p. sales Nat. Law Publishing, 1996—98; v.p. & dir. nat. advertising Am. Lawyer Media, 1998—99, v.p. & group publisher, 1999—. Office: Am Lawyer Media 345 Park Ave So New York NY 10010

VERMILYE, PETER HOAGLAND, banker; b. NYC, Jan. 17, 1920; s. Herbert Noble and Elise Trace (Hillyer) V.; m. Lucy Shaw Mitchell, Oct. 14, 1950; children: Peter H., Dana R., Andrew R., Mary S. AB, Princeton U., 1940. V.p. pension investments J.P. Morgan & Co. and Morgan Guaranty Trust, 1940-64; ptnr. State St. Research & Mgmt., Boston, 1965-69; pres. Alliance Capital Mgmt., NYC, 1970-77; sr. v.p., chief investment officer Citibank, NYC, 1977-84; chmn. Baring Am. Asset Mgmt., Boston, 1984-89; sr. advisor Baring Asset Mgmt., 1990-95, Harbor Capital Mgmt., Boston, 1996—2003, Fortis Investments, 2004—. Chmn. Huntington Theatre, 1989—96; bd. dirs. Engelhard Hanovia, Breadstreet Holdings Corp. Trustee Boston U., 1970—. Mem.: Brook, Somerset, Myopia. Home: 157 School St Manchester MA 01944-1236 Office: Fortis Investments 75 State St Ste 2700 Boston MA 02109

VERMYLEN, PAUL ANTHONY, JR., oil industry executive; b. NYC, Dec. 5, 1946; s. Paul Anthony and Nancy Primrose (Barr) Vermylen; m. Robin S. Collins, Jan. 24, 1970; children: Robert T.C., Nancy Barr Vermylen Thornton, Sarah Morgan Vermylen Trust, Paul Anthony III. AB, Georgetown U., 1968; MBA, Columbia U., 1971. V.p. Citibank N.A., NYC, 1971-78; treas. Commonwealth Oil Refining Co., San Antonio, 1978-81, v.p. fin., CFO, 1981—82; v.p., CFO, dir. Meenan Oil Co., Inc., Syosset, NY, 1982—91, pres., 1992—2001, Meenan Oil Co., L.P., 1992—2001; chmn. Kestrel Energy Co., Inc., Huntington, NY, 2002—05; pres., bd. dirs. Kestrel Energy Ptnrs. LLC, 2005—; chmn. Kestrel Heat LLC, 2006—. Bd. dirs. Petroleum Industry Rsch. Found., 1992—2002, Downeast LNG, Inc., 2005—. Bd. dirs. Huntington Arts Coun., NYC, 1983—89, v.p., 1986—87, pres., 1987—89; bd. dirs. Cold Spring Harbor Whaling Mus., 1995—2000; bd. advisors Cold Spring Harbor Lab. DNA Learning Ctr., 1991—2000; bd. regents Georgetown U., Washington, 1997—2003; trustee Girls Prep. Charter Sch., NYC, 2004—, bd. dirs., 2004—, Soc. for Preservation of Long Island Antiquities, 2006—. Mem.: Causeway Club Southwest Harbor, Maine, NY Yacht Club, Cold Spring Harbor Beach Club.

VERNARELLI, MICHAEL JOSEPH, economics professor, consultant, academic administrator; b. Rochester, NY, Nov. 24, 1948; s. S. John and Angelica Dolores (Morabito) V.; m. Joan Ann Taylor, Oct. 4, 1975; children: Jacqueline Andrea, Laurel Aileen. BA in Econs., U. Mich., 1970; MA in Econs., SUNY, Binghamton, 1974, PhD in Econs., 1978. Account analyst Travelers Ins. Co., Rochester, 1970-71; rsch. assoc. Ctrl. Adminstrn. SUNY, 1975-76; prof. econs. Rochester Inst. Tech., 1976—, chmn. dept., 1987—. Cons. econs. Rochester Downtown Devel. Corp., 1980; rsch. economist divsn. housing rsch. HUD, Washington, 1980-81, vis. scholar, 1980; pres., forensic economist Rochester Econ. Cons., 1983—; vis. prof. U.S. Bus. Sch. in Prague, 1992-96. Contbg. author: Federal Housing Policy and Desegregation, 1986. Mem. Brighton (N.Y.) Bd. Archtl. Rev., 1990-91, mem. planning bd., 1991-98. Recipient Eisenhart award Rochester Inst. Tech., 1987; grantee SUNY, Binghamton, 1974. Mem. Am. Econ. Assn., Nat. Assn. Forensic Economists, Ea. Econ. Assn., Greater Rochester C. of C. (panel mem. bus. trends com. 1987—), Omicron Delta Epsilon. Roman Catholic. Avocation: golf. Home: 133 Esplanade Dr Rochester NY 14610-3325 Office: Rochester Inst Tech Rochester NY 14623-0887 Office Phone: 585-475-2455. Personal E-mail: mjvern11@aol.com. Business E-Mail: mjvgss@rit.edu.

VERNER, JAMES MELTON, lawyer; b. Selma, Ala., Sept. 19, 1915; s. Singleton Foster and Jennie (Harris) V.; m. Gretchen Gores, Aug. 12, 1939; children: Ann Verner Picardo, James Singleton, William Melton. Student, Biltmore Coll., 1932—34; AB, U. N.C., 1936, JD, 1938. Bar: NC 1938, Tenn. 1947, D.C. 1950, Va. 1986. Assoc. firm Gover & Covington, Charlotte, NC, 1938; law clk. atty. gen. NC, 1938-40; atty. CAB, Washington, 1940-43; asst. gen. counsel Chgo. & So. Airlines, Memphis, 1946-47; atty. Air Transport Assn. Am., Washington, 1947-49; hearing examiner CAB, 1949-50, exec. asst. to chmn., 1950, exec. dir., 1950-53; from atty. to ptnr. Turney & Turney, 1953—60; ptnr. firm Verner, Liipfert, Bernhard, McPherson & Hand, Chartered (and predecessor firms), 1960-88; hon. mem. bd. dirs., spl. coun. Piper Rudnick Gray Cary (merged with Verner, Liipfert, Bernhard, McPherson & Hand, Chartered), Washington. Assoc. editor N.C. Law Rev., 1937—38. Former mem., chmn. policy bd. Legal Counsel for Elderly, Washington. Lt. (j.g.) USNR, 1943-46; legal officer Naval Air Transport Svc., 1945-46. Mem.: ABA, Cosmos Club (Washington), Order of Golden Fleece. Home: 900 N Taylor St # 2104-2106 Arlington VA 22203-1858 Office: Piper Rudnick Gray Cary 1200 Nineteenth St NW Washington DC 20003-6132 *My belief is that if you treat other people fairly and trust them, you will seldom be disappointed and will be the better for it.*

VERNEY, RICHARD GREVILLE, paper company executive; b. Providence, Aug. 24, 1946; s. Gilbert and Virginia Ruth (Piggott) Verney; m. Dorothy Howard, Aug. 26, 1967; children: Virginia F., Elizabeth I., Heather B., Eric B. AB, Brown U., 1968. Mgmt. trainee Monadnock Paper Mills, Bennington, NH, 1969-70, asst. gen. mgr., 1970, exec. v.p., 1970-76, pres., 1977-85, chmn., CEO, 1978—, Monadnock Non-Wovens, LLC, 1998—, Monadnock Specialty Coatings, LLC, 2000—07. Mem. exec. com. Crotched Mt. Found., Greenfield, NH, 1974—87, trustee, 1974—, St. George's Sch., Newport, RI, 1978—93, chmn., 1985—89, hon. trustee, 1993—, Monadnock Cmty. Hosp., 1993—2000, v.p., 1997—99; trustee Nantucket Conservation Found., Inc., 1994—, pres., 1998—. Mem.: Bus. Industry Assn. N.H. (bd. dir. 1991—, mem. exec. com. 1998—2004), Boston Paper Trade Assn., Sales Assn. Paper Industry, Am. Forest and Papers Assn. (chmn. exec. bd. pulp consumers divsn. 1980—82, chmn. splty. packaging and indsl. divsn. 1984—85, chmn. cover and text exec. com. 1989—91, bd. dir. 1991—98, chmn. printing, writing exec. com. 2002—03, co-chmn. printing, writing exec. com. 2005—07, bd. dirs. 2007—), N.Y. Yacht Club (N.Y.C.), Nantucket Yacht Club (Mass.), Algonquin Club (Boston). Republican. Episcopalian. Home: PO Box 145 The Verney Farm Bennington NH 03442-0145 Office: Monadnock Paper Mills Inc 117 Antrim Rd Bennington NH 03442-4205 Business E-Mail: rverney@mpm.com.

VERNIKOS, JOAN, science organization director; b. Alexandria, Egypt, May 9, 1934; came to U.S., 1960; d. Apostolos and Catherine (Manganari) V.; m. Constantine Danellis, June 10, 1960 (dec. Apr. 1971); children: Eftihia, George; m. Geoffrey Cyril Hazzan, Sept. 4, 1978. B Pharmacy, U. Alexandria, 1955; PhD, U. London, 1960. Asst. prof. Ohio State U. Med. Sch., Columbus, 1961-64; rsch. assoc. NAS NASA Ames Rsch. Ctr., Moffett Field, Calif., 1964-66, rsch. scientist, 1966-93, chief human studies, 1972-76, acting dep. dir. life sci., 1976, assoc. dir. space rsch. Moffet Field, Calif., 1987-93, chief life sci. divsn., 1988-93; dir. life scis. NASA HQ Code UL, Washington, 1993—. Mem. pharmacology study sect. NIH, Bethesda, Md., 1974-78; cons. Adv. Group for Aerospace R & D, Cologne, Germany, 1991; mem. aerospace medicine adv. com. NASA, Washington, 1988-93. Author: Hormones and Behavior, 1972, Neuroregulators and Psychiatric Disorders, 1977, Selye's Guide to Stress Research, Vol. 1, 1980, Strategies for Mars, 1993, Stress: Neurochemical and Molecular Approaches, 1992; author, editor: Inactivity: The Physiology of Bedrest, 1986. Mem. adv. bd. Nat. Hispanic U., San Jose, Calif., 1991-93. Recipient medal for sci. achievement NASA, 1973, medal for exceptional svcs., 1994, AIAA Jeffries Med. Rsch. award, 1994, Aerospace States Assn. honoree, 1994. Fellow World Econ. Forum, Aerospace Med. Assn. (Strughold award 1990); mem. IBRO, Internat. Acad. Astronautics, Endocrine Soc., Am. Soc. Pharmacology and Exptl. Therapeutics, Soc. Neuroscience. Greek Orthodox. Achievements include two patents; research on hormone indexes of stress; understanding brain mechanisms regulating stress response and evidence for coping mechanisms; contributor to understanding physiological responses and adaptation to weightlessness of space flight, drug treatments for postflight orthostatic intolerance; minimal requirements for artificial gravity in prolonged space missions.

VERNON, CARL ATLEE, JR., retired wholesale food distributor executive; b. Topeka, Aug. 15, 1926; s. Carl Atlee and Capitola May (Jarboe) V.; m. Marion Leila Colton, May 7, 1950; children: Mary Catherine, Matthew Fowler, Susan Elizabeth. BS, Yale U., 1947. Merchandising mgr. Fleming Cos., Topeka, 1957-61, dir. merchandising, 1961-66, dir. info. services, 1966-72, v.p. info. services, 1972-74, v.p. regional systems, 1974-79, sr. v.p. mktg. services Oklahoma City, 1979-88. Chmn. Shawnee County chpt. ARC, Topeka, Kans., 1957-58. Served to ensign USNR, 1944—46. Republican. Episcopalian. Avocations: golf, travel. Personal E-mail: cavernonjr@aol.com.

VERNON, DARRYL MITCHELL, lawyer; b. NYC, May 4, 1956; s. Leonard and Joyce (Davidson) V.; m. Lauren Lynn Bernstein, Aug. 21, 1982. BA in Math., Tufts U., 1978; JD, Yeshiva U., 1981. Bar: N.Y. 1982, U.S. Dist. Ct. (so. and ea. dists.) N.Y. 1982, U.S. Ct. Appeals (2d cir.) 1987. Assoc. Hochberg & Greenberg, NYC, 1981—82; ptnr. Greenberg & Vernon, 1982—83, Law Offices of Darryl M. Vernon, 1983—; pres., ptnr. Vernon & Ginsburg, LLP, 1989—. Spkr. in field; instr. CLE courses; bd. editors NY Real Estate Reporter. Mem. editl. bd.: NY Real Estate Reporter, 2007—; contbr. articles to profl. jours. Samuel Belkin scholar, Yeshiva U., 1979. Mem. Assn. Bar City N.Y. (com. legal issues pertaining to animals), N.Y. State Bar Assn. (mem. spl. com. on animals and the law). Office: 261 Madison Ave New York NY 10016-2303 Home Phone: 914-238-8941; Office Phone: 212-949-7300. Business E-Mail: dvernon@vernonginsburg.com.

VERNON, GARY WAYNE See LEVOX, GARY

VERNON, KAREN, art gallery owner, educator; b. El Dorado, Ark., June 11, 1948; d. William John Vernon and Clara Mae Irby-Vernon; m. Kenneth John Muenzenmayer, Mar. 7, 1992; m. Maynard Patrick Dugan (dec.); children: Michelene Dorin, Kristin Patrice, Susan Jo. BFA, U. North Tex., Denton, 1972. Art instr.; gallery dir. Coconut Grove Gallery, Miami, Fla., 2002—05; gallery owner; artist, instr., cons. Cons. Ampersano Art Supply, Austin, Tex., 1997—. Mem.: Watercolor Art Soc. Houston, Tex. Watercolor Soc., Birmingham Watercolor Soc. Office: Gallery Round Top 203 E Austin Round Top TX 78954

VERNON, MIKE, retired professional hockey player; b. Calgary, Alta., Canada, Feb. 24, 1963; Goalie Calgary Flames, 1982-94, 2000—02, Detroit Red Wings, 1994-97, San Jose Sharks, 1997-99, Florida Panthers, 1999—2000. Player NHL All-Star Game, 1988—91, 1993. Co-recipient William M. Jennings Trophy, NHL, 1996; named Most Valuable Player, Western Hockey League (WHL), 1982, Player of the Yr., 1982; named to First All-Star Team, 1982, 1983, Second All-Star Team, Ctrl. Hockey League (CHL), 1984, The Sporting News, 1989, NHL, 1989; recipient Del Wilson Trophy for top goaltender, Western Hockey League (WHL), 1982, 1983, Hap Emms Trophy, Meml. Cup, 1983, Conn Smythe Trophy, NHL, 1997. Achievements include being a member of Stanley Cup Champion Calgary Flames, 1989, Detroit Red Wings, 1997; having his number, 30, retired by Calgary Flames, 2007. *

VERNON, WESTON, III, (WES VERNON), broadcaster, writer, actor; b. NYC, Aug. 23, 1931; s. Weston, Jr. and Adelaide (Neilson) V.; m. Alida Steinvoort, Oct. 5, 1951; children: Rosanne, Weston IV, Diane, John Randall. Student, Utah State U., Logan, 1949-50, Brigham Young U., Provo, Utah, 1953-54. Early broadcasting career on staff of radio stas., in Utah and Wyo., 1950-54; news and announcer KBMY, Billings, Mont., 1954-63; news dir., polit. specialist KSL Radio-TV, Salt Lake City, Utah, 1963-68; bur. chief Bonneville Internat. Corp., Washington, 1968-72; corr. CBS Radio Stas. News Svc. CBS Radio, Washington, 1972-97; host CBS Crosstalk, 1975-97. Columnist RenewAmerica.us, US AIM Report, The High Green, The Timetable, The Accuracy In Media Report, Washington columnist Railfan & Railroad Mag., guest host Dateline: Washington Radio Am. Network, 1998—; actor:. Bd. dirs. Winding-Orchard Citizens Assn., Wheaton-Glenmont, Md., 1974—77, 1986—, pres., 1975—76. Served with AUS, 1951—52. Recipient Journalism awards, Mont. A.P. Press Stas., 1960, Utah Bar Assn., 1965, Utah Broadcasters Assn., 1965—66, Nat. Press Club. Mem. SAG, AFTRA (exec. bd. Balt.-Wash. local 1997—), Am. Legion (comdr. Yellowstone Post 4 1962-63), Chesapeake Rlwy. Assn. (pres. 1992-94, bd. dirs. 1984-2006). Office: 1605 Billman Ln Silver Spring MD 20902-1417

VERON, J. MICHAEL, lawyer, writer; b. Lake Charles, La., Aug. 24, 1950; s. Earl Ernest and Alverdy (Heyd) V.; m. Melinda Anne Guidry, Jan. 2, 1993; children: John Heyd, Katharine Leigh, Dylan Michael Earl. BA, Tulane U., 1972, JD, 1974; LLM, Harvard U., 1976. Bar: La. 1974, U.S. Dist. Ct. (we. dist.) La. 1977, U.S. Dist. Ct. (ea. dist.) La. 1979, U.S. Dist. Ct. (mid. dist.) La., 1983, U.S. Dist. Ct. (ea. dist.) Tex. 1992), U.S. Ct. Appeals (5th cir.) 1981, U.S. Ct. Appeals (fed. cir.) 1996, U.S. Tax Ct. 1988. Law clk. to presiding justice La. Supreme Ct., New Orleans, 1974-75; sole practice Lake Charles, 1976-78; ptnr. Scofield, Gerard, Veron, Singletary & Pohorelsky (formerly Scofield, Gerard, Veron, Hoskins & Soileau), Lake Charles, 1978—2005, Bice, Palermo & Veron, Lake Charles, 2005—. Instr. legal method and rsch. Boston U., 1975-76; lectr. environ. law McNeese State U., 1976-79; faculty Tulane Trial Adv. Inst., 1980; adj. prof. La. State U. Sch. Law, 1993-2000. Author: The Greatest Player Who Never Lived, 2000, The Greatest Course That Never Was, 2001, The Caddie, 2004, Shell Game, 2007; mem. bd. editors Tulane Law Rev., 1972-73, assoc. editor, 1973-74. Mem. athletic adv. com. Tulane U., 1983-86; pres. Krewe of Barataria, 1980-86. Named to La. State U. Law Ctr. Hall of Fame, 1993. Mem. U.S. Golf Assn. (regional affairs com.), La. Golf. Assn. (bd. dirs., pres. 1990), Order of Coif, Maritime Law Assn., Lake Charles Country Club (pres. 1986). Roman Catholic. Avocations: golf, gin rummy, athletics. Home: 9 Par Dr Lake Charles LA 70605-5925 Office: Bice Palerom & Veron 721 Kirby St Lake Charles LA 70601 E-mail: mike@bpvlaw.com.

VERONEAU, JOHN K., ambassador; m. Carol Svoboda; 2 children. BA, JD, U. Maine. Legis. dir. to U.S. Senator William S. Cohen; legis. dir. to U.S. Senator Bill Frist; chief of staff to U.S. Senator M. Susan Collins, 1989—97; served under sec. of def. William S. Cohen, 1997—2001; asst. sec. def. legis. affairs, 1999—2001; asst. U.S. Trade Rep. congl. affairs Exec. Office of Pres., 2001—03, gen. counsel U.S. Trade Rep., 2003—05, dep. U.S. Trade Rep., 2006—. Home: US Trade Rep 600 17th St NW Washington DC 20508 *

VERONGOS, HELEN, editor; Asst. fgn. editor, night New York Times. Office: New York Times 229 W 43d St New York NY 10036 Office Phone: 212-556-7415. Office Fax: 212-556-7278.

VERONICA, DEBRA CLARISSE, principal; b. Buffalo, Sept. 17, 1966; d. John Owczarek and Dolores Evans; m. Mark David Veronica, Apr. 7, 1989; 4 children. BSc, State U. of NY at Buffalo, 1988, MSc, 1995. Cert. Teaching NY, 1996. Tchr. St. Barnabas Sch., Depew, NY, 1988—89, St. Amelia Sch., Tonawanda, NY, 1989—91, Buffalo Pub. Sch., 1991—2003; adj. prof. Canisius Coll., Buffalo, 2001—03; asst. prin. Lancaster Pub. Sch. Sys., NY, 2003—04; elem. prin. Maryvale Sch. Sys., Cheektowaga, NY, 2004—. Summer sch. prin. Sweet Home Sch., Amherst, NY, 2003; ednl. cons. Discovery Toys. Vol. tchr. St. Amelia Religious Edn. Dept., 1988—90, 1992; pres. Mother of Twins Club of Buffalo, 2002—04, corresponding sec., 2000, 2001, club adv., 2004—06. Mem.: Internat. Reading Assn., Sch. Admin. Assn. of NY State, Assn. for Supervision and Curriculum Devleop., Nat. Assn. of Elem. Sch. Prin., Phi Alpha Theta, Kappa Delta Pi. Avocation: reading. Office: Maryvale Sch Sys 1 Nagel Dr Buffalo NY 14225

VERONIS, GEORGE, geophysics educator; b. New Brunswick, NJ, June 6, 1926; s. Nicholas Emmanuel and Angeliki (Efthimakis) V.; m. Anna Margareta Olsson, Nov. 8, 1963; m. Catherine Elizabeth, Jan. 29, 1949 (div. Nov. 1962); children: Melissa, Benjamin. AB, Lafayette Coll., 1950; PhD, Brown U., 1954; MA (hon.), Yale U., 1966; DSc (hon.) Lafayette Coll. 1997. Staff meteorologist Inst. Advanced Study, Princeton, 1953-56; staff mathematician Woods Hole Oceanographic Inst., Mass., 1956-64, mem. staff, dir. geophys. fluid dynamics summer program, 1959—, assoc. prof. MIT, Cambridge, 1961-64, research oceanographer, 1964-66; prof. geophysics and applied sci. Yale U., New Haven, 1966—, Henry Barnard Davis prof., 1985—, chmn. geology and geophysics, 1976-79, dir. applied math, 1979-93. Editor Jour. Marine Rsch., 1973—; contbr. articles to profl. jours. Served with USN, 1943-46. Fellow Am. Acad. Arts and Scis., Am. Geophys. Union; mem. NAS, Norwegian Acad. Scis. (Robert L. and Bettie P. Cody award 1989, Henry Stommel Rsch. award 1997). Greek Orthodox. Office Phone: 203-432-3148. Business E-Mail: george.veronis@yale.edu.

VERONNEAU-TROUTMAN, SUZANNE, retired ophthalmologist; b. Coaticook, Que., Can., Oct. 30, 1928; d. Sarto Veronneau and Victorine Marcoux; m. Richard C. Troutman, July 12, 1967; stepchildren: David Troutman, Anne Troutman, Richard Troutman. BA, Coll. St. Maurice, St. Hyacinthe, Que., 1951; BSc II, U. Montreal, Que., 1952, MD, 1957; postgrad. in ophthalmology/pathology, Inst. Ophthalmology, London, 1960—61. Diplomate ophthalmology Royal Coll. Physicians of London, Royal Coll. Surgeons of Eng., lic. Med. Coun. Can., physician N.Y. State, diplomate ophthalmology Coll. of Physicians and Surgeons Province of Que., Royal Coll. of Physicians and Surgeons of Can., Am. Bd. of Ophthalmology. Sr. plastic surgery, neurosurgery resident Notre Dame Hosp., Montreal, 1957—58; resident in ophthalmology Hosp. Maisonneuve, Montreal, 1958—59; asst. in ophthalmology Hosp. Edouard Herriot, Lyon, France, 1959—60; clin. asst., OPD officer Royal Eye and Moorfields Eye Hosps., London, 1961; ophthalmic surgeon Ghandi Eye Hosp., Aligarh, India, 1962; instr. basic scis. Maisoneuve Hosp., Montreal, 1963—67, clin. assoc. prof. ophthalmology SUNY Downstate Med. Ctr., Bklyn., 1971—82; clin. instr. dept. ophthalmology Cornell U. Med. Coll., NYC, 1971—74, clin. asst. prof. ophthalmology, 1974—77, clin. assoc. prof. ophthalmology, 1977—98, clin. prof. ophthalmology, 1998—2000; clin. prof. emeritus Weill Med. Coll. of Cornell U., NYC, 2000—. Dir. strabismus clinic and orthoptics Maisoneuve Hosp., Que., 1963—67; chief ocular motility clinic Manhattan Eye Ear and Throat Hosp., NYC, 1970—2000; asst. attending physician dept. surgery, divsn. ophthalmology Hosp. of the Holy Family, 1973—77, assoc. attending physician, 1977—80; asst. dir. dept. motor anomalies N.Y. Eye and Ear Infirmary, 1974—78, assoc. dir., 1978—82, assoc. attending surgeon, 1974—82; adj. attending ophthalmologist Bronx Lebanon Hosp. Ctr., 1975—77, assoc. attending ophthalmologist, 1977—79; cons. dept. ophthalmology Beth Israel Med. Ctr., 1979—87; lectr. in field. Editor, transl.: Hugonniers' textbook Strabismus, Heterophoria, Oculomotor Paralysis; author: (textbook translated in French, Japanese and Portuguese) Prisms in the Medical and Surgical Management of Strabismus; contbr. 32 chpts. to books, articles more than 35 articles to sci. jours. Established endowment of biennial internat. prize Pan Am. Assn. Ophthalmology, 1991; established ann. prize Women in Ophthalmology, San Francisco, 1997; established perpetual endowment ann. scholarships and prize dept. edn. U. Que., Montreal, 1997; established perpetual endowment ann. scholarships dept. ophthalmology U. Montreal, 2006. Recipient Residents award for outstanding tchg., N.Y. Eye and Ear Infirmary, 1970, Spl. Achievement medal, U. Montreal, 1993. Fellow: ACS (life), Royal Coll. Surgeons Can.; mem.: AMA (life), Am. Ophthalmol. Soc., Am. Acad. Ophthalmology (life Honor award 1981), Pan Am. Assn. Ophthalmology (life; bd. dirs. 1993—2003), Med. Soc. of the State of N.Y. (life), Am. Assn. Pediat. Ophthalmology and Strabismus (life; charter mem.). Home: Apt 30 A 860 United Nations Plz New York NY 10017 Personal E-mail: sveronneau@msn.com.

VERPLANK, SCOTT RACHAL, professional golfer; b. Dallas, July 9, 1964; m. Kim Verplank; children: Scottie, Hannah, Emma, Heidi. BS in Bus., Okla. State U., 1986. Profl. golfer PGA Tour, 1986—; US Amateur champion, 1984; NCAA champion, 1986; winner Western Open, 1985, Buick Open, 1988, World Cup of Golf (individual), 1998, Reno-Tahoe Open, 2000, Bell Can. Open, 2001, EDS Byron Nelson Championship, 2007. Mem. Walker Cup team, 1985, World Cup team, 1998, 2004, Ryder Cup team, 2002, 06, Presidents Cup team, 2005. Recipient Ben Hogan award, 2002. Avocations: reading, kids, sports, quail hunting. Office: PGA 100 Ave of Champions Palm Beach Gardens FL 33418 *

VERRANT, JOHN ALAN, engineering executive; b. Hibbing; s. John Carl and Marie E. Verrant; m. Sherry Lynn Smith, Aug. 28, 1982; children: John Lawrence, Katherine Marie. BS in Mech. Engring., U. Minn., Mpls., 1974, MS in Mech. Engring., 1976. Program mgr. diagnostic divsn. Abbott Labs, Santa Clara, Calif., 1989—2004; v.p. engring. Immunicon Corp, Huntingdon Valley, Pa., 2004—. Recipient Arch T. Caldwell award, Soc. Automotive Engring. Achievements include research in anti-cancer targets on circulating tumor cells; development of smart water explosion control system; discovery of sampling and physical characterization of diesel exhaust aerosols; research in dilution system for measuring diesel exhaust particulate; patents in field. Avocations: skiing, hiking, camping, fishing, hunting. Office: Immunicon Corp 3401 Masons Mill Rd Huntingdon Valley PA 19006 Home Phone: 215-862-0671; Office Phone: 215-346-8256. Office Fax: 215-830-0751. Personal E-mail: verntja@yahoo.com. Business E-Mail: jverrant@immunicon.com.

VERRECCHIA, ALFRED JOSEPH, toy company executive; b. Providence, Feb. 19, 1943; s. Alfred Augustus and Elda Lucy (Tortolani) V.; m. Geraldine Macari, June 11, 1964; children: Michael, Michele, Melisa, Lisa. BS, U. R.I., 1967, MBA in Fin., 1971; Doctorate (hon.), Johnson & Wales U., 1991. Joined as jr. accountant Hasbro, Inc., Pawtucket, RI, 1965, v.p. fin., 1980-82, sr. v.p. fin., CFO, 1982-86, exec. v.p. fin., CFO, 1986-89, exec. v.p., 1989, pres. Hasbro mfg. svcs., 1989, co-COO, 1989, COO, domestic toys, exec. v.p. global ops., CFO, 1990—96, exec. v.p., pres., global ops., 1996—99, exec. v.p., pres., global ops and develop., 1999; exec. v.p., global ops., CFO Hasbro Inc., Pawtucket, 1999—2000; pres., COO, CFO Hasbro, Inc., Pawtucket, 2000—01, pres., COO, 2001—03, pres., CEO, 2003—. Bd. dirs. Hasbro Inc., Old Stone Corp., FM Global. Chmn. Bradley Hosp., East Providence, R.I.; pres. R.I. Pub. Expenditure Coun., Providence; bd. mem. Bd. of Govs. for Higher Edn., Providence, U. R.I. Coll. Bus., Kingston, R.I. Mem. Toy Mfrs. Am. (bd. mem.). Office: Hasbro Inc 1027 Newport Ave Pawtucket RI 02862 *

VERREOS, NICK, apparel designer; b. St. Louis, Mo., Feb. 13, 1967; AA, Can. Coll.; BA, UCLA; AA Cum Laude, Fashion Inst. Design and Merchandising, LA. With Ecru, Isshu, Swell Store, Nallie and Millie; draper, patternmaker, illustrator Paris Blues, Panacea, Deborah McGuire, Friends TV show, NBC's Passions; prodn. patternmaker Lucca; wardrobe asst. Queer Eye for the Straight Guy; tailor, styling asst. Replay Italy; designer, owner Nikolaki, 2001—; instr. Fashion Inst. Design and Merchandising, LA, 2003—. Fashion design contestant Bravo's Project Runway; designer prom dress line Windsor Fashions; spokesperson Fashion Inst. Design and Merchandising; fashion commentator NBC, E! Entertainment, TV Guide Channel. Recipient Suisse du Jeune Talent award. Achievements include designing dresses for hollywood celebrities. Office: Fashion Inst Design and Merchandising 919 S Grand Ave Los Angeles CA 90015-1421 *

VERRET, DANIEL JOSEPH, otolaryngologist; s. Lee and Therese Verret. BSE summa cum laude, Tulane U., New Orleans, 1997; MD, UT S.W. Med. Sch., Dallas, 2001. Lic. Tex., 2002. Intern, gen. surgery U. Tex. S.W. Med. Sch., Dallas, 2001—02, resident, dept. otolaryngology, 2002—06; fellow, facial plastic and reconstructive surgery U. Mo., Columbia, 2006—. Presenter in field. Contbr. articles to profl. jours. Scholar, U. Tex. S.W. Med. Sch., 1997—2001. Mem.: AMA, ACS, Triologic Soc., Am. Acad. Otolaryngology Head & Neck Surgery, Am. Acad. Facial Plastic and Reconstructive Surgery, Alpha Omega Alpha. Office: 1965 S Fremont Ste #120 Springfield MO 65804 Home Phone: 214-394-8976; Office Phone: 417-887-3223. Personal E-mail: goines@sbcglobal.net.

VERRILL, CHARLES OWEN, JR., lawyer; b. Biddeford, Maine, Sept. 30, 1937; s. Charles Owen and Elizabeth (Handy) V.; m. Mary Ann Blanchard, Aug. 13, 1960 (dec.); children: Martha Anne, Edward Blanchard, Ethan Christopher, Elizabeth Handy, Matthew Lawton, Peter Goldthwait; m. Diana Baber, Dec. 11, 1993. AB, Tufts U., 1959; LLB, Duke U., 1962. Bar: D.C. 1962. Assoc. Weaver & Glassie, 1962-64, Barco, Cook, Patton & Blow, 1964-66, ptnr., 1967, Patton, Boggs & Blow, 1967-84, Wiley, Rein LLP (and predecessor firm), Washington, 1984—. Adj. prof. internat. trade law/internat. bus. transaction Georgetown U. Law Ctr., Washington, 1978—, Charles Fahy Disting. adj. prof., 1993; vis. sr. lectr. internat. trade law Duke U. Law Sch., 1998—; nat. adv. bd. Natural Resources Coun. of Maine, 2002—; panel mem. CPR Washington, 2003—. Local dir. Tufts U. Ann. Fund, 1965-69; mem. Duke Law Alumni Coun., 1972-75; trustee Internat. Law Inst., 1981—, chmn. bd. trustees, 1983-87, pres., 2002—; apptd. to roster of dispute settlement panelists World Trade Orgn., 1995, 97; adv. com. rules U.S. Ct. Internat. Trade, 1998—; chmn. D.C. Cable Television Adv. Com., 1999—; bd. visitors Duke U. Law Sch., 2000—. Recipient Charles B. Rhyne Disting. Alumni award, Duke U. Law Sch., 2007. Mem. ABA, Internat. Bar Assn., D.C. Bar Assn., Am. Soc. Internat. Law (editl. adv. com. Internat. Legal Materials, 2007-), Internat. Law Assn. (Am. br.), Order of Coif, Theta Delta Chi, Phi Delta Phi, Met. Club (Washington), Chevy Chase Club (Md.), Tarratine Club (Dark Harbor, Maine). Office: Wiley Rein LLP 1776 K St NW Washington DC 20006-2304 Office Phone: 202-719-7323. Business E-Mail: cverrill@wileyrein.com.

VERRILL, F. GLENN, advertising executive; b. NYC, Dec. 17, 1923; s. Ralph Francis and Rose (Cuva) V.; m. Jean Demar, Aug. 25, 1946; children: Gary, Joan. AB, Adelphi Coll., 1949; A.M., Harvard U., 1950. With Batten, Barton, Durstine & Osborn, Inc., 1952—98, v.p., 1964; creative dir. Batten, Barton, Durstine & Osborn, Inc. (Burke Dowling Adams div.), Atlanta, 1965-70, exec. v.p., gen. mgr., 1970-71, pres., 1971-88, chmn., 1988—98, also dir. parent co. Author: Advertising Procedure, 1983, rev. edit., 1986, 88. Mem. adv. bd. U. Ga.; vice chmn. bd. overseers Coll. Bus. Adminstrn., Ga. State U.; bd. dirs. Atlanta Humane Soc., pres., 1980-81; chmn. Advanced Advt. Inst. Atlanta, 1981; mem. Peabody award com., 1984—90; bd. dirs. Atlanta Coll. of Art, 1990. With USAAF, 1943-46. Mem. Am. Assn. Advt. Agys. (nat. dir. 1973—), Atlanta Athletic Club, Cherokee Club, Harvard Club (Atlanta). Episcopalian. Home: 1730 Winterthur Close Atlanta GA 30328

VERRILL, KATHLEEN WILLS, special education educator; b. Tucson, Jan. 4, 1938; d. William Oscar Wills and Helen Louise (Boswell) Perry; m. Thomas Anthony Verrill, July 30, 1966; 1 child, Nathan Anthony. AA, Monterey Peninsula Coll., 1958; BA, San Francisco State U., 1963, MA, 1965. Tchr. educable mentally retarded Albany (Calif.) Unified Schs., 1963-70, Sch. Dist. # 49, Fairfield, Maine, 1970-73; resource tchr. Indpls. Schs., 1973-75; tchr. learning handicapped Phila. Sch. Dist., 1975-77, ednl. evaluator, 1977-79, instructional advisor, 1979-81; resource specialist San Francisco Unified Schs., 1981-82, Alameda (Calif.) Unified Sch. Dist., 1982—. Author Food Centered Curriculum for Learning Disabled, 1965. Rep. Sch. Dist. Affirmative Action com., Alameda, 1988-90. Recipient PTA Calif. Hon. Svc. award Lum Sch., 1991; named Tchr. of Yr. Alameda Sch. Dist., 1986; Crown Zellerbach Found. fellowship, 1964, edn. grant Alameda County Schs., 1964. Mem. NEA, Coun. Exceptional Children, Alameda Edn. Assn. (rep. 1989-90), Calif. Tchrs. Assn., Delta Kappa Gamma (chmn. rsch. 1988-89, pres. Delta Zeta chpt. 1992-94, exec. bd. 1994—). Avocations: travel, classical music, reading, cooking, study of artists. Office: Alameda Unified Sch Dist 1801 Sandcreek Way Alameda CA 94501-6024

VERRILLO, RONALD THOMAS, neuroscience educator, researcher; b. Hartford, Conn., July 31, 1927; s. Francesco Paul and Angela (Forte) V.; m. Violet Silverstein, June 3, 1950; children: Erica, Dan, Thomas. BA, Syracuse U., NY, 1952; PhD, U. Rochester, 1958. Asst. prof. Syracuse U., 1957-62, rsch. assoc., 1959-63, rsch. fellow, 1963-67, assoc. prof., 1967-74, prof., 1974-94, prof. emeritus, 1995—, assoc. dir. Inst. Sensory Rsch., 1980-84, dir., 1984-93, dir. grad. neurosci. program, 1984-93. Advisor com. on hearing, bioacoustics and biomechanics NRC. Author: Adjustment to Visual Disability, 1961 (award 1962); contbr. chpts. to books, articles to profl. jours. With USN, 1945-46. Fellow Am. Found. for Blind, 1956, NATO, 1970; grantee NSF, 1969-72, 84-87, NIH, 1972—; recipient Internat. Sensory Aids award, 1998. Fellow Acoustical Soc. Am. (Silver medal 1999); mem. Soc. for Neurosci., N.Y. Acad. Scis., Sigma Xi (Rsch. award 1982). Home: 312 Berkeley Dr Syracuse NY 13210-3031 Office: Syracuse U Inst Sensory Rsch 621 Skytop Rd Syracuse NY 13244-5290 Office Phone: 315-443-4166. Business E-Mail: ron_verrillo@isr.syr.edu.

VERRONE, PATRIC MILLER, lawyer, writer; b. Glendale, NYC, Sept. 29, 1959; s. Pat and Edna (Miller) V.; m. Margaret Maiya Williams, 1989; children: Patric Carroll Williams, Marianne Emma Williams, Theodore Henry Williams. BA, Harvard U., 1981; JD, Boston Coll., 1984. Bar: Fla. 1984, Calif. 1988, US Dist. Ct. (mid. dist.) Fla. 1984, US Dist. Ct. (ctrl. dist.) Calif. 1995, US Ct. Appeals (9th cir.) 1995. Assoc. Allen, Knudsen, Swartz, DeBoest, Rhoads & Edwards, Ft. Myers, Fla., 1984-86; writer The Tonight Show, Burbank, Calif., 1987-90. Adj. prof. Loyola Law Sch., LA, 1998—2000; lectr. U. Calif., LA, 2002—05. Dir., prodr., writer The Civil War-The Lost Episode, 1991; writer: The Larry Sanders Show, 1992—94, The Critic, 1993—95; prodr., writer The Simpsons, 1994—95, 2002—06, Muppets Tonight!, 1995—97 (Emmy award Best Children's Program, 1998), Pinky and the Brain, 1998, Futurama, 1998—2002 (Environ. Media award, 2000, 2003, WGA award nominee, 2004, Emmy nominee, 1999, 2001, 2003, 2004, Emmy award for outstanding animated program, 2002, Writers Guild award nominee, 2004, Annie award nominee, 2004), 2005—07, co-exec. prodr., writer Class of 3000, 2005—, Futurama Movies, 2006—; editor: Harvard Lampoon, 1978—84, Boston Coll. Law Rev., 1983—84, Fla. Bar Jour., 1987—88, LA Lawyer, 1994—2006; issue editor Ann. Entertainment Law Issue, 1995—2006; contbr. articles to profl. jours. including Elysian Fields Quar., White's Guide to Collecting Figures, Frank Sinatra: The Man, The Music, The Legend, Bongo Comics. Bd. dirs. Calif. Confedn. of Arts, 1994-98, Mus. Contemporary Art, 1994-95; trustee Am. Film Inst., 2005—; mem. adv. bd. Hollywood Health and Soc., 2005—. Mem. ABA (vice-chair arts, entertainment and sports law com. 1995-96), Calif. Bar, Calif. Lawyers for Arts, LA County Bar Assn. (sec. barristers exec. com., chmn. artists and the law com., steering com. homeless shelter project, intellectual property and entertainment law sect., state appelate jud. evaluation com., legis. activity com.), Fla. Bar Assn., Assn. Media and Entertainment Counsel (Labor Counsel of Yr. 2006), (Writers Guild Am. West (exec. com. animation writers caucus, bd. dirs. 1999-2001, sec., treas., 2001-05, chair organizing com. 2001-05, pres. 2005—, animation writers caucus, Animation Writing award 2002), Harvard Club Lee County (v.p. 1985-86), Harvard Club So. Calif. Republican. Roman Catholic. Avocations: baseball, history. Home and Office: PO Box 1428 Pacific Palisades CA 90272-1428

VERSACE, DONATELLA, fashion designer; b. Reggio di Calabria, Italy, May 2, 1955; d. Antonio and Francesca V.; m. Paul Beck (div.); children: Allegra, Daniel. Degree in lit., U. Florence, Italy. Head designer Versus label Gianni Versace Group, 1978—97, vice chmn., style and image dir. NYC, 1997—. Released fragrance Versace Woman, 2001. Achievements include created children's line, 1993; launched fragrance Versace Woman, 2001. Office: Gianni Versace SpA Via Ges 12 20121 Milan Italy Address: Instante Vesa srl Via Spiga 25 20121 Milan Italy Office Phone: 02 7610931. Office Fax: 02 798572. *

VERSCH, ESTHER MARIE, artist; b. Santa Monica, Calif., May 27, 1927; d. Claro Contreras Santellanes and Juana Hernandez; m. Chester Ray Fraelich, Nov. 14, 1943 (div. Nov. 1964); children: Joe Fraelich, Diane Fraelich Foster Viramontes; m. Terry Lee Versch, June 21, 1969; stepchildren: Fred, Roman, Joseph, Terry Jr., Michael. Student, East L.A. Coll., Pasadena City Coll. Lic. vocat. nurse. Nurse pvt. dr.'s office, LA, 1968-69, U. So. Calif. Med. Ctr., LA, 1963-68; artist Altadena, Calif., 1972—. Artist: (front cover) Library Services L.A., 1983, Christmas card for Western Greeting Inc., (back cover) Moccasin Tracks, 1984-85; one woman shows include Republic Fed. Savings, Altadena, Calif., Pasadena Pub. Libr., Whites Art Store and Gallery, La Canada, Calif., 1979, Windmill Gallery, 1985; group exhbns.: Women Artists of the West Internat. Exhbn. and Sale, Cody Western and Wildlife Classyc, 1979, Nat. Cowgirl Hall of Fame, Hereford, Tex., 1978, Beauty for the Beast Benefit, 1980, Ducks Unltd. Invitational Art Show, Taylor, Mich., 1986-87, Lawrence (Kans.) Indian Art Show, Mus. Anthropology, 1989-90, Snake River Showcase, Lewiston, Idaho, 1992, Women Artists of the West, 1992, 98, 99, Death Valley 49's Invitational Art Show, 1994-2000, 2001, George Ohr Cultural Arts and Cultural Ctr., Biloxi, Miss., 1998, Western and Wildlife Invitational Art Show, Estes Park, Colo., 2000, WAOW Art Show Pinedale, Wyo, 2002, Art and Music Festival, Dublin, Ohio, 2002, West Wind Gallery, Casper, Wyo., 2003-04, Pomerene Ctr. for the Arts, 2004, Zanesville Ctr. for the Arts, 2004, 05, Red River Valley Mus., Vernon, Tex., 2004, Ronald Reagan Mus., Simi Valley, Calif., 2004, Johnson Humrickhouse Mus., 2004-05, Dogwood Festival Artists Tour Studio, 2006, Juliet Art Exhibit Nat. Arts Found., Skokie, Ill., 2006, Johnson Humrick Ho. Mus., 2006, West Wing Gallery, Casper, Wyo, 2006, others; collections: Johnson Humrickhouse Mus., Coshocton, Ohio, other pvt. collections; illustrator back cover Moccasin Tracks, 1984-85. Vol. nurses aide City View Hosp., L.A., 1960-63; vol. Arroyo Rep., Pasadena, Calif., St. Luke Hosp., Pasadena, 1990-94, flu immunization ARC, 1977-78. Recipient Gold medal for watercolor San Gabriel Fine Arts, 1979, Best of Show award for watercolor Am. Indian and Western, 1990, Hon. mention San Gabriel Fine Arts, 1990, 3rd Place Watercolor Women Artists of the West Saddle Back Art Gallery, 1982. Mem. Women Artists of the West (emeritus mem., treas., asst. sec., editor West Wind, membership chmn.), Ohio Art League, Coshocton Art Guild (v.p. Juried Art Show 2004-05). Republican. Roman Catholic. Avocations: walking, gardening, sewing. E-mail: everschart@newsguy.com.

VERSCHOOR, CURTIS CARL, writer, consultant; b. Grand Rapids, Mich., June 7, 1931; s. Peter and Leonene (Dahlstrom) V.; m. Marie Emilie Kritschgau, June 18, 1952; children: Katherine Anne, Carolyn Marie, John Peter, Carla Michelle. BBA with distinction, U. Mich., 1951; MBA, U. Mich., Ann Arbor, 1952; EdD, No. Ill. U., DeKalb, 1977. CPA; cert. mgmt. acctg., cert. fin. planner, cert. fraud examiner, cert. internal auditor; chartered fin. cons. Pub. accountant Touche, Ross, Bailey & Smart (C.P.A.'s), 1955-63; with Singer Co., 1963-68, asst. controller, 1965-68; controller Colgate-Palmolive Co., 1968-69; asst. controller bus. products group Xerox Corp., 1969-72; controller Baxter Internat., 1972-73; CFO, v.p. fin. Altair Corp., Chgo., 1973-74; prof. DePaul U., Chgo., 1974-94, ledger and quill alumni rsch. prof., 1994—; pres. C.C. Verschoor & Assocs., Inc., 1981—. Part-time instr. Wayne State U., 1955-60. Author: Audit Committee Briefing: Understanding the 21st Century Audit Committee Governance Roles, 2000, Audit Committee Briefing: Facilitating New Audit Committee Responsibilites, 2001, Governance Update 2003, Ethics and Compliance: Challenges for Internal Auditing, 2007: Impact of the New Initiatives, 2003, Ethics and; contbg. editor: Jour. Accountancy, 1961-62, Jour. Internal Auditing, 1985—, Strategic Fin., 1999-; editl. adv. bd. Acctg. Today, 1991-2004, Internal Auditor, 1993—. Trustee Hektoen Inst. for Medicine, Chgo., 1996—. Served with AUS, 1953-55. Recipient Elijah Watts Sells award Am. Inst. C.P.A.'s, 1953; rsch. scholar Ctr. for Bus. Ethics, Bentley Coll. Mem. AICPA, Fin. Execs. Inst., Am. Acctg. Assn., Inst. Mgmt. Accts., Inst. Internal Auditors, Nat. Assn. Corp. Dirs., Assn. Cert. Fraud Examiners, Internat. Assn. Bus. and Soc., Soc. for Bus. Ethics, Beta Gamma Sigma, Beta Alpha Psi, Delta Pi Epsilon, Phi Kappa Phi, Phi Eta Sigma. Home: 231 Wyngate Dr Barrington IL 60010-4840 Office: DePaul Univ One E Jackson Blvd Chicago IL 60604-2287 Personal E-mail: curtisverschoor@sbcglobal.net.

VERSCHUREN, ANNETTE, retail executive; b. North Sydney, NS, Can., 1956; Grad., Concordia U.; BBA, St. Francis Xavier U., Antigonish, NS; D (hon.), Mt. St. Vincent U.; LLD (hon.), St. Francis Xavier U., Antigonish, NS. Devel. officer Cape Breton Devel. Corp., Sydney, N.S., Canada; exec. v.p. Can. Devel. Investment Corp.; v.p. corp. devel. Imasco Ltd.; pres., co-owner Michael's of Can., 1993—96; mem. staff to divsn. pres. EXPO Design Ctr. to Can. Divsn. pres. Home Depot, 1996—. Bd. mem. Can. Coun. Chief Execs.; chancellor Univ. Coll. Cape Breton; mem. North Am. Competitiveness Coun., 2006—, Can. Corp. Coun. on Volunteering. Bd. mem. Habitat for Humanity. Recipient Can. 125 medal. Mem.: Retail Coun. Can. (chair, Disting. Can. Retailer of Yr. 2005). Office: Home Depot Can Inc 900-1 Concorde Gate Toronto ON M3C 4H9 Canada

VERSFELD, LEON, lawyer; s. Johannes Hendrik and Lorraine Versfeld; m. Heather Lea Hunter, Sept. 27, 2003; 1 child, Annie Grace. BLC, U. Pretoria, South Africa, 1996, LLB, 1998; tng. diploma (hon.), Law Soc. South Africa, 1999; grad., Greater Kans. City Bar Leadership Acad., 2006. Bar: The High Ct. South Africa 1999, Mo. 2003, U.S Dist. Ct. Kans. 2003, U.S Dist. Ct. (we. dist.) Mo. 2003. Law clk. to Hon. NG Manitz Dept. Justice, Pretoria, 1997, law clk. to Hon. Dep. Judge Pres. P.J. Van Der Walt, 1998—99; pvt. practice, advocate of Higher Ct. Pretoria, 1999—2003; assoc. Wirken Law Group, P.C., 2003—06; mng. mem. Versfeld & Hugo, LLC, 2006—. Grad. Greater Kansas City Bar Leadership Acad., 2005—06; mem. congress Fellows of Ctr. for Internat. Legal Studies; presenter and spkr. in field. Contbr. articles to profl. pubs. and confs. Bd. mem. Ctrl. Youth Rugby, Kansas City, 2004—05; bd. dirs. Tru-Friends, Truman Med. Ctr., 2006; chmn. fgn. rugby player com. Kans. City Rugby Football Club, Kansas City, 2003—04; barrister Kans. City Met. Bar. Assn. Inn of Ct., Kansas City, 2004—05. Nominee Best of the Bar, Kans. City Bus. Jour., 2007; scholar, Delta Motor Corp., South Africa, 1994-1998. Mem.: ABA, Am. Trial Lawyers Assn., Am. Immigration Lawyer Assn., Kans. City Met. Bar Assn. (chmn. internat. law com., barrister inns of ct. 2004—05). Avocations: rugby, tennis, golf. Office: Versfeld Hugo LLC 4740 Grand Blvd Ste 200 Kansas City MO 64112 Office Phone: 816-891-8600. Personal E-mail: lversfeld@gmail.com.

VERSFELT, DAVID SCOTT, lawyer; b. Mineola, NY, Feb. 17, 1951; s. William H. and Ruth (Gerland) V.; m. Mary Deborah Garber, Aug. 31, 1974; children: Christopher L., William S., Kathryn H. AB, Princeton U., 1973; JD, Columbia U., 1976. Bar: N.Y. 1977, U.S. Dist. Ct. (so. and ea. dists.) N.Y. 1977, U.S. Ct. Appeals (D.C. cir.) 1979, U.S. Ct. Appeals (2d and 7th cirs.) 1980, U.S. Supreme Ct. 1980, U.S. Ct. Appeals (9th cir.) 1981, U.S. Ct. Appeals (3d cir.) 1982, Ct. Internat. Trade 1990, U.S. Ct. Appeals (fed. cir.) 1994, U.S. Ct. Appeals (6th cir.) 1996. With Kirkpatrick & Lockhart LLP, NYC, 1998—2005, Kirkpatrick & Lockhart Nicholson Graham LLP, NYC, 2005—06, Kirkpatrick Lockhart Preston Gates Ellis LLP, NYC, 2007—. Mem. vol. divsn. Legal Aid Soc., N.Y.C., 1985-88, Partnership for a Drug-Free Am., 1989—. Mem. ABA, Fed. Bar Coun., Phi Beta Kappa. Office: Kirkpatrick & Lockhart Preston Gates Ellis LLP 599 Lexington Ave New York NY 10022-6030

VERSHBOW, ALEXANDER R., ambassador; b. Boston, July 3, 1952; m. Lisa (Kaufman) Vershbow; two children. BA in Russian and East European Studies, Yale Coll., 1974; MS in Internat. Rels., Columbia U., 1976. Various fgn. svc. positions, 1977—; dir. Office of Soviet Union Affairs US Dept. State, Washington, 1988-91, prin. dep. asst. to Sec. of State for European & Can. Affairs, 1993-94; spl. asst. to pres. and sr. dir. European Affairs NSC, Washington, 1995-97; US amb. to NATO and permanent rep. to North Atlantic Coun. US Dept. State, Brussels, 1998—2001, US amb. to Russian Fedn. Moscow, 2001—05, US amb. to Republic of Korea (South Korea) Seoul, 2005—. Contbr. articles to profl. jours. Recipient Anatoly Sharansky Freedom award Union of Couns. of Soviet Jews, 1990, 1st ann. Joseph J. Kruzel award, Sec. of Def. William Cohen, 1997, Disting. Honor award US Dept. State, 2001. Office: DOS Amb 9600 Seoul Pl Washington DC 20521 *

VERSLYCKE, TIM, research scientist; b. Sint-Amandsberg, Belgium, Oct. 5, 1975; s. Willy Verslycke and Rita Van Puyenbroeck; m. Patricia Pinto da Silva. PhD, Ghent U., Belgium, 2003. Investigator Woods Hole Oceanog. Instn., Mass., 2003—. Pres. AFS, Ghent, 1996—98. Recipient Ann. North Sea award, Flanders Marine Inst., 2004; fellow, Belgian Am. Ednl. Found., 2005—06; scholar, Ocean Life Inst., 2003—05. Office: Woods Hole Oceanographic Institution 45 Water St Woods Hole MA 02543 Home Phone: 508-292-0139; Office Phone: 508-289-3729. E-mail: tim@whoi.edu.

VER STEEG, DONNA LORRAINE FRANK, nurse, sociologist, educator; b. Minot, ND, Sept. 23, 1929; d. John Jonas and Pearl H. (Denlinger) Frank; m. Richard W. Ver Steeg, Nov. 22, 1950; children: Juliana, Anne, Richard B. BSN, Stanford, 1951; MSN, U. Calif., San Francisco, 1967; MA in Sociology, UCLA, 1969, PhD in Sociology, 1973. Clin. instr. U. ND Sch. Nursing, 1962-63; USPHS nurse rsch. fellow UCLA, 1969-72, asst. prof. Sch. Nursing, 1973-79, assoc. prof. Sch. Nursing, 1979-94, asst. dean Sch. Nursing, 1979-81, chmn. primary ambulatory care Sch. Nursing, 1976-87, assoc. dean Sch. Nursing, 1983-86, prof. emeritus chair primary care Sch. Nursing, 1994-96, prof. emeritus Sch. Nursing, 1996—; spl. cons., mem. adv. com. on physicians' assts. and nurse practitioner progs. Calif. State Bd. Med. Examiners, 1972-73. Co-prin. investigator PRIMEX Project Family Nurse Practitioners, UCLA Ext., 1974—76; assoc. cons. Calif. Postsecondary Edn. Commn., 1975—76; spl. cons. Calif. Dept. Consumer Affairs, 1978; chair nurse practioner/physician's asst. statewide program planning com. Calif. Area Health Edn. Ctr., 1978—89; mem. Calif. State Legis. Health Policy Forum, 1980—81; accredited visitor Western Assn. Sch. and Coll., 1985; mem. nurse practitioner adv. com. Calif. Bd. RN, 1995—97; mem. Edn. Industry Interface, Info. Devel. Mktg. Sub Com., 1995—99, recruitment, 1999—2001; archivist Calif. Strategic Planning Com. Nursing/Colleagues in Caring Project, 1995—. Contbr. chpts. to profl. books, articles to profl. jours. Recipient Leadership award Calif. Area Health Edn. Ctr. Sys., 1989, Commendation award Calif. State Assembly, 1994; named Outstanding Faculty Mem., UCLA Sch. Nursing, 1982. Fellow Am. Acad. Nursing; mem. AAAS, AAUW, ANA (pres. elect Calif. chpt. 1977-79, pres. 1979-81, interim chair Calif. 1995-96), Nat. League Nursing, Calif. League Nursing, N.Am. Nursing Diagnosis Assn., Am. Assn. History Nursing, Stanford Nurses Club, Sigma Theta Tau (Alpha Eta chpt. Leadership award Gamma Tau chpt. 1994), Sigma Xi. Home: 708 Swarthmore Ave Pacific Palisades CA 90272-4353 Office: UCLA Sch Nursing Box 956917 Los Angeles CA 90095-6917 Business E-Mail: dversteе@sonnet.ucla.edu.

VERSTEEG, ROBERT JOHN, minister, actor, writer; b. Oradell, NJ, July 7, 1930; s. John Marinus and Edna Elizabeth (Ames) Versteeg; m. Sally Maude Youngblood Creel, Feb. 17, 1951 (div. Apr. 1976); children: Cassandra Lee, John Richard, Jay Russell; m. Donna Marie Stevens, June 22, 1977; 1 child, Rick. BA, Ohio Wesleyan U., 1952; MDiv, Garrett Theol. Sem., Evanston, Ill., 1955; student, Baldwin-Wallace Coll., Berea, Ohio, 1962; MA, U. N.C., 1971. Ordained to ministry Meth. Ch., 1955. Pastor Ohio Meth. Ch., 1955-62; prof., dir. drama Louisburg (N.C.) Coll., 1962-75; assoc. prof., dir. Conservatory Acting Program, Va. Commonwealth U., Richmond, 1975-76; pastor Peebles (Ohio) United Meth. Ch., 1977-79, Point Place United Meth. Ch., Toledo, 1979-82, First United Meth. Ch., Ada, Ohio, 1982-86, Oak Hills United Meth. Ch., Cin., 1986-94, Trinity United Meth. Ch., Bowling Green, Ohio, 1994-99; writer LectionAid, 1997—99, Lectionary Homiletics, 1999—. Author: The Gracious Calling of the Lord, 1960, The Secret Life of the Good Samaritan, 1963, Whose Church is This Anyway?, 1985, Tales of Tittivillus, 1992, LectionAid, 1998, The Star Thrower, 2003; contbr. articles to profl. jours.; author, performer: (TV series) The Browning Show, 1974; Men of Faith, 1990—; (TV films) Paul A Prisoner, 1993—95; founder, dir.: Playback Theatre N.W. Ohio; Life Stage Theatrical Troupe, Inc. Named Seminarian Preacher of the Yr., Pulpit mag., 1955; named to Outstanding Young Men of Am., 1965; recipient Best Sermons award, HarperCollins, 1991; NEH fellow, 1972. Mem.: Nat. Assn. Drama Therapy, Fellowship United Meths. in Worship, Music and Other Arts. Democrat. Avocations: reading, piano, conditioning. Home and Office: 616 Flanders Ave Bowling Green OH 43402-1519 Office Phone: 419-601-0499. E-mail: bojov@wcnet.org.

VERSYP, SHARON, women's college basketball coach; BA, Purdue U, 1989. Asst. coach U. Louisville, 1996—97; asst. coach, recruiting dir. James Madison U., Harrisonburg, Va., 1997—2000; women's basektball head coach U. Maine, Orano, 2000—05, Ind. U., 2005—06, Purdue U., West Lafayette, Ind., 2006—. Recipient Coach Yr. award, America East Conf., 2003, 2005, Regional Coach Yr, NCAA, 2007. Office: Mackey Arena Rm 15 900 North University Dr West Lafayette IN 47907 *

VERTEFEUILLE, CHRISTINE SIEGRIST, state supreme court justice; b. New Britain, Conn., Dec. 10, 1950; BA in Polit. Sci., Trinity Coll., 1972; JD, U. Conn., 1975. Pvt. practice, 1975-89; judge Conn. Superior Ct., 1989—99; adminstrv. judge Waterbury Jud. Dist., 1994-99, complex litig. judge, 1999; judge Appellate Ct., 1999-2000; assoc. justice Conn. Supreme Ct., 2000—. Alternate mem. Waterbury and New Haven (Conn.) Grievance Panels, 1985-89; faculty Conn. Judges Inst., 1989-94. Recipient Jud. award Conn. Trial Lawyers Assn., 1995. Mem. Conn. Bar Assn. (mem. exec. com. real property 1988-89). Office: Conn Supreme Ct 231 Capitol Ave Hartford CT 06106 Office Phone: 860-757-2117.

VERTS, LITA JEANNE, academic administrator; b. Jonesboro, Ark., Apr. 13, 1935; d. William Gus and Lolita Josephine (Peeler) Nash; m. B. J. Verts, Aug. 29, 1954 (div. 1975); 1 child, William Trigg. BA, Oreg. State U., 1973; MA in Lingustics, U. Oreg., 1974; postgrad., U. Hawaii, 1977. Librarian Forest Research Lab., Corvallis, Oreg., 1966-69; instr. English Lang. Inst., Corvallis, 1974-80; dir. spl. svcs. Oreg. State U., Corvallis, 1980-96, faculty senator, 1988-96; ret., 1996. Editor Trio Achievers, 1986, 3rd edit., 1988; contbr. articles to profl. jours. Precinct com. Rep. Party, Corvallis, 1977-80; adminstrv. bd. 1st United Meth. Ch., Corvallis, 1987-89, fin. com., 1987-93, tchr. Bible, 1978—; bd. dirs. Westminster Ho., United Campus Ministries, 1994-95; adv. coun. Disabilities Svc., Linn, Benton, Lincoln Counties, 1990-99, vice-chmn., 1992-93, chmn. 1993-94; citizen adv. bd. on Transit, 1998—, intercity steering com., 1999—, Corvallis Downtown Parking Commn., 1999—; Oreg. Longterm Care Ombudsman, 1999—. Mem. N.W. Assn. Spl. Programs (pres. 1985-86), Nat. Coun. Ednl. Opportunities Assn. (bd. dirs. 1984-87), Nat. Gardening Assn., Alpha Phi (mem. corp. bd. Beta Upsilon chpt. 1990-96). Republican. Methodist. Avocations: gardening, photography, golf. Home: 530 SE Mayberry Ave Corvallis OR 97333-1866 Personal E-mail: l.verts@comcast.net.

VERVEER, PHILIP L., lawyer; b. Corvallis, Oreg. BSFS, Georgetown U., 1966; JD, U. Chgo., 1969. Bar: DC 1969, US Dist. Ct., DC 1969, US Ct. Appeals, DC Cir. 1971, US Ct. Appeals, 10th Cir. 1982, US Supreme Ct. 1986. Trial atty. Dept. Justice, Antitrust Div., 1969—77; supervisory atty. FTC, Bur. of Competition, 1977—78; chief FCC, Cable Television Bur., Broadcast Bur. and Common Carrier Bur., 1978—81; ptnr. telecom. dept. Willkie Farr & Gallagher LLP, Washington, DC. Mem.: ABA, Fed. Comm. Bar Assn. Office: Willkie Farr & Gallagher LLP 1875 K Street, NW Washington DC 20006 Office Phone: 202-303-1117. E-mail: pverveer@willkie.com.

VERVILLE, ELIZABETH GIAVANI, federal official; b. NYC, July 13, 1940; d. Joseph and Gertrude (Levy) Giavani. BA, Duke U., 1961; LLB, Columbia U., 1964. Bar: Mass. 1965, U.S. Supreme Ct. 1970, D.C. 1980. Assoc. Snow Motley & Holt, successor Gaston Snow & Ely Bartlett, Boston, 1965-67; asst. atty. gen. Commonwealth of Mass., Boston, 1967-69; atty. advisor for African affairs U.S. Dept. State, Washington, 1979-72, asst. legal adviser for East Asian and Pacific affairs, 1972-80, dep. legal adviser, 1980-89; dep. asst. sec. state Bur. Politico-Mil. Affairs Bur. Politico-Mil. Affairs, Washington, 1989-92, sr. coord., 1992-95; dir. for global and multilateral affairs Nat. Security Coun., Washington, 1995-98; dep. dir. Critical Infrastructure Assurance Office, Washington, 2000—01; spl. rep. Bur. Narcotics and Law Enforcement, Washington, 2000—02, 2005—; acting dep. asst. sec. Bur. Internat. Narcotics and Law Enforcement, Dept. State, Washington, 2001—02, sr. advisor, 2002—05, acting dep., asst. sec., 2005—07, dep., asst. sec., 2007—. Recipient presdl. rank of meritorious exec., 1985, 90, 2003, presdl. rank disting. exec., 1988. Mem. Am. Soc. Internat. Law, Coun. on Fgn. Rels. Home: 3012 Dumbarton Ave NW Washington DC 20007-3305 Office: Bur Internat Narcotics & Law Enforcement State Dept Washington DC 20520-0001 Home Phone: 202-337-6079; Office Phone: 202-647-9822.

VERWAAYEN, BEN J.M., communications company executive; M in Law and Internat. Politics, State U. of Utrecht. Mgr. pub. rels. to various mgmt. positions ITT Nederland, 1975-83, exec. v.p., dir. opers., 1983-88; pres. PTT Telecom BV (Royal PTT Nederland NV), 1988-97; exec. v.p., COO Lucent Technologies, Inc., Murray Hill, NJ, 1997-99, vice-chmn., 1999—2001; CEO & bd. dir. BT Group, London, 2002—. Bd. dirs. UPS. Office: BT Group BT Centre 81 Newgate St London EC1A 7AJ England

VESCIO, ROBERT ALLEN, oncologist, educator; b. Inglewood, Calif., Aug. 16, 1960; Bachelor's Degree, Pomona Coll., Claremont, Calif.; MD, U. Calif. Med. Sch., San Diego, 1986. Diplomate Am. Bd. Internal Medicine, Hematology, Med. Oncology. Intern, internal medicine U. Calif., San Diego, 1986—87, resident, internal medicine, 1987—89; fellow, hematologic oncology UCLA, 1990—93; asst. provider divsn. hematology/oncology Dept. Veteran Affairs, West Los Angeles, Calif., 1993—2001; attending physician, Outpatient Cancer Ctr., Samuel Oschin Comprehensive Cancer Inst. Cedars-Sinai Med. Ctr., LA, 2001—. Asst. prof. divsn. hematology/oncology UCLA David Geffen Sch. Medicine, assoc. prof. medicine; dir., myeloma program, Cedars-Sinai Med. Ctr. Contbr. sevearl articles to peer-reviewed jours., chapters to books; reviewer Blood, Leukemia, Leukemia/Lymphoma, Transfusion and the Am. Jour. Hematology. Named one of Top Specialists in multiple myeloma and amyloidosis, America's Top Doctors for Cancer. Office: Cedars-Sinai Med Ctr 8700 Beverly Blvd #AC-1049 Los Angeles CA 90048 Office Phone: 310-423-1825. Office Fax: 310-423-1977. *

VESELL, ELLIOT SAUL, pharmacologist, educator; b. NYC, Dec. 24, 1933; s. Harry and Evelyn (Jaffe) Vesell; m. Kristen Paige Peery, Mar. 24, 1968; children: Liane Clark, Hilary Peery. AB magna cum laude, Harvard U., 1955, MD magna cum laude, 1959; DSc (hon.), Phila. Coll. Pharmacy & Sci., 1988; PhD (hon.), Philipps U., Marburg, Germany, 1991. Intern, children's med. svc. Mass. Gen. Hosp., Boston, 1959-60; rsch. assoc. Rockefeller U., NYC, 1960-62; asst. resident medicine Peter Bent Brigham Hosp., Boston, 1962-63; clin. assoc. Nat. Inst. Arthritis Metabolic Diseases, NIH, Bethesda, Md., 1963-65; head sect. pharmacogenetics Nat. Heart Inst., NIH, Bethesda, 1965-68; Evan Pugh prof. pharmacology Pa. State U., Hershey, 1968—, asst. dean grad. edn., 1973-96, chmn. dept. pharmacology Coll. Medicine, 1968—2000, Bernard B. Brodie prof., 1991—. Pfizer vis. prof.; Burroughs Wellcome vis. prof. Editor: The Life and Works of Thomas Cole, 1964, Progress in Basic and Clin. Pharmacology, 1990, others; contbr. articles to profl. jours. Recipient Von Humboldt award, 1988. Fellow: AAAS, Royal Soc. Medicine (Frohlich vis. prof. 1985); mem.: Am. Soc. Clin. Pharmacology Therapeutics (Oscar B. Hunter Meml. award 1991), Am. Coll. Clin. Pharmacology (pres. 1980—82, Disting. Investigator award 1999), Am. Soc. Pharmacology Exptl. Therapeutics (sec.-treas. 1995—98, Exptl. Therapeutics award 1971, Harry Gold award clin. pharmacology 1985), Am. Soc. Clin. Investigation, Assn. Am. Physicians, Phi Beta Kappa, Alpha Omega Alpha. Office: Pa State U Coll Medicine Dept Pharmacology PO Box 850 Hershey PA 17033-0850 Office Phone: 717-531-8245. Business E-Mail: esv1@psu.edu.

VESELY, JEFFREY M., lawyer; b. Glendale, Calif., Feb. 23, 1950; BA, Univ. Calif., Santa Barbara, 1972; JD, San Fernando Valley Univ., 1975; MBA, Golden Gate Univ., 1982. Bar: Calif. 1975, US Supreme Ct. 1980. Ptnr., chmn. Tax practice Pillsbury Winthrop Shaw Pittman, San Francisco. Co-author: Distinctions Between Unitary & Nonunitary Businesses: A Practical Guide, 2001; contbr. articles to profl. jours., chapters to books. Office: Pillsbury Winthrop Shaw Pittman 50 Fremont St San Francisco CA 94105 Office Phone: 415-983-1075. Office Fax: 415-983-1200. Business E-Mail: jeffrey.vesely@pillsburylaw.com.

VESPA, NED ANGELO, photographer; b. Streator, Ill., May 31, 1942; s. Ned James and Evelyn Blanche (Flanigan) V.; m. Carol DeMasters, Sept. 11, 1976; 1 child, Nicole Marie; 1 son by previous marriage, James Paul. BS, So. Ill. U., 1965. Photographer Milw. Jour. Co., 1965-95, Milw. Sentinel, 1965-95; ret., 1995. Freelance, 1995—. Mem. Nat. Press Photographers Assn., Wis. News Photographers Assn. (past pres.), Milw. Press Photographers.

VESPOLI, LEILA L., lawyer, energy executive; b. Akron, Ohio, 1959; BS, Miami U., Ohio, 1981; JD, Case Western Res. U., 1984. Bar: Ohio 1984. Atty. to sr. atty. Ohio Edison, Akron, 1985—97; assoc. gen. counsel FirstEnergy Corp., Akron, 1997—2000, v.p., gen. counsel, 2000—01, sr. v.p, gen. counsel, 2001—. Bd. trustees The NEOUCOM Found. Named a Women of Profl. Excellence, YWCA. Mem.: Greater Cleve. Gen. Counsel Assn., Ohio C. of C., Energy Assn. Pa. (bd. dirs.), NJ Utilities Assn. (bd. dirs.). Office: FirstEnergy Corp 76 S Main St Akron OH 44308-1890

VESSEY, JOHN WILLIAM, JR., military officer; b. Mpls., June 29, 1922; s. John William and Emily (Roche) V.; m. Avis Claire Funk, July 18, 1945; children: John William, David, Sarah. BS, U. Md., 1963; MS, George Washington U., 1967; LLD, Concordia Coll., St. Paul, 1978, U. Md., 1983, Concordia Sem., St. Louis, 1983; DMS (hon.), Norwich U., Northfield, Vt., 1985; grad., Command and Gen. Staff Coll., 1958, Indsl. Coll. Armed Forces, 1966. Commd. 2nd lt. U.S. Army, 1944, advanced through grades to gen., 1976; comdr. U.S. Army Support Command Thailand, 1970-71; chief Mil. Assistance Adv. Group Laos, 1972-73; dir. ops. Dept. Army Washington, 1973-74; comdr. 4th Inf. Div. Ft. Carson, Colo., 1974-75; dep. chief of staff-ops. Dept. Army Washington, 1975-76; comdr.-in-chief UN Command/U.S. Forces in Korea Seoul, 1976-79; comdr.-in-chief Republic of Korea/U.S. Combined Forces Command, 1978-79; vice chief of staff U.S. Army Washington, 1979-82; chmn. Joint Chiefs of Staff, 1982-85; ret. U.S. Army, 1985; presdl. emissary to Hanoi for POW/MIA matters, 1987-93. Bd. dirs. Nat. Flag Day Com.; mem. bd. vistors UMUC; chmn. bd. Ctr. Preventive Action, Def. Sci. Bd. Decorated D.S.C., Def. D.S.M., D.S.M., AF D.S.M., Navy D.S.M., Legion of Merit, Bronze Star, Air medal, Joint Svcs. Commendation medal, Army Commendation medal, Purple Heart (U.S.), Presdl. Medal of Freedom, decorated by govts. of Austria, Belgium, Chile, Colombia, Germany, France, Greece, Honduras, Korea, Luxembourg, Norway, Pakistan, Saudi Arabia, Spain, Thailand, Uruguay; recipient State of Minn. Disting. Svc. medal, Excellence in Diplomacy award Am. Acad. of Diplomacy, Sylvanus Thayer award USMA, Alumni Achievement award and Disting. Pub. Svc. award George Washington U., Disting. Alumnus award U. Md., Golden Plate award Am. Acad. Achievement, Adm. John M. Will award N.Y. Coun. Navy League, hon. award Nat. League Families. Mem. VFW (Eisenhower medal), Assn. U.S. Army (George Marshall medal), Army Aviation Assn., U.S. Armor Assn., Coun. Fgn. Rels. (chair bd. dirs. ctr. for prevention action), Phi Kappa Phi. Lutheran.

VESSOT, ROBERT FREDERICK CHARLES, physicist, researcher; b. Montreal, Que., Can., Apr. 16, 1930; s. Robert Charles Ulysses and Marguerite Yvonne (Giauque) V.; m. Norma Newman Wight, Apr. 18, 1959; children: Judith Norma, Margaret Anne, Nancy Elizabeth. BA, McGill U., 1951, MSc, 1954, PhD, 1956. Mem. research staff MIT, 1956-60; mgr. Maser Research and Devel., Varian Assos., Hewlett Packard, Beverly, Mass., 1960-69; sr. physicist Harvard-Smithsonian Center for Astrophysics, Cambridge, Mass., 1969-2001, rsch. assoc., 2002—. Contbr. articles to profl. jours.; patentee in field. Served with RCAF, 1951-53. Recipient medal for outstanding sci. achievement NASA, 1978, I.I. Rabi award IEEE, 1993. Fellow Am. Phys. Soc.; mem. Eastern Yacht Club. Office: 60 Garden St Cambridge MA 02138-1516

VEST, CHARLES MARSTILLER, engineering educator, former academic administrator; b. Morgantown, W.Va., Sept. 9, 1941; s. Marvin Lewis and Winifred Louise (Buzzard) V.; m. Rebecca Ann McCue, June 8, 1963; children: Ann Kemper, John Andrew. BS in Mech. Engring., W.Va. U., 1963; MS in Mech. Engring., U. Mich., 1964, PhD, 1967; degree (hon.), Mich. Tech. U., 1992, W.Va. U., 1994, Ill. Inst. Tech., 1998, U. Notre Dame, 1998, Musashi Inst. Tech., 1999, NC State U., 2002, Colo. Sch. Mines, 2005, Harvard U., 2005, Ohio U., 2006; LLD (hon.), Cambridge U., Eng., 2006. Asst. prof., then assoc. prof. U. Mich., Ann Arbor, 1968—77, prof. mech. engring., 1977—90, assoc. dean acad. affairs Coll. Engring., 1981—86, dean Coll. Engring., 1986—89, provost, v.p. acad. affairs, 1989—90; pres. MIT, Cambridge, 1990—2004, pres. emeritus, prof. mech. engring., 2004—. Bd. dirs. E.I. du Pont de Nemours and Co., IBM, Math. for Am., Ithaka Harbors, Inc., Blanchette Rockefeller Neuroscis. Inst., Kavli Found., In-Q-Tel; vis. assoc. prof. Stanford (Calif.) U., 1974-75; mem. Commn. on the Intelligence Capabilities of the U.S. Regarding Weapons of Mass Destruction, 2004-05; mem. Ctr. for Strategic and Internat. Studies Commn. on Sci. Comm. and Nat. Security; mem. Mass. Gov.s Coun. on Econ. Growth and Techn. 1990-99; chmn. Presdl. Adv. Com on Redesign of Space Stat., 1993-94; chmn. U.S. Dept. Energy Task Force on Future of Sci. Programs, 1992-93; vice-chmn. Coun. on Competitiveness, 1996-04; mem. Commn. Future Higher Edn., 2005-, President's Com. Advisors on Sci. and Tech., Iraq Intelligence Commn., 2004; mem. adv. com. On Transformational Diplomacy for the U.S. Sect. State; mem. adv. bd. subcommittee Rice-Chertoff Secure Borders and Open Doors, U.S. Dept. Homeland Security.; life mem. MIT Corp., bd. trustee. Author: Holographic Interferometry, 1979, Pursuing the Endless Frontier: Essays on MIT and the Role of Research Universities, 2005; assoc. editor Jour. Optical Soc. Am., 1982-83; contbr. articles to profl. jours. Trustee Woods Hole Oceanographic Inst., 1991-2004, New England Aquarium; Univ. Corp. for Advanced Internet Devel., 2002-04; WGBH Ednl. Found., 2002-04; adv. trustee TIAX adv. bd., Environ. Rsch. Inst. Mich. Named 2006 Nat. Medal Tech. Laureate; recipient Excellence in Rsch. award, U. Mich., 1980, Disting. Svc. award, 1972, Disting. Visitor award, U. La Plata, Argentina, 1979, Centennial medal, Am. Soc. Engring. Edn., 1993, Nat. Leadership award, Phi Kappa Psi, 1999, Arthur M. Bueche award, Nat. Acad. Engring., 2000, Pres.' award Accrediation Bd. for Engring. and Tech., 2002, U. Mich. Engring. Alumni award, 2004. Fellow: ASME, Optical Soc. Am., Am. Acad. Arts and Scis., AAAS (2006 Philip Hauge Abelson prize 2007); mem.: Assn. Am. Univs. (past chmn.), NAE (councillor 2005—, pres.-elect 2007, mem. governing bd., pres. 2007—, Arthur M. Bueche Award 2000), Pi Tau Sigma, Tau Beta Pi, Sigma Xi. Presbyterian. *

VEST, GAYLE SOUTHWORTH, obstetrician, gynecologist; b. Duluth, Minn., Apr. 7, 1948; d. Russell Eugene and Brandon (Young) Southworth; m. Steven Lee Vest, Nov. 27, 1971; 1 child, Matthew Steven. BS, U. Mich., 1970. Diplomate Am. Bd. Ob-Gyn. Intern in ob-gyn. Milw. County Gen. Hosp., 1974-75, So. Ill. U. Sch. Medicine, 1975-78; pvt. practice Chapel Hill (N.C.) Ob-Gyn., 1978-80; asst. attending physician dept. ob-gyn. U. N.C. Sch. Medicine, Chapel Hill, 1978-80; clin. assoc. dept. ob-gyn. Duke U. Med. Ctr., Durham, NC, 1978-80; pvt. practice Big Stone Gap (Va.) Clinic, 1980-88, Norwise Ob-Gyn. Assocs., Norton, Va., 1988—. Fellow: ACOG; mem.: Wise County Med. Soc., Med. Soc. Va., Va. Ob-Gyn. Soc., Christian Med. and Dental Assn. Avocations: skiing, kayaking, travel.

VEST, GEORGE SOUTHALL, retired diplomat; b. Columbia, Va., Dec. 25, 1918; s. George Southall and Nancy Margaret (Robertson) V.; m. Emily Barber Clemons, June 21, 1947; children: Jeannie, George, Henry BA, U. Va., 1941, MA, 1947. Fgn. service duty SHAPE and NATO, Quito, Ottawa, Paris; dir. bur. polit. mil. affairs Dept. State, asst. sec. of state for European affairs Washington, 1977-81; ambassador to European Communities Brussels, 1981-85; dir. gen. Fgn. Svc. Dept. State, Washington, 1985-89, career amb., 1987-89, ret., 1989. Served to capt. U.S. Army, 1941-46, ETO Mem. Phi Beta Kappa Episcopalian. Avocations: bicycling, gardening. Home: 5307 Iroquois Rd Bethesda MD 20816-3104

VEST, HYRUM GRANT, JR., retired horticultural sciences educator; b. Salt Lake City, Sept. 23, 1935; s. Hyrum and Josephine Gwendolyn (Lund) V.; m. Gayle Pixton, Sept. 18, 1958; children: Kelly, Lani, Kari, Kamille, Kyle. BS, Utah State U., 1960, MS, 1964; PhD, U. Minn., 1967. Pathologist, agronomist U.S. Dept. Agr., Beltsville, Md., 1967-70; vegetable breeder Mich. State U., East Lansing, 1970-76; dept. head dept. hort. and landscape architecture Okla. State U., Stillwater, 1976-83; head dept. hort. scis. Tex A & M U., College Station, 1983-89; head dept. plants, soils and biometeorology Utah State U., Logan, 1989-95, assoc. dir. Utah Agrl. Experiment Sta., 1995-2000; mem. Nat. Plant Genetics Resource Bd., Washington, 1982-88; ret., 2000. Served to 1st lt. U.S. Army, 1960-63. Univ. research fellow Utah State U., 1963-64 Fellow Am. Soc. Hort. Sci. Republican. Mem. Lds Ch. Home: 368 Spring Creek Rd Providence UT 84332-9432 E-mail: gvest@cc.usu.edu.

VEST, STEVEN LEE, gastroenterologist, hepatologist, internist; b. Mpls., July 30, 1948; s. Lee Herbert and Marian Mize (Rains) V.; m. Gayle Maureen Southworth, Nov. 27, 1971; 1 child, Matthew Steven. BA, U. Minn., 1970, MD, 1974. Diplomate Am. Bd. Internal Medicine, Am. Bd Gastroenterology. Intern internal medicine Milw. County Hosp., 1974—75; resident internal medicine So. Ill. U., Springfield, 1975—77; fellow gastroenterology and hepatology Duke U. Med. Ctr., Durham, NC, 1978—80; cons. gastroenterology-hepatology and internal medicine Lonesome Pine Hosp., Big Stone Gap, Va., 1980—; cons. gastroenterology and internal medicine St. Mary's Hosp., Norton, Va., 1983—, Norton Cmty. Hosp., Norton, 1985—. Chmn. med. care evaluation, Lonesome Pine Hosp., Big Stone Gap, 1984-88, chmn. pharmacy, therapeutics and transfusion com., 1992-94; chief of medicine Norton Cmty. Hosp., 1991-93, 97-99, exec. com., bd. dirs., 1993-2002, 05—, mem. credentials com., 1995-97, bylaws com., 1996-97 Fellow ACP-Am. Soc. Internal Medicine, Am. Coll. Gastroenterology; mem. Am. Gastroent. Assn., Am. Soc. Internal Medicine, Va. Med. Soc. (state del. 1992), Wise County Med. Soc. (treas. 1984-86, v.p. 1991-92, pres. 1992-93), Am. Assn. Christian Counselors, Wise County C. of C. Methodist. Avocations: kayaking, jogging, skiing, photography, Karate. Home: Powell Valley 1800 Egan Rd Big Stone Gap VA 24219-4224 Office: NCH Med Arts Bldg 2 98 15th St NW Ste 202 Norton VA 24273-1600 Office Phone: 276-679-0244.

VESTAL, ALLAN W., dean, law educator; BA, Yale U., 1976, JD, 1979. Prof. partnership and corp. law, comml. law, and real estate Washington and Lee U. Sch. Law, 1989—2000; dean U. Ky. Coll. Law, Lexington, 2000—. Practiced law for ten yrs., Wis., Iowa. Publ. (treatise with Prof. Hillman and Dean Weidner) The Revised Uniform Partnership Act; contbr. chapters to books, articles to law revs. Mem.: Am. Law Inst. Office: University of Kentucky College of Law Room 209 620 S Limestone Lexington KY 40506-0048 Office Phone: 859-257-1678. E-mail: vestal@email.uky.edu. *

VETTEL, ERIC J., library director; m. Jennifer Wythes Vettel. BA in History, Stanford U.; MA in History, Standord U.; PhD in History, U. Va. Bancroft Postdoctoral Fellow in US History U. Calif., Berkeley; exec. dir. Woodrow Wilson Presdl. Libr., Staunton, Va., 2005—. Invited spkr. in field. Author: Biotech: The Countercultural Origins of an Industry, 2006. Office: Woodrow Wilson Presdl Libr 18-24 N Coalter St PO Box 24 Staunton VA 24402-0024 Office Phone: 540-885-0897. Office Fax: 540-886-9874. Business E-Mail: evettel@woodrowwilson.org. *

VETTER, DAVID R., lawyer; b. Balt., Apr. 3, 1959; BA in English and Econs., Bucknell U., 1981; JD, U. Fla., 1984. Bar: Fla. 1984, US Dist. Ct. (mid. dist. Fla.) 1985. Atty. Robbins, Gaynor and Bronstein, Tampa, Fla., 1984—93, ptnr., 1991—93; v.p., gen. counsel Tech Data Corp., Clearwater, Fla., 1993—2000, corp. v.p., gen. counsel, 2000—03, sr. v.p., gen. counsel, sec., 2003—. Mem.: ABA, Assn. Corp. Counsel, Fla. Bar Assn. Office: Tech Data Corp 5350 Tech Data Dr Clearwater FL 33760-3122

VETTER, JAMES GEORGE, JR., lawyer; b. Omaha, Apr. 8, 1934; s. James George and Helen Louise (Adams) V.; m. Mary Ellen Froelich, June 25, 1960; 1 child, James G. III. BS, Georgetown U., 1954; JD, Creighton U., 1960. Bar: Nebr. 1960, Tex. 1967. Counsel IRS, Washington, 1960-64, Dallas, 1964-67; atty. Dallas, 1967—; sr. ptnr. Vetter, Bates, Tibbals, Lee & DeBusk, P.C., 1979-89; mem. Godwin Gruber, LLC, 1989—, mng. dir., 1994-98; of counsel Godwin, Pappas, Langley & Ronquillo, LLP, Dallas. Lectr. taxation seminars; gen. counsel, bd. dirs. Pilgrim's Pride Corp.; bd. dirs. AFV Energy, Inc., VLSIP Techs., Inc. Contbr. articles to profl. jours. Asst. sgt.-at-arms Tex. Dem. Conv., 1968; adv. selection com. Georgetown U., 1970-85; scoutmaster Boy Scouts Am., 1974-75; trustee St. Monica Sch. Endowment Trust, 1999—. With USAF, 1954-57; capt. USAFR, ret. Fellow Tex. Bar Found.; mem. Nebr. Bar Assn., State Bar Tex. (cert. tax law 1983—), Coll. State Bar Tex., Dallas Bar Assn. (chmn. fee disputes com. 1985, chmn. publs. com. 1988, chmn. pictoral directory com. 1993), Real Estate Fin. Execs. Assn. (pres. 1982-83), Cash Alliance (pres. 1987-88), Creighton U. Alumni Assn. (pres. Dallas-Ft. Worth 1969-70), Ctrl. Dallas Assn. (bd. dirs. 1994-95), Park Cities Club, Delta Theta Phi. Roman Catholic. Office: Godwin & Gruber PC 1201 Elm St Ste 1700 Dallas TX 75270 Office Phone: 214-939-4817. E-mail: jvetter@godwingruber.com. *

VETTER, LAWRENCE ANTHONY, art educator, consultant; s. Anthony Lawrence and Lilly Vetter; m. Andrea Kay Oppelt, Jan. 12, 1968; 1 child, Rachel Tomeo. BA, Calif. State U., Fullerton, 1968, MA, 1970; postgrad., U.S. Internat. U., 1972, U. Calif., Irvine, 1974—75. Cert. coll. tchr. Calif., 1970, secondary tchr. Calif., 1975. Instr. and counselor Calif. State U., Fullerton, 1970—73, adj. lectr., 2000—; art educator Hacienda-LaPuente Unified Sch. Dist., City of Industry, 1973—; adj. lectr. Calif. Poly. U., Pomona, 2000—01. Ceramic chemistry cons. Laguna Clay Co., City of Industry, Calif., 1989—; ceramicist stoneware and porcelain vessels; adj. lectr. Calif. State U., Fullerton, 2000—; lead tchr. Performing Arts Acad., 2006—, advanced placement coord., 1995—2000, 2007—; spkr. in field. Vol. Calif. State Parks Sys., Dana Point, 1996—. Named Nat. Outstanding Pub. Secondary Educator in the Ceramic Arts, Studio Potter Mag. N.H., 1990—91; recipient Outstanding Secondary Educator, LA County Supervisors, 1999—2000, Outstanding Advanced Placement Tchr., City of La Puente, 1996, Outstanding Secondary Tchr., U. Calif. San Diego, 2000—01, 2001—02; grantee Instrn. of Advanced Placement Art History, Hacienda-LaPuente Unified Sch. Dist., 1997, Coll. Bd./ Mellon Found., 1998. Master: Dave Hebler's Original Am. Kenpo Karate Assn. (life seventh degree black belt); mem.: NEA, Hacienda-LaPuente Unified Tchrs. Assn., Calif. Tchrs. Assn. Achievements include research in 35 stoneware glazes and 21 Raku glazes developed for international sales for Laguna Clay Company. Avocations: art, martial arts, volleyball. Home: 33472 Intera Way Dana Point CA 92629 Office: LaPuente HS 15615 East Nelson Ave La Puente CA 91744 Office Phone: 626-934-6745. Business E-Mail: lvetter@hlpusd.k12.ca.us.

VETTORI, PAUL MARION, lawyer; b. Washington, Sept. 6, 1944; s. Mariano L. and Bessie (Southard) V.; m. Judith Ann Gersack, June 19, 1965; children: Joseph, Damon, Jason, Justin. BA, U. Md., Coll. Park, 1967; JD, U. Md., Balt., 1970. Bar: Md. 1970, U.S. Dist. Ct. Md. 1970, U.S. Ct. Appeals (4th cir.) 1970. Assoc. Frank, Bernstein, Conaway & Goldman, Balt., 1971-74; asst. atty. gen. Md. Atty. Gen.'s Office, Balt., 1974-75; ptnr. Shapiro, Vettori & Olander, Balt., 1975-81, Frank, Bernstein, Conaway & Goldman, Balt., 1981-91, Kenny, Vettori & Robinson, P.A., Balt., 1992-97, White, Miller, Kenny & Vettori, LLP, Towson, Md., 1997—2000, Kenny & Vettori, LLP, Towson, 2000—. Fellow Am. Coll. Trial Lawyers, Am. Bd. Trial Lawyers; mem. ABA, Md. State Bar Assn., Balt. County Bar Assn., Howard County Bar Assn., Rotary (pres.). Avocation: sports. Office: 502 Washington Ave 720 Towson MD 21204-4505 E-mail: vettori@wmkv.com.

VEURINK, GARY R., chemicals executive; m. Ruth Veurink; 3 children. BSChemE, SD Sch. Mines and Tech.; graduate student in Chem. Engring., U. Mich.; grad. Advanced Mgmt. Prog., INSEAD, Fontainebleau, France; D (hon.), SD Sch. Mines and Tech., 2002. Rschr. Electro Mech. Rsch. Lab. Mich. divsn. Dow Chem. Co., 1972, global mfg. dir. engring. plastics, 1995, v.p. global purchasing, 1998, site dir. Mich. ops., bus. ops. dir. performance chems., 2000, bus. ops. leader, v.p. mfg. and engring. Chems. and Intermediates Portfolio, 2004, corp. v.p. mfg. and engring., 2004—, mem. Office of the Chief Exec., 2004—. Bd. dirs. Dow Corning Corpn., Dorinco Reinsurance Co., NAM. Pres., mem. exec. coun. Lake Huron Area Coun. Boy Scouts Am.; bd. trustees Mich. chpt. Nature Conservancy. Mem.: AIChE. Office: Dow Chem Co 2030 Dow Ctr Midland MI 48674 *

VEVERKA, DONALD VICTOR, science educator; b. Cleve., Ohio, Sept. 2, 1956; s. Donald Clayton and Christine Joann Veverka; m. Joni Dee Ratliff, Sept. 19, 2004; 1 child, Mitchell C. BS, Ohio State U., 1978, MS, 1979; PhD, Colo. State U., 2001. Cons. self employed, Cleve., 1979—84; asst. prof. US Air Force Acad., Colo. Springs, Colo., 1994—. Rhodes scholarship selection bd. panel mem. US Air Force Acad., Colo. Springs, Colo., 2003. Contbr. articles various profl. jours. Vol. Wilson United Meth. Ch., Colo. Springs, Colo., 2000—03, Veteran's Standdown, Colo. Springs, 2003. Maj. USAF, 1984—2005. Mem.: Am. Soc. for Nutritional Scis., Soc. for Nutrition Edn., Phi Kappa Phi Nat. Honor Soc. Republican. Protestant. Achievements include patents for health promotion program "Lets Get Moving", 2001. Avocations: golf, fishing, trap and skeet. Office: USAF Acad Dept Biology 2355 Faculty Dr U S A F Academy CO 80840 Office Phone: 719-333-9670. Office Fax: 719-333-2420. E-mail: don.veverka@usafa.af.mil.

VEYERA, JEFFREY ALAN, bank executive; b. Providence, Jan. 12, 1971; s. George Webster and Barbara Joan Veyera; m. Anita Veyera. BS in History, US Air Force Acad., Colorado Springs, Colo., 1993. Commd. 2d lt. USAF, 1989; ret., 1998; strategic sourcing GE Med. Sys., Milw., 1998—2001; with Rhythming Connections, Denver, 2001; supplier mgr. Black & Decker, Lake Forest, Calif., 2001—03; v.p. quality productivity Bank of Am., Charloft, NC, 2003—. Mem.: Am. Soc. Quality (cert.). Republican. Roman Catholic. Avocations: photography, writing, music. Home: 717 Meadow Lake Dr Matthews NC 28105

VEYLANSWAMI, SATGURU BODHINATHA, head of religious order; b. Berkeley, Calif., Oct. 15, 1942; Spiritual studies, Self Realization Fellowship, Vedanta Soc.; studies with Gurudeva. Mgr. Gurudeva's Master Course Corr. Study; v.p. Gurudeva's several nonprofit corps., 1970—; tchr., counsellor younger monks NH; pujari Murugan Temple; sr. adminstrv. positions, tchr. Innersearch Travel-Study progs.; lectr. tours Mauritius, Malaysia, Singapore; lectr. Innersearch Travel Study Progs., UN Millenium Summit Religious and Spiritual Leaders, Alaska, Caribbean and Northern Europe, 1999—2001; sr. monk Kadavul Hindu Temple; World Hindu Leader Hinduism, 2001—. Devel., arch. Hindu Heritage Endowment, 1993—; creator Kauai Aloha Endowment. Named to 1st Acharya, Gurudeva's Order. Office: Kauai Aadheenam Ashram 107 Kaholalele Rd Kapaa HI 96746-9304

VEZEAU, TIMOTHY J., lawyer; BSEE cum laude, St. Louis U., 1966; JD, Georgetown U., 1971. Bar: Ill. 1972. Patent examiner US Patent Office, 1968—70; patent advisor US Office of Navel Rsch., 1971; founding ptnr. patent practice Katten Muchin Rosenman LLP, Chgo. Mem.: ABA, Intellectual Property Law Assn. of Chgo., Ill. Bar Assn., Chgo. Bar Assn., Eta Kappa Nu, Pi Mu Epsilon. Office: Katten Muchin Rosenman LLP 525 W Monroe St Ste 1900 Chicago IL 60661-3693 Office Phone: 312-902-5516. Office Fax: 312-577-4513. Business E-Mail: timothy.vezeau@kattenlaw.com.

VEZERIDIS, MICHAEL PANAGIOTIS, surgeon, educator; b. Thessaloniki, Greece, Dec. 16, 1943; came to U.S., 1974; s. Panagiotis and Sofia (Avramidis) V.; m. Therese Mary Statz; children: Peter Statz, Alexander Michael. MD, U. Athens, 1967; MA ad eundem (hon.), Brown U., 1989. Diplomate Am. Bd. Surgery. Fellow surg. rsch. Harvard Med. Sch./Mass. Gen. Hosp., Boston, 1974-77; resident U. Mass., Worcester, 1977-80; fellow in surg. oncology Roswell Park Meml. Inst., Buffalo, 1980-81, attending surgeon, 1981-82; staff surgeon VA Med. Ctr., Providence, 1982-84; asst. prof. surgery Brown U., Providence, 1982-88; chief surg. oncology VA Med. Ctr., Providence, 1984—, assoc. chief surgery, 1986-98, chief surgery, 1998—; cons. in surgery R.I. Hosp., Providence, 1987—; surg. oncologist Roger Williams Med. Ctr., Providence, 1989—; assoc. dir. divsn. surg. oncology Brown U., Providence, 1989—98, assoc. prof. surgery, 1988-94, prof., 1994—; prof. surgery Boston U. Sch. Medicine, 1999—. Chmn. profl. edn. com. R.I. divsn. Am. Cancer Soc., Providence, 1987-89, pres.-elect 1989-91, pres. 1991-93, del. dir. to nat. bd. dirs., 1993-96, mem. Nat. Assembly of the Am. Cancer Soc., 1997-2003, mem. internat. activities adv. com., 2003-, bd. dirs. New Eng. divsn., 1997-2005, chief med. officer New Eng. divsn., 1999-2001; chmn. R.I. State Cancer Liaison Program Am. Coll. Sugeons, 1999—, mem. commn. on cancer, 2003-, bd. dirs. Rhode Island Cancer Coun., 2004-; vis. prof. U. Patras (Greece) Med. Sch., 1988; mem. sci. adv. com. Clin. Rsch. Ctr., Brown U., Providence, 1989-91. Contbr. articles to profl. jours. and chpts. in med. books. Mem. parish coun. Ch. of Annunciation, Cranston, R.I., 1985-91; v.p. Hellenic Cultural Soc. Southeastern New Eng., Providence, 1987-89. Decorated Navy Commendation medal; named Profl. Fed. Employee of Yr., R.I. Fed. Exec. Coun., 1987; recipient St. George medal Am. Cancer Soc.; Merit Rev. Cancer Rsch. grantee VA, 1983-89. Fellow ACS (treas. R.I. chpt. 1996-2000, pres.-elect 2000-2002, pres. 2002-2004); mem. Soc. Surg. Oncology, Assn. for Acad. Surgery, Am. Soc. Clin. Oncology, N.Y. Acad. Scis. (life), Soc. for Surgery Alimentary Tract, Am. Assn. for Cancer Rsch., Collegium Internat. Chirurgiae Digestivae, Assn. Mil. Surgeons U.S., Soc. for Metastasis Rsch., New Eng. Cancer Soc., New Eng. Surg. Soc., Quidnessett Country Club. Greek Orthodox. Avocations: classical music, reading, fencing, tennis, squash, cross country skiing. Home: 50 Limerock Dr East Greenwich RI 02818-1643 Office: Univ Surg Assocs Ste 470 Two Dudley St Providence RI 02905 Office Phone: 401-331-1036. Business E-Mail: michael_vezeridis@brown.edu.

VEZINA, GILBERT, pediatric neuroradiologist; b. Montreal, Can., July 14, 1960; arrived in U.S., 1984; s. Jean Lorrain and Lise Vezina; m. Lise Marie Becker, Sept. 1, 2001; children: Annalise, Sophie. MD, McGill Med. Sch., Montreal, 1983. Staff radiologist dept. radiology Mass. Gen. Hosp., Boston, 1989—90, Children's Nat. Med. Ctr., Washington, 1992—; radiologist Wash. Metro Area Tuberous Sclerosis Rsch. Clinic, Fairfax, Va., 1997—. Integration panel mem. neurofibromatosis rsch. program U.S. Army Med. Rsch. and Material Command, Washington, 1997—2003; cons. Mgmt. of Myelomemjocele Study, NIH, Bethesda, 2003—. Pres. Am. Soc. Pediat. Neuroradiology, 2001—02; vice chair radiology com. Children's Oncology Group, 2001—. Scholar, McGill Univ. (Montreal), 1978—79. Mem.: Am. Coll. Radiology, Radiological Soc. N.Am., Am. Soc. Neuroradiology. Office: Children's Nat Med Ctr Dept Radiology 111 Mich Ave NW Washington DC 20010 Office Phone: 202-884-3651. Business E-Mail: gvezina@cnmc.org.

VEZIROGLU, TURHAN NEJAT, mechanical engineering educator, researcher; b. Istanbul, Turkey, Jan. 24, 1924; came to U.S., 1962; s. Abdul Kadir and Ferruh (Bürün) V.; m. Bengi Isikli, Mar. 17, 1961; children: Emre Alp, Oya Sureyya. A.C.G.I., City and Guilds Coll., London, 1946; B.Sc. with honors, U. London, 1947; D.I.C., Imperial Coll., London, 1948; PhD, U. London, 1951. Engring. apprentice Alfred Herbert Ltd., Coventry, U.K., 1945; project engr. Office of Soil Products, Ankara, Turkey, 1953-56; tech. dir. M.K.V. Constrn. Co, Istanbul, 1957-61; assoc. prof. mech. engring. U. Miami, Coral Gables, Fla., 1962-65, prof. Coral Fables, Fla., 1966—, dir. grad. studies mech. engring. Coral Gables, Fla., 1965-71, chmn. dept. mech. engring., 1971-75, assoc. dean research Coll. Engring., 1975-79, dir. Clean Energy Research Inst., 1974—. UNESCO cons., Paris; vis. prof. Middle East Tech. U., Ankara, 1969 Editor-in-chief: Internat. Jour. Hydrogen Energy, 1976—. Pres. Learning Disabilities Found., Miami, 1972-73, advisor, 1974-80. Recipient Turkish Presdl. sci. award Turkish Sci. and Tech. Research Found., 1975; named hon. prof. Xian Jiaotong U., China, 1982 Fellow AAAS, ASME, Instn. Mech. Engrs.; mem. Internat. Assn. Hydrogen Energy (pres. 1975), AIAA, Assn. Energy Engrs., Am. Nuclear Soc., Am. Soc. Engring. Edn., AAUP, Internat. Soc. Solar Energy, Systems Engring. Soc., Sigma Xi Office: U Miami Clean Energy Rsch Inst PO Box 248294 Miami FL 33124-8294 Home: 5783 SW 40th St # 303 Miami FL 33155 Home Phone: 305-661-1709; Office Phone: 305-284-4666. Business E-Mail: veziroglu@miami.edu. *Hydrogen energy system will provide the world with clean and abundant energy, while doing away with pollution, acid rains and the greenhouse effect. It is a noble and worthwhile goal to strive for.*

VIANDS, DONALD REX, plant breeder, educator; b. Riverdale, Md., Apr. 1, 1952; s. Walter Leroy and Lydia (Zeh) V.; m. Janice Ann Ruppelt, Aug. 7, 1976; children: Jamie Christopher, April Suzanne. BS in Agronomy, U. Md., 1974; MS in Plant Breeding, U. Minn., 1977, PhD in Plant Breeding, 1979. Undergrad. rsch. asst. U. Md., College Park, 1969-74; grad. rsch. asst. U. Minn., St. Paul, 1974-79; asst. prof. Cornell U., Ithaca, NY, 1979-85, assoc. prof., 1985-92, prof., 1992—, assoc. dir. acad. programs, 1995—2002, assoc. dean, dir. acad. programs, 2003—. Mem. adv. com. biotech. sci. adv. com. EPA, Washington, 1987-95; mem. steering com. N.Y. State North Country Devel. Program, 1990-99; adv. N.Y. State Forage and Grassland Coun., 1984-90, Alfalfa Crop Adv. Com., 1984-92. Contbr. articles to profl. jours., chpts. to books. Sunday sch. tchr. People's Bapt. Ch., Newfield, N.Y., 1988-2000, deacon, 1988-90, 93-98, Awana comdr., 1993-2000. Named Most Influential Faculty Mem. for Merrill Presdl. Scholar, Cornell U., 1991. Mem. Am. Soc. Agronomy (N.E. regional coord. mem. com. 1998-99), Crop Sci. Soc. Am., Am. Seed Trade Assn. (mem. minimum distance com. 1988-94), N.Am. Alfalfa Improvement Conf. (sec. 1984-86, v.p. 1986-88, pres. 1988-90), Ea. Forage Improvement Conf., Am. Forage and Grassland Coun. Republican. Achievements include development of 12 alfalfa varieties and 1 birdsfoot trefoil variety. Office: Cornell Univ Office Acad Programs 151 Roberts Hall Ithaca NY 14853-5905 Home Phone: 607-257-3391; Office Phone: 607-255-3081. Business E-Mail: drv3@cornell.edu.

VIANI, JAMES LAURENCE, retired lawyer; b. Kincaid, Ill., Dec. 24, 1932; s. Frank Jerome and Alfonsina V.; m. Virginia Lee Wilson, Dec. 27, 1958; children: Theresa, Diana, Deborah. BS, Millikin U., 1954; LLB, Wash. U., St. Louis, 1957. Bar: Ill. 1957, Mo. 1957. Assoc. Blackmar, Swanson, Midgley, Jones & Eager, Kansas City, Mo., 1958-59, Stinson, Mag & Fizzell, Kansas City, 1960-62; ptnr. Stinson, Mag & Fizzel, Kansas City, 1962-87, chmn. corp. dept., 1979-87, cons. ptnr., 1988-92; ret., 1988. Br. bd. chmn. YMCA, Kansas City, 1979-81. With U.S. Army, 1957-63. Mem. ABA, Phi Kappa Phi, Order of the Coif. Republican. Avocations: hiking, reading, farming. Home: 11106 Belleview Ave Kansas City MO 64114-5115

VIATER, JOHN RONALD, investment company executive; b. Mpls., 1935; s. John Anthony and Mary Agnes (Litecky) Viater; m. Eloise Maren Johnson, Feb. 5, 1991. BA, U. Santa Ana, 1954. CEO, owner ViaCo, Lake Placid, Fla., 1956—. Pfc USMC, 1953—55, Korea. Republican. Avocations: coin collecting/numismatics, art. Home and Office: 100 Brentwood Dr N Lake Placid FL 33852

VIAULT, RAYMOND G., food company executive; b. NYC, Sept. 19, 1944; m. Lucille Viault; children: Lisa, Deborah, Russell. Bachelor's degree, Brown U.; MBA, Columbia U. Pres., CEO Kraft Jacobs Suchard, Zurich, Switzerland; CEO Jacobs Suchard A.G. (acquired by Kraft Gen. Foods), 1990-93; pres. Maxwell House Coffee Co. Kraft Gen. Foods, v.p., gen. mgr. desserts divsn.; with Gen. Mills, Mpls., 1996—2004, vice-chmn., 1996—2004, also bd. dirs.; responsible for meals divsn., baking divsn. Pillsbury U.S. Bakery and Food Svc. Former bd. dirs. Cereal Ptnrs. Worldwide; bd. dirs. Newell Rubbermaid, VF Corp., Safeway Inc., 2004—. Bd. overseers Columbia Grad. Sch. Bus., N.Y.C.; trustee Lawrenceville Sch., N.J.; bd. dirs. United Way Mpls., Minn. Internat. Ctr., Technoserve. Office: PO Box 1113 One General Mills Blvd Minneapolis MN 55440-1113

VICE, ROY LEE, history professor; b. Lynchburg, Va., Oct. 12, 1950; s. Cline Lowell and Ruth Burchell (Newman) V.; m. Sara Pearsaul, June 2005. BA in History, BS in Physics, Carson-Newman Coll., 1972; MA in History, U. Chgo., 1976, PhD in History, 1984. Lectr. Continuing Edn. program U. Chgo., 1985-86, 87-88, rare books asst. univ. librs., 1986; asst. prof. Pacific Luth. U., Tacoma, 1986-87, Clemson (S.C.) U., 1988-90, Wright State U., Dayton, Ohio, 1990-95, assoc. prof., 1995—2006. Contbr. articles to profl. jours. Vol. tutor CYCLE Cabrini-Green Projects, Chgo., 1981—86; vol. lectr. LaSalle St. Ch., Chgo., 1989—98, 2000—06. With US Army, 1972—74. Mem. Am. Hist. Assn., 16th Century Studies Conf. Democrat. Baptist. Home: 111 Brown St Dayton OH 45402 Office: Wright State Univ Dept History 3640 Colonel Glenn Hwy Dayton OH 45435-0001 Business E-Mail: roy.vice@wright.edu.

VICE, SUSAN F., medicinal chemist; b. Oshawa, Ont., Can., Apr. 19, 1956; m. Andrew S. Thompson, Nov. 27, 1987. BS in Chemistry, U. We. Ont., London, Can., 1980; PhD, U. Waterloo, Ont., 1984. Postdoc. fellow U. Calif., Irvine, 1984—86; rsch. scientist Polysar Ltd., Sarnia, Canada, 1986—88; sr. prin. scientist Schering Plough Rsch. Inst., Kenilworth, NJ, 1988—2000; freelance tech. writer, 2001—05; mng. editor John Wiley & Sons, Inc., Hoboken, 2005—. Recipient Thomas Alva Edison Patent award, Rsch. and Devel. Coun. N.J., 2004; fellow Charles S. Humphrey grad. fellow, Guelph-Waterloo Ctr. Grad. Work in Chemistry, 1983, postdoc. fellow, Natural Scis. and Engring. Rsch. Coun., 1984—86, inds. postdoc. fellow, 1986; scholar, 1981—84. Mem.: Am. Soc. Microbiology, Editl. Freelancers Assn., Chem. Inst. Can. and Soc. Chemistry, Am. Chem. Soc. Home: 1144 Sawmill Rd Mountainside NJ 07092-2213 Personal E-mail: vicesf@yahoo.com.

VICHIOLA, CHRISTOPHER MICHAEL, writer, educator; b. Bridgeport, Conn., Apr. 27, 1959; s. Michael Richard and Delores (Distaci) Vichiola; m. Tracey Vichiola, Nov. 12, 1997; children: Michael, Christopher, Anthony. AS, Western Conn. State U., 1981, BA, 1983; grad., Colonel James "Bo" Gritz's Spec. Forces Green Beret On-Field Med. Surg. Sch. Cert. nursing asst. Martial arts tchr. Am. Bujinkan Dojo, Danbury, Conn., 1993—; tchr. Ctr. for Action, Kamiah, Idaho, 1997—; sales rep., safety capt. fertilizer toxic fertilizer program, power equipment specialist Home Depot, 1998—, power equipment specialist; clk. A&P Foodmart, 1999—2003; safety capt. Hazardous Waste Fertilizer Program; power equipment specialist, customer svc. program specialist Home Depot, 2006—, coord. extended warranty program, 2007—. Educator, cons. Primerica Fin. Svcs., Danbury, 1997—; educator Christic Inst. Law Firm, Washington, 1995—. *Christopher Michael Vichiola served as a key supporter and educator of the Christic Institute Law Firm's Iran-Contra LA Penca Lawsuit. As a martial arts expert, Mr. Vichiola performed exceptional and successful displays of strength such as walking over burning hot coals. During Colonel Gritz's special Forces Training, Mr. Vichiola performed major surgery by extracting bullets from injured animals. During Navy Seal Training, he mapped out underwater locations for demolition. Mr. Vichiola received a black belt in the martial art of Ninjutsu from Masaaki Hatsumi, Japan.* Author: Above the Law - The Real Story's Files, 1995, Above the Law Part II, 1995, The Real Story of Christopher Vichiola and Colonel Gritz, 1997, The Real Story of Christopher Vichiola's and Colonel Gritz's Training, 1997. Educator Rev. Jesse L. Jackson's Rainbow Coalition, Washington, 1992—, Mayor Eugene Eriquez Dem. Party, Danbury, 1987-93. Recipient Commendation award for work with mentally-ill and developmentally disabled Gov. Michael Dukakis, 1989, Commendation for work with Christic Inst. Law Firm, Rep. Jack Brooks, 1991, Eagle award Col. James "Bo" Gritz, 1997, Spike Navy Seal Scuba badge Col. James "Bo" Gritz, 1997, Nat.Outstanding Safety award Home Depot, 2006. Avocations: camping, scuba diving, basketball, football, martial arts. Office Phone: 203-730-9600.

VICINO, THOMAS JOSEPH, political science professor; b. Washington, July 18, 1980; s. Thomas Edward and Susann Elaine Vicino. BSc cum laude, U. Miami, 2002; MPP, U. Md., Balt., 2004, PhD, 2006. Rsch. asst. U. Md., Balt., 2002—04; asst. prof. urban affairs U. Tex., Arlington, 2006—. Contbr. articles to profl. jours. Policy analyst Citizens Planning and Housing Assn., Balt., 2003—06. Recipient Excellence in Govt. and Politics award, Howard County Exec., 1998, Frazer D. White award for Excellence in Comm. Studies, U. Miami, 1998—2002; fellow, U. Md., 2002—06; George Merrick scholar, U. Miami, 1998—2002. Mem.: Am. Polit. Sci. Assn., Urban Affairs Assn. Office Phone: 817-272-3356. Business E-Mail: vicino@uta.edu.

VICK, COLUMBUS EDWIN, JR., retired civil engineering design firm executive; b. Jacksonville, Fla., Nov. 8, 1934; s. Columbus Edwin Sr. and Lucretia (Dean) V.; m. Laura Anne McGowan, Mar. 28, 1964; children: Jennifer, Carolyn, Elizabeth. BSCE, N.C. State U., 1956, MSCE, 1960. Registered profl. engr., 15 states. Rsch. asst. N.C. State Civil Engring. Dept., Raleigh, 1958-60; transp. planning engr. Harland Bartholomew & Assocs., Memphis, 1960-64, office and project mgr. Raleigh, 1964-67; prin., co-founder Kimley-Horn and Assocs. Inc., Raleigh, 1967-72, pres., 1972-92; chmn., 1992-2000. Bd. dirs. Wachovia Bank, Design Profls. Coalition Am. Cons. Engrs. Coun. Co-author: North Carolina Atlas; contbr. articles to profl. jours. Past pres., bd. dirs. NC State U. Engring. Found.; past pres. bd. assocs. Meredith Coll.; past dir. NC State U. Alumni Assn.; bd. visitors NC State U.; past 2d v.p. Bapt. State Conv. of NC; bd. dirs. Assoc. Bapt. Press, past chmn.; bd. dirs. Bibl. Recorder; trustee Kenan Inst. for Engring. Tech. and Sci., Gardner Webb U., Meredith Coll.; bd. advisors Wake Forest U. Sch. Divinity; bd. trustees Cooperative Bapt. Fellowship Found., past chmn. Named Disting. Engring. alumnus, NC State U., 1991; recipient Meritorious Svc. award, 2006. Fellow ASCE (Outstanding Young Engr. award ea. br. NC sect. 1966), Inst. Transp. Engrs. (Oustanding Individual Activity award so. sect. 1978, Disting. Svc. award so. sect. 1981, Lifetime Svc. award N.C. sect. 1995); mem. NSPE (Disting. Svc. award), Am. Con. Engrs. Coun., Am. Inst. Cert. Planners, Profl. Svcs. Mgmt. Assn. (Coll. of Fellow, Leonardo da Vinci award 2005), NC Soc. Engrs. (Outstanding Engring Achievement award 1992). Baptist. Home: 2205 Nancy Ann Dr Raleigh NC 27607-3318 Office: Kimley-Horn and Assocs Inc 3001 Weston Pky Cary NC 27513-2301 Home Phone: 919-787-8859; Office Phone: 919-677-2002. E-mail: ed.vick@kimley-horn.com.

VICK, EDWARD HOGE, JR., advertising executive; b. NYC, Feb. 27, 1944; s. Edward Hoge and Margaret Jane (Sprankle) V.; m. Nancy Jane Newcomer; Children: Joshua D., Charlie, Jane. AB, U. N.C., 1966; MS, Northwestern U., 1971. With Benton & Bowles, Inc., NYC, 1971-75, Ogilvy & Mather, Inc., NYC, 1975-83; exec. v.p., dir. account service Ammirati & Puris Inc., NYC, 1983-85, pres., chief operating officer, 1985-90; pres., CEO Levine, Huntley, Vick & Beaver, NYC, 1990-94, Young & Rubicam N.Y., 1994-96, chmn., CEO, 1997—. Author: An Examination of the Creative Process, 1971. Bd. vis. U. N.C. Decorated Bronze Star (2). Mem. Am. Assn. Advt. Agys. (bd. dirs.), Advt. Edn. Found. (bd. dirs.), St. Andrew's Soc. Republican. Presbyterian. Office: Young & Rubicam 285 Madison Ave New York NY 10017 Home: 15 E Point Ln Old Greenwich CT 06870-2403

VICK, JAMES ALBERT, publishing executive, consultant; b. Norwalk, Conn., Feb. 5, 1945; s. James Albert and Madeline (Mayew) V.; m. Deborah M. Ashley, Dec. 23, 1964 (div. Oct. 1974); children: James Ashley, Guy Robert; m. Susan Jane Collins, May 14, 1977; 1 child, Jonathan Scott. BS, Boston U., 1967. Dist. mgr. McGraw Hill Pub. Co., NYC, 1969-75, Cahners Pub. Co., NYC, 1975-79; mgr. advt. ASCE, NYC, 1979-82; v.p. mktg. Bill Comm., NYC, 1982-87; pub. Thomas Pub. Co., NYC, 1987-95; v.p. Web Property Devel. Poppe Tyson, 1995-96; exec. v.p. sales/mktg. Lawyers Weekly Publs., Boston, 1996-98; v.p. publ. Phillips Publ./KIPI, White Plains, NY, 1998-2000; pub., staff dir. IEEE Spectrum Mag., NYC, 2000—. Cons. Carvajal, Calle, Colombia, 1984, McLarens, London, 1987, 2005—06; mem. pubs. com. Am. Bus. Media, 2005—06, Bus. Publ. Audit, 2005—06. Capt. USAR, 1967-70, Vietnam. Mem.: IEEE (comms. soc., computer soc.), Soc. Nat. Assn. Publs. (bd. dirs. 2005—06), Soc. Plastics Engrs., Bus. Mktg. Assn. (cert. bus. communicator), Port Royal Golf Club, Princeton Club, Elks. Episcopalian. Avocations: golf, sailing, antique restoration. Home: 473 Judd Rd Easton CT 06612 Office: IEEE Spectrum Mag 3 Park Ave Ste 1701 New York NY 10016-5997 Office Phone: 212-419-7767. Office Fax: 212-419-7589. Personal E-mail: javick@att.net. Business E-Mail: j.vick@ieee.org.

VICK, JEFFREY HARRISON, musician, educator; b. Denver, Nov. 5, 1965; s. Donald James and Sharlene Marie (Savage) Vick; m. Jacquelyn Campeau, Nov. 20, 1999; 1 child, Teresa Irene. BS in Music, U. Ariz., 1989; MEd in Music, Mont. State U., 1991. Cert. music tchr. grades K-12 Mont., secondary tchr. grades 7-12, secondary tchr. music, Office of Pub. Instrn., State Mont. Music educator Bozeman (Mont.) Pub. Schs., 1990—91, Willow Creek (Mont.) Sch., 1991—92, Anderson Sch. Dist. #41, Bozeman, 1993—. Pvt. percussion tchr., Bozeman, 1989—; prin. timpanist and percussionist Bozeman Symphony Orch., 1989—, Intermountain Opera Assn., Bozeman, 1990—, Mont. Ballet Co., Bozeman, 1993—; prin. timpanist Mont. Summer Symphony, Helena, 1998—2002, Billings Symphony, Billings, 2007—; libr., coach Mont. chamber music workshop Mont. State U., Bozeman, 1990—, adj. instr. music, 1992—96, adv. bd. Mont. chamber music workshop, 1998—2003; dist. and state music festival adjudicator, 1994—; clinician Internat. Conf. on Percussion Music, Tucson, 1995; founding dir. PercOrchestra, Bozeman, 2000—; mem. Flutes and Friends, 2000—. Editor (newsletter): Montana Percussion News, 1998—, composer numerous compositions for band, percussion, Balinese gamelan; numerous concerto and chamber music recitals. Recipient Individual Artist Fellowship award, Mont. Arts Coun., 1992—93. Mem.: NEA, Mont. Music Educators Assn., Music Educators Nat. Conf., Percussive Arts Soc. (sec. Ariz. chpt. 1986—87, v.p. Ariz. chpt. 1987—88, sec. Mont. chpt. 1998—), Am. Fedn. Musicians (exec. bd. local 709 1996—99, pres. local 709 1999—2002), Phi Delta Kappa (profl. rsch. grant 1999). Avocations: collecting instruments and masks, photography, world music. Home: 529 South Black Ave Bozeman MT 59715-5301 Office: Anderson Sch Dist #41 10040 Cottonwood Rd Bozeman MT 59718 Office Phone: 406-587-1305 110. Business E-Mail: jvick@metnet.mt.gov, jvick@andersonmt.org.

VICK, NICHOLAS A., neurologist; b. Chgo., Oct. 3, 1939; MD, U. Chgo., 1965. Diplomate Am. Bd. Neurology. Intern U. Chgo. Hosps., 1965, resident in neurology, 1966-68; fellow in neurology NIH, Bethesda, Md., 1968-70; staff Evanston (Ill.) Hosp., 1975—; prof. neurology Northwestern U. Med. Sch., Evanston, Ill., 1978—. Mem.: Am. Bd. Psychiatry and Neurology (past exec. dir.). Office: Evanston Hosp Dept Neurology 2650 Ridge Ave Evanston IL 60201-1781 Office Phone: 847-570-2570. Business E-Mail: nvick@enh.org.

VICK, SUSAN, playwright, educator, director, actress; b. Raleigh, NC, Nov. 4, 1945; d. Thomas B. Jr. and Merle (Hayes) V. MFA, So. Meth. U., 1969; PhD, U. Ill., 1979. Prof. drama/theatre and dir. theatre WPI, 1981—; playwright Excuse Me For Living Prodns., Cambridge, Mass., 1989—; exec. dramaturg WPI New Voices in NY Samuel French Festival, 2005; playwright Festival Fringe, Edinburgh, 1989—; dir. WPI New Voices in N.Y. Dreams Abridged, Samuel French Festival, 2004. Playwright Ensemble Studio Theatre, N.Y.C., 1981-83; founder WPI Ann. New Voices Festival of Original Plays, 1982. Editor: (2 vols.) Playwrights Press, Amherst, 1988—; playwright: When I Was Your Age, 1982, Ord-Way Ames-Gay, 1982, Investments, 1985, Half Naked, 1989, Quandary, 1983, Meat Selection, 1984, Give My Love to Everyone But, 1989; appeared in plays including Rip Van Winkle, 1979, Why I Live at The P.O., 1982, The Play Group, 1984-85, Present Stage, 1985, Sister Mary Ignatius Explain It All, 1986, Wipeout, 1988, Bogus Joan, 1992-93; dir. play Give My Love to Everyone But, 1990 (Edinburgh Festival); theatre editor: Sojourner The Women's Forum, 1995-98; dramatist, script cons. Clyde Unity Theatre, Glasgow, Scotland, 1992-93, 1999-2000; dir. Dreams Abridged, WPI New Voices in NY, Samuel French Festival, Chernuchin Theatre, N.Y.C., 2004. Dir., Women's Community Theatre, Amherst, 1981-84, Upstart, Wis., 1994. Faculty fellow U. Ill., 1976-77, Bd. of Trustees Award for Outstanding Tchg., WPI, 1997. Mem. U.S. Inst. for Theatre Tech., Nat. Assn. Schs. of Theatre, New Eng. Theatre Conf., Inc., Drama League, Dramatists Guild (assoc.), Soc. Stage Dirs. and Choreographers (assoc.), U.S. Inst. Theatre Tech., New England Theatre Conf., Nat. Assn. Schs. Theatre, Alpha Phi Omega (Svc. to Students award 1996). Avocations: puppets, frogs, travel. Office: WPI 100 Instit Rd Worcester MA 01609-2280 Office Phone: 508-831-5682. Business E-Mail: svick@wpi.edu.

VICKERS, DANA TATE, school psychologist, researcher; b. Hazlehurst, Ga., Nov. 14, 1970; d. Eugene Evert and Jimmie Nell Tate; m. Gregory Lee Vickers, Apr. 15, 1995; children: Lane Gregory, Jace Everet. BS in Edn., Ga. So. U., Statesboro, 1992, MEd, 1993, Edn. Specialist, 1995; D, Nova Southeastern U., Ft. Lauderdale, Fla., 2007. Sch. psychologist Coffee County Bd. Edn., Douglas, Ga., 1994—, crisis response coord., mem. dist. student support team, 2006. Pres. women's com. Jeff Dan's Farm Bur., Hazlehurst, 1998—2004; mem. women's com. Irwin County Farm Bur., Ocilla, Ga., 2004—06; sr. citizens coord. Satilla Bapt. Ch., Wray, Ga., 2006. Mem.: Profl. Assn. Ga. Educators, Nat. Assn. Sch. Psychologists, Ga. Assn. Sch. Psychologists. Avocations: reading, travel, church activities. Home: 115 Fletcher-Tate Rd Denton GA 31532 Office: Coffee County Bd Edn 1305 S Peterson Ave Douglas GA 31533 Business E-Mail: dvickers@coffee.k12.ga.us.

VICKERS, LEE LOUISE, minister; b. Suffern, NY, Dec. 20, 1954; d. Chester E. and Dorothy Jean (Allen) Vickers; 1 child, Seth. Dipl. summa cum laude, We. Bapt. Coll., 1977; A in Forestry, Flathead Valley C.C., 1979, A, 1980; BA in Liberal Arts, Regents Coll., 1988. Sec.-clk. Glacier Ch., Kalispell, Mont., 1988—91; pastor Hephzibah Heaven Ministry, Mont., 1991—. Poem, E Duo Unum, 1993; author: Earth and Sky, 2002. Firefighter, dept. sec. Marion (Mont.) Vol. Fire Dept., 1996—98. With US Army, 1982—84. Avocations: Bee Gees fan, reading, poetry. Home: PO Box 9155 Kalispell MT 59904

VICKERS, MICHAEL G., federal agency administrator; BA, U. Ala.; MA Strategic Studies and Internat. Econ., Johns Hopkins U.; MBA, Wharton Sch., U. Pa. Spl. forces officer US Army; ops. officer CIA; dir. strategic studies Ctr. for Strategic & Budgetary Assessment, sr. v.p.; asst. sec. for spl. ops. & low intensity conflict US Dept. Def., 2007—. Office: US Dept Def 1000 Def Pentagon Rm 3C683 Washington DC 20301-1000 Office Phone: 703-695-9667. Office Fax: 202-331-8019. *

VICKERS, NANCY J., academic administrator; BA, Mt. Holyoke Coll., 1967, LHD (hon.), 1999; MA, Yale U., 1971, PhD, 1976. Prof. French and Italian Dartmouth Coll., 1973—87; prof. French, Italian, and comparative literature U. Southern Calif., 1987—97, dean curriculum and instrn. Coll. Letters, Arts and Scis., 1994—97; pres. Bryn Mawr Coll., 1997—. Vis. prof. Harvard U., U. Pa., UCLA; bd. dirs. Bryn Mawr Bank Corp.; bd. govs. Coun. Dante Soc. Am. Recipient Presdl. medal Outstanding Leadership and Achievement, Dartmouth Coll., 1991; fellow vis. fellow, Princeton U. Office: Bryn Mawr Coll 101 N Merion Ave Bryn Mawr PA 19010-2899 Office Phone: 610-526-5156.

VICKERS, ROBERT EDWIN, retired military officer, historian, writer; b. Adams Mills, Ohio, Feb. 20, 1924; m. Annell Ross Waldrop, Jan. 18, 2002; children: Shelia Ross, Janace Nmi Chapman, Billie Ann Clark, Mark Rodgers. Postgrad., Indsl. Coll. Armed Forces, Wash., 1965—67, George Washington U., 1965—67. Advanced through grade to col. USAF, 1942, officer, pilot, sr. staff, comdr., 1942—75; founding charter dir. 8AF Hist. Soc., Hallendale, 1976—84; CEO, pres. Concierge Mgmt. Inc., Albuquerque, 1985—. Dir. awards & protocol 8AF Hist. Soc., Albuquerque, 1994—, dir., mgr. mil. reunion, 1981—85; cons. air historian Pueblo Hist. Aircraft Soc., Colo. Author: The Liberators from Wending, Remembrance of the Missing. Trustee AF Hist. Found., Washington, 1985—; internat. event chmn. 50th Anniversary WWII B-24 Gala Reunion, Ft. Worth, 1988—89; bd. dirs., cons. 8AF Meml. Mus. Found., Albuquerque, pres., 2004—; trustee, bd. dirs. Am. Air Mus., England, Duxford AF Mus., England. Decorated Legion of Merit, ETO Campaign medal, NATO Svc. medal, Korean War and Vietnam Svc. medals, WWII Victory medal, DFC, Meritorious Svc. medal, Air Medal with oak leaf cluster, Air Force Commendation medal with oak leaf cluster, Disting. Unit citation with oak leaf cluster, Combat Readiness medal. Mem.: Air Force Assn., Mil. Officers Assn Am., 8AF Vets. (life; historian, cons. 1979—2005, N.Mex. chpt.), Dadelians (life). Republican. Avocations: history, writing, painting, golf, travel. Home: 414 Camino de la Placita #33 Taos NM 87571 Home Phone: 505-881-1440. Personal E-mail: duganbv@aol.com.

VICKERY, ANN MORGAN, lawyer; b. Anderson, SC, June 25, 1944; d. Joseph Harold and Doris (Rogers) Morgan; m. Raymond Ezekiel Vickery, Jr., June 23, 1979; children: Raymond Morgan, Philip Dickens. AB History, Mary Baldwin Coll., 1965; JD, Georgetown U., 1978. Bar: D.C. 1978. Elem. sch. tchr., Chesterfield County, Va., 1965-66; legal pubs. specialist Nat. Archives and Record Svc., Washington, 1966-69; speech writing staff to Pres., rsch. asst., chief rschr., staff asst. The White House, Washington, 1969-74; summer clerk Graham & James, Washington, 1975; various positions Dept. Treasury, Washington, 1975-78; atty. Hogan & Hartson, LLP, Washington, 1978—, mng. ptnr.-D.C. office, dir. health practice group. Health group dir. Hogan and Hartson, LLP, Washington, 1991—, exec. com., 1992-95, 96-99, Washington office mng. ptnr., 1999—; outside legal counsel Nat. Hospice and Palliative Care Orgn., 1982— (named Woman of the Yr. 1986); spkr. in field. Contbr. articles to profl. jours. Dir. Hospice No. Va., Arlington, 1987-93; trustee Nat. Hospice Found., 1996—. Mem. ABA, Am. Health Lawyers Assn., D.C. Bar, Health on Wednesday, Phi Alpha Theta. Office: Hogan & Hartson LLP Columbia Square 555 13th St NW Ste 12E-300 Washington DC 20004-1161 Office Phone: 202-637-8605. Office Fax: 202-637-5901. Business E-Mail: amvickery@hhlaw.com.

VICKERY, EDWARD DOWNTAIN, lawyer; b. Ft. Worth, May 1, 1922; s. Charles Richard and Margaret May Vickery; children: Anne Vickery Stevenson, E.D. Jr. AS, North Tex. Agrl. Coll., 1941; BA, U. Tex., 1947, JD with honors, 1948. Bar: Tex. 1948, U.S. Dist. Ct. (so. dist.) Tex. 1948, U.S. Ct. Appeals (5th cir.) 1950, Bd. Immagration Appeals 1952, U.S. Supreme Ct. 1953. From assoc. to sr. ptnr. Royston, Rayzor, Vickery & Williams, Houston, 1948-55, sr. ptnr., 1955-98, of counsel, 1999—. Chmn. bd. dirs. Tradition Bankshares, Inc., Houston. Deacon First Presbyn. Ch., Houston, 1958-64, elder 1965-94; active Brazos Presbyn. Ch., 1972-77, chmn. 1976-77; bd. trustees Austin (Tex.) Presbyn. Theol. Sem., 1976-85, 86-95, vice-chmn. 1978-83, chmn. 1983-85, 89-95; bd. trustees Tex. Presbyn. Found. 1978-85 Fellow Am. Coll. Trial Lawyers, Internat. Acad. Trial Lawyers (Am. chpt.); mem. Internat. Assn. Ins. Counsel, Am. Judicature Soc., Maritime Law Assn. U.S. (exec. com. 1977-80), Hist. Soc. Supreme Ct. U.S., Tex. Assn. Def. Counsel (bd. dirs. 1965-67), Tex. Bar Found. (Houston chpt.), Tulane Admiralty Law Inst. (program, planning com., adv. bd., 1965-92), Propellor Club U.S. (nat. pres. 1965-66, 66-67, nat. first v.p. 1964-65, nat. exec. com. 1961-85, port of Houston pres. 1961-62), U. Tex. Littlefield Soc., Chancellor's Coun., T Assn., Longhorn Found., Law Sch. Found., Houston Club, Lakeside Country Club. Home: 22507 Blue Canyon Dr Katy TX 77450

VICKERY, JON LIVINGSTONE, neurologist; b. Freeport, Ill., May 30, 1955; s. Eugene Livingstone and Millie Margaret (Cox) V.; m. Diane Antoinetti; children: Daniel Scott, John Michael. BA, Northwestern U., 1976; MD, U. Ill., Chgo., 1980. Diplomate Nat. Bd. Med. Examiners. Resident in neurology U. Va., Charlottesville, 1980-84; staff neurologist Pinnacle Health Sys., Harrisburg, Pa., 1984—2004; v.p. Pa. Neurol. Assocs., Lemoyne, Pa., 1984—2004, pres., 2004—06; assoc. prof. of medicine Hershey Med. Ctr., Pa. State U., 1984-99; chief of medicine Holy Spirit Hosp., Camp Hill, Pa., 1992-95; with Vickery Neurodiagnostics Group Ltd., Carlisle, Pa., 2006—. Asst. coach Dickinson Coll. Fencing Team. Named to Am.'s Top Physicians Consumer Rsch. Coun., 2005. Fellow Am. Acad. Neurology; mem. AMA, Dauphin County Med. soc. (del. 1985-98), U.S. Fencing Coaches Assn., U.S. Fencing Assn. (life), U.S. Fencing Coaches Assn. (cert. moniteur de armes), Am. Orchid Soc. (cert. judge, mem. conservation com, 1989-91), Beaufort Hunt Club (bd. dirs. 1990-2000), Masons, Shriners. Avocations: fencing, photography, theater, breeding Hanoverian horses. Office: Vickery Neurodiagnostics Group Ltd 417 Village Dr Ste 6 Carlisle PA 17015 Office Phone: 717-245-2226. Personal E-mail: jvickeryvng@gmail.com.

VICKERY, RAYMOND EZEKIEL, JR., international business consultant, lawyer; b. Brookhaven, Miss., Apr. 30, 1942; s. Raymond Ezekiel and Clarene Helen (Dickens) V.; m. Raymond Clair Brown, Dec. 23, 1967 (div. June 1976); m. Ann Morgan, June 25, 1979; children: Raymond Morgan, Philip Dickens. AB, Duke U., 1964; postgrad., U. Sri Lanka, 1964-65; LLB, Harvard U., 1968. Assoc. Hogan & Hartson, Washington, 1968-77, ptnr. McLean, Va., 1985-93, Johnson & Vickery, Vienna, Va., 1977-81, Reed Smith Shaw & McClay, McLean, Va., 1981-85; asst. sec. for trade devel. U.S. Dept. Commerce, Washington, 1993-97; prin. Vickery Internat., 1977—; pvt. practice Washington, 1997—; of counsel Williams Aron & Assocs., Washington, 2002—06; sr. v.p. Stonebridge Internat. LLC, 2006—. Adj. prof. internat. transactions George Mason U., Fairfax, Va., 1997-99. Contbr. articles to profl. jours. Del. Va. Gen. Assembly, Richmond, 1974-80; mem. Dem. Com., Farifax County, Va., 1971-93; Dem. nominee for Congress, Va., 1992; mem. State Ctrl. Com., Va., 1993; mem. Libr. Bd., Fairfax County, 1972-74. Fulbright scholar, 1964. Mem. ABA, Va. Bar Assn., D.C. Bar Assn., City Club, Phi Beta Kappa, Omicron Delta Kappa. Baptist. Avocations: fishing, horseback riding. Home: 2733 Willow Dr Vienna VA 22181-5310 Office: 555 13th St NW Washington DC 20004-2514

VICKREY, ROBERT REMSEN, artist; b. NYC, Aug. 20, 1926; s. Claude Claire and Caroline (McKim) V.; m. Marjorie Elizabeth Alexander, Sept. 18, 1950 (dec. 1997); children: Remsen Scott, Elizabeth Nicole, Wendy Caroline, Alexander Sean; m. Beverly B. Rumage, July, 1999. Studied with Victoria Huntley; BA, Yale U., 1947, B.F.A., 1950; student, Art Students League. Art dealer Harmon-Meek Galleries, Naples, Fla. Co-author: New Techniques in Egg Tempera, 1973; author: Robert Vickrey-Artist at Work, The Affable Curmudgeon, 1979; one-man shows, Midtown Galleries, NYC, 1954-58, 62, 65, 69-70, 72, Columbia Mus. Art, SC, 1959, Davison Art Ctr., Wesleyan U., 1966, Va. Mus. Fine Arts, 1965, retrospective, U. Ariz. Mus. Art, 1973, San Diego Fine Arts Gallery, 1973, Harmon-Meek Gallery, Naples, Fla., 1982-2007, retrospective Thevon Liebig Art Ctr., Naples, 2006; exhibited in group shows; represented in permanent collections, Whitney Mus., Corcoran Gallery of Art, Washington, Lakeland (Fla.) Mus., Sara Roby Found., Parrish Art Mus., Southampton, Isaac Delgado Mus., Dallas Mus., Munson-Williams-Proctor Inst., Utica, NY, Met. Mus. Art, NAD, Butler Inst. Am. Art, New Britain Mus. Am. Art, Gallery Modern Art, Birmingham Mus., Spelman Coll., Newark Mus., others; illustrator mag. covers, books. Recipient award Edward Austin Abbey mural competition, 1949, top prize Fla. Internat. Art Exhbn., 1952, 2d prize Internat. Hallmark competition, 1955, Am. Artist mag. citation, 1956, Winsor and Newton award Am. Water Color Soc., 1956, S.J. Wallace Truman prize Nat. Acad. ann., 1958, Salmagundi Club award Audubon Artists, 1971, spl. prize Internat. Biennial of Sport in Fine Arts, Mus. Contemporary Art, Madrid, 1973, Gold Medal NAD, numerous others. Mem. Audubon Artists, Am. Water Color Soc., Nat. Acad. Address: 8231 Bay Colony Dr #1202 Naples FL 34108

VICTOR, A. PAUL, lawyer; b. NYC, Nov. 6, 1938; s. Samuel L. and Sophie (Ostrow) V.; m. Ellen Grabois, Aug. 30, 1959; children: Stephanie, Rebecca, Diana. BBA, U. Mich., 1960, JD with distinction, 1963. Bar: N.Y. 1964, D.C. 1964. Atty. antitrust divsn. US Dept. Justice, Washington, 1963-66; assoc. Kirkland, Ellis & Rowe, Washington, 1966-68, Weil, Gotshal & Manges, NYC, 1968-72, ptnr., 1972—2006, Dewey Ballantine, LLP, NYC, 2007—. Adj. prof. law Fordham U. Sch. of Law, NYC, 1983—; mem. adv. bd. Ctr. Am. and Internat. Law, Dallas, 1984-07; bd. dirs. Toray Industries (Am.) Inc., NYC, 1987—, vis. lectr. U. Mich. Law Sch., Columbia U. Law Sch., NYU Sch. of Law; presenter in field. Contbr. numerous articles to law revs., other legal publs. regarding U.S. internat. antitrust and trade law. Non-govtl. advisor US Del. Internat. Competition Network, 2002-04, 06-07; mem. visitors com. U. Mich. Law Sch., 1980-06, mem. dean's adv. com., 2006-; trustee Mass. Sch. Law, Andover, 1989—, chmn., 1998—; sec. Japan Soc., NYC, 1999-00; bd. dirs. NY chpt. Juvenile Diabetes Rsch. Found., 1994-99, 04—. Mem. ABA (vice-chair sect. antitrust law 1994-95, mem. coun. 1983-86, 91-94, chmn. internat. antitrust com. 1982-85, 87-90, mem. internat. task force, 2005-), Internat. Bar Assn., N.Y. State Bar Assn., Order of Coif Jewish. Avocations: golf, travel, swimming. Office: Dewey Ballantine LLP 1301 Ave of the Americas New York NY 10019 Office Phone: 212-259-6930. Business E-Mail: pvictor@deweyballantine.com.

VICTOR, ANN MICHELE, musician, educator; d. Tony and Marllys Ruth Victor. MusB, Kent State U., 1977, MusM, 1979. Tchr. cert. Univ. Tex. at Austin, 1989. Instr. cello & double bass Lamar U., Beaumont, Tex., 1980—83; orch. dir. Bowie Jr. High Ector ISD, Odessa, Tex., 1990—92, Baytown Jr. Sch., Baytown, Tex., 1992—95, Alief (Tex.) ISD, 1995—97, Macario Garcia Mid. Sch., Sugar Land, Tex., 1997—2002, Sartartia Mid. Sch., Sugar Land, Tex., 2000—. Tchr., adminstrv. co-coord. U. Tex. String Project, Austin, 1985—87; pvt. cello instr., 1990—; co-condr. strings orch. Houston Youth Symphony, 1999—. Fellow, AAUW, 1997. Mem.: Tex. Music Adjudicators Assn., Tex. Orch. Dirs. Assn., Tex. Classroom Tchrs. Assn., Tex. Music Educators Assn., Am. String Tchrs. Assn., Musician's Union Local 111. Baptist. Office: Sartartia Mid Sch Orch 8125 Homeward Way Sugar Land TX 77479 Personal E-mail: ann_victor@hotmail.com. E-mail: ann.victor@fortbend.k12.tx.us.

VICTOR, MICHAEL GARY, lawyer, physician; b. Detroit, Sept. 20, 1945; s. Simon H. and Helen (Litsky) V.; children: Elise Nicole, Sara Lisabeth. Bar: Ill. 1980, U.S. Dist. Ct. (no. dist.) Ill. 1980, U.S. Ct. Appeals (7th cir.) 1981; diplomate Am. Bd. Legal Medicine, Am. Bd. Emergency Medicine, 2003. Of counsel Bollinger, Ruberry & Garvey, Chgo., 1980—99; pres. Advocate Adv. Assocs., Chgo., 1982-95; asst. prof. medicine Northwestern U. Med. Sch., Chgo., 1982—2006; lectr. U. Ill., Chgo., 1999—. Dir. emergency medicine Loretto Hosp., Chgo., 1980-85, chief. sect. of emergency medicine St. Josephs Hosp., Chgo., 1985-87; pvt. practice med. law Barrington, Ill, 1982-; v.p. Med. Emergency Svcs. Assocs., Buffalo Grove, Ill., 1989; v.p. MESA Mgmt. Corp.; exec. leadership coach Lee Hecht Harrison, Chgo. Author: Informed Consent, 1980; Brain Death, 1980; (with others) Due Process for Physicians, 1984, A Physicians Guide to the Illinios Living Will Act, The Choice is Ours!, 1989. Recipient Svc. awards Am. Coll. Emergency Medicine, 1973-83. Fellow Am. Coll. Legal Medicine (bd. govs. 1996-97, alt. del. to AMA House of Dels. 1996-97), Chgo. Acad. Legal Medicine; mem. Am. Coll. Emergency Physicians (pres. Ill. chpt. 1980, med.-legal-ins. coun. 1980-81, 83-84), ABA, Ill. State Bar Assn., Am. Soc. Law and Medicine, Chgo. Bar Assn. (med.-legal coun. 1981-83), AMA, Ill. State Med. Soc. (med.-legal coun. 1980-86, 88), Chgo. Med. Soc. Jewish. Home and Office: 153 Aberdour Ln Palatine IL 60067-8001 Office Phone: 847-934-8404. Personal E-mail: mgv@comcast.net.

VICTOR, RICHARD STEVEN, lawyer; b. Detroit, Aug. 3, 1949; s. Simon H. and Helen (Litsky) V.; m. Denise L. Berman, Nov. 26, 1978; children: Daniel, Ronald, Sandra. Bar: Mich. 1975, U.S. Dist. Ct. (ea. dist.) Mich. 1975. Assoc. Law Offices of Albert Best, Detroit, 1975; ptnr. Best & Victor, Oak Park, Mich., 1976—80; sole practice Oak Park, 1981—85; ptnr. Law Offices of Victor, Robbins and Bassett and predecessor firms, Birmingham, Mich., 1986-93, Victor and Robbins and predecessor firms, Birmingham, 1993—98, Bloomfield Hills, Mich., 1998—2000; pvt. practice Richard S. Victor, PLLC, Bloomfield Hills, Mich., 2000—. Instr. in family law Oakland U., Rochester, Mich., 1976—; legal advisor family law Sta. Ask the Lawyer WXYT radio. Author: (column) Legally Speaking, Stepfamily Bull., 1984—; author, genera editor: Michigan Practitioners Series: Family Law and Practice, 1997; tech. advisor Whose Mother Am I? Aaron Spelling Prodns./ABC Movies; bd. editors Mich. Lawyers Weekly newspaper, 2000—. Recipient Award of Meritorious Svc. to the Children of Am., Nat. Coun. Juvenile and Family Ct. Judges, 1993, Child Advocate of Yr. award Child Abuse and Neglect Coun., 1994, Disting. Svc. award Oakland County Bar Assn., 1994, Lifetime Achievement award State Bar Mich., 1999, Disting. Alumni Award Nat. Alumni Assn. of Mich. State U.-Detroit Coll. Law, 2000, Champion of Justice award State Bar Mich, 2004; named Mich. Super Lawyer Super Lawyers Mag., 2007; named to Best Lawyers in Am. Fellow Mich. State Bar Found., Am. Acad. Matrimonial Lawyers (bd. mgrs. Mich. chpt. 1999—, sec. 1999, treas. 2000, v.p. 2001, pres. 2003, nat. CLE chair 2004—, nat bd. govs. 2004—, Fellow of Yr. 2006); mem. ABA (guest lectr. sem. 1988, exec. com. on custody 1989—), Mich. Bar Assn. (treas. family law sect. 1987-88, sec. 1988-89, chmn. continuing legal edn. com. family law sect., 1986-90, corr. sec. 1988-89, chmn. elect 1989-90, chmn. family law sect. 1990-91, Appreciation award from family law sect. 1987-89, Lifetime Achievement award family law sect. 1999, co-founder SMILE), Oakland County Bar Assn. (chmn. lawyer's admission com. 1981, unauthorized practice of law 1982, oldtimers night 1984-85, spkrs. bur. 1985), Family Law Coun. (chmn. legis. com.), Grandparent Rights Orgn. (founder, exec. dir. 1984—, newsletter editor). Jewish. Avocation: playing piano. Office: Law Offices of Richard S Victor PLLC 100 W Long Lake Rd Ste 250 Bloomfield Hills MI 48304-2721 Home Phone: 248-855-0479; Office Phone: 248-646-7177. Personal E-mail: rsvlaw@aol.com.

VICTOR, ROBERT EUGENE, real estate company executive, lawyer; b. NYC, Dec. 17, 1929; s. Louis and Rebecca (Teitelbaum) V.; m. Dorothy Saffir, Oct. 14, 1951; children: Priscilla Saffir Victor Faubel, Pandora Saffir. LL.B., St. John's U., 1953, JD, 1968. Bar: N.Y. bar 1953, Calif. bar 1965. With firm Szold and Brandwen, NYC, 1953-54; atty. Dept. Army, Phila., 1955-56; with Hughes Aircraft Co., Culver City, Calif., 1956-62; v.p., gen. counsel Packard Bell Electronics Corp., Los Angeles, 1962-70; sr. v.p., gen. counsel Cordon Internat. Corp., Los Angeles, 1970-78; also dir.; gen. counsel Am. Harp Soc., 1969-85; pres., bd. dirs. Vanowen Realty Corp., 1978-93; chmn., pres., bd. dirs. Dobere Realty, Inc., 2000—. Mem. Los Angeles County Bar Assn., Masons. Office: 722 Walden Dr Beverly Hills CA 90210-3125

VICTORSON, MICHAEL BRUCE, lawyer; b. Fairmont, W.Va., July 13, 1954; s. Morton Jerome and Deborah (Jacobson) V.; m. Janet Harris, Mar. 8, 1981; children: David Solomon, Sara Lorraine. BA, W.Va. U., 1976, JD, 1979. Bar: W.Va. 1979, U.S. Dist. Ct. (so. and no. dists.) W.Va. 1979, U.S. Dist. Ct. (ea. dist.) Ky. 1986, U.S. Ct. Appeals (4th cir.) 1980, U.S. Supreme Ct., 1992. Assoc. Love, Wise, Robinson and Woodroe, Charleston, W.Va., 1979-83, Robinson & McElwee LLP, Charleston, 1983-84, ptnr., 1985-99; mem. Jackson Kelly PLLC, Charleston, 1999—. Spkr. in field. Contbr. articles to profl. jours. Chmn. appeal bd. U.S. Selective Svc. System, So. Dist. W.Va., Charleston, 1983—; lawyers' chmn. United Way Kanawha Valley, Charleston, 1988-92, chmn. profl. divsn., 1992-93, admissions com., 1990-92; treas., bd. dirs. Med. Eye Bank W.Va., Charleston, 1989—, treas., 2000—; bd. dirs. Clay Ctr. Art Collectors Club, 2002—, v.p., 2007-; trustee B'nai Jacob Synagogue, 1992-94, 97-, v.p. 1997-01, pres. 2001-03; trustee Federated Jewish Charities of Charleston, Inc., 1998—, pres. 2004-07; vis. com. W.Va. U. Coll. Law, 1996-00. Mem. ABA, Internat. Assn. Def. Counsel, Internat. Assn. Jewish Lawyers and Jurists, Am. Law Firm Assn. (products liability steering com., bd. dirs. 1998-99), W.Va. Bar Assn., W.Va. State Bar Assn., Kanawha County Bar Assn., Def. Rsch. Inst., Def. Trial Counsel W.Va. (charter, bd. govs. 1992-98, chair product liability com. 2004-), Order of Coif, Phi Beta Kappa, Phi Delta Phi, Phi Kappa Phi, Pi Sigma Alpha. Office: Jackson Kelly PLLC PO Box 553 Charleston WV 25322-0553 Office Phone: 304-340-1079. Business E-Mail: mvictorson@jacksonkelly.com.

VICTORY, JEFFREY PAUL, state supreme court justice; b. Shreveport, La., Jan. 29, 1946; s. Thomas Edward and Esther (Horton) V.; m. Nancy Clark Victory, Jan. 20, 1973; children: Paul Bradford, William Peter, Christopher Thomas, Mary Katherine. BA in History and Govt., Centenary Coll., 1967; JD, Tulane U., 1971. Bar: La. 1971. Ptnr. Tucker, Jeter, Jackson & Victory, Shreveport, 1971-82; dist. ct. judge 1st Jud. Dist. Ct., Shreveport, 1982-90; appellate judge 2d Circuit Ct. of Appeal, Shreveport, 1991-95; assoc. justice Supreme Ct. La., 1995—. Bd. dirs. La. Judicial Coll. Bd. dirs. CODAC Drug Abuse, Shreveport; mem. La. Sentencing Commn. La. NG, 1969-75. Mem. ABA, Shreveport Bar Assn., La. Bar Assn. Republican. Baptist. Avocations: tennis, motorcycles, classic cars. Office: Supreme Ct 400 Royal St New Orleans LA 70130 *

VICTORY, NANCY J., lawyer, former federal agency administrator; b. NYC, July 19, 1962; BA, Princeton U., 1984; JD, Georgetown U., 1988. Ptnr. Wiley, Rein & Fielding, Washington; asst. sec. for comm. & info. US Dept. Commerce, Washington, 2001—03, adminstr. Nat. Telecom. & Info. Adminstrn., 2001—03. Chair FCC Advisory Com. for the 2007 World Radiocommunication Conf., 2003—. Office: Wiley Rein Fielding LLP 1776 K St NW Washington DC 20006 E-mail: nvictory@wrf.com.

VIDAILLET, HUMBERTO J., JR., physician, administrator, researcher; b. Santiago, Cuba, Sept. 24, 1954; arrived in U.S., 1968; s. Humberto J. and Caridad Vidaillet; m. Debbie Vidaillet, June 6, 1981; children: Kelsey, Daniel, Corbin. MD, U. Okla., 1981. Resident in internal medicine Mayo Clinic, Rochester, Minn., 1981-84; tng. in cardiology/electrophysiology Duke U. Med. Ctr., Durham, NC, 1984-87; dir. cardiac electrophysiology Marshfield (Wis.) Clinic, 1987—; assoc. clin. prof. medicine U. Wis. Sch. Medicine, Madison, 1994-2000, clin. prof. medicine, 2000—; dir. rsch. Marshfield Clinic Rsch. Found., 2005—. Prof. medicine U. Chile Sch. Medicine, 1994; cons. prof. medicine Inst. Med. Sci., Sch. Medicine, Medellin, Colombia, 1999; med. dir. arrhythmia svcs. St. Joseph Hosp., Marshfield, 1992—; med. dir. rsch. Marshfield Clinic; mem. hosps. and clinics bd. and authority U. Wis., 2005—; cons. in field. Contbr. articles to profl. jours. Parish coun. Our Lady of Peace Cath. Ch., Marshfield, 1996-2001; bd. dir. U. Wis. Found.; exec. com. Marshfield; vice chmn. bd. trustees Marshfield Clinic Rsch. Found., 1990-93, 2000-03, elected clin. physician rep. to bd. trustees, 2000—, vice-chair, 2003—05; coord., local prin. investigator clin. trials med. rsch., dir., Marshfield Clin. Rsch. Found., 2005-, dir. med. rsch., Marshfield Clin. Rsch. Found.; bd. dirs. New Visions Gallery, 1992-98; mem. found. bd. U. Wis. Marshfield/Wood County Campus, 1992-98. Am. Heart Assn. sr. investigator award, 1997, 15th Annual Gwen D. Sebold Rsch. Fellow ACP (chair internat. com. 1989-92, winner clin. paper competition 1984, 86, 87, faculty ann. sci. sessions, rsch. and publ. subcom.), Am. Coll. Cardiology (mem. edn. com., faculty sci. ann. sessions sr. investigator award 2000), Am. Coll. Chest Physicians, Heart Rhythm Soc. (faculty ann. sessions); mem. N.Am. Soc. Electrophysiology and Pacing (faculty ann. sci. sessions), Internat. Soc. Internal Medicine (sci. program commn.), Inter Am. Congress Cardiology (sci. program com. 2003), Intern Am. Coll. Cardiology (US rep. to sci. com., faculty ann. sci. session), Human Rights Worker Internat. Office: Marshfield Clinic 1000 N Oak Ave Marshfield WI 54449-5702 Business E-Mail: vidaillet.humberto@mcrf.mfldclin.edu.

VIDAL, DAVID JONATHAN, insurance company executive, journalist; b. Bayamón, PR, Oct. 11, 1946; s. Jesus Maria and Ercira Audacia (Mejia) V.; m. Watuza Leal, Jan. 25, 1975; 1 child, Katalyn. AB cum laude, Princeton U., 1968; student, Sch. Advanced Internat. Studies, Washington, 1982-83; MBA, Columbia U., 1991. Reporter The Caracas (Venezuela) Daily Jour., 1969-70; reporter, news editor AP, Caracas, NY and Sao Paulo, 1970-73, corr. Brasilia, Brazil, 1973-75; reporter, bur. chief N.Y. Times, NYC and Rio de Janeiro, 1975-80; spl. asst., White House fellow Dept. State, Washington, 1980-81; cons. U.S. AID, Washington, 1981-82; dept. mgr. task force Pres.'s Pvt. Sector Survey on Cost Control, Washington, 1982-83; exec. dir. Nat. Commn. Secondary Schooling for Hispanics, Washington, 1983-84; dir. pub. affairs N.Y.C. Partnership, 1984-85; asst. v.p. Continental Ins., NYC, 1985-95; v.p. Coun. on Fgn. Rels., NYC, 1995-97; dir. rsch. global corp. citizenship The Conf. Bd., NYC, 1997—; pub. Across the Board, 2001—. Adj. prof. journalism Columbia U. Grad. Sch. Journalism, N.Y.C., 1985-86; bd. dirs. Pub. Affairs Coun., Washington, 1988-95; trustee Found. for Pub. Affairs, Washington, 1989-95; mem. Contbns. Adv. Group, 1988-95, chmn., 1994-95; mem. corp. adv. group Schomburg Ctr. for Rsch. in Black Culture, 1988-95, Ad Hoc Com. on Charter Revision, 1988, Nat. Hispanic Agenda, 1988; mem. adv. group Latino Leadership Fund, 1991-95; vice-chmn. Nat. Civic League, 1999—. Author: (newspaper series) NY Times, 1980; pub. Across the Board, 2001—; contbr. articles and reports in field. Trustee N.Y. Theol. Sem., NYC, 1990—; mem. Coun. Fgn. Rels.; prin. Coun. for Excellence in Govt., Washington, 1992—; dir. Coun. on Internat. Ednl. Exch., NYC, 1997—2003; elder, trustee West End Presbyn. Ch., NYC, 1986—. Recipient Hispanic Achievement award Wall Street chpt. IMAGE, N.Y.C., 1989; Fulbright scholar, Washington and Venezuela, 1968. Fellow Royal Soc. for Encouragement of Arts, Manufacturers and Commerce; mem. N.Y. Regional Assn. Grantmakers (dir., sec. 1988-95), Nat. Inst. Industry Assn. (corp. adv. group 1990-95), Nat. Civic League, Coun. on Fgn. Rels. Democrat. Office: The Conf Bd 845 3rd Ave New York NY 10022-6601 E-mail: david.vidal@conference-board.org.

VIDAL, GORE (EUGENE LUTHER GORE VIDAL), writer; b. West Point, NY, Oct. 3, 1925; s. Eugene L. and Nina (Gore) V. Grad., Phillips Exeter Acad., 1943; DLitt (hon.), Brown U., 1988. Author: (novels) Williwaw, 1946, In a Yellow Wood, 1947, The City and the Pillar, 1948, The Season of Comfort, 1949, A Star's Progress, 1950, A Search for the King, 1950, Dark Green, Bright Red, 1950, Death in the Fifth Position, 1952, Death Before Bedtime, 1953, Thieves Fall Out, 1953, Death Likes It Hot, 1954 The Judgment of Paris, 1952, Messiah, 1954, Julian, 1964, Washington, D.C. 1967, Myra Breckinridge, 1968, Two Sisters, 1970, Burr: A Novel, 1973, Myron, 1974, Eighteen Seventy-Six, 1976, Kalki, 1978, Creation, 1981 (Prix Deauville 1983), Duluth, 1983, Lincoln, 1984, Empire, 1987, Hollywood: A Novel of America in the 1920's, 1990, Live From Golgotha: The Gospel According to Gore Vidal, 1992, The Smithsonian Institution, 1998, The Essential Vidal, 1998, The Golden Age, 2000; (non-fiction) Perpetual War for Perpetual Peace: How We Got So Hated, 2002, Dreaming War: Blood for Oil and the Cheney-Bush Junta, 2002, Inventing A Nation: Washington, Adams, Jefferson, 2003, Imperial America: Reflection on the United States of Amnesia, 2004; (memoirs) Screening History, 1992, Palimpsest, 1995, Point to Point Navigation: A Memoir, 2006; (short stories) A Thirsty Evil, 1956, Clouds and Eclipses: Collected Short Stories, 2006; (essays) Rocking the Boat, 1962, Sex, Death, and Money, 1968, Reflections upon a Sinking Ship, 1969, Homage to Daniel Shays, 1973, Matters of Fact and of Fiction, 1977, The Second American Revolution, 1982 (Nat. Book Critics Circle award for criticism 1982), Armageddon?, 1987 (London), United States: Essays 1952-1992, 1993 (Nat. Book award for nonfiction 1993), The Last Empire: Essays 1992—2000, 2001; (plays) Visit to a Small Planet, 1957, The Best Man, 1960, (Broadway revived 2000) Romulus, 1962, Weekend, 1968, An Evening with Richard Nixon, 1972, On the March to the Sea, 2005; (screenplays) The Catered Affair, 1956, I Accuse, 1958, The Left-Handed Gun, 1958, The Scapegoat, 1959, Suddenly Last Summer, 1959, The Best Man, 1964 (Cannes Critics prize 1964), Is Paris Burning?, 1966, The Last of the Mobile Hotshots, 1970; (teleplays) Barn Burning, 1954, Dark Possession, 1954, Smoke, 1954, Visit to a Small Planet, 1955, Dr. Jekyll and Mr. Hyde, 1955, A Sense of Justice, 1955, Summer Pavilion, 1955, The Turn of the Screw, 1955, Stage Door, 1955, A Farewell to Arms, 1955, The Death of Billy the Kid, 1955, Honor, 1956, The Indestructible Mr. Gore, 1959, Dress Gray, 1986, Billy the Kid, 1989; actor (films) Ritual in Transfigured Time, 1946, Suddenly, Last Summer, 1959,The Best Man, 1964, Bob Roberts, 1992, With Honors, 1994, Shadow Conspiracy, 1997, Gattaca, 1997, Igby Goes Down, 2002 Mem. Pres.'s Adv. Com. on Arts, 1961-63; Dem.-Liberal candidate for U.S. Congress, 1960, candidate for Dem. nomination from Calif., 1982; co-chmn. The New Party, 1970-71. Served with AUS, 1943-46. Named hon. citizen Ravello, Italy, 1983, Chevalier de l'Ordre des Arts et des Lettres, France, 1995; recipient Golden Plate award, Acad. Achievement, 2006. Office: Thunder Mouth Press 245 W 17th St 11th Fl New York NY 10011-5300 *

VIDAL, MARTIN ANDREAS, veterinarian; b. Boulder, Colo., May 21, 1967; s. Carl Rudolf and Jacqueline Vidal. BS, U. Wis., Madison, 1992, MS, 1995; B in Vet. Sci., Liverpool U., Merseyside, UK, 2000; PhD, La. State U., Baton Rouge, 2007. Assoc. veterinarian Minster Equine Vet. Clinic, York, Yorkshire, England, 2000—01; temp. vet. insp. Disease Emergency Control Ctr., DEFRA, UK, New Castle, 2001; vet. intern, assoc. veterinarian Goulburn Equine Vet. Hosp., Congupna, Victoria, Australia, 2001—03; equine surgery resident La. State U., Sch. Vet. Medicine, Baton Rouge, 2003—06. Temp. vet. insp. Disease Emergency Control Ctr., Dept. Environ., Food and Rural Affairs, New Castle, England, 2001. Contbr. articles to profl. jours. Recipient Storm Cat Rsch. Career Advancement award, Grayson-Jockey Club Rsch. Found., Inc., 2007, Ann. Resident award, Am. Assn. Vet. Clinicians, 2007; grantee, Wishbone Trust. Brit. Orthopaedic Assn., 1996, Protexin® Probiotic Internat., 1999, Surgeon-in-Tng. grant, Am. Coll. Vet. Surgeons, 2004, Grayson-Jockey Club Rsch. Found., Inc., 2005. Mem.; Royal Coll. Vet. Surgeons, Am. Assn. Equine Practitioners, Internat. Fedn. Adipose Therapy and Sci., Phi Zeta. Office: La State Univ Sch Vet Medicine Skip Bertman Dr Baton Rouge LA 70803 Home Phone: 225-229-6103; Office Phone: 225-578-9500. Business E-Mail: mvidal@vetmed.lsu.edu.

VIDAL, MAUREEN ERIS, theater educator, actress; b. Bklyn., Mar. 18, 1956; d. Louis and Lillian (Kaplan) Hendelman; m. Juan Vidal, June 25, 1974 (div. Sept. 1981); m. Guillermo Eduardo Uriarte, Dec. 22, 1986. BA, Bklyn. Coll., 1976, MS, 1981. From English tchr. to drama tchr. N.Y.C. Bd. Edn., 1976—, chair women's history dept., 1984—, dean, 1997—, drama tchr., 2002—. Mem PETA Humane Soc. Mem.: AFTRA, Gorilla Soc., Nat. Anti-Vivisection Soc. (mem. physicians' com. responsible medicine), Heights Players Theater Co. (arranger theatrical performance for residents of homeless shelters 1986—2003, exec. bd., sec. 1993—, actress), Doris Day Animal League, Delta Psi Omega. Avocations: travel, white-water rafting, scuba diving, skydiving, theater. Office: I S 318 101 Walton St Brooklyn NY 11206-4311 also: Heights Players 26 Willow Pl Brooklyn NY 11201-4513 Office Phone: 718-782-0589. E-mail: MVidal4942@aol.com.

VIDALE, JOHN EMILIO, geologist; b. Phila., Mar. 15, 1959; s. Guido Levi and Rosemary (Jacobson) V.; 1 child, Laura. BS, Yale U., 1981; PhD, Calif. Inst. Tech., 1986. Scientist U. Calif., Santa Cruz, 1987-90, U.S. Geol. Survey, Menlo Park, Calif., 1991-95; assoc. prof. UCLA, 1995-99, prof., 1999—, acting dir. Inst. Geophysics and Planetary Physics, 2002—03, interim dir., 2003—04. Editor Bulletin Seismology Soc. Am., 1988-93; contbr. articles to profl. jours. Gilbert fellow U.S. Geol. survey, 1994-95; co-recipient James B. Macelwane Young Investigator medal Am. Geophys. Union, 1994 Fellow Am. Geophys. Union (Macelwane medal 1994). Home: 10421 Colina Way Los Angeles CA 90077-2041 Office: UCLA Dept Earth & Space Sci PO Box 951567 Los Angeles CA 90095-1567 Business E-Mail: vidale@ucla.edu.

VIDAVER, ANNE MARIE, plant pathology educator; b. Vienna, Mar. 29, 1938; came to U.S., 1941; d. Franz and Klara (Winter) Kopecky; children: Gordon W.F., Regina M. BA, Russell Sage Coll., 1960; MA, Ind. U., 1962, PhD, 1965. Lectr. U. Nebr., Lincoln, 1965-66, rsch. assoc., 1966-72, asst. prof., 1972-74, assoc. prof., 1974-79, prof. plant pathology, 1979—, interim dir. Ctr. Biotech., 1988-89, 97-00, head dept. plant pathology, 1984-2000, 2003—06; chief scientist USDA's NRICGP, 2000—02. Contbr. articles to profl. jours. and books; patentee in field. Recipient Pub. Svc. award Nebr. Agri-Bus., 1977, Sci. award for excellence NAMA, New Orleans, 1991. Fellow AAAS, Am. Phytopath. Soc., Am. Soc. Microbiology; mem. Intersoc. Consortium for Plant Protection, Internat. Soc. Plant Pathology, Alliance for Prudent Use of Antibiotics. Avocations: indoor gardening, reading. Office: U Nebr Dept Plant Pathology Lincoln NE 68583-0722 Office Phone: 402-472-2858. E-mail: avidaver1@unl.edu.

VIDAVER, ROBERT MAXWELL, medical educator; b. Mpls., June 17, 1932; s. Robert William and Helen Mary (Ford) Vidaver; m. Virginia Moore Sewell, May 27, 1960. AB, Columbia U., 1953; MD, SUNY, 1956; MA (hon.), Dartmouth Coll., 1993. Diplomate Am. Bd. Psychiatry and Neurology, 1963. Intern in medicine U. Md., Balt., 1956—57; resident in psychiatry Yale U. Sch. Medicine, New Haven, 1957—60; asst. prof., coord. undergrad. edn. U. Md., Balt., 1962—65; state dir. psychiat. edn. Md. Dept. Health & Mental Hygiene, Balt., 1965—71; instr., asst. prof. Johns Hopkins Sch. Medicine, Balt., 1965—72; pres. First Md. Health Care Corp., Balt., 1971—72; assoc. prof. medicine and psychiatry N.J. Med. Sch., Newark, 1973—81, assoc. dean for hosp. affairs, 1979; med. dir. Martland Hosp., N.J. Med. Sch., Newark, 1974—78; prof., chmn. dept. psychiatry and behavioral sci. Ea. Va. Med. Sch., Norfolk, 1981—88; med. dir. N.H. Hosp., Concord, 1988—; prof., vice chmn. dept. psychiatry Dartmouth Med. Sch., Hanover, NH, 1988—. Bd. dirs. NH Hosp., Concord, 1988—2004. Author: Developments in Human Services' Education and Manpower, 1973; contbr. articles to profl. jours. Capt. US Army, 1960—62. NY State Regents scholar, NY State Dept. Edn., Columbia U., 1949—53, NY State Profl. scholar, SUNY Coll. Medicine, 1952—56. Fellow: Am. Psychiat. Assn. (life; Disting.); mem.: NH Psychiat. Assn. (councillor), Alpha Omega Alpha (Leonard Tow Humanism in Medicine award). Episcopalian. Office: NH Hosp 36 Clinton St Concord NH 03301-2359 Office Phone: 603-271-5202. Personal E-mail: vvidaver@hotmail.com.

VIDELA, FABIAN, investment company executive, consultant; b. Mendoza, Argentina, Aug. 20, 1972; s. Ramon Videla and Maria Dimatteo; m. Agata Di Cesare, Dec. 28, 1992; children: Alexa, Karen, Andrew, Kiara. Cert. gen. contractor Fla., 2002. CEO Smarter Investments Corp, Jacksonville, Fla., 2000—. Chmn. bd. Latin Capital Corp., Jacksonville, 2002—07, ZAZZIF SA, Mendoza, Argentina, 2006—. Chmn. Presdl. Bus. Commn., Washington, 2002—04. Named Hispanic Leader of Yr., Hispanic Bus. Conv., 2002, 2007. Avocations: travel, public speaking, soccer. Office: Smarter Investments Corp 603 King St Jacksonville FL 32204 Office Phone: 904-981-9400. Office Fax: 904-981-9499. Business E-Mail: ladevi@msn.com.

VIDELL, JARED STEVEN, cardiologist; b. Phila., Apr. 9, 1947; s. Harry and Rose (Malken) V.; m. Cyla Trocki, Dec. 27, 1969; children: Haviv Elana, Mikhael Alon, Samara Pilar. BEd, U. Miami, 1969; DO, Phila. Coll. Osteo. Medicine, 1976. Resident and chief resident in internal medicine Atlantic City (N.J.) Med. Ctr., 1976-79; fellow in cardiovascular diseases Albert Einstein Med. Ctr., Phila., 1979-81; rsch. fellow in nuclear cardiology Deborah Heart and Lung Ctr., Browns Mills, NJ, 1981-82, dir. employee health svcs., 1982-84; asst. dir. cardiology Pritikin Longevity Ctr., Downington, Pa., 1984-87; cardiologist, dir. clin. lab. Physician Care, P.C., Towanda, Pa., 1987-90; from co-chmn. intensive care to dir. cardiac stress lab. Meml. Hosp., Towanda, 1987-90; dir. house staff, intensive/cardiac care Lower Bucks Hosp., Bristol, Pa., 1992-94; dir. house staff ICU-CCU North Phila. Health Systems, 1994-97; med. dir. North Phila. Health Sys. Girard Med. Ctr., 1997—, chmn. clin. medicine, 1997—. Med. dir. Am. Cancer Soc. chpt., 1989-90; state peer rev. KEPRO, 1989-90. Contbr. rsch. articles to profl. jours. Maj. M.C. USAR, Maj. USMC. Fellow: Am. Soc. Angiology; mem.: AMA, Nat. Assn. Managed Care Physicians, Alumni Assn. Phila. Coll. Osteo. Medicine, Phila. County Med. Soc., Pa. Med. Soc., Am. Soc. Law, Medicine and Ethics, Internat. Platform Assn., Am. Coll. Physician Execs., Internat. Soc. Endovascular Surgery, Internat. Soc. Internal Medicine, Am. Soc. Internal Medicine, Am. Coll. Chest Physicians. Avocations: squash, bicycling, cross country skiing, travel, fishing. Office: 408 N Exeter Ave Margate City NJ 08402-1868 Office Phone: 609-823-1989. Office Fax: 609-823-1989.

VIDERMAN, LINDA JEAN, legal assistant, corporate financial executive; b. Follansbee, W.Va., Dec. 4, 1957; d. Charles Richard and Louise Edith (LeBoeuf) Roberts; m. David Gerald Viderman Jr., Mar. 15, 1974; children: Jessica Renae, April Mae, Melinda Dawn. AS, W.Va. No. C.C., 1983; cert. income tax prep., H&R Block, Steubenville, Ohio, 1986. Cert. surg. tech., fin. counselor; lic. ins. agt. Food prep. pers. Bonanza Steak House, Weirton, W.Va., 1981—83; ward clk., food svcs. Weirton Med. Ctr., 1982—84; sec., treas. Mountaineer Security Systems, Inc., Wheeling, W.Va., 1983—86; owner, operator The Button Booth, Colliers, W.Va., 1985—; paralegal, adminstr. Atty. Dominic J. Potts, Steubenville, Ohio, 1987—92; gen. ptnr., executrix Panhandle Homes, Wellsburg, W.Va., 1988—96; sec.-treas., executrix Panhandle Homes, Inc., 1996—; ins. agt. Milico, Mass. Indemnity, 1991—92, L&L Ins. Svcs., 1992—94; paralegal Atty. Fred Risovich II, Weirton, 1991—93; sec. The Hon. Fred Risovich II, Wheeling, 1993; paralegal Cipriani & Paull, L.C., Wellsburg, W.Va., 1993—2004; owner Wellsburg Office Supply, 1993—94; owner, operator Viderman Child Care Svcs. Co., Wellsburg, 1997—; owner, dir. Viderman & Assocs., Wellsburg, 1997—; legal asst. Cassidy, Myers, Cogan, Voegelin, & Tennant, L.C., 2004—05, Cassidy, Myers, Cogan & Voegelin, L.C., 2005—. Notary pub., 1991—. Contbr. articles to profl. jours.; author numerous poems. Chmn. safety com. Colliers (W.Va.) Primary PTA, 1985-87; founding mem. Brooke County Homeschoolers/Panhandle Homeschoolers Assn., 1999; editor Panhandle Homeschoolers Newsletter, 2000; mem., sec. LaLeche League, Steubenville, Ohio, 1978-80; vol. counselor W.Va. U. Fin. Counseling Svc., 1990—; IRS vol. Vol. Income Tax Assistance Program, 1991—. Mem. W.Va. Manufactured Housing Assn. (bd. dirs. 2001-02), W.Va. Writers Assn., Legal Assts. of W.Va., Inc., Am. Affiliate of Nat. Assn. Legal Assts., W.Va. Trial Lawyers Assn., Wellsburg Art Assn., Brooke County Genealogical Soc., Phi Theta Kappa Jehovah'S Witness. Avocations: christian ministry, home computing, camping, genealogy, home schooling. Home: RR2 Box 28 Wellsburg WV 26070-9500 Office: Panhandle Homes Inc RR 2 Box 27A Wellsburg WV 26070-9500 Personal E-mail: lviderman@aol.com.

VIDWANS, SMRUTI JAYANT, microbiologist; b. India; BS in Biology, MIT; PhD in Microbiology, U. Calif., San Francisco, 2001. Amgen rsch. fellow Irvington Inst. Immunological Rsch., 2003; postdoctoral fellow in microbiology and immunology U. Calif., San Francisco, 2004; co-founder Phenotypica. Contbr. articles to profl. jour. Named one of Top 100 Young Innovators, MIT Tech. Review, 2004. Office: U Calif Ctr Bioentrepeneurship 185 Berry St Ste 4603 San Francisco CA 94143-1016

VIE, GEORGE WILLIAM, III, lawyer; b. Tampa, Fla., Mar. 21, 1961; s. George William Jr. and Cheri Ann (Bass) V. BS magna cum laude, U. Houston, Clear Lake, Tex., 1985; JD, U. Tex., 1988. Bar: Tex. 1989, Hawaii 2002, US Dist. Ct. (so. dist.) Tex. 1990, US Ct. Appeals (5th cir.) 1990, US Mil. Ct. Appeals 1995, US Supreme Ct. 1995, US Ct. Appeals (fed. cir.) 2002; bd. cert. civil appellate law Tex. Bd. Legal Specialization. Legal asst. Bankston, Wright & Greenhill, Austin, Tex., 1985-89, atty., 1989-90; ptnr. Mills Shirley, Galveston, Tex., 1990—. Spkr. in field. Contbr. articles to legal publs. Keeton fellow, Tex. Law Sch. Found. Fellow Tex. Bar Found. (life); mem. FBA, State Bar Tex., State Bar Hawaii, Phi Kappa Phi, Sigma Phi Epsilon Office: Mills Shirley 2228 Mechanic St Ste 400 Galveston TX 77550-1591 Office Phone: 409-763-2341. Business E-Mail: gvie@millsshirley.com.

VIE, RICHARD CARL, insurance company executive; Student, St. Louis U., U. Mo. With Reliable Life Ins. Co., St. Louis, 1962-79; pres. Commonwealth Life Ins. Co., St. Louis, 1979-82; pres., chmn. bd. dirs. United Ins. Co. Am., Chgo., 1983—90; sr. v.p., bd. dirs. Unitrin, Inc., Chgo., 1990-92, pres., CEO, 1992—99, chmn., pres., CEO, 1999—2006, chmn., 2006—. Chmn. Life Insurers Conf., 1994; trustee Life Underwriters Tng. Coun. Bd. dirs. Concordia U. Found., 1985-94, Valparaiso U., 1995—. Lt. USN, 1958-62. Mem. The Racquet Club St. Louis, Execs. Club Chgo. Office: Unitrin Inc 1 E Wacker Dr Chicago IL 60601-1802 *

VIEBRANZ, CURTIS GRAY, advertising executive; b. Boston, Sept. 24, 1952; s. Alfred Colville and Elaine (Frailey) V. BA, Middlebury Coll., 1975; MBA, Harvard U., 1980. Loan officer Bank of Boston, NYC, 1975-78; mktg. mgr. Home Box Office Inc., NYC, 1980-81, mgr. corp. planning, 1981-82, dir. budgeting and planning, 1982-84, v.p., treas., 1984-85; v.p. Video Group div. Time Inc., NYC, 1985; exec. v.p. Sami/Burke Inc., Cin., 1986-87; pres. HBO Video, Inc., NYC, 1988; pres., CEO Tacoda Systems, Inc., NYC, 2004—06, CEO, 2006—. Mem. Coun. on Fgn. Rels. Pres. Middlebury Coll. Alumni Assn., 1988_; chmn. bd. trustees CEIP Fund Inc., Boston, 1984-87; bd. dirs. Boys and Girls' Clubs of Newark. Office: Tacoda Sys, Inc 345 Seventh Ave 8th Fl New York NY 10001 *

VIEGAS, JENNIFER, journalist, writer; b. Calif. BA, Wellesley Coll., Mass., 1987. Columnist Knight Ridder, McClatchy Newspapers, Sacramento, 1995—2004, Carmel Comm., Inc., Calif., 1996—98; reporter Discovery Channel News, Silver Spring, Md., 1998—, ABCNews.com, NYC, 1998—2001; journalist San Jose Mag., Calif., 1997—99; tech. writer Physicians for Social Responsibility, Washington, 1999—2001; mng. editor Studio One Networks, NYC, 2006—. Author: (book series) The 3-D Library of the Human Body, 2001, The Library of Future Medicine, 2002, Scientific American: Forces of Nature, 2007, The Declaration of Independence: A Primary Source Investigation into the Actions of the Second Continental Congress, 2003, Physics Anthology, 2004, Cell Functions, 2004, The Fort Laramie Treaty, 2005, Pierre Omidyar: The Founder of eBay, 2006, Beethoven, 2007. Mem.: Nat. Assn. Sci. Writers. Personal E-mail: reporterofnews@aol.com.

VIEHE, RICHARD B., podiatrist; m. Margaret Viehe; children: Anne, Thomas, Andrew. BS, Cornell U.; MD in Podiatric Medicine, Calif. Coll. Podiatric Medicine, 1971. Resident in podiatry Lincoln Cmty. Hosp., Calif.; staff physician Children's Hosp. of Orange County; Coastal Cmtys. Hosp., Santa Ana; Coll. Hosp., Costa Mesa; Fountain Valley Cmty. Hosp.; Hoag Meml. Presbyn. Hosp., Newport Beach; St. Joseph Hosp., Orange County, & Western Med. Ctr., Santa Ana; pvt. practice Newport Ctr. Podiatry Group, Newport Beach, Calif.; dir. surgical residency Western Medical Center, Santa Ana. Bd. trustee Calif. Coll. of Podiatric Medicine, 1987—; diplomat Am. Bd. of Podiatric Surgery & Am. Bd. of Podiatric Examiners. Fellow: Am. Coll. of Foot & Ankle Surgeons; mem.: Nat. Acad. of Practice, Am. Podiatric Med. Assn. (pres. 2002—03), Orange County Podiatric Med. Assn. (past pres.), Calif. Podiatric Med. Assn. (past pres.), Alpha Gamma Kappa, Pi Delta. Office: Newport Ctr Podiatry Group 1303 Avocado Ave Ste 195 Newport Beach CA 92660

VIEIRA, MEREDITH, television personality; b. Providence, Dec. 30, 1953; d. Edwin and Mary Elsie Vieira; m. Richard Cohen June 14, 1986; children: Benjamin, Gabriel, Lily Max. BA in English (magna cum laude), Tufts U., 1975. News announcer WORC-Radio, Worcester, Mass., 1975; reporter, anchor WJAR-TV, Providence; reporter WCBS-TV, NYC, 1979-82; from reporter, Chgo. bur. to news correspondent CBS News, NYC, 1982—84; Chgo. bur. chief, contbg. nat. corr. CBS Evening News with Dan Rather, NYC, 1982—84; substitute co-anchor Morning, 1984—85; prin. corr. West 57th, 1985—89; corr., co-editor 60 Minutes, 1989—91; contbg. corr., CBS Primetime series Verdict, 1991; co-anchor CBS Morning News, 1992—93; host, chief corr. Turning Point, 1993—97; chief correspondent ABC News, NYC, 1993; co-host, moderator The View, NYC, 1997—2006; co-host Today Show, NYC, 2006—. Narrator ABC TV special Open Sesame: The Making of Arabian Nights, 2000; host 78th Ann. Miss America Pageant, 1998, Lifetime's Intimate Portrait, 1999—, ABC special The Beatles Revolution, 2000, ABC TV Network's Countdown to Oscar, 2000, Who Wants to Be a Millionaire, 2002—, co-exec. prodr., 2005—; host ABC News Spl. Fat Like Me: How to Win the Weight War, 2003. Broadway debut Thoroughly Modern Millie, 2003, cameo appearance The Stepford Wives, 2004, guest host Larry King Live, 2005, host (spl. featurette) Desperate Housewives Season 1 DVD Set, 2005, guest appearances Sports Night, 1998, Walt Disney World Christmas Day Parade, 2002, Party Planner with David Tutera, 2005, Hi-Jinks, 2005, Celebrity Jeopardy, Between the Lions (PBS), (TV series) Healthy Kids, 1998, Spin City, 2000, All My Children, 2001, General Hospital, 2003, The Practice, 2003, (talk shows) The Tonight Show with Jay Leno, Late Show with David Letterman, Late Night with Conan O' Brien, Charlie Rose and

Live with Regis and Kelly, appeared in (nat. TV commercials) Bayer Aspirin, Got Milk?, featured on the cover of numerous magazines including TV Guide, Ladies Home Journal and others. Frequent contbr. several charitable foundations; co-founder, mem. sr. adv. bd. Club Mom's, 2004—. Recipient Front Page award Newswoman's Club of N.Y., 1991, Robert F. Kennedy journalism award, 1995, Woman of Yr. award, City of Hope, 2001, six Emmy awards for reporting; honored by Anti-Defamation League; Found. Am. Women Radio and T.V., 1997. Achievements include hosting more episodes as a game show host than any women in TV history. Office: ABC 320 W 66th St New York NY 10023-6304 *

VIELMETTI, EDWARD MARSHALL, webmaster; b. 1964; BA in Econ., U. Mich., 1988. With Cisco Systems, Inc., 1998—2001; tech. mktg. mgr. Arbor Networks, 2002—; founder The Vacume Group LLC, 2001—. Founder MSEN Inc., 1991—, Cisco Alumni Assn., 2001—, wireless.mi-.org, 2002—; bd. dirs. Jewbilation, Ann Arbor, Mich., 2002—. Author: The Revolution of Useful Web Services, 1999; contbr. PC World mag., 1994. Mem.: Internet Engring. Task Force, Internat. Network Social Network Analysis. Home: 317 S Division St PMB 218 Ann Arbor MI 48104 Personal E-mail: emv@monkey.org.

VIEN, PATRICK, music company executive; b. 1967; B. Econ., McGill U., 1989; M. Bus. Comm., U. So. Calif. Annenberg Sch. Comm., 1992. With Power Corp., 1992—2000; pres. & COO N.Am. TV, 2000—02; pres. Universal TV Networks, Calif., 2002—04; pres. Global Networks div. NBC Universal, Calif., 2004—06; chmn. & CEO Warner Music Internat., NYC, 2006—. Mem.: Young Presidents' Orgn. Office: Warner Music Group 75 Rockefeller Plaza New York NY 10019 *

VIENER, JOHN D., lawyer; b. Richmond, Va., Oct. 18, 1939; s. Reuben and Thelma (Kurtz) V.; m. Karin Erika Bauer, Apr. 7, 1969; children: John D. Jr., Katherine Bauer Viener Riordan. BA, Yale U., 1961; JD, Harvard U., 1964. Bar: N.Y. State 1965, U.S. Supreme Ct. 1970, U.S. Dist. Ct. (so. dist.) N.Y. 1974, U.S. Tax Ct. 1975. Assoc. Satterlee, Warfield & Stephens, NYC, 1964—69; sole practice NYC, 1969—76; sr. ptnr. Christy & Viener, NYC, 1976—98, Salans, Hertzfeld, Heilbronn, Christy & Viener, NYC, 1999—2000; prin., dir. BFD Capital Beteiligungs GmbH, 2001—; mng. dir. EuCap Advisors LLC, 2004—. Founder, gen. counsel Foxfire Fund, Inc., 1968—88; gen. counsel Landmark Communities, 1970—99, Am. Continental Properties Group, 1978—, NF&M Internat., Inc., 1976—2003, Singer Fund, Inc., 1979—, Immunotherapy, Inc., 1997—99, Tupper Broadcasting Group Cos., 1996—, Viener Found., 1991—, Nat. Cancer Found. Cancer Care, 1982—85, Troster, Singer & Co., 1970—77; bd. dirs. Links Fund Ltd. Bd. dirs. York Theatre Co., 1999-2001, The N.Y. Pops, 1999-2002. Mem.: Sailfish Point Golf Club, Internat. Polo Club, Palm Beach Polo Club, Washington Club, Manursing Island Club, Fairfield County Hounds, Meeker Brook Sporting Assn. Home: Los Arcos Sailfish Point Stuart FL 34996 also: Old North Rd Washington CT 06793 also: 650 Park Ave New York NY 10021

VIERA, ROBERT, SR., protective services official; b. NYC, May 30, 1958; s. Antonio Santiago and Escolastica (Moreno) V.; m. Evelyn Garcia, May 5, 1979 (div. 1981); m. Elizabeth Lee, Apr. 28, 1994; children: Robert Jr., Molly, Thomas, Melissa Marie. BA in Communications, Hofstra U., 1982; postgrad., C.W. Post Coll. Sch. Mgmt.; D in Divinity, Ch. of Gospel Ministry, 1984. Lic.: N.Y.S. (pvt. investigator). Youth services dir. Central Islip Psychiatric Ctr., Central Islip, NY, 1978-79; community relations officer Suffolk Econ. Opportunity Council, Patchogue, NY, 1979-80; community service adminstr. Town of Islip, NY, 1980-82; pub. relations officer County of Suffolk, West Babylon, NY, 1982-88; pres. RV Enterprises, East Setauket, NY, 1988—, dir. ops. Arrow Security, Islandia, NY, 1998—; pvt. investigator VSC Security, 1990—. Editor newsletter Backstage with Le Clic, 1985. Committeeman Islip Rep. Party, 1985; mem. Lowell Avenue Civic Assn., Central Islip, 1978—; chmn. bd. Central Islip Youth Devel. Corp., 1981-85; bd. dirs. U.S. Theatre Players, 1979—; pres., bd. dirs. Le Clic Theatre Players, 1985—; resident dir. East of Broadway Showcase Inc., 1985—; vol. rep. United Way of Long Island, 1980—; dir., musical dir. Carriage Ho. Players, 1986—. Recipient Presdl. Recognition award Central Islip Youth Devel. Corp., 1985. Republican. Roman Catholic. Club: Gull Haven Golf (Central Islip). Home: 26 Rosewood St Central Islip NY 11722-4738 E-mail: robertviera@aol.com.

VIERCK, CHARLES JOHN, JR., retired neuroscience educator; b. Columbus, Ohio, July 6, 1936; s. Charles John and Esther (Amadon) V.; m. Cheryl Stogner; children: Kenneth Christopher, Karl Frederick. BSc, U. Fla., Gainesville, 1959, MSc, 1961, PhD, 1963. Postdoctoral fellow U. Pa., Phila., 1963-65; asst. prof. U. Fla., Gainesville, 1965-71, assoc. prof., 1971-77, prof., 1977—2004, prof. emeritus, 2004. Adj. prof. U. NC, Chapel Hill, 1977—2007; dir. Ctr. Neurobiol. Scis. U. Fla., 1975-2005. Mem. editorial bd. Somatosensory Motor Research, Am. Pain Soc. Jour., Jour. Neurosci.; contbr. articles to profl. jours., chpts. to books Grantee NIH, NIMH, NSF, VA, 1966— Mem. Soc. Neurosci., Internat. Assn. Study Pain Democrat. Avocations: jazz, golf. Home: 6519 SW 37th Way Gainesville FL 32608-5146 Personal E-mail: vierck@mbi.ufl.edu.

VIERI, CHRISTIAN, professional soccer player; b. Bologna, Italy, July 12, 1973; s. Roberto and Nathalie V. Player Prato FC, Italy, 1989-90, Torino FC, Italy, 1990-93, Pisa FC, Italy, 1993, Ravenna FC, Italy, 1993—94, Venezia FC, Italy, 1994-95, Atalana, Italy, 1995—96, 2006—, Juventus Torino, Italy, 1996—97, Atletico Madrid, Spain, 1997—98, Lazio Roma, Italy, 1998—99, Inter Milan, Italy, 1999—2005, AC Milan, Italy, 2005, Sampdoria, Italy, 2006. Mem. Italy Nat. team, 1998—, European Super Cup Champion, Juventus Torino, 1996, European Cup Winners Cup Champion, Lazio Roma, 1999. Named to FIFA 100, 2004. Mailing: Atalanta BC Corso Europa snc Ciserano 24040 Ciserano di Zingonia Italy

VIERMETZ, KURT F., banker; b. Augsburg, Bavaria, Germany, Apr. 27, 1939; came to U.S., 1985; s. Alfons and Claire (Bruck) V.; m. Felicitas Kempe, May, 1966; 1 child, Maximilian Grad., Heilig Kreuz Coll., Germany, 1957. With Morgan Guaranty Trust Co. of N.Y., Frankfurt, Fed. Republic Germany, 1966-69, asst. v.p., 1969-71, v.p. Paris, 1971-82, sr. v.p. for Central Europe NYC, 1982-85; vice chmn. Morgan Guaranty Trust Co. N.Y., 1990—; also bd. dirs. Morgan Guaranty Trust Co. of N.Y., NYC; vice chmn. J.P. Morgan & Co., Inc., 1990—2000; gen. mgr. Saudi Internat. Bank, London, 1975-77; chmn., supervisory bd. HypoVereinsbank, Munich; treas. J. P. Morgan & Co. Inc., NY; chmn. supervisory bd. Bayerishce Hypo und Vereinsbank, AG, Munich, 1999—2003; dep. chmn., supervisory bd. Bayerishce Hypo und Vereinsbank AG, Munich, 2003—; chmn. supervisory bd. Deutsche Börse AG, Berlin, 2005—. Author books and articles on internat. fin. to profl. publs. Mem. Am. C. of C. in Germany Roman Catholic. Office: HypoVereinsbank Am Tucherpark 16 80538 Munich Germany

VIESSMAN, WARREN, JR., dean, civil engineering educator; b. Balt., Nov. 9, 1930; s. Warren and Helen Adair (Berlincke) V.; m. Gloria Marie Scheiner, May 11, 1953 (div. Apr. 1975); children: Wendy, Stephen, Suzanne, Michael, Thomas, Sandra; m. Elizabeth Gertrude Rothe, Aug. 8, 1980; children: Heather, Joshua B in Engring., Johns Hopkins U., 1952, MS in Engring., 1958, DEng, 1961. Registered profl. engr., Md. Engr. W. H. Primrose & Assocs., Towson, Md., 1955-57; project engr. Johns Hopkins U., Balt., 1957-61; from asst. to assoc. prof. N.Mex. State U., Las Cruces, 1961-66; prof. U. Maine, Orono, 1966-68, U. Nebr., Lincoln, 1968-75; sr. specialist Libr. Congress, Washington, 1975-83; prof., chmn. U. Fla., Gainesville, 1983-90, assoc. dean for rsch. and grad. study, 1990-91, assoc. dean for acad. programs, 1991—2003. Vis. scientist Am. Geophys. Union, 1970-71; Maurice Kremer lectr. U. Nebr., 1985, 2001; lectr. Harvard U. Water Policy Seminar, 1988; Wayne S. Nichols Meml. Fund lectr. Ohio State U., 1990; mem. steering com. on groundwater and energy U.S. Dept. Energy, 1979-80; mem. task group on fed. water rsch. U.S. Geol. Survey, 1985-87; mem. com. of water sci. and tech. bd. NAS, 1986-90; mem. water resources working group Nat. Coun. on Pub. Works Improvement, 1987; chmn., chief of engrs. Environ. Adv. Bd., Washington, 1991-93; chmn. solid and hazardous waste mgmt. adv. bd. State U. Sys. Fla. Co-author: Water Management: Technology and Institutions, 1984, Introduction to Hydrology, 2003, Water Supply and Pollution Control, 2005; contbr. over 167 articles to profl. jours. Mem. Water Mgmt. Com., Gainesville, 1983-88, Fla. Environ. Efficiency Study Commn., 1986-88. 1st lt. U.S. Army C.E., 1952-54, Korea. Recipient Comdr.'s award for pub. svc., U.S. Dept. Army, 1993. Diplomate Am. Acad. Water Resources Engrs. (hon. diplomate); fellow ASCE (hon. mem., Julian Hinds award 1989), Am. Water Resources Assn. (nat. pres. 1990, Icko Iben award 1983, Henry P. Caulfield Jr. medal 1996), Univs. Coun. on Water Resources (pres. 1987, Warren A. Hall medal 1994), Sigma Xi, Tau Beta Pi. Avocations: scuba diving, woodworking. Office: U Fla Coll Engring PO Box 116450 Gainesville FL 32611-6450 Office Phone: 352-392-2312. Business E-Mail: wvies@eng.ufl.edu.

VIEST, IVAN MIROSLAV, structural engineer, consultant; b. Bratislava, Slovakia, Oct. 10, 1922; came to U.S., 1947, naturalized, 1955; s. Ivan and Maria (Zacharova) V.; m. Barbara K. Stevenson, May 23, 1953. Ing., Slovak Tech. U., Bratislava, 1946; MS, Ga. Inst. Tech., 1948; PhD, U. Ill., 1951; doctorate (hon.), Tech. U. Kosice, 2002. Registered profl. engr., Pa. Research asst. U. Ill., Urbana, 1948-50, research assoc., 1950-51, research asst. prof., 1951-55, research assoc. prof., 1955-57; bridge research engr. Am. Assn. State Hwy. Ofcls., Nat. Acad. Scis., Ottawa, Ill., 1957-61; structural engr. Bethlehem Steel Corp., Pa., 1961-67, sr. structural cons., 1967-70, asst. mgr. sales engring. div., 1970-82; pvt. cons. structural engr. IMV Cons., 1983—. Cons. in field. Author: Composite Construction, 1958, History of Engineering Foundation, 1991, Composite Construction--Design for Buildings, 1997, Seventy-Five Years of the Lehigh Valley Section, 1997, An Immigrant's Story, 2006; contbr. over 130 articles to profl. jours. Recipient Constrn. award Engring. News Record, 1972, Special Achievement award, Am. Inst. Steel Constrn., 2004; named to Hall of Fame, Ga. Inst. of Tech., 1998. Fellow AAAS, Am. Concrete Inst. (Wason Rsch. medal 1956); mem. NAE, ASCE (hon., v.p. 1973-75, Rsch. prize 1958, Ernest E. Howard award 1991), Internat. Assn. Bridge and Structural Engring., Transp. Rsch. Bd. (emeritus 1999—), Czechoslovak Soc. Arts and Scis. (exec. v.p. 1992-93), Earthquake Engring. Rsch. Inst., Saucon Valley Country Club (Bethlehem). Achievements include research in steel and concrete structures as the development and promotion of composite construction for bridges and bldgs. Office Phone: 610-865-1041.

VIETH, CHRISTOPHER W., former publishing executive; BS in Acctg., St. Francis U. Various fin. positions Amerada Hess Corp., 1987—95; dir. fin. Barnes and Noble, 1995—98, dir. fin. and ops., 1998—99, v.p., corp. controller, 1998—99; comptroller Dow Jones & Co., NYC, 2000—01, v.p. fin., 2001—02, v.p., treasurer, CFO, 2002—06. Mem. adv. coun. Villanova U. Ctr. for Responsible Leadership & Governance; mem. NJ Certified Pub. Accountants.

VIETH, WILLIAM CHAPMAN, secondary school educator; b. Mauston, Wis., Feb. 12, 1954; s. Roland W. and Joan F. (Chapman) V.; m. Mara P. O'Neill, Dec. 29, 1979; children: Aaron Thoreau, Alexander O'Neill, Miles Darwin. BA, U. Wis., 1976, JD, 1979; BS, U. Minn., 1984, MEd, 1993. Cert. secondary English tchr., Minn. Tchr. English, St. Michael (Minn.)-Albertville Sch. Dist., 1984-85, Ind. Sch. Dist. 284, Wayzata, Minn., 1985—. Mem. academic standards com., Minn., 2003. Author: Hands Linking Hands to God, 2007; contbr. short stories and poetry to various publs. Recipient Whole Tchr. award Minn. Learning Disabilities, 1997, Golden Apple award (8). Home: 1740 Laurel Ave Saint Paul MN 55104-6128 Office: Wayzata HS 4955 Peony Ln N Plymouth MN 55446-1606 Office Phone: 763-745-6891. Personal E-mail: bill_vieth@wayzata.k12.mn.us.

VIETH, WOLF RANDOLPH, chemical engineering educator; b. St. Louis, May 5, 1934; s. Hans W. and Hedy (Fahrig) V.; m. Peggy Schira, July 6, 1957; children: Jane, Linda, Christopher, Mark. S.B. in Chem. Engring, Mass. Inst. Tech., 1956, Sc.D., 1961; M. Sc., Ohio State U., 1958. Registered profl. engr., N.J. From asst. prof. to assoc. prof. chem. engring. MIT, Cambridge, 1961-68, dir. Sch. Chem. Engring. Practice, 1965-68; prof. chem. and biochem. engring. Rutgers U., New Brunswick, N.J., 1968—, chmn. dept., 1968-78, now prof. emeritus. Cons. to govt. and industry; chmn. Gordon Research Conf. on Separation and Purification, 1975, Engring. Conf. on Biochem. Engring., 1978 Author: Membrane Systems, 1988, Diffusion in Polymers, 1991, Bioreactor Engineering, 1993. Mem. econ. study subcom., planning bd. Montgomery (N.J.) Twp., 1970-. Served to 1st lt. AUS, 1961. Recipient DuPont Co. Invention award, 1960, St. Albert the Great medal for sci. Aquinas Coll., 1952, Vis. Fgn. Scientist award Japan Soc. for Promotion Sci., 1975, Leadership award Biochem. Engring. Conf., 1993; Ford postdoctoral fellow, 1961. Fellow Am. Inst. Chemists, N.Y. Acad. Scis.; mem. Am. Inst. Chem. Engrs., Am. Chem. Soc., Am. Soc. Engring. Edn., Sigma Xi, Phi Lambda Upsilon. Research on applied molecular biology, semipermeable membranes, polymers. Office: Rutgers Sch Engring Dept Chem and Biochem Engring 98 Brett Rd Piscataway NJ 08854-8058

VIETOR, HAROLD DUANE, federal judge; b. Parkersburg, Iowa, Dec. 29, 1931; s. Harold Howard and Alma Johanna (Kreimeyer) V. BA, U. Iowa, 1955, JD, 1958. Bar: Iowa 1958. Law clk. U.S. Ct. Appeals 8th Circuit, 1958-59; ptnr. Bleakley Law Offices, Cedar Rapids, Iowa, 1959-65; judge Iowa Dist. Ct., Cedar Rapids, 1965-79, chief judge, 1970-79; U.S. dist. judge U.S. Dist. Ct. for So. Dist. Iowa, Des Moines, 1979-96, chief judge, 1985-92, sr. U.S. dist. judge, 1997—. Lectr. at law schs., legal seminars U.S. and Japan. Contbr. articles to profl. jours. in U.S. and Japan. Served with USN, 1952-54. Mem. Iowa Bar Assn. (pres. jr. sect. 1966-67), Iowa Judges Assn. (pres. 1975-76), 8th Cir. Dist. Judges Assn. (pres. 1986-88). Office: US Dist Ct 485 US Courthouse 123 E Walnut St Des Moines IA 50309-2035

VIETRI, LINDA SMITH, gifted and talented educator; b. Norristown, Pa., Aug. 28, 1951; d. George John (Stepfather) and Laura MacMullen Herdegen; m. Robert Vietri, Aug. 25, 1973; children: Patrick Robert, Jeffrey Thomas, Andrew Joseph. BA in English, Ursinus Coll., 1973; MSLS, Villanova U., 1974; M of Elem. Edn., Arcadia U., 1990. Cert. elem. edn. Pa., 1990. Tchr. 4th and 5th grades Centennial Sch. Dist., Warminster, Pa., 1990—98, tchr. gifted, 1998—. Curriculum resource representative-technology Centennial Sch. Dist., 1991—93; vol. tchr. students spl. needs Gen. Nash Elem. Sch., Kulpsville, 1987—90; cmty. mentor h.s. students North Penn H.S., Lansdale, 1986—87. Coord. distribs.clothing and household items Campbell Am. M.E.Ch., Phila., 2001—05. Mem.: AAUW (assoc.), ALA (assoc.), Pa. Assn. Gifted Edn. (assoc.). Lutheran. Achievements include development of distribution of needed items to less fortunate individuals and families. Avocations: volunteer and charity work, tutoring, reading, art, travel. Home: 102 Chester Cir North Wales PA 19454 Home Phone: 215-542-2420; Office Phone: 215-441-6087. Personal E-mail: vietli@centennialsd.org.

VIEUX, ALEX SERGE, computer company executive, educator, journalist, entrepreneur; b. Paris, June 30, 1957; came to U.S., 1985; s. Serge and Aliette (Ackmed) V.; children: Sarah, David. Grad., Inst. d'Etudes Politiques, France, 1978; LLM, U. Paris, 1981; degree in bus., HEC, 1982; MBA, Stanford U., 1987. Cons. Arthur Andersen, Paris, 1981—85; prof. econs. U. Paris, 1983-85; US bus. corr. Le Monde, Palo Alto, Calif., 1985; chief operating officer Cats Software, Palo Alto, 1987-88; pres. Renaissance Software, Palo Alto, 1988-89; founder, chmn., CEO DASAR, Inc., Calif., 1990—; chmn., owner Etre (European Tech. Roundtable Exhbn.) and Arte (Asian Tech. Roundtable Exhbn.), 1989—; pub. Red Herring, 2004—; CEO Red Herring, Inc., 2004—. Bd. dirs. Tandem Computers (merged with Compaq), CA, Inc., Cibox, Commerce One, BVRP, Check Point Software, 1998-, madge, Thrunet and White Pajama, PC Globe, Inc., Tempe, Ariz.; exec. dir. Daum Comm., Kyriba, Qualys; vis. prof., Univ. Paris Dauphine, 1988; lectr. Univ. de Paris Sorbonne; spl. advisor, French Minister Fin., Industry and Economics, 1991-1993; pres. French Republic's Infotech Commn., 1997-99; spkr. in field. Contbr. numerous articles to profl. jours. Fulbright scholar Stanford U., 1985-86; named one of the Top 25 People Shaping a Digital Europe, Time Europe Digital 25 Avocations: tennis, chess, reading. Home: 16 Alma Ct Los Altos CA 94022-1742 Office: DASAR Inc 19 Davis Dr Belmont CA 94002 Address: 121 Avenue des Champs Elysées 75008 Paris France also: Jinyun Bldg B1101 No 43 Xizhimen Beidajie Beijing 100044 China Office Phone: 650-321-5544. Office Fax: 650-321-5597.

VIG, VERNON EDWARD, lawyer; b. St. Cloud, Minn., June 19, 1937; s. Edward Enoch and Salley Johanna (Johnson) V.; m. Susan Jane Rosenow, June 10, 1961; 1 child, Elizabeth Karen. BA, Carleton Coll., 1959; LLB, NYU, 1962, LLM, 1963; postdoctoral studies, Univ. Paris, Fac. de Droit, 1964. Bar: N.Y. 1962; avocat, Paris, 1992. Assoc. Cleary, Gottlieb, Steen & Hamilton, Paris, 1964, Donovan, Leisure, Newton & Irvine, NYC and Paris, 1965-72, ptnr., 1972-86, LeBoeuf, Lamb, Greene & MacRae, LLP, NYC, Brussels, 1986—2001, of counsel, 2002—. Editor: NYU Law Rev. Sr. warden Grace Ch., Bklyn., 1986-2001. George F. Baker scholar, Fulbright scholar, 1963-64, Ford Found. scholar, 1963-64. Mem. ABA (internat. and antitrust sects.), N.Y. State Bar Assn. (chmn. antitrust sect. 1987-88), Assn. of Bar of City of N.Y., Internat. Bar Assn., Union Internat. des Avocats, Heights Casino (bklyn.), Merriewold Club (Forestburgh, N.Y., bd. dirs. 1985-91), Phi Beta Kappa. Episcopalian. Office: LeBoeuf Lamb Greene & MacRae LLP 125 W 55th St New York NY 10019-5369 Office Phone: 212-424-8007. Business E-Mail: vvig@llgm.com.

VIGDOR, JUSTIN LEONARD, lawyer; b. NYC, July 13, 1929; s. Irving Barton and Ida (Devins) V.; m. Louise Martin, Mar. 8, 1952; children: Robert, Jill Vigdor-Feldman, Lisa Vigdor-Peck, Wendy Vigdor-Hess. LLB magna cum laude, St. John's U., 1951; LLM, N.Y.U., 1952. Bar: N.Y. 1951, U.S. Supreme Ct 1951, Fla. 1975. Sr. counsel Boylan, Brown, Code, Vigdor & Wilson LLP, Rochester, NY, 1958—. Bd. dirs. IEC Electronics Corp.; mem. N.Y. Uniform Law Commn., Nat. Conf. Uniform Law Commrs. Contbr. articles to profl. jours. Bd. dirs. Found. for Jewish Cmty., Ames Amzalak Meml. Trust; pres. AAA N.Y. State, Inc., Al Sigl Ptnrs. Found.; chmn. N.Y. State IOLA Fund. Served with JAGC, AUS, 1952-54. Recipient Community Svc. award, 1960, award for Svc. to Community and Legal Profession, 1983, Disting. Svc. award N.Y. State Assn. County Clks., 1985. Fellow Am. Bar Found., N.Y. Bar Found. (Nathaniel award for cmty. svc. and profl. accomplishment); mem. Fla. Bar Assn., N.Y. State Bar Assn. (past pres. Ho. of Dels.), Monroe County Bar Assn. (past pres.), Estate Planning Coun., Am. Arbitration Assn. (nat. panel 1962—), N.Y. State C. of C. (Disting. Svc. award 1964), Irondequoit Country Club. Democrat. Jewish. Office: Boylan Brown Code Vigdor & Wilson LLP 2400 Chase Sq Rochester NY 14604 Home Phone: 585-381-6696; Office Phone: 585-232-5300. Personal E-mail: jvigdor@rochester.rr.com. Business E-Mail: jvigdor@boylanbrown.com.

VIGFUSSON, ROBERT JOHN, economist; b. Gimli, Man., Canada, May 20, 1971; BSc, U. Man., Winnipeg, 1994; PhD, Northwestern U., Evanston, Ill., 2002. Rsch. asst. Bank of Can., Ottawa, Ont., 1994—96; economist Fed. Res. Bd., Washington, 2002—. Contbr. articles to profl. jours. Office: Fed Res Bd 20th and C St NW Washington DC 20551 Office Phone: 202-452-2335. Business E-Mail: robert.j.vigfusson@frb.gov.

VIGIL, CHARLES J., lawyer; b. Los Alamos, N.Mex, Aug. 24, 1964; s. John Carlos and Catherine Elizabeth (Salazar) V. BBA, U. N.Mex., 1986; JD, U. Mich., 1989. Bar: N.Mex 1989, US Dist. Ct. (Dist. N.Mex) 1989, US Ct. Appeals (10th Cir.) 1989. Atty. Rodey, Dickason, Sloan, Akin & Robb, PA, Albuquerque, 1989—, pres., mng. dir. Articles editor Michigan Jour. of International Law, 1988-89. Co-chmn. N.Mex Commn. on Professionalism, 2005; mem. adv. com. N.Mex Compilation Com.; mem. H. Vearle Payne Am. Inn of Ct., 1999—2002. Mem. ABA (labor law sect., standing com. lawyers' professional liability), Albuquerque Bar Assn., N.Mex State Bar Assn. (pres.-elect 2004, pres. 2005), Nat. Conf. Bar Presidents (exec. coun.) Democrat. Roman Catholic. Office: Rodey Dickason Sloan Akin & Robb PA Ste 2200 201 3rd St NW Albuquerque NM 87103-1888 Office Phone: 505-768-7377. Office Fax: 505-768-7395. Business E-Mail: cvigil@rodey.com. *

VIGIL, DANIEL AGUSTIN, academic administrator; b. Denver, Feb. 13, 1947; s. Agustin and Rachel (Naranjo) V.; m. Claudia Cartier. BA in History, U. Colo., Denver, 1978, JD, 1982. Bar: Colo. 1982, U.S. Dist. Ct. Colo. 1983. Project mgr. Math. Policy Rsch., Denver, 1978; law clk. Denver Dist. Ct., 1982-83; ptnr. Vigil and Bley, Denver, 1983-85; asst. dean U. Colo. Coll. Law, Boulder, 1983-89, assoc. dean, 1989—2003; asst. dean U. Denver Coll. Law, 2003—. Apptd. by chief justice of Colo. Supreme Ct. to serve on Colo. Supreme Ct. Ad Hoc Com. on miniority participation in legal profession, 1988-94; adj. prof. U. Colo. Sch. Law; mem. Gov. Colo. Lottery Commn., 1990-97; mem. Colo. Supreme Ct. Hearing Bd., 1998-2002; mem. atty. regulatory adv. com. Colo. Supreme Ct., 2002—; vis. law prof. U. Denver Law Coll., 2003—04. Editor (newsletter) Class Action, 1987-88; co-editor (ethics com. column) Colo. Lawyer, 1995-97. Bd. dirs. Legal Aid Soc. Met. Denver, 1986-99, chmn. bd. dirs., 1998-99; past v.p. Colo. Minority Scholarhip Consortium, pres. 1990-91; bd. trustees Colo. Atty.'s Fund for Client Protection, 2001—; bd. trustees Boulder Bar Found., 2000-04, pres. 2003; mem. Task Force on Cmty. Race Rels., Boulder, 1989-94; past mem. jud. nomination rev. com. U.S. Senator Tim Wirth; chmn. bd. dirs. Colo. Legal Svcs., 2000-. Mem. Colo. Bar Assn. (mem. legal edn. and admissions com. 1989-94, chmn. 1989-91, bd. govs. 1991, 97—), Hispanic Nat. Bar Assn. (chmn. scholarship com. 1990-95), Colo Hispanic Bar Assn. (bd. dirs. 1985-89, pres. 1990), Denver Bar Assn. (joint com. on minorities in the legal profession 1993-95), Boulder County Bar Assn. (ex-officio mem., trustee, 1992-2003), Inns of Ct. (Penfield Tate chpt., 1993-2003), Phi Delta Phi (faculty sponsor) Roman Catholic. Avocations: skiing, cosmology. Home: 2550 Winding River Dr 0-4 Broomfield CO 80020 Office: U Denver Coll Lw 2255 E Evans Ave Denver CO 80208 Office Phone: 303-871-6208. Business E-Mail: dvigil@law.du.edu.

VIGIL-GIRON, REBECCA, former state official; b. Taos, N.Mex., Sept. 4, 1954; d. Felix W. and Cecilia (Santistevan) Vigil; 1 child, Andrew R. AA in Elem. Edn., N.Mex. Highlands U., 1978, BA in French, 1991. Sec., project monitor, customer svc. rep. Pub. Svc. Co. N.Mex., 1978-86; sec. state State of N. Mex, Santa Fe, 1987—90, 1999—2006; exec. dir. N.Mex. Commn. Status of Women, 1991; electoral observer UN, Angola, Africa, 1992, Internat. Found. Electoral Sys., Dominican Republic, 1994, Equatorial Guinea, Africa, 1996, Washington, 1996. Participant AMPART, Mex., 1991. Dem. nominee U.S. Ho. Reps., 1990. Named among 100 Most Influential Hispanics in Nation, Hispanic Bus. Mag., 1990; recipient Trio

Achievers award S.W. Assn. Student Assistance Programs, 1993, Gov.'s award Outstanding N.Mex. Women, 1994. Mem. Albuquerque Hispano C. of C. (membership rep., sr. sales mktg. rep., corp. rels. coord.) Democrat. *

VIGNALI, ROSARIO M., lawyer; b. Sept. 22, 1958; BA magna cum laude, City Coll., CUNY, 1979; JD cum laude, NY Law Sch., 1982. Bar: NY 1983, US Dist. Ct. So. Dist. NY, US Dist. Ct. Ea. Dist. NY, US Dist. Ct. No. Dist. NY. Ptnr. Wilson, Elser, Moskowitz, Edelman & Dicker LLP, White Plains, NYC. Mem.: ABA, Def. Rsch. Inst., NY State Bar Assn. Office: Wilson Elser Moskowitz Edelman & Dicker LLP 3 Gannett Dr White Plains NY 10604 Office Phone: 914-323-7000 ext. 4250. Office Fax: 914-323-7001. Business E-Mail: vignalir@wemed.com.

VIGNEAULT, ALAIN, professional hockey coach; b. Quebec City, Can., May 14, 1961; m. Josée Doucet; children: Andréanne, Janie. Player St. Louis Blues, 1981—83; head coach Can. Nat. Jr. Team, 1989-91, Trois-Rivières Draveurs, 1986—87, Hull Olympiques, 1988—92, Beauport Harfangs, 1995—97, Montreal Canadiens, 1997—2000, PEI Rocket, Charlottetown, 2003—05, Manitoba Moose (AHL), 2005—06, Vancouver Canucks, 2006—; asst. coach Ottawa Senators, 1992—95. Recipient Jack Adams Award, 2007. Office: Vancouver Canucks 800 Griffiths Way Vancouver BC Canada V6B 6G1 *

VIGNERI, JOSEPH WILLIAM, lawyer; b. Decatur, Ill., July 28, 1956; s. Joseph Paul and Thelma Lucille (Pettus) V.; 1 child: Emily Carmela. BA in Polit. Sci., Millikin U., 1980; JD cum laude, St. Louis U., 1983. Bar: Ill. 1983, U.S. Dist. Ct. (ctrl. dist.) Ill. 1983, U.S. Supreme Ct. 1990. Assoc. Rosenberg, Rosenberg, Bickes, Johnson & Richardson, Decatur, 1983-86; ptnr. Brilley & Vigneri, Decatur, 1986-88; pvt. practice, Decatur, 1988-92; ptnr. Vigneri & Robinson, Decatur, Ill., 1993-95; pvt. practice Decatur, 1995—; asst. pub. defender Macon County, Ill., 1999—. Past mem. job. svc. employer com. Ill. Dept. Employment Security. Past mem. profl. adv. com. Vis. Nurses Assn.; past bd. dirs., treas. Macon County Mental Health Assn. Mem. ABA (sect. real property, probate and trust law, com. spl. needs and tech. com., vice chmn. gen. practice com. 1991-92, family law subcom., editor newsletter), Ill. Bar Assn. (sec. individual rights sect. 1986, mem. bus. advice and fin. planning sect. coun. 1995-97), Decatur Bar Assn. (continuing legal edn. com. 1994-95, tech. com. 1996-97). Republican. Roman Catholic. Office: 136 W Washington St Decatur IL 62522-3102 Office Phone: 217-422-9992. Personal E-mail: jvigneri@gmail.com.

VIGNERON, ALLEN HENRY, theology studies educator, rector, auxiliary bishop; b. Mt. Clemens, Mich., Oct. 21, 1948; s. Elwin E. and Bernadine K. (Kott) V. AB in Philosophy, Sacred Heart Sem., Detroit, 1970; STL in Fundamental Theology, Pontifical Gregorian U., 1977; PhD in Philosophy, Cath. U. Am., 1987. Ordained deacon Roman Cath. Ch., 1973, ordained priest, 1975, titular bishop, 1996. Assoc. pastor Our Lady Queen of Peace Ch., Harper Woods, Mich., 1975-79; asst. prof. philosophy and theology Sacred Heart Major Sem., Detroit, 1985—; addetto of the secretariat of his Holiness the Pope The Holy See, Vatican City, 1991-94; rector, pres. Sacred Heart Major Sem., Detroit, 1994—; auxiliary bishop Archdiocese of Detroit, 1996—. Adj. prof. theology Pontifical Gregorian U., Rome, 1992-94. Roman Catholic. Office: Sacred Heart Major Sem 2701 W Chicago Detroit MI 48206-1704

VIGNESWARAN, WICKII THAMBIAH, cardiothoracic surgeon, educator; b. Jaffna, Sri Lanka, Jan. 25, 1955; came to U.S., 1991; s. Murugesu and Raja Poopathy (Nagalingam) Thambiah; m. Jnanarupy Thillainayagam, Dec. 3, 1984; children: Yalini, Hari, Janani. MB BChir, U. Sri Lanka, Peradeniya, 1978. Advanced cardiothoracic surg. fellow Mayo Clinic, Rochester, Minn., 1991-93; dir. gen. thoracic surgery U. Ill.-Chgo. Med. Ctr., 1994-98; dir. thoracic organ, dir. cardiothoracic transplant U. Ill.-Chgo., 1994-98; chief cardiothoracic surgery Westside VA Med. Ctr., Chgo., 1994-98; attending assoc. Michael Reese Hosp., Chgo., 1994-98; courtesy staff Mercy Hosp. Med. Ctr., Chgo., 1994-98; staff mem. Hines VA Med. Ctr., Chgo., 1998—2005; chief thoracic surgery Loyola U. Med. Ctr., Maywood, Ill., 1998—2005, dir. lung transplantation, 1998—2005; prof. surgery U. Chgo., 2006—; assoc. chief cardiac and thoracic surgery, dir. lung and heart-lung transplant U. Chgo. Hosps., 2006—. Mem. exec. com. Tamil-Nadu med. grads., Chgo., 1996-98; faculty advisor Hindu Student Coun., U. Ill.-Chgo., 1996-98. Contbr. numerous articles to med. jours. including Thorax, Jour. Cardiovasc. Surgery, Jour. Clin. Transplantation. Sen. U. Ill.-Chgo., Champaign and Rockford, Ill., 1996-98; chmn. cardiothoracic subcom. Regional Organ Bank of Ill., Chgo., 1996-97. Recipient Trainee Investigator award Midwestern Award Cen. Soc. for Clin. Investigation and Am. Fedn. for Clin. Rsch., 1993, Young Investigator award DuPont Pharm./ACP, 1993. Fellow: ACS, ACP, Royal Coll. Physicians and Surgeons Can., Royal Coll. Surgeons Edinburgh; mem.: AAAS, Am. Coll. Chest Physicians, Internat. Coll. Surgeons (v.p. 2003—06, chair coun. surg. spltys., v.p. U.S. sect., gov.), Am. Coll. Chest Physicians (gov. 2002—06,), Chgo. Surg. Soc., Gen. Thoracic Surgery Club, N.Y. Acad. Sci., Ill. Thoracic Surg. Soc. (pres. 2001), Soc. Thoracic Surgeons, Brit. Thoracic Soc., Royal Coll. Surgeons Eng., Internat. Surg. Soc., Internat. Soc. for Diseases of the Esophagus, Internat. Soc. Heart and Lung Transplantation (coun. mem. for pulmonary transplantation, coun. mem. for basic sci. and pathology), N.Am. Tamils Sci. and Tech. Soc. Hindu. Avocations: travel, martial arts, nature. Office: U Chgo 5841 S Maryland Ave MC5040 Chicago IL 60637-1470 Office Phone: 773-702-3551, 773-834-7812. E-mail: wvignesw@surgery.bsd.uchicago.edu.

VIGNOLA, ANDREW MICHAEL, SR., computer company executive; b. NYC, Sept. 6, 1938; Student in bus. adminstrn., CCNY, 1956-59. Programmer trainee Citibank, NYC, 1959-60; programmer analyst Soc. Savs., Hartford, Conn., 1960-63; mgr. on-line data ctr. NCR Corp., Boston, 1963-67; cons., sr. ptnr. Computer Assistance, Inc., Hartford, 1967-72; v.p. info. sys. svc. divsn. Soc. for Savs., Hartford, 1972-80; pres. Solar Svcs., Inc. subs. Soc. for Savings, 1977-80; sr. v.p., dir. info. svcs. Dime Savs. Bank, NYC, 1980-83; v.p. info. svcs. group Advest, inc., Hartford, 1983-85; pres. Cosine Inc., Meriden, Conn., 1985-90; exec. v.p., COO I.G.I.C., Great Neck, NY, 1993-99; mgmt. cons., 1999—. Former mem. faculty Conn. Savs. Sch. Fin. and Mgmt.; lectr. in field. Contbr. articles to profl. jours. Mem.: Data Processing Mgmt. Assn. (pres., chmn. bd. Hartford chpt. 1976—77). Achievements include invention of banking brokerage interface. Home: 30 Bonna St Beacon Falls CT 06403

VIGODA, PAUL EVAN, secondary school educator; b. Fresh Meadows, NY, July 5, 1981; s. Scott N. and Bonnie W. Vigoda. BA, postgrad., CUNY, Flushing, NY, 2003—. Social studies tchr. Mid. Sch. 216, NYC Dept. Edn., Fresh Meadows, NY, 2003—06, head basketball coach, 2003—, acad. coord., dean, 2006—. Head basketball coach Kew-Forest Sch., Forest Hills, NY, 2001—03. Author: A Class of Heroes, 2005. Dir. Jr. Knicks Cross Island YMCA, Bellerosa, NY, 2000—02; aux. police officer NY Police Dept., Flushing, 2006—. Recipient Citation of Honor, Queen's Borough Pres., 2001, Citation, NYC Coun., 2001. Mem.: Golden Key Internat. Honor Soc., Pi Sigma Alpha. Avocations: sports, politics, movies, memorabilia. Office: Mid Sch 216 64-20 175 St Fresh Meadows NY 11365

VIGODA, ROBERT A., lawyer; b. Boston, Apr. 13, 1953; BA, U. Rochester, 1975; JD, U. Miami, 1978, LLM in Estate Planning, 1979. Bar: Fla. 1978, Mass. 1979. Adj. prof., Dept. Fin. Planning and Taxation Bentley Coll.; ptnr. Edwards Angell Palmer & Dodge LLP, Boston. Mem. bd. dirs. Boston Estate Planning Coun. Named one of Mass. Super Lawyers, Law & Politics, Boston Mag., Top 100 Attys., Worth mag., 2005, 2006. Mem.: Mass. Bar Assn., Fla. Bar Assn. Office: Edwards Angell Palmer & Dodge LLP 111 Huntington Ave Boston MA 02199 *

VIGTEL, GUDMUND, retired museum director; b. July 9, 1925; came to U.S., 1948, naturalized, 1966; s. Arne Jonsen and Elisabeth (Petri) V.; m. Solveig Lund, 1951 (div. 1964); 1 child, Elisabeth; m. Carolyn Gates Smith, July 18, 1964; 1 child, Catherine Higdon. BFA, U. Ga., 1952, MFA, 1953; DFA (hon.), Atlanta Coll. Art, 1991. Adminstrv. asst. Corcoran Gallery Art, Washington, 1954-61, asst. dir., 1961-63; dir. High Mus. Art, Atlanta, 1963-91, dir. emeritus, 1991—. Contbr. articles to profl. jours. With Royal Norwegian Air Force, 1944-45. Decorated Chevalier des Arts et Lettres, Min. of Culture, France, 1985; recipient Order of Merit 1st Class, Fed. Republic Germany, 1989, The James R. Short Lifetime Achievement award, 2003. Home: 2082 Golfview Dr NW Atlanta GA 30309-1210

VIJAYAKUMAR, ASHA, ophthalmologist; b. Chitoor, Kerala, India, July 30, 1960; d. Padmanabhan and Ammu P. Menon; m. Parakkudivilakam Vijayakumar, May 27, 1984; children: Ashvin, Roshan. B in Medicine and Surgery, Bombay U., 1985, MS in Ophthalmology, 1990. Cons. ophthalmologist Olaya Med. Ctr., Riyadh, Central Province, Saudi Arabia, 1991—96; fellow in neuro-opthalmology Henry Ford Hosp., Mich., 1997—98; fellow in cornea and refractive surgery Wayne State U., 1998—99; med. officer ophthalmology Aravind Eye Hosp., Coimbatore, Tamil Nadu, India, 1999—2001; rschr. Hosp. Sick Children and Princess Margaret Hosp., Toronto, Ont., Canada, 2001—02. Presenter in field. Contbr. revs. in field. Vol. Lions Club, 1999—2001, WHO, 1999—2001, organizer, 1999—2001, Rotary Club, Palghat, Kerala. Recipient Distinction, State Bd., 1978; scholar North Bombay Sch. award, Welfare Soc., 1978. Mem.: Worth Am. Neuro-Ophthalmolgy Soc., Indian Ophthal. Soc., Am. Acad. Ophthalmology. Home: 1000 Central Ave Apt 131A Westfield NJ 07090 Home Phone: 908-232-1989.

VIJAYARATNAM, KANAPATHIPILLAI, civil and environmental engineer, consultant, director, educator; b. Analaitivu, Sri Lanka, May 10, 1948; arrived in Eng., 1979, naturalized, 1990; s. Kathirvelu Kanapathipillai and Parvathy Ponniah; m. Sakuntala Mylwaganam, Oct. 31, 1979. BSc in Engring. with honors, U. Ceylon, Peradeniya, 1971; M Engring., Asian Inst. Tech., Bangkok, 1977; MSc in Pub. Health (Environ.) Engring., Imperial Coll. U. London, 1982; cert. sustainable bus. challenge, World Bus. Coun. Sustainable Devel., 1999; Diploma, Imperial Coll., London, 1982; DEng, Irish Internat. U., 2004. Chartered engr., U.K. Instr. civil engring. U. Ceylon, Peradeniya, 1972; civil engr. Mahaweli Devel. Bd., Colombo, Sri Lanka, 1972-75, Renardet Engring., Singapore, 1977-80; engr. Chanton Engring. Ltd., Middlesex, 1984-85, S.P. Collins Assocs., Cambridge, U.K., 1985-86; cons. civil engr. Coulsdon, U.K., 1986-88; sr. engr. Neilcot Constrn. Ltd., Kent, U.K., 1988-90; engr. clean water dept. Binnie & Ptnrs., Cons. Engrs., Redhill, U.K., 1990-94; sr. engr. grade 1 SMHBinnie Cons. Engrs., K.L., Malaysia, 1995-96; dep. project mgr., prin. engr. S.S.P. Consulting Engrs., Kuala Lumpur, Malaysia, 1996-97, engring. cons., 1998-99; mng. dir. Rosebury Cons., Ltd., 1999—. Exec. dir. AITA-Net (Europe), Internat. Cons. Consortium, 2001-06; orig. contbr. to re-engring. of water ind. orgs., 1996, Broader Edu. Civil Engrs. in 21st Century, 1995, Integrated River Basin Devel., 1977, Cost and Performance Optimization of Water Treatment System (conceptual and mathematical), 1982, Mathematical Multi-Criterion & Multi-Objective Decision Approaches to Water Resources Management, 1994, Future Direction of Civil Engring. Inst. Civil Engrs., 1995, ASCE, 2003, Sustainable Development of Infrastructure in Water and Environ. Engring., 1996, Environmentally Sound Dam and Water Power Devel., 1995, Emergence and Complexity in Urban Environmental Engring Mgmt. in 21st Century, 1999, Environ. Engring. Edn. in 21st Century, 1999, 03, and Future Dir. Tech. Edn. in Asia, 1999, Project Mgmt. Water Supply and Treatment Projects in Asia, 1995, Future Direction Engring. Edn. for a Sustainable World in the New Millenium, 2000, 03, Sustainable Water Supply for Asian City, 2001, 03, Sustainable Waste Management, 2001, leading contbr. Talking Point Forum of www.bbc.co.uk on engring., sustainable devel., environment, pub. health and pub. policy issues, 2002; contbr. numerous BBC-Have Your Say (engring. and pub. policy) forum, 2003—; prof. and dean Sch. Engring. Mgmt., Sustainable Environ. Devel. and Pub. Policy Am. U. London, 2003—2006; adj. faculty Am. U. London; dean and prof. faculty engring., mgmt. and environment. Irish Internat. U., 2004-05; dir. London Engring. Sch., 2004—, exec. pres., 2005-; founder, pres., dir. gen. World Acad. Engring., 2006-; founder www.vijayaratnamfoundation.org, 2006; presenter in field. Contbr. articles to profl. jours. Named one of 500 Leaders of New Century, 1999, Asians in Millennium, 100 Eminent Tamils of 20th Century, Greatest Minds 21st Century, 2004—05; recipient Man of Yr. medal, Internat. Peace prize, 2005; UK Govt. scholar, 1976—77, NATO Advanced Inst. grantee, 1981, UNESCO/Colo. State U. grantee, 1981, 2004. Mem. ASCE, World Acad. Engring. (pres., dir. gen. 2006), Assn. Environ. Engring. and Sci. Profs., Royal Instn. London, Instn. Civil Engrs. London, Internat. Water Assn., Internat. Assn. Hydraulic Rsch. and Engring., Internat. Assn. Water Resources, Internat. Assn. Water Power, UNESCO Internat. Ctr. Engring. Edn., Chartered Inst. Water and Environ. Mgmt. Avocations: golf, travel, reading, writing, fine arts. Home: 1 Ashcroft Rise Coulsdon Surrey CR5 2SS England Personal E-mail: vijay@vijayaratnam.com. Business E-Mail: president@lesedu.co.uk, president@waeng.org, president@topmentor.co.uk.

VIKEN, LINDA LEA MARGARET, lawyer; b. Sioux Falls, SD, Oct. 27, 1945; d. Carl Thomas and Eleanor Bertha (Zehnpfennig) Crampton; m. Jerry Lee Miller, June 10, 1967 (div. 1975); m. Jeffrey Lynn Viken, Feb. 2, 1980. BS in Bus. Edn., U. S.D., 1967, JD in Law, 1977. Bar: S.D. 1978, U.S. Dist. Ct. S.D. 1978, U.S. Ct. Appeals (8th cir.) 1981. Tchr. Yankton (S.D.) High Sch., 1967-69, Edison Jr. High Sch., Sioux Falls, 1969-75; pvt. practice law Sioux Falls, 1978; ptnr. Finch, Viken, Viken, & Pechota, Rapid City, SD, 1978-92, Viken, Viken, Pechota, Leach & Dewell, Rapid City, SD, 1992—2003, Viken Law Firm, Rapid City, SD, 2003—. Part-time instr. Nat. Coll., Rapid City, 1978-80; magistrate judge Seventh Jud. Cir., Rapid City, 1983-84; chair S.D. Commn. on Child Support, 1985, 88, 96; mem. S.D. Bd. of Bar Examiners, 1987-88. Contbr. articles to profl. jours. State rep. S.D. Legislature Minnehaha County, 1973-76, Pennington County, 1988-92; state party vice chair S.D. Dem. party, 1978-80, 92-94; chair Pennington County Dem. Party, Rapid City, 1985-87. Named Woman Atty. of Yr. Law Sch. Women, 1987, Girl Scout Woman of Distinction, 1998, Fellow Am. Acad. Matrimonial Lawyers; mem. ABA, S.D. Bar, S.D. Trial Lawyers Assn. Democrat. Roman Catholic. Avocations: poetry, skiing. Office: Viken Law Firm 4200 Beach Dr Ste 4 Rapid City SD 57702 E-mail: llmv@vikenlaw.com. *

VIKER, ERIK, theater educator; b. West Islip, NY, Nov. 2, 1965; s. Arne and Patricia Viker; m. Brenda Fabian, May 27, 2006. BS, U. Fla., Gainesville, 1987; MFA, U. Tex., Austin, 2003. Asst. prof. theatre, tech. dir. Susquehanna U., Selinsgrove, Pa., 2003—. Freelance theatre prodn. mgr., Pa., 1997—. Mem.: Internat. Alliance Theatrical Stage Employees (mem., local 636). Libertarian. Roman Catholic. Home: 215 East Walnut St Selinsgrove PA 17870 Office: Susquehanna U 514 University Ave Selinsgrove PA 17870 Home Phone: 570-274-2040; Office Phone: 570-372-4548.

VILA, ADIS MARIA, lawyer, business government executive; b. Guines Habana, Cuba, Aug. 1, 1953; d. Calixto Vila and Adis C. Fernandez. BA with distinction, Rollins Coll., Winter Park, Fla., 1974; JD with honors, U. Fla., Gainesville, 1978; LLM with high honors, Institut Universitaire de Hautes Etudes Internationales, Geneva, 1981; MBA, U Chgo., 1997. Bar: Fla. 1979, DC 1984. Assoc. Paul & Thomson, 1979-82; White House fellow Office Pub. Liaison, Washington, 1982-83; spl. asst. to sec. state for inter-Am. affairs Dept. State, Washington, 1983-86; dir. Office of Mex. and Caribbean Basin, Dept. Commerce, Washington, 1986-87; sec. Dept. Adminstrn., State of Fla., 1987-89; asst. sec. for adminstrn. USDA, Washington, 1989-91; vis. fellow Nat. Def. U., Washington, 1992-93; v.p. internat. devel. Vigoro Corp., Chgo., 1994-95; v.p. govt. affairs regulatory policy, Carribean & Latin Am. Nortel Networks, 1997-2000; pres., CEO Vila & Assocs., 2001—. Vis. asst. prof. Fla. Internat. U., 1993—94; mem. adv. bd. Ams. Global Asset Mgmt. Fund, 1999—; v.p. external affairs Miami Dade C.C., 2002—03; adj. faculty bus. law various not-for-profit, for profit instns., 2002—; vis. prof. Internat. Bus. and Mgmt. Dickinson Coll., 2007—. Trustee So. Ctr. Internat. Studies, 1987—. Named one of 100 Most Influential Hispanics, 1988; Paul Harris fellow, Rotary Internat., 1983, US-Japan Leadership fellow, 1991—92, Eisenhower Exch. fellow, Beca Fiore, Argentina, 1992. Mem.: Women Execs. in State Govt. (bd. dirs. 1987—89), Am. Coun. Young Polit. Leaders (bd. dirs. 1984—), Internat. Women's Forum, Coun. Fgn. Rels. (term mem. 1987—92), Dade County Bar Assn. (bd. dirs. young and lawyers sect. 1979—87). Republican. Roman Catholic. Avocations: tennis, skiing, golf, theater, art. Personal E-mail: adisvila@comcast.net.

VILA, HECTOR, anesthesiologist, department chairman; b. Tampa; m. Claire Vila; children: John, Carmen. MD in Anesthesiology, La. State U., New Orleans, 1989. Process design engr. Exxon Co., New Orleans, 1980—85; instr. anesthesiology U. So. Fla., Tampa, 1993—94, chmn. govtl. rels., 2002—. Mem.: Am. Soc. Anesthesiologists (chair ambulatory surg. com. 2002—). Office: Moffitt Cancer Ctr 12902 Magnolia Dr Tampa FL 33612 Home Phone: 813-745-8486; Office Phone: 813-745-8486. Office Fax: 813-979-3064; Home Fax: 813-979-3064.

VILA, ROBERT JOSEPH, television personality, real estate developer, space designer; b. Miami, Fla., June 20, 1946; s. Roberto and Esperanza (Robles) Vila; m. Diana Barrett, Oct. 3, 1975; children: Christopher, Monica, Susannah. AA in Architecture, Miami Dade Jr. Coll., 1966; BS in Journalism, U. Fla., 1969. Editor English Lang. Cons., Stuttgart, Fed. Republic of Germany, 1971; stagehand Wurttemburg State Theatre, Stuttgart, 1972; project mgr. Barrett Assocs., Boston, 1973-74; pres. R.J. Vila, Inc., Boston, 1975-85; host This Old House Sta. WGBH-TV, Boston, 1978-89; host Bob Vila's Home Again, Cape Cod and Chgo., 1990—. Author: This Old House, 1980, Bob Vila's This Old House, 1982, Guide to Building Materials, 1986, Guide to Buying Your Dream House, 1990, Bob Vila's Tool Box, 1993, Bob Vila's Guide to Historic Homes of New England, 1993, Bob Vila's Guide to Historic Homes of the South, 1993, Bob Vila's Guide to Historic Homes of the Mid-Atlantic, 1993, Bob Vila's Workshop, 1994, Bob Vila's Guide to Historic Homes of the Midwest and Great Plains, 1994, Bob Vila's Guide to Historic Homes of the West, 1994 (A&E Spl.), Bob Vila's Guide to Historic Homes, 1996, Bob Vila's American Home mag., 1996, Bob Vila's Complete Guide to Remodeling Your Home, 2002. Bd. dirs. Nat. Alliance to End Homlessness, Washington, Coll. Summit. Recipient Emmy award, New Eng. Region, 1979, Nat. Region, 1985. Mem.: SAG (Screen Actors Guild), AFTRA (Am. Fedn. TV Radio Artists). Roman Catholic. Avocations: sailing, fishing, bicycling, gardening, woodworking. Office: BVTV Inc 115 Kingston St Boston MA 02111

VILA-CARRILES, WANDA HELENA, research scientist; b. San Juan, Sept. 5, 1976; d. Miguel Angel Vila-Solano and Ana Cristina Carriles-Sepulveda. PhD, Baylor Coll. Medicine, Houston, Tex., 2004. Postdoctoral fellow U. Ala., Birmingham, 2004—. ESL tchr. Houston Ind. Sch. Dist., 2001—02, sci. fair judge, ednl. outreach, parent workshop leader, sci. night organizer, 2001—03; sci. fair judge Birmingham Sch. Dist., Ala., 2007; young adult groups leader Diocese Galveston Houston, 2001—04. Recipient Young Investigator award, 4th FEBS Advanced Lecture Course, Gosau, Austria, 2003; fellow Ruth L. Kirschstein Nat. Rsch. Svc. award, NIH, 2002—04; Grad. Rsch. fellow, NSF, 1998—2001, Pre-doctoral fellow, GEM Consortium, 1998, Sci. Edn. Leadership fellow, Howard Hughes, 2001—03, Student Travel fellow, Soc. for Advancement Chicanos and Native Am. Sci., 2002. Mem.: AAAS (assoc.), Am. Chem. Soc. (assoc.), Endocrine Soc. (assoc.), Am. Physiol. Soc. (assoc.), Am. Assn. of Pharm. Scientists (assoc.). Office: Univ Ala 1918 University Blvd MCLM 705 Birmingham AL 35294-0005 Personal E-mail: wvilacarriles@yahoo.com.

VILADAS, PILAR, editor; BA, Harvard Coll., 1977. With Interiors mag., 1979—81; with Progressive Architecture, 1981—88; home design editor NY Times mag., 1997—, House & Garden, 1989—93; contbg. writer Archtl. Digest, 1993—96. Author: Los Angeles: A Certain Style, 1995, Domesticities: At Home with the NY Times Magazine, 2005; co-author: California Beach Houses: Style, Interiors, & Architecture, 1996. Office: NY Times 229 W 43rd St New York NY 10036 Office Phone: 212-556-5183. Office Fax: 212-556-7382.

VILCEK, JAN TOMAS, immunologist, medical educator; b. Bratislava, Czechoslovakia, June 17, 1933; came to U.S., 1965, naturalized, 1970. s. Julius and Friderika (Fischer) V.; m. Marica F. Gerhath, July 28, 1962 MD, Comenius U., Bratislava, 1957; CSc (PhD), Czechoslovak Acad. Sci., Bratislava, 1962. Fellow Inst. Virology, Bratislava, 1957-62, head of lab., 1962-64; asst. prof. microbiology NYU Med. Ctr., NYC, 1965-68, assoc. prof., 1968-73, prof., 1973—. Chmn. nomenclature com. WHO, 1981—86; mem. adv. com. Am. Cancer Soc., 1981—87, chmn., 1983; mem. sci. adv. bd. Max Planck Inst., Munich, 1987—95; pres. Vilcek Found., 2003—. Author: Interferon, 1969; editor in chief Archives of Virology, 1975-86, Cytokine and Growth Factor Revs., 1995-2005; editor: Interferons and the Immune System, 1984, Tumor Necrosis Factor: Structure, Function and Mechanism of Action, 1991, Cytokine Reference, 2000; mem. editl. bd. Virology, 1979-81, Archives of Virology, 1986-92, Infection and Immunity, 1983-85, Antiviral Rsch., 1984-88, Jour. Interferon and Cytokine Rsch., 1988—, Jour. Immunological Methods, 1986—, Natural Immunity and Cell Growth Regulation, 1986-92, Jour. Immunology, 1987-89, Lymphokine Rsch., 1987-94, Jour. Biol. Chemistry, 1988-90, ISI Atlas Sci., Immunology, 1988-89, Jour. Cellular Physiology, 1988—, Cytokine, 1989—, Biologicals, 1989-95, Acta Virologica, 1991—, Internat. Archives of Allergy and Immunology, 1992-98, Folia Biologica, 1993-96, Cellular Immunology, 1993-96, Jour. of Inflammation, 1994-97, Cytokines, Cellular & Molecular Therapy, 1998-2005; contbr. articles to profl. jours.; co-inventor of anti-inflammatory drug infliximab used in rheumatoid arthritis and Crohn's disease, other inflammatory disorders. Mem. rev. panel Israel Cancer Rsch. Fund, 1993-96; mem. fellowship rev. com. Am. Heart Assn., 1992-94. Recipient Rsch. Career Devel. award, USPHS, 1968—73, Recognition award, Japanese Inflammation Soc., 1989, Outstanding Investigator award, Nat. Cancer Inst., NIH, 1991—98, Elliott Osserman Disting. Svc. Cancer Rsch. award, Israel Cancer Rsch. Fund, 1996, Disting. Alumnus award and medal, Comenius U., Bratislava, 2001, Albert Gallatin medal, NYU, 2005; grantee, USPHS, others. Fellow AAAS; mem. Am. Soc. Microbiology, Am. Assn. Immunologists, Internat. Soc. Interferon and Cytokine Rsch. (hon. life), Czech Immunology Soc., Internat. Cytokine Soc. (hon. life, pres. 1997-98), Czechoslovak Soc. Microbiology. Office: NYU Med Ctr 550 1st Ave New York NY 10016-6402 Business E-Mail: jan.vilcek@med.nyu.edu.

VILCHEZ, VICTORIA ANNE, lawyer; b. Tampa, Fla., Aug. 10, 1955; d. Angel and Mary Ida (Guarisco) Vilchez; m. Louis J. Deutsch; children from previous marriage: Matthew Stephen Williams, Michael Paul Williams, Heather Margaret Williams. BA, Fla. State U., Tallahassee, 1977; JD, Mercer U., Macon, Ga., 1980. Bar: Fla. 1980. Trial atty. Office Pub. Defender, Miami, Fla., 1980-83; pvt. practice, 1983—. Traffic magistrate Palm Beach County Ct., 1991—95; mem. Class 1994 Leadership Palm

Beach County; bd. dirs. Girl Scouts coun., Palm Glades, Fla., 1995—2004, 2006—, 1st v.p., 2003—04, 2d v.p., 2006—; mem. Rep. Nat. Conf. Women and Law, Atlanta, 1978; vol. Coun. Cath. Women. Recipient cert. of achievement, 8th Nat. Conf. Juvenile Justice, 1981, Livingstone Hall award, Juvenile Justice ABA, 1998; grantee, Mercer U., 1977. Mem.: Legal Aid Soc. Palm Beach (bd. dirs. 1992—, v.p. 1999—2001, pres. 2001—03), Guild Cath. Lawyers (pres.-elect 2004—06, pres. 2006—), Palm Beach County Hispanic Bar Assn. (pres.-elect 1990—91, pres. 2005—06), Palm Beach County Bar Assn. (bd. dirs. 1990—, treas. 1993—94, 1994—97), Fla. Assn. Women Lawyers (sec., newsletter editor Palm Beach County chpt. 1985—86, mentor chair 2003, pres.-elect 2004—05, pres. 2005—06), Fla. Bar, Leadership Palm Beach County (bd. govs. 1999—2001, grad. 1994), Fla. State U. Alumni Assn. Roman Catholic. Address: PO Box 32 West Palm Beach FL 33402-0032 Office Phone: 561-471-0001. Business E-Mail: vilchezlaw@gmail.com.

VILENCHIK, MICHAEL MARC, radiobiologist, biophysicist, bio-oncologist; b. Brjansk, Russia, May 30, 1938; s. Marc and Grunja G. (Smoljakova) V.; m. Valentina I. Vasilieva, Jan. 12, 1964 (div. 1967); 1 child, Joan; m. Julia N. Runova, Mar. 6, 1968 (div. 1971); 1 child, Vera. MD, 1st Med. Inst., St. Petersburg, Russia, 1961; PhD, Inst. Virology, Moscow, 1967. Postgrad. rsch. Inst. Virology, Moscow, 1963-66; rsch. scientist, sr. biophysicist, sr. resident Inst. Biophysics, Pushchino, Moscow, 1966-90; vis. scientist Med. Rsch. Coun., Didcot, England, 1990—; rschr. Inst. for Environ. Rsch., Tel Aviv, 1991; rsch. scholar SUNY Health Sci. Ctr., Syracuse, 1991-93, Cornell U., Ithaca, N.Y., 1993-94; rsch. scientist Longevity Achievement Found. and Sally Balin Med. Ctr., Media, Pa., 1994—. Author: Biological Fundamentals of Aging and Longevity, 1976, 87, 89, Radiobiological Effects and Environment, 1983, 91, The Rules of Molecular-Genetic Action of Chemical Carcinogens, 1977, Dynamic DNA Instability and the Late Radiobiological Effects, 1987, Modification of Carcinogenic and Antitumor Actions of Ionizing Radiation, 1985; contbr. articles to profl. jours., chpts. to books. Mem.: Am. Assn. for Cancer Rsch. Achievements include research in biophysics of aging and carcinogenesis; mechanisms of radiation effects and biophyisics of the genome. Office Phone: 610-565-3300.

VILIM, NANCY CATHERINE, advertising executive; b. Quincy, Mass., Jan. 15, 1952; d. John Robert and Rosemary (Malpede) V.; m. Geoffrey S. Horner, Feb. 16, 1992; children: Matthew Edward Cajda, Megan Catherine Cajda, Margaret Horner. Student, Miami U., Oxford, Ohio, 1970-72. Media asst. Draper Daniels, Inc., Chgo., 1972—74; asst. buyer Campbell Mithun, Chgo., 1974—75; buyer Tatham, Laird & Kudner, Chgo., 1975—77; media buyer Adcom, Inc. div. Quaker Oats Corp., Chgo., 1977—79; media supr. G.M. Feldman, Chgo., 1979—81; v.p. media dir. Media Mgmt., 1981—83; v.p. broadcast dir. Bozell, Jacobs, Kenyon & Eckhardt, Chgo., 1983—88; v.p., media mgr. McCann-Erickson, Inc., 1989—2002; broadcast supr. OMD USA, Chgo., 2002—04; sr. media buyer GSD&M, Chgo., 2004—05; media dir. Jordan, Ross & Rose, Northfield, Ill., 2005—. Judge 27th Internat. Broadcast Awards, Chgo., 1987. Co-pres. Immaculate Conception Religious Edn. Parents Club, 1995-96. Recipient Media All Star awards Sound Mgmt. Mag., N.Y.C., 1987. Mem. Broadcast Advt. Club Chgo., Mus. Broadcast Communications, NAFE. Office: JRR Advt 790 Frontage Rd Northfield IL 60093

VILLA, JOHN KAZAR, lawyer; b. Ypsilanti, Mich., June 9, 1948; s. John Joseph and Susie (Hoogasian) V.; m. Ellen Ann Edwards, June 3, 1990. AB, Duke U., 1970; JD with honors, U. Mich., 1973. Bar: Mich. 1973, DC 1975, US Ct. Appeals (1st-10th dists. DC), US Ct. Appeals (fed. cir.), US Dist. Ct. DC, US Ct. Fed. Claims. Trial atty. US Dept. Justice, Washington, 1973-77; spl. asst. US atty. US Atty.'s Office DC, 1975—76; assoc. Williams & Connolly, Washington, 1977-81, ptnr., 1981—, mem. exec. com., 2001—. Adv. bd. Georgetown Corp. Counsel Inst.; adj. prof. Georgetown Law Sch. Contbr. articles to profl. jours.; assoc. editor: Mich. Law Rev., 1971—73. Mem.: Am. Law Inst., ABA. Office: Williams & Connolly 725 12th St NW Washington DC 20005-5901 Office Phone: 202-434-5117. Office Fax: 202-434-5705. E-mail: jvilla@wc.com. *

VILLABLANCA, JAIME ROLANDO, neuroscientist, medical educator; b. Chillàn, Chile, Feb. 1929; arrived in U.S., 1971, naturalized, 1985; s. Ernesto and Teresa (Hernàndez) V.; m. Guillermina Nieto, Dec. 3, 1955; children: Amparo C., Jaime G., Pablo J., Francis X., Claudio I. Bachelor in Biology, Nat. Inst. Chile, 1946; licentiate medicine, U. Chile, 1953, MD, 1954. Cert. neurophysiologist. Rockefeller Found. postdoctoral fellow in physiology John Hopkins and Harvard Med. Schs., 1959-61; Fogarty internat. rsch. fellow in anatomy UCLA, 1966-68, assoc. research anatomist and psychiatrist, 1971-72; assoc. prof. psychiatry and biobehavioral scis. UCLA Sch. Medicine, 1972-76; prof. psychiatry and biobehavioral scis. UCLA, 1976—2004, prof. neurobiology, 1977—2004, disting. prof. psychiatry and biobehavioral scis., neurobiology, 2004—07, disting. emeritus prof., 2007—. Mem. faculty U. Chile Sch. Medicine, 1954-71, prof. exptl. medicine, 1970-71; vis. prof. neurobiology Cath. U. Chile Sch. Medicine, 1974; cons. in field. Author numerous rsch. papers, book chpts., abstracts; chief regional editor Developmental Brain Dysfunction, 1988-99. Decorated Order Francisco de Miranda (Venezuela), 1987; recipient Premio Reina Sofia, Madrid, 1990, Lifetime Achievement award UCLA Sch. Medicine, 2001, Emeritus award Colegio Medico de Chile, 2004; fellow Rockefeller Found., 1959-61, Fogarty Internat. Rsch. fellow NIH, 1966-68; grantee USAF Office Sci. Rsch., 1962-65, Found. Fund Rsch. Psychiatry, 1969-72, USPHS-Nat. Inst. Child Human Devel., 1972-96, USPHS-Nat. Inst. Drug Abuse, 1981-85, USPHS-Nat. Inst. Neurol. Disorders and Stroke, 1988-92, Fgn. Scientist Traveling grant Tokyo Met. Govt., 1995. Mem. AAAS, AAUP, Sleep Rsch. Soc. (Significant Early Contbr. award 2003), Mental Retardation Rsch. Ctr., Brain Rsch. Inst., Internat. Brain Rsch. Orgn., Am. Physiol. Soc., Soc. for Neurosci., Assn. Venezolana Padres de Niños Excepcionales, Soc. Child and Adolescent Psychiatry and Neurology (Chile, hon.), Johns Hopkins Med. and Surg. Assn., Sigma Xi. Home: 200 Surfview Dr Pacific Palisades CA 90272-2911 Office: UCLA Dept Psychiatry & Biobehavioral Scis Los Angeles CA 90024-1759 Home Phone: 310-459-2452. Business E-Mail: jvillablanca@mednet.ucla.edu.

VILLACIAN, VANESSA LUISA, psychologist; b. Miami, Fla., Sept. 14, 1973; d. Fernando and Tania Luisa (Alvarez) Villacian; m. Robert Pagés, Dec. 23, 2004. Psy.D. utmost distinction, Carlos Albizu U., Miami, 2000. Cert. hypnotherapist. Pres. The Answers Centre, Miami, 2002—. Clin. dir. Oasis, Miami, 2005. Mem.: APA, Psi Chi. Avocation: exercise. Home: 199 Edgewater Dr Coral Gables FL 33133 Office: The Answers Centre 7171 SW 62nd Ave 301 South Miami FL 33143 Office Phone: 305-308-2178. Personal E-mail: drvpages@yahoo.com.

VILLACORTA, YBET, lawyer; BA, Rutgers U., 1978, MS, 1982; PhD in bioinorganic chemistry, MIT, 1987; JD, Fordham U., 1991. Bar: NJ 1992, NY 1992, DC 1999. Ptnr., patent atty. Katten Muchin Zavis Rosenman, Washington, DC. Mem.: ABA, NY Bar Assn., NJ Bar Assn., DC Bar Assn., Am. Intellectual Property Law Assn. Office: Katten Muchin Zavis Rosenman East Lobby, Ste 700 1025 Thomas Jefferson St. NW Washington DC 20007 Office Phone: 202-625-3838. Office Fax: 202-339-8292. E-mail: ybet.villacorta@kmzr.com.

VILLAGOMEZ, TIMOTHY P., lieutenant governor; b. Sept. 10, 1962; s. Jose T. and Rita P. Villagomez; m. Margaret E. Keene; children: Renaesha, Jose, Rita, Juanita, Timmy, Kinda Rose. BS, San Diego U., 1987. Rep. Dist. 1 Commonwealth No. Mariana Islands Legislature, 2004—06, vice spkr., 2004—06, chmn. Pub. Utilities, Transp., and Comm. Com., 2004—06; lt. gov. Commonwealth No. Mariana Islands, 2006—. Construction & design engr. Commonwealth Utilities Corp., dep. exec. dir., exec. dir., 1994—2002; pacific regulator Micronesia Telecommunications & Cable TV Ops., 1994—2002. Chmn. Gov.'s Declaration Task Force Water State of Emergency, 1995—99, Nat. Rehab. Adv. Coun.; mem. Housing Task Force, 1999—2001, Comml. Devel. & Capital Improvement/Fed. Projects Task Force. Named Govt. Businessman of Yr., Saipan C. of C., 2000; recipient Innovation Award, Nat. Assn. State Facilities, 1998, 1999. Mem.: ASCE, Am. Gen. Contractors, Am. Pub. Power Assn., Pacific Power Assn., Assn. Pacific Island Legislatures (pres. 2004), Jr. Golf Assn. Office: Lt Gov Office of Gov Caller Box 10007 Saipan MP 96950 Office Phone: 670-664-8876. Office Fax: 670-664-2311. E-mail: tpvillagomez@itecnmi.com.

VILLAIRE, HOLLY HENNEN HOOD, theater producer, director, actress, educator; b. Yonkers, NY, Apr. 11, 1944; d. John Wilson and Adele Jelonek (Deer) Hood. BA (summa cum laude), U. Detroit, 1964; MA, U. Mich., 1967. Cert. of studies Centre Dramatique Nat. du Sud Est, France, 1965. Assoc. artistic dir. Hamm & Clov Stage Co., Yonkers, NY, 1973—2001, producing artistic dir., 2001—; prodr. Olympic Arts Festival (Ensemble Studio Theatre), 1984; asst. prof. Allentown Coll. (now De Sales U.), 1991—92, Vassar Coll., 1992. Dir. grad. showcases Am. Musical and Dramatic Acad., 1992—95; screening, finals judge U. Resident Theatre Assn. Auditions, 1993—95; finals judge Region 2 Am. Coll. Theatre Festival, 1993—94; guest spkr. Disting. Artist Forum with James Earl Jones, U. Mich., 1993; guest artist, S.W. Gas Disting. Artist lectr. UNLV, Las Vegas, 1994; forum prodr. Actor's Ctr., 1996; casting cons. Stratford Festival Theatre, Conn., 1998; adj. prof. Mercy Coll., 2000—. Actor: Antony and Cleopatra (Pitts. Press award as Best Actress, 1989), (Off-Broadway) God Bless You, Mr. Rosewater, Bklyn. Acad. Music Theatre Company (BAM); dir.: Car, Berlin Festival, 1973; actor: Coming Around Again: A Concert in Tribute to Christopher Reeve, 1997; (Broadway plays) Habeas Corpus, Scapino, (theatre) On Borrowed Time, 1965, Our Town, 1966, Return the Rain, 1971, This Property is Condemned, 1972, Eyes of Chalk, 1972, Talk to Me Like the Rain and Let Me Listen, 1972; dir.: Anam, 2001, An Aisling Christmas, 2002, Anam Cara, 2003, Of Pubs and Parishes, 2004, Ardnaglass on the Air, 2005, A Touch of the Playright, 2006; prodr.: The Ring, 2006, Hispanic Heritage Cultural Weekend, 2006. Arts Alive grantee, Westchester Arts Coun. (NYSCA), 2003, 2004, 2005, 2006, NEA, 2006. Mem.: Actor's Equity Assn., AFTRA, SAG. Office Phone: 914-963-6222. Business E-Mail: hvillaire@hammandclov.org.

VILLA-KOMAROFF, LYDIA, molecular biologist, educator, academic administrator; b. Las Vegas, N.Mex., Aug. 7, 1947; d. John Dias and Drucilla (Jaramillo) V.; m. Anthony Leader Komaroff, June 18, 1970. BA, Goucher Coll., 1970; PhD, MIT, 1975; DSc (hon.), St. Thomas U., 1996, Pine Manor Coll., 1997; PhD (hon.), Goucher Coll., 1997. Rsch. fellow Harvard U., Cambridge, 1975-78; asst. prof. dept. microbiology U. Mass. Med. Ctr., Worcester, 1978-81, assoc. prof. dept. molecular genetics micro, 1982-85; assoc. prof. dept. neurology Harvard Med. Sch., Boston, 1986-95; sr. rsch. assoc. neurology Children's Hosp., Boston, 1985-95, assoc. dir. mental retardation rsch. ctr., 1987-94; prof. dept. neurology Northwestern U., Evanston, Ill., 1995—2002, assoc. v.p. rsch., 1995-97, v.p. rsch., 1998—2002; v.p. for rsch., COO, Whitehead Inst. for Biomed. Rsch., Cambridge, Mass., 2003—05; chief sci. officer Cytonome, Inc., 2005—; CEO Ctyonome Inc., 2006—. Mem. mammalian genetics study sect. NIH, 1982-84, mem. reviewers rsch., 1989, mem. neurol. disorders program project rev. com., 1989-94; mem. adv. bd. Biol. Sci. Directorate, NSF, 1994-99; bd. dirs. Nat. Ctr. Genome Rsch., 1995-00, TransKaryotic Therapies, 2003-05, chair 2005; mem. adv. coun. Nat. Inst. Neurol. Disorders and Stroke, NIH, 2000-04; bd. trustees Pine Manor Coll., 2004—; sr. lectr. Sloan Sch. Mgmt. MIT, 2003--05; bd. chair Pine Manor Coll., 2007-. Contbr. articles and abstracts to profl. jour.; patentee in field. Recipient Hispanic Engr. Nat. Achievement award, 1992, Nat. Achievement award Hispanic Mag., 1996; inducted Hispanic Engr. Nat. Achievement Hall of Fame, 1999; selected 50 most important Hispanics by "business & Tech., Hispanic Engr. & Info. Tech." mag. 2003; Helen Hay Whitney Found. fellow, 1975-78; NIH grantee, 1978-85, 89-96. Mem. AAAS (bd. dirs. 2000-05), Am. Soc. Microbiology, Assn. for Women in Sci., Soc. for Neurosci., Am. Soc. Cell Biology, Soc. for Advancement Chicanos and Native Ams. in Sci. (founding, bd. dir. 1987-93, v.p. 1990-93). Office Phone: 617-330-5030 ext. 354. Business E-Mail: lvk@alum.mit.edu.

VILLANO, STEPHEN PAUL, lawyer; b. Fort Meade, Md., Aug. 29, 1961; s. Michael Charles and Clair Elizabeth Villano; m. Christina Groll. BS, U. Colo., 1982; JD, Hastings Coll. Law, 1986. Assoc. Holland & Hart LLP, Denver, 1986—91, of counsel, 1997—99, ptnr., 2000—; counsel Jones Intercable, Inc., Englewood, Colo., 1992—97. Bd. dirs. Mile High chpt. ARC, Denver, 2006—. Office: Holland & Hart 555 17th St Ste 3200 Denver CO 80202 Office Phone: 303-295-8000. Office Fax: 303-295-8261.

VILLANUEVA, BENITO, physician, educator; b. Aug. 27, 1943; MD, U. Beunos Aires, 1967. Cert. Am. Bd. Ob-gyn. Pres. ob-gyn Georgetown U., Washington, 1968—72; fellow reproductive endocrinology U. Wash., Seattle, 1972—74; prof. reproductive medicine U. Calif., San Diego, 1974—79; founder IGO Med. Group, San Diego, 1979. Recipient award, Am. Soc. Reproductive Medicine, 1979, Pacific Coast Reproductive Soc., 1979. Fellow: ACOG.

VILLARAIGOSA, ANTONIO RAMON, mayor; b. East LA, Jan. 23, 1953; m. Corina Raigosa, 1987 (separated 2007); children: Marisela, Prisila, Antonio Jr., Natilia Fe. BA in History, UCLA, 1977; JD, People's Coll. of Law, 1985. Mem. Calif. State Assembly, 1995—2001, Dem. whip and mem. appropriations and budget coms., majority leader, 1997, speaker, 1998—2001; city councilman, dist. 14 LA City Coun., 2003—05; mayor City of LA, 2005—. Mem. LA Met. Transp. Bd., 1990—94; nat. co-chair Kerry Presdl. Campaign, 2003—04; chair LA City Coun. Transp. Com.; bd. dirs. Met. Transit Authority. Mem. Greater Eastside Voter Registration and Edn. Project, Jobs with Peace, LAUSD Mex. Am. Edn. Commn., L.A. Ctr. for Law and Justice. Named one of 25 Most Influential Hispanics, Time Mag., 2005; recipient Golden Plate award, Acad. Achievement, 2006. Achievements include first Latino mayor for LA since Cristobal Aguilar left office in 1872. also: Ste 3200 725 S Figueroa St Los Angeles CA 90017-5432 Office: Office of Mayor City Hall 200 North Spring St Los Angeles CA 90012 *

VILLAREAL, PATRICIA J., lawyer; b. Sonora, Calif., Aug. 27, 1951; BA in Polit. sci., Mount Vernon Coll., 1975; JD, Harvard U., 1980. Bar: Tex. 1980. Law clk. to Judge H. Barefoot Sanders U.S. Dist. Ct. (no. dist.) Tex., 1980-82; mem. Jones Day (formerly Jones, Day, Reavis & Pogue), Dallas; ptnr. and chair, new assoc. recruiting Jones Day, Dallas. Spl. asst. Ho. Reps. Judiciary Com., 1975-77 Office: Jones Day 2727 N Harwood St Dallas TX 75201-1515 Office Phone: 214-969-2973. Business E-Mail: pjvillareal@jonesday.com.

VILLAROSA, SHARI, ambassador; BA in Internat. Studies, U. NC, Chapel Hill; JD, Coll. William and Mary. Diplomat in residence East-West Ctr., Honolulu; desk officer Office Investment Affairs US Dept. State, Washington, Singapore and Indonesia desk officer, dep. dir. Office Burma, Cambodia, Laos, Thailand and Vietnam Affairs, spl. asst. to undersecretary econ. affairs, dir. Philippines, Malaysia, Brunei, Singapore Affairs, East Asia and Pacific Bur., US Chargé d'Affaires to Burma Rangoon, 2005—. Office: DOS Amb 4250 Rangoon Pl Washington DC 20521-4250 *

VILLARREAL, CARLOS CASTAÑEDA, engineering executive; b. Brownsville, Tex., Nov. 9, 1924; s. Jesus Jose and Elisa L. (Castañeda) Villarreal; m. Doris Ann Akers, Sept. 10, 1948 (dec. 1995); children: Timothy Hill, David Akers; m. June Ricchezza McElroy, Oct. 3, 2002. BS, US Naval Acad., 1948; MS, US Navy Postgrad. Sch., 1950; LLD (hon.), St. Mary's U., 1972. Registered profl. engr. Commd. ensign US Navy, 1949, advanced through grades to lt., 1956; comdg. officer U.S.S. Rhea, 1951, U.S.S. Osprey, 1952; comdr. Mine Divsn. 31, 1953; instr. elec. engring. US Naval Acad., 1954—56; resigned, 1956; mgr. marine and indsl. operation Gen. Electric Co., 1956—66; v.p. mktg. and adminstrn. Marquardt Corp., 1966—69; adminstr. Urban Mass Transit Adminstrn., Dept. Transp., Washington, 1969—73; commr. Postal Rate Commn., 1973—79, vice chmn., 1975—79; v.p. Washington ops. Wilbur Smith and Assocs., Fairfax, Va., 1979—84, sr. v.p., 1984—86, exec. v.p., 1987—, also bd. dirs. Lectr. in field; mem. industry sector adv. com. Dept. Commerce; mem. sect. 13 adv. com. Dept. Transp., 1983—86. Contbr. articles to profl. jours. Mem. devel. com. Wolftrap Farm Pk. Performing Arts, 1973—78; bd. edn. St. Elizabeth Sch.; bd. dirs. Assoc. Cath. Charities, 1983—86; chmn. fin. com. Cath. Charities, USA; coun. mem. St. Elizabeth Ch., 1982—86, chmn. fin. com.; active John Carrol Soc. Decorated knight Sovereign Mil. Hospitaller Order St. John of Jerusalem of Rhodes and Malta, knight equestrian Order of Holy Sepulchre of Jerusalem, knight comdr.; recipient Outstanding Achievement award, Dept. Transp., 1974. Fellow: ASCE, Am. Cons. Engrs. Coun. (vice chmn. interna. com.); mem.: NSPE (pres. DC soc. 1986—87, bd. dirs. 1988—91), IEEE, Intelligent Transp. Soc. Am. (chmn. fin. com., bd. dirs.), Inst. Traffic Engrs., Inst. World Politics, Internat. Bridge, Tunnel and Turnpike Assn., Washington Soc. Engrs., Transp. Rsch. Bd., Am. Rds. and Transp. Builders Assn. (chmn. pub. transp. adv. coun.), Soc. Am. Mil. Engrs., Soc. Naval Archs. and Marine Engrs., Am. Pub. Transit Assn., Army-Navy Club (pres. 1999—2004), Univ. Club. Republican. Roman Catholic. Office: Wilbur Smith Assocs 300 Williams Dr Ste 300 Fairfax VA 22031 Office Phone: 703-698-9780. Personal E-mail: cvillarreal-1@comcast.com. Business E-Mail: cvillarreal@wilbursmith.com.

VILLARREAL, CHRISTIE M., lawyer; b. Laredo, Tex., Dec. 9, 1976; BA cum laude, St. Mary's U. San Antonio, 1998, JD cum laude, 2001. Bar: Tex. 2001, US Dist. Ct. (no. dist. Tex.). Briefing atty. to Chief Justice Alma L. Lopez 4th Ct. Appeals, San Antonio, 2001—02; assoc. Godwin, Pappas, Langley & Ronquillo, L.L.P., Dallas, 2002—. Named a Rising Star, Tex. Super Lawyers mag., 2006. Mem.: Dallas Hispanic Bar Assn., Dallas Assn. Young Lawyers, Hispanic Nat. Bar Assn., ABA, Dallas Bar Assn. Office: Godwin Pappas Langley Ronquillo LLP Renaissance Tower Ste 1700 1201 Elm St Dallas TX 75270 Office Phone: 214-939-8675. E-mail: cvillarreal@godwinpappas.com. *

VILLARREAL, JUNE PATRICIA, retired sales executive; b. Atlantic City, Sept. 26, 1929; d. Edmund N. and Dorothy R. (McDowell) Ricchezza; m. Ottavio Gelmi, Dec. 16, 1954 (div. 1964); 1 child, Alessandra; m. Robert Joseph McElroy, Oct. 16, 1970 (dec. May 1974); m. Carlos Castañeda Villarreal, Oct. 3, 2002. Student, Temple U., 1947-48, Georgetown U., 1951-53. Staff mem. Am. Consulate Gen., Milan, 1954; legis. asst. U.S. Senate, Washington, 1956; social sec. Amb. of Finland, Washington, 1958; adminstrv. asst., translator Roosevelt and Clark Lobbyists, 1958—59; legis. asst. to congressman Washington, 1960-65; sr. assoc. Gillmore M. Perry Co., Washington, 1965-76; sales exec., cons., 1980-87; ptnr. Mfrs. Representatives Internat., Washington, 1987-97; ret., 1997. Pres. Spanish-Portugese Study Group, 1994—95. Mem.: Alliance Française, D.C. League Rep. Women, Pan Am. Round Table, John Carroll Soc., Georgetown U. Alumni Assn., Equestrian Order Holy Sepulchre of Jerusalem (Lady Comdr. 2003—), Army Navy Club (Washington). Republican. Roman Catholic. Home: 4000 Cathedral Ave NW Apt 208B Washington DC 20016-5254 Personal E-mail: jprvilla@verizon.net.

VILLARREAL, ROBERTO ESCAMILLA, retired political science researcher, educator, administrator; b. Karnes City, Tex., Oct. 20, 1936; s. Epifanio Sr. and Antonia (Escamilla) V.; m. Norma Pedraza, June 12, 1965; children: Marco Dante, Carlo Renato, Ethel Minerva. BS, Tex. A&I U., 1962, MS, 1966; MA, U. Okla., 1972, PhD, 1975. Tchr. Pawnee Ind. Sch. Dist., Tex., 1962-63, Pharr-San Juan-Alamo Ind. Sch. Dist., Tex., 1963-66; instr. Bee County Coll., Beeville, Tex., 1967-70, U. Okla., Norman, 1970-72; chmn. Bee County Coll., Dept. Social Seis., 1972-73; dir. Bee County Coll., Fed. Programs, 1973-76; prof. U. Tex. Polit Sci. Dept., El Paso, 1976—2003, chmn., 1987—, prof. emeritus, 2003—. Advisor U. Tex. System, Austin, 1990-91; assoc. v.p. acad. affairs U. Tex., El Paso, 1991-96; exec. dir. Internat. Consortium for Health and Environ. Security, 2003— Author: Chicano Elites and Non-Elites, 1979; author/editor: Latino Empowerment, 1988, Latinos and Political Coalitions, 1991. Mem. exec. com. Hispanic Leadership Inst., El Paso, 1989— Recipient Ford Found. fellowship, 1979-71, Disting. Svc. award U. Tex., El Paso, 1985, Outstanding Achievement award in edn. Mex. Am. Bar Assn., 1991; Fulbright scholar, Mex., 1998-99; named one of 100 Most Influential Hispanics in U.S., Hispanic Bus., Mag., 1997 Mem. Nat. Assn. Chicano Studies (exec. officer 1985-86), Am. Assn. for Higher Edn. (chair Hispanic Caucus 199), Tex. Assn. Coll. Tchrs. (v.p. 1979-80, pres. 1980-82) Democrat. Roman Catholic. Home: 172 Oak Fields Dr Floresville TX 78114 Office: AFIOH/RSRH 2513 Kennedy Cir Brooks City-Base TX 78235-5226 Office Phone: 210-710-8698. Personal E-mail: revilla@tgti.net.

VILLARRUBIA, GLENDA BOONE, reading specialist, reading coordinator, educational consultant, educator; d. Albert Jewel and Tommie Lee Boone; m. David Daniel Villarrubia, Apr. 2, 1977; children: David Daniel Jr., Steven Joseph, John Albert. BA, Southeastern La. U., 1976, MBA, 1978. La. Teaching Certificate 1976, Reading Specialist Certification 1978, Behavior Specialist Certification 2000. Tchr. Wash. Parish Schools, Franklinton, La., 1976—79; tchr./coord. Jefferson Parish Schools, New Orleans, 1979; tchr. Ouachita Parish, Monroe, La., 1980; tchr. edn. Bogalusa City Schools, La., 1981—82, tchr., 1982—96, individualized edn. program cons., 1999—2005, individualized edn. program facilitator, resource teachers spl. edn., 1998—2000, dir./supr. spl. edn., 2000—01, individualized edn. program facilitator, 2001—04, compliance monitoring facilitator, 2005—. Spl. edn. cons., 2000; owner The Tchrs. Desk, 1989—99. Mem. Crisis Prevention Inst.; troop supporter Bogalusa, La, 2002—05; tiger cub leader Boy Scouts Am., Bogalusa, 1985; 4-H leader sponsor Bogalusa City Schools, 1985; beta club leader Wash. Parish Schools, 1977. Recipient Tchr. of Yr., Bogalusa City Schools, 1983, 1993, La. Dept. Edn., 1992. Mem.: Associated Profl. Educators of La., La. Pub. Sch. Rels. Assn., La. Edn. Rsch. Assn., La. Assn. Supervision and Curriculum Devel., La. Assn. Educators, Learning Disability Assn., La. Assn. Sch. Execs., Nat. Edn. Assn., Coun. Exceptional Children, Southeastern La. Alumni Assn., Alpha Signa Tau. Avocations: travel, gardening, church, reading. Home: 21486 Hwy 436 Bogalusa LA 70427 Office Phone: 985-281-2148. Personal E-mail: glenda90@hotmail.com.

VILLARRUBIA, TODD M., lawyer; b. New Orleans, Aug. 13, 1966; BA, U. New Orleans, 1988; JD, La. State U., 1992; LLM in Taxation, Emory U., 1993. Bar: La. 1992, US Tax Ct., cert.: La. State Bar Assn. (estate planning and adminstrn.). Atty. Steeg & O'Connor; ptnr. Livaccari, Villarrubia & Lemmon, LLC; of counsel Blue Williams, LLP, Metairie, La., 2005—. Contbr. articles to profl. publs. Named one of Top 100 Attys., Worth mag., 2005—06. Mem.: New Orleans Estate Planning Coun., ABA, La. Bar Assn., New Orleans Bar Assn. Office: Blue Williams LLP 3421 N Causeway Blvd 9th Fl Metairie LA 70002 Office Phone: 504-831-4091. Office Fax: 504-837-1182. E-mail: tvillarrubia@bluewilliams.com. *

VILLAVASO, STEPHEN DONALD, lawyer, urban planner; b. New Orleans, July 12, 1949; s. Donald Philip and Jacklyn (Tully) V.; m. Regina Smith, Apr. 17, 1971; children: Christine Regina, Stephen Warner. BS in Econs., U. New Orleans, 1971, M in Urban and Regional Planning, 1976; JD, Loyola U., New Orleans, 1981. Bar: La. 1982; recognized ct. expert in land use, planning and zoning. Urban and regional planner Barnard & Thomas, New Orleans, 1976-78; dir. analysis and planning Office of Mayor, City of New Orleans, 1978-81; counsel for planning and devel. Office of City Atty., City of New Orleans, 1983-84; dir. planning and environ. affairs Tecon Realty, New Orleans, 1981-83; v.p. for planning and project mgmt. Morphy, Makofsky, Mumphrey & Masson, New Orleans, 1984-89; bus. devel. mgr. Waste Mgmt., Inc., New Orleans, 1989-96; pres. Villavaso & Assocs., LLC, New Orleans, 1996—, Brownfields Redevel. Profls. LLC, New Orleans, 2000—. Bd. dirs. Regional Loan Corp.; guest lectr., adj. prof. Coll. of Urban and Pub. Affairs, U. New Orleans, 1976—; spl. instr. grad. studies in urban planning So. U. New Orleans, 1987—. Bd. dirs. New Orleans Traffic and Transp. Bur., 1981-86, Riverfront Awareness, New Orleans, 1984-86; bd. dirs. Vols. Am. Greater New Orleans, 1987-96, vice chmn., 1990, chmn. bd., 1992-95. With USN, 1971-74. Named one of Outstanding Young Men of Am., 1980, 82. Fellow: Am. Inst. of Cert. Planners; mem.: ABA, La. Bar Assn., Urban Land Inst., Am. Planning Assn. (pres. La. divsn. 1980—84, disting. svc. award 1985), U. New Orleans Alumni Assn. (bd. dir. 1990—), Delta Sigma Pi (pres. 1971), Phi Kappa Phi, Omicron Delta Kappa. Democrat. Roman Catholic. Avocations: stamp collecting/philately, camping, travel. Business E-Mail: svillavaso1@cox.net.

VILLAVAZO, KRISTEN LEE, language educator; b. Greenfield, Mass., Nov. 15, 1968; d. John Charles and Carol Ann Graves; m. Alfredo Villavazo, July 27, 1996; children: Amelia Carolina, Ana Sofia, Adriana Isabella. BA, Smith Coll., Northampton, Mass., 1991; M Bilingual Edn., U. Tex., San Antonio, 2000. English asst. Coll. les Capuchines, Lyon, France, 1991—92; bilingual English tchr. Tec. de Monterrey, Guadalajara, Mexico, 1992—96; French tchr. St. Mary's Hall, San Antonio, 1997—. Mem.: Am. Tchrs. Fgn. Lang., Am. Assn. Tchrs. French. Home: 16515 Pemcanyon San Antonio TX 78240

VILLAVECES, JAMES WALTER, allergist, immunologist, consultant; b. San Luis Obispo, Calif., Nov. 4, 1933; s. Robert and Solita (Combariza) V. BA, UCLA, 1955; MD, U. Calif. Med. Sch., 1960. Diplomate Am. Bd. Allergy and Immunology. Intern Sawtelle VA Hosp., LA, 1960-61; preceptorship in adult allergy L.A. County Hosp., LA, 1964-66; fellow in allergy White Meml. CCM, LA, 1966-67; co-chief allergy divsn. Ventura (Calif.) Med. Ctr., 1969—87; practice medicine specializing in allergy-immunology Ventura, 1984—. Founder botanical weed allergy walks, 1970; cons. in allergy/immunology, Blue Cross, 1991-96; medical invention cons., Inventor Internat., Inc.; inventor, cons. Sprixx: Alcohol-gel Clip on Dispensers, 2001, 3M; mem. Pharmacy and Therapeutics Com., Wellpoint (Blue Cross Calif.) Inc., 1991-96; prodr. Ventura County cities street-tree guide for asthma patients; peer reviewer Blue Cross So. Calif. Wellpoint, 1980, 1994-95; cons., lectr., peer reviewer in field. Writer, prodr., editor films; contbr. articles on biology of pollens and molds of Ventura County to profl. jours.; patentee in field. Bd. dir. Am. Lung Assn., Ventura, 1969-85, pres., 1974, advisor air pollution control com., 1971-74; judge Ventura Sci. Fair, 1970-85; lectr. in field. Recipient commendation County Bd. Suprs., Ventura, 1974; named one of Am.'s Top Physicians Consumers Rsch. Coun. Am., 2003-05. Fellow Am. Acad. Allergy, Asthma, Immunology, Am. Coll. Allergy, Asthma, Immunology; mem. Calif. Soc. Allergy-Immunology, Calif. Med. Assn., Ventura County Med. Assn., Gold Coast Tri-County Allergy Soc. (pres. 1987), CAL Club (hon.), Ventura County Sports Hall of Fame (mem. founding bd.), Mensa. Republican. Achievements include development of infection protection device for hospital and food service establishments. Avocations: writing, photography, lecturing, pistol target shooting, fishing. Home: 928 High Point Dr Ventura CA 93003-1415 Office: Dudley Profl Ctr 4080 Loma Vista Rd Ste M Ventura CA 93003-1811 Office Phone: 805-656-0433. Personal E-mail: jvillavece@aol.com, jvillavece@yahoo.com, allergycare2006@yahoo.com.

VILLELLA, EDWARD JOSEPH, dancer, choreographer, performing arts association administrator; b. Long Island, NY, Oct. 1, 1936; s. Joseph and Mildred (DeGiovanni) Villella; m. Janet Greschler (div.); 1 child, Roddy; m. Linda Carbonetta; children: Christa Francesca, Lauren. BS in Marine Transp., NY State Maritime Coll., 1957; LHD (hon.), Boston Conservatory, 1985, degree (hon.), Union Coll., Schenectady, NY, 1991; DHL (hon.), St. Thomas U., Miami, Fla., 1994, U. SC, 1997; DFA (hon.), SUNY Maritime Coll., Bronx, 1998; Doctor (hon.), Fla. Atlantic U., 2000, U. NC, Asheville, 2002, Coll. Charleston, 2002; degree (hon.), LI U., 2005. Mem. N.Y.C. Ballet, 1957, soloist, 1958—60, prin. soloist, 1960—83; artistic dir. Ballet Okla., Oklahoma City, 1983—86; founding artistic dir., CEO Miami (Fla.) City Ballet, 1985—. Vis. artist U.S. Mil. Acad., West Point, 1981—82; vis. artist Salute to Balanchine residency Harvard U., 1999—2000; vis. prof. dance U. Iowa, 1981; resident Heritage chair arts and cultural criticism George Mason U.; Dorthy F. Schmidt artist-in-residence Coll. of Arts and Letters, 2000—01. Dancer Symphony C., Scotch Symphony, We. Symphony, Donizetti Variations, Swan Lake, La Source, The Nutcracker, Agon, Stars and Stripes, The Prodigal Son, The Figure in the Carpet, 1960, Electronics, 1961, A Midsummer Night's Dream, 1962, Bugaku, 1963, Tarantella, 1964, Harlequinade, 1965, The Brahms-Schoenberg Quartet, 1966, Jewels, 1967, Symphony in Three Movements, 1972, Schéhérazade, 1975, choreographer Narkissas, 1966, Shostakovitch Ballet Suite, 1972, Shenandoah, 1975, Gayane Pas de Deux, 1972, Salute to Cole, 1973, Sea Chanties, 1974, Prelude, Riffs and Fugues, 1980, dancer TV The Ed Sullivan Show, Bell Telephone Hour, Mike Douglas Show, TV spl. Harlequin, 1975 (Emmy award); co-author (autobiography): Prodigal Son, 1991. Mem. Nat. Coun. Arts, 1968—74; chmn. Commn. for Cultural Affairs, NYC, 1978; bd. visitors N.C. Sch. for Arts; mem. adv. panel Nat. Endowment for Arts; trustee Wolf Trap Found. for Arts. Named Miamian of Yr., UNICO Nat., 1993, Miracle Maker, Big Bros. Big Sisters of Greater Miami, 2003; named to Fla. Artists Hall of Fame, 1997, Dance Hall of Fame, 2004; recipient Dance Mag. award, 1964, Lions of Performing Arts award, N.Y. Pub. Libr., 1987, Capezio Dance award, 1989, Gold medal, Nat. Soc. Arts and Letters, 1990, William G. Anderson Merit award, AAHPERD, 1991, Nat. Medal of Arts award, 1997, Kennedy Ctr. Honors, 1997, Cultural Soc. award, Bklyn. Ctr. for Performing Arts at Bklyn. Coll., 1998, Am. Irreplaceable Dance Treasures: The First 100, Disting. Achievement award, U. Fla., 2005, U. Fla. Coll. Fine Arts, 2005; Robert J.H. Kiphuth fellow, Yale U., 2001, Hon. Theater Arts Br. fellow, U.S. Imperial Soc. Tchrs. Dancing, 2003. *

VILLERS, PHILIPPE, mechanical engineer; b. Paris, June 20, 1935; arrived in U.S., 1940, naturalized, 1946; s. Raymond and Garda (Schmidt) Villers; m. Annie Louise Young, July 13, 1957 (div. 1973); children: Jocelyn Anne(dec.), Renata Jane; m. Katherine Stephan, 1973; children: Noel Stephan, Carolyn Grace. AB in Applied Scis. cum laude, Harvard U., 1955; SM in Mech. Engring, MIT, 1960. Mem. mfg. tng. program GE, 1955-58; project engr. Perkin-Elmer Corp., Wilton, Conn., 1959-62; project engr. Apollo Antenna pointings sensor Barnes Engring. Co., Stamford, Conn., 1962-65; project mgr. Advanced Products Ctr., Link Group, Gen. Precision, Inc., Binghamton, NY, 1965-67; mgr. advanced products Concord Control, Inc., Boston, 1967-69; co-founder, sr. v.p., dir. Computervision Corp., Bedford, Mass., 1969-80; founder, pres., dir. Automatix, Inc., Billerica, Mass., 1980-84; chmn. bd. Automatix Inc., Billerica, Mass., 1984-86; founder, pres., dir. Cognition Inc., 1985-88. Bd. dir. Xyvision, Inc., Wakefield, Mass., chmn., 1992—94; bd. dir. Grainpro Inc., Concord, Mass., pres., 1996—; bd. dir. Voxiva Inc., 2001—07, Mercy Corps, United Villages, Herndon Alliance, 2006—. Del. Dem. Nat. Conv., 1988, 1992; mem. Dem. Town Com., Wilton, 1963, Concord, Mass., 1978—, chmn., 1984—96; mem. Harvard Com. Univ. Resources, 1981—92; mem. various vis. coms. MIT, 1981—91; mem. vis. com. Nat. Bur. Stds., 1981—84; trustee U. Lowell, 1985—91; mem. adv. bd. Inst. Global Leadership Tufts U., Medford, Mass., 2005—; founder and pres. Families U.S.A. Founds. (formerly Villers Found.), Washington, 1981—, Bay State Retiree Vol. Coun., Concord, 1989—92. Grad. fellow, NSF, 1959—60. Mem.: ACLU (pres. com. 1981—, bd. dirs. Physicians Human Rights 1991—94), ASME, IEEE, Soc. Mfg. Engrs., Unitarian-Universalist Assn. (pres. coun. 1982—86), Amnesty Internat. (bd. dirs. 1990—96, ombudsman 1992—96, mem. exec. com. 1994—96, mem. leadership coun. 1995—, coord. Concord group 15 1998—), Sigma Xi. Achievements include patents for process welding aluminum liners to steel surfaces; a horizon sensor for visible wavelength; infrared roughness testing instrument; improved thermopile construction thermal die marker; method for long term storage of a bulk biologically active commodity; solar sail applications for interpanetary probe propulsion and stabilization; method and apparatus for targetless wafer alignment; method and system for transporting and storing commodities. Home: 20 Whits End Rd Concord MA 01742-5411 Office: 200 Baker Ave Ste 309 Concord MA 01742-2170 Home Phone: 978-369-1053; Office Phone: 978-371-7400. Business E-Mail: pvillers@igc.org.

VILLFORTH, JOHN CARL, engineer, health physicist; b. Reading, Pa., Dec. 28, 1930; s. Carl and Grace L. (Fichthorn) Villforth; m. Joanne E. Heine, Sept. 12, 1953; children: Mary Jane Villforth Smith, Elaine, Jennifer Villforth Veazy. BS in San. Engring., Pa. State U., 1952, MS, 1954; MS in Physics, Vanderbilt U., 1958. Cert. Am. Bd. Health Physics. With USPHS, 1961-90; dir. Ctr. Devices and Radiol. Health, 1969-90, asst. surgeon gen., 1972-90, chief engr., 1985-89; pres. Food and Drug Law Inst., Washington, 1990—2001. Bd. dirs. Vasogen Inc., EduNeering Inc. Served to capt. USAF, 1954—61, served to rear adm. USPHS, 1961—90. Decorated DSM, Outstanding Svc. medal; recipient Outstanding Engring. Alumnus award, Pa. State U., 1987, Recognition award, HHS, 1987, Disting. Alumni award, FDA, 2000, Pa. State U., 2005; Univ. Alumni fellow, 2002. Mem.: USPHS Commd. Officers Assn. (chmn. bd. dirs. 1999—2000), Regulatory Affairs Profl. Soc., Internat. Radiation Protection Assn., Health Physics Soc. (pres. 1976—77, Elda Anderson award 1970), FDA Alumni Assn. (chmn. 2001—). Personal E-mail: jcvillforth@comcast.net. *Understand the problem! Too much energy is wasted and too many relationships are strained because we fail to understand the underlying problem before we embark on a solution.*

VILLICA-A, TAUNYA, corporate financial executive; b. 1972; Co-founder, mng. ptnr. Affinity Fin. Grp. Mem. Ariz. Town Hall; former pres. Kiwanis de Amigos; Cmty. Needs and Preparedness com. chair Am. Red Cross; bd. treasurer Tucson Hispanic Chamber of Commerce; mem. Agua Prieta Shelters. Named one of 40 Under 40, Tucson Bus. Edge, 2006. Office: Affinity Financial Group 5363 E Pima St Tucson AZ 85712 Office Phone: 520-795-3360.

VILLINES, BOBBY T., environmental services administrator, information technology manager; s. Bob M. and Sadie M. Villines; m. Annette C. Russ, Dec. 19, 1992; children: Hannah L., Sarah L. BS, East Ctrl. U., Ada, Okla., 1994; MPH, Tulane U., New Orleans, La., 2003. Registered environ. health specialist Nat. Environ. Health Assn., 1997. Field environ. health officer Indian health svc. USPHS, Many Farms, Ariz., 1995—97, Shiprock, N.Mex., 1997—2000, environ. health cons. Indian health svc. Albuquerque, 2000—04, environ. health specialist Indian health svc. Pawnee, Okla., 2004—, info. tech. specialist, 2004—. Cons. in field. Deacon Montgomery Ch. Christ, Albuquerque, 2001—04. Lt. comdr. USPHS, 1995—2007. Decorated Isolated Hardship ribbon USPHS, citation, Achievement medal, Commendation medal, Unit commendation, Outstanding Unit citation, Spl. Assignment award, Crisis Response Svc. award; named Environ. Health Specialist of Yr., Navajo Area Indian Health Svc., 1999. Mem.: Commd. Officer Assn. (assoc.), Nat. Environ. Health Assn. (assoc.). Republican. Avocations: website development, information technology, computer hardware/software maintenance. Home Phone: 405-533-1279; Office Phone: 918-762-6589.

VILLOCH, KELLY CARNEY, art director; b. Kyoto, July 22, 1950; d. William Riley and stepdaughter Hazel Fowler Carney; m. Joe D. Villoch, Aug. 9, 1969; children: Jonathan, Christopher, Jennifer. A in Fine Arts, Dade C.C., Miami, Fla., 1971; student, Metro Fine Arts, 1973-74, Fla. Internat. U., 1985-88. Design asst. Lanvin, Miami, 1971—74, Fieldcrest, Miami, 1974-77; art dir. Advercolor, Miami, 1977-78; art dir. copywriter ABC, Miami, 1978-89; writer Armed Forces Radio & TV Network; multimedia dir. ADVITEC, 1989-91; art dir. writer Miami Write, 1979—89; owner Beach Point Prodns., 1992—; editor-in-chief L'Avenue Mag., 1998—. Lectr. Miami Dade C.C., cons. Studio Masters, North Miami, 1979-89; writer Lucent Techs., Telephonetics, Algorhythm, Intertel, 1997—; creative mktg. dir. Raintree Media, 2000. Prin. works include mixed media, 1974 (Best of Show 1974), pen and ink drawing, 1988 (Best Poster 1988); writer, dir., editor, prodr. (video film) Bif, 1988, Drink + Drive = Die, 1994; scriptwriter (film) The Raft, 1994, (charity video) Rosie O'Donnell, 2002; writer, dir., prodr. (pub. svc. announcement) Reading is the Real Adventure, 1990; film editor Talent Times Mag.; author: Winds of Freedom, 1994; art dir., exec. com. Miami Hispanic Media Conf., 1992, 93, 94; editor-in-chief, film editor: In Grove Miami Mag., 1994-96; webmaster, web content provider, website design cons., writer, graphic artist Guru Comms., 1996; editor-in-chief L'Avenue Mag., Miami Mag., Fla. Journey and Miami Guide, 1998-99, Paladar mag., 2002, Decasa mag., 2002, Flash Animation: Passionate Nomad-A Journey Through Cairo, 2002, Collins Ave. Mag., Markee Mag., 2006; web content provider WEBCOM; webmaster Miami Metro Mag., 2000; sr. editor Channels Intl. Mag., 2001; web site designer, multimedia dir.; creative mktg. dir. Light Sculptor Jim Morrison, 2005. State of Fla. grantee LimeLite Studios, Inc., 1990, William Douglas Pawley Found. grantee, Frances Wolfson scholar, Cultural Consortium grantee, 1993. Mem. Am. Film Inst., Phi Beta Kappa. Avocations: animation, printmaking, skin diving, boating, painting. Personal E-mail: villochk@bellsouth.net.

VILMA, JONATHAN POLYNICE, professional football player; b. Coral Gables, FL, Apr. 16, 1982; BS finance, U. Miami, 2004. Linebacker New York Jets, 2004—. Named NFL Defensive Rookie of the Yr., 2004; named to Pro Bowl, 2005.

VILSACK, TOM (THOMAS JAMES), former governor; b. Pitts., Dec. 31, 1950; adopted s. Bud and Dolly Vilsack; m. Ann Christine Bell, Aug. 1973; children: Jess, Doug. BA in History, Hamilton Coll., Clinton, NY, 1972; JD, Albany Law Sch., 1975. Pvt. practice, Mt. Pleasant, Iowa, 1975—87; mayor City of Mt. Pleasant, Iowa, 1987—92; mem. Iowa State Senate, Des Moines, 1992-98; gov. State of Iowa, Des Moines, 1999—2007; announced bid for US President in 2008; dropped out of 2008 US President bid for fin. reasons on Feb. 23, 2007. Chmn. Midwest Gov. Conf., Dem. Gov. Assn.; mem. Nat. Gov. Assn. (exec. com.); vis. prof. Drake U., 2007—; bd. dir. Carnegie Learning Inc., 2007—. Founding mem. & former chmn. Governors Biotechnology Partnership; former chmn. Ethanol Coalition; bd. dir. United Way, Mt. Pleasant; former chmn. Midwest Governor's Conference. Mem. Mt. Pleasant C. of C. (pres.), Rotary (pres.). Democrat. Office Phone: 515-281-5211. Office Fax: 515-281-6611. *

VINAR, BENJAMIN, lawyer; b. Rock Island, Ill., Apr. 10, 1935; s. Isidore and Bessie (Sherman) Vinar; m. Rochelle Weinfeld, June 17, 1962; children: Jacqueline, Dov, Elana, Daniella. BA, U. Ill., 1957; LLB, NYU, 1960. Bar: N.Y. 1961, U.S. Dist. Ct. (so. dist.) N.Y. 1962, U.S. Ct. Appeals (2d cir.) 1964, U.S. Supreme Ct. 1966, U.S. Dist. Ct. (ea. dist.) N.Y. 1971. Assoc. Donovan, Leisure, Newton & Irvine, NYC, 1961-71; pvt. practice NYC, 1971-76, Garden City, NY and NYC, 1986—; ptnr. Siff & Newman, P.C., NYC, 1976-86; assoc. Donovan, Leisure, Newton & Irvine, NYC, 1961—71; pvt. practice NYC, 1971—76, Garden City and NYC, NY, 1986—; ptnr. Siff & Newman, P.C., NYC, 1976—86. Contbr. articles to profl. jours. Mem. nat. law com. Anti-Defamation League, NYC, 1975—2000; pres. Queens Jewish Cmty. Coun., NYC, 1979—81, Young Israel of Queens Valley, NYC, 1984—86; v.p. Nat. Coun. Young Israel, 1986—90, YM-YMHA of No. Queens, NYC, 1989—91; bd. dirs. Met. Coun. on Jewish Poverty, NYC, 1984—89. Mem.: ABA, NYU Law Rev. Alumni Assn. (pres. 1981—83), Nassau Bar Assn. (past chair appellate practice com.), Phi Kappa Phi, Phi Beta Kappa, Order of Coif. Democrat. Office Phone: 718-793-9226. E-mail: vinarlaw@cs.com.

VINATIERI, ADAM MATTHEW, professional football player; b. Yanktown, SD, Dec. 28, 1972; s. Paul and Judy; m. Valerie Vinatieri. BS in Fitness and Wellness, SD State U. Kicker New Eng. Patriots, 1996—2006, Ind. Colts, 2006—. Named to AFC Pro-Bowl Team, 2003—04. Achievements include kicking a game winning field goal in Super Bowl XXXVI, XXXVIII; being a member of Super Bowl Champion New England Patriots, 2001, 03, 04, Indianapolis Colts, 2007. Office: Indpls Colts 7001 W 56th St Indianapolis IN 46254 *

VINCE, CLINTON ANDREW, lawyer; b. Bklyn., May 31, 1949; s. Tibor Andrew and Priscilla (Ward) V.; divorced; children: Matthew McHale, Jennifer Ann. AB, Trinity Coll., 1971; JD, Georgetown U., 1974. Bar: N.Y. 1975, U.S. Dist. Ct. (so. and ea. dists.) N.Y. 1975, U.S. Ct. Appeals (2nd cir.) 1975, D.C. 1976, U.S. Dist. Ct. D.C. 1976, U.S. Ct. Appeals (D.C. and 8th cirs.) 1976, U.S. Supreme Ct. 1979, U.S. Ct. Appeals (4th and 11th cirs.) 1984, U.S. Ct. Appeals (5th cir.) 1985, U.S. Ct. Appeals (10th cir.) 1988. Ptnr. Verner, Liipfert, Bernhard, McPherson & Hand, Washington, 1984—2001; mem. and ptnr. D.C. office Sullivan & Worcester, LLP, 2001—, mng. ptnr., dir. energy group, 2001—. Chief energy cons. City of New Orleans, 1983—; gen. counsel Southeastern Power Resources Com., Tucker, Ga., 1986—. Editor in chief: Energy Law Jour. of the EBA, 2004—05. Bd. dirs. Fed. City Coun., bd. trustees Keystone Energy. Mem.: ATLA, ABA, D.C. Bar Assn, Fed. Energy Bar Assn. (former chmn. bd. dir., chmn. Fed. Energy Law Jour. Found.), Econ. Club Washington, Cosmos Club. Avocations: sailing, skiing, tennis, literature, writing. Office: Sullivan & Worcester LLP 1666 K St NW Ste 700 Washington DC 20006 E-mail: cvince@sandw.com.

VINCENSI, AVIS A., sales executive, medical educator; b. Hazardville, Conn., July 10, 1949; d. George P. Vincensi and Hilda G. (Boucher) Vincensi(dec.). AS in Bus., Holyoke C.C., Mass., 1987. Registered diagnostic med. sonographer, radiologic tech., radiography, mammography. X-ray technologist Baystate Med. Ctr., Springfield, Mass., 1969—73, Cooley Dickinson Hosp., Northampton, Mass., 1971—73, Holyoke Hosp., 1974—87, sonographer, 1973—82; sonographer, supr. Providence Hosp., Holyoke, 1982—87; sonographer Diagnostic Imaging, Springfield, Mass., 1987—90; product specialist/product mktg. sales Corometrics Med. Sys., Wallingford, Conn., 1991—96; diagnostic reagent rep. Sigma Diagnostics, St. Louis, 1996—2002; clin. adj. prof. Springfield Tech. C.C., 1999—2002, assoc. prof., 2002—06, bd. dirs., 1999—2006, chair dept. sonography, 2002—06; staff sonographer Hartford Hosp., Conn., 2006—. Recipient 2 Gold medals and 1 Silver medal Tai Chi competition, 2002. Mem.: Am. Inst. Ultrasonic Medicine, Am. Registry Diagnostic Med. Sonographers. Home: 101 Acushnet Ave Springfield MA 01105-2218 Office: 85 Jefferson St Hartford CT 06106 Business E-Mail: avincensi@harthosp.org.

VINCENT, CHARLES EAGAR, JR., sportswriter; b. Beaumont, Tex., Mar. 24, 1940; s. Charles Eagar and Hazel Ruth (Balston) V.; m. Mary Jacquelyn Bertman, Aug. 8, 1959 (div. Jan. 1969); children: Lisa Marie, Dixie Ann, Charles Joseph, John Patrick; m. Patricia Helene Skinner, Mar. 28, 1970 (div. Apr. 1985); 1 child, Susanna Lee; m. Karen Judith Peterson, Aug. 17, 1985. Student, Victoria Coll., 1958-59. Reporter Victoria (Tex.) Mirror, 1958-59, Taylor (Tex.) Daily Press, 1959-60; sports writer Beaumont (Tex.) Jour., 1960-62; sports editor Galveston (Tex.) Tribune, 1962-63; sports writer San Antonio Express-News, 1963-69, Sandusky (Ohio) Register, 1969-70, Detroit Free Press, 1970-85, sports columnist, 1985-99. Author: Welcome to My World, 1994, Broken Wings, 1998, Men of Courage; Women of Strength, 2004; co-author: (with Richard Bak) The Corner, A Century of Memories at Michigan and Trumbull, 1999. Recipient 4th Pl. award Nat. AP Sports Editors, 1981, 5th Pl., 1989, 92, Sister Mary Leila Meml. award, 1991, Mich. Columnist of Yr. award, 1991, 97; Afro-Am. Night honoree, 1991, Mich. Writer of the Yr. Nat. Sportscasters and Sportswriters, 1998. Mem.: Baseball Writers Assn. Am. Avocations: travel, cooking, genealogy. Personal E-mail: Vincentcharlie@hotmail.com.

VINCENT, CHRISTINE, academic administrator; m. David Chambers; 2 children. BA in visual arts, Ill. State U. Founder Cmty. & Cultural Resource Devel. Inc., NYC; dep. dir. Ford Found., NYC, 1991—2001; pres. Maine Coll. Art, Portland, 2001—. Office: Office of President Maine College of Art 97 Spring St Portland ME 04101

VINCENT, DAVID RIDGELY, financial consultant; b. Detroit, Aug. 9, 1941; s. Charles Ridgely and Charlotte Jane (McCarroll) Vincent; m. Margaret Helen Anderson, Aug. 25, 1962 (div. 1973); children: Sandra Lee, Cheryl Ann; m. Judith Ann Gomez, July 2, 1978; children: Amber, Jesse Joseph Flores(dec.) 1 stepchild, Micheal Flores Jr. BSBA, Calif. State U., Sacramento, 1964; MBA, Calif. State U., Hayward, 1971; PhD, Somerset U., 1991. Cert. mgmt. cons. Sr. ops. analyst Aerojet Gen. Corp., Sacramento, 1960-66; contr. Hexcel Corp., Dublin, Calif., 1966-70; mng. dir. Memorex, Vienna, 1970-74; sales mgr. Ampex World Ops., Friebourg, Switzerland, 1974-76; dir. product mgmt. NCR, Sunnyvale, Calif., 1976-79; v.p. Boole & Babbage Inc., Sunnyvale, 1979-85; gen. mgr. Inst. Info. Mgmt., Sunnyvale Calif., Calif., 1979-85; pres., CEO The Info. Group, Inc., Santa Clara, Calif., 1985—2005; fin. advisor, dist. mgr. Ameriprise Fin. Svcs., Campbell, Calif., 2005—. Author: Perspectives in Information Management, Information Economics, 1983, Handbook of Information Resource Management, 1987, The Information-Based Corporation: Stakeholder Economics and the Technology Investment, 1990, Reengineering Fundamentals: Business Processes and the Global Economy, 1994—96; contbr. articles to profl. jours. Referee emeritus U.S. Soccer Fedn. Mem.: Inst. for Mgmt. Cons., Product Devel. and Mgmt. Assn., Am. Mktg. Assn., Nat. Investor Rels. Inst., Assn. Fin. Profl., World Future Soc., Soc. Competitive Intelligence Profl., Am. Electronics Assn., Nat. Alliance Bus. Econ., Silicon Valley Roundtable, Soc. Info. Mgmt. (treas.). Home: 2803 Kalliam Dr Santa Clara CA 95051-6838 Office: Ameriprise Fin Svcs Inc 1919 S Bascom Ave Campbell CA 95008 Office Phone: 408-963-2372. Business E-Mail: david.r.vincent@ampf.com.

VINCENT, DIRK L., lawyer; b. Mar. 24, 1967; BBA, Pacific Lutheran Univ., 1988; JD, Columbia Univ., 1991. Bar: Calif. 1992, Wash. 1992. Law clk. Judge Andrew J. Kleinfeld, US Ct. Appeals Ninth Cir., 1991—92; atty. Gibson, Dunn & Crutcher, LA, 1992—96; co-founder, ptnr., bus. litigation Fairbank & Vincent, LA, 1996—. Adj. prof. Loyola Law Sch., 2001—. Editor (sr., articles): Columbia Bus. Law Rev.; contbr. articles to profl. jours. Named a Rising Star, So. Calif. Super Lawyers, 2006; recipient Thomas E. Dewey prize; Stone Scholar. Mem.: ABA, Assn. Bus. Trial

Lawyers, State Bar Calif., LA County Bar Assn. Office: Fairbank & Vincent Ste 2320 11755 Wilshire Blvd Los Angeles CA 90025 Office Phone: 310-996-5520. Office Fax: 310-996-5530. Business E-Mail: dvincent@fairbankvincent.com.

VINCENT, FRANCIS THOMAS, JR., (FAY VINCENT), former baseball commissioner; b. Waterbury, Conn., May 29, 1938; s. Francis Thomas and Alice (Lynch) V.; m. Valerie McMahon, July 3, 1965; children: Anne, William, Edward. BA cum laude, Williams Coll., 1960; LLB, Yale U., 1963. Bar: Conn. 1963, N.Y. 1964, D.C. 1969. Assoc. Whitman & Ransom, NYC, 1963-68; ptnr. Caplin & Drysdale, Washington, 1968-78; assoc. dir. div. corp. fin. SEC, Washington, 1978; pres., chief exec. officer Columbia Pictures Industries, Inc., NYC, 1978-83, chmn., chief exec. officer, 1983-87; pres., chief exec. officer entertainment bus. sect. The Coca-Cola Co., NYC, 1987; dep. commr., chief oper. officer Major League Baseball, NYC, 1989, commr., 1989-92; pres. New England Collegiate Baseball League, 1998—2003. Non-exec. dir. Westfield Am. Mgmt. Ltd., 2002—; bd. dir. Time Warner, Inc, 1993—. Author: The Last Commissioner, 2002, The Only Game in Town: Baseball Stars of the 1930s and 1940s Talk About the Game They Loved, 2006. Trustee Williams Coll., 1970-88, Hotchkiss Sch., 1975—, Carleton Coll., 1988—. Mem. NY Athletic Club, Belle Haven Club, Phi Beta Kappa. Clubs: University, Belle Haven. Roman Catholic.

VINCENT, FREDERICK MICHAEL, SR., neurologist, educator; b. Detroit, Nov. 19, 1948; s. George S. and Alyce M. (Borkowski) Vincent; m. Patricia Lucille Cordes, Oct. 7, 1972; children: Frederick Michael Jr., Joshua Peter, Melissa Anne. BS in Biology, Aquinas Coll., 1970; MD, Mich. State U., 1973. Cert. in neurology Am. Bd. Psychiatry and Neurology, 1979, Am. Bd. Electrodiagnostic Medicine, 1992, Am. Bd. Forensic Examiners, 1996, Am. Bd. Forensic Medicine, 1996, in neurology with subspecialty of clin. neurophysiology Am. Bd. Psychiatry and Neurology, 1996. Intern St. Luke's Hosp., Duluth, Minn., 1974; resident in neurology Dartmouth Med. Sch., Hanover, NH, 1975—77, instr. dept. medicine, chief resident neurology, 1977—78; chief neurology sect. Munson Med. Ctr., Traverse City, Mich., 1978—84; asst. clin. prof. medicine and pathology Mich. State U., East Lansing, 1978—84, chief sect. neurology Coll. Human Medicine, 1984—87, clin. prof. psychiatry and internal medicine, 1989—2004, clin. prof. medicine, 1990—, clin. prof. neurology and ophthalmology, 2001—; pvt. practice Lansing, Mich., 1987—. Clin. and rsch. fellow neuro-oncology Mass. Gen. Hosp., Boston, 1985; clin. fellow in neurology Harvard Med. Sch., Boston, 1985; cons. med. asst. program Northwestern Mich. Coll., Traverse City, 1983—84; neurology cons. radio call-in show Sta. WKAR, East Lansing, 1984—2000, Sta. WCMU-TV, 1987, 1993—. Author: (book) Neurology: Problems in Primary Care, 1987, 2d edit., 1993; contbr. articles to profl. jours. Fellow, NSF, 1969, Nat. Multiple Sclerosis Soc., 1971. Fellow: ACP, Am. Bd. Legal Medicine, Am. Assn. Neuromuscular and Electrodiagnostic Medicine (computer electronics com. 1995—98, profl. practice com. 1999—2000, practice rev. panel 2000—03), Am. Acad. Neurology (program accreditation devel. subcom. 1993—2001), Am. Bd. Forensic Examiners, Am. Heart Assn.; mem.: Am. Coll. Legal Medicine, Am. Coll. Physician Exec., Soc. for Neuro-Oncology, Movement Disorders Soc., Am. Clin. Neurophysiology Soc., Inuit Art Soc., Univ. Club, Alpha Omega Alpha. Independent. Roman Catholic. Avocations: art, fishing. Office: 1515 Lake Lansing Rd Ste F1 Lansing MI 48912-3752 Office Phone: 517-374-1055. Business E-Mail: vincen11@msu.edu.

VINCENT, HAL WELLMAN, retired military officer, investor; b. Pontiac, Mich., Sept. 27, 1927; s. Harold and Glenda (Wellman) V.; m. Virginia Bayler, June 9, 1951; children: David B., Dale W., Deborah K. Vincent. Student, Navy V-5 program Western Mich. Coll./Colgate U., 1945; BS in Engring., U.S. Naval Acad., 1950; postgrad., Marine Officers Basic Sch., 1950, Flight Sch., 1952, Test Pilot Sch., 1955, Navy Fleet Air Gunnery Sch., 1958, Air Force Fighter Weapons Sch., 1959, Marine Corps Command and Staff Coll., 1964, Indsl. Coll., 1969, Marine Air Weapons Tng. Unit, 1972. Commd. 2d lt. U.S. Marine Corps, 1950, advanced through grades to maj. gen., 1974; rifle and machinegun platoon comdr. Camp Lejeune, NC, 1951; fighter pilot El Toro, Calif., 1953-54, Republic of Korea, 1953—54; test pilot Flight Test Div., Patuxent River, Md., 1955-57; ops. officer, squadron asst. and fighter pilot El Toro, 1958-59; conventional weapons project test pilot Naval Air Weapons Test Ctr., China Lake, Calif., 1960-62; squadron ops. and exec. officer El Toro and Japan, 1962-64; aviation specialist Marine Corps amphibious warfare presentation team and staff officer Quantico, Va., 1965-66; comdg. officer 2d Marine Aircraft Wing fighter-attack squadron, Beaufort, SC, 1967-68; exec. officer Marine Aircraft Group, Vietnam, 1969; logistics staff officer Fleet Marine Force Pacific, Hawaii, 1970-72; comdg. officer Marine Aircraft Group, Yuma, Ariz., 1972-73; chief of staff 3d Marine Aircraft Wing, El Toro, 1973-76; dep. chief. of staff plans and policy to Comdr. in Chief Atlantic, Norfolk, Va., 1976-78; comdg. gen. 2d Marine Aircraft Wing, Cherry Point, NC, 1978-80; dep. comdg. gen. Fleet Marine Force Atlantic, Norfolk, 1980-81; ret., 1981; pvt. investor, 1981—. Weapons test pilot; preliminary pilot, evaluator new mil. aircraft. Contbr. numerous articles on tactics and conventional weapons delivery, flight test stability and control to various mil. publs. Decorated Legion of Merit with 2 gold stars, D.F.C., Bronze Star with combat V, Air medal with star and numeral 14, Honor medal 1st class, Cross of Gallantry with gold star (Republic of Vietnam); recipient Wright Bros. Master Pilot award, 2005. Mem. SAR, Soc. Exptl. Test Pilots, Early Pioneer Naval Aviators, Marine Corps Aviation Assn., Mach 2 Club, Marbella Country Club. Achievements include invention of triple ejector rack for delivery of conventional bombs, 1961; devel. of fighter tactics in F8 and F4 aircraft, 1958-69; flew 165 models of fgn. and U.S. mil. aircraft; flew 8 models of fixed wing and helicopters on 242 combat missions; first Marine to fly MACH-2; pilot for 62 years. Personal E-mail: hwvincent@webtv.net. *In all 36 years in the service I am convinced that war is bad, and little is accomplished in the long term by warfare. However when National policy dictates a war, then we must not limit what can be done. We must win! My thought "Winning isn't everything, it's the only thing!" When I must go to battle I want to be allowed to "fight to win".*

VINCENT, JAMES LOUIS, biotechnology company executive; b. Johnstown, Pa., Dec. 15, 1939; s. Robert Clyde and Marietta Lucille (Kennedy) V.; m. Elizabeth M. Matthews, Aug. 19, 1961 (div. 1998); children: Aimee Archelle, Christopher James; m. Joyce Anne Fitzgibbons, Dec. 30, 1999 (div. 2002). BSME, Duke U., 1961; MBA in Indsl. Mgmt., U. Pa., 1963; DBA (hon.), U. New Haven, 1998. Mgr. Far East divsn. Tex. Instruments, Inc., Tokyo, 1970—72; pres. Tex. Instrument Asia, Ltd., Tokyo, 1970—72; v.p. diagnostic ops., pres. diagnostics div. Abbott Labs., North Chgo., Ill., 1972—74, group v.p., bd. dirs., 1974—81, exec. v.p., COO, bd. dirs., 1979—81; corp. group v.p., pres. Allied Health and Sci. Products Co. Allied Corp., Morristown, NJ, 1982—85; CEO Biogen, Inc., Cambridge, Mass., 1985—97, 1999—2000, chmn. bd., 1997—2002; ret., 2002. Trustee Duke U., Com. for Econ. Devel.; bd. dirs. Alnylam Pharms. Recipient Young Exec. Achievement Young Execs. Club, Chgo., 1976, Disting. Alumni award Duke U., 1988, Biotech. award Wall St. Transcript, 1997. Mem. Mass. Bus. Roundtable, The Comml. Club Boston, Algonquin Club Boston, The Links (N.Y.C.). Republican. Presbyterian.

VINCENT, JIM, performing company executive; b. NJ; m. France Nguyen; children: Lena, Claire, June. Studied at, Wash. Sch. of Ballet, Harkness House of Ballet, N.C. Sch. of the Arts. Profl. dancer Jim Kylian's Nederlands Dans Theater, Nacho Duato's Compania Nacional de Danza in Spain; asst. artistic dir. Compania Nacional de Danza, 1990—94; concept designer, show dir. Disneyland Paris, 1997; artistic dir. Hubbard St. Dance Chgo., 2000—. Ballet master Nederlands Dans Theater II, Compa a Nacional de Danza, Opera National de Lyon. Office: Hubbard Street Dance Chgo 1147 W Jackson Blvd Chicago IL 60607 *

VINCENT, JOHN BERTRAM, chemist, educator; b. Cape Girardeau, Mo., July 10, 1962; s. Jack Donald and Patricia Illers Vincent; m. Sharon Ellen Nevels; children: Allisa, Christina. BS, Murray State U., Ky., 1984; PhD, Ind. U., 1988. Postdoctoral rsch. assoc. U. Va., Charlottesville, 1988-90, NIH postdoctoral fellow, 1990-91; asst. prof. chemistry U. Ala., Tuscaloosa, 1991-96, assoc. prof., 1996-2001, prof., 2001—, faculty tchg. fellow Coll. Arts and Scis., 2002—05, pres. faculty senate, 2006—. Contbr. articles to profl. jours. Recipient Outstanding Commitment to Tchg. award U. Ala. Alumni Assn., 1999, Outstanding Honor Program Faculty award U. Ala. Honors Student Assn., 1998. Mem. Am. Diabetes Assn., Ala. Acad. Sci., Coun. on Undergrad. Rsch., Soc. Biol. Inorganic Chemistry, Am. Chem. Soc. (sec. Ala. sect. 1996-97). Presbyterian. Home: 716 53d Ct E Tuscaloosa AL 35404 Office: U Ala Dept Chemistry Tuscaloosa AL 35487-0336 Office Phone: 205-348-9203. Office Fax: 205-348-9104. Business E-Mail: jvincent@bama.ua.edu. E-mail: nevels@dbtech.net.

VINCENT, MARK See DIESEL, VIN

VINCENT, NORMAN FULLER, broadcast executive; b. Boston, Oct. 5, 1930; s. Norman Harrison and Marian Bernice (Fuller) V.; m. Karen Ann Walter, June 21, 1969. BA, Denison U., 1953. Sales mgr. Sta. WMBR, Jacksonville, Fla., 1956-62; gen. mgr. Sta. WZOK, Jacksonville, 1962-66; owner, pres. Norm Vincent Sound Recording Studios, Inc., Jacksonville, 1966-75; dir. radio ops. Sta. WJCT, Jacksonville, 1975-91; announcer, narrator radio, TV film and video, talking books, 1976—. Producer, host (radio): Swing Time with Norm Vincent, 1992—. Served with USN, 1953-56; to comdr. USNR, 1958-80. Mem.: Advt. Fed. Am., Jacksonville C. of C. (armed svcs. com.), Navy League, Exch. Club, Sigma Alpha Epsilon. Republican. Episcopalian. Home: 2110 The Woods Dr Jacksonville FL 32246-1016 Office Phone: 904-221-5218. Personal E-mail: vincentswing@aol.com.

VINCENT, NORMAN L., retired insurance company executive; b. Milw., July 21, 1933; s. Victor V. Vincent and Hilda I. (Boedecker) Vincent Patlow; m. Arlene Page, Jan. 31, 1953 (div. 1978); children: J. Todd, Meg; m. Donna Jean Doll, Aug. 8, 1980. BS, U. Wis., 1957; MS, Purdue U., 1958, PhD, 1960. Diplomate Am. Bd. Profl. Psychology; registered psychologist., Ill., C.P.C.U., C.L.U. Supr. agy. research State Farm Ins. Cos., Bloomington, Ill., 1960-63, dir. agy. research., 1963-66, asst. v.p. agy., 1966-69, asst. v.p. exec., 1969-70, v.p. data processing, 1970-94; systems v.p., 1994-95. Pres. Bloomington Bd. Edn., 1974-77; bd. dirs. YMCA, Bloomington, 1971-85. Served with M.I. U.S. Army, 1953-55. Mem. AAAS Home: W332 N 5861 Meadowlark Ct Nashotah WI 53058-9528

VINCENT, RICHARD C., communications educator, researcher; b. Allentown, Pa., Mar. 1, 1949; s. Charles L. and Elizabeth A. Vincent; m. Christine LaCaruba, Jan. 29, 1971; children: Marisa Claire, Marielle Bryce. BA, Mansfield U., 1972; MA, Temple U., 1977; PhD, U. Mass., Amherst, 1983. Instr. Slippery Rock U., Pa., 1979—81; asst. prof. Western Ill. U., Macomb, 1981—83, So. Ill. U., Carbondale, 1983—86; assoc. prof. U. Hawaii-Manoa, Honolulu, 1986—2001; chairperson dept. comm. Ind. State U., Terre Haute, 2001—04, prof., 2005—. Editor: Towards Equity in Global Communication: MacBride Report Update, 1999; author: Financial Characteristics of Selected B Film Productions of Albert J. Cohen, 1980, Global Glasnost: Toward a New International Information/Communication Order?, 1992, U.S. Glasnost: Missing Political Themes in U.S. Media Discourse, 2004; contbr. chapters to books, articles to profl. jours. Chartered mem. Honolulu Cmty. Media Coun., 1999—2001; del. UN & ITU's World Summit on Info. Soc., Geneva, Tunis, 2003—05. Fulbright scholar, U.S. State Dept., USIA, Dublin (Ireland) City U., 1994—95. Mem.: HCMC Freedom of Info. Day (assoc.; co-chair 2000—01), MacBride Round Table (assoc.; pres. and past pres. 1994—2000), Broadcast Edn. Assn. (assoc.; internat. divsn. rsch. chair 2006—), Am. Edn. in Journalism and Mass Comm. (assoc.; internat. divsn. sec. 2001—02, internat. divsn. rsch. chair 2002—03), Internat. Comm. Assn. (assoc.), Nat. Comm. Assn. (assoc.), Internat. Assn. Mass Comm. Rschrs. (assoc.), Union for Dem. Comm. (assoc.). Achievements include research in mass media, information and communication technologies, and international communication. Avocations: photography, travel. Office: Indiana State University Comm Dept 218 N 6th St Terre Haute IN 47809 Home Phone: 812-298-0699; Office Phone: 812-237-3246. Office Fax: 812-237-3217. Business E-Mail: rvincent@indstate.edu.

VINCENT, SAM (JAMES SAMUEL VINCENT), professional basketball coach, former professional basketball player; b. Lansing, Mich., May 18, 1963; Grad., Mich. State U., East Lansing, 1985. Guard Boston Celtics, 1985—87, Seattle SuperSonics, 1987—88, Chgo. Bulls, 1988—89, Orlando Magic, Del., 1989—92; spl. advisor to v.p. Reggie Williams Disney Wide World of Sports, 1992—93; head coach Cape Town Kings, South Africa, 1996—99, Greek A-2 Men's Basketball League, Larissa, Greece, 1999—2000, A1 Dutch League Canoe Jeans, Den Bosch, Netherlands, NBA Devel. League Ft. Worth Flyers, 2005—06, Charlotte Bobcats, 2007—; asst. coach Dallas Mavericks, 2006—07. Head coach Men's and Women's South African Sr. Nat. Teams, 1999, Nigerian Women's Nat. Team; head coach Nigerian Nat. Team FIBA (Internat. Basketball Fedn.) World Championship, 2006. Achievements include winning a FIBA (International Basketball Federation) Championship as head coach of the Nigerian Women's National Team, 2003. Office: Charlotte Bobcats 333 E Trade St Charlotte NC 28202 *

VINCENT, THOMAS JAMES, retired manufacturing executive; b. Balt., Mar. 17, 1934; s. Thomas Alonzo and Helen Geraldine (Cloman) V.; divorced; children: Wayne S., Robin K. MS, MIT, 1968. Div. gen. mgr. Fairchild Industries, St. Augustine, Fla., 1969-72; pres. T.J. Vincent Properties Ltd., St. Augustine, 1972-75, Pacific Concrete & Rock Co., Honolulu, 1975-77, Ramsey Engring. Co., St. Paul, 1977-80, Kobe Inc., LA, 1980-84, Milchem Inc., Houston, 1984-85, York (Pa.) Internat. Corp., 1985-88, also bd. dirs., cons.; chmn., CEO Hawaii Seafood Growers, Inc., Kahuku, 1990-92. Author: Fairplan, 1962; publ.: In the Name of the Boss Upstairs, The Father Ray Brennan Story, 2004 Founder, pres. Thomas J. Vincent Found. Inc., Kaneohe, Hawaii, 1990—; founder, v.p., treas. Winter Park (Fla.) Family Health Ctr., Inc., 1995—. Named one of Outstanding Young Men in Am., Jaycees, 1965; Alfred P. Sloan fellow MIT, 1967; recipient Rsch. for Progress Achievement award, 1972. Avocations: deep sea fishing, orchid growing. Home and Office: 44-447 Kanoehe Bay Dr Kaneohe HI 96744

VINCENTI, GENE A., director, consultant; b. Elizabeth, NJ, Oct. 2, 1949; s. Charles and Lucy (Diange) Vincenti; m. Regina Abrantes, July 10, 1971; children: Michael James, Jason Luis. BA, Rutgers U., Newark, 1971, MBA, 1973; Cert., Harvard Grad. Sch. Edn., Cambridge, Mass., 1990. Student asst. Kean U., Union, NY, 1968—71, offsite program mgr. Boonton, NJ, 1971; budget resource officer Rutgers U., New Brunswick, NJ, 1973—76, asst. provost, 1973—76, Newark, 1976—80, assoc. provost, 1980—2003, exec. v.p. adminstrn., 2003—. Interfunctional and team cons. Rutgers U., 1972; mem. regional bus. partnerships evaluator mid. states, 1980; mem. gov.'s mgmt. improvement agy. State of N.J., Trenton, 1982; evaluator Middle States Assn., Phila., 1985. Many other church, state and county roles; lector, Eucharistic minister, pres. parish coun. St. Thomas More Ch., Manalapan, 1989—2003; trustee Univ. Heights Sci. Park, Newark, 1990—; mem. Recreation Commn., Manalapan, NJ, 1994—2001, chmn,., 1996—2001. Recipient Bus. Ptnrship award, N.J. Transit, 1987; grantee, N.J. Commn. on Higher Edn., 1995. Mem.: Am. Planning Assn., Nat. Assn. Coll. and Univ. Bus. Officers, Internat. Econ. Devel. Coun. Roman Catholic. Avocations: baseball, basketball, travel. Home: 15 Mt Stream Ct Barnegat NJ 08005 Office: Rutgers Univ Ste 590 123 Washington St Newark NJ 07102 Home Phone: 609-607-5299.

VINCENTI, MICHAEL BAXTER, lawyer; b. Balt., Dec. 28, 1950; s. Rudolph and Betty (Jones) V.; m. Patricia Lynn Bishopp, Apr. 14, 1984; children: Sarah, Elizabeth. BA, Johns Hopkins U., 1972; JD, NYU Sch. Law, 1975. Bar: Ill. 1975, Ky. 1979. Assoc. Sonnenschein, Nath & Rosenthal, Chgo., 1975-79; from assoc. to ptnr. Wyatt, Tarrant & Combs, Louisville, 1979—. Guest instr. Jefferson Cmty. Coll., Louisville, 1988-98, 2004—. Sec., gen. counsel Louisville Sci. Ctr., 1993-04; dir., counsel bd. trustees Chance Sch., Louisville, 1995-98; mem. Chpt. of Christ Ch. Cathedral, 2004—. Mem. ABA, Internat. Coun. Shopping Ctrs., Ill. Bar Assn., Am. Land Title Assn. (lender's counsel group), Am. Coll. Real Estate Lawyers, Am. Coll. Mortgage Attys., Ky. Bar Assn., Louisville Bar Assn., Rotary, Louisville Boat Club, Lex Mundi. Episcopalian. Avocations: squash, racquetball, tennis, travel, reading. Office: Wyatt Tarrant & Combs 500 W Jefferson St Ste 2700 Louisville KY 40202-2898 Office Phone: 502-562-7518. Fax: 502-589-0309. E-mail: mvincenti@wyattfirm.com.

VINCENTI, SHELDON ARNOLD, lawyer, educator; b. Sept. 4, 1938; s. Arnold Joseph and Mae (Burch) Vincenti; children: Matthew Lewis, Amanda Jo. AB, Harvard U., 1960, JD, 1963. Bar: Utah 1963. Sole practice law, Ogden, 1966—67; ptnr. Lowe and Vincenti, Ogden, 1968—70; legis. asst. to U.S. Rep. Gunn McKay, Washington, 1971—72, adminstrv. asst., 1973; prof., assoc. dean U. Idaho Coll. Law, Moscow, 1973—83, dean, prof. law, 1983—95, prof. law, 1995—2006; acad. dean Am. Justice Sch. Law, Paducah, Ky., 2006—. Home: 3285 W Twin Rd Moscow ID 83843-9114 Office: U Idaho Coll Law 6th & Rayburn St Moscow ID 83843

VINCENTI, WALTER GUIDO, aeronautical engineer, emeritus educator; b. Balt., Apr. 20, 1917; s. Guido A. and Agnes (Nicolini) V.; m. Joyce H. Weaver, Sept. 6, 1947; children— Margaret Anna, Marc Guido. AB, Stanford U., 1938, Aero. Engr., 1940. Aero. research scientist NACA, 1940-57; prof. aero. and astronautics and history of tech. Stanford U., 1957-83, prof. emeritus, 1983—. Cons. to industry, 1957—; mem. adv. panel engring. sec. NSF, 1960-63. Author: (with Charles H. Kruger, Jr.) Introduction to Physical Gas Dynamics, 1965, (with Nathan Rosenberg) The Britannia Bridge, 1978, What Engineers Know and How They Know It, 1990; also papers.; co-editor (with Milton Van Dyke) Annual Review of Fluid Mechanics, 1970-76. Served with USN, 1945-46. Recipient Gold medal Pi Tau Sigma, 1948, Engr.-Historian award ASME, 1997; Rockefeller Pub. Service award, 1956; Guggenheim fellow, 1963 Fellow AIAA; mem. Internat. Acad. Astronautics (corr.), Soc. History Tech. (Usher prize 1984, Leonardo da Vinci medal 1998), Nat. Acad. Engring., Phi Beta Kappa, Sigma Xi, Tau Beta Pi. Home: 555 Byron St #306 Palo Alto CA 94301 Office: Stanford U Stanford CA 94305 Business E-Mail: sts@stanford.edu.

VINECOUR, ONEIDA AGNES, nurse; b. Port Arthur, Tex., Oct. 15, 1917; d. Ernest Eugene and Gertrude Mary (Wooldridge) Thorn; m. Seymour Vinecour, Jan. 14, 1943 (dec. 1976); children: Seymour Jacob, Rebecca Leah. Diploma, St. Mary's Hosp. Sch. Nursing, Port Arthur, 1939; postgrad., cert. Surg. Tech., Anesthesia, Cook County Hosp., 1939-40; postgrad. U. Chgo., 1939-40, Tex. Coll. Mines, 1943, U. Tex. Health Ctr. R.N., cert. occupational audiometric technician, occupl. spirometric technician. Operating room supr., instr. Schumpert Meml. Hosp., Shreveport, La., 1940-41; anesthetist St. Joseph Hosp., Albuquerque, 1941-42; operating room supr., instr. Lynn City Hosp. (Mass.), 1946-48; staff anesthetist St. Mary's Hosp., Port Arthur, Tex., 1951-53, in service dir., 1971-73; staff nurse Tyler County Hosp., Woodville, Tex., 1964-65; dept. head, supr. Park Pl. Hosp., Port Arthur, 1965-71; operating room supr. Mid-County Hosp., Nederland, Tex., 1973-81; staff nurse Baptist Meml. Hosp., Beaumont, Tex., 1973-81; part time staff Health Care Svcs., Port Arthur, 1983—; indsl. nurse Synpol Inc., 1984-86; staff nurse Texaco Chem. Plant, Port Arthur, 1986-92, Olsten Health Care Svcs., 1992—, staff nurse Huntsman Petro-Chem. Corp., 1996—. Served as officer U.S. Army Nurse Corps, 1942-46. Recipient Marie Curie award Oxford U., Eng., 2006. Mem. Am. Nurses Assn., Mass. Nurses Assn., Tex. State Nurses Assn., Assn. Occupational Health Nurses. Republican. Methodist. Home: 2502 Glenwood Dr Port Arthur TX 77642-2639

VINEGRAD, ALAN, prosecutor; Grad. magna cum laude, U. Pa, 1980; JD, NYU, 1984. Bar: NY, practice before: US Ct. Appeals (2nd and 3rd Cirs.), US Dist. Cts. (Eastern and So. Dist., NY). Staff acct. Price Waterhouse & Co.; clerk for Hon. Leonard B. Sand US Dist. Ct. (So. Dist.), NY, student law clerk for the Hon. Naomi Reice Buchwald; private practice Meister Leventhal & Slade, 1985—90; chief of general crimes US Atty. Office, Brooklyn, NY, 1990—94, chief of civil rights litig., 1994—97, dep. chief of the criminal divsn., 1999, chief of the criminal divsn., chief asst. US atty.; interim US Atty. US Atty. Office, Eastern Dist., New York, 2001; ptnr., white collar def. and trial practice groups Covington & Burling, NY. Adj. prof. New York Law Sch., 1996—; guest lectr. Brooklyn Law Sch., Cardoza Sch. Law, Fordham Law Sch., Hofstra Law Sch., New York U. Law Sch., Yale Law Sch., Dept. Justice's Office of Legal Edu. Sr. editor NYU Law Review, bd. editor NY Law Journal; contbr. articles to profl. jours. and reviews. Bd. dir. Legal Aid Soc. Recipient Atty. Gen. award for Distinguished Service, Stimson Medal for Outstanding Prosecutor, US Atty. Office for Eastern Dist. of NY, Henry L. Stimson medal, Assn. Bar of City NY, 1993, Atty. General's award for Disting. Svc., 1997. Mem.: Fed. Bar Coun. (bd. trustee, chmn., com. on 2nd cir. cts.). Office: Covington & Burling 1330 Avenue of the Americas New York NY 10019 Office Phone: 212-841-1000. Business E-Mail: avinegrad@cov.com.

VINENT-CANTORAL, AIDA R., mediator; b. Havana, Cuba, Nov. 8, 1948; arrived in U.S., 1959; d. Roberto M. Vinent and Carmen; m. Ennio Cantoral, Dec. 26, 1979 (div. 1981); 1 child, Alfredo Cantoral. BA, Alverno Coll., Milw., 1969; MA, Marquette U., Milw., 1971, cert. dispute resolution, 1998; cert. negotiating labor agreements, Harvard U., Cambridge, Mass., 2000, U. Mich., 2002, Northwestern U., Evanston, Ill.; cert. mediation sys. design, U. Tex.; postgrad., U. So. Tex. Coll. Law, 2004, Fed. Mediation and Conciliation Inst., 2004. Family health asst. Milwaukee County Dept. Human Svcs. & Hosp., 1975—; human svcs. case coord. Milwaukee County Dept. Human Svcs. and Hosp., 1998—; mediator pvt. practice Milw., 1979—; mediator Milwaukee County Family Ct., 1998—, USPS, 1998—, Bus. to Bus., 1998—, CHIPS, 1997, Wis. Spl. Edn. Mediation Sys., 2001—; case mgr. Milw. Co. Disability Svs., 1996—. Cons. in field. Active ACR, 1998—, Wis. Assn. Homicide Investigators, 2000—; parent educator Centro Legal, Milw., 1998—. Named Human Svcs. Worker of Yr., Wis. Foster Parents, 1980. Mem.: Wis. Coun. Problem Gambling, Wis. Assn. Mediators. Republican. Address: PO Box 462 Greendale WI 53129-0462 Office Phone: 414-550-8772. E-mail: avinent@aol.com.

VINES, HENRY ELLSWORTH, III, lawyer, accountant, financial planner; b. Chgo., Apr. 17, 1950; s. Henry Ellsworth and Verle (Low) V.; m. Ethel Melton (div. 1977); 1 child, Tiffany Layne; m. Cindy Lou Rich, Jan. 5, 1985; 1 child, Sasha Teresa Root. BS, Menlo Sch. Bus. Adminstrn., 1972; MBA, Golden Gate Grad. Sch., 1985; CFP, Coll. Fin. Planning, Denver, 1987; JD, William F. Taft Law Sch., 1994; LLM, Wash. Sch. Law, 1998. Bar: Calif. 1996; CPA, Calif.; certified CFP. Asst. contr. Legallet Tanning, San Francisco, 1973-79; auditor Martin Schoonover & Paddock,

Orange, Calif., 1980-82; tax mgr. Helsley Mulcahy & Fesler, Santa Ana, Calif., 1982-85; v.p. fin. Catalina Furniture Co., Fullerton, Calif., 1985-94; CFO Precision Concepts, Anaheim, Calif., 1987-93; pvt. practice in tax preparation Orange, Calif., 1985—; CFO M.E. Woodworking, Riverside, Calif., 1989-93, Textured Design Furniture, Anaheim, 1994-95; corp. and tax atty. in pvt. practice, Irvine, Calif., 1996—. Author: The Greatest Athlete Athlete of All Time; contbr. articles in field. Mem.: AICPA, ABA, Calif. Inst. CPAs, Irvine Spectrum Toastmasters (pres. 2000—01), San Mateo Tennis Club (pres. 1978), Foster City Tennis Club (pres. 1977). Republican. Avocations: tennis, fishing, golf. Home: 130 N Windy Pointe Orange CA 92869-2400 Office: Ste 300 8 Corporate Park Irvine CA 92606-5196

VINES, JIM (JAMES K.), lawyer, former prosecutor; b. Dec. 1959; BS in Acctg., Washington & Lee U., 1981, JD, 1988. Law clk. to Hon. Robert R. Merhige, US Dist. Ct.; law clk. to Chief Justice William H. Rehnquist, US Supreme Ct., 1989—90; assoc. King & Spalding LLP, Atlanta, 1990—93; exec. dir., gen. counsel for environ. affairs Bridgestone/Firestone, Nashville, 1993—2000; ptnr. Baker, Donelson, Bearman & Caldwell, Nashville, 2000—02; US atty. (mid. dist.) Tenn. US Dept. Justice, Nashville, 2002—06; ptnr. King & Spaulding LLP, Washington, 2006—. Adj. prof. environ. law Vanderbilt U. Mem.: Tenn. Bar Assn., Ga. Bar Assn. Office: King & Spalding LLP 1700 Pennsylvania Ave NW Ste 200 Washington DC 20006 E-mail: jvines@kslaw.com. *

VINES, JOHN R., career military officer; BS, U. Ala.; MA, Naval War Coll. Advanced through grades to lt. gen. US Army, 2003; with 3rd Infantry Divsn., US Army Europe & Seventh Army, Ranger Dept. US Army Infantry Ctr., Ft. Benning, Ga.; comdr., specialist 1st Ranger Batallion, Hunter Army Airfield, Ga.; exec. officer 3rd Ranger Battallion, Ft. Benning, Ga., 1984—87; numerous command and staff positions Ft. Bragg, 1987—2000; comdr. 82nd Airborne Divsn., 2000—02, Coalition Task Force 82, 2002—03, Combined/Joint Task Force-180, Bagram, Afghanistan, 2003, XVIII Airborne Corps, Ft. Bragg, NC, 2003—, Multi-Nat. Corps-Operation Iraqi Freedom, Iraq, 2005—06. Decorated Def. Disting. Svc. medal, DSM, Def. Superior Svc. medal, Bronze Star (with Oak Leaf cluster), Combat Infantry Badge, Master Parachutist Badge (with Bronze Svc. Star), Pathfinder Badge, Ranger Tab.

VINET, LUC, physicist, educator; b. Montreal, Can., Apr. 16, 1953; s. Jean and Françoise (Ouellette) V.; m. Letitia Muresan, May 19, 1989; children: Jean-François, Laurent, Stéphane, Sophie Andrée. BSc, U. Montreal, 1973, MSc, 1974, PhD, 1980; D, U. P.& M. Curie, Paris, 1979. Rsch. assoc. MIT, Cambridge, 1980—82; rsch. fellow, asst. prof., assoc. prof. U. Montreal, 1982—88, prof. physics, 1992—99; vice prin. (acad.) McGill U., Montreal, 1999—2001, provost, vice prin. (acad.), 2001—05; rector U. Montreal, 2005—. Invited prof. U. Cath. de Louvain, 1980-82; vis. scholar MIT, Cambridge, 1987; vis. prof. UCLA, 1989-90; dir. Ctr. Rsch. Math., Montreal, 1993-99; prof. physics, rector U. Montreal, 2005-. Editor: Group Theoretical Methods in Physics, 1989, Quantum Groups Integrable Models and Statistical Systems, 1993, Physics and Quantum Field Theory, 1996, Symmetries and Integrability of Difference Equations, 1996. Grantee FCAR, 1984—, NSERC, 1982—, rsch. fellow, 1982-92. Mem. APS, AMS, SIAM, CAP, CMS. Achievements include contributions in theoretical physics and mathematics - symmetry studies of difference equations; algebraic interpretation of q-special functions using quantum groups; applications of Berry potentials in the nuclear collective model; identification of Lie superalgebras as dynamical algebras in quantum mechanics; development of dimensional reduction in Yang Mills theories. Office: U Montreal Cabiner du Recteur CP 6128 SLCC Centerville Montreal PQ H3C 3S7 Canada

VINGOE, D. GRANT, lawyer; b. 1957; BA, U. Toronto, Can., 1979; LLB, Osgoode Hall, Toronto, 1981; LLM, NYU, 1984. Bar: Ontario, Canada 1983, NY 1985. Counsel Toronto Stock Exchange, 1984—85; assoc. Kramer, Levin, Naftalis & Frankel, 1986—93, ptnr., 1994—96; ptnr., corp. dept. Dorsey & Whitney LLP, NYC, 1996—2004; ptnr., cross-border securities, fin. services regulation Arnold & Porter, NYC, 2004. Securities adv. com. Ontario Securities Commn., 1999—2001; bd. dir. Mkt. Regulation Services, Inc., Toronto, ON, Canada, 2004—. Mem.: ABA, Securities Industry Assn., Canadian Bar Assn., Canadian Soc. of NY, Americas Soc. Office: Arnold & Porter LLP 399 Park Ave New York NY 10022-4690 Office Phone: 212-715-1130. Office Fax: 212-715-1399. Business E-Mail: Grant_Vingoe@aporter.com.

VINIAR, DAVID A., investment company executive; BS summa cum laude in Econs., Union Coll., 1976; MBA, Harvard U., 1980. Joined Goldman Sachs, 1980, ptnr., 1992-96, mng. dir., 1992—94, dep. CFO, 1994—98, exec. v.p., CFO, 1999—, head, fin. divsn. and co-head credit risk mgmt. and adv. and firm wide risk, 2001—02, head ops., tech. and fin. divsn., 2002—. Bd. trustees Union Coll. Mem. bd. trustees Union Coll. Recipient CFO Excellence Award for Risk Management, CFO mag., 2001. Office: Goldman Sachs 85 Broad St New York NY 10004 *

VINICOMBE, CHARLES JAMES, lawyer; b. Bklyn., July 12, 1962; s. James Charles and Virginia Rose V.; m. Michele Lee Buchman, Dec. 4, 1993. BA, Seton Hall U., 1984; JD, Wake Forest U., 1987. Bar: N.J., N.C.; U.S. Dist. Ct. N.J., U.S. Dist. Ct. (mid. dist. N.C.), U.S. Ct. Appeals (3rd and 4th cirs.). Assoc. Carruthers & Roth, Greensboro, NC, 1987-89, Drinker, Biddle & Reath, Princeton, NJ, 1989-96, ptnr., 1996—. Adj. faculty Seton Hall Law Sch., Newark, 1996-97. Articles editor Wake Forest Lw Rev., 1986-87; contbr. articles to profl. jours. Law Faculty scholar Wake Forest Law Sch., Winston-Salem, N.C., 1986-87. Mem. N.J. Bar Assn., ABA, Def. Rsch. Inst., Jaycees (v.p., sec., pub. rels. dir. North Plainfield, N.J. 1980-84). Avocations: reading, hiking, fishing. Office: Drinker Biddle & Reath LLP Ste 300 105 College Rd E Princeton NJ 08540-6622 Office Phone: 609-716-6500. Office Fax: 609-799-7000. Business E-Mail: charles.vinicombe@dbr.com.

VINIKAS, VINCENT, historian, educator; b. Erie, Pa., Mar. 29, 1951; s. Matthias Vytautas Vinikas and Eva Aldona Damarodas. BA magna cum laude, Pa. State U., 1972; MA, Columbia U., 1974, PhD, 1983. Asst. prof. U. Ark., Little Rock, 1983—89, assoc. prof., 1989—98, prof., 1998—. Inst. fellow NEH, Ariz. State U., Tempe, 1984; conferee Newberry Libr., Smithsonian Instn., Washington, 1985; inst. fellow NEH, U. N.C., 1993; vis. prof. Karl Franzens U., Graz, Styria, Austria, 1994; inst. fellow NEH, Columbia U., NY, 1998; referee/cons. St. Martin's Press, Prentice-Hall, McGraw-Hill, Houghton-Mifflin, Wadsworth. Author: (monograph) Soft Soap Hard Sell: American Hygiene in an Age of Advertisement; reviewer: Am. Hist. Rev., Jour. So. History, Jour. Social History, Jour. Econ. History, The Historian, Tech. and Culture, Ark. Hist. Quar., Jour. Am. History; contbr. articles to profl. jours.; conferee Sandage Symposium, U. Ill, 2000. Mem. ACLU, Gurdjieff Found. of Ark., Little Rock. Recipient Rsch. award, U. Ark., 1984, 1996; Pres.'s fellow, Columbia U., 1974-1975. Mem.: Am. Hist. Assn., Ark. Assn. of Coll. History Tchrs. (Biennial Essay Award 1993), Phi Alpha Theta (advisor Iota Zeta chpt.), Phi Kappa Phi (exec. bd. chpt. 134 1989—92), Phi Beta Kappa. Avocations: duplicate bridge, wilderness camping, boating. Home: 3312 W Capitol Ave Little Rock AR 72205 Office: Univ Ark History Dept Little Rock AR 72204 Home Phone: 501-663-1996; Office Phone: 501-569-3235. Office Fax: 501-569-3059. Business E-Mail: vxvinikas@ualr.edu.

VINING, (GEORGE) JOSEPH, law educator; b. Fulton, Mo., Mar. 3, 1938; s. D. Rutledge and Margaret (McClanahan) V.; m. Alice Marshall Williams, Sept. 18, 1965; children: George Joseph IV, Spencer Carter. BA, Yale U., 1959, Cambridge U., 1961, MA, 1970; JD, Harvard U., 1964. Bar: DC 1965. Atty. Office Dep. Atty. Gen., Dept. Justice, Washington, 1965; asst. to exec. dir. Nat. Crime Commn., 1966; assoc. Covington and Burling, Washington, 1966-69; asst. prof. law U. Mich., 1969-72, assoc. prof., 1972-74, prof., 1974-85, Hutchins prof., 1985—. Sir Edward Youde prof., Hong Kong, 2002. Author: Legal Identity, 1978, The Authoritative and the Authoritarian, 1986, From Newton's Sleep, 1995, The Song Sparrow and the Child, 2004. NEH sr. fellow, 1982-83, Bellagio fellow Rockfeller Found., 1997. Fellow Am. Acad. Arts and Scis.; mem. ABA, D.C. Bar Assn., Am. Law Inst. (life), Century Assn., Clare Hall Cambridge U. (life). Office: U Mich 964 Legal Rsch Ann Arbor MI 48109-1215

VINKEN, PIERRE JACQUES, publishing executive; b. Nov. 25, 1927; MD, U. Utrecht, 1955; postgrad., U. Amsterdam, The Netherlands, 1957-63; D (hon.), U. Paris, 1981. Staff neurosurgeon Univ. Clinic, Amsterdam, 1964-69; pres., chief editor Excerpta Medica Found., Amsterdam and Princeton, NJ, 1962-88; mng. dir. Elsevier Pub. Co., Amsterdam, 1972-78, chmn. bd. dirs., 1979-95, Reed Elsevier, London, 1993-95. Chmn. Netherlands del. Intergovernmental Unisist Conf., Paris, 1970; mem. Netherlands Unisist Commn., 1971—79, Nat. Sci. Policy Coun., The Hague, 1983—90; prof. med. database informatics U. Leyden, 1975—93; chmn. supervising bd. Halder Holdings, The Hague, Netherlands, Blue Horse Prodns., Rotterdam, Netherlands, Medialand, Amsterdam, Optas, Rotterdam, Trust Theater Co.; bd. dirs. Wereldhave Investment Co., Logica, Aalberts Industries, Revisor, Nat. Acad. Arts, Internat. Rights-Collecting and Distbns. Agys. Founder, editor-in-chief: book Handbook of Clinical Neurology, 78 vols.; editor: sci. books; contbr. articles to profl. jours. Pres. Internat. Congress Patient Counselling, 1976—79; chmn. Netherlands Commn. Bibliography and Documentation, 1972—81; dep. chmn. European Pubs. Coun.; chmn. Hiscom, Leyden, 1987—98, The Lancet, London, 1991—95; bd. dirs. Pearson, London, 1988—91, The Economist, London, 1989—92; mem. soc. adv. coun. Tinbergen Inst., Rotterdam, 1996—2000. Recipient award, Royal Netherlands Acad. Sci., 1997. Mem.: European Info. Providers Assn. (pres. 1980—83), Peruvian Soc. Psychiat. Neurology and Neurosurgery (hon.), Amsterdam Neurol. Soc. (hon.), French Neurol. Soc. (hon.), Neurol. Soc. India (hon.), Netherlands Rep. Soc. (founder 1996), Order of Orange Nassau (comdr.), Order of Netherlands' Lion (knight), Order Hipolitó Unanue (comdr.). Home: Schubertstraat 2 1077 GS Amsterdam Netherlands Personal E-mail: vinken@quicknet.nl.

VINKEY, RACHEL BURDICK, psychiatrist; b. Rochester, NY, Aug. 13, 1965; d. Victor Fowler and Karen Farney Vinkey; m. Shriram Krishnan, July 5, 1996; 1 child, Anya Vinkey Kirshnan. BA, U. Chgo., 1988; MD, SUNY, 1997. Resident Harvard/Cambridge Hosp., Mass., 2001; clin. instr. U. Calif., San Francisco, 2001—03, asst. clin. prof., 2003—; pvt. practice psychiatrist Oakland, 2004—; assoc. psychiatrist U. Calif. Student Health, Berkeley, 2004—05. Contbr. chapters to books. Scholar, U. Chgo., 1983, Bklyn. Psych. Soc. award, 1997. Mem.: APA, No. Calif. Psychol. Soc. Avocations: running, painting, poetry.

VINOCUR, CHARLES DAVID, pediatric surgeon; b. Cleve., Jan. 18, 1947; s. Joseph Leonard and Marion B. Vinocur; m. Pamela N. Newberg, June 16, 1974; children: Jeffrey Michael, Meryl Beth. BS, U. Mich., Ann Arbor, 1969, MD, 1973. Bd. cert. gen. surgery Am. Bd. Surgery, 1978, cert. spl. competence in pediatric surgery Am. Bd. Surgery, 1982. Attending surgeon St. Christopher's Hosp. for Children, Phila., 1980—2006, surgeon-in-chief, 1998—2006, tng. dir. Pediat. Surg. Fellowship, 1998—2006; prof. surgery and pediat. Temple U. Sch. Medicine, Phila., 1988—97, Drexel U. Coll. Medicine, 1998—2006, AI duPont Hosp. for Children/Thomas Jefferson Sch. Medicine, Wilimington, Del., 2006—. Office: AI duPont Hospital for Children 1600 Rockland Rd Wilmington DE 19803 Home Phone: 610-525-5194; Office Phone: 302-651-5888. Office Fax: 302-651-5990. Business E-Mail: cvinocur@nemours.org.

VINOGRADOVA, NATALYA, mathematician, educator; b. Russia, Aug. 10, 1969; MS in Math., St. Petersburg State U., Russia, 1991; PhD in Math. Edn., SUNY, Buffalo, 2005. Cert. tchr. N.Y. Instr. math. Pedagogical U., Russia, 1991—99, Phillips Exeter Acad., NH, 2000—01; prof. dept. math. Plymouth State U., NH, 2005—. Spkr. in field. Author: (book) The First Steps in the Theory of Probability, 1996. Mem.: Math. Assn. of Am., Nat. Coun. Tchrs. of Math. Home: PO Box 433 Plymouth NH 03264 Office Phone: 603-535-3235. Personal E-mail: nvinogradova@hotmail.com.

VIÑOLY, RAFAEL, architectural firm executive; b. Montevideo, Uruguay, 1944; arrived in US, 1978; Grad. in Arch., Univ. Buenos Aires, Argentina, 1969. Founding ptnr. Estudio de Arquitectura, Argentina, 1964—78; guest lectr. Univ. Wash., Harvard Univ. Grad. Sch. Design; founder, prin. Rafael Viñoly Architects PC, NYC, 1983—, established office London, 2000. Prin. works include John Jay Coll. Criminal Justice, 1988, Tokyo Internat. Forum, 1996, Univ. Chgo. Grad. Sch. Bus., Watson Inst. for Internat. Studies, Brown U., Howard Hughes Med. Inst. Janelia Farm Rsch. Campus, Va., Porter Neuroscience Rsch. Ctr. at NIH, Md., UCLA Nanosystems Rsch. Inst., Cleve. Mus. Art, Bklyn. Children's Mus., Nasher Mus., Duke U., Jazz at Lincoln Ctr., NYC, Leicester City Theatre, Performing Arts Centre, UK, also include courthouses, private residences, athletic facilities and performing arts venues; author: Rafael Viñoly, 2003. Recipient Medal of Honor, AIA NY Chapter, 1994. Fellow: AIA; mem.: NAD (academician 1994—), Japan Inst. Architects. Office: Rafael Vinoly Architects PC 50 Vandam St New York NY 10013 Office Phone: 212-924-5060. Office Fax: 212-924-5058. Business E-Mail: RafaelVinoly@rvapc.com.

VINROOT, RICHARD ALLEN, lawyer, mayor; b. Charlotte, NC, Apr. 14, 1941; s. Gustav Edgar and Vera Frances (Pickett) V.; m. Judith Lee Allen, Dec. 29, 1964; children: Richard A., Laura Tabor, Kathryn Pickett. BS in Bus. Adminstrn., U. N.C., 1963, JD, 1966. Bar: N.C. 1966, U.S. Dist. Ct. (ea., mid. and we. dists.) N.C. 1969, U.S. Ct. Appeals (4th cir.) 1969. Ptnr. Robinson, Bradshaw & Hinson, P.A., Charlotte, 1969—. Mayor City of Charlotte, 1991-95; bd. dirs. Martin-Marietta Materials Inc. Tchr. sr. h.s. sunday sch. Myers Park Presbyn. Ch., 1970—, ruling elder, 1970-76, 1978-84, 1996-2000, chmn. of session, 1984; mem. Charlotte City Coun., 1983-91. With U.S. Army, 1967-68, Vietnam. Recipient Bronze Star, 1968; named Mcpl. Leader of the Yr. Am. City & County Mag., 1995. Mem. ABA, VFW, N.C. Bar Assn., Mecklenburg County Bar Assn. (sec. 1976, bd. dir. 1970-76), Mecklenburg County Vietnam Vets. Assn., Mecklenburg County Eagle Scouts Assn., Am. Legion, Phalanx Lodge Mason. Republican. Presbyterian. Office: Robinson Bradshaw & Hinson PA 1900 Independence Ctr 101 N Tryon St Ste 1900 Charlotte NC 28246-0103

VINSON, C. ROGER, federal judge; b. Cadiz, Ky., Feb. 19, 1940; BS, U.S. Naval Acad., 1962; JD, Vanderbilt U., 1971. Bar: Fla. 1971. Commd. ensign USN, 1962, advanced through grades to lt., 1963, naval aviator, until 1968, resigned, 1968; assoc. to ptnr. Beggs & Lane, Pensacola, Fla., 1971-83; judge US Dist. Ct. (no. dist.) Fla., Pensacola, 1983—, chief judge, 1997—; judge Fgn. Intelligence Surveillance Ct., 2006—. Mem. Jud. Conf. Adv. Com. on Civil Rules, 1993-99; mem. 11th Cir. Pattern Instrn. Com. Contbr. articles to profl. jours. Divsn. chair, area chair United Way of Escambia County; bd. dirs. Pensacola Arts Coun., also treas.; mem. corp. bd. Bapt. Hosp. of Pensacola, 1977-82; co-founder, v.p., charter bd. dirs. Escambia County Epilepsy Soc.; trustee, sec., chair Fellows Meml. Fund Found.; trustee Fla. Bapt. Found., 1979-83; Sunday sch. tchr., bd. dires. First Bapt. Ch. Pensacola. Recipient J. Nixon Daniel Leadership award, 1976, Rinehardt Holm Disting. Svc. award, 1976, Pensacola Action '76 Achievement award, 1976; Wilson Merit scholar, 1968-71. Mem. Am. Judicature Soc., Fla. Bar, Escambia-Santa Rosa Bar Assn., Soc. Bar of 1st Jud. Cir., N.W. Fla. Fed. Bar Assn. (co-founder), Rotary Club of Pensacola (bd. dirs. 1997—, pres. 1998-99), Panhandle Tiger Bay Club (co-founder, pres. 2002-03). Office: US Courthouse 5th fl 1 N Palafox St # 32501 Pensacola FL 32501-5665

VINSON, DAVID BERWICK, neuropsychologist; b. Houston, Oct. 7, 1917; s. David Berwick and Norma (Calhoun) V.; m. Helen Patricia Freiday, Dec. 28, 1940; children: David Berwick III (dec.), Helen Catharine. BA, UCLA, 1941; PhD, U. London, 1952. Dir. Tex. Acad. Advancement Life Scis., 1954-89; pres. Microset, Inc., Tex., 1978-87, Factor, Inc., Tex., 1986—2006, Assessment Systems, Inc., Tex., 1968—2005. Cons. in field. Capt. USAF, 1941-43, ETO. Fellow AIAA; mem. APA, IEEE, Soc. Biol. Psychiatry, Sigma Xi. Lutheran. Home and Office: 161 Schattenbaum Dr Fredericksburg TX 78624-6301

VINSON, LAURENCE DUNCAN, JR., lawyer; b. Gadsden, Ala., Mar. 17, 1947; BS with hons., U. Ala., Tuscaloosa, 1969; JD, U. Ala., 1973. Bar: Ala., U.S. Dist. Ct. (no., mid. and so. dists.) Ala., U.S. Ct. Appeals (11th cir.), U.S. Supreme Ct. Assoc. Bradley Arant Rose & White, LLP, Birmingham, Ala., 1973-79, ptnr., 1979—. Bar: Ala. 1973, U.S. Dist. Ct. (no. dist.) Ala. 1973, U.S. Supreme Ct. 1977, U.S. Ct. Appeals (11th cir.) 1981, U.S. Dist. Ct. (so. dist.) Ala. 1989, U.S. Dist. Ct. (mid. dist.) Ala. 1991. Chmn. Ala. Uniform Comml. Code Revisions Coms., 1991-2004. Mem. ABA, Birmingham Bar Assn., Ala. State Bar, Ala. Law Inst., Order of Coif, Phi Beta Kappa, Omicron Delta Kappa. Office: Bradley Arant Rose & White LLP One Federal Pl 1819 5th Ave N Birmingham AL 35203-2104 Office Phone: 205-521-8000. Business E-Mail: lvinson@bradleyarant.com.

VINSON, VICTORIA DEAN, middle school educator; b. Cedartown, Ga., June 19, 1952; d. BennieDean Vinson and Katherine Louise (Green) Easterwood BSEd, U. Ga., 1975; postgrad., Valdosta State U., 1976-78, Berry Coll., 1980-81, U. Maryland, Lakenheath, Eng., 1982-84, W. Ga. Coll., 1991. Cert. K-12 gifted tchr., Ga. Tchr. Tift County High Sch., Tifton, Ga., 1976-79, Elm St. Mid. Sch., Rockmart, Ga., 1980-81, 85-89, tchr. of gifted, 1991—; tchr. RAF Feltwell (Eng.)-Lakenheath Mid. Sch., 1981-84. Instr. aerobics Floyd Med. Ctr., Rome, Ga., 1985-89; tchr./asst. Baird Ballet Co., Rome, 1984-88; tchr., choreographer Rome City Ballet, 198991, Acad. Performing Arts, Cedartown, 1992-93. Mem. ASCD, NEA, Ga. Edn. Assn., Polk Edn. Assn., Nat. Coun. Tchrs. English, Ga. Supporters for Gifted, Profl. Dance Tchrs. Assn., Nat. Dance Exercise Inst. Tng. Assn., Beta Sigma Phi. Democrat. Home: 99 Seab Green Rd Cedartown GA 30125-4637 Office: Elm St Mid Sch 100 Morgan Valley Rd Rockmart GA 30153-1610

VINSON, WILLIAM THEODORE, lawyer; BS, USAF Acad., 1965; JD, UCLA, 1969. Bar: Calif. 1970. Judge advocate USAF, 1970-74; trial counsel Phillips Petroleum, San Mateo, Calif., 1974-75; atty. Lockheed Corp., Westlake Village, Calif., 1975-90, v.p., sec., 1990-92, v.p., gen. couns., 92-95; v.p., chief counsel Lockheed Martin Corp., Westlake Village, 1995-98; cons. Lockheed Corp., Westlake Village, 1998; chmn. Siemens Govt. Svcs., Inc., 2001—. Chmn. SAP Govt. Support and Svcs. Inc., 2006—. Bd. dirs. Westminster Free Clinic, 2001—. Office: 5560 E Napoleon Ave Oak Park CA 91377-4746

VINTZILEOS, ANTHONY MARK, obstetrician, gynecologist; b. Athens, Greece, Dec. 15, 1950; s. Mark and Barbara (Prokopiou) V.; m. Colleen Ann McBride, June 25, 1977 (div.); children: Mark, Matthew, Michael; m. Cathylynn Pike, Dec. 30, 1989; children: Barbara, William. MD, Athens U. Med. Sch. Intern Monmouth Med. Ctr., Long Branch, N.J., 1976-77; resident St. Josephs Hosp. Med. Ctr., Paterson, N.J., 1977-81; prof., chmn. Dept. Ob-gyn. and Reproductive Scis. Robert Wood Johnson Med. Sch. Maternal fetal medicine fellow U. Conn. Health Ctr., Farmington, N.J., 1981-83. Mem. Am. Coll. Ob-gyn. Home: 4 Sky High Ter Bridgewater NJ 08807-1201 Office: Dept OB-GYN Winthrop U Hosp 259 First St Mineola NY 11501 Home Phone: 908-722-8020; Office Phone: 516-663-8657. Office Fax: 516-663-2804. Business E-Mail: avintzileos@winthrop.org.

VIOLA, BILL, artist, writer; b. NYC, Jan. 25, 1951; s. William John and Wynne Viola; m. Kira Perov; children: Blake, Andrei. BFA, Syracuse U., 1973, DFA, 1995, Sch. Art Inst. Chgo., 1997, Calif. Coll. Arts & Crafts, Oakland, 1998, Mass. Coll. Art, 1999, Calif. Inst. of the Arts, Valencia, 2000, U. Sunderland, Eng., 2000. Tech. dir. Art/Tapes/22 Video Studio, Florence, Italy, 1974-76; artist-in-residence Sta. WNET, NYC, 1976-83, WXXI-TV, Rochester, NY, 1979, Sony Corp., Atsugi Labs., Japan, 1980-81, San Diego Zoo, 1984; instr. Calif. Inst. of Arts, Valencia, 1983; represented by James Cohan Gallery, NYC. Solo exhbns. include The Kitchen Ctr., N.Y., 1974, Everson Mus. Art, Syracuse, N.Y., 1975, Mus. Modern Art, N.Y.C., 1979, 87, Whitney Mus. Art, N.Y.C., 1982, Musee d'Art Moderne, Paris, 1983, Mus. Contemporary Art, L.A., 1985, Fukui Prefectural Mus. Art, Fukui City, Japan, 1989, Staditsche Kunsthalle Düsseldorf, 1992, Moderna Musee, Stockholm, 1993, Museo Nacional Centro de Arte Reina Sofia, Madrid, 1993, Musee Cantonal des Beaux-Arts, Lausanne, Switzerland, 1993, Whitechapel Art Gallery, London, 1993, Tel Aviv Mus. Art, 1994, Musée d'Art Contemporain, Montreal, 1993, Centro Cultural/Banco de Brazil, Rio de Janeiro, 1994, 46th Venice Biennale, 1995, Festival d'Automne Paris, 1996, Bill Viola: A 25 Year Survey Exhbn., Whitney Mus. Am. Art, N.Y., travels to Whitney Mus. Am. Art, 1997, L.A. County Mus. Am. Art, 1998, Stedelijk Mus., Amsterdam, 1998, Mus. Pur Moderne Kunst and Shirnkunstalle Dominkankloister, Germany, 1999, San Francisco Mus. Modern Art, 1999, Art Inst. Chgo., 1999-2000, 2KM, Karlsruhe, Germany, 2000, James Cohan Gallery, N.Y., 2000, Anthony d'Offay Gallery, London, 2001, Bill Viola: Going Forth By Day, Deutsche Guggenheim Berlin, 2002; group exhbns. include De Saisset Art Gallery and Mus., Santa Clara, Calif., 1972, Whitney Mus. Am. Art, 1975-87, 89, 93, Stedelijk Mus., Amsterdam, 1984, Carnegie Mus. Art, Pitts., 1988, Kölnischer Kunstverein, Cologne, Germany, 1989, Israel Mus., Jerusalem, 1990, Musée Nat. d'Art Moderne, Ctr. Georges Pompidou, Paris, 1990, Martin Gropius Bau, Berlin, 1991, Mus. Moderne Kunst, Frankfurt, Germany, 1991, Royal Acad., London, 1993, Denver Art Mus., Columbus (Ohio) Art Mus., 1994, Anthony d'Offay Gallery, London, 1995, Mus. Modern Art, N.Y.C., 1995, Tate Gallery, London, 1995, Albright-Knox Art Gallery, 1996, Fabric Workshop, Phila., 1997, MOMA, N.Y., 1999, La Beauté, Found Cartier, 2000, Tate Modern, London, 2000, Nat. Gallery, London, 2000, James Cohan Gallery, NY, 2001; spl. screening film: Dèserts, Vienna, Austria, 1994, WhiteCahpel Art Gallery, London, 2001, 49th Venice Biennale, 2001, Perth Festival, Australia, 2001, Commune di Ferrara, Italy, 2001, Musse d'Art Contemporian de Montreal, Canada, 2001; commns. include The Stopping mind, Mus. Moderne Kunst, Frankfurt, 1991, Nantes Triptych, Dèlegation aux Arts Plastiques, Nantes, France, 1992, Slowly Turning Narrative, Isnt. Comtemporary Art, Phila., Va. Mus. Fine Art, Richmond, 1992, Tiny Deaths, Biennale d'Art Contemporain de Lyon, France, 1993, Dèserts, Konzerthause, Vienna, 1994, 3e Biennale d'Art contemporaire de Lyon, Musèe d'art contemporain, Lyon, France, 1995, Helaba Main Tower, Frankfurt, Germany, 2000, Gotesborgs Musiken, Sweden, 2001, Deserts, Konzerthaus, Vienna, 2001, Deserts, Carnigie Hall, New York, 2001, Deserts, Royal Festival Hall, London, 2001, Deserts, IRCAM, Centre Pomidou Main Hall, Paris, 2001, others; composer: (album) David Tudor-Rainforest IV, 1981; (video) Chott el-Djerid, Anthem, 1983, Hatsu-Yume, 1981, The Reflecting Pool, 1977-79, The Space Between the Teeth, 1976, Bill Viola: Selected Works, 1986, I Do Not Know What It Is I Am Like, 1986, The Passing, 1991, The City of Man, 1989, Nantes Triptych, 1992, Slowly Turning Narritive, 1992, Tiny Deaths, 1993, The Greetings, 1995, The Crossing, 1996, The Quintet of Remembrance, 2000, The Quintet of the Unseen, 2000, The Quintet of the Astonished, The Quintet of the Silent, 2000, Surrender, 2001, Catherine's

Room, 2001, Five Angles for the Millenium, 2001, Going Forth By Day, 2002. Japan/U.S. Creative Arts fellow NEA, 1980, Rockefeller Found. Video Artist fellow, 1982, Visual Artist fellow NEA, 1983-89, Guggenheim Meml. Found. fellow, 1985, Intercultural Film/Video fellow Rockefeller Found., 1991; recipient Jury prize U.S. Film and Video Festival, 1982, Grand prize, 1983, Jury prize Video Culture/Can., 1983, Grand prize for video art, 1984, First prize for video art Athens (Ohio) Film/Video Festival, 1984, Maya Deren award Am. Film Inst., 1987, First prize Festival Internat. d'Art Video et des Nouvelles Images Electroniques de Locarno, 1987, John D. and Catherine T. MacArthur Found. award, 1989, Skowhegan medal, 1993, First prize Festival Internat. de Video, Cidade de Vigo, Spain, 1993, Medienkunstpreis, Siemens Kulturprogramm and Zentrum fur Kunst und Medientechnologie, Germany, 1993; scholar-in-residence The Getty Rsch. Inst. for History of Art and Humanities, L.A., 1998. Office: 282 Granada Ave Long Beach CA 90803 E-mail: info@billviola.com.

VIOLANTE, JOSEPH ANTHONY, lawyer; b. Jersey City, June 15, 1950; s. Carmine Joseph and Carmine Joseph (Cardillo) Violante; m. Linda Lee Munn, July 5, 1972 (div. May 24, 2006); m. Debra Blanken, Oct. 28, 2006. Student, St. Peter's Coll., Jersey City, 1972-74; BA, U. N.Mex., 1975; JD, U. La Verne, Calif., 1980. Bar: Calif. 1981, D.C. 1990, U.S. Dist. Ct. (cen. dist.) Calif. 1982, (6th dist.) Ohio 1992, U.S. Ct. Appeals (fed. cir.) 1990, U.S. Ct. Appeals (D.C. cir.) 1991, U.S. Ct. Vets. Appeals 1990. Sole practice, Thousand Oaks, Calif., 1981-85; atty., cons. Bd. Vet. Appeals, Washington, 1985-90; staff counsel DAV, Washington, 1990-92, legis. counsel, 1992-96, dep. nat. legis. dir., 1996-97, nat. legis. dir., 1997—. Mem. adv. com. Bowie Cable TV, 1989-91, bd. dirs., 1992-94. Co-host cable TV show Vets. Forum, 1991-94. Asst. coach Am. Youth Soccer Orgn., Thousand Oaks, 1981-84, Little League, Thousand Oaks, 1981-84; del. John Glenn Calif. Dem. Presdl. Primary, Thousand Oaks, 1984; active campaign Combined Fed., Washington, 1985; mem. presdl. del. Prisoners of War/Missing in Action, Southeast Asia, 1996. With USMC, 1969-72. Mem.: FBA (vets. com. 1991—92, at-large bd. mem., contbg. writer Tommy), KC, ABA (vice chmn. vets. benefit com. 1991—98), DAV (life; comdr. 1990—91), Coun. of 2,000, Nat. Italian-Am. Found. (nat. mentors program), Italian-Am. Bar Assn., DC Bar Assn., Fed. Cir. Bar Assn. (chmn. vets appeal com. 1992—96, chmn. legis. com. 1996—2001, bd. govs. 2001—04), Calif. Bar Assn., Nat. Found. Women Legislators (bd. dirs. 2001—), VFW (life; comdr. 1984—85), 2d Bn. 4th Marine Assn., Marine Corps League, Italian-Am. War Vets., Am. Legion, 3d Marine Divsn. Assn. (life). Democrat. Roman Catholic. Avocations: coin collecting/numismatics, reading, travel. Office: DAV Nat Svc & Legis Hdqrs 807 Maine Ave SW Washington DC 20024-2410 Office Phone: 202-554-3501. Business E-Mail: jviolante@davmail.org.

VIORST, JUDITH STAHL, writer; b. Newark, Feb. 2, 1931; d. Martin Leonard and Ruth June (Ehrenkranz) Stahl; m. Milton Viorst, Jan. 30, 1960; children: Anthony Jacob, Nicholas Nathan, Alexander Noah. BA, Rutgers U., 1952; grad., Washington Psychoanalytic Inst., 1981. Author: (children's books) Sunday Morning, 1968, I'll Fix Anthony, 1969, Try It Again Sam, 1970, The Tenth Good Thing About Barney, 1971 (Silver Pencil award 1973), Alexander and the Terrible, Horrible, No Good, Very Bad Day, 1972, My Mama Says There Aren't Any Zombies, Ghosts, Vampires, Creatures, Demons, Monsters, Fiends, Goblins or Things, 1973, Rosie and Michael, 1974, Alexander, Who Used to Be Rich Last Sunday, 1978, The Good-Bye Book, 1988, Earrings!, 1990, The Alphabet from Z to A (with Much Confusion on the Way), 1994, Alexander, Who's Not (Do You Hear Me? I Mean It!) Going to Move, 1995, Super-Completely and Totally the Messiest, 2001, Just in Case, 2006; (poetry) The Village Square, 1965-66, It's Hard to Be Hip Over Thirty and Other Tragedies of Married Life, 1968, People and Other Aggravations, 1971, How Did I Get to Be Forty and Other Atrocities, 1976, If I Were in Charge of the World and Other Worries, 1981, When Did I Stop Being Twenty and Other Injustices, 1987, Forever Fifty and Other Negotiations, 1989, Sad Underwear and Other Complications, 1995, Suddenly Sixty and Other Shocks of Later Life, 2000, I'm Too Young to be Seventy and Other Delusions, 2005; (with Milton Viorst) The Washington Underground Gourmet, 1970, Yes Married, 1972, A Visit From St. Nicholas (To a Liberated Household), 1977, Love and Guilt and the Meaning of Life, Etc., 1979, Necessary Losses, 1986, Murdering Mr. Monti, 1994, Imperfect Control, 1998, You're Officially a Grown-Up, 1999, Grown-up Marriage, 2003; (musical) Love and Shrimp (book and lyrics), 1990; (HBO children's movie) Alexander and the Terrible, Horrible, No Good, Very Bad Day (book and lyrics), 1990, (children's stage musical) Alexander and the Terrible, Horrible, No Good, Very Bad Day, 1998, Alexander, Who's Not Not Not Not Not Not Gong to Move (book and lyrics), 2003. Recipient Emmy award for poems used in Anne Bancroft Spl., 1970. Jewish.

VIORST, MILTON, writer; b. Paterson, NJ, Feb. 18, 1930; s. Louis and Betty (LeVine) Viorst; m. Judith Stahl, Jan. 30, 1960; children: Anthony, Nicholas, Alexander. BA summa cum laude, Rutgers U., 1951; student (Fulbright scholar), U. Lyon, France, 1952; MA, Harvard U., Cambridge, Mass., 1955; MS, Columbia U., NYC, 1956. Reporter Bergen Record, NJ, 1955-56, Newark StarLedger, 1956-57, Washington Post, 1957-61; Washington corr. NY Post, 1961-64; syndicated columnist Washington Evening Star, 1971-75; staff writer New Yorker, NYC, 1987-93; Ferris prof. journalism Princeton U., NJ, 1995-96. Lectr. in field. Author: (book) Hostile Allies: FDR and deGaulle, 1965, Great Documents of Western Civilization, 1965, Fall from Grace: The Republican Party and the Puritan Ethic, 1968, Hustlers and Heroes, 1971, Fire in the Streets: America in the 1960's, 1980, Making a Difference: The Peace Corps at Twenty-Five, 1986, Sands of Sorrow: Israel's Journey from Independence, 1987, Reaching for the Olive Branch: UNRWA and Peace in the Middle East, 1990, Sandcastles: The Arabs in Search of the Modern World, 1994, In The Shadow of the Prophet: The Struggle for the Soul of Islam, 1998, What Shall I Do With This People? Jews and the Fractious Politics of Judaism, 2002, Storm from the East: The Struggle Between the Arab World and the Christian West, 2006; contbr. articles to profl. jours.; contbg. corr.: Washington Quar. Mem. nat. adv. com. Mid. East Policy Coun.; chmn. Fund Investigative Journalism, 1969—78; bd. dirs. Georgetown Day Sch., 1977—80, Inst. World Affairs. Officer USAF, 1952—54. Recipient Columbia Journalism Alumni award, 1992, Human Rights award, UN Assn. DC, 2002, chevalier, Legion d'Honneur, France, 2005; scholar, Mid. East Inst.; Woodrow Wilson Sr. fellow, 1973—79, Alicia Patterson fellow, 1979. Mem.: Coun. Fgn. Rels., Author's Guild, Soc. Profl. Journalists, PEN, Am. Peace Now, Phi Beta Kappa. Office Phone: 202-966-8676. Personal E-mail: mviorst@aol.com.

VIRANI, SHANIL, data analyst; b. Penticton, B.C., Canada, Jan. 25, 1973; BS, U. Waterloo, Ont., 1996; MS, postgrad., Yale U., New Haven, Conn., 2004—. Data analyst Smithsonian Instn., Cambridge, Mass., 1999—2004. Mem.: Am. Astron. Soc.

VIRANT, PAUL, chef; b. 1970; m. Jennifer Virant; 1 child, Lincoln. Degree in Nutrition, Wesleyan Coll.; grad., Culinary Inst. Am., Hyde Park, NY. With Cascade Mountain Winery; chef March, NYC, Charlie Trotter's, Ambria, Padovani's Bistro and Wine Bar, Honolulu, Everest, Chgo., Outpost, Chgo., Blackbird, Chgo.; owner, exec. chef Vie, Western Springs, Ill. Named Best New Chef, Chgo. Mag., 2005, Rising Star Chef, Restaurant Hospitality Mag., 2005, StarChefs.com, 2005, 2006 Jean Banchet Rising Star Chef, Best New Chef, Food & Wine Mag., 2007. Office: Vie 4471 Lawn Ave Western Springs IL 60558 Office Phone: 708-246-2082. Office Fax: 708-246-2668. *

VIRDEN, FRANK STANLEY, retired military officer; b. Long Beach, Calif., Sept. 21, 1933; s. Frank and Katherine Stanley Virden; m. Jacquelin Ann Moseley, 1954 (div. 1979); children: Yvette Virden Parsons, Geoffrey Alexander; m. Elisabeth Burns Virden, 1991; stepchildren: Wesley Delwin Bonds III, Charles Cary Bonds. BA in Polit. Sci., Duke U., Durham, NC, 1955; MBA in Transp. Adminstrn., Mich. State U., East Lansing, 1966. Commdg. officer Navy Cargo Handling Bn. One, Williamsburg, Va., 1969—72; grp. supply officer Svc. Grp. Three, US Seventh Fleet, 1972—74; dir. storage & transp. Def. Constrn. Supply Ctr., Columbus, Ohio, 1974—77; commdg. officer Naval Sch., Transp. Mgmt., Oakland, Calif., 1977—79; dep. comdr. Mil. Traffic Mgmt. Command, DC, 1979—81; cons. in field, 1981—93; exec. dir. Episcopal Cmty. Svcs. Found., Cin., 1993—96; ret., 1996. Pres. US Navy League Coun., Cin., 1989—92. Dir., pres. Baldwin County Pub. Transit Coalition, Robertsdale, Ala., 1999—2007; bd mem., chair Nat. Network Lay Profls., NYC, 1994—2000; standing com. mem. Episcopal Diocese Ctrl. Gulf Coast, Pensacola, Fla., 2001—04; exec. mem. Espisc. Cmty. Svcs., 1993—96; infrastructure com. co-chair Charter Party, Cin., 1983—87. Capt. USN, 1955—81. Decorated Meritorious Svc. medal Sec. Navy, Commendation medal, Legion of Merit award; recipient Unsung Hero award, ACT II Cmty. Organizing Fedn., 2003, 2005. Mem.: Mensa, Am. Assn. Woodturners. Independent. Episcopalian. Achievements include being the driving force in the development of Baldwin County Public Transit Coalition; development of church organization being responsible for successfully curtailing drug trafficking in county public schools. Avocations: woodworking, travel. Home: PO Box 475 Gulf Shores AL 36547-0475 Personal E-mail: vivahaus@gulftel.com.

VIRELLI, LOUIS JAMES, JR., lawyer; b. Phila., Nov. 4, 1948; s. Louis James and Elsie Antoinette (Colombo) V.; m. Barbara Ann Rotella, Aug. 22, 1970; children: Louis J. III, Christopher F. BE in Mech. Engring., Villanova U., 1970; JD, U. Tenn., 1972. Bar: Pa. 1973, U.S. Patent and Trademark Office, 1973, U.S. Ct. Customs and Patent Appeals 1974, U.S. Dist. Ct. (we. dist.) Pa. 1976, U.S. Dist. Ct. (ea. dist.) Pa. 1977, U.S. Ct. Appeals (9th cir.) 1980, U.S. Ct. Appeals (D.C. cir.) 1982, U.S. Supreme Ct. 1982. Patent atty. Sperry New Holland Co., Pa., 1973—74; assoc. counsel Westinghouse Co., Pitts., 1974—76; assoc. Paul & Paul, Phila., 1976—80, ptnr., 1980—84; patent counsel Nat. Starch and Chem. Co., Bridgewater, NJ, 1984—88, asst. gen. counsel, intellectual property, 1988—92, gen. counsel, intellectual property, 1992—95; asst. gen. counsel Patents Unilever US, Inc., Edgewater, NJ, 1988—95; v.p. gen. patent counsel Unilever N.V., P.L.C., Englewood Cliffs, 1995—96, sr. v.p., gen. patent counsel, 1997—2003, sr. v.p., gen. counsel intellectual property, 2003—06; sr. counsel Morgan Lewis, NYC, 2007—. Arbitrator U.S. Dist. Ct. (ea. dist.) Pa., Phila., 1982-84. Mem.: ABA, Assn. Corp. Patent Counsel (treas., v.p., pres.), Phila. Patent Law Assn., NJ Patent Law Assn., Intellectual Property Owners Assn. (bd. dirs.). Office: Morgan Lewis 1701 Market St Philadelphia PA 19103-2921 also: Morgan Lewis & Bockius LLP 101 Park Ave New York NY 10178-0060 Office Phone: 215-963-5125. Business E-Mail: lvirelli@morganlewis.com.

VIRGO, JOHN MICHAEL, economist, researcher, educator; b. Prestbury Village, Eng., Mar. 11, 1943; s. John Joseph and Muriel Agnes (Franks) V.; m. Katherine Sue Ulmrich, Sept. 6, 1980; 1 child, Debra Marie Riekstins. BA, Calif. State U., Fullerton, 1967, MA, 1969, Claremont Grad. U., 1971, PhD, 1972. Instr. econs. Whittier (Calif.) Coll., 1970-71, Calif. State U., Fullerton and Long Beach, 1971-72, Claremont (Calif.) Grad. Sch., 1971-72; asst. prof. econs. Va. Commonwealth U., Richmond, 1972-74; assoc. prof. mgmt. So. Ill. U., Edwardsville, 1975-83, prof., 1984—. Bd. dirs., founder Internat. Health Econ. & Mgmt. Inst., Edwardsville, 1983-87. Author: Legal & Illegal California Farmworkers, 1974; author, editor: Health Care: An International Perspective, 1984, Exploring New Vistas in Health Care, 1985, Restructuring Health Policy, 1986; founder, editor-in-chief Internat. Advances in Econ. Rsch.; contbr. articles to profl. jours. Served with USN, 1965-68. Mem. AMA, Am. Econ. Assn., Am. Soc. Assn. Execs., Internat. Atlantic Econ. Soc. (founder, exec. v.p., mng. editor Atlantic Econ. jour. 1973—), European Econ. Assn., Allied Social Scis. Assn. (chmn. exec. confs. 1982-84), Western Econs. Assn., Western Econ. Assn., So. Econs. Assn., Media Club (St. Louis). Democrat. Roman Catholic. Avocations: tennis, skiing. Home: 5277 Lindell Blvd Saint Louis MO 63108-1223 Office: Internat Atlantic Econ Soc 2nd Fl 4949 W Pine Blvd Saint Louis MO 63108-1431 Office Phone: 314-454-0100. Business E-Mail: iaes@iaes.org.

VIRGO, KATHERINE SUE, medical researcher; b. East Alton, Ill., Feb. 14, 1959; d. John William and Doris Ann (Spencer) Ulmrich; m. John Michael Virgo, Sept. 6, 1980. BSBA, So. Ill. U., 1981, MBA, 1983; PhD in Health Svcs. Rsch., St. Louis U., 1991. From asst. coord. to exec. adminstr. Atlantic Econ. Soc., Edwardsville, Ill., 1976—86; co-founder, exec. adminstr. Internat. Health Econs. and Mgmt. Inst., Edwardsville, 1983—87; health sci. specialist VA Med. Ctr., St. Louis, 1986—93, clin. rsch. coord., 1993—; asst. prof. St. Louis U., 1991—96, assoc. prof., 1996—2001, prof., 2001—. Bd. dir. Internat. Health Econs. and Mgmt. Inst., Edwardsville, 1983-87. Assoc. editor: Atlantic Econ. Jour., 1994—, dep. editor: Internat. Advances in Econ. Rsch., 1995—; co-editor: Cancer Patient Follow-Up, 1997, The Bionic Patient, 2005; ad hoc reviewer: Jour. of the AMA, 1995—96, Med. Care, 1995—, Women's Health Issues, 2000—01, Jour. Spinal Cord Medicine, 2002—, Jour. Behavioral Health Svc. Rsch., 2000—, mem. editl. bd.: Surg. Oncology, 2007—, Jour. Gen. Internal Medicine, 2005, ad hoc reviewer: Internat. Jour. Oncology, 2005—; contbr. articles to profl. jours. Mem. St. Louis Cathedral Basilica Choir. VA grantee. Mem.: APHA (sect. councilor 2003—06, program chair 2005—), Soc. Internat. Geriatric Oncology, Am. Paraplegia Soc., Health Econs. Rsch. Orgn., Acad. of Health, Am. Soc. Clin. Oncology (health svcs. rsch. com. 2002—05, methods subcom., dissemination and implementation subcom.), Internat. Health Econs. Assn. Democrat. Roman Catholic. Avocations: singing, piano, travel, reading, swimming. Home: 5277 Lindell Blvd Saint Louis MO 63108-1223 Office: VA Med Ctr 112JC 915 N Grand Blvd Saint Louis MO 63106-1621 Business E-Mail: virgoks@slu.edu.

VIRKAR, ANIL V., materials engineer, educator; BTech in Metall. Engring. with honors, Indian Inst. Tech., Bombay, 1967; MS in Engring. Mechanics, La. State U., Baton Rouge, 1969; PhD in Materials Sci., Northwestern U., Evanston, Ill., 1973. Postdoctoral fellow materials sci. & engring. U. Utah, 1973—74, rsch. asst. prof., 1974—76, asst. prof., 1976—79, assoc. prof., 1979—84, prof., 1984—, chair dept. materials sci. & engring., 1998—. Founding mem. Ceramatec, 1976. Contbr. articles to sci. jours., chapters to books. Fellow: Am. Ceramic Soc. (Ross Coffin Purdy award 1993); mem.: Electrochemical Soc., Am. Soc. Metals, NAE. Achievements include patents in field. Office: Dept Materials Sci & Engring U Utah 122 S Central Campus Dr Rm 304 Salt Lake City UT 84112 Office Phone: 801-581-5396. Office Fax: 801-581-4816. E-mail: anil.virkar@m.cc.utah.edu. *

VIRKHAUS, TAAVO, symphony orchestra conductor; b. Tartu, Estonia, June 29, 1934; came to U.S., 1949; s. Adalbert August and Helene Marie (Sild) V.; m. Nancy Ellen Herman, Mar. 29, 1969. MusB U. Miami, 1955; MusM Eastman Sch. of Music, Rochester, 1957, DMA, 1967. Dir. music U. Rochester (N.Y.), also assoc. prof. Eastman Sch., Rochester, 1967-77; music dir., condr. Duluth (Minn.) Superior Symphony Orch., 1977-94; guest condr. Rochester Philharm., Minn. Orch., Balt. Symphony, Vancouver Symphony and others, 1972—; music dir., condr. Hunstville (Ala.) Symphony Orch., 1989-2003, condr. emertius, 2003—; guest condr. at Tallinn, Estonia, 1978, 88, 90, 92, 93, 94, 99; lectr. U. Minn.-Duluth, U. of Wis.-Superior. With U.S. Army, 1957-58, USAR, 1957-61. Recipient Howard Hanson Composition award, 1966, Am. Heritage award JFK Libr. for Minorities, 1974; Fulbright scholar, Musikhochschule, Cologne, 1963. Mem. Am. Symphony Orch. League, Condrs. Guild, Am. Fedn. of Musicians. Composer: Violin Concerto, 1966, Symphony No. 1, 1976, Symphony No. 2, 1979, Symphony No. 3, 1984, Symphony No. 4, 1989, Symphony No. 5, 1994, Violin Concerto No. 2, 1995. Republican. Lutheran. Personal E-mail: tvirkhaus@knology.net.

VIRTEL, JAMES JOHN, lawyer; b. Joliet, Ill., May 15, 1944; BA cum laude, Loras Coll., 1966; JD cum laude, St. Louis U., 1969. Bar: Mo. 1969, Ill. 1969. Atty. Armstrong Teasdale LLP, St. Louis, 1976—. Adj. prof. law St. Louis U., 1995-99; regent Loras Coll., Dubuque, Iowa, 1996—. Editor: St. Louis U. Law Jour., 1968-69. Fellow Am. Coll. Trial Lawyers; mem. Ill. State Bar Assn., Mo. State Bar Assn. Office: Armstrong Teasdale LLP 1 Metropolitan Sq Ste 2600 Saint Louis MO 63102-2740 Office Phone: 314-342-8088. Personal E-mail: jvirtel@sbcglobal.net. E-mail: jvirtel@armstrongteasdale.com.

VISCARDI, PETER G., risk management and environmental affairs executive; b. NYC, Dec. 28, 1947; s. Peter and Louise (Johnson) Viscardi; m. Margaret E. McGowan, Sept. 11, 1971 (div. 2001); children: Margaret, Peter; m. Linda M. Gawel, Sept. 26, 2003. BA, Hunter Coll., NYC, 1970. CPCU. Ins. mgr. Jaffie Contracting Co., Inc., NYC, 1971-73; ins. adminstr. Otis Elevator Co., NYC, 1973, supr. ins. adminstrn., 1974; dir. adminstrn. Finsure divsn. Studebaker-Worthington, Inc., NYC, 1975-78, corp. risk mgr./exec. v.p., chief oper. officer, 1978-80; mgr. corp. ins. Fortune Brands, Inc. (formerly Am. Brands), NYC, 1980-81, mgr. corp. ins. and real estate, 1981-87, dir. corp. ins. Old Greenwich, Conn., 1987-90, dir. risk mgmt. and environ. affairs, 1990-99; cons. Shirley, NY, 2000—03; sr. mgr. Ernst & Young, 2003—04; cons., 2004—05; pres. Viscardi Risk Consulting Corp., 2005—. Mem. editl. bd.: Risk and Benefits Mag., 1987—89, 1991—92, instnl. investor adv. bd.:, 1997. Mem. adv. bd. ACE Bermuda, 1999—2003. Mem.: Profl. Liability Underwriting Soc., Nat. Assn. Mfrs. (risk mgmt. and environ. quality coms. 1990—99), Am. Mgmt. Assn. (ins. and risk mgmt. coun.), Soc. CPCUs. Office Phone: 631-924-0887. E-mail: lirisk@optonline.net.

VISCLOSKY, PETER JOHN, congressman, lawyer; b. Gary, Ind., Aug. 13, 1949; s. John and Helen (Kauzlaric) Visclosky; m. Anne Marie O'Keefe; children: John, Timothy. BS in acctg., Ind. U., Indpls., 1970; JD, U. Notre Dame, 1973; LLM in internat. and comparative law, Georgetown U., 1983. Bar: Ind., D.C., U.S. Supreme Ct. Legal asst. Dist. Atty.'s Office, NYC, 1972; assoc. Benjamin, Greco & Gouveia, Merrillville, Ind., 1973-76, Greco, Gouveia, Miller, Pera & Bishop, Merrillville, Ind., 1982-84; assoc. staff appropriations com. US Ho. Reps., Washington, 1976-80, assoc. staff budget com., 1980-82; mem. US Congress from 1st Ind. dist., 1985—; mem. appropriations com., subcoms. treasury, postal svc., gen. govt. and military constrn. Democrat. Roman Catholic. Office: US Ho Reps 2256 Rayburn Ho Office Bldg Washington DC 20515-1401 also: Dist Office Ste 9 701 E 83d Ave Merrillville IN 46410 *

VISCOMI, FRANK JOSEPH, pharmaceutical executive; b. Easton, Pa., Dec. 18, 1951; s. John Dominic and Catherine Viscomi; m. Janet Lynn Wilson, Sept. 29, 1979; children: Lauren Michelle, Rebecca Elizabeth. BS in Biology, Alderson Broaddus Coll., Phillipi, W.Va., 1973; MAT in Edn., Coll. NJ, Trenton, 1988, MA in Math. Physics, 1988. Biologist Colgate Palmolive Co., Piscataway, NJ, 1977—88; mgr. Johnson & Johnson Pharm. R&D, Raritan, NJ, 1988—. Tchr. Hun Sch. of Princeton, NJ, 1998—2000. Contbr. scientific papers to profl. jours.; author: 47, 2006, The Pinhole: A Theory in n-Dimensions, 2007. Mem.: Math. Assn. of Am., Mensa (life). Achievements include patents pending for Mathematical Algorythm to Calculate the Area of and Object in n-Dimensional Space; Anti-Inflammatory Agent Extracted from Milkweed Plants; Development of Laser System to Measure Corneal Opacity; Development of Laser System to Detect Tissue Degradation. Home: 82 Knapp Ave Trenton NJ 08610 Home Phone: 609-581-3820; Office Phone: 908-704-4750. Personal E-mail: fviscomi@aol.com.

VISCOVICH, NANCY ANNE, psychologist; b. Astoria, NY, June 12, 1969; d. Jerry and Elizabeth Viscovich; m. James Allen Joyce, Sept. 10, 2005; 1 child, James Vincent Joyce. BS, Fashion Inst. Tech., NYC, 1991; MA, Queens Coll., Flushing, NY, 1996; PhD, Grad. Ctr. City NY, 2004. Cert. diplomate Am. Profl. Psychology, Splty. Bd. Cert. Clin. Neuropsychology. Neuropsychology intern North Shore U. Hosp., Manhasset, NY, 2002—03; postdoctoral resident in neuropsychology Harvard Med. Sch., Boston, 2003—05; clin. pediat. neuropsychologist Dean Health Sys., Madison, Wis., 2005—. Mem.: APA, Internat. Neuropsychol. Assn. Avocations: running, piano, travel. Office: Dean Health Sys 1313 Fish Hatchery Rd Madison WI 53719

VISCUGLIA, JENNY LOU, music educator; b. Englewood, Colo., Sept. 12, 1967; d. Dwight B and Lynda Lee Eames; m. Felix Alfred Viscuglia, Apr. 5, 1997; m. Andrew Norvelle, Nov. 19, 1989 (div. Sept. 27, 1996). BS in Music Edn., U. Nev., Las Vegas, 2003. Cert. nursing asst., Colo., 1986; music tchr. K-12 Nev., 2003. Cert. nursing asst. Cherry Creek Nursing Ctr., Aurora, Colo., 1986—87; class a alarm operator Regent Security, Englewood, Colo., 1987—88; waitress, asst. mgr. McCoy's Family Restaurant, Littleton, Colo., 1988—89; clerical Kelly Services, Las Vegas, Nev., 1989—90; adminstrv. asst. Nathan Adelson Hospice Found., Las Vegas, Nev., 1990—95; sec. Rio Suites Hotel and Casino, Wine Cellar, Las Vegas, Nev., 1996—97; libr. Nev. Symphony, Las Vegas, Nev., 1994—98; pers. mgr., libr., clarinet sub The Las Vegas Philharm., Las Vegas, Nev., 1998—2004; k-8 music tchr. Clark County Sch. Dist., Las Vegas, Nev., 2003—. Mem. Goodsprings Citizens Adv. Coun., Goodsprings, Nev., 1998—2004; treas., mem. Goodsprings Hist. Soc., Goodsprings, 2001—04. Mem.: NEA, Music Educators Nat. Conf., Am. Orff-Schulwerk Assn., Nat. Assn. Music Educators. Avocations: travel, music. Home: Post Office Box 664 Goodsprings NV 89019 Office: Sandy Valley Elem Mid Sch Sandy Valley NV 89019 Home Phone: 702-874-1411; Office Phone: 702-799-0935. Personal E-mail: viscuglia@aol.com.

VISCUSI, W(ILLIAM) GREGORY KIP, law and economics educator; b. Trenton, NJ, Oct. 3, 1949; s. William Edward and Evelyn (Martin) V.; m. Catherine Makdisi, Sep. 26, 1972 (div.); children: Kira Margaret, Michael Kip; m. Joni Hersch, Jan. 18, 1998. AB summa cum laude, Harvard U., Cambridge, Mass., 1971, MPP, 1973, AM, 1974, PhD, 1976. Prof. econs. Northwestern U., Evanston, Ill., 1976-80, 85-88; dep. dir. White House Council on Wage and Price Stability, Washington, 1979-81; prof. econs. Duke U., Durham, NC, 1981-85; John M. Olin prof. econs. U. Chgo., 1985-86; George G. Allen prof. econs. Duke U., Durham, NC, 1988-96; John M. Olin vis. prof. law and econs. Harvard Law Sch., Cambridge, Mass., 1995, John F. Cogan Jr. prof. law and econs., 1996—2006; univ. disting. prof. law, econs., mgmt. Law Sch. Vanderbilt U., Nashville, 2006—. Rsch. assoc. Nat. Bur. Econ. Rsch., 1978—, Nat. Commn. for Employment Policy, 1981; mem. EPA Sci. Adv. Bd., 1986—, econs. bd., 1992—, Clean Air Act, 1992—, Nat. Acad. Sci. Panel, 1978-79; cons. US Gen. Acctg. Office, 1981-85, Dept. Justice, 1986-87, 89-91, U.S. Office Mgmt. and Budget, 1983; assoc. reporter Am. Law Inst., 1986-91; adj. fellow in civil justice Manhattan Inst., 1987—; inaugural spkr. Geneva Risk Econ. Lectrs., Geneva Assn. Risk and Ins., 1989; John R. Commons lectr. U. Wis., 1990; Ayne Ryde lectr. Lund U., Sweden. Author: Employment Hazards, 1979 (Wells prize 1977), Risk by Choice, 1983, Reforming Products Liability, 1991, Fatal Tradeoffs, 1992, Smoking, 1992, Rational Risk Policy, 1998, Smoke-filled Rooms: A Post-mortem on the Tobacco Deal, 2002; founding editor Jour. Risk and Uncertainty; contbg. editor Regulation mag.; assoc. editor Internat. Rev. of Law Econs., Geneva

Papers on Risk and Ins. Theory, Jour. Regulatory Econs., Jour. Environ. Econs. and Mgmt., J Risk and Ins., Rev. Econs. and Stats., Am. Econ. Rev., Managerial and Decision Econs., Contemporary Econ. Policy. Recipient Article of the Yr. award Econ. Inquiry, 1988, Royal Econ. Soc., 1999; Book of the Yr. awards Am. Risk and Ins. Assn., 1992, 93, 94, 2000, Article award Am. Risk and Ins. Assn., 1999. Mem. Am. Econs. Assn., Econometric Soc., Assn. Environ. and Resource Economists, Assn. for Pub. Policy Analysis and Mgmt., So. Econs. Assn. We. Econs. Assn., Managerial and Decision Econs. Roman Catholic. Office: Vanderbilt Univ Law Sch 131 21st Ave South Nashville TN 37203-1181 Home Phone: 617-864-6560.

VISEK, WILLARD JAMES, nutritionist, animal scientist, physician, educator; b. Sargent, Nebr., Sept. 19, 1922; s. James and Anna S. (Dworak) V.; m. Priscilla Flagg, Dec. 28, 1949; children: Dianna, Madeleine, Clayton Paul. B.Sc. with honors (Carl R. Gray scholar), U. Nebr., 1947; MSc (Smith fellow in agr.), Cornell U., 1949, PhD, 1951; MD (Peter Yost Fund scholar), U. Chgo., 1957; DSc (hon.), U. Nebr., 1980. Diplomate Nat. Bd. Med. Examiners. Grad. asst., lab. animal nutrition Cornell U., 1947-51; AEC postdoctoral fellow Oak Ridge, 1951-52; research assoc., 1952-53; research asst. pharmacology U. Chgo., 1953-57, asst. prof., 1957-61, assoc. prof., 1961-64; rotating med. intern U. Chgo. Clinics, 1957-58, 58-59, 59; prof. nutrition and comparative metabolism, dept. animal sci. Cornell U., Ithaca, NY, 1964-75; prof. clin. sci. (nutrition and metabolism) Coll. Medicine and dept. food sci. U. Ill. Coll. Agr., Urbana-Champaign, 1975—; prof. dept. internal medicine U. Ill. Coll. Medicine, Urbana-Champaign, 1986-93, prof. emeritus, 1993—. Bd. dirs. Coun. Agriculture, Sci. and Tech., 1994-97; bd. sci. advisors Coun. Sci. and Health, 1994—; Brittingham vis. prof. U. Wis. Madison, 1982-83; Hogan meml. lectr. U. Mo., 1987; mem. subcom. dog nutrition com. animal nutrition NRC-Nat. Acad. Sci., 1965-71; adv. coun. Inst. Lab. Animal Resources, NRC-Nat. Acad. Sci., 1966-69; sub-com. animal care faciltities Survey Inst. Lab. Animal Resources, 1967-70; cons., lectr. in field; mem. sci. adv. com. diet and nutrition cancer program Nat. Cancer Inst., 1976-81; mem. nutrition study sect. NIH, 1980-84; chmn. membership com. Am. Inst. Nutrition-Am. Soc. Clin. Nutrition, 1978-79, 80-83, 85; cons. VA, NSF, indsl. orgns.; Wellcome vis. prof. in basic med. scis. Oreg. State U., 1991-92; bd. sci. counselors USDA, 1989-91. Mem. editl. bd. Jour. Nutrition, 1980-84, editor, 1990-97; mem. editl. bd. Physiol. Rev., 1995-2001; contbr. articles to profl. jours. Bd. dirs. Coun. for Agrl. Sci. and Tech., 1994-97; active local Boy Scouts Am. Served with AUS, 1943-46. Recipient alumni award Nebr. 4-H, 1967, 97, alumni award U. Chgo., 1997, faculty merit award U. Ill. Coll. Medicine, 1988, Alumni Achievement award U. Nebr., 1997, U. Chgo., 1997; Nat. Cancer Inst. spl. fellow MIT, rsch. fellow Mass. Gen. Hosp., 1970-71; sr. scholar U. Ill., 1988. Fellow AAAS, Am. Inst. Nutrition (Osborne and Mendel award 1985), Am. Soc. Animal Sci. (chmn. subcom. antimicrobials, mem. regulatory agency com. 1973-78); mem. Am. Physiol. Soc., Soc. Pharmacology and Exptl. Therapeutics, Am. Inst. Nutrition (council 1980-83, 85-86), Soc. Exptl. Biology and Medicine, Am. Soc. Clin. Nutrition, Am. Therapeutic Soc., Am. Gastroenterol. Assn., Am. Bd. Clin. Nutrition, Innocents Soc., Fedn. Am. Socs. Exptl. Biology (sci. steering group life scis. rsch. office, adv. com. 1986-92), Am. Bd. Nutrition (bd. dirs.), Am. Soc. Nutritional Scis. (Conrad Elvehjem award 1996), Nat. Dairy Coun. (rsch. adv. com. 1987-91, vis. prof. nutrition program 1981-92), Gamma Alpha (pres. 1948-49), Phi Kappa Phi (pres. 1981-82), Alpha Gamma Rho (pres. 1946-47), Gamma Sigma Delta. Presbyterian (elder). Home: 1405 W William St Champaign IL 61821-4406 Office: U Ill 190 Med Sci Bldg 506 S Mathews Ave Urbana IL 61801-3618 Office Phone: 217-244-2797. Business E-Mail: wvisek@uiuc.edu.

VISH, DONALD H., lawyer, writer, photographer; b. Ft. Benning, Ga., Jan. 18, 1945; s. D. H., Jr. and Dorris (Parrish) Vish; m. Catherine Pence Hamilton, Aug. 20, 1966 (div. 1986); children: Donald Hamilton, Daphne Mershon Sullivan. BA in English, Bellarmine Coll., 1968; JD cum laude, U. Louisville, 1971. Bar: Ky. 1971, Fla. 1972. Sec., gen. counsel Gen. Energy Corp., Lexington, Ky., 1978-83; ptnr. Wyatt, Tarrant & Combs, Lexington, 1980-88, Frost Brown Todd, Lexington, 1988-89, 1991-98; gen. counsel Ky. Coal Producers' Self-Ins. Fund, 1992-98; sec., gen. counsel AIK Workers Compensation Fund, 1998—2004, exec. v.p., 2002—04, Middleton, Reutlinger, 2004—. Apptd. assoc. solicitor U.S. Dept. Interior, 1989—91; adj. assoc. prof. mineral law U. Ky., Lexington, 1979—85. Author: Poems and Musings, 2001, The Kentucky Anthology: 200 Years of Writing in the Bluegrass State, 2005; contbg. author: American Law of Mining, 2d edit., 1984, bd. editors and contbg. author: Coal Law and Regulation, 1983—93, Kentucky Election Law, 1995. Trustee Syre Sch., Lexington, 1980—88, chmn. bd. dir., 1986—88; mem. Blue Grass coun. Boy Scouts Am., 1988—93; apptd. gov. Ky. Registry Election Fin., 1991—93; bd. dir. Highlands Cmty. Ministries, 2001—04; bd. dirs. Ky. Shakespeare Festival, 2005—, Interfaith Paths to Peace, 2006—. Fellow: Am. Bar Found. (life); mem.: ABA (chmn. coal com., natural resources sect. 1987), Ky. Bar Assn. (mem. ethics com. 1983—85, chair residency com. 1998—2002), Fla. Bar, Energy and Mineral Law Found. (mem. exec. com. 1979—82, trustee 1979—91, trustee emeritus 1998), Am. Law Inst., Louisville Bar Found. (life), Ky. Bar Found. (life). Home: 5020 Nitta Yuma Dr Harrods Creek KY 40027 Office: Middleton Reutlinger 2500 Brown and Williamson Tower Louisville KY 40202 Home Phone: 502-228-5316; Office Phone: 502-584-1135. Personal E-mail: donaldvish@att.net.

VISHNESKI, JOHN STANLEY, III, lawyer; b. Virginia Beach, Va., Aug. 27, 1963; s. John Stanley and Antoinette Ann (Caracciolo) V.; m. Jane Estelle Beard, May 28, 1988; children: John Joseph II, Peter Anthony, Robert Thomas, Elisabeth Katharine. BA, U. Va., 1985, JD, 1988. Bar: N.D. 1988, Ill. 1988, D.C. 1989, U.S. Ct. Appeals (7th cir.) 1991, U.S. Dist. Ct. Md. 1992, U.S. Dist. Ct. D.C. 1992. Ptnr. Mayer, Brown, Rowe & Maw, Chgo. Contbr. articles to profl. jours. Elder Fair Oaks Presbyn. Ch., Oak Park, Ill., 1989—. Mem. ABA, Chgo. Bar Assn. (orch. mem. 1988—), D.C. Bar Assn., 7th Cir. Bar Assn., Raven Soc., Jefferson Soc. (pres. 1985), Phi Beta Kappa, Omicron Delta Kappa. Avocations: clarinet, wine collecting, racquetball. Office: Mayer Brown Rowe Maw Llp 230 S La Salle St Ste 400 Chicago IL 60604-1407 E-mail: jvishneski@mayerbrownrowe.com.

VISHNIAC, ETHAN TECUMSEH, astronomy educator; b. New Haven, Sept. 29, 1955; s. Wolf Vladimir and Helen Frances (Simpson) V.; m. Ilene Joy Busch, June 13, 1976; children: Cady Anne, Miriam Rachel. BS and BA summa cum laude, U. Rochester, 1976; MA, Harvard U., 1980. Rsch. assoc. Princeton U., 1980-82; lectr. U. Tex., Austin, 1982-84, asst. prof., 1984-88, assoc. prof., 1988-93, prof., 1993-98, Johns Hopkins U., Balt., 1998—2007, McMaster U., Hamilton, 2007—. Assoc. editor Phys. Rev. Letters, 1995-97; sci. editor Astrophys. Jour., 1997-2006; editor-in-chief Astrophysical Jour., 2006-; contbr. numerous articles to profl. jours. Recipient Presdl. Young Investigator, 1985; Alfred Sloan fellow, 1986. Fellow Am. Phys. Soc.; mem. Am. Astron. Soc. (Helen B. Warner prize 1990), Internat. Astron. Union. Home Phone: 410-464-2032. Business E-Mail: ethan@pha.jhu.edu.

VISHWANATH, ARUN, information scientist, educator; arrived in U.S., 1998; s. T. Vishwanath Rajagopalan and Rajagopalan Prema; m. Leslie Anne Padgett. BS in Commerce and Econs., U. Bombay, India, 1994, MBA, 1996; PhD, SUNY, Buffalo, NY, 2001. Dir. rsch. Goldhaber Rsch. Assocs., Amhrest, NY, 1999—2004; asst. prof. Sch. Informatics U. Buffalo, 2004—. V.p. Buffalo (N.Y.) Ad Coun., 2003—; vis. asst. prof. Ind. U., Bloomington, Ind., 2001—02. Contbr. articles to profl. jours. Grantee, N.Y. Sea Grant, 2004, N.Y. State Dept. Health-Buffalo (N.Y.) Acad. Medicine, 2005, Agy. Healthcare Rsch. and Quality NIH, 2006. Mem.: Assn.Edn. in Journalism and Mass Comms., Acad. Mgmt., Internat. Comm. Assn., Brainstorm Buffalo. Office: Univ Buffalo 333 Lord Christopher Baldy Hall Buffalo NY 14260 Business E-Mail: avishy@buffalo.edu.

VISITANTE, EL (EDUARDO CABRA), singer, musician; b. Santurce, PR, Sept. 10, 1978; Co-founder, pianist & singer Calle 13; signed to White Lion Records Inc., Santurce, PR. Musician: (albums) Calle 13, 2005 (Latin Grammy award for Best Urban Music Album, 2006), (songs) Atrévete Te, Te!, 2005 (Latin Grammy award for Best Short Form Music Video, 2006). Recipient Best New Artist award, also Best Urban Music Album & Best Short Music Video awards, Latin Grammy Awards, 2006. Office: White Lion Records Inc Urb Ocean Park 2072 Calle Cacique Santurce PR 00911-1514 *

VISKANTA, RAYMOND, mechanical engineering educator; b. Lithuania, July 16, 1931; came to U.S., 1949, naturalized, 1955; s. Vincas and Genovaite (Vinickas) V.; m. Birute Barbara Barpsys, Oct. 13, 1956; children: Renata, Vitas, Tadas. BSME, U. Ill., Champaign, 1955; MSME, Purdue U., West Lafayette, Ind., 1956, PhD, 1960, DEng (hon.), 2007, Tech. U. Munich, 1994. Registered profl. engr., Ill. Asst. mech. engr. Argonne (Ill.) Nat. Lab., 1956-59, student rsch. assoc., 1959-60, assoc. mech. engr., 1960-62; assoc. prof. mech. engring. Purdue U., West Lafayette, Ind., 1962-66, prof. mech. engring., 1966-86, Goss disting. prof. engring., 1986—. Guest prof. Tech. U. Munich, Germany, 1976-77, U. Karlsruhe, Germany, 1987; vis. prof. Tokyo Inst. Tech., 1983. Contbr. over 500 tech. articles to profl. jours. Recipient Sr. U.S. Scientist award Alexander von Humboldt Found., 1975, Sr. Rsch. award Am. Soc. Engring. Edn., 1984, Nusselt-Reynolds prize, 1991, Thermal Engring. award for Internat. Activity, Japan Soc. Mech. Engrs., 1994, Alumni award for Disting. Svc. U. Ill.-Urbana-Champaign, 2000; Japan Soc. for Promotion of Sci. fellow, 1983. Fellow ASME (Heat Transfer Meml. award 1976, Max Jakob Meml. award 1986, Melville medal 1988), AIAA (Thermophysics award 1979); mem. AAAS, NAE, Acad. Engring. Scis. Russian Fedn. (fgn.), Lithuanian Acad. Scis. (fgn.), Sigma Xi, Pi Tau Sigma, Tau Beta Pi. Home: 3631 Chancellor Way West Lafayette IN 47906-8809 Office: Purdue Univ 585 Purdue Mall West Lafayette IN 47907-2088 Home Phone: 765-463-7816; Office Phone: 765-494-5632. Personal E-mail: rviskanta@insightbb.com. Business E-Mail: viskanta@ecn.purdue.edu.

VISNJIC, GORAN, actor; b. Sibenik, Croatia, Sept. 9, 1972; m. Ivana Vrdoljak, May 8, 1999; 1 adopted child, Tin. Grad., Acad. of Dramatic Arts, Zagreb. Actor: (films) Maternal Halfbrothers, 1988, Paranoia, 1993, Welcome to Sarajevo, 1997, The Peacemaker, 1997, Rounders, 1998, Practical Magic, 1998, Committed, 2000, The Deep End, 2001, (voice) Ice Age, 2002, Doctor Sleep, 2002, Long Dark Night, 2004, Elektra, 2005; (TV films) See You, 1995, Night Watch, 1995, Spartacus, 2004; (TV series) ER, 1999—, Nasa mala klinika, 2004, Duga mracna noc, 2005. Recipient Vladimir Nazor award, 2005. Avocations: fencing, diving, swimming. Office: c/o United Talent Agency 9560 Wilshire Blvd Ste 5 Beverly Hills CA 90212-2400 *

VISO, OLGA, museum director; b. Fla. MA in Art History, Emory U., 1992. Positions in dept. modern & contemporary art, office of registrar and office of dir. High Mus. Art, Atlanta, 1989—93; asst. cur. Norton Mus. Art, West Palm Beach, Fla., 1993, Hirshhorn Mus. and Sculpture Garden, Washington, 1995, assoc. cur., 1998, cur. contemporary art, 2000—03, dep. dir., 2003—06, dir., 2006—. Mem. Fed. Adv. Com. Internat. Exhibitions; co-commr., US Pavilion Venice Biennial, 2001. Arranged (exhibitions) Distemper: Dissonant Themes in the Art of the 1990s, 1996, Regarding Beauty: A View of the Late Twentieth Century, 1999—2000. Office: Smithsonian Institution PO Box 37012 Hirshhorn Mus MRC Code 350 Washington DC 20013

VISOCKI, NANCY GAYLE, information services consultant; b. Dumont, NJ, May 13, 1952; d. Thomas and Gloria Visocki. BA in Math., Manhattanville Coll., 1974; MS in Ops. Rsch. and Stats., Rensselaer Poly. Inst., 1977. Rsch. asst. Coll. Physicians and Surgeons Columbia U., NYC, 1974-75; programmer analyst R. Shriver Assocs., Parsippany, NJ, 1977-79; sr. tech. rep. GE Info. Svcs. Co., East Orange, NJ, 1979-81, mgr. project office Morristown, NJ, 1981-83, tech. dir., 1983-87, tech. mgr., 1988-89, area mgr. sys. devel. and consulting Parsippany, 1989-92, area tech. mgr. sys. devel. and cons., Fin. Info. Sys., 1992-93, sr. cons. info. svcs., 1993-98, project mgr. e-commerce sys. integration, 1998-2000; mgr. Major e-commerce Applications Practice, 2000—03. Active Western Hills Christian Ch., Tranquility, N.J., 1986—; vol. Women's Ctr., Hackettstown, N.J., 1989-93; class fundraising and gift chmn. Rensselaer Poly. Inst., Troy, N.Y., 1991-95; vol. Elfun Soc., 1981—; vol. bd. dirs., treas. NJCFS Assn., 2004— Manhattanville Coll. grantee, Purchase, N.Y., 1970-71; tuition fellow Rensselaer Poly. Inst., 1975-77. Mem. NAFE, Elfun, Women of Accomplishment. Avocations: tai chi, hiking, bicycling, reading, yoga.

VISSCHER, MARTY ORRICO, biomedical researcher; d. Frank Paul and Elizabeth Brinkley Orrico; m. Ronald Bosman Visscher, June 10, 1972; children: Paul David, Robert Christopher. PhD, Ind. U., Bloomington, Ind., 1973; student, Xavier U., Cin., Ohio, 2005—. Postdoctoral fellow chemistry Ind. U., Bloomington, 1973—74, vis. prof. chemistry, 1974—76; asst. prof. chemistry U. Cin., 1976—78; sr. scientist R&D The Procter & Gamble Co., Cin., 1978—95; co-founder, dir. The Skin Sciences Inst. Cin. Children's Hosp. Med. Ctr., 1995—, rschr. The Skin Scis. Inst., 1995—. Mem. ADHD collaborative and task force Cin. Children's Hosp. Med. Ctr., 2002—; spkr. in field. Author: The Ideas of Chemistry, Harcourt Brace Jovanovich Inc., Laboratory Manual for The Ideas of Chemistry, Harcourt, Brace, Jovanovich, Inc., New York; contbr. chapters to books, articles to profl. jours. Mem. troop com. troop 417 Boy Scouts of Am., Cin., 1992—2006, merit badge counselor troop 417, 1996—2006; pres. Glendale Youth Sports, Cin., 1994—96, coach soccer, 1990—94; pres. Princeton Aquatics Parent Bd. Princeton City Schs., Cin., 1998—2000. Mem.: WGUC Pub. Radio, Glendale Lyceum. Achievements include patents in field. Avocations: running, fashion design, sewing, art, embroidery. Office: Cincinnati Children's Hospital Medical C 3333 Burnet Avenue Cincinnati OH 45229 Home Phone: 513-771-2129; Office Phone: 513-558-0393. Business E-Mail: visschmo@email.uc.edu.

VISSER, LESLEY, sports correspondent; b. Quincy, Mass., Sept. 11, 1953; m. Dick Stockton. BA cum laude in English, Boston Coll., 1975; PhD (hon.), Coll. Our Lady of Elms, Mass., 1995. Sports staff Boston Globe, 1974-88; feature reporter, sports staff CBS Sports, 1988—94, 2000—; corr. GameDay (now NFL Countdown), SportsCenter ESPN, Bristol, Conn., 1994-98; sideline reporter ABC, NYC, 1994-00, reporter Monday Night Football, 1998-00. Sideline reporter coll. football, NFL and Super Bowl ABC, 1994—; reporter Monday Night Football, 1998—. Trustee Women's Sports Found., 1993—. Named outstanding woman sportswriter in Am., 1983, New England Newswoman of Yr., WISE Woman of the Yr., 2002; named to the New England Sports Hall of Fame; recipient Journalism award Women's Sports Found., 1992, Pioneer award AWSM, 1999, Compass award, 2003, Pete Rozelle Radio Television award, Pro Football Hall of Fame 2006, Pop Warner Female Achievement award, 2006, Gracie Allen award Am. Women in Radio & Television, 2006 Office: CBS Sports 524 W 57th St New York NY 10019-2924

VISSER, RICHARD EDGAR, minister; b. South Weymouth, Mass., Apr. 28, 1937; s. Edgar and Marjorie (McPhee) V.; m. Carol Naomi Edwards, June 21, 1958; children: Andrew, Thomas, Peter. AB, Gordon Coll., Wenham, Mass., 1958, BS, 1959; BD, Gordon Div. Sch., So. Hamilton, Mass., 1962, MRE, 1965; D Ministry, Asbury Theol. Sem., Wilmore, Ky., 1983. Ordained to ministry Am. Bapt. Chs. in U.S.A., 1962. Pastor Acton-Milton Mills Bapt. Ch., Milton Mills, NH, 1962—65, First Bapt. Ch., Derry, NH, 1966—69; min. edn. Peters Creek Bapt. Ch., Library, Pa., 1969-73; pastor 1st Bapt. Ch., Warren, Pa., 1973-79, min. ch. edn. and music St. Albans, W.Va., 1980-83, sr. pastor Waynesburg, Pa., 1983—2003; co- pastor First Baptist Church, Warren, Pa., 2003—06; interim exec. min. Pitts. Baptist Assn., 2004—05; co-interim pastor Ogunquit Bapt. Ch., Maine, 2006—07. Pres. Clergymen's Assn. of Derry, 1967-69; founder, chmn. Pitts. Ch. Edn. Conv., 1972-73; clk. Pitts. Bapt. Assn., 1971-73; pres. Ministerial Assn., Warren, 1975-76, St. Albans, 1982-83, Waynesburg, 1988-90, 99-2001; moderator Ten Mile Assn. Waynesburg, 1985-87; pres., Ten Mile Assn. Mins. and Spouses, 2001-03; co-founder, vice chmn. Ten Mile and Monogahela Assns. Lic. Lay Pastor Tng. Program, 1988-90; chairperson Am. Bapt. Ch. Leadership Inst. Western Pa., 1993-2002; pres. Am. Bapt. Chs. of Pa. and Del., 1991-92, chmn. Sunday Sch. team, 1987-90, exec. com., 1987-94, 1997-2002, chmn. Budget Commn. 2004-05; mem. gen. bd., bd. ednl. ministries Am. Bapt. Chs. U.S.A., 1997-2002, mem. comms. com., 1999-2002, com. of 100 for Renewal, 1992-98; mem. Ministers and Missionaries Benefit Bd., 1999-2002, chmn. benefits com., 2000-02. Founder, chmn. Warren (Pa.) Community Chorus, 1974-78; pres. Warren County Health and Welfare Coun., 1975-77; chmn. Forest-Warren Counties Human Svcs. Adv. Commn., 1978-79; co. chmn. Greene County Human Svcs. Adv. Commn., Pa., 1988-96, vice chmn., 2000—02, chmn. mental health com., 2000—02, mem. sr. outreach and referral coalition, 2001-03; chmn. Greene County chpt. ARC, 1989-91; bd. dirs. Greene County Meml. Hosp., 1989—02; bd. dirs. Comty. Found. Greene County, 2000—03, vice chmn. 2001—03; mem. emergency food and shelter bd. Greene County FEMA, 1985-2003. Recipient Apollo award, Alderson-Broaddus Coll., Phillipi, W. Va., 1995, Disting. Cmty. Svc. award, Greater Waynesburg C. of C., 2002. Mem. Am. Bapt. Mins. Coun. (Excellence in Ministry award 2000, v.p. Pa. and Del. chpt. 1978-79), Rotary (v.p. Waynesburg Club 1990-91, pres. 1991-92). Avocations: walking, reading, singing. Home: Apt 204 25 Thornton Way Brunswick ME 04011 Personal E-mail: cvisser15370@yahoo.com. *I feel that sometimes people avoid leadership roles because they can be demanding. I do not seek leadership roles, but when I see needs and suggest possible solutions, these roles often seem to find me. I have found that an open, ordinary person such as I can make a difference and enjoy some rich rewards.*

VISSICCHIO, ANDREW JOHN, JR., linen service company executive; b. NYC, Dec. 21, 1941; s. Andrew John and Ann (Renna) V.; m. Patricia Ann Hunken, Jan. 18, 1964; children: Andrew John III, Douglas David. BS in Bus., L.I. U., 1963; postgrad., A.T. Roth Grad. Sch. Bus., 1963-64, Harvard U., 1995-98. Gen. mgr. Allied Coat & Apron, Bklyn., 1963—72; ops. officer N.Y. Ocean Sci. Lab., Montauk, NY, 1972—76; gen. mgr. Am. Svc. Corp., Miami, Fla., 1976—79, dist. mgr., 1979—83, v.p. ops., 1983—87; gen. mgr. Nat. Linen Svc., West Palm Beach, Fla., 1987—88, dist. mgr. Atlanta, 1988—91, v.p., gen. mgr. linen supply divsn., 1991—94, regional v.p., 1994—96; v.p. FDR Svcs. Group, Hempstead, NY, 1997—99; regional v.p. Video Save Inc., NYC, 2000—01. Author: A Book of Simple Poems; Pianist recital Carnegie Hall, 1956, 57. Vice chmn. Boca Raton Fin. Adv. Bd., 1999—; bd. dir. Boca Helping Hands, 2002-06; v.p., bd. dirs. Guatemalan Tomorrow Fund, 2003. Recipient Dedicated Svc. award Montauk Fire Dept., 1976, Milliken award New Prodn. Devel. in Textile Rental Industry, 1996; Meadowbrook Bank scholar L.I. U., 1962-63; decorated Knight of Malta, 2006. Mem. Textile Rental Svc. Assn. (strategic com. 1984-86), S.Am. Explorers Club, Am. Orchid Soc., Boca Raton Orchid Soc. (fin. com.), Coalition for Species Orchid, Order of Marta (knight). Republican. Roman Catholic. Achievements include development of Prod-Q; NSure. Avocations: collecting and growing orchids, poetry, boating, fishing, classical music-opera. Home: 2350 NW 38th St Boca Raton FL 33431-5439

VISTE, ARLEN ELLARD, chemistry professor; b. Austin, Minn., Aug. 13, 1936; s. Arthur E. and Edith L. (Kehret) V.; m. Elizabeth Ann Lindbeck, June 14, 1959; children: Solveig, David, Mark. BA, St. Olaf Coll., 1958; PhD, U. Chgo., 1962. Asst. prof. chemistry St. Olaf Coll., Northfield, Minn., 1962-63; NSF fellow Columbia U., NYC, 1963-64; asst. prof. Augustana Coll., Sioux Falls, SD, 1964-68, assoc. prof., 1968-73, prof., 1973—, prof. emeritus, 2002—. Contbr. articles to profl. jours. Mem. Am. Chem. Soc., Royal Soc. Chemistry (London), S.D. Acad. Sci., Midwest Assn. Chemistry Tchrs. in Liberal Arts Colls., Phi Beta Kappa, Sigma Xi. Home: 1500 W 30th St Sioux Falls SD 57105-3622 Office: Augustana Coll Chemistry Dept Sioux Falls SD 57197-0001 Business E-Mail: arlen.viste@augie.edu.

VITA, STEVEN, poet; b. Chgo., July 16, 1960; s. John and Rosemarie V. BA in Art and English, Denison U., Granville, Ohio, 1982; MFA in English, CUNY, 1985. Founder, editor Veery, Chgo., 1991—. Author: The Heart of Tents, 1991.

VITAL, PATRICIA BEST, lawyer; b. Pitts., Mar. 26; d. Clarence D. and Billie Lorraine (Wilson) B.; m. Leo Vital, Mar. 30. BA magna cum laude, U. Tenn., Chattanooga, 1989; JD with honors, U. Tenn., 1992. Bar: Ga. 1994, Tenn. 1993, U.S. Dist. Ct. (ea. dist.) Tenn. 1993, U.S. Ct. Appeals (6th cir.) 1993, U.S. Dist. Ct. (no. dist.) Ga. 1995, U.S. Ct. Appeals (11th cir.) 1995, U.S. Supreme Ct. 1996. Legal asst. Gleason & Assoc. Law Firm, Rossville, Ga., 1981-82; med. staff coord. Hutcheson Med. Ctr., Ft. Oglethorpe, Ga., 1982-86; rsch. asst. U. Tenn. Law Coll., Knoxville, 1991-92; from law clk. to assoc. atty. Lusk, Carter & McGhehey, Chattanooga, 1990-93; pvt. practice Chattanooga, 1993—; mediator, arbitrator Vital Dispute Resolution Svcs., Chattanooga, 1996—. Law clk. Hamilton County Attys. Office, Chattanooga, 1990; devel. coun. co-chair class 1992 U. Tenn. Coll. Law, alumni network mentoring program, 1995—; deans cir., 1992—; pres. adult scholars program U. Tenn., Chattanooga, 1988-89, adult scholars program adv. coun., scholarship com., 1994—; small bus. coun. Chattanooga C. of C, 2004-; presenter in field; adj. prof. pre-trial litig., legal asst. studies program U. Tenn., 1997; instr. Law Sch. Admission Test preparation course KAPLAN, Inc., 1999-00; commn. CLE and specialization Tenn. Supreme Ct., 1996-01; panel mediator, arbitrator (ea. and mid. dists.) Tenn. Fed. Mediation Programs, Settlement Solutions LLC, 2006-, Tenn. Supreme Ct. Rule 31 civil/family domestic violence mediator U.S. Dept. Justice, Key Bridge Found., Am. with Disabilities, Chattanooga Better Bus. Bur., Coun. Better Bus. Burs. AutoLine Arbitration, Hamilton County Tenn. Divorce Mediation, Am. Health Lawyers ADR Svc.; mem. panel, chair arbitration panel Nat. Assn. Securities Dealers, US Dept. Labor/AEIDR; adv. bd. ProLex, LLC, 2003—, chair, 2004—; protection from harm mediator Tenn. Divsn. Mental Retardation Svcs., 2006-. Co-author: Tennessee Alternative Dispute Resolution Handbook, 1997; contbr. articles to profl. jours. Mentor Hamilton County Bd. Edn., 1995-96; cmty. resource person Ooltewah Mid. and Chattanooga Phoenix Mid. Schs., 1994-96; capt. attys. team presch. phon-a-thon Siskin Found., 1994-95; mem. Chattanooga Chamber Found. Leadership Chattanooga Class, 1997-98; nat. adv. bd. Ctr. for Enterprise Edn., Peabody Coll. Edn., Vanderbilt U., 1998-2000; chair accessibility subcom., planning com. S.E. Region Inst. on Deafness Conf., 2004. Mem. ABA (ethics 2000 adv. coun. 1998, dispute resolution sect. Boston Conf. Planning Com. 1998-2000, co-chair dispute resolution sect. State and Local Bar Com. 1998-2000), AAUW, Fed. Bar Assn., Nat. Inst. Dispute Resolution, Nat. Assn. Mediators in Edn., Am. Health Lawyers Assn., Nat. Assn. Women Bus. Owners (local chpt. bd. dirs. 1994), Am. Soc. Law, Medicine and Ethics, Tenn. Bar Assn. (com. chair, sec. and spkr. ho. of dels. 1995—, com. chair law related edn. 1996-97, bd. dirs. law office tech. and mgmt. 1994-96, sec-treas., chair-elect, chair dispute resolution sect. 1995-98, Merit award 1995, mem. editl. bd. TBALink), Mediation Assn. Tenn. (chair continuing mediation edn., curriculum com. 1996-98), Tenn. Trial Lawyers Assn., Tenn. Assn. Med. Staff Svcs., Nat. and Tenn. Assn. Ptnrs. in Edn., Ga. State Bar Assn., Chattanooga Bar Assn. (bd. govs. 1996-97, chair bd. govs. task force on the future Tenn. judicial sys. 1995-96, centennial planning com. 1996-97, chair continuing legal edn. com. 1994-95, chair ethics rules rev. com. 1998-99, chair dispute resolution com. 1998—, First Beyond the Call of Duty award 1995), Chattanooga Trial Lawyers Assn. (dir., gov. bd. 1995-2000), Southeast Tenn. Lawyers Assn. Women (dir. at-large 1996-97), Better Bus. Bur., S.E. Tenn. Coun. on Children & Youth, Leadership Chattanooga Alumni Assn. (mem. cmty. edn. com. 2004—, grad. program com. 2004—, dir. gov. bd., 2006, sect. gov. bd., 2007), Chattanooga Area C. of C., Phi Delta Phi. Avocations: whitewater rafting, mountain hiking, aerobics, reading. Office: Vital Law Offc & Dispute Resolution Svcs Pioneer Bldg Ste 540 801 Broad St Chattanooga TN 37402 Office Phone: 423-267-2378. Office Fax: 423-267-2376. Personal E-mail: best-law@mindspring.com.

VITALE, DICK, commentator; b. Garfield, NJ; m. Lorraine Vitale; children: Terri, Sherri. Basketball coach East Rutherford HS, NJ, 1965-71; asst. basketball coach Rutgers U., New Brunswick, NJ, 1972; basketball coach U. Detroit, 1973-77, athletic dir., 1978; basketball coach Detroit Pistons, Auburn Hills, Mich., 1978-79; TV commentator, sports analyst ESPN Sports, 1979—; sports columnist Basketball Times, 1979—, Ea. Basketball, 1979—; TV commentator ABC Sports, 1987—; sports radio commentator ABC Radio Network, 1987—. Radio commentator The J. P. McCarthy Show, Detroit; guest spkr., lectr. Co-author: (with Curay Kirk Patrick) Vitale: Just Your Average, Bald, One-Eyed Basketball Wacko Who Beat the Ziggy and Became a PTP'er, 1989, (with Dick Weiss) Time Out, Baby!, 1992, Living a Dream, 2003, (with Mike Douchant) Tourney Time, It's Awesome Baby, 1994; co-author various computer games; appeared in TV commls. for Adidas, Taco Bell. Named Sports Personality of Yr., Am. Sportscasters Assn., 1989. Roman Catholic. Achievements include earning 5 sectional and 2 consecutive state championships as a high school basketball coach. Office: ESPN ESPN Plz Bristol CT 06010 *

VITALE, JOSEPH F., state legislator; b. Elizabeth, NJ, Nov. 10, 1954; Pres. Vitale Sign Corp., Woodbridge, N.J., 1985—; mem. N.J. Senate, Dist. 19, Trenton, 1998—. Mem. environ. com. N.J. State Senate, health com., women's issues, children and family svcs. com. Vice chair Habitat for Humanity; Middlesex County chair Walk for Health, Am. Heart Assn.; mem. mayor's adv. com. Middlesex County Paraiso Assistance Project; mem. Woodbridge Twp.; chmn. Woodbridge Twp. Dem. Party, 1992-97. Named one of 2007 People to Watch, Sunday Star Ledger. Mem. Woodbridge Twp. C. of C. Democrat. Office: NJ State Senate Dist Office 87 Main St Woodbridge NJ 07095-2821 Address: NJ State Senate PO Box 098 Trenton NJ 08624-0098 E-mail: SenVitale@njleg.state.nj.us. *

VITALE, RUTH ANN, former film company executive; b. Boston, Oct. 20, 1952; d. Joseph J. and Gilda J. (Camuso) V. BA in English, Tufts U., 1974; MS in Journalism, Boston U., 1975. Account exec. Sta. WNAC-TV, Boston, 1976-78, Top Market TV/Post-Newsweek, NYC, 1978-79; v.p., media account exec. McCann Erickson, NYC, 1979-81; mgr. sales ops. Hearst/ABC Video Services, NYC, 1981-82; dir. film acquisition The Movie Channel, NYC, 1982-83; sr. v.p. prodn. Vestron Pictures, Stamford, Conn., 1983-87, ind. producer, 1987-88; sr. v.p. prodn. United Artists/Metro-Goldwyn-Mayer, Inc., Beverly Hills, Calif., 1988—95, Fine Line Features/New Line Cinema Corp., Los Angeles, Calif., 1995—97; co-pres. Paramount Classics, Los Angeles, Calif., 1997—2005; pres. First Look Studios, Inc., Los Angeles, Calif., 2005—07.

VITALE, THOMAS M., lawyer; b. NYC, Aug. 16, 1956. AB in Physics, Princeton Univ., 1977; JD, Stanford Univ., 1980. Bar: NY 1981, US Dist. Ct. (so. dist. NY) 1981. Atty. Chadbourne & Parke, NY, 1980—81, Battle Fowler, NY, 1982—85, Gaston & Snow, NY, 1985—91; ptnr. Mayer, Brown, Rowe & Maw LLP, NY, 1991—, now ptnr.-in-charge NYC Office. Assoc. editor Stanford Law Rev. Mem.: Phi Beta Kappa. Office: Mayer-Brown Rowe & Maw LLP 1675 Broadway New York NY 10019-5820 Office Phone: 212-506-2510. Office Fax: 212-849-5510. Business E-Mail: tvitale@mayerbrownrowe.com.

VITALIANO, ERIC NICHOLAS, federal judge; b. SI, NY, Feb. 27, 1948; m. Helen M. Fleming, Sept. 9, 1983; children: Michael, Emma, Abigail, Halle. AB, Fordham Coll., 1968; JD cum laude, NYU, 1971; postgrad., U. Colo., 1977. Bar: NY 1971. Law clk. to Mark A Costantino, US Dist. Ct. (Ea. dist.) NY, NYC, 1971-72; assoc. Simpson Thacher & Bartlett, NYC, 1972-79; chief staff to Congressman John M. Murphy US Ho. Reps., NYC, 1979-80; ptnr. Russo, Silverman & Vitaliano, NYC, 1982-86; mem. NY Assembly, Albany, 1982—2002; counsel Behrins & Behrins, 1999—2001; judge NY State Unified Ct. Sys., 2002—06, US Dist. Ct. (Ea. dist.) NY, 2006—. Rsch. editor NYU Law Rev., 1970-71. Co-founder Citizens Against Bus Exhaust; co-founder Bodine Creek Civic Assn.; former parish chmn. Cardinal's Archdiocesan Appeal; former mem. Dem. Com. Richmond County, NY; past pres. N. Conf. Italian-Am. State Legislators; past adv. Assumption Coun., KC. Recipient Stella Falletta Meml. award Clifton Homeowners and Tenants Assn., SI, 1986, Aldo R. Benedetto Outstanding Citizen award Am. Legion, 1994, Pub. Policy award NY State Cath. Conf., 1998; named Dem. of Yr., Young Dems. Richmond County, 1980, Friend of Edn., Susan E. Wagner HS, SI, 1983, Legislator of Yr., NY State Clks. Assn., 1987, Friend of Italian-Am. Inst. Inst., CUNY, 1990, Man of Yr., Italian Club SI, 1991, Man of the Yr., Met. Police Conf. of NY State, 1995, Legislator of the Yr. Supreme Ct. Officers, 2000, Detective Investigators Assn., 2000. Mem.: Order of Coif. Office: US Dist Ct 225 Cadman Plaza E Brooklyn NY 11201 Office Phone: 718-613-2135.

VITE, FRANK ANTHONY, realtor; b. Aurora, Ill., Feb. 9, 1930; s. Frank A. and Rose (Cosentino) V.; grad. Marmion Mil. Acad., 1948; student Sch. Mgmt., U. Notre Dame, 1958; D.B.A. (hon.), Hillsdale Coll., 1972; m. Barbara Ann Decio, Oct. 23, 1954; children: Bradley Scott, Mark Steven, Michael Lee, Leslie Ann, Lisa Ann. Plant engr. Lyon Metal Products, Aurora, 1951-52, purchasing agt., 1953-54; became sales mgr., exec. v.p., owner, dir. Skyline Homes, Inc., Elkhart, Ind., 1954; pres., owner B&F Realty, Inc., No. Ind. Appraisal Co., Golden Falcon Homes, Inc.; real estate broker; dir. 1st Nat. Bank, Elkhart, Ind. Trustee Hillsdale (Mich.) Coll., Holy Cross Coll., South Bend, Ind.; bd. dirs. Ind. Commn. Higher Edn. With AUS, 1952-53, Korea. Mem. Elkhart Bd. Realtors, Nat. Sales Execs. Assn., Ind. Real Estate Assn., Nat. Inst. Real Estate Brokers, Holy Name Soc., K.C. (4 deg.), Knight of Malta, Elks. Republican Office: 1300 Cassopolis St Elkhart IN 46514-3248 Home: 9 Colonia Miramonte Paradise Valley AZ 85253 Office Phone: 574-264-0651.

VITEK, REG(INALD) A., lawyer; b. Bakersfield, Calif., Apr. 23, 1942; BA, San Diego State Coll., 1964; JD, UCLA, 1967. Bar: Calif. 1967, US Ct. Appeals (2d, 9th cir.), US Supreme Ct. 1976. Ptnr., bus. litigation Seltzer Caplan McMahon Vitek, San Diego. Lectr. Nat. Inst. Trial Advocacy. Mem.: ABA, State Bar Calif., San Diego County Bar Assn., Fed. Bar Assn., Assn. Trial Lawyers Am., San Diego County Trial Lawyers Assn., Assn. Bus. Trial Lawyers (founding mem. San Diego chpt.), Am. Inns of Ct., Louis M. Welsh San Diego chpt. (Master, mem. exec. com.). Office: Seltzer Caplan McMahon Vitek Symphony Towers 750 B St San Diego CA 92101 Office Phone: 858-685-3075. Office Fax: 858-702-6804. Business E-Mail: vitek@scmv.com.

VITEK, VACLAV, materials scientist; b. Olomouc, Czechoslovakia, Sept. 10, 1940; came to U.S., 1978; s. Josef and Ruzena V.; m. Ludovita Stankovicova, Aug. 5, 1972; children: Adrian Joseph, Clementine Mary. BSc in Physics, Charles U., Prague, 1962; PhD in Physics, Czechoslovakian Acad. Scis., Prague, 1966; doctorate (hon.), Tech. U. Brno, 1999. Research assoc. dept. metall. materials sci. and research fellow Wolfson Coll., Oxford (Eng.) U., 1967-75; research officer Central Elec. Research Labs., Central Elec. Generating Bd., Leatherhead, Eng., 1975-78; prof. materials sci. and engring. U. Pa., 1978—. Vis. prof. U. Groningen, Netherlands, 1985-86. Recipient Humboldt award for sr. scientists, Germany, 1992-93, Acta metallurgica Gold medal, 1996, Mach medal Czech Acad. Scis., 1999. Fellow Inst. Physics (London), Am. Soc. Metals Internat., Metals, Minerals Materials Soc.; mem. NAE (elected 2006), Am. Phys. Soc., Materials Rsch. Soc. Office: U Pa Dept Materials Sci and Engring 3231 Walnut St Philadelphia PA 19104-6202 Home Phone: 610-328-4250. Business E-Mail: vitek@seas.upenn.edu.

VITELLO, PAUL, journalist; m. Carol Polsky; children: Sam, Anna. BA, Trinity Coll., Hartford, Conn. Reporter New York Newsday, 1981—2005, New York Times, 2005—. Author: (articles) Recount's Silent Stunner: Gore Should Have Won, 2001, The Eleventh of Never, 2005. Office: The New York Times 3000 Hempstead Tpke Ste 200 Levittown NY 11756-1409

VITETTA, ELLEN S., microbiologist, immunologist, educator; BA, Conn. Coll.; MS, NYU, 1966, PhD, MD, 1968. Prof. microbiology Southwestern Med. Sch., U. Tex., Dallas, 1976—; dir. Cancer Immunobiology Ctr., U. Tex., Dallas, 1988—; Sheryle Simmons Patigian Disting. chair in cancer immunobiology Southwestern Med. Sch., U. Tex., Dallas, 1989—. Bd. sci. coun. NCI Cancer Treatment Bd., 1993; sci. adv. bd. Howard Hughes Med. Inst., 1992—; Kettering selection com. GM Cancer Rsch. Foun., 1987-88; task force NIAID in Immunology, 1989-90; mem. sci. bd. Ludwig Inst., 1983—. Mem. editl. bd.: Advances in Host Defense Mechanisms, 1983—, Annual Review of Immunology, 1991—, Bioconjugate Chemistry, 1989-93, Cellular Immunology, 1984-93, Current Opinions in Immunology, 1992—, FASEB Journal, 1987—, Internat. Jour. of Oncology, 1992—, Internat. Soc. Immunopharmacology, 1989—, Jour. of Immunology, 1975-78, Molecular Immunology, 1978-93; assoc. editor Cancer Research, 1986—; Immunochemistry sect. editor: Jour. of Immunology, 1978-82; co-editor in chief: Therapeutic Immunology, 1992—. Recipient Women's Excellence in Sci. award Fedn. Am. Soc. Exptl. Biology, 1991, Taittinger Breast Cancer Rsch. award Komen Found., 1983, Pierce Immunotoxin award, 1988, NIH Merit award, 1987—, U. Tex. Southwestern Med. Sch. Faculty Teaching awards 1989, 91, 92, 93, 94, FASED Excellence in Sci. award, 1991, Abbot Clinical Immunology award Am. Soc. Microbiologists, 1992, Past State Pres. award Tex. Fed. Bus. Profl. Women's Club, 1993, Richard and Hinda Rosenthal Found. award Am. Assn. Cancer Rsch 1995, Charlotte Friend award Am. Assn. Cancer Rsch., 1995, AAAS Mentreny award, 2002. Mem. Am. Assn. Immunologists (pres. 1994), Nat. Acad. Scis., Am. Acad. Microbiology (hon.). Achievements include co-discovery of IL-4, development of immunotoxins and identification of IgD on murine B cells. Office: Univ Texas Cancer Immunobiol Ctr 6000 Harry Hines Blvd Dallas TX 75235-5303 Address: 6914 Pemberton Dr Dallas TX 75230-4260 E-mail: ellen.vitetta@utsoutheastern.edu.

VITEV, IVAN MATEEV, physicist, researcher; arrived in US, 1997; s. Matei Ivanov Vitev and Lilia Zlatkova Viteva; m. Sofiya Nikolova Micheva-Viteva, Jan. 14, 2000. MS, Sofia U., Bulgaria, 1995; PhD, Columbia U., NYC, 2002. Cert. physics tchr. Sofia U., Bulgaria, 1995. Rsch. assoc. Iowa State U., Ames, 2002—04; J. Robert Oppenheimer fellow Los Alamos Nat. Lab., N.Mex., 2004—. Grantee, Los Alamos Nat. Lab., 2005—; J. Robert Oppenheimer fellow, 2004—. Mem.: Am. Phys. Soc. Achievements include research in theoretical nuclear physics; new states of matter; jet interactions in quark-gluon plasma. Avocations: photography, hiking. Office: Los Alamos Nat Lab Mail Stop B283 Group T-16 Los Alamos NM 87545 also: Los Alamos Nat Lab Mail Stop H846 Group P-25 Los Alamos NM 87545 Home Phone: 505-920-5554; Office Phone: 505-665-8066, 505-667-1029. Office Fax: 505-665-1931, 505-665-7920. Business E-Mail: ivitev@lanl.gov.

VITEZ, MICHAEL, reporter; b. Washington, 1957; m. Maureen Fitzgerald; children: Timmy, Sally, Jonathan. Degree, U. Va., 1979. Past reporter Hartford Courant, Washington Star, Virginian-Pilot, Norfolk; reporter Phila. Inquirer, 1985—. Co-recipient Pulitzer Prize for explanatory journalism, 1997. Office: Phila Inquirer PO Box 8263 Philadelphia PA 19101-8263

VITIELLO, ANTHONY F., lawyer; b. Bklyn., Feb. 18, 1968; s. Anthony and Antoinette (Rotondo) V.; m. Stacey M. Vitiello, June 3, 1994. BA, Lehigh U., 1990; JD, NYU, 1993, LLM in Taxation, 1996. Bar: NJ 1993, NY 1994, US Tax Ct. 1994. Atty. IRS, NYC, 1993-94; assoc. Fox and Fox, NYC, 1994-96, Sills Cummis et al, Newark, 1996; ptnr. Connell Foley, LLP, Roseland, NJ. Adj. prof. Fairleigh Dickinson U. Pro bono spkr. Rutgers U. Tax Clinic, Newark, 1996. Named one of Top 100 Attys., Worth mag., 2005—06. Mem. ABA, NY State Bar Assn., NJ Bar Assn., US Tax Ct. Republican. Office: Connell Foley LLP 85 Livingston Ave Roseland NJ 07068 Office Phone: 973-535-0500. E-mail: avitiello@connellfoley.com. *

VITKOWSKY, VINCENT JOSEPH, lawyer; b. Newark, Oct. 3, 1955; s. Boniface and Rosemary (Ofack) Vitkowsky; m. Mary Gunzburg, May 16, 1981 (div. 1997); children: Vincent Jr., Victoria, Pierce; m. Pandora Strasler, Sept. 18, 1999. BA, Northwestern U., 1977; JD, Cornell U., 1980. Bar: NY 1981. Assoc. Hart and Hume, NYC, 1980-84, Kroll & Tract, NYC, 1984-87; of counsel Nixon, Hargrave, Devans & Doyle, NYC, 1988-89; ptnr. Buchalter, Nemer, Fields & Younger, NYC, 1990-95, Edwards Angell Palmer & Dodge LLP, NYC, 1996—. Mem. panel arbitration London Ct. Internat. Arbitration; lectr. in field. Contbr. articles to profl. jours. Mem. Am. Arbitration Assn. (internat. panel arbitrators), Internat. Bar Assn. (com. officer), Internat. Law Assn. (Am. br. com. on formation customary internat. law), Assn. Bar City NY, Cornell Club, Federalist Soc. Law and Pub. Policy (exec. com. internat. and nat. security practice group, mem. nat. practioners adv. coun.), IBA Human Rights Inst. (officer, com. interventions and trial observations 2000-04). Home: 422 E 72d St Apt 15E New York NY 10021 Office: Edwards Angell Palmer & Dodge LLP 750 Lexington Ave Fl 12 New York NY 10022-1253 Business E-Mail: vvitkowsky@eapdlaw.com.

VITO, RAYMOND P., engineering educator, researcher; BS, SUNY, Buffalo, 1964, MS, 1965; PhD, Cornell U., 1971. Postdoctoral fellow McMaster U., Canada; asst. prof. Ga. Inst. Tech., Atlanta, 1974, assoc. dean for academic affairs, prof., Woodruff Sch. Mech. Engring.; mem. program faculty, Wallace H. Coulter Dept. Biomedical Engring. Ga. Inst. Tech. and Emory U.; pres., CEO, co-founder Medanola Medical, Inc., 2001—. Contbr. articles to profl. publs. Recipient Outstanding Svc. award, Ga. Inst. Tech., 2000, ANAK Soc. Outstanding Faculty award, 2000, Walter H. Coulter award for Innovation and Entrepreneurship, 2002, Cardiovascular Techniques & Technologies Meeting Innovation of Yr. award, 2004; Med. Rsch. Coun. of Can. Postdoctoral Fellowship, 1973, Nat. Aeronautics and Space Adminstrn./Am. Soc. for Engring. Edn. Summer Faculty Fellowship, 1976, 1979, Am. Soc. Mech. Engrs. fellow, 1997, Am. Inst. for Med. & Biological Engring. fellow, 2006. Fellow: Am. Soc. Mech. Engrs.; mem.: Sigma Xi. Achievements include 5 US Patents. Office: Ga Inst Tech Coll Engring IBB Post Office Box 0405 Rm 2308 Atlanta GA 30332-0363 Office Phone: 404-894-2792. Office Fax: 404-894-1658. Business E-Mail: raymond.vito@me.gatech.edu.

VITRAC, JEAN-JACQUES CHARLES, international business consultant; b. Paris, May 31, 1942; came to U.S., 1972; s. Jean Bernard Vitrac and Paulette Aimée (Buisson) Mannerheim; m. Roswitha Kahling, Sept. 11, 1965; children: Emmanuel, François, Catherine. Diploma, Faculty of Law, Aix, France, 1963; post grad. in mktg., Institut National Du Marketing, Paris, 1972; post grad. in econ. scis., Institut Superieur Sciences Economiques, Paris, 1979; D in Comml. Sci. (hon.), Milan U., 2007. Devel. officer Europe-Africa Internat. Jaycees, Geneva, 1968-70; dir. econ. affairs Internat. Jaycees, Coral Gables, Fla., 1970-72; mktg. cons. Bernard Krief Internat., Paris, 1973-79; strategy cons. Euro-PacRim Internat., Walnut Creek, Calif., 1980—. Owner Domaine Becquet Winery, Valley Springs, Calif.; chair task force on multinat. strategies Ctrl. Bank of France, Paris, 1974-78; mktg. cons. Aérospatiale, Paris, 1978; bd. dirs. Capsule Française Inc., Napa, Calif.; asst. prof. mktg. Inst. Français de Gestion, Paris, 1973-79; U.S. chmn. L'Entreprise Demain, Brussels, 1982-98; no. Calif. chmn. World Tech. Execs. Network, 1987-90; founder Export-Incubator-USA, San Francisco, 2006. Author: Discover Export, 1974; co-author: Doing Business in California, 1989; editor World Tech. Execs. Network Review, 1989-90; guest columnist France-Amérique, 2005-06. Bd. dirs. E. Bay Internat. Trade Coun., 1996-97, Venetian Lakeshore, 2004-05, v.p., 2006; chair parish coun. St. Patrick's Ch., 1998, 99; trustee Mark Twain St. Joseph's Hosp. Found., 1999-2004, exec. bd. mem., pub. rels. com. co-chair, 2000-2001; elected to Calaveras County Rep. Ctrl. Com., 2001. Named knight Equestrian Order of Holy Sepulchre of Jerusalem,; recipient Ambassador for Peace award Internat. Fedn. World Peace, 2006. Mem. Nat. Bus. Incubation Assn. (profl.), KC (dep. grand knight 1998, treas. 1999-2001, grand knight 2001-02, trustee 2002-04), Am. Assn. Polit. Cons., Art Renaissance Found. (hon., chair Calif. chpt. 1994—), Classical Philharm. (v.p. 1995-96), Cal-France Coun. (v.p. 1996-97), Kiwanis Internat (gov.'s cabinet, dir. com. svc. 1996-97), French War Vets. (No. Calif. chpt. pres. 1996-97), Napa Kiwanis Club (disting. pres. 1993, bd. dirs. Calif.-Nev.-Hawaii Found. 1996-98), Wine Inst., Calaveras Wine Assn., West Calaveras Rotary (founding pres. 2000-01), Jackson Rotary. Republican. Roman Catholic. Home: Becket's Ranch PO Box 467 Valley Springs CA 95252 Office: Euro PacRim Int Corp 2173 Hwy 12 East PO Box 1418 Valley Springs CA 95252-1418 Office Phone: 209-772-3469. Personal E-mail: californieusa@yahoo.fr.

VITRANO, FRANK G., supermarket executive; b. 1955; With Pathmark Stores Inc., Carteret, NJ, 1972—, v.p., treas., exec. v.p., treas., CFO, 1998—2002, pres., CFO, 2002—05, co-pres., CFO, 2005—. Office: Pathmark Stores Inc 200 Milik St Carteret NJ 07008 *

VITT, DAVID AARON, health products executive; b. Phila., Aug. 3, 1938; s. Nathan and Flora B.; m. Renee Lee Salkever, Oct. 20, 1963; children: Nadine Lori Einiger, Jeffrey Richard. BS, Temple U., 1961. Sales engr. X-Ray Corp., Phila., 1961-65, Midwest Am., Chgo., 1965-67, product mgr., 1967-68, product mgr. regional sales, 1968-70; dir. mktg. Valtronic & Living Wills, Bronx, NY, 1970-74; v.p., gen. mgr. dental divsn. Siemens Med. Sys. Inc., Iselin, NJ, 1974—86, past corp. v.p., gen. mgr. dental divsn.; CEO, pres. Pelton & Crane, Charlotte, NC, 1986-89; v.p. govt. sales, ret. Siemens Med. Sys., 1994; founder, pres., CEO D.A.V., Inc., 1995—; founder, co-owner RealDental.com. Pres. Denx Am. Inc., 1998; industry rep. to Am. Nat. Stds. Inst.; co. rep. U.S.-USSR Trade and Econ. Coun.; co-founder Enter Am. Group Exec. Consultants. Bd. dirs. Am. Fund for Dental Health; apptd. mem. Charlotte Mecklenburg Cmty. Rels. Com.; mem. bd. visitors U. N.C., Charlotte; officer, mem. exec. com. Jr. Achievement. Served in USAR, 1961-68. Mem. Am. Mgmt. Assn. (bd. dirs. N.J. chpt.), Am. Mktg. Assn., Am. Dental Trade Assn. (bd. dirs.), Dental Mfrs. Am. (past pres.), Am. Acad. Dental Radiology, Charlotte C. of C. (bd. advisors), Acad. Gen. Dentists (bd. mem. found.), Masons (32d deg.), Shriners. Republican.

VITTAL, VIJAY, electrical engineer, educator; b. Bangalore, India, Dec. 25, 1955; arrived in U.S., 1979; s. H.S. Padmanabha and K. Shakuntala V.; m. Sunanda Vittal, June 8, 1980; children: Eknath, Vinayak. B in Engring., B.M.S. Coll. Engring., Bangalore, India, 1977; M, Indian Inst. of Tech., Kanpur, India, 1979; PhD, Iowa State Univ., 1982. Asst. prof. Iowa State Univ., Ames, 1982-86, assoc. prof., 1986-90; program dir. NSF, Washington, 1993-94; prof. Iowa State U., Ames, 1990—2004, Murray and Ruth Harpole prof., 2000—04, Anson Marston Disting. prof., 2004; Ira A. Fulton Chair prof. Ariz. State U., Tempe, 2005—. Cons. Siemens Energy Automation, Plymouth, Minn., 1992-93, G.E. Power Systems, Schenectady, N.Y., 1999. Author: Power System Analysis, 2000, Power System Transient Stability, 1992; contbr. articles to profl. jours. Recipient Presdl. Young Investigator award NSF, 1985. Fellow IEEE (chair power sys. dynamic performance com.); mem. US Nat. Acad. Engring. Office: Ariz State U Ira A Fulton Sch Engring PO Box 875706 Tempe AZ 85287-5706 Office Phone: 480-965-1879. Office Fax: 480-965-0745. E-mail: vijay.vittal@asu.edu.

VITTECOQ, GERARD R., manufacturing executive; Grad., Ecole Superieure Commerce, Rouen, France; MBA, Laval Univ., Canada. Fin. mgmt. positions Caterpillar Inc., 1975—82; fin. rep., asst. mgr. Caterpillar Overseas S.A., 1982—85, comptroller, 1985—87; strategy mgr. Caterpillar Inc., 1987—89, dir., strategy & planning, 1990—95; mng. dir. Caterpillar France S.A., 1995—98, Caterpillar Belgium S.A., 1998—2001; v.p. EAME prod. develop. & ops. Caterpillar Inc., 2001—03, group pres., 2003—. Mem. European Am. Indsl. Council; mem. mgmt. bd. Fedn. des Syndicats Patronaux, Geneva; mem. exec. com. Internat. Inst. Mgmt. Develop.; exec. mem. World Bus. Council for Sustainable Develop. Office: Caterpillar Inc 100 NE Adams St Peoria IL 61629 *

VITTER, DAVID BRUCE, senator, former congressman; b. New Orleans, May 3, 1961; s. Al and Audrey Vitter; m. Wendy Baldwin, 1991; children: Sophie, Lise, Airey, Jack BA magna cum laude, Harvard U., 1983; BA/MA in History/Econs. with highest honors, Oxford U., 1985; JD with honors, Tulane U. Sch. Law, 1988. Bar: La. 1988. Bus. atty., La., 1988—99; assoc. Golden, Kingsmill and Riess, New Orleans, Duplass, Witman, Zwain and Williams, Metairie, La., Duplass, Zwain and Bourgeois, Metairie, La.; mem. La. Ho. of Reps., 1991—99, U.S. Congress from 1st. dist. La., 1999—2005, mem. transp. and judiciary com., govt. reform com., appropriations. com. Washington, 1999—2005; US Senator from La., 2005—. Adj. prof. law Tulane U., 1993—99, Loyola U., 1993—99; mem. com. security and coop. in Europe US Senate, com. commerce, sci. and transp., com. environment and public works, com. small bus. and entrepreneurship. Articles editor Tulane Law Rev., 1987-88. Lector, St. Francis Xavier Cath. Ch., Metairie, La.; Mem. Coastal Conservation Assn., Ducks Unlimited. Rhodes scholar; Recipient Legis. of Yr., Alliance for Good Govt., Lifetime Achievement award Victims & Citizens Against Crime, Republican of Yr. award Northshore Republican Men's Club, 2005. Mem. ABA, New Orleans Bar Assn., Phi Beta Kappa, Nat. Rifle Assn.; former mem. La. Bar Assn. Republican. Roman Catholic. Office: US Senate 516 Hart Senate Office Bldg Washington DC 20510 also: District Office Ste 201 2800 Veterans Blvd Metairie LA 70002 Office Phone: 504-589-2753, 202-224-4623. Office Fax: 504-589-2607, 202-228-5061. *

VITTER, JEFFREY SCOTT, academic administrator, computer science educator, researcher; b. New Orleans, Nov. 13, 1955; s. Albert Leopold Jr. and Audrey Malvina (St. Raymond) V.; m. Sharon Louise Weaver, Aug. 14, 1982; children: Jillian St. Raymond, J. Scott Jr., Audrey Louise. BS in Math. with highest honors, U. Notre Dame, 1977; PhD in Computer Sci., Stanford U., 1980; AM (hon.), Brown U., 1986; MBA, Duke U., 2002. Asst. computer performance analyst Standard Oil Co. Calif., San Francisco, 1976—77; rsch. and tchg. asst. Stanford (Calif.) U., 1977—80, tchg.

fellow, 1979; asst. prof. computer sci. Brown U., Providence, 1980—85, assoc. prof. computer sci., 1985—88, prof. computer sci., 1988—93; Gilbert, Louis and Edward Lehrman prof. computer sci. Duke U., Durham, NC, 1993—2002, chmn. dept., 1993—2001, co-dir. Ctr. for Geometric and Biol. Computing, 1997—2002; prof. computer sci. Purdue U., 2002—, Frederick L. Hovde dean Coll. of Science, 2002—. Cons. IBM, 1981-86, Inst. for Def. Analyses, 1986, Ctr. for Computing Scis., 1992—, Lucent Technologies, Bell Labs., 1997; mem. rsch. staff Math. Scis. Rsch. Inst., Berkeley, 1986, Inst. Recherche en Informatique et en Automatique, Roquencourt, France, 1986-87, Inst. Recherche en Informatique et en Automatique, Sophia Antipolis, France, 1998-1999; vis. prof. Ecole Normale Superieure, Paris, 1986-89; vis. and adj. prof. Tulane U., 1990-2006, mem. bd. advisors Sch. Sci. and Engring., 2006—; lectr. Asian Sch. on Computer Sci., Bangkok, 1987; assoc. mem. Ctr. Excellence in Space Data and Info. Scis. Author: The Design and Analysis of Coalesced Hashing, 1987, Efficient Algorithms for MPEG Video Compression, 2002; editor Algorithmica, 1994—, guest editor, 1988, 94; editor Math. Sys. Theory: Internat. Jour. on Math. Computing Theory, 1991—, Soc. for Indsl. and Applied Math. Jour. on Computing, 1989-1997, Algorithm Engineering, 1999, External Memory Algorithms, 1999; contbr. articles to profl. jours.; patentee in field. Recipient Faculty Devel. award IBM, 1984, NSF Presdl. Young Investigator award, 1985; NSF grad. fellow, 1977-80; Guggenheim fellow, N.Y.C., 1986-87. Fellow IEEE (editor Trans. on Computers 1985, 87-91), Assn. for Computing Machinery (editor Comms. 1988-95, Jour. Exptl. Algorithmics, 2000; mem.-at-large spl. interest group on automata and computability theory 1987-91, vice chair spl. interest group on algorithms and computation theory 1991-1997, chair 1997-2001, exec. com. 2001-05, Recognition of Svc. award 1997, 2001); mem. Computing Rsch. Assn. (bd. dirs. 2000—, co-chair govt. affairs com. 2001—), Phi Beta Kappa, Sigma Xi. Avocations: reading, golf, basketball, football, genealogy. Office: Purdue U Math Sciences Bldg 150 N University St West Lafayette IN 47907-2067 Office Phone: 765-494-1730. Business E-Mail: dean@science.purdue.edu.

VITTETOE, MARIE CLARE, retired clinical laboratory science educator; b. Keota, Iowa, May 19, 1927; d. Edward Daniel and Marcella Matilda Vittetoe. BS, Marycrest Coll., 1950; MS, W.Va. U., 1971, EdD, 1973. Staff technologist St. Joseph Hosp., Ottumwa, Iowa, 1950-70; instr. Ottumwa Hosp. Sch. Med. Tech., 1957-70, St. Joseph Hosp. Sch. Nursing, Ottumwa, 1950-70; asst. prof. U. Ill., Champaign-Urbana, 1973-78; prof. clin. lab. scis. U. Ky., Lexington, 1978-94. Mem. Sisters of Humility of Mary, 1946—; chair Congregation of Humility of Mary; clin. lab. asst., lab. cons. 6 clinics in Haiti, 2000—; cons. nat. public health lab., Haiti. Author: Vittetoe Family Tree and Scrapbook, 2000, Peiffer-Berg Family Tree and Scrapbook, 2000, Lutz/Peiffer Family Tree Update, 2002, Vittetoe Family Tree Update, 2002; contbr. articles to profl. jours. Vol. hosp. labs., Haiti, 1999—; apptd. to advisory bd. CRUDEM Found., 2005—. Named Ky. Col., Marie Vittetoe award for excellence in svc. named for her, U. Ky., 1999; recipient Kingston award for Creative Tchg., Recognition award for svc. to edn., Commonwealth of Ky. Coun. on Higher Edn., disting. grad. award, Nat. Cath. Ednl. Assn., 1995, devel. of youth award, Iowa 4-H Found., 1996, award for devel. Best Little Lab. in Haiti, 2002. Mem. Am. Soc. for Med. Tech. (chmn. 1986-89, Profl. Achievement award 1991, Ky. Mem. of Yr. award 1994), Am. Soc. Clin. Lab. Scis., Am. Soc. Clin. Pathologists (assoc.), Alpha Mu Tau, Phi Delta Kappa, Alpha Eta. Avocations: walking, genealogy.

VITTOR, KENNETH MARK, lawyer; BS with honors, Cornell U., 1971; JD, U. Chgo., 1974. Assoc. Cahill, Gordon & Reindel, NYC, 1974-80; sr. v.p., assoc. gen. counsel McGraw-Hill Cos., NYC, 1980-95, sr. v.p., gen. counsel, 1995—99, exec. v.p., gen. counsel, 1999—. Chmn. Libel Def. Resource Ctr., 1999-2000. Mem. Copyright, Patent and Trademark Commn., Freedom to Read Commn., Assn. Am. Pubs., Mag. Pubs. Am. (chmn. legal affairs com.), Lawyers Commn. (chmn. libel, privacy and first admendment subcommittee 1983-86). Office: McGraw-Hill Cos 48th Fl 1221 Avenue Of The Americas New York NY 10020-1095 *

VITTORI, ROBERTO, astronaut; b. Viterbo, Italy, Oct. 15, 1964; m. Valeria Nardi; 3 children. Grad., Italian Air Force Acad., 1989; grad. undergrad. pilot tng., Reese AFB, Tex., 1989; grad., U.S. Navy Test Pilot Sch., 1995; attended, U.S. Air Force Flight Safety Sch., 1997—98. Flew Tornado GR1 aircraft 155th Squadron, 50th Wing, Piacenza, Italy, 1991—94; project pilot for devel. of European aircraft EF2000 Italian Test Ctr., 1995—98; nat. rep. Beyond Visual Range Air-to-Air Missile R&D Program, 1996—98; wing flight safety officer Italian Test Ctr., 1997; tchr. aerodynamics accident investigation course Italian Air Force; astronaut Italian Space Agy. in cooperation with ESA, 1998; joined European Astronaut Corp., ESA European Astronaut Ctr., Cologne, Germany, 1998; mission specialist candidate astronaut NASA Johnson Space Ctr., Houston, 1998—, with Astronaut Office New Generation Space Vehicles Br., 2002; tng. as bd. engr. Yuri Gagarin Cosmonaut Tng. Ctr., Star City near Moscow, 2001; participated in a taxi-flight to Internat. Space Station, 2002; mem. of crew with Salizhan Sharipov and Leroy Chiao Expedition 11, 2005. Maj. Italian Air Force. Avocations: soccer, running, swimming, reading. Office: NASA Johnson Space Ctr Astronaut Office/CB Houston TX 77058

VITTY, RODERIC BEMIS, retired financial planner, publishing executive; b. St. Johnsbury, Vt., July 28, 1933; s. Clarence Lucian and Leota (Cobleigh) V.; m. Virginia Gable, March, 1960 (div. 1983); children: Roderic G., Virginia A., David P., Suzanne L.; m. Patricia Lyster, June 21, 1986. BS, U.S. Mil. Acad., 1955; MS in Fin. Svcs., Am. Coll., Bryn Mawr, Pa., 1977, MS in Mgmt., 1987; postgrad. exec. mgmt. program, Columbia U., 1985. CLU; chartered fin. cons.; cert. fin. planner. With Conn. Gen. Life Ins. Co. (CIGNA-Lincoln Fin. Advisor), 1960, mgr. br. office Cherry Hill, NJ, 1968—, mgr. Greater Phila. office, 1981—, mktg. gen. mgr., 1983—85, gen. mgr., regional v.p., 1985—94. Pub., owner Vt. Heritage press, Caber Pub. Ltd. Trustee St. Johnsbury Acad., Vt., 1993—, co-chair capital campaign, 1999; mem assembly of overseers Dartmouth-Hitchcock Med. Ctr.; civilian aide Sec. Army State of Vt., 2005-. Served with inf. U.S. Army, 1955-59, Pa. N.G., 1961-68. Recipient GAMA Master Agy. Builder award, 1982-92, Nat. Mgmt. awards (20), 1972-92, Outstanding Agy. awards (9), CIGNA; named to CIGNA Hall of Fame, 1998. Mem. West Point Soc. Phila. (pres. 1969-71, 89-94, emeritus, 1994), Nat. Assn. Ins. and Fin. Advisors, South Jersey Fin. Planning Coun., Internat. Assn. Fin. Planners, Soc. of Fin. Svc. Profls., So. N.J. Gen. Agts. and Mgrs. Assn. (pres. 1979-80), Nat. GAMA (regional v.p. 1986-89, treas., exec. com. 1991-94), Assn. Grads U.S. Mil. Acad. (trustee 1992—2005, emeritus 2005-, pres. Class of 1955, 1995-2000), Soc. Colonial Wars, Soc. Mayflower Descendants, Army Athletic Assn., Sunnybrook Swim Club, Cherry Hill Raquet Club, Riverton Country Club, Quechee Club Vt., St. Johnsbury Country Club, Safari Club Internat., Chevaliers du Tastevin, Union League Phila., St. Andrews Soc. Vt., Masons (32 deg.), Shriners, K.T. Presbyterian. Address: Twildoon Lodge-Angell Trail PO Box 151 Quechee VT 05059-0151

VITVITSKY, JACK, physician assistant; b. White Plains, NY, Mar. 8, 1945; s. Alexander Jack and Helen Louise Virginia (Rider) V. BS, U. Rochester, 1968; AAS, Cuyahoga C.C., Cleve., 1978; postgrad., SUNY, Plattsburgh, 1964-66, 73-74, Liberty U., 1994—. Cert. first aid and CPR instr. ARC; cert. EMT instr. N.Y.; cert. ground and flight instr., instrument instr., multi-engine instr., written test examiner FAA. Physician's asst. Planned Parenthood No. N.Y., 1979-84, Dr. David P. Gorman, Malone, N.Y., 1980-81, N.Y. State Dept. Corrections, Dannemora, N.Y., 1981-84, N.Y. State Office Mental Retardation and Devel. Disabilities, Tupper Lake, N.Y., 1984-85, N.Y. State Dept. Corrections, Raybrook, NY, 1985—2002; owner Adirondack Computer Testing Ctr., 1996—2005; assoc. sales rep. Primerica Fin. Svcs., Plattsburg, NY, 2002—04; bus driver Franklin County Assn. Sr. Citizens at Saranac Lake Ctr., NY, 2002—04; med. standards officer NY Army N.G., Watervliet, 2004—05; physician asst. Post Deployment Health Reassessment Program Logistics Health, Inc., Fort Hood, Tex., 2007—. Contbr. articles to profl. jours. Active Lake Placid Vol. Ambulance Svc., Inc., 1975—, Nat. Ski Patrol System, 1975—; mem. aviation explorer program Boy Scouts Am. With U.S.Army Res., 1981-84, N.Y. Army N.G., 1984—. Mem. Am. Acad. Physician Assts. (cons. minority affairs com. 1999-2001), NY State Soc. Physician Assts., Soc. Army Physician Assts. (del. to Am. Acad. Physician Assts. Ho. of Dels.), Adirondack Soc. Physician Assts. (sec. 1996-2004), Mid-Hudson Assn. Physician Assts., Fellowship Christian Physician Assts. (sec. 1992-97), Exptl. Aviation Assn., Aircraft Owners and Pilots Assn., US Army Flight Soc. of Flight Surgeons, NRA, Gun Owners Am., Am. Legion. Republican. Avocations: snowshoeing, skiing, writing, woodworking, equine activities. Home: 132 Old Military Rd Lake Placid NY 12946-1699 Office: 466th Med Co NYARNG 147 Warren St Glens Falls NY 12801 Personal E-mail: jackvitvitsky@juno.com.

VITZ, PAUL CLAYTON, psychologist, educator; b. Toledo, Aug. 27, 1935; m. Evelyn Birge; 6 children. BA high honors in Psychology, U. Mich., 1953; PhD, Stanford U., 1962. Instr. psychology Pomona (Calif.) Coll., 1962-64; asst. prof. NYU, 1965-70, assoc. prof., 1970-85, dir. psychology dept. undergrad. program, 1973-79, prof., 1985—2004, prof. emeritus, 2004—, acting dir. master's program, 1988—91, acting dir. grad. program, 1989—90. Adj. prof. John Paul II Inst. on Marriage and Family, Washington, 1990-2003, Internat. Acad. Philosophy, 1994-98; prof./sr. scholar Inst. for Psychol. Scis., 2000—; lectr. in field. Author: Psychology as Religion: The Cult of Self-Worship, 1977, 2d edit., 1994, (with A.B. Glimcher) Modern Art and Modern Science: The Parallel Analysis of Vision, 1984, Censorship: Evidence of Bias in Our Children's Textbooks, 1986, Sigmund Freud's Christian Unconscious, 1988, Faith of the Fatherless: The Psychology of Atheism, 1999; editor: (with S. Krason) Defending the Family: A Sourcebook, 1998, (with S. Felch) The Self: Beyond the Postmodern Crisis, 2006; contbr. articles to profl. jours., chpts. to books. Grantee Nat. Inst. Mental Health, 1963-64, 64-66, 66-67, Nat. Inst. Neurol. Diseases and Blindness grantee, 1970-73, 73-74, Nat. Inst. Edn., 1983, 84-85, Dept. Edn., 1986-87. Office: Inst for the Psychol Scis Ste 511 2001 Jefferson Davis Hwy Arlington VA 22202

VIVIAN, CASSANDRA, museum administrator, writer, photographer; b. Monessen, Pa., Dec. 12, 1942; d. Alfred Arthur Vivian and Elizabeth Marie Parigi. MA, California U. Pa., 1973. Cert. tchr. Pa., 1963. Instr. Am. U. in Cairo, 1978—84; mktg. mgr. Am. U. in Cairo Press, 1984—88; CEO Monessen Heritage Mus. Greater Monessen Hist. Soc., Pa., 1995—. Guest curator Carnegie Mus. Natural History, Pitts., 1991—92; local historian, rschr. WVU Nat. Parks Svc. HABS/HAER, Monessen, 1995; cons. USS Constn. Mus., Boston, 2003; cons., photographer No. Lights Films PBS, Farmington, Pa., 2006; CEO Mid Mon Valley Indsl. Mus., Monessen, 2006. Author: The Overseer's Family: A Memoir of the Tuscan Countryside, Cairo: A Practical Guide, An Italian American Christmas in Western PA, Mid Mon Valley Postcards, The National Road in Pennsylvania, Monessen: A Typical Steel Country Town, Islands of the Blest: A Guide to the Oases and the Western Desert of Egypt, A Walking and Driving Tour of Historic Brownsville, The Western Desert of Egypt: An Explorer's Handbook, William Eaton: A Forgotten American Voice, (plays) Titanic: The Monessen Story; photography book, Egypt: Touching the Land, exhibitions include The National Road in Digital (Artist of the Pike, 2003), Carnegie Mus. Natural History, Akhnaton Gallery, Cairo, Am. Ctr. Named Disting. Steward of Cmty., Pa. Ho. of Reps., 2005; recipient Meritorious award, California U. Pa., 2003, Br. Recognition award, Mon Valley NAACP, 2005, Creative Artist stipend, Pa. Coun. on Arts, 2005; Pa. Humanities and the Arts grantee, Pa. Humanities Coun. Pa. Coun. on the Arts, 2000. Office: Greater Monessen Historical Society 505 Donner Ave Monessen PA 15062 Home Phone: 724-684-6270; Office Phone: 724-684-8460. Personal E-mail: cassandra.vivian@gmail.com. Business E-Mail: monessen@verizon.net.

VIZQUEL, OMAR ENRIQUE, professional baseball player; b. Caracus, Venezuela, Apr. 24, 1967; Grad. high sch., Caracus. With Seattle Mariners, 1989-93; shortstop Cleve. Indians, 1994—2004, San Francisco Giants, 2004—. Recipient Winner Am. League Golden Glove, 1993-2001, Nat. League Golden Glove, 2006; named to MLB All-Star game, 1998, 1999, 2002 Office: c/o San Francisco Giants Pacific Bell Park 24 Willie Mays Plaza San Francisco CA 94107 *

VLACH, JIRI, electrical engineering educator, researcher; b. Prague, Czechoslovakia, Oct. 5, 1922; arrived in Can., 1969; s. Frantisek and Bozena (Papouskova) V.; m. Dagmar Gutova, Oct. 22, 1949; 1 son, Martin. Dipl.eng., Tech. U. Prague, 1947, C.Sc., 1957. With Research Inst. for Radio Communications, Prague, 1948-67, head math. dept., until 1967; vis. prof. U. Ill., Urbana, 1967-69; prof. elec. engring. U. Waterloo (Ont., Can.), 1969—. Author: Computerized Approximation and Synthesis of Linear Networks, 1969, (with others) Computer Methods for Circuit Analysis and Design, 1983, 2nd edit., 1994, Basic Network Theory with Computer Applications, 1992; assoc. editor IEEE Trans. on Circuits and Systems, 1979-80, 87-88, 98—. Fellow: IEEE (life); mem.: Eta Kappa Nu. Home: 355 Craigleith Dr Waterloo ON Canada N2L 5B5 Office: U Waterloo 200 University Ave West Waterloo ON Canada N2L 3G1 Office Phone: 519-888-4567 ext 3671. Personal E-mail: jvlach@uwaterloo.ca.

VLADECK, BRUCE CHARNEY, healthcare educator, former academic administrator; b. NYC, Sept. 13, 1949; s. Stephen Charney and Judith (Pomarlen) V.; m. Fredda Wellin, Aug. 5, 1973; children— Elizabeth Charney, Stephen Isaiah, Abigail Sarah. BA, Harvard U., Cambridge, Mass., 1970; MA, U. Mich, 1972, PhD in Polit. Sci., 1973. Assoc. social scientist NYC-Rand Inst., 1973-74; asst. prof. Columbia U., NYC, 1974-78, assoc. prof., 1978-79; asst. commr. health planning and resources devel. NJ Dept. Health, Trenton, 1979-82; asst. v.p. Robert Wood Johnson Found., Princeton, NJ, 1982-83; pres. United Hosp. Fund, NYC, 1983-93; adminstr. HCFA, Washington, 1993-97; prof. health policy and geriatrics Mt. Sinai Med. Ctr., NYC, 1997—2004; prin. Health Scis. Adv. Svcs. Ernst & Young LLP, 2004—06; interim pres. U. Medicine and Dentistry NJ, Newark, 2006—07. Mem. NY State Coun. on Health Care Financing, Albany, 1978-92; mem. com. on nursing home regulation Inst. Medicine, Washington, 1983-85, chmn. com. on health care for homeless people, 1986-88, mem. prospective payment assessment com., 1986-93; mem. Nat. Bipartisan Commn. on Future of Medicare, 1997-98. Author: Unloving Care: The Nursing Home Tragedy, 1981. Contbr. numerous articles to profl. publs. Fellow N.Y. Acad. Medicine; mem. Inst. Medicine, Nat. Acad. Scis., Phi Beta Kappa. Office Phone: 917-583-0835. Business E-Mail: vladeck@umdnj.edu.

VLADEM, PAUL JAY, investment advisor; b. Chgo., Apr. 5, 1952; s. Arthur I. and Elaine A. (Ascher) V.; m. Sondra Joyce Berman, Dec. 27, 1981; children: Ashley Sherree, Evan David. BSBA with honors and high distinction, U. Ill., Chgo., 1974. Lic. brokerage securities, Fla., Ill., Ariz., Conn., Ga., Ind., N.C., Colo., Md., Nev., Del., N.Y., Ohio, Calif., Utah, Mich., Mo., Mass., NJ, Pa., Tenn., Va., Oreg.; registered investment advisor; lic. ins. agt., Fla., Ill., Ind., Utah, Conn., Ariz., NY, Tenn.; CPA, Fla., Ill.; lic. real estate agt., Fla. In charge acct. Peat Marwick, Fort Lauderdale, Fla., 1974-76; mgr. McGladrey & Pullen, CPA, Fort Lauderdale, 1976-85; sr. v.p. fin. Integrated Resources formerly Easter Kramer, Boca Raton, Fla., 1985-89; pres. Associated Investor Svcs., Fort Lauderdale, 1989—. Bd. dirs. Israel Bonds, Ft. Lauderdale, 1994, Jewish Family Svc., Ft. Lauderdale, 1993, Jewish Fedn. Broward County Investment Com., Coral Springs Mus. Arts; chmn. CPA Com. on Israel Bonds, Ft. Lauderdale, 1994, mem. prof. adv. com., 1992—. Named One of Top Ten Brokers of Yr. Registered Rep. Mag., 1994. Mem. AICPA (personal planning divsn.), Fla. Inst. CPAs (mem. personal fin. planning com., 1985), Internat. Platform Assn. Democrat. Jewish. Avocations: tennis, basketball, attending sporting events. Home: 6508 NW 103rd Ln Parkland FL 33076-2934 Office: Associated Investor Svcs 2699 Stirling Rd Ste A200 Fort Lauderdale FL 33312-6583 Office Phone: 954-983-5600. Business E-Mail: Paul@afc-ais.com.

VLADEM, STEVEN ALLEN, writer, film producer, motivational speaker; b. Chgo., July 24, 1949; s. Arthur and Elaine Edythe (Ascher) Vladem. BA with honors and distinction, U. Ill., Chgo., 1970; MEd in Math., Northeastern Ill. U., Chgo., 1973; MA in Ednl. Adminstrn./Supervision, Roosevelt U., Chgo., 1975; ScD, London Sch. Applied Rsch., 1993. Tchr. math. Chgo. Bd. Edn., 1971-81, statistician and evaluator dept. rsch. and evaluation, 1979; supr. program svcs. Dept. Planning, Chgo. City Hall, 1981; coord. alt. sch. without walls program Chgo. Met. HS, 1982-87, coord. computer assisted instrn., 1987-91; developer ednl. software Chgo., 1987-92; freelance computer cons., 1987-92; writer/lectr., 1994—; prodr. Image Lost Film, 2003—. Lectr. in field; mktg. cons. Enoch Searle Prodns., 2001—, Cosmic Films, 2001—; motivational spkr. Profl. Spkrs. Bur. Internat., 2001—. Author: (poetry) The Jigsaw People, 1997; exhibitions include Gallery Art, Internat. Congress Arts and Commn., Keble Coll., Oxford U., Eng.; prodr.: Image Last Films, 2003—; exec. prodr.: (films) Gein, 2003. Mem. Internat. Parliament Safety and Peace, Palermo, Italy, 1993—95; bd. dirs. Nat. Coalition health Care Reform, 1998—; founder coun. London Diplomatic Acad., Internat. Diplomatic Acad., Albert Schweitzer Inst., Chgo. Coun. Fgn. Rels., Internat. Fellowship Christians and Jews; sec.-gen. United Cultural Conv.; hon. amb. laureates Jr. Achievement and Chgo. Assn. Bus. and Industry, 1990; support group leader, outreach vol. Nat. Keratoconus Found., LA, 1995—; docent Tour of Old Town Old Town C. of C., Chgo., 1993; patron various arts orgns.; vol. Sight Savers Internat., Karen Or Ctr. Multi-Handicapped Blind Children, State of Ill. Transplant Program, 2003, Am. Transplant Assn., Cinema for Deaf Film Festival, 2003; judge Daniel Webster Acad. Poets Competition, 1998; nominator Col.'s Way Award. Finalist, U.S. Nat. Memory Championship, N.Y.C., 1997; named John W. Rogers Educator of the Yr., Jr. Achievement, Chgo., 1990; named to Wall of Tolerance, Civil Rights Meml. Ctr., 2003; recipient Congress Star of Distinction, Internat. Congress Arts and Comm./St. John's Coll., Cambridge U., 1992, medal of Merit, Republic of Peru, 1992, Alzheimers Rsch. award, Alzheimers Assn. Am., 2000, Internat. Peace prize, 2002, Congl. medal of Excellence, 2002, Am. medal of Honor, 2002. Mem. NATAS, Ill. Prodn. Alliance, Internat. Platform Assn. (bd. govs. internet team, red carpet com., Gold Ribbon Most Popular Artist 1995), United Writers Assn. (life fellow), World Univ. Roundtable, Toastmasters Internat., Internat. Order of Merit (Cambridge, Eng.), Daniel Webster Acad. Poets (Cert. of Merit 1995), Chrysopoets, Order of Templars of Jerusalem (knight), Lofsensic Ursinius Order (knight comdr.), World Order of Sci. Edn. Culture. (knight-cavalier), Am. Order Excellence, Order of San Ciriaco (count), Internat. Diplomatic Acad., Am. Legion (gold medal, sch. leadership award 1967), Rotary Club, Lions Club. Avocations: cinema, musical theatre, backgammon, architecture, world travel. Address: Profl Spkrs Bur Internat 1112 5th Ave Ste 101 Worthington OH 43085 Home: 1700 Hinman Ave Apt 2b Evanston IL 60201-4592 E-mail: stevevladem@yahoo.com.

VLADIMIROFF, MAXIM, music educator, composer; b. Sochi, Russia, Apr. 18, 1968; s. Sergey and Tatyana Vladimiroff; m. Leisa Dale Lundberg, May 15, 1995; children: Damian, Lucas. MusB, Gnessin Coll., Moscow, 1987; MA, U. Calif., Irvine, 1999. Tchr. EAMA, NYC, 2003—; accompanist Danbury Music Ctr., Conn., 2005—. Pianist VPC, Brookfield, Conn., 2006—. Composer: 12 Preludes for Piano, 1997, Quid Ploras, Mulier?, 2001, Four Pieces for Striung Trio, 2004. Mem.: ASCAP, MTNA, Am. Music Ctr. Home: 25 Stage Rd Brookfield CT 06804

VLADIMIROVICH, VINOGRADOV PAVEL, cosmonaut; b. Magadan, Russia, Aug. 31, 1953; married; 3 children. Grad. in Dept. Airborne Vehicles, Moscow Aviation Inst., 1977. Pilot-cosmonaut, 3rd class cosmonaut Russian Fedn.; specialized in software develop for automated interactive designing systems of recoverable vehicles, develop. aerodynamics and aerodyne arrangement design models, computer graphics, 1977—83; with Head Design Bur. Rocket Space Corp., Energia, 1983; joined Energia cosmonaut corp, 1992; completed generic space tng. Yu. A. Gagarin Cosmonaut Tng. Ctr., 1992—94, complete advance test-cosmonaut tng., 1994—95; flight engr. tng. of Mir-20 and EuroMir-95 back-up crew Soyuz TM and Mir Space Station, 1995; trained for Spaceflight on Soyuz TM vehicle and Mir spac e station as flight engr. Mir-22/NASA-3 and Cassiopeia programs, 1995—96; trained as flight engr. Mir-24 prime crew, 1996—97; flight engr. Soyuz TM and Mir Station, Expedition 24 (Mir-24/NASA 5. 6), 1997—98; trained for spaceflight as back-up flight engr. Mir-28, 1999—2000; trained as flight engr. Mir-29, 2000; completed tng. as test cosmonaut Internat. Space Station group, 2001—02; trained as flight engr. Internat. Space Station Taxi Back-up crew 5, 2002—03; crew comdr. Internat. Space Station, Expedition-13, Soyuz TMA-8, 2006. Avocations: game sports, astronomy, history of avaiation and cosmonautics. Office: Astronaut office CB NASA Johnson Space Center Houston TX 77058

VLADUTIU, ADRIAN O., physician, educator; b. Bucharest, Romania, Aug. 5, 1940; came to U.S., 1969, naturalized 1974; s. Octavian and Veturia (Chirescu) Vladutiu; m. Georgirene V. Dietrich; children: Christina Lynn, Catherine Joy. MD, Sch. Medicine, Bucharest, 1962; PhD in Immunopathology, Sch. Medicine, Jassy, Romania, 1968. Diplomate Am. Bd. Pathology. Asst. prof. physiopathology Sch. Medicine, Bucharest, 1968-71; assoc. prof. pathology SUNY Sch. Medicine, Buffalo, 1978-81, prof. pathology, 1981—, pathologist, 1974—2006; dir. clin. labs. Buffalo Gen. Hosp., 1982—2001, prof. microbiology, 1982—, prof. medicine, 1985—. Cons. Niagara Falls (N.Y.) Meml. Hosp., 1976—82, Tri-County Hosp., Gowanda, NY, 1991—93; acting head dept. pathology Buffalo Gen. Hosp, 1985—86; dir. lab. Deaconess Hosp. Buffalo, 1982—91, Columbus Meml., Buffalo, 1996—98. Author: Pleural Effusion, 1986; contbr. chapters to books, articles to profl. jours. Med. Rsch. Coun. Can. fellow, 1968, Buswell fellow, 1969; recipient rsch. prize Ministry Edn. Romania, 1965, rsch. award NIH, 1985. Fellow: ACP, Nat. Acad. Clin. Biochemistry, Coll. Am. Pathologists; mem.: Am. Soc. Investigative Pathology, Am. Assn. Immunologists. Achievements include first demonstration of the association of autoimmunity with major histocompability antigens; discovery of Buffalo thyroxine binding globulin gene. Home: 80 Oakview Dr Buffalo NY 14221-1420 Business E-Mail: vladutiu@buffalo.edu. E-mail: guthormones@yahoo.com.

VLAHOS, EFSTRATIOS G., retired cardiologist; b. Thessaloniki, Greece, May 21, 1924; s. George E. and Gleni (Christofa) Vlahos; children: George, Aristotelis. Lic. NY, NJ. Rotating intern Bronx Hosp., NY. With Greek Army. Greek Orthodox.

VLAHOV, DAVID, epidemiologist; b. Washington, Aug. 31, 1952; s. William John and Helga Rose Vlahov; m. Robyn Randice Mione; children: Alexander, Alexandra Gershon. BA, Earlham Coll., 1974; BSN, MS, U. Md., 1980; PhD, Johns Hopkins U., 1988. RN 1977. Prof. epidemiology Sch. Pub. Health Johns Hopkins U., Balt., 1988—2001; dir. Ctr. for Urban Epidemiologic Studies, v.p. for rsch. N.Y. Acad. Medicine, NYC, 1999—; prof. clin. epidemiology Sch. Pub. Health Columbia U., NYC, 1999—. Mem. nat. adv. coun. on drug abuse Dept. HHS. Contbr. more than 550 sci. papers to profl. jours.; editor: Jour. Urban Health, 2000—. Recipient Merit award, NIH, 1995—2005; grantee, 1990—, CDC, 1990—, Robert Wood

Johnson Found., 1990—, N.Y. Cmty. Trust, 1990—. Fellow: N.Y. Acad. Medicine, Infectious Disease Soc. of Am.; mem.: Am. Pub. Health Assn., Am. Epidemiol. Soc., Soc. for Epidemiol. Rsch. Home: 401 E 86th St Apt 12 E New York NY 10028 Office: NY Acad Medicine 1216 Fifth Ave New York NY 10029 Office Phone: 212-822-7382. Business E-Mail: dvlahov@nyam.org.

VLASAK, BRIAN EMERSON, composer; b. Binghamton, NY, July 1, 1979; s. Steven John Best and Peggy Ann Goldsberry. MusB, SUNY, Potsdam, 2003, MusM, 2004; PhD in Music, U. Iowa, Iowa City, 2007. Tchg. asst. music theory U. Iowa, 2004—07, composer, 2001—, condr., 2003—. Dance class acompanist, dept. dance and drama SUNY, Potsdam, NY, 2001—04; adv. bd. mem. Savayards, 2006—. Composer: (composition) Homage to A.M, 2005 (Henry and Parker Pelzer fellow, 2005), Three Miniatures, 2007, Chamber Concerto, 2007. Mem.: Soc. Composers Inc (chpt. officer-at-large 2004—), Am. Musicological Soc., Am. Composer's Forum. Green Party.

VLAY, STEPHEN CHARLES, cardiologist, electrophysiologist; b. NYC, July 25, 1950; s. Stephen and Rose Vlay; m. Linda C. Vlay. AB, NYU, 1971; MD, Yale U., 1975. Diplomate Am. Bd. Internal Medicine, Am. Bd. Cardiovasc. Disease, Am. Bd. Clin. Cardiac Electrophysiology; testamur NASPExAM, 1997. Intern and resident in internal medicine NYU-Bellevue Med. Ctr., NYC, 1975-78; fellow in cardiology Johns Hopkins Hosp., Balt., 1978-81, asst. in medicine, 1980-81; instr., asst. prof., then assoc. prof. medicine SUNY, Stony Brook, 1981-92, prof., 1992—. Dir. Stony Brook Arrhythmia Study and Sudden Death Prevention Ctr. Editor: Manual of Cardiac Arrhythmias, 1988, Medical Care of the Cardiac Surgical Patient, 1992, A Practical Approach to Cardiac Arrhythmias, 1996. Fellow ACP, Am. Heart Assn. (coun. on clin. cardiology), Am. Coll. Cardiology, Heart Rhythm Soc.; mem. N.Am. Soc. Pacing and Electrophysiology. Office: SUNY Health Sci Ctr N T17 020 Stony Brook NY 11794-0001

VLAZNY, JOHN GEORGE, archbishop; b. Chgo., Feb. 22, 1937; s. John George and Marie Hattie (Brezina) V. BA, St. Mary of the Lake Coll., Mundelein, Ill., 1958; STL, Pontifical Gregorian U., Rome, 1962; MA in Classics, U. Mich., 1967; MEd, Loyola U., 1972; LLD (hon.), U. Portland, 1999. Ordained priest Roman Cath. Ch., 1961, consecrated bishop Roman Cath. Ch., 1983. Assoc. pastor St. Paul of the Cross Ch., Park Ridge, Ill., 1962—63, St. Clement Ch., Chgo., 1963—68, St. Aloysius Ch., Chgo., 1968—72, pastor, 1979—81; assoc. pastor St. Sylvester Ch., Chgo., 1972—74, Precious Blood Ch., Chgo., 1974—79; faculty Quigley Prep., North Chgo., Ill., 1963—79, dean of studies, 1969—79; rector Niles Coll., Chgo., 1981—83; aux. bishop Archdiocese of Chgo., 1983—87; Episcopal vicar Vicariate I, Chgo., 1983—87; bishop Episc. Ch., Winona, Minn., 1987—97; archbishop Diocese of Portland, 1997—. Pres. Presbyteral Senate, Chgo., 1976—77; mem. Diocesan Clergy Personnel Bd., Chgo., 1981—84, chmn., 1983—84. Bd. dirs. NED, Latino Tng. Ctr., Chgo., 1980—81, Sacred Heart Sch. Theology, Hales Corners, Wis., 1986—, St. Mary's Coll., Winona, 1987—. Mem.: Nat. Conf. Cath. Bishops (various coms. 1983—), Nat. Comms. Found. (bd. dirs. 1990—). Roman Catholic. Avocations: music, running.

VLCEK, DONALD JOSEPH, JR., food products executive, wholesale distribution executive, writer; b. Chgo., Oct. 30, 1949; s. Donald Joseph and Rosemarie (Krizek) V.; m. Claudia Germain Meyer, July 22, 1978 (div. 1983); 1 child, Suzanne Mae; m. Valeria Olive Russell, Nov. 11, 1989 (div. Mar. 2006); children: James Donald, Victoria Rose. BBA, U. Mich., 1971. Cert. facilitator Adizes Inst. Gen. mgr. Popps, Inc., Hamtramck, Mich., 1969-76; sr. v.p. Domino's Pizza Inc., 1978—93; pres. Domino's Pizza Distbn. Corp., Ann Arbor, Mich., 1978-93, chmn., 1993-94, also bd. dirs.; pres. Don Vlcek & Assocs., Ltd., Plymouth, Mich., 1994—; CEO Beaver Buddies, LLC, Plymouth, Mich., 2001—04; master franchisee Beaver Tails Can., Inc., Mich., Ind., Ill., Ohio, Wis.; pres. WonderPizzaUSA, 2005—07, bd. mgrs., 2005—07, COO, 2005—07; v.p. Marco's Franchising LLC, Toledo, 2007—. Profl. speaker, personal coach, seminar leader, bus. cons., workshop facilitator; trustee Domino's Pizza Ptnrs. Found.; bd. dirs. RPM Pizza Inc., Gulfport, Miss., Dimango Corp., South Lyon, Mich.; sr. v.p. distbn. and tech. Domino's Ohio Commissary, Zanesville; pres. Morel Mountain Corp.; judge 1994 Duck Stamp contest U.S. Dept. Interior, Jr. Fed. Duck Stamp Contest, 1995; bd. dirs. Beaver Tails Can. Author: The Domino Effect, 1992 (Best of Bus. award ALA 1992, Soundview's Top 30 Business books of 1993), SuperVision, 1997, Job Planning and Review System Manual, 1997, 2001; (audio cassette tape series Super Vision); contbr. articles to profl. jours. Bd. dirs. Men's Hockey League of Oak Park, Mich., 1973-78; asst. coach Redford Scorpions Jr. Travel Hockey Team. Named Person of Yr. Bd. Franchises, Boston, 1981; recipient Teal award Ducks Unltd., 1992, State Major Gifts Chmn. award, 1992, 93, State Chmn.'s award, 1992, State Major Gifts award, 1994, Russ Bengal award, 2003, Mr. Producer award, 1997, 98, 2000, others. Mem. Am. Soc. of Tng. Dirs., Mich. Steelheaders Assn. (life), Ducks Unltd. (life, Domino's Pizza chpt. treas., sponsor, chmn. 1988—, Mich. state bd. dirs., life sponsor, chmn. 1989, 91-92, state trustee 1992-98, hon. trustee 2001—, chmn. exec. com. 1992-94, major gifts chmn. 1993-98, chmn. strategic devel. com. 1994, sponsor in perpetuity Grand Slam Life, Heritage sponsor, recipient Russ Bengal award, 2003), Mich. United Conservation Club (life), Whitetails Unltd. (life), Pheasants Forever (life), Midstates Masters Bowling Assn. (bd. dirs. 1976-85), Barton Hills Country Club (golf com., capt. dist. team), U. Mich. Alumni Assn. (life), Domino's Lodge/Drummond Island Wildlife Habitat Found. (pres., chmn. bd.), Vlcek Family Wildlife Found. (pres., chmn. bd.), Elks (life), Die Hard Cubs Fan Club, Greater Detroit C. of C., Profl. Spkrs. Assn. of Mich. (bd. dirs. 1997-99), Mich. Soc. Assn. Execs., Sm. Bus. Assn. Mich., Nat. Spkrs. Assn., Profl. Spkrs. Ill. (profl.), Internat. Coaching Fedn. (cert. master), Am. Soc. Tng. Dirs., Bus. Network Profls. Republican. Roman Catholic. Avocations: hunting, fishing, hockey, art, coin collecting/numismatics. Home: 9251 Beck Rd N Plymouth MI 48170-3336 Office: Don Vlcek & Assoc Ltd PO Box 701353 Plymouth MI 48170-0963 Office Phone: 734-266-2260. Personal E-mail: vlcek2@aol.com.

VLIET, MARNI, foundation administrator; d. James and Mary Louise Tasheff; m. Richard Wayne Vliet, Jan. 26, 1944; children: Whitney Aletia, Sasha Marie. BEd, Wichita State U., 1970, MEd, 1977. Lectr. Wichita State U., 1977—85; program cons. Kans. Health Found., Wichita, 1985—86, program officer, 1986—88, v.p. programs, 1988—92, sr. v.p., 1992—96, exec. v.p. and COO, 1996, pres. and CEO, 1996—. Mem. strategic planning com. Dept. Preventive Medicine, U. Kans. Med. Sch., Wichita, 1993—94; bd. dir. Ctrs. Disease Control Found.; spkr. in field. Co-author: Public Health Reports, Community Grantmaking: A Strategic Approach; contbr. articles to jour. Founding chair Funders Concerned Against Substance Abuse, Washington, 1989—94; chair health com. Wichita Commn. on Status of Women, 1975—80, co-chair legis. com.; vice chair bd. Women's Studies Cmty. Coun., Wichita; co-founder Old Town Assn. Wichita, mem. bd.; founding chair Wichita Farm & Art Market Com., mem.; founding dir. Parent Awareness Group and Teen Awareness Day, Robinson Jr. HS, Wichita; founder, dir. Women Alive & Well I & II, Wichita; mem. exec. bd. Women's Alcohol Treatment Services, Wichita; mem. Wichita Children's Mus., Women in the Arts, Wichita; vice chair bd. Wichita Commn. on Status of Women; mem. health promotion adv. bd. Kaiser Family Found., Menlo Park, Calif., 1988—90; bd. dir. Drug Strategies, Washington, 2002—; mem. Grantmakers in Health, 1995—2001, chair bd. dirs., 1999—2001; mem. Cmty. Anti-Drug Coalitions Am., Washington, 1992—98, chair bd. dirs., 1996—98; mem. State of World Forum, San Francisco, 1998; bd. dir. Wichita Symphony Soc., 2000—, Wichita Art Mus., 2000—; mem. bd. Clearinghouse Midcontinent Founds., Kansas City, 1993—97. Recipient President's Drug Adv. Coun. Leadership award, Exec. Office Pres. U.S., 1992, Cmty. Coun. Adv. Bd. award, Wichita State U. Ctr. Women's Studies, 1996, Bd. Trustees' award, Wichita State U., 1996, Exec. of Yr. award, Clarus, 1997—98, Nat. Leadership award, Cmty. Anti-Drug Coalitions Ams., Washington, DC, 1998, Pub. Policy award, Kans. State U. Coll. Human Ecology, 2004, Women Bus. Honoree, Wichita Bus. Jour., 2004, Brotherhood/Sisterhood award, Nat. Conf. Cmty. and Justice, 55th Annual Humanitarian award, Wichita, 2005. Mem.: Coun. Founds. (assoc.), Sigma Theta Tau Internat. (adv. coun.). Avocations: reading, gardening, travel. Office: Kansas Health Found Attn Jamie Hunt Comm Prog Assoc 309 E Douglas Wichita KS 67202 Home Phone: 316-683-0707; Office Phone: 316-262-7676. Office Fax: 316-262-2044.

VO, EVANLY, organic chemist; b. Quang Ngai, Ctrl., Vietnam, Nov. 15, 1965; parents Kim Vo and Quy Thi Nguyen; m. Quynh-Giao Thi Nguyen, May 23, 1998; children: Jennifer Nguyen Vo, Elaine Nguyen Vo BS, U. New Orleans, 1993; PhD, U. Houston, 1997. Tchg. asst. U. Houston, 1994-95, rsch. asst., 1995-97; postdoc. scientist U. Calif., Riverside, 1998; rsch. chemist Nat. Inst. Occupl. Safety and Health, Morgantown, W.Va., 1998—2001; phys. scientist Nat. Personal Protective Tech. Lab., Pitts., 2001—. Contbr. articles to profl. jours. Recipient Best Rsch. award Stockholm, 2005, Postdoctoral Scientist award U. Calif., 1998, Tchg. Assistantship award, U. Houston, 1994-95; named Internat. Scientist of Yr., Cambridge, Eng., 2004 Mem. ACS, Golden Key, Phi Kappa Phi, Alpah Theta Epsilon. Avocations: tennis, soccer. Office: CDC/NIOSH/NPPTL 626 Cochrans Mill Rd Pittsburgh PA 15236 Business E-Mail: eav8@cdc.gov.

VO, HUU DINH, pediatrician, educator; b. Hue, Vietnam, Apr. 29, 1950; arrived in U.S., 1975; s. Chanh Dinh and Dong Thi (Pham) Vo; children: Katherine Hao-An, Karyn Bao-An, Hugh Hung. MD, U. Saigon, 1975. Diplomate Am. Bd. Pediat., Am. Bd. Physician Specialties, bd. cert. pediats. and family practice Western U. Adminstr. bilingual vocat. tng. Cmty. Care and Devel. Svc., LA, 1976-77; resident in pediat. Univ. Hosp., Jacksonville, Fla., 1977-80; physician, surgeon, chief med. officer Lanterman Devel. Ctr., Pomona, Calif., 1980-92, chief med. staff, 1984-88, coord. med. ancillary svc., 1984-88, 91—; physician Pomona Valley Cmty. Hosp., 1988-90; asst. clin. prof. Loma Linda (Calif.) Med. Sch., 1983—; chief med. officer So. Reception Ctr. and Clinic., Norwalk, Calif., 1992-98; physician, surgeon F.C. Nelles Youth Facility, 1998—; med. dir. CTC - HGS Youth Facility, 2004—07, adminstr., 2004—07. Bd. dirs. Huu D. Vo M.D. Inc. Radio talk show host, 1997—. Nat. co-chair mem. Vietnamese Am. Cmty. U.S., 1993—95, chmn. bd. comptrs., 1998—2006, adviser, 2006—; pres. Vietnamese Cmty. Pomona Valley, 1983—85, 1987—95, 1999—, chmn., 1993—95; bd. dirs. YMCA, Pomona, 1988—92, Sch.-Cmty. Partnership, Pomona, 1988—92, ARC, Pomona, 1995—. Mem.: AMA (Physician Recognition award 1989, 1992, 1998, 2004), Vietnamese-Am. Physicians Assn. LA and Orange County (founding mem., sec. 1982—84, bd. dirs. 1987—90), LA Pediat. Soc. Republican. Buddhist. Avocations: tennis, soccer, reading, singing, music. Office: Huu D Vo MD Inc 1182 E Holt Ave Pomona CA 91767 Office Phone: 909-623-8502. Personal E-mail: drhuuvo@hotmail.com.

VODO, PLARENTA, physicist, researcher; b. Divjake, Albania, Mar. 24, 1975; d. Jani and Naunka Vodo. PhD in Condensed Matter Physics, Northeastern U., Boston, 2000—06. Tchg. asst. Northeastern U., 2000—02, rsch. asst., 2002—04, rsch. assoc., 2006—; tchg. asst. Poly. U., Tirana, Albania, 1998—2000. Home: 140 Calumet St #2 Roxbury MA 02120 Office: Northeastern Univ Physics Dept 120 Forsyth St Boston MA 02115 Home Phone: 617-470-8090. Personal E-mail: p.vodo@neu.edu.

VODRA, WILLIAM WILSON, lawyer; b. LA, Sept. 13, 1943; BA, Coll. of Wooster, 1965; JD, Columbia U., 1968. Bar: Ohio 1968, D.C. 1981. Atty. Bur. Narcotics and Dangerous Drugs/Drug Enforcement Adminstrn. Dept. Justice, 1971-74; atty. Office Gen. Counsel FDA Dept. Health Edn. and Welfare, 1974-79; ptnr., Pharmaceutical & Med. Tech. Practice Group Arnold & Porter, Washington, 1979—. Vice-chmn. Commn. on Federal Drug Approval Process, 1981—82; mem. Com. on Fed. Regulation of Methadone Treatment, Nat. Acad. Scis., 1992—95. Contbr. articles to profl. jours. Office: Arnold & Porter Thurman Arnold Bldg 555 12th St NW Washington DC 20004-1206 Office Phone: 202-942-5088. Office Fax: 202-942-5999. Business E-Mail: william.vodra@aporter.com.

VOEGEL, PHILLIP DONOVAN, chemistry professor; b. Ind., 1968; m. Melinda Voegel; children: Anastasia, Keven. BA in Chemistry, Wabash Coll., Crawfordsville, Ind., 1991; PhD in Analytical Chemistry, U. Louisville, 1997. Asst. prof. Midwestern State U., Wichita Falls, Tex., 1998—2005, Southeastern La. U., Hammond, 2005—. Bd. dirs. Wichita Falls Libr., Tex., 2003—05. Grantee, US EPA, 2006—. Mem.: Am. Chem. Soc. (chair Wichita Falls-Duncan sect. 2002, chair-elect Baton Rouge sect. 2007). Achievements include research in determining the potential for algal bloom in Lake Maurepas. Office: Southeastern Louisiana U Dept Chemistry and Physics SLU 10878 Hammond LA 70402 Home Phone: 225-567-1149; Office Phone: 985-549-2158. Business E-Mail: phillip.voegel@selu.edu.

VOEGELI, VICTOR JACQUE, historian, educator, dean; b. Jackson, Tenn., Dec. 21, 1934; s. Victor Jacque Voegeli and Winnie Lassiter; m. Anna Jean King, Oct. 14, 1956; children: Victor Jacque, Charles Lassiter. BS, Murray State Coll., Tishomingo, Okla., 1956; MA, Tulane U., New Orleans, 1961, PhD, 1965. Instr. history Tulane U., 1963-65, asst. prof., 1965-67; asst. prof. history Vanderbilt U., 1967-69, assoc. prof., 1969-73, prof. history, 1973-98, chmn. history dept., 1973-76, dean Coll. Arts and Sci., 1976-92, acting dean Coll. Arts and Sci., 1996-97, prof. emeritus, dean emeritus, 1998—. Author: Free But Not Equal: The Midwest and the Negro During the Civil War, 1967. Served with US Army, 1956-58. Nat. Endowment Humanities grantee, 1969-70, 72. Mem. So. Hist. Assn. Address: 2110 Golf Club Ln Nashville TN 37215-1224

VOEGTLIN-ANDERSON, MARY MARGARET, music educator, small business owner; b. Seattle; d. Joseph Walter and Veronica Margaret (Conroy) Voegtlin; m. Terry Lee Anderson, Mar. 19, 1977 (div. July 20, 1982). BA cum laude, Marylhurst U., 1963; postgrad., U. Wash., 1963—65, Oakland U., 1968, Seattle Pacific U., 1982—84. Cert. std. tchg. grades K-12 Wash. Profl. cellist Oreg. Symphony, Portland, 1962—63; tchr. music and humanities Chinook Mid. Sch., Seattle, 1963—89, gifted edn. specialist, 1983—89; tchr. music, music dept. chair Highline H.S., Seattle, 1989—2004, tchr. honors English, 1989—2004; owner, tchr. Anderson Music Studio, Seattle, 2004—. Contralto soloist Mt. Baker Pk. Presbyn. Ch., 1966—68, U. Congl. Ch., Seattle, 1968—73; profl. singer Seattle Opera Co., 1968—70; vocal coach, advisor Highline Jazz Ensemble, Seattle, 1990—2004; pvt. piano, cello and voice tchr., Seattle, 1991—; astronomy club advisor Highline H.S., Seattle, 1998—2004; dir. Highline Dist. Youth Orch., 2003—04, Burien Sr. Choir, 2003; trustee Sunlight Waters Corp., 2002—; pres., owner Anderson Music Studio. Contbr. articles to profl. jours. Officer, sec. 46th Legis. Dist. Dem. Party, Seattle, 1974—78, chairperson Initiative 314 Campaign, 1975; Wash. state conv. del. Dem. Party, Olympia, 1976, Dem. precinct chairperson Seattle, 1976—77. Fulbright Scholarship grantee, Nat. Tchrs. Performance Inst., Oberlin Coll., Ohio, 1970. Mem.: NEA, Planetary Soc., Nat. Coun. Tchrs. English, Seattle Astron. Soc., Music Educators' Nat. Conf. Roman Catholic. Avocations: astronomy, reading, bicycling, writing, hiking. Personal E-mail: mvanderson03@aol.com.

VOELLGER, GARY A., business consulting executive, retired air force officer; BS in Indsl. Rels. Pers. Mgmt., San Jose State U., 1967; grad., Squadron Officer Sch., 1971; M in Psychology, Peperdine U., 1976; grad., Air Command Staff Coll., Maxwell AFB, 1979, Air War Coll., 1988; cert. in Joint Flag Officer War Fighting, Maxwell AFB, 1997; cert.in sr. mgrs. govt. seminar, Harvard U., 1997. Commd. 2d. lt. USAF, 1967, advanced through grades to maj. gen., 1996; pers. officer 379th Combat Support Grp., Wurtsmith AFB, Mich., 1967-69; undergrad. navigator trng. Mather AFB, Calif., 1969-69; weapons sys. officer 46th Tactical Fighter Squadron, MacDill AFB, Fla., 1970-70; weapons syss. officer 91st Tactical Fighter Squadron, Royal Air Force Bentwaters, Eng., 1970-72; undergrad. pilot tng. Laredo AFB, Tex., 1972; F-111 transition tng. Nellis AFB, Nev., 1973-73; F-111 pilot 428th Tactical Fighter Squadron, Takhli Royal AFB, Thailand, 1973-74; F-111 instr. pilot, flight comdr., standardization and evaluation flight examiner 523rd Tactical Fighter Squadron, 27th Tactical Fighter Wing, Cannon AFB, N.Mex., 1974-79; air ops. staff officer, politico-mil. affairs officer, asst. dep. dir. Joint Nat. Security Coun. Matters Hdqs. USAF, Washington, 1980-84; comdr. 55th Tactical Fighter Squadron, Royal Air Force, Upper Heyford, Eng., 1984-87; asst. dep. comdr. ops. 20th Tactical Fighter Wing, Royal Air Force; dep. comdr. ops. 4450th Tactical Group, Nellis AFB, Nev., 1988-89, vice comdr., 1989-90; comdr. 552nd Air Control Wing, Tinker AFB, Okla., 1990-92, Coll. Aerospace Doctrine, Rsch. and Edn., Air U., Maxwell AFB, Ala., 1992-93, 43rd Air Refueling Wing, Malmstrom AFB, Mont., 1993-94, 92nd Air Refueling Wing, Fairchild AFB, Wash., 1994-95, 437th Airlift Wing, Charleston AFB, S.C., 1995-96; dir. ops. Hdqs. Air Mobility Command, Scott AFB, Ill., 1996-98; NATO force comdr. Hdqs. NATO Airborne Early Warning Force, Mons, Belgium, 1998-2000; ret. USAF; prin. Booz Allen Hamilton, O'Fallon, Ill. Decorated D.D.S.M., Legion of Merit with oak leaf Cluster, Bronze Star medal, Meritorious Svc. medal with two oak leaf clusters, Air medal with oak leaf cluster, Armed Forces Expeditionary medal, Rep. Vietnam Gallantry Cross with Palm. Office: Booz Allen & Hamilton Inc 1728 Corporate Crossing Ste 2 O Fallon IL 62269 Office Phone: 618-622-2333. Business E-Mail: voellger_gary@bah.com.

VOEVODSKY, VLADIMIR, mathematician; b. Russia, June 4, 1966; BS in Math., Moscow State U., 1989; PhD in Math., Harvard U., 1992. Assoc. prof. Northwestern U., 1996—99; prof. Inst. for Advanced Study, Princeton, NJ, 2002—. Mem. Inst. for Advanced Study, Harvard U., 1992—93, 1998—2001; visiting prof. Max Planck Inst. for Math., 1996—97, Harvard U., 1996—97. Co-author: Cycles, Transfers and Motivic Homology Theories, 2000. Recipient Fields medal, 2002, rsch. grants, NSF, Clay Prize fellowship, 1999, 2000. Office: Inst for Advanced Study Sch Math Fuld 116 Einstein Dr Princeton NJ 08540 E-mail: vladimir@math.ias.edu.

VOGAN, DAVID A., JR., mathematics professor; married. AB, MS, Univ. Chgo., 1974; PhD, MIT, 1976. Mem. inst. adv. study Princeton Univ., 1977—79; instr. MIT, 1976—77, asst. prof., 1979—81, assoc. prof., 1981—84, prof., 1984—. Grantee NSF grad. fellowship, 1974—76, Sloan Found. Fellow, 1983—87. Mem.: AAAS, Am. Math. Soc. (coun. mem. 1985—87, sci. policy com. 1989—91). Achievements include being one of 18 top mathematicians and computer scientists (Atlas of Lie Groups Project) from the US to successfully map E8, one of the largest and most complicated structures in mathematics. Office: Dept Math Rm 2-243 MIT 22 Massachusetts Ave Cambridge MA 02139-4307 Office Phone: 617-253-4991. *

VOGEL, ARTHUR ANTON, clergyman; b. Milw., Feb. 24, 1924; s. Arthur Louis and Gladys Eirene (Larson) V.; m. Katharine Louise Nunn, Dec. 29, 1947; children: John Nunn, Arthur Anton, Katharine Ann. Student, U. of South, 1942-43, Carroll Coll., 1943-44; B.D., Nashotah House Theol. Sem., 1946; MA, U. Chgo., 1948; PhD, Harvard, 1952; S.T.D., Gen. Theol. Sem., 1969; D.C.L., Nashotah House, 1969; D.D., U. of South, 1971. Ordained deacon Episcopal Ch., 1946, priest, 1948; teaching asst. philosophy Harvard, Cambridge, Mass., 1949-50; instr. Trinity Coll., Hartford, Conn., 1950-52; mem. faculty Nashotah House Theol. Sem., Nashotah, Wis., 1952-71, asso. prof., 1954-56, William Adams prof. philosophical and systematic theology, 1956-71, sub-dean Sem., 1964-71; bishop coadjutor Diocese of West Mo., Kansas City, 1971-72, bishop, 1972-89; rector Ch. St. John Chrysostom, Delafield, Wis., 1952-56; dir. Anglican Theol. Rev., Evanston, Ill., 1964-69; mem. Internat. Anglican-Roman Cath. Consultation, 1970-90, Nat. Anglican-Roman Catholic Consultation, 1965-84, Anglican chmn., 1973-84; mem. Standing Commn. on Ecumenical Relations of Episcopal Ch., 1957-79; mem. gen. bd. examining chaplains Episcopal Ch., 1971-72. Del. Episcopal Ch., 4th Assembly World Council Chruches, Uppsala, Sweden, 1968, and others. Author: Reality, Reason and Religion, 1957, The Gift of Grace, 1958, The Christian Person, 1963, The Next Christian Epoch, 1966, Is the Last Supper Finished?, 1968, Body Theology, 1973, The Power of His Resurrection, 1976, Proclamation 2: Easter, 1980, The Jesus Prayer for Today, 1982, I Know God Better Than I Know Myself, 1989, Christ in His Time and Ours, 1982, God, Prayer and Healing, 1995, Radical Christianity and the Flesh of Jesus, 1995; editor: Theology in Anglicanism, 1985; contbr. articles to profl. jours. Vice chmn. bd. dirs. St. Luke's Hosp., Kansas City, Mo., 1971, chmn., 1973-89. Research fellow Harvard, 1950 Mem. Am. Philos. Assn., Metaphys. Soc. Am., Soc. Existential and Phenomenological Philosophy, Catholic Theol. Soc. Am. Episcopalian. Home: 4203 W 94th Terrace Apt 111 Prairie Village KS 66207 E-mail: akvogel@swbell.net.

VOGEL, CARL E., communications executive; b. Oct. 18, 1957; BS in Fin. and Acctg., St. Norbert Coll., DePere, Wis. With Jones Intercable, 1983; exec. v.p. EchoStar Comm. Inc., 1994—97; CEO Star Choice Comm., 1998; chmn., CEO Primestar Inc., 1998—99; exec. v.p., COO AT&T Broadband, 1999; sr. v.p. Liberty Media Corp., 1999—2001; pres., CEO Charter Comm. Inc., 2001—05; vice chmn. EchoStar Comm. Corp., 2005—, pres., 2006—. Bd. dirs. C-SPAN, CableLabs, EchoStar Comm. Corp., 2005—. Mem.: Nat. Cable TV Assn. (bd. dirs.). Office: EchoStar Comm Corp 9601 South Meridian Blvd Englewood CO 80112 Office Phone: 303-723-1000. *

VOGEL, CEDRIC WAKELEE, lawyer; b. Cin., June 4, 1946; s. Cedric and Patricia (Woodruff) V. BA, Yale U., 1968; JD, Harvard U., 1971. Bar: Ohio 1972, Fla. 1973, U.S. Tax Ct. 1972, U.S. Supreme Ct. 1975. Ptnr. Vogel, Heis, Wenstrup & Cameron, Cin., 1972-96; sole practice, 1997—. Chmn. mem.'s com. Cin. Art Mus., 1987-88; chmn. auction Cin. Hist. Soc., 1985; local pres. English Speaking Union, 1979-81, nat. bd. dirs., 1981; chmn. Keep Cin. Beautiful, Inc., 1994-96; active Bravo! Cin. Ballet, 1989; chmn. Act II Nutcracker Ball, 1987-88; bd. dirs. Merc Libr., 1991-98, Cin. Preservation Assn., 1990-93, Cin. Opera Guild, 1997-99, Pro Srs., 1996-2005; vice chmn. Children's Heart Assn. Reds Rally, 1989; bd. dirs. Cin. Country Day Sch., 1983, pres. Alumni Coun. and Ann. Fund, 1983. Mem.: Fla. Bar Assn., Cin. Bar Assn., Yale Alumni Assn. (del. 1984—87), Harvard Law Sch. Assn. Cin. (pres. 1997—99, 2003—), Heimlich Inst. (trustee 1987—2001), Pro Srs. (bd. dirs. 1996—2005), Harvard Club of Cin. (bd. dirs. 1996—98, pres. 1999—2000), The Lawyers Club Cin. (pres. 1995), Cincinnatus, Cin. Yale Club (pres. 1980—81, 1996—97). Republican. Home: 3473 Forest Oak Ct Cincinnati OH 45208-1842 Office: 817 Main St Ste 800 Cincinnati OH 45202-2183 Home Phone: 513-871-7953; Office Phone: 513-421-4225. Personal E-mail: rvogel@iac.net.

VOGEL, EZRA F., sociology educator; b. Delaware, Ohio, July 11, 1930; s. Joseph H. and Edith (Nachman) V.; m. Suzanne Hall, July 5, 1953 (div.); children: David, Steven, Eva; m. Charlotte Ikels, Nov. 3, 1979. BA, Ohio Wesleyan U., 1950; MA, Bowling Green State U., 1951; PhD, Harvard U., 1958; LittD (hon.), Kwansai Gakuin, 1980, Wittenberg Coll., 1981, Bowling Green State U., 1982, U. Md., 1983, Albion Coll., 1988, Chinese

U., Hong Kong, 1992, Ohio Wesleyan, 1996; LittD (hon.), U. Mass., Lowell, 1996, Yamaguchi U., 1998, Monterrey Inst., 2002. Rsch. fellow Harvard (for work in Japan), 1958-60; asst. prof. Yale U., 1960-61; rsch. assoc., lectr. Harvard U., 1961-67, prof., 1967—2000, Henry Ford II prof. social scis., 1990—2005, emeritus, 2005—, assoc. dir. East Asian Rsch. Ctr., 1967-73, dir., 1973-77, chmn. council East Asian studies, 1977-80, dir. program on U.S.-Japan relations, 1980-87, hon. chmn. program on U.S.-Japan rels., 1988—, mem. faculty council, 1981-84, dir. Asia Ctr., 1997-99, rsch. prof., 2000—; nat. intelligence officer for East Asia Nat. Intelligence Coun., 1993-95, dir. Fairbank Ctr. East Asian Studies, 1995-99. Mem. Joint Com. on Contemporary China, 1968-75, Com. on Scholarly Communication with Peoples Republic China, 1973-75, Joint Com. Japanese Studies, 1977-79 Author: Japan's New Middle Class, 1963, Canton Under Communism, 1969, Japan As Number One, 1979, Comeback, 1985, The Impact of Japan on a Changing World, 1987, One Step Ahead in China, 1989, The Four Little Dragons, 1991, Is Japan Still Number One?, 2000; co-editor: (with Norman W. Bell) A Modern Introduction to the Family, 1960, (with George Lodge) Ideology and National Competitiveness, Living With China, 1997, (with Ming Yuan and Akihiko Tanaka) The Golden Age of the U.S.-China Japan Triangle, 2002; editor: Modern Japanese Organization and Decision-Making, 1975. Trustee Ohio Wesleyan U., 1970-75, 80-94. Served with AUS, 1951-53. Recipient Harvard faculty prize for book of year, 1970, Japan Found. prize, 1996, Japan Soc. prize 1998; Guggenheim fellow, 1972 Mem. Assn. Asian Studies (bd. dirs. 1970-72), Am. Acad. Arts and Scis. Home: 14 Sumner Rd Cambridge MA 02138-3018 Office Phone: 617-495-4014.

VOGEL, H. VICTORIA, psychotherapist, educator, writer, stress disorder and addiction recovery counselor; BA, U. Md., 1968; MA, NYU, 1970, MA, 1975; MEd, postgrad., Columbia U., 1982—; cert., Am. Projective Drawing Inst., 1983; CASAC, New Sch. U. for Social Rsch., 2000. Diplomate Am. Acad. Experts in Traumatic Stress; cert. addiction recovery counselor, expert in traumatic stress, alcohol and substance abuse counselor, addictions treatment, addiction counseling alcohol and substance abuse. Art therapist Childville, Bklyn., 1962-64; tchr. Montgomery County (Md.) Jr. H.S., 1968-69; with H.S. divsn. N.Y.C. Bd. Edn., 1970—; guidance counselor, instr., psychotherapist in pvt. practice. Guidance counselor, instr., psychotherapist in pvt. practice; clin. counseling cons. psychodiagnosis and devel. studies, art/play therapy The Modern Sch., 1984—; art/play therapist Hosp. Ctr. for Neuromuscular Disease and Devel. Disorders, 1986—; employment counselor-adminstr. N.Y. State Dept. Labor Concentrated Employment Program, 1971-72; intern psychotherapy and psychoanalysis psychiat. divsn. Ctrl. Islip Hosp., 1973-75, Calif. Grad. Inst., L.A.; intern psychol. counseling and rehab. N.J. Coll. Medicine, Newark, 1979. Author: The Never Ending Story of Alcohol, Drugs and Other Substance Abuse, 1992, Variant Sexual Behavior and the Aesthetic Modern Nudes, 1992, Psychological Science of School Behavior Intervention, 1993, Joycean Conceptual Modernism: Relationships and Deviant Sexuality, 1995, Electronic Evil Eyes, 1995 (U.S. Cert. of Recognition, 1996), Psychological Paradigms of Alcohol Violence Suicide Trauma Addiction Variant Pathologies PTSD and Schizophrenia, 1999. Mem. com. for spl. events NYU, 1989; participant clin. and artistic perspectives Am. Acad. Psychoanalysis Conf., 1990, participant clin. postmodernism and psychoanalysis, 1996; aux. police officer N.Y. Police Dept., 1994—; chair bylaws com. Columbia U., 1995—. Mem.: ACA, AAAS, APA, NY Acad. Sci., Tchrs. Coll. Adminstrv. Women in Edn., Assn. Humanistic Psychology (exec. sec. 1981), Art/Play Therapy, N.Y. Art Tchrs. Assn., Am. Acad. Experts Traumatic Stress (diplomate in expert traumatic stress), Am. Soc. Group Psychotherapy and Psychodrama (publs. com. 1984—), Am. Orthopsychiat. Assn., Am. Psychol. Soc., Phi Delta Kappa (editor chpt. newsletter 1981—84, exec. sec. Columbia U. chpt. 1984—, chmn. nominating com. for chpt. officers 1986—, rsch. rep. 1986—, pub. rels. exec. bd. dirs. 1991, NYU chpt. v.p. programs 1994—).

VOGEL, JAMES EDMOND, plastic surgeon; b. NYC, Mar. 11, 1956; BS in BioChemistry, Bowdoin Coll., Maine, 1978; MD, Mount Sinai Sch. Medicine, 1982. Intern New England Med. Ctr., Boston, 1982—83, surgery residency, 1982—84, U. NC, Chapel Hill, NC, 1984—87; fellowship plastic surgery Johns Hopkins Hospital, Balt., 1987—91, assist. chief service plastic surgery, 1989—90, assist. prof. to assoc. prof. surgery div. of plastic surgery, 1989—; pvt. practice Owings Mills, Md. Diplomat Nat. Bd. Med. Examiners, 1983. Named a Top Doc, Balt. mag. Fellow: Am. Coll. of Surgeons; mem.: Internat. Soc. of Hair Restoration Surgery (bd. of governors 1993—98, pres. 1996—97, exec. com. 1996—99, chmn. sci. com. 1993—99), Northeastern Soc. of Plastic & Reconstructive Surgeons, Nathan Womack Surg. Soc., Md. Breast Soc., Johns Hopkins Med. Soc., Balt. County Med. Soc., Am. Soc. of Aesthetic Plastic Surgery, Am. Soc. of Plastic Surgeons. Office: 4 Park Center Ct Ste 100 Owings Mills MD 21117 Office Phone: 410-484-8860. *

VOGEL, JEFFREY C., state agency administrator; m. Kathy Vogel; children: Sam, Chase. BS in Acctg., U. Wy., 1983. Acting commr. Wyo. Divsn. Banking, 1996, 2002, dep. banking commr., commr., 2002—. Vice chmn. Mo. Conf. State Bank Suprs., 2005. Office: Wyo Divsn Banking Herschler Bldg 3rd Fl E 122 W 25th St Cheyenne WY 82002 Office Phone: 307-777-7797. Office Fax: 307-777-3555. E-mail: jvogel@wyaudit.state.wy.us.

VOGEL, JENNIFER L., lawyer, air transportation executive; BBA, U. Iowa, Iowa City; JD, U. Tex. Sch. Law, Austin, 1987. Atty. Vinson & Elkins, LLP; v.p., gen. counsel Enron Global Power & Pipelines; v.p. legal, asst. sec. Continental Airlines, Inc., Houston, 1995—2001, gen. counsel, 2001—, sr. v.p., chief compliance officer, corp. sec., 2003—. Mailing: Continential Airlines Inc PO Box 4607 Houston TX 77210-4607 Office Phone: 713-324-2950. Office Fax: 713-324-2637. *

VOGEL, JOHN WALTER, lawyer; b. Dansville, NY, Sept. 19, 1948; s. Walter Earl and Betty (Elston) V.; m. Pamela Hill; children: Michael John, Jennifer Alexandra. BA, SUNY, Albany, 1970; JD, Syracuse U., 1976. Bar: N.Y. 1976, U.S. Dist. Ct. (we. dist.) N.Y. 1979, U.S. Tax Ct. 1980, U.S. Supreme Ct., 1980, U.S. Dist. Ct. (no. dist.) N.Y. 1985, U.S. Ct. Appeals (2d cir.) 1985. Assoc. Edward J. Degnan Law Offices, Canisteo, NY, 1976-77; atty. NY State Dept. Agrl. and Markets, Albany, NY, 1977-78; pvt. practice Dansville, 1978—. Legal counsel Dansville Econ. Devel. Corp., 1983—; local counsel Danville Ctrl. Sch. Dist.; atty. N.Y. State Festival of Balloons, Town of Dansville, Town of West Sparta; mem. atty. grievance com. 4th Jud. Dept. Dir. Livingston County (N.Y.) Drug Abuse Prevention Coun., 1981-82. With US Army, 1970—73. Mem.: Nat. Assn. Elder Law Attys., Livingston County Bar Assn. (sec., treas. 1980—82, v.p. 1984—85, pres. 1985—86), N.Y. State Bar Assn. Republican. Methodist. Home: 261 Main St Dansville NY 14437-1111 Office: 125 Main St Dansville NY 14437-1611 Office Phone: 585-335-2238.

VOGEL, NELSON J., JR., lawyer; b. South Bend, Ind., Oct. 13, 1946; s. Nelson J. and Carolyn B. (Drzewiecki) V.; m. Sandra L. Cudney, May 17, 1969; children: Ryan C., Justin M., Nathan J., Lindsey M. BS cum laude, Miami U., Oxford, Ohio, 1968; JD cum laude, U. Notre Dame, 1971. Bar: Ind. 1971, Mich. 1971, U.S. Dist. Ct. (no. dist.) Ind. 1971, U.S. Tax Ct. 1972, U.S. Ct. Appeals (7th cir.) 1975, U.S. Ct. Claims 1980. Acct. Coopers & Lybrand, South Bend, 1969-71; assoc. Barnes & Thornburg, South Bend, 1971-76, ptnr., 1977—. Lectr. U. Notre Dame, South Bend, 1971, 74-80; instr. Ind. U., South Bend, 1971-74; vice-chair Barnes & Thornburg, 2001—, mng. ptnr. South Bend office, 2001—. Trustee Project Future, St. Joseph Co., 2002-; pres. Big Bros./Big Sisters, South Bend, 1978-79; bd. pres. South Bend Regional Mus. Art, 1984-86; ethics com. Meml. Hosp., South Bend, 1986-94; bd. adv. Goshen Coll. Family Bus. program, 1993-99; bd. dirs. Madison Ctr., 2003-06. Mem. Nat. Employee Stock Ownership Plan Assn. (sec.-treas. Ind. chpt. 1993-95), Nat. Assn. State Bar Tax Sec. (exec. com. 1982-84), Ind. State Bar Assn. (chmn. taxation sect. 1981-82, Citation of Merit 1979), Mich. Bar Assn. (tax sect.), Ind. State HS Hockey Assn., Inc. (bd. dirs. 1998-01, treas. 1998-01), Michiana World Affairs Coun. (bd. dirs. 1992-96), Michiana World Trade Club (bd. dirs. 1992-96), Mental Health Assn. St. Joseph County (bd. dirs. 1997-01), St. Joseph County C. of C. (bd. dirs. 2005—). Home: 1146 Dunrobbin Ln South Bend IN 46614-2150 Office: Barnes & Thornburg 600 1st Source Bank 100 N Michigan St Ste 600 South Bend IN 46601-1632 Office Phone: 574-233-1171. Business E-Mail: nvogel@btlaw.com.

VOGEL, PAULA ANNE, playwright; b. Washington, Nov. 16, 1951; d. Donald Stephen and Phyllis (Bremerman) Vogel. BA, Cath. U., 1974; doctoral studies, Cornell U., 1974-77. Instr. theatre and women's studies Cornell U., Ithaca, N.Y., 1978-81; prodn. supr. Theatre on Film & Tape, NYC, 1983-85; Adele Kellenberg Seaver prof. Creative Writing Program, Brown U., Providence, 1985—. Author: (plays) Meg, 1977 (Nat. Playwright award Am. Coll. Theatre Festival), And Baby Makes Seven, 1984, Desdemona, 1985, The Oldest Profession, 1988, The Baltimore Waltz, 1992 (Obie award for best play, 1992), Hot 'N' Throbbing, 1994, The Mineola Twins, 1996, How I Learned to Drive, 1996 (Pulitzer prize, 1998, Obie award, 1997, N.Y. Drama Critics Drama Desk award for best play, 1997, Lucille Lortel award, 1997, Outer Critics' Circle award, 1997). Recipient Bunting award, Radcliffe-Harvard Colls., 1990, Pew Charitable Trust Sr. Residency award, 1995, Laura Pels award, 1999; grantee Fund for New Am. Plays, 1994; playwright fellow NEA, 1981, 1990, Guggenheim fellow, 1995. Fellow: Am. Acad. Arts & Sciences, McDowell Colony; mem.: New Dramatists. Office: Brown U PO Box 1852 Providence RI 02912-1852

VOGEL, SCOTT CHARLES, music educator; b. Mpls., Minn., Apr. 14, 1963; s. Wayne Kent Vogel and Karen Marie Vogel-Pearsal; m. Kari Ann Laine, July 25, 1992; children: Tristan, Carli, Collin. AA, No. Hennepin Cmty. Coll., 1984; BSc, Bemidji State U., 1988. Dir. bands, tchr. Princeton Pub. Schs., Minn., 1988—92, Mahnoman Pub. Schs., Minn., 1992—98, Coon Rapids HS, Minn., 1998—. Mem.: Minn. Band Dirs. Assn., Internat. Assn.of Jazz Educators (treas. 1992—95), Minn. Music Educators Assn., Music Educators Nat. Conf., Sons of the Am. Legion. Avocations: archery, fishing, camping, hunting. Home: 31512 104th St Princeton MN 55371 Office: Coon Rapids HS 2340 Northdale Blvd Coon Rapids MN 55433

VOGEL, SUSAN CAROL, nursing administrator; b. Hartford, Conn., Oct. 9, 1948; d. Morton B. and Esther (Riback) Worshoufsky. Diploma in nursing, Grace Hosp., New Haven, 1969; B in Healthcare Mgmt., U. La Verne, 1991, M in Health Adminstrn., 1994. RN Calif., cert. nephrology nurse, Nephrology Nurse Cert. Bd. Oper. rm. nurse New Britain Gen. Hosp., Conn., 1970-72; staff nurse oper. rm. Parkview Cmty. Hosp., Riverside, Calif., 1972-74; staff nurse dialysis, IV team Cedars-Sinai Med. Ctr., LA, 1974-82; clin. nurse III dialysis UCLA, 1982-88; nurse mgr. inpatient dialysis UCLA Med. Ctr., 1988-93; adminstr. South Valley Regional Dialysis Ctr., Encino, Calif., 1993—2007; pres. Renal Replacement Therapies, Inc.; chronic clin. mgr. western region NxStage Med. Inc., 2007—. Bd. dirs. End Stage Renal Disease Network 18, med. rev. bd., 1996—2000, treas.; chmn. bd. Renal Support Network, 2006—. Author (with others): Review of Hemodialysis for Nurses and Dialysis Personnel, 1993, 1999, Vascular Access, Principles and Practices, 1996, 3d edit., 2002; editor: Nephrology Nursing Jour., 2000—02. Med. rev. bd. End Stage Renal Disease Network 18, 1996—2000, treas., 2004—06; pres. Calif. Dialysis Coun., 2002—05, past pres., 2005—; trustee Am. Kidney Fund, 2005—; chmn. bd. dirs. Renal Support Network, 2006. Mem.: NAFE, Calif. Dialysis Coun. (pres.-elect 2002—), Nat. Kidney Found., Am. Nephrology Nurses Assn. (pres. L.A. chpt. 1990—92, 1996—98, nat. chairperson hemodialysis spl. interest group 1993—95), Am. Orgn. Nurse Execs. Avocations: travel, skiing. Office Phone: 310-871-4996. Business E-Mail: svogel@nxstage.com.

VOGEL, THOMAS TIMOTHY, surgeon, educator, lay worker; b. Columbus, Ohio, Feb. 1, 1934; s. Thomas A. and Charlotte A. (Hogan) V.; m. M.M. Darina Kelleher, May 29, 1965; children: Thomas T., Catherine D., Mark P., Nicola M. AB, Coll. of Holy Cross, 1955; MS, Ohio State U., 1960, PhD, 1962; MD, Georgetown U., 1965. Pvt. practice surgery, Columbus, 1971-2001; chmn. liturgy com., pres. parish coun. St. Catharine Parish, Columbus, 1971-73; chmn. diocesan adminstrn. com. Diocesan Pastoral Coun., Columbus, 1972-73, chmn., 1973-75; vice prefect Sodality of Holy Cross, 1953-55; mem. Ohio Bishop's Adv. Coun., Columbus, 1976-79. Clin. asst. prof. surgery Ohio State U., Columbus, 1974—; past trustee Peer Rev. Sys., Inc.; assoc. med. dir. United Health Care, Columbus, 1997-2000; cons. Rehabilitation Svcs.; commr., surveillance utilization rev. mem. Medicaid, State of Ohio, 1998-2000; assoc. med. dir. Palmetto GBA, 1999—. Contbr. articles to profl. jours. Chmn. coun. grad. students Ohio State U., 1961; bd. dirs. St. Vincent's Children's Ctr., 1975-83, chmn., 1981-82; past chmn. bd. trustees St. Joseph Montessori Sch. Named Knight of the Holy Sepulchre, Equestrian Order of the Holy Sepulchre of Jerusalem, 2001; recipient Layman's award, Columbus Ea. Kiwanis, 1972. Mem. ACS, Am. Physiol. Soc., Assn. for Acad. Surgery, Ohio State Med. Assn. (del. 1993—), Sigma Xi, Delta Epsilon Sigma. Roman Catholic. Home: 247 S Ardmore Rd Columbus OH 43209-1701 Office: 621 S Cassingham Rd Columbus OH 43209-2403 E-mail: vogel.3@osu.edu.

VOGEL, VICTOR GERALD, medical educator, researcher; b. Bethlehem, Pa., Mar. 14, 1952; s. Victor Gerald Jr. and Margaret Moser (Smith) V.; m. Saralyn Sue Schaffner, June 25, 1977; children: Heather Marie, Christiaan Keith. Diplomate Am. Bd. Internal Medicine, Am. Bd. Preventive Medicine, Nat. Bd. Med. Examiners. Resident in internal medicine Balt. City Hosps., 1978-81; fellow in med. oncology Johns Hopkins Oncology Ctr., Balt., 1983-86; Andrew W. Mellon fellow Johns Hopkins Sch. Hygiene Pub. Health, Balt., 1984-86; asst. prof. medicine and epidemiology U. Tex./M.D. Anderson Cancer Ctr., Houston, 1986-93, assoc. prof. clin. cancer prevention, 1993-95; asst. prof. epidemiology U. Tex. Sch. Pub. Health, Houston, 1987-95; prof. medicine and epidemiology U. Pitts. Cancer Inst./Magee-Womens Hosp., 1996—, dir. MAGEE/UPCI breast cancer program, 1996—2002, dir. MAGEE/UPCI breast cancer prevention program, 2003—. Epidemiologist Tex. breast screening project Am. Cancer Soc., 1986-93; mem. data and safety monitoring bd. Women's Health Initiative, NIH, 1994—2004; bd. dirs. Nat. Surg. Adjuvant Breast and Bowel Project Found., Inc., 1997—, AMC Cancer Ctr., Denver, 1996-99; protocol chmn. Nat. Cancer Inst. Study of Tamoxifen and Raloxifene. Contbr. articles to profl. jours. Founding mem. Nat. Surg. adjuvant Breast and Bowel Project Found., Inc.; founding pres. Internat. Soc. Cancer Risk Assessment and Mgmt., 2003. Served with USPHS, 1981-83. Named Med. Vol. of Yr., Am. Cancer Soc., 1983; recipient award, 1987, career devel. award, 1990—93; fellow, Susan G. Komen Breast Cancer Found., 1990—93. Fellow Am. Coll. Preventive Medicine, ACP; mem. Am. Soc. Clin. Oncology, Am. Soc. Preventive Oncology, Christian Med. and Dental Assn., Am. Assn. Cancer Rsch. Republican. Presbyterian. Avocation: flying. Office: U Pittsburgh Cancer Inst Magee-Womens Hosp 300 Halket St Rm 3524 Pittsburgh PA 15213-3108 Home Phone: 412-782-5585; Office Phone: 412-641-6500. Business E-Mail: vvogel@magee.edu. E-mail: vvogel@aol.com.

VOGEL, WARREN, lawyer; b. Phila., Oct. 2, 1948; BA, Temple U., 1970; JD cum laude, Temple U. Sch. Law, 1973. Bar: Pa. 1973, US Fed. Ct. 1973. Mem. Eckert Seamans Cherin & Mellott, LLC, Phila. Panelist Pa. Bar Inst. seminar. Editor, contbr. Temple U. Law Quar., 1972—73. Bd. dirs. JCCs of Greater Phila. With Pa. Air Nat. Guard, 1970—73. Named to Pa. Super Lawyers, Phila. Mag., 2004, 2005—06; recipient Corpus Juris Secundum award, 1973; sr. scholar dept. health policy, Thomas Jefferson U. Med. Sch. Mem.: Phila. Estate Planning Coun., Pa. Bar Assn. (mem. task force ltd. liability co. documents), Phila. Bar Assn. (mem. sect. on corp., bus. and banking law 1973—), ABA (subcom. on tax matters 1979—, mem. sect. bus. law). Office: Eckert Seamans Cherin & Mellott LLC 2 Liberty Pl 22nd Fl 50S 16th St Philadelphia PA 19102 Office Phone: 215-851-8400. Office Fax: 215-851-8383. Business E-Mail: wvogel@eckertseamans.com.

VOGEL, WERNER PAUL, retired machine company executive; b. Louisville, June 15, 1923; s. Werner George and Emma (Bartman) Vogel; m. Helen Louise Knapp, Oct. 2, 1954. B in Mech. Engring., U. Louisville, 1950. With Henry Vogt Machine Co., Louisville, 1942—86, asst. plant supt., 1957—60, plant supt., 1961—73, v.p., 1974—86; ret. Trustee City of Strathmoor, Ky., 1959—61; clk. City of Glenview Manor, Ky., 1967—73, trustee, 1974—75, treas., 1986—89; mem. adv. coun. Lindsey Wilson Coll., 1988—2003; bd. dirs. Louisville Protestant Altenheim, 1979—80, pres., 1985—90, ret. With USAAF, 1944—46. Mem.: ASME, Sigma Tau, Tau Beta Pi. Republican. Methodist. Home: 9118 Coventry Ln Louisville KY 40219

VOGELGESANG, SANDRA LOUISE, former ambassador, writer, consultant; b. Canton, Ohio, July 27, 1942; d. Glenn Wesley and Louise (Forry) Vogelgesang; m. Geoffrey Ernest Wolfe, July 4, 1982. BA, Cornell U., 1964; MA, Tufts U., 1965, MA in Law and Diplomacy, 1966, PhD, 1971. With Dept. State, Washington, 1975-97, policy planner for sec. state and European Bur., 1975-80, dir. Econ Policy Office, Orgn. Econ. Coop. and Devel., 1981-82, econ. minister U.S. Embassy, Ottawa, Can., 1982-86, dep. asst. sec. Internat. Orgn. Affairs Bur., 1986-89; dep. asst. adminstr. Office Internat. Activities Environ. Protection Agy., Washington, 1989-92; with Dept. State, Washington, 1992; sr. policy advisor Agy. for Internat. Devel., 1993; US amb. to Nepal Dept. State, Washington, 1994-97; pres. Everest Assocs. and Himalaya, 1997—2004. Bd. dirs. Ctr. for Econ. Devel. and Population Activities; mem. women and conservation com. World Wildlife Fund, 1997—2004, mem. Nat. Coun., 1999—2004; bd. advisors Am.'s Soc., NYC, 1986—89; mem. Pres.'s Coun. of Cornell Women Cornell U., 1998—; adv. com. Dept. of Treasury com. on Internat. Child Labor Enforcement, 1999—; mem. global coun. Internat. Mus. Women, 2004—; writer, cons. internat. devel. issues. Author: Long Dark Night of the Soul, The American Intellectual Left and the Vietnam War, 1974, American Dream-Global Nightmare: The Dilemma of U.S. Human Rights Policy, 1980. Bd. dirs. Crafts Ctr., 1999-2000. Recipient Meritorious Service awards, 1973, 74, 82, 83, 86, Disting. Honor award, 1976 Dept. State, Pres.' Disting. Service award, 1985. Mem. Council on Fgn. Relations. Office: 9009 Charred Oak Dr West Bethesda MD 20817-1923 Business E-Mail: everest.associates@erols.com.

VOGELMAN, JOSEPH HERBERT, scientific engineering company executive; b. NYC, Aug. 18, 1920; s. Jacob and Sabina (Weingarten) V.; m. Norma Schneider, Dec. 8, 1946; children: Jeffrey Allan, Leslie Sue, Linda Leigh. BS, CCNY, 1940; M.E.E., Poly. Inst. Bklyn., 1948, D.Elec. Engring., 1957. Registered profl. engr., N.Y., N.J. Project engr. Signal Corps Engr. Labs., Belmar, NJ, 1943-45; chief devel. br. Watson Labs., Eatontown, NJ, 1945-50; chief scientist Rome Air Devel. Center, Griffiss AFB, NY, 1951-52, chief electronic warfare lab., 1953-56, dir. communications, 1956-59; v.p., dir. Capehart Corp., NYC, 1959-64; dir. electronics Chromalloy Am. Corp., NYC, 1964-67, gen. mgr. pocket fone div., 1966-67, v.p., 1967-73; v.p., dir. Cro-Med Bionics Corp., 1968-73; vice chmn. bd., dir. Laser Link Corp., 1968-73; chief scientist, dir. Orentreich Found. for Advancement Sci., 1973—; pres. Vogelman Devel. Corp., 1973—. Chmn. tech. adv. com. Compupix, Inc., 1984-86. Contbr. articles to profl. jours. and encys.; patentee in field. Served with AUS, 1942-43. Recipient Outstanding Performance award USAF, 1957 Fellow AAAS, IEEE; mem. Titulaire, Societe Francaise de Electroniciens et des Radio Electriciens, N.Y. Acad. Scis., Sigma Xi, Eta Kappa Nu. Home: 48 Green Dr Roslyn NY 11576-3221 Office: 910 5th Ave New York NY 10021-4155 Personal E-mail: dr.jhv@juno.com.

VOGELMAN, LAWRENCE ALLEN, lawyer, educator; b. Bklyn., Feb. 24, 1949; s. Herman and Gertrude (Wohl) V.; m. Deborah Malka, Jan. 24, 1971 (div. Aug. 1980); m. Marcia Sikowitz, Mar. 3, 1985 (div. Nov. 1999). BA, Bklyn. Coll., 1970; JD, Bklyn. Law Sch., 1973. Bar: NY 1974, U.S. Dist. Ct. (so. and ea. dists.) NY 1975, U.S. Ct. Appeals (2d cir.) 1975, U.S. Ct. Appeals (3d cir.) 1983, U.S. Supreme Ct. 1983, NH 1994, U.S. Dist. Ct. NH 1994, U.S. Ct. Appeals (1st cir.) 2001. Trial atty. Legal Aid Soc., NYC, 1973-77; assoc. appellate counsel Criminal Appeals Bur., NYC, 1977-78; clin. prof. law Yeshiva U. Benjamin N. Cardozo Sch. Law, NYC, 1979—94; dep. dir. NH Pub. Defender, Concord, 1994—97; ptnr. Nixon, Raiche Vogelman Barry & Slawsky, Manchester, NH, 2005—. Adj. prof. law Franklin Pierce Law Ctr., 1994-98; faculty Inst. for Criminal Def. Advocacy, 1995—; program dir. Max Freund Litig. Ctr., 1984—; team leader Emory U. Trial Techniques Program, Atlanta, 1981-89, NJ region, Nat. Inst. Trial Advocacy, 1997—; faculty N.E. region, Nat. Inst. Trial Advocacy, 1985—, Boston region, 2002—, Tom C. Clark Ctr. for Advocacy, Hofstra U. Sch. Law, 1985—, Legal Aid Soc. Trial Advocacy Program, 1986-89, Widener U. Law Sch. Intensive Trial Program, 1987-91, U. San Francisco Intensive Trial Advocacy Program, 1991—; mem. indigent's assigned counsel panel, appellate div. First Dept., NYC, 1979-94; crminal justice act panel U.S. Dist. Ct. (so. and ea. dist.) NY, 1985-94, dist. NH, 1997—, 1st cir., 2003—; adminstrv. law judge NYC Environ. Control Bd., 1980-81. Author, editor: Cases and Materials on Clinical Legal Education, 1979; editor revisions to Eyewitness Identification. Pres. bd. trustees Woodward Park Sch., 1990—94; bd. dirs., legal coun. N.H. Civil Liberties Union. Fellow: Am. Bd. Criminal Lawyers; mem.: AAJ (exec. com. civil rights sect.), NH Trial Lawyers Assn., NY State Defenders Assn., NH Bar Assn. (ethics com. 1995—, dispute resolution com. 1999—, bd. law examiners 1999—, fed. ct. adv. com. 2002—, chair fed. practice sect. 2003—04, bd. govs. 2004—), NH Assn. Criminal Def. Lawyers, Nat. Assn. Criminal Def. Lawyers, Soc. Am. Law Tchrs., Assn. Legal Aid Attys. (chmn. bargaining com. 1974—79, exec. v.p. 1977—78, exec. com. 1984—86), Assn. Bar City of NY, Fortune Soc. (exec. com., bd. dirs.), Am. Inns of Ct. (master Daniel Webster Inn), Order of Barristers. Democrat. Unitarian Universalist. Home: 22 Cedar Point Rd Durham NH 03824 Office: Nixon Raiche Vogelman Barry & Slawsky 77 Central St Manchester NH 03101 Office Phone: 603-669-7070. Personal E-mail: larryvpd@aol.com. Business E-Mail: vogelmanlarry@yahoo.com.

VOGELSANG, ERIC R., language educator, basketball and soccer coach; b. Latrobe, Pa., Sept. 29, 1978; s. Keith R. Vogelsang and Shirley J. LaMantia. B in Elem. Edn., Ind. U. of Pa., 2002. Cert. elem. tchr. Pa., 2002, mid. level English tchr. Pa., 2003. 8th grade English tchr. Ligonier Valley Sch. Dist., Pa., 2002—, H.S. girls soccer coach, 2002—, H.S. girls basketball coach, 2003—; tchg. cons. Southcentral Pa. Writing Project, Indiana, Pa., 2004—. Youth soccer coach Loyalhanna United Soccer Club, Latrobe, Pa., 2000—, youth soccer camp assoc. dir., 2002—, youth soccer referee, 2003—; youth soccer camp dir. Ligonier Valley YMCA, Pa., 2004—; literacy coach Ligonier Valley Sch. Dist., Pa., 2004—; bd. mem. Southcentral Pa. Writing Project, Indiana, Pa., 2005—, young writers camp dir., 2005—. Presenter (PSSA writing assessment workshop) Changes in PSSA Writing Test. Bd. mem. Loyalhanna United Soccer Club, Latrobe, Pa., 2001—05. Nominee Young Educator of Yr., PASCD, 2006; grantee, Thoburn Found., 2004. Mem.: NEA, ACSD, Pa. State Edn. Assn., Pa. Mid. Sch. Assn., Nat. Coun. of Tchrs. of English. Democrat. Methodist. Home:

329 Bridges Rd Bolivar PA 15923 Office: Ligonie Valley Mid Sch Bell Street Extension Ligonier PA 15658 Home Phone: 724-676-2203. Personal E-mail: erv3@hotmail.com. Business E-Mail: vogelsang@iu7.wiu.k12.pa.us.

VOGELSBERG, ROSS TIMM, education educator, researcher; b. Bryn Mawr, Pa., Feb. 23, 1945; s. Robert Wilhelm Vogelsberg and Jean Byram (Fishburn) Blanchard. BS, Colo. State U., 1968; MS, Utah State U., 1974; PhD, U. Ill., 1979. Part-time assoc. Gateways Inc., Ft. Collins, Colo., 1968; master resource tchr. Utah State U., Logan, 1972-74, assoc. dir. project, 1974-77; rsch. assoc. U. Ill., Urbana, 1977-79; project dir., asst. prof. U. Vt., Burlington, 1979-85; project dir., assoc. prof. Temple U., Phila., 1985-94; exec. dir., prof. Rural Inst. Disabilities U. Mont., Missoula, 1995—. Contbr. numerous articles to profl. jours. and chpts. in books. With U.S. Army, 1969-71, ETO. Named one of Outstanding Young Men of Am., U.S. Jaycees, 1982; recipient Svc. award United Cerebral Palsy Pa., 1986. Mem. Assn. for Spl. Edn. Tech., Am. Ednl. Rsch. Assn., Assn. for Persons Analysis, Assn. for Persons with Severe Handicaps, Nat. Soc. for Performance and Instruction, Assn. for the Advancement of Behavior Therapy, Coun. for Exceptional Children, Am. Assn. on Mental Deficiency. Office: U Mont Rural Inst 634 Eddy Ave Missoula MT 59812-0001 Office Phone: 406-243-5467.

VOGELSTEIN, BERT, oncology educator; b. Balt., June 2, 1949; BS in Math., U. Pa., 1970; MD, Johns Hopkins U. Sch. Medicine, 1974. Rsch. assoc. Nat. Cancer Inst., 1976—78; pediatric intern and resident Johns Hopkins U. Sch. Medicine, Balt., 1974—76, asst. prof., 1978—83, assoc. prof., 1983—89, Clayton prof. oncology and pathology, 1989—, Howard Hughes Med. Inst. investigator, 1995—. Advisor NIH Sci. Rev. Groups, Nat. Cancer Inst.; bd. reviewing editors Science; assoc. editor Molecular Cell and Cancer Cell; sci. adv. bd. U. Calif., San Francisco, Cancer Ctr., GMP Genetics, Morphotek; sci. review bd. Pediatric Brain Tumor Found., US. Assoc. editor: Genes, Chromosomes and Cancer, mem. bd. reviewing editors: Sci. mag.; contbr. articles to profl. jours., 99 US patents in the field. Recipient William Allan award, Am. Soc. of Human Genetics, Alfred G. Knudson award, Nat. Cancer Inst., Anne & Jason Farber Lecture award, Am. Acad. Neurology, 1991, Internat. award, Gairdner Found., 1992, Medal of Honor, Am. Cancer Soc., 1992, Richard Lounsbery award, NAS, 1993, Baxter Rsch. award, Assn. Am. Med. Coll., 1994, laureates Passano Found., 1994, G.H.A. Clowes Meml. award, Am. Assn. Cancer Rsch., 1995, Charles S. Mott prize, GM Cancer Rsch. Found., 2000. Mem.: NAS, Am. Philosophical Soc., Inst. Medicine, Am. Acad. Arts and Scis. Achievements include revolutionizing our understanding of complex genetic mutations that occur when an normal bowel epithelial cell is transformed into a malignant cell. Office: Johns Hopkins U Sch Med Dept Oncology 424 N Bond St Baltimore MD 21231-1000

VOGELZANG, NICHOLAS JOHN, medical oncologist; b. Holland, Mich., Dec. 13, 1949; AB, Trinity Christian Coll., 1971; MD, U. Ill., Chgo., 1974. Diplomate Am. Bd. Internal Medicine and Med. Oncology. Intern, resident, chief resident Rush Presbyn. St. Lukes, Chgo., 1974-78; fellow, instr. U. Minn., Mpls., 1978-82; asst. and assoc. prof. U. Chgo., 1982-93, prof., attending physician, 1993—2003, dir., Cancer Rsch. Ctr.; dir. Nev. Cancer Inst., Las Vegas, 2004—; prof. medicine U. Nev. Sch. Medicine, 2004—. Attending physician Bernard Mitchell Hosp., Chgo., investigator, U. Chgo. for Cancer and Leukemia Group B, 1988-99, chmn. prostate com., 1993-99; prin. investigator, U. Chgo. Cancer Ctr. Support Grant; cons., contractor Roche, Schering, Zeneca, Bristol-Myers Squibb, U.S. Biosci., Immunex, Abbott; sci. adv. bd., Advanced Life Scis., founding bd. mem. Mesothelioma Applied Rsch. Found. (chmn. bd. dir., 2006-); invited spkr./lectr. in field. Lead editor: Comprehensive Textbook of Genitourinology, 1996, 3rd edit. 2005; editor, Malignant Mesothelioma, 2005; mem. editl. adv. bd. Cancer, Cancer Research, Clinical Genitourinary Cancer, The Prostrate Journal, Journal Clinical Oncology, Seminars in Oncology; contbr. several articles to profl. jours., chpts. to books. Named Alumnus of Yr. Trinity Christian Coll., 1991. Fellow ACP; mem. Am. Cancer Soc. (bd. dirs. Ill. divsn. 1986—, pres. 1994-96), Am. Assn. Cancer Rsch., Am. Soc. Clin. Oncology (mem. program com. 1985, European Soc. Med. Oncology, nat. bd. dirs. 1993-96), Am. Urol. Assn, Kidney Cancer Assn., Soc. Urologic Oncology. being a recognized expert in new therapies for patients with matastatic kidney cancer, including genetic therapy, new cytokine therapy and combination cytokine therapy. Office: 10000 W Charleston Blvd Ste 260 Las Vegas NV 89135 Office Phone: 702-822-5433. *

VOGL, OTTO, polymer science and engineering educator; b. Traiskirchen, Austria, Nov. 6, 1927; came to US, 1953, naturalized, 1959; s. Franz and Leopoldine (Scholz) V.; m. Jane Cunningham, June 10, 1955; children: Eric, Yvonne. PhD, U. Vienna, 1950; D (hon.), U. Jena, Germany, 1983, Poly. Inst., Iasi, Romania, 1992, Osaka U., Japan, 1996, Slovak Acad. Scis., 2001, U. Leoben, Austria, 2005. Instr. U. Vienna, 1948-55; rsch. assoc. U. Mich., 1953-55, Princeton U., 1955-56; scientist E.I. Du Pont de Nemours & Co., Wilmington, Del., 1956-70; prof. polymer sci. and engrng. U. Mass., 1970-83, prof. emeritus, 1983—; Herman F. Mark prof. polymer sci. Poly. U., Bklyn., 1983-95, prof. emeritus, 1996—. Guest prof. Kyoto U., 1968, 80, Osaka U., 1968, 96, Royal Inst. Stockholm, 1971, 87, 99, U. Freiburg, Germany, 1973, U. Berlin, 1977, Strasbourg U., 1976, Tech. U. Dresden, 1982, Wuhan U., China, 1984; Monbusho prof. Kyoto Inst. Tech., Japan, 1996; guest prof. Soviet Acad. Sci., 1973, Polish Acad. Sci., 1973, 75, Acad. Sci. Romania, 1974, 76; chmn. com. on macromolecular chemistry Nat. Acad. Sci.; cons. in field. Author: Polyaldehydes, 1967, (with Furukawa) Polymerization of Heterocyclics, 1973, Ionic Polymerization, 1976, (with Simionescu) Radical Co and Graftpolymerization, 1978, (with Donaruma) Polymeric Drugs, 1978, (with Donaruma and Ottenbrite) Polymers in Biology and Medicine, 1980, (with Goldberg and Donaruma) Targeted Drugs, 1986, (with Immergut) Polymer Science in the Next Decade, 1997, (with Kitayama and Hatada) Macromolecular Design of Polymeric Materials, My Life with Polymer Science, 2004, The History of the Pacific Polynesian Federation, 2005; contbr. articles to profl. jours. Sr. fellow Japan Soc. Promotion of Sci., 1980; recipient Fulbright award, 1976, Humboldt prize, 1977, Chemistry Pioneer award, 1985, Gold medal City of Vienna, Austria, 1986, Exner medal, 1987, Mark medal, 1989, Honor Ring, City of Traiskirchen, 1989; golden hon. diploma U. Vienna, 2000, Hon. Cross of Arts and Scis., Rep. of Austria, 2000, Culture prize City of Traiskirchen, 2002, hon. medal SAS Polymer Rsch. Inst, 2003. Fellow AAAS; mem. Am. Chem. Soc. (chmn. divsn. polymer chemistry 1974, chmn. Conn. Valley sect. 1974, award applied polymer chemistry 1990, Herman F. Mark award 2000), Am. Inst. Chemistry (chmn. Pioneer Award 1985), Austrian Chem. Soc. (hon.), Japanese Soc. Polymer Sci. (hon., award 1991), NY Acad. Sci., Austrian Acad. Sci., Royal Swedish Acad. Sci., Pacific Polymer Fedn. (pres.), Slovak Chem. Soc. (hon.), Croatian Chem. Soc. (hon.), Sigma Xi. Home: 12 Canterbury Ln Amherst MA 01002-3536 Office: U Mass Dept Polymer Sci and Engring Amherst MA 01003-4530 Office Phone: 413-577-1628. Business E-Mail: vogl@polysci.umass.edu.

VOGRIN, JOSEPH EDWARD, III, lawyer; BA magna cum laude, Duquesne U., Pitts, 1969; JD, Duquesne U., 1972. Bar: Pa. 1972, U.S. Ct. Appeals (3rd cir.) 1972, US Supreme Ct. 1984. Dep. dist. atty. Dist. Atty's Office Allegheny County, Pitts., 1972—79; ptnr. Scott, Vogrin & Riester, Pitts., 1980—96, Vogrin & Riester, P.C., Pitts., 1996—2000, Meyer Darragh Buckler Bebenek & Eck, Pitts., 2000—. Mem. curriculum rev. commn. Pa. Mcpl. Police Officer's Tng. Commn., Harrisburg, 2000—. Solicitor Ohio Twp. San. Authority, Pitts., 1983—, Twp. Shaler, Pitts., 1986—. Quaker Valley Coun. Govts., Pitts., 1987—2007, North Hills Coun. Govts., Pitts., 1989—, Boroughs Assn. Allegheny County, Pitts., 1991—92, Borough's Assn. Allegheny County, Pitts., 1994—95, Ross Twp. CSC, Pitts., 1993—; co-counsel Allegheny County and Western Pa. Assn. Twp. Commrs., Pitts., 1997—; solicitor Twp. Res., Pitts., 1998—, Borough Avalon, Pitts., 1992—2005. Mem.: Allegheny County Bar Assn. (chmn. assn. mcpl. and sch. solicitors Allegheny County 1998—99). Office: Meyer Darragh Buckler Bebenek & Eck 4850 USX Tower 600 Grant St Pittsburgh PA 15219 Personal E-mail: jvogrin@mdbbe.com.

VOGT, DOUGLAS, news cameraman, journalist; b. Alta., Canada, 1959; married; 3 children. Cameraman CBC-TV, BBC-TV; now with ABC News, NYC, Europe, Middle East, 1991—. Recipient three Emmy awards. Achievements include covering stories in Afganistan, Iraq, Croatia, Bosnia, and Somalia. Office: ABC News Press Rels 47 W 66th St New York NY 10023-6201 Home: Aix-en-Provence France

VOGT, ERICH WOLFGANG, physicist, academic administrator; b. Steinbach, Man., Can., Nov. 12, 1929; s. Peter Andrew and Susanna (Reimer) V.; m. Barbara Mary Greenfield, Aug. 27, 1952; children: Edith Susan, Elizabeth Mary, David Eric, Jonathan Michael, Robert Jeremy. BS, U. Man., 1951, MS, 1952; PhD, Princeton U., 1955; DSc (hon.), U. Man., 1982, Queen's U., 1984; LLD (hon.), U. Regina, 1986; DSc (hon.), Carleton U., 1988, U. B.C., 1999; LLD (hon.), Simon Fraser U., 1996. Rsch. officer Chalk River (Ont.) Nuclear Labs., 1956-65; prof. physics U. B.C., Vancouver, 1965-95, prof. emeritus, 1995—, assoc. dir. TRIUMF Project, 1968-73, dir. TRIUMF Project, 1981-94, v.p. univ., 1975-81; chmn. Sci. Council B.C., 1978-80. Co-editor: Advances in Nuclear Physics, 1968—; Contbr. articles to profl. jours. Decorated officer Order of Can., Order of BC; recipient Centennial medal of Can., 1967 Fellow Royal Soc. Can., Am. Phys. Soc.; mem. Can. Assn. Physicists (past pres., gold medal for achievement in physics 1988). Office: Triumf 4004 Wesbrook Mall Vancouver BC Canada V6T 2A3 Office Phone: 604-222-1047. Business E-Mail: vogt@triumf.ca.

VOGT, KATHLEEN CUNNINGHAM, musician, educator; b. Ellwood City, Pa., July 3, 1951; d. Joseph Edward and Dorothea Cunningham Vogt. BS summa cum laude in Music Edn., Duquesne U., 1973, M in Music edn., 1975. Cert. Tchr Nat. Bd., 2003. Tchr., band and choral dir. Diocese of Pitts. Schs., 1973—79; tchr., band dir. Carrick HS, 1980—84; band dir., drama tchr. Hanahan (SC) HS, 1984—2004, Sangaree Mid. Sch. Instr. percussion Duquesne U., Pitts., 1975—79; adj. prof. Charleston So. U., SC, 2001—; guest clinician and conductor, 1975—. Musician: Pitts. Symphony Orch., Charleston Symphony Orch., Lowcountry Winds, Charleston (SC) Cmty. Band. Mem. Hanahan Area Arts Coun. Mem.: Nat. Bd. Cert. Tchrs., All Berkeley County Music Educators, Nat. Band Assoc., Nat. Baton Twirling Assn., Nat. Twirling Judges Bur. (Inducted into Baton Twirling Hall of Fame 2002), Am. Sch. Band Dirs. Assn., SC Band Dirs. Assn. (Outstanding Performance award 1985—2004, SC State Marching Band Champions 1986, 1987, 1988, 1991), SC Music Educators Assn., Music Educators Nat. Conf., Pi Lambda Theta, Phi Beta Mu. Home: 504 Greenmeadow Rd Goose Creek SC 29445 Personal E-mail: katyvogt@aol.com.

VOGT, LORNA CORRINE, retired librarian, small business owner; b. Rochelle, Ill., Feb. 18, 1936; d. Chester Floyd and Vera Mae (Worthington) Patton; m. Norman E. Vogt, Aug. 18, 1957; 1 child, Cindy Jean Vogt Welch. BE, No. Ill. U., DeKalb, 1957, MA, 1972; postgrad., Western Ill. U., Macomb, 1989-90. Tchr. speech and English Harlem H.S., Loves Park, Ill., 1957-58; tchr. English, libr. Alden-Hebron Jr.-Sr. H.S., Ill., 1958-59; traffic mgr. Sta. WLBK Radio, DeKalb, Ill., 1964-65; libr. No. Ill. U., DeKalb, 1967, Malta Schs., Ill., 1968-71, Sycamore H.S., Ill., 1971-94; ret., 1994; owner Sesquicentennial Farm. Mem. Ogle County (Ill.) Farm Bur.; presenter in field. Author: The Heritage of the Lafayette Township Schools, 1990; compiler (book) James Reed Family, 1991, William Patton Family, 1987, Lafayette Township Officers, 1993; photographer (exhibits) Freeport Area Camera Club, 2004, 05. Chmn. Books South Africa Commn., DeKalb, 1991-92; co-chmn. Literary Festival Little 7 Conf., 1991-93; mem. Stephenson County Hist. Soc., 2002-; former mem. Assn. Gravestone Studies; chmn. bd. deacons Conglist. Ch., 1993-94, vice moderator, 1994-95; mem. Ill. Conf. United Ch. of Christ Bd., 1996-98, exec. bd., 1996-98, vice moderator Prairie Assn., 1996-97, moderator, 1997-98, Ill. Conf. del. United Ch. of Christ Gen. Synod, Providence, 1999, Kansas City, Mo., 2001. Mem. NEA, Popular Culture Assn. (presenter 1989), Ill. Assn. Tchrs. English (presenter 1988-90), Nat. Coun. Tchrs. English (presenter 1991, 93), Ill. Edn. Assn., Ill. Assn. Media Edn., Midwest Gilbert and Sullivan Soc., Somerset County Pa. Hist. and Geneal. Soc., Ill. Ret. Tchrs. Assn., Ret. Tchrs. Assn. Stephenson County (sec. 2004-06), Ret. Educators Assn. Sarasota, Freeport Area Camera Club, Stephenson County Hist. Soc., Ill. State Geneal. Soc. (cert. descendant civlil war svc. men), Alpha Sigma Alpha (life), Nat. Coun. Tchrs. English Ctr. of Excellence (co-dir., 1989-1991). Congregationalist. Avocations: writing, genealogy. Home: 3167 Sandy Pointe Dr Freeport IL 61032-2824 Personal E-mail: lornapat218@aol.com.

VOGT, PETER K., oncologist; b. Broumov, Czech Republic, Mar. 10, 1932; BS dr. honoris causa, U. Würzburg, Germany, 1955; PhD, U. Tübingen, Germany, 1959; postgrad., Max-Planck Inst., Tübingen, 1955—59, U. Calif., Berkeley, 1959—62. Asst. prof. pathology U. Colo. Sch. Medicine, Denver, 1962—66, assoc. prof. pathology, 1966—67; assoc. prof. microbiology U. Wash., Seattle, 1967—69, prof. microbiology, 1969—71; Hastings prof. microbiology U. So. Calif., LA, 1971—78, Hastings Disting. prof. microbiology, 1978—80, Hastings Disting. prof. microbiology and chair dept. microbiology, 1980—93; dept. molecular and exptl. medicine, head divsn. oncovirology Scripps Rsch. Inst., LaJolla, Calif., 1993—. Mem. sci. bd. advisors Nat. Cancer Inst., 1996—, German Cancer Ctr., Heidelberg. Mem. editl. bd. Virology, Current Topics in Microbiology and Immunology, Jour. Molecular Medicine, Cancer Rsch., Cell Growth and Differentiation, Archives of Biochemistry and Biophysics, 1994—99, Jour. Virology. Named McGinnis lectr., Duke U., 1999, Princess Takamatsu lectr., 1995, Calif. Scientist of the Yr., 1975; recipient Charles S. Mott prize, GM Cancer Rsch. Found., 1991, Howard Taylor Ricketts award, U. Chgo., 1991, Internat. prize in virology, ICN, 1989, Bristol Myers award, 1989, Paul-Ehrlich and Ludwig-Darmstaedter prize, 1988, Robert J. and Claire Pasarow award, 1987, Waterford Biomed. Sci. award, 1986, Ernst Jung prize for medicine, 1985, Alexander von Humboldt award, Fed. Republic Germany, 1984, Disting. Tchg. award, U. Wash., 1970—71, U. So. Calif., 1974, 1976, 1985, Irene-Vogeler prize, Max-Planck Soc., 1976, Assocs. award for creative scholarship and rsch., U. So. Calif., 1975, Studienstiftung des Deutschen Volkes, 1955. Fellow: Am. Acad. Microbiology; mem.: AAAS, NAS, Am. Philos. Soc., IOM, Deutsche Akademie der Naturforscher Leopoldina, Internat. Soc. Differentiation, Japanese Cancer Assn. (hon.), Am. Chem. Soc., Am. Assn. for Cancer Rsch., Am. Soc. Virology, Am. Soc. Microbiology (councilor 1976—77, chmn. virology divsn. 1975, vice chmn. virology divsn. 1973—74). Office: Scripps Research Inst Dept Molecular/Exptl Medicine 10550 N Torrey Pines Rd La Jolla CA 92037

VOGT, ROCHUS EUGEN, physicist, researcher; b. Neckarelz, Germany, Dec. 21, 1929; came to U.S., 1953; s. Heinrich and Paula (Schaefer) V.; m. Micheline Alice Yvonne Bauduin, Sept. 6, 1958; children: Michele, Nicole. Student, U. Karlsruhe, Germany, 1950-52, U. Heidelberg, 1952-53; SM, U. Chgo., 1957, PhD, 1961. Asst. prof. physics Calif. Inst. Tech., Pasadena, 1962-65, assoc. prof., 1965-70, prof., 1970—2002, R. Stanton Avery disting. svc. prof., 1982—2002, R. Stanton Avery disting. svc. prof. and prof. physics emeritus, 2002—, chmn. faculty, 1975-77, chief scientist Jet Propulsion Lab., 1977-78, chmn. div. physics, math. and astronomy, 1978-83, acting dir. Owens Valley Radio Obs., 1980-81, v.p. and provost, 1983-87. Vis. prof. physics MIT, 1988-94; dir. Caltech/MIT Laser Interferometer Gravitational Wave Observatory Project, 1987-94. Author: Cosmic Rays (in World Book Ency.), 1978, (with R.B. Leighton) Exercises in Introductory Physics, 1969; contbr. articles to profl. jours. Fulbright fellow, 1953-54; recipient Exceptional Sci. Achievement medal NASA, 1981, Profl. Achievement award U. Chgo. Alumni Assn., 1981. Fellow AAAS, A. Phys. Soc. Achievements include research in astrophysics and gravitation. Office: Calif Inst Tech 103-33 1200 E California Blvd Pasadena CA 91125-0001 Home Phone: 626-398-5066; Office Phone: 626-395-3800. Business E-Mail: vogt@caltech.edu.

VOHS, JAMES ARTHUR, health plan administrator; b. Idaho Falls, Idaho, Sept. 26, 1928; s. John Dale and Cliff Lucille (Packer) Vohs; m. Janice Hughes, Sept. 19, 1953 (dec. Oct. 1999); children: Lorraine, Carol, Nancy, Sharla; m. Eileen Galloway, Oct. 8, 2005. BA, U. Calif., Berkeley, 1952; postgrad., Harvard Sch. Bus., 1966. Employed by various Kaiser affiliated orgns., 1952—92; chmn., pres., CEO Kaiser Found. Hosps. and Kaiser Found. Health Plan, INc., Oakland, Calif., 1975—92, chmn. emeritus; chmn. bd. dirs. Holy Names Coll., 1981—92; chmn. Marcus Foster Inst., 1981—. Chmn. Fed. Res. Bank San Francisco, 1991—94. Mem. Oakland Bd. Port Commrs., 1993—96; bd. dirs. Oakland-Alameda County Coliseum Complex, 1986—96, Bay Area Coun., 1985—94, chmn., 1991—92. With US Army, 1946—48. Mem.: Inst. Medicine NAS. Personal E-mail: javohs@sbcglobal.net.

VOICULESCU, DAN VIRGIL, mathematics professor; b. Bucharest, Romania, June 14, 1949; m. Ioana-Maria Voiculescu, 1979. Studied Math., U. Bucharest, 1967—72, PhD in Math., 1977. Asst. U. Bucharest, 1972—73; rschr. Math. Inst., Bucharest, Romania, 1973—75, Math. Dept., INCREST, Bucharest, Romania, 1975—86; vis. assoc. prof. U. Calif., Berkeley, Calif., 1981, vis. prof., 1986—87, prof. math., 1987—, Miller prof., 1997—98. Aisenstadt Chair Centre de Recherches Mathematiques, Montreal, Canada, 1991; vis. prof. U. Paris VI, 1997, ETH Zurich, 1997, ENS Paris, CNRS and Institut H. Poincare, France, 1999; mem. Clay Math. Inst., 2000; lectr. in field. Mem. editl. bd. Advances in Mathematics, Annals of Mathematics, 1993—99, International Equations and Operator Theory, Jour. of Operator Theory, International Mathematics Research Notices, Pacific Journal of Mathematics, Infinite Dimensional Analysis, Quantum Probability and Related Topics, Journal of Functional Analysis; contbr. articles to prof. jours. Recipient NAS award in Math., 2004; Guggenheim Fellow, 1997. Mem.: NAS, Am. Math. Soc. (mem. com. on nat. meetings 1997—99). Office: U Calif Berkeley Dept Math 783 Evans Hall Berkeley CA 94720-3840 Office Phone: 510-643-7342. Business E-Mail: dvv@math.berkeley.edu.

VOIGHT, CAROLYN JEAN, administrative assistant; b. Waco, Tex., Aug. 20, 1953; d. Carroll Eugene and Wincie Iona Cannon; children: Christopher Jason Sorrels, Robyn Lynn Sorrels. BBA magna cum laude, Davenport U., 2000; MS, Ctrl. Mich. U., 2002; degree in Edn., U. Cambridge, 2003; student in Ednl. Adminstrn., Tex. A&M U., 2006—. Adj. instr. North Harris Montgomery C.C. Dist., Tomball, Tex., 1991—99; office mgr. Profl. Counseling Ctr., Lapeer, Mich., 2001—03; asst. to chief investment officer Baylor U., Waco, Tex., 2003—. Vol. Baylor U., Waco, Tex., 2003—06. Mem.: Am. Assn. C.C.s, Kappa Delta Pi (assoc.). Republican. Methodist. Avocations: reading, walking, gardening. Home: PO Box 463 Waco TX 76703 Office: Baylor University One Bear Place 97030 Waco TX 76798 Home Phone: 254-644-5663; Office Phone: 254-710-7833. Office Fax: 254-710-8798. Business E-Mail: carolyn_voight@baylor.edu.

VOIGHT, JACK C., state official; b. New London, Wisconsin, Dec. 17, 1945; s. Oscar C. and Thelma J. (Hamm) V.; m. Martha J. (Wolfe), July 14, 1973; children: Carly and Emily. BS, U. Wis., Oshkosh, 1971. Claims adjuster U.S. F and G Ins. Co., Appleton, Wis., 1971-74; ins. agy. owner Voight Ins. Agy., Appleton, Wis., 1974—; state treas. State of Wis., 1995—2006. Bank organizer Am. Nat. Bank, Appleton, Wis. 1992-94; real estate broker Voight Realty and Ins., Appleton, 1977-92. Pres. Appleton Northside Bus. Assn., 1982; alderman city coun., City of Appleton, 1983-83, pres., 1992-93; Sgt. U.S. Army, 1968-70. Decorated Bronze Star; named Citizen of Yr. Appleton Northside Bus. Assn., 1990. Mem. Nat. Assn. State Treas., Midwest State Treas. Assn. (pres. 1996-97); Appleton Noon Optimist Club (pres. 1980). Republican. Presbyterian. Avocations: gardening, politics. Office: State Treas Wis PO Box 7871 Madison WI 53707-7871 E-mail: jack.voight@ost.state.wi.us. *

VOIGHT, JERRY D., lawyer; b. Bozeman, Mont., Aug. 21, 1937; children: Janet, Jason. BS in Chem. Engring., Mont. State U., 1959; JD with hons., George Washington U., 1965. Bar: DC 1966, US Supreme Ct. 1969, US Ct. Appeals (Fed. Cir.) 1982, registered: US Patent & Trademark Office. Sr. ptnr. Finnegan, Henderson, Farabow, Garrett & Dunner LLP, Washington, 1972—, mng. ptnr. Palo Alto Office Calif. Contbr. articles to profl. jour. Named one of best lawyers in intellectual property law, Best Lawyers in Am., 2005—06. Mem.: DC Bar Assn., ABA, Am. Intellectual Property Law Assn. Avocations: skiing, collecting wood block prints. Office: Finnegan Henderson Farabow Garrett & Dunner LLP Stanford Rsch Park 700 Hansen Way Palo Alto CA 94304-1016 Office Phone: 650-849-6600. Office Fax: 650-849-6666. Personal E-mail: jerry.voight@finnegan.com.

VOIGHT, JON, actor; b. Yonkers, NY, Dec. 29, 1938; s. Elmer and Barbara (Camp) V.; m. Lauri Peters, 1962 (div. 1967); m. Marcheline Bertrand, Dec. 12, 1971 (div. 1978); children: James Haven, Angelina Jolie. BFA, Cath. U., 1960; studied with, Sanford Meisner and Samantha Harper, NYC. Stage appearances include O Oysters Revue, 1961, The Sound of Music, 1961, A View from the Bridge, 1965, Romeo and Juliet, 1966, The Tempest, 1966, Two Gentlemen of Verona, 1966, That Summer-That Fall, 1967 (Theatre World award 1967), A Streetcar Named Desire, 1973, The Hashish Club, 1975, Hamlet, 1976, The Seagull, 1992; TV appearances include Cimarron Strip, Gunsmoke; films include Fearless Frank, 1967, Hour of the Gun, 1967, Out of It, 1969, Midnight Cowboy, 1969 (Acad. award nom. best actor 1969, NY Critics Circle award 1969, L.A. Film Critics award best actor 1969, BAFTA award most promising newcomer 1969, Golden Globe award most promising newcomer 1969), Catch-22, 1970, The Revolutionary, 1970, Deliverance, 1972, The All American Boy, 1973, Conrack, 1974, The Odessa File, 1974, End of the Game, 1976, Coming Home, 1978 (Acad. Award for Best Actor 1978, Golden Globe award 1978, Cannes Internat. Film festival award 1978, NY Film Critics best actor award 1978, L.A. Film Critics award best actor 1978), The Champ, 1979 (Golden Globe award 1979), Runaway Train, 1985 (Acad. award nominee best actor 1986, London Film Critics award nominee 1986, Golden Globe best actor 1986), Desert Bloom, 1986, Eternity, 1990, The Rainbow Warrior, 1992, Heat, 1995, Mission Impossible, 1996, Rosewood, 1997, Anaconda, 1997, Most Wanted, 1997, The Rainmaker, 1997, U Turn, 1997, I Once Had a Life, 1998, Enemy of the State, 1998, Varsity Blues, 1999, A Dog of Flanders, 1999, Pearl Harbor, 2001, Lara Croft: Tomb Raider, 2001, Zoolander, 2001, Ali, 2001, Holes, 2003, Karate Dog, 2004, The Manchurian Candidate, 2004, Superbabies: Baby Geniuses 2, 2004, National Treasure, 2004, September Dawn, 2006, Transformers, 2007; (TV films) Chernobyl: The Final Warning, 1991, The Last of His Tribe, 1992, Convict Cowboys, 1995, Boys Will Be Boys, 1997, Noah's Ark, 1999, Second string, 2002, Jasper, Texas, 2003, The Five People You Meet in Heaven, 2004, Pope John Paul II, 2005; (mini-series) Return to Lonesome Dove, 1993; actor, prodr., co-writer (films) Lookin' To Get Out, 1982, The Fixer, 1998; actor, prodr. (films) Table for Five, 1983, A Tribute to Dustin Hoffman, 1999, Noah's Ark, 1999, Second String, 2000. *

VOIGT, BARTON R., state supreme court chief justice; b. Scotland, SD; BA in History, MA in History, U. Wyo., Laramie, JD. Atty., Thermopolis, Wyo.; former Hot Springs County atty.; former county ct. judge Gillette; judge Wyo. Eigth Jud. Dist., Douglas, 1993—2001; justice Wyo. Supreme Ct., 2001—, chief justice, 2006—. Mem. Bd. of Jud. Policy and Adminstrn. Mem.: Wyo. Bar Assn. Office: Wyo Supreme Ct 2301 Capitol Ave Cheyenne WY 82001 Office Phone: 307-777-7573.

VOIGT, CYNTHIA, writer; b. Boston, Feb. 25, 1942; d. Frederick C. and Elise (Keeney) Irving; married, 1964 (div. 1972); m. Walter Voigt, Aug. 30, 1974; children: Jessica, Peter. BA, Smith Coll., 1963. High sch. tchr. English, Glen Burnie, Md., 1965-67; tchr. English Key Sch., Annapolis, Md., 1968-69, dept. chmn., 1971-79, tchr., dept. chmn., 1981-88. Author: Homecoming, 1981, Tell Me If the Lovers Are Losers, 1982, Dicey's Song, 1982 (John Newbery medal 1983), The Callender Papers, 1983 (Edgar award 1984), A Solitary Blue, 1983, Building Blocks, 1984, Jackeroo, 1985, The Runner, 1985 (Silver Pencil award 1988, Deutscher Jugend Literator Preis 1989, ALAN award 1989), Come a Stranger, 1986, Izzy, Willy Nilly, 1986 (Calif. Young Reader's award 1990), Stories About Rosie, 1986, Sons From Afar, 1987, Tree by Leaf, 1988, Seventeen Against the Dealer, 1989, On Fortune's Wheel, 1990, The Vandemark Mummy, 1991, Orfe, 1992, Glass Mountain, 1991, David and Jonathan, 1992, The Wings of a Falcon, 1993, When She Hollers, 1994, Bad Girls, 1996, Bad, Badder, Baddest, 1997, Elske, 1999, It's Not Easy Being Bad, 2000, Bad Girls in Love, 2002, From Bad to Worse, 2003, Angus and Sadie, 2005.

VOIGT, ELLEN, literature educator; b. 1943; BA, Converse Coll.; MFA, U. Iowa. Prof. poetry MIT; prof. Goddard Coll., Vt.; prof. MFA program for writers Warren Wilson Coll., Asheville, NC, 1981—; Vt. State Poet, 1999—2003. Tchr. Bread Loaf Writers' Conf., Aspen Writer's Conf., Ind. Writers' Conf., Napa Writer's Conf., Catskills Writers' Conf., RopeWalk Writers' Conf. Author: (poems) Claiming Kin, 1976, The Forces of Plenty, 1983, The Lotus Flowers, 1987, Two Trees, 1992, Shadows of Heaven, 2002 (Nat. Book award finalist), (sonnet) Kyrie, 1995 (Nat. Book Critics' Circle award finalist, Teasdale Poetry prize); co-editor (with Gregory Orr): Poets Teaching Poets: Self and the World; author: The Flexible Lyric, 2001. Recipient Pushcart prize; fellow, Acad. Am. Poets, 2002; grantee, Vt. Coun. Arts, NEA, Guggenheim Found. Fellow: Am. Acad. Arts and Sciences; mem.: Acad. Am. Poets (chancellor 2003—). Achievements include developing and directing the nation's first low-residency writing program at Goddard College in 1976; the program has since been emulated by other colleges and universities. Office: Warren Wilson Coll PO Box 9000 Asheville NC 28815

VOIGT, FRANCIS, academic administrator; m. Ellen Bryant Voigt; 2 children. BA, Wesleyan U.; MA, U. Iowa. Faculty, adminstr. Goddard Coll.; co-founder, CEO, pres. New Eng. Culinary Inst., Montelier, Vt., 1980—. Mem. Vt. Human Resources Investment Coun., 2001—; mem. appeals com. Accrediting Commn. Career Schools and Colleges of Tech.; co-chair mktg. com. Vt. Higher Edn. Coun.; dir. Vt. Bus. Roundtable, Vt. Tech. Coun. Chair Vt. C. of C.; mem. Cabot, Vt. Sch. Bd. Mem.: Rsch. Chef's Assn., Am. Inst. Wine and Food, Les Amis D'Escoffier Soc., Nat. Restaurant Assn., Vt. Lodging and Restaurant Assn., Assn. Vt. Ind. Colleges (mem. exec. com.), Career Coll. Assn. (mem. bd. dirs. 2003—, chair profl. devel. com. 2003—), Rotary Internat. Club (pres.). Office: New Eng Culinary Inst 56 Coll St Montpelier VT 05602 *

VOIGT, KARL ALBERT, electrical engineer, military officer; b. Pitts., Aug. 8, 1960; s. Karl Ernest and Charlotte Ebert Voigt; m. Kimberlee Kay Miller; children: Scot Miller-Bent, Alexandria K., Sarah M., Danielle E. BSME, U. Pitts., Pitts., 1983; M in Strategic Studies, US Army War Coll., Carlisle, Pa., 2006. Commd. 2d lt. USN, 1979, advanced through grades to col., 2006; support equipment program officer Naval Air Systems Command, Washington, 1983—94; program mgr., analyst fgn. mil. sales group F/A-18 Program Office/Naval Air Systems Command, Washington, 1992—94; mem. fleet support team for support equipment Naval Air Depot, Jacksonville, Fla., 1994—96, Consolidated Automated Support Sys. offload integrated pogram team leader, 1996—99, electronic warfare fleet support team leader, 1999—2005; USN black belt trainee Fleet Readiness Ctr. SE, Jacksonville, 2006—. Contbr. articles to profl. jours. Mem., leader Indian Guide/Princess Program YMCA, Orange Park, Fla., 1996—2002; Troop 653 com. chmn. Boy Scouts Am., Orange Park, 1997—2002; fin. chair Asbury United Meth. Ch., Orange Park, 2004. Col. US Army. Mem.: Soc. Am. Mil. Engrs., Res. Officers Assn. Office Phone: 904-317-1699. Business E-Mail: karl.voigt@navy.mil.

VOIGT, PHILIP KENNETH, music educator; b. Smithtown, NY, Feb. 13, 1976; s. Roseann B. and Kenneth J. Voigt; m. Jennifer L. Mondolino. MusB, Ithaca Coll., NYC, 1994—98; MA, SUNY, Stony Brook, 1999—2002, Advanced Grad. Cert. in Sch. Dist. Adminstrn., 2002—04. Cert. tchr. State of N.Y., 1998, sch. dist. adminstr. State of N.Y., 2004. Music tchr. Kings Pk. Ctrl. Sch. Dist., NY, 1998—99, Ctrl. Islip Union Free Sch. Dist., NY, 1999—. Coord. L.I. Summer Music Workshop, Southhampton, NY, 1995—; dir. fine and performing arts Ctrl. Islip Union Free Sch. Dist., NY, 2001—; mem. adv. coun. Ea. Suffolk Bd. Coop. Ednl. Svcs., Westhampton, NY, 2002—; mem. exec. coun. N.Y. State Coun. Adminstr. for Music Edn., Islip, 2002—, Suffolk County Music Educators Assn., NY, 2003—. Roman Catholic. Avocations: jazz, theater, music. Office: Central Islip Union Free Sch Dist 545 Clayton St Central Islip NY 11722 Home Phone: 631-988-9454, 631-521-7768; Office Phone: 631-348-5111. Office Fax: 631-348-5162. Personal E-mail: pvoigt@optonline.net.

VOIGT, RICHARD, lawyer; b. Oskaloosa, Iowa, Jan. 20, 1946; s. Franz Otto Wilhelm and Minni (Heilbrunn) V.; m. Annemarie H. Riemer, Oct. 2, 1976; children: Samuel, Nicholas. BA, Conn. Wesleyan U., 1968; JD, U. Va., 1974. Bar: Va. 1974, U.S. Dist. Ct. (ea. dist.) Va. 1979, Conn. 1981, U.S. Dist. Ct. Conn. 1982, U.S. Ct. Claims 1982, U.S. Ct. Appeals (4th cir.) 1982. Assoc. counsel regional litigation Solicitor's Office Osha Div., 1978-80; staff atty. U.S. Dept. Labor, Washington, 1974-78; prin. Siegel, O'Connor, Schiff, Zangari & Kainen, P.C., 1981-88, 87-88; ptnr. Cummings & Lockwood, Hartford, 1988—2003, McCarter & English, Hartford, 2003—. Contbg. author: ABA Treatise on Occupational Safety and Health Law, 1988; contbr. articles to profl. jours. Bd. dirs. Urban League Greater Hartford, 1984-88, Isnt. for Non-Profit Tng. and Devel., 1991-95, Hartford Proud and Beautiful, 1995—, Greater Hartford Arts Coun., 2001—. Mem. ABA (labor and employment law sect., OSHA com., litigation sect.), Conn. Bar Assn. (labor employment law sect., employment discrimination com., com. on alternative dispute resolution). Avocations: acrylic design, history, sports. Office: McCarter & English LLP 36th Floor Cityplace I Hartford CT 06103 Office Phone: 860-275-6776.

VOIGT, STEVEN RUSSELL, lawyer; b. Geneva, Nebr., Dec. 29, 1952; s. James Leroy and Martha Anne (Erikson) V.; m. Barbara Jeane Molcyk, Apr. 23, 1983; children: Kelsey Marie, Katelyn Anne. BS, U. Nebr., 1975, JD, 1978. Bar: Nebr. 1978, U.S. Dist. Ct. Nebr. 1978, U.S. Tax Ct. 1980. Assoc. Nye, Hervert, Jorgensen & Watson, Kearney, Nebr., 1978-80; ptnr. Giese, Butler & Voigt, Kearney, 1980-82, Butler & Voigt, Kearney, 1982-85, Butler, Voigt & Brewster, Kearney, 1985-97, Butler, Voigt & Stewart P.C., Kearney, 1997—. Bd. dirs. Western Nebr. Legal Svcs., Scottsbluff, pres. bd. 1997-2000; pub. defender County of Kearney, Minden, Nebr., 1982—; pres. Nebr. Lawyers Trust Account Found., Lincoln, 1986-90. Bd. dir. Legal Aid Nebr., 2000—06. Mem. ABA (exec. coun. young lawyers div. 1985-86), Assn. Trial Lawyers Am., Nebr. State Bar Assn. (vice chair judiciary com.), Nebr. Criminal Defense Atty's. Assn., Sertoma (pres. Kearney chpt. 1983-84), Kearney Country Club (pres. of bd. dirs. 1995), Masons, Shriners. Avocations: golf, bicycling. Home: 5207 Avenue G Pl Kearney NE 68847-8598 Office: Butler Voigt & Stewart PC 2202 Central Ave Ste 200 Kearney NE 68847-5359 Office Phone: 308-234-5524.

VOINOVICH, GEORGE VICTOR, senator, former governor; b. Cleve., July 15, 1936; m. Janet (Allen) Voinovich; 3 children. BA in Govt., Ohio U., 1958; JD, Ohio State U., 1961; LLD (hon.), Ohio U., 1981. Bar: Ohio 1961, US Supreme Ct. 1968. Asst. atty. gen. State of Ohio, 1963-64; mem. Ohio Ho. of Reps., 1967-71; auditor Cuyahoga County, Ohio, 1971-76; commr., 1977-78; lt. gov. State of Ohio, Columbus, 1979, gov., 1991-98; mayor City of Cleve., 1979-89; US Senator from Ohio, 1999—; mem. fgn. rels. com., environment and pub. works com., fgn. relations com. homeland security and governmental affairs com. Pres. Nat. League Cities, 1984-85; trustee US Conf. Mayors; chmn. Midwestern Govs. Conf., 1991-92, Coun. Gt. Lakes Govs., 1992-94; chmn. Jobs for America's Graduates Program, 1995- (Nat. Leadership award 1993); mem. State and Local Govt. Coalition, 1994- Recipient Tree of Life award, Jewish Nat. Found., 1981, Cert. of Merit award Ohio U., Humanitarian award NCCJ, 1986, Disting. Urban Mayor award Nat. Urban Coalition, 1987, Nat. Public Svc. award SADD, 1991, Edn. Reform Pioneer award Nat. Bus. Roundtable, 1994, George Falcon Golden Spike award, Nat. Assn. Railroad Passengers, 2000; named one of Outstanding Young Men in Ohio Ohio Jaycees, 1970; one of Outstanding Young Men in Greater Cleve. Cleve. Jaycees; named to All-Pro City Mgmt. team City & State Mag., 1987. Mem. Rep. Govs. Assn. (vice chmn. 1991-92, chmn. 1992-93), Nat. Govs. Assn. (chmn. edn. action team on sch. readiness 1991, chmn. child support enforcement work group 1991-92, mem. strategic planning task force 1991-92, mem. human resources com., co-chmn. task force on edn. 1992-93, mem. exec. com. 1993-98, co-lead gov. on fed. mandates, chmn. 1997-98), Omicron Delta Kappa, Phi Alpha Theta, Phi Delta Phi. Republican. Roman Catholic. Office: US Senate 524 Hart Sentate Office Bldg Washington DC 20510-0001 also: Central Ohio Office Rm 310 37 West Broad St Columbus OH 43215 Office Phone: 202-224-3353, 614-469-6697. Office Fax: 202-228-1382, 614-469-7733. E-mail: columbus_voinovich@voinovich.senate.gov. *

VOITIER, DORIS, school system administrator; Math tchr., Chalmette HS St Bernard Parish Dist. Schools, La., superintendent La., 2004—. Recipient Woman of Yr. award, St. Bernard Bus. and Professional Women's Club, Profile in Courage award, John F. Kennedy Libr. Found., 2007. *

VOITLE, ROBERT ALLEN, dean, physiologist; b. Parkersburg, W.Va., May 12, 1938; s. Ray Christian and Ruby Virginia (Hannaman) V.; m. Linda Ellen Loveday, Dec. 5, 1975; children: Robert Allen, Elizabeth Anne, Christian Blair, Vanessa Virginia. BS, W.Va. U., 1962; MS, W.Va., 1965; PhD, U. Tenn., 1969. Asst. in poultry U. Tenn., Knoxville, 1965-69; asst. prof. physiology U. Fla., Gainesville, 1969-75, assoc. prof., 1975-79; prof., head dept. poultry Calif. Poly. State U., San Luis Obispo, 1979-81; dean Coll. Agr., Auburn U., Ala., 1981—2000, prof. poultry sci. Ala., 2000—. Cons. Columbia Bank for Coops., S.C., 1972 Contbr. articles to sci. jours. Pres., other offices Alachua County Fair Assn., Gainesville, 1969-79. Recipient Pub. Service award Alachua County Commn., 1975; recipient Tchr. of Yr. award U. Fla., 1977, Golden Feather award Calif. Poly. Inst., 1982 Mem. Poultry Sci. Assn., So. Poultry Sci. Assn., Gainesville Jaycees (JCI senatorship), Sigma Xi, Gamma Sigma Delta Clubs: Elks. Episcopalian. Home: 2247 Longwood Dr Auburn AL 36830-7105 Office: Auburn U Coll Agr Auburn AL 36849 Office Phone: 334-844-2603. Business E-Mail: rvoitle@ag.auburn.edu.

VOJCANIN, SAVA ALEXANDER, lawyer; b. Oak Lawn, Ill., Oct. 15, 1964; s. Jovan and Lili (Yovanovich) V.; m. Valerie S. Rupich, Oct. 12, 2002; 1 child: John William Diploma, Culver Mil. Acad., 1981; BA with distinction, DePauw U., 1985; JD, Washington U., 1988. Bar: Ill. 1988, US Dist. Ct. (no. dist.) Ill. 1989, US Dist. Ct. (no. dist.) Tex. 1996, US Supreme Ct. 2006. Assoc. Schaffenegger, Watson & Peterson Ltd., Chgo., 1988-91, Clausen Miller P.C., Chgo., 1991-98, ptnr., 1999—, shareholder, 2002—. Editor: Law, Culture and Values, 1989. Mem. Mayor's Adv. Coun. on Immigrant and Refugee Affairs, Chgo., 1992-97; trustee St. Basil Orthodox Ch. of Lake Forest, 1997—, sec. bd. trustees, 1999-2002, nominating com., 2002-2005. Mem.: ABA, Chgo. Bar Assn., Serbian Bar Assn. Am. (treas. 1999—2000, sec. 2000—01, v.p. 2001—02, pres. 2002—03, bd. dirs.). Orthodox. Office: Clausen Miller PC 10 S LaSalle St Chicago IL 60603-1098 Business E-Mail: svojcanin@clausen.com.

VOJNOVIC, IGOR ZORAN, geographer, urban planner, educator; b. Belgrade, Yugoslavia, Jan. 26, 1966; arrived in U.S., 1997; s. Zoran and Branislava Vojnovic; m. Ghada Georgis, June 10, 1999. BA, York U., Toronto, Can., 1990; MSc, U. Toronto, 1992, PhD, 1997. Instr. urban design U. Toronto, 1994—97; rsch. assoc. Intergovernmental Com. on Urban and Regional Rsch., Toronto, 1996—97; instr. urban-environmental policy Syracuse U., 1997—98; sr. urban planning and design cons. Pub. Sector Innovations, Halifax, NS, Canada, 1998—99; asst. prof., urban-environmental design Dalhousie U., Halifax, 1998—99; asst. prof. urban-environ. policy Tex. A&M U., College Station, 1999—2002; prin. urban planning and design cons. Paul Raff Studio, Toronto, 2001—; assoc. prof., met. environments Mich. State U., East Lansing, 2002—. Adj. prof. govt. U. Alta., Edmonton, Canada, 2004—. Author: (monograph (in english & french) Municipal Consolidation in the 1990s, 1997; contbr. articles to profl. jours. Outreach planning and design svc. staff Dalhousie U., 1998—99, Tex. A&M U., 1999—2002, Mich. State U., 2002—06. Recipient Founders Coll. Book award, York U., 1990, Griffith Taylor Meml. award in Recognition of Acad. Excellence, U. Toronto, 1996—97, The Corps of Cadets Tchg. award, Tex. A&M U., 2002; fellow, Social Sci. and Humanities Rsch. Coun. of Can., 1993—96, Syracuse U., 1997—98; grantee, Can. Donner Found., 1998—99, Tex. A&M U., 2001, Inst. Pub. Policy and Social Rsch., 2003, Land Policy Program, 2004—, Com. Vitality Program Grant, 2005—; scholar, Province of Ont., 1990—92. Achievements include research in local policy framework for regional restructuring used as a guide in the amalgamation of Halifax Regional Municipality; framework for municipal tax structure used for the Provincial-Municipal Service Exchange Amendments/General Work Plan and Guide to Principles. Avocations: music, saxophone. Home Phone: 517-664-2656; Office Phone: 517-355-7718. Business E-Mail: vojnovic@msu.edu.

VOJTA, PAUL ALAN, mathematics professor; b. Mpls., Sept. 30, 1957; s. Francis J. and Margaret L. V. B in Math., U. Minn., 1978; MA, Harvard U., 1980, PhD, 1983. Instr. Yale U., New Haven, 1983-86; fellow Math. Scis. Rsch. Inst., Berkeley, Calif., 1986-87, Miller Inst. for Basic Rsch., Berkeley, 1987-89; assoc. prof. U. Calif., Berkeley, 1989-92, prof., 1992—. Mem. Inst. for Advanced Study, Princeton, 1989-90, 96-97. Author: Diophantine Approximations and Value Distribution Theory, 1987; editor: Jour. Reine Angew Math., 2004—. Recipient perfect score Internat. Math. Olympiad, 1975. Mem. Am. Math. Soc. (Frank Nelson Cole Number Theory prize 1992), Math. Assn. Am., Phi Beta Kappa, Tau Beta Pi. Avocations: skiing, computers. Office: Univ Calif Dept Math 970 Evans Hall 3840 Berkeley CA 94720-3840

VOJTEK, ROSEANNE OBRIEN, principal; b. Salem, Oreg., Apr. 21, 1953; d. Allen William and Audrey Darlene Kraxberger; m. Robert Joseph Vojtek, Aug. 29, 1992; children: Caroline Adele O'Brien, Holly Elizabeth O'Brien. BS, Oreg. State U., Corvallis, 1976; MS, U. Oreg., Eugene, 1985, PhD, 1993. Lic. provisional educator, intermediate adminstr. and supr. Conn., 1999, cert. supt. Conn., 1999. Tchr. Winston-Dillard Sch. Dist., Oreg., 1977—89; grad. tchg. fellow U. Oreg., Eugene, 1989—93; elem. prin. Forest Grove Sch. Dist., Oreg., 1993—95; dir. instrn. Oreg. City Pub. Sch, Oreg., 1995—99; elem. sch. prin. Ivy Dr. Elem., Bristol Pub. Sch., Bristol, Conn., 1999—. Presenter in field. Contbr. articles to profl. jours. Mem.: NAESP (state rep. 2006—07, Share The Dream grant 2006—07), Conn. Assn. Sch. (bd. dirs., elem. bd. mem., com. chair 2003—07), Internat. Soc. Tech. Edn. (nat. ednl. tech. stds. com.), Nat. Staff Devel. Coun. (pres., bd. trustees 1995—2001), Phi Delta Kappa (local chpt. officer, state rep., area I-A coord. 1981—2007). Lutheran. Office: Ivy Drive Elem Sch 160 Ivy Dr Bristol CT 06010 Home Phone: 860-582-8663; Office Phone: 860-584-7843. Business E-Mail: rosievojtek@ci.bristol.ct.us.

VOKETAITIS, ARNOLD MATTHEW, bass-baritone, educator; b. East Haven, Conn., May 11, 1930; s. Mathew Joseph and Agnes Mary (Pilvelis) V.; m. Marion Lee Dever, June 1959 (div. 1967); children: Arnold Mathew Jr., Paul Stanley; m. Nijole Lipciute, Sept. 6, 1968. BS in Bus. Adminstrn, Quinnipiac Coll., 1954. Dir. opera program De Paul U., Chgo., 1987-89. Lectr. techniques for mus. stage, author singing technique Northwestern U., Evanston, Ill., 1986; mem. adv. panels in music and ethnic affairs Ill. Arts Coun.; mem. panel for opera and mus. theatre NEA; faculty mem. Brevard (N.C.) Summer Music Ctr., 1987, 88; artist-in-residence for opera and voice Auburn U., Ala., 1990-93; artist/mgr. for pianists, formed Keyboard Artists Internat., 1998. Condr. master classes in singing; author on voice technique; operatic debut with N.Y.C. Opera, 1958, European debut at Liceo, Barcelona, Spain, 1968; mem. Met. Opera Nat. Co., appeared with maj. operatic and symphonic orgns. in U.S., Can., Mex., Cen. Am., S.Am., Lyric Opera of Chgo., 1966-84, 89, rec. artist for Desto, Vox, Columbia, RCA; recitalist appearances on Pay-TV; classical soloist U.S. Army Band, Washington. Served as sgt. U.S. Army, 1954-56. Recipient 1st place award, Conn. Opera Assn. auditions, 1957, Rockefeller Found. award, 1964, Lithuanian Man of Yr. award, 1990, Disting. Alumni award, Quinnipiac U., 1991. Mem. AFTRA, Am. Guild Mus. Artists (life), Actors Equity. Avocations: golf, fishing, theater. Personal E-mail: avkey@juno.com. *I have felt very strongly over the years that opera was written to be enjoyed, not revered, and that it cried out to be acted as well as sung. With television's influence on the viewer, necessity became reality and my hopes are being realized.*

VOKIC, HEATHER MAUREEN, artist, educator; b. Euclid, Ohio, Jan. 1, 1975; d. John L. and Patricia E. Pund; m. Miroslav A. Vokic, June 21, 1997; children: Lawrence R., Alexis M., Andrew J. BS summa cum laude, Case Western Res. U., 1993; Cert. of Completion in Art Edn., Cleve. Inst. Art, 1997; MA magna cum laude, Southeastern U., Fla., 2004. Visual arts educator Ohio Dept. of Edn. Art tchr. The Andrews Sch., Willoughby, Ohio, 1997—2001; art educator Meml. Jr. H.S., Mentor, Ohio, 2002—03, Wiley Mid. Sch., University Heights, Ohio, 2003—. Exhbn. and commn., Stained Glass & Textile Work. Educator, designer Christ Luth. Ch., Willoughby, 2001—05. Recipient Silk Heros grant, Reaching Heights Found., 2004—05; Martha Holden Jennings scholar, 2005—06. Mem.: Ohio Mid. Sch. Assn. (assoc.). Lutheran. Avocations: painting, stained glass, textiles. Home: 496 E 319th St Willoughby OH 44095 Home Phone: 440-347-9877; Office Phone: 216-371-7270. Personal E-mail: vglassdesigns@adelphia.net. E-mail: h_vokic@chuh.org.

VOLANAKIS, JOHN EMMANUEL, immunologist, rheumatologist; b. Thessaloniki, Greece, Mar. 17, 1938; arrived in US, 1968, naturalized, 1978; s. Emmanuel (Manolis) John and Cleo (Agathonos) Volanakis; children: Emmanuel (Manolis) John, Marina Cleo. MD, Aristotle U., Thessaloniki, 1962; DMed, Nat. U. Athens, Greece, 1968, PhD (hon.), 2003. Cert. Bd. Internal Medicine Ministry Health, Greece, 1967. Fellow rheumatology Cleve. Met. Gen. Hosp., 1968—71; instr. dept. medicine U. Ala., Birmingham, 1971—73, asst. prof. dept. medicine, 1973—77, assoc. prof. dept. medicine, 1977—83, prof. dept. medicine, 1983—2003; pres., sci. dir. Biomedical Sciences Rsch. Ctr. Alexander Fleming, Vari, Greece, 1997—2003. Dir., rsch. component Multipurpose Arthritis Ctr., Birmingham, Ala., 1984—97. Editor: The Human Complement System in Health and Disease; contbr. articles to profl. jours. Cadet Mil. Med. Sch., 1956—61, Thessaloniki, Greece. Named Anna Lois Waters Chair of Medicine in Rheumatology, U. Ala., 1989—97; recipient Alexander von Humbolt, Rsch. award for Sr. U.S. Scientists, Alexander von Humbolt Stiftung, 1996—97; Robert M. Stecher fellow, Arthritis Found. Ohio, 1969—71, Fogarty Sr. Internat. Rsch. fellow, NIH, 1978—79. Mem.: Assn. Am. Physicians. Achievements include patents for crystals of human factor D. Avocation: literature. Home: 2900 Redmont Park C 302W Birmingham AL 35205 Office: Univ Alabama at Birmingham 1530 3rd Ave South BDB 479 Birmingham AL 35294-0012 Office Phone: 205-934-5235. Office Fax: 205-934-1477. Business E-Mail: volanaki@uab.edu.

VOLANAKIS, PETER F., manufacturing executive; B in Economics, Dartmouth Coll., 1977; M in Finance, Tuck Sch. Bus. Dartmouth Coll., 1982. Market devel. specialist optical products Corning Inc., 1982, product mgr. tech. ceramics then various comml. positions environmental products, 1985—91, dir. corp. mktg., 1991, gen. mgr. environmental products Wiesbaden, Germany, 1992—95, exec. v.p. Siecor Corp. Hickory, NC, 1995—97, sr. v.p. advanced display products, 1997—99, exec. v.p. display sector and life sciences divsn., 1999—2001, pres. Corning Technologies with responsibility info. display and advanced materials groups internat. operations and central engrng., 2001—05, COO, 2005—, pres., 2007—, bd. dirs., 2000—, Dow Corning, 2001—. Bd. trustees Corning Inc. Found., Corning Mus. Glass; bd. overseers Amos Tuck Sch. Bus. Adminstrn. Dartmouth Coll. Office: Corning Inc 1 Riverfront Plaza Corning NY 14831-0001 *

VOLBERG, HERMAN WILLIAM, electronics engineer, consultant; b. Hilo, Hawaii, Apr. 6, 1925; s. Fred Joseph and Kathryn Thelma (Ludloff) V.; m. Louise Ethel Potter, Apr. 26, 1968 (dec.); children: Michael, Lori. BSEE, U. Calif., Berkeley, 1949. Project engr. Naval Electronics Lab., San Diego, 1950-56; head solid state rsch. S.C. div. Gen. Dynamics, San Diego, 1956-60; founder Solidyne Solid State Instruments, La Jolla, Calif., 1958-60; founder, v.p. electronics divsn. Ametek/Straza, El Cajon, Calif., 1960-66; founder, cons. H.V. Cons., San Diego, 1966-69; sr. scientist Naval Ocean Systems Ctr., Oahu, Hawaii, 1970-77; chief scientist Integrated Scis. Corp., Santa Monica, Calif., 1978-80; founder, pres. Acoustic Sys. Inc., Goleta, Calif., 1980-84, Invotron, Inc., Murray, Utah, 1984—; sr. scientist Reson, Inc., Santa Barbara, Calif., 1992—. Cons. Lockheed-Martin, 1985—, U. Utah Ctr. for Engring. Design, 1991; cons. on autonomous underwater vehicle sonar systems Mitsui/U. Tokyo, 1992; lectr. solid state course UCLA and IBM, 1956-62; instr. Applied Tech. Inst., Columbia, Md., 1988—; contbr. to undersea acoustical rsch. and devel. programs European Union, 1990—; presenter in field Author: The Doppelganger Brane, 2004; contbr. articles to profl. jours. Mem. adv. panels for advanced sonar systems and for high resolution sonars, USN, 1970-77. 1st lt. U.S. Army, 1944-47, ETO. Recipient award of merit Dept. Navy, 1973, 94. Mem.: VFW, NRA, AAAS, IEEE (life), Math. Assn. Am., N.Y. Acad. Scis., Acoustical Soc. Am., Air Force Assn., Marine Tech. Soc., Mine Warfare Assn., U.S. Naval Inst., Libr. Congress Assocs. (charter), Planetary Assn., Old Crows, Am. Legion, Elks, Masons. Achievements include patents for device for detecting and displaying the response of tissue to stimuli, high rate neutralizer (HIRAN), crane high-voltage sensing sys. Home and Office: 41 W 6830 S Murray UT 84107-7124 Office Phone: 801-207-7815. Personal E-mail: hwvolberg@yahoo.com.

VOLCKER, PAUL A(DOLPH), economist, former Chairman of the Board of Governors of the Federal Reserve System; b. Cape May, NJ, Sept. 5, 1927; s. Paul A. and Alma Louise (Klippel) V.; m. Barbara Marie Bahnson, Sept. 11, 1954 (dec. June 1998); children: Janice, James. AB summa cum laude, Princeton U., 1949; MA, Harvard U., 1951; LLD (hon.), Princeton U., 1982, Harvard U., 1985, London U., 1994. Economist Fed. Res. Bank N.Y., 1952-57, pres., 1975-79; fin. economist Chase Manhattan Bank, NYC, 1957-61, v.p., dir. forward planning, 1965-68; dir., Office Fin. Analysis US Dept. Treasury, Washington, 1961—63, dep. under sec. monetary affairs, 1963-65, under sec., 1969-74; chmn. bd. govs. Fed. Res. Sys., Washington, 1979-87; chmn. James D. Wolfensohn, Inc., 1988—96. Prof. internat. econ. policy Princeton U., 1988-95, prof. emeritus, 1995-; chmn. Nat. Commn. Pub. Svc., 1987-90, 2002-03, Trilateral Commn., 1990-2001, Internat. House & Fin., 1998—, Svcs. Vol. Corps., 1998-2005, Ind. Inquiry into the UN Oil for Food Programme, 2004-05; chmn. bd. trustees Internat. Acctg. Stds. Com., 2000-06; dir. Inst. Internat. Econs. Recipient Arthur S. Fleming award, US Treasury Dept. Exceptional Svc. award, 1965, Alexander Hamilton award, 1973; Sr. fellow Woodrow Wilson Sch. Pub. and Internat. Affairs, 1974-75.

VOLENTINE, RICHARD J., JR., lawyer; b. Tampa, Fla., Apr. 2, 1955; s. Richard J. Sr. and Mary Francis (Shaw) V.; children: Rachel Elizabeth, Scott Thomas, Melissa Mary. BS, Spring Hill Coll., 1977; JD, U. Ala., 1980. Bar: Ala. 1980, Mo. 1982, Fla. 1984, Ga. 2005. Staff atty. Ala. Jud. Coll., Tuscaloosa, 1980-81; staff counsel Citicorp Person-to-Person, Inc., St. Louis, 1982; regional counsel Citicorp Person-to-Person Corp., Tampa, 1982-84; asst. gen. counsel Citicorp Savs. Fla., Miami, 1984-85; assoc. counsel Home Fed./Capital Corp., Atlanta, 1985-86; regional atty. FDIC, Atlanta, 1986-88; gen. counsel, v.p. Altus Bank, Mobile, Ala., 1988-90; v.p., assoc. gen. counsel Chase Home Mortgage Corp., Tampa, Fla., 1990-91; sr. v.p., chief legal officer Prudential Bank, Atlanta, 1991—2000; assoc. gen. counsel Fannie Mae, Atlanta, 2000—. Mem. ABA, Assn. Corp. Counsel, Ala. Jud. Coll. Faculty Assn. (hon.). Republican. Roman Catholic. Avocations: playing golf, basketball, and other sports, photography, writing. Home: Unit 201 3920 Riverlook Pky Marietta GA 30067 Office: 950 E Paces Ferry Rd Ste 1900 Atlanta GA 30326 Home Phone: 770-953-3157; Office Phone: 404-398-6022. Business E-Mail: richard_volentine@fanniemae.com.

VOLFSON-DOUBOVA, ELENA, psychiatrist, researcher; b. St. Petersburg, Russia, Oct. 27, 1971; d. Valeriy Dmitrievich Dubov and Larisa Alexandrovna Dubova; m. Ilya Alexander Volfson, Aug. 18, 2000; children: Veronique Anna Volfson, Erik Robert Volfson. BS, St. Petersburg State Pavlov Med. U., Russia, 1992, MD, 1996; MPH, SUNY, Albany, 2000. Lic. Med. NJ, St. Petersburg Acad. Postgraduate Edn., Russia. Internal medicine resident St. Petersburg State Med. Acad. Postgraduate Edn., 1996—98; psychiatry resident U. Med. Dental NJ, Robert Wood Johnson Med. Sch. Psychiatry Residency Program, Piscataway, 2001—06; fellowship addiction psychiatry U. Med. Dental NJ, 2006—. Rschr. addiction psychiatry U. Med. Dental NJ, 2004—05; rschr. mental illness, health policy Health Policy Rsch. Ctr., New Sch. U., NYC, 2000; rschr. infectious diseases epidemiology Pub. Health Rsch. Inst., NYC, 2000; med. interpreter St. Petersburg City Health Dept., 1995—98. Contbr. articles various profl. jours. Grantee, Fogarty Internat. Ctr., 1999-2000; Prof. Eichvald scolarship, St. Petersburg Med. Acad. Postgraduate Edn., 1997, Edmund S. Muskie, FREEDOM Support Act Grad. Fellowship Program, US Dept. State, Bur. Cultural, Ednl. Affairs, 1998-2000. Mem.: APHA (assoc.), NJ Psychiat. Assn. (assoc.), Am. Psychiat. Assn. (assoc.). Office: U Med Dental NJ Robert Wood Johnson Med Sch 671 Hoes Ln C 205 Piscataway NJ 08854 Home: 26110 Cherry Blossom Ct Lawrenceville NJ 08648 Home Phone: 732-316-8466, 609-799-8545; Office Phone: 732-235-4341. Office Fax: 732-235-4277; Home Fax: 732-235-4649. Personal E-mail: volfsone@yahoo.com. Business E-Mail: volfsoel@umdnj.edu.

VOLGIN, DENYS V., medical researcher; b. Melitopol, Ukraine, Apr. 19, 1973; s. Victor E. Volgin and Ludmila I. Volgina; m. Valeria Dovbik, June 12, 2003; children: Anastasia, Darya D. MS biology, chemistry (hon.), Melitopol State Pedagogical U., Ukraine, 1990—95; PhD physiology of human and animals, Bogomolets Inst. Physiology, Kiev, Ukraine, 1996—99. Asst. tchr. physiology Melitopol State Pedagogical U., Ukraine, 1995—96; postgraduate rschr. Bogomolets Inst. Physiology, Kiev, 1996—99; postdoctoral rschr. U. Pa., Phila., 1999—2002, rsch. assoc., 2002—06, rsch. asst. prof. physiology, 2006—. Recipient Faculty Career Advancement award, Am. Acad. Sleep Medicine, 2004; fellow Soros Fellowships, Internat. Renaissance Found., 1994, 1996. Mem.: Internat. Soc. Neurochemistry, Am. Acad. Sleep Medicine. Achievements include research in pharmacological correction of hypoxic states; study of the role of nitric oxide in central control of breathing in neonatal animals; single-cell gene expression profiling of upper airway motoneurons; study of GABAergic mechanisms in hypothalamic neurons involved in sleep/wake control study of GABAergic regulation of gene expression. Avocations: poetry, the arts. Office: Univ Pa 3800 Spruce St 209 E/Vet Philadelphia PA 19104 Home: 4528 Spruce St Philadelphia PA 19139 Office Phone: 215-898-6258. Business E-Mail: dvolgin@vet.upenn.edu.

VOLGMAN, ANNABELLE SANTOS, cardiologist, educator; b. Quezon City, The Philippines, Oct. 30, 1957; arrived in U.S., 1970; d. Raymundo Jocson and Purificacion Villatuya Santos; m. Keith Allen Volgman, Apr. 23, 1988; children: Robert Keith, Caroline Annabelle. BA, Barnard Coll., 1980; MD, Columbia U., 1984. Internal medicine resident U. Chgo. Hosps. and Clinics, 1984—87; cardiology fellow Northwestern Meml. Hosp., Chgo., 1987—90; asst. prof. Rush U., Chgo., 1990—2000, assoc. prof., 2001—. Cons. and spkr. in field. Contbr. articles to profl. jours. Fellow: Am. Coll. Cardiology; mem.: Am. Heart Assn. (med. chair women's legacy luncheon 2000—02, bd. dirs. 2002—, Spl. Merit award 2001—02, Women with Heart award 2005), Menomonee Club (bd. dirs. 2002—04). Avocations: running, bicycling, triathlons, reading, swimming. Office: Rush Heart Inst Ste 1159 1725 W Harrison St Chicago IL 60612 Office Phone: 312-942-6569. Business E-Mail: annabelle_volgman@rush.edu.

VOLK, AUSTIN N., retired insurance company executive; b. NYC, Dec. 28, 1918; s. Nicholas and Helen Volk; m. Rae Petigrue, Aug. 17, 1979; children: Deborah Saliba, John Glidden, James L.P. Glidden, Gordon G. Glidden. BA in Econ., Brown U., Providence, 1941. V.p. Nicholas Volk & Co. Inc., NYC, 1946—55, pres., 1955—75, ret., 1975. Pres. Nat. Naval Res. Surface Policy Bd., Omaha, 1964—66; mem. Nat. Naval Res. Policy Bd., Washington, 1967—69. Pres. Englewood Cemetery Assn., NJ, 1988—2006; trustee, chmn. Naval War Coll. Found., 1997—99; councilman, coun. pres. City of Englewood, 1955—60, mayor, 1960—64, 1966—68; assemblyman State of N.J., Trenton, 1968—72. Capt. USNR, 1941—73, PTO, WWII, ATO, Korean War. Mem.: Navy League (pres. N.Y. coun. 1982—84, Teddy Roosevelt Leadership award 1982), Naval Order U.S. (pres. 1990—92, mem. N.Y. coun.).

VOLK, KENNETH HOHNE, lawyer; b. Hackensack, NJ, Nov. 8, 1922; s. Henry L. and Constance (Brady) V.; m. Joyce Geary, May 11, 1954; children: Christopher H., Cynthia. BS, U.S. Naval Acad., 1946; LLB, Yale U., 1953. Ptnr. Burlingham, Underwood, NYC, 1955-92; of counsel McLane, Graf, Raulerson & Middleton, Portsmouth, N.H., 1992—. Speaker various symposia and confs. on maritime law. Assoc. editor Am. Maritime Cases; contbr. articles to profl. jours. Pres. Maritime Assocs., N.Y.C., 1967-68; chmn. bd. dirs. Seamen's House YMCA, N.Y.C., 1971-76; sec., bd. dirs. Seamen's Ch. Inst., N.Y.C., 1977-92; bd. dirs. Strawbery Banke Mus., Portsmouth, N.H.; mem. adv. bd. Tulane Admiralty Law Inst. Fellow Am. Bar Found., Am. Coll. Trial Lawyers; mem. ABA, Assn. Bar of City of N.Y., Maritime Law Assn. U.S. (exec. com. 1977-80, pres. 1990-92), Comite Maritime Internat. (titulary mem.), Quaker Hill Country Club (pres. 1976-78). Republican. Espicopalian. Avocations: reading, hiking, fishing. Office: McLane Graf Raulerson & Middleton 100 Market St Portsmouth NH 03801 Office Phone: 603-436-2818. E-mail: kenneth-volk@mclane.com.

VOLK, KRISTIN, advertising agency executive; b. Phila., Feb. 26, 1953; d. Richard H. and Doris (Colasanti) V. BS in Biology, Tufts U., 1976; MPH, Boston U. Sch. Med., 1981. Rsch. technician Beth Israel Hosp., Boston, 1976; rsch. asst. Dana-Farber Cancer Inst., Boston, 1976-78; sr. rsch. asst. Beth Israel Hosp., Boston, 1978-81; rsch. supr. Schneider Parker Jakuc Advt., Boston, 1981-86; v.p., assoc. rsch. dir. HBM/Creamer, Boston, 1986-88, Della Femina McNamee, Boston, 1988-90; v.p., dir. rsch. Lawner Reingold Britton & Ptnrs., Boston, 1990-93; sr. v.p., dir. consumer insight group Arnold Fortuna Lawner & Cabot, Boston, 1993-95; exec. v.p., dir. consumer insight group Arnold Comm., Inc., Boston, 1995-99; exec. v.p., dir. strategic planning Deutsch Boston, 1999—2001; exec. v.p., chief mktg. officer Arnold Worldwide, NYC, 2001—. Guest lectr. colls. and univs., Boston. Contbr. articles to profl. jours. Mem. Am. Assn. Advt. Agencies (account planning group com., chmn. conf. 1998), Ad Club N.Y. Home: 252 7th Ave Apt 15k New York NY 10001-7349

VOLK, PATRICIA GAY, writer, essayist; b. NYC, July 16, 1943; d. Cecil Sussman and Audrey Elaine (Morgen) Volk; m. Andrew Blitzer, Dec. 21, 1969; children: Peter Morgen, Polly Volk BFA cum laude, Syracuse U., 1964; student, Sch. Visual Arts, NYC, 1968, New Sch., 1975, Columbia U., 1977-88. Art dir. Appelbaum & Curtis, NYC, 1964-65, Seventeen Mag., Triangle Publs., NYC, 1966-68; copywriter Doyle, Dane, Bernbach, Inc., NYC, 1969-88, also sr. v.p., creative mgr., 1969-87, sr. v.p.- assoc. creative dir., 1987-88; columnist N.Y. Newsday, 1995-96; fiction instr. Yeshiva Coll. Fiction instr. Playwrights Horizon Theater Sch., Marymount Coll. Author: The Yellow Banana, 1985 (Word Beat Press Fiction Book award 1984), White Light, 1987, All it Takes, 1990, Stuffed: Adventures of a Restaurant Family, 2001, To My Dearest Friends, Knopf, 2007; contbr. articles to N.Y. Times mag., Redbook, Allure, Mirabella, Family Circle, The New Yorker, The Atlantic, Playboy, others; contbr. short stories to popular and small press publs. and anthologies. Recipient Stephen E. Kelly award, 1983, Various Andy, Clio, Effie and One Show awards, 1970—88, Yaddo fellow, 1983, 1999, 2001—06, MacDowell fellow, 1984, 2000. Mem.: PEN, Century Assn., Author's Guild, Juliana Berner's Anglers.

VOLK, STEPHEN RICHARD, diversified financial services company executive, investment banker, lawyer; b. Boston, Apr. 22, 1936; s. Ralph and Miriam (Rose) V.; m. Veronica J. Brown, June 19, 1959 (dec. Feb. 1989); children: Jeffrey A., Andrew M., Michael J.; m. Diane Kemelman, Apr. 22, 1990; 1 child, Anne. Grad. cum laude, Dartmouth Coll., 1957; JD, Harvard U., 1960. Bar: N.Y. 1961. Assoc. Shearman & Sterling, NYC, 1960-68, ptnr., 1968—88, dep. sr. ptnr., 1988-91, sr. ptnr., 1991—2001; vice chmn. Credit Suisse First Boston, NYC, 2001—02, mem. exec. bd. and operative com., chmn., 2002—04; mem. exec. bd. Credit Suisse Group, 2003—04; vice chmn. Citigroup Inc., 2004—. Bd. dirs. ContiGroup Cos. Inc., Consol. Edison, Inc., 1996; trustee Consol Edison Co. N.Y.C., Inc., 1998; chmn. Credit Suisse First Boston, 2002-04. Mem. dean's adv. bd. Harvard Law Sch., 1997. Fellow Am. Bar Found.; mem. Assn. Bar City N.Y., Harvard Law Sch. Assn., N.Y.C., 1999, Coun. on Fgn. Rels., Univ. Club, Phi Beta Kappa. Office: Citigroup Inc 399 Park Ave New York NY 10043

VOLK, WILLIAM R., lawyer; b. Corpus Christi, Tex., Aug. 11, 1950; BA, Vanderbilt U., 1972; JD with honors, U. Tex., 1975. Bar: Tex. 1975. Ptnr., co-head Corp. Fin. & Securities Sect. Vinson & Elkins LLP, Austin, Tex. Fellow: Texas Bar Found. (life); mem.: ABA, Austin Bar Assn. Office: Vinson & Elkins LLP 2801 Via Fortuna, Ste 100 Austin TX 78746 Business E-Mail: wvolk@velaw.com.

VOLKAY, CHRIS JOHN, investment company executive; b. Hollywood, Calif., Nov. 14, 1954; s. Robert and Yvonne Pearl Volkay. Lic. real estate agt. Calif. V.p. Rubicon Corp. Am., Van Nuys, Calif., 1986—. Mentor investment counselors and brokers Paladin Mortgage, Van Nuys, 1995—. Author: Laughing Gas, 2000; contbr. articles to profl. jours., poems, short stories to lit. publs. Mem.: Brights, Ctr. for Inquiry West, Coun. Secular Humanism. Libertarian. Secular Humanist. Office Phone: 818-765-8800. E-mail: cvolkay@aol.com.

VOLKEMA, MICHAEL A., office furniture manufacturer; Chmn., CEO Meridian Inc., Spring Lake, Mich.; pres., CEO Coro Inc., Zeeland, Mich., Herman Miller Inc., Zeeland, 1995—2004, chmn., 2000—. Office: Herman Miller Inc 855 E Main Ave Zeeland MI 49464-0302 Office Fax: 616-654-5234.

VOLKER, DALE MARTIN, state legislator, lawyer; b. Lancaster, NY, Aug. 2, 1940; s. Julius J. and Loretta (O'Neill) Volker; m. Carol A. Suchyna, Nov. 28, 1970; children: Martin Andrew, Mark Dale, Meredith Ann. BA, Canisius Coll., 1963; JD, SUNY, Buffalo, 1966. Bar: NY 1967. Police officer Village of Depew, NY, 1966—72; assemblyman NY State Assembly, Albany, 1972—74; mem. NY State Senate, Albany, 1975—, Fowler and Volker, Lancaster, NY, 1978—. Mem.: Erie County Bar Assn., Eagles, Moose, Elks. Republican. Roman Catholic. Home: 92 Center Dr Depew NY 14043-1706 Office: Rm 427 State Capitol Albany NY 12247 also: 5441 Broadway Lancaster NY 14086-2123 Office Phone: 716-685-4805. Business E-Mail: volker@senate.state.ny.us.

VOLKERS, NANCY ELAINE, writer; b. Williamson, NY, Sept. 26, 1968; d. Stewart William Volkers and Carolyn Ruth Sparks, Dorothy Mae Wilson (Stepmother); m. Matthew Allan Taylor, June 19, 2000; children: Sascha Carolyn Taylor, Zoe Mae Taylor. BA in Biology, Drew U., Madison, NJ, 1990; MA in Communication and Journalism, Stanford U., Calif., 1991. Comm. mgr. Aetna Inc., Blue Bell, Pa., 2000—; publs. dir. U. Md., Balt., 1998—99; asst. dir. pub. affairs Johns Hopkins Children's Ctr., Balt., 1997—98; press officer, writer Nat. Cancer Inst., Bethesda, Md., 1991—94; assoc. news editor Jour. Nat. Cancer Inst., Bethesda, 1992; freelance writer and editor Fairfax, Va., 1999—. Contbr. articles to profl. and Internet publs. Fellow, Stanford U., 1990—91; scholar, Drew U., 1986—90. Mem.: DC Sci. Writers Assn., Nat. Assn. Sci. Writers, Vt. Playwright's Cir., Phi Beta Kappa. Avocations: running, sewing, bicycling, quilting, playwriting. Home Phone: 802-849-9290; Office Phone: 802-849-9290. Personal E-mail: nancyvolkers@gmail.com.

VOLKHARDT, JOHN MALCOLM, retired food products executive; b. Chester, Pa., Apr. 13, 1917; s. George Thomas and Evelyn (Mitchell) V.; m. Linda J. Volkhardt; children: Michael, Jacqueline, Janet, Dana. AB cum laude, Brown U., 1939. Product mgr. Vick Chem. Co., NYC, 1939-48; gen. mgr. Northam Warren Co., Stamford, Conn., 1948-56, Rit div. Best Foods Co., NYC, 1956-58; with Best Foods div. CPC Internat. Inc., Englewood Cliffs, N.J., 1958-78, exec. v.p., 1968-71, pres., 1971-78; pres. North Am. div. CPC Internat. and exec. v.p. CPC Internat., 1978-82, group v.p., 1979; v.p. CPC, 1971-78, dir., 1977-82; pres., chmn. Full Circle Corp., Moss Creek, 1985-91; pres. Water Oak Utility, 1985-91. Dir. Storm Eye Inst., 2002—05. Chmn. bd. Keep Am. Beautiful, Inc., 1979-82, chmn. bd. trustees, 1982. Recipient Herbert Hoover award Nat. Assn. Wholesale Grocers Am.; honoree Nat. Jewish Hosp., 1976. Mem. Phi Beta Kappa.

VOLKMAN, ALVIN, retired physician, research scientist, educator; b. Bklyn., June 10, 1926; s. Henry Phillip and Sarah Lucille (Silverstein) V.; m. Winifred Joan Grinnell, June 12, 1947 (div. Aug. 1967); children: Karl Frederick, Nicholas James, Rebecca Jane Evans, Margaret Rose Werrell, Deborah Ann Falls; m. Carol Ann Fishel, Jan 26, 1973 (dec. Sept. 1992); 1 child, Natalie Fishel; 1 stepchild, Jeffrey C. Moore; m. A. Suzanne Hiss, Oct. 6, 1997. BS, Union Coll., 1947; MD, U. Buffalo, 1951; D in Philosophy, U. Oxford, Eng., 1963. Diplomate Nat. Bd. Med. Examiners, Am. Bd. Pathology. Intern Mt. Sinai Hosp., Cleve., 1951-52; rsch. fellow dept. anatomy Western Res. U. Sch. Medicine, 1952-54; resident, then sr. resident, then asst. in pathology Peter Bent Brigham Hosp., Boston, 1956-60; asst. prof. pathology Columbia U. Coll. Physicians and Surgeons, 1960-66; asst. mem., then assoc. mem. Trudeau Inst., Saranac Lake, NY, 1966-67; prof. dept. pathology East Carolina U. Sch. Medicine, Greenville, NC, 1977—, acting chmn. dept. pathology, 1989-90, assoc. dean for rsch. and grad. studies, 1989-95, prof. emeritus, 1995—, ret., 1999. Mem. NIH study sect. immunological scis., 1975-79, chmn., 1977-79. Contbr. articles to sci. jours. Served to lt. USNR, 1954-56. Am. Cancer Soc. scholar, 1961-63, Arth and Rheumat Found. fellow, 1952-54. Mem. AAAS, Am. Soc. Investigative Pathology, Am. Assn. Immunologists, Am. Soc. Hematology, Reticuloendothelial Soc., Am. Soc. Microbiologists, N.Y. Acad. Scis., Soc. Leukocyte Biology (hon. life). Personal E-mail: alvolk@suddenlink.net.

VOLKMAR, FRED ROBERT, psychiatrist, educator, director; b. Highland, Ill., Mar. 26, 1950; s. Fred Harwood and Ella Josephine (Smith) Volkmar; m. Elizabeth Anne Wiesner, Sept. 2, 1984; children: Lucy Amelia, Emily Louisa. BS, U. Ill., Urbana-Champaign, 1972; MA, MD, Stanford U., Calif., 1976. Diplomate Am. Bd. Psychiatry and Neurology. Resident psychiatry Stanford U., Calif., 1976—80; fellow child psychiatry Yale U., New Haven, 1980—82; asst. prof. Child Study Ctr., 1982—88, assoc. prof., 1988—98, prof., 1998—, Irving B. Harris chair, 2003—, chmn., dir., chief child psychiatry Yale New Haven Hosp., 2006—. Cons. psychiatrist Benhaven Sch., New Haven, 1984—, med. dir., 1982—85; mem. sci. com. Nat. Ctr. for Clin. Infant Programs, Washington, 1985. Recipient Sandoz award, 1980, Ittelson award, Am. Psychiat. Assn., Faculty Scholar award, William T. Grant Found., 1982, Rsch. Career award, NIMH, 1983, Tarjan award, Am. Acad. Child Adolescent Psychiatry, 2007; James scholar, Laughlin fellow, 1982. Mem.: Am. Acad. Child Psychiatry, Soc. for Rsch. in Child Devel., Phi Beta Kappa. Democrat. Avocations: astronomy, photography, sailing. Office: Yale U Child Study Ctr 230 S Frontage Rd PO Box 207900 New Haven CT 06519-1124 Home Phone: 203-481-0715; Office Phone: 203-785-5759. Business E-Mail: fred.volkmar@yale.edu.

VOLKOW, NORA DOLORES, medical researcher, director; b. Mexico City, Mar. 27, 1956; m. Steven Adler. BA, Modern Am. Sch., Mexico City, 1974; MD, Nat. U. Mex., 1980; postgrad. in Psychiatry, NYU, 1980-84. Diplomate Am. Bd. Psychiatry and Neurology. Rsch. asst. Registro Nacional de Anatomia Patologica, Mexico City, 1975-76, Miles Lab. Experimental Therapeutics, Mexico City, 1977-78; intern St. Anne Psychiat. Hosp., Paris, 1979-80; residency NYU Dept. Psychiatry, 1981—84; asst. prof. U. Tex. Med. Sch., Houston, 1984-87; attending physician psychiat. unit Herman Hosp., Houston, 1985-87; assoc. scientist dept. medicine Brookhaven Nat. Lab., Upton, NY, 1987-89, assoc. chief of staff, Clinical Rsch. Ctr., 1990, dir. Nuclear Medicine, 1994—2003, dir. NIDA/DOE Imaging Ctr., 1997—2003, assoc. dir. life sciences, 1999—2003; assoc. prof. dept. psychiatry SUNY, Stony Brook, 1991—2003, assoc. dean, Sch. Med., 1997—2003; lectr., Psychiatry Dept. Columbia Univ.; dir. Nat. Inst. on Drug Abuse (NIDA), Washington, 2003—. Mem. Adv. Com. for Minority Tng. in Psychiatry, Washington, 1991—; mem. study sect. in clin. neuroscis. NIH, Washington, 1992—; elected mem., Inst. Medicine, 2000. Co-editor: Positron Emission Tomography in Schizophrenia Research, 1991. Named Innovator of the Yr., U.S. News and World Report, 2000; named one of the World's Most Influential People, TIME Mag., 2007; named to Who's Next in 2007, Newsweek, 2007; recipient Premio Robins award, U. Mex., 1978, Premio Gabino Barrera award, 1981, Laughlin fellowship, Am. Coll. Psychiatry, 1984, Scanditronix scholarship, 1985, Paul C. Aebersold award, Soc. of Nuclear Medicine, 2003. Office: Nat Inst on Drug Abuse NIH Rm 5274 6001 Executive Blvd Bethesda MD 20892-9581 *

VOLL, JOHN OBERT, history professor; b. Hudson, Wis., Apr. 20, 1936; s. Obert Frank and Ruth Olivia (Seaberg) V.; m. Sarah Lynne Potts, June 12, 1965; children: Sarah Layla, Michael Obert. AB summa cum laude, Dartmouth Coll., 1958, PhD (Ford Found. fellow), 1969; AM (Danforth fellow), Harvard U., 1960. Instr. history U. N.H., Durham, 1965-69, asst. prof., 1969-74, assoc. prof., 1974-82, prof., 1982-95, chair dept., 1988-91; prof. Georgetown U., Washington, 1995—, dep. dir. Ctr. for Muslim-Christian Understanding, 1996—2004, 2006—, dir. Ctr. for Muslim-Christian Understanding, 2004—06. Mem. history and social scis. adv. com. Coll. Bd. 1983-86, chmn. European history and world cultures achievement test com., 1985-88; tchg. fellow Harvard U., 1969. Harvard Ctr. for Middle Eastern, Studies Vist. Com., 2003-05 Author: Historical Dictionary of the Sudan, 1978, 2nd edit., 1992, Islam Continuity and Change in the Modern World, 2nd edit., 1994; (with others) The Sudan: Unity and Diversity, 1985, Eighteenth Century Renewal and Reform in Islam, 1987, Sudan: State and Society in Crisis, 1991, Islam and Democracy, 1996, Makers of Contemporary Islam, 2001; contbr. articles to profl. jours. Mem. bd. Ecumenical Ministry U. N.H., 1974-78, pres., 1975-77; chmn. social action Durham Cmty. Ch., 1974-75, mem. ch. coun., 1977-78, deacon, 1986—. Sheldon traveling fellow, 1960-61, U. N.H. summer fellow, 1969, 89, NEH fellow, 1971-72, Fulbright faculty rsch. abroad fellow, 1978-79, Inst. Advanced Studies fellow Hebrew U., 1984-85; recipient Egyptian Presdl. medal, 1991. Mem. Am. Coun. Learned Socs. (del. 1989-96, del. exec. com. 1989-92, bd. dirs. 1990-92), New England Hist. Assn. (sec. 1975-78, v.p. 1981, pres. 1982), Sudan Studies Assn. (bd. dirs. 1981-82, co-exec. dir. 1990-94), N.H. Coun. on World Affairs (bd. dirs. 1978-95), World History Assn. (bd. dirs. 2005—), Am. Hist. Assn. (chmn. program com. 1999), Mid. East Studies Assn. (bd. dirs. 1987-89, pres. 1992-93), Am. Coun. for Study of Islamic Socs. (bd. dirs. 1989—, v.p. 1989-91), N.H. Humanities Coun. (bd. dirs. 1991-95). Mem. United Ch. of Christ. Home: 4000 Cathedral Ave NW Apt 652B Washington DC 20016-5205 Office: Ctr Muslim Christian Understanding Georgetown U Washington DC 20057-0001 Office Phone: 202-687-8375. E-mail: vollj@georgetown.edu.

VOLLACK, LIA, broadcast executive; Joined Sony Pictures Entertainment, 1997, sr. v.p., 1999—2000, exec. v.p., 2000, pres. worldwide music Columbia Pictures, 2002—. Named one of top women in music, Billboard, 2005, 100 Most Powerful Women in Entertainment, Hollywood Reporter, 2006. Achievements include becoming first female theatrical sound designer on Broadway. Office: Columbia Pictures 10202 West Washington Blvd Culver City CA 90232 Office Phone: 310-244-4000. Office Fax: 310-244-2626. E-mail: lia_vollack@spe.sony.com. *

VOLLBRACHT, MICHAEL, apparel designer, illustrator; b. Quincy, Ill., 1947; Grad., Parsons Sch. of Design, 1969. Designer Geoffrey Beene, 1969—71, Donald Brooks, 1971—73; illustrator Henri Bendel, 1973—75, Bloomingdales, 1975—80; designer, owner Michael Vollbracht Inc., 1980—85; designer Bill Blass Ltd., 2003—. Author: Nothing Sacred, 1985, 2d edit., 2000, Bill Blassan American Designer, 2002. Recipient Norman Norell award, J.C. Penney award, Coty award, 1980. Office: Bill Blass Ltd 550 7th Ave New York NY 10018 Office Phone: 212-221-6660.

VOLLEN, ROBERT JAY, lawyer; b. Chgo., Jan. 23, 1940; s. Ben N. and Rose (Belonsky) V.; m. Judith Paula Spector, Aug. 12, 1961; children: Steven, Neil, Jennifer. AB, U. Mich., 1961; JD, U. Chgo., 1964. Bar: Ill. 1964, D.C. 1965, U.S. Supreme Ct. 1975. Atty. appellate sect. Civil Div., U.S. Dept. Justice, Washington, 1964-65; asso. firm Schiff Hardin & Waite,

Chgo., 1965-70, partner firm, 1971-72; gen. counsel BPI (Bus. and Profl. People for Pub. Interest), Chgo., 1972-83; ptnr. Schwartz & Freeman, Chgo., 1983-87. Mem. vis. com. U. Chgo. Law Sch., 1978—81. Mem. ABA (ho. of dels. 1974-76), Chgo. Coun. Lawyers (gov. 1972-76, 79-81). Home: 2 Kingswood Ct Deerfield IL 60015-1912 E-mail: rvollen@ameritech.net.

VOLLMER, CHARLES MAHLON, JR., surgeon; b. Meadowbrook, Pa., July 25, 1967; s. Charles Mahlon and Judith Ann Vollmer; m. Beth Lucile Krankel, May 20, 1995; 3 children. BA, U. NC, Chapel Hill, 1989; MD, Jefferson Med. Coll., Phila., 1994. Diplomate Am. Bd. Surgery, 2004. Intern, resident Barnes Jewish Hosp., Washington U., St. Louis, 1994—2001; fellow HPB and transplantation surgery U. Toronto, Canada, 2001—03; asst. prof. surgery med. sch. Harvard U., Boston, 2003—; attending surgeon Beth Israel Deaconess Med. Ctr., Boston, 2003—. Contbr. articles to profl. jours. Adv. Nat. Pancreas Found., Boston, 2004—07. Named Eagle Scout, Boy Scouts of Am., 1980. Fellow: ACS; mem.: Soc. Surgery Alimentary Tract, Alpha Omega Alpha. Conservative. Lutheran. Office: Beth Israel Deaconess Medical Center 330 Brookline Ave Stoneman 9 Boston MA 02215 Office Phone: 617-667-2633.

VOLLRATH, FREDERICK E., human resources specialist, career officer; BBA in Mgmt., U. Miami; MA in Pers. Mgmt./Adminstrn., Cen. Mich. U.; grad., U.S. Army Command/Gen. Staff, U.S. Army War Coll. Commd. 2d lt. U.S. Army, 1963, chief pers. mgmt. sect., mil. pers. divsn. Off. Adj. Gen. Vietnam, 1967—68; chief pers. svcs. divsn., then dep. adjutant gen. 4th Adjutant Gen. Co., 4th Infantry Divsn., Ft. Carson, Colo., 1972—74; adjutant gen., dep. chief of staff 4th Infantry Divsn. Ft. Carson, 1977—80; ret. U.S. Army, 1998; dir. pers. svc. support, enlisted pers. mgmt. 1st pers. cmd. U.S. Army Europe and 7th Army, Germany, 1981-84, dep. comdr. 1st pers. command, 1986-88; comdg. gen. U.S. Army Pers. Info. Sys. Command, Alexandria, Va., 1988; dir. mil. pers. mgmt. Office of Dep. Chief of Staff Pers. U.S. Army, Washington, 1995-96, dep. chief of staff for pers., 1996-98, advanced through grades to lt. gen., 1996; corp. v.p. human resources Computer Sci. Corp., El Segundo, Calif. Decorated Meritorious Svc. medal with 4 oak leaf clusters. Office: Computer Sci Corp 2100 E Grand Ave El Segundo CA 90245

VOLLUM, ROBERT BOONE, management consultant; b. Abington, Pa., Sept. 13, 1933; s. Charles Milton and Marion (Yocum) V.; m. Gayle Lorraine Timmerman, July 8, 1956; children: Robert Boone III, Jeffrey Charles. BS in Engring. and Sci., U.S. Naval Acad., 1955. Sr. cons., group leader Stevenson, Jordan & Harrison, Inc., NYC, 1959—65; asst. to pres., plant supt., sales engr. W.L. Gore & Assocs., Inc., Newark, Del., 1965—69; gen. mgr. Philmont Pressed Steel subs. Gulf & Western Industries, Inc., Bethayres, Pa., 1969—72; gen. mgr. Air Shields divsn. Narco Sci. Industries, Inc., Hatboro, Pa., 1972—75; pres. Advanced Airflow Tech., Inc., Warminster, Pa., 1975—76, R.B. Vollum & Assocs., Huntingdon Valley, Pa., 1986—, RBV Mktg. Inc., Willow Grove, Pa., 1992—; chmn. bd. dirs., CEO SFM Technologies, Willow Grove, 1994—. Prin. mfg. cons. Sperry Corp., Blue Bell, Pa., 1976-84; dir. cons. Creative Output, Inc., Milford, Conn., 1984-86; spkr. in field. Contbr. articles to profl. jours. Bd. dirs. Upper Moreland Little League, 1965-76. Served to lt. USN, 1955-59. Fellow Am. Prodn. and Inventory Control Soc. (chpt. pres. 1984-85); mem. soc. Mfg. Engrs (sr. mem.), Computer and Automated Systems Assn. (sr. mem.). Republican. Episcopalian. Home: 525 Overlook Ave Willow Grove PA 19090-2818 Office: PO Box 206 Huntingdon Valley PA 19006-0206 Home Phone: 215-659-8580; Office Phone: 215-784-9011. Personal E-mail: rbvollum@rbvollum.com.

VOLLWEILER, CHERYL P., lawyer; b. NYC, Dec. 4, 1963; BA, Brandeis U., 1985; JD, Hofstra U., 1988. Bar: NY 1989, NJ 1989, US Dist. Ct. Ea. Dist. NY, US Dist. Ct. So. Dist. NY, US Dist. Ct. Dist. NJ. Ptnr. Wilson, Elser, Moskowitz, Edelman & Dicker LLP, NYC. Mem.: ABA, Internat. Alliance Exec. & Profl. Women (bd. dirs.), Assn. Profl. Ins. Women (bd. dirs.), NY State Bar Assn. (co-chair toxic tort com.). Office: Wilson Elser Moskowitz Edelman & Dicker LLP 150 E 42nd St 23rd Fl New York NY 10017-5639 Office Phone: 212-490-3000 ext. 2674. Office Fax: 212-490-3038. Business E-Mail: vollweilerc@wemed.com.

VOLNER, IAN D., lawyer; b. NYC, June 2, 1940; BA, Colgate Univ., 1962; JD (LLB), Columbia Univ., 1965. Bar: NY 1967, DC 1970. Staff atty. FCC Rev. Bd., 1968—70; ptnr., Advertising Marketing & New Media, Communications practices Venable LLP, Washington. Adj. prof. NY Law Sch., 1981—88, Catholic Univ. Am., Univ. Md. Mem.: ABA, Fed. Comm. Bar Assn., NY State Bar Assn., DC Bar Assn., Phi Beta Kappa. Office: Venable LLP 575 7th St NW Washington DC 20004 Office Phone: 202-344-4814. Office Fax: 202-344-8300. Business E-Mail: idvolner@venable.com.

VOLPE, ANGELO ANTHONY, retired academic administrator, chemist, educator; b. Nov. 8, 1938; s. Bernard Charles and Serafina (Martorana) V.; m. Jennette Murray, May 15, 1965. BS, Bklyn. Coll., 1959; MS, U. Md., 1962, PhD, 1966; M in Engring. (hons.), Stevens Inst. Tech., 1975. Rsch. chemist USN Ordnance Lab., Silver Spring, Md., 1961-66; from asst. prof. to prof. chemistry Stevens Inst. Tech., Hoboken, NJ, 1966-77; chmn. dept. chemistry East Carolina U., Greenville, NC, 1977-80, dean Coll. Arts and Scis., 1980-83, vice chancellor for acad. affairs, 1983-87; pres. Tenn. Technol. U., Cookeville, 1987-2000, ret., 2000, pres. emeritus, 2000—. Adj. prof. textile chem. N.C. State U., Raleigh, 1978-82; guest lect. Plastics Inst. Am., Hoboken, 1967-82. Contbr. articles to profl. jours. Recipient Ednl. Svc. award Plastics Inst. Am., 1973; named Freygang Outstanding Tchr., Stevens Inst. Tech., 1975. Mem. Am. Chem. Soc., Tenn. Acad. Scis., Sigma Xi, Phi Kappa Phi. Democrat. Roman Catholic. Avocations: golf, reading. Home: 734 Loweland Rd Cookeville TN 38501-2888 Office Phone: 931-372-3220. Personal E-mail: avolpe@tntech.edu.

VOLPE, DORIS, artist; b. Rockford, Ill., Dec. 22, 1930; d. August and Grace Adelaide Meenen; m. Samuel Volpe, Dec. 26, 1950 (dec. July 1994); children: Michael, Margaret. Group exhbns. include Art Inst. Chgo., Deer Path Gallery, Lake Forest, Ill., Gregoire Galleries, N.Y.C., Rhoda Sande Gallery, N.Y.C., Yolanda Kelly Gallery, Chgo., Peoria (Ill.) Regional Gallery, Old Orchard Shopping Ctr., Skokie, Ill., New Horizons, Chgo., Lake County Mus., Wauconda, Ill., Open Spectrum, Libertyville, Ill., Coll. Lake County, Grayslake, Ill., Neville-Sargent Gallery, Chgo., Sonnenschein Gallery, Lake Forest, Chgo. Botanic Gardens, Galleria Renata, Chgo., Clementi House Gallery, London, Millburn (Ill.) Gallery, Art in the Barn, Barrington, Ill., Art Expo, Lake Forest, Plaza del Lago, Wilmette, Ill., The Artists' Den, Valparaiso, Ind., Heirloom Gallery, Wilmette, North Shore Art League Fall Festival, Later Impressions, Chgo., Gallery 203, Chgo. Fountain Square, Evanston IL, Arts in Northbrook, Northbrook, Cantigny Fine Art Festival, Wheaton IL; solo exhbns. include Covenant Club, Chgo., 1st Fed. Savs. and Loan, Chgo., Lake County Court House, Waukegan, Ill., Kemper Group, Long Grove, Ill., The Stanley Gallery, Norfolk, Va., Univ. Club, Chgo., Chgo. Cultural Ctr. Avocations: gardening, art league activities.

VOLPE, EDMOND L(ORIS), retired college president; b. New Haven, Nov. 16, 1922; s. Joseph D. and Rose (Maisano) V.; m. Rose Conte, May 20, 1950; children: Rosalind, Lisa. AB, U. Mich., 1943; MA, Columbia U., 1947, PhD, 1954. Instr. NYU, 1949-54; mem. faculty CCNY, 1954-74, prof. English, 1968-74, chmn. dept., 1964-70; pres. Richmond Coll., 1974-76, Coll. S.I., NY, 1976-94; ret. Fulbright prof. Am. lit., France, 1960-61. Author: A Reader's Guide to William Faulkner, 1964, The Comprehensive College, 2001, A Reader's Guide to William Faulkner: The Novels Reissued, 2003, A Reader's Guide to William Faulkner: The Short Stories, 2004; also anthologies and coll. text books.; co-editor: Eleven Modern Short Novels. Bd. dirs. S.I. United Way, 1975—, S.I. coun. Boy Scouts Am., 1977-84, S.I. Doctors Hosp., 1977-78, Snug Harbor Cultural Ctr., 1978-83, St. Vincent's Hosp., 1979—; mem. N.Y.C. Mayor's Commn. on Bias, 1986-88. With AUS, 1943-46. Recipient Commendatore Order of Merit, Republic of Italy, Cmty. Svc. award Italian Club S.I., Humanitarian award S.I. Jewish Found. Sch., Mills G. Skinner award S.I. br. N.Y. Urban League, Christopher Columbus award Columbian Assn. Bd. Edn., Disting. Cmty. Svc. award YMCA, Cmty. Svc. award S.I. Women's divsn. Am. Com. on Italian Migration, Outstanding Achievement award Guiseppe Mazzini Lodge of Sons of Italy; named Educator of Yr. Am. Legion Richmond County. Mem. MLA, Am. Studies Assn., Assn. Dept. English (exec. com. 1969-71), Am. Assn. State Colls. and Univs. (task force ednl. opportunites for the aging, rsch. and liason com., com. internat. programs, health affairs com.), Am. Assn. Higher Edn., Am. Assn. Colls. for Tchr. Edn., Am. Assn. Univ. Profs., Am. Coun. Edn., Am. Studies Assn., Assn. Colls. and Univs. N.Y., Assn. Depts. of English (nat. exec. com.), Coll. English Assn. (nat. bd. dirs.), Consortium Internat. Programs, Inst. Internat. Edn., Inc., Mid. States Assn. Colls. and Schs., Andiron Club N.Y. (pres. 1972-75).

VOLPE, JOSEPH, Canadian government official; b. Monteleone, Puglia, Italy, Sept. 21, 1947; married; 4 children. MA in Edn., U. Toronto, Can. Mem. Can. Parliament, 1988—; parliamentary sec. to the min. health Govt. Can., 1996—98, chair standing com. on health, 1998—99, chair standing com. on natural resources and govt. ops., 1999—2000, min. human resources and skills devel., 2003—. Office: House of Commons Ottawa ON Canada K1A 0A6

VOLPE, PETER ANTHONY, surgeon; b. Columbus, Ohio, Dec. 17, 1936; s. Peter Anthony and Jeanette Katherine (Volz) V.; m. Suzanne Stephens, Sept. 5, 1959; children: John David, Michael Charles; m. Kathleen Ann Townsend, Mar. 28, 1978; 1 child, Mark Christopher; m. Theresa Ann Morse, Aug. 27, 2000. BA cum laude, Ohio State U., 1958, MD summa cum laude, 1961. Diplomate Am. Bd. Surgery, Am. Bd. Colon and Rectal Surgery (pres. 1988). Pvt. practice, San Francisco, 1969—; sr. ptnr. Volpe, Chui, Abel, Yee, Sternberg, San Francisco, 1987—; clin. prof. surgery U. Calif., San Francisco, 1995—. Asst. clin. prof. surgery U. Calif., San Francisco, 1972-95; chmn. dept. surgery St. Mary's Hosp. and Med. Ctr., San Francisco, 1978-90. Contbr. articles to profl. jours. Lt. USN, 1962—64. Fellow ACS (bd. govs. 1988-94), Am. Soc. Colon and Rectal Surgeons (treas. 1985-89, pres. 1990); mem. San Francisco Surg. Soc., San Francisco Med. Soc. Office: Volpe Chiu Abel and Yee Sternberg 3838 California St San Francisco CA 94118-1522 Office Phone: 415-668-0411.

VOLPE, RALPH PASQUALE, retired insurance company executive; b. Souderton, Pa., Sept. 20, 1936; s. Pasquale S. and Katie M. (Hartzell) Volpe; m. Marie F. Romano, Feb. 6, 1962; children: William, Anthony, Lynda. BA in Polit. Sci., Pa. State U., 1963. Claim cons. Aetna Life & Casualty Co., King of Prussia, Pa., 1964-97; litig. cons. Hartford Ins., King of Prussia, 1998—2003; ret., 2003. Bd. suprs. Upper Merion Twp., 1974—79, 1982—87, 1994—2005, chmn. bd. suprs., 1984, 1986—87, 1996—97, 2003—05, vice chmn. bd. suprs., 1985, 1995; 2d v.p. Montgomery County Assn. Twp. Ofcls., 1995—97, pres., 1997—99; exec. bd. Greater Valley Forge Transp. Mgmt. Assn., 1994—2003; study commn. Upper Merion Govt., 1974; exec. com. Rt. 202, 1994—2003; chmn. blue ribbon panel Montgomery County Waste Sys. Authority, 1997—98; sec. Montgomery County Assn. Twp. Ofcls., 2007—; chmn. Montgomery County Dem. Campaign, 1975, Upper Merion Dems., 1980—81. With US Army, 1959—61. Recipient Good Govt. award, Upper Merion Jaycees, 1977, Excellence in Govt. Svc. award, King of Prussia C. of C., 1997, Earth Day award, Upper Merion Twp., 2004, Friend of Libr. award, Upper Merion Twp. Libr., 2005, Pub. Sector award, Greater Valley Forge Transp. Mgmt. Assn., 2005. Mem.: Southeastern Assn. Twp. Ofcls., Pa. State Assn. Twp. Suprs. (chmn. rules com. 1997—2000, chmn. resolution-legislation com. 2002—05, 17th Ann. Pres.'s Leadership award 2006), Montgomery County Assn. Twp. Ofcls. (life), Chapel Four Chaplains (Legion of Honor), Valley Forge Hist. Soc., Valley Forge Order Sons of Italy Am., Optimists. Republican. Roman Catholic. Home: 240 Strawberry Ln King Of Prussia PA 19406 Personal E-mail: ralphvolpe@comcast.net.

VOLPE, RICHARD GERARD, insurance accounts executive, consultant; b. Sewickley, Pa., Apr. 10, 1950; s. Ralph Carl and Louise P. (Cosentino) V.; m. Janet Lynn Henne, May 10, 1986; 1 child, John Ralph. BA, Vanderbilt U., Nashville, 1972. CPCU 1978; fellow Life Underwriting Tng. Coun. Trainee, asst. mgr. Hartford Ins. Group, Conn., 1973-74; v.p. sales Roy E. Barker Co., Franklin, Tenn., 1975-80; asst. v.p., product mgr. comml. ins. Nat. Farmers Union Ins., Denver, 1980-82; prin. R.G. Volpe & Assocs, Denver, 1982-85; acct. exec. Millers Mut. Ins., Aurora, Colo., 1985-89; pres, CEO AccuSure, Inc., Arvada, Colo., 1989—93; acct. exec. J.R. Misken, Inc., Denver, 1990-92, The Prudential, Colorado Springs, 1992-2001; sr. fin. rep. Principal Fin., Denver, 2001—04; mng. gen. ptnr. Planning Solutions Colo., LLC, 2004—. Edn. chmn. Insurors Tenn., Nashville, 1978-79; new candidate chmn. Mid-Tenn. chpt. CPCU, Nashville, 1979-80; cons. Bennett Nat. Bank Colo., mktg. mgr., 1989-90; cons. Colo. Plains Ins., Inc., 1987-90. Contbr. articles to profl. jours. Dem. chmn. Williamson County, Tenn., 1979; campaign mgr. legis., Franklin, 1979-98; legis. chmn. Centennial Life Underwriters, 1998, 2000, 02; del. Rep. State Caucus, 1998, 2000; mem. dist. com. Arapaho Dist., Denver Area coun. Boy Scouts Am., 2000. Named Hon. Col. Gov. Tenn., 1979; recipient Hertiage Soc., Boy Scouts of Am., 2004. Fellow Life Underwriters Tng. Coun.; mem. Soc. Property and Casualty Underwriters, Centennial Life Underwriters, Million Dollar Roundtable (qualifying mem.), South Metro Denver C. of C., Order of the Arrow, KC. Roman Catholic. Avocations: skiing, camping, hiking, bicycling, sailing. Home: 10908 Snow Cloud Trl Littleton CO 80125-9210 Office: 10908 Snow Cloud Tr Littleton CO 80120 Personal E-mail: rgvolpe1@msn.com.

VOLPE, THOMAS J., corporate financial executive; b. Bklyn., Dec. 22, 1935; s. John G and Josephine (Fontana) Volpe; m. Anita Mazzei, Nov. 24, 1957; children: Lisa, Lori, John. BS in Econs., Bklyn. Coll., 1957; MBA, CCNY, 1965; degree (hon.), St. Francis Coll., 1997. Mgr. Deloitte Haskins & Sells, NYC, 1957-70; v.p., treas. Colgate Palmolive Co., NYC, 1970-85; sr. v.p., fin. ops. Interpublic Group of Cos., NYC, 1986—2001; sr. advisor Babcock & Brown, NYC, 2001—. Bd. dirs. Am. Tech. Ceramics, e-Smart Techs., Rochdale Investment Trust. Trustee St. Francis Coll., Bklyn., 1971—2001, chmn. emeritus; trustee Englewood Hosp. Found. and Hosp. Sys., NJ; bd. mem. Urban Glass. Mem.: NY State Soc CPAs (comt chmn), Fin Execs Inst (comt chmn, pres NY chpt 1995). Office: Babcock & Brown 885 Second Ave New York NY 10017 Office Phone: 212-230-0724. E-mail: tomv@babcockbrown.com.

VOLPERT, RICHARD SIDNEY, lawyer; b. Cambridge, Mass., Feb. 16, 1935; s. Samuel Abbot and Julia (Fogel) V.; m. Marcia Flaster, June 11, 1958; children: Barry, Sandy, Linda, Nancy. BA, Amherst Coll., 1956; LL.B. (Stone scholar), Columbia U., 1959. Bar: Calif. bar 1960. Atty. firm O'Melveny & Myers, Los Angeles, 1959-86, ptnr. LA, 1967-86, Skadden, Arps, Slate, Meagher & Flom, LA, 1986-95, Munger, Tolles & Olson, LA, 1995—. Pub. Jewish Jour. of Los Angeles, 1985-87. Editor, chmn.: Los Angeles Bar Jour, 1965, 66, 67, Calif. State Bar Jour, 1972-73. Chmn. cmty. rels. com. Jewish Fedn.-Coun. L.A., 1977-80; bd. dirs. Jewish Fedn.-Coun. Greater L.A., 1976-99, v.p., 1978-81; pres. Los Angeles County Natural History Mus. Found., 1978-84, trustee, 1974—, chair bd. dirs., 1992-97, pres., bd. govs., 1997—; chmn. bd. councilors U. So. Calif. Law Ctr., 1979-85; vice chmn. Nat. Jewish Cmty. Rels. Adv. Coun., 1981-84, mem. exec. com., 1978-85; bd. dirs. U. Judaism, 1973-89, bd. govs., 1973-89; bd. dirs. Valley Beth Shalom, Encino, Calif., 1964-88; mem. capital program major gifts com. Amherst Coll., 1978-86; bd. dirs., mem. exec. com. L.A. Wholesale Produce Market Devel. Corp., 1978-95, v.p., 1981-93, pres. 1993-96; mem. exec. bd. L.A. chpt. Am. Jewish Com., 1967—, pres., 1999-2002, nat bd. govs., 2000-, nat. v.p., 2006-; vice-chmn. Los Angeles County Econ. Devel. Coun., 1978-81; bd. dirs. Jewish Cmty. Found., 1981—, Brandeis-Bardin Inst., 1995-2000, L.A. Chamber Orch., 2002-04; mem. Pacific S.W. regional bd. Anti Defamation League B'nai B'rith, 1964—. Named Man of Year, 1978 Fellow Am. Bar Found.; mem. Los Angeles County Bar Assn. (trustee 1968-70, chmn. real property sect. 1974-75), Los Angeles County Bar Found. (trustee 1977-80, 96-99), Calif. Bar Assn. (com. on adminstrn. justice 1973-76), Am. Coll. Real Estate Lawyers (bd. govs. 1996-99), Anglo-Am. Real Property Inst. (treas. 1995-98), Amherst Club of So. Calif. (dir. 1968-85, pres. 1972-73). Jewish. Home: 16055 Royal Oak Rd Encino CA 91436-3913 Office: Munger Tolles & Olson 355 S Grand Ave 35th Fl Los Angeles CA 90071-1560 Office Phone: 213-683-9101. Business E-Mail: richard.volpert@mto.com.

VOLPI, MICHELE, chemicals executive; b. Florence, Italy; B in Bus. Adminstrn., Bocconi U., Milan, MBA. Cert. Six Sigma Green Belt. Mgmt. cons. The Boston Consulting Grp.; European mktg. dir., structured products bus. Gen. Electric Co., gen. mgr., Polymershapes Bus. Unit; global mgr., Assembly Bus. H.B. Fuller Co., 2002—04, grp. pres., gen. mgr., Global Adhesives grp., 2004—06, pres., CEO, 2006—. Office: HB Fuller Company 1200 Willow Lake Blvd Saint Paul MN 55110-5101 Office Phone: 651-236-5095. Office Fax: 651-236-5898. *

VOLPI, MIKE (MICHELANGELO A. VOLPI), internet television service company executive; b. Milan, 1967; BSME, MSME, MBA, Stanford U. Former product devel. engr. and product mktg. mgr. optoelectronics divsn. Hewlett Packard; v.p. bus. devel. Cisco Systems, Inc., San Jose, Calif., 1994—99, sr. v.p. bus. devel. and alliances, 1999—2000, chief strategy officer, 2000—02, chief strategy officer, v.p. internet switching and svcs. group, sr. v.p. routing tech. group, 2002—07; CEO Joost, 2007—. Bd. dirs. Equinix, Inc., TIBCO Software, Opsware Inc., Skype, 2004—05. *

VOLTZ, STERLING ERNEST, physical chemist, researcher; b. Phila., Apr. 17, 1921; s. Harry John and Gertrude Irene (Derr) V.; m. Betty Morgan, Nov. 6, 1943; children: Sandra Elizabeth, Karen Lee. BA, Temple U., 1943, MA, 1947, PhD, 1952. Rsch. chemist Houdry Process Corp., Linwood, Pa., 1951-58; group leader Sun Oil Co., Marcus Hook, Pa., 1958-60; supervising engr. GE, Phila., 1960-62, cons. liaison scientist Valley Forge, Pa., 1962-68; rsch. assoc. Mobil Rsch. & Devel. Corp., Paulsboro, NJ, 1968-80, adminstrv., 1980-86; pvt. practice Media, Pa., 1986—. Contbr. articles to profl. jours. including Jour. Phys. Chem., Jour. Am. Chem. Soc., Jour. Organic Chemistry, Analytical Chemistry, Jour. Soc. Automotive Engrs., Jour. Chem. and Engring. Data, Jour. Am. Inst. Chem. Engrs. and others. Lt. (j.g.) USN, 1943-46, ETO. Mem. AAAS, Am. Chem. Soc. (Phila. sect.), Catalysis Soc., Catalysis Club. Phila. (sec.-treas., chmn., dir. 1957-60), Am. Legion, Disabled Am. Vets., Sigma Xi. Achievements include 23 patents for Simulation of Catalytic Cracking Process, for Compatible Mixtures of Coal Liquids and Petroleum Based Fuels, for Reactivation of Automotive Exhaust Oxidation Catalyst, for Increasing Antiknock Value of Olefinic Gasoline, for Preparation of Aromatic Hydrocarbons, for Process for Dehydrocyclizing Heterocyclic Organic Compounds, for Alumina Stabilized by Thoria to Resist Alpha Alumina Formation, for Method of Treating Chromium Oxide, others; invention of plastic dry bag; co-development of commercial methanol-to-gasoline process, of fuel cell for space power applications, including first successful operation in space flight; development of catalysts and processes for petroleum and petrochemical conversions, of electronic apparatus to measure dielectric properties during oxidation reactions and establish reaction kinetics; establishment of relationship between catalytic properties, surface chemistry, and semiconductivity properties of metal oxide catalysts; research on catalytic systems for automotive emissions control including kinetic model of oxidation of carbon monoxide and hydrocarbons. Home: 6 E Glen Cir Media PA 19063-4712

VOLUSE, CHARLES RODGER, III, retired education educator; b. Balt., Oct. 14, 1943; s. Charles Rodger Jr. and Beulah (Gisriel) V.; children: Steven Michael, Andrew Craig. BS in Edn., Southwestern U., Georgetown, Tex., 1965; MEd, Boston U., 1968; EdD, U. Va., 1973. Prof. grad. reading edn. SUNY, Potsdam, 1973-77; assoc. dir. grad. reading program Xavier U., Cin., 1976-83, prof., 1977-80; cons. Hamilton County Office Edn., Cin., 1980—2000, activegifted and talented programs, 1985—2000. Dir. Curriculum Devel. Assocs., Cin., 1982—; cons. Hamilton County Bd. of Mental Retardation, Cin., 1983-85; prof. Coll. Mt. Joseph. Author: Adult Subvocalization Behaviors, 1973, Experiences in Language for the Learning Handicapped, 1985; creator ednl. programs. Mem. Internat. Reading Assn., Nat. Council Tchrs. of English, Nat. Council Tchrs. of Math, Ohio Valley Assn for the Talented and Gifted. Home: 594 Laurel Oaks Dr Loveland OH 45140-9119 E-mail: drcvoluse@fuse.net.

VOLZ, CHARLES HARVIE, JR., lawyer; b. Richmond, Va., Sept. 15, 1925; s. Charles Harvie and Mary V. (Mallory) V.; m. Constance A. Lewis, July 30, 1976; children: Charles Harvie III, Judith C. BS, U. Ala., 1950, JD, 1951. Bar: Ala. 1951, U.S. Dist. Ct. Ala., U.S. Ct. Appeals (5th cir.), U.S. Ct. Mil. Appeals, U.S. Ct. Appeals (11th cir.), U.S. Supreme Ct. 1962. Spl. agt. FBI, 1951; claim mgr. Allstate Ins. Co., 1952-54; claims atty. State Farm Ins. Co., 1954-57; ptnr. Roberts, Orme & Volz, Gadsen, Ala., 1957-59; sole practice Montgomery, 1961-63; asst. dir. Dept. Indsl. Rels., Ala., 1959-63; ptnr. Volz, Capouano, Wampold & Prestwood, 1963-84, Volz & Volz, 1984-95, Volz, Prestwood & Hanan, 1995—2001; of counsel Prestwood and Assocs., 2001—. Note editor Ala. Law Rev., 1950-51. Campaign dir. March of Dimes, 1958, Am. Cancer Soc., 1967; exec. sec. Gov.'s Com. on Employment of Physically Handicapped, 1959-62; mem. Pres.'s Com. on Employment of Physically Handicapped, 1959-62; pres., bd. dirs. Montgomery chpt. Am. Cancer Soc. 2nd lt. USAAF, 1943-45. Recipient Outstanding Service award Am. Cancer Soc., 1967 Mem. ATLA (state committeeman 1973-75), Am. Arbitration Assn. (mem. nat. panel), ABA, Ala. Bar Assn., Ala. Trial Lawyers Assn., Farrah Law Soc., Montgomery Country Club, Masons, Kiwanis, Phi Alpha Delta. Methodist. Home and Office: 1638 Cobblestone Ct Montgomery AL 36117-1713

VOLZ, WILLIAM HARRY, lawyer, educator; b. Sandusky, Mich., Dec. 28, 1946; s. Harry Bender and Belva Geneva (Riehl) V. BA, Mich. State U., 1968; MA, U. Mich., 1972; MBA, Harvard U., 1978; JD, Wayne State U., 1975. Bar: mich. 1975. Atty. pvt. practice, Detroit, 1975-77; mgmt. analyst Office of Gen. Counsel, HEW, Woodlawn, Md., 1977; from asst. prof. to prof. Wayne State U., Detroit, 1978—86, prof., 1986, dean, 1986—96; dir. Ctr. for Legal Studies Wayne State U. Law Sch., 1996-97; instr. Pa. State U., Coll. Sta., 1997—. Cons. Merrill Lynch, Pierce, Fenner & Smith, N.Y.C., 1980-83, City of Detroit Law Dept., 1982, Mich. Supreme Ct., Detroit, 1981; ptnr. Mich. CPA Rev., Southfield, 1983-85; expert witness in product liability, comml. law and bus. ethics; pres. Wedgewood Group. Author: Managing a Trial, 1982; contbr. articles to legal jours.; mem. editl. bds. bus. and law jours. Internat. adv. bd. Inst. Mgmt., L'viv, Ukraine, Legal counsel Free Legal Aid Clinic, Inc., Detroit 1976-96, Shared Ministries, Detroit, 1981, Sino-Am. Tech. Exch. coun., China, 1982; chair advt. rev. panel BBB, Detroit, 1988-90; pres. Mich. Acad. Sci., Arts and Letters, 1995-96, 98-2000, bd. dirs. Common Ground, Greater Detroit Alliance Bus., Olde Custodian Fund. Mem.: ABA, Players (bd. dirs.), Amateur Medicant Soc. (commissionaire 1981—85), Harvard Bus. Sch. Club Detroit, Econ. Club Detroit, Detroit Athletic Club, Beta Alpha Psi, Alpha Kappa Psi, Golden Key. Home: 3846 Wedgewood Dr Bloomfield

Hills MI 48301-3949 Office: Wayne State U Sch Bus Adminstrn Cass Ave Detroit MI 48202 Home Phone: 248-644-1035; Office Phone: 313-577-4694. Business E-Mail: ab9241@wayne.edu.

VOM BAUR, DAPHNE DE BLOIS, artist; d. Francis Trowbridge vom Baur and Carolyn Bartlett Laskey; m. David Verner Hamilton, Sept. 3, 1973; children: Zoe Hamilton-vom Baur, Nerissa Alexandra Hamilton-vom Baur. BFA, Boston U., 1968. Fellow Atlantic Ctr. for Arts, New Smyrna Beach, Fla., 1986; mem. acquisitions com. S.C. Arts Commn., Columbia, SC, 1989—91. Vis. artist Susquehanna Studio, Union Dale, Pa., 1985—86. Exhbn., The Frye Mus., Seattle, 2002. Recipient Purchase award, S.C. State Art Collection, 1986. Mem.: Cosmos Club (mem. arts coun. 2001—05). Avocations: cross country skiing, opera, horses, painting. Office: Verner Gallery LLC 1 West Washington St PO Box2270 Middleburg VA 20118 Home Phone: 540-349-8950; Office Phone: 540-687-6875. Business E-Mail: vombaur@earthlink.net.

VOM SAAL, WALTER, psychology professor; b. NYC, Nov. 29, 1944; s. W. Rudolf and Jane (Towle) vom S.; children: Daniel, Laura, Jeffrey. BA, Columbia U., 1966; MA, McMaster U., 1967, PhD, 1969. Asst. prof. psychology Princeton (N.J.) U., 1969-74; assoc. prof. Millersville (Pa.) U., 1974-79, prof. psychology, 1979-86, assoc. v.p., 1986-89; provost and v.p. acad. affairs SUNY, Oneonta, 1989-94, acting pres. Plattsburgh, 1993-94, prof. psychology, 1989—. Named Disting. tchg. fellow Commonwealth of Pa., 1979, Disting. Tchg. chair, 1979. Mem. Phi Beta Kappa. Home: 103 Elm St Oneonta NY 13820 Office: SUNY 502 Fitzelle Hall Oneonta NY 13820

VONA, JOHN DAVID, music educator; m. Tammy Givin, July 1, 1988; children: Philip Christopher, Courtney. B in Music Edn., Ithaca Coll., NY, 1985, M in Music Edn., 1988; cert. in Advance Study, SUNY, Brockport, 1993. Cert. educator music K-12 N.Y. State Dept. Edn., 1989, sch. dist. administr. N.Y. State Dept. Edn., 1994. Dir. band Addison (N.Y.) Ctrl. Schs., 1989—2004, tchr. music, 2004—. Judge music N.Y. State Field Band Conf., 1996—; horn instr. Dansville White Sabers Drum and Bugle Corps, NY, 2007. Asst. coach basketball YMCA; asst. coach small fry football; com. chmn. Troop 61 Boy Scouts Am., Corning, NY, 2005. Named Tchr. of Yr., Addison (N.Y.) Student Coun., 2003; recipient Eagle award, Boy Scouts Am., 1980; grantee, Steuben-Alleghany BOCES, 1999. Mem.: N.Y. State Sch. Music Assn. (adjudicator 1993—), Steuben County Music Tchrs. Assn., Music Educator's Nat. Conf., Phi Mu Alpha (treas. 1983—85). Office: Addison Central Schools 7 Cleveland Drive Addison NY 14801 Home Phone: 607-936-4632; Office Phone: 607-359-2261. Business E-Mail: jvona@addison.wnyric.org.

VONADA, NICHOLAS ANDREW, information technology educator; b. Williamsport, Pa., Dec. 10, 1951; s. Richard C. Vonada, Sr. and Joan L. Vonada; m. Linda R. King, July 27, 1949; children: Nicole L., Samantha R. BS, Lycoming Coll., Pa., 1977; MEd, Lock Haven U., Pa., 1993; postgrad., Pa. State U., 2003—. Cert. NOVELL adminstr.; sys. engr., Microsoft. With Frito Lay Corp., 1977—81, Am. Home Foods, 1981—87; prof. Pa. Coll. Tech., Winspt, Pa., 1987—. Contbr. articles to profl. jours. Chmn. planning commn. Old Lycoming Township, Williamsport, Pa., 1991—97. Maj. US Army, 1971—74, with USAR, 1977—2001, ret. Mem.: Common Am. Adv. Coun., NEA, Info. Sys. Edn. Conf., Am. Educators Rsch. Conf., Am. Educators Rsch. Assn., Common Users Group (advisor 2004—). Home: 28 Aztec Ln Williamsport PA 17701 Office: Pennsylvania College Technology One College Ave Williamsport PA 17701 Office Phone: 570-326-3761 ext. 7518. Business E-Mail: nvonada@pct.edu.

VON AHN, LUIS, computer science educator, computer scientist; b. Guatemala City, Guatemala, 1978; BS in Math. (summa cum laude), Duke U., Durham, NC, 2000; MS in Computer Sci., Carnegie Mellon U., Pitts., Pa., 2003, PhD in Computer Sci., 2005. Summer intern U. Calif., Berkeley, 2001, IBM T.J. Watson Rsch. Lab, Hawthorne, NY, 2002, Microsoft Rsch., Redmond, Wash., 2004; post-doctoral fellow, computer sci. dept., Ctr. for Algorithm Adaptation Dissemination and Integration (ALADDIN) Carnegie Mellon U., Pitts., 2005—06, asst. prof., computer sci. dept., 2006—. Tchg. asst., Abstract Algebra Duke U., 1999, tchg. asst., Software Design and Implementation, 99, tchg. asst., Algorithms, 2000; tchg. asst., Great Theoretical Ideas in Computer Sci. Carnegie Mellon U., 2001, instr., Formal Languages, Automata and Computability, 05, 05, instr., Great Theoretical Ideas in Computer Sci., 06; program com. mem. Workshop on Human Interactive Proofs, 2005; invited spkr. in field. Contbr. articles to profl. jours.; invited reviewer for conferences and jours., work has been featured in news articles, TV and Radio The Discovery Channel, AP, NY Times, BBC Worldwide, CNN, USA Today, PC Mag., Slashdot, New Scientist and several others. Named one of Brilliant 10, Popular Sci. mag., 2006; Microsoft Grad. Rsch. fellowship, 2004, MacArthur Fellow, John D. and Catherine T. MacArthur Found., 2006. Achievements include patents pending in field; research includes CAPTCHAs and novel techniques for utlizing the computational abilities of humans; credited with inventing the ESP Game. Office: Computer Sci Dept Wean Hall 4121 Carnegie Mellon U 5000 Forbes Ave Pittsburgh PA 15213 Business E-Mail: biglou@cs.cmu.edu.

VON ALLMEN, DION S., mathematics educator, department chairman, mathematics professor; s. Robert L. and Barbara K. von Allmen. BS, Ind. U. SE, New Albany, 1985. Math. dept. chair Providence H.S., Clarksville, Ind., 1986—; adj. math. lectr. Ind. U. SE, New Albany, 1991—; math. instr. Bellarmine U., Louisville, 1996—. Named Outstanding Adj. Lectr., Ind. U. SE, 2000. Mem.: Mensa Internat. Office: Providence HS 707 Providence Way Clarksville IN 47129

VON ARX, DOLPH WILLIAM, food products executive; b. St. Louis, Aug. 30, 1934; s. Adolph William and Margaret Louise (Linderer) von A.; m. Sharon Joy Landolt, Dec. 21, 1957; children: Vanessa von Arx Gilvarg, Eric S., Valerie L. BSBA, Washington U., St. Louis, 1961; LHD, St. Augustine Coll., 1988. Account exec. Compton Advt., NYC, 1961-64; v.p. mktg. Ralston Purina Co., St. Louis, 1964-69; exec. v.p. mktg. Gillette Personal Care Div., Chgo., 1969-72; exec. v.p. gen. mgmt. group T.J. Lipton Inc., Englewood Cliffs, NJ, 1973-87; pres., chief exec. officer R.J. Reynold Tobacco Co., Winston-Salem, NC, 1987-88; chmn., chief exec. officer Planters LifeSavers Co., Winston-Salem, 1988-91. Bd. dirs. Internat. Multi Food, Mpls., Hosp. Ptnrs. Am., Charlotte, N.C., No. Trust Fla. Corp., Miami, Cree Rsch. Inc., Durham, N.C., Ruby Tuesday Inc., BMC Fund Inc., Hosp. Ptnrs. Am., Charlotte, NC, Aquascent, Inc.; chmn. Morrison's Restaurant Atlanta, 1996-98. Bd. visitors U. N.C., 1988-92; chmn. bd. trustees Wake Forest U. Grad. Sch. Mgmt., 1988-96; pres. bd. trustees N.C. Dance Theater, Winston-Salem, 1989-90; bd. dirs. Forsyth Meml. Hosp., 1988-92, Naples Conservancy, Naples Philharm. Ctr. for Arts, Fla. Arts Coun., Reynolds Mus. Am. Art, Naples Cmty. Hosp., chmn., 1994-99, bd. dirs. health care sys., chmn., 1995-2005; chmn. Regional Bus. Alliance SW Fla., Naples, Fla., 2004—. Mem. Belle Haven Club (Greenwich) (bd. dirs. 1983-87), Naples Yacht Club, Univ. Club (N.Y.C.), Linville Ridge Country Club (Linville, N.C.), Royal Poinciana Club (Naples, Fla.), Port Royal Club (Naples). Avocation: tennis. Home: 3663 Rum Row Naples FL 34102

VON BAILLOU, ASTRID, executive search consultant; b. Neutitschein, Czech Republic, Mar. 2, 1944; d. Karl von Baillou and Angela Stillfried; m. Dennis Hallam Bigelow, Oct. 21, 1967 (div. Oct. 1994). BA in English, Sweet Briar Coll., 1965. Creative dir. Freeman Advt., Washington, 1969-72; on-air reporter, prodr. PBS, BBC, London Weekend TV, NYC, 1972-80; v.p. Sci. Program Group TV, Washington, 1980-82; pres. Cullen & Casey, NYC, 1982-86; sr. v.p. Ruder Finn, NYC, 1986-87; pres. Baillou Internat., NYC, 1988-94; prin., mgmt. dir. Kinser & Assocs., NYC, 1994-2000; ptnr. Kinser & Baillou, NYC, 2000—. Home: 1245 Park Ave Apt 19F New York NY 10128-1740 Office Phone: 212-534-2161. Business E-Mail: search@kinserbaillou.com.

VON BERNUTH, ROBERT DEAN, agricultural engineering educator, consultant; b. Del Norte, Colo., Apr. 14, 1946; s. John Daniel and Bernice H. (Dunlap) von B.; m. Judy M. Wehrman, Dec. 27, 1969; children: Jeanie, Suzie BSE, Colo. State U., 1968; MS, U. Idaho, 1970; MBA, Claremont Grad. U., Calif., 1980; PhD in Engring., U. Nebr., 1982. Registered profl. engr., Calif., Nebr. Agrl. product mgr. Rain Bird Sprinkler Mfg., Glendora, Calif., 1974-80; instr. agrl. engring. U. Nebr., Lincoln, 1980-82; from assoc. prof. to prof. U. Tenn., Knoxville, 1982-90; prof. Mich. State U., East Lansing, 1990—, chmn., 1992-96. V.p. Von-Sol Cons., Lincoln, 1980-82; prin. Von Bernuth Agrl. cons., Knoxville, East Lansing, 1982—. Patentee in field. With USNR, 1970—98, Vietnam. Decorated DFC (2); recipient Disting. Naval Grad. award USN Flight Program, Pensacola, Fla., 1970. Fellow Am. Soc. Agrl. Engrs.; mem. ASCE, Irrigation Assn. (Person of Yr. 1994), Naval Res. Assn. Avocations: flying, skiing, antique tractors. Office: Mich State U Sch of Planning Design & Constrn Human Ecology Bldg East Lansing MI 48824

VON BRANDENSTEIN, PATRIZIA, production designer; Prodn. designer The Mirisch Agy., LA, 1978—. Prodn. designer: (films) Heartland, 1979, Breaking Away, 1979, Ragtime, 1981 (Academy award nomination best art direction 1981), Silkwood, 1983, Amadeus, 1984 (Academy award best art direction 1984), A Chorus Line, 1985, The Money Pit, 1986, No Mercy, 1987, The Untouchables, 1987 (Academy award nomination best art direction 1987), Working Girl, 1988, The Lemon Sisters, 1990, Postcards From the Edge, 1990, Billy Bathgate, 1992, Sneakers, 1992, Leap of Faith, 1993, Six Degrees of Separation, 1993, The Quick and the Dead, 1995, Just Cause, 1995, The People vs. Larry Flynt, 1996, A Simple Plan, 1998, Man on the Moon, 1999, Shaft, 2000, It Runs in the Family, 2002, The Emperor's Club, 2002, Ice Harvest, 2006, All the King's Men, 2006, Goya's Ghosts, 2006; costume designer: (films) Between the Lines, 1977, Saturday Night Fever, 1977, A Little Sex, 1982.

VON BRAUN, PETER CARL MOORE STEWART, finance company executive; b. Greenwich, Conn., June 24, 1940; s. Carl Conrad and Martha Irwin (Moore) von B.; m. Elisabeth Esser, July 1, 1967 (div. Dec. 1980); m. Denene Jensen, Sept. 26, 1987; children: Christina Stewart, Alexander Stewart. BA with high honors, Yale U., 1964; PhD summa cum laude, U. Cologne, 1966. Assoc. McKinsey & Co., Inc., NYC, 1966-72, prin., 1972-77; chief internat. program devel. Order of St. John, London, 1977-80; exec. dir. Sight Programme, London and Sultanate of Oman, 1977-84; mng. ptnr. Leyton Assocs., Greenwich, 1980—; chmn., CEO Am. Microtrace Corp., Virginia Beach, Va., 1987-95, RusPetrol (USA), LLC, Greenwich, Conn., 1989-99. Mng. dir. LabelADD, LLC, Greenwich, Conn., 1987—99; chmn. Leix LLC, Riverside, Conn., 2000—. Author: Die Verteidigung Indiens, 1968, How to Save a Life, 1977, How to Save An Eye, 1981; contbr. articles to profl. jours.; producer (film) How to Save a Life, 1977. Chmn. Battle Harbour Found., Greenwich, 1972—; vestryman Trinity Parish, N.Y.C., 1977-84; chmn. Anglican Svc. Tng. & Relief Orgn., London, 1986—; bd. dirs. Presiding Bishop's Fund, N.Y.C., 1977-81; mem. exec. bd. Greenwich Coun. Boy Scouts Am. With USN, 1956-58, U.S. Army, 1958-64. Decorated knight of grace and knight of justice Order of St. John, companion with star Order of Merit (Cyprus), other fgn. and U.S. decorations; Fulbright scholar, 1964-66. Mem.: Cavalry, Guards Polo (London); N.Y. Yacht (N.Y.C.), Yale Club, Indian Harbor Yacht Field Club (Greenwich, Conn.), Battle Harbour Yacht (Newfoundland, Can.), Commodore, Stewart Soc. (Edinburgh). Republican. Episcopalian. Avocations: sailing, military history, cooking. Home: 36 Zaccheus Mead Ln Greenwich CT 06831-3753 Office Phone: 203-661-5442. E-mail: vonbraun@optonline.net.

VONCANNON, BRIAN EVERETT, writer, scriptwriter, radio personality, naturopath; s. Mary Jane and Charles Everett Voncannon. AA in Applied Sci., Ctrl. Piedmont C.C., 1998; D in Naturology, Am. Inst. Holistic Theology, 1996; D in Alternative Medicines, Open Internat. U. Alternative Medicines, 2004; D of Naturopathy, Clayton Coll. Natural Health, Birmingham, Ala., 2006. Cert. in gen. law enforcement, chem. analyst of breath, profl. trainer. Police officer Concord City Police Dept., Concord, NC, 1990—95; dep. sheriff/swat officer Cabarrus County Sheriff's Dept., Concord, NC, 1997—2002; author EveningStorm Enterprises, Midland, NC, 1997—; cmty. radio dj/rec. studio owner EveningStorm Radio, Midland, NC, 2002—. Swat officer Cabarrus County Sheriff's Dept., Concord, NC, 1998—2002. Author: (book) Chronic Fatigue Syndrome: Living with the Unknown, Shadows: Diary of a Ninja, Cherokee Blue Eyes: Keeping the Heritage Alive, Living Behind the Shield: A Modern Warrior's Path to Bravehood, Completing the Circle: The Hathcock Indian Blood, (screenplays) The Keepers, Orbit. Sound tech. First Bapt. Ch. of Locust, Locust, NC, 1985—2000. E-6 staff sgt. US Army Reserves, 1991—99, Concord, North Carolina. Decorated Army Achievement medal US Army, Disting. Honor Grad. award US Army Inf. Tng. Ctr., Ft. Benning, Ga., Cert. of Recognition for Cold War Svc. Dept. of Def., Nat. Def. Svc. medal US Army. Democrat. Baptist. Avocations: martial arts, physical fitness activities, outdoor activities, creating native American crafts, travel. Home: 13101 Pine Bluff Rd Midland NC 28107 Office: EveningStorm Enterprises 13101 Pine Bluff Rd Midland NC 28107 E-mail: eveningstorm@earthlink.net.

VONDERHAAR, STEVEN PAUL, counseling administrator; s. Clarence and Marlene Vonderhaar; m. Margaret Ann Korode, June 19, 1993; children: Mollie, Sean, Claire. BA, U. Cin., 1989; MA, Xavier U., 1995; MS, Miami U., 1999. Lic. sch. psychologist Ohio Dept. Edn., nat. cert. sch. psychologist NASP, lic. sch. psychologist Ohio State Bd. Psychology. Psychol. assoc. Northkey Cmty. Care, Covington, Ky., 1993—98; sch. psychologist Milford Exempted Village Schs., 1999—; mitigation specialist S.W. Ohio, 1994—. Adj. prof. Miami U., 2004—, Xavier U., 2005—; range finder com. Ohio Dept. Edn., 2004, 05. Presenter various profl. workshops. Mem.: NASP, Ohio Sch. Psychologists Assn., SW Ohio Sch. Psychologists Assn. (pres. 2004—05, rep. 2007—), Psi Chi, Phi Kappa Tau. Avocations: reading, soccer, golf, hiking, bicycling. Home Phone: 513-576-1401; Office Phone: 513-831-1314. Personal E-mail: vonderhaar_4@yahoo.com.

VON DER HEYDEN, KARL MUELLER, retired manufacturing executive; b. Berlin, July 18, 1936; arrived in U.S., 1957, naturalized, 1967; s. Werner and Erika (Mueller) von der Heyden; m. Mary Ellen Terrell, Aug. 17, 1963; children: Ellen, Eric. Student, Free U., Berlin, 1959—61; BA, Duke, 1962; MBA, U. Pa., 1964. CPA Pa., 1965. Mgmt. trainee Berliner Bank, Berlin, 1955-57; sr. staff acct. Coopers & Lybrand, Phila., 1963-66; asst. comptr., corporate comptr. Pitney-Bowes, Inc., Stamford, Conn., 1966-74; v.p., contr. PepsiCo., Inc., Purchase, 1974-77; v.p. fin. Pepsi-Cola Co., 1977-79, v.p. mfg., 1979-80; v.p. fin., treas. H.J. Heinz Co., Pitts., 1980-83, sr. v.p. fin., CFO, 1983-89; exec. v.p., CFO RJR Nabisco Inc., NYC, 1989-93, co-chmn., CEO, 1993; pres., CEO Metallgesellschaft Corp., NYC, 1993-94; vice chmn. PepsiCo, Inc., Purchase, NY, 1996—2001; sr. advisor Clipper Group, 1994-97. Chmn. Fin. Acctg. Stds. Adv. Coun., 1995—96; bd. dirs. H.J. Heinz Co., 1983—89, Macy's, NYSE Euronext, Dreamworks Animation SKG. Trustee Am. Acad. in Berlin, NY Global Ptnrs., Inc. Mem.: Univ. Club N.Y.C. Office: 25 Central Park W Apt 24K New York NY 10023

VON DER HEYDT, JAMES ARNOLD, federal judge; b. Miles City, Mont., July 15, 1919; s. Harry Karl and Alice S. (Arnold) von der H.; m. Verna E. Johnson, May 21, 1952. BA, Albion Coll., 1942; JD, Northwestern U., 1951. Bar: Alaska 1951. Pvt. practice, Nome, Alaska, 1953—59; judge superior ct. Juneau, Alaska, 1959—66; from judge to sr. judge U.S. Dist. Ct. Alaska, 1966—; U.S. commr. Nome, 1951—; U.S. atty. divsn. 2 Dist. Alaska, 1951—53; mem. Alaska Ho. of Reps., 1957—59. Author: Mother Sawtooth's Nome, 1990, Alaska, The Short and Long of It, 2000. Pres. Anchorage Fine Arts Mus. Assn. Recipient Disting. Alumni award Albion Coll., 1995, Professionalism and Ethics award Inn of Ct., 2005. Mem. Alaska Bar Assn. (bd. govs. 1955-59, pres. 1959-60), Am. Judicature Soc., Masons (32d degree), Shriners, Phi Delta Phi, Sigma Nu. Avocations: researching arctic bird life, creative writing, painting. Office: US Dist Ct 222 W 7th Ave Box 40 Anchorage AK 99513-7564 Home Phone: 907-279-4298; Office Phone: 907-677-6254.

VON DER MEHDEN, FRED R., political science professor; b. San Francisco, Dec. 1, 1927; s. Fred G. and Margaret (de Valasco) von der M.; m. Audrey Eleanor Whitehead, Dec. 27, 1954; children: Laura Davis, Victoria Margaret Fredrickson. BA, U. of Pacific, 1948; MA, Claremont Grad. Sch., 1950; PhD, U. Calif., Berkeley, 1957. Mem. faculty U. Wis. Madison, 1957-68; chmn. East Asian studies U. Wis.-Madison, 1963-65, 67-68; Albert Thomas prof. polit. sci. Rice U., 1968—2000, dir. Center for Research, 1969-70, chmn. dept., 1975-78, dir. program devel. studies, 1978-83; editor Rice U. Press, 1982-95; Albert Thomas prof. emeritus Rice U., 2000—. Cons. AID, 1967-78 Author: Politics of the Developing Nations, 1964, 2d edit., 1969, Religion and Nationalism in Southeast Asia, 1963, Comparative Political Violence, 1973; co-author: Issues of Political Development, 1967, The Military and Politics of Five Developing Nations, 1970, Southeast Asia 1930-1970, 1974, Religion and Modernization in Southeast Asia, 1986, Two Worlds of Islam, 1993; editor: (with R. Soligo) Issues on Income Distribution, 1975, Ethnic Groups of Houston, 1984, Radical Islam in Southeast Asia, 2006. Mem. Mid-West Conf. Asian Affairs (pres. 1968-69), Assn. Asian Studies, Am. Polit. Sci. Assn., SW Conf. Asian Affairs (pres. 1976-77) Home: 12530 Mossycup Dr Houston TX 77024-4937 Office Phone: 713-348-4848. Business E-Mail: fvdm@rice.edu.

VON DER SCHMIDT, EDWARD, III, neurosurgeon, veterinarian; b. Jan. 13, 1953; BS in Animal Sci., Rutgers U., 1975; DVM, Cornell U., 1979; MD, U. Medicine and Dentistry N.J., Newark, 1984. Diplomate Nat. Bd. Med. Examiners, Am. Bd. Neurol. Surgery. Veterinarian Secaucus (N.J.) Animal Hosp., 1979-82; pvt. practice vet. medicine NJ, 1980-85; gen. surg. intern Washington Hosp. Ctr., Washington, 1984-85; resident in neurosurgery George Washington U. Med. Ctr., Washington, 1985-90; pvt. practice neurosurgery Princeton (N.J.) Healthcare Ctr., 1990—. Neurosurgeon Robert Wood Johnson U. Hosp., New Brunswick, NJ, St. Peter's Med. Ctr., New Brunswick, Somerset Med. Ctr., Somerville, NJ; chief neurosurgery sect. Med. Ctr. Princeton; mem. search com. for chief divsn. neurosurgery U. Medicine and Dentistry N.J./Robert Wood Johnson Med. Sch. Mem.: AAAS, AMA, N.J. Soc. Med. Specialty (pres. 2000—02), Coun. State Neurosurgical Safety (mem. reform commn. 2001, vice chmn. N.E. quadrant 2003—), Am. Assn. Med. Transcription (bd. dirs. Ctrl. N.J. chpt.), Am. Coll. Physician Execs., Soc. Exec. Physicians, Soc. Critical Care Medicine, N.J. Neurosurgical Soc. (trustee at large 2000—, sec. treas. 1998—2000), N.Y. Acad. Sci., Middlesex Med. Soc. (sec. 2003, del.), Middlesex County Med. Soc., Med. Soc. N.J., Congress Neurol. Surgeons (mem. joint sect. disorders spine and peripheral nerves), Am. Assn. Neurol. Surgeons, Alpha Zeta (Best Freshman award). Home: 140 Hodge Rd Princeton NJ 08540-3014 Office: Princeton Healthcare Ctr 419 N Harrison St Ste 204 Princeton NJ 08540-3521

VON DRAN, RAYMOND, dean, library and information science educator; AB, Seton Hall U., 1968; MLA, U. Wis., Madison, 1971, MA in History, 1972, PhD in Info. Sci., 1976, Asst. prof. Sch. Libr. and Info. Sci., Cath. U. Am., Washington, 1976—81, assoc. chair, 1977—81, assoc. dean, 1981—83, dean, assoc. prof., 1983—87; dean, prof. Sch. Libr. and Info. Scis., U. North Tex., Denton, 1987—95, chair Info. Resources Coun., exec. asst. to provost for info. resources, 1990—95; dean, prof. Sch. Info. Studies, Syracuse U., NY, 1995—, chair Com. Info. and Comm. Tech. Issues NY, 1996—97. Sr. cons. Network Devel. Office Libr. Congress, 1978—82; coord., project mgr. Nat. Rehab. Info. Ctr., 1983—87; cons. in field. Contbr. articles to profl. jours. Mem.: ALA, Soc. Info. Mgmt., Educause (mem. Conf. Planning Com.), NY Libr. Assn., Decision Scis. Inst., Assn. Info. Sys., Assn. Computing, Assn. Libr. and Info. Sci. Edn., Am. Soc. Info. Sci. and Tech., Beta Phi Mu. Office: Syracuse U Sch Info Studies 4-206 Center for Science and Technology Syracuse NY 13244-4100 Office Phone: 315-443-2736. Office Fax: 315-443-5806. E-mail: vondran@syr.edu. *

VON DRASEK, LISA, librarian; b. Phila., Pa. MLIS, Pratt Inst., 1995. Buyer, mgr. Please Touch Mus. for Children; children's libr. Bank St. Coll. Edn., NYC, 1998—, grad. faculty mem., 2006—. Columnist: Teaching PreK-8 Mag., Nick Jr. Family Mag. Named one of the Movers & Shakers, Libr. Jour., 2007. Office: Library and Media 610 W 112th St New York NY 10025-1898

VON DREHLE, RAMON ARNOLD, lawyer; b. St. Louis, Mar. 12, 1930; s. Arnold Henry and Sylvia E. (Ahrens) Von D.; m. Gillian Margaret Turner, Sept. 13, 1980; children by previous marriage: Carin L., Lisa A., Courtney A. BS, Washington U., St. Louis, 1952; JD, U. Tex., Austin, 1957; postgrad, Parker Sch. Internat. Law, Columbia U., 1965. Bar: Tex. 1956, Mich. 1957, U.S. Supreme Ct. 1981. Sr. atty. Ford Motor Co., Dearborn, Mich., 1957-67; assoc., asst. gen. counsel Ford of Europe, Inc., Brentwood, Essex, Eng., 1967-75, v.p., gen. counsel, 1975-79; v.p. legal Ford Motor Credit Co., Dearborn, 1979-87; v.p., gen. counsel Am. Road Ins. Co., Dearborn, 1979-87; exec. dir. legal affairs Ford Fin. Services Group, Dearborn, 1987-91; leader in residence Walsh Coll., Mich., 1992. Panelist large complex case program Am. Arbitration Assn., 1993—; advisor to Czech Republic Ministry of Privatization, Prague, 1993-94; leader Russian Def. Conversion Project, 1995-96; lectr. in Ea. Europe, 1995; pres. Focus Internat. LLC, 1995—. Article editor: Tex. Law Rev, 1956-57. Trustee Birmingham Unitarian Ch., 1966-67. Served to 1st lt. AUS, 1952-54, Korea. Mem. ABA, Mich. Bar Assn., Tex. Bar Assn., Internat. Bar Assn., Am. Fin. Svcs. Assn. (chmn. 1990-91, bd. dirs. 1981-91), Fin. Svcs. Coun. (bd. dirs. 1987-91), Washington U. Alumni Club Detroit (past pres.), Order of Coif, Tower Club (Tysons, Va.), Confrèrie des Chevaliers du Tastevin (France, Washington), Royal Automobile Club (London), Cosmos Club (Washington). Mem. Christ Ch. Home and Office: 519 Princess St Alexandria VA 22314-2332 E-mail: rvond2@aol.com.

VON ESCHEN, ROBERT LEROY, electrical engineer, consultant; b. Glasgow, Mont., Oct. 3, 1936; s. Leroy and Lillian Victoria (Eliason) Von E.; m. Carolyn Kay Frampton, Dec. 14, 1965 (dec. Feb. 1999); children: Eric Leroy, Marc Alfred. BSEE, Mont. State U., 1961; postgrad., U. Liberia, Lakeland C.C., Glendale C.C. Registered profl. engr., Pa. Hydro constrn. engr. U.S. Army Corps of Engrs., Mont., 1961-62, SD, 1961—62; hdqrs. chief engr. Eagle Constrn. Co., Colo., 1962; resident transp./distbn. elec. engr. Stanley Cons., Inc., West Africa, 1962-63, hydro cons., startup engr. Manila, West Africa, 1965-66; with Stanley Cons., 1962-68, Gilbert Assoc./United Energy Svc., 1968-92; performance based assessment program sect. engr., maintenance planning engr., condition assessment survey sec. mgr. Gilbert Assocs., Inc., Tex., 1992—. Cons. engr. fossil power plant, Ky., Colo., Mo., Korea; site project mgr., Ariz., Aruba; nuclear constrn. startup engr., Pa., Ala., Ohio; safety sys. functional inspector,

Calif., Wis., Oreg.; performance based assessment program project mgr., Tex.; tech. cons. World Bank, Liberia; engring. cons. USN, Manila, 1967; founding dr. Madison Comptr. Soc., Ohio, 1983-85; v.p., dir. Boy Scouts Am., 1981-84. Founder, dir. Madison (Ohio) Computer Soc., 1983—85; v.p., bd. dirs. N.E. coun. Boy Scouts Am., Painesville, 1983—85; bd. dirs. Let's Shoot Gun Club, LLC, 2003—, Kids World Multimedia. Recipient Silver Beaver award Boy Scouts Am., 19 other awards. Mem.: AFIO, NARP, NPSE, IEEE, NRA, Tex. State Engring. Soc., Ohio State Engring. Soc., Nat. Def. Indsl. Orgn., Soc. Am. Mil. Engrs., Shriners, Masons (life). Avocations: target and skeet shooting, construction design, computers, electronics. Home: 1001 S Girl Scout Rd Amarillo TX 79124-2135 Office: BWXT Pantex LLC PO Box 30020 Amarillo TX 79120-0020

VON ESCHENBACH, ANDREW C., federal agency administrator, oncologist, urologic surgeon; b. Phila., Oct. 30, 1941; BS, St. Joseph's Univ., Phila., 1963; MD, Georgetown U., 1967. Diplomate Am. Bd. Urology. Intern U. Pa./Phila. Gen. Hosp., 1967—68; resident gen. surgery Pa. Hosp., Phila., 1971—72, resident urology, 1972—75; instructor, urology U. Pa. Sch. Medicine; fellow urol. oncology U. Tex. MD Anderson Cancer Ctr., Houston, 1976—77, prof. urology, 1980—2002, chmn. dept. urology, 1983—96, cons. prof., cell biology, prof. urology, exec. v.p., chief acad. officer, dir. program ctr. Genitourinary Cancer Ctr. Houston, 1997—2002, founding dir., Prostate Cancer Research Prog., 1996, v.p. for academic affairs, Roy M. and Phyllis Gough Huffington Clin. Rsch. Disting. Chair in Urologic Oncology; dir. Nat. Cancer Inst., NIH, Bethesda, Md., 2002—06; acting commr. FDA, Rockville, Md., 2005—06, commr., 2006—; sr. adv. to sec. US Dept. Health & Human Services., Washington, 2006—. Founding mem. C-Change. Contbr. articles to profl. jours., books, and book chpt.; mem. edit. bd. (several jours.). Lt. comdr. U.S. Navy Medical Corps, 1968—71. Named one of 100 Most Influential People, Time Mag., 2006, Best Doctors in Am., Am. Radium Soc., 2007; recipient Julie Rogers "Spirit of Love" award, Certificate of Meritorious Service for outstanding contbn. to prostate disease research, Uniformed Services U. of the Health Sci., Carpe Diem award, Lance Armstrong Found., 2007. Mem.: AMA, Am. Med. Writers Assn., Soc. Surg. Oncology, Am. Urological Assn., Am. Cancer Soc. (pres.-elect 2002), Uniformed Svcs. Univ. of Health Sciences. Office: FDA Parklawn Bldg 14-71 HF-1 5600 Fishers Ln Rockville MD 20857 Office Phone: 301-827-2410. Office Fax: 301-443-3100. Business E-Mail: andrew.voneschenbach@fda.hhs.gov.

VON FRAUNHOFER-KOSINSKI, KATHERINA, bank and advertising executive; b. NYC; m. Jerzy Kosinski, Feb. 15, 1987 (dec. May 3, 1991). Student, St. Joseph's Convent, London, Clark's Coll. Various positions Robert W. Orr & Assocs., NYC; with traffic dept. Compton Advt., Inc., NYC, 1956-63; acct. exec. J. Walter Thompson Co., NYC, 1963-69; product mgr. Natural Wonder line Revlon Co., NYC, 1969-71; pres. Scientia Factum, Inc., NYC, 1971—, Polish Am. Resources Corp., NYC, 1992—2000, pres., CEO, 1992—2002. Chmn. Am. Bank in Poland, 1990—2001. Co-founder Westchester Sports Club. Assoc. fellow Timothy Dwight Coll./Yale U., 1997—. Avocations: skiing, horse/polo, swimming, photography. Office: 60 W 57th St New York NY 10019-3909 Office Phone: 212-246-0128. Personal E-mail: sfi440@aol.com.

VON FURSTENBERG, BETSY, actress, writer; b. Neiheim Heusen, Germany, Aug. 16, 1931; d. Count Franz-Egon and Elizabeth (Johnson) von F.; m. Guy Vincent de la Maisoneuve (div.); 2 children.; m. John J. Reynolds, Mar. 26, 1984. Attended Miss Hewitt's Classes, N.Y. Tutoring Sch.; prepared for stage with Sanford Meisner at Neighborhood Playhouse. Made Broadway stage debut in Second Threshold, N.Y., 1951; appeared in Dear Barbarians, 1952, Oh Men Oh Women, 1954, The Chalk Garden, 1955, Child of Fortune, 1956, Nature's Way, 1957, Much Ado About Nothing, 1959, Mary Mary, 1965, Paisley Convertible, 1967, Avanti, 1968, The Gingerbread Lady, 1970 (toured 1971), Absurd Person Singular, 1976; off Broadway appearances include For Love or Money, 1951; toured in Petrified Forest, Jason and Second Man, 1952; appeared in Josephine, 1953; subsequently toured, 1955; What Every Woman Knows, 1955, The Making of Moo, 1958 (toured 1958), Say Darling, 1959, Wonderful Town, 1959, Season of Choice, 1959, Beyond Desire, 1967, Private Lives, 1968, Does Anyone Here Do the Peabody, 1976; appeared in Along Came a Spider, Theatre in the Park, N.Y.C., 1985; appeared in film Women Without Names, 1950; TV appearances include Robert Montgomery Show, Ed Sullivan Show, Alfred Hitchcock Presents, One Step Beyond, The Mike Wallace Show, Johnny Carson Show, Omnibus, Theatre of the Week, The Secret Storm, As the World Turns, Movie of the Week, Your Money or Your Wife, Another World; writer syndicated column More Than Beauty; contbr. articles to newspapers and mags. including N.Y. Times Sunday Arts and Leisure, Saturday Rev. of Literature, People, Good Housekeeping, Art News, Pan Am Travel; co-author: (novel) Mirror, Mirror, 1988; author, illustrator Grandmothers Surprise, 2004. Avocations: tennis, painting, photography.

VON FURSTENBERG, DIANE, fashion designer, writer, entrepreneur; b. Brussels, Dec. 31, 1946; arrived in US, 1969, naturalized, 2002; d. Leon L. and Liliane L. (Nahmias) Halfin; m. Eduard Egon von Furstenberg, July 16, 1969 (div. 1983); children: Alexandre, Tatiana; m. Barry Diller, Feb. 2, 2001; m. Barry Diller, Feb. 2, 2001. Student, U. Madrid, 1965-66, U. Geneva, 1966-68. Founder, pres. Diane von Furstenberg Studio, L.P., NYC, 1970—; pres. Diane von Furstenberg Ltd., NYC; founder Salvy, Paris, 1985. Pioneer TV shopping with creative and live on-air selling Silk Assets collection, 1992; returns to retail as designer DIANE line of signature dresses, including the wrap, 1997. Author: Diane Von Furstenberg's Book of Beauty, 1977; Beds, 1991, The Bath, 1993, The Table, 1996, DIANE: A Signature Life, 1998; contbg. editor Vanity Fair mag., 1993; exec. prodr.: (films) Forty Shades of Blue, 2005, Andy Warhol: A Documentary Film, 2006. Recipient Ellis Island Medal of Honor, 1986. Mem.: Coun. of Fashion Designers of Am. (pres. 2006—, Lifetime Achievement award 2005). *Honesty in all ways: honest products, honest and straight approach to needs.* *

VON FURSTENBERG, GEORGE MICHAEL, economics professor, researcher; b. Germany, Dec. 3, 1941; arrived in U.S., 1961; m. Gabrielle M. Koblitz von Willmburg, June 9, 1967; 1 child, Philip G. PhD, Princeton U., 1967. Asst. prof. Cornell U., Ithaca, NY, 1966-70; assoc. prof. Ind. U., Bloomington, 1970-73, prof., 1976-78, Rudy prof. econs., 1983—2006; sr. staff economist Coun. Econ. Advisors, Washington, 1973-76; div. chief rsch. dept. IMF, Washington, 1978-83; Robert Bendheim prof. econ. and fin. policy Fordham U., NYC, 2000—03; econ. program dir. NSF, Arlington, Va., 2006—. Project dir. Am. Coun. Life Ins., Washington, 1976—78; sr. advisor Brookings Instn., Washington, 1978—90; vis. sr. economist planning and analysis staff Dept. State, Washington, 1989—90; Bissell-Fulbright vis. prof. Can.-Am. rels. U. Toronto, 1994—95. Contbg. author, editor: The Government and Capital Formation, 1980, Capital, Efficiency and Growth, 1980, Acting Under Uncertainty: Multidisciplinary Conceptions, 1990, Regulation and Supervision of Financial Institutions in the NAFTA Countries and Beyond, 1997; editor: Internat. Money and Credit: The Policy Roles, 1983; co-author: Learning from the World's Best Central Bankers, 1998; co-editor: Monetary Unions and Hard Pegs: Effects on Trade, Financial Development, and Stability, 2004; assoc. editor: Rev. Econs. and Stats., 1987—92, Open Econs. Rev., 1997—2006, Jour. Econ. Asymmetries, 2004—; contbr. articles to profl. jours. Fulbright grantee, Poland, 1991—92. Mem.: Am. Econ. Assn., N.Am. Econs. and Fin. Assn. (pres. 2000). Roman Catholic. Avocation: tennis. Office: NSF Divsn Social and Econ Scis 995N 4201 Wilson Blvd Arlington VA 22230 Office Phone: 703-292-8202. Business E-Mail: vonfurst@indiana.edu, gvonfurs@nsf.gov.

VONGERICHTEN, JEAN-GEORGES, food service executive, chef; b. Strasbourg, France; arrived in US, 1985; Studied with chef Paul Hueberlin, Auberge de l'Ill. Worked with Paul Bocuse L'Oasis Market, Paris; worked with master chef Louis Outhier L'Oasis, France; chef Oriental Hotel, Bangkok; opened Meridian Hotel, Singapore, Mandarin Hotel, Hong Kong, Lafayette, Boston, 1985, exec. chef NYC, 1986; opened Jo Jo, 1991, Vong, NYC, London, 1995, Hong Kong, 1997, Chgo., 1999, Jean-Georges, NYC, 1997, Nougatine, NYC, 1997, Mercer Kitchen, NYC, 1998, The Lipstick Cafe, Prime, Las Vegas, Nev., 1998, Dune, Bahamas, 2000, V Steakhouse, NYC, 2004, 66, 2003, Spice Market, 2005, Perry St., 2005. Author: Simple Cuisine, Jean-Georges: Cooking at Home with a Four-Star Chef, 1998, Simple to Speculate, 2000; appeared Martha Stewart Show, Live! with Regis and Kathie Lee, Today Show, Good Morning Am., Food Network, (TV series) Julia's Kitchen with Master Chefs with Julia Child, 1995. Named Jo Jo Best New Restaurant of Yr., Esquire Mag., Chef of Yr., Outstanding Chef, James Beard Found., 1998; recipient four stars for Lafayette, NY Times, three stars for Jo Jo, three stars for Vong, four stars for Jean Georges, 1997, Best New Restaurant award for Jean Georges, James Beard Found., 1998. Office: Jean Georges Mgmt LLC 111 Prince St New York NY 10012 *

VON GIERKE, HENNING EDGAR, biomedical science educator, former government official, researcher; b. Karlsruhe, Germany, May 22, 1917; arrived in U.S., 1947, naturalized, 1977; s. Edgar and Julie (Braun) Von Gierke; married; 2 children. Dipl. Ing., Karlsruhe Tech., 1943, Dr. Engr., 1944. Asst. in acoustics Karlsruhe Tech., 1944—47, lectr., 1946; cons. Aerospace Med. Research Labs, Wright-Patterson AFB, Ohio, 1947—54, chief bioacoustics br., 1954—63, dir. biodynamics and bionics div., 1963—88; assoc. prof. Ohio State U., 1963—88; clin. prof. Wright State U., 1980—. Mem. com. hearing bioacoustics and biomechanics NRC, 1953—93, chmn., 1990—93, bio-astronaut com., 1959—61; mem. adv. com., flight medicine and biology NASA, 1960—61. Author numerous tech. publs., book chpts.; patentee in field. Fellow: Am. Inst. Med. and Biol. Engring., Coll. Fellows, Aerospace Med. Assn. (v.p. 1966—67, E. Liljenkrantz award 1966, A.D. Tuttle award 1974, John Paul Stapp award 2004), Inst. Environ. Scis. (hon.), Acoustical Soc. Am. (pres. 1979—80, Silver medal 1981, Gold medal 1999); mem.: Internat. Acad. Astronautics, Mil. Audiology Assn. (hon.), Biomed. Engring. Soc., Inst. Noise Ctrl. Engring., Internat. Acad. Aviation and Space Medicine, NAE. Achievements include research in bioacoustics, acoustics, biomechanics and bioengineering. Home: 1325 Meadow Ln Yellow Springs OH 45387-1219

VON HAKE, MARGARET JOAN, librarian; b. Santa Monica, Calif., Oct. 27, 1933; d. Carl August and Inez Garnet (Johnson) von Hake. BA, La Sierra Coll., 1955; MS in Library Sci., U. So. Calif., 1963. Tchr. Newbury Park Acad., Calif., 1955—60, librarian, 1957—60; circulation librarian Columbia Union Coll., Takoma Park, Md., 1962—67, library dir., 1967—2007, prof. emerita, 2007—. Pres. congress Acad. Libr. Dirs. of Md., 1999—2000; chair Md. Ind. Coll. Univ. Assn. Libr. Dirs. Round Table, 1996—98, Adventist Libr. Info. Cooperative Coun., 2005—07. Mem. ALA, Md. Libr. Assn.,Assn. Seventh Day Adventist Librs. (newsletter editor 1981-83, pres. 1989-90), Sligo Federated Music Club (pres. 1988-89, yearbook co-editor 2000—). Republican.

VON HILSHEIMER, GEORGE EDWIN, III, neuropsychologist; b. West Palm Beach, Fla., Aug. 15, 1934; s. George E. Jr. and Dorothy Sue (Bridges) Von H.; m. Catherine Jean Munson, Dec. 27, 1968 (div. Oct. 1987); children: Dana Ghermine, George E., Alexandra; m. Jonnie Mae Warner, June 29, 1991; stepchildren: Dennis Warner, Derek Warner. BA, U. Miami, 1955; PhD, Saybrook Inst., San Francisco, 1977. Diplomate Acad. Psychosomatic Medicine, Am. Bd. Behavioral Medicine, Am. Acad. Pain Mgmt., Am. Bd. Cert. Managed Care Providers, Am. Acad. Psychol. Treating Addiction, Nat. Register Neurofeedback. Sr. min. Humanitas, NYC, 1959-64; headmaster Summerlane Sch., North Branch, NY, 1964-69; supt. Green Valley Sch., Orange City, Fla., 1969-74; neuropsychologist Growth Insts., Twyman's Mill, Va., 1974-79, Growth Inst., DeLand, Fla., 1980-82; assoc. health profl. Maitland, Fla., 1982—2006; pvt. practice biofeedback trainer and hypnotist, 1998—. Cons. Pres. Kennedy's Commn. Nat. Vol. Svc., Juvenile Del., Migratory Labor, 1963-64, Sci. Adv. Bd. EPA, Washington, 1974-84; chmn. Cert. Bd., Internat. Coll. Environ. Medicine, 1991-94; mem. Bd. Assn. Diagnostic Efficiency and Brief Therapy, dir. curriculum, 1993-94; cons. Queen St. Psychiatric Hosp., 1982, Ont. Correctional Inst., Toronto, 1984-95. Author: How to Live With Your Special Child, 1970, Understanding Problems of Children, 1975, Allergy, Toxins and the LD Child, 1977, Psychobiology of Delinquents, 1978, Depression Is Not a Disease, 1989, Brief Therapy, 1993, Brief Therapy: Antecedent Scientific Principles, 1994; editor Human Learning, Washington, 1974-94; editor: Jour. of ANT, ANT Trails, 1998—. Mem. spl. bd. Fla. Symphony Orch., 1992-93. With mil. intelligence U.S. Army, 1957-59. Fellow Royal Soc. Health (life), Internat. Coll. Applied Nutrition, Acad. Psychosomatic Medicine; mem. Assn. Neurotrainers (pres. 1998), Toastmasters, Phi Kappa Phi, Omicron Delta Kappa, Alpha Sigma Phi. Mem. Ch. Of Brethren. Achievements include establishment of minor physical anomalies as significant predictor of physical and mental disease; demonstrated that treatment by neurofeedback significantly reduced criminal recidivism and that delinquency is a function of physical disease; demonstrated that ADHD and pain respond to neurofeedback; introduced treatment of schizophrenia by neurofeedback through Electro Dermal Response; introduced treatment of irritable bowel syndrome by neurofeedback; contributor to proof that alcoholism responds to EEG biofeedback. Office: AAT 125 S Swoope Ave Ste 109 Maitland FL 32751-5784 Home Phone: 407-647-5283; Office Phone: 407-644-6464. Business E-Mail: drvonh@embarqmail.com.

VON HIPPEL, ERIC ARTHUR, innovation educator; b. Boston, Aug. 27, 1941; s. Arthur Robert and Dagmar von Hippel; m. Jessie Roberta Janjigian; children: Christiana Dagmar Jessie, Eric James. BA, Harvard U., Cambridge, Mass., 1964; MS, MIT, 1966; PhD, Carnegie-Mellon U., Pitts., 1973; PhD in econ. (hon.), Ludwig Maximilans Univ., 2004; PhD in Mgmt. (hon.), Copenhagen Bus. Sch., 2007. Engring. mgr. Graphic Sciences, Inc, Danbury, Conn., 1966—69; cons. McKinsey and Co., NYC, 1970—72; prof. Sloan School of Management, MIT, Cambridge, 1973—; head Innovation and Entrepreneurship Group. Pres. Lead User Concepts Inc, Cambridge, 1996—. Author: The Sources of Innovation, 1988, Democratizing Innovation, 2005; contbr. articles to scholarly jours. Named Sir Walter Scott Disting. Prof., Australian Grad. Sch. Mgmt., 1997—98; fellow, Canadian Inst. for Advanced Rsch., 1995—97; grantee, NSF, Alfred P. Sloan Found., 3M; Nortel Networks; NYNEX; Xerox; Bush,Boake,Allen,Bell-Atlantic. Achievements include patents for facsimile technology. Avocation: industrial archaeology. Office: MIT Rm E52-566 50 Memorial Dr Cambridge MA 02141 Business E-Mail: evhippel@mit.edu.

VON HIPPEL, FRANK NIELS, public and international affairs educator; b. Cambridge, Mass., Dec. 26, 1937; s. Arthur Robert and Dagmar (Franck) von H.; m. Patricia Bardi, June, 1987; 1 child from previous marriage, Paul Thomas. S.B., MIT, 1959; PhD, Oxford U., 1962. Rsch. assoc. U. Chgo., 1962-64, Cornell U., Ithaca, N.Y., 1964-66; asst. prof. Stanford U., Calif., 1966-69; assoc. physicist Argonne Nat. Lab., Ill., 1970-73; research physicist Princeton U., NJ, 1974-83, prof. pub. and internat. affairs NJ, 1983-93, 95—, co-dir. Program on Sci. and Global Security NJ, 2005; asst. dir. for nat. security Pres.'s Office of Sci. and Tech. Policy, Washington, 1993-94. Bd. dirs. Bull. of Atomic Scientists, Chgo., 1983-86, mem. editl. bd., from 1996, chmn. editl. bd., 1991-93. Author: Advice and Dissent, 1974, Citizen Scientist, 1991; chmn. editl. bd. Sci. and Global Security, 1989—; contbr. articles to profl. jours. Rhodes scholar, 1959-62; McArthur Found. Prize fellow, 1993-98. Fellow AAAS (bd. dirs. 1987-88, Hilliard Roderick prize in Sci., Arms Control and Internat. Security 1994); mem. Fedn. Am. Scientists (chmn. 1979-84, Pub. Svc. award 1989), Fedn. Am. Scientists Fund (chmn. 1986-93, 96—). Home: 3 University Way Princeton Junction NJ 08550-1617 Office: Princeton Univ Woodrow Wilson Sch Princeton NJ 08544-1013 *

VON HIPPEL, PETER HANS, chemistry professor, researcher; b. Goettingen, Germany, Mar. 13, 1931; came to U.S., 1937, naturalized, 1942; s. Arthur Robert and Dagmar (Franck) von H.; m. Josephine Baron Raskind, June 20, 1954; children: David F., James A., Benjamin J. BS, MIT, Cambridge, Mass., 1952; MS, MIT, 1953, PhD, 1955. Phys. biochemist Naval Med. Research Inst., Bethesda, Md., 1956-59; from asst. prof. to assoc. prof. biochemistry Med. Sch. Dartmouth Coll., 1959-67; prof. chemistry, mem. Inst. Molecular Biology U. Oreg., 1967-79, dir. Inst. Molecular Biology, 1969-80, chmn. dept. chemistry, 1980-87; rsch. prof. chemistry Am. Cancer Soc., 1989—. Chmn. biopolymers Gordon Conf., 1968; mem. trustees vis. com. biology dept. MIT, 1973—76; mem. bd. sci. counsellors Nat. Inst. Arthritis, Metabolic and Digestive Diseases NIH, 1974—78, mem. coun. Nat. Inst. Gen. Med. Scis., 1982—86, mem. dir.'s adv. com., 1987—92; bd. dirs. Fedn. Am. Socs. for Exptl. Biology, 1994—98; mem. NIH-CSR panel on boundaries for sci. rev., 1998—2003, mem. joint steering com. for pub. policy, 1998—. Mem. editl. bd. Jour. Biol. Chemistry, 1967-73, 76-82, Biochem. Biophys. Acta, 1965-70, Physiol. Revs., 1972-77, Biochemistry, 1977-80, Trends in Biochem. Soc., 1987—, Protein Sci., 1990-95; editor Jour. Molecular Biology, 1986-94; contbr. articles to profl. jours., chpts. to books. Lt. M.S.C. USNR, 1956-59. Recipient Merck award Am. Soc. Biochem. and Molecular Biology, 2000; NSF predoctoral fellow, 1953-55; NIH postdoctoral fellow, 1955-56; NIH sr. fellow, 1959-67; Guggenheim fellow, 1973-74 Fellow: Biophys. Soc., Am. Acad. Arts and Scis.; mem.: AAAS, Am. Philosophic Soc., Fedn. Am. Scientists, Nat. Acad. Scis., Biophys. Soc. (coun. 1970—73, pres. 1973—74), Am. Soc. Biochem. and Molecular Biology, Am. Chem. Soc., Sigma Xi. Home: 1900 Crest Dr Eugene OR 97405-1753 E-mail: petevh@molbio.uoregon.edu.

VON HOELLE, JOHN JACOB LEWIS, publisher, commercial developer; b. Miami, Fla., Sept. 21, 1940; s. John Charles and Susan Ann (Lewis) von H.; m. Jan Behringer, Oct. 7, 1961; children: Eric, Christopher, Timothy, Andrew, Ellen. MS, U. Cambridge, Eng., 1966. V.p. MNI Corp., NYC, 1969-79, McCall's Publs., NYC, 1979-81; pres. Dyne-Am. Publs., Wilmington, 1981-95; dir. publs. Oak Knoll Press, New Castle, Del., 1995—. Bd. dirs. St. Paul's Bibliographies, Winchester, U.K., Agamemnon Corp., Wilmington, Del; cons. Smithsonian Instn., Washington; spkr. internat. antiquarian and pub. convs., 1980—. Author: Collector's Encyclopedia, 1983, 1984, 1986, Sound and Glory, 1990, Godfather of the Brandywine, 1994, Tales of the Eastern Shore, 1995, The Lewis Chronicles, 1996, In Search Of, 1999, The Silence of Them, 2000, The Bibliography of Cold War Intelligence Literature, 2002, Bio-bibliography of Ernesto Che Guevara, 2003, The Song of I'bram, 2003, various other books on history, biography and 70 short stories, Tales from a Forgotten War, 2004, Deception, 2004, Silent Shadows, 2005, Return to a Haunted Kingdom, 2006, A Boyhood of Yesteryear, 2006; editor, co-pub.: The British Libr., 1995—, Libr. of Congress, 2000—. Lt. col. USAF, 1958-62, USAFR, 1964-91. Recipient N.Y. award for scholarship and rsch. TCI, 1986, Taylor-Peabody award in Am. lit., 1995. Mem. Assn. Am. Pubs., Nat. Writers Assn., Internat. Assn. Fgn. War Corrs., Assn. Former Intelligence Officers (Washington, D.C.), Royal Cambrian Geneal. Soc., Egypt Exploration Soc., Oriental Inst. Avocations: writing, Mayan and and Near Eastern archaeology, collecting Cold War espionology books, Egyptian ushabtis and cuneiform tablets. Office: Oak Knoll Press 310 Delaware St New Castle DE 19720-5037

VON HOFFMAN, NICHOLAS, writer, retired reporter; b. NYC, Oct. 16, 1929; s. Carl and Anna (Bruenn) von H.; m. Ann Byrne, 1950 (div.); children: Alexander, Aristodemos, Constantine; m. Patricia Bennett, 1979 (div.). Grad., Fordham Prep. Sch., 1948. Assoc. dir. Indsl. Area Found., Chgo., 1954-63; mem. staff Chgo. Daily News, 1963-66, Washington Post, 1966—76; columnist N.Y. Observer, 1993—; contbg. writer Archtl. Digest, 1996—. Author: Mississippi Notebook, 1964, Multiversity, 1966, We Are The People Our Parents Warned Us Against, 1968, Two, Three, Many More, 1969, Left at The Post, 1970, (with Garry Trudeau) Fireside Watergate, 1973, Tales From the Margaret Mead Taproom, 1976, Make-Believe Presidents: Illusions of Power from McKinley to Carter, 1978, Organized Crimes, 1984, Citizen Cohn, 1988, Capitalist Fools, 1992, Hoax, 2004, Devil's Dictionary of Business, 2005; also articles.

VON HOLDEN, MARTIN HARVEY, psychologist; b. Bronx, NY, May 29, 1942; s. Leon and Gertrude (Fishbein) Von H.; m. Virginia T. Brown, Dec. 17, 1971; 1 child, Mark Walter; children by previous marriage: Sandi Gwen Bitton, David Lawrence; 1 stepchild, Theresa Ann Brilli-Rogers. BA, NYU, 1964; MA, U. Toledo, 1965; D Pub. Adminstrn., NYU, 1981. Sr. psychologist N.Y. State Dept. Mental Hygiene, Rockland State Hosp., Orangeberg, 1966-67, team leader, 1970-71, dir. interdisciplinary tng. team, 1971-73; chief of service Metro Unit Harlem Valley Psychiat. Ctr., Wingdale, NY, 1973-74, dep. dir. programs, 1974-75; dep. dir. treatment svcs. Pilgrim Psychiat. Ctr., West Brentwood, NY, 1975-76; dir. Matteawan State Hosp., Beacon, NY, 1977, Ctrl. N.Y. Psychiat. Ctr., Marcy, NY, 1977-82; exec. dir. Rochester (N.Y.) Psychiat. Ctr., 1982-97; privatization project mgr. Fla. Dept. Children & Families, Tallahassee, 1997-98; from svc. team coord. to adminstr. G. Pierce Wood Meml. Hosp., Arcadia, Fla., 1998-2000; adminstr. G. Pierce Wood Meml., Arcadia, Fla., 2000—02; ops. mgmt. cons. mgr. DeSoto Juvenile Correctional Facility, 2002—06; cons. mental health Fla. Dept. Juvenile Justice, 2006—. Assoc. dir. Inst. Motivation Rsch., Croton-on-Hudson, N.Y., 1965-73; dir. Martin H. Von Holden Assocs., motivation rsch., Fairlawn, N.J., 1970-74; cons. psychologist, group therapist Green Haven Correctional Facility, Stormville, N.Y., 1970-77; cons. psychologist, group therapist Auburn (N.Y.) Correctional Facility, 1977-94, Butler Correctional Facility, 1994-96, Willard Drug Treatment Ctr., 1997; clin. assoc. prof. dept. psychiatry Sch. Medicine, U. Rochester, 1983-97; cons. in field; spkr. in field. Contbr. articles to profl. jours. Mem. adv. coun. N.Y. State Commn. Quality Care to Mentally Disabled, 1989-97. Capt. MSC, U.S. Army, 1967-70. Recipient James Gordon Bennett prize NYU, 1964, Outstanding Achievement award United Way of N.Y. State, 1994. Fellow Am. Assn. Mental Health Adminstrs. (cert. mental health adminstr.); mem. Am. Psychol. Assn., Am. Correctional Assn., Am. Assn. Correctional Psychologists, Assn. Facility Dirs. N.Y. State Office Mental Health (pres. 1984-85), Order of Arrow, Psi Chi Jewish. Home: 1250 Peppertree Ln Port Charlotte FL 33952-1357 Office Phone: 863-990-0739. Personal E-mail: vonholden@comcast.net.

VON KAENEL, HOWARD J., army officer; b. Ft. Knox, Ky., Oct. 26, 1946; BS, U.S. Mil. Acad., 1969; Rhodes Scholar, MA in Philosophy, Politics and Econs., Oxford U., Eng., 1973. Commd. 2d lt. U.S. Army, 1969, advanced through grades to maj. gen., with field arty., 1969, regimental / DIVARTY comdr., 1989—91; comdg. gen. III Corps Arty., Ft. Sill, Okla., 1992-94; dep. under sec. for policy Office of Sec. of Def., Washington, 1994-96; dep. dir. strategy, plans and policy directorate Office of Dep. Chief Staff for Ops. and Plans, Washington, 1996, dir. strategy, plans and policy directorate, 1996-98; mil. dep. for internat. affairs Office of Dep. Under Sec. of Army, Washington, 1998—, acting dep. under Sec. of Army for Internat. affairs, 1999. MIT seminar XXI, 1986; sr. fellow Brookings Instn., 1989. Decorated Def. DSM, Legion of Merit with 2 oak leaf clusters, Bronze Star medal with 3 oak leaf clusters, others.

VON KALINOWSKI, JULIAN ONESIME, lawyer; b. St. Louis, May 19, 1916; s. Walter E. and Maybelle (Michaud) von K.; m. Penelope Jayne Dyer, June 29, 1980; children by previous marriage: Julian Onesime, Wendy Jean von Kalinowski. BA, Miss. Coll., 1937; JD with honors, U. Va., 1940. Bar: Va. 1940, Calif. 1946. Assoc. Gibson, Dunn and Crutcher, LA, 1946-52, ptnr., 1953-85, mem., chmn. exec. com., 1962—, adv. ptnr., 1985—; CEO, chmn. Litigation Scis., Inc., Culver City, Calif., 1991-94, chmn. emeritus Torrance, Calif., 1994-96, Dispute Dyamics, Inc., Torrance, Calif., 1996-2000. Instr. antitrust law So. Meth. Sch. of Law, 1982-84, bd. visitors, 1982-85; bd. dirs. W.M. Keck Found.; faculty Practising Law Inst., 1971, 76, 78-80; spkr. spl. program on antitrust litigation Columbia U. Law Sch., NYC, 1981; lawyers dels. com. to 9th Cir. Jud. Conf., 1953-67; UN expert Mission to People's Republic China, 1982. Contbr. articles to legal jours.; author: Antitrust Laws and Trade Regulation, 1969, desk edit., 1981; gen. editor: World Law of Competition, 1978, Antitrust Counseling and Litigation Techniques, 1984; gen. editor emeritus Antitrust Report. Mem. adv. bd. Salvation Army, LA. With USN, 1941-46, capt. Res. ret. Fellow Am. Bar Found., Am. Coll. Trial Lawyers (chmn. complex litigation com. 1984-87); mem. ABA (ho. of dels. 1970, chmn. antitrust law sect. 1972-73), State Bar Calif. (Anti-Trust Lawyer of Yr. award 2002), L.A. Bar Assn., U. Va. Law Sch. Alumni Assn. (mem. deans adv. coun.), Calif. Club, L.A. Country Club, La Jolla Beach and Tennis Club, Phi Kappa Psi, Phi Alpha Delta. Republican. Episcopalian. Home and Office: 12320 Ridge Cir Los Angeles CA 90049-1151 Office Phone: 310-472-1977.

VON KAPPELHOFF, DORIS See DAY, DORIS

VON KLEMPERER, KLEMENS, historian, educator; b. Berlin, Nov. 2, 1916; came to U.S., 1938; s. Herbert O. and Frieda (Kuffner) Von K.; m. Elizabeth Lee Gallaher, Dec. 19, 1953; children: Catharine Lee, James Alfred Abitur, Französisches Gymnasium, Berlin, 1934; MA, Harvard U., 1940, PhD, 1949; MA, Cambridge U., 1974. Vis. prof. Stanford U., Palo Alto, Calif., 1960; prof. history Bonn U., Fed. Republic Germany, 1963-64; L. Clark Seelye prof. history Smith Coll., Northampton, Mass., 1960-87, prof. emeritus, 1987—. Vis. prof. Amherst (Mass.) Coll., 1989, 91, 96; vis. fellow Trinity Coll., Oxford, Eng., 1982. Author: Germany's New Conservatism, 1957, Mandate for Resistance, 1969, Ignaz Seipel: Christian Statesman, 1972, German Resistance Against Hitler: The Search for Allies Abroad 1938-1945, 1992, The German Incertitudes, 1914-1945, 2000; editor: A Noble Combat. The Letters of Shiela Grant Duff and Adam von Trott, 1988, "Für Deutschland" Die Männer des 20 Juli, 1994; contbr. articles to profl. jours. Served with AUS, 1943-46, ETO Recipient Austrian Cross of Honor for Sci. and Art 1st class, 1997; Guggenheim Found. fellow, 1957-58; Fulbright fellow, 1957-58, 63-64; Overseas fellow Churchill Coll., Cambridge, Eng., 1973-74; Inst. for Advanced Study fellow, Berlin, 1986; Am. Philos. Soc. grantee, 1977-78, Am. Council of Learned Socs. grantee, 1978-79 Mem. Am. Hist. Soc. (chmn. conf. group for central European history 1982-83) Clubs: Century (N.Y.C.). Avocations: mountain climbing, hiking. Home: 23 Washington Ave Northampton MA 01060-2822 Office: Smith Coll Northampton MA 01063-0001 Home Phone: 413-586-0709; Office Phone: 413-585-3705. Business E-Mail: kvonklem@smith.edu.

VON KLITZING, KLAUS, research facility administrator, physicist; b. Schroda, Poland, June 28, 1943; s. Bogislav and Anny (Ulbrich) von K.; m. Renate Falkenberg, May 27, 1971; children: Andreas, Christine, Thomas. Diploma, Tech. U. Braunschweig, 1969; PhD, U. Wuerzburg, 1972; Habilitation, 1978. Faculty mem. Tech. U., Munich, 1980-84; dir. Max Planck Inst. FKF, Stuttgart, 1985—; hon. prof. Stuggart U., 1985. Rschr. Clarendon Lab., Oxford, 1975—76, High Magnetic Field Lab., Grenoble, 1979—80. Recipient Nobel prize in physics Royal Swedish Acad. Sci., 1985. Mem.: German Physical Soc. (hon.). Achievements include discovery of the quantized Hall effect. Office: Max Planck Inst Feskörperforschung Heisenbergstr 1 D-70569 Stuttgart Germany

VON KUSTER, LEE NORMAN, retired mathematics professor; b. Scobey, Mont., Mar. 28, 1932; s. Roger Norman and Ragnild Matilda von Kuster; m. Cleo Lorraine Forbes; children: Jeffrey Lee, Gregory Hal, Lowell Eron. BA, U. Mont., Missoula, 1954, MEd, 1967, EdD, 1971. Math. and sci. tchr. Turner Pub. Schs., Mont., 1955—56, Frazer Pub. Schs., Mont., 1958—61, Wolf Point Pub. Schs., Mont., 1961—63, Glendive Pub. Schs. and Dawson CC, Mont., 1964—67; state supr. math. Dept. Pub. Instrn., Helena, Mont., 1967—69; instr. math. U. Mont., 1969—71, prof. math. edn., 1971—94, U. Tex. Pan Am., Edinburg, 1994—2007; ret., 2007. Cons. U. Mont., 1980—88. Named Most Inspirational Prof., U. Mont., 1986; scholar NSF scholar, Boston Coll., 1963—64;, Wayne State U., Detroit, 1962. Mem.: Nat. Coun. Suprs. Math., Assn. Math. Tchrs. Eng., Nat. Coun. Tchrs. Math., Phi Delta Kappa. Republican. Home: 2808 Umbrella Bird Ave Mcallen TX 78504 Personal E-mail: lvonkuster@rgv.rr.com.

VON MANDEL, MICHAEL JACQUES, lawyer; b. Yokohama, Japan, Oct. 20, 1941; came to the U.S., 1946; s. Michael Maximillan and Suzanne (Jacques) V.M.; m. Mary Denise Bienvenue, Dec. 22, 1984; 1 child, Michelle Denise. AB in Econs., Georgetown U., DC, 1964; JD, Cath. U., 1968; LLM in Taxation, NYU, 1970. Bar: Washington 1969, Conn. 1969, U.S. Supreme Ct. 1972, Ill. 1976, U.S. Dist. Ct. (no. dist.) Ill. 1976, U.S. Ct. Appeals (7th cir.) 1976, Fla. 1977. Trial atty. FTC, Washington, 1968-69; trial atty. tax divsn. U.S. Dept. Justice, Washington, 1970-76; pvt. practice Chgo., 1976-93; ptnr. Von Mandel & Von Mandel, Chgo., 1994—. Adj. prof. grad. tax program DePaul U., Chgo., 1980-83. Contbr. chapters to books. Mem. ABA (tax and litigation sects. 1976—), Chgo. Bar Assn. (fed. tax com. 1976—), Fed. Bar Assn. (bd. dirs. 1981-93), Seventh Cir Bar Assn., Union League Club. Roman Catholic. Address: Ste 1000 79 W Monroe St Chicago IL 60603-4901 Home: 1333 N Sandburg Terr Chicago IL 60610 Office Phone: 312-726-2145. Personal E-mail: mvmtax@aol.com.

VON MEHREN, GEORGE M., lawyer; b. Boston, Nov. 2, 1950; m. Barbara A. von Mehren, Dec. 20, 2003; children: Paige E., Reed C. AB, Harvard U., 1972, JD, 1977; BA, Cambridge U., Eng., 1974, MA, 1985. Bar: Ohio 1977, registered: US Supreme Ct., US Ct. Appeals (6th cir.), US Dist. Ct. (No. Dist.) Ohio. Assoc. Squire, Sanders & Dempsey LLP, Cleve., 1977-86, ptnr., 1986—, chair Internat. Dispute Resolution Practice Group, 1998—. Contbr. articles to profl. jours.; spkr. in field. Office: Squire Sanders & Dempsey 127 Public Sq Ste 4900 Cleveland OH 44114-1304 Office Phone: 216-479-8614. Office Fax: 216-479-8777. Business E-Mail: gvonmehren@ssd.com.

VON MEHREN, ROBERT BRANDT, retired lawyer; b. Albert Lea, Minn., Aug. 10, 1922; s. Sigurd Anders and Eulalia Marion (Anderson) von M.; m. Mary Katharine Kelly, June 26, 1948 (dec. Mar. 1985); children: Carl S., John M. (dec.), Katharine, Jane, Margaret; m. Susan Heller Anderson, Apr. 2, 1988. BA summa cum laude with philosophical oration, Yale U., 1943; LLB magna cum laude, Harvard U., 1946. Bar: N.Y. 1946, U.S. Supreme Ct. 1954. Law clk. to Judge Learned Hand U.S. Ct. Appeals (2d cir.), 1946-47; law clk. to Assoc. Justice Stanley Reed U.S. Supreme Ct., 1947-48; assoc. Debevoise & Plimpton, NYC, 1946, 48-57, ptnr., 1957-93, of counsel, 1994-95, ret., 1995. Arbitrator in internat. and other matters; sr. lectr. in law Wharton Sch. U. Pa., Phila., 1985-86; legal counsel Prep. Commn. for Internat. Atomic Energy Agy., N.Y.C., 1956-57; trustee Practising Law Inst., N.Y.C., 1972-96, emeritus, 1996, pres., 1979-86, chmn. bd., 1986-96. Bd. editors Harvard Law Rev., 1944-46, Am. Jour. Internat. Law, 1981-89, hon. editor, 1990-2000; contbr. articles to profl. jours. Trustee Axe Houghton Found., N.Y.C., 1965—; bd. dirs. Legal Aid Soc., N.Y.C., 1966-70; pres. Harvard Law Sch. Assn. N.Y., 1982-83. Mem. Assn. Bar City N.Y., Internat. Law Assn. (vice chmn. 1989—, pres. Am. br. 1978-86, chmn. exec. com. 1986-92), Coll. of Comml. Arbitrators, Coun. on Fgn. Rels., Univ. Club, Century Assn. N.Y.C., The Comml. Bar Assn. (hon. mem.). Home: 925 Park Ave New York NY 10028-0210 Office: 919 3rd Ave 46th Fl New York NY 10022 Office Phone: 212-909-6588. Business E-Mail: rbvonmeh@debevoise.com.

VON MERING, OTTO OSWALD, anthropology educator; b. Berlin, Oct. 21, 1922; came to Switzerland, 1933, to U.S., 1939, naturalized, 1954; s. Otto O. and Henriette (Troeger) von M.; m. Shirley Ruth Brook, Sept. 11, 1954; children: Gretchen, Karin, Gregory, Hilary, Celia. Grad., Belmont Hill Sch., 1940; BA in History, Williams Coll., 1944; PhD in Social Anthropology, Harvard U., 1956. Instr. Belmont Hill Sch., Belmont, Mass., 1945-47, Boston U., 1947-48, Cambridge Jr. Coll., 1948-49; rsch. asst. lab. social rels. Harvard U., 1950-51, Boston Psychopathic Hosp., 1951-53; Russell Sage Found. fellow NYC, 1953-55; asst. prof. social anthropology U. Pitts. Coll. Medicine, 1955-60, assoc. prof., 1960-65, prof. social anthropology, 1965-71; prof. child devel. and child care U. Pitts. Coll. Allied Health Professions, 1969-71; prof. anthropology and family medicine U. Fla., 1971-76, prof. anthropology in ob-gyn, 1979-84, prof. anthropology and gerontology, 1986-96, prof. anthropology and gerontology emeritus, 1998, joint prof. dept. medicine, coll. medicine, 1994-96. Lectr. Sigmund Freud Inst., Frankfurt, Germany, 1962-64, Pitts. Psychoanalytical Inst., 1960-71, Interuniv. Forum, 1967-71; tech. adviser Maurice Falk Med. Fund, 1964-75; Fulbright vis. lectr. 1962-63; Richard-Merton guest prof. Heidelberg U., Germany, 1962-63; vis. prof. Dartmouth, 1970-71; vis. lectr. continuing edn. Med. Coll. Pa., 1990-92; vis. lectr. U. Sheffield, Eng., 1995, U. Liverpool, 1995, U. Augsburg, 1997, U. Heidelberg, 1997; hon. vis. prof. U. Coll. London Med. Sch., 1997; supr. grad. study program Ctr. Gerontologic Studies, U. Fla., 1983-85, assoc. dir. 1985-86, dir. 1986-96, prof. emeritus 1998; coord. com. Geriat. Edn. Ctr., Coll. Medicine, U. Fla., 1986-96; med. selection com. Coll. Medicine U. Fla., 2000-07; adv. bd. nursing programs Santa Fe CC, 2001-07; nat. tech. expert panel long-term care Health Care Financing Adminstrn., Washington; adv. bd. Internat. Exch. Ctr. Gerontology State U. System Fla., 1987-92, Second Season Broadcasting Network, Palm Beach, Fla., 1989-92, Fla. Policy Exch. Ctr. Aging, State U. System Fla., 1991-95, Assoc. Health Industries Fla., Inc., Nat. Shared Housing Resource Ctr., Balt., 1994-95; cons. in field. Author: Remotivating the Mental Patient, 1957, A Grammar of Human Values, 1961, (with Mitscherlich and Brocher) Der Kranke in der Modernen Gesellschaft, 1967, (with Kasdan) Anthropology in the Behavioral and Health Sciences, 1970, (with Maria Alvarez) Aging, Demography and Well-Being in Latin America, 1989; (with R. Binstock and L. Cluff) The Future of Long Term Care, 1996; also articles; commentary editor: Human Organization, 1974-76; corr. editor Jour. Geriatric Psychiatry, 1990-98; mem. editl. bd. Med. Anthropology, 1976-84, Ednl. Gerontology, 1990-2005, Australasian Leisure for Pleasure Jour., 1995-2000, Jour. Cross-Cultural Gerontology, 1996-2002; contbr. essays to books. Pres. Dedicated Alt. Resources for the Elderly, 1996-98; bd. dirs. No. Ctrl. Fla. chpt. Alzheimer's Assn., 1996—2002; bd. dirs. Shepherd's Ctrs. Am., Gainesville, 1998-2000. Recipient Fulbright-Hayes Travel award, 1962-63; grantee Wenner-Gren Found., N.Y., 1962-63, Am. Philos. Soc., 1962-63, Maurice Falk Med. Fund, 1970-71, US-DHHS, 1979-83, Walter Reed Army Inst. Rsch., 1987-91, US-ADA/Fla. Dept. Elder Affairs, 1993-94, Rockefeller Bros. Fund, 1950-51; spl. fellow NIMH, 1971-72. Fellow AAAS, Am. Anthrop. Assn. (mem. James Mooney award com. 1978-81, vis. lectr. 1961,-62, 71-74, 91-92), Am. Gerontol. Soc., Royal Soc. Health, Acad. Psychosomatic Medicine, Am. Ethnological Soc., Soc. Applied Anthropology, Royal Anthrop. Inst.; mem. Assn. Am. Med. Colls., Assn. Anthrop. Gerontol. (pres.-elect 1991-92, pres. 1992-93), Am. Fedn. Clin. Research, Am. Public Health Assn. (capacity proposal evaluator-reviewer, 2007), Canadian Assn. Gerontology, British Soc. Gerontology, So. Gerontol. Soc. (Gerontol. Pioneer honor 2005), Med. Group Mgmt. Assn., World Fedn. Mental Health, Internat. Assn. Social Psychiatry (regional counselor 1973-81), Internat. Hosp. Fedn., Help Age Internat. (London). Home: 818 NW 21st St Gainesville FL 32603-1027 Office: U Fla Ctr Gerontological Studies Turlington Hall Gainesville FL 32611 Office Phone: 352-376-9512. *Three guides to conduct I value most: always search for the best fit of fact, argument, and experience. Every first remedy must be amended quickly. When the past disturbs the present, more work on the future is needed.*

VON MUEFFLING, WILLIAM, investment company executive; BA, Columbia U., 1990, MBA, 1995. Analyst Deutsche Bank, Germany, France, Gabelli & co.; mng. dir. Worldwide Opportunities Hedge Funds Lazard Asset Mgmt., mng. dir. European Opportunities Hedge Funds; founder Cantillon Capital Mgmt. Adj. assoc. prof. fin. and economics Columbia U., 2001—. Office: Cantillon Capital Mgmt 25th Floor 40 W 57th St New York NY 10019 also: Columbia Univ 310 Uris 3022 Broadway New York NY 10027 Office Phone: 212-603-3300, 212-854-7903. Office Fax: 212-854-7900. E-mail: wvonmueffling@cantilloncapital.com.

VON PRINCE, KILULU MAGDALENE, retired occupational therapist, sculptor; b. Bumbuli, Lushoto, Tanzania, Jan. 9, 1929; arrived in U.S., 1949; d. Tom Adalbert and Juliane (Martini). BA in Occupl. Therapy, San Jose State U., 1958, MS in Occupl. Therapy, 1972; EdD, U. So. Calif., 1980; doctorate in Higher Edn., 1978. Registered occupl. therapist; cert. work evaluator, work adjustment specialist. Commd. 2d lt. U.S. Army, 1959, advanced through grades to lt. col., staff asst. Denver, 1959-62; hand rehab. asst., hand therapy Walter Reed Army Med. Ctr., 1962-65; hand rehab. asst. occupl. therapist 97th Gen. Hosp., U.S. Army, Frankfurt, Germany, 1965-68; sr. occupl. therapist Inst. Surg. Rsch. U.S. Army, Ft. Sam Houston, Tex., 1967-70; dir. occupl. therapy clinic, sr. dir. clinics Tripler Army Med. Ctr., Honolulu, 1972-75; adminstr. occupl. therapy clinic, cons. LAMC U.S. Army, Presido, Calif., 1975; asst. evening coll. program San Jose CC, Calif., 1976-77; fellow allied health adminstrn. SUNY, Buffalo, 1978, Commonwealth U., Richmond, Va., 1978-79; staff project devel. pre-retirement program older adults De Anza Coll., Cupertino, Calif., 1980—81; project dir. Ctr. of Design, Palo Alto, 1980; part-time instr. Stroke Activity Ctr. Cabrillo Coll., Santa Cruz, Calif., 1981; dir. occupl. therapy clinics Presbyn. Med. Ctr., 1981-86; ptnr., mgr. retail store, 1986-89; dir. rehab. therapy Merrithew Meml. Hosp. Contra Costa Med. Ctr., Martinez, Calif., 1990-93; sculptor, 1993—; activity program coord. Calif. Womens Detention Facility, Chowchilla, 1994-97; ret., 1997. Co-author: Splinting of Burned Patients, 1974; producer videos: Elbow Splinting of the Burned Patient, 1970, Self-Instruction Unit: Principles of Elbow Splinting, 1971; contbr. articles to profl. jours. With US Army, 1952—55. Decorated Legion of Merit; recipient Disting. Alumni Honors award San Jose State U., 1982, Best of Show award Nat. Veteran's Creative Arts Competition, Fresno Local Vet Art Show, 2004; honored by having Ballon painting to be first mosaic mural on Hwy. 168, Rotary Club, Fresno., 2006; scholar U.S. Surgeon Gen., 1972; fellow Kellogg Found., 1979. Mem.: Occupl. Therapy Assn. Calif. (v.p. 1981—84, state chair pers. 1981—84, state chair continuing edn. 1984—86, award of excellence 1986, Lifetime Achievement award 1994), Am. Occupl. Therapy Assn., Am. Soc. Hand Therapists (life), Alliance Calif. Artist. Avocations: stone sculpture, painting, kayaking, travel, fossil hunting. Home: 172 N Karen Ave Clovis CA 93612-0112 E-mail: kiluluv@aol.com.

VON RAFFLER-ENGEL, WALBURGA (WALBURGA ENGEL), retired language educator; b. Munich, Sept. 25, 1920; came to U.S., 1949, naturalized, 1955; d. Friedrich J. and Gertrud E. (Kiefer) von R.; m. A. Ferdinand Engel, June 2, 1957; children: Lea Maxine, Eric Robert von Raffler. DLitt, U. Turin, Italy, 1947; MS, Columbia U., 1951; PhD, Ind. U., 1953. Free-lance journalist, 1949-58; mem. faculty Bennett Coll., Greensboro, NC, 1953-55, U. Charleston (formerly Morris Harvey Coll.), W.Va., 1955-57, Adelphi U., CUNY, 1957-58, NYU, 1958-59, U. Florence, Italy, 1959-60, Istituto Postuniversitario Orgn. Aziendale, Turin, Italy, 1960-61, Bologna Center of Johns Hopkins U., 1964; assoc. prof. linguistics Vanderbilt U., Nashville, 1965-77, prof. linguistics, 1977-85, prof. emerita, sr. rsch. assoc. Inst. Pub. Policy Studies, 1985—2002, dir. linguistics program, 1978—85; chmn. com. on linguistics Nashville U. Ctr., 1978—85; Italian NSF prof. Psychol. Inst. U. Florence, Italy, 1986-87; prof. NATO Advanced Study Inst., Cortona, Italy, 1988; pres. Kinesics Internat., 1988—, ret. Vis. prof. linguistics Shanxi U., Peoples Republic China, 1988-2002; vis. prof. U. Ottawa, Ont., Can., 1971-72, Lang. Scis. Inst., Internat. Christian U., Tokyo, 1976, U. Paris, Sorbonne, 1965-67, 1978-79; grant evaluator NEH, NSF, Can. Coun.; manuscript reader Ind. U. Press, U. Ill. Press, Prentice-Hall; advisor Trinity U., Simon Frazer U.; dir. internat. seminar Cross-Cultural Comm., 1986-87; mem. Ctr. for Global Media Studies, 1999; State Dept. Italy del. to Congress of the Hague; lectr. in field; specialist in non-verbal comm. Author: Il prelinguaggio infantile, 1964, The Perception of Nonverbal Behavior in the Career Interview, 1983, The Perception of the Unborn Across the Cultures of the World, Japanese edit., 1993, English edit., 1994 (transl. into Chinese), A Traveler's Guide to Cross-Cultural Business Communications, 2000; co-author: Language Intervention Programs, 1960-75; editor, co-editor 12 books; author films and videotape; contbr. of 500 articles to profl. jours. in Engish, Itialian, French, German, Chinese, Japanese. Grantee Am. Coun. Learned Socs., NSF, Can. Coun., Ford Found., Kenan Venture Fund, Japanese Ministry Edn., NATO, UNESCO, Finnish Acad., Meharry Med. Coll., Internat. Sociol. Assn., Internat. Coun. Linguists, Tex. A&M U., Vanderbilt U., others. Mem. AAUP, Internat. Linguistic Assn., Linguistic Soc. Am. (chmn. Golden Anniversary film com. 1974, emerita 1985—), Linguistic Assn. Can. and the U.S., Internat. Assn. for Applied Linguistics (com. on discourse analyses, sessions chmn. 1978), Lang. Origins Soc. (exec. com. 1985-97, chmn. internat. congress, 1987), Internat. Sociol. Assn. (rsch. com. for sociolinguistics, session co-chmn. internat. conf. 1983, session chmn. profl. conf. 1983), Internat. Coun. Psychologists, Internat. Assn. for Intercultural Comms. Studies, Internat. Assn. for Study of Child Lang. (v.p. 1975-78, chmn. internat. conf. Tuscan Acad. Scis., Florence, Italy 1972), Inst. for Nonverbal Comm. Rsch. (workshop leader 1981), Southeastern Conf. on Linguistics, 1980— (hon. mem. 1985—), Semiotic Soc. Am. (organizing com. Internat. Semiotics Inst. 1981), Nat. Assn. Scholars, Tenn. Assn. Scholars (bd. dirs. 1998-99), Internat. Assn. for Intercultural Comms. Studies (panel organizer 1999), United Europe Movement (sect. chmn. 1944-45), Internat. Comm. Assn., Internat. Pragmatics Assn. Achievements include being instrumental in forcing Vanderbilt U. to enroll women on an equal basis with men. Home and Office: 2455 Brighton Oaks San Antonio TX 78231 *In the social sciences theories come and theories go. Carefully collected and objectively analyzed data are useful for generations and the cleanest research design in the lab does not equal a moderately neat design in the naturalistic setting.*

VON RHEIN, JOHN RICHARD, music critic, journalist, writer; b. Pasadena, Calif., Sept. 10, 1945; s. Hans Walter and Elsa Maryon (Brossmann) von R. AA, Pasadena City Coll., 1965; BA in Eng., UCLA, 1967; BA in Music, Calif. State U., Los Angeles, 1970. Music reviewer Hollywood (Calif.) Citizen-News, 1968-70; music editor and critic, dance critic Akron (Ohio) Beacon Jour., 1971-77; music critic Chgo. Tribune, 1977—; prof. music appreciation Rio Hondo Jr. Coll., Calif., 1970-71. Lectr., TV host, rec. annotator. Co-author (with Andrew Porter): Bravi; contbr. articles to World Book Ency., New Grove Dictionary of Music, mags. and papers. Music Critics Assn.-Kennedy Center for Performing Arts fellow, 1972, 75; recipient Peter Lisagor award Soc. Profl. Journalists, 1999. Mem. Music Critics Assn. N.Am. (edn. com., dir. 1988), Ravinia Critics Inst. (dir. 1988). Office: Chgo Tribune Co 435 N Michigan Ave Chicago IL 60611-4066 Home Phone: 773-561-2620; Office Phone: 312-222-3570. Business E-Mail: jvonrhein@tribune.com.

VON ROEDERN, BOLKO GRAF, energy executive, researcher; b. Johannesburg, Dec. 20, 1950; arrived in US, 1979; s. Conrad Graf and Dagmar Grafin (Lubbert) von Roedern; m. Susan Kathryn Bateman, July 6, 1982; children: Gabriele Kathryn, Meredith Margret, Christina Barbara. Diploma in physics, Tech. U. Clausthal, Germany, 1976; PhD, U. Stuttgart, 1979. Postdoctoral fellow Harvard U., Cambridge, Mass., 1979—83; sr. scientist Solar Energy Rsch. Inst., Golden, Colo., 1983—85; mgr. Glasstech Solar, Inc., Wheat Ridge, Colo., 1985—89; ptnr., co-owner MV Systems, Inc., Golden, 1989—90; sr. project mgr. Nat. Renewable Energy Lab., Golden, 1990—. Contbg. author Ency. of Energy, 2004, inventor in field. Pres. Holy Cross Luth. Ch., Wheat Ridge, 2001—03. Recipient R&D 100 award, 2003; co-finalist, World Tech. Network and The Economist, 1999. Mem.: Materials Rsch. Soc., Am. Phys. Soc., German Phys. Soc. Avocations: horseback riding, skiing, flying. Office: Nat Renewable Energy Lab 1617 Gole Blvd Golden CO 80401-3393 Office Phone: 303-384-6480. Office Fax: 303-384-6430. Business E-Mail: bolko_von_roedern@nrel.gov.

VON ROSEN, RÜDIGER, stock exchange executive; b. Grocholin, June 21, 1943; Diploma, U. Frankfurt, 1970; PhD, 1973. With Deutsche Bundesbank, 1974-86; exec. vice-chmn. Fedn. German Stock Exchanges, 1986-93; speaker bd. mng. dirs. Frankfurter Wertpapierbörse AG, Frankfurt, 1990-92; mem. bd. mng. dirs. Deutsche Börse AG, Frankfurt, 1993-94, mng. dir., 1995—, Deutsche Aktieninstitut EV, Frankfurt. Hon. prof. Frankfurt U., 1998; hon. consul of Latvia, 2004—. Office: Deutsches Aktieninstitut EV Niedenau 13-19 D-60325 Frankfurt Germany Office Phone: +49-69-92915-21. E-mail: rosen@dai.de.

VON SAUERS, JOSEPH F., lawyer; b. NYC; s. Joseph F. and Margaret von Sauers; m. June A. von Sauers. BEE, Manhattan Coll., 1980; MBA, Pepperdine U., 1987; JD, Southwestern U., 1991; LLM, Columbia U., 1995; DBA, North Central U., 2001. Bar: Calif. 1992, D.C. 1993, Minn. 1993, Tex. 1993, Colo. 1994, U.S. Patent and Trademark Office. Contracts negotiator Hughes Aircraft Co., El Segundo, Calif., 1985-92; atty. Jones, Day, Reavis & Pogue, Dallas, 1992-94, Loeb & Loeb, LLP, LA, 1995-97, Gray, Cary, Ware & Freidenrich, Palo Alto, Calif., 1997-98; dep. gen. coun. Roland Corp. U.S., LA, 1998—. Active Calif. Lawyers for Arts, L.A., 1996; guest spkr. Loyola U., L.A., 1996. Contbr. articles to profl. jours. Capt. USNR. Recipient Kuwait Liberation medal Saudi Arabian/Kuwaiti Govts., 1992, 96, Joint Svcs. Commendation medal, Navy Commendation medal (2), Navy Achievement medal; Wildman scholar Southwestern U., 1987-91. Mem.: LA County Bar Assn., Naval Res. Assn. Avocations: sailing, golf, tennis.

VON SCHACK, WESLEY W., utilities executive; b. NY, 1944; married. AB, Fordham U., 1965; MBA, St. John's U., Jamaica, NY, 1971; doctorate, Pace U., 1990. Chmn., CEO, pres. DQE, Pitts., 1986-96, ret., 1996; chmn., pres., CEO N.Y. State Electric and Gas Corp., Binghamton, 1996-99, chmn. bd. dirs., 1999—; chmn., pres., CEO Energy East Corp., New Gloucester, Maine, 1998—, lead dir. Bd. dirs. Mellon Fin. Corp., Energy East Corp., Teledyne Techs., Inc., Gettysburg Found.; chmn., dir. AEGIS Ins. Co., Inc. Trustee Gettysburg Found. Mem.: Am. Gas Assn. Found. (trustee). Office: Energy East Corp 217 Commercial St Portland ME 04101 Business E-Mail: wwvonschack@energyeast.com.

VON SELDENECK, JUDITH METCALFE, career planning administrator; b. High Point, NC, June 6, 1940; d. Frederick Maurice and Harriet (Curtis) Metcalfe; m. George Clay von Seldeneck, Apr. 8, 1972; children: Rodman Clay, Kevin Clay. BA, U. N.C., 1962; postgrad., Am. U., 1963—64. Senatorial asst., 1963—72; pres., CEO Diversified Search Cos., Phila., 1972—, Diversified Health Search. Bd. dirs. Corestates Fin. Corp.,

Keystone Life Ins. Co., Tasty Baking Co. Bd. dirs. Greater Phila. C. of C., Com. of 200; mem., co-founder, bd. dirs. Forum Exec. Women. Mem.: Assn. Search Cons., Wharton Club Phila. (bd. mem.), Sunneybrook Golf Club, Phila. Cricket Club. Democrat. Episcopalian. Avocations: golf, reading, fishing. Home: 8124 St Martins Ln Philadelphia PA 19118-4103

VON SPEYER, JACQUES, financier; b. Munich, June 12, 1950; s. Naftalie and Leah von Speyer; m. Alexa Andrea Petschek; children: Dahlia Petschek-von Speyer, Sarah Petschek-von Speyer. Degree in Internat. Fin., London Sch. Econs., 1970. Vice-chmn. Zentral Bank, Zurich, Switzerland, 1974—85; sr. adv. FDIC Mfr. Hanover Bank, Continental Ill. Bank, 1985—86; founder Seychelles Cinnamon Industry, 1986—90; chmn. Palm Beach Milk Co., 1990—94, Global Interact, 1994—99, Deerfalls Internat., Issaquah, Wash., 1999—. Amb. EEC, Brussels, 1971—73. Recipient Order Merit award, Italian Govt., 1975, Quuen's medal, Hong Kong, 1977. Republican. Jewish. Achievements include invention of micro heat technology; 747 airport catering system; 1000 meter sniper scope spotting ring. Home and Office: Deerfalls Interantional 4580 Klahanie Drive South East Issaquah WA 98029 Home Phone: 425-222-0050; Office Phone: 425-222-0050. Office Fax: 425-222-0054; Home Fax: 425-222-0054. Personal E-mail: deerfalls@comcast.net.

VON SPIEGEL, JANICE KRIEGER, mathematics educator; d. Donald and Frances Krieger; m. Charles F. von Spiegel, Mar. 20, 1971; children: Heidi Robinson, Jacqueline. BA in Edn., U. Akron, 1971, MA in Edn., 2003. Tchg. cert. OH Dept. Edn., 2005. Math tchr. Akron Pub. Schs., Ohio, 1972—76; math instr. U. Akron, 1982—85; math tchr. St. Vincent-St. Mary H.S., Akron, 1985—88, Archbishop Hoban HS, Akron, 1988—. Spkr. in field. Adviser Academic Challenge Team, Akron, 1992—2004, Future Tchrs. Club, Akron, 2004—05. Mem.: Greater Akron Math. Educators Soc. (pres. 1996—2003), Math. Assn. Am., Nat. Coun. Tchrs. Math., OH Coun. Tchrs. Math. (east dist. dir. 2000—03, spkr., gen. co chair statewide conf. 1998, 2004, Outstanding Math. Classroom Tchr. East Dist. OH 1999), Pi Mu Epsilon. Home: 202 Mineola Ave Akron OH 44313 Office: Archbishop Hoban HS 1 Holy Cross Blvd Akron OH 44306 Home Phone: 330-864-7048. Personal E-mail: jvonspiegel@neo.rr.com. Business E-Mail: vonspiegelj@hoban.org.

VON STACKELBERG, KATHERINE ELLEN, environmental scientist, consultant; d. John Roderick von Stackelberg and Steffi Heuss; m. Garth Wayne Jonson, July 14, 1995; children: Sigurgeir Temple Jonson, Bryndis LeRoy Jonson. AB, Harvard U., 1988, MS, 1998, ScD, 2006. Sr. scientist Menzie-Cura and Assoc. Inc., Winchester, Mass., 1993—2006; rsch. mgr. Harvard Ctr. for Risk Analysis, Boston, 2003—; mng. scientist Exponent Inc., Winchester, 2006—. Grantee NSF and EPA, 2003—. Mem.: Assn. Environ. and Rsch. Economists, Soc. Environ. Toxicology and Chemistry (assoc.; del. Pellston Workshop 2003, tech. com.), Soc. Risk Analysis (assoc.; program com.). Achievements include research in evaluation of alternative air pollution control strategies for Slovak Republic through the Harvard Institute for International Development; design of contingent valuation survey to value noncancer and ecological effects of exposure to PCBs in the environment; development of probabilistic modeling tools to support risk-based decision making involving environmental contaminants; providing technical leadership in developing software to support risk-based decisionmaking. Avocations: travel, Muay Thai. Office: Harvard Ctr for Risk Analysis Harvard Sch for Pub Health 401 Park Dr Landmark 404C Boston MA 02215 Home Phone: 617-783-2130; Office Phone: 617-998-1037. Home Fax: 617-783-4827. Personal E-mail: kvon@igc.org. Business E-Mail: kvon@hsph.harvard.edu.

VON STUDNITZ, GILBERT ALFRED, state official; b. Hamburg, Germany, Nov. 24, 1950; came to U.S., 1954. s. Helfrid and Rosemarie Sofie (Kreiten) von S. BA, Calif. State U., LA, 1972. Adminstrv. hearing officer State of Calif., Montebello, 1987-91, mgr. III driver control policy unit Dept. Motor Vehicles Sacramento, 1991-93; ops. mgr. Driver Safety Review, 1993-95; contract mgr. State Dept. Health Svcs., 1995-97; staff mgr. licensing ops. policy Dept. Motor Vehicles, Sacramento, 1997-2000; Welfare-to-Work regional mgr. State Health and Human Svcs. Agy., Sacramento, 2000; regional mgr. State Labor and Workforce Devel. Agy., 2002—. Author: Aristocracy in America, 1989; editor publs. on German nobility in U.S., 1986—. Active L.A. Conservancy, West Adams Heritage Assn., dir., 1989-91. Fellow: Internat. Soc. for Chivalric Rsch., Entente Cordiale for Chivalric and Heraldic Traditions; mem.: Nat. Assn. Managed Care Regulators, Driver Improvement Assn. Calif. (v.p. 1992—96, dir. media rels. 1996—), Calif. State mgrs. Assn., Orders and Medals Soc. Am., Sierra Club, Assn. German Nobility in N.Am. (pres. 1985—), Benicia Hist. Soc., Intertel, Mensa, Phi Sigma Kappa (v.p. chpt. 1978). Roman Catholic. Avocations: genealogy, collecting. Home: 1101 W 2nd St Benicia CA 94510-3125

VON VOLBORTH, ALEX (ALEXIS), geochemist, geological engineering educator; b. Viipuri, Finland, July 11, 1924; came to U.S. 1955, naturalized; m. Nadia Hasso, 1947; children: Tatyana, Swetlana, Maria, Gregory, Anna, Nicholaus H.W., Elisabeth. PhC, U. Helsinki, 1950, PhLic and PhD in Geology-Mineralogy, 1954. Mineralogist, rsch. assoc., assoc. prof., prof. U. Nev., Reno, 1956—68; Killam vis. prof. geology, Killam rsch. prof. Dalhhousie U., Canada, 1968—72; vis. prof. NASA Lunar Sci. Inst., U. Houston, 1972—73; vis. rsch. chemist U. Calif., Irvine, 1973—76; prof. geology and chemistry N.D. State U., 1975—78; prof. geology, scientist Nuc. Radiation Ctr., Wash. State U., Pullman, 1978—79; prof. geochemistry and chemistry Mont. Coll. Mineral Sci. and Tech., Butte, 1979—94, prof. geol. engring., 1987—92, dir. accelerator lab., 1983—86, sr. radiation safety officer, 1983—86; prof. emeritus Mont. Tech./U. Mont., Butte, 1995—. Prin. investigator Stoichiometry Study Lunar Rocks, NASA, 1972-73; cons. AEC, 1961-63, NASA, 1965-73, Anaconda Co., 1968, Atomic Energy Orgn. Iran, 1975, King Abdul Aziz U., Jeddah, Saudi Arabia, 1975-76, Johns Manville Corp., Chevron, 1980-83, Pegasus Gold Inc., 1987, Placer Dome Inc., Echo Bay, Inc., 1990; U.S. rep., del. 2d Conf. on Natural Reactors, IAEC, Paris, 1977; U.S. rep. Internat. Geol. Correlation Program, 1990-96; interpreter, Russian translator in Soviet Siberia for U.S. and Can. mining cos., 1990-96. One-man shows include All-Russian Geol. Rsch. Inst. and Mus. of A.P. Karpinsky, St. Petersburg, 2006, Gallery P, Las Vegas, Nev., 2006, State Geol. Mus. of V.I. Vernadsky, Moscow, 2006, Ctrl. Exhbn. Hall, St. Petersburg, 2006, Stroganov Palace - Russian Mus., 2007, Represented in permanent collections Smithsonian Nat. Mus. of Natural History, Washington, DC, Mineralogical Mus., Harvard Univ., Am. Mus. Natural History; contbr. articles to profl. jours. Traveling rsch. fellow Outokumpu Found., U. Vienna, U. Heidelberg, 1954-55, Hoover fellow Calif. Inst. Tech., 1955-56, sr. fellow Australian Acad. Sci., 1965, fellow Guggenheim Found., 1965-66; fossil Elkoceras Volborthi named in his honor. Fellow Mineral. Soc. Am., Am. Inst. Chemists; mem. Am. Chem. Soc., Am. Nuclear Soc., Soc. Econ. Geologists, Internat. Precious Metals Inst. Achievements include discovery of two new minerals, Vayrynenite and Tarkianite. Home and Office: PO Box 80 Dayton MT 59914-0080 Office Phone: 406-849-5830. Personal E-mail: aalex000@centurytel.net.

VON WALDOW, ARND N., lawyer; b. Moenchen-Gladbach, Germany, Mar. 15, 1957; came to U.S., 1966; s. Hans Eberhard and Brigitte H. (Schulze-Kadelbach) von W.; m. Esther R. Haguel, May 25, 1987; children: Rachel J., Danielle M. BA, Syracuse U., 1980; JD, U. Pitts., 1983. Bar: La. 1983, Pa. 1989. Assoc. Sessions & Fishman, New Orleans, 1983-90, Eckert, Seamans, Cherin & Mellott, Pitts., 1990-91; ptnr. Meyer, Darragh, Buckler, Bebenek & Eck, Pitts., 1991-99, Reed, Smith, Shaw & McClay, Pitts., 1999—. Mem. Product Liability Adv. Coun., Chgo., 1991—. Mem. ABA, Def. Rsch. Inst., Phi Beta Kappa. Home: 1738 Hempstead Ln Pittsburgh PA 15241-1376 Office: Reed Smith Shaw & McClay 435 6th Ave Ste 2 Pittsburgh PA 15219-1886 Office Phone: 412-288-7242. Business E-Mail: avonwaldow@reedsmith.com.

VOOGT, JAMES LEONARD, medical educator; b. Grand Rapids, Mich., Feb. 8, 1944; married; 3 children. Student, Calvin Coll., 1962-64; BS in Biological Sci., Mich. Tech. U., 1966; MS in Physiology, Mich. State U., 1968, PhD in Physiology, 1970. Fellow, lectr. dept. physiology U. Calif., San Francisco, 1970-71; asst. prof. dept. physiology and biophysics U. Louisville Sch. Medicine, 1971-77, assoc. prof. dept. physiology and biophysics, 1977; assoc. prof. dept. physiology U. Kans. Sch. Medicine, 1977-82, prof. physiology, 1982—. Assoc. dean rsch. U. Kans. Sch. Medicine, 1982—84, chmn. dept. physiology, 1993—2001; vis. prof. Erasmus U., 1985; vice chancellor rsch. U. Kans. Med. Ctr., 2006—. Mem. editl. bd. Endocrinology, 1984-86, 89-92, Am. Jour. Physiology, 1984-88, Doody's Jour., 1995-98; ad hoc reviewer Neuroendocrinology, Sci., Biology of Reproduction, Life Scis., Jour. Endocrinology, Molecular Cellular Neuroscis., Procs. Soc. Exptl. Biology and Medicine, biochm. endocrinology study sect. NIH, 1992, reproductive endocrinology study sect., 1994-98; reviewer grants NSF; editor sci. procs. Rsch. Week, 1982-83; contbr. over 120 articles to profl. publs., 4 chpts. to books. Grantee NIH, 1972-85, 88—, NSF, 1985-86, 91-94, Ctr. on Aging, 1988, Nat. Inst. Drug Abuse, 1991-93; fellow Japan Soc. Promotion of Sci., 1993; recipient Outstanding Young Alumni award Mich. Tech. U., 1974, Honors in Edn., Med. Student Voice, 1990; inducted Mich. Tech. U. Acad. of Scis. and Arts, 2000. Mem. AAAS, Endocrine Soc., Internat. Soc. Neuroendocrinology (charter mem.), Am. Physiol. Soc. (pub. affairs adv. com. 1983-87) Soc. Neuroscis., Phi Kappa Phi, Sigma Xi. Office: Dept Molecular and Integrative Physiology U Kans Med Ctr 3901 Rainbow Blvd Kansas City KS 66160-0001

VOOK, FREDERICK LUDWIG, physicist, consultant; b. Milw., Jan. 17, 1931; s. Fred Ludwig and Hedwig Anna (Werner) V.; m. Frederica Jean Sandin, Aug. 16, 1958; children: Eric Robert, Dietrich Werner. BA with honors, U. Chgo., 1951, BS, 1952; MS, U. Ill., 1954, PhD in Physics, 1958. With Sandia Labs., Kirtland AFB East, N.Mex., 1958-94; div. supr., 1962-71; mgr. dept. research, 1971-78; dir. research, 1978-94; pvt. cons. Albuquerque, 1994—. Editor: Radiation Effects in Semiconductors, 1968; co-editor: Applications of Ion Beams to Metals, 1974. Mem. coll. engring. adv. bd. U. Ill.; mem. policy bd. Nat. Nanofabrication Facility Cornell U.; mem. basic energy sci. adv. com. Panel on Value of Basic Rsch; mem. Okla. State Univ. Ctr. for Laser and Photonics Rsch. adv. bd. U. Chgo. and U. Ill. scholar and fellow. Fellow Am. Phys. Soc.; mem. IEEE (sr. mem.), Böhmische Physikalische Gesellschaft, Phi Beta Kappa, Sigma Xi. Office Phone: 505-884-4754. Personal E-mail: fandfvook@msn.com.

VOOK, RICHARD WERNER, retired physics professor; b. Milw., Aug. 2, 1929; s. Fred Ludwig and Hedwig Anna (Werner) V.; m. Julia Deskins, Sept. 7, 1957; children: Katherine, Elizabeth, Richard S., Frederick W. BA, Carleton Coll., 1951; MS, U. Ill., 1952, PhD, 1957. Staff physicist IBM Rsch. Lab., Yorktown Heights, NY, 1957—61; sr. rsch. physicist Franklin Inst. Rsch. Labs., Phila., 1961—65; assoc. prof. of metallurgy Syracuse U., NY, 1965—70, prof. of materials sci., 1970—84, prof. of physics, 1984—93, prof. emeritus, 1993—, dir. solid state sci. and tech., 1984—87, 1990—91. Physicist/chemist U. Calif., Lawrence Livermore Nat. Lab., summers 1977-81; summer faculty mem. Sandia Nat. Lab., Albuquerque, 1983, 84; bd. editors Thin Solid Films, 1985-99; cons. prof. Beijing U. Posts and Telecom., 1998-2002. Contbr. articles to profl. publs., chpts. to books. Recipient L. B. Pfeil medal and prize Metals Soc. of Great Britain, 1983. Mem. Am. Vacuum Soc., Microscopy Soc. Am., Phi Beta Kappa, Sigma Xi, Pi Mu Epsilon. Lutheran. Achievements include discovery of Auger R-factor characterization of thin film growth; development of theory of substrate-induced differential thermal expansion strains in thin films; first observation of Stranski-Krastanov growth mode in vapor deposited thin films, first use of flash evaporation to form high Tc superconducting thin films; co-discoverer of perpendicular electric field effect in copper surface electromigration. Office: Syracuse Univ 201 Physics Bldg Syracuse NY 13244-1130 Personal E-mail: rvook@hotmail.com.

VOORHEES, RICHARD LESLEY, federal judge; b. Syracuse, NY, June 5, 1941; s. Henry Austin and Catherine Adeline (Fait) V.; m. Barbara Holway Humphries, 1968; children: Martha Northrop, Steven Coerte. BA, Davidson Coll., 1963; JD, U. N.C., Chapel Hill, 1968. Bar: N.C. 1968, U.S. Dist. Ct. (we. dist.) N.C. 1969, U.S. Tax Ct. 1969, U.S. Ct. Appeals (4th cir.) 1978, U.S. Dist. Ct. (mid. dist.) N.C. 1981. Mem., ptnr. Garland, Alala, Bradley & Gray, Gastonia, NC, 1968-80; pvt. practice Gastonia, NC, 1980-88; judge U.S. Dist. Ct., Charlotte, NC, 1988—, chief judge, 1991-98, 2006—, mem. com. on adminstrn. of magistrate judges sys., 2005—. Mem. N.C. State Rep. Exec. Com., Gaston County Rep. Com., chmn., 1979-83, U.S. Jud. Conf. Com., 1993—, case mgmt. and ct. adminstrn. com., 4th Cir. Ct. Appeals Jud. Coun., 1992-93; chmn. Gaston County Bd. Elections, Gastonia, 1985-86; alt. del. Rep. Nat. Conv., Kansas City, Kans., 1976. 1st lt. U.S. Army, 1963-65, U.S. Army Res., 1963-69. Mem. N.C. Bar Assn., Fed. Judges Assn., Dist. Judges Assn. Avocation: boating. Office: US Dist Ct WDNC 250 Fed Bldg 401 W Trade St Charlotte NC 28202-1619

VOORHEES, STEPHANIE ROBIN FAUGHT, retired art educator; b. Indpls., Dec. 18, 1951; d. Edward Francis and Dorothy Marie (Teague) Faught; m. James Osborn Voorhees, June 19, 1999. BFA, Montclair State U., NJ, 1973, postgrad., 1974-76. Substitute tchr. Woodbridge (N.J.) Twp. Bd. of Edn., 1971-73, elem. art tchr., 1973-84, 85-86; middle sch. art tchr. Colonia (N.J.) Middle Sch., 1984-85; high sch. art tchr. Woodridge HS, 1986—90; middle sch. art tchr. Avenel (N.J.) Middle Sch., 1990-94; art tchr. John F. Kennedy H.S., Iselin, NJ, 1994-98, ret., 1998. Spkr. Woodbridge River Watch, 1991; pvt. art tchr., 1983-93; yearbook advisor Woodbridge H.S., 1989-90, Avenel Mid. Sch., 1991-94, John F. Kennedy H.S., 1995-98; play set designer, 1989, 94-97. Illustrator: Care of the Lower Back, 1975, Touching All the Bases, 1993; profl. muralist. Campaign vol. Rep. Party, Woodbridge, 1992; sec. to the producer Fgn. Broadcast Svc. Dem./Rep. Nat. Convs., Miami, 1972. Recipient Gov.'s Tchr. Recognition award NJ State Dept. of Edn., 1992, Excellence in Edn. award Woodbridge C. of C., 1992. Mem. AAUW, Woodbridge Twp. Fedn. of Tchrs. (v.p. 1980-83, pres. 1983-95, cert. of merit, 1982), Art Educators of N.J., Met. Mus. of Art, Manatee County Vets. Coun. (sr. v.p.), Ecology Club (advisor 1990-94), Am. Legion Aux. 325 (historian 2000-01, treas. 2001-2003), Am. Legion (sec. 2003-, treas. post 325, sec. post 30), Cabane 880 (historian 2000-01, garde de la port 2001-02, condr. 2003—), VFW Post 10141 Ladies Aux. (life, sec. 2000, sr. v.p. 2001-03). Baptist. Avocations: singing, playing piano, dance, writing, cruise travel. Home: 16211 18th Ave E Bradenton FL 34212 Office Phone: 941-375-2269. Personal E-mail: steff18@tampabay.rr.com.

VOORHEES, THEODORE, JR., lawyer; b. May 24, 1949; AB, Harvard U., 1971; JD, Catholic U., 1974. Bar: DC 1975. Ptnr. Covington & Burling, Washington, chmn. Product Liability and Toxic Tort Practice Group, co-chmn. Antitrust and Consumer Law Practice Group. Office: Covington & Burling 1201 Pennsylvania Ave NW Washington DC 20004-2401 Office Phone: 202-662-5236. Office Fax: 202-778-5236. Business E-Mail: tvoorhees@cov.com.

VOORSANGER, BARTHOLOMEW, architect; b. Detroit, Mar. 23, 1937; s. Jacob H. and Ethel A. (Arnstein) V.; m. Lisa Livingston, 1964; m. Catherine Hoover, Sept. 10, 1983 (dec. Dec. 2001); children: Roxanna Virginia (dec.), Matthew Ansley; m. Peggy Loar, June 5, 2004. AB cum laude, Princeton U., 1960; diplome, Fontainebleau, 1960; MArch, Harvard U., 1964; D (hon.), U. Architecture and Urbanism, Romania. Assoc. Vincent Ponte, Montreal, Que., Canada, 1964-67, I.M. Pei & Ptnrs., 1968-78, dir. Iran, 1975-78; co-chmn. Voorsanger & Mills (Architects), NYC, 1978-90; founder, prin. Voorsanger & Assocs., Architects, NYC, 1990—; founder Taylor/Voorsanger Urban Designers, 1991. Lectr. Bennington (Vt.) Coll., U. Pa., Columbia U., Harvard U.; guest critic, lectr. Yale U., Pratt Inst., CUNY, R.I. Sch. Design, U. Cin., Syracuse U., U. Tex., Arlington; mem. adv. bd. Parson Sch. Architecture; mem. archtl. rev. panel Port Authority of NY & NJ; advisor to Samsung Corp., Korea. Exhbns. include: NYU, Archtl. Assn., London, Harvard Grad. Sch. Design, Vacant Lots Housing Study, NY, Deutsches Architeckur Mus., Frankfurt, Mus. Finnish Architecture, Avery Lib. Centennial Exhbn. Columbia Univ., Helsinki, Bklyn. Mus.; major projects include: Le Cygne Restaurant, Neiman houseboat, NYU Midtown Ctr., NYU Bus. Sch. Library, La Grandeur housing, NYU dormitories, Hostos Cmty. Coll., NY; finalist Bklyn. Mus. masterplan internat. competition, expansion and master plan Pierpont Morgan Libr., Wethersfield Carriage Mus., Amenia, NY; Montana and Wyoming Residences; Advanced Tng. Ctr., NYU, New York Apt., NYC, Riverdale (NY) Jewish Ctr.; fellow J. Pierpont Morgan Libr., NY, Asia Soc., NY, Brody Residence, VA, Daniels/Falks Residence, Ariz., Wildcat Ridge Residence, Snowmass, Calif., Nemerever Residence, Napa, Calif., Port Authority NY/NJ Air Traffic Control Towers, Univ. Art Mus., U. Va., Asia Soc. and Mus., NYC, Olana Mus., Hudson, NY, Elie Tahari Offices, NJ; winner competition for Nat. World War II Mus., New Orleans. Mem. vis. com. RI Sch. Design, U. Tex., Arlington; mem. Pt. Authority NY/NJ Ground Zero Archive, NY Hist. Soc., also mem. archtl. cir. steering com.; chmn. bd. advisors Temple Hoyne Buell Ctr., Study Am. Architecture, Columbia U., NYC, 1989—; mem. adv. bd. Parsons Sch. Architecture; chair archtl. rev. panel Port Authority NY, NJ; bd. dirs. Worldesign Found.; mem. Regent's Panel NY State U., NY State Regents' Com. on Schs; pres. NY Found. for Architecture 2000-01. 1st lt. US Army, 1960-61. Recipient Cannon prize NAD, state and nat. awards NYC chpt. AIA, AIA/Better Homes, Bard City Club, Interiors mag., Stone Inst., AIA/Libr., Lumen, Pratt Inst., NYU, NYC Art Commn.; competition winner Nat. WWII Mus., New Orleans. Fellow: NAD, AIA (numerous offices, including pres. N.Y.C. chpt. 1987, Nat. Honor awards, N.Y. State and NYC awards); mem.: Alumni Coun. Grad. Sch. Design Harvard (editl. bd. Harvard Design mag.), Wadawanuck Club, Century Assn., Sir John Soane Mus. Found., Archtl. League NYC (bd. dirs.), Ellis Island Yacht Club (commodore 2001—). Office: 246 W 38th St Fl 14 New York NY 10018-5805 Home Phone: 212-832-1668; Office Phone: 212-302-6464. Business E-Mail: bvoorsanger@voorsanger.com.

VORA, ASHOK, financial economist; came to U.S., 1970; s. Kevalchand and Laxmi (Mehta) V.; m. Rama Kata; children: Anjali Serena, Amit Raunak. B.Sc., U. Bombay, 1967; MBA, Indian Inst. Mgmt., 1970; PhD, Northwestern U., 1973. Asst. to chmn. Vora Automotives Ltd., Bombay, 1963-67, dir., 1967-70; asst. prof. fin. CUNY, 1973-80; vis. asst. prof. fin. U. Wis., Madison, 1977; vis. assoc. prof. fin. Northwestern U., Evanston, Ill., 1979-80; assoc. prof. fin. CUNY, 1980-84, prof. fin., 1984—; dir. fin. rsch. Fed. Home Loan Mortgage Corp., Reston, Va., 1987-88; vis. prof. fin. Hofstra U., Hempstead, NY, 1990-91. Cons. in field. Contbr. articles to profl. jours. Mem. Am. Econ. Assn., Am. Fin. Assn., Fin. Mgmt. Assn., So. Fin. Assn., S.W. Fin. Assn., Western Fin. Assn., Mensa, Nat. Wildlife Fedn., Beta Gamma Sigma. Office: CUNY Dept Econs 55 Lexington Ave New York NY 10010-5518

VORA, MANU KISHANDAS, chemical engineer, consultant; b. Bombay, Oct. 31, 1945; s. Kishandas Narandas and Shantaben K. (Valia) V., m. Nila Narotamdas Kothari, June 16, 1974; children: Ashish, Anand. BSChemE, Banaras U., India, 1968; MSChemE, Ill. Inst. Tech., Chgo., 1970, PhD in ChemE, 1975; MBA, Keller Grad. Sch. Mgmt., Chgo., 1985. Grad. asst. Ill. Inst. Tech., 1969-74; rsch. assoc. Inst. Gas Tech., Chgo., 1976-77, chem. engr., 1977-79, engring. supr., 1979-82; mem. tech. staff AT&T Bell Labs. (now Lucent Techs.), Holmdel, NJ, 1983-84, Naperville, Ill., 1984—, mgr. customer satisfaction, 1990-96, voice of the customer mgr., 1997-2000; pres., CEO Bus. Excellence, Inc., 2000—. Adj. prof. Ill. Inst. Tech., Chgo., 1993—; spkr. in field. Editor: Internat. Petroleum Encyclopedia, 1980. Chmn. Save the Children Holiday Fund Drive, 1986-99; trustee Avery Coonley Sch., Downers Grove, Ill., 1987-91; pres., dir. Blind Found. for India, Naperville, 1989—. Recipient Non-Supervisory AA award Affirmative Actions Adv. Com., 1987, 92, 97, Outstanding Contbn. award Asian Am. for Affirmative Actions, 1989, Disting. Svc. award Save the Children, 1990, Ann. Merit award Chgo. Assn. Tech. Socs., 1992. Fellow Am. Soc. for Quality (standing rev. bd. 1988—, editl. rev. bd. 1989, tech. media com. 1989, mixed media rev. bd. 1994, nat. quality month regional planning com. 1989-94, nat. cert. com. 1989-94, chmn. cert. process improvements subcom. 1990-94, testimonial awards 1995, 96, 2001, 02, exec. bd. Chgo. sect., vice chmn. sect. affairs 1993-94, sect. chmn. 1994-95, nat. dir. at large, 1996-98, nat. dir. 1998-2000, v.p. 2000-2002, vice chmn. investing in quality capital campaign, spl. award 1991, Century Club award 1992, Founders' award 1993, Joe Lisy Quality award 1994, Grant medal 2001, Lancaster medal 2005); mem. Ill. Team Excellence award (chief judge 1993-99, steering com. 1993-99, award). Hindu. Avocations: reading, photography, travel, philanthropic activities. Home: 1256 Hamilton Ln Naperville IL 60540-8373 Office: Bus Excellence Inc PO Box 5585 Naperville IL 60567-5585 Home Phone: 630-637-9301; Office Phone: 630-548-5531. Personal E-mail: manuvora@yahoo.com.

VORAN, JOEL BRUCE, lawyer; b. Kingman, Kans., Mar. 24, 1952; s. Bruce H. and Venora M. (Layman) V.; m. Marsha A. Kooser, May 26, 1979; children: Erica, Ben, Ashley. BS with honors in Bus., U. Kans., 1974; JD with distinction, U. Tex., 1977. Bar: Mo. 1977, US Dist. Ct. (we. dist. Mo.) 1977, US Tax Ct. 1986. Assoc. to ptnr. Lathrop & Gage, L.C., Kansas City, Mo., 1977—. Adv. dir. Mark Twain Bank, Kansas City, 1985-89. Bd. dirs. Kansas City YMCA, 1979—; city chmn. Prairie Village Rep. Party, Kans., 1985-88; participant Kansas City Tomorrow Project, 1989-90. Named one of Top 100 Attys., Worth mag., 2006. Fellow Am. Coll. Trust and Estate Counsel; mem. ABA, Mo. Bar Assn., Kansas City Met. Bar Assn., Kansas City Lawyers Assn., Delta Tau Delta (bd. dirs., pres. 1977-87; alumni pres. Kansas City chpt. 1989-90), Friends of Art Club, Phi Delta Phi, Order of the Coif. Republican. Roman Catholic. Avocations: tennis, golf, jogging. Office: Lathrop & Gage LC 2345 Grand Blvd Ste 2800 Kansas City MO 64108-2642 Office Phone: 816-460-5625. Office Fax: 816-292-2001. E-mail: jvoran@lathropgage.com. *

VORCE-TISH, HELENE R., writer; d. Palmer Lemuel Vorce and Adelaide Catherine Miller; m. Charles Ronald VanBuren, Dec. 23, 1950 (div. Aug. 1967); children: Gail Rae, Karen Helene; m. William David Tish, Oct. 20, 1978 (dec.). BA in Psychology, Mich. State U., 1950, tchrs. cert. in English, 1961; M in English, U. N.Mex., 1968. Secondary tchr. English and creative writing Grant Unified Tchrs. Dist., Sacramento. Spkr. in field; instr. workshops in field. Author: (novels) The Wounds of Hate, 2001, Challenging the Forces of Hate, 2002, Fencing With Danger, 2006; regular contbr.: Foothill Times; contbr. articles to profl. jours. and popular mags. Fellow: Am. Soc. Journalists and Authors, Calif. Writers Club (bd. mem. 1999—2000). Avocations: tennis, swimming, jogging. Home: 3473 Santos Cir Cameron Park CA 95682 Office Phone: 530-677-3327. Personal E-mail: tish@directcon.net.

VORHEES, MARK, writer; BA in Polit. Sci., U. Wis., Madison, 1979. Editor, pub. Information Law Alert, 1993—97; editor American Lawyer Media, 1997—2004; exec. editor American Lawyer, NYC, 2004—05; sr. writer Boston Consulting Group, Inc., 2005—. Office: Boston Consulting Group 430 Park Ave New York NY 10022 also: One Exchange Place, 6th Fl Boston MA 02109 Office Phone: 212-446-2800.

VORNBERG, JAMES ALVIN, education educator; b. Corpus Christi, Tex., Nov. 23, 1943; s. Hadley F. and Gladys O. (Smith) V.; children: Scott, Mark. BS in Edn., S.E. Mo. State U., 1965; MEd, U. Ariz., 1969, PhD, 1973. Cert. tchr., prin., supt., Mo., Tex., Ariz. Tchr. Pattonville Schs., St. Ann, Mo., 1965-66; asst. to supt. Am. Sch., São Paulo, Brazil, 1971-73; asst. prof. U. Ariz., Tucson, 1973-74; from. asst. prof. to assoc. prof. Tex. A&M U., Commerce, 1974-81, prof., 1981—, head dept., 2001—06, interim dean coll. edn. and human svcs., 2006—. Co-author: The New School Leader for 21st Century: The Principal, 2002; co-author, editor: Texas Public School Organization and Administration, 10th edit., 2006. Lt. col. USAFR, 1967-94. Office: Tex A&M U-Commerce Dean's Office COEHS Commerce TX 75429 Office Phone: 903-886-5181.

VOROSMARTI, JAMES, physician; b. Palmerton, Pa., Oct. 18, 1935; s. James and Ruth Smith (Mohler) V.; m. Carol Ann Schoch, June 1959; children: James III, Richard Stefan, Erika Lynn. AB, Lafayette Coll., 1957; MD, Jefferson Coll., 1961. Diplomate Am. Bd. Preventive Medicine. Sr. med. officer USN submarine base, Pearl Harbor, Hawaii, 1964-66; med. officer Deep Submergence Project, San Diego, 1966-70; post-doctoral fellow physiology dept. SUNY, Buffalo, 1970-72; exchange med. officer Inst. Naval Medicine, Gosport, Eng., 1972-75; exec. officer Naval Med. Research Inst., Bethesda, Md., 1975-78, comdg. officer, 1980-83; program mgr. Naval Med. Research, Devel. Command, Bethesda, 1978-80; med., life scis. asst. Sec. Def., Washington, 1983-86; cons. occupational medicine Rockville, Md., 1986—. Editor: Undersea Biomedical Research, 1978-82. Recipient Def. Superior Svc. medal Sec. of Def., 1986. Fellow ACP, Am. Coll. Preventive Medicine, Am. Coll. Occupational and Environ. Medicine, Am. Acad. Family Physicians; mem. Am. Physiol. Soc., Undersea Hyperbaric Med. Soc. (Shilling award 1987, past pres.). Home and Office: 16 Orchard Way S Rockville MD 20854-6130

VORT, ROBERT A., lawyer; b. Newark, Sept. 24, 1943; s. Saul S. and Ruth J. (Jacobson) Vort; m. Elizabeth Hornstein, June 25, 1968 (div. Nov. 1979); m. Marcelle Greenstein, Nov. 18, 1979 (div. Jan. 1991); children: Joel, Abigail, Rebecca; m. Tina Kruh, Feb. 4, 1996; 1 child, Hannah. BS in Econs., U. Pa., 1965; JD, Columbia U., 1968. Bar: NJ 1968, NY 1970, US Ct. Appeals (2d and 3d cirs. 1975), US Ct. Appeals (9th cir.) 1980, US Ct. Appeals (5th cir.) 1981, US Ct. Appeals (fed. cir.) 1984, US Dist. Ct. NJ 1968, US Dist. Ct. (so. and ea. dists.) NY 1984, US Supreme Ct. 1977. Law clk. to Hon. Theodore I. Botter Superior Ct. of NJ, 1968-69; assoc. Davis & Cox, 1969-71, Israel B. Greene, 1971-73; sole practitioner, 1973-82; ptnr. Balk, Goldberger, Seligsohn, O'Connor & Rhatican, 1982-84, Kirsten, Friedman & Cherin, 1986; pvt. practice, 1984-85, 87-88; ptnr. Goldberg, Mufson & Spar, West Orange, NJ, 1988-91; counsel Donald Friedman, West Orange, 1991-92; pvt. practice Tenafly, NJ, 1997—; ptnr. Pearce, Vort & Fleisig LLC, Hackensack, 2001—04; atty. pvt. practice, 2005—. Mem.: ABA (litigation sect., family law sect., legal econs. sect.), Bergen County Bar Assn., NJ State Bar Assn. (appellate practice subcom.). Office: 2 Univ Plz Hackensack NJ 07601 Office Phone: 201-342-9501. Business E-Mail: rvort@vortlaw.com.

VORYS, ARTHUR ISAIAH, lawyer; b. Columbus, Ohio, June 16, 1923; s. Webb Isaiah and Adeline (Werner) V.; m. Lucia Rogers, July 16, 1949 (div. 1980); children: Caroline S., Adeline Vorys Cranson, Lucy Vorys Noll, Webb I.; m. Ann Harris, Dec. 13, 1980. BA, Williams Coll., 1945; LLB, JD, Ohio State U., 1949. Bar: Ohio 1949. From assoc. to ptnr. Vorys, Sater, Seymour & Pease LLP, Columbus, 1949-82, sr. ptnr., 1982-93, of counsel, 1993—. Supt. ins. State of Ohio, 1957-59; bd. dirs Vorys Bros., Inc., others. Trustee, past pres. Children's Hosp., Greenlawn Cemetery Found.; trustee, former chmn. Ohio State U. Hosps.; regent Capital U.; del. Rep. Nat. Conv., 1968, 72. Lt. USMCR, World War II. Decorated Purple Heart. Fellow Ohio State Bar, Columbus Bar Assn.; mem. ABA, Am. Judicature Soc., Rocky Fork Headley Hunt Club, Rocky Fork Hunt and Country Club, Capital Club, Phi Delta Phi, Chi Psi. Home: 5826 Havens Corners Rd Columbus OH 43230-3142 Office: Vorys Sater Seymour & Pease LLP PO Box 1008 52 E Gay St Columbus OH 43216-1008

VOS, HUBERT DANIEL, investor; b. Paris, Aug. 2, 1933; s. Marius and Aline (Porge) V.; m. Susan Hill, Apr. 18, 1958; children: Wendy, James. BA, Institut d'Etudes Politiques, U. Paris, 1954; M in Pub. Adminstrn., Princeton U., 1956. Internal auditor Internat. Packers Ltd., 1957-61, dir. fin., 1962-64; asst. to contr. Monsanto Co., 1964-66, contr. internat. div., 1966-69; v.p. planning and fin. Smith Kline Corp., 1969-72; sr. v.p. fin. Comml. Credit Co., Balt., 1972-74; sr. v.p. fin. and adminstrn., dir. Norton Simon Inc., NYC, 1974-79; sr. v.p. fin., dir. Becton Dickinson and Co., Paramus, NJ, 1979—2004; pres. Stonington Capital Corp., Santa Barbara, Calif., 1984—. Mem. Santa Barbara Mus. Art, Scholarship Found. of Santa Barbara, La Cumbre Golf and Country Club. Home: 800 Via Hierba Santa Barbara CA 93110-2222 Personal E-mail: hubertvos@aol.com.

VOSBECK, ELIZABETH JUST, retired geneticist; b. Mankato, Minn., May 24, 1925; d. Frederick William and Frances Beneta (Johnson) Just; m. William Frederick Vosbeck, Aug. 2, 1947; children: Lee, William Frederick III, Lynn, Jon Scot, James Stephen. BBA, U. Minn., 1947; MS in Anatomy, George Washington U., Washington, 1965; PhD in Human Genetics, George Washington U., 1975. Mktg. rsch. dir. Mpls. C. of C., 1947—48; embryology lab. instr., lectr., human genetics rschr. George Washington U., Washington, 1965—75; lab. dir. cell chromosome analysis Reprodn. Genetics Ctr., McLean, Va., 1976—87; ret., 1987. Grantee, NIH grantee, 1968—70. Mem.: DAR, Sigma Xi, Beta Gamma Sigma. Republican. Avocations: golf, bridge, genealogy, astrology, ice skating. Home: 7512 Fort Hunt Rd Alexandria VA 22307 E-mail: vosbeck01@aol.com.

VOSBECK, ROBERT RANDALL, architect; b. Mankato, Minn., May 18, 1930; s. William Frederick and Gladys (Anderson) V.; m. Phoebe Macklin, June 21, 1953; children: Gretchen, Randy, Heidi, Macklin. BArch, U. Minn., Mpls., 1954. Various archtl. positions, 1956-62; ptnr. Vosbeck-Vosbeck & Assocs., Alexandria, Va., 1962-66, VVKR Partnership, Alexandria, 1966-79; exec. v.p. VVKR Inc., 1979-82, pres., 1982-88; prin. Vosbeck/DMJM, Washington and Alexandria, Va., 1989-94; v.p. DMJM Arch. and Engring., 1990-94; pvt. practice archtl. cons., 1994—. Mem. Nat. Capital Planning Comm., 1976-81, U.S./USSR Joint Group on Bldg. Design and Constrn., 1974-79; mem. Nat. Park System Adv. Bd., 1984-88. Archtl. works include Pub. Safety Ctr., Alexandria, Va., 1987, Yorktown Visitors Ctr, Va., 1976, Frank Reeves Mcpl. Office Bldg., Washington, 1986, Fed. Bldg., Norfolk, Va., 1979, Jeff Davis Assocs. Office Complex, Arlington, Va., 1991, Westminster Continued Care Retirment Community, Lake Ridge, Va., 1993; author: Design Matters: The Story of VVKR, 2003. Pres. Alexandria Jaycees, 1960-61; v.p. Va. Jaycees, 1962-63; pres. Alexandria Ch. of Com., 1974-75; bd. dirs. Vail Religious Found. Engring. officer USMC, 1954-56. Recipient Plaque of Honor, Fedn. Colegios Architects, Republic of Mexico, Alumni Achievement award U. Minn. Coll. Arch., 2001, hon. fellowship Colegios Architects of Spain, Royal Archtl. Inst. Can., Soc. Architects of Mex., AIA Kemper award, 2007; named Outstanding Young Man in Va., 1963, Acadamecian, Internt. Acad. Arch. Fellow AIA (bd. dirs. 1976-78, v.p. 1979-80, pres. 1981), Internat. Union Architects (coun. 1981-87), Nat. Trust Hist. Preservation. Presbyterian. Home and Office: 770 Potato Patch Dr Unit A Vail CO 81657-4462

VOSBECK, WILLIAM FREDERICK, JR., architect; b. Mankato, Minn., May 13, 1924; s. William Frederick and Gladys (Anderson) V.; m. Elizabeth Just, Aug. 2, 1947; children: Lee, William Frederick III, Lynn, James Stephen. Student, U. Notre Dame, 1943, Cornell U., 1945; BArch, U. Minn., 1947. Ptnr. Vosbeck & Ward, Alexandria, Va., 1957-62, Vosbeck Vosbeck & Assos. (changed to Vosbeck Vosbeck Kendrick Redinger, Architects, Engrs., Planners), Alexandria, 1962-68; chmn. bd. dirs. VVKR, Inc., merged with Suter & Suter, Basel, Switzerland. Bd. dirs. Dominion Resources Va. Power, Crestar Fin. Corp. Prin. works include Nat. Automobile Dealers Assn. Hdqs., Am. Trucking Assn. Hdqs., Woodrow Wilson Rehab. Bldgs. and campus planning. Mem. Gov.'s Com. Employment Handicapped, 1973; trustee Va. Found. Ind. Colls., Va. Mus. Fine Arts, Va. C. of C.; vis. design critique, U. Va. Architecture; mem. Alexandra Hosp. Bd., pres., 1970, Mt. Vernon Presbyn. Ch. With USMCR, 1943—50. Recipient Wash. Acad. Sci. Nat. Capital award for achievement in arch., Nat. Rehab. Assn. citation tech. svcs., Gargoyle award, T. David Fitz-Gibbon Archt. Firm awrd, numerous honor and merit awards Va. Soc. AIA, Va. Mus. Fine Arts, Outstanding Achievement award Engring. News Record, 1977. Fellow AIA (pres. Va. chpt. 1971), Sigma Alpha Epsilon Found., Belle Haven Country Club, Cosmos Club, Rotary. Home: 7512 Fort Hunt Rd Alexandria VA 22307-1924 Office: Vosbeck Assocs 211 N Union St Alexandria VA 22314-2643 Home Phone: 703-765-6117; Office Phone: 703-765-5526. Fax: 703 683-4707.

VOSBURG, BRUCE DAVID, lawyer; b. Omaha, June 17, 1943; s. Noble Perrin and Dena V. (Ferrari) V.; m. Susan Simpson, May 27, 1972; children: Margaret Amy, Wendy Christine, Bruce David. BA, U. Notre Dame, 1965; BSME, 1966; JD, Harvard U., 1969. Bar: Nebr. 1969, Ill. 1970, U.S. Supreme Ct. 1974. Law clk. U.S. Dist. Ct. Nebr., 1969-70; assoc. Kirkland & Ellis, Chgo., 1970-72; ptnr. Fitzgerald & Schorr, Omaha, 1972—. Author: Financing Small Businesses, 1981, Securities Law Practice, 1987, Securities Law-Going Public, 1989, Trade Secret Protection, 1994, Protecting Intellectual Property, 1998, Intellectual Property Law, 2000. Pres. Children's Crisis Ctr., 1984-85, bd. dirs., 1973-84, Childrens Savinds Inst. 1985-86, bd. dirs. 1984-90; pres. Nebr. Tennis Assn., 1976-77; mem. Leadership Omaha, 1979; chmn. bd. dirs. City of Omaha Parks and Recreation, 1985-92; founding dir. Friends of the Parks, 1988; bd. dirs. Omaha Pub. Libr. Found., 1997—, pres., 1999—; bd. dirs. Western Heritage Mus., 1998—; exec. com. U.S. Tennis Assn., 2004—. Named to, Nebr. Tennis Hall of Fame. Fellow Nebr. Bar Found.; mem. ABA, Nat. Assn. Bond Attys., Nebr. Bar Assn. (chmn. securities com.), Omaha Bar Assn. (exec. coun. 1983-86), Rotary (dir. 1993-98), USTA/Mo. Valley Tennis Assn. (chmn. grievance com. 1978—), Nebr. Appleseed Found. (advisory bd.), Am. Intellectual Property Lawyers Assn., Tau Beta Pi. Republican. Roman Catholic. Office: Ste 400 13220 California St Omaha NE 68154-5228 Office Phone: 402-342-1000.

VOSE, KATHRYN KAHLER, marketing and communications executive; b. Denton, Tex., Aug. 18, 1953; d. James and Martha Kahler; m. William O. Vose, June 1, 1996. BA in Sociology, Sophie Newcomb Coll. Tulane U., 1975; MA in Mass Communications, U. Minn., 1977. Health/scis. reporter The Jour.-News, Nyack, NY, 1977—83; nat. corr. Newhouse Newspapers, Washington, 1983—93; comm. dir. U.S. Dept. Edn., Washington, 1993—96; dir. comm. and mktg. Campaign for Tobacco-Free Kids, Washington, 1996—99, v.p. comm. and mktg., 1999—2000; sr. v.p., worldwide dir. anti-tobacco group Porter Novelli, Washington, 2001—02, exec. v.p., 2002—, dir. health and social mktg. practice, 2002—. Panelist Washington Week In Review; vis. fellow Woodrow Wilson Nat. Fellowship Found; adviser World Health Orgn.; bd. mem., chair mktg. com. Nat. Partnership for Women and Families; mem. steering com. for the women, tobacco and cancer initiative Nat. Cancer Inst.; mem. program and comm. coms., chmn. subcom. on comm. 11th World Conf. on Tobacco and Health; contbr. Nat. Acad. Scis. Recipient Crystal Medallion award AMA, Clarion award Assn. Women Comm., Silver Inkwell award Internat. Assn. Bus. Communicators, Mercury Grand award MerComm Internat., Thoth (2) awards Pub. Rels. Soc. Am., Assoc. Press Mng. Editors Pub. Svc. award. Mem. Nat. Press Club (pres. 1991, bd. govs.), Pub. Rels. Soc. Am. Home: 3351 Tennyson St NW Washington DC 20015-2442 Home Phone: 202-966-1301; Office Phone: 202-973-5800. Personal E-mail: kkahlervose@porternovelli.com.

VOSIK, WAYNE GILBERT, lawyer; b. Phila., July 22, 1945; s. Alexander Frank and Dorothy Marie (Yarnell) V.; m. Helga Maria Kuepper, Oct. 31, 1970 (div. Nov. 1995); m. Mary Helen Welch, Mar. 21, 1997; children: Melissa Marie Vosik Osborne, Douglas Wayne, Dorothy Marie Zhen. BA, Temple U., 1967, JD, 1970. Bar: Pa. Asst. dist. atty. Phila. Dist. Atty.'s Office, 1970-72; sec., gen. counsel Ins. Fedn. Pa., Phila., 1972-74; gen. counsel, asst. sec. Acad. Ins. Group, Valley Forge, Pa., 1974-78; pvt. practice Feasterville, Pa., 1979-92; v.p. legal and govt. affairs, asst. sec., dir. human rels. Am. Travellers Corp., Bensalem, Pa., 1992-97; pvt. practice Warrington, Pa., 1997—. Cons. ins. dept. US VI, St. Thomas, 1993; bd. dirs. Greater Delaware Valley Health Underwriters Assn., Phila.; instr. Am. Coll., Brwyn Mawr, Pa., 1998. Mem. ABA, Pa. Bar Assn., Pa. Health Underwriters Assn. (mem. legis. com. 1997-2001), Life and Health Compliance Assn. (edn. com. 1996-, exec. com. 2003-06), Phi Alpha Delta. Republican. Methodist. Avocation: coaching youth soccer. Office: 1800 Street Rd 300 Warrington PA 18976-2566 Home: 55 Great Oak Dr Southampton PA 18966-1209 Office Phone: 215-491-3790. Personal E-mail: wgvosik@aol.com.

VOSK, TED W., lawyer; b. Detroit, Mich., Sept. 6, 1967; s. Stuart Allan Vosk and Susan Helen Stevens; m. Kristine Erin Kelly. BS in Physics and Math., Ea. Mich. U., 1995; Juris Doctorate, Harvard Law Sch., Cambridge, MA, 1996—99. Bar: Mass. 1999, Wash. 2000, US Dist. Ct. (we. dist.) Wash. 2003, US Supreme Ct. 2007. Acting mng. dir. NSF Sci. and Tech. Ctr. on Materials and Devices for Info. Tech. Rsch., Seattle, 2002—03; assoc. Magnuson Lowell, Redmond, Wash., 2003—04; pvt. practice, cons. Bothell, Wash., 2004—; of counsel PJC Law Group, Oreg., 2006—, Callahan Law, Wash., 2007—, Padula & Assoc., Wash., 2007—. V.p. Celestial North, Bothell, 2004—; presenter, spkr. in field. On air performer (radio broadcast) Its Over Your Head; contbr. articles to profl. pubs., chapters to books. Active voter protection program Wash. State Dem. Party, Seattle, 2004, 2006; moderator Ea. Mich. U., Ypsilanti, 2005—05. Named Wash. Rising Star in Criminal Law, Wash. Law and Politics Mag., 2005; Leib scholar, Ea. Mich. U. Dept. of Physics, 1992—94, Recognition of Excellence scholar, Ea. Mich. U., 1992—94, Goldwater scholar in math., sci. and engring., Barry Goldwater Excellence in Edn. Found., 1993—95, Sandra J. Lobbestael scholar, Ea. Mich. U. Dept. of Math., 1993—94, Campus Leader scholar, Ea. Mich. U., 1994. Mem.: ACLU, Nat. Assn. Civil Defense Lawyers, Assn. for Symbolic Logic, Wash. Alliance DUI Trial Lawyers, NW Acad. DUI Def., Wash. Assn. of Criminal Def. Lawyers (mem. legis. com. 2006—), Math. Assn. of Am., Mensa, Sigma Pi Sigma, Phi Kappa Phi. Democrat. Avocations: astronomy, mathematics, scuba diving, skydiving, motorcycling. Home Phone: 425-823-0480; Office Phone: 425-753-6343. Office Fax: 425-820-7532. Business E-Mail: tvosk@comcast.net.

VOSKA, KATHRYN CAPLES, consultant, facilitator; b. Berkeley, Calif., Dec. 26, 1942; d. Donald Buxton and Ellen Marion (Smith) Caples; m. David Karl Nehrling, Aug. 15, 1964 (div. Nov. 1980); children: Sandra E. Nehrling, Barbara M. Nehrling, Melissa A. Nehrling-Holmgren; m. James Edward Voska, Aug. 31, 1985. BS, Northwestern U., 1964; MS, Nat.-Louis U., 1989. Cert. teacher, Ill.; cert. career mgmt. fellow practitioner Inst. Career Cert. Internat. Tchr. pub. schs., Northbrook and Evanston, Ill., 1964-65; acting phys. dir. YWCA, Evanston, Ill., 1975; quality control technician Baxter Travenol, Morton Grove, Ill., 1978-80; sr. quality assurance analyst Hollister Inc., Libertyville, Ill., 1980-85; info. ctr. trainer, tech. training mgr. Rand McNally, Skokie, Ill., 1985-92; cons., facilitator Capka & Assocs., Skokie and Kansas City, 1992—; dir. edn. Nat. Office Machine Dealers, 1992-94; career and mgmt. cons. Right Mgmt., Overland Park, Kans., 1994—. Pvt. practice estate conservator. Telephone worker Contact Chgo. Crisis Hotline, 1989-90; CPR instr. trainer Amer. Heart Assn., Chgo., 1977-89; aquatic dir. YMCA, Evanston, Ill., 1969-80; rep. Alumnae Panhellenic Coun., Evanston, 1969-75; grad. Leadership Overland Park, 1996, mem. 15th anniv. special task force. Mem. ASTD (bd. dirs. Kansas City chpt. 1997-99), ASCD, Soc. Human Resource Mgmt., Midwest Soc. Profl. Cons., Assn. for Mgmt. Orgn. Design, Chgo. Orgn. Data Processing Educators, Chgo. Computer Soc., Info. Ctr. Exch. of Chgo., Assn. Quality and Participation, Am. Soc. for Quality (teller N.E. Ill. sect. 1982-84), Internat. Soc. for Performance Improvement, Assn. Career Profls. Internat. (founding pres. Kansas City chpt. 2000-02, nat. bd. dirs. 2000—, nat. bd. v.p., pres.-elect 2002-04, nat. bd. pres. 2004-06, past pres., 2006—, chmn. internat. membership drive 2004), Learning Resource Network. Presbyterian. Avocations: scuba diving, swimming, hiking, camping, travel. Home: 1001 E 118th Ter Kansas City MO 64131-3828 Office: Right Mgmt 7300 W 110th St Ste 800 Overland Park KS 66210-2387 Office Phone: 913-323-2309. Personal E-mail: kvoska@kc.rr.com. Business E-Mail: kathy.voska@right.com.

VOSS, BARRY VAUGHAN, lawyer; b. St. Paul, July 25, 1952; s. James Lee and Stella Marie (Stewart) V.; m. Marilyn Williams, Jan. 25, 1980; children: Rori, Tiffini, Aaron. BA, U. Minn., 1975; JD, Hamline U., 1978. Bar: Minn. 1978, U.S. Dist. Ct. Minn. 1980, U.S. Ct. Appeals (8th cir.) 1982. Pres. Voss and Hickman, P.A., Mpls., 1978—. Spkr. in field. Author: A Taste of Cold Steel, 1999. Bd. dirs. Ramsey County Corrections Adv. Bd., St. Paul, 1977-79, RS Eden Program, 1998—. Recipient Most Well-Prepared award Minn. Lawyers Judges' Choice, 1991, Super Lawyer, Minn. Law and Politics Survey, 2000, 01, 02, 03, others. Mem. Am. Trial Lawyers Assn. (fire loss com.), Minn. Assn. Criminal Def. Attys. (bd. dirs. 1992-96), Minn. Trial Lawyers Assn., Minn. State Bar Assn. (civil litigation and criminal law sects.), Hennepin County Bar Assn. Democrat. Lutheran. Avocations: public speaking, sports, reading. Office: 527 Marquette Ave #1050 Minneapolis MN 55402-1339 E-mail: b.v.voss@worldnet.att.net.

VOSS, JERROLD RICHARD, architecture educator; b. Chgo., Nov. 4, 1932; s. Peter Walter and Annis Lorraine (Hayes) V.; m. Jean Evelyn Peterson, Aug. 21, 1954; children: Cynthia Jean, Tania Hayes. B.Arch., Cornell U., 1955; M. City Planning, Harvard U., 1959; PhD (Bus. History fellow, Univ. fellow, IBM fellow), 1971. Asst. prof. U. Calif., 1960-61; asst. prof., asso. prof. U. Ill., 1961-69; asso. prof. Harvard U., 1969-71; prof. city and regional planning Ohio State U., Columbus, 1971—, chmn. dept. city and regional planning, 1971-79; dir. Ohio State U. (Knowlton Sch. Architecture), 1981-96, prof., 1996-2000, dir., prof. emeritus, 2000—. UN advisor to Govt. Indonesia, 1964-65; social affairs officer UN Secretariat, 1970-71; project mgr. UN Task Force on Human Environment, Thailand, 1975-76; dir. rsch. and devel. UN Ctr. for Human Settlements (Habitat), 1979-81; cons. Ill. Dept. Devel., J.S. Bolles & Assocs., UN Office Tech. Cooperation, UN Devel. Program, AID, Bechtel Nat. Inc., other pvt. and pub. orgns.; mem. external examiners team United Arab U., 1992—. Author: Human Settlements: Problems and Priorities; Contbr. articles to profl. jours. Mem. pub. policy com. Smithsonian Instn., 1970-73; bd. dirs. Champaign County United Community Council, 1965-69, Columbus Theatre Ballet Assn., 1972-75. Served to 1st lt. U.S. Army, 1955-57. Mem. Acad. for Contemporary Problems (asso.), Am. Am. Inst. Planners, Am. Soc. Engring. Edn., Internat. Center for Urban Land Policy (London). Office: 190 W 17th Ave Columbus OH 43210-1320

VOSS, LINDA I., finance company executive; b. Pigeon, Mich., Dec. 4, 1959; d. Edward and Pearl (Riffel) Ulrich; m. Timothy Voss, Aug. 9, 1980; 1 child, Jason Adam. BS in Mgmt., Oakland U., Rochester, Mich., 1982; MBA in Fin., U. Mich., 1986. Student asst. Oakland U., Rochester, 1981; acct. GMAC, Detroit, 1982-84, fin. analyst, 1985-87, asst. mgr., 1988-89, mgr., 1989-90, credit analysis mgr., 1992-93, fin. planning mgr., 1993-94, asst. treas., 1995-96, fin. dir., 1996-97; mem. fin. staff GM, Detroit, 1990-91; CFO, exec. v.p. Nuvell Fin. Svcs./Credit Corp., Little Rock, 1997—2004; mng. dir., exec. v.p. Nat. Auto Fin., Jacksonville, Fla., 2004—06; CFO, COO GMAC Comml. Fin., NYC, 2006—. Bd. dir. GMAC Comml. Fin., NYC. Author fin. software, 1988. Coach Rochester YMCA, 1988-91; bd. dirs. Luth. HS, Little Rock, 2003; tchr. St. John Sunday Sch., Rochester, 1987-91; mem. Ark. Sales Tax Adv. Com., 2000. GM fellow, 1984. Mem. Fin. Mgmt. Assn., Golden Key, Beta Gamma Sigma. Lutheran. Avocations: antiques, golf, piano. Office: GMAC Comml Fin 1290 Ave of Americas New York NY 10104 Business E-Mail: lvoss@gmaccf.com.

VOSS, OMER GERALD, farm equipment executive; b. Downs, Kans., Sept. 14, 1916; s. John and Grace (Bohlen) V.; m. Annabelle Katherine Lutz, June 30, 1940; 2 children. AB, Ft. Hays State Coll., Kans., 1937; JD, U. Kans., 1939. Bar: Kans. bar 1939. With Internat. Harvester Co., 1936-79, v.p. farm equipment div., 1962-66, exec. v.p., dir., 1966—, vice chmn., 1977-79. Served with USAAF, 1943-46 Mem.: Westmoreland Country Club, Comml. Club, Chgo. Club.

VOSS, PETER S., investment company executive; Grad., Brown Univ. CEO Security Pacific Investment Group; CEO, Europe, SE Asia Hoar Govett Cos.; Head, London merchant banking ops. Security Pacific Corp.; group exec. v.p. Bank of America; CEO, chmn. New Eng. Investment Cos. LP (now IXIS Asset Mgmt. Group NA, LP), Boston, 1992—. Bd. dir. United Way Mass. Bay. Mem.: Investment Co. Inst. (bd. dir.). Office: IXIS Asset Mgmt Group NA LP 399 Boylston St Boston MA 02116-3305 Office Phone: 617-449-2100.

VOSS, REGIS DALE, agronomist, educator; b. Cedar Rapids, Iowa, Jan. 4, 1931; s. Francis Joseph and Mary Valeria (Womichil) V.; m. Margaret Anne Mitchell, Nov. 24, 1956; children: Lori Anne, John Patrick, David James. BS, Iowa State U., 1952, PhD, 1962. cert. profl. agronomist. Agriculturist Tenn. Valley Authority, Muscle Shoals, Ala., 1962-64; prof. Iowa State U., Ames, 1964-99, prof. emeritus, 1999—. Co-contbr. chpt. to: Fertilizer Technology and Use, 1985, Soil Testing and Plant Analysis, 1990; assoc. editor Jour. Prodn. Agr., 1988-92. Pres. FarmHouse Frat. Alumni Assn. Bd., Ames, 1990. 1st lt. USAF, 1952-56, Korea., sec. treas. Iowa State U. Retirees Assn., 2003-2004 Recipient Burlington No. Found. award Iowa State U., 1990, disting. svc. award Iowa State U. Ext., 1996, Iowa Master Farmer Exceptional Svc. award, 1998. Fellow AAAS, Am. Soc. Agronomy (bd. dirs. 1976-78, Agronomic Extension Edn. award 1984, Agronomic Achievement award 1989, Werner L. Nelson award 1992), Soil Sci. Soc. Am. (bd. dirs. 1980-83). Republican. Roman Catholic. Achievements include development of field laboratory for training of crop advisors on diagnosis of crop problems; research on effects of soil amendments on chemical indices and crop yields and economic analysis of crop yield. E-mail: rvoss@iastate.edu.

VOSS, THOMAS R., electric power industry executive; B in Elec. Engring., U. Mo., Rolla, 1969. Registered profl. engr., Mo., Ill. Student engr. Union Electric (now AmerenUE), 1969, asst. engr., engr. to staff engr., supt. and dist. mgr., 1975—87, mgr. distbn. operating, 1988; v.p. region ops. AmerenCIPS Ameren Corp., 1998, sr. v.p. energy delivery/customer svcs., sr. v.p. generation, pres. AmerenEnergy and AmerenEnergy Resources, exec. v.p., COO, 2004—, pres., CEO AmerenUE, 2006—. Served in USAF. Office: Ameren Corp One Ameren Plz 1901 Chouteau Ave Saint Louis MO 63103 *

VOSSLER, DEBORAH J., mathematics and science educator; b. Portland, Oreg., May 15, 1954; d. Louis Paul and Ruth Ella Varga; m. V. Vic Vossler, June 30, 1972; children: Christopher Isaac, Erin Renee, Sierra Amira. BA in Bus. Adminstrn., U. Wash., 1977; M in Tchg., Wash. State

U., 1995. CPA Wash., 1980; profl. educator Wash., 1998. Acct. Rainier Nat. Bank, Seattle, 1977—79; bus. adminstr. Luth. Family Svcs., Portland, Oreg., 1979—81; tchr., adminstr. Maasae Girls Luth. Secondary Sch., Monduli, Tanzania, 1995—98; math, sci. tchr. Frontier Mid. Sch., Vancouver, Wash., 1998—. Math dept. chair Frontier Mid. Sch., Vancouver, Wash., 2003—; leadership tchr. Ptnr. for Reform in Secondary Sci. and Math., Vancouver, 2004—. Vol. libr. Moringe Secondary Sch., Monduli, Tanzania, 1994; chair youth and family ministry Family of Christ Luth. Ch., Vancouver, 2000—06; bd. mem. Interracial Family Assn., Portland; bd. dirs. Orgn. Developmentally Accelerated Youth, Vancouver, 1981—85; leader Camp Fire, Vancouver, 1987—90; asst.leader Boys Scouts of Am., Vancouver, 1990—95; referee Evergreen Soccer League, Vancouver, 1992—94. Mem.: Nat. Sci. Tchrs. Am., Nat. Coun. Tchrs. Math. Lutheran. Avocation: travel. Home: 3106 NE 146 Pl Vancouver WA 98682 Office: Frontier Mid Sch 7600 NE 166 Ave Vancouver WA 98682 Home Phone: 360-260-9305; Office Phone: 360-604-3200. Personal E-mail: uwdog@comcast.net. Business E-Mail: dvossler@egreen.wednet.edu.

VOST, KEVIN GERARD, psychologist; b. Springfield, Ill., Jan. 31, 1961; s. James Henry and Marjorie Margaret Vost; m. Kathy Ann Collins, Oct. 20, 1984; children: Eric Gerard, Kyle Edward. AA in Gen. Studies, Springfield Coll., Ill., 1981; BA in Psychology, Sangamon State U., Springfield, Ill., 1984, MA in Gen. Psychology, 1990; D in Clin. Psychology, Adler Sch. Profl. Psychology, Chgo., 1997. Lic. psychologist Ind. State Psychology Bd., Indpls., 1998. Disability claims adjudicator State of Ill. Dept. of Human Services, Springfield, Ill., 1984—; intern sch. medicine So. Ill. U., Springfield, Ill., 1995—96. Instr. Lincoln Land C.C., Springfield, 1991; adj. prof. gerontology U. Ill., Springfield, 1994—95; adj. instr. psychology MacMurray Coll., Jacksonville, Ill., 2000—01. Author: Memorize the Faith! (And Most Anything Else): Using the Methods of the Great Catholic Medieval Memory Masters, Full Range of Motive: The Psychology of Lifelong Lifting; contbr. articles to mags. (Writers' Contest First Pl. award Internat. Assn. Resistance Trainers, 1999), to profl. jours. Author, spkr., radio guest Sophia Inst., Manchester, NH, 2005—06. Named Commencement Marshal, Sangamon State U., 1990; recipient Outstanding Student Gen. Psychology cert., Sangagmon State U., 1990, Regional Commissioner's Excellence in Performance citation, Social Security Adminstrn., 1999, Extra-Mile award, Ill. Assn. Disability Examiners, 2006; scholar, Adler Sch. Profl. Psychology, Chgo., 1994. Mem.: Mensa (mem. rsch. rev. com. 1999—2006). Roman Catholic. Avocations: exercise, reading. Home Phone: 217-726-8091; Office Phone: 217-785-8170. Personal E-mail: drvost@ameritech.net.

VOTAW, TY M., golf association commissioner; b. Salem, Ohio; children: Sam, Caroline. BS in Journalism summa cum laude, Ohio U., 1984; JD cum laude, U. NC, 1987. Atty. Taft, Stettinius & Hollister, Cin.; gen. counsel Ladies Profl. Golf Assn. (LPGA), Daytona Beach, Fla., 1991-92, spl. asst. to commr., 1992-99, v.p. bus. affairs, 1997—99, commr., 1999—. Bd. dir. Ladies Profl. Golf Assn., World Golf Found., Golf 20/20; mem. First Tee Oversight Com. Achievements include playing a key role in the establishment of the World Congress of Women's Golf. Avocations: collector of first edition books, music. Office: c/o LPGA 100 International Golf Dr Daytona Beach FL 32124-1092 Office Phone: 386-274-6200. Office Fax: 386-274-1099.

VOTH, ALDEN H., political science professor; b. Goessel, Kans., May 4, 1926; s. John F. and Helena (Hildebrandt) V.; m. Norma E. Jost, Aug. 18, 1956; children: Susan, Thomas. BA, Bethel Coll., 1950; MS in Econs., Iowa State U., Ames, 1953; PhD in Internat. Rels., U. Chgo., 1959. Assoc. prof. polit. sci. Upland (Calif.) Coll., 1960-63; prof. polit. sci. San Jose (Calif.) State U., 1963-65, 67-91, prof. emeritus, 1991—. Vis. prof. polit. sci. Am. U. in Cairo, 1965-67; spkr. in field of crisis in Mid. East. Author: Moscow Abandons Israel, 1980, (with others) The Kissinger Legacy, 1984. Trustee Pomona (Calif.) Valley Am. Assn. UN, 1963; participant China Ednl. Exch., 1996. Am. U. in Cairo Rsch. grantee, 1966; Nat. Coun. on U.S.-Arab Rels. fellow, 1990—. Achievements include Organized four public seminars on the middle east crisis. San Jose, spring, 2005. Home: 1385 Kimberly Dr San Jose CA 95118-1426 Office: San Jose State U One Washington Sq San Jose CA 95192 Office Phone: 408-264-1662. Personal E-mail: ahvoth@aol.com.

VOTH, DOUGLAS W., dean, educator; MD, U. Kans., 1959. Diplomate Am. Bd. Internal Medicine, 1966. Intern U. Kans. Sch. Medicine, Kansas City, 1959—60, resident in internal medicine, 1960—61, 1964—65, assoc. prof. medicine, 1971—73, prof. medicine, chair dept. and dir. residency program, 1974—84, pres. corp., 1978—84; fellow in infectious diseases Upstate Med. Ctr., Syracuse, NY, 1961—64; mem. sect. infectious diseases Kans. U. Med. Ctr., 1965—73; prof. medicine U. Okla. Sch. Medicine, 1973—74; med. dir., chief med. svc. King Fahad Hosp, Al Baha, Saudi Arabia, 1985—86; overseas advisor Royal Coll. Physicians, England, 1987—; prof. medicine U. Okla. Coll. Medicine, Oklahoma City, 1987—, acting chair dept. neurology, 1990—92, exec. dean, 1992—96; dean Faculty of Medicine and Health Scis., United Arab Emirates, 1996—2000; dir. med. edn. Sheikh Zayed Hosp., Abu Dhabi, 2000—01; dir. alumni and devel. U. Okla. Health Scis. Ctr., 2001—02; dean U. Okla. Coll. Pharmacy, Oklahoma City, 2002—. Trustee U. Presbyn. Neurol. Inst., Oklahoma City, 1994—96. Fellow: ACP, Infectious Diseases Soc. Am. Office: Univ of Okla Coll of Pharmacy PO Box 26901 Oklahoma City OK 73190 Home Phone: 405-340-6267; Office Phone: 405-271-6485. Business E-Mail: douglas-voth@ouhsc.edu.

VOTO-BERNALES, JORGE, ambassador; b. Lima, Peru, Jan. 19, 1944; married; 3 children. B in Econs., M in Internat. Rels. 3rd sec. gen. divsn. planning Peruvian Ministry Fgn. Affairs, 1971, chief of cabinet to Sec. Gen. Fgn. Affairs, 1980, positions in Ecuador, Soviet Union, Germany, Spain, Austria and Argentina, dir. Ams. gen. divsn. polit. affairs, 1987—90, dir.-gen. planning, 1993, dir.-gen. bilateral polit. affairs, 1994—95, vice-min., sec. gen. fgn. affairs, 1995—97, permanent rep. to European Office of UN Geneva, 1997—2004, amb., permanent rep. to UN NYC, 2006—; non-resident permanent rep. UN Environment Programme and UN Human Settlements Programme, Nairobi, Kenya, 1998—2004; v.p. Human Rights Commn., Geneva; chmn. agr. com. World Trade Orgn., Geneva; exec. sec. Fund for Peace and Devel. Peru-Ecuador, 2004—06. Office: Permanent Mission of Peru to UN 820 2nd Ave Fl 16 New York NY 10017 Office Phone: 212-687-3336. Office Fax: 212-972-6975. E-mail: misionperu@aol.com.

VOUDOUKIS, IGNATIOS JOHN, internist, cardiologist; b. Skalohorion, Lesvos, Greece, July 8, 1927; came to U.S., 1955; s. John Ignatios and Christina (Hatzilias) V.; m. Penny Christakos, July 15, 1962; 1 child, Christine Antoinette. MD, Nat. U. Athens, 1954. Intern Meml. Hosp., Albany, NY, 1955-56; resident Episcopal Hosp., Phila., 1956-58, Hahnemann Med. Coll. and Hosp., Phila., 1958-59; fellow in cardiology Jackson Meml. Hosp. and U. of Miami, Fla., 1959-61, Jewish Gen. Hosp., Montreal, 1961-63; rsch. assoc. in cardiology Maine Med. Ctr., Portland, 1963-64; assoc. physician Henry Ford Hosp., Detroit, 1964-67; adj. instr. medicine Wayne State U., Detroit, 1969, clin. asst. prof. medicine, 1973, clin. assoc. prof. internal medicine, 1981—; pvt. practice Detroit, 1967—. Active staff Harper Hosp., Detroit, Hutzel Hosp., Detroit. Mem. lab. facilities coun. Dept. Pub. Health, State of Mich., 1968-74; pres. Hypertension Coord. and Planning Coun. of Southeastern Mich., 1974. Recipient St. Paul Medallion, Greek Orthodox Diocese and Archdiocese of N. and S. Am., Detroit, 1986. Fellow ACP, Am. Coll. Angiology; mem. Am. Soc. Nephrology, Am. Soc. Hypertension (charter), Hellenic Univ. Club (pres 1968-69), Detroit Athletic Club. Greek Orthodox. Office: Hutzel Hosp Profl Bldg 4727 Saint Antoine St Ste 402 Detroit MI 48201-1461

VOWELL, DENISE K., federal official; BS in Polit. Sci. and Philosophy with honors, Ill. State U., 1974; JD, U. Tex., 1981; MS in Nat. Resource Strategy, Indsl. Coll. Armed Forces, 1998. From mil. police officer to tort litig. atty. to prosecutor to def. counsel to chief legal officer to appellate judge to chief trial judge US Army, 1973—2006; spl. master US Ct. Fed. Claims, Washington, 2006—. Mem.: Nat. Assn. Women Judges (mem. mil. cts. com.). Avocation: backpacking. Office: Office of Spl Masters US Ct Fed Claims 717 Madison Pl NW Washington DC 20005 E-mail: Denise_Vowell@ao.uscourts.gov. *

VOWLES, RICHARD BECKMAN, literature educator; b. Fargo, ND, Oct. 5, 1917; s. Guy Richard and Ella (Beckman) V.; m. Ellen Noah Hudson, Aug. 1, 1942 (div. 1969); children: Elizabeth Ellen, Richard Hudson. BS, Davidson Coll., 1938; postgrad., U. N.C., 1938—39, U. Stockholm, 1939—40; MA, Yale U., 1942, PhD, 1950. Engr. Hercules Powder Co., Wilmington, Chattanooga, 1941—43; chemist Rohm & Haas, Knoxville, Tenn., 1943—44; econ. cons. War Dept., 1944; Am. vice consul Gothenburg, Sweden, 1945—46; asst. prof. English Southwestern U., Memphis, 1948—50, Queens U., NYC, 1950—51; asso. prof. English U. Fla., 1951—60; prof. Scandinavian and comparative lit. U. Wis., Madison, 1960—85, prof. emeritus, 1985—, chmn. comparative lit., 1962—63, 1964—67, 1971—72, chmn. Scandinavian studies, 1977—80. Am. specialist in Scandinavia Dept. State, 1963; vis. prof. NYU, 1964, U. Helsinki, Finland, 1968, Stockholm, 1969; lectr., Sydney, Australia, 1975, Paris, 1975; master ceremonies Santa Fe Scandinavian Film Festival, 1984 Editor: Eternal Smile, 1954, Dramatic Theory, 1956, Comparatists at Work, 1968; Adv. editor: Nordic Council Series, 1965-70, Herder Ency. of World Lit; contbr. articles to profl. jours. Am.-Scandinavian Found. fellow, Stockholm, 1939-40, Lassen fellow Am. Scandinavian Found., 1986, Fulbright fellow Copenhagen, 1955-56, Strindberg fellow Stockholm, 1973, Norwegian Govt. fellow, 1978; recipient Rsch. award Swedish govt., 1978. Mem. Modern Lang. Assn., Soc. Advancement Scandinavian Study (mem. exec. com.), Internat. Comparative Lit. Assn., Am. Comparative Lit. Assn. (adv. bd.), Strindberg Soc., Phi Beta Kappa. Home: 345 W Main St #8 Madison WI 53703

VOYLES, C. ROBERT, electronics executive; BSEE, post grad., S.D. Sch. Mines and Tech. Accredited sr. exec. cons. Inst. Ind. Bus., 2005. Mgr. Magnetic Peripherals, Inc.; gen. mgr. Dakota Mountain Dragway, 1978—98; mgr. engring. svcs. SCI Sys., Inc., 1987—94; v.p and founder Electronics Assembly Resource Network, Inc., 1994—. Address: 5607 Pioneer Cir Rapid City SD 57702

VOYLES, ROBB LAWRENCE, lawyer; b. Toledo, May 26, 1957; s. Lawrence E. and Marilyn L. (McQuade) V.; m. Loretta F. Herbert, July 19, 1980; children: Lindsay Ann, Erin Lynn. BBA in Acctg. summa cum laude, U. Dayton, 1979; JD magna cum laude, U. Mich., 1982. Bar: Tex. 1982, US Dist. Ct. (no. dist.) Tex. 1982, US Ct. Appeals (5th cir.) 1983, US Dist. Ct. (we. dist.) Tex. 1986, US Dist. Ct. (no. dist.) Calif. 1989. Assoc. Rain, Harrell, Emery, Young & Doke, Dallas, 1982-87, Baker Botts LLP, Dallas, 1987-88, ptnr., litigation dept. Austin, Tex., 1989—, ptnr. in charge Austin office, 1994—2005, mem. exec. com., 2000—, chair firm-wide litig. dept., 2005—. Editor U. Mich. Law Rev., 1981-82. Bd. dir. & legal counsel Greater Austin C. of C. Named a Texas Super Lawyer, Texas Monthly mag. & Law & Politics mag., 2003—04, 2006—07; named Best Lawyer in Am., 2004—07; named one of Best of Bus. & Corp. Law, Austin Bus. Jour., 2004. Fellow Tex. Bar Found., Dallas Bar Found., Travis County Bar Found.; mem. ABA (profl. liability com. litig. sect.), State Bar of Tex., Dallas Bar Assn., Dallas Young Lawyers Assn., Travis County Bar Assn., Order of Coif, Alpha Sigma Tau. Roman Catholic. Office: Baker Botts LLP Ste 600 2001 Ross Ave Dallas TX 75201 Home: 3831 Turtle Creek Blvd #19E Dallas TX 75219 Office Phone: 512-322-2626. Office Fax: 512-322-8326. Business E-Mail: robb.voyles@bakerbotts.com.

VOYNOW, JUDITH ANN, pediatric pulmonologist, educator; BA, U. Pa., Phila., 1978, MD, 1982. Lic. pediats. Am. Bd. Pediats., pediat. pulmonary Am. Bd. Pediats. Fellow, sr. staff NIH, Bethesda, Md., 1990—92; asst. prof. Children's Nat. Med. Ctr., Washington, 1992—94; assoc. prof. Duke U. Med. Ctr., Durham, NC, 1994—. Fellow: Am. Acad. Pediats.; mem.: Am. Thoracic Soc. Office: Duke U Med Ctr Dept Pediats Box 2994 Durham NC 27710

VOYTEK, MARY SULLIVAN, sculptor; b. Memphis, July 26, 1957; d. Herbert Dean and Mary Josphine Sullivan; m. Lawrence Voytek, June 30, 1986; children: Alexa, Zachary. BFA, Calif. Coll. of the Arts, Oakland, Calif., 1980; MFA, R.I. Sch. of Design, Providence, RI, 1982. Vis. prof. R.I. Sch. of Design, Providence, 1980—81, Brown Univ., Providence, 1981—82; adj. prof. Fla. Gulf Coast Univ., Ft. Myers, Fla., 2000—04, asst. prof., 2004—. Pvt. cons. Fla. Gulf Coast Univ., Ft. Myers, Fla., 2000—01. Pub. commns., Dream to Connect, 2004 (Fla. Arts in Pub. Pl. award), exhibitions include TVS Internat., Atlanta, Ga., 2000, Atla. Internat. Mus. Art and Design, 2000, Gallery Camino Real, Gallery Ctr., Boca Raton, Fla., 2004, Zenith Gallery, Washington, 2007, H.W. Gallery, Naples, Fla., 2007, Union Sq. Gallery, San Francisco, 2007, numerous others, Represented in permanent collections Hsinchu Mus. Art, Taiwan, Sherman Gallery, Chgo., R.I. Sch. Design Mus., numerous others. Art in pub. places bd. City of Ft. Myers, Fla., 2004—; bd. mem. Fla. Arts, Ft. Myers, Fla., 2002—07. Mem.: DAR, Internat. Sculptors Ctr. Avocations: hiking, travel. Office Phone: 239-590-7241.

VRABECK, KATHY PATTERSON, video game company executive; b. 1963; BA, DePauw U., 1985; MBA, Ind. U., 1989. Sales assoc. Pillsbury Co., Quaker Oats Co., Eli Lilly & Co.; sr. v.p. mktg., gen. mgr. ConAgra Grocery; exec. v.p., global brand mgmt. Activision Inc., 1999—2000, exec. v.p., global pub. & brand mgmt., 2000—03, pres. pub., 2003—06; pres., casual entertainment Electronic Arts, Inc., Redwood City, Calif., 2007—. Bd. dirs. AVP Inc., 2006—. Named one of 100 Most Powerful Women in Entertainment, Hollywood Reporter, 2003, 2004, '25 Up and Coming Media Executives, Bus. Week, 2005, Kelley Sch. Bus. Acad. Alumni Fellows, Ind. U., 2005. Office: Electronic Arts Inc 209 Redwood Shores Pkwy Redwood City CA 94065 *

VRABLIK, EDWARD ROBERT, import/export company executive; b. Chgo., June 8, 1932; s. Steven Martin and Meri (Korbel) V.; m. Bernice G. Germer, Jan. 25, 1958; children: Edward Robert, II, Scott S. BS in Chem. Engring, Northwestern U., 1956; MBA, U. Chgo., 1961; postgrad., MIT, 1970. Registered profl. engr., Ill. Dir. indsl. mktg. Eimco Corp., 1956-61; dir. indsl. mktg. and planning Swift & Co., Chgo., 1961-68; v.p., gen. mgr. Swift Chem. Co., Chgo., 1968-73; pres., chief exec. officer Estech Gen. Chems. Corp., Chgo., 1973-86; pres. Kare Internat. Inc., Chgo., 1986—. Pres. Julius and Assocs., Inc., Kare Internat., Inc.; bd dirs. Potash Phosphate Inst., Consol. Fertilizers, Ltd.; mem. mgmt. com. Esmark Inc., Korbel, Inc., Mister Lawn Care, Inc. Author; patentee in field. Bd. dirs., v.p. Northwestern U. Tech. Inst.; trustee Future Farmers Am. Mem. Internat. Superphosphate Mfrs. Assn. (dir.), Am. Inst. Chem. Engrs., Fertilizer Inst. (dir.) Clubs: Butler Nat. (Oak Brook, Ill.). Lutheran. Home: 631 Thompsons Way Palatine IL 60067-4653 Office: 141 W Jackson Blvd Chicago IL 60604-2992 Office Phone: 847-358-4948. Personal E-mail: vrabliker@aol.com.

VRANISH, JOHN MICHAEL, electrical engineer, researcher; b. Brainerd, Minn., May 20, 1939; s. John Paul and Louise Ann (Jenkins) V.; m. Dorothy Jean Ward, June 27, 1980; children: John Christopher, Anthony Brian. BS, U.S. Mil. Acad., 1962; MSEE, George Washington U., 1973. Staff engr. robotics rsch. Naval Surface Weapons Ctr., White Oak, Silver Spring, Md., 1971-82, Nat. Bur. Standards, Gaithersburg, Md., 1982-86; staff engr. space mechanisms and space robotics Goddard Space Flight Ctr., Greenbelt, Md., 1986—2006, emeritus, 2006—; pres. Vranish Innovative Techs., 2006—. Mem. tech. task force Office of Sec. Def., 1981-82, fact finding com., 1981; cons. U.S. Congress, 1983, 87, 96; spkr. in field. Contbr. articles to profl. pubs. Capt. US Army, 1962—70. Recipient Bose award, Design News Mag., 1997, 100 award, R&D Mag., 1997, 2006, Exceptional Engring. Achievement medal, NASA, Exceptional Achievement Tech. medal, Exceptional Svc. medal; grantee, Productivity Enhancement Program, Dept. of Defense, 1979. Mem. Robotics Internat. of Soc. Mfg. Engrs. (charter, award 1981). Achievements include development of actuator upgrade designee, F-35 joint strike fighter; invention of capaciflector, driven ground, virtual feel 3-D sprags, carrier-less anti-backlash transmission, robotic deriveter, magnetostrictive direct drive rotary motor, spin bearings, continuously variable planetary transmission, gear bearings, flexure wedges, stepping flexures; 3-D interactive display, screw locking clickless wrench, conformal robot gripper; world record holder in single stage gear reduction and for precision non-contact robotic assembly in space; patents pending in field. Avocations: sports, physical fitness, military history. Home and Office: Vranish Innovative Techs 900 Truro Ln Crofton MD 21114-1207 Office Phone: 410-721-2650. Personal E-mail: jmvranish@comcast.net.

VRANISH, KENNETH, electrical engineer, consultant; s. Joeseph and Luise Vranish; m. Peggy Young, July 14, 1981; children: Job, Politea, David. BEE, Mont. State U., Bozeman, 1978. Cert. athletic trainer Billings Sch. Athletic Tng. & Massage Therapy, 1973, emergency med. technician II Mont. State U., 1978. Project engr. Boeing Co., Seattle, 1979—87; cons. KVA Engring., Inc., Roundup, Mont., 1987—2000; project mgr. CDI Corp, Tempe, Ariz., 2000—02; rsch. lead Smiths Aerospace, Grand Rapids, Mich., 2002—05; cons. KVA Engring., Inc., Grand Rapids, 2005—. Mem. econ. devel. HTM Grp., Phila., 1998—2003; ceo Christian Counseling & Crisis Ctr., Federal Way, Wash., 1982—84. Recipient Pride In Excellence award, Boeing Co., 1984. Mem.: IEEE. Achievements include development of a multistage binary cycle power generation system; research in the effects of atmospheric radiation on semicondutor devices in aircraft; facilitating and negotiating agreements between the US and Philippine departments of agriculture for meat export to the US. Avocations: mountain climbing, spelunking, hiking, racquetball. Home: 6570 Burton St SE Grand Rapids MI 49546 Personal E-mail: kvranish@belcan.com.

VRATIL, JOHN LOGAN, state legislator, lawyer; b. Great Bend, Kans., Oct. 28, 1945; s. Frank and Althea (Shuss) V.; m. Kathy Hoefer, June 21, 1971 (div. Dec. 1985); m. Anne Whitfill, Mar. 7, 1986 (div. Dec. 1992); m. Teresa Hobbs, Mar. 15, 1996; children: Alison, Andy, Kurtis, Ashley. BS in Edn., U. Kans., 1967; postgrad., U. Southampton, Eng., 1967-68; JD, U. Kans., 1971; postgrad., U. Exeter, Eng., 1972. Bar: Kans. 1971, U.S. Dist. Ct. Kans. 1971, U.S. Ct. Appeals (10th and 8th cirs.) 1975, U.S. Supreme Ct. 2005. From assoc. to ptnr. Bennett, Lytle, Wetzler & Winn, Prairie Village, Kans., 1972-83; with Lathrop & Gage, Overland Park, Kans., 1983—; mem. Kans. Senate from 11th dist., 1998—, v.p., 2003—. Contbr. articles to profl. jours. Mem. recreation commn. Prairie Village, 1982-83, mem. planning commn., 1983-84; v.p. Usher Mansion Hist. Found., Lawrence, Kans., 1990—. Fellow ABA Found.; mem. ABA, Kans. Bar Assn. (pres. 1995-96, gov. 1988-97), Kans. Bar Found. (trustee 1996-2002), Johnson County Bar Assn. (pres. 1979), Kans. Sch. Attys. Assn. (pres. 1985), Overland Park C. of C. (bd. dirs. 1985-94, pres. 1988). Republican. Avocations: sports, hunting, reading. Office: Lathrop & Gage 10851 Mastin Blvd Ste 1000 Overland Park KS 66210-2007 Address: Kansas Senate State Capitol Rm 281-E Topeka KS 66612 Home Phone: 913-341-7559; Office Phone: 913-451-5100. Business E-Mail: jvratil@lathropgage.com.

VRATIL, KATHRYN HOEFER, federal judge; b. Manhattan, Kans., 1949; BA, U. Kans., 1971, JD, 1975; postgrad., Exeter U., 1971-72. Bar: Kans. 1975, Mo. 1978, U.S. Supreme Ct., 1995. Law clk. U.S. Dist. Ct., Kansas City, Kans., 1975-78; assoc. Lathrop Koontz & Norquist, Kansas City, Mo., 1978-83; ptnr. Lathrop & Norquist, Kansas City, 1984-92; judge City of Prairie Village, Kans., 1990-92, US Dist. Ct. Kans, 1992—. Bd. dirs. Kans. Legal Bd. Svcs., 1991-92; mem. com.on adminstrv. office Jud. Conf. of the U.S., 2000-06; mem. jud. coun. U.S. Ct. Appeals for the Tenth Cir., 2002-04; mem. dist. judge adv. com. Fed. Jud. Ctr., 2003—, chair, 2006—; mem. U.S. Jud. Panel on Multi Dist. Litigation, 2004—. Bd. editors Kans. Law Rev., 1974-75, Jour. Kans. Bar Assn., 1992-94. Mem. nat. adv. bd. U. Kans. Ctr. for Environ. Edn. and Tng., 1993-95. Fellow Kans. Bar Found., Am. Bar Found.; mem. ABA (editl. bd. Judges Jour. 1996-98), Am. Judicature Soc., Nat. Assn. Judges, Fed. Judges Assn., Kans. Bar Assn. (mem. bench bar com., 2000—), Mo. Bar Assn., Kansas City Met. Area Bar Assn., Johnson County Bar Assn., Assn. Women Judges, Lawyers Assn. Kansas City, Kans. State Hist. Soc., U. Kans. Law Soc. (bd. govs. 1978-81, 2005—), Kans. U. Alumni Assn. (mem. Kansas City chpt. alumni bd. 1990-92, nat. bd. dirs. 1991-96, bd. govs. Adams Alumni Ctr. 1992-95), Native Sons and Daus of Kans. (life), Jr. League Wyandotte and Johnson Counties, Order of Coif, Kans. Inn of Ct. (master 1993—, pres. 1999-2000), Phi Kappa Phi. Republican. Presbyterian. Office: Robert J Dole US Courthouse Ste 511 500 State Ave Kansas City KS 66101-2403 Office Phone: 913-551-6550.

VREDEVOE, DONNA LOU, academic administrator, microbiologist, educator, biomedical researcher; BA in Bacteriology, UCLA, 1959, PhD in Microbiology, 1963. USPHS postdoctoral fellow Stanford (Calif.) U., 1963—64; instr. bacteriology UCLA, 1963, postgrad. rsch. immunologist dept. surgery Ctr. Health Scis., 1964-65, asst. rsch. immunologist dept. surgery Ctr. Health Scis., 1964-67, asst. prof. Sch. Nursing, Ctr. Health Scis., 1967-70, assoc. prof., 1970-76; prof. Sch. Nursing, Ctr. Health Scis., 1976—, assoc. dean Sch. Nursing, 1976-78, acting assoc. dean Sch. Nursing, 1985-86, asst. dir. space planning Cancer Ctr., 1976-78, dir. space planning, 1978-90, cons. to lab. nuc. medicine and radiation biology, 1967-80, acting dean Sch. Nursing, 1995-96. Chair acad. senate UCLA, 1999—2000, vice chancellor acad. pers., 2001—06, spl. asst. to chancellor, 2006—07, prof., vice chancellor emerita, 2006—. Contbr. articles to profl. publs. Postdoctoral fellow USPHS, 1963-64; Mabel Wilson Richards scholar UCLA, 1960-61; rsch. grantee Am. Cancer Soc., Calif. Inst. Cancer Rsch., Calif. divsn. Am. Cancer Soc., NIH, USPHS, Am. Nurses Found., Cancer Rsch. Coordinating Com. U. Calif., Dept. Energy, UCLA. Mem Am. Soc. Microbiology, Am. Assn. Immunologists, Am. Assn. Cancer Rsch., Nat. League Nursing (2d v.p. 1979-81), Sigma Xi, Alpha Gamma Sigma, Sigma Theta Tau (nat. hon. mem.). Office: UCLA Sch Nursing 700 Tiverton Ave 3-232 Factor Bldg Box 951702 Los Angeles CA 90095-1702

VREDEVOOGD COMBS, PAT, real estate company executive; m. Guy Combs; 6 children. V.p. Coldwell Banker AJS Schmidt, Cascade, Mich. Chair Mich. Real Estate Commn., 2002. Named one of Real Estate's 25 Most Influential Thought Leaders, Realtor Mag., 2006. Mem.: Grand Rapids Assn. Realtors (pres. 1990), Women's Coun. of Realtors (pres. 1986), Mich. Assn. Realtors (pres. 1995, Mich. Realtor of Yr. 2002), Nat. Assn. Realtors (regional v.p. - Mich and Ohio 1997, nat. fundraising chair, polit. action com. 2003, 1st v.p. 2005, pres. 2007, leadership team mem., chair edn. com., chair equal opportunity com., chair pub. policy com.). Office: Coldwell Banker AJS Schmidt Realty 4488 Cascade Rd SE Grand Rapids MI 49546 Office Phone: 616-559-7241. E-mail: pat@patsplace.com. *

VREE, ROGER ALLEN, lawyer; b. Chgo., Oct. 2, 1943; s. Louis Gerard and Ruby June (Boersma) V.; m. Lauren Trumbull Gartside, Mar. 29, 1969; children: Jonathan Todd, Matthew David. BA, Wheaton Coll., 1965; MA,

Stanford U., 1966, JD, 1969. Bar: Ill. 1969, U.S. Dist. Ct. (no. dist.) Ill. 1969. Assoc. Sidley & Austin, Chgo., 1969—75; ptnr. Sidley Austin LLP, Chgo., 1975—. Mem.: ABA. Office: Sidley Austin LLP One South Dearborn Chicago IL 60603 E-mail: rvree@sidley.com.

VREELAND, RUSSELL GLENN, tax manager, accountant, consultant; b. Princeton, NJ, Apr. 27, 1960; s. Glenn Earl and Barbara Ann (Jungels) Vreeland; m. Traci Ann Harbold, Dec. 17, 1988 (div. 2006); children: Hans Russell, Anna Patricia. BSBA, Bloomsburg U., Pa., 1982. CPA Pa., Md. Sr. acct. Louis H. Linowitz & Co., Trenton, N.J., 1982-85; tax supr. Horty & Horty, P.A., Wilmington, Del., 1985-87; tax mgr. Stewart Waddell & Co. P.A., Columbia, Md., 1988-92; assoc. in charge of tax Hillman & Glorioso, P.L.L.C., Vienna, Va., 1993-98; ptnr. Vreeland & Assocs., LLC, 1998—2006, Vreeland & Co., Ltd., 2001—06; sr. tax mgr. Clifton Gunderson, LLP, 2006—. Spkr. in field. Author: Foreign Sales Corporations - A Primer, 1992, Exporting - Are You Ready?, 1993; contbr. articles to profl. jours. Mem. Sykesville Econ. Devel. Commn., Md., 1998—2001; chair Sykesville Budget Com., 2000—, Sykesville Capital Improvement Com., 2000—; chmn. fin. com. Woodland Village Condominium Assn., 1989—90; mem. Sykesville Town Coun., 2000—07, pres., 2002—05; mem. Sykesville Hist. Dist. Commn., 2002—07; com. chair Sykesville Centennial, 2003—04; co-chair fin. com. Messiah Luth. Ch., 2000—06. Mem.: AICPA (adv. group mem. partnership taxation com. 1997—98, apptd. mem.partnership taxation com. 1998—99, tax divsn., accredited bus. valuations), Md. Assn. CPAs (mem. fed. taxation com. 1990—91). Republican. Lutheran. Office Phone: 301-931-2050.

VRENTAS, JAMES SPIRO, chemical engineering professor; b. Danville, Ill., Apr. 14, 1936; s. Spiro and Evanthia (Guintonis) V.; m. Christine Mary Jarzebski, June 8, 1975; children: Catherine Eva, Jennifer Marie. BS, U. Ill., 1958; MSChE, U. Del., 1961, PhD, 1963. Rsch. engr. Dow Chem. Co., Midland, Mich., 1963-69, sr. rsch. engr., 1969-72; asst. prof. Ill. Inst. Tech., Chgo., 1972-73, assoc. prof., 1973-76, prof., 1976-80, Pa. State U., University Park, 1980-85, Dow prof., 1985—. Contbr. articles to profl. jours. Recipient William H. Walker Nat. Rsch. award AIChE, 1981, Charles Stein Materials Rsch. award, 1989. Mem. AIChE. Greek Orthodox. Achievements include development of theories for diffusion, rheology, and sorption in polymers. Home: 1705 Princeton Dr State College PA 16803-3260 Office: Pa State U 119 Fenske Lab University Park PA 16802-4400 Business E-Mail: jsv1@psu.edu.

VROMAN, DAVID COLE, music educator; b. Princeton, Ill., June 21, 1956; s. Russell C. and Donna J. Vroman; m. Gail S. Welch, July 11, 1981; children: Kristen M., Michael C., Matthew D. children: Katie. BA, Western Ill. U., Macomb, 1978; MS, U. Ill., Champaign-Urbana, 1984, EdD, 1994. Cert. tchr. Ill., 1985. Band dir. Riverview Grade Sch., East Peoria, Ill., 1978; band, choir tchr. Pinckneyville Cmty. HS, Ill., 1978—83; grad. asst. music edn. U. Ill., Champaign-Urbana, 1983—84, grad. asst. univ. bands, 1984—85; dir. band, chmn. dept. music Bradley U., Peoria, Ill., 1986—. Condr. Peoria Mcpl. Band, 1991—. Mem. WCBU, Peoria, 2005. Named Outstanding Young Educator, Peoria Jaycees, 1992; recipient Faculty Achievement award for excellence in scholarship, Bradley U. Slane Coll., 2006, Outstanding Prof., Alpha Chi Omega, 1997, Forty Under Forty Leadership award, WMBD and Interbusiness Issues, 1995. Mem.: Ill. Music Educators Assn., Coll. Band Dirs. Assn., Phi Beta Mu (pres. ill. chpt. 2005, Outstanding Bandmaster award Ill. chpt. 2004). Office: Bradley U 1501 W Bradley Ave Peoria IL 61625 Home Phone: 309-677-2605; Office Phone: 309-677-2605. Office Fax: 309-677-3871. Business E-Mail: dvroman@bradley.edu.

VROMAN, KENDAL, investment company executive; b. 1971; BS in Applied Computer Sci., Ill. St. Univ., 1997; MBA with emphasis in Fin., Mktg., Northwestern Univ. Kellogg Sch. Mgmt., 1999. With marchFirst, Inc.; with Am. Info. Sys. Divsn. Andersen Cons. LLP; consul. Chgo. Merc. Exch. Holdings, Inc., Chgo., 2001—02, project mgr., 2002—05, dir., co-head corp. devel., 2005—. Named one of 40 Under Forty, Crain's Bus. Chgo., 2005. Office: Chgo Merc Exch Holdings Inc 20 S Wacker Dr Chicago IL 60606 Office Phone: 312-930-1000. *

VROOM, GOVERT, finance educator; s. Rudolphus Johannes Vroom and Johanna Elisabeth Bakker. PhD, INSEAD, Fontainebleau, France, 2005. Registered fin. controller, VRC, Netherlands, 1997. Sr. cost mgmt. cons. KPN Telecom, Den Haag, Netherlands, 1991—97; asst. prof. Purdue U. Krannert Sch., West Lafayette, Ind., 2005—. Lt. Netherlands armed forces, 1989—91. Office: Purdue U Krannert Sch 403 W State St West Lafayette IN 47907-2056

VRYHOF, JOHN C., lawyer; BA in Econs. with high honors, Mich. State U., 1980; JD cum laude, U. Mich. Law Sch., 1983. Bar: Ill. 1983, Ariz. 1987, Supreme Ct. Ariz., Supreme Ct. Ill., cert.: Ariz. Bd. Legal Specialization (estate trust law, tax law). Atty. Sidley & Austin, Chgo., 1983—88, Streich Lang, P.A., Phoenix, 1988—96; ptnr. Snell & Wilmer, LLP, Phoenix, 1996—. Named one of Top 100 Attys., Worth mag., 2006. Fellow: Am. Coll. Trust and Estate Counsel. Office: Snell & Wilmer LLP 1 Arizona Ctr Phoenix AZ 85004-2202 Office Phone: 602-382-6333. E-mail: jvryhof@swlaw.com.

VU, JOSEPH DUONG, financial educator; b. Hanoi, Vietnam, Mar. 13, 1952; s. Phuong and Nhan (Trinh) V.; m. Huyen Tran T. Do, July 1, 1978; children: Christine, Daniel. BBA, Ohio U., 1973; MBA, U. Chgo., 1975, PhD in Fin., 1984. Chartered fin. analyst. Asst. prof. Loyola U., Chgo., 1981-85, U. Ill., Chgo., 1985-88; assoc. prof. fin. DePaul U., Chgo., 1988—. Fin. advisor, arbitrator Nat. Assn. Securities Dealers. Author: Investment Management, 1993. Hospice vol. Palliative Care Ctr. of the North Shore. Mem. Am. Fin. Assn., Vietnamese Assn. Ill. (pres. 1993-98), Fin. Mgmt. Assn., Midwest Fin. Assn., Chartered Fin. Analyst Inst. Avocation: tennis. Office Phone: 312-362-5121.

VUCINIC, DEJAN, neuroscientist; b. Belgrade, Yugoslavia, Dec. 27, 1969; PhD, MIT, Cambridge, 1998. Fellow Yale U., New Haven, 2002—03, Salk Inst., La Jolla, Calif., 2004—. Mem.: Am. Physiol. Soc. Achievements include research in Top Quark. Office: Salk Inst 10010 N Torrey Pines Rd La Jolla CA 92037 Office Phone: 858-453-4100. Business E-Mail: dejan@salk.edu.

VUCKOVIC, VLADETA D, retired mathematics professor; b. Subotinac, Serbia, Mar. 30, 1923; s. Dimitrije R. Vukovic and Andjelija P. Vuckovic; children: Alex, Stephanie. MSc, U. Belgrade, Yugoslavia, 1949; PhD in Math., Serbian Acad. Scis., Yugoslovai, 1953. Prof. math. Tchr. U., Zrevjanin, Serbia and Montenegro, 1951—60; asst. U. Belgrade, Serbia and Montenegro, 1950—53, assoc. prof., 1961—63; assoc. prof. math. U. Notre Dame, Ind., emeritus prof., 1990—. Author: From Rhapsody to Epitaph; editor: Naše Oelo; contbr. articles to profl. jours. Pres. Notre Dame for Nixon Com., 1972. Avocation: literature.

VUGMEISTER, BORIS, physicist, writer; b. Kiev, Ukraine, Aug. 17, 1947; s. Tauba Breytman and Khaim Vugmeister; m. Yelena Neymark, Dec. 24, 1971; children: Yulia Vugmeyster, Liliya Vugmeyster. BS (hon.), Kiev State U., 1971, MS (hon.) in Physics, 1971; PhD in Theoretical Physics, Inst. Semiconductor Physics, Kiev, 1977; DS in Physics, Council Higher Edn., Moscow, 1986. Leading rsch. scientist Inst. Material Sci., Kiev, 1980—90; vis. prof. physics Lehigh U., Bethlehem, Pa., 1991—95, Princeton U., NJ, 1995—99. Cons., referee Am. Inst. Physics, Datamir Inc. Contbr. chapters to books, articles to profl. and scientific jours. Grantee, NSF, 1991—99. Mem.: Am. Phys. Soc. Achievements include first to theory of relaxor ferroelectrics, in theory of phase transitions and energy transfer kinetics in disordered matter. Home Phone: 973-773-0776. Personal E-mail: vugmeister@datamir.net.

VUITTON, HENRY-LOUIS, designer; b. Asnieres, Seine, France, Aug. 10, 1911; s. Gaston-Louis and Renee (Versillé) V.; m. Josette Rateau, Oct. 15, 1935; children: Colette (Mrs. Jacques Novatin), Philippe-Louis (dec.), Daniele (Mrs. Philippe Masson). Student, Cours Saint-Louis, Paris. Comml. dir. Vuitton et Vuitton, Paris, 1945-75, pres. bd. mgrs., 1975-77; pres. bd. insps. Louis Vuitton (S.A.). Author: La Malle aux Souvenirs. Decorated officer Order Nat. of Merit France; Grande Medaille d'Or du Travail; recipient Silver medal City of Paris

VUKELICH, SHARON IRENE, aerospace engineer, consultant; b. 1952; d. Donald B. and Dorothy Violet Williams; m. Thomas Harvey Havens; children: Christopher Michael, Charles Edward Havens, Flora Irene Havens. BSAE, U. of Mich., 1974; MSAE, U. of Cin., 1980. Design engr. GE Aircraft Engines, Cin., 1974—82; propulsion engr. USAF/ASC/YZ, Dayton, 1982—95; propulsion structures tech. expert USAF/ASC/ENFP, Dayton, 1995—2000; chief engr. USAF/ASC/LPJ, Dayton, 2000—03; sr. rsch. engr. U. of Dayton Rsch. Inst., Ohio, 2003—. Contbr. reference book; assoc. editor (jour.) Materials Evaluation; contbr. articles to profl. jours. Decorated Outstanding Civilian Career Svc. award USAF, Exceptional Civilian Svc. award DOD, Exemplary Civilian Svc. award USAF; recipient Outstanding Profl. Achievement award, Affiliates Societies Coun., 2002, Value Engrng. Suggestion award, DOD, 1987, Value Engr. of the Yr., 1985—86, ASC Value Engr. of the Yr., USAF, 1985—86. Mem.: ASM Internat., Am. Helicopter Soc., Am. Soc. Nondestructive Testing (sec.-treas. 2003—04, v.p. 2004—05, pres. 2005—, dir. 2001—03). Office: University of Dayton Research Institute 300 College Pk Dayton OH 45469-0120 Home Phone: 513-899-2605; Office Phone: 937-229-4670. Office Fax: 937-229-2650. E-mail: sharon.vukelich@udri.udayton.edu.

VUKSTA, MICHAEL JOSEPH, surgeon; b. Pitts., Apr. 25, 1926; s. Michael and Mary Sarah (Hanulya) V.; m. Dorothy Ann Bosak, Sept. 12, 1953; children: Patricia, Michael, Carol, Janet. BA, Youngstown State U., 1949; MD, Ohio State U., 1957. Diplomate Am. Bd. Surgery. Enlisted USN, advanced through grades to capt., 1974; intern St. Elizabeth Hosp., Youngstown, Ohio, resident in gen. surgery, 1958-62; pvt. practice gen. surgery Youngstown, 1962-89; head blue team surgery Oak Knoll U.S. Naval Hosp., Oakland, Calif., 1989-93; assoc. prof. surgery NEOUCOM. Capt. USN retired. Fellow ACS, Am. Coll. Sports Medicine, Southwestern Surg. Congress; mem. Nat. Athletic Trainers Assn. (advisor). Byzantine Catholic. Home: 131 Lovett Pl Pensacola FL 32506-5265

VULGAMORE, ALLISON, performing arts association administrator; BMus, Oberlin Coll. Former gen. mgr., artistic adminstr., mgr. ops. Nat. Symphony Orch., Washington; former gen. mgr. N.Y. Philharm. Orch., NYC; pres., mng. dir. Atlanta Symphony Orch., 1993—. Hon. dir. Oberlin Coll.; mem. arts challenge panel in music NEA. Bd. dirs. Midtown Alliance; mem. Vision 2000 Econ. Devel. Collaborative; Cultural Olympiad and opening ceremonies coord. Centennial Olympic Games, Atlanta, 1996. Am. Symphony Orch. League fellow, 1980. Mem. Atlanta Rotary. Office: Atlanta Symphony Orchestra Robert W Woodruff Arts Ctr 1293 Peachtree St NE Ste 300 Atlanta GA 30309-3552

VULTAGGIO, DON J. (DOMINICK VULTAGGIO), beverage company executive; b. Bklyn., Feb. 26, 1952; 1 child, Wes. Co-founder, head Ferolito, Vultaggio & Sons, Lake Success, NY, 1971—; launched Midnight Dragon Malt Liquor, 1986, Crazy Horse Malt Liquor, 1992, AriZona Iced Tea, 1992, Miss. Mud Black & Tan Beer, 1996, Miss. Mud Lager Beer, Palm Beach Malt Flavored Beverages, 1998, Blue Luna Café, 1998. Office: Arizona Beverage Co 5 Dakota Dr Ste 205 New Hyde Park NY 11042 Office Phone: 516-812-0300. Office Fax: 516-326-4988.

VUMBACCO, JOSEPH V., health services executive; BA, Bowdoin Coll.; JD, Syracuse u. Atty. Mudge, Rose, Guthrie and Alexander; sr. v.p. F&M Schaefer Corp.; exec. v.p. The Turner Corp., 1982—96, Health Mgmt. Assocs., Inc., Naples, Fla., 1996—97, pres., 1997—2001, pres., CEO, 2001—06, vice chmn., CEO, 2006—07, vice chmn., 2007—. Office: Health Mgmt Assocs Inc Ste 500 5811 Pelican Bay Blvd Naples FL 34108-2710 Office Phone: 239-597-7161. Business E-Mail: susie.brin@hma.org. *

VUONO, CARL E., communications systems company executive, retired military officer; b. Monongahela, Pa., Oct. 18, 1934; BS in Engring., US Mil. Acad., West Point, NY, 1957; grad., Field Artillery Sch., USMC Command and Staff Coll., US Army War Coll.; MS in Pub. Adminstrn., Shippensburg State Coll., Pa., 1973; D in Pub. Adminstrn. (hon.), Shippensburg U. Commd. 2nd lt. US Army, 1957, advanced through grades to gen., 1986, dep. chief. of staff Ops. and Plans Washington, chief of staff, 1987-91; with MPRI, Alexandria, Va., 1993, pres., 1999; sr. v.p., pres. L-3 Svcs. Group L-3 Comm. Holdings, Inc. Roman Catholic. Office: L-3 Comm Holdings Inc 1215 S Clark St Ste 1205 Arlington VA 22202 *

VUOTO, ANTHONY F., corporate financial executive; BA, Princeton U.; MBA, Wharton Sch. Bus., U. Pa. Pres. consumer lending divsn. Bank One Corp., pres., COO First USA Bank; vice chmn., CFO Providian Fin. Corp., San Francisco, 2002—05; sr. v.p., CFO Card Services Washington Mutual Inc., Seattle, 2005—07, pres. Card Services, 2007—. Office: Washington Mutual 1302 2d Ave Seattle WA 98101 *

VYAS, NISHA ANNE, physician; BA, Stanford U., Palo Alto, Calif., 1995; MD, U. SD, Vermillion, 2000. Lic. dr. U. SD, 2000. Fellow maternal fetal medicine Georgetown U., DC, 2004—. Office Fax: 202-444-1757. Business E-Mail: nvyas99@yahoo.com.

VYAZOVKIN, SERGEY, chemistry professor; b. Kazan, Russia, Feb. 20, 1960; came to U.S., 1995; s. Valentin and Irma Vyazovkin; m. Sasha Vyazovkin, Oct. 1, 1983; 1 child, Polina. BS, Belorussian U., Minsk, 1982, PhD in Chemistry, 1989. Rsch. prof. U. Utah, Salt Lake City, 1998—2001; prof. U. Ala., Birmingham, 2001—. Editor: Thermochim. Acta; mem. editl. bd.: Jour. Thermal Analysis and Calorimetry. Lise Meitner Rsch. fellow Austrian Rsch. Fund, 1992-93, Rsch. fellow NATO, 1994 Mem.: ACS, N.Am. Thermal Analysis Soc. (Mettler award 2004). Office: U Ala Dept Chemistry 901 S 14th St Birmingham AL 35294 E-mail: vyazovkin@uab.edu.

VYKUKAL, EUGENE LAWRENCE, pharmaceutical executive, director; b. Caldwell, Tex., June 26, 1929; s. Henry J. and Anna P. (Polansky) V.; m. Judith Anderson, Jan. 1, 1977; children: Anna K., Mark Roman, Laura Roman, Geni. BS in Pharmacy, U. Tex., Austin, 1952. Pharmacist Scarborough's Pharmacy, Baytown, Tex., 1952-53; pharmacist Gene Vykukal's Pharmacy, Clifton, Tex., 1953-57; with Southwestern Drug Corp. (name now Bergen Brunswig Drug Co.), 1957-86; gen. sales mgr. Southwestern Drug Corp., Dallas, 1966-67, v.p., dir. sales, 1967-75, exec. v.p., dir. sales, 1975-81, exec. v.p., 1980-81, pres., chief exec. officer, 1981-86, vice chmn., 1985-86, dir., 1966-86; asst. dean for devel., lectr. Coll. Pharmacy U. Tex., Austin, 1991—, mem. adv. coun. Pharm. Found., chmn., 1978—; sr. v.p. profl. affairs Bergen Brunswig Corp., Bergen Brunswig Drug Co., 1986—. Mem. centennial endowment com. U. Tex., 1980—; bd. dirs. Baylor U. Med. Center Found., Dallas; mem. indsl. adv. coun. Coll. Pharmacy, U. Ky., 1990—. Recipient Disting. Alumni award U. Tex. Coll. Pharmacy, 1979, William J. Sheffield Disting. Alumni award U. Tex. at Austin Coll. Pharmacy, 1987, Legend of Pharmacy award U. Tex. Coll. Pharmacy Alumni Assn., 1997. Mem. Nat. Wholesale Druggists Assn. (chmn. sales mgmt. com. 1972-73, dir. 1980—, chmn. bd. 1985-86, 1st vice chmn. 1983—, chmn. exec. com. 1987—, Timothy Barry award 1990), Am. Pharm. Assn., Tex. Pharm. Assn. (long range planning com. 1983—), Wholesale Druggist Assn. Tex. (pres. 1978-79), Drug Travelers Assn. Tex. (pres. 1977-78), Sales and Mktg. Execs. Dallas (dir. 1971-72). Roman Catholic. Office: U Tex Coll Pharmacy Pharmacy Bldg Austin TX 78712-1074 E-mail: givevickacall@aol.com. *The quality of life in our great country has been enhanced by the tremendous strides made in our health care delivery system over the past three decades. To have served in the pharmaceutical segment has been very rewarding.*

VYSKOCIL, MARY KAY, lawyer; b. NYC, May 22, 1958; d. Gerard John and Kay Theresa (Murphy) V. BA summa cum laude, Dominican Coll., Blauvelt, NY, 1980; JD, St. John's U., Jamaica, NY, 1983. Bar: N.Y. 1984, U.S. Dist. Ct. (so., ea. and no. dists.) N.Y. 1984, U.S. Dist. Ct. Conn. 1988, U.S. Dist. Ct. (no. dist.) Calif. 1988, U.S. Ct. Appeals (2d cir.) 1984, U.S. Ct. Appeals (3d cir. 1985), U.S. Ct. Appeals (4th and 6th cirs.) 1993, U.S. Ct. Appeals (9th cir.) 1992, U.S. Ct. Appeals (11th cir.) 1996, U.S. Supreme Ct. 1989; cert. in secondary edn., N.Y. Assoc. Simpson Thacher & Bartlett, NYC, 1983-90, ptnr., litigation dept., 1991—. Co-chair consumer subcom., gender working group 2d cir. Task Force on Racial, Ethnic and Gender Fairness, N.Y.c., 1995-97. Co-author: Modern Reinsurance Law and Practice, 1996, 2d. edit., 2000. Trustee St. Joseph's Sem., Yonkers, N.Y., 1986—, Dominican Coll., 1987—; 2nd v.p. alumni bd. dirs. St. John's U. Sch. Law, 1996—, dean search comm., 1998—. Recipient 40 Under Forty award Nat. Law Jour., 1995. Mem. Assn. Bar City N.Y. (fed. cts. com. 1996-99, chair ins. com. 1993-96), ABA (co-chair subcom. ins. coverage com. of litigation sect. 1997—). Roman Catholic. Avocations: swimming, reading, travel, horseback riding. Office: Simpson Thacher & Bartlett 425 Lexington Ave New York NY 10017-3954 Office Phone: 212-455-3093. Office Fax: 212-455-2502.

WAAGEN, LINDA LOUISE, elementary school educator; b. Ft. Collins, Colo., Apr. 9, 1956; d. William Albert Vanderlaan and Vera Louise (Curtis) Wilson; m. Jack A. Waagen (div.); m. James Eugene Scholz, Feb. 20, 2000. BS, So. Adventist U., Collegedale, Tenn., 1976; MEd, Old Dominion U., Norfolk, Va., 1994. Profl. tchg. cert. Tchr. Greene Valley SDA Sch., Rochester, Minn., 1979—86, Ft. Smith SDA Sch., Ark., 1986—90, Tidewater Adventist Acad., Chesapeake, Va., 1990—97, Tualatin Valley Jr. Acad., Hillsboro, Oreg., 1997—2000, Portland Adventist Elem. Sch., Gresham, Oreg., 2000—. Author: Roll the Presses, 2001 (Intel's Top 50, 2001). Recipient Don Keate Acad. Excellence, N. Pacific Union SDA, 1999, 2004. Mem.: Nat. Coun. History Edn., Orgn. Am. Historians, Nat. Coun. Social Studies. Adventist. Avocations: raising and showing Arabian horses, photography. Home: PO Box 2415 Gresham OR 97030 Office: Portland Adventist Elem 3990 NW 1st St Gresham OR 97030

WAAK, PATRICIA ANN, political organization administrator, environmental association executive; b. Muskogee, Okla., Feb. 1, 1943; d. Boxly William and Anne Nell (Smith) W.; children: Cinira Anne Baldi, Rachel Nell Carter. Student Tulane U., 1961-62, U. Houston, 1964-65, George Mason U., 1976-77; diploma Mather Sch. Nursing, 1964. R.N., Va. notary public, N.Y. Peace Corps nurse, Maceio, Alagoas, 1966-68; staff nurse U. Wis. Children's Hosp., Madison, 1968-70; dir. counseling Planned Parenthood, Washington, 1973-75; spl. asst. Devel. Support Bur., U.S. AID, Washington, 1977-78; assoc. dir. Office of Population, AID, Washington, 1978-82; asst. dir. Ctr. for Population and Family Health, Columbia U., N.Y.C., 1982-85; dir. population Nat. Audubon Soc., 1985—, state chair, Colo. Dem. Party, 2005-; U.S. del. UN Population Commn., 1981-82; cons. Family Planning Internat., 1973, Global Com. of Parliamentarians on Population and Devel., 1984-85; project design team U.S. AID, Zimbabwe, 1985, evaluation team, Kenya, Uganda, Nigeria, 1987; NGO participant UN Mid-Decade Conf. of Women, Copenhagen, 1981; moderator global population anniversary Peace Corps Conf., 1981; mem. U.S. del. 2nd and 3d preparatory com. meetings UN Internat. Confs. on Population Devel.; mem. environ. strategy and planning commn. World Conservation Union; lectr. in field. Exec. producer (population videotape) What is the Limit, Sharing the Earth, Finding the Balance, Population and Wildlife. Mem. McGovern-Shriver Presdl. Campaign Staff, 1972; vice chmn. Arlington Democratic Com., 1974; chmn. Arlington Com. on Status of Women, 1975; dep. campaign mgr. Shriver for Pres. Com., 1976; del. Va. Dem. Conv., 1976, 82; mem. Population Task Force, 1986—, Internat. Union Conservation Nature and Natural Resources, NGO steering com. on Devel., Environment and Population; del. World Conservation Strategy Conf. Recipient Population Fellows award Population Ref. Bur., 1993. Mem. Am. Pub. Health Assn. (population sect. council, com. on women's rights), Nat. Council for Internat. Health (pub. policy com.), Assn. for Women in Devel., Nat. Women's Polit. Caucus, Soc. Internat. Devel., Women in Def. of Environment. Home: 4225 Weld Co Rd 1/2 Erie CO 80516 Office: 777 Santa Fe Ave Denver CO 80204 Business E-Mail: pwaak@coloradodems.org.

WAAS, GEORGE LEE, lawyer; b. NYC, July 12, 1943; s. George and Anne Waas; m. Harriet I. Waas, July 18, 1971; children: Elaine Beth Hudgins, Amy Michelle Kinsey. BS in Journalism, U. Fla., 1965; JD, Fla. State U., 1970. Bar: Fla. 1970, in state and fed. govt. law and administrv. practice, Fla., US Supreme Ct., 1973. Asst. atty. gen. State of Fla., 1970-71; staff atty. Fla. League of Cities, 1971; asst. to sec. and dir. labor Fla. Dept. Commerce, 1971-73; assoc. dir. continuing legal edn. Fla. Bar, 1973-74; asst. dean, instr. coll. law Fla. State U., 1974-75; atty. Fla. Dept. Health and Rehab. Services, 1977-80; ptnr. Slepin, Slepin, Lambert & Waas, 1981-86; counsel state elections Fla. Dept. of State, 1986-87; asst. atty. gen. State of Fla., Tallahassee, 1987—2003, sr. asst. atty. gen., 2003—04, special counsel to Fla. atty. gen., 2004—. Contbr. articles to profl. jours. Bd. dir. Big Bend Muscular Dystrophy Assn., 1980-83 (pres. 1983); mem. Leon County Cultural Resources Commn., 1985-87; mem. Gov.'s Coun. on the Voter Registration Act, 1993-96. Mem. Fla. Govt. Bar Assn. (pres. 1976-77), Fla. Bar (exec. council administrv. law sect. 1981-86, chmn. 1985-86, Fla. Govt. Lawyer Sec., fed., state and adminstrv. law cert. com., Claude Pepper Outstanding Govt. Lawyer award 2000), Masons, Capital Tiger Bay Tallahassee (dir. 1974-80), Fla. Bar Profl. Com. Democrat. Jewish. Home: 3797 Sally Ln Tallahassee FL 32312-1018 Office: Collins Bldg Tallahassee FL 32399-1050 Office Phone: 850-414-3662. Personal E-mail: waas01@comcast.net.

WAAS, HARRIET ISSNER, elementary school educator; b. Miami, Fla., July 6, 1949; d. Martin and Hildegard (Wimpfheimer) Issner; m. George L. Waas, July 18, 1971; children: Elaine Beth, Amy Michelle. BS, Fla. State U., 1971, MS, 1978. Cert. elem., reading, lang. arts, gifted-talented tchr., ESL Fla. Elem. tchr. Leon County Schs., Tallahassee; mem. Fla. Title I Statewide Team Dist. Educators, 1997—2002, ETS/Region XIV Comprehensive Ctr. Leadership Team, Pineview. Profl. reading developer Just Read Fla., 2002—; mem. Fla. Elem. Reading Adv. Bd., 2006—. Contbr. articles to profl. jours. Recipient Extra Mile award, 1986, 1987, 1988. Mem.: SACS, Internat. Reading Assn. Home: 3797 Sally Ln Tallahassee FL 32312-1018

WABBY, JAMES PATRICK, quality assurance professional, educator; b. Pitts., Apr. 20, 1976; s. James and Patricia Wabby. BSc in Biol. Scis., Duquesne U., 2000, MSc in Health Mgmt. Systems, 2002. HIPAA cons. C.C. Allegheny County, Pitts., 2002—03, adj. prof., 2003—04; clin. regulatory affairs and quality assurance Abbott Labs., Chgo., 2004—. Mem. bioethics oversight com. Abbott Labs., Chgo., 2004—, mem. human factors coun., 2004—; adj. prof. Robert Morris Coll. Ill., Chgo., 2005—. Mem. philanthropy team Abbott Labs., Pitts., 2004—; polit. campaign mgr.

Dist. Justice, Pitts., 1998. Recipient Health Sci. award, Duquesne U., 2000. Mem.: Regulatory Affairs Profl. Soc., Am. Soc. Law, Medicine, and Ethics, Am. Health Lawyers Assn. Avocations: fishing, running, exercise, reading, travel. Home: 4783 Willow Dr Pittsburgh PA 15236

WACHENHEIM, EDGAR, III, investment company executive; b. NYC, Oct. 14, 1937; s. Edgar Jr. and Elizabeth (Lewis) W.; m. Sue Wallach, June 6, 1963; children: Lance, Kim, Chris, Amy. BA, Williams Coll., 1959; MBA, Harvard U., 1966. Securities analyst Goldman, Sachs & Co., NYC, 1966-69; mng. dir. Cen. Nat. Gottesman Inc., NYC, 1969-88; chmn., chief exec. officer Greenhaven Assocs., Inc., NYC, 1988—. Bd. dirs. Cenro Corp., N.Y.C., Sejak, N.Y.C., Ctrl. Nat. Gottesman, Inc., N.Y.C.; pres. trustees Rye Country Day Sch., 1985-93; bd. dirs. Miriam and Ira D. Wallach Found.; trustee, treas. N.Y. Found., 1993—99; trustee Skidmore Coll. 1993-2001, trustee emeritus 2001-; trustee Mus. Modern Art N.Y.C.; trustee, chair exec. com. NY Pub. Libr., 1988-; chmn. Sue and Edgar Wachenheim Found. Trustee Arthur Ross Found., N.Y.C., 1978—; chmn. investment com., trustee UJA Fedn. Jewish Philanthropies, N.Y.C., 1985-97; mem. fin. com., trustee Rye Country Day Sch., N.Y., 1985-97; bd. dirs. Miriam and Ira D. Wallach Found. Mem. N.Y. Soc. Security Analysts, Beach Point Club, Harvard Club, Century Country Club. Avocations: skiing, tennis. Office: Greenhaven Assocs Inc 3 Manhattanville Rd Purchase NY 10577-2116

WACHMAN, MARVIN, retired academic administrator; b. Milw., Mar. 24, 1917; s. Alex and Ida (Epstein) W.; m. Adeline Lillian Schpok, Apr. 12, 1942; children: Kathleen M., Lynn A. BS, Northwestern U., 1939, MA, 1940; PhD, U. Ill., 1942; LLD (hon.), U. Pa., 1964, Lincoln U., Pa., 1970, Del. Valley Coll. Sci. and Agr., 1973, Med. Coll. Pa., 1982, Bloomfield Coll., 1987, Albright Coll., 1991; DHL (hon.), Gratz Coll., 1973; LittD (hon.), Jewish Theol. Sem. Am., 1973, Drexel U., 1980; LHD (hon.), Colgate U., 1975, Widener U., 1976; DSc (hon.), Thomas Jefferson U., 1980; LHD, U. New Eng., 1997; DHL, Phila. Coll. Textiles and Sci., 1999. Asst. in history U. Ill., 1940-42; instr. Biarritz Am. U., Biarritz, France, 1945-46; vis. asst. prof. San Diego State Coll., summer 1948, U. Minn., 1950; assoc. prof. history U. Md. in Europe, 1952-53; from instr. to prof. Colgate U., 1946-61, dir. upper class core program, 1956-61; pres. Lincoln (Pa.) U., 1961-70; v.p. acad. affairs Temple U., 1970-73, pres., 1973-82, chancellor, 1982-2000, Dir. Salzburg Seminar in Am. Studies, 1958-60, pres. Fgn. Policy Rsch. Inst., 1983-89; acting exec. dir. Pa. Higher Edn. Assistance Agy., 1989; acting pres. Phila. Coll. Textiles and Sci., 1991; pres. Albright Coll., 1991-92. Past chmn. Nat. Ctr. for Higher Edn. Mgmt. Sys.; specialist in Africa for State Dept., 1965, 68; mem. adv. coun. World Learning, Inc.; mem. Colgate Nat. Coun.; chmn. emeritus Collegis, Inc. Author: History of Social-Democratic Party of Milwaukee, 1897-1910, 1945, The Education of a University President, 2005; contbr. articles to profl. jours. and newspapers, also chpts. in books. Mem. adv. coun. Greater Phila. Urban Affairs Coalition, World Affairs Coun.; vice chair Fgn. Policy Rsch. Inst.; hon. dir. Phila. Contributionship; trustee emeritus Balch Inst. Ethnic Studies; mem. bd. overseers Coll. V.I.; hon. trustee Albright Coll.; hon. life trustee Temple U. With US Army, 1942—46. Mem. NAACP, Am. Studies Assn. (past mem. exec. com.), AAUP (past pres. Colgate U. chpt.), Am. Hist. Assn., ACLU, Pa. Assn. Colls. and Univs. (past chmn., pres. 1993), Phi Beta Kappa. Office: Temple U Philadelphia PA 19122-6096 Office Phone: 215-204-6275. Business E-Mail: marvin.wachman@temple.edu.

WACHOWSKI, ANDY, film director; b. Chgo., Dec. 29, 1967; s. Ron and Lynne Wachowski; m. Alisa Blasingame, 1991. Student, Emerson Coll., Boston. Motion picture dir., writer, prodr. (With brother Larry) writer Assassins, 1995 (story, hon. mention Stockholm Film Festival); exec. prodr., writer, dir. films Bound, 1996 (Internat. Fantasy Film award 1997, nominee spl. grand prize Deauville Film Festival, hon. mention Stockholm Film Festival), The Matrix, 1999 (Saturn award for best dir., Saturn award nominee for best writer, Sierra award nominee 2000, Las Vegas Film Critics Soc. Best Original Screenplay, nominee best fgn. film Norwegian Internat. Film Festival 2000), The Matrix Reloaded, 2003; writer and exec. prodr. V for Vendetta, 2006. Office: William Morris Agy One William Morris Pl Beverly Hills CA 90212

WACHOWSKI, LARRY, film director; b. Chgo., June 21, 1965; s. Ron and Lynne Wachowski; m. Thea Bloom, Oct. 30, 1993 (div. Dec. 2002). Student, Bard Coll. Motion picture dir., writer, prodr. (With brother Andy) writer Assassins, 1995 (story, hon. mention Stockholm Film Festival); exec. prodr., writer, dir. films Bound, 1996 (Internat. Fantasy Film award 1997, nominee spl. grand prize Deauville Film Festival, hon. mention Stockholm Film Festival), The Matrix, 1999 (Saturn award for best dir., Saturn award nominee for best writer, Sierra award nominee 2000, Las Vegas Film Critics Soc. Best Original Screenplay, nominee best fgn. film Norwegian Internat. Film Festival 2000), The Matrix Reloaded, 2003, The Matrix Revolutions, 2003, V for Vendetta, 2006. Address: William Morris Agy care Dave Wirtschafter One William Morris Pl Beverly Hills CA 90212

WACHS, MARTIN, urban planning educator, author, consultant; b. NYC, June 8, 1941; s. Robert and Doris (Margolis) Wachs; m. Helen Poliner, Aug. 18, 1963; children: Faye Linda, Steven Brett. BCE, CUNY, 1963; MS, Northwestern U., 1965, PhD, 1967. Asst. prof. U. Ill., Chgo., 1967-69, Northwestern U., Evanston, Ill., 1969-71; assoc. prof. urban planning UCLA, 1971-76, prof., 1976-96; dir. U. Calif. Transp. Ctr., 1996-99; prof. civil and environ. engring. and city/regional planning U. Calif., Berkeley, 1996—2005, dir. Inst. Transp. Studies, 1999—2005; dir. transp. space and tech. group RAND Corp., Santa Monica, Calif., 2006—. Vis. disting. prof. Rutgers U., New Brunswick, NJ, 1983—84; mem. exec. com. Transp. Rsch. Bd., 1995—2004, chmn., 2000; vis. fellow Oxford U., England, 1976—77. Author: Transportation for the Elderly: Changing Lifestyles, Changing Needs, 1979, Transportation Planning on Trial, 1996; contbr. articles to profl. jours.; editor: Ethics in Planning, 1984, The Car and the City, 1992. Mem. steering com. LA Parking Mgmt. Study, 1976—78; bd. dirs. LA Commuter Computer, 1978—94; mem. Calif. Commn. Transp. Investment, 1995. Served to capt. Ordnance Corps. US Army, 1967—69. Named Mem. of the Yr., San Francisco chpt. Women's Transp. Seminar, 2006; recipient Pike Johnson award, Transp. Rsch. Bd., 1976, W. N. Carey Disting. Svc. award, 2002, Disting. Tchg. award, UCLA Alumni Assn., 1986, Disting. Planning Educator award, Calif. Planners Found., 1986, Disting. Educator award, Coun. U. Transp. Ctrs., 2003, Disting. Planning Educator award, Assn. Collegiate Schs. Planning, 2006; Guggenheim fellow, 1977, Humanities fellow, Rockefeller Found., 1980, Rsch. lectr., Soc. Sigma Xi, 2004—. Fellow: Am. Inst. Cert. Planners, Am. Coun. Edn.; mem.: ASCE, Inst. Transp. Engrs., Cosmos Club (Washington). Jewish. Home: 670 Harbor St #3 Venice CA 90291-5519 Office: RAND Corp Santa Monica CA 90401-3208 Home Phone: 310-306-2080. Business E-Mail: wachs@rand.org.

WACHSBERGER, CHAIM, lawyer; b. Tel Aviv, Sept. 15, 1951; BA, Queens Coll. CUNY, 1973; JD, Columbia U., 1976. Bar: NJ 1976, NY 1977. Ptnr. Chadbourne & Parke LLP, NYC, head, Project Fin. Practice Group, mem. mgmt. com. Contbr. articles to profl. jour. Mem.: ABA (Corp., Banking & Bus. Law Sect., Am. Bar Assn.), NJ State Bar Assn., NY State Bar Assn. Office: Chadbourne & Parke LLP 30 Rockefeller Plaza New York NY 10112 Office Phone: 212-408-5232. Office Fax: 212-541-5369. Business E-Mail: cwachsberger@chadbourne.com.

WACHSMAN, HARVEY FREDERICK, lawyer, neurosurgeon; b. Bklyn., June 13, 1936; s. Ben and Mollie (Kugel) W.; m. Kathryn M. D'Agostino, Jan. 31, 1976; children: Dara Nicole, David Winston, Jacqueline Victoria, Lauren Elizabeth, Derek Charles, Ashley Max, Marea Lane, Melissa Roseanne. BA, Tulane U., 1958; MD, Chgo. Med. Sch., 1962; JD, Bklyn. Law Sch., 1976. Bar: Conn. 1976, NY 1977, Fla. 1977, DC 1978, Pa. 1984, Md. 1986, Tex. 1987, US Dist. Ct. (Conn.) 1976, US Dist. Ct. (ea. and so. dists.) NY 1977, US Dist. Ct. (we. dist.) NY 1979, US Dist. Ct. (no dist.) NY 1982, US Dist. Ct. (RI) 1978, US Dist. Ct. (DC) 1981, US Dist. Ct. (ea. and we. dists.) Pa. 1990, US Ct. Claims 1990, US Tax Ct. 1990, US Ct. Internat. Trade 1990, US Ct. Appeals (2d cir.) 1976, US Ct. Appeals (DC) 1981, US Ct. Appeals (3rd cir.) 1990, US Supreme Ct. 1980, cert.: Am. Bd. Profl. Liability Attys. 1982, Nat. Bd. Trial Advocacy (Civil Trial Adv.) 1980; diplomate Nat. Bd. Med. Examiners, Am. Bd. Legal Medicine, 1982, Am. Bd. Neurol. and Orthop. Medicine and Surgery, Am. Bd. Med.-Legal Analysts in Medicine and Surgery, lic. Conn., Fla., La., Ariz., NY, Ga., Calif., Nev. Intern surgery Kings County Hosp. Ctr., Bklyn., 1962-63; resident in surgery Kingsbrook Med. Ctr., Bklyn., 1964-65; resident in neurol. surgery Emory U. Hosp., Atlanta, 1965-69; practice medicine specializing in neurosurgery Bridgeport, Conn., 1972-74; sr. ptnr. Law Offices of Harvey F. Wachsman, MD, JD, LLP, Great Neck, NY, 2001—; of counsel firm Queller, Fisher, Dienst, Serrins, Washor & Kool, LLP, NYC, of counsel; atty., pvt. practice Law Offices Harvey F. Wachsman, Upper Brookville, NY, McGehee, Pianelli & Wachsman, LLP, Upper Brookville, NY. Trustee SUNY, Melvin M. Belli Soc., Melanoma Found.; chmn. health sci. and hosp. com.; chmn., bd. dirs. Odyssey Inst. Internat.; bd. dirs. Am. Soc. Neuroimaging, 1989-1990; pres., CEO Found. Excellence & Ethics in Medicine, 1998-; mem. sponsor Trial Lawyers Pub. Justice, 1983; adj. prof. law St. John's U., Jamaica, NY, Bklyn. Law Sch., NY; adj. prof. neurol. surgery SUNY, NY, clin. asst. prof. neurology U. South Fla., Tampa; faculty mem. Practicing Law Inst., 1983; lectr. in field. Author: American Law of Medical Malpractice, Vol. I, 1980, 2d edit., 1992, American Law of Medical Malpractice, Vol. II, 1981, 2d edit., 1993, American Law of Medical Malpractice, Vol. III, 1982, 2d edit., 1994, Cumulative Supplement to American Law of Medical Malpractice, 1981, 82, 83, 84, 86, 88, American Law of Medical Malpractice, 2d edit., Vols. I, II and II, Lethal Medicine, 1993, co-author (with S. Alschuler, and Henry Holt), 1993, contbg. author Law Book Pub.; mem. editl. bd. Legal Aspects of Med. Practice, 1978-82, editl. adv. bd. mem. Lab 79; subject adv. com. Trial Mag.; editor Trial, 1981-82, 82-83, editor, northeast editor Legal Aspects Medical Practice column. Mem. 40th anniversary Israel's com. Friends of Arts' Celebration; pres., bd. trustees Nat. Grand Opera Co., 1987—92; bd. trustees Nassau County Fine Arts, 1989; v.p. Carson Scholar Fund, Balt., 1997; chmn. bd. dirs. Deja Vu Dance Co., 1985—89, Friends of Nassau County Office of Cultural Devel., 1990—92; past bd. chmn. Bd. Police Commrs. Assn. Conn., past pres.; past chmn. Newtown Bd. Police Commrs., Conn. Fellow: Am. Acad. Forensic Scis., Am. Coll. Legal Medicine Found. (bd. trustees 1988—), Assn. Trial Lawyers Am., Royal Soc. Medicine (London), Am. Coll. Legal Medicine (mem. bd. govs. 1983—84, mem. exec. coun. 1983—84, chmn. edn. com. 1983—87, chmn. 1985, mem. bd. govs. 1986—89, chmn. nat. meeting New Orleans 1988, exec. com. 1988, nat. meeting, bd. dirs. ACLM Found.), Royal Soc. Medicine, Royal Soc. Arts (London); mem.: AMA, ABA, Am. Society Law and Medicine, Tex. Bar Assn., Md. Bar Assn., Pa. Bar Assn., NY State Trial Lawyers Assn. (parliamentarian 1989—90, bd. dirs. 1990—92), NY State Acad. Trial Lawyers, Assn. Trial Lawyers Am. (NY state del. 1989—90, mem. bd. govs. 1990—92), Am. Bd. Profl. Liability Attys. (pres. 1988—), Nat. Bd. Trial Advocacy (examination devel. com. 1981, 1982, 1983, bd. dirs. 1989), Am. Assn. Advancement Sci., Scribes: Am. Society Writers on Legal Subjects, Am. Soc. Contemporary Medicine and Surgery, Conn. State Med. Soc., Nassau-Suffolk Trial Lawyers Assn., Fairfield County Med. Soc., Nassau County Bar Assn., Pa. Trial Lawyers Assn., Wis. Acad. Trial Lawyers (hon.), Tex. Trial Lawyers Assn., Md. Trial Lawyers Assn., Fla. Acad. Trial Lawyers, Conn. Trial Lawyers Assn., NY Trial Lawyers Assn., NY Acad. Scis., DC Bar Assn., Fla. Bar Assn., Conn. Bar Assn. (med. legal com.), NY Bar Assn., Congress Neurol. Surgeons, Nat. Lawyers Club, Cosmos (Washington), Cosmos Club (Washington). also: 233 Broadway New York NY 10279 Office: McGehee Pianelli Wachsman LLP 55 Mill River Rd Oyster Bay NY 11771 Office Fax: 516-624-0667. E-mail: hwachsman@quellerfisher.com. *In my pursuit of knowledge and excellence in the fields of neurosurgery and the law, I have found that arming oneself with the power of knowledge is truly the key to helping others. Let one's goal in life be to help others, and he shall always find fulfillment, challenge and hope.*

WACHTEL, ALBERT, writer, educator; b. NYC, Dec. 20, 1939; s. Jacob and Sarah Rose (Kaplansky) W.; m. Sydelle Farber, Mar. 9, 1958; children: Sally Rose, Seth Laurence, Stephanie Allyson, Synthia Laura, Jonathan Benjamin, Jessica Eden, Jacob Ethan. BA, CUNY, 1960; PhD, SUNY, Buffalo, 1968. Instr. SUNY, Buffalo, 1963—66, asst. to dean, 1966—68; asst. prof. U. Calif., Santa Barbara, 1968—74; prof. English, creative writing Pitzer Coll., Claremont (Calif.) Colls., 1974—. Playwright: Paying the Piper, 1968, Prince Hal, 1995; co-editor Modernism: Challenges and Perspectives, 1986; author: The Cracked Looking Glass: James Joyce and the Nightmare of History, 1992; contbr. stories, creative essays to lit. jours., newspapers, and mags. NDEA fellow, 1960-63, fellow Creative Arts Inst., U. Calif., Berkeley, 1970, NEH Summer Inst., Dartmouth Coll., 1987; Danforth Found. assoc., 1978, NEH Seminar, Cornell U., 1998. Jewish. Office: Pitzer Coll Claremont Colls Claremont CA 91711-6101 Office Phone: 909-607-3641. Business E-Mail: awachtel@pitzer.edu.

WACHTELL, ESTHER, non-profit management executive, consultant; b. June 30; m. Thomas Wachtell, Jan. 27; children: Roger Bruce, Wendy Anne, Peter James. BA in Phil., Conn. Coll.; MA in Literature, Cornell U. Pres. Music Ctr. of Los Angeles County; founder, pres. The Wachtell Group, TWG, Inc. Bd. dirs. Mus. Ventura County, Ojai Music Festivals, Children's Hosp. LA; founding chair U. So. Calif Ctr. Philanthropy and Pub. Policy. Mem.: Tower Club, Regency Club (bd. dirs.). Fax: 805-649-3303.

WACHTELL, HERBERT M., lawyer; b. NYC, May 24, 1932; BS, NYU, 1952, LLB, 1954; LLM, Harvard Univ., 1955. Bar: N.Y. 1955, US Dist. Ct. (so. & ea. N.Y.), US Ct. Appeals (2d, 3d, 4th, 5th, 7th, 8th, 11th & Fed. cir.), US Supreme Ct. 1973. Asst. U.S. atty. U.S. Dept. Justice, so. dist. N.Y., 1955—57; ptnr., litigation dept. Wachtell, Lipton, Rosen & Katz, NYC, 1965—. Editor: NYU Law Rev., 1953—54; author: N.Y. Practice Under the CPLR, 1986. Root-Tilden scholar. Fellow: Am. Bar Found., Am. Coll. Trial Lawyers; mem.: ABA, N.Y. County Lawyers Assn., Assn. Bar City of N.Y., Phi Beta Kappa, Order of the Coif. Office: Wachtell Lipton Rosen & Katz 51 W 52nd St New York NY 10019-6150 Office Phone: 212-403-1216. Office Fax: 212-403-2216. Business E-Mail: hmwachtell@wlrk.com.

WACHTER, MICHAEL L., law and finance educator; b. NYC, Mar. 12, 1943; s. Abraham and Florence W.; m. Susan M. Jaffe, June 23, 1968; children: Jessica, Jonathan. BS, Cornell U., 1964; MA, Harvard U., 1967, PhD, 1970. Asst. prof. econs. U. Pa., Phila., 1969-73, assoc. prof., 1973-76, prof. econs., law and mgmt., 1976—93, William B. Johnson prof. law & econ., 1993—, co-dir. Inst. for Law and Econ., 1984—; sr. advisor Brookings Instn., Washington, 1976-90. Mem. Minimum Wage Study Commn., Washington, 1978-81; cons. U.S. Postal Svc., 1980—. Editor: Removing Obstacles to Economic Growth, 1984, Toward a New U.S. Industrial Policy, 1982; contbr. articles to profl. jours. NIH grantee, 1981-83; NSF grantee, 1974-77; 20th Century Fund grantee, 1978-82; Gen. Electric Found. grantee, 1980-83 Mem. Am. Econ. Assn., Econometric Soc., Indsl. Relations Research Assn. Office: U Pa Law Sch Inst Law & Econs 3400 Chestnut St Philadelphia PA 19104-6204 Office Phone: 215-898-7719. Business E-Mail: mwachter@law.upenn.edu. *

WACHTER, SUSAN MELINDA, finance educator; b. June 22, 1943; d. Nathaniel and Edith (Dubow) Jaffe; m. Michael Lawrence Wachter, June 23, 1968; children: Jessica, Jonathan. BA, Radcliffe Coll., 1965; PhD, Boston Coll., 1974; MA (hon.), U. Pa., 1978. Lectr. Bryn Mawr Coll., Pa., 1969-72; lectr. Wharton Sch. U. Pa., Phila., 1972-74, asst. prof. fin., 1974-78, assoc. prof., 1978-95, prof. real estate and fin., 1995—, chmn. real estate dept., 1997—99; asst. sec., policy devel. and rsch. HUD, 1999—2001; Richard B. Warley prof. fin. mgmt., 2003—. Bd. dirs. Beneficial Corp., Beneficial Mortgage Corp. Author: Latin American Inflation: The Structuralist-Monetarist Debat, 1976, Inflation and Pensions, 1987; co-author: Redlining and Public Policy, 1980; co-editor: Towards a New U.S. Industrial Policy?, 1981, Removing Obstacles to Economic Growth, 1984, Real Estate Economics, 1997, Savings and Capital Formation: The Policy Options; editor: Social Security and Private Pensions: Planning for the 21st Century, 1988; bd. editors Jour. Real Estate Rsch., Jour. Am. Real Estate and Urban Econs., Jour. Housing Econs., Jour. Real Estate Fin. and Econs. Recipient Lindbach award Lindbach Soc., 1974-75; Rsch. fellow Harvard U., 1966. Mem. Am. Econ. Assn., Am. Fin. Assn., Econometric Soc., Am. Real Estate and Urban Econs. Assn. (bd. dirs. 1984-91, pres. 1988), Lambda Alpha. Home: 355 Margo Ln Berwyn PA 19312-1453 Office: U Pa Finance Dept Philadelphia PA 19104 Office Phone: 215-898-6355. Business E-Mail: wachter@wharton.upenn.edu.

WACHTLER, SOL, lawyer, educator; b. NYC, Apr. 29, 1930; s. Philip Henry and Fay (Sobel) W.; m. Joan Wolosoff, Feb. 23, 1952; children: Lauren Jane, Marjorie Dru, Alison Toni, Philip Henry. BA, Washington and Lee U., 1951, LLB, 1952, postgrad., 1980, LLD (hon.), 1981, New Eng. Sch. Law, 1978, Bklyn. Law Sch., 1978, Hofstra U., 1980, SUNY, 1981, Syracuse U., Dowling Coll., 1990, Thomas M. Cooley Law Sch., 1990, New. Eng. Law Sch.; LHD (hon.), LIU, Coll. of St. Rose. Bar: N.Y. 1956. Justice N.Y. State Supreme Ct., 1968-72; judge N.Y. State Ct. Appeals, Albany, 1972-84; chief judge State of N.Y., Albany, 1985-93; prof. law Touro Law Sch., 1997—. Guest lectr. Bklyn. Law Sch., Hofstra Law Sch., Yale U. Sch. Law, Albany Law Sch., St. John's Law Sch., 1968-77, USIA, Munich, Germany, 1973, Stuttgart, Germany, 1977, U. Leyden, Amsterdam, Stockholm, 1988, Madrid, 1989; chmn. NY State Fair Trial/Free Press Conf., NY State Commn. on Bicentennial of US Constitution.; bd. dirs. Confs. Chief Justices; trustee Nat Jud. Coll. Author: After the Madness, 1997, Blood Brothers, 2003; critic-at-large New Yorker mag., 1996; contbr. articles to legal jours. Councilman Town of North Hempstead, N.Y., 1963-65, chief exec., 1965-67; mem. Nassau County Bd. Suprs., 1965-67, chmn. com. pub. safety, 1965-67; trustee L.I. Jewish-Hillside Med. Ctr., 1970-98, L.I. U.; exec. com. North Shore L.I. Jewish Health Sys., 1998—; bd. overseers Nelson A. Rockefeller Inst. Govt., Touro Law Sch., 2002-; dist. chmn. Boy Scouts Am., 1968-69; trustee Cerebral Palsy Assn., Assn. for Help of Retarded Children, 1966-67. Mem. Am. Law Inst., Assn. N.Y. State Supreme Ct. Justices, ABA, N.Y. State Bar Assn., Nassau County Bar Assn., Order of Coif, Phi Delta Phi. Jewish. Home: 10 Stonehill Dr N Manhasset NY 11030-4438 E-mail: SWCADRE@aol.com. *As a people, we are fond of the observation that ours is a nation of laws and not of men. It too, like the words of our great laws, seems to lend security, a sense of certainty, and a predictability to the paths we travel. In the law particularly, the thought that past generations have separated right from wrong and good from evil can be comforting. Yet, here again, if we will just scratch the surface, we will find that the greatest responsibility for our national welfare does not rest with statutes carved in stone but with the principles, conscience, and morality of the individuals who constitute this generation.*

WACHTMAN, JEANETTE MARIE, art educator, artist, writer; d. John and Margaret Wachtman. BS in Art Edn., State U. Coll., Buffalo, 1971, MS in Art Edn., 1972. Cert. permanent tchg. State U. Coll. -Buffalo, 1972, tchr. 1-5 Ga., 1991. Tchr. art Phoenix Sch. Dist., 1973—83, Suzuki Internat. Learning Ctr., Atlanta, 1984—85, Clayton State Coll., Ga., 1984—85, Chastain Art Ctr., Atlanta, 1984—86, Atlanta Coll. Art, 1988—92, Steeple Art Ctr., Marietta, Ga., 1990—92, Kennesaw State U., Ga., 1988—, Cobb County Schs., Marietta, 1991—. Mem. bd. Ga. Art Edn. Assn., 1995—2001, chair state capitol art exhibit, 1995—2000, co-chair office of govt. art exhibit, Ga., 1996—2000, chair elem. divsn., 1999—2001, art advocacy rep., 2000; mem. elem. divsn. devel. com. Nat. Art Edn. Assn., 1999—2000; presenter, lectr. in field. Author: (book) The How of It - A Cultural Program Resource Guide, 1995, Artists, Elements, and Principles of Art, 2001; co-author: Rhythm-ongs - The History of Art, 2000; one-woman shows include The Octagon House, Camillus, NY, 1977, Seneca Wall Gallery, Liverpool, NY, 1979, Woman in the Arts Festival, Syracuse, NY, 1980, Penfield Libr., SUNY, Oswego, 1981, Liverpool Art Gallery, NY, 1982, Trail of Tears Art Gallery, Atlanta, 1984, Inner Space Gallery, 1993, Istanbul Ctr. for Culture and Dialogue, Norcross, Ga., 2006, The Art Station, Big Shanty, Kennsaw, Ga., 2007. Organizer and presenter cmty. based arts edn. program Blackwell Elem. Sch., Cobb County, Marietta. Named Tchr. of Yr., Bryant Elem. Sch., 1996—97, Ga.'s Elem. Art Educator of Yr., Ga. Art Edn. Assn., 1997—98, Elem. Art Educator of Yr., Nat. Art Edn. Assn., 1999; recipient Youth Art Month award of Excellence, Ga. Art Edn. Assn., 1999, Outstanding Continuing Educator award, Kennesaw State U., 1993, Target, 2002; grantee, CVS, 2001, So. Bell, 1992—93, N.Y. State Edn. Dept., 1979. Mem.: Ga. Art Edn. Assn., Nat. Art Edn. Assn. Avocations: travel, art, writing. Home Phone: 770-894-3934. Home Fax: 770-894-3934. Personal E-mail: rajean@tds.net.

WACHTMANN, LYNN R., state legislator; m. Trudy Blue; children: Cory, Aaron. Grad., Four County Joint Vocat. Sch. Owner, pres. Maumee Valley Bottlers, Inc., Napoleon, Ohio; ptnr. Culligan Water Conditioning; former councilman City of Napoleon; mem. Ho. of Reps., Ohio, 1985—98, Ohio Senate from 1st dist., Columbus, 1999—, chmn. health, human svcs. and aging com., mem. energy, natural resources, environment, highways and transp., ins., commerce and labor coms. Vol. fundraiser Crisis Pregnancy Ctrs. of N.W. Ohio, Bryan; vol. Orphan Grain Train; mem. Rep. Ctrl. Com.; Sunday sch. tchr., usher St. Paul Luth. Ch.; bd. dirs. Ohio Water Quality Assn. Named Nat. Legislator of Yr., Am. Legis. Exch. Coun., 1994, State Legislator of Yr., Nat. Retail Fedn., 1996, Legislator of Yr., Am. Legion, 2000; recipient Bobcat Legis. award, 1993, Watchdog of the Treasury award, United Conservatives of Ohio, Oustanding Freshman Legislator of Yr. award, 2000, Grad. Wall of Fame award, Four County Joint Vocat. Sch., 1997, Legislator of Yr. Defender of Life award, Ohio Right to Life, 1997, Conservation Legis. award, League of Ohio Sportsmen Nat. Wildlife Fedn., 1997, Guardian of Small Bus. award, Nat. Fedn. Ind. Bus., 1998. Mem.: NRA, Ohio Twp. Assn., Nat. Assn. Sportsman Legislators, Am. Legis. Exch. Coun. (state chmn.), Ohio Right to Life Soc., Gideon's Internat., Ohio Farm Bur., Pheasants Forever, Ducks Unlimited. Republican. Office: Rm # 040 Senate Bldg Columbus OH 43215 Office Phone: 614-466-8150.

WACHTMEISTER, COUNT WILHELM H.F., diplomat; b. Vanas, Sweden, Apr. 29, 1923; s. Gustaf and Margaretha (Trolle) W.; m. Ulla Leuhusen, 1947; children: Anna, Erik. LLD, U. Stockholm, Sweden, 1946. Attache Swedish Ministry for Fgn. Affairs, 1946-47; attache Swedish Embassy, Vienna, Madrid and Lisbon, 1947-50; 2d sec. Swedish Ministry Fgn. Affairs, Stockholm, Sweden, 1950-55; 1st sec. Swedish Embassy, Moscow, 1955-58; personal asst. to UN Sec. Gen., 1958-61; head UN sect. Fgn. Ministry, Stockholm, 1962-65, dep. under-sec. polit. affairs, 1965-66; ambassador to Algeria Swedish Embassy, 1966-67; under-sec. for polit. affairs Swedish Ministry Fgn. Affairs, Stockholm, 1968-74; Swedish ambassador to U.S. Swedish Embassy, Washington, 1974-89; dean diplomatic corps in Washington, 1986-89. Sr. advisor to chmn. AB Volvo,

1989-94. Mem. Soc. Cincinnati (France), Nya Sällskapet, Swedish-Am. C. of C. (chmn. 1993-95), Sällskapet, Stockholm. Avocation: tennis. Address: Karlavagen 59A SE 11449 Stockholm Sweden Office Phone: 46-8-6603823.

WACK, THOMAS E., lawyer; b. Mo., 1944; AB magna cum laude, Georgetown U., 1966; JD, Northwestern U., 1969. Bar: Mo. 1969. Ptnr., mem. exec. com. Bryan Cave LLP, St. Louis. Program dir. Fed. Practice Com. U.S. Dist. Ct. (Mo. dist.). Fellow Am. Coll. Trial Lawyers; mem. ABA, Mo. Bar Assn. (mem. bus. torts com., mem. unfair competition com. 1990-92). Office: Bryan Cave LLP One Metropolitan Square 211 North Broadway, Ste 3600 Saint Louis MO 63102 Office Phone: 314-259-2182. E-mail: tewack@bryancave.com.

WACKER, JOHN M., music educator, director; s. A. Mainard and Sarah E. Wacker; m. Nancy E. Russell, Mar. 30, 1996; children: Brian R, Elizabeth I. MusB in Edn., U. No. Colo., Greeley, 1983; MusM, Ind. U. of Pa., Ind., Pa., 1999; JD, U. Wyo., Laramie, 1994. Dir. band Burns Jr. and Sr. HS, Wyo., 1983—85, Cheyenne Ctrl. HS, Wyo., 1985—90; music sales, clinician Yocum Music Co., Cheyenne, 1990—99; coord. instrumental music Laramie County C.C., Cheyenne, 1999—2001; tchg. fellow U. North Tex., Denton, 2001—04; dir. bands We. State Coll. Colo., Gunnison, 2005—. Pvt. practice music clinician, Gunnison, 1990—. Fellow, U. North Tex., 2001—04; grantee, We. State Coll. Colo., 2006. Mem.: Music Educators Nat. Conf., Internat. Trumpet Guild, Nat. Honor Soc., Phi Beta Mu, Kappa Kappa Psi. Office: We State Coll Colorado Quigley Hall Gunnison CO 81231 Home Phone: 970-641-4974; Office Phone: 970-943-2169. Personal E-mail: jwacker@musician.org. Business E-Mail: jwacker@western.edu.

WACKER, WARREN ERNEST CLYDE, internist, educator; b. Bklyn., Feb. 29, 1924; s. John Frederick and Kitty Dora (Morrissey) W.; m. Ann Romeyn MacMillan, May 22, 1948; children: Margaret Morrissey, John Frederick. Student, Georgetown U., 1946—47; MD, George Washington U., 1951; MA (hon.), Harvard U., 1968. Intern George Washington U. Hosp., 1951-52, resident in internal medicine, 1952-53; resident Peter Bent Brigham Hosp., Boston, 1953-55; Nat. Found. Infantile Paralysis fellow, 1955-57; investigator Howard Hughes Med. Inst., Boston, 1957-68; from faculty to prof. hygiene Harvard U., Cambridge, Mass., 1955-71, assoc. prof. medicine, 1968—71, 1971—89, acting master Mather House, 1974-75, acting master Kirkland House, 1975-76, master Cabot House, 1978-84; sr. med. cons. Risk Mgmt. Found., Cambridge, 1992—; Henry K. Oliver prof. hygiene emeritus Harvard U., Cambridge, 1995—. Dir. health svcs. Harvard U., Cambridge, 1971-89; vis. scholar St. Mary's Hosp. Med. Sch., 1964; vis. prof. U. Tel Aviv, 1987; chmn. bd. Applied Mgmt. Sys., Burlington, Mass., 1982-97, Millipore Corp., Bedford, Mass., 1971-94. Author: Magnesium and Man, 1981; sec., editl. adv. bd. Biochemistry, 1962-76; assoc. editor Magnesium; mem. editl. bd. Toxiogical and Environ. Chemistry, 1989-2006; contbr. articles to profl. jours. Vestryman St. Paul's Episc. Ch., Brookline, Mass., 1965-68, 76-79, 91-94; bd. dirs. Harvard Cmty. Health Plan, Boston, 1973-84, mem. fin. com., 1984-86, mem. corp., 1986-96; bd. dirs. Bishop Rhinelander Found., Cambridge, 1973-76, 78-84, Controlled Risk Ins. Co., 1976-78; pres. bd. overseers Peter Bent Brigham Hosp., Boston, 1979-84; trustee Brigham and Women's Hosp., Boston, 1984-89, Risk Mgmt. Found., 1979-92; mem. mgmt. bd. MIT, 1985-95; mem. corp. Mt. Auburn Hosp., Cambridge, 1986—2006; mem. adv. bd. hospitality program Episc. Diocese Mass., 1989-95. 1st lt. USAAF, 1942-45. Decorated Air medal, D.F.C., Liberation medal, Greece; named Disting. Alumnus, George Washington U., 1963; recipient Cert. of Merit, Soc. Magnesium Rsch., 1985. Mem. AMA, Am. Chem. Soc., Am. Soc. Biol. Chemistry, Am. Soc. Clin. Investigation, Mass. Med. Soc., ACP, Am. Coll. Health Assn. (pres. 1981, Boynton award 1986), Biochemistry Soc. (London), Am. Coll. Nutrition, Harvard Club (Boston), Sigma Xi, Alpha Omega Alpha. Home: 91 Glen Rd Brookline MA 02445-7764 Office: Risk Mgmt Found 101 Main St Cambridge MA 02142-1519 Office Phone: 617-679-1216. Business E-Mail: wwacker@rmf.harvard.edu.

WACKERMANN, WILLIAM, publishing executive; married; 3 children. Grad., Villanova U., 1989. Mktg. mgr. Bus. Week; various positions Vanity Fair, corp. mgr., 1995—96; N.Y. advt. mgr. Conde Nast Traveler, 1996—97, advt. mgr., 1997—98, assoc. pub., 1999—2000, House & Garden, 1998—99; v.p. and pub. Details mag., 2000—04, Glamour mag., 2004—. Named Mag. Pub. of Yr., Delaney Report, 2002; recipient Media Mavens award, Advt. Age, 2003. Office: Glamour Mag Conde Nast Bldg 4 Times Sq New York NY 10036-6522 *

WACKERNAGEL, MATHIS, engineering company executive, director; b. Basel, Switzerland; m. Susan Burns; 1 child, Andre. MS in Mech. Engring., Swiss Fed. Inst. Tech., Zürich, 1988; PhD in Cmty. and Regional Planning, U. BC, Vancouver, Can., 1994. Exec. dir. Global Footprint Network, Oakland, Calif., 2003—. Author: (book) Our Ecological Footprint; editl. bd. mem. (Jour. Ecol. Econs.). Recipient Conservation Merit award, WWF Internat., 2006; grantee Skoll Social Entrepreneurship award, Skoll Found., 2007. Achievements include development of eclogical footprint - a resource accounting tool that measures how much nature we have, how much we use, and who uses what. Office Phone: 510-839-8879. Office Fax: 510-251-2410.

WADDELL, DON, professional sports team executive; m. Cheryl Waddell; 1 child, Chelsea. Player No. Mich. U. Divsn. I Hockey, 1976—80, US Nat. Team, World Champs., 1983; player, coach Goaldiggers Hockey Club, Toledo, 1985—86, Flint Spirits, 1986—88; player Los Angeles Kings, 1980—83; head coach, gen. mgr. Flint Spirits, 1988—89, gen. mgr., 1989—90; v.p., exec. com. RDV Sports, San Diego Gulls, 1990—95, head coach, 1991—92; v.p., exec. com. RDV Sports, Orlando Solar Bears, 1995—97; asst. gen. mgr. Stanley Cup Champion Detroit Red Wings, 1997—98; v.p., gen. mgr. Atlanta Thrashers, Atlanta, 1998—; asst. gen. mgr. Team USA World Championships, 1999—2000, gen. mgr., 2001—02. Named First Team Internat. Hockey League All-Star, 1982, 1986, Second Team Internat. Hockey League All-Star, 1988; named to CCHA All-Decade Team, No. Mich. U., 1970. Achievements include inducted into the No. Mich. U. Sports Hall of Fame, 1992. Office: Atlanta Thrashers 1 CNN Ctr 12th Fl S Tower Atlanta GA 30303-2762

WADDELL, DOUGLAS HOWARD, family physician; b. Bluff City, TN, May 6, 1943; s. Cecil Howard and France Daisy (Boling) W.; m. Luz Isabel Garza, Jan 2, 1971; children: Amy, Christopher, Brandon. BS in Biology, Chemistry, Carson-Newman Coll., Jefferson City, Tenn., 1965; MD, U. Tenn., 1969. Diplomate Am. Bd. Family Practice. Intern Baylor U. Med. Ctr., Dallas, 1970; physician, owner Launey Med. Clinic, Dallas, 1971-82, Beltline North Med. Clinic, Dallas, 1983-85, Atrium Med. Clinic, Dallas, 1985—. Fellow Am. Acad. Family Physicians; mem. Tex. Med. Assn., Dallas County Med. Soc., Tex. Acad. Family Physicians (bd. dirs. state assn., past sec., treas., v.p., pres. Dallas chpt.), Am. Coll. Occupational and Environ. Medicine. Republican. Baptist. Avocations: gardening, cooking. Home: 10473 Epping Ln Dallas TX 75229-6310 Office: Atrium Med Clinic 14465 Webb Chapel Rd Ste 111 Dallas TX 75234-3600 Home Phone: 214-350-2370; Office Phone: 972-247-6900.

WADDELL, JOHN COMER, electronics executive; b. Bridgeport, Conn., Sept. 10, 1937; s. John and Dorothy Margot (Comer) W. BA, Yale U., New Haven, 1959; MBA, Harvard U., 1965. Assoc. R.W. Pressprich & Co., NYC, 1965-68; ptnr. Glenn, Green & Waddell, NYC, 1968-80; exec. v.p. Arrow Electronics, Inc., Melville, NY, 1969-80, chmn., CEO, 1980—86, chmn., 1986—94, vice chmn., 1994—. Mem. com. arch. & design Mus. Modern Art, NYC; mem. com. photographs Met. Mus. Art, NYC; co-chmn. Joffrey Ballet; past pres. Found. for Joffrey Ballet; dir. 55th St. Dance Theater Found., Nat. Corp. Fund for Dance, Am. Arts Alliance. Officer Office of Naval Intelligence USN. Office: Arrow Electronics Inc 50 Marcus Dr Melville NY 11747-4210 Office Phone: 631-847-2000. *

WADDELL, M. KEITH, human resources specialist; From v.p. to vice chmn., CFO, treas. Robert Half Internat. Inc., Menlo Pk., Calif., 1986—93, vice chmn., 1999—, CFO, 1999—, treas., 1999—. Office: Robert Half International Inc 2884 SandHill Rd Menlo Park CA 94025

WADDELL, MARK E., lawyer; b. Dec. 3, 1957; BSChemE, NJ Inst. Tech., 1979; JD, Seton Hall U., 1984. Bar: NJ 1985, NY 1985, US Ct. Appeals (Fed. Cir.), registered: US Patent & Trademark Office. Process develop. engr., 1979—83; patent atty. Hubbell Cohen, NYC, 1983—86; atty., patent law dept. Hoffmann-La Roche Inc., NYC, 1986—87; patent atty. Cohen, Pontani & Lieberman, NYC; ptnr. Bryan Cave LLP, NYC, 1991—2001, mem. exec. com & strategic planning com., chmn., Intellectual Property Practice Group; ptnr., intellectual property dept., litig. dept. Chadbourne & Parke LLP, NYC, 2001—07; ptnr. Loeb & Loeb LLP, NYC, 2007—. Spkr. in field; contbr. articles to profl. jour. Mem.: Intellectual Property Owners Assn., Fed. Cir. Bar Assn., NY Intellectual Property Law Assn. Office: Loeb & Loeb LLP 345 Park Ave New York NY 10154 E-mail: mwaddell@loeb.com. *

WADDELL, PHILLIP DEAN, lawyer; b. Covington, Ky., Nov. 14, 1948; s. Ewell Edward and Sarah Isobel (Dean) W.; m. Jill Annette Tolson, Aug. 23, 1975; children: Nathan Ewell, James Seth. BA, Centre Coll. Ky., 1971; JD, No. Ky. U., 1982. Bar: Ky. 1982, Ohio 1983, Tenn. 1986. V.p., mgr. escrow Eagle Savings Assn., Cin., 1973-83; v.p. Union Planters Nat. Bank, Memphis, 1983-84; sr. v.p., liason First Nat. Bank & Trust Co., Oklahoma City, 1984-86; sr. v.p., sec., gen. counsel First Mortgage Strategies Group, Inc., Memphis, 1986-92; atty. pvt. practice, Memphis, 1992—. Mem. ABA, Am. Judicature Soc., Ky. Bar Assn., Tenn. Bar Assn. Republican. Presbyterian. Home: 8436 Summerlin Cove Memphis TN 38125 Office: 9056 Stone Walk Pl Germantown TN 38138 Business E-Mail: pdw@waddell-law.com.

WADDELL, WILLIAM JOSEPH, pharmacologist, toxicologist; b. Commerce, Ga., Mar. 16, 1929; s. Daniel and Lillian Marie (Vollrath) Waddell; m. Grace Carolyn Marlowe, Oct. 19, 1974; children: William Joseph, James Glenn, Martin Christie, Amy Allison. AB in Chemistry, U. N.C., 1951, MD, 1955. Postdoctoral rsch. fellow U. N.C. Sch. Medicine, 1955-58, asst. prof. pharmacology, 1958-62, asso. prof., 1962-72, assoc. prof. oral biology Dental Rsch. Ctr., 1967-69, prof., 1969-72, assoc. dir., 1968-72; prof. pharmacology U. Ky. Coll. Medicine, Lexington, 1972-77; prof., chmn. dept. pharmacology and toxicology U. Louisville, 1977-97, emeritus chmn., 1997—, prof. emeritus, 1998—. Centennial Alumni Disting. vis. prof. U. N.C. Sch. Medicine, 1979. Contbr. articles to profl. jours. Fellow: Acad. Toxicological Scis.; mem.: Soc. Toxicology, Soc. Exptl. Biology and Medicine, Internat. Soc. Study Xenobiotics, Am. Teratology Soc., Am. Physiol. Soc., Am. Soc. Pharmacology and Exptl. Therapeutics, Sigma Xi. Home: 14300 Rose Wycombe Rd Prospect KY 40059-9024 Office: U Louisville Dept Pharmacology Louisville KY 40292-0001 Home Phone: 502-228-4220. Business E-Mail: bwaddell@louisville.edu.

WADDELL, WILLIAM ROBERT, lawyer; b. Ft. Thomas, Ky., Nov. 24, 1940; s. Ewell Edward and Sara Isabel (Dean) W.; m. Linda Kay Waddle, Aug. 25, 1962; children: Robert William, Keith Edward, Alex Watson. AB, Williams Coll., 1962; JD, U. Va., 1965. Bar: Va. 1965, U.S. Dist. Ct. (ea. dist.) Va. 1966, U.S. Ct. Appeals (4th cir.) 1966, U.S. Supreme Ct. 1966, N.C. 1991. Assoc. McGuire, Woods, Battle & Boothe, Richmond, Va., 1965—69, ptnr., 1969—. Adj. faculty Sch. Law, U. Va., 1995-; bd. dirs. Cmty. Bank Virginia Beach, Va., The George Found., Alex Lee, Inc., Hickory, N.C., Downtown Rep. Club, Norfolk, Va., Greater Norfolk Corp. Author: Virginia Corporations, 2005, Dispute Resolution: A Survey, 2006; contbr. articles to profl. jours Pres. Bon Air Cmty. Assn., Richmond, 1979-80; bd. dirs., sec. Va. Advanced Tech. Assn., Richmond, 1986-96; chmn. The Steward Sch., 1985-88, Jr. Achievement of Richmond, Inc., 1989-90. Mem. ABA (comml. code com., sales subcom. 1982—, chmn. telecomm. com. 1986-90, 94-96, vice-chmn. com. on law of commerce in cyberspace 1996-98, dispute resolution com. 1990—), Order of Coif. Avocations: tennis, history, woodworking. Office: McGuireWoods LLP 1 James Ctr 901 E Cary St Richmond VA 23219 also: McGuireWoods LLP World Trade Ctr 101 W Main St Ste 9000 Norfolk VA 23510-1655 Business E-Mail: wwaddell@mcguirewoods.com.

WADDEN, CHRISTOPHER DAVID, food products executive; b. Ridgewood, NJ, Feb. 25, 1959; s. Robert Vincent and Mary Elizabeth (Townley) W. BSME, Tex. A&M U., 1981; MBA, Keller Grad. Sch. Mgmt., 2002. Registered profl. engr., Tex. Ind. spl. project engr. Dresser Magcobar, Houston, 1981-83; staff engr. Nabisco Brands (Nat. Biscuit Co.), Houston, 1983-84, mechanical supt. St. Louis, 1984-85, sr. project engr. East Hanover, N.J., 1985-86, shift mgr. Houston, 1986-88, ops. mgr. San Francisco, 1988-89, mfg. mgr. Chgo., 1989-91; gen. mgr. Yili Nabisco Biscuit and Food Co., Ltd., Beijing, 1991-95; pres. F.W.C. Internat., Lighthouse Point, Fla., 1995-2000; gen. mgr. Laguna Cookie Co., Tustin, Calif., 2000—01, Organic Milling Co., San Dimas, Calif., 2001—03, pres., 2005—07, Veraison LLC, Pasadena, Calif., 2007—. Contbg. author: Cookie and Cracker Manufacturing, 1990. Rep. com. mem., Lisle, Ill., 1990. Roman Catholic. Avocations: aviation, oenology, acting, writing. Office: 1035 Nithsdale Pasadena CA 91105

WADDEN, RICHARD ALBERT, environmental engineer, educator, science administrator, consultant; b. Sioux City, Iowa, Oct. 3, 1936; s. Sylvester Francis and Hermina Lillian (Costello) Wadden; m. Angela Louise Trabert, Aug. 9, 1975; children: Angela Terese, Noah Albert, Nuiko Clare. Student, St. John's U., Collegeville, Minn., 1954-56; BSChemE, Iowa State U., 1959; MSChemE, N.C. State U., 1962; PhD in Chem. and Environ. Engring., Northwestern U., 1972. Registered profl. engr., Ill., cert. indsl. hygienist. Engr. Linde Co., Tonnawanda, NY, 1959-60, Humble Oil Co., Houston, 1962-65; instr. engring. Pahlavi U. Peace Corps, Shiraz, Iran, 1965-67; tech. adviser Ill. Pollution Control Bd., Chgo., 1971-72; asst. dir. Environ. Health Resource Ctr. Ill., Chgo., 1972-74; from asst. prof. to assoc. prof. environ. and occupational health scis. Sch. Pub. Health U. Ill., Chgo., 1972—79, prof., 1979—2003, dir., 1984-86, 88-92, dir. Office Tech. Transfer Ctr. Solid Waste Mgmt. and Rsch., 1987-92, dir. indsl. hygiene and hazardous waste tng. programs Occupl. Safety and Health Ctr., 1987—2002, prof. emeritus, 2003—. Vis. scientist Nat. Inst. Environ. Studies, Japan, 1978—79, invited scientist, Japan, 1983, Japan, 84, Japan, 88; cons. air pollution control, health implications energy devel., indoor air pollution. Author: (book) Energy Utilization and Environmental Health, 1978; author: (with P. A. Scheff) Indoor Air Pollution, 1983; author: Engineering Design for Control of Workplace Hazards, 1987; contbr. articles to profl. publs. Vis. scholar, Northwestern U., Evanston, Ill., 1997; Sr. Internat. fellow, Fogarty Internat. Ctr.-NIH, 1978—79, 1983, WHO fellow, 1984. Mem.: AIChE, Am. Conf. Govtl. Indsl. Hygienists, Am. Indsl. Hygiene Assn., Air and Waste Mgmt. Assn., Am. Acad. Indsl. Hygiene (diplomate), Am. Acad. Environ. Engrs. (diplomate), Am. Chem. Soc. Address: 816 16th St Wilmette IL 60091

WADDEN, THOMAS ANTHONY, psychologist, educator; b. Richmond, Va., Sept. 3, 1952; s. Thomas Antony Jr. and Mary Lloyd (Cradock) W.; m. Jan Robin Linowitz, Nov. 11, 1984; children: David Joseph, Michael James, Steven Zachary. AB magna cum laude, Brown U., 1975; PhD, U. N.C., 1981; MA (hon.), U. Pa., 1994. Psychology intern Boston VA Med. Ctr., 1980-81; instr. in psychology U. Pa. Sch. Medicine, Phila., 1981-82, asst. prof. psychology, 1982-87, assoc. prof. psychology, 1987-91, prof. psychology, 1994—; prof. psychology, dir. clin. tng. Syracuse (N.Y.) U., 1992-93. Clin. dir. Obesity Rsch. Group, U. Pa., Phila., 1983-91, dir. Weight and Eating Disorders Program, 1994—; dir. Ctr. for Health and Behavior, Syracuse U., 1992-93. Author (with K.D. Brownell): LEARN PRogram for Weight Control, 1998; assoc. editor: Annals of Behavioral Medicine, 1990—93, mem. editl. bd.: Internat. Jour. Eating Disorders, Jour. Cons. and Clin. Psychology, Obesity Rsch.; editor (with T.B. VanItallie): Treatment of the Seriously Obese Patient, 1992; editor: (with A.J. Stunkard) Obesity: Theory and Therapy, 1993, Handbook of Obesity Treatment, 2002; contbr. chapters to books; writer: numerous sci. papers. Recipient Nat. Rsch. Svc. award NIMH, 1983-85, Rsch. Scientist Devel. award, 1987-91, 94-2000, Midcareer Investigator award in patient oriented rsch., 2003—. Mem. APA, Soc. Behavioral Medicine (bd. dir. 1987-90), Assn. for Advancement of Behavior Therapy (New Rschr. award 1986), Acad. Behavioral Medicine, Obesity Soc. (v.p. 2003-04, pres. 2005-06), Germantown Cricket Club, Cosmos Club, Phi Beta Kappa, Sigma Xi. Democrat. Avocations: tennis, squash, music, guitar. Home: 433 Bolsover Rd Wynnewood PA 19096-1301 Personal E-mail: cprout_02115@yahoo.com.

WADDILL, CYNTHIA KAY, orthopaedic nurse practitioner; d. Owen Lee and Epsie Adrias Sugg; m. Dale Alin Waddill, July 16, 1993; children: Stacy Kay Emfinger, Christopher Ryan Emfinger, Jamison Matthew Emfinger. ADN, U. Ark., Little Rock, 1984; BSN, U. Phoenix, 2000, MSN, 2001, Graceland U., 2003. RN, cert. orthop. nurse, oper. rm. nurse. Orthop. trauma charge nurse U. Ark. Med Sci. Campus, Little Rock, 1991—96, Shands Hosp., Jacksonville, Fla., 1996—2001; nurse Shands U. Fla. Hosp., Jacksonville, 2004—05, Mcleod Regional Med. Ctr., 2005—. Sr. nurse cons. Orthop. Trauma Practice Cons., Jacksonville, 2001—. Mem.: ANA, Fla. Nurses Assn., Am. Acad. Nurse Practitioners, Nat. Assn. Orthop. Nurses, Sigma Theta Tau. Baptist. Avocations: scuba diving, golf, fishing. Office: McLeod Orthopaedic Assocs 901 E Cheves St Ste 500 Florence SC 29501 Personal E-mail: cbones100k@aol.com.

WADDINGTON, RAYMOND BRUCE, JR., language educator; b. Santa Barbara, Calif., Sept. 27, 1935; s. Raymond Bruce and Marjorie Gladys (Waddell) W.; m. Linda Gayle Jones, Sept. 7, 1957 (div.); children: Raymond Bruce, Edward Jackson; m. Kathleen Martha Ward, Oct. 11, 1985. BA, Stanford U., 1957; PhD, Rice U., 1963; postdoctoral (Univ. fellow in Humanities), Johns Hopkins U., 1965-66. Instr. English U. Houston, 1961-62; instr. U. Kans., 1962-63, asst. prof., 1963-65; asst. prof. English lit. U. Wis., Madison, 1966-68, assoc. prof., 1968-74, prof., 1974-82; prof. English lit. U. Calif., Davis, 1982—2005. Author: The Mind's Empire, 1974, Aretino's Satyr, 2004; co-editor: The Rhetoric of Renaissance Poetry, 1974, The Age of Milton, 1980, The Expulsion of the Jews, 1994; mem. editl. bd. The Medal, 1991; sr. editor: Sixteenth Century Jour.; editor: Praeger Series on the Early Modern World. Recipient Scaglione prize for Italian Studies, 2005; Huntington Libr. fellow, 1967, 75; Inst. Rsch. in Humanities fellow, 1971-72; Guggenheim fellow, 1972-73; NEH fellow, 1977, 83; Newberry Libr. fellow, 1978; Am. Philos. Soc. grantee, 1965. Mem. Renaissance Soc. Am., Milton Soc. Am., Am. Numismatic Soc., 16th Century Soc. and Conf. (pres. 1985), Brit. Art Medal Soc., Logos Club. Home: 39 Pershing Ave Woodland CA 95695-2845 Office: U Calif Dept English Davis CA 95616 E-mail: rbwaddington@ucdavis.edu.

WADDY, LAWRENCE HEBER, writer; b. Sydney, Oct. 5, 1914; came to U.S., 1963; s. Percival Stacy and Etheldred (Spittal) W.; m. Laurie Hancock, July 10, 1972. BA, Oxford U., 1937, MA, 1945. Asst. master Winchester Coll. Eng., 1938—42; headmaster Tonbridge Sch., England, 1949—62; edn. officer BBC, 1962—63; chaplain The Bishop's Sch., La Jolla, Calif., 1963—67; lectr. in Greek and Latin lit. U. Calif., San Diego, 1969—80; vicar Ch. of Good Samaritan, University City, Calif., 1970—74; hon. asst. St. James By The Sea Episcopal Ch., La Jolla, 1975—. Author: Pax Romana & World Peace, 1950, Symphony, 1976, A Parish By the Sea, 1988, Shakespeare Remembers, 1994, First Bible Stories, 1994, Florence Nightingale, 1996, Bible Drama, 2004. Chaplain, British Navy, 1942-46. Recipient Drama 1st prize BBC, 1964. Republican. Episcopalian. Home: 5910 Camino De La Costa La Jolla CA 92037-6550 Personal E-mail: lawrencewaddy@yahoo.com.

WADDY, PATRICIA A., historian, retired architecture educator; b. Cannelton, Ind., July 29, 1941; d. Luther and Gertrude Viola (Brandyberry) W. BA, Rice U., 1963; MA, Tulane U., 1965; PhD, NYU, 1973. Vis. lectr. Carnegie-Mellon U., Pitts., 1970-71, asst. prof., 1971-77; assoc. prof. archtl. history Syracuse U., NY, 1977-91, prof., 1991—2002, disting. prof. architecture, 2002—; prof. emeritus, 2006. Vis. lectr. Cornell U., Ithaca, N.Y., 1977, vis. assoc. prof., 1980; Frederic Lindley Morgan prof. archtl. design U. Louisville, 2006. Author: Seventeenth-Century Roman Palaces: Use and The Art of the Plan, 1990 (Alice Davis Hitchcock award 1992); co-author: (with D. DiCastro and A.M. Pedrocchi) Il Palazzo Pallavicini Rospigliosi e la Galleria Pallavicini, 2000; editor Nicodemus Tessin the Younger, Traicté dela decoration interieure (1717), 2002. Fulbright grantee, Rome, 1968-69; fellow Am. Acad. in Rome, 1970, Nat. Humanities Ctr., 1984-85, Samuel H. Kress sr. fellow Nat. Gallery Art, 1994-95, NEH fellow, 1998-99, Guggenheim fellow, 1999-00, Am. Coun. Learned Soc. fellow, 1978. Mem. Soc. Archtl. Historians (book rev. editor Jour. 1985-88, editor 1990-93, 2d v.p. 1993-94, 1st v.p. 1994-96, pres. 1996-98), Coll. Art Assn., Renaissance Soc. Am. Office: Syracuse U Sch Architecture Syracuse NY 13244-1250 Business E-Mail: pwaddy@syr.edu.

WADE, DAVID ALLEN, graphics designer; b. Memphis, Dec. 1, 1978; BFA in Graphic Design, Miss. State U., Starkville, 1997—2001, MFA in Electronic Visualization, 2001—04. Grad. instr. Miss. State U., 2002—04; assoc. environment modeler Electronic Arts - Tiburon, Orlando, Fla., 2005—. Creator (animated short) Flotsam & Jetsam (Ofcl. Selection/Honorarium, Dallas Video Festival, 2005), designer (graphic design print campaign) Spot Cleaner (PUSH Cmf. award of excellence, 2001). Mem.: Am. Mensa. Office: Electronic Arts - Tiburon 1950 Summit Park Dr Orlando FL 32810 Business E-Mail: dwade@ea.com.

WADE, DWYANE (DWAYNE TYRONE WADE JR.), professional basketball player; b. Chgo., Jan. 17, 1982; s. Dwyane and Jolinda Wade; m. Siohvaughn Funches, 2002; children: Zaire Blessing, Zion Malachi Airamis. Student, Marquette U., 2000—03. Guard Miami Heat, 2003—. Mem. US Olympic Basketball Team, Athens, 2004. Named NBA Finals MVP, 2006, Sportsman of Yr., Sports Illus., 2006; named to NBA All-Rookie 1st Team, 2004, All-NBA 2nd Team, 2005, Ea. Conf. All-Star Team, NBA, 2005—07; recipient Best Breakthrough Athlete, ESPY awards, 2005, Best NBA Player, 2006. Achievements include playing on NBA Championship team, 2006. Office: c/o Miami Heat American Airlines Arena 601 Biscayne Blvd Miami FL 33132 *

WADE, EDWIN LEE, lawyer, writer; b. Yonkers, NY, Jan. 26, 1932; s. James and Helen Pierce (Kinne) W.; m. Nancy Lou Sells, Mar. 23, 1957; children: James Lee, Jeffrey K. BS, Columbia U., 1954; MA, U. Chgo., 1956; JD, Georgetown U., 1965. Bar: Ill. 1965. Fgn. svc. officer U.S. Dept. State, 1956-57; mktg. analyst Chrysler Internat., S.A., Switzerland, 1957-61; intelligence officer CIA, 1961-63; industry analyst U.S. Internat. Trade

Commn., 1963-65; gen. atty. Universal Oil Products Co., Des Plaines, Ill., 1965-72; atty. Amsted Industries, Inc., Chgo., 1972-73; chief counsel dept. gen. svcs. State of Ill., Springfield, 1973-75; sr. atty. U.S. Gypsum Co., Chgo., 1975-84; gen. atty. USG Corp., 1985, corp. counsel, 1986, asst. gen. counsel, 1987, corp. sec., 1987-90, corp. sec., asst. gen. counsel, 1990-93; prin. Edwin L. Wade, 1993-95; instr. Roosevelt U., Chgo., 1995-96. Author: (books) Constitution 2000: A Federalist Proposal for the New Century, 2000, Talking Sense at Century's End: A Barbarous Time...Now What?, 2000; editor: Let's Talk Sense, A Pub. Affairs Newsletter, 1994-98. Fellow Chgo. Bar Assn. (life); mem. ABA, Ill. Bar Assn., Am. Philatelic Soc. Home: 434 Mary Ln Crystal Lake IL 60014-7257 Office: Let's Talk Sense Pub Co PO Box 2195 Crystal Lake IL 60039-2195

WADE, ESTELLE B., psychologist, psychoanalyst; b. Bklyn., July 20, 1938; d. David and Selma Jobyna Schwartz; m. Donald E. Wade (div.); m. Alan L. Cantor, Apr. 3, 1992. BA magna cum laude, Clark U., 1959; MA, Brandeis U., 1961; PhD, Columbia U., 1971. Lic. psychologist NY, 1972, cert. profl. qualification psychology Assn. State Provincial Bds., 2001; bd. cert. found. fellow Am. Coll. Advanced Practice Psychologists, 1999. Postdoctoral fellowship in psychoanalysis Post-grad. Ctr. Mental Health, NYC, 1980—83; counselor Inst. Crippled & Disabled, NYC, 1961—62, N.Y.C. Dept. Hosps., Bklyn., Queens, 1962—65; psychology intern VA, NYC, 1966—68; tchg. asst. Columbia U., NYC, 1968—69; lectr. psychology CUNY, 1969—70; staff psychologist Queens County Neuropsychiatric Inst., Jackson Heights, 1969—71, chief psychologist, 1971—81; supervising psychologist Fifth Ave. Ctr. Psychotherapy, NYC, 1981—84; pvt. practice psychoanalysis & psychotherapy NYC, 1977—. Host several radio programs, 1971—75. Singer: Amato Opera Chorus, 1976—77. Mem. Pinewoods Folk Music Soc., 1966—75, program chair, 1971—75; mem. Queens Ind. Democrats, Jackson Heights, 1967—69, Sloop Clearwater-NYC Chapter, 1969—75, program chair, 1973—75. Mem.: APA (life; program chair divsn. independent practice 1980—81, psychologist psychoanalyst practitioner, divsn. psychoanalysis 1984—), NY State Psychological Assn. (emeritus), Nat. Register Health Svc. Providers Psychology (platinum registrant 1994), Phi Beta Kappa. Democrat. Jewish. Avocations: classical music, opera, reading, walking. Office: 730 Fifth Ave 9th Fl New York NY 10019 Office Phone: 212-659-7799.

WADE, GARY R., state supreme court justice; b. Tenn., May 31, 1948; married; 3 children. BS, U. Tenn., 1970; JD, U Tenn. Coll. Law, 1973. Pvt. practice, 1973—87; judge Tenn. Ct. Criminal Appeals, 1987—2006; assoc. justice Tenn. Supreme Ct., 2006—. Mem. Chancellor's Assocs. U. Tenn., 1988—91, bd. visitors Coll. Arts & Sciences, mem. Coll. Law Dean's Cir., mem. devel. coun.; bd. trustees Walters State Cmty. Coll. Found.; pres. assoc. Pellissippi State Tech. Cmty. Coll.; mem. Tenn. Sentencing Commn., 1990—94. Mayor City of Sevierville, Tenn., 1977—87; pres. Friends of the Great Smoky Mountains Nat. Park; bd. dirs. East Tenn. Found.; hon. chmn. Boys & Girls Club of the Smoky Mountains; bd. dirs. AAA East Tenn., Tenn.'s Resource Valley. Named Mover & Shaker of Yr., Mountain Press, 1983—85, 1997; recipient Presdl. award, Am. Heart Assn., 1987, Key to the City of Sevierville, 1987, Sevierville C. of C. award, 1987. Fellow: Tenn. Bar Found.; mem.: Tenn. Jud. Conf. (exec. com. 1990—97, pres. 1995—96), Am. Inns of Ct., Tenn. Assn. Criminal Def. Lawyers, Tenn. Trial Lawyers Assn., Tenn. Bar Assn., Sevier County Heart Assn., Sevierville Lions, Phi Delta Theta (pres. Eta S. Province 1990—97). Methodist. Office: 505 Main St Ste 200 Knoxville TN 37902 Office Phone: 865-549-6121.

WADE, GAYLIA SUZANNE, secondary school educator; d. Paul Hamilton Garrett and Sylvia Maurice Smith; m. Lorrin Louis Dreier (div.); children: Lorri Anne Dreier(dec.), Christopher Eric Dreier; m. Richard Merrill Wade, Dec. 20, 1997; 1 stepchild, Staci Lanell Wade Watkins. BA cum laude, So. Nazarene U., Bethany, Okla., 1967; postgrad., U. N.Mex., Albuquerque, 1985—97. Secondary tchg. cert. N.Mex., Tex. Tchr. Burges HS, El Paso, Tex., 1967—68, Albuquerque Pub. Schs., 1968—70, 1985—, Socorro (Tex.) Ind. Sch. Dist., 1980—84. Mentor tchr. for students tchrs. U. N. Mex., Coll. Santa Fe, 1992—2007; coord. mid. sch. initiative at-risk students City of Albuquerque/Albuquerque Pub. Schs., 1995—97; mentor gateway to tchg. program Golden Apple Found., U. N.Mex., Albuquerque Pub. Schs., 2005—; tutor Advantage Tutoring, Albuquerque, 2005—06. Sponsor World Vision, 1992—94, Lamplighters Club, 1995—2007, Voice of Martyrs, Bartlesville, Okla., 2005—07, Homework Club, 2006, 2007; contbr., supporter Albuquerque Rescue Mission, Storehouse, Joy Junction, 2005—06, Roadrunner Food Bank. Named Best All-Around Tchr., Truman Mid. Sch., 1988; recipient Excellence in Tchg. award, N.Mex. Golden Apple Found., 1997, Grant Middle Sch., 2006, 2007. Fellow: Golden Apple Found. (life); mem.: Phi Delta Lambda. Republican. Baptist. Avocations: quilting, gardening, literature, piano. Office: Grant Mid Sch 1111 Easterday Dr NE Albuquerque NM 87112 Office Phone: 505-299-2113.

WADE, GLEN, electrical engineer, educator; b. Ogden, Utah, Mar. 19, 1921; s. Lester Andrew and Nellie (Vanderwerff) W.; m. LaRee Bailey, Mar. 20, 1945; children: Kathleen Ann, RaLee, Lisa Jean, Mary Sue. BS in Elec. Enging. U. Utah, Salt Lake City, 1948, MS, 1949; PhD, Stanford U., Calif., 1954. Research group leader, asso. prof. elec. enging. Stanford U., 1955-60; asso. dir. enging., microwave and power tube div. Raytheon Co., 1960-61, asst. gen. mgr. research div., 1961-63; dir. Sch. Elec. Enging., Cornell U., 1963-66, J.P. Levis prof. enging., 1963-66; prof. elec. enging. U. Calif. at Santa Barbara, 1966—. Indsl. advisor U. RI, 1961-63; vis. lectr. Harvard, 1963; cons. to industry, 1956—; vis. prof. Tokyo U., 1971; Fulbright-Hays lectr., Spain, 1972-73; cons. mem. Dept. Def. Adv. Group Electron Devices, 1966-73; Spl. Chair prof. Nat. Taiwan U., 1980-81, internationally renowned fgn. scholar lectureship, 1988; UN vis. prof. Nanjing Inst. Tech., 1986; UN vis. prof. S.E. U. People's Republic of China, 1989, Nat. Com. Sci. and Tech. vis. prof. U. Guanajuato, Mex., 1994—; elected mem. The Electromagnetics Acad., 1990. Editor: Transactions on Electron Devices, 1961-71, IEEE Jour. Quantum Electronics, 1965-68; series editor: Harcourt Brace Jovanovich, 1964—; contbr. articles to profl. jours. U.S. del. Tech. Cooperation Program internat. meeting, 1970. Served with USNR, 1944-46. Recipient ann. award Nat. Electronics Conf., 1959, Outstanding Teaching award Acad. Senate, U. Calif., Santa Barbara, 1977, Prof. of Yr. award U. Calif. at Santa Barbara Mortar Bd. Sr. Honor Soc., 1988, Hon. Chairmanship award Twentieth Acoustical Imaging, 1992, Disting. Alumnus award Enging. Coll. U. Utah, 1998. Fellow IEEE (life; mem. adminstrv. com. profl. group election devices 1960-71, mem. publs. bd., chmn. info. processing com., mem. exec. com. 1971-72, dir. 1971-72, chmn. edn1. activities bd. 1971-72, editor proc. 1977-80, Centennial award 1984, Millennium medal 2000); mem. Am. Phys. Soc., Phi Kappa Phi, Tau Beta Pi, Sigma Xi, Eta Kappa Nu (Outstanding Young Elec. Engr. award 1955) Home: 1098 Golf Rd Santa Barbara CA 93108-2411 Office: Rm 214 Bldg 406 U Calif Santa Barbara CA Office Phone: 805-893-2508. Business E-Mail: wade@ece.ucsb.edu.

WADE, JAMES O'SHEA, editor, writer; b. Atlanta, June 17, 1940; s. Richard J. and Mary Clare (O'Shea) W.; m. Linda Norman, June 19, 1971; 1 child, Christopher Scott. AB magna cum laude, Harvard U., 1962. Editor Blaisdell Pub. Co., NYC, 1963-65; asst. to pres., sr. editor Macmillan Co., 1966-69; editor-in-chief World Pub. Co., 1969-71; v.p., editorial dir. David McKay Co., 1971-74; founder, pres. Wade Pub. Co., Inc., NYC, 1975-78; exec. v.p. Rawson, Wade Pubs., Inc., NYC, 1978-82; sr. editor Crown Pubs., Inc., NYC, 1982-85, exec. editor, 1985-95, v.p., 1988-95; with Ind. Editors Group, 1996—. Mem. Century Club (N.Y.C.), Iroquois/D.U. Club (Harvard), Hasty-Pudding Inst. 1770 (Harvard U.). Democrat. Home and Office: 1565 Baptist Church Rd Yorktown Heights NY 10598-5812 Personal E-mail: jedit@optonline.net.

WADE, JUNE BOOTH, secondary school educator; b. St. Petersburg, Fla., Dec. 24, 1934; d. Monroe Phillippi and Julia Lenoir (Burdett) Booth; m. Charles Wade, Feb. 18, 1956; children: Susan Wade Infanzon, John Eric. BSJM, U. Fla., 1956. Tchr. English and journalism Hillsborough County Schs., Tampa, Fla. Mem. Nat. Coun. Tchrs. English, Fla. Coun. Tchrs. English, Hillsborough Coun. Tchrs. English, Ret. Educators Fla. (West Hillboraigh chpt.), Delta Kappa Gamma

WADE, LEROY GROVER, JR., chemistry educator; b. Jacksonville, Fla., Oct. 8, 1947; s. Leroy Grover and Margaret Lena (Stevens) W.; m. Sandra Martinez Kooreny; children: Christine Elizabeth, Jennifer Diane. BA summa cum laude, Rice U., 1969; AM, Harvard U., 1970, PhD, 1974. Resident rsch. fellow Du Pont Corp., Wilmington, Del., 1969; tchg. fellow in chemistry Harvard U., Cambridge, Mass., 1969-74, sr. adviser to freshmen, 1971-74; resident sci. tutor Radcliffe Coll., Cambridge, 1970-74; asst. prof. chemistry Colo. State U., Ft. Collins, 1974-80, assoc. prof., 1980-89; prof. chemistry Whitman Coll., Walla Walla, Wash., 1989—. Author: Annual Reports in Organic Synthesis, 1975-82, 8 vols., Compendium of Organic Synthetic Methods, Vols. III, IV, V, 1977, 80, 84, Organic Chemistry, 1987, 6th edit., 2005; contbr. articles to sci. jours.; reviewer profl. jours., textbooks. Mem. AAAS, Am. Chem. Soc., Am. Acad. Forensic Scis., Phi Beta Kappa (pres. chpt. 1983-84), Sigma Xi. Office: Whitman Coll Chemistry Dept Walla Walla WA 99362 E-mail: wadelg@whitman.edu.

WADE, MICHAEL ROBERT ALEXANDER, marketing specialist; b. NYC, June 29, 1945; s. Burton Jean and Celia (Handleman) W.; m. Carole Kay West, Aug. 25, 1974. AB, U. Chgo., 1967; postgrad. in pub. adminstrn., Am. U., 1967—71; MBA in Fin., NYU, 1975. Program analyst, mgmt. intern HUD, 1967—71; dep. dir. Mgmt. Comm. and Briefing Ctr. U.S. Price Commn., 1972; asst. exec. sec. policy coordination U.S. Cost of Living Coun., 1973—74; assoc. dir. U.S. Indochina Refugee Program, 1975—76; pres. China Trade Devel. Corp. Chgo., 1997—. Participant in Okla. oil and gas prodn. Recipient Meritorious Svc. award Exec. Office of Pres., 1972, Disting. Svc. award U.S. Cost of Living Coun., 1974. Mem. Soc. Contemporary Art, Internat. Bus. Coun. MidAm. (bd. dirs.). Office: China Trade Devel Corp 1110 Granville Dr 1st Fl Newport Beach CA 92660-6227 Office Phone: 949-759-6950. Business E-Mail: china-trade@worldnet.att.net.

WADE, NICOLE JENNINGS, lawyer; b. Portsmouth, Va., July 31, 1970; m. Michael Todd Wade, May 27, 1995. BA cum laude, Vanderbilt U., 1992; JD cum laude, U. Mich., 1995. Bar: Ga. 1995, US Dist. Ct. (no. dist.) Ga. 1996, US Dist. Ct. (mid. dist.) Ga. 1998, US Ct. Appeals (11th cir.) 1997, US Ct. Appeals (4th cir.) 1998. Ptnr. Powell Goldstein LLP, Atlanta, Ga., 1995—. Mem.: State Bar Ga. (chair mandatory continuing legal edn. and trial credit assistance com. 1999—2000), Bleckley Inn of Ct. (barrister 2001—03), Atlanta Bar Assn. Office: Powell Goldstein LLP 1201 W Peachtree St Atlanta GA 30309 Office Phone: 404-572-6600. Office Fax: 404-572-6999. Business E-Mail: nwade@pogolaw.com.

WADE, REBA, musician, educator; b. Dresden, Tenn., Apr. 30, 1938; d. John Buford and Willie Ruth (Todd) Tilley; m. Ronald Lee Wade, July 22, 1956; children: Tony Lee, Randy Neal. Student, U. Tenn., Martin, 1976-80. Tchr. pvt. studio, Martin, 1962-70, 76—, Sharon (Tenn.) Sch., 1968, Westview H.S., Martin, 1976--79, Greenfield (Tenn.) Sch., 1984-86; mgr., dir. Wade Bros., Martin, 1965-71, High Variety Show Mems., Martin, 1994—. Tchr., accompanist for students, shows, groups, auditions and on radio and TV; profl. pianist; trainer in field. Prodr. Wade Bros. Rec., 1969, student recs., 1988-90, 97-2005; author lyrics, music original compositions including Little Cowboy, 1963, I Love My Jesus, 1963, Christmas Time, 1964, Happy Happy Day, 1964, Love, 1964, Oh How I Love You, 1965, Dear Mis-Fortune, 1965, Red Lace, 1965, Crazy Little Feeling, 1967, All Because of Christmas Day, 1968, Mean Mean Mama, 1968, God is Like This, 1979, Little Dreams, 1992, also tnr., prodr., 1988-90, 97-2001; performer Christmas music The White House, 1997-98, Pentagon Party, 1998, World Wide Air Show RAF, Fairford, Eng., London, 1999, Jackson State Fair, Tenn., Obion Count Fair, Union City, Soybean Festival, Martin, Cherry Blossom Festival, US Capital, 2006; recorded 3CDs (total 32 songs and pieces on piano), Nasville, Tenn., 2000, 2001, Christmas CD (9 songs), 2003; recorded 18 songs and pieces on piano, Hilltop Rec. Studio, Nashville, 2000, 12 others, 2001, 10 more songs, 2003; prodr. five rec. sessions Hilltop Rec. Studio, Nashville, 2004; tnr. students Cerebral Palsy Telethon WBBJ TV, Jackson, Tenn., 1995-2002, 06. Active in civic affairs, 1947-; judge music festival U. Tenn., Martin, 2000-01, 2002, 2004-05, fall performance, 2000-01, 2002-03, 04, 05, Kiwanis Club Talent Show, 2000-01; active Martin Elem. Chorus, 2001; fundraiser Big Cypress Tree State Park, 2000-01, Dickson (Tenn.) Police Dept., 2000, Relay for Life, 1992-2006, 07; invited charter mem. 1st Women's History Mus., Washington; planner, tnr. fund raiser program local fire dept. to buy new fire truck, 2000, entertainment fund raiser local town to install new lights in town, 2000; trained and provided entertainment for various charities. Recipient Vol. Svc. award State of Tenn. Recreation and Parks Assn., 2001, Companion Honor award, 2002, Salute to Greatness award, 2005; named Internat. Woman Yr., 2001, Internat. Musician, 2004, Internat. Musician Yr., 2004; nominated for Am. Medal Honor, 2002, 03-04, Lifetime Achievement award United Cultural Convention, 2005. Fellow Internat. Biog. Assn. (life, dir. deputy gen., 2006, advisor to dir. gen., 2006, Top 100 Musicians Pinnacle Achievement award, 2006, Internat. Order Merit, 2006); mem. SAI (life, social chmn. 1979), Songwriters Guild Am., Music Tchrs. Nat. Assn., Philharm. Music Club (v.p. 1983-84, pres. 1985), Am. Coll. Musicians, Dem. Women, Am. Biog. Inst. (profl. women's adv. bd., 2006—, World Lifetime Achieve award, 2004, Woman of Yr., 2006, 500 Greatest Geniuses of 21st Century, 2006, Am. Medal Honor, 2006) Baptist. Achievements include being ivvited to become a charter member of the first women's history museum in Washington DC. Avocations: music writing, interior decorating and designing, travel, church and charity work. Home: 208 Melody Dr Martin TN 38237-5535

WADHAMS, TIMOTHY, consumer products company executive; BA in Economics, U. Mich., MBA. CPA Coopers & Lybrand, 1972; joined Masco Corp., Taylor, Mich., 1976, various positions MasocTech, 1984—2000, v.p. fin., CFO, 2001—04, sr. v.p., CFO, 2004—. Bd. trustees Ann Arbor Area Cmty. Found., Arbor Hospice Found.; bd. dir., M Club U. Mich.; cmty. adv. bd. Kellogg Eye Inst. Campaign. Office: Masco Corp 21001 Van Born Rd Taylor MI 48180 *

WADKINS, LANNY LANSTON, professional golfer; b. Richmond, Va., Dec. 5, 1949; s. Jerry Lanston and Francis Ann (Burnett) W.; m. Rachel Irene Strong, Jan. 2, 1971; 1 child, Jessica; m. Penelope Elizabeth Atwood, Nov. 11, 1978; 2 children Travis and Tucker. Student, Wake Forest U. Profl. golfer PGA, 1971—. Mem. numerous nat. teams including Walker Cup (2), 1969, 71, World Amateur Cup, 1970, Ryder Cup (8), 1977, 79, 83, 85, 87, 89, 91, 93, Ryder Cup Capt., 1995, World Cup (3), 1977, 84, 85, U.S. vs. Japan (2), 1982, 83, Nissan Cup, 1985, Dunhill Cup, 1986, Kirin Cup, 1987, Asahi Glass Four Tours, 1991; golf analyst, CBS Sports, 2003-06. Winner 1968, 70 So. Amateur champion, Sahara Invitational, 1972, PGA, 1977, World Series of Golf, 1978, Can. PGA, 1978, Tournament Players' Championship, 1979, 82, 83, (4) 1978 Victoria PGA Championship (Australia), Can. PGA Championship, 1979 Bridgestone Open (Japan), L.A. Open, 1979, 85, Phoenix Open, 1982, Greater Greensboro, 1983, Bob Hope Desert Classic, 1985, Doral Ryder, 1987, 1984 World Nissan Championship (Japan), Hawaiian Open, 1988, 91, Colonial Open, 1988, Anheuser Busch Classic, 1990, 1990 Fred Meyer Challenge, PGA of AmericaPlayer of Yr., 1985, Greater Hartford Open, 1992, 2000 ACE Group Classic, among others. Address: PGA America/Senior Tour 100 Ave of the Champions PO Box 109601 Palm Beach Gardens FL 33410-9601

WADLEY, M. RICHARD, consumer products executive; b. Lehi, Utah; s. Merlyn R. and Verla Ann (Ball) W.; children: Lisa Kathleen, Staci Lin, Eric Richard, Nicole Marie. BS, Brigham Young U., 1967; MBA, Northwestern U., 1968. Brand asst. packaged soap and detergent divsn. Procter & Gamble Co., Cin., 1968-69, asst. brand mgr. packaged soap and detergent divsn., 1970-71, brand mgr. Dawn detergent, 1972-73, copy supr. packaged soap and detergent divsn., 1974-75, brand mgr. Tide detergent, 1975-77, assoc. advt. mgr. packaged soap and detergent divsn., 1977-81; corp. product dir. Hallmark Cards, Inc., Kansas City, Mo., 1982-83, corp. product dir. Ambassador Cards divsn., 1983-85; v.p., gen. mgr. feminine protection divsn. Tambrands Inc., Lake Success, NY, 1986-88; sr. v.p. Bongrain, Inc., NYC, 1988-89, pres., CEO AltaDena Inc. divsn. City of Industry, Calif., 1989-91; pres. The Summit Group, 1991-93; chmn., CEO, bd. dirs. T-Chem Products Inc., Santa Fe Springs, Calif., 1993-99; CEO The Bayshore Group, 1999—; sr. cons. Ironwood Adv., 1999—. Bd. dirs. Legacy Interactive, Funosophy, Inc., Mellano & Co.; adj. prof. MBA program Pepperdine U., 1998—99. Bd. dirs. Long Beach Opera, 1991-95, L.I. Friends of the Arts, 1986-88; mem. adv. bd. Bus. Sch. Calif. State U., Long Beach, 1991-93. Avocations: civil war history, tennis, travel. Personal E-mail: rwbayshore@aol.com.

WADLINGTON, W. M., retired commodity futures trader, financial engineer; b. Madisonville, Ky., Oct. 28, 1944; s. W. Milton and Ellen Christine (Bryan) W.; m. Anne R. Lewis, Apr. 29, 1979; children: Andrew Stephen, Michael Edward, Thomas Scott. BA, Vanderbilt U., 1967. Commd. 2d lt. U.S. Army, 1967, advanced through grades to capt., 1970, field artillery officer, 1967-78, resigned, 1978; chmn. ChartBook.com, Ltd., San Diego, 1994-98; commodity futures trader, 1978-98; ret., 1998. Pres. Scripps Ranch Villages, 1998—2004; trustee LaJolla Country Day Sch., 2000—. Decorated Silver Star. Republican. Avocations: ancient languages, computer programming, opera, weightlifting, running. Home: 10981 Twinleaf Ct San Diego CA 92131-3643

WADLINGTON, WALTER JAMES, law educator; b. Biloxi, Miss., Jan. 17, 1931; s. Walter and Bernice (Taylor) Wadlington; m. Ruth Miller Hardie, Aug. 20, 1955; children: Claire, Charlotte, Ian(dec.), Susan, Derek Alan. AB, Duke U., 1951; LLB, Tulane U., 1954. Bar: La. 1954, Va. 1965. Pvt. practice, New Orleans, 1954—55, 1958—59; asst. prof. Tulane U., 1960—62; mem. faculty U. Va., 1962—, prof law, 1964—, James Madison prof., 1970—2002, James Madison prof. emeritus, 2002—, prof. legal medicine Med. Sch., 1979—2002, Harrison Found. rsch. prof., 1990—92. Tutor civil law U. Edinburgh, Scotland, 1959—60; vis. Tazewell Taylor prof. law Coll. William and Mary, 1986; dir. med. malpractice program Robert Wood Johnson, 1985—91, mem. adv. com. clin. scholars program, 1989—97; chmn. nat. adv. bd. Improving Malpractice Prevention and Compensation Sys., 1994—98; Disting. Health Law Tchr. Am. Soc. Law, Medicine and Ethics; trustee-at-large Edn. Commn. Fgn. Med. Grads., 1995—2003. Author (with O. Brien): Cases and Materials on Domestic Relations, 1970, 6th edit., 2007, Family Law in Perspective, 2001; author: 2d edit., 2007; author: (with Waltz and Dworkin) Cases and Materials on Law and Medicine, 1980; editor-in-chief: Tulane U. Law Rev., 1953—54; author (with Davis, Scott, and Whitebread): Children in the Legal System, 3rd edit., 2004. Fulbright scholar, U. Edinburgh, 1959—60. Mem.: Am. Law Inst., Inst. of Medicine of NAS, Found. Advancement Internat. Med. Edn. and Rsch. (bd. dirs., sec. 2001—03). Home: 1620 Keith Valley Rd Charlottesville VA 22901-3018 Office: U Va Sch Law 580 Massie Rd Charlottesville VA 22903-1738 Office Phone: 434-293-5261. Personal E-mail: wwadlington@earthlink.net. Business E-Mail: wjw@virginia.edu.

WADLOW, JOAN KRUEGER, retired academic administrator, construction executive; b. LeMars, Iowa, Aug. 21, 1932; d. R. John and Norma I. (Ihle) Krueger; m. Richard R. Wadlow, July 27, 1958; children: Dawn, Kit. BA, U. Nebr., 1953, PhD, 1963; MA, Fletcher Sch. Law and Diplomacy, 1956; cert., Grad. Inst. Internat. Studies, Geneva, 1957. Mem. faculty U. Nebr., Lincoln, 1966-79, prof. polit. scis., 1964-79, assoc. dean Coll. Arts and Scis., 1972-79; prof. polit. scis., dean Coll. Arts and Scis., U. Wyo., Laramie, 1979-84, v.p. acad. affairs, 1984-86; prof. polit. sci., provost U. Okla., Norman, 1986-91; chancellor U. Alaska, Fairbanks, 1991-99. Cons. on fed. grants; bd. dirs. Alaska Sea Life Ctr., Key Bank Alaska; mem. Commn. Colls. N.W. Assn.; pres. Lan Constrn., Inc., 1999-2004. Contbr. articles to profl. jours. Bd. dirs. Nat. Merit Scholarship Corp., 1988-97, Lincoln United Way, 1976-77, Bryan Hosp., Lincoln, 1978-79, Washington Ctr., 1986-99, Key Bank of Alaska, Alaska SeaLife Ctr.; v.p., exec. commr. North Ctrl. Assn., pres., 1991; pres. adv. bd. Lincoln YWCA, 1970-71; mem. def. adv. com. Women in the Svcs., 1987-89; mem. cmty. adv. bd. Alaska Airlines; mem. Univ. Pres.'s Mission to Israel, 1998; mem. bd. dirs. Netarts Oceanside Sanitary Dist., 2002-04. Recipient Mortar Board Tchg. award, 1976, Alumni Scholar Achievement award Rotary Internat., 1998, Alumni Achievement award U. Nebr., 2003; Seacrest Journalism fellow 1953-54, Rotary fellow, 1956-57, fellow Conf. Coop. Man, Lund, Sweden, 1956. Mem. NCAA (divsn. II pres. coun. 1997-99), Internat. Studies Assn. (co-editor Internat. Studies Notes 1978-91), Nat. Assn. State Univs. and Land-Grant Colls. (exec. com. coun. acad. affairs 1989-91, chair internat. affairs counsel 1996-97), Western Assn. Africanists (pres. 1980-82), Assn. Western Univs. (pres. 1993), Coun. Colls. Arts and Scis. (pres. 1983-84), Greater Fairbanks C. of C., Gamma Phi Beta. Republican. Congregationalist. Address: Chancellor Emerita PO Box 246 Oceanside OR 97134-0246 Personal E-mail: wadlow@hughes.net.

WADLOW, R. CLARK, lawyer; b. Providence, Nov. 30, 1946; AB, Dartmouth Coll., 1968; JD, Harvard U., 1971. Bar: Alaska 1971, DC 1972, US Ct. Appeals (9th & DC cir.), US Dist. Ct. Alaska, 1971, US Dist. Ct. DC, US Supreme Ct. 1974. Law clk. to Hon. George F. Boney Alaska Supreme Ct., 1971-72; ptnr. Sidley & Austin, Wash., DC, 1990—. Adj. prof. law Cath. U. Am., Columbus Sch. Law, 1983-87. Mem. bd. trustees Greater Wash. Ednl. Telecom. Assn., Wash., DC, 1985—90. Mem. ABA (bd. govs. 1978-81, chmn. forum com. on comm. law 1987-89, chmn. standing com. on forum coms. 1990-92, chmn. standing com. on continuing edn. of the bar 1993—, chmn. com. on scope and correlation of work 1993-94), Fed. Bar Assn. (mem. exec. com. 1989-92), Alaska, DC, Federal Comm. Bar Assn., Am. Judicature soc. Office: Sidley Austin 1501 K St NW Washington DC 20005 Office Phone: 202-736-8215. Office Fax: 202-736-8711. Business E-Mail: rwadlow@Sidley.com.

WADSWORTH, DYER SEYMOUR, minerals executive; b. NYC, June 16, 1936; s. Seymour and Phoebe Armistead (Helmer) Wadsworth; m. Beverley Allen Dunn Barringer, Feb. 2, 1963; children: Sophia, Jennifer. BA, Yale U., 1959; JD, Harvard U., 1962. Bar: N.Y. 1963, Pa. 1979. Assoc. Humes, Andrews & Botzow, NYC, 1962-64; with Inco Ltd. and subs., NYC, 1964-96; asst. gen. counsel Inco Ltd., NYC, 1982-96; pres. Inco US, Inc., NYC, 1993-96; chmn., CEO, treas., dir. Cass County Iron Co., Linden, Tex., 1992—; chmn. Barringer Crater Co., Flagstaff, Ariz., 1996—. Gen. counsel Sailors Snug Harbor, Sea Level, NC, 1987—2000, Baseline Fin. Svcs., Inc., NYC, 1997—2000. Trustee Isaac Tuttle Fund for Aged, NYC, 1968—96; bd. dirs. Frenchman Bay Conservancy, Hancock, Maine, 1997—, Amsterdam Nursing Home Corp., NYC, 1982—, chmn. bd. dirs., 1986—2000. Named Trustee of the Yr., N.Y. Assn. Homes and Svcs. for Aging, 1995. Mem.: Meteoritical Soc., Yale Club Suncoast (bd. dirs. 2001—, pres. 2002—04), Union Club (N.Y.C.), Ivy League Club (Sarasota, Fla.) (bd. dirs. 2005—07), Pilgrims Soc. (N.Y.C.). Home: 8466 Lockwood Ridge Rd PMB 304 Sarasota FL 34243-2951

WADSWORTH, FRANK WHITTEMORE, foundation administrator, literature educator; b. NYC, June 14, 1919; s. Prescott Kingsley and Elizabeth (Whittemore) W.; m. Roxalene Harriet Nevin, Oct. 22, 1943 (dec. 1979); Susan, Roxalene; m. Deborah Yohalem, Dec. 22, 1980. AB, Princeton U., 1946, PhD, 1951. Instr. English Princeton (N.J.) U., 1949-50; instr. to assoc. prof. English UCLA, 1950-61; prof. English, dean div. humanities U. Pitts., 1962-67; acad. v.p. SUNY-Purchase, 1967-78, prof. lit., 1967-89, emeritus, 1989—; nat. rep. Woodrow Wilson Nat. Fellowship Found., 1958-61, trustee, 1973—2003; vice-chmn. bd. trustees, 1992—2003; trustee Wenner-Gren Found., NYC, 1970—, chmn. bd. trustees, 1977-87, vice-chmn. bd. trustees, 1992—. Author: The Poacher from Stratford, 1958; contbr. articles to publs. Served to lt. (j.g.) USNR, 1942-45. Woodrow Wilson fellow, 1946-47; Scribner fellow, 1948-49; Folger Shakespeare Library fellow, 1961; Guggenheim fellow, 1961-62 Mem. MLA, Am. Soc. Theatre Research, Malone Soc., Phi Beta Kappa Clubs: Princeton. Home: 430 Sterling Rd Harrison NY 10528-1316

WADSWORTH, JEFFREY, metallurgist, educator; b. Hamburg, Germany, May 12, 1950; s. Frank William and Irene Wadsworth; m. Geraldine McCulley, Oct. 11, 2006; children: Emma Claire, Thomas Frank. BMet, Sheffield U., Eng., 1972, PhD, 1975, DMet, 1990, Deng (hon.), 2004. Rsch. assoc. Stanford U., Calif., 1976-80, cons. prof. Calif., 1996—2002; staff scientist, then mgr. metallurgy Lockheed R&D Div., Palo Alto, Calif., 1980-92; assoc. dir. chemistry and materials science Lawrence Livermore Nat. Lab., Livermore, Calif., 1992-96, dep. dir. sci. and tech., 1996—2002; sr. exec. Battelle Meml. Inst., Columbus, Ohio, 2002—; dir. Oak Ridge Nat. Lab., US Dept. Energy, Tenn., 2003—; distinguished rsch. prof. U. Tenn., 2005—. Contbr. numerous articles to profl. jours.; co-inventor, patentee novel steels and aluminum alloys; discoverer process to reinvent ancient discovery Damascus Steels. Recipient Brunton medal Sheffield U., 1975, Metallurgica/Aparecida, 1976. Fellow ASM Internat., AAAS, TMS; mem. NAE, Am. Inst. Mining, Metall. and Petroleum Engring., Am. Ceramic Soc., Materials Rsch. Soc. Office: Oak Ridge Nat Lab PO Box 2008 Oak Ridge TN 37831

WADSWORTH, JOHN (JACK) SPENCER, JR., investment banker; b. Ft. Thomas, Ky., Sept. 12, 1939; s. John Spencer and Mary Claire (Walker) W.; m. Bette Sue Pendery, June 17, 1961; children: Elizabeth J., John S. III, Christopher W. BA in Economics, Williams Coll., 1961; MBA in Fin., U. Chgo., 1963. Exec. v.p., bd. dirs. First Boston Corp., NYC, 1963-78; joined Morgan Stanley, NYC, 1978, mng. dir., various positions US investment banking divsn., 1978—87; pres. Morgan Stanley Japan, Tokyo, 1988—93; chmn. Morgan Stanley Asia Ltd., 1993—2000, hon. chmn.; now adv. dir. Morgan Stanley; ptnr. Manitou Ventures. Bd. dirs. Pixar Inc., 2002—; chmn. bd. Littleford Bros. Inc., Florence, Ky. Trustee Asia Soc., Williams Coll.; bd. trustees Solomon R. Guggenheim Mus., NYC. Mem.: Asia Am. MultiTechnology Assn. (charter mem.). Office: Morgan Stanley 1585 Broadway New York NY 10036

WADSWORTH, ROBERT DAVID, advertising executive; b. Prestbury, Cheshire, Eng., May 20, 1942; came to U.S., 1978; s. Eric and Irene (Thorpe) W.; m. Kathleen O'Meara, Dec. 13, 1968; children: Tracey, Charles Robert. BA, U. Natal, S. Africa, 1963. With Lever Bros. S. Africa, 1960-66, sr. brand mgr., 1964-66, Gen. Foods S. Africa, 1967; account exec. London Press Exch., S. Africa, 1968, Grant Advt., S. Africa, 1969; dir., then mng. dir. Cen. Advt., Johannesburg, S. Africa, 1970-73; dir. new bus. coord. McCann-Erickson, South Africa, 1973-78; sr. v.p., mng. rep., new bus. coord. McCann-Erickson, Inc., NYC, 1978-82; client dir., exec. v.p. Lintas, NYC, 1983-90; dir. corp. strategy, regional dir. So. Africa Lintas Worldwide, NYC, 1991-97; cons. Midlothian, Va., 1998—. Home and Office: 14018 Bayport Landing Ter Midlothian VA 23112-2038

WADSWORTH WALKER, CHERILEE, music educator; b. Port Clinton, Ohio, Mar. 15, 1961; d. Richard Vernon Wadsworth and Joyce Marie Meter Wadsworth; m. James Edward Walker, May 2, 1996. MusB in Music Theory, Baldwin Wallace Coll., 1991; MusM in Jazz Studies, Ind. U., 1993; PhD in Music Edn., U. Okla., 2005. Musician 3d class 6th fleet USN, Naples, Italy, 1994—96, musician 2d class NATO, 1996—98; asst. prof. East Ctrl. U., Ada, Okla., 1998—2001; tchg. chmn. performing arts Ill. Ctrl. Coll., East Peoria, 2001—. Adjudicator, clinician Performing Arts Cons., Keyport, NJ, 2003—; res. musician 85th Divsn. Band, US Army, Arlington Heights, Ill., 2005—; presenter in field; spkr. in field. Contbr. articles to profl. publs.; performer: Montreux Jazz Festival, 2003, Ill. Gubernatorial Inauguration, 2003, Ft. Des Moines Meml. Pk. Dedication, 2004, Nat. Boy Scout Jamboree, 2005, WCBU 35th ann. broadcast concert, 2005. Recipient Ednl. award, Harmony Found., Inc., Minn., 2001, Commn. award, Heartland Music Found., Oklahoma City, 2001, Presentation award, Peoria World Affairs Coun., 2005. Mem.: Am. Choral Dirs. Assn., Nat. Assn. Tchrs. Singing. Office: Ill Ctrl Coll 1 College Dr East Peoria IL 61635 Office Phone: 309-694-5548. Business E-Mail: cwadsworthwalker@icc.edu.

WADZINSKI, MARY BETH, administrative assistant; b. Wausau, Wis., Apr. 26, 1953; d. Erwin Fredrick Hackbart and Selma Ruth Margaret Krueger; m. William R. Wadzinski, June 20, 1987 (div. June 1997); children: Bethany Dawn, Andrew William. AS, Northcentral Tech. Coll., 1973. Typist Wausau (Wis.) Abstract and Title Co., 1973-76; adminstrv. asst. Marathon County Dept. Social Svcs., Wausau, 1977—. Author poems, songs. Recipient Poet Merit award, Am. Poetry Assn., 1989, Editors Choice awards, Nat. Libr. Poetry, 1996—98, 2001, Honorable Mention award, Iliad Press, 1996—98. Mem.: America's Registry, Famous Poets Soc. (Shakespeare Trophy of Excellence 2002, Poet of Yr. medallion 2002, Diamond Homer trophy 1996, Recognition award 1998, Poet of Yr. medallion 1999, Diamond Homer trophy 1999, Recognition award 2001), Internat. Poetry Hall of Fame, Internat. Soc. Poets. Democrat. Lutheran. Avocations: shopping, garage sales, writing, singing. Home: 1113 N 6th Ave Wausau WI 54401-2747 Home Phone: 715-675-3517; Office Phone: 715-261-7595.

WAELSCH, SALOME GLUECKSOHN, geneticist, educator; b. Danzig, Germany, Oct. 6, 1907; arrived in U.S., 1933, naturalized, 1938; d. Ilya and Nadia Gluecksohn; m. Heinrich B. Gluecksohn, Jan. 8, 1943; children: Naomi Barbara, Peter Benedict. Student, U. Konigsberg, Germany, U. Berlin, 1927—28; PhD, U. Freiburg, Germany, 1932; DSc (hon.), Columbia U., 1995. Rsch. assoc. in genetics Columbia U., 1936—55; assoc. prof. anatomy Albert Einstein Coll. Medicine, 1955—58, prof., 1958—63, prof. molecular genetics, 1963, chmn. dept. genetics, 1963—76, disting. prof. emeritus. Mem. study sects. NIH. Author: contbr. numerous articles on devel. genetics. Recipient Nat Medal of Sci., Pres. Clinton, 1993, Thomas Hunt Morgan medal, Genetics Society of America, 1999. Fellow: Am. Acad. Arts & Scis., AAAS; mem.: The Royal Soc., Am. Soc. Human Genetics, Am. Soc. Naturalists, Soc. Devel. Biology, N.Y. Acad. Scis. (hon.), Genetics Soc., Am. Assn. Anatomists, Am. Soc. Zoologists, NAS, Sigma Xi. Office: Albert Einstein Coll Med Rm 827 1300 Morris Park Ave Bronx NY 10461-1926 E-mail: gradus@aecom.yu.edu.

WAETZMAN, LARRY SAMUEL, diversified financial services company executive; b. Reading, Pa., Dec. 11, 1945; s. Joseph and Lilyan B. (Berliner) W.; m. Bonnie Lynn Samuels, July 27, 1969; children: Ross, Evan, Melissa. BA, Franklin & Marshall Coll., 1967; MA, U. Wis., 1968; postgrad., Nova U., Temple U., Harvard U. Lic. profl. planner, N.J. Dir. planning Borough of Norristown, Pa., 1972—74; dir. cmty. devel. Twp. of Haverford, Havertown, Pa., 1974—80; sr. planning cons. Govt. Studies & Sys., Phila., 1980—81; ptnr. Tredinnick/Waetzman Assocs., Havertown, 1981—87; prin. The Waetzman Planning Group, Ardmore, Pa., 1997—2001; pres. Waetleman Planning Group Inc., 2001—. Pres. Congregation Ner Tamid, Springfield, Pa., 1989-91; mem Haverford Twp. Planning Commn., 2004-06. Served to 1st lt. U.S. Army, 1969-72. Mem. Am. Soc. Consulting Planners (pres. 1998-2000), Am. Planning Assn. (pres. ea. Pa. chpt. 1981-85), AICP, Pa. Planning Assn. (bd. dirs. 1981-85), N.J. Assn. Cons. Planners. Avocation: skiing. Home: 2725 Pine Valley Ln Ardmore PA 19003-1718 Office Phone: 610-527-0600. E-mail: lsw@waetzmanplanning.com.

WAGAR, ELIZABETH ANN, microbiologist, director; d. Kenneth H. and Annabel Wagar; m. Michael Lee Gerson, Feb. 2, 1985. MD, Mich. State U., East Lansing, 1981. Diplomate Am. Bd. Pathology, 1985. Assoc. chief microbiology clin. labs. UCLA, 1989—, dir. clin. labs., 1999—. Fellow, NIH, 1985—88. Mem.: Coll. Am. Pathologists (mem. quality practices com. 2004). Office: UCLA Dept Pathology 10833 Le Conte Ave Los Angeles CA 90095-1732 Office Phone: 310-206-4003. Business E-Mail: ewagar@mednet.ucla.edu.

WAGDY, MAHMOUD F., engineering educator; BSc, Cairo U., Giza, Egypt, 1973, MSc, 1977; PhD, Kans. State U., 1983. Assoc. prof. Calif. State U., Long Beach, 1989—92, prof., 1992—. Summer faculty fellow Air Force Rsch. Lab., Dayton, Ohio, 2005. Contbr. articles to profl. jours. Recipient 145 internat. citations for rsch. Mem.: IEEE (chmn. LA chpt. on I & M, indsl. electronics 1992—96). Home: 8352 Brush Dr Huntington Beach CA 92647 Office: Calif State U Long Beach 1250 Bellflower Blvd Long Beach CA 90840 Office Phone: 562-985-5110. Business E-Mail: wagdy@csulb.edu.

WAGENER, CHRISTINE ELIZABETH, psychotherapist, educator; b. Alexandria, Va., Sept. 1, 1948; d. Harry F. and Elizabeth Whitmore Wagener; m. Lawrence L. Foust, Aug. 20, 1977. BA, Jacksonville U., 1970; MSW, Va. Commonwealth U., Richmond, 1976. LCSW Tex. Clin. asst. prof. psychiatry U. Va. Med. Sch., Charlottesville, 1976—80; asst. clin. prof. psychiatry U. Tex. Med. Sch., Houston, 1980—88; pvt. practice psychotherapist Houston, 1988—. Adj. asst. prof. U. Houston Grad. Sch. Social Work, 1980—88; field instr. Va. Commonwealth U. Sch. Social Work, Richmond, 1977—80. Mem. exec. bd. Mental Health Assn., Houston, 1991—97. Mem.: NASW, Acad. Cert. Social Workers. Avocations: sailing, travel, cooking. Office: 2 Chelsea Blvd Houston TX 77006

WAGER, CARRIE BROCKWAY, chemist, researcher; d. Jerome R. and Bonnie S. Brockway (Stepmother); m. Travis T. Wager, Apr. 18, 1988; children: Genevieve M., Cecelia G. PhD, U. Utah, Salt Lake City, 1994—2000. Isotopic labeling Pfizer, Inc., Groton, Conn., 2000—05, process tech., 2005—. Contbr. articles to profl. jours. Office: Pfizer Inc Eastern Point Rd Groton CT 06340

WAGGONER, JAMES CLYDE, lawyer; b. Nashville, May 7, 1946; s. Charles Franklin and Alpha (Noah) W.; m. Diane Dusenbery, Aug. 17, 1968; children: Benjamin, Elizabeth. BA, Reed Coll., 1968; JD, U. Oreg., 1974. Bar: Oreg. 1974, U.S. Dist. Ct. Oreg. 1975, U.S. Ct. Appeals (9th cir.) 1980, U.S. Tax Ct. 1979, U.S. Supreme Ct. 1979. Clk. to presiding justice Oreg. Supreme Ct., Salem, 1974-75; assoc. Martin, Bischoff & Templeton, Portland, Oreg., 1975-78, ptnr., 1978-82, Waggoner, Farleigh, Wada, Georgeff & Witt, Portland, 1982-89, Davis Wright Tremaine, Portland, 1990—. Contbr. articles to profl. jours. Fulbright scholar U. London, 1968-69. Mem. ABA, Oreg. Bar Assn., Multnomah Bar Assn., Reed Coll. Alumni Assn. (v.p. 1988, pres. 1989, bd. mgmt.) Alzheimers Assn. of Columbia-Willamette (v.p. 1992, pres. 1993), Order of Coif, Phi Beta Kappa. Democrat. Avocations: woodworking, calligraphy. Office: Davis Wright Tremaine 1300 SW 5th Ave Ste 2300 Portland OR 97201-5682 Home Phone: 503-284-6685; Office Phone: 503-778-5326. Business E-Mail: jimwaggoner@dwt.com.

WAGGONER, JAMES D. (J.D. WAGGONER), library director; MLS, U. SC, 1994. With W.Va. Libr. Commn., Charleston, 1971—, interim sec., 2001—02, exec. sec., 2002—. Recipient Outstanding Alumni award, U. SC Sch. Libr. & Info. Sci., 2005. Mem.: W.Va. Libr. Assn. (pres. 1993—94), Chief Officers of State Libr. Agys. (Rsch. & Stats. com.). Office: WVa Libr Commn 1900 Kanawha Blvd E Charleston WV 25305 Office Phone: 304-558-2041. Office Fax: 304-558-2044. E-mail: waggoner@wvlc.lib.wv.us.

WAGGONER, KATHLEEN ALICE, psychotherapist; b. St. Louis, Jan. 10, 1954; d. William Dale Jerry Siebe and Doris Ilene Hanson; m. Robert Douglas Clark, July 24, 1974 (div. 1980); children: Angel Mae, Andrew Miles, Jason Allen; m. Curtis Lee Waggoner, Jr., Sept. 6, 1981; children: Amanda Jane, Jennifer Lee, Elizabeth Anne, Kathleen Rose. AA, St. Louis CC, 1983; BS, Southeast Mo. State, 1989, MA, 2003. Cert. NCC, LPC. Tchr. Cinemon Bear Day Care, Cape Girardeau, Mo., 1985—87; supr. infant toddlers San Jose Hosp., Calif., 1989—91; pvt. cons. Molene, Ill., 1991—93; clin. staff Pathways Cmty. Supports, Cape Girardeau, 1995—97, Cmty. Counseling Ctr., Cape Girardeau, 1999—. Pres. WELA, 2002—; sec. Sedgewickville Luth. Ch., Mo., 2004—. E-2 USN, 1973—76, Key West, Fla. Mem.: ACA. Personal E-mail: katecila@hotmail.com.

WAGGONER, LAWRENCE WILLIAM, law educator; b. Sidney, Ohio, July 2, 1937; s. William J. and Gladys L. Waggoner; m. Lynne S. Applebaum, Aug. 27, 1963; children: Ellen, Diane. BBA, U. Cin., 1960; JD, U. Mich., 1963; PhD, Oxford U., Eng., 1966. Assoc. Cravath, Swaine & Moore, NYC, 1963; prof. law U. Ill., Champaign, 1968-72, U. Va., Charlottesville, 1972—74, U. Mich., Ann Arbor, 1974-84, Lewis M. Simes prof. law, 1987—. Dir. rsch., chief reporter joint editorial bd. for Uniform Trust and Estate Acts, 1986-94, dir. rsch., 1994—, mem. joint editl. bd. uniform trust and estate acts; reporter restatement (3d) of property, 1990—; adviser restatement (3d) of trusts, 1993—. Author: Family Property Law: Wills, Trusts, and Future Interests, 4th edit., 2006, Uniform Trust and Estate Statutes, 2007, California and Uniform Trust and Estate Statutes, 2007. Served to capt., U.S. Army, 1966-68. Fulbright scholar Oxford U., 1963-65; named to Sidney City Schs. Hall of Honor, Ohio, 2007. Mem. Am. Law Inst., Am. Coll. Trust and Estates Counsel, Internat. Acad. Estate and Trust Law. Office: U Mich Law Sch 625 S State St Ann Arbor MI 48109-1215 Business E-Mail: waggoner@umich.edu.

WAGGONER, PAUL EDWARD, agricultural scientist; b. Appanoose County, Iowa, Mar. 29, 1923; s. Walter Loyal and Kathryn (Maring) W.; m. Barbara Ann Lockerbie, Nov. 3, 1945; children: Von Lockerbie, Daniel Maring S.B., U. Chgo., 1946; MS, Iowa State Coll., 1949, PhD, 1951. From asst. to chief scientist Conn. Agrl. Expt. Sta., New Haven, 1951-71, vice dir., 1969-71, dir., 1972-87, disting. scientist, 1987—. Mem. panels on policy implications of global warming NAS, 1989-91; chmn. sci. adv. bd. Giant Sequoia Nat. Monument, 2001-02. Contbr. articles to profl. jours. Served to capt. USAAF, 1943-46 Guggenheim fellow, 1963 Fellow AAAS (chmn. climate changes and water resources com. 1986-89), Am. Phytopath. Soc.; mem. NAS, Am. Meteorol. Soc. (Outstanding Achievement in Biometeorology award 1967), Conn. Acad. Sci. and Engring. (Anton-de-Bary medal 1996). Achievements include rsch. in hydrologic role of foliar pores, climate change on agriculture and water resources, how much ten billion can spare for nature, returning forests. Home: 314 Vineyard Point Rd Guilford CT 06437-3255 Office: Conn Agrl Expt Sta PO Box 1106 New Haven CT 06504-1106 Office Phone: 203-453-2816. Personal E-mail: agwagg@comcast.net.

WAGGONNER, JOSEPH DAVID, III, architect; b. Shreveport, La., Feb. 27, 1949; s. Joseph David Waggonner, Jr. and Mary Ruth (Carter) Waggonner. BA, Duke U., Durham, NC, 1971; MArch, Yale U., New Haven, 1975. Draftsman Arch. of the Capitol, Washington, 1974; archtl. designer Bechtel Corp., San Francisco, 1976—78; staff arch. DMJM/Curtis and Davis, New Orleans, 1978—80; assoc. Labouisse, Graeber Ltd., New Orleans, 1980—82; prin. Labouisse & Waggonner, New Orleans, 1982—89, Waggonner & Ball Archs., New Orleans, 1989—. Vis. critic Tulane U., New Orleans, 1980, design prof., 1983—84. Prin. works include 400 Lafayette St. (Gambit Best Comml. Renovation award, 1984), 430 Notre Dame St. (LAA Honor award, 1984), Mignon Faget Canal Pl. (New Orleans chpt. AIA Honor award, 1987), Dominican HS (Gulf State region AIA Honor award, 1995), Dog Trot Weekend Home (AIA La. Honor award, 2005), Isidore Newman Lower Sch. Expanion (AIA La. Honor award, 2005), A.B. Freeman Sch. Bus. (AIA La. Honor award, 2005), Mem.: AIA (Honor award 1987), Assn. Preservation Tech., Soc. Archtl. Historians. Democrat. Methodist. Office: Waggonner & Ball Archs 2200 Prytania St New Orleans LA 70130-5804 Office Phone: 504-524-5308. Office Fax: 504-524-5314. E-mail: d_waggonner@wbarchitects.com. *

WAGLE, A. TINA, education educator, researcher; d. Datta and Sue Wagle. BA, Colgate U., Hamilton, NY, 1996; MA, Middlebury Coll., Vt., 1999; PhD, SUNY, Buffalo, 2003. Cert. in secondary Spanish tchg. NY, 2000. Tchr. Portsmouth Abbey Sch., RI, 1996—99; instr. Canisius Coll., Buffalo, 2000—03; asst. prof. Daemen Coll., Amherst, 2002—03; prof. SUNY Empire State Coll., 2003—. Bilingual edn. adv. com. mem. Buffalo Pub. Schools, 2004—; redesign team mem. Grover Cleve. HS, Buffalo, 2005—. Bd. trustees Cath. Charities of Western NY, Buffalo, 2005—. Mem.: Am. Ednl. Rsch. Assn. Office: 2875 Union Rd Cheektowaga NY 14227 Home Phone: 716-689-3320; Office Phone: 716-686-7800. Home Fax: 716-853-7713. Business E-Mail: tina.wagle@esc.edu.

WAGMAN, ROBERT JOHN, journalist, writer; b. Chgo., Nov. 11, 1942; s. Albert Alan and Rosamond (Horner) Wagman; m. Carol Ann Mueller, Jan. 30, 1965; children: Jennifer, Patricia, Marilyn. AB, St. Louis U., 1966, MA, 1968, JD, 1971. Analyst Dun & Bradstreet, 1965-67; with CBS News, 1967-71, 74-77; asst. to dean St. Louis U. Sch. Law, 1971-74; Washington bur. chief N.Am. Newspaper Alliance, 1977-80, Ind. News Alliance, 1980-82; columnist Newspaper Enterprise Assn., 1980-95. Sr. corr. Soccertimes, VP, Washington, SMA Global. Author, co-author: Hubert Humphrey, The Man and His Dream, 1978, Citizens Guide to the Tax Revolt, 1979, Asbestos: The Silent Killer, 1982, Lord's Justice, 1985, Instant Millionaires, 1986, The Nazi Hunters, 1988, The First Amendment Book, 1991, 2d edit., 1996, World Almanac Guide to the Supreme Court, 1993, Blood Oath, 1994, Hong Kong, 1997, And Beyond, 1997, The Engine of America, 2007; editor: World Almanac of U.S. Politics, 1994—2000. Recipient Thomas Stokes award in Journalism. Business E-Mail: mobilewag@aol.com.

WAGNER, ALAN CYRIL, television and film producer, consultant, performing arts educator; b. NYC, Oct. 1, 1931; s. Joseph and Isabelle (Chanson) W.; m. Martha Celia Dreyfus, Mar. 11, 1956; children: David Mark, Susan Jill, Elizabeth Celia. BA, Columbia U., 1951, MA in English, 1952. Mgr. network programs Benton & Bowles, Inc., NYC, 1957-61; dir. program devel. CBS, NYC, 1961-68, v.p. program devel. Hollywood, Calif., 1968-73, v.p. program planning and devel. NYC, 1973-75, v.p. nighttime programs, 1975-78, v.p. programs, 1978-82; pres., chief exec. officer The Disney Channel, NYC, 1982-83; pres., CEO Alan Wagner Prodns., Inc., NYC, 1983—; exec. v.p. feature and TV devel. and prodn. Grosso-Jacobson Entertainment Corp., NYC, 1985-90; pres. Boardwalk Entertainment, NYC, 1990-97, chmn., 1997—. Sr. program cons. Todays Cath. Cable Network, 1999—; creative cons. concert series Ctrl. Synagogue, NYC, 2004—; adj. assoc. prof. visual arts NYU, 1993—98; lectr. Met. Opera Guild, CUNY, Wagner Soc. Prodr., dir., host program Living Opera. Stas. WNYC-WNYC-FM, NYC, 1958-68; host radio broadcasts NYC Opera Co., 1978-80; panelist, commentator Met. Opera broadcasts, 1996—; contbr., Opera News, 2001—, Playbill, 2004—; exec. prodr. film Reunion at Fairborough, 1985; prodr. TV pilot We're Puttin' on the Ritz, 1986; author: Prima Donnas and Other Wild Beasts, 1961; exec. con. The Gunfighters, Diamonds; supervising prodr. Cop Talk: Behind the Shield, 1988, 89, True Blue, TV movie and series, 1989, A Family for Joe, TV movie and series, 1989-90, TV series Counterstrike, 1990-93, Top Cops, 1989-94; exec. prodr. TV movies Spenser: Ceremony, Spenser: Pale Kings and Princes, 1993, Spenser: The Judas Goat, Spenser: A Savage Place, 1994, Wounded Heart, 1995, Hearts Adrift, Reasons of the Heart, 1996, TV series The Marriage Counselor, 1994. Lt. (j.g.) USNR, 1953-57. Recipient Evelyn Burkey Meml. award Writers Guild Am., 1983, Silver Circle award NATAS, 1999. Mem. Brit. Acad. Film and TV Arts, Wagner Soc. N.Y., Columbia U. Alumni Assn. Avocations: opera, other music, sound reproduction, baseball, other sports. Office: Boardwalk Entertainment 210 E 39th St New York NY 10016-2754 *A decent and abiding respect for the opinions and talents of the creative community on one hand, and the consuming community on the other, has always served as the necessary framework for any decision making in both my professional and personal life. The doers and the thinkers are crucially important, but no more so than those for whom they do and think. If I can serve as an effective middle man, a good part of my life's objective is realizable.*

WAGNER, ALEXANDER JOHANNES, physicist, educator; m. Heather Jean Ummel-Wagner, Oct. 10, 2000. Diploma in Math., U. Bielefeld, Germany, 1990, diploma in Physics, 1990; MS in Physics, U. Bielefeld, 1994; PhD in Theoretical Physics, Oxford U., Eng., 1997. Postdoctoral rsch. asst. MIT, Cambridge, Mass., 1998—99, U. Edinburgh, Scotland, 2000—02; asst. prof. N.D. State U., Fargo, 2002—. Presenter in field. Achievements include research in lattice boltzmann; spinodal decomposition; viscoelasticity. Office: ND State Univ Dept Physics Administration Dr Box 5566 Fargo ND 58105-5566 Office Phone: 701-231-9582. Business E-Mail: alexander.wagner@ndsu.edu.

WAGNER, ALLAN RAY, psychology professor; b. Springfield, Ill., Jan. 6, 1934; s. Raymond August and Grace (Johnson) W.; m. Barbara Rae Meland, Nov. 21, 1959, (dec. Nov. 1994); children: Krystn Rae, Kathryn Rae. BA, U. Iowa, 1956, MA, 1958, PhD, 1959; MA hon., Yale U., 1970. Asst. prof. psychology Yale U., New Haven, 1959-64, assoc. prof., 1964-69, prof., 1970-89, chmn. psychology dept., 1983-89, James Rowland Angell prof. psychology, 1990—, chmn. philosophy dept., 1991-93, dir., divsn. of the soc. sci., 1992-98. Cons. NIMH, 1968-71; mem. Pres. Biomed. Research Panel, 1975-76; adv. bd. Cambridge Ctr. Behavioral Studies, 1982-2000; mem. psychobiology panel NSF, 1984-85, com. on basic research in behavioral and social scis. NRC, 1984-87. Author: Reward and Punishment, 1965; assoc. editor: Learning and Motivation, 1969-74, Animal Learning and Behavior, 1972-74; editor: Jour. Exptl. Psychology, 1974-81, Quantitative Analyses of Behavior, Vol. 3, 1982, Vol. 4, 1983, Vol. 7, 1988. Fellow, NSF, 1958, NIMH, 1963; grantee, NSF, 1960—2004. Fellow APA (Disting. Scientific Contbn. award 1998-99), AAAS (mem. coun. 1988-91), Soc. Exptl. Psychologists (Howard Crosby Warren medal 1991), Am. Psychol. Soc.; mem. NAS, Psychonomic Soc., So. Quantitative Analysis of Behavior (sec. 1983-92), Ea. Psychol. Assn. (bd. dirs. 1985-88), Sigma Xi, New Haven Lawn Club. Home: 1405 Ridge Rd North Haven CT 06473-3051 Office: Yale U Dept Psychology PO Box 208205 New Haven CT 06520-8205 Home Phone: 203-288-2338; Office Phone: 203-432-4691. Business E-Mail: allan.wagner@yale.edu.

WAGNER, ANNETTE M., dermatologist, surgeon; b. Halifax, Nova Scotia, Can., Sept. 14, 1960; d. Ronald Clarence and Thelma May Dillman; children: Hadley Ann, Kirstin Laurel, Michela Jean, Charles Norman, Madison Leah, Gavin Lewis. BSc, U. Calgary, Alberta, Can., 1984; MDCM, McGill U., Montreal, Quebec, Can., 1988. Dir. pediats. dermatol. surgery Children's Meml. Hosp., Chgo., 1994—, attending physician,

1994—. Clin. practice dir. Childrens Meml. Hosp., Chgo., 1996—98. Office: Childrens Meml Hosp 2300 Children's Plz Box 107 Chicago IL 60524 Office Fax: 708-836-4805; Home Fax: 773-327-3448.

WAGNER, ANNICE MCBRYDE, judge; b. DC; BA, JD, Wayne State U. Administrative aide to pres. Barnstable County Mental Health Assn.; with Houston and Gardner; gen. counsel Nat. Capital Housing Authority; people's counsel D.C.; assoc. judge Superior Court DC, 1977-90, DC Ct. Appeals, 1990—94, 2005—, chief judge, 1994—2005, sr. judge, 2005—. Mem. bd. directors Conf. Chief Justices; mem. bd. trustees United Planning Org., 1979—, v.p. bd. trustees, 1988—; chair Task Force On Gender Bias In The Courts, DC Judicial Conf. Arrangements Com., Com. on Selection & Tenure of Hearing Commrs.; mem. teaching team, trial advocacy workshop Harvard U. Office: DC Ct of Appeals 500 Indiana Ave NW Ste 6000 Washington DC 20001-2131 *

WAGNER, ANTHONY E., academic administrator, former state official; b. Chambersburg, Pa. m. Lisa Wagner; 2 children. BA, Pa. State Univ. Fiscal policy specialist Pa. Gov. Budget Office, 1989—91; exec. asst. Sec. of Budget, 1991—93; dep. sec. for adminstrn. Pa. Dept. Agriculture, 1993—95; dir., govt. rels. Pa. State Univ., 1995—2001, spl. asst. to sr. v.p., fin., bus., 2001—02, asst. corp. controller, 2004—05; dep. sec. budget to Pa. budget sec., 2001—03; dep. state treas. investments and programs Pa. State Treas. Dept., 2005—06; exec. dep. state treas. State of Pa., 2006—07; v.p., CFO Temple Univ., 2007—. Deep-sea diver USN. Cath. *

WAGNER, ARTHUR WARD, JR., lawyer; b. Birmingham, Ala., Aug. 13, 1930; s. Arthur Ward and Lucille (Lockheart) W.; m. Ruth Shingler, May 11, 1957; children: Celia Wagner Minter, Julia Wagner Dolce, Helen Wagner McAfee. BSBA, U. Fla., 1954, JD, 1957. Bar: Fla. 1957, U.S. Dist. Ct. (so. dist.) Fla. 1957, U.S. Dist. Ct. (mid. dist.) Fla. 1975. Ptnr. Wagner & McAfee, P.A., West Palm Beach, Fla., 1959-2000; ret., 2000—. Lectr. in field. Author: Art of Advocacy: Jury Selection, 1981; co-author: Anatomy of Personal Injury Lawsuit I & II, 1968 and 1981. Mem. 15th Jud. Nominating Com., Palm Beach City, 1979—82, 4th Dist. Nominating Commn., Palm Beach City, 1982—86; mem. pres.'s coun. U. Fla.; vestry Holy Trinity Parish, v.p., 2002—; bd. dirs., chmn. U. Fla. Found., 2004—, chmn, 2005—06. Fellow Internat. Acad. Trial Lawyers, Am. Coll. Trial Lawyers, Internat. Soc. Barristers, Am. Bd. Trial Advs.; mem. Assn. Trial Lawyers Am. (pres. 1975-76, hon. life trustee Roscoe Pound Found.), So. Trial Lawyers Assn. (pres. 1991), U. Fla. Law Coll. Alumni (mem. bd. govs.). Democrat. Episcopalian.

WAGNER, AUREEN PINTO, psychologist, educator; d. Baptist and Winifred Pinto; m. Scott C. Wagner, June 25, 1994; 2 children. BA, St. Agnes Coll., Mangalore, India, 1981; MA, Mysore U., India, 1983; PhD, U. Iowa, 1989. Lic. psychologist NY. Clin. intern Yale U. Child Study Ctr., New Haven, 1988—89; postdoctoral fellow Brown U., Providence, 1989—91; asst. prof. psychiatry/psychology U. Rochester (NY) Sch. Medicine and Dentistry, 1991—98; founder, dir. Lighthouse Press, Inc., Rochester, 1998—2006, The Anxiety Wellness Ctr., Rochester, 2006—; clin. assoc. prof. neurology U. Rochester (NY) Sch. Medicine and Dentistry, 2003—. Mem. profl. adv. bd. Tourette Syndrome Assn. Rochester, 1997—; dir. The Anxiety Wellness Ctr., Rochester, 2006—; mem. sci. adv. bd. Obsessive Compulsive Found., New Haven, 2005—; internat. spkr. in field. Author: Up and Down the Worry Hill: A Children's Book about Obsessive-Compulsive Disorder and its Treatment, 2000 (Reader's Preference Editors' Choice Award, 2003), What to Do When Your Child Has Obsessive-Compulsive Disorder: Strategies and Solutions, 2002, (manual) Treatment of OCD in Children and Adolescents, 2003, Worried No More: Help and Hope for Anxious Children, 2002, 2d edit., 2005. Grantee J.N. Tata scholar, Tata Found., Bombay, India, 1984—88; Lady Meherbai Tata scholar, Lady Meherbai Tata Edn. Trust, Bombay, India, 1984—88, Robert J. Haggerty Rsch. scholar, U. Rochester Sch. of Medicine, 1995, Nat. Merit scholar, Govt. of the State of Karnataka, India, 1981—83. Mem.: APA, Genesee Valley Psychol. Assn. (chmn. newsletter com. 2005—), Anxiety Disorders Assn. Am., Obsessive Compulsive Found. Roman Catholic. Achievements include development of conceptual framework to explain treatment of OCD to children. Avocations: travel, gardening, choral music, walking. Office: 2300 Buffalo Road #100B Rochester NY 14624 Home Phone: 585-594-5404; Office Phone: 585-594-4770. Personal E-mail: aureen@rochester.rr.com.

WAGNER, BILLY (WILLIAM EDWARD WAGNER), professional baseball player; b. Tannersville, Va., July 25, 1971; m. Sarah Wagner. Student, Ferrum Coll., Va. Draft pick Houston Astros, 1993, pitcher, 1995—2003, Phila. Phillies, 2003—05, NY Mets, 2005—. Mem. US Team World Baseball Classic, 2006. Named to Nat. League All-Star Team, Maj. League Baseball, 1999, 2001, 2003, 2005, 2007; recipient Rolaids Relief award, 1999. Achievements include holding the single-season NCAA record for most strikeouts per nine innings (19.1 in 1992); Division III mark for most career K's (327 in 182.1 innings); fewest hits allowed per game (1.58 in 1992). Office: NY Mets 123-01 Roosevelt Ave Flushing NY 11368 *

WAGNER, BRADLEY JEREMIAH, agricultural engineer; b. Hershey, Pa., Dec. 19, 1981; s. George and Sonja Wagner; m. Julie LeAnn Stone, May 22, 2004. BS in Agrl. and Biol. Engring., Pa. State U., 2004. EIT Pa., registered hydraulic specialist, Pa. Engr. CNH Am. LLC, New Holland, Pa., 2004—. Mem. crop harvesting com. Agrl. Equipment Tech. Conf., 2003—. Mem.: Fluid Power Soc., Am. Soc. Agrl. Engrs., Coaly Honor Soc., Golden Key Internat. Honor Soc., Alpha Epsilon. Mem. Ch. Of Brethren. Avocations: woodworking, mechanics, outdoor activities. Office: CNH Crop Harvesting Field Test 120 George C Delp Rd New Holland PA 17557 Business E-Mail: bradley.wagner@cnh.com.

WAGNER, BRUCE STANLEY, marketing professional; b. San Diego, Aug. 1, 1943; s. Robert Sheldon and Janet (Lowther) Wagner; m. Elizabeth Pearsall Winslow, Oct. 4, 1975; children: Sage Elizabeth, Alexander Winslow. BA, Dartmouth Coll., 1965; MBA, U. Pa., 1984. Sr. v.p. Grey Advt., Inc., NYC, 1967-81; exec. v.p., chief oper. officer Campaign '76 Media Comm., Inc., Washington, 1975-76; exec. v.p., bd. dirs. Ross Roy, Inc., Bloomfield Hills, Mich., 1981-91, Ross Roy Group, Inc., Bloomfield Hills, 1991—94; v.p. mktg. and comms. ITT Automotive Inc., Auburn Hills, Mich., 1995-99; pres. Wagner & Co., Ltd., Birmingham, Mich., 1999—2000; v.p. mktg. and corp. comms. MSX Internat. Inc., Southfield, Mich., 2001—03; pres. Wagner & Co., Ltd., Birmingham, 2004—. Mem. parents bd. Bucknell U., pres. parents bd., 1999—2000, mem. bus. adv. bd., chmn., 2003—. Mem.: Am. Assn. Advt. Agys. (chmn., bd. govs. Mich. coun. 1985—86, bd. govs. ctrl. region 1988—94), Wharton Alumni Assn. (chmn. 1983—85), Birmingham Athletic Club, Orchard Lake Country Club, Detroit Athletic Club, Wharton Club Mich. (bd. dirs. 1985—90). Office: PO Box 194 Glen Arbor MI 49636

WAGNER, CHARLENE BROOK, secondary school educator; b. LA; d. Edward J. and Eva (Anderson) Brook; children: Gordon, Brook, John. BS, Tex. Christian U., 1952; MEd, Sam Houston U., 1973; postgrad., U. Tex., Austin, 1975, Tex. A&M U., 1977. Sci. educator Spring Branch Ind. Sch. Dist., Houston, 1970-98; ret., 2000; dir. CompuKidZ, Houston, 1998—2000; cons. Scott Foresman, Addison Wesley, Ginn, Houston. Cons. Scott Foresman Pub. Co., Houston, 2000-01; owner Sci. Instrnl. Sys. Co., 1988—; dir. Compukidz. Mem. Houston Symphony League, 1992, Mus. Fine Arts, Mus. of Art of Am. West, Houston, 1989, Mus. Natural Scis., Women's Christian Home, Houston, 1991; mem. Houston Grand Opera Guild, mem. exec. bd. 1999-2000, rec./corr. sec.; social chmn. Encore, 1988; mem. Magic Circle Rep. Women's Club. Mem.: AAUW, NAFE, NEA, Internat. Platform Assn., Spring Branch Edn. Assn., Tex. State Tchrs. Assn., Heather and Thistle Soc., Wellington Soc. for Arts (Houston chpt.), Clan Anderson Soc., Art League Houston, Shepherd Soc., Watercolor Arts Soc. (Houston), Houston Highland Games Assn., Space City Ski Club. Episcopalian. Avocations: painting, watercolor media. Home: 2670 Marilee Ln Apt B54 Houston TX 77057-4264 E-mail: wagner2670@aol.com.

WAGNER, CHERI J., business owner; b. Mar. 9, 1963; Owner, mgr. Wagner Constrn., Lake Arrowhead, Calif., 1980-94, Blind Ambitions, Skyforest, Calif., 1994—. Mem. C. of C., Soroptomists, Nat. Fedn. Ind. Bus., Humane Soc., Arrowhead Bldg. Contractors Assn., Mountain Women's Assn.

WAGNER, CHERYL JEAN, elementary school educator; AS, CC Allegheny County, Pitts., 1994; BA, U. Pitts., 1998, MAT, 1999. Cert. elem. tchg. Pa. Kindergarten tchr. Bethel Park Sch. Dist., Pa., 1999—2002, 1st grade tchr., 2002—. ESL tutor Bethel Park Sch. Dist., Pa., 1999—2000, pvt. tutor, 1999—2005, homebound tutor, 1999—2005, class size reduction initiative tchr., 2000—02, stepping up tutor, 2004—05, mem. wellness com., 2004—06, mem. assessment com., 2006—07; participant Western Pa. Wellness Coll., 2004, 05, 06. Nominee Extra Mile award, Bethel Park Sch. Dist., 2005; named Keystone Tech. Integrator, Pa. Dept. Edn., 2006. Mem.: Bethel Park Fedn. Tchrs. Avocations: reading, exercise.

WAGNER, CHRISTIAN NIKOLAUS JOHANN, materials engineering educator; b. Saarbrucken-Dudweiler, Germany, Mar. 6, 1927; arrived in U.S., 1959, naturalized, 1969; s. Christian Jakob and Regina (Bungert) W.; m. Rosemarie Anna Mayer, Apr. 5, 1952; children: Thomas Martin, Karla Regine, Petra Susanne. Student, U. Poitiers, France, 1948-49; Licence es Sci., U. Saar, Ger., 1951, Diplom-Ingenieur, 1954, Dr.rer.nat., 1957. Research asst. Inst. fur Metallforschung, Saarbrucken, 1953-54; vis. fellow M.I.T., 1955-56; research asso. Inst. fur Metallforschung, 1957-58; teaching, research asst. U. Saarbrucken, 1959; asst. prof. Yale U., New Haven, Conn., 1959-62, assoc. prof., 1962-70; prof. dept. materials engring. UCLA, 1970-91, prof. emeritus, 1991—, chmn. dept., 1974-79, asst. dean undergrad. studies Sch. Engring. and Applied Sci., 1982-85, acting chmn., 1990-91. Vis. prof. Tech. U., Berlin, 1969, U. Saarbrücken, 1979—80. Contbr. articles to profl. jours. Recipient U.S. Sci. Humboldt award, U. Saarbrucken, 1989—90, 1992. Fellow Am. Soc. Metals Internat.; mem. Am. Crystallographic Assn., Minerals, Metals and Materials Soc. Home: 37621 Golden Pebble Ave Palm Desert CA 92211-1430 Office: UCLA 6532 Boelter Hl Los Angeles CA 90095-0001 Personal E-mail: cnjwagner@verizon.net.

WAGNER, CURTIS LEE, JR., judge; b. Nov. 8, 1928; m. Jeanne E. Allen (dec.); children: Curtis L. III, Rex A. Student, Tenn. Poly. Inst., 1947-49; LLB, U. Tenn., 1951. Bar: Tenn. 1952. Assoc. Kramer, Dye, McNabb and Greenwood, Knoxville, Tenn., 1951-54; atty.-adv. gen. crimes and fraud sect. Criminal Divsn. Dept. Justice, Washington, 1954-56; trial atty. Dept. Justice, Washington, 1954-60; assigned to Ct. of Claims sect. Civil Divsn., Washington, 1956-60; spl. asst. comms., transp. and utilities JAG Dept. Army, Washington, 1960-64; chief Regulatory Law Divsn., Washington, 1964-74; adminstrv. law judge FERC, Washington, 1974-79, chief adminstrv. law judge, 1979—. Mem. civilian lawyer career com., 1960-74; chmn. JAG incentive awards com. 1960-74; mem. Army Staff Awards Bd., 1964-74, Army Environ. Policy Council, 1972-74. Dist. commr. Nat. Capital Area coun. Boy Scouts Am., 1967-69; mem. Bd. Govts. Watergate of Alexandria Condo, 1996—; commr. Alexandria Redevel. and Pub. Housing Commn., 1996-2000; mem. waterfront com. City of Alexandria, 2005—. Decorated Meritorious Civilian Svc. award, Exceptional Civilian Svc. award; recipient citation for outstanding performance Dept. Army, 1961-74, Scouter's Tng. award Boy Scouts Am., 1965, Scoutmaster's Key, 1966, Commr.'s Key, 1968, Commr.'s Arrowhead Honor, 1966, Silver Beaver award 1969. Mem. Order of Arrow, Annapolis Yacht Club. Methodist. Office: Fed Energy Regulatory Commn 888 1st St NE Washington DC 20426-0002 Office Phone: 202-502-8500. Business E-Mail: curtis.wagner@ferc.gov.

WAGNER, CYNTHIA GAIL, editor, writer; b. Bethesda, Md., Oct. 3, 1956; d. Robert Cheney and Marjory Jane (Kletzing) W. BA in English, Grinnell Coll., 1978; MA in Comms., Syracuse U., 1981. Editl. asst. The Futurist/World Future Soc., Bethesda, Md., 1981—82, staff editor, 1982-85, asst. editor, 1985-91, sr. editor, 1991-92, mng. editor, 1992—. Editor: (newsletter) Futurist Update, 2000—, (book) Foresight, Innovation, and Strategy: Toward a Wiser Future, 2005; columnist: 3-2-1 Contact, 1994; contbr. Encyclopedia of the Future, 1995, The 21st Century, 1999; contbg. writer/music reviewer BeaversonIdol.com., 2004—. Mem. Theatre Comm. Group, Washington Shakespeare Reading Group. Avocation: theater. Office: The Futurist World Future Soc 7910 Woodmont Ave Ste 450 Bethesda MD 20814-3066 Business E-Mail: cwagner@wfs.org.

WAGNER, DAVID, computer scientist, educator; b. 1974; AB in Math., Princeton U., NJ, 1995; MS in Computer sci., U. Calif., Berkeley, 1999, PhD in Computer sci., 2000. Asst. prof. to assoc. prof. computer sci. U. Calif., Berkeley, Calif., 1998—. Mem. organizing com. Ctr. Discrete Math. & Theoretical Computer Sci., Rutgers U., Piscataway, NJ; mem. prog. com. Oper. Systems Design & Implementation Symposium, 2004; co-chair IEEE Security & Privacy Conf. Co-author: (numerous sci. publs. including) Cryptoanalysis of the Cellular Encryption Algorithm, 1997, Cryptanalysis of Some Recently-Proposed Multiple Modes of Operation, 1998, TAZ Servers and the Rewebber Network: Enabling Anonymous Publishing on the World Wide Web, 1998, Slide Attacks, 1999, The Boomerang Attack, 1999, Practical Techniques for Searches on Encrypted Data, 2000, Intercepting mobile communications: the insecurity of 802.11, 2001, Securing Wireless and Mobile Networks: Is It Possible?, 2002, Private Circuits: Securing Hardware against Probing Attacks, 2003, Analyzing Internet Voting Security, 2004. Named Best Academic Rschr., Info. Security Mag.; named one of Brilliant 10, Popular Sci. mag., 2002; grantee Sloan Rsch. fellowship. Expert in the field of security, wireless security, sensor network security, cryptography. Discovered flaw in Secure Sockets Layer security tool built into Netscape Navigator (with Ian Goldberg), cryptanalyzed the CMEA algorithm used in cellphones (with Bruce Schneier). Invented new form of cryptanalysis called "slide attack" (with Alex Biryukov). Office: Computer Sci Divsn U Calif Berkeley 629 Soda Hall Berkeley CA 94720-1776

WAGNER, DONALD BERT, health facility administrator; b. York, Pa., July 27, 1930; s. Bert Daniel and Mary Elizabeth (Roelke) W.; m. Janet Louise Bankert, July 12, 1952; children: Kimberly, Susan, David, John. Student, Franklin & Marshall, 1948-50; BS in Phys. Therapy, Columbia U., 1952; MHA, Baylor U., 1960. Commd. 2d lt. USAF, 1952, advanced through grades to brig. gen., 1982; physical therapist Randolph AFB, San Antonio, 1952-55; asst. adminstr. USAF/RAF S. Ruislip, London; adminstr. USAF/RAF Bentwaters, Ipswich, England, 1955-58; various adminstrv. roles USAF Hosps. and Commands, Europe and U.S., 1958-73; dep. comdr. USAF Sch. Health Care Sci., Wichita Falls, Tex., 1973-75; adminstr. Wilford Hall Med. Ctr., San Antonio, 1975-79; chief med. svc. corps Office Surgeon Gen. USAF, San Antonio, 1979-82; dep. surgeon gen. USAF Med. Svc. Ctr., San Antonio, 1981-82, ret., 1982; adminstr., assoc. v.p. M. D. Anderson/U. Tex. Cancer Ctr., Houston, 1982-85; chief exec. officer Meml. Southwest Hosp., Houston, 1985-91; v.p. Meml. Hosp. System, Houston, 1985-91, internal cons., interim hosp. CEO, 1991—2005; mem. adv. bd. Grad. Program in Healthcare Adminstrn. Texas Women's U., Houston. Adj. prof. Baylor and Trinity U., San Antonio, 1975-82; assoc. prof. U. Houston, St. Louis U., 1982-88; exec. officer Woodlands Hosp., Angleton-Danbury Hosp., Prevention and Recovery Ctr., Bellville Hosp., MHHS Long Term Acute Care Hosp., MH S.E. Hosp.; cons., El Salvador, Nicaragua, China, Saudi Arabia, Japan, Korea, 1991-02. Bd. dirs. Hospice at the Med. Ctr., 1982-2001, Child Advocates, Houston, 1985-89, Kidney Found., Houston, 1985-88, Westland YMCA, Houston, 1985-88, 90-94, Ft. Bend County YMCA, 1998-03, Greater Houston Hosp. Coun., 1983-87, Sam Houston area Alzheimer's Assn. 1990-94; mem.n. external adv. bd. Sch. Allied Health, U. Tex. Med. Br.; mem. adv. bd. gradrogram healthcare adminstrn. Tex. Women's U., Houston. Named Disting. Alumnus Baylor U. Program in Healthcare Adminstrn., 1993. Fellow Am. Coll. Healthcare Execs. (edn. com., ethics com., comm. com.), Royal Soc. Health; mem. Am. Hosp. Assn. (bd. dirs. hosp. rsch. and edn. found. 1990—), Tex. Hosp. Assn., Assn. Mil. Surgeons U.S. (Ray E. Brown award 1982, Outstanding Sr. Level Healthcare Exec. Regents award 1991, Regents Lifetime Achievement award 2004), Am. Mgmt. Soc. Republican. Methodist. Avocation: music. Home and Office: 1746 Carriage Way Sugar Land TX 77478-4201 Home Phone: 281-980-5613; Office Phone: 281-980-5613.

WAGNER, DOROTHY MARIE, retired senior creative designer, artist; b. Chgo., Jan. 12, 1926; d. William Christopher and Margaret Frances (Rowell) W. Student, Kalamazoo Coll., 1943-45; BS, Western Mich. U., 1947; BFA, Art Ctr. Coll. Design, LA, 1962. Dir. electroencephalography lab. Bronson Hosp., Kalamazoo, 1945-51; dir. EEG lab. Terr. Hosp., Kaneohe, Hawaii, 1951-55, UCLA Med. Ctr., 1955-60; sr. creative designer GM Tech. Ctr. Styling, Warren, Mich., 1962-82. Cons. in EEG, Army Hosp., Honolulu, 1950-55; dir. sales and rental gallery Pt. Huron (Mich.) Mus., 1989-93, art and painting instr., 1992-96. Recipient Best of Show award Ea. Mich. Internat. Art Show, 1992, 1st pl. award, 1988, 89, 94. Mem. Blue Water Art Assn. (pres. 1990-96), Orion Art Ctr. Episcopalian. Avocations: horseback riding, showing in dressage, breeding and raising racing greyhounds, water color and acrylic painting, stained glass design and fabrication. Home: 14841 Pine Knoll Rd Capac MI 48014-1913 E-mail: dot@glis.net.

WAGNER, EDWARD JOHN, physiologist, educator; b. Inglewood, Calif., Sept. 2, 1963; s. Edward Joseph Wagner and Jeanne Marie Stevens. BS, UCLA, 1986; PhD, Mich. State U., East Lansing, 1994. Postdoctoral fellow Oreg. Health & Sci. U., Portland, 1994—98, rsch. asst. prof., 1998—2001; asst. prof. We. U. Health Scis., Pomona, Calif., 2001—05, assoc. prof., 2005—. Grantee Rsch. Scientist Career Devel. award, Nat. Inst. Drug Abuse, 2000—03. Mem.: Bruin Bench (assoc.). Democrat. Avocations: racquetball, golf, skiing, travel. Office: Western U Health Scis 309 E Second St Pomona CA 91766 Office Phone: 909-469-5239. Office Fax: 909-469-5698. E-mail: ewagner@westernu.edu.

WAGNER, EDWARD KURT, publishing company executive; b. NYC, Sept. 29, 1936; s. Kurt Henry and Julia Marie (Selesky) W.; m. Ann Marie Philbin, Jan. 31, 1959; children: Denise, Steven, Kenneth, Jeanne. BBA, St. Francis Coll., 1961. With Pitman Pub. Corp., NYC, 1952-75, v.p., treas., 1968-71, exec. v.p., 1971-75; financial mgr. Dun-Donnelley Pub. Corp., NYC, 1975-76, contr. gen. book div., 1976-77; sr. mgr. contr.'s dept. Dun & Bradstreet, Inc., NYC, 1977-78, asst. contr., 1978-83, contr., 1983-88, v.p., contr., 1989-96; ret., 1996—. Home: 55 Shoal Rd Jackson NJ 08527

WAGNER, FREDERICK REESE, retired language educator; b. Phila., Apr. 15, 1928; m. Barbara Alexander Brady, May 9, 1959 (div. 1968); 1 child, Christopher A. BA summa cum laude, Duke U., 1948, MA, 1949, PhD, 1971. Advt mgr. Prentice-Hall, Inc., NYC, 1955-57; promotion mgr. Harper & Row, NYC, 1957-65; instr. English Duke U., Durham, NC, 1967-69; asst. prof. Hamilton Coll, Clinton, NY, 1969-73, assoc. prof., 1973-78, prof. English, chmn. dept., 1978-90, prof. English, 1990-95, ret., 1995. Author: Famous Underwater Adventurers, 1962; Submarine Fighter of the American Revolution, 1963; Patriot's Choice: The Story of John Hancock, 1964; Robert Morris, Audacious Patriot, 1976. Mem. Thoreau Soc. (pres. 1984-86), Hawthorne Soc., Phi Beta Kappa. Home: 2160 Bleecker St Apt A-215 Utica NY 13501

WAGNER, FREDERICK WILLIAM (BILL), lawyer; b. Daytona Beach, Fla., Apr. 13, 1933; s. Adam A. and Nella (Schroeder) W.; m. Ruth Whetstone; children: Alan Frederick, Darryl William, Thomas Adam. BA, U. Fla., 1955, LLB with honors, 1960. Bar: Fla. 1960, U.S. Supreme Ct. 1967, D.C. 1989; cert. civil trial lawyer, Fla. Bar; cert. aviation lawyer, Fla. Bar. Pvt. practice law, Miami, Fla., 1960-63, Orlando, Fla., 1963-65, Tampa, Fla., 1965—; ptnr. Nichols, Gaither, Beckham, Colson, Spence & Hicks, Tampa, 1965-67; ptnr., shareholder Wagner, Vaughan McLaughlin & Brennan, P.A., 1967—. Mem. Gov.'s Jud. Nominations Commn., 1971-72, Constnl. Jud. Nominations Commn., 1972-75; mem. Fla. Bd. Bar Examiners, 1974-77, emeritus mem., 1995—; chmn. Civil Procedure Rules Com. Fla. Bar, 1977-78; bd. govs. Fla. Bar, 1978-83; trustee Roscoe Pound Inst., 1984-92; mem. civil jury instrn. com. Fla. Supreme Ct., 1985-2003. Contbr. articles to profl. jours. 1st lt. USAF, 1955-57. Fellow Am. Bar Found., Am. Coll. Trial Lawyers, Internat. Acad. Trial Lawyers, Am. Bd. Trial Advs.; mem. Am. Assn. for Justice (formerly known as ATLA; bd. govs. 1973-80, 84-89, chmn. pub. affairs dept. 1984-89, treas. 1982-84, v.p. 1986-87, pres.-elect 1987-88, pres. 1988-89), Am. Inns of Ct. Found. (trustee 1996-2000), Fla. Justice Assn. (formerly known as Acad. Fla. Trial Lawyers; bd. dirs. 1965-84, pres. 1972-73), Bay Area Trial Lawyers Assn. (v.p. 1966-68), Am. Law Inst. (coun. 1993—), Lawyer-Pilots Bar Assn., Fla. Bar Found., U. Fla. Alumni Assn., Nat. Bd. Trial Advocacy (cert. civil), Assn. Personal Injury Lawyers, Australian Lawyers Alliance, Pan European Orgn. Personal Injury Lawyers, So. Trial Lawyers Assn., Tampa Bay Trial Lawyers Assn. Democrat. Methodist. Avocations: travel, flying. Home: 901 Mariner Way Tampa FL 33602-5759 Office: Wagner Vaughan McLaughlin & Brennan 601 Bayshore Blvd Ste 910 Tampa FL 33606-2786 Home Phone: 813-223-5610; Office Phone: 813-225-4000. Business E-Mail: BillWagner@WagnerLaw.com.

WAGNER, GERALDINE MARIE, nursing educator, consultant; b. Renton, Wash., Apr. 12, 1948; d. Ernest F. and Vera P. (Temiraeff) W. AA, Pasadena City Coll., 1970; BA cum laude, Calif. State U., Northridge, 1977; BSN, Calif. State U., LA, 1982; MEd summa cum laude, Azusa Pacific U., 1993. Cert. pub. health nurse, Calif. Dept. Health Svcs. In utilization mgmt. Blue Cross, Woodland Hills, Calif., 1987-88, Healthmarc, Pasadena, Calif., 1988-90; nursing educator, asst. dir. vocat. nursing program Casa Loma Coll., LA, 1991-92, dir. program planning and devel., and coord. continuing edn. Lake View Terrace, 1992-93; dir. vocal. nursing program Glendale (Calif.) Career Coll., 1994-95; with patient care rev. svcs. U. So. Calif. U. Hosp., LA, 1996—; med.-legal nurse cons., 2000—. Docent Mission La Purisima Concepcion. Capt. Nurse Corp, U.S. Army, 1979-84. Mem.: VFW, Civil War Preservation Trust, Calif. Mission Studies Assn., Assn. for Women in Math., Fellowship Cath. Scholars, Nat. Assn. Cath. Nurses, Computer Using Educators, Nat. Coun. Tchrs. Math., Am. Math. Soc., Blue Army Our Lady Fatima, Nat. Maritime Hist. Soc., Soc. Cath. Social Scientists, Civil War Soc., Order of Preachers, Mil. Officer Assn. Am., U.S. Naval Inst., Cath. War Vets, Res. Officers Assn. U.S., Army Nurse Corps. Assn., AMVETS, Assn. U.S. Army, Inst. Religious Life, Assn. Hebrew Catholics, Disabled Am. Vets., Am. Legion, Sigma Theta Tau, Pi Lambda Theta. Roman Catholic. Home: 924 Rock Rose Ln Lompoc CA 93436 Office Phone: 805-735-3575. E-mail: srgmwagnerop@earthlink.net, srgmwagnerop@verizon.net.

WAGNER, HAROLD A., retired gas industry executive; b. Oakland, Calif., Nov. 12, 1935; s. Harold A. and Lurline Frances (Madsen) Wagner; m. Marcia Kenaston, July 17, 1956; children: Sandra Wagner Boyce, Kristi Wagner Schwiering, Tracey, Eric. BS in Mech. Engring., Stanford U.,

1958, SEP, 1982; MBA, Harvard U., 1963. Regional sales mgr. ind. gases U.S. Air Products & Chems., Allentown, Pa., 1963—70; mgr. GM ind. gases U.K.Air Products & Chems., 1970—76; regional sales mgr. GM Ind. Gases Continental Europe, 1976—80, GM Ind. Gases U.S., 1980—81; v.p. sales ind. gases div. FM, 1981—82; v.p. corp. planning Air Products & Chems., 1982—87, v.p. bus. div. chems., 1987—88; pres. AP Europe, 1988—90, exec. v.p., 1990—91, pres., COO, 1991—92, past chmn. pres., CEO; chmn., pres., CEO, dir. Air Products and Chems., 1992—2001, chmn., CEO, dir., ret.; chmn. Agere Systems, 2001—. 1st lt. USAF, 1958—61. Avocations: squash, photography. Home: 4031 Savannah Trl Santa Rosa CA 95404-8897

WAGNER, JAMES MILLER, funeral director; b. Louisville, Ky., June 3, 1965; s. William Henry and Jane (Miller) Wagner. Funeral dir., Hanover Coll., 1988. Apprentice, funeral dir., embalmer Highlands Funeral Home Inc., Louisville, 1989—; funeral dir. Bosse Funeral Home, Inc., Louisville, 1995—. Sec. bd. dirs. Louisville Hist. League, 1989—99. Mem.: Falls Cities Funeral Dirs. Assn., Rotary Club Louisville. Roman Catholic. Avocation: history. Home: 3013 Tremont Dr Louisville KY 40205 Office Phone: 502-451-8440.

WAGNER, JAMES WARREN, academic administrator, engineering educator; b. Washington, July 12, 1953; s. Robert Earl and Bernice (Bittner) W.; m. Debbie Kelley, July 31, 1976; children: Kimberly Renee, Christine Kelley. BSEE, U. Del., 1975; MS, Johns Hopkins U., 1978, PhD, 1984. Electronics engr. U.S. FDA, Washington, 1975-84; asst. prof. Johns Hopkins U., Balt., 1984-88, assoc. prof., 1988-93, prof., 1993-97, chmn. dept. materials scis. and engring., 1993-97; prof. materials sci. and engring., dean Case Sch. Engring. Case Western Res. U., Cleve., 1998—2000, provost, 2000-01, interim pres., 2001—02; pres. Emory U., Atlanta, 2003—. Contbr. articles to profl. jours. Elder Presbyn. Ch. U.S.A.; bd. mem. Carter Ctr., Ga. Rsch. Alliance, SunTrust Banks, Metro Atlanta C. of C. Mem. IEEE, Optical Soc. Am., Laser & Electro-Optics Soc. Presbyterian. Achievements include scientific contributions to the field of optical metrology applied to materials characterization, especially advanced holographic and laser-based ultrasonic methods. Office: Emory U Office of Pres Atlanta GA 30322

WAGNER, JODY M., treasurer; b. Canton, Ohio; m. Alan L. Wagner; children: Rachael, Jason, Elizabeth, Maxwell. Degree in econs., Northwestern U., Evanston, Ill., 1977; grad. degree in law, Vanderbilt U., Nashville, 1980. Bar: Tenn. 1980, Va. 1984. With Kaufman and Canoles PC, Norfolk, Va., 1981—2002; state treas. Va., 2002—. Office: Commonwealth of Va Dept of Treasury 101 N 14th St Richmond VA 23218 Office Phone: 804-371-6013. Business E-Mail: jody.wagner@trs.virginia.gov.

WAGNER, JOHN EDWARD, equity specialist; b. Amarillo, Tex. BS, Tex. A&M, College Station, 1999; MHA, Trinity U., San Antonio, 2001. Adminstrv. fellow Baylor Health Care Sys., Dallas, 2001—02; mgr. ops. IQ Healthcare, Houston, 2002—05; fin. analyst Meml. Hermann Health Care Sys., Houston, 2005—06; assoc. Freestone Partners, LLC, Houston, 2006—. Mem.: Healthcare Fin. Mgmt. Assn., Am. Coll. Healthcare Adminstrs. Republican. Avocations: tennis, golf, wine.

WAGNER, JOHN LEO, lawyer, retired judge, mediator, arbitrator; b. Ithaca, NY, Mar. 12, 1954; s. Paul Francis and Doris Elizabeth (Hoffschneider) W.; m. Marilyn Modin, June 18, 1987. Student, U. Nebr., 1973-74; BA, U. Okla., 1976, JD, 1979. Bar: Okla. 1980, Calif. 1999, U.S. Dist. Ct. (we. dist.) Okla. 1980, U.S. Dist. Ct. (no. and ea. dists.) Okla. 1981, U.S. Dist. Ct. (ctrl. dist.) Calif. 2000, U.S. Ct. Appeals (10th cir.) 1982. Assoc. Franklin, Harmon & Satterfield Inc., Oklahoma City, 1980-82; ptnr. Franklin, Harmon & Satterfield, Inc., Oklahoma City, 1982; assoc. Kornfeld, Franklin & Phillips, Oklahoma City, 1982-85, ptnr., 1985; magistrate judge U.S. Dist. Ct. No. Dist. Okla., Tulsa, 1985-97; dir. Irell & Manella LLP Alt. Dispute Resolution Ctr., Newport Beach, Calif., 1997—2005. Pres. U. Okla. Coll. Law Assn., 1991-92. Fellow Am. Coll. Civil Trial Mediators, Internat. Acad. Mediators, Fed. Magistrate Judge's Assn. (dir. 10th cir. 1987-89); mem. ABA, 10th Cir. Edn. Com., Okla. Bar Assn., Council Oak Am. Inn of Cts. (pres. 1992-93), Jud. Conf. U.S. (com. ct. adminstrn. and case mgmt. 1992-97), CPR-Georgetown Commn. Ethics and Standards in ADR. Republican. Office: Judicate West ADR 1851 E 1st St Ste 1450 Santa Ana CA 92705 Office Phone: 800-488-8805. Business E-Mail: jwagner@wagneradr.com.

WAGNER, JUDITH BUCK, investment firm executive; b. Altoona, Pa., Sept. 25, 1943; d. Harry Bud and Mary Elizabeth (Rhodes) B.; m. Joseph E. Wagner, Mar. 15, 1980; 1 child, Elizabeth. BA in History, U. Wash., 1965; grad., N.Y. Inst. Fin., 1968. Registered Am. Stock Exch., N.Y. Stock Exch., investment advisor. Security analyst Morgan, olmstead, Kennedy & Gardner, LA, 1968-71, Boettcher & Co., Denver, 1972-75; pres. Wagner Investment Mgmt., Denver, 1975—. Chmn. The Women's Bank, N.A., Denver, 1977-94, organizational group pres., 1975-77; chmn. Equitable Bankshares Colo., Inc., Denver, 1980-94; pres. Equitable Bank of Littleton, Colo., 1985; lectr. Denver U., Metro State, 1975-80. Author: Woman and Money series Colo. Woman Mag., 1976, moderator "Catch 2' Sta. KWGN-TV, 1978-79. Pres. Bit Sisters Colo., Denver, 1977-82, bd. dirs., 1972-83; bd. fellows U. Denver, 1985-90; bd. dirs. Red Cross, 1980, Assn. Children's Hosp., 1985, Colo. Health Facilities Authority, 1978-84, Jr. League Cmty. ADv. Com., 1979-82, Bros. Redevel., Inc., 1979-80; mem. agy. rels. com. Mile High United Way, 1978-81, chmn. United Way Venture Way, 1978-81, chmn. United Way Venture Grant com., 1980-81; bd. dirs. Downtown Dener, Inc., 1988-95; bd. dirs., v.p., treas. The Women's Found. Colo., 1987-91; treas., trustee, v.p., Graland Country Day Sch., 1990-97, pres., 1994-97; trustee Denver Rotary Found., 1990-95, Hunt Alternatives Fund, 1992-97; trustee The Colo. Trust, 1998—, chmn., 2003-05. Recipient Making It award Cosmopolitan Mag., 1977, Women on the Go award, Savvy Mag., 1983, Minouri Yasoui award, 1986, Salute Spl. Honoree award, Big Sisters, 1987; named one of the Outstanding Young Women Am., 1979, Woman Who Makes A Difference award Internat. Women's Forum, 1987, Maverick Thinker award Urban Park, 2003; named Disting. Citizen award U. Colo., 2005. Fellow Assn. Investment Mgmt. & Rsch.; mem. Women's Forum Colo. (pres. 1979), Women's Found. Colo., Inc. (bd. dirs. 1986-91), Denver Soc. Security Analysts (bd. dirs. 1976-83, v.p. 1980-81, pres. 1981-82), Colo. Investment Advisors assn., Rotary (treas. Denver chpt. found., pres. 1993-94), Leadership Denver (Outstanding Alumna award 1987), Pi Beta Phi (pres. U. Wash. chpt. 1964-65). Office: Wagner Investment Mgmt Inc Ste 240 3200 Cherry Creek South Dr Denver CO 80209-3245 Office Phone: 303-777-1800.

WAGNER, KENNETH LYNN, lawyer; b. McPherson, Kans., Oct. 13, 1956; s. Francis D. and Mary V. (Van Buren) W.; m. Lida Jane McNearney, Oct. 22, 1983; 1 child, Elizabeth Ann. BS in Journalism, U. Kans., 1979, JD, 1983; LLM, Georgetown U., 1987. Bar: Mo. 1983, Ill. 1984, D.C. 1985. Atty. div. corp. fin. SEC, Washington, 1984-86, spl. counsel, 1986-88; assoc. Schlafly, Griesedieck, Ferrell & Toft, St. Louis, 1983-84, Stinson, Mag & Fizzell, Kansas City, Mo., 1988-89, Arent, Fox, Kintner, Plotkin & Kahn, Washington, 1989-94; assoc. counsel Banc One Corp., 1994-98; sr. counsel Goodrich Corp., 1998—2004, prin. counsel, 2004—06; assoc. gen. counsel Bank of Am. Corp., Charlotte, NC, 2006—. Mem. ABA, Soc. Corp. Secs. and Governance Profls., Mo. Bar Assn. Republican. Office: Bank of America NC1-002-29-01 101 S Tryon St Charlotte NC 28255 Business E-Mail: kenneth.wagner@bankofamerica.com.

WAGNER, LESLIE, lawyer; b. Houston, July 18, 1953; d. Jacob and Geraldine (Harris) W. BA in Am. Studies, cum laude, U. Tex., Austin, 1975; JD, U. Houston, 1980. Bar: Tex. 1980, US Dist. Ct. (so. dist.) Tex. 1981; cert. employment lawyr., Cornell, 2000. Trial atty. civil rights EEOC, Houston, 1981—84; pvt. practice Houston, 1984—85, 1987—88, 2004—; dir. law placement U. Houston Law Ctr., 1985—87; employee rels. atty, sr. employee rels. analyst The Meth. Hosp. System, Houston, 1988—97; employee rels. cons. Prudential Fin., Houston, 1997—2003; equal employment affirmative action cons., 2004—. Cons. EEOC, Houston, 1984—; v.p., treas. Houston Soc. Healthcare Human Resources Adminstrns., 1995-97; dir., gen. counsel Hematology/Oncology Assistance Resource Coalition, 1995-2002. Editor: U. Houston Law Rev., 1979, assoc. editor, 1980. Mem. health and edn. com. Jewish Cmty. Ctr., Houston, 1983-85; polit. cons. Houston, 1984-85; vol. instr. Seven Acres Jewish Home for the Aged, 2006-. Named Honors Day Honoree U. Tex., 1971; Arts and Scis. scholar U. Tex., 1971-74. Mem. ABA (com. employee and labor rels. 1983-85, employment rights com. gen. practice sect. 1986), ATLA, Houston Bar Assn., Tex. Young Lawyers Assn. (job fair com.), Tex. Hosp. Assn., Soc. of Human Resources Mgmt., Nat. Assn. Law Placement (careers com. 1986-87, minority placement com. 1987), Am. Studies Assn., Soc. Human Resources Mgmt., HR Houston, Houston Festival Dancers (treas. 1976-77), Eta Phi Sigma. Democrat. Jewish. Avocations: creative writing, dance, reading, yoga, pilates. Home: 5407 Wigton Dr Houston TX 77096-4005 Personal E-mail: leslie.wagner@earthlink.net.

WAGNER, LINDSAY JEAN, actress; b. LA, June 22, 1949; d. Bill Nowels and Marilyn Louise (Thrasher) W.; m. Alan Rider (div.); m. Michael Brandon, Dec. 1976 (div.); m. Henry Kingi, 1981 (div.); children: Dorian Henry, Alex Nathan; m. Lawrence Mortorff, 1990 (div.). Student, U. Oreg., 1967. Tchr. acting children Founders Sch. Los Angeles, 1975. Actress numerous TV shows Universal Studios, Universal City, Calif., 1971-74; motion picture picture appearances include: Two People, 1972, The Paper Chase, 1973, Second Wind, 1976, Nighthawks, 1981, Martin's Day, 1984, Ricochet, 1991, Frog and Wombat, 1998, A Light in the Forest, 2002, Buckaroo, 2005, The Surfer King, 2006; TV series include The Bionic Woman, 1976-78, Jessie, 1984, Peaceable Kingdom, 1989; appeared in TV miniseries Scruples, 1980, Princess Daisy, 1983, The Dead of the Night, 1989, Voices of the Heart, 1990, To Be the Best, 1991; TV films include: The Two Worlds of Jennie Logan, 1979, The Incredible Journey of Dr. Meg Laurel, 1979, I Want to Live, 1983, Two Kinds of Love, 1983, Callie and Son, 1983, Passion, 1984, This Child is Mine, 1985, The Other Lover, 1985, Nightmare at Bitter Creek, 1988, The Taking of Flight 847, 1988, Shattered Dreams, 1990, Babies, 1990, Fire in the Dark, 1991, She Woke Up, 1992, Treacherous Crossing, 1992, To Be the Best, 1992, A Message from Holly, 1992, Nurses on the Line: The Crash of Flight 7, 1993, Men Who Hate Women & Women Who Love Them, 1994, Once in a Lifetime, 1994, Bionic Ever After?, 1994, Fighting for My Daughter, 1995, A Mother's Instinct, 1996, Sins of Silence, 1996, Their Second Chance, 1997, Contagious, 1997, Frog and Wombat, 1998, The Fourth Horseman, 1998, Thicker Than Water, 2005; author book, video, film; (with others) Lindsay Wagner's New Beauty: The Acupressure Facelift; co-author: The High Road to Health, 1990; spokesperson for Select Comfort Sleep Number Bed.

WAGNER, MARK A., retail executive; BS, No. Ky. Univ., 1985; MBA, We. New England Coll., 1993. Joined Walgreen Co., Deerfield, Ill., 1977, mgmt. positions from dist. mgr. to operational v.p., 1993—2000, treas., 2000—02, sr. v.p., 2002—06, exec. v.p. store ops., 2006—. Office: Walgreen Co 200 Wilmot Rd Deerfield IL 60015 *

WAGNER, MARTHA JO, lawyer; b. Chgo., Apr. 6, 1951; d. Joseph Richard and Mary Marjorie W. BA summa cum laude, U. Md., 1979; JD cum laude, Georgetown U., 1982. Bar: DC 1982, Pa. 1983, Ga. 1997, U.S. Dist. Ct. D.C. 1983, U.S. Dist. Ct. (we. dist.) Pa. 1985, U.S. Ct. Appeals (3d cir.) 1985. Motions clk. DC Ct. Appeals, Washington, 1982-83; atty. Pension Benefit Guaranty Corp., Washington, 1983-85; assoc. Reed, Smith, Shaw & McClay, Pitts., 1985-88, Kilpatrick & Cody, Washington, 1988—91, ptnr., 1991, Kilpatrick & Stockton, Atlanta and Washington, 1999; ptnr., employee benefits practice Venable LLP, Washington. Editor (lead articles): The Tax Lawyer; contbr. articles to profl. jours. Fellow Am. Coll. Employee Benefits Counsel; mem. ABA (co-chmn. Employee Benefits Com., Labor & Employment Law sect.), State Bar Ga., DC Bar Assn., Phi Beta Kappa, Phi Kappa Phi, Phi Alpha Theta. Democrat. Office: Venable LLP 575 7th St NW Washington DC 20004 Office Fax: 202-344-8300. Business E-Mail: mjwagner@venable.com.

WAGNER, MARY ANN, human resources executive; b. St. Louis, May 24, 1947; d. John Gerard and Carmela Lucy (Cozza) Blethroad; 1 child, John Patrick. BA, Webster U., St. Louis, 1979, MA, 1982. Tchr. Our Lady of Fatima, St. Louis, Wetterau, St. Louis; personnel mgr. Venture, St. Louis, 1979-81, customer svc. coord. O'Fallon, Mo., 1981-84, personnel mgr., 1984-86; regional personnel mgr., 1986-88; dir. tng. and devel., 1988-92; divsn. v.p. dir. of assoc. rels. May Merchandising, St. Louis, 1995-98; sr. v.p. human resources Meier & Frank, Portland, Oreg., 1998-2001; sr. v.p. May Mdse. Co., St. Louis, 2001—06; sr. v.p. human resources Federated Retail Holdings, Inc., St. Louis, 2006—. Adj. prof. Webster U., 1990-95. Bd. of Dir., Daniel Webster Soc.; v.p. State Bd. of Dir., Interventional Svc. Orgn. for Young Women; bd. of Dir., Urban League Mem. AAIM Mgmt. Assn., Am. Soc. Tng. and Devel., Am. Mgmt. Assn. Roman Catholic. Avocations: antiques, music, sports. Home: 325 Perceval Dr Saint Charles MO 63304-5708 Office Phone: 314-342-6547.

WAGNER, MARY MARGARET, library and information scientist, educator; b. Mpls., Feb. 4, 1946; d. Harvey F.J. and Yvonne M. (Brettner) W.; m. William Moore, June 16, 1978; children: Lebohang Y.C., Nora M. BA, Coll. St. Catherine, St. Paul, 1969; MLS, U. Wash., 1973; PhD, U. Minn., 2003. Asst. libr. St. Margarets Acad., Mpls., 1969-70; libr. Derham Hall High Sch., St. Paul, 1970-71; youth worker The Bridge for Runaways, Mpls., 1971-72; libr. Guthrie Theater Reference and Rsch. Libr., Mpls., 1973-75; asst. br. libr. St. Paul Pub. Libr., 1975; prof. dept. info. mgmt. Coll. St. Catherine, St. Paul, 1975—. Del. Minn. Gov.'s Pre-White House Conf. on Librs. and Info. Svcs., 1990; mem. Minn. Pre-White House Program Com., 1989-90, Continuing Libr. Info. and Media Edn. Com. Minn. Dept. Edn., Libr. Devel. and Svcs., 1980-83, 87-2002; mem. cmty. faculty Met. State U., St. Paul, 1980—; mem. core revision com. Coll. St. Catherine, 1992-93, faculty budget adv. com., 1992-95, faculty pers. com., 1989-92, 2001-04, acad. computing com. 1991-96, ednl. policies com., 1998-01; chair curriculum subcom. Minn. Vol. Cert. Com., 1993—. Contbr. articles to profl. jours. Bd. dirs. Christian Sharing Fund, 1976-80, chair, 1977-78. Recipient Bonnie Jean Keley and Jean Kelly award Faculty Excellence, 2006; grantee U.S. Embassy, Maseru, Lesotho, Africa, Brit. Consulate, Maseru, Fed. Inst. Mus. and Libr. Scis., various founds., Upper Midwest Assn. for Intercultural Edn. travel grantee Assoc. Colls. Twin Cities. Fellow: Higher Edn Consortia for Urban Affairs (bd. dirs. 1998—2007); mem.: ALISE (chair internat. rels. com. 2001—03), ALA (libr. book fellows program 1990—91), Minn. Ednl. Media Orgn., Minn. Libr. Assn. (pres. 1981—82, chair continuing edn. com. 1987—90, steering com. Readers Adv. Roundtable 1989—91), Spl. Libr. Assn., Am. Soc. Indexers, Am. Soc. Info. Sci. Office: Coll St Catherine Dept Info Mgmt 2004 Randolph Ave Saint Paul MN 55105-1750 Office Phone: 651-690-6843. Business E-Mail: mmwagner@stkate.edu.

WAGNER, MARY S., education center administrator; b. Jamestown, ND, May 13, 1948; d. Thomas Charles Heydweiller and Lila Mae Clemens; m. David Wagner (div.); children: Kristen, James. BS, Cameron U., 1982; MBA, Okla. City U., 1984; graduate, Army Mgmt. Staff Coll., 1995; EdD, Nova Southeastern U., 1998. Cert. tchr. Okla., 1982. Adminstrv. asst. Electronics Command, Ft. Monmouth, NJ, 1972—74, Army Audit Agy., Frankfurt, Germany, 1974—80, Civilian Pers. Office, Ft. Sill, Okla., 1980—83; guidance counselor Army Edn. Ctr., Germany, 1983—86; test specialist Military Entrance Processing Sta., Springfield, Mass., 1986—88; vocat. aptitude battery, 1988—90; edn. svcs. officer 415 Base Support, Bn. Kaiserstlantern, Germany, 1990—96, Western Corridor, Republic of Korea, 1996—97, Area Support Group, Kuwait, 1997—. Named Vol. of Yr., Boy Scouts Am., 1986; recipient Outstanding Svc. award, Area Support Group, Kuwait, 2005, Commdrs. medal, U.S. Army, 1991. Avocations: reading, travel, cooking. Office: Area Support Group Kuwait Edn ASG Kuwait APO AE 09366 Business E-Mail: mary.wagner@arifian.arcent.army.mil.

WAGNER, NORMAN JOSEPH, III, chemical engineering educator, researcher; b. Phila., Aug. 7, 1962; s. Norman Joseph and Gertrude Eugene (Mamrod) Wagner; m. Sabine Banerjee, Dec. 21, 1990. BS, Carnegie Mellon U., 1984; PhD, Princeton U., 1989. Collaborator Los Alamos Nat. Lab., US Dept. Energy, 1986—96, dir.'s postdoctoral, 1990; NATO postdoctoral fellow U. Konstanz, Germany, 1988-89; asst. prof. U. Del., Newark, 1991-95, assoc. prof., 1995—99, prof., 1999—, Alvin B. and Julia O. Stiles prof., 2005—. Rschr. Ctr. for Molecular and Engring. Thermodynamics, 1995—; guest prof. Inst. Polymer Physics, Swiss Fed. Inst. of Tech., Zurich, Switzerland, 1997, Dept. Physics, U. Konstanz, Germany, 1997—98; Robert W. Vaughan Lectureship Calif. Inst. Tech., 1998; vis. scholar Dept. Physics, U. Rome, 2004. Sect. editor Current Opinion in Colloid & Interface Science, 2001—, editl. bd. Rheologica Acta, 2001—, Journal of Polymer Science Part B: Polymer Physics, 2002—, Particles & Particle Systems Characterization, 2004—, Journal of Rheology, 2005—; contbr. articles to profl. jours. Named to Upper St. Clair HS Alumni Hall of Fame, 2002; recipient Presdl. Young Investigator Award, NSF, 1991, DuPont Young Faculty Award, 1995, 1996, 1997, Fulbright Sr. Scholar Award, 1997, Paul A. Siple Meml. Award, 2002. Mem.: AAAS, Neutron Scattering Soc. of Am., Materials Rsch. Soc., Am. Physical Soc., Am. Soc. Engring. Edn., Am. Chem. Soc. (Local Sect. Award, Del. Sect. 2006), Soc. Rheology, Am. Inst. Chem. Engrs., Fulbright Soc., Delta Phi Alpha. Achievements include patents in field of Shear Thickening Fluid Containment in Polymer; Advanced Body Armor Utilizing Shear Thickening Fluids, 2005. Office: U Del Dept Chem Engring 224 Colburn Lab Newark DE 19716 Office Phone: 302-831-8079. Office Fax: 302-831-4466. E-mail: wagnernj@udel.edu.

WAGNER, PAUL ANTHONY, JR., education educator; b. Pitts., Aug. 28, 1947; s. Paul A. and Mary K. Wagner; m. Kerry Wagner; children: Nicole S., Eric P., Jason G., Emily Ryanne. BS, N.E. Mo. State U., 1969; MEd, U. Mo., 1972; MA in Philosophy, 1976, PhD in Philosophy of Edn., 1978. Internal expeditor electromotive div. GM, La Grange, Ill., 1970-71; instr. Moberly Jr. Coll., Mo., 1972-73, U. Mo., Columbia, 1973-78, acting dir. instl. rsch. and planning, 1990-92, dir. univ. self study, 1991-92; instr. Mo. Mil. Acad., 1978-79; prof. edn., philosophy U. Houston-Clear Lake, Atrium Cir. disting. rsch. prof., 1980, dir., Inst. Logical and Cognitive Studies, 1980—, chancellor's disting. svc. prof., 1985, dir., project in profl. ethics, 1989—, chmn., dept. edn. found., 2003—, founding doctoral faculty mem., 2006—. Judge Sears Intercollegiate Ethics Bowl, Dallas, 1998; pres. Wagner & Assoc. Ednl. Consulting, 1988-93; dir. Tex. Ctr. for Study Profl. Ethics in Tchg., 1988-95; rsch. assoc. Ctr. for Moral Devel., Harvard U., 1985-86; vis. scholar Stanford U., Palo Alto, Calif., 1981; cons. total quality mgmt. Golden Gate U., 1992-93, M.D. Anderson Cancer Ctr. and Hosp., 1992-93, U. Houston-Victoria, 1993; cons. strategic planning Houston Chronicle Newspaper, 1997; chair So. Accreditation of Coll. and Sch. steering com. U. Houston, Clear Lake, 1990-93, pres. faculty senate, 1999-2001; chair planning and budgeting com., 1996-98, Univ. Life com., 2003-2007, Houston Tenneco Marathon, 1992-94; dir. U. Gifted Acad.; steering com. Trilateral Conf. and Supershow Greater Human Partnership, 1994-95; cons., ethics trainer Am. Leadership Forum, 1995-98; chair Tchr. Cert. Coun. 2000-; planning com. Tex. Ethics in Govt. Ann. Conf., 1995-98;; adj. prof. ethical theory U. Houston, 2000—; faculty exec. com. U. Houston Sys., 1999-2001, chair univ. life com., 2003—, faculty senate exec. comm., 1999— dept. chair Ednl. Found., 2003—, mem. doctoral faculty, 2005—, mem. grad. faculty, 1990—; adj. prof. bus. mgmt. U. Houston, Victoria, chmn. edn. dept., 2003—; cons. in field Author: (with F. Kierstead) The Ethical Legal and Multicultural Founds. of Teaching, 1992, Understanding Professional Ethics, 1996, Wagner-Kierstead Moral Self-Assessment Protocol, 2d edit., 2002; co-author: Educational Leadership as Moral Architecture, 2007; contbr. articles to profl. jours. on sci. edn., mgmt. theory and philosophy of edn.; mem. editl. bd. Jour. of Thought, 1981-85, Focus on Learning, 1982-85; editl. cons. Instrnl. Scis., 1981-83; editl. assoc. Brain and Behavioral Scis., 1985. Vice-chmn. Human Rights Com., Columbia, Mo., 1978-79; Sunday sch. tchr. Mary Queen Cath. Ch., Friendswood, Tex., 1979-85; founding bd. dir. Bay Area Symphony Soc., 1983-85; capital campaign com. Soc. Prevention Cruelty to Animals, 1989-91; publicity com. Am. Cancer Soc., Houston chpt., 1989-92; cons. in strategic planning M.D. Anderson Cancer Ctr. vol. divsn., 1992-93; steering com. City of Houston Emerging Bus. Conf., 1994-95, Trilateral Conf., Greater Houston Partnership, 1994-95; active Houston Bus. Promise; chair strategic planning com. Leadership Houston, 1996-98; bd. dirs. Houston Vol. Ctr., Leanna Spraianno Dance Co., 1999-2002, Baker Inst., 1998-2001, chair, 1999-2001; bd. dirs. Hope Village Friendswood, Tex.; ann. leadership briefing com. Rice U., 2001-03; mem. Linda Lorelle Scholarship Com., 1995—, Project Grad Coordinating Coun., 1994-96, pres., 1995-96; emcee, expert commentator for pub. TV, Channel 8, Houston, 1989-2002. Sgt. Mo. N.G., 1970-76; mem. choir Queen of Angels Cath. Ch., Dickinson, Tex., 2003—. Recipient Cert. of Appreciation, City of Columbia, 1978; K.E. Graessle scholar, 1968, Mo. Peace Studies Inst. grantee, 1971. Mem. AAUP, Assn. Applied and Profl. Ethics, Am. Assn. Pub. Adminstrs. (ethics com.), Am. Philos. Assn., Assn. Philosophers in Edn. (exec. bd., v.p.), Philosophy of Edn. Soc. (exec. sec.-treas., hospitality chair 1995-96), Am. Ednl. Studies Assn., Philosophy Sci. Assn., S.W. Philosophy Edn. Soc., Tex. Network for Tchr. Tng. in Philosophy for Children (bd. dirs. 1983-90), Tex. Ctr. for Ethics in Edn. (bd. dirs. 1990-98), Tex. Ednl. Found. Soc. (pres. 1995-98), Tex. Assn. Coll. Tchrs., So. Assn. Colls. Coord., Houston Bar Assn. (steering com. NAFTA Conf. 1993-94), Informal Logic Assn., Leadership Houston, Friends Hermann Pk., Clearlake Cir. (chair 1979-85), Phi Delta Kappa, Kappa Delta Pi. Roman Catholic. Avocations: running, reading, opera, ballet. Home: RR 4 Box 217 Navasota TX 77868-9413 Office: U Houston 2700 Bay Area Blvd Rm 338 Houston TX 77058-1002 Office Phone: 281-283-3571. Business E-Mail: wagner@cl.uh.edu.

WAGNER, PAULA, film company executive, film producer; b. Youngstown, Ohio, 1948; m. Robin Wagner (div.); m. Rick Nicita, 1984. BFA in Drama, Carnegie-Mellon U. Agent Creative Artist Agy.; cofounder (with Tom Cruise) Cruise/Wagner Productions, 1993—; CEO United Artists Corp., 2006—. Actress on & off Broadway, (TV miniseries) Loose Change, 1978; co-author: Out of Our Father's House; prodr.: (films) Mission: Impossible, 1996, Without Limits, 1998, Mission: Impossible II, 2000, Vanilla Sky, 2001, The Last Samurai, 2003, Suspect Zero, 2004, Elizabethtown, 2005, Ask the Dust, 2006, Mission: Impossible III, 2006; exec. prodr.: The Others, 2001, Narc, 2002, Shattered Glass, 2003, War of the Worlds, 2005; prodr.: (TV miniseries) Nightmares and Dreamscapes: From the Stories of Stephen King, 2006. Bd. trustees Carnegie-Mellon U.; bd. dir. Nat. Film Preservation Found., UCLA Sch. Theater, Film and TV. Co-recipient Nova award for outstanding achievement by new or emerging prodr. in theatrical motion pictures, Producer's Guild, 1997; named one of 100 Most Powerful Women in Entertainment, Hollywood Reporter, 2006. Office: United Artists Corp 0250 Constellation Blvd Los Angeles CA 90067 *

WAGNER, RANDY SUSAN, travel company executive; b. 1952; BA Art History, U. Penn., BE; ME, Boston U.; Phd. ABD ednl. psychology, Fordham U. Staff psychologist United Cerebral Palsy Assn.; worked for Citibank, Chrysler, American Express, Exxon, Campbell Soup and Colgate-Palmolive; exec. v.p., internat. account dir. Leo Burnett; corp. v.p. of strategic global brand ktg. McDonald's Corp.; chief mktg. officer Orbitz LLC, 2005—. Spkr. in field. Named a Woman to Watch, Crain's Chgo. Bus., 2007. Office: Orbitz LLC 500 W Madison Ave Ste 1000 Chicago IL 60661 Office Phone: 312-894-5000. Office Fax: 312-894-5001. *

WAGNER, RAYMOND THOMAS, JR., lawyer, legal association administrator; b. St. Louis, June 8, 1959; s. Raymond T. and Loretto (Muenster) W.; m. Ann L. Trousdale, Feb. 20, 1987. BA, St. Louis U., 1981, MBA, 1984; JD, U. Mo., Kansas City, 1985; LLM in Taxation, Washington U., St. Louis, 1993. Bar: Mo. 1985, Ill. 1986, U.S. Supreme Ct. 1989, U.S. Tax Ct. 1989. Legal rsch. and writing instr. U. Mo., Kansas City, 1983-84; law clk. to chief justice Mo. Supreme Ct., Jefferson City, 1985-86; assoc. Gilmore & Bell, St. Louis, 1986-87, Suelthaus & Kaplan P.C., St. Louis, 1987-89; gen. counsel Mo. Dept Revenue, 1989-90; counsel to gov. State of Mo., Jefferson City, 1990-91; dir. revenue Mo. Dept. Revenue, 1991-93; counsel Armstrong Teasdale Schlafly & Davis, St. Louis, 1993; dir. revenue Ill. Dept Revenue, Springfield, 1993-95; legal and legis. v.p. Enterprise Rent-A-Car, St. Louis, 1995—; mcpl. judge City of Ballwin, Mo., 1999—2005. Adj. prof. law LLM taxation program sch. law Washington U., St. Louis, 1993—; adj. prof. tax law Fontbonne U., St. Louis, 2002-03; chmn. Gov.'s Ethics Com., 1991-92, Mo. Hwy. Reciprocity Commn., 1991-93; commr. Multistate Tax. Commn., 1991-93, Mo. Mil. Adv. Commn., 1991-93; mem. IRS Oversight Bd., 2003-, chmn., 2004-06. Precinct capt. Gravois Twp., Webster Groves, 1988; bd. dirs. Shelter the Children, St. Louis, 1988-95; bd. dirs. Foster Care Coalition St. Louis, 1995-2002, pres. 1998-2000; chmn. platform com. Mo. Rep. Conv., 1992; exec. bd. dirs. St. Louis U. Sch. Bus.; mem. chancellor's coun. U. Mo., St. Louis, 1998—. Mem. ABA, Ill. Bar Assn., Mo. Bar Assn., Bar Assn. Met. St. Louis (chmn. law student svcs. com. 1986-87, chmn. social com. 1987-88, mem. exec. com. young lawyers assn. 1988-89, co-chmn. administrv. law com., govt. liaison com. young lawyers sect. 1989-90, chmn. legis. com. 1991-2004, legal svcs. oversight commn. 2001-), Regional Commerce and Growth Assn. (vice chair pub. policy coun. 1996, chair pub. policy coun. 1998-2000, vice chair govt. affairs exec. com. 2000-02), Associated Industries Mo. (bd. dirs. 1996-2003), Mo. C.of C. (bd. dirs. 1998-2004). Republican. Roman Catholic. Home: 313 Saint Andrews Ct Ballwin MO 63011-2504 Office: Enterprise Rent-A-Car 600 Corporate Park Dr Saint Louis MO 63105-4204 Office Phone: 314-512-5000. E-mail: rwagner@erac.com.

WAGNER, RICHARD E., economist, educator; b. Jamestown, ND, Apr. 28, 1941; s. Herbert and Dorothy Mae King; m. Barbara Helen (Westgate) W., June 9, 1962; children: Stephanie Wagner Tice, Valerie Wagner Smith. AA, Fullerton CC, Calif., 1961; BS, U. So. Calif., 1963; PhD, U. Va., 1966. Asst. prof. econs. U. Calif., Irvine, 1966-68, Tulane U., New Orleans, 1968-73; prof. econs. Va. Poly. Inst. and State U., Blacksburg, 1973-79, Auburn (Ala.) U., 1979-81, Fla. State U., Talahassee, 1981-88; Holbert L. Harris prof. econs. George Mason U., Fairfax, Va., 1988—. Sr. fellow, chmn. acad. adv. bd. Pub. Interest Inst., Mt. Pleasant, Iowa, 1995—. Author: Democracy in Deficit, 1977, To Promote the General Welfare, 1989, The Economics of Smoking, 1991, Trade Protection in the United States, 1995, Fiscal Sociology and the Theory of Public Finance, 2007; editor: Public Choice and Constitutional Economics, 1988, Charging for Government, 1991, Limiting Leviathan, 1999, Federalist Government in Principle and Practice, 2001, Politics, Taxation, and The Rule of Law, 2002, Fiscal Sociology and the Theory of Public Finance, 2007. Mem. Am. Econ. Assn., So. Econ. Assn. (exec. com. 1987-88), Internat. Inst. Pub. Fin., Internat. Soc. New Indtl. Econs., Pub. Choice Soc. Home: 11845 Clara Way Fairfax Station VA 22039 Office: George Mason U Dept Econs Fairfax VA 22030 Office Phone: 703-993-1132. Business E-Mail: rwagner@gmu.edu.

WAGNER, ROBERT, actor; b. Detroit, Feb. 10, 1930; m. Natalie Wood, Dec. 28, 1957 (div. April 27, 1962); m. Marion Marshall Donen; 1 child, Kate; remarried Natalie Wood, July 16, 1972 (dec. Nov. 29, 1981); 1 child, Courtney; m. Jill St. John, 1990. Films include: Halls of Montezuma, The Frogmen, Let's Make It Legal, With a Song in My Heart, What Price Glory?, Stars and Stripes Forever, The Silver Whip, Titanic, Star of Tomorrow, Beneath the 12-Mile Reef, Prince Valiant, Broken Lance, White Feather, A Kiss Before Dying, The Mountain, The True Story of Jesse James, Stopover Tokyo, In Love and War, Say One For Me, Between Heaven and Hell, The Hunters, All the Fine Young Cannibals, Sail a Crooked Ship, The Longest Day, The War Lover, The Condemned of Altona, Harper, Banning, The Biggest Bundle of Them All, The Pink Panther, The Curse of the Pink Panther, Winning, The Affair, The Towering Inferno, Critical List, Dragon: The Bruce Lee Story, Overdrive, 1997, Austin Powers-International Man of Mystery, 1997, Wild Things, 1998, No Vacancy, 1999, Love and Fear, 1999, The Kidnapping of Chris Burden, 1999, Austin Powers: The Spy Who Shagged Me, 1999, Crazy in Alabama, 1999, Forever Fabulous, 2000, The Calling, 2001, Jungle Juice, 2001, Austin Powers in Goldmember, 2002, El Padrino, 2004, Little Victim, 2005, Hoot, 2006 (voice) Everyone's Hero, 2006; starred in TV series It Takes a Thief, Switch!, Hart to Hart (Golden Globe nominee), Lime St.; produced, starred in TV series Madame Sin; formed Robert Wagner Prodns.; other TV appearances include: Streets of San Francisco, The Ox-Bow Incident, Gun In His Hand, And Man Created Vanity, The Enemy on the Beach, Runaway Bay, How I Spent My Summer Vacation, Name of the Game, City Beneath the Sea, Cable Car Mystery, To Catch a King, Cat on a Hot Tin Roof, Indiscreet, 1988, Seinfeld, 1990, Becoming Dick, 2000, The Retrievers, 2001, Rocke's Red Glare, 2000-01; Movies of the Week There Must Be a Pony, Love Amongst Thieves, This Gun for Hire.

WAGNER, ROBERT EARL, retired agronomist; b. Garden City, Kans., Mar. 6, 1921; s. Fay Arthur and Margaret (Longbottom) W.; m. Bernice Bittner, Aug. 7, 1948; children— Robert Earl, James Warren, Douglas Alan. BS, Kans. State Coll., 1942; MS, U. Wis., 1943, PhD, 1950. Forage crops specialist Ft. Hays Expt. Sta., Hays, Kans., 1943—45; assoc. agronomist Plant Industry Sta., U.S. Dept. Agr., Beltsville, Md., 1945—48, rsch. agronomist, asst. project leader pasture and range project, 1951—54, rsch. agronomist, project leader we. pasture and range project, 1954—56; prof., head dept. agronomy U. Md., 1956—59; regional dir. Am. Potash Inst., 1959—66; v.p. Am. Potash Inst., Found. Internat. Potash Rsch., 1966—67; dir. Coop. Ext. Svc., U. Md., 1967—75; pres., bd. dirs. Potash Inst., 1975—77, Potash and Phosphate Inst., 1977—88, pres. emeritus, 1988—; chmn., bd. dirs. Potash & Phosphate Inst. Can., 1975—88; pres., bd. dirs. Found. for Agronomic Rsch., 1980—87; owner Wagner Performance Cattle, Stone Mountain, Ga., 1985—. Bd. dirs. mem. exec. com. Internat. Fertilizer Devel. Ctr., 1975-98; chmn. Nat. Ext. Com. on Orgn. and Policy; mem. U.S. del. 7th Internat. Grassland Congress, New Zealand. Author tech., popular publs.; Editor: Proc. Sixth Internat. Grassland Congress. Chmn. fin. com. Parks Springs Retirement Cmty., 2005—06. Recipient Medallion award Am. Forage and Grassland Coun., Disting. Grasslander award, 1994; award Md. Farm Bur.; Disting. Svc. award in agr. Kansas State U., 1985, Disting. Alumnus award, 1990; Cert. of Disting. Citizenship, State of Md.; Robert E. Wagner Efficient Agr. award established in his honor; Disting. Grasslander award Am. Forage and Grassland Coun., 1994; named to Am.'s Registry of Outstanding Profls., 2003. Fellow AAAS, Am. Soc. Agronomy (chmn. grassland com., exec. com., bd. dirs., pres. N.E. br.), Crops Sci. Soc. Am., Soil Sci. Soc. Am.; mem. Grassland Coun. (pres.), Am. Soc. Range Mgmt., Cosmos Club (Washington), Atlanta Athletic Club, Sigma Xi, Alpha Zeta, Gamma Sigma Delta, Phi Kappa Phi Presbyterian. Home: 1495 Parkview Blvd Stone Mountain GA 30087-1016 Office: 655 Engineering Dr Norcross GA 30092-2822

WAGNER, ROBERT WALTER, photographer, communications educator, film producer, consultant; b. Newport News, Va., Nov. 16, 1918; s. Walter George and Barbara Anne Wagner; m. Betty Jane Wiles, Nov. 21, 1948; children: Jonathan R., Jeffrey A., Jennifer J. BSc, Ohio State U., 1940, MA, 1941, PhD, 1953. Motion picture writer-dir. Office War Info., NYC and Washington, 1942-43; writer-dir. Office Coord. Interam. Affairs for South and Ctrl. Am., 1943-44; chief info. Divsn. Mental Hygiene, Ohio Dept. Pub. Welfare, 1944-46; dir. divsn. motion pictures Ohio State U., Columbus, 1946-58, prof. comms., photography and cinema, 1960—, chmn. dept. photo-cinema, 1966-74. Pres. Univ. Film Found., 1979-85; writer, dir. James Thurber's Columbus Town, 1990, Images of the Depression, 1990; writer, prodr. TV series The Last of the Silents, 1975; internat. cons. comms.; bd. dirs. Am. Film Inst., 1974-81; mem. faculty U. So. Calif., 1958-59, U. P.R., 1961, 66, 68, San Jose State U., 1967, Ariz. State U., 1971, Concordia U., Montreal, 1980, 81, Danish Nat. Film Sch., 1983, 94, Emerson Coll., Boston, 1987. Author film series: Series of Motion Picture Documents on Communication Theory and New Educational Media, 1966; co-author: The American Tintype, 1999; editor: Education of Film Maker, 1975; co-producer: Cognizant Media, Studio City, Calif., 1997, The View from Malabar, 2000; curator: The Art of Humane Propaganda, Columbus Mus. of Art, 2001, Pioneers of The American Tintype, Columbus Mus. of Art, 2003, Photography in The Midwest, Encl. of The Midwest, 2007; author: Not On Your Tintype, 2005. Recipient Disting. Svc. award Columbus Cmty. Film Coun., 1986, Disting. Svc. award Ohio State U., 1988, Ohiana Pegasus award, 1985; Ency. Brit. fellow, 1953; Sr. Fulbright fellow, Peru, 1976. Fellow Soc. Motion Picture and TV Engrs. (Eastman Gold Medal award 1981); mem. Acad. TV Arts and Scis. (Disting. Svc. award 1966), Univ. Film/Video Assn. (bd. editors jour. 1975-85, editor jour. 1956-75), Internat. Congress Schs. Cinema and TV (v.p. 1964-82), Assn Ednl. Comm. and Tech. (bd. editors jour. 1976—), Torch Club (Columbus, pres. 1996). Home: 1353 Zollinger Rd Columbus OH 43221-2939

WAGNER, ROBIN SAMUEL ANTON, stage and set designer; b. San Francisco, Aug. 31, 1933; s. Jens Otto and Phyllis Edna (Smith-Spurgeon) W.; children: Kurt, Leslie, Christie. Student, Calif. Sch. Fine Arts, 1953-54. Pres. Scarab Prodns., Inc., 1975—; prof. theatre arts Columbia U., 1988—; sr. v.p. The Design Edge, 1989—. Adv. com. Broadway Theatre Inst. Set designer (Broadway plays) The Condemned of Altona, 1966, Galileo, 1967, The Trial of Lee Harvey Oswald, 1967, Hair, 1968, Lovers and Other Strangers, 1968, The Cuban Thing, 1968, The Great White Hope, 1968, Promises Promises, 1968, The Watering Place, 1969, My Daughter, Your Son, 1969, Gantry, 1970, The Engagement Baby, 1970, Lenny, 1971 (Drama Desk award, outstanding set design, 1971), Jesus Christ Superstar, 1971, Inner City, 1971, Sugar, 1972, Lysistrata, 1972, Seesaw, 1973, Full Circle, 1973, Mack & Mabel, 1974, The Fifth Dimension with Jo Jo's Dance Factory, 1974, A Chorus Line, 1975, Hair, 1977, On the Twentieth Century, 1978 (Tony award, best scenic design, 1978, Drama Desk award, outstanding scenic design, 1978), Ballroom, 1978, Comin' Uptown, 1979, 42nd Street, 1980, Dreamgirls, 1981 (Drama Desk award, outstanding set design, 1982), Merlin, 1983, Song and Dance, 1985, Teddy & Alice, 1987, Chess, 1988, Jerome Robbins' Broadway, 1989, City of Angels, 1989 (Tony award, best scenic design, 1990, Drama Desk award, outstanding set design, 1990), Crazy for You, 1992, Jelly's Last Jam, 1992, Angels in America: Millennium Approaches, 1993, Angels in America: Perestroika, 1993, Victor/Victoria, 1995, Big, 1996, The Life, 1997, Side Show, 1997, Saturday Night Fever, 1999, Kiss Me, Kate, 1999 (Tony award, best scenic design, 2000, Drama Desk award, outstanding set design of a musical, 2000), The Wild Party, 2000, The Producers, 2001 (Tony award, best scenic design, 2001, Drama Desk award, outstanding set design of a musical, 2001), Flower Drum Song, 2002, The Boy From Oz, 2003, Never Gonna Dance, 2003, A Chorus Line, 2006, (plays) Resurrection Blues, 2006, (off-Broadway) Putting It Together, Hamlet 90, In White America, View from the Bridge, Mahogony, The Prodigal, Between Two Theives, Cages. Mem. adv. bd. Nat. Corp. Theatre Fund, Theatre Adv. Coun. for City of N.Y.; mem. art adv. com. N.Y. Internat. Festival of the Arts; bd. trustees N.Y. Shakespeare Festival. Recipient Theatre World award, 1975, Outer Circle Critics award, 1978, 90, 92, 00, Maharam award, 1973, 75, 82, Lumen award, 1975, Dramalogue award, 1980, Boston Critics award, 1974, 92, award for excellence in theatre Ensemble Studio Theatre, 1990, Dora award, 1995, New Eng. Theatre Conf. 1996 Lifetime Achievement award, En Garde Arts honoree, N.Y.C., 1996. Mem. United Scenic Artists Elected to The Theatre Hall of Fame, 1999. Office: Robin Wagner Studio 890 Broadway New York NY 10003-1211

WAGNER, ROD, library director; b. Oakland, Nebr., Sept. 14, 1948; s. Francis Lynn and Doris Jean (Egbers) W.; m. Diane Kennedy, June 14, 1969; children: Jennifer, Brian, James. BA Social Sci. Edn., Wayne State Coll., Nebr., 1970; MA Polit. Sci., U. Nebr. Lincoln, 1971; MA Libr. Sci., U. Mo., 1981. Rsch. coord. Nebr. Libr. Commn., Lincoln, 1972, planning, evaluation, rsch. coord., 1972-73, adminstrv. asst., 1973-74, dep. dir., 1974-87, dir., 1988—. Bd. dirs. Nebr. Universal Svcs., 1998-2006. Mem. state govt. coun. Nebr. Info. Tech. Commn., 1999—. With U.S. Army N.G., 1970-77. Mem. ALA (contbr. yearbook 1981-84), Assn. Specialized and Cooperative Libr. Agys. (bd. dirs. 1998-2000), Nebr. Libr. Assn. (pres.-elect 1993-94, pres. 1994-95), Chief Officers State Libr. Agys. (dir. 2006-08), Western Coun. State Librs. (pres. 1992-93). Presbyterian. Office: NE Libr Commn 1200 N St Ste 120 Lincoln NE 68508-2023 Office Phone: 402-471-4001. Business E-Mail: rwagner@nlc.state.ne.us.

WAGNER, ROY, anthropology educator, researcher; b. Cleve., Oct. 2, 1938; s. Richard Robert and Florence Helen (Mueller) W.; m. Brenda Sue Geilhausen, June 14, 1968 (div. Dec. 1994); children: Erika Susan, Jonathan Richard. AB, Harvard U., 1961; AM, U. Chgo., 1962, PhD, 1966. Asst. prof. anthropology So. Ill. U., Carbondale, 1966-68; assoc. prof. Northwestern U., Evanston, Ill., 1969-74; prof. U. Va., Charlottesville, 1974—, chmn. dept., 1974-79. Mem. cultural anthropology panel NSF, Washington, 1981-82. Author: (novels) Habu, 1972, The Invention fo Culture, 1975, Lethal Speech, 1978, Symbols That Stand for Themselves, 1986, An Anthropology of the Subject, 2001. Social Sci. Research Council faculty research grantee, 1968; NSF postdoctoral research grantee, 1979. Fellow Am. Anthropol. Assn. Avocation: flying hot air balloons. Home: 726 Cargil Ln Charlottesville VA 22902-4302

WAGNER, SAMUEL ALBIN MAR, state agency administrator; b. Brighton, Colo., Feb. 23, 1942; s. Jacob Doer and Leota Garnet (Wilson) W.; m. Donna Dee Person, Mar. 20, 1987; children: Kurt, Andrea, Autumn, Jan, Arthur. BA in History, U. Colo., 1964, MA in History, 1965; STB (MTS) in History of World Religions, Harvard U., Cambridge, Mass., 1968; cert. in archival adminstrn., U. Denver, 1978. cert. records mgr. 1983; cert. archivist 1994. Archival asst. Harvard U. & Harvard Bus. Sch., 1965-68; asst. curator we. hist. collections U. Colo., 1968-70; sr. asst. archivist Cornell U., Ithaca, NY, 1971-73; city archivist City of Providence, 1978-80; state records analyst Wyo. State Archives, Cheyenne, 1979-83; pres. Records Mgmt. Cons. Internat., 1983—; records mgr. Ft. Collins Police Dept., Colo., 1984-87; pub. records adminstr. State RI, Providence, 1987-90; asst. prof. master archival studies program U. BC, Vancouver, Canada, 1990-93; prodr. community access Sta. JCTV, Jefferson City, 1994-96; chief NJ Bur. Records Mgmt., Trenton, 1996—; pres. Historic Rsch. Svcs., Jefferson City, 1994—; dep. dir. divsn. archives and records mgmt. State NJ, Trenton, 2007—. Instr. Chapman, U., 1981-87, Colo. State U., 1985-87, Lincoln U., 1995-96, U. BC, 1990-93; speaker in field. Author: Brighton Reflections, 1976, Adams County: Crossroads of the West, 1977, Directory of Automated Records Management Systems, 1985-91, Crossroads of the West: A History of Brighton and the Platte Valley, 1977, The Fort Lupton Story, 1977, Adams County Colorado: A Centennial History, 2002, Moving Archives, 2002, Brighton Reflections, 2006; editor: Brighton Blade, Ft. Lupton Press, Colo., 1973-77; editor, records analyst Mo. State Archives, Jefferson City, 1994-96; contbr. articles to profl. jours, stories to anthologies. Officer, bd. dirs. Adams County Hist. Soc., 1973-77; county historian Adams County, Brighton, 1976-77; mem. Brighton Human Rels. Commn., 1977-78; bd. dirs. Brighton Bicentennial Com., 1975-76, Ft. Lupton Bicentennial Com., 1975-76, RI RSVP, 1978-80, mem. RI Pub. Records Adv. Coun., 1987-90, RI Hist. Records Adv. Bd., 1987-90; chmn. info. profls. legis. task force Freedom of Info. and Privacy Assn., 1991-93; chmn. oral history project Cole County Hist. Soc., 1996. Recipient Hist. Preservation award Adams County Hist. Soc., 1978, award Freedom of Info. and Privacy Assn., 1993; grantee Ethnic Heritage Project Colo. Humanities Coun., 1977, Humanities and Social Scis. U. BC, 1993, Nat. Historic Pub. & Records Commn., 1988-92; Ford Found. fellow, 1964-65. Mem. Assn. Records Mgrs. and Adminstrs. (pres. No. Colo. chpt. 1984-85, v.p. Ocean State chpt. 1987-90, bd. dirs., editor Vancouver chpt. 1991, bd. dirs. Ctrl. NJ chpt. 2000-, pres. 2002-04, bd. dirs. Ctrl. South Jersey chpt. 2004—), records mgmt. standards and glossary task forces, Mem. Yr. 1985, microcomputer/PC industry action com., chmn. 1984-86, editor Software Dir. 1985-91, co-chmn. tech. applications com. 1989-90, chmn. Archives ISG 1997-99, ISG mid-year seminar program com. 1998-2002, mgr. edn. sector 1999-2002), Inst. Cert. Records Mgrs. (regional coord., exam proctor, grader 1982-, cert. records mgr. 1983), Soc. Am. Archivists (com. automated records and techniques 1990-94, select com. task force on automated records and techniques 1994-98, chmn. MicroMARC users group 1994-96, rep. joint SAA-ARMA Com. 1995-97), Nat. Assn. Govt. Archivists an Records Adminstrs., Archives Assn. B.C. (freedom of info. and privacy legis. com. 1990-93), Assn. Can. Archivists (electronic records select com. 1991-93, Acad. Cert. Archivists (outreach com. 1996-98, mem. commn. on future of archival enterprise 1999-2000), Pub. Sector Mgrs. Assn., Am. Civil Liberties Union, Nature Conservancy, Am. Hist. Soc. of Germans from Russia (charter mem.), Mid-Atlantic Regional Archives Conf. (program com. 1999-2000, 2002-, mem. local arrangements com. 2003—). Democrat. Unitarian Universalist. Avocations: history, art, photography, filmmaking. Home: 387 N 6th Ave Brighton CO 80601 Office Phone: 609-530-3204. Business E-Mail: albin.wagner@sos.state.nj.us.

WAGNER, SANDRA M., lawyer; b. Utica, NY; BA, St. Lawrence U., Canton, NY, 1974; JD, U. San Diego, 1977. Bar: Calif. 1981, U.S. Dist. Ct. (no. dist.) Calif. 1981, U.S. Tax Ct. 1981. Assoc. Law Offices Timothy A. Tosta, San Francisco, 1981—83, Law Offices Jesse W. Jack, San Jose, Calif., 1983—87; ptnr. Froman and Wagner LLP, San Diego, 1999—2003; pvt. practice Cupertino, Calif., 1987—89, San Diego, 1990—98, 2003—. Author, editor: AILA's 12th Annual California Chapters Conference Handbooks, AILA's 15th and 16th Annual California Chapters Conference Handbooks. Cub Scout leader Boy Scouts Am., Solana Beach, Calif., 1991—97, Boy Scout leader, 1994—. Recipient Scout Leader Recognition award, Del Mar Solana Beach Optimist Club, 1993, 1994, 1998, Dist. award Merit, Boy Scouts Am., 1996, Silver Beaver award, 2002. Mem.: Am. Immigration Lawyers Assn. (chair San Diego chpt. 2002—03, vice chmn. San Diego chpt. 2006—07, chair San Diego chpt. 2007—), Order of Arrow (mem. election com. 1999—), Rotary (mem. svc. com. 2000—), Sigma Delta Pi. Avocations: camping, backpacking, rock climbing, music. Office: 12625 High Bluff Dr Ste 302 San Diego CA 92130 Business E-Mail: swagner@wagnerimmigrationlaw.com.

WAGNER, THOMAS EDWARD, academic administrator, educator; b. Lexington, Ky., Dec. 6, 1937; s. Thomas Caney and Gaynell (Waggoner) W.; m. Susan Adell Brant, Sept. 3, 1960; children: Brant, Brian, Jennifer. BS, U. Cin., 1962; MA, Miami U., Oxford, Ohio, 1967; EdD, U. Cin, 1973. Tchr. Finneytown Sch. Dist., Cin., 1962—67; admissions officer U. Cin., 1967—70, summer sch. dean, 1970—73, asst. to pres., 1973—74, asst. v.p., 1974—77, vice provost faculty affairs, 1977—85, sr. vice provost, 1985—91, dean for undergrad. and student affairs, 1987—91, v.p. student affairs and svcs., 1991—94, prof. planning, 1983—2000, prof. emeritus, 2000—. Mem. adv. com. The Collegeboard, N.Y.C., 1989-91. Author 3 books; contbr. articles to profl. jours and chpts. to books. Bd. dirs. Charter Com., Cin., 1985-88, Inroads, Cin., 1990-96, Presbyn. Child Welfare Agy., 1992-98, Buckhorn Children's Ctr., 1992-98; mem. steering com. Cin. Youth Collaborative, 1988-91; active Fernald Citizens Adv. Bd., 1993—. With USAFR, 1955-63. Fulbright fellow, 1992, USIA rsch. fellow, 1997. Fellow Ctr. for Dispute Resolution, Soc. for Values in Higher Edn. Presbyterian. Avocations: reading, sports, photography. Home: 1086 W Galbraith Rd Cincinnati OH 45231-5612 Office: Univ Cin Sch of Planning PO Box 210016 Cincinnati OH 45221-0016

WAGNER, TODD, Internet company executive; Grad., Ind. U., U. Va. CPA Tex. Co-founder, CEO broadcast.com. (now Yahoo! Broadcast), 1995—; co-owner, CEO 2929 Entertainment. Founder Todd Wagner Found., 2000—; founder, co-chmn. Content Partners, LLC; bd. trustees Am. Film Inst., Tribeca Film Inst.; spkr. in field. Guest appearances on CNBC and CNN, featured in Wall Street Journal, Fortune, NY Times, Business Week and Variety, actor, exec. prodr. (films) Akeelah and the Bee, 2006; exec. prodr.: (TV series) Star Search, 1983, The Benefactor, 2004; (films) Searching for Debra Winger, 2002; exec. prodr.: (films) Godsend, 2004; exec. prodr.: (films) Criminal, 2004, Enron: The Smartest Guys in the Room, 2005, The Jacket, 2005, Good Night, and Good Luck, 2005; exec. prodr.: (films) One Last Thing..., 2005; exec. prodr.: (films) The War Within, 2005, Herbie Hancock: Possibilities, 2006, The Architect, 2006, Diggers, 2006; exec. prodr.: (films) Fay Grim, 2006. Bd. dir. After-School All Stars Dallas. Named Man of Yr., 2000, Social Entrepreneur of Yr., Dallas Ctr. for Nonprofit Mgmt., 2002, Kappa Sigma Man of Yr., 2003; named one of Forbes' Richest Americans, 2006; recipient Trailblazer Award, Dallas Film Festival, 2004, Dallas CASA's Champion of Kids, 2005, First Star Visionary award. Office: Yahoo Broadcast 2914 Taylor St Dallas TX 75226-1908 also: Todd Wagner Found 3008 Taylor St Dallas TX 75226 E-mail: twagner@2929entertainment.com.

WAGNER, WILLIAM GERARD, dean, information scientist, consultant, physicist, investment manager; b. St. Cloud, Minn., Aug. 22, 1936; s. Gerard C. and Mary V. (Cloone) W.; m. Janet Agatha Rowe, Jan. 30, 1968 (div. 1978); children: Mary, Robert, David, Anne; m. Christiane LeGuen, Feb. 21, 1985 (div. 1989); m. Yvonne Naomi Moussette, Dec. 4, 1995. BS, Calif. Inst. Tech., 1958, PhD (NSF fellow, Howard Hughes fellow), 1962. Cons. Rand Corp., Santa Monica, Calif., 1960-65; sr. staff physicist Hughes Research Lab., Malibu, Calif., 1960-69; lectr. physics Calif. Inst. Tech., Pasadena, 1963-65; asst. prof. physics U. Calif. at Irvine, 1965-66; assoc. prof. physics and elec. engring. U. So. Calif., LA, 1966-69, prof. depts. physics and elec. engring., 1969—, dean div. natural scis. and math. Coll. Letters, Arts and Scis., 1973-87, dean interdisciplinary studies and developmental activities, 1987-89, spl. asst. automated record services, 1975-81; founder program in neural, informational & behavioral scis., 1982—. Chmn. bd. Malibu Securities Corp., L.A., 1971—; cons. Janus Mgmt. Corp., L.A., 1970-71, Croesus Capital Corp., L.A., 1971-74, Fin. Horizons Inc., Beverly Hills, Calif., 1971—; allied mem. Pacific Stock Exch., 1974-82; fin. and computer cons. Hollywood Reporter, 1979-81; mem. adv. coun. for emerging engring. techs. NSF, 1987-89; cons. Wagner Tech.

Solutions, L.A., 2001—. Contbr. articles on physics to sci. publs. Richard Chase Tolman postdoctoral fellow, 1962—65. Mem.: Am. Phys. Soc., Nat. Assn. Security Dealers, Sigma Xi. Home: 183 Beloit Ave Los Angeles CA 90049-3007 Office: U So Calif Hedco Neurosci Bldg Los Angeles CA 90089-0001 Office Phone: 213-740-7839. Business E-Mail: wwagner@usc.edu.

WAGO, MILDRED HOGAN, retired municipal official; b. NYC, Aug. 16, 1918; d. Andrew James and Gunhild (Olsen) Hogan; m. Charles Leonard Wago, Nov. 24, 1949 (dec.); children: Linda G., Richard Herbst, Charlene C., and William Decker. Grad. bus. sch., White Plains, NY. Clk. Met. Life Ins. Co., NYC, 1938-50; publican Town of North Castle, Armonk, NY, 1960—2001. Mem. N.Y. State Assn. Receivers and Collectors (v.p. 1983-2001), Westchester County Assn. Receivers and Collectors (v.p., pres. 1987—), Nat. Assn. Exec. Females. Republican. Home: 3 Wago Ave Armonk NY 10504-1447

WAGONER, ANNA MILLS S., prosecutor; b. 1949; BA, Agnes Scott Coll.; JD, Wake Forest U. Assoc. Woodson, Linn, Sayers, Lawther, Short and Wagoner, 1975—87, ptnr., 1987—90; chief judge Dist. 19-C, NC, 1990—2001; US atty. (mid. dist.) NC US Dept. Justice, 2001—. Office: US Attys Office PO Box 1858 Greensboro NC 27402 *

WAGONER, DAVID EVERETT, lawyer, arbitrator; b. Pottstown, Pa., May 16, 1928; s. Claude Brower and Mary Kathryn (Groff) W.; children: Paul R., Colin H., Elon D., Peter B., Dana F.; m. Jean Morton Saunders; children: Constance A., Jennifer L., Melissa J. BA, Yale U., 1950; LLB, U. Pa., 1953. Bar: D.C. 1953, Pa. 1953, Wash. 1953. Law clk. U.S. Ct. Appeals (3d cir.), Pa., 1955-56; law clk. U.S. Supreme Ct., Washington, 1956-57; ptnr. Perkins & Coie, Seattle, 1957-96. Panel mem. of arbitration forum worldwide including People's Republic of China, B.C. Internat. Comml. Arbitration Ctr., Hong Kong Internat. Arbitration Centre, London Ct. Internat. Arbitration, AAA's Internat. Ctr. Dispute Resolution, CPR Inst. Dispute Resolution. Mem. sch. com. Mcpl. League Seattle and King County, 1958—, chmn., 1962-65; mem. Seattle schs. citizens coms. on equal ednl. opportunity and adult vocat. edn., 1963-64; mem. Nat. Com. Support Pub. Schs.; mem. adv. com. on community colls., to 1965, legislature interim com. on edn., 1964-65; mem. community coll. adv. com. to state supt. pub. instrn., 1965; chmn. edn. com. Forward Thrust, 1968; mem. Univ. Congl. Ch. Council Seattle, 1968-70; bd. dirs. Met. YMCA Seattle, 1968; bd. dirs. Seattle Pub. Schs., 1965-73, v.p., 1966-67, 72-73, pres., 1968, 73; trustee Evergreen State Coll. Found., chmn. 1986-87, capitol campaign planning chmn.; trustee Pacific NW Ballet, v.p. 1986. Served to 1st lt. M.C., AUS, 1953-55 Fellow Coll. Comml. Arbitrators, Am. Coll. Trial Lawyers (mem. ethics com., legal ethics com.), Chartered Inst. Arbitrators, Singapore Inst. Arbitrators; mem. ABA (chmn. standing com. fed. jud. improvement, chmn. appellate advocacy com., mem. commn. on separation of powers and jud. independence), Wash. State Bar Assn., Seattle-King County Bar Assn., Acad. Experts, Swiss Arbitration Assn., Nat. Sch. Bds. Assn. (bd. dirs., chmn. coun. Big City bds. edn. 1971-72), English-Speaking Union (v.p. Seattle chpt. 1961-62), Chi Phi. Office: Internat Arbitration Chambers US BankCtr 1420 5th Ave Fl 22 Seattle WA 98101-4087 Home: 1633 Broadmoor Dr E Seattle WA 98112-3747 Office Phone: 206-224-2872. E-mail: email@davidwagoner.com.

WAGONER, DAVID RUSSELL, writer, educator; b. Massillon, Ohio, June 5, 1926; s. Walter Siffert and Ruth (Banyard) W.; m. Patricia Lee Parrott, July 8, 1961 (div. June 1982); m. Robin Heather Seyfried, July 24, 1982; children: Alexandra Dawn, Adrienne Campbell. BA in English, Pa. State U., 1947; MA in English, Ind. U., 1949. Instr. English DePauw U., 1949-50; instr. Pa. State U., 1950-53; asst. prof. U. Wash., 1954-57, assoc. prof., 1958-66, prof., 1966-2000, prof. emeritus, 2000—. Elliston lectr. U. Cin., 1968; editor Poetry NW, 1966-02; poetry editor Princeton U. Press, 1977-81, Mo. Press, 1983— Author: (poetry books) Dry Sun, Dry Wind, 1953, A Place to Stand, 1958, The Nesting Ground, 1963, Staying Alive, 1966, New and Selected Poems, 1969, Working Against Time, 1970, Riverbed, 1972, Sleeping in the Woods, 1974, Collected Poems, 1976, Who Shall Be the Sun?, 1978, In Broken Country, 1979, Landfall, 1981, First Light, 1983, Through the Forest, 1987, Walt Whitman Bathing, 1996, Traveling Light: Collected and New Poems, 1999, The House of Song, 2002, Good Morning and Good Night, 2005; (novels) The Man in the Middle, 1954, Money, Money, Money, 1955, Rock, 1958, The Escape Artist (also film 1982), 1965, Baby, Come on Inside, 1968, Where is My Wandering Boy Tonight?, 1970, The Road to Many a Wonder, 1974, Tracker, 1975, Whole Hog, 1976, The Hanging Garden, 1980; editor: Straw for the Fire: From the Notebooks of Theodore Roethke, 1943-63, 1972. Recipient Morton Dauwen Zabel prize Poetry mag., 1967, Blumenthal-Leviton-Blonder prize, 1974, 2 Fels prizes Coordinating Coun. Lit. Mags., 1975, Tietjens prize, 1977, English-Speaking Union prize, 1980, Sherwood Anderson award, 1980, Union League Prize, 1987, Ruth Lilly Poetry prize, 1991, Levinson prize, 1994, Pacific N.W. Booksellers award, 2000, Arts Fund Lifetime Achievement award, 2007; Guggenheim fellow, 1956, Ford fellow, 1964, Nat. Inst. Arts and Letters grantee, 1967, Nat. Endowment for Arts grantee, 1969 Mem. Acad. Am. Poets (chancellor 1978—2000), Soc. Am. Magicians, Nat. Assn. Blackfeet Indians (asso.) Home: 5416 154th Pl SW Edmonds WA 98026-4348 Office: U Wash PO Box 354330 Seattle WA 98195-4330 E-mail: renogawd@aol.com.

WAGONER, JENNINGS LEE, JR., historian, educator; b. Winston-Salem, NC, July 26, 1938; s. Jennings Lee and Carolyn Nelme (Phifer) W.; m. Shirley Canady, Aug. 12, 1962; children: David Carroll, Brian Jennings. BA, Wake Forest U., Winston-Salem, NC, 1960; MAT, Duke U., Durham, NC, 1961; PhD, Ohio State U., Columbus, 1968. Tchr. High Point Pub. Schs., NC, 1960-62; instr. Wake Forest U., 1963-65; tchg. assoc. Ohio State U., Ohio, 1965-68; from asst. prof. to prof. history of edn. U. Va., Charlottesville, Va., 1968—2005; dir. Ctr. for Study Higher Edn., 1975-85, chmn. leadership and policy studies, 1985-87; disting. prof. Curry Sch. Edn. U Va., Va., 1987, William C. Parrish Jr. Endowed prof. Va., 1994—96; prof. emeritus, 2005—. Vis. research scholar Harvard U., 1972, U. Calif., Berkeley, 1984; vis. prof. Monash U., Melbourne, Australia, 1992. Author: Thomas Jefferson and the Education of a New Nation, 1976, Jefferson and Education, 2004; co-author: American Education: A History, 1996, 3d edit., 2004; co-editor: Changing Politics of Education, 1978: editl. bd. History of Edn. Quar., Ednl. Studies jour.; contbr. articles to profl. jours. Recipient Disting. Prof. award Univ. of Va. Alumni Assoc., 1996, Sesquicentennial fellow U. Va., 1972, 84, 90. Mem. History of Edn. Soc. (pres. 1983-85, bd. dirs. 1979-81), Am. Ednl. Rsch. Assn. (v.p. divsn. F 1981-83), Orgn. Am. Historians, Am. Ednl. Studies Assn. (bd. dirs.), Assn. Study Higher Edn., Raven Soc., Outward Bound, Kappa Delta Pi, Phi Delta Kappa, Omicron Delta Kappa (faculty advisor), Golden Key Nat. Honor Soc. Avocations: hiking, fishing, canoeing. Home: 468 Dry Bridge Rd Charlottesville VA 22903-7456

WAGONER, MICHAEL D., ophthalmologist; b. Dallas, Tex., Aug. 7, 1953; s. Charles and Jo Ann Wagoner; life ptnr. Barbara Elias. BS, U. Tex., 1975; MD, Baylor Coll. Medicine, 1978. Cert. med. intern St. Elizabeth's Hosp. of Boston,Tufts Med. Sch., 1979, ophthalmic pathology Mass. Eye and Ear Infirmary, Harvard Med. Sch., 1980, ophthalmology residency Mass. Eye and Ear Infirmary, Harvard Med. Sch., 1983, ophthalmology cornea and external disease Masschusetts Eye and Ear Infirmary, Harvard Med. Sch., 1985, ophthalmology bd. Am. Bd. of Ophthalmology, 1985. Asst. prof. of ophthalmology Harvard Med. Sch., Boston, 1985—99; prof. of clin. ophthalmology U. of Iowa, Iowa City, 1999—2002, adj. prof. of ophthalmology, 2006—. Dir., cornea and external disease svc. Mass. Eye and Ear Infirmary, Harvard Med. Sch., Boston, 1991—94; med. dir. King Khaled Eye Specialist Hosp., Riyadh, Saudi Arabia, 1995—99, 2002—. Author: (textbook) Atlas of Cornea Disease, Excimer Laser Surgery; contbr. articles to sci. jours., chapters to books. Recipient Honor award, Am. Acad. of Ophthalmology, 1992, Secretariat award, 2003, Sr. Achievement award, 2004. Mem.: Am. Acad. Ophthalmology (licentiate). Unitarian. Avocations: running, travel, popular culture. Home: 1451 Grand Ave Iowa City IA 52246 Office: King Khaled Eye Specialist Hospital One Arruba Rd Riyadh 11462 Saudi Arabia Home Phone: 319-358-1513; Office Phone: 966-1-482-1234 x2059. Office Fax: 966-1-482-1234 x3645. Personal E-mail: michaelwagoner625@yahoo.com. Business E-Mail: mwagoner@kkesh.med.sa.

WAGONER, RALPH HOWARD, academic administrator; b. Pitts., May 30, 1938; s. Richard Henry and Charlotte (Stevenson) W.; m. Wilma Jo Staup, Dec. 21, 1961; children: Amanda Jane, Joseph Ryan. AB in Biology, Gettysburg Coll., 1960; MS in Ednl. Adminstrn., Westminster Coll., 1963; PhD, Kent State U., 1967; postgrad., MIT, 1973, Dartmouth Coll., 1979. Prin., tchr., coach Williamsfield (Ohio) Elem. and Jr. High Sch., 1960-62; dir. elem. edn. Pymatuning Valley (Ohio) Local Schs., 1962-64, asst. supt. instrn., 1964-65; acad. counselor, asst. to dean coll. edn. Kent (Ohio) State U., 1965-66, instr. edn., 1966-67; asst. prof. Drake U., Des Moines, 1967-70, assoc. prof., 1970-71, chmn. dept. elem. edn., 1968-70, chmn. dept. tchr. edn., 1970-71, acad. adminstrn. intern Am. Council Edn., Office of Pres., 1971-72, asst. to pres., 1972-77, dir. devel., 1975-77; v.p. pub. affairs and devel., prof. Western Ill. U., Macomb, 1977-87, pres., 1987-93, Augustana Coll., Sioux Falls, SD, 1993—2000, Lutheran Ednl. Conf. of N.Am. Adj. prof. San Francisco Theol. Sem., 1971; mem. senate Drake U., 1968-77; sponsor interhall council Western Ill. U., 197893, mem. BOG/UPI task force on incentives for faculty excellence, co-chmn., faculty mentor, 1985-93; cons. in field. Co-author: (with L. Wayne Bryan) Societal Crises and Educational Response: A Book of Readings, 1969, (with Robert L. Evans) The Emerging Teacher, 1970, (with William R. Abell) The Instructional Module Package System, 1971, Writing Behavioral Objectives or How Do I Know When He Knows, 1971; contbr. articles to profl. jours. Chmn. Mid-Ill. Computer Consortium, 1980, 85, Western Ill. Corridor of Opportunity, 1987-93; mem. Pres.' Regional Adv. Coun., 1977-87; mem. investments com. McDonough County YMCA; mem. exec. com. Macomb Area Indsl. Corp.; trustee Robert Morris Coll., 1983-88, Chgo. and Carthage, Ill., 1983-88; bd. dirs. Ill. Coun. Econ. Edn., 1987-93, McDonough County United Way Dr., 1980-82; bd. trustees The Cornerstone Found. LSS of Ill., 1990-96; mem. Sioux Falls Tomorrow Task Force, 1993-94; bd. dirs. S.D. Symphony, 1993—, Edn. Telecomms. State of S.D., 1993—, Sioux Falls Devel. Found., 1993—, Children's Inn, 1993—, Sioux Valley Physicians Alliance, 1995—, LECNA, 1996—; life trustee Lutheran Social Svcs., 1996—. Recipient Man of Yr. award Andover Rotary Club, 1964, Quax Honor award, 1969-70, Disting. Alumni award Gettysburg (Pa.) Coll., 1991; named McDonough County Citizen of Yr., Elks, 1982. Fellow Am. Coun. Edn. (cons. fund raising 1984-87); mem. Am. Assn. State Colls. and Univs. (com. econ. devel. 1988, com. on athletics 1987), Ednl. Computing Network (chmn. policy bd. 1985-87), Assn. Midcontinent Univs. (coun. dels. 1987-93), Gateway Conf. (coun. dels. 1987-93), Coun. for Advancement and Support of Edn. (discussion leader, speaker, 1975, 77, 80, 84, 86, 91, 92, 93, 94, Citation award 1981, 83, Grand award 1982, Bronze award 1985, Silver award 1986), Macomb C. of C. (exec. com., bd. dirs.), Ill. Chamber Econ. Devel. Policy Task Force, Blue Key (hon.), Omicron Delta Kappa, Phi Eta Sigma (hon.), Phi Mu Alpha. Lodges: Rotary. Lutheran. Office: Augustana Coll 2001 S Summit Ave Sioux Falls SD 57197-0001 Home: 6512 Evergreen Acres Dr Wentworth SD 57075-7316

WAGONER, RICK (G. RICHARD WAGONER JR.), automotive executive; b. Wilmington, Del., Feb. 9, 1953; BS in Econs., Duke U., 1975; MBA, Harvard U., 1977. Analyst in treas.'s office, mgr. Latin Am. financing, dir. Can. and overseas borrowing, dir. capital analysis and investment GM Corp., NYC, 1977-81, treas. Sao Paulo, Brazil, 1981-84, exec. dir. fin., 1984-87, v.p., fin. mgr., 1987-88, group dir. strategic bus. planning, 1988-89, v.p. fin. Zurich, Switzerland, 1989-91, pres. Brazil, 1992-93, head Worldwide Purchasing Group, 1993-94, exec. v.p., pres. N. Am. ops., 1994-98, pres., COO, 1998—2000, pres., CEO, 2000—03, chmn., CEO, 2003—. Bd. dirs GM Corp., 1998—. Chmn. bd. visitors Fuqua Sch. Bus. Duke U.; trustee Detroit County Day Sch. Mem. Soc. Automotive Engrs. (mem. VISION 2000 exec. com.). Office: GM Corp 300 Renaissance Ctr Detroit MI 48265-0001 *

WAGONER, ROBERT VERNON, astrophysicist, educator; b. Teaneck, NJ, Aug. 6, 1938; s. Robert Vernon and Marie Theresa (Clifford) W.; m. Lynne Ray Moses, Sept. 2, 1963 (div. Feb. 1986); children: Alexa Frances, Shannon Stephanie; m. Stephanie Brewster, June 27, 1987. BME, Cornell U., 1961; MS, Stanford U., 1962, PhD, 1965. Rsch. fellow in physics Calif. Inst. Tech., 1965-68, Sherman Fairchild Disting. scholar, 1976; asst. prof. astronomy Cornell U., 1968-71, assoc. prof., 1971-73; assoc. prof. physics Stanford U., 1973-77, prof., 1977—2004, emeritus prof., 2005—. George Ellery Hale disting. vis. prof. U. Chgo., 1978; mem. Com. on Space Astronomy and Astrophysics, 1979-82, theory study panel Space Sci. Bd., 1980-82, physics survey com. NRC, 1983-84; grant selection com. NSERC (Can.), 1990-93; mem., Kavli Inst. Particle Astrophysics Cosmology, 2004-; mem. visitors com. divsn. astron. scis. NSF, 2005 Contbr. articles on theoretical astrophysics and gravitation to profl. jours., mags.; co-author Cosmic Horizons, 1982; patentee in field. Sloan Found. rsch. fellow, 1969-71; Guggenheim Meml. fellow, 1979; grantee NSF, 1973-90, 2000-03, NASA, 1982-99. Fellow Am. Phys. Soc.; mem. Am. Astron. Soc., Internat. Astron. Union, Tau Beta Pi, Phi Kappa Phi Office: Stanford U Dept Physics Stanford CA 94305-4060 Home Phone: 650-493-4241; Office Phone: 650-723-4561. Business E-Mail: wagoner@stanford.edu.

WAGONER, WALTER DRAY, JR., lawyer; b. New Haven, Dec. 25, 1942; s. Walter D. and Mariana (Parcells) Wagoner; m. Rosa Nilda Morales, Jan. 22, 1980; children: David, William Carlos, Brenda, Lisa. BA, Yale U., 1965, LLB, 1970. Bar: Conn. 71, U.S. Dist. Ct. Conn. 71. Staff atty. New Haven Legal Assistance Assn., 1970—74, mng. atty., 1974—76, dir. legal edn., 1976—78; sole practice New Haven, 1978—. Chmn. New Haven City Commn. Cultural Affairs, 1977—79; trustee Conn. Pub. TV, 1977—83, U.S. Bankruptcy Ct. for Dist. Conn., 1983—87. Mem.: Conn. Bar Assn., Loizenos Club (hon.). Democrat. Office: 840 Elm St New Haven CT 06511-4010 Office Phone: 203-624-7759. E-mail: wdwagoner@yahoo.com.

WAH, BENJAMIN WAN-SANG, electrical and computer engineering educator; b. Hong Kong, Sept. 7, 1952; s. Hsien-Feng and Chi-Ching (Wong) W.; m. Christine Hai-Ling Lee, Nov. 4, 1981; children: Catherine Lih-Lien, Elaine Yin-Lien. BSEE, Columbia U., 1974, MSEE, 1975; MS in Computer Sci., U. Calif., Berkeley, 1976, PhD, 1978. Asst. prof. elec. engring. Purdue U., West Lafayette, Ind., 1979-84, assoc. prof. elec. engring., 1984-85; assoc. prof. elec. and computer engring. U. Ill., Urbana-Champaign, 1985-89, prof. elec. and computer engring., 1989—, Robert T. Chien disting. prof. engring., 1998—2003, Franklin W. Woeltge endowed prof. elec. and computer engring., 2004—. Program dir. NSF, Washington, 1988-89; Fujitsu vis. chair prof. intelligence engring. U. Tokyo, 1992; McKay vis. prof. U. Calif., Berkeley, 1994. Editor: Computers for Artificial Intelligence Applications, 1986 (Best Seller, Computer Soc. Press 1987, 88); contbr. articles to profl. jours. Recipient Lifetime Achievement award, R.T. Yeh, 2004. Fellow ACM, AAAS, IEEE (co-founder jour. 1988, editor-in-chief IEEE Trans. on Knowledge and Data Engineering, 1993-96), Soc. for Design and Process Sci.; mem. IEEE Computer Soc. (bd. govs. 1989-93, 96-97, treas. 1997, 2d v.p. publs. 1998, 1st. v.p. publs. 1999, pres. 2001, Tech. Achievement award 1998, W. Wallace-McDowell medal 2006), Pan Wen Yuan Found. (Outstanding Rsch. award, 2006, R.E. Merwin award, 2007). Avocations: bicycling, building computers, tennis. Office: Univ Ill Rm 456 CSRL 1308 W Main St Urbana IL 61801-2307 Office Phone: 217-333-3516. Office Fax: 217-244-7175. Business E-Mail: wah@uiuc.edu.

WAHINGTON, ANTHONY WILLIAM, volunteer coordinator; b. Balt., Md., July 20, 1976; s. Chester and Joyce Ann Washington. BS, Frostburg State U., 1999. Program mgr. Frostburg State U., Frostburg, Md., 2000—01; asst. dir. Frostburg State U., Ctr. for Volunteerism and Nat. Svc., 2001—02; stage crew Ctr. Stage Theatre, Balt., 2002; vol. coord. Md. Sci. Ctr., Balt., 2003—. Adv. bd. mem. Allen HallSTARS!, Frostburg State U., 2000—02; com. mem. Frostburg State U. Leadership Com., 2000—02; bd. mem. Frostburg State U. Pres. Bd on Affirmative Action and Equal Employment Opportunities, 2001—02. Com. mem. Spl. Olympics of Alleghany County, Cumberland, Md., 1999—2002, Am. Cancer Soc., Relay for Life, Frostburg, 2001—02. Recipient Pres. Student Svcs. award, Corp. for Nat. Comm. Svc., 2000, CEO award, 2001, Govs. Cert. for Volunteerism, Govs. Office on Svc. and Volunteerisms, 2000—02, Daily Point of Light award, Points of Light Found., 2004, Govs. citation, State of Md., 2004. Independent. Achievements include development of Thanksgiving sponsor a family program at Frostburg State U; the roots African Am. Theatre Org., Frostburg State U. Avocations: writing and performing poetry, volunteering, trumpet, bass, sports. Office: Md Sci Ctr 601 Light St Baltimore MD 21230 E-mail: twashington@mdsci.org.

WAHL, DONALD J., counseling administrator; BS in Transp., Travel & Tourism, St. Louis U., 1974; MA in Counseling Psychology cum laude, Chapman U., 1977; PhD in Counselor Edn. magna cum laude, St. Louis U., 1985. Lic. profl. counselor Mo., 1995, counselor Nat. Bd. Cert. Counselors, 1995, cert. group psychotherapist Nat. Registry Cert. Group Psychotherapists, 1996, sch. counselor Mo., 1999. Activities therapist St. Louis U., 1977—98; instr. Bevo Long and Nottingham Cmty. Schs., 1991—98; counselor, cons. Cath. Family Svcs., 1999, dir. Kenrick cmty. group program, 1999—2000; crisis counselor NW R-I Sch. Dist., Jefferson County, 1999—2002; dir. Youth Violence Prevention Project, St. Louis, 2002—, Family Therapy Program, 2003—; corp. cons. St. Louis Metro. Sewer Dist., 2006. Adj. prof. dept. behavioral scis. St. Louis C.C., 1999; adj. prof. U. Mo.; presenter in field. Prodr.: (website) Youth Violence Prevention Project. Cons. Youth Violence Prevention Project, 2002—07; mem. Children's Behavioral Health Coalition, 2003—07. 1st lt. USAF, 1974—76. Grantee, USAF, 1970—73. Mem.: Mo. Mental Health Counselors Assn., Partnership Against Violence Network, Am. Mental Health Counselors Assn. Achievements include development of Youth Violence Prevention Program Selection Tool. Home Phone: 314-781-6801; Office Phone: 314-652-6004 3013. Personal E-mail: jeffcoproject@hotmail.com.

WAHL, GEOFFREY MYLES, biology professor; b. LA, Apr. 6, 1948; s. Alfred Wahl and Bertha Snyder; m. Barbara Anne Parker, Apr. 6, 1948; children: Matthew, Allison. BA in Bacteriology, UCLA, 1970; PhD, Harvard U., Cambridge, 1976. Rsch. asst. prof., biology dept. U. Utah, Salt Lake City, 1975—76; postdoctoral fellow, biochemistry dept. Stanford U., Calif., 1976—79; asst. prof. Salk Inst. Biol. Studies, La Jolla, Calif., 1979—84, assoc. prof., 1984—87, sr. mem., 1987—89, prof., 1989—. Adj. assoc. prof., dept. biology U. Calif., San Diego, 1985—89, adj. prof., dept. biology, 1989—; editl. bd. mem. DNA Repair, Molecular Cancer Rsch., 2002—. Mem.: NIH (mem. mammalian genetics study section 1986—88, mem. human genome spl. study section 1989), AAAS, Am. Cancer Soc. (ad hoc reviewer 1984—), Leukemia Soc. Am., Am. Assn. Cancer Rsch. (co-chair internat. meeting with Peter Jones 2002, co-chair internat. meet with Ki Hong 2003, program chair ann. meeting 2004, pres.-elect 2005, pres. 2006—). Achievements include patents for method for isolation of extrachromosomal amplified genes; FLP medicated gene modificaiton in mammalian cells, and compositions of cells usefulness; site-specific recombination in eukaryotes and constructs; compositions and methods for treatigns cells having double-minute DNA. Avocations: cooking, travel, photography, theater. Office: Salk Inst Biol Studies 10010 N Torrey Pines Rd La Jolla CA 92037

WAHL, ROSEMARIE, biologist, educator; d. Arnold Spencer and Rosemary Doyle Wahl; m. Michael Leroy Tumlinson, May 31, 1992; m. Miroslav Synek (div.); children: Mary Rose Synek, Thomas Robert Synek. BS, MIT, 1956; MS, U. Chgo., 1961, PhD, 1967. Instr. U. Ill., Chgo., 1965—66; asst. prof. Tex. Christian U., Ft. Worth, 1967—72; assoc. prof. St. Mary's U., San Antonio, 1976—83, prof., 1983—, chair dept. biol. scis., 1979—2004. Vis. asst. prof. U. Tex., Austin, 1972—75; chief advisor health professions St. Mary's U., 1979—2004, chair premed./predental adv. com., 1979—2004. Mentor, advisor on biotechnology, mayor, city ofcl. City of San Antonio, 1984—95. Recipient Disting. Faculty award, St. Mary's U. Sch. Sci., Engring and Tech., 1986. Mem.: Tex. Genetics Soc., Tex. Assn. Advisors for Health Professions (exec. com.), Am. Soc. Microbiology, Sigma Xi. Avocations: travel, culture, welfare of children and veterans. Office: St Marys U Dept Biol Scis 1 Camino Santa Maria San Antonio TX 78228 Office Phone: 210-431-8064. Business E-Mail: rwahl@stmarytx.edu.

WAHL, WILLIAM BRYAN, marketing professional, real estate company officer; b. Aurora, Colo., Dec. 17, 1963; s. Harold Edward Wahl and Dianne (Fowler) Armstrong. BBA in Mgmt., St. Edward's U., 1987; MBA in Gen. Bus., Kent Coll., 1991; PhD in Bus., U. San Moritz, 1999. Asst. store mgr. Handy Dan, Austin, Tex., 1981-88; real estate broker Powell/Armstrong Realty, Austin, 1985—88, S&W Realty, Austin, 1988—; nat. mktg. dir. Am. Home Products, Austin, 1988—; pres. Wahl Success Systems, Austin, 1989—, project mgr. applied materials, 1995—98; procurement mgr. Dell Computer Corp., 2000—; pres. O.H.S. Prodns., 2000—, Brigadier Group LLC, 2003—, Am. Healthcare Options LLC, 2003—. Bd. dirs. Pahl Enterprises, Austin, 1988—. Named Outstanding Citizen, Berkeley Davis, Inc., Berkeley, Calif., 1988. Mem. Austin Assn. Life Underwriters, Austin Bd. Realtors, Tex. Assn. Realtors, Nat. Assn. Realtors, Nat. Assn. Life Underwiters, Mktg. and Distributive Edn. Roman Catholic. Avocations: black belt in taekwondoe, golf, weightlifting. Home: 10305 Button Quail Cove Austin TX 78758 Personal E-mail: wassys@aol.com.

WAHLBERG, MARK, actor; b. Dorchester, Mass., June 5, 1971; s. Donald and Alma Wahlberg; children: Ella Rae, Michael. Singer (albums with Marky Mark and the Funky Bunch) Music for the People, 1991, You Gotta Believe, 1992; Appeared in films Renaissance Man, 1994, The Basketball Diaries, 1995, Fear, 1995, Boogie Nights, 1997, Traveller, 1997, The Big Hit, 1998, Three Kings, 1999, The Corruptor, 1999, The Yards, 1999, The Perfect Storm, 2000, The Planet of the Apes, 2001, Rock Star, 2001, The Truth About Charlie, 2002, The Italian Job, 2003, I Heart Huckabees, 2004, Four Brothers, 2005, Invincible, 2006, The Departed, 2006 (Best Supporting Actor, Nat. Soc. Film Critics, 2007), Shooter, 2007; (TV films) The Substitute, 1993; exec. prodr.: (films) Juvvies, 2004, (TV series) Entourage, 2004-07. Office: Cortina Bus Mgmt PO Box 610287 Newton MA 02461 *

WAHLBERG, PHILIP LAWRENCE, former bishop; b. Houston, Jan. 18, 1924; s. Philip Lawrence and Ella Alieda (Swenson) W.; m. Rachel Conrad, June 1, 1946; children: David, Christopher, Pauli, Sharon. AA, Tex. Luth. Coll., 1942, DD (hon.), 1963; BA, Lenoir Rhyne Coll., Hickory, NC, 1944, DD (hon.), 2005; MDiv, Luth. Theol. Sem., Columbia, SC, 1946. Ordained to ministry United Luth. Ch. in Am., 1946. Pastor St. Luke Luth. Ch., Thunderbolt, Ga., 1946-50, Redeemer Luth. Ch., Wilmington Island, Ga., 1946-50, St. Mark Luth. Ch., Corpus Christi, Tex., 1950-59; pres. Tex.-La. Synod, United Luth. Ch. Am., Austin, Tex., 1959-62; bishop

Tex.-La. Synod, Luth. Ch. Am., Austin, Tex., 1963-87; acting dir. devel. Luth. Outdoor and Retreat Ministries Southwest, 1987-88; legis. liaison Tex. Impact, Austin, 1989-91; interim coord. Regional Ctr. for Mission Evang. Luth. Ch. in Am., Dallas, 1991-92; mem. devel. staff Luth. Sem. Program in Southwest, 1992—2005; mem. com. on appeals, also chmn. Evang. Luth. Ch. in Am., 1988-95, hearing officer, 1995-98. Also mem. exec. coun. Luth. Ch. in Am., N.Y.C., 1980-87, chmn. com. on legal matters, 1984-87; mem. mgmt. com. Divsn. for Mission in N.Am., N.Y.C., 1972-80, chmn., 1972-76; bd. dirs. Bd. Am. Missions, N.Y.C., 1963-72, chmn., 1968-72; bd. dirs. Luth. Sch. Theology, Chgo., 1967-87. Author articles in religious jours., sermons; author theol. cassette, 1973. Named Disting. churchman Tex. Luth. Coll., 1978; Disting. Alumnus, Lenoir Rhyne Coll., 1962; named Man of Year, Thunderbolt, Ga. C. of C., 1950. Democrat. Avocations: winemaking, golf, choral singing. Office: 5804 Cary Dr Austin TX 78757-3108 Personal E-mail: phiwah@yahoo.com.

WAHLEN, EDWIN ALFRED, lawyer; b. Gary, Ind., Mar. 12, 1919; s. Alfred and Ethel (Pearson) W.; m. Alice Elizabeth Condit, Apr. 24, 1943 (div. 1983); children: Edwin Alfred, Virginia Elizabeth, Martha Anne; m. Elizabeth L. Corey, Nov. 23, 1984. Student, U. Ala., 1936-38; AB, U. Chgo., 1942, JD, 1948. Bar: Ill. 1948. Practiced in, Chgo., 1948—; mem. firm Haight, Goldstein & Haight, 1948-55; ptnr. Goldstein & Wahlen, 1956-59, Arvey, Hodes, Costello & Burman (and predecessor), 1959-91, Wildman, Harrold, Allen & Dixon, 1992—. Author: Soldiers and Sailors Wills: A Proposal For Federal Legislation, 1948. Served to 2d lt. AUS, 1942-46. Decorated Silver Star medal, Bronze Star medal. Mem. ABA, Ill. Bar Assn., Chgo. Bar Assn., Order of Coif, Phi Beta Kappa, Phi Alpha Delta. Home: 1250 Breckenridge Ct Lake Forest IL 60045-3875 Office: 225 W Wacker Dr Chicago IL 60606-1224

WAHLGREN, FRANCIS J., art appraiser; MA in Art History, Queens Coll., NY, 1985; attended, Parsons Sch. Design, NY, Am. Coll., Paris. With Christie's, NYC, 1987—, specialist in books and manuscripts, internat. dept. head. Catalogued and auctioned the Fox-Bute Set of Audubon's Birds of America (2000) for $8 million, a world auction record for any printed book. Office: Christie's/NY 20 Rockefeller Plz New York NY 10020 Office Phone: 212-636-2665. Office Fax: 212-636-4928. Business E-Mail: fwahlgren@christies.com.

WAHLQUIST, ANDREW FOLKMAN, government affairs executive; b. Ogden, Utah, Jan. 29, 1940; s. Keith Campbell and Ruth (Folkman) W.; m. Myrna Helen Kasparek, July 13, 1962; children: Kristin Diane, Andrea Katherine. BS in Comm., U. Utah, 1963. Asst. news dir. KCPX-TV & Radio, Salt Lake City, 1959-67; pub. relations asst. U.S. Steel, Pitts., 1967-72; nat. coord., Let's Clean Up Am. Office Sec. Interior, Washington; spl. asst. The White House, Washington, 1973-74, deputy asst. adminstr., 1974—76; pres. Commemorative Mktg., Washington, 1976; chief of staff to Senator John Warner US Congress, Washington, 1979-86; v.p. govt. relations, v.p. corp. relations Greenwich Air Services, Miami; v.p. bus. devel. Kellstrom Industries; ptnr. Alcalde & Fay, Arlington, Va., 2002—. Dir. Wolf Trap Assocs., Vienna, Va., 1995; mem., Salt Lake City C. of C.; commr. Va. Port Authority, Norfolk, 1994-97; guest lectr. U. Va., George Mason U., Am. U. Producer, writer (documentary) Utah Hoover Commission, 1970 (Utah Broadcasters award 1970), Scrapbook of a Grand Old Lady, 1968 (1st pl. award Utah Broadcasting 1968). Dir. Claude Moore Colonial Farm, McLean, Va., 1980—; dir. emeritus Fairfax (Va.) Symphony, 1980—; adminstr. Am. Revolution Bicentennial. Recipient George Washington medal Freedoms Found., Valley Forge, Pa., 1972, Man of Yr. award Utah Jaycees, Salt Lake City, 1966. Mem. Pub. Rels. Soc. Am., Soc. Profl. Journalists, Army and Navy Club Washington, Am. League Lobbyists. Republican. Mem. Lds Ch. Office: Alcalde & Fay 2111 Wilson Blvd Ste 850 Arlington VA 22201-3058 Office Phone: 703-841-0626. Office Fax: 703-243-2874. E-mail: wahlquist@alcalde-fay.com.

WAHLQUIST, BRENT T., federal agency administrator; b. Utah, Mar. 28, 1942; BS in Botany, MA in Botany, Brigham Young U.; PhD in Biology, N.Mex. State U. Prin. investigator, project mgr. on environ. studies for electric generating stations, transmission lines and coal mines Westinghouse Electric, 1971; prin. investigator, project mgr. Rocky Mountain Energy Corp., Carbon Fuel Corp., W.Va., 1978—82; dep. dir. W. Va. State Water Resources Divsn. and Reclamation Divsn., 1982—83; asst. dir. Office Surface Mining, US Dept. Interior, 1983—95, regional dir., Mid-Continent Region, 1995—99, regional dir. Denver, 1999—2002, regional dir., Appalachian Region, 2002—07, acting dir., 2005—07, dir., 2007—. Recipient Pres. Rank award for Meritorious Exec. Svc., 2005. Office: US Dept Interior Office Service Mining Reclamation 1849 C St NW Washington DC 20240 Office Phone: 202-208-3100. *

WAHOSKE, MICHAEL JAMES, lawyer; b. Ripon, Wis., June 4, 1953; children: Jennifer, John. BA with highest honors, U. Notre Dame, 1975, JD summa cum laude, 1978. Bar: Minn. 1978, U.S. Dist. Ct. Minn. 1979, U.S. Ct. Appeals (7th cir.) 1979, U.S. Ct. Appeals (8th and 9th cirs.) 1980, U.S. Ct. Appeals (10th cir.) 1982, U.S. Supreme Ct. 1982, U.S. Ct. Appeals (6th cir.) 1988, U.S. Ct. Appeals (fed. cir.) 1989, U.S. Ct. Appeals (D.C. cir.) 1992, U.S. Ct. Appeals (4th cir.) 1994, U.S. Ct. Appeals (11th cir.) 1996, Supreme Ct. of Winnebago Tribe of Nebr., 1996. Law clk. to judge Luther M. Swygert U.S. Ct. Appeals (7th cir.), Chgo., 1978-79; law clk. to chief justice Warren E. Burger U.S. Supreme Ct., Washington, 1979-80; assoc. Dorsey & Whitney, Mpls., 1980-85, ptnr., chmn., appellate practice, 1986—. Adj. prof. law U. Minn., Mpls., 1981-83. Exec. editor U. Notre Dame Law Rev., 1977-78; co-editor: Freedom & Education: Pierce v. Society of Sisters Reconsidered, 1978. Recipient Vol. Recognition award Nat. Assn. Attys. Gen., 1993, Spl. Recognition award, 2003; Supreme Ct. Reception honors State and Local Legal Ctr., 1991, 92, 93, 95. Fellow: Am. Acad. Appellate Lawyers; mem.: FBA, ABA (standing com. on Amicus Briefs 1997—2002), Hennepin County Bar Assn., Minn. Bar Assn., U.S. Ct. Appeals (8th cir.) Bar Assn., Phi Beta Kappa. Office: Dorsey & Whitney LLP Ste 1500 50 S Sixth St Minneapolis MN 55402-1498 Office Phone: 612-340-8755. Office Fax: 612-340-2868. Business E-Mail: wahoske.michael@dorsey.com.

WAHWEAH, LINDA MCNEIL, insurance agent, writer; b. Albuquerque, Apr. 2, 1955; d. Ernest Neil and Elizabeth Ann (Murane) Lemke; m. Eugene Gerald Wahweah, Feb. 14, 1979 (div. June 2001). Bus., Cannon's Internat. Bus. Coll., 1976. Legal sec. Manpower Gen. Dynamic, San Bernardino, Calif., 1980—82; ins. c.s.r. p.l. and comml. Ctrl. City Ins. Agy., San Bernardino, 1982—84; ins. office mgr. Bankers Life Ins., Riverside, Calif., 1984—85; ind. ins. agt. Am. Family Life Ins., Redlands, Calif., 1985—88; civil rights adv. Walker River Palute Tribe, Schurz, Nev., 1989—95; freelance writer Native Am. Civil Rights, San Clemente, Calif., 1996—2003; chronical specialist Native Am. Civil Union, San Bernardino, West Cajon, Calif., 2000—03. Promotor specialist Karaoke of Inland Empire, San Bernardino, 2000—03; council mem. Native Am. Civil Rights Union, 1992—95, fellow founder, 1993; freelance writer, 1989—. Author: Poetry's "Guardian" Best Poems and Poets of 2003. Organizer cmty. workshop Strike This, 2007; lobbyist Walker River Piaute Tribe, Schurz, Nev., 1993—95, civil rights adv. San Clemente, 1995—. Named World Champion Amateur Poet, Internat. Soc. Poets, 2002, No. Am. Poet of Merit, Internat. Libr. Poetry, 2002, New Country Female Vocalist, CCMA of Inland Empire, 1999; recipient Editor's Choice award, Internat. Libr. Poetry, 2003, Outstanding Achievement in Poetry award, Internat. Soc. Poets, 2004, Poet of Merit award, Internat. Soc. Poetry, 2005, 2006, 2007. Mem.: ACLU, San Bernardino County Bar Assn., European Soc. Lit., Humane Soc., Am. Poetry Assn., Am. Lit. Guild, N.Am. Fishing Club. Democrat. Ch. Of Christ. Avocations: writing, karoake, cooking, sewing. Office Phone: 909-379-5227. E-mail: lml9m@aol.com.

WAILAND, GEORGE, lawyer; b. Munich, Mar. 14, 1947; came to US, 1951; s. Max and Bella (Grylak) W.; m. Adele M. Rosen, Aug. 20, 1972; children: J. Zachary, William J. BS, NYU, 1969, JD, 1972. Bar: NY 1973, US Supreme Ct. 1976, US Dist. Ct. (so., ea. dists.) NY 1973, US Dist. Ct. (no. dist.) NY 1981, US Claims Ct. 1979, US Tax Ct., 1979, US Ct. Appeals (2d cir.) 1973, US Ct. Appeals (fed. cir.) 1982, US Ct. Appeals (4th cir. and 9th cir.) 1986, (10th cir.) 2007, US Ct. Appeals (7th cir.) 1987. Assoc. Cahill Gordon & Reindel LLP, NYC, 1972-80, ptnr., 1980—. John Norton Pomeroy scholar NYU, 1970. Home: 1050 Park Ave New York NY 10028-1031 Office: Cahill Gordon & Reindel LLP 80 Pine St Fl 17 New York NY 10005-1790 Office Phone: 212-701-3212. Business E-Mail: gwailand@cahill.com.

WAINIO, MARK ERNEST, insurance company consultant; b. Virginia, Minn., Apr. 18, 1953; BA, Gustavus Adolphus Coll., 1975. Cert. safety profl., assoc. loss control mgmt., assoc. risk mgmt., assoc. claims, CPCU. Carpenter ABI Contracting Inc., Virginia, 1975-77; co-owner Mesabi Builders, Albuquerque and Eveleth, Minn., 1977-79; sr. engring. rep. Aetna Life & Casualty, Albuquerque, 1979-86; loss control specialist CNA Ins. Cos., Albuquerque, 1986-91, loss control cons., 1991-94, mgr. loss control svcs., 1994-95, dir. loss control svcs., 1995-97, asst. v.p. loss control svcs., 1997-98, RSKCo a bus. unit, CNA Risk Mgmt., Albuquerque, 1998—99; asst. v.p. client svcs. RSKCo Cons. Svcs., Albuquerque, 1999—2003; client svc. dir. CNA Risk Control, Albuquerque, 2003—04, consulting dir., 2004—. Owner MEW Safety and Risk Mgmt., 1989—; pres. MW Enterprises, 1990—. Mem. Am. Soc. Safety Engrs., CPCU. Avocations: golf, fishing, hunting, swimming, Karate. Office: CNA 8500 Menaul Blvd NE Ste B560 Albuquerque NM 87112-1273 Business E-Mail: mark.wainio@cna.com.

WAINSCOTT, JAMES LAWRENCE, steel industry executive; b. LaPorte, Ind., Mar. 31, 1957; s. James J. and Frances J. (Cunningham) W. BS magna cum laude, Ball State U., 1979; MBA U. Notre Dame, 1987. CPA, Ind.; cert. mgmt. acct.; cert. internal auditor; cert. info. systems auditor; chartered fin. analyst. Sr. auditor Geo. S. Olive & Co., CPAs, Indpls. and Valparaiso, Ind., 1979-82; fin. mgr. Midwest div. Nat. Steel Corp., Portage, Ind., 1982-88, mgr. pension investments, Pitts., 1988-90, asst. treas., asst. sec., Pitts., 1991-92; treas., asst. sec., Mishawaka. Ind., 1993-95, v.p. & treas., AK Steel Holding Corp., Middletown, OH, 199598, CFO, AK Steel Holding Corp., 1998-99, sr. v.p., CFO, 1999-2003, pres. & CEO, 2003-, chmn. 2006-; cons. Edward J. Wainscott, CPA, LaPorte, Ind., 1982; instr. acctg. Purdue U.-Westville, 1980-82, Valparaiso U., 1980-84. Advisor Jr. Achievement, 1984; vol. Am. Cancer Soc., Valparaiso Income Tax Assistance Program, Valparaiso Community/Univ. Campaign; pres., treas. Midwest Steel Employees Fed. Credit Union; pres. Midwest Steel Employees Assn.; mem. Ball State U. Cardinal Connection; mem. N.W. Ind. Open Housing Council; chmn. dean's adv. council Valparaiso U.; bd. dirs. Youth Svc. Bur. St. Joseph County; chmn. fin. com. Good Shepherd Parish, Cin., 1999-2001. Mem. Ind. CPA Soc. (chmn. chpt. activities com. 1985-86, chpt. bd. dirs. 1983-86, chpt. pres. 1984-85, chmn. chpt. task force, Pres. award 1994, state bd. dirs. 1987-90), Nat. Assn. Accts. (chpt. bd. dirs. 1982-86, chpt. pres. 1983-84; Past Pres. award 1984), Am. Inst. CPA's, Inst. Mgmt. Acctg., Inst. Internal Auditors, Inst. Chartered Fin. Analysts, Assn. for Investment Mgmt. and Rsch., Chgo. Soc. Fin. Analysts, U. Notre Dame Exec. MBA Alumni Assn., Mensa, Blue Key, Golden Key, Intertel, Delta Sigma Pi. Roman Catholic. Avocations: music, chess, coin collecting, sports, travel. Office: AK Steel Holding Corp 703 Curtis St Middletown OH 45043 Home: 8099 Carnaby Ln Cincinnati OH 45249-1567 *

WAINSTEIN, KENNETH L., federal agency administrator, former prosecutor; b. Alexandria, Va., 1962; BA in Govt. and Internat. Rels., U. Va., 1984; JD, U. Calif., Berkeley, 1988. Corr., caseworker Office Congressman Carl D. Perkins, Washington, 1984; paralegal securities sect. Cleary, Gottlieb, Steen & Hamilton, Washington, 1984—85; summer assoc. for litigation, environ., tax and labor teams Hunton & Williams, Washington, 1986; summer assoc. for litigation, corp. and labor depts. Gibson, Dunn & Crutcher, Washington, 1987; law clk. for Hon. Thomas Penfield Jackson U.S. Dist. Ct. D.C., Washington, 1988—89; asst. U.S. atty. (So. dist.) NY US Dept. Justice, 1989—92, line prosecutor, dep. chief homicide sect. Washington, 1994—99, prin. asst. U.S. atty. DC, 1999—2000, interim U.S. atty. DC, 2001, dir. Exec. Office U.S. Attorneys, 2001—02; gen. counsel FBI, Washington, 2002—03, chief of staff, 2003—04; interim U.S. atty. DC US Dept. Justice, 2004—05, US atty. Washington, 2005—06, asst. atty. gen. for nat. security, 2006—. Mem.: Phi Beta Kappa. Office: US Dept Justice 950 Pennsylvania Ave NW Washington DC 20530 *

WAINWRIGHT, CARROLL LIVINGSTON, JR., retired lawyer; b. NYC, Dec. 28, 1925; s. Carroll Livingston and Edith Katherine (Gould) W.; m. Nina Walker, July 2, 1948; children: Delos Walker, Mark Livingston. AB, Yale U., 1949; LL.B., Harvard U., 1952. Bar: N.Y. 1953. Atty. Milbank, Tweed, Hadley & McCloy (and predecessor), NYC, 1952-58, 60-62, ptnr., 1963—2005; ret., 2005. Asst. counsel Gov. N.Y., 1959-60; mem. State Commn. Jud. Conduct, 1974-83; hon. dir. U.S. Trust Corp.; hon. trustee U.S. Trust Co. N.Y.; adj. prof. law Washington and Lee U. Sch. Law, 1991-97; mem. governing bd. N.Y. Cmty. Trust, 1991—2004. Hon. trustee Am. Mus. Natural History; trustee Edward John Noble Found.; trustee Boys' Club N.Y., 1966—, pres., 1986-94, hon. trustee, 1999; vice-chmn. Cooper Union Advancement Sci. and Art, 1988-95, hon. trustee; trustee Ch. Pension Fund and Affiliates, 1974-91, treas. 1974-78; mem. univ. coun. Yale U., 1978-81; mem. vestry Trinity Ch., N.Y.C., 1983-90; dir. Greater Yellowstone Coalition, 1992-98, 99—. Served with USMCR, 1943-46. Mem. ABA, N.Y. State Bar Assn., Assn. Bar City N.Y. (treas. 1970-73, v.p. 1975-76), Union Club, Down Town Assn. (pres. 1985-92), Maidstone Club (pres. 1970-73). Home: 57 Dunemere Ln East Hampton NY 11937-2705

WAINWRIGHT, DALE V., state supreme court justice; b. Tenn. m. Debbie Wainwright; 3 children. Studied, London Sch. of Economics, 1981; BA, Howard U., 1983; JD, U. Chgo. Law Sch., 1988. With Andrews & Kurth, Houston, Haynes & Boone, Houston; dist. judge. Harris County, 1999—2002; justice Tex. Supreme Ct., Austin, 2002—. Mem. Am. Law Inst., Tex. Commn. on Jud. Efficiency. Co-founder Aspiring Youth Program; bd. mem. Houston Volunteer Lawyers Program, Texas Young Lawyers Assn.; former pres. Houston Young Lawyers Assn. Recipient Legal Excellence award, NAACP, 2000. Fellow: Houston Bar Found., Tex. Bar Found.; mem.: ABA, Houston Bar Assn., State Bar Tex. Office: Tex State Supreme Ct PO Box 12248 Austin TX 78711 Office Phone: 512-463-1332. *

WAINWRIGHT, DAVID STANLEY, patent agent; b. New Haven, May 23, 1955; s. Stanley Dunstan and Lillian (Karelitz) W.;m. Catherine Demetra Kefalas, Aug. 11, 1984; children: Maxwell Stanley Hector, Eric George Alexander. BSc in Physics with 1st class honors, Dalhousie U., Halifax, NS, 1976; MSc in Physics, U. BC, Vancouver, 1979. Registered patent agt., U.S., Can. Model plant supr., scientist, technician Moli Energy Ltd., Maple Ridge, BC, Canada, 1978-84, project leader cell devel., 1984-88, cell devel. mgr., 1988-90, 1990-92, mgr. intellectual property, 1992-98; patent agt. Ballard Power Sys., Burnaby, BC, 1998—2005; sr. patent agent Cardiome Pharma Corp., Vancouver, Canada, 2005—06; IP specialist Questair Techs. Inc., Burnaby, Canada, 2006—. Contbr. articles to profl. jours. Mem. Patent and Trademark Inst. Can. Home: 2585 W 1st Ave Vancouver BC Canada V6K 1G8 Office: Questair Technologies Inc 6961 Russell Ave Burnaby BC Canada V5J 4R8 Office Phone: 604-453-6896. Business E-Mail: wainwright@questairinc.com.

WAINWRIGHT, GEORGE L., JR., retired state supreme court justice; b. Wilson County, NC, Dec. 10, 1943; s. George Sr. and Susan Wainwright; m. Carol McChesney; children: Kennon, Ashton. AB in Political sci., U. N.C., 1966; JD, Wake Forest U., 1984. Agribusiness and real estate positions, Wilson, 1966-81; atty. Wheatly, Wheatly, Nobles & Weeks, Beaufort, NC, 1986-90; judge Dist. Ct., 1991—94; resident Superior Ct. judge for N.C. Jud. Dist. 3B, 1994—98; justice NC Supreme Ct., 1999—2006. Served in U.S. Coast Guard Reserve, 1966—72. Morehead scholar, 1966. Mem. N.C. Bar Assn., Lookout Rotary Club. Presbyterian. Home: 5206 Driftwood Ln Morehead City NC 28557

WAINWRIGHT, MARCUS, apparel designer; b. Eng. m. Glema Neece. Grad., Wellington Coll., Eng. Co-founder, head designer Rag & Bone, NYC, 2001—. Recipient Ecco Domani Fashion Found. award, 2006, Swarovski award for Emerging Talent Menswear, Coun. Fashion Designers Am., 2007. Office: Rag & Bone LLC 80 W 40th St New York NY 10018 Office Phone: 212-278-8214. Office Fax: 212-287-8242. *

WAINWRIGHT, PAUL EDWARD BLECH, construction company executive; b. Annapolis, Md., Jan. 28, 1917; s. Richard and Alice Sorrel (Blech) W.; m. Helen Mae Rogers, July 10, 1941; children: Richard, Paul Edward Blech, John. BS in Civil Engring, Va. Mil. Inst., 1938. Cost engr. Turner Constrn. Co., NYC, 1938-40, cost engr., asst. supt., 1945-46; cost. engr. for contractors Pacific Naval Air Bases, Honolulu, 1940-42; with Dillingham Corp., Honolulu, 1946-82, asst. v.p., then v.p., 1961-69, group v.p. constrn., 1969-82; cons. constrn. Honolulu, 1982—. Bd. dirs. Hawaii Visitors Bur., 1967, Goodwill Industries Hawaii, 1965-70; pres. Citizens Adminstrn. of Justice Found., 1968, Hawaii Epilepsy Soc., 1975. Served with AUS, 1942-45. Decorated Legion of Merit, Bronze Star, Air medal. Mem. Am. Soc. Mil. Engrs., Beavers, Gen. Contractors Assn. Hawaii (pres. 1966), Hawaii C. of C. (dir. 1964-65), Waikiki Yacht Club, Outrigger Canoe Club. Republican. Episcopalian. Home: 4301 Providence Point Pl SE Issaquah WA 98029-6270

WAINWRIGHT, RUFUS, musician, singer; b. Rhinebeck, NY, July 22, 1973; s. Loudon Wainwright III and Kate McGarrigle. Singer: (albums) Rufus Wainwright, 1998 (Juno award for Best Alternative Album, 1999), Poses, 2001 (Juno award for Best Alternative Album, 2002), Want One, 2003, Want Two, 2004, Release the Stars, 2007, (with Kate & Anna McGarrigle) Love Over & Over, 1983, Heartbeats Accelerating, 1990, McGarrigle Hour, 1998, McGarrigle Christmas Hour, 2005, (soundtracks) Myth of Fingerprints, 1997, Big Daddy, 1999, I Am Sam, 2001, Moulin Rouge, 2001, Shrek, 2001, Brokeback Mountain, 2005; composer: (films) Meet the Robinsons, 2007; actor: (films) Tommy Tricker & the Stamp Traveller, 1988, Heights, 2004, The Aviator, 2004, The Age of Ignorance, 2007. Named Best New Artist, Rolling Stone, 1998. Office: MCT Mgmt Ste 2001 520 8th Ave New York NY 10018 also: c/o Sam Kirby William Morris Agy 1325 Ave of the Americas New York NY 10019 also: c/o Carla Sacks/Krista Williams Sacks & Co 427 W 14th St New York NY 10014 *

WAISANEN, CHRISTINE M., lawyer, writer; b. Hancock, Mich., May 27, 1949; d. Frederick B. and Helen M. (Hill) W.; m. Apr. 21, 1979; children: Jeffrey Hunt, Erick Hill. BA with honors, U. Mich., 1971; JD, U. Denver, 1975. Bar: Colo. 1975, D.C. 1978. Labor rels. atty. U.S. C. of C., Washington, 1976-79; govt. rels. specialist ICI Americas, Inc., Wilmington, Del., 1979-87; dir. cultural affairs City of Wilmington, 1987; founder, chief writer Hill, Katzenstein & Waisanen, 1988—. Chmn. Delaware State Coastal Zone Indsl. Control Bd., 1993—. Mem. Fed. Bar Assn., Jr. League of Wilmington (v.p. 1985-86), Women's Rep. Club of Wilmington (bd. dirs. 1988-93), U. Mich. Club of Del. (pres. 1999—). Republican. Presbyterian. Home: 1609 Mt Salem Ln Wilmington DE 19806-1134 Personal E-mail: cwais23@aol.com.

WAIT, CHARLES VALENTINE, banker; b. Albany, NY, May 28, 1951; s. Newman Edward Jr. and Jane Caroline (Adams) W.; m. Candace Ellin Hollar, May 27, 1978; children: Charles Valentine Jr., Christopher David, Alexandra Dallas Wait. BA, Cornell U., 1973; cert. in banking, Rutgers U., 1981; LHD (hon.), SUNY Empire State Coll., 2001. Asst. v.p. The Adirondack Trust Co., Saratoga Springs, NY, 1974, treas., 1978-81, sec., treas., 1981-84, pres., 1984—. Trustee NY Bus. Devel., 1997-2003; mem. Saratoga County Indsl. Devel. Agency, 1998-2006; mem. Yaddo Corp., Saratoga Springs, 1996-2004, sec., treas., 1997-2004; class A dir. Fed. Res. Bank NY, 2003— Chmn. Saratoga Springs City Ctr. Authority, 1983—89; trustee Skidmore Coll., Saratoga Springs, NY, 1984—2002, Nat. Mus. Dance, Saratoga Springs, NY, 1987—2002, Charles R. Wood Found., 1991—98, NY Racing Assn., 1985—, Saratoga Hosp., 2003—04, Nat. Mus. Racing, 1988—91, v.p., 1989—91; with Saratoga Care, Inc., 2002—04; mem. Saratoga County Water Authority, 2007—; chmn. Face of the Future Capital Campaign. Named Outstanding New Yorker, NY State Jaycees, 1984, Disting. Citizen, Saratoga Springs Sr. Citizens, 2002; recipient Pvt. Sector Initiative award, Pres. Ronald Reagan, Commitment to Cmty. award, NY State Bus. Coun., 1983, Liberty Bell award, Saratoga County Bar Assn. for cmty. svc., Good Scout award, Twin Rivers Coun., 1997, Sam Walton Bus. Leader award, 1997, Exec. of Yr. award, Capital Dist. Bus. Rev., 1999, Denis Kemball-Cook award, 2003, Lucy Skidmore Scribner award, Skidmore Coll., Saratoga Springs, 2003, J. Michael O'Connell Cmty. Svc. award, Saratoga Jaycees, 2004, Disting. Econ. Devel. Leadership award, SEDC, Saratoga Springs, 2007; Paul Harris fellow Dist. 7190, 1997. Mem. Ind. Bankers Assn. of N.Y. State (bd. dirs., sec. 1986-87), N.Y. Bankers Assn. (bd. dirs. 1987, treas. 1995—, chmn. 1997-99), N.Y. State Bankers Retirement System (trustee 1987-95, vice chmn., chmn. 1992-94), Am. Inst. Banking (Counsel of Yr. 1976), Greater Saratoga C. of C., Pillar Soc. Republican. Home: 658 N Broadway Saratoga Springs NY 12866-1624 Office: The Adirondack Trust Co 473 Broadway Saratoga Springs NY 12866-2262 Office Phone: 518-584-5844.

WAIT, SAMUEL CHARLES, JR., academic administrator, educator; b. Albany, NY, Jan. 26, 1932; s. Samuel C. and Isabel M. (Cassedy) W.; m. Carol D. Petrie, June 6, 1957; children: Robert J., Alison R. BS in Chemistry, Rensselaer Polytechnic Inst., 1953, MS in Physical Chemistry, 1955, PhD in Physical Chemistry, 1956. Postdoc. teaching fellow U. Minn., 1958-59; visiting asst. prof. Carnegie Inst. Tech., 1959-60; rsch. sci. Nat. Bur. Standards, 1960-61; from asst. prof. to prof. of chemistry Rensselaer Poly. Inst., Troy, N.Y., 1961—, from asst. dean of sci. to assoc. dean of sci., 1974—, acting dean of sci., 1978-80, 88-89, 2005—06. Dir. Cooperative Coll. Sci. Improvement Program, Troy, 1972-73, Rsch. Participation for High Sch. Tchrs., Troy, 1962-67; asst. dir., prof. M of Sci. in Natural Scis. Program, Troy, 1962-74. Author: Scattering of Laser Radiation, 1971; contbr. articles to profl. jours. Pres. dist. 2 Niskayuna (N.Y.) Fire Co., 1970-72, mem. 1966-; mem. Niskayuna Bd. Fire Commrs., 1978-83; trustee Dudley Obs., 1978—, v.p., 1980-91, pres., 1991-2001; mem. math., sci. and tech. adv. com. Schenectady County C.C., 1976—, chmn., 1977-78; vice chmn. Schenectady County Fire Adv. Bd., 1978-79; mem. Schenectady County Hazardous Materials Team, 1991-2002. Recipient Disting Faculty award Rensselaer Alumni Assn., 1988, Alumni Key award, 1994, Rensselaer Alumni Admission award of excellence, 1993, Rensselaer Alumni Assn. Albert Fox Demers medal, 1997, Rensselaer Alumni Fellow award, 2003, Disting. Svc. award Renselaer Alumni Assn., 2005; named fellow Rsch. Corp., 1954-55, Eastman Kodak Co., 1955-56; Fulbright scholar, 1956-58. Mem. Am. Chem. Soc., Rensselaer Premed. Soc., Sigma Xi, Alpha Epsilon Delta, Phi Theta Kappa. Office: Rensselaer Poly Inst 1C 05 Sci Ctr 110 8th St Troy NY 12180-3522 Home Phone: 518-785-1518; Office Phone: 518-276-6305. Business E-Mail: waitsc@rpi.edu.

WAITE, BARBARA L. (PIXIE), lawyer; b. Columbus, Miss., July 7, 1952; BA summa cum laude, Memphis State Univ., 1980; JD, Georgetown

Univ., 1984. Bar: DC 1984, DC Ct. Appeals 1985, US Dist. Ct. (DC, Ariz.), US Ct. Internat. Trade 1985, US Ct. Appeals (DC, Fed. cir.) 1985, US Supreme Ct. 1989. Ptnr., Copyright & Unfair Trade practice Venable LLP, Washington, 2000—. Editor (mng.): Am. Criminal Law Rev. Mem.: Copyright Soc. USA. Office: Venable LLP 575 7th St NW Washington DC 20004 Office Phone: 202-344-4811. Office Fax: 202-344-8300. Business E-Mail: blwaite@venable.com.

WAITE, CHARLES MORRISON, food products executive; b. Chgo., Oct. 1, 1932; s. Norman and Lavinia M. (Fyke) W.; m. Barbara Chowning Wham, Aug. 21, 1954; children: Susan R., Charles M., John B., David T. BA, Yale, 1954; MBA, Harvard, 1958. Mgr. planning and analysis Standard Fruit & Steamship Co., New Orleans, 1958-62, v.p., exec. v.p., 1969-72, dir., 1972-76; div. mgr. Standard Fruit Co., La Ceiba, Honduras, 1962-69; dir. Standard Fruit Tropical Charities, Inc., 1970-76; sr. v.p. Castle & Cooke, Inc., Honolulu, 1972-76; exec. v.p. Castle & Cooke Foods, San Francisco, 1974-76; pres. United Fruit Co., Boston, 1976-77; sr. v.p. United Brands Co., Boston, 1976-77; pres. Genoa Packing Co., Boston, 1977-78, Catelli Foods, Inc., 1979-90, Howard Foods Inc., Danvers, Mass., 1990—, also bd. dirs. Bd. dirs. Rock of Ages Corp., Barre, Vt., Swenson Granite Co., Concord, N.H. Served to 1st lt. USAF, 1955-57. Mem. Zeta Psi. Clubs: Harvard (Boston). Republican. Episcopalian. Home: 520 Cherry Valley Rd Gilford NH 03249-7841 Office: Howard Foods Inc 5 Ray St Danvers MA 01923-3531

WAITE, CHARLES PRESCOTT, entrepreneur; b. Manchester, Conn., Mar. 30, 1930; s. Earl M. and Virginia (Clark) W.; m. Catherine Corbett, Apr. 21, 1951 (div. Feb. 1985); children: Charles P. Jr., David C., Catherine C., Patricia C.; m. Angela Peterson, Feb. 16, 1985. BS, U. Conn., 1957; MBA, Harvard U., 1959. V.p. Am. Research & Devel. Corp., Boston, 1960-66; ptnr., pres. Greylock Mgmt. Corp., Boston, 1966—. Bd. dirs. Stellar Computer Corp., Newton, Mass., Floating Point Systems, Beaverton, Oreg., Micom Sytems, Simi Valley, Calif., Data Input Output Corp., Kirkland, Wash., Lumber Mutual Ins. Co., Framingham, Mass. Trustee Kenyon Coll., Gambier, Ohio, 1985—, Dana Hall Sch., Wellesley, Mass., 1974-84. Served to lt. col. U.S. Army, USAR, 1951-73. Republican. Congregationalist. Clubs: Algonquin (Boston), Harvard (Boston and N.Y.C.). Avocation: travel. Home: 85 E India Row Boston MA 02110-3320 Office: Brett Levy 40 Court St Boston MA 02108-2202

WAITE, DENNIS VERNON, brokerage house executive, consultant; b. Chgo., Aug. 26, 1938; s. Vernon George and Marie G. Waite; m. Christine Rene Hibbs; 1 child, Kip Anthony. BA, U. Ill., 1968; MS in Journalism, Northwestern U., 1969. Fin. reporter, columnist Chgo. Sun-Times, Chgo., 1969-76; asst. prof. Northwestern U., Evanston, Ill., 1978-79; assoc. prof. Mich. State U., East Lansing, 1979-82; ptnr. Fin. Rels. Bd., Inc., Chgo., 1982-90, sr. ptnr., 1991-97, sr. counselor, 1997—. Reporter, producer econ. affairs Sta. WTTW-TV, Sta. WBBM-TV, Chgo., 1973-76; adj. faculty English, Coll. of DuPage, 1998—2004. Mem. editorial adv. bd. alumni relations U. Ill., Chgo., 1980-84, 90-94. With USAF, 1956-60, PTO. Rutgers U. fellow, 1972. Mem. Medill Alumni Assn. (bd. dirs. 1989-92). Avocations: reading, writing, history, Tae Kwon Do. E-mail: dennis_waite@yahoo.com.

WAITE, JON PHILIP, music educator; b. Madison, Wis., Nov. 28, 1973; s. John Frederick Waite and Christine Mary Waite (nee Cornwall). B of Music Edn., U. Wis., Stevens Point, 1997. Dir. bands Del Norte H.S., Albuquerque, 1997—2001; dir. bands, tchr. instrumental music Hamilton H.S., Sussex, Wis., 2001—. Home: 224 N 72nd St Milwaukee WI 53213 Office: Hamilton School District W220 N6151 Town Line Rd Sussex WI 53089 Home Phone: 414-258-1409; Office Phone: 262-246-6471 1717. Personal E-mail: saxguy73@hotmail.com. E-mail: waitjo@hamiltondist.k12.wi.us.

WAITE, LAWRENCE WESLEY, osteopathic physician, educator; b. Chgo., June 27, 1951; s. Paul J. and Margaret E. (Cresson) W.; m. Courtnay M. Snyder, Nov. 1, 1974; children: Colleen Alexis, Rebecca Maureen, Alexander Quin. BA, Drake U., 1972; DO, Coll. Osteo Medicine and Surgery, 1975; MPH, U. Mich., 1981. Diplomate Nat. Bd. Osteo. Med. Examiners; bd. cert. family practice, holistic medicine, neuromusculoskeletal medicine, Osteopathic Manipulative Medicine. Intern Garden City Osteo. Hosp., Mich., 1975—76; practice gen. osteo. medicine Garden City, 1979—82, Battle Creek, 1982—96, La Crosse, Wis., 1996—2004; emergency rm. physician, 2004—; sect. head Onalaska Family Practice, 1999—2002, coord. rsch., chmn. dept., 1996—99, chmn. integrative medicine edn./rsch. com., 2002—04, vice chair, dept. integrative medicine, 2004. Cons. Nat. Bd. Examiners Osteo. Physicians and Surgeons, 1981—88, 1998—; chief med. examiner Calhoun County, 1991—93; preceptor U. Wis. Med. Sch., 1997—2000, assoc. clin. prof., 2000—, Mich. State U. Coll. Osteo. Medicine, East Lansing, 1979—97, Lakeview Gen. Osteo. Hosp., Battle Creek, Mich., 1983—87; mem. profl. adv. coun. Good Samaritan Hosp., Battle Creek, 1982—83; exec. bd. Primary Care Network, 1994—96; assoc. clin. prof. Des Moines U. Coll. Osteo. Medicine, 2002—05; mem. evaluations registry Commn. on Osteo. Coll. Accreditation, 2006—. Writer TV program Cross Currents Ecology, 1971; editor radio series Friendship Hour, 1971-72 Bd. dirs. La Crosse YMCA, 2000-03, Internat. Log Rolling Assn., 2000-04; cert. judge U.S. Log Rolling Assn., 2006—; bd. dirs., instr. Hospice Support Services, Inc., Westland, Mich., 1981-86; exec. bd. officer Battle Creek Area Urban League, 1987-91; bd. dirs., mem. exec. com. Clearwater Farm Found., Inc., 1999-04; vestryman St. Thomas Episcopal Ch., 1990-93; bd. mem. Eagle Bluff Environ. Learning Ctr., Lanesboro, 2003-; leader Boy Scouts Am.; bd. sec. Internal Soc. Complementary Medicine Rsch., 2004-05. Served to lt. comdr. USN, 1976-79. U. Wis. fellow, Madison, 2003-04; State of Iowa scholar, 1969. Mem.: Am. Coll. Osteo. Emergency Physicians (govtl. affairs com. 2007—), Am. Acad. Osteopathy, South Ctrl. Osteo. Assn. (officer, state del. 1983—96), Am. Osteo. Assn., Internat. Soc. Complementary Medicine Rsch. (sec. 2004—05), Population Inst. (population action coun. 1984—99), Brotherhood St. Andrews (life), Bermuda Hist. Soc. (life), Nat. Eagle Scouts Assn. (life). Avocations: geography, medieval history, genealogy. Home and Office: 2110 Evenson Dr Onalaska WI 54650-8772 Business E-Mail: lwwaite@wisc.edu.

WAITE, STEPHEN HOLDEN, lawyer; b. Rochester, NY, Dec. 5, 1936; s. Richard Holden and Judith H. (Lapp) Waite; m. Sarah T. Caswell, Aug. 20, 1960 (dec. Mar. 1996); children: Sarah T., Richard H. BA, Amherst Coll., 1958; JD, Yale U., 1961. Bar: N.Y. 1961. Mem. firm Nixon, Hargrave, Devans & Doyle, Rochester, NY, 1961-69; v.p., counsel Lincoln First Banks Inc., Rochester, 1969-73, sr. v.p., 1973-77, exec. v.p., 1978-81, CFO, 1973-81; sr. v.p. Schlegel Corp., 1981-82; mem. firm Harris, Beach, Wilcox, Rubin & Levey, Rochester, 1982-88, Underberg & Kessler, Rochester, 1988—. Past chmn. Rochester Area Hosp. Assn.; strategic planning commn. Monroe Cmty. Hosp.; past bd. dirs., treas. Hosp. Trustees N.Y. State; past bd. dirs., past chmn. Ctr. Govtl. Rsch.; past treas., bd. dirs. Planned Parenthood Rochester/Syracuse Region; bd. dirs. Mercy Flight Ctrl., Inc.; past bd. dirs. Highland Hosp., Monroe County Long Term Care, Inc., Rochester Regional Rsch. Libr. Coun., Hosp. Assn. N.Y. State, Health Futures for Rochester, Harley Sch., Hearing and Speech Ctr. Rochester. With US Army, 1962. Mem.: Monroe County Bar Assn., Country Club Rochester. Home: 68 N Main St Pittsford NY 14534 Office: 300 Bausch and Lomb Pl Rochester NY 14604 Office Phone: 585-258-2826.

WAITES, ROBERT GUINN, utilities executive; b. Laurel, Miss., July 12, 1950; s. Robert Leland Waites and Ida Doris (Gordon) Robinson; m. Lynda Gay Tubertini, Nov. 25, 1972; children: Julie G. Burran, Andrea G. BS, U. So. Miss., 1972; JD, Miss. Coll., 1976. Commd. 2d lt. U.S. Army, 1972, advanced through grades to capt., 1980, res., 1980; legal counsel Miss. House Reps., Jackson, 1976-89, Legis. Environ. Protection Coun., Jackson, 1989-90; dep. dir. Miss. Pub. Utilities Staff, Jackson, 1990-96, exec. dir., 1996—. Mem. ABA, Miss. State Bar Assn., Miss. Rep. Party, Kappa Sigma (Outstanding Mem. award 1972). Methodist. Avocations: golf, biking. Home: 179 Apple Blossom Dr Brandon MS 39047-7686 Office: Miss Pub Utilities Staff 550 High St Jackson MS 39201-1113

WAITKUS, JAY, writer; b. Grosse Pointe Farms, Mich., Oct. 7, 1968; s. Gerald C. Waitkus and Sara W. Kent. BS, Charter Oak State Coll., New Britain, Conn., 2003; MA, Fla. Atlantic U., 2005. Freelance journalist Sun-Sentinel, Palm Beach Post, South Fla. Bus. Jour., others, Fla., 1998—2001. Author: (novels) In the Depths of Shadows, 2003, Dividing Line, 2006, short stories, (plays) The Fallen Angel's Redeemer, 2002. Founding sponsor Disabled Vets. LIFE Meml. Found., Washington; donor USO, Carter Ctr.; mem. Habitat Partners Coun. Habitat for Humanity, 2006—, donor; Christian missionary, ch. planter Bapt. Ch. Palm Beach, Fla., 1997—98. Named Writer of Month, Gulf Coast Writers Assn., 2002. Mem.: Nat. Writers Assn., Nat. Geog. Soc., Golden Key Internat. Honor Soc. Conservative. Home Phone: 561-733-4714.

WAITS, THOMAS ALAN, composer, actor, singer; b. Pomona, Calif., Dec. 7, 1949; s. Frank W. and Alma (Johnson) McMurray; m. Kathleen Patricia Brennan, Aug. 10, 1980; children: Kellesimone Wylder, Casey Xavier, Sullivan Blake. Composer 20 albums including Closing Time, 1973, The Heart of Saturday Nite, 1974, Nighthawks at the Diner, 1975, Small Change, 1976, Foreign Affairs, 1978, Blue Valentine, 1979, Heart Attack and Vine, 1980, One From the Heart, 1981, Swordfishtrombones, 1983, Rain Dogs, 1985, Anthology, 1985, Frank's Wild Years, 1987, Big Time, 1988, Bone Machine, 1992, Night on Earth, 1992, The Black Rider, 1993, Beautiful Maladies, 1998, Mule Variations, 1999 (Grammy Award, 1999), Alice, 2002, Blood Money, 2002, Real Gone, 2004, Orphaus, 2006; composer (film scores) One from the Heart, 1983, Streetwise, 1985, Night on Earth, 1991; co-author music and songs (with Kathleen Brennan) for Night on Earth, 1991, End of Violence, 1997, Bunny, 1999, Liberty Heights, 2000, Big Bad Love, 2002, Pollock, 2002, Dead Man Walking, film American Heart; composer songs and music for The Black Rider opera, Hamburg, Germany, 1990; composer songs and music, writer (with Kathleen Brennan) Alice Avant Garde opera, Hamburg, 1992, opera Woyzeck (recipient Italian Drama Critics award for Best Musical, 2003), Copenhagen, 2000; actor (musical) Frank's Wild Years, 1986, (stage play) Demon Wine, 1989; appeared in films Paradise Alley, 1978, The Outsiders, 1983, Rumble Fish, 1983, The Cotton Club, 1984, Down by Law, 1986, Ironweed, 1987, Candy Mountain, 1987, Big Time, 1988, Cold Feet, 1989, The Bearskin, 1991, Queen's Logic, 1991, At Play in the Fields of the Lord, 1991, Bram Stoker's Dracula, 1992, Short Cuts, 1993, Mystery Men, 1999, Coffee & Cigarettes, 2003, Domino, 2003. Recipient Acad. Award nomination Best Song Score for One from the Heart, 1983; Grammy award for best alternative album Bone Machine, 1992, Grammy award for Mule Variations as best contemporary folk music, 2000, Dramalogue award for actor Demon Wine, Danish Theater award for Woyzeck as best musical, 2001. Mem. ASCAP (Founders award for career achievement in songwriting 2001), Musicians Union Local 47, SAG, AFTRA, Motion Picture Acad. Office: care Howard Grossman 10960 Wilshire Blvd Ste 2150 Los Angeles CA 90024-3807

WAITT, THEODORE W. (TED WAITT), venture capitalist, former computer company executive; b. Sioux City, Iowa, Jan. 18, 1963; m. Joan Waitt; 4 children. Attended, U. of Iowa; PhD (hon.), U. of SD. Co-founder Gateway Inc., Poway, 1985, pres., 1985—96, 2001—04, CEO, 1993—99, 2001—04, chmn., 1993—2005; founder, chmn., CEO Avalon Capital Group. Founder, chmn. Waitt Family Found., 1993—; chair Waitt Inst. for Historical Discovery, Waitt Inst. for Violence Prevention, Waitt Inst. for Scientific Breakthroughs; trustee Salk Inst., 2005—; chmn., Founding Fathers campaign Family Violence Prevention Fund. Named one of Ten Outstanding Young Americans, U.S. Jr. C. of C., Forbes' Richest Americans, 2005, 2006; recipient Young Entrepreneur of the Year award, U.S. Small Bus. Assn.

WAJENBERG, ARNOLD SHERMAN, retired librarian, educator; b. Indpls., Apr. 11, 1929; s. Henry and Hazel L. (Johnson) W.; m. Joyce E. Dunham, Sept. 6, 1952; 1 child, Earl S. BA, Butler U., Indpls., 1951, MA, 1953, U. Chgo., 1955. Cataloger U. Chgo. Library, 1953-69; catalog librarian U. Ill., Chgo., 1969-74, asst. catalog librarian Champaign-Urbana, 1974-78, prin. cataloguer, 1979-94; ret., 1994; prof. library adminstrn. U. Ill., Champaign-Urbana. Prin. educator, Ill. Tng. Program for Implementation of Anglo-Am. Cataloguing Rules, 2d edit., 1979-80; mem. editorial policy com. Dewey Decimal, 1981-92; Ill. rep. cataloging adv. com., Online Computer Libr. Ctr. 1979-82, cataloging and database svcs. adv. com., 1989-92. Author: FLC FEDLINK AACR 2 Cataloging Manual for Federal Libraries, 1981; contbr. articles to profl. jours. Mem. ALA (com. on cataloging: description and access 1981-86, mem.-at-large exec. com. cataloging and classification sect. 1982-86, Margaret Mann citation 1995) Avocations: walking, science fiction. Home: 240 Donald Dr Goffstown NH 03045-6214

WAJER, RONALD EDWARD, management consultant; b. Chgo., Aug. 31, 1943; s. Edward Joseph and Gertrude Catherine (Rytelny) W.; m. Mary Earlene Hagan, July 5, 1969; children: Catherine, Michael. BSIE, Northwestern U., 1966; MBA, Loyola U., Chgo., 1970. Project engring. mgr. Procter & Gamble, Chgo., 1966-67; indsl. engring. mgr. Johnson & Johnson, Bedford Park, Ill., 1967-71; project mgr. Jewel Cos., Franklin Park, Ill., 1971-73; divsn. engring. mgr. Abbott Labs., North Chicago, Ill., 1973-79; pres. bus. engring. divsn. R.E. Wajer & Assocs., Northbrook, Ill., 1979—. Contbr. articles to profl. jours. Sec. Downtown Redevel. Commn., Mt. Prospect, Ill., 1977-78; fundraising vol. Maryville Acad., Des Plaines, 1985—; bd. dirs. Lattof YMCA, Des Plaines, 1994-96; profl. advisor Sch. for New Learning, DePaul U., 1994—; mem. indsl. sector com. Lincoln Found. for Bus. Excellence, 1997-99. Recipient Cmty. Svc. award Chgo. Lighthouse for the Blind, 1989, Cert. of Merit, Village of Mt. Prospect, 1978. Mem. Inst. Indsl. Engrs. (cmty. svc. chmn. 1984), Inst. Mgmt. Cons. (cert., exec. v.p., bd. dirs. 1987-94), Assn. Mgmt. Cons. (ctrl. regional v.p. 1985-87), Midwest Soc. Profl. Cons., Northwestern Club Chgo. Roman Catholic. Office: Bus Engring 5 Revere Dr Ste 200 Northbrook IL 60062-8000 Office Phone: 847-824-0809. Business E-Mail: rewajer@busnengg.com.

WAJERT, SEAN PETER, lawyer; b. Chester, Pa., Feb. 2, 1960; s. John Max and Kathleen Francella (Gorand) W.; m. Lisa Marie. AB magna cum laude, Harvard U., 1981; JD cum laude, U. Pa., 1984. Bar: Pa. 1984, US Dist. Ct. Ea. Dist. Pa. 1986, US Ct. Appeals 3rd Cir. 1985, US Ct. Appeals 10th Cir. 1986. Law clk. to Hon. Arlin M. Adams US Ct. Appeals 3rd Cir., Phila., 1984-85; assoc. Pepper, Hamilton & Scheetz, Phila., 1985-87, Hoyle, Morris & Kerr, Phila., 1988-91, ptnr., 1992-95; of counsel Dechert Price & Rhoads (now Dechert LLP), Phila., 1995—97, ptnr., 1997—, chair firm mass torts & product liability practice group. Adj. prof. U. Pa. Law Sch., 1990-98, Thomas O'Boyle hon. lectr.-in-law, 1999-2000. Editor in chief: U. Pa. Law Rev., 1983-84. Vol. Congl. campaign., Phila., 1988, Bucks City, 1989. James Finnegan Fellow, 1979; recipient Am. Jurisprudence Award, 1982, Edwin R. Keedy Award, 1984, John H. Maurer Meml. Prize, 1984. Mem. ABA, Pa. Bar Assn., Phila. Bar Assn., Def. Rsch. Inst., Order of Coif. Republican. Roman Catholic. Office: Dechert LLP Cira Centre 2929 Arch St Philadelphia PA 19104-2808 Office Phone: 215-994-2387. Office Fax: 215-994-2222. Business E-Mail: sean.wajert@dechert.com.

WAJSGRAS, DAVID C., manufacturing executive; m. Teena Wajsgras; 3 children. BS in Acctg., U. Md., College Park; MBA in Fin., Am. U. CPA. CFO Maserati Automobile, Balt.; sr. auditor Coopers & Lybrand; contr. Contellation Investments, C.G.I.; from contr. to v.p. fin. UNC Inc., Annapolis, Md.; various sr. fin. positions AlliedSignal, Inc., Morristown, NJ, 1992—97; corp. contr. Engelhard Corp., Iselin, NJ, 1997—99; v.p. contr. Lear Corp., Southfield, Mich., 1999—2002, sr. v.p., CFO, 2002—05, exec. v.p., CFO, 2005—06; CFO, sr. v.p. Raytheon Corp., Waltham, Mass., 2006—. Mem.: Fin. Execs. Inst. Office: Raytheon Corp 870 Winter St Waltham MA 02451-1449 *

WAKABAYASHI, SEIJI, chef; b. Japan; Sous chef Cafe Del Rey; chef West Channel Bar and Grill, Kihachi, Tokyo, Spago; exec. chef Ondine, Sausalito, 1999—2001; owner, exec. chef Nandina, Dallas, Bushi-Tei, San Francisco. Named one of San Francisco's Rising Stars, StarChefs.com, 2007. Office: Bushi-Tei 1638 Post Rd San Francisco CA 94115 Office Phone: 415-440-4959. *

WAKE, MADELINE MUSANTE, academic administrator, nursing educator; Diploma, St. Francis Hosp. Sch. Nursing, 1963; BS in Nursing, Marquette U., 1968, MS in Nursing, 1971; PhD, U. Wis., Milw., 1986. Clin. nurse specialist St. Mary's Hosp., Milw., 1971-74, asst. dir. nursing, 1974-77; from dir. continuing nursing edn. to provost Marquette U., Milw., 1977—2002, provost, 2002—. Mem. devel. team Internat. Classification for Nursing Practice, Geneva, 1991-99. Chmn. bd. dirs. Trinity Meml. Hosp., Cudahy, Wis., 1991-96; bd. dirs. Blood Ctr. Wis., 2003-. Recipient Profl. Svc. award Am. Diabetes Assn.-Wis. affiliate, 1978, Excellence in Nursing Edn. award Wis. Nurses Assn., 1989; named Disting. Lectr. Sigma Theta Tau Internat., 1991. Fellow: Am. Acad. Nursing; mem.: ANA, Am. Assn. Colls. and Univs., Vis. Nurs Assn. Wis. (bd. dirs.), Am. Assn. Coll. Nursing (bd. dirs. 1999—2002). Office: Marquette Univ O'Hara Hall Milwaukee WI 53201-1881 Office Phone: 414-288-7511.

WAKE, MARVALEE HENDRICKS, biology professor; b. Orange, Calif., July 31, 1939; d. Marvin Carlton and Velvalee (Borter) H.; m. David B. Wake, June 23, 1962; 1 child, Thomas A. BA, U. So. Calif., 1961, MS, 1964, PhD, 1968. Tchg. asst., instr. U. Ill., Chgo., 1964, asst. prof., 1968—69; lectr. U. Calif., Berkeley, 1969—73, asst. prof., 1973—76, assoc. prof., 1976—80, prof. zoology, 1980—89, chmn. dept. zoology, 1985—89, chmn. dept. integrative biology, 1989—91, 1999—2002, assoc. dean Coll. Letters and Sci., 1975—78, prof. integrative biology, 1989—2003, Chancellor's prof., 1997—2000, prof. of the Grad. Sch., 2004—. Mem. NAS/NRC Bd. on Sustainable Devel., 1995-99, NSF Bio Adv. Commn., 1997-2002; Smithsonian Sci. Commn., 2001-02. Editor, co-editor: Hyman's Comparative Vertebrate Anatomy, 1979, The Origin and Evolution of Larval Forms, 1999, Ecology and Evolution in the Tropics, 2005; co-author: Biology, 1978; contbr. articles to profl. jours. NSF grantee, 1978—; Guggenheim fellow, 1988-89. Fellow: AAAS (chair Biology Sect. G 1998), Calif. Acad. Sci. (trustee 1992—98, hon. trustee 1998—), Am. Acad. Arts and Scis.; mem.: Internat. Soc. Vertebrate Morphology (pres.-elect 2004—07), Am. Inst. Biol. Sci. (pres. 2005), World Congress of Herpetology (sec. gen. 1994—97), Internat. Union Biol. Scis. (U.S. nat. com. 1986—2007, chair 1992—95, sec. gen. 1994—2000, pres. 2000—04), Soc. Integrative Comparative Biology (pres. 2001—03), Am. Soc. Ichthyologists and Herpetologists (bd. govs. 1978—, pres. 1984). Office: U Calif Dept Integrative Biology 3060 VLSB Berkeley CA 94720-3140 E-mail: mhwake@socrates.berkeley.edu.

WAKE, RICHARD W., food products executive; b. 1953; BS, U of Illinois. With Aurora Eby-Brown Co., Inc., 1975—, co-pres., bd. dir. Naperville, Ill., 1983—. Office: 280 Shuman Blvd Ste 280 PO Box 3067 Naperville IL 60566-7067

WAKE, THOMAS G., food products executive; Co-pres. Eby-Brown Co., Naperville, Ill., co-chief exec., 1983—. Office: Eby Brown Co 280 Shuman Blvd Ste 280 Naperville IL 60563-2578

WAKEFIELD, ANDRE, history professor; b. Bloomington, Ind., Apr. 8, 1965; s. Ray Milan and Margrit Vogeley Wakefield; m. Rebecca Kornbluh, July 11, 1993; children: Zachary Ray, Elijah Lev. BA, St. John's Coll., Annapolis, Md., 1987; MA, U. Minn., Mpls., 1990; PhD, U. Chgo., 1999. Assoc. ICF Inc., Washington, 1991—92; prof. history Pitzer Coll., Claremont, Calif., 2001—; extended grad. faculty Claremont Grad. U., 2003—. Translator, editor with Claudine Cohen: G. W. Leibniz's Protogaea. Grantee, NEH, 2001—03; Postdoctoral fellow, Dibner Inst. for the History of Sci. and Tech., MIT, 1999—2001, Cotsen fellow, Princeton U. Soc. of Fellows in the Liberal Arts, 2001. Office: Pitzer College 1050 North Mills Ave Claremont CA 91711 Office Phone: 909-607-3068.

WAKEFIELD, MARIE A., counselor, educational association administrator; b. Elyria, Ohio, Aug. 9, 1947; stepd. Orville B. and d. Ethel A. Thomas; m. Charles F. Wakefield, Nov. 13, 1975; children: Paul, Philip, Charlene, Conya. BS in Edn., Cen. State U., Wilberforce, Ohio, 1969; MS, U. Nev., Las Vegas, 1979, adminstrv. endorsement, 1989. Cert. profl. elem. tchr., K-8 counselor, Nev. Elem. tchr. Clark County Sch. Dist., Las Vegas, elem. counselor. Pres. Am. Counseling Assn., Alexandria, Va. Editor parents newsletters. Recipient Outstanding Counseling Edn. award, Dr. Kay P. Carl, John A. Bailey Disting. Profl. award, Profl. Black Women's Rose award. Mem.: ACA (pres.), Assn. Multicultural Counseling Devel., Assn. Adult Devel. Aging (Disting. Svc. award), Western Region Governing Coun., Nev. Counseling Assn., Am. Bus. Womens Assn., Southern Nev. Sch. Counselors Assn., Nat. Self-Esteem Coun. Avocations: piano, reading. Office: 8091 Petunia Flower Way Las Vegas NV 89147 Office Phone: 702-876-5926. Business E-Mail: mawakefield@cox.net. *

WAKEFIELD, MARY KATHERINE, medical association administrator, medical educator; b. Aug. 12, 1954; BSN, Mary Coll., Bismarck, ND, 1976; MSN, U. Tex., Austin, 1978, PhD, 1985; grad. program for sr. mgrs. in govt., Harvard U., 1991. RN. Staff nurse ICU St. Alexius Hosp., Bismarck, ND, 1975-76; nurse United Hosp., Grand Forks, ND, 1976-77; acad. asst. sch. nursing U. Tex., Austin, 1977-78; instr. Brackenridge Sch. Nursing Austin Community Coll., 1978-79; mem. faculty U. ND, Grand Forks, 1979-87, assoc. prof., chairperson, 1985-87; legis. asst. health and edn. issues Senator Q. Burdick, Washington, 1987-89; chief of staff Senator Kent Conrad, Washington, 1989—96; prof., dir. Ctr. Health Policy, Rsch. & Ethics George Mason U., Fairfax, Va., 1996—2001; prof., dir. Ctr. Rural Health U. ND Sch. Medicine & Health Sciences, Grand Forks, 2001—, assoc. dean, 2001—. Bd. dirs. AcademyHealth, ND Health Care Rev., Blue Cross Blue Shield ND; mem. VA spl. med. adv. group; bd. trustees Catholic Health Initiatives; part-time staff nurse The United Hosp., Grand Forks, 1979-86; mem. faculty assoc. U. Md. Sch. of Nursing, 1990—; mem. adj. faculty George Mason U. Sch. of Nursing, Va., 1990—; selected to participate in 1991 Cong. Bundestag Staff Exchange Program, Germany; presenter in field. Editorial bd. Nursing Econs., 1990—, Jour. Rural Health, Annals of Family Medicine; contbr. articles to profl. jours. Recipient Nurse Rsch. award, Am. Orgn. Nurse Execs., 2006. Fellow Am. Acad. Nursing; mem. AAUW, ANA (coun. nursing rsch.), Inst. Medicine, ND Acad. Sci., Nat. League for Nursing, Philippine Nurses Assn. of Met. Washington (hon. 1991), Sigma Theta Tau, Sigma Xi. Office: Ctr Rural Health PO Box 9037 Grand Forks ND 58202-9037 Office Phone: 701-777-3848. Office Fax: 701-777-6779.

WAKEFIELD, TIMOTHY STEPHEN (TIM WAKEFIELD), professional baseball player; b. Melbourne, Fla., Aug. 2, 1966; m. Stacy Wakefield. Student, Fla. Tech. Pitcher NY-Pa. League, Welland, 1989,

Carolina League, Salem, 1990, So. League, South Carolina, 1991, 93, Am. Assn. League, Buffalo, 1991-92, 94, Pitts. Pirates, 1992-93, Internat. League, Pawtucket, 1995, Boston Red Sox, 1995—. Donates money to the Make-A-Wish Foundation for every strikeout and win. Named Nat. League Rookie of the Yr. The Sporting News, 1992, Am. League Comeback Player of the Yr., 1995; inducted into the Sunshine State Conference Hall of Fame, 1998 Placed 3rd in Cy Young voting, 1995. Won 16 games first year with Boston Red Sox leading them to division title. Longevity and consistency have helped him become one of the top pitchers in Red Sox history. Office: c/o Boston Red Sox Fenway Pk 4 Yawkey Way Boston MA 02215-3409

WAKELEE, DANIEL WILLIAM, academic administrator; s. Earl and Marcia Wakelee; m. Joanne Powell Wakelee, Aug. 16, 1987; 1 child, Andrew Arthur. AB, Occidental Coll., 1982; MPA, Calif. State U. Northridge, 1990; PhD, U. Calif. Santa Barbara, 1995. Coord. food and shelter Project Understanding, Ventura, Calif., 1983—84; exec. dir. FOOD Share, Oxnard, Calif., 1984—88; asst. dir. Calif. State U. Nortridge, Ventura, 1988—98; assoc. dir. Calif. State U. Channel Islands, Camarillo, 1999—2001, assoc. dean of faculty, 2001—, assoc. prof. pub. adminstrn., 2005—. Mem. Channel Islands Inter Disc Rsch. Group, 2006—. Patient vol. Camarillo Hospice, Calif., 2001—06; elder Eastminster Presbyn. Ch., Ventura, Calif., 1988—2000; bd. dirs. Project Understanding, Ventura, Calif., 1987—89. Ventura County Scholarship Project, Ventura County Cmty. Found., 1999—2001, Calif. History Social Sci. Project grant, U. Calif., 2000-2002. Mem.: Western Assn. of Br. Campus Adminstrs. (nat. conf. chair 2002—02), Calif. Intersegmental Articulation Coun. (instl. rep. 2001—03), Calif. Assn. for Bilingual Edn., Am. Assn. for Higher Edn., Coun. Colls. of Arts and Sci. (liberal arts com. 2003—05, assoc. deans commn.). Office: Calif State Univ Channel Islands One University Dr Camarillo CA 93012 Home Phone: 805-642-5582; Office Phone: 805-437-8542. Business E-Mail: dan.wakelee@csuci.edu.

WAKOSKI, DIANE, poet, educator; b. Whittier, Calif., Aug. 3, 1937; d. John Joseph and Marie Elvira (Mengel) W. BA in English, U. Calif., Berkeley, 1960. Writer-in-residence Mich. State U., East Lansing, 1976—, Univ. disting. prof., 1990—. Vis. writer Calif. Inst. Tech., 1972, U. Va., 1972-73, Wilamette U., 1973, Lake Forest Coll., 1974, Colo. Coll., 1974, U. Calif., Irvine, 1974, Macalester Coll., 1975, U. Wis., 1975, Hollins Coll., 1974, U. Wash., 1977, Whitman Coll., 1976, Emory U., 1980-81, U. Hawaii, 1978. Author: Coins and Coffins, 1962, Discrepancies and Apparitions, 1966, Inside The Blood Factory, 1968, The George Washington Poems, 1967, The Magellanic Clouds, 1969, The Motorcycle Betrayal Poems, 1971, Smudging, 1972, Dancing On The Grave of A Son Of A Bitch, 1973, Trilogy, 1974, Virtuoso Literature For Two and Four Hands, 1976, Waiting For the King of Spain, 1977, The Man Who Shook Hands, 1978, Cap of Darkness, 1980, The Magician's Feastletters, 1982, The Collected Greed: Parts I-XIII, 1984, The Rings of Saturn, 1986, Emerald Ice: Selected Poems 1962-87, 1988 (William Carlos Williams prize 1989), Medea The Sorceress, 1991, Jason the Sailor, 1993, The Emerald City of Las Vegas, 1995, Argonaut Rose, 1998, The Butcher's Apron: New & Selected Poems, 2000. Named Univ. Disting. Prof., Mich. State U., 1990, Author of Yr., Mich. Libr. Assn., 2003; recipient award, Mich. Arts Found., 1989, Disting. Faculty award, Mich. State U., 1989; grantee Cassandra Found., 1970, N.Y. State Cultural Coun., 1971—72, Guggenheim Found., 1972—73, Fullbright, 1984, Mich. Arts Coun., 1988. Office: Mich State U 207 Morrill Hall East Lansing MI 48824-1036 E-mail: dwakoski@aol.com.

WAKS, JAY WARREN, lawyer; b. Newark, Dec. 6, 1946; m. Harriet, July 27, 1969; children: Jonathan Warren, Allison Lindsay. BS, Cornell U., 1968, JD, 1971. Bar: N.Y. 1972, U.S. Ct. Appeals (2d cir.) 1972, U.S. Dist. Ct. (no. dist.) N.Y. 1972, U.S. Dist. Ct. (so. dist.) N.Y. 1973, U.S. Dist. Ct. (ea. dist.) N.Y., 1973, U.S. Ct. Appeals (3d cir.), U.S. Ct. Appeals (2d cir.), U.S. Ct. Appeals (D.C. cir.), 1983, U.S. Dist. Ct. D.C. 1985, U.S. Supreme Ct. 1991. Law clk. to Hon. Inzer B. Wyatt U.S. Dist. Ct. So. Dist. N.Y., 1971-72; assoc. Kaye, Scholer, Fierman, Hays & Handler, NYC, 1972-80; ptnr. Kaye Scholer LLP, NYC, 1981—, chmn. employment and labor law practice/litigation, chmn. ADR practice group, mem. e-commerce practice group and internat. practice group; lectr. Inst. for Workplace Studies, ILR Sch., Cornell U. Bd. dirs., exec com., gen. counsel Legal Momentum; advisor restatement of the law third-employment law Am. Law Inst., 2004—. Bus. Watch columnist Nat. Law Jour., 1990—; contbg. author numerous articles to profl. jours. Chair Work in Am. Inst., 2002—04; nat. chmn. Cornell Law Sch. ann. fund Cornell U., 2001—04, chmn. 20th, 25th and 30th reunion campaigns Cornell Law Sch., former nat. co-chair Cornell Law Sch. dean's spl. leadership com. Class of '68, major gifts com., co-chair, 2002; exec. com. Cornell U. Coun., 2000—, chmn., 2005—07; chmn. adv. coun. Cornell Law Sch., chmn., 2004—07; employment disputes com. CPR Internat. Inst. for Conflict Prevention and Resolution, 1988—, chair, 1991—, mem. CPR exec. com.; bd. dirs. Fed. Bar Found., 2004—, v.p., 2006—; mem. exec. com., chair program com. Fed. Bar Coun. Named Top of the Docket column for success in high-profile public sector case, Am. Lawyer, 2002, Among #1 Employment Def. Lawyers in NY, Chambers USA Guides, 2003—; named one of Nation's Best Litigators in Employment Law, Nat. Law Jour., 1992, Best Lawyers in NY and Among 7 Best Corp. Side Labor/Employment Lawyers, NY mag., 1995, NY Area's Best Lawyers, 2005; recipient recognition for svc. to diversity efforts, Cornell Black Alumni Assn. Fellow Am. Bar Found., Coll. Labor and Employment Lawyers; mem. ABA (spkr. ann. meetings sect. labor and employment), State Bar Calif. (assoc.), N.Y. State Bar Assn. (co-chair employment alternative dispute resolution com., labor and employment law sect., exec. com. 1995-99, spl. com. age discrimination in profession 2006-), Am. Law Inst. (elected), Assn. Bar of City of N.Y. (chmn. labor and employment law com. 1990-93), Fed. Bar. Coun. (sustaining). Avocations: swimming, tennis, skiing, fitness training, travel. Office: Kaye Scholer LLP 425 Park Ave New York NY 10022-3506 Office Phone: 212-836-8558. Business E-Mail: jwaks@kayescholer.com.

WAKS, ROBERT GILMAN, librarian; b. Bronx, NY, Dec. 22, 1947; s. Albert Leopold and Lillian Waks; m. Arlene Susan Ferris, Apr. 4, 1954; 1 child, Jason. BA in Germanic Langs. and Lit., CUNY, Queens, NY, 1970, MLS, 1983; MA in German Studies, CUNY, NYC, 1973. Cert. German tchr. NJ, profl. libr. NJ. Documentation specialist Drexel, Burnham, Lambert, NYC, 1983—88; methods and procedures analyst Israel Discount Bank, NYC, 1988—94; internat. bus. rschr. Tech. Mktg. Corp., Darien, Conn., 1994—97; English tchr., cross-cultural facilitator Global Inst. Langs. and Cultures, Plantation, Fla., 1997—98; reference and acquisitions libr. Broward County Libr. Divsn., Ft. Lauderdale, Fla., 1998—99; sr. reference libr. Irving Pub. Libr., NJ, 1999—2002; head interlibrary loan svcs. Coll. St. Elizabeth, Morristown, NJ, 2002—; pvt. German lang. instr., cross-cultural cons. Mem.: NJ Libr. Assn., NY Cir. Translators, Am. Translators' Assn., Austrian-Am. Coun., Overseas Neighbors. Avocations: reading, languages, music, hiking. Office: Coll St Elizabeth 2 Convent Rd Morristown NJ 07960

WAKSCHLAG, MILTON SAMUEL, lawyer; b. Omaha, July 4, 1955; s. Fishel and Stefa (Kleiner) W.; m. Laurie S. Weinzweig, June 15, 1980; children: Tmima, Shira, Efraim. BA, Loyola U., 1977; JD, U. Chgo., 1980; LLM in Taxation, DePaul U., 1987. Bar: Ill. 1980. Assoc. Borge and Pitt, Chgo., 1980-85, ptnr., 1986, Katten Muchin Rosenman LLP, Chgo., 1987—, chair, pub. fin. dept., chair, fin. products group, mem. pro bono com. Adv. com. on svcs. to disabled, Ill. Atty. Gen's Office; prin. faculty mem. nat. tng. seminar, Govt. Fin. Officers Assn.; co-chair Bond Buyer's Ninth Ann. Midwest Pub. Fin. Conf.; nat. conf. chmn., Ctr. Bus. Intelligence; spkr. in field. Author: Important Developments During the Year: Tax Exempt Financing, 1989; contbr. papers in field. Founder, v.p., bd. dirs., trustee Keshet: Jewish Parents of Children with Spl. Needs, 1984—2006; trustee Lincolnwood Dist. Pub. Libr., 1988-89; bd. dirs. Brisk Rabbinical Coll., 1990-2006. Recipient Pro Bono Svc. award, Katten Muchin Rosenman LLP, Guardian of Hope award, Keshet, 2006. Mem. ABA (chmn. com. on tax-exempt fin., 1999-2001), Nat. Assn. Bond Lawyers (mem. steering com. bond attys.' workshop). Office: Katten Muchin Rosenman LLP 525 W Monroe St Chicago IL 60661 Office Fax: 312-577-8897. Business E-Mail: milton.wakschlag@kattenlaw.com.

WAKSMAN, BYRON HALSTED, immunologist, educator, medical association administrator; b. NYC, Sept. 15, 1919; s. Selman A. and Bertha (Mitnik) W.; m. Joyce Ann Robertroy, Aug. 11, 1944; children: Nan, Peter. BS, Swarthmore Coll., 1940; MD, U. Pa., 1943. Intern Michael Reese Hosp., Chgo., 1944; fellow Mayo Found., 1946-48; NIH fellow Columbia U. Med. Sch., 1948-49; assoc., then asst. prof. bacteriology and immunology Harvard Med. Sch., 1949-63; rsch. fellow, then assoc. bacteriologist (neurology) Mass. Gen. Hosp., 1949-63; prof. microbiology Yale U., 1963-74, prof. pathology, 1974-78, chmn. dept., 1964-70, 72-74, prof. pathology and biology, 1979-89; v.p. rsch. programs Nat. Multiple Sclerosis Soc., NYC, 1979—87, v.p. rsch. and med. programs, 1987-89; adj. prof. pathology NYU, 1979—, rsch. prof. biomedicine and sci. edn., 2002—, dir. (ad interim) programs for prep. edn. sci. and medicine, 2002—03, sr. advisor collaborative edn. programs, 2003—; vis. scientist in neurology Harvard U., 1990—. Mem. expert panel immunology WHO, 1963—83; microbiology fellowships panel and study sect. mem. NIH, 1961—69; bd. trustees Found. for Microbiology, 1968—, pres., 1970—2000, chmn. bd. trustes, 2001—; bd. trustees Biosis, 1988—91; dir. sci. writing fellowships program Marine Biol. Lab., Woods Hole, Mass., 1990—95; Humboldt prof. Max Planck Inst., Martinsried, 1991—92; dir. European Initiative for Communicators Sci., 1992—95; chmn. bd. Sci. Counsellors Nat. Inst. Aging, 1977—79. Contbr. articles to profl. jours.; editor: Progress in Allergy/Chemical Immunology, 1962—; mem. editl. adv. bd.: Cellular Immunology, 1970—95, Immunol. Comms., 1970—95, Inflammation, 1975—90, assoc. editor: Bacteriol. Revs., 1963—67, Jour. Immunology, 1962—66, Internat. Archives Allergy and Applied Immunology, 1962—95. Served as psychiatrist AUS, 1944-46. Fellow Am. Acad Arts and Scis.; mem. Am. Assn. Immunologists (councillor 1965-70, pres. 1970-71), Brit. Soc. Immunology, Am. Soc. Microbiology (councillor 1967-71), Am. Acad. Microbiology, Am. Acad. Neurology, Am. Neurol. Assn. Home: Brookhaven at Lexington 1010 Waltham St Apt 462 Lexington MA 02421 Office Phone: 781-862-3839. Business E-Mail: bwaksman@partners.org.

WAKUMOTO, YOSHIHIKO, electronics company executive, grants executive; b. Tokyo, June 4, 1931; s. Yoshitaro and Fumie (Oka) W.; m. Reiko Tanaka, Mar. 28, 1959; children: Yoshiaki, Yoshiyuki. BA, Tokyo U., 1955; postgrad., Columbia U., 1960-61. Dep. mgr. license negotiation Toshiba Corp., Tokyo, 1964-67, mgr. overseas mfg. ops., 1967-72, mgr. fin. divsn., 1972-74, gen. mgr. internat. fin. divsn., 1974-81, gen. mgr. internat. affairs divsn., 1981-88, v.p., dep. group exec.-internat. staff group, 1988-91, exec. v.p. for corp. planning, info. sys. and group cos., 1991-95, exec. v.p. for internat. rels., 1995-96, advisor, 1996—2001; exec. dir. Japan Found. Ctr. for Global Partnership, Tokyo, 1996—2002; spl. asst. to the pres. The Japan Found., 2002—05. Mem., Japan Nat. Com. United World Colls., 1996—2002; dir. The Am. Studies Found., 1997—; chairperson CARE Japan, 2003—; pres. Japan Assn. for Cultural Exch., 2004—. Co-author: Foreign Exchange Risk and International Financial Strategy, 1973, The Run-up of 21st Century, 1991; translator: Management By Exception, 1968. Mem. Internat. House of Japan, Japan Inst. Internat. Affairs, Fgn. Corr. Club Japan (assoc.). Home: 3-43-18 Hongo Bunkyo-ku Tokyo 113-0033 Japan Office: Japan Assn for Cultural Exch 1-9-15 Akasaka No 2 Bldg 9F Minato-ku Tokyo 107-0052 Japan Home Phone: 81-3-3814-0040. E-mail: waksan@tcn-catv.ne.jp.

WALBERG, HERBERT JOHN, psychologist, educator, consultant; b. Chgo., Dec. 27, 1937; s. Herbert J. and Helen (Bauer) W.; m. Madoka Bessho, Aug. 20, 1965; 1 child, Herbert J. III. BE in Edn. and Psychology, Chgo. State U., 1959; ME in Counseling, U. Ill., 1960; PhD in Ednl. Psychology, U. Chgo., 1964. Instr. psychology Chgo. State U., 1962—63, asst. prof., 1964—65; lectr. edn. Rutgers U., New Brunswick, NJ, 1965—66; asst. prof. edn. Harvard U., Cambridge, Mass., 1966—69; assoc. prof. edn. U. Ill., Chgo., 1970—71, prof., 1971—84, rsch. prof., 1984—; external examiner, 1981. External examiner, 1981; ednl. cons. numerous orgns.; external examiner Monash U., 1974, 76, Australian Nat. U., 1977; speaker in field; former coord. worldwide radio broadcasts on Am. Edn. Voice of Am., USIA, Office Pres. U.S., cons. Ctr. for Disease Control U.S. Pub. Health Svcs., 1985-90. Author, editor 49 books; chmn. editl. bd. Internat. Jour. Ednl. Rsch., 1985—; contbr. over 350 articles to profl. jours., chpts. to books. Mem. Chgo. United Edn. Com., also other civic groups, 1971-86; bd. dirs. Family Study Inst., 1987; chmn. bd. dirs. Heartland Inst., 1995. Nat. Inst. Edn. rsch. grantee, 1973, NSF rsch. grantee, 1974, March of Dimes rsch. grantee, 1976, numerous others. Fellow AAAS, Am. Psychol. Assn., Royal Statis. Soc.; mem. Internat. Acad. Edn. (founding), Am. Ednl. Rsch. Assn., Assn. for Supervision and Curriculum Devel., Brit. Ednl. Rsch. Assn., Nat. Soc. for Study Edn., Evaluation Rsch. Soc., Internat. Acad. Scis., Phi Delta Kappa (Disting. Rsch. award U. Chgo. chpt. 1971, cert. of recognition 1985), Phi Kappa Phi (hon.). Lutheran. Avocation: travel. Home: 180 E Pearson St Apt 3607 Chicago IL 60611-2135 Office: U Ill 1040 W Harrison St Chicago IL 60607-7129 Office Phone: 312-505-0528. Personal E-mail: hwalberg@yahoo.com.

WALBERG, TIM (TIMOTHY LEE WALBERG), congressman, former state legislator; b. Chgo., Apr. 12, 1951; s. John Andrew and Alice (Wilcox) W.; m. Susan Gail Polensky, 1973; children: Matthew Lee, Heidi Gail, Caleb Paul. Grad., Western Ill. U., 1970; Diploma, Summit Christian Coll., 1973; BS, Ft. Wayne Bible Coll., 1975; MA with hons., Wheaton Coll. Grad. Sch., 1978. Pastor New Haven (Ind.) Bapt. Ch., 1973-77, Union Gospel Ch., Tipton, Mich., 1978-83; mem. Mich. Ho. of Reps. from 57th dist., 1983—98; pres. Warren Reuther Ctr. for Edn. & Cmty. Impact, 1999—2001; divsn. mgr. Moody Bible Inst., Chgo., 2001—06; mem. US Congress from 7th Mich. dist, Mich., 2007—, mem. agrl. com., edn. & labor com. Asst. minority whip Mich. Ho. of Reps., vice chmn. Corrections Com., mem. Agriculture, Forestry & Minerals, Edn. Econ. Devel. & Energy Coms., Prison Reform & Children at Risk Task Force. Mem. Tecumsoh Kiwanis Club, Lenawee County Riding for the Handicapped, Lenawee County Basic Human Needs Task Force. Republican. Protestant. Office: 800 W Garrison Jackson MI 49202 also: 325 Cannon House Office Bldg Washington DC 20515 *

WALBESSER, HENRY HERMAN, computer science educator; b. Buffalo, May 9, 1935; s. Henry Herman and Florence (Schoenl) W.; m. Diane L. Walker, Aug. 16, 1958; children: Henry, Kathleen, James. BS, SUNY, Buffalo, 1958; MA, U. Md., 1960, PhD, 1965; DSc, U. of the Republic, Uruguay, 1976. Asst. prof. U. Tex., Austin, 1961-63; assoc. dir. AAAS, Washington, 1963-68; assoc. prof. U. Md., College Park, 1968-76, assoc. dean/assoc. provost, 1971-76, prof., chair Catonsville, 1976-92, prof. emeritus, 1992—; prof. Baylor U., Waco, Tex., 1992—, dean, 1992—96; COO, provost Henry Cogswell Coll., Everett, Wash., 2005—06; dir. Human-Computer Interaction Rsch. Lab., Hewitt, Tex., 2006—. Author: Evaluation Model, 1965, Integrity and Higher Education, 2001, A Brief Primer on Teaching: For New University Personnel, 2002, Imagination, 2003, An Introduction to Data Analysis for Computer Scientists and Engineers, 2003; co-author: Descriptive Data Analysis, 1991, Inferential Data Analysis, 1994; contbr. articles to profl. jours. Active adv. bd. Gov.'s Econ. Devel. Office, Annapolis, Md., 1988-91, Strecker Mus., Waco, 1992-2006, Lyric Opera of Waco, 1997-2006; worker Habitat for Humanity, Waco, 1996—. Fulbright-Hays fellow, 1967, 68, SEAMEO fellow, 1981, 82, OECD fellow, 1988. Fellow: AAAS; mem.: Nat. Hist. Soc. Democrat. Baptist. Avocations: bioinformatics, history of university presidents, gardening. Office: PO Box 1428 Hewitt TX 76643 Home: 400 Shadow Mt Waco TX 76712 Office Phone: 254-644-0841. Personal E-mail: hhwalbesser@aol.com.

WALCH, TIMOTHY GEORGE, library director; b. Detroit, Dec. 6, 1947; s. George Louis Walch and Margaret Mary (Shields) DeSchryver; m. Victoria Irons, June 24, 1978; children: Thomas Emmet, Brian Edward. BA, U. Notre Dame, 1970; PhD, Northwestern U., 1975. Assoc. dir. Soc. Am. Archivists, Chgo., 1975-79; grants analyst Nat. Hist. Publ. Commn., Washington, 1979-81; budget analyst Nat. Archives, Washington, 1981-82, editor Prologue, 1982-88; asst. dir. Hoover Presdl. Libr., West Branch, Iowa, 1988-93, dir., 1993—. Chair Iowa Ctr. Book, 2005—07. Author: Catholicism in America, 1989, Pope John Paul II, 1989, Parish School, 1996, reprinted, 2003, others; editor: Herbert Hoover & Harry S Truman, 1992, Immigrant America, 1994, At the President's Side, 1997, Herbert Hoover & Franklin D. Roosevelt, 1998, Uncommon Americans, 2003, and others; assoc. editor: U.S. Cath. Historian, 1983—; guest columnist Cedar Rapids Gazette, 1996-2006; contbr. History News Svc., 2002—. Named to Pres.'s Club St. Ambrose U., 2005; recipient Journalism award, U.S. Cath. Press Assn., 1986, 1st place publ. award, Nat. Assn. Govt. Communicators, 1988, U.S. Archivist's award, Nat. Archives, 1993, Iowa Gov.'s Vol. award, 1995, 97, 2006, Dominican Veritas Forum award, 1996, Rogus Lecture, U. Dayton, 1999, Williams Lecture, La. State U., Shreveport, 2000, Hatfield Lecture, Oreg. Hist. Soc., 2003. Mem. Orgn. Am. Historians, U.S. Cath. Hist. Soc., State Hist. Soc. Iowa (trustee 2005—), Iowa Hist. Found. (chair 2006—), Rotary (Harris fellow 2005). Office: Hoover Presdl Libr PO Box 488 West Branch IA 52358-0488 Office Phone: 319-643-6029. Personal E-mail: twalch47@aol.com. Business E-Mail: timothy.walch@nara.gov. *

WALCHER, ALAN ERNEST, lawyer; b. Chgo., Oct. 2, 1949; s. Chester R. and Dorothy E. (Kullgren) W.; children: Dustin Alan, Michael Alan, Christopher Ray. BS, U. Utah, 1971, cert. in internat. rels., 1971, JD, 1974. Bar: Utah 1974, U.S. Dist. Ct. Utah 1974, U.S. Ct. Appeals (10th cir.) 1977, Calif. 1979, U.S. Dist. Ct. (cen. dist.) Calif. 1979, U.S. Ct. Appeals (9th cir.) 1983, U.S. Dist. Ct. (ea., no., and so. dists.) Calif. 1994. Sole practice, Salt Lake City, 1974-79; ptnr. Costello & Walcher, L.A., 1979-85, Walcher & Scheuer, 1985-88, Ford & Harrison, 1988-91, Epstein Becker & Green, 1991-2003; sole practice, 2003-; judge pro tem Los Angeles Mcpl. Ct., 1986-91; dir. Citronia, Inc., Los Angeles, 1979-81. Trial counsel Utah chpt. Common Cause, Salt Lake City, 1978-79. Robert Mukai scholar U. Utah, 1971. Mem. Soc. Bar and Gavel (v.p. 1975-77), ABA, Fed. Bar Assn., Los Angeles County Bar Assn., Century City Bar Assn., Assn. Bus. Trial Lawyers, Phi Delta Phi, Owl and Key. Home: 17933 Sunburst St Northridge CA 91325-2848 Office Phone: 310-344-6570. Personal E-mail: alan1002@earthlink.net.

WALCHER, GREG E., government agency administrator, small business owner; s. Wendell Barge and Adeline Delilah Walcher; m. Diana Schlauger, July 12, 1992; 1 child, Amber Duncan. BA in Polit. Sci. and History, Mesa State Coll., Grand Junction, Colo., 1979. Senate staff US Senator William Armstrong, Washington, 1979—89; pres., CEO Club 20, Grand Junction, 1989—99; exec. dir. Colo. Dept. Natural Resources, Denver, 1999—2004; owner, CEO Natural Resources Group LLC, Washington, 2005—. Owner Walcher Orchards, Palisade, Colo., 1992—; sr. assoc. Stillwell Group, Washington, 2006—07; sr. advisor Dawson and Assocs., Washington, 2006—07. Exec. com. mem. Aspinall Meml. Commn., Palisade, 1998—2007; commr. Colo. Wildlife Commn., Denver, 1999—2004; bd. mem. Colo. Water Conservation Bd., Denver, 1999—2004, Gt. Outdoors Colo. Trust Fund, Denver, 1999—2004, Colo. Commn. of Indian Affairs, Denver, 1999—2004; GOP nominee US Congress, Colo., 2004—04; bd. mem. Pinchot Inst. for Conservation, Millford, Pa., 2000—04. Recipient John Vanderhoof award, Club 20, 1999. Mem.: Grand Junction Rotary Club. Conservative. Methodist. Home: PO Box 1393 Palisade CO 81526 Office: Natural Resources Group 1501 Crystal Dr Ste 925 Arlington VA 22202 Office Phone: 970-640-5089. Personal E-mail: gregwalcher@aol.com.

WALCOTT, CHARLES, neurobiology and behavior educator; b. Boston, July 19, 1934; s. Charles Folsom and Susan (Cabot) W.; m. Jane Clayton Taylor, Aug. 14, 1976; children: Thomas Stewart, Samuel Cabot. AB, Harvard U., 1956; PhD, Cornell U., 1959. Asst. prof. div. engring. and applied physics Harvard U., Cambridge, Mass., 1961-65; asst. prof. biology Tufts U., Medford, Mass., 1965-67; assoc. prof. dept. biology SUNY, Stony Brook, 1967-74, prof. dept. biology, 1974-81; prof., exec. dir. Cornell Lab. of Ornithology, Ithaca, NY, 1981-93, Louis Agassiz Fuertes dir., 1992-95; prof. neurobiology and behavior Cornell U., 1981—, dir. divsn. biol. scis., 1998-99, assoc. dean of the univ. faculty, 2000—03, dean of univ. faculty, 2003—. Cons., dir. Elem. Sci. Study, Watertown, Mass., 1961-67; dir. 3-2-1- Contact, Children's TV Workshop, N.Y.C., 1978—80; dir. L.A. Fuertes. Contbr. many rsch. papers to sci. jours. Dir. sci. TV, Mass. Audubon, Lincoln, 1959—61. Avocations: gardening, sailing, photography. Home: 84 Besemer Hill Rd Ithaca NY 14850-9636 Office: Cornell U Dept Neurobiology Behavior W255 Seeley Mudd Hall Ithaca NY 14853 Office Phone: 607-254-4382. Business E-Mail: cw38@cornell.edu.

WALCOTT, JOHN L., communications executive; b. Paterson, NJ, Aug. 29, 1949; s. Henry Richards Jr. and Katharine McCauley (Fearing) W.; m. Nancy Bittles, Aug. 11, 1973; children: Jennifer James, Allison Tierney, Elizabeth Bittles. BA, Williams Coll., 1971. With Ridgewood (NJ) News, 1972, The Record, Hackensack, NJ, 1972—77; econ. corr., nat. polit. corr., chief diplomatic corr. Newsweek, 1977—86; nat. security corr. Wall St. Jour., 1986—89; fgn. editor, nat. editor US News & World Report, 1989—96; fgn. editor, news editor Knight Ridder, Inc., 1997—2002, bur. chief, 2002—06; bur. chief Washington bur. The McClatchy Co., 2006—. U.S. rep. U.N. Conf. on Media, Igls, Austria, 1983; mem. Georgetown U. Sch. Fgn. Svc. Leadership Seminar, Washington, 1985; profl. lectr. Georgetown U. Sch. Fgn. Svc., 1996—; bd. advisors SmartBrief, Inc., 1997—. Co-author: (with David C. Martin) Best Laid Plans: The Inside Story of America's War Against Terrorism, 1988. Named Disting. Friend, Georgetown U. Sch. Fgn. Svc., 1985—; recipient Edward Weintal prize Georgetown U., 1988, Edwin M. Hood award Nat. Press Club, 1983, Freedom of the Press award, 1995, Overseas Press Club award, 1983, 84, Newspaper Guild of N.Y. award, 1985, Nat. Headline award, 2005. Mem. Overseas Writers Club (pres. 1986-88), White House Correspondents Assn., Gridiron Club, Sigma Delta Chi. Presbyterian. Office: McClatchy Newspapers One Metro Ctr Ste 1000 700 12th St NW Washington DC 20005-3994 Business E-Mail: jwalcott@mcclatchydc.com.

WALD, ARNOLD, gastroenterologist; b. NYC, June 10, 1942; s. Jack and Ruth (Fox) W.; m. Ellen Faith Rashkow, June 26, 1966; children: Elissa Karen, Eric Lawrence. BA, Colgate U., 1964; MD, SUNY, NYC, 1968. Diplomate Am. Bd. Internal Medicine, Am. Bd. Gastroenterology. Intern Kings County Hosp., Bklyn., 1968-69, resident, chief resident, 1969-71; fellow in medicine Johns Hopkins Hosp., Balt., 1973-75; asst. prof. medicine U. Pitts. Sch. Medicine, 1978-83, assoc. prof., 1983-91, prof., 1991—2006; chief gastroenterology divsn. Montefiore U. Hosp., Pitts., 1991-95; assoc. chief divsn. gastroenterology and hepatology U. Pitts. Med. Ctr., 1993—2000, dir. fellowship tng. and edn. divsn. gastroenterology, hepatology and nutrition, 1999—2006, prof. medicine, obstetrics, gynecology and reproductive scis., 2005—06; prof. medicine U. Wis. Sch. Medicine and Pub. Health, Madison, 2006—. Head gastroenterology unit Montefiore Hosp., Pitts., 1985-91; mem. adv. bd. Internat. Found. Bowel

Dysfunction, 1992—; bd. dirs. Pitts. chpt. Nat. Found. Ileitis and Colitis, Inc. 1980-84. Contbr. articles to profl. jours and books. Maj. U.S. Army, 1971-73. Master Am. Coll. Gastroenterology (bd. trustees 1991-98, gov. western Pa. 1988-90, chmn. internat. rels. com. 1993); fellow ACP; mem. Am. Gastroent. Assn., Ctrl. Soc. Clin. Rsch. (councillor 1985-90, chmn. gastroent. sect. 1989-90), Am. Motility Soc., Internat. Found. for Functional Gastrointestinal Disorders, Gastroenterology Rsch. Group. Democrat. Jewish. Avocations: tennis, reading, hiking. Office: Sect GI and Hepatology H61 516 CSC 500 Highland Ave Madison WI 53792 Home: 2510 Marshall Pkwy Madison WI 53713 Office Phone: 608-263-4033. Business E-Mail: axw@medicine.wisc.edu.

WALD, BERNARD JOSEPH, lawyer; b. Bklyn., Sept. 14, 1932; s. Max and Ruth (Mencher) W.; m. Francine Joy Weintraub, Feb. 2, 1964; children— David Evan, Kevin Mitchell. B.B.A. magna cum laude, CCNY; J.D. cum laude, NYU, 1955. Bar: N.Y. 1955, U.S. Dist. Ct. (so. dist.) N.Y. 1960, U.S. Dist. Ct. (ea. dist.) N.Y. 1960, U.S. Ct. Appeals (2d cir.) 1960, U.S. Supreme Ct. 1971. Mem. Herzfeld & Rubin, P.C. and predecessor firms, N.Y.C., 1955—. Mem. ABA, N.Y. State Bar Assn., Assn. Bar City N.Y., N.Y. County Lawyers Assn. Office: Herzfeld & Rubin PC 40 Wall St Ste 5400 New York NY 10005-2301 Office Phone: 212-471-8475. Business E-Mail: bwald@herzfeld-rubin.com.

WALD, DOUGLAS L., lawyer; b. Sept. 16, 1954; AB, Harvard Univ., 1975, JD, 1979. Bar: D.C. 1979. Law clk. Judge William H. Timbers, US Ct. Appeals, 2d Cir., 1979—80; ptnr., chmn. Assoc. Com. Arnold & Porter, Washington, 1980—. Contbr. articles to profl. jours. Office: Arnold & Porter 555 Twelfth St NW Washington DC 20004-1206 Office Phone: 202-942-5112. Office Fax: 202-942-5999. Business E-Mail: douglas_wald@aporter.com.

WALD, INGEBORG, librarian, translator; children: Alexander Lieb, Gregory Lieb. Student, Freie U., Berlin, 1953—57, Friedrich Schiller U., Jena, Germany, 1952—53; MA, Boston U., 1969; MLS, Calif. State U., San Jose, 1975. Libr. Goethe Inst., Boston, 1968—71; libr. asst. Lane Med. Libr., Stanford U., Palo Alto, Calif., 1971—75; various positions Cornell U., NY, 1976—91; libr. German Sch. NY, White Plains, 1991—2000; cons. La. State Dept. Edn., 2002; gen. libr. Hill Meml. Libr., La. State U., Baton Rouge, 2004. Coun. mem. Westchester BOCES Sch. Libr. Sys., 1991—2000; lectr. in field; cons. in field. Translator: An Ark of Stars, 1989, 12 Poems, 12 Paintings, 1991. Recipient Poetic Achievement award, Arcadia Poetry Press, Editor's Choice award, Nat. Libr. Poetry, 1997; grantee, NY Coun. on the Arts, 1979, Whitney Found., 1981, Kress Found., 1984—85, Coun. of the Creative and Performing Arts, 1985, 1988, Deutscher Akademischer Austauschdienst, 1986, 1987.

WALD, MICHAEL LEONARD, public relations executive; b. Balt., Jan. 5, 1951; s. Leonard Marvin and Frances (Kosinski) Wald; m. Marlena Malmstedt, June 10, 1972. BA, Am. U., 1972; MPA, U. Ga., Athens, 2006. Mgr. Woodward and Lothrop Dept. Store, Washington, 1972-75, Hecht Co., Washington, 1975-76; store mgr. W.J. Sloane & Co., Washington, 1976-77; economist U.S. Bur. Labor Stats., Balt., 1977-85, Washington, 1985-86, Atlanta, 1986-96, S.E. regional economist, 1996—2006; pub. rels. specialist U.S. Dept. Labor, Office Pub. Affairs, Atlanta, 2007—. Lectr. fed. compensation issues. Mem. editl. bd. HR Atlanta, 1993—95; contbr. articles to profl. jours.; reviewer Monthly Labor Rev., 1992—, peer reviewer ACA Jour., 1995—99. Bd. dirs. Athens (Ga.) Habitat for Humanity, 1990—93; venue mktg. liaison mgr. 1996 Centennial Olympic Games. Recipient Commr.'s award for Outstanding Mgmt. Performance, 2000, Sec.'s Exceptional Achievement award, 2001. Mem.: Labor and Employee Rels. Assn., Atlanta Econ. Club (officer 2003—04), Atlanta Labor and Employment Rels. Assn. (bd. mem. 2005, bd. dirs. 2005—), Nat. Assn. Bus. Econ., Atlanta Compensation Assn. (v.p. 1992—94, pres. 1996), Pi Alpha Alpha, Phi Kappa Phi, Alpha Tau Omega. Avocations: reading, home improvement, travel. Home: 5015 Fawn Valley Dr Loganville GA 30052-3879 Office: US Dept Labor 61 Forsyth St SW Ste 6875 Atlanta GA 30303-8817 Home Phone: 770-267-7641; Office Phone: 404-562-2076. Business E-Mail: wald.michael@dol.gov.

WALD, NIEL, public health educator; b. NYC, Oct. 1, 1925; s. Albert and Rose (Fischel) W.; m. Lucienne Hill, May 24, 1953; children: David, Phillip. AB, Columbia U., NYC, 1945; MD, NYU, 1948. Sr. hematologist Atomic Bomb Casualty Comm., Hiroshima, Japan, 1954-57; head biologist health physics divsn. Oak Ridge Nat. Lab., 1957-58; med. rsch. and tchg. specializing in radiation medicine and cytogenetics Pitts., 1958—; mem. faculty U. Pitts. Grad. Sch. Pub. Health and Med. Sch., 1958—2004, prof. radiation health, 1962-91, prof. environ. and occupl. health, 1991—2004, prof. radiology, 1965—2004; prof. human genetics U. Pitts., 1991—2004, prof. emeritus, 2004—; chmn. dept. radiation health U. Pitts. Grad. Sch. Pub. Health and Med. Sch., 1969-76, 77-89, chmn. dept. occupl. health, 1975-76, chmn. dept. indsl. environ. health scis., 1976-77. Dir. radiation medicine dept. Presbyn.-Univ. Hosp., 1966—; med. dir. Clin. Cytogenetics Lab., U. Pitts., 1982-99, chmn. Radiation Safety Com. 1960-2005, radiation cytogenetics cons., 1999—; dir. U.S. Dept. Energy postdoctoral fellowship program in radiation scis., 1997-2004; cons. U.S. NRC Office of Nuc. Materials Safety and Safeguards, mem. adv. panel for decontamination of Three Mile Island Nuc. Power Sta. Unit 2, 1981-93, cons. adv. com. on reactor safeguards, 1989-94; mem. U.S. working group on health effects, U.S.-USSR Joint Coordinating Com. for Civilian Nuc. Reactor Safety, 1989-92; cons. USN, nuc. industries and utilities; chmn. radiol. health study sect. USPHS, 1967-71; mem. Nat. Coun. Radiation Protection and Measurements, 1969-81, consociate mem., 1981—; mem. Gov. Pa. Adv. Com. Atomic Energy Devel. and Radiation Control, 1966-84, chmn., 1974-76; mem. Pa. Dept. Environ. Protection adv. com. on low level radioactive waste disposal, 1985—; mem. U.S. nuc. tech. adv. group Internat. Stds. Orgn., 2003-. Contbr. numerous articles to sci. and med. publs. Vol. U.S. Citizens Def. Corps Air Warden Svc., 1943—45, capt. USAF, 1952—54. Recipient Health Physics Faculty Rsch. award U.S. Dept. Energy, 1992-95. Mem. Health Physics Soc. (pres. 1973-74), Am. Pub. Health Assn. (governing coun. 1971-73, program devel. bd. 1973-74), Radiation Rsch. Soc. (assoc. editor jour. 1965-68), Soc. Nuc. Medicine (assoc. editor jour. 1959-69), Am. Soc. Human Genetics, Am. Coll. Occupl. & Environ. Medicine, AAAS, AMA, Internat. Soc. Hematology. Achievements include research in the diagnosis and treatment of accidental human radiation injury, in human radiation dosimetry by automatic image analysis of radiation-induced chromosome aberrations, in the cytogenetics of murine radiation-induced leukemia and in health studies of irradiated human populations in U.S., Japan and Russia. Office: U Pitts Grad Sch Pub Health 100 Technology Dr Rm 561 Pittsburgh PA 15219-3130 Office Phone: 412-624-2735. Business E-Mail: wald@pitt.edu.

WALD, PATRICIA MCGOWAN, retired federal judge; b. Torrington, Conn., Sept. 16, 1928; d. Joseph F. and Margaret (O'Keefe) McGowan; m. Robert L. Wald, June 22, 1952; children: Sarah, Douglas, Johanna, Frederica, Thomas. BA, Conn. Coll., 1948; LLB, Yale U., 1951; HHD (hon.), Mt. Vernon Jr. Coll., 1980; LLD (hon.), George Washington Law Sch., 1983, CUNY, 1984, Notre Dame U., John Jay Sch. Criminal Justice, Mt. Holyoke Coll., 1985, Georgetown U., 1987, Villanova U., Amherst Coll., NY Law Sch., 1988, Colgate U., 1989, Hofstra U., 1991, New Eng. Coll., 1991, Vermont Law Sch., 1995; LLD, Yale U., 2001. Bar: DC 1952. Clk. to Hon. Jerome Frank US Ct. Appeals, 1951—52; assoc. Arnold, Fortas & Porter, Washington, 1952—53; mem. DC Crime Commn., 1964—65; atty. Office of Criminal Justice, 1967—68, Neighborhood Legal Svc., Washington, 1968—70; co-dir. Ford Found. Project on Drug Abuse, 1970, Ctr. for Law and Social Policy, 1971—72, Mental Health Law Project, 1972—77; asst. atty. gen. for legis. affairs US Dept. Justice, Washington, 1977—79; judge US Ct. Appeals (DC cir.), 1979—99, chief judge, 1986—91; judge Internat. Criminal Tribunal for Former Yugoslavia, The Hague, Netherlands, 1999—2001. Bd. dirs. Am. Constn. Soc., 2002—. Author: Law and Poverty, 1965; co-author: Bail in the United States, 1964, Dealing with Drug Abuse, 1973; bd. editors: ABA Jour., 1978—86; contbr. articles to profl. jours. Mem. Commn. on Intelligence Capabilities of the US Regarding Weapons of Mass Destruction, 2004—05; trustee Ford Found., 1972—77, Phillips Exeter Acad., 1975—77, Agnes Meyer Found., 1976—77, Conn. Coll., 1976—77; active Carnegie Coun. on Children, 1972—77; bd. dirs. Mental Disability Rights Internat., 2002—. Named one of 100 Most Influential Lawyers, Nat. Law Jour., 2006, The 50 Most Influential Women Lawyers in Am., 2007; recipient Lifetime Achievement award, The Am. Lawyer, 2004. Mem.: ABA-Ctrl. and Ea. European Law Inst. (exec. bd. 1994—99), Am. Constitution Soc. (bd. dirs. 2004—), Am. Philos. Assn., Inst. Justice Initiative, Am. Acad. Arts and Scis., Am. Law Inst. (coun. mem. 1979—, exec. com. 1985—99, 2d v.p. 1988—93, 1st v.p. 1993—98), Open Soc. Inst. (chair justice initiative 2002—), Phi Beta Kappa. Office: 2101 Connecticut Ave NW Washington DC 20008 Personal E-mail: patwald2@cs.com. *

WALD, PETER ALLEN, lawyer; b. 1953; AB magna cum laude, Brown U., 1974; JD magna cum laude, Harvard U., 1977. Bar: Calif. 1979. Law clk. to Hon. James R. Browning US Ct. Appeals (9th cir.), 1977—78; ptnr. Latham & Watkins, LLP, San Francisco, 1996—, global dept. chair, litig. dept. and chair, Bay Area litig. dept. Notes editor Harvard Law Rev., 1977. Named one of Top 10 Trial Lawyers in Am., Nat. Law Jour., 2006. Mem.: Phi Beta Kappa. Office: Latham & Watkins LLP Ste 2000 505 Montgomery St San Francisco CA 94111-2562 Office Phone: 415-395-8006. Office Fax: 415-395-8095. E-mail: peter.wald@lw.com. *

WALD, RICHARD CHARLES, media consultant, educator; b. NYC; s. Joseph S. and Lily (Forstate) W.; m. Edith May Leslie; children: Matthew Leslie, Elizabeth Tole, Jonathan Simon. BA, Columbia U., 1952, MA, 1953; AB, Clare Coll., Cambridge, 1955. From reporter to mng. editor NY Herald Tribune, 1951—66; asst. mng. editor Washington Post, 1967; exec. v.p. Whitney Comm. Corp., NYC, 1968; pres. NBC News, 1968-77; asst. to chmn. bd, Times-Mirror Co., LA; sr. v.p. ABC News, 1978—99, sr. v.p. editl. quality, 1993—99, now cons.; Fred Friendly Prof. Journalism Columbia U., 1999—. Annotator: (with James Bellows) The World of Jimmy Breslin, 1967; chmn. bd. Columbia Daily Spectator. Mem. adv. bd. Knight Fellowship, Stanford U.; bd. dir. Correspondents Fund, Ctr. For Comm. Mem.: Fedn. Am. Scientists. Office: Columbia Sch Journalism 2950 Broadway New York NY 10027 also: ABC News 47 W 66th St New York NY 10023-6290 E-mail: richard.c.wald@abc.com.

WALD, ROBERT LEWIS, lawyer; b. Worcester, Mass., Sept. 9, 1926; s. Lewis and Freda Ann (Rosenfield) W.; m. Patricia Ann McGowan, June 22, 1952; children: Sarah Elizabeth, Douglas Robert, Johanna Margaret, Frederica Nora, Thomas Robert. AB, Harvard U., 1947; LLB, Yale U., 1951. Bar: Mass. 1951, D.C. 1959, U.S. Ct. Appeals (4th cir.) 1957, U.S. Supreme Ct. 1957, U.S. Ct. Appeals (D.C. cir.) 1959, U.S. Ct. Appeals (6th cir.) 1975. Clerk to Judge Irving R. Kaufman U.S. Dist. Ct. (so. dist.) N.Y., 1951-52; asst. to gen. counsel, chief div. export trade FTC, Washington, 1954—56; ptnr. Wald, Harkrader & Ross and predecessors, Washington, 1961—87, Nussbaum & Wald, Washington, 1989—96; sr. counsel Baach Robinson & Lewis, Washington, 1996—. Dir., trustee Washington Lawyers' Com. for Civil Rights, Urban Affairs and predecessor, 1969—, co-chmn., 1976—78; dir. Romanian-Am. Enterprise Fund, 1994—97, chmn., 1994—96; dir. Global Rights and predecessor, 1991—, Frederic B. Abramson Mem. Found., 1998—; hon. dir. Capital Area Immigrants' Rights Coalition, 1999—; dir. Internat. Sr. Lawyers Project, 2001—; bd. mgmt. trustees Internat. Assn. Women Judges, 1997—. Served to lt. USNR, 1944-46, 52-53. Mem. ABA, D.C. Bar Assn. Home: 2101 Connecticut Ave NW Washington DC 20008-1728 Office: Baach Robinson & Lewis 1201 F St NW Ste 500 Washington DC 20004 Office Phone: 202-833-8900. Business E-Mail: robert.wald@baachrobinson.com.

WALD, SYLVIA, artist; b. Phila., Oct. 30, 1915; Student, Moore Inst. Art, Sci. and Industry. One-woman shows include U. Louisville, 1945, 49, Kent State Coll., 1945, Nat. Serigraph Soc., 1946, Grand Central Moderns, N.Y.C., 1957, Devorah Sherman Gallery, Chgo., 1960, New Sch., 1967, Book Gallery, White Plains, N.Y., 1968, Benson Gallery, Bridgehampton, L.I., 1977, Knoll Internat., Munich, 1979, Amerika Havs, Munich, 1979, Aaron Berman Gallery, N.Y.C., 1981, Hirschltadler Gallery, 1994, New Britain (Conn.) Mus., 1994, Dongah Art Gallery, Seoul, Korea, 1995, Hanlim Art Gallery, Daejun, 1995-96, Kwangju City Art Mus, Pusan, Korea, Dong Shin U., Kwangju, 1996, Chosun U. Mus., Kwangju City, 2001, Chosun Univ. Mus. Art, Kwangju, Korea, 2002, 05, Tenri Gallery, N.Y.C., 2004, 05; exhibited in group shows at Nat. Sculpture Soc., 1940, Sculpture Internat., Phila., 1940, Chgo. Art Inst., 1941, Bklyn. Mus., 1975, Libr. of Congress, 1943, 52, 58, Smithsonian Instn., 1954, Internat. Print Exhbn., Salzburg and Vienna, 1952, 2d Sao Paulo Biennial, 1953, N.Y. Cultural Ctr., 1973, Mus. Modern Art, N.Y.C., 1975, Benson Gallery, Bridgehampton, L.I., 1982, Dumon-Landis Gallery, New Brunswick, N.J., 1982-83, Suzuki Gallery, N.Y.C., 1982, Sid Deutch Gallery, N.Y.C., 1983, Aaron Berman Gallery, N.Y.C., 1983, Full House Gallery, Kingston, N.J., 1984, Nabi Gallery, Sag Harbor, N.Y., 1989, Worcester Mus., 1991, Boston Mus. Fine Arts, 1991, Hirschl & Adler Gallery, N.Y.C., 1993, Parrish Mus., Southampton, 2002, Tenri Galleru, NYC, 2005, 2x13 Gallery, 2006, Korea Gallery, 2006, others; represented in permanent collections Aetna Oil Co., AAUW, Ball State Tchrs. Coll., Bibliotheque Nat., Paris, Bklyn. Mus., Howard U., State U. Iowa, Libr. of Congress, U. Louisville, Nat. Gallery, Mus. Modern Art, Phila. Mus., N.C. Mus., Rose Mus. Art at Brandeis U., Whitney Mus., N.Y.C., Finch Coll. Mus., N.Y.C., U. Nebr., Ohio U., U. Okla., Princeton, Victoria and Albert Mus., Walker Gallery, Worcester (Mass.) Art Mus., Guggenheim Mus., N.Y.C., Grunewald Mus., UCLA, Rutgers Mus., N.J., Aschenbach Collection Mus., San Francisco, Grunewald Coll. Mus. UCLA, Wellesley Coll.; acquisitions Yale U. Art Gallery, 1998, Cleve. Mus., 1998; contbr. articles to profl. jours. Address: 417 Lafayette St New York NY 10003-7005

WALD, WAYNE A., lawyer; b. Queens, NY, Dec. 18, 1962; BS magna cum laude, SUNY, Albany; JD, NYU, 1989. Bar: NY 1990. Ptnr. Katten Muchin Zavis Rosenman, NYC. Office: Katten Muchin Zavis Rosenman 575 Madison Ave New York NY 10022 Office Phone: 212-940-8508. Office Fax: 212-940-8776. E-mail: wayne.wald@kmzr.com.

WALDA, JOHN D., educational association administrator, lawyer; b. Ft. Wayne, Ind., June 14, 1950; s. David William and Martha (Lefever) W.; m. Martha Clark Fallgatter, Sept. 21, 2002; children: Laura, Kirk. AB, Ind. U., 1972, JD, 1975. Bar: Ind. 1975, US Dist. Ct. (no. and so. dists. Ind.) 1975, US Ct. Appeals (7th cir.) 1977, US Ct. Appeals (6th cir.) 1987, US Dist. Ct. (we. dist. Mich.) 1991. Ptnr. Barrett & McNagny, Ft. Wayne, 1975—2001; chmn. Clarian Health Ptnrs., Inc., 1996—2000, dir., 1996—2004, Assn. Governing Bds. of Univs. & Colls., 2000—04, vice chmn., 2000—02, chmn., 2002—03; exec. dir. fed. rels. Ind. U. Sys., 2002—04; sr. v.p. fed. rels. BoseTreacy Assocs., LLC; ptnr. litig. group Bose McKinney & Evans, LLP; pres., CEO Nat. Assn. Coll. and Univ. Bus. Officers, 2006—. Dir. Ft. Wayne Newspapers, Inc., 1990—; master of the bench Am. Inns of Ct.; gen. counsel Jour.-Gazette (Ft. Wayne). Pres. bd. trustees Ind. U., 1990—; first chmn. Ind. Lottery Commn., 1989; bd. dirs. Ft. Wayne Civic Theatre, Ft. Wayne Mus. Art; active Allen County Pks. & Recreation Bd., Headwaters Park Commn.; bd. dirs., v.p. Jr. Achievement N.E. Ind.; Dem. candidate for US Ho. Reps., 1978, 80. Fellow Ind. Bar Found.; mem. ABA (ho. dels. 1983-86), Ind. State Bar Assn., (chmn. young lawyers sect. 1983-84), JUNTO Club Ft. Wayne (pres.). Democrat. Avocations: skiing, backpacking, golf. Office: Nat Assn Coll and Univ Bus Officers 2501 M St NW Ste 400 Washington DC 20037 Office Phone: 202-861-2500. E-mail: john.walda@nacubo.org.

WALDECK, JOHN WALTER, JR., lawyer; b. Cleve., May 3, 1949; s. John Walter Sr. and Marjorie Ruth (Palenschat) W.; m. Cheryl Gene Cutter, Sept. 10, 1977; children: John III, Matthew, Rebecca. BS, John Carroll U., 1973; JD, Cleve. State U., 1977. Bar: Ohio 1977, cert.: Ohio State Bar Assn. (in bus., comml. and indsl. real property law) 2007. Product applications chemist Synthetic Products Co., Cleve., 1969—76; assoc. Arter & Hadden, Cleve., 1977—85, ptnr., 1986—88, Porter, Wright, Morris and Arthur, Cleve., 1988—90, ptnr. in charge, 1990—96; ptnr. Walter & Haverfield LLP, Cleve., 1996—, mem. exec. com., 2003—07. Bd. advisors Litigation Mgmt., Inc., 2000—04. Chmn. Bainbridge Twp. Bd. Zoning Appeals, Chagrin Falls, Ohio, 1984-94; trustee Greater Cleve. chpt. Lupus Found. Am., 1978-91, sec., 1979-86; trustee LeBlond Housing Corp., Cleve., 1990-96, sec., 1996, Univ. Circle, Inc., 1993-97, Fairmount Ctr. for Performing and Fine Arts, Novelty, Ohio, 1993-96, sect., 1994-95; bd. dirs. Geauga County Mental Health Recovery Svc. Bd., Chardon, Ohio, 1988-97, treas., 1991-93, vice-chmn., 1993-95, chmn., 1995-97; mem. bd. advisors Palliative Care Svcs., Cleve. Clinic Cancer Ctr., 1989-91; specialization bd. Real Property Law, 2007. Named an Ohio Super Lawyer, Law & Politics Mag., 2007. Mem. Ohio State Bar Assn. (real property sect. bd. govs. 1992, real property specialty cert. bd. 2007—, cert. real property specialist, 2007—), Greater Cleve. Bar Assn. (real property, corp. banking sect, co-chair real estate law inst. 1990, 95, 96). Roman Catholic. Avocations: beekeeping, gardening, jogging. Home: 18814 Rivers Edge Dr W Chagrin Falls OH 44023-4968 Office: Walter & Haverfield LLP suite 3500 1301 E Ninth St Cleveland OH 44114 Office Phone: 216-781-1212. Business E-Mail: jwaldeck@walterhav.com.

WALDEN, DANA, broadcast executive; BA in Comm., U. So. Calif. Formerly with Bender, Goldman & Helper; former v.p. mktg. Arsenio Hall Comm., Paramount; former sr. v.p. media and corp. rels. 20th Century Fox TV, v.p. current programming, 1994—96, former v.p. drama, former sr. v.p. drama, former exec. v.p. drama devel., pres., 1999—, chmn., 2007—. Named one of 100 Most Powerful Women in Entertainment, Hollywood Reporter, 1999—2005, 2006. Mem.: Hollywood Radio and TV Soc. (v.p. 2003—). Office: 20th Century Fox TV 10201 W Pico Blvd Bldg 88 Rm 29 Los Angeles CA 90035 *

WALDEN, GREG, congressman; b. The Dalles, Oreg., Jan. 10, 1957; s. Paul Walden; m. Mylene Walden; 1 child. BS in Journalism, U. Oreg., Eugene, 1981. Press sec. Staff of US Rep. Denny Smith of Oreg., 1981—84, chief of staff, 1984—86; owner Columbia Gorge Broadcasters, Inc., The Dalles, 1986—; mem. Oreg. State Ho. Reps., 1989-95, majority leader, 1991-93; mem. Oreg. State Senate, 1995-97, asst. majority leader, 1995-97; mem. US Congress from 2nd Oreg. dist., 1999—, mem. energy and commerce com., vice chmn. oversight and investigations subcommittee, mem. energy independence and global warming com., dep. whip, 2002—. Owner MSW Comm. Bd. dirs., exec. com. Assn. Oreg. Industries; bd. dirs. Oreg. Health Scis. Found. Named Outstanding Young Oregonian, Oreg. Jaycees, 1991, Legislator of Yr., Nat. Rep. Legislators Assn., 1993, Agr. Retailers Assn., Ctrl. Oreg. Visitors Assn., Nat. Assn. Home Care, Nat. Rural Health Assn., Oreg. Assn. Home Care, Oreg. Rural Electric Coop. Assn., Hero of the Taxpayer, Ams. for Tax Reform, Friend of the Shareholder, Am. Shareholders Assn., Oreg. Person of Yr., Dorchester Conf., Perfect Voter, Info. Tech. Industry, Guardian of Small Bus., Nat. Fedn. Ind. Bus., Friend of the Pear Industry, N.W. Pear Industry, Friend of the Farm Bur., Oreg. Farm Bur., Protector of Property Rights, Property Rights Alliance, Champion of Small Bus., Small Bus. Survival Com.; recipient Legislator of Yr., Safari Club Internat., Benjamin Franklin award, 60+ Assn., Pub. Svc. award, Am. Coll. Nurse-Midwives, Thomas Jefferson award, Food Distribrs. Internat., Disting. Svc. award, Forest Counties and Schs. Coalition, Champion award, League of Pvt. Property Owners, Congl. Champion award, Nat. Assn. Svc. and Conservation Corps, Wheat Adv. award, Nat. Assn. Wheat Growers, Appreciation award, Oreg. Nat. Guard, Sr. Legis. Achievement award, Seniors Coalition, Spirit of Enterprise award, US C. of C., Golden Bulldog award, Watchdog of the Treasury. Mem. Hood River C. of C., Nat. Fedn. Ind. Bus., Elks, Rotary. Republican. Episcopalian. Office: US House Reps 1210 Longworth House Office Bldg Washington DC 20515 Office Phone: 202-225-6730. Office Fax: 202-225-5774. E-mail: greg.walden@mail.house.gov. *

WALDEN, JAMES WILLIAM, accountant, educator; b. Jellico, Tenn., Mar. 5, 1936; s. William Evert and Bertha L. (Faulkner) Walden; m. Eva June Selvia, Jan. 16, 1957 (dec. Aug. 1988); 1 child, James William; m. Hattie Nan Lamb, Jan. 6, 1990 (div. June 1992); m. Janet Faulkner, Aug. 12, 1993 (div. May 2001); m. Louise Davis, Apr. 28, 2004. BS, Miami U., Oxford, Ohio, 1963; MBA, Xavier U., Cin., 1966. CPA Ohio. Tchr. math. Middletown (Ohio) City Sch. Dist., 1963-67, Fairfield (Ohio) High Sch., 1967-69; instr. accounting Sinclair Community Coll., Dayton, Ohio, 1969-72, asst. prof., 1972-75, assoc. prof., 1975-78, prof., 1978-89, prof. emeritus, 1991—. Cons., public acct.; mem. adj. faculty in acctg. Capital U., 1980—. Group comdr., fin. officer and chief staff Ohio wing CAP; bd. dirs. Frankin Cmty. Svcs.; bd. dir. Franklin Food Pantry. With USAF, 1954—59. Mem.: Ohio Soc. CPAs, Greater Hamilton Estate Planning Coun., Nat. Soc. Pub. Accts., Pub. Accts. Soc. Ohio (pres. S.W. chpt. 1985—86), Springboro C. of C. (bd. dirs., treas.), Kiwanis (pres. Springboro chpt.), Butler County Torch Club, Lions, Rotary, Am. Legion (life), Beta Alpha Psi. Office: Sinclair CC 251 Siler St Jellico TN 37762 Office Phone: 423-784-1502. Personal E-mail: jwalden@one.net.

WALDEN, JENNIFER LEE, plastic surgeon; b. Austin, Tex., Nov. 17, 1971; d. Richard M. and Shirley T. Walden. BA, U. Tex., Austin, 1994, MD, 1998. Intern U. Tex., Galveson, 1998—99, resident in plastic surgery, 1999—2003; aesthetic surgery fellow Manhattan Eye, Ear and Throat Hosp., NYC, 2003—04, asst. attending, 2004—, Lenox Hill Hosp., NYC, 2004—. Co-dir. Nat. Student Rsch. Forum. Contbr. articles to profl. jours. Med. mission vol. surgeon Austin Smiles, 2005—06; med. vol. NYC Dept. of Health Med. Res. Corps. Recipient Mavis P. Kelsey Excellence in Medicine award, Kelsey Seybold Found., Houston, 1998, Hermann Barnett Meml. award, U. Tex., 1998, Janet M. Glasgow Meml. award, Am. Med. Women's Assn., 1998, Merck Manual award, Merck and Co., 1998, Best Sci. Exhibit award, Am. Soc. for Aesthetic Plastic Surgery, 2004; Vaughn Found. scholar, U. Tex., 1995—97, Isabella H. Brackenridge scholar, 1996, 1998, Donald P. Duncan Meml. scholar, 1997. Mem.: ACS (assoc.; plastic and maxillofacial surgery adv. coun. 2002—03), NY Med. Soc., NY County Med. Soc., Northeastern Soc. Plastic Surgeons, Assn. Women Surgeons, Am. Soc. Plastic Surgeons, Alpha Omega Alpha (Tex. alpha chpt. pres. 1997—98), Pi Beta Phi (edn1. enrichment chair 1993—94). Office: 50 E 71st St New York NY 10021 Office Phone: 212-288-9009. Office Fax: 212-737-8340. E-mail: drjenniferwalden@hotmail.com.

WALDEN, JOHN, retail executive; married; 5 children. B, U. Ill.; M, Northwestern U.; JD, Ill. Inst. Tech. Former exec. Storage Tech. Corp., Ameritech Corp.; former pres., COO Peapod, Inc., Skokie, Ill.; pres., Best Buy.com subs. Best Buy Co., Inc., 1999—2002, exec. v.p. human capital and leadership, 2002—05, exec. v.p. customer bus. group, 2005—. Office: Best Buy Co Inc 7601 Penn Ave S Minneapolis MN 55423 Office Phone: 612-291-1000. Office Fax: 612-292-4001.

WALDEN, SHELTON HARRISON, radio personality, educator; s. Herman B. Walden and Sarah Louise Harrison. BA in Polit. Sci., Fordham U., 1984. Radio broadcaster, NYC, 1986—. Prodr., radio host, jounalist

Walden's Pond. Mem.: Fighting 69th Rep. Club (pres. 2005—06). Home and Office: 65 W 96th St 24C New York NY 10025 Office Phone: 212-209-2984. Business E-Mail: shelton@waldenspond.com.

WALDENBERG, ALAN S., lawyer; b. Mineola, NY, June 19, 1953; BS magna cum laude, U. Md., 1974; JD cum laude, Harvard U., 1978. CPA Md., 1976; bar: NJ 1978, US Dist. Ct. NJ (inactive) 1978, NY 1979, US Tax Ct. 1981. Ptnr., mem. exec. com. Schulte Roth & Zabel LLP, NYC. Contbr. articles to profl. jour.; spkr. in field. Mem.: NY Bar Assn. (Taxation Sect.). Office: Scultz Roth & Zabel LLP 919 Third Ave New York NY 10022 Office Phone: 212-756-2000. Office Fax: 212-593-5955. Business E-Mail: alan.waldenberg@srz.com.

WALDERA, WAYNE EUGENE, crisis management executive; b. Cayuga, ND, Mar. 23, 1930; s. Bernard Cyril and Eleanor Nee (Kugler) W.; m. Eva Jenzene Personius, Jan. 13, 1958; children: Anthony, Lori, Mia, Shauna. BSBA, N.D. State U., 1952. With Gamble-Skogmo, 1954-88; pres. Gamble div. Gamble-Skogmo, Mpls., 1972-88; pres., CEO Retail Resource Co., Mpls., 1988-89, Amdura Corp., Denver, 1989-92, also bd. dirs.; chmn. Sullivan Waldera, Inc., Mpls., 1992-93; prin., CEO Waldera & Co. Inc., Mpls., 1993—. 1st lt. USAF, 1952-54. Home: 12125 62nd St Waconia MN 55387-9411 Office: Waldera & Co Inc 700 Twelve Oaks Ctr Dr Ste 208 Wayzata MN 55391-1435 E-mail: wwaldera@uswest.net.

WALDHAUSEN, JOHN ANTON, retired surgeon, editor; b. NYC, May 22, 1929; s. Max. H. and Agnes H. (Stettner) W.; m. Marian Trescher, June 4, 1957; children: John H., Robert Rodney, Anthony Gordon Scarlett. BS magna cum laude, Coll. Great Falls, 1950; MD, St. Louis U., 1954. Diplomate Am. Bd. Surgery, Am. Bd. Thoracic Surgery. Intern Johns Hopkins Hosp., 1954-55, resident, 1955-57; clin. asst. Nat. Heart and Lung Inst., NIH, 1957-59; resident Hosp. U. Pa., 1959, Ind. U. Med. Ctr., 1960-62; practice medicine specializing in cardiothoracic surgery Indpls., 1962-66, Phila., 1966-70; mem. staff Milton S. Hershey Med. Ctr., Hershey, Pa., 1969-96. From instr. to asst. prof. Ind. U. Med. Ctr., 1962—66; assoc. prof. surgery U. Pa., Phila., 1966—70; prof. surgery Pa. State U. Coll. Medicine/Milton S. Hershey Med. Ctr, 1966—83, chmn. dept. surgery, 1969—94, sr. mem. grad. faculty, 1970—94, interim provost, dean, 1972—73, assoc. dean health care, 1973—75, assoc. dean and dir. Univ. Physicians, 1993—96, J.W. Oswald prof., 1983—99, J.W. Oswald prof. emeritus, 1999—; trustee U. Great Falls, Mont., 2001—04. Mem. editl. bd. Jour. Cardiovasc. Surgery, 1985-93, Jour. Pediatric Surgery, 1972-78, Jour. Thoracic and Cardiovasc. Surgery, 1982, editor, 1994-2000; cons. editor Archives of Surgery, 1972-74; contbr. chpts. to books and articles to med. jours. Recipient Career Devel. award USPHS, 1964. Fellow AAAS; mem. AMA, ACS (chpt. pres. 1974-75, gov. 1979-85, chmn. adv. coun. cardiothoracic surgery 1992-97), Am. Acad. Pediat., Am. Assn. Surgery of Trauma, Am. Coll. Cardiology (sec. 1981-82, trustee 1984-89, mem. editl. bd. jour. 1983, assoc. editor 1986-89), Am. Fedn. Clin. Rsch., Am. Heart Assn., Am. Physiol. Soc., Am. Soc. Artificial Internal Organs, Am. Assn. Thoracic Surgery (1st v.p. 1990-91, pres., 1991-92), Am. Surg. Assn. (1st v.p. 1984-85), Ctrl. Surg. Assn., Internat. Cardiovasc. Soc. (chpt. recorder 1969-74), Pa. Assn. Thoracic Surgery (pres. 1977-78), Thoracic Surgery Dirs. Assn. (pres. 1977-79), Societe International de Chirurgie (membership chmn. 1987-92, treas. 1992-94), Soc. Clin. Surgery (treas. 1971-80, v.p. 1981-82, Pres. 1982-83), Soc. Surg. Chairmen, Soc. Thoracic Surgeons, Soc. Univ. Surgeons, Soc. Vascular Surgery, So. Surg. Assn., Sigma Xi, Alpha Omega Alpha. Home: 515 Bridgeview Dr Lemoyne PA 17043 Office: Pa State U Coll Med MS Hershey Med Ctr PO Box 850 Hershey PA 17033-0850 Office Phone: 717-531-8330. Personal E-mail: jwaldhausen@aol.com.

WALDINGER, ROBERT JON, psychiatrist; b. Omaha, Mar. 1, 1951; s. David and Miriam (Passman) W.; m. Jennifer Abby Stone, May 26, 1986; children: Daniel Cane, David Stone. AB, Harvard U., 1973, MD, 1978. Diplomate Am. Bd. Psychiatry and Neurology. Fellow in psychol. rsch. McLean Hosp., Belmont, Mass., 1982-85, asst. dir. residency tng., 1985-90; dir. tng. Mass. Mental Health Ctr., Boston, 1990-96; rsch. assoc. Judge Baker Children's Ctr., Boston, 1997—2003; assoc. prof. psychiatry Harvard Med. Sch., 2003—. Mem. faculty Boston Psychoanalytic Inst., 1987—; cons. Harvard U. Health Svc., Cambridge, Mass., 1984—. Author: Psychiatry for Medical Students, 1984, Effective Psychotherapy with Borderline Patients, 1987. Knox fellow Harvard U., 1973. Fellow Am. Psychiat. Assn. (Falk fellow 1980-82). Democrat. Jewish. Office: Brigham and Women's Hosp 1249 Boylston St 3rd Fl Boston MA 02215-5794 Office Phone: 617-525-6133. Business E-Mail: rwaldinger@partners.org. *

WALDKOETTER, RAYMOND OLIVER, psychologist, consultant; b. Indpls., Oct. 25, 1928; s. Raymond Oliver Waldkoetter, Sr. and Viola Simmons Waldkoetter; m. Mary Frances McBane, Sept. 25, 1953; children: Lisa K. Keenan, Greta A. Banner, Eric R., William H., Janet M. Turko, Olivia E. BS in Edn., Ind. U., 1951, MS in Edn., 1955, EdD in Psychol. Studies, 1963. Cert. psychologist Ind. Health Professions Bur. Dir. student activities U. Toledo, 1957—59; expatriate tutor Techiman Tng. Coll., Abetifi, Ghana, 1959—60; counselor Testing Bur. Depauw U., Greencastle, Ind., 1960—61; rsch. psychologist Enlisted Evaluation Ctr., Ft. Harrison, Ind., 1961—63, tech. advisor, 1965—73; dean of students Shepherd Coll., Shepherdstown, W.Va., 1963—64; sr. rsch. psychologist Army Rsch. Inst., Alexandria, Va., 1974—82; consulting psychologist U.S. Army Soldier Support Ctr., Ft. Harrison, 1982—93; pvt. practice Greenwood, Ind., 1993—. Mem. bd. advisors The Monroe Inst., Faber, Va., 1986—. Capt. USMC, 1951—59. Recipient Harry Greer award, Internat. Mil. Testing Assn., USN, 1983, Comdrs. award for Civil Svc., Dept. of the Army, 1993. Mem.: APA, Masons, Phi Delta Kappa, Theta Xi. Methodist. Achievements include personnel rating form design; sound-wave acoustic therapy; occupational analysis for performance enhancement. Avocations: reading, parapsychology, travel. Home: 906 S Haven Rd Greenwood IN 46143-2623

WALDMAN, AMY, journalist; BA, Yale U., 1991. Freelance journalist, prof. U. Western Cape, South Africa, 1992—94; editor, writer Washington Monthly; editor Washington Post; metro desk reporter NY Times, 1997—2002, co-bur. chief New Delhi, 2002—05; nat. corr. Atlantic Monthly, Washington, 2005—. Recipient Disting. Feature Writing award, NY Newspaper Pub. Assn., Front Page award, Newswomen's Club NY, Overseas Press Club award for best bus. reporting in newspapers, 2006. Office: The Atlantic Monthly 600 New Hampshire Ave NW Washington DC 20037 Office Phone: 202-266-6000.

WALDMAN, BARRY HOWARD, film producer; b. Bklyn., Oct. 23, 1963; s. Arthur Lloyd and Lee (Rothke) W. BA, U. Miami, 1984. Mgr. unit prodn. Lastraw Films, Davie, Fla., 1985; mgr. line prodn. and unit prodn. Swan Prodns., Ann Arbor, Mich., 1985, Vernon Films, Miami, Fla., 1985-86; producer Elf Prodns., Miami, 1986-87; line producer Person to Person Films, NYC, 1987—. Assoc. prodr.: Bravo Awards, Miami, 1987, SH TV Prodns., Hallandale, Fla., 1987, (films) The Rock, 1996, Armageddon, 1998,; prodr.: (films) Shallow Grave, 1987, (TV series) Key West, 1993, Without a Trace, 2002; exec. prodr.: (films) Gone in Sixty Seconds, 2000, Pearl Harbor, 2001, Kangaroo Jack, 2003, Bad Boys II, 2003, National Treasure, 2004, Domino, 2005, Deja Vu, 2006. Mem. Ind. Film Project, Fla. Film Producers. Jewish. *

WALDMAN, DANIEL, lawyer; BA, Harvard U., 1977; JD, Columbia U., 1980. Bar: D.C. 1980. Clk. to Judge William A. Norris U.S. Ct. Appeals (9th cir.), 1980-82; assoc. Arnold & Porter, Washington, 1982—87, ptnr., 1987—96; gen. counsel Commodity Futures Trading Commn., Washington, 1996—99; ptnr., Derivatives Practice Group Arnold & Porter, Washington, 1999—. Office: Arnold & Porter 555 Twelfth St NW Washington DC 20004-1206 Office Phone: 202-942-5804. Office Fax: 202-942-5999. Business E-Mail: dan.waldman@aporter.com.

WALDMAN, MICHAEL, economist, educator; b. Paterson, NJ, May 12, 1955; s. Henry and Nettie Waldman; m. Karen Voris, July 9, 1982 (div. Jan. 1992); m. Lisa Berki, July 18, 1999; children: David Henry, Emma Nicole. BS in Econs., MIT, 1977; PhD in Econs., U. Pa., 1982. From asst. prof. to prof. econs. UCLA, 1983-93; prof. econs. Cornell U., Ithaca, NY, 1991-97, Charles H. Dyson prof. in mgmt., 1997—. Vis. prof. econs. Yale U. Sch. Orgn. and Mgmt., New Haven, 1989—90, U. Chgo. Grad. Sch. Bus., 1997—99. Co-editor: Jour. Econ. Perspectives, 2000—06; assoc. editor: Quar. Jour. Econs., 2000—; contbr. articles to profl. jours. Mem.: Western Econ. Assn., Soc. Labor Economists, Royal Econ. Soc., Econometric Soc., Am. Econ. Assn. (program com. 2004). Office: Cornell U Johnson Grad Sch Mgmt Sage Hall Ithaca NY 14853 Business E-Mail: mw46@cornell.edu.

WALDMAN, SEYMOUR MORTON, lawyer; b. NYC, Aug. 6, 1926; s. Louis and Bella B. Waldman; m. Lois Citrin, Aug. 5, 1951; children: David, Daniel, Michael, Ellen. BA, Columbia U., 1948, LLB, 1950. Bar: N.Y. 1950, U.S. Ct. Appeals (1st, 2d, 3d, 4th, 5th, 6th and D.C. cirs.), U.S. Dist. Ct. (so. dist.) N.Y., U.S. Dist. Ct. (ea. dist.) N.Y., U.S. Supreme Ct. 1956. From assoc. to ptnr. Waldman & Waldman, NYC, 1950—82; ptnr., of counsel Vladeck, Waldman, Elias & Engelhard, P.C., 1982—2005. Village atty. Village of Croton-on-Hudson, NY, 1972—2005. Chair zoning bd. appeals Village of Croton-on-Hudson, 1963—72; trustee Hosp. Joint Diseases Orthopaedic Inst., 1968—93. With USN, 1944—46. Mem. ABA, N.Y. State Bar Assn., Phi Beta Kappa. Avocation: tennis. Office: Vladeck Waldman Elias & Engelhard PC 1501 Broadway Ste 800 New York NY 10036-5560 Business E-Mail: swaldman@vladeck.com.

WALDMAN, STEVEN, editor; Former advisor to CEO Corp. Nat. Svcs.; editor Washington Monthly; nat. editor US News & World Report; CEO, co-founder, editor-in-chief Beliefnet.com. Contbr. articles to numerous profl. jours.; TV Appearances CNN, Fox News, ABC News, Radio Appearances Nat. Pub. Radio; author: The Bill (a textbook used in college courses around the US); regular contbr. Slate & National Review. Named one of Nation's top "spiritual innovators", Time Mag., 2000; recipient Nat. Mag. award for General Excellence in Online Jour., Am. Soc. Mag. Editors, 2007. Office: BeliefNet Inc Box 1062 303 Park Ave S New York NY 10010 Fax: 212-533-1492. *

WALDMANN, THOMAS ALEXANDER, medical researcher, physician; b. NYC, Sept. 21, 1930; s. Charles Elizabeth (Sipos) Waldmann; m. Katharine Emory Spreng, Mar. 29, 1958; children: Richard Allen, Robert James, Carol Ann. AB, U. Chgo., 1951; MD, Harvard U., 1955; PhD (hon.), U. Med. Sch., Debrecin, Hungary, 1991. Diplomate Am. Bd. Allergy and Immunology. Intern Mass. Gen. Hosp., Boston, 1955—56; clin. assoc. Nat. Cancer Inst. NIH, Bethesda, Md., 1956—58, sr. investigator, 1958—68, head immunophysiology sect., 1968—73, chief metabolism br., 1971—. Cons. WHO, 1975, 78; bd. dirs., v.p. Found. for Advanced Edn. in Scis., Bethesda, 1980—2002, treas., 1988—90, v.p., 1990—92; William Dameshek vis. prof. U. Calif., Irvine, 1984; mem. med. adv. bd. Howard Hughes Med. Inst., 1987—93; vis. com. mem. Harvard Med. Sch., Boston, 1988—94; mem. sci. adv. com., chmn. Mass. Gen. Hosp., 1992—96; chmn. sci. adv. bd. HealthCare Investment Corp., Princeton, NJ, 1986—2003. Author: Plasma Protein Metabolism, 1970; contbr. articles to profl. jours. With USPHS, 1956—58, 1959—63, 1975—94. Named Man of Yr., Am. Leukemia Soc., 1980; recipient Henry M. Stratton medal, Am. Hematology Soc., 1977, G. Burroughs Mider award, NIH, 1980, DSM, Dept. Health and Human Svcs., 1983, Abbott Lab. award in Clin. and Diagnostic Immunology, Am. Soc. Microbiology, 2002, Debrecen prize, Debrecen Med. Sch., Hungary, 2005, Dana Found. prize, Am. Assn. Immunologists, 2007. Fellow: Am. Acad. Allergy (Bela Schick award 1974, John M. Shelton award 1984, Lila Gruber prize 1986, Simon Shubitz prize 1987, CIBA-GEIGY Drew award 1987, Milken Family Med. Found. Disting. Basic Scientist prize 1991, Artois Latour Internat. Rsch. prize 1991, Bristol-Myers Cancer prize 1992, Paul Ehrlich medal 1997), Acad. Med. Scis. (hon.); mem.: NAS (chmn. 1985—89), Clin. Immunology Soc. (pres. 1988), Am. Soc. Clin. Investigation (mem. editl. bd. 1978—80, 1983—88), Assn. Am. Physicians, Hungarian Acad. Scis. (hon.), Inst. Medicine, Am. Acad. Arts and Scis. Achievements include research in defining of structure of multisubunit IL-2 receptor; identifying novel cytokine IL-15; forms of IL-2R-directed therapy using alpha and beta-emitting radionuclide chelate versions of humanized monoclonal antibodies (Zenapax daclizumab) for treatment of cancer and Multiple Sclerosis; analysis of immunoglobulin gene rearrangements to define clonality and classifying human lymphoid neoplasia; discovery of intestinal lymphangectasia and allergic gastroenteropathy. Office: Nat Inst Health 10 Center Dr Bethesda MD 20892-1374 Office Phone: 301-496-6656. Business E-Mail: tawald@helix.nih.gov.

WALDMEIR, PETER NIELSEN, retired journalist; b. Detroit, Jan. 16, 1931; s. Joseph John and Helen Sarah (Nielsen) W.; m. Marilyn C. Choma; children— Peter William, Patti Ann, Lindsey Marilyn, Christopher Norman. Student, Wayne State U., 1949-58. From mem. staff to sports columnist Detroit News, 1949—72, gen. columnist, 1972—2004; ret., 2004. Pres. Old Newsboys Goodfellow Fund, Detroit, 1988; mem. city coun. Grosse Pointe Woods, Mich., 2005. With USMC, 1951-53. Recipient Headliners award Nat. Headliners Club, 1971, SDX Lifetime Achievement award, 2000; named Mich. Sports Writer of Yr., Nat. Sportscasters and Sportswriters, 1967, 69, 71; Heart award Variety Club Internat., 1985; inducted Mich. Journalism Hall of Fame, 2000. Mem. Sigma Delta Chi. Roman Catholic. Personal E-mail: pwaldmeir@aol.com.

WALDO, ALBERT LEON, internist, educator; b. NYC, Nov. 25, 1936; MD, SUNY Coll. Medicine, Bklyn., 1962. Cert. in internal medicine, specialty in clin. cardiac electrophysiology, specialty in cardiovasc. Intern Kings County Hosp., Bklyn., 1962-63, resident in medicine, 1965-66, Balt. City Hosps., 1963-65; fellow Coll. Physicians and Surgeons Columbia U., 1966-68, from asst. to assoc. prof. dept. pharmacy, Coll. Physicians and Surgeons, 1969—72; fellow cardiology Columbia-Presbyn. Med. Ctr., NYC, 1968-69; from assoc. prof. to prof. medicine U. Ala., 1972—86; with U. Hosps., Cleve., 1986—, dir., clin. cardiac electrophysiology program; prof. medicine Case Western U., Ohio, 1986—, Walter H. Pritchard Prof. Cardiology, prof. medicine, and prof. Biomedical Engineering Ohio. Cons., Circulatory Sys. Devices Panel of the Medical Devices Advisory Com., FDA; mem. Electrical Signaling, Ion Transport, and Arrhythmias (ESTA) Study Sect., NIH/NHLBI. Serves or has served on the editl. bds. of peer reviewed journals in the field, including Circulation, Journal American College Cardiology, American Journal Cardiology, Pacing and Clinical Electrophysiology, Journal Cardiovascular Electrophysiology, Journal Electrocardiology, Heart Rhythm, (audio journals) American College of Cardiology (ACCEL), North American Society of Pacing and Electrophysiology (NASPETapes) (also editor-in-chief); contbr. articles to profl. jours. Recipient award for Achievements in Clin. and Exptl. Cardiology, Found. Hartsvrienden RESCAR of The Netherlands. Fellow Am. Coll. Cardiology (past pres. Ohio Chpt.), ACP, Am. Coll. Chest Physicians, Am. Heart Assn.; mem. Am. Physiol. Soc., Am. Soc. Clin. Investigation, Heart Rhythm Soc. (founding mem., past pres. formally called N.Am. Soc. Pacing and Electrophysiology, Disting. Scientist award, 1997), Assn. Am. Physicians, Assn. Univ. Cardiologists, Cardiac Electrophysiology Soc. (past pres.) Office: U Hosps Cleve 11100 Euclid Ave Cleveland OH 44106-1736 Office Phone: 216-844-7690. Business E-Mail: albertwaldo@case.edu. *

WALDO, JAMES CHANDLER, lawyer; b. Seattle, Oct. 23, 1948; s. Burton Chandler and Margaret (Hoar) W.; m. Sharon B. Waldo; children: Sara K., William K., John J. Grad., Whitman Coll., 1970; JD, Willamette U., 1974. Bar: Wash. 1974, U.S. Ct. Appeals (9th cir.) 1976. Exec. asst. Dept. of Labor, Washington, 1974-76; asst. U.S. atty. Justice Dept., Seattle, 1976-79; of counsel ESTEP & LI, Seattle, 1979-80; ptnr. Gordon, Thomas, Honeywell, Malanca, Peterson & Daheim LLP, Seattle, 1981—. Chmn. N.W. Renewable Resources Ctr., Seattle, 1984-97, Wash. State Energy Strategy Com., 1991-93; spl. counsel on Water for Gov., 2001—04. Trustee Western Wash. U., 1981-93. Recipient Outstanding Alumnus of Yr. Whitman Coll., 1994, Dir.'s award Wash. Dept. Fisheries, 1986, Pres.'s award Assn. Wash. Bus., 1988, Outstanding Citizen award Western Assn. Fish & Wildlife Agys., 1987, Merit award, Am. Water Works Assn., 2005. Mem. Am. Water Works Assn. (Award of Merit 2005). Office: Gordon Thomas Honeywell Malanca Peterson & Daheim LLP PO Box 1157 Tacoma WA 98401-1157 Office Phone: 253-620-6541.

WALDO, ROBERT LELAND, retired insurance company executive; b. Pittsville, Wis., Sept. 1, 1923; s. Elmer Harley and Edith Viola (Senter) W.; m. Elaine Anne Jossie, June 4, 1947; children: Daniel Robert, Thomas Parker, Susan Jeanne. BA, U. Wis., 1949, JD, 1951. Assoc. atty. Foley & Lardner, Milw., 1951-59; asst. sec., asst. gen. counsel Wis. Gas Co., Milw., 1959-69; v.p., gen. counsel Verex Corp. and Subss., Madison, Wis., 1969-72; exec. v.p., sec. Verex Corp. and subs., Madison, Wis., 1972-78, pres., chief operating officer, 1978-82, pres., chief exec. officer, 1982-85, chmn., chief exec. officer, 1985-86. Served as sgt. U.S. Army, 1943-46, ETO. Mem. Wis. Bar Assn., Dane County Bar Assn., Mortgage Ins. Co.'s Am. (pres. 1980-82), Maple Bluff Country Club. Republican. Methodist. Avocations: travel, golf. Home: 818 Charing Cross Rd Madison WI 53704-6010

WALDOCK, WILLIAM DAVID, aerospace transportation executive, educator; b. Ft. Worth, Tex., Aug. 4, 1952; s. Wallace Gordon and Annabelle (Wolfe) W.; m. Barbara A. Wisler, Sept. 14, 1974; children: Andrew, Kathleen. BA in History, U. Fla., 1975; student, Miami-Dade Coll., Miami, Fla., 1977-78; M of Aero. Sci. with honors, Embry-Riddle Aero. U., 1982; postgrad., Kennedy-Western U. Prof. aero. sci. Embry-Riddle Aero. U., Prescott, Ariz., 1982—, chief investigator aircraft accidents, 1991—, assoc. dir. Ctr. Aerospace Safety Edn., 1986—, dir. Robertson Aviation Safety Ctr., 1995—. Pres., chief cons. Sys. Safety, Inc., Prescott, 1990—; cons. Am. West Airlines, Phoenix, 1996-99; presenter numerous safety confs. Contbr. articles to profl. publs.; guest various T.V. shows. Lt. comdr. USCG, 1975-96, ret. Mem. SAFE Assn. (Gen. Spruance award for Outstanding Contbns. to Safety Through Edn. 1990), Aircraft Owners and Pilots Assn., Aircraft Rescue and Firefighting Working Group, Am. Soc. Safety Engrs., World Safety Orgn. (cert.), Internat. Soc. Air Safety Investigators (pres. Ariz. chpt. 1987—). Achievements include over 150 field investigations; research in accident history. Office: Embry-Riddle Aero U Bldg 21 3700 Willow Creek Rd Prescott AZ 86301-3721 Home Phone: 928-776-1020; Office Phone: 928-777-6956. Personal E-mail: wwaldock@msn.com.

WALDON, ALTON RONALD, JR., judge; b. Lakeland, Fla., Dec. 21, 1936; s. Alton Ronald and Rupert Juanita (Wallace) W.; m. Barbara De Costa, June 3, 1961; children: Alton III, Dana Olive, Ian Patrick. BS, John Jay Coll., NYC, 1968; JD, NY Law Sch., 1973. Capt. NYC Housing Authority Police Dept., 1962—75; dep. commr. NY State Divsn. Human Rights, 1975—82; assemblyman NY State Assembly, 1983—86; congressman US Ho. Reps., Washington, 1986—87; commr. NY State Commn. Investigation, 1987—90; senator NY State, 1991—2000; judge Ct. of Claims State of NY, 2000—06; commr. NY State Victims Bd., 2007—. Bd. dirs. USO Met. NY. Recipient Thurgood Marshall fellow, NY State Trial Lawyers Assn., 1970-73. Mem. Met. Black Bar Assn., Macon B. Allen Bar Assn., Comus Club NY, Alumni Assn. NY Law Sch., Alumni Assn. John Jay Coll., Masons (33 deg.), Sigma Pi Phi. Democrat. Roman Catholic. Avocation: sports. Office Phone: 718-923-4400.

WALDREP, B. DWAIN, education educator; b. Decatur, Ala., Oct. 11, 1954; s. Emmett N. and Melva Jo Waldrep; m. Phyllis M. Morgan, June 9, 1971; 1 child, Matthew N. BA, Southeastern Bible Coll., 1984; MA, U. Ala., 1985; MABS, Dallas Theol. Sem., 1991; PhD, Auburn U., 2001. Prof. Southeastern Bible Coll., Birmingham, Ala., 1990—; adj. prof. U. of Ala., 2002—. Contbr. articles to profl. jours. Specialist 5 US Army, 1971—76, US and Korea. Mem.: So. Hist. Assn., Ala. Hist. Assn.

WALDRIP, KAREN MARIE, career planning administrator; b. Tacoma, Oct. 17, 1961; d. Mike and Ethel Gray; m. Edwin Thomas Waldrip, Aug. 25, 1990; 1 child, Amy Lynn Ely. BS in Psychology, U. Puget Sound, 1984, M in Edn. and Counseling, 1987. Lic. profl. counselor Alaska, 2000. Counselor, social worker Ryther Child Ctr., Seattle, 1985—87; edn. specialist Petersburg Coun. on Alcoholism, Alaska, 1987—88; adult treatment specialist Lakeside-Milam Recover Ctrs., Juneau, Alaska, 1988—90; employment career counselor State of Alaska Dept. Labor and Workforce Devel., Juneau, 1990—2006; pvt. practice DBA: Alaska's Renewable Resources and Workforce Consulting, Auke Bay, 2006—; job developer, career counselor, cmty. rehab. provider Dept. Vocat. Rehab. Supporter Big Bros., Big Sisters, Boy Scouts of Am., Girl Scouts of Am., Juneau, 2002; doner ARC Assn., Juneau, 1999—2006; active Ptnr. in Hope donor registry St. Jude's Med. Ctr., Juneau, 2005; active Paralyzed Vets. Am., Juneau, 2000—06. Recipient 15 Yr. Svc. award, State of Alaska, 2000, E-Commerce 900+ Feedback award, 2005; grantee State Tng. and Employment Program, State of Alaska, 1993, 1994, 1995, 1995—2000. Mem.: Cmty. and Econ. Devel. (licentiate). Independent. Avocations: fishing, hunting. Home: 19935 Cohen Dr Juneau AK 99801 Office: DBA: Alaska's Renewable Resources PO Box 210555 Auke Bay AK 99821 Office Phone: 907-723-6970. Personal E-mail: etwaldrip75@msn.com. Business E-Mail: alaskarenewableresources@msn.com.

WALDRON, GERARD J., lawyer; b. Nov. 20, 1960; BA, U. Va., 1982; M in Pub. Policy, with honors, Duke U., 1990, JD with high honors, 1990. Bar: Pa. 1990, DC 1997. Staff for US Rep. Edward Markey (D-MA) US Ho. of Reps, Washington, 1982—85, staff, sub-com. energy, 1985—87, staff, sub-com. telecom., 1987, sr. counsel, sub-com. telecom., 1991—95; law clk. for Judge Dickson Phillips US Ct. Appeals (4th cir.), Washington, 1990—91; ptnr., Comm. Practice Group Covington & Burling, Washington. Author: Keep States Off the Net Backbone: Only the FCC Has Authority to Regulate Interstate Web Traffic, 2000, FCC Clarifies Telemarketing Rules, 2005. Office: Covington & Burling 1201 Pennsylvania Ave NW Washington DC 20004-2401 Office Phone: 202-662-5360. Office Fax: 202-662-6291. Business E-Mail: gwaldron@cov.com.

WALDRON, JEREMY JAMES, law educator; b. Invercargill, Southland, New Zealand, Oct. 13, 1953; s. Francis Herbert and Joyce Annette (Ainge) W.; m. Helen McGimpsey, Jan. 26, 1974 (div. Oct. 1989); 1 child, Samuel James. BA with honors, U. Otago, New Zealand, 1974, LLB with honors, 1978; DPhil, Oxford U., 1986. Bar: New Zealand 1978. Asst. lectr. philosophy U. Otago, 1975-78; fellow in polit. theory Lincoln Coll., Oxford, Eng., 1980-82; lectr. in polit. theory U. Edinburgh, Scotland, 1982-87; prof. law U. Calif., Berkeley, 1987—96; Laurence S. Rockefeller Univ. prof. of politics Princeton U., 1996—97; Maurice and Hilda

Friedman prof. law Columbia U., NYC, 1997—2004, Univ. prof., 2005—06, NYU, 2006—. Editor: collection of essays Theories of Rights, 1984, Nonsense Upon Stilts, 1987; author: (textbook) The Law, 1990, (monograph) The Right to Private Property, 1988; contbr. articles to profl. jours. Avocations: romance, music, travel. Home: 19 Edwards Pl Princeton NJ 08540-5113 Office: NYU Sch Law 40 Washington Sq S, 411K New York NY 10012 Office Phone: 212-998-6573. Office Fax: 212-998-4894. E-mail: jeremy.waldron@nyu.edu.

WALDRON, KAREN, development, construction and management company executive; m. Shawn Ricci. Chairperson/sr. v.p. F&W Mgmt.; pres. Bent Tree Farm Ltd., The Ctr. at Walnut Grove; chairperson, CEO Fralin and Waldron, Inc., Roanoke, Va. Mem. bd. visitors Radford U.; mem. exec. bd. Roanoke Valley Horse Show; pub. bd. dirs., chair Va. Horse Ctr. Avocations: horse industry, Pilates instruction, yoga, dance. Office: Fralin and Waldron Inc Ste 200 PO Box 24018 3130 Chaparral Dr Roanoke VA 24018

WALDRON, THEODORE CHARLES, physician; b. West Hazleton, Pa., June 3, 1946; s. Leonard Raymond Waldron; m. Gloria Jean Koziel, June 24, 1978; children: Theodore Leonard, Darren Christopher. BS in Biology, Alliance Coll., 1968; D of Osteopathy, Phila. Coll. Osteopathic Medicine, 1978. Diplomate Am. Osteo. Coll. Gen. Practice; diplomate Nat. Bd. Examiners of Osteo. Medicine and Surgery; diplomate State Bd. Osteo. Examiners; cert. gen./family practice; lic. Pa., S.C. Gen. practice medicine, Conyngham, Pa., 1979-00; chief family practice dept. Hazleton St. Joseph Med. Ctr., 1989-90; physician specialist II White Haven (Pa.) Ctr., 1993-96; disability physician specialist Pa. Dept. Labor and Industry Bur. Disability Determination, Wilkes-Barre, 1996—; med. dir. Lattimer ICF-MR Facility, 1995—2000. Med. dir. Hazleton Nursing & Geriatric Ctr., Mountain City Convalescent Ctr., Hazleton, 1983-91; occupational health physician Workmed, Hazleton, 1991-93. Dir. vector control for Lycoming, Clinton, Snyder and Union counties, Pa. following Hurricane Agnes flooding, 1972. Served as sgt. USAR, N.G., 1969-76. Mem. Am. Osteopathic Assn., Pa. Osteopathic Med. Assn., Am. Osteopathic Coll. Family Practice, Pa. Osteopathic Gen. Practice Soc., S.C. Osteopathic Med. Assn. Republican. Roman Catholic. Avocations: fishing, photography, gardening, electronics, science. Home: 146 Hickory Rd Sugarloaf PA 18249-9556 E-mail: twaldron@gmpexpress.net.

WALDROP, FRANCIS NEIL, physician; b. Asheville, NC, Oct. 5, 1926; s. Troy Lester and Emma Louise (Ballard) W.; m. Eleanor Dorothy Wickes, June 10, 1950; children: Mark Lester, Barbara Louise. AB, U. Minn., 1946; MD, George Washington U., 1950. Intern George Washington U. Hosp., Washington, 1950-51; resident St. Elizabeth's Hosp., Washington, 1951-54, med. officer, 1951-71; dir. manpower and tng. programs NIMH, Rockville, Md., 1972-75; dep. adminstr. Alcohol, Drug Abuse and Mental Health Adminstrn., HEW, Rockville, 1975-79; ret., 1979. Clin. prof. psychiatry George Washington U. Recipient Superior Service award HEW, 1962, Disting. Service award, 1964. Fellow Am. Psychiat. Assn. (Distinguished life, Vestermark award 1980). Achievements include research, publs. in field. Home: 1775 Elton Rd Silver Spring MD 20903-1726

WALDROP, SHERRY HUTCHINSON, elementary school educator; b. Tifton, Ga., Mar. 8, 1953; d. Cecil W. and Omie Lee Hutchinson; m. William G. Waldrop; children: Cynthia Williamson, Grant, Matthew. A, Abraham Baldwin Agrl. Coll., Tifton, 1975; B, Valdosta State Coll., Ga., 1986, M, 1991; Edn. Specialist, Valdosta State U., Ga., 1996. Cert. educator, master tchr. Ga. Profl. Stds. Commn., 2006, nat. bd. cert. tchr. Ga. PSC, 2005. Tchr. Berrien County Bd. Edn., Enigma, Ga., 1986—88, Tift County Bd. Edn., Tifton, 1988—. Recipient ABAC Educators award, Alumni, 2006. Office: Eighth Street Middle School 700 W 8th St Tifton GA 31794 Home Phone: 229-386-0947; Office Phone: 229-387-2445. Business E-Mail: swaldrop@tiftschools.com.

WALEK, DAVID B., lawyer; b. Ft. Monmouth, NJ, May 18, 1954; s. Walter J. and Charlotte H. (Haag) W.; m. Elizabeth R. Gibson; children: Christopher, Emily, Merritt. BA cum laude, Yale U., 1976; JD, Harvard U., 1980. Bar: Mass., 1980. Assoc. Ropes & Gray, Boston, 1980-89, ptnr. corp. dept., 1989—, co-head tech. co. practice group. Lectr. Sloane Sch. Mgmt., MIT. Chmn. Artists for Humanity, Boston. Mem.: ABA, Boston Bar Assn. Office: Ropes & Gray 1 International Pl Boston MA 02110-2624 Home: 279 South Ave Weston MA 02493 Office Phone: 617-951-7388. Office Fax: 617-951-7050. Business E-Mail: david.walek@ropesgray.com.

WALEN, HARRY LEONARD, historian, lecturer, author; b. Winchester, Mass, June 26, 1915; s. Harry Leonard and Alice (Garland) W.; m. Elizabeth Rowe Benson, June 26, 1939; children: Harry Benson, Kimball Frederick, Robert Leonard. AB cum laude, Harvard U., 1937, AM, 1942. Tchr. Los Alamos Ranch Sch., N.Mex., 1937-42, head English dept. N.Mex., 1939-42; tchr. English Groton Sch., Mass., 1942-46; instr. English, faculty marshal Newton Jr. Coll., 1946-51; tchr. English and journalism Newton HS, Newtonville, Mass., 1946-51, adminstr., 1951-55; directing editor secondary sch. English textbooks Ginn and Co., Boston, 1955-61; prin. Needham HS, Mass., 1961-72, career and post secondary guidance counselor Mass., 1972-79. Mem. Regional Interviewing Com. for Overseas Grants and Fellowships, 1961-84; mem. planning com. Task Force on High Sch. Graduation Requirements, Mass Dept. Edn., 1976-80. Author: (books) The Family Travel-Camper, 1955, (with E. Gordon and others) Types of Literature, American Literature, English Literature, 1964, The Memory Book of the New England Association of Teachers of English, 1981, The Sons of the American Revolution 1962-82: An Historical Anthology, 1984, Images and Perceptions, 1996, The Birds of Budapest, 2004; (monographs) English Learning Environments, 1972, History of the Order of Founders and Patriots of America, 1982, Centennial History, 1996; co-author Alluring Rockport, rev. edit. 1986, The Little Old Meeting House and How It Grew; (poetry) Images and Perceptions, 1996; editor The English Leaflet, 1947-54; cons. editor on career edn. New Voices Series, 1978; poet laureate, Rockport, 1998, 99-; contbr. chpts., articles, poems to books, profl. jour. and periodicals. Alderman City of Newton, Mass., 1961-72; corp. mem. USS Mass. Meml. Com., Inc., 1972—, bd. dir., 1984-91, honorary dir., 1995—; chmn. edn. com. N.E. Conf. NCCJ, 1972-82, mem. study mission to Israel, 1974; vice chmn. New Eng. Conf. on Quality of Life, Boston, 1973; mem. Newton Regional Adv. Manpower Planning Bd., 1973-77; pres. counseling svc. YMCA, Greater Boston, 1976-7; chmn. Newton Highlands Bd. Christian Edn., 1974-75; pres. bd. trustees weekday ch. sch.; 1st Congl. Ch., Rockport, Mass., ch. historian, 1982-2002; del. Mass. Conf. United Ch. Christ, 1989-96. John Hay fellow, 1965; Mass. Dept. Edn. Commonwealth fellow, 1971; recipient citation U.S. Commr. Edn., 1971, citation New Eng. Assn. Schs. and Colls., 1984, cert. of Appreciation, City of Newton, 1971, Service award, YMCA, 1978. Mem. Nat. Council Tchr. English (assoc. chmn. nat. conv. 1965, chmn., co-founder Emeritus Assembly 1979-83, various other coms. and offices, Citation 1969), Nat. Assn. Secondary Sch. Prin., Headmasters Assn. (life), New Eng. Assn. Tchr. English (life, past pres., chmn. ann. C. S. Thomas award com. 1975-96, historian 1978—, Thomas award 1978), Mass. Secondary Sch. Prins. Assn. (diploma standards com. 1973-78, Bronze plaque 1974), Mass. Council Tchr. English (co-founder), Mass. Schoolmasters Club (past pres., hon. life), MENSA, Friends of Jackson Homestead, Newton Hist. Soc. (life, past pres.), Los Alamos (N.Mex.) Hist. Soc. (life), Sandy Bay Hist. Soc. (pres. 1983-86), Greater Boston Guidance Club (hon.), Nat. Gavel Soc., New Eng. Hist. and Geneal. Soc., SAR (pres. state 1979-81, nat. trustee 1981-83, historian gen. 1983-86, sec. Mus. Bd. 1982-88, Minuteman award 1985), Gen. Soc. Mayflower Descs. (mem. nat. exec. com. 1990-93), Mass. Soc. Mayflower Descs. (gov. 1985-88, dep. gov. gen. 1988-93), Pilgrim John Howland Soc. (pres. 1987-99, pres. emeritus 1999—, led pilgrimage to Eng., 1989), Mass. Huguenot Soc. (pres. 1990-92, nat. del. 1983-92), Descs. Colonial Clergy, Soc. Colonial Wars, Navy League US (life), Sons and Daus. of 1st Settlers of Newbury (pres. 1982-84), Piscataqua Pioneers (pres. 1990-91), Order of Crown of Charlemagne, Order Founders and Patriots (nat. treas. 1978-81, dep. gov. gen. 1981-84, exec. com. 1992-2000, councillor gen. Mass. 1984—, NH, 1987-90, 93—, gov. 1992-95, councillor gen. 1993—, Nat. Disting. Svc. award 1996), Boston Athenaeum, Harvard Club, Boston Authors Club (pres. 1995-96), English Lunch Club (pres. 1975-82), Friday Evening Club (most venerable 1979-86), Sandy Bay Yacht Club, Masons (32d degree, 50-Yr. award). Home: 16 Rockrimmon Rd Kingston NH 03848-3037

WALENDOWSKI, GEORGE JERRY, accounting and business educator; b. Han-Minden, Germany, Mar. 25, 1947; arrived in US, 1949; s. Stefan (dec.) and Eugenia (Lewandowska) W. AA, LA City Coll., 1968; BS, Calif. State U., LA, 1970, MBA, 1972; cert., Inst. Mgmt. Accts., 2004; cert. in leadership, Cornell U., 2006; master cert., Villanova U., 2006, cert. in fin. and acctg., orgnl. leadership and bus. analysis, 2007. Cert. community coll. instr. acctg. and mgmt., Calif. Acct. Unocal (formerly Union Oil Co. Calif.), LA, 1972-76, data control supr., 1976-78, acctg. analyst, 1978-79; sr. fin. analyst Hughes Aircraft Co., El Segundo, Calif., 1979-83, fin. planning specialist, 1983-84, program controls specialist, 1984-86, bus. mgmt. specialist, 1986-92, bus. analyst, 1993-95. Adj. instr. bus. math. L.A. City Coll., 1976-80, acctg., 1980-97, 99—, mem. acctg. adv. com., 1984, 87, 89, 99, acctg. and bus. Pasadena City Coll., 1996-2001, 2003—; reviewer conf. papers. Contbr. articles to profl. jours. Mem. commn. Rep. Pres. Task Force, 1986; mem. Tchrs. Acctg. Two Yr. Colls. Scholarship Com., 2007 Recipient Medal of Merit, Rep. Presdl. Task Force, 1984, cert. of merit, named registered life mem. commn., 1986, named Honor Roll life mem., 1989; recipient Vice-Presdl. Cert. of Commendation, Rep. Nat. Hall of Honor, 1992, Rep. Congl. cert. of Appreciation, 1993, Rep. Congl. Order of Freedom award Nat. Rep. Congl. Com., 1995, Recognition award LA chpt. Strategic Leadership Forum, 1983. Mem.: Tchrs. Acctg. at Two-Yr. Colls. (scholarship com. 2007), High Potentials Soc., Mysterium Soc., Internat. High IQ Soc., Midwest Fin. Assn. (program rev. com. 2002), Ea. Fin. Assn. (program rev. com. 2000), Soc. Advancement Mgmt. (editl. rev. bd. Advanced Mgmt. Jour. 1999—, selection com. mem. Internat. Conf. 2000), Nat. Bus. Edn. Assn., Am. Acctg. Assn. (Tchg. and Cirriculum Innovative Tchg. award com. 2004—05, competitive manuscript com. 1997—98, reviewer tchg. curr. sect. 1998, tchg. and curriculum sect. two-yr. coll. issues com. 1998—99), Inst. Mgmt. Accts. (author's cir. L.A. chpt. 1980, mem. editl. adv. bd. Strategic Fin. and Mgmt. Acctg. Quarterly 2002—, Robert Half author's trophy 1980, cert. of appreciation 1980, 1983), Acad. Mgmt. (reviewer social issues in mgmt. divsn. 1991, mgmt. edn. and devel. disvsn. program rev. com. 1998—99, reviewer bus. policy and strategy divsn. 2002—04, reviewer for acad. of mngmt. learning & ed. Jour. 2003, Bus. Policy and Strategy Divsn. Outstanding Reviewer award 2004), Mind Soc., Elateneos Soc., High IQ Soc. for Gifted and Talented (hon.), Nat. Scholars Honor Soc., Kappa Delta Pi, Phi Delta Kappa, Delta Pi Epsilon (proposal reviewer 2005), Beta Gamma Sigma. Republican. Roman Catholic. Home: 426 N Citrus Ave Los Angeles CA 90036-2632 Office: LA City Coll 855 N Vermont Ave Los Angeles CA 90029 Personal E-mail: geowalen@sbcglobal.net.

WALES, GWYNNE HUNTINGTON, retired lawyer; b. Evanston, Ill., Apr. 18, 1933; s. Robert Willett and Solace (Huntington) W.; m. Janet McCobb, Feb. 8, 1957; children— Thomas Gwynne, Catherine Anne, Louise Carrie. AB, Princeton U., 1954; JD, Harvard U., 1961. Bar: N.Y. 1962. Assoc. White & Case, NYC, 1961-69, ptnr., 1969-2000, resident ptnr. Brussels, 1969-75, Ankara, Turkey, 1998-2000. Served with USN, 1954-58. Mem.: Am. Law Inst. (life), Round Hill (Greenwich, Conn.). Home: 1406 Brookside Dr Fairfield CT 06824

WALES, JIMMY DONAL (JIMBO WALES), Internet company executive; b. Huntsville, Ala., Aug. 7, 1966; m. Christine Wales; 1 child, Kira. Attended, Auburn U.; attended PhD programs in finance, U. Ala., Ind. U. Faculty mem. U. Ala., Ind. U.; futures and options trader Chgo. Options Assocs., Chgo.; founder Nupedia.com, 1999—2000; CEO Bomis, Inc., San Diego, 2000—01; founder Wikipedia (Parent orgn.-Wikimedia Found., Inc.), 2001—, Wikimedia Found. Inc., St. Petersburg, Fla., 2003—, pres., dir., chmn. bd. trustee, 2005—; founder Wikia, 2004—. Nominee Rave award in Technology, WIRED, 2005; named one of 50 Who Matter Now, Business 2.0, 2007, Top 25 Web Celebs, Forbes mag., 2007; recipient 100 Most Influential People, Time Mag., 2006. Office: Wikimedia Found Inc 204 37th Ave N Saint Petersburg FL 33704 *

WALES, KEN, film producer; b. Salem, Ind., Aug. 13, 1938; s. Wales Eugene and Clara (Ferree) Smith. BA, U. So. Calif., 1961, postgrad., 1963-64. Producer Blake Edwards Prodns., LA, 1961-74, various major studios, LA, 1975-85; v.p. prodn. Walt Disney Studios, Burbank, Calif., 1985; producer various film projects, Hollywood, Calif., 1986—. Cons. and speaker in field; radio talk show host, L.A., 1986—. Prodr: (films) including Wild Rovers, 1971, The Tamarind Seed, 1974, Islands in the Stream, 1977, Revenge of Pink Panther, 1978, Door to Door, 1985, Amazing Grace, 2006; co-prodr.: (TV miniseries) John Steinbeck's East of Eden, 1979-80 (Golden Globe Winner 1981); actor, prodr: (films) The Prodigal, 1983. Recipient Walt Disney scholarship U. So. Calif., 1956-61, Centurion award Nat. Religious Broadcasters, 1986, Stairway to the Stairs award S.M. Fine Arts Soc., 1968. Mem. Dirs. Guild Am., Acad. Motion Pictures Arts & Scis., Screen Actors Guild, Soc. Motion Picture & TV Engrs., Nat. Assn. Ednl. Broadcasters, Alpha Epsilon Rho, Cinema Circulus. Presbyterian. Avocations: photography, amateur radio, music, art, tennis. Home: 1533 Michael Ln Pacific Palisades CA 90272-2022 Office: 1533 Michael Ln Pacific Palisades CA 90272-2022 *

WALES, ROSS ELLIOT, lawyer; b. Youngstown, Ohio, Oct. 17, 1947; s. Craig C. and Beverly (Bromley) W.; m. Juliana Fraser, Sept. 16, 1972; children: Dod E., J. Craig. AB, Princeton U., 1969; JD, U. Va., 1974. Bar: Ohio 1974, U.S. Dist. Ct. (so. dist.) Ohio 1974, U.S. Ct. Appeals (5th cir.) 1979. Assoc. Taft, Stettinius & Hollister, Cin., 1974-81, ptnr., 1981—. Pres. US Swimming, Inc., Colorado Springs, 1979-84, US Aquatic Sports, Inc., Colorado Springs, 1984-88, 94-98, Cin. Active to Support Edn., 1987-88; chmn. sch. tax levy campaign, Cin., 1987; trustee The Childrens Home Cin., 1987—, v.p., 1995-98, pres., 1998-02; bd. dirs., sec., v.p. FINA Bur., 1988-2000; trustee Cin. State Tech. and CC, 1994—, sec. bd., 1995-98, vice-chmn., 1998-00, chair 2000-02; pres. Cin. Arts Sch., Inc., 2000-01; sec. Greater Cin. Arts and Edn. Ctr., 1996-05; mem. Anti-Doping Rev. Bd., US Anti-Doping Agy., Colo. Springs; dir. Child Welfare League Am., 2003-, treas., 2005-06, chair, 2007-. Mem. ABA, Ohio Bar Assn., Cin. Bar Assn., Internat. Swimming Fedn. of Lausanne, Switzerland (sec. 1988-92, v.p. 1992-2000). Presbyterian. Office: 425 Walnut St Ste 1800 Cincinnati OH 45202-3957 Home Phone: 513-321-8637; Office Phone: 513-357-9351. Business E-Mail: wales@taftlaw.com.

WALES, WALTER D., physicist, researcher; b. Oneonta, NY, Aug. 2, 1933; s. Walter D. and Anna Laura (Brockway) W.; m. Margaret Irene Keiter, June 19, 1955; children: Stephen Dirk, Carolyn Sue. BA, Carleton Coll., 1954; MS, Calif. Inst. Tech., 1955, PhD, 1960. Instr. physics U. Pa., Phila., 1959-62, asst. prof., 1962-64, assoc. prof., 1964-72, prof., 1972—, chmn. dept. physics, 1973-82, assoc. dean, 1982-87, acting dean, 1987-88, assoc. dean, 1988-92, dep. provost, 1992-95, interim dean, 1996-98, ombudsman, 1999-2001, interim assoc. provost, 2002—04; assoc. dir. Princeton (N.J.)-Pa. Accelerator, 1968-71; staff physicist AEC, 1972-73. Fellow Am. Phys. Soc.; mem. Am. Assn. Physics Tchrs. Achievements include research in exptl. particle physics. Home: 404 Drew Ave Swarthmore PA 19081-2406 Office: 209 S 33rd St Philadelphia PA 19104-6317 Business E-Mail: wales@physics.upenn.edu.

WALGREN, DOUG, lawyer, former congressman; b. Dec. 28, 1940; married. BA, Dartmouth Coll.; LL.B., Stanford U. Bar: Pa., Calif. Staff atty. Neighborhood Legal Services; individual and corp. practice law, 1969-76; chmn. subcom. on sci. rsch. and tech. 98th-100th Congress from 18th Dist. Pa.; chmn. subcom. on commerce, consumer protection and competitiveness 101st Congress; of counsel Drinker Biddle & Reath LLP, Washington, 2002—. Bd. mem. Nat. Ctr. for Rehabilitation Med., NIH, Ctr. Organ Recovery and Edn. Named Nat. Sci. Found. Legislator of Yr., 1989. Mem.: Calif. Bar Assn., Pa. Bar Assn. Office: Drinker Biddle & Reath LLP Ste 1100 1500 K St NW Washington DC 20005-1209 Office Phone: 202-842-8806. Business E-Mail: douglas.walgren@dbr.com.

WALI, MOHAN KISHEN, environmental scientist, forester, educator; b. Kashmir, India, Mar. 1, 1937; came to U.S., 1969, naturalized, 1975; s. Jagan Nath and Somavati (Wattal) W.; m. Sarla Safaya, Sept. 25, 1960; children: Pamela, Promod. BS, U. Jammu and Kashmir, 1957; MS, U. Allahabad, India, 1960; PhD, U. B.C., Can., 1970. Lectr. S.P. Coll., Srinagar, Kashmir, 1963-65; rsch. fellow U. Copenhagen, 1965-66; grad. fellow U. B.C., 1967-69; asst. prof. biology U. N.D., Grand Forks, 1969-73, assoc. prof., 1973-79, prof., 1979-83, Hill rsch. prof., 1973; dir. Forest River Biology Area Field Sta., 1970-79, Project Reclamation, 1975-83; spl. asst. to univ. pres., 1977-82; staff ecologist Grand Forks Energy Rsch. Lab. U.S. Dept. Interior, 1974-75; prof. Coll. Environ. Sci. and Forestry SUNY, Syracuse, 1983-89, dir. grad. program environ. sci., 1983-85, prof. Sch. Natural Resources, 1990—, dir. Sch. Natural Resources, assoc. dean Coll. Agr., 1990-93; dir. Environ. Sci. Grad. program Ohio State U., Columbus, 2001—06. Vice chmn. N.D. Air Pollution Adv. Coun., 1981-83; co-chair IV Internat. Congress on Ecology, 1986. Editor: Some Environmental Aspects of Strip-Mining in North Dakota, 1973, Prairie: A Multiple View, 1975, Practices and Problems of Land Reclamation in Western North America, 1975, Ecology and Coal Resource Development, 1979, Ecosystem Rehabilitation-Preamble to Sustainable Development, 1992; co-editor Agriculture and the Environment, 1993; sr. editor Reclamation Rev., 1976-80, chief editor, 1980-81; chief editor Reclamation and Revegetation Rsch., 1982-87; contbr. articles to profl. jours. Recipient B.C. Gamble Disting. Tchg. and Svc. award, U. ND, 1977. Fellow AAAS, Nat. Acad. Scis. India; mem. Ecol. Soc. Am. (chmn. sect. internat. activities 1980-84), Bot. Ecol. Soc., Can. Bot. Assn. (dir. ecology sect. 1976-79, v.p. 1982-83), Am. Soc. Agronomy, Am. Inst. Biol. Sci. (gen. chmn. 34th ann. meeting), Internat. Assn. Ecolog (co-chmn. IV Internat. Congress Ecology), Internat. Soc. Soil Sci., N.D. Acad. Sci. (chmn. editl. com. 1979-81), Sigma Xi (nat. lectr. 1983-85, pres. Ohio State chpt. 1993-94, pres. Syracuse chpt. 1984-85, Outstanding Rsch. award U. N.D. chpt. 1975). Office: Ohio State U Sch Environ and Natural Resources 2021 Coffey Rd Columbus OH 43210-1044 Business E-Mail: wali.1@osu.edu.

WALK, BARBRA DENISE, customer service administrator, tutor; b. Tacoma, Wash., Aug. 29, 1969; d. Robert Edward and Connie Lee Walk. A, Pierce Coll., Tacoma, 1993; BA, Wash. State U., Pullman, 1996. Office mgr. Comcast, Douglasville, Ga., 1999—2003; warranty adminstrn. coord. Rinnai, Peachtree City, Ga., 2004—; writer Gallopade Internat., Peachtree City, 2005—06; tutor Peachtree City, 2005—. Mem. edn. com. Japanese Am. Friendship Soc., Peachtree City, 2005—06. Named Miss Congeniality, Miss TEEN pageant, 1983; recipient Scholastic Achievement award, 1983, 5 achievement awards, Dale Carnegie. Mem.: Mensa, Phi Alpha Theta. Avocations: travel, tap dancing, music. Home Phone: 678-777-7876.

WALK, CHARLIE, music company executive; BA in Bus. Adminstr., Boston U., 1990. Coll. mktg. rep. Sony Music Distribution's New England branch, 1987—90, account service rep., 1990; promotion mgr. Columbia Records, N.E. Region, 1990—94; assoc. dir. Pop Promotion, Columbia Records, 1994, dir., 1994—95, v.p., 1997—98, sr. v.p., 1998—99; v.p. Promotion, Columbia Records, 1999—2000, exec. v.p., 2000—04, Creative Mktg. & Promotion, Coumbia Records, 2004—05; pres. Epic Records, 2005—. Office: Epic Records 550 Madison Ave New York NY 10001 Office Phone: 212-833-8000. Office Fax: 212-833-4818. *

WALK, LOUIS BERNARD, physician; b. Lacona, Iowa, Apr. 8, 1930; s. William J. Walk and Veronica M. Endres. BS, Drake U., 1953, MS, 1958; DO, Coll Med. and Surgery, Des Moines, 1966. Diplomate Am. Bd. Family Practice. With med. dept. US Army, 1967—75; resident in family medicine William Beaumont Med. Ctr., El Paso, Tex., 1970—73; solo practice family practice clinic Silvis, Ill., 1975—96; physician Iowa, Ill., Mo., Nebr., 1997—. Bd. dirs. Illini Hosp., Silvis, 1986—89. Brigadier gen. spl. forces US Army, 1969—70, Vietnam. Named one of Am.'s Top Family Doctors, Am. Consumer Rsch. Coun., 2004—05. Mem.: Am. Acad. Family Physicians, Assn. Mil. Surgeons US, Sigma Phi Epsilon. Home: 21517 Arbor St Elkhorn NE 68022 Office Phone: 308-381-2224. Fax: 308-381-0793.

WALKE, GEARY LYNN, judge; b. Stephensville, Nfld., Can., Jan. 3, 1951; s. Emil Paul and Joyce Walke; m. Barbara Ann Cain, Mar. 18, 1972; children: Justin Paul, Collin Robert. BA, U. Okla., 1973; JD, Oklahoma City U., 1975. Bar: Okla. 1976, US Dist. Ct. (we. dist.) Okla. 1976, US Ct. Appeals (10th cir.) 1980, US Supreme Ct. 1981. Editl. asst. Okla. Hist. Soc., Oklahoma City, 1974-75; legal intern Legal Aid Western Okla., Oklahoma City, 1975-76; ptnr. Coleman, Walke & Briggs, Del City, Okla., 1976—; spl. judge Dist. Ct. Oklahoma County, 2000-. Chmn. bd. dirs. Hope Cmty. Mental Health Ctr., Oklahoma City, 1980-82; mem. accreditation com. Rose State Coll., Midwest City, Okla., 1984—; chmn. Del City Bd. Adjustment, 1979—. Mem. ABA, Okla. Jaycees (state legal counsel 1980-81), Del City Area C. of C. (pres. 1984), Okla. Trial Lawyers Assn., Assn. Trial Lawyers Am., Okla. Bar Assn. Democrat. Presbyterian. Home: 32 N Bradbury Dr Edmond OK 73034 Office: Oklahoma County 321 Park Ave Rm123 Oklahoma City OK 73102

WALKEN, CHRISTOPHER, actor; b. Astoria, NY, Mar. 31, 1943; s. Paul Walken; m. Georgianne Thon, Jan. 1969. Attended Hofstra U., studied with Wynn Handman, Actors Studio. Stage appearances include Broadway, off-Broadway and regional theatres throughout U.S. and Can.; Broadway debut in J.B, 1959; other stage appearances include Best Foot Forward, West Side Story, Macbeth, The Lion in Winter (Clarence Derwent award 1966), Hamlet, The Rose Tatoo (Theatre World's Most Promising Personality 1966-67), Romeo and Juliet, The Seagull, 2001, The Night Thoreau Spent in Jail (Joseph Jefferson award 1970-71), Kid Champion (Obie award 1975), Miss Julie, Sweet Bird of Youth, Hurlyburly, 1984, Cinders, 1984, A Bill of Divorcement, 1985, Coriolanus, 1988, Othello, 1992, (also playwright) Him, 1995, Mother Courage, 2006; films include The Anderson Tapes, 1971, Next Stop Greenwich Village, The Sentinel, 1977, Roseland, 1977, Annie Hall, 1977, The Deer Hunter, 1978 (N.Y. Film Critics Best Supporting Actor award 1978, Acad. award Best Supporting Actor 1979), Last Embrace, 1979, Dogs of War, 1981, Heavens Gate, 1980, Pennies From Heaven, 1981, The Happiness Cage, 1982, The Dead Zone, 1983, Brainstorm, 1983, A View to a Kill, 1984, At Close Range, 1986, Deadline, 1987, Puss in Boots, 1988, The Milagro Beanfield War, 1988, Biloxi Blues, 1988, Communion, 1989, King of New York, 1990, Homeboy, 1991, The Comfort of Strangers, 1991, McBain, 1991, All American Murder, 1992, Batman Returns, 1992, True Romance, 1993, A Business Affair, 1994, Wayne's World II, 1994, Pulp Fiction, 1994, Search and Destroy, 1995, Nick of Time, 1995, The Addiction, 1995, The Prophecy, 1995, The Funeral, 1996, Basquiat, 1996, The Wild Side, 1996, Things To

Do in Denver When You're Dead, 1995, Last Man Standing, 1996, Touch, 1997, Mousehunt, 1997, Excess Baggage, 1997, Suicide Kings, 1997, Sleepy Hollow, 1999, Blast From the Past, 1999, Kiss Toledo Goodbye, 1999, Vendetta, 1999, Antz (voice), 1998, Illuminata, 1998, New Rose Hotel, 1998, The Prophecy II, 1998, Trance, 1998, Scotland PA, 2001, Joe Dirt, 2001, America's Sweethearts, 2001, Chelsea Walls, 2001, The Affair of the Necklace, 2001, Jungle Juice, 2001, Poolhall Junkies, 2002, The Country Bears, 2002, Plots with a View, 2002, Catch Me If You Can, 2002 (Best Actor in Supporting Role, British Acad. Film Award (BAFTA) 2003), Kangaroo Jack, 2003, Gigli, 2003, The Rundown, 2003, Man on Fire, 2004, Envy, 2004, The Stepford Wives, 2004, Around the Bend, 2004, Wedding Crashers, 2005, Domino, 2005, Click, 2006, Man of the Year, 2006, Hairspray, 2007, Balls of Fury, 2007; TV films include Sarah, Plain and Tall, 1991 (Emmy nominee), Skylark, 1993, Scam, 1993; The Opportunists, 1999, The Prophecy III: The Ascent, 1999, Sarah, Plain and Tall: 3, 1999, Julius Caesar, 2002; (TV series) Saturday Night Live (Am. Comedy award 2001), Naked City, 1958, Hawaii Five-O, 1968, Kojak, 1973; (TV mini-series) Julius Caesar, 2002. Recipient Best Supporting Male Performance (True Crime: NYC), Spike TV Video Game awards, 2005. Office: c/o Toni Howard Internat Creative Mgmt 10250 Constellation Blvd Los Angeles CA 90067 *

WALKER, ALICE, writer; b. Eatonton, Ga., Feb. 9, 1944; d. Willie Lee and Minnie (Grant) W.; m. Melvyn R. Leventhal, Mar. 17, 1967 (div. 1976); 1 dau., Rebecca Walker Leventhal, 1970. Attended, Spelman Coll.; BA, Sarah Lawrence Coll., 1966; PhD (hon.), Russell Sage U., 1972; DHL (hon.), U. Mass., 1983. Co-founder, pub. Wild Trees Pr., Navarro, Calif., 1984-88. Writer in residence, tchr. black studies Jackson State Coll., 1968-69, Tougaloo Coll., 1970-71; lectr. literature Wellesley Coll., 1972-73, U. Mass., Boston, 1972-73; disting. writer Afro-American studies dept. U. Calif., Berkeley, 1982; Fannie Hurst Prof. of Literature Brandeis U., Waltham, Mass., 1982; cons. Friends of the Children of Miss., 1967. Author: Once, 1968, The Third Life of Grange Copeland, 1970, Five Poems, 1972, Revolutionary Petunias and Other Poems, 1973 (Nat. Book award nomination 1973, Lillian Smith award So. Regional Coun. 1973), In Love and Trouble, 1973 (Richard and Hinda Rosenthal Found. award Am. Acad. and Inst. of Arts and Letters 1974) Langston Hughes: American Poet, 1973, Meridian, 1976, Goodnight, Willie Lee, I'll See You in the Morning, 1979, You Can't Keep a Good Woman Down, 1981, The Color Purple, 1982 (Nat. Book Critics Circle award nomination 1982, Pulitzer Prize for fiction 1983, Am. Book award 1983; movie Steven Spielberg, The Color Purple; also staged on Broadway), In Search of Our Mothers' Gardens, 1983, Horses Make a Landscape Look More Beautiful, 1984, To Hell With Dying, 1988, Living By the Word: Selected Writings, 1973-1987, 1988, The Temple of My Familiar, 1989, Her Blue Body Everything We Know: Earthling Poems, 1965-1990, 1991, Finding the Green Stone, 1991, Possessing the Secret of Joy, 1992, (with Pratibha Parmar) Warrior Marks, 1993, (with others) Double Stitch: Black Women Write About Mothers & Daughters, 1993, Everyday Use, 1994, Alice Walker Banned: The Banned Works, 1996, Everything We Love Can Be Saved: A Writer's Activism: Essays, Speeches, Statements and Letters, 1997, The Same River Twice, 1997, By The Light of My Father's Smile, 1998, We Are the Ones We Have Been Waiting For: Inner Light in a Time of Darkness, 2006; editor: I Love Myself When I'm Laughing... And Then Again When I'm Looking Mean and Impressive, 1979, The Way Forward is With a Broken Heart, 2000, Absolute Trust in the Goodness of the Earth: New Poems, 2003. Recipient first prize Am. Scholar essay contest, 1967, O. Henry award for Kindred Spirits, 1986, Nora Astorga Leadership award, 1989, Fred Cody award for lifetime achievement Bay Area Book Reviewers Assn., 1990, Freedom to Write award PEN Ctr. USA West, 1990; Bread Loaf Writer's Conf. scholar, 1966; Merrill writing fellowship, 1967; McDowell Colony fellowship, 1967, 77-78; National Endowment for the Arts grantee, 1969, 77; Radcliffe Inst. fellowship, 1971-73; Guggenheim fellow, 1977-78. Achievements include introducing the word "womanist". Address: Random House Inc 1745 Broadway #B1 New York NY 10019-4305 *

WALKER, ALLEN LYON, engineer; b. Wellsboro, Pa., Jan. 30, 1943; s. Joseph Dewitt and Louise (Thompson) W.; m. Jean Barbara Hickson, Aug. 11, 1979 (div. Jan. 1985); 1 child, Iain Lyon Walker; m. Mary Ann Knowlton Walker, Jan. 30, 1987. A in Engring. Mech., Williamsport (Pa.) Tech. Inst., 1963; Grad., U.S. Army Aviation Sch., 1970, U.S. Army Test Pilots Sch., 1970, U.S. Army Comd./Gen. Staff, Coll., Ft. Leavensworth, Kans., 1991. Lic. comml. pilot, FAA. Exptl. lab. tech. Ille Electric Corp., Williamsport, 1963-65; commd. 2nd lt. U.S. Army, 1965, advanced through grades to maj., 1966, ret., 1995; tool engr. Ingersoli Rand Corp., Painted Post, N.Y., 1965-66; aviator, test pilot U.S. Army, Vietnam, 1966-68, aircraft maintenance officer Europe, Germany, 1969-72, co. comdr., 1969-72; maintenance engr. Ingersoll Rand Corp., Painted Post, N.Y., 1972-75; logistics mgr. Bell Helicopter Internat., Kermanshah, Iran, 1975—77; base supply mgr. Gen. Devices/Grumman, Isfahan, Iran, 1977—79; field engr. Northrop Grumman Corp., Phila., 1980—. Adv. Army of the Rep. of Vietnam, Anh-Khe, 1967, English instr., 1967. Author treatise, 1990. Founding warden Internat. Order of St. Vincent, Holy Nativity, Rockledge, Pa., 1992-98, life mem.; dist. commr. Cradle of Liberty coun. Boy Scouts Am., Phila., 1994-99, coun. commr., 1999-2004, adv. coun., 2004—. Maj. U.S. Army, 1966-72, Vietnam, Europe. Decorated Bronze Star, Air medal, Meritorious Svc. medal; recipient Silver Beaver award, Boy Scouts Am., award of merit, Cradle of Liberty coun. Boy Scouts Am., Disting. Commr. award, Daniel C. Beard Masonic Scouter's award, Boy Scouts Am.; James E. West Found. fellow. Mem.: SAR, Soc. Logistics Engrs. (vice-chmn. 1982—85), Mil. Order of Loyal Legion of US Allied Masonic Degrees (steward 2004), Lyons Family Assn. (v.p. 1972—75), Brit. Officers Club of Phila. (sec. 1990—93), York Rite (Phila. gov. 2005—06), Royal Order Scotland, Nat. Sojourners, Knights Templar, Shriners (comdr. Legion of Honor 2000), Freemasons (past master 2001—03, jr. warden 2005, 32d degree). Republican. Episcopalian. Avocations: genealogy, scouting, astronomy. Office: Naval Inventory Control Pnt 700 Robbins Ave Philadelphia PA 19111-5008 Home: 40 North Hill Ter Mansfield PA 16933

WALKER, ANN YVONNE, lawyer; b. San Francisco, Sept. 26, 1954; d. C. Richard and Athene (Henderson) Walker. BS with distinction in Math., Stanford U., 1976; JD, Stanford Law Sch., 1979. Bar: Calif. 1979. Assoc. Wilson, Sonsini, Goodrich & Rosati, Palo Alto, Calif., 1979-86, mem., 1986—. Violinist, bd. dirs. Redwood Symphony Orch., 1985—; bd. dirs. Fremont Opera, Inc., 2007—. Named to Best Lawyers in Am., 2006, 2007, Northern Calif. Super Lawyers, Law & Politics Mag., 2004—06. Mem.: ABA (mem. fed. regulation securities com. 1992—, mem. com. lawyer bus. ethics 1993—, mem. standing com. professionalism 1996—99, chair 1997—2001, mem. bus. law sect. publs. bd. 2000—04, mem. bus. law sect. coun. 2001—05, mem. standing com. tech. and info. sys. 2005—), Palo Alto Area Bar Assn., Santa Clara County Bar Assn., Calif. State Bar Assn. (mem. corps. com. 1992—96, chair 1995—96, mem. exec. com. bus. law sect. 1996—, vice chair 1998—99, chair 1999—2000, advisor 2000—05, co-chair coun. state bar sects. 2001—02, advisor emeritus 2005—), Phi Beta Kappa. Office: Wilson Sonsini Goodrich and Rosati 650 Page Mill Rd Palo Alto CA 94304-1050 Office Phone: 650-320-4643. Business E-Mail: awalker@wsgr.com.

WALKER, ANNETTE, retired counseling administrator; BS in Edn., Huntingdon Coll., 1974; MS in Adminstrn. and Supervision, Troy State U., 1977-78, MS in Sch. Counseling, 1990, AA in Sch. Adminstrn., 1992; diploma, World Travel Sch., 1990; diploma in Cosmetology, John Patterson Coll., 1992; MEd in higher Edn. Adminstrn., Auburn U., Ala., 1995. Cert. tchr., adminstr., Ala.; lic. cosmetologist, Ala.; lic. funeral dir., Ala. Tchr. Montgomery (Ala.) Pub. Sch. System, 1976-89, sch. counselor, 1989—2000; lit. tchr. Fed. Bur. of Justice, 1997—2000; ret., 2000; acad. advisor Cmty. Coll. of Air Force; acad. counselor Maxwell Air Force Base, Ala., guidance counselor edn. office, 2001—. Tchr. Fed. Govt., 1997—, US Bur. Justice, 1997—; gymnastics tchr. Cleveland Ave. YMCA, 1971-76; girls coach Montgomery Parks and Recreation, 1973-76; summer sch. sci. tchr. grades 7-9, 1977-88; chmn. dept. sci. Bellingrath Sch., 1987-90, courtesy com., 1987-88, sch. discipline com., 1977-84; recreation asst. Gunter AFB, Ala., 1981-83; calligraphy tchr. Gunter Youth Ctr., 1982; program dir. Maxwell AFB, Ala., 1983-89; vol. tchr. Internat. Officer Sch., 1985—, Adult Laubach Reading Prog., Ala. Goodwill Amb., 1985—, day camp dir., 1987, calligraphy tchr., 1988; trainer internat. law for sec. students, Ala., 1995—; sales rep. Ala. World Travel, 1990—; behavior aid Brantwood Children's Home, 1996—; computer tchr. hs diploma program Montgomery County Sch., 1995—; hotel auditor, 1995—; Am. del. to China, People to People Internat., 1998; acad. advisor CC of Air Force, Maxwell AFB, Ala., 2002—; ESL tchr., counselor, Okinawa, Japan, 2000-02, Germany, 2005-06; behavior specialist Group Homes for Children, 2006; greeter FedEx Kinko's, 2006-; leader workshops in field. Mem. CAP; vol. zoo activities Tech. Scholarship Program for Ala. Tchrs. Computer Courses, Montgomery; bd. dirs. Cleveland Ave. YMCA, 1976—80; sponsor Belle-Howe chpt. Young Astronauts, 1986—90, Pate Howe chpt., 1991—92; judge Montgomery County Children Festival Elem. Sci. Fair, 1988—90; bd. dirs. Troy State U. Drug Free Schs., 1992—; chmn. Maxwell AFB Red Cross-Youth, 1986—88; goodwill amb. sponsor to various families (award 1989, 95); State of Ala. rep. P.A.T.C.H.-Internat. Law Inst., 1995; founder Okinawa, Japan chpt., bd. dirs. People to People Internat., 2000; tchr. Sunday sch. Beulah Bapt. Ch., Montgomery. Named Tchr. of the Week, WCOV-TV, 1992, Ala. Tchr. in Space Program, summer, 1989, Local Coord. Young Astronaut Program, 1988, Citizen Amb. to China, People to People Internat., 1999; recipient Outstanding High Sch. Sci./Math. Tchr. award, Sigma Xi, 1989, Most Outstanding Youth Coun. Leader award, Maxwell AFB Youth Ctr., 1987, Outstanding Ala. Goodwill Amb. award, 1989, 1995, Tchr. of Yr. award, Paterson Sch., 1990, Career Infusion award (Most Appreciated Tchr. award), 1987, Montgomery Pub. Sch., 1982, 1984, Earthwatch Ednl. award, Israel, 1997, 20 Class award, Maxwell AFB Internat. Fgn. Officer Program, 25 Class award, 2003, 30 Class award, 2005, Ala. Goodwill Amb. award, Maxwell AFB Inernat. Officer Program 30 Class award, 2005; Fulbright scholar, Japan, 1999. Mem. NEA, Internat. Platform Assn., People to People Internat. (founder, bd. trustees, organizer, pres. Ala. chpt. 1998), Nat. Sci. Tchrs. Assn., Ala. Sch. Counselors, Montgomery Sch. Counselors Assn., Montgomery County Ednl. Assn., Space Camp Amb., Huntingdon Alumni Assn. (sec.-treas.), Ala. Goodwill Amb., Montgomery Capital City Club, Young Astronauts, Ea. Star, Japan Friends of Fulbright Meml. Fund Tchr. Prog., Water Watch, Montgomery, AL, Zeta Phi Beta, Chi Delta Phi, Kappa Pi. Avocations: international travel, calligraphy, international food, cruising. Personal E-mail: Awalker2001@yahoo.com.

WALKER, ANTOINE DEVON, professional basketball player; b. Chgo., Aug. 12, 1976; 1 child, Crystal. Student, U. Ky., 1996. Forward Boston Celtics, 1996—2003, 2005, Dallas Mavericks, 2003—04, Atlanta Hawks, 2004—05, Miami Heat, 2005—. Named to 1996-97 NBA All Rookie First Team. Avocations: dance, bowling, video games.

WALKER, AUDREY THAYER, social worker, psychotherapist; b. Quincy, Mass., June 29, 1935; d. Paul Clifton and Dorothy Ritchie Thayer; m. David A. Walker, Aug. 21, 1982; children: Elizabeth Penniman Billett Bilhartz, Matthew Thayer Billett. AB, Wheaton Coll., Ill., 1957; MSS/MSW, Smith Coll., Northampton, Mass., 1959. LCSW Acad. Cert. Social Workers, 63, LICSW DC, 1985, cert. diplomate in clin. social work 1990. Caseworker Ch. Home Soc., Boston, 1959—61; caseworker, family therapist Family Svc. Agy. of Sacramento, 1961—63; chief psychiat. social worker, supr. dept. psychiatry George Washington U., 1969—90, adj. assoc. prof., 1971—, dir. social work tng., 1975—90; adj. assoc. prof. Smith Coll. Sch. for Social Work, Northampton, Mass., 1971—2003; pvt. practice clin. social worker, psychotherapist, 1990—; adj. faculty Counseling and Psychiat. Svcs., Georgetown U., 1993—2006; field faculty advisor Smith Coll. Sch. for Social Work, Northampton, Mass., 1996—2003, adj. assoc. prof., 2006—. Adj. faculty, cons., 1999—; co-leader theoretical integrative seminar Smith Coll. Sch. for Social Work, 2003—; presenter in field; cons. Clin. Social Work Inst., 1990—. Smell Coll Sch. Social Work, 1990—. Co-sponsor Life Cycle Courses George Washington U. Dept. Psychiatry, Washington Psychoanalytic Inst., 1975—85; co-chair benefit ann. lectures Smith Coll. Sch. for Social Work Alumni Assn., Washington, 1978—88. Named Disting. Practitioner, Nat. Acads. of Practice, 2005—; recipient Day-Garreit award for significant and maj. contbns. to social work, Smith Coll. Sch. Social Work, 2005; Grad. Study scholar, Episcopal Ch. of Am., Youth Svcs. Divsn., 1957-1959, Sr. Class Grad. Study awardee and scholar, Wheaton Coll. Sr. Class, 1957. Mem.: Acad. Cert. Social Workers, Washington Psychoanalytic Inst./Smith. Coll. SSW Alumni, Nat. Academics of Practice (disting. practitioner, social work 2005—), Am. Group Psychotherapy Assn. (full clin. mem. 1982—2004), Smith Coll. Sch. for Social Work Alumni Assn. (Greater Washington chpt. steering com. 1974—93, co-chair Psychoanalytic Jour. Club 1975—76), Greater Washington Soc. for Clin. Social Work (v.p. profl. affairs 1990—94, bd. mem.-at-large, advisor 1994—2005, continuing edn. com. 1995—, founding chair consultation svcs. com. 1997—98, ad hoc ethics com. 2006—07, Cert. of Appreciation 1991—97, 2002—04), Nat. Membership Com. on Psychoanalysis in Social Work (Washington area chair 1997—2003), Smith Coll. Club (Washington) (bd. dirs. 1983—87), Pi Gamma Mu. Democrat. Avocations: travel, literature, theater, ballet. Home: 4416 Q St NW Washington DC 20007 Office: 3 Washington Cir NW Ste 406 Washington DC 20037 Home Phone: 202-363-0276; Office Phone: 202-331-1547. Business E-Mail: audrey.walker@msb.edu.

WALKER, BERNICE BAKER, artist; b. Carbondale, Pa., Dec. 25, 1928; d. William Robert and Bernice Mary (Parry) Baker; m. Joseph Henry Walker, Sept. 13, 1952. Student, Richmond Profl. Inst., 1946-47; BFA, RI Sch. Design, 1952. Artist Highlights for Children, 1952-55, Studio K, Lancaster, Pa., 1959-64; tchr. Heintzelman Art Assn., Manheim, Pa., 1975-86; owner The Design Corner, Lancaster, 1989—2003. Tchr. Lancaster County Art Assn. Mem. Pa. Watercolor Soc., Venice Art Ctr., Englewood Art Ctr., Longboat Key Ctr. of the Arts, Am. Soc. Portrait Artists, Sarasota Portrait Soc., SW Pastel Soc., Am. Portrait Soc., Manasota Weavers and Spinners. E-mail: bernspin1@aol.com.

WALKER, BETTE, automotive executive; BS in Bus. Mgmt., U. NH; student, Bosotn U.; completed Global Leadership Executive Development Program, Harvard U. Tech. dir. Latin Am. Digital Equip. Corp.; IT exec. auto. sector safety restraint sys. AlliedSignal, Inc.; v.p., CIO, energy & chassis divsn. Delphi Corp., Troy, Mich., 1997—. Office: World Hdqrs 5725 Delphi Dr Troy MI 48098-2815

WALKER, BETTE M., information technology executive; BS in Bus. Mgmt., U. NH. Various positions most recently info. tech. dir. Latin Am. Digital Equipment Corp.; head of info. tech. automotive sector's safety restraint systems divsn. AlliedSignal Inc., head of info. tech. aerospace sector's comml. avionics divsn.; chief info. officer energy & chassis divsn. Delphi Corp., Troy, Mich., 1997, exec. dir. global bus. services and ops., now v.p., chief info. officer. Named one of Premier 100 IT Leaders, Computerworld, 2005. Office: VP & CIO Delphi Corp 5725 Delphi Dr Troy MI 48098-2815

WALKER, BETTY STEVENS, lawyer; b. NYC, Feb. 3, 1943; d. Randolph Blakney and Anne (Stevens) Wood; m. Paul Thomas Walker, Aug. 27, 1942; children: Camarf, Tarik, Kumi. BA in Polit. Sci. and History, Spelman Coll., 1964; JD, Harvard U., 1967. Bar: U.S. Dist. Ct. (DC) 1981, U.S. Ct. Appeals (DC cir.) 1977, U.S. Supreme Ct. 1996. Coord. southern schs. Legal Def. and Ednl. Fund, NYC, 1964; asst. prof. polit. sci. Shaw U., Raleigh, NC, 1968-69, faculty fellow, 1969-70; corp. atty. Southern Railway Co., Washington, 1974-77; exec. asst. to adminstr. Farmers Home Adminstrn. USDA, Washington, 1977-81; assoc. Walker & Walker Assoc., P.C., Washington, 1981—. Democrat. Mem. African Meth. Ch. Office: Walker & Walker Assoc PC 7600 Georgia Ave NW Ste 203 Washington DC 20012-2205 Office Phone: 202-842-4664.

WALKER, BRIAN C., manufacturing executive; Pres., N. Am. Herman Miller, Inc., 1999—2003, pres., COO, 2003—04, pres., CEO, 2004—, bd. dir., 2003—05. Office: Herman Miller 855 E Main Ave Zeeland MI 49464-0302 Office Phone: 616-654-3000. Office Fax: 616-654-5234. *

WALKER, CARLENE MARTIN, state senator; BS, Brigham Young U., 1969. Supr. coding & data entry the Wirthlin Group, 1982-86; cons. D.K. Shifflet & Assocs., 1987-88; ptnr., mgr. Covecrest Properties, 1978-99; tech. recruiter Manpower Tech., 1999-2000; mem. Utah State Senate, Salt Lake City, 2001—. Chair, founder Women's Polit. Action Com.; chair transp. appropriations. Active AGs Task Force on ID Theft, Capitol Preservation Bd.; bd. dirs. United Way, Salt Lake Convention and Vis. Bur., Hogle Zoo. Office: 4085 E Prospector Dr Salt Lake City UT 84121 Office Phone: 801-773-4599.

WALKER, CAROLE A., advertising executive; b. 1959; m. Andrew Walker; 2 children. Multiple positions DMB&M and Young & Rubicam; media dir., dir. print services Nabisco, Inc., 1994—2001; dir. e-comm., advt. and strategy Kraft e-Commerce Divsn., 2001—05; dir. mktg. comm. Masterfoods USA, 2005—. Named a Woman to Watch, Advt. Age, 2007; recipient Numerous Silver Anvil awards in Pub. Rels., Effie. Mem.: Assn. of Nat. Advertisers (ANA). Office: Masterfoods USA 800 High St Hackettstown NJ 07840 *

WALKER, CAROLYN MAE, retired secondary school educator; b. Neptune, NJ, Apr. 29, 1941; d. Frank and Estella (Matutis) W; m. Philp A. Carr, Jan. 28, 2006. BA in Sci., Montclair State Coll., 1963; MA in Edn., Newark State Coll., 1970. Cert. tchr., N.J. Elem. tchr. Howell Twp. Bd. Edn., NJ, 1963-65, Englishtown-Manalapan Regional Schs., NJ, 1965-67, Freehold Borough Schs., NJ, 1967-70, Freehold Regional HS, 1970-73, North Brunswick Twp. Bd. Edn., NJ, 1975—2002; ret., 2002. Vol. St. Vincent de Paul. Mem. NSTA, NJ Sci. Tchrs. Assn., NJ Schoolwomen's Club, Alpha Delta Kappa (chair pres. 1972-74, state sec. 1974-76, state v.p. 1976-78), Deep Cut Bonsai Club. Roman Catholic. Avocations: cruising, dressmaking, needlecrafts, gardening, classical/popular music. Personal E-mail: caramw@verizon.net.

WALKER, CHARLES D., astronaut; b. Bedford, Ind., Aug. 29, 1948; s. Donna Lake Walker; m. Susan Y. Flowers; 1 child. BS in Aero. and Astronautical Engring., Purdue U., 1971; DSc (hon.), St. Louis Coll. Pharmacy, 1985. Civil engring. technician, land acquisition specialist, forest firefighter U.S. Forest Svc.; design engr. Bendix Aerospace Co.; project engr. Naval Sea Systems Command; test engr., Aft Propulsion Subsys. for Space Shuttle orbiters McDonnell Douglas Corp., 1977, original mem. Space Mfg. Team (laster Electrophoresis Ops. in Space, EOS), chief test engr., payload specialist, EOS commercialization project, 1979—86, spl. asst. to pres. Space Systems Co., 1986; sr. mgr., space programs bus. devel. and mktg. Boeing Co. Ops., Washington. Industry mem. numerous NASA task forces; mem. NRC Space Applications Bd.; faculty course advisor, lectr. Internat. Space U., 1988; nat. panel mem. NASA/Industry Manned Flight Awareness Program, NASA/Industry Edn. Initiative; bd. dirs. Challenger Ctr. Space Sci. Edn.; trainer various NASA astronaut crews; astronaut Space Shuttle missions 41-D, 51-D and 61-B; chmn. organizing com. World Space Congress, 1992. Contbr. articles to profl. jours. and mags., chapters to books. Bd. mem. Astronauts Meml. Found.; vol. chmn., bd. dirs. Spacecause. Named Ky. Col., Commonwealth of Ky., 1990; recipient Space Flight medals, NASA, 1984—85, Aerospace Laurels award, Aviation Week and Space Tech. Mag., 1985, Engring. Astronaut Alumnus award, Purdue U. Schs. Engring., Lindbergh award, AIAA, St. Louis sect., 1986. Mem.: Assn. Space Explorers (bd. dirs.), Nat. Space Soc. (bd. dirs., past pres.). Achievements include patents for electrophoresis apparatus with flow control. Office: Astronaut Office/CB NASA Johnson Space Ctr Houston TX 77058

WALKER, CHARLES DODSLEY, conductor, organist; b. NYC, Mar. 16, 1920; s. Marshall Starr and Maude Graham (Marriott) Walker; m. Janet Elizabeth Hayes, May 30, 1949 (dec. Feb. 1997); children: Peter Hayes, Susan Starr; m. Elizabeth Ann Phillips, Jan. 14, 2001. BS, Trinity Coll., 1940; AM, Harvard U., 1947. Organist, choirmaster Am. Cathedral, Paris, 1948-50, Ch. of the Heavenly Rest, NYC, 1951-88; music dir. Blue Hill Troupe, Ltd., NYC, 1955-90, Chapin Sch., NYC, 1961-85; mem. organ faculty Union Theol. Sem., NYC, 1962-73, NYU, NYC, 1968-80; dean, music dir. Berkshire Choral Inst., Sheffield, Mass., 1982-91; organist, choirmaster Trinity Episcopal Ch., Southport, Conn., 1988—2007. Contbr. articles to profl. jours. Lt. comdr. USNR, 1942—46. Named Artist of Yr., Fairfield Arts Coun., 2004; recipient Disting. Alumnus award, Cathedral Choir Sch., 1988. Fellow: Am. Guild Organists (nat. pres. 1971—75); mem.: Canterbury Choral Soc. (founder, condr. 1952—), Am. Fedn. Musicians, St. Wilfrid Club, Bohemians. Avocations: travel, photography. Home: 160 W 96th St Apt 15N New York NY 10025-9212 Office: Ch Heavenly Rest 2 East 90th St New York NY 10128 Office Phone: 212-289-3400. Personal E-mail: dodsley@aol.com.

WALKER, CHARLES HENRI, lawyer; b. Columbus, Nov. 11, 1951; s. Watson Hershel and Juanita Elizabeth (Webb) W.; m. Amanda Tressel Herndon, June 27, 1981; children: Katrina Della, Allison Lyles, Carlton Wesley. BA magna cum laude, Tufts U., 1973; JD, Emory U., 1976. Bar: Ohio 1976. Assoc. Bricker & Eckler LLP, and predecessors, Columbus, 1976-81, sr. counsel, 1982—. Bd. dirs. Salesian Boys Club, Columbus, 1983-89, Planned Parenthood Cen. Ohio, Columbus, 1984-85, Life Care Alliance, 1993—, Ctrl. Ohio Transit Authority, 1994—2000; mem. sports arena com. City of Columbus, 1989; chmn. Tufts Alumni Admissions Program, 1986—; legal advisor Ohio Mock Trial Advocacy Program, 1988-92; pres., bd. dirs. I-670 Corridor Devel. Corp., 1993—98. Fellow ABA; mem. Nat. Bar Assn., Ohio Bar Assn. (com. profl. conduct and legal ethics, 1988—92), Columbus Bar Assn., Nat. Assn. R.R. Trial Counsel, Columbus Acad. Alumni Assn. (past pres.), Sigma Pi Phi. Democrat. Roman Catholic. Clubs: Athletic, President's (Ohio State U.). Home: 40 E Frankfort St Columbus OH 43206-1041 Office: Bricker & Eckler LLP 100 S 3rd St Columbus OH 43215-4291 Office Phone: 614-227-2339. Office Fax: 614-227-2390. E-mail: cwalker@bricker.com.

WALKER, CHARLES URMSTON, retired university president; b. Bolivar, Pa., June 20, 1931; s. Charles William and Frances May (Urmston) W.; m. Cherie Hall Duckworth, Aug. 7, 1959; children: Douglas Leland, Christy Lynn. BA, U. Pitts., 1953; MA, Columbia U., 1958; PhD, Stanford U., 1964; LLD (hon.), Kanto Gakuin U., 1979; LHD (hon.), Linfield Coll., 1992. Asst. prof. English Rockford Coll., Ill., 1958-61; dept. head, residence dir. Menlo Coll., Menlo Park, Calif., 1961-64; v.p., dean Hamline U., St. Paul, 1964-70; pres. Russell Sage Coll., Troy, NY, 1970-75, Linfield Coll., McMinnville, Oreg., 1975-92, pres. emeritus, 1992—; ednl. cons., 1992—; vice chair, dir. Ford Family Found., Roseburg, Oreg., 1993, dir. managed programs, 1993-98. Bd. dirs. 1st Fed. Savs. & Loan, McMinnville; mem. Univ. Pres. Initiative, IIE/USIA/NATO, Brussels, 1991. Bd. dirs. South Tillamook County Libr., 1994, pres., 2004; pres. Neskowin

(Oreg.) Chamber Music; co-chair bldg. com. First Bapt. Ch., McMinnville; chair Oreg. Cultural Trust, Found. Better Oreg.; bd. dirs. Tillamook County Futures Coun., 2005; v.p. Hillside Found., 2003—; trustee James & Marion Miller Found., Portland. Warg scholar U. Pitts., 1949-51; Univ. fellow Stanford U., 1963-64; Hill Found. grantee, St. Paul, 1970; Paul Harris fellow Rotary Internat., 1987; recipient Community Svc. award Troy, N.Y. Troy C. of C., 1975, First Citizen award McMinnville, Oreg., 1989, Govs. award Oreg. Vol. of Yr., 2006; named Man of Yr., Troy C. of C., 1975. Mem. Univ. Club (Portland), Rotary (past pres. McMinnville). Home: 1324 SW Gilorr St Mcminnville OR 97128-6617 Personal E-mail: cwalkc@oregoncoast.com.

WALKER, CHARLS EDWARD, economist, consultant; b. Graham, Tex., Dec. 24, 1923; s. Pinkney Clay and Sammye D. (McCombs) W.; m. Harmolyn Hart, June 24, 1949; children: Carolyn, Charls Edward. BBA, U. Tex., 1947, MBA, 1948; PhD in Econs., U. Pa., 1955. Instr. fin. U. Tex., 1947-48, asst. prof., then assoc. prof., 1950-54; instr. fin. U. Pa. Wharton Sch., 1948-50; fin. economist Fed. Res. Bank Phila., 1953; with Fed. Res. Bank Dallas, 1954-61, v.p., econ. adviser, 1958-61; economist Republic Nat. Bank Dallas, 1955-56; asst. to sec. treasury, 1959-61; exec. v.p. Am. Bankers Assn., NYC, 1961-69; under sec. treasury, 1969-72; dep. sec., 1972-73. Adj. prof. U. Tex., Austin, 1986-96, Tex. A&M U., 2000-2003; bd. dirs. Nat. Coun. Econ. Edn.; chmn., CEO Charls E. Walker Assocs., Inc., 1973-96; disting. vis. prof. Emory U., 2000-02. Co-editor: The Bankers Handbook, New Directions in Federal Tax Policy, The Consumption Tax: A Better Alternative, 1987, Intellectual Property Rights and Capital Formation, 1988, The U.S. Savings Challenge, 1990; contbr. articles to profl. jours. and newspapers, chpts. to books. Founder, chmn. emeritus Am. Coun. for Capital Formation; co-founder, chmn. exec. com. Com. on the Present Danger, 1976; chmn. Pres.'s adv. coun. on minority enterprise, 1973-75; co-chmn. Presdl. Debates, 1976; founder chmn. Bretton Woods Com.; chmn. Ronald Reagan's Task Force on Tax Policy, 1980; sr. advisor Ctr. for Deliberative Polling, U. Tex., 1996-, Stanford U., 2003-. 2d lt. USAAF, 1943—45. Recipient Alexander Hamilton award U.S. Dept. Treasury, Urban League award, Baker award for Exemplary Svc. to Econ. Edn., 1991, Disting. Svc. award, 2002, Pro Bono Meritas award Coll. Liberal Arts U. Tex., 2003; named Disting. Alumnus, U. Tex., 1994. Mem.: Coun. Fgn. Rels., Congl. Club (Bethesda, Md.), Burning Tree Club. Home (Winter): 105 Biltmore Saint Simons Island GA 31522 Home: 9426 Thrush Ln Potomac MD 20854-4143 Personal E-mail: charlswalk@aol.com. *What's good for the public interest ultimately is good for every person, business, or other group in the nation. This, combined with modern application of the Golden Rule, about sums it up.*

WALKER, CLARENCE EUGENE, psychology professor; b. Monongahela, Pa., Jan. 8, 1939; s. Lewis G. Walker and Olga T. Brioli; div.; children: Chad Eugene, Kyle Lewis, Cass Emanuel. BS in Psychology summa cum laude, Geneva Coll., 1960; MS in Clin. Psychology, Purdue U., 1963, PhD in Clin. Psychology, 1965. Lic. psychologist, Okla. Psychology trainee West 10th St. VA Hosp., Indpls., 1962—63; intern in clin. psychology Riley Children's Hosp., West 10th St. VA Hosp., Indpls., 1963—64; asst. prof. Westmont Coll., 1964—68; pvt. practice clin. psychology Santa Barbara, Calif., 1965—68; from asst. prof. to assoc. prof. Baylor U., 1968—74; pvt. practice clin. psychology Waco, Tex., 1970—74; assoc. prof. med. sch. U. Okla., Oklahoma City, 1974—80, prof. med. sch., dir. pediatric psychology tng. program, 1980—95, prof. emeritus, 1995; chief pediatric psychology svc. Okla. Children's Meml. Hosp., 1974—80, dir. out-patient pediatric psychology clinic, 1974—80; assoc. chief mental health svcs. Children's Hosp. Okla., 1980—95; pres. Psychol. Cons., Inc., 1998—. Cons. Head Start Program, Waco, 1968-70, VA Hosp, Waco, 1969-74, VA Ctr., Temple, Tex., 1969-74, Region XII Ednl. Svc. Ctr., Waco, 1971-74, Rusk (Tex.) State Hosp., 1972-74, Bapt. Children's Home, Oklahoma City, 1975-79; rsch. cons. Los Alamos (N.Mex.) Pub. Schs., 1975-79; chmn. divsn. edn. and psychology Westmont Coll., 1966-68; consulting psychologist, 1995—. Author: Learn to Relax, 1975, 3d edit., 2001, (with P. Clement, A. Hedberg and L. Wright) Clinical Procedures for Behavior Therapy, 1981, (with B.L. Bonner and K. Kaufman) The Physically and Sexually Abused Child, 1988, others; editor: The History of Clinical Psychology in Autobiography, vol. I, 1992, vol. II, 1993, (with M.C. Roberts) Handbook of Clinical Child Psychology, 1983, 3d edit., 2001; contbr. articles to profl. jours. Fellow APA; mem. AAAS, Southwestern Psychol. Assn. (pres. 1977), Okla. Psychol. Assn. (pres. 1983), Soc. Pediatric Psychology (pres. 1986), Ctrl. Tex. Psychol. Assn. (pres. 1973), Sigma Xi. Avocations: reading, wine tasting, travel. Office Phone: 405-341-7399. Business E-Mail: genewalker@iname.com.

WALKER, CLARENCE WESLEY, lawyer; b. Durham, NC, July 19, 1931; s. Ernie Franklin and Mollie Elizabeth (Cole) W.; m. Ann-Heath Harris, June 5, 1954; children: Clare Ann, Wesley Gregg. AB, Duke U., 1953, LL.B., 1955. Bar: N.C. 1955. Assoc. Mudge Stern Baldwin & Todd, 1955-59; ptnr. Kennedy, Covington, Loddell & Hickman, Charlotte, NC, 1961—. Bd. dirs. Lawyers Mut. Liability Ins. Co., Legal Services Corp. N.C., Oakwood Homes Corp. Glendale Group, Ltd.; lectr. N.C. Bar Found. Continuing Legal Edn. Insts., N.C. Jud. Planning Com., 1978-79; pres. Pvt. Adjudication Found. Chmn. bd. mgrs. Charlotte Meml. Hosp. and Med. Ctr., 1981-87; trustee N.C. Ctrl. U., 1979-83; vice-chmn. Charlotte-Mecklenburg Hosp. Authority, 1988-99; adv. bd. Ctrl. Piedmont Paralegal Sch.; trustee Carolinas Healthcare Found., Charlotte Country Day Sch., 1977-81; state chmn. Nat. Found. March of Dimes, 1968-70; chmn. Charlotte Park and Recreation Commn., 1970-73; bd. dirs. Charlotte Symphony, 1965-71, Bethlehem Ctr., 1975-77, N.C. Recreators Found., 1973-75; adv. bd. Charlotte Children's Theatre, 1972; bd. dirs. Charlotte C. of C., 1970-72; bd. visitors Duke U. Law Sch.; dir., gen. campaign chmn. United Way Ctrl. Carolinas, 1985. Fellow Am. Bar Found.; mem. N.C. Bar Assn. (pres. 1978-79, gov. 1971-75), ABA (state del. 1980-89, assembly del. 1989-97, bd. govs. 1997-2000, chair audit com. 2000—) 26th Jud. Dist. Bar Assn., Mecklenburg Bar Found. (trustee), Am. Law Inst., Order of Coif, Phi Eta Sigma, Phi Beta Kappa. Democrat. Methodist. Home: 1047 Ardsley Rd Charlotte NC 28207-1815 Office: Kennedy Covington Lobdell & Hickman Hearst Tower 47th Fl 214 N Tryon St Charlotte NC 28202 Office Phone: 704-331-7450. Business E-Mail: cwalker@kennedycovington.com.

WALKER, COREAN JONES, evangelist; b. Marion, Ind., Mar. 27, 1952; d. Arthur Lee and Millie Mae Jones; 1 child, Jennifer Nicole. Diploma, Marion HS, Marion, Ind., 1970; diploma word processing, Ind. Bus. Coll., Marion, Ind., 1987—89. Evangelist. Dist. coord. Ind. One Ch. One Child, Marion, Ind., 1991—92; dir., fin. coord. Caring Hands Ministry, Marion, Ind., 1997—2003; editor-light centennial New Light Bapt. Ch., Marion, Ind., 2001—02; pub. rels. and mktg. mgr. In His Presence Internat. Ministry. Author: Walk With Me Lord, 2002, Inspirations of Love, 2003; editor: (newsletter) Light Centennial, 2001. Exec. sec. B for City Coun., Marion, Ind., 2003; founder Arthur Lee Jones- Millie Mae Jones Ministries; group leader Purpose Driven Women; founder His Women Outreach Ministry; active In The Way Ministries; bd. dirs. Faith Tabernacle Outreach Ministries, Am. Bus. Women, Grant County Chaplaincy Bd., Grant County Sheriff's Dept. Recipient Corean Walker Day Proclamation, City of Muncie, James P. Carey-Mayor, 1991, Ind. One Ch. One Child, Elaine Walters/South Bend Ind., 1991, Cert. of Recognition, Famous Poets-Mark Schramm/ Talent, Oreg., 2001, Editor's Choice award, Internat. Libr. Poetry, 2005. Baptist. Starting "Caring Hands" a ministry that has helped 1,600 children have a nice Christmas- also in helping 250 children with Easter baskets. Assisting in adoptions for special needs children; intercessor for Kids Hope; assistance directory of Crowned With His Glory Ministries. Home: 2125 So Florence St Marion IN 46953 Office Phone: 765-668-8871. Personal E-mail: evancjw@yahoo.com.

WALKER, COREY DAVID BAZEMORE, humanities educator; b. Norfolk, Va., Feb. 12, 1971; s. Melvin Jerome and Gloria Jean Walker; m. Carthene Rolanda Bazemore, Aug. 7, 1993; 1 child, Camryn Paris Bazemore. B.S., Norfolk State U., 1993; MDiv, Va. Union U., Richmond, 1998; M of Theol. Studies, Harvard U., Cambridge, Mass., 1999; PhD, Coll. William and Mary, Williamsburg, Va., 2001. Sr. underwriter State Farm Ins. Cos., Charlottesville, Va., 1993—96; scholar-in-residence Carter G. Woodson Inst. African-Am. and African Studies U. Va., Charlottesville, 2001—02, dir. Ctr. Study Local Knowledge, 2002—03, asst. prof. dept. religious studies, 2003—06; vis. prof. Historiches Inst. Friedrich-Schiller U. Jena, Germany, 2002; asst. prof. dept. Africana studies Brown U., Providence, 2006—. Vice rector bd. visitors Norfolk State U., 1995—99; bd. dirs. Civic Frame, Balt., 2005—. Co-dir., co-prodr. (film) Fifeville, 2005 (Internat. Competiton Selection: 52nd Internat. Short FilmFestival/Internationale Kurzfilmtage Oberhausen, 2005). Mem. Dem. Socialists Am., NYC, 2005—07. Fellow, Ford Found. and NRC, 2000—02; Stephen J. Wright Commonwealth grad. fellow, Coll. William and Mary, 1999—2000, Summer Rsch. fellow, Carter G. Woodson Inst. African-Am. and African Studies, U. Va., 2000, Rsch. Travel fellow, Inst. Anglistik und Amerikanistik, Humboldt U. Berlin, 2000, Sesquicentennial assoc., U. Va., 2006. Mem.: Soc. Study Black Religion, Am. Acad. Religion (assoc. editor jour. 2006—), Caribbean Philos. Assn., Am. Philos. Assn., Am. Hist. Assn., Am. Studies Assn., Masons, Alpha Phi Alpha. Office: Brown U 79 Laurison St PO Box 1904 Providence RI 02912 Office Fax: 401-863-3559. Business E-Mail: cdbwalker@brown.edu.

WALKER, CRAIG MICHAEL, lawyer; 2 children. BA, Williams Coll., 1969; JD, Cornell U., 1972. Bar: N.Y., 1973, U.S. Dist. Ct. (so. dist.) N.Y., 1975, U.S. Ct. Appeals (2d cir) 1975, U.S. Supreme Ct., 1976. Assoc. Alexander and Green, NYC, 1972—80, ptnr., 1980—86, chmn. litigation dept., 1985—86; ptnr. Walter, Conston, Alexander, and Green P.C., NYC, 1987—89, Rogers and Wells, LLP, NYC, 1990—99, Clifford, Chance, Rogers, and Wells, LLP, NYC, 2000—02; spl. trial counsel Clifford Chance US, LLP, NYC, 2002—03; ptnr., spl. trial counsel Walker Law, LLP, Pound Ridge, NY, 2004—. Contbr. author: New York Forms of Jury Instruction, 1992; contbr. articles to profl. journals. Fellow Am. Bar Found.; mem. ABA (contbr. articles), N.Y. State Bar Assn., Def. Rsch. Inst., Fed. Bar Coun. Democrat.

WALKER, DALE MAXWELL, city official; b. Big Rapids, Mich., Dec. 18, 1947; s. Lewis M. and Hilma I. (Windquist) W.; m. Joanne Kay Richmond, June 22, 1968; children: Christina Elizabeth, Heather Marie. BS, Ferris State U., 1970; MBA, Ctrl. Mich. U., 1981. Cert. govt. fin. mgr., credentialed city mgr. Dir. fin. City of Owosso, Mich., 1970-74; internal auditor John Wesley Coll., 1974—76; corp. treas. Mich. Bapt. Homes, Detroit, 1976-77; dir. fin. City of Cadillac, Mich., 1977—. Pres. Gospel Bookstore, Inc., Cadillac, 1983-98; bd. dirs. Workplace Ministry, 2001-05. Bd. dirs. Wexford County United Way, 1980-82, Shiawassee County United Way, 1971-72; sec.-treas. Cadillac Police and Fire Retirement System, 1977-87, bd. dirs. 1987—; chmn. Mcpl. Employees Retirement System, Mich., 1997—. Fellow Govtl. Fin. Officers Assn. U.S. and Can. (Profl. Achievement award 1984-2007); mem. Mich. Mcpl. Fin. Officers Assn. (bd. dirs. 1983-85), Internat. City Mgrs. Assn., Mich. Mcpl. Treas. Assn., Mcpl. Treas. Assn. U.S. and Can. (bd. dirs. 1982-84), McGuires Golf Club. Republican. Baptist. Avocations: golf, swimming, reading. Home: 901 Lincoln St Cadillac MI 49601-2035 Office: 200 N Lake St Cadillac MI 49601-1829 Office Phone: 231-775-0181. E-mail: finance@cadillac-mi.net.

WALKER, DANIELLE, engineering executive; Engr. Progressive Engring. Group, LLC, Phila. Named one of 40 Under 40, Phila. Bus. Jour., 2006. Office: Progressive Engring Group, LLC 3001 Market St 2nd Fl Philadelphia PA 19104-2897 Office Phone: 215-222-0606. Office Fax: 212-222-0400.

WALKER, DAVID ALAN, finance educator; b. York, Pa., Jan. 5, 1941; s. Arthur Benjamin and Alva (Strasbougher) Walker; m. Audrey Thayer, Aug. 21, 1982; children: Matthew Billett, Elizabeth Penniman Bilhartz. BA, Pa. State U., 1962; MS, Iowa State U., 1964, PhD, 1968. Asst. prof. Pa. State U., 1968-70; economist FDIC, 1970-76, 78-80; vis. assoc. prof. Northwestern U., 1976-77; dir. rsch. Office Comptroller Currency, 1977-78; assoc. prof. fin. Georgetown U., 1980-82, prof., 1982-92, assoc. dean, 1985-87, John A. Largay prof., 1992—. Chair governing bd. Credit Rsch. Ctr., 1997-05; dir. Capital Mkts. Rsch. Ctr., 1989-2005; mem. quality assessment team Israel Coun. Higher Edn., 2005-07; cons. in field. Co-author textbooks; editor Jour. Fin. Rsch., 1981-87; co-editor Jour. Small Bus. Fin., 1992-95; mem. editl. bd. Jour. Applied Fin., Jour. Fin. Rsch., Fin. Mgmt., J.F.Q.A., Fin. Rev., Quar. Rev. Econ. and Fin., Jour. Small Bus. Fin.; contbr. articles to profl. jours. NDEA fellow, 1962-64. Mem. Am. Econ. Assn., So. Fin. Assn. (bd. dirs.), Ea. Fin. Assn. (bd. dirs.), Fin. Mgmt. Assn. (v.p. 1990-91, pres. 1994-95, trustee 1995-2005, chair bd. trustees 1999-2005), Beta Gamma Sigma. Republican. Home: 4416 Que St NW Washington DC 20007 Office: Georgetown U Sch Bus Washington DC 20057-0001 Home Phone: 202-363-0276; Office Phone: 202-687-4582. E-mail: walkerd@georgetown.edu.

WALKER, DAVID ELLIS, JR., communications educator, minister, consultant; b. Richmond, Va., Oct. 5, 1938; s. David Ellis and Laura Eloise (Vaughan) W.; m. Sandra Suzanne Barnes, Feb. 3, 1964; children: David Ellis III, Virginia Suzanne Walker Frizzell, Cindy Poole Key, Michelle Poole Clark. BA, David Lipscomb U., 1960; MA, U. Fla., 1961, PhD, 1969. Ordained to ministry Ch. Christ, 1954. Instr. Jacksonville (Fla.) U., 1963-65; min. Ch. of Christ, 1954—; prof. Middle Tenn. State U., Murfreesboro, 1965—. Acting chmn. dept. speech Middle Tenn. State U., 1984, 1990, dir. debate, 1965-70, pres. faculty senate, 1983-84; coord. comm. studies,1969-81, 97-99; cons. in field. Editor Jour. of NonTraditional Education, 1992-96; contbr. articles to profl. jours. Grad. fellow U. Fla., 1961-63; grantee Mid. Tenn. State U., 1967, 72, 77-78, 88-90, 92-94, David Walker scholar Mid. Tenn. State U., 1993—. Mem. NEA, Tenn. Comm. Assn. (v.p. 1973-74, 2002-03, pres. 1974-75, 2003-04, editor jour. 1977-85, Educator of Yr. 2002-03.), Tenn. Intercollegiate Forensic Assn. (pres. 1966-67, exec. sec. 1967-68), So. States Comm. Assn., Tenn. Edn. Assn., Pi Kappa Delta (gov. province of S.E. 1966-68), Phi Kappa Phi (chpt. treas. 1989-90). Avocations: reading, walking. Home: Ste 202 910 Murfreesboro Rd Franklin TN 37064 Office: Mid Tenn State U Dept Of Speech And Theatre Murfreesboro TN 37132-0001 Home Phone: 615-599-2724; Office Phone: 615-898-2270. Business E-Mail: dwalker@mtsu.edu.

WALKER, DAVID MICHAEL, federal official; b. Birmingham, Ala., Oct. 2, 1951; s. David Sellers and Dorothy Ann (West) W.; m. Mary Carmel Etheredge, June 12, 1971; children: Carol Marie, James Andrew. BS in Acctg., Jacksonville U., 1973; Sr. Exec. Govt. Cert., Harvard U., 1986; PhD in Bus. Adminstrn. (hon.), Bryant Coll., 2002; PhD in Pub. Svc. (hon.), Lincoln Meml. U., 2004; PhD in Civil Laws (hon.), Jacksonville U., 2006, PhD (hon.) in Pub. Svc.; PhD (hon.), Am. U., 2007. CPA, Fla., Tex. Sr. auditor Price Waterhouse & Co. and Coopers & Lybrand, Jacksonville, Fla., 1973-76; dir. personnel Coopers & Lybrand, Atlanta and Houston, 1976-79; Ea. regional mgr. Source Svcs. Corp., Washington, 1979-83; acting exec. dir. and dep. exec. dir. Pension Benefit Guaranty Corp., Washington, 1983-85; dep. asst. sec. US Dept. Labor, Washington, 1985-87, asst. sec. for pension and welfare benefit programs, 1987-89, pub. trustee for social security and medicare, 1990—95; ptnr., global mng. dir. human capital svcs. practice Arthur Andersen LLP, Atlanta, 1989-98; US comptroller gen. US Govt. Accountability Office, Washington, 1998—. Author: Retirement Security-Understanding and Planning Your Financial Future, 1996; co-author: Delivering on the Promise: How to Attract, Manage and Retain Human Capital, 1998; contbr. articles, editl. adv. bd. numerous profl. jours., tv and radio programs. Gov. bd. Internat. Orgn. Supreme Audit Instns. chmn. strategic planning, acctg., reporting; chmn. US Intergovtl. Audit Forum; chmn. US Joint Fin. Mgmt. Improvement Program, Ctr. Continuous Auditing. Recipient numerous leadership pub. svc., profl. and industry awards for outstanding svc. and contbns. Mem. AICPA Group of 100 (past chmn. employee benefit plans com.), Nat. Acad. Pub. Adminstrn., Nat. Acad. Social Ins., Coun. for Excellence in Govt., Concord Coalition, Sons of Am. Revolution, Cosmos Club. Roman Catholic. Home: 9061 Tower House Pl Alexandria VA 22308-2758 Office: US Govt Accountability Office 441 G St NW Ste 7100 Washington DC 20548-0001 Office Phone: 202-512-5500. E-mail: walkerd@gao.gov.

WALKER, DEWARD EDGAR, JR., anthropologist, educator; b. Johnson City, Tenn., Aug. 3, 1935; s. Deward Edgar and Matilda Jane (Clark) W.; m. Candace J. Arroyo; children: Alice, Deward Edgar III, Mary Jane, Sarah, Daniel, Joseph Benjamin. Student, Ea. Oreg. Coll., 1953-54, 56-58, Univ. of the Americas, 1958-59; BA in Anthropology with honors, U. Oreg., 1960-61, PhD in Anthropology, 1964; postgrad., Wash. State U., 1962. Asst. prof. anthropology George Washington U., Washington, 1964-65, Wash. State U., Pullman, 1965-67, research collaborator, 1967-69; assoc. prof., chmn. dept. Sociology/Anthropology, lab. dir. U. Idaho, Moscow, 1967-69; prof. U. Colo., Boulder, 1969—, research assoc. in population processes program of inst. behavioral sci., 1969-73, assoc. dean Grad. Sch., 1973-76. Founder, v.p. Walker Rsch. Group, Ltd., Boulder, Colo., 1995. Founder, co-editor Northwest Anthropol. Rsch. Notes, 1966—; editor, Jour. Northwest Anthropology, 1967-2007, Plateau Vol.: Handbook of North American Indians, 1971-98; author of over 250 publs. Mem. tech. steering panel Hanford Environ. Dose Reconstrn. Project, 1988-95, Basalt Waste Isolation Project, Hanford, 1986-88; advisor Native Am. affairs. With U.S. Army, 1954-62. Fellow NSF, 1961, NDEA, 1961-64. Fellow Am. Anthropol. Assn. (assoc. editor Am. Anthropologist 1973-74), Soc. Applied Anthropology (hon. life, exec. com. 1970-79, treas. 1976-79, chmn. 1960-2000, cons., expert witness, editor Human Orgn. 1970-76, High Plains Applied Anthropologist); mem. AAAS, Am. Acad. Polit. and Social Scis., N.W. Anthropol. Conf. Achievements include research in Fakama, Saliskkotenai, Sioux, Calille, Washo, Shashane, Pauite, Bannock, Wreatilla, Tulolip, Black Feet, Arapaho, Navajo, Mohawk and affiliated tribes of Northwest Indians. Avocations: geology, mining, ranching. Home: PO Box 4147 Boulder CO 80306-4147 Office: U Colo PO Box 233 Boulder CO 80309-0233 Office Phone: 303-492-6719. Business E-Mail: walkerde@colorado.edu. *I have been both lucky and happy to have had the opportunities to do so many wonderful things in my life as an anthropologist.*

WALKER, DONALD BARCLAY, retired criminal justice educator, consultant, researcher, writer; b. Toledo, Jan. 19, 1935; s. Harry Charles and Elsie Marie Walker; m. Laurel Lee Ostberg, May 6, 1961; children: Dale Barclay, Scott Charles. BS, U. Mich., Ann Arbor, 1956; PhD, Wayne State U., Detroit, 1975. Probation counselor Family Ct., Toledo, 1960—64; tchg. asst. So. Ill. U., Carbondale, 1964—66, Wayne State U., Detroit, 1966—72; instr. dept. sociology and anthropology U. Mich., Flint, asst. prof. dept. sociology and anthropology; asst. prof. criminal justice Kent. State U., Ohio, 1980—88, assoc. prof., 1988—2000; ret. Ref. student disciplinary com. Kent State U., 1975—88, student advisor, 1997—2000; vis. prof. ctr. study pub. order U. Leicester, England, 1989—90, 1996—97. Contbr. articles to profl. jours.; author: (textbook) Criminal Justice In America, 1978. Child adv. Inst. Child Advocacy, Cleve., 1982—87. Named Hon. Vis. Prof., U. Leicester, Eng., 1990; grantee, Kent State U., 1987, Can. Embassy. Mem.: Am. Criminal Justice Assn., Am. Soc. Criminolgoy, Midwestern Criminal Justice Assn., Midwestern Sociol. Assn. Avocations: travel, reading, baseball.

WALKER, DONALD BURKE, retired music educator, retired archivist, composer; b. Ventura, Calif., Dec. 18, 1941; s. Marion Russell and Dorothy Burke Walker; m. Harrie Alley (div.); children: Nathaniel Burke, Anthony Cannon; m. Ellen Iris Amsterdam, Aug. 20, 1993. MA in Composition, U. Calif., Berkeley, 1966, MLS, 1974, PhD in Music, 1971; MA in History, Calif. State U., Sacramento, 1992. Vis. asst. prof. Sonoma State U., Rohnert Park, Calif., 1973—74, 1977—78, U. South Fla., Tampa, 1975—77, Oreg. State U., Corvallis, 1979; organist St. Paul's United Meth. Ch., Stockton, Calif., 1980—2000; univ. archivist U. of Pacific, Stockton, 1991—2003; ret., 2004. History columnist San Joaquin Farm Bur. News, Stockton, 1990—98. Composer: Symphony # 5, 2002, Seven Psalms, 2003, musician numerous compositions on VVM label. Archivist San Joaquin County Hist. Soc., Lodi, Calif., 1989—2003, editor quar. publ., 2000—03; historian exhbn. catalog and exhibit Italian Presence in San Joaquin Valley, 1994. Grantee, NEH, 1977, Composer in Cmty., Oakland, Calif., 1997. Mem.: Am. Music Ctr. Democrat.

WALKER, DONALD EZZELL, retired academic administrator; b. Springfield, Mo., July 13, 1921; s. Edward Everett and Cecilia (Ezzell) W.; m. Ann Lathrop, Dec. 17, 1943; 1 son, Craig Lathrop. AB, U. So. Calif., 1943, M.Th., 1947; PhD, Stanford U., 1954; L.H.D. (hon.), Southeastern Mass. U., 1973. Recreational dir. club work All Nations Found., Los Angeles, 1941-42, Wilshire Meth. Ch., Los Angeles, 1942-43; asst. minister Vincent Meth. Ch., Los Angeles, 1943-44; minister Encinitas Meth. Ch., 1945-47; teaching asst. Stanford U., 1947-49; instr. sociology San Diego State Coll., 1949-51, asst. prof. sociology, 1951-54, assoc. dean students, counseling, 1954-56, dean counseling, 1956-58, v.p. acad. affairs, 1968-71, acting pres., 1971-72; dean of students San Fernando Valley State Coll., Northridge, Calif., 1958-60; pres. Idaho State U., 1960-64; dean of students Sonoma State Coll., Rohnert Park, Calif., 1964-66; vice chancellor student affairs U. Calif., Irvine, 1966-68, sr. lectr. Grad. Sch. Adminstrn., 1967-68, fellow Univ. Coll., 1967-68; pres. Southeastern Mass. State U., N. Dartmouth, 1972-83; chancellor Grossmont-Cuyamaca Community Coll. Dist., El Cajon, Calif., 1983-92; ret., 1992. Author: (with others) Readings in American Public Opinion; The Effective Administrator: A Practical Approach to Problem-Solving, Decision-Making, and Campus Leadership, 1979; Never Try to Teach a Pig to Sing: Wit and Wisdom for Leaders, 1996; contbr. (with others) articles to profl. jours. Home: 3228 B Via Corrizo Laguna Woods CA 92637

WALKER, DORETTA ANITA, director; b. Memphis, Tenn., Feb. 21, 1942; d. Elgin and Mary Ella Walker. BS, So. Ill. U., 1970; cert. reading specialist, Harris Stowe Tchrs. U., 1978; MEd, Nat. Coll. Edn., 1989. Cert. officer African Meth. Episc. Ch., 2004. Mem. Divsn. Curriculum Com., St. Louis, Chpt. I Staff Devel. Planning Com., St. Louis; mem. curriculum com. SAT-MMA, St. Louis; coord. After Sch. Tutorial Program, St. Louis. Named to Wall Tolerance, 2005; recipient Shining Star award, 2004, Tchr. Appreciation award, Urban League of Metro, St. Louis, 1990. Mem.: NAACP, Nat. Bethou Edn. Alumni, So. Ill. U Alumni Assn., The Symner Alumni Assn. (life), Tu Gamma Delta. Democrat. Avocations: travel, photography, jazz. Home: 3026A N Taylor Ave Saint Louis MO 63115

WALKER, DUARD LEE, medical educator; b. Bishop, Calif., June 2, 1921; s. Fred H. and Anna Lee (Shumate) Walker; m. Dorothea Virginia McHenry, Aug. 11, 1945; children: Douglas Keith, Donna Judith, David Cameron, Diane Susan. AB, U. Calif., Berkeley, 1943, MA, 1947; MD, U. Calif., San Francisco, 1945. Diplomate Am. Bd. Microbiology. Intern, U.S. Naval Hosp., Shoemaker, Calif., 1945—46; asst. resident internal medicine Stanford U. Service San Francisco Hosp., 1950—52; asso. prof. med. microbiology and preventive medicine U. Wis., Madison, 1952—59, prof. med. microbiology, 1959—88, prof., chmn. med. microbiology, 1970—76, Paul F. Clark prof. med. microbiology, 1977—88, prof. emeritus, 1988—, prof., chmn. med. microbiology, 1981—88. Cons. Naval Med. Rsch. Unit,

Gt. Lakes, Ill., 1958—74; mem. microbiology tng. com. Nat. Inst. Gen. Med. Scis., 1966—70; mem. nat. adv. Allergy and Infectious Diseases Coun., 1970—74; mem. adv. com. on blood program rsch. ARC, 1978—79; mem. study group on papovaviridae Internat. Com. on Taxonomy of Viruses, 1976—90; mem. vaccines and related biol. products adv. com. FDA, 1985—89; mem. rev. panel postdoct. rsch. fellowships for physicians Howard Hughes Med Inst., 1990—93. Mem. editl. bd. Infection and Immunity, 1975—83, Archives of Virology, 1981—83, Microbial Pathogenesis, 1985—90. Served to lt. (j.g.) USNR, 1943—46, served to capt. USNR, 1953—55. Fellow NRC postdoctoral virology, Rockefeller Inst. Med. Rsch., N.Y.C., 1947—49, USPHS immunology, George Williams Hooper Found., U. Calif., San Francisco, 1949—50. Fellow: Infectious Diseases Soc. Am., Am. Acad. Microbiology, Am. Pub. Health Assn.; mem.: Arts and Letters, Wis. Acad. Sics., Am. Soc. Virology, AAUP, Reticulendothelial Soc., Soc. Exptl. Biology and Medicine, AAAS, Am. Soc. Microbiology, Am. Assn. Immunologists, NAS. Home: 618 Odell St Madison WI 53711-1435 Office: U Wis Med Sch 600 Highland Ave Madison WI 53792-1510 Office Phone: 608-233-9279. Personal E-mail: dlwalke1@facstaff.wisc.edu.

WALKER, EDWARD KEITH, JR., retired management consultant, retired military officer; b. Annapolis, Md., Jan. 23, 1933; s. Edward Keith and Miriam (Whitmore) W.; m. Carol Ann Turner, June 12, 1954 (dec. June 14, 2002); children: Lynn Walker Streett, Wendy Louise. BS, U.S. Naval Acad., Annapolis, Md., 1954; postgrad., Armed Forces Staff Coll., Norfolk, Va., 1966; MBA in Fin. Mgmt., George Washington U., Washington, 1970. Commd. ensign U.S. Navy, 1954, advanced through grades to rear admiral, 1981; force supply officer COMSUBLANT Norfolk, Va., 1975—78; exec. officer SPCC Mechanicsburg, Pa., 1978—80; comdr. Naval Supply Ctr., Puget Sound, Bremerton, Wash., 1980—81; Atlantic Fleet supply officer CINCLANTFLT Norfolk, 1981—83; asst. comptroller Navy Dept., Washington, 1983—84; comdr. Naval Supply Systems Command and 35th Chief Supply Corps Washington, 1984—88; v.p. adminstrn. and corp. strategy Resource Cons. Inc., Vienna, Va., 1989—2000, v.p. emeritus, 2000—. Vice chmn. bd. dirs. Herley Industries; bd. visitors Elon U. Decorated D.S.M., Legion of Merit (3 awards); recipient Def. Superior Service medal, 1983 Mem. Vinson Hall Corp. (bd. dirs., chmn. 2003), Naval Acad. Found. (trustee), U.S. Navy Meml. Found. (bd. dirs., treas.), Supply Corps Found. (past pres.), Supply Corps Assn. (past pres.), U.S. Naval Inst. (golden life), Naval Submarine League (life), Naval Order U.S. (life), Surface Navy Assn. (life), Navy League U.S. (life), Naval Acad. Alumni Assn. (life), Mil. Officers Assn. (life), N.Y. Yacht Club, Chesapeake Yacht Club. Republican. Episcopalian. Home: 3520 Saylor Pl Alexandria VA 22304-1831 Home Phone: 703-823-6149. *There is no greater satisfaction than to see your people succeed, and then to insure they get the credit.*

WALKER, EDWARD S., JR., think-tank executive, former ambassador; b. Abington, Pa., June 13, 1940; s. Edward Stanley and Rosabel Dunlop (Gould) W.; m. Wendy Jane Griffiths, Apr. 7, 1973; Kathryn Erica, Christopher James. BA, Hamilton Coll., 1963; MA, Boston U., 1965. Joined Fgn. Svc., US Dept. State, Washington, 1967; polit. officer Am. Embassy, Tel Aviv, 1969-73; staff asst. Nr. Ea. affairs US Dept. State, Washington, 1974-75; Arabic lang. trainee Fgn. Svc. Inst., Lebanon, Tunis, Egypt, 1975-77; polit. officer Am. Embassy, Damascus, Syria, 1977-79; spl. asst. Pres.'s personal rep., Washington, 1980-82; exec. dir. Office of Dep. Sec. US Dept. State, Washington, 1982-84; mem. Royal Coll. Def. Studies, London, 1984-85; dep. chief of mission Am. Embassy, Riyadh, Saudi Arabia, 1985-88; dep. asst. sec. Bur. Near East Affairs US Dept. State, 1988-89, U.S. amb. to United Arab Emirates Abu Dhabi, 1989-92; dept. permanent rep. to UN, NYC, 1993-94; U.S. amb. to Egypt US Dept. State, Cairo, 1994-97, U.S. amb. to Israel Tel Aviv, 1997—99, asst. sec. for Near Ea. Affairs Washington, 2000—01; pres., CEO Mid. East Inst., Washington, 2001—. With U.S. Army, 1962-65. Decorated Order of Independence (Abu Dhabi); recipient Superior Honor award Dept. State, 1975, Meritorious Honor award, 1976, Disting. Civilian Svc. award Dept. Def., 1997. Episcopalian. Office: Middle East Inst 1761 N St NW Washington DC 20036

WALKER, FRANCIS JOSEPH, lawyer; b. Aug. 5, 1922; s. John McSweeney and Sarah Veronica (Meechan) W.; m. Julia Corinne O'Brien, Jan. 27, 1951; children: Vincent Paul, Monica Irene Hylton, Jill Marie Nudell, John Michael, Michael Joseph, Thomas More. BA, St. Martin's Coll., 1947; JD, U. Wash., 1950. Bar: Wash. Asst. atty. gen. State of Wash., 1950-51; pvt. practice Olympia, Wash., 1951—. Gen. counsel Wash. Cath. Conf., 1967-76. Lt. (j.g.) USNR, 1943-46; PTO. Home and Office: 2723 Hillside Dr SE Olympia WA 98501-3460 Office Phone: 360-352-2245.

WALKER, F(RANK) BORDEN, oil industry executive; b. 1953; m. Michele Walker. BS, U. NC, 1975; MBA, Dartmouth Coll., Hanover, NH, 1977. Sr. v.p. retail mktg. Hess Corp. (formerly Amerada Hess), 1996, exec. v.p., pres. mktg. and refining, 2002—, bd. dirs., 2004—. Office: Hess Corp 1185 Avenue of the Americas New York NY 10036 Office Phone: 212-997-8500. *

WALKER, FRANKLIN CURTIS, federal agency administrator; b. Sept. 10, 1945; s. Howard and Edna Walker; m. Judy Provins, May 29, 1967; children: Mark, Kathy, Phillip. BS in Biology, N.Mex. State U., 1967. Park ranger White Sands Nat. Monument Nat. Park Svc., 1970-72, park ranger Jefferson Nat. Expansion Meml., 1972-73, park ranger Gulf Islands Nat. Seashore, 1973-77, naturalist south dist. Yellowstone Nat. Park, 1977-80, chief of interpretation Carlsbad Caverns Nat. Park, 1980-85, park supt. Ft. Clatsop Nat. Meml., 1985-90, supt. Nez Perce Nat. Hist. Park Idaho, Oreg., Wash., Mont., 1990-98, supt. Saguaro Nat. Park Tucson, 1998—. 1st lt. U.S. Army, 1967-69. Office: Saguaro Nat Park 3693 S Old Spanish Trl Tucson AZ 85730-5601 Home: PO Box 254 Yellowstone National Park WY 82190-0254

WALKER, FRED ELMER, broadcast executive; b. Trenton, NJ, May 31, 1931; s. Elmer and Adele F. (Decker) W.; m. Catharine Middleton Sullivan, Nov. 26, 1952; children: Catharine Walker Bergstrom, Elizabeth Walker Phillips, Frederick Christopher. Student, Trenton State Coll., 1952, NYU, 1953. Dir. pub. relations Sta. WPTZ-TV, Phila., 1953; v.p., gen. mgr. Sta. WTTM-AM, Trenton, 1956-59; gen. sales mgr. Sta. KYW-AM, Cleve., 1959-62; v.p., gen. mgr. Sta. KDKA-AM, Pitts., 1962-65, Sta. KYW-TV, Phila., 1965-67, Sta. KPIX-TV, San Francisco, 1967-69, Sta. WLWT-TV, Cin., 1969-71; pres. Broad St. Communications Corp., New Haven, 1971-85; v.p. radio group Westinghouse Broadcasting, NYC, 1985-88; exec. v.p. Broad St. Ventures, NYC, 1988—; mng. ptnr. Broad St. Consulting, 1997—. Pres. Broad St. TV Corp., 1988-96, Broad St. Mgmt. Corp., 1988-96; bd. dirs. Broadcast Music, Inc., 1984-87, Call for Action, Washington, 1993-2000. Bd. dirs. Long Wharf Theatre, New Haven, WXEL-TV, 1998-2005; chmn. Long Wharf Theatre Future Fund campaign, 1983-85, chmn. devel., 1986-90, chmn. and pres., 1990-97; mem. Pres.'s Coun. Albertus Magnus Coll.; trustee Hamden Hall Country Day Sch., chmn. devel. com.; chmn. 250th fund dr. United Ch. Christ, 1987-89; chmn. Call For Action, Washington, 1994-2000; trustee Fla. Stage, 1998-2000; pres. Edn. TV Fund, 2006—. Recipient Alfred P. Sloan award, 1954, Ohio State Ednl. award, 1953; fellow Berkeley Coll. Yale U., 1976. Mem. Radio Advt. Bur. (dir.), TV Bur. Advt., Nat. Assn. Broadcasters, New Haven Lawn Club. Democrat. Personal E-mail: fredewalk1@aol.com.

WALKER, GEORGE H., investment company executive; BA/BS, MBA, U. Pa., Phila. Ptnr., head alternative investment strategies, mem. partnership com. Goldman Sachs Asset Mgmt.; global head investment mgmt. divsn., mem. exec. com. Lehman Bros. Holdings, NYC, 2006—. Vice chair bd. trustees The New Sch.; mem. bd. overseers U. Pa. Sch. Arts & Sci.; bd. dirs. Local Initiatives Support Cooperation. Office: Lehman Bros Holdings 745 Seventh Ave New York NY 10019 Office Phone: 212-526-7000. *

WALKER, GEORGE HERBERT, III, former ambassador, retired investment banking company executive; b. St. Louis, Mar. 16, 1931; s. George H. and Mary (Carter) W.; m. Sandra E. Canning, Dec. 23, 1955 (div. Oct. 1962); children: Mary Elizabeth, Wendy, Isabelle; m. Kimberly Gedge, July 27, 1968 (div. Jan. 1977); children: George H. IV, Carter; m. Carol Banta, Feb. 21, 1987. BA, Yale U., 1953; LL.B., Harvard U., 1956. Bar: Conn. 1956. Gen. ptnr. G.H. Walker & Co. (later G.H. Walker, Laird Inc.), 1961-74; sr. v.p., also bd. dirs. White, Weld & Co. Inc., 1974-75; chmn. bd. dirs. G.H. Walker & Co., 1973-74; exec. v.p. Stifel Nicolaus & Co., 1976-78, pres., CEO, 1978-92, chmn., 1982—2001, chmn. emeritus, 2001—; US amb. to Hungary US Dept. State, Budapest, 2003—06. Civilian aide to sec. U.S. Army for Ea. Mo., 1973-80; bd. dirs. Laidlaw Corp., Laclede Steel Co., Eck-Adams Corp.; bd. govs. Midwest Stock Exch., 1982-88. Bd. dirs. Downtown St. Louis Inc., 1975-90, chmn., 1984-86; bd. dirs. Webster U., chmn. bd., 1987-92; trustee Mo. Hist. Soc., St. Louis Children's Hosp., 1972-92, Jefferson Nat. Expansion Meml. Assn., 1992; vestryman St. Ann's Ch., Kennebunkport, Maine; mem. Mo. Rep. Ctrl. Com., 1983—; adv. bd. St. Louis Area coun. Boy Scouts Am., 1989—; trustee investment trust Episcopal Diocese of Mo.; hon. bd. dirs. Anti-Drug Abuse Edn. Fund, Inc., 1990—; bd. dirs. St. Louis Zoo, 1992. With USAF, 1956-58. Mem. Rotary (St. Louis club). E-mail: walkergh@stifel.com.

WALKER, GEORGE HERBERT, IV, investment company executive; BA, BS, Univ. Pa.; MBA, Wharton Sch., Univ. Pa. Joined Goldman Sachs, NYC, 1992, ptnr., co-head wealth mgmt., head alternative investment strategies, CEO hedge fund strategies, 1998—2006; global head investment mgmt. div., mem. exec. com. Lehman Brothers, NYC, 2006—. Vice-chmn. bd. trustees The New Sch.; bd. dir. Local Initiatives Support Corp.; mem. bd. overseers Univ. Pa. Sch. Arts & Sciences. Mem.: Phi Beta Kappa. Office: Lehman Brothers 745 7th Ave New York NY 10019 *

WALKER, GEORGE KONTZ, law educator; b. Tuscaloosa, Ala., July 8, 1938; s. Joseph Henry and Catherine Louise (Indorf) W.; m. Phyllis Ann Sherman, July 30, 1966; children: Charles Edward, Mary Neel. BA, U. Ala., 1959; LLB, Vanderbilt U., 1966; AM, Duke U., 1968; LLM, U. Va., 1972; postgrad. (Sterling fellow), Law Sch. Yale U., 1975-76. Bar: Va. 1967, N.C. 1976. Law clk. U.S. Dist. Ct., Richmond, Va., 1966-67; assoc. Hunton, Williams, Gay, Powell & Gibson, Richmond, 1967-70; pvt. practice Charlottesville, Va., 1970-71; asst. prof. Law Sch. Wake Forest U., Winston-Salem, NC, 1972-73, assoc. prof. Law Sch., 1974-77, prof. Law Sch., 1977—, mem. bd. advisors Divinity Sch., 1991-94; Charles H. Stockton prof. internat. law U.S. Naval War Coll., 1992-93. Vis. prof. Marshall-Wythe Sch. Law, Coll. William and Mary, Williamsburg, Va., 1979-80, U. Ala. Law Sch., 1985; cons. Naval War Coll., 1976—, Nat. Def. Exec. Res., 1991—, Naval War Coll., Internat. Law Dept. Adv. Bd., 1993—. Author: The Tanker War, 1980-88, 2000; contbr. articles to profl. jours. With USN, 1959-62, capt. USNR, ret. Woodrow Wilson fellow, 1962-63; decorated Order of the long Leaf Pine; recipient Joseph Branch Alumni Svc. award, Wake Forest, 1988, Meritorious Unit Commendation, USN, 1992-93; named Hon. Atty. Gen. N.C., 1986. Mem.: ABA, Internat. Inst. Humanitarian Law, Maritime Law Assn., Am. Law Inst., Am. Judicature Soc., Internat. Law Assn. (exec. com. Am. br. 2001—), Am. Soc. Internat. Law (exec. coun. 1988—91), N.C. Bar Assn. (v.p. 1997—98), Va. Bar Assn., Order of Barristers (hon.), Piedmont Club, Phi Delta Phi, Sigma Alpha Epsilon, Phi Beta Kappa, Order of the Coif (hon.). Democrat. Episcopalian. Home: 3321 Pennington Ln Winston Salem NC 27106-5439 Office: Wake Forest U Sch Law PO Box 7206 Winston Salem NC 27109-7206

WALKER, GEORGE THEOPHILUS, JR., composer, music educator, pianist; b. Washington, June 27, 1922; s. George Theophilus Sr. and Rosa (King) W.; children: Gregory, Ian. MusB, Oberlin Coll., 1941; student of, Rudolf Serkin, Rosario Scalero; Artist Diploma, Curtis Inst. music, 1945; D of Mus. Arts, U. Rochester, 1957; DFA (hon.), Lafayette Coll., 1982; MusD (hon.), Oberlin Coll., 1983; student of, Nadia Boulanger; MusD (hon.), Curtis Inst. Music, 1997; DHL (hon.), Montclair State U., 1997; MusD (hon.), Bloomfield Coll., 1997; DFA (hon.), Spelman Coll., 2001. Instr. Dillard U., New Orleans, 1953-54; instr. Dalcroze Sch. Music, NYC, 1960-61, New Sch. Social Research, NYC, 1961; instr. to assoc. prof. Smith Coll., Northampton, Mass., 1961-68; assoc. prof. U. Colo., Boulder, 1968-69; disting. prof. Rutgers U., Newark, 1976-92, prof. emeritus, 1992. Concert pianist Nat. Concert Artists, N.Y.C., 1950-53, Columbia Artists, N.Y.C., 1959-60; adj. prof. Peabody Inst. Johns Hopkins U., Balt., 1975-78; disting. prof. U. Del., Newark, 1975-76. Composer: Sonata for 2 Pianos (Harvey Gaul prize 1963), numerous sonatas, cantatas and concertos, Concerto for Cello and Orch., 1982, Sinfonias for Orch. Bd. dirs. Am. Bach Found., 1988; mem. Mary Flagler Cary Trust Commn., 1998. Recipient award Am. Acad. and Inst. Arts and Letter, 1982, Koussevitsky award, 1988, Pulitzer prize, 1996, L.J. Govs. award 1997, Koussevitsky award 1998, Mary Flagler Cary Charitable Trust award, 1998, Dorothy Maynor Arts Citizens award, 2000, A.I. duPont award Del. Symphony, 2001, Classical Roots Lifetime Achievement award Detroit Symphony, 2001, Foils for Orch. award, Eastman Commn., 2006, Legacy award, Nat. Opera Assn., 2007; grantee Smith Coll., U. Colo., Rutger U. Rsch. Coun., NEA, NJ State Coun. for Arts; Fulbright fellow, 1957, John Hay Whitney fellow, 1958, Guggenheim fellow, 1969, 88, Rockefeller fellow, 1971, 74; Disting. scholar U. Rochester, 1996; commd. NY Philharm., Kennedy Ctr., Cleve. Orch., Boston Symphony, NJ Symphony, Am. Guild of Organists; inducted Am. Classical Music Hall of Fame, 2000. Mem. ASCAP, Am. Acad. Arts and Letters (mem.-elect), Am. Bach Found. (bd. dirs. 1988), Am. Symphony League. Democrat. Avocations: tennis, photography, audio. Home: 323 Grove St Montclair NJ 07042-4223 Personal E-mail: gtwalker@verizon.net.

WALKER, GEORGE W., bishop; Sr. bishop African Meth. Episcopal Zion Ch., Farmington. Named one of 100 Most Influential Black Americans, Ebony mag., 2006.

WALKER, GLORIA LEE, training services executive; b. Oklahoma City, Dec. 31, 1942; d. Russell Holland and Ethel Wanita (Kierig) Walker; m. Thomas William Rupprath, June 3, 1966 (div. Feb. 1995); children: Robert Rupprath, John Rupprath. BA in Sociology, U. S.C., 1965; MS in Elem. Edn., U. Nebr., 1971; EdD in Adminstrn., Fla. Atlantic U., 1986. Ops. rsch. analyst U.S. Bur. Mines, Washington, 1988-90; employment devel. specialist IRS, Dallas, 1991-92; pres. AMERITRAIN, Dallas/Lubbock, Tex., 1992—. Author: Training a Diversified Workforce, 1993, Developing Training Materials, 1995, Instructing Diversified Employee, 1995, Seminars in Training, 1995.

WALKER, GORDON BEVERLEY MOORE, JR., business educator; b. NYC, Oct. 10, 1944; s. Gordon Beverley Moore and Nancy Holton Walker; m. Jane Edwards, June 15, 1977 (div. Sept. 1983); 1 child, Emma; m. Nancy Niebuhr, Mar. 22, 1984; children: Hugh Curran, Ian Moore. BA, Yale U., 1966; MBA, U. Pa., 1976, PhD, 1982. Assoc. prof. Sloan Sch. Mgmt., MIT, Cambridge, Mass., 1981-86, Wharton Sch., U. Pa., Phila., 1986-91, Sch. of Orgn. and Mgmt., Yale U., New Haven, 1991-93; David B. Miller prof. of bus., dept. chair Cox Sch. of Bus., So. Meth. U., Dallas, 1993—. Cons. in field; bd. dirs. Alico, Inc. Co-author: Modern Competitive Strategy, 2003, 2d edit., 2006; contbr. articles to profl. jours. 1st lt. USMC, 1967-70. Decorated Bronze star; recipient numerous grants including NSF, 1987-89, 95-97. Mem.: Am. Sociol. Assn., Acad. Mgmt., Yale Club of Dallas (pres. 2001—02, 2003—05). Home: 331 Ridgebriar Dr Richardson TX 75080-1920 Office: Cox Sch Bus So Meth U Dallas TX 75275-0333 Office Phone: 214-768-2191. Business E-Mail: gwalker@mail.cox.smu.edu.

WALKER, GORDON DAVIES, government official, writer, lecturer, consultant; b. Logan, Utah, July 10, 1944; s. Rudger Harper and Fawn Lucile (Davies) W.; m. Carlene Martin, June 5, 1968; children— Kimberly Anne, Kelly Anne, Gordon Davies Jr., Bradford Martin AB, Brigham Young U., 1968; MBA, Harvard U., 1971. Project dir. Becker Research Co., Boston, 1969-71; dir. mktg. Am. Nat. Enterprises, Salt Lake City, 1971-72; v.p., dir. Sweetwater Properties, Salt Lake City, 1972-76; gen. ptnr. Covecrest Properties, Salt Lake City, 1976—; spl. asst. to sec. HUD, Washington, 1981-82, dep. under sec., 1983-86; cons. real estate, fin. Commerce Cons., Washington, 1986-87; pres., chief exec. officer Deseret Fed. Savs. and Loan, Salt Lake City, 1987-88; pres. U.S. Resources, Inc., Phoenix, 1988-92, also bd. dirs.; pres. Energy Lock Inc., Salt Lake City, 1992—2002; exec. dir. Utah chpt. Alzheimer's Assn., 2002—06; dir. housing cmty. devel. State of Utah, 2003—. Author: Finance Your Own Way to Success, 1980; Develop Your Way to Success, 1981; Hottest New Ideas of the 1980's, 1982. Rep. state del., Salt Lake City, 1974; del. Rep. Nat. Conv., 1988 Mem. Nat. Assn. Realtors Mem. Lds Ch.

WALKER, GRAHAM CHARLES, biology professor; b. Boston, Feb. 8, 1948; s. Charles Bertram and Margaret Elizabeth (Biehn) W.; m. Janet Elizabeth Haliburton, May 30, 1970; 1 child, Gordon Andrew. BSc with honors, Carleton U., Ottawa, Ont., Can., 1970; PhD, U. Ill., 1974. Asst. prof. biology MIT, Cambridge, Mass., 1976-80, assoc. prof. biology, 1980-86, prof. biology, 1986—. Rsch. prof. Howard Hughes Med. Inst., 2002—, Am. Cancer Soc., 2003—. Co-author: DNA Repair and Mutagenesis; editor-in-chief Jour. Bacteriology, 1991-2001, editor, 1985-91; editl. bd. Mutation Rsch., Amsterdam, Netherlands, 1982—; editl. bd. DNA Repair, 2002—, contbr. articles to Procs. NAS USA, Cell, Microbiology Rev., Jour. Bacteriology. Housemaster McCormick Hall, MIT, Cambridge, 1986-92, Margaret MacVicar Faculty fellow MIT, 1992-2002, John Simon Guggenheim Meml. fellow, 1984, Woodrow Wilson fellow, 1970; recipient Rita Allen Career Devel. award, 1978-83, Howard Hughes Med. Inst. grantee in biology, 2002. Fellow Am. Acad. Arts & Scis.; mem. Am. Acad. Microbiology, Am. Soc. for Microbiology, Genetics Soc. Am., Am. Chem. Soc., Environ. Mutagen Soc. Achievements include discovery of umuDC analogs on plasmid pKM101; demonstration of repetoire of SOS genes; demonstrated critical role of exopolysaccharide in nodule invasion by Rhizobium meliloti; cloning and analysis of roles of UmuDC in UV mutagenesis; demonstrated RecA-mediated cleavage activates UmuD, second symbiotically active exopolysaccharide in R. meliloti. Office: MIT Biology Dept 77 Massachusetts Ave Cambridge MA 02139-4307 Business E-Mail: gwalker@mit.edu.

WALKER, H. REED, lawyer; b. Kansas City, Mo., Dec. 3, 1952; s. Huffman Walker and Marjorie Hallier. BSBA, William Jewell Coll., Liberty, Mo., 1974; JD, Washburn U., Topeka, Kans., 1977. Bar: Kans. Supreme Ct. 1977, Colo. Supreme Ct. 1992, Mo. Supreme Ct. 1995, US Ct. Appeals (8th cir.) 1988, US Ct. Appeals (10th cir.) 2000, US Supreme Ct. 1984. Ptnr. Barnett, Walker & O'Connor, Chartered, Kansas City, 1986—96; pres. Law Offices H. Reed Walker, P.A., Mission, Kans., 1997—. Presenter in field. Contbr. articles to profl. jours. Mem.: Kans. Bar Assn. (former pres. litig. section.), Kans. Trial Lawyers Assn., Wyandotte County Bar Found. (pres. 1987—88, mem. grievance and ethics Com 1987—, sec. 2000—). Office: Law Offices H Reed Walker PA 5800 Foxridge Dr Ste 306 Mission KS 66202 Office Phone: 913-432-1826. Office Fax: 913-236-7115. Personal E-mail: hreedwalker1@aol.com.

WALKER, HENRY GILBERT, health care executive, consultant; b. Gowanda, NY, Feb. 16, 1947; s. Henry George and Grace Dayton (Moore) W.; m. Elaine Ruth Darbee, July 18, 1970 (div. Dec. 1979); 1 child, Matthew Case; m. Patricia Ann Andrade, May 14, 1983; children: Michael David, Christopher John. BS in Indsl. Engring., Cornell U., 1969; MBA, U. Chgo., 1975. Evening adminstr. Rush-Presbyn. St.-Luke's Med. Ctr., Chgo., 1973-75; mgmt. cons. Booz, Allen & Hamilton, Chgo., 1975-79; regional adminstr., v.p. S.W. Community Health Service, Albuquerque, 1979-83, adminstr., v.p., 1983-86; exec. v.p. Presbyn. Healthcare Services, Albuquerque, 1986-92; pres., CEO Tucson Med. Ctr., 1992—95, Health Ptnrs. of Ariz., 1995—97, Providence Health System, Seattle, 1997—2004; ptnr. Andrade Walker Consulting, LLC, Bellevue, Wash., 2004—. Bd. dirs. Park Dist., Elmhurst, Ill., 1978, 1979; mem. Dist. III Cmty. Action Com., Albuquerque, 1985; divsn. chmn. United Way of Albuqueque, 1985, 1988. Recipient Hosp. Survey award U. Chgo., 1975, Bachmeyer award U. Chgo., 1975, Outstanding Midshipman award Cornell U., 1969; named one of Emerging Healthcare Leaders, Healthcare Forum, 1985, 86, Healthcares Up and Comers, Modern Healthcare Mag., 1987. Mem.: Healthcare Forum (bd. dirs., chmn.), N.Mex. Hosp. Assn. (chmn. bd. dirs. 1983—85, treas.). Democrat. Presbyterian. Avocations: reading, hiking, skiing.

WALKER, HERSHEL O., history educator; b. Andrews, Tex., Dec. 30, 1957; s. H. O. Jr. and Betty Ann Walker; m. Mary H. Walker; children: Allison Robinson, Jesse K., Shawn M. BA, Tex. Tech. U., Lubbock, 1981; MA, Tex. A&M U., College Station, 1995. Cert. secondary tchr. Tex. Edn. Agy. Tchr. world and U.S. history grades 9-12 Giddings Ind. Sch. Dist., Tex., 1981—. Office: Giddings HS PO Box 389 Giddings TX 78942-0389

WALKER, HOWARD ERNEST, lawyer; b. Mobile, Ala., Mar. 3, 1944; s. Ernest W. and Denise (Kearney) W.; m. Michelle Anne Pinsonneault, June 20, 1992. BA, U. Ill., 1966; JD, Boston U., 1974. Bar: R.I. 1974. Assoc. Hinckley, Allen & Snyder, Providence, 1974-80, ptnr., 1980—2004. Trustee Providence Pub. Libr., 1978-2000, pres., 2002—, vice chmn. programs; trustee R.I. Wild Plant Soc., 1995-97—; trustee R.I. Civic Chorale & Orchestra, 1988-95; dir. South Shore Mental Health Ctr., 1997—, v.p. 2000—; trustee and sec. Hopkinton Land Trust, 2000-04; mem. Hopkinton Planning Bd., 2002—, sec., 2003-04. Lt. USNR, 1967-71. Mem. ABA, R.I. Bar Assn. (mem. ad hoc com. on future of law practice, chmn. superior ct. bench/bar com. 1990-93, 94-95, Dorothy Lohmann Cmty. Svc. award 2003), Maritime Law Assn. of US, Phi Kappa Phi, Phi Beta Kappa. Avocations: western Americana, natural history. Home: 39A Berrie Ln PO Box 118 Rockville RI 02873-0118 Office Phone: 401-539-6767. Business E-Mail: hewlaw@hughes.net.

WALKER, IGNACIO JOSE, lawyer; b. Buenos Aires, Sept. 13, 1976; s. Guillermo Jose Walker and Graciela Auge; m. Camila Failo, Mar. 6, 2004; children: Delfin, Francisco. Degree in Law, Cath. U. Argentina, Buenos Aires, 1999; LLM, So. Meth. U., Dallas, 2005. Cert.: Colegio Publico de Abogados de la Ciudad de Buenos Aires (adv.) 2000. Clk. First Instance Fed. Ct. Nr. 2, San Isidro, Argentina, 1997—2000; trainee counsel Nobleza Piccardo S.A., Buenos Aires, 2000—01; assoc. Estudio Beccar Varela, Buenos Aires, 2001—05; fgn. assoc. Latham & Watkins LLP, LA, 2005—06; counsel S.Am. Avery Dennison Corp., Pasadena, Calif., 2006, Buenos Aires, 2006—. Home: Gral Artigas 1388 Talar del Lago II Lote 52 Pacheco Buenos Aires 1617 Argentina Office: Avery Dennison Corp Av Warnes 2225 Buenos Aires C1427DPB Argentina Home Phone: 54911 6046-5222; Office Phone: 5411 4014-2216.

WALKER, IRA ALLEN, financial consultant; m. Deborah Walker; children: Mary Ashley, Joseph, Michael. Grad., Bklyn. Coll., 1978; postgraduate student, U. Pa., Phila., 1993—95. Sr. v.p., corp. svcs. specialist Morgan Stanley, Red Bank, NJ, 1987—, dir. Walker Group. Bd. trustees Montclair State U., NJ; fin. advisor for United Way NYC Morgan

Stanley. Named one of Best Brokers in Am., Registered Rep, 2002, Best 100 Brokers, Barron's, 2005—07. Office: Morgan Stanley 20 Linden Pl Red Bank NJ 07701 Office Phone: 732-936-3300. E-mail: ira.walker@morganstanley.com. *

WALKER, IRVING EDWARD, lawyer; b. Balt., Jan. 31, 1952; s. Bertram and Mildred (Shapiro) W.; m. Leslie A. Walker; children: Brandon Harris, Aaron Seth, Emily Celeste. BA, Duke U., 1973; JD, U. Md., 1978. Bar: Md. 1978, US Dist. Ct. Md. 1978, US Ct. Appeals (4th cir.) 1980, US Supreme Ct. 1995, US Ct. Appeals (3d cir.) 2001. Assoc. Frank, Bernstein, Conaway & Goldman, Balt., 1978-85, ptnr., 1986-91; prin. Miles & Stockbridge, Balt., 1991-2001; ptnr. Saul Ewing LLP, Balt., 2001—. Chmn. Bankruptcy & Creditors Rights Group, 1991-2000, vice chair Bankruptcy and Reorganization Group, 2006—. Contbg. author: Bankruptcy Deskbook, 1986. Bd. dirs. Jewish Cmty. Ctr. Greater Balt., 1986-88, Temple Emanuel of Balt., Inc., 1996-02, Homeless Persons Representation Project, 2005-, Etz Chaim Ctr., 2005-. Mem. ABA, Md. Bar Assn., Bar Assn. Balt. City (chmn. bankruptcy and bus. law com. 1989-90), Am. Bankruptcy Inst., Bankruptcy Assn. Dist. Md. (pres. 1992-93, chmn. Balt. chpt. 1989-91), Order of Coif. Avocation: weightlifting. Office: Saul Ewing LLP 500 E Pratt St Baltimore MD 21202 Home Phone: 410-484-2492. Business E-Mail: iwalker@saul.com.

WALKER, JANE STEWART, small business owner, publishing executive, educator; b. Connersville, Ind., July 9, 1938; d. George Sinks and Cornelia Stewart Tatman; m. Frank Dilling Walker, Aug. 25, 1979; m. Guy Thomas Connelly (div.); children: Kevin Connelly, Katherine Connelly. BA, Sweet Briar College, Va., 1960. Asst. tchr. The Children's Corner, Indpls., 1971—75; historic interpreter Conner Prairie Pioneer Settlement, Noblesville, Ind., 1975; staff asst. Hist. Landmarks Found. Ind., Indpls., 1975—78; classified ads, credit and purchasing Topics Newspapers, 1978—80; staff edn. docent Children's Mus., 1981—88; part owner News Examiner Co., Connersville, 1991—93, Winchester (Ky.) Sun, 1991—2005, Comml. Printing Svc., Connersville, Ind., 1989—. Dir. and v.p. Tatman, Inc., Connersville, Ind., 1983—; sec. and pres. Found. Hand Rsch. and Edn., Indpls., 1988—94; dir. and v.p. Walker Family Found., 1993—. Author: The Encyclopedia of Indianapolis, 1994. State co-chair Phillips Acad. Nat. Centennial Fund Dr., Andover, Mass., 1977—79; dir. and pres. Coleman Adoption Svcs., 1982—88; chmn. fin. devel. Arthritis Found. Ind., Indpls., 1989—97; mem. alumni coun. Phillips Acad., Andover, Mass., 1984; bd. dir. Sweet Briar Coll., Va., 1999—2006, vice chair. bd. dir., 2003—06. Co-recipient Humanitarian of Yr., Arthritis Found. Ind., 1998. Mem.: Sweet Briar Alumnas Club of Ind. (co-pres. 1990—), Univ. Park Country Club. Avocations: photography, golf, reading, travel. Office: 7361 Eaton Ct University Park FL 34201

WALKER, JENNIE LOUISE, not-for-profit fundraiser, consultant; b. Ft. Hood, Tex., Nov. 27, 1962; d. Homer Lee and Jennie Louise (Smith) Walker; m. Philip Jerome King, Apr. 23, 1994 (div. Mar. 1999). BA in Speech Comm., Columbus State U., Ga., 1984, postgrad., 1985, Mercer U., Macon, Ga., 1987-90. Intern Senator Mack Mattingly, Washington, 1984, Congressman Richard Ray, Washington, 1984; rsch. asst. Robinson Humphrey Co., Inc., Atlanta, 1985-89; mktg. asst. Norrell Corp., Atlanta, 1989-90; dir. rsch. Carter Ctr., Inc., Atlanta, 1990-94, Boys & Girls Clubs Am., Atlanta, 1994-2000; dir. philanthropic initiatives WEBMD Found., Inc., Atlanta, 2000; assoc. dir. Global Philanthropists Cir. Synergos Inst., NYC, 2000—02; pres., CEO Jennie Walker Co., Inc., NYC, 2001—04, J. Walker, Inc., 2004—. Mem. adv. bd. The Found Ctr., Atlanta, 1997—2000, Found. Ctr., Atlanta, 1997—2000. Vol. Atlanta Project, 1992, Sta. WPBA-TV, Channel 30, Musicians on Call N.Y., 2001—, Lyric Chamber Music Soc. N.Y., 2000—; mem. adv. bd. Ga. Addiction Pregnancy and Parenting Family Enrichment Ctr, 1994—96; mem. Music Mgrs. Forum U.S., 2003—; vol. World Hunger Yr., 2004—. Richard Ray for Congress Campaign Com., 1984. Mem.: ASCAP, DAR, NARAS (assoc.), Nat. Assn. Recording Industry Profls., Nashville Songwriters Assoc. Internat., Women in Music (mem. 2002—), Assn. Ind. Music Pubs., Assn. Ind. Music Publ., Nat. Acad. Popular Music, Spl. Libr. Assn., Soc. Competitive Intelligence Profls., Am. Prospect Rsch. Assn. (pres. Ga. chpt. 1993—94, 1996—97), Nat. Acad. Songwriters, Ga. Music Industry Assn. (bd. dirs. 1991—93, publicity chair 1991—93, v.p. 1992—93, 1995—98, bd. dirs. 1995—2000, fundraising chair 1995—2000, pres. 1998—2000, pres. emeritus, advisor 2000—, Pres. award for vol. svc. 1997), Nat. Soc. Fundraising Exec., Columbus State U. Alumni Assn. Methodist. Avocations: songwriting, singing. Office: 435 W 57th St #15-S New York NY 10019 Office Phone: 212-541-7456. Business E-Mail: jennie@jenniewalker.com.

WALKER, JERALD CARTER, academic administrator, minister; b. Bixby, Okla., May 22, 1938; s. Joseph Carter and Trula Tosh (Jackson) W.; m. Virginia Canfield, Apr. 14, 1963; children: Elisabeth Katherine, Anne Carter. BA in Sociology, Oklahoma City U., 1960; BD, U. Chgo., 1964; D of Religion, Sch. Theology at Claremont, 1966; LHD (hon.), Shiller U., 1994. Ordained to ministry Meth. Ch., 1964. Dir., campus minister Campus Christian Assn., Chgo., 1961-64; minister of outreach Temple Meth. Ch., San Francisco, 1965-66; chaplain, asst. prof. religion Nebr. Wesleyan U., Lincoln, 1966-69; pres. John J. Pershing Coll., Beatrice, Nebr., 1969-70; v.p. univ. rels., assoc. prof. Southwestern U., Georgetown, Tex., 1970-74; pres. Baker U., Baldwin, Kans., 1974-79, Oklahoma City U., 1979-97, chancellor Okla., 1997—. Ednl. adv. to bd. dirs. Tianjin U. Commerce, People's Republic of China; participant Okla. Ann. Conf. of United Meth. Ch. Co-author: The State of Sequoyah: An Impressionistic View of Eastern Oklahoma, 1985; contbr. chpt. book, articles to profl. jours. Bd. dirs., past chmn. Okla. Ind. Coll. Found. Recipient Alumni Recognition award Nebr. 4H Club, 1970, Okla. 4H Club, Disting. Alumnis award Oklahoma City U., 1974, Outstanding Citizen award Dist. 575 Rotary Internat., 1990, Award for Excellence Asia Soc. Okla., 1990, Humanitarian award for Okla/Ark. region NCCJ, 1992, Nat. Police Adminstrn. award for promotion or peace and order Rep. of China, 1992, Francis Asbury award for fostering United Meth. Ministries in Higher Edn., 1994, Excellent Leader award Mgmt. Devel. Inst. Singapore, 1996, Benjamin Franklin award Downtown Olka. City Sertoma Club, 1992, Excellent Leader award Mgmt. Devel. Inst. of Singapore, 1996, Nat. Medal of Honor Cherokee Nation, 2000; inducted to Okla. Higher Edn. Hall of Fame, 1999. Mem. Nat. Assn. Schs. and Colls. of United Meth. Ch. (past pres.), Nat. Assn. Colls. and Univs. (bd. dirs.). Office: Oklahoma City U 6826 E 112th St S Bixby OK 74008-2062

WALKER, JEWETT LYNIUS, clergyman, church official; b. Beaumont, Tex., Apr. 7, 1930; s. Elijah Harvey and Ella Jane (Wilson) W.; m. Dorothy Mae Croom, Apr. 11, 1965; children: Cassandra Lynn, Jewett L., Kevin, Michelle, Ella, Betty Renne, Kent, Elijah H. BA, Calif. Western U., 1957; MA, Kingdom Bible Inst., 1960; B Religious Edn., St. Stephens Coll., 1966, DD, 1968; LLD, Union Bapt. Sem., 1971; postgrad., St. Paul Sch. Theology, 1979, Southwestern Bapt. Theol. Sem., 1985-86; grad., Nat. Planned Giving Inst., 1981, Philanthropy Tax Inst., 1982; DD, Clinton Jr. Coll., 1992. Ordained to ministry African Methodist Episcopal Zion Ch., 1957. Pastor Shiloh A.M.E. Zion Ch., Monrovia, Calif., 1961-64, Martin Temple A.M.E. Zion Ch., LA, 1964-65, 1st A.M.E. Zion Ch., Compton, Calif., 1965-66, Met. A.M.E. Zion Ch., LA, 1966-73, Logan Temple A.M.E. Zion Ch., San Diego, 1973-74, Rock Hill A.M.E. Zion Ch., Indian Trail, NC, 1974-79, Bennettsville A.M.E. Zion Ch., Norwood, NC, 1979-86, Price Meml. A.M.E. Zion Ch., Concord, NC, 1986-89, Mt. Zion A.M.E. Zion Ch., Hickory Grove, SC, 1989-91, NewHope AME Zion, Lancaster, SC, 1991—92, Mt. Zion A.M.E. Zion Ch., Lancaster, SC, 1992—2001, Mt. Moriah A.M.E. Zion Ch., Richburg, SC, 2001—03, New Hope A.M.E. Zion Ch., Lancaster, SC, 2003—06, North Corner A.M.E. Zion, Lancaster, 2007—. Sec.-treas. dept. home missions, brotherhood pensions and relief African Methodist Episcopal Zion Ch., Charlotte, N.C., 1974-92; mem. exec. bd. Prophetic Justice Unit Com. Nat. Coun. Chs., co-chairperson pers. com.; mem. World Meth. Coun., del. 14th World Conf Author: Is There a Man in the House, 1975, Lets Get Serious about Missions, 1991, Issues Facing the Ministry, 1991, The Denominational Dollar, 1992, also articles. Chmn. Minority Affairs Adv. Com., Mecklenburg County; trustee Clinton Coll., dir. planned giving, 1992; trustee Rock Hill, Lomax-Hannon Coll., Greenville, Ala., Union Bapt. Theol. Sem., Birmingham, Ala.; bd. mgrs. McCrorey br. YMCA; pres. Am. Ch. Fin. Svc. Corp., Carolina Home Health Svc. Inc., Meth. Life Ins. Soc. Inc., bd. trustees State N.C. Coll. Found., Inc., 1987, del. Presbyn. Ptnrs. in Ecumenism Nat. Coun. Chs. Christ, 1986, pres., 1988—; pres. Walker Funeral Home Inc. (formerly The House of Irma Funeral Home), Concord, 1995, Am. Ch. Econ. Devel. Corp.; del. Presbyn. Ch. U.S. Gen. Assembly, 1985; mem. citizens parole accountability com. Mecklenburg County, Charlotte, 1993; mem. planned giving adv. bd. Livingston Coll., Salisbury, N.C.; pres. Jewett L. Walker & Assocs.; chmn. minority affairs adv. com. Mecklenburg County; com. mem. Charlotte Mecklenburg Citizen Parole Accountability Com., 1994, vice chmn., 1998; pres. Pardue St. Apts. Inc., Lancaster, S.C., 1997—, Am. Ch. Econ. Devel. Corp., 1999; elected to jud. coun. African Meth. Episcopal Zion Ch., 2000; mem. adv. bd. Mechanics and Farmers Bank, Charlotte, 2001 Fellow Nat. Assn. Ch. Bus. Adminstrs., Ch. Bus. Adminstrn., Presbyn. Ch. Bus. Adminstrn. Assn.; mem. NAACP (life), Nat. Soc. Fund Raising Execs., Am. Bible Soc. (state dir. vols., N.C. and S.C. dir. vol.), Nat. Spkrs. Bur., Christian Ministries Mgmt. Assn., Am. Soc. Assn. Execs., Funeral and Cremation Soc. South, Inc. (founding mem. 1998), Shriners, Masons (33 deg.), Prince Hall Affiliation. Republican. Home: 910 Bridlepath Ln Charlotte NC 28211-2022 Office: 4501 Walker Rd Charlotte NC 28211-2047

WALKER, JOAN H., insurance company executive; m. George Walker. BA, Rutgers U., New Brunswick, 1968, MA in Sociology, 1973. Sr. exec. mktg. and govt. N.J. State Govt., 1973-83; pres. Richmann & Ptnrs., 1983-88; exec. v.p. Saatchi & Saatchi, 1988-90; mng. dir. mktg. comm. NYNEX Corp., 1990-93; pres., CEO Bozell Pub. Rels., NYC, 1993-96; ptnr. Bozell Sawyer Miller Group, 1996; sr. v.p. corp. comm. Ameritech, Chgo., 1996-99; sr. v.p. global pub. affairs Monsanto (merged with Pharmacia & UpJohn, now Pharmacia), Skolie, Ill., 1999—2002; exec. v.p. corp. mktg. and comm. Qwest Comm. Internat., 2002—05; sr. v.p. corp. rels. Allstate Corp., Northbrook, Ill., 2005—, interim chief mktg. officer, 2007—. Dir. Qwest Found.; mem. bd. trustees Colo. Symphony Orch. Office: Allstate Corp 2775 Sanders Rd Northbrook IL 60062 E-mail: Joan.H.Walker@am.pnu.com. *

WALKER, JOHN E. (NED WALKER), air transportation executive; married. B in Mass Comm., U. Colo., Boulder. News dir. KLMO Radio, Colo.; various positions including reporter, weekend anchor and asst. news dir. KWGN-TV, Denver; dir. corp. comm. Frontier Horizon Frontier Airlines; with Continental Airlines, Inc., Houston, 1987—, sr. dir. comm. dept., staff v.p. corp. comm., v.p. corp. comm., 1995—2000, sr. v.p. worldwide corp. comm., 2000—. Bd. dirs. Theater Under the Stars, Houston. Named an Employee Comm. All-Star, Inside PR, 1996. Office: Continental Airlines Inc PO Box 4607 Houston TX 77210 Office Phone: 713-324-5000. Office Fax: 713-324-2637. E-mail: ned.walker@coair.com. *

WALKER, JOHN ERNEST, molecular biologist, researcher; b. Halifax, Eng., Jan. 7, 1941; s. Thomas Ernest and Elsie (Lawton) W.; m. Christina Jane née Westcott, 1963; children: Esther, Miriam. BA in Chemistry, St. Catherine's Coll., Oxford, Eng., 1964; MA, DPhil, Oxford U., Eng., 1969; doctorate (hon.), U. Buenos Aires, Argentina, 1998, U. Huddersfield, 1998, U. Manchester Inst. Sci. & Tech., 1999, Oxford U., 1999, Groningen U., 1999, U. Leeds, 1999, U. London, 2002, U. Sussex, 2003, U. Liverpool, 2004, U. East Anglia, Norwich, 2006, Moscow State U., 2007. Vis. rsch. fellow U. Wis., 1969—71; NATO rsch. fellow CNRS, Gif-sur-Yvette, France, 1971—72; EMBO rsch. fellow Pasteur Inst., Paris, 1972—74; mem. scientific staff, Molecular Biology Lab. Med. Rsch. Coun., Cambridge, England, 1982—87, sr. scientist lab. molecular biology, 1987—98, dir. Dunn Human Nutrition Unit, 1998—. Hon. prof. Peking Union Med. Coll., 2001—, U. Cambridge, 2002, prof. molecular bioenergetics, 2002—. Contbr. articles to profl. jours. Recipient Johnson Found. prize U. Pa., 1994, CIBA medal and prize Biochem. Soc., 1996, Peter Mitchell medal European Bioenergetic Congress, 1996, Gaetano Quagliariello prize U. Bari, 1997, Nobel prize in chemistry, 1997, Royal Soc. Chemistry award of Biomembrane Chemistry, 2003; named Nobel Laureate in Chemistry, 1997, hon. fellow Inst. Biology, 2002—. Fellow Royal Soc., Sidney Sussex Coll.; mem. European Molecular Biology Orgn. (Knight Bachelor 1998), Soc. Chem. Industry (Messel medal 2000); fgn. mem. L'Accademia Nazionale Dei Lincei, Rome, 2003-; fgn. assoc. NAS, 2004-. Avocations: cricket, opera music, walking. Office: Dunn Human Nutrition Unit Med Rsch Coun Cambridge CB2 2XY England Business E-Mail: walker@mrc-dunn.cam.ac.uk.

WALKER, JOHN KENT, JR., lawyer; Grad. magna cum laude, Harvard Coll.; grad. with distinction, Stanford Law Sch., 1987. Asst. US atty. US Dept. Justice, San Francisco; sr. counsel AirTouch Comm.; assoc. gen. counsel Netscape, 1998—99; sr. counsel AirTouch Comm.; exec. v.p. Liberate Technologies; dep. gen. counsel eBay Inc.; v.p., gen. counsel Google, 2006—. Office: Google Inc 1600 Amphitheatre Pky Mountain View CA 94043 *

WALKER, JOHN LOCKWOOD, lawyer; b. Atlanta, Sept. 3, 1952; s. James William and Doris (Camp) W.; m. Caroline Asher Walker, Jan. 16, 1952; children: Ann Caroline, John Lockwood Jr., Elizabeth Davis, Lindsay Eleise. BA, Duke U., 1974, JD, 1977. Atty. legal div. bd. govs. FRS, Washington, 1977-79; assoc. Simpson Thacher & Bartlett LLP, NYC, 1979-84, ptnr., 1984—. Chmn. Richina Pacific Ltd. Bd. dirs., vice chmn. Fin. Svcs. Vol. Corps. Mem. Coun. on Fgn. Rels., Bretton Woods Com., Met. Club of Washington, Univ. Club (NYC), Chevy Chase (Md.) Club, Bedford (NY) Golf and Tennis Club, Sankaty Head Golf Club (Nantucket, Mass.). Episcopalian. Office: Simpson Thacher & Bartlett LLP 425 Lexington Ave Fl 8 New York NY 10017-3954 E-mail: JWalker@stblaw.com.

WALKER, JOHN MERCER, JR., federal judge; b. NYC, Dec. 26, 1940; s. John Mercer and Louise (Mead) W.; m. Cristy West, June 20, 1980 (div. Apr. 1983); m. Katharine Kirkland, Feb. 14, 1987. BA, Yale U., 1962; JD, U. Mich., 1966. Bar: NY 1969, US Dist. Ct. (so. dist.) NY 1971, US Ct. Appeals (2d cir.) 1972, US Supreme Ct. 1977, US Ct. Appeals (DC cir.) 1982. Maxwell Sch. Pub. Adminstrn. fellow, state counsel Republic of Botswana, Africa, 1966-68; assoc. Davis, Polk and Warwell, NYC, 1969-70; asst. US atty. criminal divsn. (So. dist.) NY US Dept. Justice, NYC, 1971-75; assoc. to ptnr. Carter, Ledyard and Milburn, NYC, 1975-81; asst. sec. enforcement ops. US Dept. Treasury, Washington, 1981-85; judge US Dist. Ct. (so. dist.) NY, 1985-89, US Ct. Appeals (2d cir.), New Haven, 1989—2006, chief judge, 2000—06, sr. judge, 2006—. Adj. prof. NYU Law Sch., 1995—; gen. counsel Nat. Coun. on Crime and Deliquency, NYC, 1977-81; chmn. Fed. Law Enforcement Tng. Ctr., Washington, 1981-85; spl. counsel Adminstrv. Conf. US, Washington, 1986-92; mem. budget com. jud. conf. Inst. Jud. Adminstrn., 1992—, dir., 1992—. Del. Rep. Nat. Conv., Detroit, 1980. With USMCR, 1963-67. Recipient Alexander Hamilton award Sec. of Treas., Washington, 1985, Secret Service Honor award, 1985. Mem. ABA, DC Bar Assn., Assn. Bar City of NY, Fed. Judges Assn. (pres. 1993-95). Republican. Episcopalian. Office: US Ct Appeals 157 Church St New Haven CT 06510-2100 *

WALKER, JONATHAN LEE, lawyer; b. Kalamazoo, Mar. 8, 1948; s. Harvey E. and Olivia M. (Estrada) W. BA, U. Mich., 1969; JD, Wayne State U., 1977. Bar: Mich. 1977, U.S. Dist. Ct. (we. dist.) Mich. 1989, U.S. Dist. Ct. (no. dist.) Ill. 1991, U.S. Dist. Ct. (ea. dist.) Mich. 1983, Colo. 1996, U.S. Dist. Ct. Colo. 1996, U.S. Ct. Appeals (10th cir.) 1996. Assoc. Moore, Barr & Kerwin, Detroit, 1977-79; ptnr. firm Barr & Walker, Detroit, 1979-82; assoc. firm Richard M. Goodman, P.C., Detroit, 1983-87; hearing officer Mich. Civil Rights Commn., Detroit, 1983-86; pvt. practice Detroit, 1988-89, Birmingham, Mich., 1990—95; dep. pub. defender Office of State Pub. Defender, Colorado Springs, Colo., 1998—. Participant Detroit Bar Assn. Vol. Lawyer Program. Bd. dirs. Cmty. Treatment Ctr.-Project Rehab., Detroit, 1983-89; mem. ARC of Pikes Peak region, 2002—, pres. bd., 2004—; mem. scholarship com. Latino en Marcha Scholarship Fund, Detroit, 1984; treas. youth assistance program Citizens Adv. Coun., 1987; mem. State Domestic Violence Offenders' Mgmt. Bd., 2001-04; bd. dirs. Colorado Springs chpt. ACLU, 2002-2003; mem. allocation com. Pikes Peak United Way, 2006—. Mem. State Bar Mich. Found., Wayne County Mediation Tribunal (mediator), Nat. Lawyers Guild (exec. bd. Detroit chpt. 1988-92, pres. Detroit chpt. 1988-90), Mich. Trial Lawyers Assn. (co-chair coalition com. 1988-90, exec. bd. 1988-96, co-chair pro bono com. 1991-96), State Bar Mich. (com. on underrepresented groups in law 1980-92, chmn. 1983-85, mem. com. jud. qualifications 1985-86, Latin Am. affairs coun. 1978-96), Colo. Criminal Def. Bar, Legal Aid and Def. Assn. (bd. dirs. 1990-95), Hispanic Bar Assn., Trial Lawyers Pub. Justice (founder 1981, mem. amicus com. 1985-86, state capt. 1991-95), El Paso County Bar Assn., Ctr. Auto Safety. Office: 415 S Sahwatch Colorado Springs CO 80903 Office Phone: 719-475-1235 x 1529. Personal E-mail: jwmtnguy1@earthlink.net.

WALKER, JUDY LOU, special education educator, director; d. Charles Emil and Carolyn Hazel Carlson; m. Bernard Dee, July 8, 1989; children: Jaycie, Brendan. BA in Liberal Studies, Biola U., La Mirada, Calif., 1988; MS in Elem. Edn., Chadron State Coll., Nebr., 1996. Cert. profl. tchr. Nebr. Substitute tchr. Kimball Pub. Schs., Nebr., 1989—90, Title I tchr., 1990—92, asst. volleyball coach, 1990—94, asst. basketball coach, 1990—94, Title I dir., 1992—. AWANA leader Kimball Evang. Free Ch., 2000—01, leader TruthQuest, 2004—. Nominee Title I Disting. Schs. award, 1997—98, 1998—99. Mem.: NEA, Nebr. State Edn. Assn., Kimball Edn. Assn., Internat. Reading Orgn. Avocations: reading, sports, scrapbooks. Office: Mary Lynch Elem Sch 1000 E 6th St Kimball NE 69145 Office Phone: 308-235-4696.

WALKER, KARA, artist; b. Stockton, Calif., Nov. 26, 1969; BA in Painting/Printmaking, Atlanta Coll. Art, 1991; MFA in Painting/Printmaking, R.I. Sch. Design, 1997. Prof. art Columbia U., NYC. US representative São Paolo Bienal, Brazil, 2002. One-woman shows include Gallery 100, Atlanta, 1991, Ctr. Curaltorial Studies, Bard Coll., Annandale-on-Hudson, NY, 1995, Nexus Contemporary Arts Ctr., Atlanta, 1995, Wooster Gardens/Brent Sikkema, NYC, 1995, 1998, Bernard Toale Gallery, Boston, 1996, Huntington Beach Arts Ctr., Calif., 1997, U. Chgo., 1997, Contemporary Arts Ctr., Cin., 1997, Henry Art Gallery, U. Wash., Seattle, 1997, The Carpenter Ctr., Harvard U., Cambridge, Mass., 1997, San Francisco Mus. Modern Art, 1997, The Forum, St. Louis, 1998, Vienna State Opera House, Austria, 1998, The Print Ctr., Phila., 1998, Galleri Index, Stockholm, 1998, Contemporary Arts Mus., Houston, 1999, Calif. Coll. Arts and Crafts, Oliver Art Ctr., Oakland, 1998, Brent Sikkema, NY, 1998, McKinney Ave. Contemporary, Dallas, 1999, Des Moines Art Ctr., 2000, The Emancipation Approximation, Tel Aviv Mus. Art, 2001, Disturbing Allegories, Vanderbilt U. Fine Arts Gallery, Tenn., 2001, American Primitive, Brent Sikkema Gallery, NYC, 2001, Nat Turner's Revelation (an Important Lesson from our Negro Past You Will Likely Forget to Remember), Galerie Max Hetzler, Berlin, 2002, For the Benefit of All the Races of Mankind (Mos' Specially the Master One, Boss), Germany, 2002, Mannheimer Kunstverein, Germany, 2002, Internat. Bienal of Sao Paolo, Brazil, 2002, An Abbreviated Emancipation, U. Mich. Mus. Art, 2002, Narratives of a Negress, Tang Tchg. Mus. and Art Gallery, Skidmore Coll., 2003, Drawings, Brent Sikkema, 2003, Excavated from the Black Heart of a Negress, Studio Mus., Harlem, 2003, Centro Nazionale per le Arti Contemporanee, Rome, 2003, Fibbergibbet and Mumbo Jumbo, Fabric Workshop and Mus., Phila., 2004, Grub for Sharks: A Concession to the Negro Populace, Tate Liverpool, 2004, Museo de Arte Carrillo Gil, Mexico City, 2005, Event Horizon, New Sch. U., 2005, Song of the South, REDCAT, LA, 2005, My Complement, My Enemy, My Oppressor, My Love, 2007, exhibited in group shows at New Visions Gallery, Atlanta, 1991, MU Gallery, Boston, 1993, Sol Koffler Gallery, Providence, 1994, Paul Morris Gallery, NYC, 1995, Mills Gallery, Boston, Inst. Contemporary Art, 1996, Greg Kucera Gallery, Seattle, 1997, Stephen Friedman Gallery, London, 1998, Looking Forward Looking Backward, Elaine L. Jacob Gallery, Wayne State U., 1999, Istanbul Biennial: The Passion and the Wave, 1999, This Is Not the Place, Ramapo Coll. NJ, 2000, Blurry Lines, John Michael Kholer Arts Ctr., Wis., 2000, The Print World, Ljubljana Biennial, Slovenia, 2001, The Americans, Barbican Art Galleries, London, 2001, Form Follow Fiction, Castello di Rivoli Museo d'Arte Contemporanea, 2001, Moving Pictures, Solomon R. Guggenheim Mus., NYC, 2002, Telling Tales: Narrative Impulses in Recent Art, 2002, Tempo, MoMAQNS, NYC, 2002, Black President: The Art and Legacy of Fela Anikulapo-Kuti, New Mus., NYC, 2003, Comic Release: Negotiating Identity for a New Generation, Carnegie Mellon U., 2003, Provocations, Bronx Mus. Art, 2004, Monument to Now, DESTE Found. Contemporary Art, Athens, Greece, 2004, Fairy Tales Forever: Internat. Homage to H.C. Andersen, Copenhagen, 2005, Kiss the Frog! The Art of Transformation, Nat. Mus. Art, 2005, Getting Emotional, Inst. Contemporary Art, Boston, 2005, The Shadow, Vestsjaellands Kunstmuseum, Denmark, 2005, The World is a Stage, Mori Art Mus., Tokyo, 2005, Trials and Terrors, Mus. Contemporary Art, 2005, numerous others; author: Freedom, A Fable, A Curious Interpretation of the Wit of a Negress in Troubled Times; contbr. articles to profl. jours. Named one of 100 Most Influential People, Artists and Entertainment, Time Magazine, 2007; recipient MacArthur fellow, John D. and Catherine T. MacArthur Found., Lucelia Artist award, Smithsonian Am. Art Mus., 2004; fellow Individual Artist's fellow, Art Matters, Inc.; scholar Presdl. scholar, Atlanta Coll. Art, Ida Blank Ocko scholar. Office: c/o Sikkema Jenkins & Co 530 West 22d St New York NY 10011 *

WALKER, KAREN D., lawyer; b. Tampa, Feb. 24, 1968; BS in Comm. Studies, Fla. State U., 1990; JD with high honors, U. Fla., 1993. Bar: Fla. 1993, US Dist. Ct. (No. and So. Districts Fla.) 2000. Ptnr. Holland & Knight LLP, Tallahassee. Mng. editor U. Fla. Law Rev., 1991—92, title standards editor, 1992—93. Past chair bd. dirs. United Way of the Big Bend, Inc. Mem.: ABA (chair young lawyers divsn., com. on women in the profession 2000—02, mem. standing com. on pub. edn. 2000—02, state chair pub. contract law sect. state/local procurement divsn. 2002—, mem. sect. on pub. utilities, comm., and transp. law, chair IT procurement com.), Tallahassee Women Lawyers, Tallahassee Bar Assn., Fla. Bar (mem. adminstrv. law sect.), Order of Coif. Office: Holland & Knight LLP 315 S Calhoun St Ste 600 Tallahassee FL 32301 Office Phone: 850-425-5612. Business E-Mail: karen.walker@hklaw.com.

WALKER, KELLYE L., lawyer; b. Little Rock, Aug. 1966; BS, La. Tech. U., 1987; JD, Emory U., 1992. Atty. Boult, Cummings, Conners & Berry PLC, Nashville; assoc. Chaffe, McCall, Phillips, Toler & Sarpy LLP, New Orleans, 1995—98, ptnr., 1998—2000; mem., counsel Hill & Barlow LLP, Boston, 2000—03; sr. v.p., gen. counsel, sec. BJ's Wholesale Club Inc., Natick, Mass., 2003—07; gen counsel Diageo N. Am., 2007—. Bd. dirs. Assn. Corp. Counsel, New England Legal Found., Mus. Afro-Am. History. Office: Diageo 801 Main Ave Norwalk CT 06860 *

WALKER, KENNETH LYNN, lawyer; b. New Haven, Nov. 22, 1948; s. John Charles and Virginia Clare (Lovett) W.; m. Suzanne Kay Thompson, Jan. 27, 1979; children: Katherine Leslie, Caroline Leigh, Christine Lynn. BA, Coe Coll., 1969; MA, New Sch. Social Research, 1973; JD, U. Iowa, 1975. Bar: Ohio. Assoc. Baker & Hostetler, Cleve., 1975-79; atty. Cole Nat. Corp., Cleve., 1979-84; sr. group counsel TRW, Inc., Cleve., 1984-91; v.p., gen. coun. sec. Varity Corp., 1991-97; v.p. gen coun. sec. Sealy Corp., 1997-2000, sr. v.p., gen. counsel, sec. 2000-. Editor Jour. Corp. Law, 1974-75. Mem. ABA, Ohio Bar Assn., Cleve. Bar Assn. Office: Sealy One Office Parkway at Sealy Dr Trinity NC 27370 Business E-Mail: kwalker@sealy.com.

WALKER, KIM A., lawyer; BA, U. Va., 1988; JD, Columbia U., 1991. Spl. counsel, Intellectual Property Dept. Willkie Farr & Gallagher LLP, NYC. Mem.: ABA, Black Entertainment and Sports Lawyers Assn., Internat. Trademark Assn., Assn. Bar of City NY (mem. Com. Entertainment Law 2004—). Office: Willkie Farr & Gallagher LLP 787 Seventh Ave New York NY 10019 Office Phone: 212-728-8776. E-mail: kwalker@willkie.com.

WALKER, LELAND JASPER, civil engineer; b. Fallon, Nev., Apr. 18, 1923; s. Albert Willard and Grayce (Wilkinson) W.; m. Margaret Frances Noble, Jan. 21, 1946; children: Thomas, Margaret, Timothy. BS in Civil Engring, Iowa State U., 1944; D. Eng. (hon.), Mont. State U., 1983. Engr. with various govtl. depts., 1946-51, 53-55; v.p. Wenzel & Co. (cons. engrs.), Great Falls, Mont., 1955-58; pres., chmn. bd. No. Engring. and Testing, Inc., Great Falls, 1958-88. Pres. Ind. Labs. Assurance Co., 1977-79; bd. dirs. Applied Tech., Inc. Pres., trustee Endowment and Rsch. Found. Mont. State U., 1969-82, Mont. Deaconess Hosp., Great Falls, 1959-67. McLaughlin Rsch. Inst. Biol. Scis., 1989-92, Mont. Sch. Deaf and Blind Found., 1984—; trustee Rocky Mountain Coll., 1977-80, Dufresne Found., 1979-87; chmn., bd. dirs. Mont. Tech. Svcs. Adv. Coun. adv. coun. Engring. Coll. Mont. State U.; bd. dirs. Mont. State Fair, Engring. Socs. Commn. on Energy, 1977-79, Mont. Bd. Sci. and Tech., 1983-88, Great Falls Chamber Found., 1989-91, trustee Great Falls Public Libr. Found., 1995-2001. Named to Mont. Engrs. Hall Fame, 2003. Fellow ASCE (pres. 1976-77), AAAS, Cons. Engrs. Coun. (pres. Mont. 1971), Accrediting Bd. Engring. and Tech. (v.p. 1978-79, pres. 1980-83); mem. Nat. Acad. Engring., Am. Coun. Ind. Labs. (hon., sec. 1973-76), Meadowlark Country Club, Pachyderm Club (bd. dirs., v.p. 1992-94), Chi Epsilon (nat. hon.), Tau Beta Pi (hon.). Republican. Methodist. Home: 1200 32nd St S Apt 9 Great Falls MT 59405-5333

WALKER, LINDA LEE, lawyer; b. Phila., Jan. 24, 1954; d. M. Lorenzo and Romaine Yvonne (Smith) W.; m. Steve Collins; children: Jessica Marie McIntyre, Nicole Yvonne McIntyre. BA, U. Penn., 1975; JD, Yale U., 1978. Bar: NY 1979, US Dist. Ct. (so. and ea. dists.) NY 1982, US Ct. Appeals (1st cir.) 1982; NASD. Asst. regional atty. HHS, NYC, 1978-82; assoc. Shea and Gould, NYC, 1982-85; v.p., sr. assoc. counsel Chase Manhattan Bank, N.A., NYC, 1985-89; v.p., assoc. gen. counsel Citicorp Credit Svc., NYC, 1989-97; asst. gen. counsel Prudential Ins. Co. Am., Iselin, 1997—2000, v.p., chief compliance officer for Prudential Retirement, 2000—04; dir. compliance UBS Fin. Svcs., Inc., Weehawken, NJ, 2004—. Mem., Phi Beta Kappa. Office Phone: 201-352-4959. Business E-Mail: linda.walker@ubs.com.

WALKER, LORENZO GILES, surgeon, educator; b. Phila., June 29, 1957; s. Manuel Lorenzo and Romaine Yvonne (Smith) W.; m. Yvonne Ruiz; children: Zachary Giles, Benjamin Lee, Cassidy Leigh. BA cum laude, U. Pa., 1978; MD, Harvard U., 1982. Diplomate Am. Bd. Orthopaedic Surgery, Nat. Bd. Med. Examiners; lic. surgeon, Mass., Calif.; cert. added qualification hand surgery, 1993; recertified orthopedic surgery and hand surgery, 2003. Intern in surgery New Eng. Deaconess-Harvard Surg. Svc., Boston, 1982-83, asst. resident in surgery, 1983-84; resident in orthop. surgery Harvard U., Boston, 1985-88; fellow in hand surgery UCLA Med. Sch., 1988-89, asst. clin. prof. orthop. surgery Calif., 1988—, attending physician dept. orthop. Hand Clinic Calif., 1996-98; ptnr. Ventura Orthop. Hand and Sports Med. Group, Calif., 1994-98; solo practice hand surgery, 1998—. Staff physician St. John's Plasant Valley Hosp., Camarillo, Calif., St. John's Regional Med. Ctr., Oxnard, Calif., Cmty. Meml. Hosp., Ventura, Calif.; attending physician, cons. Sepulveda, Calif. VA Hosp.; presenter in field. Cons. reviewer Clin. Orthopaedics and related Rsch., 1990-92; contbr. numerous articles to profl. jours. Vol. Spl. Olympics, Ventura, 1994-96, Direct Relief Internat., Santa Barbara, Calif., 1994-96, Ventura County Rescue Mission, 1994-98. Recipient Cert. of Appreciation, Am. Heart Assn., 1994; UCLA faculty fellow, 1988-89. Mem. Am. Soc. for Surgery of the Hand, Am. Assn. for Hand Surgery, AMA, Calif. Med. Assn., Calif. Orthopaedic Assn., Calif. Ringside Physician, Ventura County Med. Soc., Internat. Soc. Aquatic Medicine, Western Orthopaedic Assn., Orthopaedic Overseas, UCLA Hand Club, Arthroscopy Assn. N.Am., Alpha Epsilon Delta, Onyx Honor Soc., Philomathean Soc. Avocations: photography, scuba diving, sports memorabilia, fishing, travel. Office Phone: 805-485-7764.

WALKER, MAMIE ODENA, retired secondary school educator; b. Statesville, NC, Mar. 12, 1940; d. Ernest Glen Sr. and Annie Louise Allison; m. William Paul Walker Jr.; 1 child, Daryl L. BS, Livingstone Coll., Salisbury, NC, 1963; MS in Tchg., Cath. U. Ams., Washington, 1971. Cert. in day care I and II Prince George's CC, MD, 1982. Sci. tchr. Elm City (NC) Pub. Schs., 1963—64, Mackin Cath. HS, Archdiocese of Washington, 1965—67, Washington Pub. Schs., 1967—69, 1971—74, 1988—2002; ret., 2002; lab. asst. Howard U. Coll. Medicine, Washington, 1965—67. Mem. adv. com. Sickle Cell Disease Assn., Washington, Am. Physiol. Soc.; mem. Cool Spring Terrace Assn., Adelphi, Md., 2002—; v.p. Washington Inter Alumni Coun. United Negro Coll. Fund, 1988—. Named Outstanding Biology Tchr., Nat. Assn. Biology Tchrs., 1973, 1993. Mem.: Livingstone Coll. Alumni Assn. (v.p. Washington chpt.), Delta Sigma Theta (Geraldine P. Woods award). Democrat. Avocations: cooking, reading, gardening, singing, public speaking. Home: 8410 Rambler Dr Adelphi MD 20783

WALKER, MARGARET SMITH, real estate company executive; b. Lancashire, Eng., Oct. 14, 1943; came to U.S., 1964; d. Arthur Edward and Doris Audrey (Dawson) Smith; m. James E. Walker, Feb. 6, 1992. Lic. real estate agt., Hawaii. Broker Coldwell Banker Pacific Properties/Previews, Honolulu, 1974-81; pres. Maggie Parkes & Assocs., Inc., Honolulu, 1981—. Bd. dirs. Aloha State Dressage Soc., Honolulu, 2001, Hawaii Opera Theatre, 2002—, com. chmn., chmn. Opera Ball, 1997. Mem. Am. Horse Shows Assn., Hawaii Horse Shows Assn., Outrigger Canoe Club. Episcopalian. Avocations: dressage riding, horse show management.

WALKER, MARK A., lawyer; b. NYC, June 24, 1941; s. Joseph and Eleanor (Junger) W.; m. Tania Khodjamirian; children: Marie, Andrew. BA, Stanford U., 1963; LLB, Yale U., 1966. Bar: N.Y. 1967, U.S. Dist. Ct. (so. dist.) N.Y. 1977. Assoc. Cleary, Gottlieb, Steen & Hamilton, Paris, Brussels and NY, 1966-75, ptnr. NYC, 1975—2005, mng. ptnr., 2005—. Mem. Assn. Bar City N.Y. Office Phone: 212-225-2240. E-mail: mwalker@cgsh.com.

WALKER, MARY L., lawyer; b. Dayton, Ohio, Dec. 1, 1948; d. William Willard and Lady D. Walker; 1 child, Winston Samuel. Student, U. Calif., Irvine, 1966-68; BA in Biol. Scis./Ecology, U. Calif., Berkeley, 1970; postgrad., UCLA, 1972-73; JD, Boston U. Law Sch., 1973. Bar: Calif. 1973, U.S. Supreme Ct. 1979, U.S. Dist. Ct. (no., ctrl., ea. and so. dists.) Calif. Atty. So. Pacific Transp. Co., San Francisco, 1973-76; assoc. Richards, Watson & Gershon, LA, 1976—77, ptnr., 1979-82, ptnr., chair environ. dept. San Francisco, 1989-91; prin. dep. asst. atty., environment and natural resources divsn. U.S. Dept. Justice, Washington, 1982-84; dep. solicitor U.S. Dept. Interior, Washington, 1984-85; asst. sec. for environment, safety and health U.S. Dept. Energy, Washington, 1985-88; spl. cons. to chmn. bd. Law Engring. Inc., Atlanta, 1988-89; v.p., West Coast and the Pacific Law Environ., Inc., San Francisco, 1989; ptnr. Luce, Forward, Hamilton & Scripps, San Diego, 1991-94; ptnr. and chair San Diego Environ. Law Group Brobeck, Phleger & Harrison, LLP, San Diego, 1994—2001; gen. counsel and chief of ethics, Dept. Air Force, US Dept. Def., Washington, 2001—. U.S. commr. InterAm. Tropical Tuna Commn., 1988—95; mem. adv. bd. Floresta, Inc.; instr. natural resources law U. Calif., San Diego. Author of opinion pieces on environ. regulation, energy policy and nuclear power. Bd. dirs. Endowment for Cmty. Leadership, 1987—2000, Global Involvement Through Edn., 1998—2001; chair, environ. com. San Diego C. of C., 1993—94; adv. bd. Endowment for Cmty. Leadership, Washington. Named Outstanding Young Women of Am., 1984; recipient Women Who Mean Business award, Inaugural award for Law, San Diego Bus. jour., 1994. Mem. Calif. Bar Assn., San Diego Bar Assn., BIOCOM (bd. dirs. 1991-2001, pres. 1994, chair/co-chair environ. and safety com., 1991-2001), Profl. Women's Fellowship-San Diego (co-founder, bd. dirs. 1996-2001, pres. 1996-97), World Affairs Coun., Renaissance Women. Republican. Office: Air Force Gen Counsel Rm 4E836 1740 Air Force Pentagon Washington DC 20330-1740 Office Fax: 703-693-9355, 703-697-3796. E-mail: maryl.walker@pentagon.af.mil.

WALKER, MICHAEL ANGUS, economist, director; b. Corner Brook, Nfld., Can., Sept. 11, 1945; m. Janet Walker; children: Margot, Joel. BA, St. Francis Xavier U., 1966; MA, U. Western Ont., 1967, PhD, 1971. Instr. U. Western Ont., Canada, 1968—69; with Bank of Can., 1969—72; instr. Carleton U., Canada, 1971; with Fed. Dept. Fin., Canada, 1973—74; exec. dir. The Fraser Inst., Vancouver, B.C., Canada, 1974—2005, sr. fellow, 2005—; pres. The Fraser Inst. Found., 2005—. Bd. dirs. Mancal Corp., The Milton and Rose D. Friedman Found., Canaccord Capital Inc., dir., 2006—. Office: The Fraser Inst 4th Floor 1770 Burrard St Vancouver BC Canada V6J 3G7 Office Phone: 604-688-0221. Business E-Mail: michaelw@fraserinstitute.ca.

WALKER, MICHAEL CHARLES, SR., retired services executive; b. Rochester, NY, Mar. 4, 1940; s. Charles Boyle and Evelyn Esther (Young) W.; m. Patricia Ann Camelio, Feb. 2, 1963; children: Michael Charles Jr., Lyn, Lea, Matthew. BA, U. Colo., 1962; MBA, Columbia Pacific U., 1982, DBA, 1984. Adminstrv. trainee Lincoln Rochester (N.Y.) Trust Co., 1962-64, mktg. officer, 1964-68; asst. v.p. Lincoln First Bank of Rochester, 1968-72, v.p., 1972-77; pres. M.C. Walker Co., Inc., Spencerport, NY, 1977-80; CEO, PRCC, Rochester, 1980—89; pres., CEO Presbyn. Homes and Svcs. Genesee Valley, Inc., Rochester, 1999—2002. Lectr. SUNY, Brockport, 1982—89; v.p., dir. Kilian and Caroline Schmitt Found., Rochester, 1985—; mem. adv. bd. Chase Manhattan Bank, Rochester, 1989—92; trustee Rochester Hearing and Speech Ctr., 1989—95, chmn., 1993—94; bd. dirs. Genesee Region Home Care Assn., Rochester, 1990—2000; trustee Greater Rochester C. of C., 1981—89. Author: Introduction to Bank Marketing Research, 1969, rev. edit., 1972, Practical Handbook of Marketing Definitions, 1970, 2d edit., 2004, Marketing to Seniors, 2004; contbr. articles to profl. jours. Leader task force Spencerport Ctrl. Schs. Bd. Edn., 1977, 80-81, 85; chmn. Monroe County Svs. Bond Com., Rochester, 1972-97; mem. United Way Evaluation Team, 1990-94; bus. adv. bd. SUNY, Brockport, 1993—2004; mem. N.Y. State Bd. Profl. Med. Conduct, 1993-2006; profl. adv. com. Self Help for Hard of Hearing, 1994-96; trustee Nazareth Coll., 2005—. Recipient Pres.'s Geneseekers award, Rochester Area C. of C., 1979, Innovation of Yr. award, NYAHSA, 1989, Cmty. Svc. award, Self Help for Hard of Hearing, 1997, Patriotic Svc. award, U.S. Treasury, 1997. Mem. Am. Mktg. Assn. (pres. Rochester chpt. 1969-70), N.Y. State Bankers Assn. (pres. residential mortgage com. 1975-76), N.Y. Assn. Homes and Svcs. for Aging (various coms.), Rochester Rotary, Am. Legion. Episcopalian. Avocations: golf, reading, travel, physical fitness.

WALKER, MORT, cartoonist; b. El Dorado, Kans., Sept. 3, 1923; s. Robin A. and Carolyn (Richards) W.; m. Catherine Prentice, Aug. 24, 1985; children: Greg, Brian, Polly, Morgan, Marjorie, Neal, Roger, Whitney, Cathy, Jr., Priscilla. Student, Kansas City Jr. Coll., 1941-42, Washington U., St. Louis, 1943-44; BA, U. Mo., 1948; LL.D., William Penn Coll., 1981. Designer Hallmark Greeting Cards, 1941; editor Dell Pub. Co., 1948-49; free lance cartoonist Saturday Evening Post, other popular mags., 1948-50. Scholar in residence Mo. U., 1992. Comic strip artist King Features, 1950—; creator Beetle Bailey, 1950, Hi and Lois, 1954, Sam's Strip, 1961, Boner's Ark, 1968, Sam and Silo, 1977, The Evermores, 1982, Betty Boop and Felix, 1984, (for United Features) Gamin and Patches, 1987; author: Most, 1971, Land of Lost Things, 1973, Backstage at the Strips, 1975, The Lexicon of Comicana, 1981, The Best of Beetle Bailey, 1984, The Coconut Crew, 1997, (autobiography) Mort Walker's Private Scrapbook, 2001; contbr. 92 paperback collections. Mem. Pres.'s Com. to Hire Handicapped, People to People Com. Exhbn. touring group show Met. Mus. Art, N.Y.C., 1951; chmn. Internat. Mus. Cartton Art. Served to 1st lt. AUS, 1943-46, ETO. Decorated chevalier Order Arts and Letters (France); recipient Outstanding Cartoonist award The Banshees, 1955, Il Secolo XIX award (Italy), 1972, Adamson award (Sweden), 1975, 88, Segar award, 1977, 4th Estate award Am. Legion, The Jester, 1979, Power of Printing, 1977, NCS Golden T-Square award, 1999, Disting. Civilian Svc. award U.S. Army; named Man of Yr. NCCJ, 1988, Artist of Yr., Caputhin Order, 2006. Mem. Nat. Cartoonists Soc. (pres. 1959-60, Reuben award 1953, Best Humor Strip award 1966, 69, named to Hall Fame, Nat. Cartoon Mus. 1989, Gold Key award, 2007), Artists and Writers, Newspaper Features Coun. Authors Guild, Soc. Illustrators, Nat. Press Club, Silvermine Club (Norwalk, Conn.), Greenwich Country Club, Quechee Club, Kappa Sigma (named Man of Yr. 1988). Office: King Features 300 W 57Th St New York NY 10019-3741 *If I enjoy my own life that's one life enjoyed. But if I can help others enjoy their lives more, many lives are made more enjoyable.*

WALKER, OLENE S., former governor; b. Ogden, Utah, Nov. 15, 1930; d. Thomas Ole and Nina Hadley (Smith) W.; m. J. Myron Walker, 1957; children: Stephen Brett, David Walden, Bryan Jesse, Lori, Mylene, Nina, Thomas Myron. BA, Brigham Young U., 1954; MA, Stanford U., 1954; PhD, U. Utah, 1986; HHD (hon.), Weber State U., 1997. V.p. Country Crisp Foods, 1969-92; mem. Utah Ho. of Reps. Dist. 24; lt. gov. State of Utah, 1993—2003, gov., 2003—05. Mem. Salt Lake Edn. Found. bd. dirs. 1983-90; dir. community econ. devel.; mem. Ballet West, Sch. Vol., United Way, Commn. on Youth, Girls Village, Salt Lake Conv. and Tourism Bd.; mem. adv. coun. Weber State U. Mem. Nat. Assn. Secs. of State (Western chmn., nat. lt. gov.'s conf., pres. 1997-98). Republican. Mem. Lds Ch. Achievements include becoming first female elected to office of governor of Utah.

WALKER, PAM, biology educator; BA, Ga. Coll.; MA, Ga. State Univ.; EdS, Ga. So. Univ. Sci. tchr. Telfair County, Ga., Fitzgerald City, Ga., Laurens County, Ga., Alexander H.S., Douglasville, Ga., 1990—. Named Douglas County Tchr. of Yr., 2005, Ga. Tchr. of Yr., 2007. Achievements include authoring 20 textbooks and tchr. resource books. Office: Alexander H S 6500 Alexander Pkwy Douglasville GA 30135 Business E-Mail: pam@sciencebookwriters.com. *

WALKER, PAMELA, mathematics educator; BS, Utah State U., Logan, 1974. Cert. early childhood/elem. edn. and libr. media tchr. Utah. 4th grade tchr. A.W. Johnson Elem. Sch., Firth Sch. Dist., Idaho, 1974—83, Washington Ter. Elem. Sch., Weber Sch. Dist., Ogden, Utah, 1984—89; 3rd grade tchr. Mcpl. Elem. Sch., Weber Sch. Dist., Roy, Utah, 1989—91; math tchr. Sand Ridge Jr. HS, Weber Sch. Dist., Roy, 1991—92, Roy Jr. HS, Weber Sch. Dist., Roy, 1992—2006; tchr. libr. media ctr. Sand Ridge Jr. High, Weber Sch. Dist., 2006—. Named Tchr. of Yr., Firth Sch. Dist., 1983; recipient Apple for Tchr. award, Std. Examiner Newspaper, 1992—2006, Teacher's Recognition award, Remax Realtors, 1996. Mem.: Utah Edn. Assn. (assoc.). Avocations: sewing, needlecrafts. Business E-Mail: pwalker@weber.k12.ut.us.

WALKER, PATRICIA ANN, special education educator; b. Medford, Oreg., July 29, 1962; d. Oran C. Chastain and Sadimae J. Chastain-Jones, Benjamin Jones (Stepfather); m. John Walker; 1 child, Robert Owen. BS in Elem. Edn., So. Oreg. State Coll., 1985. Store mgr. 7-Eleven Store, Costa Mesa, Calif., 1986—90; sales rep. Mclanes So. Calif., San Bernardino, 1990—93, Sales Mark, Santa Fe Springs, Calif., 1993—98; substitute tchr. San Diego City Union Sch. Dist., 2000—02; spl. edn. pre-k tchr. Escondido Union Sch. Dist., Calif., 2002—. Recipient Nicolaysen Ctr. Employee of the Yr. award, Escondido Union Sch. Dist., 2004-05, Nicolaysen Ctr. Educator of the Yr. award, Escondido Elem. Educators Assn., 2004-05; grantee, Delta Kappa Gamma, 1981; scholarship, Ben Ziri Caravan of the Alhambra, 2001, Found. of Devel. Disabilities Peterson, 2001. Mem.: Nat. PTA, Coun. for Exeptional Children, Escondido Elem. Educators Assn., Autism Soc. of Am. (San Diego chpt.). Avocations: swimming, spending time with my son. Home: 4250 Don Way San Diego CA 92117 Office: Escondido Union School District 1330 E Grand Ave Escondido CA 92027-3099 Home Phone: 858-273-4204; Office Phone: 760-432-2168. Personal E-mail: pwalker714@yahoo.com.

WALKER, PAUL R., lawyer; b. Bronx, NY, Feb. 6, 1945; AB, U. Notre Dame, 1966; LLB, U. Pa., 1969. Bar: N.Y. 1970, Calif. 1972. Former ptnr. Paul, Hastings, Janofsky & Walker, LA; ptnr., chmn. real estate practice group, mem. mgmt. com. & mng. ptnr. LA office Dewey Ballantine LLP, LA. Office: Dewey Ballantine LLP Suite 2600 333 S Grand Ave Los Angeles CA 90071-1530 Office Phone: 213-621-6200. Office Fax: 212-621-6201. Business E-Mail: pwalker@deweyballantine.com.

WALKER, PETER, landscape architect; BS in Landscape Arch., U. Calif., Berkeley, 1955; postgrad., U. Ill., 1956; M in Landscape Arch., Harvard U., 1957. Resident Am. Acad. in Rome, 1991; co-founer Sasaki, Walker Assocs., Inc., 1957—75; prin., consulting prin., chmn. The S.W.A. Group, 1975—83; founder, prin. Peter Walker & Ptnrs. Landscape Arch. Inc., Berkeley, Calif., 1983—. Instr. landscape arch. Harvard U. Grad. Sch. Design, 1958—59, adj. prof., 1976—91, acting dir. Urban Design Program, 1977—78, chmn. dept. landscape arch., 1978—81, Charles Eliot chair, 1992; vis. critic MIT, 1959; dir. The S.W.A. Group Summer Sch., 1973—83; chmn. dept. landscape arch. U. Calif., Berkeley, 1997—99; guest lectr. and spkr. in field. Co-author: Invisible Gardens: The Search for Modernism in the American Landscape; mem. editl. bd.: Landscape Arch., 1988—91. Named co-winner, World Trade Ctr. Site Meml. Competition, 2003; named to Inst. Honor, AIA, 1992. Fellow: Inst. for Urban Design, Am. Soc. Landscape Archs. Office: Peter Walker and Ptnrs 739 Allston Way Berkeley CA 94710

WALKER, PHILIP CHAMBERLAIN, II, health facility administrator; b. Big Spring, Tex., July 7, 1944; s. Philip Chamberlain and Mary Catherine (St. John) W.; m. Linda Jane Holsclaw, Jan. 21, 1978; children: Shannon M., Meghan M. BA, Cen. Wash. State Coll., 1970; MS, U. Utah, 1971. Exec. dir. Multnomah Found. for Med. Care, Portland, Oreg., 1972-81; chief exec. officer Peer Rev. Orgn. for Wash. State, Seattle, 1981-84; dir. Preferred Provider Orgn. devel. Provident Life and Accident, Chattanooga, 1984-88; v.p. Maxicare Health Plans, LA, 1988-91; v.p., gen. mgr. Maxicare Health Plans Midwest, Chgo., 1991-92; pres. Health Plus, Peoria, Ill., 1992—; CEO, chmn. bd. HCH Adminstrn., Peoria, Ill., 1992-98; sr. v.p. Health Care Horizons, Albuquerque, 1992-98; exec. v.p. Proctor Health Sys., 1998—. Bd. dirs. RMR Group, HCH Adminstrn., Health Care Horizons; cons. in field. Contbr. articles to profl. jours. Bd. dirs. Boys and Girls Club of Greater Peoria, 2003—; v.p. Boys and Girls Club Peoria, 2004—06; Ctrl. Ill. regional adv. bd. Multiple Sclerosis Assn., 2002—04; chmn. Hult Health Edn. Ctr., 1999—2003, bd. dirs., Cancer Ctr. for Health Living, 2001—03, Heart of Ill. United Way, 2004—. With USAF, 1961—66, Vietnam. Mem.: Creve Coeur Club (bd. govs., pres.). Office: 5409 N Knoxville Ave Peoria IL 61614 Office Phone: 309-689-8600. Business E-Mail: phil.walker@proctor.org.

WALKER, PHILIP DOOLITTLE, retired literature and language professor, composer; b. Newburyport, Mass., 1924; m. Corlette Rossiter, Mar. 23, 1952; children: Melissa Sokol, Laura Ragan, Barbara McMillan. BA, Yale U., New Haven, Conn., 1947, MA, 1951, PhD, 1956. Instr. Lawrence Coll., Appleton, Wis., 1954—57, U. Calif., Santa Barbara, 1957—60, asst. prof., 1960—64, assoc. prof., 1964—70, prof., 1970—90, prof. emeritus French lit., 1990—. Chair dept. French and Italian U. Calif., 1971—75. Author: (book) Germinal and Zola's Philosophical and Religious Thought, (biography) Zola; contbr. articles to profl. jours. Bd. mem. Yale Lit. Mag., New Haven, 1944—45. Lt. (j.g.) USNR, 1942—46. Fellow, John Simon Guggenheim Meml. Found., 1967—68, Fitzwilliam Coll., Cambridge, England, 1986; grantee, Fulbright Found., 1951—52. Mem.: Mil. Order Two World Wars, Yale Club Santa Barbara, Elizabethan Club Yale U. Democrat. Episcopalian. Avocation: composing.

WALKER, R. A., oil industry executive; m. Stephanie Walker; 2 children. BS, MBA, U. Tulsa. Various mcht. banking positions up to sr. mng. dir, co-head Prudential Capital Group; pres., CEO 3TEC Energy Corp.; mng. dir. Global Energy Group UBS Investment Bank; sr. v.p. fin., CFO Anadarko Petroleum Corp., 2005—. Bd. trustees United Way Greater Houston, Houston Mus. Natural Sci., treas., 2007. Office: Anadarko Petroleum Corp 1201 Lake Robbins Dr The Woodlands TX 77380-1046 Office Phone: 832-636-1000. *

WALKER, RANDALL H., air transportation executive; b. Boulder City, Nev. m. Terry Walker; 6 children. BS in Acctg. magna cum laude, Brigham Young U. Budget analyst Clark County (Nev.) Mgr.'s Office; bus. mgr. Las Vegas Met. Police Dept.; dep. city mgr. City of Las Vegas; Las Vegas rep. to Nev. State Legislature; asst. county mgr. Clark County, dir. dept. fin.; dep. dir. Clark County Dept. Aviation, now dir. Office: c/o McCarran Internat Airport PO Box 11005 Las Vegas NV 89111-1005

WALKER, RANDOLPH MEADE, minister; b. Heathsville, Va., Mar. 24, 1950; s. Levi Robeson and Elsie Tolson Walker; m. Deloris Adair Walker; children: Jennifer Michelle, John Randolph. BA, Hampton U., 1972; MA, U. Memphis, 1976, PhD, 1990; LLD, LeMoyne-Owen Coll., 2002; MDiv, Memphis Theol. Sem., 2004. Pastor Pilgrim Rest Bapt. Ch., Henning, Tenn., 1976—82; sales exec. AC-DELCO Divsn. GM Corp., Memphis, 1972—86; pastor New Phila. Bapt. Ch., Memphis, 1982—96; assoc. prof. LeMoyne-Owen Coll., Memphis, 1987—2002; pastor Castalia Bapt. Ch., Memphis, 1998—. Bd. mem. Shelby County Hist. Com., Memphis, 2002—. Mem. NAACP, Memphis, 1976—, Urban League, Inc., Memphis, 1982—, Kiwana's Inst., Memphis, 2002—. Recipient Svc. award, Memphis Theol. Sem., 2003. Mem.: So. Conf. of African Am. Studies, Memphis Bapt. Ministerial Assn., West Tenn. Hist. Soc. Democrat. Baptist. Avocations: baseball, football, basketball, reading, writing. Office: Castalia Bapt Ch 1540 Castalia St Memphis TN 38114 Office Phone: 901-276-7295. E-mail: rmwalker@midsouth.rr.com.

WALKER, RAYMOND JOHN, physicist; b. LA, Oct. 26, 1942; s. Raymond Osmund and Marie Dorothy (Peterman) W. BS, San Diego State U., 1964; MS, UCLA, 1969, PhD, 1973. Rsch. assoc. U. Minn., Mpls., 1973-77; rsch. geophysicist Inst. Geophysics and Planetary Physics UCLA, 1977—, prof. in residence Inst. Geophysics and Planetary Physics and Dept. Earth and Space Sci., 1999—. Mgr. planetary plasma interactions node NASA, 1990-, project scientist planetary data sys., 1992-96, prin. investigator virtual magnetospheric observatory, 2007—; mem. numerous coms. on space physics and the mgmt. of space physics data NRC and NASA. Contbr. articles to profl. jours. Mem. AAAS, Am. Geophys. Union (chair info. tech. com. 1990-92, Edward A. Flinn III award 1996), Am. Astron. Soc. (div. Planetary Sci.). Achievements include research in magnetospheric physics, in planetary magnetospheres, in global magnetohydrodynamic simulation of solar wind-magnetosphere interaction, in data management, in magnetic field modeling. Home: 11053 Tennessee Ave Los Angeles CA 90064-1936 Office: UCLA IGPP 405 Hilgard Ave Los Angeles CA 90095-1567 Home Phone: 310-477-3637; Office Phone: 310-825-7685. Business E-Mail: rwalker@igpp.ucla.edu.

WALKER, RICHARD BRIAN, chemistry professor; b. Quincy, Mass., May 14, 1948; s. George Edgar and Eva Mary (Taylor) W. BS in Biochemistry, U. So. Calif., 1970; PhD in Pharm. Chemistry, U. Calif., San Francisco, 1975. Rsch. assoc. Oreg. State U., Corvallis, 1975-76, U. Wash., Seattle, 1976-78; lectr. U.S. Internat. U., San Diego, 1978-81, Hamdard Sch. Pharmacy, New Delhi, 1981-82; rsch. scientist Biophysica Found., San Diego, 1982-83; assoc. prof. chemistry U. Ozarks, Clarksville, Ark., 1983-84; asst. to assoc. prof. chemistry U. Ark., Pine Bluff, 1984-96, prof. chemistry, 1996—, interim chair dept. chemistry and physics, 2007—. Prin. investigator minority biomed. rsch. support program NIH, Bethesda, Md., 1986—; project dir. Ark. Systemic Sci. Initiative; chair U. Ark. Pine Bluff Instl. Rev. Bd., 2003-, interim chair dept. chemistry and physics, 2007; rev. in field. Contbr. articles to profl. jours. Coord. home Bible fellowship The Way Internat., Pine Bluff, 1984-99, North Little Rock, 2007—; judge Ctrl. Ark. Sci. Fair, Little Rock, 1986—. NIH rsch. grantee, 1986, 89, 93, 2006. Mem. Am. Chem. Soc., Ark. Acad. Scis., Am. Assn. Pharm. Scientists, Sigma Xi (sec.-treas. ctrl. Ark. chpt. 2005-06, v.p. 2000-07). Avocations: fishing, golf, skiing. Office: 1200 University Dr Pine Bluff AR 71601-2799 Home: 2401 Lakeview Rd Apt K3 North Little Rock AR 72116-9410 Home Phone: 501-812-4110; Office Phone: 870-575-8894. Business E-Mail: walker_r@uapb.edu.

WALKER, RICHARD HAROLD, pathologist, educator; b. Cleve., Dec. 2, 1928; s. Harold Deford and Bernice Margaret (Wright) W.; m. Carolyn Franklin, Sept. 28, 1954; children: Bruce, Lynn, Cara, Leah. BS, Emory U., 1950, MD, 1953. Intern City of Memphis Hosps., 1953-54; resident in pathology Coll. Medicine U. Tenn., Memphis, 1954-55, 57-59, prof. pathology, 1966-70; Am. Cancer Soc. clin. fellow U. Tenn. Coll. Medicine, 1957-59; med. dir. blood bank and transfusion svc. City of Memphis Hosps., Memphis, 1961-70; chief of blood bank and transfusion service William Beaumont Hosp., Royal Oak, Mich., 1970-95, med. dir. Sch. Med. Tech., 1970-91. Clin. prof. pathology Sch. Medicine Wayne State U., Detroit, 1982-95. Contbr. articles on blood transfusion, blood group genetics and transfusion medicine to med. jours. Capt. USNR ret. Recipient Murray Thelin Humanitarian award Memphis chpt. Nat. Hemophilia Found., 1968. Mem. AMA, Coll. Am. Pathologists, Am. Soc. Clin. Pathologists (Disting. Svc. award 1977, Ward Burdick award 1992), Am. Assn. Blood Banks (pres. 1976-77, John Elliott Meml. award 1986), Tenn. Assn. Blood Banks (L.W. Diggs award 1986), Internat. Soc. Blood Transfusion, Am. Soc. for Histocompatibility and Immunogenetics. Republican. Presbyterian. Home: 4204 Fleet Landing Blvd Atlantic Beach FL 32233-4590

WALKER, RICHARD HENRY, lawyer; b. Wilmington, Del., Dec. 29, 1950; s. Henry H. and Mary L. (Meister) W. BA, Trinity Coll., 1972; JD cum laude, Temple U., 1975. Bar: Pa. 1976, U.S. Supreme Ct. 1977, N.Y. 1978, D.C. 1981. Law clk. to Hon. Collins J. Seitz U.S. Ct. Appeals (3rd cir.), Wilmington, Del., 1975-76; assoc., ptnr. Cadwalader, Wickersham & Taft, NYC, 1976-91; regional dir. N.E. office U.S. SEC, NYC, 1991-95, gen. counsel Washington, 1996-98, dir. enforcement, 1998—2001; global gen. counsel Deutsche Bank, 2001—. Bd. dir. MBIA Inc., 2006—; mem. legal adv. com. NYSE. Trustee Am. Folk Art Mus. Recipient Presdl. Rank Disting. Svc. award, SEC, 1997, Disting. Svc. award. Fellow Am. Bar Found.; trustee SEC Historical Soc.; mem. Phi Beta Kappa

WALKER, RICHARD HUGH, orthopaedic surgeon; b. Elgin, Ill., Jan. 29, 1951; m. Wendy Allen; children: Ashley Elizabeth, Blake Allen, Emily Paige. AB cum laude, Occidental Coll., 1973; MD, U. Chgo., 1977. Diplomate Nat. Bd. Med. Examiners, Am. Bd. Orthopaedic Surgery. Jr. resident in surgery UCLA, 1977-79; jr. resident in orthopaedic surgery Stanford (Calif.) U., 1979-81, sr. resident, 1981-82, chief resident, 1982-83; clin. mem. divsn. orthop. surgery, sect. lower extremity reconstructive surgery Scripps Clinic, La Jolla, Calif., 1983—, co-dir. lower extremity reconstructive surgery fellowship, divsn. orthopaedic surgery, 1989—, assoc. head. divsn. orthopaedic surgery, 1990-97, chmn. dept. surgery, 1998—, v.p. surg. svcs., 2001—. Staff physician dept. surgery Green Hosp. of Scripps Clinic, La Jolla, 1983—, mem. exec. com., 1994—2001, chief of staff, 1995—97; Team physician San Diego Padres, 1983—86, team physician, 1995—99; Clin. instr. dept. orthopaedics and rehab. U. Calif., San Diego, 1983—92, asst. clin. prof., 1992—; Mem. bd. dir. Scripps Clinic Med. Group, La Jolla, 1992—, mem. exec. com., 1998—, med. dir. surg. specialties, 1998—2001, mem. joint exec. bd., 1992—93. Cons. reviewer Clin. Orthopaedics and Related Rsch., 1989—, Jour. Bone and Joint Surgery, 1994—; contbr. articles to profl. jours. Mem. AMA, ACS, Am. Acad. Orthopaedic Surgeons, We. Orthopaedic Assn. (program chmn. San Diego chpt. 1994-95, treas. 1995-96, v.p. 1996-97, pres. 1997-98, Resident Paper award 1983), Calif. Orthopaedic Assn., Assn. Arthritic Hip and Knee Surgery (charter mem. 1991), Am. Assn. Hip and Knee Surgeons, Assn. Bone and Joint Surgeons (Nicholas Andry Rsch. award 1997). Office: Scripps Clinic Divsn Orthop Surgery 10666 N Torrey Pines Rd La Jolla CA 92037-1092 Office Phone: 858-554-9882. Business E-Mail: rwalker@scrippsclinic.com.

WALKER, RICHARD K., lawyer; b. Knoxville, Tenn., Oct. 21, 1948; BA with honors, U. Kans., 1970, JD, 1975; student, U. Bonn, Germany; grad. student, U Tübingen, Germany. Bar: Ariz. 1975, D.C. 1977, U.S. Supreme Ct. 1977. Asst. prof. law U. S.C., 1977-81, assoc. prof. law, 1981-82; ptnr. Bishop, Cook, Purcell & Reynolds, Washington, 1981-90, Winston & Strawn, Washington, 1990-93; dir. Streich Lang, Phoenix, 1993-2000; ptnr. Quarles & Brady Streich Lang, Phoenix, 2000—. Bd. trustees Ariz. Theatre Co., 1995-2001, 2004-; bd. dirs. Phoenix Cmty. Alliance, 2001—04. Fulbright Direct Exch. scholar. Mem. ABA, Labor and Employment Law Sec. (mem. equal employment opportunity law com. and devel. of the law under the NLRA com., 1979—), Litigation Sec. (mem. class actions and derivitive suits com. and trial pratice com., 1998—, mem. employment rels. and labor law com., 1979—), Ariz. Assn. Def. Counsel (bd. dirs. 1997-2000). Office: Quarles & Brady LLP Renaissance One 2 N Central Ave Phoenix AZ 85004-2391 Office Phone: 602-229-5219. E-mail: rwalker@quarles.com.

WALKER, ROBERT F., social studies educator; b. Van Nuys, Calif., Sept. 9, 1977; s. Carol Walker. BA, U. Calif., Davis, 2000; MA in History, Stanford U., Calif., 2002; MA in Ednl. Tech., Calif. State U., Northridge, 2005. Cert. single subject tchg. credential in Social Studies Calif. State U., 2003. Social studies tchr. Bishop Alemany HS, Mission Hills, Calif., 2003—04, Acad. Canyons, WSHUHD, Santa Clarita, Calif., 2004—. Mem.: Internat. Soc. Tech. in Edn., Nat. Coun. Social Studies, Am. Hist. Assn. Green Party. Office: Acad Canyons 26455 Rockwell Canyon Rd Santa Clarita CA 91355 Home Phone: 661-803-1966; Office Phone: 661-362-3056.

WALKER, ROBERT HARRIS, historian, writer, editor; b. Cin., Mar. 15, 1924; m. Grace Burtt; children: Amy, Rachel, Matthew. BS, Northwestern U., 1945; MA, Columbia U., 1950; PhD, U. Pa., 1955. Edn. specialist U.S. Mil. Govt., Japan, 1946-47; instr. Carnegie Inst. Tech., 1950-51, U. Pa., 1953-54; asst. prof., dir. Am. studies U. Wyo., 1955-59; asso. prof. George Washington U., 1959-63, prof. Am. civilization, 1963-94, dir. Am. studies program, 1959-66, 68-70. First dir. edn. and pub. programs NEH, 1966-68; fellow Woodrow Wilson Internat. Ctr., 1972-73, Rockefeller Rsch. Ctr., 1979, Hoover Instn., Huntington Libr., 1980; specialist grants to Japan, Germany, Thailand, Iran, Greece, Israel, Brazil, China, People's Republic of Korea, Hong Kong, 1964-91; Fulbright lectr., Australia, New Zealand, Philippines, 1971, Sweden, France, West Germany, Norway, all 1987; Am. Coun. Learned Socs. alt. del. UNESCO Gen. Info. Program, 1978—; co-founder Algonquin Books, 1982. Author: Poet and Gilded Age, 1963, Life in the Age of Enterprise, 1967, American Society, 1981, 2d edit., 1995, Reform in America (nominated for Pulitzer prize in history), 1985, (with R.H. Gabriel) Course of American Democratic Thought, 3d edit., 1986, Cincinnati and the Big Red Machine, 1988, Everyday Life in Victorian America, 1994; editor, compiler: American Studies in the U.S., 1958, American Studies Abroad, 1975, Reform Spirit in America, 1976, 85, American Studies: Topics and Sources, 1976, Friends of Raoul Wallenberg, 1987-1997, 1998; editor: Am. Quar., 1953-54; sr. editor: Am. Studies Internat., 1970-80, Am. studies series for Greenwood Press, 1972—, over 100 vols. Founding mem. Japan-U.S. Friendship Commn., 1977-80; founding pres. Friends of Raoul Wallenberg Found., 1987-99. With USNR, 1943-46, 50. Mem. Am. Studies Assn. (nat. pres. 1970-71), Cosmos Club, Phi Beta Kappa. Office: 200 Riverside Blvd #4J New York NY 10069-0907

WALKER, ROBERT R., music educator; b. Electra, Tex., Oct. 23, 1963; s. Bobby Walker and Jan Kaspar; m. Elizabeth Pond, Aug. 23, 1986; children: Emily Hamilton, Bo Hamilton, Katherine, Hannah, Michael, Matthew, Bryan. MusB, Emporia State U., 1992, MusM, 1995. Cert. interactive TV instr. Kellogg C.C. Music instr. Kellogg C.C., Battle Creek, Mich., 1995—2001; dir. music Labette C.C., Parsons, Kans., 2001—. Recipient Disting. Faculty award, Labette C.C., 2005, Exemplory Online Course Design award, Kans. Blackboard Users Group, 2003. Mem.: Am. Choral Directors Assn. (assoc.). Home: 2812 Stevens Parsons KS 67357 Office: Labette CC 200 South 14th St Parsons KS 67357 Home Phone: 620-423-3026; Office Phone: 620-820-1021. Business E-Mail: robertw@labette.edu.

WALKER, ROBERT SMITH, former congressman; b. Bradford, Pa., Dec. 23, 1942; s. Joseph Erdman and Rachael Viola (Smith) W.; m. Sue Ellen Albertson, Apr. 13, 1968 (dec. May 9, 2007). Student William & Mary, 1960—61; BS in Edn., Millersville U., Pa., 1964; MA in Polit. Sci, U. Del., 1968; LLD (hon.), Franklin & Marshall Coll., 1998. Tchr. Penn Manor High Sch., Lancaster, Pa., 1964-67; legis. asst. to Congressman Edwin D. Eshleman, 1967-74, adminstrv. asst., 1974-76; mem. US Congress from 16th Pa. dist., Washington, 1977-96, chmn. House Com. Sci.; vice chmn. house budget com., chmn. house Rep. leadership, 1995-97; chief dep. minority whip, 1989-95; spkr. pro tempore, 1996; chmn. Wexler & Walker Pub. Policy Assocs., Washington, 1997—. Chmn. Commn. on the Future of the U.S. Aerospace Industry, 2001—02; mem. Nat. Acads. Aeronautics and Space Engring. Bd., 2004—, Pres.'s Commn. on the U.S. Postal Svc., 2003, Pres.'s Commn. on Space Exploration, 2004; polit. analyst Fox News, 2005—. Co-author: Congress-The Pennsylvania Dutch Representatives, 1774-1974, Can You Afford This House, 1978, House of Ill Repute, 1987, Space: The Free Market Frontier, 2003, Crossroads: The Future of American Politics, 2003; contbr. articles to profl. jours. Trustee Aerospace Corp., 1997—; vice chmn. Space Found. 2004-06, chmn. 2006—; mem. Susquehana Valley Ctr. Pub. Policy, 1998—. With Pa. NG, 1967-73, bd. dirs. Space Devel., 2001—, Zero G, 2005—. Pa. Nat. Guard, 1967—73. Recipient NASA Disting. Svc. medal, 1996, NASA Disting. Pub. Svc. medal, 2004; fellow Millersville U., 1996-2001, Franklin & Marshall Coll., 1997-2001. Mem. Am. League of Lobbyists (bd. dirs. 2000-04). Republican. Presbyterian. Office: Wexler & Walker Pub Policy Assocs 1317 F St NW Ste 600 Washington DC 20004-1157 Office Phone: 202-638-2121. Business E-Mail: walker@wexlerwalker.com. *The revolution sweeping politics, economics, culture and technology will produce new opportunities but at the same time will demand a new way of thinking about our economy and our society. The wealth of information available to each individual means that government and business must think in terms of individualized approaches.*

WALKER, ROGER CRAIG, mathematics professor; b. Orlando, Fla., Sept. 29, 1960; s. Willie and Geraldine Walker; m. Jacqueline Marie Mumford, Apr. 25, 1987; 1 child, Roger Craig Walker II. MS in Bus. Fin. Mgmt., Naval Postgraduate Sch., Monterey, 1995. Math. educator Conway Mid. Sch., Orlando, 1997—. Capt. USMC, 1985—97. Recipient Tchr. of Yr., Conway Mid. Sch., 2002. Independent. Lutheran. Home: 3016 Ashna Lane Orlando FL 32806 Office: Conway Mid Sch 4600 Anderson Rd Orlando FL 32812 Home Phone: 407-894-7998; Office Phone: 407-249-6420. Office Fax: 407-249-6429; Home Fax: 407-894-7998. Personal E-mail: bowewalker@aol.com. Business E-Mail: walkerr3@ocps.net.

WALKER, ROGER GEOFFREY, geology educator, consultant; b. London, Mar. 26, 1939; s. Reginald Noel and Edith Annie Walker; m. Gay Parsons, Sept. 18, 1965; children: David John, Susan Elizabeth. BA, Oxford U., Eng., 1961, DPhil in Geology, 1964. NATO postdoctoral fellow in geology Johns Hopkins U., Balt., 1964-66; from asst. to assoc. prof. McMaster U., Hamilton, Ont., Canada, 1966-73, prof. geology, 1973-98, prof. emeritus, 1998—. Tchr. profl. short courses on various aspects of oil exploration in clastic reservoirs, Can., U.S., Brazil, Australia, Japan, Italy, Venezuela, Norway; grant selection com. earth scis. sect. Nat. Scis. and Engring. Rsch. Coun. Can., 1981-84; Judd A. & Cynthia S. Oualline Centennial lectr. U. Tex., Austin, 1986; vis. scientist Denver Rsch. Ctr., Marathon Oil Co., Littleton, Colo., 1973-74, Amoco Can. Petrol Co., Calgary, Alta., 1982; vis. fellow Australian Nat. U., Canberra, 1981; vis. prof. Fed. U. Ouro Preto, Brazil, 1987, 89-91, Fed. U. Rio Grande do Sul, Brazil, 1992; adj. prof. U. Regina, 1997—; pres. Roger Walker Cons., Inc., 1997-2006. Editor: Facies Models, 1979, 3d edit., 1992; contbr. over 140 articles to profl. jours. Recipient oper. and strategic grants Nat. Scis. and Engring. Rsch. Coun. Can., 1966—. Fellow: Royal Soc. Can.; mem.: Internat. Assn. Sedimentologists (Henry Clifton Sorby medal 2002), Can. Assn. Univ. Tchrs., Soc. Sedimentary Geology (Francis J. Pettijohn medal 1997), Soc. Econ. Paleontologists and Mineralogists (hon.; assoc. editor 1970—78, pres. eastern sect. 1975—76, coun. for mineralogy 1979—80), Am. Assn. Petroleum Geologists (Disting. lectr. 1979—80, Disting. Educator award 1999), Can. Soc. Petroleum Geologists (Link award 1983, R.J.W. Douglas Meml. medal 1990), Geol. Assn. Can. (assoc. editor 1977—80, Past Pres.'s medal 1975, Disting. Svc. award 1994, Logan medal 1999). Achievements include research in sedimentary facies analysis, sedimentology of turbidites, quantitative basin analysis, sedimentology of Western Canadian Cretaceous clastic wedge. Home: 83 Scimitar View NW Calgary AB Canada T3L 2B4 Home Phone: 403-208-0210. Personal E-mail: walkerrg@telus.net.

WALKER, RONALD EDWARD, psychologist, educator; b. East St. Louis, Ill., Jan. 23, 1935; s. George Edward and Marnella (Altmeyer) W.; m. Aldona M. Mogenis, Oct. 4, 1958; children: Regina, Mark, Paula, Alexis. BS, St. Louis U., 1957; MS, Northwestern U., 1959, PhD, 1961. Lectr. psychology Northwestern U., 1959-61; faculty dept. psychology Loyola U., Chgo., 1961—, asst., then asso. prof., 1961-68, prof., chmn. dept., 1965—73, prof. emeritus, 1999—, acting dean Coll. Arts and Scis., 1973-74; dean Loyola U. (Coll. Arts and Scis.), 1974-80, academic v.p., 1980-81, sr. v.p., dean faculties, 1981-89, exec. v.p., 1989-99. Cons. VA, Chgo., 1965-74; Am. Psychol. Assn.-NIMH; vis. cons., 1969; vis. scientist Am. Psychol. Assn. NSF, 1968; Cook County (Ill.) rep. from Ill. Psychol. Assn., 1969-72; cons.-evaluator North Cen. Assn., 1986-99. Contbr. articles to profl. jours. Bd. trustees St. Francis Hosp., Evanston, Ill., 1986—92, Chgo. Archdiocesan Sems., 1985—97, Loyola Acad., Wilmette, Ill., 1987—93, St. Louis U., 1988—97; bd. dirs. Holy Family Villa Nursing Home, Lemont, Ill., 2002—05. Recipient Disting. Psychologist of Yr. award Ill. Psychol. Assn., 1986. Home: Unit 5I 1630 Sheridan Rd Wilmette IL 60091-1835 Business E-Mail: rwalker@luc.edu.

WALKER, RONALD HUGH, retired management consultant; b. Bryan, Tex., July 25, 1937; s. Walter Hugh and Maxine (Tarver) W.; m. Anne Lucille Collins, Aug. 8, 1959; children: Lisa, Marjorie, Lynne. BA, U. Ariz., 1960. With Allstate Ins. Co., Pasadena, Calif., 1964-67, Hudson Co., 1967-69; asst. to sec. interior, 1969-70; founder, 1st dir., staff asst. to Pres. U.S. White House Advance Office, 1970-72; spl. asst. to Pres., 1972-73; dir. Nat. Park Service, Washington, 1973-75; cons. Saudi Arabia, 1975; assoc. dir. World Championship Tennis, 1975-77; pres. Ron Walker & Assocs., Inc., Dallas, 1977-79; sr. ptnr., mng. dir. Korn/Ferry Internat., Washington, 1979—2001; ret., 2000. Bd. dirs., chmn. Guest Svcs. Inc., Mullin Cos., Inc., Vinson & Co.; chmn. NOVAVAX, 1999-2005. Bd. dirs. U.S.S. Arizona Found. and Memorial; mem. Nat. Pk. Svc. Dirs. Coun.; founder, chmn. emeritus Order of Raft, 1972; spl. presdl. del. to Prime Min. Indira Gandhi's funeral New Delhi, 1984; spl. presdl. del. to Games of XXIV Olympiad Seoul, 1988; trustee Nat. Outdoor Leadership Sch., Nat. Fitness Found., Pres.'s Coun. on Phys. Fitness and Sports, 1981—85; bd. dirs. NCAA Found., mem. exec. com., mem. adv. bd.; bd. dirs. Meridian Internat.; mem. Ctr. for Study of Presidency, 1988—95; chmn. Freedom Found. at Valley Forge, 1989—2000; trustee Ford's Theater, Washington; men's chair Project Hope Ann. Ball, 1989, 1990, 1991; chmn. ann. dinner Boys and Girls Clubs Am., 1993; chmn. 50th Presdl. Inauguration, Dedication Richard Nixon Libr., Birthplace, 1990, bd. dirs., 1990; nat. chair Celebrities and Sports for Bush-Quayle; mem. over-site com. U.S. Rowing, 1993; mem. com. Preservation of White House, 1973—75; mem. Nat. Pk. Adv. Bd., 1973—75, Nat. Pk. Found., 1973—75, John F. Kennedy Ctr. for Performing Arts, 1973—75, Friends of Nancy Hanks Ctr.; bd. trustees Mridian House Internat., 1992—; mem. USA Gymnasium Found., 1993—99; trustee U. Ariz. Found.; chair Nat. Pk. Found. Alumni Assn.; bd. dirs Saquaro Nat. Park; mem. adv. bd. Nat. Park Sys., 2004—; vol. Nixon/Agnew Campaign, 1968, transition and inauguration team, 1969; vice chmn., mem. Pres.'s Commn. on Bicentennial U.S. Constn., 1985—88; mem. Coun. for Excellence in Govt., 1988—; mgr., CEO Rep. Nat. Conv., 1984, sr. advisor, 1988, 1992, 1996, 2000, 2004, Bush/Quayle Presdl. Campaign, 1988, Bush/Cheney Presdl. Campaign, 2000, 2004, Bush/Cheney Inauguration; hon. chmn. Cheney Inaugural Activities; co-ord. v.p. debate Cheney and Lieberman, 2000, Cheney and Edwards, 2004; mem. leadership adv. bd. NCAA; bd. dirs. Grand Teton Nat. Pk. Found., Saquaro Nat. Pk. Found. Capt. US Army, 1961—64. Recipient Disting. Citizen award U. Ariz., 1973, Outstanding Svc. award Dept. Interior, 1975, Centennial Medallion award U. Ariz., 1989, Ellis Island Congl. medal of honor, 1992, Lincoln medal Ford's Theater, 2002. Mem. NCAA (bd. dirs. 1992-2003, exec. com. 1992-2003, adv. bd.), Econs. Club of Washington, Met. Club of Washington, Congl. Country Club, Georgetown Club, City Club of Washington, Univ. Club. of N.Y., Burning Tree Club, Phi Delta Theta (named to Hall of Fame, 1991). Republican. Methodist. Home (Winter): 13535 Placita Montanas de Oro Tucson AZ 85755 E-mail: roadrunnerrhw@aol.com.

WALKER, RONALD R., editor, educator, writer; b. Newport News, Va., Sept. 2, 1934; s. William R. and Jean Marie (King) W.; m. O. Diane Mawson, Apr. 16, 1961; children: Mark Jonathan, Steven Christopher. BS, Pa. State U., 1956; postgrad., Harvard U., 1970-71. Reporter, news editor, sr. editor, editorial page editor, mng. editor San Juan Star (P.R.), 1962-73, Washington columnist, 1982-84, city editor, 1984-87; instr. journalism Pa. State U., State College, 1973-74; asst. prof. Columbia U. Grad. Sch. Journalism, NYC, 1974-76; editor The Daily News, V.I., 1976-77; press sec. Gov. V.I., 1978-79; spl. asst., chief of staff Rep. James H. Scheuer, U.S. Congress, 1980-82, Resident Commr. Jaime B. Fuster, U.S. Congress, 1987-92; spl. asst., press sec. Resident Commr. Antonio J. Colorado, 1992-93; ind. profl. writer, weekly columnist editl. page San Juan Star, 1993—; regular columnist St. John Times, 1997—. Contbr. articles to nat. mags. and jours. including The Nation, The N.Y. Times, The Washington Post, and others. Served with U.S. Army, 1957-59. Nieman fellow in journalism Harvard U., 1970-71. Mem. Soc. Nieman Fellows, Leica Hist. Soc. Am. Home: PO Box 1358 St John VI 00831-1358 Personal E-mail: rrwalker340@earthlink.net.

WALKER, RONALD TRACY, retired personnel director; b. North Wilkesboro, NC, July 27, 1937; m. Nena Watkins; children: Randy, Kirk. Student, Wilkes C.C., Wake Forest U. With CMI Industries Inc., Elkin, NC, 1967-99, plant human resource mgr.; ret., 1999; mem. N.C. Ho. of Reps., 1999—. Commr. Wilkes County, 1978-96, past mem. region "D" coun. govts., regional econ. devel. coun., indsl. park com., chmn. regional transp. com., mem. regional adv. com. to WNCREDC, liaison Advantage West and region "D" coun. govts.; past chmn. region "D" coun. govts. Wilkes County, northwestern housing authority, past mem. bd. edn., 1972-76, airport authority; past vice-chmn., chmn. Wilkes County Commrs.; past bd. dirs. Blue Ridge Water Assn.; pres. Northwestern Devel. Assn.; trustee Health Ins. N.C. Assn. County Commrs.; mem. N.C. Regional Econ. Devel. Commn.; apptd. mem. N.C. Adv. Coun. Vocat. and Technical Edn., 1972-76, N.C. Dept. Correction, 1984-92; Rep. candidate for N.C. Commr. of Labor, 1996; candidate N.C. House, 1998, 2000, N.C. House of Rep., 2001-, With USAF, 1955-59. Recipient Leadership award Western N.C., 1996. Office Phone: 919-733-5935. Personal E-mail: tracyw@ncleg.net.

WALKER, ROSLYN ADELE, retired museum director; b. Memphis, July 26, 1944; Student Gen. Studies, U. Poitiers, France, 1965; BS in Art Edn. with high honors, Hampton U., 1966; MA in History of Art, Indiana U., 1969, PhD in History of Art, 1991. Registrar Mus. African Art, Washington, 1968-69; coord. Univ. Art Gallery U. Mass., Amherst, 1969-70; temporary registrar Fed. Dept Antiquities Nat. Mus., Lagos, Nigeria, 1970; curator of collections Inst. African Studies U. Idaban, Nigeria, 1973-75; curator ethnographic art collection Univ. Mus. Ill. State U., Normal, 1975-81, interim adminstr., 1975, adminstr., 1975-77, dir., 1977-81; curator Nat. Mus. African Art Smithsonian Instn., Washington, 1981-93, sr. curator, 1993-97, dir., 1997—2002; sr. curator The Arts of Africa, the Pacific and the Americas Dallas Mus. Art, Margaret McDermott curator African art. Rsch. asst. Mus. Modern Art, N.Y.C., 1971-72, guest curator African Women/African Art, The African-Am. Inst., N.Y.C., 1976, Lakeview Mus. Arts and Scis., Peoria, Ill., 1981; instr. in primitive art U. Mass., Amherst, 1969-70, in African decorative art USDA Grad. Sch., Washington, 1984. in Art in Africa, Dept. Art History, U. Md., College Park, 1990; vis. lectr. Afro-Am. Art, Ind. U., Bloomington, 1970-71, lectr. 1971-72, summer program, U. Idaban, Nigeria, 1974; asst. prof. Art Dept., Ill. State U., Normal, 1975-81. Author: (with Roy Sieber) African Art in the Cycle of Life, 1987, Olowe of Ise: A Yoruba Sculptor to Kings, 1998; contbr. catalogs for exhibitions of African Art to Royal Acad. of Arts, London, 1995, Guggenheim Mus. N.Y. and Afro-Am. Hist. and Cultural Mus., Phila., 1996; contbr., reviews, essays and articles to profl. jours. and mags. Mem. visual arts and crafts adv. panel Washington Commn. on the Arts. Recipient Ford Found. Fgn. Study grant, 1965, Faculty Rsch. grant, U.

Mass., 1970, Fgn. Lang. fellowship Ind. U., Bloomington, 1971, Grant in Aid, Ind. U., 1972, Rsch. Fund grant (collections-based), Smithsonian Instn., Washington, 1994; named Twenty Yr. Student, Hampton U., 1986. Mem. Arts Coun. African Studies Assn. (past bd. dirs.), ArTable, Assn. Art Mus. Dirs.

WALKER, RUTH CHARLOTTA, language educator, real estate broker; b. Kirksville, Mo., Oct. 3, 1931; d. Marion S. and Fern Thomas Schott; m. Dennis O. Walker, Nov. 21, 1954 (dec.). BS in Edn., Ctrl. Mo. State Coll., Warrensburg, 1952. Lic. real estate broker Wis., 1982. Tchr. English and speech, Warrensburg, Mo., 1951—53; pvt. tutor English and speech Mexico, 1956—57, Milw., 1968—95; profl. spkr., 1970—95; real esate broker, 1982—90; writer profl. book revs., 1990—. Author: (booklet) What Does P.E. Mean?, 1983. Pres. Woman's Club of Am. Fedn. Women, So. Milw., 1975—78, P.E.O. Sisterhood, So. Milw., 1979—81; sec. Woman's Courtroom Civic Conf., Milw., 1980. Mem.: Book Club So. Milw., Delta Zeta. Republican. Presbyterian. Achievements include raising funds for police department equipment, establishing camp Wil-o-Way in Grant Park, Milwaukee, creating drive for civic auditoriums. Avocations: travel, writing, reading.

WALKER, SALLY M., writer; b. NJ; m. James Walker. Author: (children's books) Volcanoes, 1994, Rhinos, 1996, Earthquakes, 1996, Opossum at Sycamore Road, 1997, Hippos, 1997, The 18-Penny Goose, 1999, Dolphins, 1999, Seahorse Reef: A Story of the South Pacific, 2001, Wheels and Axles, 2001, Levers, 2001, Screws, 2001, Work, 2001, Inclined Planes and Wedges, 2001, Pulleys, 2001, Sea Horse's Surprise, 2001, Fireflies, 2001, Life in an Estuary: The Chesapeake Bay, 2002, Jackie Robinson, 2002, Fossil Fish Found Alive: Discovering the Coelacanth, 2002, Rays, 2002, Bessie Coleman: Daring to Fly, 2003, Secrets Of A Civil War Submarine: Solving The Mysteries Of The H. L. Hunley, 2005 (Am. Libr. Assn.'s Sibert Internat. Book award, 2006), Mystery Fish: Secrets Of The Coelacanth, 2005. Recipient Outstanding Trade Books for Children award (twice), Children's Choice award, 2001. Mailing: Author Mail CarolHoda Books Lerner Pub Group 1251 Washington Ave N Minneapolis MN 55401-1036

WALKER, SAMUEL DAVID, lawyer; b. Madison, Wis., June 21, 1958; s. William Delaney and Suzanne Jamison (Porter) W.; m. Cynthia Fiora Elizabeth Nardini, Aug. 6, 1983; children: John Renato, Samuel Alexander. AB magna cum laude, Duke U., 1980; JD cum laude, Harvard U., 1984. Bar: NC 1984, US Dist. Ct. (we. dist. NC) 1985, US Ct. Appeals (4th cir.) 1985, US Ct. Appeals (DC cir.) 1993, US Dist. Ct. (dist. DC) 1994. Law clk. to Hon. John D. Butzner Jr. US Ct. Appeals (4th cir.), Richmond, Va., 1984-85; assoc. Robinson, Bradshaw & Hinson, Charlotte, NC, 1985-89; spl. asst. to asst. sec. labor for employment stds. US Dept. Labor, Washington, 1989-90, dep. wage-hour adminstr. to acting wage-hour adminstr., 1990, acting asst. sec. labor for employment stds., 1990-91, dep. asst. sec. labor for employment stds., 1991; dep. asst. sec. edn. for intergovernmental and interagency affairs US Dept. Edn., Washington, 1991-92, acting asst. sec. edn. for intergovernmental and interagency affairs, 1992; of counsel Wiley, Rein & Fielding, Washington, 1992-93, ptnr., 1993—2002; v.p. Coors Brewing Co., Golden, Colo., 2002—05; sr. v.p., global chief legal officer, corp. sec. Molson Coors Brewing Co., Denver, 2005—. Asst. clearance coun. Pres.-elect George W. Bush, 2000—01. Fellow Am. Bar Found.; mem. ABA, Colo. Bar Assn., DC Bar Assn. Avocations: family, outdoor sports, tennis. Office: Molson Coors Brewing Co 1225 17th St Denver CO 80202 Home: 5330 S Marshall St Littleton CO 80123 Office Phone: 303-277-2164. Office Fax: 303-277-7848. Personal E-mail: samuel.walker@molsoncoors.com.

WALKER, SUZANNE ROSS, mathematics and education educator; b. Johnston, RI, Aug. 14, 1960; d. Raymond Henry Ross and Matilda Marion DeChristofaro; m. Paul Joseph Walker, Feb. 17, 1990; 1 stepchild, William Braeden Pierce. BA in Math./Math Edn. magna cum laude, Providence Coll., 1982, EdM in Guidance Counseling summa cum laude, 1992. HS math tchr. Bay View Acad., East Providence, RI, 1983—85, LaSalle Acad., Providence, 1985—87, Woonsocket Edn. Dept., RI, 1987—, math curriculum coord., 1998—. Math instr. Hall Inst. Tech. Sch., Pawtucket, RI, 1983—90; adj. faculty mem. calculus RI Coll., 1987—; advisor advanced placement calculus class Woonsocket HS, 1997—; prof. edn. Providence Coll., 2000—, math prof., 2006—. Chairperson Johnston H.S. Class of 1978, RI, 1988—. Mem.: Am. Math. Soc., Am. Tchrs. Math., R.I. Math. Tchrs. Assn. (advisor to student math team), Nat. Coun. Tchrs. Math., Math. Assn. Am., Phi Sigma Tau, Pi Mu Epsilon. Roman Catholic. Avocations: aerobics, yoga, walking, movies, music. Home: 39 Roger Williams Dr Greenville RI 02828 Office: Woonsocket HS 777 Cass Ave Woonsocket RI 02895 Office Phone: 401-767-4730. Personal E-mail: suzy814@msn.com.

WALKER, TAMMIE LEIGH, music educator; d. Dennis Edwin Behr and Elaine Rita Creager; m. Chad Lynn Walker, July 29, 1995; children: Sophia Marian, Bennett Chad, Lucy Isabel, Grace Tammie. DMA in Piano Performance, U. Ill., 2001. Tchg. asst. U. Ill., Champaign-Urbana, 1995—98; assoc. prof. music Western Ill. U., Macomb, 1998—. Musician: performances in continental U.S., Hawaii, and Western Europe. Scholar, U. Wis., 1991—95. Fellow: Ill. State Music Tchrs. Assn. (coord. music competitions 2002—); mem.: Coll. Music Soc., Music Tchrs. Nat. Assn., Pi Kappa Lambda, Phi Kappa Phi. Democrat. Presbyterian. Avocations: travel, camping, cooking, running. Home: 426 W Jackson St Macomb IL 61455 Office: Western Illinois Univ Browne Hall 219 1 University Cir Macomb IL 61455 Office Phone: 309-298-1237. Office Fax: 309-298-1968. Business E-Mail: tl-walker4@wiu.edu.

WALKER, THOMAS CARLTON, music educator; b. Rochester, Minn., Apr. 10, 1936; s. Carl and Ethel Walker; m. Alleen Logsdon, Aug. 24, 1964; children: Kurt, Craig, Garett, DeAnna. Attended, St. Paul Bible Coll., 1956; MusB, Greenville Coll., 1958; attended, U. Ariz., 1962—63, MusM, 1967; advanced grad. study, U. Mo., 1976. Cert. C.C. tchg. cert. Ariz., 1987, lic. life ins. Ariz., massage therapy Ariz. Music instr. Phoenix Christian HS, 1960—62, Elfrida Elem., Valley Union HS, Elfrida, Ariz., 1963—67; music dept. chair Ctrl. Coll., McPherson, Kans., 1967—81; choral conductor McPherson Coll., Kans., 1972—73, 1974—75; min. of music Free Meth. Ch., McPherson, 1967—73, 1974—75; music dept. chair Bartlesville Wesleyan Coll., Bartlesville, Okla., 1981—83; music instr. Phoenix Christian HS, Phoenix, 1983—85; dir. music Epworth United Meth. Ch., Phoenix, 1986—91; music instr. Glendale C. C., Glendale, Ariz., 1991—92; instr. Maricopa County Traffic Survival Sch., Phoenix, 1985—97; dir. music, choir Bethel Bapt. Ch., Phoenix, 1991—99; dir. music Lakeview United Meth. Ch., Sun City, Ariz., 1999—. Massage therapist Self Employed, Ariz., 1989—; conductor Overseas Touring Choir, 1979; choir conductor Free Meth. World Convocation, Indpls., 1979; coll. rep. Watson Colloquium-Free Meth. Ch. World Headquarters, Winona Lake, Ind., 1980; music dir. ch. & youth camps in Calif., Ariz., Kans., Ark. & Ill.; vocal & choral cons. McPherson Theatre Guild; mem. facilities planning com. McPherson Free Meth. Ch. Composer: Five Songs of Thanksgiving, 1967. With U.S. Army Air Defense Command Choral Group, 1958—60. Sgt. US Army, 1958—60, with USAR, 1960—62. Named Outstanding Educator of Am., Outstanding Educators of Am., 1972. Mem.: Ariz. Music Educators Assn., Am. Choral Dir. (life), Music Educators Nat. Conf. (life), Internat. Massage Assn. Meth. Avocation: antiques. Home: 4140 W Hayward Ave Phoenix AZ 85051 Office Phone: 623-974-5821.

WALKER, THOMAS H., real estate developer; b. Hattiesburg, Miss., Nov. 11, 1950; s. Thomas Ray and Mary Ella (Bennett) W.; m. Cynthia Kay Sherer, June 5, 1993; children: Ty, Kelly, Rachel, Stacey. BS in Engring., Miss. State U., 1972; MBA, U. West Fla., 1982; postgrad., Nat. Def. U., 1987-88, Harvard U., 1990, Fed. Exec. Inst., 1992. Registered profl. engr., Va. Indsl. engr. Navy Pub. Works Ctr., Norfolk, Va., 1973-75, Atlantic Divsn. Naval Facility Engring. Commn., Norfolk, Va., 1975-76; supervisory gen. engr. Naval Comm. Sta., Exmouth, Australia, 1976-78; indsl. engr. Western Divsn. Naval Facility Engring. Commn., San Bruno, Calif., 1978-79; head facilities mgmt. Navy Pub. Works Ctr., Pensacola, Fla., 1979-82, Subic Bay, The Philippines, 1982-85; dep. dir. facilities mgmt. USMC, Washington, 1985-89; asst. commr. GSA, Washington, 1989-92, dep. asst. regional adminstr., 1992-93, asst. regional adminstr. pub. bldgs. Kansas City, Mo., 1993-99; asst. regional adminstr. Pub. Bldgs. Svc., Atlanta, 1999—2006; sr. dir. govt. programs Opus Corp., Atlanta, 2006—; bd. dirs. Housing Corp., Starkville, Miss., 2007—. Bd. dirs. Kansas City BOMA, 1994-99. Mem. engring. adv. com. Bagley Coll. Engring, Miss. State U., 2007-; coach Little League Baseball, Fairfax, Va., 1986-92, Girls Softball Team, Lees Summit, Va., 1995; cub scout den father Boy Scouts Am., Fairfax, 1987-88. Miss. State U. Disting. Engring. fellow, 1992; recipient Arthur S. Fleming award Washington Jaycees, 1989, Presdl. rank award, 1996, v.p. Hammer award, 1996, Ga. Tech. U. Hon. Ednl. Svc. award, 2005. Mem. NSPE, Va. Soc. Profl. Engrs., Bldg. Owners and Mgrs. Assn. (mem. govt. bldgs. com. 1991—, chmn. 1993—2006, mem. corp. facilities com. 1991—, nat. adv. coun. 1995—, Atlanta bd. dirs. 2007—, Nat. Mem. of Yr. 1997, Atlanta Svc. award 2000, Bd. Chmn.'s award 2006), Internat. Facilities Mgmt. Assn. (mem. pub. sector com. 1991—, Golden Cir. award 1994), Sr. Execs. Assn., Nat. Assn. Ret. Fed. Employees, Phi Kappa Phi, Alpha Pi Mu, Gamma Beta Phi, Sigma Lambda Chi, Alpha Tau Omega. Methodist. Avocation: golf. Home: 595 Kings Grant Walk Roswell GA 30075-5528 Office: 925 North Point Pkwy Ste 305 Alpharetta GA 30005 Home Phone: 678-461-4574; Office Phone: 404-456-7089. Business E-Mail: tom.walker@opuscorp.com.

WALKER, THOMAS RAY, city aviation commissioner; AB in Art, Dartmouth Coll., 1970; BArch, Ill. Inst. Tech., 1977. Project mgr. Lohan Assocs., 1977-86; v.p. design and constrn. The Chgo. Dock and Canal Trust, 1986-91; exec. dir. Pub. Bldg. Commn. of Chgo., 1991-95; commr. dept. transp. City of Chgo., 1995-99; commr. Chgo. Dept. of Aviation, City of Chgo., 2000—. Prin. works include Soldier Field World Cup renovation, Chgo., Wright Coll. Addition, Chgo. Pub. Schs. capital improvement program, Cityfront Ctr., Chgo., MarketTower Officer Bldg., Indpls., Episcopal Sch. of Dallas Libr./Fine Arts addition, Frito-Lay Nat. Hdqs., Plano, Tex. Vice chmn. Chgo. Area Transp. Study; commr. State St. Commn.; mem. com. Newhouse arch. fellowship prgm Chgo. Arch. Found.; mem. Chgo. Planning Commn.; mem. selection com. cmty. svc. fellowship Chgo. Cmty. Trust; mem. TRB steering com. Conf. Transp. Issue in Large U.S. Cities; mem. Conf. Minority Transp. Officials; trustee Chgo. Music and Dance Theater; chmn. leadership coun. Met. Open Cmtys.; co-chmn. adv. bd./housing com. Met. Planning Coun. 1st lt. USAF, 1970-72. Mem. Intelligent Transp. Soc. of Am. (bd. dirs.), Nat. Assn. City Transp. Ofcls. (chmn.), Nat. Orgn. Minority Architects, Urban Land Inst., Lambda Alpha Internat. Office: O'Hare Internat Airport Dept of Aviation PO Box 66142 Chicago IL 60666-0142

WALKER, TIMOTHY CRAIG, transportation executive; b. Huntington, W.Va., Jan. 16, 1945; s. John Paul and Marjorie Frances (Withers) W. BA, Northwestern U., 1967; B of Fgn. Trade, Am. Grad. Sch. Internat. Mgmt., 1968. Mgmt. trainee to dir. OIM/internat. mktg. ops. NCR Corp., Dayton, Ohio, 1968—79; v.p. mktg. Do-Ray Lamp Co., Inc., Colorado City, Colo., 1979—81; v.p. sales and mktg. Truck-Lite Co., Inc., Jamestown, NY, 1984—; pres., COO Truck-Lite Internat., Inc., 1990—, also bd. dirs. Recruiter Am. Grad. Sch. Internat. Mgmt., 1971—. Bd. dirs. Valley Human Resources, United Way Agy., 1980-84, Goodwill Industries of Pueblo, Colo., 1983-84; mem. Working Group for U.S. Dept. Commerce MOSS Talks. Recipient Pres.'s award 1st alumnus Am. Grad. Sch. Internat. Mgmt., 1976, award for excellence in internat. advt., 1968; named to Automotive Hall of Fame. Mem. Transp. Safety Equipment Inst. N.Am. (chmn. mktg. and statis. com. 1980-82), European Transport Maintenance Coun. (bd. dirs. 1991-93), Heavy Duty Bus. Forum (bd. dirs.), Heavy Duty Mfrs. Assn. (bd. govs. 1987-95, sec. 1990-91, 95-96, vice chmn. 1997, chmn. 1998), Overseas Automotive Coun. (bd. dirs.), Pueblo Area C. of C. (transp. com. 1981-84), Coun. Fleet Specialists (mfrs. liaison com. 1989-91), 500 Automotive Execs. Club. Republican. Presbyterian. Home: PO Box 1263 Jamestown NY 14702-1263 Office: Truck-Lite Co PO Box 387 Jamestown NY 14702-0387 Office Phone: 716-665-6214. Personal E-mail: tcwbhx@aol.com. Business E-Mail: twalker@truck-lite.com.

WALKER, VAUGHN R., federal judge; b. Watseka, Ill., Feb. 27, 1944; s. Vaughn Rosenworth and Catharine (Miles) W. AB, U. Mich., 1966; JD, Stanford U., 1970. Intern economist SEC, Washington, 1966, 68; law clk. to the Hon. Robert J. Kelleher US Dist. Ct. Calif., LA, 1971-72; assoc. atty. Pillsbury Madison & Sutro, San Francisco, 1972-77, ptnr., 1978-90; judge US Dist. Ct. (no. dist.) Calif., San Francisco, 1990—, chief judge, 2004—. Mem. Calif. Law Revision Commn., Palo Alto, 1986-89; bd. advisors Law and Econs. Ctr., George Mason U., 1999—; mem. civil rules adv. com. Jud. Conf. U.S., 2006—. Bd. dirs. Jr. Achievement of Bay Area, San Francisco, 1979-83; bd. dirs. St. Francis Found., San Francisco, 1991-97, 98—, vice chair, 2004-06, chair, 2007—. Woodrow Wilson Found. fellow U. Calif., Berkeley, 1966-67. Fellow Am. Bar Found.; mem. ABA (jud. rep., antitrust sect. 1991-95), Lawyers' Club of San Francisco (pres. 1985-86), Assn. Bus. Trial Lawyers (dir. 1996-98), Am. Law Inst., Am. Saddlebred Horse Assn., San Francisco Mus. Modern Art, Bohemian Club, Olympic Club, Pacific-Union Club. Office: US Dist Ct 450 Golden Gate Ave San Francisco CA 94102-3482

WALKER, WALDO SYLVESTER, biologist, educator, academic administrator; b. Fayette, Iowa, June 12, 1931; s. Waldo S. and Mildred (Littelle) W.; m. Marie J. Olsen, July 27, 1952 (div.); children: Martha Lynn, Gayle Ann; m. Rita K. White, June 16, 1984. BS cum laude, Upper Iowa U., Fayette, 1953; MS, U. Iowa, 1957, PhD, 1959; D of Sci. (hon.), Upper Iowa U., 2004. Mem. faculty Grinnell (Iowa) Coll., 1958, assoc. dean coll., 1963-65, chmn. div. Natural Scis., 1968-69, dean of adminstrn., 1969-73, exec. v.p., 1973-77, dean coll., 1973-80, provost, 1977-80, exec. v.p., 1980-90, exec. v.p. and treas., 1988-90, v.p. for coll. svcs., 1990-95, prof. biology, 1968-2001, prof. emeritus, 2001—. Research assoc. U. B.C. Dept. of Botany, 1966-67. Author articles on plant physiology, ultrastructural cytology. Served with U.S. Army, 1953-55. Fellow NSF Sci. Faculty, 1966-67; recipient NSF research grants, 1960-63, 68. Mem. Am. Assn. Colls., Am. Conf. Acad. Deans (nat. chmn. 1977-78), Am. Assn. Higher Edn., Sigma Xi. Home: 1920 Country Club Dr Grinnell IA 50112-1130 Address: Grinnell Coll PO Box H2 Grinnell IA 50112-0805 E-mail: walkerws@iowatelecom.net.

WALKER, WALTER FREDERICK, professional basketball team executive; b. Bradford, Pa., July 18, 1954; m. Linda Walker. Diploma, U. Va.; MBA, Stanford U., 1987; BA, U. Va., 1976. Chartered Fin. Analyst. Player Portland (Oreg.) Trail Blazers, 1976-77, Seattle SuperSonics, 1977-82, pres., CEO, 1994—; player Houston Rockets, 1982-84; with Goldman Sachs and Co., San Francisco, 1987-94; prin. Walker Capital, Inc., San Francisco, 1994. Mem. USA gold medal World Univ. Games basketball team, 1973; broadcaster basketball Raycom Network, 1989-94; cons. Seattle SuperSonics, 1994. Bd. dirs. Advanced Digital Info. Corp., Drexler Tech. Corp. Named 1st team Acad. All-Am. U. Va.; named to Pa. State Sports Hall of Fame. Nat. trustee Boys and Girls Clubs of Am. Office: Seattle SuperSonics 351 Elliott Ave W Seattle WA 98119-4101 E-mail: wwalker@sonics-storm.com.

WALKER, WALTER HERBERT, III, lawyer, educator, writer; b. Quincy, Mass., Sept. 12, 1949; s. Walter H. Jr. and Irene M. (Horn) W.; m. Anne M. DiScuillo, June 17, 1972; children: Brett Daniel, Jeffrey St. John. BA, U. Pa., 1971; JD, U. Calif., San Francisco, 1974. Bar: Calif. 1974, Mass. 1981. Appellate atty. ICC, Washington, 1975-77; trial atty. Handler, Baker, Greene & Taylor, San Francisco, 1977-80; ptnr. Sterns and Walker and predecessor firm Sterns, Smith, Walker & Grell, San Francisco, 1981-88; ptnr. firm Walker & Durham, San Francisco, 1988—99, Walker, Hamilton & White, San Francisco, 2000—. Author: A Dime to Dance By, 1983 (Best 1st Novel by Calif. Author), The Two Dude Defense, 1985, Rules of The Knife Fight, 1986, The Immediate Prospect of Being Hanged, 1989, The Appearance of Impropriety, 1992. Finalist Calif. Trial Lawyer of Yr., 2003. Mem. ABOTA, ATLA, Consumer Attys. of Calif., Mass. Bar Assn., San Francisco Trial Lawyers Assn., Mystery Writers Am., Hastings Rugby Club. Democrat. Office: 50 Francisco St Ste 460 San Francisco CA 94133-2100 Office Phone: 415-986-3339.

WALKER, WILLIAM BOND, painter, retired librarian; b. Brownsville, Tenn., Apr. 15, 1930; s. Marshall Francis and Mary Louise (Taylor) W. BA, State U. Iowa, 1953; M.L.S., Rutgers U., 1958. Librarian-trainee Donnell br. N.Y. Public Library, NYC, 1955-57; reference librarian/cataloger Met. Mus. Art, NYC, 1957-59; chief librarian Bklyn. Mus., 1959-64; supervisory librarian Library of Nat. Collection Fine Arts and Nat. Portrait Gallery, Smithsonian Instn., Washington, 1964-80; Arthur K. Watson chief librarian Thomas J. Watson Library, Met. Mus. Art, NYC, 1980-94; ret., 1994. Adj. lectr. Columbia U. Sch. Library Service, 1987-88. Author: annotated bibliography American Sculpture, 18th-20th Century, 1979; retrospective exhbn. paintings, 1954-96, Pittsfield, Mass., 1996-97; solo and group exhbns. Columbia County, NY, Berkshire County, Mass., Rochester, NY, 1997-2007. Mem. ALA, Art Librs. Soc. N.Am (charter; pres. 1975, Disting. Svc. award, 1992), Geneal. and Biog. Soc. (corr.), Phi Beta Kappa. Home: 54 Queechy Lake Dr PO Box 237 Canaan NY 12029-0237 E-mail: lakequeechy@taconic.net.

WALKER, WILLIAM D., library director; BS, Loch Haven U.; AMLS, U. Mich. Head info. svcs. U. Ill. Med. Ctr. Libr. of the Health Scis.; dir. Med. Libr. Ctr. of NY; sr. v.p., Andrew W. Mellon dir. rsch. librs. NY Pub. Libr. Sys.; dir. librs. U. Miami, Coral Gables, Fla., 2003—. Office: U Miami Otto G Richter Libr Coral Gables Campus Coral Gables FL 33124-0320 Office Phone: 305-284-3551. Office Fax: 305-284-4027. E-mail: wwalker@miami.edu. *

WALKER, WILLIAM EASTON, surgeon, educator, lawyer; b. Glasgow, Scotland, Aug. 7, 1945; came to U.S., 1969; s. William Telfer and Josephine Blair (Easton) W.; m. Mary Fraley Cooley, June 23, 1973; children— Sarah Cooley, Blair Easton, Denton Arthur Cooley, William Easton, II MD, Glasgow U., Scotland, 1968; PhD, Johns Hopkins U., 1975; JD, South Tex. Coll Law, 1993. Diplomate Am. Bd. Surgery, Am. Bd. Thoracic Surgery, Am. Bd. Vascular Surgery. Intern, resident Johns Hopkins U., Balt., 1969-75; resident Vanderbilt U., Nashville, 1975-79; assoc. prof., dir. div. thoracic and cardiovascular surgery U. Tex. Med. Sch., Houston, 1979-94. Cons. M.D. Anderson Hosp., Houston, 1979—. Recipient Harwell Wilson award Vanderbilt U., Nashville, 1979 Fellow ACS, So. Surg. Assn., Royal Coll. Surgeons, Am. Coll. Cardiology; mem. Am. Assn. Thoracic Surgery, Coun. Fgn. Rels., Houston Country Club, Belle Meade Country Club, Cosmos Club (Washington), Krewe of Endymion (New Orleans), Phi Beta Kappa, Sigma Xi. Republican. Presbyterian. Avocations: law, bridge, Wagner, World War I history, cooking. Home and Office: 2831 Sackett St Houston TX 77098-1125 Home Phone: 713-520-0545; Office Phone: 713-520-0021. E-mail: wwalker19@houston.rr.com.

WALKER, WILLIAM O., JR., pediatrician; b. Meridian, Miss., Feb. 27, 1954; s. William Otis and Miriam Wilkerson Walker; m. Patricia Lathrop, June 7, 1975; children: William Lathrop, Kathryn Ryan. MD, Tulane U., New Orleans, 1979. Diplomate Am. Bd. of Pediat., 1984, in Neurodevelopmental Disabilities Am. Bd. of Pediat., 2001, cert. in Developmental Behavioral Pediats. Am. Bd. of Pediat., 2002. Assoc. prof., pediat. U. of Wash. Sch. of Medicine, Seattle, 2001—; dir., develomental behavioral pediat. fellowship Dept. of Pediat., U. of Wash. Sch. of Medicine, Seattle, 2002—. Col. US Army, 1979—2001. Fellow: Am. Acad. of Cerebral Palsy and Devel. Medicine, Am. Acad. of Pediat.; mem.: Child Neurology Soc. Office: Children's Hosp Med Ctr 4800 Sand Point Way NE A7938 Seattle WA 98105 Home Phone: 253-566-3288; Office Phone: 206-987-3664. Office Fax: 206-987-3824.

WALKER, WILLIAM TIDD, JR., investment banker; b. Detroit, Sept. 5, 1931; s. William Tidd and Irene (Rhode) W.; m. Patricia Louise Frazier, Sept. 10, 1953; children: Donna Louise, Carol Ann, Sally Lynn, Alyssa Jane. Student, Stanford, 1950. Stockbroker William R. Staats & Co., Los Angeles, 1952-57, sales mgr., 1957-58, syndicate partner, 1958-65; sr. v.p. Glore Forgan, William R. Staats Inc., NYC, 1965-68; partner, exec. com. Lester, Ryons & Co., Los Angeles, 1968; exec. v.p. Bateman Eichler, Hill Richards Inc., Los Angeles, 1969-85. Pres., CEO WTW Inc.; chmn., CEO Walker Assocs.; bd. dirs. Digid, Inc.; chmn. King-Thomason Group, Inc., Supralife Internat., Stone Mountain Data Ctrs. Inc.; adv. mem. Am. Stock Exch., 1981—. With USAF, 1949-52. Mem. Securities Industry Assn. (dir. nat. syndicate com., chmn. Calif. Dist. 10), Pacific Coast Stock Exch. (bd. govs. 1971-72), Investment Bankers Assn. (nat. pub. rels. com. 1966—), Bond Club L.A. (pres. 1973), Calif. Yacht Club. Office: Walker Assocs PO Box 10684 Beverly Hills CA 90213-3684 Office Phone: 310-276-8783.

WALKER, WILLIAM WOODARD, JR., management consultant, telecommunications technology executive; b. Montevideo, Uruguay, Aug. 2, 1950; s. William Woodard and Jane (Wootton) W. BA in Polit. Sci., U. N.C., Chapel Hill, 1973; MBA, Coll. of William & Mary, 1978. Acct. mgr. Jarvis Corp., Alexandria, Va., 1978-80; mgmt. cons. Daniel Penn Assocs., Schuykill Haven, Pa., 1981-82; mktg. exec. Sprint Corp., McLean, Va., 1982-84; pres. Woodard Walker Assocs., Inc., Vienna, Va., 1984—. Dir. bd. of dirs. coun. of co-owners The Colonies Condominium, McLean, 1992-94. Mem.: Soc. Telecomm. Cons., Friends Assisting the Nat. Symphony Orch., Washington (exec. com. 1996—97), Met. Club Washington. Episcopalian. Avocations: tennis, bicycling. Office: Ste 1350 8000 Towers Crescent Dr Vienna VA 22182-2700 Personal E-mail: woodwalk@mindspring.com.

WALKER, WOODROW WILSON, retired lawyer, real estate investor, farmer; b. Greenville, Mich., Feb. 19, 1919; s. Craig Walker and Mildred Chase; m. Janet K. Keiter, Oct. 7, 1950; children: Jonathan Woodrow, William Craig, Elaine Virginia. BA, U. Mich., 1943; LLB, Cath. U., 1950. Bar: D.C. 1950, U.S. Supreme Ct. 1958, Va. 1959. Operator family farm, 1937-39; dir. Libr. of Congress Fed. Credit Union, 1957-60; atty. Am. law div. legis. reference Libr. Congress, Washington, 1951-60; pvt. practice, Arlington, Va., 1960—2000. Counsel, bd. dirs. Calvary Found., Arlington, 1970-85, first pres., 1972; judge moot ct. George Mason Law Sch., 1986, Columbus Law Sch., 2007, Cath. U., 2007; owner-operator Walker Farm Front Royal, Va., 1972—. Co-author rsch. publs. for U.S. Govt.; featured in Washington Post. V.p. Jefferson Civic Assn., Arlington, 1955-61; pres. Nellie Custis PTA, Arlington, 1960-61; sec. Arlington County Bd. Equalization Real Estate Assessment, 1962, chmn. 1963; troop com. chmn. of honor Boy Scouts Am., 1964-69, life scout, sr. patrol leader troop 131; mem. Arlington County Pub. Utilities Commn., 1964-66, vice chmn., 1965-66; pres. Betschler Class Adult Sunday Sch., Calvary United Meth. Ch., Arlington, 1965. With U.S. Army, 1943-45, PTO. Cited for notable deed in conduct of his legal duties Washington Post, 1996. Mem. ABA, Arlington County Bar Assn., Va. Farm Bur., Va. Cattleman's Assn. Independent. Methodist. Home and Office: 2822 Ft Scott Dr Arlington VA 22202-2307

WALKER BONNER, LINDA CAROL, music educator; b. Nashville, Aug. 18, 1953; d. John Louis and Caronia Walker; m. Divorced; children: Jordan Bonner III, Angela Jonelle Bonner. BS, Tenn. State U., 1975; M, Vanderbilt U., 1977. Music specialist Williamson County Schools, Franklin, Tenn., 1976—. Contbr. articles to profl. jours. Vol. Habitat For Humanities, Nashville, 2000—05; v.p. Missionary Soc., Nashville, 2002—05. Mem.: WCEA (life; minority rep. 1986—92), TEA (life; minority affairs com. 1988—90). Home: 756 Garrison Dr Nashville TN 37207 Office: Grassland Elem Sch 6803 Manley Ln Brentwood TN 37027 Home Phone: 615-876-3435; Office Phone: 615-472-4480. Personal E-mail: lcwbonner@comcast.net. E-mail: lindab1@wcs.edu.

WALKER NEVE, DIANA, singer, voice educator; d. Ellis Roy Walker and Beth Swenson; m. Charles Montgomery, Jr. Neve; 1 child, Nicholas Pietro Joseph Neve stepchildren: Meisha E. Neve, Charles M. Neve, III, Robert B. Neve, Mariah A. Neve, Isaiah A. Neve. MusB Performance Highest Honors, U. Mo.-Kansas City Conservatory Music, 1977, MusM Performance High Honors, 1979. Coloratura soprano soloist St. Louis Opera, 1983—84, N.Y.C. Opera, 1983—90; soprano recitalist Carnegie Hall, Carnegie Recital Hall, NYC, 1983—94, Town Hall (Winners Cir. Series), NYC, 1984; soprano concert recitalist Internat. Art Song Festival, Petit Jean, Ark., 1985—86; coloratura soprano soloist Bklyn. Philharm., 1985—86, Balt. Renaissance Opera, 1985—86, Miami Chamber Symphony, Fla., 1986, Chattanooga Opera, 1986, Seattle Opera, 1985—87, Handel Festival Soc., Washington, 1987—88, Utah Opera, Salt Lake City, 1987—88, Chgo. Opera Theatre, 1989, Nat. Ballet Can., Toronto, 1985—89, Lyric Opera Kansas City, Mo., 1985—96, L'Opera de Nice, France, 1989; singing prin. role of Carlotta and Madame Firmin in Phantom of the Opera Live Entertainment Corp Can., Toronto, 1991—95; coloratura soprano soloist Roanoke Opera and Symphony, Va., 1994—96; guest artist The Vocal Majority (Award Winning Male Choir), Dallas, 1998—99; classical/musical theatre concert performer Utah Arts Coun., Salt Lake City, 1998—. Tchr. voice, Salt Lake City, 1997—; guest artist prof., lectr. Brigham Young U., Provo, Utah, 1995—2000; guest artist prof. U. Mass., Amherst, 1983, U. Hawaii, Honolulu and Hilo, 2002—03. Vocalist (with David Glen Hatch): CD Broadway Classics, vocalist (with Mormon Symphony & Youth Chorus): CD You'll Never Walk Alone, soprano soloist: CD A Mormon Tabernacle Choir Christmas; actor: (documentaries) The Earthquake Zone, (and singer): (films) Look at Me (Innovation in Film award, Kans. City Film Festival, 1997); soundtrack soloist: films The Ghost of Dickens Past, soundtrack artist: films Cold Mountain, guest artist: soap opera Another World, 1984. Guest artist performer The Nat. Assn. of Christians and Jews, Salt Lake City and other cities, Utah, 1993—94, Hugh O Brian Youth Found., Honolulu, 1994—95; vocal rec. guest artist Sweet Songs of Liberty CD Benefit for 9/11 Victims by MoV'N Pictures, Inc., Salt Lake City and NYC, 2001; artist Utah Arts Coun. Performing Arts Tour Broadway Classics in Concert, 1999—; guest artist performer Com. to Elect Mit Romney for Gov. of Mass.; soprano soloist Mormon Tabernacle Choir, Salt Lake City, 1988—90. Recipient 2d Pl., Naefger Competition, 1978, Met. Opera Young Artist Awards, 1979, Internat. Am. Music Competition at Carnegie Hall, 1983, Alumni Achievement award, U. Mo.-Kansas City Conservatory Music, 1985, Gov.' s Artist award, Gov. Michael Leavitt, Utah, 2000; grantee Monetary award for Career Devel., The Sullivan Found., N.Y.C, 1980—85, Monetary award for Film Project, Nat. Endowment for Arts, 1993; scholarship, Music Acad. West, Santa Barbara, Calif., 1977, fellowship, Tanglewood Music Festival, Mass., 1978, scholarship, Banff Sch. Music, Alta., Can., 1979, Aspen Summer Music Festival, 1979. Mem.: Can. Actors Equity, Nat. Assn. Tchrs. Singing (won 3 student contests Kansas City Conservatory Music 1977—79), Am. Guild Musical Artists, Actors Equity. Republican. Mem. Lds Ch. Avocations: travel, scuba diving, camping, horseback riding, violin. Home: 2763 Evergreen Ave Salt Lake City UT 84109 Personal E-mail: charles_diana@comcast.net.

WALKER TUCKER, DANA, lawyer; b. St. Louis, Oct. 23, 1963; d. Donald Edward and Mary Louise Walker; m. Mark Avery Tucker, May 29, 1998; 1 child, Jackson Miles Tucker. BS, U. Mo., 1986; JD (scholar 1991-94), St. Louis U., 1994. Bar: Mo. 1995, Ill. 2003. With Husch and Eppenberger, St. Louis, 1994—96, Banks and Assocs., 1996—2000; atty. Gary, Williams, Parenti, et. al., Stuart, Fla., 2000—02; atty., ptnr. Fox Galvin LLC, St. Louis, 2002—. Adj. prof. Washington U. Law Sch., 2004—. Mem.: Bar Assn. Met. St. Louis, Mound City Bar Assn., Def. Resource Inst., Nat. Bar Assn., Delta Sigma Theta. Democrat. Baptist. Office: Fox Galvin LLC #1 Memorial Dr Saint Louis MO 63102 Home Phone: 314-749-2365; Office Phone: 314-588-7000. Office Fax: 314-588-1965; Home Fax: 314-588-1965. Personal E-mail: dtucker@foxgalvin.com.

WALKINSHAW, NICOLE M., performing arts educator; B in Com. Processes & Disorders, U. Fla., 1988—92, B, 1988—92; M in Social Foundations in Multicultural Edn., Fla. Atlantic U., 2004—05. Cert. in Adolescent Young Adulthood/English Lang. Arts U.S. Nat. Bd. Edn., Fla., 2003, Speech, English & English for Speakers of Other Lang. Fla. Dept. Edn., 1992. Educator Nova HS, Davie, Fla., 1992—. S.t.a.r. mentoring program dir. Nova HS, 1996—, broadway series interactive achievers program dir., 2001—, e.a.g.l.e. tolerance tng. initiative program dir., 2002—. Facilitator (seminar) Integrating Literary Circles Across the Curricular Disciplines, Honae vs Tatamya: Exploring the Multifaceted & Mystical World of Japan; editor: (pub.) SNAPSHOT Entertainment Newsletter. Fundraiser project dir. Until There's A Cure, Davie, 1997—98; youth vol. coord. Read Across Am., Davie, 2002—05; fundraiser project coord. Broadway Cares Equity Fights A.I.D.S., Davie, 2003—05; vol. supr. Kids In Distress, Davie, 2003—05. Recipient Broward's Best, Broward County Sch. Bd., 2003, Alumni Assn. Appreciation award, U. Fla., 2004; Team Mentor grant, Citibank, 2002—03, Fulbright Meml. Fund. scholar, 2002. Mem.: NEA, Fla. Edn. Assn., Nat. Assn. Multicultural Edn., Fla. Humanities Coun., So. Poverty Law Ctr. Avocations: writing, travel, cinematic & arts appreciation. Office: Nova HS 3600 College Ave Davie FL 33314 Home Phone: 954-472-4935; Office Phone: 754-323-1650.

WALKOVIK, DONALD C., lawyer; b. Kenosha, Wis., 1948; BBA, U. Wis., 1970; JD, Harvard U., 1973. Bar: NY 1974. Mem. Sullivan & Cromwell, NYC, 1973—81, ptnr., 1981—92, mng. ptnr. Hongkong, 1992—97, ptnr. NYC. Mem.: ABA, NY State Bar Assn., Bar Assn. of NYC, NY County Lawyers' Assn., Internat. Bar Assn. Office: Sullivan & Cromwell 125 Broad St New York NY 10004-2489 Office Phone: 212-558-4000, 212-558-3911. Office Fax: 212-558-3588. Business E-Mail: walkovikd@sullcrom.com.

WALKOWIAK, VINCENT STEVEN, lawyer; b. Apr. 22, 1946; s. Vincent Albert and Elizabeth (Modla) W.; m. Linda Kae Schweigert, Aug., 1968; children: Jenifer, Steven. BA, U. Ill., 1968, JD, 1971. Bar: Ill. 1971, Minn. 1971, Tex. 1981, U.S. Ct. Appeals (8th cir.) 1971, (5th cir.) 1982, U.S. Dist. Ct. (ea., we., so., and no. dists.) Tex. 1982. Assoc. Dorsey, Marquart, Windhorst, West & Halladay, Mpls., 1971-74; ptnr. Fulbright & Jaworski LLP, Houston, 1982—. Prof. Fla. State U., Tallahassee, 1974-76, So. Meth. U., Dallas, 1976-84. Editor: Uniform Product Liability Act, 1980, Trial of a Product Liability Case, vol. 1, 1981, vol. 2, 1982, Preparation and Presentation of Product Liability, 1983, Attorney Client Privilege in Civil Litigation, 3d edit., 2004. Office: Fulbright & Jaworski LLP 2200 Ross Ave Ste 2800 Dallas TX 75201-2784 Home Phone: 214-692-6046; Office Phone: 214-855-8037. Business E-Mail: vwalkowiak@fulbright.com.

WALKUP, CHARLOTTE LLOYD, lawyer; b. NYC, Apr. 28, 1910; d. Charles Henry and Helene Louise (Wheeler) Tuttle; m. David D. Lloyd, Oct. 19, 1940 (dec. Dec. 1962); children: Andrew M. Lloyd, Louisa Lloyd Hurley; m. Homer Allen Walkup, Feb. 4, 1967. AB, Vassar Coll., 1931; LLB, Columbia U., 1934. Bar: NY 1935, US Supreme Ct. 1939, US Dist. Ct. DC 1953, Va. 1954. Asst. solicitor Dept. Interior, Washington, 1934-45; asst. gen. counsel UNRRA, Washington and London, 1945-48; assoc. and cons. firms Washington, 1953, 55, 60; atty., spl. asst. Office Treasury, Washington, 1961-65, asst. gen. counsel, 1965-73. Cons. Rogers & Wells, Washington, 1975-86. Editor Columbia Law Rev., 1933-34, Life Stories of a Celebrated Lawyer: Memoirs of Charles H. Tuttle, Esq., 2002. Pres. Alexandria Cmty. Welfare Coun., 1950-52; bd. dirs. Alexandria Coun. Human Rels., 1958-60, New Hope Found., 1977. Recipient Meritorious Svc. award Dept. Treasury, 1970, Exceptional Svc. award, 1973, Career Svc. award Nat. Civil Svc. League, 1973; named Hon. fellow Harry S. Truman Libr. Inst. Mem.: Columbia U. Alumni Assn., Phi Beta Kappa. Democrat. Episcopalian. Home: 4800 Fillmore Ave Apt 1251 Alexandria VA 22311-5077 Personal E-mail: walkup@comcast.net.

WALKUP, ROBERT E., mayor; b. Ames, Iowa, Nov. 14, 1936; m. Beth Walkup; 3 children; 2 stepchildren. BS in Indsl. Engring., Iowa State U. Exec. Rockwell Internat., Fairchild Republic; sr. exec. Hughes Aircraft Co.; mayor City of Tuscon, Ariz., 1999—. Chmn. Greater Tucson Econ. Coun.; founder, first chmn. Ariz. Space Commn.; vol. Tucson Cmty. Food Bank; co-founder Pima-Santa Cruz County Sch.-to-Work Program; co-founder El Centro Cultural de las Americas. Capt. U.S. Army. Republican. Avocations: playing guitar, sketching, studying astronomy, restoring antique cars and motorcycles. Office: City Hall 255 W Alameda St Tucson AZ 85701-1362 Fax: 520-791-4213. Business E-Mail: email_mayor@mail.ci.tucson.az.us. *

WALL, BRIAN RAYMOND, forest economist, business consultant, researcher; b. Jan. 26, 1940; s. Raymond Perry and Mildred Beryl (Pickert) W.; m. Joan Marie Nero, Sept. 1, 1962 (div. Aug. 1990); children: Torden Erik, Kirsten Noel. BS, U. Wash., 1962; MF, Yale U., 1964. Forestry asst. Weyerhaeuser Timber Co., Klamath Falls, Oreg., 1960; inventory forester West Tacoma Newsprint, Steilacom, Oreg., 1961-62; timber sale compliance forester Dept. Nat. Resources, Kelso, Wash., 1963; rsch. forest economist Pacific N.W. Rsch. Sta., USDA Forest Svc., Portland, Oreg., 1964-88; cons., 1989—. Co-founder, bd. dirs. Cordero Youth Care Ctr., 1970-81; owner Brian R. Wall Images and Communications; Nikken ind. distbr. Sage Mentor Lifestyles; owner Sage Mentors Bus. Consultancy; cons. to govt. agys., Congress univs., industry, small bus.; freelance photographer. Co-author: An Analysis of the Timber Situation in the United States, 1982; contbr. articles, reports to profl. publs., newspapers. Interviewed and cited by nat. and regional news media. Recipient Cert. of Merit U.S. Dept. Agr. Forest Svc., 1982. Mem. ACLU, Soc. Am. Foresters (chmn. Portland chpt. 1973, Forester of Yr. 1975), Conf. of Western Forest Economists Inc. (founder, bd. dirs. 1988-91, treas. 1982-87), Portland Photographic Forum, Common Cause, Oregon Economists Assn., Nat. Audubon Soc., Amnesty Internat., Zeta Psi. Home: 6160 SW Alice Ln # 204 B Beaverton OR 97008 Personal E-mail: brianr.wall@msn.com.

WALL, CHARLES R., lawyer; BA in History, Grinnell Coll., Iowa, 1967; JD, U. Mo. Law Sch., 1970. Assoc. and ptnr. Shook, Hardy & Bacon, Kans. City, Mo., 1970—90; v.p.,assoc. gen. coun. Philip Morris Co. Inc., NYC, 1990—94, sr. v.p. litig., 1994—95, dep. gen. coun., 1995—2000; sr. v.p., gen. coun. Altria Grp., Inc. (formerly Philip Morris Co. Inc.), NYC, 2000—. Mem.: bd. dirs. NY City Opera, Neurosciences Inst., La Jolla, Calif. Office: Altria Group Inc 120 Park Ave New York NY 10017 Office Phone: 917-663-5000. *

WALL, CHRISTOPHER READ, lawyer; b. Norfolk, Va., Oct. 6, 1952; s. Maurice E. Wall and Marilyn (Murrah) Hardin; m. Barbara L. Wartelle, June 21, 1980. BA summa cum laude, Yale U., 1974; BA, Oxford U., 1976; JD, U. Va., 1979. Bar: N.Y. 1980, U.S. Dist. Ct. (so. dist.) N.Y. 1980, U.S. Ct. Internat. Trade 1985, D.C. 1986, U.S. Dist. Ct. D.C. 1986, U.S. Ct. Appeals (fed. cir.) 2002. Ptnr. Winthrop, Stimson, Putnam & Roberts and Pillsbury Winthrop LLP, NYC & Washington, 1979—2005; ptnr., co-chmn. Internat. Trade practice Pillsbury Winthrop Shaw Pittman, Washington, 2005—. Contbr. articles to profl. jours. Vice chmn & past chmn. Swedish-Am. C. of C.; chmn. trade & investment adv. com. British-Am. Bus. Assn. Mem. ABA (chmn. spl. adv. com. internat. activities, vice chmn. internat. law & practice sect., co-chmn. internat. litigation com.), Assn. of Bar of City of N.Y., DC Bar, Phi Beta Kappa. Office: Pillsbury Winthrop Shaw Pittman 2300 N St NW Washington DC 20037 Office Phone: 202-663-9250. Office Fax: 202-663-8007. Business E-Mail: cwall@pillsburylaw.com.

WALL, CLARENCE VINSON, state legislator; b. Athens, Ga., Oct. 17, 1947; s. Clarence Jacob and Fannie Lucile (Clark) W.; m. Linda Gail Mason, Dec. 6, 1969 (div. 1980); 1 child, Jeffrey Vinson. Grad. high sch., Lawrenceville, Ga., 1965. Rep. Ga. Ho. of Reps., Lawrenceville, 1973-82, 85-96. Staff sgt. Ga. Air N.G., 1967-73. Republican. Baptist. Home: 1609 Braselton Hwy Lawrenceville GA 30043

WALL, DELLA, human resources specialist, manufacturing executive; Various positions SupeRx Drug Stores, Kroger Mfg., 1971—2000; v.p. deferred benefits Kroger Co., Cinn., 2000—01, v.p. compensation and benefits, 2001—03, corp. v.p. human resources, 2003—04, group v.p. human resources, 2004—. Bd. dirs. Profit Sharing Coun. Am. Office: Kroger Co 1014 Vine St Cincinnati OH 45202-1100 Office Phone: 513-762-4000. Office Fax: 513-762-1160.

WALL, FREDERICK THEODORE, retired chemistry professor; b. Chisholm, Minn., Dec. 14, 1912; s. Peter and Fanny Maria (Rauhala) W.; m. Clara Elizabeth Vivian, June 5, 1940; children: Elizabeth Wall Ralston, Jane Vivian Wall. B.Chemistry, U. Minn., 1933, PhD, 1937. Mem. faculty chemistry dept. U. Ill., 1937-64, dean grad. coll., 1955-63; prof., chmn. dept. chemistry U. Calif., Santa Barbara, 1964-66, vice chancellor rsch., 1965-66; vice chancellor grad. studies and research, prof. chemistry U. Calif. at San Diego, 1966-69; exec. dir. Am. Chem. Soc., Washington, 1969-72; prof. chemistry Rice U., Houston, 1972-78. Pres. Assn. Grad. Schs., 1961; trustee Inst. Def. Analyses, 1962-64; mem. governing bd. Nat. Acad. Scis.-NRC, 1963- 67. Author: Chemical Thermodynamics, 1958; editor Jour. Phys. Chemistry, 1965-69. Mem. Am. Chem. Soc. (Pure Chemistry award 1945, dir. 1962-64), Finnish Chem. Soc. (corr.), Am. Acad. Arts and Scis., Nat. Acad. Scis. Achievements include early work on Monte Carlo computer simulation of macromolecular configurations and of basic reaction probabilities. E-mail: ftwall@worldnet.att.net.

WALL, JAMES J., lawyer; b. Rutherfordton, NC; s. James G. and Hazel S. Wall; m. Susan F. Mintz, Jan. 31, 1984; children: Lauren A., Penelope-;children from previous marriage: Victoria, Jane. BA, Wofford Coll., Spartanburg, SC, 1967; JD, U. NC, Chapel Hill, 1973. Ptnr. Cherry and Wall, Wilmington, NC, 1973—79; sr. mng. atty. Legal Aid NC, Wilmington, 1979—. Lt. US Army, 1967—79. Mem.: NC Bar Assn. Democrat. Episcopal. Office: Legal Aid NC 201 S Front St Ste 1002 Wilmington NC 28402

WALL, JAMES MCKENDREE, minister, editor; b. Monroe, Ga., Oct. 27, 1928; s. Louie David and Lida (Day) W.; m. Mary Eleanor Kidder, Sept. 11, 1953; children: David McKendree, Robert Kidder, Richard James. Student, Ga. Inst. Tech., 1945-47; BA, Emory U., 1949, MDiv, 1955, LHD (hon.), 1985; MA, U. Chgo., 1960; LittD (hon.), Ohio No. U., 1969; DHL (hon.), Willamette Coll., 1978; DD (hon.), MacMurray, 1981; DHL (hon.), Coe Coll., 1987; DHL (hon.), Elmhurst Coll., 1999. Ordained to ministry United Meth. Ch., 1954. Staff writer, sports dept. Atlanta Jour., 1948-50; asst. minister East Lake Meth. Ch., Atlanta, 1953; asst. to dean students Emory U., Atlanta, 1954-55; pastor North Ga. Conf. Moreland, Luthersville Meth. Chs., Ga., 1955-57, Bethel United Meth. Ch., Chgo., 1957-59; mng. editor Christian Adv. mag., Park Ridge, Ill., 1959-63, editor, 1963-72, Christian Century mag., Chgo., 1972-99, sr. contbg. editor, 1999—. Author: Church and Cinema, 1971, Three European Directors, 1973, Winning the War, Losing Our Soul, 1991, Hidden Treasures: Searching for God in Modern Culture, 1997; author, editor: Theologians in Transition, 1981, A Century of the Century, 1987, How My Mind Has Changed, 1991. Del. Dem. Nat. Conv., 1972, 76, 80, 92, 96, 2000; mem. Dem. Nat. Com., 1976-80, Dem. State Cen. Com., 1974-86, Pres. Commn. White House Fellowships, 1976-80. Served to 1st lt. USAF, 1950-52. Mem. Alpha Tau Omega, Omicron Delta Kappa, Sigma Delta Chi. Home: 451 S Kenilworth Ave Elmhurst IL 60126-3928 Office: Christian Century 104 S Michigan Ave Ste 700 Chicago IL 60603-5905 E-mail: jimwal165@aol.com.

WALL, JOHN, manufacturing executive; Student, Ga. Inst. Tech., 1969—71; BS in Mech. Engring., MIT, 1975. Rsch. engr., engine lubricants Chevron Rsch. Co., 1978—82, sr. rsch. engr., emissions, 1982—85, unit leader, diesel & aviation fuels rsch., 1985—86; chief engr., heavy-duty projects Cummins, Columbus, Ind., 1986—87, dir., emissions rsch., 1987—88, dir., 94 heavy duty engines, 1988—89, exec. dir., adv. heavy duty engine devel., 1989—91, v.p., adv. heavy duty engine devel., 1991—92, v.p., adv. engring., tech. planning, 1992—95, v.p., rsch. & devel., 1995—2000, v.p., CTO Ind., 2000—. Office: Cummins Box 3005 Columbus IN 47202-3005 *

WALL, KAY, librarian, dean; BA, U. Miss.; MLS, La. State U. Med. libr.; reference libr. U. So. Miss., 1982, univ. libr., 2003—06; dean librs. Clemson U., SC, 2006—. Mem.: Southeastern Libr. Network. Office: Clemson U Libr 4th Fl, Rm 401A Campus Box 343001 Clemson SC 29634-3001 Office Phone: 864-656-5169. Office Fax: 864-656-0758. E-mail: kwall@clemson.edu. *

WALL, KENNETH E., JR., lawyer; b. Beaumont, Tex., Apr. 6, 1944; s. Kenneth E. and W. Geraldine (Peoples) W.; m. Marjorie Lee Hughes, Dec. 21, 1968; children— Barbara, Elizabeth, Kenneth. Grad. Lamar U., 1966, U. Tex.-Austin, 1969. Bar: Tex. 1969, U.S. Supreme Ct. 1979. Asst. city atty., Beaumont, 1969-73, city atty., 1973-84; with firm Olson & Olson, Houston, 1984—; dir. Tex. Mcpl. League Ins. Trust, 1979-84, vice chmn., 1983-84; counsel S.E. Tex. Regional Planning Commn., 1974, 76. Active Boy Scouts Am., Girl Scouts U.S.A. Mem. Nat. Inst. Mcpl. Law Officers (chmn. com. on local govt. pers. 1979-81, 82-84), State Bar Tex., Tex. City Attys. Assn. (pres. 1982-83), Jefferson County Bar Assn. (dir. 1975-77), Houston Bar Assn., Phi Delta Phi. Methodist. Office: 2727 Allen Pkwy Houston TX 77019 Home Phone: 281-359-6280; Office Phone: 713-533-3800. Business E-Mail: kwall@olsonolson.com.

WALL, M. DANNY, finance company executive; BArch, N.D. State U., 1963. Exec. dir. Urban Renewal Agy., Fargo, ND, 1964-71, Salt Lake City Redevel. Agy., 1971-75; dir. legis. Office US Senator Jake Garn, Washington, 1975-78; minority staff dir. Senate Com. Banking, Housing and Urban Affairs, Washington, 1979-80, staff dir., 1980-86, rep. staff dir., 1987; chmn. Fed. Home Loan Bank Bd./Fed. Home Loan Mortgage Corp., Washington, 1987-89; dir. Office Thrift Supervision (formerly Fed. Home Loan Bank Bd.), 1989-90; fin. svcs. cons., 1990—2003; sr. v.p. Dougherty Funding LLC, 1997—2003; chmn, pres. Capmark Bank (formerly GMAC Comml. Mortgage Bank), 2004—. Home Phone: 801-596-0650; Office Phone: 801-567-2686. Business E-Mail: dan_wall@capmark.com.

WALL, ROBERT ANTHONY, JR., lawyer; b. Hartford, Conn., Mar. 3, 1945; s. Robert Anthony and Eileen (Fitzgerald) W.; children: Andrea, Melanie, Victoria, Robert, Natalie. BA, Georgetown U., Washington, 1968; JD, Am. U., Washington, 1973. Bar: Conn. 1974, U.S. Ct. Appeals (D.C. cir.) 1974, U.S. Dist. Ct. Conn. 1974, U.S. Supreme Ct. 1977. Ptnr. Wall, Wall & Frauenhofer, Torrington, Conn., 1974-87; pvt. practice Torrington, 1987—. Mem. State of Conn. Rep. Ctrl. Com., 1976-79. Mem. Conn. Trial Lawyers Assn. (bd. govs. 1984-86), Ct. Washington #67 Foresters of Am. (trustee 1988—). Roman Catholic. Home: 55 Quail Run Torrington CT 06790-2550 Office: 8 Church St Torrington CT 06790-5247 Home Phone: 860-489-6485; Office Phone: 860-496-8383. Fax: 860-496-0128. E-mail: wallgawrych@yahoo.com.

WALL, SIMEON HENINGER, JR., plastic surgeon; b. Madison, Wis., Apr. 8, 1970; m. Holly Casey; children: Trace, Casey. Grad. with honors, U. Tex., Austin; MD, U. Tex., San Antonio, 1996. Cert. Am. Bd. Plastic Surgery, 2002, lic. La., Calif. Intern gen. surgery Stanford U. Med. Ctr., Calif., 1996—97, resident plastic surgery, 1997—99, resident, 1999—2001; active staff mem. Christus Schumpert, Shreveport, La., 2001, Doctors Hosp., Shreveport, 2001; assoc. staff mem. Willis Knighton Med. Ctr., Shreveport, 2001; clin. faculty mem. La. State U. Health Scis. Ctr., Shreveport; plastic surgeon Wall Ctr. Plastic Surgery, Shreveport, 2001—. Del. to La. State Med. Soc. Com. Med. Profl. Liability. Patients have been featured on internat. infomercials, The Discovery Channel, local news and nat. advertising campaigns. Plastic surgeon Interplast. Mem.: Shreveport Med. Soc. (bd. dir.), La. State Med. Soc. (mem. med. specialties com.), La. Soc. Plastic Surgeons (sec./treas.), Am. Soc. Plastic Surgeons, Zedplast (Stanford U. Plastic Surgery Alumni Assn.). Avocations: golf, tennis, guitar, singing, snowboarding, hunting, fishing, duck hunting. Office: Wall Ctr Plastic Surgery 1400 E Bert Kouns Ste 106 Shreveport LA 71105 Office Phone: 318-795-0801. Office Fax: 318-795-9492.

WALL, WILLIAM HERBERT, state coordinator student loan programs; b. St. Augustine, Fla., June 9, 1943; s. Harold C. and Martha D. W.; m. Hallie Josephine Wynne, July 8, 1972; 1 child, Nancy Wynn Wall. BS in Journalism, U. Fla., 1964, MEd, 1965; PhD, U. Ala., 1978. Asst. to v.p. for student affairs U. Fla., Gainesville, 1965-69, fin. aid counselor, 1969-70; asst. dir. fin. aid U. Ala., Tuscaloosa, 1970-78; sr. staff assoc. Ala. Commn. on Higher Edn., Montgomery, 1978-80, asst. dir., 1980-91, dir. grants and scholarships, 1991—2000, assoc. exec. dir., 2000—03; dir. Ala. Student Loan Program, Montgomery, 2004—. Advisor Ala. Indian Affairs Commn., Montgomery, 1989-94. Sec. bd. and chmn. nominating com. Ala. Indian Community Loan Fund, 1989-90; pres. Our Lady Queen of Mercy PTO, 1991—, Endowment Found., 1990-92. Recipient Cert. of Appreciation, Nat. Health Agys., 1987, Dist. IX State Employee of Yr. award Ala. State Employees Assn., 1999, 2000, 03. Mem. Ala. Assn. Student Fin. Aid Adminstrs. (pres. 1986-87, M. Cecil Padgett award 1981, Disting. Pres. award 1987), So. Assn. Student Fin. Aid Adminstrs. (conf. chmn. 1989, 90, exec. bd. 1981-87, recipient Disting. Svc. award 1990, Spl. Recognition plaque 1989, 80, citation 1984, 91, hon. life mem. 2004), Nat. Assn. Student Fin. Aid Adminstrs. (mem. editl. bd. jour. 1995—), Nat. Assn. State Scholarship and Grant Progs., Civitan (dist. tng. coord. 1985, lt. gov. 1987, edn. officer 1988, sec.-treas. 1989, 92, Disting. Svc. award 1988, Govs. award 1989, club honor key 1994, dist. honor key 1996, internat. honor key 2000, internat. grants and scholarships com. 1999-2002, 05-, chmn. 2002, 07), Montgomery Quarterback Club (treas. 1999-2004, mem. exec. bd. 1999-, mem. found. bd. 1999-). Episcopalian. Avocation: classical music.

Home: 1641 Prairie Ln Montgomery AL 36117-3427 Office: Student Loan Program 100 North Union St Ste 308 Montgomery AL 36104 Office Phone: 334-265-9720.

WALLACE, ALEXANDRA, broadcast executive, television producer; married; 2 children. BA, Columbia U., 1988. Assoc. prodr. NBC News, 1990—96; prodr. CBS Evening News with Dan Rather, 1996—98; sr. prodr. CBS This Morning, The Early Show, CBS News, sr. broadcast prodr.; sr. prodr. NBC News Today, 2005—06; exec. prodr. NBC News Weekend Today, 2006—07, NBC Nightly News with Brian Williams, 2007—; v.p. NBC News, 2006—. Office: NBC 30 Rockefeller Plz New York NY 10112 Office Phone: 212-664-4971. Office Fax: 212-664-6045. *

WALLACE, ANDERSON, JR., lawyer, educator; b. Cleve., Sept. 24, 1939; s. Anderson and Agatha Lee (Culpepper) Wallace; m. Kristine Lee Gough; children: Anderson III, Whitney, Nicole Belcher. BA, George Washington U., 1962, JD, 1964, LLM, 1966. Bar: Tex. 68, U.S. Dist. Ct. (no. dist.) Tex. 68, U.S. Ct. Claims 68, U.S. Tax Ct. 68, U.S. Ct. Appeals (5th cir.) 68, U.S. Supreme Ct. 71, U.S. Ct. Appeals (11th cir.) 81. Program mgmt. asst. NASA, Washington, 1962—64; atty. U.S. Dept. Treasury, Washington, 1964—66; tax atty. Price Waterhouse & Co., Atlanta, 1966—67; tax ptnr. Jackson, Walker, Winstead, Cantwell & Miller, Dallas, 1967—84; dir. in charge tax dept. Baker, Mills & Glast, P.C., Dallas, 1984—93; pres. Anderson Wallace, Jr., P.C., Attys., Dallas, 1993—. Instr. Sch. Law So. Meth. U. Trustee S.W. Mus. Sci. and Tech., Dallas, 1974—, Girls Found. Dallas Inc.; chmn. Inst. on Employee Benefits, Southwestern Found., 1976. Mem.: ABA. Office: 3328 Purdue Ave Ste 100 Dallas TX 75225-7635 Home Phone: 214-691-1499; Office Phone: 214-739-1714. E-mail: awallacejr@sbcglobal.net.

WALLACE, ANTHONY FRANCIS CLARKE, anthropologist, educator; b. Toronto, Ont., Can., Apr. 15, 1923; s. Paul A.W. and Dorothy Eleanor (Clarke) W.; m. Betty Louise Shillott, Dec. 1, 1942; children: Anthony, Daniel, Sun Ai, Samuel, Cheryl, Joseph. BA, U. Pa., 1948, MA, 1949, PhD, 1950; L.H.D. (hon.), U. Chgo., 1983. Instr. anthropology Bryn Mawr Coll., 1948-50; asst. instr. anthropology U. Pa., research sec. Behavioral Research Council, 1951-55; research asst. prof. U. Pa., 1952-55, vis. assoc. prof., 1955-61, prof., 1961—, chmn. dept., 1961-71, Geraldine R. Segal prof. Am. social thought, 1980-83, Univ. prof. anthropology, 1983-88, prof. emeritus, 1988—. Sr. rsch. assoc. anthropology Eastern Pa. Psychiat. Inst., 1955-60, dir. clin. research, 1960-61, med. research scientist, III, 1961-80; mem. tech. adv. com. N.J. Psychiat. Inst., 1958; cons. disaster studies NRC, 1956-57; cons. Phila. Housing Authority, 1952; mem. rsch. adv. com. Commonwealth Mental Health Research Found., 1960-61, U.S. Office Edn., 1965-68; mem. behavioral scis. study sect. NIMH, 1964-68; mem. NRC, 1963-66; mem. various adv. coms. NIMH, 1962—; mem. social sci. adv. council NSF, 1969-72 Author: King of the Delawares: Teedyuscung, 1700-1763, 1949, Culture and Personality, 1961, rev. edit., 1970, Religion: An Anthropological View, 1966, Death and Rebirth of the Seneca, 1970, Rockdale: The Growth of an American Village in the Early Industrial Revolution, 1978, new. edit., 2004, Social Context of Innovation, 1983, new ed., 2003. St. Clair, 1987, The Long, Bitter Trail, 1993, Jefferson and the Indians, 1999, Revitalizations and Mazeways, 2003, Modernity and Mind, 2005 Bd. mgrs. Funds. Fund for Research in Psychiatry, 1969-71. Served AUS, 1942-45. Recipient Bancroft prize in Am. History, 1979, Dexter prize in History of Technology, 1989, Caroline Bancroft prize in history, 2000; Guggenheim fellow, 1978-79 Fellow Am. Anthrop. Assn. (pres. 1971-72),; mem. Nat. Acad. Scis., Am. Philos. Soc., Am. Acad. Arts and Scis. Office: Univ Pa Dept Anthropology 33rd and Spruce Sts Philadelphia PA 19104 Home: 1922 Upper Mountain Rd Lewiston NY 14092-9707

WALLACE, ARDELIA LESLENE, elementary school educator; d. Robert J. and Billie Loyce Turner; m. Kenneth Carson Wallace, Oct. 26, 1946; 1 child, Carson Wayne. BS, SW Tex. State U., San Marcos, Tex. Cert. Tchr. State Bd. of Educators, Tex., 1997. Fifth grade tchr. Dripping Springs ISD, Dripping Springs, Tex., 1999—. Mem.: ATPE. D-Conservative. Achievements include Innovative Teaching Award for 2004. Avocations: reading, gardening. Home Phone: 512-288-3382; Office Phone: 512-858-4903 207.

WALLACE, ARTHUR, JR., retired college dean; b. Muskogee, Okla., June 12, 1939; s. Arthur and Edna (Collins) W.; m. Claudina Young, Oct. 4, 1969 (div. Nov. 2002); children: Dwayne, Jon, Charles. BS, Langston U., 1960; MS, Okla. State U., Stillwater, 1962, PhD, 1964. Dir. commodity rsch. Gen. Foods Corp., White Plains, NY, 1964-67; v.p., sr. economist Merrill Lynch & Lionel D. Edie & Co., NYC, 1968-71; econ. cons. Wall St. fin. instns. Group IV Econs., NYC, 1972-76; mgr. U.S. and Can. econs. Internat. Paper Co., NYC, 1976-78, chief economist, 1978-82, dir. corp. affairs and policy analysis, 1982-83, corp. sec. Purchase, NY, 1983-87, v.p., corp. sec., 1987-93; pres. Internat. Paper Co. Found., 1983-93; dean coll. bus. San Francisco State U., 1993-98; ret.

WALLACE, BARBARA BROOKS, writer; b. Soochow, China, Dec. 3, 1922; arrived in U.S., 1938; d. Otis Frank and Nicia Brooks; m. James Wallace, Jr., Feb. 27, 1954; 1 child, James V. BA, UCLA, 1945. Script sec. Foote, Cone & Belding, Hollywood, Calif., 1946-49; tchr. Wright MacMahon Secretarial Sch., Beverly Hills, Calif., 1949-50; head fund drive Commerce and Industry Divsn. ARC, San Francisco, 1950-52. Author: Claudia, 1969 (Nat. League Am. Pen Women Juvenile Book award, 1970), Andrew the Big Deal, 1970, The Trouble with Miss Switch, 1971, Victoria, 1973, Can Do, Missy Charlie, 1974, The Secret Summer of L.E.B. (Nat. League Am. Pen Women Juvenile Book award, 1974), Julia and the Third Bad Thing, 1975, Palmer Patch, 1976, Hawkins, 1977, Peppermints in the Parlor, 1980 (William Allen White award, 1983), The Contest Kid Strikes Again, 1980, Hawkins and the Soccer Solution, 1981, Miss Switch to the Rescue, 1981, Hello, Claudia, 1982, Claudia and Duffy, 1982, The Barrel in the Basement, 1985, Argyle, 1987, 1992, Perfect Acres, Inc., 1988, The Twin in the Tavern, 1993 (Edgar award Mystery Writers Am., 1994), Cousins in the Castle, 1996, Sparrows in the Scullery, 1997 (Edgar award, 1998), Ghosts in the Gallery, 2000, Secret in St. Something, 2001, Miss Switch Online, 2002, The Perils of Peppermints, 2003. Mem.: Authors Guild, Children's Book Guild of Washington, Alpha Phi. Episcopalian. Home: 6251 Old Dominion Dr Apt 436 Mc Lean VA 22101-4810 E-mail: bbwallace@cox.net.

WALLACE, BEN, professional basketball player; b. White Hall, Ala., Sept. 10, 1974; m. Chanda Wallace. Student, Va. Union U., Richmond, 1996. Forward-ctr. Washington Bullets, 1996—99, Orlando Magic, Fla., 1999—2000, Detroit Pistons, 2000—06, Chgo. Bulls, 2006—. Mem. USA Team. Named NBA Defensive Player of Yr., 2002, 2003, 2005, 2006; named to NBA All-Defensive Team, 2002, 2003, 2004, 2005. Achievements include being a member of NBA Champion Detroit Pistons, 2004. Office: Chgo Bulls United Ctr 1901 W Madison St Chicago IL 60612-2459 *

WALLACE, BOB (ROBERT EUGENE WALLACE JR.), lawyer; b. NYC, Mar. 1, 1956; s. Robert E. Wallace Sr. and Vivian A. (High) Wallace; m. Julia Wallace; children: Grant, Eric. BA in Am. Studies, Yale U., 1978; JD, Georgetown U., 1981. Bar: Mo. 1981, Pa. 1991. Legal intern NFL, NYC, 1980; assoc. Guilfoil, Petzall & Shoemake, St. Louis, 1981—91; asst. to the pres., gen. counsel Phila. Eagles, 1991—94; exec. v.p., gen. counsel St. Louis Rams, 1995—. Adj. prof. law St. Louis U., 1986-88. Bd. govs. downtown YMCA, St. Louis, 1985-88; bd. dirs. Payback, Inc., Urban League of Greater St.Louis, Operation Excel, Amateur Athletic Assn., St. Louis, 1985-88, Sports Lawyers Assn., St Louis Sports Commn. Recipient Dist. Service award St. Louis Pub. Schs., St. Louis, 1985-88. Mem. ABA (sports lawyer div.), Met. Bar Assn. (exec. com. young lawyers sect., chmn. media com. 1983-86). Democrat. Avocations: sports, reading, bike riding. Office: St Louis Rams One Rams Way Earth City MO 63045 Office Phone: 314-982-7265. Business E-Mail: bwallace@rams.nfl.com.

WALLACE, CANDY, Culinary Association Administrator; Exec. dir. Am. Personal & Pvt. Chef Inst. & Assn., San Diego. Co-author: The Professional Personal Chef: The Business of Doing Business as a Personal Chef, 2007. Mem.: Internat. Assn. Culinary Professionals (Businessperson/Entrepreneur of Yr., Award of Excellence 2003), Women Chefs & Restaurants, Am. Culinary Fedn. (bd. mem. San Diego chpt.), Les Dames d'Escoffier Internat. (bd. mem. San Diego chpt.). Office: Am Personal & Pvt Chef Assn 4572 Delaware St San Diego CA 92116 Business E-Mail: info@personalchef.com. *

WALLACE, CHRIS, professional sports team executive; m. Debby Wallace; 1 child, Truman. Founder Blue Ribbon Coll. Basketball Yearbook, 1981; draft cons. US Basketball League; with NY Knicks, LA Clippers, Denver Nuggets, Portland Trail Blazers; scout Miami Heat, dir. player pers.; gen. mgr. Boston Celtics, 1997—2007; v.p. basketball ops., gen. mgr. Memphis Grizzlies, 2007—. Mem. NBA Basketball Without Borders Africa Camp, Johannesburg. Named one of Most Influential Members of Coll. Basketball Media, Sports Illus., 1991. Office: Memphis Grizzlies 191 Beale St Memphis TN 38103 *

WALLACE, CHRISTOPHER, broadcast television correspondent; b. Chgo., Oct. 12, 1947; s. Mike and Norma (Kaphan) W.; m. Lorraine Smothers, Oct. 4, 1997; children: Peter Farrell, Margaret Coleman, Andrew Farrell, Catherine Farrell, Sarah Smothers, Remick Smothers. BA, Harvard U., 1969. Nat. reporter Boston Globe, 1969-73; polit. reporter Sta. WBBM-TV, Chgo., 1973-75; investigative reporter Sta. WNBC-TV, NYC, 1975-78; polit. reporter NBC News, Washington, 1978-81; anchor Today Show, 1982, NBC Nightly News (Sunday), 1982—84, 1986—87; chief corr. White House, 1982-89; anchor Meet the Press, 1987—88; sr. corr. Prime Time Live, ABC-TV, 1989-98; substitute host Nightline, ABC-TV; chief corr. 20/20 ABC-TV, Washington, 1998—2003; host FOX News Sunday with Chris Wallace, FNS, FOX News Channel, 2003—. Covered presdl. campaigns and Democratic and Republican conventions, 1980, 84, 88. Reporter, writer: documentaries NBC The Migrants, 1980, Protection For Sale: The Insurance Industry, 1981, Nancy Reagan, The First Lady, 1985. Recipient Peabody award U. Ga., 1978, Emmy award NATAS, 1981, 90, award Overseas Press Club, 1981, Humanitas Found. award, 1981, Investigative Reporters and Editors award U. Mo. Sch. Journalism, 1990, 95, George Polk award, 1992, Columbia-DuPont award, 1997. Office: FOX News Channel 1211 Avenue of the Americas New York NY 10036

WALLACE, CURTIS WILBERN, JR., music director, organist; b. Roanoke, Va., Apr. 30, 1962; s. Curtis Wilbern and Shirley Jean Wallace. BA in Sacred Music, Roanoke Coll., 1984. Organist Midland Bapt. Ch., Vinton, Va., 1977—80; music dir. Our Lady Perpetual Help Cath. Ch., Salem, Va., 1980—85; dir. music ministries Holy Redeemer Cath. Ch., Coll. Park, Md., 1985—87; organist, choir master St. Mark's Luth. Ch., Roanoke, 1988—90; dir. music St. Margaret Mary Cath. Ch., Winter Park, Fla., 1990—. Dir. music ministries divsn. Nat. Assn. Pastoral Musicians. Prodr.: (St. Margaret Mary Choir CD) Sounds of Christmas, 2002, Taizé Prayer, 2003, Jubilate Deo, 2005. Mem.: Am. Guild Organists. Republican. Roman Catholic. Achievements include leading St. Margaret Mary Catholic Church pilgrimage to Rome, Italy in November 2003. Avocations: aquarium fish, travel. Home: 648 Tuskawilla Point Lane Winter Springs FL 32708-4902 Office: St Margaret Mary Catholic Ch 526 Park Ave N Winter Park FL 32789-3208 Home Phone: 407-696-7290; Office Phone: 407-628-2346. Office Fax: 407-647-4492. Personal E-mail: curtiswallace@cfl.rr.com. Business E-Mail: curtis@stmargaretmary.org.

WALLACE, DANNY P., library and information scientist, educator; b. Monett, Colo., Oct. 23, 1950; s. Harold and Willa Wallace; m. Connie J. Van Fleet; children: Robyn Solomon, Elizabeth. BS in Edn., Mo. State U., 1973; MA in Libr. Sci., U. Mo., Columbia, 1977; PhD, U. Ill., Urbana-Champaign, 1984. Assoc. dean, prof. La. State U., Baton Rouge, 1985—95; dir., prof. Kent State U., Ohio, 1996—2000; dir. U. Okla., Norman, 2000—05, prof., 2000—. Editor: Reference and User Svcs. Quar., 2000—06; author: (book) Library Evaluation: A Casebook and Can-Do Guide. Mem.: ALA (com. accreditation 2003—), Okla. Libr. Assn. (chair-elect libr. edn. divsn. 2006—), Am. Soc. Info. Sci. and Tech. (mem. editl. bd. jour., Doctoral Dissertation scholar 1984), Assn. Libr. and Info. Sci. Edn. (bd. dirs. 1998—2001, 2003—04, Doctoral Students' Dissertation award 1986, Tchg. Excellence award 2000), Reference and User Svcs. Assn. (bd. dirs. 1991—2006). Office: Univ Oklahoma 401 W Brooks Rm 120 Norman OK 73019 Office Phone: 405-325-3921.

WALLACE, DAVID ERIC, craftsman, retired military officer; b. Portland, Maine, Dec. 7, 1949; s. Laurence Elbert and Carleen Casparius Wallace; m. Katherine Gorham, Dec. 30, 1985; children: Nicholas Gorham, Andrew Pearce Woodin, Nathan Alec Woodin. AS, C.C. of the Air Force, Keesler AFB, 1977; BS, U. Nebr., Omaha, 1981; MS in Bus. Adminstrn., Thomas Coll., Waterville, Maine, 1991. Cryptologic supt. USAF, San Antonio, 1970—91; owner, CEO David E. Wallace & Co. LLC Pipe Organ Builders, Gorham, Maine, 1982—. Adv. trustee and curator Friends of the Kotzschmar Organ, Inc., Portland, 1981—98; dean Portland chpt. Am. Guild of Organists, 1988—89; nat. chmn. Organ Hist. Soc. Ann. Conv., Lewiston, Maine, 1992; pres. Gorham Cmty. Chorus, 2005—06. Author: articles in profl. jours. Mem. fund raising bd. and bldg. com. Citizens for Auditorium Restoration, Portland, 1990—97; mem. ho. and pub. safety mgmt. Portland Symphony Orch., 1988—92. Chief master sgt. (e-9) USAF, 1970—91, San Antonio. Decorated Meritorious Svc. Medal with 3 oak leaf clusters USAF, Air Medal with 5 oak leaf clusters, Outstanding Mobilization Augmentee of Yr. Mem.: Air Force Assn., Organ Hist. Soc., Am. Guild of Organists (dean 1988—89), Am. Inst. Organ Builders. Avocations: sign language, figure skating, kayaking, hiking, travel. Home and Office: David E Wallace & Co LLC Pipe Organs 147 County Rd Gorham ME 04038-1916 Office Phone: 207-839-7621. Office Fax: 207-839-6873. E-mail: deworgans@aol.com.

WALLACE, DAVID FOSTER, writer; b. Ithaca, NY, Feb. 21, 1962; s. James Donald and Sally Foster Wallace. BA Summa Cum Laude in English and Phil., Amherst Coll., 1985; MFA in Creative Writing, U. Ariz., 1987. Eng. Prof. Ill. State U., 1992—2000; Roy E. Disney Prof. Creative Writing Pomona Coll., 2002—. Author: (novels) The Broom of the System, 1998, Infinite Jest, 1996, (books of short fiction) Brief Interviews with Hideous Men, 1999, Oblivion, 2004, (nonfiction) A Supposedly Fun Thing I'll Never Do Again, 1997, Up Simba!, 2000, Everything and More, 2003, Consider the Lobster, 2005; contbr. short fiction to numerous mags. Grantee MacArthur Found. Genius Grant, 1997. Office: Pomona Coll Dept Eng 140 W 6th St Claremont CA 91711-6335 *

WALLACE, DAVID K., musician, composer; b. Slidell, La. s. Charles B. and Marilyn L. Wallace; m. Lauri C. Galbreath, Dec. 31, 2005. MusB, U. Houston, 1992; MusM, Mannes Coll. Music, NYC, 1994; DMA, Juilliard Sch., NYC, 1999. Tchg. artist Lincoln Ctr. Inst., NYC, 1997—2002; sr. tchg. artist NY Philharmonic, NYC, 1997—; violinist The Doc Wallace Trio, NYC, 1999—; grad. faculty Juilliard Sch., 2000—; violist, composer Music Unlocked!, NYC, 2005—. Faculty Am. Symphony Orch. League, 1998—; viola, violin faculty Mark O'Connor Strings Conf., San Diego, 2002—; lead tchr. artist symposia NY Philharmonic Asia Tour, 2006; soloist and concert performer NPR, ABC-TV, McGraw Hill Young Artist's Showcase, WQXR Radio, Live from the Lamb's, Chamber Music Soc. Lincoln Ctr.; NY Viola Soc.; cons. Tanglewood Music Festival, Chamber Music Am., Meet the Composer, Young Audiences, Inc., NY Philharmonic, LA Philharmonic, Pitts. Symphony, Va. Symphony, Manhattan Sch. Music, Eastman Sch. Music, Am. Symphony Orch. League. Contbg. editor: The New York Philharmonic's Pathways to the Orchestra, 2002; author: Reaching Out: A Musician's Guide to Interactive Performance, 2007; composer: William Blake Rhapsody, 2006 (CAP award, 2006); performer: (NY premiere) Viola Concerto by Stefano Gervasoni. Performer Conservation Internat. 10th Ann. Benefit, NYC, 2006; bd. mem. The Lamb's Ch., NYC, 1999—. Named C. Halee and David Baldwin Tchg. Artist chair, NY Philharmonic; recipient J. Richard French prize, Juilliard Sch., 1999, Mannes Coll. Performance award, 1994, Robert Sherman award, McGraw-Hill Cos., 2002. Mem.: ASCAP (ASCAPLUS award 2006), Am. Music Ctr., Am. Strings Tchrs. Assn. (alternative strings com. 2004, 2006—07). Independent. Avocations: electronics, poetry, bookbinding, mountain climbing, sports.

WALLACE, DEE, actress; b. Kansas City, Mo., Dec. 14, 1948; d. Robert Stanley and Maxine (Nichols) Bowers; m. Christopher Stone, June 28, 1980 (dec.); m. Skip Belyea; 1 child, Gabrielle. BA, U. Kans., 1971. Actress feature films The Christmas Visitor, Secret Admirer, Cujo, E.T., Jimmy the Kid, The Howling, 10; actress ABC movies of the week Eminent Domain, Hostage Flight, A Whale for a Killing; actress CBS movies of the week An Enemy Among Us, Sin of Innocence, The Sky is No Limit, Happy, Surprise, Surprise, The Five of Me, Young Love, First Love; actress NBC movies of the week Wait Til Your Mother Gets Home, Child Bride of Short Creek, Skeezer; actress CBS After School Special Dad's Out of a Job; actress ABC After School Special Run Don't Walk; actress CBS series Police Story, Together We Stand/Nothing is Easy, Lou Grant; actress stage prodns. including Annie Get Your Gun, Oklahoma, My Fair Lady, Applause, Butterflies are Free, Middle of the Night. Spkr. in field; mgr. DWS Acting Studio, Burbank, Calif. Appeared in films including Nevada, 1997, Mutual Needs, 1997, Black Circle Boys, 1997, Bad As I Wanna Be: The Dennis Rodman Story, 1998, Flamingo Dreams, 1998, To Love, Honor and Betray, 1999, Invisible Mom II, 1999, Pirates of the Plain, 1999, Out of the Black, A Month of Sundays, Dead Canaries, Spice of Life, Total Rex, Abominable, Expiration Date, Rob Zombie's Halloween, 2007, others; appeared on TV shows Cold Case, 2005, Crossing Jordan, 2005, Sons and Daughters, 2005, Without a Trace, Close to Home, Bones. Fundraiser Actors and Others for Animals, L.A., 1980—, Amanda Found., L.A., 1986, 87; co-host, fundraiser Children's Hospital Telethon, Sta. KCET, L.A., 1985—; spokesperson Nat. Assn. of Children of Alcoholics, 1987—. Mem. Screen Actors Guild, Actors Equity, AFTRA. Methodist. Avocations: dance, singing. Office Phone: 818-876-0386. E-mail: totoent@aol.com.

WALLACE, DON, JR., law educator; b. Vienna, Apr. 23, 1932; s. Don and Julie (Baer) Wallace; m. Daphne Mary Wickham, 1963; children: Alexandra Creed, Sarah Anne, Benjamin James. BA with high honors, Yale U., 1953; LL.B. cum laude, Harvard U., 1957. Bar: N.Y. 1957, D.C. 1978, U.S. Supreme Ct. Assoc. Fleischmann, Jaeckle, Stokes and Hitchcock, NYC, 1959-60, Paul, Weiss, Rifkind, Wharton and Garrison, NYC, 1957-58, 60-62; rsch. asst. to faculty mem. Harvard Law Sch., Cambridge, Mass., 1958-59; regional legal adv. Middle East AID, Dept. State, 1963-65, dep. asst. gen. counsel, 1965-66; assoc. prof. law Georgetown U. Law Ctr., Washington, 1966-71, prof., 1971—2002; chmn. Internat. Law Inst., Washington, 1969—; adj./emeritus prof. Georgetown U. Law Ctr., Washington, 2002—. Cons. AID, 1966-70, UN Centre on Transnat. Corps., 1977-78; counsel Wald, Harkrader & Ross, Washington, 1978-86, Arnold & Porter, 1986-89, Shearman & Sterling, 1989-98, Morgan, Lewis & Bockius, 1998—; legal advisor State of Qatar, 1979-82; chmn. adv. com. on tech. and world trade Office of Tech. Assessment, U.S. Congress, 1976-79; mem. Sec. of State's Adv. Com. on Pvt. Internat. Law, 1979—; mem. U.S. del. UN Conf. on State Succession in Respect of Treaties, Vienna, 1978; mem. U.S. del. UN Commn. Internat. Trade Law, Vienna, 1981—; vis. com. Harvard Law Sch., 1996-97; mem. panel of judges World Trade Orgn., 1996-2000. Co-author: Internat. Business and Economics: Law and Policy; Investor-State Arbitration; author: International Regulation of Multinational Corporations, 1976, Dear Mr. President: The Needed Turnaround in America's International Economic Affairs, 1984; editor: A Lawyer's Guide to International Business Transactions, 1977-87; contbr. numerous articles on internat. trade and law to profl. jours., books revs. on law and bus. to profl. jours. Coord. Anne Arundel County (Md.) Dem. Nat. Com., 1972-79; sec. Chesapeake Found., 1972-73; nat. chmn. Law Profs. for Bush and Quayle, 1988, 92, for Dole and Kemp, 1996; v.p., bd. govs. UNIDROIT Found., Rome, 1997—. Fulbright fellow, 1967, Eisenhower Exch. fellow, 1976. Mem. ABA (chmn. sect. internat. law 1978-79, ho of dels. 1982-84, mem. adv. bd. Ctrl. European and Eurasian Law Initiative), Am. Law Inst., Repub. Nat. Lawyers Assn., Internat. Law Assn., Shaybani Soc. of Internat. Law (v.p.), Cosmos Club, Met. Club, Acad. Coun. European Ctr. Peace and Devel. (Belgrade). Republican. Home: 2800 35th St NW Washington DC 20007-1411 Office: Georgetown U Law Ctr 600 New Jersey Ave NW Washington DC 20001-2022 E-mail: wallace@ili.org.

WALLACE, DONALD JOHN, III, rancher; b. Houston, May 17, 1941; s. D. J., Jr. and Doris Jill (Gano) Wallace; m. Patricia Anne McShane, Sept. 3, 1964 (div. 1984); children: Donald John IV, Megan; m. Nena Jo Isenhower, June 1, 1985 (div. 1989); 1 child, Andrew; m. Kay Fulkerson, May 31, 1997. BBA in Mktg., Texas A&M U., 1963. Regional sales dir. Orkin Exterminating Co., Inc., Dallas, 1977-79, br. mgr., 1979-80, dist. mgr., 1980-83, comml. region mgr., 1983-85, regional sales dir., 1985-86; owner Omega Telex, Dallas, 1986-88; rancher Valley View, Tex., 1988—. Leader Big Mineral Trail Riders Club, Boy Scouts Am.; pres. Frank Buck Zool. Soc.; mem. Tex. Structural Pest Control Bd., Austin, 1983—84; bd. dirs. Frank Buck Zoo, Gainesville, Tex., 1997—98, North Tex. Med. Found., Gainesville Econ. Devel. Corp., North Tex. Med. Ctr. Republican. Methodist. Avocations: hiking, fishing, hunting, skiing, horseback riding. Home: 1034 Trails End Valley View TX 76272-6114 Personal E-mail: donandkay@cooke.net.

WALLACE, DOUGLAS C., geneticist, educator; PhD in Microbiology and Human Genetics, Yale U. Prof., dir. Ctr. for Molecular Medicine Emory U. Sch. Medicine, Atlanta, 1990—2002; Donald Bren prof. biol. scis. and molecular medicine U. Calif., Irvine, 2002—; dir. Ctr. for Molecular, Mitochondrial Medicine and Genetics, U. Calif., 2002—. Author of more than 270 rsch. papers published in various jours. including Cell, Science, Nature, Procs. of Nat. Acad. of Scis., New Eng. Jour. Medicine. Co-recipient Passano award (with Guiseppi Attardi); recipient Rsch. award for Medical Rsch. in Alzheimer's Disease, Metropolitan Life Found., Pasarow Found. award in Cardiovascular Disease. Fellow: Am. Acad. Arts and Scis.; mem.: NAS, Am. Soc. Human Genetics (William Allan award 1994). Business E-Mail: dwallace@uci.edu.

WALLACE, EDWARD CORBETT, lawyer; s. Edward Corbett Wallace; m. Pamela S. Falk; children: Richard Falk-Wallace, William Gerety Falk-Wallace. BA cum laude, Columbia U., 1971, MA, 1973; JD, Fordham U., 1977. Bar: NY 1977, US Dist. Ct. (so. dist.) NY 1980, US Ct. Appeals (2d cir.) 1994. Chief of staff to Pres. City Coun., NYC, 1983-86; v.p. Boston Properties, NYC, 1986-91; counsel Lankenau, Kovner & Kurtz, NYC, 1991-92; ptnr. Phillips, Nizer, Benjamin, Krim & Ballon, NYC, 1992; now shareholder, govt. and adminstrv. law dept. Greenberg Traurig, LLP, NYC. Councilmem.-at-large, NNY, 1981-83; mem. law com. Mcpl.

Arts Soc. Office: Greenberg Traurig LLP MetLife Bldg 200 Park Ave New York NY 10166 Office Phone: 212-801-9200. Office Fax: 212-801-6400. Business E-Mail: wallacee@gtlaw.com.

WALLACE, EMILY MITCHELL, writer, editor, educator; d. George Lafayette and Prewitt Carlisle (Evans) Mitchell; m. Gregory Merrill Harvey, June 14, 1969; m. Robert Arthur Wallace, June 8, 1954 (div. 1964). BA, Southwest Mo. State, 1958; MA, Bryn Mawr Coll., 1959, PhD, 1965. Tutor, history and lit. Curtis Inst. of Music, Phila., 1957—58, chair English dept., 1976—78, 1979—83; tchr. lit. Shipley Sch., Bryn Mawr, Pa., 1959—60; instr. to asst. prof. U. Pa., Phila., 1962—67; vis. asst. prof. Swarthmore Coll., Pa., 1967—68, 1969—70; leader interdisciplinary seminar Yale U., New Haven, 1979; rsch. assoc. Ctr. Visual Culture Bryn Mawr Coll., 2003—. Mem. sponsoring com. Marianne Moore Fund for Poetry, Bryn Mawr Coll., 1975—; mem. adv. com. Rosenbach Mus. and Libr., Phila., 1980—; curriculum cons. Cooper Union of Art, Sci. and Tech., NY, 1984—85; interdisciplinary rsch. scholar in poetry and visual arts; writer photographic essays and multimedia lectrs. scholarly and acad. audiences, double-screen lectrs. confs. and symposia univs. and mus. Author: (book) A Bibliography of William Carlos Williams, 1969; guest editor (periodical) W.C. Williams Review, Centennial Issue, 1983, PAIDEUMA (Spcl. James Laughlin Vol.), 2002; author: (photo essay) Youthful Days and Costly Hours: The Education of Ol' Ez and Billy Williams at Penn, U. Pa. Conf. Papers, 1983, Athena's Owls: The Education of Marianne Moore and Hilda Doolittle, Bryn Mawr '09 in Poesis, 1985, Some Friends of Ezra Pound in the Yale Rev., 1986, Saffron Honey: A Love Song by William Carlos Williams, in The Idea and The Thing in Modernist American Poetry, 2001, Why Not Spirits?-The Universe is Alive, in Ezra Pound and China, 2003. Mem. bd. dirs. Am. Found., Bok Tower, Fla., 1976—86; shareholder The Libr. Co., Phila., 1981—; lifetime mem. Friends of the Bryn Mawr Coll. Libr., Pa., 1996—; mem. Yale Libr. Assocs., Franklin Inn., Phila. Fellow, AAUW, 1968—69; Workman Traveling fellowship, Bryn Mawr Coll., Eng., France, Italy, 1961—62, Inaugural Beinecke fellow, Yale U., 1987, Everett Helm Vis. fellow, Lilly Libr., Ind. U., 2003. Mem.: Modern Lang. Assn., Harvard Humanities Ctr. Faculty Arts and Scis., Conn. Acad. Arts and Sci., Assn. Lit. Scholars and Critics, Emily Dickinson Soc., H.D. Soc., Ezra Pound Soc., William Carlos Williams Soc. (first pres.), Marianne Moore Soc., Wallace Stevens Soc., Henry James Soc., Ernest Hemingway Soc., Merion Cricket Club. Democrat. Avocations: chess, music, travel, gardening, tennis. Home: 1939 Panama St Philadelphia PA 19103-6609 Office Phone: 610-718-0503. Personal E-mail: emwallace@aol.com.

WALLACE, F. BLAKE, retired aerospace transportation executive, retired mechanical engineer; b. Phoenix, Jan. 10, 1933; BMechE, Calif. Inst. Tech., 1955; MS in Engring., Ariz. State U., 1963, PhD in Engring., 1967. Preliminary design engr. Pratt & Whitney, East Hartford, Conn., 1955-59; chief engr. advanced tech. Garrett Corp., Phoenix, 1959-80; mgr. advanced plans and programs Aircraft Engine Group GE, Evendale, Ohio, 1981-83; gen. mgr. Allison div. GM, Indpls., 1983-93, v.p., 1987-93; chmn. & CEO Allison Engine Co., Indpls., 1993-95; ret., 1995. Author numerous tech. papers. Fellow AIAA (chmn. air breathing propulsion tech. com. 1977-78, Air Breathing Propulsion award 1991), U.S. Advanced Ceramic Assn. (chmn. 1987-89).

WALLACE, FRANKLIN SHERWOOD, lawyer, director; b. Bklyn., Nov. 24, 1927; s. Abraham Charles and Jennie (Etkin) Wolowitz; m. Eleanor Ruth Pope, Aug. 23, 1953; children: Julia Diane, Charles Andrew. Student, U. Wis., 1943-45; BS cum laude, U.S. Mcht. Marine Acad., 1950; LLB, JD, U. Mich., 1953. Bar: Ill. 1954. Practice law, Rock Island, Ill.; ptnr. Winstein, Kavensky & Wallace. Asst. state's atty. Rock Island County, 1967-68; local counsel UAW at John Deere-J.I. Case Plants; boxing commr. State of Ill., 2005 Former bd. dirs. Tri City Jewish Ctr.; former trustee United Jewish Charities of Quad Cities; former bd. dirs. Blackhawk Coll. Found. Mem. ABA, Ill. Bar Assn. (chmn. jud. adv. polls com. 1979-84), Rock Island County Bar Assn., Am. Trial Lawyers Assn., Ill. Trial Lawyers Assn., Nat. Assn. Criminal Def. Lawyers, Ill. Appellate Lawyers Assn., Am. Judicature Soc., Blackhawk Coll. Found, Ill. State Boxing Bd. Commn. Democrat. Jewish. Home: 36571 Tallowood Dr Palm Desert CA 92211 also: 3409 20th St Rock Island IL 61201 Office Phone: 309-794-1515. Personal E-mail: fnewallace@aol.com.

WALLACE, GLADYS BALDWIN, librarian; b. Macon, Ga., June 5, 1923; d. Carter Shepherd and Dorothy (Richard) Baldwin; m. Hugh Loring Wallace Jr., Oct. 14, 1941 (dec. Sept. 1968); children: Dorothy, Hugh Loring III. BS in Edn., Oglethorpe U., 1961; MLS, Emory U., 1966; EdS, Ga. State U., 1980. Libr. pub. elem. schs., Atlanta, 1956-66; libr. Northside HS, 1966-87, Episc. Cathedral St. Philip. Author: The Time of My Life, 1994, Just a Moment, a Book of Poetry, 2005, Glorious Grass, 1999. Mem. Madison-Morgan Cultural Ctr. Recipient Poet of Merit award, 1999; Ga. Dept. Edn. grantee, 1950, NDEA grantee, 1963, 65. Mem.: Am. Assn. Ret. Persons. Home: NC 6 136 Peachtree Memorial Dr NW Atlanta GA 30309-1096

WALLACE, HARRY LELAND, lawyer; b. San Francisco, June 26, 1927; s. Leon Harry and Anna Ruth (Haworth) W.; m. Marilyn D. Wallace (dec. June 13, 2005); 1 child, Mary Ann Wallace Frantz. AB in Govt.; BS in Bus, Ind. U., 1949; JD, Harvard U., 1952. Bar: Wis. 1953. Law clk. U.S. Supreme Ct. Justice Sherman Minton, Washington, 1952-53; assoc. firm Foley & Lardner, Milw., 1953-61, partner, 1961-96, retired, 1996; officer and/or dir. various corps. Treas. Mequon-Thiensville Sch. Bds., 1966-67, 71-73, pres., 1965-66, 67-71, 73-75; bd. dirs. Milw. County Assn. for Mental Health, 1970-76, Milw. Mental Health Found., 1983-94; chmn. financing policies com. Gov.'s Commn. on Edn., 1969-70; mem. Gov.'s Task Force on Sch. Financing and Property Tax Reform, 1972-73; chmn. Gov.'s Commn. on State-Local Rels. and Fin. Policies, 1975-76; trustee Pub. Policy Forum, 1976-92, sec., 1984-86, pres., 1986-88. With USN, 1945-46. Mem. Wis. Bar Assn., Am. Law Inst., Phi Beta Kappa, Beta Gamma Sigma, Delta Tau Delta. Clubs: Milwaukee. Methodist. Home: 1913 Somerset Ln Northbrook IL 60062-6067 Personal E-mail: lelandwallace@comcast.net.

WALLACE, HENRY JARED, JR., lawyer; b. Pitts., Oct. 26, 1943; s. Henry Jared and Jane (Bowman) Wallace. BA, Harvard U., 1965, JD, 1968. Bar: Pa. 1969, U.S. Supreme Ct. 1973. With Reed Smith, Pitts., 1968—94; pvt. practice Pitts., 1995—. Served with U.S. Army, 1968-70. Mem. Duquesne Club, Fox Chapel Golf Club, Harvard-Yale-Princeton Club (Pitts.). Home and Office: 149 Ridgeview Dr New Kensington PA 15068-9389

WALLACE, J. CLIFFORD, federal judge; b. San Diego, Dec. 11, 1928; s. John Franklin and Lillie Isabel (Overing) Wallace; m. Virginia Lee Schlosser, 1957 (dec.); m. Elaine J. Barnes, Apr. 8, 1996 (dec.); m. Dixie Jenee Robison Zenger, Apr. 2, 2001. BA, San Diego State U., 1952; LLB, U. Calif., Berkeley, 1955. Bar: Calif. 1955. With Gray, Cary, Ames & Frye, San Diego, 1955—70; judge US Dist. Ct. (so. dist.), Calif., 1970—72, US Ct. Appeals (9th cir.), San Diego, 1972—96, chief judge, 1991—96, sr. judge, 1996—. Contbr. articles to profl. jours. Stake pres. San Diego East LDS Ch., 1962—67, regional rep., 1967—74, 1977—79. With USN, 1946—49. Mem.: Inst. Jud. Adminstrn., Am. Bd. Trial Advocates. Mem. Lds Ch. Office: US Ct Appeals 9th Cir 940 Front St Ste 4192 San Diego CA 92101-8918 *My principles, ideals and goals and my standard of conduct are embodied in the Gospel of Jesus Christ. They come to fruition in family life, service, industry and integrity and in an attempt, in some small way, to make my community a better place within which to live.* *

WALLACE, JANE HOUSE, retired geologist; b. Ft. Worth, Aug. 12, 1926; d. Fred Leroy and Helen Gould (Kixmiller) Wallace. AB, Smith Coll., 1947, MA, 1949; postgrad., Bryn Mawr Coll., 1949—52. Geologist US Geol. Survey, 1952—97; chief Pub. Inquiries Offices, Washington, 1964—72, spl. asst. to dir., 1974—97, dep. bur. ethics counselor, 1975—97, Washington liaison Office of Dir., 1978—97; ret., 1997. Recipient Meritorious Service award Dept. Interior, 1971, Disting. Svc. award, 1976, Sec.'s Commendation, 1988, Smith Coll. medal, 1992. Fellow Geol. Socs. Am., Washington (treas. 1963-67); mem. Sigma Xi (assoc.)

WALLACE, JESSE WYATT, pharmaceutical scientist; b. Canton, Ga., Jan. 24, 1925; s. Jesse Washington and Lula (Wyatt) W.; m. Myra Brown, Jan. 2, 1949; children: Karin, Kimberly, Stephen, David. BBA magna cum laude, U. Ga., 1954; postgrad., U. Pa., 1959; MS, Ga. Inst. Tech., 1960; postgrad., U. Va., 1978, MIT, 1984. Chmn. svc. groups Ga. Tech, Atlanta, 1953-57; adminstrv. mgr. Am. Viscose Corp., Marcus Hook, Pa., 1957-61; various exec. positions FMC Corp., Phila., 1961-85; pres., dir. Wallco Internat. Corp., Wilmington, Del., 1985-89, 96—; v.p., sec. Pharm. Svc. and Tech., Inc., Woodbury, NJ, 1989-95. Adv. bd. Pharm. Tech. Conf., 1986—99. Editor: Controlled Release Systems, 1988; contbr. Encyclopedia, 1989; contbr. articles to profl. jours; author (manual) Problem Solver, 1980. Vice chmn. Ch. Deacons, Wilmington; v.p., pres. Wilmington Gideons, 1969-71; v.p., bd. dirs. ACA Acad., 1971-73; founder, vice chmn. Del. Family Found., 1990-99. Lt. USN, 1943-46, 50-53. Recipient Publ. award Pharm. Technology, 1989. Fellow Acad. Pharm. Scis., Am. Assn. of Pharm. Scientists; mem. Internat. Platform Assn., La. Fedn. Internat. Pharm., Am. Assn. Pharm. Scientists, Mensa, Delta Sigma Pi (life), Delta Mu Delta. Republican. Avocations: reading, golf, travel, racquetball. Office: Wallco Internat Corp 1106 Grinnell Rd Wilmington DE 19803-5126 Personal E-mail: jessewallace@comcast.net.

WALLACE, JOHN E., state supreme court justice; b. Pitman, NJ, 1942; m. Barbara Wallace; 5 children. BA in Political sci., U. Del., 1964; JD, Harvard U. Sch. of Law, 1967. Atty. Trustees of Penn Central Transportation Co., Montgomery, McCracken, Walker & Rhoads, Phila.; partner Atkinson, Myers, Archie & Wallace; municipal judge Wash. Township, Gloucester County; judge NJ Superior Ct., 1984—92, judge appellate div., 1992—2003; justice NJ Supreme Ct., 2003—. Former mem. NJ Supreme Ct. Task Force for Minority Concern; mem. NJ Ethics Commn., Jud. Advisory Com. on Americans with Disabilities Act, Supreme Ct. Special Com. on Matrimonial Litigation, Appellate Div. Rules Com.; former chmn. Supreme Ct. Ad Hoc Com. on Admissions. Coach Washington Twp. H.S. Served to rank of captain US Army, 1968—70. Mem.: ABA, Garden State Bar Assn. (Van J. Clinton award 2002), NJ State Bar Assn., Nat. Bar Assn., Camden County Bar Assn., Gloucester Bar Assn. Office: Richard J Hughes Justice Complex 25 Market St PO Box 970 Trenton NJ 08625 *

WALLACE, JOHN LOYS, retired aviation services executive; b. Decatur, Tex., July 31, 1941; s. John K. and Flora Viola (Lumsden) Montgomery W.; m. Linda M. Jackson, May 18, 1962; children— John, Amy Lynn, Katherine Lea, Elizabeth D'Ann Student, U. Tex.-Arlington, 1961-65, North Tex. State U., Denton, 1960-61. V.p. acctg. svcs. Cooper Airmotive, Dallas, 1975-77, v.p. fin., 1977-80, exec. v.p., gen. mgr. Gen. Aviation div., 1980-82; exec. v.p. fin., adminstrn. Aviall, Dallas, 1982-85; exec. v.p., chief oper. officer Aviall, Inc., Dallas, 1985-89, pres. Gen. Aviation Svcs. div., 1989-93; ret., 1993. Mem. Fin. Execs. Inst., North. Dallas C. of C., U.S./Mex. C. of C. (bd. dirs.), Chif Exec.'s Round Table, Cotton Creek Club, Delta Sigma Phi. Republican. Presbyterian. Avocations: gardening, fishing, golf. Home: 3651 Pinehurst Cir Gulf Shores AL 36542-9052

WALLACE, JULIA DIANE, newspaper editor; b. Davenport, Iowa, Dec. 3, 1956; d. Franklin Sherwood and Eleanor Ruth (Pope) W.; m. Doniver Dean Campbell, Aug. 23, 1986; children: Emmaline Livingston Campbell, Eden Jennifer Campbell. BS in Journalism, Northwestern U., 1978. Reporter Norfolk Ledger-Star, Va., 1978-80, Dallas Times Herald, 1980-82; reporter, editor News sect. USA Today, Arlington, Va., 1982-89, mng. editor spl. projects, 1989-92; mng. editor Chgo. Sun-Times, 1992-1996; exec. editor Statesman Jour., Salem, Oreg., 1996—98; mng. editor Ariz. Republic, Phoenix, 1998—2000, Atlanta Jour.-Constitution, 2001—02, editor, 2002—. Mem. Am. Soc. Newspaper Editors. Mailing: Atlanta Journal-Constitution PO Box 4689 Atlanta GA 30302 *

WALLACE, KEITH M., lawyer; b. Evansville, Ind., Apr. 2, 1956; s. B. Joe and M. Joyce (Nicolaides) W.; children: Elizabeth Anne, Paul Minh BA in Psychology, Ind. U., 1978; JD, Valparaiso U., 1983. Bar: Ky. 1984, Ind. 1983, U.S. Dist. Ct. (so. dist.) Ind. 1983, U.S. Ct. Appeals (7th cir.) 1985, U.S. Supreme Ct., 1997. Comml. credit analyst Old Nat. Bank, Evansville, 1978-79; assoc. Cubbage & Thomason, Henderson, Ky., 1983-84, Perdue & Stigger, Evansville, 1984-86; ptnr. Jones & Wallace, Evansville, 1987-90; fgn. expert Peking U. Law Dept., China, 1990-91; ptnr. Wright, Evans & Daly, Evansville, 1991-95, Jones & Wallace, Evansville, 1996-2001; of counsel Bowers Harrison, 2001—. Asst. city atty., Evansville, 1984-90; hearing officer City of Evansville Dept. Code Enforcement, 1992-99. Steward Christian Fellowship Ch., 1988-90; vol. Evansville Rescue Mission, 1987-92, Habitat for Humanity, 1992-2005; bd. dirs. Impact Ministries, 1992-2006, Joint Coun. on Internat. Children Svcs., 2004—; exec. dir. Families Thru Internat. Adoptions, Inc., 1995—, Childvision, Inc., 2004—. Recipient Sagamore of the Wabash award Gov. Frank O'Bannon, 1999, Disting. Hoosier award Gov. Evan Bayh, 1996, Angel in Adoption award Congl. Coalition on Adoption Inst., 2005. Mem. Am. Acad. Adoption Attys., Ind. Bar Assn., Ky. Bar Assn., Evansville Bar Assn., Am. Immigration Lawyers Assn., Christian Legal Soc. Office: PO Box 1287 Evansville IN 47706-1287 Office Phone: 812-479-9900. Fax: 812-464-3676. E-mail: kwallace@ftia.org.

WALLACE, KIRK D., research scientist; s. D. and S. Wallace; m. R. Trousil. PhD, Washington U., St. Louis. Rsch. scientist Washington U., 2001—05; sr. scientist Washington U. Sch. Medicine, 2006—. Chmn. St. Louis Wind Symphony, 2004—. Mem.: Acoustical Soc. Am., IEEE Ultrasonics, Ferroelectrics, and Frequency Control Soc. Achievements include research in nonlinear ultrasound propagation. Home: 7263 Lindell Blvd Saint Louis MO 63130 Office: Washington U 4320 Forest Park Ave CB 8125 Saint Louis MO 63108 Home Phone: 314-721-8941; Office Phone: 314-454-5539.

WALLACE, LINDA KAY, mathematics professor; d. John Edward and Marion Sue Wallace. BS, Radford U., 1989, MS, 1991. Educator Prince William County Pub. Sch., Manassas, Va., 1991—98, math. instrnl. specialist, 1998—2001, algebra readiness coord., 2001—06; math. coord. Roanoke City Pub. Schs., Va., 2006—. Ednl. cons. Casio, Inc., Dover, NJ, 2004—. Mem.: Nat. Coun. Tchrs. Math. (assoc.), Nat. Coun. Suprs. Math. (assoc.), Phi Delta Kappa (assoc.; pres. chpt. 1448 2004—05, Outstanding Student of Yr. 1991). Office: 40 Douglass AveNW Roanoke VA 24012 E-mail: lwallace@rcps.info.

WALLACE, LORRAINE SILVER, medical educator, researcher; b. Kitchener, Ontario, Can., Jan. 13, 1970; m. William H. Wallace, Mar. 3, 2000; 1 child, Muriel E. PhD, Ohio State U., Columbus, 1998. Assoc. prof. U. Tenn., Knoxville, 2001—. Conservative. Achievements include research in health literacy and patient-physician communication. Avocations: travel, golf. Office: Univ Tenn 1924 Alcoa Hwy U-67 Knoxville TN 37920 Home Phone: 865-558-5735; Office Phone: 865-544-9352. Business E-Mail: lwallace@mc.utmck.edu.

WALLACE, MARK ALLEN, hospital administrator; b. Oklahoma City, Apr. 24, 1953; s. William Howell and Mollie Marie (Godsy) W.; children: Emily, Benjamin. BS, Okla. Bapt. U., 1975; MS, Washington U., St. Louis, 1978. Adminstrv. asst. Bapt. Med. Ctr., Oklahoma City, 1975-77; adminstrv. resident Meth. Hosp., Houston, 1977-78; asst. v.p. Tex. Meth. Hosp., Houston, 1978-80, v.p., 1980-83, sr. v.p., 1983-89; pres., CEO Tex. Children's Hosp., Houston, 1989—. Adj. instr. Washington U., 1984—; adj. asst. prof. Tex. Womans U., Houston, 1983—; bd. dirs., chmn. fin. com., treas. Greater Houston Hosp. Svc. Corp., 1986-90; bd. trustees, Nat. Assn of Children's Hospitals and Related Institutions Contbr. articles to profl. jours. Chmn. campaign drives United Way, Houston, 1984, 86, corporate walk for Juvenile Diabetes Found. Walk to Cure Diabetes, 2000; class chmn. alumni vision for excellence and growth for future campaigns Okla. Bapt. U., 1982; bd. dirs. Tex. Gulf Coast chpt. March of Dimes Birth Defects Found., 1985-91, Zoological Society of Houston, Sam Houston Area Coun. of the Boy Scouts, World Health & Golf Assn., Greater Houston Partnership (vice-chair Flood Control Task Force), Greater Houston Community Found.; bd. governors, Houston Forum; active mem. Second Baptist Ch., Houston, Young Presidents' Orgn., and Houston Country Club Recipient Emerging Leaders in Health Care award Healthcare Forum Mag. and Korn/Ferry Internat., 1987. Fellow Am. Coll. Healthcare Execs. (com. on membership, subcom. on recruitment 1990—, Robert S. Hudgens Meml. award, 1992, Young Healthcare Exec. of Yr., 1992); mem. Am. Heart Assn. (med. adv. com. 1990-91), Healthcare Forum (pres. emerging leaders alumni group 1988-91), Am. Hosp. Assn., Tex. Hosp. Assn. (bd. dirs., bd. dirs. polit. action com. 1988—, chmn. bd. trustees, 1998-1999), Greater Houston Hosp. Coun. (bd. dirs. 1991—, chmn. 1993-1994), Houston Area Health Care Coalition, Childrens Hosp. Assn. Tex. (pres. 1992—, chmn. 2002-2003), Tex. Gulf Coast Arthritis Found. (bd. dirs. 1990-91). Republican. Baptist. Office: Tex Children's Hosp 6621 Fannin St Houston TX 77030 also: PO Box 300630 Houston TX 77230-0630

WALLACE, MARK RAYMOND, physician; b. Seattle, Feb. 22, 1955; s. George Warren and Grace Joanne (Balch) W.; m. Kathleen Cornell, Jan. 19, 1985 (dec. May 10, 2003); 1 child, Luke Randall; m. Jan Garavaglia, Apr. 29, 2006. BA in Chemistry, Whitman Coll., Walla Walla, Wash., 1977; MD, St. Louis U., 1981. Diplomate Am. Bd. Internal Medicine, sub-bd. Infectious Diseases; cert. added competence in clin. tropical medicine. Intern Med. Ctr. Hosp. of Vt., Burlington, 1981-82; resident U. Wash., Seattle, 1982-84; staff physician Naval Hosp., Long Beach, Calif., 1984-85, head internal medicine dept., 1986-87, fellow in infectious diseases San Diego, 1987-89, staff physician, 1989-90, head HIV unit, 1990-93, dir. infectious disease fellowship, 1993—2003, head infectious disease, 1998—2002; dir. fellowship in infectious disease Orlando Regional Med. ctr., Fla., 2007—. Author/co-author 175 jour. articles and 145 abstracts. Capt. USN, 1984—2005. Decorated Navy Commendation medal (2), Meritorious Svc. medal (2); Nat. Merit scholar, 1973. Fellow ACP, Infectious Disease Soc. Am., Royal Soc. Tropical Medicine and Hygiene; mem. AMA, Am. Soc. Microbiology (Weigelt-Wallace award in clin. medicine named in his honor 1992), Physicians Assn. for AIDS Care, Phi Beta Kappa, Alpha Omega Alpha. Avocation: fishing. Address: 685 Palm Spring Dr Ste 2A Altamonte Springs FL 32701 Office: 86 W Underwood St Ste 102 Orlando FL 32086

WALLACE, MARYJEAN ELIZABETH, science educator; b. Cedar Grove, NJ, July 19, 1963; d. Albert Joseph and Jean Wallace. BS summa cum laude, Adelphi U., Garden City, NY, 1985; MA summa cum laude, Ind. State U., Terre Haute, Ind., 1987. Cert. elem. tchr. NJ, secondary edn. earth sci. tchr. NJ, ednl. supr. NJ. Sci. tchr. Meml. Mid. Sch., Cedar Grove, NJ, 1987—91, Burnet Mid. Sch., Union Township, NJ, 1991—2000, Briarcliff Mid. Sch., Mountain Lakes, NJ, 2000—. Eucharistic min. Notre Dame of Mt. Carmel Ch., Cedar Knolls, NJ, 2002—. Named one of Outstanding Softball Players in NJ, Star Ledger, 2000; named to Athletic Hall of Fame, Adelphi U., 2000; Postgraduate scholar, NCAA, 1985. Mem.: NSTA, NJ Sci. Tchrs. Assn., Mountain Lakes Edn. Assn. (v.p. and membership chmn. 2005—), Phi Kappa Pi, Delta Tau Alpha, Kappa Delta Phi. Roman Catholic. Avocations: photography, travel, camping, hiking. Office: Briarcliff Mid Sch 93 Briarcliff Rd Mountain Lakes NJ 07046 Home Phone: 973-285-3874; Office Phone: 973-334-0342. Personal E-mail: mjwallace15@optonline.net. Business E-Mail: mwallace@mtlakes.org.

WALLACE, MICHELE, writer, educator; b. NYC, Jan. 4, 1952; d. Robert Earl Wallace, Burdette (Stepfather) and Faith Ringgold; m. Eugene Nesmith, Dec. 22, 1989 (div. Nov. 2002). BA, CCNY, 1974, MA in English, 1990; PhD in Cinema Studies, NYU, 1998. Asst. prof. English CUNY, 1989—91; assoc. prof. English, women's studies and film CUNY and CUNY Grad. Ctr., 1991—97, prof., 1998—2006. Pres. Art Without Walls, 1974. Author: Black Macho and the Myth of the Superwoman, 1979, Invisibility Blues: Pop to Theory, 1990, Black Popular Culture, 1992, Dark Designs and Visual Culture, 2004; columnist: The Village Voice, 1996; editor: Women in Art, 1971; mem. editl. bd.: Social Identities, Souls; contbr. to newspapers and popular mags. including Ms., The Village Voice, The Nation, The N.Y. Times, Art Forum, Art In America; editor-at-large: Essence Mag., 1983. Founding mem. Nat. Black Feminist Orgn., 1974; pres. Women Students and Artists for Black Art Liberation, 1970—76. Mem.: PEN, MLA, Oscar Micheaux Soc., Soc. Cinema Studies, Am. Studies Assn., Phi Beta Kappa. Office Phone: 212-650-6367. Personal E-mail: olympiax@aol.com. Business E-Mail: awallace@ccny.cuny.edu.

WALLACE, MIKE (MYRON LEON WALLACE), newscaster, television personality; b. Brookline, Mass., May 9, 1918; s. Frank and Zina (Sharfman) Wallace; m. Lorraine Perigord, 1955 (div. 1983); children: Peter(dec.), Christopher, Pauline; m. Mary Yates, June 28, 1986. BA, U. Mich., 1939; LHD (hon.), U. Mass., 1978; LLD (hon.), U. Mich., 1987, U. Pa., 1989. Associated with radio, 1939—; TV, 1946—; commentator CBS-TV, 1951—55, TV interviewer, reporter, 1951—; CBS news corr., 1963—; corr., co-editor 60 Minutes, CBS, 1968—. Numerous TV appearances include Night Beat, 1956—57, The Mike Wallace Interview, 1957—60, anchor Biography, 1959—61 (George Foster Peabody award, 1962), CBS Reports: 1968, 1993, presenter Mike Wallace Then and Now, 1990, co-anchor Watergate: The Secret Story, 1992, In the Killing Field of America, 1995 (Robert F. Kennedy Journalism award grand prize and TV first prize, 1996, George Foster Peabody award, 1995); author: Mike Wallace Asks, 1958; co-author (with Gary Paul Gates): (memoir) Close Encounter, 1984, Between You and Me: A Memoir, 2005. Naval comm. officer USN, 1943—46. Named Broadcaster of Yr., Internat. Radio and TV Sco., 1993; named to TV Acad. Hall of Fame, 1991; recipient Robert Sherwood award, 19 ATVAS Emmy awards, Disting. Achievement award, U. So. Calif. Sch. Journalism, Robert F. Kennedy Journalism award in Internat. broadcast category, George Foster Peabody award for 60 Minutes: The CIA's Cocaine, 1993, Alfred I. DuPont Columbia U. Journalism award, 1972, 1983, 1999, Carr Van Anda award, 1977, Thomas Hart Benton award, 1978, Paul White award, Radio/TV News Directors Assn., 1991, Lifetime Achievement Emmy, 1993, Fred Friendly First Amendment award, Quinnipiac Coll., 2002, honored for lifetime contribution to radio and TV, Chgo. Mus. Broadcast Comm., 1989. Mem.: Soc. Profl. Jounalists, Century Assocs., Sigma Delta Chi.

WALLACE, NICOLLE (NICOLLE DEVENISH), former federal official; b. Orinda, Calif. m. Mark Wallace. BA, U. Calif., Berkley; MA, Medill Sch. of Journalism, Northwestern U. With Calif. Assembly Rep. Caucus, 1997—98, Calif. Rep. Party, 1998; former press aide to CEO Grassroots.com; former press secretary to Gov. Jeb Bush State of Fla.;

former communications dir. Fla. State Tech. Office; spl. asst. to Pres. & dir. of media affairs The White House, Washington, 2000—05, asst. to Pres. for comm., 2005—06. Communications dir. Bush-Cheney '04 campaign.

WALLACE, NORA ANN, lawyer; b. Phila., May 24, 1951; AB, Vassar Coll., 1973; JD cum laude, Harvard U., 1976. Bar: N.Y. 1977. Mem. Willkie Farr & Gallagher, NYC. Trustee Vassar Coll., Bklyn. Acad. Music, Bklyn. Acad. Music Endowment Trust; bd. dirs. Joseph Collins Found. Office: Willkie Farr & Gallagher 787 7th Ave New York NY 10019-6099

WALLACE, PAULA S., academic administrator; married; 4 children. BA, Furman U.; MEd, EdS, Ga. State U.; LLD (hon.), Gonzaga U. Co-founder Savannah Coll. Art and Design, 1979, pres., 2000—. Author: (children's books) World of Birthdays, World of Food, World of Holidays, World of Sports, several others. Mem. Skidaway Island United Meth. Ch., Savannah, Ga. Film and Videotape Commn., Ga. C. of C.; bd. dirs. B. B. & T. Bank, Nat. Mus. Women in the Arts. Recipient Oglethorpe Bus. and Profl. Women award, James T. Deason Human Rels. award, Principled Leadership award southeast Ernst & Young, 2004; named Outstanding Young Woman of Am., Ky. Col., One of Most Influential Georgians Ga. Trend mag., 2005; named to Savannah Bus. Hall of Fame, Chevalier dan l'Ordre des Palmes Academique, 2005. Office: Savannah Coll Art and Design PO Box 3146 Savannah GA 31402-3146 Office Phone: 912-525-5200. *

WALLACE, PETER MARSDEN, radio personality and producer, commentator, writer; b. Parkersburg, W.Va., Aug. 15, 1954; s. Aldred Pruden and Margaret Anne (Yoak) Wallace; m. Bonita Lucille Shock, Oct. 15, 1977 (div. 2005); children: Meredith Anne, Matthew Edward. AB in journalism/advt., Marshall U., 1976; ThM, Dallas Theol. Sem., 1984. Editor W.Va. Hillbilly, Richwood, W.Va., 1976-79; editl. asst. Dallas Theol. Sem., 1981-84; editl. mgr. Walk Thru the Bible Ministries, Atlanta, 1984-85, editl. dir., 1985-90; sr. copywriter & broadcast prodr. Larry Smith & Associates, Atlanta, 1990—2001; exec. prodr. Day 1 radio program (formerly The Protestant Hour), Atlanta, 2001—, host, 2005—; v.p. Alliance for Christian Media. Mem. Faith & Values Media Mem. Coun. Author: What Jesus Is Saying to You Today, 1994, What the Psalmist is Saying to You Today, 1994, What God Is Saying to You Today, 1995, Psalms for Today, 2001, TruthQuest Devotional Journal, 2002, Old Testament for Today, 2003, Out of the Quiet: Responding to God's Whispered Invitations, 2004, Living Loved, 2007; co-author: The West Virginia Picture Book, 1979; contbr. articles to religious magazines; editor: The Daily Walk Bible, 1987. Recipient Outstanding Young Men Am. Award, US Jaycees, 1984. Democrat. Avocations: reading, camping, travel. Office: Day 1 Ste 300 644 W Peachtree St Atlanta GA 30308-1925 Home: 955 Juniper St NE #4027 Atlanta GA 30309 Office Phone: 404-815-9110. Office Fax: 404-815-0495. E-mail: pwallace@day1.net.

WALLACE, R. H., JR., lawyer; b. Livingston, Tex., Oct. 9, 1943; BS, U.S. Naval Acad., 1966; JD, Baylor U., 1973. Bar: Tex. 1973, US Dist. Ct. (no., so., ea. we. dist. Tex.), US Ct. Appeals (5th cir.), US Supreme Ct.; cert. civil trial & criminal law Tex. Bd. Legal Specialization. Atty. criminal div., appellate sect. US Dept. Justice, 1973—76; asst. U.S. atty. US Dept. Justice, No. Dist. Tex., 1976-84, dep. chief criminal div., 1983-84; mem., comml. litig. practice Shannon Gracey Ratliff & Miller LLP, Fort Worth. Fellow Am. Coll. Trial Lawyers; life fellow Tex. Bar Found.; mem. ABA, State Bar Tex. Office: Shannon Gracey Ratliff & Miller Ste 3800 777 Main St Fort Worth TX 76102 Office Phone: 817-336-9333. Office Fax: 817-336-3735. Business E-Mail: rhwallace@shannongracey.com.

WALLACE, RASHEED, professional basketball player, marketing professional; b. Sept. 17, 1974; s. Jackie Wallace; m. Fatima Sanders, July 18; 3 children. Attended, U. N.C. Prof. basketball player Washington Wizards, 1995—96, Portland Trailblazers, 1996—2004, Atlanta Hawks, 2004, Detroit Pistons, 2004—; CEO Dir. Hit Studios, Phila., 2002—. Founder Rasheed A. Wallace Found., Phila., 1997. Named to NBA All-Star Team, 2000, 2001. Achievements include being a member of NBA Championship Team, 2004. Office: c/o Detroit Pistons 2 Championship Dr Auburn Hills MI 48326

WALLACE, RICHARD P., computer company executive; BSEE, Univ. Mich.; M engring. mgmt., Santa Clara Univ. Engring. positions Ultratech Stepper, Cypress Semiconductor; mgmt. positions KLA-Tencor Corp., 1988—95, v.p., gen. mgr. Wisard San Jose, Calif., 1995—98, v.p., gen. mgr. Mirage group, 1998—99, group v.p., 1999—2000, exec. v.p., 2000—05, pres., COO, 2005, CEO, 2006—. Office: KLA-Tencor Corp 160 Rio Robles San Jose CA 95134 *

WALLACE, ROBERT BRUCE, retired surgeon; b. Washington, Apr. 12, 1931; s. William B. and Anne E. W.; m. Betty Jean Newel, Aug. 28, 1955; children: Robert B., Anne E., Barbara N. BA, Columbia U., 1953, MD, 1957. Diplomate Am. Bd. Surgery, Am. Bd. Thoracic Surgery. Chmn., prof. dept. surgery Mayo Clinic and Mayo Med. Sch., Rochester, Minn.; bd. govs. Mayo Clinic, 1968-79; prof. dept. surgery Georgetown U. Sch. Medicine, 1980—96, chmn. dept. surgery, 1980-95, surgeon and chief univ. hosp., 1980-95; retired, 1996. Trustee Mayo Found., 1970—78; chmn. sci. adv. com. LeDucq Found., 2000—05. Mem. ACS (bd. govs. 1975-79), Am. Surg. Assn., Soc. Clin. Surgery, Am. Assn. Thoracic Surgery (pres. 1994-95), Internat. Cardiovascular Soc., Soc. Vascular Surgery, Thoracic Surgery Found. Rsch. & Edn. (bd. dirs. 1993-2001, pres. 1998-2001). Home: 1322 Darnall Dr Mc Lean VA 22101-3009 E-mail: rbwallace@cox.net.

WALLACE, SAMUEL TAYLOR, health system administrator; b. Blytheville, Ark., Sept. 2, 1943; m. Sara Billow, Apr. 30, 1992. BS, U. Mo., 1965; M.H.A., Washington U., St. Louis, 1970. Asst. adminstr. Hillcrest Med. Ctr., Tulsa, 1969-75; adminstr. St. Luke's Meth. Hosp., Cedar Rapids, Iowa, 1975-81, pres., 1981-95, Iowa Health Sys., Des Moines, 1995—. Bd. dirs. Vol. Hosp. Am., Dallas, 1982-94, Iowa Golf Charities, 2001-; chmn. bd. dirs. Vol. Hosp. Iowa, Cedar Rapids, 1983-87; bd. dirs. Greater Des Moines Partnershp, 1996—, Physician Mgmt. Resources, 1996—2000, Health Enterprise of Iowa, 1995-2000; mem. Cedar Rapids coun. Boy Scouts Am., 1983, Mid-Iowa coun., 1995—. Served to capt. M.S.C. U.S. Army, 1965-68, Vietnam. Recipient Silver Beaver award Boy Scouts Am., 1980, Silver Antelope award, 1992; James E. West fellow, 1994, Dist. Eagle Scout, 2002. Fellow Am. Coll. Healthcare Execs. (Iowa bd. regents 1982-84, 88-95, interim gov. Dist. 5 1999-2000); mem. Iowa Hosp. Assn. (dir. 1982-85). Lodges: Rotary (Cedar Rapids pres. 1986-87). Republican. Methodist. Office: Iowa Health Sys 1200 Pleasant St Des Moines IA 50309-1406

WALLACE, THOMAS C., editor, publishing executive; b. Vienna, Dec. 13, 1933; came to U.S., 1938; s. Don and Julia (Baer) W.; m. Lois Kahn, July 19, 1962 (div. May 2000); 1 son, George Baer; m. Barbara Shortt, Nov. 12, 2000. Grad., Peddie Sch., 1951; BA, Yale U., 1955, MA in History, 1957. Editor G.P. Putnam Sons, NYC, 1959-63; with Holt, Rinehart & Winston, NYC, 1963-81, editor-in-chief gen. books divsn., 1968-81; v.p., sr. editor Simon and Schuster, NYC, 1981; editor W.W. Norton, NYC, 1982-87; v.p. Wallace Lit. Agy., NYC, 1987-98; pres. T. C. Wallace Agy., NYC, 1998—. Bd. dirs. Roger Klein Found. Mem. PEN, Yale Club, Century Assn. (N.Y.C.). Home and Office: 2 S End Ave Apt 44 New York NY 10280 Home Phone: 212-786-4329; Office Phone: 646-478-7459. Personal E-mail: tcwallace2@aol.com.

WALLACE, TIMOTHY R., manufacturing executive; b. 1954; Grad., So. Meth. U., 1975. Joined Trinity Industries, 1975, v.p., 1984, sr. v.p., 1989, COO railcars and containers segment, chmn., pres., CEO, 1996—. Bd. dirs. VIAD Corp., Phoenix. Office: Trinity Industries 2525 Stemmon Freeway Dallas TX 75207 *

WALLACE, WALTER C., lawyer, government official; b. NYC, Mar. 25, 1924; m. Frances Helm, Apr. 5, 1963; 1 dau., Laura. BA magna cum laude, St. John's U., Hillsdale, NY, 1948; LLB with distinction, Cornell U., 1951. Bar: N.Y. 1952, Calif. 1954, D.C. 1975, U.S. Dist. Ct. (no. dist.) Calif. 1954, U.S. Ct. Appeals (9th cir.) 1954, D.C. 1975, U.S. Dist. Ct. D.C. 1975, U.S. Ct. Appeals (D.C. cir.) 1975. Assoc. Cahill, Gordan & Reindel, NYC, 1951-54; exec. asst. Sec. of Labor, Washington, 1955-60, asst. sec. of labor for manpower and employment, 1960-61; gen. counsel Presdl. R.R. Commn., Washington, 1961; v.p. labor rels. Hudson Pulp & Paper Corp., NYC, 1963-73; pres. Bituminous Coal Operators Assoc., Washington, 1974-75; ptnr. Ables & Wallace, Washington, 1977-80; prin. Law Offices Walter C. Wallace, NYC, 1981-82; mem. Nat. Mediation Bd., Washington, 1982—, chmn., 1983, 85, 88. U.S. del. Internat. Labor Orgn. Conf. on Labor Rels. in Timber Industry, Geneva, 1958; asst. to cabinet com. on oil imports chaired by John Foster Dulles, 1958. Mem. bd. editors Cornell Law Quar., 1950-51. Bd. dirs. Nat. Safety Coun., Washington, 1974-75; asst. to chmn. United Givers Fund, Washington, 1956, mem. admission and allocations com., 1957-58. Staff sgt. US Army, 1943—45. Decorated Bronze Star for meritoreous svc. in combat, 1945; recipient Presdl. commendation Pres. Eisenhower, Washington, 1961, Disting. Svc. award United Givers Fund, 1956, Disting. Svc. award Nat. Mediation Bd., 1990. Mem. Calif. Bar Assn., N.Y. State Bar Assn., D.C. Bar Assn., Order of Coif. Republican. Roman Catholic. Home: 125 W 16th St Apt 152 New York NY 10011

WALLACE, WILLIAM, III, engineering executive; b. Bklyn., June 7, 1926; s. William and Ruth (Fitch) W.; m. Dorothy Ann Reimann, Aug. 2, 1969 (dec.); 1 child, Andrew William. B.E.E., Union Coll., 1947. Registered prof. engr., 22 states. Test engr. Gen. Electric Co., Schenectady, 1947; engr. Ebasco Services Inc., NYC, 1948-67, chief elec. engr., 1967-70, mgr. projects, 1970-73, v.p. Atlanta office Norcross, Ga., 1973-76, exec. v.p. NYC, 1976-80, dir., pres., chief exec. officer, 1980-82, chmn., chief exec. officer, 1982-86, also bd. dirs.; cons., 1986—. Bd. dirs. McNab Corp. Chmn. bd. advisors Sch. engring., N.C. State U., 1986-89; mem. adv. bd. trustees Union Coll., 1997-2000; trustee Poly. Prep. Country Day Sch., 1990-2002; trustee Saddle River Day Sch.; deacon West Side Presbyn. Ch., Ridgewood, N.J., 1988-90, 96-2000, elder, 1990-93, trustee, 2000-2003. Mem. IEEE (sr.), NSPE, N.J. State Soc. Profl. Engrs., World Rehab. Fund (bd. dirs. 1986-96), N.Y.C. C. of C. and Industry (bd. dirs. 1980-88), Delta Upsilon (vice chmn. Ednl. Found. 1986-95). Republican. Home and Office: 84 Buckhaven Hl Upper Saddle River NJ 07458

WALLACE-TAYLOR, ELIZABETH, medical/surgical nurse; b. Hartford, Conn., May 24, 1951; d. Anna Flannery Wallace; m. Joseph H. Taylor (div.); children: Lauren Taylor, Julia Taylor. Student, Seattle U., 1969—70; degree, Royal Acad. Music, London, 1974; diploma in nursing, Mass. Coll. Nursing, Framingham, 2004. RN Mass. Singing tchr. Cork Sch. Music, Ireland, 1973—75; singer Coro Nacional d'España, Teatro Zarzuela, Madrid, 1975—77, Hochschule fur Musik, Frankfurt, Germany, 1977—78, Teatro Margherita, Genova, Italy, 1978—80, Boston Concert Opera, 1981—89, Tanglewood Fesitval Chorus, 1987—97; prin., owner Allegro Piano Svc.; nurse H. William Fegley, MD, 2001—06; sales rep. M. Steinert & Sons, Natick, Mass., 2007—. Singer: Tanglewood Festival Chorus, Boston Concert Opera. Named Artist of the Month, Copley Soc. Boston, 1984; recipient 1st Pl. Close Up Magic Contest award, Soc. Am. Magician's, 1996. Mem.: Nat. Assn. Tchrs. Singing, Assn. Tchrs. Singing, Mass. Assn. Nurses. Avocations: writing, magic, painting, drawing. Home: 70 Harrington Rd Framingham MA 01701 Office: M Steinert & Sons 1298D Worcester Rd Natick MA 01760 Office Phone: 508-655-7373. Business E-Mail: beth@msteinert.com.

WALLACH, ALAN, art historian, educator; b. Bklyn., June 8, 1942; s. Israel and Vivian (Esner) W.; m. Phyllis Rosenzweig, Jan. 3, 1988. BA in Math., Columbia U., 1963, MA, 1965, PhD, 1973. Assoc. prof. Kean Coll., Union, NJ, 1974-89; Ralph H. Wark prof. art and art history, prof. Am. studies Coll. William and Mary, Williamsburg, Va., 1989—. Vis. prof. UCLA, 1982-83, Stanford (Calif.) U., 1987, CUNY, 1988, U. Mich., 1989; disting. vis. prof. U. Del., 2006; co-curator Nat. Mus. Am. Art, Washington, 1991-94. Author: (with William Truettner) Thomas Cole: Landscape into History, 1994; Exhibiting Contradiction: Essays on the Art Museum in the United States, 1998; mem. editl. bd. Am. Quar., 2000-03; contbr. articles to profl. jours. Mem. Am. Studies Assn. (bd. mng. editors, 2000-03), Coll. Art Assn. (bd. dirs. 1996-2000, Disting. Tng. Art History award, 2007), Assn. Art Historians. Home: 2009 Belmont Rd NW Washington DC 20009-5449 Office: Coll William and Mary Dept Art and Art History Williamsburg VA 23187-8795 Office Phone: 757-221-2530. Business E-Mail: axwall@wm.edu.

WALLACH, ANNE JACKSON See JACKSON, ANNE

WALLACH, DAVID MICHAEL, lawyer; b. Ft. Worth, Nov. 13, 1954; s. David Edward and Zelma Jane (Gilbreath) W.; m. Susan Danell Hailey, Aug. 16, 1975; children: Landon James, Tyler Field, Carter Hailey. BA, Tex. Christian U., 1975; JD, U. Houston, 1979. Bar: Tex. 1979, U.S. Dist. Ct. (no. dist.) Tex. 1979, U.S. Ct. Appeals (5th and 11th cirs.) 1979, U.S. Dist. Ct. (so. dist.) Tex. 1986, U.S. Dist. Ct. (we. dist.) Tex. 1992. Assoc. Shannon, Gracey, Ratliff & Miller, Ft. Worth, 1979-83, ptnr., 1983-91; shareholder Wallach, Andrews & Stouffer, Ft. Worth, 1991—. Contbr. articles to profl. jours. Named Boss of Yr. Fort Worth Legal Secs. Assn., 1991, Atty. of Excellence, Ft. Worth Bus. Press, 2003, 04, 05, Tex. Super Lawyer, Tex. Monthly, 2003-06. Fellow Tex. Bar Found.; mem. Tex. Assn. Def. Counsel (v.p. programs 1993-96, bd. dirs. 1989-96, 97—, v.p. North Tex. region 1997-98, exec. v.p. 1999-2000, pres. 2001-02, pres.'s award 1992), Def. Rsch. Inst., Fedn. Def. and Corp. Counsel, Tarrant County Civil Trial Lawyers Assn. (pres. 1988-89, exec. v.p. 1987-88), State Bar Tex., Tarrant County Bar Assn., North Tex. Soc. for Health Care Risk Mgmt., Health Industry Coun. Dallas-Ft. Worth Region, Shriners, Masons. Republican. Methodist. Avocations: golf, skiing, racquetball. Office: Wallach Andrews and Stouffer PC 550 Bailey Ave Ste 500 Fort Worth TX 76107 Office Phone: 817-338-1707. Business E-Mail: m.wallach@wallach-law.com.

WALLACH, ELI, actor; b. Bklyn., Dec. 7, 1915; s. Abraham and Bertha (Schorr) W.; m. Anne Jackson, Mar. 5, 1948; children: Peter Douglas, Roberta Lee, Katherine Beatrice. AB, U. Tex., 1936; MS in Edn, CCNY, 1938; student, Neighborhood Playhouse Sch. of Theatre, 1940; doctorate (hon.), Emerson Coll., Boston, Sch. Visual Arts, 1991. Corp. mem., dir. Neighborhood Playhouse Sch. Theatre. Actor, 1945—; Broadway plays include Antony and Cleopatra, 1948, Mr. Roberts, 1949-50, Rose Tatoo, 1950-52, Camino Real, 1953, Mademoiselle Colombe, 1953, Teahouse of the August Moon, 1954-55, London prodn., 1954, Major Barbara, 1956, Rhinoceros, 1961, Luv, 1964, Promenade All, 1972, Twice Around the Park, 1983, Opera Comique, Kennedy Ctr. Performing Arts, 1987, The Flowering Peach, Fla., 1987, Broadway, 1994, Cafe Crown, 1989; appeared off-Broadway prodn. Typists and the Tiger, 1962-63, London prodn., 1964, Saturday, Sunday, Monday, 1974, (with wife and 2 daus.) Diary of Anne Frank, 1977-78, Visiting Mr. Green, 1997; off-Broadway in Tennessee Williams Remembered, 1999; on tour Down the Garden Paths, 1998-99; appeared in: nat. tour co. Waltz of the Toreadors, 1973-74; appeared in TV films Executioner's Song, 1982, Murder By Reason of Insanity, 1985, Monday Night Mayhem, 2000, Monday Night Mayhem, 2002; TV series Batman, 1966, Kojak, 1973, Highway to Heaven, 1984, Our Family Honor, 1985, L.A. Law, 1986, Law & Order, 1990, The Education of Max Bickford, 2001-02; TV miniseries Christopher Columbus, 1985, The Education of Max Bickford, 2002; motion pictures include Baby Doll, 1955, The Misfits, 1960, The Victors, 1962, Lord Jim, 1964, How To Steal a Million, The Good, the Bad and the Ugly, The Tiger Makes Out, Band of Gold, Zig-Zag, Cinderella Liberty, 1973, Crazy Joe, 1973, Movie, Movie, 1976, Sam's Son, 1985, Tough Guys, 1986, Rocket to the Moon,1986, Nuts, 1987, The Impossible Spy, 1987, Godfather III, 1990, The Two Jakes, 1990, Article 99, Mistress, 1991, Night and the City, 1991, Honey, Sweet Love, 1993, Two Much, 1995, The Associate, 1996, Keeping the Faith, 2000, Mystic River, 2003, King of the Corner, 2004, (voice) The Easter Egg Adventure, 2004, The Moon and the Son: An Imagined Conservation, 2005, A Taste of Jupiter, 2005, The Hoax, 2006, The Holiday, 2006, Mama's Boy, 2006; author: The Good, The Bad, And Me: In My Anecdotage, 2005. Served to capt. Med. Adminstrn. Corps AUS, World War II. Recipient Donaldson, Theatre World, Variety, Antoinette Perry, Drama League awards, Brit. Film Acad. award, 1956, Disting. Alumnus award U. Tex., 1989, Career Achievement Award Nat. Bd. Review, 2006. Original mem. Actors Studio. Office: Talent Works 220 E 22nd Ste 400 New York NY 10010 *

WALLACH, ERIC JEAN, lawyer; b. NYC, June 11, 1947; s. Milton Harold and Jacqueline (Goldschmidt) W.; m. Miriam Grunberger, Mar. 21, 1976; children: Katherine, Emily, Peter. BA, Harvard U., 1968, JD, 1972. Bar: N.Y. 1973, U.S. Dist. Ct. (so. and ea. dists.) N.Y. 1973, U.S. Dist. Ct. (no. dist.) N.Y. 1989, U.S. Ct. Appeals (2nd cir.) 1973, (3d cir.) 1996, U.S. Tax Ct. 1976. Assoc. Webster & Sheffield, NYC, 1972-77, Rosenman & Colin, NYC, 1977-80, ptnr., 1981-96, mem. mgmt. com., 1993-96, chmn. employment practice group, 1985-96; ptnr., chmn. employment practice group Kasowitz, Benson, Torres & Friedman LLP, NYC, 1996—. Arbitrator Internat. Ct. Arbitration, Am. Arbitration Assn., others; presenter, chmn. CLE programs, Practising Law Inst., Cambridge Inst. Mem. editl. bd. You and the Law, 1992-96; contbr. articles to profl. jours. Sec.-treas. Art Dealers Assn. Am., Inc., N.Y.C., 1985-96; trustee C.G. Jung Found. for Analytical Psychology; trustee Am. Jewish World Svc., Inc., N.Y.C., 1989-97, chmn., 1995-97; dir. N.Y. Jr. Tennis League. Named to NY Super Lawyers. Mem. Harvard Club N.Y.C. (admissions com. 1992-94), Sunningdale Country Club, Poughkeepsie Tennis Club. Democrat. Avocations: sports, travel, reading. Home: 940 Park Ave New York NY 10028 also: 16 Buttonwood Ln Rhinebeck NY 12572-3510 Office: Kasowitz Benson Torres & Friedman LLP 1633 Broadway New York NY 10019 Office Phone: 212-506-1750. Business E-Mail: ewallach@kasowitz.com.

WALLACH, HOWARD FREDERIC, psychiatrist; b. Chgo., Sept. 4, 1923; s. Leo and Mildred (Ebert) W.; m. Laurie Rochelle Gettleman, Sept. 15, 1945 (div. July 1968); children: Joan, John, Richard; m. Gloria Bunny Jackman, July 14, 1968; children: Rand, Steve, Beth. MD, U. Ill., Chgo., 1946; M.Social Psychiatry, UCLA, 1969. Diplomate Am. Bd. Psychiatry and Neurology. Intern Cook County Hosp., Chgo., 1946—47, resident internal medicine, 1947—49; pres. Mount Sinai Hosp. Med. Rsch. Found., 1952—64; asst. clin. prof. psychiatry UCLA, 1968—80, assoc. clin. prof., 1980—; chief allied mental health Brentwood VA Hosp., LA, 1970—72; chief psychiatry Sepulveda VA Hosp., LA, 1972—74; pvt. practice LA. Bd. govs. Cedars-Sinai Med. Ctr., L.A., 1985—, mem. exec. com., 2000—; cons. VA Med. Ctr., L.A., 1982-90; developer maj. high rise apts., Chgo., 1951-64. Contbr. articles to profl. jours. Sec. Am. Psychiat. Found., Washington, 1990-99; bd. dirs. Nat. Mus. Health and Medicine, Washington, 1989-99; v.p. Jewish Family Svc. of L.A., 1997-98; bd. dirs., pres. Young Men's Jewish Charities, Chgo., 1951-62; mem. Cook County Blue Ribbon Commn., 1959-63. 1st lt. U.S. Army, 1943-46. Recipient Bronze award Boys Clubs of Am., 1962, Pres.'s Spl. Achievement award So. Calif. Psychiat. Soc., 1991. Fellow Am. Coll. Psychoanalysts, Am. Psychiat. Assn. (exec. com. 1982-88), Am. Acad. Psychoanalysis; mem. Calif. Psychiat. Assn. (pres. 1986-88), So. Calif. Psychiat. Soc. (pres. 1979-80, mem. coun. 1975-83), Alpha Omega Alpha. Avocations: photography, computers, golf, walking, presidential manuscript collecting. Office: 2080 Century Pk E Ste 1809 Los Angeles CA 90067-2001 Office Phone: 310-553-2833. Personal E-mail: hfwallach@gmail.com.

WALLACH, KENNETH L., paper company executive; b. NYC, 1946; m. Susan Wallach. BA, Harvard Coll., 1968, JD, 1972. Chmn., pres., CEO Ctrl. Nat.-Gottesman Inc., Purchase, NY, 1998—. Mem. regional adv. bd, J.P. Morgan Chase. Trustee Am. Mus. Natural History; dir. 92d St. Y, Syracuse Pulp and Paper Found., Nat. Book Found. Fellow: Am. Acad. Arts & Scis. Office: Ctrl Nat-Gottesman Inc 3 Manhattanville Rd Purchase NY 10577 *

WALLACH, LESLIE ROTHAUS, architect; b. Pitts., Feb. 4, 1944; s. Albert and Sara F. (Rothaus) W.; m. Susan Rose Berger, June 15, 1969; 1 child, Aaron. BS in Mining Engring., U. Ariz., 1967, BArch, 1974. Registered arch., Ariz.; registered contractor, Ariz. Prin. Line and Space LLC, Tucson, 1978—. Mem. awards jury Sunset mag., 1997, Ariz. Homes of Yr., 1997, L.A. AIA; keynote spkr. various confs. Rep. projects include Ariz. Sonora Desert Mus. Restaurant Complex, Tucson, Elgin Elem. Sch., Ariz., Hillel Student Ctr. U. Ariz., Tucson, Boyce Thompson Southwestern Arboretum Vis. Ctr., Superior, Ariz., San Pedro Riparian Ctr., Sierra Vista, Ariz., Nat. Hist. Trails Ctr., Casper, Wyo., 2002, Vis. Ctr. and Arborteum, Flagstaff, Ariz., 2001, Regional Libr., Phoenix, 2002, Poetry Ctr. for U. Ariz., 2003, New Regional Libr. U. Ariz., Phoenix, 2006; contbr. Sunset Mag., Architecture Mag. and Fine Homebuilding; pub.: Space and Society (Italy), Hinge (Hong Kong), Wallpaper (London); exhibited at U. Ariz., AIA Nat. Conv., Washington, The Dutch Jour., Objekt, 2003; interview and profile pub. in Architecture and Urbanism, 2006. Bd. dirs Tucson Regional Plan, Inc.; pres. Civitas Sonoran (The Environ. Design Coun. of the U. of Ariz. Coll. of Arch.). Recipient Roy P. Drachman Design award, 1982, 85, 93, 2001, Electric League Ariz. Design award, 1987, 88, Gov. Solar Energy award, 1989, Desert Living awards citation, 1991, Ariz. Architect's medal, 1989, Disting. Alumni award U. Ariz., 1998, also 45 additional design awards, including 4 received in 1995, winner $25,000 prize, nat. Endowment of the Arts, 2002, Coll. of Architecture Alumni of Yr., U. Az., 2001. Fellow AIA (Ariz. Honor award 1989, 92, 96, AIA/ACSA Nat. Design award 1991, Western Mountain region Design award 1992, 96, CA AIA/Phoenix Homes and Gardens Home of the Yr. Honor award 1992, 96, Western Region Silver medal 1996, design award, 2004); mem. SAC AIA (past pres., Design award 1985, 88, 90), Western Mountain Region AIA (named Firm of Yr. 1999), Tex. AIA (jury mem. design awards, 2005—). Achievements include being selected as the architect to design the 300 acre Desert Learning Center Campus and new visitor center in Red Rock Canyon, Nevada. Office: Line and Space 627 E Speedway Blvd Tucson AZ 85705-7433 Office Phone: 520-623-1313. Business E-Mail: studio627@lineandspace.com.

WALLACH, MAGDALENA FALKENBERG (CARLA WALLACH), writer; b. Brussels; d. Carl Albert and Renee Antoinette (Meunier) Falkenberg; m. Philip Charles Wallach, Mar. 5, 1950. Student, Columbia U., NYC, Hunter Coll., New Sch. U. Ptnr. Williams-Falkenberg Advt. Assocs., Inc., NYC, 1951-55. Author: Reluctant Weekend Gardener, 1971, Interior Decorating with Plants, 1976, Gardening in the City, 1976, Garden in a Teacup, 1978; contbr. articles to NY Times, Glamour, Working Woman, Greenwich Time, Stamford Adv, others. Former bd. dirs. ARC, NYC; active Bruce Mus., 1987-2007, chmn. spl. events 75th anniversary gala, chmn. Renaissance Ball, bd. dirs., also other fundraising activities; bd. dirs., v.p., chair annual fund raiser Greenwich Adult Day Ctr. Mem. Nat. League Am. PEN Women (pres. Greenwich br. 1987-92, Owl award

1996), Authors Guild, Garden Writers Assn., English-Speaking Union (past bd. dirs. Greenwich br.). Roman Catholic. Avocations: gardening, reading, travel, music, theater. Home: 126 W Lyon Farm Dr Greenwich CT 06831-4352

WALLACH, MARK IRWIN, lawyer; b. Cleve., May 19, 1949; s. Ivan A. and Janice (Grossman) W.; m. Karla L. Wallach, 1996; children: Kerry Melissa, Philip Alexander; stepchildren: Daniel Kanter, Rachel Kanter, Adam Kanter. BA magna cum laude, Wesleyan U., 1971; JD cum laude, Harvard U., 1974. Bar: Ohio 1974, U.S. Dist. Ct. (no. dist.) Ohio, 1974, U.S. Ct. Appeals (6th cir.) 1985, U.S. Supreme Ct. 1985. Law clk. U.S. Dist. Ct., Cleve., 1974-75; assoc. Baker & Hostetler, Cleve., 1975-79; chief trial counsel City of Cleve., 1979-81; assoc. Calfee, Halter & Griswold, Cleve., 1981-82, ptnr., 1982—, co-chmn. litigation dept., 2004—. Mem. fed. ct. adv. com. U.S. Dist. Ct. (no. dist.) Ohio, 1991-95; chmn. bd. trustees Ohio Group Against Smoking Pollution, 1986-90; trustee Cleve. chpt. Am. Jewish Com., 1986—, sec. 1989-91, v.p., 1991-95, pres., 1995-97; bd. trustees Citizens League of Greater Cleve., 1978-79, 87-92. Author: Christopher Morley, 1976. Pres. Wesleyan Alumni Club, Cleve., 1983—87, 1992—2006; trustee Lyric Opera, Cleve., 1995—2006, pres., 1996—98, Ratner Schs., 1994—96, Performing Arts Together, 1997—2001; trustee The Sculpture Ctr., 2001—, pres., 2001—; trustee Bellefaire Jewish Children's Bur., 2001—06; trustee, sec. Opera Cleve., 2006—07; pres. Space Solar Power Assn., 2006—; exec. bd. Cleve. chpt. Am. Constn. Soc., 2006—. Mem.: ABA, Greater Cleve. Bar Assn., Cuyahoga County Law Dirs. Assn., Fed. Bar Assn., Ohio Bar Assn., The Club at Key Ctr., The Cleve. Racquet Club. Democrat. Jewish. Avocations: reading, bicycling, space exploration, politics. Home: 2758 Claythorne Rd Shaker Heights OH 44122-1938 Office: Calfee Halter & Griswold 1400 Key Bank Ctr 800 Superior Ave E Cleveland OH 44114-2688 Home Phone: 216-371-0287; Office Phone: 216-622-8344. Business E-Mail: mwallach@calfee.com.

WALLACH, NOLAN R., mathematician, consultant; b. Bklyn., Aug. 3, 1940; s. Morris and Pauline Wallach; m. Barbara Hawkins, Apr. 25, 1965; children: Dana, Pamela. BS, U. Maryland, 1962; MA, Wash. U., St. Louis, Mo., 1963, PhD, 1966. Instr. U. of Calif., Berkeley, 1966—69; asst. prof. math. Rutgers U., New Brunswick, NJ, 1969—70, assoc. prof. math., 1970—72, prof. math., 1972—86, Hermann Weyl prof. math., 1986—89; disting. prof. math. U. Calif.-San Diego, La Jolla, 1989—. Cons. Ctr. for Comm. Rsch., La Jolla, 1995—; mem. Mat. Math. Com., 1985—92. Author: (book) Real Reductive Groups I, II, 1988, Continuous Cohomology, 2d edit., 1999; editor: Mathematics: Theory and Applications, 2001—; co-editor: Annals of Math., 1997—2003. Recipient Sloan fellowship, Alfred Sloan Found., 1972—74, Linback award for rsch. excellence, 1977. Fellow: Am. Acad. Arts and Scis.; mem.: Am. Math. Soc. (mem. editl. com. 1991—93, editor bull. 1995—98, mem. coun. 1999—2002). Office: U Calif San Diego Dept Math La Jolla CA 92093 Business E-Mail: nwallach@ucsd.edu.

WALLACH, PATRICIA, councilman, retired mayor; b. Chgo. m. Ed Wallach; 3 children. Grad., Pasadena City Coll. Mem. city coun. City of El Monte, Calif., 1990-92, mayor, 1992-99, elected mem. of city coun., 2003—. Ret. tchr.'s aide Mountain View Sch. Dist. Past trustee El Monte Union High Sch. Dist., L.A. County High Sch. for the Arts; amb. of goodwill Zamora, Michoacan, Mex., Marcq-en-Baroeul, France, Yung Kang, Hsiang, Republic of China, Minhang, Peoples Republic of China; bd. dirs. Cmty. Redevel. Agy., El Monte Cmty. Access TV Corp.; mem. PTA, Little League Assns.; del. Foothill Transit. Mem. League of Calif. Cities, San Gabriel Valley Coun. of Govts., Independent Cities Assn., U.S./Mex. Sister Cities Assn., Sister Cities Internat., Women of the Moose, El Monte Women's Club. Office Phone: 626-580-2001.

WALLACH, STEVEN ERNST, lawyer, pilot; b. NYC, Mar. 21, 1944; s. Eduard Herbert Wallach and Karin (Wassermann) Grunebaum; m. Stefany Gay Rosehill (div. Oct. 1990); children: Shelby Karin, Shawna Beth; m. Geri Joan Grieco, Nov. 21, 1992. BS, USAF Acad., 1965; MS summa cum laude, U. So. Calif., 1971; JD magna cum laude, Nova U., 1986. Bar: Fla. 1986, D.C. 1988, U.S. Dist. Ct. (so. dist.) Fla. 1987, U.S. Dist. Ct. (mid. dist.) Fla. 1989, U.S. Dist. Ct. Ariz. 1989; cert. airline transport pilot, 1969; bd. cert. aviation law, 1998. Systems analyst Hughes Aircraft Co., LA, 1971-72; airline capt. Eastern Air Lines, Miami, 1972-91; atty. Barwick, Dillian & Lambert P.A., Miami Shores, Fla., 1987-96; atty., ptnr. Thornton Davis & Murray, P.A., Miami, 1996-98. Aviation mgmt. cons. PRC Speas, Lake Success, N.Y., 1977-83, TRAMCO, Cambridge, Mass., 1972-77, A.V. lawyer, 1997, Steven Wallach Assoc., 1998—. Trustee Karin Grunebaum Cancer Found., Cambridge, 1979—; chmn. Karin Grunebaum Cancer Rsch. Found., Cambridge, 2004—. Capt. USAF, 1965—70. Decorated DFC, 5 air medals. Avocation: flying. Home: 2600 S Ocean Blvd Apt 21-E Boca Raton FL 33432

WALLACK, RINA EVELYN, lawyer; b. Pitts.; d. Erwin Norman and Gloria A. (Schacher). AD in Nursing, Delta Coll., 1973; BS cum laude in Psychology, Eastern Mich. U., 1980; JD cum laude, Wayne State U., 1983. Registered nurse Mich.; bar: Calif. 1983. Psychiat. head nurse Ypsilanti (Mich.) State Hosp., 1973-77, instr., nursing educator, 1977-80; teaching asst. contracts Wayne State U., Detroit, 1981-83; legal asst. Wayne County Prosecutor's Office, 1982-83; atty. NLRB, L.A., 1983-86, dir. employee rels. legal svcs. Paramount Pictures Corp., L.A., 1986-89, v.p., 1989-98, v.p., sr. counsel, 1998-2002, sr. v.p., 2002-; Contbr. articles to profl. jours. Instr. ARC, Mich., 1978-80. Recipient Am. Jurisprudence Book award, 1983. Mem. ABA, L.A. County Bar Assn., Am. Trial Lawyers Assn., Mich. Bar Assn., Calif. Bar Assn., Order of Coif. Avocations: shooting, movies, dancing, reading, photography.

WALLENMEYER, WILLIAM ANTON, retired physicist; b. Evansville, Ind., Feb. 3, 1926; s. William Anton and Mindie (Madden) W.; m. Diane May Hankins, June 1, 1952; children: Wendy Kauffman, Jon, Ann Ellis, Timothy. BS, Purdue U., 1950, MS, 1954, PhD, 1957, PhD (hon.), 1989. Jr. rsch. assoc. Brookhaven Nat. Lab., LI, NY, 1954—55; asst. prof. physics Wabash Coll., Crawfordsville, Ind., 1955-56; dir. accelerator divsn. Midwestern U. Rsch. Assn., Madison, Wis., 1957-62; dir. divsn. high energy physics U.S. Dept. Energy, Germantown, Md., 1962-87; pres. Southeastern Univ. Rsch. Assn., Washington, 1987-92; spl. asst. to pres. Univ. Rsch. Assn., Washington, 1993-94. With Air Corps US Army, 1944—46. Fellow: AAAS, Am. Phys. Soc. Home: 1204 Azalea Dr Rockville MD 20850-2024 E-mail: bantonw@verizon.net.

WALLER, EDWARD MARTIN, JR., lawyer; b. Memphis, July 2, 1942; s. Edward Martin and Freda (Lazarov) W.; m. Laura Jayne Rhodes, June 18, 1982; children: Lauren, Jonathan, Melissa. BA, Columbia U., 1964; JD, U. Chgo., 1967. Bar: Fla. 1967. Assoc. Fowler, White, Boggs, Banker, P.A., Tampa, Fla., 1967-72, ptnr., 1972—. Mem.: ABA (banking and fin. transactions com. 1978—82, co-chmn. 1983—87, coun. 1990—92, litig. sect. standing com. professionalism chmn. 1995—97, budget officer 1996—2000), Bay Area Legal Svcs. (bd. dir. 2003—, pres. 2006—07), Hillsborough County Bar Assn., Fla. Bar Assn., Fla. Supreme Ct. Commn. on Professionalism. Democrat. Jewish. Office: Fowler White Boggs Banker PO Box 1438 Tampa FL 33601-1438 Office Phone: 813-222-1137.

WALLER, EPHRAIM EVERETT, retired association executive; b. Sioux City, Iowa, Aug. 10, 1928; s. Everett and Ruth Emma (Little) W.; m. Virginia Louise Harper, Oct. 3, 1959. BA, U. Iowa, 1951, MA, 1959; grad., Strategic Intelligence Sch., 1955, Army Security Agy. Sch., 1962, Nat. Cryptologic Sch., 1966, Commd. and Gen. Staff Coll., 1966; grad. with honors, State Dept. Fgn. Svc. Inst., 1967, Turkish Lang. Sch., 1968; grad., Indsl. Coll. Armed Forces, 1972; EdD with honors, U. S.D., 1981. Cert. fgn. area specialist, cryptologist. Commd. 2d lt. U.S. Army, 1951, advanced through grades to lt. col., 1967, ret., 1979; exec. dir. Midwest Agrl. Chem. Assn., Sioux City, Iowa, 1981—95; ind. cons. in field Sioux City, 1996—. Mem. sci. and regulatory oversight coun. Am. Crop Protection Assn., Washington, 1990-95; mem. interregional coord. coun. Joint Body U.S. Regional Agrl. Assns., Dawson, Ga., 1991-95 Contbr. articles to profl. jours. Mem. coms. 1st Congrl. Ch., Sioux City, 1937— Decorated Bronze Star, Cross of Gallantry with Silver Star, Legion of Merit with oak leaf cluster, Chinese and Vietnamese Honor medals, Meritorious Svc. medal with oak leaf cluster, Joint Svc. Commendation medal with oak leaf cluster, Army Commendation medal with oak leaf cluster, Army Gen. Staff badge, Vietnamese Combat Merit medal; Asia Found. scholar U. Iowa; recipient Outstanding Leadership in the Industry award Am. Crop Protection Assn., 1995, Leadership in Cmty. and Pub. Edn. award Chem. Prodrs. and Distbrs. Assn., 1993-94, Dedication and Svc. to Agrl. Industry award Ill. Fertilizer and Chem. Assn., 1987, Dean Roy Exceptional Svc. award Midwest Agrl. Chem. Assn., 1985, Industry Vision award Mid Am. Crop Protection Assn., 1995, Significant Svc. to Agr. and Agrl. Chem. Industry award So. Crop Protection Assn., 1981-95, Don Kenna Excellence in Coalition Bldg. and Pub. Rels. award Fertilizer and Ag-Chem. Affiliated Assns., 1994. Mem. Ret. Officers Assn., Siouxland C. of C. (com. 1981-95), Interprofl. Inst., Scottish Rite, Masons, Eastern Star, Phi Delta Kappa, Delta Sigma Rho Avocations: swimming, hiking, travel, stamp collecting/philately, writing. Home: 2847 Valley Dr Sioux City IA 51104-4071

WALLER, EUNICE MCLEAN, retired elementary school educator; b. Lillington, NC, June 29, 1921; d. Absolom and Mary W. (Tucker) McLean; m. William DeHomer Waller, Aug. 9, 1958; m. Henry W. Ferguson, June 29, 1942 (div. June 1954). BS summa cum laude, Fayetteville U., NC, 1942; MS in Edn., U. Pa., 1952; 6th yr. Cert., U. Vt., 1965. Tchr. Harnett H.S., Dunn, NC, 1942—46, Shawtown H.S., Lillington, NC, 1946—56; demonstration tchr. Fayetteville State U., NC, 1956—58; tchr. 2d and U. Elem. Sch., Washington, 1958—60; tchr., asst. to prin. Fitch Elem. Sch., Washington, 1960—62; 7th grade tchr. Sarah Nance Elem. Sch., Columbia, SC, 1963—64; tchr. 8th grade Clark Lane Mid. Sch., Waterford, Conn., 1969—93; ret., 1993. Instr. dept. edn. Conn. Coll., New London, 1970—2001. Corporator Lawrence Meml. Hosp., New London; commr. ethics City Coun. of New London, Conn., 1990—2001; mayor, dep. mayor New London, 1986—88; Civil Rights commr. City New London, 2006—; state convener State of Conn. Nat. Coun. Negro Women, Inc. sects., Washington, 2006—; v.p. NAACP, New London, 1990—2001; pres. Nat. Coun. Negro Women, New London, 1993—2000; trustee Mitchell Coll., New London, Waterford Country Sch., Conn. Named Woman of the Yr., Nat. Coun. Negro Women, 1993; recipient Lifetime Achievement award, W.E.B. DuBois, 1999, Cmty. Svc. award for outstanding achievement, Opportunities Industry Coun., 1983, Dr. E.E. Smith Highest Honors award, Fayetteville State U., 1942; grantee, NSF, 1965. Mem.: NEA (life; Conn. state dir. 1984—88), Conn. Edn. Assn. (Pub. Relations Achievement award 1988), New London Lions (v.p. 1989—99). Democrat. Baptist. Avocations: civic volunteer, civil rights activitst. Personal E-mail: eunicewaller@msn.net.

WALLER, GARY FREDRIC, language educator, poet; b. Auckland, N.Z., Jan. 3, 1944; came to U.S., 1983; s. Fred and Joan Elsie (Smythe) W.; m. Jennifer Robyn Denham, July 2, 1966 (div. 1980); children: Michael, Andrew; m. Kathleen Ann McCormick, Nov. 12, 1988; one child, Philip. BA, U. Auckland, 1965, MA, 1966; PhD, Cambridge U., Eng., 1970. Donaldson Bye fellow Magdalene Coll., Cambridge, Eng., 1967-69; assoc. prof. English U. Auckland, New Zealand, 1969-72, Dalhousie U., N.S., Can., 1972-78; head, prof. English Wilfrid Laurier U., Waterloo, Can., 1978-83; head, prof. lit. and cultural studies Carnegie Mellon U., Pitts., 1983-92; dean arts and scis., prof. lit. and cultural studies U. Hartford, West Hartford, Conn., 1992-95; provost, v.p. acad. affairs, prof. lit. and cultural studies Purchase (N.Y.) Coll. SUNY, 1995—2004, prof. lit. and cultural studies Purchase (N.Y.) Coll., 2005—. Author: The Strong Necessity of Time, 1976, The Triumph of Death, 1977, Pamphilia to Amphilanthus, 1977, Dreaming America, 1979, Mary Sidney Countess of Pembroke, 1979, Sir Philip Sidney and the Interpretation of Renaissance Culture, 1984, Sixteenth Century Poetry, 1986, 2d edit., 1993, Reading Texts, 1986, Lexington Introduction to Literature, 1987, Shakespeare's Comedies, 1991, Reading Mary Wroth, 1991, The Sidney Family Romance, 1993, Edmund Spenser: A Literary Life, 1994, Lady Mary Sidney's Antonie and a Discourse of Life and Death, 1996, Shakespeare's All'w Well that Ends Well: New Critical Essays, 2007; (poems) Other Flights, Always, 1991, Impossible Futures Indelible Pasts, 1983. Office: Purchase Coll Humanities Purchase NY 10577

WALLER, GEORGE DARRYL, music educator; b. Elizabeth City, NC, May 19, 1961; s. George Alexander and Jean Faye Brickhouse Waller. MusB, Greensboro Coll., NC, 1983; MA, The George Wash. U., Washington, 1996. Cert. supr. and adminstr. Va. Dept. of Edn., 1996. Choral dir. Denbigh H.S., Newport News, Va., 1983—96; program adminstr. Ctr. for the Arts at Woodside H.S., Newport News, Va., 1996—2001; min. of music Hilton Bapt. Ch., Newport News, Va., 1983—86; music dir. Deer Pk. Bapt. Ch., Newport News, Va., 1988—94, Hilton Christian Ch., Newport News, Va., 1994—. Supr. of music Newport News Pub. Schs., Newport News, Va., 2001—. Singer: (professional singer) The Chamber Singers. Bd. dirs. Peninsula Youth Orch., Newport News, Va., 2000—04; arts commr. Newport News Arts Commn., Newport News, Va., 2003—05. Mem.: ASCD, Va. Assn. Music Edn. Adminstrs. (pres. 2002—), Va. Assn. of Phys. Edn., Recreation, and Dance, Southeastern Theatre Conf., Nat. Art Edn. Assn., Nat. Assn. of Tchrs. of Singers, Va. Music Educators Assn. (sect. pres. - vamea 2002—). Christian. Avocations: travel, theater. Home: 108 Wendy Ct Newport News VA 23601 Office: Newport News Public Schools 12465 Warwick Blvd Newport News VA 23606 Home Phone: 757-595-4177; Office Phone: 757-591-4561. Office Fax: 757-595-7522. E-mail: darryl.waller@nn.k12.va.us.

WALLER, HAROLD MYRON, political science professor; b. Detroit, Oct. 12, 1940; s. Allan L. and Lillian R. (LeVine) W.; m. Diane Carol Goodman, June 28, 1966; children: Sharon, Dahvi, Jeffrey. SB, MIT, 1962; MS, Northwestern U., 1966; PhD, Georgetown U., 1968. Asst. prof. McGill U., Montreal, 1967-71, assoc. prof., 1971-93, prof., 1993—, chmn. polit. sci. dept., 1969-74, 89-90, acting chmn., 1980-81, 86-87, assoc. dean (acad.) faculty arts, 1991-94, acting dean faculty arts, 1994-95, chair N.Am. studies program, 2003—04, 2007—. Pres. McGill Assn. Univ. Tchrs., Montreal, 1978-79; fellow Jerusalem Ctr. Pub. Affairs, 1980—, Canadian Inst. for Jewish Rsch., 1988—; dir. Can. Ctr. Jewish Cmty. Studies, Montreal, 1980—; vis. scholar Hudson Inst., Washington, 2004-05. Co-author: Maintaining Consensus: The Canadian Jewish Polity in the Postwar World, 1990; co-editor: Canadian Federalism: From Crisis to Constitution; contbg. editor: Middle East Focus; mem. editorial bd. Jewish Political Studies; chmn. editorial bd. Viewpoints; contbr. numerous articles to profl. jours. and books in field. Com. chmn. Can. Jewish Congress, Montreal, 1971-74; chair, nat. exec. Can. Profs. for Peace in Middle East, Toronto, 1975-85; pres. Akiva Sch., Montreal, 1984-85; com. chmn. Jewish Edn. Council, Montreal, 1986-88. Recipient Nat. Jewish Book award Jewish Book Coun., N.Y.C., 1991; Grad. fellow NSF, Washington, 1965-66, Leave fellow Social Sci. Humanities Rsch. Coun., Ottawa, 1981-82. Fellow Can. Inst. for Jewish Rsch.; mem. Am. Polit. Sci. Assn., Can. Polit. Sci. Assn., Assn. Jewish Studies, Assn. Sociol. Study of Jewry, Assn. Israel Studies, Faculty Club, Sigma Xi, Pi Sigma Alpha. Jewish. Avocations: travel, athletics, reading, politics. Office: McGill U Dept Polit Sci 855 Sherbrooke St W Montreal PQ Canada H3A 2T7 Office Phone: 514-398-4806. Business E-Mail: harold.waller@mcgill.ca.

WALLER, JOHN HENRY, JR., state supreme court justice; b. Mullins, SC, Oct. 31, 1937; s. John Henry and Elnita (Rabon) Waller; m. Jane McLaurin Cooper, Nov. 16, 1963 (div.); children: John Henry III, Melissa McLaurin; m. Debra Ann Meares, May 9, 1981; children: Ryan Meares, Rand Ellis. AB in Psychology, Wofford Coll., 1959; LLB, JD, U. S.C., 1963. Mem. SC Ho. of Reps., 1967—77, asst. majority leader, 1973—74, majority leader, 1975—76; mem. SC Senate, 1977—80; judge SC Cir. Ct., 1980—94; assoc. justice SC Supreme Ct., 1994—. Capt. US Army, 1959—60. Recipient Disting. Svc. award, Municipal Assn. of S.C., 1968. Mem.: Millins Rotary Club (1st pres.), Shriners, Masons. Avocations: woodworking, golf, water sports, skiing. Office: SC Supreme Ct Supreme Court PO Box 11330 Columbia SC 29211-1330 *

WALLER, JOHN LOUIS, anesthesiologist, educator; b. Loma Linda, Calif., Dec. 1, 1944; s. Louis Clinton and Sue (Bruce) W.; m. Jo Lynn Marie Haas, Aug. 4, 1968; children: Kristina, Karla, David. BA, So. Coll., Collegedale, Tenn., 1967; MD, Loma Linda U., 1971. Diplomate Am. Bd. Anesthesiology. Intern Hartford (Conn.) Hosp., 1971—72; resident in anesthesiology Harvard U. Med. Sch.-Mass. Gen. Hosp., Boston, 1972—74, fellow, 1974—75; asst. prof. anesthesiology Emory U. Sch. Medicine, Atlanta, 1977—80, assoc. prof., 1980—86, chmn. dept. anesthesiology, 1986—2000, prof., 1986—2001, prof. emeritus, 2001—; chief anesthesiology Emory U. Hosp., Atlanta, 1986-94, med. dir., 1993-95; assoc. v.p. info. svcs. Woodruff Health Scis. Ctr., 1995-97; chief info. officer Emory U. System Healthcare, Atlanta, 1995-97; prof. anesthesiology Med. U. S.C., Charleston, 2002—, chmn. dept. anesthesia and perioperative medicine, 2002—05, dir. med. informatics, 2005—. Cons. Arrow Internat., Inc., Reading, Pa., 1988—; mem. adv. com. on anesthetic and life support drugs FDA, Washington, 1986—92; numerous vis. professorships and lectures; bd. dirs. Picis, Inc. Contbr. articles to med. jours. Bd. dir. Picis Inc., 2006—. Maj. MC USAF, 1975—77. Recipient cert. of appreciation Office Sec. Def., 1983. Fellow: Am. Coll. Chest Physicians, Am. Coll. Anesthesiologists; mem.: Assn. Cardiac Anesthesiologists, Soc. Acad. Anesthesia Chmn. (councillor 1989—), Assn. Univ. Anesthesiologists, Internat. Anesthesia Rsch. Soc. (trustee 1984—2002, sec. 1996—98, chair 1998—2000), Soc. Cardiovascular Anesthesiologists (pres. 1991—93), Am. Soc. Anesthesiologists. Avocations: fishing, sailing, swimming. Office: Med Univ SC Dept Anes and Perioperative Medicine 167 Ashley Ave Ste 301 Charleston SC 29425 Business E-Mail: wallerj@musc.edu.

WALLER, MARY BELLIS, educational consultant, researcher; b. Milw., May 18, 1940; d. Ernest Anthony and Hazel Mary (Addie) Bellis; m. Michael I. Waller, May 9, 1987 (dec. Nov. 1996); children: Eric B. Griswold, Andrew D. Griswold, Megan E. Griswold Simone BS, U. Wis., Milw., 1969, MS, 1971, PhD, 1992. Coord. Wis. Coalition for Ednl. Reform, Milw., 1971-74; instr. U. Wis., Milw., 1974-77; exec. dir. Worker Rights Inst., Milw., 1977-87; adj. prof. Nat. Coll. Edn., Evanston, Ill., 1981-96; preceptor, clin. program coord. U. Wis.-Parkside, Kenosha, 1987-96; Wis. lead cons. Emprise Designs, 1993-97; psychotherapist, dir. outreach programs Achievement Assocs., Ltd., 1998—; clin. assoc. prof. U. Wis., Milw., 2002—. Cons. on drug-affected children; ctr. scientist Ctr. for Addiction and Behavioral Health Rsch., 1996—; pres. Program Devel. and Evaluation, 1993—, Priority Group, Inc., 1998—. Author: Crack-Affected Children: A Teacher's Guide, 1993, Lady of the Manor: Medieval Cooking with Herbs, 1994; author numerous articles on drug-affected children. Mem. ASCD, NAEYC, Am. Ednl. Rsch. Assn., Assn. Tchr. Educators, Phi Delta Kappa (Disting. Svc. award 1992). Home: 8316 N Regent Rd Milwaukee WI 53217-2736 Office Phone: 414-352-2213. Personal E-mail: mwaller2@wi.rr.com.

WALLER, PETER WILLIAM, public relations executive; b. Kewanee, Ill., Oct. 1, 1926; s. Ellis Julian and Barodel (Gould) Waller; m. Anne-Marie Appelius van Hoboken, Nov. 10, 1950; children: Catherine, Hans. BA with honors, Princeton U., 1949; MA with honors, San Jose State U., 1978. Bur. chief Fairchild Publs., San Francisco, 1953-55; freelance writer Mountain View, Calif., 1956-57; pub. rels. coord. Lockheed Missiles and Space, Sunnyvale, Calif., 1957-64; info. mgr. 1st missions to Jupiter, Saturn, Venus NASA Ames Rsch. Ctr., Mountain View, 1964-83, mgr. pub. info., 1983-95; cons. NASA-Ames Galileo, Lunar Prospector, 1996-97; prodr. space films PacPAW Assoc., 1998—. Speechwriter to pres. Lockheed Missiles and Space, 1960—64. Prodr.: (documentaries) Jupiter Odyssey, 1974 (Golden Eagle, 1974); prodr., writer NASA Aero. program, 1984; contbr. articles to profl. jours., encyclopedias. Cons. preservation Lake Tahoe Calif. Resources Agy., Sacramento, 1984. Mem.: No. Calif. Sci. Writers Assn., Sierra Club. Democrat. Congregationalist. Avocations: skiing, travel, architecture, construction, hiking. Home: 3655 La Calle Ct Palo Alto CA 94306-2619 Personal E-mail: pwaller@sbcglobal.net.

WALLER, ROBERT JAMES, writer; b. Aug. 1, 1939; s. Robert Sr. and Ruth W.; m. Georgia Ann Wiedemeier (div. 1997); 1 child, Rachael. Student, U. Iowa, 1957-58, U. No. Iowa, 1958; PhD, Ind. U., 1968. Prof. mgmt. U. No. Iowa, Cedar Falls, 1968-91, dean bus. sch., 1979-85. Author: Just Beyond the Firelight: Stories & Essays, 1988, One Good Road is Enough: Essays, 1990, The Bridges of Madison County, 1992, Slow Waltz in Cedar Bend, 1993, Old Songs in a New Cafe: Selected Essays, 1994, Border Music, 1995, A Thousand Country Roads: An Epilogue to the Bridges of Madison County, 2002, High Plains Tango, 2005; recorded album The Ballads of Madison County, 1993, Puerto Vallarta Squeeze, 1996. Recipient Literary Lion award New York Public Library, 1993. Office: care Aaron Priest Literary Agy 708 3rd Ave Fl 23 New York NY 10017-4201

WALLER, ROBERT REX, ophthalmologist, educator, foundation administrator; b. NYC, Feb. 19, 1937; s. Madison Rex and Sally Elizabeth (Pearce) W.; m. Sarah Elizabeth Pickens, Dec. 27, 1963; children: Elizabeth, Katherine, Robert Jr. BA, Duke U., 1958; MD, U. Tenn., 1963. Diplomate Am. Bd. Ophthalmology (dir. 1982—, vice chmn. 1988-89, chmn. 1989—). Intern City of Memphis Hosps., 1963-64; resident in internal medicine Mayo Grad. Sch. Medicine, Rochester, Minn., 1966-67, resident in ophthalmology, 1967-70, faculty, 1970—; assoc. prof. ophthalmology Mayo Clinic, Rochester, Minn., 1974-78, prof., 1978—; chmn. dept. ophthalmology Mayo Med. Sch., Rochester, Minn., 1974-84, cons., 1970—, bd. govs., 1978-93, chmn., 1988-93; trustee Mayo Found., Rochester, 1978—, pres., CEO, 1988-98, pres. emeritus, 1999—. Chmn. bd. trustees Healthcare Leadership Coun., Washington, 1999—2001, mem. bd. trustees, 2001—. Contbr. chpts. to books, articles to profl. jours. Elder 1st Presbyn. Ch., Rochester, 1975-78; mem. Rochester Task Force on Pub. Assembly Facilities, 1983-84. Oculplastic Surgery fellow U. Calif. San Francisco, 1973. Mem. AMA, Minn. State Med. Assn., Zumbro Valley Med. Assn., Am. Acad. Ophthalmology, Am. Ophthalmol. Soc., Orbital Soc., Am. Soc. Ophthalmic Plastic and Reconstructive Surgery, Minn. Acad. Ophthalmology and Otolaryngology, Memphis Country Club, Old Baldy Golf Club, Augusta Nat. Golf Club, Alpha Omega Alpha, Delta Tau Delta. Presbyterian. Avocations: golf, travel, photography. Home: 199 Greenbriar Dr Memphis TN 38117-3238 E-mail: RWaller@mayo.edu.

WALLER, STACEY, psychologist; b. Charleston, W. Va., Feb. 12, 1974; d. Clarence V and Glenna J Waller. BA, W. Va. U., 1996; MA, Western Mich. U., 2000, PhD, 2004. Lic. Psychologist. Post doctoral fellow W. Va. U., 2002—04; clin. psychologist W. Va. U. Med. Corp., 2004. Contbr. articles to profl. jours. Mem.: Am. Psychological Assn. Office: W Va U

Dept Behavioral Medicine and Psychiatry 930 Chestnut Ridge Rd Morgantown WV 26506 Business E-Mail: swaller@hsc.wvu.edu.

WALLER, STEVEN R., engineer; b. Moline, Ill., June 17, 1957; m. Dawn M. Vroman, June 4, 1977. AAS, Hamilton Tech. Coll., Davenport, Iowa, 1985, student. Cert. interconnect designer, IPC, 2000. Engrng. technician Rockwell Collins, Cedar Rapids, Iowa, 1985—2004; sr. pcb designer Crystal Group, Inc., Hiawatha, Iowa, 1999—2001; sr. deployment engr. Trapeze Group, Inc., Cedar Rapids, 2005—06; engr. Rockwell Collins, 2007—. Designer's coun. IPC, Hiawatha, Iowa, 2000—01. City councilman Hiawatha City Govt., 2001—03. Mem.: Mensa (life). Achievements include patents for LCD/keyboard system; PC to K/V/M/serial port extension. Personal E-mail: s.waller@mchsi.com.

WALLER, WILLIAM LOWE, JR., state supreme court justice; b. Miss., Feb. 9, 1952; s. Bill and Carroll (Overton) Waller; m. Charlotte Brawner, Aug. 4, 1979; children: William, Jeannie, Clayton. BA in Bus., Miss. State U., 1974; JD, U. Miss., 1977; grad., U.S. Army War Coll. Bar: Miss. 1977. Ptnr. Waller and Waller, 1977-97; judge City of Jackson, Miss., 1995-96; justice Miss. Supreme Ct., Jackson, 1998—, presiding justice, 2004—. Chmn. Miss. Pub. Defenders Task Force, 2000-05; mem. Study Commn. on the Miss. Jud. Sys.; chmn. Supreme Ct. Rules Com., 2001-. Deacon First Bapt. Ch., Jackson, Miss. Recipient Chief Justice award, 2005. Mem. ABA, Miss. Bar Assn. (chmn. Lawyer Referral Service 1987-89), Miss. Trial Lawyers Assn. (bd. mem. 1979-82), Hinds County Bar Assn. (Jud. Innovation award 2003-04), Jackson Young Lawyers Assn., Christian Legal Soc., Am. Legion, Miss. Nat. Guard Assn. (sec., chmn. legis. com., bd. dirs., nat. guard Miss. Army 1975-2004). Office: PO Box 117 Jackson MS 39205-0117

WALLER, WILMA RUTH, retired secondary school educator, librarian; b. Jacksonville, Tex., Nov. 15, 1921; d. William Wesley and Myrtle (Nesbitt) W. BA with honors, Tex. Woman's U., 1954, MA with honors, 1963, MLS with honors, 1976. Tchr. English Dell (Ark.) High Sch., 1953-54, Jefferson (Tex.) Ind. Schs., 1954-56, Tyler (Tex.) Ind. Schs., 1956-68; librarian Wise County Schs., Decatur, Tex., 1969-71, Thomas K. Gorman High Sch., Tyler, 1971-74, Sweetwater (Tex.) Ind. Sch. Dist., 1974-86; ret. Lectr., book reviewer for various clubs. Active in past as vol. for ARC, U. Tex. Health Ctr. Ford Found. fellow, 1959; recipient Delta Kappa Gamma Achievement award, 1992. Mem. UDC, Smith County Ret. Sch. Pers., Bible Study Group, Delta Kappa Gamma. Republican. Baptist. Avocations: reading, gourmet cooking, piano, writing. Home: 1117 N Azalea Dr Tyler TX 75701-5206

WALLERSTEIN, MITCHEL BRUCE, dean, educator; b. NYC, Mar. 8, 1949; s. Melvin Julian and Rita Helen (Nomburg) W.; m. Susan Elyse Perlik, June 29, 1974; children: Matthew, Leah. AB, Dartmouth Coll., 1971; MPA, Syracuse U., 1972; MS, MIT, 1977, PhD, 1978. Assoc. dir. Internat. Food Policy Program MIT, Cambridge, Mass., 1978-83, lectr. dept. polit. sci., 1978-83; asst. prof. dept. polit. sci. Holy Cross Coll., Worcester, Mass., 1979-81; exec. dir. office internat. affairs NRC, NAS, Washington, 1983-89; dep. exec. officer NRC, Washington, 1989-93; dep. asst. sec. of def. U.S. Dept. Def., Washington, 1993-97; disting. rsch. prof. Nat. Def. U., Washington, 1998; v.p. John D. and Catherine T. MacArthur Found., Chgo., 1998—2003; dean, prof polit. sci. and pub. adminstrn. Maxwell Sch. Citizenship and Pub. Affairs, Syracuse U., NY, 2003—. Adj. prof. Sch. Advanced Internat. Studies, Johns Hopkins U., Washington, 1992-98; adj. prof. Sch. Fgn. Svc., Georgetown U., Washington, 1989-93. Author: Food for War--Food for Peace: The Politics of U.S. Food Aid, 1979; author, dir. reports in field including multiple NAS reports on tech. transfer and nat. security. Recipient Sec. Def. medal for Outstanding Pub. Svc., 1997, 98. Fellow Nat. Acad. Pub. Adminstrn.; mem. AAAS, Internat. Inst. Strategic Studies, Coun. on Fgn. Rels. Democrat. Office: Maxwell Sch Citizenship and Pub Affairs Syracuse Univ 200 Eggers Hall Syracuse NY 13244-1020 Office Phone: 315-443-3461. Office Fax: 315-443-3385. Business E-Mail: mwallers@maxwell.syr.edu.

WALLERSTEIN, ROBERT SOLOMON, retired psychiatrist; b. Berlin, Jan. 28, 1921; s. Lazar and Sarah (Guensberg) Wallerstein; m. Judith Hannah Saretsky, Jan. 26, 1947; children: Michael Jonathan, Nina Beth, Amy Lisa. BA, Columbia U., 1941, MD, 1944; postgrad., Topeka Inst. Psychoanalysis, 1951-58. Assoc. dir., then dir. rsch. Menninger Found., Topeka, 1954-66; chief psychiatry Mt. Zion Hosp., San Francisco, 1966-78; tng. and supervising analyst San Francisco Psychoanalytic Inst., 1966—; clin. prof. U. Calif. Sch. Medicine, Langley-Porter Neuropsychiat. Inst., 1967-75, prof., chmn. dept. psychiatry, also dir. inst., 1975-85, prof. dept. psychiatry, 1985-91, prof. emeritus, 1991—, ret. Vis. prof. psychiatry La. State U. Sch. Medicine, New Orleans Psychoanalytic Inst., Pahlavi U., Shiraz, Iran, 1977, Fed. U. Rio Grande do Sul, Portol Alegre, Brazil, 1980; mem., chmn. rsch. scientist career devel. com. NIMH, 1966—70; fellow Ctr. Advanced Study Behavioral Scis., Stanford, Calif., 1964—65, 1981—82, Rockefeller Found. Study Ctr., Bellagio, Italy, 1992. Author: 21 books; mem. editl. bd.: numerous profl. jours.; contbr. over 370 articles to profl. jours. With US Army, 1946—48. Recipient Heinz Hartmann award, N.Y. Psychoanalytic Inst., 1968, Disting. Alumnus award, Menninger Sch. Psychiatry, 1972, J. Elliott Royer award, U. Calif., San Francisco, 1973, Outstanding Achievement award, No. Calif. Psychiat. Soc., 1987, Mt. Airy gold medal, 1990, Mary Singleton Sigourney award, 1991, Outstanding Contbn. to Psychoanalytic Edn. award, Internat. Fedn. Psychoanalytic Edn., 1999. Fellow: ACP, Am. Orthopsychiat. Assn., Am. Psychiat. Assn., Am. Coll. Psychoanalysts; mem.: Group Advancement Psychiatry, Mex. Psychoanalytic Assn. (hon.), Brit. Psycho-Analytic Soc. (hon.), Internat. Psychoanalytic Assn. (v.p. 1977—86, pres. 1985—89, hon. v.p. 1999—), Am. Psychoanalytic Assn. (pres. 1971—72), Phi Beta Kappa, Alpha Omega Alpha. Home: 290 Beach Rd Belvedere CA 94920-2472 Home Phone: 415-435-3417; Office Phone: 415-435-3417. Personal E-mail: judywall@mindspring.com.

WALLEY, BYRON See CARD, ORSON SCOTT

WALLEY, JAMES MARVIN, JR., engineering executive, management consultant, real estate company executive; b. Orange, Calif., Oct. 25, 1947; s. James Marvin Sr. and Edna Amelia (Rohr) W.; m. Marynelle Lorimer Walley, Apr. 28, 1990; children: Charlotte, Elizabeth, Edward, Joseph. BSCE, Tulane U., 1970; MSCE, George Washington U., 1974; MBA in Fin., U. So. Miss., 1980. Registered profl. engr., Tex., Va.; cert. property mgr., lic. broker. Commd. ensign USN, 1970, advanced through grades to lt. comdr. Civil Engr. Corps, served in Vietnam, 1970-71, resigned, 1981; exec. v.p. SPW, Inc., Dallas, 1981-84; chief ops. officer, ptnr. Montgomery Cos., Inc., Dallas, 1984-87; sr. v.p. Law Engring., Inc., Dallas, 1988-94; pres., COO Cura, Inc., Dallas, 1995. Pres., CEO Geo. Marine, Inc., 1996; v.p. Archon Group, 1997—. Vice chmn., chmn. ARC, 1985, sec.; councilman University Park City, 1998-2002. Rear Admiral Civil Engr. Corps, USN Res. Fellow: ASCE; mem.: Soc. Am. Mil. Engrs., Seabee Meml. Scholarship Assn. (pres. 2001—03), Leadership Dallas Alumni (pres. 1986), Tulane Alumni Coun. Assn. (pres. 1989), Salesmanship Club Dallas, Masons (32d Degree, KCCH). Republican. Roman Catholic. Avocations: golf, skiing. Address: RADM CEC USNR 600 E Las Colinas Blvd Ste 400 Irving TX 75039

WALLFESH, HENRY MAURICE, communications executive, writer; b. NYC, June 15, 1937; s. David Shibe and Rose (Silk) W.; m. Suzanne Krakowitch, Dec. 26, 1960; children: Saundra Kay, Gerald Bruce. Grad. indsl. and labor rels., Cornell U., 1958. Editor, co-pub. Indsl. Rels. News, NYC and Stamford, Conn., 1960-67; pres., chief exec. officer RAI div. Hearst Bus. Communications, NYC, 1968-91, sr. v.p., editor at large, 1991; pres. Whale Communications, Inc., Stamford, Conn., 1992—. Pres. Indsl. Rels. Inst., Stamford, 1964-67; founder, bd. dirs. Internat. Soc. Pre-Retirement Planners, 1975-88; bd. dirs. VSOP Mktg., Boston. Author: Implications of the Age Discrimination in Employment, 1977, When a CEO Retires, 1978. Bd. dirs. Aging in Am., N.Y.C., 1985-90, N.Y.C. Anti-Defamation League, 1987-89; mem. alumni bd. dirs. Cornell Inst. Labor Rels., 1995—99. Capt. inf. USAR, 1958-67. Recipient Corp. Achievement award Nat. Assn. for Sr. Living Industries, 1990; inducted into Internat. Soc. Pre-Retirement Planners Hall of Fame, 1988. Mem. Roxbury Swim and Tennis Club (bd. dirs. 1975-78), Cornell Club. Jewish. Avocations: tennis, theater, writing. Home and Office: 341 Biltmore Ln Somerset NJ 08873-6004 Personal E-mail: hswhale@aol.com.

WALLIN, LELAND DEAN, artist, educator; b. Sioux Falls, SD, Oct. 14, 1942; s. Clarence Forrest and Leona Mae (McInnis) W.; m. Meredith Maria Hawkins, Mar. 26, 1977; 1 child, Jessica Hawkins. Student, Columbus Coll. Art and Design, 1961-62; BFA in Painting, Kans. City Art Inst., Mo., 1965; MFA in Painting, U. Cin. with Cin. Art Acad., 1967. Prof. drawing, painting, sculpture St. Cloud State U., Minn., 1967-86; prof. Queens Coll., CUNY, Flushing, NY, 1983-84; prof., coord. MFA painting Marywood U., Scranton, Pa., 1985-90; prof. painting and drawing East Carolina U., Greenville, NC, 1992—. Adv. Painting Guild, 1993-2006; lectr. Carnegie-Mellon U., Pitts., 1988; curator Philip Pearlstein Retrospective Exhibit, Scranton, 1988; juror Belin Arts Grant Com., Waverly, Pa., 1986-89; vis. prof. painting East Carolina U., Greenville, 1992-93; judge, juror No. Nat. Art Competition, 1993. One-man shows include Mpls. Coll. Art and Design, 1977—78, Harold Reed Gallery, NYC, 1983, Gallery Henoch, 1991, Greenville Mus. Art, NC, 2007, exhibited in group shows at Bklyn. Mus., 1983, Greenville County Mus. Art, SC, 1983, Huntsville Mus. Art, 1994, San Bernardino County Mus. Internat., Calif., 1995, Contemporary Realism, Phila., 1996, Ctr. Arts, Laredo, Tex., 1997 (Internat. First Pl. award, 1997), Downey Mus. Art, Calif., 1998, Ctr. Arts, Laredo, Tex., 1999 (Internat. First Pl. award, 1999), Palm Springs Desert Mus., 1999, Fine Arts Ctr., Sacramento, 1999, Bellevue Art Mus., Wash., 2001, Morris Mus. Art, Ga., 2001, Huntsville Mus. Art, Ala., 2002, Miss. Mus. Art, 2002, Barret Art Ctr., Poughkeepsie, NY, 2003, Myth, Magic & Metaphor, Chgo., 2004, Union St. Gallery, 2004; contbr. articles to profl. jours. Named Outstanding Tchr., East Carolina U., 1994, 1995; recipient Scholar-Tchr. award for Coll. Fine Arts and Comm., East Carolina U. Sch. Art and Design, 2005—, numerous rsch. awards, East Carolina U., 1994—. Home: 218 York Rd Greenville NC 27858-5601

WALLING, CHEVES THOMSON, chemistry professor; b. Evanston, Ill., Feb. 28, 1916; s. Willoughby George and Frederika Christina (Haskell) W.; m. Jane Ann Wilson, Sept. 17, 1940; children: Hazel, Rosalind, Cheves, Janie, Barbara AB, Harvard, 1937; PhD, U. Chgo., 1939. Rsch. chemist E.I. duPont de Nemours, 1939-43, U.S. Rubber Co., 1943-49; tech. aide Office Sci. Research, Washington, 1945; sr. rsch. assoc. Lever Bros. Co., 1949-52; prof. chemistry Columbia U., NYC, 1952-69; Disting. prof. chemistry U. Utah, Salt Lake City, 1970-91, prof. chemistry emeritus, 1991—. Author: Free Radicals in Solution, 1957, Fifty Years of Free Radicals, 1995; also numerous articles. Fellow AAAS; mem. Nat. Acad. Scis., Am. Acad. Arts and Scis., Am. Chem. Soc. (editor jour. 1975-81, James Flack Norris award 1970, Lubrizol award 1984) Home: 222 Gilson Rd PO Box 537 Jaffrey NH 03452-0537 Office Phone: 603-532-6557.

WALLING, DONOVAN ROBERT, editor, writer; b. Kansas City, Mo., Jan. 9, 1948; s. Donovan Ernest and Dorothy Jane (Goyette) W.; m. Diana Lynn Eveland, Oct. 19, 1968 (dec. 1991); children: Katherine Anne, Donovan David, Alexander James. BS in Edn., Kans. State Tchrs. Coll., 1970; MS, U. Wis., Milw., 1975. Cert. tchr., adminstr., Wis., Ind. Tchr. Sheboygan (Wis.) Area Sch. Dist., 1970-81, 83-86, coord. lang. arts and reading, 1986-91; tchr. Dept. Def. Dependents Schs., Zweibruecken, Germany, 1981-83; dir. instrnl. svcs. Carmel (Ind.)-Clay Schs., 1991-93; dir. publs. Phi Delta Kappa Internat., Bloomington, Ind., 1993—2006; sr. cons. Ctr. for Civic Edn., Calabasas, Calif., 2007—. Mem. adj. faculty U. Wis., Oshkosh, 1986-91, Silver Lake Coll., Manitowoc, Wis., 1987-91. Author: Complete Book of School Public Relations, 1982, How To Build Staff Involvement in School Management, 1984, Teachers as Leaders, 1994, Rethinking How Art Is Taught, 2000, Visual Knowing, 2005, Teaching Writing to Visual, Auditory, and Kinesthetic Learners, 2006; also numerous articles. Mem. ASCD, Nat. Coun. Tchrs. English, Nat. Art Edn. Assn., Phi Delta Kappa (v.p. Cen. Ind. chpt. 1992-93). Avocations: writing, painting. Office: Ctr for Civic Edn 5145 Douglas Fir Rd Calabasas CA 91302-1440 Home Phone: 812-335-1456.

WALLINGER, M(ELVIN) BRUCE, lawyer; b. Richmond, Va., Dec. 27, 1945; s. Melvin W. and Ellen Scott (Barnard) W.; m. Rosemary Moore Hynes, Aug. 8, 1970; children: Mary Moore, Ann Harrison, Carrie. BA, U. Va., 1968, JD, 1972. Bar: Va. 1972, U.S. Dist. Ct. (we. dist.) Va. 1972, U.S. Ct. Appeals (4th cir.) 1976, U.S. Supreme Ct. 1978, U.S. Dist. Ct. (ea. dist.) Va. 1986; mediator and arbitrator for Am. Arbitration Assn. (Comml., Employment and Large, Complex Case panels). Assoc. Wharton, Aldhizer & Weaver, Harrisonburg, Va., 1972—76, ptnr., 1976—2004, Hoover Penrod, Harrisonburg, Va., 2004—. Fellow ABA, Am. Coll. Trial Lawyers, Va. Law Found.; mem. Va. Bar Assn. (exec. com. 1996-99), Harrisonburg Bar Assn. (pres. 1984), Va. State Bar (pres. young lawyers conf. 1981-82, chmn. 6th dist. disciplinary com. 1988-89), Va. Assn. Def. Attys. (pres. 1989-90). Avocations: bicycling, scuba diving. Office: Hoover Penrod 342 South Main Street Harrisonburg VA 22801 Office Phone: 540-433-2444.

WALLINGFORD, ANNE, freelance/self-employed writer, marketing professional, consultant; b. Chgo., June 29, 1949; d. Lester Arlyn and Roseanne (Jones) W. BS in Edn., Chgo. State U., 1975. Cert. elem. and mid. sch. tchr., Ill. Profl. dressmaker Annie's Original's, Chgo., 1968-72; instr., asst. prin., St. Bonaventure Sch., Chgo., 1972-81; instr., chair sci. dept. Our Lady of Lourdes Sch., Chgo., 1981-87; product designer, catalog mgr. FSC Ednl., Inc., Mansfield, Ohio, 1988-91; interim dir. pub. rels. Shelby Meml. Hosp., 1991-92; founder, dir. Anne Wallingford WordSmith, Chgo., 1992—. Instr. English lit. and bus. writing North Ctrl. Tech. Coll., 1991-92; catalog/project developer ETA, 1992-95, Sargent-Welch, 1993-2002, Basic Sci., 2003—; permissions editor McGraw-Hill, 2000—, Eisco Electronic Instrumentation, 2007—, United Sci., 2002—; tech. writer, cons. in field. Contbr. articles to profl. jours. and newspapers. Active The Vol. Ctr., Mansfield, 1992-93, steering com. Wright Cmty. Ctr., 1991; treas. Wolfram St. Block Club, Chgo., 1975-78. Recipient Gold award Adler Planetarium, Chgo., 1985. Mem. Nat. Writers Union, Chgo., Women in Pub. (Individual Excellence in Prodn., 1994, 95), Soc. Tech. Communicators, Writers-Editors Network, Profl. Freelance Assn. (founder, pres., 1991-92), Editl. Freelancers Assn., Mensa. Avocations: telecommunications, reading, theater, museums.

WALLINGFORD, JACK W., secondary school educator; b. Schenectady, NY, Sept. 1954; s. John William Wallingford and Norma Genevieve Restofo; m. Jacqueline Sophia Wallingford (div.). Student, Akron U., Ohio, 1972—74; BA in English, Kent State U., Ohio, 1976, MA in English, 1978, tchr. cert., 2005; postgrad., Cleve. State U., 2006. Cert. tchr. Ohio, mentor David's Challenge, 2006. Contbr. articles to Archery World. Active Pedal to Point, Multiple Sclerosis Soc., Independence, Ohio, 2004—06. Mem.: Nat. Wild Turkey Fedn. (banquet chmn. 1996—), Trout Unltd., Cleve. Mus. Natural History, Rotary, Trout Club (life). Avocations: conservation, fly fishing, archery, bow hunting, photography. Home: 10831 Ambler Ln Mantua OH 44255-9276

WALLIS, BEN ALTON, JR., lawyer; b. Llano County, Tex., Apr. 27, 1936; s. Ben A. and Jessie Ella (Longbotham) W.; children from previous marriage: Ben a. III, Jessica; m. Joan Mery, 1987. BBA, U. Tex., 1961, JD, 1971; postgrad., Law Sch. So. Meth. U. Bar: Tex. 1966, U.S. Dist. Ct. (no. dist.) Tex. 1971, U.S. Ct. Appeals D.C. 1974, U.S. Dist. Ct. D.C. 1975, U.S. Dist. Ct. (we. dist.) Tex. 1975, U.S. Dist. Ct. (no. dist.) Calif. 1983, U.S. Ct. Appeals (5th cir.) 1975, U.S. Ct. Appeals (8th cir.) 1980, U.S. Ct. Appeals (11th cir.) 1981, U.S. Dist. Ct. (ea. dist.) Wis. 1983, U.S. Supreme Ct. 1974. Pvt. practice, Llano, 1966-67, Dallas, 1971-73; investigator, prosecutor State Securities Bd. Tex., 1967-71; v.p. of devel. Club Corp. Am., Dallas, 1973; assoc. counsel impeachment task force U.S. Ho. of Reps. Com. on Judiciary, Washington, 1974; prin. Law Offices of Ben Wallis, P.C., San Antonio, 1974—. Chmn. Nat. Land Use Conf., 1979-81; mem. Gov.'s Areawide Planning Adv. Com., 1975-78; pres. Inst. Human Rights Rsch., 1979-2000. Mem.: FBA, ATLA, Coll. of State Bar of Tex., State Bar Tex. (former chmn. agr. tax com.), D.C. Bar Assn., San Antonio Bar Assn., Delta Theta Phi, Delta Sigma Pi. Republican. Baptist. Office: 7800 W IH 10 Ste 100 San Antonio TX 78230 Office Phone: 210-525-1500. Office Fax: 210-525-9323; Home Fax: 210-698-6683. Business E-Mail: ben@wallislaw.com.

WALLIS, CARLTON LAMAR, librarian; b. Blue Springs, Miss., Oct. 15, 1915; s. William Ralph and Tellie (Jones) W.; m. Mary Elizabeth Cooper, Feb. 22, 1944; 1 child, Carlton Lamar. BA with spl. distinction, Miss. Coll., 1936; MA, Tulane U., 1946; B.L.S., U. Chgo., 1947; L.H.D., Rhodes Coll., Memphis, 1980. English tchr., coach Miss. Pub. Schs., 1936-41; teaching fellow Miss. Coll. and Tulane U., 1941-42; chief librarian Rosenberg Library, Galveston, Tex., 1947-55; city librarian Richmond, Va., 1955-58; dir. Memphis Pub. Library, 1958-80, ret., 1980. Author: Libraries in the Golden Triangle, 1966; contbr. articles to library jours. Trustee Belhaven Coll., 1978-82, Nat. Ornamental Metal Mus., 1989—. Served as chief warrant officer AUS, 1942-46. Decorated Bronze Star. Mem. ALA (chmn. library mgmt. sect. 1969-71), Pub. Library Assn. (dir. 1973-77), Tex. Library Assn. (pres. 1952-53), Va. Library Assn., Southwestern Library Assn. (exec. bd. 1950-55), Southeastern Library Assn. (chmn. pub. library sect. 1960-62), Tenn. Library Assn. (pres. 1969-70, Distinguished Service award 1979, Intellectual Freedom award 1998). Presbyterian (elder). Club: Egyptian (pres. 1973-74). Home: 365 Kenilworth Pl Memphis TN 38112-5405

WALLIS, DIANA LYNN, artistic director; b. Windsor, Eng., Dec. 11, 1946; d. Dennis Blackwell and Joan Williamson (Gatcombe) W. Grad., Royal Ballet Sch., Eng., 1962-65. Dancer Royal Ballet Touring Co., London, 1965-68; ballet mistress Royal Ballet Sch., London, 1969-81, dep. ballet prin., 1981-84; artistic coord. Nat. Ballet of Can., Toronto, 1984-86, assoc. artistic dir., 1986-87, co-artistic dir., 1987-89; free-lance prod., tchr. London; dep. artistic dir. English Nat. Ballet, London, 1990-94; artistic dir. Royal Acad. Dance, 1994—. Fellow Imperial Soc. Tchrs. Dancing. Office Phone: 020 7326 8012. Business E-Mail: lwallis@rad.org.uk.

WALLIS, EDWIN E., JR., lawyer; b. Memphis, Sept. 7, 1948; m. Elizabeth B. Butler, Aug. 22, 1969; children: Margaret H., Mollie W. Carter, Edwin E. III. BA, Vanderbilt U., Nashville, 1969, JD, 1972. Ptnr. Moss, Benton & Wallis, PLLC, Jackson, Tenn., 1975—. Chmn. West Tenn. Regional Blood Ctr., Inc., Jackson, Old Hickory Acad., Jackson; pres. United Way Madison. Anglican. Office: Moss Benton & Wallis PLLC 325 N Parkway Jackson TN 38305 Home Phone: 731-668-5859; Office Phone: 731-668-5500.

WALLIS, ERIC G., lawyer; b. Astoria, NY, Jan. 8, 1950; AB magna cum laude, U. Pacific, 1972; JD, U. Calif., Hasting Coll. of Law, 1975. Bar: Calif. 1975. Mem. Crosby, Heafey, Roach & May PC, Oakland, Calif., 1982—. Editl. assoc. Hastings Law Jour., 1974-75. Mem. ABA (sect. litigation), State Bar Calif., Alameda County Bar Assn. Office: Crosby Heafey Roach & May PC 1999 Harrison St Fl 26 Oakland CA 94612-3520 E-mail: ewallis@chnm.com.

WALLIS, JIM, religious speaker, activist, writer; b. Detroit, June 4, 1948; m. Joy Carroll, Oct. 25, 1997; children: Luke, Jack. BA, Mich. State U., 1970; grad., Trinity Evang. Div. Sch., Deerfield, Ill. Founder, editor-in-chief, exec. dir. Sojourners, 1971—; convener, pres. Call to Renewal, 1995—. Vis. fellow Inst. Politics, Harvard U., 2002. Author: Call to Conversion, 1981, The Soul of Politics: A Practical and Prophetic Vision for Change, 1994, Who Speaks for God? A New Politics of Compassion, Community, and Civility, 1996, Faith Works, 2000, God's Politics: Why the Right Gets It Wrong and the Left Doesn't Get It, 2005. Named one of 50 Faces for America's Future, Time mag., 1979. Office: Sojourners Ste 200 3333 14th St NW Washington DC 20010-2319 Office Phone: 202-328-8842.

WALLIS, OLNEY GRAY, lawyer; b. Llano, Tex., July 27, 1940; s. Ben Alton and Jessie Ella (Longbotham) W.; m. Linda Lee Johnson, June 29, 1963; children: Anne, Brett. BA, U. Tex., 1962, JD, 1965. Bar: Tex. 1965, U.S. Dist. Ct. (so. dist.) Tex. 1966, U.S. Ct. Mil. Appeals 1968, U.S. Surpeme Ct. 1970, U.S. dist. Ct. (we. dist.) Tex. 1976, U.S. Ct. Appeals (5th cir.) 1977, U.S. Tax Ct. 1980, U.S. Ct. Appeals (10th cir.) 1981, U.S. Ct. Appeals (11th cir.) 1983, U.S. Dist. Ct. (no. dist.) Tex. 1985, U.S. Dist. Ct. (ea. and we. dists.) Ark. 1985, U.S. Ct. Appeals (8th cir.) 1985. Assoc. Brown & Cecil, Houston, 1965-66; asst. U.S. atty. Dept. Justice, Houston, 1971-74; mem. Jefferson, Wallis & Sherman, Houston, 1975-81, Wallis & Pruitt, Houston, 1981-87, Wallis and Short, Houston, 1987—. Instr. U. Md., Keflauik, Iceland, 1968-69; mem. faculty continuing legal edn. U. Houston, 1981-84. Capt. USAF, 1969-70. Decorated Air Force Commendation medal. Mem. Assn. Trial Lawyers Am., Am. Judicature Soc., Tex. Trial Lawyers Assn., Houston Bar Found., Phi Delta Phi, Phi Kappa Tau. Office: Wallis & Short 9535 S Hwy 16 Llano TX 78643 Office Phone: 713-956-1300. Personal E-mail: ogwlawyer@earthlink.net.

WALLIS, RICHARD FISHER, physicist, researcher; b. Washington, May 14, 1924; s. William F. and Alberta (Sigelen) W.; m. Mary Camilla Williams, Aug. 20, 1955; children: Maria Fisher, Sylvia Camilla. BS, George Washington U., 1945, MS, 1948; PhD, Cath. U. Am., 1952. Postdoctoral fellow (U. Md.), College Park, 1951-53; chemist Applied Physics Lab. Johns Hopkins U., Silver Spring, Md., 1953-56; physicist Naval Rsch. Lab., Washington, 1956-66, 67-69, head semiconductors br., 1958-66, 67-69; prof. physics U. Calif., Irvine, 1966-67, 69—; prof. emeritus, 1993—; chmn. dept. physics U. Calif., Irvine, 1972-75, 80-83. Vis. prof. U. Paris, 1975-76, 79, 85. Author: (with Maradudin and Dobrzynski) Handbook of Surfaces and Interfaces, 1980, (with Balkanski) Many-Body Aspects of Solid State Spectroscopy, 1986, (with Balkanski) Semiconductor Physics and Applications, 2000; editor: Lattice Dynamics, 1965, Localized Excitations in Solids, 1968 (with Stegeman) Electromagnetic Surface Excitations, 1986, (with Birman and Sebenne) Elementary Excitations in Solids, 1992; contbr. articles to profl. jours. Served with U.S. Army, 1945-46. Recipient Pure Sci. award Naval Rsch. Lab., 1964, Disting. Alumni Achievement award George Washington U., 1991. Fellow Am. Phys. Soc., AAAS; mem. Philos. Soc. Washington, Phi Beta Kappa, Sigma Xi Home: 2635 Alta Vista Dr Newport Beach CA 92660-4102 Office: U Calif Dept Physics Irvine CA 92697-0001

WALLISON, FRIEDA K., lawyer; b. NYC, Jan. 15, 1943; d. Ruvin H. and Edith (Landes) Koslow; m. Peter J. Wallison, Nov. 24, 1966; children: Ethan S., Jeremy L., Rebecca K. AB, Smith Coll., 1963; LLB, Harvard U., 1966. Bar: N.Y. 1967, D.C. 1982. Assoc. Carter, Ledyard & Milburn, NYC, 1966-75; spl. counsel divsn. market regulation SEC, Washington, 1975;

exec. dir., gen. counsel Mcpl. Securities Rulemaking Bd., Washington, 1975-78; ptnr. Rogers & Wells, NYC and Washington, 1978-83, Jones, Day, Reavis & Pogue, NYC and Washington, 1983-98; mem. Govtl. Acctg. Standards Coun., Washington, 1984-90, Nat. Coun. on Pub. Works Improvement, Washington, 1985-88; vice chair environ. fin. adv. bd. EPA, 1988-92. Contbr. articles to profl. jours. Fellow Am. Bar Found.; mem. N.Y.C. Bar Assn.

WALLMANN, JEFFREY MINER, author; b. Seattle, Dec. 5, 1941; s. George Rudolph and Elizabeth (Biggs) W. BS, Portland State U., 1962; PhD, U. Nev., 1998. Pvt. investigator Dale Sys., NYC, 1962-63; asst. buyer, mgr., pub. money bidder Dohrmann Co., San Francisco, 1966-69; dir. pub. rels. London Films, Cinelux-Universal, Trans-European Publs., 1970-75; editor-in-chief Riviera Life mag., 1975-77; instr. U. Nev., Reno, 1990—, Regis U., 2003—. Instr. U. Nev., Las Vegas, 1998—, chair gen. studies; instr. U. Phoenix, 2001—, Regis U., 2003—. Author: The Spiral Web, 1969, Judas Cross, 1974, Clean Sweep, 1976, Jamaica, 1977, Deathtrek, 1980, Blood and Passion, 1980, Brand of the Damned, 1981, The Manipulator, 1982, Return to Conta Lupe, 1983, The Celluloid Kid, 1984, Business Basic for Bunglers, 1984, Guide to Applications Basic, 1984, The Western: Parables of the American Dream, 1999, (under pseudonym Leon DaSilva) Green Hell, 1976, Breakout in Angola, 1977, (under pseudonym Nick Carger) Hour of the Wolf, 1973, Ice Trap Terror, 1974, (under pseudonym Margaret Maitland) The Trial, 1974, Come Slowly, Eden, 1974, How Deep My Cup, 1975, (under pseudonym Amanda Hart Douglass) First Rapture, 1972, Jamaica!, 1978, (under pseudonym Grant Roberts) The Reluctant Couple, 1969, Wayward Wives, 1970, (under pseudonym Gregory St. Germain) Resistance # 1: Night and Fog, 1982, Resistance #2: Magyar Massacre, 1983, (under pseudonym Wesley Ellis) Lonestar on the Treachery Trail, 1982, numerous others, (under pseudonym Tabor Evans) Longarm and the Lonestar Showdown, 1986, (under pseudonym Jon Sharpe) Trailsman 58: Slaughter Express, 1986, numerous others in Trailsman series, also others under pseudonyms; co-author: (under pseudonym William Jeffrey) Duel at Gold Buttes, 1980, Border Fever, 1982, Day of the Moon, 1983, The Western: Parables of the American Dream, 1999; contbr. articles and short stories to Argosy, Ellery Queen's Mystery Mag., Alfred Hitchcock's Mystery Mag., Zane Grey Western, Venture, Oui, TV Guide. Mem. Mystery Writers Am., Sci. Fiction Writers Am., We. Writers Am., Nat. Coun. Tchrs. English, Crime Writers Am., Nev. state Coun. Tchrs. English, Esperanto League N.Am., We. Lit. Assn., Internacia Soc. Amikeco Kaj Bonvolo, Sci. Fiction Rsch. Assn., Internat. Assn. Fantastic in the Arts, We. Lit. Assn. Office: care of Barry Malzberg PO Box 61 Teaneck NJ 07666-0061

WALLOT, JEAN-PIERRE, archivist, historian; b. Valleyfield, Que., Can., May 22, 1935; s. Albert and Adrienne (Thibodeau) W.; m. Denyse Caron; children: Normand, Robert, Sylvie. BA, Coll. Valleyfield, 1954; lic. es lettres, U. Montreal, 1957, MA in History, 1957, PhD in History, 1965; D (hon.), U. Rennes, France, 1987, U. Ottawa, Can., 1996. Reporter Le Progres de Valleyfield, 1954—61; from lectr. to prof. dept. history U. Montreal, 1961—65, dept. chmn., 1973—75, vice-dean studies faculty arts and scis., 1975—78, vice-dean rsch. Faculty Arts and Scis., 1979—82, academic v.p., 1982—85. Nat. archivist, Can., 1985-97; historian Nat. Mus. Man, Ottawa, Ont., 1966-69, assoc. prof. U. Toronto, 1969-71; prof. Concordia U., Montreal, Que., 1971-73; vis. prof. U. Ottawa, 1997—, dir. Ctr. Rsch. en Civilisation Canadienne-Francaise, 2000-06; dir. Etude Assn. Ecole Pratique des Hautes Etudes en Scis. Sociales, Paris, 1975, 79, 81, 83, 85, 87, 89, 94. Author: French and American Intrigues in Canada, 1965; author: (with John Hare) Imprints in Lower Canada, 1967; author: Confrontations, 1971; author: (with G. Paquet) Patronage and Power in Lower Canada, 1973, A Quebec that Changed, 1973, Un Québec Moderne, 2007; editor (with R. Girard): Memoires de J.E. McComber, bourgeois de Montréal, 1981; editor: (with J. Goy) Evolution and Ruptures in the Rural World, 1986; editor: Identity Constructs and Social Practices, 2002, The Non-Existent Debate: The Pepin-Robarts Commission, 2003, Linguistic Governance, 2005; editor: (with G. Paquet) Un Quebec Moderne, 2007. Pres. internat. adv. com. on Memory of the World UNESCO, 1993—98, pres. Canadian ad hoc com. on Memory of the World, 2005; pres. ad hoc Can. Com. on Memory of the World, 2005—. Decorated officer Order Arts et Lettres, France; officer Order of Can., 1991; recipient Marie Tremaine medal, 1973, Tyrrell medal, 1982, Royal Soc. Centenary medal, 1994, Jacques Ducharme prize, 1997, Queen's Jubilee medal, 2002; Faculty of Arts and Scis. U. de Montreal Merit medal, 2004. Fellow Royal Soc. Can. (sect. pres. 1985-87, pres. 1997-99); mem. Am. Antiquarian Soc., Acad. des Lettres du Quebec, Inst. d'Histoire l'Amerique Francaise (pres. 1973-77), Can. Hist. Assn. (pres. 1982), Assn. Can.-Francaise l'Avancement Scis. (pres. 1981-83, emeritus mem.), Assn. Archivists Que., Assn. Can. Archivists, Internat. Coun. on Archives (v.p. 1988-92, pres. 1992-96, pres. emeritus). Roman Catholic. Office: U Ottawa CRCCF PO Box 450 Sta A Ottawa ON Canada K1N 6N5 Office Phone: 613-562-5800 ext 4131. Business E-Mail: jpwallot@uottawa.ca.

WALLPHER, LUIS ANTONIO, small business owner, painter, writer; b. La Paz, Bolivia, Apr. 30, 1948; s. Luis Humberto Wallpher and Hortensia Gonzalez; m. Monica Vivado De Wallpher, Oct. 13, 1991; children: John L., Anthony, Andy. BFA, Md. Inst. Coll. of Art. Owner Wallyher Galleries of Fine Arts, LaPaz, Bolivia. Author: En La Brecha Cultural, 2005. Councilman Municipal House, LaPaz, Bolivia, 1996; pres., founder Falange Democratica Boliviana, LaPaz, Bolivia, 1998; founder Momimiento Haciendo Patria. Recipient Mare of La Paz, 1994. Mem.: Am. Inst. of Conservation of Monuments. Avocations: tennis, movies, painting.

WALLS, AMOS LOUIS, III, music educator; b. Detroit, Oct. 16, 1952; s. Amos Louis Jr. and Hazel Mae (Cook) Walls; m. Candace Liticia Whaley, Mar. 25, 1995; children: Roderick Barnes, Cameron Barnes, Tawney Barnes, Tennille, Rashana. MusB, Wayne State U., Detroit, 1977, MusM, 1979; cert. tchr., Madonna U., Livonia, Mich., 1992. Owner auto repair shop, Detroit, 1980—86; tchr. vocal music Detroit Pub. Schs., 1987—. Organist Outer Drive Faith Luth. Ch., Detroit, 2002—, Cmty. Fellowship Ch., Detroit, 2003—. Mem.: Guild English Handbell Ringers, Am. Guild Organists. Seventh Day Adventist. Avocations: photography, bodybuilding, Bible reading, bicycling. Home: 13997 Coyle Detroit MI 48227 Office: Ctrl HS 2425 Tuxedo Detroit MI 48206

WALLS, MARTHA ANN WILLIAMS (MRS. B. CARMAGE WALLS), publishing executive; b. Gadsden, Ala., Apr. 21, 1927; d. Aubrey Joseph and Inez (Cooper) Williams; m. B. Carmage Walls, Jan. 2, 1954; children: Byrd Cooper, Lissa Walls Vahldiek. Student pub. schs., Gadsden. Pres., dir. Walls Newspapers, Inc., 1969-70; sec., treas., dir. Summer Camps, Inc., Guntersville, Ala., 1954-69; CEO, pres., dir. So. Newspapers, Inc., Houston, 1970—; pres., dir. So. Newspapers of Ala., Inc., Scottsboro. V.p., dir. Ft. Payne (Ala.) Newspapers, Inc., Galveston Newspapers, Inc.; dir. Monroe (Ga.) Newspapers, Inc.; bd. dirs. Jefferson Pilot Corp., Greensboro, N.C., 1990-98, Jefferson-Pilot Life Ins. Co., 1990-98, Jefferson Pilot Comm., 1990-98. Bd. dirs. Montgomery Acad., 1970-74. Mem.: Soc. Profl. Journalists. Episcopalian. Office: 5701 Woodway Ste 300 Houston TX 77057 Personal E-mail: mwalls@sninews.com.

WALLS, WILLIAM WALTON, JR., management consultant; b. Phila., Oct. 3, 1932; s. William Walton and Mary Crown (Elliott) W.; m. Nina Catherine deAngeli, July 1, 1961; 1 child, Deborah. BSME, Swarthmore Coll., 1959. With Boeing Helicopters, Phila., 1959-96, v.p. light helicopter joint venture, 1988-91, v.p. devel. programs, 1991-92, v.p. rsch. and engring., 1992-96; small high-tech. bus. cons. Ridley Park, Pa., 1996—. Cons. in field. Chmn. aerospace adv. coun. Pa. State Coll., 1974-79; mem. NATO Indsl. Advisors Group, 1988-93; mem. bd. advisors Rotocraft Ctr. Excellence, Rensselaer Polytech. Inst., 1982-84 Mem. Am. Helicopter Soc. (pres. 1988-89, chmn. 1989-90). Republican. Avocations: travel, computers, classical music, exercise. Home: 502 Harrison St Ridley Park PA 19078-3208 Personal E-mail: wwwallsjr@comcast.net.

WALLSKOG, JOYCE MARIE, nursing educator, retired psychologist; b. Melrose Park, Ill., Apr. 20, 1942; BSN, Alverno Coll., 1977; MSN, U. Wis., Milw., 1982; PhD, Marquette U., Milw., 1992. RN, Wis.; lic. psychologist; diplomate Am. Coll. Forensic Examiners. Staff nurse St. Mary's Hill Hosp., Milw., 1977—78, Waukesha (Wis.) Meml. Hosp., 1978—80, clin. nurse specialist, 1980—87; asst. prof. nursing Marquette U., Milw., 1986—2005; psychotherapist Psychiat. Assocs. Comprehensive Services, Ltd., Milw., 1982—85; nurse psychotherapist Counseling and Wellness Ctr., Waukesha, 1982—2005; adv. practice nurse prescriber, 1995—2005; guest lectr. Concordia U., Milw., 2005. Cons. Alverno Coll., Milw., 1983-84, Health Care Cons., Sussex, Wis., 1985—; coord. Waukesha Premenstrual Syndrome Program, 1980—; nurse psychotherapist Stress Mgmt. and Mental Health Svcs., Waukesha, 1991-94; co-founder Turning Point Mental Health and Cons. Svcs., Waukesha, 1994—; advanced practice nurse prescriber, 1995—. Contbr. articles to profl. jours. Bd. dirs. Waukesha County Mental Health Assn., 1982; mem. Waukesha County Unified Svcs., 1984; adv. bd. Northwest Rehab. Ctr., 1992-94; advisor Resolve Through Sharing, 1986-2001, Women's Health Svcs., 1987-2001; advisor Parish Nurse Program. Mem. APA, ANA (coun. psychiat. and mental health nursing), Wis. Nurses Assn. (rep. Wis. Coalition on Sexual Misconduct by Psychotherapists and Counselors 1988-93), Delta Upsilon Sigma, Phi Lambda Delta. Personal E-mail: wallskogj@aol.com.

WALLS PERRY, J(OYCE) LORRAINE, elementary school educator; b. Washington, Pa., Aug. 23, 1948; d. William K. and Minnie (Crockett) W.; m: Robert L. Perry; 1 child, Lisa Michelle. BA, Point Park Coll., Pitts., 1971; MA in Teaching, U. Pitts., 1972, cert. in curriculum and supervision, 1995. Cert. elem. and early childhood tchr. Pa., elem. prin. Instructional teacher leader, elem tchr. Pitts. Bd. Edn., 1988-92, resource tchr. elem. and mid. sch. social studies, 1992—2000; v.p. Belmar Elem. Sch., Pitts., 2000—02; ednl. cons., 2002—; dir. edn. Greater Allen Christian Acad., Pitts., 2006—. Tchr.-in-Residence fellow U. Pitts., 1992-93. Holmes group scholar, 1992-93. Mem. TESA. Home: 3594 Harlow Pl Pittsburgh PA 15204-1143 Home Phone: 412-771-8737. Personal E-mail: raine823@msn.com.

WALL SPITZER, SILDA, not-for-profit developer, First Lady of New York State; m. Eliot Spitzer, 1987; 3 children. BA summa cum laude, Meredith Coll., 1980; JD, Harvard Law Sch., 1984. Former atty., mergers, acquisitions, corp. fin. Skadden Arps Slate Meagher & Flom; former atty., internat legal group Chase Manhattan Bank. Founding chair Children for Children; hon. chair Women's Leadership Forum NY, Eleanor Roosevelt Legacy Found.; founding co-chair Project Cicero; adv. bd. mem. NYCharities.org; mem. NY Blue Ribbon Commn. on Youth Leadership; bd. mem. Children's Museum Manhattan, 1995—99. Office: CFC 6 E 43rd St 25th Fl New York NY 10017 *

WALMER, EDWIN FITCH, retired lawyer; b. Chgo., Mar. 24, 1930; s. Hillard Wentz and Anna C. (Fitch) W.; m. Florence Poling, June 17, 1952; children: Linda Diane Walmer Dennis, Fred Fitch. BS with distinction, Ind. U., 1952, JD with high distinction, 1957. Bar: Wis. 1957, U.S. Dist. Ct. (ea. dist.) Wis. 1957. Assoc. Foley & Lardner, Milw., 1957-65, ptnr., 1965-90, ret., 1990. Served to 1st lt. U.S. Army, 1952-54. Recipient Cal. C. Chambers award Culver (Ind.) Mil. Acad., 1948. Fellow Am. Coll. Trust and Estate Counsel; mem. Order of Coif, Dairymen's Country Club (Boulder Junction, Wis.), Vineyards Country Club (Naples, Fla.), Phi Eta Sigma, Beta Gamma Sigma. Republican. Congregationalist. Avocations: golf, fishing.

WALMSLEY, PRISCILLA HELEN, computer company executive; d. Bruno Joseph and Agnes Marie Walmsley; life ptnr. Douglas Michael Kimble. BS, U. Va., Charlottesville, Va., 1990. Software developer Platinum Tech. Inc., McLean, Va., 1990—95, dir. devel., 1995—99; v.p. devel. XMLSolutions Corp., McLean, 1999—2002; mng. dir. Datypic, Traverse City, Mich., 2002—. Mem. working group W3C, Cambridge, Mass., 1999—2004. Author: Definitive XML Schema, 2001, XML in Office 2003, 2003, XQuery, 2006. Mem.: Sierra Club (sec. 2001—06, chmn. membership 2001—06), Mensa. Home Phone: 231-929-1658. Personal E-mail: pwalmsley@datypic.com.

WALPIN, GERALD, lawyer; b. NYC, Sept. 1, 1931; s. Michael and Mary (Gordon) W.; m. Sheila Kainer, Apr. 13, 1957; children: Amanda Eve, Edward Andrew, Jennifer Hope. BA, CCNY, 1952; LLB cum laude, Yale Law Sch., 1955. Bar: N.Y. 1955, U.S. Supreme Ct. 1965, U.S. Ct. Appeals (2d cir.) 1960, (6th cir.) 1969, (3d cir.) 1976, (8th cir.) 1982, (9th cir.) 1983, (llth cir.) 1983, (7th cir.) 1984, U.S. Ct. Claims 1984. Law clk. to Hon. E.J. Dimock US Dist. Ct. (so. dist.) NY, NYC, law clk. to Hon. F.P. Bryan, 1955-57; asst. US atty., chief spl. prosecutions US Atty. Office, NYC, 1960-65; sr. ptnr. Katten Muchin Rosenman, LLP, predecessor firms, NYC, 1965—2002, chmn. litigation dept., 1985-96, counsel, 2002—07; insp. gen. Corp. Nat. and Cmty. Svc., 2007—. Adv. com. Fed. Ct. So. Dist. NY, 1991-98; co-chmn. lawyers divsn. Anti-Defamation League, NY, 1994-97; bd. dirs. Ctr. Individual Rights, 1997—2007; pres. Fed. Bar Coun., 2002-04. Editor Yale Law Jour., 1953-54, mng. editor, 1954-55; contbr. articles to profl. jours. Pres. Parker Jewish Inst. for Health Care and Rehab., New Hyde Park, N.Y., 1987-90, trustee, 1979—2007; bd. dirs. Fund for Modern Cts., N.Y.C., 1985-91; mem. law com. Am. Jewish Com., 1980-90; mem. Com. for Free World, N.Y.C., 1983-91; trustee, mem. exec. com. United Jewish Appeal-Fedn. Jewish Philanthropies, N.Y.C., 1984-96; mem. Nassau County Crime Commn., 1970; pres. Kensington Civic Orgn., Gt. Neck, N.Y., 1972-73. Recipient Quality of Life award United Jewish Appeal Fedn., 1978, Human Rels. award Am. Jewish Com., 1982, Gift of Life award Jewish Inst. Geriatric Care, 1987, Learned Hand award Am. Jewish Com., 1990, Human Rels. award Anti-Defamation League, 1998. Mem. ABA, Fed. Bar Coun. (chmn. modern cts. com. 1989, v.p. 1991-95, chmn. bench and bar liaison com. 1994-95, vice chmn. 1995-97, chmn. bd. dirs. 1997-99, pres. 2002-04, pres. emeritus 2004-2006), Federalist Soc. (chmn. litigation sect. 1996-99, mem. bd. visitors 1999—2007), Univ. Club. Republican. Jewish. Home: 875 Park Ave New York NY 10021-0341 Office: 1201 NY Ave NW Washington DC 20525 Home Phone: 212-288-5324; Office Phone: 202-606-9366. Business E-Mail: g.walpin@cncsorg.gov. *My life should be an appropriate response to God and this country for providing me with the opportunities I have had: Contribution to our society and strengthening of our country's steadfast opposition to discrimination for or against anyone based on race, religion or sex.*

WALPOLE, JIM (JAMES R.), lawyer; b. Oswego, NY, Aug. 31, 1944; s. Richard and Margaret Mary Walpole; children: Sarah, Mark, Ethan. BA, John Carroll U., 1966; JD, Case Western Res. U., 1969. Bar: Ohio 1969, D.C. 1971, Ill. 1994, U.S. Ct. Appeals (D.C., 3d, 4th, 7th, 8th and 11th cirs.), U.S. Supreme Ct. 1973. Trial atty. US Dept. Justice, Washington, 1971-74; asst. gen. counsel Am. Mining Congress, Washington, 1975—79; ptnr. Holland & Hart LLP, Washington, 1979—85, Chadbourne & Parke LLP, Washington, 1985-92; v.p. environment, safety & health FMC Corp., Chgo., 1992-95; asst. gen. counsel Sears Roebuck & Co., Chgo., 1995—2001; gen. counsel, Nat. Oceanic & Atmospheric Adminstrn. (NOAA) US Dept. Commerce, Washington, 2002—07. Mem. adv. com. U.S. C. of C., Washington, 1987-92; adj. prof. environ. law Cath. U., Washington, 1975-79. Author publs. in field. Bd. dirs. Griffin Theater Co. Roman Catholic. Avocations: civil war, fishing. *

WALRATH, HARRY RIENZI, retired minister; b. Alameda, Calif., Mar. 7, 1926; s. Frank Rienzi and Cathren (Michlar) W.; m. Dorothy M. Baxter, June 24, 1961; 1 son, Gregory Rienzi. AA, City Coll., San Francisco, 1950; BA, U. Calif., Berkeley, 1952; MDiv, Ch. Div. Sch. of Pacific, 1959. Ordained deacon Episcopal Ch., 1959, priest, 1960. Dist. exec. San Mateo area Boy Scouts Am., 1952-55; curate All Souls Parish, Berkeley, Calif., 1959-61; vicar St. Luke's, Atascadero, Calif., 1961-63, St. Andrew's, Garberville, Calif., 1963-64; assoc. rector St. Luke's Ch., Los Gatos, 1964-65, Holy Spirit Parish, Missoula, Mont., 1965-67; vicar St. Peter's Ch., Litchfield Park, Ariz., 1967-69; also headmaster St. Peter's Schs., Litchfield Park, Ariz., 1967-69; chaplain U. Mont., 1965-67; asst. rector Trinity Parish, Reno, 1969-72; coord. counciling svcs. Washoe County Coun. Alcholism, Reno, 1972-74; adminstr. Cons. Assistance Svcs., Inc., Reno, 1974-76; pastoral counselor, contract chaplain Nev. Mental Health Inst., 1976-78; contract mental health chaplain VA Hosp., Reno, 1976-78; mental health chaplain VA Med. Ctr., Reno, 1978-83, staff chaplain, 1983-85, chief chaplain svc., 1985-91, triage coord. mental health, ret., 1991. Per diem chaplain Washoe Med. Ctr., Reno, 1993; assoc. priest Trinity Episcopal Ch., Reno, 1995; assoc. Mountain Ministries, Susanville, Calif., 1995—. Author: God Rides the Rails-Chapel Cars on American Railroads at the Turn of the Century, 1994. Dir. youth Paso Robles Presbytery; chmn. Diocesan Commn. on Alcoholism; cons. teen-age problems Berkeley Presbytery; mem. clergy team Episcopal Marriage Encounter; chaplain Make A Wish Found., 1998-2000; mem. at-large Washoe dist. Nev. area coun. Boy Scouts Am., scoutmaster troop 73, 1976, troop 585, 1979-82, asst. scoutmaster troop 35, 1982-92, assoc. adviser area 3 Western region, 1987-89, regional com. Western Region, 1989-90; lodge adviser Tannu Lodge 346, Order of Arrow, 1982-87; docent coun. Nev. Hist. Sch., 1992; South Humboldt County chmn. Am. Cancer Soc.; trustee Cmty. Youth Ctr., Reno. With USNR, 1944-46. Decorated Pacific Theatre medal with star, Am. Theatre medal, Victory medal, Fleet Unit Commendation medal; recipient dist. award of merit Boy Scouts Am., St. George award Episc. Ch.-Boy Scouts Am., Silver Beaver award Boy Scouts Am., 1986, Founders' award Order of the Arrow, Boy Scouts Am., 1995; performance awards VA-VA Med. Ctr., 1983, 84; named Arrowman of Yr., Order of Arrow, Boy Scouts Am. Cert. substance abuse counselor, Nev. Mem. Ch. Hist. Soc., U. Calif. Alumni Assn., Nat. Model R.R. Assn. (life), Sierra Club Calif., Missoula Coun. Chs. (pres.), Rotary, Alpha Phi Omega. Democrat. Home: 4822 Ramcreek Trl Reno NV 89519-8029 E-mail: v7t11@aol.com.

WALRATH, PATRICIA A., state legislator; b. Brainerd, Minn., Aug. 11, 1941; d. Joseph James and Pansy Patricia (Drake) McCarvill; m. Robert Eugene Walrath, Sept. 1, 1961; children: Karen, Susan, David, Julie. BS, Bemidji State U., 1962; MS, SUNY, Oswego, 1975. Cert. secondary math. tchr., N.Y., Mass. Programmer analyst Control Data Corp., Mpls., 1962-65; crewleader dept. commerce U.S. Census, Middlesex County, Mass., 1979-80; selectman Town of Stow, Mass., 1980-85; tchr. math. Hale Jr. High Sch., Stow, 1981-82; instr. math. Johnson & Wale Coll. Hanscom AFB, Bedford, Mass., 1983-84, test examiner, 1983-84; state rep. 3d Middlesex dist. State of Mass., Boston, 1985—. Many coms. including most recently; chmn. com. long term debt and capital expenditures Mass. Ho. of Reps., 1997—2001, asst. whip, floor chair, 2001—04, chmn. healthcare financing com., 2005—. Chmn. Mass. Indoor Air Pollution Commn., Boston, 1987-88; mem. Stow Dem. Com., 1988—. Recipient Disting. Svc. award Auburn N.Y. Jaycees, 1976. Mem. LWV (pres. 1973-76, dir. fin. 1977-78), Mass. Legislators' Assn., Mass. Dem. Leadership Coun. (v.p. 1991-92, co-chmn. 1993-94, treas. 1995-99), Mass. Women's Legis. Caucus (chair 1986). Roman Catholic. Avocations: gardening, stamp collecting/philately, travel. Home: 20 Middlemost Way Stow MA 01775-1363 Office: State Capital RM 236 Boston MA 02133 Office Phone: 617-722-2430. Business E-Mail: Rep.PatriciaWalrath@hou.state.ma.us.

WALSETH, DAVID G., lawyer, insurance company executive; b. Dec. 5, 1947; BA, St. Olaf Coll.; JD, U. Minn. With Hartford Life Insurance Companies; sr. v.p., gen. counsel, corp. sec. Luth. Brotherhood Fraternal Benefit Soc.; v.p., sr. assoc. gen. counsel Thrivent Fin. for Luths.; exec. v.p., gen. counsel, corp. sec. Conseco, Inc., Carmel, Ind., 2006—. Mem.: ABA, Soc. Fin. Svc. Profls., Assn. Life Insurance Counsel, Assn. Corp. Counsel, Hennepin County Bar Assn., Minn. State Bar Assn. Office: Conseco, Inc 11825 N Pennsylvania St Carmel IN 46032 *

WALSH, ARTHUR CAMPBELL, retired psychiatrist; b. Vancouver, BC, Can., Dec. 21, 1919; came to US, 1964; s. William Charles and Kathleen (Patterson) W.; m. Bernice Martha Hessom, Dec. 26, 1944; children: Kathleen, David, Thomas. Degree, U. Alta., Edmonton, 1943. Intern Vancouver Gen. Hosp., BC, 1943; pvt. practice Vancouver, BC, 1964-67; resident psychiatry U. Pitts., clin. asst. prof. psychiatry, 1967-99; semi-ret., 1999; pvt. practice Pitts., 1969—99; ret., 1999; pres. Alzheimer Treatment Rsch. Ctr., Pitts., 1969-98. Psychiat. cons. VA, Pitts., 1969-89, Woodville State Hosp., Pitts., 1969-86. Author: Conquering Senility; co-author: Mental Capacity: Legal and Medical Aspects of Assessment and Treatment, 2nd edit., 1999; contbr. med. articles to profl. jours. With Royal Can. Army Med. Corps, 1943-45. Mem. Am. Psychiat. Assn. Achievements include development of anticoagulant therapy for dementia due to impaired brain circulation with arrest of dementia in 50% diagnosed as Alzheimers Disease with complete Alzheimer reversal in 15% of people treated; research in anticoagulant therapy combined with psychiatric care is the only treatment reported to actually not only arrest the dementing process but even reverse it almost completely in most of the alzheimer and related dementia patients. Home: 279 Norman Dr Cranberry Township PA 16066-4235 E-mail: acw@z-bzoom.net.

WALSH, BRIAN M., physicist; b. Cambridge, Mass., Oct. 21, 1962; s. Gerald Joseph and Elizabeth Helen (Yale) Walsh; 1 child, Jennifer Levesque. BA, Boston U., 1987; MS, Boston Coll., 1992, PhD, 1995. Rsch. asst. Boston Coll., Chestnut Hill, Mass., 1990—95, rsch. assoc., 1995—2002; aerospace technologist NASA, Hampton, Va., 2002—. Asst. to dir. Sch. Atomic and Molecular Spectroscopy Boston Coll., Chestnut Hill, 1995, 98; mem. Innovation Award com. NASA, Hampton, 2005; lectr. Internat. Sch. Atomic and Molecular Spectroscopy, 1998, 2002, 04, 06, Majorana Ctr., Erise, Italy. Contbr. articles to profl. jours., chpt. to book. Polit. campaign aide Anderson for Pres., Manchester, NH, 1980, Mondale for Pres., Manchester, 1984. Recipient Superior Accomplishment award, NASA, 2003, Innovation Competition award, 2004, H.J.E. Reid award, 2005. Mem.: Nat. Geog. Soc. Roman Catholic. Avocations: Karate, baseball, coin collecting/numismatics, comic book collecting, baseball card collecting. Office: NASA Langley Rsch Ctr 5 N Dryden St Hampton VA 23681 Office Phone: 757-864-7112. Office Fax: 757-864-8828. Business E-Mail: brian.m.walsh@nasa.gov.

WALSH, CHARLES RICHARD, retired banker; b. Bklyn., Jan. 30, 1939; s. Charles John and Anna Ellen Walsh; m. Marie Anne Goulden, June 24, 1961; children: Kevin C., Brian R., Gregory M. BS, Fordham U., 1960; MBA, St. John's U., 1966, D of Comml. Scis. (hon.), 1985. V.p. Mfrs. Hanover Trust Co., Hicksville, NY, 1974-80, sr. v.p., 1980-86, exec. v.p., 1986-90, group exec., mem. mgmt. com., 1990-92; exec. v.p., group exec. Chem. Banking Corp., Hicksville, NY, 1992-95, The Chase Manhattan Corp., 1995-97; ret., 1997. Bd. dirs. Mastercard Internat.; bd. dirs., former chmn. Eastern States Monetary Svcs., Lake Success, NY, 1978-88; former pres., CEO, bd. dirs. The Bankcard Assn., Hicksville, 1988-91. Vice chmn.

adv. bd. St. John's U., 1982—; sustaining mem. Rep. Nat. Com., 1978—. With USAR, 1960, 61-62. Mem. N.Y. State Bankers Assn. (former bd. dirs., mem. gov. coun., chmn. consumer banking divsn.), Am. Bankers Assn. (mem. govt. rels. coun., chmn. bank card divsn., mem. exec. com., former mem. comms. coun. and chmn. edn. com.), Am. Mgmt. Assn., N.Y. Credit and Fin. Mgmt. Assn., Soc. Cert. Consumer Credit Execs. (cert.), Beta Gamma Sigma, Omicron Delta Epsilon, North Hempstead Country Club, Gov.'s Club Kiawah Island (S.C.), Kiawah Island Club. Republican. Home: 31 Fieldstone Ln Oyster Bay NY 11771-3122 also: 107 Goldeneye Dr Kiawah Island SC 29455-5773

WALSH, CHRISTINE ANN, cardiologist; b. Bklyn., Dec. 31, 1947; d. Martin and Loretta (Lesniewski) Kull; m. Sean Michael Walsh, June 10, 1978; children: Kathleen, Sean, Stephen. BS, Fordham U., 1969; MD, Yale U., 1973. Diplomate Am. Bd. Pediatrics, Am. Bd. Critical Care Medicine, Am. Bd. Pediatric Cardiology. Intern, then resident Babies Hosp., N.Y., Columbia-Presbyn. Med. Ctr., N.Y.; fellow in pediatric cardiology Columbia U., N.Y., asst. prof. Coll. Physicians and Surgeons NYC, 1980-84; asst. prof. Albert Einstein Coll. of Medicine, NYC, 1984-91; asst. attending physician N.C. Bronx Hosp., 1984—; asst. attending pediatrician Jacobi Med. Ctr., Bronx, 1984—; dir. Pediat. Dysrhythmia Ctr. Montefiore Med. Ctr., Bronx, 1984—, from asst. to assoc. attending pediatrician, 1984-98, attending pediatrician, 1998—, chief sect. pediat. cardiology, 2002—; assoc. prof. pediat. Albert Einstein Coll. of Medicine, Bronx, 1991-98, prof., 1998—, co-chair admissions com., 1998—. Cons. Adult Arrhythmia Svc., Montefiore Med. Ctr., Pacemaker Ctr., epilepsy unit, Cranio-facial Ctr.; postdoctorate in cardiac electrophysiology and phramcology Columbia U. Coll. Physicians and Surgeons, NYC, 1978—80. Editor: Adolescent Medicine, State of Art Revs., Adolescent Cardiology; contbr. articles to profl. jours. Bd. dirs. Velo-Cardio-Facial Syndrome Ednl. Found., NYC, 1995—. Grantee, Albert Einstein Interdivisional, 1995, 1999. Fellow: Am. Acad. Pediat., Am. Coll. Cardiology; mem.: N.Y. Soc. Pediatric Critical Care Assn., Am. Heart Assn., Pediat. Electrophysiology Soc., Pediatric Cardiology Soc. (treas. 1987—88, sec. 1988—89, v.p. 1989—90, pres. 1990—91), Heart Rhythm Soc., Assn. Yale Alumni Medicine (sec.), Phi Beta Kappa. Avocations: gardening, skiing, scuba diving, piano, camping. Home: PO Box 238 Flushing NY 11363-0238 Office: Montefiore Med Ctr 111 E 210th St Bronx NY 10467-2401 Office Phone: 718-741-2310.

WALSH, DANIEL J., health products executive; MBA in Exec. Mgmt., St. John's U., NYC. CPA NY. With US Dept. Def., Loral Corp.; dir., sr. mgr. mgmt consulting divsn. PricewaterhouseCoopers, 1986—93; corp. compliance officer Smiths Grp., PLC, 1993—2003; v.p., chief compliance officer Sci.-Atlanta, Inc., 2003—05; exec. v.p., chief ethics and compliance officer Cardinal Health, 2005—. Office: Cardinal Health 7000 Cardinal Pl Dublin OH 43017

WALSH, DAVID GRAVES, lawyer; b. Madison, Wis., Jan. 7, 1943; s. John J. and Audrey B. Walsh; married; children: Michael, Katherine, Molly, John. BBA, U. Wis., 1965; JD, Harvard U., 1970. Bar: Wis. Law clk. Wis. Supreme Ct., Madison, 1970-71; ptnr. Walsh, Walsh, Sweeney & Whitney, Madison, 1971-86; ptnr.-in-charge, pres. Foley & Lardner, Madison, 1986—95. Pres., bd. regents U. Wis., 2003—; bd. dirs. Nat. Guardian Life, Madison, Thompson Investment Mgmt., Inc.; lectr. U. Wis., Madison, 1974-75, 77-78; pres. U. Wis. sys. bd. regents, 2005-. Chmn. State of Wis. Elections Bd., Madison, 1978. Lt. USN, 1965-67, Vietnam. Recipient Disting. Bus. Alumnus award U. Wis. Sch. Bus., 1997. Maple Bluff Country Club (Madison) (pres. 1987). Roman Catholic. Avocations: tennis, golf, fishing. Home: 41 Fuller Dr Madison WI 53704-5962 Office: Foley & Lardner PO Box 1497 Madison WI 53701-1497 Office Phone: 608-258-4269. Business E-Mail: dwalsh@foley.com.

WALSH, DAVID JAMES, lawyer; b. Dubuque, Iowa, Aug. 10, 1949; s. James and Helen Walsh; m. Alice Chebba; children: Elizabeth, James. BA, Loras Coll., 1971; JD, U. Wis., 1974; MBA, Alaska Pacific U., 1990; postgrad. in Internat. Bus., City U. London, 1991. Bar: Wis. 1974, Alaska 1975. Asst. dist. atty. State of Alaska, Anchorage, 1975-78; pvt. practice Anchorage, 1974-75, 78-90; co-founder, chmn. exec. com. Internat. Assn. Ins. Suprs., 1992-95; dir. ins. State of Alaska, 1990-95; gen. counsel Domestic Brokerage Group Am. Internat. Group, NYC, 1995-98; pres. Nat. Assn. Ins. Commrs., 1994; exec. v.p., corp. counsel Swiss Re Life & Health, Stamford, CT. Mem. Gov.'s Transition Team, 1982-83; mem. U.S./Alaska R.R. Transfer Team, 1982-84; vice chmn. State Rolyalty Oil and Gas Adv. Bd., 1985-87; bd. dirs. IFNY; adj. prof. law Pace U. Chmn. Anchorage Mcpl. Assembly, 1976-86; bd. dirs. Alaska Mcpl. League, 1976-86, pres., 1980; mem. exec. bd. Greater N.Y. coun. Boy Scouts Am., 1997—. Mem. Assn. Internationale de Droit des Assurances (presdl. coun. 1995—). Office: Swiss Re Life And Health 175 King St Armonk NY 10504-1606

WALSH, DAVID JOSEPH, pediatric neurologist, educator; b. St. Louis, Oct. 5, 1946; s. Joseph Lloyd and Dorothy Ann Walsh. BS, Georgetown U., Washington, DC, 1968; MD, Med. U. SC, 1973. Diplomate Am. Bd. Psychiatry and Neurology, Am. Bd. Pediat. Asst. prof. neurology and pediat. Jacksonville Health Edn. Program, U. Fla., Jacksonville, 1981—82; asst. prof. pediat. and neurology U. Kans., Kansas City, 1982—88; pvt. practice Allegheny Neurol. Assoc., Pitts., 1988—90; asst. prof. neurology Med. Coll. Wis., Milw., 1990—2004; assoc. prof. neurology St. Louis U., St. Louis, 2004—. Program dir. pediat. residency U. Kans., Kansas City, 1982—87; program dir. pediat. neurology residency program Med. Coll. Wis., Milw., 2001—03; chief med. staff, divsn. neurology Children's Hosp. Wis., Milw., 2001—04; chief sect. child neurology St. Louis U., St. Louis, 2004—. Author: (short story) Upping the Ritalin. Sec. profl. adv. bd. Epilepsy Found., 2006—; pres. Epilepsy Found. S.E. Wis., Milw., 1994—2004, chair profl. adv. bd., 1992—2004. Lt. USNR, 1974—76. Fellow: Am. Acad. Neurology; mem.: Assn. U. Profs. Neurology, Harvard Med. Alumni Assn., Med. U. SC Alumni Assn., Child Neurology Soc. Independent. Roman Catholic. Avocations: Aikido, opera, travel. Office: Cardinal Glennon Children's Hosp 1465 S Grand Blvd Glennon Hall Rm 7514 Saint Louis MO 63104 Office Phone: 314-268-4105. Business E-Mail: walshdj@slu.edu.

WALSH, DAVID M., IV, lawyer; b. Chula Vista, Calif., Feb. 6, 1969; m. Tamara Walsh. BA with honors and high distinction, U. Ky., 1991; JD with honors, U. Tex., 1994. Bar: Tex. 1994, US Dist. Ct. (no., ea. and so. dists. Tex.), US Ct. Appeals (5th cir.). Assoc. Chamblee & Ryan, P.C., Dallas, shareholder, 2007—. Named a Rising Star, Tex. Super Lawyers mag., 2006. Mem.: Def. Rsch. Inst., Tex. Assn. Def. Counsel, Dallas Bar Assn., Phi Beta Kappa. Office: Chamblee & Ryan PC 2777 Stemmons Freeway Ste 1157 Dallas TX 75207 Office Phone: 214-905-2003. Business E-Mail: dmwalsh@chambleeryan.com.

WALSH, DENNIS P., federal agency administrator; b. 1954; m. Barbara A. O'Neill; children: Steven, Rose. BA in Govt. summa cum laude, Hamilton Coll., 1976; JD cum laude, Cornell Law Sch., 1983. Atty.-adv. NLRB, 1984—87, field atty. region 4, 1987—89, chief counsel to Margaret A Browning, 1994—97, chief counsel to Wilma B. Liebman, 1997—2000, mem., 2000—01, 2002—04, 2006—; assoc. Spear, Wilderman, Borish, Endy, Browning & Spear LLP, Phila., 1989—94. Office: NLRB Franklin Court Bldg 1099 14th St NW Washington DC 20570-0001 Business E-Mail: dennis.walsh@nlrb.gov.

WALSH, DENNY JAY, reporter; b. Omaha, Nov. 23, 1935; s. Gerald Jerome and Muriel (Morton) W.; m. Peggy Marie Moore, Feb. 12, 1966; children from previous marriage: Catherine Camille, Colleen Cecile; 1 son, Sean Joseph. B.J., U. Mo., 1962. Staff writer St. Louis Globe-Democrat, 1961-68; asst. editor Life mag., NYC, 1968-70, assoc. editor, 1970-73; reporter N.Y. Times, 1973-74, Sacramento Bee, 1974—. Served with USMC, 1954-58. Recipient Con Lee Kelliher award St. Louis chpt. Sigma Delta Chi, 1962; award Am. Polit. Sci. Assn., 1963; award Sigma Delta Chi, 1968; Pulitzer prize spl. local reporting, 1969; 1st prize San Francisco Press Club, 1977; Beacon award for lifetime achievement, 1st Amendment Coalition, 2004. Office: Sacramento Bee 21st & Q Sts Sacramento CA 95816 Home Phone: 916-721-9624; Office Phone: 916-321-1189. Business E-Mail: dwalsh@sacbee.com.

WALSH, DIANA CHAPMAN, former academic administrator, sociologist, educator; b. Phila., July 30, 1944; d. Robert Francis and Gwen (Jenkins) Chapman; m. Christopher Thomas Walsh, June 18, 1966; 1 child, Allison Chapman. BA in English, Wellesley Coll., 1966; MS in Journalism, Boston U. Sch. of Pub. Comm., 1971; PhD in Health Policy, Boston U., 1983; LHD (hon.), Boston U, 1994, Amer. Coll. of Greece, Athens, 1995, U. Mass., Amherst, 1999; LHD, Northeastern U., 2003. Dir. info., edn. Planned Parenthood League, Newton, Mass., 1971—74; sr. program assoc. Dept Pub. Health, Boston, 1974—76; assoc. dir. Boston U. Health Policy Inst., 1985—90; prof. Sch. Pub. Health, Sch. Medicine, Boston U., 1987—90, adj. prof. pub. health, 1990—; Florence Sprague Norman and Laura Smart Norman prof., chair dept. health and social behavior Harvard Sch. Pub. Health, 1990—93, adj. prof., 1993—; pres. Wellesley Coll., 1993—2007. Trustee WGBH Edn. Found., Boston, 1993-2000, Amherst (Mass.) Coll., 1998—; dir. State St. Corp., Boston, 1997—; chair internat. commn. Am. Coun. on Edn., 1998; consortium on financing higher edn. Asian U. for Women. Author: Corporate Physicians, 1987; co-author: Payer, Provide, Consumer, 1977; editor: Women, Work and Health: Challenges to Corporate Policy, 1980; contbr. chpt. to book. Bd. dirs. Planned Parenthood League of Mass., 1974—79, 1981—85, bd. overseers, 1993—94; trustee Occupl. Physicians Scholarship Fund, 1987—94, WGBH Ednl. Found., 1993—2000. Recipient Book of the Yr. award Am. Jour. Nursing, 1980; Kellogg Nat. fellow, 1987-90. Mem. APHA, Am. Sociol. Assn., Soc. for the Study of Social Problems, Mass. Pub. Health Assn. Avocations: gender and health, social policy, writing, skiing. Office Phone: 781-283-2237. E-mail: president@wellesley.edu. *

WALSH, DIANE, pianist; b. Washington, Aug. 16, 1950; d. William Donald and Estelle Louise (Stokes) W.; m. Henry Forbes, 1969 (div. 1979); m. Richard Pollak, 1982. MusB, Juilliard Sch. Music, 1971; MusM, Mannes Coll., 1982. N.Y.C. debut Young Concert Artists Series, 1974; founding mem. Mannes Trio, 1983-94; solo appearances include: Kennedy Ctr. for Performing Arts, Washington, 1976, Met. Mus., N.Y.C., 1976, Wigmore Hall, London, 1980, Merkin Concert Hall, 1989, Miller Theatre, 1994, 96; with Mannes Trio: Lincoln Ctr.'s Alice Tully Hall, Libr. of Congress, 1987; appeared with maj. orchs. worldwide, including St. Louis Symphony, Indpls. Symphony, San Francisco Symphony, Am. Symphony, Austin (Tex.) Symphony, Bavarian Radio Symphony of Munich, Berlin Radio Symphony, Radio Symphony Frankfurt, Radio Symphony Stuttgart; has toured Europe, N.Am., S.Am., C.Am., Russia; Marlboro Festival, 1982, Bard Festival, 1990-99, Santa Fe (N.Mex.) Festival, 1995; recs. for Nonesuch Records, 1980, 82, Book-of-Month Records, 1985, Music and Arts, 1990, CRI, 1991, Koch, 1995, Biddulph Records, 1998, Stereophile, 1998, Newport Classic, 1998, Sony, 2000, Bridge, 2004, Jonathan Digital, 2007; artistic dir. Skaneateles Festival, 1999-2004; mem. piano and chamber music faculty Mannes Coll. Music, 1982—. Recipient 3d prize Busoni Internat. Piano Competition, Italy, 1974, 2nd prize Mozart Internat. Piano Competition, Salzburg, Austria, 1975, 1st prize Munich Internat. Piano Competition, 1975, Naumburg Chamber Music award, 1986, Classical Recording Found. award, 2004, Classical Internet award, 2004; grantee NEA, 1981, Kitteredge Fund, 2007. Office Phone: 212-580-0210.

WALSH, DON, engineer, consultant; b. Berkeley, Calif., Nov. 2, 1931; s. J. Don and Marguerite Grace (Van Auker) W.; m. Joan A. Betzmer, Aug. 18, 1962; children: Kelly Drennan, Elizabeth McDonough BS, U.S. Naval Acad., 1954; MS, Tex. A&M U., 1967, PhD, 1968; MA, San Diego State U., 1968. Commd. ensign USN, 1954, advanced through grades to capt., 1974, officer-in-charge Bathyscaph Trieste Trieste, 1959-62, comdr. in USS Bashaw, 1968-69; dir. Inst. Marine and Coastal Studies, prof. ocean engrng. U. So. Calif., LA, 1975-83; pres., CEO Internat. Maritime, Inc., 1976—; mng. dir. Deep Ocean Engrng., Inc., 1990—2000, also bd. dirs. Dir. Ctr. for Marine Transp. Studies, U. So. Calif., 1980-83, Coastal Resources Ctr., 1990-94; trustee USN Mus. Found., 1989—; mem. Nat. Adv. Com. on Oceans and Atmosphere, 1979-85; bd. govs. Calif. Maritime Acad., 1985-95; pres. Parker Diving, 1989-94. Editor, contbr.: Law of the Sea: Issues in Ocean Resource Management, 1977, Energy and Resources Development of Continental Margins, 1980, Energy and Sea Power: Challenge for the Decade, 1981, Waste Disposal in the Oceans: Minimizing Impact, Maximizing Benefits, 1983; editor Jour. Marine Tech. Soc., 1975-80; mem. editorial bd. U.S. Naval Inst., 1974-75. Bd. dirs. Charles and Anne Lindbergh Found., 1996-2005. Decorated Legion of Merit (2); Woodrow Wilson Internat. Ctr. for Scholars fellow, 1973-74. Fellow Marine Tech. Soc., Acad. Underwater Arts and Scis., Explorers Club (hon. life, bd. dirs. 1994-2000, Explorers Medal, 2001); mem. AAAS, Soc. Naval Archs. and Marine Engrs., Am. Soc. Naval Engrs., Navy Inst., Adventurers Club (hon. life), Am. Geog. Soc. (hon. life), Nat. Acad. Engring. Home and Office: Internat Maritime Inc 14758 Sitkum Ln Myrtle Point OR 97458-9726 Personal E-mail: imiwalsh@worldnet.att.net, imiwalsh@mac.com.

WALSH, DONNIE (JOSEPH DONALD WALSH JR.), professional sports team executive; b. NYC, Mar. 1, 1941; m. Judy McNamara; 5 children. B, law degree, U. NC. Bar: 1977. Draft pick Phila. Warriors; assoc. head coach U. NC; asst. coach U. SC, Denver Nuggets, head coach, 1979-81; asst. coach Ind. Pacers, 1984-86, gen. mgr., 1986-92; pres. Ind. Pacers Sports & Entertainment, 1988—, CEO. Office: Ind Pacers 125 S Pennsylvania St Indianapolis IN 46204 *

WALSH, DOUGLAS SHAWN, medical association administrator, dermatologist, director, military officer; b. Cin., May 18, 1961; s. Gerald Peter and Geraldine Lee Walsh; m. Anocha Kansorn, July 1, 2004. BS summa cum laude in Biology, Mt. St. Mary's Coll., 1983; MS in Biology and Exptl. Medicine, St. Thomas Inst. Adv. Studies, Cin., 1985; MD, George Washington U., 1989. Diplomate Am. Bd. Dermatology, Nat. Bd. Med. Examiners, ACLS, Advanced Trauma Life Support, good clin. practices; med. lic. Md., 1990-, Pa., 1993-, Hawaii, 1995-98, Thailand, 2001-2002, Ga., 2003-, drug enforcement admisntrn., 1995-, 2002-. Commd. 2d lt. U.S. Army, 1986, advanced through grades to col., 1993; intern Walter Reed Army Med. Ctr., Wash., 1989-90, resident in dermatology, 1992-95; chief dept. combat casualty and clin. rsch. divsn. surgery Walter Reed Army Inst. Rsch., Wash., 1990-92, med. rsch. fellow, 1994-95, rsch. investigator divsn. exptl. therapeutics, 1995; clin. investigator dept. immunology US Army med. component Armed Forces Rsch. Inst. Med. Scis., Bangkok, 1990-92, asst. chief, 1995—97, chief dept., 1997—2001, sr. clin. investigator, 2001—02; chief dermatology svc. dept. medicine Eisenhower Army Med. Ctr., Ft. Gordon (Augusta), Ga., 2002—05, chief dept. clin. investigation, 2003—05; asst. chief dept. clin. trials Walter Reed Army Inst. Rsch., Silver Spring, 2005—06. Rsch. asst. dept. molecular virology Gamble Inst. Med. Rsch., Cin., 1984-85; rschr. in microbial genetics George Washington U. Sch. Medicine, 1986-87; cons. in dermatology Walter Reed Army Med. Ctr., 1995—; clin. cons. Leonard Wood Meml. Ctr for Leprosy Rsch., Cebu City, Philippines, 1996—; mem. Instl. Animal Care and Use Com. Armed Forces Rsch. Inst. Med. Scis., Bangkok, 1996—; adj. assoc. clin. prof. dept. medicine sect. dermatology Med. Coll. Ga., Augusta, 2003-; adj. assoc. prof. dept. dermatology Uniformed Svcs. U. Health Scis., Bethesda, 2004-. Contbr. numerous articles to profl. jours. Decorated Army Commendation medal, 1995; Armed Forces Health Professions scholar, 1985-89; Frederick Mohs grantee Nat. Skin Cancer Found., 1993-94; grantee Dermatology Found., 1994-95. Fellow Am. Acad. Dermatology; mem. AMA (mem. com. on phys. plant resources for accreditation 1987) Am. Soc. Microbiology, Binford-Dammin Soc. for Infectious Disease Pathologists, Am. Soc. Tropical Medicine and Hygiene, Soc. Investigative Dermatology, Am. Fedn. Clin. Rsch., Monsignor Tierney Honor Soc., Delta Epsilon Sigma, Beta Beta Beta. Mailing: USAMRU-K Unit 64109 APO AE 09831-5000 Business E-Mail: dwalsh@wrp.ksm.org.

WALSH, EDWARD JOSEPH, food products and cosmetics executive; b. Mt. Vernon, NY, Mar. 18, 1932; s. Edward Aloysius and Charlotte Cecilia (Borup) W.; m. Patricia Ann Farrell, Sept. 16, 1961; children: Edward Joseph, Megan Simpson, John, Robert. BBA, Iona Coll., 1953; MBA, NYU, 1958. Sales rep. M & R Dietetic Labs., Columbus, Ohio, 1955-60; with Armour & Co., 1961-71, Greyhound Corp., 1971-87; v.p. toiletries div. Armour Dial Co., Phoenix, 1973-74, exec. v.p., 1975-77; pres., CEO Armour Internat. Co., Phoenix, 1978-84; pres. The Dial Corp. (formerly Armour-Dial Co.), Phoenix, 1984-87, chief exec. officer, 1984-87; pres., chief exec. officer Purex Corp., 1985; chmn., chief exec. officer The Sparta Group Ltd., Scottsdale, Ariz., 1988—. Bd. dirs. Nortrust Holding Corp., Phoenix, Matrixx Initiatives, Inc., Phoenix; mem. bd. advisors Brother to Brother Internat., 1988—2001, Universal Tech. Inst., Phoenix, 1996—2004, No. Trust N.A., 2006—. Trustee Scottsdale Meml. Health Found., 1995-98; pres. Mt. Vernon Fire Dept. Mems. Assn., 1960-61. Served with U.S. Army, 1953-55, Germany. Recipient Loftus Lifetime Achievement award, Iona Coll., 2004. Mem. Am. Mgmt. Assn., Nat. Meat Canner Assn. (pres. 1971-72), Cosmetic, Toiletries and Fragrance Assn. (bd. dirs. 1985—87), Nat. Food Processors Assn. (bd. dirs.). Republican. Roman Catholic. Office: The Sparta Group Ltd 6623 N Scottsdale Rd Scottsdale AZ 85250-4421

WALSH, ELIZABETH JAMESON, musician; b. Panhandle, Tex., Oct. 23, 1913; d. Edwin Reece and Lela (Blackshear) Jameson; m. Thomas Norris Walsh, Nov. 1, 1951 (dec. May 5, 1990); children: Thomas Edwin, Richard Malcolm, Lela Elizabeth. MusB, U. North Tex., Deuton, 1941, MusM, 1942. Cert. tchr. music. Piano tchr. U. North Tex., Denton, 1940-42; music tchr. Perryton HS, Tex., 1942-43, Plainview HS, Tex., 1943-45; choir dir. Presbyn. and Disciples Ch., Plainview, 1943-45; music tchr. Dallas Pub. Sch., 1945-53; organist, choir dir. Midway Hills Ch., Dallas, 1954-60; piano tchr. Hockaday Pvt. Sch., Dallas, 1960-70; music tchr. Dallas Pub. Sch., 1970-82; organist, choir dir. Greenville Ave. Christian Ch., Dallas, 1975-82, Grace Meth. Ch., Dallas, 1982-91, St. Andrews Episcopal Ch., Farmers Branch, Tex., 1991—, Christ United Meth. Ch., 2001—. Composer (operetta) Day in Mexico, 1971, various titles for choir, 1996—; author: The Echo Tower, 1987, The House on the Hill, 1989, Uncle Willie (biography); appeared as Cleopatra as Caesar and Cleopatra, Dallas Little Theatre, 1933, Jane in Jane Eyre, Amarillo Little Theatre, 1935, Anna in Anna and the King of Siam, Northway Ch. Players, 1971, Uncle Willie (biolgraphy), 2004. Mem. Dallas Civic Chorus, 1960-65, Dallas Symphony Chorus, 1970-75, Farmer's Br. Women's Club, 1995—; v.p. Mus. Arts, 2003—. Recipient 2nd prize in Nat. Recording Contest, Nat. Piano Guild, 1973. Mem. Dallas Music Tchr. Assn., Dallas chpt. Am. Guild Organists, Musical Arts Club (sec. 2001-03, 1st v.p. 2005-), Daus. Republic of Tex. (chaplain 1993-95, pres. James Butler Bonham chpt. 1997—, sec. 2005—, Mamie Wynne Cox award 1995, sec. 1995-97, 2003, chmn. yearbook), Pro Musica (pres. 1976-77, 85-86, 2001—, sec. 2003-05, asst. sec. 2003—, treas. 1980-81, 96-97), Pi Beta Phi, Mu Phi Epsilon. Avocations: reading, travel. Home: 14339 Tanglewood Dr Farmers Branch TX 75234-3855

WALSH, GEORGE WILLIAM, publishing company executive, editor, author; b. NYC, Jan. 16, 1931; s. William Francis and Madeline (Maass) W.; m. Joan Mary Dunn, May 20, 1961; children: Grail, Simon. BS, Fordham U., 1952; MS, Columbia U. Sch. Journalism, 1953. Copy editor, reporter Cape Cod Standard-Times, Hyannis, Mass., 1955; communications specialist IBM, NYC, 1955-58; editorial trainee Time, Inc., 1958-59; writer-reporter Sports Illus., NYC, 1959-62; book editor Cosmopolitan, NYC, 1962-65, mng. editor, 1965-74; editor-in-chief, v.p. Ballantine Books div. Random House, NYC, 1974-79, Macmillan Pub. Co., NYC, 1979-85; pub. cons., 1985—. Author: Gentleman Jimmy Walker, 1974, Public Enemies, 1980, Damage Them All You Can: Robert E. Lee's Army of Northern Virginia, 2002, Whip the Rebellion: Ulysses S. Grant's Rise to Command, 2004, Those Damn Horse Soldiers: True Tales of the Civil War Cavalry, 2006. Served with AUS, 1953-55. Mem. Assn. Am. Pubs. Clubs: Univ., NYC, Pamet Harbor Yacht and Tennis, Truro, Mass., Cosmos, Washington. Roman Catholic. Personal E-mail: edchief@verizon.net.

WALSH, J. MICHAEL, wholesale distribution executive; BS in Indsl. Engring., Tex. Tech U., Lubbock; MBA, Tex. A&M U. Sr. v.p. ops. Core-Mark Holding Co., Inc., 1991—96, sr. v.p. US Distbn., 1996—99, exec. v.p. sales, 1999—2003, pres., CEO, 2003—, bd. dirs., 2004—; sr. v.p. ops. Food Svcs. of Am., 1992; sr. v.p. distbn. Core Mark Internat. Inc., 1996—99. Office: Core-Mark Holding Co 395 Oyster Point Blvd Ste 415 South San Francisco CA 94080 Office Phone: 650-589-9445. *

WALSH, JAMES, retail supermarket executive; Sr. v.p., CFO Meijer, Grand Rapids, Mich. Office: Meijer 29129 Walker St NW Grand Rapids MI 49544 Office Fax: (616) 453-6067.

WALSH, JAMES HAMILTON, lawyer; b. NYC, May 20, 1947; s. Edward James and Helen Smith (Hamilton) W.; m. Janice Ausherman, Aug. 3, 1967; children: Tracy, Courtney, Eric. BA in Psychology, Bridgewater Coll., Va., 1968; JD, U. Va., Charlottesville, 1975. Bar: Va. 1975, US Dist. Ct. (ea. and we. dists.) Va. 1975, US Ct. Appeals (4th cir.) 1976, US Supreme Ct. 1982, US Ct. Appeals (3d cir.). Assoc. McGuire, Woods LLPms), Richmond, Va., 1975-82; ptnr. McGuire, Woods, Battle & Boothe (and predecessor firms), Richmond, Va., 1982—. Instr. Nat. Inst. Trial Adv.; adj. prof. U. Richmond, 1992, 93; spl. prosecutor US Dist. Ct. (ea. dist.) Va., 1979, 84. Contbr. articles to profl. jours. Mem. bd. trustees Bridgewater Coll., mem. exec. com.; mem. staff Va. Law Rev. With US Army, 1969-72. Named Best Lawyers in Am., 2003—, Va. Legal Elite, 2002, 2006, Va. Super Lawyers. Mem. ABA (mem. antitrust sect. health care com., litigation sect.), Fedn. Def. and Corp. Counsel, Va. State Bar (bd. govs. antitrust sect. 1984-90, chmn. 1986), Va. Bar Assn. (chmn. criminal law sect. 1997, 98), Richmond Bar Assn., Willow Oaks, Order Coif, Phi Delta Phi. Episcopalian. Home: 113 Adingham Ct Richmond VA 23229-7761 Office: McGuire Woods LLP 1 James Ctr 901 E Cary St Richmond VA 23219-4004 Office Phone: 804-775-4356. Business E-Mail: jwalsh@mcguirewoods.com.

WALSH, JAMES JOSEPH, lawyer; b. New Orleans, June 21, 1948; s. Francis Michael and Violet (Young) W.; m. Priscilla Robson Ferris, Oct. 12, 1972; children: Caitlin Marian, Alison Robson. BA, La. State U., 1970, JD, 1975. Bar: La. 1975, Mich. 1977, US Ct. Appeals (6th cir.) 1981, US Supreme Ct. 1991. Law clk. Mich. Ct. Appeals, Detroit, 1975-77; assoc. Bodman LLP, Detroit, 1977—84, ptnr., 1984—. Counsel Outdoor Advt. Assn. Mich. Editor: La. Law Rev., 1975. Named to Hall of Fame, La. State U. Law Sch., 1988. Mem. State Bar Mich., Washtenaw County Bar Assn., Detroit Athletic Club, Mich. C. of C., Jefferson City Buzzards. Avocations: fishing, gardening, golf. Home: 8025 Mast Rd Dexter MI 48130-9301 Office: Bodman LLP 201 S Division Ste 400 Ann Arbor MI 48104 Office Phone: 734-930-0237. Business E-Mail: jwalsh@bodmanllp.com.

WALSH, JAMES THOMAS (JIM WALSH), congressman; b. Syracuse, NY, June 19, 1947; s. William F. Walsh; m. DeDe Ryan; 3 children. BA in Hist., St. Bonaventure U., 1970. Agrl. ext. agt. Peace Corps, Nepal, 1970-72; mktg. exec. telecom. co., 1974-88; exec.-in-residence telecom. inst. SUNY Inst. Tech. Utica-Rome, 1986-87; mem. Common Coun., Syracuse, NY, 1977-85, pres., 1986-88; mem. US Congress from 25th NY dist., 1989—, mem. appropriations com., ranking mem. labor, health & human svcs. and edn. subcommittee, chmn. mil. quality of life and vets. affairs subcommittee, chmn. Friends of Ireland, 1995—, co-chair US-Irish Interparliamentary Grp., co-founder, co-chair Congl. Hearing Health Caucus. Bd. mem. Erie Canal Mus., Vera Ho., Everson Mus. Recipient Flax Trust award, 1997, Bobby Sands award, Ancient Order Hibernians, 1998, Ellis Island Medal of Honor, Nat. Ethnic Coalition Orgns., 2002, Legislator of Yr. award, Congl. Fire Svcs. Inst., 2003, Willis H. Carrier award, Ctr. Excellence in Environ. Systems, 2003. Republican. Roman Catholic. Office: PO Box 7306 Syracuse NY 13261-7306 Office Phone: 202-225-3701, 315-423-5657. Office Fax: 315-423-5669. *

WALSH, JAN, library director; MLS, U. Pitts. With Wash. State Libr., Olympia, 1978—, acting state libr., 2002, state libr., 2002—. Mem.: Wash. Libr. Assn., Chief Officers of State Libr. Agys. (Continuing Edn. com., Stats. com.), Libr. Coun. Wash. Office: Wash State Libr Divsn Wash Sec State PO Box 42460 Olympia WA 98504-2460 Office Phone: 360-704-5253. Office Fax: 360-586-7575. E-mail: jwalsh@secstate.wa.gov. *

WALSH, JOAN, editor-in-chief; Freelance writer; with In These Times, Chgo., Santa Barbara News & Review; news editor Salon.com, San Francisco, 1998—99, v.p. news, 1999—2003, v.p., co-mng. editor, 2003—04, sr. v.p., editorial ops., 2003—04, editor-in-chief, 2005. Office: Salon Media Group 101 Spear St 203 San Francisco CA 94105-1517 Office Phone: 415-645-9200. Business E-Mail: jwalsh@salon.com.

WALSH, JOHN, television show host, missing children and victims' rights advocate; b. Auburn, NY, Dec. 26, 1945; m. Revé Drew Walsh, 1971; children: Adam(dec.), Megan, Callahan, Hayden. Former hotel marketer. Author: Tears of Rage, 1997, No Mercy, 1998, Public Enemies: The Host of America's Most Wanted Targets the Nation's Most Notorious Criminals, 2001; host (TV series) America's Most Wanted, 1988—, The John Walsh Show, 2002—04, creator The New America's Most Wanted: America Fights Back, appeared in (TV) Springfield's Most Wanted, 1995, Safety Patrol, 1998, American Crime Fighter: E! True Hollywood Story, 2000, Inside TV Land: Cops on Camera, 2002, Laci Peterson: E! True Hollywood Story, 2004, co-host Hawaii's Missing Kids: Eyes of the Innocent, 2004, actor & exec. prodr. (TV films) Smart Kids, 1994, If Looks Could Kill: The John Hawkins Story, 1996; actor: (films) Jesuit Joe, 1991, Wrongfully Accused, 1998, Press Run, 1999, Grey Owl, 1999; narrator (films) The Safe Side, 2004. Founder Adam Walsh Child Resource Ctr., Straight Shooter; bd. dir. Nat. Ctr. for Missing and Exploited Children, chief exec. officers coun., nat. adv. bd., spokesperson. Named one of 50 Most Beautiful People in World, People mag., 1996, 100 Americans Who Changed History, CBS Portraits; recipient US Marshals Man of Yr. award, 1988, Spl. Recognition award, US Atty. Gen., honored in Rose Garden 4 times by 3 US Presidents, FBI Man of Yr. award, 2000. Achievements include being instrumental advocate in passage of Missing Children Act of 1982, and Missing Children's Assistance Act of 1984; testified over 55 times before Congress and state legislatures on crime, missing children and victims' issues. Office: Americas Most Wanted PO Box Crime TV Washington DC 20016-9126

WALSH, JOHN ALFRED, retired social worker; b. NYC, June 4, 1927; s. Joseph Thomas and May Catherine (Moran) Walsh; m. Gwendolyn Ann Stockton, Apr. 13, 1952; children: Ralph, Carl, Nils. BA cum laude, St. Mary's U., Balt., 1949; M in Social Svc., Fordham U., 1954. Lic. clin. social worker, nursing home adminstr., marriage/family therapist. Social worker Cath. Charities, Bklyn., 1949—56; supr. after care clinics Ancora (N.J.) Psychiat. Hosp., 1956—57; dir. social svc. Trenton (N.J.) Psychiat. Hosp., 1958—68; asst. supt. Hunterdon Devel. Ctr., Clinton, NJ, 1968—91; ret. Author: (pamphlet) Fabulous Rosts, 1982. V.p. Warren County Hist. Soc., Belvidere, NJ, 1990—, Assn. Hunterdon Devel. Ctr., Clinton, 1991—; mem. bd. edn. Belvidere Sch. Dist., 1991—2001. Capt. US Army, 1953—66. Avocation: collecting stamps and post cards. Home: 703 Oxford St Belvidere NJ 07823 E-mail: jaw703@aol.com.

WALSH, JOHN CHARLES, investment company executive, director; b. Indpls., Sept. 8, 1924; s. John Charles; children: Michael S., Carolyn Ann, Anne D. BS, Notre Dame U., 1949. Auditor Herdrich Boggs & Co., Indpls., 1949—78; with P.R. Mallory & Co., Inc., 1978—; pres. Walgang Co. Inc., Indpls., 1970—. V.p., treas. P.R. Mallory & Co., 1971. With USMCR, 1943—45. Mem. Fin. Execs. Inst., Ind. Hist. Soc., Econ. Club, Notre Dame Club, Rotary. Home: 4974 Shadow Rock Cir Carmel IN 46033-9500 Office: 160 W Carmel Dr Ste 265 Carmel IN 46032

WALSH, JOHN L., energy executive; BA, MBA, Harvard Univ. Mgmt. positions through v.p. AmeriGas indsl. gas div. UGI Corp., 1981—86; v.p. spl. gases, pres. process gas solutions No. Am., pres. process Plants BOC Group PLC, 1986—2001, exec. dir., CEO indsl. & spl. products div., 2001—05; pres., COO UGI Corp., 2005—; bd. dir. AmeriGas Propane, 2005—, UGI Utilities. Office: UGI Corp 460 N Guelph Rd King Of Prussia PA 19406 Mailing: UGI Corp PO Box 858 Valley Forge PA 19482 *

WALSH, JOSEPH HAYES, lawyer; b. Boston, Feb. 9, 1950; s. Joseph Henry and Eileen M. Walsh; m. Sandra A. Walsh; children: Catherine E., Christine A. AB cum laude, Boston Coll., 1972, JD cum laude, 1975. Bar: Mass. 1975, US Dist. Ct. Dist Mass. 1977, US Ct. Appeals (1st cir.), US Supreme Ct. Assoc. Crane, Inker & Oteri, Boston, 1975-80; ptnr. White, Inker & Aronson, Boston, 1984-92, Cuddy, Lynch & Bixby, Boston, 1992-94, Menard, Murphy & Walsh, Boston, 1994—. Named one of Top 100 Lawyers, Worth mag., 2005. Office: Menard Murphy & Walsh 60 State St Boston MA 02109-1800

WALSH, JOSEPH LEO, III, lawyer; b. St. Louis, Dec. 7, 1954; s. Joseph Leo and Joan Marie (Bocklage) W.; m. Eileen Rose Boland, June 11, 1982; children: Katie Rose, Joseph L. IV, Brian James, John Patrick, Mary Elizabeth. BS cum laude, Loras Coll., 1977; JD, St. Mary's U., 1984. Bar: Tex. 1984, U.S. Dist. Ct. (so. dist.) Tex. 1985, Mo. 1986, U.S. Dist. Ct. (ea. dist.) Mo. 1989, U.S. Ct. Appeals (8th cir.) 1989, U.S. Supreme Ct. 1991. Assoc. Chamberlain, Hrdlicka, White, Johnson & Williams, Houston, 1984-86; atty. Haley, Fredrickson & Walsh, St. Louis, 1986-88; assoc. Gray & Ritter, St. Louis, 1988-95; pvt. practice St. Louis, 1995—; mcpl. judge 21st Jud. Cir. Ct., Frontenac, 2000—01, Creve Coeur, Mo., 2003—. Pro bono legal clinic St. Patrick Ctr., 1991—, Holy Guardian Angel Settlement, 1995—; jud. clk. U.S. Dist. Ct. (we. dist.) Tex., 1984. Co-author: Missouri Bar CLE Treatise on Torts, 2d edit., 1990; sr. assoc. editor St. Mary's U. Sch. Law Jour., 1983-84. Active Holly Hills Neighborhood Assn., 1991-93; v.p. Our Lady of Pillar Men's Club, 1998, pres., 1999-2000. Recipient Torts and Evidence award Lawyers' Co-op Pub. Co., 1982; named to Nat. Order Barristers, 1984. Mem. ATLA, Am. Bd. Trial Advocates, Mo. Assn. Trial Attys., Bar Assn. Met. St. Louis, Lawyers Assn. St. Louis, Phi Delta Phi (pres. 1984). Roman Catholic. Home and Office: 10469 White Bridge Ln Saint Louis MO 63141-8415 Office: 4399 Laclede Saint Louis MO 63108 Home Phone: 314-567-6768; Office Phone: 314-535-5500. Office Fax: 314-531-1131. Personal E-mail: jlwatty@swbell.net.

WALSH, JOSEPH MICHAEL, magazine distribution executive; b. NYC, Jan. 19, 1943; s. John Redmond and Bridget Judith (Donovan) W.; m. Theresa Rose Vericker, Oct. 3, 1964; children— Joseph, Matthew, Teresa Ann, John, James. BBA in Acctg., Iona Coll., 1964. With Peat, Marwick, Mitchell & Co., C.P.A.s, NYC, 1964-70, audit supr., until 1970; asst. to chmn. bd. and pres. Cadence Industries Corp., West Caldwell, NJ, 1970-71, v.p., 1971-74, exec. v.p., 1974-87; pres. subs. Curtis Circulation Co., 1972-74, chmn., chief exec. officer, 1982—; pres. Data Services for Health, 1976-77, U.S. Pencil and Stationery Co., 1977-79, Perfect Subscription Co. (parent Perfect Sch. Plans, Perfect Telephone Plan, Moore Cottrell and Keystone Readers Service), 1980-83. Mem. AICPA, N.Y. State Soc. CPAs, K.C. Office: Curtis Circulation Co 730 River Rd New Milford NJ 07646-3048 Home Phone: 561-694-1966; Office Phone: 201-634-7401. E-mail: jwalsh@curtiscirc.com.

WALSH, JOSEPH RICHARD, lawyer; b. Atlanta, May 10, 1951; s. Joseph Radamaker and Meta Lucille (Cole) Walsh; m. Elisabeth Clare Kane, July 27, 1980; children: Lindsay Carolyn, Dana Elisabeth, Cameron Marisa. B in Indsl. Engring., Ga. Inst. Tech., 1973; JD, U. Ga., 1976; ML in Taxation, Georgetown U., 1984. Bar: Ga. 1976, U.S. Dist. Ct. (no. dist.) Ga. 1976, U.S. Ct. Appeals (5th cir.) 1976, Va. 1978, U.S. Ct. Appeals (4th cir.) 1978, DC 1979, U.S. Ct. Appeals (11th cir.) 1982, U.S. Claims Ct. 1983, U.S. Tax Ct. 1983, Calif. 1984, U.S. Dist. Ct. (no. dist.) Calif. 1984, U.S. Ct. Appeals (9th cir.) 1984. Indsl. engr. So. Rlwy. Sys., Atlanta, 1973—74; atty. ICC, Washington, 1977—78, atty., asst. rail merger coord., 1979—84; assoc. Fulbright & Jaworski, Washington, 1978—79; counsel Bank Am. Nat. Assn., San Francisco, 1984—85, sr. counsel, 1985—98, asst. gen. counsel, 1998—2006; pvt. practice law Orinda, Calif., 2006. Counselor Athens (Ga.) Legal Aid and Defender Soc., 1976; instr. comml. law San Francisco Law Sch., 1987—92. Co-author: (book) Federal Regulatory Process: Practice and Procedure, 1981. Campaign vol. Jimmy Carter Presdl. Campaign, NH, 1976. Named Outstanding Young Men Am., U.S. Jaycees, 1982; Nat. Merit scholar, Ga. Inst. Tech., 1969, NSF grantee, 1972. Mem.: ABA, World Affairs Coun., Assn. Corp. Counsel, Am. Inst. Indsl. Engrs., San Francisco Leasing Lawyers Forum, San Francisco Bar Assn., Calif. Bar Assn., Va. Bar Assn., Fed. Bar Assn., Ga. Bar Assn., DC Bar Assn., Calif. Nature Conservancy, Sierra Club, Commonwealth Club Calif., Lawyers Club (San Francisco), Alpha Pi Mu, Tau Beta Pi, Phi Kappa Phi. Office: 65 Rheem Blvd Orinda CA 94563 Business E-Mail: jrichardwalsh@comcast.net.

WALSH, JOSEPH THOMAS, retired state supreme court justice; b. Wilmington, Del., May 18, 1930; s. Joseph Patrick and Mary Agnes (Bolton) W.; m. Madeline Maria Lamb, Oct. 6, 1955; children: Kevin, Lois, Patrick, Daniel, Thomas, Nancy. BA, LaSalle Coll., 1952; LLB, Georgetown U., 1955. Bar: D.C. 1955, Del. 1955. Atty. Ho. of Reps., Dover, Del., 1961-62; chief counsel Pub. Svc. Commn., Dover, 1964-72; judge Del. Superior Ct., Wilmington, 1972-84; vice chancellor Ct. of Chancery, Wilmington, 1984-85; justice Del. Supreme Ct., Wilmington, 1985—2003. Adjunct prof. Widener U. Sch. of Law, 2003—. Capt. U.S. Army, 1955-58. Democrat. Roman Catholic.

WALSH, JOY IRENE, literature educator, language educator; d. Lloyd Dice Tennies and Phyllis Cloe Wayland. AA in Elem. Edn., Butler County CC, Pa., 1987; BS in Elem. Edn., Houghton Coll., NY, 1989; MA in English, Slippery Rock U., Pa., 1992. Tutor Butler County CC, 1990—92, instr., 1993—; devel. specialist Lifesteps, Inc., Butler, 2000—02. Mem.: Nat. Coun. Tchrs. English. Office: Butler County CC College Dr Oak Hill Butler PA 16003

WALSH, KATE, actress; b. San Jose, Calif., Oct. 13, 1967; m. Alex Young, Sept. 2007. Student, U. Ariz. Actor: (radio plays) Born Guilty; (plays) Moon Under Miami, Troilus and Cressida; (films) Normal Life, 1996, Peppermills, 1997, Night of the Lawyers, 1997, Three Below Zero, 1998, Heaven, 1998, Henry, Portrait of a Serial Killer II, 1998, The Family Man, 2000, Under the Tuscan Sun, 2003, After the Sunset, 2004, Kicking and Screaming, 2005, Inside Out, 2005, Bewitched, 2005, Veritas, Prince of Truth, 2006; (TV series) The Drew Carey Show, 1997—2002, The Mike O'Malley Show, 1999, Turks, 1999, The Norm Show, 2000—01, Mind of a Married Man, 2001, Joint Custody, 2004, Grey's Anatomy, 2005—07 (Outstanding Performance by an Ensemble in a Drama Series, SAG, 2007); (TV films) Bobby Cannon, 2005; (TV series) Private Practice, 2007—. Mailing: Grey's Anatomy Los Feliz Tower 4th Fl 4151 Prospect Ave Los Angeles CA 90027 *

WALSH, KENNETH THOMAS, journalist; b. NYC, May 29, 1947; s. Thomas Gerard and Gloria (Junior) W.; m. Barbara Barclay Howarth, June 13, 1982; children: Jean, Christopher. BA, Rutgers U., 1968; MA, Am. U., 1970. News clk. N.Y. Times, Washington, 1969-70; newsman AP, Denver, 1972-76; reporter, statehouse corr., polit. editor Denver Post, 1976-79, chief polit. writer, polit. columnist, 1979-81, Washington corr., 1981-84; congl. corr. U.S. News and World Report, Washington, 1984-86, White House corr., 1986—. Adj. prof. comm. Am. U., Washington, 1993—. Author: Feeding the Beast: The White House Versus the Press, 1996, Ronald Reagan: Biography, 1997. 1st lt. U.S. Army, 1970-72. Recipient prize for disting. reporting on the presidency Gerald R. Ford Found., Grand Rapids, Mich., 1992, 98; named Outstanding Adj. Prof. Am. U., Washington, 1998. Mem. White House Corr. Assn. (bd. mem. 1990-98, pres. 1994-95, Aldo Beckman award for disting. White House coverage 1991, 2007). Office: US News and World Report 1050 Thomas Jefferson St NW Washington DC 20007-3817 *

WALSH, KERRI LEE, Olympic athlete; b. Aug. 15, 1978; d. Tim and Margie. BA in Am. studies, Stanford U., 1999. Player BVA Tour, 2001, FIVG Internat. Tour, 2001—, AVP Tour, 2003—; beach volleyball player Team USA, Sydney Olympic Games, 2000, Team USA, Athens Olympic Games, 2004. Named First Team All-Am., 1995—99, Pro Beach Volleyball Rookie of the Yr., 2001, AVP Best Offensive Player, 2003, AVP Most Valuable Player, 2003, AVP Team of the Yr. (With Misty May), 2003. Achievements include being the second person in history named First Team All-American four years in a row, Stanford U., 1995-1999; winning FIVB World Champions with partner Misty May, 2002, 2003; winning gold medal (with Misty May) in Athens Olympic games, beach volleyball, 2004. Office: c/o USOC One Olympic Plz Colorado Springs CO 80909

WALSH, KEVIN P., energy executive, financial services executive; BS cum laude in Fin., Bus. Mgmt., Fairfield Univ.; grad., GE Fin. Mgmt. Program. Region mgr., internat. credit, collections ops. GE, 1985—86; region mgr., customer fin. programs for comm. aircraft and indsl./power generation programs GE Aircraft Engines, 1986—88; program mgr., fin. mgmt. GE, 1988—90, asst. v.p., sales, 1990—92, v.p., project fin. sales Stamford, Conn., 1992—93, dir., structured fin. London, 1993—95, mng. dir., capital mkts, 1995—96, sales originator, structured fin., 1996—98, mng. dir., structured fin. printing, paper, forest products group, 1998—2000, mng. dir., structured fin. e-bus., 2000—04, mng. dir. of portfolio, comml. fin. energy fin. svcs. Stamford, Conn., 2004—. Past bd. dir. Southern Star Ctrl. Gas Pipeline, Inc., 2005. Named one of 50 Who Matter Now, Business 2.0, 2007. Office: GE Energy Fin Svcs 120 Long Ridge Rd Stamford CT 06927 Office Phone: 203-357-4880. Office Fax: 203-357-4942. *

WALSH, LAWRENCE EDWARD, lawyer; b. Port Maitland, NS, Can., Jan. 8, 1912; came to U.S., 1914, naturalized, 1922; s. Cornelius Edward and Lila May (Sanders) W.; m. Mary Alma Porter; children: Barbara Marie, Janet Maxine (Mrs. Alan Larson), Sara Porter, Dale Edward, Elizabeth Porter (Mrs. Peter LaColla). AB, Columbia U., 1932, LLB, 1935; LLD, Union U., 1959, St. John's U., 1975, Suffolk U., 1975, Waynesburg Coll., 1976, Vt. Law Sch., 1976. Bar: N.Y. 1936, D.C. 1981, Okla. 1981, U.S. Supreme Ct. 1951. Spl. asst. atty. gen. Drukman Investigation, 1936—38; dep. asst. dist. atty. N.Y. County, 1938—41; assoc. Davis Polk Wardwell Sunderland & Kiendl, 1941—43; asst. counsel to gov. State of NY, 1943—49, counsel to gov., 1950—51; counsel Pub. Svc. Commn., 1951—53; gen. counsel, exec. dir. Waterfront Commn. of N.Y. Harbor, 1953—54; judge US Dist. Ct. (so. dist.) NY, 1954—57; dep. atty. gen. US Dept. Justice, 1957—60; ptnr. Davis, Polk & Wardwell LLP, 1961—81; counsel Crowe & Dunlevy LLP, Oklahoma City, 1981—. Ind. counsel Iran/Contra investigation, 1986-93; chmn. N.Y. State Moreland Commn. Alcoholic Beverage Control Law, 1963-64; pres. Columbia Alumni Fedn., 1968-69; dep. head with rank of amb. U.S. del. meetings on Vietnam, Paris, 1969; counsel to N.Y. State Ct. on Judiciary, 1971-72; 2d cir. mem. U.S. Cir. Judge Nominating Commn., 1978-80. Author: (Book) Firewall The Iran-Contra Conspiracy and Cover-Up, 1997, The Gift of Insecurity, 2003. Trustee emeritus Columbia U., Mut. Life Ins. Co., N.Y. Recipient medal for excellence Columbia U., 1959, Law Sch., Columbia U., 1980, John Jay award Columbia Coll., 1989. Fellow Am. Bar Found., Am. Coll. Trial Lawyers; mem. Am. Law Inst., ABA (pres. 1975-76), N.Y. State Bar Assn. (pres. 1966-67), Oklahoma County Bar Assn., Okla. State Bar Assn., Internat. Bar Assn., Assn. of Bar of City of N.Y., N.Y. County Lawyers Assn., Fed. Bar Coun., Law Soc. Eng. and Wales (hon.), Can. Bar Assn. (hon.), Mex. Bar Assn. (hon.), Century Assn., Oklahoma City Golf and Country Club, Beta Theta Pi. Presbyterian. Home: 1902 Bedford Dr Oklahoma City OK 73116-5306 Office: 1800 Mid Am Towers Oklahoma City OK 73102 Office Phone: 405-235-7700. E-mail: legalew@sbcglobal.net.

WALSH, M. EMMET, actor; b. Ogdensburg, NY, Mar. 22, 1935; BBA, Clarkson Coll., 1958; student, Am. Acad. Dramatic Arts, 1959-61. Appeared in films including Chasing 3000, The Man in the Chair, Raising Arizona, Ordinary People, The Milagro Beanfield War, Romeo and Juliet, Winterdance, My Best Friend's Wedding, Twilight, A Time To Kill, Albino Alligator, Free Willy II, Snow Dogs, Music of Chance, White Sands, Narrow Margin, The Mighty Quinn, Clean and Sober, Harry and The Hendersons, Fletch, Missing in Action, Back to School, Blood Simple, Blade Runner, Silkwood, Sundown, Brubaker, Raise the Titanic, Fast Walking, Reds, The Jerk, Straight Time, At Long Last Long, Serpico, What's Up Doc?, They Might Be Giants, Midnight Cowboy, End of the Road, Cannery Row, Slap Shot, Cold Turkey, The Traveling Executioner, Alice's Restaurant, Airport '77, Wild Wild West, Christmas in the Clouds, Poor White Trash, Random Hearts, Iron Giant, Skirty Winner, Queen of Hearts, Baggage, Me and Will, Erasable You, Carrot Top, A Time to Kill, Chairman of the Board, Retroactive, The Killing Jar, Portraits of Innocence, Criminal Hearts, Panther, Camp Nowhere, Dead Badge, Probable Cause, Glass Shield, Relative Fear, Cops and Robbersons, Bitter Harvest, Wilder Napalm, Equinox, Naked Truth, Killer Image, Red Scorpion, Chattahoochee, Thunderground, Catch Me If You Can, War Party, Sunset, No Man's Land, The Best of Times, Wildcats, Critters, The Pope of Greenwich Village, Grandview-USA, Raw Courage, Scandalous, Escape Artist, Back Roads, Bound for Glory, Nickelodeon, Mickey & Nicky, The Fish That Saved Pittsburgh, Kid Blue, Prisoner of 2nd Avenue, The Gambler, Get to Know Your Rabbit, Escape From the Planet of the Apes, Little Big Man, Loving, Stiletto, Christmas With The Kranks, Racing Stripes, Bitter Harvest, Greener Mountains, Inn Trouble, Man in the Chair, Big Stan, Your Name Here, Sherman's Way, Darkness Visible; (TV shows) include Frasier, Sandy Duncan Show, Bonanza, Mind of the Married Man, The Rockford Files, All in the Family, Bob Newhart Show, The Waltons, Little House on the Prairie, Early Edition, Tales from the Crypt, Home Improvement, The Outer Limits, X Files, The Abduction of Kari Swenson, Resting Place, The Woman Who Willed a Miracle, The Guardian, Tracy Ullman's Trailer Tales, Charlie Lawrence, Ed, Gideon's Crossing, Night Visions, Cover Me, NYPD Blue, Monster, Men in White, Nightmare in Big Sky Country, The Tracey Ullman Show, Dogs, The Lottery, The Mixed Up Files Of..., The Jackie Thomas Show, Wild Card, Four Eyes and Six Guns, Grey Fox, The Nerd, Love and Lies, Fourth Story, The Flash, Unsub, Brotherhood of the Rose II, Murder Ordained I & II, Amazing Stories, Broken Vows, Hero in the Family, The City, Deliberate Stranger, The Right of the People, Twighlight Zone, The Hitchhiker, You Are the Jury, Vanishing America, After Mash, Night Partners, High Noon Two, East of Eden I & II, Helinger's Law, French-Atlantic Affair, Countdown to Superdome, Dear Detective, Mrs. R's Daughter, James at Fifteen, Red Alert, A Question of Guilt, No Other Love, Panic On Page One, Skag, The Gift, Mississippi, Starsky and Hutch, Mary Hartman, Gibbsville, Tony Randall Show, Nancy Walker Show, Kate McShane, Joe & Sons, The Cop and the Kid, Brahmins, McMillan & Wife, N.Y.P.D., Baretta, Don Rickles Show, Nichols, Texas Wheeler, Crime Club, Prudential's "On Stage," The Doctors, Outlaws, Jimmy Stewart Show, Men at Law, Dr. Dan, Love of Life, Amy Prentiss, The Law, Arnie, Julia, Con Sawyer; HBO series includes The Mind of the Married Man; Broadway shows include That Championship Season, Does the Tiger Wear a Necktie?, The Beauty Part, Buried Child, Royal Nation Theatre, London, 2004; Off Broadway shows include Shepherds of the Shelf, Blackfriars Theatre, 1961, The Old Glory, The Outside Man, Am. Pl. Theatre, 1964, Death of the Well Loved Boy, St. Marks Playhouse, 1967, Three From Column "A", Theatre 73, 1968, Are You Now or Have You Ever Been, L.A. Ford's Theatre, D.C., 1975, Marathon '93, Ensemble Studio Theatre, 1993; Off-Off-Broadway shows at New Theatre Workshop, The Loft, Tamarack, Actors Studio, The Playbox, Ensemble Studio Theatre, The Pub. TheatreNYSF; regional theatre shows at Theatre of Living Arts, Phila., 1965, Studio Arena, Buffalo, 1966, Long Wharf Theatre, New Haven, 1967, Cin. Playhouse in Pk., 1995, La Jolla Playhouse, 1999, Arena Stage, D.C., 2000; summer stock shows at Coll. Theatre, Am. Acad. Dramatic Arts, 1954-61, Bucks County Playhouse, New Hope, Pa., 1962, Brattleboro Summer Theatre, Vt., 1963, Caravan Theatre, Dorset, Vt., 1964, U. Ky., 1966, Berkshire Theatre Festival, Stockbridge, Mass., 1967-70, Vt. Summer Theatre Festival, Johnson, 1974, U. Tulsa, 1983, Santa Barbara Theatre Festival, 1985, U. Vt., 1992; voices include The Civil War, Baseball, The Way West, The West, King of The Hill, Wild Thornberry, Muriel's Christmas Carol, Big Guy and Rusty, The Simpsons, The New Scooby Doo, BBC Radio Play, Squirrel Boy, the "X's", numerous others.

WALSH, MARIE LECLERC, nurse; b. Providence, Sept. 11, 1928; d. Walter Normand and Anna Mary (Ryan) Leclerc; m. John Breffni Walsh, June l8, l955; children: George Breffni, John Leclerc, Darina Louise. Grad., Waterbury Hosp. Sch. Nursing, Conn., 1951; BS, Columbia U., 1954, MA, 1955. Team leader Hartford (Conn.) Hosp., 1951-53; pvt. duty nurse St. Luke's Hosp., NYC, 1953-57; sch. nurse tchr. Agnes Russel Ctr., Tchrs. Coll. Columbia U., NYC, 1955-56; clin. nursing instr. St. Luke's Hosp., NYC, 1957-58; chmn. disaster nursing ARC Fairfax County, Va., 1975; course coord. occupational health nursing U. Va. Sch. Continuing Edn., Falls Church, 1975-77; mem. disaster steering com. No. Va. C.C., Annandale, 1976; adj. faculty U. Va. Sch. Continuing Edn., Falls Church, 1981; disaster svcs. nurse ARC, Wichita, Kans., 1985-90, disaster svcs. nurse Seattle-King County chpt. Seattle, 1990-96; ret. Rsch. and statis. analyst U. Va. Sch. Continuing Edn. Nursing, Falls Church, l975; rsch. libr. Olive Garvey Ctr. for Improvement Human Functioning, Inc., Wichita, l985. Sec. Dem. party, Cresskill, N.J., 1964-66; county committeewoman, Bergen County, N.J., 1965-66; pres., v.p., Internat. Staff Wives, NATO, Brussels, Belgium, 1978-80; election officer, supr. Election Bd., Wichita, 1987, 88; v.p. McLean Newcomers, 1997-99, pres., 1999-2000. Mem. AAAS, AAUW, N.Y. Acad. Sci., Pi Lambda Theta, Sigma Theta Tau. Avocations: travel, gardening. Home: 8800 Prestwould Pl Mc Lean VA 22102-2231 Personal E-mail: mlwnet@msn.com.

WALSH, MATTHEW M., construction executive; b. Chgo., Jan. 7, 1946; m. Joyce Walsh; children: Matt IV, Sean, Erin. BA in Bus., U. Notre Dame, Ind., 1968; JD, Loyola U., Chgo., 1972. CEO Walsh Group, Chgo. Bd. mem. Constrn. Industry Roundtable. Mem. bd. St. Ignatius Coll. Prep. Sch., Union League Club; mem. adv. coun. Sch. Architecture U. Notre Dame. Recipient Outstanding Achievement in Constrn. award, The Moles, 2005. Mem.: Union League Club. Office: Walsh Group 929 W Adams St Chicago IL 60607-3021 Office Phone: 312-563-5400. Office Fax: 312-563-5420. *

WALSH, MICHAEL J., lawyer; b. Portland, Oreg., Sept. 4, 1932; s. Frank M.J. and Elisemary (Derbes) W.; m. June Griffin, Nov. 28, 1959; children: Molly, Erin, Kathryn (dec.), Anne. BA, U. Portland, 1954; JD, Georgetown U., 1959. Bar: D.C. 1959, Oreg. 1959, U.S. Ct. Appeals (fed. and 9th cirs.) 1959, U.S. Tax Ct. 1959, U.S. Supreme Ct. 1968. Law ck. to presiding justice Oreg. Supreme Ct., Salem, 1959-60; mng. ptnr. Rankin, Walsh, Ragen and Roberts, Portland, 1960-75; pvt. practice Portland, 1976—81; ptnr. Walsh and Connolly, Portland, 1982—83; of counsel McEwen, Hanna, Gisvold and Rankin, Portland, 1983-85, Bullivant, Houser, Bailey, Pendergrass, & Hoffman, Washington, 1985—. Chief judge Employees Compensation Appeals Bd. US Dept. Labor, Washington, 1985—2003, sr. counsel Adminstrv. Appeals Bds., 2003—04; legal counsel Reagan-Bush '84, Nat. Hdqs., Washington, 1983—84. Chmn. legal dev. March of Dimes, 1967; chmn. admissions Georgetown U., Oreg., 1972-83; trustee Christie Sch., 1974-78; trustee Cath. Charities Oreg., 1966-72, pres. 1971; trustee Parry Ctr. for Children, 1967-73, v.p. 1970-71; trustee Portland Tennis Ctr. Assn., 1972-83, pres. 1976-82; bd. dirs. Portland Traffic Safety Commn., 1981-83. Served with JAGC, USAF, capt. res. Mem. Am. Judicature Soc., Am. Trial Lawyers Assn., Nat. Assn. Coll. and Uiv. Attys., Am. Arbitration Assn., D.C. Bar Assn., Oreg. Bar Assn. (mem. various coms.), Multnomah County Bar Assn., Portland C. of C. (bd. dirs. 1975-78, chmn. legis. coun. 1975), John Carroll Soc., Thomas More Soc. Clubs: Georgetown Univ. (Oreg.) (pres. 1966). Home: 3273 Sutton Pl NW # B Washington DC 20016-3537

WALSH, MICHAEL P., mechanical engineer; m. Evelyn Walsh. BS, Manhattan Coll., 1966; postgrad., Princeton U., 1970. Dir. motor vehicle pollution control Dept. Air Resources, NYC, 1970—74, U.S. Environ. Protection Agy., 1974—81; independent technical cons., 1981—. Co-chair mobile source advisory subcom. EPA. Author: (bimonthly publ.) Car Lines. Named MacArthur fellow, John D. and Catherine T. MacArthur Found., 2005. E-mail: mpwalsh@igc.org.

WALSH, MICHAEL S., lawyer; b. Chgo., Sept. 29, 1951; AB, Colgate U., 1973; MBA, Cornell U., 1975; JD, So. Meth. U., 1978. Bar: Ill. 1978, U.S. Dist. Ct. (no. dist.) Ill. 1978, U.S. Ct. Appeals (fed. cir.) 1983, U.S. Ct. Appeals (9th cir.) 1985. Mem. Jenner & Block, Chgo. Mem. ABA, Ill. State Bar Assn., Chgo. Bar Assn., Computer Law Assn. Office: Jenner & Block One IBM Plz Chicago IL 60611-3608 E-mail: mwalsh@jenner.com.

WALSH, MICHAEL THOMAS, historian, musician; b. Balt., Dec. 1, 1978; s. John Michael and Annette Mary Walsh; m. Jennifer Trombetta, July 7, 2007. BA in History, magna cum laude, Loyola Coll., Balt., 2000; MA in Historical Studies, U. Md., Balt. County, 2002; PhD in Public Policy, U. Md., Balt., 2002—. Profl. musician self employed, Balt., 1998—; tchg. asst. history U. Md., 2002—03, tchg. asst. polit. sci., 2003—05, acadmic advisor, 2003—, tchg. asst. history, 2005—07; transfer student evaluator Towson U., 2007—. Contbr. ency. entries; musician: Whisky Train's Automatic Sin, 2004. Supporting mem. Colonial Williamsburg Found.; sustaining mem. Rep. Nat. Com., 2006; pres. Rep. Presdl. Task Force, 2006. Recipient Outstanding Achievement Jazz Performance, 1997—98. Mem.: Orgn. Am. hist., Am. Hist. Assn., Pi Sigma Alpha, Phi Alpha Theta. Republican. Roman Catholic. Avocations: music, reading, sports, swimming. Personal E-mail: mwalsh3@umbc.edu.

WALSH, NAN, artist, painter, sculptor, consultant; b. NYC, Nov. 4, 1932; d. Joseph Edward and Mary Ellen (White) Heinl; m. Albert Anthony Walsh, July 10, 1954 (dec. Oct. 9, 2002); children: Maryellen, Nanette, Mark, Gregg (dec.). BS in Elem. Edn., Fordham U., 1954; postgrad., Nat. Acad. Sch. Fine Arts, Art Life Studio Inc., White Plains and Portchester, NY, 1984-94, V.K. Jonynas, LI, NY, 1968-88, Art Ctr. No. N.J., 1996—2002. Fashion model Martha Clyde, NYC, 1951-54; tchr. Yonkers (N.Y.) Pub. Schs., 1953-55; gallery dir. Mamaroneck Artists Guild, Larchmont, NY, 1988-95; fine artist, art juror, cons., 1995—. Membership juror Mamaroneck Artists Guild, Larchmont, 1982-84, membership juror chair, 1996-98, mem. adv. bd., 1996-98; mem. Ctr. for Contemporary Printmaking, 1998—. One-woman shows and juried exhbns. Westchester and N.Y.C., 1976—; works represented in corp. and pvt. collecitons. Hostess chairperson Citizens for John Lindsay, Gracie Mansion, N.Y., 1970; mem. Studio Twelve, pres., show chair, 1972-80; mem. Katonah Mus. Art. Recipient numerous 1st place awards for art. Mem. Nat. League Am. Penwomen (corr. sec. and membership chair 1992-96), Nat. Mus. Women in the Arts, N.Y. Soc. Women Artists, Guild Creative Art, N.J. Artists Equity, Mamaroneck Artists Guild (v.p. 1982, 83, membership chair 1992-95 Fordham U. Art Club (show chair 1965-80). Avocations: gardening, bridge, tennis, swimming, travel.

WALSH, NICOLAS EUGENE, rehabilitation services professional, educator; b. Mpls., July 1, 1947; s. Leonard Cyril and June Alice Walsh; m. Wendy Sarah Allnutt, June 1, 1973; children: Meghan, Rorey, Katlin, Alaine. BS, USAF Acad., 1969; MS, Marquette U., 1974; MD, U. Colo., 1979. Asst. prof. naval sci. Marquette U., Milw., 1972—74; from asst. prof. to assoc. prof. rehab. medicine U. Tex. Health Sci. Ctr., San Antonio, 1982—89, prof., chmn. rehab. medicine, 1989—, exec. assoc. dean Sch. Medicine, 1999—2000, disting. prof., 2001—. Dir. Am. Bd. Phys. Medicine and Rehab., Rochester, Minn., 1994—2006, sec., 1996—98, chmn., 1998—2005; pres., CEO Univ. Physician Group, 1998—2001. Author book chpts.; editor: Rehabilitation of Chronic Pain, 1991; editor-in-chief Archives of Phys. Medicine and Rehab., Chgo., 1994—2000; mng. editor: Rehabilitation Medicine: Principles and Practices, 2005. Named Health Care Profl. of Yr., Gov.'s Com. for Disabled Persons, 1989; recipient Excellence in Rsch. award, Am. Jour. Phys. Medicine and Rehab., 1991. Fellow: Am. Acad. Phys. Medicine and Rehab. (Richard and Hinda Rosenthal Found. award 1991, Zieter lectr. 2003), Am. Bd. Pain Medicine (v.p. 1993—94, sec. 1994—96); mem.: Phys. Medicine and Rehab. Edn. and Rsch. Found. (pres. 1993—2000, Excellence in Rsch. award 1991), Assn. Acad. Physiatrists (v.p. 1993—95, pres. 1996—98). Office: U Tex Health Sci Ctr Mail Code 7872 7703 Floyd Curl Dr San Antonio TX 78229-3900 Home Phone: 210-493-1174; Office Phone: 210-567-5350. Business E-Mail: walshn@uthscsa.edu.

WALSH, PATRICK CRAIG, urologist; b. Akron, Ohio, Feb. 13, 1938; s. Raymond Michael and Catherine N. (Rodden) W.; m. Margaret Campbell, May 23, 1964; children— Christopher, Jonathan, Alexander. AB, Case Western Res. U., 1960, MD, 1964. Intern in surgery Peter Bent Brigham Hosp., Boston, 1964-65, asst. resident in surgery, 1965-66; asst. resident in pediatric surgery Children's Hosp. Med. Center, Boston, 1966-67; resident in urology UCLA Med. Ctr., 1967-71; dir., chmn. James Buchanan Brady Urol. Inst., urologist-in-chief Johns Hopkins Hosp., Balt., 1974—2004; prof., dir. dept. urology Johns Hopkins U. Sch. Medicine, 1974—2004, prof. urology, 2004—. Contbr. articles to med. jours. Served to comdr. M.C. USN, 1971-73. Recipient Charles F. Kettering medal GM Cancer Rsch. Found., 1996. Mem. Soc. Univ. Surgeons, Am. Assn. Genitourinary Surgeons, Clin. Soc. Genitourinary Surgeons, Am. Urol. Assn., Endocrine Soc., Am. Surg. Assn. Inst. Medicine of NAS, Alpha Omega Alpha. Roman Catholic. Office: Johns Hopkins Med Inst 600 N Wolfe St Baltimore MD 21287-0005 Office Phone: 410-955-6101.

WALSH, PATRICK M., career military officer; b. Va. Beach, Va., 1955; s. Jim and Betty Walsh; m. Andy Walsh; children: Jennifer, Matthew. BS, US Naval Acad., 1977; MA, Ph.D, Fletcher Sch. Law & Diplomacy, Tufts U. Advanced through ranks to admiral USN, 2007; with "Golden Dragons" Attack Squadron One Nine Two; comdr. Light Attack Wing Pacific; operational test dir. Air Test & Evaluation Squadron; ops. officer "Golden Warriors" Strike-Fighter Squadron Eight Seven; comdr. "Gunslingers" Strike Fighter Squadron One Zero Five, Carrier Air Wing One, Carrier Group Seven/USS John C. Stennis Strike Group; spl. asst. to dir. Office Mgmt. & Budget, Exec. Office of the Pres.; chair Dept. Leadership, Ethics, & Law US Naval Acad.; exec. asst. to Chief Naval Pers./Dep. Chief Naval Ops. for Manpower & Pers. USN; dep. dir. for strategy & policy (J-5) The Joint Staff, The Pentagon, 2001—05; dir. Navy Quadrennial Def. Review USN, 2005, dir. Navy Programming divsn., 2005; comdr. US 5th Fleet, Combined Maritime Forces, 2005—07, US Naval Forces, US Ctrl. Command (USNAVCENT), 2005—07; vice chief naval ops. USN, Washington, 2007—. Decorated Def. Superior Svc. medal, Meritorious Svc medal, Air medal with Combat V, Strike/Flight medal (5), Navy Commendation medal (3) with Combat V, Navy Achievement medal, Presdl. Svc. badge; recipient Disting. Grad. award, Jesuit Coll. Preparatory, 1973, Disting. Alumnus award, 1995, Legion of Merit (4). Office: US Navy 2000 Navy Pentagon Washington DC 20350

WALSH, PAUL S., beverage executive; b. Manchester, May 15, 1955; 1 child. Grad., Manchester Polytechnic. Fin. planning and acct. mgr. Grand Metropolitan, Watney, Mann and Truman Brewers, 1982—86; fin. dir. Grand Metropolitan (merged with Guinness UDV in 1997), Watney, Mann and Truman Brewers, 1986; CFO Inter-Continental Hotels, 1987—88, CFO, food divsn., 1989—92; chmn., pres., CEO Pillsbury Co., Mpls., 1992—2000; COO, CEO Guinness UDV Diageo plc, London, 2000—01, CEO, 2000—. Bd. dirs. Grand Metropolitan, 1995, Diageo, 1997—, Burger King Corp.; non-exec. dir. Centrica plc, 2003—, Fed. Express Corp., General Mills, Inc.; chair ct. of govs. Henley Mgmt. Coll. Mem.: Chartered Inst. Mgmt. Accountants, Scotch Whisky Assn. (dir., vice chair). Office: Diageo plc 8 Henrietta Pl London W1G 0NB England

WALSH, PETER JOSEPH, physics professor; b. NYC, Aug. 21, 1929; s. Peter and Mary Ellen (Kelly) W.; m. Rosemarie Imundo, May 13, 1952; children: Kathleen, Mary Ellen, Susan, Carole, Karen. BS, Fordham U., 1951; MS, N.Y.U., 1953, PhD, 1960. Research physicist Westinghouse Elec. Co., Bloomfield, NJ, 1951-60; supervisory physicist Am. Standard, Piscattaway, NJ, 1960-62; prof. Fairleigh Dickinson U., 1962-93; prof. emeritus, 1993—. Vis. rsch. scientist MIT, 1977; vis. prof. electronics and elec. engring. U. Sheffield, 1978-79; NASA fellow U. Santa Clara, 1980; Am. Soc. Engring. Edn. Navy fellow Naval Rsch. Labs., 1981, 82, 86, NASA Langley, 1987, Air Force fellow Hanscom AFB, 1988, Kirtland AFB, 1990; vis. prof. U. Genoa, 1984; vis. scholar Stanford U., 1984-85, cons. physics to 20 labs., 1963—; chmn. bd. trustees EMS Ednl. Corp., 1982—. Author: Dark Side of Knowledge, articles in field; patentee in field. Mem. Am. Phys. Soc., AAAS, N.J. Acad. Sci., Sigma Xi (sec. 1969) Home: 40 Saint Josephs Dr Stirling NJ 07980-1224 Personal E-mail: peterj@gowebway.com.

WALSH, PETER JOSEPH, marketing professional; b. Newport, RI, Jan. 22, 1948; s. Alexander Ronald and Mary (O'Connell) W.; m. Virginia Diana Santore, May 11, 1978 (div. May 1992); children: Bridget, Peter, Lara, Elizabeth, Vanessa. BA, Santa Clara U., 1970; MA, Johns Hopkins U., 1978. V.p. Noblemet Internat., NYC, 1978-80; mktg. dir. Multi-Arc Scientific Coatings, St. Paul, Minn., 1980-88; sr. v.p. Projects Devel., Inc., NYC, 1988-91; pres. Kiser Rsch., Inc., Washington, 1990-93; v.p. Sonalysts, Inc., Waterford, Conn., 1993—. Bd. dirs. Conn. Tech. Coun., 2002—. Bd. dirs. Portsmouth Abbey Sch. Alumni, Portsmouth, RI, 1996—2000, Mystic Coast and Country, 2002—, Newport Internat. Film Festival, 2006—. Roman Catholic. Avocations: tennis, golf, running. Office: Sonalysts Inc 215 Parkway N Waterford CT 06385-1209 Home: 4 Barney Ct Newport RI 02840

WALSH, PHILIP CORNELIUS, retired mining executive; b. Harrison, NJ, May 23, 1921; s. Philip Cornelius and Frances (Prendergast) Walsh; m. Alexandra Somerville Tuck, May 19, 1945 (dec. Sept. 1993); children: Eugenie Philbin Flaherty, Philip C.C., Frances Cummings, Alexander Tuck, Nicholas Holladay, Elizabeth Lovering; m. Peggy Flanigan McDonnell, Oct. 13, 1996. BA, Yale U., 1943; member of the Class of 1944. With W.R. Grace & Co., Lima, Peru and NYC, 1946-71; v.p. parent co., chief operating officer Latin Am. group, 1961-71, group exec. corp. adminstrv. group, 1970-71; v.p. Cerro Corp., 1972-74, Newmont Mining Corp., 1974-80; chmn. bd. Foote Mineral Co., Exton, Pa., 1979-80; dir. Cyprus Minerals Co., 1980—85; vice chmn. St. Joe Minerals Corp., 1980-85; chmn. bd. Chilean Lithium Co. Ltd., 1980-94; dir. T. Rowe Price Assocs., Inc., 1986—2000; ret., 2000. Past dir. Peabody Coal Co., Piedmont Mining Co.; bd. advisors Fond Elec.; mem. Nat. Strategic Minerals and Metals Program Adv. Commn. Mem. Harding Twp. Bd. Edn., NJ, 1960—66, Harding Twp. Com., 1966—72, police commr., 1966—72; trustee Morristown Meml. Hosp., 1969—79; vis. com. Colo. Sch. Mines, Global Sys. and Cultures. 1st lt. US Army. Decorated Silver Star, Purple Heart. Mem.: AIME (Saunders gold medal 1992, Disting. Mem. award 1993), Am. Soc. (hon. dir.), Pan Am. Soc. U.S. (past vice chmn.), Am. Assn. Order of Malta (past chancellor), Fed. Assn. Order of Malta, Edgartown Golf Club, Essex Hunt Club, Edgartown Yacht Club (commodore 1993—95), Racquet and Tennis Club, Somerset Hills Country Club, Sigma Xi, Phi Beta Kappa. Republican. Roman Catholic. Home: Pleasant Valley Peapack NJ 07977 Personal E-mail: knobbyiv@aol.com.

WALSH, ROBERT ANTHONY, lawyer; b. Boston, Aug. 26, 1938; s. Frank and Emily Angelica (Bissitt) Walsh; m. Angela Rosalie Barile, Aug. 3, 1966; children: Maria, Robert II, Amy. SB, MIT, 1960; MS, Fla. Inst. Tech., 1967; JD, Suffolk U., 1971. Bar: Mass. 1971, U.S. Dist. Ct. Mass. 1972, U.S. Patent Office 1972, Can. Patent Office 1973, Ill. 1976, U.S. Supreme Ct. 1976, U.S. Ct. Appeals (Fed. cir.) 1982, U.S. Ct. Mil. Appeals 1983, Vt. 1996; registered profl. engr., Mass., 1970. Engr. Saturn Boeing, Michaud, La., 1964-65; program analyst RCA, Cape Canaveral, Fla., 1965-68; patent trainee, engr. Avco Research Lab., Everett, Mass., 1968-72; patent atty. GTE Labs., Waltham, Mass., 1972-73; group patent counsel Bell & Howell Co., Chgo., 1973-78; patent counsel ITT E. Coast Patents, Nutley, N.J., 1978-80, patent counsel internat., 1980-82, sr. patent counsel internat., 1982-86; dir. internat. patents ITT Corp., NYC, 1986-87; gen. patent counsel ITT Def. Tech. Corp., Nutley, 1987-89; chief patent counsel, assoc. gen. counsel Allied-Signal Aerospace Co., Phoenix, 1989-94; patent atty. IBM Corp., Essex Junction, Vt., 1994—2005, Virtual Law Firm Morgan & Finnegan, NY, 2005—. Ednl. counselor admissions MIT, No. N.J., 1978-89, Vt., 1998-2005, RI, 2005—, Ariz., 2005—; with Office of Judge Adv. Gen., Washington. Col. (ret.) USAF, 1960—92, with Res. USAF. Decorated Legion of Merit USAF, Commendation medal with two oak leaf clusters. Mem. ABA (co-chmn. subcom. PTC sect. 105), Tri-State USAFR Lawyers Assn. (Meritorious Achievement award 1980), KC (fin. sec. Scottsdale, Ariz. 1993-95), Internat. Patent Club (pres. 1988-89), Am. Intellectual Property Law Assn., Aerospace Industry Assn. (chmn. Intellectual Property com.), Chgo. Patent Law Assn., N.J. Patent Law Assn., Ariz. Patent Law Assn. (bd. dirs.), Vt. Bar Assn., Civil Air Patrol (legal officer, lt. col. Vt. wing), Sigma Xi. Roman Catholic. Home: 8100 E Camelback Rd Unit 29 Scottsdale AZ 85251 Office: 3 Govenor Ave Westerly RI 02891 Personal E-mail: walshra@aol.com.

WALSH, ROBERT K., dean; m. Kathie Walsh; 4 children. AB, Providence Coll., 1964; JD, Harvard U., 1967. Bar: Calif. 1967, Ark. 1979. Assoc. McCatchen, Black, Verleger & Shea, LA, 1967-70; asst. prof. Villanova (Pa.) U., 1970-71, assoc. prof., 1971-73, prof., 1973-76; dean U. Ark., Little Rock Sch. Law; ptnr. Friday, Eldredge & Clark, Little Rock, 1981-89; dean, prof. Wake Forest Sch. Law, Winston-Salem, NC, 1989—. Bd. trustees Nat. Assn. Law Placement Found., Am. Inns of Ct. Found. Mem. ABA (chair Accreditation Com. 1984-86, chair Standards Rev. Com. Sect. Legal Edn. 1991—, Central European and Eurasian Law Initiative Adv. Coun.), N.C. Bar Assn. (chair bar bench and law schs. com. 1990-92, v.p., bd. govs. 1994-95). Office: Wake Forest Sch Law Dean's Office PO Box 7206 Winston Salem NC 27109-7206 Office Phone: 336-758-5435. Office Fax: 336-758-4632. *

WALSH, RUSSELL W., director tutorial services; b. Phila., June 7, 1947; s. William Joseph Jr. and Virginia M. (Haman) W.; children: Elizabeth, Bruce, Megan. BS, Bloomsburg State Coll., 1969; MA, Rider Coll., 1980; postgrad., U. Pa. Cert. reading specialist, supr., history, N.J., Pa. Tchr. Bristol (Pa.) Borough Schs.; adj. prof., reading Glassboro (N.J.) State Coll.; adj. prof., grad. edn. St. Joseph's Univ., Phila.; dir., tutorial svcs. Glassboro (N.J.) State Coll. Presenter, speaker in field. Recipient Merit awards, 1985, 88, Literacy Honor award, 1983. Mem. Internat. Reading Assn., West Jersey Reading Coun., SIGNAL, NCTE, NJRA, NJRA.

WALSH, SEAN M., lawyer, computer scientist, criminologist; b. NYC, Dec. 26, 1947; s. John W. and Catherine M. Walsh; m. Christine Ann Kull, June 10, 1978; children: Kathleen, Sean, Stephen. BS, Fordham U., Bronx, NY, 1970, JD, 1973. Bar: NY 1974. Chief, asst. dist. atty. Dist. Atty.'s Office Bronx County, 1973—96; pres. Walsh Assocs. Forensic Cons., Douglaston, NY, 1997—; asst. gen. counsel FBI, 2004—. Officer/dir. Law Enforcement Video Assocs., Ft. Worth, 1989-95; counsel Office Inspector Gen., N.Y.C., 1999-2004; asst. dist. atty. Dist. Atty. Office NY County, 1999-2004. Author: Video and the Law, 1979; inventor non-linear video wire tapping rec. sys. Vice-chmn. NYC Cmty. Planning Bd., 1986-98; pres. Queens Civic Congress, NY, 1996—, past pres./dir. Douglaston Civic Assn. Recipient Outstanding Cmty. Bd. Work, NYC, 1973, Outstanding Svc. to NY State Police, 1992, Van Zandt Cmty. Svc. award, 1999; named Marshall to Little Neck Douglaston Meml. Day Parade, 1990. Mem. Assn. Bar City NY (Comm. com. 1983-85, Computer com. 1997-2000), High Tech. Crime Investigation Assn. (pres. local chpt. 1994-96, internat. pres. 2000-2001). Avocations: sailing, skiing, scuba diving. Home: PO Box 238 Douglaston NY 11363-0238 Office Phone: 202-324-0551.

WALSH, THOMAS CHARLES, lawyer; b. Mpls., July 6, 1940; s. William G. and Kathryne M. Walsh; m. Joyce Williams, Sept. 7, 1968; children: Brian Christopher, Timothy Daniel, Laura Elizabeth Smith. BS in Commerce magna cum laude, St. Louis U., 1962, LLB cum laude, 1964. Bar: Mo. 1964, U.S. Dist. Ct. (ea. dist.) Mo. 1964, U.S. Ct. Appeals (8th cir.) 1968, U.S. Supreme Ct. 1971, U.S. Ct. Appeals (6th cir.) 1972, U.S. Ct. Appeals (5th cir.) 1974, U.S. Ct. Appeals (D.C. cir.) 1980, U.S. Ct. Appeals (7th cir.) 1982, U.S. Ct. Appeals (9th cir.) 1987, U.S. Ct. Appeals (4th cir.) 1989, U.S. Ct. Appeals (11th and fed. cirs.) 1992, U.S. Ct. Appeals (2d and 10th cirs.) 1993. Jr. ptnr. Bryan, Cave, McPheeters & McRoberts, St. Louis, 1964-73; ptnr. Bryan Cave LLP, St. Louis, 1974—; mem. exec. com. Bryan Cave LLP, St. Louis, 1980-96. Mem. 8th Cir. Adv. Com., 1983-86. Bd. dirs. St. Louis Symphony Soc., 1983-95. With U.S. Army, 1965-66; lt. USNR, 1966-71. Fellow Am. Coll. Trial Lawyers, Am. Acad. Appellate Lawyers; mem. Mo. Bar Assn., St. Louis Bar Assn., Am. Law Inst., Mo. Athletic Club, Bellerive Country Club. Roman Catholic. Office: Bryan Cave LLP 1 Metropolitan Sq 211 N Broadway Saint Louis MO 63102-2750 Home Phone: 314-997-7871; Office Phone: 314-259-2284. Business E-Mail: tcwalsh@bryancave.com.

WALSH, THOMAS FRANCIS, JR., producer, writer, director; b. NYC, Aug. 15, 1956; s. Thomas Francis and Catherine Alice (May) W.; m. Adriana Mia Stastny, Oct. 19, 1996; children: Barron, Arielle, Thomas III. BFA, NYU, 1977. Pres. Tom Walsh Prodns. Inc., NYC and Del., 1977-89; chmn., CEO I.D.L. Inc., NYC and Calif., 1989-91, Wonderland Dream Factory Inc., Calif. and Del., 1991-93, Enteraktion Inc. and Enteraktion Studios, Inc., LA, 1993—, also prodr., dir. 8 new entertainment web series, prodr., dir. Kidsline (TV), 2002—. Prodr.: (feature film) Denial, 1991; (CD-ROM) The Arrival, 1996; exec. prodr.: (TV) We Dare You!, 1982, House to House, 1982, Mismatch, 1979; prodr., dir.: The Whole Truth, 1977, (TV) Global Trade with Toms Travis, 2002; prodr., dir., writer (TV) 14 Stories, 2002, Newsoes, 2003, (TV) Tower of Madness, 2004, (TV) Seahawk, 2004, (TV) The Kernies, 2005 (TV) Los Opolis; set up major co-prodn. joint venture with China animation cos., prodr., writer movies, feature films; created and developed more than 175 creatures and characters for TV, movies and computer animation; creator, dir., writer, prodr. China Co-Prodn. Joint Venture, 2007. Helena Rubenstein Co. scholar, N.Y.C., 1976-77; recipient 1st prize for best TV show Conn. Assn. Profl. Communicators, 1974, Bronze and Silver awards Nat. Forensic League, 1977, Kate Garland award NYU/Columbia Pictures, 1976. Mem. Psi Upsilon (Delta chpt.), Alpha Epsilon Rho. Avocations: boating, diving, trains. Office: Enteraktion Studios Sound City Center Stages 15466 Cabrito Rd Van Nuys CA 91406 Home: 1015 9th St Apt 104 Santa Monica CA 90403 Business E-Mail: tomwalsh@enteraktion.com.

WALSH, THOMAS JOSEPH, ophthalmologist; b. NYC, Sept. 18, 1931; s. Thomas Joseph and Virginia (Hughes) W.; m. Sally Ann Maust, June 21, 1958; children: Thomas Raymond, Sara Ann, Mary Kelly, Kathleen Meghan. BA, Coll. Fordham, 1954; MD, Bowman Gray Med. Sch., 1958; degree in Mgmt., Yale U., 1998. Intern St. Vincent's Hosp., NYC, 1958-59; resident ophthalmology Bowman Gray Med. Sch., Winston-Salem, NC, 1961-64; fellow neuro-ophthalmology Bascom Palmer Eye Inst., Miami, Fla., 1964-65; practice medicine specializing in neuro-ophthalmology Stamford, Conn., 1965—; dir. neuro-ophthalmology service, asst. prof. ophthalmology and neurology Yale Sch. Medicine, New Haven, 1965-74, assoc. prof., 1974-79, prof., 1979—, also bd. permanent officers; dir. ophthalmology Stamford Hosp., 1978-83; mem. staff St. Joseph Hosp., Yale New Haven Hosp. Cons. to surgeon gen. army in neuro-ophthalmology Walter Reed Hosp., Washington, 1966—, VA Hosp., West Haven, 1965—, Silver Hill Found., New Canaan, Conn., 1974—; adj. prof. Dartmouth Med. Sch.; telemedicine bd. ORBIS Internat.; cons. mem. of bd. Orbis Internat.; lectr. in field. Contbr. articles to various publs. Adv. bd. Stamford Salvation Army, 1972-92; med. bd. Darien Nurses Assn., Conn., 1972—; surgeon Darien Fire Dept., 1969—. With AUS, 1959-61. Decorated Knight of Malta; Centennial fellow Johns Hopkins, 1976; named one of Top Opthalmologists, Best Doctors.com, 2004 Mem. AMA, Conn., Fairfield County med. socs., Acad. Ophthalmology, Oxford Ophthal. Congress, Acad. Neurology, Am. Assn. Neurol. Surgeons, Internat. Neuro-Ophthalmology Soc., Soc. Med. Cons. to Armed Forces, Cosmos Club (Washington), Darien County Club, Yale Club (N.Y.C), Lions, Army-Navy Club, Orbis Internat. (cybermedicine bd. mem.). Office: Yale Dept Ophthalmology PO Box 208061 330 Cedar St Stamford CT 06520-8061 Home Phone: 203-866-0220; Office Phone: 203-785-6444. Personal E-mail: twalsh13@optonline.net. Business E-Mail: thomas.walsh@yale.edu.

WALSH, W. TERENCE, lawyer; b. Toledo, Nov. 18, 1943; s. Walter James and Ann (Gifford) W.; m. Patricia Jane Walker, Dec. 17, 1966; children: Christopher O'Brien, Ryan Kerrick, Ann Elisabeth. AB, Brown U., 1965; JD, Emory U., 1970. Bar: Ga., 1971, U.S. Dist. Ct. (no. dist.) Ga., 1971, U.S. Ct. Appeals (11th cir.), 1971, U.S. Supreme Ct., 2003. Assoc. Alston, Miller & Gaines, Atlanta, 1970-76, ptnr., 1976-83; ptnr., litig. trial practice group Alston & Bird LLP, Atlanta, 1983—. Lectr. various seminars on bus. litig., appellate procedure, juvenile law, ethics, and professionalism. Contbr. articles to profl. jours. Co-founder Truancy Intervention Project, 1991—; chmn. Kids In Need of Dreams, Inc., 1993-; bd. dirs. Family Connection Partnership, 2000-, Georgians for Children, 1993-2003, The Bridge, 1994-99, Ga. Justice Project, 1987-97, Juvenile Justice Fund, 2000—, Ga. Acad., 1999-2002; bd. dirs. Atlanta Legal Aid Soc., Inc., 1976-98, pres., 1987; chmn. Capital Area Mosaic, 1994-96; chmn. sch. bd. Christ the King Sch., 1982-84; alumni trustee Brown U., 1994-2001; chmn. State Bar Com. on Children and the Cts., 1996—; bd. dirs. Justice for Children Adv. Bd. Supreme Ct. Ga., 2000—. Recipient cmty. svc. award Martin Luther King, Jr. Ctr. for Nonviolent Social Change, 1995. Fellow: Ga. Bar Found.; mem.: ABA (juvenile justice sect., Livingston Hall Juvenile Justice award 1999), Atlanta Bar Assn. (Leadership award 2005), Gate City Bar Assn., Atlanta Bar Assn. (bd. dirs. 1987—93, pres. 1991—92, Charles E. Watkins award 1994, S. Phillip Heiner award 1994, David Pollard award 1995), State Bar Ga. (bd. govs. 1979—99, pres. young lawyers sect. 1980—81, H. Sol Clark award 1987, Chief Justice's award for cmty. svc. 1998), Emory Law Alumni Assn. (exec. com. 1990—98, Disting. Law Alumnus award 2000). Avocations: sports, gardening, reading. Office: Alston & Bird LLP One Atlantic Ctr 1201 W Peachtree St NW Ste 4200 Atlanta GA 30309-3449 Home Phone: 404-351-5916; Office Phone: 404-881-7161. Office Fax: 404-253-8884. Business E-Mail: twalsh@alston.com.

WALSH, WILLIAM ALBERT, management consultant, retired military officer; b. Gilman, Ill., Aug. 15, 1933; s. Lawrence Eugene and Myrtle R. (Mulder) W.; m. Joan Elizabeth Kennedy, Dec. 28, 1957; children: Kathryn, Michael, Julie. BS in Commerce, U. Notre Dame, 1955; MS in Mgmt. with distinction, U.S. Naval Postgrad. Sch., Monterey, Calif., 1962; MS in Internat. Affairs with honors, George Washington U., 1972. Commd. ensign U.S. Navy, 1955, advanced through grades to rear adm., 1981; exec. asst. to dep. chief naval ops. (Surface Warfare), Washington, 1974-76; comdg. officer USS Juneau, San Diego, 1976-78; comdr. Amphibious Squadron Three, San Diego, 1978-79; head plans and policy div., comdr. rapid deployment naval forces Comdr. in Chief U.S. Pacific Fleet, Honolulu, 1979-81; comdr. Amphibious Group Eastern Pacific, San Diego, 1981-82; dir. surface warfare div. Office Chief Naval Ops., Pentagon, Washington, 1983-85; ret., 1985; pres. Air/Space Am., San Diego, 1986-89, W.A. Walsh Enterprises, 1990—. Decorated Legion of Merit with 2 gold stars, Bronze Star, Navy Commendation medal U.S.; Disting. Service Order 2d Class Vietnam

WALSH, WILLIAM ARTHUR, JR., lawyer; b. Washington, Mar. 17, 1949; children: Jesse Creighton, Patrick McKay. BS in Econs. and Fin., U. Md., 1972; JD, U. Richmond, 1977. Bar: Va. Ptnr. Hunton & Williams LLP, Richmond, Va., 1977—. Adv. bd. for law rev. U. Richmond. Trustee, bd. dirs. Va. Commonwealth U. Real Estate Found.; mem. Va. Commonwealth U. Real Estate Circle of Excellence. Mem. Va. Bar Assn., Am. Coll. Real Estate Lawyers. Home: 4705 Leonard Pky Richmond VA 23226-1337 Office: Hunton & Williams LLP Riverfront Plz East Tower 951 E Byrd St Richmond VA 23219-4074 Home Phone: 804-359-2470; Office Phone: 804-788-8378. Business E-Mail: wwalsh@hunton.com.

WALSH, WILLIAM DESMOND, investor; b. NYC, Aug. 4, 1930; s. William J. and Catherine Grace (Desmond) W.; m. Mary Jane Gordon, Apr. 5, 1951; children: Deborah, Caroline, Michael, Suzanne, Tara Jane, Peter. BA, Fordham U., 1951; JD, Harvard U., 1955. Bar: NY 1955. Asst. US atty. So. dist. NY, NYC, 1955-58; counsel NY Commn. Investigation, NYC, 1958-61; mgmt. cons. McKinsey & Co., NYC, 1961-67; sr. v.p. Arcata Corp., Menlo Park, Calif., 1967-82; chmn. Sequoia Assocs. LLC, 1982—; pres., CEO Atacra Liquidating Trust, 1982-88. Chmn. bd. dir. Neuroscis. Inst./Scripps, Ameriscape, Inc., Cornelius, Oreg., Creativity Inc., Van Nuys; bd. dir. URS Corp., San Francisco, Am. Ireland Fund, Boston. Mem. bd. overseers Hoover Inst.; co-chmn. dean's adv. bd. Harvard Law Sch.; trustee emeritus Fordham U. Mem. NY State Bar Assn., Harvard Club (NYC and San Francisco), Fordham Club No. Calif., Knights of Malta. Office Phone: 650-321-4346. Office Fax: 650-321-4588. Business E-Mail: sequoiaassociates@gmail.com.

WALSH, WILLIAM L., JR., lawyer; b. Boston, June 21, 1941; BS, Boston Coll., 1965; JD, Cath. U. Am., 1968. Bar: Va. 1968, D.C. 1971. Trial atty. Naval Supply Systems Commd., 1968-71, dep. counsel, 1974-77; asst. counsel Naval Ordinance Systems Commd., 1971-74; staff asst. to Commn. on Govt. Procurement, 1972; asst. gen. counsel Dept. Navy, 1977-78; navy legal mem. Def. Acquisition Regulation Coun., 1977-78; chief counsel NASA's George C. Marshall Space Flight Ctr., 1978-81; ptnr., Govt. Contracts practice Venable LLP, Vienna, Va. Mem. adv. bd. George Mason Univ. Sch. Mgmt., Nat. Ctr. for Tech. & the Law; past chmn. Govt. Affairs com., No. Va. Tech. Council; bd. dir., past gen. counsel Fairfax County C. of C. Mem. ABA (chmn. Small Bus. com., Fed Regulations com.), Fed. Bar Assn., Va. State Bar Assn, DC Bar Assn., Fairfax County Bar Assn., Arlington County Bar Assn. Office: Venable LLP Suite 300 8010 Towers Crescent Dr Vienna VA 22182 Office Fax: 703-760-1685, 703-821-8949. Business E-Mail: wlwalsh@venable.com.

WALSH MITCHELL, DIANA, school psychologist, consultant; d. T. and D. Walsh. BA, Hofstra U., 1997; MA, Adelphi U., 1999; MS in Edn., Fordham U., 2002, Profl. Diploma in Sch. Psychology, 2002; D in Psychology, Fairleigh Dickinson U., 2005. Cert. sch. psychologist N.Y. State Edn. Dept., 2002. Sch. psychologist Pub. Sch., Hewlett, NY, 2002—03; psychometrician Schneider Children's Hosp., New Hyde Park, NY, 2002—04; cons. NY, 2004—; sch. psychologist NY, 2004—. Cons. Pvt. Sch., Kew Gardens, NY; presenter in field. Mem.: NASP, APA, N.Am. Assn. for the Study of Obesity, NY Assn. Sch. Psychologists. Home: 170 Sackville Rd Garden City NY 11530-1107 Home Phone: 516-328-6583. Personal E-mail: dianawmitchell@aol.com.

WALSH-PIPER, KATHLEEN A., museum director; b. Chgo., Aug. 17, 1947; d. James Clement and Jane (Burnham) W.; m. Michael G. Rubin, May 17, 1969 (div. 1978); m. Rubin H. Piper, Dec. 19, 1987. BA, Washington U., St. Louis, 1969, MA in Art History, 1973; postgrad., St. Louis U. Cert. tchr., Mo. Tchr. St. Louis Archdiocesan Schs., 1970-73; asst. prof. Mo. Bapt. Coll., St. Louis, 1973; tchr. Hazelwood Jr. High Sch., St. Louis, 1974-77; mus. tchr. St. Louis Art. Mus., 1976, coord. rsch. ctr., 1977-80; asst. dir. mus. edn. Art. Inst. Chgo., 1980—85; dir. edn. Terra Mus. Am. Art, Chgo., 1985-88; head dept. tchr. and sch. programs Nat. Gallery Art, Washington, 1988—95; cultural specialist U.S. Info. Agency, 1995; dir. edn. and pub. progs. Dallas Mus. Art, Tex., 1995—2002; dir. U. Ky. Art Mus., Lexington, 2002—. Mus. guest scholar J. Paul Getty Mus., Malibu, Calif., 1997. Author: Image to Word: Art and Creative Writing, 2002; contbr. articles to profl. jours. Robert E. Smith fellow Nat. Gallery of Art, 1994. Mem. Nat. Art Edn. Assn. (regional mus. educator 1984, nat. mus. educator 1985, dir. mus. divsn. 1992—), Am. Assn. Mus. (chair midwest edn. ccom. 1983-84). Avocation: writing. Office: U Ky Art Mus 116 Singletary Ctr Rose St and Euclid Ave Lexington KY 40506-0241 Office Phone: 859-257-1152. E-mail: kwpiper@email.uky.edu.

WALSKE, M(AX) CARL, JR., physicist; b. Seattle, June 2, 1922; s. Max Carl and Margaret Ella (Fowler) W.; m. Elsa Marjorie Nelson, Dec. 28, 1946; children: C. Susan, Steven C., Carol A. (dec.). BS in Math. cum laude, U. Wash., 1944; PhD in Theoretical Physics, Cornell U., 1951. Staff, asst. theoretical divsn. leader Los Alamos Sci. Lab., 1951-56; dep. rsch. dir. Atomics Internat., Canoga Park, Calif., 1956-59; sci. rep. AEC in U.K., London, 1961-62; theoretical physicist RAND Corp., 1962-63; sci. attache U.S. missions to NATO and OECD, Paris, 1963-65; staff mem. Los Alamos Sci. Lab., 1965-66; asst. to sec. def. for atomic energy Dept. Def., 1966—73, chmn. military liaison com. to atomic energy commn.; pres., COO Atomic Indsl. Forum, Inc., Washington, 1973-87. Chmn. Upper Hood Canal Watershed Mgmt. Com., 1994-2000; budget steering com. Kitsap County, 1996, budget com., 1997-99, participant strategic planning, 1997, planning commn., 1998-2000. Lt. (j.g.) USNR, 1943-51. Recipient Disting. Civilian Svc. medal Dept. Def. Fellow Explorers Club, Am. Phys. Soc.; mem. Am. Nuc. Soc., Phi Beta Kappa, Sigma Xi. Home: PO Box 370 Silverdale WA 98383-0370 E-mail: cwalske@wavecable.com. *To seek out positions which appeared the most challenging and personally satisfying; to gain my reward through self-respect rather than public recognition; to expend extra effort as an offset to my limitations.*

WALSTON, RICK LYLE, clergyman, seminary executive, educator; b. Longview, Wash., Sept. 3, 1954; s. Lyle Basil and Harriet Marion (Salhus) W.; m. Susan Elizabeth Insel, Oct. 29, 1988. AS in Practical Theology, Christ for the Nations Inst., 1980; BA, Warner Pacific Coll., 1982, MREL magna cum laude, 1987; STD summa cum laude, Bethany Theol. Sem., 1988, MA in Christian Counseling, 1995; cert. in Christian Apologetics, Inst. Christian Def., 1997; D in Ministry, Bakke Grad. U., Seattle, 1999; PhD in New Testament, North-West U., South Africa, 2000; MDiv, Korea Reformed Theol. Sem., Seoul, 2001. Ordained minster. Assoc. pastor Christian Life Ctr. Assemblies of God Ch., Longview, 1977-82; tchr., registrar Berean Coll. Extension Sch., Longview, 1980-82; sr. pastor Praise Song Assemblies of God Ch., Longview, 1982-86; registrars asst. Warner Pacific Coll., Portland, Oreg., 1986-87; sr. pastor Home Fellowship Assembly Ch., Longview, 1988; ednl. cons., owner Coll. Degree Cons. Svcs., Longview, 1989-92; sr. pastor Christian Assembly, Longview, 1992—; pres. Columbia Evangelical Sem., Longview, 1990—. Co-founder Clackamas (Oreg.) Bible Inst., Clackamas Christian Ctr., 1987; co-dir. edn. dept. Kelso (Wash.) First Assembly of God Ch., 1989-92. Author: Divorce and Remarriage, 1991, (with John Bear) Walston & Bear's Guide to Earning Religious Degrees Non-Traditionally, 1993, Walston's Guide to Earning Religious Degrees Non-Traditionally, 1995, Unraveling the myster of The Motivational Gifts: Your Gifts Discovery Manual, 2005, The Speaking in Tongues Controversy: The Initial, Physical Evidence of the Baptism in the Holy Spirit Debate, 2005, Something Happened on the Way to Happily Ever After: A Biblical View of Marriage, Divorce & Remarriage, 2006, (with Clarence Buckle) The Pentecostal Assemblies of Newfoundland View of Divorce and Remarriage, 2007, Walston's Guide to Christian Distance Learning, 5th edit., 2007; contbr. articles to profl. jours. Coord. religious events Christian Life Ministerial Assn., Longview, 1979-82; retirement home minister Praise Song Assembly of God Ch., 1982-86, hosp. minister, 1982-86. Recipient Cert. of Recognition, Christ for the Nations Inst., 1980, Full Gospel Fellowship Internat., 1980. Fellow Faraston Theol. Rsch. Fellowship (pres. 1990-92, Rsch. Fellow of Yr. 1990); mem. Oreg. Assn. for Psychol. Type, Evang. Theol. Soc., Evang. Philos. Soc., Assn. Christian Continuing Edn. Schs. and Sems. Republican. Avocations: writing, weight training, gardening. Office: Columbia Evang Sem PO Box 847 Longview WA 98632-7521 Office Phone: 360-802-6437. Business E-Mail: ces@columbiaseminary.edu.

WALSTON, RODERICK EUGENE, federal official; b. Gooding, Idaho, Dec. 15, 1935; s. Loren R. and Iva M. (Boyer) W.; m. Margaret D. Grandey; children: Gregory Scott W., Valerie Lynne W. AA, Boise Jr. Coll., 1956; BA cum laude, Columbia Coll., 1958; LL.B. scholar, Stanford U., 1961. Bar: Calif. 1961, U.S. Supreme Ct. 1973. Law clk to judge U.S. Ct. Appeals 9th Cir., 1961-62; dep. atty. gen State of Calif., San Francisco, 1963-91, head natural resources sect, 1969-91, chief asst. atty. gen. pub. rights div., 1991-99; spl. dep counsel Kings County, Calif., 1975-76; gen. counsel Metropolitan Water Dist. So. Calif., 2000—02; dep. solicitor U.S. Dept. Interior, 2002—; of counsel Best, Best and Krieger, LLP, Walnut Creek, Calif., 2005. Mem. environ. and natural resources adv. coun. Stanford (Calif.) Law Sch. Contbr. articles to profl. jours.; bd. editors: Stanford Law Rev., 1959-61, Western Natural Resources Litigation Digest, Calif. Water Law and Policy Reporter; spl. editor Jour. of the West. Co-chmn. Idaho campaign against Right-to-Work initiative, 1958; Calif. rep. Western States Water Coun., 1986—; environ. and natural resources adv. coun., Stanford Law Sch. Astor Found. scholar, 1956-58; Nat. Essay Contest winner Nat. Assn. Internat. Rels. Clubs, 1956, Stanford Law Rev. prize, 1961; recipient Best Brief award Nat. Assn. Attys. Gen., 1997, Burton award best article, 2007; named Pub. Lawyer of Yr., Calif. State Bar, 2004. Mem. ABA (chmn. water resources com. 1988-90, vice chmn. and conf. chmn. 1985-88, 90—), Contra Costa County Bar Assn., U.S. Supreme Ct., Hist. Soc., Federalist Soc., World Affairs Coun. No. Calif. Office: Best Best and Krieger LLP 2033 N Main St Walnut Creek CA 94596 Office Phone: 925-977-3304. Business E-Mail: roderick.walston@bbklaw.com.

WALT, MARTIN, physicist, educator; b. West Plains, Mo., June 1, 1926; s. Martin and Dorothy (Mantz) W.; m. Mary Estelle Thompson, Aug. 16, 1950; children: Susan Mary, Stephen Martin, Anne Elizabeth, Patricia Ruth. BS, Calif. Inst. Tech., 1950; MS, U. Wis., 1951, PhD, 1953. Staff mem. Los Alamos Sci. Lab., 1953-56; research scientist, mgr. physics Lockheed Missiles and Space Co., Palo Alto (Calif.) Rsch. Lab., 1956-71, dir. phys. scis., 1971-86, dir. research, 1986-93; cons. prof. Stanford U., 1986—. Mem. adv. com. NRC, NASA, Dept. Def., U. Calif. Lawrence Berkeley Lab. Author 2 books; contbr. articles to sci. jours. Served with USNR, 1944-46. Wis. Research Found. fellow, 1950-51; AEC fellow, 1951-53 Fellow Am. Geophys. Union, Am. Phys. Soc.; mem. Am. Inst. Physics (bd. govs.), Fremont Hills Country Club. Home: 12650 Viscaino Ct Los Altos Hills CA 94022-2517 Office: Stanford U Starlab Packard 352 Stanford CA 94305 Business E-Mail: walt@nova.stanford.edu.

WALTER, BURL LEROY, JR., retired music educator; b. Lawrence, Kans., Aug. 15, 1933; s. Burl Leroy and Ruth Christian Walter; m. Evelyn Ruth Shaline, Mar. 26, 1956; children: Burl Leroy III, Ellen Ruth. BS, NW Mo. State U., Maryville, 1956. Music educator Hopkins Pub. Schools, Hopkins, Mo., 1955—56; army bandsman 22nd Army Band, San Francisco, 1956—58; music educator Macksberg H.S., Macksburg, Iowa, 1958—60, Schleswig H.S., Schleswig, Iowa, 1960—63; musician Glenn Houpt Trio and Symphony Orch., Sioux City, Iowa, 1963—64; music educator Kings Canyon Unified Sch. Dist., Reedley, Calif., 1964—2000; lectr. Calif. State U., Fresno, Calif., 1974—75. Mem. Kings Canyon Edn. Assn., 1965; treas. Fresno-Madera Music Edn. Assn., Calif., 1965; v.p. Calif. Band Directors Assn., Calif., 1968; mem. Calif. Teachers Assn., Calif., 1965, Fresno Dixieland Soc., Calif., 1985, Percusive Arts Soc., Calif., 1965, Local 210 Musicians Union, Calif., 1965. Pfc US Army, 1956—58, San Francisco. Named Outstanding Music Educator, Fresno-Madera Music Edn. Assn., 1996—97, Outstanding Band Dir., 1997, Outstanding Music Educator, Calif. Music Educators Assn., 1988, 1996, State of Calif., 1996; named to Hall Of Fame, Reedley C. of C., 1999; recipient Man Of Yr., 1997, Disting. Svc. award, Calif. Band Dirs. Assn., 1968, Lifetime Svc. award, Calif. Band Dirs., 2001. Home: 1425 E St Reedley CA 93654

WALTER, CARMEL MONICA, writer; b. Dublin, July 24, 1943; arrived in U.S., 1961; d. Albert and Anastatia Woods; m. Michael William Walter, June 15, 1963; children: Coleen, Daniel, Eileen. BS magna cum laude, Madonna U., Livonia, Mich., 1987. Co-founder, co-owner Am. Security Alarm Co., Madison Heights, Mich., 1969—72, Alarm Supply Co., Inc., Livonia, Mich., 1969—89, founder, owner Milford, NJ, 2001—07; writer, 2007—. Intro.and product tng. for first wireless security sys. Resident Sentry, Madison Heights, 1967—72; co-owner CMD Co., Flemington, NJ, 1989—2002; established ongoing comprehensive tech. support sys. Alarm Supply Co., Milford, 2003—07. Co-author (with Michael Walter): (security products and application manual) The Security Store. Mem. cert. nat. emergency response teams emergency support function #13 public safety and security Am. Bd. Cert. in Homeland Security, Springfield, Mo., 2005. Mem.: Am. Coll. Forensic Examiners Inst. (life; cert. homeland security-II), Kappa Gamma Pi. Roman Catholic. Avocations: travel, golf, theater, cooking, interior design. Office Phone: 908-995-4150. Personal E-mail: carmelwalter@aol.com.

WALTER, HAROLD MARK, lawyer; b. Balt., 1957; BA, Franklin Marshall Coll., 1979; JD, U. Md., 1982. Bar: Md. 1983, N.Y. 1997, U.S. Dist. Ct. Md. 1990, U.S. Dist. Ct. (so. and ea. dists.) N.Y. 1997, U.S. Dist. Ct. D.C. 2004, U.S. Ct. Appeals (4th cir.) 1992, U.S. Ct. Appeals (3d cir.) 1997, U.S. Supreme Ct. 1995, DC 2005. Law clk. Ct. Spl. Appeals, Md., 1982—83; ptnr. Tydings & Rosenberg LLP, Balt., 1983—. Steering com. industrywide litig. Def. Rsch. Inst. Named one of Top Ten Most Winning Attys., The Nat. Law Jour., 2002. Mem.: ABA (forum com. comms. law, forum com. entertainment and sports industries), N.Y. State Bar Assn., Md. State Bar Assn., Balt. (Md.) County C. of C. Office: Tydings & Rosenberg LP 100 East Pratt St Baltimore MD 21202 Office Phone: 410-752-9720. Business E-Mail: hwalter@tydingslaw.com.

WALTER, HUGO GÜNTHER, humanities educator, poet; b. Phila., Mar. 12, 1959; s. Paul and Elli R. Walter. BA, Princeton U., 1981; MA in Humanities, Old Dominion U., 1989; MA in Lit., Yale U., 1983, MPhil in Lit., 1984, PhD in Lit, 1985; PhD in Interdisciplinary Humanities, Drew U., 1996. Adj. instr. Yale U., New Haven, 1981-85, Old Dominion U., Norfolk, Va., 1988-89; asst. prof. Washington and Jefferson Coll., Washington, Pa., 1989-92, Fairleigh Dickinson U., Madison, NJ, 1992-96, Kettering U., Flint, Mich., 1996-99; assoc. prof. Berkeley Coll., White Plains, 1999—. Vis. asst. prof. Rhodes Coll., Memphis, 1986-87, U. Mo., Columbia, 1987-88. Author: (poetry) The Fragile Edge, 1988, Velvet Rhythms, 1989, Amber Blossoms and Evening Shadows, 1990, Golden Thorns of Light and Sterling Silhouettes, 1991, Waiting for Babel Prophesies of Sunflower Dreams, 1992, Along the Maroon-Prismed Threshold of Bronze-Pealing Eternity, 1992, The Light of the Dance Is the Music of Eternity, 1993, Dusk-Gloaming Mirrors and Castle-Winding Dreams, 1994, Amaranth-Sage Epiphanies of Dusk-Weaving Paradise, 1995, 2d edit., 1996, A Purple-Golden Renascence of Eden-Exalting Rainbows, 2001, (monographs) The Apostrophic Moment in 19th and 20th Century Lyric Poetry, 1988, Space and Time on the Magic Mountain: Studies in the 19th and 20th Century European Literature, 1999. Recipient Faculty of Yr. award, Berkeley Coll., 2006. Mem. Acad. Am. Poets, Internat. Soc. Poets. Avocations: music, painting. Home: 157 Loomis CT Princeton NJ 08540-3438 Personal E-mail: hwalprin@aol.com.

WALTER, J. JACKSON, management consultant, foundation administrator; b. Abington, Pa., Nov. 6, 1940; s. Joseph Horace and Edith Wilson (Jackson) W.; m. Susan Draude, Feb. 3, 1978; 1 child, Allison K. AB, Amherst Coll., Mass., 1962; LLB, Yale U., New Haven, 1966. Sec. Fla. Dept. Bus. Regulation, Tallahassee, 1976-79; dir. US Office Govt. Ethics, Washington, 1979-82; pres. Nat. Acad. Pub. Adminstrn., Washington, 1982-84, Nat. Trust Historic Preservation, Washington, 1984-92; exec. dir. Waterford Found., Va., 1996-98. Chmn. Amendment I, Inc., 2000—06. Co-author: America's Unelected Government, 1983. Contbr. articles to profl. jours. Mem. Nat. Acad. Pub. Adminstrn., Met. (Washington) Club. Office Phone: 540-882-4116.

WALTER, JESSICA, actress; b. Bklyn., Jan. 31, 1941; d. Arturo Toscanini; m. Russ Bowman, 1966 (div. 1978); m. Ron Leibman, June, 26, 1983; 1 child, Brooke Student, Bucks County Playhouse, Neighborhood Playhouse. Actor: (Broadway plays) Advise and Consent, 1961; other stage prodns. include: Rumors, 1988; (films) include Lilith, 1964, The Group, 1966, Grand Prix, 1966, Bye Bye, Braverman, 1968, Number One, 1969, Play Misty for Me, 1971, Going Ape, 1982, Spring Fever, 1983, Flamingo Kid, 1984, PCU, 1994, Dark Goddess, 1994, Slums of Beverly Hills, 1998, My Best Friend's Wife, 2001, Dummy, 2002, Unaccompanied Minors, 2006; (TV series) Love of Life, 1962-65, For the People, 1965, Amy Prentiss, 1974-75, All That Glitters, 1977, Trapper John M.D., 1979-1986, ltd. series Amy Prentiss, 1974-75 (Emmy award for Outstanding Lead Actress in Ltd. Series) Bare Essence, 1983, (voice) Wildfire, 1986, Aaron's Way, 1988, (voice) Pirates of Darkwater, 1991-92, (voice) Dinosaurs, 1991-94, The Round Table, 1992, One Life to Live, 1996-97, Oh Baby, 1998-2000, Arrested Development, 2003-06; (TV miniseries) Wheels, 1978; (TV films) Kiss Me Kate, 1968, The Immortal, 1969, Three's a Crowd, 1969, They Call It Murder, 1971, Women in Chains, 1972, Home for the Holidays, 1972, Columbo: Mind Over Mayhem, 1974, Hurricane, 1974, Having Babies, 1976, Victory at Entebbe, 1976, Black Market Baby, 1977, Wild and Wooly, 1978, Dr. Strange, 1978, Secrets of Three Hungry Wives, 1978, Vampire, 1979, She's Dressed to Kill, 1979, Miracle on Ice, 1981, Scruples, 1981, Thursday's Child, 1983, The Return of Marcus Welby, M.D., 1984, The Execution, 1985, Killer in the Mirror, 1986, Jenny's Song, 1988, Aaron's Way: The Harvest, 1988, Leave of Absence, 1994, Mother Knows Best, 1997, Doomsday Rock, 1997, I Do (But I Don't), 2004; TV guest appearances include Route 66, 1963, The Nurses, 1964, It Takes a Thief, 1969, Mission: Impossible, 1970, The Name of the Game, 1971, Night Gallery, 1972, Banacek, 1973, Barnaby Jones, 1974, Ironside, 1974, Hawaii Five-O, 1974, McCloud, 1975, McMillan and Wife, 1976, Quincy, 1978, Knots Landing, 1982, Joanie Loves Chachi, 1982, Matt Houston, 1982, Three's a Crowd, 1984, 85, Murder, She Wrote, 1985, 91, Magnum P.I., 1986, Coach, 1994, Babylon 5, 1994, Law & Order, 1995, Just Shoot Me!, 1998, Jack & Jill, 2000, 01, Touched by an Angel, 2003. Office: Judy Shane & Assocs 606 N Larchmont Ste 309 Los Angeles CA 90004 *

WALTER, MICHAEL CHARLES, lawyer; b. Oklahoma City, Nov. 25, 1956; s. Donald Wayne and Viola Helen (Heffelfinger) W. BA in Polit. Sci., BJ Editl. Journalism, U. Wash., 1980; JD, Seattle U., 1983. Bar: Wash. 1985, US Dist. Ct. (9th cir. 1985), US Supreme Ct. 2005. Ptnr. Keating, Bucklin & McCormack, Inc., P.S., Seattle, 1985—. Instr. Bellevue (Wash.) C.C., 1983-90. FAX: 206-223-9423. Mem. ABA, Wash. State Bar Assn., Seattle-King County Bar Assn., Wash. Def. Trial Laywers Assn., Wash. Assn. Mcpl. Attys., Def. Rsch. Inst., Am. Planning Assn. Avocations: running, swimming, hiking, coin collecting/numismatics, photography. Office: Keating Bucklin & McCormack Inc PS Bank of Am Plz 800 5th Ave Seattle WA 98104 Home: 14307 SE 88th Pl Newcastle WA 98059-3485 Office Phone: 206-623-8861. Office Fax: 206-223-9423. E-mail: mwalter@kbmlawyers.com.

WALTER, PATRICIA L., psychotherapist, consultant; b. Logansport, Ind., Mar. 15, 1935; d. William Marion and Doris May (Duddleston) Sievers; m. Raymond C. Walter Jr., Mar. 28, 1968; m. Keith A. Erny (div.); children: Rodney Erny, Jeffrey Erny, Mark Erny, Troy Erny. BS in Edn., Ind. U., 1973, MS in Edn. & English, 1976, MS in Counseling, 1984. Cert. English tchr., lic. mental health counselor Ind., cert. nat. cert. addictions prevention specialist III, forensic counselors 1998. Tchr. English Logansport Sch. Corp., Ind., 1973—97; psychotherapist Four County Counseling, Peru, 1993—2000; high sch. counselor Logansport Cmty. Schs., 1997—2003; mental health cons. Texas Migrant Headstart, Kokomo, 2004—; psychotherapist RAJ Clinic, Logansport, 2004—. Coord. Adminstrv. Counsel, Logansport, 2001—03; coach Acad. Competitions, 1987—98, Girls 6th Grade Basketball, 1975—78. Vol. First Call Home Health and Hospice, 2004. Mem.: Call County Carousel, Am. Mental Health Counselors Assn., Kiwanis (sec. 1997—98, pres. 2005—), Zeta Tau Chapter of Sigma Phi Gamma Sorority. Republican. Avocations: golf, ballroom dancing, reading, exercise, gardening. Home: 5209 Canterbury Ln Logansport IN 46947

WALTER, PAUL HERMANN LAWRENCE, chemistry professor; b. Jersey City, Sept. 22, 1934; s. Helmuth Justus and Adelaide C. J. (Twardy) W.; m. Grace Louise Carpenter, Aug. 25, 1956; children: Katherine Elizabeth Walter Bousquet, Marjorie Allison Walter Moran. BS, MIT, 1956; PhD, U. Kans., 1960. Rsch. scientist DuPont Cen. Rsch. Dept., Wilmington, Del., 1960-67; prof. chemistry Skidmore Coll., Saratoga Springs, NY, 1967-96, chair chemistry and physics, 1975-85, prof. emeritus, 1996—. Translator: (book) Foundations of Crystal Chemistry, 1968; contbr. articles to profl. jours. Fellow Chem. Inst. Can.; mem. AAAS, AAUP (pres. 1984-86), Am. Chem. Soc. (bd. dirs. 1991-99, chmn. 1993-95, pres.-elect 1997, pres. 1998, Radding award 2002), Soc. Quimica de Mexico (hon.). Presbyterian. Achievements include patents in field. Home: 3 Benedictine Retreat Savannah GA 31411-1624 E-mail: phlw@alum.mit.edu.

WALTER, PETER, biochemist; b. Berlin; Diploma in Chemistry, Free U. Berlin, 1976; MSc in Organic Chemistry, Vanderbilt U., 1977; PhD in Cell Biology, Rockefeller U., 1981. Prof., chmn. dept. biochemistry & biophysics U. Calif., San Francisco; investigator Howard Hughes Medical Inst. Harvey lectr. Rockefeller U., 1996; Feodor-Lynen lectr. Mosbach Kolloquium, 1998. Co-author: Molecular Biology of the Cell, 2002, Essential Cell Biology, 2003. Recipient Searle Scholar award, 1983, Passano award, 1988, Eli Lilly award, 1988, Alfred P. Sloan award, 1989, Merit award, Nat. Insts. Health, 1990, Wiley Prize biomedical sciences, 2005. Fellow: Am. Acad. Microbiology, Am. Acad. Arts and Scis.; mem.: NAS, European Molecular Biology Orgn. (assoc.). Office: U Calif San Fransisco Dept Biochemistry & Biophysics Genentech Hall N312 600 16th St San Francisco CA 94143-2200 Office Phone: 415-476-5017. Office Fax: 415-476-5233. Business E-Mail: walter@cgl.ucsf.edu.

WALTER, ROBERT D., health products executive; b. Columbus, OH, July 13, 1945; m. Peggy McGreevey, 1967; children: Matthew, Blane, Peter. BMechE, Ohio U., 1967; MBA, Harvard U., 1970; Ph.D (hon.), Ohio U., 1997. Engr. N. Am. Rockwell, 1968; founder Cardinal Foods Inc. (acquired by Roundy's Inc. 1988), Dublin, Ohio, 1971-88; founder, CEO Cardinal Distribution, Dublin, Ohio, 1979—94; CEO Cardinal Health, Inc. (formerly Cardinal Distribution), Dublin, 1994—2006, chmn., 2006—. Bd. dirs. Viacom Inc., Am. Express; bd. trustees Battelle Meml. Inst., Ohio U. Trustee Battelle Meml. Inst. Recipient Christopher Columbus award, Greater Columbus C of C, 2001. Avocations: golf, running, skiing. Office: Cardinal Health Inc 7000 Cardinal Pl Dublin OH 43017-1092 *

WALTER, SHERYL LYNN, lawyer; b. Morris, Ill., July 18, 1956; d. C. Frank and Margaret (Juhl) W. BA in History cum laude, Grinnell Coll., Iowa, 1978; JD cum laude, U. Minn., 1984; MPA John F. Kennedy Sch. of Govt., Harvard U., 2003. Bar: Minn. 1984, U.S. Dist. Ct. Minn. 1987, U.S. Ct. Appeals (8th cir.) 1987, D.C. 1989, U.S. Dist. Ct. D.C. 1989, U.S. Ct. Appeals (D.C. cir.) 1989. Law clk. to presiding judge 3d Jud. Dist. of Minn., Rochester, 1984-85; law clk. to Chief Judge Donald P. Lay U.S. Ct. Appeals (8th cir.), St. Paul, 1985-87; assoc. Mayer, Brown & Platt, Washington, 1987-89; gen. counsel Nat. Security Archive, Washington, 1989-94, Assn. Records Review Bd., Washington, 1994-95, Commn. Protecting and Reducing Govt. Secrecy, Washington, 1995-97, dep. spl. counsel U.S. Senate Vets. Affairs com., 1997-98; minority staff dir., chief counsel U.S. Senate Jud. Com., Youth Violence Subcom., 1998-2000; with Office Legis. Affairs US Dept. Justice, Washington, 2000—03, acting asst. atty. gen., 2001, chief of staff Office Intelligence and Policy Rev., 2003—06, exec. officer Nat. Security Divsn., 2006—. Cons. Amnesty Internat., Washington, 1988-89. Vice chair bd. dirs. Rosemont Ctr. Head Start Sch., 2004—. Mem. ABA (vice chmn. adminstrv. law sect. govt. info. subcom. 1990-96), D.C. Bar Assn. (steering com., adminstrv. law sect. 1990-97), Am. Soc. Access Profls. (bd. dirs. 1990-98, pres. 1996-97), Brit.-Am. Security Info. Coun. (bd. dirs. 1994-2000), Lawyers Alliance for World Security (bd. dirs. 1994-2000). Office: US Dept Justice 9th and Pennsylvania Ave NW Washington DC 20530

WALTER, THOMAS BERNARD, music educator, conductor; b. Neenah, Wis., Apr. 23, 1952; s. Michael Milton and Marie Helen Walter; m. Susan Jane Eastman, Aug. 9, 1974; children: Aaron Thomas, Alexandria Suzanne. MusB, St. Norbert Coll., De Pere, Wis., 1974; MusM in Edn., U. Miami, Coral Gables, 1980. Music educator Menasha Pub. Schs., Wis., 1974—, coord. k-12 music, 1996—, dir. choral studies, 2001—. Accompanist Chaminade Women's Chorus, Appleton, Wis., 1974—79, music dir., 1980—; dir. music St. John the Bapt. Cath. Ch., Menasha, 1978—2000; coord. children's honor choir Wis. Choral Director's Assn., Appleton, 2001; coord. music St. Mary Cath. Ch., 2002—; mem. steering com. Fox Cities H.S. Choral Festival, 2004—; soloist holiday concert Boy Choir Orgn., 1993, 2004. Music dir. Menasha Civic Chorale, Wis., 1974—77, Liberty Choir, Appleton, 1976—80; facilitator Appleton Med. Ctr. Sing For The Cure choral project., 2002; music dir. Colors of Christmas gospel choir Fox Cities Performing Arts Ctr., 2004. Recipient Excellence in Edn. award, Menasha Pub. Schools, 1981, 1994. Mem.: Nat. Assn. Pastoral Musicians (assoc.), Music Educators Nat. Conf. (assoc.), Am. Choral Directors Assn. (assoc.), Wis. Choral Directors Assn. (assoc.). Roman Catholic. Avocations: travel, swimming, reading, history. Home: 3341 White Birch Ln Appleton WI 54915 Office: Menasha HS 420 7th St Menasha WI 54952 Home Phone: 920-739-3981; Office Phone: 920-967-1800 4533. E-mail: waltert@mjsd.k12.wi.us.

WALTER, VIRGINIA LEE, psychologist, educator; b. Temple, Tex., Oct. 30, 1937; d. Luther Patterson and Virginia Lafayette (Wilkins) W.; m. Glen Ellis, 1958 (div.); children: Glen Edward, David Walter; m. Robert Reinehr, 1963 (div.); 1 son, Charles Allen; m. Robert Bruininks, 1975 (div.). BS, U. Tex., Austin, 1959, MEd, 1967; postgrad. internship program in spl. Edn. Adminstrn., 1970; EdD, U. Houston, 1973. Prof. ednl. psychology dept. ednl. psychology U. Minn., Mpls., 1973-85; pres. Sch. Resource Ctr., Austin, Tex., 1985-90; tchr. Llano Pub. Schs., 1988-97; dir. Walter Resources, 1998—. Chmn. State Adv. Coun. for Inservice Tng. Regular Classroom Tchrs., 1977-79; cons. spl. ednl. various sch. dists., state depts. and agys. Editl. cons.: Jour. Ednl. Psychology, 1979, Reading Rsch. Quar., 1982; assoc. editor: Exceptional Children, 1979-84; assoc. editor Teaching Exceptional Children, 1985-89; contbr. articles to profl. jours., papers to profl. confs. Named Minn. Spl. Educator of Yr., 1978; recipient Svc. award Internat. Coun. Exceptional Children, 1978; HEW Office of Human Devel. Svcs. grantee, 1976-80; Dept. Edn. contractee, 1980-83 Mem. Coun. for Exceptional Children, Nat. Assn. Children with Learning Disabilities (dir. Minn. chpt. 1978-80), Nat. Assn. Retarded Citizens, AAUP, Assn. Supervision and Curriculum Devel. Home and Office: 7108 Running Rope Austin TX 78731-2128

WALTER, W. EDWARD, hotel and corporate financial executive; Ptnr. Trammell Crow Residential Co.; pres. Bailey Capital Corp.; from sr. v.p. acquisitions to exec. v.p., CFO Host Marriott Corp., Bethesda, Md., 1996—2003, exec. v.p., 2003—, CFO, 2003—. Office: Host Marriott Corp 6903 Rockledge Drive Ste 1500 Bethesda MD 20817

WALTER, WILLIAM G., consumer products company executive; V.p., gen. mgr., Specialty Chemicals Group FMC Corp., Phila., 1997—2000, exec. v.p., 2000—01, chmn., pres. CEO, 2001—. Dir. Internat. Paper Co., 2005—. Mem. The Business Roundtable; mem. exec. comm. The Philadelphia Chamber of Commerce. Office: c/o FMC 1735 Market St Philadelphia PA 19103 *

WALTER, WILLIAM PAUL, retired bioengineer; b. Youngstown, Ohio, Sept. 14, 1925; s. John William and Susan Irene (Herald) Walter; m. Rita Elizabeth Lang, Aug. 24, 1986. BS in Chemistry, Biology, English and Philosophy, Mt. St. Mary's, Emmitsburg, Md., 1948; postgrad., U. Md., 1953; MD in Statis. Engring., Loyola Coll., 1954; postgrad., U. Wis., 1963. Registered microbiologist. From microbiologist to lab chief Pilot Plant Divsn. Lab., Ft. Detrick, Md., 1951—63; project engr., prin. investigator Bioengring. Divsn., Ft. Detrick, 1963—74; prin. investigator, bioengr. chief Biol. Defense Group, Edgewood Arsenal, Md., 1971—74; ret., 1974. Cons. Pitman and Moore, Indpls., 1974-75, Johnson and Johnson, Washington, 1974-76, Merck Pharm., Rahway, NJ, 1976-77, Peebles Hosp., Brit. Virgin Islands, 1977-78, NASA, Washington, 1966. Contbr. articles to profl. jours. Supr. Monocacy Fed. Credit Union, Frederick, Md., 1969. With USN, 1944-46. Mem. Am. Soc. Microbiology, Am. Acad. Microbiology (Nat. Registry of Microbiologist), Sigma Xi (Achievement award 1965, 67, chmn. publicity com. 1966, social com. 1970). Republican. Roman Catholic. Avocations: boating, fishing, bowling, basketball referee, snorkeling. Home and Office: 101 Dreamtime Ave Lake Placid FL 33852-6290 Home Fax: 863-465-1427.

WALTERMIRE, THOMAS ALLEN, finance company executive; b. Balt., Oct. 30, 1949; s. William Everett and Emma (Barack) W.; m. Shirley Jean Flinn, June 16, 1972; children: Todd Andrew Barack Waltermire, Kevin Adam Davis Waltermire, Heidi Alexis Nicole Waltermire. BS, Ohio State U., 1971; MBA, Harvard U., 1974. Mgr. corp. fin. B.F. Goodrich Co., Akron, Ohio, 1975-76; asst. treas., 1977-78; asst. contr., 1978-80; dir. planning, analysis chem. group B.F. Goodrich Co., Cleve, 1980, dir. purchasing div., 1981-84, v.p. comml. svcs., 1984, pres. elastomers and latex div. Cleve., 1985-89, v.p. investor rels., 1989—93; CFO Geon Co., Cleve., 1993—97, COO, 1997—99, CEO, 1999—2000, PolyOne Corp. (Geon and M.A. Hanna merger), Cleve., 2000—05. Vice chmn., bd. dirs. NorTech; mem. Ohio Third Frontier Adv. Bd.; chmn. Ohio Polymer Strategy Coun. Bd. dirs., exec. com. Ohio Bus. Roundtable; bd. dirs. Greater Cleve. Partnership, Vols. Unlimited, Cleve. Orchestra, Ohio State U. Assn., 1998—2003, Nat. Inventors Hall of Fame; chmn. Ohio State U. Assn., 1999—2001; mem. Ohio State U. Alumni Adv. Coun. Republican. Methodist.

WALTERS, ARTHUR SCOTT, neurologist, educator, clinical research scientist; b. Balt., Feb. 20, 1943; s. Charles Henry and Jean Vivian (Scott) W.; m. Bokyun Kim, May 18, 1985 (div. Oct. 1992); m. Lesley J. Gill, Dec. 19, 1992. BA, Kalamazoo Coll., 1965; MS, Northwestern U., 1967; MD, Wayne State U., 1972. Diplomate Am. Bd. Psychiatry and Neurology; diplomate Am. Bd. Sleep Medicine. Intern Oakwood Hosp., Dearborn, Mich., 1972-73; resident in neurology SUNY Downstate Med. Ctr., Bklyn., 1976-79; movement disorder fellow Neurol. Inst., NYC, 1982-84; asst. prof. neurology Robert Wood Johnson Med. Sch., U. Medicine & Dentistry NJ, New Brunswick, 1984-91, assoc. prof. neurology, 1991-99, clin. prof. neurology, 1999—; asst. chief divsn. neurology Lyons VA Med. Ctr., NJ, 1985-89, neurology cons., 1984-99; prof. neurosci. Seton Hall U. Sch. Grad. Med. Edn., South Orange, NJ, 1999—, NJ Neurosci. Inst., Edison, 1999—. Nat. chmn. med. adv. bd. Restless Legs Syndrome Found., 1992-98; organizer Internat. Restless Legs Study Group, 1992—; head Restless Legs Syndrome and Periodic Limb Movement Coun. for the Nat. Sleep Found., 1994-96; neurology cons. Coney Island Hosp., Bklyn., Bklyn. Jewish Hosp., 1980-81; presenter in field. Contbr. articles to profl. publs., chpts. to books; organizer symposia. Named Rschr. of Yr. in medicine Seton Hall U. Sch. Grad. Med. Edn., 2003-04, Michael S. Aldrich hon. lectr. in sleep medicine for outstanding contbns. to patient care, rsch. and edn. U. Mich., 2006; grantee UMDNJ, 1984-86, VA RAG, 1985-86, Sandoz Corp., 1985-88, VA Merit Rev., 1989-98, Clemente Found., 1994-95, Purdue Pharma, 2000—, NIH, 2002. Fellow Am. Acad. Neurology, Am. Acad. Sleep Medicine; editl. bd., (journal) Sleep and Sleep Medicine; mem. AAAS, Am. Neurol. Assn., Sleep Rsch. Soc., Movement Disorder Soc., NY Acad. Scis., NJ Sleep Soc. (sec. 1995-96, treas. 1996-97, v.p. 1998-99). Office: NJ Neuro Sci Inst JFK Med Ctr 65 James St Edison NJ 08820-3947 Home Phone: 732-545-2905; Office Phone: 732-321-7000 ext. 68177. Personal E-mail: artumdnj@aol.com.

WALTERS, BARBARA JILL, broadcast journalist; b. Boston, Sept. 25, 1931; d. Lou and Dena (Selett) Walters; m. Robert Katz, June 21, 1955 (div. 1958); m. Lee Gruber, 1963 (div. 1976); 1 adopted child, Jacqueline; m. Merv Adelson, 1986 (div. 1992). BA in English, Sarah Lawrence Coll., 1953, LHD (hon.), Ohio State U., Marymount Coll., 1975, Wheaton Coll., 1983, Temple U., Hofstra U., Ben-Gurion U. Former producer WNBC-TV; former writer CBS News; then with Stas. WPIX and CBS-TV; writer, reporter-at-large Today Show, 1961—63, regular panel mem., 1964—74, co-host, 1974—76; moderator syndicated program Not For Women Only, 1972—76; founder, pres. Barwall Productions, NYC, 1976—; newscaster ABC Evening News (now ABC World News Tonight), 1976—78; host The Barbara Walters Spls., 1976—; co-host ABC TV news show 20/20, 1984—99, anchor, 1999—2004; host The 10 Most Fascinating People, 1993—; co-exec. prodr., co-owner, co-host The View, ABC, NYC, 1997—; exec. prodr. The Iyanla Show, 2001. Contbr. NBC Radio Network. Contbr. ABC programs Issues and Answers; author: (book) How to Talk With Practically Anybody About Practically Anything, 1970; contbr. to Reader's Digest, Good Housekeeping, Family Weekly. Honorary chair Nat. Assn. Help for Mentally Retarded Children, 1970. Named Woman Yr. Comm., 1974, Broadcaster Yr., Internat. Radio and TV Soc., 1975, Woman Yr., Theta Sigma Phi; named one of Am.'s 75 Most Important Women, Ladies' Home Jour., 1970, 200 Leaders Future, Time Mag., 1974, 10 Women Decade, Ladies' Home Jour., 1979, Most Important Women, Roper Report, 1979, Women Most Admired Am. People, Gallup Poll, 1982, 1984, Am.'s 100 Most Important Women, Ladies' Home Jour., 1983, America's 100 Most Important Women of the Century, Good Housekeeping, 2000, Ladies' Home Journal, 2000, 100 Most Powerful Celebrities, Forbes.com, 2007; named to 100 Women of Accomplishment, Harper's Bazaar, 1967, 1971, Museum of Television and Radio, Los Angeles, 2004; recipient Award Yr., Nat. Assn. TV Program Execs., 1975, Daytime Emmy award, Nat. Acad. TV Arts and Scis., 1975, Emmy award, 1980, 1982, 1983, Daytime Emmy award for outstanding talk show, 2003, Mass Media award, Am. Jewish Com. Inst. Human Relations, 1975, Barbara Walters' Coll. Scholarship in Broadcast Journalism established in her honor, Ill. Broadcasters Assn., 1975, Matrix award, N.Y. Women in Comm., 1977, Hubert H. Humphrey Freedom prize, Anti Defamation League B'nai B'rith, 1978, Pres.'s award, Overseas Press Club, 1988, inducted Hall of Fame, Acad. TV Arts and Scis., 1990, Lowell Thomas award, Marist Coll., 1990, Lifetime Achievement award, Internat. Women's Media Found., 1991, saluted, Am. Mus. Moving Image, 1992, Lifetime Achievement award, Women's Project and Prodn., 1993, honored for contbn. to broadcast journalism, Mus. TV and Radio, 1996, George Foster Peabody award for her interview with actor Christopher Reeve, 1996, Muse award, NY Women in Film and TV, 1997, Lifetime Achievement award, Daytime Emmy Awards, 2000, Nat. Acad. TV Arts and Scis., 2000, Silver Satellite award, Am. Women Radio and TV, Sherry Landing Leadership award, The Hollywood Reporter, 2005. Achievements include first woman to co-anchor the Network News, 1976; interviewed every U.S. president and first lady since Nixon; conducted several historic interviews including the Nov. 1977 joint interview with Egyptian President Anwar Sadat and Israel's Prime Minister Menachem Begin; hour-long primetime interview with Cuba's President Fidel Castro, June 9, 1977 and a second interview 25 years later in 2002; conducted the first interview with Monica Lewinsky, which became the highest-rated news program, 48.5 million viewers, ever broadcast by a single network, 1999. Office: The View 320 W 66th St New York NY 10023-6304

WALTERS, BILL, retired state senator; b. Paris, Ark., Apr. 17, 1943; s. Peter Louis and Elizabeth Cecelia (Wilhelm) W.; m. Joyce Leslie Garrett Moore, Jan. 9, 1964 (div. 1970); children: Jamie, Sherry Ann; m. Shirley Ann Dixon, Aug. 20, 1971; 1 child, Sandra. BS, U. Ark., 1966, JD, 1971. Bar: Ark. 1971, U.S. Dist. Ct. Ark. 1971. Asst. prosecuting atty. 12th Jud. Dist. Ark., Ft. Smith, 1971-74; pvt. practice Greenwood, Ark., 1975—; mem. Ark. Senate, Little Rock, 1982-2000. Bd. dirs., sec.-treas. Mineral Owners Collective Assn. Inc., Greenwood; former v.p., bd. dirs. Sebastian County Abstract & Title Ins. Co., Greenwood and Ft. Smith, Ark.; mem. Ark. Real Estate Commn., Ark. Abstract and Title Commn. Committeeman Rep. Ctrl. Com. Ark., Ft. Smith, 1980; search pilot CAP, Ft. Smith. Decorated Silver Medal of Valor; recipient Cert. of Honor Justice for Crime's Victims, 1983. Mem. Ark. Bar Assn., South Sebastian County Bar Assn. (pres. 1991-94), Profl. Landmen's Assn. Roman Catholic. Home: PO Box 280 Greenwood AR 72936-0280 Office: 1405 W Center Greenwood AR 72936-3200 Home Phone: 479-996-4520; Office Phone: 479-996-2100. Business E-Mail: bwalters@waltlaw.net.

WALTERS, CLAYTON WILLIAM, health facility administrator, rehabilitation services professional, consultant; b. Jellico, Tenn., June 7, 1951; s. Phillip Gordon and Sarah Eileen Walters; m. Susan Louise Brandau; children: David Clayton, Christopher, Matthew, Cassandra. AA in Humanities, Dutchess C.C., Poughkeepsie, NY, 1979. Exec. dir. Baldwin Rsch. Inst., Amsterdam, NY, 2003—04, v.p. cons., 2004—06; v.p. ops. St. Jude Thaddeus Inc., Des Moines, 2006—. Republican. Episcopalian. Avocations: reading, book collecting, sailing. Home: 608 North St Adair IA 50002 Office: St Jude Thaddeus Inc 3807 Thronton Ave Des Moines IA 50321

WALTERS, DANIEL L., library director; B, U. Wash., M in Librarianship. With North Ctrl. Regional Libr., Wenatchee, Wash., King County Libr. Sys., Seattle; dir. Spokane Pub. Libr., Wash., Buffalo and Erie County Pub. Libr.; exec. dir. Las Vegas-Clark County Libr. Dist., Nev. Contbr. articles to profl. publs. Mem. exec. com. ARC Inland NW Chpt.; bd. dirs. YMCA, Spokane, Wash. Named Cmty. Person of Yr., Las Vegas Asian C. of C. Mem.: ALA, NY Libr. Assn., Las Vegas Execs. Assn., Wash. Libr. Assn., Nev. Libr. Assn., Online Computer Libr. Ctr., Pub. Libr. Assn. (v.p./pres.-elect 2004). Office: Las Vegas Clark County Libr Dist 833 Las Vegas Blvd N Las Vegas NV 89101 Office Phone: 702-734-7323.

WALTERS, DANIEL RAYMOND, political columnist; b. Hutchinson, Kans., Oct. 10, 1943; s. Howard Duke and Glenna Lucille (Hesse) W.; m. Doris K. Winter, June 16, 1995; children: Danielle, Staci. Mng. editor Hanford (Calif.) Sentinel, 1966-69, Herald News, Klamath Falls, Oreg., 1969-71, Times-Standard, Eureka, Calif., 1971-73; polit. writer and columnist Sacramento (Calif.) Union, 1973-84; polit. columnist, state editor Capitol Bur., Sacramento Bee, 1984—. Author: The New California: Facing the 21st Century, 1986; founding editor Calif. Polit. Almanac, 1989. Office: The Sacramento Bee 925 L St Ste 600 Sacramento CA 95814-3763

WALTERS, FARAH M., health services company administrator, former hospital administrator; b. Feb. 10, 1945; BS, Ohio State U., 1968; MS, Case Western Res. U., 1975, MBA, 1984. Sr. v.p., gen. mgr. Univs. Hosps., Cleve., 1987-89, exec. v.p., 1989-91, exec. dir., 1991-92, pres., CEO, 1992—2002, QualHealth LLC, 2005—. Mem. Ohio Commn. to Study the Ohio Econ. & Tax Structure; bd. dirs. PolyOne Corp., Celanese, 2007—. Named to Bus. Hall of Fame, Bus. mag., 2000, Ohio Women's Hall of Fame, 2001; recipient Ellis Medal of Honor.

WALTERS, GLEN ROBERT, retired banker; b. Mpls., Sept. 11, 1943; s. Sterling Thomas and Mildred Eunice (Parkinson) W.; m. Gail Elvira Engelsen, June 11, 1966; children: Nicole Marie, Brent Aaron, Hillary Renee. BA, U. Minn., Mpls., 1965, postgrad., 1965-67; banking degree, Rutgers U., New Brunswick, NJ, 1982. Comml. banker 1st Nat. Bank, Mpls., 1967-83, sr. v.p. human resources, 1983-90; sr. v.p. Firstar Bank Minn., Mpls., 1990-2001, US Bank, Mpls., 2001—05. Served to sgt. USNG, 1967-73 Republican. Presbyterian.

WALTERS, JOHN P., federal official; b. 1952; m. Mary Walters; children: Michaela, Rebecca. BA, Mich. State U.; MA, U. Toronto. Acting asst. dir., program officer divsn. edn. programs NEH, 1982—85; asst. to sec. US Dept. Edn., 1985—88; chief of staff White House Office Nat. Drug Control Policy, Washington, 1989—91, dep. dir. supply reduction, 1991—93, dir., 2001—; pres. Philanthropy Roundtable, 1996—2001. Dir. Nat. Youth Anti-Drug Media Campaign; vis. fellow Hudson Inst., 1993; instr. polit. sci. James Madison Coll. Mich. State U., Boston Coll.; sec.'s rep. Nat. Drug Policy Bd., Domestic Policy Coun.'s Health Policy Working Group. Co-author (with William J. Bennett & John J. Di Iulio Jr.): Body Count: Moral Poverty and How to Win America's War Against Crime and Drugs, 1996. Pres. New Citizenship Program. Achievements include releasing the National Drug Control Strategy which set aggressive goals of a ten percent reduction in teen and adult drug use in two years and a twenty five percent reduction in five years; Monitoring the Future Study showed a nineteen percent reduction in teen drug use over four years exceeding the President's goal and bringing drug use to its lowest levels since the early 1990s; lead a restructuring of the federal drug control budget so that it more accurately reflects the actual dollars spent on programs aimed at reducing drug use making it a more useful tool for policymaker; oversees the creation and implementation of the Access to Recovery treatment initiative announced by President Bush in his 2003 State of the Union Address; the Access to Recovery treatment initiative approach to drug treatment funding provides vouchers for hundreds of thousands of Americans struggling with addiction. Office: Office Nat Drug Control Policy 750 17th St NW Washington DC 20503 *

WALTERS, JOHNNIE MCKEIVER, lawyer; b. Hartsville, SC, Dec. 20, 1919; s. Tommie Ellis and Lizzie Lee (Grantham) W.; m. Donna Lucile Hall, Sept. 1, 1947; children: Donna Dianne Walters Gent, Lizbeth Kathern Walters Kukorowski, Hilton Horace, John Roy. AB, Furman U., 1942, LLD, 1973; LLB, U. Mich., 1948. Bar: Mich. 1948, N.Y. 1955, S.C. 1961, D.C. 1973. Atty. office chief counsel IRS, Washington, 1949-53; asst. mgr. tax div. law dept. Texaco, Inc., NYC, 1953-61; ptnr. firm Geer, Walters & Demo, Greenville, SC, 1961-69; asst. atty. gen. tax div. Dept. Justice, Washington, 1969-71; commr. IRS, 1971-73; ptnr. firm Hunton & Williams, Washington, 1973-79, Leatherwood Walker Todd & Mann, P.C., Greenville, 1979-95; exec. v.p., gen. counsel Colonial Trust Co., Greenville, 1996—2004; ret., 2006. Bd. dirs. Textile Hall Corp., Greenville, Colonial Trust Co. Mem. S.C. Coun. on Competitiveness, 1987—91, S.C. Ethics Commn., 2005—. With USAF, 1942—45. Fellow Am. Coll. Tax Counsel (founding regent), Am. Coll. Trust and Estate Counsel, Am. Bar Found., S.C. Bar Found. (bd. dirs. 1988-92); mem. ABA (taxation sect.), S.C. Bar (chmn. taxation sect. 1983-84), Rotary (pres. local club 1968-69). Republican. Baptist. Home: 125 Hummingbird Ridge Greenville SC 29605-5305 Personal E-mail: johnniewalters@bellsouth.net.

WALTERS, MARIAN R., research administrator; b. Washington, 1948; PhD, U. Houston, 1975. Prof. physiology Tulane U. Sch. Medicine, New Orleans, 1980—2004, dir. tuxcoe leadership core, 1999—2004, dir. of grad. studies in physiology, 1983—2004; assoc. dean rsch. and grad. studies Penn State U., Harrisburg, 2004—. Author: (book chapter) Encyclopedia of Hormones: Calcium Regulating Hormones. Mem.: Soc. Exptl. Biology and Medicine (coun. mem. 2001—, treas. 2006—). Office: Penn State Harrisburg 777 W Harrisburg Pike Middletown PA 17057

WALTERS, MARK DOUGLAS, obstetrician, gynecologist, director; b. Toledo, July 21, 1954; s. Donald Walters; m. Virginia Walters; children: Samantha, Maxwell, Zoe. BS in biology, U. Cincinnati, 1976; MD, Ohio State U., 1980. Cert. Am. Bd. Ob-Gyn. Intern Tufts U. Sch. Medicine, Boston, 1980—81, resident in ob-gyn., 1981—84; asst. prof. dept. ob-gyn. U. Tex. Health Sci. Ctr., San Antonio, 1984—90; assoc. prof. dept. reproductive biology and ob-gyn. Case Western Reserve U. Sch. Medicine, Cleve., 1990—93; med. dir. Women's Health Ctr. U. Hospitals of Cleve., 1990—93; head sect. gen. gynecology, dir. urogynecology The Cleve. Clinic, 1993—, dir. fellowship program in urogynecology/reconstructive pelvic surgery, 1997—, vice-chair gynecology, 2006—; prof. surgery Cleve. Clinic Lerner Coll. Medicine, 2006—. Vice chair gynecology Cleve. Clinic, 2006—. Author: (book) Clinical Urogynecology, 1993, Urogynecology and Reconstructive Pelvic Surgery, 3d edit., 2006. Recipient Ann. Resident Tchg. award, MetroHealth Med. Ctr., 1996, 1999, 2000, 2002. Fellow: Am. Coll. of Obstetricians and Gynecologists; mem.: Cleve. Soc. of Ob-gyn., Soc. of Gynecologic Surgeons, Am. Urogynecology Soc., Jour. of Gynecologic Surgery (editl. bd.), Internat. Urogynecology Jour. (editl. bd.). Office: The Cleve Clinic Dept Ob-gyn 9500 Euclid Ave Desk A81 Cleveland OH 44195 Office Phone: 216-445-6586. E-mail: walterm@ccf.org.

WALTERS, MARTHA LEE, state supreme court justice; b. 1951; married; 2 children. JD, U. Ore. Sch. Law, 1977. Pres. Walters, Chanti & Zennache, Eugene, Oreg.; justice Oreg. Supreme Ct., 2006—. Chmn. exec. com. Nat. Conf. Commrs. on Uniform State Laws, 1992—. Recipient Pub. Justice award, Oreg. Trial Lawyers Assn., 1998. Mem.: Am. Law Inst., Oreg. Law Commn. Office: Walters Chanti & Zennache 245 E 4th St Eugene OR 97401 also: Oreg Supreme Ct 1163 State St Salem OR 97301-2563 Office Phone: 503-986-5700. Office Fax: 503-986-5730. *

WALTERS, MILTON JAMES, investment banker; b. Hornell, NY, May 21, 1942; s. James Henry and Frances Eleanor (Simmons) W.; m. Caroline Houck, May 24, 1963; children: Melissa Ann, Gregory Thomas, Timothy Allen. BA, Hamilton Coll., 1964. Trainee Mfrs. Hanover, 1964-65; with A.G. Becker Inc., NYC, 1965-84; mng. dir. Smith Barney, NYC, 1978—84, Prudential Securities, NYC, 1997-99; pres. Tri-River Capital, 1988—. Bd. dirs. Decision One, Frederick's of Hollywood, Sun Healthcare Group. Trustee Hamilton Coll., Clinton, N.Y., 1983-88, Friends Acad., Locust Valley, N.Y., 1981-91 Mem. Nat. Assn. Corp. Dirs., Nat. Assn. Cert. Valuation Analysis, Econ. Club N.Y. Republican. Presbyterian. Office: Tri-River Capital PO Box 128 New York NY 10150-0128 Office Phone: 212-581-5777. Business E-Mail: mjw@tririv.com.

WALTERS, RICHARD B., lawyer; b. Houston, Jan. 11, 1945; s. Wyatt and Norma Brooks Walters; children: William Richard, Brian Jacob Bossin, Blake Ragsdale. BS in Commerce, Washington & Lee U., Lexington, Va., 1967; JD, U. Houston, 1971. CPA Tex., 1973; bar: Tex. 1971, cert.: Tex. Bd. Legal Specialization (estate planning and probate law specialist) 1994. Sr. tax acct. Deloitte, Haskins & Sells (Now Deloitte & Touche), CPAs, Houston, 1971—74; assoc. atty. Chamberlain, Hrdlicka, White & Waters, Houston, 1974—76; participating assoc. atty. Fulbright & Jaworski, LLP, Houston, 1976—81; v.p., gen. counsel Mgmt. Compensation Group, Inc., Houston, 1981—84; sr. tax mgr. Ernst & Whinney, CPAs (Now Ernst & Young, LLP), Houston, 1984—86; investment property specialist Coldwell Banker Comml. Real Estate Svcs., Houston, 1986—89; of counsel Porter & Clements, LLP (Now Porter & Hedges, LLP), Houston, 1989—91; ptnr. Kormeier & Walters, LLP, Houston, 1991—. Bd. dirs. Houston Estate and Fin. Forum, 2001—07; personal gifts planning adv. coun. U. Houston, 2002—; adv. bd. Woodway Fin. Advisors Trust Co., Houston, 2007—. Bd. dirs. Lamar HS Alumni Assn., Inc., Houston, 2005—07; former adminstrv. bd. Chapelwood United Meth. Ch., Houston; adv. bd. Depression Bipolar Support Alliance Greater Houston, 2005—07. Fellow: Am. Coll. Trust and Estate Counsel. Office: Kormeier & Walters LLP 675 Bering Dr Ste 350 Houston TX 77057 Home Phone: 713-789-8435; Office Phone: 713-973-2777. Office Fax: 713-984-1141. Business E-Mail: rwalters@kwlawyer.com.

WALTERS, ROBERT ANCIL, physicist, mathematician; b. Russell Springs, Ky., Mar. 12, 1915; s. Robert Edmund Lee and Talitha Margaret (Wilson) W.; m. Etha Jane McKinley, Feb. 2, 1943; 1 child, Robert Ancil II; m. Sandra Faye Roy, June 29, 1969; 1 child, Forrest Wayne. BS, Western Ky. U., 1941; postgrad., George Washington U., 1943-45, Agrl. Grad. Sch., 1947-48, Am. U., 1951-52. H.S. asst. prin. Russell County Bd. Edn., 1941-42; physicist, head exterior ballistics U.S. Naval Weapons Lab., Dahlgren, Va., 1942-59; pres. Walters Ins. and Investment Counselor, Dahlgren, 1948-80; engr., head systems planning U.S. Naval Space Surveillance, Dahlgren, Va., 1959-69; R&D specialist, physicist interdisciplinary math. cons. U.S. Naval Warfare Lab., Dahlgren, 1969-75. Pres. Navel Weapons Lab. Fed. Credit Union, Dahlgren, 1968-74; bd. examiners Potomac River Naval Com., Washington, 1953-56; biology lab. instr. Western Ky. U., Bowling Green, 1935-36. Chmn. Old Dominion Eye Bank, Richmond, Va., 1975-76; co-chair Dem. Party, Ky., 1937-42; pres. Nat. Fedn. Fed. Employees, Washington, 1963-69. Recipient Nat. Quality award Nat. Assn. Life Underwriters, 1976; named Ky. Col., gov. of Ky., 1976, Outstanding Citizen of Yr., VFW, 1981, Guest of Honor King George County Fall Festival, 1994. Mem.: Lions Internat. (dep. dist. gov. 1976—77, Disting. Svc. award 1975, Melvin Jones fellow 2001, cert. for disting. leadership and svc. 2005). Baptist.

WALTERS, RONALD OGDEN, mortgage banker; b. Holcombe, Wis., July 13, 1939; s. Ogden Eugene and Josephine Ann (Hennekens) W.; m. Margaret Ellen Weisheipl, July 14, 1962; children: Laurie, Cheryl, Michael, Patrick Student, U. Wis., 1959-62. Mgr. Thorp Fin., LaCrosse, Wis., 1962-65, regional mgr. Milw., 1965-69, ITT Consumer Fin. Corp., Milw., 1969-74, sr. v.p. Brookfield, Wis., 1974-90, exec. v.p. adminstrn., 1990-92; CEO Ideal Fin. Corp., Brookfield, 1993—, USA Funding Corp., Brookfield, Wis., 1993—. Mem. Wis. Fin. Services Assn. (pres. 1980) Republican. Roman Catholic. Avocations: boating, fishing, hunting. Home: 812 Back Bay Delafield WI 53018-1528 Office: 17035 W Wisconsin Ave Brookfield WI 53005-5734 Office Phone: 262-938-9259. Business E-Mail: rwalters@usafundingcorp.com.

WALTERS, ROSS A., federal judge; BA in History, Pa. State U., 1971; JD with high distinction, U. Iowa, 1977. Law clk. to Judge William C. Hanson US Dist. Ct. (So. Dist. Iowa), 1977—79; assoc. Herrick and Langdon, Des Moines, 1979—82, ptnr., 1982—90; judge Iowa Dist. Ct. (Jud. Dist. 5-C), 1990—94; magistrate judge US Dist. Ct. (So. Dist.) Iowa, 1994—, chief magistrate judge, 1998—2005. Chief magistrate judge US Dist. Ct. (So. Dist.) Iowa, 1998—2005. Bd. editors, contemporary studies project leader Iowa Law Rev. Legal officer, adminstrv. div. officer US Navy Reserve, 1971—74, aboard USS Oklahoma City. Office: US Courthouse Rm 440 123 E Walnut St Des Moines IA 50309-2035

WALTERS, SHERWOOD GEORGE, management consultant, educator; b. Detroit, May 9, 1926; s. George Henry and Helen (Parker) Walters; m. Alexandra Sielcken, Sept. 4, 1952; children: Margaret Taylor Clifford, Karen Chapin, George Alexander II, Virginia Sherwood McFee. BA in Econ., Political Sci., and History cum laude, Western Md. Coll., 1949; MS in Internat. Trade, History, Columbia U., 1950, MBA with distinction, 1953; PhD in Govt. with distinction, NYU, 1960, cert. specialist in Latin Am. affairs, 1960. From instr. to assoc. prof. econs. sociology mktg. Coll. Bus. Econs., Lehigh U., Bethlehem, Pa., 1950—60; pres., dir. S.G. Walters Assocs. Mgmt. Cons., 1952—; exec. v.p., dir. ctrs., retail planning mgr., devel. projects mgr. Mobil Oil, NYC, 1960-65; mgr. comml. mktg. Chem. Plastics divsn., exec. officer mktg. dir. Gen. Tire & Rubber Internat. Plastics Co., Akron, Ohio, 1965-70; prof. Rutgers U. Bus. Sch., New Brunswick, 1970—93, prof. emeritus mgmt. studies, 1993—; founding dir. interfunctional mgmt. program Rutgers U., New Brunswick, 1970-88; founding dir. PhD mgmt. program, chmn. orgn. ops. mgmt. dept. Rutgers U. Grad Sch. Bus. Adminstrn., New Brunswick. Rsch. dir. US Small Bus. Devel. Coun., 1950—60; former co-dir. E.I. DuPont de Nemours Interdisciplinary Rsch. Team; dir. various internat. programs in mgmt., banking and sci. NSF, 1971—2004; educator, emissary, NSF/IUCRC program advisor, 1980—. Author (with Cmte. on Retailing, et al.): Principles of Retailing, 1955, Principles of Marketing, 1961; author: (with M.D. Snider, M.L. Sweet) Readings in Marketing, 1962; co-author (with Morris L. Sweet and Max D. Snider): (seminal books) Marketing Management Viewpoints Commentary and Readings, 2d edit., 1970; co-author: (with Morris L. Sweet) Mandatory Housing Finance Programs, A Comparative International Analysis, 1975; co-author: (with Denis O. Gray) Managing the Industry University Cooperative Research Center: A Guide for Directors and Other Stakeholders, 1998; prodr., dir., participant (commercially sponsored radio program) Breakfast with the Walters, WEST/NBC, Easton, Pa., 1953—57; contbr. 188 jour. articles and govt. rsch. reports. Adviser Nat. Rep. Congl. Com. on Tax Reform, 2001; mem. NJ Govs. Commn. Energy Task Force, NJ, 1975—76, Jud. Com. Energy Safety Stds., 1975—76, Com. Liquified Natural Gas, 1975—76; chmn. Subcom. Forecasting Demand and Supply Liquified Gas, 1975, 1976; mem. NJ R&D Coun., 1984—93; chmn. U./Indsl. Partnerships, John Von Neumann Ctr., Princeton U., 1986; hon. chmn. bus. adv. coun. Nat. Rep. Congl. Com., 2003—04; elder, trustee, co-dir. Christian Edn. Com. Topsail Presbyn. Ch., Hampstead, NC. From pvt. to 1st lt. Inf., Quartermaster Corps US Army, 1944—47, ETO. Named Internat. Educator of Yr., 2007; recipient Founders Day award, NYU, 1960, Prof. of Yr. (student selected), Rutgers Grad. Sch. Bus., 1976, Christian R. and Mary F. Lindback Excellence in Tchg. award, Rutgers U., 1983, Rep. Presdl. Legion of Merit medal, 1994, cert. signed by Ronald Reagan, Phil Gramm and W. David Harris, 1994, Excellence award, NSF, 2004, Bd. Trustees Alumni award, McDaniel Coll. (formerly Western Md. Coll.), 2005, Businessman of Yr. Winner from NC award, Bus. Adv. Coun., Nat. Rep. Congl. Com., DC, 2003, 2004, 2005, Lifetime Achievement award, World Congress Arts, Sci., Comm., Cambridge, Eng., 2006, Dr. S. George Walters Interfunctional Mgmt. Cons. Excellence award named in his honor, Rutgers Bus. School, 1999—, award, former Spkr. of House Newt Gingrich with personal congratulations by Pres. George W. Bush, 2006; DuPont fellow, 1951, Spl. Studies scholar, Ford Found., Harvard U. Bus. Sch., Cambridge, Mass., 1956. Fellow: Acad. Polit. Sci.; mem.: SAR, S.R., Newcomen Soc., Beta Gamma Sigma (sec., treas., pres. Lehigh U. chpt. 1953—60, sec., treas., pres. Rutgers U. chpt. 1970—88). Avocation: deep sea fishing. Home: 110 Topsail Watch Ln Hampstead NC 28443-2728 Office Phone: 910-329-0663. Office Fax: 910-329-0824. Personal E-mail: s.george.walters@worldnet.att.net, s.george.walter@worldnet.att.net.

WALTERS, SUE FOX, broadcast executive, accountant; b. Louisville, June 9, 1941; d. Thomas Burke and Reva Crick Fox; m. Hugh Alexander Walters (dec. 2001); children: Thomas Wade Walters, Alexandra Walters Ebling. Student, N.C. State U., Ky. Wesleyan Coll. Acct., paralegal for fin. instns. and firms; ct. adminstr. 45th Jud. Cir. Ct., Ky.; v.p., treas. Alexander and Assocs., CATV cons. firm, Greenville, Ky.; corp. adminstr., pub. corp. Bellevue, Wash.; sr. acctg. specialist Japanese/Am. Automotive Mfg. Co., Bowling Green, Ky.; land developer. Pres., Jr. Woman's Club Greenville, 1964-65, Woman's Club of Greenville, 1976-78; vice gov. 2d dist. Ky. Fedn. Women's Clubs, 1980. Avocations: historical preservation, design, antiques, dogs, flying. Home: 151 N Main St Greenville KY 42345-1503

WALTERS, WILLIAM BEN, chemistry professor; b. Highland, Kans., Apr. 26, 1938; s. Ben Guthrie and Dolly Varden (Shaw) W.; m. Barbara Lulu Sternaman, Aug. 5, 1962; children: Katharine, David. AS, Highland Coll., 1957; BS, Kans. State U., 1960; PhD, U. Ill., 1964. Asst. prof. MIT, Cambridge, 1965-70; assoc. prof. chemistry U. Md., College Park, 1970-77, prof., 1977—, assoc. chmn. dept., 1982-86. Vis. prof. U. Louvain, Belgium, 1978; chair U. Senate, 1999-00; mem. physics adv. com. Grand Accelerateur Nat. d Ions Lourds, 2003-2006. Recipient Nuc. Chemistry award Am. Chemical Soc., 2001, Rsch. award U. Md., Sigma Xi, 1998; Guggenheim fellow Oxford U., 1986-87, Von Humboldt fellow Univ. Mainz, 2001-02, 06. Mem. Am. Phys. Soc., European Phys. Soc., Am. Chem. Soc. (chmn. div. nuclear chemistry 1986), Rotary (bd. dirs. College Park 1990-91, 2000—). Office: U Md Dept Chemistry College Park MD 20742-0001 Office Phone: 301-405-1801. Business E-Mail: wwalters@umd.edu.

WALTHER, ADRIAAN, retired physics professor; s. George F. J. A. Walther and Gerrigje A. Van Donk; m. Trudy C. Huygen, May 14, 1960; children: Peter J., Ellen G. Sousa. Ph.D, Tech. U. Delft, Netherlands, 1959. Chief scientist Diffraction Ltd., Inc., Bedford, Mass., 1960—72; prof. physics WPI, Worcester, Mass., 1972—2001; ret., 2001.

WALTHER, PETER C., church musician; b. NYC, Apr. 18, 1947; s. Edmund P. Walther and Caryl Estelle Roane. B in Music Edn., Hope Coll., Holland, Mich., 1969. Cert. tchr. NY, 1973. Vocal music Sauquoit Ctrl. Schs., NY, 1973—79; music instr. Mohawk Valley C.C., Utica, NY, 1982—88; organist, choir dir. various chs., NY, Md., 1988—2003; dir. music ministries First Bapt. Ch., Rome, NY, 2003—. Lectr., instr. Annapolis Opera, Md., 1999—2001; dir. Utica Mannerchor, 2001—; chapel organist Keuka Coll., Keuka Park, NY, 2006—; presenter in field. Contbr. articles to profl. jours. Dir. NY State Sangerfests, Kingston, 2003, Binghamton, 2006; bd. mem. Fulton County Arts Coun., Johnstown, NY, 1990—94; past mem. Knights Templar. Mem.: Am. Antiquarian Soc., Am. Guild Organists, Elgar Soc., Horatio Alger Soc. (past bd. mem.), NY State Hist. Assn. Republican. Baptist. Avocations: opera, cinema history, literature. Home: 5741 Judd Rd Oriskany NY 13424 Office: First Bapt Ch 301 W Embargo St Rome NY 13440 Office Phone: 315-336-2610.

WALTHER, STEVEN T., lawyer; b. Reno, Nev., July 18, 1943; BA in Russian, U. Notre Dame, 1965; JD, U. Calif., Berkeley, 1968. Bar: Nev. 1968, US Dist. Ct. (Nev.) 1969, Calif. 1969, US Ct. Appeals (9th cir.) 1986, US Supreme Ct. 1991. Mem. US Commn. on Civil Rights, 1971—; chair Nev. Bd. CLE, 1982—90; panelist US Magistrate Judge Merit Selection Panel, 1990; pres. Western States Bar Conf., 1999—2000; mem. LexiNexis Martindale-Hubbell Legal Adv. Bd., 2001—; pres. Nat. Caucus State Bar Assn., 2002—03; guest lectr. Nat. Jud. Coll., Reno; mem. Nev. State Adv. Com.; chair internat. bus. task force Coll. Bus. Adminstrn., U. Nev., Reno; lectr., presenter on rule of law and human rights issues; mem. Am. Law Inst., mem. consultative group principles and rules of transnational civil procedures, mem. consultative group internat. jurisdiction and judgements. Author: The Globalization of the Rule of Law and Human Rights, 2000. Recipient Awards of Spl. Appreciation, 1991, 1999, Award of Spl. Appreciation, Am. Red Cross, Sierra, Nev. chpt., 1999, Pres. award, Scenic Nev., 2005. Fellow: World Acad. Art and Sci., Am. Bar Found. (chair 2003—04, del. leader, rule of law del. to Russia 2005); mem.: ABA (chair standing com.on world order under law 1993—95, bd. govs. 1995—97, fin. com. 1995—97, ho. del. 1995—97, chair spl. adv. com. on internat. activities 1997—98, mem. Cent. European and Eurasian Law Initiative 1997—98, mem. subcom. on internat. jud. relations 1997—98, rep. to UN 1998—2000, mem. UN and internat. instns. coord. com. 1998—, mem. internat. human rights com. 1999—, mem. Cent. European and Eurasian Law Initiative 2000—01, co-founder 2001, first chair 2001—03, exec. bd. mem. 2001—, coun. mem. 2002—, mem. sect. individual rights and responsibilities, mem. ctr. for human rights, mem. lit. sect., mem. exec. bd., mem. sect. on bus., mem. sect. internat. law), State Bar of Nev. (gov., bd. govs. 1978—91, pres. 1990—91), Human Rights First, Nat. Coun., State Bar of Calif., Washoe County Bar Assn., Am. Inns of Ct. (Bruce R. Thompson chpt.) (master emeritus), Am. Soc. Internat. Law, Nat. Conf. Bar Pres., Inc. (mem. sponsorship com. 1994—95), Nat. Conf. Bar Found. (trustee bd. trustees 2004—), Boalt Hall Alumni Assn., U. Calif. Law Sch. (pres. 2001—02). Office: Walther Key Maupin Oats Cox & LeGoy 4785 Caughlin Pwy Reno NV 89509

WALTHIE, THEO H., chemicals executive; Grad. summa cum laude in Chem. Engring., Tech U. Delft, Netherlands. Mem. spl. assignments prog. Dow Europe, 1970—72, prodn. engr. chlorinated solvents plant Terneuzen, Netherlands, 1972—74, various purchasing positions Rotterdam, Netherlands, 1974—78; bus. mgr. Dow Chem. Iberica, 1978—82; mgr. hydrocarbon feedstock supplies Dow Europe, Horgen, Switzerland, 1982—86, bus. v.p. hydrocarbons, 1986—89, v.p. polyurethanes, 1989—91, mgr. thermosets bus. grp., 1991—92, mgr. automotive grp., 1992—95, global v.p. hydrocarbons and energy, 1995—2000; bus. grp. pres. hydrocarbons and energy Dow Chem. Co., 2000—, mem. Office of the Chief Exec., 2006—. Mem.: Assn. Petro-Chem. Producers Europe (pres. 1998, mem. steering com. 1997, pres. 1998), Internat. Isocyanate Inst. (pres.), European Isocyanate Producers Assn. (v.p.). Office: Dow Chem Co 47 Bldg Midland MI 48067

WALTNER, BEVERLY RULAND, artist; b. Kansas City, Mo.; d. Harry George and Ruth Anna (Laitner) Waltner, Jr. Student Columbia U., 1950-51, Yale U., 1951-53; B.A., U. Miami, Fla., 1955; M.F.A., No. Ill. U., 1968; postgrad. Kent State U., summer 1968. Tchr. art pub. schs. N.Y., Fla., Mo., Ill., 1960-65; instr. art Barry Coll., Miami Shores, Fla., 1969-70; artist-designer, Coral Gables, Fla., 1972—; One-woman shows: Art Gallery, No. Ill. U., DeKalb, 1968, Lyons Meml. Library, Point Lookout, Mo., 1968, Jewish Community Ctr. Gallery, Kansas City, Mo., 1969; juried exhbns. include: New Horizons in Painting, North Shore Art League, 1966, 68, Chautauqua Exhbn. Am. Art, 1968-73, 78, 10th Midwestern Bienniel, Joslyn Mus., 1968, Mid-Am. I, Nelson Gallery and St. Louis Mus., 1968, Nat. Soc. Painters in Casein and Acrylic, 1969, 70, 72, 73, Ark. Nat., Ark. State U., 1970, 35th Ann. Mid-Yr. Show, Butler Inst. Am. Art, 1970, Ann. Exhbn. Am. Painting, Soc. Four Arts, 1971, 74, IV and V Ann. Pan. Am. Exhbns., 1972, 73; represented in permanent collections: No. Ill. U., Arlen Realty Mgmt., Inc., Alexander Muss and Sons, Equitable Life Assurance Soc. U.S., Gen. Devel. Corp., Zuckerman-Vernon Corp., also numerous pvt. collections. Recipient 1st place award Ann. Chautauqua Exhbn. of Am. Art, 1968, Louis E. Selden award, 1972; top award New Horizons in Painting Show, 1966, honorable mention, 1968. Mem. Artists Equity Assn., Cultural Execs. Council Profl. Artists Guild (treas. 1977-78, v.p. 1978-79, editorial staff newsletter 1977—79), Chautauqua Art Assn., Coral Gables C. of C. (cultural affairs com. 1979). E-mail: bob98@bellsouth.net.

WALTON, ALAN GEORGE, venture capitalist; b. Birmingham, Eng., Apr. 3, 1936; s. Thomas George and Hilda (Glover) W.; m. Jasmin Yvonne Christensen, Sept. 1, 1958 (dec. Nov. 1970); children: Kimm A., Keir D.A.; m. Elenor Jean McElliott, Aug. 6, 1977; children: Kristin M., Sherri L. PhD, U. Nottingham, Eng., 1960, DSc, 1973; LLD (hon.), U. Nottingham, Eng., 2005. Rsch. assoc. Ind. U., Bloomington, 1960-62; asst. prof. chemistry Case Western Res. U., Cleve., 1962-66, assoc. prof., 1966-69, assoc. prof. macromolecular sci., 1969-71, prof., 1971-81, dir. lab. for biol. macromolecules, 1972-81, disting. adj. univ. prof., 2007—; pres., CEO Univ. Genetics Co., 1981-86, chmn., 1986-87; sr. ptnr. Oxford Biosci Ptnrs., Westport, Conn., 1987—; chmn. Oxford Biosci. Corp., 1992—. Vis. lectr. biol. chemistry Harvard Med. Sch., 1971; mem. Pres. Carter's Task Force on Sci. and Tech.; U.S. project officer Rudjer Boskovic Inst., Zagreb, Yugoslavia, 1967—75; bd. dirs. Acadia Pharma, Alexandria R.E.I.T. Applied Cell Tech.; chmn. Avalon Therapeutics; co-founder The Inst. for Genomic Rsch., 1994; co-founder, past bd. mem. Human Genome Scis. Inc.; emeritus dir. Research!America; founder, past chmn. Gene Logic, Inc., Exelixis, Inc. Author: Formation and Properties of Precipitates, 1967, Biopolymers, 1973, Structure and Properties of Amorphous Polymers, 1980, Polypeptide and Protein Structure, 1981, Recombinant DNA, 1981, Yearbook of Genetic Engineering and Biotechnology, 1983, 85, 88, (biography) Beneath This Gruff Exterior There Beats a Heart of Plastic, 2000, How to Make Money Investing in Biotechnology, 2005. Bd. dirs. Friends of Nottingham U. Recipient Israel State medal, 1972, Case Inst. Centennial Scholar medal, 1981. Mem. Nat. Venture Capital Assn., Sigma Xi (Research award 1973), Pi Kappa Alpha. Home: 11 Beachside Common Westport CT 06880 Office: Oxford Biosci Corp 315 Post Rd W Westport CT 06880-4739 Business E-Mail: awalton@oxbio.com.

WALTON, ALICE LOUISE, bank executive; b. Newport, Ark., Oct. 7, 1949; d. Sam and Helen (Robson) Walton BBA, Trinity U., 1971; D. of Bus. Adminstrn. (hon.), S.W. Bapt. U., 1988. Investment analyst First Commerce Corp., New Orleans, 1972-75; dir., v.p. investments Walton Enterprises, Bentonville, Ark., 1975—; retail & investment broker E.F. Hutton Co., New Orleans, 1975-79; vice chair, investment dir. Walton Bank Group, Bentonville, Ark., 1982-88; founder, former pres., chair, CEO Llama Co./Llama Asset Mgmt. Co., Fayetteville, Ark. Mem. dean's adv. coun. U. Ark. Coll. Bus. Adminstrn., Fayetteville, 1989-90. Bd. trustees Amon Carter Mus., Ft. Worth, Tex. Named Disting. Bus. Lectr. Ctrl. State U., Edmond, Okla., 1989, Arkansan of Yr., Ark. Easter Seals Soc., 1990; named one of Top 100 Women in Ark., Ark. Bus., 1995, Top 200 Collectors, ARTnews mag., 2006, Forbes 400, Forbes Mag., 1999-, World's Richest People, Forbes Mag., 2001-, Richest Americans, Forbes Mag., 2006-. Mem.: Northwest Ark. Coun. (first chairperson 1990). Avocation: horse racing. *

WALTON, ANDRE PIERRE, psychologist, consultant; s. Christiane Harvey; m. Robin Walton, Aug. 20, 2000. BA, Open U., Eng., 1992; PhD, U. Nev., Reno, 2005. CEO CT Audio Group of Cos.; exec. dir. Found. Relevant Edn. About the Law, Las Vegas, Nev., 2005—. Home Phone: 702-633-5270; Office Phone: 702-388-7527. Personal E-mail: walton_andre@hotmail.com.

WALTON, ANTHONY JOHN (TONY WALTON), set designer, illustrator, writer; b. Walton on Thames, Eng., Oct. 24, 1934; s. Lancelot Henry Frederick and Hilda Betty (Drew) W.; m. Julie Andrews, May 10, 1959 (div. 1968); 1 child, Emma Kate; m. Genevieve LeRoy, Sept. 12, 1991; 1 stepchild, Bridget. Student, Oxford Sch. Tech. Art and Commerce, 1949-52, Slade Sch. Fine Art, London, 1954-55. Designer settings, costumes for theater prodns., London, off-Broadway, 1957-60, Broadway, 1961—; Broadway prodns. include Pippin, 1972 (Tony award 1972-73, Drama Desk award 1972-73), Shelter, 1973 (Drama Desk award 1972-73), Chicago, 1975, Sophisticated Ladies, 1981, The Real Thing, 1984, Hurlyburly, 1984, I'm Not Rappaport, 1985, House of Blue Leaves, 1986 (Tony award 1985-86), Drama Desk award 1985-86), Front Page, 1986, Social Security, 1986 (Drama Desk award 1985-86), Anything Goes, 1987, Grand Hotel, 1989, Six Degrees of Separation, 1990, The Will Rogers Follies, 1991, Death and the Maiden, 1992, Conversations with My Father, 1992, Four Baboons Adoring the Sun, 1992, Guys and Dolls, 1992 (Tony award 1991-92, Drama Desk award 1991-92), Tommy Tune Tonight, 1992, She Loves Me, 1993, A Grand Night for Singing, 1993, Laughter on the 23rd Floor, 1993, Picnic, 1994, A Christmas Carol, N.Y.C., 1994, Company, 1995, Moonlight, 1995, A Fair Country, 1996, A Funny Thing Happened on the Way to the Forum, 1996, The Shawl, 1996, Make Someone Happy, Bay St. Theater Festival, 1997, Not Waving, 1997, Steel Pier, 1997, King David, 1997, 1776, 1997; The Cripple of Inishmaan, 1998; Noel & Gertie, 1998; House, 1998; Ashes to Ashes, 1999; Annie Get Your Gun, 1999; On Raftery's Hill, 2000 (Dublin and London); If Love Were All, 1999; Taller Than a Dwarf, 2000, Uncle Vanya, 2000, The Man Who Came To Dinner, 2000, Our Town, 2002, Blithe Spirit, 2002, I'm Not Rappaport, 2002,

Nobody don't Like Yogi, 2003, The Boy Friend, 2003, Princesses, 2004, Well, 2006; dir., designer The Importance of Being Earnest, 1996, Major Barbara, 1997, Where's Charley?, 2004, After the Ball, 2004; dir. Noel Coward in Two Keys Bay St. Theatre Festival, 1996; dir. Missing Footage, 1999; dir., co-writer, costume designer Oops! The Big Apple Circus Stage Show, 1999; ballets, principally San Francisco Ballet Co., Am. Ballet Theatre, Peter and the Wolf, Dance Theatre of Harlem "St. Louis Woman", 2003, Lincoln Ctr., N.Y.C.; films include Mary Poppins, A Funny Thing Happened on the Way to the Forum, Murder on the Orient Express, The Wiz, All That Jazz (Acad. award with Philip Rosenberg 1980), Prince of the City, Star 80, The Glass Menagerie, 1987, Regarding Henry, 1991, Our Town, 2003; operas in London, 1963-68, Spoleto, Italy, 1965, Santa Fe, 1975, San Francisco, 1992, Chgo., 1993; author: Adelie Penguin in Wonders, 1981; illustrator (books) Wonders, 1981, The Importance of Being Earnest, 1973, Lady Windemere's Fan, 1973, Popcorn, 1972, God Is a Good friend, 1969, Witches Holiday, 1971, Dumpy the Dump Truck, 2000, The Great American Musical, 2006, and 11 more books in the continuing series. Served with RAF, 1952-54. Recipient Emmy award Death of a Salesman, 1986; named to Theatre Hall of Fame, 1991; elected to Interior Design Hall of Fame, 1993. Mem.: Acad. Motion Picture Arts and Scis., Costume Designers Guild Calif., United Scenic Artists. Office: care Martino ICM 40 W 57th St New York NY 10019-4001

WALTON, CAROLE LORRAINE, clinical social worker; b. Harrison, Ark., Oct. 20, 1949; d. Leo Woodrow Walton and Arlette Alegra (Cohen) Armstrong. BA, Lambuth Coll., Jackson, Tenn., 1971; MA, U. Chgo., 1974. lic. clin. social worker. Social worker Community Mental Health, Flint, Mich., 1971-72, clin. social worker Westchester, Ill., 1974-76; dir. self-travel program Chgo. Assn. Retarded Citizens, 1973; coord. family svcs. Inner Harbors Psych. Hosp., Douglasville, Ga., 1976-83; sr. mental health clinician Northside Mental Health Ctr., Atlanta, 1983—; pvt. practice clin. social work Atlanta, 1997—2001. Mem.: NASW, Ga. Soc. for Clin. Work (pres. 1981—82, 1993—95, ethics co-chair 2003—05). Avocation: tennis. Office: Northside Mental Health Ctr 1140 Hammond Dr Ste J-1075 Atlanta GA 30328-7145 Office Phone: 770-842-3761.

WALTON, CEDAR, musician; b. Dallas, Jan. 17, 1934; Student, U. Denver. Albums include: Cedar!, 1967, Plays Cedar Walton, 1967, Spectrum, 1968, Electric Boogaloo Song, 1969, Soul Cycle, 1969, Breakthrough, 1972, Night at Boomer's Vol. 1, 1973, Night at Boomer's Vol. 2, Firm Roots, 1974, Eastern Rebellion, Vol. 1, 1975, Mobius, 1975, Pentagon, 1976, Eastern Rebellion, Vol. 2, 1977, First Set, 1977, Second Set, 1977, Third Set, 1977, Animation, 1978, Maestro, 1980, Piano Solos, 1981, Eastern Rebellion, Vol. 3, 1982, Among Friends, 1982, Cedar Walton-Ron Carter-Jack DeJohnette, 1983, Eastern Rebellion, Vol. 4, 1983, Cedar Walton, 1985, Bluesville Time, 1985, Trio, Vol. 1, 1985, Trio Vol. 2, 1985, Trio Vol. 3, 1985, Cedar's Blues, 1985, Plays, 1986, Love Is the Thing, 1986, Cedar Walton Plays, 1986, Blues for Myself, 1986, Off Minor, 1990, As Long As There's Music, 1990, Cedar, 1990, Heart and Soul, 1991, It's Timeless, 1991, Standard Album, 1991, My Funny Valentine, 1991, Easy Does It, 1992, Maybeck Recital Hall Series, Vol. 25, Manhattan Afternoon, 1992, Ironclad, 1995, Live at Yoshi's, 1995, Composer, 1996, Art Blakey Legacy, 1997, Lush Life/Plays the Music of Billy..., 1997, Soundscapes, 1997, Eastern Rebellion, 1997, Suites from Henry V, Battle of Britain, 1997, Live at Maybeck Recital Hall, 1997; other appearances include Lucky Thompson, 1956, Heart and Soul, 1958, This Is the Moment, 1958, Giant Steps, 1959, Blue Spring, 1959, Free for All, 1964, Mode for Joe, 1966, Tender Storm, 1966, Gentle Eyes, 1972, At the Kosei Nenkin, 1976, Soldier, 1979 Bag's Bag, 1979, Easy Living, Essence, 1986, Bebop, 1988, She's Gotta Have It, 1991, Mosaic, 1992, Small Hotel, 1993, Reverence, 1993, Simple Pleasure, 1993, Yazoo, 1994, Eastern Rebellion, 1995, Once More, 1995, Jazz Profile, 1997, Jazz Club: Drums, 1997, Summer Soft, numerous others; worked with Billy Higgins, Art Blakey, Ron Carter, Milt Jackson, Curtis Fuller, Clifford Jordan, Bob Berg, Freddie Hubbard, Lee Morgan, Bobby Hutcherson, Dexter Gordon, Kenny Dorham, John Coltrane, others. Recipient Nightlife award for Outstanding Jazz Soloist, 2007. *

WALTON, CHARLES MICHAEL, civil engineering educator; b. Hickory, NC, July 28, 1941; s. Charles O. and Virginia Ruth (Hart) W.; m. Betty Grey Hughes; children: Susan, Camila, Michael, Gantt. BS, Va. Mil. Inst., 1963; MCE, N.C. State U., 1969, PhD, 1971. Research asst. N.C. State U., Raleigh, 1967-71; transp. planning engr. N.C. Hwy. Commn., Raleigh, 1970-71; asst. prof. civil engring. U. Tex., Austin, 1971-76, assoc. prof., 1976-83, prof., 1983—, Bess Harris Jones Centennial prof. natural resource policy studies, 1987-91, Paul D. and Betty Robertson Meek Centennial prof. engring., 1991-93, Ernest H. Cockrell Centennial chair engring., 1993—, chmn. dept. civil engring., 1988-96. Transp. cons., 1970—; assoc. dir. Ctr. for Transp. Rsch. U. Tex., 1980-88; chmn., exec. com. Transp. Rsch. Bd., NRC, 1991, Disting. Lectr., 1994. Contbr. articles to profl. jours. Past chmn. Urban Transp. Commn., Austin. Recipient Disting. Engring. award N.C. State U., 1995, Joe J. King Profl. Engring. Achievement award U. Tex. at Austin, 1995-96, W.N. Carey Jr. Disting. Svc. award Transp. Rsch. Bd., 1998, George S. Bartlett award AASHTO, Transp. Rsch. Bd., ARTBA, 2000, Disting. Contbns. to Univ. Transp. Edn. and Rsch. award Coun. Univ. Transp. Ctrs., 2005; named to Am.'s Top 100 Pvt. Sector Transp. Design and Constrn. Profls. of 20th Century, 2004, Am. Rd. and Transp. Builders Assn., 2005. Fellow ASCE (Harland Bartholomew urban planning award 1987, Frank M. Masters transp. engring. award 1987, James Laurie prize 1992, Francis C. Turner lectr. 1999, Outstanding Projects and Leaders award, 2005), Inst. Transp. Engrs.; mem. NSPE, NAE, Intelligent Transp. Soc. Am. (tech. coord. coun., past chair bd. dirs., past chair tech. coord. coun.), Am. Rd. and Transp. Assn. (western v.p., past pres. edn. divsn., 1st vice chair, named to Am.'s Top 100 Pvt. Sector Transp. Design and Constrn. Profls. of 20th Century), Am. Rd. and Transp. Builders Assn. (chmn.), Soc. Automotive Engrs., Urban Land Inst., Inst. for Ops. Rsch. and Mgmt. Scis., Soc. Am. Mil. Engrs., Internat. Rd. Fedn. (bd. dirs.), Internat. Rd. Ednl. Found. (bd. dirs.), Austin C. of C. (Leadership Austin program). Democrat. Methodist. Home: 3404 River Rd Austin TX 78703-1031 Office: U Tex Dept Civil Engring Dept Civil Engring ECJ Hall Ste 6 3 Austin TX 78712 Home Phone: 512-477-9258; Office Phone: 512-471-1414. Business E-Mail: cmwalton@mail.utexas.edu.

WALTON, CHRISTY R., philanthropist; b. Feb. 1949; m. John Thomas Walton (dec. June 27, 2005); 1 child, Lukas. Mem. bi-nat. advisory bd. San Diego Natural History Mus., former mem. bd. trustees; co-founder Harborside Sch., San Diego, 1996. Named one of Forbes Richest Americans (with family), 2005—. *

WALTON, CONRAD GORDON, SR., retired architect; b. Houston, June 18, 1928; s. John Edward and Evelyn Lucile (Gordon) W.; m. Rilda Ellen Akin, Dec. 10, 1954; children: Conrad Gordon Jr., Evelyn Coleman, Roberta Agnes. BS (Walsh scholar), Rice U., 1951; postgrad., U. Houston, 1955. Registered architect, Tex., NCARB, ret. Past pres. DCW Architects, Inc. Mem.: AIA (emeritus). Home: 9014 Springview Ln Houston TX 77080-1755

WALTON, DAN GIBSON, lawyer; b. Houston, Mar. 26, 1950; s. Dan Edward and Lucy Frances (Gibson) W.; m. Martha Sandlin, June 24, 1972; children: Cole Gibson, Emily Wyatt. BA with honors, U. Va., 1972; JD with honors, U. Tex., 1975. Bar: Tex. 1975, U.S. Dist. Ct. (so. dist.) Tex. 1977, U.S. Ct. Appeals (D.C. cir.) 1975, U.S. Ct. Appeals (5th cir.) 1981, U.S. Supreme Ct. 2001; bd. cert. in civil trial law. Law clk. to hon. Malcolm R. Wilkey D.C. Ct. Appeals (D.C. cir.), 1975-76; assoc. Vinson & Elkins LLP, Houston, 1976-82, ptnr., 1982—. Bd. dirs., sec. The Meth. Hosp., Houston, 1993—2003; mem. admission commn. US Dist. Cts. (so. dist.) Tex.; chair US Magistrate Judge Merit Selection Com. Bd. dirs. Tex. Equal Access to Justice Found., 2000-06, South Tex. Coll. Law, Houston, 1994—, Briarwood Sch./Brookwood Cmty., Houston, 1991—, Alley Theatre, 2003—; trustee St. John's Sch., Houston, 1997-2005, Good Samaritan Found., 1998—2006, Cullen Trust for Health Care, 2002—; chancellor Tex. Ann. Conf., United Meth. Ch., 1996—. Fellow Am. Bar Found.; mrm. Tex. Bar Found., Houston Bar Found. (chair 1994), Houston Bar Assn. (pres. 1998-99), Garland Walker Am. Inn of Ct. (master), Am. Bd. Trial Advocates (assoc.), Internat. Soc. Barristers, Internat. Assn. Def. Counsel, Tex. Assn. Def. Counsel, State Bar Tex. (bd. dirs, 1999-2002, pres. 2007—). Avocations: golf, skiing. Office: Vinson & Elkins LLP 2300 First City Tower 1001 Fannin St Ste 3201 Houston TX 77002-6706 Office Phone: 713-758-2026.

WALTON, G. CLIFFORD, physician; b. Richmond, Va., Jan. 5, 1968; s. Eugene Marion and Mary Ann (McNabb) W.; m. Tami Marie Daniel, June 26, 1998. BS summa cum laude, Hampden-Sydney Coll., 1990; MD, Med. Coll. Va., 1994. Intern Med. Coll. Va., Richmond, 1994-95; resident Blackstone (Va.) Family Practice, 1995-97; pvt. practice, Kenbridge, Va., 1997-99, Richmond, 1996—. Med. examiner Va. Dept. Health, Powhatan, 1996—; mem. housestaff coun. Med. Coll. Va., 1995-97. Sci. fair judge Southside Va. H.S., Farmville, 1988-97. Mem. AMA, Am. Acad. Family Physicians, Med. Soc. Va., Phi Beta Kappa, Sigma Xi, Omicron Delta Kappa. Avocations: baseball card collecting, gardening, photography. Home: 1640 Jeter Rd Powhatan VA 23139-6907 Office: Patient First 12101 South Chalkley Rd Chester VA 23831 Office Phone: 804-796-3636.

WALTON, GERALD WAYNE, retired university official; b. Union, Miss., Sept. 11, 1934; s. Willie Jay and Ruby Elizabeth (Williamson) W.; m. Juliet Katherine Hart, Aug. 26, 1960; children: Katherine Hart, Dorothy Elizabeth, Margaret Stevens. AA, East Central Jr. Coll., 1954; BS, U. So. Miss., 1956; MA, U. Miss., 1959, PhD, 1967. Tchr. asst. U. Miss., 1956-59, instr. English, 1959-62, asst. prof., 1962-67, assoc. prof., 1967-70, prof., 1970-99, assoc. dean Coll. Liberal Arts, 1970-76, dean, 1976-82, assoc. vice chancellor for acad. affairs, 1982-94, interim vice chancellor for acad. affairs, 1994-96, provost, 1996-99. Contbr. articles to profl. jours. Vice-pres. Oxford Human Rels. Coun., 1968; mem. adminstrv. bd. Oxford U. Meth. Ch., chmn. bd. trustees, 1971-72, lay leader, 1999-2001; bd. dirs. Yoknapatawpha Arts Coun., 1980-81; sec.-treas. So. Lit. Festival, 1965; sec. U. Miss. Friends of Libr.; v.p. U. Miss. Friends Mus. bd. trustees Miss heritage Trust. Tri-Univ. fellow in linguistics U. Nebr., 1969-70. Mem. MLA, Am. Dialect Soc., Miss. Folklore Soc., Friends of Arts in Miss., Miss. Assn. English Tchrs. (sec. 1968), Miss. Inst. Arts and Letters (sec. 1979-80), Nat. Coun. Tchrs. English, William Faulkner Soc., Miss. Hist. Soc., Oxford-Lafayette County Heritage Soc., So. Studies Adv. Coun., Rotary (sec.), Golden Key, Phi Kappa Phi, Sigma Tau Delta, Omicron Delta Kappa. Home: 106 Ole Miss Dr Oxford MS 38655-2615 Office Phone: 662-915-1598. E-mail: gww@olemiss.edu.

WALTON, JAMES MELLON, investment company executive; b. Pitts., Dec. 18, 1930; m. Ellen Carroll; 4 children. BA, Yale U.; MBA, Harvard U. With Gulf Oil Corp., Phila., Houston, Pitts., Tokyo, Rome, 1958-67; pres. Carnegie Inst., Pitts., 1968-84, Carnegie Mus. Natural History and Mus. of Art, Pitts., 1968-84, Carnegie Library, Pitts., 1968-84; life trustee, pres. emeritus Carnegie Inst. and Carnegie Library, Pitts. Bd. dirs. New Ireland Fund, Inc. Mem. sponsoring com. Penn's Southwest Assn.; trustee emeritus Carnegie-Mellon U.; treas. Carnegie Hero Fund Commn.; dir. World Affairs Coun. of Pitts., One Hundred Friends of Pitts. Art; trustee Sarah Scaife Found. Inc., Extra Mile Found.; chmn. Vira I. Heinz Endowment; mem. Cultural Dist. Devel. Com. Lt. U.S. Army, 1954-56. Office: 525 William Penn Way Ste 3902 Pittsburgh PA 15219-1710 E-mail: jmwa@earthlink.net.

WALTON, JIM, news network executive; BA in Radio, TV and Film, U. Md., 1981. Video journalist CNN, Atlanta, 1981-83; tape editor CNN Sports, Atlanta, 1983-85, exec. prodr., 1985-97; pres. CNN/SI, Atlanta, 1997—2000, CNN Networks/USA, Atlanta, 2000; pres. & COO CNN News Group, Atlanta, chmn. & CEO, 2003—. Olympic prodr. 1984 L.A. Games, remote prodr., sr. prodr. Office: CNN 1 CNN Ctr NW Atlanta GA 30303-2762

WALTON, JIM CARR, bank executive; b. 1948; s. Sam Moore and Helen Walton; m. Lynne Walton; 4 children. Grad., U. Ark. Pres., chmn., CEO Arvest Bank, Bentonville, Ark. At-large exec. com. mem. Ark. Coun. Econ. Edn.; mem. nat. bd. advisors Children's Scholarship Fund; mem. dean's exec. adv. bd. Sam M. Walton Coll. Bus. Named one of World's Richest People, Forbes, 2001—, Forbes Richest Americans, 2006—. Office: 125 W Central Ste 218 Bentonville AR 72712 *

WALTON, JON DAVID, lawyer; b. Clairton, Pa., Sept. 18, 1942; s. Thomas Edward and Matilda Lucy (Sunday) W.; m. Carol Jeanne Rowland, Sept. 15, 1964; children: David Edward, Diane Elizabeth. BS, Purdue U., 1964; JD, Valparaiso U., 1969. Bar: Pa. 1969. Atty. U.S. Steel Corp. (now USX Corp.), Pitts., 1969-73; asst. gen. counsel Harbison-Walker Refractories, Pitts., 1973-75, gen. counsel, 1975-81, v.p., gen. counsel, 1981-83; regional gen. counsel Dresser Industries, Inc., Pitts., 1983-86; gen. counsel, sec. Allegheny Ludlum Corp., Pitts., 1986-90, v.p., gen. counsel, sec., 1990-96, Allegheny Techs. Inc., Pitts., sr. v.p., gen. counsel, sec., sr. v.p., chief legal and admin. officer, 2001—03, exec. v.p. human resources, chief legal and compliance officer, gen. counsel, corp. sec., 2003—. Trustee Westminster Coll., 1997—; pres., bd. dirs. Music for Mt. Lebanon, 1996-2002, Pitts. Youth Golf Found., 1991-2001, United Way of Allegheny County, 2002-, NAM, 2002-, Pitts. Symphony Orchestra, 2003-; clk. of session Southminster Presbyn. Ch., 1998-2001, 04-. Mem. ABA, Pa. Bar Assn., Allegheny County Bar Assn., Am. Soc. Corp. Secs. (former pres. regional group), Am. Corp. Counsel Assn., Am. Arbitration Assn. (panel arbitrators), Duquesne Club, Valley Brook Country Club, Rolling Rock Club. Home: 137 Hoodridge Dr Pittsburgh PA 15228-1803 Office: Allegheny Technologies Inc 1000 Six PPG Pl Pittsburgh PA 15222-5479 Office Phone: 412-394-2836. Business E-Mail: jwalton@alleghenytechnologies.com. *

WALTON, JOSEPH PAUL, neuroscientist, audiologist; b. Kort Knox, Ky., Sept. 26, 1954; m. Debbie Walton; children: Shannon, Caitlyn. BA in Hearing Sci., U. Fla., Gainesville, 1976, MA in Audiology, 1982, PhD, 1984. Cert. audiologist Am. Speech, Hearing and Lang. Assn. (assoc.), 1984. Coll. prof. U. Rochester, NY, 1984—. V.p. Fairport Soccer Club, NY, 2000—04, Rochester Dist. Youth Soccer League, 2000—. Clin. fellow, Vets. Adminstrn., 1982—83. Mem.: Acoustical Soc. Am. (assoc.), Assn. Rsch. Otolaryngology (assoc.), Sigma Xi (assoc.). Achievements include patents for noise reduction hearing aid circuit. Office: Univ Rochester 601 Elmwood Ave Rochester NY 14642

WALTON, MORGAN LAUCK, III, lawyer; b. Woodstock, Va., July 30, 1932; s. Morgan Lauck Jr. and Frances (Allen) W.; m. Jeannette Freeman Minor, Mar. 4, 1961; children: Morgan Lauck IV, Charles Lancelot Minor, Christopher Allen, Laura Cathlyn Hirschfeld. BA, Randolph-Macon Coll., 1953; LLB, U. Va., 1959. Bar: Va. 1959, N.Y. 1959, U.S. Ct. Appeals (2d cir.) 1959, U.S. Dist. Ct. (ea. and so. dists.) N.Y. 1960, U.S. Dist. Ct. (we. dist.) Va. 1988. Assoc. Donovan Leisure Newton & Irvine, NYC, 1959-68, ptnr., 1968-84; counsel FDIC, Washington, 1989-90, asst. gen. counsel, 1990-97; dir. Advice Co., Sausalito, Calif., 2005—; ret. Contbr. articles to profl. jours. Trustee Randolph-Macon Acad., Front Royal, Va., 1987-92, trustee emeritus, 2002—; trustee Unitarian Ch. Shenandoah Valley, Stephens City, Va., 1987-2007; mem. coun. Law Sch. U. Va., 1989-92; treas. Shenandoah Valley Music Festival, Woodstock, 1986-87; chmn. bd. All Souls Ch., NYC, 1974-76; active Shenandoah County Dem. Com., 1999—; assoc.dir. Lord Fairfax Soil and Water Dist., 2004-05, dir., 2005-06. With US Army, 1953-56. Mem. Univ. Club (N.Y.C.), Collectors Club, Order of Coif, Phi Beta Kappa. Democrat. Home and Office: 908 Kern Springs Rd Woodstock VA 22664-3216 Personal E-mail: jwalton@shentel.net.

WALTON, ROBERT LEE, plastic surgeon; b. Lawrence, Kans., May 30, 1946; s. Robert L. and Thelma B. (Morgan) W.; m. Elisabeth K. Beahm, Oct. 7, 2000; children: Marc, Morgan, Lindsey. BA, U. Kans., 1968; MD, U. Kans., Kansas City, 1972. Diplomate Am. Bd. Surgery, Am. Bd. Plastic Surgery. Resident in surgery Johns Hopkins Hosp., Balt., 1972-74, Yale-New Haven (Conn.) Hosp., 1974-78; chief of plastic surgery San Francisco Gen. Hosp., 1979-83; prof. and chmn. dept. plastic surgery U. Mass. Med. Ctr., Worcester, 1983-94; prof., chmn dept. plastic surgery U. Chgo., 1994—2004, prof. dept. plastic surgery, 2004—. Contbr. articles to profl. jours. Founder Projecto Mira Found. for Handicapped Children, Santurce, P.R., 1990. Mem. ACS, Am. Assn. Plastic Surgeons, Am. Soc. Plastic and Reconstructive Surgery, Am. Soc. Reconstructive Microsurgery, Alpha Omega Alpha. Office: Plastic Surgery Chgo 60 East Delaware Pl Ste 1430 Chicago IL 60611 Home Phone: 312-944-0972; Office Phone: 312-337-7795. Personal E-mail: notlaw72@sbcglobal.net. Business E-Mail: drrwalton@sbcglobal.net. *

WALTON, (SAMUEL) ROB(SON), discount department store chain executive; b. Tulsa, 1944; s. Sam Moore and Helen Walton; m. Carolyn Walton (div.); 3 children. Student, Coll. of Wooster; BA in Acctg., U. of Arkansas, 1966; JD, Columbia U., 1969. Formerly with Conner, Winters, Ballaine, Barry & McGowen; with Wal-Mart Stores Inc., Bentonville, Ark., 1969—, sr. v.p., 1978-82, also bd. dirs., vice chmn. bd., 1982-92, chmn., 1992—. Trustee Wooster Coll. Named one of World's Richest People, Forbes Mag., 2005, Forbes Richest Americans, 2006—. Avocations: bicycling, pheasant hunting. Office: Wal-Mart Stores Inc 702 SW 8th St Bentonville AR 72716-6299 *

WALTON, RODNEY EARL, lawyer; b. Corvallis, Oreg., Apr. 28, 1947; s. Ray Daniel Jr. and Carolyn Jane (Smith) W. BA, Coll. Wooster, Ohio, 1969; JD, Cornell U., Ithaca, NY, 1976; MA in History, Fla. Internat. U., Miami, 2001. Bar: Fla. 1976, US Dist. Ct. (so. dist.) Fla. 1976, US Supreme Ct. 1980, US Ct. Appeals (11th cir.) 1981. Assoc. to jr. ptnr. Smathers & Thompson, Miami, Fla., 1976-87; ptnr. Kelley, Drye and Warren, Miami, 1987-93; atty. Heinrich Gordon Hargrove Weihe & James, P.A., Ft. Lauderdale, 1994-97. Adj. instr. US mil. history Fla. Internat. U., 2001, adj. instr. modern U.S. history, 2003—04, 2006, adj. instr. contemporary US history, 07, adj. instr. history of the US Supreme Ct., 07. Sec. bd. dirs. Kings Creek Condominium Assn., Miami, 1984-89, treas., 1984, pres., 1990-91. 1st lt. U.S. Army, 1969-73, Vietnam. Decorated Bronze Star. Mem. ABA, Fla. Bar Assn. Republican. Methodist. Avocations: travel, reading, tennis, history. Home: 7985 SW 86th St Apt 430 Miami FL 33143-7014 Personal E-mail: rodneyearlwalton@aol.com.

WALTON, SHIRLEY DAWN, retired medical technician; b. Jamestown, NY, Dec. 12, 1935; d. Kenneth Everett and Wilma Alene Lewis; m. Okley Homa Walton, May 3, 1963 (dec.); 1 child, William W. Cert. respiratory care practioner Fla., 1993. Trainee Women's Christian Hosp., Jamestown, 1956—61; nurse's aid St. Joseph's Hosp., Tampa, Fla., 1963—64, cardiology technician, 1964—74; cardiology tech. U. Hosp., Tampa, 1975—82, respiratory therapist, 1982—88; cardiology tech. East Pasco Med. Ctr., Zephyrhills, Fla., 1988—98; ret., 1998. Methodist. Home: 6801 Woodsman Dr Zephyrhills FL 33544 Personal E-mail: wwaltonz@aol.com.

WALTON, STANLEY ANTHONY, III, lawyer; b. Chgo., Dec. 10, 1939; s. Stanley Anthony and Emily Ann (Pouzar) W.; m. Karen Kayser, Aug. 10, 1963; children: Katherine, Anne, Alex. BA, Washington and Lee U., 1962, LLB, 1965. Bar: Ill. 1965, U.S. Dist. Ct. (no. dist.) Ill. 1966, U.S. Ct. Appeals (7th cir.) 1966. Ptnr. Winston & Strawn, Chgo., 1965-89, Sayfarth Shaw Fairweather, Chgo., 1989-96. Trustee Village of Hinsdale (Ill.), 1985-89; bd. dirs. Washington and Lee Law Sch., Lexington, Va., 1975-78, bd. dirs. univ. alumni, 1983-87, pres., 1986-87; bd. dirs. UNICEF, Chgo., 1983; pres. Hinsdale Hist. Soc., 1979-81, 2001—, St. Isaac Jogues PTA, 1980; sec. Hinsdale Cmty. Svc., 2000—; bd. dirs. Hinsdale Ctrl. Found., 2000—. Mem. Ill. State Bar Assn., Phi Alpha Delta, Hinsdale Golf Club. Republican. Roman Catholic. Home and Office: 6679 Snug Harbor Dr Willowbrook IL 60527 Office Phone: 630-887-9216.

WALTRIP, DARRELL LEE, race car driver; b. Owensboro, Ky., Feb. 5, 1947; s. Leroy and Margaret Jean (Evans) Waltrip; m. Stephanie Hamilton Rader, Aug. 15, 1969; children: Jessica Leigh, Sarah. Student, Ky. Wesleyan Coll. Driver for Junior Johnson & Assocs., Rick Hendrick Motor Sports; owner Darrell Waltrip Honda Volvo, 1994—. Author (with Jade Gurss): DW: A Lifetime Going Around in Circles, 2004; (with Jay Carty) Darrell Waltrip: One on One: The Faith That Took Him to the Finish Line, 2004; actor(voice): (films) Cars, 2006, Talladega Nights: The Ballad of Ricky Bobby, 2006. Named Driver of Yr., Nat. Motorsports Press Assn., 1977, Olsonite Driver of Yr., 1979, winner, Winston Cup, 1982, Nat. Assn. Stock Car Auto Racing Championship, 1985, Winston Cup Championship, 1981, 1982, 1985, Coca Cola 600, 1985, 1988, 1989, Wrangler 500, 1985, Bisch 500, 1986, Budweiser 400, 1986, Holly Farms 400, 1986, Goody's 500, 1987, 1988, 1989, Motorcraft 500, 1989, Daytona 500, 1989, Champion Spark Plug 500, 1991. Mem.: Nat. Assn. Stock Car Auto Racing. Republican. Presbyterian. Achievements include being the top motor sport money winner worldwide with more than 7.5 million dollars.

WALTRIP, MICHAEL CURTIS, professional race car driver; b. Owensboro, Ky., Apr. 30, 1963; m. Elizabeth Buffy Waltrip; children: Caitlin Marie, Margaret Carol. Stock car racer, 1981—. Owner, pres. Michael Waltrip Racing, Inc. Appearances: (several televesion and radio commercials). Recipient Most Popular Driver awards, NASCAR Dash Series, 1983, 1984, Driver of the Race, Pocono 500, 2006. Achievements include Mini-Modified divsn. track championship Ky. Motor Speedway, 1981; NASCAR Touring Goody's Dash Series, 1982-84, including series title 1983; NASCAR Winston Cup Series, 1985—, including 2d-place in Rookie of Yr. race, 1986; 2d-place 1988 Miller 500 at Pocono; 1st place, Daytona 500, 2001, 2003, Pepsi 400, 2002; NASCAR Busch Series Grand Nat. divsn. career includes 11 victories. Avocations: golf, tennis. Office: 222 Raceway Dr Mooresville NC 28117-6510 *

WALTRIP, ROBERT L., environmentalist, funeral company executive; b. Austin, Tex., 1931; BBA in Mgmt., U. Houston, 1954. With Heights Funeral Home, 1954—62; founder, chmn. bd. Service Corp. Internat., Houston, 1962—, CEO, 1962—2005; founder, chmn. bd. dirs. Waltrip Enterprises Inc., Houston, 1982—; with Tanknology Corp. Internat., Houston, 1988—, Tanknology Environ. Inc., Houston, 1989—. Office: Service Corp International 1929 Allen Pky Houston TX 77019-2507 also: Tanknology Environ Inc 5225 Hollister St Houston TX 77040-6205

WALTUCK, DAVID, chef, restaurant owner; m. Karen Waltuck. Student, CCNY, Culinary Inst. Am. Lunch chef La Petite Ferme, NYC; chef, co-owner (SoHo, Grand St) Chanterelle, NYC, 1979—89, chef, co-owner (TriBeCa, Harrison St.), 1989—. Author: Staff Meals from Chanterelle, 2000. Named Best Chef: NYC, James Beard Found., 2007; recipient Best Restaurant award for Chanterelle, 2004. Office: Chanterelle 2 Harrison St New York NY 10013-2810 *

WALTZ, JOSEPH MCKENDREE, neurosurgeon, educator; b. Detroit, July 23, 1931; s. Ralph McKinley and Bertha (Seelye) W.; m. Janet Maureen Journey, June 26, 1954; children: Jeffrey McKinley, Mary Elaine, David Seelye, Stephen McKendree; m. Marilyn Liska, June 5, 1967; 1 child, Tristana McKendree. Student, U. Mich., 1950; BS, U. Oreg., 1954, MD, 1956. Diplomate Am. Bd. Neurol. Surgery. Surg. intern U. Mich. Hosp., 1956-57, gen. surg. resident, 1957-58, clin. instr. neurosurgery, 1960-63; neurosurg. assoc. St. Barnabas Hosp., NYC, 1963—; assoc. dir. Inst. Neurosci., 1974—, dir. dept. neurol. surgery, 1977—2002; attending Neurosci. Inst. Our Lady of Mercy, 1998—. Assoc. cons. in neurosurgery Englewood (N.J.) Hosp., 1964—; assoc. prof. neurosurgery NYU Med. Str., 1974—; asst. prof. dept. surgery (neurosurgery) N.Y. Coll. Osteo. Medicine, 1989—; mem. alumni bd. U. Mich. Med. Ctr., 1995; dir. Med. Ct. Graphics. Author: (chpt.) Cryogenic Surgery, Neurology, 1982, Advances in Neurology, 1983, Textbook of Stereotactic and Functional Neurosurgery, 1997; contbr. articles to profl. jours. Mem. sci. adv. bd. Dystonia Med. Research Found., 1980—; trustee St. Barnabas Hosp., 1980—. Served to capt. M.C. AUS, 1958-60. Recipient Bronze award Am. Congress Rehab. Medicine, 1967, World Cmty. Svc. award Rotary, Disting. Trustee award United Hosp. Fund, 1995. Mem. AMA, Am. Paralysis Assn., World Soc. Stereotactic and Functional Neurosurgery, Congress Neurol. Surgeons, Math. Assn. Am., Internat. Neural Network Soc., Soc. for Cryobiology, N.Y. State Med. Soc., Bronx County Med. Soc., N.Y. State Neurosurg Soc., Nat. Ski Patrol, Phi Beta Pi. Achievements include spl. rsch. on neurophysiology and treatment of epilepsy, basal ganglia disorders, abnormal movement disorders, cerebral palsy, also neurosurg. application stereotactic thalamic surgery and spinal cord stimulation. Home: Four B Island South 720 Milton Rd Rye NY 10580-3258 Office: 150 Purchase St Ste 7 Rye NY 10580 Home Phone: 914-967-8958; Office Phone: 914-967-6577. Personal E-mail: joemwaltz@aol.com.

WALTZ, KATHLEEN M., publishing executive; b. Mar. 6, 1954; m. Bill Raffel, 1990; stepchildren: Jamie, Jenny. BA, DePaul U., 1985; postgrad., Northwestern U. Telemarketer Chgo. Tribune, 1973, mgr. recruitment advt., 1987, dir. customer satisfaction, 1989—90, dir. classified advt., 1990—95, v.p./dir. of developing bus., 1995—97; v.p., gen. mgr. Sun-Sentinel Co., Fla., 1997—98; CEO, pres., pub. Daily Press, Newport News, Va., 1998—2000; pub. Orlando Sentinel, 2000—; CEO & pres. Orlando Sentinel Comm., 2000—. Bd. dirs. United Way of Va. Peninsula, Peninsula Allice for Econ. Devel. WHRO Found. and Greater Peninsula Now; bd. dirs., exec. com. Hampton Roads Partnership; ABC/NAA liaison com., sr. exec. resource corps. Coll. of William and Mary. Mem. So. Newspapers Pub. Assn. (diversity com.). Avocations: travel, golf, gardening. Office: Orlando Sentinel 636 N Orange Ave Orlando FL 32801 Office Phone: 407-420-5070. E-mail: kwaltz@orlandosentinel.com.

WALTZ, SUSAN, political scientist, educator; Former chmn. Amnesty Internat., London, England, 1993-98; prof. internat. pub. policy Gerald Ford Sch. Pub. Policy U. Mich., Ann Arbor, 2001—. Bd. dirs. Am. Friends Svc. Com., 2000—. Office: Ford Sch Public Policy Michigan Univ 3227 Weill Hall 735 S State St Ann Arbor MI 48109 Office Phone: 734-615-8683. Business E-Mail: swaltz@umich.edu.

WALTZER, GARRETT J., lawyer; b. Nashville, 1961; BA, Colorado College, 1983; JD, University of California, Los Angeles School of Law, 1987. Bar: Calif. 1987. Law clerk to the Hon. Ferdinand F. Fernandez, U.S. Dist. Ct. for Central Dist. of Calif., 1987—88; ptnr. Skadden, Arps, Slate, Meagher & Flom LLP. Office: Skadden 525 University Avenue Suite 1100 Palo Alto CA 94301

WALZ, ANGELA, retired secondary school educator; b. Salt Lake City; d. Albert Richard and Emma (Boehnke) Riedel; m. Marvin Gideon Walz, Nov. 21, 1967; children: Gregory Marvin, Richard David. BS, U. Utah, Salt Lake City, 1959; student, Brigham Young U., Provo, Utah, 1963—81, Utah State U., Logan, 1985, Boston U., 1987—92, U. San Diego, 1994—97, U. Md., Ramstein, Germany, U. Minn., Hanan, Germany. Sec. MIA music com. LDS Ch., 1955—64; elem. tchr. SLC, 1959—60; tchr. Eval. Utah Dep. Pub. Instr., 1960—61, Kelly Girl Agy., 1961—64; adminstrv. asst. music dept. Brigham Young. U., 1963, U. Utah Ednl. Rsch., 1966; sec. Am. Embassy, Germany, 1964—65; bus. tchr. Granite H.S., Salt Lake City, 1961—64, Dept. Def. Overseas Sch., Sasebo, Japan, 1966—67, Bitburg H.S., 1967—84, Baumholder H.S., Germany, 1985—94; bus. and work experience tchr. Hanau H.S., Germany, 1994—2001. Mem. curriculum develop. com. Dept. Def. Dependent Sch., Wiesbaden, Germany, 1995—2000, Washington, 1995—2000; prin. adv. bd. Baumholder H.S., 1990—91; admin. asst. music programs Ch. of Jesus Christ Latter Day Saints, Salt Lake City, 1956—64. Soloist: various musical prodns. Mem. cmty. choral groups Rheinlandpfalz Internat. Choir, Germany, 1961—90; ch. pianist and organist Latter Day Saints Ch., 1953—2006. Recipient Outstanding Tchr. award, Bitburg Sch. Dist., 1971, Baumholder Sch. Dist., 1991, Hanau Sch. Dist., 1995, Outstanding FBLA adv., Future Bus. Leaders of Am., 1990. Republican. Ch. Jesus Christ. Avocations: music, swimming, skiing, travel, community involvement. Home: 477 E Peak Ridge Way Draper UT 84020

WALZ, DEBORAH SUE, application developer, musician; b. Washington, June 21, 1958; d. Ernest Ferdinand Walz and Barbara Jean Brugliera; m. Daniel Peter Bourquard, Apr. 7, 1984 (div. May 21, 1998); 1 child, Noelle Laurin Bourquard. BS in Math., Bucknell U., Lewisburg, Pa., 1980. From programmer I to programmer II Data Gen. Corp., Westboro, Mass., 1980—82; programmer, analyst CSPI, Billerica, Mass., 1982—84; from software engr. II to prin. software engr. Digital Equipment Corp., Nashua, NH, 1984—98; prin. software engr. Compaq Computer Corp., Nashua, 1998—2000, Progress Software Corp., Nashua, 2000—. Mem., lead trumpet Hollis Town Band, NH, 1986—2007, v.p., 1989—90, sec., 1994—95; mem. Actorsingers, Nashua, NH, 1999—2007, dir., 2001—03. Recipient Outstanding Devel. award, Data Gen. Corp., 1981, Outstanding Devel. Contbn., Digital Equipment Corp., 1996. Mem.: Mensa, Buglers Across Am. Avocations: trumpet, reading. Home: 9 Kodiak Rd Brookline NH 03033 Office: Progress Software Corp One Indian Head Plz Nashua NH 03060 Home Phone: 603-673-9124; Office Phone: 603-578-6874. Office Fax: 603-595-9318. Personal E-mail: debwalz@hotmail.com.

WALZ, EDWARD GEORGE, protective services official; s. George Francis and Margaret Ellen Walz; m. Christine Ann Dallago, Apr. 23, 1992; life ptnr. Linda Periera; children: Kelly Ann, Edward George Jr., Christopher Joseph. Diploma, Big Bend CC, Washington, 1984. Police officer NYC Police Dept., 1988—2005, Dept Army Police, Fort Hamilton, NY, 2005—. Staff sgt. US Army, 1983—99. Decorated Army Achievment Medal US Army, SW Asian Svc. medal, Army Commedation Medal; recipient Cert. Achievment, Soc. Prevention Cruelty to Children, 2003, Nat. Law Enforcement Mus., 2006, Meritorious award, NYC Police Dept., 1986—2005, Excellant Police Duty award, 1988—2005, Silver Star For Bravery, Am. Fedn. Police, 1992, Cert. Achievment, Assn. US Army, 1986, Cert. Appreciation, Nat. World War II Mus., 2006, Cert. Commendation, Nat. Mus. US Army, 2007. Mem.: US Army Hist. Soc., NYC Patrolman Benevolent Assoc., Am. Legion, VFW (life; sr. vice comdr. 2005—06). Home Phone: 631-839-8400; Office Phone: 718-630-4456.

WALZ, JEFF (JEFFREY J. WALZ), women's college basketball coach; b. 1971; s. Roger and Janine Walz; m. Kim Kumfer, May 17, 2003; children: Kaeley Thöney, Jacob Joseph. BS in Secondary Edn. and Bus., No. Ky. U., 1995; MEd, Western Ky. U. Adminstrv. asst. Western Ky. U., asst. coach, 1995—97, U. Nebr., 1997—2001, U. Minn., 2001—02, U. Md., 2002—06, assoc. head coach, 2006—07; head coach U. Louisville, 2007—. Office: U Louisville Womens Basketball Athletic Dept 2100 S Floyd St Louisville KY 40292

WALZ, LEO R., conductor; b. Denver, Colo., Sept. 10, 1960; s. Edward and Edna Walz. MusM, Colo. State U., 1985; MusD, U. Miami, 1992. Conductor, music dir. The Alhambra Orch., Miami, Fla., 1990—2000; tchr. Miami-Dade Pub. Sch., Miami, Fla., 1997—; conductor So. Fla. Youth Symphony, Miami, Fla., 2000—. Guest conductor, Romania, Russia, Bulgaria, Ukraine. Mem.: Conductors Guild, Am. Symphony Orch. League. Achievements include founder, The Alhambra Orch. Miami Fla. 1990. Home: 6261 Sunset Dr G8 Miami FL 33143

WALZ, THOMAS, biology professor; b. Basel, Switzerland, Nov. 4, 1967; s. Dieter and Dorothea Walz. PhD, U. Basel, Switzerland, 1996. David Phillips rsch. fellow U. Sheffield, England, 1998—99; asst. prof. Harvard Med. Sch., Boston, 1999—2004, assoc. prof., 2004—06; adj. assoc. prof. U. Tex. Med. Br., Galveston, 2004—06, prof., 2007—. Dir. Harvard Med. Sch., 2002—. Office: Harvard Med Sch 240 Longwood Ave Boston MA 02115 Office Phone: 617-432-4090.

WALZ, TIM (TIMOTHY J. WALZ), congressman, social science educator; b. West Point, Nebr., Apr. 6, 1964; m. Gwen Whipple, 1994; children: Hope, Gus. BS in Social Sci. Edn., Chadron State Coll., Nebr., 1989; MS in Edn. Leadership, St. Mary's U., Winona, Minn., 2001. High sch. tchr. People's Rep. China, 1989—90; tchr. Alliance Pub. Schools, 1991—96, Mankato West High Sch., Mankato, Minn., 1996—2006; mem. US Congress from 1st dist. Minn., 2007—, mem. agrl. com., vets affairs com., transp. & infrastructure com. Advanced to Sgt. Major US Army Nat. Guard, 1981—2005, served in Operation Enduring Freedom, 2005. Named Neb. Citizen Soldier of Yr., 1989, Outstanding Young Nebraskan, Nebr. Junior C. of C., 1993, Mankato Tchr. of Yr., 2003, Minn. Tchr. of Excellence, 2003; recipient Minn. Ethics in Edn. award, 2002. Democrat. Lutheran. Office: 1529 Longworth House Office Bldg Washington DC 20515 also: 1134 7th St NW Rochester MN 55901 *

WALZER, JAMES HARVEY, lawyer, author; b. Neptune, NJ, Jan. 24, 1949; s. Elwood John and Mary Elizabeth (Harvey) W.; m. Gloria Jean Demkowski, May 29, 1971; children: Sara, Emily, Amanda, Adam. BA, Bowdoin Coll., 1972; JD, Cleve. State U., 1975. Bar: N.J. 1975, U.S. Dist. Ct. N.J. 1975. Pvt. practice, Newark, 1975-78, Livingston, N.J., 1978-81, Boonton, N.J., 1981—. Legal forms editor All-State Legal, a div. of All-State Internat., Inc., Cranford, NJ, 1978—96. Author: Employment, Agency, Service Agreements, 1986, Motor Vehicle Law and Practice-Forms, 1988, 2000, Civil Practice Forms, 5 vols., 4th edit., 1990, 8 vols., 6th edit., 2006, Agents & Independent Contractors, 2003; editor, author: Legal Forms, 1995-96. Mem. Manville Bd. Adjustment, NJ, 1976; bd. dirs. Somerset-Sussex Legal Svcs. Mem. NJ Bar Assn., Morris County Bar Assn. Democrat. Home: 18 Magda Ln Hillsborough NJ 08844-4217 Office: 103 William St PO Box 675 Boonton NJ 07005-0675 Office Phone: 973-299-1990. Personal E-mail: jhwalzer@aol.com.

WALZER, MICHAEL, retired political science professor; b. NYC, Mar. 3, 1935; s. Joseph P. and Sally (Hochman) W.; m. Judith Borodovko, June 17, 1956; children: Sarah, Rebecca. BA, Brandeis U., 1956; PhD, Harvard U., 1961. Fulbright fellow Cambridge U., England, 1956-57; asst. prof. Princeton U., 1962-66; faculty Harvard U., 1966-80, prof. govt., 1968-80; prof. Sch. Social Scis., Inst. Advanced Study, Princeton, NJ, 1980—2007, UPS found. prof., 1986—2007. Editor, Dissent Magazine; author: The Revolution of the Saints, 1965, Obligations: Essays on Disobedience, War and Citizenship, 1970, Political Action, 1971, Regicide and Revolution, 1974, Just and Unjust Wars, 1977, Radical Principles: Reflections of an Unreconstructed Democrat, 1980, Spheres of Justice: A Defense of Pluralism and Equality, 1983, Exodus and Revolution, 1985, Interpretation and Social Criticism, 1987, The Company of Critics: Social Criticism and Political Commitment in the Twentieth Century, 1988, What It Means To Be an American, 1993, Thick and Thin: Moral Argument at Home and Abroad, 1994, (with David Miller) Pluralism, Justice, and Equality, 1995, On Toleration, 1997; Arguments From the Left, 1997, Reason Politics and Passion, 1999, Exilic Politics in the Hebrew Bible, 2001, War Politics and Morality, 2001, Arguing About War, 2004, Politics and Passion, 2005; editor: (with others) The Jewish Political Tradition, Vol. I, 2000, Vol. II, 2003; contbg. editor New Republic, 1976—; mem editl bd. Philosophy and Public Affairs, Political Theory. Bd. govs. Hebrew U., Jerusalem, 1975—; trustee Brandeis U., 1983-88; chmn. faculty adv. cabinet United Jewish Appeal, 1977-81. Home: 103 Linwood Cir Princeton NJ 08540-3625

WALZER, NORMAN CHARLES, retired economics professor; b. Mendota, Ill., Mar. 17, 1943; s. Elmer J. and Anna L. Walzer; m. Dona Lee Maurer, Aug. 22, 1970; children: Steven, Mark. BS, Ill. State U., Normal, 1966; MA, U. Ill., 1969, PhD, 1970. Rsch. dir. Cities and Villages Mcpl. Problems Com., Springfield, Ill., 1974-84; vis. prof. U. Ill., Urbana, 1977-78; prof. econs. Western Ill. U., Macomb, 1978—2005, chmn. dept. econs., 1980-89, dir. Ill. Inst. Rural Affairs, 1988—2005, interim dean coll. bus. and tech., 1993-95; prof., dir. emeritus, 2005—. Author: Cities, Suburbs and Property Tax, 1981, Government Structure and Public Finance, 1984; editor: Financing State and Local Governments, 1981, Rural Community Economic Development, 1991; co-editor: Financing Local Infrastructure in Non Metro Areas, 1986, Financing Economic Development in The 1980s, 1986, Financing Rural Health Care, 1988, Rural Health Care, 1992, Rural Community Economic Development, 1992, Local Economic Development: International Trends and Issues, 1995, Community Visioning Programs: Practice and Principles, 1996, Public-Private Partnerships for Local Economic Development, 1998, Cooperative Approach to Community Economic Development, 2000, Local Government Innovations, 2000, American Midwest: Managing Change in Rural Transition, 2003, Cooperatives and Development: Applications for the 21st Century, 2003, Entrepreneurship as a Local Development Strategy, 2006. Mem. Am. Econs. Assn., Ill. Econs. Assn. (pres. 1979-80), Mid-Continent Regional Sci. Assn. (pres. 1985-86). Office: Western Ill U Ill Inst Rural Affairs 518 Stipes Hall Macomb IL 61455

WAMBACH, ABBY (MARY ABIGAIL WAMBACH), Olympic athlete; b. June 2, 1980; Grad., Univ. of Florida. Mem. U.S. Nat. Soccer Team, 2001—; professional soccer player Washington Freedom, 2002—03; mem. U.S. Women's Olympic Soccer Team, Athens, 2004. Named WUSA All-Star game MVP, 2002, WUSA Rookie of the Year, 2002, WUSA First Team All-Star, 2003, MVP Founders Cup Champions match, 2003; named to WUSA All-Star Team, 2002—03. Achievements include member of US Women's Gold medal Soccer Team, Athens Olympic games, 2004; scored overtime game winning goal in Olympic gold medal game, Athens Olympic games, 2004; member of Founders Cup Championship Team, Washington Freedom, 2003. Office: c/o US Soccer Federation 1801 S Prairie Ave Chicago IL 60616

WAMBOLD, RICHARD LAWRENCE, manufacturing executive; b. Wilbraham, Mass., Jan. 19, 1952; s. Richard A. and Virginia M. (Reid) W.; m. Patricia Bentley, Aug. 24, 1974; children: Lauren, Carolyn, Robin. BA, U. Tex., 1974, MBA, 1977. From systems cons. to strategic planning mgr. Tenneco, Inc., Houston, 1977-81, asst. to chmn. and chief exec. officer, 1981-84, pres. Tenneco Ventures Inc., 1984-88, v.p. corp. planning and devel., 1988—; exec. v.p., gen. mgr. Internat. Bus. Group, J.I. Case Co., Racine, Wis., 1988—99; chmn. and CEO Pactiv Corp., 1999—. Mem. Nat. Venture Capital Assn., Bus. Roundtable, Comml. Club Chgo. Avocation: sailing. Office: J I Case 700 State St Racine WI 53404-3392 also: Headquaters 1900 West Field Court Lake Forest IL 60045 *

WAMP, ZACHARY PAUL, congressman; b. Ft. Benning, Ga., Oct. 28, 1957; m. Kim Watts; 2 children. Student, U. NC, Chapel Hill, 1977—78, student, 1979—80, U. Tenn., 1978—79. Chmn. Hamilton County Rep. Party, 1987; regional dir. Tenn. Rep. Party, 1989; v.p. Charter Real Estate Corp., 1989-92; comml. and indsl. real estate broker Fletcher Bright Co., 1992-94; mem. US Congress from 3rd Tenn. dist., 1995—, mem. appropriations com., founder, co-chmn. Congl. Fitness Caucus. Bd. dirs. United Negro Coll. Fund, Am. Diabetes Assn., Boy Scouts Am., Chattanooga Urban League. Named Chattanooga Bus. Leader of Yr., Chattanooga Bus. Jour., 1993; recipient Disting. Svc. award, Chattanooga C. of C., Brainerd-East Hamilton County Br., 1999, Energy Leadership award, US Energy Assn. and Johnson Controls, Inc., 2003. Republican. Baptist. Office: US Ho Reps 1436 Longworth Ho Office Bldg Washington DC 20515 Office Phone: 202-225-3271. *

WAMPLER, WESLEY ALLEN, chemist; b. Amarillo, Tex., Oct. 28, 1959; s. Bobby Lee and Grace June (Smith) Wampler; m. Dorothy Marie Wampler; children: Kristen, Vance. BS in Chemistry and Biology, Tarleton State U., Stephenville, Tex., 1981; MS in Chemistry, U. Tex., Arlington, 1987, PhD in Chemistry, 1995. Scientist Alcon Labs., Ft. Worth, 1981—85; analytical lab. mgr. Sid Richardson Carbon Co., Ft. Worth, 1985—89, sr. rsch. chemist, 1989—95, mgr. Ft. Worth Rsch. Ctr., 1995—2002, v.p. R&D, 2002—. Contbr. chapters to books, articles to profl. jours. Asst. scoutmaster Boy Scouts Am., Weatherford, Tex., 2001—06; sch. bd. mem. St. Lukes Episcopal Sch., Ft. Worth, 1990—94; vestry mem. St. Lukes Episcopal Ch. Avocations: golf, hunting, camping, chemistry magic show. Office: Sid Richardson Carbon Co 201 Main St Ste 3000 Fort Worth TX 76102

WAMUTOMBO, DIKEMBE MUTOMBO MPOLONDO MUKAMBA JEAN JACQUE **See MUTOMBO, DIKEMBE**

WAN, FREDERIC YUI-MING, mathematician, educator; b. Shanghai, Jan. 7, 1936; arrived in U.S., 1947; s. Wai-Nam and Olga Pearl (Jung) W.; m. Julia Y.S. Chang, Sept. 10, 1960. SB, MIT, 1959, SM, 1963, PhD, 1965. Mem. staff MIT Lincoln Lab., Lexington, 1959—65; instr. math. MIT, Cambridge, 1965—67, asst. prof., 1967—69, assoc. prof., 1969—74; prof. math., dir. Inst. Applied Math. and Stats. U. B.C., Vancouver, 1974—83; prof. applied math. and math. U. Wash., Seattle, 1983—95; prof. math., prof. mech. and aero. engrng. U. Calif., Irvine, 1995—. Chmn. Dept. Applied Math. U. Wash., 1984-88, divsn. dean scis. Coll. Arts and Scis., 1988-92; vice chancellor rsch., dean grad. studies U. Calif. Irvine, 1995-2000, faculty athletics rep., 2000-04, dir. math. and computational biology grad. program, 2006—; program dir. divsn. math. sci. NSF, 1986-87, divsn. dir., 1993-94; mem. MIT Ednl. Coun. for B.C. Area Can., 1974-83; trustee NSF Inst. Pure and Applied Math., chmn., 1999-2001; cons. in field Assoc. editor Jour. Applied Mechanics, 1991-95, Can. Applied Math. Quar., Studies in Applied Math., Jour. Dyn. Discrete, Continuous and Impulsive Sys., 1994-97, Natural Resource Modeling 1985-88, Internat. Jour. Solids & Structures, 1996-2005, Jour. Mechanics of Material and Structures, 2005—; contbr. articles to profl. jours. Killam Sr. fellow, 1979; recipient Sloan Found. award, 1973, Phys. Scis. Tchg. Excellence award 2004. Fellow AAAS, ASME; mem. Russian Acad. Natural Scis. (fgn.), Am. Acad. Mechanics (sec. fellows 1984-90, pres. 1993-94), Soc. Indsl. and Applied Math., Can. Applied Math. Soc. (coun. 1980-83, pres. 1983-85, Arthur Beaumont Disting. Svc. award 1991), Am. Math. Soc., Math. Assn. Am., Sigma Xi (pres. U. Calif. Irvine chpt. 2005—) Home: 22 Urey Ct Irvine CA 92612-4077 Office: U Calif Irvine Dept Math Rm 267 MST Bldg Irvine CA 92697-3875 Business E-Mail: fwan@uci.edu.

WAN, GUOFANG, education professor; 1 child, M. W. Cheng. MA, U. Warwick, UK, 1996; PhD, Pa. State U., State College, 1996. Assoc. prof. curriculum and instrn. Bradley U., Peoria, Ill., 1996, Ohio U., Athens, 2004—. Author: Media Literacy Education, 2007, TV Takeover, 2007, Virtually True, 2007. Mem.: Am. Edn. Rsch. Assn. (Best Presented Paper award 2001). Achievements include research in the education of diverse populations.

WAN, JULIA CHANG, retired science educator; b. Hong Kong, Oct. 13, 1937; d. Charles S.Y. and Lucy (Wong) Chang; m. Frederic Y.M. Wan, Sept 10, 1960. BA, Wellesley Coll., 1960, MA, 1970; EdD, Boston Coll., 1978. Mem. staff Bio Rsch. Inst., Cambridge, Mass., 1960-64; physics tchr. Watertown (Mass.) H.S., 1970-73; sci. dir. Watertown Pub. Schs., 1973-79; curriculum dir. Fed. Way Sch. Dist., Fed. Way, Wash., 1979-83; asst. supt. Bainbridge Island (Wash.) Sch. Dist., 1983-93; program dir. NSF, Washington, 1993-95; dir. Ctr. for Excellence in Sci. and Math. Edn. Calif. State U., Fullerton, 1995-2000. Mem. accreditation com. N.W. Assn. Schs. and Colls., Boise, Idaho, 1981-95; mem. edn. opportunity coun. AAAS, Washington, 1995-99; bd. dirs. Challenger Ctr., Alexandria, Va., 1997-2000. Author: Designing School Health Education Curricula, 1992, 2d edit. 1995; contbr. articles and revs. to sci. mags. Bd. dirs. NOW, 1985-88; mem. Commn. on Asian-Am. Affairs, Olympia, Wash., 1990-93; bd. trustees Girls, Inc., Orange County, Calif., 1995-2000. Recipient award profl. excellence We. Wash. U., Bellingham, 1988, exemplary program award Met. Life Found., N.Y.C., 1989; grantee: NSF (numerous), Arlington, Va., 1989-2000, Beckman Found., Irvine, Calif., 1998-2000. Mem. ASCD, Am. Ednl. Rsch. Assn., Nat. Sci. Tchrs. Assn. E-mail: Jwan@fullerton.edu.

WANAGER, CHARLES RAYMOND, JR., reporter, editor; b. Decatur, Ill., Aug. 3, 1949; s. Charles R. R. and Martha Joan Wanager; divorced; children: Benjamin, Luke. BS in Journalism, So. Ill. U., Carbondale, 1971, MS in Journalism, 1982. Reporter, editor Banner-Graphic, Greencastle, Ind., 1972—75, Courier and Press, Evansville, Ind., 1975—80; vis. lectr. So. Ill. U., Carbondale, 1980—82; instr. journalism Ea. Ill. U., Charleston, 1982—84; reporter, editor Walton Tribune, Monroe, Ga., 1990—95; pub. info. dir. Gordon Coll., Barnesville, Ga., 2005—06; reporter, editor Carrollton Star News, Ga., 2006—. Vol. Habitat for Humanity, Carrollton, 2004—; active Carroll Meth. Assurance Coalition, Carrollton, 2007. Recipient 1st pl. feature writing, Ga. Press Assn., 2004, 1st pl. edn. reporting, Carroll County Educators Assn., 2004. Mem.: Soc. Profl. Journalists (v.p. 1975—80), Sierra Club. Northern Baptist. Avocations: painting, reading, hiking, creative writing, photography. Home: 104e Danny Dr Carrollton GA 30117 Office: Carrol Star-News 961 Maple St Carrollton GA 30117

WAND, PATRICIA ANN, librarian; b. Portland, Oreg., Mar. 28, 1942; d. Ignatius Bernard and Alice Ruth (Suhr) W.; m. Francis Dean Silvernail, Dec. 20, 1966 (div. Jan. 19, 1986); children: Marjorie Lynn Silvernail, Kirk Dean Silvernail. BA, Seattle U., 1963; MAT, Antioch Grad. Sch., 1967; AMLS, U. Mich., 1972. Vol. Peace Corps, Colombia, S.Am., 1963-65; secondary tchr. Langley Jr. High Sch., Washington, 1965-66; asst. libr. Wittenberg U. Libr., Springfield, Ohio, 1967-69; secondary tchr. Caro (Mich.) High Sch., 1969-70; assoc. libr. Coll. of S.I. (N.Y.) Libr., 1972-77; head, access svcs. Columbia U. Librs., NYC, 1977-82; asst. univ. libr. U. Oreg., Eugene, 1982-89; univ. libr. The Am. U., Washington, 1989—. Cons. Bloomsburg (Pa.) U. Libr., 1990, Banco Ctrl., Ecuador, 1998, Am. U. Sharjah, UAE, 1999-2003; bd. dirs. CAPCON, 1997-2003, chair, 2002-03; bd. dirs. ERIC Clearinghouse on Higher Edn. Adminstrn. Contbr. articles to profl. jours. Pres. West Cascade Returned Peace Corps Vols., Eugene, 1985-88; v.p. Friends of Colombia, Washington, 1990—; speaker on Peace Corps, 1965—, libr. and info. svcs., 1979—; bd. mem. Nat. Peace Corps Assn., 2005—. Honors Program scholarship Seattle U., 1960-62, Peace Corps scholarship Antioch U., 1965-66; recipient Beyond War award, 1987, Fulbright Sr. Lectr. award Fulbright, 1989, Disting. Alumnus award Sch. of Info. and Libr. Studies, U. Mich., 1992. Mem. ALA (chmn. com. on legislation 1997-98, coun. 2001-04, internat. rels. com. 2004—), Assn. Coll. and Rsch. Librs. (chair budget and fin. bd. dirs. 1987-89, 2001-04, chair WHCLIS task force 1989-92, chair govt. rels. com. 1993-94, chair internat. rels. com. 1996-98), On-line Computer Librs. Ctr. (adv. com. on coll. and univ. librs. 1991-96), D.C. Libr. Assn. (bd. dirs. 1993-98, pres. 1996-97, Disting. Svc. award 2003). Home: 4854 Bayard Blvd Bethesda MD 20816-1785 Office: Am Univ Libr 4400 Massachusetts Ave NW Washington DC 20016-8046 Office Phone: 202-885-3237.

WANDEL, SHARON LEE, sculptor; b. Bemidji, Minn., Mar. 19, 1940; d. Roy J. and Bonnie (Englund) Opsahl; m. Thaddeus Ludwik Wandel, Oct. 17, 1970; children: Holly, Erika. BA, Gustavus Adolphus Coll., 1962; MSW, Columbia U., 1965; Cert. in Arts Mgmt., SUNY, Purchase, 1993. Caseworker Manhattan State Hosp., NYC, 1963-64; caseworker/rschr. Cmty. Svc. Soc., NYC, 1965-67; teaching asst. dept. medicine NYU Med. Ctr., NYC, 1967—71. Adv. bd. Lamia, Inc., NYC, 1999—2003. One-woman shows at Silvermine Guild of Artists, New Canaan, Conn., 1993, 97, 2000, Pen and Brush, NYC, 1994, Clark Whitney Gallery, Lenox, Mass., 1994, James Cox Gallery, Woodstock, NY, 1994, 96, Cortland Jessup Gallery, Provincetown, Mass., 1998, NYC, 2000, 02, Gallery Marya, Osaka, Japan, 1999, Laura Barton Gallery, Westport, Conn., 2000, Firehouse Gallery, Damaviscotta, Maine, 2000, Gallery Irohane, Osaka, Japan, 2001; exhibited in group shows at Nat. Acad. Design, NYC, 1988, 90, 92, 94-95, 97-2000, 04-07, Cortland Jessup Gallery, Provincetown and NYC, 1998-2002, Canyon Ranch, Lenox, Mass. 1999-2003, Chesterwood, Lenox, Mass., 2000-01, Butler Inst. Am. Art., Youngstown, Ohio, 2000, Cavalier Gallery, Nantucket, Mass., 2001, Berkshires Bot. Garden, Mass., 2001, Paesaggio Gallery, West Hartford, Conn., 2001-04, Leighton Gallery, Blue Hill, Maine, 2001-07, Munson Gallery, Chatham, Mass., 2002-07, Sakai (Japan) City Mus., 2002, Craven Gallery, Martha's Vineyard, Mass., 2002-07, Berta Walker Gallery, Provincetown, Mass., 2002, Elan Fine Arts, Rockport, Maine, 2003-07, Clarke Galleries, Stowe, Vt., 2003-07, Palm Beach, Fla., 2003-04, NYC, 2003-04, Westchester Arts Coun., White Plains, NY, 2004, Gallery Yellow, Cross River, N.Y., 2006-07, Flinn Gallery, Greenwich, Conn., 2006-07; permanent collections at Art Students League, Westinghouse Corp. Collection, Pitts., Nat. Acad. Design, Housatonic Mus., CT, C. of C., Toyamura, Japan, Pfizer Corp. Collection, Armonk, NY; commns. include two 8' bronze figures for Ihilani Resort, Kapolei, Hawaii, 1993, 2 5" figures Silvermine Galleries, 1993. Mem. rsch. com. Arthritis Found., N.Y.C., 1968-69. Recipient N.Am. Sculpture Exhbn. 2d place, 1991, Three River Arts Festival (Carnegie Inst.) Purchase award, 1990, Hakone Open Air Mus. (Japan) 3d and 4th Rodin Grand Prize Exhbn. Excellent Maquettes, 1990, 92, Marietta Gallery 1st prize for sculpture, 1990, Ariel Gallery Internat. Competition Group Show award, 1989, Salmagundi Club McReynolds award, 1989, Barret Coleco award, 1988, 1st place nat. competition Sundance Gallery, Bridgehampton, N.Y., 1997; Vt. Studio Ctr. fellow, 2000; elected Nat. Academician Nat. Acad. Design, 1994, Ellint Speyer prize, 2007. Mem. Silvermine Guild of Artists (Solo Show award 1992), N.Y. Soc. Woman Artists (past pres.), Knickerbocker Artists USA, The Pen and Brush (Meisner award 1990, Solo Show award 1993), Nat. Acad. Design (elected nat. academician 1994, Cleo Hartwig award 1990), Nat. Sculpture Soc. (Meisner award 1994, Hexter award 1993, Spring award 1991, Meiselman award 1990), Audubon Artists (Chaim Gross Found. award 1993), Sculptors Guild (past bd. dirs.). Avocations: travel, cooking, reading. Studio: PO Box 314 Croton On Hudson NY 10520-0314 E-mail: wandel_s@hotmail.com.

WANDELL, BRIAN A., neuroscientist, educator; BS in Math. and Psychology, U. Mich., 1973; PhD in Social Sci., U. Calif., Irvine, 1977. Postdoctoral fellow U. Pa.; from asst. to assoc. prof. Stanford U., Calif., 1979—88, prof., 1988—, Isaac and Madeline Stein family prof., 2002—. Author: Foundations of Vision; assoc. editor: Jour. Vision, Jour. Neuroscience and Neural Networks; contbr. articles to profl. jours. Named McKnight Sr. Investigator, 1997; recipient Edridge-Green Medal in Ophthalmology for work in visual neurosciences, 1997, Macbeth prize, Inter-Soc. Color Coun., 2000. Fellow: Optical Soc. Am.; mem.: NAS (Troland Rsch. award 1986). Office: Jordan Hall Stanford Univ Stanford CA 94305 Office Phone: 650-725-2466. Fax: 801-409-3254. E-mail: wandell@stanford.edu.

WANDELL, KEITH E., manufacturing executive; BBA, Ohio Univ.; MBA, Dayton Univ. Mgmt. positions Johnson Controls, Inc., Milw., 1988—97, corp. v.p., 1997—2005, pres. battery group, 1997—2003, pres., automotive group, 2003—06, exec. v.p., 2005—06, pres., COO, 2006—. Office: Johnson Controls Inc 5757 N Green Bay Ave Milwaukee WI 53201 *

WANDELL, MORGAN, broadcast executive; b. Feb. 17, 1971; Grad. with honors in Econs., Claremont Coll., Calif., 1993. Writer-prodr. Channel One, pres. programming, 1999—2004; dir. creative affairs Touchstone TV, Burbank, Calif., 1997—99, sr. v.p. drama, 2004—; with Digital Entertainment Network, 1999. Achievements include overseeing the release of the TV shows Grey's Anatomy, Desperate Housewives and Lost and the development of the shows Criminal Minds, Ghost Whisperer, Kyle XY and Ugly Betty. Office: Touchstone TV 500 S Buena Vista St Burbank CA 91521-0001 *

WANDER, HERBERT STANTON, lawyer; b. Cin., Mar. 17, 1935; s. Louis Marvin and Pauline (Schuster) W.; m. Karen Woloshin, Aug. 2004; children: Daniel Jerome, Susan Gail, Lois Marlene. AB, U. Mich., 1957; LLB, Yale U., 1960. Bar: Ohio 1960, Ill. 1960. Law clk. to judge US Dist. Ct. (no. dist.) Ill., 1960—61; ptnr. Pope Ballard Shepard & Fowle, Chgo., 1961—78, Katten Muchin Rosenman LLP, Chgo., 1978—. Chair Michael Reese Health Trust, 2006; bd. dirs. Tel. & Data Systems, Chgo.; mem. legal adv. com. to bd. govs. NY Stock Exch., 1989—92; mem. legal adv. bd. Nat. Assn. Securities Dealers, Inc., 1996—99; spkr. in field. Editor: (jour.) Bus. Law Today, 1992-93; editor-in-chief: (jour.) The Bus. Lawyer, 1993-94; contbr. numerous articles to profl. jour. Bd. dir. Jewish Fedn. Met. Chgo., 1972—, pres., 1981-83; bd. dir. Jewish United Fund, 1972—, pres., 1981-83, chmn. pub. affairs com., 1984-87, gen. campaign chmn., 1993; former regional chmn. nat. young leadership cabinet United Jewish Appeal; vice-chmn. large city budgeting conf. Coun. Jewish Fedns., 1979-82, bd. dir., 1980—, exec. com., 1983-84. Mem.: ABA (sec. bus. law sect. 1992—93, vice-chair 1993—94, chair-elect 1994—95, chair 1995—96, apptd. to commn. on multidisciplinary practice 1998, task force on atty.-client privilege 2004, task force on fed. sentencing guidelines 2004, co-chair SEC adv. com. on smaller pub. cos. 2004), Chgo. Bar Assn., Ill. State Bar Assn., Yale Law Sch. Assn. (exec. com. 1982—86), Northmoor Country Club, Std. Club, Econ. Club, Phi Beta Kappa. Home: 70 Prospect Ave Highland Park IL 60035-3329 Office: Katten Muchin Rosenman LLP 525 W Monroe St Ste 1700 Chicago IL 60661-3693 Business E-Mail: hwander@kattenlaw.com.

WANDERMAN, SUSAN MAE, lawyer; b. Mar. 12, 1947; d. Leo and Muriel D. Wanderman. AB, Wheaton Coll., Norton, Mass., 1967; JD, St. John's U., 1970; LLM, NYU, 1976. Bar: N.Y. 1971, U.S. Dist. Ct. (ea. and so. dists.) N.Y. 1972, U.S. Ct. Appeals (2d cir.) 1973, U.S. Supreme Ct. 1974. Asst. legal officer, legal dept. Chem. Bank, NYC, 1972—75; 2d v.p. legal dept. Chase Manhattan Bank N.A., NYC, 1975—82; asst. gen. counsel Citicorp Svcs., Inc., NYC, 1982—84; v.p. Citibank, N.A., NYC, 1984—. Instr. bus. law and law for the layman LaGuardia C.C., 1976—77; law day spkr. Queens County Supreme Ct., 1979—83; mem. Cmty. Bd. 6, Queens County, NYC, 1987—. Contbr. articles to legal publs. Past vol. N.Y. State Bar Assn. Lawyers in the Classroom. Mem.: ABA, Queens County Bar Assn., N.Y. State Bar Assn. Office: Citibank NA One Court Sq Long Island City NY 11120

WANDERS, HANS WALTER, banker; b. Aachen, Germany, Apr. 3, 1925; came to US, 1929, naturalized, 1943; s. Herbert and Anna Maria (Kusters) W.; m. Elizabeth Knox Kimball, Apr. 2, 1949; children: Crayton Kimball, David Gillette. BS, Yale U., 1947, Ga. Inst. Tech., 1945; postgrad., Rutgers U., 1961—64. With GE, 1947-48, Libbey-Owens-Ford Glass Co., 1948-53, Allied Chem. Co., 1953-55, McKinsey & Co., Inc., 1955-57; from asst. cashier to v.p. No. Trust Co., Chgo., 1957-65; v.p. Nat. Blvd. Bank, Chgo., 1965-66, pres., 1966-70; exec. v.p. Wachovia Bank & Trust Co., N.A., Winston-Salem, NC, 1970-74, chmn., 1977-85, vice chmn., 1985-88, also bd. dirs.; pres. Wachovia Corp., Winston-Salem, 1974-76, 85-87, chmn., 1977-85, vice chmn., 1987-88, also bd. dirs.; pres., chief exec. officer 1st Wachovia Corp. Services, Inc., Winston-Salem, 1986-88; dir. Exxon Supply Co., 1989-94, Goody's Mfg. Corp., 1989-94, Gulf Resources, Inc., 1989-92, Turnpike Properties, Inc., 2001—. Chmn. Winston-Salem Found. Com., 1981-82; bd. dirs. NC Textile Found., NC Engrng. Found., Inc., 1971-88; trustee, mem. exec. com. Salem Coll. and Acad., 1986-91, Tax Found., 1982—, vice chmn., 1984-86, chmn., 1986-88, chmn. exec. com., 1989; mem. bd. visitors Fuqua Sch. Bus., Duke U., 1978-89, NC Japan Ctr., 1982—; mem. nat. corps. com. United Negro Coll. Fund; mem., chmn. NC Bd. Econ. Devel., 1989-93; corporator Belmont Hill Sch., 1996—. Lt. USNR, 1943-46, 51-53. Mem. Am. Bankers Assn. (chmn. mktg. divsn. 1979-80, dir. 1971-73), Assn. Res. City Bankers, Conf. Bd. (So. regional adv. coun.), Assn. Bank Holding Cos. (bd. dirs., exec. com. 1981-83), Chgo. Club, Commonwealth Club Chgo., Twin-City Club Winston Salem, Old Town Club Winston-Salem, Roaring Gap Club NC Home: 10 Graylyn Pl Winston Salem NC 27106 Office: Wachovia Corp 420 W 4th St Ste 202-A Winston Salem NC 27101-2837 Office Phone: 336-761-5016.

WANDYCZ, PIOTR STEFAN, historian, educator; b. Krakow, Poland, Sept. 20, 1923; s. Damian Stanislaw and Stefania (Dunikowska) W.; m. Maria Teresa Chrzaszcz, Aug. 13, 1963; children: Anna, Joanna, Antoni. BA, Cambridge U., 1948, MA, 1952; PhD, London U., 1951; MA (hon.), Yale U., 1968; DHC, Wroclaw U., 1993, Sorbonne U., Paris, 1997, Jagiellonian U., 2000, Cath. U. Lublin, 2004. Instr. to assoc. prof. history Ind. U., 1954-66; fellow Harvard's Russian Rsch. Ctr., 1963-65; assoc. prof. history Yale U., 1966-68, prof., 1968-89, chmn. Russian and East European coun., 1974-76, 81-83, Bradford Durfee prof., 1989-97, prof. emeritus, 1997—. Vis. prof. history Columbia U., 1967, 69, 74 Author: Czechoslovak-Polish Confederation and Great Powers, 1956, France and Her Eastern Allies, 1962, Soviet-Polish Relations, 1969, The Lands of Partitioned Poland, 1974, United States and Poland, 1980, August Zaleski, 1980, Polska i Zagranica, 1986, The Twilight of French Eastern Alliances, 1988, Z Dziejow dyplomacji, 1988, Polish Diplomacy 1914-1945, 1988, The Price of Freedom, 1992, 2nd edit., 2001, Die Freiheit und ihr Preis, 1993, Pod zaborami, 1994, Cena wolnosci, 1995, 2d edit., 2003, Laisves Kaina, 1997, Stredni Evropa v Dejinach, 1998, Tsenata na svobodata, 1999, Z Pilsudskim i Sikorskim, 1999, Il prezzo della liberta, 2001, O Federalizmie i emigracji, 2003, Pax Europaea, 2003; co-author: Historia Europy Srodkowo-Wschodniej, 2000, Histoire de l'Europe du Centre-Est 2004, Tsina Slobody, 2004, A Szabaeag Ara, 2004, Aleksander Skrzynski, 2006; contbr. articles to profl. jours.; mem. editl. bd. Slavic Rev., Internat. History Rev., Polish Rev., Polin., East European Politics and Society, Acta Poloniae Historica. Served as 2d lt. Polish Army, 1942-45. Decorated Comdr.'s Cross of Polonia Restituta; recipient Alfred Jurzykowski Found. award in history, 1977; fellow Guggenheim Found., Ford Found., Rockefeller Found., Am. Philos. Soc., Am. Coun. Learned Socs., Social Sci. Rsch. Coun., Internat. Rsch. and Exchs. Bd. Mem. AAAS (hon., Wayne Vucinich prize 1989), Am. Hist. Assn. (George Louis Beer prize 1962, 89), Polish Hist. Assn. (hon.), Polish Acad. Arts and Scis., Polish Acad. Scis., Polish Inst. Arts and Scis. (pres. 1999—), Polish Soc. Abroad (A. Lenkszewicz prize 1991, Oscar Halecki History award 1997), Czechoslovak Acad. of Scis. (Hlavka medal 1992, A. Gieysztor prize 2004, J. Nowak Jezioranski prize, 2006), Czechoslovak Soc. Arts and Scis. Home: 27 Spring Garden St Hamden CT 06517-1913 Office: Yale U Dept History New Haven CT 06520-8324 Office Phone: 203-432-1382. Business E-Mail: piotr.wandycz@yale.edu.

WANEBO, HAROLD J., surgeon, educator; b. Denver, Feb. 12, 1935; s. Clifford P. and JoAnn (Curtin) W.; m. Claire Anne Wanebo, Oct. 27, 1964; children: John Eric, Michael David, Jacqueline Elise. BS, Regis Coll., 1957; MD, U. Colo., 1961. Intern Cornell Med. divsn. Bellevue Hosp., N.Y., 1961-62, resident N.Y., 1962-63; surg. resident U. Calif. Med. Ctr., San Francisco, 1963-65, 67-69; fellow in tumor immunology Meml. Sloan-Kettering Cancer Ctr., N.Y., 1965-67, sr. surg. fellow N.Y., 1971-73, clin. asst. attending surgeon N.Y., 1973-74, assoc. N.Y., 1973-77, asst. attending surgeon N.Y., 1974-77, assoc. scientist N.Y., 1977-83, cons. clin. immunology svc. N.Y., 1977-90; instr. surgery Cornell U.-N.Y. Hosp. Med. Ctr., 1973-75, asst. prof. surgery, 1975-77; chief divsn. surg. oncology Med. Ctr., prof. surgery U. Va., Charlottesville, 1977-87; prof. surgery, dir. surg. oncology Brown U., Providence, R.I., 1987—; prof. surgery Boston U. Med. Sch., 2006—. Spkr. surg. oncology clinics, 2005. Editor: Hepatic and Biliary Cancer, 1987, Common Problems in Cancer Surgery, 1990, Colorectal Cancer, 1993, Surgery for Gastrointestinal Cancer, 1996; contbr. numerous chpts. to books and articles to profl. jours. Maj. U.S. Army, 1969-71, Vietnam. Decorated Bronze star; recipient Commendation medal V device. Mem. ACS, Am. Assn. Cancer Edn., Am. Assn. Cancer Rsch., Am. Assn. Immunologists, Am. Cancer Soc. (Jr. Faculty Clin. Fellowship award 1974-77), Am. Surg. Assn., Am. Soc. Clin. Oncology, Assn. Am. Vol. Physicians, Med. Soc. State of N.Y., Med. Soc. R.I., Med. Soc. Va., Nafzigger Surg. Soc., New Eng. Surg. Soc., N.Y. Acad. Scis., N.Y. Surg. Soc., Soc. Surgery of Alimentary Tract, Soc. Surg. Oncology, Soc. Univ. Surgeons, Southeastern Surg. Congress, So. Surg. Assn., Soc. Head and Neck Surgery. Office: Landmark Med Ctr Divsn Surg Oncology 206 Cass Ave Woonsocket RI 02895 Office Phone: 401-767-1595. Business E-Mail: hwanebo@rwme.org.

WANEK, WILLIAM CHARLES, public relations executive; b. Ridgewood, NY, Oct. 21, 1932; s. William John and Anna (Benes) W.; m. Robbie Gene Fairbanks, Feb. 14, 1974; children: William Robert, Jennifer Leigh. BA in English, CCNY, 1954; MA in Psychology, The New Sch. Social Rsch., NYC, 1982. Asst. editor Soap Chem. Spltys. Mag., NYC, 1956-58; editor in chief Maintenance Supplies Mag., NYC, 1958-60; acct. exec. O.S. Tyson & Co. Inc., NYC, 1960-62; dir. advt. and pub. rels. Pa. Glass Sand Corp., NYC, 1962-64; sr. acct. exec. McCann-Erickson Inc., NYC, 1964-66; acct. supr. Burson-Marsteller Assocs., NYC, 1966-71; exec. v.p. Gibbs & Soell Inc., NYC, 1971—. With U.S. Army, 1954-56. Mem. Am. Agrl. Editors Assn., Nat. Agri-Mktg. Assn. (bd. dirs. ea. chpt. 1974-76), Nat. Assn. Farm Broadcasters. Presbyterian. Avocations: horticulture, classical music, theater, reading, swimming. Office: Gibbs & Soell Inc 600 3rd Ave Fl 6 New York NY 10016-1903

WANG, AIXUE, translator, writer; b. Taoyuan, Hunan, China; arrived in U.S., 1988; s. Gaokun Wang and Yunhuang Xia; m. Lingling Li, May 7, 1986; 1 child, Haoming. MA, U. Houston, 1990, PhD, 1995. Tchr. No. 4 HS, Taoyuan, 1976—82; instr. Beijing Coll. Internat. Rels., 1984—88; tchg. asst. U. Houston, 1988—95; internat. program specialist and adj. prof. English William Woods U., Fulton, Mo., 1995—2002; freelance translator, writer St. Paul, 2002—. Author: A Comparison of the Dramatic Work of Cap Yu and J. M. Synge, 1999; translator (to Chinese): 1850 "The Prelude" (Wordsworth), 2004. Home and Office: 5046 Eastwood Mounds View MN 55112 Office Phone: 651-283-8655. Personal E-mail: wangax@hotmail.com.

WANG, ALBERT HUAI-EN, lawyer; b. Tainan, Taiwan, Feb. 21, 1967; s. Tien-Yu Wang and Shiu-Yin Chen. BA in Bus. Econs. magna cum laude, MA in Bus. Econs. magna cum laude, UCLA, 1990; JD, Cornell U., 1994. Bar: NY 1995. Tax specialist KPMG Peat Marwick, LA, 1990-91; tchr. asst. Cornell Law Sch., 1993; assoc. Willkie Farr & Gallagher LLP, NYC, 1994-99; sr. assoc. Schulte Roth & Zabel LLP, NYC, 1999—2001; ptnr. Phillips Nizer LLP, NYC, 2001—. Legal counsel, adv. coun. Asian Am. Bus. Devel. Ctr., NYC, 1999—2007; dir. Baldor Splty. Foods, Inc., 2001—. U. Calif. regent scholar, 1986-90, Alumni scholar UCLA, 1986, Departmental scholar, 1989. Mem.: ABA, Am. C. of C., Asian Fin. Soc. (adv. coun. mem. 2002—), Orgn. Chinese Ams. (NY chpt. adv. coun.), US-China Lawyers Soc. (bd. dirs. 2002—), Chinese Fin. Soc. (dir., legal counsel 2000—02), NY State Bar Assn., Chinese Am. Voters Assn. of Queens (dir. NY chpt. 1999—2001), Asia Soc., China Inst., Phi Beta Kappa, Omicron Delta Epsilon, Phi Delta Phi. Democrat. Office: Phillips Nizer LLP 666 Fifth Ave New York NY 10103-0084 Home: 13810 Franklin Ave Apt 5n Flushing NY 11355-3305 Office Phone: 212-977-9700. Business E-Mail: awang@phillipsnizer.com.

WANG, ALBERT JAMES, violinist, educator; b. Ann Arbor, Mich., Nov. 19, 1958; s. James and Lydia (Ebenhoch) Wang; m. Bridget Renee Becker, June 30, 1987 (div. 2000); children: Ona Lenore, Kevin Lewis. MusB, Ind. U., 1979; MusM, U. Mich., 1981; DMA, Am. Conservatory, 1993. Prin. second violin Baton Rouge Symphony Orch., 1981-82; first violin Valcour String Quartet, Baton Rouge, 1981-82, Loyola String Quartet, 1982-83; mem. Lyric Opera Chgo. Orch., 1982—; mem. Orch. Ill., Chgo., 1982-88; prin. 2d violin Internat. Symphony Orch., Port Huron, Mich., 1984; 1st violin Internat. String Quartet, Port Huron, 1984; concertmaster, soloist Chgo. Chamber Orch., 1985-88, Chgo. Philharm., 1985—; mem. Grant Park Symphony Orch., Chgo., 1986-87; concertmaster, soloist Birch Creek Music Festival, Wis., Woodstock (Ill.) Mozart Festival Orch., 1988-90; concertmaster Rockford (Ill.) Symphony Orch., 1990-91, Northwestern Music Festival Orch., 1990—; soloist, concertmaster Pro Musica Orch. of Mauritius, 1992-93; soloist, concertmaster China tour Classical Symphony Orch., 1994, 95; soloist, concertmaster Midwest Symphony Orch., 1995-96; music dir. Baroque Masterplayers, 1994—; soloist, concertmaster Met. Arts Orch., 1995-98. Artist-in-residence St. Clair Coll., Port Huron, 1984, Elgin C.C., 1994—97; lectr. Am. Conservatory Music, Chgo., 1989—92; Fulbright lectr. Francois Mitterand Conservatory of Music, Quatre Bornes, Mauritius, 1992—93; asst. prof. violin Roosevelt U., 1993—2002; adj. prof. violin Wheaton (Ill.) Coll., 1997—2000; adj. asst. prof. violin Moody Bible Inst., Chgo., 1997—2000; v.p. sales and mktg. Music Edn. Publs., Inc., Coral Springs, Fla., 1997—98. Numerous solo, recital and chamber music appearances and master classes throughout U.S., Can., France, Mauritius and China; recs. and broadcasts by Mauritian Nat. Radio and WFMT Chgo. Fine Arts Sta., PBS, Nat. Pub. Radio, and Chinese Nat. Radio and TV; numerous world premieres; recs. on New World Records and with Slavic Projection Ensemble; N.Y. recital debut at Carnegie Hall, 1998; adjudicator for state and nat. music competitions; contbr. articles and revs. to profl. jours. Vol. ARC, Literacy Vols. Am., Chgo. Pub. Librs., United Way; bd. advisors Prism Music Festival, 1984—, Am. Chamber Symphony, 1985, Symphony II, 1993-94. Fulbright grantee, 1992-93; recipient 1st prize Ann Arbor (Mich.) Symphony Competition, 1976, Soc. Am. Musicians Competition, Chgo., 1984, Internat. Concerts Atlantique Competition, N.Y.C., 1989, Chgo. Park Dist. Competition, 1991, 2nd prize Biennial Adult Artist Competition, 1992, Helmuth Fuchs Performance award 1998; selected to Arts Am. Touring Artist Roster, 1993; finalist Lilly Fellows Program in Humanities and the Arts, Valparaiso U., 1994, Harry and Sarah Zelzer Fellowship and prize; recipient Leo Sowerby medal, 1994; Christian Performing Artists' fellow. Mem. ASCAP, Am. Fedn. Musicians, Am. String Tchrs. Assn., Coll. Music Soc., Chamber Music Am., Am. Music Ctr., Music Tchrs. Nat. Assn., Christian Performing Artists' Fellowship. Avocations: powerlifting, fishing, travel, woodworking. Home: 6110 N Glenwood Ave Chicago IL 60660-1804 Office: Lyric Opera Chgo 20 N Wacker Dr Chicago IL 60606-2806 Office Phone: 312-332-2244. Personal E-mail: aw_dma@hotmail.com.

WANG, ANDREW HSING-JEN, marketing professional, information technology executive, journalist, librarian; b. Tainan, Taiwan, June 12, 1939; came to U.S., 1966. s. John Chin-Yuan and Ping Huang W. m. Miaw-Jen Lin Wang, Nov. 21, 1979; children: Sherry, Stanley, Jeffrey, Justina. BA in Journalism, Nat. Chengchi U., Taipei, Taiwan, 1962; MLS, Atlanta U., 1967; MBA, Ohio State U., 1984. News reporter and internat. news wire translator China Times, Taipei, Taiwan, 1964-66; head cataloging dept. St. Mary's (Md.) Coll., 1967-69; asst. univ. libr. Denison U., Granville, Ohio, 1969-76; exec. dir. Asia Pacific svcs. and new initiatives Online Computer Libr Ctr, Dublin, Ohio, 1976—2007; v.p. OCLC Asia Pacific, Dublin, 2007—. Advisor Nat. Ctrl. Libr., Taiwan, 1995-2000; master's degree examination com. mem. East China Normal U., Shanghai, 2000; cons., sr. tech. advisors recruitment UN Devel. Program Transfer of Knowledge Through Expatriate Nationals, 2002. Contbr. articles to profl. jours. Mem.: Beta Phi Mu. Office: OCLC Online Computer Libr Ctr 6565 Kilgour Pl Dublin OH 43017-3395 Business E-Mail: wanga@oclc.org.

WANG, ARTHUR CHING-LI, judge, educator; b. Boston, Feb. 4, 1949; s. Kung Shou and Lucy (Chow) W.; m. Wendy F. Hamai, May 22, 1976 (div. 1981); m. Nancy J. Norton, Sept. 1, 1985; children: Alexander Xinglin, Sierra Xinan. BA, Franconia Coll., 1970; JD, U. Puget Sound, 1984. Bar: Wash. 1984. Printer Carmel Valley (Calif.) Outlook, 1970-73; project coord. Tacoma (Wash.) Cmty. House, 1973-76; rsch. analyst Wash. Ho. of Reps., Olympia, 1977-80, mem., 1981-94; of counsel Davies Pearson, P.C., Tacoma, 1984-94; mem. Pers. Appeals Bd., Olympia, 1994—96; chief adminstrv. law judge Wash. Office Adminstrv. Hearings, 1997—2006; judge Wash. Ct. Appeals, 2000. Adj. prof. U. Puget Sound Law Sch., Tacoma, 1987—94, Seattle U. Law Sch., 1995—98, 2006—; chmn. commerce and labor com. Wash. Ho. Reps., Olympia, 1985—88, chmn. revenue com., 1989—92, chmn. capital budget com., 1993—94; chair Nat. Ctrl. Panel Dir.'s Conf., 2004. Assoc. editor U. Puget Sound Law Review, 1983-84. Vista vol. Tacoma Urban League, 1973—74; del. Dem. Nat. Conv., 1976; bd. dirs. Pierce County AIDS Found., 1999—2005, pres., 2002; bd. dirs. Planned Parenthood of Western Wash., 2001—, chair, 2005—06. Named Chinese Am. Man of Yr., Seattle Chinese Post, 1991, Legislator of Yr., Wash. Health Care Assn., 1992, Alumni of Yr., U. Puget Sound Law Sch. Alumni Assn., 1993; recipient Exemplary Leadership award, Wash. State Access to Justice Bd., 1999, Profl. Excellence award, Nat. Assn. Asian Am. Profls., Seattle, 2001, State Leadership award, Wash. State Combined Fund Dr., 2003. Democrat. Avocation: birding. Home: 3319 N Union Ave Tacoma WA 98407-6043

WANG, BIXIANG, mathematician; BS, Lanzhou U., China, 1988, MS, 1991, PhD, 1994; MS, McMaster U., Can., 2003. Postdoctoral rschr. Beijing Inst. Applied Physics and Computational Math., 1994—96; asst. prof. Tsinghua U., Beijing, 1996—97; rsch. fellow U. Complutense de Madrid, 1997—98; postdoctoral rschr. Brigham Young U., Provo, Utah, 1998—99, vis. asst. prof., 1999—2000, U. Kans., Lawrence, Kans., 2003—05; asst. prof. N.Mex Inst. Mining and Tech., Socorro, N.Mex., 2005—. Contbr. over 35 articles to profl. jours. Fellow, Spanish Ministry Edn. and Sci., 1997—98; scholar, German Academic Exch. Svc., 1998,

McMaster U., 2001—02, Natural Scis. and Engring. Rsch. Coun. Can., 2002—04. Mem.: Soc. Indsl. and Applied Math., Am. Math. Soc. Office: New Mexico Institute of Mining and Tech 801 Leroy Place Socorro NM 87801 Office Phone: 505-835-5787.

WANG, CHAO-CHENG, mathematician, engineer; b. Peoples Republic of China, July 20, 1938; came to U.S., 1961; s. N.S. and V.T. Wang; m. Sophia C.L. Wang; children: Ferdinand, Edward. BS, Nat. Taiwan U., 1959; PhD, Johns Hopkins U., 1965. Registered profl. engr., Tex. Asst. prof. Johns Hopkins U., Balt., 1966-68, assoc. prof., 1968-69; prof. Rice U., Houston, 1968-79, Noah Harding prof., 1979—, chmn. math. sci. dept., 1983-89, chmn. mech. engring. and materials sci., 1991-94. Author numerous books in field; contbr. articles to profl. jours. Named Disting. Young Scientist Md. Acad. Sci., 1968. Mem. ASME, Soc. Natural Philosophy (treas. 1985-86), Am. Acad. Mechs. Office: Rice Univ Dept Mech Engring Materials Sci Houston TX 77251

WANG, CHARLES B., professional sports team executive, former computer company executive; b. Shanghai, Rep. China, Aug. 19, 1944; arrived in U.S., 1952; BS in Math., Queens Coll., 1967. Programming trainee Columbia U. Riverside Rsch. Inst., Islandia, NY; v.p. sales Std. Data Corp.; CEO Computer Assocs., Islandia, 1976—2000, chmn., 1980—2002, chmn. emeritus; owner, CEO NY Islanders, Uniondale, 1999—, Bridgeport Sound Tigers; co-owner NY Dragons (arena football). Author: Techno Vision, 1994, Techno Vision II: Every Executive's Guide to Understanding and Mastering Technology and the Internet, 1997. Founder The Smile Train; active Nat. Ctr. for Missing and Exploited Children, Make-A-Wish Found. Avocations: cooking, basketball. Address: NY Islanders Nassau Veterans Meml Coliseum 1255 Hempstead Turnpike Uniondale NY 11553

WANG, CHEN CHI, electronics executive, real estate company executive, diversified financial services company executive; b. Taipei, Taiwan, Aug. 10, 1932; came to U.S., 1959, naturalized, 1970; s. Chin-Ting and Chen-Kim Wang; m. Victoria Rebisoff, Mar. 5, 1965; children: Katherine Kim, Gregory Chen, John Christopher, Michael Edward. BA in Econs., Nat. Taiwan U., 1955; BSEE, San Jose State U., 1965; MBA, U. Calif., Berkeley, 1961. With IBM Corp., San Jose, Calif., 1965-72; founder, CEO Electronics Internat. Co., Santa Clara, Calif., 1968-72, owner, gen. mgr., 1972-81; reorganized as EIC Group, 1981-2000; chmn. bd., CEO EIC Investment Corp., 1982—2004; dir. Systek Electronics Corp., Santa Clara, 1970-73; founder, sr. ptnr. Wang Enterprises (name changed to Chen Kim Enterprises 1982), Santa Clara, 1974-75, Hanson & Wang Devel. Co., Woodside, Calif., 1977-85; chmn. bd. Golden Alpha Enterprises, San Mateo, Calif., 1979-99; mng. ptnr. Woodside Acres-Las Pulgas Estate, Woodside, 1980-85; founder, sr. ptnr. DeVine & Wang, Oakland, Calif., 1977-83, Van Heal & Wang, West Village, Calif., 1981-82; founder, chmn. bd. EIC Fin. Corp. (now EIC Investment Corp.), Redwood City, Calif., 1985-90; chmn. bd. Maritek Corp., Corpus Christi, Tex., 1988-89; chmn. EIC Internat. Trade Corp., Lancaster, Calif., 1989-90, EIC Capital Corp., Redwood City, 1990-91. Mng. mem. Sixtieth West, LLC, 1997—2004, Land Investment Co. Calif., LLC, 1998—, Aceh Capital, LLC, 1998—. Author: Monetary and Banking System of Taiwan, 1955, The Small Car Market in the U.S., 1961. Mem. nat. adv. coun. Brigham Young U. 2d lt. Nationalist Chinese Army, 1955—56. Mem. Internat. Platform Assn., Tau Beta Pi. Mem. Christian Ch. Home: 195 Brookwood Rd Woodside CA 94062-2302 Office: ACE Group Head Office Bldg 2055-2075 Woodside Rd Redwood City CA 94061-3355 Office Phone: 650-364-3330. Business E-Mail: chenwang@acecapgroup.com.

WANG, CHEN-KU, retired library director; b. Peiping, China, July 18, 1924; s. Bing-fong Wang and Fong-gen Hsia; m. Shuo-fen Wang, Aug. 15, 1946; children: Pei-chi, Sheng-shiang, Sheng-Wen. MA, Peabody Coll. Tchrs., 1959; LLD (hon.), Ohio U., 1988. Prof. Nat. Taiwan Normal U., Taipei, 1960-94; dir. Nat. Ctrl. Libr. Republic of China, 1977-89, ret., 1994. Dir. Ctr. for Chinese Studies, 1977—89. Author: Selection and Acquisition of Library Materials, 1978; hon. editor Jour. Libr. and Info. Sci., 1975—. Decorated knight comdr. Silvestri, Vatican; recipient Disting. Svc. award Chinese-Am. Libr. Assn.and Libr. Assn. China, 1986, 87. Mem. Libr. Assn. China (pres. 1992-97, hon. pres. 2003-06).

WANG, DAVID, finance educator; BBA, Feng Chia U., Taiwan, 1994; MS in Bus. Adminstrn., San Francisco State U., 2000; D of Bus. Adminstrn., Golden Gate U., 2003. Adj. prof. of fin. Golden Gate U., San Francisco, Calif., 2002—04; asst. prof. of fin. Hsuan Chuang U., Hsinchu, Taiwan, 2004—, dir. of academic program devel., 2004—05. Internat. affairs com. mem. Decision Sciences Inst., 2005—; editl. adv. bd. mem. Internat. Rsch. Jour. of Fin. and Economics, 2005—, Internat. Bull. of Bus. Adminstrn., 2005—; cons. Info. Ctr. on Schools Abroad, Taipei Pub. Libr., Taiwan, 2005—. Author: (journal article) Journal of Academy of Business and Economics, Vol. 5, No. 2, pp. 53-61, Journal of American Academy of Business, Cambridge, Vol. 6, No. 1, pp. 272-277 (Best Author Award, 2005), Corporate Finance Review, Vol. 9, No. 3, pp. 33-38, Journal of Academy of Business and Economics, Vol. 3, No. 1, pp. 79-86, Journal of American Academy of Business, Cambridge, Vol. 5, No. 1&2, pp. 203-209. Recipient Rsch. Award, Hsuan Chuang U., Taiwan, 2005, Tutoring Award, 2005; grantee Rsch. Grant, 2004-2005, 2005-2006, Nat. Sci. Coun., Taiwan, 2004-2005. Mem.: Taiwan Fin. Assn., Fin. Engring. Assn. of Taiwan, Internat. Assn. of Fin. Engineers, Decision Sciences Inst., Global Assn. of Risk Professionals, Assn. for Fin. Professionals, Fin. Mgmt. Assn. Internat., Am. Fin. Assn. Achievements include research in Author of several journal articles in the field of financial engineering. Office: Hsuan Chuang University 48 Hsuan Chuang Road Hsinchu 300 Taiwan Home Phone: 886-2-23633416; Office Phone: 886-3-5302255 ext.2265. Office Fax: 886-3-5391235. E-mail: dwang@hcu.edu.tw.

WANG, DELIANG, computer scientist, educator; b. He County, China, Jan. 27, 1963; came to U.S., 1988; s. Shiwu Wang and Xianzheng Song; m. Ping Bai, Jan. 19, 1991 BS, Peking U., Beijing, 1983, MS, 1986; PhD, U. So. Calif., 1991. Asst. rsch. fellow Inst. Computing Tech. Academia Sinica, Beijing, 1986—87; rsch. asst. U. So. Calif., LA, 1988—90; asst. prof. Ohio State U., Columbus, 1991—96, assoc. prof., 1997—2001, prof., 2001—. Vis. scientist Harvard U., Cambridge, 1998-99 Assoc. editor (jour.) Neurocomputing, 1995—, Neural Computing and Applications, 1996—, IEEE Trans. Neural Networks, 1998—; contbr. articles to profl. jours NSF rsch. initiation award, 1992, Office of Naval Rsch. young investigator awardee, 1996 Fellow IEEE; mem. Internat. Neural Networks Soc. (pres. 2006), IEEE Signal Processing Soc., IEEE Computational Intelligence Soc Achievements include contributions to temporal sequence learning/processing, revealing learning mechanisms in anuran visual perception and oscillatory associative memory; co-discovered mechanism of selective gating and co-originated LEGION networks; applying LEGION networks to visual and auditory scene analysis. Office: Ohio State U Dept Computer Sci and Engring 2015 Neil Ave Columbus OH 43210 Office Phone: 614-292-6827. E-mail: dwang@cse.ohio-state.edu.

WANG, DONG, history professor, director; b. Luoyang, China, Apr. 23, 1967; d. Zhiyang Wang and Yuehua Gao. PhD, U. Kans, Chinese Acad. Social Scis., Beijing. Assoc. prof history, exec. dir. dept. history East-West Inst. Internat. Studies, Gordon Coll., Wenham, Mass., 2002—; assoc. in rsch. Fairbank Ctr. for East Asian Rsch., Harvard U., Cambridge, Mass., 2002—. Author: China's Unequal Treaties: Narrating National History, 2005, Managing God's Higher Learning: U.S.-China Cultural Encounter and Canton Christian College (Lingnan University), 1888-1952, 2007; assoc. editor: Jour. Am.-East Asian Rels., 2006—. Recipient Yat-sen award, 1996; grantee, Pew Charitable Trusts, 1993—97. Mem.: Assn. for Asian Studies, European Assn. Chinese Studies. Office: Gordon College 255 Grapevine Rd Wenham MA 01984 Office Phone: 978-867-4842.

WANG, ELISE, political science scholar; d. David and Beth W. Student, Univ. Pa.; student in Mandarin, immigration issues, Chinese history, Beijing Univ.; BA in Women, Gender and Sexuality Studies and Comparative Religion, Harvard Univ., 2007; MSc. student in Forced Migration, Oxford Univ., 2007—. Works for Mass. Com. on Status of Women. Rhodes Scholar. Avocations: viola, violin, crew. *

WANG, FEI, pharmacist, educator; d. Ke-Chiang and Iok Meng Lee Wang; m. Cunegundo Manuel Vergara; children: Leander Vergara, Chiu Yen Vergara. BS in Pharmacy, St. John's U., Jamaica, NY, 1983, MS in Pharmacy, 1994, PharmD, 1996. Cert. pharmacotherapy specialist Am. Pharm. Assn., DC, 1998, smoking cessation specialist Nat. Smoking Cessation Program, U. Pitts., 1998. Cmty. pharmacist Genovese Drug Stores, Inc., Fort Lee, NJ, 1983—84, supervising pharmacist Astoria, NY, 1985—90; hosp. pharmacist Cornell Med. Ctr., NY Hosp., NYC, 1990—93, target drug clin. coord., 1993—95; specialty residency in adult internal medicine Med. U. SC, Charleston, 1996—97, clin. pharmacist in surgery & trauma, 1996—97; clin. specialist in ambulatory care Hartford Hosp., Conn., 1997—. Adj. preceptor St. John's U., NYH-CMC, 1993—94; adj. instr. Med. U. SC, 1996—97; clin. preceptor U. Conn., 1997—2005, asst. clin. prof. Sch. Pharmacy, 1997—, dir. ambulatory care residency and fellowship program, 2001—; presenter in field; lectr. in field. Contbr. articles to profl. jours. Grant, Hartford Hosp. & Boehringer Ingelheim, 2002—05. Mem.: Conn. Soc. Health Sys. Pharmacists, Am. Soc. Health Sys. Pharmacists, Am. Coll. Clin. Pharmacy. Office: U Conn 69 North Eagleville Rd Unit 3092 Storrs Mansfield CT 06269-3092 Home Phone: 860-571-0465; Office Phone: 860-545-4125. Business E-Mail: fwang@harthosp.org.

WANG, FEN, adult education educator, researcher; arrived in US, 2002; BS in Mgmt. Info. Systems, Tianjin U., China, 2002, BS in Sci. and Tech. English, 2002; D in Mgmt. Info. Systems (hon.), U. Md., Balt., 2005. Rsch./tchg. asst. U. Md. Balt. County, Balt., 2002—05; asst. prof. Ea. Nazarene Coll., Quincy, Mass., 2005—. Com. mem. IRMA. Dir. missionary soc. Quincy Chinese Nazarene Ch., 2006—07. Finalist 1st Ann. Jessica Soto-Perez award, U. Md. Balt. County; Grad. Rsch. and Tchg. scholar, 2002—05, Dissertation fellow, 2005. Mem.: Info. Resources Mgmt. Assn., Decision Sci. Inst. Achievements include research in intelligent decision support technologies.

WANG, FRANCIS WEI-YU, biomedical materials scientist, researcher; b. Pei-Kang, Yun-Lin, Taiwan, July 21, 1936; came to U.S,. 1956; s. Yin-Kwei and Tsai-Wei Wang; m. Susan Shu-Huei Liao, June 18, 1966; children: Anthony, Andrea, Edwin. BSChemE, Calif. Inst. Tech., 1961, MSChemE, 1962; PhD in Chemistry, U. Calif., San Diego, 1971. Chemist Pacific Soap Co., San Diego, 1962—66; rsch. asst. U. Calif.-San Diego, La Jolla, 1966—71; USPHS postdoctoral fellow Polytechnic U., Bklyn., 1971—72; sr. rsch. chemist Nat. Inst. Stds. and Tech., Gaithersburg, Md., 1972—. Contbr. numerous articles to profl. jours. Recipient W.P. Slichter award Dept. Commerce, 1997, Bronze medal, 1985. Mem. Soc. Biomaterials, Am. Chem. Soc., Am. Phys. Soc. Achievements include patents on non-destructive method for fluorescence monitoring of polymerization and solidification of thermoplastic polymer, fluorescence monitoring of polymer injection molding, and fluorescence monitoring of polymer viscosity and orientation. Office: Nat Inst Stds and Tech 100 Bureau Dr Stop 8545 Gaithersburg MD 20899-8545 E-mail: francis.wang@nist.gov.

WANG, FREDERICK MARK, pediatrician, ophthalmologist, educator; b. NYC, Feb. 17, 1948; Student, Northwestern U., 1968; MD, Yeshiva U., 1972. Diplomate Am. Bd. Ophthalmology, Am. Bd. Pediats., Nat. Bd. Med. Examiners. Intern in pediats. H.C. Moffitt-U. Calif. San Francisco Hosps., 1972-73; resident in pediats. Bronx Mcpl. Hosp. Ctr.-Albert Einstein Coll. Medicine, 1973-74, resident in ophthalmology, 1976-79; Heed fellow in ophthalmology and strabismus Children's Hosp. Nat. Med. Ctr., Washington, 1979-80; asst. prof. ophthalmology Albert Einstein Coll. Medicine, Bronx, 1980-82, asst. clin. prof., 1982-85, assoc. clin. prof., 1985-95, clin. prof., 1995—, asst. prof. pediats., 1980-82, asst. clin. prof. pediats., 1982-92; dir. pediat. ophthalmology and strabismus svc. Montefiore Med. Ctr., Bronx, 1980-90. Cons. ophthalmologist Children's Evaluation & Rehab. Ctr., Rose Kennedy Ctr. for Rsch. in Mental Retardation and Human Devel., Bronx, 1980—, Craniofacial Ctr., Montefiore Med. Ctr., Bronx, 1980—; attending physician in ophthalmology Bronx Mcpl. Hosp./Montefiore Med. Ctr., 1980—; asst. attending physician in ophthalmology North Ctrl. Bronx Hosp., 1980-98; attending physician Strabismus Svc., N.Y. Eye & Ear Infirmary, N.Y.C., 1982-99, attending surgeon, 1999—; mem. dept. ophthalmology Lenox Hill Hosp., N.Y.C., 1988—; sci. reviewer Jour. Am. Acad. Ophthalmology, 1980-86; mem. profl. adv. bd. Found. for Children with Learning Disabilities, N.Y.C., 1983-89; mem. sci. adv. bd. The Glaucoma Found., N.Y.C., 1986-92; mem. profl. adv. bd. Nat. Assn. for Visually Handicapped, N.Y.C., 1988—; coord. pediat. sect. Greater N.Y. Ophthalmology Clin. Lectr. Series, 1990-93; mem. Velo-Cardio-Facial Syndrome Ednl. Found., 1994—, nominating com., 1995—. Mem. editl. bd. Jour. Pediat. Ophthalmology and Strabismus, 1998—; contbr. articles to profl. jours., chpts. to books. Referee, U.S. Soccer Fedn. Maj. med. officer USAF, 1974-76. Mem. Am. Acad. Pediats., Am. Acad. Ophthalmology, Am. Assn. for Pediat. Ophthalmology and Strabismus, N.Y. Soc. for Pediat. Ophthalmology and Strabismus (program chmn. 1987-89, pres. 1990-92), N.Y. Soc. for Clin. Ophthalmology (corr. sec. 1988-90, membership chmn. 1990-91, program chmn. 1991-92, pres. 1992-93), N.Y. Acad. Medicine (sec. sect. on ophthalmology 1993-94, sect. chmn. 1995-96), Alpha Omega Alpha. Avocations: fishing, chess, swimming, soccer refereeing. Office: Pediat Ophthalmology NY 30 E 40th St New York NY 10016-1201 Home Phone: 914-723-7122; Office Phone: 212-684-3980.

WANG, GUANGYA, ambassador, international organization official; b. Jiangsu Province, China, Apr. 1950; married; 1 child. Studied, Student Ctr. of British Coun., Wales Atlantic Untied Coll. and London Sch. Econ. and Polit. Sci., United Kingdom of Great Britain and Northern Ireland, 1972—75, John Hopkins U., 1981—82. Sect. mem., dept. of translation and interpretation Ministry of Foreign Affairs, 1975—77, third sec. and then dep. divsn. chief,, dept. internat. orgns. and conf., 1983—88, counselor and then dep. dir., dept. internat. orgns. and conf., 1992—93, dir., dept. of internat. orgns. and conf., 1993—98, asst. min. foreign affairs, 1998—99, vice min. foreign affairs, 1999—2003; staff mem. to attache Chinese Mission to UN, 1977—81, attache, 1982—83, counselor, 1988—92, amb. and perm. rep, 2003—. Office: 350 East 35th St New York NY 10016 Office Phone: 212-655-6100, 212-655-6191. Office Fax: 212-634-7626, 212-481-2998. *

WANG, GWO JAW, orthopedic surgery educator; Lillian T. Pratt prof. and chmn. orthopedic surgery U. Va. Sch. Medicine, Charlottesville, 1992—2000; pres. Kaohsiung Med. U., Taiwan, 2000—06. Vis. prof. Kaohsiung Med. U., Taiwan, 2006—. Recipient U. Va. Pres.'s Report award, 1992, Otto Aufranc award, Hip Soc. and Am. Acad. Orthop. Surgeons, 1992, 1997, Stinchfield award, 1986, Nicholas Andry award, 1998, Va. career award, 2006. Office: Kaohsiung Med Univ 100 Shih Chuan 1st Rd Kaohsiung Taiwan Home Phone: 886-7-537-1179; Office Phone: 886-7-3121101 ext.5390. Business E-Mail: gwojaw@cc.kmu.edu.tw.

WANG, JAW-KAI, bioengineering educator; b. Nanjing, Jiangsu, China, Mar. 4, 1932; arrived in U.S., 1955; s. Shuling and Hsi-Ying (Lo) W.; m. Kwang Mei Chow, Sept. 7, 1957 (div. Oct. 1989); children: Angela C.C., Dora C.C., Lawrence C.Y.; m. Bichuan Li, Sept. 25, 1999. BS, Nat. Taiwan U., 1953; MS in Agrl. Engring., Mich. State U., 1956, PhD, 1958. Registered profl. engr., Hawaii. Faculty agrl. engring. dept. U. Hawaii, Honolulu, 1959-93, assoc. prof., chmn. dept. agrl. engring., 1964-68, prof., chmn. dept. agrl. engring., 1968-75, prof. biosys. engring., 1994—2000, prof. molecular bioscis. dept., 2000—02; prof. emeritus U. Hawaii-Manoa, Honolulu, 2004—, dir. Aquaculture Program, 1990-96; spl. asst., Internat. Rsch. Dept., Office of Internat. Cooperation and Devel. U.S. Dept. Agr., 1988; pres. Aquaculture Tech., Inc., 1990—; academic cons. Chinese Acad. Fishery Scis., 2004—, chief sci. advisor, fishery, machinery and instrument rsch. inst., 2004—, chief tech. expert, rsch. inst. fisheries machinery and instrument, 2005—, mem. nat. open lab. for control of aquaculture water quality, 2005—. Co-dir. internat. sci. and edn. coun. USDA; vis. assoc. dir. internat. programs and studies office Nat. Assn. State Univs. and Land-Grant Colls., 1979; vis. prof. Nat. Taiwan U., 1964-65, 2000-01, U. Calif., Davis, 1980; hon. prof. coll. pharmacology Tianjing U., China, 2003; cons. U.S. Army Civilian Adminstrn., Ryukus, Okinawa, 1965, Internat. Rice Rsch. Inst., Philippines, 1971, Pacific Concrete and Rock Co. Ltd., 1974, AID, 1974, Universe Tankships, Del., 1980-81, World Bank, 1981, 82, ABA Internat., 1981-85, Internat. Found. for Agrl. Devel./World Bank, 1981, Rockefeller Found., 1980, Orizaba, Inc., 1983, Agrisys./FAO, 1983, Info. Processing Assocs., 1984, County of Maui, 1984, 85, Dept. of State, 1985, Alexander and Baldwin, 1986; mem. expert panel on agrl. mechanization FAO/UN, 1984-90; sr. fellow East-West Ctr. Food Inst., 1973-74; dir. Info. Sys. and Svcs. Internat., Inc., 1986-90; mem. bd. on agr. and natural resources The Nat. Acads., 2004—; panel mem. Vietnam Edn. Found., 2004-06; acad. cons. Chinese Acad. Fishery Scis., 2004-06; mem. bd. agrl. and natural resources Nat. Acads., 2004-06. Author: Irrigated Rice Production Systems, 1980; editor: Taro-A Review of Colocasia Esculenta and its Potentials, 1983; mem. editl. bd. Aquacultural Engring., 1982—. Recipient Exemplary State Employee award State of Hawaii, 1986, State of Hawaii Disting. Svc. award Office of Gov., 1990. Fellow Am. Soc. Agrl. Engrs. (chmn. Hawaii sect. 1962-63, chmn. grad. instrn. com. 1971-73, various coms., Engr. of Yr. 1976, Tech. Paper award 1978, Kishida Internat. award 1991), Am. Inst. Med. and Biol. Engring.; mem. NAE, Aquaculture Engring. Soc. (pres. 1993-95), Sigma Xi, Gamma Sigma Delta (pres. Hawaii chpt. 1974-75), Pi Mu Epsilon. Office: U Hawaii MBBE Dept 1955 East West Rd Honolulu HI 96822 Home Phone: 808-377-5087; Office Phone: 808-956-8154. Personal E-mail: jawkai@gmail.com. Business E-Mail: jawkai@hawaii.edu. *To be allowed a continuing search for truth even when you are doubting its existence, is to be blessed.*

WANG, JIA, research scientist; b. Wenzhou, Zhejiang, China, Dec. 25, 1968; came to the U.S., 1990; p. KeQiang Wang and DanPing Cai. BA, Wenzhou Tchrs.' U., 1988; MS, Ft. Valley State U., 1992; PhD, UCLA, 1996. Sr. statistician Applied Mgmt. and Planning Group, LA, 1995-97; asst. dir., sr. rsch. assoc. Ctr. for Pacific Rim Studies UCLA, 1997—2002, sr. rsch. and project dir. Ctr. for Study of Evaluation, 2002—07; v.p. rsch. Pub. Works, Inc., Pasadena, Calif., 2006—. Cons. The World Bank, Washington, 1997—, WHO, Geneva, Switzerland, 1999-2002. 1st author: (book) Measuring Country Performance on Health: Selected Indicators for 115 Countries, 1999; contbr. articles to profl. jours. Univ. fellow UCLA, 1992-96. Mem. AAAS, Am. Ednl. Rsch. Assn., Comparative and Internat. Edn. Soc. Avocations: reading, hiking, travel. Office: Pub Works Inc 90 North Daisy Ave Pasadena CA 91107 E-mail: jiawang@ucla.edu.

WANG, JIAN, materials scientist, researcher; b. Weiyuan, Sichuan, China, Mar. 3, 1971; s. Fengyan Wang and Shufen Deng; m. Lingyun Zhu, Apr. 16, 1974. BS, Peking U., Beijing, China, 1992, PhD, 1998. Postdoctoral fellow U. Tex., Austin, 1999—2001; rsch. assoc. Boston U., 2001—04; scientist Nanostellar, Menlo Park, Calif., 2004—. Contbr. articles Jour. of Am. Chem. Soc., Jour. of Physical Chemistry, to profl jours. Co-founder Austin Peking U. Alumni Assn. Mem.: Am. Chem. Soc. Achievements include development of nanocatalyst formulation and synthesis for automobile exhaust control in a nanotechnology start up co; patents pending in field. Avocations: reading, badminton, ping pong/table tennis, classical music.

WANG, JIE, computer science educator; b. Guangzhou, Guangdong, China, Aug. 28, 1961; s. Yeu-Yun and Lian-Fang (Hu) W.; m. Helen Hong Zhao, Dec. 26, 1986; 1 child, Jesse. BS, Zhongshan U., Guangzhou, 1982, ME, 1984; PhD, Boston U., 1990. Asst. prof. Wilkes U., Wilkes-Barre, Pa., 1990-93; asst. prof. math. dept. U. N.C., Greensboro, 1993-96, assoc. prof. Director Network and Systems Security Laboratory, Lowell, MA, 2001—. Contbr. articles to profl. confs.; referee jours. Boston U. Presdl. fellow 1989-90; grantee NSF, 1991—. Mem. IEEE Computer Soc., Assn. Computing Machinery (spl. interest group on algorithms and computation theory 1988—), European Assn. Theoretical Computer Sci. Avocation: painting. Office: U NC Dept Math Scis Greensboro NC 27412-0001

WANG, JINLIN, chemical engineer; b. Beijing, Apr. 12, 1957; s. Longji Wang and Enting Cai; m. Lifu Jiang, Mar. 15, 1986; children: Yuhong, John Yuming. BSE, Beijing Inst. Chem. Tech., 1982; PhD in Chem. Engring., Purdue U., 1995. Postdoctoral fellow Bisco Inc., Itasca, Ill., 1996—97; rsch. chemist Cargill Inc., Wayzata, Minn., 1997—98; sr. materials analyst Intel Corp., Chandler, Ariz., 1998—. Presenter in field. Contbr. articles to profl. jours. Mem.: The Soc. of Rheology. Achievements include research in packaging materials and processes developments for microelectronic packages, especially flip chip packaging technology; rheology and wettability of packaging materials; solder joint reliability; metrology developments; patents in field. Avocations: reading, table tennis. Office: Intel Corp CH5-232 5000 W Chandler Blvd Chandler AZ 85226 Business E-Mail: jinlin.wang@intel.com.

WANG, JIONGJIONG, neuroscientist, educator; s. Jinhai Wang and Fengxian Fu; m. Bo Peng, Dec. 22, 1998; 1 child, Eric. BS, Fu Dan U., Shanghai, 1993; PhD, U. Sci and Tech. China, Beijing, 1998. Staff scientist U. Pa., Phila., 2001—03, asst. prof., 2003—. Fellow Inst. on Aging, U. Pa., Phla., 2004—; cons. Hong Kong Rsch. Grants Coun., China, 2004—. Contbr. chapters to books. Fellow, Gordon Rsch. Conf., 2002; grantee, Thrasher Rsch. Fund, 2004, NIMH, 2005; scholar, Fu Dan U., 1990—93, Hongkong Dong's Found., 1997. Mem.: Cognitive Neurosci. Soc., Orgn. Human Brain Mapping (Student Stipend award 1999), Internat. Soc. Magnetic Resonance in Medicine (Student Stipend award 2000—03). Achievements include patents pending for multi-contrast hemodynamic imaging using arterial spin labeling. Avocations: music, reading, sport, movie, travel. Office: Univ Pa 3 W Gates 3400 Spruce St Philadelphia PA 19104 Home Phone: 856-428-4232; Office Phone: 215-614-0631. Office Fax: 215-349-8260. E-mail: wangj3@mail.med.upenn.edu.

WANG, JOHN CHENG HWAI, communications engineer, researcher; b. Beijing, Feb. 12, 1934; s. Hwa Lung and Shu Shiang (Shia) W.; m. Rosa Jenny Chu, Sept. 9, 1967; children: Sophia, Maria, Nina, Amy. BS, U. Md., 1959; MS, U. Pitts., 1968. Engr. Chesapeake Instrument Corp., Shadyside, Md., 1959-64; rsch. scientist Rsch. Ctr. U.S. Steel Corp., Monroeville, Pa., 1964-67; asst. prof. Pa. State U., New Kensington, 1967-69; rsch. engr. FCC, Washington, 1969—. Cmn. working party ionospheric propogation, Internat. Telecom. Union (ITU), Geneva, 1983-. Contbr. articles to profl. jours. Fellow IEEE. Avocations: astronomy, bridge, Chinese history. Office: FCC 445 12 St SW Washington DC 20554-0001 Office Phone: 202-418-2435. Business E-Mail: john.wang@fcc.gov.

WANG, JOHN XIAOWU, computer company executive; b. Hefei, Anhui, China, July 6, 1958; arrived in U.S., 1982; s. Zhi Dao Wang and Xian Zhen Fang; m. Lin Hu, Aug. 24, 1985; children: Fanny, Kathy, Bill. B in Physics, U. Sci. and Tech. China, Hefei, 1982; MS, NYU, 1984, PhD in Physics, 1990. Sr. engr. Micromath, Salt Lake City, 1990-92; chmn., chief engr. Poly Software Internat. Ltd., Salt Lake City, 1992-95, pres., CEO, 1995—, software engr. Pearl River, NY, 2000—. Contbr. articles to profl. jours. James Arthur fellow, NYU, 1990. Home: 7 Kerry Ct Pearl River NY 10965-3034 Business E-Mail: wang@polysoftware.com.

WANG, JUI HSIN, biochemistry educator; b. Beijing, Mar. 16, 1921; arrived in U.S., 1946; s. Lieh and Sun Li (Sun) W.; m. Yen Chan Yang, Apr. 2, 1949 (dec. 1993); children: Jane, Nancy. BS, Nat. S.W. Assoc. U., Kunming, China, 1945; PhD, Washington U., St. Louis, 1949; MA (hon.), Yale U., 1960. Postdoctoral fellow radiochemistry Washington U., 1949-51; mem. faculty Yale U., New Haven, 1951-72, prof. chemistry, 1960-62, Eugene Higgins prof. chemistry, 1962-65, Eugene Higgins prof. chemistry and molecular biophysics, 1965-72; Einstein prof. sci. SUNY, Buffalo, 1972—. Rschr. molecular structure and biochem. activity, superconductivity. Contbr. articles to profl. jours., chpts. to books. Guggenheim fellow Cambridge U., 1960-61. Fellow AAAS, Am. Acad. Arts and Scis.; mem. Am. Chem. Soc., Am. Soc. Microbiology, Yale Chemists Assn., Am. Soc. for Biochemistry and Molecular Biology, Am. Phys. Soc., Biophys. Soc., Am. Assn. Cancer Rsch., Academia Sinica, Materials Rsch. Soc., Am. Assn. Cancer Rsch., Sigma Xi. Home: 755 Renaissance Dr Apt 206 Williamsville NY 14221-8046 Office: SUNY Dept Chemistry Buffalo NY 14260-0001 Business E-Mail: juiwang@buffalo.edu.

WANG, JUN, process engineer, materials scientist; s. Youfa Wang and Yulian Chen; m. Wenyun Yang, Dec. 23, 2002; 1 child, Barry K. BS, U. Sci. and Tech. China, Hefei, 1996; MS, Shanghai Inst. Ceramics, China, 1999; PhD, Pa. State U., University Park, 2004. Adj. rsch. assoc. Pa. State U. Material Rsch. Inst., University Park, 2004—06; sr. rsch. engr. Saint-Gobain HPM Northboro R&D Ctr., Northboro, Mass., 2004—. Contbr. articles to profl. jours. Mem.: IEEE, Am. Chem. Soc., Materials Rsch. Soc., Am. Ceramic Soc. (program chair, sec. New England section 2005—). Achievements include patents pending for unagglomerated core-shell nanoparticles for functional applications; transition alumina nanoparticle abrasives for chemical mechanical planarization; improved stability of transition alumina slurry used for copper chemical mechanical planarization; methods and apparatus for minimizing the aging effect on alumina particles in slurry solutions; development of balidate HPLC as a powerful tool to separate and disperse nanoparticle for medical applications. A startup company called Keystone Nano was formed based on this core technology in 2005; developed and commercializing next generation of soft alumina abrasive for chemical mechanical planarization (CMP) application. Home: 47 Sheridan Dr #6 Shrewsbury MA 01545 Office: Saint-Gobain HPM Northboro R&D Ctr 9 Goddard Rd Northborough MA 01532 Office Phone: 508-351-7952. Office Fax: 508-351-7740. Business E-Mail: jun.wang@saint-gobain.com.

WANG, KAIHONG, mechanical engineer, researcher; MS, So. Ill. U., Carbondale, 2000; PhD, Va. Tech, Blacksburg, 2004. Mfg./mech. engr. Capital Steel and Iron Inc., Beijing, 1990—98; mech. engr. AREVA NP Inc., Lynchburg, Va., 2005—. Mech. design/mfg. processes Capital Steel and Iron Inc., Beijing, 1990—98; structural analysis AREVA NP Inc., Lynchburg, Va., 2005—. Rsch. Assistantship, Va. Tech, 2000—04, So. Ill. U., 1998—2000. Mem.: AIAA, ASME, Soc. for Exptl. Mechanics. Office: AREVA NP Inc 3315 Old Forest Rd OF-50 Lynchburg VA 24501 Office Phone: 434-832-4653. Office Fax: 434-832-2831.

WANG, KIM, commissioner, librarian; m. Harry Wang; children: Elaine, Steve, Leslie. BA in History, U. Colo.; MLS, U. Calif., Berkeley. Former libr. U. So. Calif., Hughes Aircraft; property mgr. and real estate broker. Mem. Nat. Mus. & Libr. Services. Bd., Inst. Mus. & Libr. Services, Washington, 2004—. V.p. La Terrazza Homeowners Assn.; former parks and recreation commr., planning commn. mem. City of Rancho Palos Verdes; bd. mem. Libr. Calif. Bd.; mem. Cultural Arts Commn., Torrance, Calif.; trustee Marymount Coll., Palos Verdes, Calif.; former bd. mem. Am. Heart Assn., Torrance. Mem.: AARP, AAUW (Torrance br.), LWV (Torrance br.), Am. Contract Bridge League, Torrance Sister City Assn., Torrance Hist. Soc., Torrance Hist. Assn., Torrance Chamber Toastmasters, Torrance Area C. of C. Office: Inst Mus and Libr Svcs 1100 Pennsylvania Ave NW Washington DC 20506 *

WANG, LEI, biochemist; b. China; BS in Organic Chemistry, Peking U., 1994, MS in Physical Chemistry, 1997; PhD in Bioorganic Chemistry, U. Calif., Berkeley, 2002. Postdoctoral rschr. biochemistry U. Calif., San Diego, 2002—. Contbr. articles to profl. jour. Named one of Top 100 Young Innovators, MIT Tech. Review, 2004; recipient Grand prize, Collegiate Inventors Competition, Nat. Inventors Hall Fame, Young Scientist prize, Amersham Biosciences, 2003; Merck fellow, Damon Runyon Cancer Rsch. Found., 2002. Office: The Salk Inst 10010 N Torrey Pines Rd La Jolla CA 92037 Business E-Mail: lewang@ucsd.edu.

WANG, LU-HAI, medical educator, biochemist; b. Tonan Jien, Yuin Lin Shien, Taiwan, Sept. 2, 1947; s. Bun-Chin Wang and Tsoo Huang; m. Mei-Hui Teng; children: Sophia F., Sandra T. PhD, U. Calif., Berkeley, 1976. Postdoctoral fellow Univ. Calif., Berkeley, 1976—77, Rockefeller U., NYC, 1977—79, asst. prof., 1979—85, assoc. prof., 1985—88; assoc. prof. with tenure The Mt. Sinai Sch. Medicine, NYC, 1988—92, prof., 1992—. Study sect. mem., reviewers reserve NIH, Bethesda, Md., 1988—; sci. cons. Nat. Health Rsch. Inst., Taipei, Taiwan, 1996; hon. prof. Peking Union Med. Coll., China, 1998; rschr. of molecular oncogenesis in field; bd. mem. oncogene rsch., edn. bd. The Mt. Sinai Sch. Medicine, NYC, 1986—90. Recipient Jr. Faculty award, Am. Cancer Soc., 1979, Career Rsch. Devel. award, NIH; scholar Am. Leukemia Soc. Mem.: Soc. Chinese Biochemists in Am. (virology edn. bd. 1997—, chief edn., biotech. & biopharm divsn. 2005—05), Am. Soc. Advancement Scis., N.Y. Acad. Sci., Am. Soc. Microbiology. Office: Mount Sinai Sch Medicine Dept Microbiology 1 Gustave Levy Pl New York NY 10029 Home Phone: 201-967-2484; Office Phone: 212-241-3795.

WANG, LUMIN, nuclear engineer; s. Z.Y. Wang; m. Lily Li Zhao; children: Diana, Teresa, Emily. PhD in Materials Sciences, U. Wis., Madison, 1988. Rsch. scientist U. N.Mex, Albuquerque, 1990—97; prof. nuc. engring., materials sci. and engring. U. Mich., Ann Arbor, 1997—. Dir. electron microbeam analysis lab. U. Mich. Contbr. over 300 articles to profl. jours. Office: Univ Michigan 2355 Bonisteel Blvd Ann Arbor MI 48109 Home Phone: (734) 414-0095; Office Phone: 734-647-8530. Business E-Mail: lmwang@umich.edu.

WANG, MICHAEL LEE, ophthalmologist; s. Chan Huan and Katherine Tsang Wang; m. Susan Carol Wong, Oct. 25, 1986; children: Jonathan Chu, Matthew Lee, Kira Lin. MD, U. Calif., San Francisco, 1982—86. Diplomate Am. Bd. Ophthalmology, 1986. Ophthalmologist Eye Physicians E.Bay, Oakland, Calif., 1990—. Office: Eye Physicians E Bay 80 Grand Ave #700 Oakland CA 94612 Home Phone: 510-652-7826. Office Fax: 510-893-1108. Business E-Mail: myeyemds@netscape.net.

WANG, MIN, electronics engineer; b. Qishan, Shaanxi, China, Sept. 20, 1977; arrived in U.S., 1999; s. Enquan Wang and Huanqin Li; m. Jiang-Jiang Cheng, Aug. 30, 2003. BS, Tsinghua U., Beijing, 1999; MSEE, U. Wash., 2001, PhDEE, 2004. Pre-doctal rsch. assoc. U. Wash., Seattle, 1999—2004; software engr. Intel Corp., Hillsboro, Oreg., 2003; rschr. Intel Corp. - Intel Rsch., Seattle, 2003; sr. signal integrity engr. Intel Corp., Folsom, Calif., 2004—. Mem.: IEEE (Best Paper award 2002, 2006). Home: 4453 Lick Mill Blvd Santa Clara CA 95054 Mailing: Intel Corp 2200 Mission College Blvd MS SC12-108 Santa Clara CA 95054 Office Phone: 408-765-7127. E-mail: min.wang@gmail.com.

WANG, MINGYU, hydrologist, environmental scientist; B in Hydrogeology, Liaoning Tech. U., China, 1982; M in Hydrogeology, China U. of Geoscis., 1988; PhD, U. Ariz., 2000. Cert. Ground Water Profl. Nat. Ground Water Assn., USA, 2002. Lectr. & rsch. hydrogeologist Liaoning Tech. U., Fuxin, Liaoning, China, 1988—95, assoc. prof., 1995—96; vis. rsch. scientist U. of Ariz., Tucson, 1996—97; sr. project scientist US EPA's Ctr. for Subsurface Modeling Support, Ada, Okla., 2000—. Contbr. articles to profl. jours. Mem. of editl. bd. Jour.: Hydrogeology and Engring. Geology, Beijing, 2002—; oversea expert reviewer Nat. Natural Sci. Found. of China (NSFC), Beijing, 2004—. Named to Hundreds of Talents list, Chinese Acad. Scis., 2005; recipient Extraordinary Ability Outstanding Scientist, US Govt., 2003, Sr. Tech. Leader, Shaw Environ., Inc., 2004, Pres. award for Excellence, ManTech Environ. Tech., Inc, 2001, Nat. Outstanding Rsch. award, Chinese Govt., 1995, Excellent Grad. Student, China U. of Geoscience Beijing, 1988. Mem.: Nat. Ground Water Assn. (NGWA), Internat. Assn. of Hydrogeologists (IAH), Am. Geophys. Union. Achievements include research in Practical & Cost-Effective Discrete Fracture Fluid Flow-Equivalent Continuum Approach; Practical & Cost-Effective Discrete Fracture Network Fluid Flow Approach; Groundwater protection optimal management; Control of groundwater bursting into mines; Pumping test design in fractured rocks; integrated and systematic groundwater modeling approach. Office: EPA's Ctr Subsurface Modeling 919 Kerr Research Dr Ada OK 74820 Home Phone: 1-405-310-2205; Office Phone: 1-580-436-8656. Office Fax: 1-580-436-8718. Personal E-mail: mingyuwpan@yahoo.com. E-mail: wang.mingyu@epa.gov.

WANG, NANCY, pathologist, educator; b. An-Wei, China, Sept. 2, 1944; m. Tingchung Wang; children: Jessie, Melissa. BS, Nat. Taiwan U., 1966; MS, U. Minn., 1968, PhD, 1978. Diplomate Am. Bd. Med. Genetics. Instr. Dept. Pathology & Lab. Med. U. Minn., Mpls., 1978-79, asst. prof., 1980-82, Dept. Pathology, Tulane Med. Sch., 1982-83, assoc. prof., 1984-86, U. Rochester, NY, 1986-93, prof. NY, 1993—. Mem.: Am. Assn. Human Gennetics. Office Phone: 585-275-6597. Business E-Mail: nancy_wang@urmc.rochester.edu.

WANG, NING, education educator; b. Jingzhou, China, Dec. 25, 1971; PhD, U. Chgo., 2002. Rsch. assoc. U. of Chgo. Law Sch., 2002—05; asst. prof. Ariz. State U., Tempe, 2005—. Summer Fellow, Ctr. for Advanced Study in Behavioral Sci., 2006. Office: Sch of Global Studies Ariz State Univ 675 S Myrtle Ave Tempe AZ 85287-4802 Office Phone: 480-727-0738. Office Fax: 480-727-8292. Business E-Mail: ningwang@asu.edu.

WANG, PEILING, information scientist, educator; d. Yongping and Junming Wang. BEngring in Chemistry, East China Sci. Tech. U., 1982; MS in Info. Sci., Inst. Scientific Tech. Info., China, 1986; PhD, U. Md., College Park, 1987—94. Libr., dir. Agrl. Resource and Econ. Dept. Info. Ctr. U. Md., 1990—95; assoc. prof. U. Tenn., Knoxville, 1995—. Contbr. articles to profl. jours. Recipient Best Paper award, Am. Soc. Info. Sci. & Tech., 1999; Rsch. & Demonstration grant, Inst. Mus. & Libr. Svcs., 2005. Mem.: Am. Soc. Info. Sci., Assn. Libr. and Info. Sci. Edn. (Rsch. grant 2005). Office: Univ Tenn Knoxville 1345 Circle Park Dr Knoxville TN 37996 Home Phone: 865-692-3547; Office Phone: 865-974-2148. Office Fax: 865-974-4967. Business E-Mail: peilingw@utk.edu.

WANG, RUN, research scientist; b. Yinchuan, China, Mar. 31, 1980; m. Zhiming Chen, June 28, 2001. BS, Tsinghua U., 2001; PhD, Case Western Res. U., Cleve., 2006. Rsch. asst. Case Western Res. U., 2001—06, rsch. assoc., 2006—. Contbr. articles to profl. jours. Case Prime fellow. Mem.: Electrochem. Soc., Chinese Scholar and Student Assn. (coord. 2001—), Sigma Xi. Office: Case Western Res U 10900 Euclid Ave Glennan 508 Cleveland OH 44106 Office Phone: 216-368-4947. Business E-Mail: rxw54@cwru.edu.

WANG, SHELDON, information technology executive, insurance company executive; BS in Physics, Fuzhou Univ., China; MS in Physics, Idaho State Univ.; PhD in Med. Informatics, Univ. Utah. Exec. v.p., rsch., devel., COO HealthVision (acquired by Eclipsys); sr. v.p., rsch., devel. Eclipsys Corp.; sr. v.p. engring eHealthInsurance, Mountain View, Calif., 1999—2007, chief tech. officer, 1999—, and exec. v.p. tech., 2007—; also pres., CEO eHealth China, 2003—. Named one of Top 25 Chief Tech. Officers, InfoWorld mag., 2007. Office: eHealthInsurance 440 E Middlefield Rd Mountain View CA 94043 Office Phone: 877-456-7180.

WANG, SHIH-HO, electrical engineer, educator; b. Kiangsu, China, June 29, 1944; arrived in US, 1968; BEE, Nat. Taiwan U., Taipei, 1967; MEE, U. Calif., Berkeley, 1970, PhD in Elec. Engring., 1971. Asst. prof. elec. engring. U. Colo., Colo. Springs, 1973-76, Boulder, 1976-77; asst. prof. electrical engring. U. Md., College Park, 1977-78, assoc. prof., 1978-84; prof. U. Calif., Davis, 1984—. Cons. Lawrence Livermore (Calif.) Nat. Lab., 1986-88; scientific officer Office Naval Research, Arlington, Va., 1983-84. Assoc. editor Internat. Jour. Robotics and Automation, 1986—90. Served to 2d lt. China Air Force, Taiwan, 1967-68. Mem. IEEE (hon. mention award control systems soc. 1975). Office: Univ Calif Dept Elec Computer Engring Davis CA 95616 Business E-Mail: shwang@ucdavis.edu.

WANG, SUSAN S., manufacturing executive; BA in Acctg., U. Tex.; MBA, U. Conn. CPA, Calif. With Price Waterhouse & Co., NYC; various fin. and acctg. mgmt. positions Xerox Corp., Westvaco Corp.; dir. fin. Solectron Corp., Milpitas, Calif., 1984, v.p. fin., CFO, 1986, sr. v.p., 1990—, also bd. dirs. Mem. adv. bd. YWCA, Santa Clara County; chairperson Fin. Exec. Rsch. Found. Recipient Top Women in Industry award YWCA; named one of San Francisco Bay Area's most powerful corp. women. Mem. AICPA, N.Y. State Soc. CPA, Fin. Execs. Inst. Office: Solectron Corp 777 Gibraltar Dr Milpitas CA 95035-6328

WANG, TIAN, immunologist, educator; d. Hengqi Wang and Yanqiu Pan; m. Tong Han, 1995 (div. 1998); m. Thomas Welte, 2005. PhD, U. Tex., Galveston, 1995—2000. Postdoctoral fellow Yale U. Sch. Medicine, New Haven, 2000—04, assoc. rsch. scientist, 2004—05; asst. prof. Colo. State U., Ft. Collins, 2005—. Grantee Kempner Postdoctoral fellowship, U. Tex. Med. Br., 2001, 2003, Jr. Faculty award, Am. Fedn. Aging Rsch., 2005; Rsch. grant, NIH, 2006, Coll. Coun. grant, Colo. State U., 2006. Mem.: AAAS (corr.), Am. Assn. Virologist (assoc.), Am. Assn. Immunologist (life AAI Travel award 2005, 2006), Sigma Xi (assoc.). Achievements include patents for comprising West Nile Virus polypeptides. Office: Campus Delivery 1690 Colo State Univ Fort Collins CO 80523 Office Fax: 970-491-8707. Business E-Mail: tian.wang@colostate.edu.

WANG, TING, mechanical engineering educator; BSME, Tatung Inst. Tech., Taipei, Taiwan, 1977; MSME, SUNY, Buffalo, 1981; PhD in Mech. Engring., U. Minn., 1984. Dir. Energy Conversion and Conservation Ctr., U. New Orleans, prof. dept. mech. engring.; dir. gas turbine lab. Clemson (S.C.) U. Contbr. articles to profl. publs. Endowed chair Jack and Reba Matthy Energy Rsch. Fellow ASME (mem. gas turbine com., heat transfer com., biomass and alternative fuels com., George Westinghouse Silver medal 1998). Achievements include research in gas turbine application, integrated gasification combined cycle, mist/steam cooling for advanced turbine systems, heat transfer enhancement and drag reduction on micro-structured surfaces, impingement cooling on a moving surface, turbulent and transitional flows, energy conservation in residential housing. Office: Energy Conversion & Conservation Ctr Univ New Orleans New Orleans LA 70148-2220 Business E-Mail: twang@uno.edu.

WANG, TSUEY TANG, science educator, venture capitalist; b. Tainan, Taiwan, Nov. 12, 1932; came to U.S., 1958; s. Shih-Neng and Tsun (Chen) W.; m. Margaret Mei-Tieh Lin, June 12, 1965; children: David, Marjorie, Vanessa. BS, Cheng Kung U., Tainan, 1955; PhD, Brown U., 1965. Asst. prof. Poly. U. N.Y., Bklyn., 1965-67; disting. mem. tech. staff AT&T Bell Labs., Murray Hill, NJ, 1967-88; vis. prof. Rutgers U., New Brunswick, NJ, 1988—; pres., chmn. bd. dirs. Transpac Capital Corp., Springfield, NJ, 1988—. Vis. prof. Tokyo U. Agr. and Tech., 1984; mem. indsl. adv. bd. Nat. Ctr. Composite Materials, U. Del., 1986-89; bd. dirs. Internat. Power Devices, Inc., Boston, 1989-99; spl. invited vis. prof. Japan Ministry Edn., Tokyo, 1992; bd. dirs., sr. advisor Metal Industries R&D Ctr., Taiwan, 2005-06; advisor Nat. Applied Rsch. Labs., Taiwan, 2007—; bd. dirs. HDM Systems Corp., Boston, 2007—; sr. advisor Indsl. Tech. Rsch. Inst., Taiwan, 2007—. Author: (chpt.) Polymer Blends, 1978, (chpt.) Optical Telecommunications, 1979; editor: The Applications of Ferroelectric Polymers, 1988; patentee in field. Recipient Borden Corina Keen fellow Brown U., 1961. Fellow Am. Phys. Soc.; mem. ASME, Soc. Advancement Material and Process Engring., Materials Rsch. Soc., N.Y. Acad. Scis. Achievements include research in spinodal decomposition in polymer blends; melting point depression in compatible polymer blends. Office: Rutgers Univ Chem and Biochem Engring Piscataway NJ 08854 Business E-Mail: tsuey@rci.rutgers.edu.

WANG, VERA, fashion designer; b. NYC, June 27, 1949; d. Cheng Ching Wang; m. Arthur Becker, June 22, 1989; children: Cecilia, Josephine. BA in Art History, Sarah Lawrence Coll., New York, 1978. Various positions including accessories editor, European editor, sr. fashion editor Vogue mag., NYC, 1969—85; design dir. Ralph Lauren Women's Wear, NYC, 1987-89; prin. Vera Wang Bridal House Ltd., NYC, 1990—; expanded to ready-to-wear, fragrance, eyewear, footwear, fine jewelry, and a home collection. Designer for Olympic figure skaters including Nancy Kerrigan's silver medal performance at the 1994 Olympics. Costume designer (films) The Parent Trap, 1998, First Daughter, 2004; author: Vera Wang on Weddings, 2001. Recipient Womenswear Designer of the Yr., Coun. Fashion Designers Am., 2005, André Leon Talley Lifetime Achievement award, Savannah Coll. Art and Design., 2006. Achievements include first to successfully fuse high style and fashion with the tradition and symbolism of the bridal industry; designing wedding and red carpet gowns for Hollywood's elite. Office: Vera Wang Bridal House 225 W 39th St Fl 10 New York NY 10018-3103 Office Phone: 212-575-6400. *

WANG, WAYNE, film director; b. Hong Kong, Jan. 12, 1949; arrived in U.S., 1967; m. Cora Miao. Student, Calif. Coll. Arts and Crafts. Dir., writer: A Man, a Woman, and a Killer, 1975, Blue in the Face, 1995, Chinese Box, 1997; dir., writer, prodr., editor: Chan is Missing, 1982; dir., prodr.: Dim Sum: A Little Bit of Heart, 1985; dir.: Slamdance, 1987, Dim Sum Take Out, 1988, Eat a Bowl of Tea, 1989, Life is Cheap...But Toilet Paper is Expensive, 1989, The Joy Luck Club, 1993, Smoke, 1995, Anywhere But Here, 1999, Maid in Manhattan, 2002, Because of Winn-Dixie, 2005, Last Holiday, 2006; prodr. Lanai-Loa, 1998; dir., writer, prodr. Center of the World, 2001. Office: 916 Kearny St San Francisco CA 94133 also: ICM c/o Bob Walker 40 W 57th St Fl 16 New York NY 10019-4001

WANG, WILLIAM KAI-SHENG, law educator; b. NYC, Feb. 28, 1946; s. Yuan-Chao and Julia Ying-Ru (Li) W.; m. Kwan Kwan Tan, July 29, 1972; 1 child, Karen You-Chuan. BA, Amherst Coll., Mass., 1967; JD, Yale U., New Haven, Conn., 1971. Bar: Calif. 1972. Asst. to mng. partner Gruss & Co., NYC, 1971-72; asst. prof. law U. San Diego, 1972-74, asso. prof., 1974-77, prof., 1977-81, Hastings Coll. Law, U. Calif., San Francisco, 1981—. Vis. prof. law U. Calif., Davis, 1975—76, Hastings Coll. Law, U. Calif., 1980, UCLA, 1990, Villanova U., 1999, Bklyn. Law Sch., 2000, Leiden (Netherlands) U., 2004; cons. White Ho. Domestic Policy Staff, Washington, 1979; chair investment policy oversight group, bd. participant Law Sch. Admissions Coun.; nat. adjudicatory coun. NASD; mem. then chair com. on audit and assn. investment policy Assn. Am. Law Schs., 1995—98. Co-author: Insider Trading, 2d edit., 2006; mem. editl. bd.: Internat. and Comparative Corp. Law Jour.; contbr. articles to newspapers, mags., profl. jours. Mem. State Bar Calif., Am. Law Inst. Home: 455 39th Ave San Francisco CA 94121-1507 Office: U Calif Hastings Coll Law 200 McAllister St San Francisco CA 94102-4978 Office Phone: 415-565-4666. Business E-Mail: wangw@uchastings.edu.

WANG, WILLIAM WEIQI, physician; b. Shanghai, June 3, 1962; arrived in U.S., 1989; s. Junmin Wang and Shanlai Gan. MD, Shanghai Med. U., 1985; PhD, U. Medicine and Dentistry N.J., Newark, 1995. Fellow NIMH, Bethesda, Md., 1995—96; rsch. assoc. Baylor Coll. Medicine, Houston, 1997—98; resident psychiatry Washington U., St. Louis, 1998—2002; attending psychiatrist SSM Healthcare, St. Louis, 2002—; clin. instr. St. Louis U. Med. Sch., 2003—. Dir. med. rsch. Advent Rsch. Inst., 2006—; bd. dir. Impact Group, LLC; med. dir. geriatric transitional program SSM St. Joseph Health Ctr., 2007—. Author: Psychiatry Pearls of Wisdom, 1999, Psychiatry for the Boards, 2002, 2007; contbr. articles to profl. jours. Recipient Clin. Rec. award, Shanghai Bur. Pub. Health, 1988. Mem.: AMA, Am. Psychiat. Assn. Avocations: fine arts, history. Office: 255 Spencer Rd Saint Peters MO 63376 Office Phone: 636-939-2550. Personal E-mail: wwwang@rocketmail.com.

WANG, XIAO, language educator; d. ZhiYuan Wang and Yu Lang Huang. BA, NW Tchrs. U., China, 1979—83; MA, St. Cloud State U., Minn., 1990—92; PhD, Ball State U., Muncie, Ind., 1992—97. Cert. tchr. Xian Jiao Tong U., 1986. English instr. Ariz. State U., Tempe, 1997—98; prof. English Broward CC, Ft. Lauderdale, Fla., 1998—. Program chair TYCA-SE Conf., Ft. Lauderdale, 2001—01. Author: (book) English Composition (Tchg. Excellence award, 2001). Doner Ball State U., Muncie, Ind., 2000—06. Mem.: NCTE. Achievements include research in interlanguage characteristcis in the texts by Chinese-American freshman composition students at UCLA. Home: 9230 Lagoon Pl #211 Davie FL 33324 Office: Broward CC 3501 SW Davie FL 33314 Home Phone: 754-422-9990; Office Phone: 954-201-6515. Office Fax: 954-202-6646. Business E-Mail: xwang@broward.edu.

WANG, XIAODONG, biomedical researcher, educator; b. 1963; BS in Biology, Beijing Normal U., 1984; PhD in Biochemistry, U. Tex. Southwestern Med. Ctr., Dallas, 1991. Fellow Damon Runyon-Walter Winchell Cancer Rsch. Fund, 1991; George L. MacGregor disting. chair, prof. biomedical sci. U. Tex. Southwestern Med. Ctr., Dallas, 1991—; investigator Howard Hughes Med. Inst., 1997—. Contbr. article to profl. jours. Recipient Wilson S. Stone Meml. award, Anderson Cancer Ctr., Eli Lilly award, Am. Chem. Soc., 2000, Paul Marks prize, Meml. Sloan-Kettering Cancer Ctr., 2001, Norman Hackerman award in Chemical Rsch., Welch Found., 2002, Shaw prize in Life Sci. and Medicine, Shaw Found., Hong Kong, 2006. Mem.: NAS (Award in Molecular Biology 2004, Richard Lounsbery award 2007), Soc. Chinese Biomed. Scientists in Am. (Young Investigator award 1999), Ray Wu Soc., Am. Soc. Cell Biology, Am. Soc. Biochemistry and Molecular Biology (Schering-Plough award 2000), Am. Assn. Cancer Rsch. (Outstanding Achievement in Cancer Rsch. 2004). Office: Univ Tex Southwestern Med Ctr Dallas/Biomed Sci 5323 Harry Hines Blvd Dallas TX 75390-9038 also: Howard Hughes Med Inst 4000 Jones Bridge Rd Chevy Chase MD 20815-6789 *

WANG, XINSHENG, lawyer; b. Da Tong, Shan Xi, China, May 20, 1975; arrived in US, 1997; d. Zhifang Wang and Fumei Zhang; m. Jiaher Tian, Jan. 9, 1999; 1 child, Caleb Y. Tian. BS, Peking U., Beijing, China, 1997; MS, U. Kans., Lawrence, 1999, JD, 2002. Rsch. asst. Higuchi Biosci. Ctr., Lawrence, 1997—99; patent atty. Lathrop & Gage, LC, Kansas City, Mo., 2002—05, NYC, 2005—. Corp. gen. counsel, dir. Christian Worldwide Worship Ministries, Omaha, 2002—05. Active Lawrence Chinese Evang. Ch., 2002—05. Mem.: ABA, US-China Lawyers Soc. (bd. dirs. 2005—06). Avocations: fishing, tai chi. Office: Ste 1847 230 Park Ave New York NY 10169 Office Phone: 212-650-6236. Personal E-mail: xinshengw@hotmail.com.

WANG, XIUBIN, transportation educator; s. Zhaoxian Wang and Meihua Ren; m. Fenghuan Wang; children: Kelvin, Benjamin Z. PhD, U. Calif., Irvine, 2001. Asst. prof. U. Wis., Superior, 2002—07, rschr. Madison, 2007—. Recipient Excellence in Rsch. award, U. Wis., Superior, 2006. Mem.: Transp. Rsch. Bd. Home Phone: 608-262-6639. Personal E-mail: xbwang@gmail.com. Business E-Mail: wangx@engr.wisc.edu.

WANG, YANG, cardiologist, educator, medical researcher; b. Tangshan, China, May 12, 1923; arrived in U.S., 1949; s. Yu-Shen and Jun-Rong (Bo) Wang; m. Helen S. Huang; children: Dale, Cynthia, Jennifer, Heather. MB, Nat. Shanghai Med. Coll., 1948; MD, Harvard U., 1952. Diplomate Am. Bd. Internal Medicine, cert. cardiovasc. diseases. Intern, resident Mass. Gen. Hosp., Boston, 1952—57, fellow in cardiology, 1957—58; fellow in cardiovasc. physiology Mayo Found., Rochester, Minn., 1958—59; dir. cardiac catherization lab., program dir. cardiovasc. fellowship tng. U. Minn. Hosp., 1959—86; from instr. to prof. med. cardiology U. Minn. Med. Sch., Mpls., 1959—93, prof. emeritus, 1993—. Contbr. chapters to books, articles to profl. jours. Bd. dirs. Minn. Mus. Art, St. Paul, 1984—90, MacPhail Music Ctr., 2002—05; bd. dirs. China Ctr. U. Minn.; session elder House of Hope, Presbyn. Ch., St. Paul. Capt. MC USAF, 1954—56. Recipient Lifetime Educator award, U. Minn. Med. Sch. Cardiology, 1999. Fellow: AAAS, ACP, Am. Heart Assn. (pres., bd. dirs. Minn. chpt. 1973—74, cons., internat. program com., Gt. Plains com., Lifetime Achievement award 2004), Am. Coll. Cardiology; mem.: Am. Fedn. Clin. Rsch., Minn. Acad. Medicine (pres. 1997—98), Ctrl. Soc. Clin. Rsch., Assn. Univ. Cardiologists, Alpha Omega Alpha. Achievements include development of rate-pressure product as an index of cardiac work and coronary blood flow; research in cardiovascular response to exercise in normal subjects and in heart disease; in vivo assessment of cardiac valve protheses; treatment of adult congenital heart disease and of coronary disease in diabetes mellitus. Office: FUMC MMC 508 420 Delaware St SE Minneapolis MN 55455-0374 Business E-Mail: wangx002@umn.edu.

WANG, YINMIN, materials scientist, educator; s. Zhenhua Wang and Aixiang Sheng. BS, Nat. U. Def. Tech., China, 1991; MS in Materials, Shanghai Jiao Tong U., China, 1994, Johns Hopkins U., Balt., 1999, MS in Computers, 2003, PhD in Materials, 2003. Harold Graboske fellow Lawrence Livermore Nat. Lab., Livermore, Calif., 2004—06, staff scientist, 2006—. Reviewer panel Singapore Sci. and Engring. Rsch. Coun., Singapore, 2004—; reviewer various jours. Contbr. articles to profl. jours. Recipient CMS Excellence in Publ. awards, Lawrence Livermore Nat. Lab., 2005—06, MRS medal, Materials Rsch. Soc., 2002; Disting. Harold Graboske fellow, Lawrence Livermore Nat. Lab., 2004—05. Mem.: TMS (assoc.), Materials Rsch. Soc. (assoc.). Achievements include discovery of using bimodal nanostructure to achieve high strength and high ductility in nanostructured materials; patents pending for high strength and high performance nanostructured materials and the method of making the same; research in finding of superplastic behavior in carbon nanotubes; ultrahigh strength nanostructured materials under shock loading; fast mass transport in sub-2nm carbon nanotube pores. Home Phone: 209-830-1966.

WANG, YUCONG, engineering executive; s. Hezhang and Lingmei Wang; m. Lin Cao, July 4, 1987; children: Linda J., Daniel J. BS, Shanghai Jiaotong U., 1982, MS, 1984; PhD, Mich. Tech., 1990; MBA, Ctrl. Mich. U., 2000. Faculty Shanghai Jiaotong U., 1984—87; sr. engr. advanced mfg. engring. GM Powertrain, Saginaw, Mich., 1990—96, staff engr. quality assurance, 1996—99; prin. engr., leader Surface Engring. and Tribology Ctr., GM, Pontiac, Mich., 1999—2006, program mgr. China tech. mgmt., 1999—2006; pres. Detroit Chinese Engrs. Assn., Detroit, 2005—06, GM CAG, Detroit, 2006—; dept. mgr. materials engring. GM Pontiac, 2006—. Adj. prof. engring. Oakland U., Mich.; guest prof. Shanghai Jiaotang U. Author over 60 articles to tech. publs. Vice chmn. Tri-City Am. Chinese Assn., Saginaw, Mich., 1992—93; pres. Detroit Chinese Engr. Assn., GM CAG. Recipient Appreciation award, U.S. Dept. of Energy, 2002, Herman H. Doehler award, N.Am. Diecasting Assn., 2005, Asian Am. Engr. of Yr. award, Chinese Inst. of Engrs., USA, 2006. Fellow: ASM Internat. (Saginaw Valley chpt. vice-chmn. 1998—99, chmn. 1999—2000, 5-Star chpt. award 2000); mem.: Soc. Automotive Engring., Am. Soc. Materials, Nat. Soc. of Collegiate Scholars (life), Beta Gamma Sigma (life). Achievements include invention of 35 Patents In Automotive Engineering, Materials Engineering, Surface Engineering And Tribology Areas. Office: Gen Motors Corp MC 483-730-312 823 Joslyn Ave Pontiac MI 48340 Home Phone: 248-788-4563; Office Phone: 248-508-8122. Business E-Mail: yucong.wang@gm.com.

WANG, YUEJIAN, research scientist; s. Gaoke Wang and Guimei Zhao; m. XinXin Liu; 1 child, Janice. MS, Stephen F. Austin State U., Nacogdoches, Tex., 2002; PhD, Tex. Christian U., Ft. Worth, 2006. Engr. 7th Rsch. and Design Inst., China Nat. Nuc. Corp., TaiYuan, 1996—2000; rsch./tchg. asst. Tex. Christian U., Los Alamos, 2002—06; rsch. assoc. Los Alamos Nat. Lab., N.Mex., 2006—07, postdoctoral rsch. assoc., 2007—. Presenter in field. Mem. editl. adv. bd.: Sci. Jours. Internat., 2007; contbr. articles to profl. jours. Nuc. Energy Qi-fei scholar, China Nat. Nuc. Corp., 1996. Mem.: Am. Phys. Soc. (assoc.). Home: Trinity Dr 3000 Apt 43 Los Alamos NM 87544 Office: Los Alamos National Laboratory Los Alamos NM 87545 Home Phone: 505-661-4126; Office Phone: 505-665-6054. Personal E-mail: wang_yuejian@hotmail.com.

WANG, YUFENG, science educator; arrived in U.S., 1995; d. Qiancai Wang and Jinzhu Chen. BS in Genetics, Fudan U., Shanghai, China, 1993; MS in Stats. and Genetics, Iowa State U., 1998, PhD in Bioinformatics and Computational Biology, 2001. Grad. asst. Iowa State U., Ames, 1995—2001; rsch. scientist Am. Type Culture Collection, Manassas, Va., 2001—03; asst. prof. U. of Tex., San Antonio, 2003—. Author to profl. jours. albums. Fellow James Cornette Rsch. fellowship, Iowa State U., 2001. Mem.: Am. Statis. Assn., Internat. Soc. Computational Biology, Genetics Soc. Am. Achievements include research in functional divergence and age distribution of human gene families, computational approach in drug discovery, evolutionary and population genetics of infectious diseases. Office: University of Texas San Antonio Dept of Biology 6900 N Loop 1604 West San Antonio TX 78249 Home: 12222 Vance Jackson Rd Apt 1538 San Antonio TX 78230-5947 Office Phone: 210-458-6492. Business E-Mail: ywang@utsa.edu.

WANG, YUHANG, science educator; b. Xian, China, Nov. 3, 1968; s. Zhizhong Wang and Helan Cheng; m. Yiqun Bai; children: Clara, Ella. BS, Peking U., 1990; PhD, Harvard U., Cambridge, Mass., 1997. Rsch. scientist II Ga. Inst. Tech., Atlanta, 1997—99, assoc. prof., 2002—; asst. prof. atmospheric chemistry and air pollution Rutgers U., New Brunswick, NJ, 2000—02. Mem.: Am. Aerosol Assn., Am. Meteorol. Soc., Am. Geophys. Union. Office: Ga Inst Tech 311 Ferst Dr Atlanta GA 30332-0340 Office Phone: 404-894-3995. Office Fax: 404-894-5638. E-mail: yuhang.wang@eas.gatch.edu.

WANG, YU-PING, computer science educator, engineering educator; arrived in US, 1999, permanent resident, 2003; s. Jinxuan Wang and Aiqing Zhao; m. Ping Xie; children: Aubrey, Macie. PhD, Xi'an Jiaotong U., China, 1996—96. Sr. rsch. engr. Perceptive Sci. Instrument Inc., League City, Tex., 2000—01, Advanced Digital Imaging Rsch., LLC, League City, 2001—03; asst. prof. computer sci. and elec. engring. U. Mo., Kansas City, 2003—. Contbr. articles to profl. jours. Rsch. grantee, U. Mo. Mem.: IEEE (mem. machine learning for signal processing tech. com. 2006—). Achievements include research in image processing and biimaging analysis. Home Phone: 913-488-8212; Office Phone: 816-235-5223. Office Fax: 816-235-5159. Business E-Mail: wangyup@umkc.edu.

WANG, ZENG-YU, neurologist, immunologist; b. Dongan, Hunan, China, July 27, 1962; came to U.S., 1993; s. Xian-Zhun and Yue (Lu) W.; m. Jianhua, Oct. 1, 1989; 1 child, Rachel. MD, Hunan Med. U., China, 1984, M in Neurology, 1987; PhD, Karolinska Inst., Stockholm, Sweden, 1993. Resident, attending physician Hunan Med. U., 1985-90; rsch. asst. Karolinski Inst., Stockholm, 1990-93; postdoctoral assoc. U. Minn., St. Paul, 1994-98; resident NYU Med. Ctr., NYC, 1999—. Contbr. articles to profl. jours. Recipient Rsch. fellowship Karolinska Inst., 1991, Rsch. fellowship Swedish NHR-fonden, 1992, Rsch. fellowship Muscular Dystrophy Assn., 1994. Mem. AAAS, N.Y. Acad. Scis. Achievements include induction of oral tolerance to experimental myasthenia gravis, T cell autoimmunity in myasthenia gravis, T cell epitope repertoire and immunopathogenesis in myasthenia gravis. Home: 14914 Hollywood Ave Flushing NY 11355-1720

WANG, ZHI, biomedical researcher; b. Lanchou City, Ganshu, China, June 2, 1950; m. Xia Zhang, June 24, 1953; 1 child, Ruibing. MD, Xi'an Sch. Medicine, 1981. Action dir., asst. prof. Tufts U. Sch. Medicine, Boston, 1999—2000; dir., prof. Boston U. Sch. Medicine, 2001—. Recipient Assn. Rsch. award, Am. Laryngol. Assn., 1994; grantee, NIH, 2001. Fellow: Am. Acad. Otolaryngology Head and Neck Surgery. Achievements include research in less side-effects in cancer treatment/surgery. Office: Boston Univ Sch Medicine 88 E Newton St D616 Boston MA 02118 Home: 9 Hialeah Lane Framingham MA 01701 Office Phone: 617-414-1590. Personal E-mail: zhiw@hotmail.com. Business E-Mail: zwang@bu.edu.

WANGARD, GREGG, chef; b. Wis. m. Kelly Wangard. Studied, Wauesha Tech. Coll., Wis. Apprentice Am. Culinary Fedn.; intern Rosewood Caneel Bay Resort, St. John, US Virgin Islands; chef de cuisine Cucina Restaurant, Kohler, Wis., The Immigrant Room & Winery Bar, The Am. Club; head, culinary ops. Ocean and Vine Restaurant, Loews Santa Monica Hotel, 2004—. Named one of LA's Rising Stars, StarChefs.com, 2006. Avocations: bicycling, basketball, tennis, Green Bay Packers. Office: Ocean and Vine at the Loews Santa Monica Hotel 1700 Ocean Ave Santa Monica CA 90401 Office Phone: 310-458-6700. *

WANGER, EUGENE GILKISON, retired lawyer; b. Chgo., May 16, 1933; s. Eugene Miles and Roka Gilkison Wanger; m. Marilyn Rose Morris, July 14, 1962. AB cum laude, Amherst Coll., Mass., 1955; JD, U. Mich., Ann Arbor, 1958. Bar: Mich. 1958, US Supreme Ct. 1968. Assoc. Fraser, Trebilcock, Davis & Foster, Lansing, Mich., 1958—61, Snyder Loomis & Ewert, Lansing, 1962—65; city atty. Lansing, 1965—67; prin. Wanger Law Offices, Lansing, 1968—95. Contbr. articles to profl. jours. Del. Mich Constl. Conv., 1961—62; nat. bd. dirs. Am. Truck Hist. Soc., 1987—2002; mem. Ingham County Bd. Commrs., Mich., 1965—73, chmn., 1972; co-chmn. Mich. Com. Against Capital Punishment, 1972—. Recipient Legacy of Life award, Ctrl. United Meth., Detroit, 2000, conf. rm. in state office bldg. named in his honor, 2001. Mem.: ABA (mem. death penalty com. sect. on individual rights and responsibilities), State Bar Mich. (past vice chmn. com. constl. law, Champion of Justice award 2005), Am. Judicature Soc., Hist. Soc. Mich. (life), Mich. Supreme Ct. Hist. Soc. (life), Mich. Bar Found. (life), Ingham County Hist. Commn. (pres. 1977—78). Republican. Congregational. Achievements include wrote Michigan's constitutional ban of death penalty. Avocation: history.

WANGLER, WILLIAM CLARENCE, retired insurance company executive; b. Buffalo, Dec. 7, 1929; s. Emil A. and Viola M. (Roesser) W.; m. Carol B. Sullivan, Aug. 17, 1957; children: Jeffrey W., Eric J. BS, SUNY, Cortland, 1951. Claims adjuster Liberty Mut. Ins. Co., Buffalo, 1954-60, claims supr. Miami, Fla., 1960-65, home office examiner Boston, 1965-68, asst. claims mgr. Cleve., 1968-69, claims mgr. Cleve, 1969-73, div. claims service mgr. Pitts., 1973-79, div. claims mgr., 1979-86, v.p. asst. gen. claims mgr. adminstrn. Boston, 1986-94, ret., 1994. Pres. Claims Mgrs. Counsel, Cleve., 1970; chmn. Nationwide Intercompany Arbitration, Cleve., 1969-70. Loaned exec. Mass. Bay United Way, Boston, 1964; account exec. Pitts. United Way, 1985-86. Served to capt. USMC, 1951-54. Republican. Roman Catholic. Home: 64 Trout Farm Ln Duxbury MA 02332-4609 Personal E-mail: vcwangler@webtv.net.

WANGSNESS, GENNA STEAD, retired hotel executive, innkeeper; b. Detroit, Feb. 2, 1942; d. William Allen Stead and Genevieve Josephine Schreiber; m. Roger Carroll Wangsness, Dec. 1, 1967; children: Alison Lee Clement, Bijali Anne, Brian William. BA in Liberal Studies, Georgetown U., 1995. Vol. Peace Corps, Tehran, Iran, 1965—67; sec. Office of Pres. Georgetown U., Washington, 1984—86, coord. adminstrv. svcs. Office of Pres., 1986—89, adminstrv. officer dept. surgery, 1989—92, adminstrv. office Sch. Summer and Continuing Edn., 1992—95; exec. asst. to exec. v.p. Am. Soc. Clin. Oncology, Alexandria, Va., 1995—96; innkeeper The Inn at Folkston, Ga., 1997—2006; ret., 2006. Author: Folkston Then and Now 1881-2003, A Self-Guided Walking Tour of Historic Downtown, Folkston, Georgia, 2003. Mem.: Alpha Sigma Lambda. Achievements include establishment of womens studies section at Charlton Public Library.

WANI, MANSUKHLAL CHHAGANLAL, chemist; b. Nandurbar, Maharastra, India, Feb. 20, 1925; came to U.S., 1958, naturalized, 1977; s. Chhagnalal Kikabhai and Maniben Chhanganlal (Shah) W.; m. Ramila Mansukhlal Dalal, Dec. 4, 1954; 1 child, Bankim M. BS with honors, St. Xavier's Coll., Bombay U., 1947, MS, 1950; PhD, Ind. U., 1962. Lectr. chemistry Bhavan's Coll., Bombay, 1951-58; rsch. asst. Ind. U., Bloomington, 1958-61; rsch. assoc. U. Wis., Madison, 1961-62; prin. scientist Rsch. Triangle Inst., Rsch. Triangle Park, NC, 1962—. Inventor anticancer drugs. Recipient B.F. Cain Meml. award Am. Assn. Cancer Rsch., 1994, City of Medicine award Durham, N.C., 1994, Award of Recognition Nat. Cancer Inst., 1996, Charles E. Kettering prize GM Cancer Rsch. Found., 2000, Ranbaxy Rsch. award. Mem. AAAS, Am. Chem. Soc., Am. Soc. Pharmacognosy, N.Y. Acad. Scis., India Assn. (pres. 1970-72), Hindu Soc. (dir. 1976-81), Assn. Indians in Am., Indo-Am. Forum, Sigma Xi, Phi Lambda Upsilon. Democrat. Avocations: reading, travel, sports. Home: 2801 Legion Ave Durham NC 27707-1921 Office: Rsch Triangle Inst 3040 W Cornwallis Rd Research Triangle Park NC 27709-2194 Home Phone: 919-489-2573; Office Phone: 919-541-6685. Business E-Mail: MCW@rti.org.

WANK, GERALD SIDNEY, periodontist, educator; b. Bklyn., Jan. 20, 1925; s. Joseph and Sadie (Ikowitz) W.; m. Gloria Baum, June 4, 1949; children: David, Stephen, Daniel. BA, NYU, 1945, DDS, 1949; cert. in orthodontia, Columbia U., 1951, cert. in periodontia, 1956. Intern Bellevue Hosp., 1949-50; pvt. practice NYC, Great Neck, N.Y., 1949—; instr. dept. periodontia, oral medicine NYU Dental Sch., 1956-63, asst. clin. prof. dept. periodontia, 1963-67, asst. prof. periodontia, oral medicine, former postgrad. dir. periodontal-prosthesis dept. fixed partial prosthesis, 1970—, clin. assoc. prof. periodontia and oral medicine, 1970-77, clin. prof. dept. periodontia and implantology, 1977—, postgrad. dir. periodontia, 1968-71, Disting. prof. periodontics, 2002; lectr. periodontology Harvard U. Sch. Dental Medicine, 1971—74; vis. lectr. N.Y.C. C.C. Sch. Dental Hygiene, 1960-65, Albert Einstein Coll. Medicine, 1967-96; sr. asst. attending staff North Shore U. Hosp., 1974-77, sr. asst. attending divsn. surgery, 1977—. Cons. orthodontic panel N.Y. State, N.Y.C. depts. health, 1953-80; cons. periodontal prosthesis, Goldwater Meml. Hosp., N.Y.C.; former postgrad. instr. 1st Dist. Dental Soc. Postgrad. Sch., dist. claims com.; lectr. in field; mem. com. admissions N.Y. U. Coll. Dentistry, 1975-86, chmn. fund raising, 1976-77; cons. N.Y. VA Hosp., 1996—. Contbr. to: Practice of Periodontia, 1960, Dental Clinics of North America, 1972, 81, Manual of Clinical Periodontics, 1973; contbr. articles to profl. jours. Capt. USAF, 1953-55. Recipient Alumni Meritorious Service award NYU, 1981, Coll. Dentistry Alumni Achievement award NYU, 1983, Disting. Prof. Periodontics award NYU Coll. Dentistry, 2002, named to Leaders in Am. Sci., 1963-64. Fellow APHA, Am. Acad. Oral Medicine, Acad. Gen. Dentistry, N.Y. Acad. Dentistry (life), Internat. Coll. Dentists (life), Am. Coll. Dentistry (life), Am. Acad. Oral Medicine (pres. N.Y. sect. 1971-72); mem. N.Y. Coll. Dentists (dir.), ADA, Dental Soc. N.Y.C. (dir. 1st dist., chmn. ethics com. 1985-86, peer rev. com.), Fedn. Dentaire Internat., Am. Assn. Dental Schs., N.Y. State Pub. Health Assn., AAUP, Pan Am. Med. Assn. (life), AAAS, ADA, Am. Acad. Periodontology, Sci. Rsch. Soc. Am., Northeastern Soc. Periodontia (life), Am. Acad. Dental Medicine, Acad. Gen. Dentistry, Internat. Acad. Orthodontia, Am. Assn. Endodontists (life), Am. Acad. Periodontia (life), Am. Acad. Oral Medicine (life), NYU Coll. Dentistry Alumni Assn. (dir., sec. 1973-74, v.p. 1974-75, pres. 1976-77), Am. Assn. Endodontists, NYU Coll. Dentistry Dental Assocs. (charter), Acad. Oral Rehab. (hon.), First Dist. Dental Soc. (program chmn. 1984, chmn. continuing edn. 1983, sec., 1985, v.p. Eastern Dental Soc. br. 1986, pres.-elect 1987, pres. br. 1988, bd. dirs. 1989—, Meritorious Svc. award 1997), NY County Dental Soc. (peer rev. com.), Am. Acad. Osseointegration (life), NYU Gallatin Assocs., Alumni Fedn. NYU (dir. 1976-81), N.Y. County Dental Soc. (Dist. Claims Com.), Soc. of the Torch, Masons, Century Club, NYU Club, Fresh Meadow Country Club, Omicron Kappa Upsilon (life), Alpha Omega. Jewish. Home and Office: 40 Bayview Ave Great Neck NY 11021-2819 Office: 30 E 40th St New York NY 10016-1201 Personal E-mail: g.wank@aol.com.

WANKAT, PHILLIP CHARLES, chemical engineering educator; b. Oak Park, Ill., July 11, 1944; s. Charles and Grace Wankat; m. Dorothy Nel Richardson, Dec. 13, 1980; children: Charles, Jennifer. BS in Chem. Engring., Purdue U., 1966, MS in Edn., 1982; PhD, Princeton U., 1970. From asst. prof. to C.L. Lovell disting. prof. chem. engring Purdue U., West Lafayette, Ind., 1970—, head freshman engring., 1987-95, interim dir. continuing engring. edn., 1996, head interdisciplinary engring., 2000—04. Cons. pharm. firm, 1985-94. Author: Large Scale Ads and Chromatog, 1986, Equil Staged Separations, 1988, Rate Controlled Separations, 1990, Teaching Engineering, 1993, The Effective, Efficient Professor, 2002, Separation Process Engineering, 2007. With AUS, 1962-64. Recipient award in Separations Sci. and Tech., Am. Chem. Soc., 1994. Mem. AIChE, Am. Soc. Engring. Edn. (Union Carbide Lectr. award 1997), Am. Chem. Soc. Achievements include patents in field. Avocations: fishing, canoeing, camping. Office: Purdue U Dept Chem Engring 480 Stadium Mall Dr West Lafayette IN 47907-2100 Business E-Mail: wankat@ecn.purdue.edu.

WANN, LAYMOND DOYLE, retired petroleum research scientist; b. Magazine, Ark., Apr. 25, 1924; s. Vernon Cecil and Emma (McCrary) W.; m. Betty Lou Brown, Nov. 6, 1948; children: Jacqueline, Lyndall Doyle. BS in Physics (Phi Eta Sigma scholar), Okla. State U., 1949, MS, 1950. With Conoco Inc., Ponca City, Okla., 1951-84, sr. rsch. scientist, 1957-60, rsch. group leader, 1960-81, assoc. rsch. dir., 1981-84, staff scientist, 1984-85, ret., 1985. Cons. in disciplines of phys. Contbr. articles on elec. and radioactive well-logging, elec. design to profl. jours. Patentee in field. Mem. Mcpl. Airport Bd., Ponca City. Served with AUS, 1942-46; ETO. Decorated Bronze Star. Mem. Am. Petroleum Inst. (chmn. well logging subcom.), IEEE, Aircraft Owners and Pilots Assn., Seaplane Pilots Assn., VFW, Am. Legion, Phi Kappa Phi, Pi Mu Epsilon, Sigma Pi Sigma. Republican. Episcopalian (vestryman). Home: 1501 Monument Rd Ponca City OK 74604-3522 Office: 1000 S Pine St Ponca City OK 74601-7509 E-mail: ldwann@yahoo.com.

WANNER, ERIC, foundation executive; b. Wilmington, Del., Mar. 14, 1942; s. Edwin and Isabel Smith (Speakman) W.; m. Patricia Attix, June 13, 1964 (div. 1976); children: Noel Edwin, Erin Cole; m. Carla Francesca Seal, June 18, 1983; children: Lindzay Elizabeth. BA, Amherst Coll., 1963; PhD, Harvard U., 1969. Asst. to assoc. prof. Harvard U., Cambridge, Mass., 1968-76; behavioral sci. editor Harvard U. Press, Cambridge, Mass., 1976-82; program officer Alfred P. Sloan Found., NYC, 1982-84, v.p., 1984-86; pres. Russell Sage Found, NYC, 1986—. Trustee Ctr. for Advanced Study in Behavioral Scis., 1993-99; bd. dirs. Dogan Found., Paris, Am. Acad. Polit. Social Sci. Fulbright fellow Sussex U., Brighton, Eng., 1979, N.Y. Inst. for Humanities fellow, NYU, 1985-93, Am. Acad. Arts and Scis. fellow, 1994—. Mem.: Century Assn., Sigma Xi. Office: Russell Sage Found 112 E 64th St New York NY 10021-7383 Business E-Mail: ew@rsage.org.

WANNIER, MARIO MARC-ANTOINE, oil industry executive, multimedia specialist, director; b. Basle, Switzerland, Sept. 16, 1951; arrived in U.S., 2000; s. Willy Wannier and Aurelie Wannier-Bourquard; m. Clemencia Bello, Jan. 6, 1975; children: Catherine, Marianne. Vordiplomexamen, Basle U., Switzerland, 1973, Diplomexamen, 1975, PhD in Earth Scis., 1979. Asset mgr. Sarawak Shell Berhad, Miri, Malaysia, 1994—99; subsurface projects mgr. Shell Oil Co., Houston, 2000—07, head rsch. projects The Hague, Netherlands, 2007—. Author (dir.): Destination Miri: A Geological Tour, 1998 (Multimedia CD Title of Yr. award Pikom-Computimes IT, 1999), Northern Sarawak's National Parks and Giant Caves. Designer geol. exhbn. on the jura mountains Musee d'Histoire, Delemont, Switzerland, 1973—75. With Swiss AF, 1971—78. Personal E-mail: mwannier@yahoo.com.

WANNSTEDT, DAVID RAYMOND, college football coach, former professional football coach; b. Pitts., May 21, 1952; m. Jan Wannstedt; children: Keri, Jami. Grad., U. Pitts., 1974. Player Green Bay Packers, 1974; grad. asst. U. Pitts. Panthers, 1975—76, receivers & spl. teams coach, 1977—78; defensive line coach Okla. State U. Cowboys, 1979-82, U. So. Calif. Trojans, 1983-85; defensive. coord. U. Miami Hurricanes, 1986-89; def. coord. Dallas Cowboys, 1989-93; head coach Chgo. Bears, 1993-98; asst. head coach Miami Dolphins, 1999-2000, head coach, 2000—04, U. Pitts. Panthers, 2004—. Named to NCAA 2nd team All-East, NFL Coach of the Year UPI, Football News, 1994; inducted into Western Pa. Hall of Fame, 1990. Office: U Pitts Football Team PO Box 7436 Pittsburgh PA 15213 Office Phone: 412-648-8711.

WANORIE, TEKLE O., finance educator; s. Orshiso Wanorie and Ruth Doboch; m. Haimi T. Kelborro; children: Nep T. Orshiso, Betty T. Orshiso, Ben T. Orshiso. MBA, Andrews U., Berrien Springs, Mich., 1988; MA, U. Alabam, Tuscaloosa, 2000; PhD, U. Ala., 2002. Prof. Solusi U., Bulawayo, Zimbabwe, 1989—96; asst. prof. bus. NW Mo. State U., Maryville, 2004—. Chair, dean Solusi U., 1995—96. Contbr. articles to profl. jours. Spkr., tchr. Seventh-day Adventist Ch., Bedford, Iowa, 2005—07. Recipient Abundant Energy & Enthusiasm award, Mktg. & Mgmt. Dept., 2006, Tchr. of Yr. award. Mem.: Prodn. & Ops. Mgmt. Soc. (assoc.). Home: 1166 Brentwood Dr Maryville MO 64468 Office: NW Mo State Univ 800

University Dr Maryville MO 64468 Office Phone: 660-562-1283. Office Fax: 660-562-1731; Home Fax: 660-562-1731. Personal E-mail: tekleow@aol.com. Business E-Mail: tekleow@nwmissouri.edu. E-mail: towanorie@gmail.com.

WANTLAND, WILLIAM CHARLES, retired bishop, lawyer; b. Edmond, Okla., Apr. 14, 1934; s. William Lindsay and Edna Louise (Yost) W. BA, U. Hawaii, 1957; JD, Okla. City U., 1967; D in Religion, Geneva Theol. Coll., Knoxville, Tenn., 1976; DD (hon.), Nashotah House, Wis., 1983, Seabury-Western Sem., Evanston, Ill., 1983. With FBI, various locations, 1954-59, Ins. Co. of N.Am., Oklahoma City, 1960-62; law clk.-atty. Bishop & Wantland, Seminole, Okla., 1962-77; vicar St. Mark's Ch., Seminole, 1963-77, St. Paul's Ch., Holdenville, Okla., 1974-77; presiding judge Seminole Mcpl. Ct., 1970-77; atty. gen. Seminole Nation of Okla., 1969-72, 75-77; exec. dir. Okla. Indian Rights Assn., Norman, 1972-73; rector St. John's Ch., Oklahoma City, 1977-80; bishop Episcopal Diocese of Eau Claire, Wis., 1980-99; interim bishop of Navajoland, 1993-94; ret., 1999. Adj. prof. Law Sch. U. Okla., Norman, 1970-78; instr. canon law Nashotah House, 1983-97, 2004—; nat. coun. Evang. and Cath. Mission, Chgo., 1977-90; mem. Episcopal Commn. on Racism, 1990-92, Episcopal Coun. Indian Ministries, 1990-95, Standing Commn. on Constn. and Canons, 1992-95; assisting bishop Diocese of Dallas, 2002—04, of Ft. Worth, 2000—. Author: Foundations of the Faith, 1982, Canon Law of the Episcopal Church, 1984, The Prayer Book and the Catholic Faith, 1994; The Catholic Faith, The Episcopal Church and the Ordination of Women, 1997; co-author: Oklahoma Probate Forms, 1971; contbr. articles to profl. jours. Pres. Okla. Conf. Mcpl. Judges, 1973; v.p. South African Ch. Union, 1985-95; trustee Nashotah House, Wis., 1981—, chmn., 1992-98; bd. dirs. SPEAK, Eureka Springs, Ark., 1983-89; Wis. adv. com. US Civil Rights Commn., 1990-91; support com. Native Am. Rights Fund, 1990—; coun. mem. City of Seminole, Okla., 2002—, vice mayor, 2003—; co-chmn. Luth.-Anglican-Roman Cath. Commn. of Wis., 1989-95; pres. Wis. Episc. Conf., 1995-97, Wis. Coun. Chs., 1985-86; active Living Ch. Found., 1981-02; bd. dirs. Seminole Nation Hist. Soc., 1999—, pres., 2006—; adv. bd. Seminole Hist. Soc., 2003—. Recipient Most Outstanding Contbn. to Law and Order award Okla. Supreme Ct., 1975, Outstanding Alumnus award Okla. City U., 1980, Wis. Equal Rights Coun. award, 1986, Manitou Ikwe award Indian Alcoholism Coun., 1988, Episcopal Synod Pres.'s award, 1995, 2004. Mem. Okla. Bar Assn., Okla. Indian Bar Assn., Oklahoma City Law Sch. Alumni Assn. (pres. 1968), Ct. Indian Offenses Seminole Nation Okla. (chief magistrate 2006—). Democrat. Episcopalian. Avocations: canoeing, skin-diving, cross country skiing. Personal E-mail: puca382@mbo.net. *If we truly believe that God reigns, we will so order our lives that such a belief is clearly reflected in all that we do and say; further, such a belief will shape our relations, not only with all other people, but all of God's created order.*

WANZENBERG, ALAN, architect; Grad. cum laude, U. Calif., Berkeley; grad., Harvard U., Cambridge, Mass. Cert. Nat. Coun. Archtl. Registration Bds., lic. Colo., Conn., Idaho, Fla., Mass., NJ, NY, Pa., Vt. With I.M. Pei and Ptnrs.; founder, ptnr. Johnson & Wanzenberg, 1982—96; owner, prin. Alan Wanzenberg Arch., PC and Alan Wanzenberg Design, LLC, NYC, 1996—. Mem.: AIA. Office: Alan Wanzenberg Arch PC 333 W 52nd St New York NY 10019 Office Phone: 212-489-7980. Office Fax: 212-489-7981. *

WAPIENNIK, CARL FRANCIS, manufacturing executive, planetarium and science institute administrator; b. Donora, Pa., Oct. 10, 1926; s. Karl and Rose (Kidzinski) W.; m. Elva Louise Bartron, Nov. 27, 1953; children: Carl Eric, Ellen Louise. BS, U. Pitts., 1953. Prodn. supr. RCA, Canonsburg, Pa., 1953—54; staff physicist Buhl Planetarium and Inst. Popular Sci., Pitts., 1954—64, exec. dir., 1964—82; owner, operator Work-O-Art Miniatures (small mfg. firm), 1983—2003. Patentee means for controlling liquid flow. Mem. Rostraver Twp. Planning Commn., 1965-67; mem. adv. bd. Allegheny C. of C. (formerly North Side Pitts. C. of C.), 1966-67, dir., 1968-73, pres., 1970; mem. adv. coun. Salvation Army, 1978-82; bd. dirs. Bapt. Homes, Pitts., 1982-94; chmn. Rostraver Twp. Mcpl. Water Authority, 1990-94. With USNR, 1945-46. Recipient Man of Yr. award in sci. Pitts. Jaycees, 1969. Mem. Pitts. Bapt. Assn. (bd. dirs. 1976-82), Phi Beta Kappa, Sigma Pi Sigma. Home: 602 Salem Church Rd Belle Vernon PA 15012-2906

WARAKOMSKI, ALPHONSE WALTER JOSEPH, JR., sales executive, marketing professional; b. NYC, Apr. 1, 1943; s. Alphonse Walter and Mary (Dupnock) Warakomski. BS in Chemistry, St. Bonaventure, 1968; MBA in Mktg., Keller Grad. Sch., 1981. Chemist, lab. mgr. Purification Sci., Geneva, NY, 1968—73; applications engr. Pollution Control Industries, Stamford, Conn., 1973; mgr. sales Kopper's Environ. Elements, Balt., 1974; mktg. specialist, regional mgr. Union Carbide Linde, Chgo., 1975—79; sales engr. Dorr Oliver, Chgo., 1980—81; dir. mktg. and sales Linde AG Lotepro, Valhalla, NY, 1981—2000; ptnr. Mixing and Mass Transfer Techs., Inc., 2000—. Contbr. articles to profl. jours. Mem.: AIChE, Am. Chem. Soc., Water Environment Fedn., Internat. Ozone Assn., Am. Water Works Assn. Home: 8833 N Congress Apt 818 Kansas City MO 64153 Home Phone: 816-584-1969; Office Phone: 816-665-1931. Business E-Mail: awarakomski@m2ttech.com.

WARBERG, WILLETTA, concert pianist, music educator; b. Twin Falls, Idaho, June 2, 1932; d. George William Warberg and Ethel Margaret (Sargent) Warberg-Chandler; m. David Jacob Bar-Illan, Sept. 3, 1954 (div.); children: Daniela, Jeremy Oscar. Student, Colo. Women's Coll., 1950-51, Aspen Music Camp, 1951; studied with, Rudolph Firkusny, 1951-53; BS, Mannes Coll. Music, NYC, 1954. Assoc. food editor Look mag., NYC, 1956-61; food editor Status mag., NYC, 1961-62, Ladie's Home Jour., NYC, 1964-66; photog. stylist Gourmet mag., NYC, 1961-64, freelance writer, photog. stylist, 1965-75; pres., owner Willetta Enterprises, advt. agy., Twin Falls, 1976-84; food columnist, music and arts critic Times News, 1978-87; duo-piano ptnr. with Robert Starer, NYC, Woodstock, 1991—2000; piano coach Saugerties, NY, 1991—. Made feasibility study of restaurant situation in Israel, U.S. Dept. State ICA Point 4 Program, Washington and Israel, 1960; artist-in-residence Holy Cross Concert Series, Kingston, N.Y., 1994—. Concert pianist, Idaho, Oreg., Utah, Wash., Colo., N.Y.C., N.Y. State, 1940—; author: Cooking from Scratch, 1976, Space Age Cookery, 1977; syndicated food columnist Willetta Says, 1978-87; contbr. food and sci. articles to Cosmopolitan, Modern Maturity, Esquire, Sun Valley, Sci. Diegest, also other mags. Bd. dirs. N.W. Opera Assn., 1984-87; pres. bd. dirs. Woodstock Lyric Theatre, 1994-2000; v.p. bd. dirs. Woodstock Chamber Orch., 1993—; chmn. Friends of the Maverick Concerts Inc., Woodstock, N.Y., 1999—. Winner Rocky Mountain talent search contest Salt Lake Tribune and Salt Lake Telegram, 1949. Mem. Nat. Fedn. Music Clubs, Music Tchrs. Nat. Assn. (cert.), Kingston Music Soc. Avocations: designing and sewing clothes, painting still lifes, swimming, developing recipes, writing.

WARBURTON, RALPH JOSEPH, architect, educator, engineer; b. Kansas City, Mo., Sept. 5, 1935; s. Ralph Gray and Emma Frieda (Niemann) W.; m. Carol Ruth Hychka, June 14, 1958; children: John Geoffrey, Joy Frances W. Tracey. BArch, MIT, 1958; MArch, Yale U., 1959, M.C.P., 1960. Registered arch., Colo., Conn., Fla., Ill., La., Md., NJ, NY, Tex., Va., DC; registered profl. engr., Conn., Fla., NJ, NY; registered cmty. planner, Mich., NJ; lic. interior designer, Fla. With various archtl. planning and engring. firms, Kansas City, Mo., 1952-55, Boston, 1956-58, NYC, 1959-62, Chgo., 1962-64; chief planning Skidmore, Owings & Merrill, Chgo., 1964-66; spl. asst. for urban design HUD, Washington, 1966-72, cons., 1972-77; prof. architecture, archtl. engring. and planning U. Miami, Coral Gables, Fla., 1972-2000, chmn. dept. architecture, archtl. engring. and planning, 1972-75, assoc. dean engring. and environ. design, 1973-74, dir. grad. urban and regional planning program, 1973-75, 81, 87-93, prof. emeritus, 2000—. Advisor govt. Iran, 1970, govt. France, 1973, govt. Ecuador, 1974, govt. Saudi Arabia, 1985; cons. in field, 1972—, lectr., critic design juror in field, 1965—; mem./chmn. Coral Gables Bd. Archs., 1980-82. Author: Space for Urban Activity, 1960; assoc. author: Man-Made America: Chaos or Control, 1963; editor: New Concepts in Urban Transportation, 1968, Housing Systems Proposals for Operation Breakthrough, 1970, Focus on Furniture, 1971, National Community Art Competition, 1971, Defining Critical Environmental Areas, 1974; contbg. editor: Progressive Architecture, 1974-84; editl. adv. bd.: Jour. Am. Planning Assn., 1983-88, Planning for Higher Edn., 1986-94, Urban Design and Preservation Quar., 1987-94; contbr. over 130 articles to profl. jour.; mem. adv. panel Industrialization Forum Quar., 1969-79, archtl. portfolio jury Am. Sch. and Univ., 1993. Mem. Met. Housing and Planning Coun., Chgo., 1965-67; mem. exec. com. Yale U. Arts Assn., 1965-70; pres. Yale U. Planning Alumni Assn., 1983-89; mem. ednl. adv. com. Fla. Bd. Architecture, 1975; mem. grievance com. The Fla. Bar, 1996-99; mem code commn.'s Nat. Fire Protection Assn., 1998-. Recipient W.E. Parsons medal Yale U., 1960; recipient Spl. Achievement award HUD, 1972, commendation Fla. Bd. Architecture, 1974, Fla. Trust Hist. Preservation award, 1983, Group Achievement award NASA, 1976; Skidmore, Owings & Merrill traveling fellow MIT, 1958; vis. fellow Inst. Architecture and Urban Studies, NYC, 1972-74; NSF grantee, 1980-82. Fellow AIA (nat. housing com. 1968-72, nat. regional devel. and natural resources com. 1974-75, nat. sys. devel. com. 1972-73, nat. urban design com. 1968-73, bd. dirs. Fla. S. chpt. 1974-75, Edn. Leadership award Miami chpt. 2000, Test of Time Design award Fla. Assn. 2002), ASCE (archtl. engring. and structural engring. insts.), Fla. Engring. Soc. (bd. dirs. 1984-85, Miami chpt. bd. dirs. 1982-83, 84-85), Nat. Acad. Forensic Engrs.; mem. Am. Inst. Cert. Planners (exec. com. dept. environ. planning 1973-74), Am. Soc. Engring. Edn. (chmn. archtl. engring. divsn. 1975-76), Dade Heritage Trust (Cmty. Svc. award 2002), Nat. Sculpture Soc. (allied profl.), Nat. Soc. Archtl. Engrs. (founding), NSPE, Nat. Trust Hist. Preservation (principles and guidelines com. 1967), Am. Soc. Landscape Archs. (hon., chmn. design awards jury 1971, 72), Am. Planning Assn. (Fla. chpt. award excellence 1983), Am. Soc. Interior Designers (hon.), Omicron Delta Kappa, Sigma Xi, Tau Beta Pi. Home and Office: 2825 Cascade Dr Plano TX 75025-4106 Office Phone: 214-495-9892. Personal E-mail: ProfRJWarc@aol.com. *My contribution to society is made through comprehensive determination, design, development and research activity leading to habitats most suited to the optimum continuing progress of mankind.*

WARCHOL, JUDITH MARIE, secretarial service company executive; b. Chgo., Apr. 20; d. Michael Henry and Rose Therese (Vito) Schmidt Fitpold; m. Daniel August Warchol, Aug. 17, 1963 (dec.); children—Kathleen Louise, Raymond Michael, Sherry Lynn. Exec. sec. N.W. Malt & Grain, Chgo., 1958-63; pres. Judy's Mailing & Secretarial Service, Northbrook, 1968—, Americano Motor Inn, Beaumont, Tex., 1976—; owner Jovies Family Restaurant, Beaumont, 1977-78, Chances R, Beaumont, 1978-80; v.p. Golden Triangle Limo Service, Beaumont, 1982—; mng. ptnr. Warchol Investments, Beaumont, Tex., 1982—. V.p. Band Booster Club, Stanley Field Jr. High Sch., Northbrook, 1975-77; leader Blue Bird Group, Camp Fire Girls, Northbrook, 1971-76; bd. dirs. Stanley Field Jr. High Parent Tchr. Club, Northbrook, 1976-78; foster parent, Sierra Leone, 1978-85. Mem. Women in Mgmt., Nat. Assn. Secretarial Services, Mail Advertisers Assn., Northbrook C. of C. (bd. dirs. 1984-86). Republican. Roman Catholic. Avocations: boating, golf, tennis, fitness programs, self-improvement studies. Home: 3493 Techny Rd Northbrook IL 60062-5066 Office: Judy's Mailing & Secretarial Service 33863392 Commercial Ave Northbrook IL 60062-1833

WARCKEN, NANCY B., elementary school educator; d. Marvin and Geanice Bell; children: Mark, Lindsay, Jeff. BS in Elem. Edn., U. Tex.-Austin, 1973. Tchr. Old Town Elem., Round Rock, Tex., 1988—97; math. tchr. Cedar Valley Mid. Sch., Austin, Tex., 1998—; campus coord. Ptnrs. Edn. Cedar Valley Mid. Sch., 2000—. Named one of Outstanding Am. Tchrs., Nat. Honor Roll, 2007; recipient Tchr. of Yr., Cedar Valley Mid. Sch., 2002—03. Mem.: Austin Area Council Tchrs. Math., Tex. Council Tchrs. Math., Nat. Council Tchrs. Math. Avocations: hiking, travel, scrapbooks.

WARD, AARON, professional hockey player; b. Windsor, Ont., Can., Jan. 17, 1973; Attended, U. Mich. Defenseman Detroit Red Wings, 1993—2001, Carolina Hurricanes, 2001—06, NY Rangers, 2006—07, Boston Bruins, 2007—. Achievements include being a member of Stanley Cup Champion Detroit Red Wings, 1997, 1998, Carolina Hurricanes, 2006. Office: Boston Burins 100 Legends Way Boston MA 02114 *

WARD, BILL, musician; b. Birmingham, England, May 5, 1948; Founding mem., drummer Black Sabbath, 1969—80, 1983, 1994, 1997—. Musician: (albums) Ward One: Along the Way, 1985, When the Bough Breaks, 1997, Two Hands Clapping, 1999; musician: (with Black Sabbath) Black Sabbath, 1970, Paranoid, 1971, Master of Reality, 1971, Black Sabbath, vol. 4, 1972, Sabbath Bloody Sabbath, 1973, Sabotage, 1975, Technical Ecstasy, 1976, Never Say Die!, 1978, Heaven & Hell, 1980, Born Again, 1983, Sabbath Stones, 1996, Reunion, 1998. Named to Rock and Roll Hall of Fame, 2006. Office: Sanctuary Records Group Ltd Sanctuary House 45-53 Sinclair Rd London W14 0NS England

WARD, CAM, professional hockey player; b. Sherwood Park, Atla., Can., Feb. 29, 1984; Goalie Lowell Lock Monsters (AHL), 2004—05, Carolina Hurricanes, 2005—. Recipient Conn Smythe Trophy, 2006. Achievements include being a member of Stanley Cup Champion Carolina Hurricanes, 2006; tying the record for playoff wins by a rookie goalie, 2006. Office: Carolina Hurricanes RBC Ctr 1400 Edwards Mill Rd Raleigh NC 27607

WARD, CHARLES A., federal agency administrator; b. Huntsville, Ala., Oct. 14, 1931; s. Hosie and Barbara Ward; 1 child, Pamela A. BA, Talladega Coll., 1954. Distbn. clk. Post Office Dept., Chgo., 1954—65, foreman mails, 1966—68, gen. foreman, 1968—70; mgr. quality control U.S. Postal Svc., 1973—78, mgr. distbn., 1973—80, officer-in-charge Ft. Lauderdale, Fla., 1980, sect. ctr. mgr., postmaster Binghamton, NY, 1980—82, acting mgr. sect. com. Va., 1982, mgr. sect. ctr., postmaster Memphis, 1982—84, Greensboro, NC, 1984—87. Mem. United Negro Coll. Fund; co-chair Combined Fed. Campaign, Memphis; mem. Piedmont Interfaith Coun.; bd. dirs. Broome County Urban League, Binghamton, NY, United Way; bd. visitors Oak Ridge Mil. Acad.; bd. advisers Friends Home, Inc.; mem. Shepherds Ctr. Greensboro, McIver Ednl. Ctr., Hayes-Taylor YMCA, United Svc. for Older Adults. Mem.: NAACP, Greensboro Housing Coalition, So. Poverty Law Ctr., Nat. Assn. Postmasters of US, Nat. League Postmasters, Nat. Assn. Ret. Fed. Employees, Nat. Assn. Postal Supvs., Midwest Assn. Sickle Cell Anemia, United Negro Coll. Fund, N.C. A&T Aggie Club, Greensboro Civitan Club, Rotary, Talladega Coll. Alumni Club, Omega Psi Phi. Home: 219 Village Ln Unit E Greensboro NC 27409-2523

WARD, CHARLES RAYMOND, systems engineer; b. Lansing, Mich., Oct. 23, 1949; s. George Merrill and Dorothy Irene (Hupp) W.; m. Sarah Hopkins Eddy, June 23, 1979; children: Katherine Emily, Rachel Elizabeth. BS in Math., Purdue U., 1971; MSEE, Naval Postgrad. Sch., 1977. Commd. ensign USN, 1971, advanced through grades to lt. commdr., served on USS Barbel, 1972-75, served on USS James Madison, 1978-81, served on USS Alabama, 1983-85; strategic navigation project mgr. Strategic Systems Programs, Arlington, Va., 1985-91; surveillance towed array sensor sys., mgr. sys. engring. Govt. Info. Sys. divsn. TRW, McLean, Va., 1991-95; integrated undersea surveillance sys., mgr. internat. programs TRW, San Diego, 1995-2000; integrated undersea surveillance, mgr. fixed surveillance Command, Control and Intelligence divsn. TRW, 2000—02; asst. program mgr. sys. integration Command Control and Intelligence Divsn. Northrop Grumman Mission Sys., 2002—04; program mgr. Maritime Surveillance Sys., Def. Mission Sys. Divsn., Northrop Grumman Mission Sys., 2004—. Editor: Trident Navigation Standard Operating Procedures, 1991, Acoustic Warfare Operating Doctrine, 1992, Surveillance Towed Array Sensor Passive User's Guide, 1994. Chmn. grounds com. Burke (Va.) United Meth. Ch., 1989-97, chmn. worship com., 1993-94; chmn. United Meth. Conf. Campsites Com., 2006—; chmn. Camp Va. site adv. com., 2001—; chmn. Julian Retreat Ctr. Task Force, 2002-06, chmn. conf. campside com., 2006—. Mem. IEEE, Eta Kappa Nu, Sigma Xi. Republican. Achievements include research in automatic depth and pitch control for a near surface submarine. Office: Northrop Grumman Mission Systems 1843 Hotel Circle S San Diego CA 92108-3320 E-mail: chuck.ward@ngc.com.

WARD, CHARLIE, professional basketball player; b. Thomasville, Ga., Oct. 2, 1970; Student, Tallahassee C.C., Fla., Florida State U. Basketball player N.Y. Knicks, 1994—2004, Phoenix Suns, 2004—. Recipient Heisman Trophy, 1993, Coll. Football Player of the Yr. award Sporting News, 1993; named to Coll. All-America First Team Sporting News, 1993; Coll. Football Hall of Fame, 2006.

WARD, CHESTER LAWRENCE, physician, consultant; b. Woodland, Calif., June 8, 1932; s. Benjamin Briggs and Nora Elizabeth Ward; m. Sally Diane Ward, Dec. 10, 1960; children: Katharine, Lynda. BA, U. Calif., Santa Barbara, 1955; MPH, U. Calif., Berkeley, 1966; MD, U. So. Calif., 1962; grad., Indsl. Coll. Armed Forces, 1978. Commd. 2d lt., inf. U.S. Army, 1954, advanced through grades to brig. gen., 1980; surgeon 5th Spl. Forces, Ft. Bragg, NC, Vietnam, 1963-64; chief aviation medicine, preventive medicine and aeromed. consultation service Ft. Rucker, Ala., 1967-68; surgeon Aviation Brigade and USA Vietnam Aviation Medicine Cons., 1968-69; flight surgeon Office of U.S. Army Surgeon Gen., 1970-71; physician The White House, Washington, 1971-75, 76; dir. environ. quality rsch. U.S. Army Med. Rsch. and Devel. Commd., 1975-76; comdr. Womack Cmty. Hosp., 1978—80; surgeon XVIII Airborne Corps, Ft. Bragg, 1978-80; comdr. William Beaumont Army Med. Ctr., El Paso, Tex., 1980-82; med. dir. Union Oil Co., Schaumburg, Ill., 1982-83, dir. domestic medicine LA, 1983-84; exec. dir. continuing med. edn. and clin. prof. emergency medicine U. So. Calif. Sch. Medicine, LA, 1984-85; dir., health officer Dept. Pub. Health, Butte County, Calif., 1985-95; cons., contractor, pvt. practice medicine, 1996—; med. dir. NorCal EMS, 2001—05. Trustee, pres. Oroville Union HS Dist., 1998—2002; chmn. Citizen's Bond Oversight Com., 2003—05; dir. The Estuary Owners' Assn., 2006—, pres., 2006—; apptd. by Gov. Wilson Calif. Commn. Emergency Med. Svcs., past commr. Decorated DSM, Legion of Merit (2), Bronze Star, Air medal (5). Fellow: Aerospace Med. Assn., Am. Coll. Preventive Medicine (past regent); mem.: No. Calif. Emergency Med. Svcs. Inc. (governing bd. 1987—2006, dir.), Calif. Med. Assn. (past del.), Butte-Glenn County Med. Soc. (past pres.), Mil. Officers Assn. (past chpt. pres.). Personal E-mail: tvldoc@sbcglobal.net.

WARD, CHRISTOPHER, computer scientist, researcher; b. London, Eng., Aug. 17, 1959; s. Michael Ward and Jean Mary Potter; m. Kathleen M McWilliams, Sept. 1, 1990; children: Keegan D McWilliams-Ward, Eva J McWilliams-Ward, Christina C McWilliams-Ward. BSc in Computer Sci., U. Hertfordshire, Eng., 1983; MSc in Computer Sci., U. Fla., Gainesville, 1985, PhD in Computer Sci., 1987. Asst. prof. Auburn U., Ala., 1988—93; assoc. prof. Hunter Coll., CUNY, NYC, 1993—96; sr. mem., tech. staff and group head Sarnoff Corp., Princeton, NJ, 1996—2000; rsch. staff mem. IBM T.J. Watson Rsch. Ctr., Hawthorne, NY, 2000—. Author: (textbook) Computer Organization and the MC 68000; contbr. articles to profl. jours. Mem. bd. edn. Glen Ridge Sch. Dist., NJ, 2001—07. Recipient Presdl. Recognition award, U. Fla., 1985, Authors award, Auburn U., 1993, Achievement award, Sarnoff Corp., 1998, Rsch. award, IBM Corp., 2005—06. Mem.: IEEE (sr.), Internat. Broadcasters Conv. (coun. mem. 1997—2000), Assn. Computing Machinery, Upsilon Pi Epsilon (chpt. pres. 1987—88). Achievements include patents in field. Office: IBM TJ Watson Research 19 Skyline Drive 1S-D60 Hawthorne NY 10532 Office Phone: 914-784-7186. Personal E-mail: christopher_ward@ieee.org. Business E-Mail: cw1@us.ibm.com.

WARD, DANE MICHAEL, academic administrator; b. Dallas, Apr. 29, 1958; s. Gerald George and Carol Sue (Underhill) Ward; m. Jennifer Anne Stringham, Aug. 8, 1987; children: William Brandon, Wesley Barnes. BA in Anthropology, Ind. U., Bloomington, 1976—80; MS in Social Studies Edn., Fla. State U., Tallahassee, 1981—83; MLS, Ind. U., Bloomington, 1990—93. Qualified Myers Briggs type indicator practitioner Ctr. Applications Psychol. Type, Fla., 1997. Anthropology, edn., social work libr., Purdy/Kresge Libr. Wayne State U., Detroit, 1993—97, coord. info. literacy Adamany Undergrad. Libr., 1997—99; coord. instrn. svcs. U. Librs., Ctrl. Mich. U., Mt. Pleasant, 1999—2002; assoc. dean pub. svcs. Milner Libr., Ill. State U., Normal, Ill., 2002—. Participant Assn. Coll. and Rsch. Librs. Think Tank III: Info. Literacy and Technol. Transformation Higher Edn., New Orleans, 1999; faculty mem. Assn. Coll. & Rsch. Librs. Info. Literacy Inst., New Orleans, 2002—; founding dir. sch. librarianship program Ill. State U., Normal, 2004—; chair Consortium Academic and Rsch. Librs. in Ill., Pub. Svcs. Working Group, 2006—. Editor: (book) The Collaborative Imperative: Librarians and Faculty Working Together in the Information Universe, 2000. Vol. US Peace Corps, Senegal, 1984—86. Named one of Top 20 Libr. Instrn. Articles award, ALA Libr. & Info. Tech. Round Table, 2001; recipient Academic Staff Outstanding Contbr. award, Wayne State U., 1997, Info. Literacy award, Mich. Libr. Assn. Info. Literacy Round Table, 2000. Mem.: ALA, Ill. Sch. Libr. Media Assn., Assn. Coll. & Rsch. Librs., Ind. Hist. Soc. Achievements include development of effective collaboration between academic librarians and faculty, redefining and implementing information literacy instruction and facilitating emergence of future academic libraries. Home: 3211 Eagle Crest Rd Bloomington IL 61704 Office: Ill State Univ Milner Libr Campus Box 8900 Normal IL 61790-8900 Home Phone: 309-661-9754. Office Fax: 309-438-3676. Business E-Mail: dmward@ilstu.edu.

WARD, DAVID, educational association administrator, former academic administrator; b. Manchester, Eng., July 8, 1938; arrived in US, 1960; s. Horace and Alice (Harwood) Ward; m. Judith B. Freifeld, June 11, 1964; children: Michael J.H., Peter F.B. BA, U. Leeds, Eng., 1959, MA, 1961; MS, U. Wis., 1961, PhD, 1963; LittD, U. Leeds, 1992. Lectr. Carleton U., Ottawa, Ont., 1963—64; asst. prof. U. Brit. Columbia, Vancouver, 1964—66, U. Wis., Madison, 1966—67, assoc. prof., 1967—70, prof., 1970—, chmn. geography dept., 1974—77, assoc. dean Grad. Sch., 1980—88, provost and vice chancellor acad. affairs, Andrew Clark prof. geography, 1989—94, chancellor, 1994—2000; pres. Am. Coun. Edn., Washington, 2000—. Mem. exec. com. Argonne Nat. Lab., Ill., 1990—93; dir.-at-large Social Sci. Rsch. Coun., 1991—93; mem. Kellogg Commn. on Future of Land Grant Univs.; chair Internet 2, Consortium Advances Network Devel.; mem. coun. UN U., 2004—; mem. Sec. of Edn.'s Commn. on Future of Edn., 2005. Author: Cities and Immigrants, 1970, Geographic Perspectives on Americas Past, 1978, Poverty Ethnicity and the American City, 1989, Landscape of Modernity, 1992; contbr. articles to profl. jours. Fellow Guggenheim fellow, 1970, Einstein fellow, Hebrew U., 1980, Fulbright fellow, Australian Nat. U., 1979. Fellow: Am. Acad. Arts and Scis.; mem.: Assn. Am. Geographers (pres. 1989). Office: Am Council on Edn One Dupont Circle NW Washington DC 20036-1193 Office Phone: 202-939-9311. Office Fax: 202-659-2212. E-mail: president@ace.nche.edu. *

WARD, DAVID ALLEN, sociology educator; b. Dedham, Mass., June 21, 1933; s. Theodore Allen and Jessie Miller (Ketchum) W.; m. Carol Jane Barton, June 10, 1957 (div. 1964); children: Douglas Allen, Andrew Barton; m. Reneé Ellen Light, Mar. 10, 1967. BA, Colby Coll., 1955; PhD, U. Ill., 1960. Asst. prof. Wash. State U., Pullman, 1960-61; asst. research sociologist UCLA, 1961-64; assoc. prof. U. Minn., Mpls., 1965-68, prof., 1968—2002, chmn. dept. sociology, 1984-88, 92-95. Chmn. Salzburg (Austria) Seminar in Am. Studies, 1977; cons. jud. com. U.S. Ho. Reps., Washington, 1984. Co-author: Women's Prison, 1965, Prison Treatment, 1971; co-editor: Delinquency, Crime and Social Process, 1969, Confinement in Maximum Custody, 1981; editorial cons. Jour. Criminal Law and Criminology, 1968-97. Mem. Mpls. Civilian Police Rev. Bd., 1991-94. Liberal Arts fellow Harvard U. Law Sch., 1968-69; Fulbright research fellow, 1971-72; research fellow Norwegian Fgn. Office, Oslo, 1976. Mem.: Am. Soc. Criminology, Am. Sociol. Assn. (chmn. sect. criminology 1976—77). Office: Univ of Minn Dept of Sociology 909 Social Sci Bldg Minneapolis MN 55455

WARD, DAVID SCHAD, scriptwriter, film director; b. Providence, Oct. 24, 1947; s. Robert McCollum and Miriam (Schad) W.; children: Joaquin Atwood, Sylvana Soto. BA, Pomona Coll., 1967; M.F.A., UCLA, 1970. Scriptwriter: films include Steelyard Blues, 1971, The Sting, 1973 (Acad. award best original screenplay 1973), The Milagro Beanfield War, 1988, (with Nora Ephron and Jeff Arch) Sleepless in Seattle, 1998 (Academy award nominee Best Original Screenplay 1998), (with John Eskow, Ted Elliott and Terry Rossio) The Mask of Zorro, 2006, (with Phil Sears and Blake T. Evans) Flyboys, 2006; writer, dir. films include Cannery Row, 1981, Major League, 1989, King Ralph, 1991, The Program, 1993, Major League II, 1995, Down Periscope, 1996. Mem.: Acad. Motion Picture Arts and Scis., Dirs. Guild Am. Office: c/o Ben Smith 8942 Wilshire Blvd Beverly Hills CA 90211

WARD, DOREE MAXINE, secondary school educator; b. Des Moines, Oct. 17, 1955; d. Jeane and Wesley Ward. BSE in Edn., Drake U., 1977, MSEd, 1997. Tchr. Thomas Jefferson H.S., Council Bluffs, Iowa, 1978—82; tchr./coach Floyd Valley H.S., Alton, Iowa, 1982—84, Newton H.S., Newton, 1987—. Del. Russia and Hungary People to People Internat., 1993. Mem.: NEA, Iowa Assn. Safety Edn. (pres. 1994—2002), Iowa State Edn. Assn. Avocations: swimming, horseback riding, softball, basketball. Home: 515 E 10th St S Newton IA 50208 Office: Newton High School 800 E 4th St S Newton IA 50208 Home Phone: 641-791-9697. Business E-Mail: wardd@newton.k12.ia.us.

WARD, ERICA ANNE, lawyer, educator; b. Okiyama, Japan, Oct. 20, 1950; d. Robert Edward and Constance Regina (Barnett) Ward; m. Ralph Joseph Gerson, May 20, 1979; children: Stephanie Claire Gerson, Madeleine Ward Gerson. BA, Stanford U., 1972; JD, U. Mich., 1975. Bar: Calif. 1975, DC 1976, US Ct. Appeals (5th and DC cir.) 1977, Temp. Emergency Ct. Appeals 1983, Mich. 1989. Assoc. Wilmer, Cutler & Pickering, Washington, 1975—77; staff counsel US Senate Ethics Com., Washington, 1977—78; exec. asst. gen. counsel Dept. Energy, Washington, 1978—79; counsellor to dep. sec., 1980; assoc. dir. energy and natural resources, domestic policy staff White House, Washington, 1980—81; counsel Skadden, Arps, Slate, Meagher & Flom., Washington, 1981—87; ptnr., 1987; adj. prof. law U. Mich., Ann Arbor, 1984—85; Editor Mich. Law Rev., 1975; commr. Mackinac Is. State Pk. Commn., Mich., 1989—95. Recipient Outstanding Svc. medal, Dept. Energy, 1981. Mem.: Women's Bar Assn. DC, ABA, U. Mich. Law Sch., Cranbrook Ednl. Cmty., Children's Hosp. Mich. Democrat. Jewish. Office: Skadden Arps Slate Meagher Flom 1440 New York Ave NW Ste 600 Washington DC 20005-6000 Office Phone: 202-371-7050. Business E-Mail: eward@skadden.com.

WARD, GEOFFREY CHAMPION, writer, editor; b. Newark, Ohio, Nov. 30, 1940; s. Frederick Champion and Rachel Duira (Baldinger) W.; m. Diane Raines; children: Nathan, Kelly; 1 stepchild, Garrett. BA, Oberlin Coll., 1962, DHL (hon.), 2004, Wilkes U., 1995. Sr. picture editor Ency. Britannica, Chgo., 1964-68; co-founder, editor Audience mag., Boston, 1969-73; mng. editor Am. Heritage Mag., NYC, 1976-78, editor, 1978-82. Author: Lincoln's Thought and the Present, 1978, Treasures of the Maharajas, 1983, Before the Trumpet: Young Franklin Roosevelt, 1882-1905, 1985, A First-Class Temperament: The Emergence of Franklin Roosevelt, 1989 (Nat. Book Critics Cir. award, Francis Parkman prize Soc. Am. Historians, L.A. Times biography prize, Ohioana award), The Civil War: An Illustrated History, 1990, American Originals: The Private Worlds of Some Singular Men and Women, 1991; (with Diane Raines Ward) Tiger Wallahs, Encounters with the Men Who Tried to Save the Greatest of the Great Cats, 1993, Baseball: An Illustrated History, 1994, Closest Companion: The Unknown Story of the Intimate Friendship between Franklin Roosevelt and Margaret Suckley, 1995, The West: An Illustrated History, 1996, (with Michael Nichols) The Year of the Tiger, 1998, Not for Ourselves Alone: Elizabeth Cady Stanton and Susan B. Anthony, 1999, Jazz: A History of America's Music, 2000, (with Dayton Duncan) Mark Twain, 2001, Unforgivable Blackness: The Rise and Fall of Jack Johnson, 2004 (Anisfield/Wolf Book award, 2005, William Hill Sports Book of Yr. 2006), The War: An Intimate History 1941-1945, 2007; editor: The Best American Essays of 1996; (TV documentaries) Huey Long, 1985, Thomas Hart Benton, 1989, Lindbergh, 1990, Nixon, 1990 (Writer's Guild Am. award), The Civil War, 1990 (Emmy award), Reminiscing in Tempo, 1991, Empire of the Air, 1992, The Kennedys, 1992 (Emmy award), George Marshall and the American Century, 1993, Baseball, 1994 (Emmy award), Daley: The Last Boss, 1995, The West, 1996, Theodore Roosevelt, 1996 (Emmy award), Thomas Jefferson, 1997, Frank Lloyd Wright, 1998, Not for Ourselves Alone, 1999, Jazz, 2000, (with Dayton Duncan) Mark Twain, 2001, Unforgivable Blackness: The Rise and Fall of Jack Johnson, 2005 (Emmy award, Writers Guild award), The War, 2007; contbr. articles to mags., jours. Bd. dirs. Save the Tiger Fund. Recipient Christopher awards for The Statue of Liberty, Theodore Roosevelt, Not For Ourselves Alone, Mark Twain, The Civil War, New Eng. Booksellers Assn. award, Am. Booksellers award, Lila Acheson Wallace Readers Digest writers award. Mem. Soc. Am. Historians (Friend of History award), Orgn. Am. Historians, Serengeti Club, Writers Guild Am., East Inc., Century Assn. Home: 17 C 290 W End Ave New York NY 10023-8106 Office: Brandt &Hochman care Carl Brandt 1501 Broadway Ste 2310 New York NY 10036-5689

WARD, GEORGE FRANK, JR., international programs executive, ambassador; b. Jamaica, NY, Apr. 9, 1945; s. George Frank and Hildegard Louisa (Evans) W.; m. Peggy Elizabeth Coote, June 12, 1965; 1 child, Pamela Ward Priester. BA, U. Rochester, 1965; MPA, Harvard U., 1980. U.S. vice consul Am. Consulate, Hamburg, Germany, 1970-72; ops. officer Office Sec. State, Washington, 1972-74; U.S. consul Am. Consulate Gen., Genoa, Italy, 1974-76; polit. officer Am. Embassy, Rome, 1976-77, exec. asst., 1977-79, polit. officer Bonn, Germany, 1984—85, dep. chief mission, 1989—92; polit.-mil. officer US Dept. State, Washington, 1980-84, 1985—88, prin. dep. asst. sec. Bur. Internat. Orgn., 1992-96, US amb. to Namibia, 1996-99, US coord. for humanitarian assistance to Iraq, 2003; v.p., dir. profl. tng. program US Inst. Peace, Washington, 1999—2005; sr. v.p. internat. programs World Vision, 2005—. Capt. USMC, 1965-69, maj. USMCR, 1969-78. Decorated Vietnamese Cross Gallantry, Naval Commendation medal with combat V; recipient Presdl. Meritorious Svc. award, 1992, 1994, Disting. Honor award, U.S. State Dept., 1992. Fellow: Phi Beta Kappa; mem.: Am. Fgn. Svc. Assn., Washington Inst. Fgn. Affairs, Cosmos Club. Anglican. Home: 3404 Walnut Hill Ct Falls Church VA 22042-3546 Home Phone: 703-560-8295; Office Phone: 202-572-6318. Business E-Mail: gward@worldvision.org.

WARD, GEORGE TRUMAN, architect; b. Washington, July 24, 1927; s. Truman and Gladys Anna (Nutt) W.; m. Margaret Ann Hall, Sept. 10, 1949; children: Carol Ann Ward Dickson, Donna Lynne Ward Solomon, George Truman, Robert Stephen. BS, Va. Poly. Inst., 1951, MS, 1952; postgrad., George Washington U., 1966. Registered profl. arch., Va., Md., D.C., W.Va., Del., N.C. Archtl. draftsman Charles A. Pearson, Radford, Va., 1950; head archtl. sect. Hayes, Seay, Mattern & Mattern, Radford and Roanoke, 1951-52; with Joseph Saunders & Assocs., Alexandria, Va., 1952-57, assoc. arch., 1955-57; ptnr. Vosbeck-Ward & Assocs., Alexandria, 1957-64, Ward/Hall Assocs., Fairfax, 1964—. Dir. Crestar Bank/Greater Washington Region, 1967-99. Pres. PTA Burke (Va.) Sch., 1970-71; mem. bd. mgrs. Fairfax (Va.) County YMCA, 1964-76; chmn. adv. com. Coll. Arch., Va. Poly. Inst., 1984-90; bd. dirs., mem. investment com. Va. Tech. Found., Inc., 1986-91, 93-98; pres. Springfield Rotary Found., 1978-79; chmn. county adv. bd. Salvation Army, 1978-79, 89-95, co-chmn. Fairfax County Salvation Army Capital Campaign, 1991-95; mem. Gen. Bd. Va. Bapts., deacon, moderator; mem. bd. vis. Va. Poly. Inst. & State U., 1984-87; trustee Fairfax County Pub. Schs. Edn. Found., Inc. With AUS, 1946-47. Paul Harris fellow; recipient Disting. Svc. award Va. Tech. Alumni Assn., 1988; recipient William H. Ruffner medal Va. Tech., 1996, VSAIA William C. Noland award, 1998, Va. Tech. Coll. Arch. and Urban Studies Lifetime Contbn. award, 1998. Fellow Coll. AIA; mem. AIA (corp., charter Octagon Soc.), No. Va. Soc. AIA (chmn. polit. action com. 1991-93, Disting. Svc. award 1990, treas. Va. soc. 1994-98, Outstanding Achievement award 1996), Rowe Fellowship (charter mem. 1988), Alumni Assn. Va. Poly. Inst. & State U. (bd. dirs., v.p 1992, pres. 1994), Interfaith Forum on Religion, Art and Arch., Va. Found. for Arch. (trustee), Va. Assn. Professions, Va. C. of C., No. Va. Angus Assn. (pres. 1987-88), Va. Tech. Alumni Assn. (hon., life, bd. dirs. Disting. Svc. award 1988), Masons, Shriners, KT, Rotary (charter mem., pres. Springfield 1973-74, Disting. Svc. award dist. 7610 1995), Tau Sigma Delta, Omicron Delta Kappa, Phi Kappa Phi, Pi Delta Epsilon, Ut Prosim. Baptist. Office: Ward Hall Assocs AIA Ste 125 14900 Conference Center Dr Chantilly VA 20151 Business E-Mail: gtward@wardhall.com.

WARD, HARRY MERRILL, history professor; b. West Lafayette, Ind., July 30, 1929; s. Hiley L. and Agnes Ward. Student, U. Ill., 1947-49; BA, William Jewell Coll., 1951; MA, Columbia U., 1954, PhD, 1960. Social investigator NYC Dept. Welfare, 1958—59; asst. prof. Georgetown Coll., Ky., 1959—61; from asst. to assoc. prof. Morehead State U., 1961—65; vis. assoc. prof. So. Ill. U., Carbondale, 1967—68; assoc. prof. history U. Richmond, Va., 1965—77, prof. history, 1977—93, William Binford Vest prof. history, 1993—99, William Binford Vest prof. history emeritus, 1999—. Co-founder Am. Revolution Roundtable, Richmond; cons. in field. Author: The United Colonies of New England, 1643-1690, 1961, Department of War, 1781-1795, 1962, 1981, Unite or Die: Intercolony Relations, 1690-1763, 1971, Statism in Plymouth Colony, 1973, Duty, Honor or Country: General George Weedon and the American Revolution, 1979, Richmond: An Illustrated History, 1985, 1988, Charles Scott and the Spirit of '76, 1988, Major General Adam Stephen and the Cause of American Liberty, 1989, Colonial America, 1607-1763, 1990, American Revolution: Nationhood Achieved, 1763-1788, 1994, General William Maxwell and the New Jersey Continentals, 1997, The War for Independence and the Transformation of American Society, 1999, Between the Lines: Banditti of the American Revolution, 2002, George Washington's Enforcers: Policing the Continental Army, 2006; co-author: Richmond During the Revolution, 1775-1783, 1977; contbr. articles to profl. jours.; assoc. editor: Encyclopedia of the American Revolution, 2006. With USMC, 1951—53. Recipient Fraunces Tavern Mus. Book award, 1990, Scholar award in history, Va. Social Sci. Assn., 1992, History prize for disting. achievement, Soc. of the Cin. in the State of N.J., 2004, LTG Richard Trefry Book award, Army Hist. Found., 2005. Fellow: Pilgrim Soc.; mem.: Am. Hist. Assn., So. Hist. Assn., Orgn. Am. Historians, Am. Revolution Roundtable. Office: U Richmond Dept History Richmond VA 23173-0180 Office Phone: 804-289-8345. Business E-Mail: dgovoruh@richmond.edu.

WARD, HARRY PFEFFER, hematologist, retired academic administrator; b. Pueblo, Colo., June 6, 1933; s. Lester L. and Alysmai (Pfeffer) W.; m. Betty Jo Stewart, Aug. 20, 1955; children— Stewart, Leslie, Elizabeth, Mary Alice, Amy. AB, Princeton U., 1955; MD, U. Colo., 1959; MS, U. Minn., 1963. Intern Bellevue Hosp., NYC, 1959; resident Mayo Clinic, Rochester, Minn., 1960-63; practice medicine specializing in hematology; chief medicine Denver VA hosp., 1968-72; dean, asso. v.p. U. Colo. Sch. Medicine, 1972-78, prof. medicine, 1972; chancellor U. Ark. Med. Sci., Little Rock, 1979-2000, chancellor emeritus, 2000—. Clin. investigator VA, 1964-67 Chmn. Assn. Acad. Health Ctr., 1993-94. Mem. ACP, AMA, Am. Fedn. Clin. Research, Central Soc. Clin. Investigation, Am. Soc. Hematology, Internat. Soc. Hematology, Western Soc. Clin. Research. Home: 369 Valley Club Cir Little Rock AR 72212-2900 Office: U Ark Med Scis 4301 W Markham St Little Rock AR 72205-7101 E-mail: hpward1@msn.com.

WARD, HILEY HENRY, journalist, educator; b. Lafayette, Ind., July 30, 1929; s. Hiley Lemen and Agnes (Fuller) W.; m. Charlotte Burns, May 28, 1951 (div. 1971); children: Dianne, Carolee, Marceline, Laurel; m. Joan Bastel, Aug. 20, 1977. BA, William Jewell Coll., 1951; MA, Berkeley Bapt. Div. Sch., 1953; MDiv, McCormick Theol. Sem., Chgo., 1955; student, Northwestern U., 1948, 54, 56-57; PhD, U. Minn., 1977. News asst. Christian Advocate, 1953-55; editor jr. publs. David C. Cook Pub. Co., 1956-59; editor Record, Buchanan, Mich., 1960; religion editor Detroit Free Press, 1960-73; asst. prof. journalism Mankato (Minn.) State U., 1974-76; assoc. prof. journalism Wichita (Kans.) State U., 1976; prof. journalism Temple U., Phila., 1977-96, prof. emeritus, 1997—, dir. news-editorial sequence, journalism dept., 1977-80, chmn. dept., 1978-80. Instr. journalism Oakland U., Rochester, Mich., evenings 1963-66. Author: Creative Giving, 1958, Space-age Sunday, 1960, Documents of Dialogue, 1966, God and Marx Today, 1968, Ecumania, 1968, Rock 2000, 1969, Prophet of the Black Nation, 1969, The Far-out Saints of the Jesus Communes, 1972, Religion 2101 A.D., 1975, Feeling Good About Myself, 1983, Professional Newswriting, 1985, My Friend's Beliefs: A Young Reader's Guide to World Religions, 1988, Reporting in Depth, 1991, Magazine and Feature Writing, 1993, Mainstreams of American Media History, 1997; editor: Media History Digest, 1979-94; exec. editor: Kidbits, 1981-82; book editor: Editor and Publisher, 1989-98; contbr. articles to profl. jours., feature articles to newspapers and mags.; also short stories and poems. Religious Pub. Rels. Coun. fellow, 1970; recipient citation Religious Heritage Am., 1962, Leidt award Epsic. Ch., 1969, citation U.S. Am. Revolution Bicentennial Adminstrn., 1976, Text and Acad. Authors citation, 1997. Mem. Religion Newswriters Assn. (pres. 1970-72), Am. Soc. Journalists and Authors, Am. Journalism Historians Assn. (bd. dirs. 1994-96, Kobre lifetime achievement award 1999), Overseas Press Club. Home: PO Box 399 1263 Folly Rd Warrington PA 18976-1422 E-mail: bastel@voicenet.com.

WARD, HINES, JR., professional football player; b. Seoul, Republic of Korea, Mar. 8, 1976; s. Hines Ward Sr. and Kim Young-hee; m. Simone Ward; 1 child, Jaden. BA in consumer economics, U. Ga., 1997. Wide receiver Pitts. Steelers, 1998—. Named Super Bowl XL MVP, 2006; named to NFL Pro-Bowl, 2001—04. Achievements include being a member of Super Bowl XL Champion Pittsburgh Steelers, 2006; being the first Korean-American Super Bowl MVP, 2006. Office: c/o Pittsburgh Steelers 3400 S Water St Pittsburgh PA 15203

WARD, HORACE TALIAFERRO, federal judge; b. LaGrange, Ga., July 29, 1927; m. Ruth LeFlore (dec.); 1 son (dec.). AB, Morehouse Coll., 1949; MA, Atlanta U., 1950; JD, Northwestern U., 1959. Bar: Ga. 1960. Instr. polit. sci. Ark. A.M. and N. Coll., 1950-51, Ala. State Coll., 1951-53, 55-56; claims authorizer U.S. Social Security Adminstrn., 1959-60; assoc. firm Hollowell Ward Moore & Alexander (and successors), Atlanta, 1960-69; individual practice law Atlanta, 1971-74; judge Civil Ct. of Fulton County, 1974-77, Fulton Superior Ct., 1977-79; U.S. Dist. Ct. judge No. Dist. Ga., Atlanta, 1979-93; sr. judge U.S. Dist. Ct. No. Dist. Ga., Atlanta, 1993—. Lectr. bus. and sch. law Atlanta U., 1965-70; dep. city atty., Atlanta, 1969-70, asst. county atty., Fulton County, 1971-74 Former Trustee Friendship Baptist Ch., Atlanta; mem. Ga. adv. com. U.S. Civil Rights Commn., 1963-65; assisting lawyer NAACP Legal Def. and Edn. Fund, Inc., 1960-70; mem. Jud. Selection Commn., Atlanta, 1972-74, Charter Commn., 1971-72; mem. Ga. Senate, 1964-74, jud. com., rules com., county and urban affairs com.; mem. State Democratic Exec. com., 1966-74; former bd. dirs. Atlanta Legal Aid Soc.; bd. dirs. Atlanta Urban League, Fed. Defender Program, No. Dist. Ga.; trustee Met. Atlanta Commn. on Crime and Delinquency, Atlanta U., Fledgling Found. Mem. Am. Bar Assn., Nat. Bar Assn. (chmn. jud. council 1978-79), State Bar Ga., Atlanta Bar Assn., Gate City Bar Assn. (pres. 1972-74), Atlanta Lawyers Club, Phi Beta Kappa, Alpha Phi Alpha, Phi Alpha Delta, Sigma Pi Phi. Office: US Dist Court 1252 US Courthouse 75 Spring St SW Atlanta GA 30303-3309 Home Phone: 404-588-0641; Office Phone: 404-215-1330.

WARD, JAMES A., lawyer; b. Waukesha, Wis. BA in Polit. Sci., Carroll Coll., Waukesha, 1971; JD, So. Meth. U., 1974. Bar: Wis. 1974, U.S. Dist. Ct. (ea. and we. dists.) Wis. 1974, U.S. Supreme Ct. 1979. Atty. Krause & Ward, Waukesha, 1974-78; sole practitioner Waukesha, 1978-80; atty. Congdon, Ward & Walden, S.C., Waukesha, 1981—2002; sole practitioner, 2003—. Mem. Waukesha County Bd. Adjustment, 1992—. Mem. Rotary Office: 161 W Wisconsin Ave Pewaukee WI 53072-2400 Office Phone: 262-691-3000. E-mail: james@jwardlaw.com.

WARD, JOE HENRY, JR., retired lawyer; b. Childress, Tex., Apr. 18, 1930; s. Joe Henry and Helen Ida (Chastain) W.; m. Carlotta Agnes Abreu, Feb. 7, 1959; children: James, Robert, William, John. BS in Acctg., Tex. Christian U., 1952; JD, So. Meth. U., 1964. Bar: Tex. 1964, Va. 1972, D.C. 1974; CPA, Tex. Mgr. Alexander Grant & Co. CPA's, Dallas, 1956-64; atty. U.S. Treasury, 1965-68; tax counsel U.S. Senate Fin. Com., 1968-72; pvt. practice Washington, 1972-83; asst. gen. counsel, tax mgr. Epic Holdings, Ltd. and Crysopt Corp., 1983-87; pvt. practice Washington and Va., 1987-95; ret., 1995. Lt. USNR, 1952-56. Mem.: AICPA, Univ. Club. Home: 2639 Mann Ct Falls Church VA 22046-2721

WARD, JON DAVID, retired insurance company executive; b. Marshalltown, Iowa, Nov. 30, 1944; s. Wiley Granger and Maxine Lucille (Culbertson) W.; children: Wendy, Stacey, Christine. BS in Acctg., U. No. Iowa, 1969; MBA, Ill. State U., 1973. Cert. internal auditor; CLU. Audit dir. State Farm Ins. Cos., Bloomington, Ill., 1969—2006; ret., 2006. Contbr. articles to profl. jours. and chpts. to books. Ct.-apptd. spl. advocate Child Protection Network and Children's Advocacy Ctr., Bloomington, 1997-2001; sec. Bloomington-Normal Sister Cities Commn., 1989-95. Fellow Life Mgmt. Inst.; mem. Inst. Internal Auditors (bd. dirs. 1984-97). Methodist. Avocations: racquetball, running, skiing, travel, reading. Home: 19319 Great Crane Rd Bloomington IL 61704-5231

WARD, JONATHAN P., investment banker; b. May 6, 1954; BSChemE, U. N.H., 1976; grad. advanced mgmt. program, Harvard Bus. Sch. With R.R. Donnelley, 1977—2001, pres. Merchandise Media and Fin. Svcs. bus. units, mgr. comml. printing operation, v.p., dir. Spartanburg, S.C., mfg. divsn., exec. v.p. Comml. Print Sector, 1995—97, pres., COO, 1997—2001; pres., CEO ServiceMaster, Downers Grove, Ill., 2001—02, chmn., CEO, 2002—06; mng. dir. investment banking, chmn. Chgo. office Lazard Ltd., Chgo., 2006—. Dir. Metromail Corp., Siegwerk Inc. USA, J. Jill Group Inc., First Horizon. Trustee Goodman Theatre, Chgo.; dir. Chgo. Youth Ctrs., Evanston Northwestern Hosp. Mem.: Nat. Assn. Mfr., Direct Mktg. Assn. Office: Lazard Ltd 200 W Madison St Ste 2200 Chicago IL 60606 Office Phone: 312-407-6600. Office Fax: 312-407-6620. *

WARD, KECA B., small business owner, consultant; b. Pitts., Feb. 21, 1970; d. David and Keca Ward; m. David C. Bertolotti, Oct. 4, 1997; children: Gianna Nicole, Giacomo Christopher. BS, Ind. U. Pa., 1992. Account mgr. Bell Atlantic Mobile (now Verizon Wireless), Wayne, 1993—97, Devon Consulting, Wayne, 1997—2004; co-owner Green Apple Corp., Wayne, 2004—. R-Conservative. Office: Green Apple Corp 122 E Lancaster Ave St 300A Wayne PA 19087 Business E-Mail: kward@greenapplecorp.com.

WARD, KEN, JR., journalist; Environ. reporter Charleston Gazette, W.Va. Recipient Edward J. Meeman award for environ. reporting, Scripps Howard Found., 2006. Mem.: Soc. Environ. Journalists (chair First Amendment task force 2002—, David Stolberg Meritorious Svc. award 2004). Office: The Charleston Gazette 1001 Virginia St E Charleston WV 25301 Office Phone: 304-348-1702. Office Fax: 304-348-1233. E-mail: kward@wvgazette.com.

WARD, L. TAYLOR, III, lawyer; b. Birmingham, Ala., May 29, 1959; m. Theresa Ward; 2 children. BA, Samford Univ., 1981, MBA, JD, Samford Univ., 1984. Bar: Ala. 1984, Fla. 1987. V.p., gen. counsel JM Family Enterprises, Deerfield Beach, Fla., 2000—. Bd. dir. JM Assoc. Credit Union. Mem.: ABA, Assn. Corp. Counsel, Ala. State Bar, Fla. State Bar, Broward County Bar Assn., So. Palm Beach County Bar Assn. Office: JM Family Enterprises 100 Jim Moran Blvd Deerfield Beach FL 33442 Office Phone: 954-429-2000. Office Fax: 954-429-2601.

WARD, LARRY THOMAS, social program administrator; b. Abington, Va., Sept. 10, 1951; s. Manuel Thomas and Virginia June (Meade) W.; m. Jacqueline June Moore, Aug. 7, 1982 (div. June 1995); 1 child, Nicholas Lawrence; m. Kathleen Denise McCaslin, July 14, 1998. BSW cum laude, U. Md., 1983, MSW, 1984; PhD in Counseling Psychology, Columbia State U., 1997. Lic. social worker. Legis. lobbyist Citizen Action Coalition, Balt., 1982-83; mgmt. cons. United Way Md., Balt., 1983-84; program adminstr. Adams County Office Aging, Gettysburg, Pa., 1985-86; dir. social work Margaret E. Moul Home, York, Pa., 1986-87; coord. employee assistance program, family svc. supr. Family and Children's Svcs., Harrisburg, Pa., 1987-92, cons. drug & alcohol Gettysburg, 1984-86; pres., CEO Impact Sems., Guffey, Colo., 1988-97; pub. Guffey Co., 1992-97; pres., CEO Family Adv., Guffey, 1997—2001; CEO Internat. Child Advocacy Resource Enterprise, Inc., Guffey, 2002—. Author: Meditatinos on Descartes, 1979, A Philosophical Perspective, 1979, Heracles Reborn, 1983, Protective Services for the Elerly, 1984, Why A Psychiatrist, 1985, The blue ridge Summit Project, 1986, The Effects of Office Design on the Delivery of Therapeutic Social Work Services, 1987, Emotional Disorders of the Chronically Disabled Adolscent, 1987, Resistance to School-based EAPs, 1989, 2d edit., 1993, What Healthy Couples Seem to Know, 1990, Good Relationships Have Certain Traits, 1991, Truth, Justice, and the American Way: The Life and Times of Noel Neill, 2003, Noel Neill: Lois Lane Goes West, 2003, Noel Neill: The Original Lois Lane, 2003, Canon City, Colorado: Every Picture Tells a Story, 2005, Truth, Justice, and the American Way: Expanded Collector's Edition, 2006; exec. prodr. film on courtroom survival techniques, 1996, Canon City Colorado: Every Picture Tells A Story, 2005. Ex-officio bd. dirs. Grass Roots, Inc., Columbia, Md., 1984; del. Gov.'s Youth Adv. Coun., Annapolis, Md., 1970-72; mem. consumer adv. coun. Met. Edison Co., Harrisburg, 1986-87. Recipient Original Art award Md. Pub. Broadcasting, 1969. Democrat. Avocations: tennis, baseball. Home: 932 Clover Ave Canon City CO 81212

WARD, LESLIE ALLYSON, journalist, editor; b. LA, June 3, 1946; d. Harold Gordon and Marilyn Lucille (Dahlstead) W.; m. Robert L. Biggs, 1971 (div. 1977); m. Colman Robert Andrews, May 26, 1979 (div. 1988); m. John P. Lindsay, Oct. 10, 2003. AA, Coll. San Mateo, 1966; BA, UCLA, 1968, MJ, 1971. Reporter, researcher L.A. Bur. Life mag., 1971-72; reporter, news asst. L.A. bur. N.Y. Times, 1973-76; sr. editor New West mag., LA, 1976-78, 79-80; L.A. bur. chief US mag., 1978-79; Sunday style editor L.A. Herald Examiner, 1981-82, editor-in-chief Sunday mags., 1982-83, Olympics editor, 1984, sports editor, 1985-86, sr. writer, 1986; sr. editor L.A. Times Mag., 1988-90; travel editor L.A. Times, 1990—2003. Democrat. Office: LA Times Times Mirror Sq Los Angeles CA 90053

WARD, LIESL HOPE, language educator; d. Joseph Edward and Gara Lovorn Ward. PhD, U. Ill., Urbana-Champaign, 2000. Chair comm. dept. Jefferson State C.C., Birmingham, Ala., 2003—. Mem. Bapt. Ch. Covenant, Birmingham, 2001—. Mem.: Ala. Edn. Assn., Am. Assn. C.C. Women, Phi Theta Kappa (faculty advisor 2002—, faculty scholar 2006, Pargon Advisor award 2005). Office: Jefferson State Community College 4600 Valleydale Rd Birmingham AL 35242 Home Phone: 205-933-0873; Office Phone: 205-520-5956. Office Fax: 205-520-5981. E-mail: lward@jeffstateonline.com.

WARD, LLEWELLYN ORCUTT, III, oil industry executive; b. Oklahoma City, July 24, 1930; s. Llewellyn Orcutt II and Addie (Reisdorph) W.; m. Myra Beth Gungoll, Oct. 29, 1955; children: Casidy Ann, William Carlton. Student, Okla. Mil. Acad., 1948—50; BS, U. Okla., 1953; postgrad., Harvard U., 1986. Registered profl. engr., Okla. Dist. engr. Delhi-Taylor Oil Corp., Tulsa, 1955-56; ptnr. Ward-Gungoll Oil Investments, Enid, Okla., 1956—; owner L.O. Ward Oil Ops., Enid, 1963—; chmn., CEO Ward Petroleum Corp. Mem. Okla. Gov.'s Adv. Coun. on Energy; rep. to Interstate Oil Compact Commn.; dir. Hydril Corp; chmn., CEO Ward Petroleum Corp. Chmn. Indsl. Devel. Commn., Enid, 1968—; active YMCA; mem. bd. visitors Coll. Engring., U. Okla.; mem. adv. coun. Sch. Bus., trustee Phillips U., Enid, Univ. Bd., Pepperdine, Calif.; Okla. chmn. U.S. Olympic Com., 1986—; Rep. nat. committeeman from Okla., 1982-88; mem. Pres.'s adv. com. on arts Kennedy Ctr. Served with C.E., U.S. Army, 1953-55. Named Chief Roughneck of Yr., Lone Star Steel, 1999, Disting. Alumnus, Okla. Mil. Acad., 1993; named to Hall of Fame, Enid Pub. Sch. Found., 2006; recipient Gov.'s Arts award, 2006. Mem. Ind. Petroleum Assn. Am. (chmn. 1996-98), Okla. Ind. Petroleum Assn. Am. (pres., bd. dirs.), Nat. Petroleum Coun., Enid C. of C. (Businessman of Yr. 1988, Citizen of Yr. 2006), U. Okla. Coll. Engring. Disting. Grads. Soc., Am. Bus. Club (pres. 1964), Masons, Shriners, Rotary (pres. Enid 1990-91), Alpha Tau Omega. Methodist. Home: 900 Brookside Dr Enid OK 73703-6941 Office: 502 S Fillmore St Enid OK 73703-5703 Home Phone: 580-234-8779; Office Phone: 580-234-3229.

WARD, LOUIS EMMERSON, retired physician; b. Mt. Vernon, Ill., Jan. 19, 1918; s. Henry Ben (Pope) and Aline (Emmerson) Ward; m. Nan Talbot, June 5, 1942; children: Nancy, Louis, Robert, Mark; m. Marian Mansfield, Jan. 27, 1979. AB, U. Ill., 1939; MD, Harvard, 1943; MS in Medicine, U. Minn., 1949. Intern Ill. Research and Ednl. Hosp., Chgo., 1943; fellow medicine Mayo Found., 1946—49; cons. medicine, rheumatology Mayo Clinic, 1950—83, chmn. bd. govs., 1964—75. Contbr. articles to profl. jours. Vice chmn. bd. trustees Mayo Found., 1964—76; past bd. dirs. Fund for Republic, Ctr. for Study Dem. Instns., Arthritis Found., Northwestern Bell Telephone Prin. Fin. Group; mem. Nat. Coun. Health Planning and Resource Devel., 1976—83. With M.C. US Army, 1944—46. Recipient Achievement award, U. Ill., 1968, Disting. Alumnus award, Mayo Found., 1983. Master: Am. Coll. Rheumatology; mem.: So. Minn. Med. Assn., Zumbro Valley Med. Soc., Minn. Med. Soc., Ctrl. Soc. Clin. Rsch., Nat. Soc. Clin. Rheumatologists, AAAS, AMA, Phi Delta Theta, Alpha Omega Alpha, Sigma Xi, Phi Beta Kappa. Home: Apt 916 211 2nd St NW Rochester MN 55901-2820

WARD, MICHAEL J., rail transportation executive; b. Balt., Sept. 2, 1950; BS, U. Md., 1972; MBA, Harvard U., 1976. Rsch. analyst Chessie Sys., Balt., 1977—80, mgr., coord. analysis-fin., 1980—81, mgr. bus. rsch. Cleve., 1981—82, dir. nat. accts., 1982—84, asst. v.p. coal mktg., 1984—85, Balt., 1984—86; v.p. coal mktg. CSX Distbn. Svcs., Balt., 1986—88; v.p. coal CSX Transp., Jacksonville, 1988—94, gen. mgr. C&O Bus. Unit, v.p. coal Huntington, W.Va., 1994—95, sr. v.p. fin. Jacksonville, 1995—96, CFO, 1995—98, exec. v.p. fin., 1996—98, exec. v.p. coal and merger planning, 1998—99, exec. v.p. coal svc. group, 1999—2000, exec. v.p. ops., 2000, pres., 2000—03, CEO, 2002—03; pres. CSX Corp., Jacksonville, 2002—, chmn., pres., CEO, 2003—. Bd. dirs. Ky. Coal Coun., Ashland, Inc., CSX Corp. Bd. dirs. Ctr. Energy Econ. Devel., Take Stock in Children. Mem.: Fla. Coun. 100, Assn. Am. Railroads (bd. dirs.), Phi Kappa Phi, Beta Gamma Sigma. Office: CSX Corp 500 Water St C 900 Jacksonville FL 32202 *

WARD, MICHAEL W., lawyer; b. Chgo., Aug. 16, 1950; s. John Francis and Mary Frances (Brophy) W.; m. Amy Louise Alsopiedy, June 29, 1974; children: Daniel Joseph, James Patrick. BA, U. Notre Dame, 1972; JD, Ill. Inst. Tech., 1976. Bar: Ill. 1976, U.S. Dist. Ct. (no. dist.) Ill. 1976, U.S. Ct. Appeals (7th cir.) 1976, U.S. Supreme Ct. 1980, U.S. Dist. Ct. (no. dist.) Ill. 1982, U.S. Ct. Appeals (6th cir.) 1985. Asst. state's atty. Cook County, Chgo., 1976-80; assoc. O'Keefe, Ashenden, Lyons & Ward, Chgo., 1980-85, ptnr., 1986—99; pres. Michael W Ward P.C., 1999—. V.p. Northshore Fellowship League, Evanston, Ill., 1982-84; mem. St. Nicholas Sch. Bd., Evanston, 1984-86; bd. dirs. New Horizons Youth Group, Evanston, 1979-85; mem. adv. bd. Cath. Charities, 1989—; mem. fin. coun. St. Nicholas Ch., Evanston, 1988-97. Mem. Ill. State Bar Assn. (pub. utilities section council 1988-90, Chgo. Bar Assn., Fed. Comm. Bar Assn. (charter mem. midwest coordinating com.). Roman Catholic. Home: 1012 Mulford St Evanston IL 60202-3317 Office: Michael W Ward PC 1608 Barclay Blvd Buffalo Grove IL 60089-4523

WARD, PERRY W., college president; BS, Miles Coll.; MSW, PhD, U. Ala. Pres. Lawson State CC, 1987—; exec. dir. basic edn. Birmingham Pub. Schls., Ala., 1979-87, dir. fed. programs adminstrn., 1975-79; adj. prof. U. Ala. Grad. Schl. Soc. Work, 1977-82; dir. emerg. schl. aid act program Miles Coll., 1973-75, assoc. dir. emerg. schl. assistance progam 1972-73, instr. adult edn. program, 1969-71. Cons. in field. Bd. dirs. U. Ala., Health Svcs. Found.; Birmingham Urban League (pres.), Ala. Coll. Assn. (pres.), Central Ala. Athletic Assn. (v.p.); mem. Pres.'s roundtable; participant AACC Pres. Acad. Fellow I-D-E-A Acad. Disting. Educators award; recipient Kermit Mathison Ounstanding Cmty. Coll. Administrator award, NAACP Boy Scouts Am. Appreciation award, Headstart Recognition for Outstanding Svc. award. Bd. dir. Compass Bk. Ala.; mem. Leadership Birmingham, Leadership Ala., C. of C. Birmingham Edn. roundtable, Nat. bd. Am. Assoc. Cmty. Colls. (regional accreditation coms.). Office: Lawson State Com Coll 3060 Wilson Rd SW Birmingham AL 35221-1717

WARD, PETER ALLAN, pathologist, educator; b. Winsted, Conn., Nov. 1, 1934; s. Parker J. and Mary Alice (McEvoy) Ward. BS, U. Mich., 1958; MD, U. Mich. Med. Sch., 1960. Diplomate Am. Bd. Anatomic Pathology, 1964, Am. Bd. Immunopathology, 1983. Intern Bellevue Hosp., NYU, NYC, 1960—61; resident dept. pathology U. Mich. Med. Sch., Ann Arbor, 1961—63; postdoctoral fellow Scripps Clinic and Rsch. Found., divsn. Exptl. Pathology, La Jolla, Calif., 1963—65; chief, immunology br. Armed Forces Inst. Pathology, Wash., 1965—71; prof. dept. pathology U. Conn. Health Ctr., Farmington, 1971—80, prof. and chmn. dept. pathology, 1973—80; prof. and chmn. dept. of pathology U. Mich. Med. Sch., Ann Arbor, 1980—2005, interim dean, 1982—85. Mem. pathology study sect. NIH, Bethesda, Md., 1974—76, chmn. pathology study sect., 1976—78; mem. rsch. rev. com. NHLBI/NIH, Bethesda, Md., 1978—82; sci. adv. bd. Armed Forces Inst. Pathology, Wash., 1978—83; cons. VA Hosp., Ann Arbor, 1980—; first Godfrey D. Stobbe prof. of pathology U. Mich. Med. Sch., 1987—; bd. dir. Univs. Associated for Rsch. and Edn. in Pathology, Inc., 1988—90; disting. faculty lectr. U. Mich. Biomedical Rsch. Coun., Ann Arbor, 1989—; pres.-elect U.S./Can. Acad. Pathology, Inc., 1991—92, pres., 1992—93; past pres. and chair nominating com. U.S./Can. Acad. of Pathology, Inc., 1993—94; mem. Inst. Lab. Animal Resources, 1993—96; coun. chair Inst. Lab. Animal Rsch. Coun., 1999—; chmn. nominating com. Soc. Med. Consultants to the Armed Forces, 1989—93; mem. Inst. Medicine/NAS, 1990—; trustee Am. Bd. Pathology, 1988—97, bd. dirs., 1996—97, life trustee, 1998—; treas. Soc. Leukocyte Biology, 2000—03, pres., 2004—05; bd. dirs. Fedn. Am. Socs. for Exptl. Biology, 2004—. Capt. M.C. US Army, 1965—67, Armed Forces Inst. Pathology, Wash. Recipient R & D Achievement award, U.S. Army, 1969, Meritorious Civilian Svc. award, 1970, Parke-Davis award, Am. Soc. Exptl. Pathology, 1971, Borden Rsch. award, U. Mich. Med. Sch., 1990, Merit award, NIH, 1990-97, Nat. Pres. award in recognition of leadership as pres., Mich. State Med. Soc., 1992, Rous-Whipple award, Am. Soc. Investigative Pathology, 1996, Lifetime Nat. Assoc., Nat. Academies Sci., 2001, Gold-Headed Cane award, Am. Soc. Investigative Pathology, 2001, J. Burns Amberson Lectr., Am. Thoracic Soc., 2003, Disting. Svc. award, Assn. Pathology Chairs, 2004, Chugai award for excellence in mentoring and scholarship, Am. Soc. Investigative Pathology, 2005. Fellow: AAAS, Am. Heart Assn. (fellow, coun. on cardiopulmonary, perioperative & critical care 2003); mem.: Inst. Lab. Animal Rsch. Coun. (coun. chair 1999—), Assn. Pathology Chairmen (rsch. com. mem. 1982), Am. Soc. Investigative Pathology (rep. to faseb bd./faseb fin. com. 2004), Am. Thoracic Soc. (sci. adv. com. 1989), Am. Bd. Pathology (pres. 1996—97), Am. Assn. Immunologists (nominating com. 1992), Am. Assn. for Advancement of Sci., U.S. and Can. Acad. Pathology, Inc., NIH (mentored scientist spl. emphasis panel 2001), Nat. Heart, Lung, and Blood Inst. (com. mem. 1990, rev. com. 1990), Mich. Thoracic Soc., A. James French Soc. Pathologists (charter mem.), Am. Soc. Clin. Investigation. Achievements include patents for sulfatides as anti-inflammatory compounds, U.S. Patent No. 5, 486, 536; compositions and methods for the treatment of sepsis, U.S. Patent No. 6, 673, 346. Office: Univ Mich Med School 1301 Catherine M5240 Med Sci 1 Ann Arbor MI 48109-0602 Home Phone: 734-996-3992; Office Phone: 734-763-6384. Office Fax: 734-763-4872. Business E-Mail: pward@umich.edu.

WARD, PHILIP J., lawyer; b. NYC, Dec. 11, 1949; AB with distinction, Stanford U., 1971; JD magna cum laude, Harvard U., 1974. Bar: Calif. 1975, Wis. 1977, DC 1979, US Ct. Appeals (10th and 11th cirs.), US Dist. Ct. Md., US Dist. Ct. (ea. dist.) Wis., US Bankruptcy Ct. DC and Md. Law clk. to Hon. Marvin E. Frankel US Dist. Ct. (so. dist.) NY, 1974-75; spl. asst. gen. counsel US DOT, 1975—77; mem. Williams & Connolly, Wash., ptnr. Wash. adv. Coun. Lawyers Com. Human Rights; bd. dirs. CARA Georgetown U., Carroll Pub.; bd. govs. John Carroll Soc. Mem. ABA, State Bar Calif., State Bar Wis., DC Bar Assn., Phi Beta Kappa. Office: Williams & Connolly 725 12th St NW Washington DC 20005-5901 Office Phone: 202-434-5250. Office Fax: 202-434-5029. Business E-Mail: pward@wc.com.

WARD, R. LAWRENCE, lawyer; b. Kans. City, May 19, 1936; BBA, Univ. Mo., Kans. City, 1959, JD, 1961. Bar: Mo. 1961, US Dist. Ct. (Kans., we. Mo., ea. Mich. dist.), US Ct. Appeals (8th, 10th cir.), US Supreme Ct. Firm chmn. & chmn. bus. litigation group Shugart Thomson & Kilroy, Kans. City, Mo. Mem. Mo. 16th Cir. Judicial Commn., 1979—85, Mo. Appellate Judicial Commn., 1992—97. Trustee Donnelly Coll. Named one of Top Ten Trial Lawyers in Am., Nat. Law Jour., 1994, Top Ten Kans. City Legal Leaders, Daily Record, 2004; recipient Lon O. Hocker Mem. Trial Lawyer award, Mo. Bar Found., Purcell Professionalism award, 1997, Herbert Hartley award, Am. Judicial Soc., 2001. Fellow: Am. Bar Found., Am. Coll. Trial Lawyers; mem.: ABA (Mo. state del. to Ho. Del. 1992—98), Mo. Bar (mem. bd. gov. 1973—77), Kans. City Met. Bar Assn. (pres. 1983, Lifetime Achievement award 1997). Office: Shugart Thomson & Kilroy 12 Wyandotte Plz 120 W 12th St Kansas City MO 64105 Office Phone: 816-374-0571. Office Fax: 816-374-0509. Business E-Mail: lward@stklaw.com.

WARD, RICHARD HURLEY, education educator, writer; b. NYC, Sept. 2, 1939; s. Hurley and Anna C. (Mittasch) W.; children from a previous marriage: Jeanne M., Jonathan B.; m. Michelle Pierczynski, June 15, 1987; 1 child: Michelle Sophia. BS, John Jay Coll., CUNY, 1968; M in Criminology, U. Calif., Berkeley, 1969, D in Criminology, 1971. Detective NYC Police Dept., 1962—70; coord. student activities John Jay Coll., NYC, 1970—71, dean students, 1971—75, v.p., 1975—77, vice chancellor, 1977—93; assoc. chancellor and prof. internat. criminology U. Ill., Chgo., 1993—98; exec. dir. Office Internat. Criminal Justice, 1985—99; exec. v.p. MBF Edn. Group, Malaysia, 1996—97; dean Coll. Criminal Justice, Sam Houston State U., Huntsville, Tex., 1999—2006, assoc. v.p. rsch. and spl. programs, 2006—. Vis. prof. Zagazig U., Egypt, Egyptian Police Acad., 1986, East China Inst. Politics and Law, Shanghai, 1990-91; lectr., various confs. in China, Egypt, Russia, Italy, Eng., Peru, Germany, Saudi Arabia, Finland, Taiwan, Vietnam, Turkey, Korea, United Arab Emirates and U.S., 1983—. Author: (with others) Police Robbery Control Manual, 1975; Introduction to Criminal Investigation, 1975, (with Robert McCormack) An Anti-Corruption Manual for Administrators in Law Enforcement; Quest for Quality, 1984; gen. editor Foundations of Criminal Justice, 46 vols., 1972-75; editor: (with Austin Fowler) Police and Law Enforcement, Vol. I, 1972; Police and Law Enforcement, Vol. II, 1975; (with Harold Smith) International Terrorism: The Domestic Response, 1982, International Terrorism: Operational Issues, 1988; co-author: (with James Osterburg) Criminal Investigation: A Method for Reconstructing the Past, 1992, 5th edit., 2007, (with K. Kiernan and D. Mabrey) Introduction to Homeland Security, 2006. Mem. Mayor of Chgo.'s Blue Ribbon Pannel on Police Promotion; varsity baseball coach U. Ill., Chgo., 1980-82, John Jay Coll. Criminal Justice, CUNY, 1971-72; chief investigator Mayor's Commn. Police Integrity, 1998; mem. Houston Crime Lab. Com., 2005. Cpl. USMC, 1957-61. Recipient Leonard Reisman award John Jay Coll. Criminal Justice, 1968, Alumni Achievement award, 1978, Richard McGee award U. Calif., Berkeley Sch. Criminology, 1971, Friendship medal Peoples Republic of China, 1994, Hans Mattick award Ill. Acad. Criminology, 1999; Justice Dept. fellow U. Calif., Berkeley, 1971. Mem. ASPA, Acad. Criminal Justice Scis. (pres. 1977-78, Founder's award 1985), Internat. Assn. Chiefs of Police (chmn. edn. and tng. sect. 1974-75), Sigma Delta Chi. Office: Sam Houston State U Houston Police Dept Crime Lab Coll Criminal Justice Huntsville TX 77341 Office Phone: 936-294-1755. Business E-Mail: ward@shsu.edu.

WARD, RICHARD JOSEPH, university dean, educator, author; b. Beverly, Mass., Nov. 7, 1921; s. Ralph Woodbury and Margaret (Lyons) W.; m. Cecilia Butler, Sept. 1, 1951; children: Timothy, Mary, Richard, Christopher. BS, Harvard U., 1945; MA, U. Mich., 1948, PhD, 1958. Dir. planning AID Mission to Jordan, 1961-63; chmn. econ. dept. C.W. Post Coll., LI U., 1960-61, 63-65; chief planning Bur. for Near East and South Asia, AID, 1965-69; mgr. internat. cons. Peat, Marwick, Mitchell & Co., Washington, 1969-75; dean U. Mass. Coll. Bus., Dartmouth, 1975-87, dean, dir. rsch., prof., 1990-96, Chancellor prof. emeritus, 1996; dir. US Internat. U. Sch. Bus., London, 1988-89; cons. in field. Author: Principles of Economics, 1967, Development Problems, 1973, The Palestine State, 1978, Development Horizon '80, 1980; editor: The Challenge of Development, 1967, Grampas Are For All Seasons, 2005, The Fragrance of Heliotrope the Presence of Cecilia, 2007; contbr. articles to profl. jours. Bd. dirs. Indsl. Found., 1976-82; bd. dirs. Jr. Achievement, 1977-99, also past pres.; mem. exec. com. World Congress on Violence and Human Coexistence. Lt. USNR, WWII. Recipient Disting. Svc. award AID, Jordan Mission, 1963, Univ. Svc. award U. Mass. Alumni Assn., 1983, Gov.'s Citation for Svc., 1987; Harvard fellow Ford Found., 1957. Mem. Assn. Social Econs. (pres. 1970-71), Ea. Econ. Assn. (exec. com.), Am. Econ. Assn., Harvard Club (pres. 1984-87, regional bd. dirs. SE Mass. and RI 1989-92), US Signatory/Found. for Human Co-Existence. Home: 20 Pleasant St South Dartmouth MA 02748-3813 Personal E-mail: wardjrichard@comcast.net.

WARD, RICHARD VANCE, JR., management consultant; b. Montreal, Quebec, Canada, June 19, 1929; s. Richard Vance Ward and Isobel Eugene Mosley; m. Elizabeth Anne Gareau, Aug. 15, 1953; children: Carolyn, Jennifer, Philip, Karen, Katherine. BSc, McGill U., Montreal, 1951; diploma in bus. adminstrn., U. Western Ont., London, Can., 1952. Indsl. engr. CIL Inc., Montreal, Canada, 1952-63, prodn. mgr., 1963-65; prodn. dir. ICI Am. Inc., Stamford, 1965-73, CIL Inc., Montreal, Canada, 1973-76, v.p., 1976-84; pres. CIL Corp. of Am., Stamford, Conn., 1984-89, Ward Assoc. Mgmt. Cons., 1989—. Chmn., pres., dir. Friends of McGill, Inc., NYC; bd. dirs. Chlorine Inst. Washington, mem. exec. com., 1984—86; bd. dir. Cornwall Chem. Inc., CIL Corp. Am., Cansco Chems. Inc., Canada. Mem. Chem. Mfrs. Assn., Friends of McGill U. (dir, pres.), Sr. Men's Club (dir., pres.), SCORE (chmn.), Exchange Club (dir.). Avocations: sailing, hiking, curling, skiing. Home: 45 Brushy Ridge Rd New Canaan CT 06840-4207 Personal E-mail: wardllc@aol.com.

WARD, ROBERT, composer, educator, conductor; b. Cleve., Sept. 13, 1917; s. Albert E. and Carrie (Mollenkopf) W.; m. Mary Raymond Benedict, June 19, 1944; children: Melinda, Johanna, Jonathon, Mark, Timothy. B.Mus., Eastman Sch. Music, 1939; cert., Juilliard Grad. Sch. Music, 1946; student composition with, Bernard Rogers, Howard Hanson, Frederick Jacobi, Aaron Copland; conducting with, Albert Stoessel, Edgar Schenkman; D.F.A., Duke, 1972; Mus.D., Peabody Inst., 1975; D.F.A., U. N.C., Greensboro, 1992. Tchr. Juilliard Sch. Music, 1946-56; mng. editor, exec. v.p. Galaxy Music Corp., until 1967, dir., 1967—; exec. v.p. Highgate Press, 1967; pres. N.C. Sch. Arts, Winston-Salem, 1967-74, tchr. composition, 1974-79; prof. composition Duke U., Durham, NC, 1978-87, Mary Duke Biddle prof. music, 1978-87; composer Mus. Natural Sci., NC, 1999—. Chmn. bd. Triangle Music Theater Assocs. Composer: 1st Symphony, 1942, Hush'd Be the Camps Today, 1943, Second Symphony, 1947, First Sonata for Violin and Piano, 1950, Third Symphony, 1951, Fourth Symphony, 1958, Arisso and Tarantelle, Violin and Piano, 1955, Fantasia for Brass Choir and Timpani, 1956, Prairie Overture, 1957, Divertimento for Orchestra, 1961, Earth Shall Be Fair, 1960, He Who Gets Slapped (Pantaloon) (opera in 3 acts); opera in 4 acts The Crucible, 1962 (Pulitzer Prize in music); Hymn and Celebration (for orch.), 1962; for orch. Invocation and Toccata, 1963; opera in 2 acts The Lady From Colorado, 1964; Let the Word Go Forth, 1965; cantata Sweet Freedom's Song, 1965, Hymn To The Night, 1966; First String Quartet, 1966, Sacred Songs for Pantheists, 1966, Festive Ode, 1966, Fiesta Processional, 1967, Antiphony for Winds, 1967 Concerto for Piano and Orchestra, 1968, Four Abstractions, 1977; opera Claudia Legare, 1974; Fifth Symphony-Canticles for America, 1976, Sonic Structure (for orch.), 1980; opera Abelard and Heloise, 1981, Minutes Till Midnight, 1982, Dialogues for Violin, Cello and Orchestra, 1983, Concerto for Saxophone and Orchestra, 1984, Raleigh Divertimento for Wind Quintet, 1986, Festival Triptych, 1987, Sixth Symphony, 1988, First Symphonic Set for the New South, 1988, Fanfare, 1988, Second Symphonic Set, 1988, Appalachian Ditties and Dances, 1988, 5x5, 1989, Images of God, 1989, Ballet Music on The Scarlet Letter, 1990, Second Sonata for Violin and Piano, 1990, Bath County Rhapsody, 1991, Serenade for Mallarmé, 1991, By The Way of Memories for Orchestra, 1997, one act opera Roman Fever, 1993, Love's Seasons, 1994, song cycle Sacred Carticles, 1994, The Hill Song, 1996, Brass Ablaze for British Brass Band, 1996, Night Under the Big Sky for Wind Quintet and Piano, 1997, Echoes of America, Trio for Clarinet, Cello and Piano, 1997, Cherish Your Land-Chorus, 2000, Bayou Rhapsody, 2001, Cherish Your Land, 2001, Dialogues: A Triple Concerto for Violin, Cello and Piano and Orch., 2002, Seventh Symphony, 2003, Nonet arrangement of Raligh Divertimento, 2003, A Friend of Napoleon, 2005. Bd. dirs. Martha Baird Rockefeller Fund for Music, 1971-82, Am. Symphony Orch. League, 1977-89, Nat. Inst. Music Theatre, 1977-85; mem. music com. Henry St. Settlement; bd. dirs. Durham Arts Coun. Served with AUS, 1942-46. Decorated Bronze Star; MacDowell Colony fellow, 1938; recipient Juilliard Pub. award, 1942, Fine Arts award State of N.C., 1975, Gold Baton award Am. Symphony Orch. League, 1991, Disting. Faculty Alumnus award U. N.C., 1992, A.I. DuPont award of Del. Symphony, 1995; Alice M. Ditson fellow Columbia U., 1944, Guggenheim fellow, 1950, 52, 66-67; Am. Acad. Arts and Letters grantee, 1946. Mem. Nat. Acad. Arts and Letters. Home: The Forest at Duke 2701 Pickett Rd # 4022 Durham NC 27705-5688 Home Phone: 919-493-8468; Office Phone: 919-493-8468.

WARD, ROBERT ALLEN, JR., advertising executive; b. Summit, NJ, Sept. 25, 1937; s. Robert Allen and Edith Allen (Edith) Seiberling; m. Nancy Prescott, Oct. 3, 1964; children: Victoria, Jennifer, Robert. BA, Yale U., 1959. Electronics analyst and account exec. U.S. Trust Co., NYC, 1959-62; v.p., dir. Progressive Mktg. Svcs., NYC, 1962-63, Coin Depot Corp., Elizabeth, NJ, 1963-68; pres. J.S. Riley Co., Wayne, NJ, 1964-70; pres., dir. C.G.W. Enterprises, Butler, NJ, Carelli, Glynn & Ward Advt. Co., 1969-95, All Hours Answering Svc., Pompton Lakes, NJ, 1969-93; v.p., dir. N.J. Exch., 1969-93; v.p. direct Anserve Inc., 1993—. Pres., dir. B.E.K., Inc., real estate mgmt. co., Wayne, NJ, Litho Four Printers, 1970-88, Healthserve, 1996—; dir. Devon Pubs., Butler, N.J., 1977-78; owner 1250 Rt # 23 LLC, 817 Ringwood Ave. LLC. Pres. Kinnelon PTA, N.J., 1972-73; councilman Kinnelon Borough Coun., 1978-83; police commr., Kinnelon, 1978-83; mem. Kinnelon Drug Adv. Coun., 1978-83; vestry St. David Episc. Ch., Kinnelon, 1969-72, 78-87, 90-93, sr. warden, 1978-87; bd. dirs. Morris Area Coun. Girl Scouts U.S.A., 1977-80, Morris Land Conservancy, 2002—, Inner City Ensemble, 1983-90; bd. dirs. Willing Hands, 1989—, chmn., 2000—; mem. sports awards dinner com. North Jersey March of Dimes, 1986-90; chmn. Yale Alumni Schs. Commn., 1984—; dir. Morris Land Conservancy, 2002—; mem. Christmas Cove Improvement Assn. With USMC, 1959-60, served to capt. USAR and NYNG, 1960-72. Mem. No. N.J. Advt. Club (bd. dirs. 1970-72), Commerce and Industry Assn. of N.J. (Penpac bd. dirs. 1982-90), N.J. Home Builder Assoc. (bd. dirs. 1967-70), Bank Mktg. Assn., Huguenot Soc., S.A.R., Inner City Ensemble/NJ.J. Dance Troupe (bd. dirs. 1983-89), Yale Club (trustee, v.p. 1981—, pres. 1993-96, Montclair), Smoke Rise Club (Kinnelon), Smoke Rise Paddle Tennis Club (pres. 1988—). Republican. Home: 393 Ski Trl Kinnelon NJ 07405-2247 Office: Anserve 1250 State Rt 23 Butler NJ 07405-2002 Office Phone: 973-838-2242. E-mail: robert_ward@amserve.com.

WARD, ROBERT EDWARD, retired political science professor, academic administrator; b. San Francisco, Jan. 29, 1916; s. Edward Butler and Claire Catherine (Unger) W.; m. Constance Regina Barnett, Oct. 31, 1942; children: Erica Anne, Katherine Elizabeth. BA, Stanford U., 1936; MA, U. Calif.-Berkeley, 1938, PhD, 1948. Instr. in polit. sci. U. Mich., 1948-50, asst. prof. polit. sci., 1950-54, assoc. prof., 1954-58, prof., 1958-73, Stanford U., 1973-87, dir. Center for Research in Internat. Studies, 1973-87. Cons. in field; advisor Center for Strategic and Internat. Studies, Washington, 1968-87 Author: Modern Political Systems: Asia, 1963, Political Modernization in Japan and Turkey, 1964. Mem. nat. council Nat. Endowment for Humanities, Washington, 1968-73; mem. Pres.'s Commn. on Fgn. Lang.-Internat. Studies, 1978-79; chmn. Japan-U.S. Friendship Commn., 1980-83; mem. Dept. Def. Univ. Forum, 1982-87. Served to lt. (j.g.) USN, 1942-45. Decorated Legion of MErit, 1945; recipient Japan Found. award Tokyo, 1976, Order of Sacred Treasure (Japan), 1983 Fellow Am. Acad. Arts and Scis.; mem. Am. Polit. Sci. Assn. (pres. 1972-73), Assn. Asian Studies (pres. 1972-73), Social Sci. Research Council (chmn. 1969-71), Am. Philos. Soc. Home: Box 8129 501 Portola Rd Portola Valley CA 94028

WARD, ROBIN A., mathematics professor; b. Bryn Mawr, Pa., Jan. 26, 1965; d. Hugh J. Ward and Regina Dorothy Cruice; m. Christopher Michael DelConte, Aug. 21, 1999; children: Sienna Olivia DelConte, Sophia Arabella DelConte. PhD, U. Va., Charlottesville, 1997. Asst. prof. Calif. Poly. State U., San Luis Obispo, 1997—2000, U. Ariz., Tucson, 2000—07; clin. asst. prof. Rice U., Houston, 2007—. Ednl. cons. NASA, Lancaster, Calif., 1998—2002. Author: Numeracy and Literacy. Recipient Outstanding Tchg.aAward, U. Ariz., 2005; fellow, NASA and ASEE1, 1998, 1999; grantee Edn. grantee, NASA, 1998—2002, PT3 grantee, US Dept Edn., 2000—04. Mem.: AWM, RCML, NCTM. Home: 3511 Cason St Houston TX 77005 Personal E-mail: robinanneward@gmail.com.

WARD, RODMAN, JR., lawyer, director; b. Wilmington, Del., Apr. 8, 1934; s. Rodman and Dorcas (Andrews) W.; m. Susan Speakman Hill, Oct. 10, 1959; children: Margery Ward Garnett, Emily Ward Neilson, Rodman III, Jennifer Ward Oppenheimer. BA, Williams Coll., 1956; LLB, Harvard U., 1959. Bar: Del. 1959, D.C. 1959. Partner Prickett, Ward, Burt & Sanders, Wilmington, 1967-79, Skadden, Arps, Slate, Meagher & Flom, Wilmington, 1979—2002, of counsel, 2002—. Bd. dirs. WMB Holdings, Inc. Author: (with Folk and Welch) Folk on the Delaware General Corporation Law, 1987; contbr. Trustee Winterthur Mus. Gardens and Libr., exec. com. chmn. acad. affairs com.; bd. dirs. The Del. Art Mus.; exec. com., bd. dirs. The Garden Conservancy. Capt. USAF, 1960—63. Fellow: Am. Coll. Trial Lawyers; mem.: ABA, Am. Judicature Soc., Assn. of Bar of City of N.Y., D.C. Bar Assn., Am. Bar Found. (life), Del. State Bar Assn. (pres. 1989—90), Am. Law Inst., Vicmead Hunt Club, Wilmington Country Club, Wilmington Club. Home: 52 Selborne Dr Wilmington DE 19807-1216 Office: PO Box 636 Wilmington DE 19899-0636 Office Phone: 302-651-3000. Business E-Mail: rward@skadden.com.

WARD, ROGER COURSEN, lawyer; b. Newark, June 19, 1922; s. Waldron Merry and Aline Toppin (Coursen) W.; m. Katharine More Stevens, Oct. 22, 1949; children: James Olney, Alexander More. Grad., Phillips Exeter Acad., 1940; AB, Princeton U., NJ, 1943; LL.B., Columbia U., NYC, 1949. Bar: N.J. 1949. Law clk. to justice N.J. Supreme Ct., 1951; since practiced in Newark, Morristown, Montclair, NJ; ptnr. Pitney, Hardin, Kipp & Szuch, 1959-91, counsel, 1991-92, Schwartz, Tobia, Stanziale, Sedita & Campisano, LLP, 1993—2005, McElroy Deutsch, Mulvaney & Carpenter, LLC, 2005—. Bd. advisors Am. Inst. Law Tng. Within Office, Phila. 1986-88, Law Hiring and Tng. Report, Chgo., 1983-88. Bd. dirs. United Hosps. Newark, 1965-78, pres., 1973; trustee, v.p. Newark Mus. Assn., 1969-92; bd. dirs. Better Bus. Bur. Greater Newark, 1970-84; mem. Summit Zoning Bd. Adjustment, 1966-70; trustee Eye Inst. N.J., 1973, Pingry Sch., 1966-68, Summit YMCA, 1960-62, Newark Council Social Agys., 1956-60; vice chmn. Newark Mayor's Commn. on Youth, 1958-60. Served to lt. (j.g.) USNR, 1943-46, PTO, ETO. Harlan Fiske Stone scholar Columbia U., 1949. Mem. Essex County Bar Assn., Short Hills (N.J.) Club, Phi Beta Kappa. Office: McElroy Deutsch Mulvaney and Carpenter LLP Gateway Three Ctr 100 Mulberry St Newark NJ 07102-4079 Office Phone: 973-565-2019. Business E-Mail: rward@mdmc-law.com.

WARD, RONALD R., lawyer; b. Sacramento, June 12, 1947; BA, Calif. State U., 1973; JD, U. Calif., 1976. Bar: Calif. 1977, Wash., U.S. Dist. Ct. Calif. (No. Dist.) 1979, U.S. Dist Ct. (We. Dist.) Wash., U.S. Ct. Appeals (9th cir.). Asst. atty. gen. State of Wash., 1979—82; atty., shareholder Levinson Friedman PS, Seattle, 1982—2005, Jones & Ward, PLLC, Seattle, 2005—. Vol. reading tutor, tchr. asst. Hawthorne Sch., Seattle, mem. parent bd., mem. annual giving steering com.; mem. long-range planning com. Holy Names Acad., Seattle; bd. trustees N.W. Chamber Orch. Named Super Lawyer, Washington Law & Politics Mag., 2003—; named one of Top 40 Who's Who in Washington Plaintiff's Personal Injury Law, 2006, Top 40 Lawyers, Seattle Mag., 2007; recipient President's award, Washington State Trial Lawyers, 2006, Outstanding Plaintiff Trial Lawyer award, Washington Def. Trial Lawyers, 2006. Mem.: ABA (mem. Ho. of Dels. 2004—, mem. commn. for renaissance of idealism in the profession, mem. standing com. on pro bono and pub. svc., Partnership award 2005), Am. Bd. Trial Advocates, Loren Miller Bar Assn., Nat. Bar Assn. (Disting Svc. award 1994), Assn. Trial Lawyers Am., Wash. State Trial Lawyers Assn. (mem. bd. govs. 1989—96, co-chmn. Seattle downtown roundtable 1993—96, v.p. west 1994—96, Spl. Pres. Recognition award 1995), State Bar Calif., Fed. Bar Assn., Wash. State Bar Assn. (mem. bd. govs. 2002—03, pres.-elect 2003—04, pres. 2004—05), King County Bar Assn. Office: Jones & Ward PLLC 1000 Second Ave Ste 4050 Seattle WA 98104-1023 Office Phone: 206-957-1272. Office Fax: 206-957-1275. Business E-Mail: rrw@joneswardlaw.com. *

WARD, ROSCOE FREDRICK, engineering educator; b. Boise, Idaho, Dec. 5, 1930; s. Roscoe C. W. and Alice E. (Ward); m. Julia Duffy, June 8, 1963; children: Eric R., David C. Student, U. Oreg., 1949-50; BA, Coll. of Idaho, 1953; postgrad., U. Wash., 1955-57; BS, Oreg. State U., 1959; MS, Wash. State U., 1961; Sc.D., Washington U., St. Louis, 1964. Registered profl. engr., Ohio. Asst. prof. civil engring. U. Mo., Columbia, 1963-65, Robert Coll., Istanbul, Turkey, 1965-67; assoc. prof. civil engring. Asian Inst. Tech., Bangkok, 1967-68; assoc. prof. civil engring., assoc. dean Sch. Engring. U. Mass., Amherst, 1968-75; prof. Bogazici U., Istanbul, 1974-75; br. chief biomass energy Dept. Energy, Washington, 1975-79; interregional advisor UN/World Bank, NYC, 1979-83; dean Sch. Applied Scis. Miami U., Oxford, Ohio, 1983-88, prof. paper and chem. engring. Sch. Engring. and Applied Scis., 1983—. Vis. scientist Csir, Republic of South Africa, 1990-91. Contbr. chapters to books, articles to profl. jours. Fellow: ASCE. Home: 4818 Bonham Rd Oxford OH 45056-1423 Business E-Mail: wardrf@muohio.edu.

WARD, SELA, actress; b. Meridian, Miss., July 11, 1956; d. Granberry Holland and Annie Kate Ward; m. Howard Sherman May 23, 1992; children: Austin, Anabella. BA, U. Ala. Actor: (TV series) Emerald Point, N.A.S., 1983-84, Cameo By Night, 1987, Sisters, 1991—96 (Emmy award for Lead Actress in Drama Series 1994), Once and Again, 1999-2002 (winner lead actress in a drama series, Emmy award 2000, winner lead actress in a drama series, Golden Globe award 2001), House, 2005-; (TV films) The King of Love, 1987, Bridesmaids, 1989, The Haunting of Sarah Hardy, 1989, Rainbow Drive, 1990, Child of Darkness, Child of Light, 1991, Double Jeopardy, 1992, Killer Rules, 1993, Almost Golden: The Jessica Savitch Story, 1995 (winner lead actress in drama movie Cableace award 1996), The Rescuers: Stories of Courage: Two Women, 1997, Catch a Falling Star, 2000, Suburban Madness, 2004; (films) Rustler's Rhapsody, 1985, Nothing in Common, 1986, Steele Justice, 1987, Hello Again, 1987, The Fugitive, 1993, My Fellow Americans, 1996, 54, 1998, 54, 1998, Runaway Bride, 1999, The Reef, 1999, The Badge, 2002, Dirty Dancing: Havana Nights, 2003, The Day After Tomorrow, 2004, The Guardian, 2006; prodr. (Lifetime cable network) documentary Changing Face of Beauty, 2000, Lifetime "Intimate Portrait", 2001. Office: 289 S Robertson Blvd Ste 469 Beverly Hills CA 90211-2834

WARD, SOLVEIG MARIA, marketing professional; b. Stockholm, Aug. 22, 1954; d. Ingvar Erik and Inga Kronman; m. Edward L. Ward, Jan. 20, 1997; children: Johan Fredrick Mahrs, Lars Richard Mahrs. MSEE, Royal Inst. of Tech., Stockholm, 1977. Sales engr. Asea Ab, Vasteras, Sweden, 1977—80; supr. dept. sales ASEA SA de CV, Mexico City, 1980—82; product mktg. mgr. Abb (Asea) Ab, Vasteras, 1982—92; mgr. consulting engring. ABB Inc., Coral Springs, Fla., 1992—99, product mgr. Allentown, Pa., 1999—2002; dir. product mktg. RFL Electronics Inc., Boonton Twp., NJ, 2002—. Mem.: IEEE. Achievements include patents for high speed single pole trip logic for use in protective relaying. Office: RFL Electronics Inc 353 Powerville Rd Boonton NJ 07005 Home Phone: 973-506-4576; Office Phone: 973-334-3100. Office Fax: 973-334-3863. Business E-Mail: solveig.ward@rflelect.com.

WARD, STEPHEN M., JR., computer company executive; BSME, Calif. Polytech. State U., San Luis Obispo. Joined IBM Corp., Tucson, 1978; v.p. info. tech., gen. mgr. IBM ThinkPad; gen. mgr. IBM's Global Indsl. Sector; chief info. officer, v.p. bus. transformation IBM Corp., sr. v.p., gen. mgr. regional systems group Armonk, NY, 2003—04; sr. v.p., gen. mgr. personal sys. group IBM, Armonk, NY, 2004—05; CEO Lenovo Group Ltd., Purchase, NY, 2005, cons., 2005. Past bd. dir. e2open; bd. dir. Carpenter Technology Corp. Recipient NY Ten Award, Exec. Coun., 2005. Office: Lenovo Group Ltd The Centre at Purchase 1 Manhattanville Rd Purchase NY 10577

WARD, THOMAS, research scientist; BS, U. Mo., Rolla; MS, Stanford U.; PhD, U. Calif., Santa Barbara. Rschr. Harvard U., Cambidge, Mass., 2003—05. Mem.: Am. Phys. Soc. Office Phone: 310-825-1087.

WARD, TOM L., energy executive; BBA, U. Okla., 1981. Pres., COO, dir. Chesapeake Energy Corp., 1989—2006; CEO, chmn. bd. dirs. Riata Energy, Inc., 2006—. Bd. trustees Anderson U., Ind. Named one of Forbes' Richest Americans, 2006. Office: Riata Energy, Inc Ste 1600 1601 Northwest Expressway Oklahoma City OK 73118 Office Phone: 405-753-5500.

WARD, VERNON GRAVES, retired internist; b. Palisade, Nebr., Mar. 5, 1928; s. Charles Bennett and Mildred Belle (Graves) W.; m. Eleanore Mae Farstveet, Aug. 28, 1952; children: Margo, Alison, Barry. BA, Nebr. Wesleyan U., 1948; MD cum laude, U. Nebr., Omaha, 1954. Diplomate Am. Bd. Internal Medicine. Instr. in anatomy Columbia U., NYC, 1948—50; intern U. Wis., Madison, 1954—55, resident internal medicine, 1955—58, chief resident, physician, 1957—58; fellow in neurophysiology and psychosomatic medicine U. Okla., Oklahoma City, 1960—61; asst. clin. prof. medicine U. Wis., Madison, 1961—62; pvt. practice internal medicine Kearney, Nebr., 1962—67; asst. prof. U. Nebr. Coll. Medicine, Omaha, 1967—69; assoc. clin. prof. medicine U. Nebr., Omaha, 1969—; pvt. practice internal medicine Omaha, 1969—2005; ret. Chmn. dept. internal medicine Clarkson Hosp., Omaha, 1976-78, 96-98. Contbr. articles to profl. jours. including JAMA, Nebr. State Med. Jour., Wis. State Med. Jour., Am. Heart Jour., Postgrad. Medicine. Pres. Nebr. chpt. Arthritis Found., 1969-71. Lt. comdr. USNR, 1958-60. Recipient Cmty. Based Tchg. award ACP-ASIM, 2000; named Hutton Traveling Scholar Coll. of Physicians, 1965. Fellow ACP, Am. Coll. Rheumatology; mem. AMA, Nebr. State Med. Soc., Omaha Med. Soc., Am. Soc. Internal Medicine (Cmty.-Based Tchg. award 2000), Am. Psychosomatic Soc., Nebr. Soc. Internal Medicine (pres. 1980-82, Disting. Internist award 1990), Phi Kappa Phi, Alpha Omega Alpha (pres. Nebr. chpt. 1984-85), Phi Chi (grand sec.-treas. 1986—2006, co-chmn. nat. conv. Omaha 1953, emeritus trustee 2006—), Phi Kappa Tau. Republican. Lutheran. Home: 302 N 54th St Omaha NE 68132-2813 Home Phone: 402-558-7641.

WARD, WAYNE CONRAD, music educator, conductor; b. Newport, RI, Apr. 2, 1948; s. Abner Stoddard Ward and Elsie Irene Stewart. BA, Tufts U., Medford, Mass., 1970; MusM, Eastman Sch. Music, Rochester, NY, 1973. Music tchr. Dansville Ctrl. Schs., NY, 1973—75; prof. music edn. Berklee Coll. Music, Boston, 1975—. Music dir. Turtle Ln. Playhouse, Newton, Mass., 1981—; asst. music dir., music dir. Longwood Opera Co., Needham, Mass., 1988—. Mem.: Internat. Assn. Jazz Educators, Am. Choral Dirs. Assn., Music Educators Nat. Conf. Avocations: reading, movies, sports, classical and contemporary concerts. Office: Berklee Coll Music 1140 Boylston St Boston MA 02215-3693 Home: 612 Norfolk St Holliston MA 01746-2336

WARD, WILLIAM E. (KIP WARD), career military officer; b. Balt., 1949; m. Joyce L. Ward; 2 children. BA in Polit. Sci., Morgan State U., 1971; student, US Army Infantry Sch., 1976; MA in Polit. Sci., Pa. State U., 1979; grad., US Army Command & Gen. Staff Coll., 1982—83, US Army War Coll., 1991—92. Commd. 2d lt. US Army, advanced through grades to gen., 2006; rifle platoon leader A Co., 3rd Bn. 325th Infantry 82nd Airborne Divsn., Ft. Bragg, NC, 1971—72, anti-tank platoon leader, 1972—74, liaison officer, 1974; rifle platoon leader B Co. 1st Bn., 17th Infantry, 2nd Infantry Divsn. Eighth Army, Republic of Korea, 1974—76; instr. then asst. prof. social scis. US Mil. Acad., West Point, NY, 1978—82; logistics staff officer 210th Field Arty. Group US Army Europe & 7th Army, Herzo Base, Germany, 1983-85, exec. officer US Army Community Activity Aschaffenburg, Germany, 1985—86, exec. officer 1st bn. (mechanized), 7th infantry, 3rd divsn., 1986—87; comdr. 5th bn. 9th Inf. Rgt. 6th Infantry Divsn., Ft. Wainwright, Alaska, 1988—91; comdr. 2d Commando Brigade 10th Mt. Divsn., Ft. Drum, 1992—94; exec. officer to vice chief of staff US Army, Washington, 1994—95; dep. dir. ops. Nat. Mil. Command Ctr., The Joint Staff (J-3), Washington, 1995-96; asst. divsn. comdr. for support 82d Airborne Divsn., Ft. Bragg, 1996-98; chief, Office Mil. Ops. Am. Embassy, Cairo, 1998—99; comdr. 25th Inf. Divsn. U.S. Army Hawaii, Ft. Shaffer, Hawaii, 1999—2000; vice dir. ops. The Joint Staff, Washington, 2000—02; comdr. Stabilisation Force, Operation Joint Force, Sarajevo, Bosnia-Herzegovina, 2002—03; dep. commdg. gen., chief of staff US Army Europe & 7th Army, 2003—05; spl. security coord. for Mid. East US Dept. State, 2005—06; dep. comdr. US European Command (USEUCOM), Stuttgart, Germany, 2006—. Decorated Def. Superior Svc. medal with oak leaf cluster,Def. Disting. Svc. medal, Disting. Svc. medal, Legion of Merit with 2 oak leaf clusters, Def. Meritorious Svc. medal, Meritorious Svc. medal with 6 oak leaf clusters, Joint Service Commendation medal, Army Commendation medal with three oak leaf clusters, Army Achievement medal with oak leaf cluster, Presdl. Order of Merit (Arab Rep. of Egypt). Achievements include participation in OPERATION RESTORE HOPE in Mogadishu, Somalia, 1992-93. Office: US European Command (USEUCOM) Unit 30400 Patch Barracks APO AE 09131 Stuttgart Germany *

WARD, WILLIAM FRANCIS, JR., real estate investment broker; b. Everett, Mass., Aug. 23, 1928; s. William Francis and Helen (Schriber) W.; m. Elaine L. Wilson, June 11, 1950 (dec. Oct. 1993); children: Jeffrey W., Gary T., Michelle A., Gregory W., Suzanne M.; m. Marie-Louise Buchheit, Nov. 5, 1994. BS, US Mil. Acad., 1950; MBA, Harvard U., Cambridge, Mass., 1956; LLB, La Salle U., Chgo., 1966; LLD (hon.), So. Vt. U., Benington, 1996; HHD (hon.), NY Coll. Podiatric Medicine, 2003. Commd. 2d lt. US Army, 1950; resigned, 1956; econ. analyst E.I. duPont de Nemours & Co., Inc., Wilmington, Del., 1956-58; sec. N.Y. State Bridge Authority, Poughkeepsie, 1958-60; div. contr., dir. mktg. svcs. GAF Corp., NYC, 1960-63; asst. to pres. Grosset & Dunlap, Inc., 1963-65, v.p., 1965-67; contr. Dun & Bradstreet, 1967-71, v.p., 1968-71; chmn. bd., pres. Dun-Donnelley Pub. Corp., 1971-77; exec. v.p. Am. Cancer Soc.; from v.p., treas. to pres. Gestam, Inc., 1981-86; chief Army Res., 1986-91, comdr. US Army Res. Command, 1990—91; chmn., pres. Realicam, 1985—. Bd. dirs. Quotron Electronics, Inc., Empire Nat. Bank, Eastern Savs. Bank, Apple Bank for Savs., Corinthian Broadcasting, Greater NY Bank for Savs.; trustee All-City Funds; mem. adv. bd. Astoria Fin. Bank, Podia Ins. Co.; mem. faculty Dutchess C.C., 1958-60, NYU Sch. Commerce, 1960-64; trustee NYC Foot Clinics, 2004—; hon. col. 70th tank regiment US Army. Pres. Ramapo Central Sch. Dist., 1966-72, 1982-87; mem. facilities and planning bd. Good Samaritan Hosp., 1980-85; chmn. United Way, Rockland County, 1992-94; county chmn. Citizen for Kennedy and Johnson, 1960; Dem. candidate for Ho. of Reps., 1962; chmn. Young Citizens for Johnson and Humphrey, 55 counties NY, 1964; exec. v.p. Am. Cancer Soc., 1976-81; bd. dirs. NYC divsn. Aerospace Edn. Found., US Army War Coll. Found., West Point Fund, 1979, Franciscan Sisters of the Poor Found., 1980-92; trustee NY Mil. Acad., 1982-86, 91-96, trustee emeritus, 1996—; trustee Assn. Grads. US Mil. Acad., 1993-2003, trustee emeritus, 2003—, exec. com., 1996-2003, chmn. audit com., 1996-2004; trustee Hist. Soc. Rockland County, 1993-95, NY Coll. Podiatric Medicine, 2000, chmn. bd. trustees, 2004—. Capt. AUS, 1950-54; to maj. gen. 1978-91. Decorated D.S.M. with 1 oak leaf cluster, Legion of Merit, Meritorious Svc. medal with oak leaf cluster, Air medal with 3 oak leaf clusters, Army Commendation medal with oak leaf cluster, Purple Heart, Army Achievement medal. Mem. West Point Soc. (Washington chpt., Space Coast chpt., NY chpt., pres. 1974-76), Antrim Players, Soc. Harvard Engrs. and Scientists, Fin. Execs. Inst., Newcomen Soc., Res. Officers Assn., Am. Friends of Viet Nam (nat. chmn.), VFW, Am. Legion, Knight of Holy Sepluchre, Disabled Am. Vets., Pilgrim Soc., Army and Navy Club, Squadron "A" Club, Univ. Club (NY), Harvard Club (Washington), Nat. Press Club. Roman Catholic. Home: 1271 Continental Ave Melbourne FL 32940 also: 10 Debbie Ct Chester NY 10918 Personal E-mail: wward15@cfl.rr.com, wmfward@optonline.net.

WARD BLACK, JANET, lawyer; b. Kannapolis, NC; BA in Econs. cum laude, Davidson Coll., 1982; JD, Duke U., 1985. Asst. dist. atty. Cabarrus and Rowan Counties, 1985—88; atty. Wallace Whitley Pope & Black, Salisbury, NC, 1989—92, Donaldson & Black PA, Greensboro, NC, 1992—2006, Ward Black Law, Greensboro, NC, 2006—. Mem. Women's Profl. Forum, Greensboro; nat. adv. com. Win-Win Resolutions Inc., Greensboro; steering com. NC Inst. Govt. Judicial Edn. Fund; adv. panel mem. Legal Services NC, Greensboro, 2002—, co-chair Access to Justice, 2006. Bd. dirs. Women's Resource Ctr. Greensboro, Mercy Mission Teams, Greensboro; bd. trustees Hood Theological Seminary, Salisbury; vol. Appalachian Svc. Project, Save a Generation, Nicaragua, El Salvador, Habitat for Humanity, Honduras. Master: Joseph Branch Inn of Ct.; mem.: NC Assn. Women Attys., ABA, Acad. Catastrophic Injury Attys., NC Acad. Trial Lawyers (chair polit. action com. 2004—06), Assn. Trial Lawyers of Am. (bd. gov. 2005—), NC Bar Assn. (pres.-elect 2006—07). Office: Ward Black Law 208 W Wendover Ave Greensboro NC 27401 Office Phone: 800-531-9191. Office Fax: 336-379-9415. E-mail: jwblack@wardblacklaw.com.

WARDELL, TAMARA LYNN, critical care nurse; b. Terre Haute, Ind., Feb. 19, 1952; d. Donald Meredith Wardell, Jr. and Patricia Ernestine Cooksey Wardell. BSN, Duke U., Durham, NC, 1974; MSN in Nursing Edn., U. Pitts., 1986; postgrad., Duquesne U., Pitts., 1995—. Cert. basic life support Am. Heart Assn., 2005. Instr. St. Francis Med. Ctr., Sch. Nursing, Pitts., 1986—87; critical care instr. We. Pa. Hosp., Pitts., 1987—88; staff nurse, surg. icu St. Francis Med. Ctr., Pitts., 1988—92; nurse mgr., patient care coord., supr. VA Med. Ctr., Pitts., 1992—94; grad. rsch., tchg. asst. Duquesne U., Sch. Nursing, Pitts., 1996—2001. Clin. instr. Carlow U., Sch. Nursing, Pitts., 1995—99. Editor: (newsletter) Western Pennsylvania Mensa Phoenix; contbr. monthly column. Mem. svc. unit mgr., daisy leader Trillium Coun. Girl Scouts Am., Pitts., 1989—2007; sec. Pleasant Ridge Resident's Coun., McKees Rocks, Pa., 2007—; interviewer Duke U. Alumni Admissions Adv. Com., Pitts., 1991—2007. Kuhnel scholar, Mensa Edn. and Rsch. Found., 2005. Mem.: Oncology Nursing Soc. (chair awards and oncology nursing found. com. 2002—03), Nurse Healers Profl. Assoc. Internat., Inc. (nursing initiative on aging task force 2006—07), Am. Assn. Critical Care Nurses (nat. scholar rev. com. 2006), Am. Mensa (proctor 1992—, scholar chair 1997—2004, publicity chair 2006—07, scholar chair 2006—07), Coll. Club Carnegie, Sigma Theta Tau (media guide health care experts 1997—2007, pres.-elect 2006—07, Creative Arts Competition winner 2003). R-Conservative. Lutheran. Avocations: cats, gardening, reading, needlecrafts, bridge. Home: 702 Overlook Pl Mc Kees Rocks PA 15136-2096 Home Phone: 412-331-0934.

WARDEN, GAIL LEE, healthcare executive; b. Clarinda, Iowa, May 11, 1938; s. Lee Roy and Juanita (Haley) W.; m. Lois Jean Johnson, Oct. 9, 1965; children: Jay Christopher, Janna Lynn, Jena Marie. BA, Dartmouth Coll., 1960; MHA, U. Mich., 1962; PhD in pub. adminstrn., Cent. Mich. U., 1995. Adminstrv. asst. Blodgett Meml. Ctr., Grand Rapids, Mich., 1962; adj. Dewitt Hosp., Ft. Belvoir, Va., 1963-65; exec. v.p./COO Rush-Presbyn.-St. Luke's Med. Ctr., Chgo., 1965—76; exec. v.p. Am. Hosp. Assn., Chgo., 1976-81; pres., CEO Group Health Coop. Puget Sound, Seattle, 1981-88, Henry Ford Health Sys., Detroit, 1988—2003, pres. emeritus, 2003—. Past chmn. Am. Hosp. Assn., HRET, Steering Com. Transformational Leadership Project in Health Mgmt. Edn. and Practice; former chmn. Nat. Quality Forum; chair Nat. Ctr. Healthcare Leadership, IOM Com. on Future Emergency Medicine in US, Detroit Wayne County Health Authority; bd. dirs. Comerica Bank, Nat. Rsch. Corp.; mem. RAND Health Bd. Advisors; dir. emeritus Nat. Com. on Quality Assurance, former chmn.; former mem. Bd. Health Care Svcs., Inst. Medicine, Com. Quality Health Care in Am., Fed. Adv. Commn. Consumer Protection and Quality in Health Care Industry, Nat. Commn. Civic Renewal, Pew Health Professions Comms., IOM, gov. coun.; vice chair bd. dirs. Rosalind Franklin U. Medicine and Sci.; chair campaign com., mem. dean's adv. bd. U. Mich. Sch. Pub. Health. Contbr. articles to profl. jours. Former bd. dirs. Robert Wood Johnson Found., 1965; bd. dirs. Citizens Rsch. Coun. Mich.; chair Detroit Zoological Soc.; former mem. bd. dirs. Detroit Econ. Growth Corp.; former mem. Detroit Met. Wayne County Airport Commn.; former chmn. Greater Detroit Area Health Coun.; bd. dirs. Bon Secours Cottage Health Svcs., co-chair capital campaign; past mem. Fed. Adv. Commn. on Consumer Protection and Quality in the Health Care Industry. Capt. USAR. Named one of Ten Outstanding Young Men in Chgo., Jr. Assn. Commerce and Industry, 1968; named on e of 100 Most Powerful People in Healthcare, Modern Healthcare, 2002-04; recipient Nat. Health Care award, B'nai B'rith Internat., 1992, CEO award Am. Hosp. Assn.'s Soc. for Healthcare Planning and Mktg., 1993, Gold Medal award, Am. Coll. Health Care Execs., 1999; first recipient Thompson Vis. Fellowship award, Yale, Health Quality award, Nat. Com. Quality Assurance, Disting. Svc. award, AHA, Walter J. McNerney Fellowship award for Health System Improvement, HRET. Mem. APHA, NAS Inst. Medicine (governing coun.), Am. Coll. Hosp. Adminstrs. (named Young Adminstr. of Yr. 1972), Am. Healthcare Systems, Inst. Healthcare Improvment, Nat. Resource Ctr. on Chronic Care Integration, Alpha Chi Rho. Office: Henry Ford Health System 1 Ford Pl Detroit MI 48202-3450

WARDEN, JOHN LEHMAN, lawyer; b. Evansville, Ind., Sept. 22, 1941; s. Walter Wilson and Juanita (Veatch) W.; m. Phillis Ann Rodgers, Oct. 27, 1960; children: Anne W. Clark, John L., W. Carson. AB, Harvard U., 1962; LLB, U. Va., 1965. Bar: N.Y. 1966, U.S. Ct. Appeals (2d cir.) 1966, U.S. Dist. Ct. (so. and ea. dists.) N.Y. 1967, U.S. Ct. Appeals (10th cir.) 1971, U.S. Supreme Ct. 1972, U.S. Ct. Appeals (D.C. cir.) 1980. Assoc. Sullivan & Cromwell, NYC, 1965-73, ptnr., 1973—. Commr. US Antitrust Modernization Commn., 2004—07. Editor-in-chief: Va. Law Rev., 1964-65. Hon. trustee U. Va. Law Sch. Found.; trustee Am. Ballet Theatre. Fellow Am. Coll. Trial Lawyers; mem. ABA, Am. Law Inst., NY State Bar Assn., Assn. Bar City NY, NY County Lawyers Assn., Knickerbocker Club, Down Town Assn. Club, Doubles Club, Bedford Golf and Tennis Club, Lyford Cay Club. Republican. Episcopalian. Office: Sullivan & Cromwell 125 Broad St Fl 28 New York NY 10004-2489 Office Phone: 212-558-3610. E-mail: wardenj@sullcrom.com.

WARDEN, RICHARD DANA, government labor union official; b. Great Falls, Mont., Dec. 10, 1931; s. Robert Dickinson and Helen (Leach) W.; m. Barbara Freeman; children from previous marriage: Denise, Michael, Joseph, Jerome. BA, U. Mont., 1957, MA, 1958. Reporter, then state editor Gt. Falls (Mont.) Tribune, 1959-61; legis. asst. to U.S. Senator Lee Metcalf of Mont., 1962-63; adminstrv. asst. to U.S. Congressman James G. O'Hara of Mich., 1963-67; dep. dir. Office Civil Rights, HEW, 1967-68; legis. rep. AFL-CIO, 1969-70; dir. Washington Research Project Action Council, 1970-72; asst. legis. dir. UAW, 1972—75, legis. dir., 1975-77, 79-91, ret., 1991. Asst. sec. legis. HEW, 1977-79 Served with USN, 1950-54. Congressional fellow, 1961-62; recipient Pub. Affairs Reporting award Am. Polit. Sci. Assn., 1960 Mem.: Am. Polit. Sci. Assn. Home: 211 Marina Dr Lewes DE 19958

WARDEN, WALDIA ANN, retreat center administrator, director; b. New Orleans, Jan. 15, 1933; d. Walter Emmer and Lydia Eugenie (LeBlanc) W BS, St. Mary's Dominican Coll., 1961; MS Dietetics, St. Louis U., 1964; JCL, Cath. U. Am., 1988. Joined Dominican Sisters, Congregation of St. Mary, Roman Cath. Ch., 1953, coun. mem., 1976-84, 96-2004. Tchr. elem. schs., 1954—62; instr. foods and nutrition Dominican Coll., New Orleans, 1964—66, chmn. home econs. dept., 1966—69, asst. dean students, 1969—75, chmn. dept. home econs., 1975—78, chmn. Coll. Planning Coun., 1972—76; dir. Rosaryville Ctr., Ponchatoula, La., 1979—81; pres. St. Mary's Dominican Coll., New Orleans, 1983—86; defender Bond for Tribunal Archdiocese of New Orleans, 1989—2005; dir. Rosaryville Spirit Life Ctr., Ponchatoula, 2005—. Pres. St. Mary's Dominican H.S., 1990-94; coord. First Ct. Met. Tribunal, Archdiocese of New Orleans, 1994-2005 Trustee St. Mary's Dominican Coll., 1973-79, 83-86, 90-93; bd. regents Our Lady of Holy Cross Coll., New Orleans, 1992-98; bd. dirs. Henriette deLille Mid. Sch. for Girls, 2000-04, chair, 2004-05 Mem. La. Dietetic Assn. (editor jour. 1966-68), La. Leadership Conf. Women Religious, Am. Dietetic Assn., Am. Home Econs. Assn., Canon Law Soc. Am., Dominican Leadership Configuration (cluster coord. com. 2002-06, chair reconfiguration subcom. 2002-06) Home: 39003 Rosaryville Rd Ponchatoula LA 70454-7001 Office: Rosaryville Spirit Life Ctr Ponchatoula LA 70454-7001 Office Phone: 225-294-5039. Personal E-mail: dawaldia@aol.com.

WARDER, LAWRENCE A., federal agency administrator; b. Akron, Ohio, 1944; m. Dianne Warder; 2 children. BS, U. Akron; MBA, Kent State U., 1969. CPA, cert. mgmt. acct., mgmt. cons. Pilot plant operator Gen. Tire and Rubber Co., supr. fin. sys.; cons. Touche Ross & Co., Clev., 1969—70, Detroit, 1970—77, ptnr., 1977—81; mng. dir. Ctrl.-S.W. Group, Dallas, 1981—92, mgr. NY and N.E. region, 1992—96; dir. ops. cons. Deloitte Cons. LLP, 1996—98, head European ops. London, 1998—2000, global dir. ops., 2000—01, NYC, 2001—02; cons. to sys. chancellor U. Tex., 2002—05, cons. instl. audit and compliance com.; with O'Donnell Found., Dallas, Austin Ind. Sch. Dist.; CFO US Dept. Edn., Washington, 2006—, acting COO Fed. Student Aid, 2007—. Office: US Dept Edn 400 Maryland Ave SW Washington DC 20202

WARDER, MICHAEL YOUNG, academic administrator; b. Buffalo, June 29, 1946; s. Thomas Grayston and Norma A. (Young) W.; m. Cheryl Lynn Gilkerson, Feb. 8, 1975; children: Maureen, Amy, Michael Jr. BA, Stanford U., 1968. Tchr. Drew Sch., San Francisco, 1968—69; pres. Internat. Re-edn. Found., San Francisco, 1970—73; sec.-gen. Internat. Conf. on Unity of Scis., NYC, 1974—79; pres., pub. Newsworld Comm., NYC, 1976—79; dir. adminstrn. Heritage Found., Washington, 1980—83; exec. v.p. Ethics and Pub. Policy Ctr., Washington, 1983—84, The Rockford Inst., Ill., 1985—95; v.p. devel. Claremont Inst., Calif., 1995—2001; exec. dir. So. Calif. Children's Scholarship Fund, 2001—05; vice chancellor Pepperdine U., Malibu, Calif., 2005—. Radio commentator (bi-weekly) Sta. WNIJ-FM NPR Affiliate, DeKalb, Ill., 1991—95; del. leader People to People, USSR, 1991, Rockford Inst., Lithuania, Latvia, Estonia, 1994; del. leader to London Claremont Inst., 1996, del. leader to Hong Kong, 97, del. leader to Israel, 98, del. leader to Rome, 2000, del. leader to China, 06; guest TV programs Politically Incorrect/ABC, Fox News Channel, MSNBC, others; spkr. in field; polit. analyst in field. Op-ed columnist The Wall Street Jour., USA Today, L.A. Times, The Chgo. Tribune, Chgo. Sun Times, San Francisco Chronicle, San Diego Union Tribune, St. Louis Post Dispatch, Indpls. Star, 1985—; host, prodr. (TV) Stateline Newsmakers, 1990-92; columnist (weekly) Rockford Register Star, 1991-92. Recipient Silver Dome award Ill. Broadcasters Assn., 1993, 95, 96; grantee Earhart Found., 1988. Mem.: L.A. World Affairs Coun., Phila. Soc., Coun. for Nat. Policy, Americanism Ednl. League (bd. dirs.). Republican. Avocations: travel, history, geography. Office: Pepperdine U 24255 Pacific Coast Hwy Malibu CA 90263 Office Phone: 310-506-4486. Business E-Mail: michael.warder@pepperdine.edu.

WARDER, RICHARD CURREY, JR., dean, mechanical aerospace engineering educator; b. Nitro, W.Va., Sept. 30, 1936; s. Richard Currey and Edith Irene (Moser) W.; m. Carolyn Strickler, Mar. 7, 1964 (div. Dec. 1978); children: Jennifer, Jeffrey W.; m. Marjorie Dianne Forney, Jan. 10, 1981. BS, S.D. Sch. Mines, 1958; MS, Northwestern U., 1959, PhD, 1963. Registered profl. engr., Mo., Tenn. Asst. prof. Northwestern U., Evanston, Ill., 1963-65; mgr. energy processes research Litton Industries, Beverly Hills, Calif., 1965-68; assoc. prof. mech. and aerospace engring. U. Mo., Columbia, 1968-72, prof., 1972-94, James C. Dowell prof., 1989-94, chmn. mech. aerospace engring., 1988-94; dean U. Memphis Herff Coll. Engring., 1994—. Program mgr., head resources sect. NSF, Washington, 1974-76; mem. Engring. Accreditation Commn., 2003—; cons. to industry U.S. govt. Bd. dirs. Columbia Montessori Soc., 1971-73; bd. dirs. Columbia Soccer Club, 1976-80, pres., 1978-80; referee Maj. Indoor Soccer League, 1979-83. Fellow: AAAS, ASME, AIAA (assoc.); mem.: Am. Soc. Engring. Edn., Am. Phys. Soc. Methodist. Office Phone: 901-678-4306.

WARDLAW, KIM A. MCLANE, federal judge; b. San Francisco, July 2, 1954; m. William M. Wardlaw Sr., Sept. 8, 1984. Student, Santa Clara U., 1972—73, Foothill C.C., Los Altos Hills, Calif., 1973—74; AB in Comm. summa cum laude, UCLA, 1976, JD with honors, 1979. Bar: Calif., US Dist. Ct. (ctrl. dist.) Calif. 1979, US Dist. Ct. (so. dist.) Calif. 1982, US Dist. Ct. Nev. 1985, US Dist. Ct. (no. dist.) Calif. 1992, US Dist. Ct. Mont. 1993, US Dist. Ct. Minn. 1994, US Dist. Ct. (no. dist.) Ala. 1994, US Dist. Ct. (so. dist.) Miss. 1995, US Supreme Ct. Law clk. US Dist. Ct. Ctrl. Dist. Calif., 1979—80; assoc. O'Melveny and Myers, 1980—87, ptnr., 1987—95; judge US Dist. Ct. Calif., LA, 1995—98, US Ct. Appeals (9th cir.), 1998—. Presdl. transition team Dept. Justice, Washington, 1993; mayoral transition team City of LA, 1995—; bd. govs. UCLA Ctr. for Comm. Policy, 1994—, vice-chair, 1994—; cons. in field. Co-author: The Encyclopedia of the American Constitution, 1986; contbr. articles to profl. jours. Pres. Women Lawyers Pub. Action Grant Found., 1986—87; founding mem. LA Chamber Orch., 1992—; active Legal Def. and Edn. Fund Calif. Leadership Coun., 1993—; active Blue Ribbon of LA Music Ctr., 1993—; del. Dem. Nat. Conv., 1992. Named one of Most Prominent Bus. Attys. in LA County, LA Bus. Jour., 1995; recipient Buddy award, NOW, 1995. Mem.: NOW, ABA, Orgn. Women Execs., Assn. Bus. Trial Lawyers (gov. 1988—), LA County Bar Assn. (trustee 1993—94), Women Lawyers Assn. LA, Calif. Women Lawyers, Mex.-Am. Bar Assn. LA County, Hollywood Womens Polit. Com., Downtown Women Ptnrs., City Club Bunker Hill, Breakfast Club, Chancery Club, Phi Beta Kappa. Office: US Ct Appeals 9th Cir 125 South Grand Ave Pasadena CA 91105 *

WARDLOW, BENJAMIN FRANKLIN, III, sales executive; b. Lebanon, Ohio, Sept. 17, 1946; s. Benjamin Franklin Wardlow II and Blanche Lee Hardwick; m. Barbara Ann Wardlow, Sept. 17, 2002. BS, U. Cin., 1984. Corp. sales mgr. Marquette Mfg., Minn., 1968—76; br. mgr. Netherland Rubber Co., Charlestow, W.Va., 1976—78; airline acct. adminstr. Gen. Elec., Cin., 1978—81; sales mgr. Twyman Templeton Co., Columbus, 1981—87; owner A/C Sys., Cin., 1987—93; sales exec. Keidel Supply, 1993—. With US Army, Vietnam. Mem.: Disabled Veterans Am., Lexington Valley Scottish Rite, Lebanon Elks, Montgomery Lodge F & AM. Republican. Mem. Soc. Of Friends. Avocations: golf, marathon running, tennis.

WARDRIP, ELIZABETH JANE, retired librarian; b. Lawrenceburg, Ind., Dec. 12, 1925; d. Estal Joseph Ackerman and Dorothy Leona Unthank; m. Schuyler Clark Wardrip, Dec. 20, 1953 (div. Dec. 24, 1981); children: Gregory Clark, Elizabeth Jane, Margaret Louise, Laura Anne, Mary Ann. BS in Gen. Studies, Columbia U., 1951; MLS, U. Md., 1972. Cert. libr. Md., 1972. Libr. adult svcs. Prince George's County Meml. Libr. Sys., Hyattsville, Md., 1972—92, ret., 1992. Fellow, U. Rochester, 1951. Mem.: DAR (regent 1999—2001). Democrat. Roman Catholic. Avocations: reading, theater, travel, museums, art galleries. Home: 6103 Sutters Place Bowie MD 20720

WARDROPPER, IAN BRUCE, museum curator, educator; b. Balt., May 11, 1951; s. Bruce Wear and Joyce (Vaz) W.; stepmother: Nancy Hélène (Palmer) W.; m. Laurel Ellen Bradley, May 22, 1982 (div. 1996); 1 child, Chloe Bradley; m. Sarah Anne McNear, June 21, 1997. BA, Brown U., 1973; MA, NYU, 1976, PhD, 1985. Asst. curator European sculpture Art Inst. Chgo., 1982-85, assoc. curator European decorative arts and sculpture, 1985-89, Eloise W. Martin curator European decorative arts and sculpture, and classical art, 1989-2001; Iris and B. Gerald Cantor curator in charge dept. European sculpture and decorative arts Met. Mus. Art, NYC, 2001—05, chmn., 2005—. Adj. instr. Drew U., NJ, 1982; vis. asst. prof. Northwestern U., Evanston, Ill., 1986, Sch. of Art Inst. Chgo., 1988; guest scholar J. Paul Getty Mus., Malibu, Calif., 1995; Rhoades lectr. U. Chgo., 1997; exhbns. panelist NEA, 1993, creation and presentation panelist, 98, indemnity panelist, 1998—2001. Co-author: European Decorative Arts in the Art Institute of Chicago, 1991, Austrian Architecture and Design beyond Tradition in the 1990s, 1991, News from a Radiant Future: Soviet Porcelain from the Collection of Craig H. and Kay A. Tuber, 1992, Chiseled with a Brush: Italian Sculpture, 1860-1925, from The Gilgore Collections, 1994, From the Sculptor's Hand: Italian Baroque Terracottas from the State Hermitage Museum, 1998; contbr. articles to profl. jours. NEA fellow, 1976-77, Chester Dale fellow Met. Mus. Art, 1978-79; Kress Found. rsch. grantee, Paris, 1979-81, Am. Philos. Soc. grantee, 1991; named Chicagoan of the Yr. in Arts Chicago Tribune, 1994. Mem. Phi Beta Kappa. Office: Met Mus Art 1000 Fifth Ave New York NY 10028-0198 Office Phone: 212-879-5500 ext. 4980. Business E-Mail: Ian.wardropper@Metmuseum.org.

WARD-STEINMAN, DAVID, composer, music educator, pianist; b. Alexandria, La., Nov. 6, 1936; s. Irving Steinman and Daisy Leila (Ward) W.-S.; m. Susan Diana Lucas, Dec. 28, 1956 (div. 1993); children: Jenna, Matthew; m. Patrice Dawn Madura, May 28, 2001. MusB cum laude, Fla. State U., 1957; MusM, U. Ill., 1958, DMA, 1961; studies with Nadia Boulanger, Paris, 1958-59; postdoctoral vis. fellow, Princeton U., 1970. Grad. instr. U. Ill., 1957-58; mem. faculty San Diego State U., 1961—2003, prof. music, 1968—, disting. prof. music, emeritus prof., 2004, dir. comprehensive musicianship program, 1972—2003, composer in residence, 1961—, univ. rsch. lectr., 1986-87. Faculty Eastman Sch. Music Workshop, 1969, Coll. Music Soc. Nat. Inst. for Music in Gen. Studies, U. Colo., 1983-84, Calif. State Summer Sch. for the Arts, Loyola Marymount U., 1988; Ford Found. composer in residence Tampa Bay (Fla.) Area, 1970-72, Brevard Music Ctr., N.C., 1986; acad. cons. U. North Sumatra (Indonesia), 1982; concert and lecture tour U.S. Info. Agy., Indonesia, 1982; master tchr. in residence Atlantic Ctr. for the Arts, New Smyrna Beach, Fla., 1996; vis. artist in residence Victorian Ctr. for the Arts, Melbourne, Australia, 1997, faculty Coll. Mus. Soc. Nat. Insts., San Diego, 1999, 2001, 2003, Ind., 2003; adj. prof. music Ind. U., Bloomington, 2004—. Composer: Symphony, 1959, Prelude & Toccata for orch., 1962, Concerto No. 2 for chamber orch., 1962, ballet Western Orpheus, 1964, Cello Concerto, 1966, These Three ballet, 1966, The Tale of Issoumbochi chamber opera, 1968, Rituals for Dancers and Musicians, 1971, Antares, 1971, Arcturus, 1972, The Tracker, 1976, Brancusi's Brass Beds, 1977; oratorio Song of Moses, 1964; Jazz Tangents, 1967, Childs Play, 1968; 3-act opera Tamar, 1977; Golden Apples, 1981; choral suite Of Wind and Water, 1982; Christmas cantata And In These Times, 1982; Moiré for piano and chamber ensemble, 1983, And Waken Green, song cycle on poems by Douglas Worth, 1983, Olympics Overture for orchestra, 1984, Children's Corner Revisited, song cycle, 1984, Summer Suite for oboe and piano, 1984, Quintessence for double quintet and percussion, 1985, Chroma concerto for multiple keyboards, percussion and chamber orch., 1985, Winging It for chamber orchestra, 1986, Elegy for Astronauts for orchestra, 1986, What's Left for piano, 1987, Gemini for 2 guitars, 1988, Intersections II: Borobudur, Under Capricorn, 1989, Voices from the Gallery, 1990, Cinnabar for viola and piano, 1991, Seasons Fantastic for chorus and harp, 1992, Cinnabar Concerto for Viola and Chamber Orchestra, 1993, Night Winds Quintet # 2 for woodwinds, 1993, Double Concerto for Two Violins and Orchestra, 1995, Prisms and Reflections (3rd Piano Sonata), 1996, Millennium Fanfare for symph. orch., 2000, Millennium Dances for symph. orch., 2001, FIESTA! for symphony orch., 2002, FLIGHT! for 2 Pianos, 2002, I Am the Wind for voice and chamber ensemble, 2002, Songs of the Seasons for voice and piano, 2006, Hildegard's Apothecary for chorus and piano, 2007; recs. include Fragments from Sappho, 1969; Duo for cello and piano, 1974, Childs Play for bassoon and piano, 1974, The Tracker, 1989, Brancusi's Brass Beds, 1984, concert suite from Western Orpheus, 1987, Sonata for Piano Fortified, 1987, Moiré, 1987, 3 Songs for Clarinet and Piano, 1987, Concerto #2 for Chamber Orchestra, 1990, Prisms and Reflections, 1999, Cinnabar, 1999, Sonata for Piano Fortified, 1999, Night Winds, 1999, Borobudur, 1999, Cello Concerto, 2000, Cinnabar Concerto, 2000, Chroma Concerto, 2000, Skyline and Under Capricorn, 2005, Seasons Greetings for symphony orch, 2006; commd. by Chgo. Symphony, Joffrey Ballet, San Diego Ballet, San Diego Symphony, numerous others; author: (with Susan L. Ward-Steinman) Comparative Anthology of Musical Forms, 2 vols, 1976, Toward a Comparative Structural Theory of the Arts, 1989. Recipient Joseph H. Bearns prize in Music Columbia U., 1961, SAI Am. Music award, 1962, Dohnanyi award Fla. State U., 1965, ann. BMI awards, 1970—, Broadcast Music prize, 1954, 55, 60, 61; named Outstanding Prof., Calif. State Univs. and Colls., 1968, Outstanding Alumnus of Yr., Fla. State U., 1976; Fulbright sr. scholar La Trobe U. and Victorian Coll. Arts, Victorian Arts Ctr., Melbourne, Australia, 1989-90. Mem. Coll. Music Soc. (nat. bd. for composition 1991-93), Broadcast Music, Inc., Soc. of Composers, inc., Nat. Assn. of Composers U.S.A., Golden State Flying Club. Presbyterian. Home: 1159 E Winners Cir Bloomington IN 47401 Personal E-mail: dwardste@indiana.edu.

WARDY, JOE, former mayor; b. El Paso, Tex., 1953; s. Joe and Mary Rodriguez Wardy; m. Delores Prouse Wardy; children: Kaleb, David. B in fin., U. of Tex. at El Paso, 1976. With Herman/Miles Trucking, Inc., 1985, ptnr., pres.; COO Miles Group, Inc., 2000; mayor City of El Paso, Tex., 2003—05. Mem. Frank Manning Little League Bd.; pres. Franklin Football Booster Club; mem. Tex. Assn. of Football Ofcls.; exec. com. Greater El Paso C. of C.; chmn. El Paso Leadership and Rsch. Coun.; adv. bd. Liberty Mutual Ins. Southwest; bd. dir. North Am. Transp. Alliance, Candlelighters of El Paso; exec. com. Tex. Motor Transp. Assn.; mktg. and mgmt. adv. bd. U. of Tex. at El Paso; v.p. at large Am. Trucking Assn. Office: Joe Wardy, Mayor of El Paso 2 Civic Ctr Plaza, 10th Fl El Paso TX 79901

WARE, D. CLIFTON, vocalist, educator; b. Newton, Miss., Mar. 15, 1937; s. Durward Clifton and Emma Edna (Blount) W.; m. Elizabeth Jean Oldham, June 20, 1958; children: Jon Clifton, David Michael, Stephen Alan. BA, Millsaps Coll., 1959; MusM, U. So. Miss., 1962; MusD, Northwestern U., 1970. Voice instr. U. So. Miss., Hattiesburg, 1964-69; prof. voice and pedagogy U. Minn., Mpls., 1970—2007, chmn. Roy A. Schuessler Vocal Arts Ctr., 1970—2007, prof. emeritus, 2007—. Clinician, cons., adjudicator. Author: (book, song collection and video) Voice Adventures, 1988, (text, song collection, audio cassette, CD) Adventures in Singing, 1995, 2d edit., 1998, 3rd edit., 2004, Basics of Vocal Pedagogy, 1998, The Singer's Life: Goals and Roles, 2005; made recs. St. Nicolas, 1977, Paul Bunyan, 1988, Vocal Explorations: The Bad, the Good, and the Other, 2003; tenor soloist opera, oratorio, recitals. Mem. Nat. Assn. Tchrs. Singing (pres. Minn. chpt. 1972-73, 81-82, found 1995-2006), Nat. Opera Assn. (pres. 1978-79), Pi Kappa Lambda, Phi Kappa Delta, Phi Mu Alpha Sinfonia, Pi Kappa Alpha. Avocations: travel, hiking, reading.

WARE, DONALD R., lawyer; b. Hinsdale, Ill., May 31, 1949; AB magna cum laude, Yale U., 1971; JD magna cum laude, Harvard U., 1974. Bar: Mass. 1974, US Dist. Ct. Dist. Mass., US Ct. of Appeals Fed. Cir., US Ct. of Appeals (1st cir.), Supreme Ct. US. Law clk. to Hon. Paul C. Reardon Supreme Jud. Ct. Mass., Boston, 1974-75; mem. Foley, Hoag & Eliot, Boston. Spkr. in various feilds. Contbr. Adv. bd. Am. Repertory Theatre; mem. Master Plan Com., Hopkinton, NH. Recipient Best Lawyers in Am., Mass. leading intellectual property lawyers, Chambers USA: America's Leading Lawyers for Bus., Mass. Super lawyers, Highly Recommended for intellectual property, Global Counsel 3000. Mem.: Boston Bar Assn., Boston Patent Law Assn., Am. Intellectual Property Law Assn., Fed. Cir. Bar Assn. Office: Foley Hoag & Eliot LLP Seaport World Trade Center W 155 Seaport Blvd Boston MA 02210-2600 Office Phone: 617-832-1000. Office Fax: 617-832-7000. Business E-Mail: dware@foleyhoag.com.

WARE, FREDERICK, internist, educator, nephrologist; b. Omaha, June 16, 1928; s. Frederick John and Clara Louise (Abbott) Ware; m. Charlott Rae Johnson, Sept. 15, 1978; children: Andrea Johnson, Nicholas Harper; m. Elizabeth Diane Thomas (div.); children: Frederick, Mary(dec.), Sally, Tom, Dana. BSc with high distinction, U. Nebr., Lincoln, 1949; MS, U. Nebr., Omaha, 1953; PhD, U. Nebr., 1956, MD cum laude, 1956. Diplomate Am. Bd. Internal Medicine, 1965, Am. Bd. Nephrology, 1976. Co-founder, ptnr. Internal Medicine Assocs., Omaha, 1970—91; prof. internal medicine U. Nebr. Coll. Medicine, Omaha, 1968—91, prof. physiology-biophysics, 1968—91, acting chief nephrology, 1976—87, prof. emeritus, 1991—. Med. dir. Renal Disease Ctr. Clarkson Hosp., Omaha, 1973—91; med. dir. Woodman & World Life Ins. Soc., Omaha, 1976—; co-founder, med. dir., pres. Nebr. Organ Recovery Sys., Omaha, 1977—2004. Capt. USAF, 1959—61. Named Disting. Alumnus, U. Nebr. Coll. Medicine, 2003, Legend of Clarkson, Clarkson Hosp., 2005; recipient Golden Apple award, U. Nebr. Coll. Medicine, 1970; Conkling scholar, 1950. Fellow: ACP; mem.: Alpha Omega Alpha, Sigma Xi, Phi Beta Kappa. Avocations: carpentry, classical music, reading. Home: 6040 Mary Nelson Ln Fort Calhoun NE 68023

WARE, GEORGE HENRY, botanist; b. Avery, Okla., Apr. 27, 1924; s. Charles and Mildred (Eshelman) W.; m. June Marie Gleason, Dec. 21, 1955; children: David, Daniel, Patrick, John. BS, U. Okla., 1945, MS, 1948; PhD, U. Wis., 1955. Asst. prof. Northwestern State U. of La., Natchitoches, 1948-56, assoc. prof., 1956-62, prof., 1962-67; dir. Conservation Sect., No. La. Supplementary Edn. Ctr., Natchitoches, 1967-68; dendrologist Morton Arboretum, Lisle, Ill., 1968-92; adminstr. Urban Vegetation Lab., 1986-92, rsch. fellow in dendrology, 1992-94, dendrologist emeritus, rsch. assoc., 1995—. Vis. prof. U. Okla., Norman, 1957, 61, 63-64; adj. prof. Western Ill. U., 1972-85; ext. faculty George Williams Coll., Downers Grove, Ill., 1969-76, Nat. Coll. Edn., Evanston, Ill., 1972-76, adj. prof. Aurora U., 2003—. Trustee nomination caucus Coll. of DuPage, Glen Ellyn, Ill., 1974-78; bd. dirs. Kane-DuPage Soil and Water Conservation Dist., 1969-81, DuPage Environ. Commn., 1992—, Openlands Project, 1996—; pres. La. Acad. Scis., 1966-67; dir. La. State Sci. Fair, 1966. With USN, 1942-46. Recipient Gold Seal award, Nat. Coun. State Garden Clubs, 1991, Am. Forests Urban Forestry Rsch. medal, 1994, Lifetime Svc. award, Nat. Urban and Cmty. Forestry Adv. Coun., 1995, Hutchinson medal, Chgo. Botanic Garden, 1997, Norman J. Colman award, Am. Nursery and Landscape Assn., 1998, award of merit, Am. Assn. Botanic Gardens and Arboreta, 2000, Liberty Hyde Bailey award, Am. Horticultural Soc., 2002, Conservation Leadership award, Openlands Project, 2005. Mem.: Am. Forests, Nature Conservancy, Ill. Arborist Assn. (pres. 1987—88), Am. Assn. Bot. Gardens and Arboreta, Internat. Soc. Arboriculture (Pres. Commendation award 2000), Southwestern Assn. Naturalists (treas. 1963—69). Office: Morton Arboretum Lisle IL 60532-1293 Home Phone: 630-879-1606; Office Phone: 630-968-0074. Business E-Mail: gware@mortonarb.org.

WARE, GUILFORD DUDLEY, lawyer; b. Dunnsville, Va., Apr. 15, 1925; s. Catesby and Lila (Maddox) W.; m. Nancy Smith, Jan. 17, 1959 (dec. Dec. 1974); children: Elizabeth Latane, Guilford Dudley Jr., David Burwell; m. Gay Dantzler, Sept. 17, 1977. BS in Commerce, U. Va., 1949, LLB, 1952. Bar: Va. 1952, US Dist. Ct. (ea. dist.), US Ct. Appeals (4th cir.) 1957, US Ct. Appeals (5th cir.), US Ct. Appeals (fed. cir.), US Supreme Ct. 1956. Ptnr. Crenshaw, Ware & Martin, P.L.C., Norfolk, Va. Lectr. in field. Editor: The Law of Damages In Virginia. Pres. YMCA, Norfolk, 1966-67, The Va. Symphony Orch., Norfolk, 1967-68; bd. dirs., treas. Va. Inst. Marine Sci. Found., 2001—. Lt. col. USAF, 1943-46. Recipient Eggleston/I'Anson Profl. award, 2003. Fellow Am. Bar Found., Va. Law Found., Va. Legal Elite, Virginia State Bar, Virginia Bar Assn., Ctr. Applied Sci. & Tech. (bd. dirs.), Norfolk Dredging Co. (pres. 1970-98), I'Anson-Hoffman Amer. Inn of Court (pres., 1999—), Best Lawyers of Am.; mem. ABA, ATLA, Norfolk/Portsmouth Bar Assn. (pres. 1987-88), Maritime Law Assn., Southeast Admiralty Law Inst. (seminar chmn. 1983, 89, gen. chmn. 1985), Am. Judicature Soc., Norfolk Yacht and Country Club, Harbor Club (pres. 1994-96), The Whitehall Club, Norfolk German Club (pres., gen. chmn. 1985), Princess Anne Country Club. Home: 7457 St Francis Ln Norfolk VA 23505-1757 Office: Crenshaw Ware & Martin PLC 1200 Bank of Am Ctr Norfolk VA 23510 Office Phone: 757-623-3000. Office Fax: 757-623-5735. Business E-Mail: gware@cwm-law.com.

WARE, GWENDOLYN C., retired counseling administrator; m. Roy Ware, Mar. 28; 1 child, Sonja. BA in English magna cum laude, U. Ark., Pine Buiff, 1970; MEd in Secondary Counseling with honors, U. Nev., Las Vegas, 1975. English instr. Clark County Sch. Dist., Las Vegas, 1971—77, guidance counselor, 1977—95, scholarship and coll. prep counselor, 1996—2003, ret., 2003. Fin. aid/scholarship workshop presenter Clark County Sch. Dist., Las Vegas, 1997—2003; coll. preparation workshop facilitator and presenter Kappa Alpha Psi Kappa League, Las Vegas, 2002—. Mem. Black Cmty. Orgn. Network, Las Vegas, 1988—. Mem.: AAUW, NAFE, Clark County Sch. Counselors' Assn., Western Assn. Coll. Admissions Counselors, Sickle Cell Anemia Found. (scholarship rev. and selection 1987—88), Phi Delta Kappa Internat., Phi Delta Kappa (2nd v.p. membership 1997—99, Mem. of Yr. 1997). Avocations: theater, literature, music, interior decorating. Home Phone: 702-876-3053.

WARE, MARILYN, ambassador, former utilities company executive; b. Lancaster, Pa., Nov. 4, 1943; d. John III and Marian Ware; children: Mark Strode, Amy Strode, Scott Strode. D of Pub. Services., Thaddeus Stevens Coll. Tech., 1998; LittD (hon.), Franklin & Marshall Coll., 2003. Vice-chmn. Am. Water Works Co., Inc., Voorhees, NJ, 1984-88, chmn., 1988—2003, chmn. emeritus Vorhees, NJ, 2003; US amb. to Finland US Dept. State, Helsinki, 2005—. CEO Ware Family Offices, Strasburg, Pa., 1991; dir. CIGNA Corp., Phila., 1993-2005, IKON Office Solutions, Malvern, Pa., 2000—2005, Am. Enterprise Inst., Washington, 1994, PENJERDEL Coun., Phila.; mem. Nat. Infrastructure Advisory Coun., 2002, Pew Oceans Commn., 2000-03 Editor: The Oxford Press, Lancaster, Pa., 1978-82. Trustee Nat. Osteoporosis Found., Washington, 1996-2000, U. Pa. Health Sys., Phila., 1991—, Gannon U., Erie, Pa., 1996-2000, Nat. Coun. of Conservation Fund, Washington, 1999—, Eisenhower Exch. Fellowships, Phila., 1995—, chmn. exec. com., 2000; founding mem., bd. dirs. Lancaster Farmland Trust, 1987—; founder, adv. bd. dirs. Janus Sch., Mt. Joy, Pa., 1991—; v.p., sec. Oxford Found., Strasburg, 1981—; chmn. Tom Ridge for Gov. Campaign, Harrisburg, Pa., 1993-94, Rep. Com. of Lancaster County, 1978-80, Woman for Bush, Pa., 1987-88; mem. Rep. State Com. of Pa., 1985-90. Recipient Samuel S. Baxter Meml. award Water Resources Assn., 2000, Paradigm award Greater Phila. C. of C., 1999, Dir.'s Choice award Nat. Women's Econ. Alliance Found., 1992; named Bus. Leader of Yr., Rep. Caucus, Pa. Ho. of Reps., 1993, Disting. Daus. of Pa., Gov. Tom Ridge, 2000. Office: Am Embassy 5310 Helsinki Pl Washington DC 20521

WARE, PAUL F., JR., lawyer; b. Boston, Feb. 24, 1944; AB, U. Notre Dame, 1966; LLB, U. Pa., 1969. Bar: Mass. 1969, U.S. Supreme Ct. 1973, D.C. 1974. Law clk. to Hon. Andrew Caffrey U.S. Dist. Ct., 1969-70; asst. U.S. atty. Dept. Justice, Washington, 1970-73, spl. asst. U.S. atty., 1973-74; spl. asst. atty. gen. Commonwealth of Mass., Boston, 1982-83; atty. Goodwin, Procter & Hoar, Boston; ptnr. Goodwin Procter LLP, Boston, 1978—, and chmn., litig. dept., mem. exec. com. Clin. assoc. instr. Harvard Law Sch., Cambridge, Mass., 1976, trial advisor, 1977-80, 83-88; mem. faculty Mass. Continuing Legal Edn., 1990; active U.S. Magistrate Selection Panel; trial counsel Iran Contra Investigation, 1992-93. Fellow Am. Coll. Trial Lawyers; mem. ABA, Mass. Bar Assn., Boston Bar Assn. Office: Goodwin Procter LLP Exchange Pl 53 State St Boston MA 02109-2803 Office Phone: 617-570-1280. Office Fax: 617-523-1231. Business E-Mail: pware@goodwinprocter.com.

WARE, RICHARD ANDERSON, foundation executive; b. NYC, Nov. 7, 1919; s. John Sayers and Mabelle (Anderson) W.; m. Lucille Henney, Mar. 20, 1942 (div. 1972); children: Alexander W., Janet M., Bradley J., Patricia E.; m. Beverly G. Mytinger, Dec. 22, 1972. BA, Lehigh U., 1941; M in Pub. Adminstrn., Wayne State U., 1943; D in Social Sci. (honoris causa), Francisco Marroquin U., Guatemala, 1988. Research asst. Detroit Bur. Govt. Research, 1941-42; personnel technician Lend-Lease Adminstrn., Washington, 1942-43; research asso. to asst. dir. Citizens Research Council, Detroit, 1946-56; sec. Earhart and Relm Founds., Ann Arbor, Mich., 1951-70, trustee, pres., 1970-84, trustee emeritus, pres. emeritus. Prin. dep. asst. sec. def. for internat. security affairs, Washington, 1969-70; cons. Office Asst. Sec. Def., 1970-73; dir. Citizens Trust Co., 1970-87. Vice pres. Ann Arbor United Fund and Cmty. Svcs., 1968, pres., 1969; asst. dir. Mich. Joint Legis. Com. on State Reorgn., 1950-52; sec. Gov.'s Com. to Study Prisons, 1952-53; com. to chmn. Ann Arbor City Planning Commn., 1958-67; mem. Detroit Com. on Fgn. Rels., 1971-87; mem. coun. Woodrow Wilson Internat. Center for Scholars, 1977-85; vis. com. divsn. social scis. U. Chgo., 1977-85; mem. adv. com. The Citadel, 1977-85; mem. adv. coun. internat. studies program Fletcher Sch., Tufts U., 1979-85; trustee Greenhills Sch., 1973-80, Ann Arbor Area Found., 1977-83, Inst. Fgn. Policy Analysis, 1985-2003, Inst. Polit. Economy, 1985—2005, Ctr. for Study Social and Polit. Change Smith Coll., 1988—2005, Pequawket Found., 1989—, Intercollegiate Studies Inst., 1996-2004; polit. analyst Rep. Nat. Com., Washington, 1964; bd. dirs. The Liberty Fund, Inc., Indpls., 1980—2004, Bd. Fgn. Scholarships, 1984-90, chmn., 1987-89. With USAAF, 1943-46. Recipient Civilian Meritorious Service medal Dept. Def., 1970, Charles H. Hoeflich Lifetime Achievement award Intercollegiate Studies Inst., 2006; Paul Harris fellow Rotary, 1997. Fellow Mont Pelerin Soc.; mem. Govtl. Research Assoc. (trustee, v.p. 1955-56), Am. Polit. Sci. Assn., Ann Arbor Club, North Conway Country Club, Cosmos Club (Washington), Phi Beta Kappa, Phi Alpha Theta Congregationalist. Home: PO Box 310 Intervale NH 03845-0310 Office: 2200 Green Rd Ste H Ann Arbor MI 48105-1569

WARE, SUSAN W., historian; b. Washington, Aug. 22, 1950; d. Charles Kline and Charlotte McConnell Wolfe; m. Donald R. Ware, June 10, 1972. BA, Wellesley Coll., 1968—72; MA, Harvard U., 1973, PhD, 1978. Asst. to assoc. prof. NYU, 1986—95; hon. vis. scholar Radcliffe Coll., 1996—97; editor, Notable Am. Women Radcliffe Inst. for Advanced Study, Harvard U., 1997—2005; vis. lectr., history Harvard U., 2002—05. Adv. bd. Schlesinger Libr., Cambridge, Mass., 1988—97, Franklin and Eleanor Roosevelt Inst., Hyde Park, NY, 1986—; assoc. Clio, Inc., Charlotte, Vt., 1996—; exec. bd. Soc. of Am. Historians, NYC, 1990—2002. Author: (books) Beyond Suffrage: Women in the New Deal, 1981, Letter to the World: Seven Women Who Shaped the Am. Century, 1998; editor: Forgotten Heroes: Inspiring Am. Portraits from our Leading Historians, 1998; author: Holding Their Own: Am. Women in the 1930s, 1982, Ptnr. and I: Molly Dewson, Feminism, and New Deal Politics, 1987, Still Missing: Amelia Earhart and the Search for Modern Feminism, 1993, It's One O'Clock and Here Is Mary Margaret McBride! A Radio Biography, 2005. Home: 16 Hilliard St Cambridge MA 02138 Personal E-mail: sdware@aol.com.

WARE, THADDEUS VAN, retired government official; b. High Point, NC, Mar. 31, 1935; s. Elsec and Irene (Myers) W.; m. Doretha Ardella Lee, June 18, 1960; children— Kimberly Melissa, Chrystal Lynn. BA cum laude, Va. Union U., 1957; JD, Howard U., 1960. Bar: Va. bar 1961, D.C. bar 1970, U.S. Supreme Ct. bar 1970. Gen. atty. Office of Solicitor, Dept. Labor, 1961—66; trial counsel Chief Counsel's Office, Fed. Hwy. Adminstrn., 1966—69; staff asst. to Pres. Richard M. Nixon, 1969—70; chief adminstrv. judge, chmn. Bd. Contract Appeals, Dept. Transp., 1987—2003; ret., 2003. Appt. bd. contract appeals Dept. Trans., 1970. Served with AUS, 1960-61. Mem. Va., D.C., U.S. Supreme Ct., Fed. Bar Assns., Urban League, NAACP, Bd. Contract Appeals Judges Assn. (pres. 1988-89), Alpha Phi Alpha, Sigma Delta Tau, Alpha Kappa Mu (Disting. Career Svc. award). Home: 2213 Parallel Ln Silver Spring MD 20904-5446 E-mail: tvanddlware@msn.com.

WAREHAM, ELLSWORTH EDWIN, cardiothoracic surgeon, educator; b. Avinger, Tex., Oct. 3, 1914; s. Dayton and Goldie Leah Wareham; m. Barbara Nell Nix, May 7, 1950; children: Martin, Robert, Julie, John, Scott. At, Can. Jr. Coll., Coll. Heights, Alta., 1931—33, at, 1935—36, Can. Union Coll., Lacombe, Alta., 1936; MD, Loma Linda U., Calif., 1942; LLD (hon.), Andrews U., Berrien Springs, Mich., 1971. Cert. Am. Bd. of Surgery, 1954, Am. Bd. of Thoracic Surgery, 1955. Intern Seattle Gen. Hosp., 1942; indsl. surgeon Good News Bay Mining Co., Platinum, Alaska, 1942—45; resident fellow in surgery Loma Linda U. Med. Ctr., Calif., 1947—50; resident surgery Bellevue Hosp. Columbia U., NYC, 1950—52; resident thoracic and cardiovasc. surgery Queens Med. Ctr., NYC, 1952—53; resident cardiovasc. surgery svcs. St. Francis Hosp. Cardiac Children, Roslyn, NY, 1954—55; prof. surgery Loma Linda U., 1964—2006, prof. emeritus surgery, 2006—; chief cardiothoracic surgery Loma Linda U. Med. Ctr., 1964—86; acting chmn. dept. of surgery Loma Linda U., 1973—75; staff Loma Linda U. Med. Ctr., 1964—86, Riverside Gen. Hosp., Calif., 1973—75; prof. cardiac surgery King Saud U., Riyadh, Saudi Arabia, 1986—88; admin. dir. Hong Kong Heart Ctr., 1988—. Surgeon and dir., Loma Linda U. mission to Pakistan, India, Thailand and Formosa U.S. Dept. of State, 1963; surgery team Govt. of Greece, Athens, 1967—73; organizer heart surgery affiliation Evangelismos Hosp. and Loma Linda U. Sch. Medicine, 1970—76; surgeon, heart team Loma Linda U., China, 1981. Performer: (films) Atrial Septal Defect, 1964 (Golden Eagle Cine award, Venice Film Festival, 1964); contbr. articles to profl. jours. Lt.(j.g.) USN, 1945—47, PTO. Recipient Outstanding Educator of Am., 1970, award for svc. to people of Pakistan, City of Karachi, 1963, Medallion award for svc. to Greek People, Evangelismos Hosp., Athens, 1967, Golden Medal of Health, Republic of Vietnam, 1974, Outstanding Alumnus, Loma Linda U. Sch. of Med., 1974, Outstanding Contbn. to Medicine, San Bernardino County Med. Soc., 1986, Outstanding Achievement award in medicine, Ministry of Def. and Aviation, Saudi Arabia, 1986, Pres. Commendation, US, 1984, Alumnus of the Yr., Loma Linda U., 1994, Outstanding Contbn., Pasadena divsn., Am. Heart Assn., 1999. Fellow: Am. Coll. of Cardiology, Am. Coll. Surgeons; mem.: AMA, Western Assn. of Thoracic Surgery, Pacific Coast Surg. Assn., Am. Assn. for Thoracic Surgery, San Bernardino County Med. Soc., Calif. Med. Assn., Soc. of Thoracic Surgeons, Alpha Omega Alpha. Republican. Adventist. Achievements include development of heart surgery programs in Greece, Saudi Arabia, Hong Kong, developing countries. Mailing: Box 1068 Loma Linda CA 92354

WAREHAM, RAYMOND NOBLE, brokerage house executive; b. Rochester, NY, Nov. 20, 1948; s. Simon Harold and Barbara (Snell) W.; m. Cornelia Lee Clifford, June 28, 1975; children: Ellinor Park, Laura Stewart, Cornelia Ashley. BS in Indsl. Engring., Northwestern U., 1970; MBA, Harvard U., 1975. With J.P. Morgan & Co., NY, 1975-80, mgr. dir., head banking industry group NY, 1988-92, head-corp. fin. Tokyo, 1980-85; exec. dir. J.P. Morgan Securities Ltd., London, 1986-87; mng. dir. corp. fin. dept. J.P. Morgan Securities, NYC, 1992-98; sr. portfolio mgr. Sanford C. Bernstein Alliance Capital, NYC, 1999—, sr. mng. dir., 1999—. Trustee Am. Sch., Tokyo, 1982-85; bd. dir. Brick Ch. Day Sch., 1989-92, Juvenile Diabetes Found., 1997-98, Stanley Isaacs Neighborhood Ctr., 2006—; pres. bd. trustees Spence Sch., NYC, 1995-2003, life trustee, 2002—; dir. 1148 Corp., 2006—; elder Brick Presbyn. Ch., NYC, 1989-92. Lt. Supply Corps, USN, 1970-73. Mem. DERU (Northwestern hon.), Naval War Coll. Found., Union Club (NY), Duxbury (Mass.) Yacht Club, Century Club (Harvard Bus. hon.), Eagle Scouts. Republican. Avocations: sports, antique furniture. Home: 1148 5th Ave New York NY 10128-0807 Office: Alliance Capital/Sanford C Bernstein 17th Fl 1345 Ave of Americas New York NY 10105-0096

WAREJCKA, DEBRA J., research scientist; b. Evanston, Ill., Mar. 16, 1953; d. Venzel J. and Muriel M. Warejcka; m. Mark J. Welden, May 3, 1981; children: Benjamin G. Welden, Tyler J. Welden. BA, Kalamazoo Coll., Mich., 1975; PhD, Duke U., Durham, NC, 1981. Rsch. assoc. Med. Ctr. Ctrl. Ga., Macon, 1991—99; rsch. scientist Med. Coll. Wis., Milw., 2001—. Office: Med Coll Wis 8701 W Watertown Plank Rd Milwaukee WI 53226 Home Phone: 414-963-1917; Office Phone: 414-456-8444. Personal E-mail: djwarejcka@hotmail.com. Business E-Mail: djwarejck@mcw.edu.

WAREN, STANLEY ARNOLD, academic administrator, performing company executive; b. NYC, Mar. 22, 1919; s. Maurice and Minnie (Rosen) W.; m. Florence Rigal, Nov. 21, 1949; 1 child, Mark BSS., CCNY, 1938; MA, Columbia U., 1939, PhD, 1953. Exec. producer, dir. theatre, 1953-70; prof., chmn. dept. speech and theatre CCNY, 1967-72; prof., exec. officer Ph.D. program theatre CUNY, 1972-81, v.p., provost, dep. pres. Grad. Sch., 1981-84; dir. Ctr. for Advanced Study in Theatre Arts, NYC, 1979-82, 84-86. Reviewer NEH, 1978—91; advisor humanities com. Bklyn. Acad. Music, NYC, 1980—81; spl. edn. cons. Dougle Image Theatre, NYC, 1982—90; mem. adv. coun. Roundabout Theatre, NYC, 1985—93; Fulbright-Hayes vis. prof. Nat. Taiwan U., 1986—87; vis. prof. Shanghai Drama Inst., 1988; USIS grant, lectr., Hong Kong, 88, Ctr. for Living and Learning, Marymount Manhattan, 1998—2007, New Sch. U., 2000—03. Dir. musical The Chess King (Taiwan) 1987, Old B Hanging on the Wall (Shanghai), 1988, Judas, Mexico (NY), 1989, Seasoned Citizens Theatre Co., 2003-. Bd. dirs. Women's Inter. Art Ctr., NYC, 1978-82; mem. grants panel NYC Dept. Cultural Affairs, 1979; bd. dirs. Frank Silvera Workshops for Writers, NYC, 1979-81. Served to capt. USAF, 1942-46 Grantee Herman Goldman Found., 1980-82, NEH, 1980-81, NY Coun. Humanities, USIA/Arts Am., Singapore, 1990. Mem. AAUP, Assn. Theatre in Higher Edn., Soc. Stage Dirs. and Choreographers, Actors Equity Assn., Profl. Staff Congress CUNY, The Drama League (mem. awards nominating com. 1997—). Clubs: The Century Assn. (resident 1984—). Democrat. Avocations: art, tennis, swimming. Home: 465 W End Ave #11D New York NY 10024-4926 Office: CUNY Theatre PhD Program Grad Sch 365 5th Ave New York NY 10016-4309

WARENSKJOLD, DOROTHY, singer, educator; d. William Earl and Mildred Lorraine (Stombs) Warenskjold. BA, Mills Coll., 1943. Soprano San Francisco Opera Co., 1949—58, Columbia Artists Mgmt., NYC, 1950—72; adj. prof. UCLA, Westwood, 1984—97, 1999; master class instr. numerous orgns., 1999—. Master class instr. concert state presentations. Singer numerous recs. Named Woman of Yr., Opera Guild, 1988. Mem.: Nat. Assn. Tchrs. of Singing (adv. bd. 2004—). Achievements include 1st American singer asked to appear at the Rebild Festival in Denmark. Home: 7716 Oakview Ln Lenexa KS 66216 Personal E-mail: dwkc1@yahoo.com.

WARFEL, M(ARTHA) KAY, speech pathology/audiology services professional; b. Lancaster, Pa., Mar. 2, 1955; d. Orlene Dickenhart and Martha (Herr) W.; m. George Jay Malley, Jr., Sept. 21, 1978 (div. 1979); m. C. Robert Paul III, Aug. 15, 1987 (div. Mar. 2000); 1 child, Thomas Matthew Warfel Paul. BS in Speech Pathology/Audiology, Pa. State U., Univ. Pk., 1976; MEd in Speech Pathology, U. Oregon, Eugene, 1979; MBA in Mktg., Iona Coll., New Rochelle, NY, 1986; PhD in Health Adminstrn., Kennedy-Western U., Thousand Oaks, Calif., 2004. Cert. clinician. Speech lang. pathologist Lancaster-Lebanon #13, East Petersburg, Pa., 1970—78, Douglas ESD, Roseburg, Oreg., 1979—80, Bethel Sch. Dist. #52, Eugene, 1980—81, NY Bd. Edn., Bronx, 1981—93, Sch. Dist. Lancaster, Pa., 2003—04, Avon Grove Sch. Dist., West Grove, 2004—06; speech pathologist Hickory House Nursing Home, Honey Brook, Pa., 2006, Oxford Area Sch. Dist., Pa., 2006—. Speech pathologist Eugene Speech and Hearing Ctr., 1980; speech cons. Margaret Chapman Sch., Hawthorne, NY, 1988-89; instr. sensory impairments Manhattan Coll., Riverdale, NY, 1987-88; adj. instr. lang. disorders of children Coll. New Rochelle, NY, 1988-89; with press The Athletics Congress, Indpls., 1981-88; press officer 1988 USA Men's and Women's Olympic Track and Field Teams, 1988. Contbr. dissertation. Vol. Rep. Nat. Com., Lancaster, 1972, Spl. Olympics, 1976-83, Lane County Prisons, Eugene, 1979; bd. dirs. Meml. Meth. Early Childhood Ctr., advt. chairperson, 1994—. Mem. Am. Speech-Lang.-Hearing Assn., Am. Mktg. Assn., Coun. Exceptional Children, NY Speech-Lang.-Hearing Assn. Republican. United Methodist. Avocations: gardening, jogging, reading, raising poultry, cross stitch. Personal E-mail: kaypsu76@kennett.net.

WARFIELD, GERALD ALEXANDER, composer, writer; b. Ft. Worth, Feb. 23, 1940; s. George Alexander and Geraldine (Spencer) Warfield. Student, Tex. Christian U., 1958-61; BA, N. Tex. State U., 1963, MMus, 1965; postgrad., Tanglewood, 1963—64; MFA, Princeton U., 1967. Instr. Princeton U., 1968-71; assoc. dir. Index New Mus. Notation, NYC, 1971-75. Lectr. contemporary music notation; mem. conf. com. Internat. Conf. New Mus. Notation, Belgium, 1974; chmn. program com. 2d Nat. Conf. Music Theory, 1977. Author: A Beginner's Manual of Music 4B, 1967, Layer Analysis: A Primer of Elementary Tonal Structures, 1976, Writings on Contemporary Music Notations, 1977, How to Write Music Manuscript, 1977, The Investor's Guide to Stock Quotations, 1982, How to Buy Foreign Stocks and Bonds, 1984, How to Read Financial News, 1986, No Nonsense Guides to the Stock Market, Mutual Funds, Tax-Free Bonds, 1999, Managing Your Stock Portfolio, Money Market Funds, 1993; co-author: Grove's Dictionary of Music and Musicians, 1976; author (with others): Layers Dictation, 1978, Export-Import Financing, 1986, Feng Shui Revealed, 1997; editor: Longman Music Series, 1976—85; contbr. articles to profl. jours.; composer: Variations and Metamorphoses, 1973 (1st prize Ariz. Cellos Soc.), filmstrip introduction Musical Notation, 1976, Fantasy Quintet, 1978 (2d prize New Music Young Ensembles). Adv. bd. Boyce Ditto Pub. Libr., 2005—. Mem.: Broadcast Music Inc., Coll. Music Soc. (coun., conf. chmn. 1981), Am. Composers Alliance (treas. 1979—96), Soc. Composers, Inc. (chmn. exec. com. 1972—74, conf. chmn. 9th Ann. Conf. 1974, founding editor Jour. Music Scores, gen. mgr. 1977—2000, 2002—). Home: 410 SW 4th Ave # 4 Mineral Wells TX 76067-5840 Personal E-mail: geraldwarfield@cox-internet.com.

WARFORD, PATRICIA, psychologist; d. Eldon J. Jameson and Rosa Kirschenman; m. Gary W. Warford, Sept. 5, 1955; children: Candice C. Zaniewski, Nathanael A. BS, S.D. State U., 1991; MS, George Fox Coll., 1993, D of Psychology, 1996. Lic. psychologist Oreg. Bd. Psychologist Examiners, 1998. Psychologist Western Psychol. & Counseling, Beaverton, Oreg., 1994—98, Yamhill County Adult Mental Health, McMinnville, 1998—2000, pvt. practice, Newberg, 2001—; co-owner Life Strategies Domestic Abuse Program, McMinnville, 2005—. Faculty State Victims Assistance Acad., Salem, Oreg., 2004—; presenter Boston Coll., Boston, 2002, George Fox U., Newberg, 2004. Co-author: (training manual chapter) Trauma Bonding. Oregon State Victims Assistance Academy Training ManualNumber 2002-VF-GX-KO23 awarded by the Office for Victims of Crime, Office of Justice Programs, U.S. Department of Justic, 2004. Appointee Oreg. Gov.'s Coun. Domestic Violence, Salem, 2004. Mem.: APA, Tri-County Batterers Intervention Providers, Yamhill County Domestic Violence Task Force. Office: 1013 N Springbrook PO Box 3279 Newberg OR 97132 Home Phone: 503-538-9601; Office Phone: 503-554-8172. Office Fax: 877-892-6114.

WARGA, JACK, mathematician, educator; b. Warsaw, Dec. 5, 1922; came to U.S., 1943, naturalized, 1944; s. Herman and Czarna (Lichtenstein) W.; m. Faye Kleinman, Feb. 27, 1949; children: Charna Ruth Schakow, Arthur David. Student, Brussels U., 1939-40; BA, Carleton Coll., 1944; PhD, NYU, 1950. Assoc. mathematician Reeves Instrument Corp., NYC, 1951-52; Chief engring. computing sect. Republic Aviation Corp., Farmingdale, NY, 1952-53; head math dept. Burroughs Corp., Pasadena, Calif., 1954-56; mgr., math dept. Avco Research and Devel., Wilmington, Mass., 1957-66; prof. math. Northeastern U., Boston, 1966-93, prof. emeritus, 1993—. Author: Optimal Control of Differential and Functional Equations, 1972, expanded Russian transl., 1977; contbr. articles to profl. jours. Served with AUS, 1944-46. Weizmann Meml. fellow, 1956-57 Fellow AAAS; mem. Am. Math. Soc., Soc. Indsl. and Applied Math. (editor Jour. on Control and Optimization 1963-89). Home: 7356 Falls Rd W Boynton Beach FL 33437-6316 E-mail: warga@neu.edu.

WARIAN, CHRISTINE BARBARA, elementary school educator; b. Somerville, NJ, May 7, 1967; d. Terence and Loretta Warian. MusB in Music Edn. and Therapy, Immaculata Coll., 1989; MA in Reading Specialization, Kean U., 2003. Cert. reading specialist, elem. tchr. NJ. Tchr. Christ the King Sch., Manville, NJ, 1997—2000, Our Lady of Peace Sch., Fords, NJ, 2000—01; substitute tchr. Edison and Woodbridge Sch. Dists., 2001—04; reading specialist James Madison Intermediate Sch., Edison, 2004—05; tchr. Huntington Learning Ctr., Edison, NJ, 2005—06; substitute Woodbridge Sch. Dist., 2005—06; reading specialist Franklin Elem. Sch., South Plainfield, 2006—. Mem.: NJ Reading Assoc., Kappa Delta Pi. Avocations: singing, exercise, reading.

WARICHA, JOAN, publishing executive; BA, Boston U., 1967; MBA, Columbia U., 1980. V.p., editor-in-chief, assoc. pub. Scholastic, Inc., 1968-83; pres. Parachute Press, 1983-96; chmn., CEO Parachute Properties, 1996—; pres. Parachute Pub., 1996—, Parachute Entertainment, 1996—, Parachute Consumer Products, 1996—. Office: Parachute Properties 322 Eighth Ave Ste 500 New York NY 10001 Office Phone: 212-691-1421. Business E-Mail: jwaricha@parachuteproperties.com.

WARIN, ROGER E., lawyer; b. Des Moines, June 14, 1945; s. Roger Francis and Mary (Gray) Warin; m. Diane Whyte-Warin, May 31, 1974; children: Elizabeth, Patricia, Christopher, Michael. BA, Creighton U., 1967; JD, Georgetown U., 1970. Bar: Nebr. 1970, DC 1971. Law clk. for Judge Oliver Gasch US Dist. Ct., DC, Washington, 1970-71; assoc. Steptoe & Johnson LLP, Washington, 1971-77, ptnr., litig. & ins. dept., 1978—, mem. exec. com. Adj. prof. ins. law Am. U., Washington, 1978—81; bd. mem. Washington Lawyers Com. for Civil Rights. Contbr. articles to profl. jour.; spkr. in field. Fellow: Am. Coll. Trial Lawyers; mem.: ABA (Litig., Tort & Ins. Practice Sect.). Avocation: skiing. Office: Steptoe & Johnson LLP 1330 Connecticut Ave NW Ste 700 Washington DC 20036-1704 Office Phone: 202-429-6280. Office Fax: 202-429-3902. Business E-Mail: rwarin@steptoe.com.

WARINER, JEREMY, Olympic track and field athlete; b. Irving, Tex., Jan. 31, 1984; Student, Baylor Univ. Mem. U.S. Olympic Track Team, Athens, 2004. Named Mondo Outdoor Track Athlete of the Yr., USA Track Coaches Assoc., 2004. Achievements include winning gold medal, 400m, Athens Olympic games, 2004; being NCAA Champion, Indoor 400m, Indoor 4x400m relays, Outdoor 400m, Outdoor 4x400m relay, 2004. Office: c/o USOC 1 Olympic Plaza Colorado Springs CO 80909

WARING, BRADISH J., lawyer; b. New Orleans, Mar. 6, 1952; s. Simons Vanderhorst and Mary Barnwell (Rhett) W.; m. Amelia B., May 27, 1978; children: Amelia S., Mary B.R., Louisa V. BA, U. S.C., 1975, JD, 1977. Bar: SC 1978, US Dist. Ct. (Dist. SC) 1978, US Ct. Appeals (4th Cir.) 1978, US Supreme Ct. 1978. Assoc. Young, Clement, Rivers & Tisdale, Charleston, SC, 1978—81, ptnr., 1981—2003, Nexsen Prue & Adams Kleemeier, Charleston, SC, 2003—. Corp. counsel Town of Sullivan's Island, SC, 1979-81; chair emeritus Am. Law Firm Assn. Sch. Law., LA, 1998—; mem. U. SC Law Sch. Assn.; bd. dirs. U. SC Law Sch. Partnership. Bd. dirs., treas. Charleston Day Sch., 1996, chmn. bd.; vestry mem., sec. St. James Episcopal Ch., Goose Creek, SC, 1991; apptd. chair Commrs. Plottage Charleston Br., 1993-94. Fellow SC Bar Found.; mem. ABA, SC Bar Assn. (bd. govs. 1997—, ho. dels. 1985—, pres. 2007), Fedn. Ins. & Corp. Counsel, Am. Judicature Soc., Charleston County Bar Assn., Def. Rsch. Inst., Historic Charleston Found. (v.p.), Port of Charleston Pilotage Commn., SC Def. Trial Attys. Assn. Avocations: sailing, golf, hunting, travel. Office: Nexsen Prue & Adams Kleemeier PO Box 486 Charleston SC 29402 Office Phone: 843-577-9440. Office Fax: 843-720-1777. E-mail: bwaring@nexsenpruet.com.

WARING, WILLIAM WINBURN, pediatric pulmonologist, educator; b. Savannah, Ga., July 20, 1923; s. Antonio Johnston and Sue Cole (Winburn) W.; m. Nell Pape Williams, July 19, 1952; children: William Winburn, Benjamin Joseph, Antonio Johnston, Peter Ayraud, Patrick Houstoun Grad., Hotchkiss Sch., Lakeville, Conn., 1942; student, Yale U., 1942-43; MD, Harvard U., 1947. Diplomate Am. Bd. Pediatrics (subbd. of pediatric pulmonology 1985-89). Intern Children's Hosp., Boston, 1947-48; intern, then resident Johns Hopkins Hosp., Balt., 1948-52; practice medicine specializing in pediatrics Jacksonville, Fla., 1955-57; instr. dept. pediatrics

Sch. Medicine, Tulane U., New Orleans, 1957-58, asst. prof., 1958-61, assoc. prof., 1961-66, prof. emeritus, 1966—, Jane B. Aron Prof. Pediatrics, 1987-96. Dir. Pediat. Pulmonary Ctr., New Orleans, 1969-88, Cystic Fibrosis Ctr., Tulane U., New Orleans, 1963-88; chmn. profl. tng. com. Cystic Fibrosis Found., 1978-86; cons. La. State Handicapped Children's Assn., 1963-88; mem. pulmonary diseases adv. com. NIH, 1978-80. Co-author: Pro Parvulis: On Behalf of the Little Ones. A History of the Department of Pediatrics, Tulane Medical School, 1834-2003, 2003; co-author, editor: Practical Manual of Pediatrics, 1975, 2d edit., 1982; editor: Harriet Lane Handbook: A Manual for Pediatric House Officers, 1952, Hospital Pediatric Manual, 1958; contbg. author books on pediatric pulmonary disease, also articles in field; assoc. editor Am. Jour. Diseases of Children, 1989-91; mem. editl. bd. Pediatric Pulmonology, 1985-94. Served to capt. M.C., U.S. Army, 1952-54. Recipient Rsch. Career Devel. award, NIH, 1970—72, Edwin L. Kendig, Jr. award for outstanding achievement in pediatric pulmonology, 2004. Fellow Am. Acad. Pediatrics (exec. com. 1966-71, Edwin L. Kendig Jr. award), Am. Coll. Chest Physicians; mem. Am. Pediatric Soc., Am. Thoracic Soc. (v.p. 1977). Clubs: Boston, So. Yacht, Wyvern (New Orleans). Republican. Roman Catholic. Avocations: fly fishing, running, computers. Office: Tulane U Sch of Medicine Dept of Pediatrics 1430 Tulane Ave New Orleans LA 70112-2699 E-mail: wwaring@bellsouth.net.

WARITZ, RICHARD STEFAN, toxicologist, researcher; b. Portland, Oreg., Apr. 1, 1929; s. Anton John and Theresa (Stegelmaier) W.; m. Ruth Evelyn White, June 7, 1950; children: Joyce E., Gary S., Sharon J., Carol L. BA, Reed Coll., 1951; PhD, Stanford U., 1957. Diplomate Am. Bd. Toxicology, Acad. Toxicological Scis. Sr. rsch. scientist E.I. DuPont de Nemours & Co., Wilmington, Del., 1957-64, mgr. inhalation toxicology, 1964-72, mgr. bio-scis., 1972-75; sr. toxicologist Hercules Inc., Wilmington, 1975-80, mgr. toxicology, 1980-92; pres. BioSante Internat., Inc., 1992—2005. Grad. toxicology edn. adv. bd. Rutgers U., Piscataway, N.J., 1980-2005, vis. prof. toxicology, 1993-2005; life scis. adv. bd. U.S. Army, Aberdeen, Md., 1982-92; toxicology peer rev. bd. U.S. Army Ctr. for Health Promotion and Preventive Medicine, 1992—; vis. prof. toxicology Rutgers U., 1993-2005. Contbr. articles to profl. jours. Mem.: Am. Chem. Soc., Am. Conf. Govtl. Indsl. Hygienists, Am. Indsl. Hygiene Assn., Internat. Union Toxicol. Socs. (councillor 1983—88), Soc. Toxicology (treas. 1981-85, pres. Mid-Atlantic chpt. 1989). Roman Catholic. Avocations: golf, fishing, bowling. Home: 2613 Turnstone Dr Wilmington DE 19808-1638 Home Phone: 302-998-3915. Personal E-mail: waritztox@verizon.net.

WARKEL, HARRIET G., curator; d. Samuel H. and Shirley K. Mamlin; m. Raphael L. Warkel; 1 child, Randall S. MA, Ind. U., Bloomington, 1989. Assoc. curator Am. art Indpls. Mus. Art, 2000—06, curator Am. art, 2006—. Author: (book) A Shared Heritage: Art by Four African Americans, Herron Chronicle; contbr. articles to profl. jours. Mem.: Am. Assn. Mus. Avocations: antiques, American illustration collector, exercise. Office: Indianapolis Museum of Art 4000 Michigan Rd Indianapolis IN 46208 Office Phone: 317-920-2662 137. Office Fax: 317-926-8931. E-mail: hwarkel@ima.museum.

WARKENTIEN, MARK, professional sports team executive; m. Maureen Warkentien; children: Kreigh, Aubrie. Grad., Calif. State U., Fullerton, 1976. Coach Riverside City Coll., Saddleback Coll., U. Calif., Irvine, coach women's prog. Riverside; asst. coach Calif. State. U., Fullerton; asst. coach/recruiting coord., asst. athletic dir. UNLV, 1980—91; scout Seattle SuperSonics, 1991—94, Portland Trail Blazers, 1994—95, dir. scouting, 1995—98, asst. gen. mgr., 1998—2003, dir. player pers., 2003—04, Cleve. Cavaliers, 2004—05, interim gen. mgr., 2004—05; dir. player pers. Denver Nuggets, 2005—06, v.p. basketball ops., 2006—. Office: Denver Nuggets 1000 Chopper Cir Denver CO 80204 *

WARLEN, STEPHEN CLARENCE, forensic specialist, consultant; s. Clarence Milford and Elinor Elizabeth Warlen; m. Yvonne Marie Dercher, Oct. 21, 1946; children: Christopher Stephen, Jennifer Lynn Harvey, Michelle Renee, Melissa Anne. AA, Maple Woods C.C., Kansas City, Mo., 1970; BS, Ctrl. Mo. State U., Warrensburg, 1975, MS, 1977. Forensic sci. specialist Kansas City Police Dept., Crime Lab., 1997—, police officer, latent prints & photography. Cons. in field, Kansas City, 1976—. Mem.: Internat. Assn. Identificaiton (assoc.; pres., chmn. bd. 1988), Am. Acad. Forensic Scis. (assoc.). Achievements include development of ultraviolet photography & infra red photograph in the forensic sciences. Home: 4100 NW 75th St Kansas City MO 64151 Office: Kansas City Police Crime Laboratory 6633 Troost Ave Kansas City MO 64131 Home Phone: 816-349-3273; Office Phone: 816-349-3273. Office Fax: 816-349-3240. Personal E-mail: swarlen@sbcglobal.net. E-mail: swarlen@kcpd.org.

WARMAN, EDUARDO NORBERTO, research scientist; arrived in US, 1985; s. Israel Miguel and Renee Celia Warman; m. Berta Estela Feingold, Dec. 14, 1984; children: Cynthia, Leo, Max. Licenciado, U. Buenos Aires, 1985; PhD, Case Western Res. U., 1992. Staff scientist Medtronic, Mpls., 1994—99, sr. prin. scientist, 1999—. Medtronic tech. fellow, Sci. and Tech. Bd., 2000. Achievements include patents in field; patents pending in field. Office: Medtronic 7000 Central Ave NE Minneapolis MN 55432 Office Phone: 763-514-3569.

WARMAN, GUY LEE, lawyer; b. Lambert, Pa., July 11, 1929; s. Guy B. and Ida Grace (Lee) W.; m. Katherine V. Baldridge, Nov. 6, 1954; children: Katherine L., Cynthia V. BA, Pa. State U., 1953; JD, U. Pitts., 1956. Bar: Pa. 1957, U.S. Dist. Ct. (we. dist.) Pa. 1957, U.S. Ct. Appeals (3d cir.) 1976, U.S. Supreme Ct. 1971. Assoc. Metz, Cook, Hanna & Kelly, Pitts., 1957-63, ptnr. 1963-78; mem. Guy L. Warman and Assocs., P.C., Pitts., 1978-82; ptnr. Warman, Crone and Studeny, Pitts., 1982-98; spl. counsel Reed Smith LLP, 1998—. Republican county committeeman, 1970-80. Served with USAAF, 1946-49; 1st lt. USAFR 1953-56. Recipient Robert L. Vann award U. Pitts. Sch. Law, 1956. Mem. ABA, Pa. Bar Assn., Allegheny County Bar Assn. (chmn. membership com. 1968-69, chmn. ct. rules com. 1969-78, chmn. judiciary com. 1985). Republican. Presbyterian. Clubs: Longue Vue (Verona, Pa., pres. 1995-97), Duquesne Club (Pitts.), Masons, Shriners. Editor: The Allegheny County Common Pleas Court Manual, 1969-78. Contbr. articles to U. Pitts. Law Rev. Home and Office: 720 Shady Ave Pittsburgh PA 15232-2911 Office Phone: 412-956-0308. E-mail: gwarman@glwpc.com.

WARMAN, LINDA K., retired secondary school educator; b. Indiana, Pa., Mar. 25, 1942; d. James Edward and Elizabeth Josephine (Hawk) Warman. BA, Moravian Coll., Bethlehem, Pa., 1964. Tchr. Easton Area Sch. Dist., Pa., 1964—2001, chair dept. English, 1986—2001; ret., 2001. Contbr.: book Religious Literature of the West, 1970, mem.: Bach Choir of Bethlehem, 1963—78. Named Outstanding Instr. U. Honors Students, Pa. State U., 1985. Avocations: travel, reading, home decorating, gardening.

WARMAN, LYNNETTE R., lawyer; b. Willmar, Minn., Oct. 1, 1955; BA, U. Nebr., 1983; JD, Creighton U., 1986. Bar: Nebr. 1986, Tex. 1987, US Ct. Appeals 5th Cir., US Dist. Ct. No., Ea., We. & So. Districts Tex. Shareholder Jenkens & Gilchrist, P.C., Dallas, head bus. dept.; ptnr. Hunton & Williams LLP, 2007—. Mem.: ABA, Tex. Bar Assn., Dallas Bar Assn. (bankruptcy sect.), John C. Ford. Am. Inn of Ct., Am. Bankruptcy Inst. (bd. dirs.). Office: Hunton & Wiliams LLP Energy Plz 30th Fl 1601 Bryan St Dallas TX 75201-3402 Office Phone: 214-855-4792. Office Fax: 214-855-4300. Business E-Mail: lwarman@jenkens.com. *

WARMBROD, CATHARINE PHELPS, educational researcher, consultant; b. Lost Nation, Iowa, July 2, 1929; d. Paul Edward and Ruth Dorthea Phelps; m. J. Robert Warmbrod, Jan. 30, 1965. BA, U. Iowa, Iowa City, 1952; MS, U. Ill., Urbana, 1965, advanced cert. in edn., 1967. Head supr. student tchrs. in bus. edn. U. Ill., Urbana, 1966-67; chmn. office adminstrn. Columbus (Ohio) State Community Coll., 1970-77; rsch. specialist NCRVE Ohio State U., Columbus, 1977-88, rsch. specialist emeritus, 1988—; prin. Warmbrod Ednl. Svcs., Columbus, 1988-2001. Bd. dirs. Nat. Assn. Industry/Edn. Cooperation, Buffalo, 1980-88. Author: Retraining and Upgrading Workers, 1983; editor: VocEd Insider for Tech. Edn., 1981; contbr. articles to profl. jours. Bd. dirs. Ohio Women, Inc., Columbus, 1986—92, Friendship Village, Dublin, Columbus, 1990—2004. Mem. Am. Vocat. Assn. (policy com. 1980-83), Assn. Faculty and Profl. Women Ohio State U. (pres. 1984-85), Am. Assn. Cmty. Colls., Am. Tech. Edn. Assn., Delta Pi Epsilon. United Methodist. Office: Warmbrod Ednl Svcs 6000 Riverside Dr A 358 Dublin OH 43017 Home Phone: 614-798-2050. Business E-Mail: warmbrod.2@osu.edu.

WARNATH, MAXINE AMMER, psychologist, arbitrator; b. NYC, Dec. 3, 1928; d. Philip and Jeanette Ammer; m. Charles Frederick Warnath, Aug. 20, 1952; children: Stephen Charles, Cindy Ruth. BA, Bklyn. Coll., 1949; MA, Columbia U., 1951, EdD, 1982. Lic. psychologist Oreg. Various profl. positions Hunter Coll., U. Minn., U. Nebr., U. Oreg., 1951-62; asst. prof. psychology Oreg. Coll. Edn., Monmouth, 1962-77; assoc. prof. psychology, chmn. dept. psychology & spl. edn. Western Oreg. U., Monmouth, 1978-83, prof., 1983—96, prof. emeritus, 1996—. Dir. organizational psychology program, 1983—96; pres. Profl. Perspective Internat., Salem, Oreg., 1987—; cons., dir. Orgn. R&D, Salem, Oreg., 1983—87; seminar leader Endeavors for Excellence program. Author: Power Dynamism, 1987. Mem.: APA (com. pre-coll. psychology 1970—74), Western Psychol. Assn., Oreg. Psychol. Assn. (pres. 1980—81, pres.-elect 1979—80, legis. liaison 1977—78), Oreg. Acad. Sci., N.Y. Acad. Scis., Am. Psychol. Soc. Office: Profl Perspectives Internat PO Box 2265 Salem OR 97308-2265 Office Phone: 503-371-6451. Personal E-mail: mwarnath@comcast.net. Business E-Mail: warnatm@wou.edu.

WARNE, ALAN M., continuing education educator, consultant; b. Pierre, SD, Aug. 24, 1945; s. Maynard L. and Ione P. Warne; m. Joan Caulfield, Sept. 7, 1996; children: Alan, Jr. M., Andrea W. White, Amy N. BA in Polit. Sci., Ariz. State U., 1963—67; MA in Ednl. Psychology, Ea. Ky. U., 1969—70; EdD in Continuing Edn., Temple U., 1972—78. Fgn. student advisor Ariz. State U., Tempe, 1966—68; dir. internat. student services U. of Ky., Lexington, 1968—71; dir. office internat. services Temple U., Phila., 1971—77; exec. dir. Phila. Coun. Internat. Visitors, 1977—81, Nat. Coun. Internat. Visitors, Washington, 1981—85; chief exec. officer/vice pres. for programs People to People Internat., Kans. City, Mo., 1986—99; pres. & ceo Entrepreneurial Edn. Found., Kans. City, 2000—01; sr. program mgr. Med. Ctr. U. Kans., Kans. City, 2002—07; v.p. ops. Silver Fox Assoc., Kans. City, 2007—. Mng. dir. The Brain Inc., Kans. City, Mo., 2000—; planning cons. Kauffman Ctr. for Entrepreneurial Leadership, Kans. City, Mo., 2000; academic program cons. Rockhurst U., Kans. City, Mo., 2000; mem. continuing med. edn. adv. com. U. Kans., 2002—, mem. continuing med. ctr. statewide adv. bd. and governing com., 2002—; peer grant reviewer U.S. Dept. Edn., 2005—. Contbr. curriculum guide Expo 92 (Kans. City-Seville), nat. profl. newsletter Mgmt./Program Planning Articles, admissions guide - internat. student A Model for the Edn. of Fgn. Students. Bd. mem./arts com. Mayor's UN Day Com., Kans. City, Mo., 1990—96; site planning com. Kans. City Sch. Dist., Kans. City, Mo., 1990—91; bd. mem./vice chair Nat. Coun. for Internat. Visitors, Washington, 1978—81; founding bd. mem. Consortium for Internat. Citizen Exch., Washington, 1981—85, Caruthers' Arts Alliance, Kans. City, Mo.; scholarship committees rep. U. of Mo., Kans. City, Mo., 1986—2005; pres./vice pres. Pk. U. Bd. of Visitors, Parkville, Mo., 1995—2001. Recipient Del. Leader - Baltic Nations, Ambassadors, Inc., 1999, Thematic Specialist -Citizen Initiatives (6-US Cities), Inst. of Internat. Edn., 1981; grantee Ednl. Travel Grant, Republic of China Ministry of Edn., 1975. Fellow: Rotary Club Internat. (ednl./scholarship/planning committees 1999—2006); mem.: Soc. Govt. Meeting Profls., Assn. of Internat. Educators (regional chair, coord. of nat. job registry, exec. com. 1967—2000), Kans. City Club (membership com. 1993—2006). Avocations: volunteerism, travel, cinema, theater, organizational development. Home: 431 West 70th St Kansas City MO 64113 Office: U Kans Med Ctr 3901 Rainbow Blvd Kansas City KS 66160-7108 Personal E-mail: kcawarne@aol.com.

WARNECK, ROBERT TOWNSEND, religious studies educator; b. Pitts., Jan. 15, 1952; s. John Loweth and Virginia Carter Warneck; m. Diane Marshall Dickson, Dec. 17, 2005. B of Liberal Arts, Syracuse U., NY, 1973. Cert. tchr. Christian Sci. The First Ch. of Christ, Scientist, Boston. Rschr. writer The First Ch. Christ Scientist, Boston, 1973—99. Author: (book) Mary Baker Eddy: Christian Healer, 1998. Avocations: reading, movies. Office: 1 Main St #216 Burlington VT 05401

WARNECKE, JOHN CARL, architect; b. Oakland, Calif., Feb. 24, 1919; s. Carl I. and Margaret (Esterling) W.; children by previous marriage: John Carl, Rodger Cushing, Margaret Esterling, Frederic Pierce. AB, Stanford U., 1941; MA, Harvard U., 1942. Asso. Miller & Warnecke, architects, 1944-46; prin. John Carl Warnecke, AIA, 1947-58; partner Warnecke & Warnecke, 1954-62; pres., dir. design John Carl Warnecke & Assoc., 1958—. Works include U.S. Naval Acad. Master Plan, Michelson and Chauvenet Halls, Annapolis, Md., U. Calif. at Santa Cruz Master Plan and Library, Lafayette Sq., Washington, Georgetown U. Library, Washington, Kaiser Center for Tech., Pleasanton, Calif.; bldgs., Stanford U., Hawaii State Capitol, Honolulu, Philip A. Hart Senate office bldg., USSR Embassy, Hennepin Govt. Center, Mpls., J.F. Kennedy Meml. Grave, Arlington Nat. Cemetery, Va., Neiman Marcus and Bergdorf Goodman Stores, Logan Airport, Boston, Am. Hosp, Paris, The Sun Co. Hdqrs, Radnor, Pa., King Abdulaziz U. Med. Center, Jedda, Saudi Arabia, Yanbu Town Ctr. Master Plan, Hilton Hotel & Casino, Atlantic City. Mem. Fine Arts Commn., Washington, 1963-67. Recipient Arnold Brunner prize in architecture Nat. Inst. Arts and Letters, 1957; also 70 nat., regional awards for excellence. Fellow AIA; Mem. NAD (assoc., 1958-94, academician, 1994-) Office: 300 Broadway St San Francisco CA 94133-4587 also: 1707 H St NW Ste 1100 Washington DC 20006-3919 also: 462 Broadway New York NY 10013-2618 also: 1180 S Beverly Dr Los Angeles CA 90035-1153 also: Warnecke-Sonoma Vineyard 13427 Chalk Hill Rd Healdsburg CA 95448-9043

WARNER, BARRY GREGORY, ecologist, educator; b. Cambridge, Ont., July 20, 1955; s. Gregory O. and Alma (Jansen) W. B in Environ. Studies, U. Waterloo, 1978, MS, 1980; PhD, Simon Fraser U., Burnaby, Can., 1984. Rsch. asst. prof. U. Waterloo, Ont., 1985-89, rsch. assoc. prof. Ont., 1989-91, assoc. prof. geography Ont., 1991-96, prof. biology, earth sci. and geography Ont., 1996—; dir. Wetlands Rsch. Inst., 1991—; U. Neuchatel. Vis. prof. U. Neuchatel, 1993, U. Franche-Comte, Bescon, France, 2002; chair Can. Nat. Wetlands Working Group, 1993—; bd. dirs. Internat. Mire Conservation Group. Editor: Methods in Quaternary Ecology, 1990; co-editor: Wetlands: Envigradients, Boundaries and Buffers, 1996; contbr. articles to profl. jours. Postdoctoral fellow Natural Scis. and Engring. Rsch. Coun. of Can., 1984-85, rsch. fellow, 1985-90; fellow Suisse Nat. Res. Fond, 1993; Sr. Scientist Fellowship, Ministere de la Recherche, France. Fellow Geol. Assn. Can., Soc. Wetland Scientists (pres., v.p. 2000-2003). Office: U of Waterloo Wetlands Rsch Ctr Waterloo ON Canada N2L 3G1 Home Phone: 519-884-9619; Office Phone: 519-888-4567 3607. Business E-Mail: bwarner@uwaterloo.ca.

WARNER, BRIAN HUGH See MANSON, MARILYN

WARNER, CAROL M., mathematics professor; b. Ft. Smith, Ark., Oct. 08; d. Claude and Gwendolyn; m. Drew Warner. AA, U. Ark., Ft. Smith, 1990, BA in Math., 1992, MEd in Math. Edn., 1998; EdD in Higher Edn., U. Ark., Fayetteville, 2005. Cert. web instr. U. Ark. Ft. Smith. Asst. prof. U. Ark., Ft. Smith, 1994—2007. Instr. Vet. Upward Bound, Ft. Smith, 2006—. Mem. Jr. League of Ft. Smith, 1982—2007, Seb. County Rep. Com., Ft. Smith, 1982—2007; advisor Alpha Sigma Lambada, U. Ark. Named Cub Camp Namesake, U. Ark., 2006; recipient Master Tchr. award, 2006. Mem.: Am. Math. Soc., Math. Assn. Am., Golden Key, Phi Kappa Phi, Phi Beta Kappa. Office: Univ Ark 5210 Grand Ave Fort Smith AR 72913

WARNER, CARRIE, architectural engineer; b. 1973; m. Jonathan Sladek, 2006. MArch, U. Ill., Urbana-Champaign, 1998. Sr. project engr. Halvorson & Ptnrs., Chgo. Named one of 40 Under 40, Crain's Chgo. Bus., 2006. Office: Halvorson & Ptnrs Ste 650 600 W Chgo Ave Chicago IL 60610 Office Phone: 312-274-2400. Office Fax: 312-274-2401.

WARNER, CHARLES COLLINS, lawyer; b. Cambridge, Mass., June 19, 1942; s. Hoyt Landon and Charlotte (Collins) W.; m. Elizabeth Denny, Aug. 24, 1964; children: Peter, Andrew, Elizabeth. BA, Yale U., 1964; JD cum laude, Ohio State U., 1970. Bar: Ohio 1970. Assoc. Porter, Wright, Morris & Arthur and predecessor, Columbus, 1970-76, ptnr., 1976—, also mgr. labor and employment law dept., 1988-92. Pres. Peace Corps Svc. Coun., Columbus, 1974—76, Old Worthington (Ohio) Assn., 1976—78, Worthington Edn. Found., 1994—96, Opera Columbus, 1999—2001, Alliance for Quality Edn., Worthington, 1987—89; chmn. lawyers sect. United Way, Columbus, 1983—84; mem. alumni adv. coun. Ohio State U., 1998—2004; pres. Chamber Music Columbus, 2007—. Recipient Disting. Svc. award, Ohio State U., 2003, Cmty. Svc. award, Columbus Bar Assn., 2003. Fellow: Ohio Bar Found., Coll. Labor and Employment Lawyers, Am. Bar Found., Columbus Bar Found. (trustee 1996—, pres. 2007—); mem.: Ohio State U. Alumni Advisory Coun., Yale Club (pres. 1979—81), Lawyers Club, Capital Club, Nat. Coun. Ohio State U. Coll. Law (pres. 2002—04), Ohio State U. Law Alumni Assn. (pres. 1996—97, Disting. Svc. award 2003), FBA, Ohio Assn. Civil Trial Attys. (exec. bd. 1988—97, Frank Hurd Mem. of Yr. award 1998), Ohio Mgmt. Lawyers Assn. (chair 2004—06), Columbus Bar Assn. (bd. govs. 1982—93, pres. 1991—92, Cmty. Svc. award 2003), Ohio Met. Bar Assn. (pres. 1991—92), Ohio State Bar Assn. (chmn. fed. cts. com. 1992—94, coun. of dels. 1993—), ABA (exec. com. Met. Bar Caucus 1992—94, chmn. state and local bar ADR com. 1995—98, co-chair EEO com. 2000—02). Avocations: clarinet, singing, tennis. Home: 145 E South St Columbus OH 43085-4129 Office: Porter Wright Morris & Arthur 41 S High St Ste 2800 Columbus OH 43215-6194 Home Phone: 614-846-1160; Office Phone: 614-227-2013. E-mail: cwarner@porterwright.com.

WARNER, CHARLES DAVID, III, academic administrator; b. Hagerstown, Md., Feb. 2, 1957; s. Charles David Jr. and Ivy Ella Warner; m. Debra Jean Teter, May 25, 1985; children: Betsy, Molly, Charles. B in Music Edn., Shepherd Coll., 1980; M in Music Edn., Towson U., 1985; EdD, Va. Poly. Inst. and State U., 1999. Prof. music Hagerstown C.C., Md., 1989—2001, chair humanities divsn., 2000—03, dir. instrn., 2003—04; exec. dir. Univ. System Md., 2004—. Author: Opinions of Administrators, Faculty, and Students Regarding Academic Freedom and Student Artistic Expression, 2001. Mem. NEA, Phi Kappa Phi. Republican. Lutheran. Avocations: sailing, reading. Home: 17729 Bluebell Dr Hagerstown MD 21740 Office: Univ Sys Md Hagerstown Edn Ctr 32 W Wash St Hagerstown MD 21740 Office Phone: 240-527-2727. Office Fax: 240-527-2781. Business E-Mail: dwarner@hagerstown.usmd.edu. E-mail: d.warner@myactv.net.

WARNER, CHRISTOPHER HUGH, psychiatrist; b. Steubenville, Ohio, Apr. 2, 1974; s. William Norman and Diana Lynn Warner; m. Carolynn Marie Stocum, Mar. 3, 1997; children: Timothy Jordan children: Jacob Thomas, Aaron Christopher, Matthew Dylan. BS, U.S. Mil. Acad., West Point, NY., 1996; MD, Uniformed Svcs. U. of Health Sci., Bethesda, Md., 2000. Lic. physician Ind., 2000, diplomate Am. Bd. of Family Practice, 2005. Resident in family practice and psychiatry Walter Reed Army Hosp., Washington, 2000—05; chief resident NCC Family Practice-Psychiatry, Washington, 2003—05; divsn. psychiatry 3rd Inf. Divsn., Fort Stewart, Ga., 2005—. Maj. US Army, 1992—, Fort Stewart, GA. Decorated Bronze Star US Army; named Martin Fenton Nat. Resident of the Yr., Assn. of Medicine and Psychiatry, 2005, Resident Tchr. of the Yr., Soc. of Tchrs. of Family Medicine, 2005; recipient Award for Outstanding Leadership in Psychiatry, Assn. of Acad. Psychiatry, 2004, George Ginsberg Award for Accomplishment in Edn. and Tng. in Psychiatry, Am. Assn. of Dirs. of Psychiat. Residency Tng., 2004, Gen. Graves B. Erskine Award for Most Outstanding Resident, Walter Reed Army Med. Ctr., 2005, Al Glass Award for Outstanding Leadership in Mil. Psychiatry, 2005, Physician Recognition award, US Army Surgeon Gen., 2006. Mem.: Assn. for Acad. Psychiatry (assoc.), Am. Psychiat. Assn. (assoc.; regional chpt. jr. devel. officer 2005), Am. Acad. of Family Physicians (assoc.). Christian. Achievements include research in examining the ethics training of psychiatric residents; on eating disorders in military recruits; on depression in military recruits; on the characteristics and practices of FP/Psych trained individuals; on leadership development in medical residency training; psychological effects of combat exposure on soldiers. Home: 373 Steeple Chase Ln Richmond Hill GA 31324 Office: Division Mental Health Bldg 601E Fort Stewart GA 31314 Home Phone: 912-756-8304; Office Phone: 912-767-2620. Personal E-mail: christopher.h.warner@us.army.mil.

WARNER, DENNIS ALLAN, psychology professor; b. Idaho Falls, Idaho, Apr. 27, 1940; s. Perry and Marcia E. (Finlayson) W.; m. Charyl Ann DeHart, Dec. 12, 1962; children: Lisa Rae, Sara Michelle, David Perry, Matthew Arie. BS, Brigham Young U., 1964; MS with honors, U. Oreg., 1966, PhD, 1968. Asst. prof. edn. Wash. State U., Pullman, 1968-72, assoc. prof. edn., 1972-78, prof. edn., 1978-85, dir. tchr. edn., 1983-85, prof., chmn. ednl. counseling psychology, 1985-93, interim dir. Partnership Ctr., 1993—94, 2004—06, prof. edn. leadership and counseling psychology, 1994—, assoc. dean Coll. Edn., 1999—2005, exec. assoc. dean Coll. Edn., 2006—, dir. H.S. equivalency program, 2004—. Vis. asst. prof. psychology U. Idaho, Moscow, 1971. Author: Interpreting and Improving Student Test Performance, 1982; contbr. articles to profl. jours. Postdoctoral research assoc. U. Kans., 1976-77. Fellow: APA. Mem. Lds Ch. Home: 645 SW Mies St Pullman WA 99163-2057 Office: Wash State Univ Coll Edn Cleveland Hl Rm 160B Pullman WA 99164-2114 Office Phone: 509-335-1738. Business E-Mail: dawarner@wsu.edu.

WARNER, DON LEE, dean emeritus; b. Norfolk, NB, Jan. 4, 1934; s. Donald A. and Cleo V. (Slagel) W.; m. Patricia Ann Walker, Feb. 24, 1957; children: Mark J., Scott Lee. BS in Geol. Engring., Colo. Sch. Mines, 1956, MSc in Geol. Engring., 1961; PhD in Engring. Sci., U. Calif., Berkeley, 1964. Registered profl. engr., Mo., geologist, Mo., Miss., Tex. Geol. engr. Gulf Oil Corp., Casper, Wyo., 1956, Calif. Exploration Co., Guatemala, 1957-58; civil engr. U.S. Forest Svc., Gunnison, Colo., 1958-59; teaching asst. Colo. Sch. Mines, Golden, 1959-61; rsch. asst. U. Calif., Berkeley, 1962-64; rsch. geologist and engr. U.S. Pub. Health Svc., Cin., 1964-67; chief, earth scis. Ohio Basin Region Fed. Water Pollution Control Adminstrn., 1967-69; prof. geol. engring. U. Mo., Rolla, 1969-92, prof. emeritus geol. engring., 1992—, dean emeritus Sch. Mines and Metallurgy, 1992—, chmn., geol. engring., 1980-81, dean Sch. Mines and Metallurgy, 1981-93. Bd. dirs. Underground Injection Practices Coun., 1985-89; mem. adv. com. to Sec. of Interior for Mineral Resources Rsch., 1985-92; vice chmn. Mo.

Bd. Geologist Registration, 2006—. Author: Subsurface Wastewater Injection, 1977. Special award scholarship Colo. Sch. Mines, 1951-56, grad. fellowship Colo. Sch. Mines, 1959-51, rsch. fellowship U. Calif., 1962-64; recipient Best Paper award Am. Water Works Assn., 1971. Fellow Geol. Soc. Am.; mem. Am. Inst. Profl. Geologists (cert.), Am. Assn. Petroleum Geologists, Geol. Soc. Am., Nat. Ground Water Assn. (sci. award 1984, disting. lectr. 1986), Blue Key, Soc. Petroleum Engrs., Scabbard and Blade, Theta Tau, Tau Beta Pi. Avocations: fishing, boating, tennis, golf. Office: Univ Mo Sch Materials Energy and Earth Resources 1870 Miner Cir Rolla MO 65409-0001 Personal E-mail: dlw@fidmail.com.

WARNER, H. TY, entrepreneur, manufacturing executive; b. Chgo., Sept. 3, 1944; s. Harold and Georgia Warner. Student, Kalamazoo Coll. Salesman Dakin Toys, Applause Inc., San Francisco; founder, owner, pres. Ty Inc., Westmont, Ill., 1985—; owner Four Seasons, NYC, 1999—, San Ysidro Ranch, 1999—, Four Seasons Biltmore, 2000—, Sandpiper Golf Course, 2003—. Founder Ty Warner Park, Ty Warner Sea Ctr. Named one of Forbes' Richest Americans, 1999—, World's Richest People, Forbes Mag., 2001—. Achievements include invention of Beanie Babies. Office: Ty Inc 280 Chestnut Ave Westmont IL 60559 *

WARNER, HAROLD CLAY, JR., banker, investment company executive; b. Knoxville, Tenn., Feb. 24, 1939; s. Harold Clay and Mary Frances (Waters) W.; m. Patricia Alice Rethorst, Sept. 1, 1961; children: Martha Lee, Carol Frances. BS in Econs, U. Tenn., 1961, PhD, 1965. Asst. to pres. First Fed. Savs., Savannah, Ga., 1965-67; v.p. and economist No. Trust Co., Chgo., 1967-73; sr. v.p. and chief economist Crocker Nat. Bank, San Francisco, 1974-79, sr. v.p. liability mgmt., 1979-82; exec. v.p., dir. fixed income mgmt. BA Investment Mgmt. Corp., 1982-84, dir., pres., COO, 1984-86; dir., pres. Montgomery St. Income Securities, Inc., 1984-86; sr. v.p. Bank of Am., San Francisco, 1982-86; chmn. BA Investment Mgmt. Internat., Ltd., 1985-86; pres. Arthur D. Gimbel, Inc., San Mateo, Calif., 1986-87; exec. v.p., chief investment officer Riggs Nat. Bank Washington, 1987-88; chmn. Riggs Investment Mgmt. Corp., 1988-89; sr. v.p., chief economist Bank of Calif., San Francisco, 1989-93; pres., chief investment officer MERUS Capital Mgmt., San Francisco, 1989-93; pres. Govett Asset Mgmt. Co., 1993-95, Govett Fin. Svcs. Ltd., 1993-95; pres., COO Fisher Investments, Inc., Woodside, Calif., 1996; pres. Warner Fiduciary Counsel, LLC, San Francisco, 1997; 1st v.p., sr. dir. portfolio mgmt. Mellon Pvt. Wealth Mgmt., San Francisco, 1998—2007; sr. portfolio mgr., economist Mt. Eden Investment Advisors, San Francisco, 2007—. Lectr. dept. econs. U. Tenn., 1962-63, Grad. Sch. Bus., Loyola U., Chgo., 1969-73; lectr. Pacific Coast Banking Sch., U. Wash., 1978-79; bd. dirs. Children's Hosp. and Rsch. Ctr., 2007—. NDEA fellow, 1961-64 Mem. Burlingame Country Club, Pacific-Union Club, Phi Gamma Delta, Phi Eta Sigma, Beta Gamma Sigma, Omicron Delta Kappa, Phi Kappa Phi. Home: PO Box 2449 Yountville CA 94599-2449 Office: 2 Embarcadero Ctr Ste 1320 San Francisco CA 94111 Home Phone: 650-347-7809; Office Phone: 415-288-3018. Business E-Mail: hcwarner@mtedeninvest.com.

WARNER, ISIAH MANUEL, chemistry professor; b. DeQuincy, La., July 20, 1946; s. Humphrey and Irma (St. Romain) W.; m. Della Blount, June 1, 1968; children: Isiah Jr., Chideha, Edward. BS chemistry, Southern Univ., 1968; PhD, Univ. Wash., 1977. Teaching asst. Univ. Wash., Seattle, 1973-75, rsch. asst., 1975-77; asst. prof. Tex. A&M Univ., College Station, Tex., 1977-82; assoc. prof. Emory Univ., Atlanta, 1982-86, prof., 1986, 1987-92; Philip W. West prof., analytical and environ. chem. La. State Univ., Baton Rouge, 1992—, chair, dept. chem., 1994—97, Boyd prof., chem., 2000—, vice chancellor, strategic initiatives, 2001—. Cons. Nat. Sci. Found., 1980—, Coca Cola, Atlanta, 1984-92, Nat. Insts. Health, Bethesda, Md., 1979—, Eli Lilly & Co., Indpls., 1988, 89; rsch. prof., Howard Hughes Med. Inst., 2002-. Contbr. articles to profl. jours. Recipient Charles Holmes Herty award, 1992, Benedetti Pichler award, 1994, NY SAS Gold medal, 1991, Presdl. Young Investigator award, 1984, Outstanding Tchr. award, 1993, AAAS Lifetime Mentor award, Banneker Legacy award, 2006; grantee, Howard Hughes Med. Inst., 2002; Fulbright fellow for rsch., tchg. in Kenya. Mem.: Internat. Chemometrics Soc. (N.Am. chpt.), Soc. Applied Spectroscopy, Nat. Orgn. Black Chemists and Chem. Engrs., Am. Chem. Soc. (So. Chemist award 2006, award for encouraging disadvantaged students into the scis. 2003), Sigma Xi. Avocations: racquetball, chess, cards. Office: La State Univ Dept Chemistry Baton Rouge LA 70803-0001 Office Phone: 225-578-2829. Office Fax: 225-578-3971. Business E-Mail: iwarner@lsu.edu.

WARNER, JOHN ARNAN, state supreme court justice; b. Great Falls, Mont., Jan. 22, 1943; s. James Arnan and Cleo (Schaedler) W.; m. Katherine Warner; children: Matthew, Marion, Ann, Jeffrey, Jonathan, Katherine. BA, U. Mont., 1965, LLB, 1967. Bar: Mont. 1967, U.S. Dist. Ct. Mont. 1967, U.S. Ct. Appeals (9th cir.) 1982. Law clk. Mont. Supreme Ct., Helena, Mont., 1967-68; ptnr. Bosch, Kuhr, et al, Havre, Mont., 1968-88; atty. City of Havre, 1984-88; dist. judge 12th Judicial Dist., Mont., 1988—2003; justice Mont. Supreme Ct., 2003—. Former chmn. Supreme Ct. Sentence Review Div.; former mem. Dist. Ct. Council; former chmn. Mont. Jud. Standards Commn.; mem. teaching staff Commn. on Cts. of Limited Jurisdiction; mem. Supreme Ct. Commn. to Review Canons of Jud. Ethics. Past pres. Mont. Swimming, Inc.; past chmn. Hill Top Recovery Bd.; past bd. dirs Mont. AAU; del. Mont. Officials Assn. Mem. ABA, Mont. Bar Assn. (trustee 1980-88, pres. 1987-88, mem. jud. relations com.), 12th Judicial Dist. Bar Assn. (past pres.), Def. Rsch. Inst., Lions (past pres. Havre chpt. swim team). Roman Catholic. Avocations: fishing, hunting, hiking. Office: Mont Supreme Ct Justice Bldg PO Box 203003 Helena MT 59620-3003 Office Phone: 406-444-5494. Business E-Mail: jwarner@mt.gov.

WARNER, JOHN EDWARD, advertising executive; b. Troy, NY, Mar. 26, 1936; s. George Edward and Ann Frances (Teson) W.; m. Anne Elizabeth Hibbard, Sept. 19, 1959; children: Matthew J., Barbara A., Peter J., Christopher J. BS in Chemistry and Philosophy, Coll. Holy Cross, 1957. Promotion mgr. Union Carbide Corp., NYC, 1957-62; acct. exec. McCann-Erickson, Inc., NYC, 1962-64; pres. Warner, Bicking & Fenwick, Inc., NYC, 1964-84; chmn. Warner, Bicking, Morris & Ptnrs. Inc., 1984-97; pres. Transworld Advt. Agy. Network, 1987-97, Quatrefoil, Inc., 1998—. Bd. dirs. Thomas Pub. Co., N.Y.C. Author: (non-fiction) Decorating Time Savers by Jack Warner, 2001, (fiction) Tom Never's Ghost, 2006. Home: 706 Hillcrest Rd Ridgewood NJ 07450-1110 E-mail: jawarner@optonline.net.

WARNER, JOHN HILLIARD, JR., technical services company executive; b. Santa Monica, Calif., Mar. 2, 1941; s. John Hilliard and Irene Anne (Oliva) W.; m. Helga Magdalena Farrington, Sept. 4, 1961; children: Tania Renee, James Michael BS in Engring. with honors, UCLA, 1963, MS in Engring., 1965, PhD in Engring., 1967. Mem. staff Marquardt Corp., Van Nuys, Calif., 1963; mem. faculty West Coast U., LA, 1969-72; mem. staff TRW Sys. Group, Redondo Beach, Calif., 1967-70, sect. mgr., 1970-73; mem. staff Sci. Applications Internat. Corp., San Diego, 1973-75, asst. v.p., 1975-77, v.p., 1977-80, corp. v.p., 1980-81, sr. v.p., 1981-87, sector v.p., 1987-89, exec. v.p., 1989-96, bd. dirs., 1988—2006, corp. exec. v.p., 1996—2005, chief adminstrv. officer, 2003—06, exec. v.p., 2005—07. Cons. Rand Corp., Santa Monica, 1964—66; bd. dirs. AMSEC LLC, Mimix Broadband. Contbr. articles to profl. jours. Trustee Scripps Health, 2001-06; bd. dirs. Corp. Dirs. Forum, 2001—. AEC fellow, 1963, 66, NSF fellow, 1964, 65. Mem. AIAA, NDIA, Nat. Assn. Corp. Dirs., Healthcare Info. and Mgmt. Sys. Soc., Assn. US Army, Air Force Assn., Armed Forces Comm. and Electronics Assn., Navy League US, La Jolla Chamber Music Soc. (bd. dirs. 1990-97, adv. bd. 1998-2001), San Diego C. of C. (bd. dirs. 2000-04, 07), Calif. C. of C. (bd. dirs. 2000—07), Calif. Bus. Roundtable, Sigma Nu, Tau Beta Pi. Methodist. Avocations: bicycling, golf, fishing, music. Office: SAIC 10260 Campus Point Dr San Diego CA 92121-1522

WARNER, JOHN WILLIAM, senator; b. Washington, Feb. 18, 1927; s. John William and Martha Stuart (Budd) W.; m. Catherine Conover Mellon, Aug. 7, 1957 (div. 1973) children: Mary Conover, Virginia Stuart, John William IV.; m. Elizabeth Taylor, Dec. 4, 1976 (div. Nov. 7, 1982); m. Jeanne Vander Myde, Dec. 15, 2003 BS Engring., Washington and Lee U., 1949; LL.B., U. Va., 1953. Law clk. to Hon. E. Barrett Prettyman US Ct. Appeals (DC cir.), 1953-54; spl. asst. to U.S. atty. US Dept. Justice, 1956-57, asst. U.S. atty., 1957-60; ptnr. Hogan & Hartson, 1960-68; owner, operator Atoka Cattle Farm, 1961—94; under sec. Dept. Navy, US Dept. Def., Washington, 1969-72, sec., 1972-74; adminstr. Am. Revolution Bicentennial Adminstrn., 1974-76; US Senator from Va., 1979—. Chmn. armed services com.; mem. com. on homeland security & govtl. affairs, environment and pub. works com., rules and adminstrn. com., nat. Rep. senatorial com.; rep. to sec. def., Law of the Sea Talks, 1969-73, prin. US negotiator & signatory, Incidents at Sea Exec. Agreement, 1970-72, exec. branch rep., Am. Revolution BiCentennial Adminstrn., 1974-76, US del. to 12th Spl. Session of UN Gen. Assembly, 1982, observer, Geneva Arms Control Talks, 1985 Served with USNR, 1944-46; USMC, 1951-52; USMCR, 1952-64. Recipient Edmund S. Muskie Disting. Pub. Svc. award, Ctr. for Nat. Policy, 1999, Harry S. Truman award, Nat. Guard Assn. of the US, 2000, James Forrestal Meml. award, Nat. Def. Industrial Assn., 2000, Wings of Liberty award, Aerospace Industries Assn., 2001, VFW Congl. award, VFW, 2001, Arthur T. Marix Congl. Leadership award, The Retired Officer Assn., 2001, Leadership award, Pvt. Sector Coun., 2003, Spirit of Hope award, United Svc. Organizations, 2003, Congl. Am. Spirit Medallion, Nat. D-Day Mus., 2004. Mem. DC Bar Assn., Am. Legion, Veterans Fgn. Wars (Va. chpt.) Republican. Episcopalian. Office: US Senate 225 Russell Senate Bldg Washington DC 20510-0001 also: Federal Bldg Rm 235 180 West Main St Abingdon VA 24210-2844 Office Phone: 202-224-2023, 276-628-8158. Office Fax: 202-224-6295, 276-628-1036. *

WARNER, KARL K., former prosecutor; b. 1952; BS, U.S. Mil. Acad.; JD, W.Va. U. Gen. counsel to 10th Mountain Div. U.S. Army, 1994—96; legal counsel to Multi-Nat. Force Joint Chiefs of Staff, Haiti, 1994—95, legal counsel to two chmn., joint chiefs staff, 1996—98; gen. counsel U.S. Spl. Ops. Command, 1998—2001; U.S. atty. (So. dist.) W.Va. U.S. Dept. Justice, 2001—05.

WARNER, KENNETH E(DGAR), dean, public health educator, consultant; b. Washington, Jan. 25, 1947; s. Edgar W. Jr. and Betty (Strasburger) W.; m. Patricia A. Hilty, Oct. 1, 1977; children— Peter, Andrew AB, Dartmouth Coll., 1968; MPhil, Yale U., 1970, PhD, 1974. Lectr. dept. health mgmt. and policy Sch. Pub. Health, U. Mich., Ann Arbor, Mich., 1972—74, asst. prof., 1974—77, assoc. prof., 1977—83, prof., 1983—, chmn., 1982—88, 1992—95, Richard D. Remington Collegiate prof. pub. health, 1995—2001, dir. Tobacco Rsch. Network, Avedis Donabedian Disting. Univ. prof. pub. health, 2001—, dean, 2005—. Cons., Washington, 1976—95, Office on Smoking and Health, USPHS, Rockville, Md., 1978—, Inst. Medicine, Nat. Acad. Scis., Washington, 1984—, numerous additional pub. and pvt. orgns.; mem. bd. sci. counselors divsn. cancer prevention and control Nat. Cancer Inst., Bethesda, Md., 1985—89. Author: (with Bryan Luce) Cost-Benefit & Cost Effectiveness Analysis in Health Care, 1982; contbr. articles to profl. jours. Trustee Am. Lung Assn., Mich., Lansing, 1982; mem. subcom. on smoking Am. Heart Assn., Dallas, 1983-87; mem. com. on tobacco and cancer Am. Cancer Soc., N.Y.C., 1984-92; bd. dirs. Am. Legacy Found., 1999-2003. Hon. Woodrow Wilson fellow, 1968; W.K. Kellog Found. fellow, 1980-83; vis. scholar Nat. Bur. Econ. Research, Stanford, Calif., 1975-76; recipient Surgeon Gen.'s medallion Dr. C. Everett Koop, 1989. Fellow Assn. Health Svcs. Rsch.; mem. APHA (leadership award 1990), Inst. Medicine, Phi Beta Kappa. Office: U Mich Dept Health Sch Pub Health 109 Observatory St Ann Arbor MI 48109-2029 Office Phone: 734-763-5454. Business E-Mail: kwarner@umich.edu.

WARNER, KENNETH WILSON, JR., editor, publishing executive; b. Chgo., Dec. 22, 1928; s. Kenneth Wilson and Ann S. (Knapp) W.; m. Deborah Ann Bollo, Dec. 28, 1982 (div. Apr. 1995); 1 child, Joseph; children by previous marriages: Sara, Seth, Katharin. BS Ed., No. Ill. State Teachers Coll., 1950. Staff editor Bldg. Supply News, Chgo., 1953-56; staff editor Elec. Merchandising, 1956-60; free-lance writer Sarasota, Fla., 1960-66; editor Gunsport Mag., Alexandria and Falls Church, Va., 1966-67, Gunfacts Mag., Arlington, Va., 1968-70, pub., 1968-70; exec. editor Am. Rifleman, Nat. Rifle Assn., Washington, 1971-78, asst. dir. publs. div., 1972-78; editor Am. Hunter, 1973-78, Am. Rifleman, 1976-78; dir. publs. NRA, Washington, 1977-78; editor in chief Gun Digest, Knives Annual-Krause Publs., Inc., Greenville, W.Va., 1979-99; editor, pub. Knives Digest Two Knife Guys Pub., Inc., Chattanooga, 2000—01; pres. Knifeware, Inc., Greenville, W.Va. Cons. firearms and cutlery cos.; co-founder Am. Knife and Tool Inst., 1997. Author: The Practical Book of Knives. 1976; The Practical Book of Guns, 1978. Editor: The Bolt Action, 1976. Contbr. articles to profl. jours. Cpl. U.S. Army. 1951-53. Recipient Cutlery Hall of Fame; inducted into Am. Bladesmith Soc. Hall of Fame, 1999. Mem.: NRA (life), Knifemaker's Guild Am. (assoc.). Office: Prin Office PO Box 52 Greenville WV 24945-0052 Office Phone: 304-832-6878. Personal E-mail: info@knifeware.com.

WARNER, KERSTIN JULIANNA, gifted and talented educator; d. Kerstin and John Warner; m. Louis Weinberg, June 23, 1995 (separated); 1 child, Sofia Weinberg. BS in Fine Art, Vassar Coll., Poughkeepsie, NY, 1986; MS in Spl. Edn., Bank St. Coll. Edn., 1994. Cert. tchr. K-8, spl. edn. 1-12, art 1-12 Conn., tchr. elem. K-6, art 1-12, spl. edn. 1 - 12 NY. Asst. tchr. St. Anne's Sch., Bklyn., 1987—90; tchr. spl. edn. preschool The League Sch., Bklyn., 1990—92; 2d grade tchr. Berkeley Carroll Sch., Bklyn., 1992—95; tchr. gifted St. Paul Pub. Schs., 1995—99, Bedford Mid. Sch., Westport, Conn., 1999—. Coach mock trial team Bedford Mid. Sch., Westport, 2002—; book discussion trainer Westport Pub. Libr., 2001—; Conn. chair Nicholas Green award, 2005—. Pres. Vassar Club of Fairfield County, Westport, Conn., 2002—. Recipient Golden Apple Achiever award, Ashland, 1998; Inter-district Archaeology Program, Conn. Assn. for the Gifted, 2004—05. Mem.: ASCD, Nat. Assn. for Gifted Children (Conn. chair Nicholas Green award selection 2006—), Conn. Assn. for the Gifted, Nat. Coun. Tchrs. Math., Vassar Club (pres. 2002—). Democrat. Avocations: creative writing, drawing, international travel. Office: Bedford Middle School 88 North Ave Westport CT 06880 Home Phone: 203-256-8909; Office Phone: 203-341-1582. Business E-Mail: kerstin_warner@westport.k12.ct.us.

WARNER, KURT(IS), professional football player; b. Burlington, Iowa, June 22, 1971; m. Brenda Warner; 4 children. BA in Comm., No. Ill. U. Quarterback Iowa Barnstormers (Arena Football League), 1995—97, Amsterdam Admirals (NFL Europe), 1998, St. Louis Rams (NFL), 1998—2004, N.Y. Giants, East Rutherford, NJ, 2004—05, Arizona Cardinals, 2005—. Founder First Things First Found., 1999—. Named NFL MVP, 1999, 2001, Super Bowl XXXIV MVP, 2000; named to, NFL Pro-Bowl, 1999—2001. Achievements include led NFL in passing touchdowns, 1999, 2001, passing yards, completions, 2001; quarterback Super Bowl Championship Team, Super Bowl XXXIV, 2000; tied the NFL record with six consecutive 300-yard passing games during 2000-01 season; set record for highest rated passer in NFL history, 2002; holds Super Bowl record with 414 passing yards; only player in NFL history to record perfect passer rating of 158.3 twice in his career. Office: 8701 S Hardy Dr Tempe AZ 85284

WARNER, MALCOLM JOHN, curator; b. Aldershot, England, May 17, 1953; arrived in US, 1988; s. Ronald Henry and Vera Eileen Warner; m. Sara Enne Ryan, Aug. 6, 1988; children: Madeline Rose, Charles Godfrey. BA with honors, U. London, 74; PhD, U. London, 1985. Rsch. curator dept. European painting Art Inst. Chgo., 1988—90; curator prints and drawings San Diego Mus. Art, 1990—92, curator European art, 1992—96; curator paintings Yale Ctr. Brit. Art, New Haven, 1996—99, 1999—2001; sr. curator Kimbell Art Mus., Ft. Worth, 2001—; Assoc. editor Oxford Dictionary Nat. Biography, Oxford U. Press, England, 1997—2001; vis. asst. prof. U. Manchester, 1984—85. Author: Portrait Painting, 1979, Tissot, 1982; co-author (with Michael Jacobs): The Phaidon Companion to Art and Artists in the British Isles, 1980; co-author: (with Susan Wise) French and British Paintings from 1600 to 1800 in the Art Institute of Chicago. A Catalogue of the Collection, 1996; co-editor (with Mary Lutyens): Rainy Days at Brig o 'Turk. The Highland Sketchbooks of John Everett Millais, 18531, 1983, author numerous exhbn. catalogs; contbr. articles, essays to profl. publs. Mem.: Assn. Art Mus. Curators, Print. Coun. Am., River Crest Country Club. Avocation: guitar. Office: Kimbell Art Mus 333 Bowie Blvd Fort Worth TX 76107

WARNER, MINER HILL, investment banker; b. NYC, Aug. 13, 1942; s. Bradford Arnold and Nancy (Hill) W.; m. Ellen C. Murphy, Mar. 18, 1972; children— Alix Mallet-Prevost, Lily Wolcott. AB, Harvard U., 1964; C.E.P., Institut d'Etudes Politiques, Paris, 1963; M.Sc. in Econs., London Sch. Econs., 1965; LL.B., U. Pa., 1968; postgrad., NYU. Grad. Sch. Bus. Adminstrn., 1971-73. Bar: N.Y. 1969. Assoc. Shearman & Sterling, NYC, 1968-71; assoc. Salomon Bros. Inc., NYC, 1971-73; v.p. Salomon Bros. Internat. Ltd., London, 1974-78; v.p., mgr. Salomon Bros. Inc., NYC, 1979-87; dir. Merrill Lynch & Co., NYC, 1988-92; pres. Pub. Resources Internat., NYC, 1992-95, chmn., 1996—. Adv. dir. Coun. of the Americas, 1991-93. Mem. Pres.'s Pvt. Sector Survey on Cost Control, Washington, 1982-83; mem. coun. Grad. Theol. Union, Berkeley, Calif., 1998-; vestryman St. John's Ch., Fishers Island, N.Y., 1980-99, sr. warden, 1994-99; regent Cathedral of St. John the Divine, N.Y., 1995-97, trustee, 1997—, mem. exec. com.; English-Speaking Union U.S. bd. dirs., mem. exec. com., 2002-06, mem. task force Gen. Theol. Sem., N.Y., 2000-02; pres. Pilgrims of US; trustee N.Y. Hist. Soc., 1985—, chmn. 1994-99, chmn. emeritus, 1999—; trustee Hispanic Soc. Am., 2005-. Decorated Order of St. John of Jerusalem. Mem. Pub. Securities Assn. (guaranteed loan com. 1980-86), Mayflower Soc. (former gov.), Brook Club (v.p.), River Club, Links Club, Met. Club (Washington), Fishers Island Club, Hay Harbor Club (Fishers Island) (former dir.), Econ. Club N.Y. Republican. Episcopalian. Home: 148 E End Ave New York NY 10028-7503 Office: Pub Resources Internat 780 3d Ave Ste 2805 New York NY 10017-2024

WARNER, PATRICIA ANN, secondary school educator; b. Wooster, Ohio, Dec. 21, 1949; d. Kent Branson and Irene Mae (Graves) W. BA in English, Coll. of Wooster, Ohio, 1972, MAT in English, 1973. Cert. tchr., Ohio; nat. bd. cert. tchr. adolescence and young adulthood English lang. arts. Instr. in English Orrville H.S., Ohio, 1974—, Wayne Col., Orrville, Ohio, 1988-91. Named Orrville City Schs. Tchr. of Yr., 1987-88, Jennings Scholar Jennings Found., 1994-95. Mem. NEA, NCTE, Ohio Coun. Tchrs. English and Language Arts, Coun. English Leadership. Office: Orrville HS 841 N Ella St Orrville OH 44667-1154 Office Phone: 330-682-4661.

WARNER, PAUL L., lawyer; b. Washington, Aug. 16, 1947; AB magna cum laude, U. Calif., Riverside, 1969; JD magna cum laude, Harvard U., 1972. Bar: Calif. 1972, US Ct. Appeals (9th cir.), US Dist. Ct. (ctrl. dist.) Fla., US Dist. Ct. (no. and ctrl. dists.) Calif., Calif. State Cts., Calif. Supreme Ct. Law clk. to Hon. Charles M. Merrill US Ct. Appeals (9th cir.), 1972-73; atty. Jeffer, Mangels, Butler & Marmaro, San Francisco; ptnr. Jeffer Mangels Butler & Marmaro, San Francisco. Judge pro tem San Francisco Superior Ct. Contbr. Mem. Bar Assn. San Francisco (mem. law firm econs. sect.), LA County Bar Assn., Phi Beta Kappa. Office: Jeffer Mangels Butler & Marmaro 2 Embarcadero Center 5th Fl San Francisco CA 94111 Office Phone: 415-398-8080. Office Fax: 800-808-5071. Business E-Mail: pwarner@jmbm.com.

WARNER, PAUL MICHAEL, federal judge, former prosecutor; b. 1952; BA, Brigham Young U., 1973, JD, 1976, MPA, 1984. Atty. judge advocate general's corps USN, 1976—82; asst. atty. gen. State of Utah, Salt Lake City, 1982—83; asst. US atty. Dist. Utah US Dept. Justice, Salt Lake City, 1983—96, US atty., 1996—2006; magistrate judge US Dist. Ct., Salt Lake City, 2006—. With USNR, 1976—82, advanced through ranks to col. Nat. Guard, 1983—, Utah. Office: US Dist Ct 350 S Main St Salt Lake City UT 84101 *

WARNER, PETER DAVID, publishing executive; b. Phila., Aug. 15, 1942; s. Robert and Myra (Spector) W.; m. Ruth Bluestein (div. 1982); m. Jill Sansone, 1983; children: Emily, Cynthia, Nicholas. BA, NYU, 1964. Asst. dir. membership and devel. Mus. Modern Art, NYC, 1973-76; editor, promotion dir. Book-of-the-Month Club, NYC, 1976-79; pres. Thames and Hudson, NYC, 1979—. Author: Loose Ends, 1972, Lifestyle, 1986. Mem. The Writers Room (bd. dirs.), The Century Assn. Office: Thames & Hudson Inc 500 5th Ave New York NY 10110-0002

WARNER, ROBERTA ARLENE, retired accountant, financial services executive; b. Binghamton, NY, Dec. 31, 1938; d. Murrilan Earl and Ethel Margaret (Bell) W. BA, SUNY, Binghamton, 1960; MBA, Ind. U., 1962, MHA with highest distinction, 1973. CPA, N.Y.; lic. nursing home adminstr., N.Y. Sr. acct. Arthur Young & Co., CPA, Buffalo, 1962—66; acctg. supr. Children's Hosp., Buffalo, 1966—68; contr. King Manor Nursing Homes-Ave. Bldg. Corp., Buffalo, 1968—71; asst. dir. health fin. Hosp. Assn. N.Y. State, Albany, 1973—80, dir. health fin., 1980—93, Healthcare Assn. N.Y. State, Albany, 1994—97, dir. data analysis and stds., 1997—98; pres. Roberta A. Warner Co., 1999—2003, ret., 2003. Author articles in field. Trustee Ednl. Found. of Am. Women's Soc. CPA, Am. Soc. Women Accts., 1985-87. Fellow Healthcare Fin. Mgmt. Assn.; mem. AICPA, Am. Acctg. Assn., Am. Soc. Women Accts. (pres. Buffalo chpt. 1967-68), Am. Women's Soc. CPA, N.Y. State Soc. CPA, Ind. U. Alumni Assn. (life), SUNY Binghamton Alumni Assn. (life), Grange. Methodist. Home: 569 NY Rte 79 Windsor NY 13865-2714

WARNER, ROLLIN MILES, JR., economics educator, real estate broker; b. Evanston, Ill., Dec. 25, 1930; s. Rollin Miles Warner Sr. and Julia Herndon (Polk) Clarkson BA, Yale U., 1953; cert. in law, Harvard U., 1956; MBA, Stanford U., 1960; cert. in edn. adminstrn., U. San Francisco, 1974; cert., Coll. Fin. Planning, 1977. Lic. real estate broker Real Estate Cert. Inst., Calif. Asst. to v.p. fin. Stanford U., 1960—63; instr. history Town Sch., San Francisco, 1963—70, instr. econs. and history, dean, 1975—; prin. Mt. Tamalpais, Ross, Calif., 1972—74; dir. devel. Katharine Branson Sch., Ross, 1974—75. Author: America, 1986, Europe, 1986, Africa, Asia, Russia, 1986, Greece, Rome, 1981, Free Enterprise at Work, 1986 From scoutmaster to summer camp commr. Boy Scouts Am., San Francisco, 1956—. Served to lt. USNR, 1953—55, Korea, Pacific, Vietnam. Recipient Silver Beaver award Boy Scouts Am., 1986, medal Town Sch. for Boys Alumni Coun., 1995. Mem.: U.S. Naval Inst., Marines Meml. Assn., South End Rowing Club (San Francisco), San Francisco Yacht Club (Belvedere, Calif.), Grolier Club NY. Office: Town Sch 2750 Jackson St San Francisco CA 94115-1195 E-mail: warnerrollinm1960@alumni-gsb.stanford.edu.

WARNER, SALLY SLADE, musician; b. Worcester, Mass., Sept. 6, 1932; d. Harold Stephen and Anna Mae (Snow) Slade. Diploma, Royal Carillon Sch., Mechelen, Belgium, 1979. Record libr. music dept. Phillips Acad.,

Andover, Mass., 1974—. Composer: Passacaglia on E-A-C, 1979, Variations on Die Alder Soeste Jesus, 1979. Organist, dir. music Ch. St. John the Evangelist, Boston, 1960—85; carillonneur St. Stephen's Episcopal Ch., Cohasset, Mass., 1985—. Recipient Berkeley medal, U. Calif., Berkeley, 1988. Mem.: Soc. Companions of Holy Cross, Am. Guild Organists (ChM 1963, AA 1964), Guild Carillonneurs N.Am. Home: 7 Crescent Dr Andover MA 01810

WARNER, SCOTT DENNIS, investment banker; b. York, Pa., July 13, 1963; s. Earl Dennis and Sandra Glee (Barnhart) W. SB in Elec. Engring., MIT, 1986, SB in Computer Sci. and Engring., 1986, SM in Elec. Engring. and Computer Sci., 1986; MBA in Fin., U. Chgo., 1990. Intern IBM Corp., Yorktown Heights, NY, 1983-86; fin. analyst Merrill Lynch & Co., NYC, 1986-88, assoc., 1990-94, v.p., 1994-95; assoc. Goldman, Sachs & Co., NYC, 1989; v.p. Lipper & Co., L.P., NYC, 1995-98, Gerard Klauer Mattison & Co., Inc., NYC, 1998—2002; sr. cons. avantage Capita Ltd., London, 2006—. Pres. Internat. Capital LLC, Luxembourg, 2003—05, Warner Capital S.E.C.S., Luxembourg, 2003—05. Nat. Merit scholar, 1981, ROTC scholar, 1981, teaching asst. scholar MIT, 1985, 86; Leon C. Marshall scholar U. Chgo., 1988. Mem. Nat. Eagle Scout Assn., Delta Upsilon Frat. Republican. Presbyterian. Office: 17 Cranley Mews London SW7 3BX England Personal E-mail: scottdwarner@yahoo.com.

WARNER, TEDDY FLEMING, lawyer; b. Findlay, Ohio, Jan. 3, 1932; s. Freeman Dininger and Marjorie (Fleming) Warner; m. Carolyn Jean Warner, June 12, 1958; children: Wendy Ann, Randall Scott. AA, Phoenix Coll., 1955; BA with distinction, Ariz. State U., 1956; JD, U. Ariz., 1959. Bar: Ariz. 1959, U.S. Dist. Ct. Ariz. 1959, U.S. Supreme Ct. 1971. Prin. Warner Angle Roper Hallam Jackson & Formanek, Phoenix, 1962—82; sr. ptnr., pres. Warner Angle Roper & Hallam PC and predecessors, Phoenix, 1982—. Com. on fitness and character Ariz. Supreme Ct., 1983—90, spl. com. legal aid and indigent defendants, ho. resolutions com., 1992—; bd. vis. Ariz. State U. Sch. Law, Ariz., 1979; lectr. in field. Bd. dirs. Phoenix and Valley of Sun YMCA, 1970—84, pres., 1977; bd. dirs. Sagauro-Grand Canyon chpt. March of Dimes, 1968—82, chmn., 1972—73, state chmn., 1974—82, nat. council chpt. vols., 1979—82; bd. dirs. Vol. Bur., 1975; active Fiesta Bowl Com., 1979—84; chmn. bd. trustees Ariz. Perinatal Trust, 1980—; active Ariz. Acad. With USAF, 1951—54. Fellow: Ariz. Bar Found. (Pro Bono Svc. award 1987), Am. Bar Found. (founding); mem.: ABA (ho. of dels. 1981—91, assembly del. 1992—), Law Coll. Assn. U. Ariz., Ariz. State Law Soc., State Bar Ariz. (chmn. com. on del. legal svcs. com.), Maricopa County Bar Found. (charter), Maricopa County Bar Assn. (pres., bd. dirs. 1981), Pinetop Country Club, Ariz. Country Club (sec., bd. dirs. 1971—73), Delta Sigma Phi, Phi Delta Phi. Republican. Office: Ste 1500 3550 N Central Ave Phoenix AZ 85012-2112

WARNER, WILLIAM HAMER, mathematician; b. Pitts., Oct. 6, 1929; s. John Christian and Louise (Hamer) W.; m. Janet Louise West, June 29, 1957; 1 dau., Katherine Patricia. Student, Haverford Coll., 1946-48; BS, Carnegie Inst. Tech., 1950, MS, 1951, PhD, 1953. Research asso. grad. div. applied math. Brown U., Providence, 1953-55; asst. prof. dept. aerospace engring. and mechanics U. Minn., Mpls., 1955-58, asso. prof., 1958-68, prof., 1968-95, prof. emeritus, 1995—. Author: (with L.E. Goodman) Statics, 1963, Dynamics, 1964; contbr. articles to profl. jours. Mem.: Soc. Natural Philosophy, Math. Assn. Am., Soc. Indsl. and Applied Math., Am. Math. Soc. E-mail: warner@aem.umn.edu.

WARNER, WILLIAM KENT, JR., religious organization administrator, consultant; b. Chgo., June 14, 1933; children: William Kent III, Robert David, Steven Bradley. BA in Biblical studies, Wheaton Coll., Ill., 1953; MA summa cum laude, Columbia Internat. U., SC, 1954; MS, U. Ill., Urbana, 1960; PhD, U. Iowa, Iowa City, 1972. Ordained Evang. Free Ch. Am., 1954. Missionary, tchr. and prin. Tchg. Tng. Inst., Zimbabwe, 1955—59; founder, dir. publ. house, 1961—67; founder, exec. dir. Christian Coll. So. Africa, Wheaton, Ill., 1969—. Prin. Tchg. Tng. Inst., Zimbabwe, 1959; founder, pub. Pub. House, Harare, 1961—67; founder, exec. dir. CCOSA, 1969—. Avocations: writing, speaking, table tennis. Office: CCOSA c/o M Mahoney CPA/MBA 416 E Roosevelt Rd Ste 110 Wheaton IL 60187 Business E-Mail: drwkwarner@hotmail.com.

WARNICK, HOWARD JAMES, retired church musician, educator; b. Frankenmuth, Mich., Mar. 23, 1935; s. Martin Frederick and Maybelle Ruth Warnick; m. Harriet Helen Lange, July 17, 1960; children: Laura, Julie, Paul. BS, Concordia Tchrs. Coll., River Forest, Ill., 1960, MA, 1965. Cert. tchr. Mich. Dept. Edn., 1973. Tchr., musician Messiah Luth. Ch., Chgo., 1960—69, interim prin., 1963—64; tchr., musician East Bethlehem Luth. Ch., Detroit, 1969—70, St. Paul Luth. Ch., Flint, Mich., 1971—85, interim prin., 1984—85; tchr., musician St. Lorenz Luth. Ch., Frankenmuth, Mich., 1985—97; ret., 1997. Election officer Twp. Precinct, Birch Run, Mich., 2000—. Mem.: Am. Guild Organists (sub dean 1980—84). Avocations: gardening, reading. Home: 10520 Dehmel Birch Run MI 48415

WARNKE, GORDON E., lawyer; b. Wetaskiwin, Alta., Canada, Nov. 3, 1957; BS, U. Alta., 1978, LLB, 1981; SJD, Harvard Univ., 1984. Bar: NY 1984. Co-mng. ptnr., mem. exec. com., co-chmn. tax group Dewey Ballantine LLP, NYC. Mem.: ABA (past chmn. com. on affiliated & related corp.), NY State Bar Assn. (mem. exec. com.), Assn. of the Bar of the City of NY. Office: Dewey Ballantine LLP 1301 Ave of the Americas New York NY 10019-6092 Business E-Mail: gwarnke@dbllp.com.

WARNOCK, JOHN EDWARD, computer company executive; b. Salt Lake City, Oct. 6, 1940; BS in Math. and Philosophy, U. Utah, 1961, MS in Math., 1964, PhD in Elec. Engring. and Computer Sci., 1969; DSc (hon.), Univ. Utah. With Evans & Sutherland Computer Corp., Computer Scis. Corp., IBM; prin. scientist Xerox Palo Alto Rsch. Ctr., Calif., 1978-81; co-founder, chmn. Adobe Sys., Inc., San Jose, Calif., 1982—, CEO, 1982—2000. Bd. dir. Octavo Corp. Patentee in field; contbr. articles to profl. jours. and industry mags.; spkr. in field. Bd. mem., past chmn. Tech Mus. Innovation; mem. entrepreneurial bd. adv. com. Am. Film Inst. Recipient Computer Achievement award Assn. for Computing Machinery SIGGRAPH, 1989, Tech. Excellence award Nat. Graphics Assn., 1989, ACM Software Sys. award, 1989, Lifetime Achievement award for tech. excellence, PC Mag., 1989, J. Anderson Disting. Achievement award, 1991, Disting. Alumnus award U. Utah, 1995, Cary award Rochester Inst. Tech., 1995, Fellow award, Computer History Mus., 2002; named Entrepreneur of Yr. Ernst & Young, Merril Lynch, Inc., 1991; named to Computer Reseller News Hall of Fame, 1998. Fellow ACM; mem. NAE, Utah Info. Tech. Assn. Office: Adobe Sys Inc 345 Park Ave San Jose CA 95110-2704

WARNOCK, WILLIAM REID, lawyer; b. Detroit, July 25, 1939; s. William G. and Margery E. (Ford) W.; m. Sandra L. Klarich, Dec. 27, 1961; children: Cheryl Lynn, Laura Ellen. BBA, U. Mich., 1961, JD with distinction, 1964. Bar: Ill. 1964, U.S. Dist. Ct. (no. dist.) Ill. 1965, U.S. Supreme Ct. 1972, Mich. 1995. With Ross & Hardies, Chgo., 1964-70; regional counsel U.S. Dept. HUD, Chgo., 1970-73; ptnr. Roan & Grossman, Chgo., 1973-82; sole practice Chgo., 1982-85; ptnr. Siegel & Warnock, Chgo., 1985-91; of counsel Donovan & Olsen, Chgo., 1991; pres. William R. Warnock P.C., LaGrange, Ill., 1992—2002, Three Rivers, Mich., 2002—03. Cons. Ill. Dept. Bus. and Econ. Devel., Chgo., 1977-78, Ill. Housing Devel. Authority, Chgo., 1973-78, Council State Housing Financing Agys., Washington, 1975-78; past pres., chmn. Atty.'s Title Guaranty Fund, Inc., Chgo., 1986-88, bd. dirs., 1976—2003. Author: (legal references) Land Use and Zoning, 1974-88, Ward on Title Examination, 1975, Illinois Real Property Service: Real Estate Exchanges, 1988, Environmental Law and the Real Estate Lawyer, 1989-90. Mem. Ill. State Bar Assn., Am. Coll. Real Estate Lawyers. Republican. Methodist. Avocations: boating, woodworking. Personal E-mail: warnockwr@aol.com.

WARNSTADT, JACQUELINE RAE, elementary school educator; m. Steve Warnstadt. BA, Morningside Coll., 1972. Tchr., 1972—, Leeds Elem. Sch., Sioux City, Iowa. Named Iowa Tchr. of Yr., 2006. Mem.: Sioux City Mus. & Hist. Assn. Office: Leeds Elem Sch 3919 Jefferson St Sioux City IA 51108 *

WARPEHA, RAYMOND LEONARD, surgeon, educator; b. Mpls., Dec. 5, 1934; s. Frank Joseph and Sophie Helen (Fryzlewicz) Warpeha; m. Ivy Lee Kloth; children: Katherine, John, Joseph, Frank. BS, U. Minn., 1956, DDS, 1958; MD, Northwestern U., 1965, PhD in Anatomy, 1966. Cert. Am. Bd. Surgery, 1971, plastic surgery Am. Bd. Surgery, 1973. Instr. anatomy Northwestern U. Med. Sch., Chgo., 1963—65, instr. surgery, 1969—72; asst. prof. surgery and anatomy Loyola U. Stritch Sch. Medicine, Maywood, Fla., 1973—75, assoc. prof. surgery and anatomy, 1975—80, prof. surgery and anatomy, 1981—2000, prof. emeritus, 2000—. Cons. surgery Cook County Hosp., Chgo., 1970—72; founder, dir. Burn Ctr. Loyola U. Hosp., 1972—91; dir. surg. anatomy dept. surgery Loyola Med. Sch., 1972—2000. Author: 59 articles and 9 book chpts., Clinics of Plastic Surgery North America, 1981; mem. editl. bd.: Chgo. Medicine. Chmn. Ill. Burn Surgeons adv. group Ill. Dept. Med. Svcs., Springfield, 1973—80; chmn. burn surgeons adv. group Divsnl. Med. Svcs., Washington, 1975; mem. bd. trustees Ill. Trauma Soc.; trustee Am. Soc. Maxillofacial Surgery. Recipient award for Lifetime Med. Contbns. and Pub. Svc. to Burn and Fire Victims and Survivors, Knapp Burn Found., Chgo., 1999; postdoctoral Am. Heart Assn. fellow, Northwestern Med. Sch., 1962—63. Fellow: Am. Coll. Surgeons (chmn. membership com. Dist. 3 1995—99); mem.: Am. Soc. Plastic and Reconstructive Surgeons, Soc. Head and Neck Surgeons, Am. Assn. Plastic Surgeons, Am. Soc. Maxillofacial Surgeons, Am. Burn Assn., Chgo. Soc. Plastic Surgery (pres. 1983—84, treas. 1981—82, v.p. 1982—83). Roman Catholic. Avocations: fishing, botany. Office: Loyola Med Ctr Dept Surgery 2160 S First Ave Maywood IL 60153

WARREN, ALVIN CLIFFORD, JR., law educator; b. Daytona Beach, Fla., May 14, 1944; s. Alvin Clifford and Barbara (Barnes) Warren; m. Judith Blatt, Aug. 20, 1966; children: Allison, Matthew. BA in English, Yale U., 1966; JD, U. Chgo., 1969. Bar: Conn. 1970, Pa. 1975. Asst. to assoc. prof. law U. Conn., West Hartford, 1969-73, assoc. prof., Duke U., Durham, NC, 1973-75, prof. U. Pa., Phila., 1975-80, prof. Harvard Law Sch., Cambridge, Mass., 1980—98, Ropes & Gray prof., 1998-, dir. fund for tax and fiscal rsch. policy, 1985-. Vis. assoc. prof., U. Pa., 1974-75; vis. prof. Harvard Law Sch., 1979-80. Author: Integration of Individual and Corporate Income Taxes, 1993; contbr. articles to law journals. Mem.: ABA (tax sect.). Office: Harvard Law Sch 1563 Massachusetts Ave Cambridge MA 02138 Office Phone: 617-495-3186. Office Fax: 617-496-4880. E-mail: warren@law.harvard.edu.

WARREN, ANDREW C., apparel executive; Joined GE Fin. Mgmt. Program; exec. v.p., CFO NBC Universal TV Grp.; sr. ops. leader GE Audit Staff; CFO Liz Claiborne Inc., 2007—. Office: Liz Claiborne Inc 1441 Broadway New York NY 10018 Office Phone: 212-354-4900. Office Fax: 212-626-1800.

WARREN, ARETE BERNICE, art historian; b. Chgo., July 23, 1946; d. Lyle Dwight Swartz and Phyllis Elizabeth Coffman; m. William Bradford Warren, Sept. 20, 1985. BA, Northwestern U., 1968; MA, U. N.C. Chapel Hill, 1970. Cert. secondary sch. tchr. Ill. Rsch. asst. Victoria and Albert Mus., London, 1970—73; lectr. Tate Gallery, London, 1973; coord. program/edn. Cooper-Hewitt Mus., NYC, 1973—74; exec. dir. Royal Oak Found., NYC, 1974—82; asst. to dir. N.C. Mus. Art, Raleigh, 1982—85; ind. writer, lectr., 1985—. Chmn. N.Y. com. Am. Mus. in Britain, 1995—2006, U.S. /U.K. coun. chmn., 1999—, trustee, 2004—; mem. Mayor's Commn. for Protocol, City of N.Y., 1995—2002; mem. steering com. N.Y. Bot. Garden, 1995—97; mem. N.Y. State Bd. for Hist. Preservation, 1998—, N.Y. State Empire Plaza Art Commn., 2000—; lectr. in field. Co-author: Glass Houses, 1988; contbr. articles to profl. jours. V.p. Royal Oak Found., Inc., 1982—86, sec., 1986—90, bd. dirs., 1987—93; bd. dirs., mem. strategic planning com. Keep N.C. Beautiful, Inc., 1983—85; trustee Preservation League N.Y. State, 1990—96, 1998—2004, trustee coun., 1996—98, 2004—, exec. com., 1998—2006; bd. visitors/nat. adv. coun. Ackland Art Mus., U. N.C., Chapel Hill, 1991—2005, chmn., 1996—2000; mem. coun. of fellows Morgan Libr., NYC, 2003—. Mem.: Internat. Coun. Mus., Am. Assn. Mus., Soc. Archtl. Historians, Millbrook (N.Y.) Garden Club, Sharon (Conn.) Country Club, Garden Club Am. (zone III N.Y. rep. 1999—2001, vice chmn. zones I, II, III, IV 2001—03, nat. chmn. 2004—06, garden history and design com.), Women's Nat. Rep. Club (bd. govs. 1989—92, pres. 1990—91), Colony Club. Avocations: gardening, writing, travel, cooking. Home: 520 E 86th St New York NY 10028

WARREN, ARTHUR LEE, secondary school educator, school system administrator; b. Newark, Sept. 6, 1947; s. Arthur and Mattie Kate Warren; m. Marvine Marshall, Oct. 10, 1970; children: Jeremy Lee, Ashlee Kathryn. BA, Rutgers U., 1978; MEd, Kean U., 1988. Cert. Adminstr./Supr. NJ., 1978, Tchr. History NJ., 1988. History tchr. Fords Jr H.S., NJ, 1978—81; tchr. Woodbridge H.S., NJ, 1984—88, vice prin., 1989—93, prin., 1996—; tchr. John F. Kennedy H.S., Iselin, NJ, 1988—89; prin. Ross St. Elem. Sch., Woodbridge, NJ, 1993—95, Fords Mid. Sch., Fords, NJ, 1995—96. Trustee Principal's Ctr. for the Garden State, Coll. of N.J., Ewing, NJ, 2004—, Prodigal Found., Woodbridge, NJ, 2000—. Com. mem. Citizen's Adv. Com., Plainfield, NJ, 1975—78, Census 2000, Twp. of Woodbridge, NJ, 1999—2000. Recipient Prin. of the Yr., N.J. Prins. & Suprs. Assn., 2000. Mem.: Nat. Assn. Secondary Sch. Prins., Assn. for Supervisory and Curriculum Devel., Nat. Assn. of Secondary Prins., N. J. Prins., Kappa Betta Pi. Office: Woodbridge HS Samuel Lupo Pl Woodbridge NJ 07095 Home Phone: 732-815-9839; Office Phone: 732-602-8600. Office Fax: 732-602-8612. Business E-Mail: arthur.warren@woodbridge.k12.nj.us.

WARREN, CHARLES DAVID, library administrator; b. Martin, Tenn., June 12, 1944; s. Charles Alton and Evelyn (Bell) W.; children: Aaron David, Meredith Hild, Julia Myers. BS, U. Tenn., 1967; MS, U. Ill., Urbana, 1969. cert. pub. library adminstr. Dir. Shiloh Regional Library, Jackson, Tenn., 1969-72, Cumberland County Pub. Library, Fayetteville, NC, 1973-79; exec. dir. Richland County Pub. Library, Columbia, SC, 1979—. Bd. dirs. Civic Music Assn., Fayetteville, N.C., 1973-79, Fayetteville Symphony, 1973-78, Fayetteville Arts Commn., 1975; v.p. Friends of Librs. U.S.A., 1994—; mem. Columbia Coord. Coun., 1987-88; chmn. Richland County History Commn., 1987-93; mem. John Cotton Dana Awards Commn., 1994-99. Recipient Lucy Hampton Bostick award, 1993, S.C. Pub. Adminstr. Yr. award, 1993; named Young Man of Yr., Fayetteville Jaycees, 1977, S.C. Libr. of Yr., 1991, Internat. Fedn. Librs., 1997-2001, Order of Silver Crescent, 1999. Mem. ALA (pres. Jr. Member Roundtable 1977, chmn. awards com. 1984), Southeastern Libr. Assn. (pres. pub. libr. sect. 1978), S.C. Libr. Assn. (bd. dirs. 1980), Friends Libraries USA (bd. dirs. 1992-), Southeastern Libr. Network (bd. dirs. 2002-), Rotary, Kiwanis, Beta Phi Mu. Democrat. Episcopalian. Home: 619 King St #806 Columbia SC 29205 Office: Richland County Pub Libr 1431 Assembly St Columbia SC 29201-3101

WARREN, DANIEL CHURCHMAN, health facility administrator; b. Washington, Sept. 23, 1939; s. Walter Thomas and Laura Kathrine W.; m. C. Frederica Lescure, June 5, 1958; 1 child, Christopher C. BS, Roanoke Coll., 1960; MD, Med. Coll. Va., 1964; MPH, U. N.C., 1971; MMAS, U.S. Army Command & Gen. Coll., 1974. Diplomate Nat. Bd. Med. Examiners, Am. Bd. Preventive Medicine, lic. physician VA; ordained Anglican Cath. priest 2002. Intern Georgetown U. Hosp., 1964-65; resident in surgery Med. Coll. Va., 1967-68, William Beaumont Gen. Hosp., 1968-69; resident in preventive medicine Walter Reed Army Inst. Rsch., 1971-73; commd. 2d lt. U.S. Army, 1965, advanced through grades to col., 1986; asst. med. dir. HealthAm. Va., 1986; pvt. practice travel, 1987-89; dir. Peninsula Health Dist., Newport News, Va., 1990—2001; warden Holyrood Sem., 2001—; rector St. Matthews Anglican Cath. Ch., 2002—; warden Scott Sch. Theology, 2003—. Clin. asst. prof. family and cmty. medicine Ea. Va. Med. Sch., Norfolk; cons. Riverside Regional Med Ctr., Newport News. Active Gloucester County Rep. Com., 1987-96, chmn. 1992-95, Gloucester County Redistricting Adv. Com., 1991, 2001; hon. chmn. Combined Va. Campaign United Way the Va. Peninsula, 1992. Fellow: Am. Coll. Preventive Medicine; mem.: Med. Soc. Va., Mid-Tidewater Med. Soc., Ret. Officers Assn., Cremona Fiddlers. Republican. Anglican. Avocation: English and Virginia history. Office: 215 Main St Newport News VA 23601 Business E-Mail: dwarrenmd@cox.net.

WARREN, DAVID LILES, educational association administrator; b. Goldsboro, NC, Sept. 15, 1943; s. James Hubert and Katherine (Liles) W.; m. Ellen Elizabeth LeGendre, Mar. 1, 1969; children— Jamison, Mackenzie, Katrin BA in English, Wash. State U., 1965; M in Urban Studies, Yale U., 1970, MDiv, 1970; PhD, U. Mich., 1976; LittD (hon.), Elmhurst Coll., 1994, Moravian Coll., 1994; LLD (hon.), Rider U., 1996, Mt. Union Coll., 1997, Centre Coll., 1997, Mercer U., 1998, Franklin and Marshall Coll., 1999; D of Pub. Svc. (hon.), Rocky Mountain Coll., 1999; LLD (hon.), Ky. Wesleyan Coll., 2000; LHD (hon.), U. New Haven, 2001; LittD (hon.), Middlebury Coll., 2001. Gen. sec. Yale U. Dwight Hall, New Haven, 1969—76, bd. dirs., 1976; assoc. dir. cmty. rels. Yale U., New Haven, 1976—78; sr. v.p., provost Antioch U., NYC and Yellow Springs, Ohio, 1978—82; chief adminstrv. officer City of New Haven, 1982—84; pres. Ohio Wesleyan U., Delaware, 1984—93, Nat. Assn. Ind. Colls. and Univs., Washington, 1993—. Cons. to hosps., sch. systems, colls., univs.; bd. dirs. Delaware County Bank; chmn. NCAA Pres. Commn., Divsn. III, 1990-92. Contbr. chpts. to books, articles to Yale Alumni Mag. Mem. New Haven Bd. Alderman, 1973-75; vice chmn. New Haven Commn. Poverty, 1981-82; pres. North Coast Athletic Conf., 1988-90; justice of peace New Haven Dem. Party, 1974-76; state chmn. People to People, 1987; chmn. Gov.'s Task Force on Dep. Registrar, 1987; chmn. Ohio Five Coll. Commn., 1985-95, Campus Compact Nat. Exec. Com., 1987-88; bd. dirs. US Health Corp., Coun. Ethics and Econs.; exec. com. Great Lakes Colls. Assn., Ctrl. Ohio Symphony Orch.; chmn. Ohio Ethics commn. Fulbright scholar Wash. State U., 1965-66, disting. Centennial Alumnus; Rockefeller fellow Yale U., 1966. Mem. Am. Assn. Higher Edn., Assn. Ind. Colls. Univs. (sec. 1987-88), Univ. Club (Columbus, Ohio), Grad. Club (New Haven), Cosmos Club (Washington), Phi Beta Kappa. Democrat. Presbyterian. Avocations: running, writing, tennis. Office: Nat Assn Ind Colls & Univs 1025 Connecticut Ave NW Ste 700 Washington DC 20036-5409 Office Phone: 202-785-8866. Office Fax: 202-835-0003. E-mail: david@naicu.edu. *

WARREN, DAVID P., stock exchange executive; b. 1954; BA, Wesleyan U.; MBA, Yale Sch. Mgmt., 1988. Investment banker CS First Boston, 1987—95; dep. treas. State of Conn., 1995—98; CFO Long Island Power Authority (LIPA), 1998—2000; chief adminstrv. officer NASDAQ Stock Market, Inc., NYC, 2001, CFO, 2001—. Office: NASDAQ Stock Market Inc 1 Liberty Plz New York NY 10006 Office Phone: 212-401-8912. Office Fax: 212-401-1014. Business E-Mail: david.warren@nasdaq.com.

WARREN, DEAN STUART, artist; b. Mpls., June 30, 1949; s. Jefferson Trowbridge and Dorothy Ann (Edin) Warren; m. Betty Sharon Poe, Aug. 14, 1971; children: Jeremy, Adam. BFA, Fla. Atlantic U., Boca Raton, 1973; MA, Northwestern State U., Natchitoches, La., 1975; MFA, Stephen F. Austin State U., Nacogdoches, Tex., 1980. Instr. art Cisco Jr. Coll., Tex., 1976-78; staff craftsworker Walt E. Disney Show Prodn. Walt Disney World, Lake Buena Vista, Fla., 1981-83, staff craftsworker staff shop, 1983, property craftsworker, 1983-87, artist preparator animation dept., 1987—; lead prodn. artist Marvac, Inc., Seminole County, Fla., 1983. Founder Dean S. Warren Studio, 1991—; cons. children's edn. program Mt. Dora Ctr. Arts, Fla.; instr. Bok Tower Gardens Edn. Ctr. Workshop, Lake Wales, Fla., 1996. Author: Runemaster, 1991; Youth Art Symposium, U. Ctrl. Fla., 1993, Children's Art program Atlantic Ctr. Arts, 1995, Edn. Ctr., 1996, one-man shows include Ormond Beach Meml. Art Gallery and Gardens, Fla., 1987, U. Ctrl. Fla. Art Gallery, Orlando, 1991, Harris House Atlantic Ctr. Arts, New Smyrna Beach, Fla., 1993, D'Ars Studio Gallery, Milan, 2000, numerous group shows including most recently, exhibited in group shows at Warehouse Gallery, Orlando, 1999—2000, D'Ars Studio Gallery, Milan, 1999—2002, Crealdé Sch. Art Sculpture Garden, Winter Park, 2000, 2003, Walt Disney World, 2000, Alice and William Jenkins Gallery, Crealdé Sch. Art, 2001, 2007, Banca Popalare di Milano, Bergamo, Italy, 2001, Postart Gallery, Milan, 2002, Galleria Blanchaert, 2002, Church St. Gallery Contemporary Art, Orlando, 2003, Deland Mus. Art, Fla., 2004, 2006, Art 6 Gallery, Richmond, Va., 2005, Albin Polasek Mus., Winter Park, Fla., 2006, Alliance for the Arts, Ft. Myers, Fla., 2007, Ormond Meml. Art Mus., Ormond Beach, Fla., 2007. Recipient award, U. Ga. Bot. Gardens, Athens, 1980, Valencia CC, 1983, Arts on The Park, Lakeland, Fla., 1995; Artsits in Schs. grantee, Tex. Commn. Arts, 1980. Mem.: Order of Merovingian Dynasty, Order of Crown of Charlemagne. Home: 8069 Wellsmere Cir Orlando FL 32835-5361 Personal E-mail: wwwarrenitaly@aol.com.

WARREN, DIANE, lyricist; Staff writer Jack White, 1983; founder, owner RealSongs, LA. Author over 100 top ten pop songs including I'll Never Get Over You (Getting Over Me), How Do I Live, I Don't Want to Miss a Thing, If You Asked Me To, Don't Turn Around, Set The Night To Music, I'll Still Love You More, Because You Loved Me (Grammy award, song written specifically for a motion picture or TV, 1996), Rhythm of the Night, Nothing's Gonna Stop Us Now, Unbreak My Heart, Music of My Heart, My First Night With You (Nashville Songwriters Assn. Internat. award, superior creativity in the words and music of a song, 2000), I Will Get There (Nashville Songwriters Assn. Internat. award, superior creativity in the words and music of a song, 2000), There You'll Be, and many others. Hon. com. mem. PETA; founder, David S. Warren Weekly Entertainment Series, Jewish Home for the Aging; donor Wildlife Waystation, 10th Ann. Life Found., The Lange Found. Named Songwriter of Yr., Nat. Acad. Songwriters, 1996, No. 1 Pop Songwriter of Yr., Am. Songwriter Awards, 1997, Songwriter of Yr., Nashville Songwriters Assn. Internat., 2000; named one of 100 Most Powerful Women in Entertainment, Hollywood Reporter, 2006; named to Songwriters Hall of Fame, 2001, Hollywood Walk of Fame, 2001; recipient Songwriter of Yr., Am. Soc. Composers, Authors & Publishers, 1990, 1991, 1993, 1998, 1999, Billboard, George and Ira Gershwin award, outstanding musical achievement, 1998, New Millennium Visionary award, Am. Cinema Awards Found., 1999, Legacy award, Orgn. For the Needs of the Elderly, 1999, Dream Maker's Cir. Award, Dream Found., 2000, Lifetime Achievement award, Bill Gavin Heritage Found., 2000, Angel award, Angels on Earth, 2000, Musician's Adv. award, Am. Soc. Young Musicians, 2001, Telly award, Found. for a Better Life, 2003. Achievements include songs features in over 80 motion pictures. Office: Realsongs 6363 W Sunset Blvd Fl 8 Hollywood CA 90028-7330 Mailing: c/o The Chasen Co 8899 Beverly Blvd Ste 405 West Hollywood CA 90048 *

WARREN, DONALD WILLIAM, medical and dental educator; b. Bklyn., Mar. 22, 1935; s. Sol B. and Frances W.; m. Priscilla Girardi, June 10, 1956; children: Donald W. Jr., Michael C. BS, U. N.C., 1956, DDS, 1959; MS, U. Pa., 1961, PhD, 1963; D in Odontology (hon.), U. Kuopio, Finland, 1991. Asst. prof. dentistry U. N.C., Chapel Hill, 1963-65, dir. Craniofacial Ctr., 1963-2000, assoc. prof., 1965-69, prof., 1969-80, chmn. dept. dental ecology, 1970-85, Kenan prof., 1980—2004, Kenan prof. emeritus, 2004—, rsch. prof. otolaryngology, 1985—2004; ret. Cons. NIH, Bethesda, Md., 1967-2000, R. J. Reynolds-Nabisco, Winston-Salem, N.C., 1986-99. Contbr. articles to profl. jours. Recipient Honor award Am. Cleft Palate Assn./Craniofacial Assn., 1992, O. Max Garner award U. N.C. Bd. Govs., 1993, honors award Angle Orthodontic Soc., 1998. Fellow AAAS, Internat. Coll. Dentists, Am. Speech and Hearing Lang. Assn. (Editors award 1998, Honors award 2003), Internat. Assn. Dental Rsch., Acoustical Soc. Am., Am. Cleft Palate Assn. (pres. 1981-82, Disting. Svc. award 1984), Am. Cleft Palate Edn. Found. (pres. 1976-77). Avocations: horse related activities, running, farming. Home: PO Box 1356 Southern Pines NC 28388-1356 Business E-Mail: don_warren@dentistry.unc.edu.

WARREN, ELIZABETH A., law educator; 1 child, Amelia Warren Tyagi. BS, U. Houston, 1970; JD, Rutgers U., 1976. Bar: NJ, Tex. Lectr. law Rutgers Sch. Law, Newark, 1977—78; asst. prof. law U. Houston Law Ctr., 1978—80, assoc. dean academic affairs, 1980—81, assoc. prof. law, 1981—83; rsch. assoc. Population Rsch. Ctr. U. Tex., Austin, 1983—87; prof. law U. Tex. Sch. Law, 1983—87, Conoco Faculty Fellow in Law, 1985—86, Jay H. Brown Centennial Fellow in Law, 1986—87; prof. law U. Pa. Law Sch., Phila., 1987—90, William A. Schnader Prof. Comml. Law, 1990—95; Leo Gottlieb prof. law Harvard Law Sch., Cambridge, Mass., 1995—. Vis. assoc. prof. law U. Tex. Sch. Law, 1981—82; vis. prof. law U. Mich., 1985; Robert Braucher Vis. Prof. Comml. Law Harvard U., 1992—93; proposal reviewer NSF, 1985—; bd. editors Am. Bankruptcy Law Jour., 1989—92; editl. adv. bd. Little Brown & Co. Law Sch. Divsn. (now Aspen Press), 1990—; com. on jud. edn. Fed. Jud. Ctr., 1990—99; bd. trustees Am. Bankruptcy Bd. Certification, 1992—96; exec. com. Nat. Bankruptcy Conf., 1993—95, 2002—05; advisor German Govt. Task Force on Bankruptcy Reform, 1993; reporter, cons., sr. advisor Nat. Bankruptcy Rev. Commn., 1995—97; regular commentator All Things Considered program Nat. Pub. Radio. Co-author: (books) As We Forgive Our Debtors: Consumer Credit and Bankruptcy in America, 1989 (Silver Gavel Award, ABA, 1990), The Law of Debtors and Creditors, 1991, 1996, 2001, Secured Transactions: A Systems Approach, 1995, 1998, 2000, 2003, Comml. Law: A Systems Approach, 1998, 2003, The Fragile Middle Class: Americans in Debt, 2000 (Scholarship Award, Am. Coll. Consumer Fin. Services Lawyers, 2000); co-author: (with Amelia Warren Tyagi) The Two-Income Trap: Why Middle-Class Mothers and Fathers Are Going Broke, 2003; author: numerous books chapters and jour. articles. Named one of The 50 Most Influential Women Lawyers in Am., Nat. Law Jour., 1998, 2007; recipient Frankel Publ. Award for Outstanding Writing, 1982, Commedation for Svc., Am. Bankruptcy Bd. Certification, 1998, Brown Award for Jud. Scholarship and Edn., Fed. Jud. Ctr., 1998, Champion of Consumer Rights Award, Nat. Assn. Consumer Bankruptcy Attorneys, 2000, Excellence in Edn. Award, Nat. Conf. Bankruptcy Judges, 2001, Lawrence P. King Award, Comml. Law League Am., 2002, Outstanding Tchr. Award, U. Houston Law Ctr., 1981, L. Hart Wright Teaching Excellence Award, U. Mich. Sch. Law, 1986, Harvey Levin Award for Excellence in Tchg., U. Pa. Sch. Law, 1989, 1992, Lindback Award for Disting. Tch., U. Pa., 1994, Albert A. Sacks-Paul A. Freund Award for Tchg. Excellence, Harvard Law Sch., 1997. Fellow: Am. Coll. Bankruptcy (Commendation for Outstanding Pub. Svc. 1998); mem.: Assn. Am. Law Schools (chair comml. and related consumer law sect. 1983—84, chair comml. law workshop 1984, planning com. conf. on tchg. contract law 1989, profl. devel. com. 1988—91, chair debtor-creditor sect. 1989—90, chair legislation com. debtor-creditor sect. 1990—93), Am. Law Inst. (exec. com. coun. 1994—95, US Adviser, Transnat. Insolvency Project 1995—, mem. nominating com. 1995—, exec. com. coun. 1998—, 2nd v.p. coun. 2000—04). Office: Harvard U Law Sch Hauser 200 Cambridge MA 02138 *

WARREN, FRANK, blogger, small business owner; Small bus. owner, Md.; weblog creator, host PostSecret, 2004—. Appearances (media) Today, 20/20, CNN, MSNBC, NPR, Fox News, others; author: PostSecret: Extraordinary Confessions from Ordinary Lives, 2005, The Secret Lives of Men and Women. Named third most popular blog, NY mag.; named one of 50 Coolest Websites (postsecret.com), Time mag., 2005, Top 25 Web Celebs, Forbes mag., 2007, Top 50 Best Websites, Chgo. Tribune, Top 5 Websites, Technorati; recipient record 5 Bloggies: Weblog of Yr., Best Topical Weblog, Best Cmty. Weblog, Best New Weblog, Best Am. Weblog, 2006. Mailing: PostSecret 13345 Copper Ridge Rd Germantown MD 20874-3454 *

WARREN, IRWIN HOWARD, lawyer; b. NYC, May 16, 1950; s. Milton and Shirley (Glatman) W.; m. Elizabeth Vogel, Aug. 11, 1974. BA, Columbia U., 1971, JD, 1974; Harlan Fiske Stone Scholar. Bar: NY, 1975, US Ct. Appeals (2nd (1979), 1st (1980), 4th (1981), 3rd (1982), 8th (1985), 5th (1996), 6th (1996) cirs.), US Dist. Ct. (So. and Ea. dists.), 1975. Assoc. Weil, Gotshal & Manges LLP, NYC, 1974-82, ptnr., co-head bus. and securities litigation dept., 1982—. Spkr. in field; litigation sect. rep. US Jud. Conference's Civil Rules Styles Com., 2003—. Contbr. articles to profl. jours. and publs. Mem. ABA (lectr., tchr., co-author of articles, co-chair, ethics subcommittee of committee on corp. counsel, sect. of litigation 1984-85, co-chair of com. on class actions and derivative suits, sect. of litigation 1986-89, mem. sect. of litigation task force on ancillary bus. activities of lawyers 1989-94, dir., divsn. III - programs, sect. of litigation 1989-90, divsn. dir., divsn. VI - sect. of litigation The Profession 1991-92, co-chair of securities litigation com., sect. of litigation 1990-91, co-chair of the ethics and professionalism com., sect. litigation 1992-95, mem., coun. of the sect. of litigation 2004-, mem., sect. of litigation fed. practice task force 2000-2004); life mem. Fellows of the Am. Bar Found. 1990-. Office: Weil Gotshal & Manges LLP 767 5th Ave New York NY 10153-0023 Office Phone: 212-310-8648.

WARREN, J. RICHARD, editor, retired humanities educator; b. Sanford, Apr. 27, 1925; s. Ralph Moore Warren and Demarius Kate Musson-Warren; m. Mabel Martin, Aug. 21, 1949; children: Barbara Anne Tucker, J. Richard Jr., Mary Jane Cowen. BA in French, Stetson U., Deland, Fla., 1949, MA in Secondary Sch. Guidance, 1951; PhD in Music Edn. Supervision and Adminstrn., Fla. State U., Tallahassee, 1961; at, Tex. A&M U., Bryan, U.Ill., Urbana, Ctrl. Signal Corps Sch., Camp Crowder, Mo., Marbach Tutoring Inst. Fgn. Langs., Frankfort, Germany, Biarritz Am. U., France, U. Fla., Gainesville, Fla. State u., Tallahassee, U. W. Fla., Pensacola. Cert. edn. adminstrn. and supervision Fla., 1951, music Fla., 1951, French Fla., 1951, coll. academic adminstrn. and supervision Fla., 1961. Tchr. music Washington County H.S., Chipley, Fla., 1950—53, Bay H.S., Panama City, 1952—59, Fla. State U., Tallahassee, 1959—61, Brevard C.C., Cocoa, 1961; cons. fine arts curriculum Fla. Dept. Edn. Instrnl. Svcs., Tallahassee, 1961—67; dean humanities Fla. Jr. Coll., Jacksonville, 1967—70; dir. continuing edn. Jacksonville U., 1970—72; dean humanities Piedmont C.C., Charlottesville, Va., 1972—73; dean humanities, divsn. dir. and chmn. fine and performing arts dept. Okaloosa-Walton C.C. (now Okaloosa-Walton Coll.), Niceville, Fla., 1973—93; ret., 1993; exec. officer Fla. League of the Arts, Inc., 1993—. Min. music First Meth. Ch., New Smyrna Beach, Fla., 1950—51, First Baptist Ch., Chipley, 1951—53, First Meth. Ch., Panama City, 1953—59, First Baptist Ch., Merritt Island, 1961, Southside Baptist Ch., Jacksonville, 1970—72; tchr. summer sch. Fla. State U., Tallahassee, 1952—59; clinician music camp Bapt. Harmony Bay, 1952—59; cons. Duval Magnet Sch., Jacksonville, 1970—72, Mattie Kelly Arts Ctr., Destin, 1975—90; editor Arts & Humanities jour. of Fla. League Arts, Niceville, 1993—. Contbg. editor: Fla. Sch. Bull., 1961—68; contbr. articles to profl. jours. Deacon Southside Bapt. Ch., Jacksonville, Fla.; mem. First Bapt. Ch., Vaparaiso, Fla.; ednl. and choir cons. Cath. Ch., Panama City, Fla., St. Augustine Diocese, Jacksonville, Fla. Sgt. Signal Corps US Army, 1943—47, ETO. Mem.: Fla. League Arts, Fla. Vocal Music Assn. (life; past pres.), Fla. Music Educators Assn. (life), Music Educators Nat. Conf. (life), Rotary (J.U. rep. 1970—72), Kiwanis (pres. Valparaiso chpt. 2005—, Cir. K advisor Okaloosa-Walton Coll. chpt., Legion of Honor), Lions, Lambda Chi Alpha (founder Stetson U. chpt.), Pi Kappa Lambda. Republican. Avocations: gardening, piano, writing. Home: 2408 Edgewater Dr Niceville FL 32578-2304

WARREN, JACK HAMILTON, retired diplomat, banker, trade policy advisor; b. Apr. 10, 1921; m. Hilary J. Titterington; children: Hilary Warren Nicolson, Martin, Jennifer Warren Part, Ian. Student, Queens U., Kingston, Ont., Can., 1938-41. Joined Dept. External Affairs, Canada, 1945; assigned London, 1948-51; fin. counsellor Washington, 1952—54; alt. Canadian dir. Internat. Monetary Fund; dir. Internat. Bank for Reconstruction & Development, Washington; fin. counsellor, del. OECD NATO, Paris, 1954—57; asst. dep. minister trade and commerce Ottawa, 1958-64; dep. minister, trade and commerce, 1964-68; dep minister industry, trade & commerce, 1968-71; high commr. to U.K., 1971-75; ambassador to U.S., 1975-77; Can. coord. Gatt multilateral trade negotiations, 1977-79; vice-chmn. Bank of Montreal, 1979-86; prin. trade policy advisor Govt. Que., 1986-94; N. American deputy chmn. Trilateral Comm. Served with Royal Canadian Navy, 1941-45; officer Order of Can., 1982. Recipient Pub. Svc. Outstanding Achievement award, 1976. Home: Ottawa 301 C-997 N River Rd Ontario Canada K1K 3V5

WARREN, JAMES I., lawyer; b. Trenton, NJ, Dec. 7, 1950; BA, Stanford U., 1971; JD, NYU, 1975, LLM, 1979, MS in Acctg., 1980. CPA; bar: NJ 1976, NY 1979. Ptnr., co-chmn. tax dept. Reid & Priest; chmn., Nat. Utility Tax Practice Group Price Waterhouse Cooper; sr. tax ptnr., Nat. Energy Tax Svc. Practice Group Deloitte & Touche; ptnr., tax, benefits, trusts & estates dept. Thelen Reid & Priest LLP, 2003—. Spkr. in field. Office: Thelen Reid & Priest LLP 875 Third Ave New York NY 10022-2001 Office Fax: 212-603-2001, 212-603-2072. Business E-Mail: jwarren@thelenreid.com.

WARREN, JAMES RONALD, retired museum director, journalist; b. Goldendale, Wash., May 25, 1925; stepson H.S. W.; m. Gwen Davis, June 25, 1949; children: Gail, Jeffrey. BA, Wash. State U., 1949; MA, U. Wash., 1953, PhD, 1963. Adminstrv. v.p. Seattle Community Coll., 1965-69; pres. Edmonds Community Coll., Lynnwood, Wash., 1969-79; dir. Mus. of History and Industry, Seattle, 1979-89. Lectr. in field. Author history books; columnist Seattle Post Intelligencer, 1979-92, Seattle Times, 1992-96. Served with U.S. Army, 1943-45, ETO, prisoner-of-war, Germany. Mem. VFW, Am. Ex-POW Assn., 42d (Rainbow) Div. Vets., Rotary, also others. Home and Office: 3235 99th Ave NE Bellevue WA 98004-1803 Personal E-mail: jrgwarren@msn.com.

WARREN, JANE CAROL, psychologist; b. Dec. 25, 1938; d. George Stafford Harris and Helen Virginia (Swift) Swift-Harris; m. Philip Clinton Warren (div.); children: Charles, Susan Warren Sohn; m. Richard Karl Hertel, July 19, 2001. BA, U. Mich., Ann Arbor, 1961, MA, 1964, PhD, 1985. Lic. psychologist Mich. Tchg. asst. in botany U. Mich., Ann Arbor, 1960—61, asst. in counseling, 1967—68; sci. tchr. Belleville (Mich.) HS, 1961—63; clin. psychologist Huron Valley Cons. Ctr., Ann Arbor, 1980—85; pvt. practice Ann Arbor, 1985—. Past pres. Mich. Psychoanalytic Found., Farmington Hills; founding mem. Allen Creek Presch., Ann Arbor. Fellow, U. Mich., 1963—64. Mem.: APA, Mich. Psychol. Assn., Am. Psychoanalytic Assn. (assoc.; steering com. 2004—07, chair com. on psychotherapist assoc.). Office: 555 E William #16-I Ann Arbor MI 48104 Office Phone: 734-662-5110. Business E-Mail: jmail@umich.edu.

WARREN, JENNIFER ELIZABETH, family nurse practitioner; b. Clovis, N.Mex., Nov. 13, 1964; d. Ronald Dwayne and Lillian Ann (Reed) Carter; m. Johnny Lynn Warren Jr., May 18, 1991. BSN, West Tex. State U., 1988; MSN-FNP, West Tex. A&M U., 1998. RN, Tex.; cert. family nurse practitioner. Clin. asst. Northwest Tex. Hosp., Amarillo, 1987—88; neonatal ICU nurse Meth. Children's Hosp., Lubbock, Tex., 1988—98, Covenant Med. Ctr., Lubbock, 1999—2000; family nurse practitioner Covenant Family Health Care Ctr., 2000—03, Garza County Health Clinic, Post, Tex., 2003—05, Spur (Tex.) Clinic, 2005—. Family nurse practitioner Primestaff, 2004—, Physicians Network Svcs., 2001—05, Spur (Tex.) Clinic, 2005—. Mem. Am. Acad. Nurse Practitioners, Tex. Nursing Assn., Endometriosis Assn. (organizer/contact, Lubbock leader 1993—), South Plains Nurse Practitioners Assn. Democrat. Methodist. Avocations: gardening, cross stitch, latch hook, swimming. Home: 1002 W 10th St Post TX 79356-2450 Office: Spur Clinic 907 E Hill Spur TX 79370 Office Phone: 806-271-3306. Office Fax: 806-495-3576, 806-271-4256. Personal E-mail: jewarren@caprock-spur.com. Business E-Mail: jewarren@teamumc.com.

WARREN, JOHN COOLIDGE, educational administrator; b. Boston, May 16, 1956; s. William Bradford and Mary-Elizabeth (Coolidge) W.; m. Laura Parker Appell, June 18, 1983; children: Ethan Reynolds Appell, Amanda Pfaltzgraff Appell. BA, Stanford U., 1978, MA, 1980; MEd, Harvard U., 1991, EdD, 1994. Tchr. history Robert Louis Stevenson Sch., Pebble Beach, Calif., 1979-81, Milton Acad., Mass., 1981, chmn. dept. history, 1992-95, acad. dean, 1995—2001, spl. asst. head sch., 2001—06; head sch. St. Mark's Sch., 2006—. Faculty cons. Ednl. Testing Svc., Princeton, 1990—, William Joiner Ctr., Boston, 1992—; editl. cons. Longman Inc., White Plains, NY, 1991—. Editor: America's Intervention in Vietnam, 1987. NEH fellow, 1985, advanced doctoral fellow, Harvard U., 1993. Mem. Am. Hist. Assn., Orgn. Am. Historians, Assn. Asian Studies, World History Assn., Boston Athaneum, Colonial Soc. Mass., Mass. Hist. Soc., Phi Beta Kappa. Avocations: canoeing, fishing. Home and Office: St Mark's Sch 25 Marlborough Rd Southborough MA 01772

WARREN, JOHN WILLIAM, professional society administrator; b. Clarksville, Ark., June 27, 1927; s. Frederick H. and Fannie Emiline (Casey) W.; m. Marguerette Christine Cohoon, Oct. 9, 1948 (dec. Dec. 1987); children: Catherine Gail, Carolyn Anne, Eve Colette; m. Anna Jane Taylor, Feb. 10, 1990. BA, Abilene Christian U., 1949; MA, U. Ark., 1951; PhD, U. Tenn., 1961. Instr. U. Tenn., Knoxville, 1954—61; assoc. prof. David Lipscomb Coll., Nashville, 1961—62; prof., chmn. English Tenn. Tech. U., Cookeville, 1962—88; assoc. exec. dir. Phi Kappa Phi, Baton Rouge, 1988—92, exec. dir., 1992—99, exec. dir. emeritus, 1999—; v.p. Assn. Coll. Honor Socs., 1999—2001, pres., 2001—03. Author Ofcl. Lit. Map of Tenn., 1976; author: Tennessee Belles-Lettres-Guide to Tennessee Literature, 1976. Mem. Rotary (Cookeville pres. 1972-73), Phi Kappa Phi (Tenn. Tech. U. chpt. pres. 1980, SE region v.p. 1982-88, nat. bd. dirs. 1982-88). Republican. Mem. Ch. of Christ. Avocations: gardening, travel. Home Phone: 479-754-2678. Personal E-mail: warrenjohn@centurytel.net.

WARREN, KATHERINE VIRGINIA, art gallery director; b. Balt., Aug. 10, 1948; d. Joseph Melvin and Hilda Virginia (Thiele) Heim; m. David Hardy Warren; 1 child, Gabriel Kristopher Coy; 1 stepchild, Michael Jonathan Warren. BA, U. Calif., Riverside, 1976, MA, 1980. Asst. curator Calif. Mus. Photography, Riverside, 1979-80, acting dir., 1980-81, asst. dir., curator of edn., 1981-84; dir. univ. art gallery U. Calif., Riverside, 1980—2003, ret., 2003—. Bd. dirs. Riverside Arts Found., 1980-89, chmn. bd., 1986-88. Marius De Brabant fellow U. Calif., 1977-79. Mem. Am. Assn. Mus., Western Mus. Conf. Office: Sweeney Art Gallery U Calif Riv Side Riverside CA 92521-0001

WARREN, KELCY L., energy executive; b. Gladewater, Tex., Nov. 9, 1955; s. Hugh Brinson and Bertie (Robinson) W. BSCE, U. Tex., Arlington, 1978. Pipeline design engr. Lone Star Gas Co., Dallas, 1978-81; pres., chief oper. officer Cornerstone Natural Gas, Inc., Dallas, 1993—96; pres. Energy Transfer Partners, Energy Transfer Equity, Dallas, 1996—2004, co-chmn., co-CEO, 2004—07, chmn., CEO, 2007—. Mem. Natural Gas Transp. Assn., Natural Gas Soc. North Tex. (pres. 1981—), Energy Club Dallas (bd. dirs. 1985—). Office: Energy Transfer Partners 2838 Woodside St Dallas TX 75204 *

WARREN, MAREDIA DELOIS, music educator; d. Odis Franklin and Mary Velma Lewis; m. Charles Augustus Warren, July 9, 1966; children: John Charles, Maredia Dionne. B in Music Edn. magna cum laude, Howard U., 1965; MA, Columbia U., 1967, EdD, 1989. Tchr. elem. music Hartford Pub. Schs., 1965—66; adj. faculty Herbert H. Lehman Coll., CUNY, 1972—79, Fairleigh Dickinson U., 1975—79, Montclaire State U., 1984—93; tchr. music grades K-6 Teaneck Pub. Schs., NJ, 1979—87; dir. vocal music Teaneck H.S., 1987—99; asst. prof. music educator William Paterson U., Wayne, NJ, 1999—2000; assoc. prof., coord. music edn. N.J. City U., Jersey City, 2000—. Condr. N.J. All-State Chorus, N.J. State Music Tchrs. Assn., 1994, 2006, Mass. Am. Choral Dirs. Assn. Women's Honor Choir, Amherst, Mass., 2003, Cape Cod H.S. Festival, 2005; dir. music, organist Presbyn. Ch. Teaneck, 1995—; presenter Choral Music Workshop, Ghana, 1995; presenter in field. Bd. mem., cons. Bergen County Divsn. Hist. and Cultural Affairs, 2002—; People to People amb. to China, 1998. Named Disting. Secondary tchr., Princeton U., 1993; recipient Trailblazer award in arts and culture, Nat. Coalition of 100 Black Women, 2005. Mem.: NEA (life), Coll. Music Soc., N.J. Music Educators Assn., Am. Choral Dirs. Assn., Am. Orff Schulwerk Assn., Orgn. Am. Kodaly Educators, Music Educators Nat. Conf. (collegiate advisor 2003—), N.J. Am. Choral Dirs. Assn. (Repertoire and Standards chair multicultural 1999—2003, bd. mem.), N.J. Edn. Assn. (life), Alpha Kappa Alpha, Inc. (Women Who Make Difference Arts award 2007). Office: NJ City Univ 2039 Kennedy Blvd Jersey City NJ 07305 Office Phone: 201-200-2158. E-mail: mdlwarren@aol.com.

WARREN, MARK EDWARD, cruise line executive, lawyer; b. Rochester, Minn., Nov. 26, 1951; s. Edward Joseph and Eunice (Golberg) W.; m. Jasmine Margaret Syracuse, Feb. 18, 1984; children: Natalie, Stephanie. Cert., Instituto de Estudios Europeos, Madrid, 1972; BA, Gustavus Adolphus Coll., St. Peter, Minn., 1974; JD, U. Minn., 1977. Bar: Calif. 1977, U.S. Dist. Ct. (no. and cen. dists.) Calif. 1978, U.S. Ct. Appeals (9th cir.) 1985, U.S. Dist. Ct. (ea. dist.) Calif. 1986, U.S. Dist. Ct. (so. dist.) Calif. 1987, D.C. 1989, U.S. Supreme Ct. 1989, U.S. Ct. Appeals (D.C. cir.) 1989, U.S. Dist. Ct. (D.C. dist.) 1989, U.S. Dist. Ct. Md. 1991, Va. 1992. Assoc. Gibson, Dunn & Crutcher, LA, 1977-78; spl. asst. to U.S. Vice Pres. Walter Mondale The White House, Washington, 1979-80; assoc. Gibson, Dunn & Crutcher, LA, 1980-84, ptnr. L.A. and Washington, 1985-93; sr. v.p., gen. counsel Princess Cruises, LA, 1993-96; exec. v.p., gen. counsel NCL Corp., Miami, Fla., 2003—. Mem. U. Minn. Law Alumni Assn. (bd. dirs. 1990-98), U.K. P&I Club (bd. dirs. 1995-96), West of Eng. P&I club 2005—). Office: 7665 Corporate Center Dr Miami FL 33126

WARREN, MELISSA ALLISON, lawyer; BA magna cum laude, Duke U., Durham, NC, 1983; JD cum laude, U. Pa. Law Sch., 1988. Bar: Md. 1988. Ptnr. bus. transactions, securities, practices Venable LLP, Balt. 2001—. Office: Venable LLP 1800 Mercantile Bank & Trust Bldg 2 Hopkins Plz Baltimore MD 21201 Office Phone: 410-244-7695. Office Fax: 410-244-7742. Business E-Mail: mawarren@venable.com.

WARREN, MICHELLE PALMIERI, internist, endocrinologist; b. NYC, 1939; MD, Cornell U. Med. Coll., 1965. Cert. Internal Medicine with subspecialty in endocrinology and reproductive endocrinology. Intern, medicine Bellevue Hosp. Ctr., NYC, 1965—66, resident, 1966—68; resident, endocrinology Meml. Hosp. Cancer, NYC, 1966—68; fellow Columbia U., Coll. Physicians & Surgeons, 1968—71, asst. prof., 1971—75, assoc. prof. clin. ob/gyn & clin. medicine, 1975—96, prof. ob/gyn & medicine, 1996—; attending St. Luke's Roosevelt Hosp., NYC, 1975; founder, med. dir., Ctr. for Menopause, Hormonal Disorders and Women's Health Columbia U. Med. Ctr., NYC, 1997—, prof. medicine and obstetrics and gynecology, Wyeth Ayerst prof. women. Cons. Wyeth Pharm.; lectr. in field. Contbr. articles to profl. jours., chapters to books; publ;ished a book on sports and hormones. Named Best Doctors in NYC, NY Mag.; named one of Best Doctors In America, 2004—05. Achievements include first to identify skeletal problems, including scoliosis and stress fractures that occur in young women because of menstrual irregularities. Address: Ctr. for Menopause, Hormonal Disorders and Women's Health Dept Ob/Gyn Columbia U Med Ctr 622 W 168th St PH 16 New York NY 10032 Office: 16 E 60th St Ste 490 New York NY 10022 Office Fax: 212-737-4664, 212-744-9353.

WARREN, PAMELA A., psychologist; d. James Herbert Trail, Jr. and Jacqueline Joann Trail; m. Bruce E. Warren, 1982; 1 child, Rachel M. B.A., MA, So. Ill. U., PhD, 1991. Lic. clin. psychologist Ill., 1993. Counselor So. Ill. U., Carbondale, 1986—89, instr., 1989—91; faculty U. Ill. Med. Sch., Dept. Psychiatry, 1994—; clin. supr. Resolutions Employee Assistance Program, Champaign, 1996—2001; faculty U. Ill., Psychology Dept., 2000—; head psychology dept. Carle Clinic Assn., Urbana, 2001—. Faculty SmithKline-Beecham Pharms., 1993—96; mem. work injury network steering com. Carle Clinic Assn., Urbana, 1999—; nat. psychol. cons. Work Injury Network, 1999—; cons. WebilityMD.com, Wayland, Md., 2001—04, Blue Cross Blue Shield Ins., Dallas, 2002—, CompPartners, Irvine, Calif., 2003—; psychol. cons. Ill. State Univs. Retirement Sys., Champaign, 2001—; mem. supported employment com. Disability Mgmt. Employer Coalitions, San Diego, 2002—; mem. complimentary and alternative medicine steering com. Carle Clinic Assn., Urbana, 2003—; adv. bd. Reed Group Med. Disability, Colo., 2004—; mem. adv. bd. Job Demands Project, Disability Rsch. Inst.; presenter in field. Author: The Management of Workplace Mental Health Issues and Appropriate Disability Prevention Strategies, 2005; contbr. articles to profl. jours. and newsletters. Hospice vol. Meml. Hospice, Carbondale, Ill., 1984—91; ticket to work adv. bd. Social Security Adminstrn., 2004—. Scholar, So. Ill. U., 1983—91. Mem.: APA, Disability Mgmt. Employee Coalition, Internat. Assn. Rehabilitation Profls. (bd. mem. Profl. Case Mgmt. sect.), Am. Coll. Occupational & Environ. Medicine (newsletter adv. bd., aadv. com.), Assn. Applied Psychophysiology and Biofeedback, Assn. Behavior Analysis, Prescribing Psychologists' Register (founding mem.), Psi Chi. Achievements include patents for state-of-the-art model to assess and manage psychological concerns in order to prevent psychological disability. Avocations: travel, art, reading, sports. Office: Carle Clinic Assn 602 W Univ E-6 Urbana IL 61801 Office Phone: 217-383-3442. E-mail: pawarren@mchsi.com.

WARREN, PETER GIGSTAD, financial planner; b. Mankato, Minn., Sept. 29, 1958; s. ValGene Lee and Lynette Elizabeth (Grane) Gigstad. BS in Computer Sci. with honors, Mich. Tech. U., 1981; MBA magna cum laude, U. Dallas, 2007. Registered investment advisor. Jr. programmer IBM, Charlotte, NC, 1981; staff cons. Duke U., Durham, NC, 1981-82; v.p., gen. mgr. Intelligent Statements Inc., Chapel Hill, NC, 1982; systems programmer Datapoint Corp., San Antonio, 1982-84; systems engring. mgr.

COMPAQ Computer Corp., Dallas, 1984-87; v.p. fin. cons., cert. fin. planner, portfolio mgr. Personal Investment Adv. Program Merrill Lynch, Ft. Worth, 1987—2007; fin. advisor, v.p., investment officer, PIM portfolio mgr. Wachovia Securities, Ft. Worth, 2007—. Exhbns. include premier photography exhbn., Nature Photography, Ft. Worth Botanic Gardens, 2001; artist States of Mind exhbn., Arlington, Tex., 2002. Named one of Ams. Top 100 Fin. Planner, 2005, 2006. Mem. Internat. Platform Assn., Ft. Worth Execs. Club (sec. 1991, v.p. 1992, pres. 1993, 2000), Lions (membership com. 1992, bd. dirs.), Sigma Iota Epsilon. Avocations: travel, gourmet cooking, public speaking, photography. Address: 4062 Hildring Dr W Fort Worth TX 76109-4720 Office Phone: 817-877-9808. Business E-Mail: peter.g.warren@wachoviasec.com.

WARREN, RICHARD WAYNE, obstetrician, gynecologist; b. Puxico, Mo., Nov. 26, 1935; s. Martin R. and Sarah E. (Crump) W.; m. Rosalie J. Franzoia, Aug. 16, 1959; children: Lani Marie, Richard W., Paul D. BA, U. Calif., Berkeley, 1957; MD, Stanford U., Calif., 1961. Diplomate Am. Bd. Ob-Gyn. Intern Oakland Naval Hosp., Calif., 1961-62; resident on ob-gyn. Stanford Med. Ctr., 1964-67; pvt. practice specializing in ob-gyn. Mountain View, Calif., 1967—. Mem. staff Stanford Hosp., El Camino Hosp.; pres. Warren Medical Corp.; assoc. clin. prof. ob-gyn. Stanford Sch. Medicine. Contbr. articles to profl. jours. With USN, 1961-64. Fellow Am. Coll. Ob-Gyn.; mem. AMA, Am. Fertility Soc., Am. Assn. Gynecologic Laparoscopists, Calif. Med. Assn., San Francisco Gynecol. Soc., Peninsula Gynecol. Soc., Assn. Profs. Gynecology and Obstetrics, Royal Soc. Medicine, Shufelt Gynecol. Soc. Santa Clara Valley. Home: 102 Atherton Ave Menlo Park CA 94027-4021 Office: 2500 Hospital Dr Mountain View CA 94040-4106 Office Phone: 650-961-8111. Personal E-mail: warren423@sbcglobal.net.

WARREN, RICK DUANE, minister, writer; b. San Jose, Calif., Jan. 28, 1954; s. James Russell and Dorothy Nell (Armstrong) W.; m. Elizabeth Kay Lewis, June 21, 1975; children: Amy Rebecca, Joshua James, Matthew David. BA, Calif. Bapt. Coll., 1977; MA of Divinity, Southwestern Bapt. Theol. Sem., 1979; D of Ministry, Fuller Theol. Sem., 1989. Youth evangelist Calif. So. Bapt. Convention, Fresno, 1970-74; assoc. pastor First Bapt. Ch., Norwalk, Calif., 1974-76; asst. to pres. Internat. Evangelism Assn., Fort Worth, 1977-79; founding pastor Saddleback Valley Cmty. Ch., Mission Viejo, Calif., 1980—; founder Pastors.com. Lectr. Saddleback Ch. Growth Seminars. Author: The Purpose-Driven Church, 1995, Personal Bible Study Methods, 1997, The Power to Change Your Life, 1998, Answers to Life's Difficult Questions, 1999, Planned for God's Pleasure, 2002, The Purpose-Driven Life, 2002 (Gold Medallion award, ECPA Book of the Yr, 2003), The Emerging Church, 2003, Daily Inspiration for the Purpose-Driven Life, 2004. Named Outstanding Preacher of 1977, McGregor Found; named one of 100 Most Influential People of 2005, Time mag. Mem. No. Am. Soc. for Ch. Growth. Baptist. Office: Saddleback Valley Comm Ch 24194 Alicia Pky Ste M San Juan Capistrano CA 92691-3927 also: Pastors.com 20 Empire Dr Lake Forest CA 92630-2244 *

WARREN, ROBERT STEPHEN, lawyer; b. Pasadena, Calif., Dec. 9, 1931; s. Harry Ludwig and Maxine Winifred (Hopkins) W.; m. Betty Lou Soden, June 11, 1955 (dec. Sept. 1991); children: Kimberly Ann, Stephen Hopkins; m. Anna Marie Pretzel, Dec. 28, 1993. BA in Econs., U. Southern Calif., 1953, LLB, 1956. Bar: Calif. 1956, Del., U.S. Ct. Appeals (9th cir.), U.S. Dist. Ct. (ctrl. dist.) Calif., U.S. Ct. Mil. Appeals, U.S. Dist. Ct. (so. dist.) Calif., U.S. Dist. Ct. (ea. dist.) Calif., U.S. Dist. Ct. (no. dist.) Calif., U.S. Dist. Ct. Wyo., U.S. Dist. Ct. Colo., U.S. Dist. Ct. (ea. dist.) Wash., U.S. Supreme Ct. From assoc. to ptnr. Gibson, Dunn & Crutcher, LA, 1956, 59—. Contbr. articles to profl. jours.; assoc. editor Southern Calif. Law Rev.; speaker in field. Mem., former chair bd. councilors U. So. Calif. Law Ctr.; past pres., exec. com. mem. Western Justice Ctr. Found. 1st lt. US Army, 1957—59. Recipient Learned Hand award Am. Jewish Com., 1988, Shattuck-Price award Los Angeles County Bar Assn., 1989, Joseph A. Ball award Brennan Ctr. for Justice/NYU, 1997, Trial Lawyer Hall of Fame award Calif. State Bar Assn., 1998. Mem. Am. Coll. Trial Lawyers, Assn. Bus. Trial Lawyers, Order of Coif, City Club on Bunker Hill, Phi Beta Kappa. Republican. Presbyterian. Avocations: hiking, reading, tennis. Office: Gibson Dunn & Crutcher 333 S Grand Ave Ste 4400 Los Angeles CA 90071-3197 Office Phone: 213-229-7326. Business E-Mail: rwarren@gibsondunn.com.

WARREN, ROSANNA, poet; b. Fairfield, Conn., July 27, 1953; d. Robert Penn Warren and Eleanor Clark; m. Stephen Scully, 1981; children: Katherine, Chiara; stepson, Benjamin. BA summa cum laude, Yale U., 1976; MA, Johns Hopkins U., 1980. Pvt. art tchr., 1977-78; clerical worker St. Martin's Parish, NYC, 1977-78; asst. prof. English Vanderbilt U., Nashville, 1981-82; vis. asst. prof. Boston U., 1982-88, asst. prof. English and modern fgn. langs., 1989-95, assoc. prof. English, 1995—, Emma MacLachlan Metcalf prof. humanities, 2000—. Poetry cons., contbg. editor Partisan Rev., 1985-98; poet-in-residence Robert Frost Farm, 1990. Author: The Joey Story, 1963, Snow Day, 1981, Each Leaf Shines Separate, 1984, Stained Glass, 1993, Departure, 2003; editor, contbr.: The Art of Translation: Voices from the Field, 1989; editor: Eugenio Montale's Cuttlefish Bones, 1993, Satura, 1998; translator (with Stephen Scully) Euripides' Suppliant Women, 1995, poetry anthologies include In Time, 1995, From This Distance, 1996, Springshine, 1998; contbr. to periodicals including Agni Rev., Am. Poetry Rev., Antioch Rev., Atlantic Monthly, Chelsea, Chgo. Rev., Georgia Rev., Nation, New Republic, New Yorker, N.Y. Times, Paris Rev., Threepenny Rev., Partisan Rev., Ploughshares, Southern Rev., Washington Post. Recipient McLaughlin English prize Yale U., 1973, Charles E. Clark award Yale U., 1976, Nat. Discovery award in poetry 92nd St. YMHA-YWCA, 1980, Newton Arts Coun. award, 1983, Lavan Younger Poets prize Acad. Am. Poets, 1992, Lamont Poetry prize Acad. Am. Poets, 1993, Lila Wallace Writers' Fund award, 1994, Witter Bynner prize in poetry Acad. Arts and Letters, 1994, May Sarton award New Eng. Poetry Club, 1995, Pushcart prize, 2004, 06, award of merit in poetry Am. Acad. Arts and Letters, 2004, Ellen Maria Gorrissen Berlin prize Am. Acad. Berlin, 2006; named Scholar of House Yale U., 1975-76; Yaddo fellow, 1980, Lannan Found. fellow, 2005; Ingram Merrill grantee, 1983, 93; Guggenheim fellow, 1985-86; Am. Coun. Learned Socs. grantee, 1989-90. Fellow: Am. Acad. Arts and Sci.; mem.: AAAL, PEN, ALTA, MLA, Acad. Am. Poets (chancellor 1999—2005), Assn. Literary Scholars and Critics (v.p. 2004, pres. 2005). Office Phone: 617-358-1782.

WARREN, RUSS C., artist, educator; b. Washington, Dec. 29, 1951; s. Thomas Wayne and Dona Marie Warren; m. Carolyn Bolen Warren, Oct. 22; children: Tasha, Tanya Marie Hegland. BFA, U. N.Mex., 1973; MFA, U. Tex., San Antonio, 1977. Prof. art Davidson (N.C.) Coll., 1978—. Home: 841 Wolf Trap Rd Charlottesville VA 22911

WARREN, RUSSELL FREDERICK, orthopedist; b. Burlington, Vt., June 18, 1939; MD, SUNY, Syracuse, 1966. Bd. cert. orthopedic surgery. Intern St. Lukes Hosp. Ctr., NYC, 1966—68; resident orthopedic surgery Hosp. for Spl. Surgery, NYC, 1970—73, surgeon in chief, 1993—2003, surgeon-in-chief emeritus, 2003; fellow in shoulder surgery Columbia Presbyn. Med. Ctr., NYC, 1977; prof. surgery, chmn. divsn. orthopaedic surgery Weill Med. Coll., Cornell U.; physician New York Giants. Sci. adv. bd. KFx Med. Corp., 2006—. Editor-in-chief Techniques in Shoulder and Elbow Surgery. Recipient Neer award for shoulder rsch., 1989, 1995, 2005, 2006, O'Donohue award for sports medicine rsch., 1982, 1991, 1994, Humana award for sports medicine, 1992, Mr. Sports Medicine award, Am. Orthopaedic Soc. Sports Medicine, 2003. Mem.: Am. Orthop. Soc. Sports Medicine (pres. 1994—95), Am. Shoulder and Elbow Soc. (pres. 1994—95). Achievements include research in shoulder and knee instability; ligament reconstruction and arthroscopy; joint replacement-knee and shoulder; rotator cuff disease and sports injuries. Mailing: Hosp for Spl Surgery 535 E 70th St New York NY 10021 Office: Belaire Bldg 1st Fl 525 E 71st St New York NY Office Phone: 212-606-1178. Business E-Mail: warrenr@hss.edu.

WARREN, RUSSELL GLEN, educational consultant; b. Balt., Apr. 29, 1942; s. Clarence N. and Kathryn (Butler) W. BBA, U. Richmond, 1964; PhD, Tulane U., 1968. Asst. prof. to assoc. prof. U. Richmond, Va., 1971—74, dean, 1974—76, asst. v.p. to asst. pres., 1976—78; v.p. acad. affairs U. Montevallo, Ala., 1978-84, James Madison U., Harrisonburg, Va., 1984-90, v.p. acad. affairs, acting pres., 1986—87; pres. N.E. Mo. State U., Kirksville, 1990—94; disting. prof. econs., mgmt. Hardin-Simmons U., Abilene, Tex., 1995-97, dir. Ctr. for Rsch. Tchg. and Learning, 1995-97; exec. v.p., provost Mercer U., Macon, Ga., 1997—2002; prof. econs. So. Wesleyan U., 2003—06; pvt. practice cons. Chmn. adv. bd. Coll. Humanities, Social Sci. Coll. Charleston, SC, 1999—2007. Author: Antitrust in Theory and Practice, 1976, Carpe Diem, 1995. Bd. dirs. Va. Rural Devel. Corp., Richmond, 1988-90, Am. Coll. Bldg. Arts, 2005—; v.p. Kiawah Island Cmty. Assn., 2006-07, chmn. bd., 2007-. Capt. US Army, 1969—71. Named One of Outstanding Young Men of Va., Va. Jaycees, 1976. Mem.: Am. Coun. on Edn. (coun. of fellows), Am. Assn. Colls. and Univs. (bd. dirs. 1994—95). Methodist. Avocations: golf, collecting cars. Home and Office: 175 Marsh Island Dr Kiawah Island SC 29455 E-mail: kiawahwarren@cs.com.

WARREN, RUSSELL JAMES, investment banker, consultant; b. Cleve., July 28, 1938; s. Harold Fulton and Agnes Elmenah (Hawkswell) Warren; m. Doris Helen Kenyeres, June 6, 1964. BS, Case We. Res. U., 1960; MBA, Harvard U., 1962. CPA Ohio. With Ernst & Whinney, Cleve., 1962—87, ptnr. in charge merger and acquisition svcs., 1976—87, pres. TransAction Group, 1987—. Bd. dirs. Seneca Capital Mgmt., Inc. Co-author: (book) Implementing Mergers and Acquisitions in the Financial Services Industry, 1985; assoc. editor: Jour. Corp. Growth, 1986—87, mem. editl. bd.:, 1988; contbg. editor: Jour. Buyouts and Acquisitions, 1984—86; contbg. author: venture capital financing study conducted in five countries for Asian Devel. Bank, Malaysia, Indonesia, Pakistan, Sri Lanka, Thailand, 1986. Trustee Case We. Res. U., 1980—2005, chmn. audit com., 1991—2005; trustee Cleve. Bot. Garden, 1995—2002, We. Res. Hist. Soc., 1996—2002, chmn. investments com., 1999—2002; trustee Cmty. Improvement Corp. Summit, Medina and Portage Counties, 1992—2000, Cascade CDC, 1992—2000, Brit.-Am. C. of C., Great Lakes Region, 2001—05; dir. Univ. Tech., Inc., 1986—88; adv. bd. Shaker Investments, 1992—; v.p. M&A Internat. Inc., 1990—91, pres., 1992; bd. zoning appeals City of Lyndhurst, 1978—, chmn., 1980—82, 1991—93, 2000—01, 2006—; mem. vis. com. Case Sch. Engring., 1990—2004, Weatherhead Sch. Mgmt., 1998—2004; deans advisory coun. Case Sch. Engring., 2005—, Weatherhead Sch. Mgmt., 2005—; trustee Town Hall of Cleve., 2005—, Fairmont Presbyn. Ch., 1987—93, elder, 1991—93. Mem.: AICPA, Cleve. World Trade Assn., Cleve. Com. Fgn. Rels., Assn. Corp. Growth, Ohio Soc. CPAs, Harvard Club NYC, Catawba Island Club, Mayfield Sand Ridge Club, Union Club, Jesters. Office: The TransAction Group 500 Hanna Bldg Cleveland OH 44115 Home Phone: 440-461-2725; Office Phone: 216-348-1666.

WARREN, STEPHEN THEODORE, human geneticist, educator; b. Grosse Point, Mich., Nov. 30, 1953; s. Theodore Stephen and Frances (Fedo) W.; m. Karen Lee Pierce, Aug. 27, 1978; 1 child, Thomas. BS, Mich. State U., 1976, PhD, 1981. Diplomate Am. Bd. Med. Genetics. Grad. asst. Mich. State Univ., East Lansing, 1976-81; rsch. assoc. Univ. Ill., Chgo., 1981-83, instr., 1983-85; asst. prof. Emory U. Sch. of Medicine, Atlanta, 1985-91, assoc. prof., 1991-93, W.P. Timmie prof. human genetics, 1993—, chmn. dept. human genetics, 2001—; investigator Howard Hughes Med. Inst., 1992—2002. Vis. scientist European Molecular Biol. Lab., Heidelberg, Germany, 1984-; cons. Ctrs. for Disease Control, Atlanta, 1988-89, NIH, Bethesda, Md., 1989—; collaborator Ctr. D'Etude du Polymorphysme Humain, Paris, 1989—. Editor-in-chief Am. Jour. Human Genetics, 2000-2005; mem. editl. bd. Human Molecular Genetics, Am. Jour. Human Genetics, Cytogenetics, Cell Genetics, Mammalian Genome, others; contbr. chpts. to books and more than 200 articles to profl. jorus. Recipient Sigma Xi prize Mich. State Sigma Xi, East Lansing, 1981, NIH fellowship NIH, Bethesda, 1982, Basil O'Connor award March of Dimes, N.Y.C., 1986, Albert E. Levy award Emory Univ., Atlanta, 1987, William Rosen Rsch. award Nat. Fragile X Found., 1996; inductee Nat. Inst. Child Health and Human Devel. Hall of Fame Honor, 2003. Fellow Am. Coll. Med. Genetics; mem. Am. Soc. Human Genetics (nominating com. 1991, awards con. 1992—, bd. dirs. 1997—, William Allan award 1999), Am. Soc. Biochemistry and Molecular Biology, Am. Soc. Microbiology, Genetics Soc. Am., Am. Soc. Human Genetics (pres., 2005), Human Genome Orgn., Inst. Medicine., Nat. Academies. Achievements include research on molecular genetic studies of the fragile X syndrome and other human genetic diseases. Home: 2305 Kimbrough Ct Atlanta GA 30350-5635 Office: Emory Univ Sch Medicine 301 Whitehead Bldg 615 Michael St Atlanta GA 30322-4218

WARREN, TOMMY MELVIN, petroleum engineer; b. Tallassee, Ala., Aug. 26, 1951; s. Henry M. and Christene (Jones) W.; m. Carolyn Milam; children: Lisa, Wesley, Eric. BS in Mineral Engring., U. Ala., Tuscaloosa, 1973, MS in Mineral Engring., 1976. Ops. engr. Amoco Prodn. Co., Lafayette, La., 1973-75, rsch. engr. Tulsa, 1976-86, rsch. supr., 1986-94; spl. rsch. assoc., 1994-99; dir. rsch. and devel. Casing Drilling Rsch., Tesco Corp., 1999—. Mem. steering com. Nat. Program for Advanced Drilling and excavation Techs., 1992. Contbr. articles to Jour. Petroleum Tech., Soc. Petroleum Engrs. Jour., SPE Drilling Engring. Recipient Rossiter Raymond award AIME, 1982, SPE Drilling Engring. award, 1997, SPE Disting. lectr., 1998-99. Mem. NAE, So. Petroleum Engrs. (chmn. tech. coverage drilling com. 1985, com. chmn. Drilling Engring. award 1984-86, tech. editor 1987-90, rev. chmn. 1990-92) Cedrick K. Ferguson medal 1985) Republican. Baptist. Achievements include patents for drilling tools and methods. Office: Tesco Corp 11330 Brittmoore Park Dr Houston TX 77041

WARREN, WILLIAM BRADFORD, lawyer; b. Boston, July 25, 1934; s. Minton Machado and Sarah Ripley (Robbins) W.; children: John Coolidge, Sarah; m. Arete B. Swartz, Sept. 20, 1985. AB magna cum laude, Harvard U., 1956, LLB cum laude, 1959. Bar: N.Y. 1960. Assoc. Dewey Ballantine, NYC, 1959-68; ptnr. Dewey Ballantine, LLP, 1968—2002, of counsel, 2002—. Lectr. Inst. Fed. Taxation, NYU, So. Fed. Tax Inst., Practicing Law Inst. Pres. Cintas Found., N.Y.C.; bd. dirs. St. John's Coll., Annapolis and Santa Fe; bd. dirs. John Carter Brown Libr., Providence; adv. bd. dirs. Met. Opera Assn., N.Y.C. Mem. Am. Law Inst., Am. Coll. Trust and Estate Counsel (former regent), Acad. Am. Poets (bd. dirs., vice chair), Internat. Acad. Estate and Trust Law (former exec. com.), N.Y. State Bar Assn. (chmn. com. taxation of trust and estates sect. 1980-83), Assn. Bar City N.Y., Soc. Mayflower Descs., Harvard Club, Knickerbocker Club, Century Club, Grolier Club (past pres.). Home: 520 E 86th St New York NY 10028-7534 Office: Dewey Ballantine LLP 1301 Avenue Of The Americas New York NY 10019-6022 Home Phone: 212-734-2779; Office Phone: 212-259-8700. Business E-Mail: wwarren@dbllp.com.

WARREN, WILLIAM L., lawyer; b. Trenton, NJ, Mar. 14, 1948; BA, Colgate U., 1969; JD, NYU, 1973. Law clk., Hon. John R. Bartels US Dist. Ct. (ea. dist.), NYC, 1974; litigation assoc. Dewey Ballantine, NYC, 1975-81; ptnr. Warren Goldberg Berman & Lubitz, Princeton, NJ, 1982-87, Cohen Shapiro Polisher Shiekman & Cohen, Lawrenceville, NJ, 1987-95; ptnr., chair, NJ environ. law group Drinker Biddle & Reath LLP, Princeton, 1995—, mng. ptnr., mem. mgmt. com. Office: Drinker Biddle Reath LLP Ste 300 105 College Rd E Princeton NJ 08540-6622 Office Phone: 609-716-6603. Office Fax: 609-799-7700. Business E-Mail: william.warren@dbr.com.

WARRICK, KIMBERLEY KAYE, language and social studies educator; b. Lake Wales, Fla., Apr. 13, 1963; d. Bonnie Dawn and Edward Milo Dunagin (Stepfather); m. Robert Kelly Warrick, Nov. 30, 1986 (div. Apr. 0, 1995); 1 child, Kalegh Rebekah. BA, Capital U., 1989; MA, Ohio State U., 1999. Cert. elem. tchr. Mont., Ohio, learning disablities tchr. Mont., Ohio. Tchr. kindergarten/kindergarten afterschool program Columbus Torah Acad., Ohio, 1990—96, tchr. resource/ESL, 1990—96, tchr. 1st grade, 1990—96; tchr. 6th grade English/Social Studies Groveport Madison Local Schs., Ohio, 1996—2003; tchr. spl. edn. 8th grade Bozeman Pub. Schs., Mont., 2003—05, tchr. spl. edn. 9th grade, 2005—. English curriculum com. Bozeman Pub. Schs., Mont., 2004—05; Ind. edn. lead tchr. Social Studies Curriculum Leadership Team, 2006. Facilitator Ctr. for Civic Edn., Bozeman, Mont., 2004—05; del. Mont. Rep. Party State Conv., Big Sky, 2004. Mem.: Phi Delta Kappa (pres. MSU chpt. 2006), Coun. Tchr. Cert. Profl. Develop. (state bd. pub. edn. 2005—), Nat. Coun. for History Edn., Bozeman Edn. Assn. (bldg. rep. 2004—), Gallatin County Rep. Women. Office: Bozeman HS 205 N 11th Ave Bozeman MT 59715 Office Phone: 406-522-6354. Office Fax: 406-522-6222. Business E-Mail: kwarrick@bsd7.org.

WARRICK, PAUL DAVID, otolaryngologist; b. Peterborough, Ont., Canada, May 15, 1972; s. Dennis Alfred and Lois Eleanor Warrick; m. Rebecca Ruth Whitt, Dec. 23, 1994; 1 child, Zachary Everett Whitt. MD, McMaster U., Hamilton, Ont., 1995—99. Diplomate Am. Bd. Otolaryngology, 2005. Intern dept. surgery U. Toronto, 1999—2000, resident dept. otolaryngology, 2000—04; otolaryngologist Affinity Med. Group, Appleton, Wis., 2004—. Fellow: Royal Coll. Surgeons Can., Am. Acad. Otolaryngology-Head and Neck Surgery; mem.: ACS (assoc.), Am. Acad. Otolaryngic Allergy. Achievements include research in vocal tremor. Avocations: golf, baseball, volleyball, stamp collecting/philately. Office: Affinity Medical Group 1501 S Madison St Appleton WI 54915 Office Phone: 920-730-4968. Office Fax: 920-730-4916. Business E-Mail: pwarrick@affinityhealth.org.

WARRING, DOUGLAS FRANKLIN, education educator, psychologist; b. Braham, Minn., Aug. 16, 1949; s. Herbert Franklin and Maxine (Anderson) W.; m. Tonya Huber, Aug. 8, 2004; children: Jana, Leah, Andrew. BA, Bethel Coll., 1971; MA in Tchg., Coll. St. Thomas, 1975; PhD, U. Minn., 1983. Lic. social studies tchr., secondary sch. prin., Minn. Instr. bus. Inver Hills C.C., Inver Grove Heights, Minn., 1980-83; instr. psychology Concordia Coll., St. Paul, 1983; asst. prof. psychology U. Minn., 1982-84; asst. prof. edn. U. St. Thomas, St. Paul, 1984-90; dir. tchr. edn. Coll. St. Thomas, St. Paul, 1989-90, assoc. dean, 1990-95; prof. in edn. and psychology Univ. St. Thomas, 1996—, dir. continuing edn., 2005—, chair tchr. edn., 2006—. Mem. bd. examiners Nat. Coun. on Accreditation for Tchr. Edn., 1997—. Jour. Critical Issues in Curriculum & Instrn., 1999-2004, Jour. Action in Tchr. Edn., 2000—. Mem. editl. bd.: Internat. Jour. Critical Inquiry into Curriculum and Instrn., 2004—06. Mem. Curriculum Com., Bloomington, Minn., 1985-89; vice chair Planning, Evaluation and Reporting Com., Bloomington, 1985-87, chair, 1988-89. Served with USAR, 1972-96. Named one of Outstanding Young Men of Am., 1985. Mem. ASCD, Am. Assn. Tchr. Edn. (exec. bd., pres. Minn. chpt. 1985, nat. resolutions com. 1988, nat. rsch. com. 1997), Minn. Assn. Tchr. Edn. (exec. bd. 1984-93, pres. 1990-92), Minn. Human Rels. Assn., Internat. Coun. of Edn. for Teaching (life), Internat. Soc. for Tchr. Edn., Am. Legion, Met. Wrestling Ofcls. Assn. (v.p. 1982-86), Minn. Assn. Supervision and Curriculum Devel. (bd. dirs. 1994-2004), Soc. Psychol. Study of Social Issues, World Coun. Curriculum Instrn., Am. Edn. Rsch. Assn. Office: U St Thomas 1000 La Salle Ave Minneapolis MN 55403-2009 Home: 2698 Lake Ct Dr Mounds View MN 55112-4106 Office Phone: 651-962-4877. Business E-Mail: dfwarring@stthomas.edu.

WARRING, JEROME THOMAS, management consultant; b. Bloomington, Ind., Feb. 2, 1941; s. Thomas Edward Warring and Ellen Chase Hanna Murphy; 1 child, Frank Anthony. AB in Polit. Sci., Ind. U., 1962, MBA in Fin., 1972. Sr. cons. KMPG/Peat Marwick & Co., LA, 1969-70; v.p. and original equity ptnr. Korn/Ferry Internat., LA, 1971-78; pres. Warring & Assocs., Anaheim Hills, Calif., 1978—, Warring Internat. Ins. Adv. Svcs., Ltd., Anaheim Hills, 1987—. Retained sr. advisor Asia-Pacific bus. devel. strategy, negotiation, and fgn. regulatory affairs Citicorp Global Consumer Ins. Ops., NYC, 1989-93; internat. spkr. in field. Mem. nat. task force com. Boys & Girls Clubs Am., Inc., NYC, 1980—82; founder, pres. nonprofit Sonshine Youth Svcs., Inc., Bell Gardens, Cudahy, Commerce, Calif., 1976—; pres. Rio Hondo Boys & Girls Club, Bell Gardens, 1978—80; bd. dirs. Bell Gardens Assn. Mchts. and Commerce, The Home Ministry Fellowship, Inc., 1971—80, 2006—. Named Man of Yr., Federated Vol. Orgns., Downey, Calif., 1981, Bd. Vol. of Yr., United Way Greater LA, 1995. Mem. Newport-Irvine Rotary, Alexis de Tocqueville Soc. Republican. Reformed Ch. of Am. Avocations: volunteer public service, mountain biking, running, boating, global Christian and Rotary Internat. missions. Office: Warring Internat Adv Svcs Ltd 5673 Stetson Ct Anaheim CA 92807

WARRINGTON, GEORGE D., former transportation executive; b. Sept. 19, 1952; BA cum laude, Syracuse U., 1974, MPA, 1975. Asst. to dir. divsn. commuter svcs. N.J. Dept. Transp., 1975-77, spl. asst. to commr., 1977-80; dep. exec. dir./chief of staff N.J. Transit Corp. Ops., 1980-88; v.p., gen. mgr. N.J. Transit Rail Ops., 1988-90; dep. commr. N.J. Dept. Transp., 1990-92; exec. dir., pres. Del. River Port Authority and Port Authority Transit Corp., 1992-94; pres. N.E. Corridor Strategic Bus. Unit, Nat. R.R. Passenger Corp. (Amtrak), 1994-98, pres., CEO, 1998—2002; exec. dir. N.J. Transit Corp., 2002—07. Bd. dirs. Phila. Belt Line R.R., U. Del. Intermodal Transp. Inst., Mineta Internat. Inst. Surface Transp. Policy Studies; mem. adv. bd. Voorhees Transp. Ctr. Bloustein Sch. Planning and Pub. Policy Rutgers U. Named Pub. Official of Yr., Meadowlands C of C, 2007; recipient Salzberg Medallion, Syracuse U., 2000.

WARRINGTON, WILLARD GLADE, retired university official; b. Macomb, Ill., Oct. 24, 1920; s. Henry K. and Farie V. (Prather) W.; m. A. Irene Windser, Aug. 9, 1945 (dec. 1969); m. Janette Moffatt Cooper, Apr. 26, 1972; children: David, Steven, Douglas, Jane Ann, Stephen Cooper. B.Ed., Western Ill. State Tchrs. Coll., 1941; MS, U. Ill., 1949, MS, 1950, Ed.D., 1952. Tchr. public high schs., Ill., 1941-42, 45-48; mem. faculty Mich. State U., 1952-58, dir. office evaluation services, 1958-74, asso. dean Univ. Coll., 1974-78, acting dean Univ. Coll., 1978-80, dir. undergrad. univ. div., 1980-85, dir., prof. emeritus, 1986—. Cons. edn.; Ford Found. cons. U. Philippines. Contbr. articles on ednl. measurement to profl. publs.; editorial bd.: Ednl. and Psychol. Measurement, 1968-85. Active Boy Scouts Am., 1957-68. Served to lt. col. USAAF, 1942-45. Mem. Nat. Council on Measurement in Edn. (pres. 1973-74), Am. Ednl. Research Assn., Assn. for Gen. and Liberal Studies (sec.-treas. 1973-79) Methodist. Home: 1211 Ascot Pl Haslett MI 48840

WARRIOR, PADMASREE, communications executive; b. Oct. 22, 1960; BSChemE, Indian Inst. Tech., New Delhi, India; MSChemE, Cornell U. Joined Motorola, Inc., Schaumburg, Ill., 1984, v.p., gen. mgr., energy sys. group, corp. v.p., chief technology officer, semiconductor products sector, v.p., 1999, corp. officer, 2000, sr. v.p., 2003—05, chief tech. officer, 2003—, exec. v.p., 2005—. Gen. mgr. Thoughtbeam, Inc. (subsidiary of Motorola); mem. coun. digital economy Tex. Gov.; mem. rev. panel Tex. Higher Edn. Bd.; dir. Ferro Corp. Named one of Top 25 Chief Tech.

Officers, InfoWorld mag., 2007; recipient Women Elevating Sci. and Tech. award, Working Woman Mag., 2001. Office: Motorola Inc 1303 E Algonquin Rd Schaumburg IL 60196 Office Phone: 847-576-5000. *

WARRO, EDWARD A., library director, dean; MLS, Simmons Coll., 1979. Libr. Simmons Coll., S.W. Tex. State U.; dean librs. Loyola U., Chgo; dean univ. librs. Boston U., 2001—. Bd. mem. Boston Libr. Consortium Inc., New England Libr. Network (NELINET). Office: Northeastern U Librs 360 Huntington Ave Boston MA 02115 Office Phone: 617-373-5001. Office Fax: 617-373-5409. E-mail: e.warro@neu.edu. *

WARSH, KEVIN MAXWELL, federal official; b. Albany, Apr. 13, 1970; m. Jane Lauder. AB with honors in Pub. Policy, Stanford U., Calif., 1992; JD cum laude, Harvard U., Cambridge, Mass., 1995. Exec. dir., v.p. mergers & acquisitions, investment banking divsn. Morgan Stanley & Co., Inc., 1996—2002; spl. asst. to Pres. for econ. policy, exec. sec. Nat. Econ. Coun., Washington, 2002—06; mem. bd. govs. Fed. Res. Sys., Washington, 2006—. Office: Fed Res Sys 20th St & Constitution Ave NW Rm 2010 Washington DC 20551 Home: 3259 N St NW Washington DC 20007-2845 Office Phone: 202-452-3200. Office Fax: 202-452-2271. *

WARSHAW, ALLEN CHARLES, lawyer; b. Harrisburg, Pa., Aug. 27, 1948; s. Julius and Miriam (Nepove) W.; m. Shirley Anne Nes, Aug. 23, 1970; children: Christopher James, Andrew Charles, William Robert. BA, U. Pa., 1970; JD, Villanova U., 1973. Bar: Pa. 1973, U.S. Dist. Ct. (ea. and mid. dists.) Pa. 1974, U.S. Ct. Appeals (3d cir.) 1975, U.S. Supreme Ct. 1977, Calif. 1978. Staff atty. Office Atty. Gen., State of Pa., Harrisburg, 1973-79, chief civil litig., 1979-85, dir. civil law, 1985-86; ptnr. Duane, Morris & Heckscher, Harrisburg, 1986—2002; shareholder Klett, Rooney, Lieber & Schorling, Harrisburg, 2002—06; chief counsel Dept. Pub. Welfare Commonwealth of Pa., 2006—. Past pres. Mechanicsburg Soccer Assn.; Dem. committeeperson Cumberland County; past bd. dirs. Mechanicsburg Area Sch. Dist. Fellow: Am. Bar Found.; mem.: ABA, FBA, ABA Coun. Appellate Lawyers, Am. Bankruptcy Inst., Pa. Bar Assn., Dauphin County Bar Assn., Wildcat Found. (bd. dirs.). Home: 1035 Mccormick Rd Mechanicsburg PA 17055-5970 Office: Dept Pub Welfare 7th and Foster Sts Harrisburg PA 17120 Office Phone: 717-783-2800. Business E-Mail: awarshaw@state.pa.us.

WARSHAW, ANDREW LOUIS, surgeon, researcher; b. NYC, Feb. 18, 1939; s. David and Florence (Rand) W.; m. Brenda Rose Flavin, Jan. 4, 1986; children: Jordan, Abigail, Daniel; stepchildren: Heather, Gretchen, Brenda. AB, Harvard U., 1959, MD, 1963. Diplomate Am. Bd. Surgery. Intern in surgery Mass. Gen. Hosp., Boston, 1963-64, resident in surgery, 1964-65, 67-70, rsch. fellow in medicine, 1970, chief resident in surgery, 1971; clin. assoc. in gastroenterology NIH, Bethesda, Md., 1965-67; from instr. surgery to prof. surgery Harvard Med. Sch., Boston, 1972-90, Harold & Ellen Danser prof. surgery, 1990-97, W. Gerald Austen prof. surgery, 1997—; assoc. chief surg. svcs. Mass. Gen. Hosp., Boston, 1990-97, chief gen. surgery, 1992-97, chmn. dept. surgery, surgeon-in-chief, 1997—. Editor: Pancreatitis, 1989, Current Practice of Surgery, 1993, The Pancreas, 1998; contbr. more than 400 articles to med. jours., revs.; contbr. to 8 med. ednl. films, videos; editor-in-chief Surgery, 1997—. Trustee Mass. Gen. Hop., Boston, 1999—. Lt. comdr. USPHS, 1965-67. Mem. ACS (pres. Mass. chpt. 1991-92, gov. 1997-2003, health policy steering com. 2001-, 1st v.p. 2004-), Am. Bd. Surgery (chmn. 1992-93, dir. 1985-93), New Eng. Surg. Soc. (pres. 1993-94), Soc. for Surgery of Alimentary Tract (pres. 1997-98), Internat. Assn. Pancreatology (pres. 1998-), Boston Surg. Soc. (pres. 1999-2000), Halsted Soc. (pres. 2002-03). Avocations: photography, fly fishing. Office: Mass Gen Hosp White 506 Boston MA 02114 Business E-Mail: awarshaw@partners.org.

WARSHAW, CAROLE KLEIN, retired education educator; d. Irving and Frieda Patlis Klein; m. Gerald Jay Warshaw, June 9, 1956; children: Ms. Jodie Sharon Arrington, Howard Gary, Dr. Joel David. BA, Hunter Coll., NYC, 1957; MS in Spl. Edn., Hofstra U., 1976; Profl. Diploma- Adminstrn., St. John's U., Queens, NY, 1987, EdD, 1993. Cert. elem. sch. tchr. N.Y.C. Bd. Edn., 1957, asst. prin. N.Y.C. Bd. Edn., 1989, adminstrn./supr. N.Y. State Dept. Edn., 1987, clin. edn. trainer Fla. Dept. Edn., 2000. Tchr. N.Y.C. Bd. Edn., Queens, 1957—84, tchr. trainer, 1984—89, dir. testing, 1989—90; coord. master's program and evening edn. programs Lynn U., Boca Raton, Fla., 1994—2005, assoc. prof., 1994—2006; ret., 2006; adj. prof. Lynn U., 2006—, Kaplan U., 2006—. Liaison to dept. of edn. Lynn U., Boca Raton, 1995—2006; cons. Florence Fuller Child Devel. Ctrs., Boca Raton, 1999—, Toussaint L'Ouverture H.S., Delray Beach, Fla., 2001—; clin. supervision trainer Fla. Dept. Edn., Boca Raton, 1999—. Contbr. articles to profl. jours. V.p. Coalition of Boynton Beach (Fla.) Residents, 1992—94, Temple Beth Emeth, Bklyn., 1964—65; pres. Palm Shores Homeowners Assn., Boynton Beach, 1993—94. Impact II grantee, N.Y.C. Bd. Edn., 1981. Mem.: Coun. Adminstrs. and Suprs., Coun. for Exceptional Children, Phi Delta Kappa, Kappa Delta Pi (counselor 1997—2006). Independent. Hebrew. Avocations: bridge, travel, music. Personal E-mail: jecawa@adelphia.net. Business E-Mail: cwarshaw@kaplan.edu.

WARSHAW, DALIT HADASS, composer, educator; b. New City, NY, Aug. 6, 1974; BA, Columbia U., NYC, 1996; MusM, Juilliard Sch., NYC, 1997, D in Musical Arts, 2003. Mem. faculty Juilliard Sch., NYC, 2000—05; prof. composition and theory Boston Conservatory, 2004—; composer-in-residence Bowdoin Internat. Music Festival, Brunswick, Maine, 2004. Composer, pianist, thereminist, Sweden; vis. prof. composition Middlebury Coll., Vt., 2003—04; resident Yaddo Colony, MacDowell Arts Colony, 1998, 2002, 06. Composer: After the Victory (commn., 2006), 12 orchestral works, numerous vocal and solo works, works for chamber ensemble; performer: over 26 orchs. including the NY Philharm. Orch. and Israel Philharm. Orch. (Zubin Mehta conducting). Grantee, ASCAP; Fulbright scholar. Mem.: Coll. Music Soc., Am. Composers Forum, Am. Music Ctr., BMI (awards). Home: 235 Commonwealth Ave Apt #5 Boston MA 02116 Office: Boston Conservatory 8 The Fenway Boston MA 02215 Home Phone: 646-645-7885. Business E-Mail: dwarshaw@bostonconservatory.edu.

WARSHAW, MARVIN D., conductor, educator, musician; s. Norman Maurice Warshaw and Heartha Joyce Levinson; m. Carol A. Pendleton, May 25, 1986. M in Musical Arts, Yale U., 1980. Pers. mgr., libr., prin. violist, soloist New Haven Symphony Orch., 1977—; pvt. lessons tchr. Wesleyan U., Middletown, Conn., 1997—; faculty instr. Ednl. Ctr. for Arts, New Haven, 1997—; strings tchr. Coop. HS for Arts and Humanities, New Haven, 1999—2004; condr. Greater New Haven Concert Orch., 2001—; founding mem., mgr. Wall St. Chamber Players, 1980—; orch. pers. mgr., libr. violist Bellingham Festival, 2004—06. Head orch. libr. Aspen (Colo.) Music Festival, 1981—98. Office: New Haven Symphony Orch 70 Audubon St New Haven CT 06510

WARSHAW, STANLEY IRVING, federal official, consultant; b. Boston, Nov. 5, 1931; s. Alec and Sarah (Laserson) W.; m. Wanda Faye Capino, Feb., 12, 1992; 1 child from previous marriage, Karen Beth. BS in Ceramic Engring, Ga. Tech. Inst., 1957; Sc.D. in Ceramics, M.I.T., 1961; grad., Advanced Mgmt. Program, Harvard Bus. Sch., 1978. Sr. scientist research div. Raytheon Co., Waltham, Mass., 1961-64; with Am. Standard, Inc., New Brunswick, N.J., 1964-75, gen. mgr. engring. and devel., 1972-75; dir. Ctr. for Consumer Product Tech., Nat. Inst. Stds. and Tech. (formerly Nat. Bur. Stds.), Washington, 1975-80, dir. Office Product Standards Policy, 1981-86, assoc. dir., 1987-89, dir. Office Standards Svcs. Gaithersburg, Md., 1989-93; sr. policy advisor for stds. and tech. U.S. Dept. Commerce, Gaithersburg, 1994-99. Served to capt. U.S. Army, 1951-53. Fellow N.Y. Acad. Scis., Washington Acad. Scis. Home: 11783 Haddon Pkwy Boynton Beach FL 33437-1665 Home Phone: 561-740-4045; Office Phone: 561-740-4045. E-mail: swarshaw@adelphia.net.

WARSHAWSKY, MARK JOEL, human resources specialist, former federal agency administrator; b. Chgo., Mar. 26, 1958; s. Arthur and Dorothy (Chislof) W.; m. Laura Beth Margolis, June 28, 1987; children: David, Hannah, Avi, Sarah. BA, Northwestern U., 1979; PhD, Harvard U., 1984. Actuary Combined Ins., Chgo., 1979-80; rsch. asst. Nat. Bur. Econ. Rsch., Cambridge, Mass., 1981—84; tutor Harvard U., Cambridge, 1983-84; economist Fed. Res. Bd., Washington, 1984-88, dir. Credit Union, 1988—89, sr. economist, 1989—92; sr. economist employee plans and exempt orgns. IRS, 1992—95; dir., strategic and pension rsch. Teachers Ins. & Annuity Assoc. Coll. Retirement Equity Fund, NYC, 1995—98; dir. rsch. Teachers Ins. & Annuity Assoc. Coll. Retirement Equity Fund Inst., NYC, 1998—2001; dep. asst. sec. for econ. policy & microeconomic analysis US Dept. Treasury, Washington, 2002—04, asst. sec. for econ. policy, 2004—06; dir. retirement rsch. Watson Wyatt Worldwide, Inc., Arlington, Va., 2006—. Mem. Social Security Adv. Bd., 2006—. Contbr. articles to profl. jours; author/editor several books. Trustee Actuarial Found., 2000—02. Sloan scholar Harvard U., 1983-84. Mem. Am. Econ. Assn., Am. Risk and Ins. Assn., Nat. Assn. Bus. Economists, Nat. Assn. Soc. Ins. Republican. Jewish. Office: Watson Wyatt Worldwide Inc 901 N Glebe Rd Arlington VA 22203 Business E-Mail: mark.warshawsky@watsonwyatt.com.

WARTELL, MICHAEL ALAN, academic administrator; b. Albuquerque, Nov. 4, 1946; s. Richard H. and Betty D. (Davis) Wartell; m. Ruth E. Beachy, Dec. 3, 1977; children: Justin Davis, Richard Harrison. BS, U. N.Mex., 1967; MS, Yale U., 1968, PhD, 1971. Asst. prof. chemistry Met. State Coll., 1971—75, assoc. prof., chmn. dept., 1975—78; dean sch. natural scis., prof. chemistry James Madison U., 1979—84; provost, v.p. acad. affairs Humboldt State U., Arcata, Calif., 1984—89, prof. chemistry, 1984—94; chancellor Ind U. - Purdue U., Ft. Wayne, 1994—. Mem. U.S. Army Sci. Bd., 1981—87; participant various study groups on chem. warfare, decontaminatin, biodefense; cons. U.S. Army, IRT Corp., Sandia Nat. Labs., SRI Internat., JAYCOR, HERO, Boeing Elecs., Battelle; mem. Def. Intelligence Agy. Sci. Adv. Com., 1984—; chmn. bd. visitors Def. Systems Mgmt. Coll., Ft. Belvoir, Va., 1984—, chair, 1985—. Co-author: Engineering Education and A Lifetime of Learning, 1975, Introduction to Chemistry, 1975, Fundamentals of Chemistry, 1980; contbr. articles to profl. jours. Bd. dirs. Humboldt State U. Found., 1984—. Fellow: Am. Acad. Forensic Scis.; mem.: Kappa Nu Epsilon, Am. Assn. Univ. Adminstrs. (evaluation task force 1978—79, stds. and rev. com. 1983—84), Am. Phys. Soc., Am. Chem. Soc., Phi Kappa Phi, Phi Beta Kappa, Sigma Xi. Jewish. Office: Ind U Purdue U 2101 E Coliseum Blvd Fort Wayne IN 46805-1445 E-mail: wartell@ipfw.edu.

WARTENBERG, KATJA ELTRIEDE, neurologist; b. Berlin, May 4, 1973; arrived in US, 2000; d. Jan Reinhardt and Monika Elisabeth (Kathe) Wartenberg. MD, Humboldt U., Berlin, PhD, 1998. Diplomate Am. Bd. Neurology. Intern in internal medicine Met. Hosp., NYC, 2000—01; resident in neurology Georgetown U., Washington, 2001—04; fellow in neurocritical care Columbia U., NYC, 2004—06; attending neurocritical care U. Dresden, Germany, 2006—. Author: Stroke Book, 2006. Mem.: Neurocritical Care Soc., Critical Care Soc., Am. Acad. Neurology. Avocations: dance, jazz. Office: U Carl Gustav Carus Fetscherstrasse 74 01307 Dresden Germany Office Phone: 011-49-351-4582564. Office Fax: 011-49-351-4585353. Personal E-mail: kwartenberg@neuro.columbia.edu. Business E-Mail: katja.wartenberg@neuro.med.tu-dresden.de.

WARTH, ROBERT DOUGLAS, history professor; b. Houston, Dec. 16, 1921; s. Robert Douglas and Virginia (Adams) W.; m. Lillian Eleanor Terry, Sept. 18, 1945. BS, U. Ky., 1943; MA, U. Chgo., 1945, PhD, 1949. Instr. history U. Tenn., Knoxville, 1950-51; instr. Rutgers U., Newark, 1951-54, asst. prof., 1954-58; vis. prof. Paine Coll., Augusta, Ga., 1960; asso. editor Grolier, Inc., NYC, 1960-62, 63-64; lectr. Hunter Coll., NYC, part time, 1962-63; asso. prof. S.I. C.C., 1964-68; prof. history U. Ky., Lexington, 1968-92, prof. emeritus history, 1992—. Pres. So. Conf. Slavic Studies, 1982-83 Author: The Allies and the Russian Revolution, 1954, Soviet Russia in World Politics, 1963, Joseph Stalin, 1969, Lenin, 1973, Leon Trotsky, 1977, Nicholas II: The Life and Reign of Russia's Last Monarch, 1997. Served with AUS, 1943-44. Sr. scholar award So. Conf. Slavic Studies, 1992. Mem. Am. Hist. Assn., Am. Assn. Advancement Slavic Studies, AAUP Office: U Ky Dept History Lexington KY 40506-0001 Home: 2069 Fontaine Rd Apt 4 Lexington KY 40502

WARTHEN, HARRY JUSTICE, III, lawyer; b. Richmond, Va., July 8, 1939; s. Harry Justice Jr. and Martha Winston (Alsop) W.; m. Sally Berkeley Trapnell, Sept. 7, 1968; children: Martha Alsop, William Trapnell. BA, U. Va., 1961, LLB, 1967. Bar: Va. 1967, U.S. Ct. Appeals (4th cir.) 1967, U.S. Dist. Ct. (ea. dist.) Va. 1969. Law clk. to judge US Ct. Appeals (4th cir.), Richmond, Va., 1967-68; assoc. Hunton & Williams, Richmond, 1986—2005, sr. counsel, 2005—. Lectr. in field U. Va. Law Sch., Charlottesville, 1975—77. Trustee exec. com. Hist. Richmond Found., 1986-95, 96—, pres., 2000-02; trustee Woodrow Wilson Presdl. Libr., 1997-2003, 05—; dir. exec. com. Preservation Alliance of Va. (now part of APVA Preservation Va.), 1991-97, pres., 1994-96; Va. rep. bd. advisors The Nat. Trust for Historic Preservation, 2003—; dir. The Corp. for Jefferson's Poplar Forest, 2005—; elder, trustee endowment fund Grace Covenant Presbyn. Ch.; moderator Hanover Presbytery, Presbyn. Ch. (USA), 1988. Lt. US Army, 1962—64. Fellow Am. Coll. Trust and Estate Counsel, Va. Law Found.; mem. Va. Bar Assn. (chmn. sect. on wills, trusts and estates 1981-89), Antiquarian Soc. Richmond (pres. 1977-78, 98-99), Country Club Va., Deep Run Hunt Club. Home: 1319 Shallow Well Rd Manakin Sabot VA 23103-2305 Office: Hunton & Williams Riverfront Plz E Tower 951 E Byrd St Richmond VA 23219 Home Phone: 804-784-5245; Office Phone: 804-788-8414. Business E-Mail: hwarthen@hunton.com.

WARTLUFT, DAVID JONATHAN, retired librarian, minister; b. Stouchsburg, Pa., Sept. 22, 1938; s. Cleaver Milvard and Dorothy (Stump) W.; m. Joyce Claudia Dittmer, June 15, 1963 (div. Sept. 1988); children: Elizabeth Marie, Deborah Joy, Rebecca Janet, Andrew Jonathan. AB (Trexler scholar), Muhlenberg Coll., 1960; MDiv (Danforth scholar), Luth. Theol. Sem., Phila., 1964; MA (scholar), U. Pa., 1964; MS (Lilly Found. scholar), Drexel U., 1968; DD, Luth. Theol. Sem., Phila., 2003. Asst. chaplain, instr. religion Springfield Coll., Mass., 1962-63; ordained minister Luth. Ch., 1964; pastor Jerusalem Luth. Ch., Allentown, Pa., 1964-66; cataloger, reference libr. Luth. Sem. Phila., 1966-68, asst. libr., 1968-77, dir. libr., 1977—2002, chaplain, 1978-79, dir. 1st yr. field edn., 1979-81, 82-83, dir. 1st yr. field edn., faculty sec., 1985—2002; interim pastor New Jerusalem (Pa.) Luth. Ch., 2003—04, New Bethel Union Ch., Pa., 2004, Maiden Creek (Pa.) Union Ch., 2005—06, Friedens Luth. Ch., Stony Run, Pa., 2006. Comms. com. Northeastern Pa. Synod, 1967—78; archivist Northeastern Pa. Synod, Luth. Ch. Am., 1970—87; conv. com. Northeastern Pa. Synod, 1976; v.p. Luth. Archives Ctr., Phila., 1979—85, 1998—2005, bd. dirs.; libr. cons. Gurkul Luth. Ch., Madras, India, 1989, Huria Kristen Batak Protestant Sem., Pematang Siantar, Sumatra, Indonesia, 1989, Luther Sem., Adelaide, Australia, 1996; chair archives adv. bd. Evang. Luth. Ch. Am., 2000—03; adv. bd. Resource Ctr. Northeastern Pa. Synod, 2003—; archivist Northeastern Pa. Synod, Evang. Luth. Ch. Am., 1988—91, 2002—. Editor: Teamwork, 1970—84, The Periodical, 1979—84, Luth. Hist. Soc. Eastern Pa.; contbr. articles to profl. jours. Mem.: Drexel U. Grad. Sch. Libr. and Info. Sci. Alulmni Assn. (bd. dirs. 1978—80), Mid. States Assn. (accreditation visitor), Assn. Uniting Religion and Art (chmn. membership com., treas. 1995—2002), Paradise Falls Luth. Assn. (chmn. religious activities 1985—86, bd. dirs. 1985—87), Assn. Theol. Schs. in US and Can. (selection panel for libr. grants), Luth. Hist. Conf. (com. on scholarly rsch. and pub. 1981—, constl. revision com. 1984—86, membership chair 1994—96, editor essays and reports 1996—2000, bd. dirs., treas., 1988-94 1996—2002), Coun. on Study Religion (liaison com. 1974—77, nominating com. 1978—80, liaison com. 1981—82), Coun. Nat. Libr. and Info. Assn. (counselor 1978—81), Southeastern Pa. Theol. Librs. Assn. (sec. 1970—73, chair planning com. 1986—89), Am. Theol. Libr. Assn. (exec. sec., editor procs. 1971—81, bd. dirs. 1991—94, recording sec. 1995—97, devel. officer 1998—99), Luth. Hist. Soc. Ea. Pa. (life; bd. dirs. 1991—94, v.p. 1994—96), Beta Phi Mu, Phi Sigma Tau, Eta Sigma Phi. Democrat. Home Phone: 610-693-5073. Personal E-mail: djwartluft@aol.com. Business E-Mail: dwartluft@ltsp.edu. *By God's grace I am freed to live a life of joyful service in gratitude.*

WARTMAN, STEVEN A., medical association administrator; Grad., Cornell U., 1966; MD, Johns Hopkins U., 1970, PhD Sociology, 1979. Diplomate Am. Bd. Internal Medicine. Dir. med. svs., chmn. medicine Mount Sinai Med. Ctr., Miami Beach; prof. medicine U. Miami; sr. residency in internal medicine Baltimore City Hosp.; intern in internal medicine Stanford U. Med. Ctr.; resident in internal medicine Yale-New Haven Hosp.; prof. medicine Albert Einstein Coll. Medicine; physician-in-chief L.I. Jewish Med. Ctr.; with Edward Meilman Disting. Chair Medicine; dir. Ctr. Quality Rsch. North Shore-L.I. Jewish Health Sys.; dean U. Tex. Med. Sch. San Antonio, 2000—05; pres. Assn. Acad. Health Centers, Washington, 2005—. Contbr. more than 120 peer-reviewed jour. articles, abstracts, chapters to books. Recipient Leadership and Achievement award, Soc. Gen. Internal Medicine, 1997, Excellence award, U.S. Health Resources and Svcs. Adminstrn., 1999; fellow Internat. in Health Care, Yugoslavia, 1969, Primary Care Policy, USPHS, 1991; scholar Henry Luce, Indonesia, 1975—76, Robert Wood Johnson Clin., Johns Hopkins U., 1976—78. Fellow: ACP; mem.: Alpha Omega Alpha, Phi Beta Kappa. Office: Assn Academic Health Centers Ste 720 1400 Sixteenth St NW Washington DC 20036

WASAN, DARSH TILAKCHAND, academic administrator, chemical engineer, educator; b. Sarai, Salah, West Pakistan, July 15, 1938; came to U.S., 1957, naturalized, 1974; s. Tilakchand Gokalchand and Ishari Devi (Obhan) W.; m. Usha Kapur, Aug. 21, 1966; children: Ajay, Kern. BSChemE, U. Ill., 1960; PhD, U. Calif., Berkeley, 1965. Asst. prof. chem. engring. Ill. Inst. Tech., Chgo., 1964-67, assoc. prof., 1967-70, prof., 1970—, chmn. dept., 1971-77, 78-87, acting dean, 1977-78, 87-88, v.p. rsch. and tech., 1988-91, provost, 1991—, provost and sr. v.p., 1995-96, v.p., internat. and Motorola chair, 1996—. Cons. Inst. Gas Tech., 1965-70, Chgo. Bridge & Iron Co., 1967-71, Ill. EPA, 1971-72, NSF, 1971, 78-79, 87-89, Nelson Industries, 1976—, B.F. Goodrich Chem. Co., 1976-78, Exxon Rsch. & Engring. Co., 1977-89, Stauffer Chem. Co., 1980-88, ICI Ams., 1988-92, Westinghouse Savannah River Co., 1995-2004, Monsanto, 1999-2004, Dow Chem., 2006-07; Procter & Gamble lectr. U. Cin. Editor-in-chief Jour. colloid and Interface sci.; mem. publs. bd. Chem. Engring. Edn. Jour.; mem. adv. bd. Jour. Separations Tech., Current Opinion in Colloid and Interface Sci., Jour. of Dispersion Sci. and Tech.; contbr. articles to profl. jours. Recipient Donald Gage Stevens Disting. Lectureship award Syracuse U., 1991, Jakob J. Bikerman Lectureship award Case Western U., 1994, Robert Gilpin Lectr. award Clarkson U., 1995, MacMoran Disting. Lectureship award Tulane U., 1996, Sidney Ross lectr. award, 1996, Bonnet Dodge Disting. Lectureship award Yale U., 1998, Dinesh O. Shah Lectureship award U. Fla., 2004, Norman N. Li Disting. Lectureship award Wayne State U., 2005, Bird-Stewart-Lightfoot Lectureship award U. Wis., 2007; Spl. citation U.S. FDA, 2000. Fellow AIChE (Ernest Thiele award 1989, Thomas Baron award in fluid-particle systems 2002, Alpha Chi Sigma award for chem. engring. rsch. 2005); mem. AAAS, NAE, Indian NAE, Am. Chem. Soc. (award in colloid chemistry 2000, Langmuir Lectureship award 2004), Am. Soc. Engring. Edn. (Western Electric award 1972, 3M Lectureship award chem. engring. divsn. 1991), Fine Particles Soc. (pres. 1976-77, Hausner award 1982), Sigma Xi. Home: 8705 Royal Swan Ln Darien IL 60561-8433 Office: Ill Inst Tech 3300 S Federal St Chicago IL 60616-3793 Office Phone: 630-985-8180. Business E-Mail: wasan@iit.edu.

WASCH, WILLIAM KARL, gerontologist, consultant; b. Mt. Vernon, NY, May 11, 1931; s. Karl F. and Lina M. (Krauth) W.; m. Susan Beck Wasch, Aug. 23, 1958; children: Christina, William K. Jr., Heidi, Frederick. BA with honors, Wesleyan U., 1952; MS in Bus., Columbia U., 1953. Fin. analyst Std. Oil of N.J., 1956-59; mktg. rep. Esso Std., NYC, 1959-61; mktg. economist Sinclair Refining Co., NYC, 1961-64; dir. devel. and alumni rels. Wesleyan U., Middletown, Conn., 1965-84; pres. William K. Wasch Assocs., Middletown, 1985—. Builder accessible housing. Author: Home Planning for Your Later Years, 1996. Trustee Wesleyan U., Middletown, 1997-2000, Nat. Coun. on the Aging, Inc., Washington, 1994-96, 98-2005, leadership coun., 2006-, host CPTV show, In Our Prime, 2005, Seabury Retirement Cmty., Bloomfield, Conn., 1984-2002; chair Middletown Sr. Affairs Comm., 1996-2002; alt. del. White House Conf. on Aging, 2005; host PBS Nat. Show In Our Prime, 2006. Lt. j.g. USNR, 1953-56. Mem. Hartford Club, Adelphic Ednl. Fund (sec., treas.), Am. Assn. for Support of Ecological Initiatives (sec., treas.), Phi Beta Kappa. Episcopalian. Avocation: squash. Home and Office: 150 Coleman Rd Middletown CT 06457-5065 Office Phone: 860-346-2967. Business E-Mail: wkwasch@gmail.com.

WASDEN, LAWRENCE, state attorney general; m. Tracey Wasden; children: Sean, Ashley, Cassidy, Blake. BA, Brigham Young U., 1982; JD, U. Idaho, 1985. Bar: Idaho 1985. Dep. pros. atty. Canyon County, Idaho; dep. atty. gen. Idaho State Tax Commn.; dep. chief of staff State of Idaho, Boise, chief of staff to atty. gen., atty. gen., 2003—. Mem.: Idaho State Bar (founding mem., immediate past chmn. govt. and pub. lawyers sect.). Republican. Office: Office Atty Gen PO Box 83720 700 W Jefferson St Boise ID 83720

WASENDORF, RUSSELL R., SR., brokerage house executive; Dir. pub. affairs Am. Soybean Assn.; head Wasendorf & Son Co., 1980—, Wasendorf & Assoc., Inc.; chmn., CEO Peregrine Fin. Group, Inc., 1980—. Founder Stocks, Futures and Options mag., 2001, Ctr. Futures Edn.; ptnr. Allen's New Am. Cafe, Chgo. Author: (books) Commody Trading: The Essential Primer, 1985, All About Futures From The Inside Out, 1992, All About Commodities From The Inside Out, 1992, All About Options from the Inside Out, 1993, All About Managed Futures From The Inside Out, 1993, The Complete Guide To Single Stock Futures, 2003. Office: PFG Inc 190 S LaSalle St 7th Fl Chicago IL 60603 Office Phone: 800-333-5673.

WASHBURN, CAROLYN K., editor-in-chief; b. 1963; m. Perry Washburn; 3 children. Grad., Ind. U. Bus. reporter Lansing State Jour., Mich., 1984—87; bus. reporter, bus. editor, asst. mng. editor news, metro editor Rochester (NY) Democrat & Chronicle, 1987—93, mng. editor, 1995—99, Idaho Statesman, Boise, 1993—95, exec. editor, 1999—2005; v.p., editor Des Moines Register, 2005—. Recipient Pres.'s ring, Gannett Co., Inc., 2001. Mem.: Am. Soc. Newspaper Editors. Office: Des Moines Register PO Box 957 Des Moines IA 50306-0957 Office Phone: 515-284-8502. E-mail: cwashburn@dmreg.com. *

WASHBURN, DAVID THACHER, lawyer; b. Claremont, NH, May 2, 1930; s. Walter Henry and Josephine Emmeline (Dana) W.; m. Joycemarie Springer, June 10, 1957 (div. Dec. 1975); children: Margaret Dana, David Thacher Jr., Robert Springer, John Putnam. BA, U. Vt., 1952; JD, NYU,

1955. Bar: N.Y. 1956, D.C. 1970, U.S. Supreme Ct 1970. From assoc. to ptnr. Paul, Weiss, Rifkind, Wharton & Garrison, NYC, 1955—95, of counsel, 1996—. Adj. prof. CUNY Law Sch., 1997-98. Trustee Rye Neck Bd. Edn., Mamaroneck, NY, 1971-73, Cambridge (Mass.) Coll., 1980-88, The Yard, NYC, 1986-95, ARIA Found., Inc., Williston, Vt., 1991—; trustee, mem. exec. com. Rare Ctr. for Tropical Conservation, Phila., 1979-80; dir. Sanctuary for Families, Inc., NYC, 1994-2003, mem. exec. com., treas. 1995-2000, mem. pres. coun. 2006—. Mem. ABA, N.Y. State Bar Assn., Assn. of Bar of City of N.Y., The Coffee House, Westchester Country Club. Home: 10 W 66th St New York NY 10023-6206 Office: Paul Weiss Rifkind Wharton & Garrison Fl 2 1285 Ave of the Americas New York NY 10019-6064 Home Phone: 212-799-9265; Office Phone: 212-373-3301. Business E-Mail: dwashburn@paulweiss.com.

WASHBURN, DONALD ARTHUR, retired transportation executive, investor; b. Mankato, Minn., Sept. 24, 1944; s. Donald and Geraldine Helen (Pint) W.; m. Christine Carvell, Aug. 24, 1968; children: Timothy, Abigail. BBA cum laude, Loyola U., Chgo., 1971; MBA, Northwestern U., 1973, JD cum laude, 1978. Bar: Ill. 1978. With prodn. mgmt. dept. J.T. Ryerson/Inland Steel, Chgo., 1963-68; asst. to the pres. G.B. Frank, Inc., 1969-70; cons. Intec, Inc., 1970-72; mktg. mgmt., atty. Quaker Oats, Co., 1972-79; sr. cons. Booz, Allen & Hamilton, 1979-80; from corp. v.p. to exec. v.p. Marriott Corp., Washington, 1980-90; sr. v.p. N.W. Airlines, Mpls., 1990-94, exec. v.p., 1994-98; pres. chmn. N.W. Cargo, 1997—98; chmn. N.W. Aerospace Tng. Corp., 1996—98. Bd. dirs. LaSalle Hotel Properties, Greenbrier Cos., Inc., Key Tech., Inc., Amedisys, Inc., Draper & Kramer, Inc., Victor Plastics, Inc., Paulson Oil Co., LAI Co., Inc.; law bd. Northwestern U., alumni adv. bd. Kellogg Grad. Sch.; adv. bd. Spell Capital Ptnrs. Fund II, LP, Fund III, LP. Contbr. articles to profl. jours. Chmn., mem. nat. bd. dirs. Friends of the Children; bd. dirs. Portland Citizens Crime Commn., Citizens Commn. on Homeless, Oreg. Bus. Assn.; dir. emeritus Childrens Cancer Rsch. Fund; chmn. nat. bd. Stand for Children. Mem.: ABA, Ill. Bar Assn., Alpha Sigma Nu, Beta Gamma Sigma. Unitarian Universalist.

WASHBURN, GLADYS HAASE, retired church musician, educator, director; b. San Antonio, Feb. 19, 1919; d. Henry August and Rosa Sophie (Sundermeyer) Haase; m. Jost Brainard Washburn, Dec. 29, 1942 (dec.); children: Yvonne Rosalind, Henry Brainard, Diane Louise. Tchg. cert. in piano/organ, St. Louis Coll. Music, 1940. Cert. piano St. Louis Coll. Music, 1940. Ch. pianist Friedens Evang. Ch., 1932—38; organist, choir dir. St. Martin's Ch., High Ridge, Mo., 1939—40; choir dir. Bethany Evang. and Ref. Ch., San Antonio, 1940—42, organist, choir dir. New Orleans, 1952—55, St. Paul's Evang. and Ref. Ch., Corpus Christi, Tex., 1944—51, Bethlehem United Ch. of Christ, Buffalo, 1964—70, First Congl. United Ch. of Christ, Dwight, Ill., 1970—72, St. Michael's Episcopal Ch., Independence, Mo., 1985—92; dir. jr. choir Bethlehem Evang. and Ref. Ch., Buffalo, 1956—61; interim organist, choir dir. St. Paul's and St. Marks Ch., Buffalo, 1963, Village United Ch. of Christ, Blue Springs, Mo., 1992—93; interim organist chs. Greater Kansas City area, 1993—97; ret., 1997. Cons. chs. seeking organists, Buffalo, Blue Springs, Mo. Organ recitalist S.W. Conf. Nat. PTA Meeting, San Antonio, 1941, 1942; accompanist Harlandale Sch. Dist., San Antonio, 1941, 1942. Recipient Cert. in Ministry in Music, United Ch. Christ, 1992. Mem.: Am. Guild Organists. Republican. United Ch. Of Christ. Avocations: sewing, cooking, reading. Home: 300 SW 19th Terr Blue Springs MO 64015

WASHBURN, GLADYS RICE, photojournalist, educator; d. Pincus and Johanna Rice. BS in Comm. Arts summa cum laude, CUNY, 1978; MA in English Edn., NYU, 1981. Photographer Conde Nast Publications, NYC, 1944—47; freelance photographer NYC, 1948—2007; photography instr. Germain Sch. Photography, NYC, 1958—65; cinematographer and editor for film Dynamic II GE Time Life Ednl., NYC, 1969—70; pres. Washburn Films, NYC, 1972—81; writing instr. Borough of Manhattan CC, NYC, 1985—2001. Exhibiting photographer Balt. Mus. Art, 1946; writer in residence Lexington for Performing Arts, NY, 1976; exhibiting filmmaker The Swing Tours Film Festival, France, 1966. Film maker (short film) The Swing (Golden Eagle award, 1965); one-woman shows include Hunter Arts Gallery, NYC, 1977, Gallery One, Hillsdale, NY, 1977; photographer (one-woman shows), Bronxville, 2004; exhibition, Bronxville Pub. Libr., NY, 2007—; author: (book) Fortune's Hand; contbg. author: Hudson River, 1988—91, 1993, designer, editor: art book Portfolio, 1994. Recipient Film Collection award, Mus. Modern Art, 1965—2007.

WASHBURN, JERRY MARTIN, accountant, corporate executive; b. Powell, Wyo., Dec. 31, 1943; s. Roland and Lavon (Martin) W.; divorced; children: Garth, Gavin, Kristina; m. Mary Scatterday. BS in Acctg., Brigham Young U., 1969. CPA, Wash., Idaho, Oreg. Staff acct. Arthur Andersen & Co., Seattle, 1969-70, from sr. auditor to audit mgr. Boise, Idaho, 1971—79; v.p. contr. Washburn Musicland, Inc., Phoenix, 1980-82; mgr., ptnr. Washburn Enterprises, Phoenix, 1977-90; pres. Total Info. Systems, Inc., Phoenix, 1984-90; v.p. KJ Mktg., Inc., Phoenix, 1990-91; dir. mktg. IPRO, Inc., Phoenix, 1991-94; assoc. Perfect Strategies, Inc., Phoenix, 1994—95; v.p., CFO Global Indsl. Products, Inc., Scottsdale, Ariz., 1995—96. Pres., CEO OneSource Techs., Inc., Scottsdale, 1996-2002, dir., chmn. 1999; ptnr. Tatum Ptnrs. LLP, 2002—; mng. mem. Ptnrs. Resource Mgmt., LLC, 2003-05; CFO Blue Sun Biodiesel, Inc., 2007; founding dir. Internat. and Commerce Bank, Phoenix, 1985-86; chmn. audit com. 1source Techs., 2000-03, AmeriFirst Found., 2004. Mem. AICPA, Inst. Internat. Auditors (pres. Boise chpt. 1974, bd. dirs. Boise and Portland chpts. 1975-77), Am. Mgmt. Soc., Wash. Soc. CPAs, Idaho Soc. CPAs. Independent. Office: Tatum Partners LLP PO Box 25881 4800 N Scottsdale Rd Scottsdale AZ 85255 Personal E-mail: washburn3@cox.net. Business E-Mail: jerry.washburn@tatumpartners.com.

WASHBURN, JOAN THOMAS, small business owner; b. NYC, Dec. 26, 1929; d. Frank B. and Josephine (Hartman) Thomas; m. Alan Lindsay Washburn, Sept. 26, 1953; children: Brian, Susan. BA, Middlebury Coll., Vt., 1951. Asst. Kraushaar Gallery, NYC, 1951—53; dir. pub. rels. Wadsworth Atheneum, Hartford, Conn., 1953—55; dir. contemporary art Graham Gallery, NYC, 1955—67; asst. Cordier-Ekstrom Gallery, NYC, 1967—69; dir. Am. painting dept. Sotheby Parke-Bernet, NYC, 1973—75; pres., dir. Washburn Gallery, NYC, 1971—. Mem. Art Dealers Assn. (bd. dirs., v.p. 1991—) Home: 20 W 57th St New York NY 10019-3917 Office Phone: 212-397-6780. Personal E-mail: jwashburn@earthlink.net.

WASHBURN, JOHN ROSSER, entrepreneur; b. Hopewell, Va., July 24, 1943; s. Winthrop Doane and Mary Virginia (Overstreet) W.; m. Rebecca m. Wells, Sept. 1991; 1 child, Amanda Ashley Washburn; stepchildren: Eric Joseph Harrison, Leo M. Cicone, Suzann R. Weldon. Student, Louisburg Jr. Coll., 1963-64, U. Richmond Ext., 1967-69, Williams Coll., 1985, Stanford U., 1986-87. Asst. mgr. Liberty Loan Corp., Richmond, Va., 1965-67; loan interviewer Ctrl. Fidelity Bank, Richmond, Va., 1967-69; regional credit/sales supr. Moores Bldg Supplies, Inc., Roanoke, Va., 1969-74; corp. credit mgt. Owens & Minor, Inc., Richmond, 1974-88; fin., investment cons. JA-GO Enterprises, Richmond, 1982-98; prin. agt., owner Washburn Ins. and Fin. Svcs. Group, Richmond, 1996—2005. Instr., lectr. investment fin., credit mgmt. Washburn Enterprises, 1970—; sec.-treas. Multi-Enterprises, Inc., Richmond, 1988-98; ind. agt. N.Y. Life Ins. Co., Richmond, 1994-98; dir., v.p. Forbes Clin. Rsch. Group, Richmond, 1995-2005; exec. sr. v.p. E-Com Cons., Inc., Richmond, 1998—; charter mem., ptnr. Nations Bus. Cons. Group, Tysons Corner, Va., 1998-2003; pres., CEO Washburn & Assocs., 2003—; sr. v.p. Am. Wellness Alliance Immune Health Mgmt. Group LLC, 2005—; vessel examiner officer Dept. Homeland Security US Coast Guard Aux., 2007—. Active YMCA, 1979—, Am. Mus. Nat. History, 1982—, Nat. Rep. Congl. Com., 1980—, U.S. Def. Com., 1981—; vessel examination officer, dept. homeland security, USCG Aux., 2007—; mem. Credit Rsch. Found. Mem. Internat. Platform Assn., Nat. Assn. Credit Mgmt. (Appreciation cert. for outstanding svc. 1980-81, pres. ctrl. Va. sect. 1979-80, chmn. legis. com. 1977-79, dir. 1983—), Am. Mgmt. Assn., Nat. Wildlife Fedn., Nat. Assn. Life underwriters (Nat. Quality award 1996, 97), Va. Assn. Life Underwriters, Am. Pharmacists Assn., Congressional Club, Hopewell Yacht Club, Mathews Yacht Club. Episcopalian. Office: Washburn Enterprises PO Box 477 Dutton VA 23050-0477 Home Phone: 804-725-1790; Office Phone: 804-725-2614. Business E-Mail: jack@washburnandassociates.com.

WASHBURN, STEWART PUTNAM, management consultant; b. Claremont, NH, Apr. 6, 1929; s. Walter Henry and Josephine (Dana) W.; m. Josephine F. Foster, Aug. 20, 1960 (dec. 1980); children: Patricia, Alice. BS in Commerce and Econs., U. Vt., 1951; MBA, Harvard U., 1953. Cert. comml. lender. V.p. Worcester County Nat. Bank, Worcester, Mass., 1955-74; v.p., sr. loan officer First Nat. Bank, New Bedford, Mass., 1974-77; sr. v.p., sr. loan officer Durfee Attleboro Bank, Fall River, Mass., 1977-90; mgmt. cons. in comml. lending Fall River and Dartmouth, Mass., 1990—. Dir. Bristol Workforce Investment Bd., Fall River, 1982-2006, chmn., 1987-99; dir. Southeastern Econ. Devel. Corp., Taunton, Mass., 1983—, treas., v.p., pres., 1995-98; dir. Jobs for Fall River 1981—, chair loan com. 1997—; mem. coun., loan com. New Bedford Econ. Devel. Coun.; mem. town mtg., fin. com. Dartmouth, Mass. With U.S. Army, 1953-55. Mem. Inst. Mgmt. Cons. (treas. New Eng. chpt. 1997-2001), Risk Mgmt. Assn. (life, bd. govs. N.E. chpt. 1973-75, chmn. credit policy roundtable 1989, Spl. Svc. award 1989). Avocations: bowling, gardening, fishing. Home and Office: 5 Middle St Dartmouth MA 02748-3427 Office Phone: 508-993-1044. Personal E-mail: spwashburn@verizon.net.

WASHINGTON, ALLYN JARVIS, writer; b. Manchester, Conn., July 15, 1930; s. Joseph Senior and Ruby Moore Washington; m. Mildred Irene Jones, June 7, 1958; 1 child, Joanne Washington Baron 1 stepchild, Margaret Ann Schroeder. BS, Trinity Coll., Hartford, Conn., 1953; ScM, Brown U., 1956. Instr. Trinity Coll., 1955—57, Boise (Idaho) Jr. Coll., 1957—58; prof. Dutchess C.C., Poughkeepsie, NY, 1958—79, acting exec. dean, 1974—75; textbook author Addison-Wesley pub., Boston, 1964—. Author: Basic Technical Mathematics with Calculus, 1964, 8th edit., 2005, Technical Calculus with Analytic Geometry, 1966, 4th edit., 2002, Introduction to Technical Mathematics, 1969, 4th edit., 1988. Sgt. US Army, 1950—51. Allyn J. Washington Ctr. Sci. and Art bldg. named in his honor, Dutchess C.C., 2000. Mem.: NY State Math. Assn. Two Yr. Colls. (pres. 1974—75, award for exemplary svc. 1978), Math. Assn. Am., Am. Math. Assn. Two Yr. Colls., Phi Beta Kappa. Avocations: bridge, travel, stamp collecting/philately. Home and Office: 160 Starling Cir Grass Valley CA 95945 Personal E-mail: allynjw@foothill.net.

WASHINGTON, DENNIS R., contracting company executive; b. Spokane, Wash., 1934; Equipment operator Guy F. Atkinson Co., Alaska; with King & McLaughlin Construction Co.; founder Washington Construction Co., Missoula, Mont., 1964; chmn., pres., CEO Morrison-Knudsen, 1999; chmn. Washington Group Internat., Inc (formerly Morrison-Knudsen), Boise, Idaho. Founder Dennis & Phyllis Washington Found., 1998. Named one of Forbes' RIchest Americans, 2006; recipient Entrepreneurial award, Montana Ambassadors, Moles award outstanding achievement construction, Am. Soc. Civil Engineers, Lewis and Clark Pioneer award, Mont. Acad. Disting. Entrepreneurs, Golden Plate award, Acad. Achievement, Metal of Honor, Nat. Ethnic Coalition Organizations. Mem.: Horatio Alger Assn. (Norman Vincent Peale award), Am. Acad. Of Achievement. Office: Washington Group Internat Inc 720 Park Blvd Boise ID 83729 Mailing: The Dennis and Phyllis Washington Found PO Box 16630 Missoula MT 59808-6630 Office Phone: 208-386-5000. Office Fax: 208-386-7186.

WASHINGTON, DENZEL, actor; b. Mt. Vernon, NY, Dec. 28, 1954; s. Denzel and Lynn Washington; m. Pauletta Pearson, June 25, 1983; children: John David, Katia, Malcolm, Olivia. BA in Drama & Journalism, Fordham U., 1977; student, Am. Conservatory Theatre, San Francisco. With N.Y. Shakespeare Festival, Manhattan Theatre Club, New Fed. Theatre. Stage appearances include Coriolanus, 1979, Spell No. 7, The Mighty Gents, Richard III, One Tiger to a Hill, Ceremonies in Old Dark Men, When the Chicken Comes Home to Roost (Audelco award), A Soldier's Play (Obie award 1981), Checkmates, 1988, Split Second, Julius Caesar, 2005; actor: (films) Carbon Copy, 1981, A Soldier's Story, 1981, Power, 1986, Cry Freedom (NAACP Image award, 1987), 1987, For Queen and Country, 1988, The Mighty Quinn, 1989, Glory, 1989 (Golden Globe award 1989, Acad. award for Best Supporting Actor, 1990, NAACP Image award, 1990), Heart Condition, 1990, Mo' Better Blues, 1990, Ricochet, 1991, Mississippi Masala, 1992, Malcolm X, 1992, Much Ado About Nothing, 1993, Philadelphia, 1993, The Pelican Brief, 1993, Crimson Tide, 1995, Virtuosity, 1995, Devil in a Blue Dress, 1995, Courage Under Fire, 1996 (NAACP Image award, 1997), The Preacher's Wife, 1996, Fallen, 1998, He Got Game, 1998, The Siege, 1998, The Bone Collector, 1999, The Hurricane, 2000 (nominee Best Actor Acad. award 2000, Golden Globe award for Best Performance by Actor in Motion Picture Drama 2000), Remember the Titans, 2000, Training Day, 2001 (Acad. award for Best Actor, 2002, nominee Golden Globe award for Best Performance by Actor in Motion Picture Drama 2002), John Q, 2002, Out Of Time, 2003, Man on Fire, 2004, The Manchurian Candidate, 2004, Inside Man, 2006, Déjà Vu, 2006; actor, dir. prodr. The Antwone Fisher Story, 2002; actor (TV movies) Wilma, 1977, License to Kill, 1984, The George McKenna Story, 1986; (mini-series) Flesh and Blood, 1979; (TV series) St. Elsewhere, 1982-88; co-author (with Daniel Paisner) A Hand to Guide Me, 2006. Spokesperson Boys and Girls Clubs Am. Recipient Harvard Found. award, 1996, Whitmey M. Young award, L.A. Urban League, 1997, Herbert Hoover Humanitarian award, The Boys & Girls Clubs of Am., 2004, Golden Plate award, Acad. Achievement, 2005, Stanley Kubrick Britannia Award for Excellence in Film BAFTA/LA Cunard Britannia awards, 2007; Am. Conservatory Theater scholar; named one of 50 Most Powerful People in Hollywood Premiere mag., 2002-06. Avocations: basketball, reading, cooking. *

WASHINGTON, DONALD W., prosecutor; b. 1955; m. Yvonna Malonson; children: Tiffany, Greg, Donny. BS in Mech. Engring., U.S. Mil. Acad., 1977; JD, S. Tex. Coll. Law, 1989. Assoc. Alexander & McEvily, Houston, 1990—91; gen. litig. counsel Conoco Inc., 1993—96, div. counsel, Gulf of Mex. divsn., 1993—96; ptnr. Jeansonne and Redmondet, Lafayette, La., 1996—2001; US atty. (we. dist.) La. US Dept. Justice, Shreveport, La., 2001—. US Army, 1977—82 USAR, 1983—87. Office: US Attys Office 300 Fannin St Ste 3201 Shreveport LA 71101 *

WASHINGTON, ERIC T., judge; b. NJ, 1953; BA, Tufts U., 1976; JD, Columbia U. Sch. of Law, 1979. Assoc. Fulbright and Jaworski, Houston and Washington, 1979—82, 1985—87; legis. dir., counsel Rep. Michael Andrews, 1983—85; spl. corp. counsel Washington, 1987—88; prin. dep. corp. counsel, 1988—90; ptnr. Hogan & Hartson, Washington, 1990-95; judge Superior Ct., 1995—99, DC Ct. Appeals, 1999—2005, chief judge, 2005—. Former co-chair, strategic planning leadership council DC Courts; mem. Standing Com. on Fairness and Access to Courts, Access to Justice Commn. Mem.: DC Bar Assn. (mem. criminal justice act counsel for child abuse and neglect com., mem. standing com. on federal judiciary). Office: DC Ct Appeals 6th Fl 500 Indiana Ave NW Fl 6 Washington DC 20001-2138 Mailing: 3159 Tennyson St NW Washington DC 20015 E-mail: ewashington@dcca.state.da.us. *

WASHINGTON, GLORIA DUNN, secondary school educator; d. Percy and Eleanor McCoy Dunn; m. Leroy Roosevelt Washington; children: Cheryl Lynn Ford, Gloria Candacy, Daphne Dena Reddick. BA, Baber-Scotia Coll., 1966; MA, U. South Fla., 1978, Edn. Specialist, 1981. Tchr. Newfane Ctrl. Sch., NY, 1966—67, Auburndale H.S., Fla., 1976—97, North Ctrl. Adult Sch., Auburndale, 1980—88, Lakeland Sr. H.S., Fla., 1997—. Youth dir. St. Mark, Lakeland, Fla., 1985—; founder/sponsor Unified Culture Club, Lakeland, 1991—; co-chair English curriculum for English tchrs. Polk County, 1997; pres. Polk County Coun. Tchrs. English, 2002—04. Editor: (poems) Polk County Poetry Contest Booklet; co-author: (curriculum) English Curriculum for North Central Adult School, 1984-1985. Chairperson adminstrv. coun. St. Mark United Meth. Ch., Lakeland, 1996—2004. Named English Tchr. Yr., Polk County Coun. Tchrs. English, 1995—96, 1999—2000, 2003—04, 2004—05, Tchr. of Excellence, Fla. Coun. Tchrs. English, 2005—06. Mem.: Delta Kappa Gamma (pres. 1998—2000, Plague-Outstanding Pres. 2000), Phi Delta Kappa (publicity 2003—). St. Mark United Meth. Achievements include est. Peace and Unity Walk, 1999-. Avocations: reading, writing, playing the piano, collecting clocks. Office: Lakeland High School 726 Hollingsworth Rd Lakeland FL 33813 Home Phone: 863-644-5450. Office Fax: 863-499-2917. Personal E-mail: gjwash1@acninc.net. E-mail: gloria.washington@polk-fl.net.

WASHINGTON, ISAIAH, actor; b. Houston, Aug. 3, 1963; m. Jenisa Marie Washington, Feb. 14, 1999; 3 children. Attended, Howard U. Actor: (films) The Color of Love, 1991, Land Where My Fathers Died, 1991, Strictly Business, 1991, Alma's Rainbow, 1994, Crooklyn, 1994, Stonewall, 1995, Clockers, 1995, Girl 6, 1996, Dead Presidents, 1995, Get on the Bus, 1996, Love Jones, 1997, Mixing Nia, 1998, Bulworth, 1998, Rituals, 1998, Out of Sight, 1998, True Crime, 1999, A Texas Funeral, 1999, Veil, 2000, Romeo Must Die, 2000, Dancing in September, 2000, Kin, 2000, Tara, 2001, Exit Wounds, 2001, Sacred Is the Flesh, 2001, Welcome to Collinwood, 2002, Ghost Ship, 2002, Hollywood Homicide, 2003, This Girl's Life, 2003, Blood on a Happy Face, 2004, Wild Things 2, 2004, Dead Birds, 2004, Trois 3: The Escort, 2004, The Moguls, 2005, Step Up, 2006; guest appearances (TV series) Law & Order, 1991, Homicide: Life on the Street, 1994, Lifestories: Families in Crisis, 1994, NYPD Blue, 1995, New York Undercover, 1996, Living Single, 1996, High Incident, 1997, Ally McBeal, 1998, Soul Food, 2002, Touched by an Angel, 2001; actor: (TV films) Strapped, 1993, Mr. & Mrs. Loving, 1996, Soul of the Game, 1996, Joe Torre: Curveballs Along the Way, 1997, Always Outnumbered, 1998; (TV series) Grey's Anatomy, 2005—07 (Outstanding Actor in a Drama Series, NAACP Image Awards, 2006, Outstanding Performance by an Ensemble in a Drama Series, SAG, 2007, Actor in a Drama Series, NAACP Image Awards, 2007). Office: Gray's Anatomy / ABC-TV Los Feliz Tower, 4th Fl 4151 Prospect Ave Los Angeles CA 90027 also: c/o Innovative Artists 1505 10th St Santa Monica CA 90401 *

WASHINGTON, JAMES WINSTON, JR., artist, sculptor; b. Gloster, Miss., Nov. 10, 1909; s. James and Lizie (Howard) W.; m. Janie R. Miller, Mar. 29, 1943. Student, Nat. Landscape Inst., 1944-47; D.F.A., Center Urban-Black Studies, 1975. Tchr. summer class N.W. Theol. Union Seattle U., 1988. One man shows U.S.O. Gallery, Little Rock, 1943, Foster-White Gallery, Seattle, 1974, 78, 80, 83, 89 (also at Bellevue Art Mus., 89), Charles and Emma Frye Art Mus., Seattle, 1980, 95, Mus. History and Industry, Seattle, 1981; exhibited in group shows Willard Gallery, N.Y.C., 1960-64, Feingarten Galleries, San Francisco, 1958-59, Grosvenor Gallery, London, Eng., 1964, Lee Nordness Gallery, N.Y.C, 1962 Woodside Gallery, Seattle, 1962-65, Foster-White Gallery, Seattle, 1974, 76, 89, 92, Smithsonian Instn., 1974, San Diego, 1977, others; retrospective exhbn. Bellevue Art Mus., Washington, 1989; represented in permanent collections Seattle, San Francisco, Oakland art museums, Seattle First Nat. Bank, Seattle Pub. Libr. YWCA, Seattle, Meany Jr. H.S., Seattle World's Fair, Expo 70 Osaka, Japan, Whitney Mus. Am. Art, N.Y.C.; commd. sculpture: Bird With Covey, Wash. State Capitol Mus., Olympia, 1983, Obelisk with Phoenix and Esoteric Symbols of Nature in granite, Sheraton Hotel Seattle, 1982, Life Surrounding the Astral Alter, In Matrix, owner T.M. Rosenblume, Charles Z. Smith & Assocs., Seattle, 1986, The Oracle of Truth (6 1/2 ton sculpture) Mt. Zion Bapt. Ch., Seattle, 1987, commd. sculptures King County Arts Commn., 1989, Bailey Gatzent Elem. Sch., Seattle, 1991, Twin Eaglets of the Cosmic Cycle (Quincy Jones), 1993, Fountain of Triumph (Bangasser Assocs. Inc.), 1992-93, Seattle, 1993-94, 94-95, Child in Matrix, 1995, Blunt Tail Owl, 1996, Bunny Rabbit and Robbin, 1996; author book of poetry Poems of Life, 1997 (Internat. Hall of Fame Nat. Soc. Poets). Passover leader Mt. Zion Baptist Ch., Seattle, 1974-87; founder James W. Washington, Jr. and Mrs. Janie Rogella Washington Found. Recipient Spl. Commendation award for many contbns. to artistic heritage of state Gov., 1973, plaque City of Seattle, 1973, plaque Benefit Guild, Inc., 1973, arts service award King County Arts Commn., 1984, cert. of recognition Gov. of Wash., 1984, Editor's Choice award Outstanding Achievement in Poetry Nat. Libr. Poetry, 1993; named to Wash. State Centennial Hall of Honor, Wash. State Hist. Soc., 1984; home and studio designated historic landmark (city and state), 1991; Dr. James W. Washington Jr. and Mrs. Janie Rosella Washington Found. established, 1997. Mem. Internat. Platform Assn., Internat. Soc. Poets (life, awards 1993), Profl. Artists Phila., Masons (33d degree).

WASHINGTON, KERRY, actor; b. Bronx, NY, Jan. 31, 1977; BFA theatre, George Washington Univ., 1998. Actor: (TV films) Magical Make-Over, 1994; (films) Our Song, 2000, 3D, Save the Last Dance, 2001, Lift, 2001, Take the A Train, Bad Company, 2002, United States of Lelan, 2003, The Human Stain, 2003, Sin, 2003, Against the Ropes, 2004, Strip Search, 2004, She Hate Me, 2004, Ray, 2004, Sexual Life, 2005, Mr. & Mrs. Smith, 2005, Fantastic Four, 2005, Wait, 2005, Little Man, 2006, The Last King of Scotland, 2006, The Dead Girl, 2006, I Think I Love My Wife, 2007. Nominee Best Female Actress, Ind. Spirit Awards, 2002. *

WASHINGTON, LINDA JACOBS, federal agency administrator; b. Annapolis, Md., 1948; m. Mark Washington; 1 child, Lisa. BA, Morgan State U., 1970; MA, U. North Tex. Various sales mktg. positions Xerox Corp., 1982—94; chief of the photoduplication service Libr. of Congress, 1994—97, dir. of integrated support services (ISS), 1997—2003; dep. asst. sec. for adminstrn. US Dept. Transp., 2003—07, asst. sec. for adminstrn., 2007—. Apptd. Bd. Grad. Sch., US Dept. Agr., 2003—07; vice-chmn. Local Fed. Coord. Com. for the Combined Fed. Campagin's Nat. Capitol Region; rep. sec. of transp. Fed. Coun. on Arts and Humanities. Office: US Dept Transp 400 7th St SW Washington DC 20590 *

WASHINGTON, MICHELE, educational consultant; BA in Edn., Capitol U., 1978, MA in Edn. and Counseling, 1993. Instr., counselor, reading tutor Oakland Cmty. Jr. Coll., St. Louis, 1975—88; counselor student career planning, advisement, sexual harassment, tchr. Dallas Ind. Sch. Dist., 1988—90; instr. Dallas CC Dist., 1990—99; owner Elehcims Art Works, Lewisville, Tex., 2000—. Spkr., presenter in field. Bd. dirs. YWCA, Womens Halfway House; program devel. com. Pheonix House. Mem.: ASTD.

WASHINGTON, OLIVIA GRACE MARY, psychotherapist, educator, counselor, researcher; m. Lewis Washington, Sept. 21, 1970. BS, SUNY, Buffalo, 1966, MS, 1968; PhD, Wayne State U., 1997. Diplomate Am. Psychotherapy Assn.; ANCC bd. cert. advance psychiat. RN, cert. nurse practitioner, Mich. Treatment rm. nurse Roswell Pk. Meml. Cancer Inst., Buffalo, 1966—68; team leader, staff nurse E. J. Meyer Meml. Hosp., Buffalo, 1966—68; insvc. educator Lane Bryant Psychiat. Hosp., Buffalo, 1968—69; clin. specialist, adult psychiat. nursing/supt. 10 Lafayette Clinic, Detroit, 1968—69; asst. DON, chair dept. psychiat. nursing Grace Hosp. Sch. Nursing, Detroit, 1971—75; assoc. prof. Wayne State U., Detroit, 1979—; internat. nursing edn. external examiner, cons. U. Botswana,

Gaborone, 1995—97; site liaison John A. Hartford Ctr. Geriatric Nursing excellence and the Gerontological Nursing Interview Rsch. Ctr Regional Tng. Consortium, 2003—; assoc. prof. Wayne State U. Coll. Nursing and Inst. Gerontology, 2003—. Contbr. articles to profl. jours. Active rsch. and svc. to homeless various orgns., 1998—; bd. dirs. Renaissance Home Health Care, Vis. Nurse Assn. of S.E. Mich., Inc., Detroit, 1997—. Recipient Pillar award, 2005, Devel. chair award, Wayne State U., 2005—06; grantee, Wayne State U. Ctr. for Health Rsch., 1999, Nat. Inst. Aging and Mich. Ctr. for Urban African Am. Aging Rsch., 1999—2000, NIH/Nat. Ctr. on Minority Health and Health Disparities, Nat. Inst. of Nursing Rsch., 2001—, Rsch. Grant award, Wayne State U. Alumni Assn., 2003, Nat. Inst. Aging, 2001—04; Brookdale fellow, 2000, Humanities Ctr. Faculty fellow, Wayne State U. Mem.: APHA, Internat. Soc. Psychiat.-Mental Health Nurses, Gerontol. Soc. Am., Am. Counseling Assn. (licentiate), Midwest Nursing Rsch. Soc. (licentiate Harriet H. Werley New Investigator award 2003). Avocations: travel, tennis, racquetball, playing alto saxophone, reading. Office: Wayne State U 5557 Cass Ave Detroit MI 48202 Home Phone: 313-213-9420; Office Phone: 313-577-4133.

WASHINGTON, REGINALD LOUIS, pediatric cardiologist; b. Colorado Springs, Colo., Dec. 31, 1949; s. Lucius Louis and Brenette Y. (Wheeler) W.; m. Billye Faye Ned, Aug. 18, 1973; children: Danielle Larae, Reginald Quinn. BS in Zoology, Colo. State U., 1971; MD, U. Colo., 1975. Diplomate Nat. Bd. Med. Examiners, Am. Bd. Pediat., Pediatric Cardiology. Intern U. Colo. Med. Ctr., Denver, 1975—76, resident in pediat., 1976-78, chief resident, instr., 1978-79, fellow in pediatric cardiology, 1979-81, from asst. prof. pedit. to assoc. clin. prof. pediat., 1982—2005, clin. prof. pediat., 2005—; staff cardiologist Children's Hosp., Denver, 1981-90; v.p. We. Cardiology Assocs., Divsn. for Fetal, Pediatric and Adult Congential Heart Disease, Denver, 1990—2004; med. dir. Rocky Mountain Pediatrix Cardiology, Denver, 2004—; chief of staff Presbyn./St. Lukes Med. Ctr., 1999-2001. Admissions com. U. Colo. Sch. Medicine, Denver, 1985-89; chmn., bd. dirs. Coop. Health Care Agreements, 1994-98; chmn. dept. pediatrics Presbyn./St. Lukes Med. Ctr, Denver, 1996-99, 2003-05, pres.-elect med. staff, 1997-99, chmn. ethics com., 2003-07; adv. coun. Nat. Heart Lung Blood Inst., NIH, 1996-986 Cons. editor Your Patient and Fitness, 1989-92; mem. editl. bd. Jour. Pediats., 2004—, Congenital Heart Disease, 2006-. Chmn. Coop. Health Care Agreements Bd., State of Colo., 1994-98; adv. bd. dirs. Equitable Bank of Littleton, Colo., 1984-86; bd. dirs. Rocky Mountain Heart Fund for Children, 1984-89, Rainbo Ironkids, 1989-95, Ctrl. City Opera, 1989-95, Cleo Parker Robinson Dance Co., 1992-94, Nat. Coun. Patient Info. and Edn., 1992-98, Children's Heart Alliance, 1993-94, Colo. State U. Devel. Coun., 1994-2003, Caring for Colo. Found., 1999-2001; nat. bd. dirs. Am. Heart Assn., 1992-96; trustee Denver Ctr. Performing Arts, 1994—, Regis U., 1994-99; mem. Gov.'s Coun. Phys. Fitness, 1990-91; bd. govs. Colo. State U., 1996-2004, pres., 2001-03; trustee Colo. Trust, 2002-; trustee Helen Bonfils Found., 2003—, Temple Hoyne Buell Found., 2007-. Recipient William E. Morgan Alumnus Achievement award Colo. State U., 2004, Cardiologist of Yr., HCA, 2004; named Salute Vol. of Yr. Big Sisters of Colo., 1990; honoree NCCJ, 1994, Physician of Yr., Nat. Am. Heart Assn., 1995, Civis Princeps award Regis U., 2007. Fellow Am. Acad. Pediat. (cardiology subsect., chmn. sports medicine and fitness com. 2000-2004, chmn. task force on obesity 2003—, Thomas Shaffer award 2007), Am. Coll. Cardiology, Am. Heart Assn. (coun. on cardiovasc. disease in the young, exec. com. 1988-91, nat. devel. program com. 1990-94, vol. of yr. 1989, pres. Colo. chpt. 1989-90, Torch of Hope 1987, Gold Heart award Colo. chpt. 1990, bd. dirs. Colo. chpt., exec. com. Colo. chpt. 1987-2000, grantee Colo. chpt. 1983-84, mem. editl. bd. Pediat. Exercise Scis. 1988-2002), Soc. Critical Care Medicine; mem. Am. Acad. Pediat. Perinatology, Am. Acad. Pediat./Pediat. Cardiology (exec. com. 1996-2004), N.Am. Soc. Pediat. Exercise Medicine (pres. 1986-87), Colo. Med. Soc. (chmn. sports medicine coun. 1992-94), Leadership Denver 1990, Glenmoor Golf Club. Democrat. Roman Catholic. Avocations: golf, fishing. Office: Rocky Mountain Pediat Cardiology 10099 Ridgegate Pkwy Ste 300 Lone Tree CO 80124 Office Phone: 303-860-9933. Business E-Mail: rlwash@aol.com.

WASHINGTON, RON, professional baseball manager; b. New Orleans, Apr. 29, 1952; Infielder LA Dodgers, 1977, Minn. Twins, 1981—86, Balt. Orioles, 1987, Cleve. Indians, 1988, Houston Astros, 1989; with coaching staff NY Mets, 1990—95; first base coach Oak. Athletics, 1996, infield coach, third base coach, 1997—2006; mgr. Tex. Rangers, 2006—. Office: Texas Rangers Baseball Club 1000 Ballpark Way Arlington TX 76011 Office Fax: 817-273-5174. *

WASHINGTON, WARREN MORTON, meteorologist; b. Portland, Oreg., Aug. 28, 1936; s. Edwin and Dorothy Grace (Morton) W.; m. LaRae Herring, July 30, 1959 (div. Aug. 1975); children: Teri, Kim, Marc (dec.), Tracy; m. Jona Ann, July 3, 1978 (dec. Jan. 1987); m. Mary Elizabeth Washington, Apr., 1995. BS in Physics, Ore. State U., 1958, MS in Meteorology, 1960; PhD in Meteorology, Pa. State U., 1964; degree (hon.), Oreg. State U., 2006. Dir. of climate and global dynamics div. Nat. Center Atmospheric Research, Boulder, Colo., 1978-95; affiliate prof. meteorology oceanography U. Mich. at Ann Arbor, 1968-71; mem. Nat. Adv. Com. for Oceans and Atmospheres, 1978-84. Mem. sec. of energy adv. bd. U.S. Dept. Energy, 1990-93; mem. Nat. Sci. Bd., 1994-2006, chair, 2002-06. Contbr. articles to meteorol. jours. Mem. Boulder Human Rels. Commn., 1969-71; mem. Gov.'s Sci. Adv. Com., 1975-78. Recipient Disting. Alumni award Oreg. State U., 1991, E.B. Lemon Disting. Alumni award Pa. State U., 1991, Le Verrier medal Soc. Meteorol. France, 1995, Bonfils-Stanton Found. award, 2000, Vollum award Reed Coll., 2005; inductee NAS portrait collection African Am. in Sci., Engring., and Medicine, 1997; named Sigma Xi Disting. lectr., 1998-99. Fellow AAAS (bd. dirs.), Am. Meteorol. Soc. (pres. 1994, Anderson award 2000, Charles Brook award 2007); mem. NAE, Am. Philosophy Soc., Am. Geog. Union, Nat. Sci. Bd. (chmn. 2002-06). Office: PO Box 3000 Boulder CO 80307-3000 Home: 8633 E Iliff Dr Denver CO 80231-3810

WASHKEWICZ, DONALD E., manufacturing executive; b. Cleve. m. Pam Washkewicz; children: Dawn, Tiffany, Bryan. BME, Cleve. State U., 1972; MBA, Case Western Res. U., Cleve., 1979. Lic. profl. engr., OH. With Parker Hannifin Corp., Cleve., 1972—, from engr. to gen. mgr. Parflex Divsn., 1972—82, v.p. ops. fluid connectors group, 1994-97, v.p., pres. hydraulics group, 1997-2000, COO, 2000—01, pres., 2000—04, 2007—, CEO, chmn., 2001—. Bd. Mfr. Alliance/MAPI. Bd. Greater Cleve. Growth Assn., Cleve. Tomorrow. Recipient Disting. Alumni Award, Cleve. State U., 2002, Ellis Island Medal Honor, 2003. Mem.: Nat. Assn. Mfr., Nat. Soc. Profl. Engr. Office: Parker Hannifin Corp 6035 Parkland Blvd Cleveland OH 44124-4141 *

WASIK, BARBARA HANNA, psychologist, educator; b. Douglas, Ga., May 29, 1942; d. Frank Joseph and Josephine (Nahoom) Hanna; m. John L. Wasik, June 24, 1966; children— John Gregory, Mark Timothy, Jeffrey Joseph AB, U. Ga., 1963; MA, Fla. State U., 1965, PhD, 1967. Lic. psychologist, N.C. Postdoctoral research fellow Duke U., Durham, NC, 1967-68; dir. research Ford Found. grant, Durham, NC, 1968-69; from asst. prof. to assoc. prof. U. N.C., Chapel Hill, 1969-77, prof., 1977—, William R. Kenan Jr. disting. prof., 2003—, assoc. dean Grad. Sch., 1972-75, chmn. div. human devel. and psychol. services, 1975-77, assoc. dean Sch. Edn., 1977-83, 1988—92, sr. investigator Child Devel. Ctr., 1972—. Mem. commn. NAS, 1998—2000; co-facilitator Nat. Forum Home Visiting, 1999—2006. Assoc. editor Jour. Applied Behavior Analysis, 1972; mem. editorial bd. Behavioral Assessment, 1984-85; contbr. chpts. to books and articles to profl. jours. Mem. N.C. Psychological Assn. (sec. 1982-85, pres. 1988-89), Am. Psychol. Assn. (divsn. 25 sec-treas. 1983-86, coun. rep. 1994-99, bd. edn. affairs 1999-2001, chair bd edn. affairs 2001), Soc. Research in Child Development, Southeastern Psychol. Assn., Assn. Advancement Behavior Therapy. Democrat. Roman Catholic. Home: 609 Brookview Dr Chapel Hill NC 27514-1402

WASKO, STEVEN E., lawyer; b. Chgo., May 10, 1954; s. Theodore J. and Beverly W.; m. Elaine L. Enger, Oct. 3, 1981 (div. Aug. 1996); 1 child, Christine; m. Deborah Wasko; stepchildren: Tara, Raef, Brooke and Christopher. B in Spl. Studies cum laude, Cornell Coll., 1976; JD cum laude, Kent U., 1979. Bar: Ill. 1979, U.S. Dist. Ct. (no. dist.) Ill. 1979. Assoc. atty. Blanshan & Summerfield, Park Ridge, Ill., 1979-81; ptnr. Summerfield & Wasko, Park Ridge, 1981-86; sole practitioner Steven Wasko and Assocs., Park Ridge, 1986-90, mng. ptnr., 1992-95; ptnr. Wasko & Michaels, Park Ridge, 1990-91, Steponate & Wasko Ltd., Park Ridge and Chgo., 1995—. Dir. Kolan Corp., Park Ridge, 1988—. Great Books leader Field Sch. Dist., Park Ridge, 1997—. Avocations: weight training, watercolors, fine art. Office: 1580 N Northwest Hwy Park Ridge IL 60068-1444

WASKO-FLOOD, SANDRA JEAN, artist, educator; b. NYC, Mar. 12, 1943; d. Peter Edmund and Margaret Dalores (Kubek) Wasko; m. Michael Timothy Flood, June 28, 1969. BA, UCLA, 1965, postgrad., 1968-69, Calif. State U., Northridge, summer 1968; student, Otis Art Inst., LA, 1969, Marie Kaufman, Rio de Janeiro, 1970-72, Museo de Arte Moderno, 1970-73, Foothill Coll., Los Altos, Calif., 1973-74, Claremont Coll., Calif., 1975, U. Wis., Janesville, 1977, Beloit Coll., Wis., 1977-78, U. Wis., 1977-78; grad. etching student, Warrington Colescott. Instr. printmaking Washington Women's Arts Ctr., 1983; artist-in-residence U. Md., College Park, 1985; instr. printmaking Arlington Arts Ctr., Va., 1984-85; prof. St. Mary's Coll., Md., 1985; instr. printmaking Arlington County Lee Arts Ctr., 1989-97; workshop coord. cultural affairs div. Arlington County Cultural Affairs, 1989-97; printmaking instr. Home Studio, Alexandria, Va., 1987—2005; founder, pres. Living Labyrinths Peace, Inc., 2005—. Condr. workshops Washington Performing Arts Soc., 2002—. One woman shows include Wisconsin Women in the Arts Gallery, Madison, 1977, Mbari Art, Washington, 1981, Miya Gallery, Washington, 1981, Slavin Gallery, Washington, 1982, Stuart Mott House, Washington, 1983, Washington Printmakers Gallery, 1986, 88, 91, St. Peter's Ch., NYC, 1989, Montana Gallery, Alexandria, Va., 1991, Montpelier Cultural Arts Ctr., Laurel, Md., 1992, Gallery 10, Washington, 1994, 96, Sch. 33, Balt., 1996; mus. and internat. shows include Boston Printmakers: The 39th North Am. Print Exhbn., Framingham, Mass., Jan.-Mar., 1986, Internat. Graphic Arts Found. and Silvermine Guild Arts Ctr., New Canaan, Conn., Feb., 1988, Prints: Washington, The Phillips Collection, Washington, Sept.-Oct., 1988, Contemporary Am. Graphics, Book Chamber Internat., Moscow, 1990, Gallery 10 Artists of Washington DC Vartai Gallery, Lithuania, 1994, Peninsula Fine Arts Ctr., Newport News, Va., 1995-96, Riva Sinistra Arte, Florence, Italy, 1997, Contemporary Art Ctr. Va., Virginia Beach, 2000, Charles Sumner Sch. Mus., Washington, DC, 2001, numerous others; numerous juried shows including most recently Cannon Rotunda, US House of Reps., Washington, 2000, Charles Sumner Sch. Mus., Washington, 2001, Washington Women Artists Marching into the Millennium, Women's Caucus for Art, 2001, Washington Women Artists, Women's Caucus for Art, 2001, Rockville Art Place, Md., 2002, Internat. Photography, 2003, Anne C. Fisher Gallery, Wash., 2005, Md. Printmakers Foundry Gallery, Washington, 2007; galleries: Slavin Gallery, Washington, D.C., 1981-83, Washington Printmakers Gallery, Washington, 1985-96, White Light Collaborative, Inc., NYC, 1988-89, Montana Gallery, Alexandria, Va., 1989-91, Gallery 10, Washington, 1992-97, Charleuoix Gallery, Albuquerque, NM, 1999, and numerous others; collections include Nat. Mus. of Women in the Arts, Washington, Corcoran Gallery of Art, Washington, Museo de Arte Moderno, Buenos Aires, Cultural Found., USSR, Coll. Notre Dame, Balt., Potomac Hosp., Woodbridge, Md.; dir. Labyrinths for Peace 2000, US Capitol, 2002; featured artist Kali Guide: A Directory of Resources for Women, 2d reprint, 2002. Pres. Washington Area Printmakers, Washington, D.C., 1985-86; pub. rels. dir. Washington Women's Arts Ctr., 1980; bd. dirs. Washington Women's Arts Ctr., 1981-82; program chair DC chpt. Women's Caucus for Art, 1998—; founding mem. the Labyrinth Soc., 1998-; spl. projects dir. Labryinth Soc., 2000; cons. Labyrinth Making and Products. Recipient Award of Honorable Mention Nat. Gallery of Art, 1989, Best of Show, Artists Equity Exhibit, Gallery 901, Washington, 1997; grantee Friends of the Torpedo Factory Art Ctr., Alexandria, Va., 1989, DC Commn. on Arts and Humanities Summer Edn. and Sports Program Artist in Schs., 2000, 01, 05, Wash. Performing Arts Soc., 2002-07; individual artists fellow Va. Commn. for Arts, 1994. Mem.: Arts/Sci. Collaborative, Inc. (NYC), Artists Using Sci. and Tech. (San Francisco), YLEM, The Labyrinth Soc., Washington Sculpture Group, Am. Print Alliance, Md. Printmakers, Women's Caucus for Art, So. Graphics Coun., Pyramic Atlantic, Nat. Print Orgn., Corcoran Gallery/Washington Project for the Arts. Avocations: classical music, hiking, reading. Studio: Living Labyrinths Peace Ctr 57 N St NW Washington DC 20001-1254 Home: 2229 Lake Ave Baltimore MD 21213-1015 Office Phone: 703-217-6706. Personal E-mail: waskoart@comcast.net.

WASKOW, ARTHUR OCEAN, theologian, educator; b. Balt., Oct. 12, 1933; s. Henry B. and Hannah (Osnowitz) W.; m. Irene Elkin, 1956 (div. 1978); children: David, Shoshana; m. Phyllis Ocean Berman, 1986. BA, Johns Hopkins U., Balt., 1954; MA, U. Wis., 1956, PhD, 1963. Legis. asst. Ho. of Reps., Washington, 1959-61; sr. staff mem. Peace Rsch. Inst., Washington, 1961-63; fellow Inst. Policy Studies, Washington, 1963-77; colleague Pub. Resource Ctr., Washington, 1977-82; faculty Reconstructionist Rabbinical Coll., Phila., 1982-89; founder, dir. Shalom Ctr., 1983—. Fellow ALEPH Alliance for Jewish Renewal, 1990-93, pathfinder, 1993-2005; mem. adv. bd. Temple of Understanding; vis. prof. religion Swarthmore Coll., 1982-83, Temple U., 1976-77, 87-88, Drew U., 1997-98, Vassar Coll., 1998; sec.-treas. Conf. On Peace Rsch. in History, 1969-74. Author: The Limits of Defense, 1962, (with Stanley L. Newman) America in Hiding, 1962, Worried Man's Guide to World Peace, 1963, From Race Riot to Sit-In, 1966, The Freedom Seder, 1969, Running Riot, 1970, The Bush Is Burning, 1971, Godwrestling, 1978, Seasons of Our Joy, 1982, These Holy Sparks, 1983, (with David and Shoshana Waskow) Before There Was a Before, 1984, (with Howard Waskow) Becoming Brothers, 1993, Down-to-Earth Judaism: Food, Money, Sex, and the Rest of Life, 1995, Godwrestling—Round 2: Ancient Wisdom, Future Paths, 1996, (with Phyllis O. Berman) Tales of Tikkun: New Jewish Stories to Heal the Wounded World, 1996, (with Phyllis O. Berman) A Time for Every Purpose Under Heaven: The Jewish Life-Spirit as a Spiritual Path, 2002, (with Ari Elon and Naomi Mara Hyman) Trees, the Earth, and Torah: A To B'Shvat Anthology, 1999, Torah of the Earth: Exploring 4,000 Years of Ecology in Jewish Thought, 2000, (with Jean Chittster and Saadi Swather-Chisti) The Text of Abraham: Stories of Hope and Peace for Jews, Christians and Muslims, 2006; editor: Debate Over Thermonuclear Strategy, 1965, Menorah Jour., 1979-2001; screenwriter: In Every Generation, 1988; editl. bd. Tikkun. Alt. del. Dem. Nat. Conv., 1968; fellow Chs. Ctr. for Theology and Pub. Policy, 1977-82; Gamaliel chair Luth. Student Ctr., Milw., 1996; wisdom-keeper UN Conf. on Habitat II, 1996; initiator A.J. Heschel 25th Yohrzeit Observance, 1998. Coolidge fellow Assn. Religion and Intellectual Life, 1983; named one of the Top 50 Rabbis in America, Newsweek Mag., 2007. Fellow Am. Acad. Arts and Scis. (colloquium on disarmament 1962); mem. Nat. Writers Union, Fabrangen, Nat. Havurah Com. (bd. dirs. 1979-80, 83-87), P'nai Or (bd. dirs. 1984-93, Aleph bd. dirs. 1993-95), Internat. Coord. Com. on Religion and Earth (steering com. 1990-93), Phi Beta Kappa. Address: 6711 Lincoln Dr Philadelphia PA 19119-3119 Office Phone: 215-844-8494. E-mail: awaskow@shalomctr.org. *For about 500 years the human race has made no "Sabbath" from ceaseless working, making, producing, doing and it therefore has raced to the brink of destroying itself and much of life on the planet. Just as individuals need rhythmic rest, so do societies—a spiritual truth that we should again learn from Torah. Time to be!.*

WASMUTH, CARL ERWIN, retired physician, lawyer; b. Pitts., Feb. 16, 1916; s. Edwin Hugo and Mary Blanche (Love) W.; m. Martha Conn., Aug. 25, 1939; children: Carl Erwin; m. Gertrude White Ruth, June 19, 1984; m. Wilhelmina Waterman Devine, May 12, 1990. BS, U. Pitts., 1935, MD, 1939; LLB, Cleve.-Marshall Law Sch., 1959. Diplomate Am. Bd. Anesthesiology. Bar: Ohio 1959. Intern Western Pa. Hosp., Pitts., 1939-40; fellow anesthesiology Cleve. Clinic Found., 1949-51, mem. emeritus staff, 1976—; pvt. practice medicine Dry Run, Pa., 1942-45, Scottdale, Pa., 1945-49; mem. dep. anesthesia Cleve. Clinic, 1951—, head dept., 1967-69; asso. prof. law Cleve.-Marshall Law Sch., 1959-66; adj. prof. Cleve. Marshall Law Sch., 1966-73. Author: Anesthesia and the Law, 1961, Law for the Physician, 1966, Law and the Surgical Team, 1968; Editor: Legal Problems in the Practice of Anesthesiology, 1973; contbg. editor: Hale's Anesthesiology; editorial bd.: Med. World News; Contbr. articles to profl. jours. Trustee Cleve.- Marshall Law Sch., chmn., 1969-71; bd. dirs. Scottdale Hosp. Found; chmn. bd. govs. Cleve. Clinic, 1969-77; trustee Cleve. Clinic Found., 1969-76, v.p., 1973-76; trustee Cleve. Clinic Ednl. Found., 1969-76, v.p., 1973-76; chmn. bd. trustees, pres. Cleve. Marshall Ednl. Found., 1972-81; bd. overseers Coll. Law, Cleve. State U., 1972-76; vis. com. Coll. Law, Case-Western Res. U., 1973-76; trustee United Torch Svcs.; hon. trustee Tucson Symphony Soc., 1983-84, 88; trustee Santa Cruz Med. Found., 1977, pres., 1978; bd. govs. Ohio World Trade Center; trustee Cancer Center Cleve., Ohio Coll. Podiatric Medicine, 1976, Am. Coll. Legal Medicine Research Found., 1984—; mem. U. Ariz. Found., 1978, World Congress Med. Law, 1967—, Keynoter 3d World Congress, 1971; sec. Commn. Med. Malpractice, HEW, 1972-73; vestryman St. Francis-in-the-Valley Episcopal Ch., Green Valley, 1990-93. Named Distinguished Eagle Scout Nat. Council Boy Scouts Am., 1977; named Outstanding Citizen Eagle Cuyahoga council, 1976; Citizen of Year Cleve. Area Bd. Realtors, 1976 Fellow: ACP, Law Sci. Acad., Am. Coll. Chest Physicians, Am. Coll. Legal Medicine (pres. bd. govs. 1966—69), Am. Coll. Anesthesiologists; mem.: ABA, AAAS, AMA, NRC, Cleve. Bar Assn., Cuyahoga County Bar Assn., Ohio Bar Assn., Transplantation Soc. (charter), Cleve. Acad. Medicine, Com. Cadaver Utilization, Nat. Acad. Sci., N.Y. Acad. Scis., Ohio Med. Assn., Acad. Anesthesiology (chmn. program com. 1967), World Fedn. Anesthesiologists (vice chmn. Am. del. 1967), Internat. Anesthesia Rsch. Soc., Cleve. Soc. Anesthesiologists (pres. 1963), Ohio Soc. Anesthesiologists (dir. 1960—69), Am. Soc. Anesthesiologists (dir., pres. 1968, spkr. ho. of dels.), Ariz. Sr. Acad., Gainey Ranch Golf Club (Scottsdale), Old Pueblo Club, The Lakes Club, Mt. Kenya Safari Club (Nanyuki, Kenya), Pleasant Valley Country Club, Tucson Club, Country Club of Green Valley, Lions (past pres. local clubs), Masons, Delta Theta Phi, Phi Rho Sigma. E-mail: cwasmuth@cox.net.

WASOW, OMAR, Internet company executive; BA in Race and Ethnic Rels., Stanford U., Calif., 1992. Coord. voter registration Freedom Summer '92, 1992; asst. dir. Strictly Bus., 1992—93; founder, owner New York Online, 1993—; internet analyst NewsChannel4, NYC, 1995—; exec. dir. BlackPlanet.com at Community Connect, NYC, 1999—. Co-chair Coalition for Ind. Pub. Charter Schs.; bd. dirs. N.Y. Software Indusry Assn., WorldStudio, The Refugee Project. Fellow Next Generation Leadership program, Rockefeller Found. Office: NBC 30 Rockefeller Plz New York NY 10112 also: BlackPlanet (dot) com Community Connect 205 Hudson St New York NY 10013

WASS, HANNELORE LINA, educational psychology educator; b. Heidelberg, Germany, Sept. 12, 1926; came to U.S., 1957, naturalized, 1963; d. Hermann and Mina (Lasch) Kraft; m. Irvin R. Wass, Nov. 24, 1959 (dec.); 1 child, Brian C.; m. Harry H. Sisler, Apr. 13, 1978. BA, Tchrs. Coll., Heidelberg, 1951; MA, U. Mich., 1960, PhD, 1968. Tchr. W. Ger. Univ. Lab. Schs., 1958-60; mem. faculty U. Mich., Ann Arbor, 1958-60, U. Chgo. Lab. Sch., 1960-61, U. Mich., 1963-64, Eastern Mich. U., 1965-69; prof. ednl. psychology U. Fla., Gainesville, 1969-92, prof. emeritus, 1992—, faculty assoc. Ctr. for Gerontol. Studies Gainesville. Cons., lectr. in thanatology. Author: The Professional Education of Teachers, 1974, Dying-Facing the Facts, 1979, 2d edit., 1988, 3d edit., 1995, Death Education: An Annotated Resource Guide, 1980, vol. 2, 1985, Helping Children Cope With Death, 1982, 2d edit., 1984, Childhood and Death, 1984; founding editor (jour.) Death Studies, 1977-92; cons. editor: Ednl. Gerontology, 1977-92, (book series) Death Education, Aging and Health Care, 1980-96; contbr. approximately 200 articles to profl. jours. and chpts. in books. Mem. Am. Psychol. Assn., Gerontol. Soc., Internat. Work Group Dying, Death and Bereavement (bd. dirs.), Assn. Death Edn. and Counseling. Home: 6014 NW 54th Way Gainesville FL 32653-3265 E-mail: wass@nersp.nerdc.ufl.edu.

WASSELL, STEPHEN ROBERT, mathematics professor, researcher; b. Santa Monica, Calif., Jan. 17, 1963; s. Desmond Anthony and Catherine Ann (Stephens) W. BS in Arch., U. Va., Charlottesville, 1984, MS in Math, 1987, PhD in Math, 1990, M in Computer Sci., 1999. Programmer, analyst UNISYS, McLean, Va., 1984-85, graphics artist, 1986; tutor summer transition program U. Va., Charlottesville, 1987-88, tchg. asst., 1986-90; asst. prof. math. Sweet Briar (Va.) Coll., 1990-96, assoc. prof. math., 1996—2002, prof. math., 2002—, dept. chmn., 1996—97, 1999—2002, 2004—05. Prof. of record Ctr. for the Liberal Arts, U. Va., 1991; vis. asst. prof. math., U. Va., Charlottesville, 1992, vis. assoc. prof. computer sci., 1998-99; doctoral cons., Charlottesville, 1989-90. Author: (with Kim Williams) On Ratio and Proportion, 2002; editor: The Golden Section, 2003, (with Branko Mitrovic) Villa Cornaro, 2006. Recipient Grad. assistantship award U. Va., 1986-90; Gordon T. Whyburn fellow, 1985-86. Mem. AAUP (Sweet Briar chpt. sec.-treas. 1993-99), Am. Math. Soc., Math. Assn. Am., Am. Solar Energy Soc., Soc. Arch. Historians, Sigma Nu. Achievements include patents for solar powered lawnmover, solar shed, ear muffs. Office: Sweet Briar Coll Dept Math Scis Sweet Briar VA 24595 Home: PO BOX 1112 Sweet Briar VA 24595 Office Phone: 434-381-6214. Business E-Mail: wassell@sbc.edu.

WASSENICH, LINDA PILCHER, retired health policy analyst, social worker; b. Washington, Aug. 27, 1943; d. Mason Johnson and Vera Bell (Stephenson) Pilcher; m. Mark Wassenich, May 14, 1965; children: Paul Mason, David Mark. BA magna cum laude with honors, Tex. Christian U., Fort Worth, 1965; MSW, U. N.C., Chapel Hill, 1970. Licensed advanced practitioner, cert. social worker, Tex. Counselor family ct. Dallas County Juvenile Dept., 1970-73, 75-76; dir. govt. rels. Vis. Nurse Assn., Dallas, 1980-84, exec. officer of hospice, 1984-85; exec. dir. Incest Recovery Assn., Dallas, 1985-86; assoc. exec. dir. Lone Star Coun. Camp Fire, Dallas, 1986-89; exec. v.p. Vis. Nurse Assn. Found., Dallas, 1989-91; dir. policy and resource devel. Vis. Nurse Assn. Tex., 1992-99; ret. Field instr. U. Tex. Arlington Sch. Social Work, 1993-99. Contbr. articles to profl. publs. Mem. Leadership Dallas, 1988—89; bd. dirs. Women's Coun. Dallas County, 1986—95, 1999—2001, pres., 1992—93; mem. adv. bd. Maternal Health and Family Planning Dallas, 1990—94; chmn. Dallas County Welfare Adv. Bd., 1991—95; bd. dirs. United Way of Met. Dallas, 1992—94, Youth Impact Ctrs., Dallas, 1993—94; trustee Simmons Family Found., Dallas, 2000—; mem. Cmty. Coun. Greater Dallas, 2004—, sec., 2007—; chair governance com. Human Rights Initiative of North Tex., Dallas, 2004—; chair adv. coun. Dallas Area Agy. on Aging, 2005—. Recipient Heart award Lone Star Coun. Camp Fire USA, 1990, Laurel award AAUW, Dallas, 1995, Valuable Alumna award Tex. Christian U. Alumni Assn., 2003, Women of Spirit award Am. Jewish Congress, Dallas, 2005; named Field Inst. of Yr., U. Tex. Arlington Sch. Social Work, 1999,

Golden Rule award finalist JC Penney, 2000. Mem.: LWV (bd. dirs. Dallas 1974—80, pres. 1995—99, bd. dirs. Tex. 1999—, Tex. v.p. pub. rels. 2001—, Myrtle Bales Bulkley award 2000, Pres. award 2005), NASW (co-chmn. Dallas unit 1981—82, chair Tex. nominating com. 1990—92, Tex. bd. dirs., Social Worker of Yr. award 1988, Lifetime Achievement in Social Work award 2002), Assn. Fundraising Profls. (bd. dirs. Dallas chpt. 1994—97, v.p. governance 1995—96, cert., Outstanding Fund Raising Exec. of Yr. 1999), Acad. Cert. Social Workers. Home: 5221 Pebblebrook Dallas TX 75229-5504

WASSER, DENNIS MATTHEW, lawyer; b. Bklyn., Aug. 27, 1942; BA with honors, U. Calif. LA, 1964; JD, U. So. Calif., 1967. Bar: Calif. 1968, cert.: State Bar Calif. Bd. Legal Specialization (specialist in family law). Ptnr. Wasser, Cooperman & Carter, LA. Lectr. in field; co-instr. advanced profl. program family law U. So. Calif., 1989; instr. U. Calif. LA. Contbr. articles to profl. jours. Mem.: ABA, Am. Acad. Matrimonial Lawyers, LA County Bar Assn. (chmn. 1984, mem. exec. com. family law sect. 1978—88), Beverly Hills Bar Assn. (chmn. family law sect. 1978—79). Office: Wasser Cooperman & Carter Ste 1200 One Century Plz 2029 Century Park E Los Angeles CA 90067 Office Phone: 310-277-7117. Office Fax: 310-553-1793. *

WASSER, HENRY, retired American literature and sociology educator; b. Pitts., Apr. 13, 1919; s. Nathan and Mollie (Mendelson) W.; m. Solidelle Felicité Fortier, Aug. 20, 1942; children: Michael Frederick (dec.), Eric Anthony (dec.), Frederick Anthony, Felicity Louise. BA, MA, Ohio State U., 1940; PhD, Columbia U., 1951. Teaching fellow George Washington U., 1940-42; analyst USAAF intelligence, 1941-43; chemist Goodyear Synthetic Rubber Co., 1943-45; from tutor to assoc. prof. City Coll., CUNY, 1946-66; prof. English, dean faculties Richmond Coll., CUNY, 1966-73; v.p. for acad. affairs Calif. State U., Sacramento, 1973-74; prof. English Coll. S.I., CUNY, 1974-89; dir. Center for European Studies, Grad. Sch. CUNY, 1979-93, prof. emeritus of sociology and English, 1989—. Fulbright prof. U. Salonika, Greece, 1955-56; Higher Edn. Seminar assoc. Columbia U., 1961—, co-chair, 1982-87, chair, 1987-89; mem. Colloquium on Higher Edn., Yale U., 1974-75; Fulbright prof. Am. Lit. U. Oslo, 1962-64, dir., prof. Am. Inst., 1963-64; vis. prof. U. Warsaw, 1964, U. Sussex, Eng., 1972, U. Salonika, 1955-56; Fulbright prof. Am. Lit. and Civilization U. Bergen, Norway, 1989-90, U. Aveiro, Portugal, 1993; steering com. Internat. Conf. Higher Edn., 1989-; rsch. scholar comparative higher edn. CUNY, 1989—; lectr. in field. Author: The Scientific Thought of Henry Adams, 1956, (with others) Higher Education in Western Europe and North America: A Selected and Annotated Bibliography, 1979, American Literature and Language: A Selected and Annotated Bibliography, 1980; editor: (with Sigmund Skard) Americana Norvegica; Norwegian Contributions to American Studies, 1968, (with others) The Compleat University, 1983, Problems of the Urban University: A Comparative Perspective, 1984, Impact of Changing Labor Force on Higher Education, 1987, Higher Education Policy: Europe and USA, 2007; editor (with Ulrich Teichler) German and American Universities: Mutual Influences, 1992, Diversification in Higher Education: A Comparative View, 1999; mem. bd. editors History of European Ideas, 1986—, guest editor, summer, 1987; guest editor Higher Edn. Policy, spring, 1994, contbr. articles to newspapers and profl. jours. Faculty trustee CUNY, 1981-86, trustee emeritus, 1986—, chair senate; bd. dirs. Scandinavian Seminar, 1978-86, sec., 1980-83, vice chmn., 1983-86. Recipient Am. Scandinavian Found. award, 1969, 71, German Acad. Exch. Svc. award, 1973, 80, 2004, Swedish Info. Svc. award, 1979, Norwegian Ministry of Culture award, 1983, NEH award, 1984, Foscolo medal U. Pavia, Italy, 1986, German Marshall Fund award, 1985, 87, Atheneum medal U. Pavia, Italy, 1988, Disting. Senator award CUNY Faculty Senate, 1994. Mem. Am. Studies Assn. (pres. Met. N.Y. chpt. 1961-62, nat. exec. coun. 1968-74), Melville Soc. Am. (historian 1969-74), MLA, Am. Scandinavian Found. (fellow 1971), Internat. Assn. Univ. Profs. English, Assn. Upper Level Colls. and Univs. (2d v.p. 1971-72), Assn. for World Edn. (internat. coun.), Phi Beta Kappa (sec. City Coll. chpt. 1957-62, 1964-67, internat. advisory bd., U. Aegean, 1991-93, pres. CUNY Acad. for Humanities and Scis. 1991-2004, exec. dir. 2004-), Henry Adams Soc. (exec. coun. 1994—, pres. 1996-2003, dir. 2004-), Mass. Hist. Soc. (fellow 2001). Home: 333 E 34th St Apt 16C New York NY 10016-4950 also: 5517 Fieldston Rd Bronx NY 10471-2503 Office: CUNY Academy Grad Sch 365 Fifth Ave New York NY 10016-4309 Office Phone: 212-817-7594. Business E-Mail: hwasser@gccuny.edu.

WASSER, LAURA ALLISON, lawyer; b. LA, May 23, 1968; d. Dennis Wasser. BA, U. Calif. Berkeley, 1991; JD, Loyola Law Sch., 1994. Bar: Calif. 1994. Ptnr. Wasser, Cooperman & Carter, LA. V.p. fin. devel., bd. dirs. Harriet Buhai Ctr. Family Law. Mem.: Calif. State Bar Assn., LA County Bar Assn., Beverly Hills Bar Assn. Office: Wasser Cooperman & Carter Ste 1200 One Century Plz 2029 Century Park E Los Angeles CA 90067 Office Phone: 310-277-7117. Office Fax: 310-553-1793.

WASSER, MARILYN J., lawyer, real estate company executive; m. Eric Wasser; 3 children. AB in Govt., Smith Coll.; JD with honors, Case Western Reserve U. Atty. private practice; atty. AT&T Corp., 1983—91, chief atty., 1991—94, v.p. law, corp. sec., 1994—2002; exec. v.p., assoc. gen. counsel AT&T Wireless, 2002—05; exec. v.p., gen. counsel, corp. sec. Telcordia Technologies, 2005—07; exec. v.p., gen. counsel Realogy Corp., Parsippany, NJ, 2007—. Office: Realogy Corp 1 Campus Dr Parsippany NJ 07054 *

WASSERBURG, GERALD JOSEPH, geology and geophysics educator; b. New Brunswick, NJ, Mar. 25, 1927; s. Charles and Sarah (Levine) W.; m. Naomi Z. Orlick, Dec. 21, 1951; children: Charles David, Daniel Morris. Student, Rutgers U., 1946—48; BS in Physics, U. Chgo., 1951, MSc in Geology, 1952, PhD, 1954, DSc (hon.), 1992; D (hon.), Brussels U., 1985, U. Paris, 1986; DSc (hon.), Ariz. State U., 1987, U. Rennes, 1998, U. Turino, Italy, 2000. Rsch. assoc. Inst. Nuc. Studies U. Chgo., 1954-55; asst. prof. Calif. Inst. Tech., Pasadena, 1955-59, assoc. prof., 1959-62, prof. geology and geophysics, 1962-82, John D. MacArthur prof. geology and geophysics, 1982—2001, prof. emeritus, 2001—. Served on Juneau Ice Field Rsch. Project, 1950; cons. Argonne Nat. Lab., Lamont, Ill., 1952-55; former mem. U.S. Nat. Com. for Geochem., com. for Planetary Exploration Study, NRC, adv. coun. Petroleum Rsch. Fund, Am. Chem. Soc.; me. lunar sample analysis planning team (LSAPT) manned Spacecraft Ctr., NASA, Houston, 1968-71, chmn., 1970; lunar sample rev. bd., 1970-72; mem. Facilities Working Group LSAPT, Johnson Space Ctr., 1972-82; mem. sci. working panel for Apollo missions, Johnson Space Ctr., 1971-73; advisor NASA, 1968-88, phys. scis. com., 1971-75, mem. lunar base steering com., 1984; chmn. com. for planetary and lunar exploration, mem. space sci. bd. NAS, 1975-78; chmn. divsn. Geol. and Planetary Scis., Calif. Inst. Tech., 1987-89; vis. prof. U. Kiel, Fed. Republic of Germany, 1960, Harvard U., 1962, U. Bern, Switzerland, 1966, Swiss Fed. Tech. Inst., 1967, Max Planck Inst., Mainz and Heidelberg, Fed. Republic of Germany, 1985, others; invited lectr., Vinton Hayes Sr. fellow Harvard U., 1980, Jaeger-Hales lectr. Australian Nat. U., 1980, Harold Jeffreys lectr. Royal Astron. Soc., 1981, Ernst Cloos lectr. Johns Hopkins U., 1984, H.L. Welsh Disting. lectr. U. Toronto, 1986, Danz lectr. U. Wash., 1989, Goldschmidt Centennial lectr. Norwegian Acad. Sci. and Letters, 1989, Lindsay lectr. Goddard Space Flight Ctr., 1996, other lectureshipss; plenary spkr. 125th Anniversary Geol. Soc. Sweden, 1996; 60th Anniversary Symposium spkr. Hebrew U., Jerusalem, 1985, 75th Anniversary Symposium spkr., 2000; Lezione Magistrale, Umbria Libri, Perugia, 2003. Served with U.S. Army, 1944-46. Decorated Combat Inf. badge; recipient Group Achievement award NASA, 1969, Exceptional Sci. Achievement award NASA, 1970, Disting. Pub. Svc. medal NASA, 1973, J.F. Kemp medal Columbia U., 1973, Profl. Achievement award U. Chgo. Alumni Assn., 1978, Goldschmidt medal Geochem. Soc., 1978, Disting. Pub. Svc. medal with cluster NASA, 1978, Wollaston medal Geol. Soc. London, 1985, Sr. Scientist award Alexander von Humboldt-Stiftung, 1985, Crafoord prize Royal Swedish Acad. Scis., 1986, Holmes medal, 1987, Regents fellow Smithsonian Inst., Gold medal Royal Astron. Soc., 1991; named Hon. Fgn. fellow European Union Geoscis., 1983. Fellow Am. Acad. Arts and Scis., Geol. Soc. London (hon.), Geol. Soc. Am., Am. Geophys. Union (planetology sect., Harry H. Hess medal 1985), Geol. Soc. Am. (life, Arthur L. Day medal 1970), Meteoritical Soc. (pres. 1987-88, Leonard medal 1975), Am. Chem. Soc., Geochemical Society and the European Assn. for Geochemistry, 1996; mem. Nat. Acad. Scis. (Arthur L. Day prize and lectureship 1981, J. Lawrence Smith medal 1985), Norwegian Acad. Sci. and Letters, Am. Phil. Soc. Achievements include research in geochemistry and geophysics and the application of the methods of chemical physics to problems in the earth scis. Major researches have been the determination of the time scales of nucleosynthesis, connections between the interstellar medium and solar material, the time of the formation of the solar system, the chronology and evolution of the earth, moon and meteorites, the establishment of dating methods using long-lived natural radio-activities, the study of geologic and cosmic processes using nuclear and isotopic effects as a tracer in nature, the origin of natural gases, and the application of thermodynamic methods to geologic systems. Office: Calif Inst Tech Divsn Geol & Planetary Scis Pasadena CA 91125-2500 Business E-Mail: gjw@gps.caltech.edu.

WASSERMAN, BARRY L(EE), architect; b. Cambridge, Mass., May 25, 1935; s. Theodore and Adelaide (Levin) Wasserman; m. Wilma Louise Greenfield, June 21, 1957 (div. 1971); children: Tim Andrew, Andrew Glenn; m. Judith Ella Michalowski, Apr. 22, 1979. BA, Harvard U., 1957, M. Arch., 1960. Registered arch., Calif. Assoc. John S. Bolles Assocs., San Francisco, 1960-69; prin. Wasserman-Herman Assocs., San Francisco, 1969-72; prin., dir. Office Lawrence Halprin U Assocs., San Francisco, 1972-76; dep. state architect State of Calif., Sacramento, 1976-78, state architect, 1978-83; prof. dept. architecture, dir. Inst. Environ. Design, Sch. Environ. Design Calif. State Poly. U., Pomona, 1983-87, chair dept. architecture, Coll. Environ. Design, 1988-96, prof. emeritus, 1997—. Program advisor Fla. A&M U., Tallahassee, 1981—83; adv. com. Interior Design Program Calif. State U., Sacramento, 2004—; bd. dirs. Environ. Coun. Sacramento; design rev. adminstr. Sacramento County, 2006—; cons. in field. Prin. works include Wasserman House, San Rafael, Calif., 1963 (AIA-Sunset Mag. award of Merit, 1965), Anna Waden Libr., San Francisco, 1969 (AIA award of Merit, 1970), Capitol Area Plan, Sacramento, 1977 (Ctrl. Valley chpt. AIA Honor award, 1979); co-author: Ethics and the Practice of Architecture, 2000. Mem. City of Sacramento Planning Commn., 2004—. Recipient awards citation, Prog. Architecture 26th Awards Program, 1979, Octavius Morgan award, Calif. Archs. Bd., 2000. Fellow: AIA (chmn. architecture govt. com. 1979, bd. dirs. environ. coun. Sacramento 2004—). Democrat. Jewish. Home: 6456 Fordham Way Sacramento CA 95831-2218 E-mail: blw2@mindspring.com.

WASSERMAN, CASEY, management consultant; b. 1974; s. Lynne Wasserman; m. Laura Ziffren. BA, UCLA, 1996. Chmn., CEO, founder Wasserman Media Group, LLC, 1998—. Pres., CEO Wasserman Found.; chmn. Arena Football League; owner LA Avengers Arena Football League team. Bd. dirs. NYU, William Jefferson Clinton Presdl. Libr. Found., LA Philharmonic, Jules Stein Eye Inst. Named an Forty Under 40, Sports Bus. Jour.; named one of 25 Most Power Angelenos, LA Bus. Jour. Office: Wasserman Media Group LLC 12100 W Olympic Blvd Los Angeles CA 90064-1052 *

WASSERMAN, EDWARD ARNOLD, psychology professor; b. LA, Apr. 2, 1946; s. Albert Leonard and May (Sabin) W. BA, UCLA, 1968; PhD, Ind. U., 1972. Postdoctoral fellow U. Sussex, Brighton, Eng., 1972; from asst. prof. to prof. psychology U. Iowa, Iowa City, 1972-83, prof., 1983—, Stuit prof. exptl. psychology, 1997—. Pres. faculty senate U. Iowa, 1997-98; vis. scientist CNRS, Marseille, France, 1999. Contbr. articles to profl. jours., chpts. to books; editor several books; assoc. editor several jours. Bd. dirs. Big Bros., Big Sisters, Johnson County, Iowa, 1982-85 Ind. U. fellow, 1968, U. Iowa fellow, 1975, 82, NAS fellow, former USSR, 1976, James Van Allen Natural Scis. fellow, 1994-95. Fellow APA, Assn. Psychol. Sci.; mem. Psychonomic Soc., Midwestern Psychol. Assn., Soc. Exptl. Psychologists, Phi Beta Kappa. Office: U Iowa Dept Psychology Iowa City IA 52242

WASSERMAN, KAREN BOLING, clinical psychologist, nursing consultant; b. Olney, Ill., July 29, 1944; d. Kenneth G. and Betty Jean (Varner) Boling; m. James M. Wasserman, Apr. 14, 1965; children: Nicole C., Michael B. RN, Barnes Hosp. Sch. Nursing, St. Louis, 1965; BA, Antioch Coll., Yellow Springs, Ohio, 1977; PsyD in Psychology, Wright State U., Dayton, Ohio, 1986. RN Mo., Ohio; lic. psychologist Ind., Ohio, nat. registered psychologist, cert. life success coach Profl. Woman Network, 2005. Staff nurse various med. facilities, 1965-76; instr. practical nurse program Ind. Vocat. Tech. Coll., Richmond, 1976-77; staff, float nurse Good Samaritan Hosp., Dayton, Ohio, 1977-78; pub. health nurse coord. Bur. Alcoholism Svcs., Dayton, 1978-79, alcoholism counselor IV, 1979-82; practicum student Wright State U. Sch. Profl. Psychology, Dayton, 1983-85; psychology intern Balt. VAMC Consortium, 1985-86; clin. psychologist Dayton VAMC, 1987-89; founder, ptnr., dir. clin. svcs. Fairhaven Clinic, P.A., Biloxi, Miss., 1989-98; clin. psychologist Gulf Oaks Hosp., Biloxi, 1989-98, Sand Hill Hosp., Gulfport, Miss., 1993-98, chief psychol. svcs., 1998; cons. psychologist Sr. Life Cons., Dublin, Ohio, 2000; exec. dir. The Ridge Counseling Ctr., Columbus, Ohio, 2001—05; cons., reviewer Bur. Disability Determination, Ohio Rehab. Svcs. Commn., 2005—. Psychiat. nursing cons. Mercy Hosp., Omaha, Council Bluffs, Iowa, 1987; instr. William Carey Coll. on the Coast, 1993; owner/propr. Angel Garden, Ocean Springs, 1996—98; founder, co-owner Ebenezer's Antiques, Springfield, Ohio, 1999—. Author: (book chpt.) Self-Esteem and Empowerment for Women, 2006. Chmn. cmty. svcs. Altrusa Internat., Biloxi, 1990—94, treas., 1993—94; Friend of the Rainbow Warrior, Greenpeace, 1986—93; mem. adminstrv. bd. Gulf Coast Ctr. for Nonviolence, 1996—98; mem. adv. bd. Ohio Coalition for Suicide Prevention, 2002; mem. Health & Wellness Com. Scioto Ridge United Meth. Ch., 2003; disaster response trainer FEMA, 2004—; trainer of trainers for disaster responders Ohio Dept. Mental Health, 2004; mem. evangelism com. First United Meth. Ch., Gulfport, Miss., 1991—93, mem. coun. on ministries, 1994—95; mem. libr. com., ch. and soc. com. Worthington (Ohio) United Meth. Ch., 1999—2001; co-convener Fairhaven OSL Chpt., North Broadway United Meth. Ch., Columbus, Ohio, 2005—; mem. Internat. Order of St. Luke the Physician, 1997—. Recipient Alumnae award in Acads., Barnes Hosp. Sch. Nursing, 1965, Career Woman of Yr. award, Lighthouse of Biloxi chpt., Bus. and Profl. Women, 1994. Fellow: Am. Acad. Psychologists Treating Addiction; mem.: Profl. Women's Network, Miss. Psychol. Assn. (region IV rep. exec. coun., continuing edn. com. 1990—95, chair 1994—95, chair membership com. 1997—98), Ohio Psychol. Assn. (legis. com. 1998—2000, profl. practice com. 2004). Avocations: architecture, gardening, travel, movies. Office: Columbus Psychol Ctr 4700 Reed Rd Columbus OH 43220 Office Phone: 614-296-3522. Fax: 614-457-0026.

WASSERMAN, MARCIA WATSON, legal administration consultant; b. Bklyn., Dec. 17, 1949; d. Stanley and Seena (Klein) Watson; m. Charles Wasserman, Mar. 23, 2003. Student, UCLA, 1967-71, 80-81, UCLA Grad. Sch., 1987-88. Dir. adminstrn. Kadison, Pfaelzer, LA, 1983-87; exec. dir. Richards, Watson and Gershon, LA, 1987-93; legal mgmt. cons. Wainess & Co., LA, 1993-99; dir. law firm svcs. Duitch Franklin Bus. Svcs., Inc., 1999-2000; dir. client adv. svcs. Green Hasson & Janks LLP, LA, 2000—03; pres. Comprehensive Mgmt. Solutions, Inc., 2003—06; COO Nossaman, Guthner Knox & Elliott LLP, LA, 2006—. Adj. faculty U. West L.A. Sch. Paralegal Studies, 1997-98. Mem. ABA, State Bar Calif. (exec. com. law practice mgmt. and tech. sect. 2002-), Assn. Legal Adminstrs. (mem. editl. adv. bd. 1998-2005, bd. dirs. 1990-92, asst. regional v.p. Calif. 1987-88, regional v.p. 1988-89, pres. Beverly Hills chpt. 1985-86, membership chair 1984-85, chair new adminstrn. sect. 1982-84, mktg. mgmt. sect. com. 1989-90, internat. conf. com.), Beverly Hills Bar Assn. (chair law practice mgmt. sect. 1998-00, chair women in legal profession co. 2000-01, co-chair mng. ptnrs. forum 2005-). Avocations: historic preservation, antiques, interior design. Office: Nossaman Guthner Knox & Elliott LLP 445 S Figueroa St 31st Fl Los Angeles CA 90071 Office Phone: 213-612-7800. Business E-Mail: mwasserman@nossaman.com.

WASSERMAN, PAUL, library and information science professor; b. Newark, Jan. 8, 1924; s. Joseph and Sadie (Ringelescu) W.; m. Krystyna Ostrowska, 1973; children: Jacqueline R., Steven R. BBA, Coll. City N.Y., 1948; MS in L.S., Columbia, 1949, MS, 1950; PhD, U. Mich., 1960; postgrad., Western Res. U., 1963-64. Advt. mgr. Zuckerberg Co., NYC, 1946-48; asst. to bus. libr. Bklyn. Pub. Library, 1949-51, chief sci. and industry div., 1951-53; librarian, asst. prof. Grad. Sch. Bus. and Pub. Adminstrn., Cornell U., 1953-56, libr., assoc. prof., 1956-62, librarian, prof., 1962-65; dean U. Md. Coll. Library and Info. Scis., 1965-70, prof., 1970-97, prof. emeritus, 1997—. Vis. prof. U. Mich., summers 1960, 63, 64, Asian Inst. Tech., U. Hawaii, U. Hong Kong, summer 1988, Chulalongkorn U., Bangkok, 1990, U. Wash., summer 1991, U. Wis., summer 1992, C.W. Post Coll., L.I. U., 1993, Inst. Sci. and Tech. China, Beijing, 1996; Isabel Nichol lectr. Denver U. Libr. Sch., 1968; market rsch. cons. Laux Advt., Inc., 1955-59, Gale Rsch. Co., Detroit, 1959-60, 63-64; rsch. planning cons. Ind. U. Sch. Bus., 1961-62; cons. to USPHS as mem. manpower tng. rev. com. Nat. Libr. Medicine, 1966-69, Ohio Bd. Regents, 1969, Omngraphics Inc., 1988-91, VITA, summer 1987; dir. Documentation Abstracts, Inc., 1970-73, v.p., 1971-73; Fulbright prof. Warsaw U., 1993-94; rsch. project dir. Kellogg Study, 1996-98. Author: Information for Adminstrators, 1956, (with Fred Silander) Decision Making, 1958, Measurement and Evaluation of Organization Performance, 1959, Sources of Commodity Prices, 1960, 2d edit., 1974, Sources for Hospital Administrators, 1961, Decision Making: An Annotated Bibliography, supplement, 1958-63, 1964, Librarian and the Machine, 1965; Book rev. editor: Adminstrv. Sci. Quar, 1956-61; editor: Service to Business, 1952-53, Directory of University Research Bureaus and Institutes, 1960, Health Organizations of the U.S. and Canada, 1961, and 2d to 4th edit., 1977, Statistics Sources, 1962 and 4th to 8th edits., 1984, (with Bundy) Reader in Library Adminstration, 1968, Reader in Research Methods in Librarianship, 1969; mng. editor: Mgmt. Information Guide Series, 1963-83, Consultants and Consulting Organizations, 1966, 4th edit., 1979, 5th edit., 1982, Who's Who in Consulting, 1968, 2d edit., 1974, Awards, Honors and Prizes: A Sourcebook and Directory, 1969, 2d edit., 1972, 4th edit. Vol. 1, 1978, International and Foreign Awards, 1975, New Consultants, 1973-74, 76-77, 78-79, Readers in Librarianship and Information Science, 1968-78, Ency. Bus. Information Sources, 1971, 3d edit., 1976, 4th edit., 1980, 5th edit., 1983, Library and Information Services Today, 1971-75, Consumer Sourcebook, 1974, 2d edit., 1978, 3d edit., 1980, 4th edit., 1983; series editor: Contributions in Librarianship and Information Science, 1969-99; coordinating mgmt. editor: Information Guide Library, 1971-83, The New Librarianship-A Challenge for Change, 1972; mng. editor: Museum Media, 1973, Library Bibliographies and Indexes, 1975, Ethnic Groups in the United States, 1976, 2d edit., 1982, Training and Development Organizations, 1978, 2d edit., 1983, Speakers and Lecturers: How to Find Them, 1979, 2d edit., 1982, Learning Independently, 1979, 2d edit., 1983, Recreation and Outdoor Life Directory, 1979, Law and Legal Information Directory, 1980, 2d edit., 1982, Ency. Health Info. Sources, 1986, Ency. Sr. Citizen Info. Sources, 1987, Ency. Pub. Affairs Info. Sources, 1987, Ency. Legal Info. Sources, 1987; mem. editorial bd. Social Scis. Citation Index, Inst. Scientific Info., 1972-95, Jour. Library Adminstrn., 1979-89, Social Sci. Info. Studies, 1979—, 1991 Education for Info.: The Internat. Rev. of Education and Tng. in Library and Info. Sci., 1983-88, The Best of Times: A Personal and Occupational Odyssey, 2000, New York from A to Z, 2002, Washington DC from A to Z, 2003, Weasel Words, The Dictionary of American Doublespeak, 2005. Active U.S. Com. on Edn. and Tng. for Internat. Fedn. for Info. and Documentation, 1993-94. Served with U.S. Army, 1943-46. Decorated Purple Heart, Bronze Star; recipient ALA Ref. Svcs. Divsn./Gale Rsch. Bus. Libr. award, 1997; Fulbright scholar, Sri Lanka, 1986-87, Poland, 1995. Mem. AAUP, ALA, Am. Soc. Info. Sci., Spl. Librs. Assn. (editor, chmn. publ. project., Disting. Mem. award bus. divsn. 1996—). Home: 4940 Sentinel Dr Apt 203 Bethesda MD 20816-3552 Office: U Md Coll Info Studies College Park MD 20742-0001 E-mail: pw11@umail.umd.edu.

WASSERMAN, RICHARD LEO, lawyer; b. Balt., Aug. 6, 1948; s. Jack B. and Claire (Gutman) W.; m. Manuele Delbourgo, May 13, 1973; children: Alexander E., Lauren E. AB, Princeton U., 1970; JD, Columbia U., 1973. Bar: N.Y. 1975, Md. 1978, U.S. Dist. Ct. (so. and ea. dists.) N.Y. 1975, U.S. Dist. Ct. Md. 1978, U.S. Ct. Appeals (2d cir.) 1975, U.S. Ct. Appeals (4th cir.) 1979, U.S. Supreme Ct. 1982. Law clk. to hon. Roszel C. Thomsen U.S. Dist. Ct. Md., Balt., 1973-74; assoc. Proskauer Rose Goetz & Mendelsohn, NYC, 1974-78, Venable LLP, Balt., 1978-81, ptnr., Bankruptcy & Creditors' Rights practice, 1982—. Bd. dirs. Legal Aid Bur., Inc., 2004—. Co-author, editor in chief: Bankruptcy Appeals Manual, 1998; editor: Bankruptcy Appeals Manual, 2d edit., 2005; contbr. chapters to books. Recipient Pro Bono Svc. award, US Dist. Ct. Md., 2005. Fellow Am. Coll. Bankruptcy, Md. Bar Found.; mem. ABA (bus. bankruptcy com.), Md. Bar Assn. (sec. coun. bus. law sect. 1989-92), Bar Assn. Balt. City (chmn. banking, bankruptcy and bus. law com. 1987-88), Bankruptcy Bar Assn. Dist. Md. (bd. dirs. 1988—, pres. 1990-91), Assn. Bar City N.Y., Am. Bankruptcy Inst., Princeton U. Alumni Assn. Md. (bd. dirs. 1980-98, pres. 1985-87), Suburban Club Baltimore County (bd. govs. 1982-89, 94-98, 2d v.p. 1986-87, sec. 1987-88, pres.-elect 1994-95, pres. 1995-97). Democrat. Jewish. Avocations: tennis, golf, bridge. Office: Venable LLP 1800 Mercantile Bank & Trust Bldg 2 Hopkins Plz Baltimore MD 21201 Office Phone: 410-244-7505. Office Fax: 410-244-7742. Business E-Mail: rlwasserman@venable.com.

WASSERMAN, ROBERT HAROLD, biology professor; b. Schenectady, Feb. 11, 1926; s. Joseph and Sylvia (Rosenberg) W.; m. Marilyn Mintz, June 11, 1950; children: Diane Jean, Arlene Lee, Judith Rose. BS, Cornell U., 1949, PhD, 1953; MS, Mich. State U., 1951. Research assoc. AEC project U. Tenn., Oak Ridge, 1953-55; sr. scientist med. div. Oak Ridge Inst. Nuclear Studies, 1955-57; assoc. prof. dept. phys. biology N.Y. State Vet. Coll., Cornell U., 1957-63, prof., 1963—, James Law prof. physiology, 1989-97, James Law prof. emeritus, 1998—, acting head phys. biology dept., 1963-64, 71, 75-76, chmn. dept. /sect. physiology, 1983-87, mem. exec. com. div. biol. sci., 1983-87. Vis. fellow Inst. Biol. Chemistry, Copenhagen, 1964-65; chmn. Conf. on Calcium Transport, 1962; co-chmn. Conf. on Cell Mechanisms for Calcium Transfer and Homeostasis, 1970; mem. adv. bd. Vitamin D Symposia, 1976—; adv. bd. Symposia Calcium-Binding Proteins, 1977-2001, chmn., 1977; food and nutrition bd. NRC; cons. NIH, Oak Ridge Inst. Nuclear Studies; pub. affairs com. Fedn. Am. Socs. Exptl. Biology, 1974-77; chmn. com. MPI, NRC; pre-doctoral fellowship panel Howard Hughes, 1999-2000, 03. Bd. editors: Calcified Tissue Research, 1977-80, Procs. Soc. Exptl. Biol. Medicine, 1970-76, Cornell Veterinarian, Jour. Nutrition; contbr.: articles to profl. jours. Served with U.S. Army, 1944-45. Recipient Mead Johnson award, 1969, Andre Lichtwitz prize INSERM, 1982, W.F. Neuman award Am. Soc. Bone and Mineral Rsch., 1990, Merit award NIH, 1993-96, Brown U. Rsch. award, 2004; Guggenheim fellow, 1964-65, 72, fellow NSF-OECD, 1964-65.

Fellow Am. Inst. Nutrition, mem. Am. Physiol. Soc., Soc. Exptl. Biology and Medicine, AAAS, Nat. Acad. Scis., Sigma Xi, Phi Kappa Phi, Phi Zeta Home: 207 Texas Ln Ithaca NY 14850-1758 Business E-Mail: rhw2@cornell.edu.

WASSERMAN, STEPHEN ALAN, lawyer; b. Cleve., Apr. 7, 1948; s. Myron Earl and Eve Ruth (Milstein) W.; m. Sandra Shulamith Moltz, Oct. 20, 1978. BA, U. Wis., 1970; JD, Northeastern U., Boston, 1978. Bar: Mass. 1978, U.S. Dist. Ct. Mass. 1978. Housing atty. Neighborhood Legal Svcs., Lynn, Mass., 1978-83; ptnr. Barmack, Boggs and Wasserman, Lynn, 1983-91; pvt. practice Salem, Mass., 1991—97, 1998—2006; ptnr. Wessler and Wasserman, Lawrence, Mass., 2007—. Bd. dirs. North Shore Cmty. Action Program, Peabody, Mass., 1995—. Avocations: reading, baseball, jogging. Office: 439 S Union St #201 Lawrence MA 01843 Office Phone: 978-689-3806. Personal E-mail: s.a.wasserman@verizon.net.

WASSERMAN, STEPHEN IRA, allergist, immunologist, educator; b. LA, Dec. 17, 1942; m. Linda Morgan; children: Matthew, Zachary. BA, Stanford U., 1964; MD, UCLA, 1968. Diplomate Am. Bd. Internal Medicine, Am. Bd. Allergy and Immunology. Intern, resident Peter B. Brigham Hosp., Boston, 1968-70; fellow in allergy, immunology Robert B. Brigham Hosp., Boston, 1972-75; asst. prof. medicine Harvard U., Boston, 1975-79, assoc. prof., 1979, U. Calif.-San Diego, La Jolla, 1979-85, prof., 1985—, chief allergy tng. program Sch. Medicine, 1979-85, chief allergy div. Sch. Medicine, 1985-93, acting chmn. dept. medicine, 1986-88, chmn. dept. medicine, 1988-2000, Helen M. Ranney prof., 1992—2001, chief allergy tng.program Sch. Medicine, 2001—05. Co-dir. allergy sect. Robert B. and Peter B. Brigham Hosps., 1977-79; dir. Am. Bd. Allergy and Immunology; dir. Am. Bd. Internal Medicine., chair, 1999-2000. Contbr. articles to profl. jours. Served to lt. comdr. USPHS, 1970-72, San Francisco. Fellow Am. Acad. Allergy and Immunology (pres. 1997-98); mem. Am. Soc. Clin. Investigation, Assn. Am. Physicians, Am. Assn. Immunologists, Collegium Internationale Allergologicum, Phi Beta Kappa, Alpha Omega Alpha. Office: U Calif San Diego Stein Clin Rsch Bldg Rm 244 9500 Gilman Dr MC 0637 San Diego CA 92093-0637

WASSERMAN, STEPHEN MILES, communications director; b. Chgo., Apr. 26, 1945; s. Samuel Isreal and Rayna (Krassner) W.; m. Faye Rita Samuelson, Oct. 17, 1971; children: Rayna, Alyssa. BA in Journalism, Bradley U., 1968. Mgr. corp. comm. Underwriters Labs., Inc., Northbrook, Ill., 1991-98, corp. mgr. global comm. svcs., 1997-98, dir. global comm. svcs., 1998-2001, mem. steering com. home fire sprinkler coalition, 1998-2001; dir. comms. group Am. Optometric Assn., Creve Coeur, Mo., 2001—. Mem. pub. rels. and fundraising com. Ill. Math. and Sci. Acad., Aurora, 1992-96; comms. chair Nat. Electric Safety Found., Washington, 1994-96; mem. steering com. Home Fire Sprinkler Corp. Campaign chmn. United Way, Buffalo Grove, Ill., 1991-93, pres., 1994-95. Mem. SAE, Am. Soc. Assn. Execs., Am. Mktg. Assn., Nat. Press Club. Office: Am Optometric Assn 243 N Lindbergh Blvd Creve Coeur MO 63141 Office Phone: 314-983-4212. Business E-Mail: smwasserman@aoa.org.

WASSERMAN, STEVE, literary agent; b. Vancouver, Wash., Aug. 3, 1952; s. Abraham and Ann (Dragoon) W.; m. Michelle Krisel, Mar. 7, 1982 (div. Dec. 2001); children: Claire, Paul, Isaac; m. Jodi Faith Cahn, Aug. 11, 2002; 1 child, Mira. AB in Criminology, U. Calif., Berkeley, 1974. Asst. editor City Mag. of San Francisco, 1975—76; dep. editor opinion sect. L.A. Times, 1977—83; editor-in-chief New Republic Books The New Republic, NYC, 1984—87; pub., editl. dir. Hill and Wang divsn. Farrar, Straus and Giroux Inc., NYC, 1987—90; pub. The Noonday Press divsn. Farrar, Straus and Giroux Inc., NYC, 1987—90; editl. dir. Times Books divsn. Random House, NYC, 1990—96; editor L.A. Times Book Rev., 1996—2005; mng. dir. Kneerim & Williams at Fish & Richardson, NYC, 2005—. Cons. editor The Threepenny Rev., Berkeley, Calif., 1980—86, Tikkun, Oakland, Calif., 1986—90; founder, co-dir. L.A. Inst. for Humanities, U. So. Calif., 1998—2005; fellow NY Inst. for Humanities, NYU, 2006—; Donald and Doris Fischer lectr. Grad. Sch. of Journalism U. Calif. Berkeley, 1999; instr., master profl. writing program U. So. Calif., 2000—05; adj. prof. dept. journalism NYU, 2007—; co-dir. L.A. Times Festival of Books, 1997—2005; chair Pulitzer Prize Nominating Jury for Gen. Nonfiction, 2001; mem. Pulitzer Prize Nominating Jury for Fiction, 2003; bd. dirs. Nat. Book Critics Cir., 1997—2005; mem. jury lit. prizes Commonwealth Club Calif., 2001—06. Contbr. articles and revs. to mags. and newspapers. Mem. PEN. Office: Kneerim & Williams at Fish & Richardson Citigroup Ctr 52nd Fl 153 E 53rd St New York NY 10022-4611 Business E-Mail: wasserman@fr.com.

WASSERMAN, SUSAN VALESKY, accountant, artist, small business owner; b. St. Petersburg, Fla., June 5, 1956; d. Charles B. Valesky and Jeanne I. (Schulz) Morgan; m. Fred Wasserman, III, May 19, 1990; 1 child, Sara Elisabeth. BS in Merchandising, Fla. State U., Tallahassee, 1978; BA in Acctg., U. South Fla., Tampa, 1983. CPA Fla.; ChFC, cert. yoga tchr. Fla. Inst. for Integrated Yoga Studies, 2002, yoga therapist Integrated Yoga Therapy, 2004. Store mgr. Levi Strauss Inc., San Francisco, 1979; pvt. practice acct. St. Petersburg, 1980—; acct., tax and fin. planning specialist Barber, Stowe & Co., St. Petersburg, 1997—98; owner White Egret Yoga Studio, South Pasadena, Fla., 2002—. Owner White Egret Yoga Studio, South Pasadena, Fla., 2002—, Yoga Flow Essential Oils, South Pasadena, Fla., 2007—; yoga therapist; aromatherapist. Exhibitions include Longboat Key (Fla.) Art Ctr., 1993, Fla. Suncoast Water Color Soc., Sarasota, 1994, South Pasadena Artspring, 1998—2000 (Judges award, 1998), 2005. Mem.: Nat. Ayurvedic Med. Assn., Internat. Assn. Yoga Therapists, Suncoast Yoga Tchrs. Assn. (pres.), Yoga Alliance. Home and Studio: 7015 Grevilla Ave S Saint Petersburg FL 33707-2050 Office: 5800 4th St N Saint Petersburg FL 33703-1402 Home Phone: 727-347-5353; Office Phone: 727-347-7354. E-mail: yogisue@tampabay.rr.com.

WASSERMAN, WILLIAM PHILLIP, lawyer; b. LA, Sept. 13, 1945; s. Al and Ceil (Diamond) W.; married; children: Sam, George. BA, U. Calif., Berkeley, 1967; JD, U. Calif., 1970. Bar: Calif. 1971, U.S. Tax Ct. 1971. Ptnr. Ernst & Young LLP, Los Angeles, 1970—. Lectr. in field.; participant in numerous programs, confs., and workshops in field in field. Mem. Editorial adv. bd.: Real Estate Taxation: A Practitioner's Guide, 1984—, Federal Tax Annual: Real Estate, 1982; contbr. numerous articles to profl. jours. Mem. ABA (nat. chmn Tax Sect. com. on real estate problems 1985-87), State Bar Calif., Los Angeles County Bar Assn., Calif. Bd. Legal Specialization (cert. taxation law specialist). Office: Ernst & Young LLP 725 S Figueroa St Los Angeles CA 90017-5524

WASSERMAN-SCHULTZ, DEBBIE, congresswoman; b. Forest Hills, NY, Sept. 27, 1955; BA in Polit. Sci., U. Fla., 1988, MA, 1990. Mem. Fla. Ho. of Reps., 1992—2004, US Congress from 20th Fla. dist., 2005—; mem. Ho. Judiciary com. Mem. Gov.'s Commn. on Edn., 1996—; mem. legis. adv. coun. So. Regional Edn. Bd., 1995—; bd. dirs. Fla. Distance Learning Network, 1994; mem. Classrooms First Task Force, 1993. Recipient award for outstanding family advocacy Dade County Psychol. Assn., 1993, Giraffe award Women's Advocacy Majority Minority, 1993, Legis. Svc. award Fla. Assn. Women Lawyers, 1993, Quality Floridian award Fla. League of Cities, 1994, AMIT Woman of Yr. award, 1994, Outstanding Legislator of Yr. award Fla. Fedn. Bus. and Profl. Women, 1994, Rosemary Barkett award Acad. Fla. Trial Lawyers, 1995, Woman of Vision award Weizmann Inst. Sci., others; named one of Six Most Unstoppable Women, South Fla. Mag., 1994. Mem. Omicron Delta Kappa. Democrat. Jewish. Avocations: bowling, golf, politics, old houses. Office: US House of Representatives 118 Cannon House Office Bldg Washington DC 20515-0920 also: 10100 Pines Blvd Pembroke Pines FL 33026 Office Phone: 202-225-7931. *

WASSERSTEIN, BRUCE, investment banker; b. Bklyn., Dec. 25, 1947; s. Morris and Lola (Schleifer) Wasserstein; m. Claude Becker; 5 children, 1 adopted child BA with honors, U. Mich., 1967; MBA with high distinction, Harvard U., 1971, JD cum laude, 1971; diploma in law, Cambridge U., 1972. Assoc. Cravath, Swaine & Moore, NYC, 1972-77; mng. dir. The First Boston Corp., NYC, 1977-88; pres. Wasserstein, Perella and Co., NYC, 1988—2000; exec. chmn. Dresdner Kleinwort Wasserstein, NYC, 2000—01; chmn., CEO Lazard Ltd., NYC, 2001—; chmn. Am. Lawyer Media, 1997—; owner The Daily Deal, 1999—, NY Mag., 2003—; chmn. Wasserstein & Co., 2001—. Author: Corporatwe Finance Law: A Guide for the Executive, 1978, Big Deal: Mergers and Acquisitions in the Digital Age, 1988 Mem. SEC Adv. Comm. Tender Offers; mem. vis. com. Harvard Law Sch., Harvard Bus. Sch., U. Mich., Columbia Journalism Sch., Cambridge U. Bus. Sch. Mem. Coun. on Fgn. Rels. Democrat. Office: Lazard Ltd 30 Rockefeller Plaza New York NY 10020

WASSHAUSEN, DIETER CARL, botanist; b. Jena, Germany, Apr. 15, 1938; came to U.S., 1950, naturalized, 1957; s. Heinz P. and Elizabeth A. (Mueller) W.; m. Merrilee M. Locklin, Dec. 23, 1961; children— Lisa A., David B. BS, George Washington U., 1962, MS, 1965, PhD, 1972. Assoc. curator dept. botany Smithsonian Instn., Washington, 1969-76; chmn., curator dept. botany Nat. Mus. Natural History, Washington, 1976—. Recipient Smithsonian Rsch. Found. award, 1974—75, Willdenow medal, 1979. Mem. Am. Soc. Plant Taxonomists, Internat. Assn. Plant Taxonomy, Neotropical Field Botanists Assn., Am. Inst. Biol. Scis., AAAS, Assn. Tropical Biology, Sigma Xi. Presbyterian. Achievements include research on systematics of neotropical Acanthaceae, floristic studies in Graminea of Brazil, floristic studies in Begoniaceae, revision of Nat. List Sci. Plant Names. Home: St James Plantation 2931 Legends Dr Southport NC 28461 Office: Nat Mus Natural History 10th St and Constitution Ave NW Washington DC 20560-0001 Office Phone: 202-633-0944. Personal E-mail: dmwasshausen@2khiway.net.

WASSMER, RUDOLF ANDREAS, entrepreneurial engineer; b. Berne, Switzerland, Nov. 27, 1941; s. Hans Erich and Margaretha Katharina (von Mandach) W.; m. Janine Antoinette Georgine Koch, Aug. 24, 1978; 1 child, Alexandra Janine. Diploma mech. engring., Fed. Inst. of Tech., 1967; diploma, European Inst. Bus. Adminstrn., 1971. Jr. project engr. internat. Polysius, Paris, 1968; del. project engr. SungShin Cement, Seoul, 1969-70; with Swiss Aluminium Ltd., Zuerich, 1971-72; cons. Portland Cement Werk, 1973; works engr. Würenlingen AG, 1973-74; tech. dir., rep., 1974-76; mem. staff Cementia Engring and Cons., Zurich, 1976-78, sr. engr. internat., 1981-87, 92; works dir., improvement plan Bamburi Portland Cement Co. Ltd., Kenya, 1978-81; enterpreneurial engr. Swiss secretariat Holdit, Leadership and Devel. Activities Internat., Zurich, 1987—. Capt. Swiss Army Res., 1964-91. Mem. INSEAD (alumnus), ETHZ, Swiss Engring. and Arch., Eur Ing Feani (cert.), Seoul Club, Mobasa Club. Avocation: sports. Office: Holdit & Studio P-C-W Hdqs 4th floor Asylstrasse 64 8032 Zurich Switzerland Office Fax: 41443830975.

WASSNER, STEVEN JOEL, pediatric nephrologist, educator; b. NYC, Dec. 16, 1946; s. Abraham and Clara (Weitzner) W.; m. Enid K. Kling, June 11, 1972; children: Adam Jacob, Nancy Shane. BS, CCNY, 1968; MD, NYU, 1972. Diplomate Am. Bd. Pediatrics, Am. Bd. Pediatrics Nephrology. Intern, resident Children's Hosp. L.A., 1972-74, fellow in pediatric nephrology, 1974-75; rsch. fellow in pediatric nephrology UCLA, 1975-77; asst. prof. pediat. Pa. State U. M.S. Hershey Med. Ctr., Hershey, 1978—83, chief divsn. pediat. nephrology and hypertension, 1978—, assoc. prof., 1983—91, dir. pediat. residency program, 1988—2006, dir. med./pediat residency program, 1989—94, vice chmn. dept., 1989—99, prof., 1991—, chief divsn. pediatric nephrology and diabetes, 1991—99, vice chmn. edn., 1999—, interim chief divsn. endocrinology, physician lead safety and quality, 2006—. Vis. prof. human biochemistry Hebrew U., Hadassah Hosp., 1985-86; dir. Pediatric Diabetes Svc., 1998-99. Contbr. articles to med. jours. Mem. adv. bd. Kidney Found. South Ctrl. Pa., Harrisburg, 1980-90, sci. adv. coun. for pediatric nephrology/urology Nat. Kidney Found., 1986-92, Harrisburg com. for Hebrew U.; bd. dirs. Jewish Family Svc., Harrisburg, 1979-85, pres., 1983-85; bd. dirs. United Jewish Fedn., 1983-85, 94-97, Yeshiva Acad., 1987-90. Recipient Rsch. Career Devel. award NIH, 1983; Musclar Dystrophy Assn. grantee, 1979-81, Disting. Educator award, 2005; Sr. Internat. fellow Fogarty Internat. Ctr. NIH, 1985. Fellow Am. Acad. Pediatrics (exec. com. sect. on nephrology, chair program subcom. 1998-2002, chmn. exec. com. sect. on nephrology 2002-06), Am. Bd. Pediatrics; mem. Am. Pediatrics Soc., Am. Soc. Nephrology, Internat. Soc. Nephrology, Am. Soc. Pediatrics, Nephrology, Internat. Soc. Pediatric Nephrology, Internat. Pediatric Nephrology Assn. (counsellor 1989-95). Office: MS Hershey Med Ctr PO Box 850 Hershey PA 17033-0850 Office Phone: 717-531-5707. Business E-Mail: swassner@psu.edu.

WASSON, GREGORY D., retail executive; B pharmacy, Purdue Univ., 1981. Various positions Walgreen Co., Deerfield, Ill., 1980—86, dist. mgr., 1986—99, regional v.p. store ops., 1999—2001; exec. v.p. Walgreens Health Initiatives Inc., 2001—02, pres., 2002; v.p. Walgreen Co., Deerfield, Ill., 2001—04, sr. v.p., 2004—05, exec. v.p., 2006—07, pres., COO, 2007—. Office: Walgreen Co 200 Wilmot Rd Deerfield IL 60015 *

WASSON, JEFFREY, music educator; b. Evanston, Ill., Aug. 24, 1948; s. Newton Oliver and Hilda Crowell Wasson. MusB, Northwestern U., 1970, MusM, 1973, PhD, 1987. Instr. music Northwestern U., Evanston, Ill., 1980-85; asst. prof. music Barat Coll., Lake Forest, Ill., 1986-92; dir. music St. Mary of the Angels, Chgo., 1992-97, Barat Coll., Lake Forest, Ill., 1987—, assoc. prof. music, 1992-99, prof. music, 1999-2001, Barat Coll. DePaul U., 2001—02; prof. musicianship DePaul U., Chgo., 2002—. Vis. prof. music, Northwestern U., 1990, 93; bd. mem. New Music Chgo., 1987, 92-94, v.p., 1987-88, pres., 1988-92; bd. dirs. Mozart Sinfonia; bd. dirs. Ars Musica Chgo., 2000-05, v.p., 2003-04, pres., 2004—; NEH summer seminar participant Brandeis U., 1995, Boston U., 2000; lectr. Yale U., U. Leuven, Belgium, U. Mich., Ann Arbor, U. Minn., U. Pitts., Mich. State U., Loyola U. of Chgo., U. Nebr. Editor: A Compendium of American Musicology, 2000; contbr. articles to profl. jours., chpts. to books. Summer seminar grantee NEH, U. Rochester (declined). Mem. NARAS, Am. Musicol. Soc., Am. Guild Organists, Internat. Musicol. Soc., Coll. Music Soc., Organ Hist. Soc., Club Internationale, Phi Kappa Lambda. Episcopalian. Avocations: fine art collecting, Lionel trains. Office: DePaul U Sch Music 804 W Belden Ave Chicago IL 60614-3296 Office Phone: 773-325-4378. Business E-Mail: jwasson@depaul.edu.

WASSON, ROBERT E., state agency administrator; b. Charleston, W.Va. s. James Edward and Marian Ruth Wasson; m. Joyce Marie Brewer, Oct. 22, 1955; children: Steven Edward(dec.), David Bradford, Thomas Robert(dec.). BS, Purdue U., West Lafayette, Ind., 1951. Commd. 2d lt. US Army, 1951, advanced through grades to lt. col., ret., 1979; dir. procurement Dept. Health & Social Svcs., State of Del., New Castle, 1975—90; commr. Commn. Vets. Affairs, Del., 2001—. Independent. Presbyterian. Avocations: woodworking, travel. Home: 507 W Clearview Ave Wilmington DE 19807-1617

WASTA, VANESSA A., media specialist, web site designer; d. Peter S. and Myrna E. Gatto; m. Sean C. Wasta, Sept. 4, 1999; 1 child, Christian C. BS in Biology, U. Md., Balt., 1996; MBA, Loyola Coll. Md., Balt., 1999. Mktg. and pub. rels. grad. resident U. Md. Greenebaum Cancer Ctr., Balt., 1995—98; assoc. dir. media rels. and web projects Johns Hopkins Kimmel Cancer Ctr., Balt., 1998—. Active music ministry mem. St. Mark Ch., Catonsville, Md., 2000—07; mem. Our Lady of Fields, Millersville, Md., 2007—. Mem.: Nat. Cancer Inst. Cancer Ctrs. Pub. Affairs Network, Nat. Assn. Sci. Writers. Achievements include development of first electronic tracking method for media inquiries at the Johns Hopkins Kimmel Cancer Center; first e-newsletter for Kimmel Cancer Center; coordinated and implemented first database-driven content management system (CMS) for Kimmel Cancer Center Web site; among first CMS systems at Johns Hopkins; coordinated first comprehensive database of clinical trials on external Web site integrated with the Kimmel Cancer Center's Clinical Research Office. Avocations: singing, piano. Office: Johns Hopkins Kimmel Cancer Center 901 S Bond St Ste 573 Baltimore MD 21231 Home Phone: 443-257-2042; Office Phone: 410-614-2916. Office Fax: 410-614-2611. Business E-Mail: wastava@jhmi.edu.

WASTBERG, OLLE M., cultural organization administrator; b. Stockholm, May 6, 1945; s. Erik and Greta (Hirsch) Wastberg; m. Inger Claesson, Feb. 21, 1968; children: David, Elias. BA, U. Stockholm, 1972. Tchr. polit. sci. U. Stockholm, 1967-68; journalist polit. dept. Expressen, 1968-71; editor-in-chief, 1994-95; rsch. fellow Bus. and Soc. Rsch. Ctr., 1971-76; pres. Aktieframjandet, 1976-82; mem. Parliament, 1976-82; pres. Swedish Newspaper Promotion Assn., 1983-91; undersec. of state for fin. affairs Ministry of Fin., Stockholm, 1991-93; pres. bd. Nordic Investment Bank, 1992-94, Swedish Broadcasting Corp., 1996-99; consul gen. for Sweden in NY, 1999—2004; dir. gen. Swedish Inst. Bd., 2005—. Bd. dirs. Swedish Inst., Alexandria, 2007; group 10 deps. IMF, 1991—93; Swedish del. meeting mins. fin., 1992; mem. govt. com. South Africa consumer politis and stock market; pres. Bertil Ohlin Inst., 1996—2000. Author: books on African problems, immigration politics and econ. topics; contbr. articles to profl. jours. Bd. dirs. Friends Hebrew U. Jerusalem; polit. sec. Liberal Youth Sweden, 1966, v.p., 1969—71; bd. dirs. Liberal Party, 1972—93, 1997—2000, pres. exec. com., 1982—83. Named Swedish Man of the Yr., NY, 2003; recipient Gold medal, Swedish Mktg. Group, 1982. Home: Bellmansgatan 6 11820 Stockholm Sweden Office: Swedish Inst Skeppbron 2 16391 Stockholm Sweden Office Phone: +4684537810. Business E-Mail: olle@wastberg.se.

WASTERLAIN, CLAUDE GUY, neurologist; s. Desire and Simone (De Taeye) W.; m. Anne Marguerite Thomsin, Feb. 28, 1967; 1 child, Jean Michel. Cand. Sci., U. Liege, 1957, MD, 1961; degree in Libr. Sci., Molecular Biology summa cum laude, Free U. Brussels, 1969. Resident Cornell U. Med. Coll., NYC, 1964-67, instr. neurology, 1969-70, asst. prof., 1970-75, assoc. prof., 1975-76, UCLA Sch. Medicine, 1976-79, prof., 1979—2005, vice-chair dept. neurology, 1976—, disting. prof., 2005—; chief neurology svc. VA Med. Ctr., Sepulveda, Calif., 1976—98; chair neurology Greater LA VA Health Care Sys., 1998—. Attending neurologist UCLA Ctr. Health Scis., 1976—. Author, editor: Status Epilepticus, 1984, Neonatal Seizures, 1990, Molecular Neurobiology and Epilepsy, 1992, Progressive Nature of Epileptogenesis, 1996, Status Epilepticus: Mechanism Management, 2006; contbr. articles to med. jours. Recipient N.Y. Neurol. Soc. Young Investigator award, 1965; Rsch. Career Devel. award NIH, 1973-76; William Evans fellow, U. Auckland, New Zealand, 1984; Worldwide AES award for rsch. in epilepsy, 1992; Golden Hammer Tchg. award, 1996; Amb. for Epilepsy, Internat. League Against Epilepsy, 2003; Pierre Gloor award Am. Clin. Neurophysiology Soc., 2006. Fellow Am. Acad. Neurology; mem. Am. Neurol. Assn., Am. Soc. Neurochemistry (coun. mem. 1991-97), Internat. Soc. Neurochemistry, Am. Epilepsy Soc., Royal Soc. Medicine. Avocations: tennis, skiing, jazz, theater. Office: West LA Va Med Ctr 127 11301 Wilshire Blvd Los Angeles CA 90073 Home Phone: 818-368-1116; Office Phone: 310-268-3595. Business E-Mail: wasterla@ucla.edu.

WATABE, NORIMITSU, marine biologist, educator; b. Kure, Hiroshima, Japan, Nov. 29, 1922; came to U.S., 1957; s. Isamu and Matsuko (Takamatsu) W.; m. Sakuko Kobayashi, Dec. 12, 1952; children: Shoichi, Sachiko. BS, 1st Nat. High Sch., Tokyo, 1945; MS, Tohoku U., Sendai, Japan, 1948, DSc, 1960. Rsch. investigator Fuji Pearl Co., Mie-ken, Japan, 1948-52; instr. Prefect U. Mie, Tsu, Mie-ken, 1952-55, asst. prof., 1955-59; rsch. assoc. Duke U., Durham, N.C., 1957-70; assoc. prof. U. S.C., Columbia, 1970-72, prof. biology and marine sci., 1972-93, disting. prof., 1993-94, disting. prof. emeritus, 1994—. Cons. Ford Found., 1968; vis. prof. U. Bonn, Germany, 1976-77; dir. Electron Microsciopy Ctr., 19770-95; cons. in field. Author: Studies on Pearls, 1959; editor: Mechanisms of Mineralization, 1976, Mechanisms of Biomineralization, 1980, Hard Tissue Mineralization and Demineralization, 1991; assoc. editor, Jour. Morphology, 1999—; contbr. articles to profl. jours. Recipient Pearl Rsch. award Elmer W. Ellsworth, 1952, Alexander Von Humboldt award Govt. of Germany, Russel award U. SC, 1981; grantee NIH, 1971-76, NSF, 1973-95. Fellow AAAS; mem. Am. Micros. Soc. (life). Avocations: music, piano playing. Office: Dept Biol Sci U South Carolina Columbia SC 29208-0001

WATANABE, AUGUST MASARU, physician, educator, retired pharmaceutical executive; b. Portland, Oreg., Aug. 17, 1941; s. Frank H. and Mary Y. W.; m. Margaret Whildin Reese, Mar. 14, 1964; children: Nan Reiko, Todd Franklin, Scott Masaru. BS, Wheaton Coll., Ill., 1963; MD, Ind. U., 1967. Diplomate Am. Bd. Internal Medicine. Intern Ind. U. Med. Center, Indpls., 1967-68, resident, 1968-69, 71-72, fellow in cardiology, 1972-74; clin. asso. NIH, 1969-71; clin. instr. medicine Georgetown U. Med. Sch., Washington, 1970-71; mem. faculty Ind. U. Sch. Medicine, Indpls., 1972—2003, prof. medicine and pharmacology, 1978—2003, chmn. dept. medicine, 1983-90; dir. Regenstrief Inst. for Health Care Ind. U. Sch. of Medicine, Indpls., 1984-90; from v.p. to group v.p. rsch. labs. Eli Lilly & Co., Indpls., 1990-94, v.p., pres. labs, 1994-95; exec. v.p. sci. and tech. Eli Lilly and Co., Indpls., 1996—2003; chmn. bd. BioCrossroads, 2003—. Mem. pharmacology study sect. NIH, 1979-81, chmn., 1981-83; cardiovasc.-renal adv. com. FDA, 1982-85; mem. com. A, Nat. Heart, Lung and Blood Inst., 1984-88, chmn., 1986-88; bd. dir. QuatRx, Endocyte, Reliant, Kalypsys, Ambrx, Marcadia Biotech; cons. in field. Contbr. articles to profl. jours.; editorial bds. sci. jours. Bd. dir. Ind. U. Found., 1989—, Indpls. Symphony Orch., 1994—, Regenstrief Found., 1995—. NIH grantee, 1972-92. Fellow ACP, Am. Coll. Cardiology, Am. Heart Assn. (councils on clin. cardiology and circulation, research rev. com. Ind. affiliate 1978-82, research and adv. com. North Central region 1978-82, adv. com. cardiovascular drugs 1976-79, chmn. com. 1979-81, chmn. program com. council on basic sci. 1982-84, chmn. com. on sci. sessions programs 1985-88, bd. dirs. 1985-88), Am. Coll. Cardiology (govt. relations com. 1979-81, trustee 1982-87); mem. Am. Fedn. Clin. Research (councilor Midwest sect. 1976-77, chmn.-elect Midwest sect. 1977-78, chmn. sect. 1978-79, chmn. sect. nominating com. 1979-80), Am. Soc. Clin. Investigation, Am. Soc. Clin. Pharmacology and Therapeutics, Am. Soc. Pharmacology and Exptl. Therapeutics (exec. com. div. clin. pharmacology 1978-81), Cardiac Muscle Soc., Central Soc. Clin. Research (councillor 1983-86, pres.-elect 1989, pres. 1990), Internat. Soc. Heart Research, Assn. Am. Physicians, Assn. Profs. of Medicine, Sigma Xi. Office: BioCrossroads Baker and Daniels Bldg 300 N Meridian St Ste 950 Indianapolis IN 46204

WATANABE, CORINNE KAORU AMEMIYA, judge, state official; b. Wahiawa, Hawaii, Aug. 1, 1950; d. Keiji and Setsuko Amemiya; m. Edwin Tsugio Watanabe, Mar. 8, 1975; children: Traciann Keiko, Brad Natsuo, Lance Yoneo. BA, U. Hawaii, 1971; JD, Baylor U., 1974. Bar: Hawaii 1974. Dep. atty. gen. State of Hawaii, Honolulu, 1974-84, 1st dep. atty. gen., 1984-85, 87-92, atty. gen., 1985-87; assoc. judge Hawaii Intermediate Ct. Appeals, Honolulu, 1992—. Mem. ABA, Hawaii Bar Assn. Office: Hawaii Intermediate Ct Appeals 426 Queen St 2d Fl Honolulu HI 96813

WATANABE, KEN, actor; b. Koide, Niigata, Japan, Oct. 21, 1959; m. Kaho Minami, Dec. 2005; 2 children from previous marriage. Actor: (films) Setouchi shonen yakyu dan, 1984, Kekkon annai mystery, 1985, Tampopo, 1985, Umi to dokuyaku, 1986, Bakumatsu jyunjyoden, 1991, Rajio no jikan, 1997, Kizuna, 1998, Supêsutoraberâzu, 2000, Oboreru sakana, 2001, Sennen no nyo-Hikaru Genji monogatari, 2001, Hi wa mata noboru, 2002, T.R.Y., 2003, The Last Samurai, 2003 (Acad. Award nomination for best supporting actor, 2004), Year One in the North, 2005, Batman Begins, 2005, Memoirs of a Geisha, 2005; (TV series) Kimitachi ga ite boku ga iru, 1992, Ikebukuro West Gate Park, 2000, Hojo Tokumune, 2001, Suna no utsuwa, 2004.

WATANABE, MAMORU, internist, researcher; s. Takazo and Nao W.; m. Marie Watanabe, June 1, 1974; 1 child, David. MD, McGill U., 1957, PhD, 1963. Intern Royal Victoria Hosp., Montreal, 1957—58, resident in medicine, 1958—63; prof. medicine U. Alta., Edmonton, 1967—74, U. Calgary, Alta., 1974—97, head internal medicine Alta., 1974—76, assoc. dean edn. Alta., 1976—80, assoc. dean research Alta., 1980—81, acting dean medicine Alta., 1981—82, dean faculty medicine Alta., 1982—92, prof. emeritus Alta., 1997—. Fellow Royal Coll. Physicians and Surgeons (Can.). Home: 162 Pumpridge Place SW Calgary AB Canada T2V 5E6 Office: U Calgary 3330 Hospital Dr NW Calgary AB Canada T2N 1N4 Home Phone: 403-253-5482; Office Phone: 403-220-8725. Business E-Mail: watanabe@ucalgary.ca.

WATANABE, MARK DAVID, pharmacist, educator; b. Santa Monica, Calif., Dec. 7, 1955; s. Jack Shigeru and Rose Nobuko (Iida) W. BA in Chemistry, U. Calif., Irvine, 1977, BS in Biol. Sci., 1978; PharmD, U. Calif., San Francisco, 1982, PhD in Pharm. Chemistry, 1990. Lic. pharmacist Calif., Oreg., Ill., Mass. Pharmacy intern various locations, San Francisco, 1979-82; pharmacist Kaiser Permanent, San Francisco, 1981-87; clin. scis. rsch. fellow in psychiat. pharmacy U. Tex., Austin, 1987-89; clin. asst. prof. pharmacy practice U. Ill., Chgo., 1989-98. Rsch. asst. U. Calif., San Francisco, 1980-87; clin. pharmacy cons. Ill. Dept. Mental Health & Devel. Disabilities, 1994-98; med. sci. mgr. Bristol-Myers Squibb, 1998-99; clin. pharmacy specialist, Alameda Co., Calif., 1999-2003; asst. cli. prof. clin. pharmacy, U. Calif., San Francisco, 1999-2003; asst. clin. specialist Northeastern U., 2003-07, asst. clin. prof., 2007—. Regents scholar U. Calif., San Francisco, 1979-82; recipient Excellence in Teaching award Long Found., San Francisco, 1984. Mem.: Am. Pharm. Assn., Am. Soc. Health-Sys. Pharmacists, Am. Coll. Clin. Pharmacy, Mensa, Phi Lambda Sigma, Rho Chi. Unitarian Universalist. Avocations: individual and fitness sports, reading, travel, music. Office: Northeastern U Sch Pharm 206 Mugar Boston MA 02115 Office Phone: 617-373-8172. Business E-Mail: m.watanabe@neu.edu.

WATCKE, THOMAS C., art educator; b. Bridgeport, Conn., Aug. 12, 1951; AA in Art, Housatonic CC, Bridgeport, 1973; BFA in Sculpture, U. Bridgeport, 1975; MFA in Art, U. Mass., Amherst, 1977. Prof. art Albright Coll., Reading, Pa., 1977—. Office: Albright Coll PO Box 15234 Reading PA 19612

WATED, GUILLERMO, psychology educator; s. Guillermo F. and Eugenie Wated. BS in Bus. Adminstrn., U. Miami, Coral Gables, 1992, MBA, 1994; MS, Fla. Internat. U., Miami, 1999, PhD in Indsl. Orgnl. Psychology, 2002. Instr. Fla. Internat. U., 2002—05; asst. prof. psychology Barry U., 2005—. Cons. Skyversity, Inc., Miami, 2000—04. Contbr. articles to profl. jours. Mem.: APA, Soc. Tchg. Psychology, Soc. Indsl./Orgnl. Psychology. Office: Barry Univ Psychology Dept 11300 NE 2d Ave Miami FL 33161

WATERBURY, JOHN, academic administrator, political science professor, writer; PhD in Pub. Law and Govt., Columbia U., 1968. Asst. prof. polit. sci. U. Mich., 1968; mem. Am. Univs. Field Staff, Cairo, 1971—77; prof. politics and internat. affairs Woodrow Wilson Sch. Pub. and Internat. Affairs, Princeton U., NJ, dir. Ctr. Internat. Studies NJ; pres. Am. U. of Beirut, 1998—. Vis. prof. U. of Aix-Marseilles III, 1977—78; editor World Politics jour. Princeton U., 1992—98. Author: Commander of the Faithful: The Moroccan Political Elite-a Study in Segmented Politics, Vol. 2, 1970, North for the Trade: The Life and Times of a Berber Merchant, 1972, Egypt: Burdens of the past, Options for the Future, 1978, Hydropolitics of the Nile Valley, 1979, Egypt of Nasser and Sadat: The Political Economy of Two Regimes, 1983, Exposed to Innumerable Delusions: Public Enterprise and State Power in Egypt, India, Mexico, and Turkey, 1993, Nile Basin: National Determinants of Collective Action, 2002; co-editor: Patrons and Clients, 1977; co-author: Middle East in the Coming Decade: From Wellhead to Well-Being, 1978; co-editor: The Political Economy of Risk and Choice in Senegal, 1987; co-author: Political Economy of the Middle East: State, Class, and Economic Development, 1990; co-editor: Political Economy of Public Sector Reform and Privatization, 1990, Peasants and Politics in the Modern Middle East, 1991; co-author: Core and Periphery: A Comprehensive Approach to Middle Eastern Water, 1997; contbr. articles to profl. jours. Fellow: Am. Acad. Arts & Scis. Office: Am U of Beirut Office of Pres PO Box 11-0236 Riad El Solh 1107 2020 Lebanon Office Phone: 961 1 350000. Office Fax: 961 1 744474. E-mail: waterbury@aub.edu.lb. *

WATERER, BONNIE CLAUSING, retired secondary school educator; b. Toledo, Sept. 25, 1940; d. Kermit Henry and Helen Ethel (Waggoner) Clausing; m. Louis P. Waterer, June 17, 1961; children: Ryan, Reid. BS in Home Econs. Edn., Ohio State U., 1962; MA in Home Econs. Edn., San Jose State U., 1966. Tchr. James Lick H.S., San Jose, 1963-67, 1973-76; adult edn. instr. Met. Adult Edn. Program, San Jose, 1968-75; home econs. instr. Independence H.S., San Jose, 1976-99, home econs. dept. chair, 1976-80; home econs. coord. East Side Union H.S. Dist., San Jose, 1980-99, coord. coll. and career resource ctrs., 1995-99, ret., 1999—. Child care occupations instr. Ctrl. County Occupl. Ctr., San Jose, 1989-99; child devel. instr. Evergreen Valley Coll., San Jose, 1995. Bd. dirs. NAMI Yavapai County, Ariz., 2001—, West Yavapai Guidance Clinic, 2005—; mem. Family Resource Ctr. adv. coun. Yavapai Regional Med. Ctr., 2004—. Mem.: AAUW (v.p. Prescott br. 2004—06), Home Econs. Tchrs. Assn. Calif. (pres. 1989—91, Outstanding Tchr. award 1987), Calif. Assn. Family and Consumer Sci. (Tchr. of Yr. award 1994), Am. Assn. Family and Consumer Sci., Phi Upsilon Omicron, Delta Kappa Gamma (sec. Prescott br. 2002—06), Omicron Nu. Democrat. Methodist. Avocations: travel, computers, cooking, sewing. Home: 1052 Vantage Pt Cir Prescott AZ 86301 E-mail: bh2oer@aol.com.

WATERHOUSE, KEITH, urologist, educator, retired surgeon; b. Derby, England, May 10, 1929; arrived in U.S., 1953, naturalized, 1964; s. Arthur Reginald and Marion (Tock) Waterhouse; m. Anne Therese Milotzky, Jan. 14, 1955; children: Katherine-Anne, Vincent, Maria-Ursula, Isabelle, Christopher. BA, Cambridge U., Eng., 1950; MD, Oxford U. Med. Sch., Eng., 1953; MA, Cambridge U., Eng., 1957. Cert. urology 1964. Intern Bklyn. Hosp., 1953—54; resident Kings County Hosp., Bklyn., 1957—59; instr. surgery SUNY, Bklyn., 1959—61, asst. prof. urology, 1961—62, assoc. prof. urology, 1962—65, prof. surgery, 1965—84, chmn. dept. urology, 1969—84, prof. emeritus, 1984—. Dir. urology Kings County Hosp., 1962—84; urologist-in-chief Downstate Med. Ctr., Bklyn., 1962—84; chmn. Residency Rev. Com., 1975—76, Registry Genito Urinary Pathology, 1975—76. Contbr.: 86 articles to med. jours., mem. editl. bd.: 6 med. jours. including Jour. Urology, Urology, Nephrology, and Urologic Radiology. Capt. Royal Army Med. Corps, 1955—57, Berlin. Recipient Valentine medal, NY Acad. Medicine, 1992, William Bureau award, NJ Acad. Medicine, 1973. Fellow: Royal Coll. Surgeons, Am. Coll. Pediatrics, Am. Coll. Surgeons; mem.: Clin. Soc. Genito Urinary Surgeons, Australian Urol. Soc. (hon.), Italian Urol. Soc. (hon.), Panamanian Urol. Soc. (hon.), Am. Soc. Genito Urinary Surgeons, Am. Urol. Soc., S.W. Fla. Archaeol. Soc. (pres. 1989—90, dir. 1987—93). Personal E-mail: rkwiuhs@aol.com.

WATERHOUSE, LYNETTE, mathematics educator; m. Robert Waterhouse; 1 child. BA in Sociology, Iona Coll., New Rochelle, NY, 1973; MS in Edn., Lehman Coll., Bronx, NY, 1987, Manhattan Coll., NY, 1991. Teacher NY State, 1984, Special Education Teacher NY State, 1991, Teacher 7-12 Social Studies NY State, 1995. Tchr. N.Y.C. Bd. Edn., 1984—93; math specialist Greenburgh Ctrl. Sch. Dist. 7, Hartsdale, NY, 1994—. Pres. Greenburgh Teachers Fedn., Hartsdale, NY, 2005—. Mem. Ethics Com., Yorktown, NY, 2005; pres., trustee John C. Hart Meml. Libr., Shrub Oak, NY, 2001—06; dir. NY State Theatre Inst., 2005—06. Scholarship, Manhattan Coll., 1989—91. Mem.: ASCD, Nat. Coun. for Social Studies, Nat. Coun. of Teachers of Math (assoc.), Kappa Delta Pi. Office: Greenburgh Ctrl Sch Dist#7 33 West HIllside Ave White Plains NY 10607 Home Phone: 914-948-8107; Office Phone: 914-948-8107. Business E-Mail: lwaterhouse@greenburgh7.com.

WATERHOUSE, RICHARD, museum administrator, artist; b. Chattanooga, July 16, 1958; s. James Franklin Waterhouse and Susan Gelsthorpe Bryan; life ptnr. Caleb Anthony Brown. BA, Centre Coll., Danville, Ky., 1981. Visual arts mgr. Ga. Coun. for the Arts, Atlanta, 1988—2002; exec. dir. Southeastern Museums Conf., Atlanta, 2002—. Ceramics, Faces (Cairo, Egypt Ceramics Biennal, 2000). Office: Southeastern Museums Conference 1860 N Rock Springs Rd Ste 100 Atlanta GA 30324 Home Phone: 404-876-9374; Office Phone: 404-378-3153. Office Fax: 404-370-1612. Business E-Mail: director@semcdirect.net.

WATERMAN, CHRISTOPHER, dean; MusB in Composition and Electric Bass, Berklee Coll. Music; PhD in Anthropology, U. Ill. Assoc. prof. music U. Wash., head ethnomusicology program, chair African studies com.; prof. dept. world arts and cultures UCLA, 1996—, chair dept., 1997—2002, acting dean, 2002—03, dean Sch. Arts and Arch., 2003—. Author: Juju: A Social History and Ethnography of an African Popular Music, 1990; co-author: American Popular Music: From Minstrelsy to MP3, 2006. Recipient Ethel Curry Disting. Lectureship in Musicology, U. Mich. Achievements include cited by Rolling Stone magazine for his innovative course on world popular music, 1992. Office: UCLA Sch Arts and Arch Box 951427 303 E Melnitz Los Angeles CA 90095-1427

WATERMAN, DANIEL, mathematician, educator; b. Bklyn., Oct. 24, 1927; s. Samuel and Anna (Robson) W.; m. Mudite Upesleja, Nov. 4, 1960; children: Erica, Susan, Scott. BA, Bklyn. Coll., 1947; MA, Johns Hopkins U., 1948; PhD, U. Chgo., 1954. Research assoc. Cowles Commn. Research in Econs., Chgo., 1951-52; instr. Purdue U., West Lafayette, Ind., 1953-55, asst. prof., 1955-59, U. Wis.-Milw., 1959-61; prof. Wayne State U., Detroit, 1961-69, Syracuse (N.Y.) U., 1969-96, prof. emeritus, 1996—, chmn. math dept., 1988-94. Cons. Martin-Marietta, Denver, 1960-61; rschr. in real and Fourier analysis, rsch. prof. Fla. Atlantic U., 1997—. Author: Homeomorphisms in Analysis, 1997; editor: Classical Real Analysis, 1985; editl. advisor Sarajevo Jour. Math.; contbr. articles to profl. jours. Fulbright fellow U. Vienna, 1952-53 Mem. Math. Assn. Am., Am. Math. Soc. (coun. mem.-at-large 1975-78), JMAA (assoc. editor 1997—), Sigma Xi. Home: 7739 Majestic Palm Dr Boynton Beach FL 33437-5413 Personal E-mail: dan.waterman@gmail.com.

WATERMAN, MICHAEL SPENCER, mathematics and biology professor; b. Coquille, Oreg., 1942; s. Ray S. and Bessie E. Waterman; m. Vicki Lynn Buss, 1962 (div. 1977); 1 child, Tracey Lynn BS, Oreg. State U., 1964, MS, 1966; MA, Mich. State U., 1968, PhD, 1969. Assoc. prof. Idaho State U., Pocatello, 1969-75; mem. staff Los Alamos Nat. Lab., 1975-82, cons., 1982—; prof. math. and biology U. So. Calif., LA, 1982—, U. So. Calif. Assocs. Endowed Chair, 1991—. Vis. prof. math. U. Hawaii, Honolulu, 1979-80; vis. prof. structural biology U. Calif., San Francisco, 1982; vis. prof. Mt. Sinai Med. Sch., NYC, 1988; 150th anniversary vis. prof. Chalmers U., 2000; Aisenstadt chair U. Montreal, 2001 Author: Introduction to Computational Biology, 1995; editor: Mathematical Methods for DNA Sequences, Calculating the Secrets of Life, 1995, Genetic Mapping and DNA Sequencing, 1996, Mathematical Support for Molecular Biology, 1999; Annals of Combinatories, Methodology and Computing in Applied Probability, Genomics, Computational Methods in Science and Technology, Acta Biochimica et Biophysica Sinca; editor-in-chief: Jour. Computational Biology; contbr. articles to profl. jours. Recipient Internat. award, Gardner Found., 2002; fellow, Guggenheim Found., 1995; grantee, NSF, 1971, 1972, 1975, 1988—, Los Alamos Nat. Lab., 1976, 1981, Sys. Devel. Found., 1982—87, NIH, 1986—99, Sloan Found., 1990—91. Fellow AAAS, Am. Acad. Arts and Scis., Inst. Math. Stats.; mem. NAS, French Acad. Sci., Am. Statis. Assn., Soc. Math. Biology, Soc. Indsl. and Applied Math. Office: U So Calif Dept Biol Sci Los Angeles CA 90089-1340

WATERMAN, MILLICENT ADORA, education educator, minister; b. Guyana, Feb. 1, 1940; arrived in US, 1996; d. Midmund Ashley and Eleanor Zelecca Johnson; 1 child, Adunnola Odilia Waterman French. BA, postgrad. diploma in edn., U. Guyana, 1972, MEd, 1978. Cert. tchr. Guyana, 1963, ordained assoc. minister African Meth. Episc. Ch. Elem. sch. tchr. Ministry Edn., Guyana, 1963—74, secondary sch. tchr., 1974—76, lectr., tchr. edn., 1976—78, sr. lectr., shpt., 1978—85, dep. prin. Tchrs. Coll., 1985—90, prin. Tchrs. Coll., 1991—95, coord. Hinterland tchr. edn. program, 1985—96; coord., dir. writing ctr. Nyack Coll., NYC, 2002—. Vol. Feed the Children, Food for Poor; missionary Morris Arullo World Evangelism. Recipient award, Ministry Guyana, 1998, 2003. Mem.: Nat. Coun. Tchrs. English. Home: 2126 Strauss St # 1 Brooklyn NY 11212 Office: Nyack Coll 361 Broadway 3d Fl New York NY 10013

WATERMAN, ROBERT A., lawyer; b. LA, Jan. 4, 1954; m. Leslie Waterman; 2 children. BA summa cum laude, Calif. State U., Long Beach, 1976; JD, U. Calif., Berkeley, 1979. Bar: Calif. 1979. Mem. McCutchen, Doyle, Brown & Enersen, San Francisco; ptnr. Latham & Watkins, San Francisco, 1993—97; sr. v.p., gen. counsel HCA, Nashville, 1997—. Assoc. editor Calif. Law Rev., 1977-78, note and comment editor, 1978-79. Mem. State Bar Calif. Office: HCA Inc 1 Park Plaza Nashville TN 37203 *

WATERS, ALICE, executive chef, restaurant owner, writer; b. Chatham, NJ, Apr. 28, 1944; 1 child. Grad. in French Cultural Studies, U. Calif., Berkeley, 1967; postgrad., Montessori Sch., London; degree (hon.), Mills Coll., Oakland, Calif., 1994. Exec. chef, owner Chez Panisse, Berkeley, Calif., 1971—, Chez Panisse Cafe, Berkeley, Calif., 1980—, Cafe Fanny, Berkeley, Calif., 1984—. Mem. adv. bd. U. Calif., Berkeley; active The Garden Project, San Francisco; spkr. in field of food safety and health. Author: Chez Panisse Menu Cookbook, Chez Panisse Vegetables, (storybook and cookbook for children) Fanny at Chez Panisse. Developer Martin Luther King Jr. Mid. Sch. Edible Schoolyard, Berkeley. Named Best Chef in Am., James Beard Found., 1992, Best Restaurant in Am., 1992, Humanitarian of Yr., 1997, Mother of Am. Cooking, N.Y. Times; named one of 10 Best Chefs in the World, Cuisine et Vins du France, 1986; recipient Spl. Achievement award, James Beard Found., 1985, Restaurant and Bus. Leadership award, Restaurants and Instns. Mag., 1987, Barbar Boxer Top Ten Women award, 1991, Le Tour du Monde en 80 Toques, Metziner & Varaut, 1991, Nat. Edn. Diplomate award, 1996. Fellow: Am. Acad. Arts & Scis. Office: Chez Panisse 1517 Shattuck Ave Berkeley CA 94709-1598 *

WATERS, BETTY LOU, newspaper reporter, writer; b. Texarkana, Tex., June 13, 1943; d. Chester Hinton and Una Erby (Walls) W. AA, Texarkana Jr. Coll., 1963; BA, East Tex. State U., 1965. Gen. assignment reporter Galveston County Pub. Co., Galveston and Texas City, 1965-68; news and feature writer Ind. and Daily Mail, Anderson, S.C., 1968-69; reporter Citizen-Times newspaper, Asheville, N.C., 1969-74; edn. and med. reporter News Star World Pub. Co., Monroe, La., 1974-79; reporter, writer Delta Democrat Times, Greenville, Miss., 1980-89; staff writer Tyler (Tex.) Morning Telegraph, 1990—. Named Citizen of Yr., Sigma Sigma chpt. Omega Psi Phi, 2001; recipient hon. mentions, Tex. AP, 1966, news media award, N.C. Easter Seal Soc., 1973, 1st place award for articles, La. Press Women's Contest, 1978, 1st place for interview, 1979, for gen. news, Miss. Press Assn., 1983, 3d place award for feature writing, 1984, for investigative reporting, 1988, 1st place for best series of articles, 1990, Sch. Bell award for outstanding series, 1997, award for outstanding edn. series, Tex. State Tchrs. Assn., 1998, Tex. Coll. Women Changing the World award, 2000, Sch. Bell award for outstanding continuous coverage, Tex. State Tchrs. Assn., 2004. Mem. Tex. Tchrs. Assn. (Sch. Bell award 2006).

WATERS, CHRIS HAROLD, literature and language professor, poet; b. Wilmington, NC, Nov. 8, 1926; s. Harold Carlton and Theodora Beatrice (Baring-Gould) Waters; m. Lenore Paley Waters (div.); children: Gwyneth, Jennifer; m. Dora Vera Mancinelli, Aug. 12, 1979; 1 child, Matthew. AB, Harvard Coll., Cambridge, Mass., 1949; MA, U. Wash., Seattle, 1954, PhD, 1956. Instr. Salisbury Sch., Conn., 1951—52; tchg. asst. U. Wash., Seattle, 1952—55; instr. to asst. prof. Coll. William and Mary, Williamsburg, Va., 1955—60; asst. prof. Carlton Coll., Northfield, Minn., 1960—62; prof. U. R.I., Kingston, 1962—91, prof. emeritus, 1991—. Co-founder, head South County French Speaking Union, RI, 1982—; co-founder Paul Claudel Soc. Author: Senegal, Poems on Africa, 1999, Hatteras Symphony, Poems, 2001, Outer Banks Sonata, Poems, 2005. Pfc. US Army, 1945—46. Mem.: R.I. Fgn. Lang. Assn., Am. Assn. Tchrs. French, African Lit. Assn. Avocations: tennis, bicycling, swimming. Home: PO Box 233 Saunderstown RI 02874

WATERS, DONALD JOSEPH, data processing executive; b. Balt., Sept. 16, 1952; s. Richard Hunter and Annette Catharine (Hannan) W.; m. Beverly Ann Brent, Apr. 5, 1974; children: Laura Elizabeth, Sarah Elizabeth. BA, U. Md., 1973; M Phil, Yale U., 1976, PhD, 1982. Resource specialist Yale Computer Ctr., New Haven, 1982-84; dir. computer services Yale Sch. Mgmt., New Haven, 1984-87; head, systems office Yale U. Library, New Haven, 1987-92, dir., libr. and adminstrv. systems, 1992-93, assoc. univ. librarian, 1993-97; dir. Digital Libr. Fedn., Coun. Libr. & Info. Resources, New Haven, 1997-99; program officer Andrew W. Mellon Found., N.Y., 1999—. Author: Strange Ways and Sweet Dreams: Afro-American Folklore From the Hampton Institute, 1983. Fellow AAAS; mem. Am. Soc. Info. Sci. Roman Catholic. Avocations: jazz, rowing, cabinet making. Home: 40 Overbrook Rd Madison CT 06443-1834 Office: 140 E 62nd St New York NY 10021-8124 Home Phone: 203-421-4320; Office Phone: 212-500-2470.

WATERS, JACK, artist, filmmaker; life ptnr. Peter M Cramer, Dec. 14, 1976. BFA, Juilliard, NYC, 1981. Co-dir. ABC No Rio, NYC, 1983—90; co-founder Allied Productions, Inc., NYC, 1980—. Mem. Collaborative Projects, Inc., NYC, 1983—. Dir.: (films) The Male GaYze. Pres. Mix NYC, 2005—07. Personal E-mail: jacwat2000@yahoo.com.

WATERS, JENNIFER NASH, lawyer; b. Bridgeport, Conn., Dec. 21, 1951; d. Lewis William and Patricia (Cousins) W.; m. Todd David Peterson, Sept. 19, 1981; children: Elizabeth, Andrew. BA, Radcliffe, 1972; JD, Harvard, 1976. Bar: D.C. 1977, U.S. Supreme Ct. 1980. Clk. U.S. Ct. Appeals (D.C. cir.), Washington, 1976-77; assoc. Jones, Day, Reavis & Poque, Washington, 1977-79, Crowell & Moring, Washington, 1979-83, ptnr., 1983—. Mem. ABA (ho. of dels. 1997-99), Fed. Energy Bar Assn. (bd. dirs. 1988-99, v.p. 1994-95, pres. 1996-97). Office: Crowell & Moring LLP 1001 Pennsylvania Ave NW Fl 10 Washington DC 20004-2505

WATERS, JOHN B., lawyer; b. Sevierville, Tenn., July 15, 1929; s. J. B. and Myrtle (Paine) W.; m. Patsy Temple, Apr. 8, 1953; children: John B., Cynthia Beth BS, U. Tenn., 1952, JD, 1961; D in Environ. Sci. (hon.), Milligan Coll., 1993. Bar: Tenn. 1961, U.S. Dist. Ct. (ea. dist.) Tenn. 1961, U.S. Supreme Ct. 1969, U.S. Dist. Ct. D.C. 1970. Of counsel Long, Ragsdale & Waters, P.C., Knoxville, Tenn.; mng. ptnr. Waters and Co. Investment Mgmt., 1993—. Mem. hearing com. Bd. Profl. Responsibility Supreme Ct., 1974—80, 1995—2001, Fed. co-chmn. Appalachian Regional Commn., 1968—71; chmn. Sevier County Indsl. Bd., Sevierville Libr. Found.; mem. Gov.'s Com. Econ. Devel.; Tenn. rep. to So. Growth Policies Bd., 1970—74; appointed dir. by Pres. Reagan TVA, Knoxville, 1984, appointed chmn. bd. dirs. by Pres. Bush, 92; bd. dirs. Inst. Nuc. Power Ops., 1985—93; trustee East Tenn. Bapt. Hosp., Knoxville; mem. Tenn.-Tombigbee Waterway Authority, 1993—2000; bd. dirs. East Tenn. Found.; chmn. Leadership Sevier, 1996—2001. Author: Downbound, The Memoirs of John B. Waters, Jr., 2004. Dir. Friends of Great Smoky Mountain Nat. Pk. Lt. USN, 1952—55. Fellow Am. Bar Found.; mem. Tenn. Bar Assn. (pres. 1983-84), Sevier County Bar Assn. (past pres.). Republican. Baptist. Home: Waters Edge 405 Burridge Dr Sevierville TN 37862-3202: 107 Joy St Sevierville TN 37862-3524 Office Phone: 865-453-1051. Business E-Mail: jbwaters@esper.com.

WATERS, JOHN W., minister, educator; b. Atlanta, Feb. 5, 1936; s. Henry and Mary Annie (Randall) W. Cert., U. Geneva, Switzerland, 1962; BA, Fisk U., Nashville, 1957; STB, Boston U., 1967, PhD, 1970; DD, St. Thomas Christian Coll., Jacksonville, Fla., 2006. Ordained to ministry Bapt. Ch., 1967. Min. religious edn. Ebenezer Bapt. Ch., Boston, 1965-67, assoc. min., 1967-69; min. Myrtle Bapt. Ch., West Newton, Mass., 1969, Greater Solid Rock Bapt. Ch., Atlanta, 1980—2005, sr. min. emeritus, 2005—. Prof. Interdenominational Theol. Ctr., Atlanta, 1976-86, trustee, 1980-83, adj. prof., 2005-; bd. dirs. Habitat for Humanities, Atlanta, 1984-90; chmn. South Atlanta Joint Urban Ministries, 1983-93; chairperson Coun. Overseers New Era Bapt. Conv. Ctr., 1996-2001; pres. Clayton County Ministers Conf., 2000 Contbr. articles to profl. jours. Mem. Va. Highlands Neighborhood Assn., Atlanta, 1977-87, Butler St. YMCA, 1980-86, South Atlanta Civic League, 1983, others; treas. Prison Ministries with Women, Inc.; v.p. South Met. Ministries Fellowahip, Atlanta, 1990-94; mem. bd. overseers Sch. Theology, Boston U., 2006—. Fund for Theol. Edn. fellow, 1965-67, Nat. Fellowship Fund fellow, 1968-70, Rockefeller doctoral fellow, 1969. Mem. AAUP (chpt. pres. 1971-72), Am. Acad. Religion, Soc. Bibl. Lit., Blacks in Bibl. Studies, New Era Missionary Bapt. Conf. Ga., So. Bapt. Conv., Am. Legion Home: 1516 Niskey Lake Trl SW Atlanta GA 30331-6318 Address: PO Box 310416 Atlanta GA 30331 Personal E-mail: jwwatersphd@yahoo.com. *In life, each of us faces a variety of choices. The choices made determine our destiny, fate. When more of us assume responsibility and accountability for the choices made, the world in which we live will be decisively better.*

WATERS, LOU, news correspondent; b. Mpls., July 7, 1938; s. Louis Joseph and Anne Marie Riegert; m. Martha Lee Morin, Feb. 15, 1975; children: Scott, Christopher, Alexander. Student, U. Minn. Reporter Sta. KDWB, Mpls., 1959, Sta. WWTC, Mpls., Sta. KFWB, LA, Sta. WLBS-FM, NYC, Sta. KNEW, San Francisco; reporter, anchor Sta. KVOA-TV, Tucson, news dir., Sta. KCST-TV, San Diego; asst. sta. mgr., evening anchor Sta. KOLD-TV, CBS, Tucson; co-anchor CNN Today CNN, Atlanta, 1980—89, co-anchor Earlyprime, 1991—. Avocations: golf, photography, music.

WATERS, MARY A., literature and language professor; d. John Elvin and Myrtle Waters; m. Noel Phipps, May 31, 1994. PhD, U. Calif., Davis, 1994—2001. Faculty fellow U. Calif., 2001—03; vis. prof. Temple U., Phila., 2003—04; asst. prof. Wichita State U., Kans., 2004—. Author: British Women Writers and the Profession of Literary Criticism, 1789-1832, 2004. Grantee Seminar grant, Nat. Endowment for Humanities, 2005; Travel grant, Fulbright Program, 1997—98. Mem.: MLA, North Am. Soc. Study Romanticism, Phi Kappa Phi Honor Soc. Avocation: dance. Office: Wichita State Univ 1845 Fairmount Wichita KS 67260-0014 Business E-Mail: mary.waters@wichita.edu.

WATERS, MARY CATHERINE, sociology educator; b. Bronx, NY, Nov. 18, 1957; d. Michael Francis and Margaret Mary (O'Carroll) W.; m. Ric W. Bayly, Sept. 10, 1993. BA in Philosophy, Johns Hopkins U., 1978; MA in Sociology, U. Calif., Berkeley, 1981, MA in Demography, 1983, PhD in Sociology, 1986. Acting instr. dept. Sociol. U. Calif., Berkeley, 1983—85; asst. prof. dept. Sociol. Harvard U., Cambridge, Mass., 1986—90, John L. Loeb assoc. prof., 1991—93, prof., 1993—, chmn. dept. Sociol., 2001—05; prof. Harvard Coll., 1999—2004, M.E. Zukerman prof. sociology, 2006—. Mem. immigration com. Social Sci. Rsch. Coun., NYC, 1994; bd. dirs. Population Assn. Am., 2005—; cons. US Census Bur., Washington, 1993—95, adv. com. profl. associations, 1999—2005; cons. Bklyn. Children's Mus., 1994—98; cons. radio coverage of immigration WGBH Radio; cons. exhibits on African Am. history, immigration Strong Mus. of History, Rochester, NY, 1994; cons. project on social context of Puerto Rican child health and growth Wellesley Coll. Ctr. Rsch. on Women, 1995—97; internat. adv. bd. Ethnicities; consulting editor Am. Jour. Sociology, 1995—98; editl. bd. mem. Internat. Migration Rev. Author: (books) From Many Strands: Ethnic and Racial Groups in Contemporary America, 1990, Ethnic Options: Choosing Identities in America, 1990, Black Identities: West Indian Immigrant Dreams and American Realities, 1991 (Mira Komorovsky award Ea. Sociol. Soc., Otis Dudley Duncan award, Am. Sociol. Assn., Best Book in Ethnic Incorporation Am. Polit. Sci. Assn., Disting. Book award Cornell U. Ctr. Study Inequality, Thomas and Znaniecki award best book internat. migration Am. Sociol. Assn., 1999); co-editor (with Peggy Levitt): The Change Face of Home: The Transnational Lives of the Second Generation, 2002; co-editor: (with Joel Perlmann) The New Race Question: How the Census Counts Multiracial Individuals, 2002; co-editor: (with Fiona Devine) Social Inequalities in Comparative Perspective, 2003; co-editor: (with Philip Kasinitz and John H. Mollenkopf) Becoming New Yorkers: Ethnographies of the New Second Generation, 2004; contbr. articles to profl. jour., chapters to books. Bd. trustees Russell Sage Found., 2002—07; adv. bd. Ctr Rsch. on Immigration U. Houston; mem. Rsch. Network on Transition to Adulthood MacArthur Found., 2001—. Recipient Gertrude Jaeger prize, U. Calif. Berkeley, 1984, Hoopes award excellence in teaching, 1990, 1996, George R. Kharl award excellence in teaching, 1991, Shannon award, Nat. Inst. Child Health and Human Development, 1995—97; fellow Walter Channing Cabot Faculty, 2003—04; grantee Radcliffe Inst. Advanced Study, 2005—06; vis. scholar Russell Sage Found., 1991—92; Guggenheim fellow, 1993—94. Fellow: Am. Acad. Arts and Sciences; mem.: Regional Sci. Assn., Soc. for Study of Social Problems, Sociol. Rsch. Assn., Am. Philosophical Soc., Population Assn. Am., Ea. Sociol. Soc. (chair Candace Rogers award com. 1994, disting. contribution to scholarship com. 2002), Am. Sociol. Assn. (nom. com. mem. sect. race and ethnic minorities 1992, coun. mem. sect. race and ethnic minorities 1994—96, nom. com. mem. sect. race and ethnic minorities 1995, coun. mem. sect. population 1995—97, nominations com. 1995—97, chair sect. internat. migration, Thomas and Znaniecky Book Award Com. 2000). Democrat. Office: Dept Sociology Harvard Univ 540 William James Hall Cambridge MA 02138-2044 Office Phone: 617-495-3947. Office Fax: 617-496-5794. E-mail: mcw@wjh.harvard.edu.

WATERS, MAXINE, congresswoman; b. St. Louis, Aug. 15, 1938; d. Remus and Velma (Moore) Carr; m. Sidney Williams, July 23, 1977; children: Edward, Karen. Grad. in sociology, Calif. State U., LA; doctorate (hon.), Spelman Coll., NC Agrl.& Tech. State U., Morgan State U. Former tchr. Head Start. Mem. Calif. Assembly from dist. 48, 1976-91, Dem. caucus chair, 1984; mem. U.S. Congress from 35th Calif. dist., 1991—; mem. Banking, Fin., Judiciary, Urban Affairs com., Ho. subcom. on banking, capitol subcom. on banking, employment and tng. subcom. on vets., veterans affairs com., banking and fin. svcs. com., ranking house subcom. on gen. oversight and investigations; chair Congl. Black Caucus. Mem. Dem. Nat. Com., Dem. Congrl. Campaign com.; del. Dem. Nat. Conv., 1972, 76, 80, 84, 88, 92, mem. rules com. 1984; mem. Nat. Adv. Com. for Women, 1978—; bd. dirs. TransAfrica Found., Nat. Women's Polit. Caucus, Ctr. Nat. Policy, Clara Elizabeth Jackson Carter Found. Spellman Coll., Nat. Minority AIDS Project, Women for a Meaningful Summit, Nat. Coun. Negro Women, Black Women's Agenda; founder Black Women's Forum; dep. City Councilman David Cunningham, 1973-76, chief dep. Minority Whip; mem. Congl. Children's Working Group, Congl. Progressive Caucus, Dem. Nat. Com.; chair Dem. Caucus Spl. Com. election Reform; vice chair Steering Com. Mem. Calif. Peer Counseling Assn., Nat. Com. Econ. Conversion and Disarmament; mem. bd. Ctr. Study Sport in Soc., L.A. Women's Found. Named one of 100 Most Influential Black Americans, Ebony mag., 2006. Democrat. Office: US Ho Reps 2344 Rayburn Ho Office Bldg Washington DC 20515-0535 also: 10124 S Broadway Ste 1 Los Angeles CA 90003 Office Phone: 202-225-2201, 323-757-8900. Office Fax: 202-225-7854, 323-757-9506. *

WATERS, RICHARD, retired publishing executive; b. Sterling, Mass., May 13, 1926; s. Sherman Hoar and Viola (Arnold) W.; m. June Hollweg Dorer, Aug. 27, 1949; children: Karl (dec.), Kurt, Kris. BA, Hobart Coll., 1950, LLD hon., 1970; MBA, Harvard U., 1951. Assoc. acct. Hunter & Weldon, NYC, 1953-55; exec. v.p., CFO Reader's Digest Assn., Pleasantville, NY, 1955-77; assoc. dean Harvard U. Bus. Sch., Boston, 1977-81; pres., CEO Sporting News, St. Louis, 1981-90, ret., 1990. Bd. dirs. Republic Nat. Bank, N.Y.C., Spectrum Pet Care, Inc. Trustee Hobart Coll., 1971-91, William Smith Coll., 1971-91; regional v.p. Associated Industries N.Y. State, Albany, 1965-79; chmn. bd. Westchester Heart Assn., Port Chester, N.Y., 1975-76; bd. dirs., vice-chmn. Gateway chpt. Nat. Multiple Sclerosis Soc., 1991-95, chmn., 1996-98, chair emeritus 1999—; mem. St. Louis Sports Commn., 1985—; hon. trustee Hobart and William Smith Colls., 1992—; bd. dirs. Buddy Fund, St. Louis, 2001—. With USN, 1944-46, PTO; 1st lt. USAF, 1951-53. Mem. Baseball Writers Assn. Am. Clubs: Old Warson Country, St. Louis Club. Republican. Home: 20 Somerset Downs Saint Louis MO 63124-1007 E-mail: somersetdw@aol.com.

WATERS, ROBYN, writer, marketing consultant; V.p. trend, design, and product devel. Target; founder, cons. RW Trend LLC, 2002—. Juror BusinessWeek IDEA Design Awards, Nat. Design Awards, Cooper-Hewitt Mus., Internat. Housewares Assn.; spkr. in field. Author: The Trendmaster's Guide: Get a Jump on What Your Customer Wants Next, 2005, The Hummer and the Mini: Navigating the Contradictions of the New Trend Landscape, 2006. Named one of Top Twenty Creative Mavericks, Fast Company mag., 2004. Office: c/o BrightSight Group 268 Wall St Princeton NJ 08540 *

WATERS, RONALD V., III, candy company executive; m. Ann Waters. BA in History & Economics, Trinity Coll.; M in Acctg., NYU. Ptnr. KPMG Peat Marwick; v.p. fin. & adminstrn. Gillette Co., 1993—99, v.p., controller, 1999, v.p. fin. & strategic planning, Grooming & Batteries, 1998—99; sr. v.p., CFO William Wrigley Jr., Inc., Chgo., 1999—2003, COO, 2004—. Bd. dir. The Joffrey Ballet, 2003—, treas., chmn. fin. com., co-chmn., 2004; bd. dir. HNI Corp., 2002—, Greater N. Mich. Ave. Assn., Goodman Theatre, Latin School of Chgo. Office: William Wrigley Jr Co 410 N Michigan Ave Chicago IL 60611

WATERS, RONALD W., theology studies educator, church administrator, pastor; b. Kokomo, Ind., July 23, 1951; s. Ronald Lee and Carolyn Elizabeth (Myers) W.; m. Norma Lee Grumbling Waters, June 16, 1973; 1 child, Melinda Ronee Waters. BA magna cum laude, Ashland U., Ohio, 1973; MA in Comms. with high honors, Wheaton Coll., Ill., 1975; MDiv with high honors, Ashland Theol. Sem., Ohio, 1985; postgrad., Asbury Theol. Seminary, 1993—2002. Ordained elder Brethren Ch., 1986; lic. minister, 1985-86. Asst. to dir. Bd. of Christian Edn. The Brethren Ch., Ashland, Ohio, 1971-74; mng. editor of publs. Brethren Pub. Co., Ashland, Ohio, 1975-78, asst. to dir. and gen. mgr., 1978-80, exec. dir., 1980-82; dir. of Denom. Bus. The Brethren Ch. Nat. Office, Ashland, Ohio, 1982-84; cons. in mgmt. and computer applications, 1984-85; pastor Mt. Olive Brethren Ch., McGaheysville, Va., 1985-89; dir. Brethren Ch. Ministries The Brethren Ch. Nat. Office, Ashland, Ohio, 1989-95; asst. prof. evangelism Ashland Theol. Sem., 1996-2001; cons. for evangelism and ch. growth The Brethren Ch. Nat. Office, Ashland, 1996—2001; pastor Hammond Ave. Brethren Ch., Waterloo, Iowa, 2002—. Bd. dirs. corp. sec. Brethren Printing Co., Ashland, 1989-96; mem. mission bd. Brethren Ch. Southeastern Dist., 1987-89; mem., sec. exec. bd. Ctrl. Dist., The Brethren Ch., 2002—; mem. statement of faith task force Gen. Conf. Brethern Ch., 1981-84, polity com. 1986-91, 2004—; bd. ref. congl. adv. The Andrew Ctr., Elgin, Ill., 1994-97; founder, tchr. Young Adult Sunday Sch. class Park St Brethren Ch., Ashland, 1990-93; adv. com. Ashland Theol. Sem., 1990-95; mem. evangelism mgmt. team New Life Ministries, Mt. Joy, Pa., 1992-2001; adj. prof. Bethany Theological Seminary, 2002—; spkr. in field. Author: Promise for the Future, 1993, Leader's Manual for Inviting and Welcoming New People, 1995; editor: The Brethren Evangelist mag., 1975-78, New Beginnings mag., 1995-97; contbg. editor LIFE process, 1998-99; contbr. numerous articles to religious jours.; webmaster, www.newlifeministries-nlm.org, 2000—. Mem. adv. coun. World Relief Corp., Wheaton, Ill., 1990-92; dir. vol. ministries Park St. Brethren Ch., 1998-99; sec.-treas. Ohio dist. Mission Bd., 1996-2001. Mem. Am. Soc. Ch. Growth, Nat. Assn. Brethern Ch. Elders, Black Hawk Assn. Evangelicals (pres. 2005-07). Mem. Brethren Ch. Office: Hammond Ave Brethren Ch 1604 Hammond Ave Waterloo IA 50702

WATERS, ROSEMARY R., biology professor; d. Leon H. and Margaret M. Rockwell; m. Jerry Waters, July 3, 1964; children: Craig R., David W. BA in Zoology magna cum laude, Calif. State U., Fresno, 1966, MA in Microbiology with distinction, 1972. Cert. ALS instr. Am. Heart Assn., 1975; dental asst. ADAA, 1962, registered Calif., 1972, cert. CC instr. Calif., 1972. Asst. quality control dir. Burton Parsons Pharmaceuticals, Seat Pleasant, Md., 1966—69; HS biology tchr. Queen of the Valley Acad., Fresno, 1969—72; dental assisting coord. Reedley Coll., Calif., 1972—94; biology prof. Fresno City Coll., 1994—. Infection control cons., Fresno, 1989—94. Author: (manual) Microbiology-A Manual of Laboratory Experiments. Mem. Chancellors Cir. State Ctr. C.C. Dist., Fresno, 2003—06; marriage ministry facilitator St. Paul Parish Newman Ctr., Fresno, 1984—96. Mem.: Calif. State U. Fresno Alumni (life), Cath. Bus. and Profl. Breakfast Club, Kappa Alpha Theta (Gamma Chi facility corp. sec. 1998—2006), Phi Kappa Phi (life). Avocations: marriage ministry, travel. Home: 1754 West Dovewood Ln Fresno CA 93711 Office: Fresno City Coll 1101 East University Ave Fresno CA 93741 Home Phone: 559-438-8663; Office Phone: 559-442-4600. Personal E-mail: rwatersfcc@comcast.net. Business E-Mail: rosemary.waters@fresnocitycollege.edu.

WATERS, SYLVIA, dance company artistic director; BS in Dance, Juilliard Sch.; studied with, Antony Tudor and Martha Graham; PhD (hon.), SUNY, Oswego, 1997. Prin. dance Alvin Ailey Am. Dance Theater, NYC, 1968—74; artistic dir. Alvin Ailey Repertory Ensemble, NYC, 1974—. Panelist Nat. Endowment for the Arts, N.Y. State Council on the Arts. Office: Ailey II Joan Weill Ctr for Dance 405 W 55th St New York NY 10019 *

WATERS, WILLIAM CARTER, III, retired internist, educator; b. Atlanta, Dec. 12, 1929; s. William Carter and Nannie Ellen (Starr) W.; m. Sarah Ann Bankston; children: William Carter IV, Sarah Walker Waters McEntire. AB, Emory U., 1950, MD, 1958. Diplomate Am. Bd. Internal Medicine (internal medicine and nephrology). Resident in internal medicine Grady Meml. Hosp./Emory U., Atlanta, 1958-60, 61-62; fellow in nephrology New Eng. Med. Ctr., 1960-61; practice medicine specializing in internal medicine and nephrology, Atlanta, 1962—2002; from instr. to assoc. prof. Emory U. Sch. Medicine, 1962-70, clin. assoc. prof., 1970-85, clin. prof., 1985—. Chief staff internal medicine Piedmont Hosp., Atlanta, chmn. bd., 1991-94; 1st chmn. bd. Promina Health Sys., Atlanta, 1994-96; med. dir. internal. medicine divsn. Multiple Sclerosis Clinic, Atlanta, 2005—. Contbr. articles to med. jours. Chmn. Piedmont Hosp. Found., 2002—05, chmn. bd. visitors, 2004—. With USAF, 1951—52. Fellow ACP (master: gov. for Ga.); mem. AMA, Med. Assn. Ga., Med. Assn. Met. Atlanta, Am. Soc. Nephrology, S.E. Clin. Club, Atlanta Country Club, Piedmont Driving Club, Big Canoe Club. Methodist. Personal E-mail: drwaters@mindspring.com.

WATERS, ZENOBIA PETTUS, retired finance educator; b. Little Rock, Mar. 4, 1927; d. Henry Augustus and Lillie Liddell (Edwards) Pettus; m. Willie Waters, Jr., Jan. 29, 1949 (div. Feb. 1955); children: Pamela E. Reed, Zenobia W. Carter. BA cum laude, Philander Smith Coll., Little Rock, 1964; MEd, U. Wash., 1968. Cert. tchr. Ark., 1966. Office mgr. United Friends of Am., Little Rock, 1946—52; sec. State Dept. Edn., Little Rock, 1958—64; lectr. bus. Philander Smith Coll., Little Rock, 1965—67, asst. prof. bus., 1968—88, assoc. prof. bus. adminstrn., 1988—92, bd. dirs., faculty rep., 1976—80; asst. prof. bus. Ark. Bapt. Coll., Little Rock, 1970—84. Asst. bus. mgr. Philander Smith Coll., Little Rock, 1970—74, dir. summer sessions, 1970—81; spkr. in field. Mem. adv. bd.: Two Centuries of Methodism in Arkansas, 2000; contbr. articles to profl. jours. Dean West Gulf Regional Sch., 1975—77; founder Nat. Campaign Tolerance, Mont, Ala., 2005; vol. Dem. Party, Little Rock, 1986—92; contact person U.S. Presdl. Campaign, Little Rock, 1992; cert. lay spkr. United Meth. Ch., 1979—; pres. so. ctrl. juris United Meth. Women, 1984—88; bd. dirs. Gen. Bd. of Global Ministries, NYC, 1984—88, Aldersgate Camp, Little Rock, 1976—79, St. Paul Sch. Theology, Kansas City, Mo., 1984—88, Mount Sequoyah, Fayetteville, Ark., 1984—88. Named Legend, Union Am. Meth. Ch., 2005; recipient Edn. Found. award, AAUW, 1983, Svc. award, Gen. Bd. Global Ministries/Women's Divsn., 1988; fellow, Nissan, 1989; grantee Ford Found. grantee, 1967. Mem.: AAUW, Nat. Campaign for Tolerance (founding mem.), Nat. Trust for Historic Preservation, United Meth. Women (pres. recognition pins 1963—2004, recognition pins 1963—2005), Phi Delta Phi, Iota Phi Lambda. Mem. Ame Ch. Avocations: reading, walking, writing. Home: 1701 Westpark Dr Apt 219 Little Rock AR 72204

WATERSTON, ROBERT HUGH, medical educator, researcher, medical geneticist, department chairman; b. Detroit, Sept. 17, 1943; BSE, Princeton U., NJ, 1965; PhD, MD, U.Chgo., 1972. Postdoctoral fellow divsn. cell biology MRC Lab Molecular Biology, Cambridge, England, 1972—74; intern in pediatric medicine Children's Hosp. Med. Ctr., Boston, 1974—75; postdoctoral fellow divsn. cell biology MRC Lab Molecular Biology, Cambridge, England, 1975—76; asst. prof. dept. anatomy and neurobiology Washington U., St. Louis, 1976—89; asst. prof. genetics Washington U. Sch. Medicine, St. Louis, 1980—81, assoc. prof. genetics, 1981—87, prof. genetics, 1987—91, prof. and acting head dept. genetics, 1991—93, James S. McDonnell prof. and chmn. dept. genetics, 1993—2003, head, dept. genetics Seattle, dir., Genome Sequencing Ctr., chmn. dept. genome sci., 2002—, William B. Gates III endowed chair biomed. scis., 2003—. Founder Genome Sequencing Ctr., St. Louis; ad hoc mem. Molecular Cytology Study Sect., 1977, 83; regular mem. Molecular Cytology Study Sect., NIH, 1987—88, chmn., 1989—91; mem. NIH, 1985—86, mem. adv. coun., chmn. Molecular Cytology Study Sect., mem. nat. adv. coun. for human genome rsch., 1998—2002; mem. fellowship rev. subcom. Molecular Dystrophy Assn., 1982—87, mem task force on genetics, 1983; mem. organizing com. Fourth Internat. C. elegans Meeting, Cold Spring Habor, NY, 1985. Contbr. over 80 articles to profl. jours.; mem. editl. bd. Jour. Cell Biology, 1988—91. Named NIH predoctoral trainee, 1968—71, Am. Heart Assn. Established Investigator, 1980—85; recipient Beadle award, Gen. Soc. Am., Dan David Prize, Peter H. Raven Lifetime award, 2000, Internat. Gairdner award, 2002, Alfred P. Sloan, Jr. prize, GM Cancer Rsch. Found., 2003, Genetics prize, Peter Gruber Found., 2005; fellow Am. Cancer Soc. (postdoctoral), 1972—74, Muscular Dystrophy Assn. (postdoctoral), 1975—76, John Simon Guggenheim, 1985—86; grantee, NIH, 1997—99, 1998—2001, Merck & Co., 1994—99. Fellow: Am. Acad. Arts & Sciences; mem.: NAS (coun. mem. Inst. Medicine 2006—), Am. Soc. Cell Biology: STS, Genetics Soc., Alpha Omega Alpha, Sigma Xi. *

WATERSTON, SAMUEL ATKINSON, actor; b. Cambridge, Mass., Nov. 15, 1940; s. George Chychele and Alice Tucker (Atkinson) W.; m. Lynn Louisa Woodruff, Jan. 26, 1976; children: Graham C., Elisabeth P., Katherine B.; child by previous marriage: James S. BA, Yale U., 1962; student, Sorbonne, Paris, 1960-61. Actor: (theatre) Indians, Oh Dad Poor Dad, Halfway Up the Tree, Lunch Hour, Hamlet, The Tempest, Measure for Measure, Much Ado About Nothing (Obie, Drama Desk awards), Benefactors, 1986, A Walk in the Woods, 1988, Abe Lincoln in Illinois, 1993-94 (Drama League award 1994), Shakespeare & Szekspir, 1994; (film) The Great Gatsby, 1975, Rancho Deluxe, 1976, Capricorn One, 1978, Interiors, 1978, Sweet William, 1978, Heaven's Gate, 1979, Eagle's Wing, 1983, The Killing Fields, 1984 (Acad. nomination best leading actor), Warning Sign, 1985, Savages, Hopscotch, 1980, Hannah and Her Sisters, 1986, Just Between Friends, 1986, The Devil's Paradise, September, 1987, Welcome Home, 1989, Crimes and Misdemeanors, 1990, Captive in the Land, 1990, Crimes and Misdemeanors, The Man in the Moon, 1991, Mindwalk, 1991, Serial Mom, 1994, Nixon, 1995, The Proprietor, 1996, Shadow Conspiracy, 1997, Le Divorce, 2003; (TV films) Much Ado About Nothing, 1974, The Glass Menagerie, 1975, Diabolique, 1975, Friendly Fire, 1978, Oppenheimer, 1982, Exiled, 1998, A House Divided, 2000, The Matthew Shepard Story, 2002; (TV series) Q.E.D., 1982, Terrorist on Trial: The United States vs. Salim Ajami; (TV miniseries) Oppenheimer, 1980, 82, Gore Vidal's Lincoln, 1988, Nightmare Years, 1989, Lost Civilizations, 1995 (Emmy award for best documentary 1996), Ken Burns' The Civil War, 1990, Thomas Jefferson, 1997; TV series Q.E.D., 1979, I'll Fly Away, 1991-93 (Emmy award nomination, Lead actor, Drama, 1993), I'll Fly Away: Then and Now, 1993 (Emmy nomination, Lead Actor - Special, 1994), Law and Order. 1994— (Screen Actors Guild award 1999), Miracle at Midnight, 1998. Law and Order: Special Victims Unit, 1999, (documentary) Unfinished Journey, 1999. Mem. Actors Equity Assn., Screen Actors Guild, AFTRA Address: care Addis/Wechsler & Assocs 955 Carrillo Dr Fl 3 Los Angeles CA 90048-5400

WATFORD, DOLORES, elementary school educator; b. Feb. 26, 1951; BS in Edn., U. Hartford, 1973; MA in Psychol. Remedial Reading, Tchrs. Coll. Columbia U., 1974; MS in Spl. Edn., LI U., 1990, MS in Edn., 1993, profl. diploma in Sch. Adminstrn., 1997. Tchr. asst. Dalton Sch., Manhattan, NY, 1974—76; tchr. Pub. Sch., Conn., 1976—77; elem. tchr. Pub. Sch. 169, Bklyn., 1981—85; reading tchr. Pub. Sch. 167, Bklyn., 1985—2005; tchr. Pub. Sch. 191, Bklyn., 1985—99, Pub. Sch. 255, Bklyn., 1999—. Sec. Sch. Leadership Team, Bklyn., 2004—05. Pres. Bklyn. Reading Council, 2002. Recipient Svc. award, Bklyn. Reading Coun., 2004. Mem.: Internat. Reading Assn., NY State Reading Assn. (v.p. 2005—, pres. 2007—). Avocations: singing, aerobics, volleyball, reading. Home: One Rundle Ct Hempstead NY 11550 Personal E-mail: doloresbrc2002@msn.com.

WATJEN, THOMAS ROS, insurance company executive; With investment and corp. fin. depts. Aetna Life and Casualty, 1981-84; ptnr. Conning and Co., ins. cons. firm, 1984-87; mng. dir. responsible for ins. practice group Morgan Stanley & Co., 1987-94; exec. v.p., CFO Provident Cos., Inc., Chattanooga, 1994—97, vice chmn., dir., 1997—99; exec. v.p., fin. UnumProvident Corp., Chattanooga, 1999—2002; vice chmn., COO UnumProvident Corp. (now Unum Group), Chattanooga, 2002—03; pres., CEO Unum Group, Chattanooga, 2003—. Office: Unum Group One Fountain Sq Chattanooga TN 37402 E-mail: twatjen@unumprovident.com. *

WATKINS, ANN ESTHER, mathematics professor; b. LA, Jan. 10, 1949; d. Rex Devere and Burnice Gordine (Duckworth) Hamilton; m. William Earl Watkins, Oct. 5, 1973; children: Mary Ann, Barbara Lee. BA, Calif. State U., Northridge, 1970, MS, 1972; PhD, UCLA, 1977. Instr. math. Los Angeles Pierce Coll., Woodland Hills, Calif., 1975-90; prof. math. Calif. State U., Northridge, 1990—. Editor: (with Albers, Rodi) New Directions in Two Year College Mathematics, 1985; co-author: (with Landwehr) Exploring Data, 1986, 2d edit., 1994, (with Landwehr, Swift) Exploring Surveys, 1987, (with Albers, Loftsgaarden, Rung) Statistical Abstract of Undergraduate Programs in the Mathematical Sciences and Computer Science, 1992, (with Scheaffer, Gnanadesikan, Witmer) Activity-Based Statistics, 1996, 2d edit., 2004, (with Scheaffer, Cobb) Statistics in Action, 2d edit., 2007; assoc. editor: American Mathematical Monthly, 1996-00; editor Coll. Math. Jour., 1989-94; co-editor: (with Apostol, Mugler, Scott and Sterrett) A Century of Calculus, Part II, 1992; mem. editl. bd. Jour. Statis. Edn., 1992-95; mem. adv. bd. Math. Horizons mag., 1992-01. Grantee NSF, 1987-90, 92—. Fellow Am. Statis. Assn.; mem. Math. Assn. Am. (2d v.p. 1987-88, pres. 2001-03, chair So. Calif. sect. 1988-89, gov. So. Calif. sect. 1995-98), Nat. Coun. Tchrs. Math. Home Phone: 818-347-1509. Business E-Mail: ann.watkins@csun.edu.

WATKINS, BIRGE SWIFT, real estate investment executive; b. Grand Rapids, Mich., May 2, 1949; s. Robert Goodell and Betty Jane (Swift) W.; m. Elizabeth Beverly Price, Nov. 28, 1985; children: Elizabeth Porter, Benjamin Thorne Swift, Robert William MacIntosh. BA, Alma Coll., 1971; MBA, London Bus. Sch., 1981; MPA, Harvard U., 1989. Staff asst. to Pres. of U.S., Washington, 1974-77; congl. press sec. U.S. Ho. of Reps., Washington, 1977; v.p. Arbor Internat. Inc., McLean, Va., 1980-81; asst. office dir. AID, Washington, 1982-88; asst. dir. Pres.'s Task Force on Internal Pvt. Enterprise, Washington, 1983-85; dep. asst. sec. USDA, Washington, 1989-90; dir. investor outreach Resolution Trust Corp., Washington, 1991-94; ptnr. Benton Resources, Washington, 1994-95; mng. dir. Thornfalcon Internat., 1996-99; sr. v.p. Lifecare Mgmt. Ptnrs., 1999—2002, Friedman, Billings, Ramsey Group, Inc., 2002—03; v.p. Landmark Atlantic Holdings, LLC, 2003—. Cons. Washington Campus Inc., 1977, Va. Med. Assocs. Inc., Springfield, 1988, U.S. C. of C. Mem. campaign staff Reagan-Bush campaign, Washington, 1980, Bush for President, 1988; mem. transition team office of Pres.-elect Bush, 1988; chmn. bd. trustees Partnership Warrenton Found.; bd. dirs., founder John Singleton Mosby Found. and Mus., Land Trust of Va.; coun. mem. Town of Warrenten, Va., 2002--. Avocations: skiing, running, contemporary art. Home: 832 Blackwell Rd Warrenton VA 20186-2216 Office: Arlington VA Office Phone: 703-998-5200.

WATKINS, BRENDA L., music educator; b. Norfolk, Va., Apr. 18, 1946; d. Rosser Lee and Constance Norsworthy Jones; m. Claude William Watkins, Nov. 1, 1964; 1 child, Kimberly Lynn, Cynthia Anne, Katherine

Lee. Student, William & Mary Coll., 1964, Old Dominion U., 1964-68. Adminstrv. asst. Va. Nat. Bank, Norfolk, 1964-71; pre-sch. tchr. asst. Westwood Hill Bapt. Ch., Virginia Beach, 1972-74; pre-sch. music tchr. Bellamy Manor and Broad Bay Manor, Virginia Beach, 1993-96; music tchr. Court House Pre-Sch., Virginia Beach, 1994-97, Great Neck Pre-Sch., Virginia Beach, 1994-97; ind. music tchr. Music and Arts Music, Chesapeake, Va., 1998—. Author, editor: Childhood Memories, 1994. Vol. info. desk Assn. for Rsch. and Enlightment, Virginia Beach, 1999. Mem. Music Tchrs. Nat. assn., Tidewater Music Tchrs. Assn., Order of Ea. Star (Kempsville chpt.), Ladies Oriental Shrine N.Am. (Zulekia Ct. #35), U.S. Amateur Ballroom Dancers Assn., Inc., Va. Dept. Game and Inland Fisheries (cert. boat safety). Lutheran. Avocations: writing, music, boating, walking. Home: 612 Cardamon Ct Virginia Beach VA 23464-1901

WATKINS, CAROLE S., human resources specialist, medical products executive; b. 1960; BA in Bus., Franklin U., Columbus, Ohio. With O.M. Scott & Sons, Lazarus, Huntington Banks; mem. staff Ltd. Brands, Columbus, Ohio, 1989—96; v.p. human resources Pharm. Distbn. Cardinal Health, Inc., Columbus, Ohio, 1996—2000, sr. v.p. pharm. distbn. and provider svcs., 2000, exec. v.p. human resources, 2000, chief human resources officer. Office: Cardinal Health 7000 Cardinal Pl Dublin OH 43017

WATKINS, CHARLES BOOKER, JR., mechanical engineering educator; b. Petersburg, Va., Nov. 20, 1942; s. Charles Booker and Haseltine Lucy (Thurston) W. BS in Mech. Engring. cum laude, Howard U., 1964; MS, U. N.Mex., 1966, PhD, 1970. Registered profl. engr., D.C. Mem. tech. staff Sandia Nat. Labs., Albuquerque, 1964-71; asst. prof. dept. mech. engring. Howard U., Washington, 1971-73, prof., chmn. dept. mech. engring., 1973-86; prof. mech. engring. CCNY, 1986—, dean Sch. Engring., 1986—99; dir. CREST Ctr., 2002—. Cons. U.S. Army, U.S. Navy, NSF, pvt. industries, 1984-85. Rsch. grantee NSF, USN, Nuclear Regulatory Commn., Dept. Energy, NASA; Sandia Labs. doctoral fellow; NDEA fellow. Fellow ASME, AIAA (assoc.); mem. AAAS, Soc. Automotive Engrs. (Ralph R. Teetor award 1980), Am. Soc. Engring. Edn., Am. Soc. Safety Engrs., Sigma Xi, Omega Psi Phi, Tau Beta Pi. Home: 130 Buckingham Dr Hackensack NJ 07601 Office: CCNY Sch Engring Convent Ave New York NY 10031

WATKINS, CRAIG, prosecutor; b. Dallas, Nov. 16, 1967; m. Tanya Watkins; children: Taryn Michelle, Cale Marcus, Chad Marcus. BA, Prairie View A&M U., 1990; JD, Texas Wesleyan U., 1994. Dist. atty. intern. Tarrant County Dist. Atty., Tex.; prosecutor City Atty. Office, Dallas; atty. Dallas County Pub. Defender's Office; founder, prin. Craig Watkins Atty. at Law, Dallas, 1997—2007; dist. atty. Dallas, 2007—. Instr. El Centro Jr. Coll., Univ. Tex., Arlington. Democrat. Office: Dallas Districy Atty Frank Crowley Courts Bldg LB19 133 N Industrial Blvd Dallas TX 75207-4399 Office Phone: 214-653-3600. Office Fax: 214-653-5774.

WATKINS, CURTIS WINTHROP, artist; b. Pontiac, Mich., Apr. 9, 1946; s. Robert James and Arvella Marquitta (Chenoweth) W.; m. Gayle Lynn Blom, Dec. 19, 1975; 1 dau., Darcy Ann. Student, Ann Arbor Art Ctr., 1964-66, Kendall Sch. Design, 1966-68, Kraus Hypnosis Ctr., 1966-70, Arons Ethical Hypnosis Tng. Ctr., 1977. Illustrator, instr. Ann Arbor Art Ctr., 1969-71; owner, dir. Hypno-Art Rsch. Ctr. and Studio, Howell, Mich., 1971—. Research on visualization process of subconscious by doing art work under hypnosis; lectr. hypnosis convs. and schs. One-man shows include LeVern's Gallery, 1969, Rackham Gallery, 1973, Hartland Gallery, 1974, Platt Gallery, 1975, Detroit Artists Guild Gallery, 1975, Golden Gallery, 1977, Cromaine Gallery, 1982, Driggett Gallery, 1982, Mill Gallery, 1983, Walnut Street Gallerya, 1983, Merrill Gallery, 1986, Corbino Gallery, 1986, VanAntwerp, 1991; group shows include Mich. All-State Show, 1980, Mich. State Fine Arts Exhibit, 1980, Washington Internat., 1981, Lansing (Mich.) Art Gallery, 1981, Capitol City Arts Show, 1981, Mich. Ann., 1981, Mich. Ann., 1982-83; illustrator: Handbook of Hypnotic Techniques, 1988. Bd. dirs. 9th Ann. Hartland Art Show, 1975, Livingston Arts and Crafts Assn., 1977-79, Hartland Art Coun., 1974-78. Recipient Dr. Garland H. Fross award, 1989, numerous awards of excellence in art. Mem. Internat. Soc. Artists, Assn. Advance Ethical Hypnosis, Am. Assn. Profl. Hypnologists, Internat. Soc. Profl. Hypnosis, Internat. Platform Assn. Presbyterian. Home: 1749 Pinckney Rd Howell MI 48843-7874 Office Phone: 517-546-6648.

WATKINS, DEAN ALLEN, electronics executive, educator; b. Omaha, Oct. 23, 1922; s. Ernest E. and Pauline (Simpson) W.; m. Bessie Ena Hansen, June 28, 1944; children— Clark Lynn, Alan Scott, Eric Ross. BS, Iowa State Coll., 1944; MS, Calif. Inst. Tech., 1947; PhD, Stanford, 1951. Engr. Collins Radio Co., 1947-48; mem. staff Los Alamos Lab., 1948-49; tech. staff Hughes Research Labs., 1951-53; asso. prof. elec. engring. Stanford, 1953-56; prof., dir. Electron Devices Lab., 1956-64, lectr. elec. engring., 1964-70; co-founder, pres., chief exec. officer, dir. Watkins Johnson Co., Palo Alto, Calif., 1957-67, chmn., chief exec. officer, dir., 1967-80, chmn., dir., 1980-2000. Cons. Dept. Def., 1956-66; mem. White House Sci. Coun., 1988-89. Patentee in field; contbr. articles to profl. jours. Legis. chmn., dir. San Meteo County Sch. Bds. Assn., 1959-69; gov. San Francisco Bay Area Coun., 1966-75; Rep. precinct capt. Portola Valley, 1964; vice chmn. San Mateo County Fin. Com., 1967-69; mem. Calif. Rep. Ctrl. Com., 1964-68; trustee Stanford, 1966-69; regent U. Calif., 1969-96, chmn., 1972-74; mem. governing bd. Sequoia Union H.S. Dist., 1964-68, chmn., 1967-68; mem. governing bd. Portola Valley Sch. Dist., 1958-66; mem. bd. overseers Hoover Instn. on War, Revolution and Peace, Stanford, 1969—, chmn., 1971-73, 85-86; adv. policy commn. Santa Clara County Jr. Achievement; trustee Nat. Security Indsl. Assn., 1965-78. Served from pvt. to 1st lt. C.E., O.R.C. AUS, 1943-46. Fellow IEEE (7th region Achievement award 1957, Frederik Philips award 1981), AAAS; mem. Am. Phys. Soc., Am. Mgmt. Assn., Western Electronic Mfrs. Assn. (chmn. San Francisco coun. 1967, v.p., dir.), Calif. C. of C. (dir. 1965-92, treas. 1978, pres. 1981), Nat. Acad. Engring., Mounted Patrol San Mateo County (spl. dep. sheriff 1960-70), San Mateo County Horseman's Assn., San Benito County Farm Bur., Calif. Cattlemen's Assn., Delta Upsilon. Clubs: Palo Alto (Palo Alto), University (Palo Alto); Shack Riders (San Mateo County); Commonwealth (San Francisco); Rancheros Visitadores.

WATKINS, DONALD V., lawyer, entrepreneur; b. 1949; s. Levi Watkins Sr. and Lillian Watkins; m. DeAndra Watkins; 4 children. Grad., So. Ill. U., U. Ala. Law Sch., 1973. Atty. Fred Gray; elected Montgomery City Coun.; rep. atty. Birmingham Ala.; trial lawyer NAACP, SCLC; major equity stake Masada Oxynol, LLC, 1998; founder, chmn. Alamerica Bank, Birmingham, 2000—; founder, CEO Donald V. Watkins, P.C. (more commonly known as The Children's Bank), 2006—. Bd. dirs. State Mut. Life Ins. Co., Rome. Mem.: Alpha Phi Alpha Fraternity, Inc. Achievements include winning 37 of 38 lawsuits as rep. for the city of Birmingham during the 1980s and 1990s; becoming the first and only litigator to successfully defend a NYSE co. CEO (Richard Scrushy) against Sarbanes-Oxley charges in 2005. Office: The Children's Bank 2170 Highland Ave Ste 100 Birmingham AL 35205 *

WATKINS, EUGENE LEONARD, surgeon, educator; b. Worcester, Mass., Jan. 4, 1918; s. George Joseph and Marcella Katherine (Akels) W.; AB with honors in biology, Clark U., 1940; MD (Hood scholar), Harvard U., 1943; m. Victoria Peake, Sept. 23, 1944; children: Roswell Peake, Priscilla Welles. Intern, Roosevelt Hosp., NYC, 1944; resident in surgery, 1944-46, 49-50, asst. resident in surgery, 1948-49; fellow in surgery, clin. rsch. fellow Mass. Gen. Hosp., Boston, 1947-48; practice medicine specializing in surgery, NYC, 1950-56, Morristown, NJ, 1950-90, Denville, NJ, 1956-85, Boonton, NJ, 1961-85; mem. staff Morristown Meml. Hosp., 1950, vice chmn. dept. surgery, 1974-77, chmn., 1959-61, mem. corp.; cons. surgeon St. Clare's Hosp., Denville, NJ, Riverside Hosp., Boonton, NJ, Community Med. Ctr., Morristown; courtesy surg. staff St. Luke's-Roosevelt Hosp. Ctr., NYC; asst. clin. prof. surgery Rutgers U. Coll. Medicine and Dentistry, New Brunswick, NJ, 1972-85; asst. clin. prof. surgery Columbia U. Coll. Phys. and Surg., 1985-90; v.p. chmn. fin. com. Morristown Bd. Health, 1954-56. Served to 1st lt., AUS, 1946. Diplomate Am. Bd. Surgery. Fellow ACS (chmn. NJ Adv. Com. 1965-77, chmn. NJ State com. Trauma, 1960); mem. NJ, Morris County med. socs., AMA, Soc. Surgeons NJ (1st v.p. 1982, pres. 1983), Am. Thoracic Soc., AAAS, Harvard Med. Soc. NY (pres. 1960-61), West Side Med. Soc., Roosevelt Hosp. Alumni Assn. Republican. Presbyterian. Clubs: Harvard (NYC), Morristown, Morristown Field. Achievements include development of spring-loop surgical suture holder. Home: Unit 419 7501 E Thompson Peak Pkwy Scottsdale AZ 85255-4537

WATKINS, FREDERICK HARVEY, plastic surgeon; s. Frederick Harvey and Barbara Jane Watkins; m. Teresa Marie Rubio, May 31, 1997; children: Brendan R., Logan R. BA, U. Va., Charlottesville, 1993, MD, 1997. Diplomate Am. Bd. Plastic Surgery. Resident gen. surgery and plastic surgery Case Western Res. U., Cleve., 1997—2003; attending surgeon Washington Plastic Surgery Group, Rockville, Md., 2003—. Contbr. articles to profl. jours. Echols scholar, U. Va., 1989—93. Fellow: ACS; mem.: AMA, Am. Soc. Plastic Surgery, Phi Beta Kappa. Office: Washington Plastic Surgery Group 3203 Tower Oaks Blvd Rockville MD 20852

WATKINS, GEORGE DANIELS, physics professor; b. Evanston, Ill., Apr. 28, 1924; s. Paul F. and Lois V. (Daniels) W.; m. Carolyn Lenore Nevin, June 19, 1949; children: Lois Roberta, Paul Brent, Ann Romaine. BS, Randolph-Macon Coll., 1943; D.Sc. (hon.), 1976; MA, Harvard U., 1947, PhD, 1952. Research physicist Gen. Electric Research Lab., Schenectady, 1952-75; adj. prof. Rensselaer Poly. Inst., 1962-65, SUNY-Albany, 1969-72; Sherman Fairchild prof. physics Lehigh U., Bethlehem, Pa., 1975-95, prof. emeritus, 1995—; chmn. Gordon Research Conf. on Defects in Semiconductors, 1981; mem. solid state adv. com. Oak Ridge Nat. Lab., 1980-85. Mem. editl. bd. Phys. Rev. B, 1978-82; contbr. articles to profl. jours. Served to lt. (j.g.) USNR, 1943-46. NSF fellow, 1966-67; named Virginian of Yr. Va. Press Assn., 1980; recipient Alexander von Humboldt sr. U.S. Scientist award, 1983, 91. Fellow Am. Phys. Soc. (Oliver E. Buckley award 1978), AAAS, Nat. Acad. Scis. Democrat. Unitarian Universalist. Home Phone: 804-474-8654. Business E-Mail: gdw0@lehigh.edu.

WATKINS, H. THOMAS, biopharmaceutical company executive; B, Coll. William & Mary; MBA, U. Chigo. Grad. Sch. Bus. With Arthur Anderson Co., 1974; mgmt. cons. McKinsey and Co., Inc., 1979—85; bus. unit dir., physicians office diagnostics Abbott Labs., 1985—88, divisional v.p., pharma. products divsn., 1988—93; divisional v.p., sector gen. mgr., benchtops sys. Abbott Diagnostics Divsn., 1993—94, area v.p., Asia/Pacific, 1994, pres., Japanese subs., corp. v.p., 1996—98; v.p. Abbott Healthsystems, 1998; pres. TAP Pharma. Products Inc. (jointly owned by Abbott Labs. abd Takeda Pharma. Co. Ltd., 1998—2004; CEO, bd. dir. Human Genome Sciences, Inc., Rockville, Md., 2004—. Bd. dir. Lake Forest Hosp. Found. and Lake Forest Hosp., Ill.; trustee William & Mary Bus. Sch. Found., Coll. William & Mary, Williamsburg, Va. Office: Human Genome Sciences Inc 14200 Shady Grove Rd Rockville MD 20850 Office Phone: 301-309-8504. Office Fax: 309-309-8512.

WATKINS, HAROLD ROBERT, minister; b. Wauseon, Ohio, July 30, 1928; s. Orra Lynn and Florence Margaret (Bruner) W.; m. Evelyn Norma Earlywine, June 18, 1950; children: Mark Edwin, Nancy Jo Watkins. AB, Bethany Coll., 1950; MDiv, Lexington Theol. Sem., 1997; DD, Phillips U., 1985, Christian Theol. Sem., Indpls., 1995; BD, Coll. of Bible, 1953. Ordained minister Disciples of Christ, 1950. Min. Park Ave. Christian Ch., Tucson, 1953-56, First Christian Ch., Tuscaloosa, Ala., 1956-57; gen. ch. adminstr. Bd. Ch. Extension of Disciples of Christ, Indpls., 1958-95, pres., 1980-95, pres. emeritus, 2004—; mem. faculty Lexington Theol. Sem., 1996-97, 98-99, interim pres., 2001—02. Chmn. bd. dirs. Discipledata, Inc., Indpls., 1980—94; bd. dirs. United Church Ins. Co. Author: Continuity, Conservation and The Cutting Edge, 2005. Trustee Bethany (W.Va.) Coll., 1976—, Nat. City Christian Ch. Corp., Washington, 1981—; bd. dirs. Ecumenical Ch. Loan Fund, Geneva; pres. World Conv. Chs. of Christ, Nashville, 1988-92; bd. dirs. United Ch. of Christ Ins. Bd., 1997—. Recipient Outstanding Alumnus award Bethany Coll., 1975. Mem. Interfaith Forum on Religion, Art and Arch. (dir. officer 1979-95, pres. 1981-82, Elbert M. Conover award 1989). Home: 7402 Somerset Bay Apt 118 Indianapolis IN 46240-3495 Office Phone: 317-251-2977. Personal E-mail: hwatkins28@aol.com.

WATKINS, HAYS THOMAS, retired railroad executive; b. Fern Creek, Ky., Jan. 26, 1926; s. Hays Thomas Sr. and Minnie Catherine (Whiteley) W.; m. Betty Jean Wright, Apr. 15, 1950; 1 son, Hays Thomas III. BS in Acctg., Western Ky. U., 1947; MBA, Northwestern U., 1948; LLD (hon.), Baldwin Wallace Coll., 1975, Alderson Broaddus Coll., 1980, Coll. of William and Mary, 1982, Va. Union U., 1987. CPA, Ill., Ohio. With C. & O. Ry. Cleve., 1949-80, v.p. fin., 1964-67, v.p. adminstrv. group, 1967-71, pres., CEO, 1971—73, chmn. bd., CEO, 1973—80; with B. & O. R.R., 1964-80, v.p. finance, 1964-71, pres., CEO, 1971—73, vice chmn. bd., CEO, 1973—80; chmn., CEO Chessie System, Inc., 1973—80; pres. and co-CEO CSX Corp. (merger of Chessie System, Inc. and Seaboard Coast Line Industries, Inc.), Richmond, Va., 1980—82, chmn. bd., CEO, 1982—89, chmn. bd., 1989-91; chmn. emeritus, 1991—. Vice-rector bd. visitors Coll. William & Mary, 1984-87, rector, 1987-93. With AUS, 1945-47. Named Man of Yr., Modern R.R. mag., 1984; recipient Excellence in Mgmt. award Industry Week mag., 1982. Mem. Nat. Assn. Accts., Am. Inst. C.P.A.'s. Clubs: Commonwealth (Richmond, Va.); Country of Va. (Richmond). Home: 22 Lower Tuckahoe Rd W Richmond VA 23238-6108 Office: CSX Corp 901 E Cary St Ste 1605 Richmond VA 23219 Office Phone: 804-782-1411.

WATKINS, JAMES DAVID, federal official, military officer; b. Alhambra, Calif., Mar. 7, 1927; s. Edward Francis and Louise Whipple (Ward) Watkins; m. Sheila Jo McKinney, Aug. 19, 1950 (dec. Sept. 1996); m. Janet L. McDonough, June 17, 2000; children: Katherine Marie, Laura Jo, Charles Lancaster, Susan Elizabeth, James David, Edward Francis stepchildren: John Christopher McDonough, Sean Charles McDonough, Robert Edward McDonough, Siobhan McDonough. BS, U.S. Naval Acad., 1949; MSME, Navy Postgrad. Sch., 1958; LHD (hon.), Marymount Coll., 1982, N.Y. Med. Coll., 1988; DSc (hon.), Dowling Coll., 1983, U. Ala., 1991; LLD (hon.), Cath. U. Am., 1985, Mt. Sinai Sch. Medicine, 1993, Calif. U. Pa., 1994; DS (hon.), Coll. William and Mary, 1999. Commd. ensign USN, 1949, advanced through grades to adm., 1979, comdg. officer U.S.S. Snook, 1964-66, exec. officer U.S.S. Long Beach, 1967-69; head submarine/nuclear power distbn. control br. Bur. Naval Pers., Dept. Navy, Washington, 1969-71, dir. enlisted pers. div., 1971-72, asst. chief naval pers. for enlisted pers. control, 1972-73; comdr. Cruiser-Destroyer Group 1 USN, 1973-75; dep. chief naval ops. manpower Dept. Navy, Washington, 1975-78, chief of naval pers., 1975-78, chief Bur. Naval Pers., 1975-78; comdr. U.S. Sixth Fleet USN, 1978-79; vice chief naval ops. Dept. Navy, Washington, 1979-81, comdr.-in-chief U.S. Pacific Fleet, 1981-82, chief naval ops., 1982-86; ret. USN, 1986; chmn. Presdl. Commn. Human Immunodeficiency Virus Epidemic, 1987-88; sec. Dept. Energy, Washington, 1989-93; pres. Joint Oceanographic Instn., 1993-2000, Consortium Oceanographic Rsch. and Edn., 1993-2001. Chmn. Presidentially Apptd. Commn. Ocean Policy, 2001—04; co-chair Joint Ocean Commn. Initiative with Mr. Leon Panetta, 2004—07. Decorated DSM with 1 gold star, Legion of Merit with 2 gold stars, Bronze Star medal with combat v; recipient Disting. Alumni award, Naval Postgrad. Sch., 1958, Chmn.'s award, Am. Assn. Engring. Socs., 1991, Disting. Grad. award, U.S. Naval Acad., 2001, Scientific Am. 50 award, 2004, Senator. John H. Chafee Coastal Stewardship award, 2005, Internat. Sea Keepers award, 2005, Lifetime Achievement award, Nat. Marine Sanctuary Found., 2006. Mem.: The Army Navy Country Club, The Alfalfa Club, Knights of Malta. Roman Catholic.

WATKINS, JAMES KELLEY, retired urologist; b. Milford, Mich., Mar. 25, 1930; s. Ralph Nelson and Georgia Eileen Watkins; m. Janet Elizabeth Weber, Dec. 29, 1956; children: Katherine Harrison, William, Christopher, Bridget Hannock. AB in History, U. Mich., Ann Arbor, 1952, MD, 1959. Diplomate Am. Bd. Urology. Head dept. urology Butterworth Hosp., Grand Rapids, Mich., 1973—74; renal transplant surgeon St. Mary's Hosp., Grand Rapids, 1973—94; chief of staff Ferguson Hosp., Grand Rapids, 1992—94; ret., 1994. Mem. Gerontology Network, Grand Rapids, 1996—2005. Bd. dirs., mem. allocations com. United Way, Grand Rapids, 1989—92; trustee YMCA, Grand Rapids. Lt. (j.g.) USN, 1952—55. Recipient Holloway scholar, USN, 1948—52. Fellow: ACS; mem.: Kent Med. Found. (pres. 1990), Kent County Med. Soc. (pres. 1989, editor monthly bull. 1989—2005). Democrat. Roman Catholic. Avocations: rowing, running, golf, bicycling, tennis. Home: 252 Pearl St NW # 3D Grand Rapids MI 49503

WATKINS, JERRY WEST, retired oil company executive, lawyer; b. Vernon, Tex., Dec. 10, 1931; s. Terrell Clark and Daisy (West) W.; m. Elizabeth Jill Cole, Sept. 3, 1955. Student, Hendrix Coll., 1949-50, La. Poly. Inst., 1950-51; JD, U. Ark., 1954. Bar: Ark. 1954. Law clk. Supreme Ct. Ark., Little Rock, 1954-55; with Murphy Oil Corp., El Dorado, Ark., 1955-89, sec., gen. atty., 1966-71, sec., gen. counsel, 1971-88, v.p., dir., 1975-88, exec. v.p., 1991-92, also bd. dirs., 1975-89. CEO, bd. dirs. Ocean Drilling and Exploration Co., New Orleans, 1989-91; mem. Ark. Bd. Law Examiners, 1969-74; bd. dirs. Simmons First Bank of El Dorado, N.A., Simmons First Nat. Corp. Mem. Barton Libr. Bd., El Dorado, 1966—89; trustee Ark. State U., 1982—87; bd. dirs. South Ark. Arts Ctr., El Dorado, 1979—82, 1985—88, Warner Brown Hosp., El Dorado, 1984—87, South Ark. Med. Sys., 1987—89, Presbyn. Found. Ark., 1998—, Union County Cmty. Found., 2001—. Mem. ABA, Ark. Bar Assn., Union County Bar Assn. Home: 111 Watkins Dr El Dorado AR 71730-2752

WATKINS, JOAN MARIE, retired osteopath, retired physician; b. Anderson, Ind., Mar. 9, 1943; d. Curtis David and Dorothy Ruth (Beckett) W.; m. Stanley G. Nodvik, Dec. 25, 1969 (div. Apr. 1974). BS, West Liberty State Coll., 1965; Cert. of Grad. Phys. Therapy, Ohio State U., 1966; DO, Phila. Coll. Osteo., 1972; M of Health Professions Edn., U. Ill., Chgo., 1986; MPH, U. Ill., 1989. Diplomate Osteo. Nat. Bds., Am. Bd. Preventive Medicine, Am. Bd. Occupl. and Environ. Medicine, Am. Bd. Emergency Medicine. Resident in phys. medicine and rehab. U. Pa., 1973—74; emergency osteo. physician Cooper Med. Ctr., Camden, 1974-79, Shore Meml. Hosp., Somers Point, NJ, 1979-81, St. Francis Hosp., Blue Island, Ill., 1981-82, Mercy Hosp. and Med. Ctr., Chgo., 1982-90, dir. emergency ctr., 1984-88; resident in occupl. and preventive medicine U. Ill., 1988-90; corp. med. dir. occupl. health svc. Univ. Cmty. Hosp., Tampa, 1992—2006; cons. in field, 2006—. Fellow Am. Coll. Occupl. and Environ. Medicine, Am. Soc. Preventive Medicine, Fla. Assn. Occupl. and Environ. Medicine (pres. 1999-2001). Avocations: sailing, needlecrafts, swimming. Home: 4306 Harbor House Dr Tampa FL 33615-5408

WATKINS, JOE BILL, lawyer; b. Llano, Tex., July 21, 1943; BA, U. Tex., 1965, LLB with high honors, 1965. Bar: Tex. 1968. Exec. asst. to atty. gen. State of Tex., 1973—74; ptnr., head Pub. Policy Sect. Vinson & Elkins LLP, Austin, Tex. Fellow: Am. Leadership Forum. Office: Vinson & Elkins LLP Ste 100 2801 Via Fortuna Austin TX 78746 Office Phone: 512-542-8460. E-mail: jwatkins@velaw.com.

WATKINS, JOHN B., lawyer; b. Feb. 4, 1956; BA, Johns Hopkins Univ., 1977; JD, Univ. Mich., 1981. Bar: Md. 1981, DC 1988. Ptnr., vice chmn. Corp. dept. Wilmer Cutler Pickering Hale & Dorr, Baltimore. Mem.: ABA, Md. Bar Assn. Office: Wilmer Cutler Pickering Hale & Dorr 100 Light St Baltimore MD 21202 Office Phone: 410-986-2820. Office Fax: 410-986-2828. Business E-Mail: john.watkins@wilmerhale.com.

WATKINS, JOHN FRANCIS, management consultant; b. Alhambra, Calif., May 21, 1925; s. Edward F. and Louise (Ward) W.; divorced; children— Stephen, Katherine, John Francis, William. BSCE, U. Tex., Austin, 1947. With Earle M. Jorgensen Co., Lynwood, Calif., 1947-90, sr. v.p. adminstrn., 1978-90, ret.; owner John F. Watkins Assocs., Pasadena, Calif., 1990—. Pres. bd. Poly. Sch., Pasadena, 1978—80, Holy Family Sch., 1994—2002; adv. bd. mem. Serra H.S., Verbum Dei H.S., Dolores Mission Sch., 1996—; mem. Coll. Sci. and Engring. Coun. Loyola Marymount U., bd. visitors Sch. Edn.; adv. bd. Bishop Mora Salesian H.S., 1994—; mem. Cath. Edn. Found. Archdiocese L.A., 1995—; St. Gabriel pastoral region bd. dirs. Cath. Charities, 1994—; bd. dirs. Boys Republic, Chino Hills, Calif., 1970—, pres., 1977—80; bd. dirs. St. Luke Hosp., Pasadena, 1979—86, chmn. bd., 1982—86; bd. dirs. Econ. Literacy Coun. Calif., 1980—87, Pasadena Mus. of History, 1990—99. Mem. U.S. Navy League (nat. bd. dirs. 1989—, pres. Pasadena coun. 1992-93), Calif. Club, Annandale Golf Club, Serra Club (pres. 1995-97), Valley Club (San Marino, Calif.), Twilight Club (pres. 2002-03). Republican. Roman Catholic. Home and Office: 410 California Ter Pasadena CA 91105-2419 Home Phone: 626-432-4712; Office Phone: 626-432-4712. E-mail: jwatkins@pacificnet.net.

WATKINS, JOHN GOODRICH, psychologist, educator; b. Salmon, Idaho, Mar. 17, 1913; s. John Thomas and Ethel (Goodrich) W.; m. Evelyn Elizabeth Browne, Aug. 21, 1932; m. Doris Wade Tomlinson, June 8, 1946; m. Helen Verner Huth, Dec. 28, 1971; children: John Dean, Jonette Alison, Richard Douglas, Gregory Keith, Rodney Philip, Karen Stroobants, Marvin R. Huth. Student, Coll. Idaho, 1929-30, 31-32; BS, U. Idaho, 1933, MS, 1936; PhD, Columbia U., 1941. Instr. high sch., Idaho, 1933-39; faculty Ithaca Coll., 1940-41; prof. Auburn U., 1941-43; assoc. prof. Wash. State U., 1946-49; chief clin. psychologist U.S. Army Welch Hosp., 1945-46; chief clin. psychologist VA Hosp., American Lake, Wash., 1949-50; chief clin. psychologist VA Mental Hygiene Clinic, Chgo., 1950-53, VA Hosp., Portland, Oreg., 1953-64; prof. psychology U. Mont., Missoula, 1964-84, prof. emeritus, 1984—, dir. clin. tng., 1964-80. Lectr. numerous univs.; clin. asso. U. Oreg. Med. Sch., 1957; pres. Am. Bd. Examiners in Psychol. Hypnosis, 1960-62. Author: Objective Measurement of Instrumental Performance, 1942, Hypnotherapy of War Neuroses, 1949, General Psychotherapy, 1960, The Therapeutic Self, 1978, (with others) We, The Divided Self, 1982, Hypnotherapeutic Techniques, 1987, rev. edit., 2006, (with others) Hypnoanalytic Techniques, 1992, (with others) Ego States: Theory and Therapy, 1997, Adventures in Human Understanding, 2001, Emotional Resonance, 2005; contbr. articles to profl. jours. Mem. Internat. Soc. Clin. and Exptl. Hypnosis (co-founder, pres. 1965-67, awards 1960-65), Internat. Soc. Hypnosis (Benjamin Franklin Gold medal award), Soc. Clin. and Exptl. Hypnosis (pres. 1969-71, Morton Prince award), Am. Psychol. Assn. (pres. divsn. 30 1975-76, award 1993), Phi Delta Kappa. Home and Office: 8258 Greenwood Pl Longmont CO 80503 Office Phone: 303-652-6556. Office Fax: 303-652-6525. *For a complete life one needs a job, a home, a love, a friend, and an enemy. My "enemies" are injustice, war, poverty, illness, and suffering, not people. Make your existence as meaningful as possible. Enjoy life fully, and when it comes time to leave, have no fear or regrets. Seek to leave this world a little better off because you lived. These are my values. Would that I were mature enough always to live up to them.*

WATKINS, KELLEE DILLARD, literature and language educator; m. Trent Elliott Watkins; 1 child, Jaeden. BA in Elem. Edn., Livingstone Coll., Salisbury, NC, 1995; MEd in Reading, Lang. and Literacy, U. NC, Charlotte, 2000. Coord. reading first Livingstone Coll., Salisbury, NC, 2002—06, dept. chairperson, 2003—05. Bd. mem. Black Achievers, Salisbury, 2002—04. Office: Livingstone Coll 701 W Monroe St Salisbury NC 28144 Office Phone: 704-216-6891.

WATKINS, LEROY J., III, entrepreneur; B in Fin., Northeastern U., Boston, 2004. Mgmt. position JPG Mktg., Malden, Mass.; pres., co-founder MyBike Inc., Boston, 2005—. Named one of Best Entrepreneurs Under 25, BusinessWeek mag., 2006. Office: My Bike Apt 5 888 Huntington Ave Boston MA 02115-2322 Office Phone: 617-216-3437. E-mail: info@mybikeonline.com. *

WATKINS, M(ARTHA) ANNE, family practice nurse practitioner; b. Vicksburg, Mich., Feb. 9, 1961; d. George H. and Coleene M. (Shearer) W. ADN, S.W. Mich. Coll., 1984; BSN, U. Mich., 1988, MSN, 2003. RN, Mich. Staff nurse Lee Meml. Hosp., Dowagiac, Mich.; clin. nurse II thoracic intensive care U. Mich. Hosps., Ann Arbor; emergency nurse Lee Meml. Hosp., Dowagiac, Mich.; critical care nurse Mercy Meml. Hosp., St. Joseph, Mich.; house supr. Lee Meml. Hosp., Dowagiac, Mich., dir. med. surg. pediat., 1995, v.p. patient care svcs., 1996—2001; family nurse practioner Planned Parenthood Mid Mich. Alliance, Benton Harbor, Mich., 2004—06, After Hours Clinic Watervliet Cmty. Hosp., Mich., 2006—. Mem. Phi Theta Kappa. Home: 303 Mcphil Dr Dowagiac MI 49047-1012 Office: After Hours Clinic Watervliet Cmty Hosp 420 Medical Park Dr Watervliet MI 49098 Office Phone: 269-463-3600. Business E-Mail: marthawatkins@borgess.com.

WATKINS, STEPHEN EDWARD, accountant, publishing executive; b. Oklahoma City, Sept. 1, 1922; s. Ralph Bushnell and Jane (Howell) W.; m. Suzanne Fowler, Aug. 16, 1976; children— Elizabeth Ann Watkins Racicot, Stephen Edward, Jr. BBA, U. N.Mex., 1944. C.P.A., N.Mex. With Peat, Marwick, Mitchell & Co., 1944-67; pres. The New Mexican daily newspaper, Santa Fe, 1967-78, 90—; pvt. practice pub. acctg. Santa Fe, 1978—. Vestryman Ch. of Holy Faith; trustee St. Vincent Hosp., 1979-85, Orchestra Santa Fe, 1976-82, Hist. Santa Fe Found. (pres. 1990). Mem. AICPA, Sons of Am. Revolution, Rotary. Home: 1325 Don Gaspar Ave Santa Fe NM 87505-4627 Office: 223 E Palace Ave Santa Fe NM 87501-1947

WATKINS, THOMAS LINNANE, lawyer; b. Richmond, Va., July 16, 1952; s. Alfred Plummer Watkins and Delia Linnane; m. Wrengay Rawls, Apr. 8, 1952; 1 child, Erin Delia. JD, William & Mary U., Williamsburg, Va., 1974—77. Bar: Va. State Bar 1977. Asst. commonwealth's atty. Chesapeake Commonwealth's Atty., Va., 1978—83; asst. com. atty. Va. Beach Commonwealth's Atty., 1983—90; pvt. practice law, 1990—94; dep. pub. defender Va. Beach PD, 1994—2003; pub. defender Franklin Pub. Defender, Va., 2003—. Recipient Am. Jurisprudence award, William & Mary Law Sch., 1975. Mem.: Southampton Bar Assoc. (assoc.). Democrat-Npl. Cath. Avocations: photography, astronomy, history, philosophy, birdwatching. Home: 22450 Barrett Town Rd Zuni VA 23898 Office: Public Defender 223 N Main St Franklin VA 23851 Home Phone: 757-242-3498. Personal E-mail: watkins991@aol.com. Business E-Mail: twatkins@idc.virginia.gov.

WATKINS, WESLEY WADE, retired congressman; b. DeQueen, Ark., Dec. 15, 1938; s. L. V. and Mary J. W.; m. Elizabeth Lou Rogers, June 9, 1963; children: Sally, Martha, Wade. BS, Okla. State U., 1960, MS, 1961. With USDA, Washington, 1961; asst. dir. admissions Okla. State U., 1963-66; exec. dir. Kiamichi Econ. Devel. Dist. of Okla., 1966-68; founder, owner constrn. and land devel. bus., 1968-76; mem. Okla. Senate, 1975-76, U.S. Congress from 3d Okla. Dist., 1977—91, 1997—2002; mem. ways and means com., human resources suncom., budget com.; pres. World Export Services, Stillwater, Okla., 1991—96. Pres. Higher Edn. Alumni Council of Okla.; Okla. chmn. Nat. Future Farmers Am. Found.; mem. Okla. Health Planning Council.; Pres. Ada (Okla). Growth and Devel. Assn. Served with Air N.G., 1960-66. Recipient Nat. Security Leadership award U.S. Air N.G., 1967, Okla. 4-H Alumni Recognition award, 1978, Disting. Alumnus award Okla. State U. Alumni Assn., 1978, others; named Policymaker of the Yr. Am. Vocational Assn., One of 3 Outstanding Young Men in Okla., Okla. Jaycees, 1968; named to Okla. State U. Hall of Fame, 1989. Mem. C. of C. Clubs: Masons, Lions. Republican. Presbyterian.

WATKINS, WILLIAM, JR., electric power industry executive; b. Jersey City, Aug. 12, 1932; s. William James and Willie Ree (Blount) W.; m. Sylvia I. Mulzac, Oct. 16, 1955; children: Cheryl, Rene, Linda. BBA, Pace U., 1954; MBA, NYU, 1962; postgrad. advanced mgmt. program, U. Mich., 1979; postgrad. exec. program, Edison Electric Inst., 1988. Staff asst. Consol. Edison Co. N.Y., NYC, 1957-64; sys. mgr. Volkswagen Am., Englewood Cliffs, N.J., 1964-71; v.p., dir. adminstrn. New Eng. Power Svc. Co., Westboro, Mass., 1972-82, v.p., dir. human resources, 1986-92; v.p., dist. mgr. Narragansett Electric Co., Providence, 1982-86, exec. v.p., 1992-97; retired. Bd. dirs. Peerless Precision Corp., Lincoln, R.I., 1982-91; mem. bd. advisors Sarasota Pvt. Bank, Fleet Fin. Group, 2001. Chmn. R.I. Urban Project, Providence, 1984, R.I. Coun. for Econ. Edn., Providence, 1984; mem. Gov.'s Commn. on Health Care Reform, 1993-94; trustee R.I. Hosp., 1995-96, Lifespan, 1996-99, Roger Williams U., Bristol, R.I., 1991-94; bd. dirs. R.I. Hosp. Fin. Corp., Providence, 1987-91, Inroads, 1993-97, Leadership R.I., 1993-95, NCCJ, 1993-97; mem. resource and devel. commn. Episcopal Diocese Mass., 1988-92; chmn. bd. trustees RISD, 1998-2000. Recipient Cmty. Svc. award Urban League R.I., 1986, Paris V. Sterett award John Hope Settlement House, 1987, Small Bus. Adminstrn. Adv. of the Yr. award, 1994; named Developer of Yr., Am. Econ. Devel. Coun., 1996. Mem. N.E. Econ. Developers Assn. (bd. dirs. 1993-97), R.I. Urban Bankers Assn., Kappa Alpha Psi, Sigma Pi Phi. Avocations: swimming, biking, hiking, travel, golf. Home: 5114 87th Ct E Bradenton FL 34211-3743 E-mail: wwatkin5114@aol.com.

WATKINS, WILLIAM D., computer hardware company executive; BS in Polit. Sci., U. Tex. Exec. Domain Tech., 1990-96; sr. v.p. Conner Peripherals, 1996-98; COO, exec. v.p. Seagate Technology, Milpitas, Calif., 1998—2000, COO, pres. Scotts Valley, Calif., 2000—04, pres., CEO, 2004—. Avocation: racing. Office: Seagate Tech 920 Disc Dr Scotts Valley CA 95066

WATKINS, W(ILLIAM) KEITH, federal judge; b. Troy, Ala., July 5, 1951; s. William Harold and Emily Joanne (Davis) W.; m. Teresa Marie Madigan, Sept. 11, 1976; children: William Scott, Emily Anne. BS, Auburn U., 1973; JD, U. Ala., 1976. Bar: Ala. 1976, US Dist. Ct. (no., mid., and so. dists.) Ala. Ptnr. Studwick & Watkins, Troy, Ala., 1976—78, Clower & Watkins, 1978—85, Clower, Watkins & Douglas, 1985—86, Calhoun, Watkins & Clower, 1987—90, Calhoun, Faulk, Watkins, Clower & Cox, 1990—94, Calhoun, Faulk, Watkins & Faircloth, LLC, 1994—2006; judge US Dist. Ct. (mid. dist.) Ala., 2006—. Baptist. Office: US Dist Ct PO Box 711 Montgomery AL 36101-0711 Office Phone: 334-954-3760. *

WATLER, PAUL C., lawyer; b. Beaumont, Tex., June 23, 1954; BJ, Univ. Tex., 1976, JD, 1981. Bar: Tex. 1981, cert.: Tex. Bd. Legal Specialization (civil trial law). Shareholder, comml. litigation Jenkens & Gilchrist, Dallas. Named a Tex. Super Lawyer; named one of Top Dallas / Fort Worth Lawyers, D Mag. Fellow: Tex. Bar Found.; mem.: ABA, Libel Def. Resource Ctr., Media Law Resource Ctr., Coll. of State Bar Tex., State Bar Tex., Dallas Bar Assn., Freedom of Information Found. Tex. (past pres., James Madison award). Office: Jenkens & Gilchrist Ste 3200 1445 Ross Ave Dallas TX 75202-2799 Office Phone: 214-855-4393. Office Fax: 214-855-4300. Business E-Mail: pwatler@jenkens.com.

WATNE, DARLENE CLAIRE, county official; b. Minot, ND, Feb. 11, 1935; d. Charles A. and Anna Marie Widdel (Fjeld) W.; m. Clair A. Watne, Mar. 27, 1954; children: Carmen, Steven, Nancy, Matthew. Court reporting diploma, 1975; grad., Real Estate Inst., 1991. Cert. residential real estate specialist, N.D. Exec. sec. Grand Exalted Ruler Elks, Minot, ND, 1964-75; pres. Bus. Coll., Minot, 1974—76; ct. reporter NW Jud. Dist., Minot, 1976—90; real estate broker Watne Realtors Better Homes & Gardens, Minot, 1990—99; mem. ND Senate from 5th dist., Bismarck, 1994—2001; commr. Ward County, ND, 1994—. Active Joint Civil Svcs. to the Poor, 1995-2001. Commr. ND State Lottery, 2002—07; mem. Souris Basin Planning Coun., 2004—07, Ward County Libr. Bd., 2006—; dir. Minot Area Devel. Corp., 2006—; numerous state polit. interim senate coms.; bd. dirs. Salvation Army, Red Cross; bd. dir. ND Credit Union, 2007—. Named Minot Woman of Distinction in Bus. and Industry, 1993, Liberty award ND Bar Assn., 2000, named Citizen of Yr. ND Builders Assn., 2001. Republican. Avocations: reading, laking. Home: 520 28th Ave SW Minot ND 58701-7065

WATNE, DONALD ARTHUR, retired accountant, educator; b. Gt. Falls, Mont., Jan. 18, 1939; BA with high honors, U. Mont., 1960, MA, 1961; PhD, U. Calif., Berkeley, 1977. CPA, Oreg. Acct. Piquet & Minihan, Eugene, Oreg., 1961-65; mgr. capital investment analysis Weyerhaeuser Co., Tacoma, 1965-68; mktg. rep. IBM Corp., Portland, Oreg., 1968-70; dir. EDP Ctr. in Concejo Mcpl., Barquisimeto, Venezuela, 1971-72; prof. acctg. Portland State U., 1976-2001, prof. emeritus, 2001—. Vis. prof. Xiamen (Fujian, People's Rep. China), 1985-86, U. Otago, Dunedin, New Zealand, 1985-86, U. Newcastle, Australia, 1985-86; cons. in field; acctg. qualifications com. Oregon State Bd. Acctg., 1989-98, CPE com., 1998-2001 Author: (with Peter B.B. Turney) Auditing EDP Systems, 2d edit. 1990; contbr. chpts. to books, articles to profl. jours. Del. to Soviet Union citizen amb. program People to People Internat., 1990; active Tng. the Trainers Program, Vilnius, Lithuania, 1993; trustee, treas. First Unitarian Ch. of Portland, 2002—; mem. bd. stewards First Unitarian Ch. of Portland Found., 2002-07, treas., 2004-07. Mem.: AICPA, Oreg. Soc. CPAs, Mensa, Mazamas Mountain Climbing Club. Home: 2826 NE 26th Ave Portland OR 97212-3503 E-mail: dawatne@msn.com.

WATROS, CYNTHIA, actress; b. Lake Orion, Mich., Sept. 2, 1968; d. Bruce and Nancy Watros; m. Curtis Gilliland, 1996; 2 children. Student, Macomb CC, Mich.; BFA, Boston U. Actor: (films) Cafe Society, 1995, His and Hers, 1997, Mercy Streets, 2000, Yellow Bird, 2001, P.S. Your Cat is Dead, 2002, Duane Incarnate, 2004, American Crude, 2005, Just Pray, 2005; (TV series) The Guiding Light, 1994 (Daytime Emmy award, 1998), Titus, 2000, Drew Carey Show, 2002—04, Lost, 2005— (Outstanding Performance by an Ensemble in a Drama Series, Screen Actors Guild award, 2006). Avocations: snow skiing, dancing. Address: care Innovative Artists 1505 10th St Santa Monica CA 90401

WATROUS, ROBERT THOMAS, academic director; b. Cleveland, Apr. 20, 1952; s. Frank Thomas and Marie Anne (Kmeicik) W.; m. Robin Joyce (Braun), Mar. 14, 1981 (div. 1993); 1 child, Michael Francis; m. Susan J. (Rupp), Mar. 8, 2003. BS, U. Dayton, Ohio, 1974, MS, 1977. Dir. student ctr. for off campus cmty. rels. U. Dayton, Ohio, 1974—76, resident dir., 1976—78; dir. of housing St. Bonaventure U., Olean, NY, 1978—81; asst. dean of student life housing U. Pa., Kutztown, 1981—86, dir. commuter and jud. affairs, 1986—2004, dean, student svcs. and campus life, 2004—. Faculty senate Kutztown U. Pa. 1986-89, 92-95; mem. Pa. Task Force on Intergroup Behavior in Higher Edn., 1991-94; trainer Pa. Interagy. Task Force on Civil Tension, Harrisburg, Pa., 1989-2001; exec. coun. Adult Learners Consortium, Bloomsburg, Pa., 1990-91; mem. Lehigh Valley Svc. Learning Consortium, 1994—. Bd. mgr. Tri Valley YMCA, Fleetwood, Pa., 1983-94; adv. bd. Crossroads, Kutztown, 1989-94; bd. dir. Jr. Achievement of Berks County, Reading, Pa., 1990, Reading, Pa., 1990, Reading and Berks Coun. YMCA, 1992-96; mem. Leadership Berks, Reading, 1990; bd. dir. Leadership Berks, 1995—, sec. 1998-99, pres., 2000-04; co-founder Leading Sch. Bd., 1994—; mem. Leadership Alliance Berks, 2004-, YMCA cultural diversity and internat. awareness com., 1994—; mem. Berks County Conflict Resolution Task Force, 1996-2004; v.p. Fleetwood Activities Booster Club, 1998-2002, pres., 1999-2001. Mem. Nat. Assn. Student Pers. Adminstr. (profl. affiliate), Hawk Mt. Coun. Boy Scouts Am. (sustaining mem.), Berks County C. of C. (sch. bd. governance com. 1993-2000), Fleetwood Youth Soccer Club (v.p., pres. 1999), Fleetwood Youth Basketball Assn. (coach 1995-96), Leadership Alliance of Berks, 2003-, Greater Reading Leadership Alliance, 2004-. Avocations: golf, sports, gardening. Business E-Mail: watrous@kutztown.edu.

WATSON, ANTHONY L., health facility executive; b. 1942; Supervising pub. health advisor dept.health edn. and welfare Ctr. for Disease Control, Pub. Health Svc., 1966-70; dep. dir. Comprehensive Health Planning Agy., NYC, 1970-76, Health Planning, NYC, 1976—85; exec. v.p., COO HIP Health Plan of NY, NYC, 1985—91, chmn., CEO, 1991—, Emblem Health, Inc., 2006—. Mem. Cmty. Coun. Greater NY. Mem. Am. Health Planning Assn., Am. Hosp. Assn. Office: HIP Health Plan of NY 55 Water St New York NY 10041

WATSON, ARTHUR DENNIS, federal official; b. Brownsville, Pa., May 11, 1950; s. Arthur Francis and Margaret Teresa (Mastile) Puglia, John Leslie Watson (Stepfather); m. Kathleen Frances Zaccardo, July 16, 1983; 1 child, Fiona Kathleen. BSBA, U. Richmond, 1972; MS in Bus.-Govt. Rels., Am. U., 1977, MA in Lit., 1979; PhD in English Lang. and Lit., Cath. U., 1987. Statis. asst. U.S. Postal Svc. Hdqrs., Washington, 1972—73, economist assoc., 1973—74, staff economist, 1974—77, mktg. analyst, 1977; rate analyst U.S. Postal Rate Commn., Washington, 1977—79, dir. pub. affairs, 1979—82; pub. affairs officer ICC, Washington, 1982—89, dep. dir. pub. affairs, 1989—93, assoc. dir. congl. and pub. affairs, 1993—95; dir. media affairs surface transp. bd. Dept. Transp., Washington, 1996—. Pres. Arthur D. Watson and Co., Clifton, Va., 1983—; Washington corr. Linn's Stamp News, Sidney, Ohio, 1983—84. Contbr. articles to profl. jours. With USCG, 1972—78. Recipient Meritorious Svc. medal, USCG Res., Pub. Svc. award, ICC, 1989, Spl. Achievement award, Surface Transp. Bd., 1999, Merger Response Team Performance award, 2000, Performance award for media and pub. affairs, 2000, Second Pl. award, Internat. Plastic Modelers Soc. (No. Va. divsn.), 2000, Merger Response Team Performance award, Surface Transp. Bd., 2001, Agy. Performance award Merger team, 2001, Performance award for website enhancements, 2002, Performance award for media and pub. affairs, 2002. Mem.: Assn. Transp. Law Profls., Nat. Assn. RR Passengers, E. Clairborne Robins Sch. Bus. Alumni Assn. Avocations: classical music, reading, writing, model building, travel. Home: 6521 Rockland Dr Clifton VA 20124-2415 Office: Surface Transp Bd 395 E St SW Ste 1208 Washington DC 20423-0001 Office Phone: 202-245-0234.

WATSON, BERNARD CHARLES, foundation administrator, educator; m. Lois Lathan, July 1, 1961; children: Barbra, Bernard Jr. BS, Ind. U., 1951; MEd, U. Ill., 1955; PhD, U. Chgo., 1967; postdoctoral work, Harvard U., 1968; LHD (hon.), Allen U., 1981, LaSalle U., 1987, Spring Garden Coll., Elizabethtown Coll, Beaver Coll., 1988, Harris-Stowe State Coll., Morris Brown Coll., 1989, Millersville U., 1991, N.C. Ctrl. U., 1999; LLD (hon.), Lincoln U., 1974, Fla. Meml. Coll., 1984, Temple U., 1986, Med. Coll. Pa., 1986, Tuskegee U., 1991, Lincoln U., 1992, Morgan State U., 1992, Phila. Coll. Pharmacy and Sci., 1994, Bethune-Cookman Coll., 1995; HHD (hon.), Wilberforce U., 1979; DFA, Univ. of the Arts, 1992; D of Pedagogy, Drexel U., 1992. Tchr., prin. Roosevelt Jr. and Sr. H.S., Gary, Ind., 1955-65; staff assoc. Midwest Adminstrn. Ctr. U. Chgo., 1965-67; assoc. supt. innovative programs Sch. Dist. Phila., 1967-68, dep. supt. for planning, 1968-70; prof., chmn. dept. urban edn. Temple U., Phila., 1970-75, also prof. social foundations Coll. Edn. and prof. urban studies Coll. Liberal Arts, 1970-75, v.p. acad. adminstrn., 1976-81, presdl. scholar, 1994—; pres., CEO William Penn Found, Phila., 1982-93; chmn. HMA Found., Phila., 1994-97. Bd. dirs. Comcast Corp., First Union Bancorp North, First Union Bank, Keystone AAA Club, Keystone Ins. Co., Phila. Contributionship; assoc. edn. Grad. Sch. Edn. Harvard U., 1970-72, mem. vis. com., 1981-87; mem. vis. com. dept. Afro-Am. studies Harvard Coll., 1974-78. Author: In Spite of the System: The Individual and Educational Reform, 1974; editor in chief Cross Reference: A Jour. Pub. Policy and Multi-Cultural Edn., 1976-79, Testing Its Origin, Use and Misuse, 1997, Colored, Negro, Black: Chasing the American Dream, 1997; contbr. numerous articles to profl. jours., chpts. to books. Mem. steering com., mem. exec. com. Nat. Urban Coalition, 1973-89; vice chmn. Nat. Adv. Coun. Edn. Professions Devel., 1967-70, Pa. Coun. on Arts, 1986-93; mem. Nat. Coun. Ednl. Rsch., 1980-82, William T. Grant Found. Commn. Work, Family and Citizenship, 1987-88; sr. vice chmn. bd. trustees Nat. Urban League, 1983-96; vice chmn. bd. dirs. Pa. Conv. Ctr. Authority, 1986-2000; trustee Thomas Jefferson U., 1993-95; sec. bd. N.J. State Aquarium, 1988-93; chmn. Ave. the Arts Inc., 1992—; mem. fed. judiciary nominating com. Pa., 1981-89; bd. dirs. Friends of the Nelson Mandela Children's Fund, 1996—, Marian Anderson Hist. Soc., 1998—, Pa. Conv. Ctr. Authority, 2001-02; mem. adv. com. Frederick D. Patterson Rsch. Inst., 1998—; chmn. bd. dirs. Barnes Found., 1999—. Recipient numerous honors and awards for leadership in edn., the arts, and civil rights. Mem. Am. Philosophical Soc., Am. Acad. Polit. and Social Sci., Phi Delta Kappa, Kappa Delta Pi. Home Phone: 941-351-7933; Office Phone: 215-820-6825.

WATSON, BRENDA BENNETT, insurance company executive; b. Decatur, Ga., Aug. 26, 1940; d. Robert Joseph and Clarissa Mae (Weekes) Bennett; m. James H. Pair Jr., Apr. 4, 1969 (div. Aug. 1993); children: Richard S. Pair, Randall J. Pair, Ronald G. Pair; m. James Leigh Watson, Sept. 9, 1995. Student, DeKalb Coll., 1971. Lic. property and casualty agt. Underwriter W. K. Stringer Co., Atlanta, 1961-65, Tharpe & Assocs., Atlanta, 1965-68; sr. v.p. Alexander - Howden, Atlanta, 1968-82; exec. v.p., ptnr. Pair Underwriting Mgrs. Inc., Atlanta, 1982-86; pres. Walkingstick-LaGere-Pair Underwriting Mgrs., Inc., Chandler, Okla., 1986-88; exec. v.p., dir. LaGere-Walkingstick Ins. Agy., Chandler, Okla., 1988—2002; exec. v.p., bd. dirs. Chandler Ins. Mgrs. Inc., 2003—06; pres., CEO, mng. ptnr. TIP Natl. Inc., 2007—. Exec. v.p. Nat. Am. Ins. Co., Chandler, Okla., 1987-2006, Austin, Tex., 1999-2003; exec. v.p., bd. dirs. Chandler Ins. Ltd., Cayman Islands, 1985-2004. Dir., past pres. Gateway to Prevention and Recovery, 1994-98. Mem. Nat. Assn. Ins. Women (pres. Atlanta chpt. 1978-79, Woman of Yr. 1979-80). Republican. Episcopalian. Office: 1900 NW Expressway Ste 860 Oklahoma City OK 73118 Home Phone: 405-340-1196; Office Phone: 405-848-8888. Business E-Mail: brenda.watson@tipnational.com.

WATSON, CATHERINE ELAINE, journalist; b. Mpls., Feb. 9, 1944; d. Richard Edward and LaVonne (Slater) W.; m. Al Sicherman (div.); children: Joseph Sicherman, David Sicherman. BA in Journalism, U. Minn., 1966; MA in Teaching, Coll. of St. Thomas, 1971. Reporter Mpls. Star Tribune, 1966-72; editor Picture mag., 1972-78, Travel sect., 1978—2004; editor in chief Galena (Ill.) Gazette, 1990-91. Instr., online mentor Split Rock Arts Program, U. Minn., 1996-2006; sr. travel editor Star Tribune, 2001-04. Author: Travel Basics, 1984, Roads Less Traveled: Dispatches from the Ends of the Earth, 2005 (named Best Book Soc. Am. Travel Writers - Ctrl. States, 2001); contbr. articles to newspapers and travel mags. and books. Recipient Newspaper Mag. Picture Editor's award Pictures of Yr. Competition, 1974, awards for writing and photography Soc. Am. Travel Writers, 1983-2004, Photographer of Yr. award, 1990, Alumna of Notable Achievement award U. Minn. Coll. Liberal Arts, 1994; rsch. grant Jerome Found./Gen. Mills Found., 2004; named Lowell Thomas Travel Journalist of Yr., 1990, Lowell Thomas Bronze awards 1994, 96, 2003. Mem. Am. Newspaper Guild, Soc. Am. Travel Writers, Phi Beta Kappa, Alpha Omicron Pi.

WATSON, CHARLES M., financial consultant; b. Ft. Sill, Okla., May 6, 1952; s. Wendell D. and Saraethel Watson; m. Mary E. Green, May 22, 1976; children: Angie, Emily. BS, Ind. U., 1974. V.p. corp. accts. Coulter Corp., Hialeah, Fla., 1979—97; dir. integrated health networks Beckman Coulter, Brea, Calif., 1997—2003; fin. advisor Smith Barney, Red Bank, NJ, 2004—. Founder Monmouth Network, Middletown, NJ, 2004—; chmn. How Firm a Foundation, Middletown, 2005—; chmn. fundraising Calico Cat Refurbishment, Middletown, 1999—2001; profl. tennis tchr. USPTA; stewardship chmn. vestry Christ Ch., Middletown, 2004—06. Mem.: No. Monmouth C. of C., Rotary (sgt.-at-arms Red Bank Club 2005—). Episcopalian. Avocation: Karate. Office: Smith Baney 55 Broad St Red Bank NJ 07701

WATSON, CHRISTOPHER, dean; BA, Bowdoin Coll.; MEd, Boston U. Regional dir. Found. for Foreign Study, Cambridge, Mass., 1991—94; assoc. dir. internat. admissions Boston U., 1994—2000; assoc. dir. admission Princeton U., NJ, 2000—01, assoc. dir. admissions NJ, 2001—05, dir. admissions NJ, 2006—07; dean undergraduate admissions Northwestern U., Evanston, Ill., 2007—. Office: Northwestern U Office of Dead of Undergrad Admissions 633 Clark St Evanston IL 60208 *

WATSON, CLAUDE ARMSTEAD, counselor; b. Marshall, Tex., Mar. 9, 1937; s. Andrew Polk and Lena Holloway Watson; m. Marie Ann Coleman, Jan. 21, 1994; children: Claudia Marie Coleman, Stephanie Colleen Swan, Andrea Maude Kelly, Mary Teresa Ricketts. BA, Wiley Coll., Marshall, Tex., 1955—61. Social ins. adminstr. Social Security Adminstrn., Dallas, 1964—87; exec. dir. Dallas County Cmty. Action Com., Inc., 1974—2006, 1989—90, Pvt. Industry Coun. Greater Dallas, Inc., 1990—91; spl. projects coord. Dallas Area Agy. Aging, 2003—. Bd. pres. Sickle Cell Anemia Found. Dallas, Inc., 1987—91; cons. to gen. supt. Wilmer-Hutchins Ind. Sch. Dist., Tex., 2002—03. Columnist (weekly newspaper) The Dallas Examiner, Perspectives. Founder, pres. Right Alternatives for People, Inc., Dallas, 1979—2001; mem. state bd. ACLU, Austin, 1994—96. Sp-4, e-4 US Army, 1958—61, Asian nations. Finalist Quarter World Speech Competition, Toastmasters Internat., 1979; recipient Silver Beaver award, Boy Scouts Am., 1983, Whitney M. Young Svc. award, 1993, Regional Dirs. Quality award, US Bur. Census, 2000, For Polit. Commentary award, Nat. Newspaper Publishers Assn., 2005. D-Liberal. Meth. Avocations: literature, bridge. Home: 1811 Dolores Way Dallas TX 75232-4102 Home Phone: 972-228-3701. Office Fax: 214-871-7442. Personal E-mail: kascole@sbcglobal.net. Business E-Mail: cwatson@ccgd.org.

WATSON, DENNIS WALLACE, microbiologist, educator; b. Morpeth, Ont., Can., Apr. 29, 1914; came to U.S., 1938, naturalized, 1946; s. William and Sarah (Verity) W.; m. Alicemay Whittier, June 15, 1941; children: Catherine W., William V. BSA, U. Toronto, 1934; MS, Dalhousie U., 1937; PhD, U. Wis., 1941, DSc (hon.), 1981. Rsch. assoc. U. Wis., 1942, asst. prof., 1946-49; vis. investigator Rockefeller Inst., 1942; investigator Connaught Lab. Med. Rsch. U. Toronto, 1942-44; assoc. prof. U. Minn., Mpls., 1949-52, prof., 1953-63, head dept. microbiology, 1964-84, Regents prof. microbiology, 1980-84, Regents prof. emeritus, 1984—. Vis. prof. Med. Sch. U. Wash., 1950; mem. Commn. Immunization Armed Forces Epidemiology Bd., 1946-59; bd. sci. counselors, divsn. biol. standards NIH, 1957-59, allergy and immunology study sect., 1954-58; chmn. tgn. grant com. Inst. Allergy and Infectious Diseases, 1964, adv. coun., 1967-71; microbiology panel Office Naval Rsch., 1963-66 Mem. editl. bd.

Infection and Immunity, 1971-72; editl. cons. Medcom Faculty Medicine, 1973— Bd. dirs. Nat. Found. Infectious Diseases, 1976-81; vice chmn. Am. Soc. Microbiology Found., 1973. With AUS, 1944-46. Recipient Rsch. Career award USPHS, 1962-64; Spl. Rsch. fellow, 1960-61 Mem. AAAS, Am. Assn. Immunologists, Am. Chem. Soc., Am. Acad. Microbiology (vice chmn. bd. govs. 1967), Am. Soc. Microbiology (pres. 1969, v.p. Found. 1972-73), Internat. Endotoxin Soc. (hon., life), Soc. Exptl. Biology and Medicine (coun. 1977-79, pres. 1976-77), Lancefield Soc., Sigma Xi, Phi Zeta. Home: 2106 Hendon Ave Saint Paul MN 55108-1419 Office: U Minn Med Sch Dept Microbiology PO Box 196 Minneapolis MN 55440-0196 Personal E-mail: watsondw651@msn.com.

WATSON, DIANE EDITH, congresswoman; b. LA, Nov. 12, 1933; d. William Allen Louis and Dorothy Elizabeth (O'Neal) Watson. AA, L.A. City Coll., 1954; BA, UCLA, 1956; MS, Calif. State U., LA; PhD, Claremont Grad. Sch., 1987. Tchr., sch. psychologist L.A. Unified Sch. Dist., 1960-69, 73-74; assoc. prof. Calif. State U., LA, 1969-71; health occupations specialist Bur. Indsl. Edn., Calif. Dept. Edn., 1971-73; mem. L.A. Unified Sch. Bd., 1975-78, Calif. Senate from dist. 26, 1978-98, chairperson health and human svcs. com.; US amb. to Micronesia US Dept. of State, 1999-2001; mem. U.S. Congress from 33d Calif. dist., 2001—, mem. govt. reform com. and internat. rels. com. Mem. Legis. Black Caucus, edn. com., budget and fiscal rev. com., criminal procedure com., housing and land use com. Calif State Sen.; del. Dem. Nat. Conv., 1972—; mem. Dem. Nat. Com.; mem. exec. com. Nat. Conf. State Legislators Author: Health Occupations Instructional Units-Secondary Schools, 1975, Planning Guide for Health Occupations, 1975; co-author: Introduction to Health Care, 1976. Recipient Mary Church Terrell award, 1976, Brotherhood Crusade award, 1981, Black Woman of Achievement award NAACP Legal Def. Fund, 1988; named Alumnus of Yr., UCLA, 1980, 82. Mem. Calif. Assn. Sch. Psychologists, L.A. Urban League, Calif. Tchrs. Assn., Calif. Commn. on Status Women. Democrat. Roman Catholic. Office: US Ho Reps 125 Cannon HOB Washington DC 20515-0533 also: 4322 Wilshire Blvd Ste 302 Los Angeles CA 90010 Office Phone: 202-225-7084, 323-965-1422. Fax: 202-225-2422; Office Fax: 323-965-1113. *

WATSON, DOC (ARTHEL LANE WATSON), vocalist, guitarist, banjoist, recording artist; b. Deep Gap, NC, Mar. 2, 1923; s. General Dixon and Annie (Greer) Waston; m. Rosa Lee Carlton; children: Eddy Merle(dec.), Nancy Ellen. Ind. rec. artist, touring performer. First appearance Boone (N.C.) Fiddler's Conf., rec. artist Folkways in 1960's, signed with Vanguard Records, 1964, recorded for United Artists, Columbia, Poppy, Sugar Hill, Verve and Flying Fish labels; performer: Newport Folk Festival, 1963, Smithsonian Inst., White House, 1980, Carnegie Hall, 1985; toured in Africa for Dept. State, 1970, also Europe and Japan, albums (many with Merle Watson) Southbound, Red Rocking Chair, The Guitar Album, Riding the Midnight Train (Grammy award for Best Traditional Folk album, 1986), Portrait, Songs for Little Pickers, On Praying Ground, 1999 (Grammy award for Best Traditional Folk Album, 1990); performer (music): (films) Places in the Heart. Recipient Grammy award for Best Traditional Recording, 1973, 1974, 1986, 1990, Grammy award for Best Country Instrumental Performance, 1979, 2007, Grammy award for Best Traditional Folk Album, 2002, Grammy award for Lifetime Achievement, 2004, NC award, State of NC, 1985, Carolina prize NY Times Corp., 1985, Nat. Medal of Arts, Pres. of U.S. with NEA, 1997, Nat. Heritage award, NEH, 1988. Office: care Folklore Prodns 1671 Appian Way Santa Monica CA 90401-3258 Fax: 310-458-6005. E-mail: info@folkloreproductions.com.

WATSON, DONALD CHARLES, JR., cardiothoracic surgeon, educator; b. Fairfield, Ohio, Mar. 15, 1945; s. Donald Charles and Pricilla H. Watson; m. Susan Robertson Prince, June 23, 1973; children: Kea Huntington, Katherine Anne, Kirsten Prince. BA in Applied Sci., Lehigh U., 1968, BSME, 1969; MSME, Stanford U., 1969; MD, Duke U., 1972; MBA, Vanderbilt U., 1992. Diplomate Am. Bd. Thoracic Surgery, Am. Bd. Surgery. Intern Stanford U. Med. Ctr., Calif., 1972-73, resident in cardiovasc. surgery Calif., 1973-74, resident in surgery Calif., 1976-78, chief resident in heart transplant Calif., 1978-79, chief resident in cardiovasc. and gen. surgery Calif., 1978-80; clin. assoc. surgery br. Nat. Heart and Lung Inst., 1974-76, acting sr. surgeon, 1976; assoc. cardiovasc. surgeon dept. child health and devel. George Washington U., Washington, 1980-84, asst. prof. surgery, asst. prof. child health and devel., 1980-84, attending cardiovasc. surgeon dept. child health and devel., 1984-89, assoc. prof. surgery, 1984-89; assoc. prof. pediats. U. Tenn.-Memphis, 1984-90, prof. surgery, 1990—2006, prof. pediats., 1990—2006, chmn. cardiothoracic surgery, 1984-99, assoc. chief med. officer, 1999—2001. Mem. staff Le Bonheur Children's Med. Ctr., Memphis, 1984—2006, chmn. cardiothoracic surgery, 1984-99; cons. in field; instr. advanced trauma life support; profl. cons., program reviewer HHS. Contbr. chpts., numerous articles, revs. to profl. publs. Bd. dirs. Airlift Hope Am., Internat. Children's Heart Found., Child Health Alliance Mid-South. Served to lt. comdr. USPHS, 1974-76. Smith Kline & French fellow Lehigh U., 1967; NSF fellow Lehigh U., 1968; univ. interdepartmental scholar and univ. scholar Lehigh U., 1968. Fellow Am. Coll. Cardiology, ACS; mem. Am. Assn. Thoracic Surgery, Soc. Thoracic Surgeons, So. Thoracic Surg. Assn., Andrew G. Morrow Soc., Norman E. Shumway Soc. (multiple bd. dirs.), NIH Alumni Assn., Stanford U. Med. Alumni Assn., Stanford U. Alumni Assn., Lehigh U. Alumni Assn., Smithsonian Assocs., U. Tenn. Pres.'s Club, LeBonheur Pres's Club, Pilots Internat. Assn., Nat. Assn. Flight Instrs., Aircraft Owners and Pilots Assn., Biltmore Forest Country Club, Phi Beta Kappa, Tau Beta Pi, Pi Tau Sigma, Phi Gamma Delta. Republican. Presbyterian. Achievements include established a regional referral center for the treatment of congenital heart disease. Avocations: golf, sailing, mountain climbing, flying. Office Phone: 828-277-0677. Personal E-mail: dcwbusi@aol.com. Business E-Mail: dwutmem@aol.com.

WATSON, DONALD RALPH, architect, dean, writer, artist; b. Providence, Sept. 27, 1937; s. Ralph Giles W. and Ethel (Fletcher) Pastene; m. Marja Palmqvist, Sept. 8, 1966 (div. Jan. 1984); children: Petrik, Elise; m. Judith Criste, Jan. 3, 1986 (dec. Oct. 8, 2000). AB, Yale U., 1959, BArch, 1962, MEd, 1969. Lic. architect Nat. Council Archtl. Registration Bds. Architect Peace Corps, Tunisia, 1962-64; archtl. cons. Govt. of Tunisia, 1964-65; pvt. practice, Trumbull, Conn., 1969—; dean Sch. Architecture, Rensselaer Poly. Inst., Troy, NY, 1990-95, prof., 1990—2001. Frederick C. Baker vis. prof. U. Oreg., 1995; chmn. environ. design program, Yale U., 1979-90; vis. prof. Yale U., 1995-2000. Author: Designing and Building a Solar House, 1977, Energy Conservation Through Building Design, 1979, Climatic Design, 1983, Energy Design Handbook, 1993; editor-in-chief Time Saver Standards: Architectural Design Data, 1997, 2005, Time-Saver Standards: Urban Design, 2003. Bd. dirs. Save the Children Fedn., 1979-82. Recipient Honor Design award Conn. Soc. Architects, 1974, Honor Design award region AIA, 1978, 84, 1st award Owens Corning Energy Conservation Bldg. Design Program, 1983, Excellence in housing award Energy Efficient Bldg. Assn., 1988, Lifetime Achievement award Passive and Low Energy Architecture, 1990, Best in Show Watercolors, Soc. Creative Artists, 1999, Green Bldg. Design award NESEA, 2002, Disting. Prof. award ACSA, 2002, James Haecker Disting. Leadership award, Archtl. Rsch. Centers Consortium, 2004; Assn. of Collegiate Schs. of Archtecture/Am. Metals Climax rsch. fellow, 1967-69; rsch. fellow Rockefeller Found., 1978. Fellow: AIA. Home and Office: 54 Larkspur Dr Trumbull CT 06611-4652

WATSON, DOUG, information technology executive; Asst. v.p. mgmt. info. sys. Bacardi-Martini; v.p. info. sys., chief info. officer Bacardi USA Inc., Miami, Fla. Named one of Premier 100 IT Leaders, ComputerWorld, 2003. Office: Bacardi USA Inc 2100 Biscayne Blvd Miami FL 33137-5028 Office Phone: 305-573-8511. Office Fax: 305-573-7507.

WATSON, E BRUCE, science educator; b. Nashua, NH, Oct. 16, 1950; m. M. Susan Watson; 1 child, Jonah. Student, Williams Coll., 1968—69; BA in Geology, U. N.H., 1972; PhD in Geochemistry, MIT, 1976. Postdoctoral fellow Carnegie Inst., 1976-77; from asst. to full prof. Rensselaer Polytechnic Inst., Troy, NY, 1977—, chmn. dept. earth and environ. scis., 1990-95, Inst. prof. sci., 1995—. Vis. scientist Max Planck Inst. Chemistry, Mainz, Germany, 1984; original mem. highly-cited rschrs. ISI Thomsen Sci.; Qualline lectr. U. Tex. at Austin, 2004. Assoc. editor Geochimica et Cosmochimica Acta, 1985-88; editor petrology and geochemistry Neues Jahrbuch fur Mineralogie, 1988-96; editor Chem. Geology, 1991-95; mem. editl. bd. Geochimica et Cosmochimica Acta, 1997—; contbr. articles to profl. jours., chpts. to books. Vis. rsch. fellow Macquarie U., Australia, 1981, geochemistry fellow European Assn. Geochemistry and Geochem. Soc.; named Disting. alumnus U. N.H., 1999. Fellow AAAS, Am. Geophys. Union (fellows com. 1992-95, nominating com. 1997-98, R.A. Daly lectr. 1999, W.H. Bucher medal), Mineral. Soc. Am. (pres. 1998), Geol. Soc. Am. (Arthur L. Day medal 1998); mem. NAS, Geochem. Soc. (budget com. 1990, councilor 1991-94, F.W. Clarke medal 1983, V.M. Goldschmidt award 2005), ISI Thomsen Sci. (original mem.). Office: Rensselaer Polytechnic Inst 110 8th St Troy NY 12180-3522 Office Phone: 518-276-8838. Business E-Mail: watsoe@rpi.edu.

WATSON, EASTER JEAN, psychotherapist, financial program consultant; b. Leland, Miss., Mar. 15, 1948; d. Tom and Louise B. Watson; m. Boisie Lee Watson, Oct. 24, 1965 (div. Apr. 1983); children: LaTonia Deonnette, Lorenzo Tomas, Derek Ondrea(dec.). BA in Sociology & Minority Studies, U. Notre Dame, 1974; MSW, Atlanta U., 1987. Psychotherapist Oak Park & River Forest Mental Health Ctr., Ill., 1991—92; program cons. child welfare program Assn. House of Chicago, Chicago, Ill., 1993—94; exec. dir. Easter Watson, MSW & Assoc., Chicago, Ill., 1994—95; child welfare admin. Kinara Com. Svcs., Chicago, Ill., 2000—01; psycho-therapist cons. Self employed, Chicago, Ill., 2001—03; asst. dir. of child welfare YMCA of Metro, Chicago, Ill., 1996—2000. Cons. alternative sch. Chgo. Pub. Sch., Mgmt. Planning Inst., Chgo., 2001—; field instr. Chgo. State U., Chgo., 2001—, Nat. Louis U., Chgo., 2001—, Roosevelt U., 2001. Coord. (parent conference) The Power of Parents, 2003. Mem. Operation PUSH, Chgo., 1996—. Grantee, U. Notre Dame, 1972. Protestant.

WATSON, EMMA, actress; b. Oxford, England, Apr. 15, 1990; Actor: (films) Harry Potter and the Sorcerer's Stone, 2001, Harry Potter and the Chamber of Secrets, 2002, Harry Potter and the Prisoner of Azkaban, 2004, Harry Potter and the Goblet of Fire, 2005, Harry Potter and the Order of the Phoenix, 2007; appearances (TV) The Oprah Winfrey Show, 2002, The Tonight Show with Jay Leno, 2002. Office: c/o Leavesden Studios PO Box 3000 Leavesden WD2 7LT England *

WATSON, GEORGE HENRY, JR., broadcaster, journalist; b. Birmingham, Ala., July 27, 1936; s. George Henry and Grace Elizabeth (Carr) W.; m. Ellen Havican Bradley, July 13, 1979; children: George H., III, Ellen Havican (dec.). BA, Harvard U., 1959; MS, Columbia U., 1960. Reporter Washington Post, 1960-61; corr. ABC News, 1962-75, Moscow bur. chief, 1966-69, London bur. chief, 1969-75, v.p., Washington bur. chief, 1976-80; v.p., mng. editor Cable News Network, 1980; v.p. news ABC News, NYC, 1981-85, exec. in charge ABC News Viewpoint, 1981-85, v.p., Washington bur. chief, 1985-93, sr. contbg. editor, 1993-2001; freelance broadcast journalist. Served with U.S. Army, 1958. Recipient Peabody award, 1982, DuPont Columbia award, 1983, nat. news Emmy award, 1984. Mem. Radio Television News Dirs. Assn., Soc. Profl. Journalists, Nat. Press Club, Overseas Press Club (award for best television documentary 1971, citation for excellence 1974), Nat. Press Club, Com. to Protect Journalists, Fgn. Policy Assn., Cosmos Club. Personal E-mail: ghwjr727@hotmail.com.

WATSON, GEORGE W., energy executive; BSEE, Queen's U., Kingston, Can., 1970, MBA in Fin. Mktg., 1972; grad. advanced mgmt. program, Harvard U., 1988. With Can. Imperial Bank Commerce, Toronto; asst. gen. mgr. worldwide, oil and gas divsn. Calgary, 1981; dir. fin. Dome Petroleum, v.p. fin.; v.p., treas. Amoco Can.; pres., CEO Intensity Resources, 1988-90; CFO TransCanada, 1990-93, pres., 1993-99, CEO, 1994-99; ptnr. Northridge Can. Inc., 1999—2002. CEO Critical Control Solutions Corp.; chmn. bd. dirs. Badger Daylighting Inc.; chmn. Zebas Energy Corp., Calgary Olympic Devel. Assn.; bd. dirs. Can. Spirit Resources Corp., Teekay LNG LLP, Repeat Seat Ltd., Recap Energy Inc., Signal Energy Corp. Bd. dirs. Queen's U., TGS N. Am. Real Estate Investment Trust. Address: PO Box 122 Niagara Falls Canada L2E 6S8 Office Phone: 403-705-7510. Business E-Mail: george.watson@criticalcontrol.com. E-mail: georgewwatson@shaw.ca.

WATSON, GEORGIANNA, retired librarian; b. Lock Haven, Pa., Feb. 18, 1949; d. George and Anna (Eisenhower) Rhine; children: Sharga Nicolle, George Winfield-Martin. BS in Edn., Lock Haven State U., 1971; MLS, Brigham Young U., Provo, Utah, 1978; M in Pub. Adminstrn., John Jay Coll. Criminal Justice, NYC, 1986. Lic. realtor NY. Tchr. Mifflin County Sch. Dist., Lewistown, Pa., 1971—72; libr. Shiprock Boarding Sch. Bur. Indian Affairs, N.Mex., 1972—79, libr. Ft. Sill Indian Sch. Lawton, Okla., 1979—80; libr. U.S. Mil. Acad., West Point, 1980—83, head pub. svcs., libr., 1983—2006; ret., 2006. Owner The Paint Pony, Walden, NY; weekly talk show host WTBQ Radio; real estate salesperson Exclusively Equine Properties, Goshen, NY, 2006—. Mem. Am. Quarter Horse Assn., Internat. Arabian Horse Assn., Am. Paint Horse Assn., NY State Horse Coun. (Mid-Hudson dir.), Pi Alpha Alpha. Republican. Home: 8 St Michaels Ln Walden NY 12586-2466 Office: Exclusively Equine Properties LLC 349 Sarah Wells Tr Goshen NY 10924 Office Phone: 845-294-4224. Personal E-mail: gwatso@hvc.rr.com.

WATSON, GLENN ROBERT, lawyer; b. Okla., May 2, 1917; s. Albert Thomas and Ethel Amelia W.; m. Dorothy Ann, Feb. 25, 1945; 1 dau., Carol Ann. Student, East Cen. State U., Okla., 1933-36; LL.B., Okla. U., 1939. Bar: Okla. 1939, Calif. 1946. Pvt. practice law, Okla., 1939-41; founding ptnr. Richards, Watson & Gershon, Los Angeles, 1946—2002; ret., 2002; city atty. Industry, Calif., 1958-65, 78-83, Commerce, Calif., 1960-61, Cerritos, Calif., 1956-64, Victorville, Calif., 1962-63, Carson, Calif., 1968-2000, Rosemead, Calif., 1960-76, Seal Beach, Calif., 1972-78, South El Monte, Calif., 1976-78, Avalon, Calif., 1976-80, Artesia, Calif., 1976-97. Served with USNR, 1942-46. Mem. ABA, Los Angeles County Bar Assn., Am. Judicature Soc., Lawyers Club of Los Angeles (past pres.), Los Angeles World Affairs Council, Internat. Cir., La Canada C. of C. (past pres.), Order of Coif, Phi Delta Phi, Delta Chi. Home: 522 Paulette Pl La Canada CA 91011 Office: Richards Watson & Gershon 355 S Grand Ave 40th Flr Los Angeles CA 90071-3101 E-mail: gwatson@rwglaw.com.

WATSON, HARLAN L(EROY), federal agency administrator, physicist, economist; b. Macomb, Ill., Dec. 17, 1944; s. Joseph Carroll and Helen Louise (Sanders) Watson; m. Sharon Ann Rinkus Diguette, Apr. 22, 1977. BA in Physics, Western Ill. U., 1967; PhD in Physics, Iowa State U., 1973; MA in Econs., Georgetown U., 1981. Postdoctoral fellow Argonne (Ill.) Nat. Lab., 1973-75; project scientist, then sr. scientist B-K Dynamics, Inc., Rockville, Md., 1975-78; tech. staff TRW Energy Systems Planning Group, Mc Lean, Va., 1978-80; profl. staff mem. subcom. on energy nuclear proliferation and govt. processes Com. on Govtl. Affairs, U.S. Senate, Washington, 1980-81; tech. and sci. cons. Com. on Sci. and Tech., U.S. Ho. of Reps., 1981-86; rep. energy and environ., coord. Com. on Sci., Space and Tech., U.S. Ho. of Reps., 1986-89; sci. adviser to sec. Dept. Interior, Washington, 1989-93, dep. asst. sec. for sci.-water and sci., 1989-90, prin. dep. asst. to sec. for water and sci., 1990-93; rep. spl. asst. subcom. energy, com. sci., space, tech. U.S. Ho. of Reps., Washington, 1993-95, staff dir. subcom. energy and environment, com. sci., 1995—2001; sr climate negotiator, spec rep US Dept State, Washington, 2001—. Contbr. articles to profl jours. Home: 6719 Tomlinson Ter Cabin John MD 20818-1328 Office: 2201 C St NW Rm 2480 Washington DC 20520-0001 E-mail: WatsonHL@state.gov.

WATSON, JACK CROZIER, retired state supreme court justice; b. Jonesville, La., Sept. 17, 1928; s. Jesse Crozier and Gladys Lucille (Talbot) W.; m. Henrietta Sue Carter, Dec. 26, 1958; children: Carter Crozier (dec.), Wells Talbot. BA, U. Southwestern La., 1949; JD, La. State U., 1956; completed with honor, Appellate Judges Seminar, NYU, 1974, Sr. Appellate Judges Seminar, 1980. Bar: La. 1956. Atty. King, Anderson & Swift, Lake Charles, La., 1956—58; prosecutor City of Lake Charles, 1960; asst. dist. atty. Calcasieu Parish, La., 1961—64; ptnr. Watson & Watson, Lake Charles, 1961—64; judge 14th Jud. Dist., La., 1964—72; judge ad hoc Ct. Appeals, 1st Cir., Baton Rouge, 1972—73; judge Ct. Appeals, 3d Cir., Lake Charles, 1973—79; assoc. justice La. Supreme Ct., New Orleans, 1979—96, ret., 1996; of counsel Baggett, McCall, Burgess, Watson & Gaughan, Lake Charles, 2004—. Faculty advisor Nat. Coll. State Judiciary, Reno, 1970, 73; adj. prof. law summer sch. program in Greece, Tulane U., 1988-00, 05-07; adj. prof. law So. U., Baton Rouge, 1998-99; del. NEH Seminar, 1976; La. del to Internat. Conf. Appellate Magistrates, The Philippines, 1977; mem. La. Jud. Coun., 1986-92. 1st lt. USAF, 1950-54. Mem. ABA, La. Bar Assn., S.W. La. Bar Assn. (pres. 1963), Law Inst. State of La., La. Coun. Juvenile Ct. Judges (pres. 1969-70), Am. Judicature Soc., S.W. La. Camellia Soc. (pres. 1973-74), Am. Legion (post comdr. 1963), Lake Charles Yacht Club (commodore 1974), Blue Key, Sigma Alpha Epsilon, Phi Delta Phi, Pi Kappa Delta. Democrat. Baptist. Home (Summer): Grand West Village Leadville CO 80461 Office Phone: 337-478-8888.

WATSON, JAMES DEWEY, molecular biologist, educator; b. Chgo., Apr. 6, 1928; s. James Dewey and Jean (Mitchell) W.; m. Elizabeth Lewis, 1968; children: Rufus Robert, Duncan James. BS, U. Chgo., 1947; PhD in Zoology, Ind. U., 1950; DSc (hon.), U. Chgo., 1961, Ind. U., 1963; LLD (hon.), U. Notre Dame, 1965; DSc (hon.), L.I. U., 1970, Adelphi U., 1972, Brandeis U., 1973, Albert Einstein Coll. Medicine, 1979, Hofstra U., 1976, Harvard U., 1978, Rockefeller U., 1980, Clarkson Coll., 1981, SUNY, 1983; MD (hon.), U. Buenos Aires, Argentina, 1986; DSc (hon.), Rutgers U., 1988, Bard Coll., 1991, U. Cambridge, 1993, Fairfield U., 1993, U. Stellenbosch, 1993, U. Oxford; MD, Charles Univ., Prague, 1998; DSc (hon.), Washington Coll., 1999, U. Judaism, 1999, U. Coll. London, 2000, Ill. Wesleyan U., 2000, Widener U., 2001, Dartmouth, 2001, Trinity Coll., Dublin, 2001. Rsch. fellow NRC, U. Copenhagen, 1950-51; Nat. Found. Infantile Paralysis fellow Cavendish Lab., Cambridge U., 1951-52, 55-56; sr. rsch. fellow biology Calif. Inst. Tech., 1953-55; asst. prof. biology Harvard U., 1955-58, assoc. prof., 1958-61, prof., 1961-76; dir. Cold Spring Harbor Lab., Watson Sch. Biol. Sci., NY, 1968—94, pres. NY, 1994—2004, chancellor NY, 2004—; assoc. dir. Nat. Ctr. for Human Genome Rsch., NIH, 1988-89, dir. Nat. Ctr. for Human Genome Rsch., 1989-92. Newton-Abraham vis. prof. Oxford U., 1994; inst. advisor Allen Inst. for Brain Sci., Seattle, Washington. Author: Molecular Biology of the Gene, 1965, 4th edit., 1986, The Double Helix, 1968, (with John Tooze) The DNA Story, 1981, (with others) The Molecular Biology of the Cell, 1983, 2nd edit., 1989, 3rd edit. 1994, (with John Tooze and David Kurtz) Recombinant DNA, A Short Course, 1983, 2nd edit., 1992, A Passion for DNA, 2000, Genes, Girls and Gamow, 2001, DNA: The Secret of Life, 2003. Named Hon. fellow Clare Coll., Cambridge U., hon. knight of Brit. Empire, 2002; recipient (with F.H.C. Crick) John Collins Warren prize Mass. Gen. Hosp., 1959, Eli Lilly award in biochemistry Am. Chem. Soc., 1959, Albert Lasker prize Am. Pub. Health Assn., 1960, (with F.H.C. Crick) Rsch. Corp. prize, 1962, (with F.H.C. Crick and M.H.F. Wilkins) Nobel prize in medicine, 1962, Presdl. Medal of Freedom, 1977, Kaul Found. award for excellence, 1993, Nat. Biotech. Venture award, 1993, Copley Medal, 1993, Charles A. Dana award, 1994, Lomonosov medal Russian Acad. Sci., 1995, Nat. medal of Sci., 1997, Liberty medal City of Phila., 2000, Benjamin Franklin medal for disting. achievement in scis. Am. Philos. Soc., 2001, Gairdner award for merit, 2002, Lotos Club Medal of Merit, 2004. Mem. NAS (Carty medal 1971), Am. Philos. Soc., Am. Assn. Cancer Rsch., Am. Acad. Arts and Scis., Am. Soc. Biol. Chemistry, Royal Soc. (London), Acad. Scis. Russia, Danish Acad. Arts and Scis. Achievements include co-discovery of Double-Helix DNA; has become the first person to receive his own personal genome map in 2007. Office: Cold Spring Harbor Lab PO Box 100 Cold Spring Harbor NY 11724-0100 *

WATSON, JERRY CARROLL, advertising executive; b. Greenville, Ala., Aug. 22, 1943; s. William J. and Georgia Katherine (Mixon) W.; m. Judith Zeigler Brooks, Sept. 16, 1988; 2 child, Theodore William, Hunter Brooks. BS, U. Ala., Tuscaloosa, 1967; MS, U. Va., 1995. Staff writer Phillips, Eindhoven, The Netherlands, 1967-68; mgr. mktg. Fuller & Dees Mktg., Montgomery, Ala., 1968-70; v.p. Nat. Student Mktg., Washington, 1970-73; pres. Coll. & Univ. Press, Washington, 1973-80; ptnr. Direct Response Consulting Svcs., McLean, Va., 1981-96. Bd. dirs. Foxhall Corp., The Art Co., Mustique Co. Founding mem. Am. Inst. Cancer Rsch. Mem. Direct Mktg. Assn., Non-Profit Mailer Fedn., Promotional Mktg. Assn., Nature Conservancy, Sierra Club, Falls Church (Va.) C. of C. (bd. dirs.). Avocations: forestry, gardening, astronomy, photography. Home: 850 Dolley Madison Blvd Mc Lean VA 22101-1821 Office: Direct Response Cons Svcs 6849 Old Dominion Dr Ste 300 Mc Lean VA 22101-3791 E-mail: watson@drcs.com, watson@mouselink.net.

WATSON, JOANN FORD, theology studies educator; b. Ashland, Ohio, Apr. 11, 1956; d. Laurence Wesley and Edna Lucille (Garber) Ford; m. Duane Frederick Watson, June 2, 1984; 1 child, Christina Lucille. BA, DePauw U., 1978; MDiv, Princeton Theol. Sem., 1981; PhD, Northwestern U., 1984. Ordained to ministry Presbyn. Ch. Asst. prof. hist. theology Ashland (Ohio) Theol. Sem., 1984-86, assoc. prof. theology, 1989-95, chair dept. ch. history and theology, 1989—95, 2003—, H.R. Gill prof. theology, 1996—; chaplain Grady Meml. Hosp., Atlanta, 1986-87; co-pastor Tri-Ch. Parish United Meth. Chs. Northwestern, NY, 1987-89; pastor Camroden Presbyn. Ch., Rome, NY, 1987-89; parish assoc. First Presbyn. Ch., 1985—86. Clergy commr. del. Gen. Assembly Presbyn. Ch., 1995; parish assoc. First Presbyn. Ch., Ashland, 2004—05. Author: Manna for Sisters in Christ, 1989, Mutuality in Christ, 1991, Meditations in Suffering, 1993, Study of Karl Barth's Doctrine of Man and Woman, 1995, Sister to Sister, 1998, Healed to Serve, 2001, Selected Spiritual Writings of Anne Dutton Vol. 1: Letters, 2003, Hymns, Poetry, Memoirs, Discourses, Vol. II, 2004, Vol. III, 2006, Vol. IV, 2007. Mem. Hospice Ashland County chpt., 1989—93; assoc. mem. Women's Symphony League, Ashland Symphony Orch., 1989—94; missionary vol. Mother Teresa's Missionaries of Charity, Calcutta, 1988. Recipient Outstanding Faculty Mentor of Yr. award, Ashland Sem., 2004, Disting. Alumni Hall of Fame award, Ashland H.S., 2005;, Northwestern U. fellow, 1982—84. Mem.: Am. Acad. Religion, Soc. Bibl. Lit., Nat. Assn. Presbyn. Clergywomen, Presbyn. Women in Leadership, Internat. Assn. Women Mins. (mem. exec. bd., trustee 1990—95), Phi Beta Kappa (Outstanding Faculty Mentor award 2001, 2002, Women's Achievement award, Ashland County, Ohio 2003, Outstanding Faculty

Mentor award 2004, 2005, 2007), Alpha Lambda Delta. Republican. Avocations: travel, music, water sports. Office: Ashland Theolog Sem 910 Center St Ashland OH 44805-4007 Office Phone: 419-289-5182. Business E-Mail: jwatson@ashland.edu.

WATSON, JOHN ALLEN, lawyer; b. Ft. Worth, Sept. 18, 1946; s. John and Mary (Barlow) W.; m. Patricia L. Clardy, Oct. 24, 1946; 1 child, Virginia E. BA, Rice U., 1968; JD, U. Tex., Austin, 1971. Bar: Tex. 1971. Assoc. Fulbright & Jaworski, Houston, 1971-78, ptnr., 1978—. Mem. ABA. Office: Fulbright & Jaworski LLP 1301 McKinney St Ste 5100 Houston TX 77010-3031 Home Phone: 713-459-4928; Office Phone: 713-651-5151. E-mail: jwatson@fulbright.com.

WATSON, JOHN LAWRENCE, III, former trade association executive; b. Rome, Ga., Jan. 14, 1932; s. John Lawrence and Mary (Cowen) W.; m. Dorothy Palmer McLanahan, Aug. 9, 1958; children: Mary Palmer Watson Gard, Valerie Catherine Watson Bilbrough, John Lawrence IV. BS, Auburn U., 1954. Trader-over the counter J.C. Bradford & Co., Atlanta, 1957-58; with Robinson Humphrey & Co., Atlanta, 1958-64, dept. head-over the counter, 1964-74, dir. equity trading, 1974-83, dir. capital markets, 1983-85; pres. Security Traders Assn., NYC, 1985-96, ret., 1996. Past mem. bd. visitors Babcock Sch. Mgmt. Wake Forest U.; past chmn. Parent's Coun. Wofford Coll.; life trustee Pace Acad.; former trustee Securities Industry Found. for Econ. Edn.; pres. trustees The City Ch., N.Y., 2005-. Named Man of Yr., Equities mag. Mem. Nat. Assn. Securities Dealers (dist. chmn. 1982, bd. govs. 1983-85), Am. Mus. Fin. History (trustee), Capital City Club, Piedmont Driving Club (Atlanta), Ponte Vedra Club, Sawgrass Country Club (Ponte Vedra), Univ. Club (N.Y.C.). Home: 505 Ponte Vedra Blvd Ponte Vedra Beach FL 32082-2317

WATSON, JOHN S., oil company executive; b. Oct. 1956; BA, U. of Calif., Davis, 1978; MBA, U. of Chicago, 1980. Mgr. credit card, products, investor relations Chevron, 1993—95; pres. Chevron Canada, Ltd., 1996—98; dir. Caltex Corp.; v.p. strategic planning Chevron Corp., 1998—2001, v.p. fin., CFO, 2001—. Office: Chevron Corp 6001 Bollinger Canyon Rd San Ramon CA 94583-2324

WATSON, JOYCE MORRISSA, forensic and clinical psychologist; d. Joseph Morris and B. Joyce Watson; 1 child, Matthew Joseph. BA, Maryville Coll., 1985; MSc summa cum laude, Troy State U., 1989; D magna cum laude in Psychology, Forest Inst. Profl. Psychology, 1994. Cert.: Fed. Bur. Prisons (fed. law enforcement officer) 1996; lic. psychologist Dept. Health, Fla., 1996. Sr. psychologist Fla. Dept. Corrections, Zephyrhills, 1995—96, regional mental health cons. Ft. Lauderdale, 1997—2000, dir. mental health Tallahassee, 1999—2002; staff psychologist, fed. law enforcement officer Fed. Bur. Prisons, Sumterville, Fla., 1996—97; dir. Sarasota Psychol. Svcs., Fla., 2002—. Faculty U. Sarasota, Tampa, 1997—2000; adv. coun. Governor's Commn. Mental Health and Substance Abuse, Tallahassee, 1999—2000; coun. mem. Fla. State Mental Health Planning Coun., Tallahassee, 1999—2001; bd. mem. hosp. North Fla. Reception Ctr. Hosp., Lake Butler, 1999—2001; presenter in field. Author jour. articles, book articles, essays in book. Vol. tchr. Fruitville Elem. Sch., Sarasota, 1989; vol. Bright Beginnings, Sarasota, 2003—05, Little League, Sarasota, 2005. Recipient Exceptional Performance award, Dept. Justice, Time-Off award, Bureau of Prisons; grantee, Pfizer, Glaxo Wellcome. Mem.: APA, Fla. Psychol. Assn., Soc. Personality Assessment. Avocations: show dogs, music, water sports. Office: J Morrissa Watson PsyD 4411 Bee Ridge Rd #353 Sarasota FL 34233 Business E-Mail: morrissawatson@aol.com.

WATSON, JULIAN See BLAKE, BUD

WATSON, KENNETH MARSHALL, physics professor; b. Des Moines, Sept. 7, 1921; s. Louis Erwin and Irene Nellie (Marshall) W.; m. Elaine Carol Miller, Mar. 30, 1946; children: Ronald M., Mark Louis. BS, Iowa State U., Ames, 1943; PhD, U. Iowa, Iowa City, 1948; ScD (hon.), U. Ind., 1976. Rsch. engr. Naval Rsch. Lab., Washington, 1943-46; staff Inst. Advanced Study Princeton U., 1948-49; rsch. fellow Lawrence Berkeley Lab., Calif., 1949-52, staff Calif., 1957-81; asst. prof. physics U. Ind., Bloomington, 1952-54; assoc. prof. physics U. Wis., Madison, 1954-57; prof. physics U. Calif., Berkeley, 1957-81, prof. oceanography, dir. marine physics lab. San Diego, 1981-93. Cons. Sci. Application Corp., 1981-2004; mem. US Pres.'s Sci. Adv. Com. Panels, 1962-71; adviser Nat. Security Coun., 1972-75; mem. JASON Adv. Panel, 1959-2001; sci. adv. bd. George C. Marshall Inst., 1989—. Author: (with M.L. Goldberger) Collision Theory, 2004; (with J. Welch and J. Bond) Atomic Theory of Gas Dynamics, 1966; (with J. Nutall) Topics in Several Particle Dynamics, 1970; (with Flatté, Munk, Dashen) Sound Transmission Through a Fluctuating Ocean, 1979. Mem.: Nat. Acad. Scis. Home: Unit 2008 8515 Costa Verde Blvd San Diego CA 92122-1150 Office: U Calif Marine Physics Lab La Jolla CA 92093-0213 Office Phone: 858-534-6620. Business E-Mail: kmw@mpl.ucsd.edu.

WATSON, LUCIA, chef; b. Mpls., Minn. BA in French, U. Minn.; attended, Sch. Am. Chefs. Cert. Master Sommelier. Staff 510 Groveland; kitchen head Minnetonka Art Ctr.; owner, exec. chef Lucia's Restaurant and Wine Bar, Mpls., 1985—, Lucia's Bakery and Cafe, Mpls. Bd. mem. Chef's Collaborative; mem. organic adv. task force Minn. Dept. Agr. Columnist In-Fisherman mag., 1990—; co-author: Savoring the Seasons of the Northern Heartland, 1995; author: In-Fisherman Presents...Cooking Freshwater Fish. Bd. chair Youth Farm Farmers Youth Project. Nominee Best Chef: Midwest, James Beard Found.; recipient Commitment to Cmty. award, Inst. Agr. and Trade Policy, 2006. Avocations: fishing, cooking. Office: Lucia's Restaurant and Wine Bar 1432 W 31st St Minneapolis MN 55408 *

WATSON, NOEL G., construction executive; b. Bison, SD, 1936; BSChemE, U. N.D., 1958; postgrad., Colo. Sch. Mines, 1958-60. With AMAX Inc., 1962-65, Jacobs Engring. Group, Pasadena, Calif., 1960-62, 1965—, pres., 1987—2002, CEO, 1992—2006, chmn., 2004—. Office: Jacobs Engineering Group PO Box 7084 1111 S Arroyo Pkwy Pasadena CA 91109 *

WATSON, OLIVER LEE, III, aerospace engineer, manufacturing executive; b. Lubbock, Tex., Sept. 18, 1938; m. Judith Valeria Horvath, June 13, 1964; 1 child, Clarke Stanford. BSEE, U. Tex., 1961; MSEE, Stanford U., 1963; MBA, Calif. State U., Fullerton, 1972; cert., U. So. Calif., 1980. Mgr. ballistic analysis Rockwell Internat. Autonetics Divsn., Anaheim, Calif., 1973-78, mgr. minuteman systems, 1978-83, mgr. preliminary engring., 1983-84; mgr. analysis group autonetics divsn. Rockwell Internat., Anaheim, Calif., 1984-85, mgr. aircraft sys. autonetics dept., 1985-93, dep. dir. integrated product devel. N.Am. aircraft aircraft modification divsn., 1993-94, dep. dir. engring. N.Am. aircraft modification divsn., 1994-96; dep. dir. engring. comm. and combat sys. divsn. Boeing N.Am., Anaheim, 1996-98; skills, process and metrics mgr. Comm. and Battle Mgmt., Anaheim, 1998-99; process, metrics and tools dir. Anaheim Site Engring., Integrated Def. Sys., Anaheim, Calif., 1999—, 2001—06; engring. performance metrics dir. C3 Networks Divsn., 2006—. Lectr. engring. Calif. State U., Fullerton, 1981—90, guest prof., 2005—06, mem. indsl. adv. bd., 1994—, vice-chmn., 1995—97; adv. com. Accreditation Bd. for Engring. and Tech., 2000; sec. Elec. Engring. Indsl. Adv. Bd., 2001—; spkr. in field. Co-author Digital Computing Using Fortran IV, 1982; Fortran 77, A Complete Primer, 1986; contbg. author: The World's Best Shortest Stories, 2001. Bd. dirs. Olive Little League, Orange, 1980; vol. Stanford U. Engring. Fund, Orange County, Calif., 1983, regional chmn. 1984-86, So. Calif. chmn. 1986-91; mem. Stanford Assocs., 1988—. Recipient Stanford Assocs. Centennial Medallion award, 1991; fellow N.Am. Aviation Sci.-Engring., L.A., 1962-63, Inst. Advancement Engring., L.A., 1976. Mem. IEEE (sr., sec. v.p. 1974-75, sect. chmn. 1975-76), Nat. Mgmt. Assn. (exec. advisor for fin. Boeing Anaheim chpt. 2002), Jaycees (v.p. Orange chpt. 1973-74), Rockwell-Calif. State U. Alumni Club (v.p. 1993, pres. 1993-94), Lido Sailing Club. Republican. Avocations: sailing, swimming, humor writing, scriptwriting, reading. Office: Boeing NAm C3ISR PO Box 3105 MC-CA92 Anaheim CA 92803-3105

WATSON, PATRICIA PULLUMS, school system administrator; b. Chgo., June 3, 1949; d. James and Aletha (Pearline) Pullums; m. Charles Michael Watson, Aug. 10, 1985; 1 child, Kevyn Charles. BA, Chgo.State U., 1973; MS in Edn. and Reading, Chgo. State U., 1981; MA in Adminstrn. and Supervision, Gov.'s State U., University Park, Ill., 1997; postgrad., Ill. State U., 2004—. Cert. tchr. Ill. Tchr. Theodore Herzl Sch., Chgo., 1973—74; program dir. Accounters Cmty. Ctr., Chgo., 1974—83, asst. exec. dir., 1989—98, exec. dir., 1998—2002, pres., CEO, 2002—03; head tchr., asst. prin. Accounters Prep. Acad., Chgo., 1980—89; tchr., dept. chair., program coord. Cullen Elem. Sch., Chgo., 1991—98; asst. prin. Shoesmith Elem. Sch., Chgo., 1998—. Mem. People To People Citizen Amb. Program, Spokane, Wash., 1997—. Grantee grant, Chgo. Found. for Edn., 1996. Mem.: NAACP, Chgo. Area Alliance Black Sch. Educators, Assn. Supervision and Curriculum Devel., Nat. Assn. Secondary Sch. Prins., Nat. Coun. Negro Women, Internat. Reading Assn., Nat. Alliance Elem. Sch. Prins., Chgo. Prins. and Adminstrs. Assn., Chgo. Asst. Prin. Assn., Phi Delta Kappa, Delta Sigma Theta. Avocation: golf. Home Phone: 773-471-9267; Office Phone: 773-535-1764. Office Fax: 773-535-1877. Personal E-mail: wats1612@sbcglobal.net. E-mail: ppwatson@cps.k12.il.us.

WATSON, PATTY JO, anthropology educator; b. Superior, Nebr., Apr. 26, 1932; d. Ralph Clifton and Elaine Elizabeth (Lance) Andersen; m. Richard Allan Watson, July 30, 1955; 1 child, Anna Melissa MA, U. Chgo., 1956, PhD in Anthropology, 1959. Archaeologist-ethnographer Oriental Inst.-U. Chgo., 1959—60, rsch. assoc., archaeologist, 1964—70; instr. anthropology U. So. Calif., Los Angeles, 1961, UCLA, 1961, L.A. State U., 1961; asst. prof. anthropology Washington U., St. Louis, 1969—70, assoc. prof., 1970—73, prof., 1973—2004, Edward Mallinckrodt disting. univ. prof., 1993—2004, prof. emerita, 2004—; faculty affiliate anthropology U. Mont., 2003—. Mem. rev. panel NSF, Washington, 1974-76; fellow Ctr. Advanced Study in Behavioral Scis., Stanford, Calif., 1981-82, 91-92. Author: The Prehistory of Salts Cave, Kentucky, 1969, Archaeological Ethnography in Western Iran, 1979; author: (with others) Man and Nature, 1969, Explanation in Archeology, 1971, Archeological Explanation, 1984, Girikihaciyan, A Halafian Site in Southeastern Turkey; author: (editor) Archeology of the Mammoth Cave Area, 1974, Prehistoric Archeology Along the Zagros Flanks, 1983; co-editor: The Origins of Agriculture, 1992, Of Caves and Shell Mounds, 1996, Archaeology of the Middle Green River Region, Kentucky, 2005. Recipient Arthur Holly Compton Faculty Achievement award Washington U., St. Louis, 2000, Peter H. Raven award for lifetime achievement Acad. Sci. St. Louis, 2002; grantee NSF, 1959-60, 68, 70, 72-74, 78-79, NEH, 1977-78, Nat. Geog. Soc., 1969-75, Southeastern Arch. Conf. Lifetime Achievement award, 2004. Fellow Am. Anthropol. Assn. (editor archaeology 1973-77, Disting. Lectr. award 1994, Disting. Svc. award 1996), AAAS (chair sect. H 1991-92); mem. Cave Rsch. Found., Am. Acad. Arts and Scis., Am. Philos. Soc., Soc. Am. Archaeology (exec. com. 1974-76, 82-84, editor Am. Antiquity 1984-87, Fryxell medal 1990), Assn. Paleorient (sci. bd.), Nat. Speleological Soc. (hon. life, editorial bd. bull. 1979—, Sci. award), Archaeol. Inst. Am. (Gold medal Disting. Archaeol. Achievement 1999, Pomerance award 2007), Nat. Acad. Scis. Business E-Mail: pjwatson@artsci.wustl.edu.

WATSON, PAUL, photojournalist, correspondent; b. Dec. 2, 1950; Photographer The Toronto Star, 1986—, Africa bur. chief, 1992—94, Asian bur. chief, 1994—98; staff writer L.A. Times, 1998—, South Asia bur. chief New Delhi, 2001—. Recipient Robert Capa gold medal for photography, 1993, Nat. Newspaper award for spot news photography, 1994, Pulitzer Prize for spot news photography, 1994, Nat. Newspaper award for internat. reporting, 1996, George Polk award for internat. reporting, 1999, 2000, Freedom of Press award, Nat. Press Club, 2000. Office: D 7/10 Vasant Vihar New Delhi India Fax: 91-11-2617-7-709. E-mail: paulrwatson@yahoo.com. *

WATSON, PAULA D., retired librarian; b. NYC, Mar. 6, 1945; d. Joseph Francis and Anna Julia (Miksza) De Simone; m. William Douglas Watson, Aug. 23, 1969; children— Lucia, Elizabeth AB, Barnard Coll., 1965; MA, Columbia U., 1966; MSLS, Syracuse U., 1972. Libr. reference U. Ill., Urbana, 1972—77, libr. city planning and landscape architecture, 1977—79, head documents libr., 1979—81; asst. dir. gen. svcs. U. Ill. Libr., Urbana, 1981—88, acting dir. gen. svcs., 1988—93, dir. ctrl. pub. svcs., 1989—93, asst. libr., 1993—95, dir. electronic info. svcs., 1995—2004, dir. scholarly comm., 2003—04; ret., 2004. Author: Electronic Journals: Acquisition and Management, 2003, E-Publishing Impact on Acquisition and Interlibrary Loan, 2004; contbr. articles to profl. jours. N.Y. State Regents fellow Columbia U., N.Y.C., 1965-66; Council on Library Resources profl. edn. and tng. for librarianship grantee, 1983 Mem. ALA (sec. univ. librs. sect. ALA-Assn. Coll. and Rsch. Librs. 1989-91, com. on instnl. coop., chair pub. svcs. dirs. group, 1997-99, mem. com. inst. coop./OCLC virtual electronic libr. steering com.), Ill. Library Assn. Avocation: gardening. Home: 715 W Delaware Ave Urbana IL 61801-4806

WATSON, PETER S., former federal agency administrator; married. LLB, Auckland U.; LLM, McGill U.; MIBA, West Coast U. Pvt. practice internat. and bus. law, L.A., Washington, 1976, 78-88; spl. advisor to Pres. Overseas Pvt. Investment Corp.; dir. Asian affairs NSC, Washington, 1989-91; commr. U.S. Internat. Trade Commn., 1991—96, vice chmn., 1992-94, chmn., 1994-96; sr. advisor Armitage Associates, L.C.; counsel Pillsbury Winthrop LLP; pres., CEO Overseas Private Investment Corp., 2001—05, Dwight Group, 2005—. Vis. prof. St. Peter's Coll., Oxford U., The Brookings Instn.; bd. trustees Woodrow Wilson Internat. Ctr. for Scholars, bd. visitors Peter F. Drucker Grad. Sch. of Mgmt. at Calremont Graduate U., Friend of Aukland U.; mem. advisory bd., Georgetown U. Journal of Internat. Law; didting. lecturer Georgetown U. McDonough Sch. Bus., co-chair Ar. Internat. Apointements Com. ABA; mem. Coun. Fgn. Relations Author Completeing the World Trading System: Proposals for a Millenium Round, 1999, Free Trade: Risks and Rewards, 2000, The Economic Arsenal in the War Against Terrorism, 2002; Co-author National Conformity Assessment Schemes: Non-Tariff Trade Barriers in Information Technology, 1999; Contbr. articles to profl. jours. Recipient New Zealand Order of Merit, 2002 Republican. Office: The Brookings Instn 1775 Massachusetts Ave NW Washington DC 20036

WATSON, RALPH EDWARD, internist, educator; b. Cin., Apr. 4, 1948; s. John Sherman and Evelyn (Moore) W.; m. Demetria Rencher, Sept. 9, 1972; children: Ralph Edward, Monifa. BS, Xavier U., 1970; MD, Mich. State U., East Lansing, 1976. Diplomate Am. Bd. Internal Medicine; cert. clin. hypertension specialist. Intern U. Cin. Med. Ctr., 1976-77, resident in internal medicine, 1977-79, asst. clin. prof. internal medicine, 1980-88; asst. prof. internal medicine Mich. State U., East Lansing, 1988-94, assoc. prof., 1994—. Attending physician in hypertension clinic Mich. State U., 1988-91, assoc. dir. hypertension clinic, 1991-94, dir. hypertension clinic, 1995—, program dir. transitional yr. residency, 1990-96, assoc. program dir. internal medicine residency, 1996-2003; mem. U.S. HHS Office Minority Health Resource Person Network. Fellow ACP, Internat. Soc. Hypertension in Blacks, Am Assn. Black Cardiologists; mem. Nat. Med. Assn., Am. Soc. Internal Medicine, Lansing Area Am. Heart Assn., Am. Black Cardiologists (chair rsch. com.), Am. Soc. Hypertension, Xavier U. Alumni Assn., Alpha Omega Alpha. Office: Mich State U 338B Clinical Ctr East Lansing MI 48824-1313 Office Phone: 517-353-4811.

WATSON, RAYMOND COKE, JR., engineering executive, consultant, academic administrator; b. Anniston, Ala., Aug. 31, 1926; BS, Jacksonville State U.; MSE, U. Ala.; MS, U. Fla.; MBA and PhD in Engring. Sci., Calif. Coast U. Chief engr. Dixie Svc. Co., 1948-54; head dept. physics and engring. Jacksonville State U., 1954-60; v.p. engring. and rsch. Teledyne Brown Engring., 1960-70, chief engr., chief scientist, 1990—2001; dir. continuing edn., engring. and math. U. Ala., Huntsville, 1970-76; pres., prof. engring. and math. Southeastern Inst. Tech., Huntsville, 1976—; owner RC Watson & Assocs., 1980—; pres., CEO Vision Techs. Kinetics, 2000—03. Adj. assoc. prof. U. Ala., Huntsville, 1961-70. Contbr. more than 450 articles and reports to profl. jours. Chmn. elec. engring. adv. bd. Ala. A&M U. Recipient NASA Pub. Svc. award; NSF Sci. Faculty Fellow. Mem. IEEE, AIAA, Optical Soc. Am., Ops. Rsch. Soc. Am., Inst. Mgmt. Sci., Internat. Soc. Optical Engrs., Inst. Indsl. Engrs. Achievements include research in defense systems, space systems and electro-optics. Home: 1801 Inspiration Ln SE Huntsville AL 35801-1150 Office: RC Watson & Assocs PO Box 1485 Huntsville AL 35807

WATSON, REBECCA WUNDER, federal agency administrator, lawyer; b. Chgo., Feb. 17, 1952; d. David Hart and Shirley May (Dahlin) Wunder; m. Keith C. Thomson, Oct. 6, 1979 (div. Dec. 1989); m. Gregory B. Watson, Jan. 20, 1996. BA, U. Denver, 1974, MA in LS, 1975, JD, 1978. Bar: Bar: Wyo. 1978, Colo. 1989, D.C. 1995, Mont. 1995. Law clk. U.S. Dist. Ct. for Dist. Wyo., Cheyenne, 1978-80; assoc., then ptnr. Burgess & Davis, Sheridan, Wyo., 1980-88; pvt. practice, Denver, 1988-90; asst. gen. counsel for energy policy US Dept. Energy, Washington, 1990-93; of counsel Crowell & Moring, Washington, 1993-95; ptnr. Gough Shanahan Johnson & Waterman, Helena, Mont., 1995—2002; asst. sec. land & minerals mgmt. US Dept Interior, Washington, 2002—. Contbr. author: ABA Natural Resource Law Handbook, 1993; contbr. articles to law jours. Mem. ABA (chmn. natural resource com. sect. adminstrv. law 1994-97, chmn. pub. lands com. sect. natural resources, energy and environ. law 1997-99), Wyo. Bar Assn., Mont. Bar Assn., Phi Beta Kappa. Republican. Avocations: cooking, reading, travel, hunting. Office: US Dept Interior Land and Materials Mgt 1849 C St NW Washington DC 20240 Home: 72 W Ranch Trl Morrison CO 80465-9503 Office Phone: 202-208-6734. E-mail: Rebecca_Watson@ios.doi.gov.

WATSON, RICHARD THOMAS, lawyer; b. Lakewood, Ohio, Aug. 21, 1933; s. Thomas Earl Watson and Sara Lucille (Whapham) Hadfield; m. Judith C. Briggs, Aug. 6, 1960; children: David, Andrew, Susan (dec.). AB, Harvard U., 1954, JD, 1960. Bar: Ohio 1960. Assoc. Spieth, Bell, McCurdy & Newell, Cleve., 1960, ptnr., 1965, mng. ptnr., 1987—. Bd. dirs. numerous corps. Chancellor Episcopal Diocese of Ohio, Cleve., 1986—; mem. Harvard U. com. on univ. resources, 1992—; bd. trustees Cleve. Mus. Art, 1991—. Mem. Union Club Cleve. Office: Spieth Bell McCurdy & Newell 925 Euclid Ave Ste 2000 Cleveland OH 44115-1408 Office Phone: 216-696-4700. Personal E-mail: richardtwatson@att.net.

WATSON, ROBERT FRANCIS, lawyer; b. Houston, Jan. 9, 1936; s. Louis Leon and Lora Elizabeth (Hodges) W.; m. Marietta Kiser, Nov. 24, 1961; children: Julia, Melissa, Rebecca. BA, Vanderbilt U., 1957; JD, U. Denver, 1959. Bar: Colo. 1959, U.S. Dist. Ct. (no. dist.) Tex. 1967, U.S. Supreme Ct. 1968, Tex. 1973, U.S. Ct. Appeals (5th cir.) 1973, U.S. Dist. Ct. (so. dist.) Tex. 1980, U.S. Ct. Appeals (11th cir.) 1981. Law clk. U.S. Dist. Ct. Colo., 1960-61; trial atty. SEC, Denver, 1961-67, asst. regional adminstr. Ft. Worth, 1967-72, regional adminstr., 1972-75; ptnr. Law, Snakard & Gambill, P.C., Ft. Worth, 1975-98, of counsel, 1998—2005, shareholder, 2005—; exec. v.p., gen. counsel First Command Fin. Svcs., Inc., Ft. Worth, 1998—2005. Counsel City of Ft. Worth Police Investigation Commn., 1975; spl. counsel Office Atty. Gen. State Ariz., 1977-78. Contbr. articles to profl. jours. Mem. Ft. Worth Crime Commn., 1987-93. Honoree 27th Ann. Rocky Mountain State-Fed.-Provincial Securities Conf. Fellow: Coll. of State Bar Tex., U. Denver Law Sch. Alumni Coun., Colo. Bar Assn., Tex. Bar Found. (life), Tarrant County Bar Assn. (charter), Ft. Worth Club; mem.: ABA, Tarrant County Bar Found., Tex. Bus. Law Found. (bd.dirs. 1988—93), State Bar Tex., Fed. Bar Assn., Shady Oaks Country Club (Ft. Worth), Phi Delta Phi. Republican. Presbyterian. also: Law Snakard & Gambill PC 1600 W 7th St Ste 500 Fort Worth TX 76102-3819 Office Phone: 817-878-6374. Business E-Mail: bwatson@lawsnakard.com.

WATSON, ROBERT JOE, retired health facility administrator, retired career officer; b. Wellington, Kans., Nov. 12, 1934; s. Charles Bruce and Marguerite B. (Scholes) W.; m. Ursula Eschenroeder, Dec. 26, 1983; children: Stephanie Watson-Zollinger, Stacy Watson Bruce, Susannah Watson Gold; stepchildren: Jurgen Wanke, Claudia Beeck. MS in Edn., Kans. State Tchrs. Coll., 1963; MBA, U. Hawaii, 1969; MHA, George Washington U., 1973, EdD, 1976; student, Command-Gen. Staff Coll., 1973, U.S. Army War Coll., 1986. Commd. 2nd lt. U.S. Army, 1963, advanced through grades to col., 1989; stationed at Tripler Army Med. Ctr., Honolulu, 1967-69, USARV Surgeons Office, Long Binh, Vietnam, 1969-70, Surgeon Gen.'s Office, Washington, 1970-74, Walter Reed Med. Ctr., Washington, 1974-76, Acad. Health Svcs., Ft. Sam Houston, Tex., 1976—80, 68th Med. Group, Ziegenberg, Germany, 1980-82, U.S. Army Hosp., Ft. Riley, Kans., 1982-84, 34th Gen. Hosp., Augsburg, Germany, 1984-87; assoc. dean USA Med. Field Svc. Sch., Ft. Sam Houston, Tex., 1987—89; assoc. dir. Student Health Ctr. U. Fla., Gainesville, 1989—2005; ret., 2005. Fellow Am. Coll. Healthcare Execs. (adv., regent 1982-84). Episcopalian. Avocations: tennis, golf, gardening. Home Phone: 352-371-8365.

WATSON, ROBERT WINTHROP, poet; b. Passaic, NJ, Dec. 26, 1925; s. Winthrop and Laura Berdan (Trimble) W.; m. Elizabeth Ann Rean, Jan. 12, 1952; children: Winthrop, Caroline. BA, Williams Coll., 1946; postgrad., U. Zurich, 1947; MA, Johns Hopkins, 1950, PhD in English, 1955. Instr. English Williams Coll., 1946, 47-48, 52-53, Johns Hopkins, 1950-52; mem. faculty U. N.C., Greensboro, 1953—, prof. English, 1963-90. Vis. poet, prof. English Calif. State U., Northridge, 1968-69 Author: (poetry) A Paper Horse, 1962, Advantages of Dark, 1966, Christmas in Las Vegas, 1971, Selected Poems, 1974, Island of Bones, 1977, Night Blooming Cactus, 1980, The Pendulum: New and Selected Poems, 1995; (novels) Three Sides of the Mirror, 1966, Lily Lang, 1977, (art book) Betty Watson Paintings, 1999; co-founder The Greensboro Rev., 1966. Swiss-Am. exch. fellow, 1947; grantee Nat. Endowment for Arts, 1973; recipient Am. Scholar Poetry prize, 1959, Lit. award Am. Acad. Inst. Arts Letters, 1977. Home: 4321 Galax Trail Greensboro NC 27410

WATSON, ROBERTA CASPER, lawyer; b. Boise, Idaho, July 11, 1949; d. John Blaine and Joyce Lucile (Mercer) C.; m. Robert George Watson, July 22, 1972; 1 child, Rebecca Joyce. BA cum laude, U. Idaho, 1971; JD, Harvard U., 1974. Bar: Mass. 1974, U.S. Dist. Ct. Mass. 1975, U.S. Supreme Ct. 1979, U.S. Ct. Appeals (1st cir.) 1979, U.S. Tax Ct. 1979, Fla. 1985, U.S. Dist. Ct. (mid. dist.) Fla. 1985, U.S. Dist. Ct. (so. dist.) Fla. 1987. Assoc. Peabody & Brown, Boston, 1974-78, Mintz, Levin, Cohn, Ferris, Glovsky & Popeo, Boston, 1978-84; sr. dir. Wolper Ross & Co., Miami, 1983-85; assoc. Trenam, Kemker, Scharf, Barkin, Frye, O'Neill & Mullis, P.A., Tampa, Fla., 1985-87, ptnr., 1988—. Co-author: A Physician's Guide to Professional Corporations; co-editor-in-chief COBRA Adv. Newsletter, 1997-2000; contbr. articles to profl. jours. Pres. Performing Arts Ctr. Greater Framingham, Mass., 1983; bd. dirs., Northside Mental

Health Ctr., 1987—, pres. 1999-2001; trustee Unitarian Universalist Found., Clearwater, Fla., 1986—; bd. dirs. Dist. 6 Cmty. Health Purchasing Alliance, pers. com. chair, 1998-2000. Named Bd. Mem. of Yr. Fla. Cmty. Mental Health, 1994; listed in Best Lawyers in Am., 1995-. Mem.: ABA (chair employee benefit com sect. taxation 1995—96, chair employee benefits interest group health law sect. 1998—2001, chair joint com. on employee benefits 2002—03), Fla. West Coast Employee Benefits Coun. (bd. dirs. 1996—2003, treas. 1997—98, v.p 1998—2001, pres. 2001—02), Am. Coll. Employee Benefits Counsel (charter mem.), Tampa Club (com. mem. 2006—07), Harvard Club (bd. dirs. West Coast Fla. chpt., sec./treas. 2007), Order Ea. Star. Democrat. Avocations: music, metaphysics, Lincoln historian, genealogy. Home: 55 Martinique Ave Tampa FL 33606-4029 Office: Trenam Kemker Scharf Barkin Frye O'Neill & Mullis PA 2700 Bank of Am Plz 101 E Kennedy Blvd Tampa FL 33602 Office Phone: 813-227-7487. Business E-Mail: rcwatson@trenam.com.

WATSON, RUBIE S., museum director; BS in Archaeology and Anthropology, U. Calif., Berkeley; MS in Anthropology, Rice U.; PhD in Social Anthropology, London Sch. Econs. Assoc. prof. anthropology, acting dir. Asian Studies program U. Pitts.; assoc. curator Peabody Mus. Archeology & Ethnology, sr. lectr. dept. anthropology Harvard U., Cambridge, Mass., 1992-95, assoc. dir., then Howells dir. Peabody Mus., 1995—. Author several books including Inequality Among Brothers: Class and Kinship in South China, 1985; editor: Memory, History, and Opposition under State Socialism, 1994; co-editor: Marriage and Inequality in Chinese Society, 1990, Harmony and Counterpoint: Ritual Music in Chinese Context, 1996. Fellow: Am. Acad. Arts. & Sci. Office: Peabody Mus Archeology Harvard U 11 Divinity Ave Cambridge MA 02138-2019

WATSON, S. MICHELE, school nurse; b. Selma, Ala., Apr. 21, 1965; d. Kenneth and Linda (Bishop) Wilds; m. H. Alan Watson, May 30, 1987. AAS, Cleveland State Community Coll, Tenn., 1987, AS, 1985. RN, Tenn. ICU staff Meml. Hosp., 1987-88; emergency rm. staff Cleveland (Tenn.) Cmty. Hosp., 1988; team leader Bradley Meml. Home Health, Cleveland, 1988-2001; sch. nurse Cleveland City Schs., 2001—06; nurse St. Mary's Hosp., 2006—. Home: 316 Mountain Crest Dr La Follette TN 37766 Business E-Mail: watson343@bellsouth.net.

WATSON, S.A., lawyer, retired judge; b. Hot Springs, Ark., July 11, 1942; s. Sterl A. and Naomi Pauline (Thrasher) W.; m. Wanda Batt, May 2, 1968; children: Angel Watson Brothers, Clinton Jeremy. JD, U. Ala., 1966. Bar: Ala. 1967, U.S. Dist. Ct. Ala. 1968, U.S. Supreme Ct. 1970. Assoc. Humphrey, Lutz & Smith, Huntsville, Ala., 1967-68; asst. dist. atty. 23d Jud. Cir., Huntsville, Ala., 1968-69, chief asst. dist. atty., 1969-72, dist. judge, 1972-74, cir. judge, 1974-87; ptnr. Hornsby, Watson, Hornsby and Blackwell, Huntsville, Ala., 1988—. Chair Madison County jud. commn. 23d Jud. Cir., 1978-83; faculty advisor Nat. Jud. Coll., Reno, 1982; spl. judge Ala. Ct. Criminal Appeals, Montgomery, 1983; spl. justice Ala. Supreme Ct., Montgomery, 1996-97; mem. faculty trial advocacy tng. program La. State U. Sch. Law, 1996, 97, 99, 2001. Home: 1929 Cherry Tree Rd Gurley AL 35748-9318 Office: Hornsby Watson Hornsby and Blackwell 1110 Gleneagles Dr SW Huntsville AL 35801-6404

WATSON, SHARON GITIN, psychologist; b. NYC, Oct. 21, 1943; d. Louis Leonard and Miriam (Myers) Gitin; m. Eric Watson, Oct. 31, 1969; 1 child, Carrie Dunbar. BA cum laude, Cornell U., 1965; MA, U. Ill., 1968, PhD, 1971. Psychologist City NY Prison Mental Health, Riker's Island, 1973-74, Youth Svcs. Ctr., LA County Dept. Pub. Social Svcs., 1975-77, dir. clin. svcs., 1978, dir., 1978-80; exec. dir. Crittenton Ctr. for Young Women and Infants, LA, 1980-89, Assn. Children's Svcs. Agys. So. Calif., LA, 1989—92, LA County Children's Planning Coun., 1992—99; cons. LA County Chief Exec. Office, 2001—04, Edn. Coordinating Coun., 2004—; mem. LA City Commn. for Children, Youth and Their Families, 2000—06, LA County Children's Planning Coun., 2001—. Mem. LA delegation Pres.'s Summit for Am.'s Future, 1997. Mem. Commn. for Children's Svcs. Family Preservation and Family Support Policy Com., 1989—99, Interagy. Coun. Child Abuse and Neglect Policy Com., 1993—99, Mayor's Com. on Children, Youth and Families, 1993—95; bd. dirs. Adolescent Pregnancy Childwatch, 1985—89, LA Ednl. Partnership, 1999—2003, LISC Health Sector, 1996—99, LA Roundtable for Children, 1988—94; trustee LA Ednl. Alliance for Restructuring Now, 1992—99. Recipient award honoree, LA County Children's Planning Coun. 'Improving Children's Lives', 2001. Mem.: Assn. Children's Svcs. Agys. So. Calif. (sec. 1981—83, pres. elect 1983—84, pres. 1984—85), Calif. Assn. Svcs. for Children (sec.-treas. 1983—84, pres. elect 1985—86, pres. 1986—87), US Figure Skating (bd. dirs. 1992—2006, chmn. sanctions and eligibility 1993—96, membership com. 1996—99, strategic planning com. 2000—02, regional vice chmn. competitions com. 2000—02, sec. 2002—06, mem. exec. com. 2002—06, nat. competition judge: singles, pairs, and synchronized skating), US Olympics Com. (Jr. Olympics com. 1998—2000), Pasadena Figure Skating Club (pres. 1985—87, 1989—90), So. Calif. Inter-Club Assn. of Figure Skating Clubs (vice chair 1989—91, chair 1991—93). Home and Office: 4056 Camino Real Los Angeles CA 90065-3928 Personal E-mail: sharonla12@aol.com.

WATSON, SOLOMON BROWN, IV, lawyer, publishing executive; b. Salem, NJ, Apr. 14, 1944; s. Solomon Brown and Denise Amelia W.; m. Bernadette Aldrich, Mar. 18, 1967 (div.); children: Katitti Madrid, Kira Pallis (twins); m. Brenda J. Wilson, Apr. 28, 1984. BA in English, Howard U., 1966; JD, Harvard U., 1971. Bar: Mass. 1972, N.Y. 1977. Assoc. Bingham, Dana & Gould, Boston, 1971-74; with legal dept. The N.Y. Times Co., NYC, 1974—76, asst. sec., 1976—79, corp. sec., asst. gen. counsel, 1979-89, gen. counsel, 1989-90, v.p., gen. counsel, 1990-96, sr. v.p., gen. counsel, sec., 1996—2005, sr. v.p., chief legal officer, 2006—. Active Vols. Legal Svc., Jobs for Youth Inc., until 1989; v.p. N.Y. Vietnam Vets. Leadership Program, Inc., until 1992, Agent Orange Assistance Fund, Vets. Adv. Bd. Lt. U.S. Army, 1966-68. Decorated Bronze Star with oak leaf cluster, Army Commendation medal with oak leaf cluster and V; recipient Nat. Equal Justice award Legal Def. Fund, 2002. Mem. ABA (com. on corp. law depts., mem. task force on corp. responsibility 2002—), Nat. Bar Assn., Assn. Bar City N.Y., Mass. Bar Assn., Newspaper Assn. Am. (mem. legal affairs com.), N.Y. Stock Exch. Office: NY Times Co 229 W 43rd St New York NY 10036-3959 Office Phone: 212-556-7534. Business E-Mail: watsons@nytimes.com.

WATSON, STANLEY ELLIS, clergyman, small business owner; b. New Orleans, July 25, 1957; s. Joseph and Dorothy (Jones) W. EdB, Jarvis Christian Coll., Hawkins, Tex., 1977; MRE, Tex. Christian U., Ft. Worth, 1979; spl. edn., So. U. A&M, Baton Rouge, 1986; grad., U.S. Acad. Pvt. Investigation, 1991; DD (hon.), Charter Ecumenical Ministries, 1994; student in Christian Counseling, Christian Bible Coll. and Sem., 2005—. Cert. tchr.; registered notary Mich.; lic. pvt. investigator, La. Asst. min. Jarvis Christian Coll., Hawkins, Tex., 1974-77; tchr. pub. sch., Daingerfield, Tex., 1977-78; sr. pastor Truevine Christian Ch., 1977—79; asst. min. Park Manor Christian Ch., Chgo., 1980-81; asst. mgr. K- Mart, Shreveport, La., 1981-82; min. United Christian Ch., Jackson, Miss., 1982-83; tchr. pub. sch., Napoleonville, La., 1986-87, Zachary, La., 1987-88; min. Vt. Christian Ch., Flint, Mich., 1988—92, sr. pastor, 1990; assoc. min. Buena Vista Bapt. Ch., St. James, La. Owner, mgr. Watson Diversified Fin. Co., 1989—, Watson Detective Agy., Donaldsonville, La., 1992—; v.p. DVY Sys., Inc., 1997—; CEO Watson and Julien Cmty. Mission, Inc., Donaldsonville, La.; clin. pastoral counseling, christian counseling, 2001.e Mem. NAACP, NEA. Recipient Presdl. citation Nat. Assn. for Equal Opportunity in Higher Edn.; Christian Women's fellow, 1975-77, St. Louis Bd. Edn. fellow, 1977-79, Tex. Christian U. Brite Div. Sch. scholar, 1977; Jarvis Christian Coll. cert. of Honor and Merit, 1974-77; named Rev. Stanley Watson Day City of Flint, Mich., 1989, Disting. Alumnus, Jarvis Christian Coll., 1995. Mem. Nat. Assn. Investigative Specialists, Am. Inst. Profl. Bookkeepers, Am. Fin. Coord. Assn. (fin. coord.), Christian Counselors Assn., Nat. Assn Investigative Specialist, Nat. Assn. Federated Tax Preparers, Am. Soc. Notaries, Aircraft Owners and Pilots Assn. Coun. for Exceptional Children, Forgotten Man Ministries, Jarvis Christian Coll. Alumni Assn. (v.p.), NAACP, Urban League of Flint, Urban Coalition of Greater Flint, Flint C. of C., Internat. Reading Assn., NEA, Am. Sailing Assn., Phi Beta Sigma, Kappa Delta Pi. Mem. Tex. Christian U. Alumni Assn. Democrat. Avocations: beekeeping, collecting coins, stamps, sports cards, coffees. Home and Office: PO Box 668 Donaldsonville LA 70346-0668 Office Phone: 225-473-3364. Personal E-mail: jarvis19771@yahoo.com.

WATSON, STEVEN L., investment company executive; Pres., CEO Valhi Corp., 2002—, dir., 1998—. Vice chmn. bd. Kronos Worldwide, 2004—; bd. dir. CompX, Keystone, TIMET. Office: Valhi Inc 5430 Lyndon B Johnson Fwy Ste 1700 Dallas TX 75240 Office Phone: 972-233-1700. *

WATSON, STEWART CHARLES, construction executive; b. Brock, Sask., Can., Sept. 17, 1922; s. Samuel Henry and Elva Jane (St. John) W.; m. Irene Lillian Ahrens, Aug. 4, 1943; children: Judith Gail (Mrs. David Stafford), Wendy Carolyn (Mrs. Rocco Amuso), Ronald James, Candyce Louise. Student, U. Buffalo. With Acme Steel & Malleable Iron Works, Buffalo, 1940—42, Acme Hwy. Products, Buffalo, 1946—55, internat. mktg. mgr., 1955—69; pres. Watson-Bowman Assocs. Inc., Buffalo, 1970—, Kinematics, 1984—. Chmn. bd. Air Stewart Inc.; Internat. lectr. on kinetics of civil engring. structures; mem. U.S. Transp. Rsch. Bd.; bd. dirs. Internat. Bridge of Peace for Bering Strait Crossing. With AUS, 1943-45, ETO. Fellow Am. concrete Inst. (dir. 1984—, Delmar Bloehm award 1984, Charles S. Whitney medal 1987, hon. mem.); mem. ASTM, NAS, Internat. Jts. and Bearings Rsch. Coun. (chmn. 1988—), Internat. Activities Commn., Masons (32 degree), Shriners. Home: 3 Chicory Ln East Amherst NY 14051

WATSON, THOMAS C., lawyer; b. Poplar Bluff, Mo., Feb. 26, 1945; s. William C. and Dorothy E. (Whitson) Watson; children: Thomas, Nathan, Edward. BS, U. Memphis, 1967, MEd, 1968; JD, Washington U., St. Louis, 1972. Bar: Mo. 1972, DC 1973. Assoc. Morgan, Lewis & Bockius, Washington, 1973-78, ptnr., 1978-79, Crowell & Moring, Washington, 1979-95, Watson & Renner, Washington, 1996—. Avocations: hiking, bicycling, computers, hunting. Office: Watson & Renner 1400 16th St NW Ste 350 Washington DC 20036 Office Phone: 202-737-6301. Personal E-mail: tw@w-r.com.

WATSON, THOMAS ROGER, lawyer; b. Concord, NH, May 14, 1951; s. Roger Edward and Mary (Hannigan) W. BA in Polit. Sci. cum laude, U. N.H., 1973; JD, Franklin Pierce Law Ctr., 1978. Bar: N.H. 1978, U.S. Dist. Ct. N.H. 1978, U.S. Ct. Appeals (1st cir.) 1978, Maine 1982, U.S. Dist. Ct. Maine 1982, U.S. Supreme Ct. 1986. Ptnr. Tybursky & Watson, Portsmouth, N.H., 1979-86, Tybursky, Watson & Harman, Portsmouth, 1987-88, Taylor, Keane, Blanchard, Lyons & Watson, P.A., Portsmouth, 1988-94, Watson, Lyons, & Bosen, P.A., Portsmouth, 1994-99, Watson & Bosen, P.A., Portsmouth, 2000—01, Watson, Bosen, Harman, Venci & Lemire, P.A., Portsmouth, 2001—04, Watson & Lemire, P.A., Portsmouth, 2004—05, Wiggin & Nourie, PA, Portsmouth, 2005—. Del. N.H. Constl. Conv., Concord, 1974. Mem. Maritime Heritage Commn., 1986-95, City of Portsmouth Hist. Dist. Commn., 1992, City of Portsmouth Planning Bd., 1992-94; bd. dirs. N.H. Small Bus. Devel. Ctr., 1993-95, N.H. Main St. Ctr., 1998-2002, sec., 2001-02; mem. adv. bd. Ballet New England, 1997—; bd. advisors N.H. Small Bus. Devel. Ctr., 1992-95; bd. trustees Strawberry Banke Mus., 2000-06, sec., 2001-02, chmn., 2002-04. Named Portsmouth Citizen of Yr., 1995. Mem. ABA, ATLA (state del. 1996-2005, chair-elect 1997-98, chair 1998-99, exec. com. 1998-99, co-chair coordinating com. on state rels. 1999-2000, mem. pub. affairs com. 1999-2003, mem. key person com., 2003—, bd. govs. 2005-, Outstanding State Del. 1997, Wiedeman-Wysocki citation of excellence, 1999, 2000, 2002), NH Bar Assn. (bd. govs. 1985-90), NH Trial Lawyers Assn. (bd. govs. 1989—, sec. 1982-92, treas. 1993-94, pres. elect 1994-95, pres. 1995-96, chair legis. com. 1992-95, 96-2000, exec. com. 1992-, recipient Pres.'s award 1993, 97, 2007, Spl. Recognition award 2000, Bd. Govs. award 2006), Rockingham County Bar Assn. (Profl. award 2001), Franklin Pierce Law Ctr. Alumni Assn. (pres. 1985-86), NH Bar Found. (bd. govs. 1987-90), Greater Portmouth C. of C. (bd. dirs. 1988-92, chmn. 1990-92, Portsmouth Citizen of Yr. 1995), Portsmouth Hist. Soc. (trustee 1994-99, pres. 1995-97), Portsmouth Atheneum (propr. 1991-). Office: Wiggin & Nourie PA PO Box 469 Portsmouth NH 03802-0469 Office Phone: 603-629-4703. Business E-Mail: twatson@wiggin-nourie.com.

WATSON, WILLIAM DOUGLAS, astrophysicist; b. Memphis, Tenn., Jan. 12, 1942; s. William Douglas and Antoinette Lovejoy Watson; m. Paula D. DeSimone, Aug. 23, 1969; children: Lucia Anne, Elizabeth Lovejoy. BS in Physics, MIT, 1960—64, PhD in Physics, 1964—68. Rsch. assoc. Ctr. Radioastronomy & Space Rsch., Cornell U., Ithaca, NY, 1970—72; asst. prof. physics, asst. prof. astronomy U. Ill., Urbana, 1972—74, assoc. prof. physics, assoc. prof. astronomy, 1974—77, prof. physics, prof. astronomy, 1977—2002, rsch. prof. physics, 2002—. Home: 715 W Delaware Ave Urbana IL 61801 Office: Univ Ill Loomis Lab 1110 W Green St Urbana IL 61801 Home Phone: 217-367-0712; Office Phone: 217-333-7240.

WATSON-BOONE, REBECCA A., dean, researcher, library and information scientist, educator; b. Springfield, Ohio, Mar. 7, 1946; d. Roger S. and Elizabeth Boone; m. Dennis David Ash, 1967 (div. 1975); m. Frederick Kellogg, 1979 (div. 1988); m. Peter G. Watson-Boone, May 26, 1989. Student, Earlham Coll., 1964-67; BA, Case Western Res. U., 1968; MLS, U. N.C., 1971; PhD, U. Wis., 1995. Asst. reference libr. Princeton (N.J) U., 1970-76; head cen. reference dept. U. Ariz., Tucson, 1976-83, assoc. dean Coll. Arts and Scis., 1984-89. Loaned exec. Ariz. Bd. Regents, 1988-89; pres. Ctr. for Study of Info. Profls., 1995—2002. Author: Constancy and Change in the Worklife of Research University Librarians, 1998, A Good Match: Library Career Opportunities for Graduates of Liberal Arts Colleges, 2007; contbr. articles to profl. jours. Mem. ALA (div. pres. 1985-86, councilor 1988-92), NAFE, Assn. for Libr. and Info. Sci. Edn. Mem. Religious Soc. Of Friends. Office: 30 Camino de la Vina Vieja Placitas NM 87043 Business E-Mail: rebeccawb@earthlink.net.

WATT, DOUGLAS (BENJAMIN WATT), writer, drama critic; b. NYC, Jan. 20, 1914; s. Benjamin Douglas and Agnes Rita (Neimann) W.; m. Ray Mantel, Nov. 5, 1937 (div.); children— Richard David, James Douglas; m. Ethel Madsen, Aug. 13, 1951; children— Patricia, Katherine. AB, Cornell U., 1934. Copy boy N.Y. News, 1936-37, radio columnist, 1937-40, drama reporter, 1940-71, sr. drama critic, 1971-87, critic-at-large, 1987-93; staff writer New Yorker mag., 1946-95; profl. song writer; columnist Small World, 1955-70. Nominating com. Tony Awards, Pulitzer Awards, Theater World Awards; co-founder Drama Desk; chmn. Astarre Awards. Pres. Hampton Animal Shelter, 1965-79. Served with USAAF, World War II. Mem. ASCAP, N.Y. Drama Critics Circle (pres. 1975-77) Clubs: Dutch Treat (N.Y.C.) (bd. govs.). Home: 27 W 86th St New York NY 10024-3615 E-mail: patricia_watt@msn.com. *To say one has achieved success, except perhaps in isolated instances, is an exercise in vanity and contrary to man's experience. At best, some satisfaction can be gained in one's career, and then almost always because of intense effort.*

WATT, (ARTHUR) DWIGHT, JR., computer programming and microcomputer specialist; b. Washington, Jan. 25, 1955; s. Arthur Dwight and Myrtle Lorraine (Putnam) W.; m. Shari Elizabeth Gambrell, July 30, 1988. BA, Winthrop U., Rock Hill, SC, 1977, MBA, 1979; EdD, U. Ga., Athens, 1989. Cert. computer and internet profl. Inst. Cert. Computer Profls., Microsoft; cert. home fire arms safety, NRA; cert. A+ personal computer technician, CompTIA; cert. sys. engr., sys. adminstr., office user specialist instr.; i-net plus cert. Comptia; Network + cert.; cert. network adminstr. and acad. instr., Cisco; Server + cert. CompTIA. Data processing instr. York Tech. Coll., Rock Hill, SC, 1977-78; computer ctr. asst. Winthrop U., Rock Hill, SC, 1976-79; data processing instr. Brunswick Coll., Ga., 1979-80; system operator, asst. programmer Sea Island Co., The Cloister, Ga., 1981; pvt. practice data processing cons. Swainsboro, Ga., 1981; computer programming/microcomputer specialist instr. Swainsboro Tech. Inst., 1981-96; sr. programmer/analyst Policy Mgmt. Sys. Corp., Columbia, SC, 1996-97; microcomputer specialist instr. Athens Tech. Coll.-Elbert County Campus, Elberton, Ga., 1997-2001; chmn. IT dept. Heart of Ga. Tech. Coll., Dublin, 2001—05; CIO Ga. Healthcare Sys., Atlanta, 2001; instr. Peirce Coll., Phila., 2005—, So. Wesleyan U., Central, SC, 2005—06, Savannah River Coll., Augusta, Ga., 2006; dir./instr. database program Northwestern Tech. Coll., Rock Spring, Ga., 2007—. Chmn. exec. bd. computer curriculum Ga. Dept. Tech. and Adult Edn., 1990-92, 2002-05, exec. bd. computer curriculum, 1994-96, vice chair, 2000-02, CIS cons. for curriculum, 2006—07; chmn. East Ctrl. Ga. Consortium for Computer Occupations, 1990-96; co-facilitator CIS curriculum rev. and update Ga. Tech. Colls., 2001; spkr. in field; cons. in field. Author: District Revenue Potential and Teachers Salaries in Georgia, 1989, Structured COBOL for Technical Students, 1998; co-author: District Property Wealth and Teachers Salaries in Georgia, 1990, Factors Influencing Teachers Salaries: An Examination of Alternative Models, 1991, Local Wealth and Teachers Salaries in Pennsylvania, 1992, School District Wealth and Teachers' Salaries in South Carolina, 1993, Test Yourself A+ Certification Practice Exams, 1998, GDTAE CIS Curriculum Standards and Guides Revision Problems, 2001. Chmn. Emanuel County chpt. ARC, Swainsboro, 1989-90, 92-93, bd. dirs., 1989-96; pres. United Meth. Men. Swainsboro, 1984-86; trustee Greater Swainsboro Tech. Inst. Found., Inc., 1995-96; bd. dirs. Emanuel Arts Coun., 2004-07. Recipient Nat. Tech. Tchr. of Yr. finalist award Am. Tech. Edn. Assn., 1994; Olympic Cmty. Hero Torchbearer, 1996 Mem. Inst. Cert. Computing Profls., Ga. Bus. Edn. Assn. (dir. dist. 1 1986, 96, dist. sec.-treas. 1993-95, dist. 1 dir.-elect 1995-96, Dist. 1 Postsecondary Tchr. Yr. 1985, State Postsecondary Tchr. Yr. 1995), Profl. Assn. Ga. Educators, Swainsboro Jaycees (Outstanding Young Citizen 1985, treas. 1984-89, pres. 1987-88, pres. S.E. Ga. Jaycee Fair 1995, treas. S.E. Ga. Jaycee Fair 1993-94), Ga. Jaycees (v.p. area C 1988-89, chaplain 1989-90, dir. region 6 1990-91, chmn. state shooting edn. 1991-92, chair Internat. BB Gun Match Championship 1999, co-chair match 2000, treas. match 2002), US Jr. C. of C. (nat. rep. shooting edn. program 1992-95, Shooting Edn. State Program Mgr. Yr. 1992, webmaster Internat. BB Gun Championship match 1999—), Swainsboro-Emanuel County C. of C. (webmaster 2002—), Ga. Kiwanis (tech. chair, webmaster 2002-2007), Emanuel Artist Guild (v.p. 2003—05), Swainsboro Kiwanis (bd. dirs., 2005—07, webmaster, 2003—), Walker County C. of C., Ft. Ogolthorne Kiwanis. Methodist. Home: PO Box 1637 206 Hereford Rd Swainsboro GA 30401 Office Phone: 706-764-3837. Personal E-mail: dwight-watt@att.net.

WATT, JOSEPH MICHAEL, state supreme court justice; b. Austin, Tex., Mar. 8, 1947; m. Cathy Watt; children: Justin, Christopher, Jennifer, Michael. BA in History, Tex. Tech U., 1969; JD, U. Tex., 1972. Bar: Tex. 1972, Okla. 1974. Pvt. practice, Altus, Okla., 1972-85; judge Dist. Trial Ct., 1985-91; gen. counsel to gov. State of Okla., Oklahoma City, 1991-92; justice Okla. Supreme Ct., Okahoma City, 1992—2003, chief justice, 2003—. Liaison to Okla. Bar Assn. Okla. Supreme Ct., 1997—98; mem. Appellate Div. of Ct. on Judiciary, 1997—98, Truth in Sentencing Commn., Supreme Ct. Long Range Planning Commn.; chmn. Supreme Ct. Com. for Time Standards. Mem.: Okla. Bar Assn. Office: Okla Supreme Ct State Capitol Rm 245 Oklahoma City OK 73105 Office Phone: 405-521-3848. Fax: 405-521-6982. E-mail: joseph.watt@oscn.net. *

WATT, KENNETH EDMUND FERGUSON, zoology educator; b. Toronto, July 13, 1929; s. William Black Ferguson Watt and Irene Eleanor (Hubbard) Dodd; m. Genevieve Bernice Bendig, Oct. 28, 1955; children: Tanis Jocelyn, Tara Alexis. BA with honor, U. Toronto, 1951; PhD in Zoology, U. Chgo., 1954; LLD, Simon Fraser U., 1970. Biometrician Rsch. div. Dept. Lands and Forests, Ont., Canada, 1954-57; sr. biometrician Can. Dept. Agr., Ottawa, Ont., 1957-60; head, statis. rsch. and svcs. Canadian Dept. Forestry, Ottawa, 1960-63; from assoc. prof. to prof. Dept. Zoology, U. Calif., Davis, 1963-93. Author: Ecology and Resource Management, 1968, Principles of Environmental Sciences, 1973, Understanding the Environment, 1982, Taming the Future, 1991. Recipient Gold medal Entomol. Soc., 1969. Achievements include development of new approach to forecasting future based on exhaustive statistic testing of nonlinear math. equations to long runs of historical data; discovery that change through time in real world systems violates Markov principles. Home: 2916 Quail St Davis CA 95616-5711 Office: U Calif Dept Evolution & Ecology Davis CA 95616 Office Phone: 530-750-3253. Personal E-mail: kenwatt@sbcglobal.net. *The actual causes of present events are much further back in time than most people suspect. Failure to understand this is why forecasting is such a disaster area.*

WATT, MELVIN LUTHER, congressman, lawyer; b. Steele Creek, NC, Aug. 26, 1945; m. Eulada Paysour; children: Brian, Jason. BS in Bus. Adminstrn., U. NC, Chapel Hill, 1967; JD, Yale U. Law Sch., 1970; degree (hon.), NC A&T State U., Johnson C. Smith U., Bennett Coll. Atty. Ferguson, Stein, Watt, Wallas, Adkins, & Gresham, 1971-92; mem. NC State Senate, 1985-86; co-owner East Towne Manor, 1989—; mem. US Congress from 12th NC dist., 1993—, mem. fin. svcs. com., 1993—, mem. judiciary com., 1993—, chmn. oversight and investigations subcommittee, chmn. Congl. Black Caucus, 2004—07, mem. joint econ. com. Pres. Mecklenburg County Bar. Active Ctrl. Piedmont CC Found., Legal Aid of Southern Piedmont, NC NB Cmty. Devel. Corpn., Auditorium-Coliseum-Civic Ctr. Authority, United Way, Mint Mus., Family Housing Svcs., Pub. Edn. Forum, Dilworth Cmty. Devel. Assn., Cities in Schs., Housing Authority Scholarship Bd., Morehead Scholarship Selection Com.; bd. visitors Johnson C. Smith U. Named one of 100 Most Influential Black Americans, Ebony mag., 2006. Mem. NAACP (life), NC Assn. Black Lawyers, NC Acad. Trial Lawyers, Charlotte C. of C. (sports action coun.), West Charlotte Bus. Incubator, Inroads Inc., Phi Beta Kappa. Democrat. Presbyterian. Office: US House Reps 2236 Rayburn House Office Bldg Washington DC 20515-3312 Office Phone: 202-225-1510. Office Fax: 202-225-1512. *

WATT, RONALD G., archivist; b. Spring Canyon, Utah, Jan. 2, 1939; s. George L. and Norma L. Watt; m. Barbara Fluckiger, Jan. 1, 1940; children: Ronda Matthew, Andrew, Gardner, April, Kennan. BA, Utah State U., Logan, 1963; MA, Utah State U., 1967; PhD, U. Minn., Mpls., 1975. Cert. archivist Calif., 1989. Social studies tchr. Canbar HS, Price, Utah, 1964—65; history instr. So. Utah State Coll., Cedar City, 1966—68; archivist hist. dept. LDS Ch., Salt Lake City, 1972—. Author: (book) A History of Carbon County, 1997, City of Diversity, A History of Price, Utah, 2001. Mem.: Cert. Archivists (treas. 1991—93), Utah Manuscripts Assn. (Dr. Everett L. Cooley Distinguished Archival Career award 2005), Utah State Hist. Soc. (bd. editors 2000—, Nick Yengich Editors Choice award 2001), Soc. Am. Archivists (chmn. subcom. world mission records 1982—85, editl. com. religious archives newsletter 1983—87, program com. newsletter 1984—85), Conf. Intermountain Archivists (newsletter editor 1976—80, coun. mem. 1980—83, pres. 1983—84, chmn. nominating com. 1984—85, mem. nominating com. 1992—93). Democrat. Mem. Lds Ch. Avocations: photography, writing, travel. Home: 4493 Thayn Dr Salt Lake City UT 84120 Office: LDS Ch Family and Ch History Dept 50 E N Temple Salt Lake City UT 84150

WATT, STEPHANIE DENISE, musician, educator, department chairman; d. Edmund Hudson and Joan Elizabeth (Patterson) Watt. BFA in Music Performance, LI U., 1984, MA in Composition and Performance, 1988, MS in Computer Sci. and Engring., 1999. Adj. asst. prof. music LI U., C.W. Post Campus, Brookville, NY, 1988—97, assoc. prof. music, 1997—; adj. asst. prof. music Suffolk County CC, Ammerman Campus, Selden, NY, 1988—97; adj. asst. prof. music Dowling Coll., Oakdale, NY, 1989—91; guest lectr. in music history Alvin Ailey Am. Sch. Dance, NYC, 1996—98. Founder EastWest Sch. Performing Arts, NY, 1979—2006; coord. seminar divsn. LI U. Chamber Music Program, Brookville, 1994—97; dir. piano studies LI U., C.W. Post Campus, 1988—, co-dir. student concert series, 1990—96, dir. theory studies, 1999—; adjudicator LI Philharm. Young Artist Piano Competition, 1994—2004, Music Lovers Club Young Artist Competition, 1994—2006, 8th and 9th NY Young Artist Piano and Violin Competition, 2005, 06; piano master classes Müvészeti Szakközepiskola és Gimnázium, Szombathely. Author: Information Theory Analyses of Bach Chorales and a Learning Classifier System, 1999; musician: (CD recording on Capstone Records) Duo for Cello and Piano by Allen Brings, 2006; dancer (dance exhbn.) Argentine Tango & Salsa Exhbn.; performer: Camerata Pro Musica, 2000, Carnegie Hall, 2005, The Hecksher Mus. Art, 2005, Park Ave. United Meth. Ch., 2005, Brick Gallery, 2005, LI U., C.W. Post Campus, 2005, 2006, Clarinet & Piano Concert, 2006, Concert Tour of Hungary, Communidad de Palermo Symphony Orch., 2006; guest artist, clinician LI Choral Festival and Inst., 2004, 2005, (DuoLeo performace) Weill Hall Carnegie Hall, NYC, 2005, Park Ave. United Meth. Ch., 2005, LI U., C.W. Post Campus, Brookville, 2005, 2006, (DuoLeo performace and solo performance) Brik Gallery, Catskills, NY, 2005, (Martino and Watt duo performace) Steinway Hall, NYC, 2006, Blueport Libr., 2006, LI Philharm. Choir, 2006, (DuoLeo performace one-woman shows) The Heckscher Mus. Art, Huntington, NY, 2005; dancer (dance exhbns.) Babylon Village Fair, NY, 2005, New Life Cmty. Ch., Sachem, NY, 2006, LI U., C.W. Post, 2006; featured Strings mag., 2002; contbr. articles to profl. confs. Recipient First Pl. award Foxtrot Exhbn., Kings Ball Dancesport Championships, SI, NY, 2001, First Pl. award Am. Tango Exhbn., 2001, First Pl. award Viennese Waltz Exhbn., Stardust Ball Competition, Melville, NY, 2002, First Pl. award Open Tango Exhbn., Stardust Ball, Melville, NY, 2002, Cert. of Recognition music performance, Mayor of Inc. Village of Hempstead, 1995, Second Pl. award slow waltz exhbn., NJ Open Championships, Rutherford, 2003, Third Pl. award Dance Team Exhbn., Northeastern Open Championships, Weston, Conn., 2003. Mem.: AAUW (assoc.), NY State Music Assn. (assoc.), Coll. Music Soc. (assoc.), Phi Eta Sigma. Achievements include research in the history of the tango and its political influence in Argentina. Home Phone: 631-491-9399; Office Phone: 516-299-2474. Office Fax: 516-299-2884. Personal E-mail: stefani1435@aol.com.

WATTA, DAVID ANTHONY, product manager; b. Detroit, Jan. 8, 1967; s. Watta D. Phillip and Elizabeth V. Watta. BA, We. Mich. U., Kalamazoo, 1993; MFA, Emerson Coll., Boston, 1996. Prodr. new media The Atlantic Monthly, Boston, 1993—97; mgr. internet program Banking website, North Palm Beach, Fla., 1997—99; exec. prodr. site Hard Rock Cafe Internat., Orlando, Fla., 1999—2000; sr. mgr. program Intel, Hillsboro, Oreg., 2000—06; dir. product mgmt. AARP, Washington, 2006—. Mem.: Mensa (life). Home: 4410 Churchman Ct Alexandria VA 22310 Office Phone: 202-434-3557. Personal E-mail: davewatta@aol.com.

WATTEL, HAROLD LOUIS, economics professor; b. Bklyn., Sept. 30, 1921; s. David Max and Carolyn (Abrams) W.; m. Sara Gordon, Sept. 1, 1946; children: Karen, Jill. BA, Queens Coll., 1942; MA, Columbia U., 1947; PhD magna cum laude, New Sch. Social Research, 1954. Jr. economist WPB, 1942; economist Dept. Agr., 1946; econ. cons. Boni, Watkins & Mounteer, 1952; economist Bur. Bus. and Community Research, Hofstra U., 1954, 57, dir., 1957-58; prof. econs. Bur. Bus. and Community Rsch., Hofstra U., 1957-86, prof. emeritus, 1986—, chmn. dept. econs., 1957-61, chmn. div. bus., 1961—, dean Sch. Bus., 1965-73. Econ. cons. to consumer counsel Staff Gov. N.Y., 1956—58; cons. N.Y. State Moreland Commn. on Alcoholic Beverage Control Law, 1963—64, Legislative Refernce Bur. U. Hawaii, 1966, Schenley Industries, 1967—, Ralston Purina Co., 1967—, Am. Can Co., 1965—; econ. cons. Nat. Millinery Planning Bd., 1959—70; ednl. cons. U.S. Merchant Marine Acad., Kings Point, 1972; cons. Bulova Watch Co., 1975—82. Author ann. publ.: The Millinery Industry; Editor: Planning in Higher Education, 1975, Chief Executive Officer Compensation, 1978, The Gross Personal Income Tax, 1981; Contbr. chpts. to books, encys., dictionaries, also reports.; Editor, contbr.: L.I. Bus, 1954-59. Mem. Comprehensive Health Planning Coun., 1970-75; bd. dirs., v. p., N.Y. State unit Am. Lung Assn.; pres. Nassau-Suffolk unit; bd. dirs. Comprehensive Health Planning Coun., Nassau-Suffolk, N.Y., N.Y. State Citizen Coun., Regional Med. Program Nassau-Suffolk, consumer rep., bd. dirs. Island Peer Rev. Orgn., 1990; treas. Parodneck Found.; chair Pronet Citizens Advocacy Ctr., 1997—. Lt. USNR, 1942-46. Edn. fellow, 1949; Hazen Found. fellow, 1952; Ford Found. regional fellow, 1960 Mem. AAUP (chpt. pres. 1953), Middle Atlantic Assn. Colls. Bus. Adminstrn. (pres. 1970-71), Am., Met. econs. assns., N.Y. State Environ. Health Assn. (v.p.), Island Peer Rev. Orgn. (consumer/AARP rep. 1990—), Pi Gamma Mu, Omicron Chi Epsilon, Beta Gamma Sigma (hon. assoc.). Home: 181 Shepherd Ln Roslyn Heights NY 11577-2525 Office: Hofstra U Dept Econ Hempstead NY 11550 E-mail: phdhlw@juno.com.

WATTENMAKER, RICHARD JOEL, archivist, director; b. Phila., Feb. 22, 1941; s. Nathan H. and Frances (Rynes) W.; m. Eva Augusta Oscarsson, June 25, 1968; children: Adrian Ezra, Barnaby Leo. BA, U. Pa., 1963; MA, NYU Inst. Fine Arts, 1965, PhD, 1972; student, The Barnes Found., 1959-66. Dir. Rutgers U. Art Gallery, New Brunswick, NJ, 1966-69; chief curator Art Gallery Ont., Toronto, Canada, 1972-78; dir. Chrysler Mus., Norfolk, Va., 1979-80, Flint (Mich.) Inst. Arts, 1980-88, Archives of Am. Art, Smithsonian Instn., Washington, 1990—2005, sr. scholar, 2006—. Lectr. Barnes Found., 1991-92. Author: The Art of Charles Prendergast, 1968, The Art of Jean Hugo, 1973, Puvis de Chavannes and the Modern Tradition, 1975, The Fauves, 1975, The Dutch Cityscape in the 17th Century and it's Sources, 1977, William Glackens' Beach Scenes at Bellport, 1988, Dr. Albert C. Barnes and The Barnes Foundation, 1993, Maurice Prendergast, 1994. Trustee Intermus. Conservation Lab., Oberlin, Ohio, 1982-88. Recipient Founders Day award NYU, 1972 Office: Smithsonian Instn Archives of Am Art Victor Bldg Ste 2200 MRC937 PO Box 37012 Washington DC 20013-7012 Home Phone: 301-779-0804; Office Phone: 202-275-1922. Office Fax: 202-275-1955. Business E-Mail: wattenmakerr@si.edu.

WATTERS, ANN OLIVA, psychologist, educator; d. George Verdelli II and Dorothy Austin Oliva; m. Thomas A. Watters, Aug. 30, 1975; children: Andrew George, Michael Thomas. BA in English, U. Calif., Berkeley, 1974; MA in English Lit., Washington U., St. Louis, 1976; MA in Health Psychology, Calif. Sch. Profl. Psychology, 1997, PhD in Psychology, 1999. Lectr. rhetoric and English Stanford U., Calif., 1987—; pvt. practice clin. psychology San Mateo, Calif., 1999—; asst. clin. prof. psychiatry U. Calif., San Francisco, 2005—. Author, editor: Global Exchange: Reading/Writing in a World Context, 2005; co-author: Creating America: Reading & Writing Arguments, 4th edit., 2005, Writing for Change: A Community Reader. Chair bd. dirs. San Mateo Med. Ctr. Found. Mem.: AAUP, APA, Calif. Psychol. Assn. Office Fax: 650-375-8398. Business E-Mail: watters@stanford.edu.

WATTERS, EDWARD MCLAIN, III, lawyer; b. 1943; s. Edward and Lucy F. (Disston) W.; m. Susan Secor, May 12, 1979; children: Jennifer Susan, Ann Elizabeth. BA cum laude, Yale U., 1965; JD cum laude, U. Pa., 1970. Bar: Pa. 1970. Ptnr. Pepper Hamilton LLP, Phila., 1977—. Lectr. programs on uniform trust act, estate planning and will drafting Pa. Bar Inst. Bd. dirs. Children's Cruise and Playground Soc. Pa., Sanitarium Playgrounds of NJ, others. Lt. USNR, 1965-75; chair Decedents Estate Adv. Com. to Pa. Legislature's Joint State Govt. Commn. Fellow Am. Coll. Trust and Estate Counsel; mem. ABA, Phila. Bar Assn., Pa. Bar Assn. (past chmn. legis. com. probate sect.), Phila. Estate Planning Coun. (past pres.), Yale Club of Phila., Penn Club, Merion Golf Club. Office: Pepper Hamilton LLP 400 Berwyn Park 899 Cassatt Rd Berwyn PA 19312-1183 Office Phone: 610-640-7809. Business E-Mail: watterse@pepperlaw.com.

WATTERS, KEITH W., lawyer; Ptnr. Keith Watters & Associates, Washington. Mem.: Bar Assn. DC (pres. 2006—07). Office: Keith Watters & Assoc Ste 1112 1717 K St NW Washington DC 20036 Office Phone: 202-887-1990. Office Fax: 202-293-2368. E-mail: keithwatters@verizon.net.

WATTERS, LINDA A., state agency administrator; m. Ronald E. Watters. BA in Bus. Adminstrn., Bowling Green State U.; MBA, U. Dayton. Analyst to positions in internat. mkt. and analysis group GM; various positions including loan analyst, corp. banking officer, asst. v.p. Comerica Bank, 1988—96, sr. loan analyst corp. banking, 1990, v.p. regional met. corp. banking, 1994—96; v.p., relationship mgr. comml. fin. svcs. Std. Fed. Bank, 1996—98; v.p., relationship mgr. Mich. Nat. Bank (now LaSalle Bank); pres., CEO Detroit Commerce Bank; commr. Mich. Office Fin. and Ins. Svcs., 2003—. Bd. trustees Capital Region Cmty. Found., 2007—. Office: Mich Office Fin and Ins Svcs PO Box 30220 Lansing MI 48909 Office Phone: 517-373-0220. Office Fax: 517-335-4978.

WATTERS, RAYMOND WENDELL, family medicine physician; b. Cin., Apr. 14, 1948; s. Lawrence Lauder and Lelia Wanda (Odell) W.; m. Vicki Jean Caccia, July 20, 1985 (div. May 1988). Student Union Coll., 1966-67; BS, Purdue U., 1970; MD, U. La Laguna, Spain, 1981, MPH, Harvard U., 1996. Diplomate Am. Bd. Family Practice. Intern St. Elizabeth Med. Ctr., Covington, Ky., 1981-82; resident U. Louisville Affiliated Hosp., 1982-85; physician emergency medicine Ireland Army Hosp., Fort Knox, Ky., 1983-85; physician Prewett and Watters Family Physicians, Corbin, Ky., 1985-1991; active duty, US Army, 1991—; team physician Cumberland Coll., Williamsburg, Ky. Vol. missions Bd. Global Missions United Methodist Ch., Ganta Liberia, 1984; bd. dirs. Area Health Edn. Ctr.; mem.-at-large Mid-Am. Coll. Health Assn. Col. M.C. U.S. Army, 1985,1991—. Recipient Research award Year U. Louisville, 1985, Army Achievement award, 1987; named Hon. Ky. Col., 1989; Union Coll. scholar, 1966, Bronze Star medal, 1991, Legion of Merit medal, 2006. Mem. AMA (participant Appalachian project Va. 1972-73), Am. Acad. Family Physicians, Ky. Acad. Family Practice, Christian Med. Fellowship (London), Am. Heart Assn. (instr. advanced cardiac life support, bd. dirs.), Am. Coll. Surgeons (instr. advanc trauma life support), Am. Coll. Health Assn. (bd. dirs.), Honorable Order Ky. Col. (hon. 1989), Am. Coll. Exec. Physicians. Republican. Avocations: racquetball, reading, running, hiking, music. Office Phone: 202-679-1313. Personal E-mail: watters408@aol.com. Business E-Mail: raymond.watters@us.army.mil.

WATTERS, RICHARD DONALD, lawyer; b. Midland, Mich., May 3, 1951; s. Donald Wayne and Madalyn Bird (Tinetti) W.; m. Ann Elizabeth Hutchison, May 24, 1975; children: Kelly E., Nathan Paul. BS in Indsl. Engring., Bradley U., 1973; JD cum laude, St. Louis U., 1976. Bar: Mo. 1976, U.S. Dist. Ct. (we. and ea. dists.) Mo. 1976, Ill. 1977, U.S. Ct. Appeals (8th cir.) 1981; cert. healthcare mediator. Assoc. Lashly & Baer, P.C., St. Louis, 1976-81, ptnr., 1981—, dept. chmn., 1989—. Instr. St. Louis U. Sch. Law, 1977-79. Chmn., pres. United Cerebral Palsy Assn. St. Louis, 1985-88; bd. dirs. Canterbury Enterprises, sheltered workshop, St. Louis, 1988-94, participant Leadership St. Louis, 1988-89; ethics com. DePaul Health Ctr., 1990-96. Mem. Am. Health Lawyers Assn., Mo. Soc. Hosp. Attys. (bd. dirs. 1988-94, pres. 1990-91), Mo. Bar Assn. (vice chmn. health and hosp. com. 1988-90), Bar Assn. Metro. St. Louis (co-chmn. med.-legal com.). Republican. Avocation: sailing. Office: Lashly & Baer PC 714 Locust St Saint Louis MO 63101-1699 Office Phone: 314-621-2939. Business E-Mail: rdwatters@lashlybaer.com.

WATTLETON, (ALYCE) FAYE, educational association administrator, advocate; b. St. Louis, July 8, 1943; d. George and Ozie (Garrett) Wattleton; m. Franklin Gordon (div.); 1 child, Felicia. BS in Nursing, Ohio State U., 1964; MS in Maternal and Infant Health Care, Columbia U., 1967; LHD (hon.), St. Paul's Coll., 1985, Spelman Coll., 1986; LLD (hon.), Northeastern Univ. Law Sch., 1990; LHD (hon.), Long Island Univ., 1990, U. Pa., 1990, Bard Coll., 1991; HHD (hon.), Oberlin Coll., 1991; LLD (hon.), Wesleyan Univ., 1991; LHD (hon.), Hofstra U., 1992, Haverford Coll., 1992, Meadville-Lombar Sem./U. Chicago, 1992; D in Pub. Svc. (hon.), Simmons Coll., 1993. Tchr. Miami Valley Hosp. Sch. Nursing, Dayton, Ohio, 1964-66; asst. dir. Montgomery County Combined Pub. Health Dist., Dayton, 1967-70; exec. dir. Planned Parenthood, Dayton, 1970-78; pres. Planned Parenthood Fedn. Am., Inc., NYC, 1978-92, Ctr. for Advancement of Women, NYC, 1995—. Author: How to Talk to Your Child About Sexuality, 1986, Life on the Line, 1996. Bd. dirs. Pardee Rand Grad. Sch., Quidel Corp., Savient Pharm., Jazz at Lincoln Ctr., Well Choice Inc., Eisenhower Fellowship, UNA/USA; trustee Columbia U. Recipient Am. Humanist award, 1986, John Gardner award, 1987, APHA award of excellence, 1989, Humanitarian award Congrl. Black Caucus Found., 1989, Claude Pepper Humanitarian award Internat. Platform Assn., 1990, Pioneer of Civil Rights and Human Rights award Nat. Conf. Black Lawyers, 1990, Florina Lasker award NY Civil Liberties Union Found., 1990, Whitney M. Young Jr. Svc. award Boy Scouts Am., 1990, Ministry of Women award Unitarian Universalist Women's Fed., 1990, Spirit of Achievement award Albert Einstein Coll. Medicine Yeshiva U., 1991, 20th Anniversary Advocacy award Nat. Family Planning and Reproductive Health Assn., 1991, Women of Achievement award Women's Projects and Prodn., 1991, Margaret Sanger award, 1992, Jefferson Pub. Svc. award, 1992, Dean's Disting. Svc. award Columbia Sch. Pub. Health, 1992, Fries prize, 2004; named one of Best Mgrs. of Non-Profit Orgns. in Am., Bus. Week, Outstanding Mother Nat. Mother's Day Com., 1997; named to Nat. Women's Hall of Fame, 1993. Office: Ctr for Advancement of Women 25 W 43rd St Ste # 1120 New York NY 10036 Office Phone: 212-391-7718. Business E-Mail: fwattleton@advancewomen.org.

WATTLEWORTH, ROBERTA ANN, physician; b. Sioux City, Iowa, Dec. 26, 1955; d. Roland Joseph and Elizabeth Ann (Ahart) Eickholt; m. John Wade Wattleworth, Nov. 7, 1984; children: Adam, Ashley. BS, Morningside Coll., Sioux City, 1978; D of Osteopathy, Coll. Osteo. Medicine/Surgery, Des Moines, 1981; M.Healthcare Adminstrn., U. Osteo. Med. and Health Scis., Des Moines, 1999; MPH, Des Moines U., 2004. Intern Richmond Heights (Ohio) Gen. Hosp., 1981-82, resident in anesthesiology, 1982-84; anesthesiologist Doctor's Gen. Hosp., Plantation, Fla., 1984-85; resident in family practice J.F. Kennedy Hosp., Stratford, NJ, 1985-87; educator family practice U. Osteo. Medicine and Health Scis., Des Moines, 1987-89; family practitioner McFarland Clinic, P.C., Jewell, Iowa, 1989-94; lectr. family practice Osteopath. Med. Ctr., Des Moines U., 1999—, prof., chair dept. family medicine, 2003—. Med. dir. nursing home Bethany Manor, Story City, Iowa, 1990-99, Jewell Vol. Fire and Rescue Squad, 1990-99. Bd. dirs. Heartland Sr. Svcs., 1995—99, Iowa Rural Health Assn. Named Nat. Outstanding Osteo. Educator of Yr., Nat. Student Osteo. Med. Assn., 2001—02. Fellow Am. Coll. Osteo. Family Physicians; mem. Am. Osteo. Assn., Am. Med. Dirs. Assn. (sec.-treas. Iowa chpt. 1997-99), Am. Coll. Osteo. Family Physicians (pres. Iowa chpt. 1995-96), Iowa Osteo. Med. Assn. (trustee 1995-99, v.p. 1999—, pres.-elect 2000-01, pres. 2001-02, Physician of Yr. 2004-05), Soc. Tchrs. Family Medicine. Lutheran. Avocations: gardening, cooking, painting. Office: 3200 Grand Ave Des Moines IA 50312-4104 Office Phone: 515-271-7816. E-mail: Roberta.Wattleworth@dmu.edu.

WATTS, ANTHONY LEE, bank executive; b. Griffin, Ga., Jan. 24, 1947; s. Edgar Lee and Eula Mae (Benton) W.; m. Barbara Malinda Harp, Oct. 11, 1969; children: Natalie Paige, Barbara Leigh, Melanie Marie. AA, Gordon Mil. Coll., 1967; ABJ, U. Ga., Atlanta, 1969. Conventional loan rep. Fed. Nat. Mortgage Assn., Atlanta, from 1971, asst. regional appraiser, quality control and property mgr., to 1976; v.p., dir. ins. svcs. Ticor Mortgage Ins. Co., Atlanta, 1976-82; v.p., regional sales and exec. v.p. Ticor Indemnity Co., 1982-85; sr. v.p., regional mgr. Ticor Mortgage Ins. Co., Atlanta, 1984, sr. v.p., ea. divsn. mgr., 1984-85; pres. Mt. Vernon Fed. Savs. Bank, Dunwoody, Ga., 1985-95, Mt Vernon Fin. Corp., 1993-95; prin., dir. Banc Mortgage Fin. Corp., 1996-99, vice chmn., co-CEO, 1999—2002, co-pres., 2003—04; ret., 2004. Lectr. to trade assns. Founder, pres, Watts Family Enterprises, Inc., 1995; elder, bd. Peachtree Christian Ch.; bd. dirs. Ga. Spl. Olympics. With US Army, 1969—71. Recipient Bronze Star. Mem.: Phoenix Soc. (bd. dirs.), Gridiron Club, Rotary Club (Paul Harris fellow 1987).

WATTS, CLAUDIUS ELMER, III, retired military officer; b. Bennettsville, SC, Sept. 22, 1936; s. Claudius Elmer and Blanche Robey (Wannamaker) Watts; m. Patricia Jane Sims, July 23, 1960; children: Claudius Elmer IV, Patricia Watts Heck. AB in Polit. Sci., The Citadel, 1958; postgrad. (Fulbright scholar), London Sch. Econs. and Polit. Sci., 1958-59; MBA, Stanford U., 1967. Commd. officer USAF, 1958, advanced through grades to lt. gen., 1986, comdr. 438th Mil. Airlift Group McGuire AFB, NJ, 1979-80, comdr. 63d Mil. Airlift Wing Norton AFB, Calif., 1980-82, asst. dep. chief staff plans Mil. Airlift Command Scott AFB, Ill., 1982-83, dep. chief staff plans Mil. Airlift Command, 1983-84; dir. budget Hdqrs. U.S. Air Force, Washington, 1984-85; sr. mil. asst. to dep. sec. def. U.S. Dept. Def., Washington, 1985-86; compt. USAF, Washington, 1986-89; pres. Citadel, Charleston, SC, 1989-96; ret., 2000. Former adv. coun. grad. sch. bus. Stanford U.; former bd. visitors Air U.; former chmn. peer rev. teams, mem. coun. NCAA Coun.; former trustee Aerospace Edn. Found.; bd. dirs., chair audit com. Cmty. First Bank S.C.; bd. dirs. Crescent Mortgage Co., Carolina Fin. Corp. Past trustee Palmetto Partnership; past chmn. Marion Sq. Commn.; former bd. dirs., mem. fin. com. Air Force Aid Soc.; mem. bd. advisors Am. Leadership Found. Decorated Def. Disting. Svc. medal, USAF Disting. Svc. medal, Legion of Merit with oak leaf cluster, DFC with two oak leaf clusters, Air medal with 10 oak leaf clusters, Gallantry Cross with Palm, Vietnamese Svc. medal with 2 svc. stars Vietnam; Paul Harris fellow, Rotary. Mem.: VFW, Mil. Officers Assn. Am., Am. Soc. Mil. Comptrs., Airlift Assn., Air Force Sgts. Assn., Air Force Assn., Am. Legion, Order of Daedalians, Mil. Order World Wars. Methodist. Avocations: golf, reading. Office: 229 Country Club Ln Charleston SC 29412-2208 Business E-Mail: wattsc@citadel.edu.

WATTS, DAVID H., construction company executive; b. Newark, 1938; Grad., Cornell U., 1960. Pres., CEO Ford, Bacon & Davis, Inc, Granite Constrn. Inc., Watsonville, Calif., 1987—2003; chmn. Granite Contrn. Inc., Watsonville, Calif., 1999—. Office: Granite Constrn Inc PO Box 50085 Watsonville CA 95077-5085

WATTS, DORIS EARLENE, retired librarian; b. Palatka, Fla., Jan. 7, 1923; d. Charles Franklin and Elouise A.C. (Hagler) Foster; m. Fernand Cortez Watts, Aug. 30, 1950 (dec. 1955); children: Varick Steven, Franklin Cortez. AB, Howard U., 1950; postgrad., Cath. U. Am., 1960-61, postgrad., 1965. Clk. War Dept., Washington, 1942-46, VA, Washington, 1949; editorial clk. Dept. Army, Washington, 1950-52, clk., 1953-59, Dept. Commerce, Washington, 1959; with ICC, Washington, 1959—, librarian, to 1983. Recipient Spl. Achievement award ICC, 1983; recipient Spl. Achievement award, 1984 Mem. ALA, Delta Sigma Theta. Democrat. Methodist.

WATTS, DUNCAN J., social sciences educator; b. 1971; BSc in Physics (honors, 1st class), Univ. Coll., Univ. New South Wales, Australian Def. Force Acad., 1991; PhD in Theoretical and Applied Mechanics, Cornell Univ., 1997. Midshipman Royal Australian Navy, 1988—91, sub-lt., 1993—97; tchg. asst., rsch. asst., dept. theoretical and applied mechanics Cornell Univ., 1993—97; postdoctoral fellow, Lazerfeld Ctr. for the Soc. Scis. Columbia Univ., 1997—98, asst. prof., sociology, 2000—02, dir., Collective Dynamics Group, 2002—, assoc. prof., sociology (without tenure), 2002—03, assoc. prof., sociology (with tenure), 2003—06, prof., sociology, 2006—; postdoctoral fellow Santa Fe Inst., 1998—99, Sloan Sch. Mgmt., MIT, 1999—2000; head, rsch. in human soc. dynamics Yahoo!, NY, 2007—. Author: Small Worlds: The Dynamics of Networks Between Order and Randomness, 1999, Six Degrees: The Science of a Connected Age, 2003; co-editor: The Structure and Dynamics of Complex Networks, 2006; contbr. articles to peer-reviewed publications. Recipient Chief Def. Force Navy prize for academic and mil. performance, 1990, Am. Sociological Assn. award for best paper in Math. Sociology, 1999, NSF Early Career award, 2000; vis. scholar Fulbright Scholar, 1993. Office: Dept Sociology 815 International Affairs Bldg 420 W 118 St New York NY 10027 also: Yahoo! 1065 Avenue of the Americas #9 New York NY 10018 Office Phone: 212-854-4343. Office Fax: 212-854-2963. Business E-Mail: djw24@columbia.edu. *

WATTS, EMILY STIPES, retired English language educator; b. Urbana, Ill., Mar. 16, 1936; d. Royal Arthur and Virginia Louise (Schenck) Stipes; m. Robert Allan Watts, Aug. 30, 1958; children: Benjamin, Edward, Thomas. Student, Smith Coll., 1954-56; AB, U. Ill., 1958, MA (Woodrow Wilson Nat. fellow), 1959, PhD, 1963. Instr. English U. Ill., Urbana, 1963-67, asst. prof., 1967-73, assoc. prof., 1973-77, prof., dir. grad. studies dept. English, 1977—2005, prof. emerita, 2005—; bd. dirs. U. Ill. Athletic Assn., chmn., 1981-83; mem. faculty adv. com. Ill. Bd. Higher Edn., 1984—, vice chmn., 1986-87, chmn., 1987-88. Author: Ernest Hemingway and The Arts, 1971, The Poetry of American Women from 1632 to 1945, 1977, The Businessman in American Literature, 1982; contbg. editor: English Women Writers from the Middle Ages to the Present, 1990; contbr. articles on Jonathan Edwards, Anne Bradstreet to lit. jours. John Simon Guggenheim Meml. Found. fellow, 1973-74 Mem. Am. Inst. Archaeology, Assn. Lit. Scholars Critics, Authors Guild, Ill. Hist. Soc., The Phila. Soc., Phi Beta Kappa, Phi Kappa Phi. Presbyterian. Home: 1009 W University Ave Champaign IL 61821-3317

WATTS, GINNY (VIRGINIA C. WATTS), artist; b. Chester, Pa., Jan. 24, 1931; d. Edwin Swoope Craig and Ruth Irene Tonge; m. Lynch S. Watts, Jr., July 21, 1951 (wid.); children: L. Kenneth, Karen Elizabeth Watts Dick, Monica Faye Watts Malandruccolo, Dawn Ellen Watts Eller; m. Alfred E. Meeds, May 5, 1948 (div. Nov. 1950); children: Brenda Joyce Meeds Parker, Edwin Lewis, Michael Alfred. Student, Del. Tech. and C.C., Georgetown, 1998—99. County coord. Easter Seals, Wilmington, Del., 1985-86; resident advisor Dept. Mental Retardation Kencrest Svcs., Dover, 1986-87, program mgr., 1987-90; fine arts instr. Del. Tech. and C.C., Georgetown, 1998—, 2002—. Instr. workshops Millsboro Art League, Del., 1998—. One person shows include Millsboro Art Gallery, 2000;

exhibited in group shows at Del. Art Ctr., 1942—, Del. Tech. and C.C., 1997—, Millsboro Art League and Gallery, Del., 1997—, Fine Arts Event, Rehoboth Beach, Del., 2000, Geyers Art Gallery, Milford, Del., 2000, 01, 2002, Del. Tech. CC., 2007, others; artist oil, graphite and watercolor paintings, 1942—; group mural: wall of Art Gallery/Del. Tech. C.C., 1998; mural for lobby of Presentations, 2000; fine art work exhibited in offices of US Sen. from Del.; contbr. articles to area newspapers. Vice-pres. Adult Art League, Del. Tech. C.C., 1997—; bd. dirs. Millsboro Art League, 1998—, pres., 2001—; mem. Sussex County Arts Coun., 1997—, Nat. Mus. Women in the Arts; bd. advisors Del. Tech. adult plus program Del. Tech. and C.C.; pres. Adult PLUS Art League, 1998—; pres. Millsboro Art League, 2001-. Recipient Excellence of Artistic Achievement award DAPA and Del. Tech. C.C., award for excellence Del. Tech. C.C., 2006. Avocations: swimming, hiking, bicycling, camping, gardening. Personal E-mail: vrcmw@aol.com.

WATTS, HAROLD WESLEY, economist, educator; b. Salem, Oreg., Sept. 30, 1932; s. Elton and Claire W.; m. Doris A. Roth, Sept. 28, 1951 (div. 1973); children— Michael Lee, Suzanne, Jane Marie, Kristin. BA, U. Oreg., 1954; MA, Yale U., 1956, PhD, 1957. From instr. to assoc. prof. Yale U., New Haven, 1957-63; from assoc. prof. to prof. econs. U. Wis., Madison, 1963-76, dir. Inst. Research on Poverty, 1966-71; prof. econs. and pub. policy Columbia U., NYC, 1976-98, prof. econs. and pub. policy emeritus, 1998—, dir. Pub. Policy Rsch. Ctr., 1988-93; sr. fellow Mathematica Policy Research Princeton, N.J., 1979-92; sr. rsch. assoc. Urban Inst., 1994-95. Recipient Paul Lazarsfeld award, 1980; Guggenheim fellow, 1975 Fellow Assn. Pub. Policy Analysis and Mgmt., Econometric Soc.; mem. Am. Econ. Assn., L.I. Wine Coun. (pres. 2000-02, sec. 2004-06). Democrat. Home: 144 Bay Ave Greenport NY 11944-1404 Office Phone: 516-384-7186. Personal E-mail: hwesleyw@aol.com.

WATTS, J. C., JR., former congressman, retired professional football player; b. Eufaula, Okla., Nov. 8, 1957; m. Frankie Watts; 5 children. BA in Journalism, U. Okla., 1981. Profl. football player Ottawa and Toronto Teams Can. Football League, 1981-86; youth min. to assoc. pastor Sunnylane So. Bapt. Ch., Del City, 1987-94; mem. Okla. Corp. Commn., 1990—95, chmn., 1992—95; mem. U.S. Congress from 4th Okla. dist., 1995—2003; mem. armed svcs. com.; mem. special oversight panel on terrorism; chmn. GOPAC, 2003—. Mem. Nat. Drinking Water Adv. Coun.; mem. electricity com. Nat. Assn. Regulatory Utility Commrs; hon. co-chmn. Rep. Nat. Conv., 2000. Bd. of rep. Fellowship of Christian Athletes, Okla.; leader Orphan Found. of Am., Boy Scouts of Am.; guest preacher; co-chair Coalition for AIDS Relief in Africa. Named Most Valuable Player (Orange Bowl), 1980, 1981; named to Orange Bowl Hall of Fame, 1992. Republican. Address: GOPAC 600 13th St Ste 790 Washington DC 20005

WATTS, JOHN S., JR., insurance company executive; BA in English, UCLA. Various mgmt. positions HealthNet, Northwestern Nat. Life Ins. Co.; regional dir. LA sales office Blue Cross of Calif., 1995—97, gen. mgr. large grp. svcs., 1997; acting sr. v.p. UNICARE comml. accounts large grp. divsn. ea., so. and ctrl. regions WellPoint Health Networks, Inc.; sr. v.p. large group divsn. Blue Cross and Blue Shield of Ga. (subs. WellPoint Health Networks, Inc.), 2001—03, pres., CEO, 2003—04; pres., CEO nat. accounts strategic bus. unit WellPoint, Inc, Indpls., 2004—06; pres., CEO comml. and consumer bus. strategic bus. unit WellPoint, Inc., Indpls., 2006—. Office: WellPoint Inc 120 Monument Cir Indianapolis IN 46204 *

WATTS, KISHA MANN, school system administrator, secondary school educator; b. Pensacola, Fla., June 3, 1980; d. Robert Darryl and Karen Theresa Watts. BA, Williams Coll., Williamstown, Mass., 2002. Membership intern Assn. Women in Sci., Washington, 2000; rsch. asst. Marine Biol. Lab., Woods Hole, Mass., 2001; sci. tchr., admissions coord., diversity dir. Thayer Acad., Braintree, Mass., 2002—. Del. for diversity Nat. Assn. Ind. Schs., India. Co-chair call to action NAIS People Color Conf., 2007. Named to Wall of Tolerance, So. Poverty Law Ctr., 2003. Mem.: NAACP, Assn. Ind. Schs. in New Eng. (mem. diversity bd.), Tchg. Tolerance, Nat. Mus. Am. Indian Art, Nat. Scholars Honor Soc. Avocations: yoga, travel, reading, fitness. Office: Thayer Academy 745 Washington St Braintree MA 02184 Home Phone: 781-356-8737; Office Phone: 781-664-2271. Office Fax: 781-843-2916. Personal E-mail: kishamw2002@yahoo.com. Business E-Mail: kwatts@thayer.org.

WATTS, LINDA SUSAN, humanities educator; BA, U. Del., 1981, MA in History, 1983; MA in Am. Studies, Yale U., 1986, PhD in Am. Studies, 1989. Instr. history and Am. studies U. Del., Newark, 1981—83; instr. English and Am. studies Yale U., New Haven, 1984—86, coord. sr. essays and projects in Am. studies, 1987—89; vis. asst. prof. English, Am. studies, and Afro-Am. studies Wesleyan U., Middletown, Conn., 1989—90; asst. prof. Drake U., Des Moines, 1990—95, asst. prof., assoc. dir. women's studies program, 1992—93, assoc. prof. English, 1995—96, assoc. prof. English, assoc. dean Coll. of Arts and Scis., 1996—99; prof. Am. studies, dir. interdisciplinary arts and scis. program U. Wash., Bothell, 1999—2001, prof. Am. studies, interdisciplinary arts and scis. program, 2001—. Author: Rapture Untold: Gender, Mysticism, and 'The Moment of Recognition' in the Writings of Gertrude Stein, 1996, Gertrude Stein: A Study of the Short Fiction, 1999, Encyclopedia of American Folklore, 2006; contbg. author: The World Is Our Home: Society and Culture in Contemporary Southern Writing; contbr. articles to profl. jours. HIV/AIDS cmty. edn. instr. ARC, Des Moines, 1992—99, HIV/AIDS instr. trainer, 1996—99; vol. literacy tutor Adult Literacy Ctr., Des Moines, 1998—99; vol. mus. visitor svcs. Experience Music Project, Seattle, 2000—01; vol. AIDS Greater Des Moines, 1992—93, SELFHELP Crafts of the World, Des Moines, 1992—94; vol. curriculum cons. and co-instr. Operation Peer Helper, ARC Youth Program, Des Moines, 1993—93; vol. edn. com. mem. AIDS Project of Greater Des Moines, 1993—95; chair HIV/AIDS edn. program com. ARC, Des Moines, 1994—95, vol. mem. HIV/AIDS edn. program com., 1995—99; vol. planning com. mem. World AIDS Day Observance, State of Iowa, Des Moines, 1997—98. Finalist Woodrow Wilson Dissertation Grant in Women's Studies, Woodrow Wilson Found., 1988, Ill.-Nat. Women's Studies Assn. Manuscript award, 1990; nominee Poet of the Yr., Internat. Soc. Poets, 2001; named Semi-Finalist N.Am. Open Poetry Contest, Internat. Libr. of Poetry, 2000, Internat. Libr. Poetry, 2001; recipient Editor's Choice Award for Outstanding Achievement in Poetry, poetry.com, 2000, Internat. Poet of Merit award, Internat. Soc. Poets, 2002, Open Poetry Competition award, King County Pub. Art Program, State of Wash., 2000; Grad. fellow, U. Del., 1981—83, Grad. Sch., Yale U., 1983—87, Marcia Brady Tucker fellow, 1984—85, Sterling fellow, Yale U., 1983—84. Mem.: Phi Beta Kappa, Phi Alpha Theta, Phi Kappa Phi. Office: Univ Wash Bothell Box 358511 11136 NE 180th St Bothell WA 98011-8246 E-mail: lswatts@u.washington.edu.

WATTS, MARK EDWIN, secondary school educator, professional volleyball player; b. Indpls., Dec. 8, 1957; s. William Joseph Watts and Clare Michelle Courtney; m. Kristi K. Kovach (div.); m. Kelley Diane Watts, Dec. 22, 2001. BS in Geology, Purdue U., West Lafayette, Ind., 1982. Cert. earth and space sci., math. Ind. Tchr. West Lafayette H.S., 1986—88, Mishawaka H.S., Ind., 1988—91, Penn H.S., Mishawaka, 1991—. Named #1 Rank Player, Midwest Assn. Volleyball Players, 1996. Mem.: Ind. State Tchrs. Assn. (rep. 1986—), Mensa, Acad. Model Aeronautics. Avocations: radio controlled aircraft, skiing, computers, antique tractors. Home: 10398 Heather Lake Dr Osceola IN 46561 Office: Penn Harris Madison Sch Coop 56100 Bittersweet Rd Mishawaka IN 46545

WATTS, MARY ANN, retired elementary school educator; b. Harrisburg, Pa., Sept. 13, 1927; d. Major Allan and Ellana Susan (Robinson) Brown; m. Spencer R. Watts, June 23, 1951; children: Shelley Lynn, Allison Dee, Howard Allan. BS, Cheyney U., 1949; postgrad., Temple U., 1965—67, Pa. State U., 1969—72, student, 2003—. Tchr. Harrisburg Sch. Dist., 1949-51, 59-69, Balt. Sch. Dist., 1951-57, Reading (Pa.) Sch. Dist., 1969-89. Mem. sch. dist. dress and discipline code com., 1977-79. Corr. Hamburg Item. Bd. dirs. Pa. State Assn. Boroughs, mem. resolutions and policy com.; mem. Bernville Borough Coun., 1976-2003, v.p., 1988-93, 96-98; sec., treas. Berks County Borough Assn., 1977-2003; Reach to Recovery vol. Am. Cancer Soc. Recipient Disting. Alumna award for achievement in govt. and politics Cheyney U., 1999. Mem. NAACP, Pa. State Edn. Assn. (life), Pa. Assn. Sch. Retirees, Reading Assn. Sch. Retirees, Bernville Woman's Club (pres. 1978-80, 86-88, Woman of Yr. 1985, Grange Cmty. Svc. award 1988), Pa. State U. Alumni Assn., Cheyney Alumni Assn. Democrat. Mem. United Ch. Of Christ.

WATTS, MICHAEL H., real estate company executive; b. 1967; B. in Mktg., SUNY Buffalo; MBA, U. Mich. Downtown regional leasing dir. Jones Lang LaSalle Inc., 1991—2000; sr. v.p. J.F. McKinney & Assocs., Chgo., 2000—. Named one of 40 Under 40, Crain's Chgo. Bus., 2006. Office: JF McKinney & Assocs Ste 3565 71 S Wacker Dr Chicago IL 60606 Office Phone: 312-819-4439. E-mail: mwatts@jfmckinney.com.

WATTS, MIKAL C., lawyer; b. Corpus Christi, Tex., July 17, 1967; BA with high honors, U. Tex., 1987, JD with honors, 1989. Bar: Tex. 1989, U.S. Dist. Ct. (so., ea., we. and no. dists.) Tex., US Ct. Appeals (5th and 6th cirs.), US Supreme Ct. Atty. for Hon. Thomas R. Phillips, Chief Justice of Supreme Ct., Tex., 1989—90; assoc. David L. Perry & Assocs., Corpus Christi, 1990—91, ptnr., 1991, Perry & Haas, L.L.P., 1991—97; founder Harris & Watts, P.C., 1997, Watts & Heard, L.L.P., 2001; founder, ptnr. Watts Law Firm, L.L.P., 2002—. Named Impact Player of the Yr., Tex. Lawyer, 2001, rising star of the plaintiff's bar, The Wall St. Jour., 2004; named one of Tex. Super Lawyers, Tex. Monthly, 2001, best trial lawyers in the country, Nat. Law Jour., 2002, 40 Under 40, 2005; recipient Niemann Cup, 1989, noted favourably, USA Today, 2004, nation's first jury awards in various cases. Mem.: ABA (mem. Tort and Insurance Practice Com.), Trial Lawyers Pub. Justice (mem. bd. dirs.), State Bar Tex., Coll. of State Bar of Tex., Reynaldo G. Garza Am. Inn of Ct. (charter mem.), Corpus Christi Young Lawyers Assn., Tex. Trial Lawyers Assn. (mem. bd. dirs., mem. Statewide Fund raising Com.), Attys. Info. Exchange Group (co-chair Chrysler Minivan Liftgate Latch Litig. Subgroup, mem. bd. dirs.), Assn. Trial Lawyers of Am., Corpus Christi Bar Assn. Office: Watts Law Firm LLP Bank of Am Plz Ste 100 300 Convent St San Antonio TX 78205 Office Phone: 361-887-0500, 888-887-0560. Office Fax: 361-887-0055. Business E-Mail: mcwatts@wattslawfirm.com. *

WATTS, NAOMI, actress; b. Shoreham, Kent, Eng., Sept. 28, 1968; d. Peter Watts and Myfanwy Watts; one child, (with Liev Schreiber) Alexander Pete Schreiber Spl. envoy on HIV/AIDS UN, 2006—. Actor: (films) For Love Alone, 1986, Flirting, 1991, Matinee, 1993, Wide Sargasso Sea, 1993, Gross Misconduct, 1993, The Custodian, 1993, Tank Girl, 1995, Children of the Corn IV: The Gathering, 1996, Persons Unknown, 1996, Under the Lighthouse Dreaming, 1997, Dangerous Beauty, 1998, A House Divided, 1998, Strange Planet, 2001, Ellie Parker, 2001, Down, 2001, Mulholland Drive, 2001, The Ring, 2002, Plots with a View, 2002, Rabbits, 2002, Ned Kelly, 2003, Le Divorce, 2003, 21 Grams, 2003 (Acad. Award nomination for best actress, 2004, Screen Actors Guild Award nomination for best actress, 2004), We Don't Live Here Anymore, 2004, The Assassination of Richard Nixon, 2004, I Heart Huckabees, 2004, Ellie Parker, 2005, The Ring Two, 2005, Stay, 2005, King Kong, 2005, The Painted Veil, 2006, (voice) Inland Empire, 2006,: (TV films) Bermuda Triangle, 1996, Timepiece, 1996, The Christmas Wish, 1998, The Hunt for the Unicorn Killer, 1999, The Wyvern Mystery, 2000, The Outsider, 2002; (TV miniseries) Brides of Christ, 1991; (TV series) Home and Away, 1991, Sleepwalkers, 1997. Mailing: Creative Artists Agy 9830 Wilshire Blvd Beverly Hills CA 90212-1825

WATTS, OLIVER EDWARD, engineering company executive; b. Hayden, Colo., Sept. 22, 1939; s. Oliver Easton and Vera Irene (Hockett) W.; m. Charla Ann French, Aug. 12, 1962; children: Erik Sean, Oliver Eron, Sherilyn. BS, Colo. State U., 1962. Registered profl. engr., Colo., Calif.; profl. hand surveyor, Colo. Crew chief Colo. State U. Rsch. Found., Ft. Collins, 1962; with Calif. Dept. Water Resources, Gustine and Castaic, 1964-70; land and water engr. CF&I Steel Corp., Pueblo, Colo., 1970-71; engring. dir. United Western Engrs., Colorado Springs., Colo., 1971-76; ptnr. United Planning and Engring Co., Colorado Springs, 1976-79; owner Oliver E. Watts, Cons. Engr., Colorado Springs, 1979—. Dir. edn. local Ch. of Christ, 1969-71, deacon, 1977-87, elder, 1987-96. 1st lt. C.E., AUS, 1962-64. Recipient Individual Achievement award Colo. State U. Coll. Engring., 1981. Fellow ASCE (life; v.p. Colorado Springs br. 1975, pres. 1978); mem. NSPE (pres. Pike's Peak chpt. 1975, sec. Colo. sect. 1976, v.p. 1977, pres. 1978-79, Young Engr. award 1976, Pres.'s award 1979), Cons. Engrs. Coun. Colo. (bd. dirs. 1981-83), Am. Cons. Engrs. Coun., Profl. Land Surveyors Colo., Colo. Engrs. Coun. (del. 1980—), Colo. State U. Alumni Assn. (v.p., dir. Pike's Peak chpt. 1972-76), Lancers, Lambda Chi Alpha. Home: 7195 Dark Horse Pl Colorado Springs CO 80919-1442 Office: 614 Elkton Dr Colorado Springs CO 80907-3514

WATTS, ROBERT ALLAN, publisher, lawyer; b. July 4, 1936; s. Richard P. and Florence (Hooker) W.; m. Emily Stipes, Aug. 30, 1958; children: Benjamin H., Edward S., Thomas J. Student, DePauw U., 1954-55; BA, U. Ill., 1959, JD, 1961. Bar: (Ill.) 1961. Assoc. Stipes Pub. Co., Champaign, Ill., 1962-67, ptnr., editor, 1967—. Treas. Planned Parenthood, 1976—80; mem. Pres.'s Coun., U. Ill.; pres. Friends of Libr., U. Ill., 1980—82; treas. Campaign Rep. Party, 1976—80; bd. dirs. local United Way, 1972—81, City of Champaign Libr. Found., 1993—2007. Mem. Ill. Bar Assn., U. Ill. Found., Nat. Acad. Arts (bd. dirs. 1983-89), Champaign Country Club, Saugatuck Yacht Club (commodore), Lake Shore Bath & Tennis Club (pres. 1983-85). Home: 1009 W University Ave Champaign IL 61821-3317 Office: Stipes Publishing Co 204 W University Ave Champaign IL 61820-3912

WATTS, ROBERT GLENN, retired pharmaceutical executive; b. Norton, Va., Apr. 28, 1933; s. Clifford Amburgey and Stella Lee (Cornette) Watts; m. Doris Juanita Slaughter, Aug. 29, 1953 (dec. 1980); children: Cynthia L. Watts Waller, Robert Glenn, Kelly L.; m. Sara Lowry Childrey, Aug. 20, 1982; 1 child, Matthew R. Alexander 1 stepchild, J. Eric Alexander. BA, U. Richmond, 1959. Dir. ops. A.H. Robins Co., Inc., Richmond, Va., 1967-71, asst. v.p., 1971-73, v.p., 1973-75, sr. v.p., 1975-79, exec. v.p., 1979-92; ret., 1992. Bd. dirs. Little Oil Co., BB&T Bank, Fidelity Group. Mem. Pvt. Industry Coun., Richmond, 1983—; sec. YMCA, Richmond, 1984—; bd. dirs. United Way, Richmond, 1982—. With USN, 1952—56. Mem.: Met. Richmond C. of C. (chmn. 1985—86). Episcopalian. Home: 2407 Islandview Dr Richmond VA 23233-2525 E-mail: RGW433@aol.com.

WATTS, ROSS LESLIE, finance educator; b. Hamilton, Australia, Nov. 10, 1942; came to U.S., 1966; s. Leslie R. and Elsie B. (Horadam) W. m. Helen Clare Firkin, Jan. 15, 1966; children: Andrew David, James Michael. B in Commerce with honors Commonwealth Govt. scholar 1960-65), U. Newcastle, Australia, 1966; MBA Ford Found. fellow 1967-68, U. Chgo., 1968, PhD, 1971. Audit clk. Forsythe & Co., Newcastle, Australia, 1960-64, acct., 1964-66; instr. Grad. Sch. Bus., U. Chgo., 1969-70; asst. prof. Simon Sch. Mgmt., U. Rochester, NY, 1971-78, assoc. prof. NY, 1978-84, prof. NY, 1984-86; endowed chair Rochester Telephone Corp., 1986-98; William H. Meckling prof. U. Rochester, NY, 1998—2005; prof. Sloan Sch. MIT, Cambridge, Mass., 2005—. Prof. commerce U. Newcastle, 1974-76; hon. prof. City U. Hong Kong, 1996—, Xiamen U., China, 1999—; disting. lectr. Hong Kong U. Sci. and Tech., 1994; vis. prof. MIT, 2002; cons. in field. Contbr. articles on acctg. rsch. to profl. jours.; assoc. editor Jour. Acctg. Rsch., 1972-78, Jour. Fin. Econs., 1974-89, Australian Jour. Mgmt., 1976-81; co-editor Jour. Acctg. and Econs., 1979—; editor Jour. Acctg. Abstracts, 1995-97; dir., editor Acctg. Rsch. Network, 1997—; mem. adv. bd. Midland Corp. Fin. Jour., 1983-88, Continental Bank Jour. of Applied Corp. Fin., 1988-94, Bank Am. Jour. Applied Corp. Fin., 1994—; mem. editorial bd. Contemporary Acctg. Rsch., 1983-85; cons. editor Asia Pacific Jour. Acctg. Econs., 1998-2005; cons. editor Jour. Contemporary Acctg. and Econs., 2005-. Recipient Notable Contbn. award AICPA, 1979, 80, award Alpha Kappa Psi Found., 1985. Mem. Am. Acctg. Assn. (Outstanding Educator award 2000, Seminal Rsch. award 2004), Am. Fin. Assn., Inst. Chartered Accts. in Australia. Home: 22 Park St Arlington MA 02474 Office: MIT Sloan Sch 50 Memorial Blvd Cambridge MA 02142-1347 Office Phone: 617-253-2668. Business E-Mail: rwatts@mit.edu.

WATTS, STEPHEN HURT, II, lawyer; b. Lynchburg, Va., Feb. 21, 1947; s. James Owen Jr. and Sarah Webb (Key) W.; m. Beverley Allan Brockenbrough, July 16, 1969 (div. 1986); children: Day Lowry, Stephen Hurt Jr.; m. Sally Yates Wood, May 24, 1986 (div. 1995); m. Mollie Crawford Talbott;, March 24, 1999. BA, Washington & Lee U., 1968; JD, U. Va., 1972. Bar: Va. 1972, W.Va. 1973. Law clk. Taylor, Michie & Callahan, Charlottesville, Va., 1970-72; assoc. Spilman, Thomas, Battle & Klostermeyer, Charleston, W.Va., 1972-75; ptnr. Watts & Watts, Lynchburg, Va., 1975-77; v.p., counsel Commonwealth Gas Pipeline Corp., Richmond, 1977-81; gen. counsel Commonwealth Natural Resources, Inc., Richmond, 1980-81; assoc. McGuire Woods LLP (formerly McGuire, Woods, Battle & Boothe, LLP), Richmond, 1981-83, ptnr., 1983—. Bd. dirs. Lower Fan Civic Assn., Richmond, 1987-91, TheatreVirginia, Richmond, 1992-93, Va. Oil and Gas Assn., 1993; pres., bd. dirs. Studio Theatre Richmond, 1991-93; chmn. outreach com. Grace and Holy Trinity Episcopal Ch., Richmond, 1993. Mem. ABA, Va. State Bar (dir. adminstrv. law sect., chmn. 1995-96), Fed. Energy Bar Assn. Office: McGuire Woods LLP One James Center 901 E Cary St Richmond VA 23219-4057 E-mail: swatts@mcguirewoods.com.

WATTS, STEVEN RICHARD, lawyer; b. Toledo, Oct. 5, 1955; s. James Hupp and Lona Jane Katherine (Miller) W.; m. Marcia Ann Jackson, Mar. 6, 1982; children: Lauren Brooke, Madison Ann. BA in History, Ohio State U., 1978; JD summa cum laude, U. Dayton, 1981. Bar: Ohio 1981, U.S. Dist. Ct. (so. dist.) Ohio 1981. Assoc. Smith & Schnacke, Dayton, Ohio, 1981-84, Porter, Wright, Morris & Arthur, Dayton, 1984-89, ptnr., 1990, Chernesky, Heyman & Kress P.L.L., Dayton, 1990—. Mem. ABA, Ohio State Bar Assn., Dayton Bar Assn. Presbyterian. Avocation: golf. Home: 1101 Viewpoint Dr Dayton OH 45459-1442 Office: Chernesky Heyman & Kress PLL 1100 Courthouse Pla SW Dayton OH 45402 Office Phone: 937-449-2832.

WATTS, SUSAN HELENE, theater educator; d. Howard Harold and Madelyn Rebecca (Moore) Watts. BA, Mich. State U., 1963; MS, U. Kans., 1984. Tchr. Douglas County Schs., Castle Rock, Colo., 1964—74; owner/mgr. Old Bank Cafe, Oskaloosa, Kans., 1976—80; tchr. Valley Falls H.S., 1984—86; instr. Highland C.C., 1986—89; tchr. Oskaloosa H.S., 1986—89; communication coord./actor Omaha Magic Theatre, 1989—90; instr./divsn. chair McCook C.C., 1990—. Charter mem. Leadership McCook, 1990—; bd. mem. S.W. Nebr. Cmty. Theater Assn., 1990—2001; del. Nebr. Transfer Initiative, 1995—; chair local integrity subcom. North Ctrl. Accreditation Com., 1998—2001; adv. bd. Bright Beginnings, 1997—2001; mem. Campus Pres.'s Adv. Coun., 1993—97. Actor: (plays) Marvin's Room, Pools Paradise, Morning's At Seven, (stand up comedy) An Evening with Cassandra; author: (humor column) Dear Cassandra; dir.: (over sixty plays and musicals) (Outstanding Kans. Theatre Tchr., 1983). Banquet com. writer/performer McCook C. of C., 1998—2002; mem. goal setting task force McCook City Coun., 1998—98; mem. McCook Humane Soc., McCook, 1995—2003; bd. dirs. SpringFest, 1998—2000. Named Outstanding Kans. Theatre Tchr., Assn. Kans. Theatre, 1983. Mem.: NEA, Soc. Stage Dir. Choregraphers, Mid-Plains Edn. Assn., Nebr. State Edn. Assn., Kiwanis, Alpha Delta Kappa, Delta Kappa Gamma. Avocations: golf, gardening. Office: McCook Cmty Coll 1205 E Third Mc Cook NE 69001 Office Phone: 308-345-8173.

WATTS, THOMAS PARRISH, history educator, consultant; m. Judy Marie Griffith, Nov. 24, 1968; 1 child, Shelly Dawn Watts-Dognazzi. BS, U. of So. Miss., Hattiesburg, 1971; MEd, U. of So. Calif., LA, 1978; M of Strategic Studies, Nat. Def. U., Washington, 1994. Nat. bd. cert. profl. tchr. Nat. Bd. for Profls. Tchg. Stds. Bn. comdr. 1313th Transp. Ocean Port Bn., Seattle, 1990—92; mil. adviser to sec. of def. Office of the Sec. of Def., Washington, 1992—93; mil. adviser to U.S. amb. U.S. Mission to NATO, Brussels, 1994—97; dir., instr. U.S. Army War Coll., Carlisle Barracks, Pa., 1997—99; dep. dir. Miss. Dept. of Human Svcs., Jackson, Miss., 1999—2000; tchr. Am. history Madison Mid. Sch., Miss., 2000—. Editor: (ednl. package) Tracing Our Trace (Nat. Geog. Soc. grant, 2002). Col. US Army, 1971—99. Decorated Legion of Merit, Def. Meritorious Svc. Medal, Army Meritorious Medals (4), Joint Svc. Commendation Medal, Army Commendation Medal (4) US Def. Dept. and US Army; named Disting. Mem. of U.S. Army Transp. Corps' Rgt., 2006, Gilda - Lehrman History Tchr. of Yr. for Miss., Gilda - Lehrman History Inst., 2005, 2002 - 2003 Tchr. of Yr., Madison County Sch. Dist., 2003. Mem.: VFW (life), Miss. Hist. Soc., Nat. Def. Transp. Assn., Am. Legion, Nat. Assn. of Social Studies Educators. Independent. United Methodist. Avocations: history, travel. Office: Madison Midd Sch 1365 Mannsdale Rd Madison MS 39110 Home Phone: 601-605-2281; Office Phone: 601-605-4171. Office Fax: 601-853-2254; Home Fax: 601-853-2254. Personal E-mail: tomw1048@aol.com. Business E-Mail: twatts@madison.k12.ms.us.

WATTS, VIRGINIA AGNES, retired special education educator; b. Hampstead, Md., Mar. 14, 1925; d. Thomas Leister and Anna (Freyer) Beam; m. Ervin Olman Watts., Sr., Feb. 9, 1946 (dec. 1972); 1 child, Ervin. RN, St. Agnes Hosp. Sch. Nursing, Balt., 1945; BS, U. Md., 1969, MS, 1974. Nurse St. Agnes Hosp., 1945-46; spl. edn. tchr. Anne Arundel Bd. Edn., Annapolis, Md., 1958-85. Recipient Richard H. Carter award, Glen Burnie Improvement Assn., 2006. Mem. AARP (state housing coord. 1992-93, local health coord. 1993-96, bd. dirs. Capitol City task force 1997—, state legis. coun. 1997—, pres. Md. chpt. 2006), Anne Arundel County Retired Tchrs. Assn. (pres. elect 1997), Md. Sr. Citizen Hall of Fame (bd. dirs. 1999-). Republican. Home: 714 Cotter Rd Glen Burnie MD 21060-7330

WATZ, MARTIN CHARLES, brewery consultant; b. St. Louis, Oct. 31, 1938; s. George Michael and Caroline Theresa (Doggendorf) Watz; m. Deborah Perkowski; children: Pamela, Kathlene, Karen. BS in Chemistry and Microbiology, SE Mo. State U., 1961; MBA, Washington U., 1966—67. Safety engr. McDonnell-Douglas, 1962-64; sr. brewing chemist Anheuser-Busch, Inc., St. Louis, 1965-68, asst. brewmaster Columbus, Ohio, 1968-79, sr. asst. brewmaster St. Louis, 1979-82, resident brewmaster Baldwinsville, NY, 1982-84, Williamsburg, Va., 1984-87; v.p. bakers yeast divsn. Anheuser-Busch Indsl. Products Corp., St. Louis, 1987-88, dir. brewing ops., 1988-89; sr. brewmaster Anheuser-Busch, Ft. Collins, Colo., 1989-99; brewing cons., 1999—. Patentee in field. With USAF, 1962—65. Mem.: Profl. Assn. Diving Instrs., U.S. Pilots Assn., Internat. Food Tech. Assocs., Am. Soc. Brewing Chemists, Master Brewers Assn. Am. (pres., nat. bd. govs.), Aircraft Owners and Pilots Assn. Avocations: flying, collectible cars. Home and Office: 1417 N County Rd # 3 Fort Collins CO 80524-9312 Office Phone: 970-482-5360. Personal E-mail: satin@frii.com.

WAUD, ROGER NEIL, economist, educator; b. Detroit, Mar. 26, 1938; s. Othneil Stockwell and Mary Josephine (Gough) Waud; children: Heather,

Neil. BA, Harvard U., 1960; MA, U. Calif., Berkeley, 1962; PhD (Ford Found. fellow), U. Calif., Berekley, 1965. Asst. prof. bus. econs. Grad. Sch. Bus. U. Chgo., 1964-69; assoc. prof. econs. U. N.C., Chapel Hill, 1969-72, prof., 1972-97, prof. emeritus, 1997—; sr. economist, bd. govs. Fed. Res. Sys., Washington, 1973-75; prof., dir. grad. econs. program Va. Tech., 1997—2002. Cons. Dept. Labor; mem. adv. bd. Taxpayers Ednl. Coalition, 1981; rsch. assoc. Nat. Bur. Econ. Rsch., 1982—92; vis. scholar Cambridge U., 1983; mem. N.C. Energy Policy Coun., 1986—92; vis. prof. Duke U., 1992—94. Author: Macroeconomics, 5th edit., 1992, Microeconomics, 5th edit., 1992; mem. editl. bd. So. Econ. Jour., 1970—73, Studies Econs. and Fin., 1995—97; contbr. articles to profl. jours. Mem.: So. Econ. Assn. (exec. com. 1977—79), Am. Econ. Assn.

WAUGAMAN, RICHARD MERLE, psychiatrist, educator; b. Easton, Pa., Apr. 27, 1949; s. Charles Hoffmeier and Ruth Alviene (Melee) W.; m. Elisabeth Leone Pearson, June 20, 1970; children: Adele Marie, Garrett Dennis. AB, Princeton U., 1970; MD, Duke U., 1973. Cert. psychiatry, 1978, psychoanalysis, 1984. Resident in psychiatry Sheppard-Pratt Hosp., Towson, Md., 1973-76; mem. faculty Washington Sch. Psychiatry, 1983-96; grad. Washington Psychoanalytic Inst., 1984, tng. and supervising analyst, 1989-2001, tng. and supervising analyst emeritus, 2001—; from clin. instr. to clin. assoc. prof. Georgetown U. Sch. Medicine, Washington, 1978-92, clin. prof. psychiatry, 1992—; staff psychiatrist Chestnut Lodge, Rockville, Md., 1986-99. Cons. psychiat. residency program Nat. Naval Med. Ctr., Bethesda, Md., 1994—96; adj. prof. psychiatry Uniformed Svcs. U. of Health Scis., 1999—; reader Folger Shakespeare Libr. Contbr. articles to profl. jours. Mem. Washington Psychoanalytic Soc., Am. Psychoanalytic Assn. (exec. coun. 1993-97, com. on certification 1998-2002), Internat. Psychoanalytic Assn., Am. Psychiat. Assn., Cosmos Club. Home: 8109 Horseshoe Ln Potomac MD 20854-3834 Office Phone: 301-654-9771. Personal E-mail: rwmd@comcast.net.

WAUGH, JOHN STEWART, chemist, educator; b. Willimantic, Conn., Apr. 25, 1929; s. Albert E. and Edith (Stewart) W.; married 1983; children: Alice Collier, Frederick Pierce. AB, Dartmouth Coll., 1949; PhD, Calif. Inst. Tech., 1953; ScD (hon.), Dartmouth Coll., 1989. Rsch. fellow in physics Calif. Inst. Tech., 1952-53; mem. faculty MIT, Cambridge, 1953—, prof. chemistry, 1962—, Albert Amos Noyes prof. chemistry, 1973-88, inst. prof., 1989—, emeritus, 1996—. Vis. prof. U. Calif.-Berkeley, 1963-64, Max Planck Inst., Heidelberg, 1972; sr. fellow Alexander von Humboldt-Stiftung; vis. scientist Harvard U., 1976; mem. chemistry adv. panel NSF, 1966-69, vice chmn., 1968-69; mem. rev. com. Argonne Nat. Lab., 1970-74; mem. sci. and edn. adv. com. Lawrence Berkeley Lab., 1980-86; exchange visitor USSR Acad. Scis., 1962, 75; mem. vis. com. Tufts U., 1966-69, Princeton, 1973-78; mem. fellowship com. Alfred P. Sloan Found., 1977-82; Joliot-Curie prof. École Supérieure de Physique et Chemie, Paris, 1985, 96; lectr. in field. Author: New NMR Methods in Solid State Physics, 1978; editor: Advances in Magnetic Resonance, 1965-87; assoc. editor: Jour. Chem. Physics, 1965-67, Spectrochimica Acta, 1964-78; mem. editl. bd. Chem. Revs., 1978-82, Jour. Magnetic Resonance, 1989—, Applied Magnetic Resonance, 1989—. Recipient Irving Langmuir award, 1976, Gold Pick Axe award, 1976, Pitts. award Spectroscopic Soc. Pitts., 1979, Wolf prize in chemistry, Wolf Found., 1984, Pauling medal, 1985, Calif. Inst. Tech. distingu. alumnus award, 1987, Killian award, 1988, ISMAR prize, 1989, Richards medal, 1992, Evans award, 1994, Ea. Analytical Symposium award 1996, Russell Varian prize, 2006; Sloan fellow, 1958-62, Guggenheim fellow, 1963-64, 72; Sherman Fairchild scholar Calif. Inst. Tech., 1989. Fellow: AAAS, Am. Phys. Soc. (chmn. divsn. chemistry and physics 1983—84); mem.: NAS, Slovenian Acad. Sci. and Arts (fgn. corr.), Nat. Magnetic Resonance Soc. India (hon.), Internat. Soc. Magnetic Resonance (coun. mem. 1989—95, exec. com. 1996—, v.p. 1997—, pres. 1999—2002), Sigma Xi, Phi Beta Kappa. Office: MIT 6-231 77 Massachusetts Ave Cambridge MA 02139-4307 Home Phone: 781-259-8030; Office Phone: 617-253-1901. Business E-Mail: jswaugh@mit.edu.

WAUGH, THEODORE ROGERS, orthopedic surgeon; b. Montreal, Sept. 21, 1926; s. Theodore Rogers and Anne Maude (Lawlor) W.; children: Susanne Rogers, Margaret Stewart, Theodore Rogers. BA, Yale U., 1949; MD, CM, McGill U., 1953; DMS, U. Goteborg, Sweden, 1968. Diplomate Am. Bd. Orthop. Surgery. Intern Royal Victoria Hosp., Montreal, 1953-54; asst. resident in pathology McGill U., 1954-55; asst. resident in surgery NYU Bellevue Med. Ctr., 1955-56; asst. resident, resident, fellow N.Y. Orthop. Hosp., Columbia U., 1958-62, instr., clin. asst. prof. orthop. surgery, 1962-68; asst. attending Presbyn. Hosp., NYC, 1962-68; prof., chief divsn. orthop. surgery U. Calif., Irvine, 1968-78; prof., chmn. dept. orthop. surgery NYU Med. Ctr., 1978-96, emeritus prof., 1997—. Adj. prof. surgery Dartmouth U. Sch. Medicine, 1998-2003, adj. prof. orthopaedics, 2003—. Contbr. numerous articles to profl. jours. Capt., M.C. USAF, 1956-58. Fellow ACS, Royal Coll. Surgeons (Can.), Am. Acad. Orthop. Surgeons, Scoliosis Rsch. Soc., Assn. Bone and Joint Surgeons, Am. Orthop. Assn., Am. Orthop. Soc. Sports Medicine; mem. Soc. Colonial Wars (sec. 2005-06), 20th Century Orthopedic Club, Alpha Omega Alpha. Presbyterian. Achievements include developing designer surgical devices used in orthopaedic surgery. Office: Dartmouth-Hitchcock Med Ctr One Medical Center Dr Lebanon NH 03756 E-mail: trwmd3@comcast.net.

WAUGH, WILLIAM HOWARD, physician, research scientist; b. NYC, May 13, 1925; s. Richey Laughlin and Lyda Pearl (Leamer) W.; m. Eileen Loretta Garrigan, Oct. 4, 1952; children: Mark Howard, Kathleen Cary, William Peter. Student, Boston U., 1943, W.Va. U., 1944; MD, Tufts U., 1948, postgrad., 1949—50. Cardiovascular rsch. trainee Med. Coll. Ga., Augusta, 1954-55, asst. rsch. prof. physiology, 1955-60, assoc. medicine, 1957-60; assoc. prof. medicine U. Ky., Lexington, 1960-69; Ky. Heart Assn. Chair in cardiovascular rsch. Ky. Heart Assn., Lexington, 1963-71; prof. medicine U. Ky., Lexington, 1969-71; prof. medicine and physiology East Carolina U., Greenville, 1971—2001, rsch. prof. physiology, 2001—04, prof. emeritus, 2001—. Head renal sect. U. Ky. Coll., Lexington, 1960-68; chmn. dept. clin. scis. East Carolina U., Greenville, 1971-75, chmn. policy and rev. com. on human rsch., 1972-90. Contbr. articles to profl. jours. With AUS, 1943-46; capt. USAF, 1952-54. Recipient NC Med. Soc. award, 1998. Fellow: ACP; mem.: AAAS, Microcirculatory Soc. (50-Yr. club), Am. Physiology Soc., NC Med. Soc. (life). Achievements include basic advances in excitation contraction coupling in vasc. smooth muscle; basic advances in autoregulation of renal blood flow and urine flow; adj. therapy in acute lung edema; noncovalent antisickling agents and amino acid nutrient in sickle cell hemoglobinopathy; oral citrulline as dietary supplement in man; daily intermittent peritoneal dialysis. Home: 119 Oxford Rd Greenville NC 27858-4954 Personal E-mail: egnwhwangh@webtv.net.

WAVLE, JAMES EDWARD, JR., pharmaceutical company executive, lawyer; b. NYC, July 19, 1942; s. James Edward and Florence Marie (Kehoe) W.; children from previous marriage: James Edward, William Patrick, Robert Thomas, Stephanie Elizabeth; m. Elizabeth Edith Symons Tallett; 1 child, Christopher Andrew; stepchildren: James E. Tallett, Alexander M. Tallett. BA, Adelphi U., 1964; JD, Georgetown U., 1967; LLM, NYU, 1968. Bar: N.Y. bar 1967. With Warner-Lambert Co., Morris Plains, N.J., 1968-87, internat. counsel, 1971-74, assoc. gen. counsel, 1974-77, v.p., gen. counsel, 1977-80, sr. v.p., gen. counsel, 1980-81; corp. sr. v.p. and pres. Parke-Davis Group, 1982-87; pres., CEO Centocor Inc., Malvern, Pa., 1987-92; chmn. Dioscor Inc., Stockton, N.J., 1993-97; chmn., pres., CEO Therics, Inc., Princeton, NJ, 1997—2003. Mem. ABA, Lookaway Golf Club, Stamford Yacht Club.

WAWRYTKO, SANDRA ANN, humanities educator; b. Chgo., Oct. 18, 1951; d. Stanley Andrew Wawrytko and Alyce Valerie Cioch-Wawrytko; m. Charles Wei-hsun Fu, Sept. 29, 1994 (dec. Oct. 15, 1996). BA in Philosophy, Knox Coll., 1972; MA in Philosophy, Washington U., 1975, PhD in Philosophy, 1976. Instr. Washington U., St. Louis, 1973—77; prof. San Diego State U., 1980—. Vis. prof. Chinese Culture U., Yangmingshan, Taiwan, 1984, Fo Guang Buddhist Coll., Kaohsiung, Taiwan, 1990—2007; prin. investigator San Diego State U. Lang. Acquisition Rsch. Ctr., San Diego, 1994—2003; vis. prof. U. San Diego, San Diego, 1978—81; founder, exec. dir. Internat. Soc. for Philosophy and Psychotherapy; founder, pres. Charles Wei-hsun Fu Found. Author: The Undercurrent of Feminine Philosophy in Eastern and Western Thought, 1981, CRYSTAL: Spectrums of Chinese Culture Through Poetry, 1995; editor: North American Institute of Zen Buddhist Studies, Rethinking the Curriculum: Toward an Integrated Interdisciplinary Education, 1990, The Problem of Evil, 2000, (book series) Asian Thought and Culture, Philosophy and Psychotherapy; co-author: The Buddhist Religion, 1996; narrator: interactive CD-ROM Crystals of Chinese Culture, 2000; author (and editor): Saving the Elephant: Asian Encounters with Imperialism, Orientalism, and Gloablization, 2004. Edn. rep. San Diego Sister City Program, Yantai, China, 1985; bd. dirs. San Diego Chinese Hist. Soc. and Mus., 2002—; pres. Charles Wei-hsun Fu Found., San Diego, 1997—. Recipient univ. fellowship, Washington. U., 1974—75, Humanities Advancement Poetry Contest award, Humanities Advancement Com., 1983. Mem.: World Congress of Logotherapy (sec.-gen. 1982—85), Internat. Soc. for Chinese Philosophy (sec., exec. bd. mem. 1990—2003), Phi Beta Delta (governing bd. 2002—06), Phi Beta Kappa (Faculty Lectr. Nu chpt. 2002—03). Avocations: poetry, translating classical Chinese poetry, collecting Asian art and books, creating culinary adventures. Office: San Diego State U Dept Philosophy San Diego CA 92182-0303 E-mail: wawrytko@mail.sdsu.edu.

WAWRZASZEK, SUSAN V., university librarian; MSLS, SUNY Buffalo. With Brandeis U., Mass., 1995—, assoc. univ. libr. Mass., 2002—03, acting univ. libr. Mass., 2003—05, univ. libr. Mass., 2005—. Office: Brandeis U Mailstop 045 PO Box 549110 Waltham MA 02454-9110 Office Phone: 781-736-4700. Office Fax: 781-736-4719. E-mail: wawrzaszek@brandeis.edu.

WAWRZYNIAK, CYNTHIA, biology professor; b. Mich. PhD, U. Tenn., Knoxville, 1986. Sect. head hair and skin care tech. Proctor and Gamble, Cinn., 1991—98; assoc. prof. Pellissippi State Tech. Comm. Coll., Knoxville, 1998—. Vol tchr., organizer local food can drive, Tenn. Achievements include patents for hair growth technology. Office: Pellissippi State Tech Comm Coll 10915 Hardin Valley Rd Knoxville TN 37933 Office Phone: 865-971-5227.

WAX, ARNOLD, physician; b. Bklyn., Mar. 11, 1949; s. Emanuel and Eleanor (Greenfield) W.; m. Francine Wax; children: Erin, Rachael, Adam, Benjamin. BS in Pharm. Scis., Columbia U., 1971; MD, SUNY, Buffalo, 1976. Diplomate Nat. Bd. Med. Examiners, Am. Bd. Internal Medicine, Am. Bd. Quality Assurance and Utilization Rev. Physicians, Am. Acad. Pain Mgmt.; lic. physician, Fla., Calif., N.D., Minn., N.Y., Nev., Ariz. Intern, resident Millard Fillmore Hosp., Buffalo, 1976-79; clin. asst. instr. SUNY, 1977-79; instr. medicine U. Rochester, NY, 1979-81; dir. internal medicine U. N.D., Grand Forks, 1982-83, clin. asst. prof., 1982-85; pvt. practice Las Vegas, Nev., 1987—. Mem. staff Sunrise Hosp., Las Vegas, Desert Springs Hosp., Las Vegas, Nathan Adelson Hospice, Las Vegas, So. Hills Hosp., Spring Valley Hosp. Contbr. articles to profl. jours. Grantee So. Nev. Cancer Rsch. Found., Ea. Coop. Oncology Group, Gynecol. Oncology Group, North Ctrl. Cancer Treatment Group, S.W. Oncology Group. Fellow Am. Coll. Physicians; mem. AMA, Am. Cancer Soc. (fellow 1979), Am. Soc. Clin. Oncology, Am. Coll. Physicians (gov. State of Nev.), Nev. Oncology So. (v.p.), Nev. Med. Soc., Clark County Med. Soc. (trustee, peer rev. com., treas.), Nev. Peer Rev. Orgn., U. Nev. Las Vegas Found., Nev. Dance Theater, Nev. Opera Theater, Las Vegas Symphony, Nev. Inst. Contemporary Art, Lied Mus., Allied Arts Coun., James Platt White Soc., U. Buffalo Found., Rho Chi (Bronze medal 1971). Home: 2224 Chatsworth Ct Henderson NV 89074-5309 Office Phone: 702-952-1251. Business E-Mail: arnold.wax@usoncology.com. E-mail: arnoldwax@cox.net.

WAX, NADINE VIRGINIA, retired bank executive; b. Van Horne, Iowa, Dec. 7, 1927; d. Laurel Lloyd and Viola Henrietta (Schrader) Bobzien; divorced; 1 child, Sharlyn K. Wax Munns. Student, U. Iowa, 1970-71; grad. Nat. Sch. Real Estate and Fin., Ohio State U., 1980-81. Jr. acct. McGladrey, Hansen, Dunn (now McGladrey-Pullen Co., CPAs), Cedar Rapids, Iowa, 1944-47; office mgr. Iowa Securities Co. (now Wells Fargo Mortgage Co.), Cedar Rapids, 1954-55; asst. cashier Mchts. Nat. Bank (now U.S. Bancorp.), Cedar Rapids, 1956-75; asst. v.p. Mchts. Nat. Bank (now U.S. Bancorp), Cedar Rapids, 1976-78, v.p., 1979-90; ret., 1990. Vol. St. Luke's Hosp. Aux., Cedar Rapids, 1981—85, SCORE, 1999—2007; bd. dirs., v.p. Kirkwood C.C. Facilities Found., 1970—2007; bd. dirs., treas. Kirkwood C.C., 1984—91; trustee Indian Creek Nature Ctr., Cedar Rapids, 1974—2007, pres., 1980—81; mem. Linn County Regional Planning Commn., 1982—92, Cedar Rapids-Marion Fine Arts Coun., 1994—97; bd. suprs. Compensation Commn. for Condemnation, 1987—92; bd. dirs. Am. Heart Assn., Cedar Rapids, 1983—94; mem. Iowa Employment and Tng. Coun., Des Moines, 1982—83. Recipient Outstanding Woman award, Cedar Rapids Tribute to Women and Industry, 1984. Mem. Fin. Women Internat. (state edn. chmn. 1982-83), Am. Inst. Banking (bd. dirs. 1968-70), Soc. Real Estate Appraisers (treas. 1978-80), Linn County Bankers Assn. (pres. 1979-80), Cedar Rapids Bd. Realtors, Cedar Rapids C. of C. (bus.-edn. com. 1986-91), Cedar Rapids Country Club. Lutheran. Avocations: travel, reading, walking. Home: 147 Ashcombe SE Cedar Rapids IA 52403-1700

WAX, WILLIAM EDWARD, photojournalist; b. Miami, Fla., Dec. 7, 1956; s. Ira and Rita (Gunshor) W. AS, Berry Coll., Rome, Ga., 1976; BS in Engring., U. Fla., 1983. With Ind. Fla. Alligator, Gainesville, Fla., 1977-79; staff photographer Gainesville (Fla.) Sun, 1979-87; photo cons. N.Y. Times regional newspapers, 1984—; freelance photographer Miami, 1987—; pres. Wax & Co. Inc., Miami Beach, Fla., 1989—, Waxcom, Miami Beach, 1996—. Owner Studio SoBe, Miami Beach, 1992—; faculty So. Short Course in News Photography, 1985—; lectr. in field. Named Photographer of Yr., NPPA/U. Mo. and Nikon, 1980, So. Photographer of Yr., 1980, Regional Photographer of Yr., 1979, 82, 85; nominated Pulitzer prize, 1979, 89, STC Internat. Design, 1996-97; recipient Mark of Excellence, Sigma Delta Chi, 1978, Best of Show award Atlanta Seminar on Photojournalism, 1982, Best of Show and Silver medal Hearst awards, 1978, Design Gold award Fla. Tech. Writers Assn., 1992, Design award, Gold award, Excellence award Soc. Tech. Comm. Internat. Tech. Art Competition, 1993, 94, 97-03, Best of Show, 1994, 98, 01, Disting. Design award, 1993, 97, 99-03, Excellence Design award, 1993, 98, 99, Design Excellence awards and award of merit, 1995, 00, Best of Show award Ann. Report Fla. Pub. Rels., 1995, Gold, Silver and Bronze awards Fla. Mag. Assn., 1994, 96-04, Merit award STC, 1995, Apex Design awards 1996-06, Global award/Ann. Report, 1996, Maggie award Best Newsletter in the West, 2004, Healthcare Advt. award, 2002-06, SIAA awards, 2004-06. Mem. Nat. Press Photographers Assn., Fla. Mag. Assn., Profl. Photographers Am., Nikon Profl. Svcs., Fla. Press Photographers Assn. Office: Wax & Co 350 Lincoln Rd Ste 516 Miami FL 33139-3148 Office Phone: 305-674-9542.

WAXENBERG, JAY DAVID, lawyer; b. NYC, Aug. 29, 1956; s. Milton J. and Edith (Balter) W.; m. Gayle D. Waxenberg, Mar. 3, 1985; children: Michael Ian, Alex Evan. BA, SUNY, Stony Brook, 1978; JD, Boston U., 1981; LLM in Taxation, NYU, 1987. Bar: NY 1982. Estate adminstr. US Trust Co., NY, 1981-84; assoc. personal planning dept. Proskauer Rose, LLP, NYC, 1984-90, partner, chmn. personal planning dept., 1991—, former exec. com. mem. Faculty mem. Fordham U. Sch. Law, continuing edn. prog. Estate Planning Beyond the Basics; faculty mem. Practising Law Inst. Intro. to the Adminstrn. of NY Estates; lectr. in will drafting. Contbr. articles to profl. jours. Mem. health sci. profl. advisor cir. Columbia U.; mem. Bankers and Lawyers adv. com. NY Philharmonic; mem. profl. adv. com. Mus. Arts and Design; mem. planning giving adv. com. Mus. Modern Art; mem. planning giving profl. adv. com. Blythedale Children's Hosp.; mem. planned giving adv. coun. NY-Presbyterian Hosp.; mem. planned giving adv. com. NY Pub. Libr.; mem. trust and estate adv. com. Meml. Sloan Kettering Cancer Ctr. Named Leader in Field, Chambers USA, NY Super Lawyer, Law and Politics, Best in Class Atty.; named one of Best Lawyers in Am., Top 100 Estate Planning Attys., Worth Mag., 2006. Fellow Am. Coll. of Trust & Estate Counsel; mem. Assn. Bar of City of NY, NY State Bar Assn. Office: Proskauer Rose LLP 1585 Broadway Fl 24 New York NY 10036-8299 Office Phone: 212-969-3606. Business E-Mail: jwaxenberg@proskauer.com. *

WAXMAN, ALLEN, pharmaceutical executive; AB magna cum laude, Dartmouth Coll., 1984; JD magna cum laude, Harvard U., 1987. Law clk. for Hon. Thomas Penfield Jackson US Dist. Ct., Washington; ptnr. Williams & Connolly, LLP, Washington; sr. asst. gen. counsel, chief litig. Pfizer, Inc., 2003—05, sr. v.p., assoc. gen. counsel, 2005—06, sr. v.p., gen. counsel, 2006—. Chmn. bd. Thurgood Marshall Acad., Washington; adj. prof. law Georgetown U. Law Ctr.; mem. US policy governance com. Pfizer, Inc. Recipient Champion of Children & Families Award, 2006. Mem.: NY Legal Aid Soc. (bd. mem.), Equal Justice Works (vice chmn.). Office: Pfizer Inc 235 E 42nd St New York NY 10017 *

WAXMAN, ANITA, theater producer; Prodr. (plays) Mrs. Klein, Below the Belt, Wild Honey (Drama Desk award nomination), The Foreigner, Music Man, 2000-01, One Flew Over the Cuckoo's Nest, 2001 (Tony award for Best Revival of a Play), Noises Off, 2001-02, Top Dog/Underdog, 2002 (Tony award for Best Play and Pulitzer Prize), The Elephant Man, 2002, Flower Drum Song, 2002-03, Gypsy, 2004 (Tony award for Best Revival of a Musical), Bombay Dreams, 2004—; co-prodr. (plays) Present Laughter (Tony award nomination), Breaking the Code, Circle & Bravo, Long Day's Journey Into Night, Annie get Your Gun, Mr. & Mrs. Nobody. Founder Noah's Ark Found.; creator Passin-Waxman Ctr., Moscow. Office: Waxman Williams Entertainment 260 W 44th St Ste 500 New York NY 10036-3900

WAXMAN, BRUCE I., lawyer; b. NYC, July 30, 1942; m. Sarah Jane Elpern, Mar. 17, 1974. BS, Cornell U., 1964; JD, Columbia U., 1967. Bar: D.C. 1970. Atty. Am. Fedn. of Govt. Employees, Washington, 1970—72; exec. dir. D.C. Pub. Employee Rels. Bd., 1972—80; dir. collective bargaining Assn. of Flight Attendants, Washington, 1980—82; atty. U.S. Dept. Commerce, Washington, 1983—2000; assoc. gen. counsel Exec. Office of Immigration Rev. U.S. Dept. Justice, Washington, 2000—06. Capt. US Army, 1967—69. Mem.: DC Bar (co-chair labor and employment law sect.), Soc. Fed. Labor Relations Professionals, Fed. Bar Assn. Office: US Dept Justice Exec Office for Immigration Rev 5107 Leesburg Pike Ste 2600 Falls Church VA 22041

WAXMAN, HENRY ARNOLD, congressman; b. LA, Sept. 12, 1939; s. Louis and Esther (Silverman) Waxman; m. Janet Kessler, Oct. 17, 1971; children: Carol Lynn, Michael David. BA in Polit. Sci, UCLA, 1961, JD, 1964. Bar: Calif. 1965. Practicing atty., 1965—68; mem. Calif. State Assembly, 1969-74, US Congress from 30th Calif. dist. (formerly 29th), 1975—, chmn. Commerce Subcommittee on Health and Environment, 1979-94, ranking minority mem. Govt. Reform Com., 1997—, mem. Energy and Commerce Com., chmn. Oversight and Govt. Reform Com., 2007—. Pres. Calif. Fedn. Young Dems., 1965-67. Recipient Excellence in Pub. Svc. award, Am. Acad. Pediat., 1983, Pub. Svc. award, Am. Assn. Pub. Health Dentistry, 1985, James Madison award, ALA, 1990, Leadership award, Nat. Gay and Lesbian Task Force, 1991, Pub. Policy on Aging award, Jewish Home for the Aging, LA, 1992, Leadership in Govt. award, Keystone Ctr., 2001, Nat. Health Leadership award, Nat. Orgn. Rare Disorders, 2002, Excellence in Immunization award, Nat. Partnership for Immunization, 2002, Nat. Leadership award, Nat. Citizens' Coalition for Nursing Home Reform, 2002, Claude Pepper award, Nat. Inst. Cmty.-Based Long-Term Care, 2004, Pub. Svc. award, Internat. Found. Employee Benefit Plans, 2004. Mem. Calif. Bar Assn., Guardians of Jewish Home for the Aged, Am. Jewish Congress, Am. Civil Liberties Union, Sierra Club, B'nai B'rith, Phi Sigma Alpha. Democrat. Jewish. Office: US Ho Reps 2204 Rayburn Ho Office Bldg Washington DC 20515-0530 Office Phone: 202-225-3976. Office Fax: 202-225-4099. *

WAXMAN, RONALD, computer engineer; b. Newark, Nov. 28, 1933; s. Benjamin and Rose (Lifson) Waxman; m. Pearl Latterman, June 19, 1955; children: David, Roberta, Benjamin. BSEE, NJ Inst. Tech., Newark, 1955; MEE, Syracuse U., NY, 1963. Engr. IBM, Poughkeepsie, NY, 1955-56, 58-64, East Fishkill, NY, 1964-70, Poughkeepsie and Kingston, NY, 1970-80, sr. engr. Manassas, Va., 1980-87; prin. scientist U. Va., Charlottesville, 1987-97; cons. pvt. practice, Reston, Va., 1997—. IEEE rep. and tech. advisor to Internat. Elec. Commn. US tech. activities group for internat. design automation stds., 1994—98; steering com. very high speed integrated circuits hardware description lang. VHDL Users Group, 1987—91; panel for assessment of Nat. Inst. Stds. and Tech. Measurement and Stds. Labs. NRC, 2002—; presenter in field. Contbr. articles to profl. jours. 1st lt. USAF, 1956-58. Fellow IEEE, IEEE Computer Soc. (bd. govs. 1989-94, 96-98, 2000-02, chmn. fellows evaluation com. 1995-96, chmn. audit com., 1997, founder, chmn. design automation stds. subcom. 1983-88, steering com. 1989-2003, chmn. design automation tech. com. 1988-90, steering com. 1991—, vice-chmn. tech. activities bd. 1991-92, 99, chmn. awards com. 1993, disting. visitor 1986-88, chmn. disting. visitor program 2004—, v.p. activities bd. 1994, v.p. tech. activities, 1998, Meritorious Svc. cert. 1988, Disting. Svc. cert. 1994, TAB Pioneer award 1989, 3d. Millennium medal 2000), Internat. Fedn. Info. Processing Orgns. (CS rep. 2000—, sec. tech. reps. com., 2000—, vice chmn. 2004—, Outstanding Svc. award 2005, tech. com. chmn. IFIP TC5, 2006—), Assn. for Computing Machinery (spl. interest group DA). Achievements include patents in field. E-mail: r.waxman@computer.org.

WAXMAN, SETH PAUL, lawyer; b. Hartford, Conn., Nov. 28, 1951; s. Felix H. and Frieda (Goodman) W.; m. Debra F. Goldberg, Mar. 20, 1977; children: Noah, Sarah, Ethan. AB summa cum laude, Harvard U., 1973; JD, Yale U., 1977. Bar: D.C. 1978, U.S. Dist. Ct. D.C. 1979, U.S. Ct. Appeals (D.C. cir.) 1979, U.S. Ct. Appeals (1st cir.) 2000, (2d cir.) 1998, (3d cir.) 1983, (4th cir.) 1982, (5th cir.) 1997, (6th cir.) 1998, (7th cir.) 1998, (8th cir.) 1998, (9th cir.) 1989, (10th cir.) 1998, (11th cir.) 1989, U.S. Ct. Appeals (fed. cir.) 1998, U.S. Supreme Ct. 1982. Law clk to Judge Gerhard A. Gesell, Washington, 1977-78; ptnr. Miller Cassidy Larroca & Lewin, Washington, 1978-94; assoc. dep. atty. gen. U.S. Dept. Justice, Washington, 1994-96, dep. solicitor gen., 1996-97, acting dep. atty. gen., 1997, solicitor gen., 1997-2001; ptnr. Wilmer, Cutler, Pickering, Hale and Dorr, LLP, 2001—06. Disting. vis. from practice Georgetown U Law Ctr., 2001—; vis. prof. Georgetown U. Law Ctr., 2001; vis. fellow Harvard U. JFK Sch. Govt., 2001; dir. Supreme Ct. Inst., Georgetown U. Law Ctr.; chmn. Legal Affairs Mag., 2004—06. Editor Yale Law Jour., The Combatant Detention Trilogy Through the Lenses of History, 2005; contbr. articles to profl. jours. Trustee Supreme Ct. Hist. Soc.; overseer Harvard U. Named hon. spl. agt., FBI, 2001; named one of 75 Best Lawyers in Washington, Washingtonian mag., 2002, 100 Most Influential Lawyers, Nat. Law Jour., 2006; recipient

Pro Bono Publico award, ABA, 1988, Edmund J. Randolph award, U.S. Dept. Justic, 2001, Benjamin L. Cardozo Cert. of Merit, Anti-Defamation League, 1987, Thomas Jefferson Found. medal in law, U. Va., 2002, Pursuit of Justice award, Internat. Assn. Jewish Lawyers and Jurists, 2001, BYU Rex Lee Advocacy Award, 2002; fellow Michael C. Rockefeller, Harvard U., 1973—74. Master: Edmund Coke Appellate Inn Court; fellow: Am. Acad. Arts & Sciences, Am. Coll. Trial Lawyers, Am Acad. Appellate Attys., Am. Bar Found.; mem.: Am. Law Inst. Office: Wilmer Cutler Pickering Hale and Dorr LLP 1875 Pennsylvania Ave Washington DC 20006 Office Phone: 202-663-6000. Fax: 202-663-6000. E-mail: seth.waxman@wilmerhale.com.

WAXMAN, SHELDON ROBERT, lawyer; b. Chgo., Apr. 22, 1941; s. Henri and Ann (Sokolsky) W.; m. Katherine Slamski, Aug. 23, 1979; children: Josiah, Zoe. BA, U. Ill., 1963; JD, DePaul U., 1965. Bar: Ill. 1965, U.S. Supreme Ct. 1976, Mich. 1985. Staff atty. Argonne (Ill.) Nat. Lab., 1968-71; asst. U.S. Atty., Chgo., 1971-74; owner firm Waxman Tax & Legal Network, Chgo. and South Haven, Mich., 1976—. Owner Ind. Contractor Cons. Svcs. Author: In the Teeth of the Wind, 2002, All Anybody Needs to Know About Independent Contracting, 2003; (screenplays) Black Messiah Murders, 2003, Chicago Piranhas, 2003; co-author: Black Messiah Murders, A Sam Cohen Case Adventure, Number 1, 2003, Piranhas on the Loose, A Sam Cohen Case Adventure Number 2, 2003, The Josephus Enigma, A Sam Cohen Case Adventure, Number 3, 2005; editor-in-chief New Z Letter; contbr. articles to profl. jours. Founder Freedom Lawyers of Am., People for Simplified Tax Law, Nukes to the Sun. Mem.: Mystery Writers Am. Office: PO Box 309 South Haven MI 49090-0309 Office Phone: 269-207-6219. E-mail: shelly@cybersol.com.

WAXMAN, STEPHEN GEORGE, neurologist, neuroscientist; b. Newark, Aug. 17, 1945; s. Morris and Beatrice (Levitch) Waxman; m. Merle Applebaum, June 25, 1968; children: Matthew, David. AB, Harvard U., 1967, PhD, 1970, MD, 1972; MA (hon.), Yale U., 1986. Rsch. fellow in neurosci. Albert Einstein Coll. Medicine, Bronx, NY, 1970—72; clin. fellow Boston City Hosp., 1972—75; asst. prof. neurology Med. Sch. Harvard U., Boston, 1975—77, assoc. prof., 1977—78; prof. Stanford U., 1978—86, vice chmn. dept. neurology, 1981—86, chmn. neuroscis. program, 1982—86; chief neurology unit Palo Alto VA Hosp., Calif., 1978—86; chmn. dept. neurology Yale U., New Haven, 1986—, Bridget Marie Flaherty prof. neurology, neurobiology and pharmacology, 1986, 2005—; chief neurology Yale-New Haven Hosp., 1986; dir., Ctr. for Neuroscience and Regeneration Rsch. Yale U. Med. Sch. Vis. asst. prof. biology MIT, Cambridge, 1975—77, vis. assoc. prof., 1977—78; vis. prof. U. Coll. London, 1998—, Inst. Neurology, Queen Square, England, 1998—; vice chmn. dept. neurology Stanford U., 1981—86, chmn. neuroscis. program, 1982—86; mem. adv. bd. Regeneration Programs VA, Washington, 1982—86; mem. sci. adv. com. Nat. Spinal Cord Injury Assn., 1982—87, Paralyzed Vets. Am., 1981—91; dir. Ctr. Rsch. Neurol. Disease VA Med. Ctr., West Haven, Conn., 1986—; mem. corp. Marine Biol. Labs., Woods Hole, Mass., 1988; mem. sci. adv. coun. Am. Paralysis Assn., 1988—92; mem. bd. sci. counselors NINDB, 1990—92; mem. bd. neurosci. and behavior Inst. Medicine, 1990; Geschwind vis. prof. Harvard U., 1996; dir. PVA/EPVA Neurosci. Rsch. Ctr. VA Hosp., West Haven, 1986—; numerous vis. lectureships. Author: Spinal Cord Compression, 1990, Correlative Neuroanatomy, 1995, 2d edit., 2000, The Axon, 1995, Diseases of the Spinal Cord, 2000, Form and Function in the Brain and Spinal Cord, 2001; editor: Physiology and Pathobiology of Axons, 1978; editor-in-chief: The Neuroscientist; editor-in-chief Neurosci. Letters; editor: Jour. Physiology; assoc. editor: Muscle and Nerve, Jour. Neurol. Scis., mem. editl. bd.: Brain, Ann. Neurology, Trends in Molecular Medicine, Brain Rsch., Internat. Rev. Neurobiology, Jour. Neurol. Rehab., Devel. Neurosci., Jour. Neurotrauma, Neurobiology of Disease, Cerebrovascular Disease, Synapse, Restorative Neurology and Neurosci.; editor: Jour. of Physiology. Named Nat. Multiple Sclerosis Soc. established investigator, 1987; recipient Trygve Tuve Meml. award, NIH, 1973, Rsch. Career Devel. award, 1975, Disting. Alumnus award, Albert Einstein Coll. Medicine, 1990; rsch. fellow, Univ. Coll., London, 1969. Fellow: NAS, Am. Acad. Neurology (Wartenberg award 1999, Dystel prize 2003), Am. Heart Assn. (stroke coun.), Inst. Medicine, Royal Soc. Medicine (Gt. Britain); mem.: Nat. Multiple Sclerosis Soc. (Reingold award 2005), Am. Univ. Profs. Neurology, Assn. Rsch. in Nervous and Mental Diseases (trustee, pres. 1992), World Fedn. Neurology, Am. Neurol. Assn. (councillor 1980), Soc. Neurosci., Internat. Brain Rsch. Orgn. (U.S. nat. com.), Dana Alliance for Brain Initiatives, Am. Soc. Cell Biology. Office: Yale U Sch Medicine 33 Cedar St New Haven CT 06519-2314 Business E-Mail: stephen.waxman@yale.edu.

WAXSE, DAVID JOHN, judge; b. Oswego, Kans., June 29, 1945; s. I. Joseph and Mary (Poole) W.; m. Linda Schilling (div.); children: Rachel, Ryan, Rebecca; m. Judy Pfannenstiel, May 29, 1982; 1 child, Elayna. BA, U. Kans., 1967; teaching cert., Columbia U., 1968, JD, 1971. Bar: Kans. 1971, U.S. Ct. Appeals (10th cir.) 1971, U.S. Supreme Ct. 1975, U.S. Ct. Appeals (8th Cir.) 1998. Dean of students Intermediate Sch. 88, NYC, 1968-70; spl. edn. tchr. Peter Cooper Sch., NYC, 1970-71; assoc. Payne & Jones, Olathe, Kans., 1971-74, ptnr., 1974-84; of counsel Shook, Hardy & Bacon, Overland Park, Kans., 1984-86, ptnr., 1986-95; shareholder Shook, Hardy & Bacon P.C., Overland Park, 1993-95; ptnr. Shook, Hardy & Bacon L.L.P., Overland Park, Kans., 1995-99; shareholder Shook, Hardy & Bacon P.C., Overland Park, 1993-95, v.p., asst. gen. counsel, 1995-99; U.S. magistrate judge Kansas City, 1999—. Mcpl. judge City of Shawnee, Kans., 1974-80; atty. City of DeSoto, Kans., 1972-79; adj. prof. U. Kans. Sch. Law, Lawrence, 1981-82; mem. juv. code adv. com. Kans. Jud. Coun., 1979-83, guardianship adv. com., 1982-83, atty. fees adv. com., 1986-87; mem. Civil Justice Reform Act Adv. Com., U.S. Dist. Ct. for Dist. Kans., 1991-95; mem. Kans. Commn. on Jud. Qualifications, 1992-99, vice-chmn. 1994-97, chair, 1997-99; v.p. Kans. Legal Svcs., Inc., 1980-82, pres., 1985-87; bd. advisors Kans. Coll. Advocacy, 1979-80; bd. trustees, Lawyer's Com. Civil Rights Under Law, 1997-99. Author: (with others) Kansas Employment Law, 1985, Litigating Employment Law Cases, 1987, Kansas Employment Law Handbook, 1991, supplements, 1992, 95, Kansas Annual Survey, 1990-2000; contbr. articles to profl. jours. Mem. Kan. Gov.'s Adv. Com. on Criminal Justice, 1974-77; mem. Kans. Justice Commn., 1997-99; gen. counsel Western Mo. Dist. ACLU, 1976-78, 86-97, v.p., 1983-86, nat. bd. dirs., 1979-86, 91-99, chmn. children's rights com., 1980-86; mem. AIDS Pol. Network, 1987-99, med. treatment issues com., 1991-96, constn. com., 1991-99; mem. med./tech. com. AIDS Coun. Greater Kans. City, 1986-98, ethics com. consortium Midwest Bioethics Ctr., 1990-2002; bd. dirs. Parents Anonymous Kans., 1978-83, pres., 1979; bd. dirs., mem. fin. com. Kans. Com. for Prevention Child Abuse, 1980-83. Fellow Am. Bar Found., Kans. Bar Found.; mem. ABA (chmn. children's rights com. and family law sects. 1985-86, mem. ho. of dels. 2000—, professionalism com. 2000-05, bd. of editors The Profl. Lawyer, 2000-05, mem. exec. com. nat. conf. fed. trial judges 2005—), Am. Judicature Soc. (bd. dirs. 1997-2003, adv. com. for ctr. for judicial conduct 1997—), Kans. Bar Assn. (chmn. legal aid com. 1978-83, bd. govs. 1988—, v.p. 1996-97, pres.-elect 1997-98, pres. 1998-99, mem. ABA ho. dels. 2000—, Pres.' Outstanding Svc. award 1982, 2006), Kans. City Met. Bar Assn., Johnson County Bar Assn. (chmn. legal aid com. 1975-82, 92-96), Earl E. O'Connor Am. Inn of Ct. (counselor, pres.-elect 2002, pres. 2003). Office: U S Courthouse 500 State Ave Rm 219 Kansas City KS 66101-2400 E-mail: judge_waxse@ksd.uscourts.gov.

WAY, BARBARA HAIGHT, retired dermatologist; b. Franklin, NJ, Dec. 27, 1941; d. Charles Padley and Alice Barbara (Haight) Shoemaker; m. Anthony Biden Way; children: Matthew Shoemaker Way, Sarah Shoemaker Way. AB in Music cum laude, Bryn Mawr Coll., 1962, postgrad., 1963-64; MD, U. Pa., 1968. Diplomate Am. Bd. Dermatology. Systems engr. IBM, Balt., 1962—63; mem. dean's staff Bryn Mawr (Pa.) Coll., 1963—64; med. intern U. Wis. Hosps., Madison, 1968—69, resident in dermatology, 1969—72; physician emergency rm. St. Francis Hosp., La Crosse, Wis., 1969—72, founder dept. dermatology, 1972; asst. prof. dept. dermatology Tex. Tech U. Sch. Medicine, Lubbock, 1972—73, from asst. clin. to assoc. clin. prof., 1973—74, asst. prof., assoc. chair, 1974—76, assoc. prof., chair, 1976—81, assoc. clin. prof., 1981—92; clin. prof. Tex. Tech. U. Health Scis. Ctr., Lubbock, 1995—2005, founder, dir. dermatology residency tng. program, 1978—81, pvt. practice, 1973—74, 1981—2006; acting dir. Lubbock City Health Dept., 1982—83; ret., 2006. Mem. credentials com. Covenant Hosp., Lubbock, 1990, 92, 94, 95, founding dir. phototherapy unit, 1990-91, 93, exec. com., 1991, 93, 98, chief dermatology sect., 1991, 93, 98, subsect. chief, 1992, 94. Alumna admissions rep. Bryn Mawr Coll., 1972-75, 87-96; mem. selection com. outstanding physician Lubbock chpt. Am. Cancer Soc., 1991-94, chmn., 1991; bd. dirs. Tex. Tech. U. Med. Found., 1987-89, Double T. Connection, 1988-90. Fellow Am. Acad. Dermatology (reviewer jour.); mem. Tex. Dermatol. Soc. (chmn. roster com. 1980), Tex. Med. Assn. (mem. sexually transmitted diseases com. 1986-90, mem. coun. pub. health 1990-92, vice councillor dist. III 1992-98, councillor dist. III 1998-2000, chmn. reference com. fin. and orgnl. affairs ann. session 1992), Lubbock County-Garza County Med. Soc. (mem. various coms. 1980-2000, chmn. sch. and pub. health com. 1983, mem. bd. censors 1983-85, chair 1985, sec. 1986, v.p. 1987, liaison with Tex. Tech. U. Health Scis. Ctr. com. 1988-91, co-chmn. pub. rels. com. 1988-89, alt. Tex. Med. Assn. del. 1988-89, del. 1990-95, 98-2000, pres.-elect 1989, pres. 1990, chmn. ad hoc bylaws com. 1991-94, chmn. Hippocratic award 1991), Women's Dermatologic Soc. (founding sec.). Personal E-mail: anthony.way@ttuhsc.edu.

WAY, DANNY, professional skateboarder; b. Portland, Ore., Apr. 15, 1974; Skateboarder H-Street, 1988—90, Blind, 1990—91; founder, skateboarder Plan B, 1991—. Named Skater of Yr., 1991, 2004. Achievements include being the first person to build and use a skateboarding megaramp, 2003; setting a distance record of 75 feet, 2004; jumping over the Great Wall of China using a megaramp, 2005. Office: c/o Plan B 1410 Vantage Ct Vista CA 92081

WAY, E(DWARD) LEONG, pharmacologist, toxicologist, educator; b. Watsonville, Calif., July 10, 1916; s. Leong Man and Lai Har (Shew) Way; m. Madeline Li, Aug. 11, 1944; children: Eric, Linette. BS, U. Calif., Berkeley, 1938, MS, 1940; PhD, U. Calif., San Francisco, 1942. Pharm. chemist Merck & Co., Rahway, NJ, 1942; instr. pharmacology George Washington U., 1943-46, asst. prof., 1946-48; asst. prof. pharmacology U. Calif., San Francisco, 1949-52, assoc. prof., 1952-57, prof., 1957-87, prof. emeritus, 1987—, chmn. dept. pharmacology, 1973-78. USPHS spl. rsch. fellow U. Berne, Switzerland, 1955-56, China Med. Bd.; rsch. fellow, vis. prof. U. Hong Kong, 1962-63; Sterling Sullivan disting. vis. prof. Martin Luther King U., 1982; hon. prof. pharmacology and neurosci. Guangzhou Med. Coll., 1987; adv. com. Pharm. Rsch. Mfrs. Assn. Found., 1968-98; mem. coun. Am. Bur. for Med. Advancement in China, 1982; bd. dirs. Li Found., 1970—, pres., 1985-98, bd. dirs. Haight Ashbury Free Clinics, 1986-93; Tsumura prof. neuropsychopharmacology med. sch. Gunma U., Maebashi, Japan, 1989-90; sr. staff fellow Nat. Inst. on Drug Abuse, 1990-91; rschr. on drug metabolism, analgetics, devel. pharmacology, drug tolerance, drug dependence and Chinese materia medica; presenter in field. Editor: New Concepts in Pain, 1967, (with others) Fundamentals of Drug Metabolism and Drug Disposition, 1971, Endogenous and Exogenous Opiate Agonists and Antagonists, 1979; mem. editl. bd. Clin. Pharmacology, Therapeutics, 1975-87, Drug, Alcohol Dependence, 1976-87, Progress in Neuro-Psychopharmacology, 1977-91, Research Communications in Chem. Pathology and Pharmacology, 1978-91, Alcohol and Drug Dependence, 1986-91, Asian Pacific Jour. Pharm., 1985—, Jour. Chinese Medicine, 1993—; contbr. numerous articles and revs. to profl. pubs. Recipient Faculty Rsch. Lectr. award, U. Calif., San Francisco, 1974, San Francisco Chinese Hosp. award, 1976, Cultural citation and Gold medal, Ministry of Edn., Republic of China, 1978, Nathan B. Eddy award, Coll. on Problems in Drug Dependence, 1979, Mentorship award, Coll. on Problems in Drug Dependence, San Juan, 2004, Chancellor's award, U. Calif., 1986, Disting. Alumnus award, U. Calif., San Francisco, 1990, Asian Pacific Am. Systemwide Alliance award, 1993, Lifetime Achievement award, Chinese Hist. Soc., 2001, Outstanding Overseas Chinese award, Chinese Cons. Benevolent Assn., Chinese Womens Assn., 2005, Cert. of Honor, Mayor Gavin Newsome, San Francisco, 2005. Fellow Am. Coll. Neuropsychopharmacology (life, emeritus), Am. Coll. Clin. Pharmacology (hon.), Coll. on Problems of Drug Dependence (exec. com. 1978-92, chmn. bd. dirs. 1978-82, Nathan B. Eddy award 1979, Mentorship award 2004); mem. AAAS, Am. Soc. Pharmacology, Exptl. Therapeutics (bd. editors 1957-65, pres. 1976-77, Torald Sollman award 1992), Fedn. Am. Socs. Exptl. Biology (exec. bd. 1975-79, pres. 1977-78), Am. Pharm. Assn. (life, Rsch. Achievement award 1962), AMA, Soc. Aid and Rehab. Drug Addicts (Hong Kong, life), Western Pharmacology Soc. (pres. 1963-64), Japanese Pharm. Soc. (hon.), Coun. Sci. Soc. Pres.' (exec. com. 1979-84, treas. 1980-84), Chinese Pharmacology Soc. (hon.), Academia Sinica (academician). Office: Univ Calif Dept Cellular and Molecular Pharmacology U64 PBX 0622 San Francisco CA 94143-0001 Office Phone: 415-476-2722.

WAY, JACOB EDSON, III, museum director; b. Chgo., May 18, 1947; s. Jacob Edson Jr. and Amelia (Evans) W.; m. Jean Ellwood Chappell, Sept. 6, 1969; children: Sarah Chappell Quiroga, Rebecca Stoddard, Jacob Edson IV. BA, Beloit Coll., 1968; MA, U. Toronto, 1971, PhD, 1978; postgrad., Episcopal Theol. Sem. S.W., 2005—. From instr. to assoc. prof. Beloit (Wis.) Coll., 1972—85; dir. Logan Mus. Anthropology, Beloit, 1980-85, Wheelwright Mus. Am. Indian, Santa Fe, 1985-89; interim dir. N.Mex. Mus. Natural History, Albuquerque, 1990-91; exec. dir. Space Ctr. Internat. Space Hall of Fame, Alamogordo, N.Mex., 1991-94; dir. N.Mex. Farm and Ranch Heritage Mus., 1994-99; cultural affairs officer State of N.Mex., Santa Fe, 1997—2003; realtor Margo Cutler, Ltd., Santa Fe, 2003—05. Evaluator Nat. Park Service, Denver, 1986. Contbr. articles to profl. jours. Mem. Nuke Watch, Beloit, 1983-84; cultural affairs officer State of N.Mex., 1997-2003. Research grants Wis. Humanities Com., 1984, NSF, 1981; grantee Cullister Found., 1978-84; fellow U. Toronto, 1971. Mem. Am. Assn. Mus., Am. Assn. Phys. Anthropology, Can. Assn. for Phys. Anthropology, N.Mex. Assn. Mus. (pres. 1994-96), Soc. Am. Archaeology, Wis. Fedn. Mus. (adv. bd. 1982-85). Avocations: camping, skiing, fishing, reading, horseback riding. Home Phone: 512-832-6652. Personal E-mail: jeway@earthlink.net.

WAYANS, MARLON, actor, film producer, writer; b. NYC, July 23, 1972; s. Howell and Elvira Wayans; children: Arnai Zachary, Shawn Howell. Grad., Howard U. Actor: (films) I'm Gonna Git You Sucka, 1988, Mo' Money, 1992, Above the Rim, 1994, The Sixth Man, 1997, Senseless, 1998, Requiem for a Dream, 2000, (voice) The Tangerine Bear, 2000, Dungeons & Dragons, 2000, The Ladykillers, 2004, Norbit, 2007; (TV series) In Living Color, 1990—94, (voice) Waynehead, 1996—97, (prodr., writer): (films) Don't Be a Menace to South Central While Drinking Your Juice in the Hood, 1996, Scary Movie 2, 2001, White Chicks, 2004, Little Man, 2006, (dir., prodr., writer): (TV series) The Wayans Brothers, 1995—99; writer (films) Scary Movie, 2000, Scary Movie 3, 2003, Scary Movie 4, 2006. Office: William Morris Agy One William Morris Place Beverly Hills CA 90212 *

WAYANS, SHAWN, actor, film producer, writer; b. NYC, Jan. 19, 1971; s. Howell and Elvira Wayans. Actor: (films) I'm Gonna Git You Sucka, 1988, New Blood, 1999; (TV series) In Living Color, 1990—94, (voice) Waynehead, 1996—97, (dir., prodr., writer) The Wayans Brothers, 1995—99, (prodr., writer): (films) Don't Be a Menace to South Central While Drinking Your Juice in the Hood, 1996, Scary Movie, 2000, White Chicks, 2004, Little Man, 2006, (co-exec. prodr., writer) Scary Movie 2, 2001; writer (films) Scary Movie 3, 2003, Scary Movie 4, 2006. Office: William Morris Agy One William Morris Pl Beverly Hills CA 90212

WAYBOURN, KATHLEEN ANN, lawyer, consultant; BA magna cum laude, Queens Coll., Flushing, NY, 1978; JD, St. John's U. Law Sch., Jamaica, NY, 1984. Bar: N.Y. 1985, U.S. Supreme Ct. 2000, U.S. Dist. Ct. (so. dist.), N.Y. 2002; cert. chemist Am. Chem. Soc. Ind. legal cons. Office of Corp. Counsel City N.Y., 1985—86; atty. Aaron J. Broder, PC, NYC, 1988—92; pvt. practice, 1991—; assoc. atty. Mangiatordi, Maher and Lemmo, LLC, 1998—99; contract atty. Steven R. Harris and Assocs., 2000—. Pres. Toxic Tort Cons., Inc., NYC, 2001—. Author: St. John's Law Balance, 1984. Pro bono homeless shelter advocacy project NY County Lawyers Assn., 1991—92, with sex discrimination clinic and no sweatshop coalition, 1994—98. Tchg. fellow scholarship, NYU Grad. Sch. Arts and Scis., 1978—79. Mem.: Am. Assn. for Justice, NY County Lawyers Assn. (recipient Appreciation certs.), Assn. Trial Lawyers Am., NY State Trial Lawyers' Assn., Beta Delta Chi. Avocations: photography, swimming, scuba diving. Office: 110 E 59th St Ste 3200 New York NY 10022 Office Phone: 646-735-1442.

WAYLAND-SMITH, ROBERT DEAN, retired banker; b. Oneida, NY, July 2, 1943; s. Robert and Prudence Cragin W.-S.; m. Kathleen Anne Schultz, Aug. 24, 1968 (dec. Oct. 1999), m. Linda M. Amendola, July 21, 2002; children: Kristin, Debra. BA in Econs., U. Rochester, 1965. Mgr. equipment svc. Strong Meml. Hosp., Rochester, NY, 1965-67; mgmt. trainee Chase Lincoln First Bank, N.A., Rochester, 1967-68, mgr. mcpl. securities, 1968-81, mgr. portfolio mgmt. depart., 1981-84, mgr. fin. and investment svc. dept., 1984-87, mgr. trust and fin. svc. dept., 1987-88; pres. and CEO Rochester region Chase Manhattan Bank, N.A., 1988-93, upstate trust and investment divsn. exec., 1993-98; ret., 1998. Mem. adv. bd. Roberts Wesleyan Coll., Rochester, 1989-99; mem. adv. coun. J.W. Jones Sch. Bus. SUNY, Geneseo, 1990-99. Trustee Ctr. for Govtl. Rsch., 1985—; dir. Greater Rochester Visitors Assn., 1990-93, Rochester Downtown Devel. Corp., 1991-93, United Neighborhood Ctrs., Greater Rochester Found., 1992-2002; mem. fin. execs. adv. bd. Coll. Bus. Rochester Inst. Tech., 1994-97; mem. United Way Greater Rochester Corp., 1998-2003; bd. dirs. Oneida Cmty. Mansion House, 1988—; bd. dir. Via Health, 1999-2001; bd. govs. The Genesee Hosp., 1992-2001; mem. bd. trustees Rochester Inst. Tech., 2003—; chair coll. coun. SUNY Coll. Geneseo, 1999—; bd. dirs. Greater Rochester Enterprise, 2004—. Fellow: Assn. for Investment Mgmt. and Rsch.; mem.: Greater Rochester Met. C. of C. (bd. dirs. 1992—95), Greater Rochester Ind. Practice Assn. (bd. dirs. 2000—), Rochester Soc. Security Analysts, Oak Hill Country Club, Genesee Valley Club (treas. 2002—05, pres. 2005—07). Avocations: golf, gardening, reading. Office: JP Morgan Chase One Chase Sq Rochester NY 14643 Home Phone: 585-381-1248; Office Phone: 585-797-1938. Business E-Mail: robert.d.wayland-smith@chase.com.

WAYNE, EARL ANTHONY, ambassador, former federal agency administrator; b. 1950; married; 2 children. BA, U. Calif., Berkeley; MA, Princeton U., Stanford U.; MPA, Harvard U., 1984. Joined Fgn. Svc., 1975, various positions; spl. asst. to sec. US Dept. State, 1981—83; first sec. US Embassy, Paris, 1984—87; nat. security corr. Christian Sci. Monitor, 1987—89; dir. regional affairs U.S. Amb. at Large for Counter-Terrorism, 1989—91; dir. Western European affairs Nat. Security Coun., 1991—93; dep. chief mission U.S. Mission to European Union, 1993—96; dept. asst. sec. for Europe and Can. US Dept. State, Washington, 1996—97, prin. dep. asst. sec. for European affairs, 1997—2000, asst. sec. for econ. & bus. affairs, 2000—06, interim under sec. for econ. bus. and agrl. affairs, 2005, US amb. to Argentina Buenos Aires, 2006—. Recipient Presdl. Disting. Svc. award, 2001, Disting. Honor award, US Dept. State, 2005, Presdl. Meritorious Svc. award. Office: US Embassy 3130 Buenos Aires Pl Washington DC 20521 Office Phone: 57774533.

WAYNE, JEANETTE MARIE, auditor; b. Mt. Clemens, Mich., Apr. 17, 1965; d. Robert Thomas W. and Sharon Elaine (Mominee) Nole; m. Ronald Edward Klicki, Sept. 14, 1985 (div. Oct. 1989). Asst. mgr. Little Caesars, Mt. Clemens, Mich., 1981-83, Cheese & Co., Birmingham, Mich., 1984; courier Chevrolet, Detroit, 1984; libr. EDS Chevorlet, Detroit, 1985-86, migration specialist, 1987; software support EDS Saturn, Troy, 1988-89, ops. tech., 1990-93; ops. tech. cons. EDS Tech. Architecture, Plano, Tex., 1993-2000; sr. auditor EDS Corp. Audit, Plano, Tex., 1997-2000, program mgr., 2000—. Program mgr. Bus. Process Leadership SAP Deployment. Republican. Office: EDS 5400 Legacy Dr Plano TX 75024-3199

WAYNE, JUNE CLAIRE, artist; b. Chgo., Mar. 7, 1918; d. Albert and Dorothy Alice (Kline) LaVine. DFA (hon.), Rutgers U., 2005. Indsl. designer, NYC, 1939-41; radio writer, mem. staff sta. WGN, Chgo., 1942-43; founder, 1959; since dir. Tamarind Lithography Workshop, Inc. (funded by Ford Found.), Los Angeles; Tamarind Inst., U. N.Mex., 1970—. Mem. vis. com. Sch. Visual and Environ. Studies, Harvard, 1972-74, chancellors adv. com., arts mgmt. program Grad. Sch. Adminstrn., U. Calif. at Los Angeles, 1969-80, Calif. Confederation of Arts adv. bd., 1988, Calif. State U. dept. of art adv. coun., Long Beach, 1988, Rutgers U. Mason Gross Sch. Arts prof. of rsch. printmaking and paper, New Brunswick, NJ, 2002-. Contbr. articles to profl. publs.; subject TV programs.; Numerous one-woman exhbns., 1935—, latest being, Art Mus., U. N.Mex., 1968, Cin. Art Mus., 1969, Iowa Art Mus., U. Iowa, 1970, Grunwald Graphics Arts Found., U. Calif. at Los Angeles, 1971, Municipal Art Gallery, Barnsdall Park, LA, 1973, Van Doren Gallery, San Francisco, 1974, La Demeure, Paris, 1974, Musée de Brest, France, 1976, Montgomery Gallery, Pomona Colls., Calif., 1978, Ariz. State U. Galleries, 1978, ICA travelling exhbn., Rennes, 1976, Nancy, 1977, Brussels, 1978, Reims, 1978, Lyons, 1979, Neuberger Mus., Purchase, NY, 1997, Skirball Mus., Cin., 1998, LA County Mus. Art, 1998, Palm Springs Desert Mus., Calif., 1999, A.R.T. Gallery, NY, 2003, Rutgers U., Newark, 2005, The Armory Ctr. for Arts, Pasadena, Calif., 2005, Stedman Gallery, Newark, 2005, Mason Gross Galleries, New Brunswick, NJ, 2006, Birmingham Mus. and Art Gallery, UK, 2006, Tama Art U. Mus., Tokyo, 2006; rep. permanent collections, Library of Congress, The British Mus., London, Mus. Modern Art, NYC, Art Inst. Chgo., Houghton Library at Harvard, Smithsonian Instn., Rosenwald Collection, The Victoria and Albert Mus., London, Nat. Gallery Art, NY Pub. Library, Cin. Art Mus., Pasadena (Calif.) Mus. Art, Phila. Mus. Art, Phila. Print Club, Birmingham Mus. and Art Gallery, Walker Art Center, Mpls., Zimmerli Art Mus., New Brunswick. Bd. dirs. Grunwald Center Graphic Arts, 1965-80. Recipient numerous prizes, 1950—, latest being Prix de la Biennal Internat. de L'Estampe d'Epinal, France, 1971; Purchase prize Biennal d'Epinal, 1973; Golden Eagle Cine award and Acad. award nomination for film Four Stones for Kanemitsu, 1974; Silver Life Achievement award YWCA, 1983; Communicator award Women in Media, 1983; Woman of the Year, Palm Springs Desert Mus., 1999; Zimmerli award Women in Arts Com., Coll. Arts Assn., 2003; Mason Gross Sch. Disting. Svc. Arts award, 2004. Mem. Writers Guild Am., Women in Film, AFTRA, Women's Caucus for Art, Soc. Am. Graphic Artists, Soc. Washington Printmakers, LA Printmakers Soc., The Trusteeship, Internat. Women's Forum. Address: 1108 Tamarind Ave Los Angeles CA 90038-1906

WAYNE, KYRA PETROVSKAYA, writer; b. Crimea, USSR, Dec. 31, 1918; arrived in U.S., 1948, naturalized, 1951; d. Prince Vasily Sergeyevich and Baroness Zinaida Fedorovna (Fon-Haffenberg) Obbolensky; m. George J. Wayne, Apr. 21, 1961; 1 child, Ronald George. BA, Leningrad Inst. Theatre Arts, 1939, MA, 1940. Actress, concert singer,

Russia, 1939-46; actress, 1948-59; enrichment lectr. Royal Viking Line cruises, Alaska-Can., Greek Islands-Black Sea, Russia/Europe, 1978-79, 81-82, 83-84, 86-8, 88. Author: Kyra, 1959, Kyra's Secrets of Russian Cooking, 1960, 1993, The Quest for the Golden Fleece, 1962, Shurik, 1971, 1992, 2007, The Awakening, 1972, The Witches of Barguzin, 1975, Max, The Dog that Refused to Die, 1979 (Best Fiction award Dog Writers Assn. Am., 1980), Rekindle the Dreams, 1979, Quest for Empire, 1986, Li'l Ol' Charlie, 1989, Quest for Bigfoot, 1996, Pepper's Ordeal, 2000, The Chaperone, 2006, Memoirs of a Piano, 2007. Founder, pres. Clean Air Program, Los Angeles County, 1971—72; mem. Seattle Art Mus.; mem. women's coun. Sta. KCET-Ednl. TV; mem. Monterey County Symphony Guild, 1989—91, Monterey Bay Aquarium, Monterey Peninsula Mus. Art, Friends of La Mirada, Fresno Art Mus., Fresno Met. Mus., Valley Children's Hosp. Served to lt. Russian Army, 1941—43. Decorated Red Star, numerous decorations USSR; recipient award, Crusade for Freedom, 1955—56, Los Angeles County, 1972, Merit award, Am. Lung Assn. Los Angeles County, 1988, award of Merit, Congress Russian Ams., 1999. Mem.: Seattle Art Mus., Idyllwild Sch. Music, Carmel Music Soc. (bd. dirs. 1992—94), Authors Guild, Soc. Children's Book Writers, PEN, Fresno Philharm., UCLA Affiliates (life), L.A. Lung Assn. (life; pres. and founder clean air program 1972—74), Art and Theatre Assn. (trustee 1987), Friends Lung Assn. (pres. 1988), UCLA Med. Faculty Wives (pres. 1970—71, dir. 1971—75), Club 25, Los Angelenos Club (life). *Personal philosophy: I believe in total loyalty. Loyalty to one's family and friends, to one's colleagues and to one's country. In my case - to my chosen country, the U.S.A.*

WAYNE, LESLIE, reporter; Spl. projects reporter NY Times, bus. day reporter. Recipient Bus. Reporter of Yr. award, Knight-Bagehot, 1997. Office: NY Times 229 West 43rd St New York NY 10036 Office Phone: 212-556-7192. Office Fax: 212-556-1448.

WAYNE, ROBERT JONATHAN, lawyer, educator; b. Fresno, Calif., Apr. 4, 1951; s. William W. and Blanche Wayne; m. Dorothy A. Madden, Oct. 23, 1981; children: Daniel, Julia. BS, U. Oreg., 1971; JD, UCLA, 1974. Bar: Calif. 1974, Wash. 1975, U.S. Dist. Ct. (we. dist.) Wash. 1975, U.S. Ct. Appeals (9th and D.C. cirs.) 1975, U.S. Supreme Ct. 1979. Law clk. U.S. Ct. Appeals (D.C. cir.), 1974-75; assoc. Perkins, Coie, Stone, Olsen & Williams, Seattle, 1975-76; dep. prosecutor King County Prosecutor's Office, Seattle, 1976-78; pvt. practice Seattle, 1978—. Instr. trial advocacy U. Wash., Seattle, 1977—, Nat. Inst. Trial Advocacy, 1980—2004, asst. team leader, 1990, team leader, 1991—2004, team leader nat. session, 1993, program dir. N.W. region, 1998—2004, lectr. implementing technology in trials; mem. faculty tchr. tng. program Harvard U., Colo. Mem. ATLA, NACDL (life, chmn. lawyers assistance strike force 1993-94), Wash. State Trial Lawyers Assn. (chmn. tort sect. 1983-85), Wash. State Bar Assn. (chmn. criminal law sect. 1982-83, 86-87, exec. com. 1980-88), King County Bar Assn. (jud. screening com. 1988-91), Wash. Assn. Criminal Def. Lawyers (founder, bd. govs. 1986-89, 99-2001, chmn. lawyers assistance strike force 1986-90, 91-93, chmn. ann. meeting 1989-90, 2001), Order of Coif, Order of Barristers. Avocation: flying. Office: 2110 N Pacific St Ste 100 Seattle WA 98103-9181 Office Phone: 206-343-5100. Business E-Mail: bwayne@trialsnw.com.

WAYNE, STEPHEN J., government educator, writer; b. NYC, Mar. 22, 1939; s. Arthur G. and Muriel Wayne; m. Cheryl Beil, May 22, 1982; children: Jared B., Jeremy B. BA with honors, U. Rochester, 1961; MA, Columbia U., 1963, PhD, 1968. Instr. polit. sci. U.S. Naval Postgrad. Sch., 1963-65; instr. politics and govt. Ohio Wesleyan U., 1966-68; asst. prof. to prof. polit. sci. and pub. affairs The George Washington U., 1968—88; prof. govt. Georgetown U., Washington, 1989—. Presenter and lectr. in field. Author: The Legislative Presidency, 1978, The Road to the White House, 1980, 7th edit., 2004, (with George C. Edwards) Presidential Leadership: Politics and Policy Making, 1985, 7th edit., 2006 (with Cal MacKenzie, David O'Brien and Richard L. Cole) The Politics of American Government, 1995, 3d edit., 1999; editor: Investigating the American Political System: Problems, Methods, and Projects, 1974, (with George C. Edwards) Studying the Presidency, 1983, (with Clyde Wilcox) The Quest for National Office, 1992, (with Wilcox) The Election of the Century and What It Tells Us About the Future of American Politics, 2002, Is This Any Way to Run a Democratic Government?, 2004, Is This Any Way To Run A Democratic Election?, 2007, (with G. Cal Mackenzie) Conflict and Consensus in America, 2007; appeared on 3 one-hour programs on presidency Every Four Years, sta. WHYY-TV, PBS, 1980; election night analyst ARD-German TV, 1992; contbr. numerous articles, chpts. and book revs. to books and profl. jours. Office: Georgetown U Dept Govt 37th And O NW Washington DC 20057-0001 Office Phone: 202-687-5908. Business E-Mail: waynes@georgetown.edu.

WAYTE, ALAN (PAUL), lawyer; b. Huntington Park, Calif., Dec. 30, 1936; s. Paul Henry and Helen Lucille (McCarthy) W.; m. Beverly A. Bruen, Feb. 19, 1959 (div. 1972); children: David Alan, Lawrence Andrew, Marcia Louise; m. Nancy Kelly Wayte, July 5, 1975. AB, Stanford U., 1958, JD, 1960. Bar: Calif. 1961, U.S. Dist. Ct. (so. dist.) Calif. 1961, U.S. Supreme Ct. 1984. Ptnr. Adams, Duque & Hazeltine, LA, 1966-85, Dewey Ballantine, LA, 1985—2004; of counsel DLA Piper LLP, LA, 2004—. Mem. L.A. County Bar Assn. (chmn. real property sect. 1981-82), Am. Coll. Real Estate Lawyers (bd. govs. 1989—, pres. 1994), Am. Coll. Mortgage Attys., Anglo-Am. Real Property Inst. (bd. govs. 1989-91), L.A. Philharm. Assn. (exec. com. bd. dirs. 1973—), Chancery Club, Calif. Club (L.A.), Valley Hunt Club (Pasadena). Office: DLA Piper LLP Suite 2300 550 S Hope St Los Angeles CA 90071 Home Phone: 626-792-8187; Office Phone: 213-330-7734. Office Fax: 213-330-7534. Business E-Mail: alan.wayte@dlapiper.com.

WAZIRI, GHAUS GHULAM, diplomat; b. Kabul, Afghanistan, Mar. 3, 1935; arrived in U.S., 1984; s. Abdul Wadood and Noorj-ehan Waziri; m. Anisa Barak Waziri, Nov. 25, 1963; children: Omar, Homaira, Zahra. B in Law and Polit. Sci., Kabul U., Afghanistan, 1957; grad. degree in Law and Polit. Sci., Sorboune U., Paris, 1968—70. Afghan del. UN, NYC, 1962—65; dir. law and treaties Dept. Fgn. Ministry, 1966—67, dep. dir. econ. rels., 1970—72; 1st sec., charge d'affairs Embassy Afghanistan, Beijing, 1973—77, Dacca, Bangladesh, 1980—81; dir. Inst. Diplomacy, Ministry Fgn. Affairs, 1977—80. Author: Afghan-Soviet War I and II, 1982, Afghanistan at High Crisis, 2004, Shelter, 2004. Dept. dir. Afghanistan Resistant Groups, Peshawar, Pakistan, 1981—88; dir., polit. advisor, pres. Peshawar based Afghan Govt., 1988—91; chief cabinet, advisor Former King Afghanistan, Rome, 1992—2000. Sgt. Afghan Mil. Infantry, 1957—59. Mem.: ACLU, Carter Ctr. Peace, Health, Acad. Polit. Sci. Avocations: music, travel, literature, studying philosophy. Home: 2941 W Lowell Ave Apt 198 Tracy CA 95377 Home Fax: 209-836-8825.

WEABER, TERRY LEE, information scientist; b. Decatur, Ill., Feb. 9, 1961; s. Jerry Lee and Bonnie Lee Weaber; m. Genevieve Rose Lenertz, Sept. 26, 1987; children: Lauren Elizabeth, Elijah Lee. A in Avionics Tech., CC Air Force, Austin, Tex., 1984; BS in Info. Tech. with honors, U. Phoenix, 2003. Air res. technician Dept. Def., Austin, Tex., 1984—91; computer, electronics, info. tech. mgr. NOAA, Ft. Worth, 1991—. Leader Boy Scouts Am., Las Vegas, Nev., 2001—03; youth group leader Bapt. Ch., Las Vegas, 2001—03. Staff sgt. USAF, 1980—84. Mem.: Nat. Space Soc., Planetary Soc. Republican. Avocations: reading, art, computers, motorcycling. Office: Nat Weather Svc 819 Taylor St Rm 10A24 Fort Worth TX 76102

WEADON, DONALD ALFORD, JR., lawyer; b. Brisbane, Australia, Sept. 15, 1945; arrived in U.S., 1946; s. Donald Alford and Ellen Martha (Salisbury) Weadon; m. Suzanne Hayden Cameron, Sept. 9, 1995. BA, Cornell U., 1967; JD, U. Calif., 1975; MBA, Harvard U., Iran Ctr. Mgmt. Studies, Tehran, 1976. Bar: Calif. 1976, D.C. 1988. Assoc. Hancock, Rothert & Bunshoft, San Francisco, 1977-80; ptnr. Bryan Cave, Washington, 1980—84; prin. Weadon & Assocs., Washington, 1984—. Adj. prof. internat. law Golden Gate U., San Francisco, 1979—82, George Mason U., Arlington, Va., 1989—; spkr., cons. U.S. Dept. Commerce, 1980—83; cons. Internat. Mktg. Assn., 1980—, Sci. Apparatus Mfg. Assn., 1983—, Valve Mfrs. Assn., 1983—; internat. counsel Am. Electronics Assn., 1986—. Contbr. articles to profl. jours. and newspapers. Trustee coun. Cornell U., 2000—, Cornell Hotel Soc., 2002—, hon. mem. Lt. comdr. USNR, 1968—72. Named Cornell U. Disting. Alumnus, 2000, 2005. Mem.: ABA (chmn. China trade law com. 1982—84, chmn. software and tech. data com. 1983—85), Press Club, Harvard Club, Savage Club, Metropolitan Club Washington DC, Olympic Club, Sovereign Mil. Order Temple Jerusalem (Grand Cross, Order of Merit), Delta Kappa Epsilon (alumni pres. 1997—, nat. bd. dirs. 1998—). Episcopalian. Office: Weadon & Assocs Internat House 3338 N St NW Washington DC 20007 Business E-Mail: dweadon@weadonlaw.com.

WEAKLAND, REMBERT G., retired archbishop; b. Patton, Pa., Apr. 2, 1927; s. Basil and Mary (Kane) Weakland. AB, St. Vincent Coll., Latrobe, Pa., 1948, DD (hon.), 1963, LHD (hon.), 1987; MS in Piano, Juilliard Sch. Music, 1954; postgrad., Columbia U., 1954—56, PhD in Musicology, 2000; LHD (hon.), Duquesne U., 1964, Belmont Coll., 1964, Cath. U. Am., 1975, Xavier U., Cin., 1988, DePaul U., 1989, Loyola U., New Orleans, 1991, Villanova U., 1992, Dayton U., 1993, Marian Coll., Fond du Lac, Wis., 1995, St. Anselm Coll., Manchester, NH, 1996, St. Norbert Coll., De Pere, Wis., 1996, U. San Francisco, 1997, Scholastica Coll., 1998; HHD (hon.), St. Ambrose U., Davenport, 1990, Aquinas Inst. Theology, St. Louis, 1991, St Mary's Coll., Notre Dame, Ind., 1994; LLD (hon.), Cardinal Stritch Coll., Milw., 1978, Marquette U., 1981, Loyola U., Chgo., 1986, U. Notre Dame, 1987, Mt. Mary Coll., Milw., 1989, John Carroll U., Cleve., 1992; LLD (hon.), Fairfield U., 1994; D of Sacred Music (hon.), St. Joseph's Coll., Rensselaer, Ind., 1979; DST of Sacred Music (hon.), Jesuit Sch. Theology, Berkeley, Calif., 1989; DST (hon.), St. John's U., Collegeville, Minn., 1991, Santa Clara U., 1991; DST (hon.), Yale U., 1993; DD (hon.), Lakeland Coll., Sheboygan, 1991, Ill. Benedictine Coll., Lisle, Ill., 1992, Regis Coll., Toronto, 1993, Trinity Coll., Hartford, 1996, Trinity Lutheran Sem., Columbus, Ohio, 1998; D of Ministry (hon.), Catholic Theol. Union, Chgo., 1999. Joined Benedictines Roman Cath. Ch., 1945, ordained priest 1951. Faculty music dept. St. Vincent Coll., 1957—63, chmn., 1961—63, chancellor chmn. of bd. of Coll., 1963—67; elected co-adjutor archabbot, 1963; abbot primate Benedictine Confederation, 1967—77; archbishop Archdiocese of Milw., 1997—2002, archbishop emeritus, 2002—. Mem.: Ch. Music Assn. Am. (pres. 1964—66), Am. Guild Organists. Roman Catholic. Office: PO Box 070912 Milwaukee WI 53207-0912

WEAKLEY, ALAN STUART, curator; b. Mongomery County, Md., Feb. 19, 1957; s. William Vanner and Jean Antoinette (Hensley) Weakley; m. Allison Elizabeth Schwarz; children: Rhiannon Leila Fay, Vanner Waldron. BA in Botany & Comparative Lit. (with highest honors), U. NC, Chapel Hill, 1978; attended grad. sch. in the Botany Dept., Duke U., 1980—84. With Coastal Zone Resources, Inc., Wilmington, NC, 1978—80; various positions including botanist, ecologist, asst. coord. & acting coord. NC Natural Heritage Prog., NC Dept. Natural Resources & Cmty. Develop., NC Divsn. Parks & Recreation, Dept. Environ. & Natural Resources, 1984—94; sr. regional ecologist, dep. chief ecologist & chief ecologist The Nature Conservancy, 1994—99; chief ecologist NatureServe (originally called Assn. for Biodiversity Info.), 2000—02; curator U. NC Herbarium, Dept. NC Botanical Garden, Chapel Hill, 2003—. Author: Flora of the Carolinas, Virginia, Georgia & Surrounding Areas, 2006; contbr. articles to profl. jours. James B. Duke Fellow, 1980—84, NSF Fellow, 1980—83. Mem.: Phi Beta Kappa Hon. Soc., Sigma Xi Hon. Scientific Soc. Office: U NC Herbarium CB 3280 Coker Hall University North Carolina Chapel Hill NC 27599-3280 Office Phone: 919-962-6931. Office Fax: 919-962-6930.

WEAKLEY, CLARE GEORGE, JR., insurance company executive, theologian, entrepreneur; b. Dallas, Apr. 14, 1928; s. Clare George and Louise (Cunningham) Weakley; m. Jean C. Burrow, July 20, 1962; children from previous marriage: Clare George III, Carol J.(dec.), Charles E. BBA, So. Meth. U., 1948, ThM, 1967. Ordained to ministry Christian Cmty., 1977. With Employers Ins., Dallas, 1948-52; owner Weakley & Co., Dallas, 1952-2001. Founder, pres. Am. Svc. Found., Inc., 1967—, Cornerstone Ministries, 1982—, Small Bus. Assn., Inc., 1988—, Christian Cmty., 1977—, founder, leader; vis. prof. western bus. theory and Christian ethics St. Petersburg (Russia) Internat. Mgmt. Inst. (formerly Leningrad Internat. Mgmt. Inst.), 1990—. Author: In God We Trust, 1997, God 101, 1998; author, editor: The Wesley Library Series for Today's Reader, The Nature of the Kingdom, 1976, The Nature of Spiritual Growth, 1977, The Nature of Revival, 1987, The Nature of Salvation, 1988, The Nature Holiness, 1988. Republican. Home: 13731 Goldmark Dr Apt 1207 Dallas TX 75240-4220 Office: Christian Cmty 13731 Goldmark Dr #1207 Dallas TX 75240 E-mail: clare@christian-community.org, weakley_co@earthlink.net.

WEARLY, WILLIAM LEVI, retired manufacturing executive; b. Warren, Ind., Dec. 5, 1915; s. Purvis Gardner and Ethel Ada (Jones) W.; m. Mary Jane Riddle, Mar. 8, 1941; children: Patricia Ann, Susan, William Levi, Elizabeth. BS, Purdue U., 1937, Dr Engring. (hon.), 1959. Student career engr. C.A. Dunham Co., Michigan City, Ind., 1936; mem. elec. design staff Joy Mfg. Co., Franklin, Pa., 1937-39, v.p., gen. sales mgr., 1952-56, exec. v.p., 1956-57, pres., dir., 1957-62; v.p., dir. Ingersoll-Rand Co., 1964-66, exec. v.p., 1966-67, chmn., chief exec. officer, 1967-80, chmn. exec. com., 1981-85. Dir. ASA Ltd., Med. Care Am.; trustee LMI; speaker engring. groups. Author tech. publs. relating to mining; patentee in field. Bd. dirs. Boys Clubs Am. Mem. NAE, IEEE, AIME, Nat. Acad. of Engring., C. of C., Sky Club N.Y.C., Blind Brook Golf Club, Desert Forest Golf Club, Minikahda Club, Ariz. Club, Masons, Shriners, Eta Kappa Nu, Tau Beta Pi, Beta Theta Pi. Republican. Methodist. Mailing: PO Box 1072 Carefree AZ 85377-1072 Home Phone: 480-488-9288. Personal E-mail: wwearly@peoplepc.com.

WEART, SPENCER RICHARD, historian; b. Detroit, Mar. 8, 1942; s. Spencer Augustus and Janet (Streng) W.; m. Carole Ege, June 30, 1971; children: Lara Kimi, Spencer Gen. BA, Cornell U., 1963; PhD, U. Colo., 1968. Postdoctoral fellow Calif. Inst. Tech., 1968-71, U. Calif., Berkeley, 1971-74; dir. Ctr. for History Physics, Am. Inst. Physics, College Park, Md., 1974—. Author: Scientists in Power, 1979, Nuclear Fear, 1988, Never at War, 1998, Discovery of Global Warming, 2003; contbr. articles to profl. jours. Recipient Andrew Gemant award Am. Inst. of Physics, 1994 Fellow AAAS. Home: 12 Buena Vista Dr Hastings On Hudson NY 10706-1104 Office: Am Inst Physics One Physics Ellipse College Park MD 20740-3843 Office Phone: 301-209-3174. E-mail: sweart@aip.org.

WEARY, PEYTON EDWIN, retired medical educator; b. Evanston, Ill., Jan. 10, 1930; s. Leslie Albert and Conway Christian (Fleming) W.; m. Janet Edsall Gregory, Aug. 23, 1952; children: Terry, Conway Christian, Carolyn Fielder. BA, Princeton U., 1970; MD, U. Va., 1955. Diplomate: Am. Bd. Dermatology (dir. 1978-88, pres. 1987-88). Intern, case Western Res. U. Hosps., Cleve., 1955-56; rotating intern Univ. Hosp. Cleve., 1955-56; asst. resident dermatology U. Va., Charlottesville, 1958-60, resident dermatology, 1960-61, instr. dept. dermatology, 1961-62, asst. prof., 1962-65, asso. prof., 1965-70, prof., chmn. dept. dermatology, 1970-93; mem. staff Univ. Hosp., mem. cancer com., 1979—98, ret., 2001, prof. emeritus, 2001—. Univ. Hosp. house staff, 1960-61, clin. staff, 1965-66, pres. clin. staff, 1966-67; co-chair Nat. Coun. on Skin Cancer Prevention, Fed. Coun. on Skin Cancer Prevention, 1997-2001, Ctr. for Disease Control, 1997-2000. Mem. editorial bd. Jour. Am. Acad. Dermatology, 1978-87; editorial adv. bd. Skin and Allergy News, 1978—; contbr. articles to profl. jours. Bd. dirs. Lupus Found. Am., 1980-84; trustee, mem. exec. com. Dermatology Found., 1975-79; pres. Albermarle County unit Am. Cancer Soc., 1967-69. Served from 1st lt. to capt., M.C. U.S. Army, 1956-58. Recipient Walter Reed Disting. Achievement award U. Va. Alumni Assn., 2001 Master: Am. Acad. Dermatology (hon. bd. dir. 1973—76, pres. 1993—95, elected master in dermatology 2000, Gold medal 1990); mem.: Coun. Med. Splty. Socs. (bd. dir. 1989—92, sec. 1992—95), Am. Bd. Med. Spltys. (v.p. 1988, pres.-elect 1989, pres. 1990—92, Disting. Svc. award 1999), Raven Soc., So. Med. Assn., Med. Soc. Va. (Cmty. Svc. award 2001), Albermarie County Med. Soc., Dermatology Found., Am. Dermatol. Assn. (bd. dir. 1987—93, pres. 1992—93), Assn. Profs. Dermatology (sec.-treas. 1976—79), Soc. Investigative Dermatology (bd. dir. 1976—81, v.p. 1985, hon. mem. 1996), Va. Dermatol. Soc. (sec.-treas. 1965—71), Nat. Assn. Physicians Environ. (pres. 1995—97), Alpha Omega Alpha, Sigma Xi. Presbyterian. Home: 204 Magnolia Dr Charlottesville VA 22901

WEATHERBURN, STEPHEN JAMES, humanities educator; b. Horsham, Sussex, Eng., Dec. 11, 1959; s. Walter Thomas and Elsie May Weatherburn; m. Bonnie Kay Grace, Feb. 16, 1997; children: Vincent Grace, Kyle Grace. BA in US Studies, U. Essex, Colchester, Eng., 1984; MA in English, U. No. Ariz., Flagstaff, 2005. Cert. tchr. Ariz., 1998, N.Mex., 1998. Tchr. Monument Valley HS, Kayenta, Ariz., 1998—2000, Tuba City HS, Ariz., 2000—04; instr. No. Ariz. U., Flagstaff, Ariz., 2004—06; tchr. Red Mesa HS, Teec Nos Pos, Ariz., 2006; instr. Dine Coll., Kayenta, Ariz., 2007—. Author: (haibun) Yomping to Dorridge, 2007, (collected haiku) Words from the Peaks, 2007. Mem.: ASCD, Nat. Coun. Tchrs. English, Acad. Am. Poets. Avocations: hiking, motorcycling, photography. Home Phone: 928-814-1683; Office Phone: 928-656-4100.

WEATHERFORD, CAROLE BOSTON, publications specialist; b. Balt., Feb. 13, 1956; d. Joseph Alexander and Carolyn Virginia (Whitten) Boston; m. Ronald Jeffery Weatherford, Feb. 2, 1985. BA in Pub. Rels., Am. U., 1977; MA in Publs. Design, U. Balt., 1982; MFA in Creative Writing, U. N.C., Greensboro. English lang. tchr. Balt. City Pub. Schs., 1978; field rep. Blood Services Dept. ARC, Balt., 1978-79; account exec. Art Litho Co., Balt., 1981; dir. communications Nat. Bar Assn., Washington, 1981-85; v.p., creative dir. B&C Assocs. Inc., High Point, N.C., 1985-88; freelance writer, publicist, 1985—. Cons. Dudley Products Co., Greensboro, N.C., 1986—; publicist, cons. Black Classic Press, Balt., 1985—, Guilford County Schs., 1992—, The Chronicle, 1990—; prof. Fayetteville State U., 2002—. Author: The Tan Chanteuse, 1995, Juneteenth Jamboree, 1995, My Favorite Toy, 1997, Me & My Family Tree, 1997, Grandma & Me, 1997, Mighty Menfolk, 1997; contbr. articles to various mags., newspapers; creator, producer, host radio talk show Black Arts Rev., 1979, Sink or Swim: African-American Lifesavers of the Outer Banks, 1999, The Sound That Jazz Makes, 2000, Remember the Bridge: Poems of a People, 2002, Sidewalk Chalk: Poems of the City, 2002, The African-American Struggle for Legal Equality, 2002, Stormy Blues, 2003, Great African-American Laughs, 2004, Freedom on the Main: The Greensboro Sit-Ins, 2005, A Negro League Scrapbook, 2005, The Carlina Parakeet, 2005, Moses: When Harriet Tubman Led her People to Freedom (NAACP Image award for children's book, 2007). Named to Outstanding Young Women of Am., 1986; winner N.C. Writers Network Black Writers Competition, 1991, N.C. Writers Network Chapbook Competition, 1995; N.C. Arts Coun. fellow, 1995. Mem. N.C. Writers Network (v.p. 1996-97), Phi Kappa Phi, Delta Sigma Theta. Democrat. Methodist. Avocations: sewing, swimming. Home and Office: 3313 Sparrowhawk Dr High Point NC 27265-9350 *

WEATHERHEAD, LESLIE R., lawyer; b. Tacoma, Sept. 28, 1956; s. A. Kingsley and Ingrid A. (Lien) W.; m. Anali C. Torrado, June 24, 1985; children: Spencer, Madeleine, Audrey. BA, U. Oreg., 1977; JD, U. Wash., 1980. Bar: Wash. 1980, Oreg. 1996, U.S. Ct. Appeals (9th cir.) 1981, U.S. Dist. Ct. (ea. dist.) Wash. 1984, U.S. Ct. Internat. Trade 1984, Hawaii 1987, U.S. Dist. Ct. (we. dist.) Wash. 1989, Idaho 1989, U.S. Dist. Ct. Idaho 1989, U.S. Supreme Ct. 1994, Colville Tribal Ct. 1993, U.S. Ct. Appeals (10th cir.) 1995, U.S. Ct. Fed. Claims 1995, U.S. Ct. Appeals (fed. cir.) 1999. Asst. terr. prosecutor Territory of Guam, Agana, 1980-83; spl. asst. U.S. Atty. Dist. of Guam and No. Marianas, Agana, 1982-83; atty. Witherspoon, Kelley, Davenport & Toole, Spokane, 1984—. Lawyer-rep. 9th cir. jud. conf., 1989-95, lawyer-rep. chmn., 1995, 9th cir. adv. bd., 2001-04, chair, 2004-05; adj. faculty Gonzaga U. Sch. of Law, 1994-95, 2001—. Contbr. articles on Indian law, administrv. investigations and fed. jurisprudence to profl. jours. Bd. dirs. Spokane Opera Co., 1989-96, pres., 1992-94; bd. trustees Spokane Symphony Orch., 2006-. Fellow Am. Coll. Trial Lawyers; mem. ABA, Fed. Bar Assn. (pres. ea. dist. 1996-97), Hawaii Bar Assn., Idaho Bar Assn., Wash. State Bar Assn., Oreg. State Bar Assn. Avocations: sailing, scuba, skiing. Office: Witherspoon Kelley Davenport & Toole 428 W Riverside Ave Spokane WA 99201-0301 Office Phone: 509-755-2011.

WEATHERLY, ALVIS MORRISON, JR., retired association developer; b. Atlanta, Nov. 19, 1925; s. Alvis Morrison and Frances Louise (Stocks) W.; m. Mary Elizabeth Hyndman, Dec. 27, 1947; children: Mary Ann Weatherly Cobb, Elizabeth Louise Weatherly Williamson, Alvis Morrison III. Student, Ga. Inst. Tech., 1942-44; BBA, U. Ga., 1947; LLB, Atlanta Law Sch., 1952. Treasury cashier for Ga. So. Bell Tel. Co. (now AT&T), Atlanta, 1948—82; devel. dir. Atlanta Area Coun. Boy Scouts Am., 1984—93. Author, editor: History of Georgia Jaycees 1921-1962, 1962. Club pres., dist. pres., state chmn., state treas., state historian Ga. Jaycees, 1955-63, past asst. coun. comm., coun. adv. bd.; instr. commr. conf. Boy Scouts Am., 1982, coun. commr. sci., wood badge, asst. course dir., nat. exec. tng. inst., pres. basic training course class, coun. encampment chief, 1976, mem. exec. bd. Altanta area coun.; past dean Coll. of Commr. Sci., 1980-1983; Jr. Achievement, Atlanta, 1951, 63; loaned exec. Atlanta United Appeal, 1964, 65; mem. Selective Svc. Bd., Atlanta, 1964-74; mem. staff Atlanta Olympics, 1996; del. 17th World Meth. Conf., Rio de Janeiro, 1996; bd. dirs., past pres. Ga., Nat. Meml. Day Assn. and Ave. of Flags; adv. bd. Hist. Oakland Found., past adminstrv. bd. mem., usher, Funeral and Meml. Guild, past sec. fin. com., past tchr. youth Sunday sch., past pres. adult Sunday sch. class, trustee, past ch. sch. membership cultivation supt., past asst. ch. sch. supt., past mem. commn. on edn., past mem. evangelism commn., past ch. sch. greeter adminstrv. bd. Peachtree Rd. United Meth. Ch. Sgt. USAAC, 1946, WWII; 1st lt. USAFR, 1961 Named Jaycee of Yr. North DeKalb chpt., Jaycees, Outstanding Dist. Pres.-Ga., Key Man of Ga., Hal Salfen Outstanding State Com. Chmn., M. Keith Upson Outstanding State V.P.; recipient Silver Beaver award, Boy Scouts Am., 1974, James E. West fellow, 1996, Whitney M. Young Jr. Svc. in Urban Scouting award, 1996, Scout Show honoree, 1996, Dist. Award of Merit, Disting. Commr. award, Vigil honor, Order of the Arrow, Spirit of Op. 1st class, 2001, Internat. Scouter's award 40 Yr. Vet. Scouter, Willing Svc. banner, WSB Radio, Atlanta, 1974, 1976, Cert., Indian Creek Garden Club, Atlanta, Cross of Mil. Svc., United Daus. of the Confederacy, Cross and Flame award, Peachtree Rd. United Meth. Ch., 11 Alive Cmty. Svc. award, Atlanta WXIA-TV, 2005. Master Mason (50 Yr. pin, Daniel Carter Beard Masonic Scouter award); mem. SAR (past pres. Atlanta chpt., War Svc. medal, Meritorious Svc. medal, Silver Good Citizenship medal), Rotary (bd. dirs., treas. Sandy Springs club, bd. dirs., sec., v.p. Smyrna-Cumberland club, sgt.-at-arms, bd. dirs., treas., sec., past pres. Buckhead Atlanta Club, Paul Harris fellow, Will Watt fellow, Otis Jackson fellow,

Tom Slaughter fellow, Cmty. Svc. award, Svc. Above Self award, Rotarian of Yr., Rotary Found. Disting. Svc. award, Buckhead (Atlanta) Boy of Yr. 2002), Tel. Pioneers Am., Shrine, 1st Families of Ga., SCV (War Svc. medal), Mil. Order of Stars and Bars (past comdr.), Huguenot Soc. in Town of Manakin in Colony of Va. (past state pres.), Jamestowne Soc. (past 1st Ga. Co. Gov.), Sons and Daus. of the Pilgrims (past 2d dep. gov.), Sons and Daus. of Antebellum Planters (founding), Order of Indian Wars of U.S., Soc. of Descs. of Washington's Army at Valley Forge, Gen. Soc. War of 1812, Sons of Revolution (2d v.p.), Order of Washington, Soc. Colonial Wars in State of Ga., Magna Charta Barons, Magna Charta Dames and Barons (past state chmn.), Sovereign Colonial Soc., Ams. Royal Descent, Colonial Order of the Crown, Soc. Descs. of Knights of the Most Noble Order of the Garter, Plantagenet Soc., Old Guard of Gate City Guard (past comdt. col., Hancock medal, Charles Gavin Trophy, The Dr. George Turnbull Pursley award, Guardsman Yr. Award 2002, 2004), Scabbard and Blade, Gridiron Secret Soc., Mil. Officers Assn. Am., Sigma Nu, Beta Gamma Sigma (past pres. Atlanta chpt.), Alpha Phi Omega, Delta Sigma Pi, Omicron Delta Kappa (alumni). Home: 710 Starlight Ln NE Atlanta GA 30342-2838

WEATHERLY, ROBERT STONE, JR., banker; b. Birmingham, Ala., May 12, 1929; s. Robert Stone and Gladys (Manning) W.; m. Mary Anne Burr, May 1, 1954; children: Robert Stone, III, Henry, William. AB, Princeton U., 1950; LL.B., Harvard U., 1953, grad. advanced mgmt. program, 1972. Bar: Ala. 1953. Assoc. firm Burr, McKamy Moore & Thomas, Birmingham, 1955-62; asst. gen. atty. Vulcan Materials Co., Birmingham, 1962-69, v.p. chems. div. Wichita, Kans., 1969-71, treas., 1971-74, v.p. and controller, 1974-77, pres. metals div. Birmingham, Ala., 1977-87, pres. Middle East div., 1982-87; chmn., chief exec. officer Jefferson Fed. Savings, Birmingham, 1987-91; dir., sec. All Seasons Travel, Birmingham, 1991—. Disting. lectr.-practitioner U. Ga. Served with U.S. Army, 1953-55. Mem. Nat. Assn. Accts. (cert. mgmt. acct.), Beta Gamma Sigma. Clubs: Country of Birmingham, Chattooga (Cashiers, N.C.). Presbyterian. Home: 4608 Old Leeds Rd Birmingham AL 35213-1802 Office: All Seasons Travel 120 Office Park Dr Birmingham AL 35223-2422

WEATHERMON, SIDNEY EARL, retired elementary school educator; b. Abilene, Tex., Jan. 20, 1937; s. Sidney Elliot Weathermon and Evelyn Marie (Landreth) Parker. BA, U. Colo., 1962, MA, 1968, EdD, 1976. Cert. K-12 reading tchr., elem. edn. tchr., K-12 reading specialist. Tchr. grades 4-6 Jefferson County Pub. Schs., Colo., 1963—66; tchr. grades 5-6 Boulder Valley Pub. Schs., Colo., 1962—63, tchr. reading, 1968—71, consortium dir. right-to-read project Louisville Mid. Sch., 1974—75, coord. comm. skills program Vocat.-Tech. H.S., 1976, K-12 dist. reading specialist, 1971—85, chpt. 1 tchr. grades 1-6, 1985—89, coord. chpt. 1 kindergarten project, 1985—89, tchr. grade 1, 1989—95; ret., 1995. Instr. U. Colo., Boulder, 1971-72, U. No. Colo., Greeley, 1977; adj. faculty Regis U., Denver, 1972-95, dept. edn. instr., 1982. Contbr. articles to profl. jours. Recipient Celebrate Lit. award Boulder Coun. Internat. Reading Assn., 1986; named Tchr. of Yr., IBM Corp., 1989, Colo./Nat. Educator, Milkin Family Found., 1990; NDEA fellow, 1966-68. Mem. NEA, Internat. Reading Assn., Colo. Edn. Assn., Boulder Valley Edn. Assn. (chair tchr. adv coun., assoc. rep., tchrs. rights and activities commn., negotiations team, profl. leave com.), Phi Delta Kappa (certs. of recognition 1987, 90), Kappa Delta Pi. Democrat. Avocation: southwest Indian art. Home: 449 S Shore Dr Osprey FL 34229-9657 E-mail: drsidw@comcast.net.

WEATHERS, MILLEDGE WRIGHT, retired economics professor; b. Augusta, Ga., May 11, 1926; s. Robert Edward Lee and Margaret Elizabeth (Johnson) W.; m. Anna-Maria Helene von Bertrab; children: Helene, Martin, Margarete, Benjamin. BA, George Washington U., 1949, MA, 1957; doctor oeconomiae publicae, U. Munich, 1961. Rsch. analyst U.S. Dept. Air Force, Washington, 1951-57, Gen. Electric Co., Santa Barbara, Calif., 1959-62; pvt. practice cons. Munich, 1962-64; cons. Gesellschaft fuer Anlagewerte, Munich, 1964-66; sr. staff analyst Lockheed-Ga. Co., Marietta, 1966-68; prof. econs. Adrian (Mich.) Coll., 1968-91. Contbr. articles to profl. jours. With U.S. Army, 1944-46. Mem. Am. Econs. Assn., Assn. for Evolutionary Econs., Nat. Tax Assn., Economists for Peace and Security, Kappa Sigma. Avocations: music, walking. Home: 930 Lincoln Ave Adrian MI 49221-3230 Personal E-mail: mweathers@adrian.edu.

WEATHERSBY, GEORGE BYRON, management company executive; b. Albany, Calif., Dec. 9, 1944; s. Byron and Fannie A. Weathersby; m. Connie J. Titone, Mar. 31, 2007; children from previous marriage: Deborah Jane, Geoffrey Byron. BS, U. Calif., Berkeley, 1965, MS, 1966, MBA, 1967; MS, Harvard U., 1968, PhD, 1970; DHL (hon.), U. San Francisco, 1987; LLD (hon.), U. So. Ind., 1992. Mem. faculty, assoc. dir. analytical studies, dir. Ford Found. rsch. program U. Calif., Berkeley, 1969-72; spl. asst. to U.S. Sec. of State Washington, 1972-73; dir. rsch. Nat. Commn. on Financing Higher Edn., Washington, 1973-74; assoc. prof. mgmt. Harvard U., Cambridge, Mass., 1974-78; commr. higher edn. State of Ind., 1977-83; pres. Curtis Pub. Co., 1983-86, New UPI Inc., Washington, 1985-86; corp. v.p. fin. Ontario Corp., Muncie, Ind., 1986-88, pres., 1988-91, also bd. dirs.; ptnr. Founders Court Inc., Princeton, NJ, 1991-93; independant cons., 1975—; pres. Oxford Mgmt. Corp., 1993-98, Cambridge Parallel Processing, 1994-98, Electronic Retailing Syss. Internat., 1996-98; pres., CEO, bd. dirs. Am. Mgmt. Assn., NYC, 1998—2002; chmn., CEO Genesys Corp., LLC, 2002—. CEO, Quisic, Inc., 2001-02; chmn. bd. dirs. Otis Conner Cos., 1984-86, Curtis Media Corp., 1984-86, Curtis Internat. Ltd., 1985-86, Prince Gardner, Inc., 1991-93, Alma Industries, 1992-93, Hanes Holding Co., 1992-93; bd. dirs. Holcim (US), Inc., Farm Fans Inc., Delta Consol. Industries, Cambridge Parallel Processing, Advanced Retail Mktg., ERS, Inc., AOI Med., Inc. Author: Financing Postsecondary Education in the U.S, 1974, Colleges and Money, 1976; contbr. numerous articles to profl. jours.; cons. editor: Jour. Higher Edn., 1974—; exec. editor: Change mag., 1980-84. Bd. dirs. Nat. Ctr. for Higher Edn Mgmt. Sys., 1980-83, U.S.A. Group, 1989—96; mem. steering com. Edn. Commn. of States, 1978-82; mem. Ind. Com. Humanities, 1981-87; trustee U. So. Ind., 1985-91, Park Tudor Sch. Indpls., 1986-91, Butler U., 1987-93; mem. adv. coun. Invest in New Zealand, 2001-, MicroNets, 2005-; mem. adv. coun. for leadership and mgmt. for U.S. Dept. State, 2004-06. Calif. Regents scholar, 1963-65; NSF fellow, 1966-67; AEC fellow, 1966-67; Kent fellow, 1967-70; White House fellow, 1972-73; named 1 of 100 Outstanding Young Leaders in Higher Edn. Change Mag., 1978, 1 of Top 100 CEOs, C10 Mag., 2000. Mem. Am. Mgmt. Assn., Am. Coun. Edn., Ops. Rsch. Soc. Am., Inst. Mgmt. Scis., Econometrica, Young Pres. Orgn. Republican. Office Phone: 908-400-2774. Business E-Mail: gweathersby@genesysllc.com.

WEATHERSTONE, SIR DENNIS, retired bank executive; b. London, Nov. 29, 1930; s. Henry Philip and Gladys (Hart) W.; m. Marion Blunsum, Apr. 4, 1959; children— Hazel, Cheryl, Gretel, Richard Paul Student, Northwestern Poly., London, 1946-49. Sr. v.p. Morgan Guaranty Trust Co. N.Y., NYC, 1972-77, exec. v.p., 1977-79, treas., 1977-79, vice chmn., 1979-80, chmn. exec. com., 1980-86; pres. J.P. Morgan & Co., Inc. (formerly Morgan Guaranty Trust Co. N.Y.), NYC, 1987-90, chmn., chief exec. officer, 1990-95. Staff mem. Internat. Monetary Fund, 1970-94, dep. dir. rsch., 1987-94; bd. dirs. GM Corp., 1986-2001, Merck & Co., Inc., 1991-2001, L'Air Liquide, NY Stock Exch., 2003-05; mem. bd. banking supervision Bank of Eng., 1995-2001; sr. fellow Inst. for Internat. Economics. Trustee Alfred P. Sloan Found., Internat. Acctg. Standards Com. Found. Decorated Knight Comdr. Order Brit. Empire. Office: Inst for Internat Econ 1750 Massachusetts Ave NW Washington DC 20036 Office Phone: 212-270-7691.

WEATHERUP, ROY GARFIELD, lawyer; b. Annapolis, Md., Apr. 20, 1947; s. Robert Alexander and Kathryn Crites (Hesser) W.; m. Wendy Gaines, Sept. 10, 1977; children: Jennifer, Christine. AB in Polit. Sci., Stanford U., 1968, JD, 1972. Bar: Calif. 1972, U.S. Dist. Ct. 1973, U.S. Ct. Appeals (9th cir.) 1975, U.S. Supreme Ct. 1980. Assoc. Haight, Brown & Bonesteel, LA, Santa Ana, 1972—78, ptnr., 1979—2003, Lewis Brisbois Bisgaard & Smith, LA, 2004—. Judge Moot Ct. UCLA, Loyola U., Pepperdine U.; arbitrator Am. Arbitration Assn.; mem. com. Book Approved Jury Instrns. LA Superior Ct. Mem. ABA, Calif. Acad. Appellate Lawyers, LA County Bar Assn., Town Hall Calif. Republican. Methodist. Home: 17260 Rayen St Northridge CA 91325-2919 Office: Lewis Brisbois Bisgaard & Smith 221 N Figueroa St Los Angeles CA 90012 Home Phone: 818-993-0542; Office Phone: 213-680-5130. E-mail: royweatherup@aol.com.

WEAVER, CHARLES LYNDELL, JR., marketing executive, educational consultant; b. Canonsburg, Pa., July 5, 1945; s. Charles Lyndell and Georgia Lavelle (Gardner) W.; m. Ruth Marguerite Uxa, Feb. 27, 1982; children: Charles Lyndell III, John Francis. BArch, Pa. State U., 1969; cert. in assoc. studies, U. Florence, Italy, 1968. Registered architect, Pa., Md., Mo., Va., Mass., Ga.; cert. Nat. Coun. Arch. Registration Bd.; cert. designee, Design Build Inst. Am., 2002. With Celento & Edson, Canonsburg, part-time 1966-71; project architect Meyers & D'Aleo, Balt., 1971-76, corp. dir., v.p., 1974-76; ptnr. Borrow Assocs.-Developers, Balt., 1976-79, Crowley/Weaver Constrn. Mgmt., Balt., 1976-79; pvt. practice arch. Balt., 1976-79; cons., project mgr. U. Md., College Park, 1979-80; corp. cons. architect Bank Bldg. & Equipment Corp., Am., St. Louis, 1980-83; dir. archtl. and engring. svcs. Ladue Bldg. and Engring. Inc., St. Louis, 1983-84; v.p., sec. Graphic Products Corp.; pres. CWCM Inc. Internat., 1987-2000. Dir. K-12 Edn. Market Ctr. and sr. program mgr. Sverdrup Corp., 1989-95; prin. Benham Internat. Eurasia, 1995, v.p., dir. mktg. and bus. devel. The Benham Group, St. Louis, 1995-96; v.p. Chiodini Assocs., 1997-98; asst. lectr. Washington U., 1997-2000, 01-; cons. Stifel Cap. Start Up Venture Capital Fund; ops. mgr., generations cons. Stifel Capco Venture Capital, 1998, Cert Inst. ABU, 2005; dir. mktg. sys. The Maiman Co., 1998-99; dir. edn. program mgmt. The Integral Group, Atlanta, 1999-2001; vis. Alpha Rho Chi lectr. Pa. State U., 1983; vis. lectr. Washington U. Lindenwood Coll., 1987, Wentworth Inst., Boston, Am. Assn. Cost Engrs., So. Fla., 1994, with U. Houston, 2002; mem. panel Assn. Univ. Architects Conv., 1983; v.p. program mgmt. and ednl. facilities Kennedy Assoc. Inc.; participant K-12 Nat. Summit, San Diego, 2002; URS Corp. dep. project mgmt. Phila. Sch. Improvement Team, 2003-04; demonstration ednl. facilities program svcs. coord.-design/build Joseph, Jingoli and Sons, 2004—, East Orange, Trenton & Vineland Abbott Demonstration Schs., 2004—; spkr. and presenter in field. Contbr. Planning Guide for Maintaining Facilities, U.S. Dept. Edn. Project bus. cons. Jr. Achievement, 1982-85, 2001-2003; mem. cluster com., advisor Explorer Program, 1982-85; mem. Design Build Inst. Am., 1998—, splty. contractor task force chmn., 2000-02. Recipient 5 brochure and graphic awards Nat. Assn. Indsl. Artists, 1973; 1st award Profl. Builder/Am. Plywood Assn., 1974; Honor award, 2 articles Balt. chpt. AIA, 1974; Better Homes and Gardens award Sensible Growth, Nat. Assn. Home Builders, 1975; winner Ridgely's Delight Competition, Balt., 1976. Mem. ASCD, AACE (conv. spkr. So. Fla. sect. 1994), Vitruvius Alumni Assn., Pa. State Alumni Assn., AIA, Constrn. Specifications Inst., Am. Assn. Sch. Adminstrs. (nat. coun., panel moderator 1994), Coun. Ednl. Facilities Planners, Assn. Sch. Bus. Ofcls., Alpha Rho Chi (nat. treas. 1980-82, dir. nat. found. treas. 1989-97), Optimists Internat. Office: Bldg 4 Ste 216 3131 Princeton Pike Lawrenceville NJ 08648 Home Phone: 609-620-0911. Business E-Mail: cweaver@jingoli.com.

WEAVER, CLIFFORD LEE, retired lawyer, winery owner; b. Chgo., Mar. 11, 1945; s. Thomas E. and Thera A. (Ramey) Cash; m. Donna Rae Florence, Aug. 20, 1966; 1 child, Megan R. AB with honors, U. Chgo., 1966, JD with honors, 1969. Bar: Ill. 1969, U.S. Dist. Ct. (no. dist.) Ill. 1969, U.S. Ct. Appeals (7th cir.) 1969, U.S. Supreme Ct. 1975. Sr. clk. U.S. Ct. Appeals, Chgo., 1969-71; assoc. Ross & Hardies, Chgo., 1971-75, ptnr., 1976-83, Burke, Weaver & Prell, Chgo., 1983-99, mng. ptnr., 1990-99; owner, operator Azienda Agricola Le Miccine vineyard and winery, 1996—. Gen. counsel N.W. Water Commn., 1978—99, DuPage Water Commn., DuPage County, Ill., 1987—99, Lake County (Ill.) Forest Preserve, 1991—99; village atty. Village of Bannockburn, Ill., 1977—99, Village of Northbrook, 1977—99, Village of Glencoe, Ill., 1978—99, Village of Hinsdale, Ill., 1985—99, Village of Libertyville, Ill., 1990—99. Co-author: Special Districts in Illinois, 1977, City Zoning, 1979; contbr. numerous articles to profl. jours. Trustee Kenilworth (Ill.) Libr. Dist., 1987-89; mem. Kenilworth Zoning Bd., 1985-2006. Mem.: ABA, Order of Coif, Phi Beta Kappa. Republican. Home: 144 Woodstock Ave Kenilworth IL 60043-1262 Office Phone: 847-256-7258. E-mail: clw@lemiccine.com

WEAVER, DELBERT ALLEN, retired lawyer; b. Shoshone, Idaho, May 28, 1931; s. Arlo Irving and Kate Rosamond (McCarter) W.; m. Jeanne Carol Alford, June 1959; children: Tobin Elizabeth, Michael Andrew, Matthew Stewart, Edward Malcolm. BA, U. Oreg., 1953, LLB, 1956. Bar: Oreg. 1956, U.S. Dist. Ct. Oreg. 1956, U.S. Ct. Appeals (9th cir.) 1968. Ptnr. Weaver & Oram, Eugene, Oreg., 1956-59; dep. atty. City of Portland, Oreg., 1959-68; assoc. Winfree, Latourette, Murphy, et al., Portland, 1968-71; stockbroker Dupont Glore Forgan, Portland, 1971-73; securities examiner corp. div. State of Oreg., Salem, 1973-75, dep. commr. corp. div., 1975-80; pvt. practice Portland, 1980-87; counsel Schwabe, Williamson & Wyatt, Portland, 1987-90, sr. ptnr., 1991-96; pvt. practice Portland, 1996-2000; counsel Dunn, Carney, Portland, 2000—04; ret., 2005. Personal E-mail: dweaver1091@charter.net.

WEAVER, DIANNE JAY, lawyer; b. Kansas City, Mo., June 28, 1944; d. Thomas G. and Anna Jeanette Jay; m. Benjamin J. Weaver, Sept. 16, 1970; children: Jay, Jenny, Scott, Elizabeth. BS, U. Kans., 1965; JD, Ind. U., 1970. Bar: Ind., Fla., Colo.; bd. cert. trial lawyer. Ptnr. Weaver & Weaver, P.A., Ft. Lauderdale, Fla.; of counsel Krupnick Campbell Malone Roselli Buser Slama & Hancock P.A., Ft. Lauderdale; ptnr. Harrell & Johnson, P.A., Jacksonville, 2002—. Speaker in field. Contbr. articles to profl. jours. Trustee Civil Justice Found.; bd. dirs. Trial Lawyers for Pub. Justice; chmn. publicity com. Civil Justice Found. Fellow Roscoe Pound Found. (life); mem. ATLA (bd. govs., sec.), Acad. Fla. Trial Lawyers (bd. dirs.), So. Trial Lawyers Assn. (bd. govs.), Fla. Bar Assn. (chair trial advocacy com.),. Fed. Bar Assn., Broward County Women Lawyers Assn. (founding pres.). Office: Harrell & Harrell PA 4735 Sunbeam Rd Jacksonville FL 32257 Office Phone: 904-251-1111. Business E-Mail: dweaver@forjustice.com.

WEAVER, DONNA RAE, winery executive; b. Chgo., Oct. 15, 1945; d. Albert Louis and Gloria Elaine (Graffis) Florence; m. Clifford L. Weaver, Aug. 20, 1966; 1 child, Megan Rae. BS in Edn., No. Ill. U., 1966, EdD, 1977; MEd, De Paul U., 1974. Tchr. H.L. Richards High Sch., Oak Lawn, Ill., 1966-71, Sawyer Coll. Bus., Evanston, Ill., 1971-72; asst. prof. Oakton Community Coll., Morton Grove, Ill., 1972-75; vis. prof. U. Ill., Chgo., 1977-78; dir. devel. Mallinckrodt Coll., Wilmette, Ill., 1978-80, dean, 1980-83; campus dir. Nat.-Louis U., Chgo., 1983-90, dean div. applied behavioral scis., 1985-89; dean Coll. Mgmt. and Bus., 1989-90; pres. The Oliver Group, Inc., Kenilworth, Ill., 1993-97; mng. ptnr. Le Miccine, Gaiole-in-Chianti, Tuscany, Italy, 1996—. Cons. Nancy Lovely and Assocs., Wilmette, 1981-84, North Ctrl. Assn., Chgo., 1982-90. Contbr. articles to Am. Vocat. Jour., Ill. Bus. Edn. Assn. Monograph, Nat. Coll. Edn.'s ABS Rev., Nat. View. Mem. Ill. Quality of Work Life Coun., 1987-90, New Trier Twp. Health and Human Svcs. Adv. Bd., Winnetka, Ill., 1985-88; bd. dirs. Open Lands Project, 1985-87, Kenilworth (Ill.) Village House, 1986-87. Recipient Achievement award Women in Mgmt., 1981; Am. Bd. Master Educators charter disting. fellow, 1986. Mem. Nat. Bus. Edn. Assn., Delta Pi Epsilon (past pres., mem. Bears Care Gala com.). Avocations: reading, travel, decorating. Home and Office: 144 Woodstock Ave Kenilworth IL 60043-1262 Address: Azienda Agricola Le Miccine S Traversa Chiantigiana 53013 Gaiole in Chianti Italy E-mail: drw@lemiccine.com.

WEAVER, EARL D., theater educator; b. Maywood, Calif., Aug. 24, 1956; s. Earl Douglas Weaver and Celia Faye Hyatt; life ptnr. Thomas G. Keetch. AA in Journalism, East LA C.C., 1977; BA in Theatre and Dance, U. Redlands, Calif., 1979; MFA, U. Calif., Irvine, 1990. Asst. prof. theatre Point Pk. U., Pitts., 1992—98; instr. theatre Las Positas C.C., Livermore, Calif., 2000—01; asst. prof. theatre U. Ctrl. Fla., Orlando, 2003—. Mng. dir. Theatre Factory, St. Louis, 1991—92. Dir.: (theatre production) Sunday in the Park with George (Outstanding Dir./Am. Coll. Theatre Festival, 1998), Tintypes (Outstanding Dir./Am. Coll. Theatre Festival, 1997). Recipient Outstanding Photography award, Internat. Libr. Photography, 2004—05. Mem.: Assn. Theatre Higher Edn. (assoc.), United Faculty Fla. (assoc.), Southeastern Theatre Conf. (assoc.), Nat. Educators Assn. (assoc.), Nat. Assn. Schs. Theatre (assoc.), Ednl. Theatre Assn. (assoc.), Actors Equity Assn. (assoc.). D-Liberal. Avocations: travel, photography. Office: University of Central Florida 12501 Research Parkway Suite 180 Orlando FL 32816 Home Phone: 407-277-9131; Office Phone: 407-823-3638. E-mail: eweaver@mail.ucf.edu.

WEAVER, ELIZABETH A., state supreme court justice; b. New Orleans; d. Louis and Mary Weaver. BA, Newcomb Coll.; JD, Tulane U. Elem. tchr. Glen Lake Cmty. Sch., Maple City, Mich.; French tchr. Leelanau Sch., Glen Arbor, Mich.; pvt. practice Glen Arbor, Mich.; law clk. Civil Dist. Ct., New Orleans; atty. Coleman, Dutrey & Thomson, New Orleans; atty., title specialist Chevron Oil Co., New Orleans; probate and juvenile judge Leelanau County, Mich., 1975—86; judge Mich. Ct. Appeals, 1987—94; justice Mich. Supreme Ct., Lansing, 1995—. Chief justice Mich. Supreme Ct., 1999—2000, re-elected, 2002—; chief justice Peter Rellected Superior Ct. Justice, 2002—; instr. edn. dept. Ctr. Mich. U.; mem. Mich. Com. on Juvenile Justice, Nat. Conv. State Adv. Groups on Juvenile Justice for U.S.; chair Gov.'s Task Force on Children's Justice, Trial Ct. Assessment Commn., Office Juvenile Justice and Delinquency Prevention; jud. adv. bd. mem. Law and Orgnl. Econs. Ctr. U. Kans.; treas. Children's Charter of Cts. of Mich. Chairperson Western Mich. U. CLE Adv. Bd.; mem. steering com. Grand Traverse/Leelanau Commn. on Youth; mem. Glen Arbor Twp. Zoning Bd.; mem. charter arts north Leelanau County; mem. citizen's adv. coun. Arnell Engstrom Children's Ctr.; mem. cmty. adv. com. Pathfinder Sch. Treaty Law Demonstration Project; active Grand Traverse/Leelanau Mental Health Found. Named Jurist of Yr., Police Officers Assn. of Mich.; named one of five Outstanding Young Women in Mich., Mich. Jaycees; recipient Eastern award, Warren Easton Hall of Fame, Lifetime Dedication to Children award, Mich. Champions in Childhood Injury Prevention, 2000, Recognition award for outstanding svc. to Mich. children and families, Gov. Engler and Family Independence Agy., 2000, Profls. award, Mich. Assn. Drug Cts., 2002, Mary S. Coleman award, Ctr. for Civic Edn. Through Law, 2002. Fellow: Mich. State Bar Found.; mem.: ABA, Antrim County Bar Assn., Leelanau County Bar Assn., Grand Traverse County Bar Assn., La. Bar Assn., Nat. Coun. Juvenile and Family Judges, Mich. Bar Assn. (chair CLE adv. bd., chair crime prevention ctr., chair juvenile law com.), Delta Kappa Gamma (hon.). Office: Mich Supreme Ct 3300 Grandview Plz 10850 E Traverse Hwy Traverse City MI 49684-1364 *

WEAVER, ERIC JAMES, educational administrator; b. Purley, Surrey, Eng., May 14, 1938; came to U.S., 1947, naturalized, 1963; s. Edward Arthur and Amelia Cecily (Ealden) W.; m. Joyce Lynn McKean, Aug. 19, 1973; children: Stephanie Lynn, Heather Elizabeth, Jonathan Eric, Christopher James. AB, Princeton U., 1958; STB, Gen. Theol. Sem., 1961; MDiv, 1972; MS, CCNY, 1968; profl. diploma, Hofstra U., 1973; EdD, 1980. Rsch. assoc. Meadow Brook Nat. Bank, West Hempstead, N.Y., 1957-61; dir. Christian edn. and youth work Ch. Holy Cross, Bklyn., 1958-61; vicar Ch. Messiah, Ctrl. Islip, N.Y., 1961-63, St. Michael and All Angel's Ch., Gordon Heights, N.Y., 1961-63; tchr. spl. edn. Nassau County Vocat. Edn. and Extension Bd., N.Y., 1963-67; supr. ctrl. adminstrn. Nassau Bd. Coop. Ednl. Svcs., 1967-70; asst. prin. Rosemary Kennedy Sch. for Trainable Mentally Retarded, Wantagh, N.Y., 1970-73; dir. spl. edn. Middle County Schs., Suffolk County, N.Y., 1973-81, dir. spl. ednl. svcs., 1981—98. Vice chmn. Project EQUALS, 1983-86; ednl. cons., instr. Spl. Edn. Tng. Resource Ctr., 1986-98; impartial hearing officer State of N.Y., 1982-97; chmn. com. spl. edn. Middle County Schs., 1973-98, com. preschool spl. edn., 1990-98; mem. Spl. Edn. Adminstrv. Leadership Tng. Acad., 1989-98; adj. asst. prof. spl. edn. C.W. Post Coll., 1979-80; ednl. cons., 1998-. Author monographs: The Sources of the First Gospel, 1958, Rudolf Bultman and Entmythologisierung, 1961, Ocular, Manual and Podiatric Dominance in a Severely Retarded Older Adolescent Population, 1968, Efforts of Special Education Administrators to Meet the Needs of Special Education Teachers by Inservice Training, 1980. Capt. Aux Police, County of Suffolk, N.Y., 1962-69; bd. dirs. Traffic Safety Bd., County of Nassau, N.Y., 1969-71, RobinPark Civic Assn.,Huntington, N.Y., 1963-66; trustee Police Hall of Fame; hon. mem. steering com. ann. art auction Lake Grove (N.Y.) Sch., 1985-90; asst. to rector Grace Ch., Huntington Sta., N.Y., 1963-66, Trinity Episc. Ch., Northport, N.Y., 1966-, rector 1999-. Fellow Am. Assn. Mental Deficiency; mem. Interagy. Coun. on Recreation for Handicapped (dir. 1970-73), Coun. Exceptional Children (pres. 1973-74), Coun. Adminstrs. Spl. Edn. (treas. 1985-89), Internat. Assn. Sci. Study Mental Deficiency, Long Island Assn. Spl. Edn. Adminstrn. (sec. 1975-76, v.p. 1976-77, pres. 1977-78, exec. com. 1978—), Assn. to Help Retarded Children, Am. Ednl. Rsch. Assn., am. assn. sch. Adminstrs, Sch. Adminstrs. Assn. N.Y. State, Phi Delta Kappa. Republican. Episcopalian. Home: 8 Oceanside Ct Northport NY 11768-1301 Office: 130 Main St Northport NY 11768-1723 E-mail: eweaver@optonline.net.

WEAVER, FRANKLIN THOMAS, retired newspaper executive; b. Johnstown, NY, Oct. 11, 1932; s. Edwin K. and Bertha J. (Wendt) W.; children: Thomas, James, Michael, David, Tammy, Kelly, Anna; m. Joyce W. Phelps, Oct. 23, 1991. BA with high honors in Journalism, Mich. State U., 1954. Advt. sales rep. Grand Rapids Press, Mich., 1955-64; controller Muskegon (Mich.) Chronicle, 1964-66; mgr. Bay City (Mich.) Times, 1966-73, Jackson (Mich.) Citizen Patriot, 1973-84, pub., 1984—99; ret. Mem.: Mich. Press Assn. (pres. 1991), Newspapers Assn. Am., Greater Jackson C. of C., Ella Sharp Mus. (pres. 1995—96), Jackson Country Club.

WEAVER, HOWARD C., newspaper executive; b. Anchorage, Oct. 15, 1950; s. Howard Gilbert and Lurlene Eloise (Gamble) W.; m. Alice Laprele Gauchay, July 16, 1970 (div. 1974); m. Barbara Lynn Hodgin, Sept. 16, 1978. BA Johns Hopkins U., 1972, MPhil Cambridge U., 1993. Reporter, staff writer Anchorage Daily News, 1972—76, columnist, 1979—80, mng. editor, 1980—83, editor, 1983—95; editor, owner Alaska Advocate, 1976—79; asst. to pres. McClatchy Newspapers, 1995—97, editor of editl. pages, 1997—2001; v.p. news The McClatchy Co., 2001—. Internat. co-chair Northern News Svc., 1989—94; disting. lectr. journalism U. Alaska, Fairbanks, 1991. Pulitzer Prize juror, 1988, 1989, 1994, 1995, 2002; bd. visitors John S. Knight Fellowship Stanford U.; Pulitzer Prize juror, 2003. Recipient Pulitzer prize, 1976, 1989, Headliner award, Press Club of Atlantic City, 1976, 1989, Gold medal, Investigative Reporters and Editors, 1989, Pub. Svc. award, AP Mng. Editor's Assn., 1976, 1989. Mem.: Investigative Reporters and Editors, Am. Soc. Newspaper Editors, Upper Yukon River Press Club (pres. 1972), Alaska Press Club (bd. dirs. 1972—84), Sigma Delta Chi (Nat. award 1989). Avocations: hockey, travel, opera.

WEAVER, JACQUELYN KUNKEL IVEY, artist, educator; b. Richmond, Ky., Mar. 14, 1931; d. Marion David and Margaret Tabitha (Brandenburg) Kunkel; m. George Thomas Ivey Sr., 1951 (dec. 1989); children: George Thomas Ivey Jr., David Richard Ivey; m. Harrell Fuller Weaver, 1991. BFA, Wesleyan Coll., 1987. Owner J.K. Ivey Art, Macon, Ga., 1974-91, J.K. Ivey Bookkeeping and Tax Svc., Macon, Ga., 1976-84, J.K. Ivey-Weaver Art Studio, Macon, 1991—. Tchr. drawing, painting and sculpture, 1991—. Exhibitions include Mid. Ga. Art Assn. Gallery, Macon, 1980—2007, Stofko-Dixon Fine Arts, Bolingbroke, Ga., 1996—2001, Self Family Art Ctr., Hilton Head Island, SC, 2001, Mus. Arts and Scis., Macon, 2002, 2005, Brazier Art Gallery, Richmond, Va., 2002, Gallery 51, Forsyth, Ga., 2003—05, Roundtree Gallery, Seaside, Fla., 2003—04, Monroe County Arts Alliance, Forsyth, Ga., 2004—05, 2006, 2007, Richard Schmid Fine Art Auction, Bellvue, Colo., 2004, 2005, 2006, 2007, Macon Arts Alliance Gallery, Ga., 2005, 2006, 2007. Bd. dirs., treas. Mid. Ga. Art Assn., Macon, 1981-84, 92, publicity chmn., 1988-89, chmn. nominating com., 1997, mem. fin. com., 1998-99, audit com., 1998. Mem.: Monroe County Arts Alliance, Hilton Head Island Art League, Oil Painters of Am., Portrait Painters Am., Inc., Mid. Ga. Art Assn., Catherine Lorillard Wolf Art Club, Mus. Arts and Scis., Wesleyan Coll. Alumnae Assn., Nat. Mus. Women in Arts (charter). Presbyterian. Avocations: ballroom dancing, reading, walking, music. Office: JK Ivey-Weaver Art Studio 6183 Hwy 87 Macon GA 31210 Office Phone: 478-477-1385. Office Fax: 478-744-0983. Business E-Mail: jweav550@bellsouth.net.

WEAVER, JANET See COATS, JANET

WEAVER, JERED, professional baseball player; b. Northridge, Calif., Oct. 4, 1982; s. Dave and Gail Weaver. Attended, Long Beach State U. Pitcher LA Angels of Anaheim, 2006—. Achievements include being the third pitcher to go undefeated in his first 12 major league starts in the last 100 years. Mailing: Angel Stadium of Anaheim 2000 Gene Autry Way Anaheim CA 92806 Office Phone: 714-940-2000. *

WEAVER, JOHN BORLAND, musician, department chairman, composer; b. Palmerton, Pa., Apr. 27, 1937; s. David Williams and Bertha Brownlee (Borl) W.; m. Marianne Carol Gruhn, Apr. 30, 1942; children: Jonathan Kirk, Kirianne Elizabeth. Diploma, Curtis Inst. Music, Phila., 1959; M in Sacred Music, Union Theol. Sem., 1968; MusD (hon.), Westminster Coll., 1995, MusD (hon.), 1995, Curtis Inst. Music, 2003. Head organ dept. Curtis Inst. Music, 1972—2003; chmn. organ dept. Manhattan Sch. Music, 1983-84, Juilliard Sch. Music, NYC, 1986—2004. Mem. faculty Westminister Choir Coll., Princeton, N.J., 1970-72, Union Theol. Sem. Sch. Sacred Music, 1970-73 Organist, choirmaster, Holy Trinity Lutheran Ch., N.Y.C., 1959-70, Temple Beth-El, Manhattan Beach, N.Y., 1970-80; dir. music, Madison Ave. Presbyn. Ch., N.Y.C., 1970—2005; solo organ recitalist, U.S., Can., Western Europe, U.K., Brazil; composer: Psalm 100, 1958, Toccatafor Organ, 1959, Epiphany Alleluias, 1967, Rhapsody for Flute and Organ, 1968, Good Christian Men, Rejoice, 1978, Introit for Pentecost, Fantasia for Organ, Passacaglia on a Theme by Dunstable, all 1981, The Joyful Feast, 1988, Psalm 46, 1989, Dialogues for Flute and Organ, 1991, Prayer for Transfiguration Day, 1991, Prelude and Fugue in E Minor, 1994, Prayer From Psalm 139, 1995, Variations on Three Hymn Tunes, 1997, Restore Us, O Lord of Hosts, 1995; contbr. articles to jours. including Reformed Liturgy and Music. Served with AUS, 1961-63. Decorated Army Commendation medal; recipient Disting. Svc. in the Field of Music award, Peabody chpt. Johns Hopkins U., 1989. Mem.: Presbyn. Assn. Musicians (pres. 1984—86), Am. Guild Organists (voted Internat. Performer of Yr., NYC chpt. 2005), N.Am. Acad. Liturgy, St. Wilfrid Club (NYC). Home: 23 Rowell Rd West Glover VT 05875 Office Phone: 802-525-4491. Personal E-mail: marianneweaver@juno.com. *By hard work and good fortune I have been able to do that which I decided, at age ten, to do with my life.*

WEAVER, KARL E., psychiatrist; b. Lakewood, Ohio, July 1, 1950; m. Christine R. Weaver. BA in Psychology, Haverford Coll., Pa., 1972; MD, Case Western Res. U., 1978. Diplomate in forensic psychiatry Am. Bd. Psychiatry and Neurology, lic. physician Calif. Flexible intern Mt. Sinai Hosp., Cleve., 1978-79; psychiatry resident Univ. Hosps. Cleve., 1979-82; pvt. practice Cleve., 1982-94; staff psychiatrist Calif. Men's Colony, San Luis Obispo, 1994-95, sr. psychiatrist, supr., 1995, chief psychiatrist, 1995—. Chmn. dept. psychiatry St. John & St. John Westshore Hosps., Cleve., 1985—90, Fairview Gen. Hosp., Cleve., 1992—94; pres., bd. dirs. St. John & St. John Westshore Profl. Corp., 1989—90; contract psychiatrist San Luis Obispo County Mental Health, 1997—, TeleCare, Santa Maria, Calif., 1998—. Address: PO Box 12826 San Luis Obispo CA 93406-2826 Office: PO Box 8101 San Luis Obispo CA 93403-8101 Personal E-mail: karlweaver@msn.com.

WEAVER, KENNETH NEWCOMER, geologist, state agency administrator; b. Lancaster, Pa., Jan. 16, 1927; s. A. Ross and Cora (Newcomer) W.; m. Mary Elizabeth Hoover, Sept. 9, 1950; children: Wendy Elaine, Matthew Owen. BS, Franklin and Marshall Coll., 1950; MA, Johns Hopkins U., 1952, PhD, 1954. Instr. geology Johns Hopkins, 1953- 54; ops. analyst Ops. Rsch. Office, Washington, 1954-56; chief geologist, then mgr. geology and quarry dept. Medusa Portland Cement Co., Wampum, Pa., 1956-63; dir., state geologist Md. Geol. Survey, Balt., 1963-92; chmn. Md. Land Reclamation Com., 1978-92. Gov.'s rep. Interstate Oil Compact Commn., Interstate Mining Compact Commn.; mem. outer shelf adv. com. U.S. Dept. Interior; chmn. Md. Topographic Mapping Com.; mem. com. on surface mining and reclamation NAS, 1978, vice chmn. com. on disposal of excess spoil, 1980-81, mem. com. on geologic mapping, 1983, liaison mem. bd. earth scis., 1982-88, mem. com. on water resources rsch., 1989-92, chmn. com. on abandoned minelands rsch. priorities, 1987; mem. subcom. on mgmt. of maj. underground constrn. projects Nat. Acad. Engring.; mem. Md. Commn. on Artistic Property, 1988-92. With U.S. Maritime Svc., 1944—46, with AUS, 1954—56. Recipient John Wesley Powell award USGS, 1994; named hdqr. bldg. The Kenneth N. Weaver Bldg. Md. Geol. Survey, 1994. Fellow Geol. Soc. Am. (sec. N.E. sect. 1985-2001), AAAS (sr.); mem. Am. Assn. Petroleum Geologists (Ea. sect., George V. Cohee Pub. Svc. award 1991), Am. Inst. Mining Engrs., Am. Inst. Profl. Geologists (editor 1983-84, Martin Van Couvering Meml. award 1992), Am. Geol. Inst. (governing bd. 1973, exec. com. 1989-90, medal in memory of Ian Campbell 2001), Am. Water Rsch. Assn., Geol. Soc. Washington, Assn. Am. State Geologists (pres. 1973, hon. mem. 1992), Johns Hopkins Club (Balt.). Republican. Presbyterian (elder). Office: Md Geol Survey 2300 St Paul St Baltimore MD 21218-5210 Home: 2525 Pot Spring Rd Unit S322 Lutherville Timonium MD 21093-2862 Home Phone: 410-252-0181; Office Phone: 410-554-5532. Personal E-mail: kweaver418@aol.com.

WEAVER, KITTY DUNLAP, author; b. Frankfort, Ky., Sept. 24, 1910; d. Arch Robertson and Rebecca (Johnson) Dunlap; m. Henry Byrne Weaver, June 29, 1933. Student, Sorbonne, Paris, summer 1930; AB, William and Mary Coll., 1932; MA, George Washington U., 1933; BS, U. Md., 1947; postgrad., Georgetown U., U. Pa., George Washington U., 1964-67, Moscow U., 1983; studied with Alfred Adler, Vienna, 1932. Jr. H.S. tchr., 1931-32; poultry farmer, 1947-55; author, 1970—. Author: Lenin's Grandchildren, 1971, Russia's Future, 1981, Bushels of Rubles, 1992. Mem. Aldie Hort. Soc., Chevy Chase (Md.) Club, Met. Club (Washington), Garden Club Am., Fauquier Londoun Garden Club. Home: 40820 John Mosby Hwy Aldie VA 20105-2820

WEAVER, LINDA MARIE, pharmacist, education educator; d. John William and Lorraine Marie Miller; m. Daniel Jacob Weaver. BA in Edn. and Spanish, Western Mich. U., 1974; BS in Pharmacy, Ferris State U., 1984; PharmD, Midwestern U., Chgo. Coll. of Pharmacy, 2000. Registered Pharmacist Mich., 1984. Ambulatory pharmacist Perry Drugs, Midland, Mich., 1984—87, Revco Drugs, Tucson, 1987—89, Walgreens Drug, Tucson, 1989—93; compliance officer Ariz. State Bd. of Pharmacy, Phoenix, 1993—99; clin. hosp. pharmacist John C. Lincoln Hosp., Phoenix, 1999—2001; med. sci. liaison Wyeth Pharmaceuticals, Scottsdale, 2001—03; med. liaison Abbott Labs., Scottsdale, 2003—04, clin. sci. mgr., 2004—. Adj. faculty mem. Midwestern U. Coll. of Pharmacy, Glendale, Ariz.; instr. Rio Salado C.C., Phoenix, 1997—98, Ariz. Pharmacy Assn., 1987—; adv. bd. mem. SCP Comm., Inc., Phoenix, 2001—01. Vol. Am. Diabetes Assn., Scottsdale, 1994—2004, Am. Heart Assn., Scottsdale, 1994—2004, Am. Cancer Assn., Scottsdale, 1994—2004. Recipient Golden Key Nat. Honor Soc., Mich. State U., 1981, Rho Chi Honor Soc., Midwestern U., 2000. Mem.: Am. Soc. of Health Sys. Pharmacists (licentiate), Am. Colleges of Clin. Pharmacists (licentiate), Am. Pharmacists Assn. (licentiate; del. 2001—03), Ariz. Pharmacy Assn. (licentiate; co-chair profl. affairs com. 1999—2000, maricopa rep. 2001—02, 2nd v.p. 2002—03, cert. of appreciation for outstanding svc. to Ariz. pharmacy assn. 2000, exec. bd. mem. award 2003). Avocations: scuba diving, cooking, jazz, travel, wine tasting. Home: 6120 E Gold Dust Ave Scottsdale AZ 85253 Office: Abbott Laboratories 6120 E Gold Dust Ave Scottsdale AZ 85253 Office Phone: 480-951-0366. Personal E-mail: lwpharmd@juno.com.

WEAVER, LOIS JEAN, physician, educator; b. Wheeling, W.Va., May 23, 1944; d. Lewis Everett and Ann Weaver. BA, Oberlin Coll., 1966; MD, U. Chgo., 1970. Pulmonary fellow Northwestern U., Evanston, Ill., 1975-77; trauma fellow U. Wash. Harborview Hosp., Seattle, 1977-79, research assoc., instr. medicine, 1979-81, clin. asst. prof. medicine, 1983—; clin. research fellow Virginia Mason Med. Research Ctr., Seattle, 1981-82; mem. med. staff Swedish Hosp., Seattle, 1984-92. Pulmonary cons. Fred Hutchinson Cancer Research Inst., Seattle, 1984-86, regional med. advisor and med. cons., disability quality br. Social Security, Seattle, 1985—. Contbr. sci. articles to profl. jours. La Verne Noyes scholar U. Chgo., 1966; Parker B. Francis fellow Northwestern U., 1975. Mem. AMA, Wash. Lung Assn., Sigma Xi. Avocations: gardening, music. Home: PO Box 2098 Kirkland WA 98083-2098 Office: 701 5th Ave Ste 2900 MIS 105 Seattle WA 98104-7075

WEAVER, LYNN EDWARD, academic administrator, consultant, editor; b. St. Louis, Jan. 12, 1930; s. Lienous E. and Estelle F. (Laspe) W.; m. JoAnn D., 1951 (div. 1981); children: Terry Sollenberger, Gwen, Bart, Stephen, Wes; m. Anita G. Gomez, Oct. 27, 1983. BSEE, U. Mo., 1951; MSEE, So. Meth. U., 1955; PhD, Purdue U., 1958. Devel. engr. McDonnell Aircraft, St. Louis, 1952-53; aerophysics engr. Convair Corp., Ft. Worth, 1953-55; instr. elec. engring. Purdue U., Lafayette, Ind., 1955-58; assoc. prof., then prof., dept. head U. Ariz., Tucson, 1959-69; assoc. dean coll. engring. U. Okla., Norman, 1969-70; exec. asst. to pres. Argonne Univs., Chgo., 1970-72; dir. sch. nuclear engring. and health physics Ga. Inst. Tech., 1972-82; dean engring., disting. prof. Auburn (Ala.) U., 1982-87; pres. Fla. Inst. Tech., Melbourne, 1987—2002, pres. emeritus, prof. elec. engring., 2002—. Cons. Ga. Power; bd. dirs. DBA Systems, Inc., Melbourne, Fla.; chmn. pub. affairs coun. Am. Assn. Engring. Soc., Washington, 1984-87; bd. adv. Ctr. for Sci., Tech. and Media, Washington; chmn. Ind. Colls. and Univs. Fla., 1999-2001. Author: (textbook) Reactor Dynamics & Control, State Space Techniques, 1968; exec. editor Annals of Nuclear Energy; contbr. numerous articles to tech. jours. U.S. rep. World Fedn., Engring. Orgn. Energy Com., 1981-86; bd. dirs. myregion.org, 2001-. Served to lt. USAF, 1951-53. Recipient Mo. Honors award for disting. svc. in engring., 1996. Fellow Am. Nuclear Soc.; mem. IEEE (sr.), Am. Soc. Engring. Edn., Sigma Xi, Eau Gallie Yacht Club. Republican. Roman Catholic. Avocations: tennis, jogging. Office: Fla Inst Tech 150 W University Blvd Melbourne FL 32901-6975 Office Phone: 321-674-8099. Business E-Mail: lweaver@fit.edu.

WEAVER, MICHAEL F., internist, researcher; MD, N.E. Ohio U. Coll. Medicine, Rootstown, Ohio, 1993. Cert. internist Am. Bd. Internal Medicine, 1996, addiction medicine Am. Soc. Addiction Medicine, 1998, med. rev. officer Am. Soc. Addiction Medicine, 1999. Assoc. prof. internal medicine and psychiatry Va. Commonwealth U., Richmond, 1996—. Med. dir. Human Resources, Inc., Richmond, 1998—. Contbr. articles to profl. jours. Grantee Mentored Clin. Scientist Devel. award, Nat. Inst. Alcohol Abuse and Alcoholism Nat. Inst. Health, 1998—2003. Fellow: Am. Soc. Addiction Medicine (chmn. exam. com. 2004); mem.: Am. Pain Soc., Coll. Problems Drug Dependence, Va. Soc. Addiction Medicine (bd. mem. 2005), Alpha Omega Alpha Honor Med. Soc. Achievements include research in treatment of alcohol withdrawal; disseminate guidelines for treatment of chronic pain and addiction. Office: Virginia Commonwealth Univ 1200 East Broad St P O Box 980109 Richmond VA 23298-0109 Office Phone: 804-828-1283.

WEAVER, MICHAEL GLENN, pharmacist; b. Tuscola, Ill., Sept. 11, 1955; s. Glen H. and Margaret I. (Long) W.; m. Catherine A. (Paynic), Sept. 30, 1978; children: Jennifer L., Michelle R., Gregory M. BS, St. Louis Coll. of Pharmacy, 1978; MBA, So. Ill. U., 1989. Registered pharmacist Ill. Clin. coordinator, staff pharmacist St. Elizabeth Med. Ctr., Granite City, Ill., 1975-87; dir. pharmacy Freeport Meml. Hosp. (now Freeport Health Network), Ill., 1987-92, dir. pharmacy and info. systems, 1992-97, dir. info. and telecom. svcs., 1997—2002; dir. pharmacy Freeport Health Network, 2002—; dir. Ill. Bd. Pharmacy, 1995-99, AeroComputing, Inc., 2001—02. Allocations com. United Way of NW Ill., 2000-, bd. dirs. 2006-, Girl Scouts, Green Hills, 2005-, exec. com., 2006-. Mem.: Am. Coll. Healthcare Execs., Ill. Coun. Hosp. Pharmacists (dir. ednl. affairs 1991—94, dir. orgnl. affairs 2004—05, pres.-elect 2005—06, pres. 2006—07), Am. Soc. Hosp. Pharmacists, Kiwanis (bd. dirs. Lincoln-Douglas chpt. 2002—, v.p. 2003—04, pres. elect 2004—05, pres. 2005—06), Delta Sigma Theta, Beta Gamma Sigma, Phi Kappa Phi. Republican. Mem. United Church of Christ. Avocations: computer, music. Home: 1346 Carriage Hill Ln Freeport IL 61032-6168 Office: Freeport Health Network 1045 W Stephenson St Freeport IL 61032-4899 Personal E-mail: mgw01@aol.com. Business E-Mail: mweaver@fhn.org.

WEAVER, MICHAEL JAMES, lawyer; b. Bakersfield, Calif., Feb. 11, 1946; s. Kenneth James and Elsa Hope (Rogers) W.; m. Valerie Scott, Sept. 2, 1966; children: Christopher James, Brett Michael, Karen Ashley. AB, Calif. State U., Long Beach, 1968; JD magna cum laude, U. San Diego, 1973. Bar: Calif., 1973, U.S. Dist. Ct. (so. dist.) Calif. 1973, U.S. Ct. Appeals (9th cir.) 1975, U.S. Supreme Ct. 1977. Law clk. to chief judge U.S. Dist. Ct. (so. dist.) Calif., San Diego, 1973-75; with Latham & Watkins, San Diego. Judge pro tem San Diego Superior Ct.; master of the Bench of the Inn, Am. Inns of Ct., Louis M. Welch chpt.; lectr. Inn of Ct., San Diego, 1981—, Continuing Edn. of Bar, Calif., 1983—, Workshop for Judges U.S. Ct. Appeals (9th cir.), 1990; mem. task force on establishment of bus. cts. sys. Jud. Coun. Calif., 1996-97; adv. com. U.S. Ct. Appeals (9th cir.), 2006—. Editor-in-chief: San Diego Law Rev., 1973; contbr. articles to profl. jours. Bd. dirs., pres. San Diego Kidney Found., 1985-90; bd. dirs. San Diego Aerospace Mus., 1985-97; trustee La Jolla (Calif.) Playhouse, 1990-91. lt. USNR, 1968-74. Fellow Am. Coll. Trial Lawyers; mem. San Diego Assn. Bus. Trial Lawyers (founding mem., bd. govs.), San Diego Def. Lawyers Assn. (dir.), Am. Arbitration Assn., 9th Cir. Jud. Conf. (del. 1987-90, mem. adv. com. 2006—), Calif. Supreme Ct. Hist. Assn. (bd. dirs. 1998—), Safari Club Internat. (San Diego chpt.), San Diego Sportsmen's Club, Coronado Yacht Club. Republican. Presbyterian. Avocations: reading, flying, skiing. Office: Latham & Watkins 600 West Broadway Ste 1800 San Diego CA 92101-8197 Business E-Mail: mike.weaver@lw.com.

WEAVER, MOLLIE LITTLE, lawyer; b. Alma, Ga., Mar. 11; d. Alfred Ross and Annis Mae (Bowles) Little; m. Jack Delano Nelson, Sept. 12, 1953 (div. May 1970); 1 dau., Cynthia Ann; m. 2d, Hobart Ayres Weaver, June 10, 1970; stepchildren: Hobart Jr., Mary Essa, Robert. BA in History, U. Richmond, 1978; JD, Wake Forest U., 1981. Bar; N.C. 1982, Fla. 1983; Cert. profl. sec.; cert. adminstrv. mgr. Supr., Western Electric Co., Richmond, Va., 1952-75; cons., owner Cert. Mgmt. Assocs., Richmond, 1975-76; sole practice, Ft. Lauderdale, Fla., 1982-86, Emerald Isle, N.C., 1986-89, Richmond, 1989—. Author: Secretary's Reference Manual, 1973. Mem. adv. coun. to Bus. and Office Edn., Greensboro, N.C., 1970-73, adv. com. to bus. edn. Va. Commonwealth U., Richmond, 1977. Recipient Key to City of Winston-Salem, N.C., 1963; Epps award for scholarship, 1978. Mem. ABA, N.C. Bar Assn., Fla. Bar Assn., Word Processing Assn. (v.p., founder Richmond 1973-75), Adminstrv. Mgmt. Soc. (com. chmn. Richmond, 1973-75), Phi Beta Kappa, Eta Sigma Phi, Phi Alpha Theta. Republican. Home: 12301 Renwick Pl Glen Allen VA 23059-6959 E-mail: Legal311@aol.com.

WEAVER, PAMELA ANN, education educator; b. Little Falls, NY, July 7, 1947; d. Floyd Aron Weaver and Norma May (Putnam) Hoyer; m. Ken Ward McCleary, Mar. 2, 1947; children: Brian Wilson, Blake McCleary, Ryan McCleary. AA, Fulton Montgomery C.C., Amsterdam, NY, 1968; BA, SUNY, 1970; MA, U. South Fla., 1973; PhD, Mich. State U., East Lansing, 1978. Mem. math. dept. Riviera Jr. H.S., Miami, Fla., 1970-72; grad. asst. Office Med., Edn. R & D Mich. State U., East Lansing, 1973-74, grad. asst. dept. mktg., 1974-75, instr. mktg.; asst. prof. mktg., hospitality svcs. adminstrn. Ctrl. Mich. State U., Mt. Pleasant, 1978-79, 1982-86, chair acad. senate, 1985-86, prof. mktg., hospitality svcs. adminstrn., 1986-89; prof., undergrad. program coord. dept. hospitality and tourism mgmt. Va. Poly. Inst. and State U., Blacksburg, 1989—, undergrad. program coord., 2005—. Contbr. over 100 articles to profl. jours. Mem. Coun. on Hotel, Restaurant and Instl. Edn. (John Wiley & Sons, Inc. award for Litetime Achievement to Hospitality Industry 1994). Office: Va Poly Inst and State U Wallace Hall Blacksburg VA 24061-0429 Business E-Mail: weaver@vt.edu.

WEAVER, PAULINE ANNE, lawyer; b. Hornchurch, Eng., Mar. 31, 1949; came to U.S., 1960; d. George Henry and Eunice Mary (Obee) W.; m. Charles Franklin Scribner, Mar. 2, 1974. BA, Memphis State U., 1971, JD, 1979. Bar: Tenn. 1979, Calif. 1980, U.S. Dist. Ct. (no. dist.) Calif. 1980. Law clk. Shelby County Office Pub. Defender, Memphis, 1977-79, Alameda County (Calif.) Office Pub. Defender, Oakland, 1980-82, atty., 1982—. Adj. prof. law John F. Kennedy U., Orinda, Calif. Legal advisor LWV, Fremont, Calif., 1980-83, Parent Info. Network, Fremont, 1979-84, bd. dirs., 1981-84; bd. dirs. Shelter Against Violent Environs., Fremont, 1981—; consumer rep. Alameda County Emergency Med. Care com., 1980-83; mem. Fremont/Newark Philharm. Guild, 1981—; vol. Parole Project, 1984—; vol. tutor Alameda County Adult Literacy Project; past pres. Washington Hosp. Healthcare Found.; bd. dir. Eden Housing. Donnelly J. Hill Meml. scholar Memphis State U. Law Alumni Assn., 1978. Mem. ABA (chmn. domestic violence com. 1984-85, screening subcom., Outstanding State Membership chmn. 1981, Gavel awards, ho. del., bd. gov. 2003-2006), State Bar Calif. (past v.p.), Found. of State Bar Calif. (pres. 2004-), So. Alameda County Bar Assn., Women Lawyers of Alameda County (treas. 1983—), Nat. Women's Polit. Caucus (chmn. 1982-83), Calif. Women Lawyers (past pres.), Nat. Conf. Women's Bar Assn. (past pres.), Alameda County Pub. Defenders Assn., Alameda County Dem. Lawyers Club, Order of Barristers, Alpha Gamma Delta (pres. 1981-83), Delta Theta Phi, Omicron Delta Kappa. Office: Alameda County Public Defender 1401 Lakeside Dr 4th Fl Oakland CA 94612

WEAVER, PEGGY (MARGUERITE MCKINNIE WEAVER), plantation owner; b. Jackson, Tenn., June 7, 1925; d. Franklin Allen and Mary Alice (Caradine) McKinnie; children: Elizabeth Lynn, Thomas Jackson III, Franklin A. McKinnie. Student, U. Colo., 1943-45, Am. Acad. Dramatic Arts, 1945-46, S. Meisner's Profl. Classes, 1949, Oxford U., 1990-91. Actress, 1946-52; mem. staff Mus. Modern Art, NYC, 1949-50; woman's editor radio sta. WTJS-AM-FM, Jackson, Tenn., 1952-55; editor, radio/TV Jackson Sun Newspaper, 1952-55; columnist Bolivar (Tenn.) Bulletin-Times, 1986—2000; chmn. Ho. of Reps. of Old Line Dist., Hardeman County, Tenn., 1986—91, 1994—97, sec., 2000—. Pres. Hardeman County chpt. Assn. Preservation of Tenn. Antiquities, 1991—95; charter mem. adv. bd. Tenn. Arts Commn., Nashville, 1967—74, Tenn. Performing Arts Ctr., Nashville, 1972—; chmn. trustees br. Tenn. Libr. Assn., Nashville, 1973—74; Henry County regional chmn. Opera Memphis, 1979—91; mem. nat. coun. Met. Opera, NYC, 1980—92, Tenn. Bicentennial Com., Hardeman County, 1993—96; bd. sec. Memphis Brooks Mus. League, 1997—98; docent Dixon Gallery and Gardens, Memphis; founder Paris-Henry County (Tenn.) Arts Coun., 1965. Mem. DAR, Nat. Soc. Colonial Dames Am. (chmn. Memphis Town com. 2002-04), Oxford Alumni Assn. NY, English Speaking Union (London chpt.), Jamestown Soc., Crescent Club, Dilettantes. Methodist. Avocations: horseback riding, travel, theater. Office: 402 Heritage Plantation Hickory Valley TN 38042 Office Phone: 731-764-6009. Personal E-mail: pweaver@heritageplantation.net. Business E-Mail: pweaver@heritagecompanies.net.

WEAVER, PETER DAVID, bishop, religious organization administrator; b. Greenville, Pa., Jan. 15, 1945; s. Adolph Peter and Dorothy Selina (Barbor) W.; children: Rebecca Hope, Sarah Joy, Rachel Faith. ThD, Boston U., 1975; MDiv, Drew U., 1969; BA, W.Va. Wesleyan U., 1966. Ordained deacon and elder United Meth. Ch. Pastor Whitaker (Pa.) U. Meth. Ch., 1971-77; sr. pastor Smithfield United Ch., Pitts., 1977-88, First United Meth. Ch., Pitts., 1988-96; bishop United Meth. Ch., Phila., 1996—2004, pres. coun. of bishops, 2003—, bishop, New Eng. conference Boston, 2004—. Adj. faculty Drew U., Madison, N.J., 1980's, Pitts. Theol. Seminary, 1990's; co-founder, pres. Bethlehem Haven, Pitts., 1981-88; chair mission divsn. Gen. Coun. on Ministries United Meth. Ch., Dayton, Ohio, 1992-96. Bd. dirs. YMCA, Pitts., 1978-88, Goodwill Industries, Pitts., 1981-93, One Voice Against Racism, Pitts., 1990-96, Vintage Inc., Pitts., 1989-96; trustee W.Va. Wesleyan Coll., Buckannon, 1980-96, Drew U., 1996—, Wesley Coll., 1996-04, Lebanon Valley Coll., 1996-04, Boston U., 2004-. Avocations: woodworking, music, water sports. Office: Box 249 Lawrence MA 01842

WEAVER, REG(INALD), educational association administrator; b. Danville, Ill. BS, Ill. State U.; MS, Roosevelt U., Chgo.; LHD (hon.), NC Shaw U.; D in Pub. Svc. (hon.), SC State U. Tchr. Danville HS, Ill.; local NEA pres. Harvey, Ill., 1967—71; pres. Ill Edn. Assn., 1981—87; mem. NEA exec. com., 1989—95; v.p. NEA, 1996—2002, pres., 2002—; v.p. Edn. Internat. Mem. exec. bd. Nat. Coun. for Accreditation of Tchr. Edn.; chair IEA Political Action Com. for Edn. (IPACE); appointed to Ill. Commn. for Improvement of Elementary and Secondary Edn., Ill. Project for Sch. Reform Adv. Coun., Ill. Literacy Coun., Task Force on At-Risk Youth; mem. Ill. State Bd. of Edn. Blue Ribbon Comm. on Improvement of Tchg. as a Profession; address conferences and forums sponsored by US Conf. Mayors, NAACP, Nat. Coun. LARaza, Rainbow Push Coalition, League United Latin Citizens, ASPIRA; advocate for public schs. Hon. mem. adv. bd. Dept. Edn. Leadership, Roosevelt U.; bd. govs. Joint Ctr. Polit. and Econ. Studies; bd. dirs. Nat. Bd. Profl. Tchg. Stds. Named one of Outstanding Men of Am., Most Influential Black Ams., Ebony mag., 2006; named to Wall of Fame, Danville HS, The Ebony Power 150, Ebony mag., 2007; recipient Ebony Mag. Influential Black Educators award, Ill. Edn. Assn. Human Rels. award, People for Am. Way Spirit of Liberty award, 2005, Chmn. award for Ednl. Leadership, 100 Black Men in Am. Inc., 2006, Congl. Gt. Points of Light award, Congl. Black Caucus, 2006, George Meany Latino Leadership award, US Hispanic Leadership Inst.,

2006, US Action Progressive Leadership award, Pres. award, Nat. Conf. Black Mayors, Excellence in Leadership award, MALDEF, 2007. Mem.: PTA (hon. life). Office: NEA 1201 16th St NW Washington DC 20036-3290 Office Phone: 202-802-7000. E-mail: rweaver@nea.org.

WEAVER, RICHARD L., II, writer, educator; b. Hanover, NH, Dec. 5, 1941; s. Richard L. and Florence B. (Grow) W.; m. Andrea A. Willis; children: Richard Scott, Jacquelynn Michelle, Anthony Keith, Joanna Corinne. AB, U. Mich., 1964, MA, 1965; PhD, Ind. U., 1969. Asst. prof. U. Mass., 1968-74; assoc. prof. speech comm. Bowling Green State U., 1974-79, prof., 1979-96, dir., basic speech comm. course, 1974-96. Vis. prof. U. Hawaii-Manoa, 1981-82, Bond U., Queensland, Australia, 1990, St. Albans, Melbourne, Australia, 1990, Western Inst., Perth, Australia, 1990. Author: (with Saundra Hybels) Speech/Communication, 1974, 2d edit., 1979, Speech/Communication: A Reader, 1975, 2d edit., 1979, Speech/Communication: A Student Manual, 1976, 2d edit., 1979, Understanding Interpersonal Communication, 1978, 7th edit., 1996, (with Raymond K. Tucker, Cynthia Berryman-Fink) Research in Speech Communication, 1981, Foundations of Speech Communication: Perspectives of a Discipline, 1982, Speech Communication Skills, 1982, Understanding Public Communication, 1983, Understanding Business Communication, 1985, Understanding Speech Communication Skills, 1985, Readings in Speech Communication, 1985, (with Saundra Hybels) Communicating Effectively, 1986, 8th edit., 2007, Skills for Communicating Effectively, 1985, 4th edit., 1993, rev. edit., 1995, (with Howard W. Cotrell) Innovative Instructional Strategies, 1987, 6th edit., 1993, (with Curt Bechler) Listen to Win: A Guide to Effective Listening, 1994, Study Guide to Accompany Communicating Effectively, 1995, 2d edit., 1998, Essentials of Public Speaking, 1996, 2d edit., 2001, (with Edgar E. Willis) How to be Funny on Purpose: Creating and Consuming Humor, 2005, And Then Some: Essays to Entertain, Motivate & Inspire, 3 vols., 2007. Mem. emeritus Nat. Comm. Assn., Ctrl. States Speech Assn., Ohio Speech Assn. Home and Office: 9583 Woodleigh Ct Perrysburg OH 43551-2669 Home Phone: 419-874-2124; Office Phone: 419-874-2124. E-mail: weaverii@sbcglobal.net.

WEAVER, ROBIN GEOFFREY, lawyer, educator; b. Columbus, Ohio, Aug. 19, 1948; BA, Ohio State U., 1970; JD, U. Mich., 1973. Bar: Ohio 1974, U.S. Dist. Ct. (no. dist.) Ohio 1974, U.S. Ct. Appeals (6th cir.) 1980, U.S. Ct. Appeals (3d cir.) 1998, U.S. Ct. Appeals (2d, 7th, and 11th cirs.) 2002, U.S. Supreme Ct., 2002, U.S. Dist. Ct. (so. dist.) Ohio 2004. Assoc. Squire, Sanders & Dempsey, Cleve., 1973-83, ptnr., 1983—; mem. faculty Nat. Inst. for Trial Adv. Northwestern U., Chgo., 1983—. Mem. Ohio Supreme Ct. Bd. of Commrs. on Grievances and Discipline, chair, 1996-97, master commr., 2002-. With U.S. Army, 1974. Fellow Am. Coll. Trial Lawyers, Internat. Soc. Barristers; mem. Cleve. Bar Assn. (pres. 2002-03); mem. ABA, Ohio Bar Assn., Cleve. Assn. Trial Attys. (life), 8th Appellate Jud. Conf., Am. Inns of Ct. (master bencher Cleve. chpt.). Office: Squire Sanders & Dempsey 4900 Key Tower Cleveland OH 44114 Office Phone: 216-479-8500. Business E-Mail: rweaver@ssd.com.

WEAVER, SIGOURNEY (SUSAN ALEXANDRA WEAVER), actress; b. NYC, Oct. 8, 1949; d. Sylvester (Pat) Weaver and Elizabeth Inglis; m. Jim Simpson, Oct. 1, 1984; 1 child, Charlotte. BA in English, Stanford U., 1971; MA in Drama, Yale U., 1974. Actress: (theatre) including Watergate Classics, 1973, The Frogs, 1974 The Nature and Purpose of the Universe, 1974, Daryl and Carol and Kenny and Jenny, The Constant Wife, 1975, Titanic, 1976, Das Lusitania Songspiel (also co-writer), 1976, Marco Polo Sings a Song, 1977, A Flea in Her Ear, 1978, Conjuring an Event, 1978, Beyond Therapy, 1981, As You Like It, 1981, Hurlyburly, 1984-85, Sex and Longing, 1996, The Merchant of Venice, 1986, The Guys, 2002, The Mercy Seat, 2002, Mrs. Farnsworth, 2004, Crazy Mary, 2007; (films) Annie Hall, 1977, Madman, 1978, Alien, 1979, Eyewitness, 1981, The Year of Living Dangerously, 1982, Deal of the Century, 1983, Ghostbusters, 1984, Une femme ou deux, 1985, Aliens, 1986 (Acad. Award nomination for best actress, 1987), Half Moon Street, 1986, Gorillas in the Mist, 1988 (Acad. Award nomination for best actress, 1989, Golden Globe for best actress - drama, 1989), Working Girl, 1988 (Acad. Award nomination for best supporting actress, 1989, Golden Globe for best supporting actress in a motion picture, 1989), Ghostbusters II, 1989, 1492: Conquest of Paradise, 1992, Dave, 1993, Death and the Maiden, 1994, Jeffrey, 1995, Copycat, 1995, Snow White: A Tale of Terror, 1997, The Ice Storm, 1997 (BAFTA Film Award for best supporting actress, 1998), A Map of the World, 1999, Galaxy Quest, 1999, Airframe, 1999, Company Man, 2000, Speak Truth to Power, 2000, Heartbreakers, 2001, Big Bad Love (voice), 2001, Tadpole, 2002, The Guys, 2002, Holes, 2003, The Village, 2004, Imaginary Heroes, 2004, Snow Cake, 2006, The TV Set, 2006, Infamous, 20006, Happily N'Ever After (voice), 2007, (TV series) Somerset, 1976, (TV miniseries) The Best of Families, 1977, (TV movies) 3 by Cheever: The Sorrows of Gin, 1979, 3 by Cheever: O Youth and Beauty!, 1979; co-prodr., actress: (films) Alien 3, 1992, Alien: Resurrection, 1997. Recipient Star on the Walk of Fame, 1999, Lifetime Achievement award, Chicago Internat. Film Festival, 2001. Office: William Morris Agy One William Morris Pl Beverly Hills CA 90212 *

WEAVER, TIMOTHY ALLAN, lawyer; b. Elkhart, Ind., Nov. 30, 1948; s. Arthur and Joan Lucile (Yoder) W.; m. Catherine Anne Power, Nov. 23, 1974; children: Daniel Timothy, Christopher Matthew, David Colwell. AB, Brown U., 1971; JD, U. Ill., 1974. Bar: Ill. 1974, Wis. 1999, U.S. Dist. Ct. (no. dist.) Ill. 1975, U.S. Ct. Appeals (7th cir.) 1975, U.S. Dist. Ct. (no. dist. trial bar) Ill. 1982, U.S. Dist. Ct. (ea. dist.) Wis. 1999. Asst. pub. defender Cook County Pub. Defender, Chgo., 1974-75; trial atty. Chgo. Transit Authority, 1975-78; assoc. Philip E. Howard Ltd., Chgo., 1978, Pretzel & Stouffer, Chartered, Chgo., 1978-82, ptnr., 1982—. Editor: Medical Malpractice, 1989, 92, 96; contbr. chpts. to books. Mem. ABA, Ill. State Bar Assn., Ill. Assn. Def. Trial Counsel, State Bar of Wis., Civil Trial Counsel of Wis., The Lawyers Club of Chgo. Office: Pretzel & Stouffer Chartered One S Wacker Dr #2500 Chicago IL 60606 Office Phone: 312-578-7416. E-mail: tweaver@pretzel-stouffer.com.

WEAVER, WILLIAM CHARLES, manufacturing executive; b. Nov. 10, 1941; s. Curtis D. and Mary (Yahres) W.; m. Karla Lee Kottas, June 13, 1964; children: Michael, Kelli. BS in Bus. Edn., Indiana U. of Pa., 1963; postgrad. in acctg., Tex. Christian U., 1964-65. CPA, Pa. With Price Waterhouse & Co., Pitts., 1965-73, audit mgr., 1970-73; corp. contr. Kennametal Inc., Latrobe, Pa., 1973-78, v.p., contr., 1978-83, v.p., treas., 1983-86, v.p., CFO, 1987-89; sr. v.p., CFO Oak Industries, Inc., Waltham, Mass., 1990-95; ret., 1995. Bd. dirs. Gemini Precision Products; chmn. bd. dirs. Weaver Enterprises, Inc., 1996—, Weaver Properties, LLC. Pres. Mountain View Parent Tchrs. Orgn., 1976—77; bd. dirs. East High Acres Civic Assn., 1976—77; treas. Greater Latrobe Hockey Club, 1982—87; chmn. bd. dirs., mem. adv. coun. Jr. Achievement, Latrobe, 1982—85; chmn. bd. trustees Latrobe United Way, 1988—89; trustee Hampton United Presbyn. Ch., 1972—73. 1st lt. US Army, 1963—65. Mem.: Fin. Execs. Inst., Palmetto Dunes Club Inc. (pres. 1998—2001). E-mail: kbweaver@hargray.com.

WEAVER, WILLIAM CLAIR, JR., (MIKE WEAVER), human resources development executive; b. Ind., Pa., Apr. 11, 1936; s. William Clair and Zaida (Bley) W.; m. Janet Marcelle Boyd, Sept. 18, 1963 (div. 1978); 1 child, William Michael; m. Donna June Hubbuch, Feb. 10, 1984. B Aero Engring., Rensselaer Poly. Inst., 1958; MBA, Washington U., St. Louis, 1971; postgrad., Rutgers U.; grad., Armed Forces Indsl. Coll. Registered profl. engr. Engr. aerodynamics N.Am. Aviation, LA, 1959-60; engr. flight test ops. Boeing/Vertol, Phila., 1963-66; engr. flight test project Lockheed Electronics, Plainfield, NJ, 1966—69; project engr. advanced systems, sr. staff engr. Emerson Electric Co., St. Louis, 1969—72; pres. Achievement Assocs., Inc., St. Louis, 1972—. Founder, charter mem. Catalyst, 1978—; faculty Leadership Mgmt., Inc.; spkr. in field. Author: Winning Selling, 1983; contbr. articles to profl. jours. Adv. com. Boy Scouts Am., Bridgeton, Mo., 1974. Capt. USAF, 1960-63, USAFR. Mem. AIAA, NSPE, Cato Inst., Am. Soc. Tng. and Devel., Am. Soc. Bus. and Mgmt. Cons., Am. Ordnance Soc., Assn. MBA Execs., Air Force Assn., Am. Helicopter Soc., Acacia Frat., St. Louis C. of C., Mensa, Mo. Athletic Club, Beta Gamma Sigma. Republican. Lutheran. Avocations: photography, music, sports. Home and Office: 1016 Evergreen Rd Yardley PA 19067-1018 Office Phone: 215-428-3400. Personal E-mail: acacia@aol.com.

WEAVER, WILLIAM SCHILDECKER, retired electric power industry executive; b. Pitts., Jan. 15, 1944; s. Charles Henry and Louise (Schildecker) W.; m. Janet Kae Jones, Mar. 7, 1981. BA, Hamilton Coll., 1965; JD, U. Mich., 1968. Bar: Wash. 1968. Assoc. Perkins Coie, Seattle, 1968-74, ptnr., 1975-91; exec. v.p., CFO Puget Sound Power & Light Co., Bellevue, Wash., 1991-97; vice chmn., chmn. unregulated subs. Puget Sound Energy, 1997, pres., COO, 1997, pres., CEO, 1998—2002, chmn., 2001—02, ret. Bd. dirs. Wash. Rsch. Coun., Seattle, 1991-97, chmn., 1995-97; trustee Seattle Repertory Theatre, 1992-95, 99-00, chmn., 2000-02, Corp. Coun. Arts, 1995-02, Pacific Sci. Ctr., 1997-02; bd. dirs. Edison Electric Inst., 1998-02. Mem. ABA, Wash. State Bar Assn., Sovren, The Soc. of Vintage Racing Enthusiasts, Sports Car Club Am., Seattle Yacht Club, Flounder Bay Yacht Club.

WEAVER-GARDNER, PRISCILLA, library director; m. Tony Weaver-Gardner; 1 child, Curtis. Head libr. ops. Jersey City Free Pub. Libr., 2001, dir., 2002—. Mem.: NJ Libr. Assn. Office: Jersey City Free Pub Libr 472 Jersey Ave Jersey City NJ 07302 Office Phone: 201-547-4788. Office Fax: 201-547-4584. E-mail: pgardner@jclibrary.org.

WEAVER-STROH, JOANNE MATEER, education educator, consultant; b. May 21, 1930; d. Kenneth Hall and Jean (Weakley) Mateer; children: Karen, Mark, Laurie. BS in Edn., U. Pa., 1952, elem. and secondary prin. cert., 1979; MS in Psychology Reading, Temple U., 1968. Tchr. Paoli (Pa.) Sch., 1952-53, Somerville Sch., Ridgewood, NJ, 1953-55, Bryn Mawr (Pa.) Sch., 1955-57, Erdenheim Sch., Springfield, Pa., 1957-58; reading specialist Abington (Pa.) Sch. Dist., 1966-67, curriculum specialist, 1967-73, coord. human rels. programs, 1973-80; prin. Rydal Elem. Sch., Abington, 1980-88, Willow Hill Elem. Sch., 1988-96; ret., 1996. Cons., tchr. Marywood Coll., Scranton, Pa., 1972—; coord. drug and alcohol abuse program Abington Sch. Dist., 1989-96; cons. Conflict Resolution, 1996—. Chmn. Abington Human Rels. Adv. Coun., 1973-88; chmn. Cmty. Rels. Com. Abington Twp., 1978—; mem. Ea. Montgomery County Human Rels. Adv. Coun., 1981-83, 2006—; chmn. No Place for Hate project Abington Twp., 2003—; mediator Abington Twp.; leader Stephen Ministry program Abington Presbyn. Ch.; mem. ctr. internat. leadership and comm. bd. advisors Pa. State U., Abington, 2006—. Named Citizen of the Week Times Chronicle Newspaper, 1976; recipient award Four Chaplains Temple U., 1979, Disting. Citizens award Roslyn Jr. C. of C., 1981, Citizens for Progress Humanitarian award, 1982, Cmty. award Abington YMCA, 1987, Dr. Martin Luther King Jr. award Abington Twp., 1989, East Montgomery County/Pa. State Human Rels. Intergroup award, 2000, Citizens That Care award Abington Cmty. Taskforce, 2003, Disting. Cmty. Svc. award Intersvc. Clubs of Glenside, 2003. Mem. ASCD, NASEP, Internat. Coop. Learning Assn., Pa. Assn. Elem. Prins., Phi Delta Kappa, Delta Kappa Gamma. Republican. Home: 109 Durham Ct Maple Glen PA 19002-2854 Home Phone: 215-793-9434. Personal E-mail: rwstroh@att.net.

WEBB, ANTHONY ALLAN, banker, director; b. Lincoln, Nebr., May 24, 1943; s. Robert McGraw and Ruth Irene (Good) W.; m. Micheline Touchette, July 10, 1971; children— Annie, Christian BA, U. Colo., 1965; B.Internat. Mgmt., Am. Grad. Sch. Internat. Mgmt., 1970. Various positions Royal Bank Can., Montreal and London, 1970-77, assoc. mgr. Toronto, Ont., Canada, 1977-80, v.p., 1980-83, sr. v.p. merchant banking, 1983-84, dir. gen. Geneva, 1984-88, sr. v.p. personal fin. svcs. Montreal, 1988-93; chmn. Royal Bank Can. Suisse, Royal Bank Can., Channel Islands; pres., CEO Royal Trust, Toronto, 1993-99; chair The Exec. Com., 2000—. Served to lt. comdr. USNR, 1965-69 Home: 90 Binscarth Rd Toronto ON Canada M4W 1Y4 E-mail: tonywebb@rogers.com.

WEBB, BRANDON TYLER, professional baseball player; b. Ashland, Ky., May 9, 1979; m. Alicia Webb. Attended, U. Ky., Lexington. Pitcher Ariz. Diamondbacks, 2003—. Named to Nat. League All-Star Team, 2006; recipient Nat. League Cy Young award, Major League Baseball Writers Assn., 2006. Office: Arizona Diamondbacks 401 E Jefferson St Phoenix AZ 85004 *

WEBB, CARL B., banker; BA, W. Tex. State U., 1972; attended, Tex. Tech. U., Masters Bus.; grad., Southern Methodist U., 1981. Corp. banking divn. InterFirst Bank, Dallas; v.p., dir. Gerald Ford's First United Bank Group, 1983; pres., COO First Nat. Bank, Lubbock, Tex., 1983-88, First Gibraltar Bank, 1988-93, First Nationwide Bank, 1994-97, Ca. Federal Bank, 1997—.

WEBB, CHARLES HAIZLIP, JR., retired dean; b. Dallas, Feb. 14, 1933; s. Charles Haizlip and Marion (Gilker) W.; m. Kenda McGibbon, June 21, 1958; children: Mark, Kent, Malcolm, Charles Haizlip III. AB, MMus, So. Meth. U., 1955; DMus, Ind. U., 1964; DMus (hon.), Anderson. Coll., 1979. Asst. to dean Sch. Music, So. Meth. U., 1957-58; mem. faculty Sch. Music, Ind. U., 1960-97, dean, 1973-97, Disting. prof., 1997—. Adv. bd. Classical Insites. Dir. Indpls. Symphony Choir, 1967-81; guest condr. chorus and orch. festivals throughout U.S.; duo-pianist with Wallace Hornibrook in U.S. and Australian tour, 1973; organist First Meth. Ch., Bloomington, 1961-, mem. hymnal revision com. Meth. Ch.; mem. jury Chopin competition; mem. jury internat. piano competitions in Munich, Budapest, South Africa, Paris, Chile, Warsaw, Bolzano, London, Cologne, Japan, Israel. Chmn. adv. bd. Internat. Music Festivals, Inc.; mem. Ind. Arts Commn., 1975-83, U.S.-USSR Commn. on Music Performance Edn., Am. Coun. Learned Socs./USSR Ministry of Culture; adv. panel Music Found.; recommendation bd. Avery Fisher Prize Program; bd. dirs. Busoni Found.; bd. adv. Van Cliburn Internat. Piano Competition; nat. adv. bd. Am. Guild Organists; trustee Indpls. Symphony Orch.; mem. Nat. Recording Preservation Found., 2002; adv. com. on cultural diplomacy U.S. Dept. State, 2004; active Nat. Rec. Preservation Found. With U.S. Army, 1955-57. Decorated D.S.M.; recipient Disting. Alumni award So. Meth. U., 1980, Sagamore of Wabash Gov. award, 1987, 89, 97, Thomas Hart Benton medal Ind. U., 1987, Disting. Alumni award Highland Park HS, Dallas, 1989, Disting Alumni award Ind. U., 2005, Ind. Gov. award for arts, 1989, Rocking Chair award, Ind. U., 1997, Sterling Patron award Mu Phi Epsilon Internat., 1989, Ind. Gen. Assembly House Resolution # 39 for meritorious svc., 1997, Pres.'s award Ind. U., 2000; subject of tribute in U.S. Congl. Record, 1997; Rockefeller scholar Bellagio Study Ctr., 1997; named Ind. Living Legend, 2004, named to Congl. Com. to Advise the Sec. of State on Cultural Diplomacy, 2004, Living Treasure Bloomington Area Arts Coun., 2007, Monroe County Arts Coun., 2007; Paul Harris fellow, Rotary Internat., 1997. Mem. Ind. Acad., Century Assn. of N.Y., Pi Kappa Lambda, Phi Mu Alpha, Phi Delta Theta. Home: 648 S Woodcrest Dr Bloomington IN 47401-5417 Personal E-mail: webbc@indiana.edu.

WEBB, CHARLES RICHARD, retired university president; b. Berkeley, Calif., Oct. 4, 1919; s. Charles Richard and Adele (McDaniel) W.; m. Andrée Bonno; 1 child, Charles Richard III. AB, U. Calif., Berkeley, 1942, MA, 1944, Harvard U., 1947, PhD, 1949. Faculty San Diego State Coll., 1949-64, prof., 1958-64, chmn. dept. history, 1956-58; dean acad. affairs Stanislaus State Coll., Turlock, Calif., 1964-66; prof. history San Diego State Coll., 1966-70; pres. Eastern Conn. State U., Willimantic, 1970-88; ret., 1988; former assoc. dean acad. planning Calif. State Colls., 1966-69, former dep. state coll. dean acad. planning. Author: Workbook in Western Civilization, 2 vols, 1959, Western Civilization vol. 1 (with Schaefer), vol. 2 (with Palm), 1958, (with Crosby) The Past as Prologue, 2 vols, 1973; contbr. articles to profl. jours. Mem. pers. com. Santa Rosa Symphony Assn., New Eng. Program, Windham Meml. Cmty. Hosp.; mem. Commn. on Conn.'s Future. With USNR, 1941-45. Mem. AAUP, Am. Hist. Assn., Am. Fedn. Musicians, Nat. Pks. and Conservation, Sonoma Land Trust, Sierra Club, Nature Conservancy, New Eng. Hist. Assn., Assn. Calif. State Coll. Profs. (v.p. 1958-60), Save the Redwoods League, Conn. Employees Assn., Am. Assn. State Colls. and Univs., Phi Alpha Theta, Kappa Delta Pi, Omicron Delta Pi, Alpha Delta Phi. Clubs: University (San Diego), Commonwealth of Calif., Willimantic Country, Saddle Club, Santa Rosa, Montecito Heights Health & Racquet Club, Santa Rosa. Home: 6495 Timber Springs Dr Santa Rosa CA 95409-5900

WEBB, DAN K., lawyer; b. Bushnell, Ill., Sept. 5, 1945; s. Keith L. and Phyllis I. (Clow) W.; student Western Ill. U., 1963-66; JD cum laude, Loyola U., 1970; m. Laura A. Buscemi, Mar. 15, 1973; children: Jeffrey, Maggie, Michael, Melanie, Megan. Bar: Ill. 1970, US Dist. Ct. (no. dist. Ill.), US Ct.Appeals (6th-8th cirs., fed. cir.), US Supreme Ct. Chief spl. prosecutions divsn. US Atty.'s Office, Chgo., 1970-76; ptnr., Cummins, Decker & Webb, Chgo., 1976-79; dir., Ill. Dept. Law Enforcement, Chgo., 1979-80; ptnr. Pierce, Webb, Lydon & Griffin, Chgo., 1980-81; US atty. (no. dist. Ill.), US Dept. Justice, Chgo., 1981-85; ptnr. Winston & Strawn LLP, Chgo., 1985—, chmn., 2006-, head litig. dept., mem. exec. com.; Iran-Contra spl. trial counsel; instr. John Marshall Law Sch., 1975—, Loyola U. Sch. Law, 1980—. Vice chmn. Met. Fair and Expn. Authority, 1978—81; bd. advs. Mercy Hosp. and Med. Ctr.; mem. Chgo. Coun. on Arson. Contbr. articles to profl. jours. Recipient spl. commendation award US Dept. Justice, 1975; named one of 10 Outstanding Young Chicagoans, Chgo. Jaycees, 1979, 100 Most Influential Lawyers, Nat. Law Jour., 2006. Fellow. Internat. Acad. Trial Lawyers, Am. Coll. of Trial Lawyers; mem. ABA, Ill. Bar Assn., Chgo. Bar Assn., Fed. Bar Assn., Legal Club Chgo., Execs. Club Chgo., Nat. Inst. Trial Advocacy, 1979-. Republican. Office: Winston & Strawn LLP 35 W Wacker Dr Ste 4200 Chicago IL 60601-9703 Office Phone: 312-558-5856. Office Fax: 312-558-5700. E-mail: dwebb@winston.com. *

WEBB, DARRELL D., retail executive; MBA, Portland State U., 1980. Group v.p. procurement The Kroger Co.; pres. Quality Food Ctr., Inc., 1999—2002, Fred Meyer, Inc., 2002—06; chmn., pres., CEO Jo-Ann Stores, Inc., Hudson, Ohio, 2006—. Office: Jo-Ann Stores Inc 5555 Darrow Rd Hudson OH 44236-4011 Office Phone: 330-656-2600. Office Fax: 330-463-6675. *

WEBB, DARRYL WILLARD, systems engineer; s. La Verne Willard and Jeraldine Marie Webb; m. Christina Denise Kowalski, Aug. 27, 1971; children: Shannon J., Meagan C. AA in Liberal Arts, Fullerton Coll., Calif., 1973; BA in Bus. Ops. Rsch., Calif. State U., Fullerton, 1974. Life cycle cost analyst Northrop Corp., Anaheim, Calif., 1975—79; exec. advisor Rockwell Internat., Anaheim, 1979—86; prin. investigator ACS, Inc., Tustin, Calif., 1986—91; project mgr. Boeing Co., Huntington Beach, Calif., 1991—2000; tech. dir. Econ Inc., Huntington Beach, 2000—01; mgr. we. region Price Sys., Inc., El Segundo, Calif., 2001—03; sr. engring. specialist Aerospace Corp., El Segundo, 2003—. Mem. adv. bd. Cost Credibility Team NASA, Marshall Space Flight Ctr., Ala., 2002; presenter in field. Contbr. articles to profl. publs. Cpl. USMC, 1968—70, Vietnam. Mem.: Internat. Soc. Parametric Analysts (pres. So. Calif. chpt. 1981—83, bd. dirs. 1986—87, tech. dir. So. Calif. chpt. 1980, Parametrician of Yr. 1984, Freiman award 2003), Phi Tau Sigma (hon. Student Mentor award 1996). Avocations: collecting historical photography, music, research in technology. Office: The Aerospace Corp 2350 E El Segundo Blvd El Segundo CA 90245 Office Fax: 310-336-5581. Business E-Mail: darryl.w.webb@aero.org.

WEBB, DONALD ARTHUR, minister; b. Wales, May 4, 1926; came to U.S., 1958; s. Arthur and Emily W.; m. Renee Mowbray, May 18, 1946; children— Cheryl, Marian, Christopher, Alison, Ian. Student, Queen's Coll., Cambridge U., Eng., 1944-45; BA, Ohio Wesleyan U., 1960; MDiv, Methodist Theol. Sch. in Ohio, 1963; PhD, Drew U., 1966; postdoctoral, Lincoln Coll., Oxford U., Eng., 1969-72; LLD, Centenary Coll. La., 1991. Ordained to ministry Methodist Ch., 1960. Insp. Brit. Social Services, 1953-58; pastor various chs. Ohio and N.J., 1958-68; dean admissions, asst. prof. theology and lit. Meth. Theol. Sch. in Ohio, 1968-75, v.p. adminstrn., 1975-77; pres. Centenary Coll. La., Shreveport, 1977-91; sr. pastor First United Meth. Ch., Shreveport, 1991-92, scholar-in-residence, 1992—. Author: The Flame and Dusty Miller, 1970, We Hold These Truths, 1960; author: Dostoevsky and Christian Agnosticism, 1971, Deep Calls to Deep, 1998, The Best Year Yet, 2004. With Brit. Royal Navy, 1945-53. Mem. Shreveport C. of C. (bd. dirs. 1978-80). Home: 5709 Lakefront Dr Shreveport LA 71119-3913 Office: First United Meth Ch Head of Tex Shreveport LA 71165-1567 Office Phone: 318-636-0630.

WEBB, DONNA LOUISE, academic director, educator; b. Yakima, Wash., Aug. 12, 1929; d. Manuel Lawrence and Rena May (Sewell) Matson; (div.); children: Marlene Park, Ed Webb III. AA in Vocat. Edn., Portland CC, Oreg., 1976; BA in Psychology, Warner Pacific Coll., 1980; MEd in Career and Vocat. Edn., Oreg. State U., Corvallis, 1980, EdD in Career and Vocat. Edn., 1983. Dir. placement Andrews U., Mich., 1969-74; dir. career edn. and coop. work experience Portland, 1976-78; coord. youth program Fed. Experiment/Chronically Unemployed Youth, Vancouver, Wash., 1979; dir. career counseling Clark Coll., Vancouver, 1979; tchr. coop. edn. project Multnomah County ESD, Portland, 1981; pvt. practice counselor Portland, 1982-84; dir. career devel. & coop. edn. Walla Walla (Wash.) Coll., 1984-87; assoc. dir. Ctr. for Lifelong Learning Loma Linda (Calif.) U., 1987-91; corp. trainer Pacific Inst., Seattle, 1991-94, account mgr. consulting and rsch., 1994—. Home decorator Frederick & Nelson; payroll and computerized bookkeeper Hilo Care Ctr.; with pers. office Flour-Utah Mining; employment counselor Snelling & Snelling Employment Agy.; tchr. bus. edn. Portland Adventist Acad. Contbr. articles to profl. jours. Mem. ASTD, Assn. Per. Adminstr. (columnist San Bernardino Sun newspaper), Coun. for Adult and Exptl. Learning, Calif. Assn. for Counseling and Devel., Coop. Edn. Assn., Nat. Commn. for Coop. Edn., Phi Delta Kappa. Office: 4501 W Powell Blvd Apt 72 Gresham OR 97030-5070 Personal E-mail: dlwbythesea@yahoo.com.

WEBB, EMILY, retired plant morphologist; b. Charleston, SC, Apr. 10, 1924; d. Malcolm Syfan and Emily Kirk (Moore) W.; m. John James Rosemond, Apr. 23, 1942 (div. 1953); 1 child, John Kirk; m. Julius Goldberg, Sept. 9, 1954; children: Michael, Judith. *In our family we have a tradition of educating our women. Great-grandmother, Emily Kirk, graduated from a women's college in South Carolina, in the 1850's, going on to graduate school for French, in Charleston, for two years. Grandmother, Will Emma Buchanan, graduated from a women's college in South Carolina at age 19. My mother, Emily Kirk Moore, graduated from a women's college in Virginia at age 19. My daughter, Judi, represents the fifth generation of well-educated women in the family in having a Master's Degree in film.* Student, Coll. Charleston, 1951—54; AB in Liberal Arts and Sci. with honors, U. Ill., Chgo., 1968, MS in Biol. Scis., 1972, PhD in Biol. Scis., 1985. Undergrad. fellow in bacteriology Med. Coll. S.C., Charleston, 1952-54; teaching asst. U. Ill., Chgo., 1969-72, 77-84, rsch. asst., 1977; teaching fellow W.Va. U., Morgantown, 1974, instr., 1974-75.

Rsch. in N.Am. bot. needlework art, 1986—. Author: Studies in Several North American Species of Ophioglossum, 1986; translator Nat. Transl. Ctr., Chgo., 1976; contbr. articles to profl. jours. James scholar U. Ill., 1968-69. Mem. DAR, ACLU. Democrat. Episcopalian. Avocations: gardening, writing, money management. Home and Office: 1356 Mandel Ave Westchester IL 60154-3433

WEBB, JACK M., lawyer; b. Monroe, La., Feb. 23, 1936; s. Sam L. and Lillian Etta (McCowen) W.; m. Diane Adele Waterman, Aug. 22, 1964; children: Julia Lillian Pogue, Kathryn Joy Shively, Samuel Logan. BS in Geology, Centenary Coll. La., 1957; JD, Tulane U., 1960; student, JFK Sch. Govt. Harvard U., 1999. Bar: La. 1960, Tex. 1962. Atty. Standard Oil Co. Tex., Houston, 1961-66; staff atty. Trunkline Gas. Co., Houston, 1966-71; sr. atty. M.W. Kellogg Co., Houston, 1971-73; sec., asst. gen. counsel Gulf Resources & Chem. Corp., Houston, 1973-78, v.p. govt. rels., adminstrv. asst. to chmn. bd., 1978-82; pres. Jack M. Webb & Assocs., 1983—; U.S. spl. amb. to Bolivia, 1985, to Finland, 1986, to Haiti, 1991, to Angola, 1992, to Ghana, 1993; hon. consul gen. Ghana, 1995—. Bd. dirs. Bradmark, Inc., Am. Meridian Ins. Co., Scotia Pacific Holding Co., Veri Med Rsch. Corp., Crystal Fuels, Inc. Bd. dirs. U.S. Peace Corps, 1985-86, Nat. Park Found., 1986-92, Boy Scouts Am., 1975—. Capt. U.S. Army, 1960-61. Mem. Tex. Bar Assn., La. Bar Assn. Methodist. Home: 3434 Locke Ln Houston TX 77027-4139 Office Phone: 281-586-7166. E-mail: jackw@jackwebb.com.

WEBB, JIM (JAMES HENRY WEBB JR.), senator, former civilian military employee; b. St. Joseph, Mo., Feb. 9, 1946; s. James Henry and Vera Lorraine (Hodges) Webb; m. Barbara Samorajczyk (div.); 1 child, Amy; m. Jo Ann Krukar (div.); children: Sarah C., James Robert, Julia A.; m. Hong Le Webb; 1 child, Georgia LeAnh. Attended, U. Southern Calif., 1963—64; BA, US Naval Acad., 1968; JD, Georgetown U., 1972. Cons. to Gov. US Territory of Guam; asst. minority counsel House Com. on Veterans Affairs, Washington, 1977-78, chief minority counsel, 1979-81; asst. sec. for reserve affairs US Dept. Def., Washington, 1984-87, sec. Dept. Navy, 1987—88; US Senator from Va., 2007—. Instr. tactics and weapons Marine Corps Officer Candidates Sch.; vis. writer US Naval Acad. Journalist covering US Marines in Beirut, PBS, 1983 (Emmy award); author: Micronesia and US Pacific Strategy: A Blueprint for the 1980s, 1974, Field of Fire, 1978, A Sense of Honor, 1981, A Country Such As This, 1983, Something To Die For, 1991, The Emperor's General, 1999, Lost Soldiers, 2001, Born Fighting: How the Scots-Irish Shaped America, 2004; story writer and exec. prodr. (films) Rules of Engagement, 2000. Served in USMC, 1968—72, 2nd lt., platoon comdr., Vietnam. Decorated Order Iron Mike award US Marine Corp League, Navy Cross, Silver Star, 2 Bronze Stars, 2 Purple Hearts; recipient Disting. Pub. Svc. award, Dept. Def., Patriot award, Medal of Honor Soc., Nat. Commander's Pub. Svc. award, Am. Legion, Media Svc. award, VFW, John Russell Leader-ship award, Robert L. Denig Disting. Svc. award; fellow Harvard Inst. Politics, 1992. Democrat. Office: US Senate 144 Russell Senate Office Bldg Washington DC 20510 also: 507 E Franklin St Richmond VA 23219 *

WEBB, JOHN GIBBON, III, lawyer; b. Flint, Mich., June 1, 1944; s. John Gibbon Jr. and Martha W.; m. Fain Murphey, July 6, 1968; children: Jennifer Horn, Philip, Andrew Aidan, John Matthew. AB, Davidson Coll., 1966; JD, Vanderbilt U., 1970. Bar: N.Y. 1971, N.J. 1981. Assoc. Curtis, Mallet-Prevost, Colt & Mosle, NYC, 1970—80; gen. counsel, v.p., sec. J.M. Huber Corp., Edison, NJ, 1980—95; pvt. bus. law practice Budd Lake, NJ, 1996—. Mem. exec. com. Sussex County CC Found., Episcopal Cmty. Devel. Inc. Mem.: ABA, Warren County C. of C., Mt. Olive C. of C., NJ State Bar Assn., NYC Bar Assn. Episcopalian. Office: Ste 125 500 International Dr N Budd Lake NJ 07828 Office Phone: 973-426-8435. Personal E-mail: webbgc@aol.com.

WEBB, JULIA JONES, elementary school educator, minister; b. Portsmouth, Va., Apr. 3, 1962; d. William Edward Jones Jr. and Fannie Ford Jones; m. Alexander Maurice Webb Sr., Nov. 17, 1990; children: Brittany Alexandria, Alexander Maurice II. BA in Early Childhood Edn., Norfolk State U., 1988; postgrad., Va. Union U., 2004—. Lic. early edn. Va. Educator Chesapeake (Va.) Pub. Schs., 1988—, chmn. grade level II Southwestern Elem., 2005—. Assoc. minister First Bapt. Ch. Gilmerton, Chesapeake, 1999—2002, New Hope Bapt. Ch., Chesapeake, 2002—05, Grove Bapt. Ch., Portsmouth, Va., 2005—. USAA All-Am. scholar, Norfolk State U., 1989. Mem.: Va. Edn. Assn. (del. 1990—91), Chesapeake Tchr. Forum. Democrat. Baptist. Avocations: coaching cheerleading, gardening, cooking, interior decorating, reading. Home: 2701 Dockside Ct Chesapeake VA 23323 Office: Southwestern Elem Sch 4410 Airline Blvd Chesapeake VA 23321 Office Phone: 757-465-6310.

WEBB, KARRIE, professional golfer; b. Ayr, Queensland, Australia, Dec. 21, 1974; Profl. golfer, 1994—; mem. LPGA Tour, 1996—; mem. Australian Team Women's World Cup of Golf, 2005. Named Rookie of Yr., Women Profl. Golfers' European Tour, 1995, Rolex Rookie of Yr., LPGA, 1996, Rolex Player of Yr., 1999, 2000, Outstanding Women's Golf Performer of Yr., ESPN Espy awards, 1997, 2001, Female Player of Yr., Golf Writers Assn. Am., 2000, Queensland Sportswomen of Yr., 2000—02, 2001, 2002; recipient Vare Trophy, LPGA, 1997, 1999, 2000, Crowne Plaza Achievement award, 2000. Achievements include winning LPGA Tour events including the Weetabix Women's Brit. Open, 1995, 97, 2002, Healthsouth Inaugural, 1996, Sprint Titleholders Championship, 1996, SAFECO Classic, 1996, 1997, ITT LPGA Tour Championship, 1996, Susan G. Koman Internat., 1997, Australian Ladies Masters, 1998, 99, 2000; winner, LPGA Tour events including the City of Hope Myrtle Beach Classic, 1998, Wegmans Rochester Internat., 1999, Mercury Titleholders Championship, 1999, Standard Register PING, 1999, The Office Depot, 1999, 2000; winner, LPGA Tour events including the du Maurier Classic, 1999, Nabisco Championship, 2000, Oldsmobile Classic, 2000, LPGA Takefuji Classic, 2000, AFLAC Champions presented by Southern Living, 2000, US Women's Open, 2000, 01; winner, LPGA Tour events including the McDonald's LPGA Championship presented by AIG, 2001, Tyco/ADT Championship, 2001, Wegmans Rochester LPGA, 2002, John Q. Hammons Hotel Classic, 2003, Kellogg-Keebler Classic, 2004, Kraft Nabisco Championship, 2006, Michelob Ultra Open, 2006, Evian Masters, 2006; winner, international events including the Women's Australian Open, 2000, 02, 07, ANZ Ladies Masters on the Robe di Kappa Ladies European Tour, 2005; inducted into World Golf Hall of Fame, 2005; first LPGA player to achieve the Super Career Grand Slam by winning all 5 majors available in her career, 2002. Avocations: reading, basketball, fishing. Office: c/o LPGA 100 Internat Golf Dr Daytona Beach FL 32124-1092 *

WEBB, LAMAR THAXTER, architect; b. Hapeville, Ga., Sept. 13, 1928; s. Eugene Garnette and Sara Ethel (Moore) W.; m. Bettye Jayne Jackson, Dec. 6, 1957; children: Mark Maynard, Robin Lynn. BBA in Fin., U. Ga., 1950; BS, Ga. Inst. Tech., 1959, BArch, 1960. Reg. arch. Ga., Fla., Tenn. Intern architect Abreu and Robeson, Inc., Brunswick, Ga., 1960-66; architect, pres. Webb & Baldwin, Inc., St. Simons Island, Ga., 1966-72; pres., owner Lamar T. Webb, Arch., Inc., St. Simons Island, 1972—. 1st lt. USAF, 1953—55. Mem. AIA (State bd. dirs. 1985-91, v.p. Golden Isles chpt. 1988-89, pres. 1989-90), Am. Soc. Interior Designers, Am. Soc. Landscape Architects (affiliate), Audubon Soc., Nat. Hort. Soc., Humane Soc. (local bd. dirs. 1985-87), Smithsonian Assocs., Coastal Alliance for Arts, Nat. Trust for Hist. Preservation, Ga. Trust for Hist. Preservation, Coastal Ga. Hist. Assn., Met. Mus. Art, Golden Isles Gourmet Club (bd. dirs.) Chien de Rotessieurs, G.I. Chap. Avocations: cooking, drawing, painting, travel. Home: 121 Runnymede Saint Simons Island GA 31522 Office: 13 Retreat Pl Saint Simons Island GA 31522 Home: Willow Creek 654 Brice Station Rd Silver Creek GA 30173 Office Phone: 912-638-8621. Personal E-mail: ltwarch@hotmail.com.

WEBB, LISA MICHELLE, regulatory affairs manager; b. Ft. Irwin, Calif., Feb. 9, 1970; d. Albert Joseph Velasquez and Susan Jane Lindsey; m. Charles Haizlip Webb III, Sept. 18, 1993; children: Charles Haizlip IV children: Wesley Grant. BA in Human Biology, Stanford U., Palo Alto, Calf., 1993; MBA, Ind. Wesleyan U., Marion, 2000. Regulatory affairs cert., US Regulatory Affairs Profl. Soc., 1998, regulatory affairs cert., European Union Regulatory Affairs Profl. Soc., 2002, regulatory affairs cert., Can. Regulatory Affairs Profl. Soc., 2004, cert. regulatory affairs San Diego State U., 2004. Regulatory affairs specialist Cook Inc., 1997—2005, regulatory affairs mgr., 2005—. Presenter in field. Sunday sch. tchr. First United Meth. Ch., Bloomington, 2000—06. Mem.: Food and Drug Law Inst., Regulatory Affairs Profl. Soc., Sorosis Philanthropic Soc., Stanford U. Alumni Assn., Psi Iota Xi, Kappa Alpha Theta (mem. alumni assn.). Home: 1618 Greenfield Ct Bloomington IN 47401 Office: Cook Inc 750 Daniels Way Bloomington IN 47404 Home Phone: 812-339-5723; Office Phone: 812-339-2235 ext. 2643. Business E-Mail: lisa.webb@cookmedical.com.

WEBB, MARK RUSSELL, music educator; b. Lansing, Mich., May 12, 1953; s. Russell Nathan and Vadah Ann Webb; m. Susan Joan Hanna, May 27, 1978; children: Natalie Lauren, Ashley Victoria. MusB, U. Mich., 1975, MusM, 1976. Cert. music tchr. K-12 Mich. Vocal music tchr. Kentwood Pub. Schs., Kentwood, Mich., 1976—95; choral coord., dir. internat. choir Blue Lake Fine Arts Camp, Twin Lake, Mich.; dir. coll. chorus Aquina Coll., Grand Rapids, Mich.; dir. chancel choir Mayflower Congregational Ch., Grand Rapids, Mich.; dir., choral activities East Grand Rapids Pub. Schs., East Grand Rapids. Named Tchr. of Yr., Mich. Sch. Vocal Music Assn., 2003, Arts Educator of Yr., ArtServe of Mich., 2003. Mem.: Mich. Sch. Vocal Music Assn. (pres. 1999—2005). Avocations: reading, music arranging. Home: 2851 Oakwood Dr SE Grand Rapids MI 49506 Office: E Grand Rapids HS 2211 Lake Dr SE Grand Rapids MI 49506 Office Phone: 616-235-7555 X5135. Office Fax: 616-235-7592. E-mail: mwebb@egrps.org.

WEBB, MARTY FOX, principal; b. Des Moines, July 15, 1942; d. Joseph John and Jean (Way) Fox; m. Andrew H. Rudolph, Aug. 17, 1963 (div. Jan. 1988); children: Kristen Ann, Kevin Andrew; m. Eugene J. Webb, Nov. 23, 1991. BS, U. Mich., 1964; MEd, Houston Bapt. U., 1982; EdD, U. San Francisco, 1993. Cert. adminstr., Tex., elem. and spl. edn. educator, Mich., Tex. Tchr. spl. edn. Hawthorn Ctr., Northville, Mich., 1964-70; tchr. Bellaire (Tex.) Sch. for Children, 1977-80; prin. Corpus Christi Sch., Houston, 1980-97; founder, head of sch. The Monarch Sch., Houston, 1997—. Spkr. in field. Bd. dirs. DeBusk Found. Recipient Elem. Sch. Recognition award U.S. Dept. Edn., 1989-90, Blue Ribbon Sch. award, 1990, Outstanding Doctoral Student award, 1994. Mem. ASCD, U. Mich. Alumni Assn. Avocations: reading, fly fishing, camping, hiking, bodybuilding. Home: 3531 Sun Valley Dr Houston TX 77025-4148 Office: The Monarch Sch 1231 Wirt Rd Houston TX 77055-6852 Office Phone: 713-479-0800. Business E-Mail: mwebb@monarchschool.org.

WEBB, MARY CHRISTINE, reading recovery and in-class educator; b. Ames, Iowa, Jan. 3, 1947; d. Howard Darrell and Lorena Faye (North) Webb; m. Harlen DuWayne Groe, Dec. 29, 1989 (div. Oct. 1997). BS in Elem. Edn., Iowa State U., 1969, MS in Emotional Disabilities, 1980, MEd in Learning Disabilities, 1986. Cert. tchr. K-9, learning disabilities, behavioral disabilities, multicategorical, Iowa; cert. in reading endorsement, Iowa, 2001; lic. brain gym instr. cons. 2006. 1st grade tchr. Holy Spirit Sch., Carroll, Iowa, 1970; severe behavior disabilities tchr. Area Edn. Agy 7, Waterloo, Iowa, 1979-85; tchg. and rsch. assistantship Iowa State U., Ames, 1985-86; multicategorical 3-8 self contained with integration tchr. Madrid Elem. and Jr. HS, 1986-87; behavior disability self contained with integration tchr. Des Moines Pub. Schs., 1987-88, resource rm. tchr., 1988-95, multicategorical self contained with integration tchr., 1995-99, in-class reading recovery tchr., behavior interventionist, 1999-2000, in-class reading recovery tchr., title reading tchr., 2000—02, in-class reading recovery tchr., reading tchr., 2002—. Lic. brain gym cons., 2006—. Active People to People Spl. Edn. Del. to Mainland China, 1993. Mem.: NEA, ASCD, Iowa State Edn. Assn., Des Moines Edn. Assn. Office: King Acad Math and Sci 1849 Forest Ave Des Moines IA 50314-1336 Personal E-mail: mcwebb47@yahoo.com.

WEBB, MAYNARD G., JR., Internet company executive; BA, Fla. Atlantic U. With Thomas Conrad, figgie Internat., IBM; dir., info. tech. Quantum Corp., 1991—95; v.p., CIO Bay Networks Inc., 1995—98; sr. v.p., CIO Gateway, Inc., 1998—99; pres. eBay Techs. Ebay Inc., San Jose, Calif., 1999—2002, COO, 2002—06; CEO LiveOps Inc., Palo Alto, Calif., 2006—. Bd. dir. Hyperion, 2006—. Office: LiveOps Inc 3340 Hillview Ave Palo Alto CA 94304 Office Phone: 650-461-1000. Office Fax: 650-745-3756. *

WEBB, O. GLENN, retired farm supplies company executive; b. 1936; married BS, U. Ill., 1957; PhD, So. Ill. U., 1973. With Growmark, Inc., Bloomington, Ill., 1966—2000, sec., 1968-72, v.p., 1972-80, pres., 1980—2000, chmn., 1980—2000; dir. Archer Daniels Midland Co., 1991—. Trustee, chmn. Am. Inst. Coop.; dir. St. Louis Farm Credit Banks, Farmers Export Co., Nat. Coop. Refinery Assn., Ill. Agr. Leadership Found.; trustee Grad. Inst. Coop. Leadership.

WEBB, ORVILLE LYNN, retired physician, pharmacologist, educator; b. Tulsa, Okla., Aug. 29, 1931; s. Rufus Aclen and Berla Ophelia (Caudle) W.; m. Joan (Liebenheim), June 1, 1954 (div. Jan. 1980); children: Kathryn, Gilbert, Benjamin; m. Jeanne P. (Heath), Aug. 24, 1991. BS, Okla. State U., 1953; MS, U. Okla., 1961; PhD in Pharmacology, U. Mo., 1966, MD, 1968. Diplomate Nat. Bd. Med. Examiners, Am. Bd. Family Practice; cert. med. examiner, 1999. Rsch. assoc. in pharmacology U. Okla., 1959—61; rsch. fellow NIH, 1962—66; instr. pharmacology U. Mo., Columbia, 1966—68, asst. prof., 1968—69; intern U. Mo. Med. Ctr., 1968—69; family practice New Castle, Ind., 1969—89; med. dir. VA Clinic, Lawton, Okla., 1989—94, Comanche County Hosp., Lawton, Okla., 1994—98; pvt. practice medicine Lawton, Okla., 1998—2002; owner Comanche County Med. Clinic, Lawton, Okla., 1998—2002, Okla. Med. Clinic, Lawton, 1999—2003; ret., 2003. Clin. assoc. prof. family medicine U. Okla. Coll. Medicine, 1989—; adj. assoc. prof. pharmacology U. Okla. Coll. Medicine, 1989—; mem. U. Okla. Medicine Admissions Bd., 1995-98; mem. staff Henry County Meml. Hosp., New Castle, Ind. 1969-89; guest prof. pharmacy and pharmacology Butler U. Coll. Pharmacy, Indpls., 1970-75; owner, dir. Carthage Clinic, 1975-89; clin. assoc. prof. family medicine Ind. U. Coll. Medicine, 1986-89; county physician, jail med. dir. Henry County, Ind., 1976-89. Author: (with Blissitt, Stanaszek, Lea, and Febiger) Clinical Pharmacy Practice, 1972; contbr. numerous articles to profl. journals. Bd. dir. Lawton Philharm., 1990-95. Recipient Cert. of Merit in Pharmacol. and Clin. Med. Rsch., 1970, Med. Student Rsch. Essay Award Am. Acad. Neurology, 1968. Fellow Am. Acad. Family Physicians, Am. Coll. Physician Exec.; mem. AMA (ann. award recognition 1975-2001), AAAS, Ind. State Med. Assn., Am. Coll. Sports Medicine, Am. Coll. Occupl. and Environ. Medicine, N.Y. Acad. Sci., Am. Soc. Contemporary Medicine and Surgery, Okla. State Med. Assn., Festival Chamber Music Soc. (bd. dirs. Indpls. 1981-87), Nat. Fraternity Eagle Scouts, Mensa, Columbia Club, Skyline Club, Country Club, Kiwanis, Elks, Sigma Xi, Phi Sigma. Achievements include research in harmful effects of anabolic steroids on athletes; cholesterol and other lipids. Home: 85 Quail Creek Dr NW Lawton OK 73507-9026 Personal E-mail: olynnwebb@earthlink.net.

WEBB, OTIS D., retired underwriter; b. Moticello, Ky., Aug. 4, 1937; s. Ova H. and Margaret E. Webb; m. Rita K. Webb, Aug. 13, 1984; m. Patty P. Phillips (div.); children: Terri L. Hendon, Richard A., Michael D., Christa L. Cons. mgr. Met Life, Louisville, 1958—72; sales mgr. Star Furniture TV and Appliance, Owensboro, Ky., 1972—83; regional mgr. Zee Med., Sheperedville, Ky., 1983—89; sales cons. Met Life, Owensboro, 1989—2000; ret., 2000; owner,operator Webb 1st Aid Safety Supply, 2003—. Instr. Life Underwriter Tng. Coun., Wash., DC, 1990—99; pres. Life Underwriters Assn., Owensboro, Ky., 1968—70, Owensboro, 1992—94. Mem. Young Dem., 1959—64; conf. bd. mem. St. Vincent DePaul, Owensboro, 2005—06. Mem.: Fraternal Order of Moose, Fraternal Order of Eagles. Democrat. Cath. Avocations: fishing, hunting, golf. Home: 3810 Broadleaf Ct Owensboro KY 42301 Office: Webb First Aid and Safety 3810 Broadleaf Ct Owensboro KY 42301 Office Phone: 270-684-2605. E-mail: rkwebb@peoplepc.com.

WEBB, PAUL, physiologist, educator, researcher, consultant; b. Cleve., Dec. 2, 1923; s. Monte F. and Barbara (Webb) Bourjaily; m. Eileen Whalen, Mar. 13, 1948; children: Shaun P., Paul S. Womacks. BA, U. Va., 1943, MD, 1946; MS in Physiol., U. Wash., 1951. Asst. prof. physiology U. Okla. Sch. Medicine, Oklahoma City, 1952—54; chief environ. sect. Aeromed. Lab., Wright-Patterson AFB, Ohio, 1954-58; prin. assoc. Webb Assocs., Yellow Springs, Ohio, 1959-82; vis. scientist INSERM, Paris, 1983; vis. prof. U. Limburg, Maastricht, The Netherlands, 1986, U. Uppsala, Sweden, 1988-89; clin. prof. cmty. health Wright State U. Sch. Medicine, Dayton, Ohio, 1980—; rsch. prof. bioengring. Wright State U., Dayton, 2005—. Cons. aerospace and undersea medicine, energy balance and thermal physiology, Yellow Springs, 1980—. Author: Human Calorimeters, 1985; contbr. articles to profl. jours. Village councilman Village of Yellow Springs, Ohio, 1969-75; mem. Air Force Scientific Adv. Bd., Washington, 1984-88. Recipient Ely award Human Factors Soc., 1972. Fellow Aerospace Med. Assn. (Aerospace Indsl. Life Scis. Assn. award 1969), Am. Inst. Med. and Biol. Engring.; mem. Am. Physiol. Soc., Am. Soc. for Clin. Nutrition, Undersea Med. Soc. (oceaneering internat. award 1979, pres. 1980-81). Home and Office: 370 Orton Rd Yellow Springs OH 45387-1321

WEBB, RICHARD C., engineering company executive; b. Omaha, Sept. 2, 1915; m. Virginia; 1 son. BSE.E., U. Denver, 1937, DSc (hon.), 1996; MSE.E., Purdue U., 1944, PhD, 1951; DSc (hon.), U. Denver, 1996. Registered profl. engr., Colo. Traffic engr. Mountain States Telephone and Telegraph Co., Denver, 1937-39; research engr. RCA Labs. Div., Princeton, N.J., 1945-53; pres., founder, tech. dir. Colo. Research Corp. (subs. Carrier Corp.), Syracuse, N.Y., 1956-61; pres., founder. tech. dir. Colo. Instruments, Inc., Broomfield, Colo., 1961-71; pres., gen. mgr. Colo. Instruments div. Mohawk Data Scis. Corp., Utica, NYC, 1971-73; pres. Webb Engring. Co. (name changed to Data Ray Corp.), Boulder, Colo., 1973-85. Vis. lectr. U. Colo., 1962-82; prof. elec. engring. U. Denver, 1953-56, Iowa State Coll., 1950 Author: Tele-Visionaries: The People Behind the Inventin of Television, 2005; contbr. articles pub. to profl. jours. Recipient Disting. Engring. Alumnus award Purdue U., 1970, Profl. Achievement award U. Denver Alumni Assn., 1983, Outstanding Elec. Engr. award Purdue U., 1992. Fellow IEEE; mem. Soc. Motion Picture and TV Engrs., Acoustical Soc. Am., Inst. Aerospace Scis., Am. Ordnance Assn., Western Electronics Mfrs. Assn. (past v.p., dir.), Sigma Xi, Tau Beta Pi, Eta Kappa Nu. Achievements include patents in field. Home: PO Box 3078 Estes Park CO 80517-3078

WEBB, RICHARD STEPHEN, manufacturing executive; b. Nottingham, Eng., Aug. 3, 1944; came to U.S., 1988; s. Sydney and Kathleen Florence (Day) W.; m. Pamela Anne Fowlds, Sept. 3, 1966 (dec. July 1976); children: Jane, Simon, Elizabeth; m. Anne Hessel, Aug. 19, 1978 (div. 1997); children: Clare, Penelope; m. Cynthia Draper, Mar. 1, 2003. BSc, U. Sheffield, Eng., 1966, PhD, 1970. Chartered scientist U.K., 2005. Rsch. scientist U. Sheffield, 1966-69; tech. asst. C.E. Ramsden & Co. Ltd., Stoke-on-Trent, Eng., 1969-74; mktg. exec. Magnesium Elektron Ltd., Manchester, Eng., 1974-80, mktg. mgr., 1980-84; bus. devel. mgr. Alcan Aluminium, Mont., Can., 1984-88; bus. mgr. Alanx Products Inc., Newark, Del., 1988-91, pres., 1992-95, Lanxide Coated Products divsn. Lanxide Performance Materials, Newark, Del., 1995-97; dir. sales and mktg. ESL ElectroSci., King of Prussia, Pa., 1997—. Chmn. Del. Mfg. Alliance, 1993-95. Contbr. articles to profl. jours. Fellow: Inst. Materials, Minerals, Mining (U.K.); mem.: Am. Chem. Soc., Am. Ceramic Soc. Avocation: marathon and road running. Office: ESL ElectroSci 416 E Church Rd King Of Prussia PA 19406-2625 Business E-Mail: rwebb@electroscience.com.

WEBB, ROBERT W., lawyer; BS, U. Ill.; JD, Chgo. Kent Coll. Law, Ill. Inst. Tech., 1970. Bar: Ill. 1970. Asst. gen. counsel Beatrice US Food Corp., gen. counsel, sec., 1986, v.p., gen. counsel, sec.; sr. v.p., gen. counsel, sec. holdings The Marmon Group Inc., Chgo., 2001—, mem. bd. dirs., 2003—. Mem. bd. overseers Chgo. Kent Coll. Law. Office: Marmon Group Inc Ste 1900 225 W Washington St Chicago IL 60606 Office Phone: 312-372-9500. Office Fax: 312-845-5305.

WEBB, ROBERT W., JR., lawyer; b. Thomasville, Ga., Mar. 16, 1950; BA magna cum laude, Vanderbilt Univ., 1972; JD, Univ. Va., 1975. Bar: Ga. 1975. Assoc. Troutman Sanders LLP, Atlanta, 1975—80, ptnr., 1981—, mng. ptnr., 1992—, and mem. exec. com. Mem.: ABA, State Bar Ga., Atlanta Bar Assn., Phi Beta Kappa. Office: Troutman Sanders LLP One Logan Sq Ste 5200 600 Peachtree St NE Atlanta GA 30308-2216 Office Phone: 404-885-3240. Office Fax: 404-962-6716. Business E-Mail: robert.webb@troutmansanders.com.

WEBB, THOMAS IRWIN, JR., lawyer, director; b. Toledo, Sept. 16, 1948; s. Thomas Irwin and Marcia Davis (Winters) W.; m. Polly S. DeWitt, Oct. 11, 1986; 1 child, Elisabeth Hurst. BA, Williams Coll., 1970; postgrad., Boston U., 1970—71; JD, Case Western Res. U., 1973. Bar: Ohio, Mich. Assoc. Shumaker, Loop & Kendrick, Toledo, 1973—79, ptnr., 1979—, chmn. corp. law dept., 1992—94, 1994mgmt. com., 1994—99. Dir. Calphalon Corp., 1990-98, Yark Automotive Group, Inc. Coun. mem. Village of Ottawa Hills, Ohio, 1979-85, adviser Ohio Securities, 1979-85, Village of Ottawa Hills, 1999—; bd. dirs. Kiwanis Youth Found. Toledo, 1982-2002, Toledo Area Regional Transit Authority, 1989-91, Arts Commn. Greater Toledo, 1993-2003, exec. com., 1994-99, v.p., 1994-96, pres., 1996-97; bd. dirs. Jr. Achievement of Northwestern Ohio, Inc., 1992-2005, Lourdes Coll. Found., 1995-2001, Toledo Orch. Assn., 1999—, Med. Coll. Ohio, 2001-05, Lourdes Coll., 2001—, Maumee Valley Country Day Sch., 2005—. Mem. ABA, Ohio Bar Assn. (corp. law com. 1989—), Toledo Bar Assn., Mich. Bar Assn., Northwestern Ohio Alumni Assn. of Williams Coll. (pres. 1974-83), Toledo-Rowing Found. (trustee 1985-2001), Toledo Area C. of C. (trustee 1991-98, exec. com. 1993-98, fin. com. 1993—), Order of Coif, Crystal Downs Country Club, Toledo Country Club, The Toledo Club (trustee 1984-90, pres. 1987-90), Williams Club NY, Crystal Lake Yacht Club. Republican. Episcopalian. Office: Shumaker Loop & Kendrick 1000 Jackson St Toledo OH 43604 Office Phone: 419-321-1237, 231-352-7542. Business E-Mail: twebb@slk-law.com.

WEBB, THOMAS J., utilities executive; b. Alexandria, Va., Oct. 3, 1952; m. Donna; 3 children. B in Fin. with honors, George Mason U.; MBA. Various fin. mgmt. positions Ford Motor Co. and subs.; controller Electronics divsn., Large Front-Wheel Drive Vehicle Ctr.; CFO Visteon Corp.; chief fin. info. officer Ford Motor Co.; exec. v.p., CFO Kellogg Co., Battle Creek, Mich., 2000—02, CMS Energy, Dearborn, Mich., 2002—. Bd. dirs.

Conix, Can., Hall Climate Control, Korea, Halla Electronics, Korea, Samcor, South Africa, Yan Feng, China, Toledo (Ohio) Molding and Die, Climate Sys., India, others. Office: CMS Energy 1 Energy Plaza Dr Jackson MI 49201-2357 *

WEBB, WATTS RANKIN, surgeon; b. Columbia, Ky., Sept. 8, 1922; s. Frank Elbert and Susie Josephine (Rankin) W.; m. Frances Luella Cooke, Aug. 19, 1944; children: Michael Andrew, Paul Alan, Harvey Elbert, Gordon Lewis. BA, U. Miss., 1942; MD, Johns Hopkins U., 1945. Diplomate Am. Bd. Surgery, Am. Bd. Thoracic Surgery, Am. Bd. Surg. Critical Care. Intern Barnes Hosp., St. Louis, 1945-46; resident in surgery VA Hosp., Biloxi, Miss., 1946-48; resident in gen. and thoracic surgery Barnes Hosp., 1948-52; chief surgeon Miss. State Sanatorium, 1952-63; instr. surgery U. Miss., 1955-56, asst. prof. surgery, 1956-58, prof., 1958-63; prof., chmn. div. thoracic and cardiovascular surgery U. Tex. Southwestern Med. Sch., Dallas, 1964-70; prof., chmn. dept. surgery SUNY Upstate Med. Center, Syracuse, 1970-77; chmn. dept. Tulane U., New Orleans, 1977-89, prof. surgery, 1977-93, La. State U., New Orleans, 1993—, Huey P. Long Hosp., Alexandria, 2007. Author: Pulmonary Problems in Surgery, 1974, Surgery in Acute Coronary Problems, 1974, Aneurysms, 1983, Cardiovascular Emergencies, 1986, Atlas of Pulmonary Resections, 1988, (with others) Surgical Management for Chest Injuries, Vol. VII, 1990; mem. editl. bd.: Annals of Thoracic Surgery, 1968-79, Surg. Rounds, 1978-82, Surgery Clinics, 1980-82, Microcirculation, 1983-84, Brit. Jour. Surgery, 1981-89; contbr. articles to profl. jours. Recipient award Hadassah, 1965, Knockers Soc. Outstanding Tchr. award SUNY Upstate Med. Ctr., 1972, Owl Club Clin. Tchr. of Yr. award Tulane U. Med. Sch., 1978, 86, 88-93, Gloria P. Walsh award for best tchr. in Med. Sch., 1992, Aesculapian Tchr. of Yr. award La. State U., 1995, 96. Fellow ACS, Am. Coll. Chest Physicians; mem. AMA, Am. Assn. Thoracic Surgery, Am. Coll. Cardiology, Am. Fedn. Clin. Research, Am. Heart Assn. (Silver medal 1963), Am. Physiol. Soc., Am. Surg. Assn., Am. Thoracic Soc., Halsted Soc., La. Med. Soc., Orleans Parish Med. Soc., New Orleans Surg. Soc., Societe International de Chirurgie, Soc. Cryobiology, Soc. Thoracic Surgeons, Soc. Univ. Surgeons, Southeastern Surg. Congress, So. Med. Assn., So. Soc. Clin. Research, So. Surg. Assn. (Shipley medal 1961), So. Thoracic Soc., So. Thoracic Surg. Assn., Surg. Assn. La., Surg. Biology Club II, Internat. Soc. Heart Transplantation, Gulf Coast Vascular Soc., Sigma Xi, Alpha Omega Alpha, Pi Kappa Pi, Beta Beta Beta, Alpha Epsilon Delta. Methodist. Office: La State U Huey P Long Hosp PO Box 5352 Pineville LA 71361-5352 Office Phone: 318-542-1812. Personal E-mail: wattsrwebb@yahoo.com.

WEBB, WELLINGTON EDWARD, political organization administrator, former mayor; b. Chgo., Feb. 17, 1941; m. Wilma J. Webb; 4 children. BA in Edn., Colo. State Coll., 1964; MA in Edn., U. No. Colo., 1971. Tchr., 1964-76; mem. Colo. Ho. of Reps., 1973—77; regional dir. HEW, 1977-81; exec. dir., Dept. Regulatory agencies State of Colo., 1981-87; auditor City of Denver, 1987-91, mayor, 1991—2003; vice chair Democratic Nat. Com., 2004—. V.p. Nat. Conf. Dem. Mayors; bd. dir. Nat. League Cities, mem. adv. bd., Brookings Inst. Ctr. Urban and Met. Policy; mem. Nat. Infrastructure Assurance Coun.; bd. dirs. Cenveo, Inc., Maximus Corp.; founder Webb Group Internat. Cons., 2003. Pres. U.S. Conf. of Mayors, 1993—2003, Nat. Conf. Black Mayors, 2000—. Named One of Top 25 Mayors in Nation, Newsweek, 1996, Chevalier of the Legion of Honor, Country of France, 1999; recipient Nat. Wildlife Fedn. Achievement award, 1999, Govt. Leadership in the Arts award, Ams. for the Arts, 2001, Bridge Builders award, Disting. Pub. Svc. award, US Conf. of Mayors, 2003. Office Phone: 303-893-9322. E-mail: wew@webbgroupintl.com.

WEBB, WILLIAM LOYD, JR., retired military officer; b. Mineral Wells, Tex., Sept. 30, 1925; s. William Loyd and Francis (Mayer) W.; m. Muriel Emma Hinson, Dec. 27, 1947; children: George Sidney, William Loyd III, Lucinda Adrienne, Alicia Muriel. Student, Tex. A & M Coll., 1942-44; BS, U.S. Mil. Acad., 1947; MA, U. Pa., 1958. Commd. 2d lt. U.S. Army, 1947, advanced through grades to maj. gen., 1974; co. comdr. Korea, 1950, Ft. Riley, Kans., 1951-52, Germany, 1953-54; assoc. prof. English U.S. Mil. Acad. West Point, N.Y., 1958-61; regimental comdr., dep. comdt. of cadets U.S. Mil. Acad., 1969-71; squadron comdr. 14th Armored Cavalry Germany, 1963-64; mem. faculty U.S Army War Coll., 1965-68; comdr. support command 1st Inf. Div. mut. assistance command Vietnam, 1968—69; dep. comdg. gen. Ft. Ord, Calif., 1971-73; ops. officer 8th Army, U.S. Forces Korea, UN Command Korea, 1973-75; sr. mem. UN Command Mil. Armistice Commn., 1975; comdr. 1st Armored Div., U.S. Army Europe W.Ger., 1975-78; dep. comdg. gen. V Corps, U.S. Army Europe W. Ger., 1978; asst. dep. chief of staff for personnel Dept. Army Washington, 1978-82. Decorated D.S.M., Legion of Merit with oak leaf cluster, D.F.C., Bronze Star medal with oak leaf cluster, Air medal with 5 oak leaf clusters, Army Commendation medal with 2 oak leaf clusters, Purple Heart. Mem. Assn. U.S. Army, Armor Assn. Anglican. Office: 10148 Hillington Ct Vienna VA 22182-2908

WEBB, WILLIAM TIMOTHY, mobile communications professional; b. Walton-on-Thames, England, May 4, 1967; s. Christopher David and Genebeth Carol W.; m. Alison Margaret Porter, June 17, 1995; children: Katherine, Hannah. B of Engring., U. Southampton, 1989, PhD, 1992; MBA, Southampton Mgmt. Sch., 1997. Chartered engr. Tech. dir. Multiple Access Technologies, Southampton, England, 1990—94; prin. cons. Smith System Engring., Guildford, England, 1994—98; dir. strategy Motorola, Schaumburg, Ill., 1998—2001; mng. cons. PA Cons., 2001—03; head R & D Ofcom, England, 2004. Mem. innovation awards judging panel Wall St. Jour.; vis. prof. U. Surrey, England, 2003—, U. DeMontfort, England, 2007—. Author: Modern Quadrature Amplitude Modultion, 1994, Introduction to Wireless Local Loop, 1998, Understanding Cellular Radio, 1998, The Complete Wireless Communications Professional, 1999, Single and Multi-Carrier QAM, 2000, Narrowband and Broadband Wireless Local Loop, 2000, The Future of Wireless Communications, 2001, Wireless Communications--The Future, 2007, Essentials of Modern Spectrum Management, 2007; contbr. articles to profl. jours. Fellow: Royal Acad. Engring., Inst. Engring. and Tech. Engrs. (v.p. 2004—); mem.: IEEE (sr.). Office Phone: 44 20 7981 3770. Business E-Mail: william.webb@ofcom.org.uk.

WEBB, WILLIAM YERICK, lawyer; b. Mont Estoril, Portugal, Apr. 13, 1935; came to U.S., 1939; s. Leslie A. and Laura E. (Detrich) W.; m. Jeannette L. Richardson, June 20, 1959; children: Elizabeth T., Douglas L., Philip N. AB, Dartmouth Coll., 1956; JD cum laude, U. Mich., 1961. Bar: Pa. 1961, U.S. Dist. Ct. (ea. dist.) Pa. 1961. Assoc. Ballard, Spahr, Andrews & Ingersoll, Phila., 1961-69, ptnr., 1969—2000; sr. v.p., gen. counsel Phila. Phillies, 2000—. Adj. prof. law Widener U. Law Sch., 1989; adj. prof. sports law Villanova Law Sch.; sec., dir. AMR Internat. Inc. and subs., 1971-81; gen. counsel Opera Co. Phila., 1975-81. Asst. editor U. Mich. Law Rev. Bd. dirs., sec., counsel Children's Country Week Assn., 1978-85; bd. dirs., chmn. Schuylkill Ctr. Environ. Edn, 1989-95; pres., bd. dirs. Radnor A Better Chance, Inc., 1982-88; chmn., bd. dirs. History Ctr. in Phila., 1996. Lt. (j.g.) USNR, 1956-58. Mem. Sports Law Assn. (bd. dirs. 1984—, past pres.), Lake Paupac Club Greentown, Pa., (bd. dirs. 1990—, past pres.), Applebrook Golf Club. Episcopalian. Office: The Phillies One Citizens Bank Way Philadelphia PA 19148-5249

WEBB, YVONNE M., secondary school educator; b. Watertown, SD, May 27, 1954; d. Lloyd T. and Rose V. Hanks; m. Melvin R. Webb; children: Justin, Grant, Forrest, Grace. BSc, No. State U., 1974. Tchr. German S.D. Sch. Visually Handicapped, Aberdeen, SD, 1974—77; tchr. Roscoe (S.D.) H.S., 1977—79, Cheyenne Eagle Butte (S.D.) H.S., 1994—, chmn. Dept. English, 1994—. Adv. student coun. Cheyenne Eagle Butte (S.D.) H.S., 1990—92, adv. H.S. class, 1983—2006. Vol. YMCA, Eagle Butte, 1996—2004, All Saints Cath. Ch., Eagle Butte, 1996—2000. Named Tchr. of Yr., Indian Office Edn., 2000. Mem.: Eagle Butte (S.D.) Edn. Assn. (sec. 1995, treas. 1995). Democrat. Roman Cath. Avocations: reading, gardening. Home: Box 27 Eagle Butte SD 57625

WEBBER, ADAM BROOKS, science educator; b. Chapel Hill, NC, Dec. 20, 1962; s. Howard Rodney and Helen Margaret Webber; m. Kelly Shawn Autrey, Dec. 27, 1984; children: Fern Athena, Fox Pythagoras. BA, Dartmouth Coll., 1984; PhD, MS, Cornell U., 1993. Design engr. True BASIC, Inc., Hanover, NH, 1985—88; asst. prof. Western Ill. U., Macomb, Ill., 1993—97, U. Wis., Milw., 1998—2000, assoc. scientist, 2000—; assoc. prof. Monmouth (Ill.) Coll., 2005—07. Prin. investigator NSF-funded projects at U. Wis.-Milw. and Western Ill. U., 1997—2004. Author: (textbook) Programming Languages: A Practical Introduction, Fluent Pascal: the Pascal Trainer Laboratory Guide, Formal Language: A Practical Introduction. Organist, composer Open Prairie United Ch. of Christ, Princeton, Ill., 2003—. Grantee, NSF, 2000—04, 1997—2000. Mem.: Songwriters Guild of Am., Assn. for Computing Machinery, Upsilon Pi Epsilon. Avocation: Karate. Home: 316 Park Ave W Princeton IL 61356 Home Phone: 815-876-1106. Personal E-mail: adam@webber-labs.com.

WEBBER, CARL MADDRA, lawyer; b. Champaign, Ill., May 23, 1944; s. Charles Maddra and Lucille Ethelyn (Rankin) W.; children: Wendy Elizabeth, Christopher Maddra, Alexandra Sandeen. BS, Northwestern U., 1966; JD, U. Ill., 1973. Bar: Ill. 1974, U.S. Dist. Ct. (cen. dist.) Ill. 1974, U.S. Ct. Appeals (7th cir.) 1979. Pres. Webber & Thies PC, Urbana, Ill., 1974—. Adj. prof. Coll. Commerce U. Ill., 1987-90. Contbr. articles to profl. jours. Active Champaign County Jail Cts. Tech. Adv. Com., 1978-79, Downtown Devel. & Redevel. Commn., Urbana, 1978-79, U. Ill. Pres. Coun., 1984—; pres. Downtown Urbana Promotion Com., 1981-82; bd. dirs. Prairielands Coun. Boy Scouts Am., 1974-2005, v.p., 1979-82, pres., 1997-99; bd. dirs. U. Ill. Libr. Friends Bd., v.p., 1984-86, pres., 1986-88; bd. visitors U. Ill. Coll. Law, 1980—. Lt. USN, 1966-70. Recipient Appreciation award City of Urbana, 1980. Fellow Am. Bar Found., Ill. Bar Found.; mem. ABA, Urbana C. of C. (dir. 1978-81, 87-89, chmn. bd. 1989-90), Champaign County Bar Assn. (bd. dirs. 1980-83, pres. 1981-82), Ill. Bar Assn. (family law sect. coun. 1978-79, real estate sect. coun. 1983-87, co-chmn. contract drafting com. 1984-88), Rotary (dir. local club 1980-82). Home: 1910 Woodfield Rd Champaign IL 61822 Office: Webber & Thies PC 202 Lincoln Square PO Box 189 Urbana IL 61801 Office Phone: 217-367-1126.

WEBBER, CHRIS (MAYCE EDWARD CHRISTOPHER WEBBER), professional basketball player; b. Detroit, Mar. 1, 1973; s. Mayce and Doris Webber. Student, U. Mich., 1991—93. Drafted Orlando Magic, Fla., 1993; forward Golden State Warriors, San Francisco, 1993—94, Washington Bullets, 1994—98, Sacramento Kings, 1998—2005, Phila. 76ers, 2005—07, Detroit Pistons, 2007—. Founder Timeout Found. Named Nat. H.S. Player of Yr., 1990—91, Mr. Basketball, State of Mich., 1991, Coca-Cola Classic NBA Player of Yr., 1994, Brut Bullets Player of Yr., 1994—95; named to NBA All-Rookie 1st team, 1994. Achievements include being drafted 1st round Orlando Magic, 1993. Avocation: collecting signed historical documents of prominent African-Am. Office: Detorit Pistons 4 Championship Dr Auburn Hills MI 48326 *

WEBBER, DEREK, aerospace executive, space tourism entrepreneur; arrived in U.S., 1993, naturalized, 2000; s. George and Joan Webber; m. Freda Joyce Phillips (dec.); m. Sarah L. Fisher; 1 child, Grace Phillippa. BS with honors in Physics and Math., U. Newcastle upon Tyne, Eng., 1966; diploma in Space Sci., U. Coll. London, 1969; diploma in Mgmt. Studies, U. Westminster, London, 1973; Cdip in Acctg. and Fin., Assn. Cert. Accts., London, 1980. Satellite and launch vehicle design engr. EADS/Astrium, Stevenage, England, 1966—69; product planning mgr. Rank Xerox Internat., London, 1974—81; dir. satellite procurement Internat. Mobile Satellite Orgn., London, 1982—93; pres., CEO, Intonations Cons., Inc., San Diego, 1993—2000; mng. dir. Tachyon Europe, Inc., 2000—01; program dir. Futron Corp., Bethesda, Md., 2001; dir. Spaceport Assocs., Bethesda, Md., 2001—. Adj. prof. U.S. Internat. U., San Diego, 1996—97; vis. lectr. summer sch. Internat. Space U., 1989, 90, 92, 93; keynote spkr. Washington Space Bus. Roundtable, 2003; presenter TV series on satellite comm., England, 1988; lectr. in field. Contbr. articles to profl. jours.; co-author: Kids to Space, 2006, Beyond Earth, 2006. Mem. internat. trade coalition Greater San Diego C. of C., 1995—99; tchr. summer camp Fedn. Galaxy Explorers, Saunders Mid. Sch., Va., 2002. Recipient Formation of Space Tourism recognition, Orbit Awards, 2006. Fellow: Brit. Interplanetary Soc.; mem.: AIAA (sr.), Soc. of Satellite Profls. Internat., Space Tourism Soc. (life), United Socs. in Space (chair coun. of regents 1996). Office: Spaceport Associates 5909 Rolston Rd Bethesda MD 20817 Office Phone: 301-493-2550. Personal E-mail: dwspace@aol.com.

WEBBER, DIANA L., management consultant executive, engineering educator; b. Sacramento, May 12, 1960; d. Ralph and Mary P. (Chace) Van Tuyl. BS, Tex. A&M U., Coll. Station, 1983; M in Computer Systems Mgmt., Creighton U., Omaha, 1987; PhD, George Mason U., Fairfax, Va., 2001. Aerospace engr. USAF, Crystal City, Va., 1978—2001, Scitor Corp., Chantilly, Va., 1995—2001; adj. prof. George Mason U., Fairfax, Va., 2001—; prin. Booz Allen Hamilton, McLean, Va., 2001—. Mem. adv. bd., assoc. editor: Booz Allen Tech. Jour.; contbr. articles to profl. jours. Capt. USAF, 1978—94, Pentagon. Mem.: ACM, IEEE Computer Soc. Democrat. Achievements include research in The Variation Point Model. Avocations: walking, reading, swimming. Office: Booz Allen Hamilton 8283 Greensboro Dr Mc Lean VA 20191 Home Phone: 703-391-5050; Office Phone: 703-902-4062. Personal E-mail: drwebber@comcast.net. Business E-Mail: webber_diana@bah.com.

WEBBER, HELEN, artist; b. NYC; d. David and Frieda (Berlin) Ross; children: Joel Benjamin (dec.), Daniel Saul, Rachel Frieda. BA, Queens Coll., 1951; postgrad., Columbia U., 1953; MA, RI Sch. Design, 1963. Site specific artist in tapestry, clay, metal, wood and glass; tchr. in design dept. Calif. Coll. Arts, Oakland, 1982, 1984, 1987; lectr. U. Calif. Keynote spkr. ASID, San Diego and Kansas City, 1983, Nat. Home Furnishings League, San Ferancisco, 1980, Chgo., 1982; lectr., exhibitor Internat. Congress Women Archs., Paris, 1983, U. Calif., Santa Cruz, 1988, Commnwealth Club, San Francisco, 1989, guest lectr. RI Sch. Design Alumni Conf., 1996; instr. Hussian Coll. Art, Phila., 2003-04. Author, illustrator: Good-Night, The Sea Is My Blanket, 1963, My Kite it the Magic Me, Summer Sun; prin. commissions for 6 Carnival Cruise Line ships; Festival, Tropical Fantasy, Holiday, Celebration, Destiny, Pittsburg Calif. Civic Ctr., Metro Commerce Bank, San Francisco, Statendam/Holland Am. Cruise Lines, VA Med. Ctr., Cleve., Vets. Cemetery, Riverside, Calif., VA Hosp., Lyons, NJ, East Tex. Med. Ctr., Tyler, St. Patrick's Hosp., Lake Charles, La., Gatwick Penta Hotel, London, Jewish Home for the Aged, Houston, Jewish Home for Aging, Riverdale, NY, Betty Ford Pavilion, Palm Springs, Fla., Sphohn Hosp., Corpus Christi, Tex., St. Agnes Hosp., Fresno, Calif., Chevron Corp., San Ramon, Calif., Merck & Co., Rahway, NJ, Kodak, Kingsport, Tenn., Kaiser Permanente, Bristol Hosp., Conn., Sacramento and San Jose, Calif., Quail Lodge Resort, Carmel Valley, Calif., Episcopal Homes Found., San Francisco, Menorah Manor, Dunedin, Fla., Hyatt Regency, Phoenix, 1st United Meth. Ch., Wichita Falls, Tex., Ctrl. Maine Hosp., Lewiston; designer, artist textile, wallpaper, sheets, towels, children's games for Collins & Aikman, Burlington, Covington, Peerage of Eng., Edward Fields, Pastime Industries. Mem. Design Internat. (pres., co-founder San Francisco 1984-85), Women -in-Design Internat. (founder, pres. 1977-83, Outstanding Contbn. to Design award 1980), Urban Art Internat. (bd. dirs.). Office: Helen Webber Art Design 103 S Village Ave Exton PA 19341-1216 Office Phone: 610-363-9241. Personal E-mail: helenwebber@comcast.net.

WEBBER, JOHN BENTLEY, orthopedic surgeon; b. Morristown, NJ, Jan. 27, 1941; s. George Bentley and Gladys (Moody) W.; m. Mary Christina Thometz, Feb. 25, 1978; children: John Bentley, Edward Alan BA, Lehigh U., 1962; MD, Temple U., 1966. Intern Rochester Gen. Hosp., NY, 1966-67; resident Temple U. Med. Ctr., Phila., 1967-70; Stelrling Bunnell fellow in hand surgery Pacific Med. Ctr., San Francisco, 1971; assoc. prof. orthopedic surgery and rehab. Hahnemann Med. Coll. and Hosp., Phila., 1973—, chief sect. on hand surgery, 1973—; attending surgeon St. Christopher's Hosp. for Children, Phila., 1996—. Cons. in hand surgery Mcpl. Med. Svcs., Phila., 1973-87, USPHS, Phila., 1973-76, burn ctr. St. Agnes Med. Ctr., Phila., 1973—, Phila. unit Shriners' Hosp. for Crippled Children, 1979-95. Served to maj. USAF, 1971-73. Fellow ACS (Pa. com. on trauma), Am. Acad. Orthopedic Surgeons; mem. AMA, Am. Soc. for Surgery of Hand, Bunnell Hand Club (pres. 1978-80), Assn. for Acad. Surgery, Eastern Orthopedic Soc., Pa. Med. Soc., Phila. Orthopedic Soc., Phila. Hand Soc. (pres. 1987-89), Phila. County Med. Soc., Phila. Coll. Physicians, Meigs Med. Assn., Rotary, Union Leauge, Riverside Yacht Club (fleet surgeon), Phila. Country Club, Delaware Valley Ducks Unltd. (chmn. 1983-88), U.S. Coast Guard (cert. master). Republican. Congregationalist. Home: 1139 Rock Creek Rd Gladwyne PA 19035-1439 Personal E-mail: handweb@aol.com.

WEBBER, RICHARD JOHN, lawyer; b. Mpls., July 27, 1948; s. Richard John and Mary Lee (Moore) W.; m. Susan Barbara Listerman, Jan. 8, 1972; children: Hillary, Joanna. BA, Princeton U., 1970; JD, U. Mich., 1973. Bar: D.C. Ct. Appeals 1974, U.S. Ct. Appeals (9th and D.C. cirs.) 1980, U.S. Dist. Ct. D.C. 1980, U.S. Claims Ct. 1974, U.S. Supreme Ct. 1980. Law clk. U.S. Ct. Claims, Washington, 1973-75; trial atty. U.S. Dept. Justice, Washington, 1975-80; assoc. Arent, Fox et al, Washington, 1980-85, ptnr., 1985—. Mem. ABA (chmn. fed. contract claims and remedies com. sect. pub. contract law 1986-91), Fed. Bar Assn. (chmn. govt. contracts sect. 1992-94, 1994-96, chmn. ADR sect. 2002-03). Office: Arent Fox Washington Sq 1050 Connecticut Ave NW Ste 500 Washington DC 20036-5303 Office Phone: 202-857-6254. E-mail: webberr@arentfox.com.

WEBBER, ROSS ARKELL, management educator; b. New Rochelle, NY, July 18, 1934; s. Richard and Muriel (Arkels) W.; m. Mary Louise Foradora, Sept. 29, 1956; children: Sarah Ruth, Judith Mary, Gregory Ross, Jennifer Louise, Stephen Andrew. BSE, Princeton U., 1956; PhD, Columbia U., 1966; MS (hon.), U. Pa., 1972. Indsl. engr. Eastman Kodak Co., Rochester, NY, 1959-61; instr. Columbia U., NYC, 1961-64; lectr. Wharton Sch. U. Pa., Phila., 1964-65, asst. prof., 1965-70, assoc. prof., 1970-76, prof., 1976-2000, chmn. dept. mgmt., 1992-95, prof. emeritus, 2000—; v.p. U. Pa., Phila., 1981-86. Dir. Wharton-Industry Exec. Program, U. Pa., 1966-68, chmn. Wharton Internat. Bus. com., 1968-69, coord. Orgn. Behavior and Mgmt. Group, 1968-75, asst. dept. chmn., PhD com., 1972-75, coord. Orgnl. and Mgmt. Component, Advanced Mgmt. Program in Health Care Adminstrn., 1973-74, mem. Univ. Coun., 1975-77, adv. com. Pub. Mgmt. Unit, The Wharton Sch., 1977-81, chmn. Grad. Admissions com.; mem. editl. bd. The Wharton Mag. Author: Organizational Behavior and the Practice of Management, 1968, 5th rev. edit., 1987; Spanish lang. edit., 1982, Culture and Management: Text and Reading in Comparative Management, 1969, Management: Basic Elements of Managing Organizations, 1979, 3rd rev. edit., 1984, Polish lang. edit., 1984, Management Pragmatics: Readings and Cases on Managing Organizations, 1979, Time is Money!: The Key to Managerial Success, 1980, Japanese lang. edit. 1983, Swedish edit. 1983, Spanish lang. edit., 1985, Portugese lang. edit., 1989, To Be a Manager, 1981, A Guide to Getting Things Done, 1984, Becoming a Courageous Manager: Overcoming Career Problems of New Managers, 1991, Breaking Your Time Barriers: Becoming a More Effective Strategic Time Manager, 1992; contbr. over 55 articles to profl. jours. Past mem. bd. dirs. United Way Southeastern Pa., Am. Water Sys., Arcadis, New Zealand; coach youth athletics, fund raiser for ch., religious educator. Lt. (j.g.) USN, 1956-59. Avocations: painting, tennis, skiing. Office: U Pa Wharton Sch 2000 Steinberg Hall Philadelphia PA 19104 Office Phone: 215-898-9368. Business E-Mail: webber@wharton.upenn.edu.

WEBB JR., JAMES HENRY See WEBB, JIM

WEBEL, CHARLES PETER, human science and psychology educator; b. LA, Dec. 23, 1948; s. James Webel and Jeanne (Herbert) Mackavanagh. BA, U. Calif., Berkeley, 1969, PhD, 1976; postgrad. in pub. health/social medicine, Harvard U., 1989-91. Chair Ctr. Ednl. Change, Berkeley, 1968-70; filmmaker Nat. Ednl. TV, NYC, 1969-70; lectr. social scis. U. Calif., Berkeley, 1976-78; dir. grad. programs Western Inst. Social Rsch., Berkeley, 1977-78; asst. prof. sociology New Coll., Sarasota, Fla., 1978-79; exec. editor social scis. Columbia U. Press, NYC, 1980-83; asst. prof. philosophy Calif. State U., Chico, 1984-89; teaching fellow gen. edn. Harvard U., Cambridge, Mass., 1990-91; gen. editor scholarly book series Peter Lang Pub., NYC, 1990—. Rsch. assoc. dept. anthropology U. Calif., Berkeley, 1990—94, lectr. Sch. Social Welfare, 2002-03; prof. human sci. and psychology Saybrook Inst., San Francisco, 1990—2001; Fulbright prof. U. Heidelberg, Germany, 2002-03l dir. Ctr. for Peace Studies, prof. social scis. U. Tromso, Norway, 2004-05; UNESCO chair for the philosophy of people U. Castellon, Spain, 2005-06; Fulbright sr. specialist and prof. U. Rome. Author: Terror, Terrorism and the Human Condition, 2004; author, editor: Marcus Critical Theory and The Promise of Utopia, 1988; co-editor: Handbook of Peace and Conflict Studies, 2007; filmmaker: Lifestyle, 1969. Organizer Congress Racial Equality, N.Y.C., 1965-66; West Coast sec. Internat. Philosophers for Prevention Nuclear Omnicide, 1985-89. Fulbright scholar Fulbright Commn., Germany, 1971-72; regents fellow U. Calif., Berkeley, 1972-73, dissertation fellow Social Sci. Rsch. Coun., N.Y.C., 1974-76, grad. fellow Harvard U., 1989-91, NEH summer fellow Harvard U., 1986, NEH fellow Cornell U., 1998. Mem. Am. Philos. Assn., Am. Sociol. Assn., Internat. Soc. Polit. Psychology, Commonwealth Club Calif., World Affairs Coun. Avocations: classical music, film, global travel, sports, humor.

WEBER, ALFONS, physicist; b. Dortmund, Germany, Oct. 8, 1927; PhD, Ill. Inst. Tech., 1956. Instr. physics Ill. Inst. Tech., Chgo., 1953-56; from asst. prof. physics to prof. Fordham U., Bronx, NY, 1957-81, prof. physics and chemistry, 1976-81, chmn. dept. physics, 1964-70; rsch. physicist Nat. Inst. Stds. and Tech., Gaithersburg, Md., 1977-98, acting chief molecular spectroscopy divsn., 1980-81, chief molecular physics divsn., 1982-95, sr. scientist physics lab., 1995-98, scientist emeritus, 1999—; program mgr. condensed matter physics divsn., materials rsch NSF, 1998—2001, program dir. exptl. phys. chemistry, chemistry divsn., 2001—04. With chem scis. divsn. U.S. Dept. Energy, 1991-92, chem. divsn. NSF, 1992-95. Editor: Raman Spectroscopy of Gases and Liquids, 1979; Structure and Dynamics of Weakly Bound Molecular Complexes, 1987, Spectroscopy of the Earth's Atmosphere and Interstellar Medium, 1992; former mem. editl. bd. Jour. of Raman Spectroscopy, Jour. Chem. and Phys. Reference Data. V.p. Union Free Dist. # 1 Sch. Bd., Eastchester, N.Y., 1970-73. Postdoctoral fellow NRC Can., U. Toronto, 1956-57. Fellow AAAS, Am. Phys. Soc. (councillor 1987-91); mem. Coblentz Soc., Soc. Applied Spectroscopy, Am. Chem. Soc. Office: Nat Inst Stds & Tech Gaithersburg MD 20899 Business E-Mail: aweber@nist.gov.

WEBER, ANN, pharmaceutical executive, researcher; married; 3 children. BS in Chemistry, U. Notre Dame, 1982; PhD in Organic Chemistry,

Harvard U., 1987. Sr. rsch. chemist, medicinal chemistry Merck & Co., Inc., NJ, 1987—91, rsch. fellow, medicinal chemistry NJ, 1991—94, assoc. dir., medicinal chemistry NJ, 1994—97, dir., medicinal chemistry NJ, 1997—2002, sr. dir., medicinal chemistry NJ, 2002—05, exec. dir., medicinal chemistry NJ, 2005—. Contbr. articles to profl. jours. Mem.: Am. Chem. Soc. (North Jersey Sect.). Achievements include being one of the scientists who led the research and testing team responsible for the development of Merck's Type 2 diabetes drug, Januvia. Office: Merck & Co Inc One Merck Dr PO Box 100 Whitehouse Station NJ 08889-0100 *

WEBER, ARNOLD I., lawyer; b. Little Cedar, Iowa, Oct. 4, 1926; divorced; children: Katherine Weber Hickle, Thomas, Margaret Weber Robertson. PhB magna cum laude, Marquette U., 1949; MA, Harvard U., 1950; JD, George Washington U., 1954, LLM, 1956. Bar: D.C. 1954, Md. 1961, Calif. 1962, U.S. Dist Ct. D.C. 1954, (no. dist.) Calif. 1962, (cen. dist.) Calif. 1992, U.S. Ct. Claims 1960, U.S. Tax Ct. 1965, U.S. Ct. Appeals (D.C. cir.) 1954, (9th cir.) 1962, (fed. cir.) 1991, U.S. Supreme Ct. 1959. Lawyer Housing and Home Fin., Washington, 1954; pvt. practice Washington, 1954-55; lawyer Tariff Commn., Washington, 1954-55, FCC, Washington, 1955-56, IRS, Washington, 1956-61; assoc. Brobeck, Phleger & Harrison, San Francisco, 1961-64; sr. gen. atty. So. Pacific Transp., San Francisco, 1964-84; western tax counsel Santa Fe Pacific Corp., San Francisco, 1985-88; pvt. practice San Francisco, 1988—. With USNR, 1944-54, PTO. Mem. ABA, Olympic Club, Bar Assn. San Francisco, State Bar of Calif. Office: PO Box 638 San Francisco CA 94104-0638 Office Phone: 415-752-7465. Personal E-mail: aiweber@sbcglobal.net.

WEBER, ARNOLD ROBERT, academic administrator; b. NYC, Sept. 20, 1929; s. Jack and Lena (Smith) W.; m. Edna M. Files, Feb. 7, 1954; children: David, Paul, Robert. BA, U. Ill., 1951; MA, MIT, 1958, PhD in Econs., 1958; DHL (hon.), U. Notre Dame, 2005, U. Ill., 2005, Northwestern U., 2005, Loyola U., 2005, Ripon Coll., 2005, U. Colo., 2005. Instr., then asst. prof. econs. MIT, 1955-58; faculty U. Chgo. Grad. Sch. Bus., 1958-69, prof. indsl. relations, 1963-69; asst. sec. for manpower Dept. Labor, 1969-70; exec. dir. Cost of Living Council; also spl. asst. to Pres. Nixon, 1971; Gladys C. and Isidore Brown prof. urban and labor econs. U. Chgo., 1971-73; former provost Carnegie-Mellon U.; dean Carnegie-Mellon U. (Grad. Sch. Indsl. Adminstrn.), prof. labor econs. and pub. policy, 1973-80; pres. U. Colo., Boulder, 1980-85, Northwestern U., Evanston, Ill., 1985-95, chancellor, 1995-98, pres. emeritus, 1998—. Cons. union, mgmt. and govt. agys., 1960—; cons. Dept. Labor, 1965; mem. Pres.'s Adv. Com. Labor Mgmt. Policy, 1964, Orgn. Econ. Coop. and Devel., 1987; vice chmn. Sec. Labor Task Force Improving Employment Svcs., 1965; chmn. rsch. adv. com. U.S. Employment Svc., 1966; assoc. dir. OMB Exec. Office of Pres., 1970—71; chmn. Presdl. R.R. Emergency Bd., 1982; trustee Com. for Econ. Devel., Nat. Multiple Sclerosis Soc.; bd. dirs. Diamond Cluster Inc.; asst. sec. manpower U.S. Dept. Labor, 1969—70. Contbr. articles to profl. jours. Laureate, Lincoln Acad. Ill.; Ford Found. Faculty Rsch. fellow, 1964-65. Mem. Am. Acad. Arts and Scis., Indsl. Rels. Rsch. Assn., Nat. Acad. Pub. Adminstrn., Comml. Club Chgo. (pres., civic com. 1995-2000), Econ. Club Chgo. (pres. 1995-97), Phi Beta Kappa. Jewish. Office: Northwestern U Office of Pres Emeritus 555 Clark St 209 Evanston IL 60208-0805 Business E-Mail: arnold-weber@nwu.edu.

WEBER, BRUCE EDWARD, art historian; b. Bklyn., Dec. 29, 1951; s. Harry and Sylvia Weber; m. Joanne Pagano. PhD, CUNY, 1985. Curator U. Ky. Art Mus., Lexington, 1979—81; curator of collections Norton Mus. Art, West Palm Beach, Fla., 1981—88; dir. rsch. and exhbns. Berry-Hill Galleries, NYC, 1990—. Faculty NYU, NYC, 1999—. Author: Paintings of New York, 1800-1950, 2005, (exhbn. catalog) Homage to the Square: Picturing, Washington Square, 1890-1960, Heart of the Matter: The Still Lifes of Marsden Hartley, (poetry) Poetic Justice, 2004, Chase Inside and Out: The Aesthetic Interiors of William Merritt Chase, 2003. Fellow Smithsonian fellow, Smithsonian Instn., Washington, 1977. Mem.: Assn. Am. Mus.

WEBER, CARL, publishing executive, retail bookstore executive, writer; b. Queens, 1966; married; 3 children. MBA in Mktg., Univ. Va. Former bus. teacher, NYC; book retailer Black Facts I, Bklyn., Black Facts II, Queens, Horizon Books, Newark; pres., founder, editl. dir. Urban Books LLC (subs. Kensington Publishing), Long Island, 2002—; founder, owner Urban Knowledge bookstore (and five other locations), Balt., 2005—; pres. Q-Boro Books (acquired by Urban Books), 2006—. Author: (novels) Lookin' for Luv, 2001, Married Men, 2001, Baby Momma Drama, 2003, Player Haters, 2004, The Preacher's Son (debuted No. 1 Essence Bestseller list), So You Call Yourself a Man, 2005. Named Blackboard Bookseller of Yr., 2000. Office Phone: 631-643-6828.

WEBER, CHARLES S., mechanical engineer; b. Albany, NY, Apr. 16, 1966; s. Charles H and Joyce M Weber; 1 child, Raeann. BS in Mech. Engring., Union Coll., Schenectady, 1988; MBA, Rensselaer Poly. Inst., Troy, 1992. Maintenance engr. Albany Internat., East Greenbush, NY, 1988—94, dept. mgr. St. Stephen, SC, 1994—98; project engr. Oak-Mitsui, Hoosick Falls, NY, 1998—2001; program mgr. SuperPower, Inc., Schenectady, NY, 2001—. Office: SuperPower Inc 450 Duane Ave Schenectady NY 12304 Office Phone: 518-346-1414. Office Fax: 518-346-3060. Business E-Mail: cweber@superpower-inc.com.

WEBER, DAVID J., history educator; b. Buffalo, Dec. 20, 1940; s. Theodore Carl and Frances (Maronska) W.; m. Carol Sue Bryant, June 16, 1962; children: Scott David, Amy Carol. BS in Social Sci., SUNY, Fredonia, 1962; MA in History, U. N.Mex., 1964, PhD in History, 1967. Asst. to full prof. history San Diego State U., 1967-76; prof. history So. Meth. U., Dallas, 1976-79, prof. history and dept. chmn., 1979-86, Robert and Nancy Dedman prof. history, 1986—. Fulbright-Hays lectr. Universidad de Costa Rica, 1970. Author: The Taos Trappers: The Fur Trade in the Far Southwest, 1540-1846, 1971, The Mexican Frontier, 1821-1846: The American Southwest Under Mexico, 1982 (Ray Billington award 1983), Richard H. Kern: Expeditionary Artist in the Far Southwest, 1848-1853, 1985 (Nat. Cowboy Hall of Fame 1985), The Spanish Frontier in North America, 1992; bd. editors: So. Meth. U. Press, 1983—; contbr. articles to profl. jours. Recipient United Meth. U. Scholar/Tchr. of Yr. award, 1986, Spain and America prize Spanish Ministry of Culture, 1993, Real Orden de Isabel la Católica, King of Spain, Juan Carlos, 2003, Orden Mexicana del Aguila Azteca (the Order of the Aztec Eagle), Govt. Mexico, 2005; postdoctoral fellow Am. Philos. Soc., 1975, Huntington Libr., 1975, Am. Coun. Learned Socs., 1980, Ctr. for Adv. Study in Behavioral Scis., Stanford U., 1986-87, NEH, 1974-75, 90-91. Fellow Soc. Am. Historians, Am. Acad. Arts & Scis.; mem. Academia Mexicana de la Historia, Tex. Inst. Letters, Tex. Hist. Assn. (lifetime fellow), Western History Assn. (pres. 1990-91), Mexico-U.S. Historians (pres. 1990), Am. Hist. Assn., Orgn. Am. Historians. Democrat. Avocations: running, bicycling, gardening, reading. Office: Dept History So Meth U Dallas TX 75275 Business E-Mail: dweber@mail.smu.edu. *

WEBER, DONALD B., advertising executive, marketing professional; b. Jersey City, Nov. 6, 1932; s. John William and Rose Ann (Saroshi) Weber; m. Ann McDermaid, 1955 (div. 1975); children: Martha Elizabeth, Margaret Ann; m. Jean Host, 1980; children: Kimberly Elizabeth, Kristen Ann. BA, Rollins Coll., Winter Park, Fla., 1954; MBA, Kellog/Northwestern U., Evanston, Ill., 1959. Account exec. Leo Burnett Co., Inc., Chgo., 1958-63; sr. v.p., mgmt. supr. Foote, Cone & Belding, Chgo., 1963-76; pres. Blau Bishop Assocs., 1976-79; v.p. Russell Reynolds Assocs., Chgo., 1979-82; sr. v.p., regional mgr. MSL Internat., Chgo., 1982-85; exec. v.p. Rumrill-Hoyt, Inc., Rochester, N.Y., 1985-88; sr. v.p. D'Arcy Masius Benton & Bowles, Chgo., 1988-95; sr. v.p., group mgmt. dir. Cramer-Krasselt, Chgo., 1996-99; pres. Intact, Inc., 1999—. Lectr. Northwestern U. Chmn. bd. Am. Cancer Soc., Chgo., 1996—99, pres., cons.; bd. dirs., chmn. comm. exec. com. Ill. divsn. Am. Cancer Soc., 1999—2001; bd. dirs. Am. Inst. Wine and Food, 1995—97; chmn. Chgo. coun. Boy Scouts Am., 1991—95. Lt. comdr. USNR, 1955—58. Mem.: Chgo. Advt. Fedn. (bd. dirs. 1988—93), Tavern Club, Exmoor Country Club. Republican. Episcopalian. Personal E-mail: intactdbw@aol.com.

WEBER, FREDERICK D., information technology executive; BS, Harvard U. Mem. founding team Kendall Sq. Rsch.; corp. v.p., chief tech. officer AMD, Sunnyvale, Calif. Spkr. in field. Contbr. articles to profl. jours. Named Innovator of Yr., EDN mag.; named one of 25 Most Influential CTOs, InfoWorld, 2004. Mem.: NAE.

WEBER, FREDRIC ALAN, lawyer; b. Paterson, NJ, July 31, 1948; s. Frederick Edward and Alida (Hessels) W.; m. Mary Elizabeth Cook, June 18, 1983. BA in History, Rice U., 1970; JD, Yale U., 1976. Bar: Tex. 1976, U.S. Dist. Ct. (so. dist.) Tex. Assoc. Fulbright & Jaworski LLP, Houston, 1976-80, participating assoc., 1980-83, ptnr., 1983—, and head, public fin. and adminstrn. dept. Dir. Houston Symphony Soc., 1993—, v.p. devel., 2001-03, 2005-. Mem. ABA, Am. Coll. Bond Counsel (treas. 2003-04, v.p. 2004-06, pres. 2006-), Nat. Assn. Bond Lawyers (bd. dirs. 1988-89, treas. 1989-90, pres.-elect 1991, pres. 1991-92), Houston Bar Assn. Office: Fulbright & Jaworski LLP 1301 McKinney St Ste 5100 Houston TX 77010-3095 Office Phone: 713-651-5151. Office Fax: 713-651-5246. Business E-Mail: fweber@fulbright.com.

WEBER, GEORGE, oncology and pharmacology educator, researcher; b. Budapest, Hungary, Mar. 29; came to U.S., 1959; s. Salamon and Hajnalka (Arvai) W.; m. Catherine Elizabeth Forrest, June 30, 1958; children: Elizabeth Dolly Arvai, Julie Vibert Wallace, Jefferson James. BA, Queen's U., 1950, MD, 1952; MD (hon.), U. Chieti, Italy, 1979, Med. Faculty, Budapest, 1982, U. Leipzig, Fed. Republic of Germany, 1987, Tokushima U., Japan, 1988; degree, Kagawa U., Japan, 1992. Rsch. assoc. Montreal Cancer Inst., 1953-59; prof. pharmacology Ind. U. Sch. Medicine, Indpls., 1959—; dir. Lab for Exptl. Oncology Sch. Medicine, Ind. U., Indpls., 1974—; Milan Panič prof. oncology Ind. U., Indpls., 1994—, Wellcome prof., 1995—; prof. Lab. for Exptl. Oncology Sch. Medicine, Ind. U., Indpls., 1974-90, disting. prof. Lab. for Exptl. Oncology, 1990—. Chmn. study sect. USPHS, Washington, 1976-78; sci. adv. com. Am. Cancer Soc., N.Y.C., 1972-76, 94-98, Damon Runyon Fund, N.Y.C., 1971-76; mem. U.S. Nat. Com., Internat. Union Against Cancer, Washington, 1974-80, 90-94, NAS, Washington, 1974-80, 90-94, U.S. Army Med. Rsch. and Breast Cancer Rsch. Program, 1996-97; prof. Brit. cancer campaign U. Oxford, Oxford, Eng., 2001; vis. prof. U. Bologna, Italy, 2001—. Editor: Advances in Enzyme Regulation, Vols. 1-48, 1962—; assoc. editor Jour. Cancer Rsch., 1969—80, 1982—89. Recipient Alecce Prize for cancer rsch. Tiberine Acad., Rome, 1971, Best Prof. award Student AMA, Indpls., 1966, 68, G.F. Gallanti prize for enzymology Internat. Soc. Clin. Chemists, 1984, Outstanding Investigator award Nat. Cancer Inst., NIH, 1986-94, Semmelweis medal & diploma Budapest, Hungary, 2001, medal Gastroenterological Soc., Aliga, Hungary, 2001, Prestigious External Award Recognition Ind. U., Indpls., Ind., 2002. Mem. Am. Soc. for Pharmacology and Exptl. Therapeutics, Am. Assn. Cancer Rsch. (G.H.A. Clowes award 1982), Russian Acad. Sci. (hon.), Hungarian Cancer Soc. (hon.), Hungarian Acad. Scis. (hon.), Acad. Scis. Bologna (Italy) (hon.). Home: 7307 Lakeside Dr Indianapolis IN 46278-1618 Office: Ind U Sch Medicine Lab Exptl Oncology 699 West Dr Indianapolis IN 46202-5119 Office Phone: 317-274-7921.

WEBER, GEORGE RICHARD, financial and internet marketing executive, writer; b. The Dalles, Oreg., Feb. 7, 1929; s. Richard Merle and Maud (Winchell) W.; m. Nadine Hanson, Oct. 12, 1957; children: Elizabeth Ann Weber Katooli, Karen Louise Weber Zaro, Linda Marie. BS, Oreg. State U., 1950; MBA, U. Oreg., 1962. CPA, Oreg. Sr. trainee U.S. Nat. Bank of Portland (Oreg.), 1950-51; jr. acct. Ben Musa, CPA, The Dalles, Oreg., 1954; tax and audit asst. Price Waterhouse, Portland, 1955-59; sr. acct. Burton M. Smith, CPA, Portland, 1959-62; pvt. practice Portland, 1962-99; assoc. World Mktg. Alliance, 1996-99, Waterman and Assocs., 2000—01, Allstate Fin. Svcs., 2001—03, Legacy for Life, 2004—, Extras Casting, 2005—. Lectr. acctg. Portland State Coll.; expert witness fin. and tax matters. Author: Small Business Long-term Finance, 1962, A History of the Coroner and Medical Examiner Offices, 1963, CPA Litigation Service References, 1991, Letters to a Friend, 1995; contbr. to profl. publs. and poetry jours. Sec.-treas. Mt. Hood Kiwanis Camp, Inc., 1965; exec. counselor SBA; mem. fin. com., powerlifting team U.S. Powerlifting Fedn., 1984, amb. People to People, China, 1987. Arty. officer AUS, 1951-53. Decorated Bronze Star. Mem. AICPA, Internat. Platform Assn., Oreg. Hist. Soc., Oreg. City Traditional Jazz Soc., Order of the Holy Cross Jerusalem, Order St. Stephen the Martyr, Order St. Gregory the Illuminator, Knightly Assn. St. George the Martyr, World Literary Acad., Portland C.S. Lewis Soc., Beta Alpha Psi, Pi Kappa Alpha. Clubs: Kiwanis, Portland Track, City (Portland); Multnomah Athletic; Sunrise Toastmasters. Republican. Lutheran. Home and Office: 3715 NE Alberta Ct Portland OR 97211-8144 Home Phone: 503-288-3328; Office Phone: 503-288-3328. E-mail: grweber@earthlink.net. *My basic beliefs are in faith, family and freedom through limited government and personal responsibility, with personal responsibility including development and use of capabilities.*

WEBER, GLORIA RICHIE, retired minister, retired state legislator; married; 4 children. BA, Washington U., St. Louis; MA, MDiv, Eden Theol. Sem., Webster Groves, Mo. Ordained to ministry Evang. Luth. Ch. Am., 1974. Family life educator Luth. Family and Children's Svcs. Mo.; mem. Mo. Ho. of Reps., 1993-94. Mo. state organizer, dir. comm. Mainstream Voters C.A.R.E., 1995. Editor: Interfaith Voices for Peace and Justice, 1996—2000. Exec. dir. Older Women's League, 1990—95. Named Woman of the Yr., Variety Club, 1978, Woman of Worth, Older Women's League, 1993; recipient Woman of Achievement award, St. Louis Globe-Dem., 1977, Unselfish Cmty. Svc. award, St. Louis Sentinel Newspaper, 1985. Faith in Action award, Luth. Svcs. St. Louis, 1994. Mem.: Older Wiser Luths. in Svc. (devotion leader), Assn. Lutheran Older Adults (mem. nat. bd. 2004—), N.Am. Interfaith Network (bd. dirs. 1993—2003), Phi Beta Kappa. Democrat. Personal E-mail: gloriaweber9@aol.com.

WEBER, H. PATRICK, lawyer; b. Cin., Jan. 25, 1949; s. Harry P. and Peggy (Sebastiani) W.; m. Marilyn Bykowski, Nov. 30, 1974; children: Kevin, Carmen, Courtney. BBA, U. Notre Dame, 1971, JD, 1974. Bar: Ohio 1974, US Dist. Ct. (so. dist. Ohio) 1974, US Tax Ct. 1975, Ky. 1990, US Claims Ct. 1991. Ptnr. Strauss & Troy, Cin., 1974-90, Barrett & Weber, Cin., 1990—. Bd. dirs. Ea. Hills Med. Billing, Inc. Trustee Med. Found. Cin., 1983—, Mercy Hosp. Anderson Found., 1990—. Named an Ohio Super Lawyer, Law & Politics Mag., 2004—06; named one of Top 100 Attys., Worth mag., 2005. Mem. ABA, Ohio Bar Assn., Cin. Bar Assn., Ky. Bar Assn., Notre Dame Alumni Assn. (trustee Cin. 1976—). Office: Barrett & Weber 500 Fourth & Walnut Ctr 105 E 4th St Cincinnati OH 45202 Office Phone: 513-721-2120. Office Fax: 513-721-2139. *

WEBER, HANNO, architect; b. Barranquilla, Colombia, Sept. 24, 1937; arrived in US, 1952; s. Hans and Ester (Oks) Weber. BA magna cum laude, Princeton U., 1959, MArch, 1961. Registered arch., Ill., Fla., Mo., Pa., NJ, Va. Urban designer, rsch. assoc. Guayana project MIT and Harvard U., Caracas, Venezuela, 1961-63; project arch. Paul Schweikher Assocs., Pitts., 1963-67; asst. prof. architecture Princeton U., NJ, 1967-73; assoc. prof. Washington U., St. Louis, 1973-80; sr. design arch., studio head, assoc. Skidmore, Owings & Merrill, Chgo., 1980-83; prin. Hanno Weber & Assocs., Chgo., 1984—. Vis. lectr. Escuela Nacional de Arquitectura Universidad Nacional de Mex., 1975; rsch. assoc. Rsch. Ctr. Urban and Environ. Planning, Princeton; project dir. Cmty. Design Workshop Washington U. Sch. Architecture, St. Louis, 1973—78; prof. architecture U. Wis., Milw., 1983—. Contbr. articles to profl. jours. Mem. Pres.'s Commn. Edn. Women Princeton U., 1968—69. Finalist, Okla. City Meml. Internat. Design Competition, 1997, Green Homes for Chgo. Design Competition, 2000; recipient 1st prize winner, Flagler Dr. Waterfront Master Plan Design Competition, West Palm Beach, Fla., 1984, Mcpl. Ctr. Design Competition, Leesburg, Va., 1987, Chgo. AIA Disting. Bldg. award Citation of Merit, 1987, Urban Design award Mcpl. Govt. Ctr., Leesburg, AIA, 1992; fellow, NEH, 1970, Graham Found., 1973. Mem.: Nat. Coun. Arch. Registration Bds., Phi Beta Kappa. Office: Hanno Weber & Assocs 11 E Adams St # 702 Chicago IL 60603-6301 Home Phone: 312-664-7556; Office Phone: 312-922-5589. Business E-Mail: weber@hannoweber.com.

WEBER, HANS JÜRGEN, physics professor; b. Berlin, May 3, 1939; came to U.S., 1966; naturalized, 1993; s. Hans Gustav Wilhelm and Hedwig Bertha Elisabeth (Angermann) W.; m. Edith E. Enzian, Aug. 19, 1966; 1 child, Chris H. MS in Math., U. Frankfurt, Fed. Republic Germany, 1961, PhD in Physics, 1965. Postdoctoral rsch. assoc. U. Frankfurt, 1965-66, Duke U., Durham, NC, 1966-67, U. Va., Charlottesville, 1967, asst. prof. physics, 1968-71, assoc. prof., 1971-77, prof., 1977—2003. Vis. scientist U. Mainz, Fed. Republic Germany, 1972, 77, 91, U. Paris-Sud, Orsay, France, 1979; vis. prof. U. Lyon, France, 1978. Co-author: Mathematical Methods for Physicists, 1995, 2001, 2005, Essentials of Math Methods for Physicists, 2003; contbr. to Physics Reports, Springer Tracts, Phys. Letters, Phys. Rev. Rsch. grantee NSF, 1971-95. Mem. Am. Phys. Soc., Am. Assn. Physics Tchrs., Sigma Xi. Lutheran. Achievements include development of a nuclear force (NN interaction) from quark models and a possible connection between quantum chromodynamics and meson dynamics; research on isobars in nuclei. Office: U Va Inst Nuclear and Particle Physics Mccormick Rd Charlottesville VA 22904-0001 Business E-Mail: hw@virginia.edu.

WEBER, HERMAN JACOB, senior district judge; b. Lima, Ohio, May 20, 1927; s. Herman Jacob and Ada Minola (Esterly) W.; m. Barbara L. Rice, May 22, 1948; children: Clayton, Deborah. BA, Otterbein Coll., 1949; JD summa cum laude, Ohio State U., 1951. Bar: Ohio 1952, U.S. Dist. Ct. (so. dist.) Ohio 1954. Ptnr. Weber & Hogue, Fairborn, Ohio, 1952-61; judge Fairborn Mayor's Ct., 1956-58; acting judge Fairborn Mcpl. Ct., 1958-60; judge Greene County Common Pleas Ct., Xenia, Ohio, 1961-82, Ohio Ct. Appeals (2d dist.), Dayton, 1982-85, U.S. Dist. Ct. (so. dist.) Ohio, Cin., 1985—2002, sr. judge, 2002—. Chmn. Sixth Cir. Dist. Judges Conf., 1988, Ohio Jud. Conf., Columbus, 1980-82; pres. Ohio Common Pleas Judges Assn., Columbus, 1975. Vice-mayor City of Fairborn, 1955-57, council mem., 1955-59. Served with USNR, 1945-46. Office: US Dist Ct 801 100 E 5th St Cincinnati OH 45202-3905

WEBER, HUGH, professional sports team executive; m. Julie Weber; children: Brenna, Zoë, Hugh III, Jackson. Grad., U. Puget Sound, Wash. Various positions in comml. products divsn. Proctor & Gamble; v.p. Ventura Foods; v.p. bus. ops. New Orleans/Okla. City (formerly Charlotte) Hornets, COO, 2006—. Avocations: running, golf, reading. Office: New Orleans Okla City Hornets 210 Park Ave Ste 1850 Oklahoma City OK 73102 *

WEBER, IDELLE, artist, educator; b. Chgo., Mar. 12, 1932; d. J. Earl and Min (Wallach) Feinberg; m. Julian L. Weber, Apr. 17, 1957; children: Jonathan Todd, Suzanne. BA, UCLA, 1954, MA, 1955. Adj. assoc. prof. art, grad. div. NYU, 1974-88; assoc. prof. Carpenter Ctr. Harvard U., 1988-91; prof. Nat. Acad., 2004-2006. Exhibited one-woman shows: Bertha Schaefer Gallery, N.Y.C., 1963, 64, Hundred Acres Gallery, N.Y.C., 1973, 75, 77, Chatham Coll., Pitts., 1979, O.K. Harris Gallery, N.Y.C., 1979, 82, Ruth Siegel Gallery, N.Y.C., 1984, 85, 87, Antony Ralph Gallery, N.Y.C., 1989, Arts Club of Chgo., 1986, Homart, Houston, 1987, Barbara Fendrick Gallery, Washington, 1987, Jean Albano Gallery, Chgo., 1994, Victorian Coll. of Arts, Melbourne, U., Australia, 1995, Contemporary Arts Forum, San Francisco, 1995, Nassau Mus. Art, 2004, Ferregut Tower Gallery, N.Y., 2005; group shows: Pa. Acad. Fine Arts, San Antonio Mus., Larry Aldrich Ctr. for Contemporary Arts, Ridgefield, Conn., 1981, Mus. Modern Art, N.Y.C., 1956, Guggeheim Mus., N.Y.C., 1964, Wadsworth Atheneum, Hartford, Conn., 1964, 66, Darnstadt (W.Ger.) Mus., Yale U. Mus., New Haven, 1975, Va. Mus., Richmond, Nat. Collection Fine Art, Washington, Butler Inst., Youngstown, Ohio, Fendrick Gallery, Washington, 1978, 85, Nat. Acad. 2002, 05, 06, 07, Danforth Mus., Framington, Mass, 1980, San Francisco Mus. Art, 1985-86, Contemporary Art Ctr., New Orleans, 1986, Indpls. Mus. Art, 1986, Graham Modern Mus., N.Y.C., 1986, Ft. Wayne Mus. Art, 1988, Carpenter Ctr. Harvard U., 1988, Met. Mus. Art, N.Y.C., 2001, U. Va. Art Mus., 2002, Gracie Mansion, Chelsea, N.Y.C., 2002, Nat. Acad. Design Mus., 2003, Neuberger Mus. Art, 2004, Nat. Acad., 2004, 05, 06, 07, Ferregut Tower Gallery, Southampton, N.Y., 2005; represented permanent collections: Nat. Collection Fine Art, Va. Mus., Sydney and Francis Lewis Found., Richmond, Yale U. Art Gallery, Albright Knox Gallery, Buffalo, Worcester (Mass.) Art Mus., Rochester (N.Y.) U. Mus., McNay Art Inst., N.Y. Pub. Library, Met. Mus. Art, N.Y.C., Pacific Bell, Calif., Bklyn Mus., Albright-Knox Gallery, Buffalo, Nelson -Atkins Mus. Art, Kansas City, Mo., Met. Mus. Art, Art Inst. Chgo., Kranert, U. Ill., Urbana, Whitney Mus. Art, Nat. Acad. and Sch. Fine Arts. Recognized in various publs. including: Arts Mag., 1979, 82, 84, 86, Photo Realism (L. Meisel), 1980, San Antonio Mus. Catalogue (L. Nochlin), 1981, Art in Am. (E. Lubell), Am. Women Artists (C.S. Rubenstein), 1982, Wall St. Jour., 1985, Christian Sci. Monitor, 1985, 86, Art in America, 1986, Washington Post, 1986, Chgo. Tribune, 1986, Washington Post, 1986, 87, Art Examiner, 1986; subject of work: American Realist Painting, 1945-1980 (John L. Ward), 1989; Scholastic Arts mag. scholar, 1950. Mem. Coll. Art Assn., Women's Caucus for Art, Artists Equity, Nat. Acad.

WEBER, JANICE ANN, library director, grant writer; b. Baytown, Tex., Aug. 28, 1952; d. James Thelmer Jr. and Doris Geraldine (Bush) Foster; m. Louis Haldane Weber, Feb. 1, 1983; 5 stepchildren. BS, Tex. Woman's U., Denton, 1982, MLS, 1985. Cert. county libr. Tex. Libr. dir. Dimmit County Libr., Carrilo Springs, Tex., 1985, Val Verde County Libr., Del Rio, Tex., 1986—89, Laredo Pub. Libr., Tex., 1989—. Sec., bd. dirs. Lit. Vol. Am., Laredo, 1989-95, bd. dirs. Webb County Heritage Found., Laredo, 1990-94; chmn. Webb County Hist. Commn., 1989-94; mem. Tuesday Music & Lit. Club, Laredo, 1997—, past pres. Mem. ALA, Nonprofit Mgmt. Assn., Tex. Libr. Assn., Tex. Mcpl. Libr. Dirs. Assn. (Libr. of Yr. 1999), Pub. Libr. Assn., Tex. City Mgrs. Assn., Reforma, Nat. Hispanic Network, AARP (pres. Laredo chpt. 965 2004-, Woman of Yr. 2001). Avocations: gourmet cooking, weaving, book making, scrapbooks, genealogy, gardening. Office: Laredo Pub Libr 1120 E Calton Rd Laredo TX 78041-7328 Office Phone: 956-795-2400. E-mail: janice@laredolibrary.org. *

WEBER, JEAN MACPHAIL, museum director; b. Boston, Apr. 2, 1933; d. Harold Percy and Dorothy Norma (Mutch) MacPhail; children: Julia Lee, Karin MacPhail, Laurie Stewart. Student, Brown U. and R.I. Sch. Design, 1950-52, Edinburgh U., Scotland, 1952-53; BA magna cum laude, Brown U., 1954; postgrad. Danforth scholar, State U. Iowa, 1954-55. Mgr. Lane Bryant Splty. Shop, Denver, 1956-57; campus advisor Saratoga Springs Council Chs., Skidmore Coll., NY, 1960-64; art dir. Our Lady of Peace Hosp., Louisville, 1964-65; dir. Jr. Art Gallery, Louisville, 1965-69, Parrish Art Mus., Southampton, NY, 1969-79, Rochester Mus., NY, 1979-80, Rochester Mus. and Sci. Ctr., NY, 1979-80, Mus. N.Mex., Sante Fe, 1981-85; co-dir. Mus. Mgmt. Inst., U. Calif.-Berkeley, 1981; dir. hist. sites State Hist. Soc. Wis., 1985-90; dir. Marine Maritime Mus., 1990-94, Mus. Art, U. Maine, 1994—. Dir. Maine Maritime Mus., 1990-94; mem.

mus. studies adv. com. Tufts U., Medford, Mass., 1993; interim dir. U. Maine Mus. of Art, 1994; adv. bd. Maine Crafts Coun., 1995; exec. dir. Nantucket Hist. Assn., 1995-2000; mem. Maine State Archives Commn., mem. mus. panel Maine Arts Commn., 2000-04. Contbr. articles to profl. jours. Mem. cultural affairs adv. com. Suffolk County, NY, 1974; trustee Inter Pueblo Cultural Ctr., 1981-82, Brown U., 1983, trustee emeritus, 1983-;; bd. dirs. Maine Community Cultural Alliance, 1991; bd. trustees ABBE Mus., 1999-2006, Hudson Mus., 1999-2003, Sir Andrew Macphail Found., 2000-. Met. Mus. grantee, 1971 Mem. Am. Assn. Mus. (accreditation commn. 1976-85, chmn. 1982-85, mem. coun. 1979-81, v.p. 1985, bd. dirs. 1993, named to Centennial Honor Roll, 2006), N.E. Mus. Conf. (v.p. 1978-79, pres. 1979-80), Internat. Coun. Mus., NY State Assn. Mus. (coun. 1977-80), Phi Beta Kappa. Mem. Soc. Of Friends.

WEBER, JOANNA, curator; Baccalaureate A4 in Philosophy, French, African Lit. with honors, Acad. Nantes, Lyceé Jean-Bedel Bokassa, Bangui, Ctrl. African Empire, 1978; diploma in religious studies, Cambridge U., Eng., 1980; BA in History and Philosophy, Wheaton Coll., Ill., 1983; MA in Religion and the Visual Arts, Yale U., New Haven, 1989. Asst. dir. Archives Couturier, Paris, 1990—91; asst. dir. religion and the arts Yale Div. Sch., New Haven, 1991—94, curator Couturier, 1991—94; asst. curator dept. European and contemporary art Yale U. Art Gallery, New Haven, 1996—99, acting curator dept. European and contemporary art, 1999—2000, asst. curator dept. European and contemporary art, 2000—02, acting asst. curator dept. African art, 2002; assoc. curator The John and Mable Ringling Mus. Art, Sarasota, Fla., 2003—. Yale Gallery rep. French Regional Mus., Lyon, France, 1999; co- project dir. exhbn., catalogue Rediscovering Fra Angelico: A Fragmentary History, 2002; co-project mgr. complete phys. collection inventory Ringling Mus., Sarasota, Fla., 2003; mem. steering com. New Colls. Conf. on Medieval-Renaissance Studies, 2004, 05; panelist John Ringling Individual Artist Grant, 2005—06; mem. Yale Slifka Ctr. for Jewish Life Arts Group, Ringling Libr. Collections Com.; grant writer; presenter in field. Author: (catalogues) Philip Guston: A New Alphabet: the Late Transition, 2000, Of Lions and Red Hats: St. Jerome at the Ringling Museum of Art, 2004, Josef Albers: Color Genius, 2006; co-editor (with John Hollander): (catalogues) Words for Imagery: A Gallery of Poems, 2001; contbr. articles to profl. jours. Participant Leadership Sarasota, 2004—05. Nominee Lannan Found. Marfa, Tex. residency, 2000; recipient Religion and the Arts prize, Yale Div. Sch., 1989, Faculty prize, Yale Inst. Sacred Music, Worship and the Arts, 1989; grantee, Menil Found., 1990—94, Lannan Found., 1999; Menil scholar, Yale U., 1987—89. Mem.: Assn. Am. Museums, Coll. Art Assn., Am. Acad. Religion. Achievements include organized complete re-installation of Yale Art Gallery's permanent collection of African art; organized insurance appraisal process for Ringling Museum of Art with Southby's. Office: John and Mable Ringling Mus Art 5401 Bay Shore Rd Sarasota FL 34243-2161

WEBER, JOHN WALTER, insurance company executive; b. Rochester, NY, Jan. 10, 1959; BS, U. Conn., 1984. Claims supr. Hartford Ins. Group, Southington, Conn., 1986-90; regional claims mgr. Housing Authority Risk Retention Group, Cheshire, Conn., 1990—. Contbr. articles to tech. publs. Mem. U. Conn. Alumni Assn. Avocations: running, reading, softball, cooking. Personal E-mail: jweber6@charter.net.

WEBER, KATIE, retired special education educator; b. Delhi, La., Dec. 6, 1933; d. Sullivan and Teresa McClain Aytch; m. Hilliard Weber Jr., June 16, 1956; children: Barrett Renwick, Sandra Anita, Dawna Lynn, Thaddeus Marc. BA, So. U., 1957; MEd, Tex. So. U., 1982. Cert. elem. and spl. edn. tchr., La., Tex. Elem. tchr. Port Arthur Ind. Sch. Dist., Tex., 1957-73, elem. spl. edn. tchr. Tex., 1974-85, secondary spl. edn. tchr. Tex., 1985—93; ret., 1993. Part-time prin. Port Arthur Ind. Sch. Dist., 1976-83, interim prin., 1983-85; mem. Tex. assessment acad. skills test Tex. Edn. Agy., Austin, 1988-90, scorer master tchr. test, 1990; also curriculum writer. Candidate for city coun. City of Port Arthur, Tex., 1974; active Brentwood Bapt. Ch., Houston, Tex., 1998-, Bapt. Women Mission III, Sr. Adult Ministry, Class 10 Sunday Sch, Buchanan Cir., 1980—, Port Child Svc. League, Port Arthur, 1989—, Life PTA-Tex. PTA, 1985, Clean Cmty. Commn., Port Arthur, 1990—. Named One of Top 20 Tchrs. in Tex., Leadership Edn., 1984-85, Bus. Assoc. of Yr. plaque Energy City chpt. Am. Women Bus. Assn., 1984. Mem. Assn. Tex. Profl. Educators (Leadership cert. 1989), Zeta Phi Beta. Democrat. Avocations: walking, gardening, cooking, reading, classical music. Address: 1819 Thornbrook Dr Missouri City TX 77489-2207

WEBER, KENNETH J., hotel executive; b. 1946; With Arthur Young & Co., NYC, 1968-71, ITT-Grinnell Corp., Providence, 1971-73, Farmbest Foods Internat., Jacksonville, 1973-74; regional contr. Marriott Corp., Washington, 1974-76, group contr., 1976-77, divsn. contr., 1977-79, pres., CEO Farrell's Ice Cream divsn., 1983-86; exec. v.p., CFO Isaly Co., Pitts., 1979-80; v.p., contr. Country Kitchens Internat. divsn. Carlson Cos., Inc., Mpls., 1980-81; sr. v.p. Poppin Fresh Restaurant divsn. Pillsbury Co., Mpls., 1981-83; sr. v.p., corp. contr. Red Lion Hotels Corp., Vancouver, Wash., 1987-92; sr. v.p., CFO Omni Hotels Corp., Hampton, N.H., 1992—; also v.p., treas. Omni Ctr. Corp., Richmond, Va.

WEBER, LISA M., insurance company executive; BA in Psychology, SUNY, Stony Brook. With Painewebber, 1988—98; sr. v.p. human resources MetLife, Inc., NYC, 1998—2003, sr. v.p., 1999, exec. v.p., 1999—2001, sr. exec. v.p., chief adminstrv. officer, 2001—04, pres. individual bus., 2004—. Bd. dirs. New Eng. Fin., Gt. Am. Fin., Reinsurance Grp. of Am.; bd. dirs. benefits com. MetLife, Inc.; mem. social responsibility com. MetLife Found. Bd. Named one of 50 Most Powerful Women in Bus., Fortune mag., 2006. Mem.: Phi Beta Kappa. Office: MetLife Inc 200 Park Ave New York NY 10166 *

WEBER, MARK, apparel executive; With Phillips-Van Heusen, NYC, 1972—2006, sr. v.p., gen. merchandise mgr., exec. v.p. merchandising, 1995—98, pres., COO, 1998—2005, CEO, 2005—06, LVMH Inc, NYC, 2006—; chmn., CEO Donna Karan Internat. Inc., NYC, 2006—. Office: LVMH Inc 19 E 57th St New York NY 10022 *

WEBER, MARK R., automotive executive; B in Indsl. Engring., Kettering U.; M in Mgmt. (Sloan fellow), MIT, 1983. Various pers. and labor rels. pos. GM Fisher Body, Elyria, Ohio, 1971—78, administr. pers. svcs. Columbus, Ohio, 1978—79, pers. dir. Syracuse, NY, 1979—82; adminstr. exec. compensation GM Pers. and Devel. Staff, Detroit, 1982—83, dir., classified employee compensation, 1983—85; dir. gen. offices pers. Chevrolet-Pontiac-GM of Can. Group, Warren, Mich., 1985—88, dir. human resources, salaried pers., 1985—88, dir. indsl. rels., 1988—91; gen. dir. pers. Inland Fisher Guide, Warren, Mich., 1991—93, gen. dir. pers. and pub. affairs, 1993—98; v.p. in charge human resources Delphi Corp., Troy, Mich., 1998—2000, exec. v.p., ops., human resource mgmt. and corp. affairs, 2000—06, exec. v.p. global bus. services, 2006—. Office: World Hdqrs Delphi Corp 5725 Delphi Dr Troy MI 48098-2815 *

WEBER, MARK W., library director, dean; BS, U. Wis., 1968, MLS, 1972; MA in Hist. and Edn., Colgate U., 1970. Dir. pub. svcs. Clifford Libr. and Learning Resources U. Evansville, 1975—79, tchr. reference and libr. mgmt., 1976—79; archives asst. Case Western Res. U., 1979—80; pub. svcs./outreach libr. Cuyahoga CC, 1981—85, tchr. labor hist. and collective bargaining, 1984—88, asst. pers. dir./EEOC officer, 1985—88; tchr. labor hist. Cleve. State U., 1983; asst. univ. libr. for pers. U. Cin., 1988—91; tchr. libr. mgmt. Ind. U., 1990; dir. staff svcs. Kent State U. Librs., 1991—2000, dean librs. and media svcs., 2001—. Contbr. articles to profl. jours. Founding bd. mem. Ethical Soc. of Cleve. Mem.: ALA, Assn. Jewish Librs., Greater Cleve. Labor Hist. Soc., Jewish Secular Cmty. Office: Kent State U Librs and Media Svcs PO Box 5190 Kent OH 44242-0001 Office Phone: 330-672-2962. E-mail: markw@lms.kent.edu. *

WEBER, MATTHEW GEORGE, lawyer; s. Robert H. and Helena K. Weber; m. Ann Ralston Weber, Aug. 31, 1996; children: Caroline, Lindsey, Thomas. BA magna cum laude, Colo. Coll., Colorade Springs, 1985; JD, Northwestern U. Sch. Law, Evanston, Ill., 1988. Bar: US Dist. Ct., Dist. of Colo., DC Ct. Appeals 1988, US Dist. Ct., DC 1989, Colo. Supreme Ct. 1989, US Ct. Appeals, D.C. Circuit 1989, US Supreme Ct. 1992, US Ct. Appeals, 10th Circuit 1995. Assoc. atty. Dow, Lohnes & Albertson, Washington, 1988—90, Baker & Hostetler, Washington, 1991—94, Hoskin, Farina, Aldrich & Kampf, P.C., Grand Junction, Colo., 1994—99, shareholder, 1999—2003; atty. Holland & Hart, LLP, Denver, 2004—06, ptnr., 2007—. Chair of law day com. Mesa County Bar Assn., Grand Junction, 2002. Author: (68 den. u. l. rev. 57) Media Liability for the Publication of Advertising: When to Kill the Messenger; contbr. (ABA book) Managed Care Litigation. Bd. dirs. Mesa County Chpt. of ARC, Grand Junction, Colo., 1995—96; bd. trustees Mesa County Pub. Libr. Dist., Grand Junction, 1999—2003. Mem.: ABA, Am. Health Lawyers Assn., Denver Bar Assn. Office: Holland & Hart LLP 555 17th St Ste 3200 Denver CO 80202 Office Phone: 303-295-8565.

WEBER, MICHAEL A., physician, researcher; m. Sandra Du Bro, Sept. 12, 1971; children: Mark S., David S. BS, Sydney U., Australia, 1967; MD, Sydney U. Sch. of Medicine, Australia, 1967. Cert. Medicine Royal Australasian Coll. of Physicians, 1977, ACP, 1977. Resident in medicine NYU Med. Ctr., 1968—71; rsch. fellow Sydney Hosp., U. Sydney, 1971—75; asst. prof. medicine Cardiovasc. Ctr., Cornell U. Med. Ctr., NYC, 1975—77; chief, sect. clin. pharmacology and hypertension, Irvine Coll. Medicine U. Calif., 1977—95, assoc. prof. medicine, 1977—82, prof. medicine, 1982—85; chmn., dept. medicine Brookdale U. Med. Ctr., Bklyn., 1995—2000; prof. medicine SUNY Downstate Coll. Medicine, Bklyn., 1995—, assoc. dean clin. rsch., 2000—04. Served on Cardiovascular and Renal Drugs Adv. Bd. FDA; cons. FDA; serves on steering committees of several nat. and internat. clin. outcomes trials; retained cons. and mem. speakers bur. Novartis, Merck, Boehringer Ingelheim, Bristol-Myers Squibb and Sanofi. Author: (jour. articles) Lancet; editor: (med. ref. book) Hypertension Medicine, Ambulatory Blood Pressure Monitorins; senior editor (jour. article) Am. Jour. of Geriatric Cardiology, consulting editor Am. Jour. of Hypertension, assoc. editor Jour. of Clinical Hypertension, mem. editl. bd. Med Reviews; contbr. several articles to profl. jours. Pres. Am. Soc. of Hypertension, NYC, 1998—2000; chmn. ASH Specialists Program in Hypertension, NYC; cons., ctr. for drug evaluation and rsch. FDA, Washington, 1993—2005. Fellow: Am. Coll. Clin. Pharmacology, Am. Coll. Physicians, Am. Heart Assn. (fellow, coun. for high blood pressure rsch.), Am. Coll. of Cardiology; mem.: Am. Soc. Hypertension (founder, past pres., chair, hypertension specialists program). Office: SUNY Downstate Coll Medicine 450 Clarkson Ave Box 97 Brooklyn NY 11203 Home Phone: 212-935-6421; Office Phone: 212-584-9191. Office Fax: 212-584-9192. Personal E-mail: michaelwebermd@cs.com. *

WEBER, MICHAEL ALLEN, school librarian; b. Reading, Pa. s. Walter Paul and Mary Ellen Weber; m. M. Jacqueline Weber, 1995; 1 child, Theresa. BA in Chemistry, Gettysburg Coll., Pa., 1982; MS in Chemistry, U. Ga., Athens, 1984; M in Librarianship, Emory U., Atlanta, 1986. Asst. libr. Crawford Long Hosp., Atlanta, 1986—88; catalog libr. Morehouse Sch. Medicine, Atlanta, 1990—91; asst. libr. dir. Alvernia Coll., Reading, 1991—2000; web designer De Lage Landen, Wayne, Pa., 2000—01; tech. svcs. libr. Kutztown U., Pa., 2001—. Rsch. grant, Libr. Svcs. and Tech. Act, 2005—06. Roman Cath. Avocation: languages. Office: Kutztown Univ 15200 Kutztown Rd Bldg 5 Kutztown PA 19530 Business E-Mail: weber@kutztown.edu.

WEBER, PAULA M., lawyer; b. Washington, Pa., June 6, 1959; BA magna cum laude, Colgate Univ., 1981; JD with high honors, George Washington Univ., 1985. Bar: Calif. 1985. Ptnr., chmn. Employment & Labor practice Pillsbury Winthrop Shaw Pittman, San Francisco. Mem.: Phi Beta Kappa, Order of the Coif. Office: Pillsbury Winthrop Shaw Pittman 50 Fremont St San Francisco CA 94105 Office Phone: 415-983-7488. Office Fax: 415-983-1200. Business E-Mail: paula.weber@pillsburylaw.com.

WEBER, RAY EVERETT, engineering executive, consultant; b. Kenton, Ohio, Dec. 11, 1946; s. Mervin Clarence and Phylis Jean Weber; m. Carolyn Antinoro, Aug. 16, 1980; children: David Charles, Stephen Ray. BS in Physics, Ohio State U., 1973. Lic. real estate agt. N.Y., 1992-1997. Project engr. Erie Lackawanna R.R., Hoboken, NJ, 1974—75; nuclear engring. adminstr. ASME, NYC, 1975—78; cognizant engr. Burns & Roe Inc., Oradell, NJ, 1978—80; supervising engr. Impell Corp., Melville, NY, 1980—88; pres. Webtor Inc., Northport, NY, 1988—; owner Weber Real Estate, Northport, NY, 1978—. Pres. Forest Ventures Inc., Northport, N.Y., 1987—. Author: Nuclear Codes/Standards. With USN, 1966—70. Mem.: ASME (nuclear subcom.), Marco Island Yacht Club, Northport Yacht Club, Am. Legion. Avocations: boating, fishing, skiing, golf. Office: Forest Ventures Inc 115 Soundview Ter Northport NY 11768-1231 Office Phone: 516-885-8059. Personal E-mail: rweber3@optonline.net.

WEBER, ROBERT CARL, lawyer; b. Chester, Pa., Dec. 18, 1950; s. Robert Francis and Lucille (Nobili) W.; m. Linda Brediger, June 30, 1972; children: Robert F., Mary Therese, David P., Joseph T. BA cum laude, Yale U., 1972; JD, Duke U., 1976. Bar: Ohio 1976, U.S. Dist. ct. (no. dist.) Ohio 1976, U.S. Ct. Claims 1980, U.S. Ct. Appeals (6th cir.) 1981, U.S. Ct. Appeals (5th cir.) 1995. Assoc. Jones, Day, Reavis & Pogue (now Jones Day), Cleve., 1976—83, ptnr., 1983—2006; sr. v.p. legal and regulatory affairs IBM Corp., Armonk, NY, 2006—. Bd. dirs. United Way Svcs. of Cleve., 1992-2002. Named one of Top 10 Trial Lawyers in Am., Nat. Law Jour., 2000, 2004. Fellow Am. Coll. Trial Lawyers, Internat. Acad. Trial Lawyers; mem. Ohio Bar Assn., Am. Law Inst., Product Liability Adv. Coun., Cleve. Bar Assn. (chmn. jud. selection com. 1985-86, trustee 1990-93, pres.-elect 1994-95, pres. 1995-96), Jud. Conf. for 8th Jud. Dist. Ohio (life), Order of Coif. Roman Catholic. Office: IBM Corp 1 New Orchard Rd Armonk NY 10504-1722 Home Phone: 216-470-6254. Business E-Mail: rcweber@us.ibm.com. *

WEBER, ROBERT MAXWELL, cartoonist; b. LA, Apr. 22, 1924; p. Milton and Edith (Huston) W.; m. Marilyn Baum, Oct. 11, 1953 (div.); children— Peter, Lee; m. Debora Graves, Dec. 24, 1988. Student, Pratt Inst., 1945-48, Art Students League, 1948-50. Fashion illustrator, 1949-54; artist New Yorker mag., 1962—; work commd. by IBM, N.Y. Telephone, Am. Airlines, Mobil, Blue Cross/Blue Shield, U.S. Healthcare, Goodyear Co., J.C. Penney Co., Air Canada, Swissair, others; contbr. cartoons to nat. mags. Served with USCGR, 1942-45. Office: New Yorker 4 Times Sq New York NY 10036-6522

WEBER, STEPHEN LEWIS, academic administrator; b. Boston, Mar. 17, 1942; s. Lewis F. and Catherine (Warns) W.; m. Susan M. Keim, June 27, 1965; children: Richard, Matthew. BA, Bowling Green State U., 1964; postgrad., U. Colo., 1964-66; PhD, U. Notre Dame, 1969; EdD (hon.), Capital Normal U., China, 1994. Asst. prof. philosophy U. Maine, Orono, 1969—74, assoc. prof., 1974—79, asst. to pres., 1976-79; dean arts and scis. Fairfield U., Conn., 1979-84; v.p. acad. affairs St. Cloud State U., Minn., 1984-88; pres. SUNY Oswego, 1988—96; interim provost SUNY Albany, 1995-96; pres. San Diego State U., 1996—. Contbr. numerous articles on philosophy and acad. adminstrn. to profl. jours. Mem. Commn. on Internat. Edn. and Commn. on Govtl. Rels.; bd. govs. The Peres Ctr. for Peace, San Diego Found.; bd. dirs. San Diego Regional Econ. Devel. Corp.; mem. internat. adv. bd. Found. for the Children of the Californias; bd. dirs. NCAA Divsn. 1 hon. mem. Asia Desk, San Diego Trade Ctr.; mem. adv. bd. Union Bank Calif. Named Outstanding Humanities Tchr., U. Maine, 1975. Mem. Am. Philos. Assn., Am. Assn. Higher Edn. Democrat. Avocations: art, woodworking, swimming, boating. Office: San Diego State Univ Office Pres 5500 Campanile Dr San Diego CA 92182-8000 E-mail: presidents.office@sdsu.edu.

WEBER, STEPHEN VANCE, physics researcher; b. Wooster, Ohio, Oct. 31, 1951; s. Dale Sarge and Lucy June (Smith) W.; m. Marie Christensen (dec. 2005), June 21, 1980; children: Erik, Kristina. AB in Physics, Princeton U., 1973; MA in Astronomy, U. Calif., Berkeley, 1974, PhD, 1978. Rsch. fellow Calif. Inst. Tech., Pasadena, 1978-80; asst. prof. Dartmouth Coll., Hanover, NH, 1980-82; rsch. scientist, physicist Lawrence Livermore Nat. Lab., Livermore, Calif., 1982—. Contbr. articles to profl. jours. Mem. Am. Phys. Soc. (excellence in plasma physics award 1995). Achievements include investigations of Rayleigh-Taylor instability and implosions in inertial confinement fusion. Office: Lawrence Livermore Nat Lab L-477 PO Box 808 Livermore CA 94551-0808 Home Phone: 925-447-9114. Business E-Mail: svweber@llnl.gov.

WEBER, SUSAN A., lawyer; b. 1958; BA, Drake U., 1984; JD, MBA, SUNY, Buffalo, 1989. Bar: Pa. 1990, D.C. 1992, Ill. 1993, U.S. Ct. Appeals (4th cir.) 1990, U.S. Ct. Appeals (3d cir.) 1991, U.S. Ct. Appeals (7th cir.) 1992. Clk. to Justice Byron White U.S. Supreme Ct.; clk. to Judge James Sprouse U.S. Ct. Appeals (4th cir.); with Sidley Austin Brown & Wood, Chgo., 1993—, ptnr., 1997—.

WEBER, THOMAS WILLIAM, chemical engineering professor; b. Orange, NJ, July 15, 1930; s. William A. and Dorothy (Negus) W.; m. Marianne S. Hartmann, June 4, 1966; children: Anne Louise, William Alois B.Chem. Engring., Cornell U., 1953, PhD, 1963; MS in Chem. Engring., Newark Coll. Engring., 1958. Registered profl. engr., N.Y. Chem. engr. econs. and planning Esso Research & Engring., Linden, NJ, 1955-58; instr. Cornell U., 1961-62; asst. prof. SUNY-Buffalo, 1963-66, assoc. prof. chem. engring., 1966-82, prof., 1982-2000, assoc. chmn. dept., 1980-82, chmn. dept., 1982-89, acting chmn., 1996-97, prof. emeritus, 2000—. Author: An Introduction to Process Dynamics and Control, 1973 Named Prof. of Yr., Tau Kappa Chi, 1965; recipient Chancellor's award for excellence in teaching, 1981, Tchr. of Yr. award Tau Beta Pi, 1982 Fellow AIChE (chmn. western N.Y. sect. 1969-70, Profl. Achievement award western N.Y. sect. 1978), Am. Soc. Engring. Edn. (chmn. instrumentation divsn. 1975-77, chmn. St. Lawrence sect. 1979-80, 92-94, chmn. divsn. experimentation and lab.-oriented studies 1985-86, chmn. Zone I 1999-2001, Outstanding Zone Campus Rep. award 1988, AT&T Found. award 1987-88); mem. Tech. Socs. Coun. Niagara Frontier (sec. 1973-75, pres. 1975-76, treas. 1978-2004), Swedish Club of Buffalo (pres. 1974-76), U.S. Masters Swimming Club, Sigma Xi, Phi Kappa Phi, Tau Beta Pi, Theta Xi. Presbyterian. Business E-Mail: twweber@eng.buffalo.edu.

WEBER, WILLIAM WESLEY, accountant; b. Columbus, Ohio, Dec. 2, 1951; s. Richard Dick and Donna Marie (Inboden) W.; m. Kay Ruth Swope, Feb. 14, 1976; children: Kristen Marie, Richard Stewart. BS, Ohio State U., 1973; MBA, Baldwin-Wallace Coll., Berea, Ohio, 1983. CPA, Tex.; cert. internal auditor, cert. fraud examiner, cert. info. tech. prol. Staff acct. Arthur Andersen, Cin., 1973-74; staff auditor Federated Dept. Stores, Cin., 1974-75, Diamond Shamrock, Cleve., 1975-77, sr. auditor, 1977-83, audit supr. San Antonio, 1983-97; acctg. mgr. Ultramar Diamond Shamrock, San Antonio, 1997-2000, bus. process specialist, 2000-01, mgr. fin. sys., 2001—04, Valero Energy Corp., 2002—04; mgr. info. sys. Governance, 2004—. Treas. Holy Trinity Presbyn. Ch., San Antonio, 1986-95. Mem. AICPA, Assn. Cert. Fraud Examiners, Inst. Internal Auditors (adj. faculty 1988-97, internat. seminars com. 1996-97), Tex. Soc. CPAs. Avocations: reading, watching auto racing. Home: 14307 Rowe Dr San Antonio TX 78247-3122 Office: Valero PO Box 696000 San Antonio TX 78269-6000 Business E-Mail: bil.w.weber@valero.com.

WEBER, YVONNE ROEBUCK, research administrator; educator; b. McKeesport, Pa., Oct. 22; d. Raymond Henry and Clara Maria (Roberts) Roebuck; B.A., U. Pitts., 1947, M.Litt., 1952, Ph.D., 1973; postgrad. Kent State U., 1950; Ecole Normale, Paris, 1953, Goethe Institut, 1960; m. William Frederick Weber, June 16, 1961; children— Laurel, Wendy. Tchr. French, German, English, history Carrollton (Ohio) High Sch., 1947-51, Canton, Ohio, 1951-52, Munhall (Pa.) High Sch., 1952-58, Wilkinsburg (Pa.) High Sch., 1958-61, Upper St. Clair (Pa.) High Sch., 1963-65; asst. prof. French and German, California (Pa.) State Coll., 1965-66, Point Park (Pa.) Coll., 1968-72; asst. prof., supr. edn. Washington and Jefferson Coll., 1976-79; scholar/discussion leader Pa. Humanities Coun., 1993. Recipient Good Citizenship award DAR, 1943, Doctoral Assn. Outstanding Svc. award U. Pitts., 1989; U. Pitts. scholar, 1943-47, Panhellenic Assn. scholar, 1946-47, disting. alumni award Sch. Edn., U. Pitts., 1985, Alumnae award, 1993; Fulbright grantee to Germany, 1960; program scholar Nat. Endowment for the Humanities, Am. Library Assn., 1986; named Disting. Alumna, U. Pitts., 1971-82; initial inductee hall of fame McKeesport High Sch., 1987. Mem. Modern Lang. Assn., Doctoral Assn. Educators, Pa. State Modern Lang. Assn., Pa. Assn. Tchr. Educators, U.Pitts. Alumni Council, Delta Kappa Gamma Soc. Internat. (Scholarship 1972-73, Eunah Temple Holden Golden Anniversary award 1979, head internat. research project, 1979-82), Mensa Internat., Pi Lambda Theta, Phi Delta Gamma, Zeta Tau Alpha. Club: McKeesport Coll. Author: A Beacon to the Future: Charting a Course for Advancement; contbr. articles to profl. jours. Home: 444 S Higley Rd Apt 301 Mesa AZ 85206-2174

WEBRE, SEPTIME, performing company executive, choreographer; b. New Orleans, Dec. 7, 1961; s. Alfred L. and Juanita (Chisholm) Webre. BA, U. Tex., 1984. Dancer Merce Cunningham Dance Co., NYC, 1991, Am. Repertory Ballet/Princeton (N.J.) Ballet, 1987—99, choreographer, 1988—99, artistic dir., 1993-99, The Washington Ballet, 1999—. Freelance choreographer with Les Grands Ballets Canadienne, 1988—, Pacific N.W. Ballet, 1988—, Sacramento Ballet, 1988—, N.C. Dance Theatre, 1988—, Columbia City Ballet, 1988—, Ballet Austin, 1988—, Dayton Ballet, 1988—, Eglevsky Ballet, 1988—, The Aspen Ballet, the Carslile Project, 1988—, others, 1988—; guest master tchr. various ballet cos., 1990—. Former mem. exec. bd. Young Dems. Am., Austin. Choreographic fellow, N.J. Coun. on Arts, 1992. Roman Catholic. Office: The Washington Ballet 3515 Wisconsin Ave NW Washington DC 20016-3085 *

WEBSTER, CATHERINE T., telecommunications industry executive; B in Econs., NJ City U. CPA. With Bell Atlantic NJ, 1978, dir. fin. planning and analysis for Telecom/Network, 1993; asst. v.p. fin. planning Corp. Fin. Grp. Bell Atlantic, 1996; v.p. fin. Network Svcs. and Wholesale Markets Verizon Comm., v.p. fin., sr. v.p. investor rels., 2005—. Office: Verizon Comm 140 West St New York NY 10007

WEBSTER, CHRISTOPHER WHITE, foreign service officer; b. Boston, Oct. 30, 1953; s. Henry deForest and Marion (Havas) W. BA cum laude, Amherst Coll., 1975; MA, Johns Hopkins U., 1977. Asst. comml. attache Am. Embassy, Buenos Aires, 1977-79; econ. comml. officer Georgetown, Guyana, 1979-81; desk officer for Jamaica and Guyana, 1982—84; econ. officer Office of Energy, Washington, 1984-86, fin. and devel. officer Lisbon, Portugal, 1986—89, econ. sect. chief Algiers, Algeria, 1989—92; dep. dir. Office of Pakistan, Afghanistan and Bangladesh Affairs, Washington, 1992—95; dep. chief of mission Khartoum, Sudan and Addis Ababa, Ethiopia, 1995-96; chief, developed Country Trade Divsn., Washington, 1996-98; dep. dir. Office of Ctrl. Am. and Panamanian Affairs, Washington, 1998-00, dep. chief of mission Dhaka, Bangladesh, 2000—03, Oslo, 2003—06; dir. Office of Devel. Fin., Washington, 2006—. Recipient Superior Honor award Dept. State, 1983, 91, 98-2000, Meritorious Honor award Dept. State, 2007. E-mail: webstercw@state.gov.

WEBSTER, DAVID ARTHUR, retired life insurance company executive; b. Downs, Ill., July 20, 1937; s. Harold Sanford and Carmen Mildred (Moore) W.; m. Anna Elizabeth Prosch, June 10, 1956; children: Theodore David, Elizabeth Anna, Arthur Lee, William Harold. BS, U. Ill., 1960. Actuarial asst. Mass. Mut. Life Ins. Co., Springfield, 1960-64; cons. actuary George Stennes & Assocs., Mpls., 1964-68; v.p., actuary Piedmont Life Ins. Co., Atlanta, 1968-72, Pacific Fidelity Life Ins. Co., Los Angeles, 1972-74; v.p., chief actuary U.S. Life Corp., NYC, 1974-76, exec. v.p., 1976-78, dir., 1976-78; pres., dir. Beneficial Pension Svcs, BPS Agy., Inc.; v.p., treas., dir. Beneficial Assurance Co., 1978-82; asst. sec., dir. Beneficial Computer Svcs., Inc.; treas. Tel-Assurance Corp.; exec. v.p., dir. Beneficial Standard Life, 1978-82; pres., dir. U.S. Life Ins. Co. of Calif., 1982-84, Western World Fin. Group Inc., 1984-86; exec. v.p., COO R.W. Durham and Co., 1987-99. Fellow Soc. Actuaries. Home: 1150 Ladera Ln Paso Robles CA 93446 E-mail: SLODavidPaso@aol.com.

WEBSTER, DAVID MACPHERSON, lawyer; b. Chgo., June 22, 1950; s. Robert Fielden and Julia Orendorff (Macpherson) Webster; m. Lucia Maxwell Blair, Oct. 3, 1987; 1 child, Jessie Maxwell. BA in History magna cum laude with honors, Williams Coll., 1972; JD, U. Va., 1975; DD (hon.), Seabury-Western Theol. Sem., 2000. Bar: Ill. 1975. Assoc. Winston & Strawn, Chgo., 1975-81, ptnr., 1981-87; White House fellow Washington, 1987-88; spl. asst. to dir. FBI, Washington, 1988-89; asst. gen. counsel for multilateral negotiations U.S. Arms Control and Disarmament Agy., Washington, 1989—94; v.p., gen. counsel A.T. Kearney, Inc., Chgo., 1994—2002; of counsel Butler Rubin Saltarelli & Boyd, Chgo., 2002—03; sr. v.p., gen. counsel Hawaiian Airlines, Honolulu, 2003—05; v.p., gen. counsel, sec. DeVry Inc., Oakbrook Terrace, Ill., 2005—07; v.p., gen. counsel Hwy. Techs., Inc., Oak Brook, 2007—. Mem. adv. com. Ill. Bus. Corp. Ill. Sec. of State, Chgo., 1982—87. Bd. dirs. Ill. Soc. Prevention Blindness, Chgo., 1980—87, 1997—2004, pres., 1999—2001; trustee Village of Winnetka, Ill., 2003—05; bd. dirs. Better Govt. Assn., Chgo., 1997—99; trustee Episc. Charities and Profl. Svcs., Chgo., 1980—87; bd. dirs. WBEZ Alliance, Inc., Chgo., 1996—2004; chair bd. trustees Seabury-Western Theol. Sem., Evanston, Ill., 1993—96, trustee, 1988—96, 2002—05. Mem.: Manuscript Soc., Ill. State Hist. Soc. (life), White House Fellows Assn., Abraham Lincoln Assn., Phi Beta Kappa (mem. exec. com. Chgo. chpt. 1996—98). Episcopalian. Avocations: history, writing. Home: 596 Arbor Vitae Rd Winnetka IL 60093-2302 Personal E-mail: davidmwebster@comcast.net. Business E-Mail: david.webster@hwy-tech.com.

WEBSTER, ERNEST WESLEY, musician, educator; b. Mt. Vernon, Ill., Oct. 30, 1932; s. Melvin Harold and Nora Mae (Wimberley) Webster; m. Arlene Waite (div. 1972); m. Judith Ann Hichman (dec. 1995); children: Elizabeth Ann Webster Kennedy, Victoria Christina; m. Lindsey Carvalho Campos, Oct. 4, 2003. Diploma in ch./conducting, Moody Bible Inst., Chgo., 1953; student, Northwestern Schs., Mpls., 1953—54; diploma in music edn. and piano, U. Ariz., 1957. Owner Webster Sch. Music, Ft. Lauderdale, 1957—. Instr. Barry U. Mem.: Accordion Tchrs. Guild Internat. (v.p.), Fla. State Music Tchrs. Assn. (pres. dist. 6). Home: 105 Lake Emerald Dr #112 Fort Lauderdale FL 33309 Office: Webster Sch Music 3058 N Federal Hwy Fort Lauderdale FL 33304 Home Phone: 954-717-8967; Office Phone: 954-537-5309.

WEBSTER, GORDON VISSCHER, JR., minister; b. Huntington, NY, Oct. 2, 1947; s. Gordon Visscher and Marion Beatrice W.; m. Gloria Marie Farwagi, May 31, 1975; children: David Gordon (dec.), Daniel Farwagi, Diana Alexandra. AB, Hamilton Coll., 1969; postgrad., St. Andrews Div. Sch., 1970-71, McCormick Theol. Sem., 1982-87; MDiv, Union Theol. Sem., 1973. Ordained to ministry Presbyn. Ch. (USA), 1973. Staff assoc. Met. Ch. Bd., Syracuse, NY, 1973-75; assoc. pastor 1st Presbyn. Ch., 1975-83; missionary Mid. East Coun. of Chs., Limassol, Cyprus, 1983-84; missionary-in-residence Presbyn. Ch. (USA), Stony Point Center, NY, 1984-86; interim pastor 1st Presbyn. Ch., Oneida, 1988-89, United Presbyn. Ch., Cortland, 1989-91; pastor Ogden Presbyn. Ch., Spencerport, 1991-2001, Downtown United Presbyn. Ch., Rochester, 2001—. Exec. dir. Am. Coalition Mid. East Dialogue, Jamesville, NY, 1986-88, Common Good Planning Ctr. Rochester Area Cmty. Found., 1998-2001; v.p. Greater Rochester Cmty. Chs., 1992-93, pres., 1994-97, exec. team, 2002-2007; chair Interfaith Forum Greater Rochester, 1995, 99; pres. Interfaith Alliance Rochester, 1998-99; mem. Mayor's Stewardship Coun. Comprehensive Planning, City of Rochester, 1996-2006; mem. Mayor's Commn. on Race and Ethnicity, 2000-05; bd. dirs. Odyssey Humanity, 2006—, Ctr. for Interfaith Study and Dialogue, 2005—; Presbyn. Commr. to Gen. Assembly Nat. Coun. of Chs. of Christ in USA, 2000—; mem. Nat. Strategy Team Let Justice Roll 2005-2006, Martin Luther King Jr. Commn. of Monroe County, 1995-2000; mem. pub. policy commn. NY State Cmty. Chs., 1996-99; mem. Presbytery Genesee Valley, 1991—, trustee, 2003-06; commr. PC (USA) Gen Assembly, 2004, mem. Jud. Commn., 2007, exec. presbyter search team, 2007-; leader workshops on Mid. East, 1983-89; moderator Syracuse Mid. East Dialogue Group, 1981-83; mem. gen. coun. Presbytery of Utica, 1988-89. Gen. coun. Cayuga-Syracuse Presbytery, 1975-83; nat. bd. mem. Am. Friends of Neve Shalom Wahat al Salam, 2004—, co-chair, 2007—; presbyn. commr. Gen. Assembly Presbyn. Ch., 1987. Grantee George Gund Found., 1987, Presbyn. Women's Opportunity Giving, 1987, Joan and Harold Feinbloom Supporting Found. of the Rochester Area Cmty. Found., 1998-2002. Mem. Witherspoon Soc. (steering com. 1974-76), Presbyn. Peace Fellowship (bd. advisors, nat. com. 1972-83). Democrat. Office: Downtown United Presbyn Ch 121 N Fitzhugh St Rochester NY 14614 Office Phone: 585-325-4000. E-mail: revgvw@aol.com.

WEBSTER, HAROLD FRANK, physicist; b. Buffalo, June 25, 1919; s. Stephen and Florence Kathryn (Frank) W.; m. Helen Voorhis, Sept. 15, 1951; children: Sue Helen, Kenneth Harold, Jean Phyllis. BA magna cum laude, U. Buffalo, 1941, MA, 1944; PhD, Cornell U., 1953. Staff mem. Radiation Lab. MIT, Cambridge, 1943-45; rsch. assoc. Rsch. Lab. GE, Schenectady, N.Y., 1951-85, cons. R&D Ctr., 1985-90; ret. Contbg. author: Packaging of Power Semiconductor Devices, 1986, Advances in Electronics, Vol. 17, 1962; patentee in field. U.S. del. to XIII Gen. Assembly of Internat. Sci. Radio Union, London, 1960. Mem. IEEE (WRG Baker award 1958), Am. Phys. Soc., Phi Beta Kappa, Sigma Xi. Achievements include discovering vortex instability in electron sheet beams, deriving current/voltage characteristics of thermionic diodes from space charge distribution, measuring dependence of thermionic emission and wetting on crystal face of metal crystals in cesium vapor. Personal E-mail: websterh@gleneddy.com.

WEBSTER, HENRY DE FOREST, neuroscientist; b. NYC, Apr. 22, 1927; s. Leslie Tillotson and Emily (deForest) W.; m. Marion Havas, June 12, 1951; children: Christopher, Henry, Sally, David, Steven. AB cum laude, Amherst Coll., 1948; MD, Harvard U., 1952. Diplomate in Neurology Am. Bd. Psychiatry Neurology. 1959. Intern Boston City Hosp., 1952-53, resident, 1953-54; resident in neurology Mass. Gen. Hosp., 1954-56, rsch. fellow in neuropathology, 1956-59, prin. investigator NIH rsch. grants, electron micros. studies peripheral neuropathy, 1959-69, mem. staffs; instr. neurology Harvard Med. Sch., Boston, 1959-63, assoc. in neurology, 1963-66, asst. prof. neuropathology, 1966; assoc. prof. neurology U. Miami Sch. Medicine, Fla., 1966-69, prof., 1969; chief sect. cellular neuropathology Nat. Inst. Neurol. Diseases and Stroke, Bethesda, Md., 1969-97; chief Lab. Exptl. Neuropathology, 1984-97; scientist emeritus NIH, 1997—; mem. staff Newton-Wellesley Hosp. Disting. scientist, lectr. dept. anatomy Tulane U. Sch. Medicine, 1973; Royal Coll. lectr. Can. Assn. Neuropathologists, 1982; Saul Korey lectr. Am. Assn. Neuropathologists, 1992; chmn. Winter Conf. on Brain Rsch., 1985-86; head neuropathology del. to visit China in 1990, Citizen Amb. Program, People to People Internat.; exec. com. rsch. group on neuromuscular disease World Fedn. Neurology, 1986-93. Author: (with A. Peters and S.L. Palay) The Fine Structure of the Nervous System, 1970, 3rd edit., 1991, Cellular Neuroscience: Projects and Images, 2006; contbr. sci. articles, revs. to profl. jours. and books. With USNR, 1945—46. Recipient Superior Svc. award USPHS, 1977, A. von Humboldt award Germany, 1985, Sci. award Peripheral Neuropathy Assn., 1994; named hon. prof. Norman Bethune U. of Med. Scis., Chanchun, China, 1991. Mem. Am. Assn. Neuropathologists (v.p. 1976-77, pres. 1978-79, Weil award 1960, Meritorious Contbns. to Neuropathology award 2001), Internat. Soc. Neuropathology (hon., councillor 1976-80, v.p. 1980-84, exec. com. 1980-84, 86-94, pres. 1986-90), Internat. Congress Neuropathology (sec. gen. VIII 1978), Peripheral Nerve Study Group (exec. com. 1975-93, chmn. 1977 meeting), Japanese Soc. Neuropathology (hon.), Am. Neurol. Assn., Am. Acad. Neurology, Royal Soc. Medicine, Am. Soc. Cell Biology, Soc. Neurosci., Rotary Internat., Ausable Club (exec. com. 1964-67). Office: NIH Rm 5B-16 Bldg 10 MSC 1400 Bethesda MD 20892-1400 Office Phone: 301-496-4747. Business E-Mail: websterh@ninds.nih.gov.

WEBSTER, JAMES RANDOLPH, JR., physician; b. Chgo., Aug. 25, 1931; s. James Randolph and Ruth Marian (Burtis) W.; m. Joan Burchfield, Dec. 28, 1954; children: Susan, Donovan, John. BS, U. Chgo.-Northwestern U., 1953; MD, MS, Northwestern U., 1956. Diplomate: Am. Bd. Internal Medicine (sub bd. pulmonary disease and geriatrics). Intern Phila. Gen. Hosp., 1956-57; resident in medicine Northwestern U., 1957-60, NIH fellow in pulmonary disease, 1962-64; chief medicine Northwestern Meml. Hosp., Chgo., 1976—88; prof. medicine Northwestern U. Med. Sch., 1977—, chief gen. med. sect. dept. medicine, 1987-88; chief exec. officer Northwestern Med. Group Practice, 1978-88; dir. Buehler Ctr. on Aging Northwestern U. Med. Ctr., 1988-2000. Chief staff Northwestern Meml. Hosp., 1988-90; pres. Chgo. Bd. Health, 2002—, Inst. Medicine, Chgo., Ill., 2002-04, exec. dir., 2004—; chair Ill. Ad Hoc Com. to Defend Health Care. Contbr. chpts. to books, articles to med. jours. Capt. U.S. Army, 1960-62. Recipient Outstanding Clin. tchr. award Northwestern U. Med. Sch., 1974, 77, 84, 86, Alumni Merit award Northwestern U., 1979, Henry P. Russe-Inst. of Medicine award for exemplary compassion in health care, 1997, Aeschulapian award as Physician of Yr., Anti Defamation League, 1998. Master: ACP (gov. for Ill. 1988—92, chair sub-com. on aging 1993, Clayppole award 1994); mem.: Ill. Geriatrics Soc. (pres. 1992—94), Am. Geriatrics Soc., Alpha Omega Alpha. Office: Inst Medicine Chgo Ste 525 332 S Michigan Ave Chicago IL 60604 Home: PO Box 274 Lakeside MI 49116 Office Phone: 312-663-0040. Business E-Mail: j-webster@northwestern.edu. *Life should best be measured not by how long you live, but how well you function.*

WEBSTER, JEFFREY LEON, graphic designer; b. Idaho Falls, Idaho, Nov. 23, 1941; s. Leon A. and Marjory M. (McAllister) Webster; m. Judith Kess, Apr. 17, 1965; children: Eric J., Marjorie P. Student, Sch. Associated Arts, St. Paul, 1962. Sci. illustrator Mayo Clinic, Rochester, Minn., 1963—66; layout artist Brown & Bigelow, St. Paul, 1966; graphic designer U. Minn., Mpls., 1966—67, U. Calgary, Alta., Canada, 1967—68; sr. artist Control Data Corp., St. Paul, 1968—70; graphic designer Idaho State U., 1970—78; owner, operator studio, Harmony, Minn.; mktg. and advt. cons. to 45 regional and nat. firms, 1978—. Mem. Idaho State U. Meml. Lectureship Com.; artist pub. ednl. exhibits. Mem. Idaho Civic Symphony Bd.; chairperson pub. rels. Unitarian Ch. Rochester, 1991—; bd. dirs. Gift of Life Transplant Ho., Rochester, 1996, Rochester Orch. and Chorale, 1996, Rochester Music Guild, 2007. Recipient Profl. citation, Libr. Congress, 1976, 1st pl. best trucking ad, Overdrive Mag., 1990. Mem.: Sierra Club (nat. agrl. com. 2003—). Home and Office: 13020 241st Ave Harmony MN 55939 Personal E-mail: jlweb@mleaf.net.

WEBSTER, JOHN CROSBY BROWN, minister, educator; b. NYC, July 14, 1935; s. Leslie Tillotson and Emily Johnston (deForest) Webster; m. Ellen Low Purdy (div.); children: Elizabeth Low Webster Shillington, Marilyn White; m. Penelope Stearns, Jan. 3, 1988. BA, Amherst Coll., Mass., 1957; MDiv, Union Theol. Sem., NYC, 1960; MA, Lucknow U., India, 1962; PhD, U. Pa., Phila., 1971. Ordained minister Presbyn. Ch. Supply pastor La Bagh Meth. Ch., Lucknow, 1960—62; lectr. Baring Union Christian Coll., Batata, India, 1963—68, 1971—76; dir. Christian Inst. Sikh Studies, Batata, 1971—76; asst. prof., prof. United Theol. Coll., Bangalore, India, 1977—81; vis. prof. Pitts. Theol. Sem., 1981—83; pastor Crossroads Presbyn. Ch., Waterford, Conn., 1984—94; diaconal worker in India Presbyn. Ch. USA, Louisville, 1994—2001; ret., 2001. Lectr. in ecumenics Union Theol. Sem., 1985—; vice moderator Presbytery So. New England, Presbyn. Ch. (USA), 2003—04, moderator, 2004—05. Editor: The Study of History and College History Teaching, 1965, History for College Students, 1966, History and Contemporary India, 1971, Popular Religion in the Punjab Today, 1974; author: The Christian Community and Change in Nineteenth Century North India, 1976, An Introduction to History, 1977, 2d edit., 1981, The Nirankari Sikhs, 1979, The Dalit Christians: A History, 1992, 2d edit., 1994, Hindi edit., 2004, The Pastor to Dalits, 1995, Studying History, 1997, Religion and Dalit Liberation: An Examination of Perspectives, 1999, 2d edit., 2002; co-author: From Role to Identity: Dalit Christian Women in Transition, 1997; co-editor: Local Dalit Christian History, 2002; editor: Bangalore Theol. Forum, 1977—81, Dalit Internat. Newsletter, 1996—2006. Bd. dirs. Drop-In Learning Ctr., New London, Conn., 1985—91, pres., 1990—91; bd. dirs. Habitat for Humanity Southeastern Conn., 1986—92, Union Theol. Sem., 1989—; mem. Waterford Housing Partnership, 1990—93; bd. dirs. Southeastern Conn. AIDS Project/Alliance for Living, New London, 1993—98, Opportunities Industrialization Ctr. New London County, 2004—; bd. mgrs. Am. Bapt. Hist. Soc., Valley Forge, Pa., 2005—. Recipient Human Rights award, Dalit Liberation Edn. Trust, Chennai, India, 1997; travel grantee, Am. Coun. Learned Socs., NEH, 1981. Mem.: Assn. Profs. Mission (v.p. 1991—92, pres. 1992—93), Assn. Presbyterians in Cross-Cultural Mission (pres. 1984—94). Democrat. Avocations: tennis, hiking.

WEBSTER, JOHN GOODWIN, biomedical engineering educator, researcher; b. Plainfield, NJ, May 27, 1932; s. Franklin Folger and Emily Sykes (Boody) W.; m. Nancy Egan, Dec. 27, 1954; children: Paul, Robin, Mark, Lark BEE, Cornell U., 1953; MSEE, U. Rochester, 1965, PhD, 1967. Engr. North American Aviation, Downey, Calif., 1954-55; engr. Boeing Airplane Co., Seattle, 1955-59, Radiation Inc., Melbourne, Fla., 1959-61; staff engr. Mitre Corp., Bedford, Mass., 1961-62, IBM Corp., Kingston, NY, 1962-63; asst. prof. elec. engring. U. Wis., Madison, 1967-70, assoc. prof. elec. engring., 1970-73, prof. elec. and computer engring., 1973-99, prof. biomed. engring., 1999—2001, prof. emeritus biomed. engring., 2001—. Author: (with others) Medicine and Clinical Engineering, 1977, Sensors and Signal Conditioning, 1991, 2d edit., 2001, Analog Signal Processing, 1999; editor: Medical Instrumentation: Application and Design, 3d edit., 1998, Clinical Engineering: Principles and Practices, 1979, Design of Microcomputer-Based Medical Instrumentation, 1981, Therapeutic Medical Devices: Application and Design, 1982; Electronic Devices for Rehabilitation, 1985; Interfacing Sensors to the IBM-PC, 1988, Encyclopedia of Medical Devices and Instrumentation, 2d edit., 2006, Tactile Sensors for Robotics and Medicine, 1988, Electrical Impedance Tomography, 1990, Teaching Design in Electrical Engineering, 1990, Prevention of Pressure Sores, 1991, Design of Cardiac Pacemakers, 1995, Design of Pulse Oximeters, 1997, The Measurement Instrumentation, and Sensors Handbook, 1999, Encyclopedia of Electrical and Electronics Engineering, 1999, Mechanical Variables Measurement, 2000, Minimally Invasive Medical Technology, 2001, Electrical Measurement, Signal Processing and Displays, 2004, Bioinstrumentation, 2004. Recipient Rsch. Career Devel. award NIH, 1971-76; NIH fellow, 1963-67; recipient Western Electric Fund award Am. Soc. Engring. Edn., 1978, Best Reference Work award, 1999, Theo C. Pilkington Outstanding Educator award, 1994. Fellow IEEE (3d Millennium medal 2000, IEEE-EMBS Career achievement award 2001), Am. Inst. Med. and Biol. Engring., Inst. Physics, Instrument Soc. Am. (Donald P. Eckman Edn. award 1974), Assn. for Advancement Med. Instrumentation (Found. Laufman-Greatbatch prize 1996). Democrat. Unitarian Universalist. Office: Univ Wis Dept Biomed Engring 1550 Engineering Dr Madison WI 53706-1609 Home Phone: 608-233-8410; Office Phone: 608-263-1574. Business E-Mail: webster@engr.wisc.edu.

WEBSTER, LARRY RUSSELL, artist; b. Arlington, Mass., Mar. 18, 1930; s. James Burpee and Ethel (Hughes) W.; m. Rosemary Siekman, June 13, 1953; children: Wendy Lyn, Ricky Stewart, Holly Jean. B.F.A., Mass. Coll. Art, 1952; MS, Boston U., 1953. Package designer Union Bag & Paper Co., NYC, 1953-54; art dir., graphic designer, v.p., dir. Thomas Todd Co., Boston, 1956-78; asst. prof. design Mass. Coll. Art, 1964-66. Paintings in permanent collections including, DeCordova Mus., Lincoln, Mass., Grand Rapids (Mich.) Art Mus., Springfield (Mo.) Art Mus., Davenport (Iowa) Municipal Gallery, Colby Coll. Art Mus., Waterville, Maine, Peabody Mus. Salem, Mass.; work represented in The Best of Watercolor 2, 1997. Served with U.S. Army, 1954-56. Recipient Silver medal Am. Watercolor Soc., 1968, 72; recipient C.F.S. award, 1963, Ed Whitney award, 1973, High winds medal, 1983, Rhinehold award, 1967, Ranger Fund Purchase prize, 1965, Adolph and Clara Obrig prize in watercolor NAD, 1970, gold medal Allied Artists Am., 1971, Washington Sch. Art award, 1977, Lena Newcastle award, 1978, Colo. Watermedia award, 1978, Golden award Rocky Mountain Nat. Watermedia Exhbn., 1979, Lorraine Fetzer Meml. award, 2d prize N.Am. Open Competition, 1990. Mem. NAD (assoc. 1974-91, academician, 1991-), Soc. Printers Boston (past mem. council), Am. Watercolor Soc. (Dolphin fellow 1981), Boston Watercolor Soc. (pres. 1974-75), Guild of Boston Artists.

WEBSTER, LESLIE TILLOTSON, JR., pharmacologist, educator; b. NYC, Mar. 31, 1926; s. Leslie Tillotson and Emily (de Forest) W.; m. Alice Katharine Holland, June 24, 1955; children: Katharine White, Susan Holland Webster Van Drie, Leslie Tillotson III, Romi Anne. BA, Amherst Coll., 1947, Sc.D. (hon.), 1982; student, Union Coll., 1944; MD, Harvard U., 1948. Diplomate: Am. Bd. Internal Medicine. Rotating intern Cleve. City Hosp., 1948-49, jr. asst. resident in medicine, 1949-50; asst. resident medicine Bellevue Hosp., NYC, 1952-53; research fellow medicine Harvard and Boston City Hosp. Thorndike Meml. Lab., 1953-55; from demonstrator to instr. medicine Sch. of Medicine Western Res. U., 1955-60; research assoc. to sr. instr. biochemistry Case Western Res. U. Sch. Medicine, 1957—60, asst. prof. medicine, 1960-70, asst. prof. biochemistry, 1960-65, asst. prof. pharmacology, 1965-67, assoc. prof., 1967-70, prof. pharmacology, 1976-92, chmn. pharmacology dept., 1976-91, prof. medicine, 1980-86, prof. emeritus pharmacology dept., 1992—; rsch. prof. pediat., divsn. pediat. pharmacology and critical care Rainbow Babies and Children's Hosp., Case Western Res. U. Sch. Medicine, 1992—2006, cons. dept. pharmacology, 2007—. Prof., chmn. pharmacology dept. Northwestern U. Med. and Dental Sch., 1970—76; dir. med. scientist tng. program Case Western Res. U. Sch. Medicine, 1979—92; mem. gastroenterology nutritional tng. grants com. NIAMD, NIH, 1965—69; mem. sci. working group on schistosomiasis WHO, 1977—83, chmn. subsect. on chemotherapy biochemistry, 1977—83; mem. exec. com. Gt. Neglected Diseases Network, Rockefeller Found., 1978—86; mem. cellular and molecular basis of disease rev. com. NIGMS, NIH, 1984—88; cons. World Bank, Laos, 2003. Contbr. articles to sci. jour. Served to lt. med. corps. USNR, 1950-52. Russell M. Wilder fellow Nat. Vitamin Found., 1956-59; Sr. USPHS Research fellow, 1959-61; USPHS Rsch. Career Devel. awardee, 1961-69; Macy faculty scholar, 1980-81. Mem. ACP (life), Central Soc. Clin. Rsch. Coalition (emeritus), Am. Soc. Clin. Investigation (emeritus), Am. Soc. Biochemistry and Molecular Biology (emeritus), Assn. Med. Sch. Pharmacology (emeritus), Am. Soc. Pharmacology and Exptl. Therapeutics (emeritus), Alpha Omega Alpha (hon.). Home: 12546 Cedar Rd No 4 Cleveland Heights OH 44106-3294 Office: Dept Pharmacology Case We Res U 10900 Euclid Ave Cleveland OH 44106-4965 Home Phone: 216-932-6219. Business E-Mail: ltw2@case.edu.

WEBSTER, MURRAY ALEXANDER, JR., sociologist, educator; b. Manila, Philippines, Dec. 10, 1941; s. M.A. and Patricia (Morse) W. AB, Stanford U., 1963, MA, 1966, PhD, 1968. Asst. prof. social rels. Johns Hopkins U., Balt., 1968-74, assoc. prof., 1974-76; prof. sociology, adj. prof. psychology U. S.C., Columbia, 1976-86; vis. prof. sociology Stanford U., 1981-82, 85, 88-89; sr. lectr. San Jose State U., 1987-89; dir. sociology program NSF, 1989-91,99-2000; prof. sociology U. N.C., Charlotte, 1993—. Author (with Barbara Sobieszek): Soruces of Self-Evaluation, 1974; author: Actions and Actors, 1975; author: (with Martha Foschi) Status Generalization: New Theory and Research, 1988; author: (with Jane Sell) Laboratory Experiments in the Social Sciences, 2007; mem. editl. bd. Social Sci. Rsch., 1975—, Am. Jour. Sociology, 1976—79, Social Psychology Quar., 1977—80, 1993—. Recipient First Citizens Bank Scholars award, 2003; NIH fellow, 1966-68; grantee NSF, Nat. Inst. Edn. Mem.: N.Y. Acad. Scis., So. Sociol. Soc., Am. Sociol. Assn. Office: Univ NC Dept Sociology Charlotte NC 28223 Office Phone: 704-687-4079. Business E-Mail: mawebste@email.uncc.edu.

WEBSTER, NORMAN ERIC, journalist, foundation administrator; b. Summerside, PEI, Can., June 4, 1941; s. Eric and Elizabeth (Paterson) W.; m. Pat Roop, 1966; children: David, Andrew, Derek, Gillian, Hilary. BA, Bishop's U., Que., Can.; MA, St. John's Coll., Oxford, Eng. Corr. Globe and Mail, Que. and Ottawa, Ont., Canada; editor Globe Mag., Toronto, Ont.; corr. Globe and Mail, Peking, China, 1969-71, columnist Ont. affairs Toronto, European corr. London, editor-in-chief Toronto, 1983-89, Montreal (Que.) Gazette, 1989-93; pres. R. Howard Webster Found., Montreal, 1993—. Chancellor U. P.E.I., 1996-2005; chmn. North-South Inst., Ottawa, 1998-2000; bd. dirs. Internat. Press Inst., Vienna, Montreal Children's Hosp. Found., McGill U. Health Ctr. Found., Asia Pacific Found. Can., Commonwealth Journalists Assn., Can. Inst. for Advanced Rsch., Bishop's U., Michener Found. Recipient Nat. Newspaper award for Peking corr., 1971, for editl. writing, 1988; Rhodes scholar; mem. Order of Can. Office: R Howard Webster Found Ste 2912 1155 Rene Levesque Blvd W Montreal PQ Canada H3B 2L5 Office Phone: 514-866-2424.

WEBSTER, OWEN WRIGHT, chemist; b. Devils Lake, ND, Mar. 25, 1929; s. Daniel Milton and Maude May (Wright) W.; m. Lillian Brostek; children: Ellen, Anne, John, James, Mary. BS in Chemistry, N.D. U., 1951, DSc (hon.), 1986; PhD in Chemistry, Pa. State U., 1955. Research chemist E.I. Du Pont de Nemours, Wilmington, Del., 1955-74, group leader, 1974-79, research supr., 1979-84, research leader, 1984-95, Du Pont fellow, 1986-95; ret., 1995. Adj. prof. dept. chemistry U. Ala., 2003. Patentee in field; contbr. articles to profl. jours. Recipient Chem. Pioneer award Am. Inst. Chemists, 1995. Fellow AAAS, Am. Chem. Soc. (chmn. Del. sect.

1975-76, Excellence in Resch. award 1987, Applied Polymer Sci. award 1993); mem. Sigma Xi. Republican. Roman Catholic. Avocations: chess, bridge, golf. Personal E-mail: owwebster@aol.com.

WEBSTER, PETER BRIDGMAN, lawyer; b. Boston, Jan. 11, 1941; s. John Archibald and Mildred (Bridgman) W.; m. Elaine Gerber, Dec. 20, 1964 (dec.); m. Margaret Dana, Dec. 28, 2004; children: Amy Elizabeth, Peter Bridgman, Timothy James. AB, Bowdoin Coll., Brunswick, Maine, 1962; LLB, Cornell U., Ithaca, NY, 1965. Bar: Maine 1965, U.S. Dist. Ct. Maine 1965. From assoc. to of counsel Verrill Dana, LLP, Portland, Maine, 1965—. Mem. grievance commn. Maine Bd. Bar Overseers, Augusta, 1979-88, chmn., 1984-88, mem. 1986-94, chmn. 1990-92; adj. prof. law U. Maine, Portland, 1981; mem. Maine Commn. on Ethics and Govtl. Practices, 1991-2002, chair 1997-2002, chair Lawyers' Fund for Client Protection, 1997—. Recipient Alumni Svc. award Bowdoin Coll., 1999. Home: 1 Ship Channel Rd South Portland ME 04106 Office Phone: 207-774-4000. Business E-Mail: pwebster@verrilldana.com.

WEBSTER, PETER DAVID, judge; b. Framingham, Mass., Feb. 12, 1949; s. Waldo John and Helen Anne (Borovek) W.; m. Michele Page Hernandez, Jan. 13, 1989; 1 stepchild, Alana Perryman. BS, Georgetown U., 1971; JD, Duke U., 1974; LLM, U. Va., 1995. Bar: Fla. 1974, U.S. Dist. Ct. (mid. dist.) Fla. 1975, U.S. Ct. Appeals (5th cir.) 1975, U.S. Dist. Ct. (so. dist.) Fla. 1977, U.S. Dist. Ct. (no. dist.) Fla. 1978, U.S. Supreme Ct. 1978, U.S. Ct. Appeals (11th cir.) 1981. Law clk. U.S. Dist. Judge, Jacksonville, Fla., 1974-75; assoc. Bedell, Bedell, Dittmar, Smith & Zehmer, Jacksonville, 1975-78; ptnr. Bedell, Bedell, Dittmar & Zehmer, Jacksonville, 1978-85; cir. judge State Fla., Jacksonville, 1986-91; judge Dist. Ct. of Appeal, First Dist., State of Fla., Tallahassee, 1991—. Master of bench Chester Bedell Am. Inn Ct., 1988-91; master of bench Tallahassee Am. Inn Ct., 1992-2002, pres. 1999-2000; master of bench E. Robert Williams Am. Inn Ct., 2007—; adj. prof. Fla. Coastal Sch. Law, 1997—; mem. com. standard jury instrns. civil cases Fla. Supreme Ct., 1979-2001, chmn. 1999-2000, mem. com. trial ct. info. sys., 1986-91, com. confidentiality records jud. br., 1993-95, task force mgmt. cases complex litig., 2006—, mem. jud. mgmt. coun. Fla., 2006—, chmn. com. jud. evaluations, 2006—. Contbg. author: Sanctions: Rule 11 and Other Powers, 1986, Florida Criminal Rules and Practice Manual, 1990. Bd. dirs. Jacksonville Area Legal Aid, Inc., 1978-82, River Region Human Svcs., Inc., Jacksonville, 1986-88; mem. adv. bd. P.A.C.E. Ctr. for Girls, Inc., Jacksonville, 1986-91; com. mem. Shawnee dist. North Fla. coun. Boy Scouts Am., 1974-78; mem. delinquency task force Mayor's Commn. on Children and Youth, City of Jacksonville, 1988-91; officer, mem. exec. bd. Suwanee River Area coun. Boy Scouts, 1991-96. Mem. Am. Judicature Soc. (bd. dirs. 2002—), Fla. Conf. Appellate Judges, Jacksonville Bar Assn., Tallahassee Bar Assn., Phi Beta Kappa, Phi Alpha Theta, Phi Eta Sigma. Office: 1st Dist Ct Appeal 301 Martin Luther King Blvd Tallahassee FL 32399-1850 Home Phone: 850-668-0079; Office Phone: 850-487-1000.

WEBSTER, ROBERT BYRON, lawyer; b. Mar. 9, 1932; s. Don B. and Glennie E. (Cole) Webster; children: Anne Elizabeth, Allison Dee, Peter Hey, James Byron. BA, U. Mich., Ann Arbor, 1955, JD, 1957. Bar: Mich. 1958, U.S. Dist. Ct. (ea. dist.) Mich., 1958, U.S. Dist. Ct. (we. dist.) Mich. 1972, U.S. Ct. Appeals (6th cir.) 1958, U.S. Supreme Ct. 1972. Law clk. U.S. Dist. Ct., 1957-59; assoc., ptnr. Hill, Lewis, Adams, Goodrich & Tait, 1959-73; judge Cir. Ct., Oakland County, 1973—82; chief judge, 1977; ptnr. Hill Lewis PC, 1982—95; chmn. Clark Hill PLC, 1995—2002; shareholder Giarmarco, Mullins & Horten, PC, Troy, Mich., 2003—. Chmn. Supreme Ct. Com. to Revise Ct Rules, 1975-78; mem. Mich. Ct. Rule Adv. Com., 1984; chair, State Bar Appellate Task Force, 1993; trustee, chmn. Horizon Health Systems, 1983-2002; co-chair Legis. Commn. on Cts. in 21st Century, 1990. Chmn. Oakland Rep. Com., 1970-71, commr. Nat. Commn. on Uniform State Laws, 1995—; chmn. State Officers Compensation Commn., 1998-2002; trustee Family and Children Svcs. Oakland County, 1976-84; mem. Oakland Cmty. Mental Health Bd. 1971-73; trustee Henry Ford Health Sys., 1995-2002; co-chair jud. qualifications com. State Bar, 1990—. With USAF, 1951-53. Fellow Am. Bar Found. (life), State Bar Mich. Found. (life), Am. Coll. Trial Lawyers; mem. ABA (mem. ho. dels. 1990-2004), Am. Law Inst.,State Bar Mich. (commr. 1982-90, v.p. 1987-88, pres. elect 1988-89, pres. 1989-90), Oakland Bar Assn. Republican. Office: 101 W Big Beaver Rd 10th Fl Troy MI 48084-5280 Office Phone: 248-457-7050. Personal E-mail: rbwebster@ameritech.net. Business E-Mail: rwebster@gmhpc.com.

WEBSTER, ROBERT G., virologist, educator; b. Balclutha, New Zealand, July 5, 1932; BSc, Otago U., New Zealand, 1955, MSc, 1957; PhD, Australian Nat. U., Canberra, 1962. Virologist New Zealand Dept. Agr., 1958—59; postdoctoral fellow (Fulbright scholar) dept. epidemiology U. Mich. Sch. Pub. Health, Ann Arbor, Mich., 1962—63; rsch. fellow dept. microbiol. Australian Nat. U. John Curtain Med. Sch., Canberra, 1964—66, fellow dept. microbiol., 1966—67; assoc. prof. dept. microbiol. U. Tenn. Med. Units, Memphis, 1968—74; prof. dept. microbiol. U. Tenn. Ctr. Health Scis., Memphis, 1974—78, prof. depts. microbiol. and immunology, 1978—85; Rose Marie Thomas chair dept. virology and molecular biology St. Jude Children's Rsch. Hosp., Memphis, 1988—. Assoc. mem. lab. immunology St. Jude Children's Rsch. Hosp., Memphis, 1968—69, mem. labs. virology and immunology, 1969—75, mem. divsn. virology, 1975—78, mem. depts. virology and molecular biology, 1978—88; Fogarty internat. sr. fellow Nat. Inst. Med. Rsch., Med. Rsch. Coun., London, 1978—79; dir. WHO Collaborating Ctr. Studies on the Ecology of Influenza Viruses in Lower Animals and Birds. Contbr. articles to sci. jours. Named a Rsch. Leader within Sci. Am. 50, 2005; recipient Bristol-Meyers Squibb award, 2002, Disting. Biotechnologist of Yr. award, New Zealand Biotechnology Assn., 2006. Fellow: Royal Soc. Medicine, Royal Soc., London, Royal Soc., New Zealand (hon.); mem.: AAAS, Am. Soc. Virology, Am. Soc. Microbiol., NAS. Achievements include research in the emergence and control of influenza; viral immunology; discovery of link between human and avian influenza viruses. Office: St Jude Childrens Rsch Hosp 332 N Lauderdale St Memphis TN 38105-2794 Office Phone: 901-495-3400. E-mail: robert.webster@stjude.org. *

WEBSTER, ROBERT KENLY, lawyer; b. NYC, May 16, 1933; s. Francis Kenly and Mary Louise (Rathbone) W.; m. Sally Irene Stratton, Apr. 16, 1960; children: Timothy Kenly, Kimberly Anne. AB, Princeton U., 1955; LLB, U. Va., 1960. Assoc. Cadwalader, Wickersham & Taft, NYC, 1960-65; asst. U.S. atty. Dept. of Justice, Washington, 1965-68; prin. dep. gen. counsel Dept. of Army, Washington, 1968-73; ptnr. Kennedy & Webster, Washington, 1973-81, Shaw, Pittman, Potts & Trowbridge, Washington, 1981-98; sole practice Washington, 1999—. Spl. investigator Iran FMS program Sec. of Def., Washington, 1977; advisor conflict of interest issues Watergate defendants Dept. Justice, Washington, 1977. Gen. counsel Princeton (N.J.) Project 55, Inc., 1989—. Lt. j.g. USN, 1955—57. Mem. ABA, ATLA, Fed. Bar Assn., Met. Club. Avocations: pottery, reading, travel, tennis.

WEBSTER, ROBERT LEE, accounting educator, researcher; b. Little Rock, Oct. 4, 1946; s. Daniel and Mildred LaNette (Patishall) W.; m. Mary Katherine Fiske, Aug. 26, 1967; children: Elizabeth Ashley, Jessica Lee. BA, Ouachita Bapt. U., 1968; MBA, Syracuse U., 1975; MS, L.I. U., 1986; DBA, La. Tech. U., 1993. Cert. govt. fin. mgr. Commd. 2d lt. U.S. Army, 1968, advanced through grades to lt. col., 1985; dep. contr. U.S. Army Electronics R&D Command, Adelphi, Md., 1975-80; chief of ops., comms. security NATO, Mons, Belgium, 1980-83; asst. prof. acctg. and fin. U.S. Mil. Acad., West Point, N.Y., 1983-86; prof. mil. sci. Henderson State U., Arkadelphia, Ark., 1986-88; ret. U.S. Army, 1988; asst. prof. acctg. Henderson State U., 1988-91, chair dept. acctg., econs. and bus. edn., 1991-93; chair dept. acctg. Ouachita Bapt. U., Arkadelphia, 1993—, George Young chair bus., 1995—. Bd. dirs. Hospitality Care Ctr., Arkadelphia, 1992-93; speaker in field. Editor Jour. Bus. & Behavioral Scis., 1995; author articles. Recipient Dean's award for acad. achievement, L.I. U., 1986; Army scholar, Syracuse U., 1974—75, Exch. Educator to Republic of Kazakhstan, 1994—95. Mem. Nat. Social Sci. Assn. (bd. govs. 1992-2002, Outstanding Conf. Paper award 1992), Am. Acctg. Assn. (pres. Southwest region 2006-07), Assn. Govt. Accts., Beta Gamma Sigma, Sigma Beta Delta. Avocations: coin collecting/numismatics, exercise. Home: 724 Colonial Dr Bryant AR 72022 Office: Ouachita Bapt U PO Box 3689 Arkadelphia AR 71998 Office Phone: 870-245-5254. Business E-Mail: websterb@obu.edu.

WEBSTER, RONALD D., diversified financial services company executive; b. Richwood, W.Va., Aug. 9, 1949; s. Ralph D. and Victoria M. (Cisek) Webster; m. Donna M. Falkenthal, Aug. 9, 1975; 1 child, Kathryn E. BSBA with high distinction, U. Ill., Chgo., 1971; MBA, U. Chgo., 1980. CPA Ill. Sr. auditor Arthur Andersen & Co., Chgo., 1970-75; dir. corp. reporting Trans Union Corp., Lincolnshire, Ill., 1975-77; asst. group contr. Union Tank Car Co. subs. of Trans Union Corp., Chgo., 1977-83; treas. Tel. and Data Sys., Inc., Chgo., 1983-87, 88-97, v.p., 1992-97; v.p., CFO Ideal Sch. Supply Corp., Oak Lawn, Ill., 1987-88; sr. v.p., CFO 21st Century Telecom. Group, Inc., Chgo., 1997-2000; sr. v.p. ctrl. region RCN Corp., Chgo., 2000-01; exec. v.p., CFO 02wireless Solutions, INc., Atlanta, 2001—02, NuVox Comms., St. Louis, 2002—04; ptrn. Tatum LLC, 2004—. Mem.: Ill. CPA Soc., Am. Soc. CPAs (Elijah Watt Sells nat. honorable mention 1973), Fin. Execs. Internat., Beta Gamma Sigma. Personal E-mail: ronwebster@comcast.net.

WEBSTER, RONIE RUTH, secondary school educator; b. Springfield, Mass., Oct. 2, 1951; d. Walter H. and Veronica M. Renner; m. Lawrence Webster, July 16, 1977. BA in French, Westfield State Coll., Mass., 1969—73. Cert. tchr. Mass., 1973. Spanish tchr. Monson HS, Mass., 1973—. Recipient Global Educator of Yr. award, Global Edn. Ctr., U. Mass., 1993, 1995, Christa's Tchrs. Honor Roll award, Framingham State Coll., 1996, Stanford Tchr. Tribute award, Stanford U., 2003, Pioneer Valley Excellence in Tchg. award, Grinspoon Found., 2005. Mem.: Mass. ASCD, ASCD, NEA, Mass. Fgn. Lang. Assn., Nat. Network Early Lang. Learning, Mass. Tchrs. Assn., Am. Assn. Tchrs. French, Am. Assn. Tchrs. Spanish & Portuguese, Am. Coun. Tchg. Fgn. Langs., Fgn. Lang. Tchrs. We. Mass. Collaborative (clk. 1988—91), Mass. Fgn. Lang. Assn. (life; newsletter editor 1990—, comm. dir. 2001—, Disting. Svc. award 2001). Home: 41 Glenn Dr Wilbraham MA 01095-1439 Office: Monson HS 55 Margaret St Monson MA 01057 Home Phone: 413-596-9284. Personal E-mail: ronie@mafla.org. Business E-Mail: websterr@monsonschools.com.

WEBSTER, SHARON B., economist; b. Wildwood, Fla., Aug. 23, 1937; d. James McWilliams and Marion (Hallbrook) Boen. BA in Polit. sci., Econ. and Psychology, U. Fla., 1959; vis. doctoral fellow, Princeton U., 1964—65; PhD, U. Va., 1965. Asst. prof. No. Mich. U., Marquette, 1962—64, U. Md., 1964—66, Hollins Coll., Roanoke, Va., 1966—71; prof. Fed. Exec. Inst., Charlottesville, Va., 1971—72; mgr. internat. program Dept. Treasury, Washington, 1972—74; economist Econ., Stats. and Coop. Svc. U.S. Dept. Agr., Washington, 1974—79; mem. Presdl. Commn. for Exec. Exch., 1979—80; dir. internat. econ. Occidental Petroleum Corp., LA, 1980—83; investment banker, account exec. Johnston, Lemon and Co., Inc., Washington, 1983—88; fin. cons. Shearson Lehman Hutton, Washington, 1988—. Mem. adv. bd. Pres.'s Caribbean Basin Initiative, 1982; chmn. bd. dirs. NATA, Inc.; bd. dirs. Genta, Inc., NABE; pres., CEO A.A. Global; bd. advisors Sintal Comm. USA, Inc., Internat. Trade Coun.; bd. advisors Patterson Sch. Diplomacy and Internat. Commerce U. Ky.; bd. advisors Consumer Health and Svcs. Am., Inc. Contbr. articles to profl. jours. Recipient Presdl. award Pvt. Sector Iniative, 1982; NDEA fellow. Mem.: AAUP, Assn. Polit. Risk Analysts, Washington Soc. Money Mgrs., Soc. Internat. Devel., Internat. Studies Assn., Nat. Assn. Bus. Economists, Am. Polit. Sci. Assn., Am. Assn. Agrl. Economists, Internat. Assn. Energy Economists, Internat. Policy Inst. (v.p. 1977—), Fed. Exec. Inst. Alumni Assn., Pres.'s Exec. Exch. Assn., Nat. Coun. Career Women, Internat. Club, Army Navy Club, Capital Spkrs. Club. Home: The Winthrop # 602 1727 Massachusetts Ave NW Washington DC 20036-2153 Office: AA Global 9039 Furrow Ave Ellicott City MD 21042-1841

WEBSTER, STEPHEN BURTIS, dermatologist, educator; b. Chgo., Dec. 3, 1935; s. James Randolph Webster and Ruth Marion (Burtis) Holmes; m. Katherine Griffith Webster, Apr. 4, 1959; children: David Randolph, Margaret Elizabeth, James Lucian. BS, Northwestern U., 1957, MD, 1960. Diplomate Am. Bd. Dermatology (bd. dirs. 1992—, v.p. 1997-98, pres.). Intern Colo. Gen. Hosp., Denver, 1960-61; resident Walter Reed Gen. Hosp., Washington, 1962-65; staff physician Henry Ford Hosp., Detroit, 1969-71, Gundersen Lutheran Med. Ctr., La Crosse, 1971—; assoc. clin. prof. U. Wis., Madison, 1976—; clin. prof. U. Minn., Mpls., 1978—. Lt. col. U.S. Army, 1962-69. Fellow Am. Acad. Dermatology (sec.-treas. 1985-88, pres. 1991); mem. AMA, Am. Dermatol. Assn. (pres. 1996-97), Am. Bd. Dermatology (v.p. 1997-98, pres. 1999-2000, assoc. exec. dir. 2001—), Wis. Med. Soc., La Crosse County Med. Soc., Soc. Investigative Dermatology, Alpha Omega Alpha. Republican. Congregationalist. Avocations: bagpipes, model trains. Home: N2062 Wedgewood Dr E La Crosse WI 54601-7175 Office: Gundersen Clinic Ltd 1836 South Ave La Crosse WI 54601-5494 Business E-Mail: sbwebste@gundluth.org.

WEBSTER, SUSAN, lawyer; b. Hartford, Conn., Dec. 21, 1956; BA, Wesleyan U., 1977; JD, Fordham U., 1984. Bar: N.Y. 1985. Ptnr., corp. Cravath, Swaine & Moore, NYC. Mem. ABA, N.Y. State Bar Assn., Assn. of Bar of City of N.Y. Office: Cravath Swaine & Moore Worldwide Plz 825 8th Ave Fl 38 New York NY 10019-7475 Office Phone: 212-474-1660. Office Fax: 212-474-3700. Business E-Mail: swebster@cravath.com.

WEBSTER, THOMAS GLENN, psychiatrist, educator; b. Topeka, Jan. 23, 1924; s. Guy Welland and Iva Amanda (Keefover) W.; m. Mary Tupper Dooly, June 27, 1948; children— Warnie Louise, Guy Weyman, David Michael AB, Ft. Hays State Coll., 1946; MD, Wayne State U., 1949. Intern Los Angeles County Gen. Hosp., Calif., 1949-50; resident in psychiatry Mass. Mental Health Ctr., Boston, 1953-55, resident in child psychiatry, 1955-56, James Jackson Putnam Children's Ctr., Boston, 1956-58; dir. presch. program for retarded children Greater Boston, 1958-62; coordinator 3d yr. med. student psychiatry clerkship Harvard U. Med. Sch.-Mass. Mental Health Ctr., Boston, 1960-63; practice medicine specializing in psychiatry Boston, 1953-62, Bethesda, Md., 1963-72, Washington, 1972—; tng. specialist psychiatry, then chief continuing edn. br. NIMH, Bethesda, Md., 1963-72; prof. psychiatry George Washington U., Washington, 1972-86, chmn. dept. psychiatry and behavioral scis., 1972-75, prof. emeritus, 1986-96. Vis. prof. Harvard U. Med. Sch., 1980-83, McLean Hosp., 1980-86; U.S.-Poland exchange health scientist, 1981 Pres. Woodhaven Citizens Assn., 1971-72. Served with AUS, 1943-46; as sr. asst. surgeon USPHS, 1951-53 Fellow Am. Coll. Psychiatrists, Am. Coll. Psychoanalysts; mem. Assn. Acad. Psychiatry (pres. 1976-78), Group Advancement Psychiatry Home: 8506 Woodhaven Blvd Bethesda MD 20817-3117

WEBSTER, WILLIAM G., JR., career military officer; b. Baton Rouge, La., July 3, 1951; BS, U.S. Mil. Acad., 1974. Commd. 2d lt. U.S. Army, 1974, advanced through grades to brig. gen., tank co. comdr. Fort Polk, La., 1974—78, ops. and plans officer Seventh Army Combined Arms Tng. Ctr., 1979—82, ops. officer 3-64 Armor, 3d Inf. Divsn. Germany, 1979—82, asst. G-3 and brigade ops. officer 24th Inf. Divsn. Ft. Stewart, Ga., 1984—87, joint staff War Plans Divsn. Washington, 1988—91, comdr. 3d bn., 77th armor in 4th inf. divsn., 1991-93; sr. armor observer contr. Cobra Team Nat. Tng. Ctr., Ft. Irwin, Calif., 1993-94; comdr. 1st brigade, 1st cavalry divsn. Ft. Hood, 1995-97; asst. divsn. comdr. 3d Inf. Divsn., Ft. Stewart, Ga., 1997-98; comdr. Ft. Irwin and Nat. Tng. Ctr., 1998—2000; deployed Ops. Desert Thunder U.S. Army, 1998, Army's dir. tng. Office Dep. Chief of Staff G-3, 2000—01, dep. J-3 U.S. Ctrl. Command Operation Enduring Freedom Afghanistan, 2001—02, dep. comdg. gen. for ops. Third U.S. Army, Combined Forces Land Component Command, Operation Iraqi Freedom Kuwait, 2002—03, Iraq, 2002—03, comdg. gen. 3d Inf. Divsn. Ft. Stewart and Hunter Army Airfield, 2003—. Decorated Legion of Merit with 4 oak leaf clusters, Air Assault badge, Parachutist badge, Def. Superior Svc. medal, Armed Forces Expeditionary medal; recipient Bronze Star.

WEBSTER, WILLIAM HEDGCOCK, lawyer, former CIA director; b. St. Louis, Mar. 6, 1924; s. Thomas M. and Katherine (Hedgcock) W.; m. Drusilla Lane, May 5, 1950 (dec. 1984); children: Drusilla Lane Busch, William Hedgcock, Katherine Hagee Roessle; m. Lynda Clugston, Oct. 20, 1990. AB, Amherst Coll., 1947; JD, Washington U., 1949; LLD (hon.), Amherst Coll., 1975, Washington U., 1978, William Wood Coll., 1978, DePauw U., 1978, Drury Coll., Columbia Coll., U. Dayton, U. Notre Dame, Center Coll., Dickinson Coll., U. Miami, DePaul U., Am. U., John Jay Coll., Westminster Coll., Georgetown U., Rockhurst Coll., Pepperdine U. Bar: Mo. 1949, US Supreme Ct. 1960, DC 1981. With Armstrong, Teasdale, Kramer & Vaughan (and predecessors), St. Louis, 1949-50, 52-59, 61-70; US atty. ((ea. dist.) Mo US Dept. Justice, 1960-61; judge US Dist. Ct. (ea. dist. Mo.), 1971-73, US Ct. Appeals (8th cir.), 1973-78; dir. FBI, 1978-87, CIA, 1987-91; sr. ptnr. Milbank, Tweed, Hadley & McCloy, LLP, Washington, 1991—2005, consulting ptnr., 2005—; chair Homeland Security Adv. Coun., 2006—. Mem. Mo. Bd. Law Examiners, 1964-69, mem. adv. com. on criminal rules, 1971-78, mem. ct. adminstrs. com., 1975-78; bd. dirs. Anheuser-Busch Cos., Maritz Inc., Pinkertons Inc., T.L.C. Beatrice Internat. Holdings Inc., Nextwave, Inc., Regulatory DataCorp Internat.; mem. adv. bd., Diligence LLC; chmn. Pub. Co. Acctg. Oversight Bd., 2002. Trustee Washington U., 1974; bd. dirs. Atlantic Coun., Nat. Legal Ctr. Pub. Interest, Nat. Symphony Assn., Coun. Fgn. Rels.; bd. dirs., chmn. Police Found.; hon. life pres. Big Bros. Orgn. St. Louis; bd. dirs. Big Bros. Am., 1966, hon. bd. dirs., 1978. Lt. USN, 1943—46, WWII, lt. USN, 1950—52, Korean War. Recipient Disting. Alumnus award Washington U., 1977, Stein award Fordham U., Law award U. Va., Theodore Roosevelt award for Excellence in Pub. Svc., Internat. Platform Assn., 1983, Jefferson award for the Greatest Pub. Svc. by an Elected or Apptd. Ofcl., 1984, Freedoms Found. Nat. Svc. medal, 1985, Disting. Intelligence medal, 1991, Presdl. Medal of Freedom, 1991, Nat. Security medal, 1991, Silver Buffalo award Boy Scouts Am., Disting. Svc. award, Am. Legion, Justice award, Am. Judicature Soc., 2001, Am. Bar Assn. medal, 2002; named Father of Yr., 1986, Man of Yr., St. Louis Globe Dem., 1980. Fellow Am. Bar Found., Am. Coll. Trial Lawyers (hon.); mem. ABA (chmn. sect. on corp. banking and bus. law 1977-78), FBA, Mo. Bar Assn., St. Louis Bar Assn., Am. Law Inst. (mem. coun. 1978), Wash. U. Alumni Fedn. (pres. 1956-57), Rotary, St. Louis Country Club, Noonday Club (St. Louis), Met. Club, Chevy Chase Club, Alfalfa Club, St. Alban's Tennis Club, Order of the Coif, Psi Upsilon, Delta Sigma Rho, Phi Delta Phi. Office: Milbank Tweed Hadley & McCloy LLP 1850 K St NW Ste 1100 Washington DC 20006-2213 Office Phone: 202-835-7500. E-mail: wwebster@milbank.com. *

WECHSLER, GIL, lighting designer; b. NYC, Feb. 5, 1942; s. Arnold J. and Miriam (Steinberg) W. Student, Rensselaer Poly. Inst., Troy, NY, 1958—61; BS, NYU, NYC, 1964; MFA, Yale U., New Haven, 1967. Lighting designer Harkness Ballet, NYC, 1967—69, Pa. Ballet, Phila., 1969—70, Stratford Shakespeare Festival, Ont., Canada, 1969—78, 1997—2004, Guthrie Theatre, Mpls., 1971, Lyric Opera, Chgo., 1972—76, Met. Opera, NYC, 1976—96, Equus, Stratford Shakespeare Festival, 1997, Macbeth, Stratford Festival, 2004, Coriolanus, Stratford Festival, 2006. Tchr. NYU, Rensselaer Poly. Inst., 1998; guest lectr. Teatro Colon, Buenos Aires, 1985, Yale U., 1980, Broadway Lighting Designers, 1994—98; guest lighting designer Am. Ballet Theatre, NYC, 1980, Paris Opera, 1983, Chatelet Theatre, Paris, 1991; dean's adv. coun. Rensselaer Poly. Inst. Cons. editor Opera Quar., 1983-90. Recipient Emmy award nominations, Illuminating Engring. Soc., United Scenic Artists. Avocations: collecting ocean liner memorabilia, gardening, kayaking. Home: PO Box 283 Upper Black Eddy PA 18972 E-mail: gillights@aol.com.

WECHSLER, MARY HEYRMAN, lawyer; b. Green Bay, Wis., Jan. 8, 1948; d. Donald Hubert and Helen (Polcyn) Heyrman; m. Roger Wechsler, Aug. 1971 (div. 1977); 1 child, Risa Heyrman; m. David Jay Sellinger, Aug. 15, 1981; 1 stepchild, Kirk Benjamin; 1 child, Michael Paul. Student, U. Chgo., 1966-67, 68-69; BA, U. Wash., Seattle, 1971; JD cum laude, U. Puget Sound, Tacoma, Wash., 1979. Bar: Wash. 1979. Assoc. Law Offices Ann Johnson, Seattle, 1979-81; ptnr. Johnson, Wechsler, Thompson, Seattle, 1981-83; pvt. practice Seattle, 1984-87; ptnr. Mussehl, Rosenberg et al, Seattle, 1987-88, Wechsler, Becker LLP, Seattle, 1988—. Mem. Bd. Ct. Edn., 1998—2007, sec., 2003—05, vice chair, 2006—07; bd. dirs. U. Wash. Law Sch. Child Advocacy Clinic, 1996—99; mem. Wash. State Commn. on Domestic Rels., 1996—97, 1999—2004; chair edn. com. Access to Justice Bd., 1996—99, mem. pub. trust and confidence com., 2000—05; chair Wash. State Coalition on Jud. Selection, 2005—07; mem. Jud. Coll. Bd. Trustees, 2005—; moderator Wash. State Summit on Jud. Independence and Jud. Selection, 2005; presenter in field. Author: Family Law in Washington, 1987, rev. edit., 1988, Marriage and Separation, Divorce and Your Rights, 1994; contbr. articles to legal publs. Mem. Wash. State Ethics Adv. Com., 1992-95; bd. dirs. Seattle LWV, 1991-92. Fellow Am. Acad. Matrimonial Lawyers (Wash. state chpt., sec.-treas. 1996, v.p. 1997-98, pres. 1999-2000, nat. arbitration com. 1999-2000, nat. interdisciplinary com. 1999-2000, nat. admissions procedure com. 2000-02, nat. long range planning com. 2003-05, chair 2003—, nat. bylaws com. 2005, nat. budget com. 2004-07); mem. ABA (chmn. membership Wash. state 1987-88), Wash. State Bar Assn. (exec. com. family law sect. 1985-91, chair family law sect. 1988-89), profl. devel. com. 2002-03, media project com. 2001, ct. improvement com. 1998-2000, legs. com. 1991-96, Outstanding Atty. of Yr. family law sect. 1988, comms. com. 1997-98, disciplinary hearing officer 1998—), Wash. Women Lawyers, King County Bar Assn. (legis. com. 1985-2000, vice-chair 1990-91, chair family law sect. 1986-87, chair domestic violence com. 1986-87, trustee 1988-90, policy planning com. 1991-92, 2d v.p. 1992-93, 1st v.p. 1993-94, pres. 1994-95, long-range planning com. 1998-99, awards com. 1997-99, nominations com. 2003, co-chair Bench-Bar Conf. 2003, Outstanding Atty. award 1999), Nat. Conf. of Bar Pres., King County Bar Found. (trustee 1997-2000), Am. Judicature Soc. (v.p. Washington chpt. 2000-03, pres. 2003-05, nat. bd. dirs. 2006-07). Office: Wechsler Becker LLP Ste 4550 701 5th Ave Seattle WA 98104-7097 Home Phone: 206-789-3657; Office Phone: 206-624-4900. Business E-Mail: mhwechsler@wechslerbecker.com.

WECHSLER, SERGIO, automotive executive, consultant; b. Rio de Janeiro, Aug. 10, 1944; arrived in US, 1965; s. Michael and Gertrud (Putziger) W.; children: Mark, Andrew. Student, Mackenzie U., 1962, Kettering U., Flint, Mich., 1967; MBA in Internat. Bus., NYU, 1974; PhD in Internat. Bus., Kennedy-Western U., 1996. Quality supr. GM do Brasil, Sao Paulo, 1963-65, quality control supt., 1967-70; quality control mgr. Gillette Corp., Berlin, 1970-71; project mgr. GM, NYC, 1971-76; plant mgr. GM de Portugal, Lisbon, 1976-79; project mgr. Adam Opel AG, Russelheim, Fed. Republic of Germany, 1979-81; quality dir. GM, Linden,

NJ, 1981-85, dir. ops. and quality control Warren, Mich., 1985-93, mgr. internat. programs, 1985-95, program mgr. Cadillac Luxury Car divsn. Flint, Mich., 1995-96. Pres., CEO Marswex Global Enterprises, Palm Harbor, Fla., 1982—, Hudson Plaza, 1984-99; chmn. Auto Exchange Club, Clearwater, Fla., 1997-2001, MSX Internat., Detroit, 1996-99, v.p. German ops., 1999-2001; regional dir. South Am. Schiller Internat. U., 2007. V.p. Temple Beth Jacob, Pontiac, Mich., 1986, pres., 1987—89. Mem. Am. Soc. Quality Control (cert. quality engr. 1992), Radio Club. Republican. Avocations: amateur radio, travel, auto restoration. Office Phone: 727-403-1599. Personal E-mail: marswex@aol.com.

WECHTER, IRA MARTIN, tax specialist, financial planner; b. Bkyn., June 26, 1947; s. Nathan Harris and Mollie (Bauer) W.; m. Myrna Ellen Rosenbaum, Dec. 22, 1968; 1 child, Megan Jill. BA, CCNY, 1969; MPA, Bernard Baruch Coll., 1973. CFP; cert. practitioner of taxation; accredited tax advisor; registered investment advisor; lic. gen. securities prin.; enrolled to practice before IRS; lic. gen. securities prin., life, health and disability ins., N.J., N.Y. Dir. adminstrv. svcs. N.Y.C. Dept. City Planning, 1971-77; dep. asst. budget dir. N.Y., N.Y.C. Office Mgmt. and Budget, 1977-81; dep. commr. N.Y.C. Dept. Environ. Protection, 1981-84; pres. Wechter Fin. Svcs., Inc., Parsippany, NJ, 1984—. Mem. Community Bd. No. 1 S.I., 1973-76, 1st v.p., 1976-77; treas. S.I. Coun. on Arts, 1974-75. Recipient Outstanding Citizenship award Borough Pres. of S.I., 1977. Mem. Nat. Assn. Enrolled Agts., Inst. Cert. Fin. Planners, Nat. Assn. Tax Practitioners, Nat. Soc. Tax Preparers, Nat. Soc. Pub. Accts. Republican. Jewish. Avocations: stamp collecting/philately, organ. Office: Wechter Fin Svcs Inc 1719 State Rt 10 Ste 310 Parsippany NJ 07054-4507 also: 1719 Route 10 Ste 224 Parsippany NJ 07054-4507 Home Phone: 973-394-1188, 973-605-1448; Office Phone: 973-605-1448. Business E-Mail: wfs@wechterfinancial.com.

WECK FARRAG, KRISTIN W., bank executive; b. Elgin, Ill., Nov. 5, 1959; d. John Francis and Florence Elaine (Ebel) W.; married Nov. 6, 2004. BBA, Augustana Coll., Rock Island, Ill., 1981. Lic. real estate broker, Ill., life/health ins. producer; registered securities rep. (series 7 and series 24); registered uniform investment advisor series 65. Intern with investment banking group First Chgo. Bank, London, 1980; intern Prudential-Bache Co., Ft. Lauderdale, Fla., 1981; residential appraiser Fox Valley Appraisal Counselors, Ltd., West Dundee, Ill., 1982-84; asst. real estate loan officer First Nat. Bank, Barrington, Ill., 1982-84; savs. and loan field examiner III Office of Thrift Supervision, Chgo., 1984-90; mng. agt. Resolution Trust Corp., Elk Grove Village, Ill., 1990-91; pres., treas., bd. dirs. Cardunal Savs. Bank, West Dundee, Ill., 1991—; dir. Prairie State Bank, Marengo, Ill., 1998—2002. Project Bus. cons. Jr. Achievement, 1992-96; literacy tutor Vols. of Am., 1998-99; dist. chmn. Found. Ednl. Excellence, 2003-04. Recipient Outstanding Achievement award Fed. Home Loan Bank Bd., 1985, Leading Us In Commerce and Industry award for fin. svcs., 1998, Sam Walton Bus. Cmty. Leader award, 1999. Mem. Nat. Assn. Securities Dealers (registered rep., registered prin.), Rotary Club Dundee Twp. (pres. 2001-02, Rotarian of Yr. 1997-98, Disting. Pres. 2002). Republican. Lutheran. Avocations: scuba diving, golf, walking, reading. Home: PO Box 930 Dundee IL 60118-0930 Office: Cardunal Savings Bank PO Box 839 Dundee IL 60118-0839 Personal E-mail: kweck@cardunal.net.

WEDDING, CHARLES RANDOLPH, architect; b. St. Petersburg, Fla., Nov. 16, 1934; s. Charles Reid and L. Marion (Whitaker) W.; m. Audrey Whitsel, Aug. 18, 1956 (div. Apr. 1979); children: Daryl L., Douglas R., Dorian B.; m. Vonnie Sue Hayes, June 22, 1984 (div. Dec. 1991); stepchildren: Stephanie W., Brian E.; m. June A. Free, Mar. 31, 1993; stepchildren: Gregory, Kristine. BArch, U. Fla., 1957. Registered arch., Fla., Ga., N.C., S.C., Del., Va., Tex., Ill., Ind., Kans., La., Mo., Okla., Tenn. Arch. in tng. Harvard & Jolly AIA, St. Petersburg, 1957-60; arch., prin., pres. Wedding & Assocs., St. Petersburg, 1960—. Mayor City of St. Petersburg, 1973-75; past chmn. Pinellas County Com. of 100, Bldg. Dept. Survey Team, City of St. Petersburg; trustee All Children's Hosp., 1968-70; sect. leader St. Petersburg United Fund, 1965-70; mem. city coun. Action Team for Pier Redevel., 1967-68; mem. exec. com. Goals for City of St. Petersburg, 1970-72; den leader Webelos, Boy Scouts Am., 1971-72; chmn., trustee Canterbury Sch. YMCA, 1968-72; mem. adv. com. Tomlinson Vocat. Sch., 1969-79; past trustee Mus. Fine Arts; past bd. dirs. Neighborly Ctr., Jr. Achievement Pinellas County; chair Downtown Partnership, 2001—. Served to 1st lt. U.S. Army, 1958-60. Fellow AIA (5 Silver Spike awards, Merit of Honor, Medal of Honor); mem. Am. Soc. Landscape Archs., St. Petersburg Assn. Archs. (past pres.), Fla. Assn. Archs. (8 Merit Design awards), St. Petersburg Yacht Club, Suncoasters Club. Republican. Episcopalian. Avocations: sailing, hunting, golf, tennis. Home: 6900 10th Ave N Saint Petersburg FL 33710-6152 Office: Wedding/Stephenson/Ibargüen Archs Inc 300 1st Ave S Saint Petersburg FL 33701-4209 Office Phone: 727-821-6610. Business E-Mail: randy@weddingarchitects.com.

WEDDINGTON, SARAH RAGLE, lawyer, educator; b. Abilene, Tex., Feb. 5, 1945; d. Herbert Doyle and Lena Catherine Ragle. BS magna cum laude, McMurry Coll., 1965, PhD (hon.), 1979; JD, U. Tex., 1967; PhD (hon.), Hamilton Coll., 1979, Southwestern U., 1989, Austin Coll., 1993, Nova Southeastern U., 1999; PhD in Human Letters (hon.), Fitchburg State Coll., 2004. Bar: Tex. 1967, D.C. 1979, U.S. Dist. Ct. (we., no. and ea. dists.) Tex., U.S. Ct. Appeals (5th cir.), U.S. Supreme Ct. Pvt. practice law, Austin, 1967-77; gen. counsel USDA, Washington, 1977-78; spl. asst. to Pres. The White House, Washington, 1978—79, asst. to Pres., 1979—81; chmn. Interdepartmental Task Force on Women, 1978-81; mem. Pres.'s Commn. on Exec. Exchange, 1981; Carl Hatch prof. law and pub. adminstrn. U. N.Mex., Albuquerque, 1982-83; pvt. practice law Austin, Tex., 1985—; dir. Tex. Office State-Fed. Rels., Austin, Washington, 1983-85. Vis. prof. govt. Wheaton Coll., Norton, Mass., 1981-83; sr. lectr. Tex. Woman's U., Denton, 1981-90, 93, U. Tex., Austin, 1986-1989, adj. assoc. prof. 1989-2001, adj. prof., 2001-. Author: A Question of Choice, 1992; contbr. articles to various mags.; contbg. editor Glamour mag., 1981-83. Mem. Tex. Ho. of Reps., 1973-77; named hon. chair San Francisco Bar Assn. Breast Cancer Hotline/Network, 2001, named hon. chair ann. benefit for Breast Cancer Rsch. Ctr., Austin, 2002, named lecture showcase presenter Nat. Assn. Campus Activities, 2003. Named Lectr. of Yr., Nat. Assn. Coll. Activities, 1990, Tex. Woman of Century, Tex. Women's C. of C., 1999, Face of Century, San Antonio Express News, 1999, 2000, Outstanding Alumnus, McMurry U., 2004, Nat. Pub. Health Hero, U. Calif., Berkeley, 2005, Keynote Spkr., China's Women Fedn., U.S. Conf. on Women in Leadership, Beijing, 2004; named one of Most Influential Lawyers of the 20th Century, Tex. Lawyer, 2000; recipient Woman of Yr. award, Tex. Women's Polit. Caucus, 1973, Outstanding Young Am. Leaders, Time Mag., 1979, Leadership award, Ladies Home Jour., 1980, Spl. Recognition award, Esquire mag., 1984, Elizabeth (Betty) Boyer award, Equity Action League, 1992, Woman Who Dares award, Nat. Coun. Jewish Women, 1993, Woman of Distinction award, Nat. Conf. for Coll. Women Student Leaders, 1993, Colby award for Pub. Svc., Sigma Kappa, 1996, Hummingbird award, Leadership Am., 1998, Tallest Texan award, Houston Chronicle, 2000, Speaking Out for Justice award, AAUW Legal Advocacy Fund, 2001, AAUW Ednl. Found., 2001, Ally award, Possible Woman Leadership Conf., 2001, Sarah Weddington Leadership Conf. named in her honor, Tex. Woman's U., 2001, Humanitarian of Yr. award, Planned Parenthood, Tex., 2003, Courage award, Women Lawyers LA, 2004, Reproductive Equity award, Lilith Orgn., 2005. Mem. Tex. Bar Assn. Office: The Weddington Ctr 709 W 14th St Austin TX 78701-1707 Business E-Mail: sw@weddingtoncenter.com.

WEDDINGTON, STACEY LEE, not-for-profit developer; m. Jerry Leon Weddington; 1 child, Alexander. Dir. ann. giving Casady Sch., Okla. City, 2000—03; dir. devel. Okla. City Nat. Meml. & Mus., 2003—. Youth educator St. Elijah Orthodox Ch., Okla. City, 2002—07. Mem.: Okla. Mus. Assn., Assn. Fundraising Profls. (dir. 2006—), Jr. League Okla. City. Avocations: travel, reading. Office: Oklahoma City Nat Meml & Mus 620 North Harvey Ave Oklahoma City OK 73102 Home Phone: 405-752-4342; Office Phone: 405-235-3313.

WEDEL-COWGILL, MILLIE REDMOND, secondary school, performing arts, communication and education educator; b. Harrisburg, Pa., Aug. 18, 1939; d. Clair L. and Florence (Heiges) Aungst; m. T.S. Redmond, 1956 (div. 1967); children: T.S. Redmond II; m. Frederick L. Wedel, Jr., 1974 (div. 1986); m. Paul R. Cowgill, May 19, 2001. BA, Alaska Meth. U., 1966; MEd, U. Alaska, Anchorage, 1972; postgrad. in comm., Stanford U., Calif., 1975-76. Lic. third class broadcasting, FCC. Profl. actress Charming Models & Models Guild of Phila., 1954-61; asst. dir. devel. in charge pub. rels. Alaska Meth. U., Anchorage, 1966, part-time lectr., 1966, 73; comm. tchr. Anchorage Sch. Dist., 1967-96; owner Wedel Prodns., Anchorage, 1976-86; cons. comms., media and edn., owner Cowgill Cons., 2003—. Pub. rels. staff Alaska Purchase Centennial Exhibit, U.S. Dept. Commerce, 1967; writer gubernatorial campaign, 1971; instr. Chapman Coll., 1990-93; adj. instr. U. Alaska, Anchorage, 1972, 77-79, 89-2001; cons. Cook Inlet Native Assn., 1978, No. Inst., 1979; judge Ark. Press Women's Writing Contest, 1990-91; sec. exec. bd. Alaska Dept. Edn. Profl. Tchg. Practices Commn., 1993-94. Bd. dirs. Sta. KAKM, Alaska Pub. TV, membership chmn., 1978-80, nat. lay rep. to Pub. Broadcasting Svc. and Nat. Assn. Pub. TV Stas., 1979; bd. dirs. Ednl. Telecom. Consortium for Alaska, 1979, Mid-Hillside Cmty. Coun., Municipality of Anchorage, 1979-80, 83-88, Hillside East Cmty. Coun., 1984-88, pres., 1984-85; rsch. writer, legal asst. Vinson & Elkins, Houston, 1981; v.p., bd. dirs. Inlet View ASD Cmty. Sch., 1994-95, pres., 1995-97; Valley Forge Freedoms Found., Murdoch Scholarships; bd. dirs. Rev. Richard Gay Trust, Alaska and Pa., 1992-2000. Recipient awards for newspapers, lit. mags.; award Nat. Scholastic Press Assn., 1981, 82, 83, 84; Alaska Coun. Econs., 1982, Merits award Alaska Dept. Edn., 1982-93, Legis. commendation State of Alaska, Nat. Blue Ribbon Outstanding Sch. award, 1993. Mem. NEA (AEA bldg. rep., state del. 70s, 80s, 94-95), Assn. Pub. Broadcasting (charter mem., nat. lay del. 1980), Indsl. TV Assn. (San Francisco and Houston 1975-81), Alaska Press Club (chmn. high sch. journalism workshops, 1968-69, 73, awards for sch. newspapers 1972, 74, 77), Alaska Fedn. Press Women (dir. 1978-86, 94-95, pres. 1995-96, h.s. journalism competition youth projects dir., award for brochures 1978, chair youth writing contest 1994-95), World Affairs Coun., Chugach Electric (chair 1990, nomination com. for bd. dirs. 1988-90), Hood Coll. Alaska Alumni Assn., Stanford U. Alumni Club (Alaska pres. 1982-84, 90-92, 99-2000, v.p. 1998-99), Rotary Club of Naples (photographer and asst. program chair 2003), Imperial Golf Course Country Club, Club at Pelican Bay, Naples (Fla.) Philharm. League (newsletter editor, 2007—, bd. dirs., 2007—), Naples Fla. U. Pa. Club, English Speaking Union. Presbyterian. Home: PO Box 111489 Anchorage AK 99511-1489 Office: Cowgill Cons PO Box 770662 Naples FL 34107-0662 Home Phone: 907-345-7793.

WEDEPOHL, LEONHARD MARTIN, electrical engineering educator; b. Pretoria, South Africa, Jan. 26, 1933; s. Martin Willie and Liselotte B.M. (Franz) W.; m. Sylvia A.L. St. Jean; children: Martin, Graham. BSc in Engring., Rand U., 1953; PhD, U. Manchester, Eng., 1957. Registered profl. engr., BC. Planning engr. Escom, Johannesburg, 1957-61; mgr. L.M. Erricson, Pretoria, South Africa, 1961-62; sect. leader Reyrolle, Newcastle, England, 1962-64; prof., head dept. Manchester U., 1964-74; dean engring. U. Man., Winnipeg, Canada, 1974-79; dean applied sci. U. BC, Vancouver, Canada, 1979-85, prof. elec. engring., 1985-97, prof. emeritus, 1998—, dean applied sci. emeritus, 1998—. Mem. Sci. Rsch. Coun., London, 1968-74; dir. Man. Hydro, Winnipeg, 1975-79, BC Hydro, Vancouver, 1980-84, BC Sci. Coun., 1982-84; cons. Horizon Robotics, Saskatoon, 1986; chmn. implementation team Sci. Place, Can., 1985; cons. CEPEL, Rio de Janeiro; adv. Man. High Voltage DC Rsch. Ctr.; tech. advisor RTDS Techs., Inc., Winnipeg, 1994—; head protection devel. Rolls Royce Indsl. Power Group, 1995-96; adj. prof. U. Man., 2002-; co-chair Knowledge Cluster, Okanagan Partnership, Kelowna, Can., 2004-; bd. dirs. Okanagan Partnership; co-chair faculty engring. adv. com. UBC-O. Contbr. articles to sci. jours.; patentee in field. Named Hon. Citizen, City of Winnipeg, 1979. Fellow Instn. Elec. Engrs. (premium 1967), Engring. Inst. Can.; mem. Assn. Profl. Engrs. BC. Avocations: music, cross country skiing, hiking. Office: 1511 Chardonnay Pl Westbank BC Canada V4T 2P9 Business E-Mail: wedepohl@shaw.ca.

WEDER, ALAN B(RIAN), internist, medical educator; b. Abington, Pa., Sept. 19, 1949; s. Howard H. and Dorothy L. Weder; m. Kimberly Weber, June 14, 1975; children: Alyson E., Christian D. BA, U. Chgo., 1971; MD, Hahnemann Med. Coll., Phila., 1975. Diplomate Am. Bd. Internal Medicine, 1975. Resident internal medicine U. Chgo., 1975—78, post-doctoral, 1978—80; faculty internal medicine U. Mich., Ann Arbor, 1980—82, prof., 1982—. Home: 2030 Hill St Ann Arbor MI 48104 Office: U Mich Med Sch 24 Frank Lloyd Wright Dr Lobby M Ann Arbor MI 48106 Office Phone: 734-998-7956. Office Fax: 734-998-7941. Business E-Mail: aweder@umich.edu.

WEDGE, CHRIS, animation director, studio executive; b. 1958; Grad., SUNY, Purchase, 1981; MA, Ohio State U. Stop-motion animator; with MAGI/SynthaVision; v.p. creative devel., founder Blue Sky, Ossining, N.Y. Animator: (films) Tron, 1992, Joe's Apt., 1996, Alien Resurrection, 1997, Bunny, 1998 (Best Animation Oscar award 1999); actor, dir.: (films) Ice Age, 2002, Robots, 2005, Ice Age: The Meltdown, 2006; creator: (films) The Daymaker, Tuber's Two Step, Balloon Guy. Office: c/o Jayson Engquist Blue Sky Studios Inc 44 S Broadway 17th Fl White Plains NY 10601 also: Blue Sky Prodns 100 Executive Blvd Ossining NY 10562-2557 Fax: (914) 259-6505. E-mail: christ@blueskystudios.com.

WEDGE, ERIC, archbishop; b. Fort Wayne, Ind., Jan. 27, 1968; m. Kate Wedge; 1 child, Ava Catherine. Garduate, Wichita St. Univ. Profl. baseball player Boston Red Sox, 1991—92, 1994, Colo. Rockies, 1993; mgr. AAA Buffalo Bison, 2000—03, Cleve. Indians, 2003—. Vol. First Energy Grand Slam Summer Reading Literacy Program, Feed the Need at Cleve. St. Augustine Church, Ronald McDonald House. Office: Cleveland Indians Jacobs Field 2401 Ontario St Cleveland OH 44115-4003

WEDGEWORTH, ANN, actress; b. Abilene, Tex., Jan. 21, 1935; m. Rip Torn, 1955 (div.); 1 child, Danae; m. Ernest Martin; 1 child, Dianna. Attended, U. Tex.; BA in Drama, So. Methodist U. Actor: (Broadway debut) Make A Million, 1958, (Broadway appearances) Chapter Two (Tony award), Thieves, Blues for Mr. Charlie, The Last Analysis, (off-Broadway appearances) Line, Chapparal, The Crucible, Days and Nights of Beebee Fenstermaker, Ludlow Fair, The Honest to God Shnozzola, A Lie of the Mind, Elba, The Aunts, The Debutante's Ball, (premiers) In the Moonlight Eddie at Pasadena Playhouse, Natural Affection in Pheonix, The Dream in Phila., (toured with nat. cos.) The Sign in Sidney Brustein's Window and Kennedy's Children, (appeared in TV series) Three's Company, The Edge of Night, Another World, Somerset, Filthy Rich, Evening Shade, (TV appearances) All That Glitters, The Equalizer, Roseanne, Bronk, Twilight Zone, Trapper John, M.D.; (TV films) The War Between the Tates, Right to Kill, Cooperstown, Fight for Justice: The Nancy Conn Story, Bogie, A Stranger Waits; (films) Handle With Care (Nat. Soc. Film Critics award), Thieves, Bang the Drum Slowly, Scarecrow, Catamount Killing, Law and Disorder, One Summer Love, Dragon-Fly, Birch Intervals, Soggy Bottom, USA, No Small Affair, Sweet Dreams, The Mens Club, A Tiger's Tale, Made in Heaven, Far North, Miss Firecracker, Green Card, Steel Magnolias, Love and a 45, The Whole Wide World, The Hunter's Moon, Hard Promises, Andy, My Science Project, The Hawk is Dying; (plays) Mother and Child, The Glass Menagerie, Period of Adjustment, Come Blow Your Horn, Goodbye Again, The Tender Trap; TV host Evening at the Improv, A&E.

WEDGLE, RICHARD JAY, lawyer; b. Denver, Dec. 2, 1951; s. Joseph M. and Lillian E. (Brown) W.; m. Susan R. Mason, Oct. 17, 1987. BA, U. Calif., Berkeley, 1974; JD, U. Denver, 1978. Bar: Colo. 1978, U.S. Dist. Ct. Colo. 1978, U.S. Ct. Appeals (10th cir.) 1980. Ptnr. Cox, Wedgle & Padmore, P.C., Denver, 1978-85, Barnes, Wedgle & Shpall, P.C., Denver, 1986-87, Wedgle and Shpall, P.C., Denver, 1987-98, Wedgle and Friedman, P.C., Denver, 1998-2000, Wedgle and Assoc. P.C., Denver, 2000—02, Wedgle and Kukreja, P.C., Denver, 2002—. Vol. coord. Dick Lamm for Gov., 1974, citizen adv. office, 1975; bd. dirs. Cherry Creek Improvement Assn., 1985-88. Mem.: ABA, Colo. Bar Assn., Denver Bar Assn., Jewish Cmty. Ctr. Avocations: running, biking, gardening. Home: 365 Marion St Denver CO 80218-3927 Office: Wedgle & Kukreja PC 730 17th St Ste 230 Denver CO 80202-3546 Office Phone: 303-893-3111.

WEDHSLER, LAWRENCE RICHARD, neurologist, educator; b. Phila., July 2, 1952; s. Richard Lawrence Wechsler; m. Phyllis Cook, Mar. 10, 1980; children: Samuel Wayne, Thomas Lawrence, Paul Matthew. MD, U. Pa., Phila., 1974—78. Lic. neurologist ABPN, 1983. Dir. UPMC Stroke Inst., Pitts., 1996—2006; prof. neurology U. Pitts., 2000—. Office: UPMC Stroke Inst C426 PUH 200 Lothrop St Pittsburgh PA 15213

WEDIG, REGINA SCOTTO, lawyer; b. Pensacola, Fla., July 30, 1955; d. Anthony P. and Janet (Treadway) Scotto; m. Eric M. Wedig. BA magna cum laude, Loyola U., 1977; MA, Tulane U., 1979; JD, La. State U., 1984. Bar: Tenn. 1984, U.S. Dist. Ct. (ea., mid. and we. dists.) Tenn. 1984, La. 1985, U.S. Dist. Ct. (ea., mid. and we. dists.) La. 1985, U.S. Ct. Appeals (5th cir.) 1985, U.S. Ct. Appeals (11th cir.) 1998. Assoc. Harkavy, Shainberg, Kosten, et al, Memphis, 1984-88, Bordelon, Hamlin & Theriot, New Orleans, 1988-94, ptnr., 1994—2004; pvt. practice Law Offices of Regina Scotto Wedig, New Orleans, 2004—, Amite, La., 2005—. Chmn. moot ct. bd. Paul M. Herbert Law Sch., La. State U., Baton Rouge, 1983-84. Editor: (newsletter) LSU-Coastal Law Newsletter, 1983-84; author: (law jour.) La. Bar Jour., 1996. Mem. La. Bar Assn., Tenn. Bar Assn., New Orleans Bar Assn. Office: PO Box 185 Amite LA 70422 Business E-Mail: rswedig@hotmail.com.

WEDLAKE, MARTINE, application developer; b. Guelph, Can., Dec. 13, 1968; s. George Bruce and Barbara Wedlake; m. Linda Cunningham, Dec. 29, 1995; children: Jamie, Peter. PhD, U. Victoria, Can., 1999. Software engr. Informix Software, Portland, Oreg., 1991—2001, IBM, Beaverton, Oreg., 2001—. Mem.: IEEE. Achievements include patents in field. Office: IBM 15400 SW Koll Pky Beaverton OR 97006 Office Phone: 503-578-3072. Business E-Mail: martinew@us.ibm.com.

WEDLICK, DENNIS, architect, writer; With Philip Johnson, 1980—92; founder, prin. Dennis Wedlick Arch. LLC, 1992—. Tchr. architecture U. Pa., Phila., Parsons Sch. Design; founding mem. Congress Residential Architecture. Author: The Good Home, 2001, Good House Parts: Creating a Great Home Piece by Piece, 2003; Designing the Good Home, 2004; author: Good House Hunting: 20 Steps to Your Dream Home, 2005. Mem.: AIA. Office: Dennis Wedlick Arch LLC 85 Worth St New York NY 10013 Office Phone: 212-625-9222. Office Fax: 212-625-8885. *

WEE, CHRISTINE DIJOS, elementary school educator; b. Honolulu, Jan. 8, 1968; d. Cosme Wayne and Victoria Amparo Dijos; m. Phillip Ying Kin Wee, July 15, 2000; children: Deanna Rae Patacsil, Logan Wayne. BEd, U. Hawaii, Manoa, 1991. Cert. tchr. Hawaii, prof. diploma in elem. edn. Univ. Hawaii, 1992. Kindergarten tchr. Island Paradise Sch., Honolulu, 1992—93, Pauoa Elem. Sch., Honolulu, 1993—94, choral dir., 1997—2005, 6th grade tchr., 1994—2002, 5th grade tchr., 2003—04, 3d grade tchr., 2004—; spl. edn. summer sch. aide Wailupe Valley Elem. Sch., Honolulu; Challenger Ctr.-trained educator, NASA program Barber's Point Elem. Sch., Kapolei, Hawaii, 1996—2002. Regional conf. del. Sch.-to-Work, Honolulu, 1998; cadre mem. Roosevelt Complex Writing Inst., Honolulu, 1999, student svcs. coord., 2002—03; mem. music action rsch. team Hawaii State Dept. Edn., 1999—2001. Mem. com. Sch. Cmty.-Based Mgmt. Coun., Pauoa Elem. Sch., 2001—03; vol., chmn. Honolulu Dist. Choral Festival, 1994—2002, 2005; mem. ch. choir; asst. dir. Sweet Adelines Internat.; bd. dirs. Pauoa Elem. Sch. PTA, 1996—97, 2005—06. Mem.: Hawaii Orff-Schulwerk Assn., Am. Choral Dirs. Assn., Hawaii State Tchrs. Assn. (union rep. 1995—96, 2000—01), Hawaii Music Educators Assn. (3d v.p. 2000—02, chmn. 2001—02), Delta Kappa Gamma. Avocations: walking, collecting keychains and unicorns, singing. Home: 823 9th Ave Honolulu HI 96816 Office: Pauoa Elem Sch 2301 Pauoa Rd Honolulu HI 96813 E-mail: tiniwee86@hawaii.rr.com.

WEED, MELVIN L., retired railroad conductor, small business owner; b. Detroit, Jan. 25, 1947; s. Merrill L. and Flora McMillan Galbraith (Thornton) W.; m. Malinda D. Ward-Corey, Jan. 29, 1966 (div. Feb. 1982). Railroad condr. Pennsylvania Railroad, Melvindale, Mich., 1966-68, Pen Cen. Railroad, Detroit, 1968-76, ConRail, Detroit, 1976-86, Amtrack, Detroit, 1986-88; proprietor Mel's Snow Removal, Madison Heights, Mich., 1978-84, Mel's Bldg. and Landscape Supply, Madison Heights, 1979-84. Local chmn., union steward United Transp. Union, Detroit, 1967-69, local v.p., 1970-76. Author: (books) Do You Feel Like Me?, 1991; contbg. poet: (anthology) Reflections of Light, 1995; singer/songwriter/composer: Cloud Nine With an Angel, 1993, (album) Faces of Love, 1996. Guardianship/foster parent State of Mich., Oakland County, 1985. Recipient citation for citizen arrest, City of Madison Heights, 1987. Avocations: writing, singing, composing music. Office: Earnest Stone Publs PO Box 1288 Sterling Heights MI 48311-1288

WEED, ROGER OREN, rehabilitation services professional, educator; b. Bend, Oreg., Feb. 2, 1944; s. Chester Elbert and Ruth Marie (Urie) W.; m. Paula J. Keller BS in Sociology, U. Oreg., 1967, MS in Rehab. Counseling, 1969; PhD in Rehab. Counseling, U. Ga., 1986. Cert. rehab. counselor; cert. disability mgmt. specialist; lic. profl. counselor; cert. case mgr., cert. life care planner. Vocat. rehab. counselor State of Alaska, Anchorage, 1969-71; instr. U. Alaska, Anchorage, 1970-76; counselor Langdon Psychiat. Clinic, Anchorage, 1971-74; from asst. dir. to exec. dir. Hope Cottages, Anchorage, 1974-79; owner Profl. Resources Group, Anchorage, 1978-80; mng. ptnr. Collins, Weed & Assocs., 1980-84; assoc. dir. Ctr. for Rehab. Tech. Ga. Tech. U., Atlanta, 1986-87; catastrophic injury rehab. Weed & Assocs., Atlanta, 1984—; from asst. prof. to prof. Ga. State U., Atlanta, 1987—. Adj. faculty Ga. Inst. Tech.; courtesy faculty U. Fla., 1996—. Co-author: Vocational Expert Handbook, 1986, Transferable Work Skills, 1988, Life Care Planning: Spinal Cord Injured, 1989, 2d edit. 1994, Life Care Planning: Head Injured, 1994, Life Care Planning for the Amputee, 1992, Rehab Cons. Handbook, 1994, rev. edit., 2001; editor: Life Care Planning and Case Mgmt. Handbook, 1999 (rev., 2004); assoc. editor Jour. Lifecare Planning, 2002—; mem. editl. bd. Jour. of Pvt. Sector Rehab., 1986—, Jour. Forensic Vocational Analysis; contbr. articles to profl. jour. Bd. dirs. Found. for Life Care Planning Rsch. Recipient Gov.'s award Gov.'s Com. on Employment, Alaska, 1982, Goldpan Svc. award Gov.'s Com. on Employment, Alaska, 1978, Profl. Svc. award Am. Rehab. Counselors Assn., 1993. Fellow Nat. Rehab. Assn. (chmn. legis. com., bd. dir. met. Atlanta chpt. 1987-89, pres. Pacific region 1983-85, Pres.'s award Pacific region 1986), Internat. Assn. Rehab. Profls. (chmn. resh. and tng.

com. 1988-93, pres. 1994-95, named Educator of Yr. 1991, 97, Lifetime Achievement award 2004), Internat. Life Care Planning (Ann. Conf. Lifetime Achievement award 2005, Disting. Prof. award 2006), Pvt. Rehab. Suppliers Ga., Anchorage Amateur Radio Club Republican. Methodist. Avocations: sailing, skiing, bicycling, flying, computers. Office: Ga State U Coll Edn Dept Counseling/Psychol Svc 9th Fl Atlanta GA 30303

WEEDEN, JEFFREY BLANE, bank executive; b. Nevada, Iowa, Oct. 4, 1956; s. Russell Reece and Betty Arlene (Miller) W.; m. Sharon Jean Ziegler, Dec. 23, 1977; children: Jamie Jo, Jacob Bryan. BS, Iowa State U., 1979. CPA, Iowa. Tax supr. Ernst & Whinney, Des Moines, 1979-84; asst. v.p. corp. tax Banks of Iowa, Inc., Des Moines, 1984-86, v.p., 1986-87, v.p. fin. and treas., 1987-90; sr. v.p., treas., chief fin. officer Firstar Corp. of Iowa (formerly Banks of Iowa, Inc.), 1990; pres., COO MFN Fin. Corp., 1999—2001, pres., CEO, 2001—02; sr. exec. v.p., CFO KeyCorp, Cleve., 2002—. Treas. Ankeny (Iowa) United Ch. Christ, 1984-86, bd. trustees, 1984-87; mem. fin. com. Covenant Presbyn. Ch., 1988—, treas., 1989-92. Mem. AICPA, Iowa Soc. CPAs, Fin. Execs. Inst. (sec. 1993—). Lodges: Optimists (bd. dirs. Ankeny club 1985-86). Republican. Avocations: boating, golf, fishing. Office: KeyCorp 127 Public Sq Cleveland OH 44114-1306 *

WEEDEN, NORMAN FRANK, geneticist, educator; b. San Francisco, Calif., Feb. 12, 1948; s. William Frank and Patricia Chubbuck Weeden; m. Catherine Louise Ray, Oct. 6, 1975; children: Alan Matthew, Charles Edward. BS in Chemistry, Stanford U., Menlo Park, Calif., 1969; MS in Biology, Humboldt State U., Arcata, Calif., 1973; PhD in Genetics, U. Calif., Davis, 1981. Prof. Cornell U., Geneva, NY, 1982—99, Mont. State U., Bozeman, 1999—. Disting. vis. prof. South China Inst. Botany, Guangzhou, 1998—99. Author: (book) A Sierra Nevada Flora; editor: Pisum Genetics. Pres. Weeden Found., NY, NY, 1993—2007, bd. dirs., 1993—2007. Recipient Outstanding Svc. award, North Am. Pulse Improvement Assn., 2003. Mem.: Pisum Genetics Assn. (pres. 2000—07). Independent. Achievements include patents for the Matrix Mill, a DNA extraction machine; improved biocontrol agent-Trichoderma harzianum; research in genetic studies in pea, apple, grape, and common bean. Avocations: hiking, botany, swimming, flute, guitar. Office: Dept Plant Sci and Plant Pathology Montana State Univ Bozeman MT 59717 Office Phone: 406-994-7622. Office Fax: 406-994-7600. Business E-Mail: nweeden@montana.edu.

WEEDFALD, PETER C., retail executive; Mgmt. positions Ziff-Davis Publishing, 1989—98; exec. v.p. ViewSonic Corp., 1998—2000; COO Bigfoot Interactive, 2000—01; v.p. strategic mktg. No. Am. Samsung Electronics Am., 2001—03, sr. v.p. strategic mktg. No. Am., 2003—05, sr. v.p. sales & mktg., 2005—06; sr. v.p., gen. mdse. mgr. Circuit City, Richmond, Va., 2006, sr. v.p., chief mktg. officer, 2006—. Office: Circuit City 9950 Mayland Dr Richmond VA 23233 *

WEEDIN, JAMES FRANK, biology professor, researcher; b. San Antonio, Tex., Dec. 17, 1949; m. Teresa Faye Johnson, Dec. 30, 1972. AS, San Antonio Coll., Tex., 1969; BA, U. Tex., Austin, 1975; MS, Sul Ross State U., Alpine, Tex., 1976. Prof. C.C. of Aurora, Colo., 1981—, sci. divsn. chair, 1985—93. Bot. cons. Tex. Natural Areas Survey, Austin, 1976—77. Author: (book) Cacti of the Trans-Pecos and Adjacent Areas, 2004 (SW Book award Border Regional Libr. Assn., 2005, Donovan D. Correll award Native Plant Soc. Tex., 2007), (profl. papers) American Jour. Botany, Southwestern Naturalist, Annals of the Mo. Botanical Gardens; sci. advisor: Chihuahuan Desert Trilogy Film Series, Nat. Edn. TV, 1980. Mem. nursing adv. bd. Pickens Tech. Ctr., Aurora, 1982—2006. Named Faculty of Yr., C.C. of Aurora, 1990; recipient Excellence award, U. Tex. Nat. Inst. Staff and Orgnl. Devel., 1991, Master Tchr. award, U. Tex. Nat. Inst. Staff and Faculty Devel., 1991; grantee, U. Tex.-Austin, 1971, Chihuahuan Desert Rsch. Inst., 1975, Cmty. Colls. Colo., 1985. Mem.: Cactus and Succulent Soc. Am. (assoc.), Southwestern Assn. Naturalists (assoc.), Western Interior Paleontol. Soc. (assoc.), Colo. Cactus and Succulent Soc. (assoc.; v.p. 1988—89, grantee 1998, 2006). Avocations: hiking, camping, photography, travel. Home: 1189 Norfolk St Aurora CO 80011 Office: Cmty Coll of Aurora 16000 E CentreTech Pkwy Aurora CO 80011 Home Phone: 303-366-7843; Office Phone: 303-361-7398. Office Fax: 303-361-7374. Personal E-mail: weedin@comcast.net. Business E-Mail: jim.weedin@ccaurora.edu.

WEEKLEY, FREDERICK CLAY, JR., lawyer; b. San Antonio, Aug. 29, 1939; s. F. Clay and Topsy (Stevens) W.; m. Lynda Freeman; children: Amber Lee Carothers, Caroline Lee. BBA, Baylor U., 1962, JD, 1963; LLM, NYU, 1969. Bar: Tex. 1963. Ptnr. Bracewell & Patterson, Houston, 1974-90; atty. Bank One, Tex., N.A., 1990-98; ptnr./counsel Shannon, Gracey, Ratliff & Miller, LLP, Ft. Worth, 1999—. Mem. coun. real property, probate and trust law sect., State Bar of Tex., 1987-90; mem. adminstrv. coun. trust divsn. Tex. Bankers Assn., 1992-95, chmn. legis. com., 1992-95. Mem. Commn. Probate Law Examiners, Tex. Bd. Legal Specialization, 1978-82. Fellow Am. Coll. Trust and Estate Counsel. Home: 1821 Mossy Oak St Arlington TX 76012-5619 Office Phone: 817-882-7698. Business E-Mail: fweekley@shannongracey.com.

WEEKLEY, JUDY LIDDINGTON, special education educator; b. Tacoma, Wash., Dec. 18, 1956; d. William Raymond and Shirley Charlotte Liddington; m. John Weekley, June 27, 1980 (dec. Feb. 1996). BA, Southeastern La. U., 1978, MEd, 1984. Tchr. Jefferson Parish Pub. Sch. Sys., Harvey, La., 1978—2002, Individual Edn. plan specialist, 2002—; instr., lectr. Our Lady Holy Cross Coll., New Orleans, 1992—. Presenter in field; cons. in field. Dir. area games, coach Spl. Olympics, La., 1978—92. Recipient Excellence in Tchg. award, C. of C., 1988, 1990, Spl. Edn. Tchr. of Yr., 1999; grantee, Jefferson Parish Pub. Sch. Sys., 1990, 1995. Mem.: Coun. Exceptional Children (Tchr. of Yr. La. 2001), Phi Delta Kappa (bd. dirs. 1992—2003, editor 1992—2003). Methodist. Avocations: gardening, cooking, music, dance, computer and video creations. Home: 3817 Lake Providence Dr Harvey LA 70058 Office Phone: 504-349-8668. Personal E-mail: judyweek@aol.com.

WEEKS, ALBERT LOREN, writer, educator, journalist; b. Highland Park, Mich., Mar. 28, 1923; s. Albert Loren and Vera Grace (Jarvis) W. Student, U. Mich., 1942-43; MA, U. Chgo., 1949; PhD, Columbia U., 1965; cert., Russian Inst., 1960. Reporter Chgo. City News Bur., 1946; polit. analyst U.S. Dept. State, 1950-53, Free Europe Com., Inc., 1953-56; editorial asst. Newsweek mag., 1957-58; Russian tech. glossary compiler McGraw-Hill Book Co., 1960-61; prof. continuing edn. NYU, 1959-89. Lectr. U.S. diplomatic history and soviet govt. Columbia U., 1951-52; mem. adv. coun. Nat. Strategy Info. Ctr., 1979-89; instr. Ringling Sch. Art and Design, 1991—; pub. spkr. S.W. Fla. Host: A Week's View of Red Press, Sta. WNBC, 1965-68; series Myths That Rule America, NBC-TV, 1979-82; author: Reading American History, 1963, The First Bolshevik: A Political Biography of Peter Tkachev, 1968, The Other Side of Coexistence: An Analysis of Russian Foreign Policy, 1970, Richard Hofstadter's The American Political Tradition and the Age of Reform, 1973, Andrei Sakharov and the Soviet Dissidents, 1975, The Troubled Detente, 1976, Solzhenitsyn's One Day in the Life of Ivan Denisovich, 1976, Myths That Rule America, 1980, War and Peace: Soviet Russia Speaks, 1983; editor/compiler Brassey's Soviet and Communist Quotations, 1987, The Soviet Nomenklatura, 1987-1991, Stalin's Other War: Soviet Grand Strategy 1939-1941, 2002, Russia's Life-Saver: Lend-Lease Aid to the USSR in World War II; internat. affairs editor Def. Sci. mag., 1982-85; columnist Def. Report, 1982-90; contbr. articles to N.Y. Times, New Republic, New Leader, Annals, Russian, Slavic revs., Christian Sci. Monitor, Problems of Communism, Survey, Mil. Intelligence, Strategic Rev., World War II mag., Air Univ. Rev., L.A. Times, Washington Times, Orbis, Global Affairs, Panorama, Sarasota Herald-Tribune, Bradenton Herald, Defense and Diplomacy, Am. Intelligence Jour., USA Today, Rossiiskiye Vesti, Vechernii Vladimir, CityTempo mag., Modern Age mag. Home: 4884 Kestral Park Cir Sarasota FL 34231-3369 Personal E-mail: aweeks1@compuserve.com.

WEEKS, ARTHUR ANDREW, lawyer, educator; b. Hanceville, Ala., Dec. 2, 1914; s. A.A. and Anna S. (Seibert) W.; m. Carol P. Weeks; children: John David, Carol Christine, Nancy Anna. AB, Samford U., 1936; LL.B., JD, U. Ala., 1939; LL.M., Duke U., 1950; LL.D. (hon.), Widener U., 1980. Bar: Ala. 1939, Tenn. 1948. Sole practice, Birmingham, Ala., 1939-41, 1946-47, 1954-61; dean, prof. law Cumberland U. Sch. Law, 1947-54; dean, prof. Samford U., 1961-72, prof. law, 1972-74, Cumberland Sch. Law, Samford U., 1984—, Del. Sch. Law of Widener U., Wilmington, 1974-82, dean, 1974-80, interim dean, 1982-83, dean emeritus, prof., 1983—; ret. Served to capt. AUS, 1941-46. Mem. ABA, Tenn. Bar Assn., Ala. Bar Assn., Birmingham Bar Assn., Del. Bar Assn. (assoc.), Phi Alpha Delta, Phi Kappa Phi, Delta Theta Phi Home: 400 University Park Dr Apt 445 Birmingham AL 35209-6482

WEEKS, CLIFFORD MYERS, musician, academic administrator; b. NYC, Apr. 15, 1938; s. Vernal C. and Adeline (Campbell) W.; m. Ethel Lynn Fleming, Oct. 26, 1963 (dec. 1982); children: Clifford M. Jr., Michele Lynn. Diploma in Arranging and Composition, Berklee Coll. Music, 1962; MusB magna cum laude, Boston Conservatory Music, 1963, MusM, 1975; cert. in edn. adminstrn., Boston State Coll., 1977. Cert. secondary sch. adminstr. and tchr. music, Mass. Tchr. music Boston Pub. Schs., 1964-74, condr. All-City Stage Band, 1972-79, adminstrv. asst. to asst. supt., 1974-75, coordinator instrumental music, 1975-79, asst. prin., 1979, adminstrv. asst. to asst. supt., 1979-96, acting cmty. supt., 1983, cluster coord., 1996-2001, exec. asst. supt. office, 2001—03; fellow Boston U., 1989; ret., 2003. Arranger, composer, trombonist, 1963—; condr. Boston Coll. Jazz and Stage Band, Chestnut Hill, Mass., 1976-78; part-time city music faculty coord., lead tchr. Berklee Coll. Music, 2006—. Composer Tryptych for tuba and piano, 1971, (oratorio) The King-Life and Teachings of Dr. Martin Luther King Jr., 1976; composer, arranger various jazz compositions, 1975. Mem. Medford (Mass.) Jaycees, 1975-76; adv. bd. Roxbury (Mass.) Boys and Girls Club, 1970—, Berklee Coll. Music, Boston, 1972. Recipient Mayor's Parkman Club award, 1999, Suskind Young at Art award, Wang Ctr. Boston Theatres, 2001; fellow, Boston U., 1989. Mem. Boston Assn. Sch. Adminstrs. and Suprs. (adminstrs. union 1997—), Boston Tchrs. Union, Black Educators Alliance Mass. (treas. 1972-76, award 1976), ASCAP, Adminstrv. Assts. Assn. (chmn. local chpt. 1982—), Assn. for Supervision and Curriculum Devel., Omega Psi Phi. Methodist.

WEEKS, DAVID FRANK, foundation administrator; b. Salt Lake City, Sept. 9, 1926; s. Frank Harold and Myrtle June (Larsen) W.; m. Betty Alice Tellin, Aug. 14, 1949; children: David Rice, Clayton Frank. Student, So. Meth. U., Dallas, 1945, U. Tex., 1946; BS (Union Pacific Carl Raymond Gray scholar), U. Idaho, Moscow, 1949; HHD (hon.), U. Louisville, Ky., 1993. Pres. Assoc. Students U. Idaho, 1948-49; announcer Sta. KBIO, Burley, Idaho, 1949; Idaho rep. Nat. Found. for Infantile Paralysis, Boise, 1949-53, asst. to nat. dir. fund raising NYC, 1953-57; asst. nat. dir. March of Dimes, NYC, 1957-59; account exec. Kersting, Brown & Co., NYC, 1959-61; exec. dir. Rsch. to Prevent Blindness, Inc., NYC, 1961-70, exec. v.p., 1970-83, pres., 1983-99, chmn. bd. dirs., 1999—; pres., trustee RPB Endowment Fund Inc., NYC, 1988—2002; mem. borough coun. Borough of Ho-Ho-Kus, NJ, 1966-68, mayor, 1968-75; consumer rep. subcom. ophthalmic prostheses HEW, 1976-79; chmn., trustee RPB Endowment Fund, Inc., NYC, 2002—. Cons. Bur. Med. Devices, FDA, 1977-80; mem. nat. adv. eye coun. NIH, HHS, 1985-90. Mem. Ho-Ho-Kus Planning Bd., 1962-65, chmn., 1965; mem. Zoning Bd., 1975-85, Bergen County Ethics Bd., NJ, 1977-82; founder, pres. Ho-Ho-Kus Republican Club, 1983-86. Served with USN, 1944-46. Recipient Bronze Palm Eagle Scout award Boy Scouts Am., 1941, Disting. Pub. Svc. award Am. Acad. Ophthalmology and Otolaryngology, 1976, cert. of recognition Johns Hopkins U. Schs. Medicine, Hygiene and Pub. Health, 1984, Nat. Vision Rsch. Leadership award Assn. U. Profs. Ophthalmology, 1989, Disting. Svc. award Johns Hopkins Med. Instns.-Wilmer Ophthal. Inst., 1989, Disting. Svc. award Am. Acad. Ophthalmology, 1995; named Ky. col., 1969, U. of Idaho Alumni Hall of Fame award, 1992. Mem. Assn. Rsch. in Vision and Ophthalmology (hon., Disting. Public Svc. award 2006), Pan Am. Ophthalmol. Assn. (assoc.), Am. Soc. Assn. Execs., Internat. Assn. Eye Rsch., Bergen County Mayors Assn. (pres. 1975-77), Assn. U. Profs. Ophthalmology (hon.), Met. Club. Home: 4058 NW Northcliff Bend OR 97701-8248 Office: Rsch Prevent Blindness 645 Madison Ave New York NY 10022-1010 Office Phone: 212-752-4333, 541-385-6088.

WEEKS, GERALD, psychologist, educator; b. Morehead City, NC, Nov. 20, 1948; s. Marion G. and Ada (Willis) W. BA in Philosophy and Psychology, East Carolina U., 1971, MA in Gen. Psychology, 1973; PhD in Clin. Psychology, Ga. State U., 1979. Diplomate Am. Bd. Profl. Psychology (pres. 1987-88, bd. dirs. 1982-87), Am. Bd. Family Psychology, Am. Bd. Sexology; cert. marital and family therapist; lic. practicing psychologist, Nev., Pa.; bd. cert. sexologist. Intern in family therapy Harlem Valley Psychiat. Ctr., Wingdale, NY, 1978-79; assoc. prof. psychology U. N.C., Wilmington, 1979-85; dir. tng. Penn Coun. for Relationships, 1985—; clin. asst. prof. psychology Sch. Medicine U. Pa., Phila., 1985-87, clin. assoc. prof., 1988-98; chair, prof. dept. counseling U. Nev.-Las Vegas, 1999—. Pvt. practice Carolina Ob-gyn. Ctr., Wilmington, 1980-85. Author: Paradoxical Therapy, 1982, Treating Couples: The Intersystem Model of the Marriage Council of Philadelphia, 1989, Promoting Change through Paradoxical Therapy, 1991, Paradoxical Psychotherapy: Theory and Practice with Individuals, Couples, and Families, 1982; co-author: (with L. L'Abate) Family Therapy: Basic Concepts and Terms, 1985, (with L. L'Abate) Integrating Sex and Marital Therapy: A Clinicians Guide, 1987, Erectile Dysfunction, 2000, (with N. Gambescia) Couples in Treatment, 1992, rev. edit., 2001, Integrative Solutions: Treating Common Problems in Couple's Therapy, 1995, (with Hof and Trent) Focused Genograms: Intergenerational Assessment of Individuals, Couples and Families, 1999, (with Demaria & Ltof) Hypoactive Sexual Desire, 2002, Treating Infidelity, (with Gambescia and Jenkins) Handbook of Family Therapy, 2003, (with Odell and Methuen) If Only I Had Known: Common Mistakes in Couples Therapy, 2004; contbr. articles to profl. jours. Fellow Am. Assn. Marital and Family Therapy (clin. mem., nat. adv. bd., approved supr.); mem. APA, Acad. Family Psychology, Interpersonal and Social Skills Assn. (founding mem.), Acad. Psychologists in Marital, Sex, and Family Therapy, Am. Assn. of Sex Educators (clin. mem.), Counselors of Therapists. Office: Dept Marriage and Family Therapy PO Box 453045 4505 S Maryland Pky Las Vegas NV 89154-3045 Office Phone: 702-895-1392. Business E-Mail: gerald.weeks@unlv.edu.

WEEKS, JANET HEALY, retired supreme court justice; b. Quincy, Mass., Oct. 19, 1932; d. John Francis and Sheila Josephine (Jackson) Healy; m. George Weeks, Aug. 29, 1959; children: Susan, George. AB in chemistry, Emmanuel Coll., Boston, 1954; JD, Boston Coll., 1958; LLD (hon.), U. Guam, 1984. Bar: Mass. 1958, Guam 1972. Trial atty. U.S. Dept. Justice, Washington, 1958-60, Trapp & Gayle, Agana, Guam, 1971-73; ptnr. Trapp, Gayle, Teker, Weeks & Freidman, Agana, 1973-75; judge Superior Ct. Guam, Agana, 1975-96; assoc. justice Guam Supreme Ct., Guam, 1996-99, retired assoc. justice Guam, 1999. Chmn. task force cts., prosecution and def. Terr. Crime Commn., 1973-76; mem. Terr. Crime Commn. Bd., 1975-76, Guam Law Revision Commn., 1981—; rep. Nat. Conf. State Trial Judges, 1982. Mem. Cath. Sch. Bd. Guam, 1973. Mem. ABA, Nat. Assn. Women Judges (charter), Am. Judges Assn., Fed. Bar Assn. (chpt. sec. 1974), Guam Bar Assn., Internat. Club (Guam). Office: 120 W Obrien Dr Hagatna GU 96910-5174

WEEKS, JEFFREY R., mathematician, researcher, educator; b. Coronado, Calif., Dec. 10, 1956; married. BA, Dartmouth Coll., 1978; MA, Princeton U., 1980, PhD, 1985. Tchr. Stockton State Coll., Ithaca Coll., Middlebury Coll.; ind. scholar; freelance mathematician part to full time; worked with Geometry Ctr., NSF, Sci. Museums, Middlebury Coll., MacArthur Found., 1999—2004. Author: The Shape of Space; contbr. articles to profl. jours. Recipient high honors Internat. Congress Mathematicians, Levi L. Conant prize for article titled: The Poincaré Dodecahedral Space and Mystery of Missing Fluctuations, Am. Math. Soc., 2007. Achievements include research on describing the topology of knots and hyperbolic structures; developed a general-purpose computer program SnapPea.

WEEKS, JOHN ROBERT, geographer, social studies educator; b. Sacramento, June 1, 1944; s. Robert Louis and Thelma Hope (Evans) W.; m. Deanna Jean Hosea, May 16, 1965; children: John Robert, Gregory, Jennifer. AB, U. Calif., Berkeley, 1966, MA, 1969, PhD, 1972. Asst. prof. sociology Mich. State U., East Lansing, 1971-74, San Diego State U., 1974-78, assoc. prof., 1978-81, prof., 1981-92, prof. geography, 1992—, chmn. dept., 1978-85; adminstrv. dir. Internat. Population Ctr., 1985—; clin. prof. family & preventive medicine U. Calif. Sch. Medicine, San Diego, 1998—. Vis. rsch. demographer U. Calif., Berkeley, 1972; cons. Allied Home Health Assn., 1978-80, Area Agy. on Aging, San Diego, 1979-81, Los Angeles Regional Family Planning Coun., 1986—, East County Econ. Devel. Coun., 1986—, UN Food and Agrl. Orgn., 2002—. Author: Teenage Marriages, 1976, Population, 9th edit., 2005, Aging, 1984, Demography of Islamic Nations, 1988, High Fertility Among Indochinese Refuges, 1989, Demographic Dynamics of the U.S.-Mex. Border, 1992. Grantee USPHS, 1983-84, 87-88, 88-89, 90—, U.S. Adminstrn. on Aging, 1979-80, U.S. Bur. of Census, 1988-89, Andrew W. Mellon Found., 1998-2001, NSF, 2001—, NICHD, 2004—; trainee USPHS, 1967-71. Mem. Population Assn. Am., Am. Sociol. Assn., Internat. Union for Sci. Study Population, Am. Assn. Geographers. Democrat. Office: San Diego State U Dept Geography San Diego CA 92182 Office Phone: 619-594-8040. E-mail: john.weeks@sdsu.edu.

WEEKS, LORI D., elementary school educator; b. Clinton, NC, Aug. 21, 1980; d. Tony B. and Connie S. Weeks. BS, Mount Olive Coll., NC, 2002. Cert. tchr. East Carolina U., 2002. Tchr. Union Mid. Sch. Sampson County Sch. Sys., Clinton, 2002—. Cheerleading coach Union Mid. Sch., Clinton, NC, 2005—. Named Tchr. of Yr., Union Mid. Sch., 2005—06.

WEEKS, MARTA JOAN, retired priest; b. Buenos Aires, May 24, 1930; arrived in U.S., 1932; d. Frederick Albert and Anne (Newman) Sutton; m. Lewis Austin Weeks, Aug. 17, 1951; children: Kermit Austin, Leslie Anne. BA in Polit. Sci., Stanford U., 1951; MDiv, Episcopal Theol. Sem. S.W., 1991; LHD (hon.), U. Utah, 2005; DDiv (hon.), Episcop. Theol. Sem. of the S.W., 2006. Ordained priest Episcopal Ch., 1992. Legal libr., sec. Mene Grande Oil Co., Caracas, Venezuela, 1948; English tchr. Centro-Venezolano Americano, Caracas, 1948; sec. Household Fin. Corp., Salt Lake City, 1951; legal sec. McKelvey & McKelvey Attys., Durango, Colo., 1952; sec., dir. Weeks Air Mus., Miami, Fla., 1985—2001; chaplain Jackson Meml. Hosp., 1992-93; interim asst. St. James Episcopal Ch., Salt Lake City, 1994-95; assisting priest St. Andrew's Episcopal Ch., Miami, Fla., 1999—2002, 2007—; priest-at-large Episcopal Diocese of S.E. Fla., 2002—04. Trustee Beloit Coll., Wis., 1980—82, U. Miami, 1983—88, 1995—, Bishop Gray Inns, Lake Worth and Davenport, Fla., 1992—2002; advisor Ctr. for Sexuality and Religion, 1997—; nat. adv. coun. U. Utah, 1998—; trustee assoc. Am. Assn. Petroleum Geologists, 2005—; dir. S.E. Fla. Episcopal Found., 2002—05. Mem.: Am. Soc. Order St. John of Jerusalem. Address: 7350 SW 162nd St Palmetto Bay FL 33157-3820 Personal E-mail: msweeks24@bellsouth.net.

WEEKS, NANCY KAY, psychologist, educator; b. Wheeling, W.Va. d. Michael and Helen Kubachka; m. Bradley Corzier Weeks, June 29, 1991; 1 child, Marcus A. AB in Elem./Spl. Edn., West Liberty State Coll., W.Va., 1979; MS in Spl. Edn., W.Va. U., Morgantown, 1983; MS in Sch. Psychology, W.Va. Coll. Grad Studies, Charleston, 1988, EdS in Sch. Psychology, 1992. 1st grade tchr. Ohio County Bd. Edn., Wheeling, 1979—80, spl. edn. tchr., 1980—89; sch. psychologist Belmont County Ednl. Svc. Ctr., St. Clairsville, Ohio, 1989—. Adj. prof. W.Va. U., 1997—2001, West Liberty State Coll., 2004—. Mem., past chmn. funds adv. com. W.Va. 4-H, Morgantown, 1980—; bd. dirs. Ohio Country Fair, Wheeling, 1983—, pres., 2004—; mem. Ohio County Devel. Authority, Wheeling, 1999—. Named Outstanding Leader, Ohio Co., 2005; named to, W.Va. 4-H Hall of Fame, 2003; recipient Presdl. Svc. award, AmeriCorp, 2003, 30 Yr. award, 4-H, 2005. Mem.: Ohio Sch. Psychologists Assn., Nat. Assn. Sch. Psychologists. Lutheran. Home: RR 1 Box 120 C-1 Wheeling WV 26003 Office: Shadyside Local Sch Dist 3890 Lincoln Ave Shadyside OH 43947 Personal E-mail: nbmweeks@peoplepc.com.

WEEKS, PATSY ANN LANDRY, librarian, educator; b. Luling, Tex., Mar. 3, 1930; d. Lee and Mattie Wood (Callihan) Landry; m. Arnett S. Weeks, Dec. 2, 1950; children: Patsy Kate, Nancy Ann, Janie Marie. BS, Southwest Tex. State U., 1951; MLS, Tex. Woman's U., 1979. Tchr. art, reading, math. Grandview Ind. Sch. Dist., Tex., 1950—52; tchr. phys. edn. Beaumont Ind. Sch. Dist., Tex., 1953; tchr. art, coll. algebra Cisco Jr. Coll., Tex., 1957—58; tchr. remedial reading Taylor County Schs., Tuscola, Tex., 1965—66, Anson Ind. Sch. Dist., Tex., 1971—73; libr. Bangs Ind. Sch. Dist., Tex., 1973—79, learning resources coord., 1979—90; dir. Heart of Tex. Ctr. for the Rev. and Exam. of Children's and Young Adults' Lit., 1988—2001; cons. Heart of Tex. Lit. Ctr., 2001—03. Bd. dirs. Anson Pub. Libr., Tex., 1971—72, Brownwood Pub. Libr., 2003—; mem. adv. com. Edn. Svc. Ctr., 1978—83; coord. Reading is Fundamental Program, 1978—83; counsilor Children's Round Table, 1993—; cons. Heart of Tex. Lit. Ctr., 2000—03, dir. projects, 2003—. Exhibitions include oil paintings, pastels various Tex. Fairs (1st prize, 1952, 1960), Gary Air Force Base, San Marcos, 1952. Named Coming Home Queen, Howard Payne U., 2006. Mem.: ALA, Tex. Assn. Sch. Libr. Adminstrs., Teenage Libr. Assn. Tex. (chmn. audio-visual award com. 1984), Tex. Assn. Improvement Reading, Tex. Assn. Sch. Librs. (media prodns. award com. 1985—86), Tex. Libr. Assn. (mem. intellectual freedom and profl. responsibility com. 1979—81, mem. Tex. Bluebonnet award com. 1982—85, chair adv. com. 1987, chair children's round table 1987, sec. young adult round table 1991—92, publs. com. 1991—, round table coun. 1993—95), Intellectual Freedom Round Table, Am. Assn. Sch. Librs., Young Adult Libr. Svcs. Assn. (chair Baker and Taylor award jury com. 2006—, outstanding books for coll.bound-fine arts com., publ.'s liaison com.), Assn. Libr. Svc. to Children (Caldecott award com. 1986, Grosset and Dunlap Group award selection com. 1988, nominating com. 1989, chair 1989—91, Newbery award com. 1999, Disting. Svc. award com. 2002—, Disting. Svc. award com. chair 2003—, cons. priority gorup II profl. devel.), Tex. State Tchr. Assn. (life), Bangs Prog. Women's Club (treas. 1974—76), Delta Kappa Gamma, Beta Phi Mu, Alpha Chi, Kappa Pi, Phi Delta Kappa. Bapt. Office: Howard Payne Univ Sta Walker Memorial Library Heart of Tex Ctr Brownwood TX 76801 Home Phone: 325-752-7315; Office Phone: 325-649-8606. Business E-Mail: pweeks@hptux.edu.

WEEKS, ROBERT ANDREW, materials science researcher, educator; b. Birmingham, Ala., Aug. 23, 1924; s. William Andrew and Annie Bell (Hammond) W.; m. Jane Sutherland, Mar. 20, 1948; children: Kevin Dale, Robin Dee, Loren Hammond, Kerry Andrew. BS, Birmingham-So. Coll.,

1947; MS, U. Tenn., 1951; PhD, Brown U., 1966. Sr. physicist Union Carbide Corp., Oak Ridge, Tenn., 1951-84; rsch. prof. material sci. Vanderbilt U., 1984-99, prof. emeritus, 1999—. Disting. vis. prof. Am. U. in Cairo, 1970-71; invited prof. Ecole Poly. Fed. de Lausanne, Switzerland, 1981; vis. prof. Cath. U., Leuven, Belgium, 1983; cons. numerous pvt. corps. and fed. agys.; prin. investigator lunar materials, 1968-74; co-prin. investigator expdn. Western desert of Egypt to desert glass site, 1981; CEO Oak Ridge Cons., 1993—. Co-editor: Effects of Modes of Formation on Structure of Glass, 1985, 88, Editing the Refereed Scientific Journal, 1994; assoc. editor Jour. Geophys. Rsch., 1968-74; editor Jour. Noncrystalline Solids, 1988-98; conf. editor Jour. Non-Crystalline Solids, 1998-2000; contbr. numerous articles to profl. jours. Served with U.S. Army, 1943-46. Union Carbide fellow, 1964; Fulbright lectr., 1980, Rsch. fellow Reading U., 1971, USIA Am. participant Egypt, India, Nepal and Sri Lanka, 1986; Sir Neville Mott award, Jour. Non-Crystalline Solids, 2006. Fellow Am. Ceramic Soc. (symposium hon. chmn. 2004, 06, R. A. Weeks Symposium named in his honor, Honolulu 1993, 2004, George W. Morey award 1998, Sir Neville Mott award 2006); mem. AAAS, Am. Phys. Soc., Sigma Xi. Avocation: photography. Home and Office: 509 Shannondale Way Maryville TN 37803 Personal E-mail: e1e2e4@aol.com.

WEEKS, ROSS LEONARD, JR., museum executive; b. Jamestown, NY, Sept. 11, 1936; s. Ross Leonard and Cecile Forbes (Carrie) W.; m. Patricia Ann Earley, June 10, 1961 (div.); children: Susan Woodall, Ross Leonard III, William Andrew, David James. AB, Colgate U., Hamilton, NY, 1958; MS, George Wash. U., Washington, DC, 1971; cert., Fed. Exec. Inst., 1988. Reporter Jamestown Post-Jour., Va., 1958-60, Richmond News Leader, 1960-65; dir. pub. info. Coll. William and Mary, Williamsburg, Va., 1965-71, asst. to exec. v.p., 1971-74, asst. to pres., dir. univ. comms., 1974-81; exec. dir. Jamestown-Yorktown Found., 1981-91, Hist. Crab Orchard Mus., Inc., Tazewell, Va., 1992—2002; ret., 2002; pres. Blue Ridge Concepts, Ltd., 1999—. Editor William and Mary Alumni Gazette, 1966-81; author: Virginia's Tazewell County: A Last Great Place, 2000; editor: 'Cause I'm Colored-The Black Heritage of Tazewell County, 2001; columnist: Clinch Valley News, 1998-2004. Chmn. Williamsburg-James City Bicentennial, 1975-77; treas. Coalfield Regional Tourism Devel. Authority S.W. Va., 1993-97; Va. S.W. Blue Ridge Highlands, Inc., 1993-97, v.p., 1996-97, pres., 1997-99; sec., treas. Frontier Culture Found., 1982-86; exec. dir. Va. Independence Bicentennial Commn., 1981-83; trustee coun. Thirteen Original States, 1982-87; chair Tazewell County Tourism Devel. Commn., 1993-97; mem. regional grant panel Va. Com. on the Arts, 1998—; mem. Gov.'s Va. History Initiative, 1995-2002; mem. parish coun., parish adminstr. Tazewell-Buchanan Cath Ch., 2003-. Mem. Am. Assn. Mus. (mus. assessment cons. 1988—), Am. Assn. State and Local History, Masons, Rotary (Paul Harris fellow 1987), Clan Ross Assn., SAR (pres. Clinch Mountain Militia chpt. 2001-03), Sigma Delta Chi, Kappa Delta Rho (Ordo Honora 1986). Avocations: travel, landscaping, antiques, history. Home: 205 View Hill Tazewell VA 24651 Personal E-mail: ross@4sw.us.

WEEKS, STEVEN WILEY, lawyer; b. Topeka, Mar. 7, 1950; s. Glen Wiley and Grace Aileen (West) W.; m. Lee Nordgren, Aug. 1, 1974 (div. 1985); 1 child, Kirstin Nordgren. BS summa cum laude, Washburn U., 1972; JD cum laude, Harvard U., 1977. Bar: Ohio. Project leader Nat. Sanitation Found., Ann Arbor, Mich., 1972; engr. Kans. Dept. Health and Environ., Topeka, 1972-74; ptnr. Taft, Stettinius & Hollister, Cin., 1977—. Dir. The Myers Y. Cooper Co., Cin.; adj. faculty Chase Coll. Law, 1987-88. Mem. adv. com. prosecuting atty., Hamilton County, Cin., 1992; mem. Hamilton County Rep. Ctrl. Com., 1994—. Mem. Ohio State Bar Assn., Cin. Bar Assn. Republican. Methodist. Avocations: computers, golf. Home: 3560 Traskwood Cir Cincinnati OH 45208

WEEKS, THEODORE R., history professor; BA, U. Colo., 1980, MA, 1984; PhD, U. Calif., Berkeley, 1992. Asst. prof. So. Ill. U., Carbondale, Ill., 1993—97, assoc. prof., 1997—2007, prof., 2007—. Assoc. editor: Kritika: Explorations in Russian and Eurasian History, 1999—; author: Nation and State in Late Imperial Russia, 1996, From Assimilation to Antisemitism: The Jewish Question in Poland, 1850-1914, 2006. Office: So Ill Univ History Dept MC 4519 1000 Faner Dr Rm 3374 Carbondale IL 62901 Office Phone: 618-453-7874.

WEEKS, WILFORD FRANK, retired geophysics educator, glaciologist; b. Champaign, Ill., Jan. 8, 1929; married; 2 children. BS, U. Ill., 1951, MS, 1953; PhD in Geology, U. Chgo., 1956. Geologist mineral deposits br. U.S. Geol. Survey, 1952-55; glaciologist USAF Cambridge Research Ctr., 1955-57; asst. prof. Washington U., St. Louis, 1957-62; adj. prof. earth scis. Dartmouth Coll., Hanover, NH, 1962-85; glaciologist Cold Regions Rsch. and Engring. Lab., Hanover, 1962-89; chief scientist Alaska Synthetic Aperture Radar Facility, Fairbanks, 1986-93; prof. geophysics Geophys. Inst. U. Alaska, Fairbanks, 1986-96. Cons. in field, 1996—; vis. prof. Inst. Low Temperature Sci. Hokkaido U., Sapporo, Japan, 1973; chair Arctic marine sci. USN Postgrad. Sch., Monterey, Calif., 1978-79; mem. earth sys. sci. com. NASA, Washington, 1984-87; advisor U.S. Arctic Rsch. Commn., divsn. polar programs NSF, Washington, 1987-88; chmn. NAS Com. on Cooperation with Russia in Ice Mechanics, 1991-92; mem. environ. task force MEDEA Cons. Group, 1992-2002. Capt. USAF, 1955—57. Recipient Emil Usibelli Prize for Rsch., 1996, U. Ill. Dept. Geology Alumni Achievment award, 1999. Fellow Arctic Inst. N.Am., Am. Geophys. Union; mem. NAE, Internat. Glaciological Soc. (v.p. 1969-72, pres. 1973-75, Seligman Crystal award 1989), Am. Polar Soc. (hon.). Avocations: contrabassist, geophysics. Home and Office: 6533 SW 34th Ave Portland OR 97239-1077 Office Phone: 503-244-1695. E-mail: w-f-weeks@comcast.net.

WEEKS, WILLIAM RAWLE, JR., oil industry executive; b. Denver, Oct. 23, 1920; s. William Rawle Sr. and Besse Elizabeth (Griffith) W.; m. June Suzanne Stephens, Jan. 22, 1944 (div. 1980); children: Stephen R., Tacy A. Weeks Hahn. BA, Stanford U., 1943. With book prodn. divsn. Stanford U. Press, 1948-49; advt. exec. Palo Alto, Calif., 1949-50; with CIA, 1951—; gen. ptnr. Weeks, Brewer & Assocs., 1971; CEO Fort Collins Consol. Royalties, Inc., Cheyenne, Wyo., 1983—. Author: Knock and Wait Awhile, 1957 (Edgar Allan Poe award 1958, Commonwealth award 1958). Nat. press and media advance man Muskie Vice Presdl. Campaign, 1968. 2nd lt. U.S. Army, 1943-46. Mem. Nat. Press Club, Denver Petroleum Club. Avocations: flying, skiing, golf, hiking.

WEEMS, HELEN RACHEL, musician, educator; d. David Burnola and Charys Weems; m. Robert Raymond Provine. BA, Sch. of the Ozarks, Point Lookout, Mo., 1986; MM, Peabody Conservatory of Music, Balt., 1991; MA, U. Md. Baltimore County, Balt., 1996. Cert. piano tchr. Music Tchrs. Nat. Assn., 2004. Radio host Sta. KSOZ, Point Lookout, 1985-86, Sta. WJHU, Balt., 1994-96; freelance pianist, tchr., singer, 1975—. Balinese dancer UMBC Gamelan, Balt., 1993—96; coord. Harper's Glen Watch, Columbia, 1998—; Choir dir. St. Luke's Episcopal Ch., Brookeville, Md., 1997—. Neighborhood improvement grantee, Gov.'s Office of Crime Control and Prevention, 1999—2002. Mem.: Greater Columbia Music Tchrs. Assn. (v.p. 1997—2000, pres. 2005—), Howard County Music Tchrs. Assn. (pres. 1999—2003, concert mgr. 2002—06). Democrat. Episcopalian. Avocations: running, gardening. Office: Helen R Weems Piano Studio 5473 Green Dory Ln Columbia MD 21044-1912

WEEMS, KERRY N., federal agency administrator; b. Portales, N.Mex., 1956; BA in Philosophy, N.Mex. State U., 1978, BBA in Mgmt., 1978; MBA, U. N.Mex., 1981. Staff mem. Appropriations Com. US Senate, 1981—83; program & budget analyst US Dept. Health & Human Svcs., Washington, 1983—88, program analyst Office of Budget, 1988—91, chief budget planning br., 1991—96, dir. divsn. budget policy, execution & mgmt., 1996—2002, acting dep. asst. sec. budget, 2001—02, acting asst. sec. for budget, tech. & fin., 2003—05, dep. chief staff, 2005—. Office: US Dept Health & Human Svcs 200 Independence Ave SW Rm 609-FW Washington DC 20201 *

WEEMS, LORI K., lawyer; b. Lubbock, Tex., Sept. 26, 1968; BA magna cum laude, Baylor Univ., 1990, JD summa cum laude, 1994. Bar: Fla. 1996. Law clerk to Hon. Sam D. Johnson U.S. Ct. Appeals, 5th Cir., Fla., 1994—96; assoc. to ptnr. Holland & Knight, Miami, 1996—2005; prin. Prieguez & Weems, LLC, Tallahassee, 2005—. Recipient Lynn Futch Most Productive Young Lawyer, Fla. Bar, 2003, Vol. Atty. of Yr., Lawyers for Children Am., 2004. Mem.: Dade County Bar Assn., ABA (bd. gov. 2002—04, ho. of delegates 2004—06), Phi Beta Kappa. Office: Prieguez & Weems LLC 112 E Jefferson St Fl 2 Tallahassee FL 32301

WEEN, MARTIN M., lawyer; b. Bklyn., Aug. 31, 1946; BA in English cum laude, SUNY, Buffalo, 1967; JD, NYU, 1971. Bar: NY 1971, US Dist. Ct. So. Dist. NY, US Dist. Ct. Ea. Dist. NY, US Dist. Ct. No. Dist. NY. Ptnr. Wilson, Elser, Moskowitz, Edelman & Dicker LLP, NYC. Mem.: ABA (tort & ins. practice sect.), NY State Bar Assn. (corp., banking & bus. law sections). Office: Wilson Elser Moskowitz Edelman & Dicker LLP 150 E 42nd St 23rd Fl New York NY 10017-5639 Office Phone: 212-490-3000 ext. 2290. Office Fax: 212-490-3038. Business E-Mail: weenm@wemed.com.

WEERACKODY, VIJITHA, electrical engineer, researcher; BSc in Engring. with 1st class honors, U. Moratuwa, Sri Lanka, 1983; PhD, U. Pa., Phila., 1984—89. Mem. tech. staff Bell Laboratories, Lucent Technologies, Murray Hill, NJ, 1990—2001; pres. PetaNetworks, NYC, 2002—05; sr. profl. staff Johns Hopkins U./APL, Laurel, Md., 2005—. Cons. TLVentures, Wayne, Pa., 2004—; adj. assoc. prof. U. Pa., Phila., 2004—. Achievements include patents for About 25 US Patents on Wireless/Communication Systems. Office: Johns Hopkins Univ/APL 11100 Johns Hopkins Rd Laurel MD 20723 Home Phone: 917-705-2049. Personal E-mail: vijitha@ieee.org. Business E-Mail: vijitha.weerackody@jhuapl.edu.

WEERTMAN, JOHANNES, materials science educator; b. Fairfield, Ala., May 11, 1925; s. Roelof and Christina (van Vlaardingen) W.; m. Julia Ann Randall, Feb. 10, 1950; children: Julia Ann, Bruce Randall. Student, Pa. State Coll., 1943-44; BS, Carnegie Mellon U., 1948, DSc, 1951; postgrad., Ecole Normale Superieure, Paris, 1951-52. Solid State physicist U.S. Naval Rsch. Lab., Washington, 1952-58, cons., 1960-67; sci. liaison officer U.S. Office Naval Rsch., Am. Embassy, London, 1958-59; faculty Northwestern U., Evanston, Ill., 1959—, prof. materials sci. dept., 1961-68, chmn. dept., 1964-68, prof. geol. scis. dept., 1963—, Walter P. Murphy prof. materials sci. and engring. emeritus, 1999—. Vis. prof. geophysics Calif. Inst. Tech., 1964, Scott Polar Rsch. Inst., Cambridge (Eng.) U., 1970-71, Swiss Fed. Inst. Reactor Rsch., 1986; cons. Cold Regions Rsch. and Engring. Lab., U.S. Army, 1960-75, Oak Ridge (Tenn.) Nat. Lab., 1963-67, Los Alamos (N.Mex.) Sci. Lab., 1967—; co-editor materials sci. books MacMillan Co., 1962-76. Author: Dislocation Based Fracture Mechanics, 1996, (with Julia Weertman) Elementary Dislocation Theory, 1964, 2d edit., 1992; mem. editorial bd. Metal. Trans., 1967-75, Jour. Glaciology, 1972—; assoc. editor Jour. Geophys. Rsch., 1973-75, 2000-01; contbr. articles to profl. jours. With USMC, 1943-46. Honored with naming of Weertman Island in Antarctica.; Fulbright fellow, 1951-52; recipient Acta Metallurgica gold medal, 1980; Guggenheim fellow, 1970-71 Fellow Am. Acad. Arts and Scis., Am. Soc. Metals, Am. Phys. Soc., Geol. Soc. Am., Am. Geophys. Union (Horton award 1972, AIME Mathewson Gold medal 1977); mem. AAAS, NAE, Am. Inst. Physics, Internat. Glaciol. Soc. (Seligman Crystal award 1983), Arctic Inst., Am. Quaternary Assn., Explorers Club, Fulbright Assn., Sigma Xi, Tau Beta Pi, Phi Kappa Phi, Alpha Sigma Mu, Pi Mu Epsilon. Home: 834 Lincoln St Evanston IL 60201-2405 Office: Northwestern U Materials Sci Dept Evanston IL 60208-0001 Home Phone: 847-328-8718; Office Phone: 847-491-3197. Business E-Mail: j-weertman2@northwestern.edu.

WEERTMAN, JULIA RANDALL, materials engineering educator; b. Muskegon, Mich., Feb. 10, 1926; BS in Physics, Carnegie-Mellon U., 1946, MS in Physics, 1947, DSc in Physics, 1951. Physicist U.S. Naval Rsch. Lab., Washington, 1952-58; vis. asst. prof. dept. materials sci. and engring. Northwestern U., Evanston, Ill., 1972-73, asst. prof., 1973-78, from asst. prof. to assoc. prof., 1973-82, prof., 1982-99, Walter P. Murphy prof., 1989, chmn. dept., 1987-92, asst. to dean grad. studies and rsch. Tech. Inst., 1973-76, Walter P. Murphy prof. emeritus, 1999—. Mem. various NRC coms. and panels. Co-author: Elementary Dislocation Theory, 1964, 1992, also pub. in French, Japanese and Polish; contbr. numerous articles to profl. jours. Mem. Evanston Environ. Control Bd., 1972-79. Recipient Creativity award NSF, 1981, 86; Guggenheim Found. fellow, 1986-87. Fellow Am. Soc. Metals Internat. (Gold medal 2005), Minerals, Metals and Materials Soc. (leadership award 1997, Robert Mehl lectr. 2006); mem. NAE, Am. Acad. Arts and Scis., Am. Phys. Soc., Materials Rsch. Soc. (Von Hippel award 2003), Soc. Women Engrs. (Disting. Engring. Educator award 1989, Achievement award 1991). Home: 834 Lincoln St Evanston IL 60201-2405 Office: Northwestern U Dept Material Sci & Engring 2220 Campus Dr Evanston IL 60208-0876 Office Phone: 847-491-5353. Business E-Mail: jrweertman@northwestern.edu.

WEERTS, RICHARD KENNETH, music educator; b. Peoria, Ill., Oct. 7, 1928; s. Gerhard Nicholas and Ellen Marie (Lindeburg) W. BS, U. Ill., 1951; MA, Columbia U., 1956, EdD, 1960; MA, N.E. Mo. State U., 1973. Tchr. Lyndhurst (N.J.) Pub. Schs., 1956-57; dir. instrumental music Scotch Plains (N.J.) Pub. Schs., 1957-61; prof. music Truman State U., Kirksville, 1961—, chair dept. music, 1994—. Author: Handbook for Woodwinds, 1965, Developing Individual Skills for the High School Band, 1969, How to Develop and Maintain a Successful Woodwind Section, 1972, Original Manuscript Music, 1973, Handbook of Rehearsal Techniques for Band, 1976; numerous papers and monographs; nat. bd. editors The Quarterly, jour. of Ctr. for Rsch. in Music Learning and Teaching, 1989. Dir. music First United Meth. Ch., Kirksville, 1970—. Served with U.S. Army, 1951-55. Mem. Coun. for Rsch. in Music Edn., Nat. Assn. Coll. Wind and Percussion Instrs. (nat. exec. sec./treas. 1971—, editor jour. 1968—), Music Educators Nat. Conf., Phi Delta Kappa. Office: NACWPI Truman State U Divsn Fine Arts Kirksville MO 63501

WEESE, BENJAMIN HORACE, architect; b. Evanston, Ill., June 4, 1929; s. Harry Ernest and Marjorie (Mohr) W.; m. Cynthia Rogers, July 5, 1963; children: Daniel Peter, Catharine Mohr. B.Arch., Harvard U., 1951, M.Arch., 1957; cert., Ecole des Beaux Arts, Fontainebleau, France, 1956. Assoc., Harry Weese & Assocs., Architects, Chgo., 1957-77; prin. Weese Langley Weese, Chgo., 1977—. Co-founder, pres. Chgo. Arch. Found., Glessner House, Chgo., 1966. Trustee Graham Found. for Advanced Studies in Fine Arts, 1988-2006, pres. 1995-99; mem. Commn. Chgo. Landmarks, 1998—. Fellow: AIA. Home: 2133 N Hudson Ave Chicago IL 60614-4522 Office: Weese Langley Weese Ltd 9 W Hubbard St Chicago IL 60610-4630 Office Phone: 312-642-1820. Business E-Mail: bweese@wlwltd.com.

WEESE, CYNTHIA ROGERS, architect, educator; b. Des Moines, June 23, 1940; d. Gilbert Taylor and Catharine (Wingard) Rogers; m. Benjamin H. Weese, July 5, 1963; children: Daniel Peter, Catharine Mohr. BSA.S., Washington U., St. Louis, 1962; B.Arch., Washington U., 1965. Registered architect, Ill. Pvt. practice architecture, Chgo., 1965-72, 74-77; draftsperson, designer Harry Weese & Assocs., Chgo., 1972-74; prin. Weese Langley Weese Ltd., Chgo., 1977—; design critic Ball State U., Muncie, Ind., Miami U., Oxford, Ohio, 1979, U. Wis.-Milw., 1980, U. Ill.-Chgo., 1981, 85, Iowa State U., Ames, 1982, Washington U., St. Louis, 1984, U. Ill., Champaign, 1987-92, Kans. State U., 1992; dean sch. architecture Washington U., St. Louis, 1993—. Bd. regents Am. Architecture Found., 1990-93; bd. mem. Landmarks Commn. St. Louis.; mem. Mayor's Task Force Downtown Now, St. Louis, 1997—. Recipient Alpha Rho Chi award Washington U., 1965, Met. Chgo. YWCA Outstanding Achievement award, 1990. Mem. AIA (bd. dirs. Chgo. chpt. 1980-83, v.p. 1983-85, 1st v.p. 1986-87, pres. 1987-88, regional dir. 1990-92, Disting. Bldg. awards 1977, 81-83, 86, 91, 95, Interior Architecture award 1981, 90, 92, nat. v.p. 1993, chmn. urban design task force St. Louis 2004 1997—), AIA/ACSA Coun. on Archtl. Rsch. (chair 1991-92), AIA Found. (pres. Chgo. chpt. 1988-89), Soc. Archtl. Historians (bd. dirs. 1992-94), Chgo. Women in Architecture, Chgo. Network, Nat. Inst. Archtl. Edn. (bd. dirs. 1988-90), Chgo. Archtl. Club (pres. 1988-89), Washington U. Sch. Architecture Alumni (nat. coun. 1988-93), Lambda Alpha. Clubs: Arts, Chgo. Archtl. Democrat. Office: Washington U Sch Architecture PO Box 1079 Saint Louis MO 63188-1079

WEESE, JOHN AUGUSTUS, retired mechanical engineer; b. Topeka, July 24, 1933; s. Ray Augustus and Margaret Maureen (Richmond) Weese; m. Betty Kay Dietrich, June 5, 1955; children: Carol Ann, Katherine Lynn. BSME, Kans. State U., 1955; MS, Cornell U., 1958, PhD, 1959. Asst. prof. USAF Acad., Colo., 1960-62; assoc. prof. mech. engring. U. Denver, 1963-67, prof., 1967-74, chmn. mech. sci. and environ. engring., 1968-70, dean engring., 1970-74, Old Dominion U., Norfolk, Va., 1974-83; dir. mech. engring. and applied mechanics NSF, Washington, 1983-85, dir. mechanics structures and materials engring., 1985-86; prof. mech. engring. Tex. A&M U., College Station, 1986—2005, head dept. engring. tech., 1986-97, coord. accreditation, regents prof., 1997—2005, interim head mech. engring. dept., 2001—03, prof. emeritus, 2005—. Structural dynamics engr. Boeing Co., Wichita, Kans., 1959—60, rsch. specialist, 1962—63; rsch. engr. Martin-Marietta Corp., Denver, 1963. Co-author: (book) Mechanics of Materials, 4th edit., 1985; contbr. articles to profl. jours. Fellow: ASME (ad hoc visitor 1977—83, Ben C. Sparks medal 1994), Am. Soc. Engring. Edn. (projects bd. engring. rsch. coun. 1982—85, chmn. publs. com. 1983—86, exec. com. 1984—90, chmn. engring. rsch. coun. 1988—90, v.p. pub. affairs 1995—97, pres.-elect 1998—99, pres. 1999—2000, Outstanding Educator mechanics divsn. 1989, Frederick J. Berger award 1997, W. Leighton Collins award 2004, Presdl. Disting Svc. award 2005). Republican. Congregationalist. Avocations: fishing, photography. Home: 34 Harness Creek View Ct Annapolis MD 21403-1678

WEFALD, JON, academic administrator; b. Nov. 24, 1937; s. Olav and Walma (Ovrum) W.; m. Ruth Ann; children— Skipp, Andy. BA, Pacific Lutheran U., Tacoma, 1959; MA, Wash. State U., Pullman, 1961; PhD, U. Mich., Ann Arbor, 1965. Teaching asst. Wash. State U., Pullman, 1959—61; teaching fellow U. Mich., Ann Arbor, 1961—64; assoc. prof. Gustavus Adolphus Coll., St. Peter, Minn., 1965—70; commnr. agr. State of Minn., St. Paul, 1971—77; pres. Southwest State U., Marshall, Minn., 1977—82; chancellor Minn. State Univ. System, St. Paul, 1982—86; pres. Kans. State U., Manhattan, 1986—. Author: A Voice of Protest: Norwegians in American Politics 1890-1917, 1971. Mem. Mid-Am. Internat. Agri-Trade Council (pres. 1974-75), Midwest Assn. State Depts. of Agr. (sec.treas. 1976-77), U.S. Dept. Agr. Joint Council on Food and Agrl. Scis. Office: Kans State U Office of Pres 110 Anderson Hall Manhattan KS 66506-0100 Office Phone: 785-532-6221. E-mail: pres@ksu.edu. *

WEG, JOHN GERARD, physician; b. NYC, Feb. 16, 1934; s. Leonard and Pauline M. (Kanzleiter) W.; m. Mary Loretta Flynn, June 2, 1956; children: Diane Marie, Kathryn Mary, Carol Ann, Loretta Louise, Veronica Susanne, Michelle Celeste. BA cum laude, Coll. Holy Cross, Worcester, Mass., 1955; MD, N.Y. Med. Coll., 1959. Diplomate: Am. Bd. Internal Medicine. Commd. 2nd lt. USAF, 1958, advanced through grades to capt., 1967; intern Walter Reed Gen. Hosp., Washington, 1959-60; resident, then chief resident in internal medicine Wilford Hall USAF Hosp., Lackland AFB, Tex., 1960-64, chief pulmonary sect., 1964-66, chief inhalation sect., 1964-66, chief pulmonary and infectious disease service, 1966-67; resigned, 1967; clin. dir. pulmonary disease div. Jefferson Davis Hosp., Houston, 1967-71; from asst. prof. to assoc. prof. medicine Baylor U. Coll. Medicine, Houston, 1967-71; assoc. prof. medicine U. Mich. Med. Sch. Univ. Hosp., Ann Arbor, 1971-74, prof., 1974—2001, prof. emeritus, 2001—. Physician-in-charge pulmonary divsn., 1971-81, physician-in-charge pulmonary and critical care med. divsn., 1981-85, co-chair instnl. review bd., 2004—; cons. Ann Arbor VA, 1971—. Wayne County Gen. Hosps., 1971-84; mem. adv. bd. Washtenaw County Health Dept., 1973—; mem. respiratory and nervous sys. panel, anesthesiology sect. Nat. Ctr. Devices and Radiol. Health, FDA, 1983—, chmn., 1985-88. Contbr. med. jours., reviewer, mem. editorial bds. Decorated Air Force Commendation medal; travelling fellow Nat. Tb and Respiratory Disease Assn., 1971; recipient Aesculpaius award Tex. Med. Assn., 1971 Master ACP (chmn. Mich. program com. 1974); fellow Am. Coll. Chest Physicians (chmn. bd. govs. 1976-79, gov. Mich. 1975-79, chmn. membership com. 1976-79, prof.-in-residence 1972—, chmn. critical care coun. 1982-85, chmn. ethics com. 1998, master fellow, 2002, master FCCP, 2002, master), Am. Coll. Chest Physicians and Internat. Acad. Chest Physicians (master, exec. council 1976-82, pres. 1980-81); mem. AAAS, Am. Fedn. Clin. Rsch., AMA, Am. Thoracic Soc. (sec.-treas. 1974-76), Am. Assn. Inhalation Therapy, Air Force Soc. Internists and Allied Specialists, Soc. Med. Consultants to Armed Forces, Internat. Union Against Tb, Mich. Thoracic Soc. (pres. 1976-78), Mich. Lung Assn. (dir., Bruce Douglas award 1981), Am. Lung Assn., Rsch. Club U. Mich., Assn. Advancement Med. Instrumentation, Central Soc. Clin. Rsch., Am. Bd. Internal Medicine (subsplty. com. on pulmonary disease 1980-86, critical care medicine test com. 1985-87, critical care medicine policy com. 1986-87), N.Y. Med. Coll. Alumni Assn. (medal of honor 1990), Alpha Omega Alpha. Home: 3060 Exmoor Rd Ann Arbor MI 48104-4132 Office: B I H 245 Box 0026 1500 E Medical Center Dr Ann Arbor MI 48109-0005 Home Phone: 734-971-6156; Office Phone: 734-763-2540. Business E-Mail: jweg@umich.edu.

WEGENER, MARK DOUGLAS, lawyer; BA cum laude, Cen. Coll., Pella, Iowa, 1970; JD, Rutgers U., 1973. Assoc. Howrey & Simon, Washington, 1973-79; ptnr., mem. exec. com. Howrey LLP, Washington, 1979—, chmn. global litigation practice group. Office: Howrey LLP 1299 Pennsylvania Ave NW Washington DC 20004-2400

WEGERSON, EDWARD J., lawyer; b. Chgo. Heights, Mar. 25, 1953; s. Edward Louis and Eileen W. Wegerson; m. Mary D. Simonett, July 19, 1980; children: Paul Edward, Sarah Maria. BA, U. Minn., Duluth, 1975; JD, U. Minn., Mpls., 1978. Assoc. Fryberger Buchanan, Duluth, 1978—81, Weise & Cox. Ltd., Mpls., 1981—83, Lindquist & Vennum, Mpls., 1983—87, ptnr., 1987—. Recipient Disting. Alumni award, U. Minn. Duluth Dept. Econs., 2001. Office: Lindquist & Vennum LLP 80 S 8th St Minneapolis MN 55402 Office Phone: 612-371-3549. Office Fax: 612-371-3707. Business E-Mail: ewegerson@lindquist.com.

WEGGE, LEON LOUIS FRANÇOIS, retired economics educator; b. Breendonk, Antwerp, Belgium, June 9, 1933; came to U.S., 1959; s. Petrus Maria and Alberta (De Maeyer) W.; m. Beate Maria Teipel, Nov. 22, 1962; children: Simone, Robert, Elizabeth. B in Thomistical Philosophy, Cath. U. Louvain, Belgium, 1957, Licentiate in Econ. Sci., 1958; PhD in Indsl. Econs., MIT, 1963. Assoc. lectr. U. New S. Wales, Kensington, Australia, 1963-66; prof. econs. U. Calif., Davis, 1966-94, retired, 1994. Vis. prof. U. Bonn, Fed. Republic Germany, 1980-81. Assoc. editor Jour. Internat.

Econs., 1971-84; contbr. articles to profl. jours. Rsch. fellow Ctr. for Ops. Rsch. and Econometrics, 1972-73, fellow The Netherlands Inst. for Advanced Study, 1987-88. Mem. Econometric Soc., Am. Statistical Assn. Roman Catholic. Home: 26320 County Rd # 98 Davis CA 95616

WEGMAN, COLLEEN, food service executive; m. O'Donnell Chris Wegman; 2 children. Grad., U. Colo., 1994; MBA, Simon Sch., U. Rochester, 2000. With Wegmans Food Markets, Inc., Rochester, 1991—, various positions, including store mgr. to dir., e-commerce, 1991—2002, sr. v.p., merchandising, 2002—05, pres., 2005—. Developed Wegmans' Nature's Marketplace depts. Named one of Rochester's Influential Women, Rochester Bus. Jour., 2005. Avocation: skiing. Office: Wegmans Food Markets Inc 1500 Brooks Ave Rochester NY 14624

WEGMAN, DANIEL R., food service executive; m. Stency Wegman; children: Colleen, Nicole. BA in Economics, with honors, Harvard U., 1969. Joined Wegman's Food Markets, Rochester, NY, 1969, pres., 1976—2005, CEO, 2005—. Chmn. bd. govs. Uniform Code Coun. Named Supermarket Impresario, Self Mag., 1998; recipient Friend of Extension award, Cornell Cooperative Extension, 1997. Mem.: Food Mktg. Inst. (chmn. 1999—2001). Office: Wegmans Food Markets 1500 Brooks Ave Rochester NY 14624

WEGMAN, WILLIAM GEORGE, artist; b. Holyoke, Mass., Dec. 2, 1943; s. George W. and Eleanor (Vezina) W. BFA in Painting, Mass. Coll. Art, 1965; MFA, U. Ill., 1967. One-man shows include Gallerie Sonnabend, Paris, 1971, Pomona Coll. Art Gallery, 1971, Sonnabend Gallery, N.Y.C., 1972, 77, Galerie Ernst, Hanover, Ger., 1972, Situation, London, 1972, Konrad Fischer Gallery, 1972, 75, 79, Courtney Sale Gallery, 1972, Tex. Gallery, Houston, 1973, 75, 79, L.A. County Mus. of Art, Calif., 1973, 112 Greene St., N.Y.C., 1974, Mayor Gallery, London, 1975, Galleria Alessandra Castelli, Milan, 1975, The Kitchen, N.Y., 1976, Bruna Soletti Gallery, Milan, 1977, 82, Rosamund Felsen Gallery, 1978, Holly Solomon Gallery, N.Y.C., 1979, 80, 82, 84, 86, 88, 90, 92, Arnolfini Gallery, Eng., 1979, U. Wis., Milw., 1979, U. Colo. Art Galleries, Boulder, 1980, Marianne Deson Gallery, Chgo., 1980, Vivianne Esders Gallery, Paris, 1981, Magnuson Lee Gallery, Boston, 1981, Robert Hull Fleming Mus., Burlington, Vt., 1981, Locus Solus, Genoa, Italy, 1982, Dart Gallery, Chgo., 1982, Fraenkel Gallery, San Francisco, 1982, 88, 90, 92, 93, James Corcoran Gallery, Los Angeles, 1982, 90, Nancy Drysdale Gallery, Washington, 1982, 87, 94, Walker Art Ctr, Mpls., 1982, Ft. Worth Art Mus., Tex., 1982, De Cordova & Dana Mus. & Park, Mass., 1982, Southeastern Ctr. for Contemporary Art, Winston-Salem, N.C., 1982, The Contemporary Arts Ctr., Ohio, 1982, Newport Harbor Mus., Calif., 1982, Inst. Contemporary Arts at Va. Mus., Richmond, 1983, Fine Arts Gallery, U. Mass., Amherst, 1983, Tex. Gallery, Houston, 1983, 86, Greenville County Mus. Art, 1984, Lowe Mus. Art, Miami, Fla, 1985, Cleve. Mus. Art, 1986, Honolulu Acad. Arts, 1987, Mass. Coll. Art, Boston, 1987, U. San Diego, La Jolla, Calif., 1988, Pace MacGill Gallery, N.Y., 1988, 90, 92, 93, San Francisco Mus. Modern Art, Calif., 1988, Galerie Durand-Dessert, Paris, 1989, Budoin Lebon, Paris, 1989, Maison de la Culture et de la Communication de Saint Etienne, France, 1989, Linda Cathcart Gallery, L.A., 1990, 92, 94, The Taft Mus. Cin., 1990, The Butler Inst., Ohio, 1990, Sperone Westwater Gallery, N.Y., 1992, Kunstmuseum, Lucerne, Switzerland, 1990, ICA, London, 1990, Stedelijk Mus., The Netherlands, 1990, Frankfurt Kunstverein, Germany, 1990, Pompidou Ctr., Paris, 1990, ICA, Boston, 1990, Ringling Mus., Fla., 1990, Whitney Mus., N.Y., Contemporary Arts Mus., Tex., 1990, Neuberger Mus., SUNY, 1991, Galerie Andreas Binder, Germany, 1992, Athenaeum Music & Arts Library, Calif., 1992, Lisa Sette Gallery, Phoenix, 1994, Greg Kucera Gallery, Seattle, 1994, George Eastman House: Internat. Mus. Photography and Film, 1995, Aspen Art Mus., ACC Galerie, Weimar, Germany, 1995, Pace Wildenstein, L.A., 1995, Anderson Gallery, Pitts., 1995, Pace/MacGill Gallery, N.Y., 1995, Tex. Gallery, Houston, 1996, Jay Gorney Gallery, N.Y., 1996, Galleri Larsen, Stockholm, 1996, Ehlers Caudill Gallery, Chgo., 1996, Gallery Art Point, Tokyo, 1997, Isetan Mus. Art, Tokyo, 1997, Saks 5th Ave., N.Y.C., 1998, Geral Peters Gallery, Dallas, 1998, Mass. Coll. Art, Boston, 1999, SOMA Gallery, La Jolla, Calif., 1999, ACC Gallery Weimar, Germany, 1999, Birmingham (Ala.) Mus. Art, 1999, Durant-Dessert Gallery, Paris, 1999, Springfield (Mass.) Mus., 1999, others; exhibited in group shows at Walker Art Ctr., Mpls., 1968, N.J. State Mus., Trenton, 1968, Detroit Inst. Art, 1969, Mus. Contemporary Art, Chgo., 1969, 77, Allen Meml. Mus., 1970, L.A. County Mus., Calif., 1971, Pasadena Art Mus., 1972, Contemporary Arts Mus., Houston, 1972, Whitney Mus. Am. Art, N.Y.C., 1973, 81, 89, Sonnabend Gallery, N.Y.C., 1974, Milw. Art Ctr., 1975, Sarah Lawrence Coll. Gallery, 1975, Phila. Mus. Art, 1976, San Francisco Mus. Modern Art, 1976, U. Calif.-Berkeley Art Mus., 1976, U. Chgo., 1976, Ringling Mus. Art, Sarasota, Fla., 1977, Walker Art Gallery, Eng., 1978, Holly Solomon Gallery, N.Y.C., 1978, 82, 87, Mus. Fine Arts, Houston, 1978, Aspen Ctr. Visual Arts, 1979, Santa Barbara Mus. Art, 1979, Mus. Modern Art, N.Y.C., 1980, 82, 83, Sidney Janis Gallery, 1981, Art Inst. Chgo., 1981, 82, Young Hoffman Gallery, Chgo., 1983, Inst. Contemporary Art, Boston, 1983, Castelli Graphics, N.Y.C., 1983, Queens Mus., N.Y., 1986, James. Madison U., Harrison, Va, 1987, Fay Gold Gallery, Atlanta, 1988, Hudson River Mus., 1989, Volcano Arts Ctr., 1989, Pace/MacGill, N.Y.C., 1990, The History of Travel, The Taft Museum, Cin., The Butler Inst. Youngstown, Ohio, 1990, William Wegman: Paintings, Drawings, Photographs, Videotapes, Kunstmuseum, Luzern, Stedelijk Museum, Amsterdam, Frankfurt Kunstverein Frankfurt, Centre Nat. d'Art et cle Culture Georges Pompidou, Paris, Inst. of Contemporary Art, London, Inst. of Contemporary Arts, Boston, Contemporary Arts Mus., Houston, J.M. Ringling Mus., Sarasota, Whitney Mus., of American Art, N.Y., 1990-92, Outdoor Photographs, Neuberger Mus., State U. of N.Y. at Purchase, 1991, William Wegman: L'oeuvre photographique, 1969-76, Fonds Regional d'Art Contemporary, Limousin, France, 1991, New Polaroids, Holly Solomon Gallery, N.Y.C., Early Black and White Photographs, Pace/MacGill Gallery, N.Y.C., New Paintings, Sperone Westwater Gallery, N.Y.C., 1992, Turner/Krull Galleries, L.A., 1993, Calif. Ctr. Arts, Escondido, 1994, Drawing Space, N.Y., 1995, Found. Cartier pour l'art Contemporain, Paris, 1996, Lance Fung Gallery, N.Y., 1997, Huntingdon Beach (Calif.) Art Ctr., 1998, Art: Concept, Paris, 1999, many others; contbr. articles to profl. jours.; videography: Reel 1, 1970-72, Reel 2, 1972, Reel 3, 1972-73, Reel 4, 1973-74, Reel 5, 1975, Reel 6, 1975-76, Reel 7, 1976-77, Reel 8, 1997-98, Reel 9, 1999, Spit Sandwich, 1970, Gray Hairs, 1974-75, World History, 1976, Man Ray, Man Ray, 1978, Accident, 1979, How to Draw, 1983, The World of Photography, 1985, Blue Monday Music Video, 1988, Alive From Off Center, 1988, Sesame Street Videos, 1989, 92, 93, 94, 95, 96, 97, 98, 99; film: Dog Baseball, 1986, The Hardly Boys in Hardly Gold, 1995; publications: Man's Best Friend, 1982, Everyday Problems, 1984, William Wegman: Paintings, Drawings, Photographs, Videotapes, 1990, Cinderella, 1993, Little Red Riding Hood, 1993, ABC, 1994, 1, 2, 3, 1995, Triangle, Circle, Square, 1995, Mother Goose, 1996, Farm Days, 1997, Puppies, 1997, My Town, 1998, What Do You Do?, 1999, Pup, 1999, Fay, 1999, William Wegman, Orange Co Mus Art, Newport Beach, Calif, 2000, Pillbury & Peters Gallery, Washington, DC, 2000, Grant Selwyn Fine Art, Calif, 2003, David Adamson Gallery, Wash DC, 2003, Sperone Westwater, NY, 2003, Pace-Macgaill Gallery, NY, 2003, many others; represented in numerous pub. collections including Kunstaus, Zurich, Mpls. Inst. Art, Mus. Fine Art, Houston, Bklyn. Mus., L.A. County Mus. Art, Mus. Fine Art, Houston, St. Louis Mus. Modern Art, Walker Art Ctr., Mpls., Whitney Mus. Am. Art, N.Y., Albright-Knox Gallery, Buffalo, Austrlian Nat. Gallery, Canberra, others; exhibited in numerous film and video festivals. Recipient Creative Artists Pub. Svc. award, 1979; Guggenheim Found. fellow, 1975, 86, Nat. Endowment for the Arts grantee, 1976, 82.

WEGNER, GARY ALAN, astronomer; b. Seattle, Dec. 26, 1944; s. Herbert Edward and Melba Jean (Gardner) W.; m. Cynthia Kay Goodfellow, June 25, 1966; children: Josef, Kurt, Christian, Peter-Jürgen, Emma. Student, Wash. State U., Pullman, 1963-65; BS, U. Ariz., 1967; PhD, U. Wash., Seattle, 1971. Fulbright fellow Mount Stromlo Obs., Camberra, A.C.T., 1971-72; departmental demonstrator in astrophysics Oxford U., England, 1972-75; sr. sci. rsch. officer South African Astron. Obs., Capetown, Republic of South Africa, 1975-78; Annie J. Cannon fellow U. Del., Newark, 1978-79; asst. prof. Pa. State U., State College, 1979-82; asst. prof. to assoc. prof. physics and astronomy Dartmouth Coll., Hanover, NH, 1982-88, Margaret Anne and Edward Leede Disting. prof. physics and astronomy, 1988—; dir. Mich.-Dartmouth-MIT Obs., 1991-99. Vis. astronomer Cornell U., 1992; vis. fellow St. Catherine's Coll., Oxford, 2002. Editor: White Dwarfs, 1989; contbr. articles to jours. in field. Keeley fellow Wadham Coll., Oxford, 1992-93, vis. fellow in astrophysics Oxford U., 1992-93; vis. prof. Astron. Inst. Ruhr U. Bochum, Germany, 1993-94; recipient rsch. prize The Alexander von Humboldt Found., Germany, 1993-94, numerous grants NSF, NASA. Mem. Am. Astron. Soc., Internat. Astron. Union. Luthran. Office: Dartmouth Coll Dept Physics & Astronomy Wilder Lab Hanover NH 03755 Business E-Mail: gary.wegner@dartmouth.edu.

WEGNER, JOHN MARK, historian; b. Toledo, May 5, 1956; s. John Albert Wegner and Roxanna Marion Fulk. BA, U. Toledo, 1979; MA, Bowling Green State U., Ohio, 1982, PhD, 1992; MS, Ea. Mich. U., Ypsilanti, 2006. Pub. rels. writer Evergreen Local Schs., Metamora, Ohio, 1977—79; prodr. WBGO-TV, Bowling Green, 1980—81; lectr. history Ea. Mich. U., Ypsilanti, 2003—. Spkr. in field; adj. instr. Monroe CC, Toledo, 1992—2003. Contbr. articles to profl. jours. Trustee Ea. Mich. U. Fedn. Tchrs., Ypsilanti, 2005—. Recipient Leo Steinem Journalism award, U. Toledo; fellow, Bowling Green State U., 1982—92. Mem.: Nat. Trust Hist. Preservation, Ohio Acad. History. Independent. Lutheran. Avocations: photography, cooking, gardening, landscape design. Home: 4131 Grantley Rd Toledo OH 43613 Office: Ea Mich U 701-K Pray-Harrold Ypsilanti MI 48197

WEGNER, JUDITH WELCH, lawyer, educator, dean; b. Hartford, Conn., Feb. 14, 1950; d. John Raymond and Ruth (Thulen) Welch; m. Warren W. Wegner, Oct. 13, 1972. BA with honors, U. Wis., 1972; JD, UCLA, 1976. Bar: Calif. 1976, D.C. 1977, N.C. 1988, U.S. Supreme Ct. 1980, U.S. Ct. Appeals. Law clk. to Judge Warren Ferguson, U.S. Dist. Ct. for So. Dist. Calif., LA, 1976-77; atty. Office Legal Counsel and Land & Natural Resources Divsn. U.S. Dept. Justice, Washington, 1977-79; spl. asst. to sec. U.S. Dept. Edn., Washington, 1979-80; vis. assoc. prof. U. Iowa Coll. Law, Iowa City, 1981; asst. prof. U. NC Sch. Law, Chapel Hill, 1981-84, assoc. prof., 1984-88, assoc. dean, 1986-88, prof., 1988—2007, dean, 1989-99, Burton Craige prof., 2007—; sr. scholar Carnegie Found. for Advancement of Tchg., 1999—2001; chmn. faculty U. NC, 2003—06. Spkr. in field. Chief comment editor UCLA Law Rev., 1975-76; co-author Educating Lawyers, 2007, State and Loval Government in a Federal System, 6th edit., 2007; contbr. articles to legal publs. Mem. Bd. Alderman, Carrboro, NC, 1984—89; mem. planning bd. Orange County, NC, 2006—; mem. bd. dir. Carol Woods Retirement Ctr., 2006—. Recipient Ernest Bell award, NC Assn. Mcpl. Attys. Mem.: ABA, Assn. Am. Law Schs. (pres. 1995), Internat. Mcpl. Lawyers Assn., Women's Internat. Forum, NC Assn. Women Attys., NC State Bar Assn., Order of the Coif, Phi Beta Kappa. Democrat. Office: U NC Sch Law Van Hecke Wettach Hall Campus Box 3380 Chapel Hill NC 27599-3380 Home Phone: 919-929-5024; Office Phone: 919-962-4113. Business E-Mail: judith_wegner@unc.edu.

WEGNER, MARY, state librarian; Degree in Hist., Iowa State U., 1971; MLS, U. Iowa, 1973. Reference libr. Waterloo Pub. Libr.; caucus staffer Iowa Ho. of Reps.; dir. Iowa Meth. Libr., Iowa Luth. Libr., Blank Children's Hosp., Des Moines; asst. state libr. State Libr. Iowa, Des Moines, 2000, state libr., 2001—. Mem. bd. trustees Bibliog. Ctr. for Rsch., 2000—. Mem.: Chief Officers State Libraries Assn. (vice chair, legis. com.), Iowa Libr. Assn. (pres. 1999). Office: State Library of Iowa Ola Babcock Miller Bldg 1112 E Grand Ave Des Moines IA 50319-0233 Office Phone: 515-281-4105. Office Fax: 515-281-6191. Business E-Mail: mary.wegner@lib.state.ia.us. *

WEH, ALLEN EDWARD, aviation executive; b. Salem, Oreg., Nov. 17, 1942; s. Edward and Harriet Ann (Hicklin) W.; m. Rebecca Ann Roberton, July 5, 1968; children: Deborah Susan, Ashley Elizabeth, Brian Roberton. BS, U. N.Mex., 1966, MA, 1973. Asst. to chief adminstrv. officer Bank N.Mex., Albuquerque, 1973; pres. N.Mex. Airways, Inc., Albuquerque, 1974; dep. dir. N.Mex. Indochina Refugee Program, Santa Fe, 1975-76; dir. pub. affairs UNC Mining & Milling Co., Albuquerque, 1977-79; pres., CEO, CSI Aviation Svcs., Inc., Albuquerque, 1979—. Chmn. New Mex. State Republican Party, 2004—. Bd. dir. N.Mex. Symphony Orch., Albuquerque Conv. and Visitors Bur., 1982; mem. Albuquerque Police Adv. Bd., 1977-78; co-chmn. fin. com. Rep. Heather Wilson (Rep.-N.Mex.) Re-Election Campaign, 1999-2004; mem. state fin. com. G.W. Bush for Pres.; co-chmn. N.Mex. Victory, 2000; chmn. N.Mex. Rep. Party, 2004—; mem. nat. adv. bd. U. N.Mex. Anderson Sch. Bus.; elected del. GOP Nat. Conv., 2000, 04; chmn. Nat. Com. Employer Support of the Guard and Res., 2002-03. Capt. USMC, 1966-71, Vietnam; Col. USMCR, 1971-97, active duty, 1990-91, Persian Gulf, 1992-93, Somalia, 2003-04, Iraq. Decorated Silver Star, Legion of Merit, Bronze Star with V device, Purple Heart with two gold stars, Meritorious Svc. medal with gold star, five Air medals. Mem. Marine Corps Res. Officers Assn. (life, bd. dir. 1973, 86), Res. Officers Assn. U.S. (life), SCV (life), N.Mex. Retail Assn. (chmn. 1999-2000). Episcopalian. Office: CSI Aviation Svcs Inc 3700 Rio Grande Blvd NW Albuquerque NM 87107-2876 Office Phone: 505-761-9000.

WEHDE, ALBERT EDWARD, lawyer; b. Milw., Feb. 14, 1935; s. Albert Christian and Mary Hubbel (Dewey) W.; m. Joan M. Forney, Nov. 4, 1978; children: John C., Edward T. BS, Marquette U., 1956, JD, 1960. Bar: Wis. 1960, Calif. 1968. Atty. AEC, Albuquerque, 1963-66; counsel Lockheed Aircraft Co., Sunnyvale and Redlands, Calif., 1966-73; assoc. Schultz & Manfield, Palo Alto, Calif., 1973-74; sr. counsel FMC Corp., Santa Clara, Calif., 1974-95; atty. AEW Internat. Cons., Sunnyvale, 1995—. Bd. dirs. Tech. Credit Union, San Jose, Calif., 1982—, chmn., 1994-96. Pres. Mountain View (Calif.) Babe Ruth League, 1976; trustee Mid-Peninsula Family Services Assn., Palo Alto, 1973-74. Served to capt. U.S. Army, 1960-63. Mem. ABA (chmn. region VII pub. contracts sect. 1977-81), Santa Clara County Bar Assn. (co-chmn. corp. counsel sect. 1983-84, mem. exec. com.), Am. Corp. Counsel Assn. (chpt. sec., pres. 1988, bd. dirs. 1983-93), Wis. Bar Assn. (bd. dirs. non resident lawyers divsn. 2002-03, pres. 2004-05, bd. govs. 2003-06). Democrat. Roman Catholic. Avocations: gourmet cooking, music, sports. Home: 1106 Lorne Way Sunnyvale CA 94087-5157 Personal E-mail: wehde@aol.com.

WEHN, KAREN SWANEY, education educator, consultant; b. Chillicotne, Ohio, Mar. 1, 1950; d. Glenn Warren and Joyce Wood Swaney; m. David Carl Wehn, Apr. 8, 1989; 1 child, Glenn Ian Taylor. BA, Ohio State Univ., Columbus, Ohio, 1980; MS, Kent State Univ., Kent, Ohio, 1986. Cert. Profl. Geologist 1996. Rsch. asst. Ohio State Univ., Columbus, Ohio, 1976—92; project geologist Conestaga Rover 3 Assoc., Niagara Falls, NY, 1992—97, Golder Assoc., Niagara Falls, NY, 1997—; lectr. Buffalo State Coll., Buffalo, 1997—; asst. prof. Erie CC, Buffalo, 2000—. Rschr., Antarctica, 1980—85; pres. Buffalo Assn. of profl. Geologists, Buffalo, 1997—98. Contbr. articles pub. to profl. jour. Lay leader Warrens Corners United Meth. Ch., 2004—05. Grantee travel to Australia, Nat. Sci. Found., 1982, travel and work in Nigeria, Earth Watch, 1990—91. Mem.: Air and Waste Mgmt. Assn. (bd. mem.). Meth. Business E-Mail: wehnks@bscmail.buffalostate.edu.

WEHR, MATTHEW, music educator; b. Allentown, Pa., Sept. 7, 1980; s. Mark and Julie Wehr. BS in Music Edn., Lebanon Valley Coll., Annville, Pa., 2002. Assoc. organist First Presbyn. Ch., Allentown, Pa., 2003—; music tchr. No. Lehigh Sch. Dist., Slatington, Pa., 2002—06, So. Lehigh Sch. Dist., Center Valley, Pa., 2006—. Sec. No. Lehigh Edn. Assn., Slatington, 2005—06. Mem.: Am. Guild Organists. Presbyterian. Avocations: travel, golf, theater. Home: 2209 W Walnut St Allentown PA 18104 Office: Southern Lehigh High Sch 5800 Main St Center Valley PA 18034 Home Phone: 484-221-8390; Office Phone: 610-282-1421.

WEHRING, BERNARD WILLIAM, nuclear engineering educator; b. Monroe, Mich, Aug. 3, 1937; s. Bernard Albert and Alma Christina (Graf) W.; m. Margaret Mary Robinson, Sept. 5, 1959; children: Mary Ann, James, Susan, Barbara. BSE. in Physics, U. Mich., 1959, BSE. in Math, 1959; MS in Physics, U. Ill., 1961, PhD in Nuclear Engring, 1966. Asst. prof. nuc. engring. U. Ill., Urbana, 1966-70, assoc. prof., 1970-77, prof., 1977-84, asst. dean engring., 1981-82; prof. nuc. engring. N.C. State U., Raleigh, 1984-89; dir. nuc. reactor program NC State U., Raleigh, 1984-89; prof. mech. engring. U. Tex., Austin, 1989-2000, dir. Nuc. Engring. Tchg. Lab., 1989-2000; adj. prof. nuc. engring. NC State U., Raleigh, 2000—. Cons. Argonne and Los Alamos nat. labs.; mem. crosssect. evaluation working group Brookhaven Nat. Lab. Contbr. sects. to books, articles to profl. publs. AEC fellow, 1963-65; NSF grantee, 1968— Fellow Am. Nuc. Soc.; mem. Am. Nuclear Soc. (standards com.), Am. Phys. Soc. Achievements include contributing in the generation of basic nuc. data and develop. of new instruments and exptl. techniques. Home: 516 Westbrook Dr Raleigh NC 27615-7321 Business E-Mail: bwwehrin@eos.ncsu.edu.

WEHRLE, LEROY SNYDER, economist, educator; b. St. Louis, Feb. 5, 1932; s. Fred Joseph and Eleanor (Snyder) W.; m. JoAnn Griffith, Aug. 29, 1959; children— Chandra Lee, Lon Joseph. BS, Washington U., St. Louis, 1953; MA in Econs, Yale, 1956, PhD with honors, 1959. Asst. instr. Yale, 1958-59; with econ. sect. AID mission to Laos, 1960-61; sr. staff economist President's Council Econ. Advisers, 1961-62; spl. econ. adviser to U.S. Ambassador Unger, Vientiane, 1962; dep. dir. AID mission to Laos, 1963-64; asst. dir. AID mission, also econ. counsellor to U.S. ambassador, Saigon, 1964-67; asso. dir. AID Mission, Saigon, 1964-67; dept. asst. adminstr. Vietnam, AID, Dept. State, 1967-68; univ. fellow Harvard, 1968-69; sr. fellow Brookings Instn., 1969-70; dir. Ill. Inst. for Social Policy, Springfield, 1970-72; aide to Lt. Gov. Paul Simon, 1972; prof. economics Sangamon State U., 1972-88; founding ptnr., chief exec. officer Health Econs. and Mkt. Analysis Inc., Springfield, 1987-94; pres. Healthcare Cost Analysis, Inc., 1994—. Chmn. bd. Tie Collar, Ltd. Mem. spl. study group Alliance Progress, 1962; mem. Rockefeller Latin Am. Mission, 1969; chmn. study team world food and nutrition study Nat. Acad. Sci., 1976-77. Served with AUS, 1953-55. Recipient William A. Jump meml. award, 1966 Home and Office: 2001 S Bates Ave Springfield IL 62704-3304 Office Phone: 217-206-7781. Personal E-mail: wehrle@springnet1.com.

WEHRMAN, ELIZABETH ANN, music educator; b. Nelson, Nebr., July 18, 1932; d. Homer Ballard and Esther May (Long) W. BA, Hastings Coll., 1953; MusM in Edn., U. Colo., 1962, PhD, 1980. Educator music Hyannis Pub. Schs., Nebr., 1953—56; acct. Mountain States Lumber Assn., Denver, 1956-57; tchr. Ft. Benton Pub. Schs., Mont., 1957—61; grad. asst. U. Colo., Boulder, 1961-62, teaching assoc., 1972-74; teaching supr. Sheridan Pub. Schs., Wyo., 1962—66; tchr. Nelson Pub. Schs., Nebr., 1967—72; prof. music Western Ill. U., Macomb, 1974—. Clinician, condr. schs., Ill., Iowa, Minn., 1970—. Dir. ch. choir Bushnell Presbyn., Ill., 1986—, St. George's Episcopalian, Macomb, Ill., 1976-80. Mem. Music Educators Nat. Conf., Coll. Music Soc. (life), Am. Choral Dirs. Assn., Am. Orff Schulwerk Assn., Nat. Band Assn., Aft Tchrs. Union, PEO Internat., Order Eastern Star, Delta Kappa Gamma, Sigma Alpha Iota, Blue Key. Republican. Presbyterian. Avocations: music, bowling, photography, gardening. Home: 7320 N 1200th Rd Colchester IL 62326-1709 Office: We Ill U Browne Hall 120 Macomb IL 61455 Office Phone: 309-298-1405.

WEHRWEIN, AUSTIN CARL, freelance/self-employed reporter; b. Austin, Tex., Jan. 12, 1916; s. George S. and Anna (Ruby) W.; m. Judith Oakes, 1950; children: Sven Austin, Paul, Peter, Joanna Judith. AB, U. Wis., 1937; LL.B., Columbia U., 1940; student, London Sch. Econs., 1948. Reporter Washington Bur., UP, 1941-43, 46-48; information specialist E.C.A., London, Copenhagen, Oslo, Stockholm, 1948-51; financial writer Milw. Jour., 1951-53; staff corr. Time, Inc., Chgo., 1953-55; reporter Chgo. Sun-Times, 1955-56, fin. editor, 1956-57; chief Chgo. bur. N.Y. Times, 1957-66; editorial writer Mpls. Star, 1966-82. Editor The Observer, 1984-87. Served with USAAF, 1943-45; mem. staff Stars and Stripes 1945-46, Shanghai, China. Recipient Pulitizer prize for internat. reporting, 1953; Disting. Journalism award U. Wis., 1963; cert. of merit ABA Gavel competition, 1968, 80; Gavel award, 1969, 71 Home and Office: 2309 Carter Ave Saint Paul MN 55108-1640 E-mail: wehr2309@msn.com.

WEI, BINGQING, engineering educator; b. Changchun, Jinlin Province, China; PhD, Tsinghua U., Beijing, 1992. Asst. prof. La. State U., Baton Rouge, 2003—07; assoc. prof. U. Del., Newark, 2007—. Mem.: Internat. Soc. Optical Engring., Electrochem. Soc., Materials Rsch. Soc. Office: U DE 126 Spencer Lab Newark DE 19716 Office Phone: 302-831-6438. Office Fax: 302-831-3619. Business E-Mail: weib@udel.edu.

WEI, HENG, engineering educator; BS in Civil/Hwy. and Traffic Engring., Beijing U. Tech., 1985, ME in Civil/Hwy. and Traffic Engring., 1988; MS in Civil Engring., U. Kans., 1996, PhD, 1999. Cert. profl. engr., Mich. Lectr., scientist Beijing U. Tech., 1988—93; rsch. and tchg. asst. U. Kans., Lawrence, 1993—98; sr. its transp. sys. engr. Iteris, Inc. and TranSmart Technologies, Inc., Anaheim, Calif., 1998—2004; lectr. Calif. State Poly. U. Pomona, 2003—04, U. So. Calif., LA, 2003—04; asst. prof. U. Cin., 2004—. Editor-in-chief U. Kans. Transp. Ctr., Lawrence, 1994—98; trb rep. U. Cin., Transp. Rsch. Bd., Washington, 2004—. Recipient Outstanding Undergrad. Student award, Beijing U. Tech., 1985; grantee, NSF, 2005, TEC Engring., Inc., 2005. Mem.: N.Am. China Overseas Transp. Assn., Internat. Chinese Transp. Profls. Assn., Engring. Soc. Detroit, Inst. Transp. Engrs. (corr.; advisor to UC student chpt.), Transp. Rsch. Bd. (corr.). Achievements include development of a new method using video-capture technique to extract vehicular trajectory and supportive software, Vehicle Video-Capture Data Collector (VEVID); strategies for large Urban Intermodal Hubs and Radiator Rodway Systems; research in methodology for prioritizing locations of Urban Transit Transfer Centers; planning on Beijing Urban Intermodal Transportational Systems; China Metropolitan Comprehensive Transportation System Planning Modes; Heuristic-Optimization Models for Service Request Vehicle/Crew Routing with Time Windows in a GIS Environment; Iteris Transportation Systems projects. Office: Dept of Civil & Environ Engring Univ of Cincinnati Cincinnati OH 45221 Office Fax: 513-556-2599. Business E-Mail: heng.wei@uc.edu.

WEI, JAMES, chemical engineering professor, academic dean; b. Macao, China, Aug. 14, 1930; came to U.S., 1949, naturalized, 1960; s. Hsiang-chen and Nuen (Kwok) W.; m. Virginia Hong, Nov. 4, 1956; children: Alexander, Christina, Natasha, Randolph (dec.). BS in Chem. Engring, Ga. Inst. Tech., 1952; MS, MIT, 1954, ScD, 1955; grad., Advanced Mgmt.

Program Harvard, 1969. From rsch. engr. to rsch. assoc. Mobil Oil, Paulsboro, NJ, 1956-62, sr. scientist Princeton, NJ, 1963-68, mgr. corp. planning NYC, 1969-70; Allan P. Colburn prof. U. Del., Newark, 1971-77; Sherman Fairchild distinguished scholar Calif. Inst. Tech., 1977; Warren K. Lewis prof. MIT, Cambridge, 1977-91, head dept. chem. engring., 1977-88; Pomeroy and Betty Smith prof. chem. engring. Princeton (N.J.) U., 1991—, dean Sch. Engring. and Applied Sci., 1991—2002. Vis. prof. Princeton, 1962-63, Calif. Inst. Tech., 1965; cons. Mobil Oil Corp.; cons. com. on motor vehicle emissions Nat. Acad. Sci., 1972-74, 79-80; mem. sci. adv. bd. EPA, 1976-79; mem. Presdl. Pvt. Sector Survey Task Force on Dept. Energy, 1982-83. Bd. editors Chem. Tech, 1971-80, Chem. Engring. Communications, 1972—; cons. editor chem. engring. series, McGraw-Hill, 1964—; editor-in-chief: Advances in Chemical Engineering, 1980; Contbr. papers, monographs to profl. lit., The Structure of Chemical Processing Industries, 1979. Trustee Am. U. Beirut, 1998—, Smith Coll., 1999—. Recipient Am. Acad. Achievement Golden Plate award, 1966. Mem. AIChE (dir. 1970-72, Inst. lectr. 1968, Profl. Progress award 1970, Walker award 1980, Lewis award 1985, v.p. 1987, pres. 1988, Founders award 1990), Am. Chem. Soc. (award in petroleum chemistry 1966), Nat. Acad. Engring. (nominating com. 1981, 96, peer com. 1980-82, membership com. 1983-85, Draper award com. 1995-97, chair chem. engring. sect. 1998-99), AAAS, Am. Acad. Arts and Scis., Academica Sinica of Taiwan, Sigma Xi. Home: 571 Lake Dr Princeton NJ 08540 Office: Princeton U Engring Quadrangle Princeton NJ 08544-5263 E-mail: jameswei@princeton.edu.

WEI, XIANGDONG, physicist, researcher; s. Bo and Jinzhi Wei. BS in Astrophysics, Peking U., Beijing, 1982; MS in Physics, Syracuse U., NY, 1992, PhD in Physics, 1994. From tchg. asst. to rsch. assoc. Syracuse U., 1988—98; asst. physicist Brookhaven Nat. Lab., Upton, NY, 1998—2000, assoc. physicist, 2000—03, physicist, 2003—. Presenter in field. Contbr. articles to profl. jours. Mem.: Am. Phys. Soc. Achievements include development of highly polarized frozen-sipn HD targets for both nuc. physics and inertial-confinement-fusion experiments; design of utilizing the polarized HD target sys. for nuc. physics measurements; research in spin-lattice relaxation time of HD-hydrogen deuteride. Office: Brookhaven Nat Lab 20 Pennsylvania Ave Upton NY 11973 Home Phone: 631-928-5844; Office Phone: 631-344-8012.

WEI, XINZHOU, engineering educator; b. China; PhD, CUNY, NYC, 2002. Lectr. CUNY, Coll. Tech., Bklyn., 2002—03, asst. prof., 2003—. Program com. Internat. Symposium on Knowledge Comm. and Conf., Orlando, Fla., 2006—; session chair The 8th World Multi-Conf. on Systemics, Cybernetics and Informatics, Orlando, 2004; Asian Am. high edn. coun. Asian Rsch. Inst., NYC, 2004—; info. tech. com. CUNY Coll. Tech., Bklyn., 2003—; reviewer IEE Jour. of Info. Security, 2006—. Recipient Sue Rosenberg Zalk Student Rsch. and Travel award, CUNY, 2002, Best Paper award, 6th World Multi-Conf. Systemics, Cybernetics and Informatics, 2002, 8th World Multi-Conf. Systemics, Cybernetics and Informatics, 2004, 2d prize, Chinese Nat. Higher Edn. Com., 1991; grantee Perkins grantee, N.Y. State, 2006—, PSC-CUNY grantee, Rsch. Found. of the CUNY, 2006—, 2005—06, 2004—05. Mem.: Internat. Soc. of Systemics, Cybernetics and Informatics, Asian Rsch. Inst. (ny 2004—06), IEEE. Office: City University of New York / CityTech Dept of Electrical Eng 300 Jay Street Brooklyn NY 11201

WEIANT, ELIZABETH ABBOTT, retired biology professor; b. New Britain, Conn., July 4, 1913; d. William Armstrong and Flora (Abbott) W. BS, MS, Tufts U., 1943; MA, Radcliffe Coll., 1952; EdD, Boston U., 1970. Instr. biology Tufts Coll., Medford, Mass., 1943-56, asst. prof., 1957-61; asst. prof. biology Simmons Coll., Boston, 1961-71, assoc. prof., 1972-79, chmn. dept., 1977-79, ret., 1979; corr. Evening Citizen, Laconia, N.H., 1987-98, Franklin-Tilton Telegram, Franklin, N.H., 1990-2000. Rschr. OSRD, USPHS, NSF, 1943-61; sr. rsch. fellow Max-Planck Inst., Seewiesen, Fed. Republic Germany, 1958; physiologist for product validation Cordis Corp., Miami, Fla., 1970 Contbr. articles to profl. jours. Active Hist. Dist. Commn., Sanbornton, NH, 1979-83; sec., Sanbornton Conservation Commn., 1979-83, Trustees of Trust Fund, Sanbornton, 1985-96; bd. dirs., sec. NH affiliate Am. Heart Assn., Manchester, 1981-85; bd. dirs., com. mem. Franklin, NH, Regional Hosp., 1984-91; pres. Sanbornton Hist. Soc., 1980-82; publicity chmn. Friends NH Music Festival; alumna trustee Tufts U., 1974-81, trustee emeritus, 1981—. Recipient Disting. Svc. award Tufts U., 1970, Tower award Westbrook Coll., Portland, Maine, 1974, Woman of Yr. award Tilton-Northfield Bus. and Profl. Women, 1980, Heart of Gold award Am. Heart Assn., 1986, award for Pub. Svc. Belknap County Pomona Grange, 1990, Gov.'s Outstanding Vol. award, 1992. Mem.: Am. Inst. Biol. Scis., Grange, Sigma Xi (sec. Tufts U. chpt. 1947—59). Republican. Home: PO Box 11 Sanbornton NH 03269-0011

WEICHER, JOHN CHARLES, economist, research director; b. Chgo., Mar. 8, 1938; s. John Jr. and Ruth Agnes (Waits) W.; m. Alice Jean Landt, Sept. 30, 1972; children: John Victor, Stephany Jean Ruth. AB, U. Mich., 1959; PhD, U. Chgo., 1968. Acting asst. prof. U. Calif., Irvine, 1965-67; assoc. and asst. prof. econs. Ohio State U., Columbus, 1967-77; with div. policy rsch. OEO, Washington, 1972-73; dir. div. econ. policy HUD, Washington, 1973-74, dep. asst. sec. econ. affairs, 1975-77, asst. sec. policy devel. and rsch., 1989—93, asst. sec. housing, commr. FHA, 2001—05; dir. econs. and fin. markets program Urban Inst., Washington, 1977-81; F.K. Weyerhaeuser scholar in pub. policy Am. Enterprise Inst, Washington, 1981-87; assoc. dir. econ. policy Office Mgmt. and Budget, Washington, 1987-89; dir. urban polity studies Hudson Inst., Washington, 1993—2001, dir. Ctr. Housing and Fin. Markets, 2005—. Author: Urban Renewal: Federal Program for Local Problems, 1972, Housing: Federal Policies and Programs, 1980, Maintaining the Safety Net, 1984; contbr. articles to profl. jours. Mem. Am. Econ. Assn., Am. Real Estate and Urban Econs. Assn. (pres. 1982, George Bloom award career achievement, 1993). Republican. Presbyterian. Avocation: sports. Office: Hudson Inst 1015 15th St NW Washington DC 20005 Home Phone: 202-327-0966, 202-244-1706; Office Phone: 202-974-2420. Office Fax: 202-974-2410. Business E-Mail: john@hudson.org.

WEICK, CYNTHIA WAGNER, business educator; b. Lincoln, Nebr., Jan. 29, 1957; d. Richard and Gloria Jean (Larsen) W. PhD, The Wharton Sch. U. of Pa, Phila., PA, 1982—86; MS, The Ohio State U., Columbus, OH, 1979—80, BS, 1975—79. Corp. planner Pioneer Hi-Bred, Internat., Des Moines, 1987—90; cons. United Nat. Devel. Program, Manhattan, NY, 1984—85; rsch. scientist Battelle Columbus Laboratories, Columbus, Ohio, 1980—82; prof. U. Pacific, Stockton, Calif., 1990—, Neven C. Hulsey chair in bus. excellence, 2006—. Contbr. articles on mgmt. of tech. to profl. jours. Dean's fellow Wharton Sch., U. Pa., 1983-84. Mem. AAAS. Avocations: art, philosophy, kayaking. Office: Univ of the Pacific 3601 Pacific Avenue Stockton CA 95211 Office Phone: 209-946-2631. Business E-Mail: cwagner@uop.edu.

WEICKERT, WANDA OPAL, child welfare and attendance counselor, psychotherapist, educator; b. LaCygne, Kans., Apr. 10, 1941; d. Frank W and Opal M Weickert. BS in Phys. Edn., Kans. State Coll., 1959—63, MS in Phys. Edn., 1963—66; MA in Marriage and Family Therapy, Phillips Grad. Inst., 1983—85; Pupil Personnel Services Credential, Calif. Luth. Coll., 1987—89. Marriage Family Child Therapist Bd. of Behavioral Sciences-California, 1991; Teaching Credential Kans., 1963, Calif., 1969. Health phys. edn. tchr. Circle HS, Towanda, Kans., 1963—69; phys. edn. tchr. Nightingale Mid. Sch., LA, 1969—73; coach & phys. edn. tchr. Reseda Sr. HS, LA, 1973—81; career edn., coach, tchr. Kennedy Sr. HS, LA, 1981—89; child welfare & attendance counselor LA Unified Sch. Dist., 1989—; marriage family child therapist Self Employed, LA, 1991—; dist. counselor LA Unified Schs., 1994—2001. Coord. cheerleaders, kayettes and pep club Circle HS, Towanda, Kans., 1963—69; dir. camp waterfront Young Women's Christian Assn., Wichita, Kans.; counselor San Fernando Valley Mental Health Clinic, Van Nuys, Calif., 1985—88; drug prevention program dir. Kennedy HS, LA, 1987—89; counselor Valley Cmty. Clinic, North Hollywood, Calif., 1989—92; adv. bd. Sch. Attendance Rev. Bd. LAUSD, LA, 1991—2001; coach 1st pl. gymnast fl. exercise, city championships LA Unified Schs., 1976, coach 3d pl. volleyball team city championships, 79, coach 3d pl. gymnast all-around events, city championships, 80, crisis team leader, 1996—2001. Choreographer (drill team performance) LA Coliseum, 1977, Hollywood Christmas Parades, 1984—86, (1st pl. band and drill team championships) LA Unified Schs., 1978. Vol. Girl Scouts, LA, 1994—95; contbr. Civitan, Burbank, Calif.; presidents club contbr. Pitts. State U., Kans. Recipient Commendation for 32 years Pub. Sch. Svc., Mayor Jim Hahn, LA, 2001. Mem.: Calif. Assn. of Marriage and Family Therapists, Calif. Teachers Assn., Delta Psi Kappa (life), Alpha Sigma Alpha (life). Avocations: quilting, gardening, camping, swimming, walking. Home Phone: 818-893-2756; Office Phone: 818-893-2756. Personal E-mail: res1fosk@verizon.net.

WEIDA, JOHNNY A., career military officer; BS, USAF Acad., 1978; MPA, Golden Gate Univ., 1987; M in nat. security & strategic studies, Naval War Coll., 1993. Commd. 2d lt. USAF, advanced through grades to brig. gen., 2003—; pilot training, instr. pilot, flight examiner Williams AFB, Ariz., 1978—83; F-16 student pilot MacDill AFB, Fla., 1983—84; F-16 pilot 35th Tactical Fighter Squadron, Kunsan Air Base, Republic of Korea, 1984—85; F-16 instr. pilot & flight examiner 33rd Tactical Fighter Squadron, Shaw AFB, SC, 1985—88; Thunderbird pilot & ops. officer Nellis AFB, Nev., 1988—91; comdr. Cadet Squadron 27 USAF Acad., Colorado Springs, Colo., 1991—92; exec. officer, comdr. 20th Ops. Support Squadron Shaw AFB, SC, 1992—95; comdr. 12th Ops. group, Randolph AFB, Tex., 1995—97; dep. asst. chief of staff U.S. Forces Korea, Yongsan Army Garrison, Republic of Korea, 1997—99; chief combat forces div. USAF HQ, Washington, 1999—2000; comdr. 388th Fighter Wing, Hill AFB, Utah, 2000—01, Squadron Officer Coll., Maxwell AFB, Ala., 2001—03; comdt. of cadets & comdr. 34th training wing USAF Acad., Colorado Springs, Colo., 2003—. Decorated Def. Superior Svc. medal, Legion of Merit with oak leaf cluster, Disting. Flying Cross, Air Force Meritorious Svc. medal with 4 oak leaf clusters, Air Force Commendation medal, Air Force Achievement medal.

WEIDEMANN, CELIA JEAN, social sciences educator, management consultant, financial consultant; b. Denver, Dec. 6, 1942; d. John Clement and Hazel (Van Tuyl) Kirlin; m. Wesley Clark Weidemann, July 1, 1972; 1 child, Stephanie Jean. BS, Iowa State U., 1964; MS, U. Wis., Madison, 1970, PhD, 1973; post grad., U. So. Calif., 1983. Advisor UN FAO, Ibadan, Nigeria, 1973—77; ind. rschr. Asia and Near East, 1977—78; program coord., asst. prof., rsch. assoc. U. Wis., Madison, Wis., 1979—81; chief inst. and human resources US AID, Washington, 1982—85; team leader, cons. Sumatra, Indonesia, 1984; dir. fed. econ. program Midwest Rsch. Inst., Washington, 1985—86; founder, pres. emeritus Weidemann Assoc., Arlington, Va., 1986—2000; pres. Weidemann Found., Arlington, Va., 2000—. Cons. U.S. Congress, Aspen Inst., Ford Found., World Bank, Egypt, Nigeria, Gambia, Pakistan, Indonesia, AID, Thailand, Jamaica, Panama, Philippines, Sierra Leone, Kenya, Jordon, Poland, India, Egypt, Russia, Finnish Internat. Devel. Agy., Namibia, pvt. client Estonia, Latvia, Russia, Japan, Internat. Ctr. Rsch. on Women, Zaire, UN FAO, Ghana, Internat. Statis. Inst., The Netherlands, Global Exch., 1986-87, Asian Devel. Bank, Mongolia, Nepal, Vietnam, Bangladesh, Indonesia, Philippines; peer reviewer NRC, NAS Author: (book) Planning Home Economics Curriculum for Social and Econ. Develop., Agrl. Ext. for Women Farmers in Africa, 1990, Fin. Services for Women, 1992, Egyptian Women and Micro.: The Invisible Entrepreneurs, 1992, Small Enterprise Development in Poland: Does Gender Matter?, 1994, Micro. and Gender in India, 1995, Supporting Women's Livelihoods: Micro Fin. That Works for the Majority, 2002; contbr. chapters to books and articles to profl. journals. Bd. visitors Sch. Human Ecology, U. Wis., 2002—; bd. dirs. Women's Polit. Com., Santa Barbara, Cmty. Counseling Ctr., Santa Barbara, Calif., 2004—, Cmty. Counseling and Edn. Ctr., Santa Barbara, Calif. Am. Home Econ. Assn. Fellow, 1969-73; grantee Ford Found., 1987-89. Mem. Soc. Internat. Devel., Am. Sociol. Assn., Assn. for Women in Devel. (pres. 1989, founder, bd. dirs.), Women in Devel. (steering com.), Coalition for Women's Econ. Devel. and Global Equality, Internat. Devel. Conf. (bd. dirs., exec. com.), Internat. Platform Assn., Pi Lambda Theta, Omicron Nu. Avocations: mountain trekking, piano and pipe organ, canoeing, photography, poetry. Office: Weidemann Found 749 Westwood Drive Santa Barbara CA 93109 Home Phone: 805-637-7988; Office Phone: 805-965-2902. Personal E-mail: jweidemann@aol.com.

WEIDEMEYER, CARLETON LLOYD, lawyer; b. Hebbville, Md., June 12, 1933; BA in Polit. Sci., U. Md., 1958; JD, Stetson U., DeLand, Fla., 1961. Bar: Fla. 1961, DC 1971, US Dist. Ct. (mid. dist.) Fla. 1963, US Ct. Appeals (5th cir.) 1967, US Ct. Appeals (DC cir.) 1976, US Supreme Ct. 1966, US Ct. Appeals (11th cir.) 1982. Rsch. asst. Fla. 2d Dist. Ct. Appeals, 1961-65; ptnr. Kalle and Weidemeyer, St. Petersburg, Fla., 1965-68; asst. pub. defender 6th Jud. Cir., Fla., 1966-69, 81-83; ptnr. Wightman, Weidemeyer, Jones, Turnbull and Cobb, Clearwater, Fla., 1968-82; pres. Carleton L. Weidemeyer, P.A. Law Office, 1982—; pres. So. Mcpl. Corp., 1997—. Guest lectr. Stetson U., 1978—80; lectr. estate planning seminars. Author: (handbook) Arbitration of Entertainment Claims, Baltimore County's Second District, The Emerging Thirties, 1990, Area History, Baltimore County, 1990, History of Musicians' Association of Clearwater, Local 729, AFM, 1999; editor Ad Lib mag., 1978-81; pub. Weidemeyer World Quar., 2000—; contbr. articles to profl. jours.; performer This Is Your Navy Radio Show, Memphis, 1951-52; leader Polka Dots, The Jazz Notes, 1976—; mem. St. Paul Ch. Orch., Fla. Hist. Soc., 1973-1976, Md. Hist. Soc., 1990—, Pinellas County Estate Planning Assn., 1997—; performer Clearwater Jazz Holiday, 1980, 81. Bd. advisors Musician Ins. Trust; trustee Francis G. Prasse Meml. Scholarship Trust, 1984—; mem. planned giving com. Upper Pinellas Assn. Retarded Citizens, 1996-2001; trustee Tampa Bay Rsch. Inst., 2001—; adv. com. Fla. Sheriff Youth Ranches, 1997—2001; bd. dirs. Pinellas Ctr. for Visually Impaired, 1999-2000; bd. dirs. Watson Ctr. for the Blind, 2000-05. Served with USN, 1951-54 Recipient Shriners Hosp. award, Upper Pinellas Assn. Retarded Citizens, 1992, Pres.'s award, 1998, Patron of Jazz award, Suncoast Classic Jazz Soc., Inc., 2003, Sertoma Centurian award, Fla. Sheriff's Assn., 1991—95. Mem. Musicians Assn. Clearwater (pres. 1976-81, emeritus 1981), Fla.-Ga. Conf. Musicians (sec., treas. 1974-76), NRA, ABA (sr. bar sect.), Fed. Bar Assn., Fla. State Hist. Soc., Md. Hist. Soc., Greater St. Petersburg Musicians Assn., Clearwater Bar Assn. (probate divsn.), Am. Fedn. Musicians (internat. law com. pres. so. conf. musicians 1979-80), Nat. Geneal. Soc., Clearwater Genealogy Soc., Md. Geneal. Soc., Augustan Soc., Lancaster Geneal. Soc. (Pa.), Pinellas Geneal. Soc. (lectr. 1995—), Carroll County Geneal. Soc. (Md.), Balt. County Geneal. Soc. (Fla.), Lancaster Mennonite Hist. Soc., Navy Hurricane Hunters, Sons Am. Revolution, Sons Union Vets. Civil War, Md. Hist. Soc., Catonsville (Md.) Hist. Soc., Am. Legion, German Am. Geneal. Assn., DAV, Fleet Res., Masons, Scottish Rite (Tampa), Egypt Temple Shrine, Moose, Sertoma (bd. dirs. Clearwater chpt. 1984-2006, v.p. 1989-92), Phi Delta Phi, Sigma Pi, Kappa Kappa Psi Home: 2261 Belleair Rd Clearwater FL 33764-2761 Office: Legal Arts Bldg Ste 1 501 S Fort Harrison Ave Clearwater FL 33756-5317

WEIDENAAR, DENNIS JAY, retired economics professor; b. Grand Rapids, Mich., Oct. 4, 1936; s. John and Jennie (Beukema) W.; m. Kristin Andrews, July 14, 1943; children: Kaarin Jaye, John Andrews. AB, Calvin Coll., Grand Rapids, 1958; MA, U. Chgo., 1961; PhD, Purdue U., 1969. Asst. prof. econs. Purdue U., West Lafayette, Ind., 1966-72, assoc. prof., 1972-77, prof., 1977-83; interim dean Krannert Sch. of Mgmt., West Lafayette, 1983-84, assoc. dean, 1984-99; dean Krannert Grad. Sch. Mgmt., West Lafayette, 1990-99, prof. econs., 1999—. Cons. TRW, B.F. Goodrich, Ea. Panhandle; bd. dirs. Lafayette Ins. Co. Author: Economics. Contbr. articles to profl. jours. Bd. dirs. Ind. Coun. on Econ. Edn., Lafayette, 1974-83. Recipient The Leavey Awd for Excellence in Pvt. Enterprise Edn., Freedom's Found., Valley Forge, 1983, Distinguished Service Awd., Joint Council on Econ. Edn., N.Y., 1986, Golden Key Nat. Honor Soc., 1985. Mem. Rotary, Delta Sigma Pi, Beta Gamma Sigma (bd. dirs.), Phi Delta Kappa. Presbyterian. Home: 217 Rosebank Ln West Lafayette IN 47906-8614

WEIDENBAUM, MURRAY LEW, economist, educator; b. Bronx, NY, Feb. 10, 1927; s. David and Rose (Warshaw) Weidenbaum; m. Phyllis Green, June 13, 1954; children: Susan, James, Laurie. BBA, CCNY, 1948; MA, Columbia U., 1949; MPA, Princeton U., 1954, PhD, 1958; LLD, Baruch Coll., 1981, U. Evansville, 1983, McKendree Coll., 1993. Fiscal economist Bur. Budget, Washington, 1949—57; corp. economist Boeing Co., Seattle, 1958—62; sr. economist Stanford Rsch. Inst., Palo Alto, Calif., 1962—63; mem. faculty Washington U., St. Louis, 1964—, prof., chmn. dept. econs., 1966—69, Mallinckrodt prof., 1971—, dir. Ctr. for Study Am. Bus., 1974—81, Washington U., St. Louis, 1982—95; chmn. Ctr. for Study Am. Bus. Washington U., St. Louis, 1995—2000; asst. sec. econ. policy US Dept. Treasury, Washington, 1969—71; chmn. Coun. of Econ. Advisors The White House, Washington, 1981—82; hon. chmn. Weidenbaum Ctr. on the Economy, Govt. and Pub. Policy, St. Louis, 2001—. Chmn. rsch. adv. com. St. Louis Regional Indsl. Devel. Corp., 1965—69; exec. sec. Pres.'s Com. on Econ. Impact of Def. and Disarmament, 1964; mem. U.S. Fin. Investment Adv. Panel, 1970—72; cons. various firms and instns.; chmn. U.S. Commn. to Rev. the Trade Deficit, 1999—2000. Author: Federal Budgeting, 1964, Modern Public Sector, 1969, Economics of Peacetime Defense, 1974, Economic Impact of the Vietnam War, 1967, Government-Mandated Price Increases, 1975, The Future of Business Regulation, 1980, Rendezvous With Reality: The American Economy After Reagan, 1988, Rendezvous With Reality: The American Economy After Reagan, paperback edit., 1990, Business, Government, and the Public, 1990, Small Wars, Big Defense, 1992, The Bamboo Network, 1996, Business and Government in the Global Marketplace, 2004, One-Armed Economist, 2004, Advising Reagan: Making Economic Policy, 1981-82, 2005; mem. editl. bd.: Publius, 1971—2004, Jour. Econ. Issues, 1972—75, Challenge, 1974—81, 1983—, Business and the Contemporary World, 1997—2000. With US Army, 1945. Named Banbury fellow, Princeton U., 1952—54; named to Free Market Hall of Fame, 1983; recipient Alexander Hamilton medal, U.S. Dept. Treasury, 1971, Disting. Writer award, Georgetown U., award for disting. tchg., Freedoms Found., 1980, award for best book in econs., Assn. Am. Pubs., 1993. Fellow: AAAS, Internat. Acad. Mgmt., Am. Acad. Arts & Scis., Assn. for Pvt. Enterprise Edn. (Adam Smith award 1986), City Coll. Alumni Assn. (Townsend Harris medal 1969), Soc. Tech. Comm., Nat. Assn. Bus. Economists, Cosmos. Office: Washington Univ Weidenbaum Ctr 1 Brookings Dr Saint Louis MO 63130-4899 Home Phone: 314-727-8950; Office Phone: 314-935-5662.

WEIDENBAUM, RHODA SUSSMAN, history educator, researcher; d. Carl and Celia Sussman; m. Sherman S. Weidenbaum, Oct. 30, 1948; children: Karen Tali Menkin, Mark, Abigail Eve Dishi. AB cum laude, Barnard Coll., NYC, 1951; MA in History of China, Columbia U., NYC, 1953; MA in US and European History, U. Conn., Storrs, 1974, PhD in Polit. Sci., 1981. Fellow Chinese history Yale U., New Haven, 1987—90; assoc. in rsch. Fairbank Ctr., Harvard U., Cambridge, Mass., 1990—. Rsch. scholar Beijing U., 1987—88, Qinghua U., Beijing, 1988; lectr. in field. Contbr. rsch. papers to profl. publs. Svc. leader, reader Torah scroll Beth El and Beth Jacob Synagogues, New London and Norwich, Conn. Named most disting. fgn. scholar, Nankai U., Tianjin, China, 1998; recipient 1st prize ann. meeting, Psychohistory Assn., 1990; Travel grantee, U. Alaska, Fairbanks, 1984. Mem.: Assn. Asian Studies (hon.; panel organizer, chmn. ann. meeting 1985). Jewish. Avocations: vocal studies, musical composition for synagogue services, travel, cooking. Home: 17 Fifth Ave Waterford CT 06385 Office: 17 Fifth Ave Waterford CT 06385 Office Phone: 860-442-2235. Personal E-mail: drrhoda81@sbcglobal.net.

WEIDENFELD, EDWARD LEE, lawyer; b. Akron, Ohio, July 15, 1943; s. Sam and Beatrice (Cooper) W.; m. Sheila Rabb, Aug. 11, 1968; children: Nicholas, Daniel. BS, U. Wis., 1965; JD, Columbia U., 1968. Bar: NY 1968, admitted to practice: US Supreme Ct. 1972, bar: DC 1973. Pvt. practice, NYC, 1969-71, 73-82, Washington, 1982—. Spl. cons. N.Y.C. Dept. Bldgs., 1967; counsel, dir. energy staff Com. on Interior and Insular Affairs, U.S. Ho. of Reps., 1971—73; mem. faculty Am. Law Inst.-ABA CLE Programs; mem. Internat. Del. to Observe Philippine Election, 1986, Internat. Del. to Observe Republic Korea Election, 1987, Pakistan Election, 1988, Chilean Election, 1989, Albanian Election, 1997; mem. D.C. Bar Task Force on the Omnibus Trusts and Estates Amendment Act of 2000, 1999—2001; lectr. to profl. groups. Editor in chief Atomic Energy Law Jour., 1975-76; contbg. author: Generations: Planning Your Legacy, 1999. Mem. Pres.'s Commn. on White House Fellowships, 1977; nat. chmn. Lawyers for Reagan/Bush, 1980; chief counsel Reagan/Bush Campaign, 1980; chmn. Reagan/Bush '84 Legal Adv. Bd., 1984; mem. D.C. Rep. Com., 1984-92, vice chmn., 1984-88; mem. Coun. Adminstrv. Conf. of U.S., 1981-92, sr. fellow, 1992-95; overseer dept. def. regional ctrs., sec. Salvation Army Adv. Bd.; trustee Danny Kaye and Sylvia Fine Kaye Found.; chmn. bd. visitors Nat. Def. U. Named one of 75 Best Lawyers in Washington, Washingtonian mag., 2002; recipient medal of Peter the Great, Russian Fedn., 2000. Mem. ABA, D.C. Bar Assn., Am. Law Inst. (life), Assn. Bar City N.Y., Met. Club (bd. govs., Washington). Office: 888 17th St NW Washington DC 20006 Office Phone: 202-785-2143. Business E-Mail: edward@weidenfeldlaw.com.

WEIDENFELD, SHEILA RABB, television producer, writer; b. Cambridge, Mass., Sept. 7, 1943; d. Maxwell M. and Ruth (Cryden) Rabb; m. Edward L. Weidenfeld, Aug. 11, 1968; children: Nicholas Rabb, Daniel Rabb. BA, Brandeis U., 1965. Assoc. prodr. Metromedia, Inc., Sta. WNEW-TV, NYC, 1965-68; talent coord. That Show with Joan Rivers, NBC, NYC, 1968-71; coord. NBC network game programs, NYC, 1968-71; prodr. Metromedia, Inc., Sta. WTTG-TV, Washington, 1971-73; creator/prodr. Take It From Here, NBC (WBC-TV), Washington, 1973-74; press sec. to first lady Betty Ford, spl. asst. to Pres. Gerald R. Ford, 1974-77; mem. Pres.'s Adv. Commn. on Hist. Preservation, 1977-81; TV prodr., moderator On the Record, NBC-TV, Sta. WRC-TV, Washington, 1978-79; pres. D.C. Prodns., Ltd., 1978; prodr., host Your Personal Decorator, 1987; mem. sec. State's Adv. Commn. on Fgn. Svc. Inst., 1972-74; founding mem. Project Censured Panel of Judges, 1976—. Bd. dirs. First Star. Author: First Lady's Lady, 1979. Mem. US Holocaust Meml. Coun., 1987-97; corporator Dana Hall Sch., Wellesley, Mass.; bd. dirs. Wolf Trap Found., Women's Campaign Fund, 1978-79; bd. dirs. DC Contemporary Dance Theatre, 1986-88, DC Rep. Ctrl. Com., 1984—, DC Preservation League, 1987-90, Am. Univ. Rome, 1988—96, Friends of the Scuola San Rocco, 2002—, Ctr. for Sci. in the Pub. Interest, 2007—; chmn. C&O Canal Nat. Hist. Park Commn., 1988—. Recipient awards for outstanding achievement in the media AAUW, 1973, 74, Silver Screen award A Campaign to Remember for the U.S. Holocaust Meml. Coun., 1989, Bronze medal Internat. Film and Video Festival N.Y., 1990; named hon. consul gen. of Republic of San Marino to Washington; knighted by Order of St. Agatha, Republic of San Marino, 1986. Mem. NATAS (Emmy award 1972), Washington Press Club, Am. Newspaper Women's Club, Am. Women in Radio and TV, Cosmos Club, Consular Corps, Sigma Delta Chi. Home: 3059 Q St NW Washington DC 20007-3081 E-mail: Sheila.Weidenfeld@verizon.net.

WEIDENKOPF, THOMAS W., human resources specialist; b. 1959; married; 2 children. BS, Cornell U. Various human resources positions Pepsi-Cola, Pizza Hut; mgr. orgn. and staffing GE, 1981—83; dir. global staffing and devel. Honeywell Internat., Inc., 1995—97; v.p. human resources Honeywell Aerospace, 1999—2002; sr. v.p. human resources and comm. Honeywell Internat., Inc., Morristown, NJ, 2002—. Office: Honeywell Internat 101 Columbia Rd Morristown NJ 07962 *

WEIDENTHAL, MAURICE DAVID (BUD), academic administrator, journalist; b. Cleve., Nov. 26, 1925; s. William and Evelyn (Kolinsky) W.; m. Grace Schwartz, Apr. 14, 1957; 1 child, Susan Elizabeth Weidenthal Saltzman. BA, U. Mich., 1950. Mem. staff Cleve. Press, 1950-81, editl. writer, 1950-51, asst. city editor, 1956-58, edn. editor, 1958-81; v.p. pub. affairs Cuyahoga C.C. Dist., Cleve., 1981-88; dir. Urban Colls. Project, Cleve., 1989—. Editor The Urban Report, Cleve., 1989-2005. Pub. affairs com. Greater Cleve. Growth Assn., 1981-88; bd. advisors Coun. for Advancement and Support of Edn., 1981-88, Nat. Coun. Mktg. and Pub. Rels., 1981-2005; alt. bd. dirs. St. Vincent Quadrangle, 1983-88; trustee Hebrew Free Loan Assn., 1975-86. With AUS, 1944-45. Decorated Air medal. Mem. Edn. Writers Assn., Soc. Profl. Journalists, (bd. dirs. 1996-2003), Cleve. City Club (bd. dirs. 1969-76), Cleve. Press Club. Home: 25858 Fairmount Blvd Cleveland OH 44122-2214 Office: 4250 Richmond Rd Cleveland OH 44122-6104 Personal E-mail: u2w@adelphia.net. Business E-Mail: bud.weidenthal@tri-c.edu.

WEIDHAAS, JOANNE BARNES, medical educator; d. John Edgar and Helen Barnes; m. Andrew John Weidhaas, Sept. 3, 1995; children: Lillian Jean, Andrew William. MD, PhD, Tufts U., Boston. Lic. radiation oncology Am. Bd. Radiolgoy, 2004. Asst. prof. Yale U., New Haven, Conn., 2004—. Recipient Young Investigator award, Breast Cancer Alliance; grantee Rsch. grant, Conn. State Tobacco Settlement. Office: Yale Univ 333 Cedar St New Haven CT 06520 Office Fax: 203-785-6309.

WEIDMAN, DAVID N., chemicals executive; m. Rachel Weidman; 6 children. BSChE, Brigham Young Univ., 1978; MBA, Univ. Mich., 1980. Positions with Am. Cyanamid, 1980—87; mng. dir. Cyanamid Nordiska, Stockholm, 1987—89; v.p., gen. mgr. Cyanamid Canada, 1989—90; v.p., gen. mgr. fibers div. Am. Cyanamid, 1990—94; v.p., gen., mgr. performance additives Allied Signal, 1994—95, pres., gen. mgr. fluorine products, 1995—98, pres. performance polymers & mem. corp. exec. council, 1998—2000; CEO Celanese Chemicals, 2000—02; COO Celanese AG, 2002—04, vice-chmn. bd. mgmt., 2003—04; pres., CEO Celanese Corp., Dallas, 2004—07, chmn., CEO, 2007—. Bd. mem. Am. Chemistry Council. Mem. Nat. Adv. Council Marriott Sch. Mgmt. Mem.: Soc. Chem. Industry (hon. treas.). Office: Celanese Corp 1601 W LBJ Freeway Dallas TX 75234 *

WEIDMAN, JOHN CARL, II, education and sociology educator, consultant; b. Ephrata, Pa., Oct. 3, 1945; s. John Carl and Mary Elizabeth (Grube) W.; m. Carla Sue Fassnacht, Aug. 20, 1967; children: Jonathan Scott, Rebecca Mary. AB in Sociology cum laude, Princeton U., 1967; AM, U. Chgo., 1968, PhD, 1974. Acting asst. prof. edn. U. Minn., Mpls., 1970-74, asst. prof. edn., sociology and Am. studies, 1974-77; sr. rsch. assoc. Bur. Social Sci. Rsch., Inc., Washington, 1977-78; assoc. prof. edn. and sociology U. Pitts., 1979-86, prof. edn. and sociology, 1986—, chmn. dept. adminstrv. and policy studies, 1986-93, dir. Inst. for Internat. Studies in Edn., 2004—. Cons. Nat. Ctr. Adminstrv. Justice, Youthwork, Inc., Upper Midwest Tri-Racial Gen. Assistance Ctr., Acad. for Ednl. Devel., Egypt, Mongolia, Asian Devel. Bank, Indonesia, Laos, Kyrgyz Republic, Mongolia, German Acad. Exch. Svc., Mongolia, Sema-Belgium, Mongolia, Uzbekistan, CRA Internat., Saudi Arabia; UNESCO chair higher edn. rsch. Maseno U. Coll., Kenya, 1993. Author: rsch. monographs; mem. editl. bd. Rev. of Higher Edn., 1984-88, Am. Ednl. Rsch. Jour., 1991-92, 96-98; co-author: Research on Higher Education in Developing Countries: Suggested Agendas and Research Strategies, 1991, Implementing a Faculty Assessment System: A Case Study of the University of Pittsburgh-USA, 1994, Higher Education Costs and Tuition, 1996, Higher Education in Korea: Tradition and Adaptation, 2000, Socialization of Graduate and Professional Students: A Perilous Passage?, 2001, Finance Higher Education, 2001; asst. editor Comparative Edn. Rev., 2003—; cons. editor Jour. Higher Edn., 1989—; contbr. chpts. to books, articles to profl. jours. Bd. dirs. Sch. Vol. Assn. Pitts., 1982-90, pres., 1984-87. Grantee U.S. Office Edn., 1971-73, Spencer Found., 1973-76, Nat. Inst. Edn., 1976-79, NEH, 1985-86, Asian Devel. Bank, Laos, 1995-96, Mongolia, 1997-2000, 2005, Indonesia, 2001, Kyrgyz Republic, 2003; Fulbright scholar U. Augsburg, Germany, 1986-87. Mem. Am. Ednl. Rsch. Assn. (sec. postsecondary divsn. 1987-89), Am. Sociol. Assn., Assn. Study of Higher Edn., Comparative and Internat. Edn. Soc., Sigma Psi, Phi Delta Kappa. Office: U Pitts 5910 Posvar Hall 230 S Bouquet St Pittsburgh PA 15260

WEIDMAN, SHEILA, marketing professional; b. Bradenton, Fla., July 11, 1961; BS in sci., Journalism and Comm., U. Fla., 1983. Mgr. comm. ASHRAE, 1983—88; mgr. corp. comm. Georgia-Pacific Corp., 1988—90, dir. external comm. and corp. advt., 1990—98, dir., spl. asst. to chmn. and CEO, 1998—2000, sr. dir. corp. mktg. and sales excellence, 2000—01, v.p. corp. mktg., 2001—02, v.p. corp. comm. and mktg. Atlanta, 2002—. Com. mem. Am. Heart Assn., Atlanta Hist. Soc.; mem. Leadership Atlanta, Class of 2004. Recipient Women of Achievement awards, YWCA, 1995. Mem.: Atlanta Sports Coun. (bd. dirs., chmn. mktg. com.), Atlanta CMO Roundtable, CMO Group of N.Am., Ga. Press Assn., Ga. State CMO Roundtable, Met. Atlanta C. of C. (vice chair chmn.'s campaign 2003), Mktg. Leadership Coun. (vice chair chmn.'s campaign 2004), Pub. Rels. Soc. Am., Sales and Mktg. Execs., Atlanta Press Club. Office: Georgia-Pacific Corp 133 Peachtree St NE Atlanta GA 30303

WEIDNER, DONALD J., dean, law educator; BS, Fordham U., 1966; JD, U. Tex., Austin, 1969. Bar: SC, U.S. Tax Ct., U.S. Dist. Cts. for No. Dist. Ohio and Dist. SC, Supreme Ct. U.S. Assoc. Willkie Farr & Gallagher, New York, NY, 1969—70; Bigelow Fellow U. Chgo. Law Sch., 1970—71; asst. prof. U. SC Sch. Law, 1971—74; assoc. prof. Cleveland State U., 1974—76, Fla. State U. Coll. Law, 1976—78, prof., 1978—, assoc. dean, 1984—85, dean, 1991—97, interim dean, 1998—2000; dean, 2000—. Vis. prof. U. Tex. Sch. Law, 1978, U. N.Mex, 1979, Stanford Law Sch., 1981, U. NC Sch. Law, 1991; prof in residence Ruden McClosky Smith Schuster & Russell, PA, 1997; reporter Uniform Partnership Act (1994) Nat. Conf. Commrs. on Uniform State Laws, 1987—94. Co-author: Real Estate: Taxation and Bankruptcy, 1979, General and Limited Liability Partnerships Under the Revised Uniform Partnership Act, 1996, The Revised Uniform Partnership Act, 1998, 1999, 2000, 2001, 2002, 2003, 2004. Order of Coif. Mem.: Am. Law Inst., Assoc. Am. Law Schs. (mem. Membership Review (Accrediation) Com. 2001—03), Fla. Supreme Ct. Hist. Soc. (Bd. Trustees), Fla. Supreme Ct. Commn. on Professionalism. Avocations: boating, fishing, scuba diving, reading, exercise. Office: Coll Law Fla State U Rotunda Rm R201 Tallahassee FL 32306-1601 Office Phone: 850-644-3071. Office Fax: 850-644-5487. E-mail: dweidner@law.fsu.edu. *

WEIDNER, JACQUE GOODIN, educational consultant, not-for-profit developer; d. Tom and Mary Goodin; m. Dale Weidner, Oct. 3, 2000; children: Martin, Jack. BSc, Winona State U., Minn., 1992; MEd, St. Cloud State U., Minn., 1999; degree in K-12 Adminstrn., St. Mary's U., Mpls., 2004. Tchr. spl. edn. Anoka-Hennepin Sch. Dist., Minn., 1992—2000, tchg. and learning specialist, 2000—. Cons. Don Johnston, Inc., Volo, Ill., 2006—. Founder The Game, Anoka, 2006—. Dfl. Office: Anoka-Hennepin School District LC/DC 2d Fl 2727 Ferry St Anoka MN 55303 Office Phone: 763-506-1351. Business E-Mail: jacque.weidner@anoka.k12.mn.us.

WEIDNER, MARK, environment research executive; b. 1952; MS in Analytical Chemistry, Purdue U., 1976. With Mich. State U., East Lansing, 1976-78; instr. Finnigan Corp., San Jose, Calif., 1978-80; sr. chemist Metro Lab., Seattle, 1980-85; now pres., treas. Analytical Resources, Inc., Seattle, 1985—. Office: Analytical Resources Inc 4611 S 134th Pl #100 Tukwila WA 98168-3212

WEIERSTALL, RICHARD PAUL, retired pharmaceutical chemist; b. Jersey City, Nov. 5, 1942; s. William August and Emily (Haughey) W.; m. Gail Janet Thomsen, Aug. 17, 1968; children: Eric, Kurt, Karen. BS, Rutgers U., 1966, MS, 1969; PhD, U. Calif., San Francisco, 1973. Unit head drug metabolism Sandoz Pharm., East Hanover, N.J., 1973-74; dir. tech. svc. Banner Gelatin Products, Chatsworth, Calif., 1974-76; v.p. tech. svc. Banner Gelatin Prod., Chatsworth, Calif., 1976-81; dir. pharm. sci. Ayerst Labs Inc., Rouses Point, N.Y., 1981-87; asst. v.p. Wyeth Ayerst Rsch., Rouses Point, 1987-95, asst. v.p. quality assurance, 1995-99; ret., 1999. Mem. Am. Assn. Pharm. Sci., Am. Pharm. Assn. Home: 7 Stewart St Rouses Point NY 12979-1511 E-mail: rweiers@northnet.org.

WEIGEL, GEORGE SHILLOW, JR., theologian; b. Balt. m. Joan Balcombe; children: Gwyneth, Monica, Stephen. BA, St. Mary's Seminary, Balt., 1973; MA, U. St. Michael's Coll., Toronto, Can., 1975. Asst. prof. theology, from asst. to dean of studies St. Thomas Sem. Sch. of Theology, Kenmore, 1975-77; scholar-in-residence World Without War Coun. Greater Seattle, 1977-84; founding pres. James Madison Found., 1986-89; pres. Ethics and Pub. Policy Ctr., Washington, 1989—96, sr. fellow, 1996—. Author: Tranquillitas Ordinis: The Present Failure & Future Promise of American Catholic Thought on War & Peace, 1987, American Interests, American Purpose; Moral Reasoning & US Foreign Policy, 1989, Catholicism and the Renewal of American Democracy, 1989, Freedom and its Discontents, 1991, The Final Revolution: The Resistance Church and the Collapse of Communism, 1992, Idealism Without Illusions: US Foreign Policy in the Nineties, 1994, Soul of the World, 1996, Witness to Hope: The Biography of Pope John Paul II, 1999, The Truth of Catholicism, 2001, The Courage to Be Catholic, 2002, Letters to A Young Catholic, 2004, The Cube and the Cathedral, 2005, God's Choice: Pope Benedict XVI and the Future of the Catholic Church, 2005; co-author (with James Turner Johnson): Just War and the Gulf War, 1991; co-editor (with Robert Royal): Building the Free Society, 1993; columnist Catholic Northwest Progress, 1993—, mem. editl. bd. First Things. Recipient papal cross Pro Ecclesia et Pontifice; fellow Woodrow Wilson Internat. Ctr. for Scholars, 1984—85. Fellow: Ethics & Pub. Policy Ctr. (sr.). Office: Ethics and Pub Policy Ctr 1015 15th St NW Washington DC 20005-2605 Office Phone: 202-682-1200.

WEIGEL, KENNETH GEORGE, lawyer; b. Neptune, NJ, Aug. 28, 1954; s. Hugo Karl and Dolores May (Ambrose) W. BA, U. Mich., 1976; JD, George Washington U., 1979. Bar: DC 1979. Assoc. Barnes, Richardson & Colburn, Washington, 1979-83, Bayh, Tabbert & Capehart, Washington, 1983-85, Morgan, Lewis & Bockius, Washington, 1985-89; ptnr. Webster & Sheffield, Washington, 1989-1990, Baker & Hostetler, Washington, 1991—93, Kirkland & Ellis, 1993—2002; ptnr., co-chmn., internat. trade and regulatory group Alston & Bird LLP, Washington, 2002. Mem. ABA (chmn. customs law com., internat. law and practice sect. 1988-91). Office: Alston & Bird LLP 950 F St NW Washington DC 20004 Office Phone: 202-756-3431. Office Fax: 202-756-3333. Business E-Mail: ken.weigel@alston.com.

WEIGEL, PAUL HENRY, biochemistry educator, researcher, consultant; b. NYC, Aug. 11, 1946; s. Helmut and Jeanne Weigel; m. Nancy Shulman, June 15, 1968 (div. Dec. 1987); 1 child, Dana J.; m. Janet Oka, May 17, 1992 BA in Chemistry, Cornell U., 1968; MS in Biochemistry, Johns Hopkins U., Balt., 1969, PhD in Biochemistry, 1975. NIH postdoctoral fellow Johns Hopkins U., Balt., 1975-78; asst. prof. U. Tex. Med. Br., Galveston, Tex., 1978-82, assoc. prof., 1982—87, prof. biochemistry and cell biology, 1987-94, vice chmn. dept. human biol. chemistry and genetics, 1990-93, acting chmn. dept. human biology, chemistry and genetics, 1992-93; prof., chmn. dept. biochemistry and molecular biology U. Okla. Health Scis. Ctr., Oklahoma City, 1994—, George Lynn Cross rsch. prof., 2004—, Ed Miller chair in molecular biology, 2006—; co-founder Hyalose LLC, 2000—. Mem. NIH Pathobiochemistry Study Sect., Washington, 1985-87; cons. Teltech, Mpls., 1985—, Hyalose LLC 2000—. Contbr. articles to profl. jours. Treas. Bayou Chateau Neighborhood Assn., Dickinson, Tex., 1981-83, v.p., 1983-84, pres., 1984-86. With U.S. Army, 1969-71. Grantee NIH, 1979—, Office Naval Rsch., 1983-87, Tex. Biotech., 1989-94, Okla. Ctr. Advancement Sci. and Tech., 2000-03; recipient Disting. Tchr. award U. Tex. Med. Br., 1989, Disting. Rsch. award, 1989. Mem.: Internat. Soc. for Hyaluronan Scis. (founding mem. 2004, sec. 2004—07, acting pres. 2007), Soc. for Glycobiology (mem. nominations com. 2004—), Assn. Med. and Grad. Depts. Biochemistry (webmaster 2002—06, bd. dirs. 2002—, pres. 2007), Am. Soc. Biochemistry and Molecular Biology (mem. pub. affairs adv. com. 2000—03), Am. Soc. Cell Biology, Am. Chem. Soc. Democrat. Lutheran. Achievements include 23 patents in field. Avocations: racquetball, basketball card collecting, poetry, camping. Home: 817 Hollowdale Edmond OK 73003-3022 Office: U Okla Health Scis Ctr Dept Biochem & Mol Biology Bmsb Rm 860 Oklahoma City OK 73190-0001 Office Phone: 405-271-2227. Business E-Mail: paul-weigel@ouhsc.edu.

WEIGEL, RUSSELL H., headmaster; m. Jane Reynolds Weigel; children: Pia, Nick. BA in Psychology, Bowdoin Coll., 1965; MA in Clinical Psychology, George Washington U., 1967; PhD in Social Psychology, U. Colorado, 1973. Prof. of psychology Amherst Coll., Amherst, Mass., 1975—95, James E. Ostendarp prof. psychology, 1992, dean of students; head of sch. Loomis Chaffee Sch., Windsor, Conn., 1995—; pres. The Loomis Inst., Windsor, Conn., 1995—. Co-author: (jour. articles) Ecological Beliefs and Behaviors: Assessment and Change, Race Relations on Prime Time Television Reconsidered: Patterns of Continuity and Change. Fellow: Am. Psychological Soc., APA (Gordon Allport prize). Office: Loomis Chaffee Sch 4 Batchelder Rd Windsor CT 06095 *

WEIGEND, GUIDO GUSTAV, geographer, educator; b. Zeltweg, Austria, Jan. 2, 1920; came to U.S., 1939, naturalized, 1943; s. Gustav F. and Paula (Sorgo) W.; m. Areta Kelble, June 26, 1947 (dec. 1993); children: Nina, Cynthia, Kenneth. BS, U. Chgo., 1942, MS, 1946, PhD, 1949. With OSS, 1943-45; with mil. intelligence U.S. War Dept., 1946; instr. geography U. Ill., Chgo., 1946-47; instr. then asst. prof. geography Beloit Coll., 1947-49; asst. prof. geography Rutgers U., 1949-51, assoc. prof., 1951-57, prof., 1957-76, acting dept. chmn., 1951-52, chmn. dept., 1953-67, assoc. dean, 1972-76; dean Coll. Liberal Arts, Prof. geography Ariz. State U., Tempe, 1976-84, prof. geography, 1976-89; ret., 1989. Fulbright lectr. U. Barcelona, 1960-61; vis. prof. geography Columbia U., 1963-67, NYU, 1967, U. Colo., summer 1968, U. Hawaii, summer 1969; liaison rep. Rutgers U. to UN, 1950-52; invited by Chinese Acad. Scis. to visit minority areas in Chinese Cent. Asia, 1988; mem. U.S. nat. com. Internat. Geog. Union, 1951-58, 61-65; chmn. Conf. on Polit. and Social Geography, 1968-69 Author articles, monographs, bulls. for profl. jours.; contbr.: (4th edit.) A Geography of Europe, 1977; geog. editor-in-chief: Odyssey World Atlas, 1966. Bd. adjustment Franklin Twp., N.J., 1959; mem. Highland Park (N.J.) Bd. Edn., 1973-75, v.p., 1975; mem. Ariz. Coun. on Humanities and Pub. Policy, 1976-80; vice chmn. Phoenix Com. on Fgn. Rels., 1976-79, chmn., 1979-81; mem. exec. com. Fedn. Pub. Programs in Humanities, 1977-82; bd. dirs. Coun. Colls. Arts and Scis., 1980-83; commr. N. Cen. Assn. Colls. and Schs., 1976-80, bd. dirs. commn. on instns. of higher edn., 1980-83. Research fellow Office Naval Research, 1952-55, Rutgers Research Council, 1970-71; grantee Social Sci. Research Council, 1956, Ford Found., 1966, Am. Philos. Soc., 1970-71, German Acad. Exchange Service, 1984; Fulbright travel grantee Netherlands, 1970-71. Mem. Assn. Am. Geographers (chmn. N.Y. Met. divsn. 1955-56, editl. bd. 1955-59, mem. coun. 1965-66, chmn. N.Y.-N.J. divsn. 1965-66), Am. Geog. Soc., Phoenix Chamber Mus. Soc. (bd. dirs. 1995-2003, pres. 2000-03), Sigma Xi (pres. Ariz. State U. chpt. 1989-91). Office: Ariz State U Dept Geography Tempe AZ 85287 Home: 7550 N 16th St Apt 3103 Phoenix AZ 85020-4618

WEIGER, JOHN GEORGE, foreign language educator; b. Dresden, Germany, Feb. 6, 1933; came to U.S., 1938, naturalized, 1945; s. Willy and Elisabeth (Prinz) W.; m. Leslie Lawrence Carpenter, Dec. 28, 1955; children: Robert Boyden, Mark Owen, Heidi Elaine. BA, Middlebury Coll., 1955; MA, U. Colo., 1957; PhD (NDEA fellow), Ind. U., 1966. Instr. U. Colo., Boulder, 1955-57, Lawrence Coll., Appleton, Wis., 1957-58; instr. Romance langs. U. Vt., Burlington, 1958-62, asst. prof., 1964-67, assoc. prof., 1967-73, prof., 1973-98, prof. emeritus, 1998—, vice chmn. Romance lang. dept., 1964-68, chmn., 1994-98, asst. dean Coll. Arts and Scis., 1968-69, assoc. dean, 1969-71, dean, 1971-76; instnl. rep. for Rhodes scholarships, Danforth fellowships, Turrell Fund scholarships, 1971-76; program chmn. George Aiken lecture series, 1975; vis. lectr. U. Bologna, 1978, 87, U. Venice, Italy, 1987, U. Valencia, Spain, 1987; Cervantes lectr. Fordham U., 1990. Cons. Eirik Borve, Inc., 1979-80. Author: Introduction to the Youthful Deeds of the Cid, 1969, The Valencian Dramatists of Spain's Golden Age, 1976, Cristobal de Virues, 1978, Hacia la Comedia, 1978, The Individuated Self: Cervantes and the Emergence of the Individual, 1979, The Substance of Cervantes, 1985, In the Margins of Cervantes, 1988; editor: Las Hazañas del Cid, 1981, La Infelice Marcela, 1985; mem. editl. bd.: Bull. of Comediantes, 1978-2000; editl. bd.: Hispania, 1993-01; contbr. articles to profl. jours., also chpts. to books. U. Vt. Faculty Research fellow, 1967, 83, 86; Am. Council Learned Socs. grantee, 1978; U. Vt. Univ. scholar for the humanities, 1985-86. Mem. MLA (chmn. comedia sect. 1970-71), Renaissance Soc. Am., Am. Assn. Tchrs. Spanish and Portuguese (chmn. com. hon. mems. and fellows 1984), The Comediantes, Internat. Assn. Hispanists, Cervantes Soc. Am., Phi Beta Kappa, Phi Sigma Iota, Phi Eta Sigma (hon.). Home: 63 Woodbine Rd Shelburne VT 05482-6702 E-mail: jweiger@adelphia.net.

WEIGERT, ANDREW JOSEPH, sociology educator; b. NYC, Apr. 8, 1934; s. Andrew Joseph and Marie Teresa (Kollmer) W.; m. Kathleen Rose Maas, Aug. 31, 1967; children: Karen Rose, Sheila Marie. BA, St. Louis U., 1958, PhL, 1959, MA, 1960; BTh, Woodstock Coll, Md., 1964; PhD, U. Minn., 1968. NIMH trainee U. Minn., Mpls., 1965-67; asst. prof. sociology U. Notre Dame, Ind., 1968-72, assoc. prof. Ind., 1972-76, prof. Ind., 1976—, chmn. dept. Ind., 1980-84, 88-89. Vis. assoc. prof. Yale U., New Haven, 1973-74. Co-author: Family Socialization, 1974, Interpretive Sociology, 1978, Society and Identity, 1986; author: Everyday Life, 1981, Social Psychology, 1983, Life and Society, 1983, Mixed Emotions, 1991, Self, Interaction, and Natural Environment, 1997, Religious and Secular Views on Endtime, 2004; adv. editor various sociology jours.; contbr. articles to profl. jours., chpts. to books. Recipient tchg. awards, 1999, 2002, 05; NSF grantee, 1969. Avocation: woodlot and prairie management. Office: U Notre Dame Dept Sociology Notre Dame IN 46556 Office Phone: 574-631-7408. Business E-Mail: aweigert@nd.edu.

WEIGHT, DOUG, professional hockey player; b. Warren, Mich., Jan. 21, 1971; Student, Lake Superior State Coll., Mich. Center NY Rangers, 1990-93, Edmonton Oilers, 1993—2001, St. Louis Blues, 2001—06, 2006—, Carolina Hurricanes, 2006. Mem. U.S. Olympic Hockey Team, Nagano, Japan, 1998, Salt Lake City, 2002, Team U.S.A., World Cup of Hockey, 1996, 2004. Named to NHL All-Star Game, 1996, 1998, 2001, 2003. Achievements include being a member of World Cup Champion Team USA, 1996; being a member of silver medal winning USA Hockey Team, Salt Lake City Olympics, 2002; being a member of Stanley Cup Champion Carolina Hurricanes, 2006. Office: St Louis Blues Savvis Ctr 1401 Clark Ave Saint Louis MO 63101-2709

WEIGHT, MICHAEL ANTHONY, lawyer, former judge; b. Hilo, Hawaii, Jan. 5, 1940; s. Leslie A. and Grace B. (Brown) W.; m. Victoria Noel; children: Rachael R., Elizabeth G., Thomas P. BA in History, U. Rochester, 1961; LLB, Vanderbilt U., 1967. Bar: Hawaii 1967, U.S. Ct. Appeals (9th cir.) 1968, U.S. Supreme Ct. 1972. Pvt. practice, Honolulu, 1974-97; former judge Dist. Ct. (1st cir.) Hawaii; asst. fed. pub. defender Dists. of Hawaii and Guam, 1997—. Bd. dirs. Bishop Mus. Assn. 1st lt. USMC, 1961—63. Mem.: Hawaii Assn. Criminal Def. Lawyers (pres. 1986), Hawaii Bar Assn. Office: Fed Pub Defenders Office 300 Ala Moana Blvd Honolulu HI 96850-0001 E-mail: miolb5440@yahoo.com.

WEIGHT, WILLIS D., geologist, writer, engineering educator, consultant; s. Robert and Charlotte Weight; m. Stephanie Weight, Aug. 19, 1977; children: Shilo, Calvin, Jared, Audrey Floyd, Levi, Ryan, Josie. BS in Engring. Geology, Brigham Young U., Provo, Utah, 1980; PhD in Math. Geology, U. Wyo., Laramie, 1989. Cert. profl. engr., Bd. Profl. Engrs. and Land Surveyors, Mont., Idaho, 1992. Mine geologist Kiewit Mining and Engring., Sheridan, Wyo., 1982—85; dept. head Dept. Geol. Engring., Butte, Mont., 1991—96; head hydrogeology program Tech. U. Mont., Butte, 1996—. Expert witness WDW & Assocs., Boulder, 1994—2006, con., 1989—. Author: (book) Manual of Applied Hydrogeology, 2001. Grantee Rsch. grant, Dept. of Agr., 2006—, EPA, 2007. Mem.: Nat. Ground Water Assn. (assoc.). Office: Mont Tech Univ 1300 West Park St Butte MT 59701 Home Phone: 406-498-0530; Office Phone: 406-496-4329. Business E-Mail: wweight@mtech.edu.

WEIGNER, BRENT JAMES, secondary school educator; b. Pratt, Kans., Aug. 19, 1949; s. Doyle Dean and Elizabeth (Hanger) W.; m. Sue Ellen Weber Hume, Mar. 30, 1985; children: Russell John Hume, Scott William Hume. BA, U. No. Colo., 1972; MEd, U. Wyo., 1977, PhD, 1984. Cert. Nat. Bd. for Profl. Tchg. Stds. Counselor, coach Olympia Sport Village, Upson, Wis., 1968; dir. youth sports F.E. Warren AFB, Cheyenne, 1973—74; instr. geography Laramie County Comm. Coll., Cheyenne, 1974-75; tchr. social sci. McCormick Jr. HS, Cheyenne, 1975—, Laramie County Sch. Dist. 1, Cheyenne, 1975—; head social studies dept. McCormick Jr. HS, 1987-99, 2001—02; curriculum adv. coun. chmn. Laramie County Sch. Dist. No. 1, 1988-89. Lectr. ednl. methods U. Wyo., 1989, clin. faculty, 1992-94; nat. chmn. Jr. Olympic cross-country com. AAU, Indpls., 1980-81; pres. Wyo. Athletic Congress, 1981-87; tchr. cons. Nat. Geog. Soc. Geography Inst., 1991, North Pole Marathon cons. Global Expdns. 2002-03; South Pole marathon cons. and guide Adventure Network Internat., 2001-02; alt. cert. assessor Wyo. State Dept. Edn., 2001-02; cons. Adventure Network Internat., 1999-02; cons. North Pole marathon, Polar Running Adventures, 2003-04, Arctic Watch, 2004—; presenter, cons. in field. Fgn. exch. student U. Munich, 1971-72; head coach Cheyenne Track Club, 1976—, pres., 1980; race dir. Wyo. Marathon, 1978—; deacon 1st Christian Ch., Cheyenne, 1987-90, elder, 1991-93; rep. candidate gen. election Wyo. Legis., 1991; bd. dirs. United Med. Ctr. of Wyo. Found., 1995—, Cheyenne Boys and Girls Club, 1999-2005; keynote spkr., Okla. Marathon, 2002. Named Wyoming State bd. edn. Disting. Educator, Wyo. U.S. West Outstanding Tchr., 1989, Wyo. Coun. for the Social Studies K-8 Tchr. of Yr., 1994-95, Jr. High Coach of Yr., Wyo.

Coaches Assn., 1996, Vol. of Yr., office Youth Alternatives, 2000; fellow Taft Found., 1976, Earthwatch-Hearst fellow, Punta Allen, Mex., summer 1987, Christa McAuliffe fellow, 1991-92, Wyo. Christa Mcauliffe Fellowship Selection Com., 1994, 95, 01; Fulbright grantee, Israel, summer 1984; Fulbright scholar Ghana and Senegal, 1990; People-to-People Internat. Ambassador to Vietnam, 1993; recipient Masons of Wyo. Disting. Tchr. award 1994. Mem. NEA, Nat. Network for Ednl. Renewal, Nat. Coun. Social Studies, Nat. Coun. Geog. Edn., Dominican Rep. Nat. Coun. for Geog. Edn. (Cram scholarship 1992), Wyo. Geog. Alliance (steering com., Amazon Workshop Fellowship 1998), Cheyenne Tchrs. Edn. Assn. (govtl. rels. com., instrn. and profl. devel. com.), U. No. Colo. Alumni Assn., Cheyenne C. of C., Wyo. Heritage Soc., Wyo. Edn. Assn. (World Book Ency. classroom rsch. project cons. 1976—, accountability task force 1989-90), Fulbright Alumni Assn. (life), U. Wyo. Alumni Assn. (life), Cheyenne Sunrise, Lions (bd. dirs. Cheyenne 1987, pres. 1995-96, 1st v.p. 1993-94, Melvin Jones Fellowship, 1995), Phi Delta Kappa (life, bd. dirs. Cheyenne 1989—, v.p., edn. award for rsch. 1990, pres. 1992-93, ednl. found. rep. 1993-94, area 4-D coord. 1994-95, Gerald Read Internat. Seminar scholar 1994; mem. outstanding doctoral dissertation com. 1994, 96), Phi Delta Kappa (Ed. award 2000). Achievements include first to run ultramarathon races on all seven continents, 1999; South Pole Ultramarathon champion, 2002; sr. men's nat. snowshoe champion, 2003, 05; North Pole Ultramarathon champion, 2003; first person in the world to run ultramarathons at both the North Pole, 2003, and the South Pole, 2002. Home: 402 W 31st St Cheyenne WY 82001-2527 Office: McCormick Jr HS 6000 Education Dr Cheyenne WY 82009-3991 Office Phone: 307-771-2650. Personal E-mail: runwyo@msn.com.

WEIHAUPT, JOHN GEORGE, geophysics educator, academic administrator; b. La Crosse, Wis., Mar. 5, 1930; s. John George and Gladys Mae (Ash) W.; m. Audrey Mae Reis, Jan. 28, 1961. Student, St. Norbert Coll., De Pere, Wis., 1948-49; BS, U. Wis., 1952, MS, 1953, U. Wis.-Milw., 1971; PhD, U. Wis., 1973. Exploration geologist Am. Smelting & Refining Co., Nfld., 1953, Anaconda Co., Chile, S.Am., 1956-57; seismologist United Geophys. Corp., 1958; geophysicist Arctic Inst. N.Am., Antarctica, 1958-60, Geophys. and Polar Research Center, U. Wis., Antarctica, 1960-63; dir. participating Coll. and Univ. program, chmn. dept. phys. and biol. sci. U.S. Armed Forces Inst., Dept. Def., 1963-73; assoc. dean for acad. affairs Sch. Sci., Ind. U.-Purdue U., Indpls., 1973-78, prof. geology, 1973-78; asst. dean (Grad. Sch., prof. geoscis. Purdue U.), 1975-78; prof. geology, assoc. acad. v.p., dean grad. studies and research, v.p. Univ. Research Found., San Jose (Calif.) State U., 1978-82; vice chancellor for acad. affairs U. Colo., Denver, 1982-86, prof. geoscis., 1987—. Sci. cons., mem. sci. adv. bd. Holt Reinhart and Winston, Inc., 1967—; sci. editor, cons. McGraw-Hill Co., 1966—; hon. lectr. U. Wis., 1963-73; geol. cons., 1968—; editorial cons. John Wiley & Sons, 1968; editorial adv. bd. Dushkin Pub. Group, 1971— Author: Exploration of the Oceans: An Introduction to Oceanography; mem. editorial bd. Internat. Jour. Interdisciplinary Cycle Research, Leiden; co-discoverer USARP Mountain Range (Arctic Inst. Mountain Range), in Victoria Land, Antarctica, 1960; discoverer Wilkes Land Meteorite Crater, Antarctic. Mem. Capital Community Citizens Assn.; mem. Madison Transp. Study Com., Found. for Internat. Energy Research and Tng.; U.S. com. for UN Univ.; mem. sci. council Internat. Center for Interdisciplinary Cycle Research; mem. Internat. Awareness and Leadership Council; mem. governing bd. Moss Landing Marine Labs.; bd. dirs. San Jose State U. Found. Served as 1st lt. AUS, 1953-55, Korea. Mt. Weihaupt in Antarctica named for him, 1966; recipient Madisonian medal for outstanding community service, 1973; Outstanding Cote Meml. award, 1974; Antarctic medal, 1968 Fellow Geol. Soc. Am., Explorers Club; mem. Antarctican Soc., Nat. Sci. Tchrs. Assn., Am. Geophys. Union, Internat. Council Corr. Edu., Soc. Am. Mil. Engrs., Wis. Alumni Assn., Soc. Study Biol. Rhythms, Internat. Soc. for Chronobiology, Marine Tech. Soc., AAAS, Univ. Indsl. Adv. Council, Am. Council on Edn., Expdn. Polaire France (hon.), Found. for Study Cycles, Assn. Am. Geographers, Nat. Council Univ. Research Adminstrs., Soc. Research Adminstrs., Man-Environ. Communication Center, Internat. Union Geol. Scis., Internat. Geog. Union, Internat. Soc. Study Time, Community Council Pub. TV, Internat. Platform Assn., Ind., Midwest assns. grad. schs., Western Assn. Grad. Schs., Council Grad. Schs. in U.S., Wis. Alumni Assn. of San Francisco, Kiwanis, Carmel Racquet Club (Rinconada), The Ridge at Hiwan (Evergreen, Colo., pres. 1991-93). Achievements include discovery of the Wilkes Land Anomaly and of the USARP Mt. Range in Victoria Land, both in Antarctica; also credited with revision of the discovery date of Antarctic continent by 3 centuries. Home: 30296 Snowbird Ln Evergreen CO 80439-9469 Office: U Colo Campus Box 172 PO Box 173364 Denver CO 80217-3364

WEIHERER, PATRICIA DEE, retired librarian; b. West Reading, Pa., Sept. 17, 1933; d. Robert Peter and Marguerite (Sprout) Weiherer. BA, Albright Coll., Reading, Pa., 1955; MLS, Rutgers U., New Brunswick, NJ, 1961. English tchr. Manheim Ctrl., Pa., 1955—56; br. libr. Reading Pub. Libr., 1956—60, asst. ref. libr., 1961—95, ref. libr., 1995—. Democrat. United Ch. Of Crist. Avocations: piano, genealogy, needlepoint, reading.

WEIHMULLER, PATRICIA ANN, minister, artist, retired executive secretary; m. Fred H. Weihmuller, Aug. 31, 1957; children: Fredric, Susan Steven, Amy Kovanda. Secretarial Diploma, Blair Bus.Coll., Colorado Springs, 1955; cert., William Rainey Harper Coll., Palatine, Ill., 1983, Mgmt. Cert., 1992; leadership diploma, Stephen Ministries, St. Louis, 1993. Cert. profl. sec. Profl. Secs. Internat., 1983. Exec. sec. State Farm Ins. Co., Dearborn, Mich., 1959—60; exec. sec. Unocal, Schaumburg, Ill., 1971—92, Motorola (temp.), Schaumburg, Ill., 1993—94; Stephen ministry leader Prince of Peace Luth. Ch., Schaumburg, Ill., 1993—98, Stephen min., 1991—2006; oil painter Hoffman Estates, Ill., 1996—. Active Star, Schaumburg, 1967—2006; election judge Cook County Bd. of Elections, Schaumburg Twp., 1995—2005; exec. sec. parish planning coun. Prince of Peace Luth. Ch., Ill., 1989—92, bible study leader, mem. Naomi Cir., 1967—. Avocations: bridge, painting, reading, sewing, travel. Personal E-mail: fpweih@aol.com.

WEIHRICH, HEINZ, management educator; b. Germany; came to US, 1959; s. Paul and Anna Weihrich; m. Ursula Weihrich, Aug. 3, 1963. BS, UCLA, 1966, MBA, 1967, PhD, 1973; Dr. (hon.), San Martin de Porres U., Peru, 2000. Assoc. Grad. Sch. Mgmt. UCLA, 1968-73; from asst. to assoc. prof. Ariz. State U., Tempe, 1973-80; prof. global mgmt. and behavioral sci. U. San Francisco, 1980—. Vis. prof. China Europe Internat. Bus. Sch., Shanghai, Grad. Sch. Bus. Adminstrsn., Switzerland, Peking U., Beijing; global mgmt. cons. in field; vis. prof. U. Applied Sci., Ludwigshafen, Germany. Author: Administración una perspectiva global, 1988 (best seller), Administracão Fundamentos da Teoriae da Cienca, Primeiro Volume, 1986, Administracão Organizacão Planejamento e Controle, Segundo Volume, 1987, Administracão Recursos Humanos: Desenvolvimento de Administradores, Terceiro Volume, 1; author: (with Harold Koontz and Cyril O'Donnell) Management, 1980, Japanese, Chinese and Indonesian edits., 1984, Singapore edit., 1985, Indonesian edit., 1986, Philippines edit., Bengali edit., 1989, Taiwan edit., 1985; author: (with Harold Koontz) 9th edit., 1988, Singapore edit., 1988, Chinese edit., 1989, Spanish edit., 1990 (best-seller Spanish speaking world), Korean edit., 1990, Pengurusan (Malaysian) edit., 1991, Czech edit., 1993, Hungarian edit., 1992; author: (with Harold Koontz and Cyril O'Donnell) Management: A Book of Readings, 1980, Essentials of Management, 1982, Taiwan, Philippines, Chinese and India edits., 1986, with Harold Koontz and Cyril O'Donnell: 6th edit., 2004, Chinese edit., Adminstracion Moderna, 1986; author: (with Harold Koontz) Management: A Global Perspective, 1993, Spanish edit., 1993 (best-seller Spanish speaking world), Singapore edit., 1993, Croatian edit., 1995, Chinese, 1998, Measuring Managers--A Double-Barreled Approach, 1981, Manajamen, Jilid 1, 1987, Manajamen, Jilid 2, 1986, Elementos de Administracion, 1983, with Harold Koontz: 6th edit., 2002, Management Excellence--Productivity through MBO, 1985, Japanese edit., 1990, Greek edit., Produttivita con L' Italian edit., 1987, Administracion, 1985, Management Basiswissen, 1986, Excelencia Administrativa (Mex.), 1987, Chinese edit., 1997, Management: A Global Perspective, internat. edit., 1993, 1993, Administración: Una Perspectiva Global, 1994, 12th edit., 2005 (best seller), Korean edit., 1996, 2006, Croatian edit., 1996, Czech edit., 1996, Elementos de Administracion - Enfoque Internactional, Exta Edicion, 2002; author: (with George Odiorne and Jack Mendleson) Executive Skills: A Management by Objectives Approach, 1980, with George Odiorne and Jack Mendleson: 6th edit., 2002;; author: (with Harold Koontz and A. Ramachandra Aryasri) Principles of Management, 2004; editor (with Jack Mendleson): Management: An MBO Approach, 1978; author (with Harold Koontz): Essentials of Management: Au International Perspective, 7th edit., 2007; contbr. articles to profl. jour. Grantee Am. Mgmt. Assn., 1970. Fellow Internat. Acad. Mgmt., mem. Acad. Mgmt., Assn. Mgmt. Excellence (trustee 1985-87), Assn. Bus. Simulation Exptl. Learning, Acad. Internat. Bus., Beta Gamma Sigma, Sigma Iota Epsilon. Roman Catholic. Office: U San Francisco 2130 Fulton St San Francisco CA 94117-1080

WEIKSNER, SANDRA S., lawyer; b. Washington, Nov. 9, 1945; d. Donald B. and Dick (Cutter) Smiley; m. George B. Weiksner, Aug. 19, 1969; children: Michael, Nicholas. BA in Psychology, Stanford U., Calif., 1966, JD, 1969. Tchg. fellow Stanford U., 1969-70; assoc. Cleary, Gottlieb, Steen & Hamilton, NYC, 1970-77, ptnr., 1978—2003, sr. counsel, 2004—. Vis. lectr. Yale Law Sch., 1991-92. Bd. dirs. N.Y. Law Sch.; mem. Union Theol. Sem. Fellow Am. Bar Found., Am. Coll. Trusts and Estates Counsel, Internat. Acad. Estate and Trust Law; mem. Assn. Bar City of N.Y. Democrat. Unitarian Universalist. Home: 164 E 81st St New York NY 10028-1804 Office: Cleary Gottlieb Steen & Hamilton 1 Liberty Plz Fl 43 New York NY 10006-1404

WEIL, ANDREW THOMAS, physician, educator; b. Phila., June 8, 1942; s. Daniel Pythias and Jenny (Silverstein) Weil. BA, Harvard U., 1964, MD, 1968. Intern Mt. Zion Hosp. Med. Ctr., San Francisco, 1968-69; assoc. Harvard Bot. Mus., Cambridge, Mass., 1971-84; fellow Inst. Current World Affairs, NYC, 1971-75; lectr. U. Ariz., Tucson, 1983—, dir. program in integrative medicine, clin. prof. medicine, 1996—. Dir. integrative health and healing Miraval Resort. Author: Natural Mind, 1972, Marriage of the Sun and Moon, 1980, From Chocolate to Morphine, 1983, Health and Healing, 1984, Natural Health, Natural Medicine, 1990, Spontaneous Healing, 1995, 8 Weeks to Optimum Health, 1997, Eating Well for Optimum Health, 2000, The Healthy Kitchen, 2002, Healthy Aging, 2005, (newsletter) Self-Healing, (website) drweil.com. Served to lt. USPHS, 1969-70. Fellow Linnean Soc. London; mem. Am. Acad. Achievement, Sigma Xi. Democrat. Buddhist. Avocation: gardening. Home: 6700 S X9 Ranch Rd Vail AZ 85641-6202 Office: Ariz Health Scis Ctr PO Box 245153 Tucson AZ 85724-5153 Office Phone: 520-647-7865. Personal E-mail: nancy@x9ranch.com.

WEIL, CASS SARGENT, lawyer; b. NYC, Nov. 6, 1946; s. Theodore and Ruth Frances (Sargent) W. BA, SUNY, Stonybrook, 1968; JD cum laude, William Mitchell Coll. of Law, 1980. Bar: Minn. 1980, U.S. Dist. Ct. Minn. 1980, U.S. Ct. Appeals (8th cir.) 1980, Wis. 1984, U.S. Ct. Appeals (7th cir.) 1984; cert. bankruptcy law specialist, consumer and bus. Am. Bd. Certification. Assoc. J.R. Kotts & Assoc., Mpls., 1980-81, Wagner, Rutchick & Trojack, St. Paul, 1981-83; ptnr. Zohlmann & Weil, Wilmar, Minn., 1983, Peterson, Franke & Riach, P.A., St. Paul, 1983-91, O'Connor & Hannan, Mpls., 1991-94, Moss & Barnett, P.A., Mpls., 1994—. Editor: Minn. Legal Forms, Bankruptcy, 1983, 1987, 1991, 1992, 1993. Recipient Leading Am. Atty. award Am. Rsch. Corp., 1994, 96, 98, 2000, 02-07; named one of Minn. Top Lawyers Mpls. St. Paul Mag., 1998, 2005; named Super Lawyer Minn. Jour. Law and Politics, 2005-07. Mem. Minn. Bar Assn. (vice chmn. bankruptcy sect. 1984-88, chmn. 1988-89), Wis. Bar Assn., Hennepin County Bar Assn. (co-chmn. debtor/creditor law sect. 2006-07), Am. Bankruptcy Inst., Turnaround Mgmt. Assn., Comml. Law League Am., Order of Barristers. Democrat. Jewish. Office: Moss & Barnett PA 4800 Wells Fargo Ctr Minneapolis MN 55402 also: 90 S 7th St Ste 4800 Minneapolis MN 55402 Office Phone: 612-877-5000. Business E-Mail: weilc@moss-barnett.com.

WEIL, D(ONALD) WALLACE, business administration educator; b. Cleve., July 20, 1923; s. Laurence J. and Carol S. (Wallace) W.; m. Jane A. Bittel, Dec. 29, 1947; children— John Wallace, Charles Andrew, Margaret Jane, Carol Wyn. BA, Oberlin Coll., 1947; JD, Willamette U., 1950. Pres. James Foundry Corp., Fort Atkinson, Wis., 1960-70; faculty bus. adminstrn. U. Wis., Eau Claire, 1971-74, chmn. dept. bus. adminstrn., 1974-77, prof., 1985—2003, ret. prof. emeritis, 2003—; pres. Diversified Industries, Inc., St. Louis, 1977-81, UHI Corp., Los Angeles, 1981-85. Dir. U.H.I. Corp. Diversified Industries, Inc., St. Louis, Sales Investments, Mgmt. Inc., Elmwood, Wis., Jane B. Inc., Eau Claire Served with AUS, 1942-45. Mem. Nat. SAR (life), Wis. SAR, Am. Security Council, Nat. Council Small Bus. Mgmt. Devel., Phi Kappa Phi, Beta Gamma Sigma. Republican. Congregationalist. Office: U Wis-Eau Claire Dept Bus Adminstrn Eau Claire WI 54701 Home: 11201 Fairfield Rd Apt 300A Minnetonka MN 55305

WEIL, EDWARD DAVID, chemist, researcher, consultant, inventor; b. Phila., June 13, 1928; s. Irving E. and Minna M. (Stainbrook) W.; m. Barbara Joy Hummel, Sept. 11, 1952; children: David L., Claudia E. BS in Chemistry, U. Pa., Phila., 1950; PhD in Organic Chemistry, U. Ill., 1953; MBA, Pace U., NYC, 1982. Chemist, supr. Hooker Chem. Co., Niagara Falls, NY, 1950-65; supr., sr. scientist Stauffer Chem. Co., Dobbs Ferry, NY, 1965-86; ind. cons., patent agt., propr. Intertech. Svcs., 1986—; dir. exploratory rsch. Adelphi Rsch. Ctr., Garden City, 1986-87; rsch. prof. Poly U., Bklyn., 1987—; IP fellow U. Akron Rsch. Found., 2006—. Contbr. articles to Kirk-Othmer Ency., Ency. Polymer Sci., Rsch. Mgmt., others. Recipient IR-100 award Indsl. Rsch. Mag. Mem. Am. Chem. Soc. (chmn. profl. rels. com. NY sect. 1980-95), Assn. Cons. Chemists and Chem. Engrs., Sigma Xi. Achievements include more than 220 patents for commercial flame retardants, processes, agricultural chemicals, others. Home: 850 Sumner Pkwy Apt 301 Copley OH 44321 Office Phone: 330-664-1075. E-mail: eweil@poly.edu.

WEIL, FRANK A., investment banker, lawyer; b. Bedford, NY, Feb. 14, 1931; s. Sylvan and Ruth Alice (Norman) W.; m. Denie Sandison, Feb. 10, 1951; children: Deborah Weil Harrington, Amanda, Sandison, William. AB cum laude, Harvard U., 1953, LL.B., 1956. Bar: N.Y. 1956. Practiced in, NYC, 1957-60; gen. partner Loeb, Rhoades & Co., NYC, 1960-71; pres. Abacus Fund, Inc., 1968-72; chief fin. officer, dir. Paine, Webber, Jackson & Curtis, NYC, 1972-77; asst. sec. industry and trade Dept. Commerce, Washington, 1977-79; partner firm, bd. chmn., Ginsburg, Feldman, Weil & Bress, Washington, 1979-83, Wald, Harkrader & Ross, Washington, 1983-85; chmn., chief exec. officer, dir., Abacus and Assocs., Inc., 1985—; chmn. bd. SyVox Corp., Exxel/Atmos, Inc. Dir. Geico, Dorr-Oliver, Inc., Stamford, Conn., 1968-77, Hamburg Savs. Bank, N.Y.C., 1975-77, J.B. Lippincott Co., Phila., 1975-77, Govt. Research Corp., 1975-77, 79-85; dir., pres. Norman Found., 1953-77, 79, 92, chmn. bd. trustee, Ednl. Alliance. Trustee Tchrs. Coll., Columbia U., 1976-79, Montefiore Hosp., 1960-77; trustee, vice chmn. No. Westchester Hosp., 1971-77; past vice chmn. bd. govs. Atlantic Inst. Internat. Affairs; past pres. Ednl. Alliance, trustee, 1957-77; trustee, sec. Fedn. Jewish Philanthropies, N.Y.C., 1965-77; trustee, chmn. Harvey Sch., 1969-76; trustee Hurricane Island Outward Bound Sch., 1974—, Washington Opera, 1984-85, Asia Soc., 1993—; bd. dirs., pres., vice chmn., Hickrill Found., Inc., 1953-77, 79—; chmn. bd. dirs. Coun. Excellence in Govt., 1984—, chmn., 1988-93, Am. Assembly, 1992—, Smithsonian Inst., 1994—, chmn., 1997—; mem. vis. com. Kennedy Sch. Govt., Harvard U., chmn., 1998—; chmn. tax com., mem. N.Y. State Econ. Devel. Bd., 1975-77, mem. Appleseed Found. bd., 1995—; chmn., mem. N.Y. State Bd. Equalization and Assessment, 1976-77; adv. bd. Sch. Advanced Internat. Studies, Johns Hopkins U., 1979-88; mem. N.Y. State Council on Fiscal and Econ. Priorities, 1985-89, N.Y. Coun. Fgn. Rels.; mem. N.Y. State Adv. Commn. on Liability Ins., 1986. Mem. Century Assn., Harvard Club, Met. Club. Home: 1516 28th St NW Washington DC 20007-3058 Office: Abacus & Assocs Inc 147 E 48th St # 3fl New York NY 10017-1223 Home Phone: 202-338-6007; Office Phone: 212-230-9801. Business E-Mail: fweil2@abacusny.com.

WEIL, GARY RONALD, lawyer; b. NYC, Oct. 1, 1953; s. Leopold and Margarete (Ofsijowitz) W. BS in Acctg., NYU, 1974; JD, NY Law Sch., 1978. Bar: N.Y. 1978, N.Y. (U.S. Dist. Ct. (so. dist.)) 1980, (U.S. Supreme Ct.) 2004. Asst. county atty. Westchester County Atty.'s Office, White Plains, N.Y., 1978-81; asst. dist. atty. Bronx (N.Y.) Dist. Atty.'s Office, 1981—, Spl. Narcotics Prosecutor's Office, NYC, 1985-87. Mem. ABA, N.Y. State Bar Asn. Democrat. Jewish. Avocations: stamp collecting/philately, photography. Office: Bronx Dist Attys Office 198 E 161st St Bronx NY 10451-3506 Business E-Mail: geedubs@aol.com, weilg@bronxda.nyc.gov.

WEIL, IRWIN, literature and language professor; b. Cin., Apr. 16, 1928; s. Sidney and Florence (Levy) W.; m. Vivian Weil, Dec. 27, 1950; children: Martin, Alice, Daniel. AB, U. Chgo., 1948, MA, 1951; PhD, Harvard U., 1960; doctorate (hon.), Nevsky Inst., St. Petersburg, Russia, 1999, Russian State U. Humanities, Moscow, 2007. Sr. social sci. research analyst Library of Congress, 1951-54; teaching fellow Harvard U., 1956-58; mem. faculty Brandeis U., 1958-65; mem. faculty dept. Slavic langs. and lit. Northwestern U., Evanston, Ill., 1966—, chmn. dept., 1976-82. Vis. prof. U. Moscow, Soviet Acad. Scis.; set up series of internat. symposia between Am. scholars and USSR Acad. Scis.; founder 1st Soviet-Am. TV Student Competition in Lit., 1988-89; active in establishment of American Studies Ctr. Humanities U., Moscow, Russia. Author books and articles pub. in field; lectr. recordings, 36 Lectures on Russian Lit., 2006. Recipient Pushkin Internat. gold medal for outstanding teaching and research, 1984, Outstanding Teaching award Northwestern U. Alumni Assn., 1987, Tempo All-Professor Team, Humanities, Chicago Tribune, 1993; Ford Found. fellow, 1954-55. Mem. Am. Assn. Tchrs. Slavic and East European Langs. (exec. sec. 1962-68, Excellence in Teaching award 1993), Am. Coun. Tchrs. Russian (v.p. 1975-79, pres. 1980-84), Internat. Assn. Profs. Russian (founding U.S. mem.). Jewish. Achievements incude establishing TV competition on American and Russian literature between American and Russian high schoolers. Office: Northwestern U Slavic Dept Evanston IL 60208-0001 Home Phone: 847-864-4835; Office Phone: 847-491-8254. Business E-Mail: i-weil@northwestern.edu. *As a scholar and teacher trying hard to develop mutual understanding and cultural exchange with the USSR, I have discovered how important and fruitful it is to apply the normal standards of friendly discourse with people from an entirely different country and historical background.*

WEIL, JEFFREY GEORGE, lawyer; b. Allentown, Pa., Apr. 28, 1951; s. Russel G.E. and Irene Marie (Kozlowski) W.; children: Michael, Stephen, Brooke, Lauren, Kristen. AB, Princeton U., 1973; JD, Harvard U., 1976. Bar: Pa. 1976, U.S. Dist. Ct. (ea. dist.) Pa. 1976, U.S. Ct. Appeals (3d cir.) 1976, U.S. Supreme Ct., 1988. Assoc. Dechert, Phila., 1976—84, ptnr., 1984—, chmn. firm hiring com., 1987—89, mem. firm exec. com., 1990—94. Chmn. com. United Way Southeastern Pa., Phila., 1982-85, trustee, 1983-89, funding policy com., 1987-90; participant Cmty. Leadership Seminar Program, Phila., 1986; bd. dirs. Hawk Mountain Sanctuary 1993—, chmn. bd. dirs., 2000-05; bd. dirs. Pa. Wildlife Fedn., 1996-99. Mem. ABA (vice-chmn. adminstrn. law com. on pub. advs. and pub. representation 1985-88, antitrust sect. pvt. litig. subcom. 1991-2002), Pa. Bar Assn., Phila. Bar Assn. (fed. cts. com. 1985—), Princeton U. Alumni Schs. Com., Phila. Athenaeum, Princeton Club Phila. Avocations: fly fishing, reading. Home: 195 Shelbourne Ln Phoenixville PA 19460-5710 Office: Cira Centre 2929 Arch St Philadelphia PA 19104-2808 Home Phone: 610-935-0538; Office Phone: 215-994-2538. Business E-Mail: jeffrey.weil@dechert.com.

WEIL, JOHN WILLIAM, technology management consultant; b. NYC, Feb. 3, 1928; s. Frank Leopold and Henrietta Amelia Weil; m. Joan Leatrice Landis, June 15, 1950; children: Nancy Ellen, Linda Jill. BS, MIT, Cambridge, 1948; PhD, Cornell U., Ithaca, NY, 1953. Various positions in nuclear reactors and computers Gen. Electric Co. (various locations), 1953-70; v.p. advanced systems and tech. Honeywell Info. Systems, Inc., Waltham, Mass., 1970-74; v.p., chief tech. officer Bendix Corp., Southfield, Mich., 1974-77, sr. v.p., chief tech. officer, 1977-83; v.p. advanced tech. and engring. Allied Corp., Southfield, 1983; pres. Modular Bio Systems, Inc., 1983-85, Weil Assocs., Inc., Bloomfield Hills, Mich., 1985-97. Founder Met. Detroit Sci. and Engring. Coalition, 1977, sec., 1977-80, pres., 1980-82; chmn. Mich. Biotech. Inst., 1981-85, trustee, 1985-92; mem. Army Sci. Bd., 1982-84. Contbr. articles to prof. jours. AEC fellow, 1950-51 Home and Office: 218 Guilford Rd Bloomfield Hills MI 48304-2737 Personal E-mail: johnww@weilhome.com.

WEIL, LEONARD, banker; b. 1922; married With U.S. Dept. State, Vienna, Austria, 1946; with Union Bank, Los Angeles, 1946-62; pres., CEO Mfrs. Bank, Los Angeles, 1962-86, pres. emeritus, 1986—. Adj. asst. prof. fin. Anderson Grad. Sch. Mgmt., UCLA (ret.) Trustee UCLA Found.; bd. visitors UCLA Grad. Sch. Mgmt.; past pres. Town Hall; bd. dirs. Braille Inst. Served with U.S. Army, 1943-45 Mem. Calif. Bankers Assn. (bd. dirs., past pres.), Am. Mgmt. Assn., Am. Econs. Assn., Am. Bankers Assn. (past dir.). Office: PO Box 571150 Tarzana CA 91357-1150 Address: 4501 La Barca Pl Tarzana CA 91356-5029 Home Phone: 818-344-3271; Office Phone: 818-344-3183.

WEIL, LOUIS ARTHUR, III, retired newspaper publishing executive; b. Grand Rapids, Mich., Mar. 14, 1941; s. Louis Arthur, Jr. and Kathryn (Halligan) W.; m. Mary Elizabeth Buckingham, Sept. 7, 1963 (div. June 1977); children: Scott Arthur, Christopher Davison, Timothy Buckingham; m. Daryl Hopkins Goss, Jan. 26, 1980. BA in English, Ind. U., 1963; DHL (hon.), Mercy Coll., Grand Valley State U. Various positions Times Herald, Port Huron, Mich., 1966-68; personnel dir., pub. Journal and Courier, Lafayette, Ind., 1968-73; gen. mgr., pub. Gannett Westchester Rockland Newspapers, White Plains, N.Y., 1973-74, pres., gen. mgr., 1974-77, pres., pub., 1977-79; v.p. devel. Gannett Co., Inc., NYC, 1979-83, sr. v.p. planning and devel., 1982-86; chmn., pub. Gannett Westchester Rockland Newspapers, White Plains, 1984-86; pres. The Detroit News, 1986-89, pub., 1987-89; U.S. pub. Time Mag., 1989-91; pub., chief exec. officer, exec. v.p. Ariz. Republic, Phoenix Gazette, Ariz. Bus. Gazette, 1991-96; chmn., pres., CEO Central Newspapers, Inc., Phoenix, 1996-2000. Bd. dirs. Ctrl. Newspapers, Inc., Prudential. Trustee Garvin Sch. Internat. Mgmt. Thunderbird; campaign chmn. Valley of the Sun United Way, 1992; past chmn. Greater Phoenix Leadership; past pres. bd. trustees Phoenix Art Mus. With USN. Office: 15974 N 77th St #102 Scottsdale AZ 85260

WEIL, LYNNE AMY, communications executive, writer; b. Santa Monica, Calif., Apr. 29, 1963; d. Robert Harry and Miriam Ruth Weil; m. Nils Johan Axel Bruzelius, Aug. 10, 2002; 1 child, Emilie Anna Bruzelius. BA in Comm., U. Calif., LA, 1985; M in Pub. Policy, Princeton U., 2001. Freelance fgn. corr. Nat. Pub. Radio, Monitor Radio, Marketplace pub. radio, BBC, various others, Bonn, Germany, 1993—96; prodr., reporter Radio Deutsche Welle, Cologne, 1991—92; European corr. Cath. News

Svc., Rome, 1996—99; reporter UPI, LA, 1986—88; prodr., reporter Calif. Pub. Radio Network, Long Beach, 1988—91; press sec. Senate Fgn. Rels. Com., Washington, 2001—03; comm. dir. Ho. Internat. Rels. Com. Dem. staff, 2003—. Cons. Woodrow Wilson Sch., Princeton U., NJ, 2003. Contbr. articles to profl. jours. Recipient Coll. journalism award with stipend, Pub. Interest Radio and TV Soc., 1985; scholar, Woodrow Wilson Sch., Princeton U., 2000—01; Congl. fellow, Am. Polit. Sci. Assn., 1999—2000. Mem.: Fgn. Corr. Assn. Germany (pres. 1995—96, v.p. 1994—95), Women in Internat. Security. Avocations: skiing, tennis, various musical instruments. Office Phone: 202-225-6735.

WEIL, MAX HARRY, internist, cardiologist, educator, researcher; b. Baden, Switzerland, Feb. 9, 1927; arrived in U.S., 1937, naturalized, 1944; s. Marcel and Gretl (Winter) Weil; children: Susan Margot, Carol Juliet. AB, U. Mich., Ann Arbor, 1948; MD, SUNY, NYC, 1952; PhD, U. Minn., Mpls., 1957; DSc (hon.), SUNY Downstate Med. Ctr., 2004. Diplomate Am. Bd. Internal Medicine and Critical Care Medicine, Nat. Bd. Med. Examiners. Intern in internal medicine U. Cin. Med. Ctr., 1952-53; resident U. Minn. Hosps., Heart Hosp., VA Hosp., Mpls., 1953-55; rsch. fellow U. Minn., Mpls., 1955-56; sr. fellow Nat. Heart Inst., Mayo Clinic, Rochester, Minn., 1956-57; chief cardiology City of Hope Med. Ctr., Duarte, Calif., 1957-59; asst. clin. prof. U. So. Calif. Sch. Medicine, LA, 1957-59, asst. prof., 1959-63, assoc. prof., 1963-71, clin. prof., 1971-81; chmn. L.A. Com. on Emergency Med. Svcs., 1968-73; prof., chmn. Dept. Medicine, chief divsn. cardiology Chgo. Med. Sch. U. Health Scis., North Chgo., 1981-91, disting. univ. prof., 1992-94, disting. univ. prof. emeritus Weil Inst. Critical Care Medicine, 1994—. Adj. prof. medicine Northwestern U. Med. Sch., Chgo., 1992—; prof. clin. med. bioengring. U. So. Calif., LA, 1972-91, adj. prof. medicine, 1981-94, clin. prof. anesthesiology, 1995—, rsch. prof. surgery, 1996—; disting. univ. prof. Weil Inst. Critical Care Medicine, Rancho Mirage, Calif., 1995—. Sect. editor Archives Internal Medicine, 1983-86, JAMA, 1969-72; guest editor Am. Jour. Cardiology, 1982, Critical Care Medicine, 1985; mem. editl. bd. Am. Jour. Medicine, 1971-79, Chest, 1980-95, Jour. Circulatory Shock, 1979-92, Clin. Engring. Newsletter, 1980—, Methods of Info. in Medicine, 1977-91, Jour. Clin. Illness, 1986—, Clin. Intensive Care, 1989—; mem. editl. adv. bd. Emergency Medicine, 1978—, Issues in Health Care Tech., 1983-86; assoc. editor Critical Care Medicine, 1973-74, mem. editl. bd., 1973-91, 94-96, sr. editor, 1997; editor-in-chief Acute Care, 1983-90, Jour. Cardiovasc. Pharmacol. Theories, 2003-; contbr. over 1100 articles to profl. jours.; patentee in field. Pres. Temple Brotherhood, Wilshire Blvd. Temple, LA, 1967-68; bd. dirs. Hollywood Presbyn. Med. Ctr., 1976-81, LA chpt. Met. Am. Heart Assn., 1962-67, Chgo. chpt. Met. Am. Heart Assn., 1982-88; active City Health and Med. Welfare Commn., Rancho Mirage, 2002—. With US Army, 1946-47. Recipient prize in internal medicine SUNY, 1952, Alumni medallion SUNY, 1970; Disting. Svc. award Soc. Critical Care Medicine, 1984; numerous rsch. grants, 1959—; named Disting. Alumni Lectr., 1967, Oscar Schwindetzky Meml. Lectr. Internat. Anesthesia Rsch. Soc., 1978; recipient Lawrence R. Medoff award Chgo. Med. Sch., 1987, Morris L. Parker Rsch. award, 1989, Mission of Mercy award Israeli Nat. Emergency Svcs., 2001; Lilly scholar, 1988-89. Master ACP; fellow Am. Coll. Cardiology (chmn. emergency cardiac care com. 1974-81); master, fellow Am. Coll. Chest Physicians, Am. Coll. Clin. Pharmacology, Am. Coll. Critical Care Medicine (Disting. Investigator award 1990, 96, A.S. Laerdal Lifetime Achievement award 2000, Lifetime Achievement award 2001), Am. Heart Assn. (coun. circulation, coun. basic sci., coun. cardiopulmonary and critical care, coun. clin. cardiology, Dickinson W. Richards Meml. lectureship 1998, Emergency Cardiac Care Lifetime Achievement award 2000), Vet. Emergency Critical Care Soc. (Knowles Meml. lectr. 2002), NY Acad. Sci., Chgo. Soc. Internal Medicine; mem. AMA (sect. editor jour. 1969-72), IEEE, LA County Med. Assn., Am. Physiol. Soc. Am. Soc. Pharmacology and Exptl. Therapeutics, Am. Trauma Soc. (founding mem.), Assn. Computing Machinery, Assn. Am. Med. Colls., Ctrl. Soc. Clin. Rsch., Chgo. Cardiol. Group (sec.-treas. 1986-88, chmn. 1988-90), Chgo. Soc. Internal Medicine, Lake County Heart Assn. (bd. govs. 1983-86), Intensive Care Soc. UK, LA Soc. Internal Medicine, Soc. Exptl. Biology and Medicine, Western Soc. Clin. Rsch., Fedn. Am. Socs. Exptl. Biology, Am. Soc. Parenteral and Enteral Nutrition, Nat. Acad. Practice (disting. practitioner), Skull and Dagger, Sigma Xi, Alpha Omega Alpha. Jewish. Avocations: swimming, tennis, photography, philosophy-economics. Office: Chgo Med Sch U Health Scis Weil Inst Critical Care Medicine 35100 Bob Hope Dr Rancho Mirage CA 92270 Office Phone: 760-778-4911. Business E-Mail: weilm@weiliccm.org.

WEIL, PETER HENRY, lawyer; b. NYC, Nov. 20, 1933; s. Frank L. and Henrietta Amelia Weil; m. Helen Fay Kolodkin, Dec. 18, 1960; children: Karen L., Frank L. BA cum laude, Princeton U., 1954; LLB cum laude, Harvard U., 1957. Bar: N.Y. 1957, U.S. Dist. Ct. (so. and ea. dists.) N.Y. 1972. Assoc. Weil, Gotshal & Manges, NYC, 1958-62; from assoc. to ptnr. Kaye Scholer, NYC, 1962-95; ret., 1995. Lectr. SMU Inst. Comml. Financing, 1985—94, Banking Law Inst., 1987—89. Author: Asset Based Lending: An Introductory Guide to Secured Financing, P.L.I., 1989, 3d edit., 1996. Former chmn. N.Y. bd. overseers, former bd. govs. Hebrew Union Coll., Jewish Inst. Religion, Cin., NYC, LA, Jerusalem. With US Army, 1957—58. Recipient U.S. Nat. Sr. Champions Ringwood Golden Master Volleyball Team award, 1983. Mem.: ABA, Assn. Bar of City of N.Y. (mem. banking law com. 1975—78). Personal E-mail: phweil@aol.com.

WEIL, RANDOLPH ALLEN, engineering executive; b. Champaign, Ill., Nov. 23, 1951; s. Nicholas Andrew and Audrey Florence W.; m. Susan Kay Rostad, Feb. 26, 1977; children: Alexandra, Aaron. BS in Econs., U. Ill., Chgo., 1973; MBA, U. Calif., Berkeley, 1974. Gen. sales mgr. Cummins Engring. Co., Downers Grove, Ill., 1975-83; gen. mgr. ops. Sub of Cummins Engine. Co., Chgo., 1983-85; v.p., gen. mgr. Global Parts, Inc. (sub-co. of The Budd Co.), Dallas, 1985—87; dir. coastal ops. Allied Tube & Conduit, Harvey, Ill., 1987-88; dir. distbn. ops. Square D. Co., Florence, Ky., 1988-92; v.p. logistics AT&T Network Systems, Morristown, NJ, 1992-94; v.p. svc. logistics NCR Corp., Dayton, Ohio, 1994—2000; pres., COO IHS Engring., 2001—03; exec. v.p. IHS Group, 2003—04; pres., CEO Weil Operations West, LLC, 2004—; pres. Highlands Ranch Parks and Rec. Found., 2005—; dir. comm. St. Mary's Acad. Parents, 2005—; dir. Power Kure, Inc., 2005—. Dir. Jr. Achievement, Dayton, 1996—99, Boy Scouts Am., Columbus, 1978—80. Mem. Am. Prodn. & Inventory Control Soc., Coun. Logistics Mgrs. Avocations: bicycling, swimming, opera, remodelling, gardening. Office Phone: 303-425-3255. Personal E-mail: raweil@att.net.

WEIL, ROLF ALFRED, economist, retired university president; b. Pforzheim, Germany, Oct. 29, 1921; arrived in U.S., 1936, naturalized, 1944; s. Henry and Lina (Landauer) W.; m. Leni Metzger, Nov. 3, 1945; children: Susan Linda, Ronald Alan. BA, U. Chgo., 1942, PhD, 1950; D Hebrew Letters, Coll. Jewish Studies, 1967; DHL, Loyola U., 1970, Bowling Green State U., Ohio, 1986; LHD, Roosevelt U., 1988. Rsch. asst. Cowles Commn. for Rsch. in Econs., 1942-44; rsch. analyst Ill. Dept. Revenue, 1944-46; mem. faculty Roosevelt U., Chgo., 1946—, prof. fin. and econs., also chmn. dept. fin., 1954-65, dean Coll. Bus. Adminstrn., 1957-64, acting pres., 1965-66, pres., 1966-88, pres. emeritus, 1988—. Past pres. Selfhelp Home for the Aged, Chgo. Author: Through these Portals-from Immigrant to College President, 1991; contbr. articles on fin. to profl. jours. Bd. dirs. trustees Roosevelt U., Selfhelp of Chgo., Inc. Mem. Am. Econ. Assn., Cliff Dwellers Club. Office Phone: 312-341-4330. Personal E-mail: rolfleniweil@aol.com. Business E-Mail: rweil@roosevelt.edu.

WEIL, SUSAN ELLEN, dietician, consultant; b. Cleveland, Ohio, May 9, 1954; d. Alexander and Ruth Weil. BS, Miami U., Oxford, Ohio, 1976; Dietetic Internship, Barnes Hosp., St. Louis, Mo., 1976—77. Registered dietitian Am. Dietetic Assn., 1977, Bd. Cert. Specialist in Renal Nutrition Commn. on Dietetic Registration, Am. Dietetic Assn., 2001. Renal dietitian UCLA Med. Ctr. Kidney and Pancreas Transplant Program and UCLA DaVita Dialysis Ctr., Los Angeles, Calif., 1979—; speakers' bur. Amgen, Inc., Thousand Oaks, Calif., 2003—; renal dietitian U. Hospitals of Cleve., Cleveland, Ohio, 1977—79; clin. instr. of nutrition edn. program Gen. Internal Medicine Residency Tng. Program, UCLA Sch. of Medicine, LA, Calif., 1982—92, co-ordinator of nutrition edn., 1990—92. Cons. (temp.) Amgen, Inc., Thousand Oaks, Calif., 2004—04; cons. Nephrology Ednl. Svcs. & Rsch., Inc., Tarzana, Calif., 2001—04; steering com., speaker's bureau Crescent Initiative, 2007. Author: (medical textbook on transplantation) Nutrition in the Kidney Tranplant Recipient, in Handbook of Kidney Transplantion, 1992, 2nd edit., 1996, 3rd edit., 2001, 4th edit., 2005, (textbook for dialysis nurses) Nutrition Management, in Review of Hemodialysis for Nurses and Dialysis Personnel, 1993, 6th edit., 1999; co-author: (interactive computer tchg. program) Renaltouch(TM); contbr. dietetics manual; co-author: Diet and Medications, in Living Well With Kidney Disease, 2006, National Kidney Foundation of Southern California, 2007. Planning com. U.S. Transpl. Olympics Nat. Kidney Found., LA, Calif., 1992; planning com. Gift of Life dinner Nat. Kidney Found. of So. Calif., LA, Calif., 2004. Mem.: Coun. on Renal Nutrition, Nat. Kidney Found., Am. Dietetic Assn. Avocation: singing. Home Phone: 310-823-0847; Office Phone: 310-794-9687.

WEIL, THOMAS ALEXANDER, retired electronics engineer; b. NYC, Jan. 22, 1930; s. Frank Leopold and Henrietta Amelia (Simons) W.; m. Dianne Isaacs; children: Deborah, Elizabeth, Alexander. BSEE, MIT, 1951. Engr. modulator sect. Raytheon Co., Watertown, Mass., 1951-55, sect. mgr. transmitters, 1955-69, dept. mgr. transmitters, 1969-77, staff scientist equipment devel. labs., 1972-95, lab. mgr. radar systems, 1977-79, lab. mgr. advanced devel., 1979-80, program mgr. oil shale program, 1980-84, sr. sci., 1985—95; ret., 1995. Cons. in field. Contbr. chapters to books, articles to profl. jours. Recipient Excellence in Tech. award Raytheon co., 1990; Raytheon Co. fellow, 1989. Fellow IEEE (tech. papers com. Modulator Symposia, Microwave Tube Symposia, Germeshausen award 1994). Universalist-Unitarian. Achievements include 11 patents in field. Avocations: classical music, photography, mountain climbing, cosmology. Home: 14 Lanark Rd Wellesley MA 02481-3029 Personal E-mail: taweil@aol.com. *Evolution and survival of the fittest have left mankind aggressive and prone to make war. Peace depends on finding how to overcome this heritage. Shouldn't we be working on how to resteer mankind's instincts?.*

WEIL, THOMAS P., retired health services consultant; b. Mount Vernon, NY, Oct. 2, 1932; s. H.M. and Alice (Franc) W.; m. Janet Whalen, Feb. 13, 1965. BA, Union Coll., 1954; MPH, Yale U., 1958; PhD, U. Mich., 1964. S.S. Goldwater fellow Mount Sinai Med. Ctr., NYC, 1957-58; assoc. cons. J.G. Steinle Assocs., Garden City, NY, 1958-61; asst. prof. UCLA, 1962-65; assoc. dir. Touro Infirmary, New Orleans, 1964-66; prof., dir. U. Mo., 1966—71; v.p. E.D. Rosenfeld Assocs., NYC, 1971-75; pres. Bedford Health Assocs. Inc., N.Y., N.C., 1975-2000; ret. Chmn. Health Edn. & Applied Rsch. Found., Washington, 1981-83; bd. dirs. Albany (N.Y.) Med. Ctr., Inc., 1974-77; cons. to numerous hosps., med. schs., health related orgs., 1958-2000. Contbr. articles profl. jours. Named vis. prof. W.K. Kellogg Found., Sydney, Australia, 1969; recipient svc. award Am. Assn. Healthcare Cons., 1982; Weil Disting. Prof. in Health Svcs. Mgmt., U. Mo., 1991-2001. Fellow APHA (emeritus), Am. Assn. Healthcare Cons. (emeritus), Am. Coll. Healthcare Execs. (emeritus). Jewish. Avocations: Appaloosa and Quarter Horses, Pointers. Office Phone: 828-252-1616. Personal E-mail: Tpweil@aol.com.

WEILAND, SCOTT RICHARD, singer; b. Santa Cruz, Calif., Oct. 28, 1967; m. Mary Forsberg, 2000 (div. 2003); children: Noah, Lucy Olivia. Founder, lead singer Mighty Joe Young, 1987—92; lead singer Stone Temple Pilots, 1992—, Velvet Revolver, 2003—; founder Softdrive Records, 2003. Singer: (albums) (with Stone Temple Pilots) Core, 1992, Purple, 1994, Tiny Music...Songs From the Vatican Gift Shop, 1996, No. 4, 1999, Shangri-La Dee Da, 2001, Thank You, 2003, (solo) 12 Bar Blues, 1998, (with Velvet Revolver) Contraband, 2004, Libertad, 2007; co-prodr.: (albums) Break Your Silence, Cinder, 2003.

WEILER, JEFFRY LOUIS, lawyer; b. NYC, Dec. 31, 1942; s. Kurt and Elaine (Kabb) W.; m. Susan Karen Goodman, June 8, 1964; children: Philip K., June M. BS, Miami U., Oxford, Ohio, 1964; JD, Cleve. State U., 1970. Bar: Ohio 1970, Fla. 1981; CPA, Ohio 1968; bd. cert. specialist in estate planning trust and probate law, Ohio; bd. cert. tax specialist, Fla., 1983—. Acct. Meaden & Moore, CPAs, Cleve., 1964-65; IRS agt. U.S. Dept. Treasury, Cleve., 1965-70; assoc. Ulmer & Berne, Cleve., 1970-71; ptnr. Benesch, Friedlander, Coplan & Aronoff, LLP, Cleve., 1971—. Adj. assoc. prof. Cleve.-Marshall Coll. Law, Cleve. State U., 1980-87. Contbr. to profl. pubs. Named Disting. Estate Planner, Estate Planning Coun. Cleve., 2004; named one of Top 50 in Cleve., Ohio Super Lawyers, 2004—07, Top 100 in Ohio, 2004—07. Fellow Am. Coll. Trust and Estate Counsel; mem. ABA (sect. taxation), Ohio State Bar Assn. (coun. estate planning trust and probate law sect. 1999—), Cleve. Estate Planning Inst. (chmn. 1980), Cleve. Tax Inst. (chmn. 1983), Cleve. Bar Assn. (treas. 1993-96, trustee 1988-91), Tax Club of Cleve. (sec. 1996-97, v.p. 1997-99, pres. 1999-2000). Avocations: photography, sailboat racing. Office: Benesch Friedlander Coplan & Aronoff LLP 2300 BP Tower 200 Public Sq Cleveland OH 44114-2378 Home: 451 Muirfield Dr Highland Heights OH 44143 Home Phone: 440-446-8081; Office Phone: 216-363-4551. Business E-Mail: jweiler@bfca.com.

WEIL-GARRIS BRANDT, KATHLEEN (KATHLEEN BRANDT), art historian; b. Surrey, Eng. d. Kurt Hermann and Charlotte (Garris) Weil; m. Werner Brandt (dec. 1983). BA with honors, Vassar Coll., Poughkeepsie, NY, 1956; postgrad., U. Bonn, Germany, 1956-57; MA, Radcliffe U., 1958; PhD, Harvard, 1966; MA, Oxford U., 1998. Asst. prof. NYU, NYC, 1963-67, assoc. prof., 1967-72, prof., 1973—; asst. prof. NYU Inst. Fine Arts, NYC, 1966-67, assoc. prof., 1967-72, prof., 1973—; vis. prof. Harvard U., Cambridge, Mass., 1980; editor in chief The Art Bulletin, NYC, 1977-81; Slade prof. Oxford U., 1998. Cons. on Renaissance art Vatican Mus., 1987—; vis. fellow Bibliotheca Hertziana (Max-Planck Inst.) Rome; faculty fellow Z. M. Remarque Inst., 2006. Author: Leonardo and Central Italian Art, 1974, Problems In Cinquecento Sculpture, 1977; author: (with J. d'Amico) The Renaissance Cardinal's Ideal Palace, 1981, (with C. d'Acidini, J. Draper, N. Penny) Giovinezza di Michelangelo, 1999-2000; editor: Michelangelo: la Cappella Sistina: documentazione e interpretazione, vol. III, 1996; contbr. articles to profl. jours. Mem. Am. com. Medici Archive Project, 1996—; bd. dirs. Raccolta Vinciana, 1997—. Decorated officer Order of Merit (Italy); recipient Rsch. award Humboldt Found., 1985, Disting. Tchg. award Lindback Found., 1967, Golden Dozen Tchr. award NYU, 1993, Alumni Great Tchr. award, 1996; Guggenheim fellow, 1976; grantee Henkel Found., 1987, Samuel H. Kress Found., 1999. Mem. Coll. Art Assn. (bd. dirs. 1973-74, 77-81), Renaissance Soc. Am. (editl. bd. 1992—), Soc. Archtl. Historians, Friends of the Frances Lehman Loeb Art Ctr. (bd. mem. 2005—), N.Y. Acad. Scis., Phi Beta Kappa (v.p. NYU chpt. 1979-81). Avocations: art films, conservation, music, dance. Office: NYU Inst Fine Arts 1 E 78th St New York NY 10021-0119 Business E-Mail: kathleen.brandt@nyu.edu.

WEILL, GEORGES GUSTAVE, mathematics professor; b. Strasbourg, France, Apr. 9, 1926; arrived in US, 1956; s. Edmond and Germaine (Falck) W. Student, Ecole Polytechnique, Paris, 1950; E.N.S., Telecom., Paris, 1952; Licence de Mathematiques, U. Paris, France, 1954, D.Sc. in Physics, 1955; PhD in Math, U. Calif. at Los Angeles, 1960. Research scientist Compagnie Generale de Telegraphie Sans Fil, France, 1952-56; rsch. fellow dept. elec. engring. Calif. Inst. Tech., Pasadena, 1956-59; tchg. assoc. math. UCLA, 1959-60; rsch. fellow math. Harvard, 1960-62; lectr., rsch. assoc. Yale, 1962-64; vis. asst. prof. Belfer Grad. Sch. Sci., Yeshiva U., 1964-65; assoc. prof. math. Poly. U., Bklyn., 1964-65, prof., 1966-95, prof. math. emeritus, 1995—. Adj. prof. math. Cooper Union, NYC. Mem. Am. Math. Soc., Societe Mathematique de France, IEEE (sr. mem.), Sigma Xi, Pi Mu Epsilon. Office: Polytechnic Univ 333 Jay St Brooklyn NY 11201-2990

WEILL, HANS, medical educator; b. Berlin, Aug. 31, 1933; came to U.S., 1939; s. Kurt and Gerda (Philipp) W.; m. Kathleen Burton, Apr. 3, 1958; children: Judith, Leslie, David. BS, Tulane U., 1955, MD, 1958. Diplomate: Am. Bd. Internal Medicine. Intern Mt. Sinai Hosp., NYC, 1958-59; resident Tulane Med. Unit, Charity Hosp. La., New Orleans, 1959-60, chief resident, 1961-62, sr. vis. physician, 1972—; NIH research fellow dept. medicine and pulmonary lab. Sch. Medicine Tulane U., New Orleans, 1960-61, instr. medicine, 1962-64, asst. prof. medicine, 1964-67, assoc. prof., 1967-71, prof. medicine, 1971—, Schlieder Found. prof. pulmonary medicine, 1985-97; chief Environ. Medicine sect. Tulane Med. Center, 1980-96; dir. univ. Ctr. for Bioenviron. Rsch., 1989-93; dir. interdisciplinary research group in occupational lung diseases Nat. Heart, Lung and Blood Inst., 1972-92, mem. nat. adv. council, 1986-90, chmn. pulmonary disease adv. com., 1982-84; active staff Tulane Med. Center Hosp., 1976—; program dir. Nat. Inst. for Environ. Health Sci., 1992-96. Cons. pulmonary diseases Touro Infirmary, New Orleans, 1962—; cons. NIH, Nat. Inst. Occupational Safety and Health, Occupational Safety and Health Adminstrn., USN, NAS, EPA; lectr., participant workshops and confs. profl. groups in U.S., France, Can., U.K.; dir. Nat. Inst. Environ. Health Scis Superfund. Basic Rsch. Program, 1992-96. Mem. editorial bd. Am. Rev. of Respiratory Disease, 1980-85, CHEST, 1987-91; editor Respiratory Diseases Digest, 1981; guest editor Byssinosis conf. supplement, CHEST, 1981. Fellow Am. Acad. Allergy, Royal Soc. Medicine, ACP; mem. Am. Thoracic Soc. (pres. 1976), Am. Lung Assn. (bd. dirs. 1975-78), New Orleans Acad. Internal Medicine (sec., treas. 1973-75), Am. Coll. Chest Physicians (gov. for La. 1970-75), Am. Fedn. Clin. Research, So. Soc. Clin. Investigation, N.Y. Acad. Scis., Brit. Thoracic Assn., Internat. Epidemiol. Assn., Am. Heart Assn. (task force on environment and cardiovascular system 1978), Brit. Thoracic Soc., Phi Beta Kappa, Alpha Omega Alpha. Home and Office: 110 Bellshire Dr Flat Rock NC 28731 Personal E-mail: hweill@earthlink.net.

WEILL, SANDY (SANFORD I. WEILL), former diversified financial services company executive; b. Bklyn., Mar. 16, 1933; s. Max and Etta (Kalika) W.; m. Joan Mosher, June 20, 1955; children: Marc P., Jessica M. Bibliowicz. BA, Cornell U., 1955, student Grad. Sch. Bus. and Pub. Adminstrn., 1954-55. Chmn. bd., CEP Carter, Berlind & Weill (name changed to CBWL-Hayden, Stone, Inc. 1970, to Hayden Stone, Inc. 1972, to Shearson Hayden Stone 1974, to Shearson Loeb Rhoades), NYC, 1960-84, dir., chmn. exec. com., 1981-83, pres., 1983-85, Am. Express Co., 1983—85, chmn., CEO Fireman's Fund Ins. Co. subs., 1984-85; chmn., CEO Am. Express Ins. Services., Inc., 1984—85; chmn., pres., CEO Comml. Credit Co., Balt., 1986—88; chmn., CEO Primerica Corp., NYC, 1988—93, pres., 1988—92; chmn. Primerica Holdings Inc., NYC; chmn., CEO Travelers Group, NYC, 1986—98; CEO Citigroup, Inc., NYC, 1998—2003, chmn., 1998—2006, chmn. emeritus, 2006—. Bd. dirs. Citigroup, Inc., 1986-2006, AT&T Corp., 1998-2002, I. Du Pont Nemours & Co., 1998-2001, United Technologies Corp., 1999-2003, Fed. Res. Bank N.Y., 2001-06; vice chmn. adv. council The Johnson Grad. Sch. of Mgmt.; founder Acad. of Fin. Co-author (with Judah S. Kraushaar): The Real Deal: My Life in Business and Philanthropy, 2006. Mem. bd. overseers Joan and Sanford I. Weill Med. Coll. and Grad. Sch. Med. Scis. of Cornell U. (formerly Cornell Med. Coll.), 1982-, chmn., 1996-; chmn. bd. trustees Carnegie Hall, N.Y.C., 1991-; trustee N.Y. Presbyn. Hosp.; bd. overseers Meml. Sloan-Kettering Cancer Ctr.; bd. dirs. Balt. Symphony Orch.; bd. gov. NY Hosp.; mem. adv. coun. Cornell Univ. Johnson Grad. Sch. Mgmt.; mem. US Dept. Treasury Working Group on Child Care. Named one of the halls in honor of at Carnegie Hall, CEO of the Yr., Chief Exec. mag., 2002; named one of Top 25 Managers of Yr., BusinessWeek, 2001, 50 Most Generous Philanthropists, 2005, 400 Richest Americans, Forbes, 2006; named to Acad. of Achievement, Washington, D.C., 1997; recipient NY State Gov.'s Art award, 1997. Mem. N.Y. Soc. Security Analysts Clubs: Cornell (N.Y.C.), Century Country (Purchase, N.Y.), Harmonie (N.Y.C.); chmn. Nat. Acad. Found. Office: Citigroup Inc 399 Park Ave New York NY 10022-4614 also: Citigroup Inc 153 E 53rd St New York NY 10043-0001 *

WEIMER, JOHN L., state supreme court justice; b. Thibodaux, La., Oct. 2, 1954; m. Penny Hymel; 3 children. BS (with honors), Nicholls State U., 1976; JD, La. State U., 1980. Pvt. practice law, 1980—95; judge 17th Judicial Dist. Ct., 1995—98, 1st Cir. Ct. of Appeal, Dist. 1, Divsn. B, 1998—2001; assoc. justice La. Supreme Ct., 2001—. Adj. prof. law Nicholls State U., 1982—97; regional co-chmn. Citizens' Summit for Justice Reform, 1997. Mem. Thibodaux Vol. Fire Dept., Rotary Club, Nicholls State U. Alumni Bd., Thibodaux Chamber of Commerce, Houma-Terrebonne Chamber of Commerce, Assumption Chamber of Commerce; established Lafourche Parish Student Govt. Day Program. Recipient Crimefighter's Outstanding Jurist award, Outstanding Jud. award, Victims & Citizens Against Crime. Mem.: Lafourche Parish Bar Assn., La. State Bar Assn. (delegate). Achievements include development of Lafourche Parish Drug Treatment Court. Office: La Supreme Ct 400 Royal St New Orleans LA 70130 *

WEIMER, ROBERT JAY, geology educator, energy consultant, civic leader; b. Glendo, Wyo., Sept. 4, 1926; s. John L. and Helen (Mowrey) Weimer; m. Ruth Carol Adams, Sept. 12, 1948; children: Robert Thomas, Loren Edward(dec.), Paul Christner, Carl Scott. BA, U. Wyo., Laramie, 1948, MA, 1949; PhD, Stanford U., Calif., 1953. Registered profl. engr., Colo. Geologist Union Oil Co. Calif., 1949-54; cons. geologist U.S. and fgn. petroleum exploration, 1954—; prof. geology Colo. Sch. Mines, 1957-83, prof. emeritus, 1983—, Getty prof. geology, 1978-83; vis. prof. U. Colo., 1961, U. Calgary, Can., 1970, Inst. Tech., Bandung, Indonesia, 1975. Fulbright lectr. U. Adelaide, South Australia, 1967; disting. lectr. and continuing edn. lectr. Am. Assn. Petroleum Geologists, Soc. Expl. Geophysicists; ednl. cons. to petroleum cos., 1964—; mem. energy rsch. adv. bd. Dept. Energy, 1985-90, Bd. on Mineral and Energy Resources, Nat. Rsch. Coun., 1988. Editor: Guide to Geology of Colorado, 1960, Symposium on Cretaceous Rocks of Colorado and Adjacent Area, 1959, Denver Earthquakes, 1968, Fossil Fuel Exploration, 1974, Studies in Colorado Field Geology, 1976, Petroleum System, Denver Basin, 1996. Trustee Colo. Sch. Mines Research Found., 1967-70; pres. Rockland Found., 1982-83; bd. dirs. Foothills Art Ctr., 1997-2002. With USNR, 1944-46. Recipient Disting. Alumnus award U. Wyo., 1982, Mines medal Colo. Sch. Mines, 1984, Brown medal, 1990, Parker medal Am. Inst. Profl. Geologists, 1986, Exemplary Alumni award U. Wyo., 1994, ISEM Hedberg award, 2001, Carla Coleman Conservation award, 2005, Hall of Fame award IPAMS, 2006. Fellow Geol. Soc. Am. (chmn. Rocky Mountain sect. 1966-67, Sloss award 2003), AAAS; mem. Am. Assn. Petroleum Geologists (hon. pres. 1992, Sidney Powers medal 1983, Dist. Educator award 1996), Soc. for Sedimentary Geology (hon., sec.-treas. 1966-67, v.p. 1971, pres. 1972, Twenhofel medal 1995), Colo. Sci. Soc. (hon., pres. 1981),

Rocky Mountain Assn. Geologists (hon., pres. 1969, found. bd. 1976-86, Scientist of Yr. 1982, Legend award 2003), Nigerian Mining and Geoscis. Soc. (hon.), Can. Soc. Petroleum Geologists (hon.), Wyo. Geol. Assn. (hon.), Colo. Sch. Mines Alumni Assn. (hon., Coolbaugh award 1996), Am. Geol. Inst. Found. (sec., treas. 1984-88, Legendary Geosci. award 2006-), Geol. Soc. Am. Found. (bd. dirs. 1999-04), Nat. Acad. Engring. (ch. sec. 11 1999), Northwoodside Inc. Land Conservancy Found. (v.p. 1995-96, pres. 1997—, Carla Coleman Conservation award 2005), Mt. Vernon Country Club (Golden, bd. dirs. 1956-59, 81-84, pres. 1983-84). Home: RR 3 25853 Mt Vernon Rd Golden CO 80401-9699 Office Phone: 303-526-0247. Business E-Mail: rweimer@mines.edu.

WEIMER, THOMAS R. (R. THOMAS WEIMER), federal agency administrator; BS, ME, Harvey Mudd Coll., Claremont, Calif., 1972; MEE, U. Wash., Seattle, 1976. Subcom. staff dir., com. on sci. US Ho. of Reps; legis. dir. Nat. Lab. Affairs, Office of Fed. Govt. Relations U. Calif.; chief of staff to sec. US Dept. Interior, 1989—93, prin. dep. asst. sec. water & sci., 2001—04, acting asst. sec. water & sci., 2004—05, asst. sec. policy mgmt. & budget, 2005—. Office: US Dept Interior Rm 5113 1849 C St NW Washington DC 20240 Office Phone: 202-208-1927. Business E-Mail: tom_weimer@ios.doi.gov.

WEIN, ALAN JEROME, urologist, educator, researcher; b. Newark, Dec. 15, 1941; s. Isadore R. and Jeanette Frances (Abrams) Wein. AB cum laude, Princeton U., 1962; MD, U. Pa., 1966; PhD (hon.), U. Patras, Greece, 2005. Diplomate Am. Bd. Urology (trustee emeritus). Intern mixed surgery Hosp. U. Pa., Phila., 1966-67, resident surgery, 1967-68; resident urology U. Pa., Phila., 1969-72, fellow Harrison Dept. Surg. Rsch. Urology Sch. Medicine, 1968-69, asst. instr. surgery Sch. Medicine, 1967-68, asst. instr. urology, 1969-71, instr., 1971-72, asst. prof., 1974-76, assoc. prof., 1976-83, prof., 1983—, asst. chief urology, 1974-79, dir. Urodynamic Evaluation Ctr., 1974—, chmn. div. urology, 1981—, chief urology, 1981—. Dir. resident edn. com. div. urology Sch. Medicine U. Pa., 1976—, coord. program urologics oncology, 1976—; chief urology VA Hosp., Phila., 1974-82, attending urologist, 1982-96; asst. surgeon Children's Hosp. Phila., 1974—; cons. CDC Coun. Incontinence, 1990—; assoc. surgeon Pa. Hosp., Phila., 1977—; attending urologist Grad. Hosp., Phila., 1980-97. Author: (with D.M. Barrett) Controversies in Neuro-Urology, 1984, Voiding Function and Dysfunction: A Logical and Practical Approach, 1988, 2d edit., 1995, (with A.R. Mundy and T.P. Stephenson) Urodynamics: Principles, Practice and Application, 1984, 2d edit., 1994, (with P.M. Hanno) A Clinical Manual of Urology, 1987, 2d edit., 1994, (with Hanno, Staskin and Krane) Interstitial Cystitis, 1990, Common Problems in Urology: Comon Problems in Infertility and Impotence, 1990, (with Abrams) The Overactive Bladder: A Widespread and Treatable Concition, 1998, (with Abrams and Khourys) Incontinence, 1999, (with Flanigan and Resnick) Objectives for Urologic Residency Education, 2001, (with Walship, REtika, Vaughan) Campbell's Urology, 8th edit., 2002, others; editl. bd. asst. Urol. Survey, 1978-81; editl. bd. cons. Investigative Urology, 1978-81; mem. editl. bd. World Jour. Urology, 1982—, Am. Urol. Assn. Update series, 1983—, Urol. Survey, 1987—, Internat. Jour. Impotence Rsch.: Basic and Clin. Studies, 1989-99, Urology, 1991—; ad hoc reviewer Cancer, 1985—; cons. editor Sexuality and Disability, 1985—; asst. editor Jour. Urology, 1980-89, ad hoc reviewer clin. sect., 1989—, editl. bd. investigative sect., 1989—; assoc. editor Neurourlogy and Urodynamics, 1982—; contbr. chpts. to 21 books; contbr. over 600 articles and abstracts to profl. jours. Mem. coun. urology Nat. Kidney Found., Inc.; mem lectrs. bur. Am. Cancer Soc., 1984—; mem. adv. panel Nat. Assn. for Incontinence, 1987—; mem. adv. bd. Simon Found., 1987—; mem. med. adv. bd. Institial Cystitis Assn., 1987—; chmn. bladder health coun. Am. Found. Urologic Disease, 1990-95; trustee Am. Bd. Urology, 1990-96. Maj. MC, U.S. Army, 1972-74. Grantee VA, 1974-79, 79, 81, 81-84, 82-85, 85-88, 88-92, Eaton Labs., 1975-76, 78-80, McCabe Rsch. Fund, 1975-82, 87-88, Merrell Nat. Labs., 1979-82, 1980-82, Nat. Kidney Found., 1980-81, NIH, 1980-83, 83-88, 84-87, 87—, Roche Labs., 1981, Smith Kline and French Labs., 1982, 86-88, Eli Lilly Labs., 1986-88, 91, Found. Interstitial Cystitis, 1986-87, 87-88, Sterling Drug Co., 1991; recipient F. Brantley Scott award Am. Found. for Urologic Disease, 1996, Hugh Hampton Young award, 1997, AUA Disting. Svc. award, 2000, AUA Disting. Contbn. award, 2001, Legion of Honor Gold Medallion award Chapel of Four Chaplains, VAlley Forge, Pa., 2001. Fellow ACS; mem. AAAS, AMA (cons. com. drug evaluation 1977-90), Am. Acad. Clin. Neurophysiology, Am. Assn. Surgery of Trauma, Am. Assn. Clin. Urologists, Am. Assn. Genito-Urinary Surgeons, Am. Surg. Assn., Am. Soc. Pharmacology and Exptl. Therapeutics, Am. Soc. Andrology, Am. Soc. Clin. Oncology, Am. Urol. Assn. (chmn. practical cases urology 1982—, rsch. com. 1985—, editl. com. mid-Atlantic sect. 1988—, pub. rels. adv. bd. 1998—, Disting. Svc. award 2000), Assn. Acad. Surgery, Can. Urol. Assn., Clin. Soc. Genito-Urinary Surgeons, Ea. Coop. Oncologic Group, Endourol. Soc., Internat. Continence Soc., Nat. Assn. VA Physicians, N.Y. Acad. Scis., Coll. Physicians Phila., John Morgan Soc., Pa. Med. Assn., Pa. Oncologic Soc., Phila. Acad. Surgery, Phila. County Med. Soc., Phila. Profl. Standards Rev. Orgn., Phila. Urologic Soc. (pres. 1990-91), Ravdin-Rhoads Surg. Soc., Urol. Assn. Pa., Radiation Therapy Oncology Group (genitourinary working com. 1980—), Royal Soc. Medicine, Soc. Internat. d'Urologie, Soc. Basic Urologic Rsch., Soc. Sex Therapy and Rsch., Soc. Govt. Svc. Urologists, Soc. Pelvic Surgeons, Soc. Univ. Surgeons, Soc. Univ. Urologists (counselor 1996—, pres. 1999-2000), Soc. Urologic Oncology, Univ. Urologic Forum, Urodynamics Soc. (exec. com. 1980—, Lifetime Achievement award 1996), Urologic Rsch. Soc., Urologist's Corr. Club, Sigma Xi. Home: 1224 Mirabeau Ln Gladwyne PA 19035-1048 Office: Hosp U Pa 9 Penn Tower 34th and Civic Center Blvd Philadelphia PA 19104-4206 Home Phone: 610-525-5545; Office Phone: 215-662-6755. Business E-Mail: alan.wein@uphs.upenn.edu.

WEINBACH, ARTHUR FREDERIC, computer company executive; b. Waterbury, Conn., May 3, 1943; s. Max and Winifred (Eckstein) Weinbach; m. Joanne Kaplan, Nov. 22, 1970; children: Michael Scott, Jonathan David. BS in Econs., U. Pa., 1965, MS in Acctg., 1966. CPA. With Touche Ross & Co., NYC, 1966—75, ptnr. Stamford, Conn., 1976—79; from v.p. to pres. Automatic Data Processing, Inc., Roseland, 1980—98, CEO, 1996—2006, chmn., 1998—. Chmn. Broadridge Fin. Solutions, Inc., 2007—. Bd. dirs. Schering-Plough Corp., First Data Corp., NJ Seeds, NJ Inst. Tech., 1998—2005, Boys Hope, 1991—2003, Overlook Hosp. Found., 1991—98, Metro N.J. U. Pa. Club, 1993—99, United Way of Tri-State, 1998—2004. Jewish. Office: ADP Inc 5 ADP Blvd Roseland NJ 07068-1786 *

WEINBERG, ADAM D., museum director; b. NYC, Dec. 10, 1954; s. James Lionel and Edith (Zickerman) Weinberg; m. Lorraine Ferguson; children: Zoé, Kira. BA, Brandeis U., 1977; MFA, SUNY, Buffalo, 1981. Dir. edn., asst. curator Walker Art Ctr., Mpls., 1981-88; dir., equitable ctr. Whitney Mus. Am. Art, NYC, 1988-90; artistic and program dir. Am. Ctr., Paris, 1990—92; sr. curator, curator of permanent collection Whitney Mus. Am. Art, NYC, 1993—99, mus. dir., 2003—; dir. Addison Gallery of American Art, Andover, Mass., 1999—2003. Author: (catalog) On the Line: The New Color Photojournalism, 1986, (book & catalog) Vanishing Presence, 1989, (exhbn. catalogs) Aldo Crommelynck: Master Prints with Am. Artists, 1989, Contingent Realms, 1990. Trustee Whitney Mus. Am. Art, Alice Pratt Brown Dir. Mem.: Coll. Art Assn., Am. Assn. Mus. Office: Whitney Mus Am Art 945 Madison Ave New York NY 10021 Business E-Mail: director@whitney.org.

WEINBERG, DAVID B., investor; b. Chgo., Feb. 19, 1952; s. Judd A. and Marjorie (Gottlieb) W.; m. Lynne Ellen Mesirow, July 6, 1980. AB cum laude, Harvard U., 1974; JD, Georgetown U., 1977. Bar: Ill. 1977, U.S. Dist. Ct. (no. dist.) Ill. 1977, U.S. Ct. Appeals (7th cir.) 1978. Law clerk to Hon. William G. Clark Supreme Ct. Ill., 1977-79; assoc. Lord, Bissell & Brook, Chgo., 1979-84, ptnr., 1985-89, Mayer, Brown & Platt, Chgo., 1989-96; chmn., CEO Judd Enterprises, Inc., Chgo., 1996—; pres. Digital BandWidth LLC, Chgo., 1996—. Ill. Supreme Ct. com. Profl. Responsibility, Chgo., 1984-94, chmn. subcom. lawyers certification. Chmn. bd. trustees Ravinia Festival Assn., Highland Park, Ill., 1998—2001; vice chmn. bd. trustees Northwestern U., 1999—. Mem. Chgo. Club, Econ. Club Chgo., Lake Shore Country Club, Arts Club Chgo. Office: Judd Enterprises Bank One Plz 21 S Clark St Ste 3140 Chicago IL 60603-2090

WEINBERG, EUGENE DAVID, microbiologist, educator; b. Chgo., Mar. 4, 1922; s. Philip and Lenore (Bergman) W.; m. Frances Murl Izen, Sept. 5, 1949; children— Barbara Ann, Marjorie Jean, Geoffrey Alan, Michael Benjamin. BS, U. Chgo., 1942, MA, 1948, PhD, 1950. Instr. dept. microbiology Ind. U., Bloomington, 1950-53, asst. prof., 1953-57, asso. prof., 1957-61, prof., 1961—, head microbiology sect., med. sci. program, 1978—92. Mem. sci. adv. bd., chair publs. Iron Disorders Inst., 1998—. Served with AUS, 1942-45. Mem.: Am. Soc. Microbiology. Office: Ind U Biology Dept Jordan Hall Bloomington IN 47405 Office Phone: 812-336-5556. Fax: 812-855-6705. Business E-Mail: eweinber@indiana.edu.

WEINBERG, GERHARD LUDWIG, history professor; b. Hannover, Germany, Jan. 1, 1928; came to U.S., 1940, naturalized, 1949; s. Max Bendix and Kate Sarah (Gruenebaum) W.; m. Janet Kabler White, Apr. 29, 1989. BA, N.Y. State Coll. Tchrs., Albany, 1948; MA, U. Chgo., 1949, PhD, 1951; LHD honoris causa, SUNY, Albany, 1989; PhD (hon.), U. Hannover, 2001. Rsch. analyst War Documentation Project Columbia U., 1951-54; vis. lectr. history U. Chgo., 1954-55, U. Ky., Lexington, 1955-56; dir. project microfilming captured German documents Am. Hist. Assn., 1956-57; asst. prof. U. Ky., 1957-59; mem. faculty U. Mich., Ann Arbor, 1959-74, prof. history, 1963-74, chmn. dept., 1972-73; William Rand Kenan, Jr. prof. history U. N.C., Chapel Hill, 1974-99, prof. emeritus, 1999—, acting chmn. dept., 1989-90. Vis. prof. Bonn U., 1983, USAF Acad., 1990-91; Shapiro sr. scholar-in-residence U.S. Holocaust Meml. Mus., 2001-02; bd. dirs. World War II Studies Assn., 1968—; cons. in field. Author: Guide to Captured German Documents, 1952, Germany and the Soviet Union, 1939-41, 1954, 1972, The Foreign Policy of Hitler's Germany, 1933-36, 1970, The Foreign Policy of Hitler's Germany, 1937-39, 1980, World in the Balance: Behind the Scenes of World II, 1981, A World at Arms: A Global History of World War II, 1994, 2005, Germany, Hitler and World War II, 1995, Visions of Victory, The Hopes of Eight World War II Leaders, 2005, Hitler's Foreign Policy 1933-1939: The Road to World War II, 2005; co-author: Soviet Partisans in World War II, 1964; editor: Hitlers zweites Buch, 1961, 95, Transformation of a Continent, 1975, Hitler's Second Book, 2003; bd. editors Jour. Modern History, 1970-72, Central European History, 1970-72, Kansas Humanities Series, 1987—, Internat. History Rev., 1990-2000, Jour. Intelligence History, 2001—. Chmn. Ann Arbor Dem. Com., 1961-63; mem. Mich. Dem. Ctrl. Com., 1963-67; mem. adv. com. on the air force history program Sec. of Air Force, 1987-90; mem. adv. com. army history program Sec. Army, 1996-2003, chmn., 1998-2003; mem. dept. defence Hist. Records Declassification Adv. Panel, 1996-02; chmn. hist. adv. panel to interagy. working group on Nazi War Crimes and Imperial Japanese Records Disclosure, 1999-07. With AUS, 1946-47. Fellow Social Sci. Research Council, 1962-63; fellow Am. Council Learned Socs., 1965-66; fellow Guggenheim Found., 1971-72; fellow Nat. Endowment Humanities, 1978-79 Mem. Am. Hist. Assn. (George Louis Beer prize 1971, 95, v.p. rsch. 1982-84), So. Hist. Assn. (chmn. European sect. 1989), Conf. Group for Ctrl. European History (chmn. 1982), Coordinating Com. Women in Hist. Profession, German Studies Assn. (exec. com. 1989-92, Halverson prize 1981, v.p. 1994-96, pres. 1996-98), World War II Studies Assn., Am. Acad. Arts and Scis., Phi Beta Kappa. Jewish. Home: 1416 Mount Willing Rd Efland NC 27243-9646 E-mail: gweinber@email.unc.edu.

WEINBERG, H. BARBARA, art historian, educator, curator; b. NYC, Jan. 23, 1942; d. Max and Evelyn Kallman; m. Michael B. Weinberg, Aug. 30, 1964. AB, Barnard Coll., 1962; MA, Columbia U., NYC, 1964, PhD, 1972. Prof. art history Queens Coll. Grad. Sch., CUNY, 1972—94; curator Am. paintings sculpture Met. Mus. Art., NYC, 1990—98; Alice Pratt Brown curator Am. paintings sculpture Met. Mus. Art, NYC, 1998—. Author: The Decorative Work of John La Farge, 1977, The American Pupils of Jean-Léon Gérome, 1984, The Lure of Paris: Nineteenth-Century American Painters and Their French Teachers, 1991, Thomas Eakins and the Metropolitan Museum of Art, 1994, co-author: American Impressionism and Realism: The Painting of Modern Life, 1885-1915, 1994, American Drawings and Watercolors in The Metropolitan Museum of Art: John Singer Sargent, 2000, John Singer Sargent in The Metropolitan Museum Art, 2000, Childe Hassam, American Impressionist, 2004, Americans in Paris, 1860-1900, 2006; mem. editl. bd. Am. Art Jour., 1984—. Mem.: Phi Beta Kappa. Office: Met Mus Art 1000 5th Ave New York NY 10028-0198 Office Phone: 212-879-5500 ext 8001.

WEINBERG, JEFFREY J., lawyer; b. NYC, Aug. 27, 1948; s. Arnold Mitchell and Lucile (Barton) W.; m. Bonnie J. Sandhaus, Aug. 23, 1970; children: Seth, Andrew. BA, SUNY, Stony Brook, 1969; JD, Georgetown U., 1973. Bar: N.Y., U.S. Dist. Ct. (so. and ea. dists.). Assoc. Weil, Gotshal & Manges, NYC, 1973-81, ptnr., 1981—. Acting judge Village of Roslyn Estates. Author: Sales of Troubled Business, 1991, 92, 93, 94. Former trustee Village of Roslyn Estate. Mem.: Friars Club. Avocation: sailing. Office: Weil Gotshal & Manges 767 5th Ave Fl Concl New York NY 10153-0119

WEINBERG, JERROLD GLADSTONE, lawyer; b. Norfolk, Va., Apr. 5, 1928; s. Charles Paul and Reba Gladstone Weinberg; m. Marcia Ellen Moress (dec.); children: Ellen Jane(dec.), Nancy Louise von Auersperg, Andrew Steven; m. Ruth A. Hofheimer, Feb. 6, 1999. BS in Comm., U. Va., Charlottesville, 1947, LLB, 1950. Bar: Va. 1949. Atty. pvt. practice, Norfolk, 1950—78; pres. Weinberg & Stein PC, Norfolk, 1978—. Lectr. law William & Mary Law Sch., Williamsburg, Va., 1980; mem. Jud. Conf. US Ct. Appeals (4th cir.). With US Army, 1951—53. Master: James Kent Am. Inn Ct. (pres. 1996—97); fellow: Va. Law Found., Am. Bar Found., Am. Coll. Trial Lawyers; mem.: ABA, Norfolk and Portsmouth Bar Assn. (pres. 1973—74), Va. Bar Assn., Norfolk Yacht and Country Club. Republican. Jewish. Home: 7310 Woodway Ln Norfolk VA 23505 Office: Weinberg & Stein 1825 Dominion Tower 999 Waterside Dr Norfolk VA 23510

WEINBERG, JOHN LEE, federal judge; b. Chgo., Apr. 24, 1941; s. Louis Jr. and Jane Kitz (Goldstein) W.; m. Sarah Kibbee, July 6, 1963; children: Ruth, Leo. BA, Swarthmore Coll., 1962; JD, U. Chgo., 1965. Bar: Ill. 1966, Wash. 1967, U.S. Dist. Ct. (we. dist.) Wash. 1967, U.S. Ct. Appeals (9th cir.) 1967. Law clk. to Hon. Henry L. Burman Ill. Appellate Ct., Chgo., 1965-66; law clk. to Hon. Walter V. Schaefer Ill. Supreme Ct., Chgo., 1966; law clk. to Hon. William T. Beeks U.S. Dist. Ct. Wash., Seattle, 1967-68; atty. Perkins Coie Law Firm, Seattle, 1968-73; magistrate judge U.S. Dist. Ct.; U.S. Magistrate judge Seattle, 1973—2003; ret., 2003; recalled, 2003—. Author: Federal Bail and Detention Handbook, 1988. Mem. ABA, Am. Judicature Soc., Wash. State Bar Assn., Seattle-King County Bar Assn., Fed. Magistrate Judges Assn. (nat. pres. 1982-83). Avocations: sports and physical fitness activities, bridge, jazz piano. Office: US Magistrate Judge 12th Fl United States Courthouse 700 Stewart St Seattle WA 98101 Office Phone: 206-370-8910.

WEINBERG, JOHN SIDNEY, investment banker; m. Amy Marie Shepherd, Mar. 3, 1984. BA in History, Princeton U., 1979; MBA, Harvard U. Mgmt. trainee Knight-Ridder Newspapers, Miami; assoc. corp. fin. dept. Goldman, Sachs & Co., 1983, co-head of investment banking services, 1997—2001; mem. mgmt. com. The Goldman Sachs Group, Inc., 2002—, co-head global investment banking, 2002—, vice chmn. NYC, 2006—. Bd. dirs. Steppingstone Found.; trustee NY-Presbyterian Hosp., 2000—. Office: The Goldman Sachs Group Inc 85 Broad St New York NY 10004

WEINBERG, JUSTIN PETER, lawyer; b. 1976; married; 2 children. BA magna cum laude, St. Cloud State U., 1998; JD, William Mitchell Coll. Law, 2001. Bar: Minn. 2001, US Dist. Ct. (dist. Minn.) 2001, US Ct. Appeals (8th cir.) 2006. Assoc. Gislason & Hunter, L.L.P., New Ulm, Minn. Named a Rising Star, Minn. Super Lawyers mag., 2006. Mem.: Minn. Bar Assn. (mem. litig. and constrn. law sects.), ABA (mem. litig. and bus. sects.). Office: Gislason & Hunter LLP 2700 S Broadway PO Box 458 New Ulm MN 56073 Office Phone: 507-354-3111. E-mail: jweinberg@gislason.com. *

WEINBERG, LEONARD BURTON, political scientist; b. NYC, Nov. 10, 1939; s. Max R. and Rose (Levin) W.; m. Ellen Bach, Aug. 23, 1966 (div.); 1 son, David; m. Sinikka Palomaki, June 4, 1986. BA, Syracuse U., 1961, PhD, 1967; MA, U. Chgo., 1963. Instr. polit. sci. U. Wis., Milw., 1966-67; asst. prof. polit. sci. U. Nev., Reno, 1967-71, assoc. prof., 1971-78, prof., 1978—, chmn. dept., 1979-82. Vis. prof. U. Florence, Italy, 1992. Author: Comparing Public Policies, 1977, After Mussolini, 1979, The Rise and Fall of Italian Terrorism, 1987, Introduction to Political Terrorism, 1989; editor: Political Parties and Terrorist Groups, 1992, Revival of Right-Wing Extremism in the 1990s, 1996, Political Violence and the Democratic Experience. 2000; co-editor: Encounters with the Radical Right, 1992, The Transformation of Italian Communism, 1994, Revival of Right-Wing Extremism in the 1990s, 1997, The Emergence of a Euro-American Radical, 1998. Recipient Fulbright Rsch. award, 1984; Italian Govt. Borsa di Studio, 1965-66; Fulbright grantee, 1965-66, Harry F. Guggenheim grantee, 1995-96. Mem. Am. Polit. Sci. Assn., Internat. Polit. Sci. Assn. (political sociology com.), Conf. Group on Italian Politics of Am. Polit. Sci. Assn., Phi Kappa Phi. Jewish. Office: U Nev Dept Polit Sci Reno NV 89557-0001 Business E-Mail: weinbrl@unr.nevada.edu.

WEINBERG, LILA SHAFFER, editor, writer; d. Sam and Blanche (Hyman) Shaffer; m. Arthur Weinberg, Jan. 25, 1953; children: Hedy, Anita, Wendy Clare. Editor Ziff-Davis Pub. Co., 1944—53; assoc. chief manuscript editor jours. U. Chgo. Press, 1966—80, sr. manuscript editor books, 1980—98; mem. faculty Sch. for New Learning DePaul U., Chgo., 1973—89. Vis. faculty continuing edn. programs U. Chgo., 1984-92. Author: (with A. Weinberg) The Muckrakers, 1961 (selected for White House Library 1963), Verdicts Out of Court, 1963, Instead of Violence, 1963, Passport to Utopia, 1968, Some Dissenting Voices, 1970, Clarence Darrow: A Sentimental Rebel, 1980; contbr. articles and revs. to various publs. Bd. dirs. Hillel Found. U. Chgo., 1988-96. Recipient Friends of Lit. award Chgo. Found. Lit., 1980, Social Justice award Darrow Community Ctr., 1980, Disting. Body of Work award Friends of Midwest Authors, 1987, John Peter Altgeld Freedom of Speech award, 2001. Mem. Soc. Midland Authors (dir. 1977-83, pres. 1983-85, Best Midwest Biography award 1980), ACLU, Clarence Darrow Commemorative Com., YIVO, Authors' League, Work in Progress. Home: 5421 S Cornell Ave Chicago IL 60615-5646 Personal E-mail: l-weinberg@sbcglobal.net.

WEINBERG, LORETTA, state legislator; b. NYC, Feb. 6, 1935; d. Murray Isaacs and Raya Hamilton; m. Irwin S. Weinberg, July 25, 1960 (dec. Feb. 1999); children: Daniel J., Francine S. BA, UCLA, 1956. Former aide NJ Assemblyman D. Bennett Mazur, Trenton; mem. NJ Assembly, Trenton, 1992—, NJ State Senate, 2005—. Mem. Teaneck Coun., 1990-94. Recipient Legis. Leadership award No. NJ Chiropractic Assn., 1992, Woman of Achievement award Bus. and Profl. Women's Club of East Bergen, 1993, Carrie Chapman Catt award No. NJ NOW, 1997, Ethical Recognition award Ethical Culture Soc. of Bergen County, 1998, Barbara Boggs Sigmund award, Women's Polit. Caucus, 2004, Legis. Recognition, Consumers for Civil Justice; named Citizen of Yr. NJ Jewish War Vets., Legislator of Yr., NJ State Nurse's Assn., 2000; named Women in Govt., Good Housekeeping, 2005. Mem. Nat. Coun. Jewish Women (life mem., Hannah G. Solomon award 1995, Disting. Achievement award Women's Commn.). Democrat. Jewish. Office: State of NJ 545 Cedar Ln Teaneck NJ 07666-1740 Home Phone: 201-928-0155; Office Phone: 201-928-0100. Business E-Mail: senweinberg@njleg.org.

WEINBERG, LOUISE, law educator, writer; b. NYC; m. Steven Weinberg; 1 child, Elizabeth. AB summa cum laude, Cornell U.; JD, Harvard U., 1969, LLM, 1974. Bar: Mass. Sr. law clk. Hon. Chas. E. Wyzanski, Jr., Boston, 1971-72; assoc. in law Bingham, Dana & Gould, Boston, 1969-72; teaching fellow Harvard Law Sch., Boston, 1972-74; lectr. law Brandeis U., Waltham, Mass., 1974; assoc. prof. law Suffolk U., Boston, 1974-76, prof., 1977-80; vis. assoc. prof. law Stanford U., Palo Alto, Calif., 1976-77; vis. prof. law Sch. Law, U. Tex., Austin, 1979, prof. law, 1980-84, Thompson prof. law, 1984-90, Andrews and Kurth prof. law, 1990-92, Fulbright and Jaworski regents rsch. prof., 1991-92, Angus G. Wynne, Sr. prof., 1992-97, Fondren chair faculty excellence, 1995—, Eugene R. Smith Centennial rsch. prof. law, 1993-97, holder William B. Bates chair, 1997—. Vis. scholar Hebrew U., Jerusalem, 1989; Forum fellow World Econ. Forum, Davos, Switzerland, 1995—; cons. PBS; pub. spkr., lectr. in field. Author: Federal Courts: Judicial Federalism and Judicial Power, 1994; co-author: Conflict of Laws, 1990, 2d edit., 2002; contbr. chpts. to books and encyclopedias, articles to profl. jours. Bd. dirs. Ballet Austin, 1986-88, Austin Coun. on Fgn. Affairs, 1985—, Austin Civil War Round Table, 1998—. Recipient Disting. Educator award Tex. Exes Assn., 1996. Mem.: Supreme Ct. Hist. Soc., Am. Constn. Soc., Maritime Law Assn., Tex. Asian C. of C., Assn. Am. Law Schs. (chair sect. on conflict laws 1991—93, chair sect. on fed. cts. 2003—05, chair sect. admiralty 2005—06), The Philos. Soc. Tex., Am. Law Inst. (consultative com. complex litigation 1989—93, consultative com. enterprise liability 1990—95, adv. group fed. judicial code revision project 1996—2001, mems.' consultative group, intellectual property 2004—, internat. jurisdiction and judgments 2004—, aggregate litigation 2006—), Phi Kappa Phi, Phi Beta Kappa. Office: U Tex Sch Law 727 Dean Keeton St Austin TX 78705-3224 Business E-Mail: lweinberg@law.utexas.edu. *Personal philosophy: The right thing is usually also the humane and liberal thing.*

WEINBERG, MARTIN GARY, lawyer; b. NYC, Mar. 8, 1946; s. Jerome and Sarah (Rothman) W.; m. Michele Brady, Sept. 6, 1985. BA, U. Wis., 1968; JD, Harvard U., 1971. Bar: Mass. 1971, NY 1971. Assoc. Crane, Inker & Oteri, Boston, 1972-74, ptnr., 1974-75, Oteri, Weinberg & Lawson, Boston, 1975; pvt. practice atty. Boston, 1996—2007. Mem. ABA, Assn. Trial Lawyers Am., NACDL (past dir.), Mass. Bar Assn., Mass. Assn. Criminal Def. Lawyers. Office: 20 Park Plz Ste 905 Boston MA 02116-4317 Office Phone: 617-227-3700, 617-969-3624. E-mail: owlmgw@att.net.

WEINBERG, MILTON, JR., retired cardiovascular and thoracic surgeon; b. Sumter, SC, Aug. 8, 1924; s. Milton and Ethel (Harper) W.; m. Joan Ehrenstrom, Nov. 24, 1956; children: Caryl, Susan, Amy. Student, Duke U., 1941-43, MD, 1947. Diplomate Am. Bd. Surgery, Am. Bd. Thoracic Surgery. Attending surgeon Rush Presbyn.-St. Luke's Med. Ctr., Chgo., 1957-90, emeritus attending, 1990—; attending surgeon Cook County Hosp., Chgo., 1956-80, Luth. Gen. Hosp., Park Ridge, Ill., 1986—2003, mem. governing coun., 1996—2001; assoc. prof. Rush Med. Coll., Chgo., 1969-78, prof. surgery, 1978-90, emeritus prof., 1990—; clin. prof. U. Chgo., 1990-99; ret., 2003. Chmn. dept. surgery Luth. Gen. Hosp., Park Ridge, 1988-94, vice-chmn. dept. surgery, 1994-2003; pres. med. staff

Rush Med. Ctr., Chgo., 1977-79; presenter movies at mtgs. ACS. Mem. editorial bd. Annals of Thoracic Surgery, 1968-79; contbr. articles to profl. jours., chpts. to surg. textbooks. Trustee The Presbyn. Home, Evanston, Ill., 1984—; bd. dirs. Chgo. Symphony Orch., 1985-95; advocate Charitable Found. Bd., 1996-2002. Maj. U.S. Army, 1951-53. Decorated Bronze Star. Fellow: ACS, Am. Coll. Cardiology, Am. Coll. Chest Physicians; mem.: Ctrl. Surg. Soc., Soc. Vascular Surgery, Soc. Thoracic Surgeons, Am. Assn. Thoracic Surgery. Avocations: fly fishing, fly rod building. Home: 983 Kirkhill Ln Lake Forest IL 60045-4209 E-mail: mw983@yahoo.com.

WEINBERG, PETER AMORY, investment banker; s. Sidney J. Weinberg Jr.; m. Deborah Beth Lindenauer, June 1, 1986; 3 children. BA, Claremont McKenna Coll., 1979; MBA, Harvard U., 1983. With Morgan Stanley, 1983—88, Goldman Sachs Internat., 1988—2005, ptnr., 1992, co-head global investment banking divsn. London, co-head partnership com., CEO; co-founder Perella Weinberg Partners, NYC, 2006—. Non-exec. dir. BAE Systems plc, 2005—. Trustee Brunswick Sch., Greenwich, Conn., Deerfield Acad., Mass., Kravis Leadership Inst., Claremont McKenna Coll., King's Academy, Jordan. Office: Perella Weinberg Partners LP 767 Fifth Ave New York NY 10153

WEINBERG, RICHARD ALAN, psychologist, educator; b. Chgo., Jan. 28, 1943; s. Meyer and Mollie I. (Soell) W.; m. Gail E. Blumberg, Aug. 25, 1964; children: Eric, Brett. BS, U. Wis., 1964; MAT, Northwestern U., 1965; PhD, U. Minn., 1968. Lic. psychologist, Minn. Asst. prof. Tchrs. Coll., Columbia U., NYC, 1968-70; prof. ednl. psychology, psychology and child psychology U. Minn., Mpls., 1970—, Birkmaier professorship, 1994-97, U. disting. tchg. prof., 1999—. Former dir. Inst. Child Devel.; former chair adv. coun. Children, Youth, and Family, chair steering com. U. Minn. Pres.'s Initiative on Children, Youth, and Family Consortium; cons. EPA; reviewer Office of Edn., NSF, NRC; guest speaker TV and radio shows. Author: (with A. Boehm) The Classroom Observer: Developing Observation Skills in Early Childhood Settings, 1997, (with Scarr and Levine) Understanding Development, 1986; former assoc. editor Contemporary Psychology; former editor: Applied Developmental Science. Bd. dirs. Children's Mus. Minn.; past pres. Am. Assn. State Psychol. Bds.; trustee Am. Assn. State Psychol. Bds. Found.; liaison Nat. Register Health Care Providers in Psychology. Grantee Bush Found., NSF, NIH. Fellow APA, Am. Psychol. Soc.; mem. Soc. Rsch. in Child Devel. (former chair pub. policy coun., chair fin. comm.), Behavior Genetics Assn., Am. Psychol. Soc. (bd. dirs.), NCAA Championship Cabinet, Phi Beta Kappa, Phi Kappa Phi. Office: U Minn 180 Child Devel 51 E River Rd Minneapolis MN 55455-0365 Business E-Mail: weinb002@umn.edu.

WEINBERG, ROBERT ALLAN, biochemist, educator; b. Pitts., Nov. 11, 1942; s. Fritz E. and Lore (Reichhardt) Weinberg; m. Amy Schulman Weinberg, Nov. 19, 1976; children: Aron, Leah Rosa. S.B., MIT, 1964, Ph.D, 1969; PhD (hon.), Northwestern U., 1984. Instr. Stillman Coll., Tuscaloosa, Ala., 1965—66; research fellow Weizmann Inst., Rehovoth, Israel, 1969—70, Salk Inst., LaJolla, Calif., 1970—72; from asst. prof. to assoc. prof. dept. biology & ctr. cancer rsch. MIT, Cambridge, 1973—82, prof. biology, 1982—, Daniel K. Ludwig prof. for cancer rsch., 1997—. Mem. Whitehead Inst., Cambridge, 1982—; rsch. prof. Amer. Cancer Soc., 1985; elected mem. Inst. of Medicine, 2000; mem. adv. bd. GM Cancer Rsch. Found. Author: (books) Racing to the Beginning of the Road: The Search for the Origin of Cancer, 1996, One Renegade Cell: How Cancer Begins, 1998, One Renegade Cell: The Quest for the Origin of Cancer, Vol. 3; contbr. articles articles to profl. jours. Named Scientist of Yr., Discover mag., 1982; recipient Bristol Myers award, 1984, Brown-Hazen award NY State Dept. Health, 1984, Sloan prize, GM Cancer Rsch. Found., 1987, Rsch. Recognition award, Samuel Roberts Noble Found., 1990, Gairdner Found. Internat. award, 1992, Harvey Prize, Technion, 1994, G.H.A. Clowes Meml. award, 1996, Nat. Medal of Sci., 1997, Wolf Prize in Medicine, Wolf Found., 2004. Fellow: Am. Acad. of Arts & Sciences; mem.: NAS (sci. award 1984). Avocations: genealogy, house building. Office: Whitehead Inst 9 Cambridge Ctr Cambridge MA 02142-1479 Office Phone: 617-258-5159. Fax: 617-258-5213. E-mail: Weinberg@wi.mit.edu.

WEINBERG, STEVEN, physics professor; b. NYC, May 3, 1933; s. Fred and Eva (Israel) Weinberg; m. Louise Goldwasser, July 6, 1954; 1 child, Elizabeth. BA, Cornell U., 1954; postgrad., Copenhagen Inst. Theoretical Physics, 1954—55; PhD, Princeton U., 1957; AM (hon.), Harvard U., 1973; ScD (hon.), Knox Coll., 1978, U. Chgo., 1978, U. Rochester, 1979, Yale U., 1979, CUNY, 1980, Clark U., 1982, Dartmouth Coll., 1984, Columbia U., 1990, U. Salamanca, 1992, U. Padua, 1992, Bates Coll., 2002, McGill U., 2003, U. Waterloo, 2004; D (hon.), U. Barcelona, 1996; PhD (hon.), Weizmann Inst., 1985; DLitt (hon.), Washington Coll., 1985. Rsch. assoc., instr. Columbia U., 1957-59; rsch. physicist Lawrence Radiation Lab., Berkeley, Calif., 1959-60; mem. faculty U. Calif., Berkeley, 1960-69, prof. physics, 1964-69; vis. prof. MIT, 1967-69, prof. physics, 1969-73; Higgins prof. physics Harvard U., 1973-83; sr. scientist Smithsonian Astrophys. Lab., 1973-83; Josey prof. sci. U. Tex., Austin, 1982—; sr. cons. Smithsonian Astrophys. Obs., 1983—. Cons. Inst. Def. Analyses, Washington, 1960—73, ACDA, 1973; Sloan fellow, 1961—65; chair in physics Coll. de France, 1971; mem. Pres.'s Com. on Nat. Medal of Sci., 1979—82, Coun. of Scholars, Libr. of Congress, 1983—85; sr. adv. La Jolla Inst.; mem. Com. on Internat. Security and Arms Control, NRC, 1981, Bd. on Physics & Astronomy, 1989—90; adv. coun. Tex. Superconducting Supercollider High Energy Rsch. Facility, 1987; Loeb lectr. in physics Harvard U., 1966—67, Morris Loeb vis. prof. physics, 1983—; Richtmeyer lectr., 1974; Scott lectr. Cavendish Lab., 1975; Silliman lectr. Yale U., 1977; Lauritsen Meml. lectr. Calif. Inst. Tech., 1979; Bethe lectr. Cornell U., 1979; de Shalit lectr. Weizmann Inst., 1979; Cherwell-Simon lectr. Oxford U., 1983; Bampton lectr. Columbia U., 1983; Einstein lectr. Israel Acad. Arts and Scis., 1984; Hilldale lectr. U. Wis., 1985; Clark lectr. U. Tex., Dallas, 1986; Dirac lectr. U. Cambridge, 1986; Klein lectr. U. Stockholm, 1989; Brittin lectr. U. Colo., 1994; Sackler lectr. U. Copenhagen, 1994; Gibbs lectr. Am. Math. Soc., 1996; Bochner lectr. Rice U., 1997; Sanchez lectr. Tex. A&M Internat. U., 1998; Witherspoon lectr. Washington U., 2001; Hamilton lectr. Royal Irish Acad., 2005; Messenger lectr. Cornell U., 2007; mem. Supercollider Sci. Policy Com., 1989—93; bd. dirs. Fedn. Am. Scientists. Author: Principles and Application of the General Theory of Relativity, 1972, The First Three Minutes: A Modern View of the Origin of the Universe, 1977, The Discovery of Subatomic Particles, 1982, revised edit., 2003; author: (with R. Feynman) Elementary Particles and the Laws of Physics; author: Dreams of a Final Theory, 1992, The Quantum Theory of Fields - Vol. I: Foundations, 1995, Modern Applications, Vol. II, 1996, Supersymmetry, Vol. III, 2000, Facing Up: Science and Its Cultural Adversaries, 2001, Glory and Terror: The Growing Nuclear Danger, 2004; rsch. and publs. on elementary particles, quantum field theory, cosmology, coeditor monographs on math. physics Cambridge U. Press, mem. adv. bd. Issues in Sci. and Tech., 1984—87, mem. sci. book bom. Sloan Found., 1985—91, editl. bd. Jour. Math. Physics, 1986—88, mem. bd. editors Daedalus, 1990—, Jour. Math. Physics, 1998—, mem. bd. assoc. editors Nuc. Physics B, —. Bd. advisors Santa Barbara Inst. Theoretical Physics, 1983—86; bd. overseers SSC Accelerator, 1984—86; bd. dirs. Headliners Found., 1993—. Named Hon. Citizen, Padua, Italy, 2007; recipient J. Robert Oppenheimer Meml. prize, 1973, Dannie Heineman prize in math. physics, 1977, Am. Inst. Physics U.S. Steel Found. sci. writing award, 1977, Nobel prize in Physics, 1979, Elliott Cresson medal, Franklin Inst., 1979, Madison medal, Princeton U., 1991, Nat. medal of Sci., NSF, 1991, Andrew Gemant prize, Am. Inst. Physics, 1997, Piazzi prize, Govts. Sicily and Palermo, 1998, Lewis Thomas prize, Rockefeller U., 1999. Mem.: NAS, Royal Irish Acad., Tex. Inst. Letters, Philos. Soc. Tex., Royal Soc. London, Am. Philos. Soc. (Benjamin Franklin medal 2004), Coun. Fgn. Rels., Internat. Astron. Union, Am. Phys. Soc., Am. Acad. Arts and Scis., Cambridge Sci. Soc., Headliners Club (Austin), Saturday Club (Boston), Tuesday Club (Austin), Phi Beta Kappa. Business E-Mail: weinberg@physics.utexas.edu.

WEINBERG, SYLVAN LEE, cardiologist, educator, editor, writer; b. Nashville, June 14, 1923; s. Abraham J. and Beatrice (Kottler) W.; m. Joan Hutzler, Jan. 29, 1956; children: Andrew Lee, Leslie. BS, Northwestern U., 1945, MD, 1948. From intern to resident, fellow Michael Reese Hosp., Chgo., 1947—51; attending physician Good Samaritan Hosp., Dayton, Ohio, 1953—99, chief of cardiology, 1966—99, founding dir. coronary care unit, 1967—99; clin. prof. medicine Wright State U., Dayton, 1975—; dir. med. edn. Dayton Heart Hosp., 2000—. Former panelist Med. Affairs, nat. TV; pres. Weinberg Marcus Cardiomed. Group, Inc., 1970-99; pres. Arts & Comms. Internat., Inc., 1995—. Author: An Epitaph for Merlin and Perhaps for Medicine, 1983, The Golden Age of Medical Science and the Dark Age of Health Care Delivery, 2000; founding editor Dayton Medicine, 1980—, Heart & Lung, 1972-87, Am. Heart Hosp. Jour., 2002—; contbr. articles to profl. jours. Capt. U.S. Army, 1951-53, Korea. Recipient Army Commendation medal, Richard A. DeWall MD award for excellence in cardiology, Am. Heart Assn., 2001, Outstanding Pub. Svc. award, Ohio State Senate, 1980. Fellow ACP (Ohio Laureate award 1997), Am. Coll. Cardiology (editor in chief jour. ACCEL 1985-2000, pres. 1993-94), Am. Coll. Chest Physicians (pres. 1984); mem. Montgomery County Med. Soc. (pres. 1980). Avocations: writing, travel, golf. Home: 4555 Southern Blvd Dayton OH 45429-1118 Office: Dayton Heart Hosp 707 S Edwin Moses Blvd Dayton OH 45408 Personal E-mail: slwjal@aol.com.

WEINBERG, TERI ELLEN, television executive, television producer; b. June 29, 1960; TV talent agent ICM; exec. v.p. scripted programming Reveille Prodns., 2002—07; exec. v.p. NBC Entertainment, 2007—. Prodr.: (TV series) Nashville Star, 2003, Coupling US, 2003; exec. prodr.: The Office, 2006, Ugly Betty, 2006—07; (TV miniseries) The Tudors, 2007. Office: NBC Entertainment 100 Universal City Plaza Universal City CA 91608 *

WEINBERG, WALTER S., lawyer; b. Chgo., Sept. 12, 1956; BA in Econs., with hon., U. Chgo., 1978; JD cum laude, Northwestern U., 1981. Bar: Ill. 1981. Ptnr., Chmn. Corp. Group Katten Muchin Rosenman LLP, Chgo. Named one of Am. Leading Lawyers for Bus., Chambers USA, 2005—06, 2006—07, Ill. Super Lawyers, 2007. Mem.: ABA, Chgo. Bar Assn., Order of the Coif, Phi Beta Kappa. Office: Katten Muchin Rosenman LLP 525 W Monroe St Chicago IL 60661 Office Phone: 312-902-5405. Office Fax: 312-577-8771. Business E-Mail: walter.weinberg@kattenlaw.com.

WEINBERG, WILLIAM HENRY, chemical engineer, physicist, educator; b. Columbia, SC, Dec. 5, 1944; s. Ulrich Vivian and Ruth Ann (Duncan) W. BS, U. SC, 1966; PhD in Chem. Engring, U. Calif., Berkeley, 1970; NATO postdoctoral fellow in phys. chemistry, Cambridge U., Eng., 1971. Asst. prof. chem. engring. Calif. Inst. Tech., 1972-74, assoc. prof., 1974-77, prof. chem. engring. and chem. physics, 1977-89, Chevron disting. prof. chem. engring. and chem. physics, 1981-86; prof. chem. engring. and chemistry U. Calif., Santa Barbara, 1989—, assoc. dean Coll. Engring., 1992-96; chief tech. officer Symyx Techs., Santa Clara, Calif., 1996—. Vis. prof. chemistry Harvard U., 1980, U. Pitts., 1987-88, Oxford U., 1991; Alexander von Humboldt Found. fellow U. Munich, 1982; cons. E.I. DuPont Co. Author: (with Van Hove and Chan) Low-Energy Electron Diffraction, 1986; editor 4 books in field; mem. editl. bd. Jour. Applications Surface Sci., 1977-85, Handbook Surfaces and Interfaces, 1978-80, Surface Sci. Reports, 1980—, gen. editor, 1992—, Applied Surface Sci., 1985—, Langmuir, 1990-96, Surface Sci., 1992—, Jour. Combinatorial Chemistry, 1998—; contbr. articles to profl. jours., chpts. to books. Recipient Giuseppe Parravano award Mich. Catalysis Soc., 1989, Disting. Teaching award Coll. of Engring., U. Calif. Santa Barbara, 1995; fellow NSF, 1966-69, Alfred P. Sloan Found., 1976-78, Camille and Henry Dreyfus Found., 1976-81. Fellow AAAS, Am. Phys. Soc. (Nottingham prize 1972), Am. Vacuum Soc.; mem. AIChE (Colburn award 1981), Am. Chem. Soc. (LaMer award 1973, Kendall award 1991, Arthur W. Adamson award 1995), N.Am. Catalysis Soc., Nat. Acad. Engring., Phi Beta Kappa. Office: Symyx Technologies 415 Oakmead Pkwy Sunnyvale CA 94085 Office Phone: 408-764-2000. Business E-Mail: hweinberg@symyx.com.

WEINBERGER, ADRIENNE, artist, art appraiser; b. Washington, Apr. 28, 1948; d. Samuel Aaron and Marta (Barta) W.; m. Edward Herschel Egelman, Mar. 21, 1980; children: Serge Maurice, Liana Dora. BA, Goucher Coll., Balt., 1970; MEd, Johns Hopkins U., Balt., 1973; MA, Northwestern U., Evanston, Ill., 1974; postgrad., Sch. of Mus. of Fine Arts, Boston, 1979—82. Lectr. Art Inst. Chgo., 1973-75; lectr., docent trainer Mus. of Fine Arts, Boston, 1978-82; mus. educator Yale Ctr. Brit. Art, Yale Art Gallery, New Haven, 1984-86; instr., coord. alumni coll. Albertus Magnus Coll., New Haven, 1987-89; instr. Mpls. C.C., 1989-94; propr. Studio 95, Edina, Minn., 1995-99, Charlottesville, Va., 1999—. Panelist New England Regional Confs., Am. Assn. Muss., Mass., Conn., 1976-77; workshop leader New Haven Green Found., New Haven 350 Com., 1987-88; pres. Cmty. Art Fund., 2000—. Author, illustrator: New Haven Coloring Book, 1987, CulchaMan Visits New York City, 1988, CulchaMan Visits Washinton, D.C., 1988. Participant Edina Futures Forum, 1990; dir. Edina-Woodhill Assn., 1997—98; active State Affirmative Action Commn., 1996—98; del. chair, mem. nominating com. Dem. State Conv., St. Paul, 1994, del., chair Rochester, 1996, St. Cloud, 1998, del. Norfolk, 2000, Roanoke, 2004; active Dem. State Exec. Com., 1997—99; sec. Dem.-Farmer Labor Party, Edina, Eden Prairie, 1990—94, chair, 1994—96, treas. 3d Congl. Dist., 1996—99; active Dem. State Cen. Com., 1994—99, Albemarle County Dem. Com., 2005; adv. bd. gifted edn. svcs. Edina Pub. Schs., 1993—96; bd. dirs. Consortium for Advancement of Arts, 2001—03, Leadership Charlottesville, 2002—, mem. leadership cir., 2002—; bd. dirs. Northwestern U. Alumni Club, 2003—, Northwestern U. Club Va. Recipient Juror's award Berkshire Mus., Pittsfield, Mass., 1981, New Haven Brush & Palette Club, 1985, Edina Art Ctr., 1991. Mem. Am. Soc. Appraisers (accredited sr. appraiser; sec. Twin Cities chpt. 1997-99, pres. Richmond chpt. 2000-01, 3d v.p. Richmond chpt. 2001-03), Charlottesville C. of C. (Amb. Corps. 2000, legis. action com. 2000—2006, legal action com. 2000-2006), U. Va. Art Mus.(vol. bd. 2003-), Leadership Charlottesville Alumni Assn. (bd. dirs. 2006—), Northwestern U. Alumni Club Va. (bd. dirs. 2003—, Vol. award 2007), Alumni Assn. Avocations: travel, reading, politics. Office: Studio 95 3100 Waverly Dr Charlottesville VA 22901-9576 Office Phone: 434-297-0694. Business E-Mail: studio95@guanotronic.com.

WEINBERGER, ALAN DAVID, lawyer, business executive; b. Washington, July 31, 1945; s. Theodore George and Shirley Sunshine (Gross) W.; m. Lauren Myra Kaminski, Dec. 2, 1979; children: Mark Henry, Benjamin Charles. BA, NYU, 1967, JD, 1970; LLM, Harvard U., 1973. Bar: N.Y. 1971, D.C. 1978, U.S. Supreme Ct. 1980. Assoc. White & Case, NYC, 1970-72; founding law prof. Vt. Law Sch., South Royalton, 1973-75; atty. SEC and Fed. Home Loan Bank Bd., Washington, 1977-81; founder, chmn. bd. dirs., CEO The ASCII Group Inc., Washington, 1984—; founder, chmn. bd. dirs. Tech. Net. Inc., Bethesda, Md., 1995. Adv. bd. Ashton Tate Inc., Torrance, Calif., 1986—87; sponsor, agt. All Union Fgn. Trade Acad., Acad. Nat. Economy of USSR in USA, 1988—90; chmn. US adv. bd. Moscow State U. of Commerce, 1992—; chmn. govt. affairs com. Computer Tech. Industry Assn.; founder Internat. Tech. Channels Assn., Germany, 2007. Author: White Paper to Reform Business Education in Russia, 1996; law rev. editor NYU Sch. Law, 1970. Named one of Top 25 Most Influential Execs. in Computer Industry, Computer Reseller News, 1988; recipient CEO of Yr. award Cyber Chanels, 1999; named eInnovator of Yr. Cyber Channels Assn., 2000. Mem. Nat. Orgn. on Disability (CEO coun.), Internat. Tech. Channels Assn. (founder 2007), D.C. Bar Assn., Order of Coif, Kenwood Country Club. Avocation: tennis. Office: ASCII Group Inc 7101 Wisconsin Ave Bethesda MD 20814-4871 Business E-Mail: aw@ascii.com.

WEINBERGER, ARNOLD, retired electrical engineer; b. Bardejov, Czechoslovakia, Oct. 23, 1924; came to U.S., 1939; s. Henry C. and Bina (Shapira) W.; widowed; children: Paul I., Ronda B., Keith A. BSEE, CCNY, 1950. Engr. Nat. Bur. Standards, Washington, 1950-60; rsch. staff mem. IBM, Yorktown Heights, N.Y., 1960-66, engr., Poughkeepsie, N.Y., 1966-91, ret., 1991. Contbr. articles on computer arithmetic, logic, large-scale integration, system organization, memories, design automation. Patentee in field. With U.S. Army, 1944-46, ETO. Fellow IEEE (Outstanding sect. award 1981). Avocation: ping pong/table tennis.

WEINBERGER, DANIEL R., psychiatrist, neurologist; b. NYC, May 24, 1947; married; 1 child. BA, Johns Hopkins U., 1969; MD, U. Pa., 1973. Diplomate Am. Bd. Psychiatry and Neurology. Intern L.A. County-Harbor Gen. Hosp., Torrance, Calif., 1973-74; grad. fellow in medicine UCLA Sch. Medicine, 1973-74; clin. fellow in psychiatry Harvard U., 1974-77; resident in psychiatry Mass. Mental Health Ctr., Boston, 1974-76, chief resident, 1976-77; assoc. in medicine, divsn. psychiatry Peter Bent Brigham Hosp., Boston, 1974-76; asst. clin. prof. psychiatry George Washington U., Washington, 1978-81, assoc. clin. prof., 1982, assoc. clin. prof. neurology and psychiatry, 1984; resident in neurology George Washington U. Med. Ctr., Washington, 1980-83; dir. rsch. ward adult psychiatry br., intermural rsch. program NIHM, Washington, 1977-78, staff psychiatrist, 1977-81; head clin. neuropsychiatry and neurobehavior unit NIMH/St. Elizabeth's Hosp., Washington, 1981-82, chief sect., 1983-86, chief clin. brain disorders br., 1986—; dir. movement disorder, dementia clinic, experimental therapeutics br. Nat. Inst. Neurol. Diseases and Stroke, Washington, 1983-86; dir. behavioral neurology svc. St. Elizabeth's Hosp., Washington, 1983-88. Part-time gen. practice Bridgewater Med. Ctr., East Bridgewater, Mass., 1974-76; emergency rm. physician Cardinal Cushing Gen. Hosp., Brockton, Mass., 1974-77; examiner Am. Bd. Psychiatry and Neurology; part-time gen. practice psychiatry and neurology, Washington, 1978—; scientists promotion review com. NIMH, 1984-87; elected to coun. Assembly of Scientists NIMH/Nat. Inst. Neurological Diseases and Stroke, 1985-88; Roerig vis. prof. U. N.Mex., 1990, U. Mich., 1992; adv. bd. Alzheimer Disease Found., 1990—, Adams Super Ctr. Brain Studies, Tel Aviv, 1993—; Neal Mysell lectr. Harvard Med. Sch., 1993; steering com. in vivo NMR Ctr., NIH, 1993—. Mem. editorial bd. Biol. Psychiatry, 1986—, Internat. Jour. Schizophrenia Rsch., 1987—, Jour. Neuropsychiatry and Clin. Neurosci., 1987—, Psychiatry, 1987—, Progress in Neuropsychiatry and Psychopharmacology, 1989—, Jour. Clin. Brain Imaging, 1989—, Psychiatry Research: Neuroimaging, 1990—, Jour. Psychiatry and Neurosci., 1990—, Neuropsychopharmacology, 1991—, Development and Psychopathology, 1991—, Harvard Review of Psychiatry, 1992—; contbr. articles to profl. jours.; patentee in field. Capt. USPHS, 1977-86. Recipient Morton Prince award Am. Psychopathol. Assn., 1984, Judith B. Silver award Nat. Alliance for Mentally Ill, 1985, Arthur S. Flemming award Washington Jaycees, 1986, Established Investigator award NARSAD, 1990, Lieber award, 1993, Dean award Am. Coll. Psychiatrists, 1994. Fellow Am. Coll. Neuropsychopharmacology (Joel Elkes internat. award 1989); mem. AMA, AAAS, Am. Psychiat. Assn. (Found. Fund prize for rsch. 1991), Am. Acad. Neurology (sci. program com. 1993—), Am. Neuropsychiatric Assn., Soc. Biol. Psychiatry (A.E. Benett Found. award clin. science 1981), Behavioral Neurology Soc., Soc. Neurosci. (pub. lectr. 20th ann. meeting 1990), Washington Neurology Soc., Washington Psychiat. Soc., Phi Beta Kappa, Alpha Omega Alpha, Inst. Medicine. Office: NIMH Clinical Brain Disorders Branch 10 Center Dr Rm 4S235 Bldg 10 Bethesda MD 20892-1379

WEINBERGER, FRANK, information management consultant; b. Chgo., Sept. 18, 1926; s. Rudolph and Elaine (Kellner) W.; m. Beatrice Natalie Fixler, June 27, 1953; children: Alan J., Bruce I. BSEE, Ill. Inst. Tech., Chgo., 1951; MBA, Northwestern U., 1959; DBA, U.S. Internat. U., San Diego, 1996. Registered profl. engr., Ill, Calif. Engr. Admiral Corp., Chgo., 1951-53; sr. engr. Cook Rsch., Chgo., 1953-59; mem. tech. staff Rockwell Internat., Downey, Calif., 1959-80, info. sys. advisor, 1980-95; info. mgmt. cons., 1995—. Pres. Temple Israel, Long Beach, Calif., 1985-87, bd. dirs. 1973-85. With USN, 1944-46. Mem. Assn. for Computer Machinery. Democrat. Jewish. Avocation: microcomputers. Home and Office: 3231 Yellowtail Dr Los Alamitos CA 90720-5253 Personal E-mail: weinberger@covad.net. *Don't ask "what can I do?" Instead, survey the needs, prepare the information, and give your best recommendation.*

WEINBERGER, HAROLD PAUL, lawyer; b. NYC, Mar. 12, 1947; s. Fred and Elaine (Schonfeld) W.; m. Toby Ann Strassman, Dec. 15, 1968; children: James David, Karen Ellen. BA, CCNY, 1967; JD, Columbia U., 1970. Bar: N.Y. 1971, U.S. Dist. Cts. (so., ea., and no. dists.) N.Y. 1972, U.S. Ct. Appeals (2d cir.) 1972. Law clk. to presiding justice U.S. Ct. Appeals (2d cir.), NYC, 1970-71; assoc. Kramer Levin Naftalis Frankel LLP, NYC, 1971-77, ptnr., 1978—; lectr. in law Columbia U. Sch. Law, NYC, 2005—. Recipient John Ordronaux prize Columbia U. Law Sch., 1970. Mem. ABA (intellectual property law sect. 1999—), Assn. Bar City N.Y. (com. fed. legislation 1975-78, com. on products liability 1983-86, mem. com. on trademarks and unfair competition 1995-97). Democrat. Jewish. Home: 336 Central Park W New York NY 10025-7111 Office: Kramer Levin Naftalis & Frankel LLP 1177 Ave of the Americas New York NY 10036 Office Phone: 212-715-9132. E-mail: hweinberger@kramerlevin.com.

WEINBERGER, MARK ALAN, corporate financial executive, former federal agency administrator; b. 1961; m. Nancy Weinberger; children: Rachel, Noah, Sean, Benjamin. Grad., Emory U.; MBA, Case We. Res., 1987; LLM in Taxation, Georgetown U., 1987. Chief tax & budget counsel to Senator John Danforth US Senate, 1993—96; co-founder, ptnr. Washington Counsel, P.C. (merged with Ernst & Young), 1996—2000; dir. U.S. nat. tax practice Ernst & Young LLP, 2000—01, dep. vice chmn., tax services The Americas, 2002—; asst. sec. for tax policy US Dept. Treasury, Washington, 2001—02. Chief of staff, counsel Pres. Bipartisan Commn. on Entitlement and Tax Reform; sr. advisor Kemp Commn.; commr. Nat. Commn. on Retirement Policy; mem. Social Security Adv. Bd., 2000—01. Office: Ernst & Young LLP 5 Times Sq 14th Fl New York NY 10036

WEINBRENNER, GEORGE RYAN, aeronautical engineer; b. June 10, 1917; s. George Penbrook and Helen Mercedes (Ryan) W.; m. Billie Marjorie Elwood, May 2, 1955. BS, MIT, Cambridge, 1940, MS, 1941; AMP, Harvard U., Cambridge, Mass., 1966; ScD (hon.), Mapua Inst. Tech., Manila, 1994. Commd. 2d lt. USAAF, 1939, advanced through grades to col., 1949; def. attaché Am. Embassy, Prague, Czech Republic, 1958—61; dep. chief staff intelligence Air Force Sys. Command, Washington, 1962—68; comdr. fgn. tech. divsn. USAF, Wright-Patterson AFB, Ohio, 1968—74; comdr. Brooks AFB, Tex., 1974—75; ret., 1975; exec. v.p. B.C. Wills & Co., Inc., Reno, 1975—84; chmn. bd. Hispaño-Technica S.A. Inc., San Antonio, 1977—. Lectr. Sch. Aerospace Medicine Brooks AFB, Tex., 1975-84; adv. dir. Plaza Nat. Bank, San Antonio; cons. Def. Dept., 1981, Dept. Air Force, 1975-84. Decorated D.S.M., Legion of Merit, Bronze Star, Air medal, Purple Heart, Ordre Nat. du Merite, Médaille de la Resistance, Croix de Guerre (France). Fellow AIAA (assoc.); mem. World Affairs Coun., Air Force Assn. (exec. sec. Tex. 1976-94), Assn. Former Intelligence Officers (nat. dir.), Air Force Hist. Found. (dir.), U.S. Strategic Inst., Nat. Mil. Intelligence Assn., Tex. Aerospace & Nat. Def. Tech. Devel.

Coun., Am. Astron. Soc., Aerospace Ednl. Foun. (trustee), Disabled Am. Vets. (life), Mil. Order World Wars, Am. Legion, Assn. Old Crows, Army-Navy Club (Washington), Kappa Sigma. Roman Catholic.

WEINBROT, HOWARD DAVID, language educator; b. Bklyn., May 14, 1936; s. William and Rose (Shapiro) W.; m. Dawn Simon. BA, Antioch Coll., Yellow Springs, Ohio, 1958; MA with honors (Woodrow Wilson fellow 1959, grad. fellow 1959-63), U. Chgo., 1959; PhD, 1963. Tchg. fellow U. Chgo., 1962-63; instr. English Yale U., 1963-66; asst. prof., then assoc. prof. U. Calif., Riverside, 1966-69; mem. faculty U. Wis., Madison, 1969—, prof. English, 1972-84, Ricardo Quintana prof., 1984-87, Vilas prof., 1987—. Andrew W. Mellon vis. prof. Inst. Advanced Study Princeton Visitor Insts., NJ, 2002—03. Author: The Formal Strain, 1969, Augustus Caesar in Augustan England, 1978, Alexander Pope and the Traditions of Formal Verse Satire, 1982, Essays on 18th-Century Satire, 1988, paperback, 2007, Britannia's Issue, 1993, paperback, 2007, Aspects of Samuel Johnson, 2005, Menippean Satire Reconsidered, 2005, 07; also numerous articles, revs.; editor: New Aspects of Lexicography, 1972, Northrop Frye and 18th Century Studies; co-editor: The 18th Century: A Current Bibliography for 1973, 1975, Poetry in English, An Anthology, 1987, Eighteenth-Century Contexts, 2001. Fellow, NEH, 1975—76; Guggenheim fellow, 1988—89, Andrew Mellon fellow, Huntington Libr., 2007—, vis. mem., Inst. for Advanced Study, Princeton. Mem. Am. Soc. 18th Century Studies (mem. editl. bd. 1977-80, exec. com. 96-99), Internat. Soc. 18th Century Studies UCLA (planning com. 2003), Johnsonians, Johnson Soc. (sec.-treas. 1970-75, v.p. 2000-01, pres. 2002-03), Midwest Am. Soc. Eighteenth Century Studies, Eighteenth Century Scottish Studies. Home: 1505 Wood Ln Madison WI 53705-1456 Office: U Wis English Dept 600 N Park St Madison WI 53706-1403 Office Phone: 608-263-3819. Business E-Mail: weinbrot@wisc.edu.

WEINEL, PAMELA JEAN, nurse administrator; b. Olney, Md., Dec. 14, 1956; d. Clarence Dawson and Jean Elizabeth (Woodward) Weinel; m. Nathan Richards, May 6, 1995. AA in Edn., Montgomery Coll., Rockville, Md., 1976; BSN, U. Md., Balt., 1986, M in sci. Adminstrn., 1998; MBA, U. Balt., 2001. Oncology staff nurse George Washington U. Med. Ctr., Washington, 1986—88, Bone Marrow Transplant coord., 1988—90; adminstrv. coord. Walter Reed Army Med Ctr., Washington, 1990—98; advice nurse Kaiser Permanente, Kensington, Md., 1991—98; rsch. program mgr. Clin. Rsch. and Protocol Mgmt. Office U. Md. Greenebaum Cancer Ctr., Balt., 1999—2002; IVF nurse Shady Grove Fertility Ctr., Rockville, Md., 2003—04; project mgr. Social and Sci. Sys., Inc. CODA Divsn. FDA MedSun Project, Silver Spring, Md., 2004—06; nurse cons. Ctr. for Devices and Radiol. Health, FDA, Rockville, 2006—; faculty assoc., grad. nursing program U. Md., Balt., 2006—. Cons., mem. People to People Internat., Russia, 1992, Vietnam, 93; roundtable facilitator Internat. BMT Symposium, Omaha, 1992; lectr. Contemporary Forums, San Francisco, 1994. Contbr., 1993—94. Sponsor for adults Resurrection Roman Cath. Ch., Burtonsville, Md., 1997—2000, CCD instr. 7th grade, 2001—02. Named an Outstanding Young Woman in Am., 1997. Mem.: NAFE, Oncology Nursing Soc. (Bone Marrow Transplant spl. interest group), Am. Soc. for Reproductive Medicine, Sigma Iota Epsilon, Phi Kappa Phi, Phi Theta Kappa, Sigma Theta Tau (scholar 1996). Avocations: travel, photography, writing, Tae Kwon Do. Office: FDA CDRH ODE Divsn DRARD 9200 Corporate Blvd 310R Rockville MD 20850 Business E-Mail: pam.weinel@fda.hhs.gov.

WEINER, ALLEN SYDNEY, law educator; b. 1963; AB in Social Studies magna cum laude, Harvard U., 1985; JD, Stanford U., 1989. Law clk. to Judge John Steadman US Ct. Appeals DC Cir., 1989—90; atty.-adviser Office of Legal Adviser, US Dept. State, 1990—96, Office Internat. Claims and Investment Disputes, 1990—92, Office Inter-Am. Affairs, 1992—95, Office Politico-Mil. Affairs, 1995—96; attaché US Embassy, The Hague, Netherlands, 1996—98, counselor for legal affairs, 1998—2001; rsch. fellow TMC Asser Inst., The Hague, 2002—03; Warren Christopher prof. of practice of internat. law and diplomacy Stanford Law Sch. & Stanford Inst. Internat. Studies, 2003—. Vis. lectr. faculty law U. Amsterdam, 2001, 02, U. Leiden, 2002; mem. adv. com. Amsterdam-Nyenrode Law Sch., 2001—03. Office: Stanford Law Sch Crown Quadrangle 559 Nathan Abbott Way Stanford CA 94305-8610 Office Phone: 650-724-4818. Business E-Mail: aweiner@stanford.edu.

WEINER, ANDREW JAY, lawyer; b. Hartford, Conn., Dec. 19, 1950; m. Debra Lewin, May 29, 1977; children: Joshua Isaac, Hannah Leah. BA, Yale Coll., 1972; JD, Harvard U., 1976. Bar: N.Y. 1977. Planner N.Y.C. Dept. City Planning, 1972-73; assoc. Shearman & Sterling, NYC, 1976-84; ptnr. Gordon Hurwitz Butowsky Weitzen Shalov & Wein, NYC, 1984-89, Morrison & Foerster LLP, NYC, 1990—. Office: Morrison & Foerster LLP 1290 Avenue Of The Americas Fl 40 New York NY 10104-0050 Office Fax: 212-468-7900. Business E-Mail: aweiner@mofo.com.

WEINER, ANNE LEE, social worker; b. Chelsea-Malden, Mass., Nov. 2, 1932; d. Nathan and Edith E. (Sigel) Varnick; m. Paul J. Weiner, Jan. 25, 1959; children: Berdine R., Ronald M. Diploma in med. sec., Chandler Sch. for Women, 1952; AA in Social Work, Middelsex C.C., 1974; BSW, Salem Coll., 1987. Med. sec. New Eng. Med. - Boston U. Hosp., Boston, 1952-1960; social worker Lynn-Union Hosp., Lynn, Mass., 1968-1982; home care social worker Mass. Elder Care, Peabody, 1982-1987; dir. Dept. Social Work Logan Homes, Wingate Homes, Hill Haven Homes, Mass., 1987-99. Mem. region bd. Hadassah steering com. social work, Hadassah Boston and Fla. Atlantic region; pres. Chessed, 2003—06; active Hist. Soc. Peabody; organizer social work support groups North Shore, Mass., 2003—04. Personal E-mail: lighthousealw@bellsouth.net.

WEINER, ANTHONY DAVID, congressman; b. Bklyn., Sept. 4, 1964; BA, SUNY, Plattsburgh, 1985. Budget dir., press-fgn. affairs asst., dist. office liaison Staff of US Rep. Charles E. Schumer from NY, 1985—91; mem. City Coun. from Dist. 48, NYC, 1991-98, mem. pub. safety, consumer affairs, transp. coms., chmn. subcommittee crime in pub. housing; mem. US Congress from 9th NY dist., 1999—, mem. energy & commerce com., judiciary com. Bd. dirs. Bklyn. Bd. Boys Town Jerusalem, Shaare Zedek Hosp., Israel. Named Legislator of Yr., Jewish Cmty. Coun. Rockaway Peninsula, 2002, Friend of the Nat. Pks., Nat. Pks. Conservation Assn., 2003; recipient Breaking the Silence award, Rachel's Children Reclamation Found., 2003, Friends of RESOLVE award, RESOLVE (Nat. Infertility Assn.), 2003. Democrat. Jewish. Office: US House Reps 1122 Longworth House Office Bldg Washington DC 20515-3209 Office Phone: 202-225-6616. *

WEINER, BRADLEY KENNETH, surgeon, researcher; b. Cleve., Oct. 7, 1964; s. Dennis and Sally Weiner; m. Anna Peri, Aug. 1, 1987; children: Jacob, Olivia, Simon. BA, Allegheny Coll., Meadville, Pa., 1987; MD, NEOUCOM, Rootstwon, Ohio, 1991. Diplomate Am. Bd. Orthopedic Surgery, 1999. Chief spinal surgery Pa. State Coll. Medicine, Hershey, Meth. Hosp., Houston, 2006—. Contbr. more than 50 articles to profl. publs. Recipient numerous awards. Office: Meth Hosp 6550 Fannin Houston TX 77030 Home Phone: 713-463-4803. Personal E-mail: bkweiner@tmh.tmc.edu.

WEINER, CARL DORIAN, retired historian; b. NYC, Mar. 26, 1934; s. Alexander and Ann (Goodson) Weiner; m. Ruth Ann Feinglass, Sept. 6, 1959; children: Nicholas, Kevin, Daniel. BA, Queens Coll., 1955; postgrad., U. Wis., 1958-61; MA, Columbia U., 1959. Instr. U. Pitts., 1961-62; mem. faculty Carleton Coll., Northfield, Minn., 1964—2004, chmn. dept. history, 1974-77, 95-98, prof., 1982—2002, William H. Laird prof. history and the liberal arts, 2002—04, prof. emeritus, 2004. With US Army, 1957. Recipient 2d Century award, Carleton Coll., 1968; Bush grantee, 1983—84. Jewish. Home: 403 Laurel Ave Saint Paul MN 55102-2015 Office Phone: 507-646-4209. Personal E-mail: cweiner@carleton.edu.

WEINER, CHARLES, historian, educator; b. Bklyn., Aug. 11, 1931; s. Louis and Minnie (Florman) W.; m. Shirley Marks (div. 1976); 1 child, Susan; m. JoAnn Hughes, 1993. BS, Case Inst. Tech., 1960, MA, 1963, PhD, 1965. Asst. editor Tooling and Production mag., Cleve., 1958-60, asso. editor, 1961; editor The Explorer, Cleve. Museum of Natural History, 1960-62; dir. Project on History of Recent Physics in the U.S., Am. Inst. Physics, NYC, 1964-65, Center for History of Physics, 1965-74; prof. history of sci. and tech. Mass. Inst. Tech., 1974—96, dir. oral history program, 1975—86, prof. emeritus, 1996—. Vis. prof. U. Calif., Berkeley, 2001, Regents lectr., 03; vis. prof. NYU, 2007. Co-editor: The Legacy of George Ellery Hale, 1972, Robert Oppenheimer: Letters and Recollections, 1980; editor: Exploring the History of Nuclear Physics, 1972, History of 20th Century Physics, 1977; mem. editorial council: Bull. of Atomic Scientists, 1979-84. Mem. com. social orgn. sci. Social Sci. Research Council, 1968-71; adv. com. to Library of Congress on Nat. Union Catalog of Manuscript Collections, 1965-71; mem. editorial adv. bd. Joseph Henry Papers, Smithsonian Instn., 1968-86; com. on history of recent biochemistry and molecular biology Am. Acad. Arts and Scis., 1968-80, project dir. com. history contemporary physics, 1966-74; mem. adv. bd. Center for the Study of Consumer Movement, Consumers Union; mem. humanities adv. bd. Sta. WGBH, Boston, 1978-79; mem. adv. bd. Sci. in Am. Life, Smithsonian Inst., 1990-94; cons. Pres. Adv. Com. Human Radiation Experiments, 1994-95. Served with U.S. Army, 1951-53. Recipient Disting. Service citation Am. Assn. Physics Tchrs., 1974; Case fellow, 1961-64; Guggenheim fellow, 1970-71; NSF grantee, 1965, 68, 70, 73, 75, 77, 81, 86; Nat. Endowment Humanities grantee, 1976, 77, 81, 86. Fellow AAAS (council 1969-75, com. on meetings 1969-72), History of Sci. Soc. (council 1968-70, chmn. Met. N.Y. Sect. 1969-70), Soc. for History of Tech. (adv. council 1977-79). Office: 56 Main St Yarmouth Port MA 02675

WEINER, EARL DAVID, lawyer; b. Balt., Aug. 21, 1939; s. Jacob Joseph and Sophia Gertrude (Rachanow) W.; m. Gina Helen Priestley Ingoglia, Mar. 30, 1962; children: Melissa Danis Balmain, John Barlow. AB, Dickinson Coll., 1960; LL.B., Yale U., 1968. Bar: NY 1969. Assoc. Sullivan & Cromwell LLP, NYC, 1968—76, ptnr., 1976—2006, of counsel, 2007—; gen. coun. Mcpl. Art Soc. NY, NYC, 2007—. Adj. prof. Rutgers U. Sch. Law, 1987—88; bd. dirs. AllianceBernstein Funds, The Acting Co., vice chmn., 1992—2003, chmn., 2003—. Gov. Bklyn. Heights Assn., 1980—87, pres., 1985—87, adv. com., 1987—; gov. The Heights Casino, 1979—84, pres., 1981—84; trustee Green-Wood Cemetery, 1985—, Bklyn. Hosp. Ctr., 1998—, vice chmn., 1991—96; bd. advisors Dickinson Coll., Carlisle, Pa., 1986—90, chmn., 1988—90, trustee, 1988—2002, vice chmn., 1998—2002; trustee Theatre Devel. Fund, 2005—; mem. adv. com. East Rock Inst., 1988—; bd. visitors U. Md. Ctr. Environ. Sci., 2002—. Lt. USN, 1961—65. Fellow Fgn. Policy Assn. (sr.); mem. ABA, N.Y. State Bar Assn., Assn. Bar City N.Y. Office: Sullivan & Cromwell 125 Broad St Fl 32 New York NY 10004-2498

WEINER, FERNE, psychologist; b. NYC, June 14, 1928; d. Irving Kapp and Peggy (Finkelstein) Hessberg; m. Howard Weiner, July 20, 1948; children: Irving Kenneth, Laurie. BA, Skidmore Coll., 1965; MA, Sarah Lawrence Coll., 1971; PhD, U. Hawaii, 1975. Lic. psychologist, Calif., Hawaii. Asst. prof. West Oahu Coll. U. Hawaii, Honolulu, 1975—77; staff psychologist Cmty. Guidance Clinic, Manchester, Conn., 1978—83; chief cons. psychologist Consultation and Evaluation Ctr., Meriden, Conn., 1984—85; psychologist cons. Disability Determination Svcs., Hartford, Conn., 1986—87, Honolulu, 1988—; police psychologist Honolulu Police Dept., 1988. Pvt. practice, Greenwich, Conn., 1983-87, Honolulu, 1988—; cons. Adopt-A-Sch. Project, Honolulu, 1991-94; interviewer, therapist Sexual Abuse Treatment Team, Manchester, 1979-83; cons., trainer Conn. schs., day care, ch. groups, 1979-87. Contbr. articles to profl. jours. Active Disaster Assistance Mgmt. Team, Hawaii, 1994-95; v.p., sec. Queens Court at Kapiolani Bd., Honolulu, 1992-95; admissions rep. Hawaii Sarah Lawrence Coll., Honolulu, 1970-80; cons. to adoptees search Orphan Voyage, Conn., 1980-87; mentor Girl Scout Coun. Am., Oahu, 1993-94. Mem. Am. Psychol. Assn. (clin. psychotherapy and neuropsychology divsn.), Hawaii Psychol. Assn., Nat. Registry Health Svcs. Providers, Outrigger Canoe Club, Shiley Sports Club. Democrat. Jewish. Avocations: aerobics, interior design, property renovation, gourmet cooking, travel. Personal E-mail: wferne1@san.rr.com.

WEINER, GERALD ARNE, stockbroker; b. Chgo., Dec. 20, 1941; s. Irwin S. and Lilyan (Stock) W.; m. Barbara I. Allen, June 18, 1967; children: Rachel Anne, Sara Naomi. BSS, Loyola U., Chgo., 1964; student, U. Vienna, 1962-63; MS, Georgetown U., 1966; postgrad., Ind. U., 1966-72, S.E. Asian Areas Cert., 1967. Pacification specialist AID, Laos, 1965; instr. polit. sci. Loyola U., Chgo., 1970-72; asst. v.p. A.G. Becker & Co., Chgo., 1973-78; sr. v.p. Oppenheimer & Co., Chgo., 1978-83, J. David Securities, Inc., Chgo., 1983-84, Morgan Stanley, Chgo., 1984—. Exec. edn. for securities industry Wharton Sch. Bus. U. Pa., 1988-90. Trustee Highland Park Police Pension Fund, 1991-2004. Mucia fellow, 1969. Mem. Midwest Bonsai Soc., Equinox Club. Republican. Jewish. Office: Morgan Stanley 70 W Madison St Ste 300 Chicago IL 60602-4278 Office Phone: 312-827-6634. Business E-Mail: gerald.weiner@morganstanley.com.

WEINER, H. RICHARD, internist; MD, U. Tex. Diplomate Am. Bd. Internal Medicine, 1998, Am. Coll. Foroensic Medicine, 1998, Am. Coll. Med. Examiners, 1997. Sr. physician U. Wis., Milw., 1994—2007, lab. dir. Reviewer Am. Bd. Internal Medicine. Achievements include research in HIV; West Nile virus; Lyme disease. Home Phone: 414-229-4716.

WEINER, HOWARD MARC, physician; b. Feb. 25, 1946; BSc, Marietta Coll., 1967; MD, U. Cin., 1971; MPH, Med. Coll. Wis., 1994. Diplomate Am.Bd. Allergy, Asthma and Immunology, Am. Bd. Preventive Medicine/Occupl. Medicine, Am. Bd. Ind. Med. Examiners. Intern medicine Temple U. Hosp., Phila., 1971—72, resident internal medicine, 1972—74; fellow allergy and clin. immunology Hosp. U. Pa., Phila., 1974—76; pres., physician Allergy & Asthma Assocs. West Boca, Boca Raton, Fla., 1988—; pres., med. dir. Med. Assessment Inst. Inc., Boca Raton, Fla., 1997—. Chmn. ethics com. Palm Beach County Med. Soc., West Palm Beach, Fla., 1994-97; bd. dirs. Primus Physicians Svcs., Inc., So. Fla. Mem. Omicron Delta Kappa Soc., Pi Kappa Epsilon. Office: 2385 NW Executive Ctr Dr Ste 100 Boca Raton FL 33431 Office Phone: 561-451-0200.

WEINER, IRVING BERNARD, psychologist; b. Grand Rapids, Mich., Aug. 16, 1933; s. Jacob H. and Mollie Jean (Laevin) W.; m. Frances Shair, June 9, 1963; children: Jeremy Harris, Seth Howard. BA, U. Mich., Ann Arbor, 1955, MA, 1957, PhD, 1959. Diplomate Am. Bd. Profl. Psychology. From instr. to prof. psychiatry and pediat. U. Rochester, NY, 1959-72; head divsn. psychology U. Rochester Med. Center, 1968-72; prof. psychology, chmn. dept. Case Western Res. U., 1972-77, dean grad. studies, 1976-79; vice chancellor for acad. affairs U. Denver, 1979-83, prof. psychology, 1979-85; v.p. for acad. affairs Fairleigh Dickinson U., Teaneck, NJ, 1985-89, prof. psychology, 1985-89; prof. psychiatry U. South Fla., Tampa, 1989—. Adv. editor John Wiley & Sons, 1967-93, 99—, Lawrence Erlbaum Assocs., 1993-99; psychology edn. rev. com. NIMH, 1977-81. Author: Psychodiagnosis in Schizophrenia, 1966, Psychological Disturbance in Adolescence, 1970, rev. edit., 1992, Rorschach Handbook, 1971, Child Development, 1972, Principles of Psychotherapy, 1975, rev. edit., 1998, Development of the Child, 1978, Child and Adolescent Psychopathology, 1982, Rorschach Assessment of Children and Adolescents, 1982, rev. edit., 1995, Adolescence, 1985, rev. edit., 1995, Handbook of Forensic Psychology, 1987, rev. edit., 2006, Principles of Rorschach Interpretation, 1998, rev. edit., 2003, Handbook of Psychology, 2003; editor: Readings in Child Development, 1972, Clinical Methods in Psychology, 1976, 83, Adult Psychopathology Case Studies, 2004, Jour. Personality Assessment, 1985-93, Rorschachiana, 1989-96; mem. editl. bd. Profl. Psychology, 1971-76, Jour. Adolescent Health Care, 1979-87, Children and Youth Svcs. Rev., 1979-91, Jour. Pediat. Psychology, 1981-87, Devel. and Behavioral Pediat., 1985-96, Studi Rorschachiani, 1985—, European Jour. Psychol. Assessment, 1985—, Jour. Adolescent Rsch., 1986-91, Jour. Personality Disorders, 1986-92, Psychol. Assessment, 1994—2003, Jour. Personality Assessment, 2003—, Assessment, 2004—, Jour. Child Custody, 2005—. Recipient Disting. Profl. Achievement award Genesee Psychol. Assn., 1974 Fellow APA, Acad. Clin. Psychology, Acad. Forensic Psychology, Acad. of Assessment Psychology (Lifetime Achievement awrd 2001); mem. Assn. Advancement Psychology, Soc. Personality Assessment (pres. 1976-78, 2005—, Disting. Contbn. award 1983), Assn. Internship Ctrs. (exec. com. 1971-76), Soc. Rsch. in Adolescence, Soc. for Rsch. in Child and Adolescent Psychopathology, Soc. for Exploration Psychotherapy Integration, Soc. Pediat. Psychology, Am. Psychol. Law Soc., Internat. Rorschach Soc. (pres. 1999-2005), Assn. Psychol. Sci., Soc. Clin. Psychology (pres.-elect, 2007—), Phi Beta Kappa, Sigma Xi, Phi Kappa Phi. Home and Office: 13716 Halliford Dr Tampa FL 33624-6903 Office Phone: 813-961-8032. Business E-Mail: iweiner@health.usf.edu.

WEINER, JACK H., lawyer; b. Phila., Nov. 21, 1934; s. Samuel A. and Sophie S. (Snyderman) W.; m. Diana M. Wiess, June 12, 1960; children—Scott, Edward, Hope. A.B., U. Pa., 1956; LL.B., Yale U., 1959. Bar: D.C. 1959, Pa. 1960, N.Y. 1973. Trial atty. U.S. Dept. Labor, 1960-65, civil div., appellate sect. U.S. Dept. Justice, 1965-68, NLRB, 1970-72; v.p., counsel Bankers Trust Co., N.Y.C., 1973—99; mem. Interglobal Entertainment Co. LLC, 1999—. Mem. ABA, N.Y. State Bar Assn., Assn. Bar City of N.Y. Republican. Club: Yale (N.Y.C.). Home: 1488 State Route 203 Chatham NY 12037-1706 Office Phone: 518-392-2426. E-mail: jackweiner@hotmail.com.

WEINER, JEROME HARRIS, mechanical engineering educator; b. NYC, Apr. 5, 1923; s. Barnet and Dora (Muchar) W.; m. Florence Mensch, June 24, 1950; children: Jonathan David, Eric Daniel. B. Mech. Engring., Cooper Union U., 1943; A.M., Columbia U., 1946, PhD, 1952. Mem. faculty Columbia U., NYC, 1952-68, prof. mech. engring., 1960-68, acting chmn. dept., 1961-62; L. Herbert Ballou Univ. prof. Brown U., Providence, 1968-93; L. Herbert Ballou Univ. prof. emeritus, 1993—. Author: (with B.A. Boley) Theory of Thermal Stresses, 1960, Statistical Mechanics of Elasticity, 1983. Fulbright research scholar Rome, Italy, 1958-59, Haifa, Israel, 1965- 66; Guggenheim fellow, 1965-66 Mem. Am. Phys. Soc., Am. Math. Soc., ASME Home: 24 Taber Ave Providence RI 02906-4113 Office: Brown U 79 Waterman St Providence RI 02912-9079 Business E-Mail: jerome_weiner@brown.edu.

WEINER, KAREN COLBY (KAREN LYNN COLBY), psychologist, lawyer; b. Oak Park, Ill., Oct. 28, 1943; d. Leonard L. and Mildred Irene (Berman) Colby; m. J. Laevin Weiner, July 26, 1964; children: Joel Laevin, Doren Robin, Anthony Justin. BA, Mich. State U., East Lansing, 1964; JD, U. Detroit, 1977, MA, 1986, PhD, 1988. Bar: Mich. 1977, D.C. 1978. Speech therapist Oak Park Sch. Dist., 1965-68; law clk. justice G. Mennen Williams Mich. Supreme Ct., Lansing, 1977-79; assoc. Dickinson, Wright, Moon, Van Dusen & Freeman, Detroit, 1979-83; intern in psychology Detroit Psychiat. Inst., 1986-88; psychologist Northland Clinic, Southfield, Mich., 1987-88; postdoctoral intern Wyandotte (Mich.) Hosp. and Health Ctr., 1988-90; psychologist Counseling Assocs., Southfield, 1988—2004, dir. psychol. svcs., quality assurance coord., 1991-99; bd. dirs. Mich. Psychoanalytic Inst. Found., 2004—. Hearing panelist Atty. Discipline Bd., Detroit, 1982-95; hearing referee Mich. Civil Rights Commn., Detroit, 1983-91; mem. Mich. Bd. Psychology, 1999—2007, vice chair, 2004-07; adj. prof. U. Detroit Mercy, 2001-03; adj. prof. Inst. Life Coach Tng., 2004—. Author: The Little Book of Ethics for Coaches, rev. edit., 2007; contbr. articles to profl. jours. Mem. adv. bd. Mich. chpt. Anti-Defamation League, 1981-90. Fellow Mich. Psychol. Assn. (mem. ethics com. 1992-2000, chmn. legis. com. 1993, chmn. ethics com. 1997-99, pres.-elect 2007—); mem. APA, Internat. Coach Fedn. (ethics and stds. com.), Mich. Soc. for Psychoanalytic Psychology (pres. 1995-97, sec. 1991-92, treas. 1992-94), Women Lawyers Assn. Mich. (pres. 1981-82, pres. Found. 1982-83), Mich. Bar Assn. Jewish. Home: 2501 Long Lake Rd West Bloomfield MI 48323 Office: 29260 Franklin Rd Ste 115 Southfield MI 48034-1144 Office Phone: 248-353-1020. Personal E-mail: drkcw@comcast.net.

WEINER, LAWRENCE, lawyer; b. Phila., Aug. 20, 1942; s. Robert A. and Goldie Weiner; m. Jane M. Coulthard, Feb. 28, 1976; 1 child, Kimberly. BS in Econs., U. Pa., 1964, JD, 1967. Bar: Pa. 1967, U.S. Dist. Ct. (ea. dist.) Pa. 1967, Fla. 1970, U.S. Dist. Ct. (so. dist.) Fla. 1976, U.S. Ct. Appeals (5th cir.) 1976, U.S. Tax Ct. 1984. Assoc., ptnr. Blank, Rome, Klaus & Comisky, Phila., 1967-71, 1975-77; ptnr. Weiner & Weisenfeld, P.A., Miami Beach, Fla., 1971-73, Pettigrew & Bailey, Miami, Fla., 1973-75; pres. Lawrence Weiner, P.A., Miami, 1977-83; ptnr. Spieler, Weiner & Spieler, P.A., Miami, 1983-89, Weiner & Cummings, P.A., Miami, 1989-94, Weiner, Cummings & Vittoria, Miami, 1994—. Lectr. Wharton Sch. U. Pa., Phila., 1968-70; instr. bus. law and acctg. Community Coll. Phila., 1967-70; lectr. estate planning various non-lawyer groups, Miami, 1972—. Mem. Fla. Bar (liaison non-lawyers groups 1980-87), Pa. Bar Assn., Phila. Bar Assn., Dade County Bar Assn. (chmn. ins. com. 1977-78, probate law com. 1992-2002). Democrat. Jewish. Office: Weiner Cummings & Vittoria 1428 Brickell Ave Ste 400 Miami FL 33131-3436 Office Phone: 305-371-7800. E-mail: lweiner@wcvlaw.com.

WEINER, LAWRENCE CHARLES, artist; b. Bronx, NY, Feb. 10, 1942; One-man shows include Hirshhorn Mus. and Sculpture Garden, Washington, 1990, San Francisco Mus. Modern Art, 1992, Walker Art Ctr., Mpls., 1994, Städtische Galerie Chemnitz, Germany, 1994, Phila. Mus. Art, 1994, Radio Düsseldorf, Germany, 1994, Leo Castelli Gallery, NY, 1994, NY Pub. libr., 1995, Mus. Ludwig Köln, 1995, Mus. Boijmans Van Beuningen, Rotterdam, 1996, The Lawrence Weiner Poster Archive, Kunsthalle Nüurnberg, 1998, Yvon Lambert Gallery, Paris, 2003, Galleri Susanne Ottesen, Copenhagen, 2003, The Wrong Gallery, 2004, Cristina Guerra Contemp. Art, 2004, Mus. Tamayo Arte Contemp., 2004, Davis Mus. Cult. Ctr., 2004, Mai 36 Gallery, 2004, Yvon Lambert Gallery, 2004, Gallery Rose Marie, 2004, Marian Goodman Gallery NYC, 2005, Regen Projects, LA, 2005, Lisson Gallery, London, 2005, Wolfsonian Mus., Miami, 2006, Nat. Maritime Mus., Greenwich, London, 2007, Parasite Art Space, Hong Kong, 2007, others; exhibited in group shows Mus. Modern Art, NY, 1970, Art Inst. Chgo., 1974, Tate Gallery, London, 1982, Mus. Contemporary Art, LA, 1983, Deutsche Guggenheim, Berlin, 2000, Kunstmuseum Rolfsburg, 2000, Reyjkavik Arts Festival, 2005; represented in permanent collections Mus. Modern Art, N.Y., Guggenheim Mus., NY, Van Abbe Mus., Eindhoven, The Netherlands, Staatliches Mus. Mönchengladbach, Germany, Ctr. Georges Pompidou, Paris, Nat. Gallery Australia, Canberra, others. Recipient Arthur Köpcke prize, Copenhagen, 1991, Wolfgang Hahn prize, 1995, Skowhegan medal for painting, 1999; fellow Nat. Endowment Arts, 1976, 83; John Simon Guggenheim fellow, 1994. Home: 297 W 4th St New York NY 10014-2207

WEINER, LESLIE PHILIP, neurology educator, researcher; b. Bklyn., Mar. 17, 1936; s. Paul Larry and Sarah (Paris) W.; m. Judith Marilyn Hoffman, Dec. 26, 1959; children: Patrice, Allison, Matthew, Jonathan.

BA, Wilkes Coll., 1957; MD, U. Cin., 1961. Diplomate Am. Bd. Psychiatry and Neurology. Intern in medicine SUNY, Syracuse, 1961-62; resident in neurology Johns Hopkins Hosp., Balt., 1962-65, fellow, 1967-69; resident Balt. City Hosp., 1962-63; fellow in virology Slow Virus Lab., Nat. Inst. Neurol and Communicative Disorders-Stroke, NIH, Balt., 1969; asst. prof. neurology Johns Hopkins U., 1969-72, assoc. prof., 1972-75; prof. neurology and microbiology U. So. Calif. Sch. Medicine, LA, 1975—, chmn. dept. neurology, 1979—2003, Richard Angus Grant Sr. chair in neurology, 1987—. Chief neurologist U. So. Calif. Univ. Hosp., 1991-96, mem. bd. govs.; chief neurologist L.A. county-U. So. Calif. Med. Ctr., 1979-94,; chmn. U. So. Calif. Gen. Clin. Res. Ctr., 1994-95; mem. neurosci. tng. study sect. NIH, 1990-93; mem. sci. adv. bd. Hereditary Disease Found., 1992—, chmn., 1994-96; mem. programs rsch. adv. com. Nat. Multiple Sclerosis Soc., 2000—; cons. in field. Editor: Neural Stem Cells Methods and Protocols, 2007; assoc. editor: Neurobase, 1994-95, Neuronet; mem. editl. bd. Infectious and Geographic Neurol., 1994—; contbr. chpts. to books; contbr. over 140 articles to profl. jours. Bd. dirs. Starbright Found., LA, 1991—99. Capt. M.C. US Army, 1965—67. Grantee, Conrad Hilton Found., 1995—97, Kenneth Norris Found., 1995—, NIH, 1999—, Race to Erase MS Nancy Davis Ctrs. Without Walls, 2000—, McDonald Found., Oxnard Found., Gogian Found., Heron Found. Fellow: Am. Acad. Neurology; mem.: AAAS, Nat. MS Soc. (mem. adv. com. rsch. program 2000—, grant 2000—), Coalition Advancement Med. Rsch., Assn. Univ. Profs. Neurology, L.A. Acad. Medicine, Johns Hopkins U. Soc. Scholars, Soc. Neurosci., Am. Neurology Assn., Am. Health Assistance Found., Alpha Omega Alpha. Democrat. Jewish. Avocations: collecting books, concerts, plays. Office: RMR 506 2025 Zonal Ave Los Angeles CA 90089 Home Phone: 323-934-0633; Office Phone: 323-442-3020. Office Fax: 323-442-5500. Business E-Mail: lweiner@usc.edu.

WEINER, MARCIA MYRA, justice of the peace; b. Apr. 12, 1934; BA, St. Mary's U., San Antonio, 1965, JD, 1970. Bar: Tex. 1971. Atty-advisor HUD, San Antonio, 1971—84, chief counsel, 1984—97; elected justice of the peace Precinct 2 Pl., Bexar County, Tex., 2000—. Recipient Spl. Achievement awards, HUD, 1972, 1975, 1977, Hub Fed. Women's Program award, Leigh Curry award, Fed. Women's Program Coun. Mgmt. award, Outstanding Bus. Woman of Yr., 2000. Mem.: Coll. State Bar Tex., San Antonio Bar Assn., Bexar County Women's Bar Assn., Fed. Bar Assn., Tex. Bar Assn., Greyhound Pets of Am., Tex. Wanderers, Randolph Roadrunners, Alamo Unit #2 of Am. Legion Aux. Jewish. Office: Justice Ct Precinct 2 6715 Bandera Rd San Antonio TX 78238 Office Phone: 210-335-4814. E-mail: msweiner@sbcglobal.net.

WEINER, MAX, psychology professor; b. Hartford, Conn., May 7, 1926; s. Harry Sam and Gertrude (Cohen) W.; m. Gloria Sall, Feb. 24, 1960; children: William Ronald, Jennifer Sharon. BA, U. Conn., 1950; MA, Trinity Coll., 1953; PhD, Yale U., 1957. Sci. tchr. Meriden (Conn.) Pub. Schs., 1952-55; guidance dir. White Plains (N.Y.) Pub. Schs., 1956-59; assoc. prof. Bklyn. Coll., CUNY, 1959-68; prof. Grad. Sch. CUNY, 1968-81, acting univ. dean, tchr. edn., 1973-74, exec. officer PhD program edn. psychology, 1970-76, dir. Ctr. for Advanced Study Edn., 1970-78, acting dean rsch. Grad. Sch., 1978-79; dean edn. Fordham U., NYC, 1981-93, prof. ednl. psychology, 1981-97, prof. and dean emeritus, 1997—. Cons. psychologist SUNY Health Sci. Ctr., Bklyn., 1967-89; mem. nat. commn. on excellence in edn. adminstrn. Univ. Coun. for Edn. Adminstrn., 1985-87; mem. nat. adv. commn. Coll. Bd. Equity 2000, 1993-2000. Contbr. articles to profl. jours. Treas. N.Y. Alliance for Pub. Schs., N.Y.C., 1987-93; mem. Mayor's Commn. on Spl. Edn., N.Y.C., 1984-85; bd. dirs. Arthritis Found., Atlanta, 1974-76; trustee Beth El Synagogue, New Rochelle, N.Y., 1985-2001, La Scuola, N.Y., 1986-2003; bd. visitors Scranton U. Sch. Edn., 1992-2002. Fellow, Japan Soc. Promotion Scis., 1978. Fellow APA, Am. Psychol. Soc., N.Y. Acad. Scis.; mem. ACA (life), AAAS, Arthritis Health Professions Assn. (pres. 1974-75), Am. Ednl. Rsch. Assn., Assn. Colls. and Schs. Edn. in State Univs. and Land Grant Colls. and Affiliated Pvt. Univs. (mem. exec. com. 1986-89, 92-93), Assn. for Measurement and Evaluation in Guidance (senator 1966-72, sec. 1973-75), Nat. Coun. Measurement in Edn., Westchester Assn. Hebrew Schs. (pres. 1982-84), Sigma Xi, Phi Delta Kappa, Kappa Delta Pi. Office: Fordham U Grad Sch Edn Neparan Rd Tarrytown NY 10591 Personal E-mail: maxglow22@aol.com.

WEINER, MICHAEL W., neuroscientist, researcher, educator; BA, Johns Hopkins U., Balt., 1961; MD, SUNY Upstate Med. Ctr., Syracuse, 1965. Diplomate in internal medicine and nephrology Am. Bd. Internal Medicine, 1972. Intern, asst. resident medicine Mt. Sinai Hosp., NYC, 1965—67; clin. fellow metabolism Yale-New Haven Med. Ctr., 1967—68; rsch. fellow Yale U. Sch. Medicine, 1968—70, U. Wis. Inst. Enzyme Rsch., Madison, 1970—72, joint appointment renal sect. dept. medicine, 1970—72, asst. prof., 1972—74; rsch. and edn. assoc. VA, 1971—74, clin. investigator, 1974—77; asst. prof. medicine U. Wis. Sch. Medicine, 1971—74, Stanford U. Sch. Medicine, 1974—80; asst. chief artificial kidney ctr. Palo Alto VA Hosp., Calif., 1974—80; chief metabolism svc. VA Hosp., Madison, 1973—74; assoc. prof. medicine in residence U. Calif., San Francisco, 1980—90, assoc. prof. radiology in residence, 1983—90, assoc. staff mem. Cardiovasc. Rsch. Inst., 1988—93, sr. staff mem. Cardiovasc. Rsch. Inst., 1994, prof. medicine, radiology and psychiatry, 1990—, mem. Alzheimer's Ctr. exec. com., 1994; chief hemodialysis unit San Francisco Vets. Affairs Med. Ctr., 1980—83, sci. dir. Magnetic Resonance Unit, 1985—, dir. Ctr. Imaging of Neurodegenerative Diseases, prin. investigator Neuroscience Ctr. Excellence. Mem. magnetic resonance com. Am. Coll. Radiology, 1989—; mem. sci. rev. bd. Alzheimer's Drug Discovery Found. (formerly Inst. for Study of Aging), 2000—; prin. investigator Alzheimer's Disease Neuroimaging Initiative. Contbr. articles to profl. publs., chapters to books; mem. editl. bd.: Nuc. Magnetic Resonance in Biomedicine, 1988—2003. Recipient Young Investigator award, Am. Coll. Cardiology, 1976, William S. Middleton award, Dept. Vets. Affairs, 2006. Fellow: Internat. Soc. Magnetic Resonance in Medicine (chair com. for affiliated sects. - SMRT 1997—98), Am. Coll. Physicians; mem.: AAAS, AAUP, Western Assn. Physicians, NY Acad. Scis., Radiol. Soc. N.Am. (Editor's Recognition award with Spl. Distinction 1993—95), Soc. Magnetic Resonance Imaging, Soc. Magnetic Resonance in Medicine, Internat. Soc. Magnetic Resonance, Internat. Soc. Artificial Organs, Western Soc. Clin. Investigation, Soc. Exptl. Biology and Medicine, Am. Soc. Pharmacology and Exptl. Therapeutics, Am. Soc. Biol. Chemists, Am. Physiol. Soc., Biophysical Soc., Am. Soc. Artificial Internal Organs, Am. Diabetes Assn., Am. Heart Assn. Coun. on Kidney in Cardiovasc. Disease, Internat. Soc. Nephrology, Am. Soc. Nephrology, Am. Fedn. Clin. Rsch., Bay Area Animal Resonance Club (founder), Mid-West Salt and Water Club, Sigma Xi. Achievements include patents in field. Office: VA Med Ctr MRS Unit 114M 4150 Clement St San Francisco CA 94121 Office Phone: 415-750-2146. Office Fax: 415-668-2864. E-mail: michael.weiner@ucsf.edu.

WEINER, PERRIE M., lawyer; b. Beverly Hills, Calif., 1961; BA summa cum laude, UCLA, 1982; JD, Loyola Law Sch., 1985. Bar: Calif. 1988. Judicial extern Judge Ralph J. Geffen, US Dist. Ct. ctrl. dist. Calif., 1985; law clk. Judge John R. Kronenberg, US Dist. Ct. ctrl. dist. Calif., 1986—87; atty. Brobeck, Phleger & Harrison, 1988—2002; mng. ptnr., internat. co-chmn. securities litig. practice group DLA Piper US LLP, LA, 2002—. Conf. spkr. in field. Contbr. articles to profl. jours. in field. Named a So. Calif. Super Lawyer, L.A. mag., 2004—07; named one of Calif. Top Mega-Rainmakers, L.A. Daily Jour., 2004—06, Top 10 Securities Litigators in US, Securities Law 360, 2006; recipient Burton award, 2006. Mem.: LA County Bar Assn., Phi Beta Kappa. Office: DLA Piper US LLP 1999 Ave of the Stars 4th Fl Los Angeles CA 90067-6022 Office Phone: 310-595-3024. Office Fax: 310-595-3324. Business E-Mail: perrie.weiner@dlapiper.com.

WEINER, RICHARD, public relations executive; b. Bklyn., May 10, 1927; s. George M. and Sally (Kosover) W.; m. Florence Chaiken, Dec. 9, 1956; children: Jessica Weiner Lampert, Stephanie Weiner Iosbaker. BS, U. Wis., 1949, MS, 1950. Pres. Creative Radio Assocs., Madison, Wis., 1951-52, Weiner-Morton Assocs., Madison, 1952-53; sr. v.p. Ruder & Finn, Inc., NYC, 1953-68; pres. Richard Weiner, Inc., NYC, 1968-86; pres. N.Y. divsn. Porter/Novelli, NYC, 1987-88, sr. counselor, 1988—. Author: Professional's Guide to Public Relations Services, 1968, News Bureaus in the U.S., 1970, Syndicated Columnists, 1972, Professional's Guide to Publicity, 1979, Military Publications, 1979, College Alumni Publications, 1980, Investment Newsletters, 1981, Webster's New World Dictionary of Media and Communications, 1996, The Skinny About Best Boy: Dollies, Green Rooms, Leads and other Media Lingo, 2006. Bd. dirs. Shake-A-Leg Miami, Fla. Fellow Pub. Rels. Soc. Am. (accredited counselor, Silver Anvil award 1965, 84, 86, 87, John Hill award 1984, Gold Anvil award 1990). Jewish. Office Phone: 305-865-3262. E-mail: rweiner522@aol.com. *The essence of life is growth, adaptation, change. I hope to continue to succeed in living vigorously.*

WEINER, RICHARD DAVID, psychiatrist, researcher; b. NYC, Nov. 25, 1945; BS, MIT, 1967; M of Systems Engring., U. Pa., 1969; MD, PhD, Duke U., 1973. Diplomate Am. Bd. Psychiatry and Neurology. Prof. psychiatry Duke U. Med. Ctr., Durham, NC, 1997—, dir. electroconvulsive therapy program, 1991—; chief, mental health svc. line VA Med. Ctr., Durham, 1993—. Office: Duke U Med Ctr PO Box 3309 Durham NC 27702-3309

WEINER, ROBERT NEIL, lawyer; b. San Antonio, May 20, 1952; s. Arthur and Sheila (Freedman) W.; m. Cheryl Toubin, May 29, 1977; children: Courtney, Lindsay. AB summa cum laude, Princeton U., 1974; JD, Yale U., 1977. Bar: D.C. 1979, U.S. Supreme Ct. 1983, N.Y. 1993. Law clk. to Hon. Henry J. Friendly US Ct. Appeals (2nd Cir.), 1977—78; law clk. to Justice Thurgood Marshall US Supreme Ct., Washington, 1978—79; from assoc. to ptnr. Arnold & Porter LLP, Washington, 1979—97, ptnr., chair bus. litig. practice group, 1998—; sr. counsel to Pres. The White House, Washington, 1997—98. Adj. prof. Georgetown U. Law Ctr., Washington, 1984-86; lectr. Univ. Va. Law Sch., 1994; assoc. ind. counsel, 1987; chmn. hearing com. D.C. Bd. Profl. Responsibility. Recipient Servant of Justice award, Legal Aid Soc., William Reece Smith Jr. award, Nat. Assn. Pro Bono Profls. Mem. ABA, DC Bar Assn. (co-chmn. ct., lawyers and adminstrn. of justice 1987-90, chmn. coun. on sects. 1989-90, bd. govs. 1990-92, gen. counsel 1992-94, pres 1995-96, bd. dir. product liability adv. coun., 2005), Am. Law Inst., Lawyers' Commn. on Civil Rights (bd. dir.), Am Bar Found., DC Bar Found. (pres.), Phi Beta Kappa. Home: 4248 50th St Washington DC 20016 Office: Arnold & Porter 555 12th St NW Washington DC 20004-1206 Office Phone: 202-942-5855. Office Fax: 202-942-5999. Business E-Mail: robert.weiner@aporter.com.

WEINER, ROBERT STEPHEN, federal agency administrator; b. Paterson, NJ, Apr. 3, 1947; s. Jess Joseph Weiner and Dorothea Violet (Slavin) Tabor. BA, Oberlin Coll., Ohio, 1969; MA, U. Mass., 1974. Student coord. Hampshire County, dir. telephone bank Kennedy for U.S. Senate, Amherst, Mass., 1970; dir. nat. voter registration Young Dems. Am., Washington, 1971-72; dir. voter registration, media dir. get out the vote Dem. Nat. Com., Washington, 1972; legis. asst. Congressman Edward Koch, Washington, 1974-75; staff dir. subcom. health and long-term care US Ho. of Reps., Washington, 1975-76, staff dir. com. aging, 1976-80; sr. assoc. Mgmt. Recruiters Internat., Springfield, Mass., 1981-83; dir. Robert Weiner Assocs., Amherst, 1983-86; media dir., press sec. com. narcotics US Ho. of Reps., Washington, 1987-90, press sec./comms. dir. com. on govt. ops., 1990-95; dir. comm. Ho. Judiciary com. Minority and Cong. John Conyers Jr., 1995; dir. pub. affairs White House Drug Policy Office, Washington, 1995—2002; pres. Robert Weiner Assocs., Pub. Affairs and Issues, 2002—. Dir. gen. press rm. Dem. Nat. Conv., Atlanta, 1988, NYC, 1992, Chgo., 1996, LA, 2000, Boston, 2004; cons. Carter-Mondale Transition, Washington, 1976-77, Congressman Claude Pepper, Washington, 1975-89. Represented in permanent exhbns. Nat. Mus. Am. History, Smithsonian Instn., Washington; contbr. numerous articles to profl. jours. Dem. nominee for US Congress, Mass., 1986; chmn. Road Runners Am. Nat. 10 Mile Championship, Amherst, 1984; vice chmn. Dem. Town Com., Amherst, 1984-87; legis. chmn. Pioneer Valley Gray Panthers, Amherst, 1981-87; nat campaign aide Kennedy for Pres., Washington, 1980. Named Communicator of Yr., Washington Crime News Svcs., 1988, 89, 90; 2d place US Nat. Masters Track Championship, 1994, 97, 2003, 04, 06. Mem. Nat. Dem. Club (bd. govs. 2002—), Sugarloaf Mountain Athletic Club (pres. 1984-86), White House Athletic Ctr. (exec. bd. 1995-2001), Potomac Valley Track Club, Capitol Hill Runners (pres. 1991—). Avocations: running, attending performing arts, hiking. Home: 1104 Sanford Ln Accokeek MD 20607-2324 Office: PO Box 28271 1750 Pennsylvania Ave NW Washington DC 20038-8271 Office Phone: 202-329-1700.

WEINER, SAMUEL, lawyer; b. Phila., Feb. 2, 1955; s. Paul David Weiner and Evelyn Ruth Monash; m. Sondra A. Petteruti, Aug. 20, 1983; children: Evonne, Alexis, Nikki. BS, U. Vt., 1977; JD, Vt. Law Sch., 1980; LLM in Taxation, Boston U. Sch. Law, 1981. Bar: Mass. 1980, NJ 1982, US Dist. Ct. (dist. NJ) 1982, US Tax Ct. 1982. Tax cons. Price Waterhouse, Boston, 1981-83; atty. Klein Chapman, Clifton, NJ, 1983-84; atty. to co-mng. shareholder Cole, Schotz, Meisel, Forman & Leonard, P.C., Hackensack, NJ, 1984—. Author: Starting a Limited Liability Company, 1995; contbr. articles to profl. jours. Bd. trustees Tomorrow's Children Fund, Hackensack, 1993—. Named one of Top 100 Attys., Worth mag., 2006. Mem. ABA, NJ State Bar Assn., Passaic County Bar Assn. Avocations: triathons, running, skiing, travel, reading. Office: Cole Schotz Meisel Forman & Leonard PC Court Plz N 25 Main St Hackensack NJ 07601 Office Phone: 201-525-6260. Office Fax: 201-678-6260. E-mail: sweiner@coleschotz.com. *

WEINER, SANDRA SAMUEL, critical care nurse, consultant; b. NYC, Jan. 12, 1947; d. Herbert A. and Ruth (Wallerstein) Samuel; m. Neil D. Weiner, June 15, 1969 (div. June 1980); 1 child, Jaime Michelle. BS in Nursing, SUNY, Buffalo, 1968; cert. in critical care, Golden West Coll., 1982; postgrad., UCLA, U. West L.A. Sch. Law, 1992—95. RN, Pa., Calif. Staff nurse N.Y. Hosp.-Cornell Med. Ctr., 1968-69; head nurse med.-surg. nursing Abington (Pa.) Hosp., 1969; assoc. prof. Sch. Nursing, U. Pa., Phila., 1970; instr. nursing Coll. Med. Assts., Long Beach, Calif., 1971-72; surg. staff nurse Med. Ctr. of Tarzana, Calif., 1978-79, Cedars-Sinai Med. Ctr., LA, 1979-81; supr. recovery rm. Beverly Hills Med. Ctr., LA, 1981-92; post anesthesia care unit nurse Westside Hosp., 1992-96, Midway Hosp., Beverly Hills, Calif., 1996-99, Encino (Calif.) - Tarzana Med. Ctr., 1996—, Four Seasons Surgery Ctr., 2001—. Med. cons. RJA & Assocs., Beverly Hills, Calif., 1984-92; instr. CPR, L.A., 1986-95. Mem. women's aux. Ctr. Theater Group Vols., L.A., 1986-94, Maple Ctr., Beverly Hills, 1987-96. Mem. ANA, Am. Soc. Post-Anesthesia Nursing, Am. Assn. Critical Care Nurses, Heart and Lung Assn., Post Anesthesia Nurses Assn., U.S. Ski Assn. Democrat. Jewish. Avocations: skiing, aerobics, travel, theater, ballet. Home: 12633 Moorpark St Studio City CA 91604-4537 Office Phone: 818-793-2050.

WEINER, SANFORD ALAN, lawyer; b. Houston, Aug. 21, 1946; s. Abe I. and Zelda C. (Caplan) Weiner; m. Leslie Eve Grenadier, Aug. 16, 1970; children: Edward, David, Evan, Rebecca. BA, U. Tex., 1968; JD, Harvard U., 1971. Bar: Tex. 1971. Ptnr. Vinson & Elkins, Ltd. Liability Partnership, Houston, 1971—. Pres. Am. Coll. Real Estate Lawyers, 2003. Mem. Houston Bar Assn., Tex. Bar Assn., Houston Real Estate Lawyers Council, Anglo-Am. Real Property Inst. Jewish. Office: Vinson & Elkins LLP 1001 Fannin St Ste 2500 Houston TX 77002-6760 Office Phone: 713-758-2558. Business E-Mail: sweiner@velaw.com.

WEINER, STEPHEN ARTHUR, lawyer; b. Bklyn., Nov. 20, 1933; s. Joseph Lee W. and Ruth Lessall (Weiner); m. Mina Rieur, Sept. 1, 1958; children: Karen, James. BA summa cum laude, Harvard U., 1954; JD cum laude, Yale U., 1957. Bar: N.Y. 1958, U.S. Supreme Ct. 1963. Assoc. Winthrop, Stimson, Putnam & Roberts, NYC, 1958-65, ptnr., 1968—2000, vice chmn. mgmt. com., 1984-97; acting prof. law U. Calif., Berkeley, 1965-68; ptnr. Pillsbury Winthrop LLP, NYC, 2001, sr. counsel, 2002—04, Pillsbury Winthrop Shaw Pittman LLP, NYC, 2005—. Arbitrator NASD Dispute Resolution, 2002—; mem. com. on character and fitness 1st dept. appellate divsn. N.Y. Supreme Ct., 1998—, spl. master, 1999—; mem. N.Y. State Jud. Inst. on Professionalism in the Law, 1999—; adj. prof. law Bklyn. Law Sch., 2003—. Contbr. articles to legal publs.; comment editor Yale Law Jour., 1956—57. Fellow Am. Coll. Trial Lawyers, Am. Bar Found., N.Y. Bar Found.; mem. Assn. of Bar of City of N.Y. (chmn. recruitment of lawyers com., chmn. com. on Stimson medal), Fed. Bar Coun. (chmn. com. on 2d cir. cts., trustee), Order of Coif, Phi Beta Kappa. Home: 190 Harbor Rd Sands Point NY 11050-2636 Office: Pillsbury Winthrop Shaw Pittman LLP 1540 Broadway New York NY 10036 Office Phone: 212-858-1749. Business E-Mail: stephen.weiner@pillsburylaw.com.

WEINER, STEPHEN FRANCIS, academic administrator, communications educator; b. Bklyn., June 22, 1955; s. Martin Joseph and Phyllis (Barrett) W.; m. Mary Thelma Lanier, June 5, 1982; children: Sarah Jane, Abraham Joshua. BA, Gallaudet U., 1978, MA, 1980; EdD, Am. U., 1992. Asst. to dean Gallaudet U., Washington, 1982-84; coord. student life and tng. Tex. Sch. for the Deaf, Austin, 1984-87; dep. dir. NorCal Ctr. on Deafness, Sacramento, 1987-89; dir. The Career Ctr. Gallaudet U., Washington, 1990-93, exec. dir. student devel., 1993-94, dean Sch. Undergrad. Studies, 1995—2001, asst. prof., 1995—2001, assoc. prof. Dept. Comm. Studies, 2001—, provost, 2007—. Commr. Calif. Atty. Gen. Commn. on Disability, Sacramento, 1988-90; bd. mem., adv. bd. Md. Rehab. Dept., Balt., 1993-94; bd. dirs. Camp Mark Seven, Old Forge, N.Y.; spkr. in field. Recipient Cmty. Svc. award Sacramento (Calif.) Deaf Citizens, 1989. Mem. ACA, Nat. Assn. Sch. Pers. Adminstrs., Md. Assn. of the Deaf. Avocations: radio controlled model airplane, boats and cars. Office: Gallaudet Univ 800 Florida Ave NE Washington DC 20002-3660 Office Phone: 202-651-5755. E-mail: Stephen.Weiner@gallaudet.edu. *

WEINER, STEPHEN MARK, lawyer; b. Boston, Mar. 20, 1943; s. Meyer and Esther (Lowenstein) W.; m. Roslyn G. Weiner, Dec. 19, 1967 (div. 1992); children: Jeremiah, Ben, Miriam, Isaac. AB magna cum laude, Harvard U., 1964; LLB, Yale U., 1968. Bar: Mass. 1968. Teaching fellow Boston Coll. Law Sch., Chestnut Hill, Mass., 1968-69; assoc. Goodwin, Proctor & Hoar, Boston, 1969-71; spl. asst. to Gov. Francis W. Sargent Commonwealth of Mass., Boston, 1971-74; chmn. Mass. Rate Setting Commn., Boston, 1972-78; assoc. prof. Boston U. Sch. Law, 1978-81, adj. prof. law, 1993—94, dir. Ctr. for Law and Health Scis.; adj. prof. law Yale Law Sch., 1994—95, Suffolk U. Sch. Law, 1997—; mem. Goulston & Storrs, Boston, 1981-90, Mintz, Levin, Cohn, Ferris, Glovsky and Popeo, PC, Boston, 1990—, ptnr., chmn., health law practice. Mem. editl. bd. New Eng. Jour. Human Svcs., 1979-81; adv. bd. Hosp. Risk Mgmt., 1979-83; contbr. articles to profl. jours. Legal adv. com. AIDS Action Com., Washington; dir., treas. AIDS Action Com., Mass., 1989—97; bd. dirs. GLAD, Inc., 1999—2000, Boston Film Video Found., 1986—2003; del. Mass. Easter Seal Soc.; trustee Beth Israel Hosp., Boston, 1979—95, Spaulding Rehab. Hosp., Boston, 1979—95, Corp. Ptnrs. Healthcare Sys., Inc., Boston, 1994—2001, Boston Ballet, dir., 2000—, treas., 2001—05; overseer Boston Lyric Opera, 2000—04; dir. New Eng. Conservatory Lab. Charter Sch. Found.; trustee Huntington Theater Co., Boston; pres. HealthWell Found., 2003; mem. govt. task force to evaluate Mass. Determination of Need Program, 1979—80; profl. adv. coun. Mass. Dept. Elder Affairs, 1979—81; Mass. atty. gen. Mass. Adv. Com. on Health Care and Tobacco Control. Mem.: Mass. Bar Assn., Nat. Health Lawyers Assn., ABA, Boston Bar Assn., Phi Beta Kappa. Office: Mintz Levin Cohn Ferris Glovsky and Popeo PC 1 Financial Ctr Boston MA 02111-2657 Home Phone: 508-660-7640; Office Phone: 617-348-1757. Office Fax: 617-542-2241. Business E-Mail: sweiner@mintz.com.

WEINER, WALTER HERMAN, bank executive, lawyer; b. Bklyn., Aug. 29, 1930; s. Harry and Sylvia (Freifeld) W.; m. Nina Ester Avidar, Oct. 11, 1966; children: Thomas Field, Jon Michael. BA, U. Mich., 1952, JD, 1953. Bar: N.Y. 1953. Sr. ptnr. Kronish, Lieb, Weiner & Hellman, NYC, 1965-79; chmn. exec. com., CEO Republic N.Y. Corp., 1980-81, pres., CEO, 1981-83, chmn. bd., CEO, 1983—; chmn. exec. com., CEO Republic Nat. Bank of N.Y., 1980-82, pres., CEO, 1981-86, chmn. bd., CEO, 1986-99, also bd. dirs.; pres. WHW Mgmt. Corp., NYC. Bd. dirs. Republic N.Y. Corp., Republic Nat. Bank of N.Y. Assoc. editor U. Mich. Law Rev. Bd. dirs. Interant. Sephardic Edn. Found.; mem. N.Y. Holocaust Meml. Commn.; bd. visitors U. Mich. Law Sch. Recipient Humanitarian award NAACP, 1987, Human Rels. award Accts., Bankers, Factors and Fin. divsn. Am. Jewish Com., 1988, Man of Yr. award Bklyn. Sch. for Spl. Children, 1988, Good Scout award Greater N.Y. Couns./Boy Scouts Am., 1994, Jewish Theol. Sem.'s Louis Marshall award, 1994, numerous others. Mem. ABA, N.Y. State Bar Assn., Assn. of Bar of City of N.Y. Office: WHW Management Corp Ste 1401 477 Madison Ave New York NY 10022-5836

WEINER, WENDY L(OU), elementary school educator, writer; b. Milw., Jan. 2, 1961; d. Kenneth J. and Jessie M. Weiner. AA, U. Wis. Washington County, West Bend; BS, MS, U. Wis., U. Wis., Milw., 1993; prin. lic., Marian Coll. Cert. nat. cert. early childhood edn. Nat. Bd. Profl. Tchg. Standards, tchr. Wis. Tchr. Milw. Pub. Schs. Contbr. articles to profl. jours. Mem. Milw. Pub. Mus. Tchr. Adv. Coun., TV and Tech. Com., Vision and Tech. Com., Learning Mag.'s Student Best Adv. Coun. Recipient Presdl. Award in Sci. Tchg. Excellence, AT&T Recognition in Sci. Tchg. Excellence, Wis. Aerospace Educator of Yr., Milw. Tchr. of Yr., Grad. Last Decade award U. Wis. Milw. Alumni Assn., Warner Cable-Tchg. Creativity with Cable award, Excellence in Sci. Tchg. award. Wis. Elem. Sci. Tchrs. Assn., Nat. Urban Tech. in Edn. award Coun. Great City Schs., Sen. Herb Kohl Tchr. Achievement award, Ameritech-Wis. Bell Gold Tchr. Recognition award, Presdl. award for elem. sci. tchg. excellence; grantee Greater Mil. Edn. Trust, Wis. Space Grant Consortium/NASA, NSF. Mem. PTA, Wis. Aerospace Edn. Assn. (instr. mag. adviser, Sam's Club Tchr. of Yr.), YMCA-Young Astronauts, Nat. Arbor Day Assn., NSTA, Wis. Elem. Tchrs. Assn., Milw. Kindergarten Assn., Wis. Secondary Sci. Assn., Wis. Assn. Sch. Adminstrs., Milw. Reading Assn., Midwest Devel. Corp., Assn. Presdl. Awardees in Sci., Soc. for Elem. Presdl. Awardees, Coun. Elem. Sci. Internat., Civil Air Patrol (sr. officer). Avocations: crafts, walking. Office: Parkview Sch 10825 W Villard Milwaukee WI 53225 Personal E-mail: wlw23@prodigy.net.

WEINFURTER, DANIEL JOSEPH, business services executive; b. Milw., Apr. 16, 1957; s. Joseph Thomas and Betty E. (Stanton) W.; m. Martha Marie Brennan, May 14, 1983; children: Amy Jordan, Andrea Taylor. BSBA, Marquette U., Milw., 1979, MBA, 1984; postgrad., George Wash. U., Washington, DC, 1984-85. Account rep. Gen. Electric Info. Svcs., Milw., 1979-81, sr. account rep., 1982-84, project mgr. Rockville, Md., 1984-86; acting regional sales mgr. Gen. Electric Corp., Morristown,

N.J., 1986, dist. sales mgr. Bensonville, Ill., 1986-87; regional sales mgr. Intelogic Trace, Inc., Schaumburg, Ill., 1987-89, area sales mgr., 1989; dir. bus. devel. Alternative Resources Corp., Lincolnshire, Ill., 1989-90, v.p. ops., 1990-93; pres. Alternative Resources Corp. Ventures, Lincolnshire, Ill., 1993—; CEO and founder Parson Group, Chgo., 1995—2002; CEO Capital H Group, Chgo., 2003—. Ad-hoc com. Riverwoods (Ill.) Village Coun., 1990—; mem. YMCA. Named number 1 of INC 500, INC Mag., 2000. Democrat. Avocations: running, raquetball, bicycling, golf, reading. Office: Capital H Group 225 W Washington St Chicago IL 60606 Home: 123 W Delaware Pl Chicago IL 60610

WEINGAND, DARLENE ERNA, librarian, educator; b. Oak Park, Ill., Aug. 13, 1937; d. Edward Emil and Erna (Heidenway) W.,; m. Wayne Anthony Weston, Sept. 7, 1957 (div. June 1976); children: Kathleen Mary, Lynda Anne, Judith Diane, Barbara Jeanne; m. James Elberling, May 1977 (div. 1980); m. Roger Paul Couture, Apr. 7, 1984. BA in History and English, Elmhurst Coll., 1972; MALS, Rosary Coll., 1973; PhD in Adult Edn./Libr. Sci., U. Minn., 1980. Asst. prof. U. Wis., Madison, 1981-86, assoc. prof., 1986-92, prof., 1992-99, prof. emerita, 1999—, SLIS acting dir., 1991, summer 86, SLIS asst. dir., 1990-94, adminstr. SLIS Continuing Edn. Svcs., 1981-99; adj. prof. and mem. affiliate grad. faculty. U. Hawaii Manoa, Manoa, 1999—2006. Cons. in mktg., continuing edn., libr. futures, info. issues, and mgmt., 1980—; invited mentor Snowbird Leadership Inst., 1990, 92; vis. fellow Curtin U. Tech. Perth, Australia, 1990; Fulbright lectr. U. Iceland, 1988; lectr. 2d World Conf. on Continuing Edn. for Libr. and Info. Sci., Barcelona, 1993, Internat. Fedn. Libr. Assn. Author: Customer Svc. Excellence: A Concise Guide for Librarians, 1997, Future Driven Library Marketing, 1998, Marketing/Planning Library and Information Services, 1999, 4th edit., 2001, Administration of the Small Public Library, 4th edit., 2001, Budgeting and the political Process in Libraries, Simulation Games, 1992 (with others), Connections: Literacy and Cultural Heritage: Lessons from Iceland, 1992, Managing Today's Public Library: Blueprint for Change, 1994, author (with others) Continuing Professional Education and Internat. Fed. of Libr. Assoc.: Past, Present, and a Vision for the Future, 1992; contbr. articles to profl. jours. Recipient excellence award Nat. Univ. Continuing Edn. Assn., 1989, Econ. and Cmty. Devel. award, 1989, outanding achievement in audio applications award Internat. Teleconferencing Assn., 1991, LITA/Libr. Hi-Tech award, 1996, disting. alumna award Dominican U., 1998; Russia project fellow Assn. Libr. and Info. Sci., 1994. Mem. ALA, AAUW, Wis. Assn. for Adult and Continuing Edn. Personal E-mail: weingand@lava.net.

WEINGART, ROBERT PAUL, financial consultant; b. East Orange, NJ, Oct. 3, 1937; s. Paul Edward and Loretta Madeline (Heagney) W.; m. Susan Beresford Lyman, July 22, 1967 (div.); children: Nicole, Melinda, Deborah, Lindsey. BA in Sci., U. Notre Dame, 1959, BSME, 1960; MBA, U. Mich., 1970. Lic. securities rep.; cert. investment specialist; registered fin. planner, fin. cons. Sales engr. New Departure Hyatt (Divsn. GMC), Sandusky, Ohio, 1960-70; dist. mgr. Xerox Corp., Pasadena, Calif., 1970-73; fin. cons. Troy, Mich., 1973—. Chmn. U.S. Navy Recruiting Dist. Assistance Coun. for State of Mich. Contbr. articles to profl. jours. Chmn. St. Alan's Parish Coun., Troy, Mich., 1997-98; precinct del., candidate Mich. Rep. Party, Troy. Comdr. USNR, 1962-94. Mem. USN Inst., Assn. Naval Aviation, Internat. Assn. Fin. Planning, Internat. Assn. Registered Fin. Cons., Knight Sovereign Mil. Order of Temple of Jerusalem. Republican. Roman Catholic. Avocations: golf, reading. Home: 2020 Somerset Blvd Apt 106 Troy MI 48084-3902 Office: Ste 201A 2820 W Maple Rd Troy MI 48084 Office Phone: 248-614-2700.

WEINGART, S. LEN, foundation administrator; s. Max Joseph Weingart and Rose Gertrude Weigart; m. Roberta J. Doyne, Jan. 28, 1963; 1 child. BA, NYU, NYC, 1953; MA, U. Miami, Fla., 1956; PhD, U. Calif., Davis, 1964. Tchg. asst. U. Miami, 1953—56; editl. asst. Oxford Encyclopaedia, NYC, 1956—57; English instr. La. State U., Baton Route, 1957—59, U. Minn., Mpls., 1959—61; fellow in English U. Calif., Davis, 1961—64; prof. English Fla. State U., Tallahassee, 1964—71; fellow psychol. Yale U., New Haven, 1971—73; dir. Elem. Shakespeare Found., Ft. Pierce, Fla., 1998—. Cons. Fox Sporting Goods, Miami, 1973—2000; comm. specialist Philip Morris Cos., NYC, 1976—78; spl. cons. St. Lucie County Sch. Dist., Fla. Author: (poetry chapbook) Seasons in Connecticut, 1979 (Art Found. award, 1979). With US Army, 1952—53. Mem.: ACLU, Nat. Coun. Tchrs. English. Republican. Avocation: tennis. Office: Elem Shakespeare 288 Kingfisher Ave Ste A Fort Pierce FL 34982

WEINGARTEN, JOSEPH LEONARD, aerospace engineer; b. NYC, June 5, 1944; s. Herman H. and Irene Jane (Binzer); m. Cindy L. Carter; 1 child, Toby stepchildren: Mark Carter, Jill Supancik. B Mech. Engring., NYU, 1966; postgrad., Air War Coll., 1976. Chief engr. Air Transportability Test Loading Agy. Wright-Patterson AFB, Wright-Patterson AFB, Ohio, 1972-74; project engr. dept. engring. USAF, Wright-Patterson AFB, 1966-72, sr. project engr. dept. engring., 1974-76, planning and project engr. dept. engring., 1976-81, chief mgmt. ops. dept. engring., 1981-83, sr. tech. planner dept. engring., 1983-92; tech. asst. DCS Engring. and Tech. Mgmt. Air Force Material Command, Wright-Patterson AFB, 1992-93; founder, CEO Huffman Wright Inst., 1993-98; cons. Main Net Inc., Urbana, Ohio, 1997—2002; exec. dir. MAC Reseller Assn., 2002—; pres. Weingarten & Winburn, LLC, Inc., 2005—. CEO Weingarten Gallery, Dayton, Ohio, 1967—; pres., v.p., sec., treas., bd. dirs. Ohio Designer Craftsmen, Columbus; sec. Ohio Designer Craftsmen Enterprise, Columbus, 1982-90; chmn. continuing edn. design dept. Affiliate Socs. Coun., Dayton, 1971-74, chmn. edn. coord. com. Kettering Inst., Wright State U., 1974-76, chmn. scientist and engr. awards panel, 1990-91, mem., 1992-94; cons. Gerson Lehrman Group, 2005-; scholar adv. Gerson Lehrman Group, 2006; bd. dirs. Geist United Opposition NW, 2006. Contbr. articles on systems engring. to Aeronautical Sys. divsn. Mech. Engring. Jour. (1st place award nat. contest 1970), Procs. 4th Intersoc. Conf. on Transp., Air Force Sys. Command, USAF Spl. Purpose Report, Gems and Minerals, Friends Jour. USAF Mus., Ceramics Monthly, The Crafts Report, Macintosh Software. Scoutmaster Troop 81, Boy Scouts Am., Kettering, Ohio, 1985—91, com. mem., 1991—93, dist. chmn. Wright Bros. Dist., 2000—04, dist. chmn. Sequoia Dist. Miami Valley Coun., 1991—93, asst. coun. commr., 1993—2000, exec. bd. Miami Valley Coun., 2004—; pres. Friends of Montessori Sch., South Dayton, Ohio, 1978—94. Capt. USAF, 1967—71. Recipient Disting. Eagle award Boy Scouts Am., 1992, Silver Beaver award Boy Scouts Am., 1995, Pinnacle award Eastern Region Microage, Inc., 1999; named as one of 5 bus. execs. of yr. Miami Valley Bus. Advisor/Cox Pub., 1998; decorated with Meritous Civilian Svc. award, US Govt., 1973. Mem. AIAA (sr. mem., air transport systems tech. com. 1976-78, 80-82, Lawrence Sperry award 1977), ASME (sr. mem.), Am. Nat. Standards Inst. (materials handling 5 com. 1968-70), Soc. Automotive Engrs. (aircraft ground support equiment com. 1969-75). Achievements include 11 patents for expendable air cargo pallet, mail container, collapsible air cargo container, process for reinforcing extruded articles, process for large scale extrusions, air flotation cargo handling system, integral aircraft barrier net, load distributive cargo platform, laminated plastic packaging material, computer printer paper support, and investment casting mold base; development of 3g cargo restraint criteria used on aircraft/spacecraft/shuttles, rope extraction system for C-5A, system for large scale structural plastics extruxions, advanced planning documents for Air Force, report in new type of DOD procurement system; holds Department of Defense authorization for manufacture of military insignia. Personal E-mail: mrmac@aol.com.

WEINGARTEN, MARC, lawyer; b. Phila., Mar. 24, 1950; BS, U. Pa., 1971; JD, Georgetown U., 1974. Bar: NY 1975. Ptnr., corp. dept. Schultz Roth & Zabel LLP, NYC, mem. exec. com. Case & notes editor Georgetown Law Rev., 1973—74. Named a Dealmaker of Yr., Am. Lawyer mag., 2007. Mem.: Assn. of Bar of City of NY (corp. law com. 1984—87, 1989—92, spl. com. on mergers, acquisitions and corp. control contests 1995—2001), ABA (Bus Law Sect, com. on long range issues affecting bus. law practice 1991—95), NY State Bar Assn. Office: Schulte Roth & Zabel LLP 919 Third Ave New York NY 10022-3902 Office Phone: 212-756-2280. Office Fax: 212-593-5955. Business E-Mail: marc.weingarten@srz.com. *

WEINGARTEN, RANDI (RHONDA), labor union administrator, lawyer; b. NYC, Dec. 18, 1957; d. Gabriel and Edith (Appelbaum) W. BS, Cornell U., 1980; JD cum laude, Benjamin N. Cardozo Sch. Law, 1983. Bar: N.Y. 1984, U.S. Dist. Ct. (so. and ea. dists.) N.Y. 1984. Legis. asst. Labor Com. N.Y. State Senate, Albany, 1979-80; assoc. Stroock, Stroock and Lavan, NYC, 1983-86; counsel to pres. United Fedn. Tchrs., NYC, 1986—98; tchr. Clara Barton HS, Brooklyn, 1991—97; asst. sec. United Fedn. Teachers, NYC, 1995, treas., 1997, pres., 1998—; v.p. Am. Fedn. Teachers. Bd. dirs. N.Y. State United Teachers; adj. instr. Cardozo Sch. Law, N.Y.C., 1986; mem. Mayor Bloomberg's transition com., N.Y.C., 2001. Mediator Bklyn. Mediation Ctr. Victim Services Agy., 1981-82 (outstanding achievement award, 1981); mem. N.Y. Com. Safety and Health, 1986, Park Slope Safe Homes Project, 1984—, Dem. Nat. Com.; bd. dirs. Justice Resource Ctr., Coun. for Unity, N.Y. Com. on Occupational Safety and Health, N.Y. Region Anti-Defamation League, United Way Greater N.Y., Internat. Rescue Com. Named one of NY Influentials, NY Mag., 2006. Mem. ABA (labor and employment sect.), N.Y. State Bar Assn., Women's Bar Assn., Council N.Y. Law Assocs., Cardozo Sch. Law Alumni Assn. (treas., bd. dirs. 1983—). Democrat. Jewish. Avocations: gardening, running, music, theater. Office: United Fedn Tchrs 52 Broadway New York NY 10004 *

WEINGARTEN, REID H., lawyer; b. Newark, Mar. 9, 1950; divorced; 1 child, Ross. BS, Cornell U., 1971; cert., Hague Acad. Internat. Law, The Netherlands, 1974; JD, Dickinson Law Sch., 1975. Bar: Pa. 1975, DC 1981, US Ct. Appeals (4th, 5th, 11th, and DC cirs.) 1981. Dep. dist. atty. Dauphin County, Harrisburg, Pa., 1975-77; trial atty. Pub. Integrity Sect. US Dept. Justice, Washington, 1977-87; ptnr., head white collar def. group. Steptoe & Johnson LLP, Washington, 1987—. Instr. FBI, Washington, 1978—; assoc. ind. counsel, Iran Contra Affair, 1988; spl. prosecutor, US Atty.'s Office (dist. Alaska), 1988; spl. counsel to the Senate fgn. rels. com. subcommittee on Near Eastern and South Asian Affairs, October Surprise Investigation, 1992; adj. prof. law, Georgetown U. Law Ctr. Co-founder, bd. dirs. See Forever Found., 1995—, chair, 1997—2003. Named one of 75 Best Lawyers in Washington, Washingtonian survey mag., 2002, 100 Most Influential Lawyers, Nat. Law Jour., 2006, The Nation's Top Litigators, 2007. Fellow Am. Coll. Trial Lawyers; mem. ABA (mem. coun. criminal justice sect. 1996-97, chair white collar crime com. 1992-94), Fed. Bar Assn. (Young Fed. Lawyer Award 1984), DC Bar Assn. Office: Steptoe & Johnson LLP 1330 Connecticut Ave NW Washington DC 20036 Office Phone: 202-429-6238. Office Fax: 202-429-3902. E-mail: rweingarten@steptoe.com. *

WEINGARTNER, H(ANS) MARTIN, finance educator; b. Heidelberg, Germany, Apr. 4, 1929; came to U.S., 1939, naturalized, 1944; s. Jacob and Grete Weingartner; m. Joyce Trellis, June 12, 1955; children— Steven M., Susan C. De La Paz, Eric H., Kenneth L. AB, SB, U. Chgo., 1950, AM, 1951; MS, Carnegie Mellon U., 1956, PhD, 1962. Economist Dept. Commerce, 1951—53; instr. Grad. Sch. Indsl. Adminstrn., Carnegie Mellon U., 1956—57; instr., then asst. prof. Grad. Sch. Bus., U. Chgo., 1957—63; assoc. prof. fin. Alfred P. Sloan Sch. Mgmt., Mass. Inst. Tech., 1963—66; prof. Grad. Sch. Mgmt., U. Rochester, NYC, 1966—77, Brownlee O. Currey prof. fin. Owen Grad. Sch. Mgmt., Vanderbilt U., Nashville, 1977—98, Brownlee O. Currey Prof. of Fin., emeritus, 1998—; dir. Computer Consoles, Inc., 1974—89. Cons. to industry. Author: Mathematical Programming and the Analysis of Capital Budgeting Problems, 3d edit, 1974, (with George Benston and Dan Horsky) An Empirical Study of Mortgage Redlining, 1978; also articles.; Deptl. editor: Mgmt. Sci, 1967-73. Served with AUS, 1953-54. Mellon fellow, 1954-55; Ford Found. fellow, 1955-56, recipient first prize Dissertation Competition, 1963. Fellow: Inst. for Ops. Rsch. and the Mgmt. Scis.; mem.: Coun. Sci. Soc. Pres. (alumni mem.), Inst. Mgmt. Scis. (v.p. fin. 1978—84, pres. 1985—86), Harbor Island Yacht Club (bd. mem. 2005—), Beta Gamma Sigma. Home: 1616 Ash Valley Dr Nashville TN 37215-4202 Office: Vanderbilt U Owen Grad Sch Mgmt 401 21st Ave S Nashville TN 37203

WEINGARTNER, RUDOLPH HERBERT, philosophy educator; b. Heidelberg, Germany, Feb. 12, 1927; came to U.S., 1939, naturalized, 1944; s. Jacob and Grete (Kahn) W.; m. Fannia Goldberg-Rudkowski, Dec. 28, 1952 (dec. Nov. 4, 1994); children: Mark H., Eleanor C.; m. Regitze E.G. Winkelhorn Hamburger, June 13, 1997. AB, Columbia U., 1950, MA, 1953, PhD, 1959. Fellow Inst. Philos. Rsch., San Francisco, 1953—55; instr. philosophy Columbia U., 1955—59; from asst. prof. to prof., chmn. dept. philosophy San Francisco State Coll., 1959—68; prof. philosophy Vassar Coll., Poughkeepsie, 1968—74, chmn. dept., 1969—74, Taylor prof. philosophy, 1973—74, dean Coll. Arts and Scis.; prof. philosophy Northwestern U., Evanston, Ill., 1974—87; provost U. Pitts., 1987—89, prof. philosophy, 1987—94, chmn. dept. philosophy, 1991—93. Author: Experience and Culture: The Philosophy of Georg Simmel, 1962, The Unity of the Platonic Dialogue: The Cratylus, The Protagoras, The Parmenides, 1973, Undergraduate Education: Goals and Means, 1992 (Frederick W. Ness book award 1993), Fitting Form to Function: A Primer on the Organization of Academic Institutions, 1996, The Moral Dimensions of Academic Administration, 1999, Mostly About Me: A Path Through Different Worlds, 2003, A Sixty-Year Ride through the World of Education, 2007; editor: (with Joseph Katz) Philosophy in the West, 1965; exhibited sculptures in Mendelson Gallery, 1992, 94, UP Gallery, 1992, Assoc. Artists Pitts. Gallery, 2000, Internat. Images Gallery, 2002-03; contbr. articles to profl. jours. Bd. dirs. Chamber Music Chgo., 1982—87, pres., 1986—87; mem. bd. advisors Pitts. Symphony, 1991—2000, bd. dirs., chmn. artistic com., mem. exec. com., 2000—05. Social Sci. Rsch. Coun. fellow, 1958—59, Guggenheim fellow, 1965—66, Am. Coun. Learned Socs. fellow, 1971—72, residency, Rockefeller Found. Study and Conf. Ctr. in Bellagio, 1994. Mem. Am. Philos. Assn., Assn. Am. Colls. (bd. dirs. 1985-89, task force on gen. edn. 1985-88, editl. bd. liberal edn. jours. 1986-94), Assoc. Artists Pitts. (artist), Phi Beta Kappa. Home: 5448 Northumberland St Pittsburgh PA 15217-1129 E-mail: rudywein@pitt.edu.

WEINGER, MATTHEW B., anesthesiologist, educator; m. Michele Weinger. BS in Elec. Engring., Stanford U., Calif., 1978, MS in Biology, 1978; MD, U. Calif., San Diego, 1982. Diplomate Am. Bd. Anesthesiology, 1987. Prof. anesthesiology U. Calif. San Diego Sch. Medicine, La Jolla, 1990—2004; prof. anesthesiology, biomed. informatics and med. edn. Vanderbilt U. Sch. Medicine, Nashville, 2004—. Assoc. examiner Am. Bd. Anesthesiology, 1994—; pres. Soc. for Tech. in Anesthesiology, 2000—01; co-chair human factors com. Assn. for Advancement Med. Instrumentation, Phila., 2000—; exec. bd. dirs. Anesthesia Patient Safety Found., Indpls., 2004—. Contbr. articles to profl. jours.; mem. editl. bd. Human Factors, 2005—. Named Norman Ty Smith Chair in Med. Simulation and Patient Safety, Vanderbilt U., 2006; named one of Top 100 Notable People in Med. Device Industry, Med. Device and Diagnostic Industry mag., 2004; recipient James S. Todd Meml. award for patient safety rsch., Nat. Patient Safety Found., 1998. Office: Vanderbilt U Med Ctr 1211 21st Ave S MAB 732 Nashville TN 37212 Office Phone: 615-936-6598. Business E-Mail: matt.weinger@vanderbilt.edu.

WEINGER, STEVEN MURRAY, lawyer; b. Chgo., Feb. 7, 1954; s. Paul and Joan (Taxay) W.; children: Blake, Paige, Haley. BA, Hampshire Coll., 1975; JD, U. Chgo., 1978. Bar: Fla. 1979, Ill. 1979, U.S. Dist. Ct. (so. dist.) Fla. 1979, U.S. Ct. Appeals (5th cir.) 1980, U.S. Ct. Appeals (11th cir.) 1981, U.S. Supreme Ct. 1982, U.S. Dist. Ct. (mid. dist.) Fla. 1989. Mem. faculty U. Miami Sch. Law, Coral Gables, Fla., 1978-79; ptnr. Kurzban, Kurzban & Weinger, P.A., Miami, Fla., 1979—. Bd. dirs. Sunrise Cmty. for Mentally Retarded, Miami, United Cerebral Palsy Tallahassee, Inc., Palmer-Trinity Sch., Miami, GobleStage, Inc., 1999—. Recipient Chmn.'s award Sunrise Cmty. for Mentally Retarded, 1987; honoree United Cerebral Palsy in South Fla., 1995, Fla. Assn. Rehab. Facilities, 1996, United Cerebral Palsy Assn., 1997. Mem. ABA, Assn. Trial Lawyers Am., Fla. Assn. Trial Lawyers. Office: Kurzban Kurzban & Weinger 2650 SW 27th Ave Fl 2D Miami FL 33133-3003 E-mail: swmiami@aol.com.

WEINGOLD, MARJORIE NASSAU, retired special education educator; b. Hartford, Conn., Oct. 27, 1929; d. Joseph Nassau and Ruth Klein; m. Allan Byrne Weingold, Dec. 21, 1952; children: Beth Plavner, Roberta Greenberg, Matthew, Daniel. BA, Oberlin Coll., 1951; MA, Columbia U., 1952; cert. diagnostic therapeutic reading disability, George Washington U., 1974. Elem. edn. tchr. Hartsdale (NY) Bd. Edn., 1952—55, USN Sch. Sys., San Juan, 1958—59; presch. tchr. White Plains (NY) Sch. Sys., 1959—60; diagnostician, remediator George Washington U. Reading Ctr., Washington, 1978—83. Pvt. tutor, Potomac, Md., 1981—90. Founder, chmn. Com. for George Washington Med. Ctr., Washington, 1992—2003; trustee George Washington U. Club, Washington, 1998—2003; chmn. host com. ACOG, Washington, 1984—88; mem. women's bd. George Washington Hosp., Washington, 1997—2006; trustee Contemporary Am. Theater, 1999—, Luther Brady Art Gallery, George Washington U., 2002—; bd. dirs. Literacy Vols. Am., Washington, 1988—97, Watergate East Inc., Washington, 1996—2001. Mem.: Heritage Soc. George Washington U. Avocations: reading, travel, tennis, swimming. Home: 2510 Virginia Ave NW Washington DC 20037-1904

WEINGROW, HOWARD LOUIS, finance company executive; b. NYC, Dec. 6, 1922; s. Nathan and Anna (Mintzes) W.; m. Muriel Corrine Franzblau, Nov. 24, 1946; children: Terry Vaccaro, Caron Abby Haim. DHL (hon.), Hofstra U., Hempstead, NY, 2004. Owner Legion Fluorescent Corp., NYC, 1946-56; ptnr. Hechler & Weingrow, Inc., NYC, 1956-58, Hechler, Lifton & Weingrow, Inc., NYC, 1958-78; exec. v.p. Tanscontinental Investing Corp., NYC, 1960-67, pres., 1967-70; prin. Lifton & Weingrow, NYC, 1958—; co-chmn. Marcade Group, Inc., NYC, 1986-91, bd. dirs., 1986-93; pres. Medis Techs., Ltd. (MDTL), 1992—, dep. chmn., 2002—07; pres. Stanoff Corp., 1980—, Wesak Internat., 1992-94, dep. chmn., 1992—94; chmn. Wesak Chrysler, 1992-94; pres. Medis Techs. Ltd., 1992—2006, 2007; dep. chmn., COO Cell Kinetics, 2006—. Bd. dirs. Preferred Health Care, NYC, Four Winds Inc., NYC, Medis-El, Medis Techs. Ltd., Xilas Med., Inc.; founder Ctr. for Chilhood Asthma Schneider Children's Hosp., 2002, Weingrow Family Pediatric Urology Lab., LI Jewish Hosp., 1989, The Howard L. and Muriel Weingrow Collection of Avant-Garde Art and Lit., Hofstra U., 1972; chmn. Vision Telemedia, Inc., 1995-98; founder endowed scholarship program Hofstra U., 2005., Treas. Dem. Nat. Com., Washington, 1970-72; bd. govs. Hofstra U. Law Sch., 1977-79; dep. fin. chmn. Pres. Carter, Washington, 1976, 80; trustee Hofstra U., 1973-76, James S. Brady Presdl. Found., 1982, Children's Med. Fund, L.I. Jewish Children's Hosp., Lake Success, NY, 1986—, Am. Jewish Congress, 1988-96; treas. Nassau County Mus. Fine Arts, 1988—, North Shore, LI Jewish Hosp. Sys., 1999—; advisor to Pres. Lyndon Johnson, OEO, Washington; fin. advisor Govt. of Grenada and Office of Prime Minister Gairy, 1977-79. Decorated DFC, Air medal, 2 bronze, 2 silver clusters; recipient Presdl. medal, Hofstra U., 1985. Office: Stanoff Corp 805 3rd Ave Fl 15 New York NY 10022-7513 Office Phone: 212-935-8484. Business E-Mail: hweingrow@medistechnologies.com.

WEINHOLD, LINDA LILLIAN, psychologist, researcher; b. Reading, Pa., Nov. 9, 1948; d. Aaron Zerbe Weinhold and Nancy Louise (Spotts) Weikel; m. Jack Wayne Prisk, Jan. 21, 1967 (div. 1969). Lic. practical nurse, AVTS, 1970; BS, Penn State U., 1975; MS, C.W. Post Ctr., 1982; PhD, Fordham U., 1986. LPN; cert. profl. counselor. Instr., asst. prof. Gettysburg Coll., Pa., 1985-86; post doc. fellow John Hopkins U., Balt., 1986-88; staff fellow NIH NIDA Addiction Rsch. Ctr., Balt., 1988-93; cons. NIH NIDA Medications Devel., Rockville, Md., 1993-94; soc. sci. program coord. Med. Ctr. NIDA Rsch., Washington, 1994-95; cons. The Clin. Cons. Group Antech, Inc., Balt., 1995; substance abuse counselor Hope Village, Inc., Washington, 1996—. Various presentations. Mem. Am. Psychol. Assn., Am. Counseling Assn., Bah'a'i', Phi Kappa Phi, Sigma Xi. Avocations: singing, dance, painting, photography, reading. Home: 2611 Bowen Rd SE Apt 203 Washington DC 20020-6623 Office: Hope Village Inc 2840 Langston Pl SE Washington DC 20020-3241 Office Phone: 202-678-1077.

WEINIG, RICHARD ARTHUR, lawyer; b. Durango, Colo., Mar. 23, 1940; s. Arthur John and Edna (Novella) W.; m. Barbara A. Westerlund, June 16, 1964. BA in Polit. Sci., Stanford U., 1962, postgrad. in Soviet Studies, 1962-65; JD, U. Calif., San Francisco (Hastings), 1971. Bar: Alaska 1971, U.S. Dist. Ct. Alaska 1971, U.S. Ct. Appeals (9th cir.) 1978, U.S. Supreme Ct. 1979. Assoc. Burr, Pease & Kurtz, Anchorage, 1971-73, Greater Anchorage Area Borough, 1973-75, Municipality of Anchorage, 1975-82; ptnr. Pletcher & Slaybaugh, Anchorage, 1982-88, Pletcher, Weinig & Merriner, Anchorage, 1988-99, 1999—2001. Mem. editl. bd. Hastings Law Jour. Active Stanford U. Young Republicans, 1961-65, Sierra Club, Mountaineering Club, Knik Canoyers and Canoers of Alaska, Alaska Ctr. for Environ. Mem.: NRA, ABA, Anchorage Bar Assn., Alaska Bar Assn. Republican. Presbyn. Office: Pletcher & Weinig 800 E Dimond Blvd Ste 3-615 Anchorage AK 99515-2045 Office Phone: 907-349-1900. E-mail: richard@akinsurancedefense.com.

WEINKAUF, MARY LOUISE STANLEY, retired clergywoman, educator; b. Eau Claire, Wis., Sept. 22, 1938; d. Joseph Michael and Marie Barbara (Holzinger) Stanley; m. Alan D. Weinkauf, Oct. 12, 1962 (dec. Nov. 2000); children: Stephen, Xanti. BA, Wis. State U., 1961; MA, U. Tenn., 1962, PhD, 1966; MDiv, Luth. Sch. Theology, Chgo., 1993. Grad. asst., instr. U. Tenn., 1961-66; asst. prof. English Adrian Coll., 1966-69; prof., head dept. English Dakota Wesleyan U., Mitchell, SD, 1969-89; instr. Columbia Coll., 1989-91. Pastor Calvary Evang. Luth. Ch., Siloa Luth. Ch., Ontonagon Faith, White Pine, Mich., Gowrie, Iowa, dir. Lay Sch. for Mission, Sayner Campus, 2006—. Author: Hard-Boiled Heretic, 1994, Sermons in Science Fiction, 1994, Murder Most Poetic, 1996. Trustee Ednl. Found., 1986-90; bd. dirs. Ontonagon County Habitat for Humanity, 1995-97, Luth. Campus Ministry for Wis. and Upper Mich., 1996-2002, Lakeland Area Food Pantry, 2000—, Fortune Lake Bible Camp, 2003-04, Pastime Club Adult Day Care Ctr., North Ctrl. Wis. Thrivent Fin. for Lutherans, 2006, pres., 2007. Mem. AAUW (divsn. pres. 1978-80), Nat. Coun. Tchrs. English, S.D. Coun. Tchrs. English, Sci. Fiction Rsch. Assn., Popular Culture Assn., Milton Soc., S.D. Poetry Soc. (pres. 1982-83), Delta Kappa Gamma (pres. local chpt., mem. state bd. 1972-89, state v.p. 1979-83, state pres. 1983-85), Sigma Tau Delta, Pi Kappa Delta, Phi Kappa Phi.

WEINKE, CHRIS, professional football player; b. St. Paul, July 31, 1972; Attended, Fla. State Univ. Quarterback Carolina Panthers, 2001—; winner Heisman Trophy. Achievements include ranking second in NFL history for passing yards as a rookie. Office: Carolina Panthers 800 S Mint St Charlotte NC 28202

WEINKOPF, FRIEDRICH J., lawyer; b. Bautsch, Germany, Feb. 17, 1930; Referendar, U. Marburg, Germany, 1954; LLM, U. Pa., 1958; JD, Chgo.-Kent Coll. Law, 1967. Bar: Ill. 1967. Sr. counsel Baker & McKenzie, Chgo. Office: Baker & McKenzie 1 Prudential Plz 130 E Randolph St Fl 3600 Chicago IL 60601-6315

WEINMAN, GLENN ALAN, lawyer; b. NYC, Dec. 9, 1955; s. Seymour and Iris Rhoda W. BA in Polit. Sci., UCLA, 1978; JD, U. So. Calif., 1981. Bar: Calif. 1981. Assoc. counsel Mitsui Mfrs. Bank, LA, 1981-83; assoc. McKenna, Conner & Cuneo, LA, 1983-85, Stroock, Stroock & Lavan, LA, 1985-87; sr. counsel Buchalter, Nemer, Fields & Younger, LA, 1987-91; ptnr. Keck, Mahin & Cate, LA, 1991-93, Dongell Lawrence Finney LLP, 2006—; sr. v.p., gen. counsel Western Internat. Media Corp., LA, 1993-96; v.p. gen. counsel and human resources, sec. Guess?, Inc., LA, 1996-2000; chief adminstrv. officer Competitive Knowledge, Inc., 2000; v.p., gen. counsel, sec. Luminent, Inc., Chatsworth, Calif., 2000-01; exec. v.p., COO Insolvency Svcs. Group, Woodland Hills, Calif., 2001—03; v.p., gen. counsel, sec. Inter-Con Security Sys., Inc., Pasadena, Calif., 2003—05; ptnr. Dongell Lawrence Finney LLP, 2006—. Mem. ABA (corp. banking and bus. law sect., com. on savs. instns., com. on banking law corp. counsel sect.), Calif. Bar Assn. (bus. law sect., com. fin. instns. 1989-91, com. consumer svcs. 1991-94), LA County Bar Assn. (corp. legal depts. sect., bus. and corps. law sect., subcom. on fin. instns.), Calif. Fashion Assn. (exec. bd. 1997-2000), Am. Apparel Mfrs. Assn. (govt. rels. com. 1997-2000), Legion Lex, U. So. Calif. Law Alumni Assn., Phi Alpha Delta. Avocation: tennis. Office Phone: 213-943-6106. Personal E-mail: gaweinman@aol.com. Business E-Mail: gweinman@dflawyers.com.

WEINMAN, HOWARD MARK, lawyer; b. NYC, May 6, 1947; s. Joseph and Kate (Dorn) Weinman; m. Pamela Eve Brodie, Jan. 6, 1980; children: David Lewis, Nathaniel Saul. BA magna cum laude, Columbia U., 1969; MPP, Harvard U., 1973, JD cum laude, 1973; LLM with highest hons. in Taxation, George Washington U., 1981. Bar: D.C. 1973. Assoc. Fried, Frank, Harris, Shriver & Kampelman, Washington and NYC, 1973—78; legis. atty. Joint Com. on Taxation U.S. Congress, Washington, 1978—80; assoc. Sachs, Greenebaum & Tayler, Washington, 1980—82, Crowell & Moring LLP, Washington, 1982—84, ptnr., 1984—. Adj. prof. internat. tax Georgetown U. Law Ctr., Washington, 1988—89. Contbr. articles to profl. jours. Mem.: ABA (taxation sect.), Phi Beta Kappa. Jewish. Home: 5404 Center St Chevy Chase MD 20815-7101 Office: Crowell & Moring LLP 1001 Pennsylvania Ave NW Fl 10 Washington DC 20004-2595

WEINMANN, ERIC, retired lawyer; b. Teplice, Czech Republic, July 29, 1913; came to US, 1942; s. Ing Edmund and Josefine (Taussig) W.; m. Camilla Behn, May 4, 1946 (div. 1953); children: Edward Marvin, Gail Greenwood; m. Mary Ethel de Limur Carothers, Dec. 21, 1974. Diploma, Handelshochschule, Berlin, 1935; MA, Columbia U., 1943, JD, 1957; LLM, Georgetown U., 1963. Bar: NY 1957, DC 1958, US Supreme Ct. 1963. Assoc. counsel Legal and Monetary Subcom. Ho. of Reps., Washington, 1957—60; atty. SEC, Washington, 1960—63; asst. dep., counsel SBA, Washington, 1963—89; ret., 1989. Contbr. articles to profl. jours. Trustee emeritus Folger Shakespeare Libr., Washington, 1985. Mem. Met. Club City of Washington Home: Washington, DC. Died Aug. 19, 2007.

WEINMANN, ROBERT LEWIS, neurologist; b. Newark, Aug. 21, 1935; s. Isadore and Etta (Silverman) Weinmann; m. Diana Weinmann, Dec. 13, 1980 (dec. Dec. 1989); children: Paul, Chris, Dana, Paige. BA, Yale U., 1957; MD, Stanford U., 1962. Diplomate Am. Bd. EEG and Neurophysiology (v.p.), Am. Acad. Pain Mgmt., Am. Bd. Forensic Medicine. Intern Pacific Presbyn. Med. Ctr., San Francisco, 1962-63; resident in neurology Stanford (Calif.) U. Hosp., 1963-66, chief resident, 1965-66; pvt. practice San Jose, Calif., 1969—. Former clin. instr. neurology Stanford U. Chmn. editl. bd. Clin. EEG Jour., mem. editl. bd. Clin. Evoked Potentials Jour.; contbr. articles to various publs. Capt. M.C. US Army, 1966—68. Recipient award, State of R.I., Santa Clara County Med. Soc., Calif. State Assembly, U.S. Congress, other orgns.; fellow, U. Paris, 1957—58. Fellow: Am. Coll. Forensic Medicine; mem.: Ind. Practice Assn., Union Am. Physicians and Dentists (bd. dirs. 1972—, pres. Calif. fedn. 1989—2006, pres. 1993—, pres. Ind. Practice Assn. 2007—). Avocations: softball, tennis, music, theater, martial arts. Mailing: 2040 Forest Ave San Jose CA 95128-4810 Home Phone: 408-741-5626; Office Phone: 510-839-0193, 408-292-0802. Personal E-mail: uapdhq@aol.com.

WEINREB, HERBERT L., physician; b. NYC, May 26, 1929; s. Morris and Paula Weinreb; m. Phyllis Posner; children: Daniel, William, David. BA, NYU, 1948; MD, Washington U. Sch. Medicine, St. Louis, 1952. Intern Bellevue Hosp., NYC, 1952—53; resident Maimonides Hosp., Bklyn., 1953—55; chief resident VA Hosp., Bklyn., 1955—56; fellow in cardiology Mt. Sinai Hosp., NYC, 1958—59; attending physician Maimonides Hosp., Bklyn., 1960—2001; ret. Capt. US Army, 1956—58. Mem.: Alpha Omega Alpha, Phi Beta Kappa. Avocations: tennis, bridge.

WEINREB, LLOYD LOBELL, law educator; b. NYC, Oct. 9, 1936; s. Victor and Ernestine (Lobell) Weinreb; m. Ruth Plaut, May 5, 1963; children: Jennifer, Elizabeth, Nicholas. BA in History, Dartmouth Coll., 1957; BA in Philosophy, Politics, and Economics, U. Oxford, 1959, MA in Philosophy, Politics, and Economics, 1963; LLB, Harvard U., 1962. Bar: NY 1963, Mass. 1969. Atty. US Dept. Justice, Washington, 1964—65; asst. prof. law Harvard Law Sch., Cambridge, Mass., 1965—68, prof., 1968—, Dane prof., 1993—. Author: Denial of Justice, 1977, The Law of Criminal Investigation, 1982, Natural Law and Justice, 1987, Oedipus at Fenway Park: What Rights Are and Why There Are Any, 1994, Criminal Process, 1998, 2004, Criminal Law: Cases, Comments, Questions, 2003, Leading Constitutional Cases on Criminal Justice, 2003, 2004, Legal Reason, 2005; co-author (with James D. Whaley): The Field Guide to Law Enforcement, 2003. Office: Harvard Law Sch 1563 Massachusetts Ave Cambridge MA 02138 Office Phone: 617-495-3191. Office Fax: 617-496-4865. Business E-Mail: weinreb@law.harvard.edu.

WEINREB, MICHAEL PHILIP, physicist; b. Lakewood, NJ, Feb. 2, 1939; s. Sol and Lillian (Bolotsky) W.; m. Alice Kogan, Aug. 28, 1966; children: Jenya, Elizabeth. BA, U. Pa., 1960; MA, Brandeis U., 1963, PhD, 1966. Physicist NASA, Cambridge, Mass., 1965-70, U.S. Dept. Transp., Cambridge, 1970, Nat. Oceanic and Atmospheric Adminstrn., Washington, 1970—2004, Gen. Dynamics Advanced Info. Sys., Washington, 2004—. Adj. prof. math. Am. U., Washington, 1984-85. Contbr. articles to profl. jours. Recipient Gold medal U.S. Dept. of Commerce, 1998, Bronze medal, 1994, 2003. Mem. Am. Meteorol. Soc., Am. Geophys. Union, Phi Beta Kappa. Avocation: music. Business E-Mail: michael.weinreb@noaa.gov.

WEINREICH, GABRIEL, physicist, minister, educator; b. Vilnius, Lithuania, Feb. 12, 1928; came to U.S., 1941, naturalized, 1949; s. Max and Regina (Szabad) W.; m. Alisa Lourié, Apr. 19, 1951 (dec. 1970); m. Gerane Siemering Benamou, Oct. 23, 1971; children: Catherine, Marc, Daniel, Rebecca, Natalie. AB, Columbia U., 1948, MA, 1949, PhD, 1954. Ordained priest Episcopal Ch., 1986. Mem. staff Bell Telephone Labs., Murray Hill, NJ, 1953-60; mem. faculty U. Mich., Ann Arbor, 1960—, prof. physics, 1964-95; prof. emeritus, 1995—; Collegiate prof. U. Mich., 1974-76. Adj. min. St. Clare's Episcopal ch., Ann Arbor, 1985-90; rector St. Stephen's Episcopal Ch., Hamburg, Mich., 1993-96. Author: Solids: Elementary Theory for Advanced Students, 1965, Fundamental Thermodynamics, 1968, Notes for General Physics, 1972, Geometrical Vectors, 1998, Confessions of a Jewish Priest: From Secular Jewish War Refugee to Physicist and Episcopal Clergyman, 2005; editor: Mechanics of Musical Instruments, 1995. Recipient Disting. Teaching award U. Mich., 1968, Klopsteg award Am. Assn. Physics Tchrs., 1992, Internat. medal French Acoustical Soc., 1992, Hutchins Gold medal for lifetime achievement in mus. acoustics, 2002. Fellow Acoustical Soc. Am. (assoc. editor Jour. 1987-89). Home: 2116 Silver Maples Dr Chelsea MI 48118-1189 Home Phone: 734-433-1426. Business E-Mail: weinreic@umich.edu.

WEINREICH, GADI, lawyer; b. Tel Aviv, Apr. 25, 1962; BA magna cum laude, Brown U., 1983; JD cum laude, Harvard U., 1987; LLM, Cambridge U., 1992. Bar: Mass. 1987, DC 1988. Ptnr. Shaw Pittman LLP, Washington; ptnr., health care practice group Sonnenschein Nath & Rosenthal LLP, Washington, 2003—. Mem. The Shakespeare Theatre Lawyers Com. Mem.: ABA (health law sect.), Gerson Lehrman Law Coun., DC Bar Assn. (health law sect.), Health Care Compliance Assn., Am. Health Lawyers Assn. Office: Sonnenschein Nath & Rosenthal LLP Ste 600, E Tower 1301 K St NW Washington DC 20015 Office Phone: 202-408-9166. Office Fax: 202-408-6399. Business E-Mail: gweinreich@sonnenschein.com.

WEINRICH, BRIAN ERWIN, mathematician, computer scientist; b. Passaic, NJ, Jan. 8, 1952; s. Erwin H. and Ann E. (Gall) Weinrich. BS, Pa. State U., 1974, MA, 1978; MS, Shippensburg U., Pa., 1983; PhD, U. Fla., Gainesville, 2007. Mathematician US Dept. Agr., Agrl. Rsch. Svc., University Park, Pa., 1974-80; instr. math. and computer sci. Shippensburg U., 1980-84; assoc. prof. math. and computer sci. California U. of Pa., 1984-97, assoc. prof. emeritus math. and computer scis., 1997—. Cons. in field; mem. Wall St. Jour. Panel, 1990—; devel. articulation agreements in Malaysia California U. of Pa., 1992—2001; vis. sr. lectr. computer sci. Inti Coll., Subang Jaya, Malaysia, 1993—2001; cons. in math., sys. and database programming, 1981—2002. Author (with A. S. Rogowski): (book) Water Movement and Quality on Strip-Mined Lands: A Compilation of Computer Programs, 1984; author: (with others) Surface Mining, 1990; contbr. articles to profl. jours. Mem. mission bd. Calvary Bapt. Ch., State College, Pa., 1975—80; visitation team Prince St. United Brethren Ch., Shippensburg, 1982—84; Bible study leader, asst. Sunday sch. tchr. Libr. Bapt. Ch., 1986—92; workshop leader, follow-up trainer Gator Christian Life, Cypress Ch., 2002—. Fellow, U. Fla., 2002—; grantee, U.S. Dept. Age, 1982—89. Mem.: Assn. Computing Machinery, Am. Biog. Inst. (bd. advisors 1989—), Computer Soc. of IEEE. Republican. Home: 1001 SW 16th Ave Apt 67 Gainesville FL 32601 Office: U Fla Dept Computer and Info Sci and Engring PO Box 116120 Gainesville FL 32611 Office Phone: 352-392-1200. Personal E-mail: brianew@earthlink.net.

WEINROTH, LOIS L., lawyer; b. NYC, 1941; AB cum laude, Barnard Coll., 1963; LLB cum laude, Columbia U., 1968. Bar: N.Y. 1968. Ptnr., co-adminstrv. ptnr., structured fin. practice area Stroock & Stroock & Lavan LLP, NYC. Office: Stroock & Stroock & Lavan LLP 180 Maiden Ln New York NY 10038-4982 Office Phone: 212-806-5868. Office Fax: 212-806-6006. Business E-Mail: lweinroth@stroock.com.

WEINSCHEL, ALAN JAY, lawyer; b. Bklyn., Feb. 9, 1946; m. Barbara Ellen Schure, Aug. 20, 1967; children: Lawrence, Adam, Naomi. BA, Bklyn. Coll., 1967; JD, NYU, 1969. Bar: N.Y. 1970, U.S. Dist. Ct. (so. and ea. dists.) N.Y. 1973, U.S. Ct. Appeals (2d cir.) 1979, U.S. Ct. Appeals (9th cir.) 1986, U.S. Ct. Appeals (3d cir.) 1993, U.S. Ct. Appeals (7th cir.) 1996. Assoc. Breed, Abbott & Morgan, NYC, 1969-74, Weil, Gotshal & Manges, NYC, 1974-78, ptnr., 1978—. Lectr. Practising Law Inst., Ohio Legal Ctr., Am. Mgmt. Assn., Law Jour. Seminars, Law and Bus. Seminars, Glasser Legalworks, Insight Seminars, Mfrs.' Alliance. Author: Antitrust Intellectual Property Handbook, 2000. Trustee N.Y. Inst. Tech., Old Westbury, N.Y., 1969-76, Temple Sinai, Roslyn, N.Y., 1981-87, 89-95. Capt. U.S. Army res., 1969-74. Mem. ABA (editl. bd. Antitrust Devels. 1981-87), NY State Bar Assn. (chmn. antitrust sect. 1993-95, Dting. Svc. award 2006), Assn. Bar of City of NY. Office: Weil Gotshal & Manges 767 5th Ave New York NY 10153-0119 Office Phone: 212-310-8550.

WEINSHALL, IRIS, academic administrator; b. Bklyn., Sept. 5, 1953; m. Charles E. Schumer, 1980; children: Jessica Emily, Alison. Grad., Bklyn. Coll., 1975; MPA, NYU. Various positions NYC Dept. Citywide Adminstrv. Svcs., NYC Dept. Environ. Protection; commr. NYC Dept. Transp. (DOT), 2000—07; vice chancellor for facilities planning, constrn. & mgmt. CUNY, 2007—. Apptd. to Taxi and Limousine Commn., NYC; spl. transp. advisor to Mayor, NYC, 2003. *

WEINSHEIMER, WILLIAM CYRUS, lawyer; b. Chgo., Jan. 12, 1941; s. Alfred John and Coress (Searing) W.; m. Roberta Limarzi, June 5, 1965; children: William C. Jr., Kurt R., Robert L. BBA in Mktg., U. Notre Dame, 1962; JD, Northwestern U., 1965. Bar: Ill. 1965, U.S. Dist. Ct. (no. dist.) Ill. 1967, U.S. Tax Ct. 1968. Ptnr. Foley and Lardner LLP, Chgo., 2001—, co-chmn. estates & trusts practice group, 2001—. Lectr. continuing legal edn. programs; mem. estate planning adv. coun. Northwestern U. Author: (with others) The New Generation Skipping Tax; Analysis, Planning & Drafting, 1987; Drafting Wills and Trust Agreements, 1990; contbr. articles to profl. jours. Bd. dirs. The Ragdale Found., Lake Forest, Ill., 1987-93, Lawyers for Creative Arts, 1973-90, Winnetka United Way, 1989-92; pres. Family Svc. Winnetka-Northfield, Inc., 1978-79. Capt. U.S. Army, 1965-67. Fellow Am. Coll. Trust and Estate Coun. (bus. planning com. 1993-2002, internat. estate planning com., 1997-99, chair Ill. chpt. 1989-92, editor Actec Notes 1991-92, bd. regents 1992-96, chair edit. bd. 1993-96), chair practice com., 2004-07; mem. ABA (vice chmn. con. on generation-skipping tax 1988-92), Ill. Bar Assn., Chgo. Bar Assn. (chmn. probate practice com. 1989), Chgo. Bar Found. (bd. dirs. 1992-96), Ill. Bar Found. (bd. dirs. 1985-91), Lawyers Club, Econ. Club, Mid-Day Club, Skokie Country Club, Notre Dame Club Chgo. (bd. govs. 1984-90). Roman Catholic. Avocations: golf, visual arts, performing. Office: Foley and Lardner LLP 321 N Clark St Ste 2800 Chicago IL 60610 Office Phone: 312-832-4590. Business E-Mail: wweinsheimer@foley.com.

WEINSHENKER, NAOMI JOYCE, clinical psychiatrist, educator, researcher; b. Ridgewood, NJ, Mar. 28, 1961; d. Theodore and Anne Betty (Jaffe) W. BA summa cum laude, Yale U., 1983; MD, U. Pa., 1989. Diplomate Am. Bd. Psychiatry and Neurology. Rotating intern Overlook Hosp., Summit, N.J., 1989-90; resident in adult psychiatry Mass. Mental Health Ctr., Harvard U. Med. Sch., Boston, 1990-92, fellow in child and adolescent psychiatry, 1992-93, Boston Childrens Hosp., Harvard Med. Sch., 1993—94; staff psychiatrist Choate Health Systems, Woburn, Mass., 1994-96; asst. prof. clin. psychiatry U. Medicine and Dentistry of N.J., Newark, 1996-2000; asst. prof. clin. psychiatry Sch. Medicine NYU, 2000—; pvt. practice psychiatry, 2006—; freelance medical reporting News12, Norwalk, Conn., 2006—; med. corr. Med. Missions Children, 2007—. Staff psychiatrist Univ. Behavioral HealthCare, Newark, 1996—97; asst.dir. Univ.Hosp. Psychiat. Outpatient Ctr., 1998—2000; mem. faculty NYU Child Study Ctr., 2000—06; cons. child outpatient svcs. Tri-City Mental Health and Retardation Ctr., Inc., Medford, Mass., 1996; dir., young adult inpatient program Tisch Hosp., 2000—04. Contbr. articles to profl. jours.; editl. asst. Emergency Medicine mag., 1983-84. Vol. psychiatry unit, coord. psychiatry vols., Yale-New Haven Hosp., 1979-83; vol. recruitment coord. Phila. Adult Spl. Olympics, 1985. Mem. Am. Psychiat. Assn., Am. Acad. Child/Adolescent Psychiatry, NJ Psychiat. Assn. (Essex County rep. Tri-County chpt. 1997-98, treas. 1998-99, sec. 1999-00, v.p. 2000-2001, pres.-elect 2001-02), NJ Coun. Child/Adolescent Psychiatry, Phi Beta Kappa, Sigma Xi. Democrat. Jewish. Avocations: theater, nutrition, vegetarianism, weightlifting, aerobics. Office Phone: 973-471-4448. Personal E-mail: naomi_weinshenker@yahoo.com.

WEINSTEIN, ALAN EDWARD, lawyer; b. Bklyn., Apr. 20, 1945; s. John and Matilda W.; m. Patti Kantor, Dec. 18, 1965; children: Steven R., David A. AA, U. Fla., 1964; BBA, U. Miami, Fla., 1965, JD cum laude, 1968. Bar: Fla. 1968, U.S. Dist. Ct. (so. dist.) Fla. 1968, U.S. Ct. Appeals (5th cir.) 1969, U.S. Supreme Ct. 1973, U.S. Ct. Appeals (4th and 11th cirs.) 1981. Assoc. Cohen & Hogan, Miami Beach, Fla., 1968-71; pvt. practice Miami Beach, 1972-81; sr. ptnr. Weinstein & Preira, Miami Beach, 1981-92; prin. Law Offices of Alan E. Weinstein, Miami, 1992—. Lectr. in field. Mem. ABA (criminal and family law sect. 1968—, white collar crime commn. 1986—), Nat. Assn. Criminal Def. Lawyers, 1st Family Law Am. Inn of Court, Fla. Bar Assn. (criminal and family law sect. 1968—, ethics com. 1987-88, bench/bar com. 1988-89, grievance com. 1999-2002, chmn. 2002, unlicensed practice of law com. 2002-05), Fla. Criminal Def. Attys. Assn. (pres. 1978-79), Fla. Assn. Criminal Def. Lawyers (treas. 1989-90), Miami Beach Bar Assn., Soc. Wig and Robe, Phi Kappa Phi. Avocations: marlin fishing, reading, travel. Office: 1801 West Ave Miami FL 33139-1431 Office Phone: 305-534-4666. Personal E-mail: defense1@bellsouth.net.

WEINSTEIN, ALLEN, archivist; b. NYC, Sept. 1, 1937; s. Samuel and Sarah (Popkoff) W.; m. Adrienne Dominguez, June 14, 1995; children: Andrew Samuel, David Meier. BA, CCNY; MA, Yale U., PhD, 1967. Prof. history Smith Coll., Northampton, Mass., 1966-81; editl. staff The Washington Post, 1981; exec. editor, The Washington Quarterly Georgetown Ctr. for Strategic and Internat. Studies, Washington, 1981—83; prof. Georgetown U., Washington, 1981—84; pres. Ctr. for the Study of Democratic Institutions, Santa Barbara, 1984; editor The Ctr. Magazine, 1984; prof. history Boston U., 1985-89; founder, pres. The Ctr. for Democracy, Washington, 1985—2003; sr. adv. for democratic institutions & dir. Internat. Found. for Elections Sys., Washington, 2003—; archivist of the US The Nat. Archives & Records Admin., Washington, 2005—. Author: Prelude to Populism:Origins of the Silver Issue, 1970, Freedom and Crisis: An American History, 1974, Perjury: The Hiss-Chambers Case, 1978 (NISC award 1978), new edit., 1998, Between the Wars: American Foreign Policy From Versailles to Pearl Harbor, 1978; co-author: The Haunted Wood: Soviet Espionage in America-The Stalin Era, 1999, The Story of America, 2002; editor: American Negro Slavery, 1968, 3d edit., 1981, Harry S Truman and the American Commitment to Israel, 1981. Exec. dir. The Democracy Program, Washington, 1982-83; acting pres. Nat. Endowment for Democracy, Washington, 1983-84; chmn. edn. com. U.S. Inst. Peace, Washington, 1986-2001; mem. U.S. Observer del., Feb., 1986 Philippines election, co-author report; vice chmn. U.S. del. UNESCO World Conf. on Culture, 1982, UNESCO/IPDC meeting, 1983; chmn. Internat. IMPAC/Dublin Lit. award, 1996-2003. Recipient Meade prize in history CCNY, 1960, Egleston prize Yale U., 1967, Binkley-Stephenson prize Orgn. Am. Historians, 1968, UN Peace medal, 1986, Coun. of Europe Silver medal, 1990, 96; Fulbright lectr., Australia, 1968, 71; Commonwealth Fund lectr. U.S. History, U. London, 1981; Fourth of July Orator Faneuil Hall, Boston, 1987. Fellow Woodrow Wilson Ctr., NEH; mem. Soc. Am. Historians, Cosmos Club. Democrat. Jewish. From 1982-84 directed the rsch. study which led to the creation of the Nat. Endowment for Democracy (NED). Office: The Nat Archives & Records Adminstrn 8601 Adelphi Rd Rm 4200 College Park MD 20740 *

WEINSTEIN, ANDREW H., lawyer; b. Pitts., Oct. 5, 1943; s. Adolph J. and Meta I. (Schwarz) W.; m. Susan Balber, Aug. 11, 1968; children: Jodi L., Toby M., Jamie M. BSBA, Duquesne U., 1965; JD, U. Pitts., 1968; LLM in Taxation, NYU, 1969. Bar: Pa. 1969, U.S. Tax Ct. 1969, Fla. 1970, U.S. Dist. Ct. (so. dist.) Fla., U.S. Ct. Fed. Claims. Trial atty. IRS, LA, 1969-70, Miami, Fla., 1970-73; ptnr. Glass, Schultz, Weinstein & Moss, Coral Gables, Fla., 1973-80, Holland & Knight, Miami, 1980—. Contbr. articles to profl. jours. Bd. dirs. Zool. Soc. Fla., Red Cross. Fellow Am. Coll. Tax Counsel, Am. Coll. Trusts and Estates Counsel; mem. ABA (tax sect., bd. cert. tax law), ARC, Fla. Bar., Best Lawyers in Am. Avocations: golf, travel. Office: Holland & Knight 701 Brickell Ave Ste 3000 Miami FL 33131-2898 Home Phone: 305-740-9888; Office Phone: 305-789-7755. Business E-Mail: andrew.weinstein@hklaw.com.

WEINSTEIN, ANNA, music educator; d. Naum and Revekka Goykhman; m. David Weinstein, Dec. 30, 1972; children: Yana, Anthony. BS (hon.), Melitopol Pedagogical Inst., Melitopol, Ukraine, 1992. Lic. tchr. Ohio. Piano instr., pvt. piano tchr. Sch. Creative and Performing Arts, Cin., 1999—. Music dir. Russian Amateur Theatre JCC, Cin., 2004—06; judge World Piano Competition. Musician: (teaching piano) Regional Judge For World Piano Competition. Music dir. Jewish Cmty. Ctr., Cin., 2004—06. Recipient Talent award for tchg., World Piano Competition, 2000, Bronze medal, 2001. Mem.: Am. Music Scholarship Assn. Office: Sch Creative and Performing Arts 1310 Sycamore St Cincinnati OH 45202 Home Phone: 513-624-6328; Office Phone: 513-363-8000.

WEINSTEIN, ARTHUR GARY, lawyer; b. NYC, May 11, 1946; s. Jacob and Ada (Ambutter) W.; m. Judith Marilyn Rothstein, Dec. 24, 1969; children: Stephen, Marc. BA, Bklyn. Coll., 1967; JD, U. Pa., 1970. Bar: N.Y. 1971, N.J. 1977, U.S. Dist. Ct. (so. dist.) N.Y. 1973, U.S. Dist. Ct. N.J. 1977, U.S. Ct. Appeals (2d cir.) 1972, U.S. Supreme Ct. 1973. Asst. dist. atty. New York County, 1970-74, 85-86; asst. counsel Office of Ct. Adminstrn., N.Y., 1974-76; spl. asst. atty. gen. Dep. Atty. Gen.'s Office, NYC, 1976—2001, counsel, 1981-85, spl. counsel, 1989-95; spl. asst. dist. atty. Monroe County, 2001—. Editor U. Pa. Law Sch. Yearbook Report, 1969-70. Business E-Mail: aweinstein@monroecounty.gov.

WEINSTEIN, BOB (ROBERT WEINSTEIN), film company executive; b. Queens, NY, Oct. 18, 1954; s. Max and Miriam (Postel) Weinstein; m. Annie Clayton, Apr. 29, 2000. Student, SUNY, Fredonia, 1971—73. Co-founder, co-chmn. (with Harvey Weinstein) Miramax Films Corp., NYC, 1979—2005; co-founder (with Harvey Weinstein) The Weinstein Co., 2005—. Prodr. (films) Playing for Keeps (also dir.), 1986, Gandahar, 1988, Mimic, 1997, Reindeer Games, 2000; exec. prodr. (films) Hardware, 1990, Strike It Rich, 1990, The Pope Must Die, 1991, Into the West, 1992, Benefit of the Doubt, 1993, Map of the Human Heart, 1993, The Night We Never Met, 1993, True Romance, 1993, Hour of the Pig, 1993, Mother's Boys, 1994, Road Killers, 1994, Prêt-à-Porter, 1994, The Englishman Who Went Up a Hill But Came Down a Mountain, 1995, Things to Do in Denver When You're Dead, 1995, Smoke, 1995, The Crossing Guard, 1995, A Month by the Lake, 1995, The Journey of August King, 1995, Blue in the Face, 1995, Beautiful Girls, 1996, Flirting with Disaster, 1996, The Pallbearer, 1996, Emma, 1996, I Love You, I Love You Not, 1996, The Crow: City of Angels, 1996, The English Patient, 1996, Scream, 1996, Sono pazzo di Iris Blond, 1996, Nightwatch, 1997, Addicted to Love, 1997, Robinson Crusoe, 1997, Mononoke-hime, 1997, Air Bud, 1997, Cop Land, 1997, Wings of the Dove, 1997, Good Will Hunting, 1997, Scream 2, 1997, Jackie Brown, 1997, Wishful Thinking, 1997, A Price Above Rubies, 1998, Phantoms, 1998, Senseless, 1998, Wide Awake, 1998, Ride, 1998, Velvet Goldmine, 1998, The Mighty, 1998, 54, 1998, Heaven, 1998, Rounders, 1998, Talk of Angels, 1998, The Faculty, 1998, Shakespeare in Love, 1998, Playing by Heart, 1998, She's All That, 1999, Guinevere, 1999, My Life So Far, 1999, Teaching Mrs. Tingle, 1999, Outside Providence, 1999, In Too Deep, 1999, Mansfield Park, 1999, Holy Smoke, 1999, Music of the Heart, 1999, Cider House Rules, 1999, Allied Forces, 1999, Down to You, 2000, Committed, 2000, The Crow: Salvation, 2000, Scream 3, 2000, Love's Labour's Lost, 2000, Takedown, 2000, The Yards, 2000, Boys and Girls, 2000, Scary Movie, 2000, Highlander: Endgame, 2000, Backstage, 2000, Malèna, 2000, Bounce, 2000, Chocolat, Dracula 2000, 2000, Spy Kids, 2001, Texas Rangers, 2001, Daddy and Them, 2001, Scary Movie 2, 2001, The Others, 2001, Shu shan zheng zhuan, 2001, Jay and Silent Bob Strike Back, 2001, Lord of the Rings: The Fellowship of the Ring, 2001, Shipping

News, 2001, Kate & Leopold, 2001, Only the Strong Survive, 2002, Full Frontal, 2002, Spy Kids 2: Island of Lost Dreams, 2002, Below, 2002, Equilibrium, 2002, Waking Up in Reno, 2002, Lord of the Rings: The Two Towers, 2002, Gangs of New York, 2002, Chicago, 2002, Confessions of a Dangerous Mind, 2002, Spy Kids 3-D: Game Over, 2003, The Human Stain, 2003, Duplex, 2003, Kill Bill: Vol. 1, 2003, Scary Movie 3, 2003, Bad Santa, 2003, Lord of the Rings: The Return of the King, 2003, Cold Mountain, 2003, Ella Enchanted, 2004, Kill Bill: Vol. 2, 2004, Fahrenheit 9/11, 2004, Finding Neverland, 2004, Shall We Dance, 2004, The Aviator, 2004, Cursed, 2005, Sin City, 2005, The Adventures of Sharkboy and Lavagirl 3-D, 2005, The Great Raid, 2005, The Brothers Grimm, 2005, Proof, 2005, Derailed, 2005, Scary Movie 4, 2006, Pulse, 2006, Breaking and Entering, 2006, School for Scoundrels, 2006, Factory Girl, 2006, The Ex, 2007, Grindhouse, 2007, others; co-exec. prodr. (films) Scandal, 1989, The Lemon Sisters, 1990, The Big Man, 1990, Dust Devil, 1992, Pulp Fiction, 1994, Victory, 1995, Jane Eyre, 1996, She's So Lovely, 1997, Halloween H20: 20 Years Later, 1998, B. Monkey, 1998, Halloween: Resurrection, 2002; prodr. (TV series) The Real Magees, 1973, Wasteland, 1999, Clerks, 2000, Project Greenlight, 2001, Glory Days, 2002, Tokyo Pig, 2002. Named one of 50 Most Powerful People in Hollywood, Premiere mag., 2004—06. Office: Weinstein Co 345 Hudson St 13th Fl New York NY 10014 Office Phone: 646-862-3400. Office Fax: 917-368-7000. *

WEINSTEIN, DAVID A., endocrinologist, director; m. Geraldine Weinstein. MD, Harvard U., Boston, 1990—94, MSc, 2000—02. Lic. pediatric endocrinology Am. Bd. Pediat. Dir. glycogen storage disease program Children's Hosp., Boston, 2001—05, U. Fla., Gainesville, 2005—. Contbr. articles to profl. jours., chapters to books. Recipient George Sacher award for biol. rsch., Gerontol. Soc. Am., 1991, Sydney Farber award, Children's Hosp. Boston, 1998, Jan Albrecht award, Am. Assn. Study Liver Disease, 2001, Dominique Belcourt Lectr. award, Montreal Children's Hosp., McGill U., 2005. Mem.: Assn. Glycogen Storage Disease (bd. dirs. 2002). Office: Univ Fla Coll Medicine Box 100296 Gainesville FL 32610 Home Phone: 352-273-5823. Office Fax: 352-265-0857. Business E-Mail: weinsda@peds.ufl.edu.

WEINSTEIN, DAVID M., not-for-profit organization executive; b. 1970; Grad., U. Wis. Madison; MBA, Kellogg Grad. Sch. Mgmt. Northwestern U. Tech. adv. Mayor of Chgo., 1998—2000; pres., CEO BlueMeteor, 2000—01; pres. David Weinstein & Assoc., LLC, Chgo., Chicagoland Entrepreneurial Ctr., Chgo. Bd. dirs. Target Grp., Mayor's Coun. Tech. Advisors. Bd. dirs. Chgo. Cultural Ctr. Found., Chgo. Transit Authority Citizens Adv. Bd., M5 Artist Collective. Named to Who's Who in Chgo. Bus., Crain's Chgo. Bus., 2005, 2006. Office: Chicagoland Entrepreneurial Center Aon Ctr 200 E Randolph St Ste 2200 Chicago IL 60601-6436 Office Phone: 312-494-6742. Business E-Mail: david@chicagolandec.org. *

WEINSTEIN, EDWARD MICHAEL, architect, consultant; b. Bklyn., May 5, 1947; s. Hyman and Freda (Rochkes) W.; m. Melanie Jane Ross, June 22, 1969; children: Valerie, David. BS, CCNY, 1969. Registered architect; lic., NJ; NY. Jr. architect N.Y.C. Dept. Ports and Terminals, 1970-72, architect, 1972-75, sr. urban designer, 1975-80, dir. waterfront devel., 1980-84, asst. commr., 1984-87; pres. EMW Assocs., Hastings-On-Hudson, NY, 1984—; ptnr. The Hastings Design Group, Hastings-On-Hudson, 1987—2001; prin. Edward M. Weinstein, Planning and Architecture, 2001—02, Edward M. Weinstein, Architecture and Planning, P.C., 2002—. Adv. bd. Metro Marine Express Ltd., N.Y.C., 1989-91. Active Planning Bd., Hastings-on-Hudson, 1990-2000, Waterfront Ctr.; trustee Greenburgh Hebrew Ctr., Dobbs Ferry, N.Y., 1986-89, 92—; v.p. N.Y. Port Promotion Assn., N.Y.C., 1984-87; adv. com. on waterfront devel. N.Y. State Assembly; chair Village of Hastings-on-Hudson Waterfront Revitalization Com., 1999—. Recipient Gold Key award House Plan Assn., 1969. Mem. AIA, Am. Assn. Port Authority, N.Y. Soc. Architects, The Waterfront Ctr., CCNY Alumni Assn., Bklyn. Tech. H.S. Alumni Assn. (life), Am. Inst. of Cert. Planners, Mcpl. Art Soc. Democrat. Jewish. Avocations: tennis, art. Office: EMW Architecture and Planning PC 14 Spring St Hastings On Hudson NY 10706 Office Phone: 914-478-0800, 914-478-0800. Business E-Mail: edward@emweinsteinpc.com.

WEINSTEIN, HARRIS, lawyer; b. Providence, May 10, 1935; s. Joseph and Gertrude (Rusitzky) W.; m. Rosa Grunberg, June 3, 1956; children: Teme Ring, Joshua, Jacob. SB in Math., MIT, Cambridge, Mass., 1956, SM in Math., 1958; LLB, Columbia U., NYC, 1961. Bar: DC 1962. Law clk. to Judge William H. Hastie US Ct. Appeals (3d cir.), Phila., 1961-62; with Covington & Burling LLP, Washington, 1962-67, 69-90, 1993—; chief counsel Office of Thrift Supervision US Dept. Treasury, Washington, 1990-92; asst. to solicitor gen. US Dept. Justice, 1967-69. Pub. mem. Adminstrv. Conf. of US, 1982—90; lectr. U. Va. Law Sch., 1996; mgmt. com. Undiscovered Mgrs., LLC, 1998—2001; disting. lectr. Columbus Sch. Law, Cath. U. Am., 2007—. V.p. Jewish Social Svc. Agy., 1995—98; mem. MIT Corp., 1989—95; bd. dirs. Jewish Cmty. Rels. Coun. Greater Washington, 2004—. Mem. Nat. Press Club. Home: 7717 Georgetown Pike Mc Lean VA 22102-1411 Office: Covington & Burling 1201 Pennsylvania Ave NW Washington DC 20004

WEINSTEIN, HARVEY, film company executive, film producer; b. Queens, NY, Mar. 19, 1952; s. Max and Miriam (Postel) Weinstein; m. Eva Chilton, 1987 (div. 2004); 3 children. Student, SUNY, Buffalo, 1969—73. With Harvey & Corkey Presents, Buffalo, 1973—79; co-founder, co-chmn. (with Bob Weinstein) Miramax Films Corp., NYC, 1979—2005; co-founder (with Bob Weinstein) The Weinstein Co., 2005—. Bd. dirs. Six Flags Inc., 2005—. Dir.: (films) Playing for Keeps (also writer), 1986, The Gnome's Great Adventure, 1987, Gandaharm, 1988; prodr. (films) The Burning, 1981, Deep End, 1985, Playing for Keeps, 1986, Shakespeare in Love, 1998 (Academy award best picture, 1998, Golden Globe award best picture, 1998, Golden Satellite award best picture, 1998, BAFTA award best picture, 1999), Malena, 2000, Gangs of New York, 2002; exec. prodr. (films) including Hardware, 1990, Strike It Rich, 1990, The Pope Must Die, 1991, Benefit of the Doubt, 1993, Map of the Human Heart, 1993, The Night We Never Met, 1993, The Hour of the Pig, 1993, Mother's Boys, 1994, The Road Killers, 1994, Pret-a-Porter, 1994, The Englishman Who Went Up a Hill But Came Down a Mountain, 1995, Things to Do in Denver When You're Dead, 1995, Smoke, 1995, The Crossing Guard, 1995, A Month by the Lake, 1995, Blue in the Face, 1995, Beautiful Girls, 1996, Flirting With Disaster, 1996, The Pallbearer, 1996, Emma, 1996, I Love You, I Love You Not, 1996, The Crow: City of Angels, 1996, The English Patient, 1996, Nightwatch, 1997, Addicted to Love, 1997, Robinson Crusoe, 1997, Air Bud, 1997, Cop Land, 1997, The Wings of the Dove, 1997, Good Will Hunting, 1997, Scream 2, 1997, Jackie Brown, 1997, Wishful Thinking, 1997, The Prophecy II, 1998, A Price Above Rubies, 1998, Phantoms, 1998, Senseless, 1998, Wide Awake, 1998, Ride, 1998, Velvet Goldmine, 1998, The Mighty, 1998, 54, 1998, Heaven, 1998, Rounders, 1998, Talk of Angels, 1998, The Faculty, 1998, She's All That, 1999, Teaching Mrs. Tingle, 1999, Mansfield Park, 1999, Music of the Heart, 1999, The Cider House Rules, 1999, Down to You, 2000, The Crow: The Salvation, 2000, Scream 3, 2000, Love's Labour's Lost, 2000, Reindeer Games, 2000, Scary Movie, 2000, Highlander: Endgame, 2000, Bounce, 2000, Chocolat, 2000, Dracula, 2000, Spy Kids, 2001, Texas Rangers, 2001, Daddy and Them, 2001, Scary Movie 2, 2001, The Others, 2001, Jay and Silent Bob Strike Back, 2001, The Lord of the Rings: The Fellowship of the Ring, 2001, Iris, 2001, The Shipping News, 2001, Kate & Leopold, 2001, Spy Kids 2: Island of Lost Dreams, 2002, Waking Up in Reno, 2002, The Lord of the Rings: The Two Towers, 2002, Chicago, 2002, Confessions of a Dangerous Mind, 2002, Spy Kids 3-D: Game Over, 2003, The Human Stain, 2003, Duplex, 2003, Kill Bill: Vol. 1, 2003, Scary Movie 3, 2003, Bad Santa, 2003, The Lord of the Rings: The Return of the King, 2003, Cold Mountain, 2003, Ella Enchanted, 2004, The Aviator, 2004, Cursed, 2005, Sin City, 2005, The Adventures of Sharkboy and Lavagirl 3-D, 2005, The Great Raid, 2005, The Brothers Grimm, 2005, Proof, 2005, Derailed, 2005, Scary Movie 4, 2006, Pulse, 2006, Breaking and Entering, 2006, School for Scoundrels, 2006, Miss Potter, 2006, The Ex, 2007, Grindhouse, 2007, Sicko, 2007; co-exec. prodr. (films) including Scandal, 1989, The Lemon Sisters, 1990, Into the West, 1992, Pulp Fiction, 1994, Restoration, 1995, Jane Eyre, 1996, Scream, 1996, She's So Lovely, 1997, Mimic, 1997, Imposter, 2002; exec. prodr. (TV series) Clerks, 2000, Project Greenlight, 2001, Glory Days, 2002, Tokyo Pig, 2002; recipient BAFTA Britannia award (with Bob Weinstein, 1996, IFP Gotham Lifetime Achievement award (with Bob Weinstein), 1997. Named Comdr., Order of British Empire, 2004; named one of 50 Most Powerful People in Hollywood, Premiere mag., 2004—06. Office: Weinstein Co 345 Hudson St 13 Fl New York NY 10014 Office Phone: 646-862-3400. Office Fax: 917-368-7000. *

WEINSTEIN, HERBERT, chemical engineer, educator; b. Bklyn., Mar. 10, 1933; s. Abraham and Pauline (Feldman) W.; m. Judith Cooper, Apr. 6, 1957; children: Michael Howard, Edward Marc, Ellen Rachel. B.Engring. in Chem. Engring, Coll. City N.Y., 1955; MS in Chem. Engring, Purdue U., 1957; PhD, Case Inst. Tech., 1963. Staff mem. Los Alamos Sci. Lab., 1956-58; research engr. NASA Lewis Research Center, Cleve., 1959-63; asst. prof. chem. engring. Ill. Inst. Tech., 1963-66, assoc. prof., 1966-72, prof., 1972-77; dir. Center for Biomed. Engring., 1973-77; prof. CUNY, 1977—2005, Herbert G. Kayser prof. of chem. engring., 1987—2003, dep. exec. officer PhD program, 2003—05, prof. emeritus, 2005—. Vis. rsch. assoc., mem. Med. Rsch. Inst. Michael Reese Hosp. and Med. Ctr., Chgo., 1965-77; vis. prof. mech. engring. Technion-Israel Inst. Tech., 1972-73; vis. prof. biomed. engring. Rush Med. Coll., Chgo., 1973-76; summer prof. Exxon Rsch. and Engring. Co., annually, 1981-92; Lady Davis vis. prof. Technion-Israel Inst. Tech., 1985; cons. to industry, rsch. labs. Mem.: Am. Inst. Chem. Engrs., Sigma Xi. Achievements include research publs. and patents on fluidization, chem. reactor engring., fluid mechanics, biomed. engring. Office: CUNY Dept Chem Engring New York NY 10031 Business E-Mail: hweinst@att.net, hweinst@ccny.cuny.edu.

WEINSTEIN, HERSCHEL S., lawyer, pharmaceutical executive; b. Kingston, NY, June 24, 1955; AB magna cum laude, Brandeis U., 1977; JD, Harvard U., 1980. Ptnr. Dornbush Schaeffer Strongin & Venaglia LLP, NYC; v.p., gen. counsel Forest Labs., Inc., 2006—. Mem.: Phi Beta Kappa. Office: Forest Labs, Inc 909 Third Ave New York NY 10022 *

WEINSTEIN, I. BERNARD, oncologist, geneticist, director, educator; b. Madison, Wis., Sept. 9, 1930; married, 1952; 3 children. BS, U. Wis., 1952, MD, 1955, DSc (hon.), 1992. Nat. Cancer Inst. spl. rsch. fellow bacteriology/immunology Harvard Med. Sch./MIT, Boston, 1959-61; career scientist Health Rsch. Coun., City of N.Y., 1961-72; assoc. vis. physician Francis Delafield Hosp., 1961-66; from asst. attending physician to assoc. attending physician Presbyn. Hosp., 1967-81, attending physician, 1981—; from asst. to assoc. prof. medicine Columbia U. Coll. Phys. and Surg., NYC, 1978-90; prof. medicine Columbia U., NYC, 1973—, prof. pub. health, 1978—, prof. genetics and devel., 1990—, Frode Jensen prof. medicine, 1990—, dir. comprehensive cancer ctr., 1985-96. Advisor Lung Cancer Segment, Carcinogenesis Program, Nat. Cancer Inst., 1971-74, Chem. and Molecular Biol. Segment, 1973-76; mem. interdisciplinary comm. program Smithsonian Inst., 1971-74, Pharmacology B Study Sect., NIH, 1971-75, numerous sci. and adv. coms. Nat. Cancer Inst., Am. Cancer Soc., 1976-88; advisor Roswell Park Meml. Inst., Buffalo, Brookhaven Nat. Lab., Divsn. Cancer Cause and Prevention, Nat. Cancer Inst., Coun. on Analysis and Projects, Am. Cancer Soc., Internat. Agy. for Rsch. on Cancer, WHO, Lyon, France; Nakasone vis. prof., Tokyo, 1987; GM Cancer Rsch. Found. vis. prof. Internat. Agy. Rsch. Cancer, Lyon, 1988; mem. adv. coun. Nat. Inst. Environ. Health Scis., 1995—; chmn. Bristol-Myers Squibb Cancer Awards, 1993-96; mem. adv. coun., GM Cancer Rsch. Found. Assoc. editor Cancer Rsch., 1973-76, 86-95, Jour. Environ. Pathology and Toxicology, 1977-84, Jour. Cellular Physiology, 1982-89, Oncogene, 1989-99, Clin. Cancer Rsch., 1998—. Named Louise Weissberger lectr., U. Rochester, 1981, Mary Ann Swetland lectr., Case Western Res. U., 1983, Daniel Laszlo Meml. lectr., Montefiore Med. Ctr., 1983, Samuel Kuna Disting. lectr., Rutgers U., 1985, Ester Langer lectr., U. Chgo., 1989, Harris Meml. lectr., MIT, 1989, Rufus Cole lectr., 1997, travel fellow, European Molecular Biology Orgn., 1970—71; recipient Meltzer medal, 1964, Clowes award, Am. Assn. Cancer Rsch., 1987, Silvio O. Conte award, Environ. Health Inst., 1990, Nakahara award, 1996, Anthony Dipple Carcinogenesis award, 2000, Disting. Achievement award, Am. Soc. Preventive Oncology, 2001, Am. Assn. Cancer Rsch./Am. Cancer Soc. award, 2001, Charles Heidelberger award, 2004. Mem.: AAAS (coun. del. 1985—88), N.Y. Acad. Sci., Am. Soc. Clin. Investigation, Internat. Soc. Quantum Biology, Am. Soc. Microbiology, Am. Assn. Physicians, Am. Acad. Arts and Scis., Inst. Medicine/Nat. Acad. Sci., Am. Assn. Cancer Rsch. (pres. 1990—91). Achievements include research in cellular and molecular aspects of carcinogenesis, environmental carcinogenesis, molecular epidemiology, cancer prevention. Office: Cancer Ctr Columbia Univ 701 W 168th St New York NY 10032-2704 Office Phone: 212-305-6921. Business E-Mail: ibw1@columbia.edu.

WEINSTEIN, JACK BERTRAND, federal judge; b. Wichita, Kans., Aug. 10, 1921; s. Harry Louis and Bessie Helen (Brodach) W.; m. Evelyn Horowitz, Oct. 10, 1946; children: Seth George, Michael David, Howard Lewis. BA, Bklyn. Coll., 1943; LLB, Columbia U., 1948, LLD (hon.), 2004, Yeshiva U., Albany U., Hofstra U., L.I. U., Yale U., NYU, St. Francis Coll., 2007. Bar: N.Y. 1949. Assoc. Columbia Law Sch., 1948-49; law clk. N.Y. Ct. Appeals Judge Stanly H. Fuld, 1949-50; ptnr. William Rosenfeld, NYC, 1950-52; mem. faculty Columbia Law Sch., 1952-67, prof. law, 1956-67, adj. prof., 1967-97; U.S. judge (Eastern Dist. N.Y.), 1967-93, chief judge, 1980-88; sr. judge Ea. Dist. N.Y., 1993—. Vis. prof. U. Tex., 1957, U. Colo., 1961, Harvard U., 1982, Georgetown U., 1991, Bklyn. Law Sch., 1988-97, others; counsel N.Y. Joint Legis. Com. Motor Vehicle Problems, 1952-54, State Sen. Seymour Halpern, 1952-54; reporter adv. com. practice and procedure N.Y. State Temp. Commn. Cts., 1955-58; adv. com. practice N.Y. Judicial Conf., 1963-66; adv. com. rules of evidence U.S. Jud. Conf., 1965-75, mem. com. jurisdiction, 1969-75, mem., 1983-86; mem. 2d Cir. Jud. Coun., 1982-88, U.S. Jud. Conf., 1983-86, others in past. Author: (with Morgan and Maquire) Cases and Materials on Evidence, 4th edit., 1965, (with Maguire, Chadbourne and Mansfield, 5th edit.), 1971, 6th edit., 1975, (with Mansfield, Abrams and Berger), 9th edit., 1997, (with Rosenberg) Cases and Materials on Civil Procedure, 1961, rev. edit, (with Smit), 1971, (with Smit, Rosenberg and Korn), 1976, (with Korn and Miller) New York Civil Procedure, 9 vols., rev. edit, 1966, Manual of New York Civil Procedure, 1967, Basic Problems of State and Federal Evidence, 1976, (with Berger) Weinstein's Evidence, 7 vols., 1967, rev. edit., 1993, Revising Rule Making Procedures, 1977, A New York Constitution Meeting Today's Needs and Tomorrow's Challenges, 1967, Disaster, A Legal Allegory, 1988, (with Greenawalt) Readings for Seminar on Equality and Law, 1979, (with Murphy) Readings for Seminar in Individual Rights in a Mass Society, 1990-91, (with Berger) Readings for Seminar in Science and Law, (with Feinberg) Mass Torts, 1992, 94, Individual Justice in Mass Litigation, 1995. Chmn. N.Y. Dem. adv. com. on Constl. Conv., 1955; bd. dirs. N.Y. Civil Liberties Union, 1956-62, Cardozo Sch. Law, Conf. on Jewish Social Studies, 1980-88; nat. adv. bd. Am. Jewish Congress, 1960-67, CARE, 1985-90, Fedn. Jewish Philanthropies, 1985-94; chmn. lay bd. Riverside Hosp. Adolescent Drug Users, 1954-55. Lt. USNR, 1943-46. Mem. ABA, N.Y. State Bar Assn., Assn. of Bar of City of N.Y., Nassau County Bar Assn., Am. Law Inst., Soc. Pub. Tchrs. Law (Eng.), Am. Acad. Arts and Scis. Jewish. Office: US Dist Ct US Courthouse 225 Cadman Plz E Brooklyn NY 11201-1818 Office Phone: 718-613-2520.

WEINSTEIN, JAY A., social sciences educator, researcher; b. Chgo., Feb. 23, 1942; s. Lawrence E. and Jacqueline L. (Caplan) W.; m. Diana S. Staffin, Sept. 16, 1961; m. Marilyn L. Schwartz, Nov. 25, 1972; children—Liza, Bennett. AB, U. Ill., 1963, PhD, 1973; MA, Washington U., St. Louis, 1965. Teaching fellow U. Ill., Urbana, 1963-64; teaching asst. McGill U., Montreal, Que., Canada, 1966-68; instr. Sir George Williams U., Montreal, Que., Canada, 1967-68; lectr. Simon Fraser U., Vancouver, B.C., Canada, 1968; asst. prof. North Central Coll., Naperville, Ill., 1970-71, U. Iowa, 1973-77; prof. social sci. Ga. Inst. Tech., Atlanta, 1977-86; head dept. sociology Eastern Mich. U., 1986-90, 2004—, faculty rsch. fellow, 1990-91; grantee ednl. devel. project USIA-Soros Found., Albania, 1992—; dir. Applied Rsch. Unit, 1996—. Cons. World Bank Study Social and Econ. Vulnerability in Albania, 1997, World Bank Study on Closing the Vulnerability Gap, Albania, 1997—98; project dir. Ea. Mich.-U-Ypsilanti Cmty. Outreach Partnership Ctr.; cons. pvt. and pub. agencies; rschr. in field. Author: Madras: An Analysis of Urban Ecological Structure in India, 1974, Demographic Transition and Social Change, 1976, Sociology-Technology: Foundations of Postacademic Social Science, 1982, The Grammar of Social Relations: The Major Essays of Louis Schneider, 1984; editor: Paradox and Society, 1986; (with Vinod Tewari and V.L.S. Prakash Rao) Indian Cities: Ecological Perspectives, Social and Cultural Change: Social Science for a Dynamic World, 1997, 2005, The Holocaust: A Sociological Analysis, 1997, Demography: The Science of Population, 2000; Studies in Comparative International Development, 1978-88; mem. editorial bd. Social Development Issues, 1977-85; specialized contbr. Calcutta Mcpl. Gazette, 1979—; editor: Social and Cultural Change, 1974-75; editor Mich. Soc. Rev., 1997-2003, Jour. Applied Sociology, 2004—, editl. reviewer Jour. Asian Studies, Social Devel. Issues, Tech. and Culture, Am. Sociologist, Technol. Forecasting and Social Change; contbr. chpts. to book, articles to profl. jours. Recipient Charles Horton Cooley award for outstanding contbns. to sociology in Mich., 1998, Alex Boros award, 2005; Fulbright prof. Ahmedabad, India, 1975-76, Hyderabad, India, 1981-82; grantee Ga. Tech. Found., 1981-82, World Order Studies Course, 1994-97, State of Mich. Rsch. Excellence Fund; Steinberg fellow, 1967. Mem. Am. Sociol. Assn. (pres. 2002-03), Soc. for Applied Sociology (v.p. 1998-99, chair sociol. practice sect., 2004-05), mem. exec. bd. 2000, pres. 2002-03), Mich. Sociol. Assn. (pres. 1988-89, v.p. 1994-95), North Ctrl. Sociol. Assn. (pres. 2007-08, John F. Schnabel award for tchg. excellence), Sigma Xi. Jewish. Office: Eastern Mich U Sociology Dept Ypsilanti MI 48197 Home Phone: 313-563-5292; Office Phone: 734-487-0012. E-mail: weinst@aol.com, jay.weinstein@emich.edu.

WEINSTEIN, JOYCE, artist; b. June 7, 1931; d. Sidney and Rose (Bier) W.; m. Stanley Boxer, Nov. 28, 1952. Student, CCNY, 1948-50, Art Students League, 1948-52. Exec. coord. Women in Arts Found., Inc., 1975-79, 81-82, coord. bd., 1983-87. One-person shows include Perdalma Gallery, NYC, 1953-56, L.I. U., Bklyn., 1969, U. Calif., Santa Cruz, 1969, T. Bortolazzo Gallery, Santa Barbara, Calif., 1972, Dorsky Gallery, NYC, 1972, 74, Galerie Ariadne, NYC, 1975, Gloria Cortella Gallery, NYC, 1976, Meredith Long Contemporary Gallery, NYC, 1978-79, 88-90, Martin Gerard Gallery, Edmonton, Alta., Can., 1981-82, 84, Galerie Wentzel, Cologne, Fed. Republic of Germany, 1982, 87, Haber Theodore Gallery, NYC, 1983, 95, Gallery One, Toronto, Ont., Can., 1983, 2002, Paul Kuhn Gallery, Calgary, 1985, Eva Cohn Gallery, Highland Park, Ill., 1985, Meredith Long & Co., Houston, 1988, 90, Alena Adlung Gallery, NYC, 1989, Flanders Contemporary Art, Mpls., 1999, 2005, Harmon-Meek Gallery, Naples, Fla., 2000, Gallery One, Toronto, 2002, Flanders Contemporary Art, Mpls., 2005, Ezair Gallery, NYC, 2007; exhibited in group shows at Marlborough Gallery, NYC, 1968, Bula Mus. Art, Calcutta, India, 1970, Phoenix Gallery, NYC, 1988, Provident Nat. Bank, 1988, Alena Adlung Gallery, 1989-90, Edmonton Art Mus., 1975, 77, 83, 85, 89, Rose Fried Gallery, NYC, 1970, Hudson River Mus., 1971, Dorsky Gallery, 1972, 94, Suffolk Mus., Stony Brook, NY, 1972, NY Cultural Ctr., 1973, Stamford (Conn.) Mus., 1973, Landmark Gallery, NYC, 1974, Women's Interart Ctr., NYC, 1974-75, 78, New Sch. Social Rsch., NYC, 1975, Bklyn. Mus., 1975, Galerie Ariadne, 1975, Mus. Modern Art, NYC, 1981, Queens Mus. NY, 1984, Centre de Creacio Contemporania, Barcelona, Spain, 1987, Fairleigh Dickinson U., Hackensack, NJ, 1976, Gloria Cortella, Inc., 1976, Northeastern U., Boston, 1977, Lehigh (Pa.) U., 1977, Meredith Long Contemporary Gallery, 1977, 78, 79, 80, Galerie Wentzel, 1981-85, Martin Gerard Gallery, 1981-84, Gallery One, 1983-84, Haber Theodore Gallery, 1982-85, Jerald Melberg Gallery, Charlotte, NC, 1984, Richard Green Gallery, NYC, 1986, Rosel Art Fair, Basel Switzerland, 1986, Meredith Long & Co., 1988-90, Broome St. Gallery, NYC, 1991, 97, Andre Zarre Gallery, NYC, 1990, Cork Gallery, NYC, 1990, Chgo. Internat. Art Exbn., 1990, Queens Coll., NYC, 1991, Miami Art Fair, 1993, Bklyn. Botanic Gardens, 1994, Dorothy Blau Gallery, Bay Harbor Islands, Fla., 1997-98, Harmon-Meek Gallery, Naples, Fla., 1998-99, Flanders Contemporary Art, Mpls., 1999, 2005, Hubert Gallery, NYC, 2003; represented in permanent collections: Pa. Acad. Fine Arts, NJ State Mus., Ciba-Geigy Corp., New Sch. Social Rsch., Bula Mus. Art, U. Calif., Mus. Modern Art, NYC, McMullen Gallery, Edmonton, Ga., De Spisset Mus., U. Santa Clara, Edmonton Art Gallery Mus., The Hines Collection, Boston, others; represented by Flanders Contemporary Art, Mpls., Gallery One, Toronto, Yellow Bird Gallery, Newburg, NY, Amy Simon Fine Art, Westport, Conn. Recipient Lambert Fund award Pa. Acad. Fine Arts, 1955, Susan B. Anthony award NOW, 1983. Home: 46 Fox Hill Rd Ancramdale NY 12503-5311 Office Phone: 518-329-0614. Personal E-mail: weinsteinjoyce@aol.com.

WEINSTEIN, KENNETH N., federal government administrator; b. NYC, Sept. 29, 1946; BS, Yale U., 1968, JD, 1974. Bar: Conn. 1974, DC 1980. Honors atty. Dept. Transp., Wash., DC, 1974—75; trial atty. (aeronautics) Fed. Aviation Adminstrn., 1975—78; trial atty. office of gen. counsel Dep. Transp., 1978—81; dep. asst. gen. counsel Dept. Transp., Wash., 1981—88, asst. chief, coun. of law, 1988-97, assoc. adminstr., 1997—2005; counsel Mayer, Brown, Rowe & Maw LLP, 2005—. Recipient SES Performance awards, 1990—2001, Presidential Rank award, 2002. Office: Mayer Brown Rowe & Maw LLP 1909 K Street NW Washington DC 20006-1101 Office Phone: 202-263-3259. Office Fax: 202-263-3300. Business E-Mail: kweinstein@mayerbrownrowe.com.

WEINSTEIN, LISA, marketing executive; b. Indianapolis, 1974; BA Journalism, Polit. Sci., U. of Ind., 1996. Media supr. Leo Burnett, 1996—2001; planning dir. Ogilvy (now MindShare), 2001—03; media dir. GMR Mktg. LLC, 2003—04; grp. planning dir. OMD USA Inc., 2004; sr. ptnr. MindShare, 2004—07, mng. dir., 2007—. Named one of 40 Under 40, Advt. Age, 2007. Avocation: real estate. Office: MindShare 350 W Mart Ctr Dr Ste 1270 Chicago IL 60654-1270 Office Phone: 312-242-1100. Office Fax: 312-242-1350. E-mail: lisa.weinstein@mindshareworld.com. *

WEINSTEIN, MARGO, lawyer; b. Chgo., July 25, 1960; BA with honors, Yale U., 1982; JD, Northwestern U., 1987. Bar: Ill. 1988. Law clk. US Ct. Appeals (7th cir.), Ill., 1987—88; ptnr. Sonnenschein Nath & Rosenthal, Chicago. Named one of Top 500 Leading Litigators in Am., Lawdragon mag., 2006; named to Order of the Coif, Northwestern U. Mem.: Women's Bar Assn. Ill. Office: Sonnenschein Nath & Rosenthal 7800 Sears Tower 233 S Wacker Dr Chicago IL 60606-6404 Office Phone: 312-876-3158. E-mail: mweinstein@sonnenschein.com. *

WEINSTEIN, MARTA, packaging services company executive; V.p. ops. Logo Co.; co-founder iLogistix (formerly Logistix), Fremont, Calif., 1984—, exec. v.p., v.p. ops., co-chairwoman, 1998—99, CEO, 2001—.

WEINSTEIN, MARTIN, aerospace transportation executive, manufacturing executive, materials scientist; b. Mar. 3, 1936; s. Benjamin and Dora (Lemo) Weinstein; m. Sandra Rebecca Yaffie, June 5, 1961; children: Hilary Ann, Sarah Elizabeth, Joshua Aaron. BS in Metals Engring., Rensselaer Poly. Inst., Troy, NY, 1957; MS, MIT, Cambridge, 1960, PhD, 1961. Mgr. materials sci. Tycolabs., Waltham, Mass., 1961-69; tech. dir. turbine support divsn. Chromalloy Am. Corp., San Antonio, 1968-71, v.p., asst. gen. mgr., 1971-74, pres., 1975-79, Chromalloy Compressor Techs., San Antonio, 1979-82; group pres. Chromalloy Gas Turbine, San Antonio, 1982-86, chmn., CEO NYC, 1986—; vice chmn., exec. officer SEQUA Corp., NYC, 2004—05, vice chmn., CEO, 2005—. Supervisory mng. dir. Turbine Support Europe, Tilburg, Netherlands, 1975—; bd. dirs. Sequa Corp., NYC, 1999—, vice chmn., CEO, 2004; bd. dirs. Turbine Support Thailand, Bangkok, Chromalloy UK, Nottingham, England, Malichaud Orleans, France. Contbr. articles to profl. jours. Bd. dirs. Chamber Players San Antonio, 1979—83, NCCJ, 1982—85, Jewish Fedn., 1981—85; mem. vis. com. dept. metallurgy and materials sci. MIT, 1992—2001. Recipient Turner Meml. award, Electrochem. Soc., 1963, Achievement award, NASA, 1963, Fellows award, Rensselaer Alumni Assn., 2006; Am. Iron and Steel Inst. fellow, 1960. Mem.: NY Acad. Sci., Am. Inst. Metall. Engrs., Am. Soc. Metals, Sigma Xi. Achievements include patents for diffusion coating of jet engine materials. Home: 111 Sheffield San Antonio TX 78213-2626 Office: Sequa Corp 200 Park Ave New York NY 10166-0005 Business E-Mail: mweinstein@chronalloy.com.

WEINSTEIN, MELVIN PHILLIP, physician educator; b. Long Branch, NJ, Apr. 27, 1944; s. Joseph and Selma Joyce (Nathanson) W.; m. Dustra Lee Anderson, July 13, 1969; children: Joanna Lee, Michael Jacob. BA in Zoology with distinction, Rutgers U., 1966; MD, George Washington U., 1970. Diplomate Nat. Bd. Med. Examiners, Am. Bd. Internal Medicine, Am. Bd. Infectious Diseases, Am. Bd. Pathology (Med. Microbiology). Intern Hartford (Conn.) Hosp., 1970-71, resident, 1973-75; fellow in infectious diseases U. Colo. Health Sci. Ctr., Denver, 1975-77, fellow in clin. microbiology, 1983; asst. prof. medicine U. Medicine and Dentistry N.J., New Brunswick, 1977-83, assoc. prof. medicine and pathology, 1983-91, prof. medicine and pathology, 1991—; staff Robert Wood Johnson U. Hosp., New Brunswick, 1977—. Cons. staff St. Peter's U. Hosp., 1998-2005; cons. Roosevelt Hosp., Edison, N.J., 1986-89; vis. assoc. prof. Rutgers U., New Brunswick, 1986-98; vis. prof. Rutgers U. Coll. Pharmacy, 1998—; trustee Am. Bd. Med. Microbiology, Washington, 1991-97; mem. area com. on microbiology, 1997-2003, mem. subcom. antimicrobial susceptibility testing Clin. and Lab. Stds. Inst., Wayne, Pa., 1993—, vice chair area com. on microbiology, 1998-2002; dir. Microbiology Lab., Robert Wood Johnson U. Hosp., New Brunswick, 1983—, HIV-Antibody Counselling and Testing Svc., 1985-87, 91—; chief divsn. of allergy, immunology and infectious diseases Robert Wood Johnson Med. Sch., 2001—; lectr. in field. Mem. editl. bd. Jour. Clin. Microbiology, 1984-99, Am. Jour. Infection Control, 1987-2000, Diagnostic Microbiology and Infectious Disease, 1989—, Clin. Microbiol. Rev., 2002-; sect. editor Clin. Infectious Diseases, Manual Clin. Microbiology, 8th and 9th edit.; contbr. chpts. to books, articles to profl. jours. Comdr. USPHS, 1971-73. Henry Rutgers Rsch. fellow, 1965-66. Fellow ACP, Infectious Diseases Soc. Am., Am. Acad. Microbiology; mem. Am. Fedn. Clin. Rsch., Am. Soc. Microbiology (BD award for rsch. in Clin. Microbiology 2004), Soc. Hosp. Epidemiologists Am., N.J. Infectious Disease Soc. (founding mem.), Alpha Omega Alpha. Avocation: golf. Office: Robert Wood Johnson Med Sch 1 Robert Wood Johnson Pl New Brunswick NJ 08901-1928 Home Phone: 609-799-4286; Office Phone: 732-235-7713.

WEINSTEIN, MICHAEL ALAN, political science professor; b. Bklyn., Aug. 24, 1942; s. Aaron and Grace W.; m. Deena, May 31, 1964. BA summa cum laude, NYU, 1964; MA in Polit. Sci., Case Western Res. U., 1965, PhD, 1967. Asst. prof. polit. sci. Case Western Res. U., summer 1967, Va. Poly. Inst., 1967-68; asst. prof. Purdue U., 1968-70, assoc. prof., 1970-72, prof., 1972—; Milward Simpson disting. prof. polit. sci. U. Wyo., 1979; sr. conflict analyst Power and Interest News Report, 2004—. Author: (with Deena Weinstein) Living Sociology, 1974, The Polarity of Mexican Thought, 1976, The Tragic Sense of Political Life, 1977, Meaning and Appreciation, 1978, The Structure of Human Life, 1979, The Wilderness and the City, 1982, Unity and Variety in the Philosophy of Samuel Alexander, 1984, Finite Perfection, 1985, Culture Critique: Fernand Dumont and New Quebec Sociology, 1985, (with Helmut Loiskandl and Deena Weinstein) Georg Simmel's Scopenhauer and Nietzsche, 1986; (with Deena Weinstein) Deconstruction as Cultural History/The Cultural History of Deconstruction, 1990, La Déconstruction un Jeu Symbolique, 1990, (with Deena Weinstein) Georg Simmel: Sociological Flâmeur/Bricoleur, 1991, Photographic Realism as a Moral Practice, 1992, (with Deena Weinstein) Postmodern(ized) Simmel, 1993, (with Arthur Kroker) Data Trash: The Theory of the Virtual Class, 1994, Culture/Flesh: Explorations of Postcivilized Modernity, 1995, Peter Viereck Reconciliation and Beyond, 1997, East/West: Globalizing Civilization, 2000, (with Deena Weinstein) Hail to the Shrub: Mediating the President, 2002, The Power of Silence and the Limits of Discourse at Oliver Wendell Holmes's Breakfast Table, 2005, The Imaginative Prose of Oliver Wendell Holmes, 2006; artist in residence Columbia Coll., 2002; mem. editl. bd. Humanitas, Social Philosophy Rsch. Book Series. Recipient Best Paper prize Midwest Polit. Sci. Assn., 1969; Guggenheim fellow, 1974-75; Rockefeller Found. humanities fellow, 1976; fellow Center Humanistic Studies, Purdue U., 1981, Lily Endowment Tchg. grant, 2001. Mem. Phi Beta Kappa. Home: 800 Princess Dr West Lafayette IN 47906-2038 Office: Dept Polit Sci Purdue U West Lafayette IN 47907 *And which is worse, to be arbitrary or to be contradictory? I have attempted to be the most consistent rationalist of all by refusing to harmonize what is irreconcilable in the name of reason.*

WEINSTEIN, MICHAEL P., marine scientist, administrator; s. Jack and Beatrice Weinstein; m. Yael Sisso, Dec. 22, 1991; children: Heather Ann Campbell, Lee Thomas. BA, Hofstra U., 1966; MS, Rutgers U., 1969; PhD, Fla. State U., 1975. Pres. TEVA Environ. Associates, Millburn, 1984—96; pres., CEO NJ. Marine Sciences Consortium, Fort Hancock, 1996—. Author: Concepts and Controversies in Tidal Marsh Ecology, 2000 (Gov.'s Tourism award, 2004, Coastal Am. Spirit award, 2006, Gov.'s Environ. Quality award, 2006); contbr. chapters to books, more than 150 articles to profl. jours. Mem. working group, bd. dirs. Nat. Transp. Rsch. Bd., Nat. Acads., Washington, 2003—04. Grantee, various fed. and state agys., 1970—. Office Phone: 732-872-1300 ext. 21.

WEINSTEIN, MILTON CHARLES, decision scientist, educator; b. Brookline, Mass., July 14, 1949; s. William and Ethel (Rosenbloom) W.; m. Rhonda Kruger, June 14, 1970; children: Jeffrey William, Daniel Jay. AB, AM, Harvard U., 1970, MPP, 1972, PhD, 1973. Asst. prof. John F. Kennedy Sch. Govt., Harvard U., Cambridge, Mass., 1973-76, assoc. prof., 1976-80; prof. policy and decision scis. Harvard Sch. Pub. Health, Boston, 1980-86, Henry J. Kaiser prof. health policy and mgmt., 1986—; prof. medicine Harvard Med. Sch., Boston, 1992—2005; v.p. Innovus Rsch. Inc., Medford, Mass., 1998—; prin. cons. i3 Innovus, Medford, 2005—. Adj. prof. cmty. and family medicine Dartmouth Med. Sch., Hanover, N.H., 1981-87; vis. lectr. Intermountain Health Care, Salt Lake City, 1997—; cons. U.S. Office Tech. Assessment, 1979-87, HHS, 1979—, VA, 1984-86, EPA, 1983—, New Eng. Med. Ctr., 1986-87, Intermountain Health Care, 1987—; mem. adult treatment panel Nat. Cholesterol Edn. Program, NIH; co-chair Panel on Cost-Effectiveness in Health and Medicine, USPHS, 1993-96. Author: Clinical Decision Analysis, 1980, Hypertension: A Policy Perspective, 1976, Cost-Effectiveness in Health and Medicine, 1996, Decision Making in Health and Medicine, 2001; mem. editl. bd. Med. Decision Making, 1981-94, Jour. Environ. Econs. and Mgmt., 1986-88, Jour. Clin. Oncology, 1996-99; assoc. editor Med. Decision Making, 1994-2001. NSF fellow, 1972. Mem. Inst. Medicine of NAS (com. on priorities new vaccine devel., com. to evaluate the NIH artificial heart program), Soc. Med. Decision Making (trustee 1980-82, pres. 1984-85), Internat. Health Econs. Assn., Internat. Soc. Pharmacoens. and Outcomes Rsch., Am. Med. Joggers Assn., US Speedskating (bd. dirs. 1996-00), Phi Beta Kappa.

WEINSTEIN, PHILIP MERRILL, lawyer; b. Providence, Nov. 12, 1942; s. Sidney and Isabelle W.; m. Nancy F. Freedman; children: Benjamin, Noah. BS, Boston U., 1965; JD, Howard U., 1968. Bar: Mass., R.I., U.S. Dist. Ct. Mass., U.S. Dist. Ct. R.I. Ptnr. Decof, Weinstein & Mandell, Providence, 1972-80; sole practice Providence, 1980-87; ptnr. Weinstein & Doren, Providence; pvt. practice. Mem. bd. trustees Gordon Sch., Providence, 1985—, Cmty. Prep Sch., Providence, 1999—; past pres. Temple Beth David. Fellow (life) RI Bar Found.; mem. ABA, Assn. Trial Lawyers Am., RI Trial Lawyers Assn, Mass. Bar Assn. (mem. exec. com., ho. of delegates, 1985-), RI Bar Assn. (mem. ho. of delegates, 1972-, mem. exec. com., v.p., pres.), Phi Sigma Delta. Avocations: sports, flute, cooking. Office: Law Office Philip M Weinstein One Providence Washington Plz Providence RI 02903-7104 Office Phone: 401-521-3500. E-mail: pweinst@aol.com. *

WEINSTEIN, RAYMOND, sculptor; b. Alexandria, Va., Jan. 6, 1920; s. Louis and Edna Brill Weinstein; m. Helene Weinstein, Mar. 26, 1950; children: Anne Simpson, Ellen Flaherty. Student, Pratt Inst., Bklyn., 1945—50, Ednl. Art Sch., NYC, 1976—2006. Machinist, toolmaker Ford Instrument Co., NY, 1941—50, Mergenthaler Co., NY, 1950—56, Singer Corp., NJ, 1956—66, Transit Authority, NYC, 1966—86. Represented in permanent collections Michael Goodman, NYC, Pace Coll., Gallery One. Pres. Sculptors Alliance, NYC, 1989—98. Recipient Alice McReynolds award, Salmagundi Club, NYC, 1990, Doris Kriedler award, ASLA, NYC, 2002. Mem.: Audubon Artists, Am. Soc. Contemporary Art (membership dir. 1991—2006). Avocations: nature, travel, camping. Home: 453 FDR Dr New York NY 10002

WEINSTEIN, ROY, physics professor; b. NYC, Apr. 21, 1927; s. Harry and Lillian (Ehrenberg) W.; m. Janet E. Spiller, Mar. 26, 1954 (dec. 1995); children: Lee Davis, Sara Lynn; m. Gail A. Birdsell, July 26, 1996. BS, MIT, 1951, PhD, 1954; ScD (hon.), Lycoming Coll., 1981. Rsch. asst. Mass. Inst. Tech., 1951-54, asst. prof., 1956-59, Brandeis U., Waltham, Mass., 1954-56; assoc. prof. Northeastern U., Boston, 1960-63, prof. physics, 1963-82, exec. officer, chmn. grad. div. of physics dept., 1967-69, chmn. physics dept., 1974-81; spokesman MAC Detector Stanford U., 1981-82; dean Coll. Natural Scis. and Math. U. Houston, 1982-88; prof. physics, 1982—; dir. Inst. Beam Particle Dynamics U. Houston, 1985-95; assoc. dir., spokesman Tex. Ctr. for Superconductivity, 1987-89. Vis. scholar and physicist Stanford (Calif.) U., 1966-67, 81-82; bd. dirs. Perception Tech., Inc., Winchester, Mass., Omniwave Inc., Gloucester, Mass., Wincom Inc., Woburn, Mass.; cons. Visidyne Inc., Burlington, Mass., Houston Area Rsch. Ctr., Stanford U., Hodotector Inc., Houston, Park Square Engring., Marietta, Ga., Harvard U., Cambridge, Mass., Cambridge Electron Accelerator, mem. adv. com., 1967-69; adv. com. and portfolio evaluation com. Houston Venture Ptnrs., 1990-99; chmn. bd. dirs. Xytron Corp., 1986-91; dir., mem. exec. com. Houston Area Rsch. Ctr., 1984-87; chmn. organizing com. Internat. Conf. on Meson Spectroscopy, 1974, chmn. program com., 1977, mem. organizing com., 1980; chmn. mgmt. group Tex. Accelerator Ctr., Woodlands, 1985-90; chmn. Tex. High Energy Physicists, 1989-91; keynote spkr. MIT Alumni series, 1988; permanent mem. exec. com. Large Vol. Detector (Underground Neutrino Telescope, Italy), 1988—; organizer session High Temperature Superconducting Magnets 3d and 4th World Congress on Superconductivity, Munich, 1993, Orlando, 1994. Author: Atomic Physics, 1964, Nuclear Physics, 1964, Interactions of Radiation and Matter, 1964; editor: Nuclear Reactor Theory, 1964, Nuclear Materials, 1964; editor procs.: 5th Internat. Conf. on Mesons, 1977; contbr. over 200 articles to profl. jours. Active Lexington (Mass.) Town Meeting, 1973-84; vice chmn. Lexington Coun. on Aging, 1977-83. With USNR, 1945-46. Recipient Founders award World Congress Superconductivity, 1988, Materials/Devices award Internat. Superconductivity Technology Ctr., Japan, and Materials Rsch. Soc., 1995, High Current award, 1997, Excellence award Internat. Program Com. Processing and Applications of Large Superconducting Rare Earth Grains Worshop, 1999, NSF Rsch. awards, 1961-96, Tex. Rsch. award, 1986-87, 90—, US Dept. Energy award 1974, 77, 87-97, NASA award, 1990-98, 2004—, ARO award, 1994—, Elec. Power Rsch. Inst. award, 1990-95, Welch Found. award, 1997—, Nat. Cancer Inst. award, 2000-04; NSF fellow Bohr Inst., Copenhagen, 1959-60, Stanford U. 1969-70, Guggenheim fellow Harvard U., 1970-71. Fellow Am. Phys. Soc. (organizer session SSC and High Energy Physics 1984); mem. Am. Assn. Physics Tchrs., Masons, Sigma Xi, Phi Kappa Phi (chpt. pres. 1977-79, Nat. Triennial Disting. Scholar prize 1980-83), Pi Lambda Phi (pres. Theta chpt. 1949-50). Unitarian Universalist. Achievements include measurement of fine structure of positronium; first measurement of rho meson coupling to gamma rays, of phi meson decay to two muons; early observation of break down in SU3 symmetry; demonstration of electron-muon universality, discovery of non-applicability of Lorentz contraction to length measured by a single observer; disproof of splitting of A2 meson; independent discovery of upsilon meson (bottom quark); achievement of highest magnetic field for any permanent magnet, in YBa2Cu307, 10.1 Tesla; achievement of highest current density in textured superconductor, 0.8 megA/cm2; development of MILD pinning centers for high temperature superconductor. Home: 4368 Fiesta Ln Houston TX 77004-6603 Office: U Houston IBPD 632 SR1 Houston TX 77204-5005 Business E-Mail: weinstein@uh.edu.

WEINSTEIN, SIDNEY, retired university program director; b. NYC, July 1, 1920; s. Jacob and Yetta W.; m. Celia Kahn, Mar. 6, 1943 (dec.); children: Risa, Jeri; m. Florence Landau, June 21, 1988. BA, Bklyn. Coll., 1951; MA, Columbia U., 1955; DPA, Indsl. Coll. Armed Forces, 1964. Contract adminstr. U.S. Corps Engrs., 1941-43; mgmt. analyst Dept. Army, NYC, 1946-55; dir. data processing procurement GSA, 1956-68, dep. asst. commr. automated data mgmt. services Washington, 1968-72, asst. commr. automated data and telecommunications, 1972-75; exec. dir. Assn. Computing Machinery, NYC, 1975-85; assoc. prof., dir. affiliates program Ctr. Research Info. Systems, Leonard N. Stern. Sch. Bus. NYU, 1985-99, ret., 1999. Cons. to chmn. U.S. CSC. Served with USAF, 1943-46. Recipient Exceptional service award, U.S. Govt., 1975. Mem. ABA (arbitrator 1989—), Coun. Engring. and Sci. Soc. Execs. (dir.), N.Y. Soc. Assn. Execs., Assn. Indsl. Coll. Armed Forces, Assn. Fed. Execs. Inst., Assn. Computing Machinery, Soc. Info. Mgmt. Home: 360 E 72nd St New York NY 10021-4753 Home Phone: 212-288-4004. Personal E-mail: s_weinstein@msn.com.

WEINSTEIN, STANLEY, Buddhist studies educator; b. Bklyn., Nov. 13, 1929; s. Louis Arthur and Ruth (Appleson) W.; m. Lucie Ruth Krebs, Sept. 23, 1951; 1 son, David Eli. BA, Komazawa U., Tokyo, 1954-58; MA, U. Tokyo, 1960; PhD, Harvard U., 1966; MAH (hon.), Yale U., 1974. Lectr. Sch. Oriental and African Studies, London, 1962-68; assoc. prof. Buddhist studies Yale U., New Haven, 1968-74, prof., 1974—2003, prof. emeritus, 2003—, chmn. coun. East Asian studies, 1982-85. Author: Buddhism under T'ang, 1987. Served with U.S. Army, 1952-54. Ford Found. fgn. area fellow, 1958-62; NEH sr. fellow, 1974-75 Mem. Am. Oriental Soc., Assn. Asian Studies Home: 270 Ridgewood Ave Hamden CT 06517-1426 Business E-Mail: stanley.weinstein@yale.edu.

WEINSTEIN, STEPHEN BRANT, communications executive, researcher, writer; b. NYC, Nov. 25, 1938; s. Max S. and Evelyn A. (Brandt) W.; m. Judith Louise Benham, June 10, 1961; children: Brant M., Anna M. SB, MIT, 1960; MS, U. Mich., 1962; PhD, U. Calif., Berkeley, 1966. Mem. tech. staff Philips Rsch. Labs., Eindhoven, The Netherlands, 1967-68, Bell Labs., Holmdel, N.J., 1968-79; v.p. tech. strategy Am. Express Co., NYC, 1979-84; exec. dir. subscriber systems rsch. Bellcore, Morristown, N.J., 1984-93; fellow, mgr. comm. tech. rsch. C&C Rsch. Lab., NEC USA, Inc., 1994—2001; pres. Comm. Theory & Tech. Cons., 2002—. Editor-in-chief KICS Jour. Comms. and Networks, 1999-2001; adj. prof. Columbia U., 2002-06. Author: Getting the Picture: A Guide to CATV and the New Electronic Media, 1986, The Multimedia Internet, 2005; co-author: Data Communication Principles, 1992; contbr. articles to profl. jours.; patentee in field. Recipient Basic Rsch. award, Eduard Rhein Found., 2006. Fellow IEEE (div. III dir. 2002-03, chmn. Press 1979-82, Centennial medal 1984), IEEE Comms. Soc. (pres. 1996-97, v.p. tech. affairs 1994-95, dir. publs. 1990-93, chief info. officer 2006—, editor-in-chief Comms. mag. 1984-89). Avocations: skiing, digital photography. Home and Office: 150 Woodland Ave Summit NJ 07901-2029 Personal E-mail: s.weinstein@ieee.org.

WEINSTEIN, STEVEN D., lawyer; b. Phila, May 3, 1946; s. Leon and Elizabeth (Evantash) W.; m. Karin Elkis, Feb. 16, 1986. BA, Rutgers U., 1968, JD, 1975. Bar: NJ 1975, Pa. 1975, US Dist. Ct. 1975, US Dist. Ct. (ea. dist.) Pa. 1975, US Supreme Ct. 1979, US Ct. Appeals (3d cir.) 1981, US Ct. Claims 1986, US Dist. Ct. (NJ) (mediator). Assoc. Lewis Katz P.C., Cherry Hill, NJ, 1975-78; pvt. practice law Collingswood, NJ, 1978-84; ptnr. Blank Rome LLP, Cherry Hill, 1984—. Counsel Camden County, NJ, 1982—84. Trustee Camden County Coll., Blackwood, NJ, 1983, West Jersey Hosp. Found., Camden, 1984-96, chmn. 1989-91, Rowan Coll., NJ, 1990-96, chmn. 1992-94, trustee devel. fund. bd., 1989-90; mem. N.J. Bus. Higher Edn. Forum; mem. cmty. impact bd. United Way of Camden County, 2004—, chmn. workplace campaign, 2006—; bd. dir. NJ Alliance for Action; mem. bd. trustees NJ Future; mem. NJ Commn. Hihgher Edn., 2007—. Mem.: NJ County Counsels Assn. (pres. 1983), Haddonfield Bd. Edn. (v.p. 2002—07, pres. 2007—), Camden County Bar Assn., Israel-Am. Affiliates (South Jersey chpt.), Ben Gurion U. of the Negev (chair 1998—2002), NJ Higher Edn. Alliance (chair), NJ Governing Bd. Assn. (sec. 1993—94, vice-chair 1996). Democrat. Jewish. Office: Blank Rome LLP Woodland Falls Corporate Park 210 Lake Dr E Ste 200 Cherry Hill NJ 08002-1163 Office Phone: 856-779-3601. Business E-Mail: weinstein@blankrome.com.

WEINSTEIN-BACAL, STUART ALLEN, lawyer, educator; b. Stuttgart, Germany, May 23, 1948; s. Marvin Stuart and Mae (Beal) W.; m. Holly Laurette Thompson, Aug. 7, 1982; children: Rachel Lee, Maximillian II, Sarah Nicole. BA, U. Va., 1970, MEd, 1973; JD cum laude, U. Miami, 1979. Bar: D.C. 1979, Va. 1981, V.I. 1985, P.R. 1988. Tchr., pvt. tutor various schs., Conn., Fla., Costa Rica, 1973-76; mem. prof. staff Merchant Marine and Fisheries Com. U.S. Ho. of Reps., Washington, 1978; assoc. Cameron, Hornbostel & Adelman, Washington, 1979-80, Burch, Kerns & Klimek, PC, Washington, 1980-81; staff atty. C.A.C.I., Washington, 1982-83; sr. assoc. Dudley, Dudley & Topper, St. Thomas, U.S. Virgin Islands, 1984-85; v.p., gen. counsel Redondo Construction Corp., San Juan, 1985-89; founder Indiano, Williams & Weinstein-Bacal, San Juan, 1989-2000; owner Weinstein-Bacal & Miller, P.S.C., Old San Juan, PR, 2000—. Contbr. articles to profl. jours. Capt. USAR, 1970-85. Mem. ABA, Am. Arbitration Assn. (pres., Caribbean region adv. coun. 1988-2000, arbitrator 1989—), Res. Officers Assn., Colegio de Abogados de P.R., U. Va. Alumni Assn., Nature Conservancy, Sovereign Order of the Oak (knight comdr.), Rotary Club of San Juan (bd. dirs. 1991-95), Middleburg Forum, Middleburg Tennis Club, Bankers Club P.R., Loudoun Golf & Country Club, Phi Alpha Delta. Avocations: sailing, golf, tennis, riding, gourmet cooking, travel. Home: Villas Del Mar E # 7D Carolina PR 00979 also: Mallory Chase Farm 35919 Turkey Roost Rd Middleburg VA 20117-3401 Office: Gonzalez Padin Bldg-Penthouse 154 Rafael Cordero St Plz Armas Old San Juan PR 00901 Home Phone: 540-687-3901; Office Phone: 787-977-2550. Personal E-mail: swb@hotmail.com. Business E-Mail: swb@w-bmlaw.com.

WEINSTOCK, GEORGE DAVID, financial services company executive; b. Vienna, Jan. 31, 1937; came to U.S., 1940; s. Paul and Ernestine Esther (Stark) W.; m. Lorna Smith, July 17, 1965; children: Pamela Ellen, Andrea Joan. AB, Columbia U., 1958, BSEE, 1959, MS, 1962; cert., Coll. for Fin. Planning, Denver, 1985. cert. fin. planner; accredited estate planner. Sr. engr. ITT, Nutley, N.J., 1959-61; sr. mem. tech. staff RCA, NYC, 1961-65; project dir. Computer Scis. Co., Paramus, N.J., 1965-69; v.p., dir., sec. Ultimacc Systems, Inc., Maywood, N.J., 1969-78; v.p. Satnick Devel. Group, Hoboken, N.J., 1978-84; sr. v.p. Knitwaves, Inc., Moonachie, N.J., 1984-85; chmn. bd. Bancroft Group, Inc., Paramus, 1985-88; pres. Atrium Adv. Group, Inc., Paramus, 1990—. Mem. faculty Fairleigh Dickinson U., Baruch Coll., Coll. Fin. Planning. Author: System 360/DOS Operation, 1971, Multi-Taxation of Retirement Plans, 1991, Retirement Planning and Employee Benefits, 1992, Solving the Pre-59 1/2 Distribution Ten Percent Penalty Tax, 1992. Com. mem. United Jewish Cmty. Bergen County, 1988; pres. N.J. Estate Planning Coun., 1993-95, trustee, 1995—. Mem. IEEE, Inst. for CFPs, Nat. Assn. Accts. Jewish. Home and Office: Atrium Adv Group Inc 6th Fl 400 Kelby St Fort Lee NJ 07024 Home Phone: 201-445-8758; Office Phone: 201-592-2537. Personal E-mail: georgelorn@aol.com.

WEINSTOCK, GEORGE MATTHEW, biology educator, researcher; b. Chgo., Feb. 6, 1949; BS, U. Mich., 1970; PhD, MIT, 1977. Staff scientist Nat. Cancer Inst.-Frederick (Md.) Cancer Rsch. Facility, 1980-83, sr. scientist, 1983-84; assoc. prof. U. Tex. Med. Sch., Houston, 1984-90, prof., 1990—. Instr. Internat. Ctr. for Gen. Engring., Trieste, Italy, 1990—, Cold Spring Harbor (N.Y.) Lab., 1986-90. Recipient Jane Coffin Childs fellowship Bank of Am.-Giannini Found., 1977-79, 79-80, Outstanding Tchr. award Grad. Sch. of Biomed. Sci., Houston, 1987. Mem. AAAS, Genetics Soc. Am., Am. Soc. for Biochemistry and Molecular Biology, Am. Soc. for Microbiology. Achievements include patents for system for expressing foreign genes in bacteria, vaccine against bovine Pasteurella haemolytica. Office: U Tex Med Sch Dept Biochemistry 6431 Fannin St Houston TX 77030-1501

WEINSTOCK, LEONARD, lawyer; b. Bklyn., Aug. 18, 1935; s. Samuel Morris and Evelyn (Reiser) W.; m. Rita Lee Itkowitz, May 25, 1963; children: Gregg Douglas, Valerie Lisa, Tara Diane. BS, Bklyn. Coll., 1956; JD, St. John's U., Bklyn., 1959. Bar: N.Y. 1961, U.S. Supreme Ct. 1964, U.S. Ct. Appeals (2d cir.) 1963, U.S. Dist. Ct. (ea. and so. dists.) N.Y. 1963, U.S. Tax Ct. 1963. Assoc. Bernard Helfenstein law practice, Bklyn., 1962-63; supr. All State Ins. Co., Bklyn., 1963-64; atty. Hertz Corp., NYC, 1964-65; ptnr. Nicholas & Weinstock, Flushing, NY, 1965-68; v.p., ptnr. Garbarini & Scher, P.C., NYC, 1968—. Lectr. Practicing Law Inst., N.Y.C., 1975—; arbitrator Nassau County Dist. Ct., Mineola, N.Y., 1979—, U.S. Dist. Ct. (ea. dist.) N.Y. 1986—; mem. Med. Malpractice Mediation Panel, Mineola, 1978—. Legal counsel Massapequa Soccer Club, N.Y., 1981—; county committeeman Dem. Party, Massapequa Park, N.Y., 1979—. With U.S. Army, 1959-62. Mem. ABA, N.Y. State Bar Assn., Nassau County Bar Assn. (mem. med. jurisprudence ins. com. 1978), N.Y. Trial Lawyers Assn. Avocations: stamp collecting/philately, softball, racquetball. Home: 38 Barstow Rd Great Neck NY 11021-2218 Office: Garbarini and Scher PC 432 Park Ave S New York NY 10016-8013 Office Phone: 212-689-1113.

WEINSTOCK, WALTER WOLFE, systems engineer; b. Phila., Aug. 18, 1925; s. Abraham and Jeanne (Feldman) W.; m. Doris Alpert, Sept. 21, 1946; children— Steven Eric, Bruce Alan. BSE.E., U.Pa., 1946, MSE.E., 1954, PhD, 1964. Design engr. Philco, 1946-49; with RCA Corp., 1949-87; prin. scientist RCA Corp. (Missile and Surface Radar div.), Moorestown, N.J., 1979-87; cons., 1987—. Mem. planning and steering adv. group Surface Ship Security Panel, Dept. Navy, 1979-82 Contbg. author: Modern Radar, 1965, Practical Phased Array Antenna Systems, 1991; contbr. articles to profl. jours. Recipient David Sarnoff award for Outstanding Achievement in Engring. RCA, 1972 Fellow IEEE (Pioneer Recognition award 2004); mem. Tau Beta Pi, Eta Kappa Nu, Sigma Tau, Pi Mu Epsilon. Achievements include patents in field. Home: 6 Beryl Rd Cheltenham PA 19012-1206 E-mail: walt1925@earthlink.net.

WEINTRAUB, BEVERLY, editor; married; 2 children. Grad., Barnard Coll. Copy editor & headline writer NY Daily News, NYC, 1990—97, copy desk chief, 1997—2004, editl. bd., 2004—. Co-recipient Pulitzer Prize for Editl. Writing, 2007. Mem.: Newswomen's Club NY. Office: NY Daily News 450 W 33rd St New York NY 10001 *

WEINTRAUB, JOSEPH BARTON, publishing executive; b. Phila., Dec. 2, 1945; s. George and Edith (Lubner) W.; m. Denise Waters, June 14, 1974. BA, U. Pitts., 1966; MA, U. Chgo., 1967, PhD, 1973. Assoc. faculty U. Ind., Gary, Ind., 1970-74; mktg. specialist journalism div. U. Chgo. Press, 1974-75, sr. copywriter journalism div., 1975-78; periodical specialist ABA, Chgo., 1978-80, mktg. mgr., 1980-92, dir. publ. planning, 1992-97, dir. book publ., 1997-99; mgr. dir. mktg. U. Chgo. Press, 1999—. Writer You, 2000; contbr. essays, translations, plays, poems, short fiction to lit. revs. and small press anthologies. Recipient award Literary awards, Ill. Art Coun., 1984, 2004, Barrington Art Coun., 1994. Mem. Phi Beta Kappa. Avocations: writing, language study, running. Office: U Chgo Press 1427 E 60th Street Chicago IL 60637-5418

WEINTRAUB, NEAL L., medical educator, cardiologist; Student, Tulane u., 1977-80, MD, 1984. Diplomate Am. Bd. Internal Medicine, Am. Bd. Cardiovasc. Diseases. Resident Emory U., Atlanta, 1984-86, U. Ill., Urbana-Champaign, 1986-87, clin. instr. medicine Coll. Medicine, 1987-88, asst. clin. prof. medicine Coll. Medicine, 1988-90; staff physician VA Med. Ctr., Danville, Ill., 1987-90, St. Louis, 1990-91; asst. prof. medicine Sch. Medicine St. Louis U., 1990-95, postdoctoral fellow clin. pharmacology, 1992-94; asst. cardiology divsn. U. Iowa Coll. Medicine, Iowa City, 1995-97, assoc. prof. cardiology, 1997—. Contbr. articles to profl. jours. Recipient Travel award Am. Coll. Cardiology/Bristol-Myers Squibb, 1994, Clinician Scientist award Am. Heart Assn., 1996. Mem. Alpha Omega Alpha. Achievements include research in vascular biology and physiology and lipid biochemistry. Office: U Iowa Coll Medicine CV Div Dept Internal Medicine 200 Hawkins Dr Iowa City IA 52242-1009

WEINTRAUB, RUSSELL JAY, lawyer, educator; b. NYC, Dec. 20, 1929; s. Harry and Alice (Lieberman) W.; m. Zelda Kresshover, Sept. 6, 1953; children: Sharon Hope, Harry David, Steven Ross. BA, NYU, 1950; JD, Harvard U., 1953. Bar: Tex. 1980. Tchg. fellow Harvard U. Law Sch., 1955-57; asst. prof. law U. Iowa, 1957-61, prof., 1961-65, U. Tex., 1965—, Marrs McLean prof. law, 1970-80, Bryant Smith chmn., 1980-82, John B. Connally chmn., 1982-98, Powell chmn., 1998—2003, emeritus, 2004—. Vis. prof. law U. Mich., 1965, UCLA, 1967, U. Calif., Berkeley, 1973-74, Bklyn. Law Sch., 1990, 95, Inst. Internat. Comparative Law, Paris, 1975, Florence, Italy, 1997, Barcelona, 1999, 2002, London, 2000, U. Houston, 1979-80, Inst. Internat. and Comparative Law, Oxford, Eng., 1982-83, 86-87, 92, 2003, Dublin, Ireland, 1991, La. State U., Aix-en-Provence, France, 1993, Tulane U., Spetses, Greece, 1998, Australian Nat. U., 2001; Ronald Graveson Meml. lectr. King's Coll., London, 2000, lectr. Hague Acad. Internat. Law, 1984; cons. U.S. Dept. State, 1995-2000, European Union Parliament, 2005; cons. in field. Author: International Litigation and Arbitration, 1994, 5th rev. edit., 2006, ann. supplement; (with Eugene Scoles) Cases and Materials on the Conflict of Laws, 1967, 2d rev. edit., 1972, supplement, 1978, Commentary on the Conflict of Laws, 1971, 5th rev. edit., 2006, ann. supplement; (with Hamilton and Rau) Cases and Materials on Contracts, 1984, 2d rev. edit., 1992; (with Hay and Borchers) Cases and Materials on the Conflict of Laws, 12th rev. edit., 2004, annual supplement; contbr. articles to profl. jours. Trustee U. Iowa Sch. Religion, 1960-65. With U.S. Army, 1953-55. Recipient Disting. Prof. award U. Tex. Sch. Law, 1977, Teaching Excellence award, 1979, cert. of meritorious service Am. Bar Assn., 1977, cert. of meritorious service Tex. Bar Assn., 1978, Best Tchr. award U. Houston, 1980, Carl Fulda award scholarship in internat. law, 1993. Mem. Am. Law Inst. (life), Am. Bar Found. (life), Tex. Bar Found. (life), Scribes. Jewish. Office: U Tex Sch Law 727 E Dean Keeton Austin TX 78705-3224 Office Phone: 512-232-1370. E-mail: rweintraub@law.utexas.edu. *The only true happiness lies in useful work done to the best of your ability.*

WEINTRAUB, SAM, retired reading educator; b. St. Louis, Apr. 24, 1927; s. Julius and Jeannette (Schwartz) W.; 1 child, Robert. BA, Ohio State U., 1948, BS, 1950, MEd, 1954; EdD, U. Ill., 1960. Tchr. Wyandotte Pub. Schs., Mich., 1950-53, Campus Sch. Wis. STate Coll., La Crosse, 1953-54; asst. prof. Case Western Res. U., Cleve., 1960-61, U. Chgo., 1964-68; assoc. prof. Ind. U., Bloomington, 1968-74; prof. SUNY-Buffalo, Amherst, 1974-95, prof. emeritus, 1995—. Vis. prof. Tex. Woman's U., Denton, 1980-81; cons. in field. Author, editor: Ann. Summary of Investigations Relating to Reading, 1968-97; co-editor: Improving Reading Research, 1976; co-editor jour. Reading Rsch. Quar., 1969-79. Recipient Legacy Builder award Family and Children's Svc. of Niagara, Inc., 2003; named to Reading Hall of Fame. Fellow Nat. Conf. Rsch. in English (pres. 1978-79); mem. Internat. Reading Assn. (Spl. Svc. award 1987, Wm. S. Gray citation of merit 1997), Nat. Coun. Tchrs. English, Am. Ednl. Rsch. Assn., Niagara Frontier Reading Coun. (v.p. 1990-91, Spl. Svc. award 1990). Avocations: reading, travel.

WEINTRAUB, SIDNEY, economist, educator; b. NYC, May 18, 1922; s. Reuben and Anna Weintraub; m. Gladys Katz, Aug. 11, 1946; children: Jeffrey, Marcia Weintraub Plunkett, Deborah Weintraub Chilewich. BBA, CCNY, 1943; B, MA in Journalism, U. Mo., 1948; MA in Econs., Yale U., 1958; PhD in Econs., Am. U., 1966. Commd. fgn. svc. officer Dept. State, 1949, dep. asst. sec. of state for internat. fin. and devel. Washington, 1969-74; asst. adminstr. for interagy. devel. coordination AID, 1974-75, exec. dir. interagy. devel. coordination com., 1974-75; ret., 1975; sr. fellow Brookings Instn., Washington, 1978-79; Dean Rusk prof. Lyndon B. Johnson Sch. Pub. Affairs, U. Tex., Austin, 1976-96, prof. emeritus, 1996, also co-dir. Program for U.S.-Mex. Policy Studies; William E. Simon chair in polit. economy Ctr. Strategic and Internat. Studies, 1993—. Disting. vis. scholar Ctr. for Strategic and Internat. Studies, Washington, 1990. Author: Free Trade with Mexico, 1984, A Marriage of Convenience: Relations Between Mexico and The United States, 1990, NAFTA: What Comes Next, 1994, NAFTA at Three: A Progress Report, 1997, Financial Decision-Making in Mexico: To Bet a Nation, 2000, Commentaries on International Political Economy: Constructive Irreverence, 2004, NAFTA's Impact on North America: The First Decade, 2004, Energy Cooperation in the Western Hemisphere: Benefits and Impediments, 2007; contbr. articles to profl. jours. Served with U.S. Army, 1943-46. Recipient Disting. Career Svc. award AID, 1975 Mem.: Am. Econ. Assn., Am. Fgn. Service Assn., Coun. on Fgn. Rels., Cosmos (Washington). Office: Ctr Strategic and Internat Studies 1800 K St NW Washington DC 20006-2202 Home Apt 2E 3900B Watson Pl NW Washington DC 20016 Home Phone: 202-337-2715; Office Phone: 202-775-3292. Personal E-mail: sidney.weintraub@gmail.com. *Once having been thrust into the Second World War, my main intellectual interest has been in foreign affairs. I had concluded, as President Kennedy did later, that domestic issues can hurt but misplaced foreign policy can kill. My drive has been to understand what motivates nations, what stimulates people within different nations, what is the U.S. national interest, and to become as expert as my talents would allow about such crucial issues as domestic security, international economic interaction, social mobility, and human development generally. This remains my ambition.*

WEINTRAUB, STANLEY, arts and humanities educator, writer; b. Phila., Apr. 17, 1929; s. Ben and Ray (Segal) W.; m. Rodelle Horwitz, June 6, 1954; children: Mark, David, Erica. BS, West Chester State Coll., Pa., 1949; MA, Temple U., 1951; PhD, Pa. State U., 1956. Instr. Pa. State U., University Park, 1953-59, asst. prof., 1959-62, asso. prof., 1962-65, prof. English, 1965-70, research prof., 1970-86, Evan Pugh prof. Arts and Humanities, 1986-99, Evan Pugh prof. Emeritus, 2000—; dir. Inst. for Arts and Humanistic Studies, 1970-90. Vis. prof. U. Calif. at Los Angeles, 1963, U. Hawaii, 1973, U. Malaya, 1977, Nat. U. Singapore, 1982 Author: Private Shaw and Public Shaw, 1963, The War in the Wards, 1964, Reggie, 1965, The Art of William Golding, 1965, Beardlsey, 1967, The Last Great Cause, The Intellectuals and the Spanish Civil War, 1968, Evolution of a Revolt: Early Postwar Writings of T.E. Lawrence, 1968, The Literary Criticism of Oscar Wilde, 1968, Journey to Heartbreak, 1971, Whistler: A Biography, 1974, Lawrence of Arabia: the Literary Impulse, 1975, Four Rossettis, A Victorian Biography, 1977, Aubrey Beardsley: Imp of the Perverse, 1976, The London Yankees: Portraits of American Writers and Artists in England, 1894-1914, 1979, The Unexpected Shaw. Biographical Approaches to G.B. Shaw and His Work, 1982, A Stillness Heard Round the World: The End of the Great War, 1985, Victoria. An Intimate Biography, 1987, Long Day's Journey into War: December 7, 1941, 1991, Bernard Shaw: A Guide to Research, 1992, Disraeli: A Biography, 1993, The Last Great Victory-The End of World War II, July/August 1945, 1995, Shaw's People. Victoria to Churchill, 1996, Uncrowned King: The Life of Prince Albert, 1997, MacArthur's War: Korea and the Undoing of an American Hero, 2000, The Importance of Being Edward. King in Waiting, 1841-1901, 2000, Silent Night. The Remarkable 1914 Christmas Truce, 2001, Charlotte and Lionel: A Rothschild Love Story, 2003, General Washington's Christmas Farewell: A Mount Vernon Homecoming, 1783, 2003, Iron Tears: America's Battle for Freedom, Britain's Quagmire: 1775-1783, 2005; editor: An Unfinished Novel by Bernard Shaw, 1958, C.P. Snow: A Spectrum, 1963, The Yellow Book: Quintessence of the Nineties, 1964, The Savoy: Nineties Experiment, 1966, The Court Theatre, 1966, Biography and Truth, 1967, Evolution of a Revolt: Early Postwar Writings of T.E. Lawrence, 1968, The Literary Criticism of Oscar Wilde, 1968, Shaw: An Autobiography 1856-1898, 1969, Shaw: An Autobiography, The Playwright Years, 1898-1950, 1970, Bernard Shaw's Nondramatic Literary Criticism, 1972, Directions in Literary Criticism, 1973, Saint Joan Fifty Years After: 1923/24-1973/74, 1973, The Portable Bernard Shaw, 1977, (with Anne Wright) Heartbreak House. A Facsimile of the Revised Typescript, 1979, (with Richard Aldington) The Portable Oscar Wilde, 1981, Modern British Dramatists, 1900-1945, 1982, The Playwright and the Pirate. Bernard Shaw and Frank Harris: A Correspondence, 1982, British Dramatists Since World War II, 1983, Bernard Shaw, the Diaries, 1885-1897, 1986, Bernard Shaw on the London Art Scene, 1885-1950, 1989, (with Rodelle Weintraub) Dear Young Friend. The Letters of American Presidents to Children, 2000, 11 Days in December. Christmas in the Bulge, 2006, 15 STars. Eisenhower, MacArthur, Marshall: Three Generals Who Saved the American Century, 2007; also editor Comparative Literature Studies, 1987-92, Shaw, The Ann. of Bernard Shaw Studies, 1956-89. Pres. Jewish Community Council of Bellefonte (Pa.) State Coll., 1966-67. Served to 1st lt. AUS, 1951-53, Korea. Decorated Bronze Star medal.; Guggenheim fellow, 1968-69; recipient Disting. Humanist award Pa. Humanities Council, 1985 Mem. The Authors' Guild, PEN. Home: 4 Winterfield Ct Newark DE 19711-2957 Office Phone: 302-235-2859. Personal E-mail: sqw4@comcast.net. *I subscribe to Bernard Shaw's declaration in the Preface to Man and Superman that "This is the true joy in life, the being used for a purpose recognized by yourself as a mighty one; the being thoroughly worn out before you are thrown on the scrap heap; the being a force of Nature instead of a feverish selfish little clod of ailments and grievances complaining that the world will not devote itself to making you happy".*

WEINTRAUT, STEVEN JAMES, lawyer; b. East Moline, Ill., Apr. 16, 1968; BBA in Fin., U. Iowa, 1991; JD with high distinction, U. Iowa Coll. Law, 1994. Bar: Minn. 1994. Shareholder Siegel, Brill, Greupner, Duffy & Foster, P.A., Mpls. Asst. dir. Trial Advocacy Bd. Served in USNR, 1987—92. Named a Rising Star, Minn. Super Lawyers mag., 2006; recipient Internat. Acad. Trial Lawyers award. Office: Siegel Brill Greupner Duffy & Foster PA 100 Washington Ave S Ste 1300 Minneapolis MN 55401 Office Phone: 612-337-6100. E-mail: stevenweintraut@sbgdf.com. *

WEINTZ, JACOB FREDERICK, JR., retired investment banker; b. NYC, June 27, 1926; s. Jacob Frederick and Grace (Cortelyou) W.; m. Elisabeth Hamlin Brewer, Nov. 26, 1955; children: Elizabeth Weintz Cerf, Polly Weintz Sanna, Eric Cortelyou, Karl Frederick. Student, Norwich U., 1943—44, D (hon.) in Fin. Mgmt., 2001; BA, Stanford U., 1948; MBA, Harvard U., 1951. Salesman Vick Chem. Co., NYC, 1948-49; assoc. buying dept. Goldman, Sachs & Co., NYC, 1951-54, assoc. new bus. dept., 1954-65, ptnr., 1965-84; ltd. ptnr. Goldman, Sachs Group L.P., 1984—99; ret., 1999; with BCRS Assocs. LLC, NYC. Pres., chmn. bd. dirs. Stonebridge Condominium Assn., Snowmass Village, Colo., 1978-85; trustee Pace U., 1981-97, Norwich U., Stanford U., 1985-95, Sierra Club Found., 1984-90, 92—98; trustee Harbor Lights Found., N.Y.C., Nat. Lighthouse Mus., S.I.; leadership coun., Harvard Sch. Pub. Health, Pace U. Fin. and Audit and Investment com., 1997-; bd. vis., Stanford Inst. Internat. Studies; vice chmn. bd. dirs. Guiding Eyes for Blind, 1984-93; bd. dir. The Forum World Affairs, Stamford, Conn., 1988-94; pres. Harvard U. Bus. Sch. Alumni Assn., 1988-90; former del. Coun. Governing Bds., Albany, N.Y.; chmn. bd. dirs. N.Y. Young Rep. Club, 1957-58; mem. exec. com. Greenwich Rep. Town Com., Conn., 1962-69, The Task Force on Def. Spending, The Economy and the Nation's Security, BENS-ED Commn. on Fundamental Def. Mgmt. Issues, 1991-92; mem. Stanford in Washington Coun. With USAAF, 1944-45. Recipient La Medaille de la Ville de Paris, 1990, Stanford Gold Spike award, 1992. Mem. Ambs. Round Table (Stamford), Bond Club (N.Y.), Newcomen Soc. N.Am., Down Town Assn., Harvard Club (NYC), Riverside Yacht Club, Flying Scot Sailing Assn. (pres. 1968-69), Theta Chi. Republican. Episcopalian. Home: Harbor Lights 43 Jones Park Dr Riverside CT 06878-2205 Office: BCRS Assocs LLC 100 Wall St New York NY 10005 Home Phone: 203-637-3577; Office Phone: 212-440-0849. Business E-Mail: fweintz@mkllp.com, fweintz@bcrsllc.com.

WEIR, ALEXANDER, JR., chemical engineer, consultant; b. Crossett, Ark., Dec. 19, 1922; s. Alexander and Mary Eloise (Field) W.; m. Florence Forschner, Dec. 28, 1946; children: Alexander III, Carol Jean, Bruce Richard BSChemE, U. Ark., 1943; MChemE, Poly Inst. Bklyn., 1946; PhD, U. Mich., 1954; cert., U. So. Calif. Grad. Sch. Bus. Adminstrn., 1958. Chem. engr. Am. Cyanamid Co., Stamford Rsch. Labs., 1943-47; with U. Mich., 1948-58; rsch. assoc., project supr. Engring. Rsch. Inst., U. Mich., 1948-57; lectr. chem. and metall. engring. dept. U. Mich., 1954-56, asst. prof., 1956-58; cons. Ramo-Woolridge Corp., LA, 1956-57; mem. tech. staff, sect. head, asst. mgr. Ramo-Wooldridge Corp., LA, 1957-60, incharge Atlas Missile Captive test program, 1956-60; tech. adv. to pres. Northrop Corp., Beverly Hills, Calif., 1960-70; prin. scientist for air quality So. Calif. Edison Co., LA, 1970-76, mgr. chem. sys. R & D, 1976-86, chief rsch. scientist, 1986-88; utility cons. Playa Del Rey, Calif., 1988—. Rep. Am. Rocket Soc. to Detroit Nuc. Coun., 1954-57; chmn. session on chem. reactions Nuc. Sci. and Engring. Congress, Cleve., 1955; U.S. del. AGARD (NATO) Combustion Colloquium, Liege, Belgium, 1955; Western U.S. rep. task force on environ. R & D goals Electric Rsch. Coun., 1971; electric utility advisor Electric Power Rsch. Inst., 1974-78, 84-87; industry advisor dept. chemistry and biochemistry Calif. State U., L.A., 1981-88. Author: Two and Three Dimensional Flow of Air through Square-Edged Sonic Orifices, 1954; (with R.B. Morrison and T.C. Anderson) Notes on Combustion, 1955, also some 60 tech. papers; inventor acid rain prevention device used in 5 states. Sea scout leader, Greenwich, Conn., 1944-48, Marina del Rey, Calif., 1965-70; bd. govs., past pres. Civic Union Playa del Rey, chmn. sch., police and fire, nominating, civil def., army liaison coms.; mem. Senate, Westchester YMCA, chmn. Dads sponsoring com., active fundraising; chmn. nominating com. Paseo del Rey Sch. PTA, 1961; mem. LA Mayors Cmty. Adv. Com.; asst. chmn. advancement com., merit badge dean Cantinella dist. LA Area coun. Boy Scouts Am. Recipient Nat. Rsch. Coun. Flue Gas Desulfurization Industrials Scale Reliability award NAS, 1975, Power Environ. Achievement award EPA, 1980, Excellence in Sulfur Dioxide Control award EPA, 1985; named Arkansas Traveler by Gov. Bill Clinton, 1989. Mem.: AIChE, Am. Geophys. Union, Navy League U.S. (v.p. Palos Verdes peninsula coun. 1961—62), NY Acad. Scis., Sci. Rsch. Soc. Am., Am. Chem. Soc., U.S. Power Squadron (navigator), St. Andrew Soc. So. Calif. (hon. capt. of fleet 1997, mem. bd. govs., chair scholarship com.), Clan Buchanan Soc. Am., Ark. Soc. Children of Am. Revolution (past pres.), Betty Washington Lewis Soc. Children of Am. Revolution (past pres.), Clan MacFarlane Soc., Clan Chattan of the US, Clan Farquharson Assn., Clan Macnachtan Assn., Santa Monica Yacht Club (lifetime hon. cannoneer, chief of protocol, vice chmn. marina mgmt. com.), Sigma Xi, Phi Kappa Phi, Phi Lambda Upsilon, Alpha Chi Sigma, Lambda Chi Alpha. Office: 8229 Billowvista Dr Playa Del Rey CA 90293-7807

WEIR, ANNE, writer; b. Boston, Feb. 9, 1942; d. John Weir and Martha (Kingman) Perry; children: Emily Weir, Sarah Noel, Katherine Joy. BA, Swarthmore Coll., Pa., 1964; MEd, U. Maine, Orono, 1984. Cert. elem. and secondary edn. tchr. Editor: Marlowe: Being In the Life of the Mind, 1996, A Book of Certainties, 1998, The Color Book, 1998, Marlowe, corrected and augmented, 1999, Christopher's Journey, Acts & Scenes, News, The Bird's Eye, 1996-2000, A Native Woman poems, 1999, American City, 2000, A Codebook for the Plays, 2000, Waking, An Academic Celebration, 2001, A Teacher's Holiday, "Streamlines" A Study in Bibliography, New Songs, 2001, The Reincarnation of Love, 2002, Literary Picture Notebooks, And in Aftertimes, 2003, Songs for the 20th Century, 2004, Summer Poems, Notes and Notice, 2005, Film, a study, 2006. Office: Writings Press PO Box 10364 Portland ME 04104-0364

WEIR, BRYCE KEITH ALEXANDER, neurosurgeon, neurologist, educator; b. Edinburgh, Apr. 29, 1936; arrived in U.S., 1992, arrived in Can., 2002; s. Ernest John and Marion Weir; m. Mary Lou Lauber, Feb. 25, 1976; children: Leanora, Glyncora, Brocke. BSc, McGill U., Montreal, Que., Can., 1958, MD, CM, 1960, MSc, 1963. Diplomate Am. Bd. Neurol. Surgery, Nat. Bd. Med. Examiners. Intern Montreal Gen. Hosp., 1960-61; resident in neurosurgery Neurological Inst., Montreal, 1962-64, 65-66, NY Neurol. Inst., NYC, 1964—65; neurosurgeon U. Alta., Edmonton, Can., 1967-92, dir. div. neurosurgery, 1982-86, Walter Anderson prof., chmn. dept. surgery, 1986-92; surgeon-in-chief U. Alta. Hosps., 1986-92; Maurice Goldblatt prof. surgery and neurology U. Chgo., 1992—2002, dir. Brain Rsch. Inst., 1993—2001, interim dean biol. scis. divsn. and Pritzker Sch. Medicine, v.p. med. affairs, 2001—02. Past pres. V Internat. Symposium on Cerebral Vasospasm; mem. neurology A study sect. NIH, 1991—93; invited speaker at over 135 profl. meetings; vis. prof. over 68 univs., including Yale U., Cornell U., Columbia U., Duke U., U. Toronto, U. Calif., San Francisco; lectr. in field. Author: Aneurysms Affecting the Nervous System, 1987, Subarachnoid Hemorrhage-Causes and Cures, 1998, Cerebral Vasospasm, 2001; co-editor: Primer on Cerebrovascular Diseases, 1997, Stroke: Pathophysiology, Diagnosis and Management, 4th edit., 2004; mem. editl. bd. Jour. Neurosurgery, chmn. bd, 1993—94, mem. editl. bd. Neurosurgery Quar., Jour. Cerebrovascular Disease, Neurosurgery; contbr. over 275 articles to profl. jours. Named Officer of the Order of Can., 1995. Fellow: ACS, Royal Coll. Surgeons Can., Royal Coll. Surgeons Edinburgh (hon.); mem.: Can. Neurosurg. Soc. (Inaugural Lifetime Achievement award 2006), Interurban Neurosurg. Soc. (chmn.), Nat. Acad. Scis., Inst. Medicine, Japan Neurosurg. Soc. (hon.), Soc. Neurol. Surgeons (Grass gold medal 1992), Am. Acad. Neurol. Surgeons, James. IV Assn. Surgeons, Am. Surg. Assn. Achievements include rsch. in cerebral vasospasm and the surgical management of intracranial aneurysms. Home: 1262 Saturna Dr Parksville BC V9P 2X6 Canada

WEIR, DAME GILLIAN CONSTANCE, musician; b. Martinborough, New Zealand, Jan. 17, 1941; d. Cecil Alexander and Clarice M. Foy (Bignell) W. Grad., Royal Coll. Music, London, 1965; Mus D (hon.), U. Victoria of Wellington, New Zealand, 1983; DLitt (hon.), Huddersfield U., 1997; Mus D (hon.), Hull U., 1999, Exeter U., 2001; Doctorate (hon.), U. Ctrl. Eng., 2001; Mus D (hon.), Leicester Univ., 2003; MusD (hon.), U. Aberdeen, Scotland, 2004. Artist-in-residence numerous univs. including Yale U, Washington U., St. Louis, U. Western Australia, Johns Hopkins U., 2005, others; vis. lectr. Royal No. Coll. Music, Manchester, Eng., 1974-89; vis. prof. organ Royal Acad. Music, London, 1997-98; Prince Consort prof. Royal Coll. of Music, London, 1999—; spkr. BBC programs on music and performance; subject of Melvyn Bragg's TV documentary South Bank Show, 2000; apptd. Disting Artist-in-residence Peabody Inst., John Hopkins U., Balt., 2005; internat. chair in organ Royal No. Coll. Music, 2006. Concert appearances with leading Brit. Orchs. and Boston Orch., Seattle Orch., Australian ABC Orch., Wurttemberg Chamber and other fgn. orch.; appeared in major internat. festivals including Edinburgh, Flanders, Aldeburgh, Bath, Proms, Europalia; appeared at concert halls including Royal Festival Hall, Royal Albert Hall, Lincoln Ctr., NY, Sydney Opera House; numerous radio and TV appearances in Brit. and world-wide including Royal Festival Hall Jubilee; organ cons.; adjudicator internat. competitions; contbr. The Messiaen Companion, 1995; contbr. articles to profl. jour.; recs. include complete organ works of Olivier Messiaen, others; TV documentary film on career, 1982, BBC TV programs The King of Instruments, 1989. Decorated comdr., dame comdr. Order Brit. Empire; recipient Turnovsky award 1985, Evening Std. award for outstanding solo performance, 1998-99, Lifetime Achievement award The Link Found., London, 2005; winner 1st prize St. Albans Internat. Organ Competition, 1964. Fellow Royal Coll. Organists (hon., mem. coun. 1977—, mem. exec. 1981-85, pres. 1994-96, 1st Woman pres.), Royal Can. Coll. Organists (hon.), Royal Coll. Music (London); mem. Royal Acad. Music (hon.), Inc. Soc. Musicians (1st woman pres. 1992-93), Albert Schweitzer Assn. (Silver medal 1998). Office: care Karen McFarlane Artists 2385 Fenwood Rd Cleveland OH 44118-3803 Office Phone: 440-542-1882. Personal E-mail: gillianweir@gillianweir.com.

WEIR, MARGARET, sociologist, political science professor; BA in Polit. Sci., Antioch Coll., 1975; MA, Brandeis Univ., 1978; PhD, Univ. Chgo., 1986. Asst. prof., govt. Harvard Univ., 1985—89, assoc. prof., 1989—90, John L. Loeb assoc. prof. social sci., 1990—92; sr. fellow, govtl. studies Brookings Inst., 1992—97, non-resident sr. fellow; and prof., dept. social, polit. sci. Univ. Calif., Berkeley, 1997—. Co-author (with Ira Katznelson): Schooling for All, 1985; author: Politics and Jobs, 1992. Fellow: Am. Acad. Arts & Scis. Office: Depts Sociology & Polit Sci 410 Barrows Hall #1980 Univ Calif Berkeley CA 94720 Office Phone: 510-643-1602. Business E-Mail: mweir@socrates.berkeley.edu, mweir@berkeley.edu. *

WEIR, PETER LINDSAY, film director; b. Sydney, Aug. 21, 1944; s. Lindsay Weir and Peggy Barnsley; m. Wendy Stites, 1966; 2 children. Educated, Scots Coll., Sydney, Vaucluse Boys H.S., Sydney U. Worked in real estate until 1965; worked as stagehand in TV, Sydney, 1967; dir. film sequences in variety show, 1968; dir. amateur univ. revs., 1967-69; dir. for Film Australia, 1969-73; made own short films, 1969-73, ind. feature film producer, dir. and writer, 1973—. Films include: Cars That Ate Paris, 1973, Picnic at Hanging Rock, 1975, The Last Wave, 1977, The Plumber (TV), 1978, Gallipoli, 1980 (Australian Film Inst. award for best dir., 1981), The Year of Living Dangerously, 1982, Witness, 1985, The Mosquito Coast, 1986, Dead Poets Society, 1989, Green Card, 1990, Fearless, 1993, The Truman Show, 1997 (David Lean award for best dir., BAFTA, 1999, London Critics Circle Film award for best dir., 1999), Master and Commander: The Far Side of the World, 2003. Raymond Longford Award, Australian Film Inst., 1990, Douglas Sirk Award, 1998. Mem. Australia A.M. Office: Creative Artists Agy care John Ptak 9830 Wilshire Blvd Beverly Hills CA 90212-1804

WEIR, RICHARD DALE, elementary school educator; b. Diamond Springs, Calif., Oct. 2, 1940; s. Martin Gaines and Phyllis Lorene (Sargent) W.; m. Carol Jean Baker, Dec. 25, 1976; children:; David Richard, Barbara Anne, Susan Michelle, Roger Allen. BS in Elem. Edn., Oklahoma City U., 1976, MEd, 1988; BS in Mgmt. Info. Sys., Coleman Coll., LaMesa, Calif., 1987. Cert. tchr. K-8, Okla. Joined USCG, 1961, advanced through grades to chief warrant officer, 1976, adminstrv. officer Washington, 1976-82, ret., 1982; platform instr. IBM Corp., Oklahoma City, 1985-86; mid. sch. tchr. Archdiocese Oklahoma City, 1987-88; adj. prof. Oklahoma City U., 1988-91; elem. tchr. Oklahoma City Pub. Schs., 1988—, adminstrv. intern, 1997-98; math. supr. Okla. State Dept. Edn., 1998-99; math. coord. Putnam City Pub. Schs., Warr Acres, Okla., 1999—. Cons. in tng. math.-sci. tchrs.; trainer for Activities Integrating Math./Scis. Nat. Leadership Network. Recipient Presdl. award for excellence in sci. and math. teaching NSF, Washington, 1993, Okla. Outstanding Tchr. award Math. Assn. Am., Washington, 1996. Mem. ASCD, Nat. Sci. Tchrs. Assn., Nat. Coun. Tchrs. Math., Coun. Presdl. Awardees Math., Okla. Coun. Tchrs. Math. (advisor Metro Oklahoma City), Soc. Elem. Presdl. Awardees. Republican. Methodist. Avocation: golf. Home: 18218 Paradise Mountain Rd Spc 77 Valley Center CA 92082-7009 Office: Putnam City Academy 5604 NW 41st St # 300 Warr Acres OK 73122-3204

WEIR, SONJA ANN, artist; b. Hazleton, Pa., Oct. 12, 1934; d. Stephen and Anna (Prehatny) Tatusko; m. Richard Clayton Weir, Jan. 14, 1956; children: Robert, Carl, Donna, Lisa, and Nancy. Studied with Mary Ellen Silkotch, 1963—83; student, Art Students League, NYC, 1985—87. Artist Knickerbocker Toy Co., Middlesex, NJ, 1980; represented by Agora Gallery, Soho, NY, 1999. Guest spkr. career day Bridgewater H.S., 1993-94; tchr. adult art edn. in Jointure, Raritan, NJ, 2001-03; mem. staff Jointure Cmty. Adult Edn. Inc., Raritan, NJ, 2002-07. One-woman shows include Johnson & Johnson, Piscataway, NJ, 1992, Stillman, NJ, 2003 (Meml. award), Somerset County Libr., Bridgewater, NJ, 1992—94, Manville Pub. Libr., NJ, 1994—99, Somerset County Libr., 2007, Morris County Libr., 2007, exhibited in group shows at Raritan Valley Art Assn., 1982—83, 1995, 1998 (Best in Show award, 1983, 2d prize, 1995, 1st pl. for oil, 1998), Ariel Gallery, NYC, 1991, Am. Artists Profl. League, 1991, 1994, Barren Art Ctr., Woodbridge, N.J., 1993, Agora Gallery, NYC, 1995—99, 2001, Somerset County Libr., 1998—99, Am. Artists Profl. League, 1999, Atrium Gallery, Morristown, NJ, 2001, Somerset County Cultural and Heritage Gallery, 2003, Johnson & Johnson, Stillman, NJ, 2003, Children's Specialized Hosp., NJ, 2003, Barrons Art Ctr., Woodbridge, NJ, 2003, Art Extraordinaire, Bernardsville, N.J., 2004, NJ Soc. Watercolor Show, 2004 (award of excellence, 2004), Amsterdam Whitney Gallery, NYC, 2005, Taiwan Ctr., Flushing, NY, 2006, Lamington Ch., Bedminster, NJ, 2006, Taiwan Ctr. Ann. Internat., 2006, Represented in permanent collections N.W.B. Bank of South Bound Brook, NJ, Summit Bank, Star Ledger, 2003, Chronicle, Bound Brook, NJ, 2003, juried mem. show, Salmagundi Club, NYC, 2007; featured in Artis Apectrum mag., vol. 11/6, 1999, Star Ledger, 2000. Judge Essex Watercolor Soc. Recipient Peter Matulavage award Salmagundi Club, Meml. award Am. Artists Profl. League, NYC, Samual Lightment Meml. award Salmagundi Club, 2003; Sr. Artist Exhbn. Citation award, Bd. of Chosen Freeholders in Somerset County, NJ, 2005. Fellow: Nat. Am. Artists Profl. League (v.p. NJ chpt. 1988—91, publicity com. 1988—91, show chmn. 1989—91, pres. NJ chpt. 1992—95, editor newsletter 1992—99, nat. exec. bd. 1998—2000, show chmn. 2001—04, nat. pres. 2001—05); mem.: Am. Artists Profl. League (nat. pres. 2002—06), Miniature Art Soc. Fla., Nat. Miniature Assn. (assoc.), Raritan Valley Arts Assn. (pres. 1982—84), Nat. Mus. Women in the Arts (charter mem.), Salmagundi Club (NYC). Home: 25 Madison St South Bound Brook NJ 08880-1244

WEIR, WILLIAM BRADLEY, emergency physician; b. Aurora, Ill., July 31, 1975; s. William H. and Marilyn J. Weir; m. Brishen M. Lewis, June 23, 2001; 1 child, Isabelle M. BA in Rhetoric & Physiology with high distinction, U. Ill., Urbana-Champaign, 1993—98; MD, U. Ill., Chgo., 1999—2003. Lic. emergency medicine Ind. U. Emergency Medicine Residency, 2006. Emergency medicine resident physician Ind. U. Emergency Medicine Residency, Indpls., 2003—06; emergency physician Carle Found. Hosp., Urbana, 2006—. Author: (medical textbook) American Academy of Emergency Medicine Resident and Student Association Toxicology Handbook; contbr. articles to profl. jours. Physician Army National Guard, N.Riverside, Ill., 1999—2003, Camp Atterbury, Ind., 2003—06, Air National Guard, St. Louis, 2006. Grantee Michael Spadafora Med. Toxicology scholarship, Soc. Academic Emergency Medicine. Mem.: Am. Coll. Emergency Physicians, Am. Acad. Emergency Medicine, Nat. Assn. EMS Physicians, Alpha Omega Alpha. Avocations: scuba diving, snow skiing, martial arts. Office: Carle Found Hosp 602 W University Ave Urbana IL 61801 Home Phone: 217-586-7969.

WEIR, SIR WILLIAM H., lawyer, judge, educator; b. East Orange, N.J., Mar. 16, 1947; s. William F. and Nela (Stinnett) W.; m. Marilyn Fowler, Dec. 6, 1969; 1 child, William Bradley. B.S., Eastern Ill. U., 1969; J.D., John Marshall Law Sch., 1977. Bar: Ill. 1977, U.S. Dist. Ct. (no. dist.) Ill. 1977. Field rep. Aetna Casualty, Chgo., 1972-76; assoc. Tomlinson & Thomas, Arlington Heights, Ill., 1976-77; ptnr. Brittain, Ketcham, Strass, Terlizzi, Flanagan, Weir & Johnson, P.C., Elgin, Ill., 1977—2003; prof. bus. law Elgin Community Coll., 1980—89; judge 16th Judicial Cir., 2003—. Author Tort Law Newsletter, 1981. Pres., Elgin YMCA, 1982-84. Served to capt. USMC, 1967-72.; Knited, 2000; Mem. Assn. Trial Lawyers Am., Ill. Trial Lawyers Assn., ABA, Ill. State Bar Assn. (speaker, co-editor tort laws newsletter 1981-83), Kane County Bar Assn. (treas., civil practice com., speaker), Navy League, Am. Legion. Lodge: Kiwanis (Elgin).

WEIS, CHARLIE, college football coach; b. Trenton, NJ, Mar. 30, 1956; m. Maura Weis; 2 children. BA speech, drama, Notre Dame Univ, 1978; MA education, South Carolina Univ, 1989. Asst. coach Boonton High School, NJ, 1979, Morristown High School, NJ, 1980—84; grad. asst., defensive backs coach South Carolina U., 1985, 1986, defensive ends coach, 1987, asst. recruiting coord., 1988; head coach Franklin Township High School, 1989; def. asst., asst. special teams coach NY Giants, 1990, running backs coach, 1991—92; tight ends coach New England Patriots, 1993—94, running backs coach, 1995, wide receivers coach, 1996, NY Jets, 1997, offensive coord., wide receivers coach, 1998—99; offensive coord., running backs coach New England Patriots, 2000, offensive coord., quarterbacks coach, 2001—02, offensive coord., 2003—05; head football coach Notre Dame U., South Bend, Ind., 2005—. Co-author (with Vic Carucci): No Excuses: One Man's Incredible Rise Through the NFL to Head Coach of Notre Dame, 2006. Achievements include being a coach for Super Bowl Champion New York Giants, 1990, New England Patriots, 2000, 2003, 2004. Office: C112 Joyce Center Notre Dame IN 46556 *

WEIS, FREDERICK M., academic administrator; m. Mary Fraser Weis; children: Matt, Marianna. Grad., Claremont McKenna Coll., 1965, MBA in Mgmt. and Fin., MA in Higher Edn. Dir. fin. and bus. affairs, treas. Scripps Coll., Claremont, Calif., 1980—82, interim pres., 2007—; v.p., treas. Claremont McKenna Coll., 1982—2002, exec. practitioner in residence, 2003—. Bd. mem. EDFUND, Rancho Cordova, Calif. Contbr. articles to profl. jours. Office: Scripps Coll Office of Pres 1030 Columbia Ave Claremont CA 91711 Office Phone: 909-621-8000.

WEIS, JOSEPH FRANCIS, JR., federal judge; b. Pitts., Mar. 12, 1923; s. Joseph Francis and Mary (Flaherty) Weis; m. Margaret Horne Weis, Dec. 27, 1958; children: Maureen, Joseph Francis, Christine. BA, Duquesne U., 1947; JD, U. Pitts., 1950; LLD (hon.), Dickinson Coll., 1989. Bar: Pa. 1950. Pvt. practice, Pitts., 1950—68; judge Ct. Common Pleas, Allegheny County, Pa., 1968—70, US Dist. Ct. (we. dist.), Pa., 1970—73, US Ct. Appeals (3d cir.), Pitts., 1973—88, sr. judge, 1988—. Lectr. trial procedures, 1965—; adj. prof. law U. Pitts., 1986—; chmn. Fed. Cts. Study Com., Jud. Conf. Com. on Expt. to Videotape Trial Procs. within the 3rd Cir., Internat. Jud. Conf. the Joint Am.-Can. Appellate Judges Conf., Toronto, 1986, London, 85; futurist subcom. bicentennial com. Ct. Common Pleas, Allegheny County, Pa., 1988; participant programs legal medicine, Rome, London; mem. Am.-Can. Legal Exch., 1987; apptd. by Chief Justice Rehnquist US Jud. Conf., Com. on Internat. Jud. Rels., 1998—2004; com. on adminstrn. bankruptcy sys., subcom. on jud. improvements Jud. Conf. US, 1983—87, chmn. civil rules com., 1986—87, chmn. standing com. rules of practice and procedure, 1988. Contbr. articles to profl. jours. Active Mental Health and Mental Retardation Bd., Allegheny County, 1970—73, Leukemia Soc., 1970—73, Disabled Am. Vets., Cath. War Vets, Mil. Order of the World Wars; trustee Forbes Hosp. Sys., Pitts., 1969—74; bd. adminstrn. Cath. Diocese Pitts., 1971—83. Capt. US Army, 1943—48. Decorated Bronze Star, Purple Heart with oak leaf cluster, French War Cross with palm; recipient St. Thomas More award, 1971, Phillip Amram award, 1991, Edward J. Devitt Disting. Svc. to Justice award, 1993, History Makers award, 1997. Fellow: Am. Bar Found., Internat. Acad. Trial Lawyers (hon.); mem.: ABA (chmn. appellate judges' conf. 1981—83), Inst. Jud. Adminstrn., Am. Judicature Soc., Acad. Trial Lawyers Allegheny County (past pres., Disting. Svc. award 1997, Jud. Leadership and Excellence award 2004), Allegheny Bar Assn. (past v.p.), Pa. Bar Assn., French Legion of Honor (knight), 4th Armored Divsn. Assn., Am. Legion, Knights of Malta, KC. Office: US Ct Appeals 5200 US PO and Ct House 7th Ave & Grant St Pittsburgh PA 15219 *

WEIS, JUDITH SHULMAN, biology professor; b. NYC, May 29, 1941; d. Saul B. and Pearl (Cooper) Shulman; m. Peddrick Weis; children: Jennifer, Eric. BA, Cornell U., 1962; MS, NYU, 1964, PhD, 1967. Lectr. CUNY, 1964-67; asst. prof. Rutgers U., Newark, 1967-71, assoc. prof., 1971-76, prof., 1976—. Congl. sci. fellow U.S. Senate, Washington, 1983—84; mem. grant rev. panel NSF, Washington, 1976—82, program dir., 1988—90; mem. rev. panel EPA, 1984—92; mem. NOAA Nat. Sea Grant Rev. Panel, 1997—; vis. scientist EPA Lab., Gulf Breeze, Fla., 1992. Mem. marine bd. NAS, 1991—94. Grantee NOAA, 1977—, N.J. EPA Rsch., 1978-79, 81-83, N.J. Marine Scis. Consortium Rsch., 1987—; NSF fellow, 1962-64, U.S. Geol. Survey, 1996—, NSF, 1998—. Mem.: NOW (pres. Essex County 1972), AAAS (chair biology sect. 1999), Assn. Women in Sci. (councilor 2002—05), Ecol. Soc. Am., Estuarine Rsch. Fedn., Soc. Environ. Toxicology and Chemistry (bd. dirs. 1990—93), Am. Inst. Biol. Scis. (bd. dirs. 1986—88, 1989—91, 1997—99, pres.-elect 2000—01, pres. 2001), Sierra Club (bd. dirs. N.J. chpt. 1986—88). Avocations: choral singing, swimming, light opera. Office: Rutgers U Dept Biol Scis Newark NJ 07102 Office Phone: 973-353-5387. Business E-Mail: jweis@andromeda.rutgers.edu.

WEIS, MARGARET EDITH, writer, editor; b. Independence, Mo., Mar. 16, 1948; d. George Edward and Francis Irene (Reed) W.; m. Robert William Baldwin, Aug. 22, 1970 (div. 1981); children: David William (dec.), Elizabeth Lynn; m. Donald Bayne Stewart Perrin, 1996 (div. 2003). BA in Creative Writing, U. Mo., 1966-70. Proofreader Herald Pub. House, Independence, Mo., 1970-73, advt. dir., 1973-82; dir. div. Independence Press, 1977-82; editor TSR Inc, Lake Geneva, Wis., 1982-86. Freelance writer; owner Sovereign Press, Williams Bay, Wis., margaretweis.com, Margaret Weis Prodns., Ltd. Author: (short story) The Test of the Twins, 1984, (books) The Endless Catacombs, 1984, Tower of Midnight Dreams, 1984, (with Tracy Hickman) The Dragonlance Chronicles, Vols. 1-3, 1984, 85, Dragonlance Legends, Vols. 1-3, 1985, 86, The Darksword Trilogy, Vols. 1-3, 1987, (with Roger Moore) Riddle of The Griffon, 1985, (under Margaret Baldwin) The Boys Who Saved The Children, 1982, Kisses of Death, 1983, (with Pat O'Brien) Wanted: Frank and Jesse James, The Real Story, 1981, (with Janet Pack) Children of The Holocaust, 1986, My First Thanksgiving, 1983, (with Gary Pack) Computer Graphics, 1984, Robots and Robotics, 1984, (short story) The Thirty Nine Buttons, 1987, (novella) (with Tracy Hickman) The Legacy, 1987, Wanna Bet?, 1987; editor: The Art of Dungeons and Dragons, 1985, Leaves of the Inn of the Last Home, 1987, The Art of Dragonlance, 1987, Dragonlance Tales, vol. 1, 2, 3, 1987, (with Tracy Hickman) The Rose of the Prophet, 1989, (with Tracy Hickman) Death's Gate, vol. 1, 1990, vols. 2, 3, 4, 5, 6, 7, Star of the Guardian, vol. 1, The Lost King, 1990, King's Test vol. 2, 1991, King's Sacrifice Vol. 3, 1991, Ghost Legion Vol. 4, 1991, Dragons of Summer Flame, 1996, (with Don Perrin), Doom Brigade, 1997, Mag Force 7 novels, 3 vols., The Soulforge, 1998, Brothers in Arms, 1999, (with Tracy Hickman) Starshield, Vols. 1-3, 1997, Legacy of the Darksword, 1997, War of Souls, 3 vols., 2000; editor: Kender, Gully Dwarves and Gnomes, 1989, Love and War, 1991, Reign of Istar, 1993, Dragons of War, 1996, Dragons of Chaos, 1997, Relics and Omens, 1998, Sovereign Stone Role-Playing Games, 1999, Sovereign Stone novels, (with Tracy Hickman) vol. 1, Well of Darkness, 2000, vol. 2, Guardians of the Lost, 2001, Journey Into the Void, vol. 3, 2003, Mistress of Dragons, 2003, Draconian Measures, 2000, Dragon's Son, 2004, Ashes and Amber, 2004, Master of Dragons, 2005, Ashes and Iron, 2005, (with Tracy Hickman) The Lost Chronicles, vol. 1 Dragons of the Dwarven Depths, Lost Chronicles, Dragons of Highland Skies, 2007, (movie) Dragon of Autumn Twilight. Named to Writer's Hall of Fame, 2002, Adventure Gaming Hall of Fame, 2002; recipient Origins award, 2001. Avocations: flyball, agility. Office Phone: 262-725-3518.

WEIS, ROBERT FREEMAN, supermarket company executive; b. Sunbury, Pa. m. Patricia Ross; children: Jennifer, Colleen, Jonathan. Grad., Mercersburg Acad., 1937; BA, Yale U., 1941. With Weis Markets, Sunbury, Pa., 1946—, v.p., treas., bd. dirs., treas., 1995—, chmn. bd. dirs., 2002—. Chair steering com. capital campaign Susquehanna U., Selinsgrove, Pa., past vice chmn. bd. trustees; past pres. bd. trustees Sunbury Cmty. Hosp., trustee; bd. dirs. Lown Cardiovascular Rsch. Found., Brookline, Mass. Past pres. Sunbury C. of C.; past chmn. bd. dirs. First Nat. Trust Bank Sunbury, emeritus dir.; past dir. Susquehanna Bancshares; treas. Sunbury chpt. United Jewish Appeal. Office: Weis Markets Inc 1000 S 2d St PO Box 471 Sunbury PA 17801-0471

WEISBERG, BARBARA, writer, editor; b. Phila., Apr. 3, 1946; d. Samuel Weisberg and Miriam (Rosenbach) Weisberg-Kind; m. David Black, June 20, 1996; stepchildren: Susannah Black, Tobiah Black. BA, U. Pa., 1968; MPhil, Yale U., 1972; MFA, Bklyn. Coll., 1992. Prodr., writer Harcourt Brace Jovanovich, NYC, 1973-77; writer WNET/Thirteen, NYC, 1977-80; assoc. dir. TV devel. Scholastic, NYC, 1980-83; dir. TV devel. Consumer Reports, Mt. Vernon, N.Y., 1983-87; writer, prodr., editor NYC, 1987—. Poetry editor Bklyn. Review (lit. jour.), 1992. Co-creator (TV series) Charles in Charge, 1984; author: (children's books) Susan B. Anthony, 1989, Coronado's Golden Quest, 1993, Knights and Castles, 1994, (adult nonfiction) Talking to the Dead, Kate and Maggie Fox and the Rise of Spiritualism, 2004, paperback, 2005. Mem. Hadassah, 1970—, NOW, 1970—, Planned Parenthood, 1985—. Recipient fellowship Yale U., 1971, MacArthur scholarship in poetry Bklyn. Coll., 1991, Wallace fellow for creative artists and writers Am. Antiquarian Soc., 1998, D. Scott Rogo award for Parapsychol. Lit., Parapsychology Found., 1998. Mem. Writers Guild of Am. East, Am. Antiquarian Soc., Authors Guild, Phi Beta Kappa. Democrat. Jewish.

WEISBERG, DAVID CHARLES, lawyer; b. NYC, June 25, 1938; s. Leonard Joseph and Rae M. (Kimberg) W.; m. Linda Gail Kerman, Aug. 27, 1960; children: Leonard Jay, Risa Beth. AB, U. Mich., 1958; LLB, Harvard U., 1961. Bar: N.Y. 1962, U.S. Dist. Ct. (so. and ea. dists.) N.Y. 1965, U.S. Supreme Ct. 1970. Assoc. Dreyer & Traub, Bklyn., 1962, Lee Franklin, Mineola, NY, 1962-65; pvt. practice, Patchogue, NY, 1965-67, 77-80; ptnr. Bass & Weisberg, Patchogue, 1967-77, Davidow, Davidow, Russo & Weisberg, Patchogue, 1981-82, Davidow, Davidow, Weisberg & Wismann, Patchogue, 1982-87, Davidow, Davidow & Wismann, Patchogue, 1988-92, Weisberg & Wismann, Patchogue, 1992-98; propr. The Lawyer's Equalizer, 2000—. Assoc. justice and justice Village of Patchogue, 1968-70, village atty., 1970-85; spl. asst. dist. atty. Suffolk County, Patchogue, 1970-85; assoc. estate tax atty., appraiser N.Y. State Dept. Taxation and Fin., Hauppauge, N.Y., 1975-85; lectr. estate tax Suffolk County Acad. Law, 1976-84, negligence law, 1994; cons. in field. Law chmn. Suffolk County Dem. Com., N.Y., 1975-85; bd. dirs. Temple Beth El of Patchogue. With USAR, 1961-62. Mem. ATLA, N.Y. State Bar Assn., Suffolk County Bar Assn., Nassau-Suffolk Trial Lawyers Sect., Lions (pres. Medford 1978-79, 2d v.p. 1984-85). Avocations: bicycling, skiing. Office Phone: 631-476-6752. Personal E-mail: dcw608@yahoo.com. Business E-Mail: dcw@lawyersequalizer.com.

WEISBERG, DAVID STEVEN, environmental scientist; s. Harry and Rena Weisberg; children: Maya Tubwon, Heather Tubwon. BA magna cum laude, Dartmouth Coll., 1969. Registered sanitarian Minn. Prin. lab. tech. U. Minn., Mpls., 1969—80, asst. scientist, 1980—91; assoc. rschr. U. Wis., River Falls, 1991—93; environ. health inspector City of St. Paul, 1994—2000, environ. health specialist, 2000—. Contbr. articles to profl. jours. Treas. Bicking for City Coun., Mpls., 2005. Recipient Marcus Heiman award, Dartmouth Coll., 1968. Mem.: Minn. Environ. Health Assn. (mem. legis. com. 2000—), Nat. Environ. Health Assn. (registered environ. health specialist). Home: 2425 Franklin Ave E Minneapolis MN 55406 Office: City of St Paul Dept Safety and Inspections 8 E 4th St Ste 200 Saint Paul MN 55101

WEISBERG, HERBERT FRANK, political science professor; b. Mpls., Dec. 8, 1941; s. Nathan R. and Jean (Schlessinger) W.; m. Judith Ann Robinson, Dec. 16, 1979; 1 child, Bryan Bowen. BA, U. Minn., 1963; PhD, U. Mich., 1968. Asst. prof. polit. sci. U. Mich., Ann Arbor, 1967-73, assoc. prof. polit. sci., 1973-74, Ohio State U., Columbus, 1974-77, prof. polit. sci., 1977—, chmn. Dept. Polit. Sci., 2005—. Author: Central Tendency and Variation, 1992, The Total Survey Error Approach, 2005; co-author: Theory Building and Data Analysis, 1984, Controversies in Voting Behavior, 2001, Survey Research Polling and Data Analysis, 1996, Classics in Congressional Politics, 1999; editor: Political Science: Science of Politics, 1985, Democracy's Feast: Elections in America, 1995; co-editor Am. Jour. Polit. Sci., 1979-82, Great Theatre: The American Congress in the 1990's, 1998, Reelection 1996: How Americans Voted, 1999, Models of Voting in Presidential Elections, 2004. Mem.: Am. Polit. Sci. Assn. (program chmn. 1983), Midwest Polit. Sci. Assn. (pres. 2001—02), Phi Kappa Phi, Pi Sigma Alpha, Phi Beta Kappa. Home: 742 Gatehouse Ln Columbus OH 43235-1732 Office: Ohio State U Dept Polic Sci 2140 Derby Hall 154 N Oval Mall Columbus OH 43210-1330

WEISBERG, LEONARD R., retired engineering executive, researcher; b. NYC, Oct. 17, 1929; s. Emanuel E. and Esther (Raynes) W.; m. Frances Simon, Mar. 23, 1980; children: Glenna Weisberg Andersen, Orren Weisberg Falk, Frances Weisberg Brookner. BA magna cum laude, Clark U., 1950; MA, Columbia U., 1952. Rsch. asst. Watson Labs. IBM, NYC, 1953-55; with RCA Labs., Princeton, NJ, 1955-71, mem. tech. staff, 1955-66, head rsch. group, 1966-69, dir. semicondr. device rsch. lab., 1969-71; dir. materials rsch. lab. Itek Corp., Lexington, Mass., 1972-74, v.p., dir. ctrl. rsch. lab., 1974-75; dir. electronics tech U.S. Dept. Def., Washington, 1975-79; v.p. rsch. and engring. Honeywell Inc., Mpls., 1980-94, ret., 1994. Adv. group on electron devices US Dept. Def., 1981—99. Contbr. articles to profl. jours. Recipient award for initiating VHSIC program U.S. Dept. Def., 1979. Fellow IEEE; mem. Am. Phys. Soc., Sigma Xi. Home and Office: 1250 S Washington St # 202 Alexandria VA 22314-4455 Office Phone: 703-549-8151. Personal E-mail: LenW5678@aol.com.

WEISBERG, MORRIS L., retired lawyer; b. Phila., June 7, 1921; s. Alexander and Hilda (Lichtenstein) W.; m. Mildred Norma Lubich, July 7, 1948; children— Richard, James, John BA, U. Pa., 1943, LL.B., 1947; MA, Yale U., 1944. Bar: Pa. 1950, U.S. Dist. Ct. (ea. dist.) Pa. 1950, U.S. Supreme Ct. 1962. Bigelow teaching fellow U. Chgo. Law Sch., 1947-48, Raymond grad. fellow, 1948-49; Gowen fellow U. Pa. Law Sch., Phila., 1948-49; ptnr. Harry Norman Ball, Phila., 1950-56; assoc. Blank, Rome, Comisky & McCauley, and predecessor, Phila., 1956-60, ptnr., 1960-93. Permanent mem. Jud. Conf. 3d Cir. Fellow Am. Bar Found.; mem. Order of Coif, Phi Beta Kappa Assocs. Office: Blank Rome 1 Logan Sq Fl 3 Philadelphia PA 19103-6998

WEISBERG, RICHARD CHARBOURN, lawyer; b. Phila., Oct. 3, 1952; s. Morris L. Weisberg and Mldred L. Lubich; m. Marie-Laure D. Ducamp, 1990; 1 child, Maximilien V. AB with highest honors, Princeton U., 1974; MLitt, Oxford U., Eng., 1976; JD, Yale U., 1979. Bar: Calif. 1979, DC 1985, NY 1998, Pa. Assco. Latham & Watkins, NYC, 1979—86, ptnr., 1986—92, Simpson, Thatcher & Barlett, 1992—97; pvt. practice Bala Cynwyd, Pa. Editor: Yale U. Law Jour., 1978-79. Recipient Marshall Scholar, 1974—76, Albert G. Milbank Memorial prize, Borden Found., John A. Larkin Jr. Memorial prize. Mem. Calif. Bar Assn., DC Bar Assn., Bar Assn. of NYC, Phi Beta Kappa. Editor: Yale U. Law Jour., 1978-79. Office: 33 Derwen Rd Bala Cynwyd PA 19004 Office Phone: 610-664-9405. Office Fax: 215-689-1504.

WEISBERG, ROBERT, ambassador; Grad., Haverford Coll., U. NC Sch. Law, Nat. War Coll. Bar: NY, NH. Devel. officer Dartmouth Coll.; fgn. svc. officer US Consulate Gen., Bombay, 1982—84, US Embassy, Moscow, 1984—86, various other cities including Miton, Geneva, Bishkek, Oslo, Warsaw, C, dep. chief mission Helsinki, Finland; US amb. to Republic of Congo US Dept. State, Brazzaville, 2006—. Recipient Medal for Outstanding Y2K Svc., Pres.'s Coun. on Year 2000 Conversion, Ellis Island Medal of Honor, award, Estrella de Carabobo, Venezuela, Disting. Gold Alumnus award, U. NC Law Sch., Presdl. award for meritorious svc. Office: DOS Amb 2090 Brazzaville Pl Washington DC 20521 *

WEISBERG, RUTH, artist; Laurea in Painting and Printmaking, Acad. di Belle Arti, Perugia, Italy, 1962; BA, U. Mich., 1963, MA, 1965. Lectr., demonstrator, juror, curator U. Mich., 1987, 88, U. Hawaii, Honolulu, 1988, Pa. Acad., Phila., 1987, Queens Coll., N.Y.C., 1987, CCNY, 1987, U. Iowa, 1978, 87, U. N.D., Grand Forks, 1987, Fresno (Calif.) Arts Ctr. and Mus., Carnegie Mellon U., Pitts., 1986, 87, U. Tenn., Knoxville, 1986, U.

Calif., Santa Cruz, 1985, U. Washington, Seattle, U. Kans., Lawrence, Skirball Mus. Hebrew Union Coll., Los Angeles, Calif. Inst. Arts, Valencia, Otis Art Inst., Los Angeles, Mass. Coll. Art, Boston, Norwegian Graphic Artists' Assn., Oslo, Coll. Art Assn. Conf., Detroit, many others; current chairperson art dept., U. So. Calif. Solo and two-person exhibitions include: Pollack Gallery, Toronto, 1969, 71, Richard Nash Gallery, Seattle, 1971, 72, 74, Seaberg-Isthmus Gallery, Chgo., 1972, Mcpl. Art Gallery, Oslo, 1972, Triad Gallery, Los Angeles, 1974, Norwegian Graphic Arts Assn., Oslo, 1976, Palos Verdes (Calif.) Art Gallery, 1976, El Camino Coll., Los Angeles, 1977, Oglethorpe U., Atlanta, 1978, Peppers Art Gallery, U. Redlands (Calif.), 1980, Kellas Gallery, Lawrence, Kans., 1979-81, M. Shore and Sons, Santa Barbara, Calif., 1981, U. Richmond, Va., 1985, U. Tenn., Knoxville, 1986, Sierra Nev. Mus. Arts Reno, 1987, The Alice Simsar Gallery, Ann Arbor, Mich., 1968, 69, 72, 74, 77, 88, Associated Am. Artists, N.Y.C., 1987, Jack Rutberg Fine Arts, Los Angeles, 1983, 85, 88; group exhibitions include: Chgo. Art Inst., 1978, E.B. Crocker Art Mus., 1978-80, Contemporary Arts Ctr., New Orleans, 1980, Pratt Graphic Ctr., N.Y.C., 1978-80, U. Art Mus., U. N.M., 1981, Loyola Marymount U., Los Angeles, 1982, Kenkeleba House, N.Y.C, 1984, The Design Ctr., Los Angeles, 1984, Palos Verdes Art Ctr., 1984, Gallery in the Plaza, Security Pacific Bank, Las Angeles, 1985, Thomas Ctr. Gallery, Gainesville, Fla., Associated Am. Artists, N.Y.C, 1987, many others; works published in The Survey Exhibition Catalogues, 1968-88; permanent collections include: The Achenback Found. for Graphic Arts, Fine Arts Mus., San Francisco, Ariz. State U. Mus., Tempe, The Art Inst. Chgo., The Dance Collection, Lincoln Ctr., N.Y.C., Detroit Inst. Arts, Grunwald Found. for Graphic Arts, U. Calif., Los Angeles, The Bibliotheque Nat. France, Paris, Los Angeles County Mus. Art, The Jewish Mus. N.Y.C, The Nat. Gallery, Washington, The Nat. Musl Women in the Arts, many others; contbr. articles to profl. jours. Mem.: L.A. Printmaking Soc., L.A. Artists Equity (adv. bd.), Tamarind Inst., Coll. Art Assn. (past pres., co-chair studio sessions, nat. adv. bd.). Office: Sch Fine Arts U S Calif Watt Hall 104 Los Angeles CA 90089-0001

WEISBERGER, BARBARA, artistic director, advisor, educator; b. Bklyn., Feb. 28, 1926; d. Herman and Sally (Goldstein) Linshes; m. Sol Spiller, Sept. 3, 1945 (div. 1948); m. Ernest Weisberger, Nov. 15, 1949; children: Wendy, Steven. BS in Edn., Psychology, Pa. State U., 1945; L.H.D. (hon.), Swarthmore Coll., 1970; D.F.A. (hon.), Temple U., 1973, Kings Coll., 1978, Villanova U., 1978, U. New England, 1996. Founder, dir., tchr. Wilkes-Barre (Pa.) Ballet Theater, 1953-63; founder, dir. Pa. Ballet, Phila., 1962-82, Carlisle (Pa.) Project, 1984—96; artistic advisor Peabody Dance, Balt., 2001—. Vice chmn. dance panel Nat. Endowment for the Arts, Washington, 1975-79. Performed with Met. Opera Ballet, N.Y.C., 1937, 38, Mary Binney Montgomery Co., Phila., 1940-42, ballet mistress, choreographer, Ballet Co. of Phila. Lyric Opera, 1961-62; choreographic works include Italian Concerto, Bach, Symphonic Variations, Franck; also operas for, Phila. Lyric Opera Co. Named Disting. Dau. of Pa., 1972, Disting. Alumna, Pa. State U., 1972; recipient 46th ann. Gimbel Phila. award, 1978. Mem. Psi Chi. Home and Office: 571 Charles Ave Kingston PA 18704-4711 Home Phone: 570-287-8349; Office Phone: 570-287-8349.

WEISBERGER, JAMES DAVID, hematopathologist; b. Wilkes-Barre, Pa., Aug. 25, 1955; s. Seymour and Sally Weisberger; m. Linda Ellen Cohen, May 20, 1984; children: Nicholas, Laura. BS, Stanford U., 1977, MS, 1978; MD U. Pa., 1983. Intern, resident internal medicine Calif. Pacific Med. Ctr., San Francisco, 1983—86; internist Fairmount Med. Group, El Cerrito, Calif., 1986—89, Cmty. Health Care Plan, New Haven, 1988—89; resident pathology NY Med. Coll., Valhalla, NY, 1990—94; fellow hematopathology NY Hosp. Cornell Med. Ctr., NYC, 1994—95; asst. prof. pathology and medicine NY Med. Coll., Valhalla, 1995—99, clin. asst. prof. pathology, 1999—; dir. hematopathology IMPATH, Inc., NYC, 1999—2003; v.p. chief med. officer Bio-Reference Labs., Elmwood Park, NJ, 2003—. Contbr. articles various profl. jours. Office: Bio-Reference Labs 481 Edward Ross Dr Elmwood Park NJ 07407

WEISBERGER, JOSEPH ROBERT, retired state supreme court justice; b. Providence, Aug. 3, 1920; s. Samuel Joseph and Ann Elizabeth (Meighan) W.; m. Sylvia Blanche Pigeon, June 9, 1951; children: Joseph Robert, Paula Ann, Judith Marie. AB, Brown U., Providence, 1942, LLD (hon.), 1992; JD, Harvard U., Cambridge, Mass., 1949; LLD (hon.), RI Coll., Providence, Suffolk U., Boston, Mt. St. Joseph Coll.; DCL (hon.), Providence Coll.; DHL (hon.), Bryant Coll., Smithfield, RI; LLD (hon.), Roger Williams Coll., 1992, Constantine U., 1997; LLD, So. New England Sch. Law, 1998; DHL (hon.), Salve Regina U., Newport, RI, 2001. Bar: Mass. 1949, R.I. 1950. With Quinn & Quinn, Providence, 1951-56; solicitor Glocester, RI, 1953-56; judge Superior Ct. RI, Providence, 1956-72; presiding justice RI Superior Ct., Providence, 1972-78; justice RI Supreme Ct., Providence, 1978—, chief justice, 1993—2001; ret., 2001; vol. mediator, 2001—. Adj. prof. U. Nev., 1986—; mem. faculty Nat. Jud. Coll.; vis. lectr. Providence Coll., Suffolk Law Sch., Roger Williams Coll.; chmn. New Eng. Regional Conf. Trial Judges, 1962, 63, 65, New Eng. Regional Commn. Disordered Offender, 1968-71, RI Com. Adoption on Rules Criminal Procedure, 1968-72, RI Adv. Com. Corrections, 1973; bd. dirs. Nat. Ctr. for State Cts., 1975-81; chmn. bd. dirs., bd. overseers Roger Williams U.; chmn. bd. dirs. Roger Williams U. Sch. Law, Joseph R. Weisberger endowed faculty chair, 2007. Chmn. editl. bd. Judges Jour., 1973-75. Pres. RI Health Facilities Planning Coun., 1967-70; chmn. Gov. RI Coun. Mental Health, 1968-73; moderator Town of East Providence, 1954-56; mem. RI Senate, 1953-56, minority leader, 1955-56; vice chmn. bd. trustee RI Hosp., hon. trustee, 2006—, 1968-92, St. Joseph's Hosp., trustee, 1962—. Lt. comdr. USNR, 1941-46. Named to R.I. Hall of Fame; recipient Erwin Griswold award, Nat. Jud. Coll., 1989; Paul Harris fellow, Rotary Internat. Fellow Am. Bar Found.; mem. ABA (ho. of dels., task force on criminal justice stds. 1977-79, exec. com. appellate judges' conf. 1979-95, nat. conf. state trial judges 1977-78, exec. com. appelate judges conf. 1979—, vice chmn., 1983-85, chmn., 1985-86), KC, RI Bar Assn. (Jud. Excellence award 2007), Am. Judges Assn. (gov.), Inst. Jud. Adminstrn., Am. Judicature Soc. (Herbert Harley award 1990), Am. Law Inst., Order of St. Gregory (knight comdr. with star 1989, Goodrich award for Svc. 1995), Phi Beta Kappa (past pres. Alpha chpt. Brown U.). Home: 60 Winthrop St Riverside RI 02915-2624 Office: RI Supreme Ct 250 Benefit St Ste 7 Providence RI 02903-2724 Office Phone: 401-222-7691. *My professional life for the last 50 years has been occupied with judicial duties. I have been blessed with the opportunity to meet ever changing challenges and to attempt to solve a myriad of problems. These opportunities have been rewarding and absorbing. I consider judicial work to be a great privilege.*

WEISBERG-SAMUELS, JANET S., psychologist; b. NYC, Mar. 21, 1940; d. Morris and Vivian (Wank) Weisberg; m. Richard Samuels, Jan. 16, 1983; children: Debra Samuels, David Samuels. BBA, CCNY, 1960; MS, CUNY, 1967; PhD, Yeshiva U., 1984. Lic. psychologist, cert. sch. psychologist N.Y. Psychologist, adminstr. Bklyn. Jewish Hosp., 1969—75, Beth Israel Hosp., NYC, 1975—87; dir. edn. Interfaith Med. Ctr., Bklyn., 1987—; pvt. practice psychology, NYC, 1985—. Program dir. Brotherhood Synagogue, NYC, 1968—75, dir. edn. and tng., 1987—, dept. psychiatry Interfaith Med. Ctr.; team leader N.Y. State Dept. Mental Hygiene, NYC, 1977; cons. N.Y.C. Bd. Edn., 1977, Parent-Child Consultation Ctr., 1980—, Westchester Jewish Comm. Svcs., 2000—06. Pres. singles divsn. Park Ave. Synagogue, NYC, 1980—83; bd. dirs. Couples Club, 1986—, pres., 1988—90. Mem.: APA, Manhattan Psychol. Assn. (exec. bd. 1993—, pres. 1997—98), Ea. Psychol. Assn., N.Y. State Psychol. Assn. (chair internship dirs. 2003—06). Avocations: opera, museums, ballet. Office: 160 E 89th St Apt 1B New York NY 10128-2306 Office Phone: 212-410-4391.

WEISBROD, BURTON ALLEN, economist, educator; b. Chgo., Feb. 13, 1931; s. Leon H. and Idelle C. (Chernoff) W.; m. Shirley Lindsay, Dec. 23, 1951; children: Glen, Linda. BS, U. Ill., 1951; MA in Econs, Northwestern U., 1952, PhD, 1958. Lectr. econs. Northwestern U., Evanston, Ill., 1954-55; instr. econs. Carleton Coll., Minn., 1955-57, Washington U., St. Louis, 1957-58, asst. prof. econs., 1958-62, assoc. prof. econs., 1962-64; vis. assoc. prof. Princeton (N.J.) U., 1962-63; sr. staff mem. Council of Econ. Advs., Pres. U.S., 1963-64; assoc. prof. dept. econs. U. Wis., Madison, 1964-66, prof., 1966-91, Evjue-Bascom prof. econs., 1985—91; dir. Ctr. for Urban Affairs and Policy Rsch. Northwestern U., Evanston, Ill., 1990-95, John Evans prof. econs., 1990—. Vis. prof. SUNY, Binghamton, 1972; sr. Fulbright lectr. U. Autonoma de Madrid, summer, 1970; vis. prof. Yale U., 1976-77; Ziskind vis. prof. Brandeis U., 1982-83; vis. scholar, Brotman fellow J.F. Kennedy Sch., Harvard U., 1982-83; tchg. fellow Australian Nat. U., 1986; mem. rsch. adv. com. Econ. Devel. Adminstrn., U.S. Dept. Commerce, 1967-69; mem. adv. com. Commn. on Pvt. Philanthropy and Pub. Needs, 1973-75; cons. various fed. and state govt. agys., 1964—; also IBM, Econ. Coun. Can., 1969, 71, 76, 78; mem. bd. econ. advs. Public Interest Econs. Ctr., 1973-86; mem. adv. com. med. care and med. econs. to 3d Nat. Cancer Survey, 1969-71; U.S. del. UN World Population Conf., Belgrade, Yugoslavia, 1965; bd. dirs. Nat. Bur. Econ. Rsch., Inc., 1979-90; vis. scholar Phi Beta Kappa Soc., 1998-99; mem. nat. rsch. resources coun. NIH, 1999-03; mem. panel on nonmarket activity NRC, 2002-04; chair com. on philanthropy and the nonprofit sector Social Sci. Rsch. Coun., 2002-04; mem. IRS stats income divsn. Users Adv. Group, 2004-. Author: Economics of Public Health, 1961, External Benefits of Public Education, 1964, (with W. Lee Hansen) Benefits, Costs, and Finance of Public Higher Education, 1969, (with Ralph L. Andreano) American Health Policy, 1974, The Voluntary Nonprofit Sector: An Economic Analysis, 1978, (with Joel F. Handler and Neil K. Komesar) Public Interest Law: An Economic and Institutional Analysis, 1978; contbg. author: (with others) Disease and Economic Development: The Case of Parasitic Diseases in St. Lucia, West Indies, 1974, Economics and Medical Research, 1983, The Nonprofit Economy, 1988; editor (with James Worthy) The Urban Crisis, 1997; author, editor: To Profit or Not to Profit, 1998; contbr. nearly 200 articles on econs. of edn., program evaluation, health care and econs. of pvt. non-profit sector to profl. jours.; mem. editl. bd.: Jour. Human Resources, 1966-86, Internat. Jour. Social Econs, 1972—, Jour. Public Econs, 1971-87, Pub. Fin. Rev., 1990—, Nonprofit and Voluntary Sector Quar., 1997—; assoc. editor: Public Fin. Quar, 1972-87. Guggenheim fellow, 1969-70; Ford Faculty fellow, 1971-72; Sr. research fellow Brookdale Inst., Jerusalem, 1978—; recipient Disting. Lifetime Rsch. award Assn. Rsch. Nonprofit Orgns. and Voluntary Assns., 1997; co-recipient Carl Taube award Disting. Rsch., APHA, 1992. Fellow AAAS; mem. Am. Econ. Assn. (exec. com. 1975-77, com. status of assn. jours. 1973-74, chmn. budget com. 1977), Midwest Econs. Assn. (pres. 1980-81), Nat. Acad. Scis. Inst. Medicine, Public Choice Soc., Internat. Inst. Public Finance, AAUP (exec. com. Washington U. chpt. 1961-62). Office: Northwestern U Econs Dept 2003 Sheridan Rd Evanston IL 60208-0826 Business E-Mail: b-weisbrod@northwestern.edu.

WEISBROD, CARL, lawyer, public official; b. NYC, Oct. 5, 1944; s. Walter and Hilda (Pelzer) W.; m. Jody Adams, Jan. 21, 1979; 1 child, William. BS, Cornell U., 1965; JD, NYU, 1968. Bar: N.Y., 1968; U.S. Dist. Ct. (so. dist.) N.Y., 1969, Asst. commr. N.Y.C. Housing Dept., 1970-72; counsel, chief exec. officer Wildcat Svc. Corp., NYC, 1972-77; gen. counsel Manpower Demonstration Rsch. Corp., NYC, 1977-78; dir. Mayor's Office of Midtown Enforcement, NYC, 1978-84; exec. dir. City Vol. Corps, NYC, 1984-86, N.Y.C. Planning Comm., 1986-87; pres. 42d St. Devel. Project, NYC, 1987-90; pres., chief exec. officer N.Y.C. Econ. Devel. Corp., 1990-94; pres. Alliance for Downtown N.Y., 1995—2005, Trinity Real Estate, NYC, 2005—; dir. Sept. 11 Fund, 2001—. Chmn. N.Y.C. Loft Bd., 1982-84, chmn. Wildcat Svc. Corp., 2002-. Contbr. articles to profl. jours. Trustee The Ford Found., 1996-, NYU Downtown Hosp., 1999-2005; dir. Tarragon Realty Advisors, Inc., Lower Manhattan Devel. Corp., Convention Ctr. Devel. Corp. Office: Trinity Real Estate 74 Trinity Pl New York NY 10006 Office Phone: 212-602-0814. Business E-Mail: cweisbrod@trinitywallstreet.org.

WEISBROD, JOHN, former professional sports team executive; b. Syosset, NY, Oct. 8, 1968; Degree, Harvard U. Exec. v.p., dir. hockey ops., alt. gov. Albany (N.Y.) River Rats, 1993—97; v.p., gen. mgr. Orlando (Fla.) Solar Bears, 1997—2000; COO Orlando (Fla.) Magic, 2000—04, gen. mgr., 2004—05. Mem. Nat. Championship Hockey Team, 1989. Recipient Donald Angier trophy, Harvard U.

WEISBROD, KEN (JOSEPH LOUIS WEISBROD), marketing professional; b. LA, July 31, 1957; s. Louis Isadore and Dolores Joan (Adamczyk) W.; m. Kary Lin Shirley, Jan. 25, 1992 (div. Apr. 2004); children: Katherine Irene, Benjamin Joseph. Cert., Gemological Inst. Am, 1988. Jewelry designer House of Time Jewelers, Granada Hills, Calif., 1968-79; pres. Ken Weisbrod Prodns., Inc., Chatsworth, Calif., 1979-85; v.p. The Ramolap Co., Chatsworth, 1985—. Dir. prodn. Katherine's of Broadway Market, Chatsworth, 1987-, The Sch. of the Arts, 2003-. Designer jewelry for numerous art exhibits, 1969-75. Mem. Advt. Prodn. Assn. L.A., Greater L.A. Zoo Assn., Advertising Prodn. Assn. L.A. Republican. Roman Catholic. Office: Sch of the Arts PO Box 4778 Chatsworth CA 91313-4778 Personal E-mail: louischatsworth@aol.com.

WEISBROD, STEPHEN ADAM, lawyer; s. David and Carol Weisbrod; m. Elizabeth Anne Singer. BA, U. Mich., 1987; JD, Harvard Law Sch., 1991. Bar: DC, Ill., NY. Law clk. to Justice Alan B. Handler NJ Supreme Ct.; law clk. to Chief Judge James B. Moran US Dist. Ct. (no. dist. Ill.); atty. Wilmer, Cutler & Pickering, Paul, Hastings, Janofsky & Walker, LLP; of counsel Gilbert, Heintz & Randolph, LLP, Washington. Faculty mem. Georgetown U. Law Ctr. Grantee Irving R. Kaufman fellowship. Mem.: Nat. Assn. Securities Dealers. Office: Gilbert Heintz & Randolph LLP 1100 New York Ave NW Ste 700 Washington DC 20005 Office Phone: 202-772-1962. E-mail: weisbrods@ghrdc.com. *

WEISBROT, DEBORAH MARCIA, psychiatrist; BA (hons.), Cornell U. Coll. of Arts and Scis., 1975; MD, SUNY, 1979. Cert. diplomate adult, child and adolescent psychiatry 1991. Unit chief, long term treatment unit program Dept. Psychiatry Albert Einstein Coll. of Medicine, Bronx, 1986—91, assoc. dir. residency tng., 1988—91; child, adolescent and adult psychiatry pvt. practice, NYC and Long Island, 1986—98; dir. child and adolescent outpatient svcs. Univ. Hosp., 1998—. Dir. child and adolescent outpatient svcs. Univ. Hosp. Author multiple jour. articles on mood and anxiety disorders in chi. Mem.: Greater L.I. Psychiat. Soc. (bd. dirs.), Acad. Child and Adolescent Psychiatry, Am. Psychiatric. Office: Divsn Child and Adolescent Psychiatry Putnam Hall S Campus SUNY Stony Brook NY 11790-8794 Office Phone: 631-632-8840.

WEISBUCH, ROBERT ALAN, academic administrator; b. Rochester, NY, Nov. 22, 1946; s. Irving Arthur and Ferne (Paull) W.; m. Candy Jaye Cooper, Aug. 27, 1994; 1 child, Gabriel; children from previous marriages: Michael, Sarah, Max. BA magna cum laude, Wesleyan U., Middletown, Conn., 1968; MPhil in English, Yale U., 1970, PhD in English, 1972. Asst. prof. English U. Mich., Ann Arbor, 1972-76, assoc. prof., 1976-85, prof., 1985—, assoc. chmn. dept. English, 1981-84, chmn., 1987-94, assoc. v.p. rsch., assoc. dean faculty programs Rackham Sch. Grad. Studies, 1994-95, assoc. v.p. rsch., 1994-95, interim dean Grad. Sch., 1995-96; pres. The Woodrow Wilson Nat. Fellowship Found., 1997—2005; dir. Mellon Fellowships Humanistic Studies, 1998—2005; pres. Drew U., Madison, NJ, 2005—. Author: Emily Dickinson's Poetry, 1975, Atlantic Double-Cross, 1986; co-editor Dickinson and Audience, 1995. Am. Coun. Learned Socs. fellow, 1976-77, Rackham fellow, U. Mich., 1983; recipient Amoco teaching award U. Mich., 1986 Mem. Phi Beta Kappa. Office: Drew U Office of Pres 36 Madison Ave Madison NJ 07940 Office Phone: 973-408-3100. E-mail: rweisbuc@drew.edu.

WEISBURGER, ELIZABETH KREISER, retired chemist; b. Greenlane, Pa., Apr. 9, 1924; d. Raymond Samuel and Amy Elizabeth (Snavely) Kreiser; m. John H. Weisburger, Apr. 7, 1947 (div. May 1974); children: William Raymond, Diane Susan, Andrew John. BS, Lebanon Valley Coll., 1944, DSc (hon.), 1989; PhD, U. Cin., 1947, DSc (hon.), 1981. Rsch. assoc. U. Cin., 1947-49; col. USPHS, 1951-89; postdoctoral fellow Nat. Cancer Inst., Bethesda, Md., 1949-51, chemist, 1951-73, chief carcinogen metabolism and toxicology br., 1972-75, chief Lab. Carcinogen Metabolism, 1975-81, asst. dir. chem. carcinogenesis, 1981-89, ret. Cons. in field; lectr. Found. for Advanced Edn. in Scis., Bethesda, 1980-95; adj. prof. Am. U., Washington, 1982-83. Asst. editor-in-chief Jour. Nat. Cancer Inst., 1971-87; mem. editl. adv. bd. Chem. Health and Safety, 1994-99, Jour. Applied Toxicology, 1996-2006; contbr. articles to profl. jours. Trustee Lebanon Valley Coll., 1970—, pres. bd. trustees, 1985—89. Recipient Meritorious Svc. medal USPHS, 1973, Disting. Svc. medal, 1985; Hillebrand prize Chem. Soc. Washington, 1981, Charles Gordon award, 1999. Fellow AAAS (nominating com. 1978-81); mem. Am. Chem. Soc. (Garvan medal 1981, Tillmanns-Skolnick award divsn. chem. health and safety 2001), Am. Assn. Cancer Rsch., Soc. Toxicology, Am. Soc. Biochem. and Molecular Biology, Royal Soc. Chemistry, Am. Conf. Govtl. Indsl. Hygienists (Herbert Stokinger award 1996, William Wagner award 2003), Grad. Women in Sci. (hon.), Iota Sigma Pi. Lutheran. Office Phone: 301-309-0078.

WEISBURGER, JOHN HANS, medical researcher; b. Stuttgart, Germany, Sept. 15, 1921; came to U.S., 1943, naturalized, 1944; s. William and Selma (Barth) W.; children: William, Diane, Andrew. AB, U. Cin., 1947, MS, 1948, PhD, 1949; MD (hon.), U. Umeå, Sweden, 1980. Officer USPHS, 1950-72; mem. staff Nat. Cancer Inst., NIH, Bethesda, Md., 1950-61, head carcinogen screening sect., 1961-72; dir. bioassay segment, Carcinogenesis Programs Nat. Cancer Inst., Bethesda, Md., 1971-72; v.p. rsch. Am. Health Found., Valhalla, NY, 1972-87; dir. Naylor Dana Inst. for Disease Prevention, Valhalla, 1972—87; rsch. prof. pathology N.Y. Med. Coll., Valhalla, 1974—; pres. Weisburger Assocs., North White Plains, NY, 1987—2007. Mem. biochemistry and nutrition study sect. NIH, 1957—58; mem. interdepartmental panel on carcinogens FDA, USDA, USPHS, 1962—71; chmn. carcinogenesis subcom. Nat. Large Bowel Cancer Project, 1972—75; mem. expert panel on nitrites and nitrosamines USDA, 1973—77; mem. Nat. Cancer Inst. Clearinghouse on Environ. Carcinogens, 1976—78; co-chmn. organizing com. US-Japan Coop. Workshop on GI Tract Cancer, 1979; chmn. sci. rev. panel NJ State Commn. Cancer Rsch., 1988—90; co-chmn. internat. symposium on health effects of tea, NY, 1991; chmn. nutrition and cancer sect. 3d Anticarcinogenesis & antimutagenesis conf., Italy, 1991; chmn. study sect. NIH-Nat. Cancer Inst., Bethesda, Md., 1991; rsch. fellow Japanese Found. for Promotion of Cancer Rsch. Nat. Cancer Ctr. Rsch. Inst., Tokyo, 1992; adv. com. rev. RDA Food & Nutrition Bd. NAS, 1993; lectr. numerous lectures in field; chmn. numerous confs. national & internat. Assoc. editor Jour. Nat. Cancer Inst., 1960-62, Xenobiotica, 1971—2004, Archives of Toxicology, 1977-87, Internat. Jour. Toxicology, 1982-2002, Preventive Medicine, 1988-2004; mem. internat. editl. adv. bd. Food and Chem. Toxicology, 1967—2004; assoc. editor Cancer Rsch., 1969-80, mem. cover editl. bd., 1987-99; mem. editl. bd. Chemico-Biol. Interactions, 1969-88, Carcinogenesis, 1979-87, Inst. Sci. Info. Atlas of Sci., 1987-89, Cancer Epidemiology Biomarkers Prevention, 1991-98, Cancer Detection Prevention, 1994-2004; mem. guest editl. bd. Japanese Jour. Cancer Rsch., 1987—; hon. editor Protective Effects of Tea on Human Health, 2006; contbr. articles to profl. jours. With US Army, 1944—46, Italy, Austria, ret. col. USPHS. Decorated D.S.M.; recipient Meritorious Svc. medal USPHS HEW, 1970, Outstanding Service award Westchester div. Am. Cancer Soc., 1984, Meyer and Anna Prentis award Mich. Cancer Ctr., 1987; named one of 1000 most cited scientists, ISI List, 1981. Leadership plaque N.J. State Commn. Cancer Rsch., 1990. Fellow N.Y. Acad. Scis., Am. Coll. Nutrition; mem. Am. Assn. Cancer Rsch. (hon. mem., rep. to European Assn. Cancer Rsch. 1985-89), Am. Chem. Soc. (hon., com. environ. improvement 1992-94, chmn. lectr. chemistry and health 31st Middle Atlantic regional meeting 1997, chmn. symposium tea and health, N.Y., 2003), Am. Gastroent. Assn., Am. Soc. Biochem. Molecular Biologists, Am. Soc. Preventive Oncology (founding mem., bd. dirs. 1983-90, Disting. Svc. award 1990), Biochem. Soc. (London, emeritus), Environ. Mutagen Soc., European Assn. Cancer Rsch. (coun. 1985-90), Japan Cancer Assn. (hon. life), Soc. Exptl. Biol. Medicine, Soc. Toxicology (chmn. bd. publs. 1968-71, councilor 1972-74, amb. toxicology Mid-Atlantic divsn. 1990, hon. mem. 1995, Award of Merit 1981), Westchester Chem. Soc. (Disting. Scientist 1996), Sigma Xi, Alpha Chi Sigma (pres. Washington profl. chpt. 1967-68), Phi Lambda Upsilon. Achievements include rsch. in lifestyle and chronic disease prevention, relevant mechanisms, and medical care cost reduction. Home: 4 Whitewood Rd White Plains NY 10603-1137 Personal E-mail: johnweisburger@aol.com. *In my lifetime a revolutionary change occurred in our knowledge of the causes and the mechanisms involved in the major premature killing diseases—heart disease, hypertension, stroke, many forms of cancer. These key advances stemmed from the partnership between the federal government, public-supported societies and academic institutions that encourage health research. The impact of these diseases can be reduced in virtually all countries of the world provided their political bodies can agree that peaceful endeavors and cooperation in fostering better health for their people can be made a high priority goal. Medical science now can implement successful prevention efforts. I am glad I have lived through this period and have played a role in this development.*

WEISEL, MICHAEL LLOYD, lawyer, educator; m. Deborah Lamm Weisel, June 6, 1987; children: Avery Christiana, Schuyler McFall. BS in Bus. Mgmt. and History, Guilford Coll., 1977; JD, Campbell U., 1980; postgrad., Duke U., 2002—; MA in History, N.C. State U., 2003. Bar: N.C. 1980; lic. securities arbitrator Nat. Assn. Securities Dealers, 1998, securities license Series 7, 24 Nat. Assn. Securities Dealers. V.p. equity Wells Fargo Bank, NA, Washington, 1988—90; v.p., portfolio mgr. Kemper Fin. Svcs., Chgo., 1990—95; atty. Allen & Pinnix, Raleigh, 1996—2003, Taylor, Penry, Rash & Riemann PLLC, Raleigh, 2003—07; gen. counsel to spkr. pro tempore N.C. Ho. Reps., NC, 2006; atty. Bailey & Dixon LLP, Raleigh, 2007—. Bd. mem. NC State Banking Commn., Raleigh, 1993—97; trustee N.C. Tchrs. and State Employees' Retirement Systems, Raleigh, 1993—95, N.C. Local Govt. Employees' Retirement Sys., Raleigh, 1993—95; chair Fgn. Trade Zone #93, Raleigh, 1997—; sec. N.C. R.R. Co., 1999—2004, N.C. Devel. Fin. Corp., 2000—, bd. dirs. Local bd. dirs. US SSS, NC, 2003—; commn. mem. Legislative Sch. Capital Constrn. Study Commn., Raleigh, 1993—95; bd. dirs., vice chair fin. com. N.C. Bd. Cmty. Colls., Raleigh, 1997—2000; com. mem. NC Legislative Fin. Institutions Com., Raleigh, 1998—99; chair Wake County Smart Start, Inc., NC, 1997—; elected chair Wake County Dem. Party, NC, 1999—2003; mem. N.C. Dem. Party State Exec. Com., 1997—; candidate Office N.C. State Treas., 1995—96. Named one of Outstanding Young Man of Am., Nat. Jaycees; fellow, Inst. Polit. Leadership; History Departmental fellow, Duke U., 2002—, Summer Seminar in Mil. History fellow, West Point Mil. Acad., 2004. Mem.: Penn Club NY, Union League Club Chgo., Phi Alpha Theta. Office: Bailey & Dixon LLP PO Box 1351 Raleigh NC 27602

WEISEL, THOMAS W., investment company executive; Founder, chmn. & CEO Montgomery Securities, San Francisco, 1978—98, Thomas Weisel Partners, San Francisco, 1999—. Co-author (with Lance Armstrong & Richard Bryant): Capital Instincts: Life As an Entrepreneur, Financier & Athlete, 2003. Trustee Mus. Modern Art, NYC, San Francisco. Office: Thomas Weisel Ptnrs 1 Montgomery St San Francisco CA 94104

WEISENBERGER, ANDREW, lawyer; b. Cin., Sept. 12, 1977; BS, Miami U., Ohio, 1999; JD, Louis D. Brandeis Sch. Law, U. Louisville, 2002; LLM, Georgetown U., 2003. Bar: Ohio 2002, US Dist. Ct. Southern Dist. Ohio 2003, Ky. 2004. Assoc. Santen & Hughes, Cin. Named one of Ohio's Rising Stars, Super Lawyers, 2006. Office: Santen & Hughes Ste 3100 312 Walnut St Cincinnati OH 45202 Office Phone: 513-721-4450. Office Fax: 513-721-0109.

WEISENBURGER, RANDALL J., advertising executive; b. 1958; With Coopers & Lybrand, 1980-85, First Boston Corp., 1987-88; mng. dir. to pres. & CEO Wasserstein Perella & Co., 1988-99; CEO Wickes Mfg. Co., Inc., Southfield, Mich., 1990-93; co-chmn. Collins & Aikman Corp., Charlotte, NC, 1993-99; exec. v.p. & CFO Omnicom Group, Inc., NYC, 1999—. Vice-chmn. Maybelline, Inc.; chmn. Yardley of London; bd. dir. Alliance Entertainment Corp. Office: Omnicom Group Inc 437 Madison Ave New York NY 10022 also: 701 Mccullough Dr Charlotte NC 28262-3318 Office Phone: 212-415-3600. Office Fax: 212-817-6551. E-mail: ir@omnicomgroup.com. *

WEISENBURGER, THEODORE MAURICE, retired judge, poet, educator; b. Tuttle, ND, May 12, 1930; s. John and Emily (Rosenau) W.; children: Sam, Jennifer, Emily, Todd, Daniel, Dwight, Holly, Michael, Paul, Peter; m. Maylyne Chu, Sept. 19, 1985; 1 child, Irene. BA, U. N.D., 1952, LLB, 1956, JD, 1969; BFT, Am. Grad Sch. Internat. Mgmt., Phoenix, 1957. Bar: N.D. 1963, U.S. Dist. Ct. N.D. 1963. County judge, tchr. Bensen County, Minnewaukan, ND, 1968-75, Walsh County, Grafton, ND, 1975-87; trial judge Devils Lake Sioux, Ft. Totten, ND, 1968-84, Turtle Mountain Chippewa, Belcourt, ND, 1974-87; U.S. magistrate U.S. Dist. Ct., Minnewaukan, 1972-75; Justice of the Peace pro tem Maricopa County, Ariz., 1988-92; instr. Rio Salado C.C., 1992—. Tchr. in Ethiopia, 1958-59. Author: Poetry and Other Poems, 1991. 1st lt. U.S. Army, 1952-54. Recipient Humanitarian award U.S. Cath. Conf., 1978, 82, Right to Know award Sigma Delta Chi, 1980, Spirit of Am. award U.S. Conf. Bishops, 1982. Home: 4353 E Libby St Phoenix AZ 85032-1732 Office Phone: 602-992-0492. Personal E-mail: tweisenburger@cox.net.

WEISER, MARC, venture capitalist; b. 1973; BS in Aerospace Engring., U. Mich., 1995, MBA, 1998. Mem., road show team MessageMedia, 1996; bus. devel. Dell Computer Corp.; assoc. Arbor Partners; founder QuantumShift, 1997; founder, mng. dir. RPM Ventures L.L.C., 2000—. Bd. mem. McKinley Associates, Ann Arbor Area Cmty. Found., McKinley Found., AutoTradeCenter, Oxlo Systems, Xtime, RiverGlass. Named one of 40 Under 40, Crain's Detroit Bus., 2006. Office: RPM Ventures 320 N Main St Ste 400 Ann Arbor MI 48104 Office Phone: 734-332-1700. Office Fax: 734-332-1900.

WEISER, MARTIN JAY, lawyer; b. NYC, Mar. 20, 1943; s. Jack J. and Esther (Attias) Weiser; m. Pamela D. Morgan, Sept. 4, 1966; children: Nicole, Jennifer. BA, Temple U., 1964; JD, Bklyn. Law Sch., 1967; LLM, NYU, 1975. Bar: N.Y. 1967, U.S. Dist. Ct. (ea. dist.) N.Y. 1975, U.S. Dist. Ct. (so. dist.) N.Y. 1990; cert. tchr. N.Y. Assoc. Newman & O'Malley, NYC, 1967-69; ptnr., pres. Raiskin, Weiser & Donofrio, P.C., NYC, 1970—99; pres. Weiser & Assocs., P.C., NYC, 1999—. Counsel Metro N.Y. Oldsmobile Dealers Assn., 1988. Bd. dirs. East Hills, N.Y. Assn., 1986—87; v.p. Rio Assn., 1988, bd. dirs., pres., 1988—2002. Mem.: ATLA, Inst. Safety Analysis, Car and Truck Leasing Assn. Am., N.Y. State Trial Lawyers Assn., Nassau Bar Assn., N.Y. County Lawyers Assn., Nob Hill Club (v.p. 1985—86). Office: Weiser & Assocs PC 215 Lexington Ave New York NY 10016-6023 Office Phone: 212-213-3111. Business E-Mail: martin@weiserlaw.com.

WEISER, RALPH RAPHAEL, oil industry executive; b. NYC, May 25, 1925; children: Jane, Jeffrey. BA, NYU, 1947; JSD, Harvard U., 1950. Bar: N.Y. 1950. Ptnr. Lotterman & Weiser, Esq., NYC, 1955-64; pres. Dragor Shipping Inc., NYC, 1964-65; chmn. Nat. Equipment Rental, NYC, 1965-67; exec. v.p. Am. Export Industries, NYC, 1967-69; pvt. practice investment, 1970-84; chmn. World Fuel Svc. Corp. (NYSE-INT), Miami, Fla., 1984—. Sgt. USAAF, 1943-45, PTO. Office: World Fuel Services Corp 9800 NW 41st St Ste 400 Miami FL 33178

WEISER, SHERWOOD MANUEL, hotel and corporation executive, lawyer; b. Cleve., Mar. 9, 1931; s. Aaron A. and Helen (Scheiner) W.; m. Judith A. Zirkin, July 31, 1955; children: Douglas J., Warren P., Bradley A. BS, Ohio State U., 1952; LLB, Case Western Res. U., 1955. Bar: Ohio 1955. Ptnr. Weiser & Weiser, Attys., Cleve., 1955-65, Weiser & Lefton, Attys., Cleve., 1965-69; chmn., chief exec. officer TCC, Miami, Fla., 1970—. Bd. dirs. Mellon United Bank, Miami, Interstate Hotels, Watsco. Trustee Fla. Internat. U. Found., Miami, 1984-94, U. Miami, 1988—, New World Symphony, Miami, 1987—; trustee, chmn. bd. Ransom-Everglades Sch., Miami, 1974-84; co-chmn. bd. advisors Coconut Grove Playhouse, 1986-90; chmn. Performing Arts Ctr. Found., 1994—. Mem. Cleve. Bar Assn., Soc. of Benchers, Order of Coif. Jewish. Avocations: tennis, sailing, art. Office: The Continental Companies LLC 3250 Mary St Miami FL 33133-5232 Home Phone: 305-663-5766; Office Phone: 305-445-4220. E-mail: weiser@tcchotels.com.

WEISERT, KENT ALBERT FREDERICK, lawyer; b. Passaic, NJ, Sept. 9, 1949; s. Frederick William and Waleska Anna Sophia (Bischoff) W.; m. Deborah Jean Searing, Mar. 12, 1983; 1 child, Christianna Lillian. BA magna cum laude, Rutgers U., 1971, JD, 1974. Bar: NJ 1974, US Dist. Ct. NJ 1974, US Tax Ct. 1975, US Ct. Appeals (3d cir.) 1978, US Supreme Ct. 1987. Adminstrv. asst. trust dept. Howard Savs. Bank, Newark, 1973-74; ptnr. Schwartz, Tobia & Stanziale, Montclair, NJ, 1975—2001; pvt. practice law Bloomfield, NJ, 2001—. Arbitrator U.S. Dist. Ct., Newark, 1985—. Contbr. chpt. to book New Jersey Transaction Guide, 1987. Pres. ch. coun. Holy Trinity Luth. Ch., Nutley, NJ, 1982-83; session mem., elder Watchung Presbyn. Ch., Bloomfield, NJ; mem. Greater NJ Estate Planning Coun.; trustee, v.p. Oakeside Bloomfield Cultural Ctr. Mem. NJ State Bar Assn., Essex County Bar Assn., Rutgers Law Sch. Alumni Assn., Nat. Trust Hist. Preservation, NJ Hist. Soc., Phi Beta Kappa, Phi Alpha Theta, Pi Delta Epsilon. Republican. Presbyterian. Avocations: classical music, antiques, tennis, historical preservation, military and general history. Home and Office: Kent AF Weisert Esq 51 Fairway Bloomfield NJ 07003 Office Phone: 973-338-5533. E-mail: kentw07@verizon.net.

WEISFELD, SHELDON, lawyer; b. McAllen, Tex., Feb. 20, 1946; s. Morris and Pauline (Horwitz) W.; m. Eve F. Weisfeld, Jan. 23, 1994; 1 child, Raquel Paolina. BBA, U. Tex., 1967; postgrad., Nat. U. Mex., 1969; JD, U. Houston, 1970. Bar: Tex. 1971, U.S. Dist. Ct. (so. dist.) Tex. 1978, U.S. Dist. Ct. (we. dist.) Tex. 1995, U.S. Dist. Ct. (ea. dist.) Tex. 2001, U.S. Ct. Appeals (5th cir.) 1978, U.S. Ct. Appeals (11th cir.) 1981, U.S. Supreme Ct. 1982. Pvt. practice, Austin, Tex., 1973—77; pvt. practice law Brownsville, Tex., 1980—. Asst. fed. pub. defender U.S. Dist. Ct. (so. dist.) Tex., Brownsville, 1977-80. Fellow Tex. Bar Found. (life); mem. ABA, Nat. Assn. Criminal Def. Lawyers (life), Tex. Criminal Def. Lawyers (dir.), Fed. Bar Assn., State Bar Tex., Cameron County Bar Assn., Hidalgo County Bar Assn., B'nai B'rith. Democrat. Office: 855 E Harrison St Brownsville TX 78520-7173 Office Phone: 956-546-2727. Fax: 956-544-7446. E-mail: isweisfeld@aol.com.

WEISFELDT, MYRON LEE, cardiologist, educator; b. Milw., Apr. 25, 1940; s. Simon Charles and Sophia (Price) W.; m. Linda Nan Zaremski, Dec. 29, 1963; children— Ellyn Joy, Lisa Janel, Sara Michelle Student, Northwester U., 1958-60; BA, Johns Hopkins U., 1962, MD, 1965. Intern and resident Columbia-Presbyn. Med. Ctr., NYC, 1965-67; fellow in cardiology Mass. Gen. Hosp., Boston, 1970-72; asst. prof. medicine Johns Hopkins U., Balt., 1972-78, prof. medicine, 1978-91, Robert L. Levy prof. cardiology, 1979-91; Samuel Bard prof. medicine, chair dept. Columbia-Presbyn. Med. Ctr., NYC, 1991—2001; William Osler prof. medicine, dir. dept. medicine Johns Hopkins Med. Sch., 2001—; physician in chief Johns Hopkins Hosp., 2001. Dir. cardiology Johns Hopkins Med. Inst., Balt., 1975-91, Peter Belfer Lab. for Johns Hopkins, Ischemic Heart Disease Spl. Ctr. Rsch., 1977-91; nat. pres. Am. Heart Assn., 1989-90; cardiology adv. com. Nat. Heart, Lung and Blood Inst., 1986-90, chmn., 1988-90; mem. adv. coun. Nat. Inst. on Aging, 1999-2002; study chair resuscitation outcomes consortium Nat. Heart Lung and Blood Inst., 2004—. Editor: The Aging Heart, 1980; editorial bd. Jour. Clin. Investigation, 1984-88, Circulation, 1980-86, 88—2004, Jour. Am. Coll. Cardiology, 1987-93, Jour. Molecular and Cellular Cardiology, 1975-80, 86-89, Circulation Rsch., 1988-94. With USPHS, 1967—69. NIH grantee, 1977-91; recipient Golden Heart award Am. Heart Assn., 1998, Harrick award, 2004. Fellow AAAS, ACP (Phillips award in clin. medicine 2006), Am. Coll. Cardiology; mem. Assn. Univ. Cardiologists, Am. Soc. Clin. Investigation, Assn. Am. Physicians, Assn. Prof. Medicine, Inst. of Medicine, Phi Beta Kappa, Alpha Omega Alpha, Interurban Clin. Club. Jewish. Office: Johns Hopkins Medicine 1830 E Monument St Ste 9026 Baltimore MD 21287 Home Phone: 410-588-2481; Office Phone: 410-955-6642. Business E-Mail: mlw5@jhmi.edu.

WEISGALL, JONATHAN MICHAEL, lawyer; b. Balt., Mar. 17, 1949; s. Hugo David and Nathalie (Shulman) W.; m. Ruth Macdonald, June 3, 1979; children: Alison, Andrew, Benjamin. BA, Columbia Coll., 1970; JD, Stanford U., 1973. Bar: D.C. 1974, N.Y. 1974, U.S. Supreme Ct. 1982, Marshall Islands 1983. Law clk. to judge U.S. Ct. Appeals (9th cir.), San Francisco, 1973-74; assoc. Covington & Burling, Washington, 1974-79; from assoc. to ptnr. Ginsburg, Feldman, Weil & Bress, Washington, 1980-83; pvt. practice Washington, 1983-99; v.p. Legis. and Regulatory Affairs MidAmerican Energy Holdings Co., 1995—. Adj. prof. Georgetown U. Law Ctr. Author: Operation Crossroads: The Atomic Tests at Bikini Atoll, 1994; exec. prodr. documentary film Radio Bikini. Chmn. bd. dirs. Ctr. for Energy Efficiency and Renewable Techs.; trustee Arena Stage, Washington; bd. dirs. Meet the Composer, Geothermal Resources Coun. Mem. Geothermal Energy Assn. (past v.p., bd. dirs., pres.), Geothermal Resources Coun. (bd. dirs.), Phi Beta Kappa. Jewish. Home: 5309 Edgemoor Ln Bethesda MD 20814-1323 Office: Ste 300 1200 New Hampshire Ave NW Washington DC 20036-6812 Office Phone: 202-828-1378. Personal E-mail: jmweisgall@midamerican.com.

WEISKOPF, WANDA, mezzo soprano, writer, poet; b. Jefferson City, Mo., Aug. 2, 1921; d. Elmer and Stella Jane (Buster) Connell; m. Herbert Weiskopf (dec.); children: Douglas McK., Marta Jane. Student, L.A. Conservatory, 1950—55. Pvt. practice, Portland, Oreg., 1970—80. Activities dir., editor Skylines Portland Ctr., 1970—85; adjudicator Met. Opera Auditions, Seattle, 1990. Singer: (Operas) Portland Cathedral and St. Michael's, 1970—85, appeared in maj. opera houses, leading roles in Mo., Calif., Oreg., Italy, San Remo; author: All Is Not Winter, 1976, On the Wings of Song: My Life with the Maestro, 1995, Listen To The River, 2001. Organizer meml. concert Am. Heart Assn., Portland, 1971; active Dem. Party, Burbank, Calif., 1990. With US Army, 1942. Mem.: Nat. Assn. Tchrs. Singing, Nat. Writers Assn. (sec. LA chpt. 1989—2005). Democrat. Avocation: walking. Home: 1207 N Cordova St #105 Burbank CA 91505-2218

WEISMAN, ERIC, music company executive; With Premier Artists Svcs., 1985, Bassin Distbr., 1985—90, Alliance Entertainment Corp., Minnetonka, Minn., 1990, pres., CEO, 1997—2003; CEO Musicland Holding Corp., 2003—05, advisor, 2005—. Office: Musicland Holding Corp 10400 Yellow Circle Dr Minnetonka MN 55343

WEISMAN, GARY, sculptor, educator; b. Chgo., May 19, 1952; s. Nathan and Betty Weisman; m. Treacy Ziegler, Nov. 26, 1989; 1 child, Jack. BFA, Columbia U., Chgo., 1974; postgrad., Art Inst. Chgo., 1974—76. Mem. faculty Penns. Acad. Fine Arts, Phila., 1986—. Prin. works include, Duluth, Minn., Chgo., Phila., Elmira Coll., NY, exhibitions include US State Dept., US Energy, Arnot Art Mus., Johnson Mus. Art, Am. Mus. Art, Berry Hill Galleries, NYC, US Embassy, Darussalam, Brunei, North Vietnam. Recipient honor, US White House, 2005. Mem.: Nat. Sculpture Soc.

WEISMAN, GARY ANDREW, biochemist; b. Bklyn., June 18, 1951; s. Joseph Herman and Elaine (Melman) W.; m. Sandra Kay Hille, Aug. 4, 1979; children: Laura Joanne, Pamela Michelle, Veronica Evelyn. BS, Polytechnic U., 1972; postgrad., U. Bordeaux, France, 1972-74; PhD, U. Nebr., 1980. Postdoctoral rsch. assoc. Cornell U., NYC, 1980-85; asst. prof. U. Mo., Columbia, 1985-92, assoc. prof., 1992-98, prof., 1998—. Spl. reviewer NIH, mem. ODCS Study Section; reviewer NSF, Am. Jour. Physiology, Jour. Biol. Chemistry, Molec. Pharmacology, Euro. Jour. Pharmacol. GLIA; editl. bd. Purinergic Signalling. Contbr. articles to profl. jours. Grantee USDA, 1987—, NIH, 1988—, CF Found., 1994-2000, Am. Diabetes, 1995-2002, Am. Heart Assn. 1994-. Mem. AAAS, Am. Chem. Soc., Am. Soc. Biochem. and Molecular Biology, Am. Diabetes Assn., Am. Heart Assn., NY Acad. Scis., Soc. for Neurosci., Am. Soc. Nutr. Scis., Am. Soc. Pharmacol. and Exptl. Therapeut. Home: 1804 University Ave Columbia MO 65201-6004 Office: U Mo Dept Biochemistry 540E Life Scis Ctr Columbia MO 65211-7310 Home Phone: 573-443-8270. Business E-Mail: weismang@missouri.edu.

WEISMAN, JOEL, retired engineering educator; b. NYC, July 15, 1928; s. Abraham and Ethel (Marcus) W.; m. Bernice Newman, Feb. 6, 1955; 1 child, Jay (dec.) B.Ch.E., CCNY, 1948; MS, Columbia U., 1949; PhD, U. Pitts, 1968. Registered profl. engr., N.Y. Plant engr. Etched Products, NYC, 1950-51; from jr. engr. to assoc. engr. Brookhaven Nat. Lab., Upton, NY, 1951-54; from engr. to fellow engr. Westinghouse Nuclear Energy Systems, Pitts., 1954-59, from fellow engr. to mgr. thermal and hydraulic analysis, 1960-68; sr. engr. Nuclear Devel. Assocs., White Plains, NY, 1959-60; assoc. prof. nuclear engring. U. Cin., 1968—96, prof. nuclear engring., 1972-96, dir. nuclear engring. program, 1977-86, dir. lab. basic and applied nuclear research, 1984-94, prof. emeritus nuclear engring., 1996—. Coauthor: Thermal Analysis of Pressurized Water Reactors, 1970, 2d edit., 1979, Chinese edit., 1981, 3rd edit., 1996, Introduction to Optimization Theory, 1973, Modern Power Plant Engineering, 1985; editor: Elements of Nuclear Reactor Design, 1977, Chinese edit., 1982, 2d edit., 1983; contbr. tech. articles to profl. jours.; patentee in field. Mem. Cin. Environ. Adv. Council, 1976-78; mem. Cin. Asian Art Soc., 1977—, v.p., 1980-82, pres., 1982-84; mem. exec. bd. Air Pollution League Greater Cin., 1980-90. Sr. NATO fellow, Winfrith Lab., U.K. Atomic Energy Authority, 1972; sr. fellow Argonne Nat. Lab., Ill., 1982; NSF research grantee, 1974-78, 82-85, 86-89; recipient Dean's award U. Cin. Coll. Engring., 1987. Fellow Am. Nuclear Soc. (v.p. Pitts. sect. 1957-58, mem. exec. com. thermal-hydraulics div. 1989-92); mem. Am. Inst. Chem. Engrs., Sigma Xi Democrat. Jewish. Avocation: Japanese art. Office: U Cin Dept Mech Ind & Nuclear Engr Cincinnati OH 45221-0001

WEISMAN, PAUL HOWARD, lawyer; b. LA, Oct. 14, 1957; s. Albert L. and Rose J. (Zimman) W. BA cum laude, U. Calif., Davis, 1979; JD, Loyola U., Los Angeles, 1982. Bar: Calif. 1982. Tax atty. legis. and regulations div. office of chief counsel Dept. of Treasury IRS, Washington, 1982-83, tax atty. dist. counsel/office of chief counsel LA, 1983-87; tax atty. Law Offices of Paul H. Weisman, LA, 1987—. Registered players contract rep. Can. Football League Players Assn. Co-author BNA Tax Mgmt. Portfolio 637 and 638 Federal Tax Collection Procedure; contbr. publs. in field. Participant vol. Income Tax Assistance, L.A., 1981-83; alt. mem. Los Angeles County Assessment Appeals Bd. Mem. San Fernando Valley Bar Assn., Beverly Hills Bar Assn. (co-chmn. tax ct. prose program). Republican. Avocations: sports, running, art, music, politics. Personal E-mail: pweisman1@socal.rr.com.

WEISMAN, RICHARD SCOTT, lawyer; b. NYC, Nov. 3, 1956; s. Harold and Sarah (Delaney) Weisman. AB, Harvard Coll., 1978, JD, 1982. Bar: N.Y. 1983. Spl. asst. Senator Daniel Patrick Moynihan, Washington, 1978-79; assoc. Cahill Gordon & Reindel, NYC, 1982-84, Sidley & Austin, NYC, 1984-87, Winthrop Stimson Putnam & Roberts, NYC, 1987-90; atty. Richard S. Weisman, Esq., NYC and Westchester, N.Y., 1990-91, Beller & Keller, NYC, 1992-95; mng. ptnr. Weisman & Calderon LLP, Mt. Vernon, N.Y., 1996—. Mem.: Bronx County Bar Assn. (bd. dirs.), Westchester County Bar Assn., Nat. Guardianship Assn., Mt. Vernon Bar Assn., N.Y. State Trial Lawyers Assn., N.Y. State Bar Assn. Office: Weisman & Calderon LLP 6 Gramatan Ave Ste 206 Mount Vernon NY 10550-3209 Office Phone: 914-668-8900. E-mail: weismanr@erols.com.

WEISMAN, STEVEN ROGER, newspaper editor; b. LA, Nov. 10, 1946; s. Joseph Harris and Etta Gladys (Sugarman) W.; m. Elisabeth Bumiller, Oct. 23, 1983; children: Madeleine Elisabeth, Theodore Joseph. BA, Yale, 1968. Reporter N.Y. Times, NYC, 1968—, City Hall bur. chief, 1976-78, Albany bur. chief, 1978, White House corr., 1979-81, sr. White House corr., 1981-85, New Delhi bur. chief, 1985-88, Tokyo bur. chief, 1989-92, dep. fgn. editor, 1992-95, mem. editl. bd., 1995—2002, chief diplomatic corr., Washington bur., 2002—. Bd. dirs. Yale Alumni Publs., New Haven, Conn., 1983—. Author: The Great Tax Wars, 2002 (Sidney Hillman book award, 2003). Recipient award Silurian Soc., N.Y.C., 1975, Edward Weintal Prize, 2004. Jewish. Office: NY Times Washington Bur 7th Fl 1627 I St Washington DC 20006 Home: 5212 Falmouth Rd Bethesda MD 20816-2913 Office Phone: 202-862-0353. Office Fax: 202-862-0340. E-mail: weisman@nytimes.com.

WEISMANTEL, GREGORY NELSON, management consultant, computer company executive; b. Houston, Sept. 8, 1940; s. Leo Joseph and Ellen Elizabeth (Zudis) W.; m. Marilyn Ann Fanger, June 18, 1966; children: Guy Gregory, Christopher Gregory, Andrea Rose. BA in English, U. Notre Dame, 1962; MBA in Internat. Bus., Loyola U., Chgo., 1979. With mgmt. staff Gen. Foods Corp., White Plains, NY, 1966-80; pres., chief exec. officer Manor House Foods, Inc., Addison, Ill., 1980-82, Weismantel & Assocs., Downers Grove, Ill., 1982-84; v.p. perishable div. Profl. Marketers, Inc., Lombard, Ill., 1984-86, group v.p. sales and mktg. services, dir. corp. strategy, 1986-87; v.p. mng. prin. CPG Industry, Louis A. Allen Assoc. Inc., Palo Alto, Calif., 1987-88; pres., chief exec. officer The Vista Tech. Group, Ltd., St. Charles, Ill., 1989-2000, chmn. bd., 2001—02; pres. Epic Global Technol., 2002—. Bd. dirs. Epicurean Foods, Ltd., Chgo., 2004; pres. Aquitec, Inc., Chgo. Chmn. fin. St. Edward's High Sch. Jubilee, Elgin, Ill., 1982-85; bd. dirs. Dist. 301 Sch. Bd., Burlington, Ill., 1980-84, St. Edward's Found., Elgin, 1982—. Capt. U.S. Army, 1962-66. Recipient ICP/Chgo. Software Assoc. Re-Engring. award, 1994-96; State of Ill. grantee, 1989, Build Ill. Investment Fund, finalist KPMG Hi-tech. Entrepreneur award, Vista Technology, 2001. Mem. Grocery Mfg. Sales Execs., Chgo. Software Assn., Chg. C. of C. (small bus. com.). Clubs: Merchandising Execs., Food Products, Am. Mktg. (Chgo.). Roman Catholic. *Success can only occur when a person realizes that life is not a rehearsal.*

WEISNER, DAVID, illustrator; b. Bridgewater, NJ; married; 2 children. BFA, Rhode Island Sch. Design. Illustrator: children's books Night of the Gargoyles, 1994, Sector 7, 2000, The Three Pigs, 2001 (Caldecott Medal Winner, 2002), June 29, 1999, Tuesday (Caldecott Medal Winner, 1992), Hurricane, Flotsam, 2006 (Caldecott Medal Winner, 2007). Office: c/o Houghton Mifflin Co Trade Div Adult Edl 8th Fl 222 Berkely St Boston MA 02116-3764 *

WEISS, ALVIN HARVEY, chemical engineer, educator, research scientist, consultant; b. Phila., Apr. 28, 1928; s. Louis and Helen F. (Wilinsky) W.; m. Devorah Schwartz, June 10, 1979; child: Linda. BSChemE, U. Pa., 1949, PhD in Phys. Chemistry, 1965; MSChemE, Newark Coll. Engring., 1955. Registered profl. engr., Mass., Del. Chem. engr. Fiber Chem. Corp., Cliffwood, NJ, 1949-51, US Army Chem. Corps, Edgewood, Md., 1951—53, Colgate-Palmolive Co., Jersey City, 1953-55, Houdry Process and Chems. Co., Linwood, Pa., 1956-63; rsch. assoc., lectr. U. Pa., Phila., 1963-66; prof. chem. engring. Worcester (Mass.) Poly. Inst., 1966-94, prof. emeritus, 1994—. NASA-ASEE summer faculty fellow Stanford U. Ames Rsch. Ctr., 1967—68; affiliate scientist Worcester Found. Exptl. Biology, 1972—74; Fulbright-Hays sr. faculty fellow to dept. chem. engring. Ben-Gurion U. of Negev, Beersheva, Israel, 1973—74, vis. prof. chem. engring., 1974; U.S. coord. U.S.-USSR Coop. Sci. Program in Chem. Catalysis, Topic IV, 1973—76, prin. investigator (with M.M. Sakharov), 1976—78; prin. investigator (with K.I. Ione) U.S.-USSR Coop. Sci. Program in Chem. Catalysis, Topic III, 1978—80; Fulbright-Hays vis. lectr. dept. chem. engring. Mid. East Tech. U., Ankara, Turkey, 1974, vis. prof., 91; vis. rsch. scientist dept. organic chemistry Weizmann Inst., Rehovoth, Israel, 1974; vis. lectr. Inst. Isotopes and Ctrl. Inst. Chemistry, Hungarian Acad. Scis., Budapest, 1976; vis. prof. Inst. Cultural Rels. and Inst. Isotopes, Hungarian Acad. Scis., 1978—80; UNIDO chief tech. advisor to Petrochem Complex of Bahia Blanca, Argentina, 1980; sr. rsch. fellow chem. sys. lab. Army Chem. Ctr., Md., 1981; UNIDO expert in chem. process devel. Rsch. Inst. for Chem. Industry, Beijing, 1982; UNIDO expert in catalysis to YARPET Petrochem. Complex, Yarimca, Turkey, 1986—87; bd. dirs. U.S. com. for sci. coop. with Vietnam; vis. lectr. Nat. Ctr. for Sci. Rsch., Hanoi Inst. of Indsl. Chemistry, Ho Chi Minh City, 1986; vis. prof., vis. scientist Ctr. for Advanced Microgravity Materials Processing, Northeastern U., Boston, 2000—02. Translator: (with M. Delleo, G. Dembinski and J. Happel) Catalysis by Non-Metals (O.V. Krylov), 1970; author (autobiography): Chemistry, Engineering and Other Stories, 2006; contbr. 125 articles to profl. jours.; patentee in field. With chem. corps US Army, 1951—53. Recipient Sci. Achievement award Worcester Engring. Soc., 1984, Founder's award, Catalysis Soc. New Eng., 1990, Outstanding Rschr. and Creative Scholar award, Worcester Poly. Inst., 1984; Rsch. grantee NSF, PRF, NASA, DOD, DOE, EPA. Fellow AIChE (rsch. com. 1968-80, symposia chmn. 1973-84); mem. AAUP, Catalysis Soc. (bd. dirs., sec. 1968-88), Catalysis Soc. New Eng. (founding pres. 1967-68, bd. dirs. 1968—), Am. Chem. Soc. (New Eng. petroleum divsn. rep. 1970-88, session chmn. 1973—), Deutsche Gesellschaft fur Chemische Apparatwesen Avocations: writing, photography. Personal E-mail: ahweiss@yahoo.com.

WEISS, ARMAND BERL, economist, association management executive; b. Richmond, Va., Apr. 2, 1931; s. Maurice Herbert and Henrietta (Shapiro) W.; m. Judith Bernstein, May 18, 1957; children: Jo Ann Michele, Rhett Louis. BS in Econs., Wharton Sch. Fin., U. Pa., 1953, MBA, 1954; DBA, George Washington U., 1971. Cert. assn. exec. Officer USN, 1954—65; spl. asst. to auditor gen. Dept. Navy, 1964—65; sr. economist Ctr. for Naval Analyses, Arlington, Va., 1965—68; project dir. Logistics Mgmt. Inst., Washington, 1966—74; dir. sys. integration Fed.

Energy Adminstrn., Washington, 1974—76; sr. economist Nat. Commn. Supplies and Shortages, 1976—77; tech. asst. to v.p. Sys. Planning Corp., 1977—78; chmn. bd., pres., CEO Assns. Internat. Inc., 1978—; chmn. bd. dirs., CFO Rail Digital Corp., 1988—91; v.p., treas. Tech. Frontiers, Inc., 1978—80; sr. v.p. Weiss Pub. Co., Inc., Richmond, 1960—. V.p. Condo News Internat., Inc., 1981; v.p., bd. dirs. Leaders Digest inc., 1987—88; sec., bd. dirs. Mgmt. Svcs. Internat. Inc., 1987—88, 1989—90; vis. lectr. George Washington U., 1971; assoc. prof. George Mason U., 1984; treas. Dranesville (Va.) Dist. Dem. Com., 1989—93, 2003—06, Fairfax County (Va.) Dist. Dem. Com., 1992—94; assisted Pres. Clinton, v.p. Gore transition at White Ho., 1993—; pres. Washington Mgmt. and Bus. Assn., 1993—; chmn. US del., session chmn. NATO Symposium on Cost-Benefit Analysis, The Hague, Netherlands, 1969, NATO Conf. on Operational Rsch. in Indsl. Sys., St. Louis, 1970; pres. Nat. Coun. Assns. Policy Scis., 1971—77; chmn. adv. group Def. Econ. Adv. Coun. Dept. Def., 1970—74; resident assoc. Smithsonian Instn., 1973—; expert cons. Dept. State, GAO; undercover agt. FBI, 3 yrs.; del. conf. UN, 2004. Co-editor: Systems Analysis for Social Problems, 1970, The Relevance of Economic Analysis to Decision Making in the Department of Defense, 1972, Toward More Effective Public Programs: The Role of Analysis and Evaluation, 1975; editor: Cost-Effectiveness Newsletter, 1966-70, Operations Rsch./Systems Analysis Today, 1971-73, Operation Rsch./Mgmt. Sci. Today, 1974-87, Feedback, 1969-93, Condo World, 1981, The Democrat, 1997-2000; assoc. editor Ops. Rsch., 1971-75; pub. IEEE Scanner, 1983-89, Spl. and Individual Needs Tech. (SAINT) Newsletter, 1987-88, Jour. Parametrics, 1984-88. Del. Pres.'s Mid-Century White House Conf. on Children and Youth, 1950; scoutmaster Japan, U.S.; leader World Jamborees, France, Can., U.S., 1945-61; Eagle scout, 1947; U.S. del. Internat. Conf. on Ops. Rsch., Dublin, Ireland, 1972; organizing com. Internat. Cost-Effectiveness Symposium, Washington, 1970; spkr. Internat. Conf. Inst. Mgmt. Scis., Tel Aviv, 1973, del., Mexico City, 1967; mem. bus. com. Nat. Symphony Orch., 1968-70, Washington Performing Arts Soc., 1974-88; bus. mgr. Nat. Lyric Opera Co., 1983—, Internat. Assn. Med. Sci. Educators, 1997-98, Data Adminstrv. Mgmt. Assn. Nat. Capital, 1992-2001, Potomac Pedalers Touring Club, 1990-2001, Am. Friends of London Sch. Econs., 1988-97; mem. mktg. com. Fairfax Symphony Orch., 1984-91; bd. dirs. McLean (Va.) Orch., 1992-94; exec. com. Mid Atlantic coun. Union Am. Hebrew Congregations, 1970-79, treas., 1974-79, mem. nat. MUM com., 1974-79; mem. dist. com. Boy Scouts Am., 1972-75; bd. dirs. Nat. Coun. Career Women, 1975-79; pres. Jewish temple, 1970-72; adminstr. Daniel Heumann Fund for Spinal Cord Rsch., 2000-; treas. Quest for the Cure, 2000-; mem. Coalition for Advancement of Med. Rsch., 2002-; del. UN Sci. Conf., 2004; mem. adv. bd. U. Pa. Mid. Atlantic Region, 2003- Named Hero of Hope, Rutgers U. Rally for Cure, 2004; recipient Silver medal 50-yard free style and half mile swimming meet, No. Va. Sr. Olympics, 1990, Gold, 2 Silver, 3 Bronze medals, 2001. Fellow AAAS, Washington Acad. Scis. (gov. 1981-92, v.p. 1987-88, pres.-elect 1989-90, pres. 1990-91, past pres. 1991-92), Va. Acad. Scis., Nat. Assn. Acad. Sci. (del. 1991-93), Ops. Rsch. Soc. Am. (chmn. meetings com. 1969-71, chmn. cost-effectiveness sect. 1969-70), Washington Ops. Rsch./Mgmt. Sci. Coun. (editor newsletter 1969-93, sec. 1971-72, pres. 1973-74, trustee 1975-77, bus. mgr. 1976-93, Moving Spirit award 1994), Internat. Inst. Strategic Studies (London), Am. Soc. Assn. Execs. (membership com. 1981-82, assn. mgmt. co. sect. coun. 1995-98, cert.), Inst. Ops. Rsch. and Mgmt. Scis., Am. Econ. Assn., Wharton Grad. Sch. Alumni Assn. (exec. com. 1970-73), Nat. Eagle Scout Assn., VFW, Am. Legion, Navy League U.S., Greater Washington Soc. Assn. Execs. (new ventures com. 1995-97), Alumni Assn. George Washington U. (governing bd. 1974-82, chmn. univ. publs. com. 1976-78, Alumni Svc. award 1980), Alumni Assn. George Washington U. Sch. Govt. and Bus. Adminstrn. (exec. v.p. 1977-78, pres. 1978-79), George Washington U. Doctoral Assn. (sr. v.p. 1968-69), Wharton Sch. Washington (sec. 1967-69, pres. 1969-70, exec. dir. 1987-2001, Joseph Wharton award 1991, Lifetime Svc. award 2000). Home: 6516 Truman Ln Falls Church VA 22043-1821 Office Phone: 703-237-1104. Personal E-mail: aiboss@aol.com.

WEISS, AVI, rabbi; b. 1944; m. Toby Weiss, June 18, 1964. Rabbi Hebrew Inst. of Riverdale, Bronx, NY; founder, dean Yeshivat Chovevei Torah (Open Orthodox), NYC. Spkr. in field. Contbr. articles to profl jours. Named Rabbi of Yr., NY Bd. Rabbis, 1993—94; named one of Fifty Jewish Leaders to Watch in Yr. Ahead, Forward newspaper, 1994, 1997, Am. Top 50 Rabbis, Newsweek Mag. Office: Hebrew Inst Riverdale 3700 Henry Hudson Pkwy Bronx NY 10463 Office Phone: 718-796-4730. Fax: 718-884-3206. *

WEISS, CARL, aerospace company executive; b. Bklyn., Dec. 6, 1938; s. Morris Harold and Sonia B. (Botwinick) W.; m. Judith Fellner, Jan. 27, 1963; children: Daniel Oren, Jonathan Michael. BBA, CUNY, 1961, MBA, 1968; postgrad., Harvard U., Boston, 1971. CPA, NY. Acct. Joseph Warren & Co., NYC, 1965-68; asst. contr. Fisher Radio Corp., LI, NY, 1968-69; sr. v.p. Deutsch Relays, Inc., East Northport, NY, 1969-83; owner, exec. v.p. Logical Solutions, Inc., Melville, NY, 1983-92; owner, pres., COO G&H Tech., Inc., Camarillo, Calif., 1992—. Bd. dirs. Deutsch Dagan, Inc. With U.S. Army, 1961-67. Mem. AICPA (future issues com. 1985-88); NY Soc. CPA. Office: G & H Tech Inc 750 W Ventura Blvd Camarillo CA 93010-8382

WEISS, CAROL JULIET, psychiatrist; b. NYC, Mar. 5, 1957; d. Eugene and Rose (Schwartz) Weiss. BA, Wesleyan U., 1977; MD, Johns Hopkins U., 1983. Diplomate Am. Bd. Psychiatry and Neurology. Intern N.Y. Hosp., NYC, 1983—84; resident Payne Whitney Clinic, N.Y. Hosp., NYC, 1984—87; asst. psychiatrist Payne Whitney Clinic - N.Y. Hosp., NYC, 1983—87; clin. fellow Cornell U., NYC, 1987—89, instr. and clin. affiliate in psychiatry and pub. health, 1989—91, clin. asst. prof. in psychiatry and pub. health NYC, 1992—; pvt. practice NYC, 1987—. Cons. in field. Contbr. articles to profl. jours., chpts. to books. Mem. Am. Psychiat. Assn., Am. Soc. Addiction Medicine, Phi Beta Kappa. Office: 1044 Madison Ave New York NY 10021-0138 Office Phone: 212-988-1209.

WEISS, CHARLES, JR., educator; b. San Francisco, Dec. 20, 1937; s. Charles and Dorothy (Wilkes) W.; m. Edith Gayle Brown, July 24, 1969; children: Jed Ariel, Tamara Ginger. BA summa cum laude, Harvard U., 1959, PhD, 1965. Post-doctoral fellow U. Calif., Berkeley, 1967-69; chemist Lawrence Berkeley Lab., U. Calif., Berkeley, 1969; staff scientist IBM Watson Lab., Columbia U., NYC, 1969-71; sci. and tech. advisor World Bank, Washington, 1971-86; prin. Internat. Tech. Mgmt. and Fin., 1987-91, Innovation Ptnrs., 1987-91; pres. Global Tech. Mgmt., 1991—. Lectr. U. Pa., Phila., 1986-90; vis. lectr. Woodrow Wilson Sch., Princeton U., 1989-94; professorial lectr. Sch. Advanced Internat. Studies, Johns Hopkins U., 1994-97; disting. prof. Sch. Fgn. Svc., Georgetown U., 1997—, chair sci., tech. and internat. affairs, 1997—2006, adj. prof. Georgetown U. Med. Ctr., 2006—; corp. bd. mem. Vols. in Tech. Assistance, Arlington, Va., 1974-85; mem. US Nat. Climate Adv. Com., Washington, 1978-81, Coun. of Fgn. Rels., 1985—; assoc. trustee Ctr. for Econ. Initatives, 2004-. Editor: Mobilizing Technology for World Development, 1979, Technology, Finance and Development, 1984, Choice and Management of Technology, 1987; contbr. articles to profl. jours. Land use chmn. Bannockburn Cmty. Assn., 1990-94. Capt. U.S. Army, 1965-67. Fellow NSF, 1959-62, NIH, 1962-65, 67-69, Woodrow Wilson Found. (hon.); Internat. scholar Open Soc. Inst., U. Nat. and World Economy, Sofia, Bulgaria, 2005-06. Fellow AAAS; mem. Internat. Orgn. Chem. Scis. for Devel. (exec. officer biotic exploration fund 1995-06), Soc. Internat. Devel., Georgetown U. Faculty Senate, US State Dept. Adv. Com. on Internat. Comm. and Info. Policy, Phi Beta Kappa. Avocation: ethnographic art and music. Office: Sch Fgn Svc Georgetown Univ 37th & O Sts NW Washington DC 20057-0001 Office Phone: 202-687-9184. Business E-Mail: weissc@georgetown.edu.

WEISS, CHARLES ANDREW, lawyer; b. Perryville, Mo., Jan. 24, 1942; s. Wallace Francis and Iola Francis Weiss; m. Marie Suzanne Desloge, June 10, 1972; children: Christopher, Robert, Julie, Anne. BJ with highest honors, U. Mo., 1964, AB with hons. in History, 1965; JD cum laude, Notre Dame U., 1968. Bar: Mo. 1968, US Dist. Ct. (ea. dist.) Mo. 1968, US Ct. Appeals (8th cir.) 1968, U.S. Supreme Ct. 1972, US Ct. Appeals (9th cir.) 1974, U.S. Ct. Appeals (2d cir.) 1977, US Ct. Appeals (1st cir.) 1987, US Ct. Appeals (5th cir.) 1992, US Ct. Appeals (fed. cir.) 2003, US Ct. Appeals (7th cir.) 2003. Law clk. to chief judge U.S. Ct. Appeals (8th cir.), 1968; ptnr. Bryan Cave LLP, St. Louis, 1969—. Lectr. St. Louis U. Law Sch., 1970-73; chmn. Legal Aid Mo. Statewide, Inc., 2003—. Supr. Red Cross Water Safety Program, Perry County, Mo., 1962-64; dir. Neighborhood Youth Corps., Perry County, 1965-66; pres. Perry County Young Dems. Club, 1965-67; committeeman Boy Scouts Am., 1982-86; mem. St. Louis Met. Sewer Dist. Civil Svc. Commn., 1999—; bd. dirs. United Way of Greater St. Louis, 1988-90. Fellow Am. Coll. Trial Lawyers; mem. ABA (ho. of dels. 1986-02, 04-, bd. govs. 2006-), Met. Bar Assn. St. Louis (pres. 1984-85), Mo. Bar Assn. (bd. govs. 1985, v.p. 1994-95, pres.-elect 1995-96, pres. 1996-97), St. Louis Bar Found. (pres. 1983), Mo. Lawyers Trust Account Found. (pres. 1992), Mo. Athletic Club (St. Louis), The Riverlands Assn., Inc. (pres. 1991-93), Jefferson Nat. Parks Assn. (chmn. 1993-2000), Notre Dame Club St. Louis (dir.), Notre Dame Law Assn. (dir., pres. 1997—). Roman Catholic. Office: Bryan Cave 211 N Broadway, Ste 3600 Saint Louis MO 63102-2733 Home Phone: 314-991-2170; Office Phone: 314-259-2215. Business E-Mail: cweiss@bryancave.com. *

WEISS, CHRISTOPHER JOHN, lawyer; b. Oswego, NY, Sept. 1, 1952; s. Robert Leo and Flora Elizabeth Weiss; children: Allison Ardis, Natalie Elizabeth, Christine Corinne, Kathryn Creigh. BS, Fla. State U., 1970, JD, 1977. Bar: Fla. 1977, U.S. Dist. Ct. (mid. and so. dists.) Fla. 1977, U.S. Supreme Ct. Ptnr. Holland and Knight (and predecessor firm), Orlando, Fla., 1977—. Lectr., author various constrn. litigation issues, 1977—. Mem. Orlando Rep. Com., 1975—. Mem. Fla. Bar, Orange County Bar Assn. (constrn. com. 1987—), Am. Arbitration Assn. (nat. panelist 1982—), Assoc. Gen. Contractors, Assoc. Builders and Contractors, Constrn. Fin. Mgrs. Assn. Avocations: reading, travel. Office: Holland & Knight PO Box 1526 Orlando FL 32802-1526 Office Phone: 407-244-1110. Business E-Mail: cweiss@hklaw.com.

WEISS, DANIEL EDWIN, minister, educator; b. Kenosha, Wis., June 9, 1937; s. Edwin and Ruth J. (Stromquist) Weiss; m. Rachel A. Johnson, Aug. 9, 1958 (div. 2004); children: Daniel E. Jr., Kristen R.; m. Barbara A. Williams, Oct. 30, 2004. BA, Wheaton Coll., 1959, MA, 1962; MDiv, Gordon Conwell Theol. Sem., South Hamilton, Mass., 1962; PhD, Mich. State U., 1964; DD (hon.), Judson Coll., 1976, Franklin Coll., 1990; DHL (hon.), Ottawa U., Kans., 1997; STD (hon.), Linfield Coll., 2000. Ordained to ministry Am. Bapt. Ch., 1962. Prof. ministry Gordon Div. Sch., Wenham, Mass., 1964—69; v.p. Gordon Coll., 1969—73; pres. Eastern Coll., St. Davids, Pa., 1973—81, Eastern Bapt. Theol. Sem., Phila., 1973—81; exec. v.p. Pace U., NYC, 1981—83; exec. dir. Am. Bapt. Bd. Edn. and Publ., Valley Forge, Pa., 1983—88; gen. sec. Am. Bapt. Chs. U.S.A., 1988—2000. Mem. ctrl. com. World Coun. Chs., Geneva, 1989—98; mem. gen. bd. Nat. Coun. Chs., NYC, 1989—2000; mem. gen. coun. Bapt. World Alliance, Washington, 1985—2000. Home: 4401 Gulf Shore Blvd N #1506 Naples FL 34103

WEISS, DANIEL H., academic administrator, former dean; m. Sandra Jarva; children: Teddy, Joel. BA, George Washington U., 1979; MA, Johns Hopkins U., 1982, PhD, 1992; MBA, Yale U., 1985. With Booz, Allen & Hamilton; chair Art Hist. Dept. Johns Hopkins U., Balt., 1998—2001, dean faculty, 2001—02, dean Zanvyl Krieger Sch. Arts and Scis., 2002—05; pres. Lafayette Coll., Easton, Pa., 2005—. Bd. mem. Walter Art Mus., John Hopkins, Shriver Hall Concert Series; trustee Park School, Baltimore. Office: Lafayette Coll 316 Markle Hall Easton PA 18042 Office Phone: 610-330-5200. E-mail: weiss@lafayette.edu. *

WEISS, DAVID I., real estate company executive, lawyer, writer; s. Kurt George and Phyllis Lee Weiss; m. Lynn Alice Epstein, Apr. 5, 1987; 1 child, Alexander Jacob. BS in Fin., U. Fla., 1983; JD, Nova Southeastern U., 1986. Bar: State Fla. Bar Assn. 1987, U.S. Dist. Ct. Fla. (so., mid. and no. dists.) 1987, U.S. Tax Ct. 1988, U.S. Ct. Appeals (11th cir.) 1988, U.S. Supreme Ct. 1990. Law clk. to Hon. Joe Eaton U.S. Dist. Ct. (so. dist.) Fla., 1986—87; ptnr. Herzfeld & Rubin, Miami, Fla., 1988—95; CEO Am. Coastal Corp., Plantation, Fla., 1995—; v.p., gen. counsel Nat. Gen. Corp., Ft. Lauderdale, Fla., 1997—; pres. Hawks Landing, Plantation, 1997—; CEO Design Safety Corp., Plantation, 2000—; ptnr. SouthStar Storage LLC, Boca Raton, Fla., 2001—, Security Storage, Delray Beach, Fla., 2003—; pres. Bluewater Groves, Inc., Ft. Pierce, Fla., 2003—; mng. mem. RPS Properties, LLC, Plantation. Mem. bd. editors U.S. Dist. Ct. So. Dist. Digest, Miami, 1987; CEO Organon Wireless, Inc., Ft. Lauderdale, 2000—; mng. mem. Royal Palm Square Properties, Inc., Coral Springs, Plantation, Fla., 2005—. Author: (children's book) When I Was A Duck, 2004; co-author: (law review article) On the Differences Between Blood and Red Ink: Economic Loss Rule (Outstanding Law Review Article, Product Liablity Jour., 1996), Conflicts of Interest under ERISA (Outstanding Law Review Article, West Pub., 1986). Bd. dirs. youth tennis program City of Plantation, 2001—; bd. dirs. Soref Jewish Cmty. Ctr. Mem.: Fla. Bar Assn. (YLD bd. govs. 1994), Dade County Bar Assn., Broward County Bar Assn., Fed. Bar Assn., Nat. Leukemia and Lymphoma Soc. (bd. reps. 2004—05, bd. trustees 2004—05), Leukemia and Lymphoma Soc. (nat. del. 2004, South Fla. bd. dirs. 2004—). Democrat. Achievements include patents for lid closure mechanism; lid closure design; retractable water protective device; patents pending for wireless interaction, meta and collection system-PageJump. Avocations: swimming, running, tennis, weight training. Office: Bluewater Groves 151 N Nob Hill Rd Ste 233 Fort Lauderdale FL 33324 Home Phone: 954-309-6082; Office Phone: 954-472-4000 303. Business E-Mail: bluewatergroves@aol.com.

WEISS, DONALD S., real estate developer; b. St. Petersburg, Fla., Aug. 18, 1947; s. Jonas Weiss and Miriam Kahan; m. Anne M. Weiss, Feb. 1978 (div. Jan. 1991); children: Laurie Blumstein, Melissa, Jason. BSBA, U. Fla., 1969. Lic. real estate broker N.Y. Asst. portfolio mgr. Chase Manhattan Bank, NYC, 1969—70; office space leasing salesperson Williams & Co., NYC, 1971—74, Sylvan Lawrence & Co., NYC, 1974—78; pvt. real estate investor NYC, 1978—; developer, creator Sugar Hill Art Ctr., NYC, 2001—. Dir. Com. for a New Am., Com. for Rational Housing Laws and Econ. Devel. in N.Y.C. and N.Y. State, various web sites. Exhibited in group shows. With US Army, 1969—73. Avocations: skiing, bridge, photography. Office: 555 W 151 St #26 New York NY 10031 Home: 8051 Mulholland Dr Los Angeles CA 90046 Home Phone: 917-923-2441; Office Phone: 212-283-1278. Personal E-mail: dweiss5348@aol.com.

WEISS, EARLE BURTON, physician; b. Waltham, Mass., Nov. 23, 1932; s. Murray E. and Ruth R. (Pill) W.; m. Ruth Lithwick, Dec. 1, 1963; children: Ilana, Joshua. BS with honors, Northeastern U., Boston, 1955; MS, MIT, Cambridge, 1957; MD, Albert Einstein Coll. Medicine, NYC, 1961. Intern King's County Hosp., Bklyn., 1961—62; resident Boston City Hosp., 1962—64, Nat. Heart Inst. fellow, 1964—66; sr. rsch. assoc. Tufts Lung Sta., 1964—71; founder/first dir. respiratory ICU, sr. attending physician pulmonary & med. svc. Boston City Hosp., 1964—71, dir. Pulmonary Physiology Lab., 1966—71; assoc. chief of medicine Tufts Med. Svc./Boston City Hosp., 1969—71; dir. divsn. respiratory diseases St. Vincent Hosp., Worcester, Mass., 1971—89, also acting med. dir., 1985—87; prof. medicine U. Mass. Med. Sch., 1977—; sr. pulmonary rsch. scientist, dept. anesthesia Rsch. Labs. Brigham and Womens Hosp., Boston, 1989—. Cons. medical devices adv. panel FDA, 1975-77; cons. in physiology Norfolk County Sanitorium, 1966-69; lectr. medicine Tufts Med. Sch., 1978-; assoc. prof. life scis. Worcester Poly. Inst., Mass., 1976—; vis. prof. Faculty of Medicine, dept. of anesthesia Harvard Med. Sch., 1990-2002, vis. prof. U. Guadalajara, Mexico, 1973, 77, prof. extraordinario faculty medicine, 1977, 82; med. dir. Found. Rsch. in Bronchial Asthma and Related Diseases, 1980—; Tb cons. Commonwealth of Mass., 1972-89; dir. regional inpatient Tb and outpatient Tb clinic, Worcester County, 1972-89 Author: Bronchial Asthma, 1976, 2d edit., 1985, 3d edit., 1993, Status Asthmaticus, 1978; contbr. (with artist Frank H. Netter) Ciba Collection: The Respiratory System Anatomy of Lung and Asthma Sections and Clinical Symposia Bronchial Asthma, Acute Respiratory Failure in COPD, 1969; contbr. over 90 articles to profl. jours., abstracts, audio tapes and book chpts. Capt. USAFR, 1965-70. Named one of Am.'s Top Physicians, 2003—; recipient 1st Dr. J. McKeever Meml. award for outstanding med. educator, 1970, The Acad. Honor Soc., Tchg. and Patient Care award, Boston City Hosp. (I-III), 1971. Fellow ACP, Am. Coll. Chest Physicians, Royal Coll. Physicians; mem. AAAS, AMA, Mass. Thoracic Soc. (pres. 1976-78, Chadwick medal for meritorious contbn. in Respiratory Diseases 1990), Am. Thoracic Soc. (co-founder clin. assembly, rep. councilor 1979-82, founder, chmn. med. devices com. 1972-79, rep. ANSI med. tech. adv. bd. 1973-75, med. edn. com. 1972-74), Am. Assn. Clin. Scientists, Am. Soc. Internal Medicine, Soc. Free Radical Rsch., NY Acad. Scis., Am. Acad. Med. Dirs., Interasthma, Astron. Soc. of the Pacific, Soc. for Astron. Scis., Royal Astron. Soc. Can., Planetary Soc., Sigma Xi. Achievements include introduction and pioneering use of controlled mechanical ventilation in acute respiratory failure of chronic lung disease, arterial blood gas profiles in status asthma, "cross-over" point in status-severe asthma, recording of breath sounds, the theory of the role of calcium and oxygen toxic products in causing asthma and airways reactivity 1979, percutaneous lung biopsy for diagnosis of respiratory infections, effect thyroid hormones upon cerebral cortex maturation and first isolation of alpha-hydroxy acid oxidase; establishment student research fellowship at Albert Einstein College of Medicine. Home: 57 South St Natick MA 01760-5526 Office: Brigham and Womens Hosp Dept Anesthesia Rsch L Boston MA 02115 Personal E-mail: drwe@comcast.net. Business E-Mail: eweiss@bics.bwh.harvard.edu.

WEISS, GEORGE HERBERT, mathematician, consultant; b. NYC, Feb. 19, 1930; s. Morris and Violet (Mayer) W.; m. Delia Esther Orgel, Dec. 20, 1961; children: Miriam Judith, Alan Keith, Daniel Jonathan. BA, Columbia U., 1951; MA, U. Md., 1953, PhD, 1958. Physicist USN, White Oak, Md., 1951-61; asst. prof. U. Md., College Park, 1959-63; fellow Rockefeller U., NYC, 1963-64, Weizmann Inst., Rehovot, Israel, 1958-59; mathematician NIH, Bethesda, Md., 1964—. Cons. GM, IBM, GE. Author: Lattice Dynamics in the Harmonic Approximation, 1963, 2d edit., 1971, The Master Equation in Chemical Physics, 1977, Contemporary Problems in Statistical Physics, 1994, Aspects and Applications of the Random Walk, 1994, Introduction to Crystallographic Statistics, 1995. With U.S. Army, 1954-56. Recipient Disting. Svc. in Math. award Washington Acad. Sci., 1967, Disting. Svc. award NIH, 1970. Avocations: photography, music, chess, philately. Office: NIH Bethesda MD 20892 Business E-Mail: weissgh@mail.nih.gov.

WEISS, GERHARD HANS, German language educator; b. Berlin, Aug. 6, 1926; came to US, 1946; s. Curt Erich and Gertrud (Grothus) W.; m. Janet Marilyn Smith, Dec. 27, 1953; children: John Martin, Susan Elizabeth Weiss Spencer, James David. BA, Washington U., St. Louis, 1950, MA, 1952; PhD, U. Wis., 1956. Prof. German U. Minn., Mpls., 1956—98, assoc. dean, 1967—71, 1979, chmn. dept. German, 1987-95, prof. emeritus, 1998—, interim dir. Ctr. Austrian Studies, 1999-2001. Mem. German-Am. Textbook Commn., Braunschweig, Fed. Republic Germany, 1985-88. Author: Begegnung mit Deutschland, 1970; editor: Unterrichtspraxis, 1975-80, Minn. Monographs in the Humanities, 1964-70; contbr. articles to profl. jours. Served to lt. col. USAR, 1946-75. Recipient Cross Merit, Fed. Republic Germany, 1982, Austrian Cross of Honor 1st Class Sci. and Arts, Republic of Austria, 2004. Mem. MLA, Am. Assn. Tchrs. German (pres. 1982-83, cert. of merit 1981, Disting. German Educator award 1991, elected hon. mem. 1995), German Studies Assn. (v.p. 1997-98, pres. 1999-00), Am. Coun. Tchg. Fgn. Langs. (Nelson Brooks award 1987). Methodist. Home: 4101 Abbott Ave S Minneapolis MN 55410-1004 Business E-Mail: weiss003@umn.edu.

WEISS, GERSON, endocrinologist, educator; b. NYC, Aug. 1, 1939; s. Samuel and Lillian (Wolpe) Weiss; m. Linda Gordon, Dec. 24, 1959; children: Jonathan, David, Michele, Andrew. BA, NYU, 1960, MD, 1964. Diplomate Am. Bd. Ob-Gyn. Intern, fellow dept. medicine Johns Hopkins Sch. Medicine, 1964-65; resident ob-gyn NYU Med. Ctr., 1964-69; rsch. fellow physiology U. Pitts. Sch. Medicine, 1971-73; asst. prof. ob-gyn NYU Med. Ctr., 1971-76, assoc. prof., 1976-80, prof., 1980-85; dir. div. reproductive endocrinology NYU Med. Center, 1975-85; prof. ob-gyn U. Med. and Dentistry NJ-NJ Med. Sch., 1986—, chmn. dept., 1986—; dir. divsn. reproductive endocrinology Hackensack U. Med. Ctr., NJ, 1996—2002. Rep. Am. Bd. Med. Spltys., bd. dirs., 2004—. Mem. editl. bd.: Fertility and Sterility Jour., 1986—93, Gyn.-Ob. Investigation; contbr. scientific papers to profl. jours. Served to maj. MC US Army, 1969—71. Rsch. grantee, NIH, 1975—, United Cerebral Palsy Found., 1977—83, Mellon Found., 1982—85, Rsch. fellow, John Polachek Found. Mem.: ACOG, Soc. Study Reprodn., NY Gynecol. Soc. (pres. 1989—90), NY Obstet. Soc. (pres. 1990—91), Soc. Gynecol. Investigation (pres. 2005—06), Endocrine Soc., Am. Bd. Ob-Gyn. (mem. divsn. reproductive endocrinology 1985—90, mem. ob-gyn. residency rev. com. 1995—2000, bd. dirs., treas. 1997—98, pres. 1998—2002, chmn. 2002—06), Am. Gyn.-Ob. Soc., Alpha Omega Alpha, Sigma Xi, Phi Beta Kappa. Home: 185 West End Ave Apt 7MN New York NY 10023 Office: UMDNJ NJ Med Sch Dept Ob-Gyn 185 S Orange Ave Newark NJ 07103-2757 Business E-Mail: weissge@umdnj.edu.

WEISS, HARLAN LEE, lawyer; b. Washington, Dec. 6, 1941; s. Richard Stanley and Ethel (Shulman) Weiss; m. Elaine Sharon Schooler, Feb. 14, 1971; children: Rachel Shayna, Brian Adam. BA, U. Md., College Park, 1963; JD with honors, U. Md., Balt., 1966. Bar: Md. 1967, DC 1967, US Dist. Ct. Md. 1967, US Dist. Ct. DC 1967, US Ct. Appeals (DC cir.) 1968, US Ct. Appeals (4th cir.) 1977, US Supreme Ct. 1970. Law clk. Thomas B. Finan Ct. Appeals of Md., 1966-67; assoc. Surrey & Morse and predecessors, Washington, 1967-72, Sachs, Greenebaum & Tayler, Washington, 1972-76, ptnr., 1976-90; mem. Kivitz & Liptz, LLC, Chevy Chase, Md., 1990. Mem. Jud. Conf. DC, 1978—79; mem. peer rev. com. Atty. Grievance Commn. Md., 2002—. Home: 12017 Cheyenne Rd Gaithersburg MD 20878-2011 Office: 650 Barlow Bldg 5454 Wisconsin Ave Chevy Chase MD 20815-6901 Office Phone: 301-951-3400. Personal E-mail: harlanlweiss@yahoo.com.

WEISS, HOLLY ANNE, music educator, singer; b. Camden, NJ, Dec. 23, 1950; d. Nicholas John Weiss and Dorothy Lora Sloan; m. Ernest Libby Whitehouse, June 26, 1996. BS in Music Edn. summa cum laude, West Chester U., 1973; Master of Music, Northwestern U., 1974. Cert. tchr. music K-12 Pa., N.J. Instr. Northeastern Bible Coll., Essex Fells, NJ, 1974—79, choir dir. and tour dir., 1975—76; instr. Utica Coll., NY, 1999—2001; pvt. practice vocal studio NYC, 1974—96, NJ, 1974—96, New Hartford, NY, 1996—. Singer: (Operas) The Opening, 2003, A Game of Chance, 2005, Salvatore Rosa, Carmen, Don Giovanni, Il Trovatore, Madame Butterfly, La Boheme, (oratorio) Elijah, Festival Te Deum, Requiem, La Nativité, Requiem, Christmas Oratorio, La Fiesta de la Posada, Magnificat, (oratorio radio broadcast) Gloria, (oratorio) Magnificat, 1993, Messiah, 1995, 1996; singer: (appearances include) Everson Mus., 1999, Munson Williams Proctor Inst., 1999, 2003, Utica Symphony, 2001, numerous others; accompanist: for students in studio and performance, resident soloist: First Presbyn. and Trinity Ch., 1980—85, Temple Emanu-El, 1980—85; singer: (TV) State of the Arts, 1983. Active Post Polio Support Group; contbr. Compassion Internat., 1989—; chair Trinity Covenant Ch., Livingston, 1990—96; chair 2d svc. task force First United Meth. Ch., New Hartford, 1997—98. Mem.: Nat. Assn. Tchrs. of Singing, B-Sharp Musical Club, Phi Beta Kappa. Avocations: gardening, art, reading, cooking, lay speaking. Office: Holly Weiss Vocal Studio 43 South Hills Dr New Hartford NY 13413

WEISS, JACK MEYAR, lawyer; b. New Orleans, Jan. 5, 1947; s. J.M. and Louise (Feitel) W.; m. Ann Robinson, June 21, 1969; children: David, Eli, Anne. AB cum laude, Yale Coll., 1968; JD magna cum laude, Harvard U., 1971. Bar: La. 1971, D.C. 1972, U.S. Ct. Appeals (5th cir.) 1972, U.S. Dist. Ct. (ea., mid. and we. dists.) La. 1975, U.S. Supreme Ct. 1973. Law clk. to Hon. John M. Wisdom U.S. Ct. Appeals, New Orleans, 1971-72; sr. law clk. chief justice Warren Burger U.S. Supreme Ct., Washington, 1972-73; legis. asst. Office U.S. Senator J.B. Johnston, Washington, 1973-75; assoc. Stone, Pigman, Walther, Wittmann & Hutchinson, New Orleans, 1975-77, ptnr., 1990—, Phelps Dunbar et al, New Orleans, 1977-90, Correro Fishman Haygood Phelps Weiss Walmsley & Casteix, L.L.P, New Orleans, Gibson, Dunn & Crutcher LLP, NYC, 1998—. Adj. prof. La. State U., Baton Rouge, 1984—; adj. asst. prof. Law Sch. Tulane U., New Orleans, 1980—. Author: (ann. survey) La. Defamation and Privacy Law; co-author: (survey) La. Pub. Records and Open Meeting Law, 1988. Trustee Isidore Newman Sch., New Orleans, 1982—, Children's Hosp., New Orleans, 1982-86. Named Am's. Leading Bus. Lawyers, by Chambers USA, 2006. Mem. ABA, DC, NYC, Am. Law Inst., NY State Bar Assn., La. State Bar Assn. (chmn. sect. corp., bus. law 1987-88), Phi Beta Kappa. Democrat. Jewish. Treas. & mng. editor: Harvard Law Review. Office: Gibson Dunn & Crutcher LLP 200 Park Ave 47th Fl New York NY 10166-0193 Office Phone: 212-351-3890. Office Fax: 212-351-5224. E-mail: JMweiss@gibsondunn.com.

WEISS, JAMES LLOYD, cardiology educator; b. Chgo., Jan. 15, 1941; s. Edward Huhner and Ruth (Wingerhoff) W.; m. Susan Forscher Weiss, July 23, 1967; children: Ethan James, Lisa Fleur. BA, Harvard Coll., 1963; MD, Yale U., 1968. Intern, resident U. Mich. Hosp., Ann Arbor, 1968-70; staff fellow NIH, Bethesda, Md., 1970-72; resident medicine Johns Hopkins Hosp., Balt., 1972-73, fellow cardiology, 1973-75, dir. Heart Station, 1976—, asst. prof. Medicine, 1975-81, assoc. prof. Medicine, 1981-90, prof. Medicine, Cariology, 1990—, Michael J. Cudahy prof. of cardiology, 1992—, assoc. dean admissions and acad. affairs, 1999—, dir. cardiology fellowship and tng. program, 1999—. Mem. editl. bd.: Johns Hopkins Med. Letter, 1991—, Jour. Am. Coll. Cardiology, 1995—; contbr. 120 articles to profl. jours. Recipient Harvard Book prize, 1959. Fellow Am. Coll. Cardiology, AHA Coun. on Circulation; mem. Harvard Club N.Y.C., Ctr. Club. Office: Cardiology Divsn Johns Hopkins Hosp 600 N Wolfe St Baltimore MD 21287-0005 Home Phone: 410-321-1145; Office Phone: 410-955-6834. E-mail: jlweiss@jhmi.edu.

WEISS, JAMES MICHAEL, financial analyst, portfolio manager; b. Chgo., July 20, 1946; s. Harold Cornelius and Elizabeth Josephine (Jesse) W.; m. Kathleen Jane Postorino, July 18, 1970; children: Elizabeth, Ann, Jane, William. BA, Marquette U., 1968; MBA, U. Pa., 1972. CFA; chartered investment counselor. Credit analyst Provident Nat. Bank, Phila., 1972; ptnr., sr. portfolio mgr. Stein Roe & Farnham Investment Counsel, Chgo., 1972—87, 1st v.p., prin., sr. portfolio mgr., 1987—90, sr. v.p., prin., sr. portfolio mgr., 1991—92; exec. v.p., sr. portfolio mgr. IDS Adv. Group, Inc., Mpls., 1993—95; pres., chief investment officer IDS Equity Advisors, 1995; sr. v.p., dep. chief investment officer Equities, State St. Rsch. & Mgmt. Co., Boston, 1995—97, exec. v.p., mem. mgmt. com., dep. head of equities, 1998—99, exec. v.p. mem. mgmt. com., chief invest. officer, bd. dirs., 1999—2002; pres. Weiss Capital Mgmt., Inc., 2002—. Bd. dirs. Tropp & Co., Chgo.; v.p. Stein Roe Cash Reserves Fund, Chgo., 1982-87; mem. investment com. Pro Mutual Group, Boston, Mass., 2004—. Author: (with others) Handbook of Cash Flow and Treasury Management, 1987; contbr. articles to profl. jours. Commr. Glenview (Ill.) Zoning Bd., 1978-80; trustee Glenview Village Bd. Trustees, 1980-86; chmn. Marquette U. Exec. Senate, Chgo., 1984-87; active Glenview Bus. Area Redevel. Com., 1990-93; bus. adv. coun. Elmhurst (Ill.) Coll., 1986-93; founding bd. dirs. Glenview Edn. Found., 1990-93; bd. trustees Fenn Sch., Concord, Mass., 1996-2002, Fenn Sch. investment com., 1996—; co-chmn. Fenn Sch. Capital Campaign, 1997-2000; bd. dirs. Gaining Ground, Concord, 2003—, bd. mem. Wright Farm Condo Assn., 2007-, South Love Assn., 2007-. With U.S. Army, 1968-70. With US Army, 1968—70. Recipient Cert. Merit Village of Glenview, 1987. Mem.: Investment Counsel Assn., CFA Inst., Boston Analysts Soc., Marquette U. Alumni Assn. (nat. bd. dirs. 1989—91, liberal arts bd. 2000—05, Nat. Svc. award 1995), Indian River Country Club (Vero Beach, Fla.), Boston Coll. Club, Wedgewood Pines Club (Stow, Mass.), North Shore Country Club (Glenview, Ill.). Avocations: golf, travel, writing. Office: Weiss Capital Mgmt PO Box 1128 Concord MA 01742-1128 Home: 13 Wright Farm Rd Concord MA 01742-1528 Home Phone: 978-369-9063; Office Phone: 978-505-5435. Business E-Mail: jweiss6@earthlink.net.

WEISS, JERRY KENNETH, sales executive, consultant, marketing professional; BA, State U. Ohio, Toledo, 1968; MA, State U. Ohio, 1968; postgrad., NYU, 1976—80. Sales and mktg. rep. Panasonic Corp., 1968—70; v.p. mktg. Danville Industries, 1970—79; sales and mktg. mgr. Sharp Electronics, 1980—82; dir. nat. sales Mattel Corp., 1982—84; sr. ptnr. The CE Group, Inc., 1984—2004. Bd. dirs. CE2, Inc., Cedarhurst. Author: (audio cassette/cd) Sales Directions. Fundraiser Westchester Reform Temple, Scarsdale, NY, 1998—2003. Scholar, State U. Ohio. Fellow: Sigma Alpha Mu (sec.), Acad. Mktg. Sci. (founding assoc.); mem.: Phi Beta Kappa, Phi Alpha Theta. Avocations: motorcycling, auto racing, white-water rafting. Office Phone: 914-948-1866. Personal E-mail: jerryweiss6@aol.com.

WEISS, JOHN ROBERT, lawyer; b. Chgo., May 7, 1961; s. Robert Gordon and Elizabeth Jean (Malecki) W.; m. Elizabeth Anne Zur, Dec. 5, 1987. BA, Northwestern U., 1982, JD, 1985. Bar: Ill. 1985, US Dist. Ct. (no. dist.) Ill. 1985, US Dist. Ct. (ctrl. dist.) Ill., 1997, US Ct. Appeals (7th cir.) 1987, US Ct. Appeals (8th cir.), 1999, US Supreme Ct. 1989. Assoc., ptnr. Chapman & Cutler, Chgo., 1985—96; ptnr. Katten Muchin Rosenman, Chgo., 1996—2006, Duane Morris LLP, Chgo., 2006—. Tchr. Chgo. Coalition for Law-Related Edn., 1985—; atty. Chgo. Vol. Legal Services, 1985—. Mem. ABA, 7th Cir. Bar Assn., Am. Judicature Soc., Ill. Bar Assn., Am. Bankruptcy Inst., Turnaround Mgmt. Assn. Roman Catholic. Avocations: golf, billiards, chess. Office: Duane Morris LLP 227 West Monroe St Chicago IL 60606 Office Phone: 312-499-6700. Office Fax: 312-499-6701. Business E-Mail: jrweiss@duanemorris.com.

WEISS, JONATHAN ARTHUR, lawyer, writer; b. May 1, 1939; s. Paul and Victoria Brodkin Weiss. BA, Yale U., New Haven, Conn., 1960, LLB, 1963; student, U. Chgo. Law Sch., 1960—61. Bar: NY 1967, DC 1994, Vet.'s Ct. (2d and 3d cirs.), U.S. Supreme Ct. 1964. Mng. atty. Neighborhood Legal Svcs., Washington, 1964-66, Mobilization for Youth Legal Svcs., NYC, 1969-71; with Ctr. on Welfare Law, Columbia U. Law Sch., NYC, 1967-69; dir. Legal Svcs. for Elderly, NYC, 1971—. Lectr. Hebrew U., Jerusalem, 1966; vis. prof. Tex. So. U. Law Sch., Houston, 1971; adj. prof. Yeshiva U. Cardozo Law Sch., NYC, 1983—85; mem. Admin. Com. Conf. US, 1986—92; extern prof. Pace Law Sch., 2003, adj. prof., 07. Co-author, editor: The Law and the Elderly, 1976; co-author: Right and Wrong a Philosophical Dialogue Between Father and Son (in Italian), 1968, translator (French and Russian) novels, plays and screen plays; contbr. articles and revs. to law and philos. periodicals US and Italy. Bd. dir. Disability Legal Def. Fund, World Trust Fund Inc. Recipient Disting. Scholar medal, Hofstra U., 1972; Fulbright scholar, 1966, archived at U. Ind. Libr., Indpls. Fellow: Am. Bar Found.; mem.: ABA (adv. coun. ethics 2000 com., Centennial com.), Am. Trial Lawyers, NY County Bar Assn. (Public Interest award, Pro Bono Lawyer of Yr.), NY State Bar (internat. sect. human rights), Native Am. Bar Assn. Democrat. Office: 142 W 87th St New York NY 10024 Personal E-mail: dostoyesty@juno.com.

WEISS, JOSEPH JOEL, consulting company executive; b. Newark, July 27, 1931; s. Harry H. and Belle (Sass) W.; m. Leah Kneller, Apr. 10, 1954 (div. 1961); children: Sara, Daniel; m. Carol Lynn Seegott, Sept. 29, 1967; children: Laura, John. BSBA, Rutgers U., 1953, MBA, 1958. Dist. mgr. N.J. Bell Telephone Co., 1955-61; asst. comptroller ITT P.R. Telephone Co., San Juan, 1964-68; sr. cons. NYC, 1968-71; v.p. data services Rio De Janeiro, 1971-74; dir. ops. NYC, 1975-80; v.p. Control Data Corp., Rio De Janeiro, 1974-75; exec. v.p., chief adminstrv. officer Burger King Corp., Miami, 1980-89; chief oper. officer Goode, Olcott, Knight & Assocs., Coral Gables, Fla., 1989-90; pres. Contraband Detection Internat., Miami, Fla., 1990-92; sr. v.p. Seegott Inc., Streetsboro, Ohio, 1992—. Bd. dirs. Sta. WPB-TV. Author: How to Get from Cubicle to Corner Office, The Quotable Manager. Pres. Civic Betterment Assn., Franklin Twp., N.J., 1961; trustee U. Miami Citizens Bd., 1987—; bd. dirs. Boy Scouts Am., 1982—. Recipient Strategic Planning Achievement award Boy Scouts Am., 1985. Mem. Hist. Soc. Fla. (bd. dirs. 1986—). Clubs: Fisher Island. Republican. Presbyterian. Avocations: painting, tennis. Home: 6682 Brookside Woods Ct Se Ada MI 49301-8219

WEISS, KENNETH ANDREW, lawyer, educator; b. New Orleans, Jan. 16, 1951; s. Irving and Julia (Mayer) Weiss. BA, Tulane U., 1972, JD with honors, 1975; LLM in Taxation with highest honors, George Washington U., 1981. Bar: La. 1975, DC 1976. Editl. writer, Washington corr. The Times-Picayune, New Orleans and Washington, 1973-79; news editor Congl. Quarterly, Washington, 1979-81; mng. editor Reporters Com. for Freedom of the Press, Washington, 1981-82; assoc. McGlinchey Stafford, New Orleans, 1982-84, dir., 1984—. Prof. Tulane U. Law Sch., New Orleans, 1987—, La. State U. Law Sch., 2000—; mem. trust code com. La. Law Inst., Baton Rouge, 1993—, mem. successions and donations com., 1996—; mem. planning com. Tulane Tax Inst., 1996—; chair Tulane U. Law Sch. Ann. Estate Planning Seminar, 1995—2001, Tulane U. Estate Planning Inst., 2002—; dean's adv. coun. Tulane Law Sch., 2003—. Co-author: Bankers' Guide to Establishing, Managing and Operating Common Trust Funds, 1986, Business Uses of Life Insurance, 1986, Executive Compensation, 1990; assoc. editor Tulane Law Rev., 1974-75, mem. bd. adv. editors, 1992—; contbr. articles to profl. jours. Bd. dirs. Longue Vue House and Gardens Adv. Corp., 1993-95, bd. dirs. Longue Vue Found., 1995—2003; trustee Greater New Orleans Ednl. TV Found., Sta. WYES-TV, 1994-98; bd. dirs. So. Repertory Theatre, 1996-2001, pres., 1998-99; bd. advisors Project Lazarus, 1996-2000, pres. 1997-99; mem. profl. adv. com., Jewish Endowment Found., 1982—; mem. planned gifts adv. com. Tulane U., 1989—; active Met. Area Com. Leadership Forum, New Orleans, 1983; fellow Inst. Politics Loyola U., New Orleans, 1989-90; mem. devel. com. Greater New Orleans Found., 1995—. bd. dirs., Innocence Project New Orleans, 2002-05, treas., 2002-04. Recipient Addy award for polit. advt., 1989, awards for investigative reporting; Phi Delta Phi scholar, 1972-73. Fellow Am. Coll. Trust and Estate Counsel; mem. La. State Bar Assn. (taxation sect., bd. cert. tax atty., bd. cert. estate planning and adminstrn. specialist), New Orleans Bar Assn. (chair taxation law com. 2003), Nat. Coun. Planned Giving (greater New Orleans chpt.), New Orleans Estate Planning Coun., Order of the Coif. Republican. Jewish. Office Phone: 504-596-2751.

WEISS, KENNETH R., newswriter; b. Calif. B in Folklore, U. Calif., Berkeley. Washington corr. NY Times Regional Newspapers; reporter States New Svc., Washington, LA Times, 1990—. Co-recipient John B. Oakes award for Outstanding Environmental Journalism, Columbia U. Grad. Sch. Journalism, 2006, George Polk award for Environmental Reporting, 2006, Walter Sullivan award for Excellence in Sci. Journalism, Am. Geophys. Union, 2007, Pub. Comm. award, Am. Soc. Microbiol., 2007, Print Media award, Am. Inst. Biol. Scis., 2007, Pulitzer Prize for Explanatory Reporting, 2007. Avocation: surfing. Office: LA Times 202 W 1st St Los Angeles CA 90012 Office Phone: 213-237-7733. E-mail: ken.weiss@latimes.com. *

WEISS, LAWRENCE N., lawyer; b. NYC, Aug. 9, 1942; s. Joseph and Martha (Guggenheimer) W.; m. Osnat Gad. BA, CCNY, 1963; LLB summa cum laude, Columbia U., 1966. Bar: NY 1966, US Ct. Appeals (2d cir.) 1967, US Dist. Ct. (so. and ea. dists) NY 1968, US Supreme Ct. 1971, US Ct. Appeals (3d cir.) 1968, US Ct. Appeals (6th cir.) 1980, US Tax Ct. 1977. Assoc. Kaye, Scholer, Fierman, Hays & Handler, NYC, 1966-67, 67-73; law clk. to judge NY Ct. Appeals, Albany and NYC, 1967; assoc. Botein, Hays, Sklar & Herzberg, NYC, 1973-76, Weisman, Celler, Spett, Modlin & Wertheimer, NYC, 1976, ptnr., 1977-79, counsel, 1979-81; prin. Lawrence N. Weiss, P.C., NYC, 1981—, Pantaleoni & Weiss, NYC, 1993—2003. Arbitrator Civil Ct., NYC, 1985—; mediator US Dist. Ct. (ea. dist.) NY and NY Supreme Ct. Author: (newsletter) Review of the Shakespeare Wars, 2006. Mem. NY County Lawyers Assn. (arbitrator joint com. fee disputes), Assn. Bar of City of NY (com. on legal edn. and admission to bar, arbitrator joint com. fee disputes), NY State Bar Assn. (chair com. CLE, com. on fed. judiciary, spl. com. on copyright, vice chair com. on UN, subcom. internat. cts., litig. sect., judiciary com.), Shakespeare Assn. Am. Avocation: shakespearean studies. Home: 107 E 37th St New York NY 10016-3065 E-mail: larry@lweiss.net.

WEISS, LEONARD, mathematician, consultant; b. NYC, Mar. 14, 1934; s. Max and Sadie (Albert) W.; m. Sandra Joyce Raynes, June 15, 1958; children: Madelyn, Eugene. B.E.E., CCNY, 1956; MS, Columbia U., 1959; PhD, Johns Hopkins U., 1962. Lectr. CCNY, 1956-59; staff scientist Research Inst. for Advanced Studies, Balt., 1962-64; asst. prof. Brown U., Providence, 1964-66, assoc. prof., 1966-68; prof. U. Md., College Park, 1968-78; legis. asst. to Senator John Glenn of Ohio, 1976-77; cons. Naval Research Lab., Washington, 1970-77; staff dir. Senate Subcom. on Energy, Nuclear Proliferation and Govt. Processes, 1977-86, Senate Com. Govtl. Affairs., 1987-99; sr. sci. fellow Ctr. Internat. Security and Cooperation, Stanford U., 2006—07. Cons. Lawrence Livermore Nat. Lab., 1999—. Editor: Ordinary Differential Equations, 1972; contbr. articles to profl. jours. and mags.; author legislation on nuclear proliferation, energy, health and safety, govt. orgn., and govt. mgmt. Alfred P. Sloan research fellow, 1966-68, IEEE Congl. fellow, 1976, Stennis Congl. fellow, 1997. Home and Office: 11701 Auth Ln Silver Spring MD 20902-1644 Office Phone: 301-593-1699.

WEISS, LISA ANN, lawyer; b. Chgo., Dec. 6, 1958; d. Benjamin B. and Suzanne (Harris) W. BA, Yale U., 1980; JD, Columbia U., 1983. Bar: N.Y. 1984. Assoc. Stroock Stroock & Lavan, NYC, 1983-86, Rosenman & Colin, NYC, 1986-92, ptnr., 1992—2000; dep. gen. counsel Sony Music, 2000—01, gen. counsel, 2001—05, Sony BMG, 2005—06; ptnr. Morrison & Foerster LLP, NYC, 2006—. Bd. dirs. Lightspeed Audio Labs., 2006—. Mem. NYC Bar Assn. (corp. law com. 1992-95). Office: Morrison & Foerster LLP 1290 Ave of the Americas New York NY 10104-0050 Office Phone: 212-468-8003. E-mail: lweiss@mofo.com.

WEISS, LYN DENISE, physician; b. Bethpage, NY, Apr. 13, 1959; d. Eugene and Lois Zanger; m. Jay M. Weiss, Apr. 7, 1984; children: Ari, Helene, Stefan, Richard. BA, U. Va., 1981; MD, SUNY, Bklyn., 1985. Diplomate Am. Bd. Electrodiagnostic Medicine, Nat. Bd. Med. Examiners, Am. Bd. Phys. Medicine and Rehab. Resident Dept. Phys. Medicine & Rehab. Nassau U. Med. Ctr., East Meadow, NY, 1985—89; attending physician Dept. Phys. Medicine & Rehab. Nassau U. Med. Ctr., 1989—94, dir. Electrodiagnostic Medicine Dept. Phys. Medicine Rehab., 1991—; dir. residency tng. Dept. Phys. Medicine & Rehab. Nassau U. Med. Ctr., 1993—; acting chmn. Dept. Phys. Medicine & Rehab. Nassau U. Med. Ctr., 1994—96; chmn. Dept. Phys. Medicine & Rehab. Nassau U. Med. Ctr., 1996—. Bd. dirs. Ctr. for Rehab. Rsch. Tech., Massapequa, N.Y., 1996— Author: Cumulative Trauma Disorders, 1997, Skin Care Triad, 2000, Easy EMG, 2004, Easy Injections, 2007.

WEISS, LYNNE S., pediatrician, educator; MD, Hahnemann Med. Coll., Phila., 1974. Diplomate Pediatrics Am. Bd. Pediatrics, 1979, Pediatric Nephrology Am. Bd. Pediatrics, 1982. Intern in Pediatrics Michael Reese Hosp., Chgo., 1974—75, resident in Pediatrics, 1975—77, fellow in Nephrology (pediatric), 1977—79; physician, chief divsn. pediat. nephrology & hypertension UMDNJ-Robert Wood Johnson Med. Sch., New Brunswick, NJ, 1985—. Prof. Pediatrics Robert Wood Johnson Univ. Hosp., New Brunswick, NJ, 1987—, dir. Pediatric Nephrology Ctr., 1987—. Office: UMDNJ-Robert Wood Johnson Med Sch Pediatric Nephrology and Hypertension 89 French St New Brunswick NJ 08901 Office Phone: 732-235-7880.

WEISS, MARIANNA SHRENGER, psychotherapist; b. Pakrac, Croatia, Dec. 10, 1941; arrived in U.S., 1951; d. Edoardo and Vanda Schrenger Weiss; 1 child, Jacob Solomon. BA, MA, U. Calif., Berkeley, 1966; MS, Calif. State U., Hayward, 1985. Lic. marriage, family, and child counselor Bd. of Behavioral Scis., Calif. Workshop leader, hotline response worker Rape Crisis Ctr., Richmond, Calif., 1987—89; coord., group facilitator, newsletter editor and contbr. Tikvah, Holocaust survivors self-help group, San Francisco and Berkeley, 1989—94; therapist Family and Children's Svcs. of Contra Costa County, Walnut Creek and Richmond, Calif., 1989—93; therapist, dir. svcs. to Holocaust survivors Family Svc. of Silicon Valley, Los Gatos, Calif., 1999—2001; therapist Ctr. for Cmty. Counseling, Eugene, Oreg., 2002—; leader chronic illness workshop PeaceHealth Med. Ctr., Eugene, 2003—. Actor: (residential theater). Office: CCC 1465 Coburg Rd Eugene OR 97401 Home Phone: 541-607-4442.

WEISS, MARK ANSCHEL, lawyer; b. NYC, June 20, 1937; s. George and Ida (Galin) W.; m. Joan Roth, June 8, 1958; children: Rebecca, Sarabeth, Jonathan, Deborah. AB, Columbia U., 1958; LLB magna cum laude, Harvard U., 1961. Bar: N.Y. 1961, D.C. 1962, U.S. Supreme Ct. 1965. Assoc. Covington & Burling, Washington, 1961-66, 69-70, ptnr., 1970—; spl. asst. to Under Sec. Treasury Dept. Washington, 1966-68; spl. asst. to sec., 1968-69. Mem. editl. adv. bd. Electronic Banking Law and Commerce Report. Mem. ABA, D.C. Bar, Fed. Bar Assn. (chmn. banking law com.). Office: Covington & Burling 1201 Pennsylvania Ave NW Washington DC 20004-2401 Home Phone: 301-657-4094; Office Phone: 202-662-5308. Business E-Mail: mweiss@cov.com.

WEISS, MARTIN HARVEY, neurosurgeon, educator; b. Newark, Feb. 2, 1939; s. Max and Rae W.; m. R. Debora Rosenthal, Aug. 20, 1961; children: Brad, Jessica, Elisabeth. AB magna cum laude, Dartmouth Coll., 1960, BMS, 1961; MD, Cornell U., 1963. Diplomate Am. Bd. Neurol. Surgery (bd. dirs. 1983-89, vice chmn. 1987-88, chmn. 1988-89). Intern Univ. Hosps., Cleve., 1963-64, resident in neurosurgery, 1966-70; sr. instr. to asst. prof. neurosurgery Case Western Res. U., 1970-73; asso. prof. neurosurgery U. So. Calif., 1973-76, prof., 1976-78, prof., chmn. dept., 1978—2004, Martin H. Weiss chair in neurol. surgery, 1997—. Chmn. neurology B study sect. NIH; mem. residency rev. com. for neurosurg. Accreditation Commn. for Grad. Med. Edn., 1989—, vice chmn., 1991—93, chmn., 1993—95, mem. appeals coun. in neurosurg., 1995—; vis. prof. U. Mich, 1987; vis. prof. Med. Sch. Harvard U., 1988; vis. prof. U. Wash., 1988, U. Calif., San Francisco, 1994, U. Oreg., 1995, Tufts U., 1996, U. Melbourne, 1996, U. Sydney, 1996, U. Erlangen/Nurnberg, 1999, U. Geneva, 1999, U. Tex., 2004, U. Oreg., 2004, Stanford U., 2005; vis. prof., Bronson Ray lectr. Cornell U., 2005—06; Afrox traveling prof. South African Congress Neurol. Surgeons, 1989; hon. guest Royal Coll. Physicians Endocrine Sect., London, 2001; lectr. in field. Author: Pituitary Diseases, 1980; editor-in-chief Clin. Neurosurgery, 1980-83; assoc. editor Bull. L.A. Neurol. Socs., 1976-81, Jour. Clin. Neurosci., 1981—; mem. editl. bd. Neurosurgery, 1979-84, Neurol. Rsch., 1980—, Jour. Neurosurgery, 1987—, chmn., 1995—, assoc. editor, 1996—. Served to capt. USAR, 1964—66, assoc. in gen. surgery USAH, USMA, 1964—66, West Point, NY. Spl. fellow in neurosurgery NIH, 1969-70; recipient Jamieson medal Australasian Neurosurg. Soc., 1996. Mem. ACS (adv. coun. neurosurgery 1985-88), Soc. Neurol. Surgeons (v.p. 1999, pres.-elect 2000—, pres. 2001-02), Neurosurg. Soc. Am., Am. Acad. Neurol. Surgery (exec. com. 1988-89, v.p. 1992-93, Kurze Lectr. 2005, Cushing medal 2005), Rsch. Soc. Neurol. Surgeons, Am. Assn. Neurol. Surgeons (bd. dirs. 1988-91, sec. 1994-97, pres.-elect 1998-99, pres. 1999-00, past pres. 2000-01, Cushing Medalist, 2005), Congress Neurol. Surgeons (v.p. 1982-83), Western Neurosurg. Soc. (Cloward medal 2006), Neurosurg. Forum, So. Calif. Neurosurg. Soc. (pres. 1983-84), Neurosurgeon Rsch. & Edn. Found. (chmn., exec. com. 2004-), Phi Beta Kappa, Alpha Omega Alpha. Home: 357 Georgian Rd La Canada Flintridge CA 91011-3520 Office: 1200 N State St Los Angeles CA 90033-1029 Home Phone: 818-790-7467; Office Phone: 323-226-7421. Business E-Mail: weiss@usc.edu.

WEISS, MELVYN I., lawyer; b. NYC, Aug. 1, 1935; s. Joseph and Jean Weiss; m. Barbara Joan Kaplan, Dec. 27, 1958; children: Gary Michael, Stephen Andrew, Leslie Caryn. BBA, CCNY, 1957; JD, NYU, 1959. Bar: NY 1960, US Dist. Ct. (so. dist.) NY, US Dist. Ct. (ea. dist.) NY, US Ct. Appeals (2d, 3rd, 4th, 5th, 6th, 8th, 9th and 10th cirs.) 1975, US Supreme Ct. 1976. Assoc. Strasser, Spiegelberg, Fried & Frank, NYC, 1959-61, Galef & Jacobs, NYC, 1962-65; founding ptnr. Milberg Weiss Bershad & Schulman LLP, 1966—, Milberg Weiss & Bershad LLP, La., 1966. Lectr. panelist univs., bar groups, CLE orgns.; vice chair bd. Drum Major Inst.; bd. dirs. ActiVote, Washington, NYU Sch. Law, Lawyer's Com. for Civil Rights Under Law; hon. prof. U. Argentine, Buenos Aires. Contbr. articles to profl. jours. Founder Melvyn and Barbara Weiss Pub. Interest Student Loan Repayment Assistance Program, NYU; mem. exec. com. Israel Policy Forum; internat. chmn. Hatikvah Project; former bd. mem. Am. Jewish Congress, Salzburg Seminar. Named 1 of 13 Attys. in Am. Who Stand Out from the Crowd, Nat. Law. Jour., 2003; named one of Most Influential Leaders in Bus., Crain's NY, 2002; named to Top 100 Most Influential People in Acctg., Accounting Today, 2001, 2002, 2003, 2004; recipient Gotham and Humanitarian award, Anti Defamation League, 1976, Outstanding Alumni Assn. Achievement award, 1982, Arthur T. Vanderbilt medal, NYU Law Sch., 1993, Proskauer award, United Jewish Appeal, 1997. Fellow Am. Coll. Trial Lawyers, NY Bar Found.; mem. ABA, B'nai B'rith (Human Rels. award Anti Defamation League 1976), CCNY Alumni Assn. (Oustanding Alumni award 1982), NYU Sch. Law (trustee, Vanderbilt medal 1993), Glen Oaks Golf and Country Club, Boca Rio Golf Club. Office: Milberg Weiss & Bershad LLP Ste 4900 1 Pennsylvania Plz New York NY 10119-0165 Office Phone: 212-594-5300. Office Fax: 212-868-1229. Business E-Mail: mweiss@milbergweiss.com. *

WEISS, MICHAEL ALLEN, retired retail executive; b. NYC, Apr. 21, 1941; s. Robert and Estelle (Kirchner) W.; m. Arlene Markman, Dec. 25, 1962; children: Eloise Kyle, Katherine Jane. BA, Syracuse U., 1962. Buyer Abraham & Straus, Bklyn., 1965-72, Casual Corner, Enfield, Conn., 1972-74; merchandiser Apparel Industries, NYC, 1974-81; pres., CEO Limited Express, Columbus, Ohio, 1981-93; vice chmn. The Limited, Inc., Columbus, 1993—2004. Bd. dirs. Chicos, FAS, Inc., 2005—. Bd. dirs. United Way of Franklin County, ARC. Mem. Winding Hollow Country Club, Capitol Club, New Albany Country Club.

WEISS, MITCHELL JOSEPH, librarian; b. Chgo., Nov. 12, 1942; s. Harry Edward and Gertrude Plotkin Weiss. ScB in Biology with high honors, Brown U., 1964; PhD in Zoology, U. Mich., 1970; MLS, Rutgers U., 1988. NIH postdoctoral rsch. fellow U. Wash., Seattle, 1970—73; postdoctoral instr. in zoology U. Iowa, Iowa City, 1973—74; asst. prof. biology Rutgers U., New Brunswick, NJ, 1974—81, vis. asst. prof., 1981—82, guest investigator, 1982—2000; sci. writer New Brunswick, 2001—02; reference libr., digital/global access libr. coord. Fairleigh Dickinson U., Teaneck, NJ, 2002—07, asst. libr. online libr., 2007—. Cons. Oriel Corp., Stamford, Conn., 1983, Knoll Pharm. Co., Mt. Olive, NJ, 1999—2000. Contbr. articles to sci. jours. Grad. fellow, NSF, 1964—69, rsch. grantee, 1976—78. Mem.: Internat. Assn. Meiobenthologists, Am. Microscopical Soc. Achievements include research in structure and development of insect brain centers at microscopic and ultrastructural levels; biology of phylum Gastrotricha, with current emphasis on sexuality, life cycles and systematics of freshwater gastrotrichs. Avocations: classical music, swimming. Office: Fairleigh Dickinson U 1000 River Rd T-WL1-01 Teaneck NJ 07666 Office Phone: 201-692-2139. E-mail: mjweiss@fdu.edu.

WEISS, MORRY, greeting card company executive; b. Czechoslovakia, 1940; m. Judith Stone. Grad., Wayne State U. Salesman, field mgr. Am. Greetings Corp., Cleve., 1961-66, advt. mgr., 1966-68, v.p., 1969-73, group v.p. mktg. and sales, 1973-78, pres., 1978—2003, COO Cleve., 1978—87, bd. dir., chief exec. officer, 1987—2003, chmn., 1992—. Office: Am Greetings Corp 1 American Rd Cleveland OH 44144-2301 *

WEISS, MYRNA GRACE, management consultant; b. NYC, June 22, 1939; d. Herman and Blanche Ziegler; m. Arthur H. Weiss; children: Debra Anne Huddleston, Louise Esther Pennington. BA, Barnard Coll., 1958; MA, Hunter Coll., 1968; MPA, NYU, 1978; cert. in Mktg., U. Pa. Tchr., NYC and Vallejo, Calif., 1959-68; dir. admissions Columbia Prep. Sch., NYC, 1969-72; dir. PREP counselling NYU, NYC, 1973-74; dept. head Hewitt Sch., NYC, 1974-79; mgr. Met. Ins. Co., NYC, 1979-84; mktg. exec. Rothschild, Inc., NYC, 1984-85; pres. First Mktg. Capital Group Ltd., NYC, 1985—; mng. dir. Wrap Co. Internat. N.V., 1992-97; advisor Lared Group, NYC, 1987-97; CEO, pres., bd. dirs. Ibnet, 1998—2002. Adv. Gov.'s Hwy. Safety Com., NYC, 1985-88; pres. Fin. Women's Assn. NY, 1984-85; faculty SUNY, 2005—. Bd. dirs. 92nd Y, NYC, 1972—90, ARC, NYC, 1989—2006, asst. treas., 1993—. Mem. Internat. Women's Forum (bd. dirs. 1990-92), Econ. Club N.Y., Women's Econ. Roundtable (bd. dirs. 1988-90). Office: 1st Mktg Capital Group Ltd 1056 5th Ave New York NY 10028-0112 E-mail: mzweiss@nyc.rr.com.

WEISS, PAUL RICHARD, plastic surgeon; b. Bklyn., July 4, 1942; s. Marray and Belle (Edelman) W.; m. Linda Wayne, Aug. 23, 1964; children: Fredda Susan, Jonathan Michael. BS, Tufts U., Medford, Mass., 1964; MD, Tulane U., New Orleans, 1969. Diplomate Am. Bd. Plastic Surgery, 1977, Am. Bd. Surgery, 1975. Intern Bronx Muni Hosp Ctr., NY, 1969—70, resident surgery, 1970—72, Montefiore Hosp. Med. Ctr., NY, 1972—74, resident plastic surgery, 1974—76; attending plastic surgeon Montefiore Med. Ctr., NY, 1976—, Albert Einstein Coll. Med. Hosp., NY, 1976—, Beth Abraham Hosp., NY, 1976—, Jewish Home & Hosp., NY, 1976—, Beth Israel Med. Ctr., NY, 1986—; clin. prof. plastic surgery Albert Einstein Coll. Medicine, Bronx, NY, 1994—. Adv. bd. FOJP Medical Malpractice, N.Y.C., 1988—. Named one of Top Doctor, NY Mag. Fellow ACS (Bronx chpt., pres. 1995-96); Am. Soc. Plastic Surgeons, Am. Assn. Plastic Surgeons (pres. 1992-93), Montefiore Med. Ctr. Staff Alumni Assn. (pres. 1994-97), Am. Assn. Hand Surgery, Northeastern Soc. Plastic Surgeons, Harry Benjamin Soc. Jewish. Avocations: landscape gardening, vintage automobiles, stamp collecting/philately, collecting and restoring antique furniture. Office: 1049 5th Ave Ste 2D New York NY 10028-0115 Office Phone: 212-861-8000. Office Fax: 212-861-8376. Personal E-mail: pweissmd@verizon.net. *

WEISS, PAUL STORCH, chemistry educator; b. Ithaca, NY, Oct. 10, 1959; s. Lionel Ira and Rhoda (Storch) W.; children: Walter Paul, Lucien Everett, Maxwell Kendall; m. Anne Milasincic Andrews, June 7, 2005. SB, SM, MIT, 1980; PhD, U. Calif., Berkeley, 1986. Vis. scientist Universite de Claude Bernard, Lyon I, CNRS, Villeurbanne, France, 1980; postdoctoral mem. tech. staff AT&T Bell Labs., Murray Hill, N.J., 1986-88; vis. scientist IBM Almaden Rsch. Ctr., San Jose, Calif., 1988-89; from asst. prof. to disting. prof. chemistry and physics Pa. State U., University Park, 1989—2005, disting. prof. chemistry and physics, 2005—. Named Presdl. Young Investigator NSF, 1991; fellow Sloan Found., 1995-97, Guggenheim Found., 1997-98. Fellow AAAS, Am. Phys. Soc., Am. Vacuum Soc.; mem. IEEE (editor-in-chief jour. 2005-07), Am. Chem. Soc. (editor-in-chief jour. 2007—), Phi Lambda Upsilon (MIT chpt. pres. 1978-79), Sigma Xi. Office: Pa State U 104 Davey Lab University Park PA 16802-6300 Business E-Mail: stm@psu.edu.

WEISS, RAINER, physics educator; b. Berlin, Sept. 29, 1932; BS, MIT, 1955, PhD, 1962. Instr. physics Tufts U., Medford, Mass., 1960-61, asst. prof. physics, 1961-62; rsch. assoc. physics Princeton U., NJ, 1962-64; asst. prof. physics MIT, Cambridge, 1964-67, assoc. prof., 1967-73, prof. physics, 1973—2001, prof. emeritus, 2001—. Mem. NASA phys. sci. com., 1970-74, SSSC com., 1982, infrared detector panel, 1978, others; mem. Panel on Joint Inst. of Lab. Astrophysics, Bd. on Assessment of NBS Progs., NAS, 1985—; coord. NSF Panel on Interferometric Obs. for Gravitational Waves, 1986; mem. NAS space sci. bd., 1983-86, others; adj. prof. physics, La. State U., 2001-. Recipient MIT Baker award for excellence in teaching, 1968; NASA Achievement Award (Monolithic Bolometers), 1984, Exceptional Sci. Achievement medal, 1991, Group Achievement medal, 1991; NASA/GSFC Group Achievement award, 1990. Fellow AAAS, Am. Phys. Soc. (Einstein prize 2007), Am. Acad. Arts & Scis.; mem. Am. Astron. Soc., NY Acad. Scis., NAS, Sigma Xi. Achievements include research in experimental atomic physics, atomic clocks, laser physics, experimental gravitation, millimeter and sub-millimeter astronomy, cosmic background measurements. *

WEISS, RANDALL A., television and radio producer, supermarket executive, television station owner; b. Gary, Ind., Sept. 3, 1952; s. Arthur and Sylvia Weiss; m. Adrienne J. Weiss, Feb. 5, 1973; children: Benjamin, Caleb, Joshua, James, Abigail, Emma. AA, Coll. DuPage, 1977; BA, Dallas Bapt. U., 1993; MA in Religious Studies, Greenwich U., 1994; diploma of practical theology, Christ for the Nations Inst., 1993; PhD, Greenwich U., 1995; MS in Jewish Studies, Spertus Inst. Jewish Studies, 1996; DMin, Faraston Theol. Sem., 1996. Ordained to Ministry, Christ for Nations Alumni Ministers Fellowship. Gen. mgr. We Care Food Stores, Inc., Knox, Ind., 1975-84; pres., CEO We Care Food Stores, Inc. subs. Five Star Foods, Knox, Ind., 1984—; prodn. mgr. Excellence in Christian Broadcasting; comml. real estate developer Magnum Value Properties, LLC; TV sta. owner KUOT-CA, Oklahoma City, WCTVB-LP, Pensacola, Fla., 2007, KTBV-LP, Bakersfield, Calif., 2007, KMSX-LP, Redding, Calif., 2007, K64GQ, Paris, Tex., 2007, KVFR-LP, Redding, Calif., 2007, KHVM-LP, Mankato, Minn., 2007, KTCJ-LP, Royalton, Minn., 2007. Songwriter, pub. Lordship Music Pub., BMI; asst. prof. on adj. faculty Global U.; dean Jewish studies dept. Columbia Evang. Sem.; bd. regents Columbia Evangelical Sem. (formerly Faraston Theol. Sem.); Am. rep. Australian Christian Channel. Author: Jewish Sects of the New Testament Era, Does Jacob's Trouble Wear a Cross?, Christianity: A Jewish Religion, In Search of the Lost Jewish Atonement, The Passion Conspiracy: Did the Jews Kill Christ of Was Jesus the Victim of Identity Theft?, 2004; writer, artist: TV Crosstalk, 1994—, Passover: The Jewish Connection to the Last Supper, Hanukkah: It's Not a Jewish Christmas, Days of Awe: The Jewish High Holidays, Father's Day, Beyond the Manger, Independence Day: Our Divine Right of Freedom, Iraq: Were We Correct; writer, artist (TV series) Today With God TV, 2006, writer, prodr. (albums) Munchy Manna, Never Seen a U-Haul on a Hearse, Lead Me to the Rock: Worship in the Holy Land, Good News Jew's Blues, I Don't Need No Designer Jeans; writer, prodr.: Jesus is Lord, The Ballad of Jess B. Notwhite (NRB Program Showcase Music Video of Yr., 2004), My Boys, 2005 (NRB Program Showcase Music Video of Yr., 2005); radio host Crosstalk; contbg. editor: World Evangelism mag. Bd. dirs. World Missionary Evangelism; founder CrossTalk Internat. Ministry Alliance. Mem. Full Gospel Bus. Men's Fellowship Internat. (life, banquet spkr.), Soc. for Pentecostal Studies, Evang. Theol. Soc., Nat. Religious Broadcasters (exec. officer TV com.), Alliance for Cmty. Media, Fellowship of European Broadcasters. Avocations: fishing, travel, reading, music. Office: Five Star Foods 1209 S Heaton St Knox IN 46534-2398

WEISS, RENÉE KAROL, editor, musician; b. Allentown, Pa., Sept. 11, 1923; d. Abraham S. and Elizabeth (Levitt) Karol; m. Theodore Weiss. BA, Bard Coll., 1951; student, Conn. Sch. Dance; studied violin with, Sascha Jacobinoff, Boris Koutzen, Emile Hauser, Ivan Galamian. Mem. Miami U. Symphony Orch., 1941, N.C. State Symphony, 1942-45, Oxford U. Symphony, Opera Orchs., Eng., 1953-54, Woodstock String Quartet, 1956-60, Bard Coll. Chamber Ensemble, 1950-66, Hudson Valley Philharmonic, 1960-66, Hudson Valley String Quartet, 1965, Princeton Chamber Orch., 1980-93; orchestral, chamber work, 1966—. Participant Theodore and Renée Weiss poetry writing workshops Princeton U., 1985, Hofstra Coll., 1985, modern poetry workshop Cooper Union, 1988, Princeton Adult Edn.; tchr. modern dance to children Bard Coll., Kindergarten Tivoli, NY Pub. Sch., 1955-58 Author: (children's books) To Win A Race, 1966, A Paper Zoo, 1968 (best books for children N.Y. Times, Book World 1968, N.J. Author's award 1968, 70, 88), The Bird From the Sea, 1970, Biography: David Schubert: Works and Days, 1984; co-editor, mgr. Quar. Rev. Lit., 1945-2005; author: (with Theodore Weiss) The Always Present Present, 2005; author of poems. Mem.: PEN (Nora Magid Lifetime Achievement award with Theodore Weiss 1997). Office: Q R L Poetry Series Princeton U 185 Nassau St Princeton NJ 08544-4914 Business E-Mail: qrl@princeton.edu.

WEISS, RHETT LOUIS, lawyer; b. Kyushu, Japan, May 22, 1961; came to U.S., 1961; s. Armand Berl and Judith (Bernstein) W.; m. Kristen Sue Krieger, Oct. 11, 1987; children: Aaron Bradford, Alexander Donald, Andrew Franklin, Alison Judith. BS in Mgmt. cum laude, Tulane U., New Orleans, 1983; JD, Coll. William and Mary, Williamsburg, Va., 1986; exec. internat. bus. cert., Georgetown U., DC, 1996; postgrad., U. N.C., Chapel Hill, 2000. Bar: Va. 1986, D.C. 1993, N.Y. 1995, U.S. Ct. Appeals (4th cir.) 1986, U.S. Tax Ct. 1987, U.S. Dist. Ct. (we. dist.) Va. 1989, U.S. Bankruptcy Ct. (we. dist.) Va. 1989, U.S. Dist. Ct. (ea. dist.) Va. 1989, U.S. Bankruptcy Ct. (ea. dist.) Va. 1996. Prin., dir. Adamson, Crump, Sharp & Weiss, P.C., Front Royal, 1987—92; chief ops. officer First Fed. Savs. Bank Shenandoah Valley, Front Royal, Va., 1990-92; sr. atty. Weil, Gotshal & Manges LLP, Washington, 1992-97; dir. strategic relocation/expansion svcs., mem. mgmt. com. Bus. Incentives Group, KPMG Peat Marwick LLP, McLean, Va., 1997-99; founder, CEO, chmn. DEALTEK, Ltd., Skaneateles, NY, 1999—; sr. team leader strategic devel. Google Inc., 2005—. Adj. prof. entrepreneurship and emerging enterprises Syracuse (NY) U. Sch. Mgmt., 2002-03; bd. dirs. Assns. Internat. Inc., McLean, Va., Weiss Pub. Co., Inc., Richmond, Va.; asst. town atty., counsel to Front Royal Planning Commn., 1987-90; presenter in field. Author: Portfolio Transactions: The Anatomy of a Deal, 1994, The Basics of Successful Negotiating, 1994, The Negotiating Process: Optimizing Give and Take, 1995, 3rd edit., 1997, Doing Global Business in a United States Foreign-Trade Zone, 1996, 97, Sales and Use Tax-Exempt Construction: An Innovative Economic Development Tool to Help Land the Deal, 1997, Facility Development, Expansion and Operations: The Major Tax and Related Cost Aspects, 1998, Doing a Deal in the U.S.: Incentives and the Project Negotiation Process, 1998, Business Expansion and Facility Development: Incentives and the Project Development Process, 1999, 2000, Working With Economic Developers, 2000, Web-Enabled Site Selection: Getting the Information You Need at Internet Speed, 2000, Economic Development in the Electronic Age, 2001, 3rd edit., 2003, Use Incentives to Make the Best Location Choice, 2001, Using the Internet in Technology Transfer and Economic Develpment, 2002, 3rd edit., 2005, Engineering Entrepreneurship and Economics, 2003, 2d edit. 2004, Technology-Driven Entrepreneurship, 2005, Hosting Effective Site Visits: It's a Key Economic Development Strategy, Not Just an Event, 2005, 2d edit., 2006, Negotiations for Entrepreneurs: The Process of Going From Nothing to Something, 2004-07, Site Selection for High Tech Companies, 2007; contbr. articles to profl. jours. Bd. dirs. Blue Ridge Arts Coun., Inc., 1987-92, v.p., 1989-90, pres., 1990-91; bd. dirs. Front Royal Little Theatre, Inc., 1988-89, Front Royal Warren County Unit Am. Heart Assn., 1991-92, Lord Fairfax C.C. Ednl. Found., 1991-94, Build-A-Future Found., 1994-98, v.p., 1997-98; Shenrapawa dist. chmn. Shenandoah area coun. Boy Scouts Am., 1988-89, coun. treas., 1991-92, coun. bd. dirs., 1987-94; adv. com. Small Bus. Assistance Ctr., Lord Fairfax C.C.; mem. Seaton Elem. Sch. devel. team D.C. Pub. Schs. Ptnrs. In Edn. Program, 1994-96; soccer coach Southwestern Youth Assn., 1998-2001, Skaneateles Youth Soccer Orgn., 2001-05. Recipient Nat. Quality Dist. award 1988, 89, Statuette award, 1992, Boy Scouts Am., Tech. Project of Yr. award, Tech. Alliance Ctrl. N.Y., 2003. Fellow John Marshall Soc. of Va. Bar Assn.; mem. Internat. Econ. Devel. Coun., DC Bar (vice chmn. comml. trans. com. 1994-96, vice chmn. real property trans. com. 1996-97, chmn. 1997-98, real estate, housing and land use sect.), Va. State Bar, NY State Bar Assn., Va., Econ. Developers Assn., Greater Syracuse C. of C. (entrepreneurial coun., technology coun. 2002-06), Ctrl. NY Internat. Bus. Alliance (founding dir. 2002—), Tech. Alliance Ctrl. NY (bd. dir. 2003-), Valley Estate Planning Coun. (bd. govs. 1989-92, pres. 1992), Front Royal-Warren County C. of C. (bd. dirs. 1989-92, chmn. 1990-91), Skaneateles Youth Soccer Orgn. (bd. dirs. 2005-), Skaneateles Sunrise Rotary Club (bd. dirs. 2002—, pres. 2003-04), Delta Tau Delta (sec. 1980-81), Beta Gamma Sigma, Beta Alpha Psi. Avocations: cars, outdoors, travel, music, sports. Office: Google Inc 1600 Amphitheatre Pkwy Mountain View CA 94043 Home PO Box 3214 Los Altos CA 94024 Business E-Mail: rhett.weiss@gmail.com.

WEISS, RICHARD A., state official; b. Africa; m. Jan Weiss; 3 children. Grad. in liberal arts, Baylor U. Adminstr. Office of Budget, Dept. Fin. and Adminstrn., Little Rock, dep. dir., dir., 1994-97; CFO, State of Ark., Little Rock, 1994—; dir. Ark. Dept. Fin. and Adminstrn., Little Rock, 2001—. Office: Fin and Adminstrn Dept PO Box 3278 Little Rock AR 72203-3278 Office Phone: 501-682-2242. E-mail: richard.weiss@dfa.state.ar.us.

WEISS, RICK, reporter; married; 1 child. BS in Biology, Cornell U., 1974; M in Journalism, U. Calif. Berkeley, 1985. Lic. med. technologist various hosp. labs., 1974—84; biology and biomedicine writer Sci. News Mag., Wash.; staff writer Health Mag., San Francisco; sci. and med. reporter health sect. Wash. Post, 1993—96, sci. and med. reporter nat. news desk, 1996—. Contbg. writer: NY Times, L.A. Times, Science, Discover. Recipient Sci. Journalism award, AAAS, 2000, Sci. in Soc. Journalism award, Nat. Assn. Science Writers, Inc., 2002, Victor Cohn Prize for Excellence in Medical Science Reporting, 2005. Office: Wash Post 1150 15th St NW Washington DC 20071-0070 Office Phone: 202-334-5514. Business E-Mail: weissr@washpost.com.

WEISS, ROBERT EDWARD, urologist, educator; b. Manchester, Conn., Sept. 17, 1959; BS magna cum laude, Brown U., 1981; MD, NYU, 1985. Intern Mt. Sinai Med. Ctr., NYC, 1985-86, resident surgery, 1986-87, resident urology, 1987-91; fellow urol. surgery Meml. Sloan-Kettering Cancer Ctr., NYC, 1991-94; assoc. prof. urology R.W. Johnson Hosp. Med. Ctr., New Brunswick, NJ, 1994—. Fellow ACS; mem. Am. Urol. Assn., Soc. Urologic Oncology, Soc. Surg. Oncology, N.Y. Urol. Assn., N.J. Urol. Assn., Soc. of Basic Urologic Rsch. Office: RW Johnson Med Ctr 1 RW Johnson Pl CN-19 New Brunswick NJ 08903 Office Phone: 732-235-7776.

WEISS, ROBERT FRANCIS, retired academic and religious organization administrator, consultant; b. St. Louis, Aug. 27, 1924; s. Frank L.G. and Helen M. (Beck) Weiss. BA, St. Louis U., 1951, Ph.L., MA, St. Louis U., 1953, S.T.L., 1961; PhD, U. Minn., 1964. Joined Soc. of Jesus, 1946; ordained priest Roman Catholic Ch., 1959; tchr. Rockhurst H.S., Kansas City, Mo., 1953—56; adminstrv. asst. to pres. St. Louis U., 1961—62; asst. dean Rockhurst Coll., Kansas City, Mo., 1964—66, dean, v.p., asst. prof. edn., 1966—72, pres., 1977—88, St. Louis U. HS, 1973—77, interim pres., 1992; asst. higher edn. and continuing formation Mo. Province S.J., St. Louis, 1989—92, treas., 1992—2003, asst. higher edn. and continuing formation, 1997—2005, asst. to treas., 2003—05, del. higher edn., 2005—. Mem. Commn. on Govtl. rels. Am. Coun. Edn., 1985—87; bd. dirs. Kansas City Regional Coun. for Higher Edn., 1987—88, Boys Hope Girls Hope, 1977—. Contbr. chapters to books, articles to profl. jours. Trustee St. Louis U., 1973—87, 1991—2003, Loyola U., New Orleans, 1973—82, 1985—88, United Student Aid Funds, Inc., 1977—94, U. San Francisco, 1987—99, Marymount Coll., Salina, Kans., 1986—88, St. Louis U. H.S., 1989—99, 2003—, Fontbonne Coll., St. Louis, 1973—77, Sacred Heart Program, Radio and TV Apostolate, St. Louis, 1990—96, pres., 1992—96, bd. mem., 2000—05; bd. dirs. Creighton U., Omaha, 1981—97, Our Little Haven, St. Louis, 1992—, St. Elizabeth Acad., St. Louis, 1997—2004, DeSmet Jesuit HS, 2003—, Loyola Acad., St. Louis, 2003—, chmn. bd. mems., 2005—; bd. dirs. St. John's Coll., Belize City, Belize, 2003—; bd. trustees St. Louis (Mo.) Archdiocesan Fund, 2006—; bd. regents Conception Sem. Coll., Mo., 2004—. 1st sgt. US Army, 1943—46. Decorated Bronze Star. Mem.: Am. Assn. for Higher Edn., Vets. Assn. Rainbow divsn. (nat. chaplain 1976—84, 1988—90, pres.-elect 1990—91, pres. 1991—92, assoc. nat. chaplain 1992—, found. pres. 2003—05), Alpha Phi Omega, Alpha Sigma Nu. Office: Mo Province SJ 4511 W Pine Blvd Saint Louis MO 63108-2109 Home Phone: 314-633-4425; Office Phone: 314-361-7765. Business E-Mail: rweiss@jesuits-mis.org. *The only way for me to look at life is in the light of faith, which I consider one of God's greatest gifts. Life for me is an opportunity to serve God and as many of my neighbors as I can. I am basically an optimist. There is so much beauty around us, so many good people, so many marvels to behold— that I thank the Lord for giving me the ability to know and experience this life and to look forward to eternal life with God, the Source of all life. Any success I have had I attribute to taking advantage of the opportunities that God has put in my path.*

WEISS, ROBERT JEROME, retired psychiatrist, educator; b. West New York, NJ, Dec. 9, 1917; s. Harry and Dora (Samuels) W.; m. Minnie Thompson Moore, Apr. 21, 1945; children— Scott Tillman, James Woodrow, Elizabeth Thompson. Student, Johns Hopkins, 1937; AB, George Washington U., 1947; MD, Columbia, 1951, MA (hon.), Dartmouth, 1964. Intern Columbia div. Bellevue Hosp., 1951, asst. resident medicine, 1953; resident psychiatry N.Y. Psychiat. Inst., 1954-56; asst. attending Vanderbilt Clinic, 1957-58, Presbyn. Hosp., NYC, 1958-59; chief psychiatry Mary Hitchcock Meml. Hosp., 1959-70; career tchr. trainee Nat. Inst. Mental Health, 1956-58; tchr., research Columbia Coll. Phys. and Surg., 1956-59; prof. psychiatry, founder dept. psychiatry, chmn. dept. Dartmouth Med. Sch., 1959-70; psychiatrist Beth Israel Hosp., 1988-90; attending physician Presbyn. Hosp., 1975-85, cons., 1985—. Vis. prof. cmty. medicine Harvard Med. Sch., 1970-75, assoc. dir. cmty. health, 1970-75, assoc. dean health care planning; prof. psychiatry and social medicine Columbia Coll. Physicians and Surgeons, 1975-86, also dir. Ctrs. for Cmty. Health, 1975-86; De Lamar prof. pub. health practice, dean Columbia U. Sch. Pub. Health, 1980-86, dean and De Lamar prof. of pub. health practice, prof. psychiatry, prof. social medicine, prof. emeritus, 1986—, dean emeritus, 1996—; vis. prof. cmty. medicine U. N.Mex. Med. Sch., 1986-89; adj. prof. arts and sci. U. Maine, Orono, 1997—; cons. Nat. Ctr. for Health Svcs. Rsch., 1975-86, NIMH, 1977-86; chmn. psychiatry tng. com. NIMH, 1967-68, mem. coord. panel, 1965-67, ad hoc com. interdisciplinary tng. program, 1966, mem. agenda com., 1966; cons. AT&T, 1990-92; chmn. bd. Academica, 1992, Employee Managed Care Corp., 1994-96; prin. Weiss, Baldacci & Fletcher; mem. com. trade treaties State Senate, 2004—. Co-editor: Columbia U. Coll. Physicians and Surgeons Complete Home Medical Guide, 1986, editor emeritus 2d and 3d edits., 1989; contbr. articles to profl. jours., chpts. to books. Founder dept. psychiatry Dartmouth Med. Sch., 1959. Served to maj. AUS, 1941-46. Recipient Bi-Centennial medal Columbia Coll. Phys. and Surg., 1967. Fellow Am. Psychiat. Assn. (life); mem. Am. Assn. Chmn. Depts. Psychiatry (pres. 1979-80). Achievements include first telemedicine 2-way transmission between medical centers; demonstrated social supports reduce disability due to mental illness; research in special health care delivery, health care preventive psychiatry. Home: 10 Cromwell Dr Orono ME 04473-3639 Personal E-mail: rjw4007@verizon.net.

WEISS, ROBERT M., urologist, educator; b. NYC, Jan. 13, 1936; s. David and Laura W.; m. Ilana Shemer, May 20, 1973; children: Erik Daniel, Dana Alexandra. BS magna cum laude, Franklin and Marshall Coll., Lancaster, Pa., 1957; MD, SUNY, Bklyn., 1960; MA (hon.), Yale U., New Haven, Conn., 1976. Diplomate: Am. Bd. Urology, Nat. Bd. Med. Examiners. Intern Cornell Med. Divsn., Bellevue Hosp., NYC, 1960-61; resident in gen. surgery Beth Israel Hosp., NYC, 1961-62; resident in urology Squier Urol. Clinic, Presbyn. Hosp., NYC, 1963-64, 65-67; vis. fellow Columbia U. Coll. Physicians and Surgeons, NYC, 1964-65, adj. assoc. prof. pharmacology, 1975-77, adj. prof. pharmacology, 1977—; mem. faculty Yale U. Med. Sch., New Haven, 1967—, prof. urology, 1976-88, prof., chief sect. of urology, 1988—, Donald Gutherie prof. surgery, 2001—, interim chmn. dept. surgery, 1999-2001; attending urology Yale-New Haven Hosp., New Haven, 1967-88, head sect. of urology, 1988—, interim chief dept. surgery, 1999—2001, pres. med. staff, 2004—06. Cons. West Haven VA Hosp. Contbr. articles to profl. jours. Trustee Am. Bd. Urology, 1998-2004. With USAR, 1962-63. Fellow ACS, Am. Acad. Pediat.; mem. AAAS, Am. Assn. Genito-Urinary Surgeons, Am. Surg. Assn., Am. Physiol. Soc., Soc. Gen. Physiologists, Assn. Univ. Urologists, Soc. Pediatric Urology, Am. Urol. Assn., Clin. Soc. Genito-Urinary Surgeons, New Eng. Surg. Soc., New Eng. Urol. Assn., Phi Beta Kappa, Sigma Xi. Office: Yale U Sch Medicine Dept Urology PO Box 208041 New Haven CT 06520-8041 Office Phone: 203-785-2815. Business E-Mail: robert.weiss@yale.edu.

WEISS, ROBERT ORR, speech educator; b. Kalamazoo, Apr. 8, 1926; s. Nicholas John and Ruth (Orr) W.; m. Ann Lenore Lawson, Sept. 16, 1951; children: Elizabeth Ann, John Lawson, James Robert, Virginia Lenore. BA, Albion Coll., 1948; MA, Northwestern U., 1949, PhD, 1954. Instr. speech Wayne State U., Detroit, 1949-51; instr. pub. speaking Northwestern U., Evanston, Ill., 1954-55; mem. faculty DePauw U., Greencastle, Ind.,

1955—2002, H.B. Gough prof. speech, 1965-97, head comm. arts and scis., 1963-78, 85-86, 93. Author: Public Argument, 1995; editor: Speaker and Gavel, 1968-75, Speaking Across the Curriculum, 1990-2006; co-editor: Current Criticism, 1971; contbr. articles to profl. jours. Served with AUS, 1945-46. Recipient Fred C. Tucker Disting. Career award, 1995, Lifetime award, Nat. Ednl. Debate Assn., 1997, Presdl. citation Nat. Communication Assn., 1999. Mem. AAUP (pres. DePauw U. chpt. 1961-62), Nat. Communication Assn. (legis. assembly 1966-68), Am. Forensic Assn. (sec.-treas. 1958-59), Ctrl. States Communication Assn., Phi Beta Kappa, Delta Sigma Rho-Tau Kappa Alpha (nat. v.p. 1981-83, pres. 1983-85), Sigma Nu. Home: 210 W Poplar St Greencastle IN 46135-2638 Home Phone: 765-653-5497; Office Phone: 765-658-4490. Business E-Mail: robertweiss@depauw.edu.

WEISS, RONALD PHILLIP, lawyer; b. Springfield, Mass., Apr. 28, 1947; s. Kermit Paul and Fay Roslyn (Robinovitz) W.; m. Janet Faye Landon, June 15, 1969; children: Emily, Katherine. BA, Dartmouth Coll., 1968; JD, U. Pa., 1972. Bar: Mass. 1972, U.S. Dist. Ct. Mass. 1975, U.S. Tax Ct. 1979, U.S. Ct. Appeals (1st cir.) 2000. Assoc. Bulkley, Richardson and Gelinas, Springfield, Mass., 1972-78; ptnr. Bulkley, Richardson and Gelinas, LLP, Springfield, 1978—. Pres. Estate Planning Coun. Hampden County, 1979-81; trustee Mass. Continuing Legal Edn. Inc., 1978-81. Author: (with others) Drafting Wills and Trusts in Massachusetts, 1990, 92, 94; editor: (with others) Massachusetts Corporate Tax Manual, 1986. Trustee Springfield Symphony Orch., 1986—, v.p., 1988—89, pres., 1989—91, chmn., 1991—94; mem. bd. advisors U. Mass. Family Bus. Ctr., 1992—; mem. adv. panel Hanson Initiative for Lang. and Literacy, MGH Inst. Health Professions, 2001—; counsel Cmty. Found. of Western Mass.; appropriations com. Town of Longmeadow, Mass., 1990—96, chmn., 1991—92, 1995—96; trustee Jewish Fedn. Greater Springfield, 1986—90. Mem. ABA, Mass. Bar Assn. (chmn. taxation sect. 1978-81, bd. dels. 1979-81), Mass. Bar Found., Hampden County Bar Assn., Rotary. Office: Bulkley Richardson and Gelinas LLP 1500 Main St Ste 2700 Springfield MA 01115-5507 Office Phone: 413-272-6259.

WEISS, SAMUEL ABRAHAM, psychologist, psychoanalyst; b. NYC; m. Alice Langer, May 20, 1958; children: Benjamin Z., Naomi E., Susan J. BA, Yeshiva U., 1944; MA, NYU, 1948, PhD, 1957. Diplomate in clin. psychology, Am. Bd. Profl. Psychology. Intern Bellevue Psychiat. Hosp., NYC, 1955—56; assoc. rsch. scientist NYU Med. Ctr., NYC, 1956—59, rsch. scientist, 1959—68, assoc. dir. amputee psychology rsch., 1958—66; assoc. prof. psychology Yeshiva U., NYC, 1961—71, psychol. cons. Stern. Coll. for Women, 1960—71; psychologist, psychotherapist, psychoanalyst in pvt. practice NYC, 1972. Cons. N.Y. State Div. Vocat. Rehab., 1958-73. Contbr. articles to profl. jours. Fellow AAAS (Rosette award 1991), APA (editl. cons. rehab. psychology 1972-80), Am. Psychol. Soc. Jewish. Achievements include new research on medical factors in phantom limb pain and rehabilitation. Home: 80-40 Lefferts Blvd Kew Gardens NY 11415-1723 Office: 7 Park Ave Apt 66 New York NY 10016-4356 Office Phone: 212-686-8324.

WEISS, SHIRLEY F., retired urban and regional planner, economist, educator; b. NYC, Feb. 26, 1921; d. Max and Vera (Hendel) Friedlander; m. Charles M. Weiss, June 7, 1942. BA, Rutgers U., 1942; postgrad., Johns Hopkins U., 1949-50; M in Regional Planning, U. NC, 1958; PhD, Duke U., 1973. Assoc. research dir. Ctr. for Urban and Regional Studies U. N.C., Chapel Hill, 1957-91, lectr. in planning, 1958-62, assoc. prof., 1962-73, prof., 1973-91, prof. emerita, 1991—; joint creator-sponsor Charles and Shirley Weiss Urban Livability Program, U. N.C., Chapel Hill, 1992—; rsch. assoc. Inst. for Rsch. in Social Sci. U. N.C., 1957—73, rsch. prof. Chapel Hill, 1973—91, acting dir. women's studies program Coll. Arts and Scis., 1985, faculty marshal, 1988-91. Grad. edn. advancement bd. U. NC, Chapel Hill, 2001—, tech. com. Water Resources Rsch. Inst., 1976-79; adv. com. on housing for 1980 census Dept. Commerce, 1976-81; cons. Urban Inst., Washington, 1977-80; rev. panel Exptl. Housing Allowance Program, HUD, 1977-80; adv. bd. on built environ. Nat. Acad. Scis.-NRC, 1981-83, program coordinating com. fed. constrn. coun. of adv. bd. on built environ., 1982-83; mem. Planning Accreditation Bd., Site Visitation Pool, Am. Inst. Cert. Planners and Assn. Collegiate Schs. Planning, 1985—; discipline screening com. Fulbright Scholar awards in Architecture and City Planning, Coun. for Internat. Exchange of Scholars, 1985-88; N.Mex. adv. bd. Enterprise Found., Santa Fe, 1997-2002; governing bd. Acad. Freedom Fund, AAUP, 1997-2000. Author: The Central Business District in Transition: Methodological Approaches to CBD Analysis and Forecasting Future Space Requirements, 1957, New Town Development in the United States: Experiment in Private Entrepreneurship, 1973; co-author: A Probabilistic Model for Residential Growth, 1964, Residential Developer Decisions: A Focused View of the Urban Growth Process, 1966, New Communities U.S.A., 1976; co-author, co-editor: New Community Development: Planning Process, Implementation and Emerging Social Concerns, vols. 1, 2, 1971, City Centers in Transition, 1976, New Communities Research Series, 1976-77; mem. editl. bd.: Jour. Am. Inst. Planners, 1963-68, Rev. of Regional Studies, 1969-74, 82-92, Internat. Regional Sci. Rev., 1975-81. Trustee Friends of Libr., U. N.C., Chapel Hill, 1988-94, Santa Fe Chamber Music Festival, adv. coun., 1990-91, 97-98, trustee, 1991-97, 98-2004, trustee emerita, 2004-; bd. dirs. Triangle Opera, 1986-89, 91-2002, Chamber Orch. of the Triangle, 1997-2005, hon. life mem., 2005-. Recipient Cornelia Phillips Spencer Bell award U. NC, Chapel Hill, 1996, Disting. Alumni award Alumni Assn. Dept. City and Regional Planning, U. NC, Chapel Hill, 1996, Mary Turner Lane award Assn. Women Faculty, 1994, (with Charles M. Weiss) Gifford Phillips award Santa Fe Chamber Music Festival, 2000, Disting. Alumni and Alumnus award U. NC, Chapel Hill, 2003; Adelaide M. Zagoren fellow Douglass Coll., Rutgers U., 1994. Emeritus fellow Urban Land Inst. (sr. fellow, exec. group, cmty. devel. coun. 1978—); mem. Am. Inst. Planners (sec., treas. southeast chpt. 1957-59, v.p. 1960-61), Am. Inst. Cert. Planners, Am. Planning Assn., Am. Econ. Assn., So. Regional Sci. Assn. (pres. 1977-78), Regional Sci. Assn. (councillor 1971-74, v.p. 1976-77), Nat. Assn. Housing and Redevelopment Ofcls., Interamerican Planning Soc., Internat. Fedn. Housing and Planning, Town and Country Planning Assn., Internat. Urban Devel. Assn., Econ. History Assn., Am. Real Estate and Urban Econs. Assn. (regional membership chmn. 1976-82, 84-85, dir. 1977-80), AAUP (chpt. pres. 1976-77, pres. N.C. Conf. 1978-79, mem. nat. coun. 1983-86, William S. Tacey award Assembly of State Confs.), Douglass Soc., Order of Valkyries, Phi Beta Kappa. Home: 750 Weaver Dairy Rd # 2114 Chapel Hill NC 27514-1483

WEISS, SIMONA, retired paralegal; d. Leon and Rose Weiss; m. Morton B. Elliot, Apr. 14, 1951 (div. May 10, 1972); children: Russell Wayne Elliot, Linda Beth Elliot-Morris. Student, Columbia U., NYC, 1968—70; BA cum laude, Fairligh Dickinson U., Teaneck, NJ, 1974; postgrad., NYU, NYC, 1974—76, William Patterson U., Wayne, NJ, 2001—03. Cert. paralegal NJ, 1980. Paralegal adminstr. Witco Chem. Corp., NYC, 1980—81; paralegal supr. Pitney, Hardin, Kipp & Szuch, Morristown, NJ, 1982—82; real estate paralegal Willkie Farr & Gallagher, NYC, 1983—84; real estate and corp. paralegal Robinson Silverman Pearce Aronsohn & Berman, NYC, 1984—90; real estate paralegal Freddie Mac, New York, NY, 1991—91; legal asst. Gen. Investment Sect. Legal Dept. The Prudential Ins. Co. of Am., Newark, 1992—94; comml. real estate paralegal Cleary, Gottlieb, Steen & Hamilton, NYC, 1994—96; real estate and corp. paralegal Hannoch Weisman, Roseland, NJ, 1996—98; comml. real estate paralegal Unilever Bestfoods, Englewood Cliffs, NJ, 1998—2002. Chmn. Haworth (N.J.) Parks & Playgrounds Com., 1972—78; county com. mcpl. chmn. Haworth (N.J.) Rep. Orgn., 1973—79; candidate Non-Partisan Bergen County (N.J.) Charter Study Commn., 1973—74; primary candidate Bergen County (N.J.) Bd. of Chosen Freeholders, 1977—77; fin. and corr. sec. Temple Beth El, Closter, NJ, 1968—72; program and publicity chmn. 1st Bergen County Women's Ctr., Teaneck, NJ, 1972—74; v.p. fund raising Haworth (N.J.) Home and Sch. Assn., 1967—69. Recipient Mayor's Cert., Borough of Haworth, 1979; scholar, Fairleigh Dickinson U., 1971—74. Mem.: Legal Asst. Mgmt. Assn., Nat. Paralegal Assn., Phi Omega Epsilon. Independent. Avocations: theater, movies, opera, ballet, reading. Home: 2000 Linwood Ave 19U Fort Lee NJ 07024 Personal E-mail: simona_wei@msn.com.

WEISS, STEFAN CRAIG, dermatologist, director; b. Mar. 6, 1974; BA in Philosophy cum laude, Yale U., New Haven, 1996; MS in Clin. Rsch., Duke U., Durham, NC, 2000, MD, 2001. Diplomate dermatology 2005, lic. Calif., Fla. Intern Tufts U., Sch. Medicine, Burlington, Mass., 2001—02; dermatology resident Stanford U., Sch. Medicine, Calif., 2002—05; staff dermatologist Kaiser Permanente Med. Group, Stockton and Santa Clara, Calif., 2004—; sr. med. dir. Connetics Corp., Palo Alto, Calif., 2005—. Mem. internat. sci. com. for edn. and rsch. in ethics UNESCO, 1999—2004; mem. gov. coun. Am. Pub. Health Assn., 2001—03; mem. organizing com. SID Basics of Skin: Pharmaceutics and Pharmacology, 2005—06, program chaird, 2006—07; vol. Camp Wonder for Kids with Skin Diseases, 2006; founder, coord. Duke U. Med. Ctr. Program for Humanities in Medicine; state chair jour. reclamation project NC Med. Soc., del. state com. aging; presenter in field. Reviewer: Jour. of Am. Acad. Dermatology, 2004—; contbr. articles to profl. jours. Chair quarter century fund Yale U. Alumni Fund, 1996—; chair of agents Yale U. Class of 1996, 2001—; mem. young profl. com. Am. Conservatory Theatre, 2005—06. Recipient 1st place Young Investigators Writing Competition, Am. Soc. Dermatol. Surgery, 2003, 1st place Psoriasis Rsch. Competition, Biogen-Idec Dermatology Resident and Fellow Forum, 2004, Resident Edn. award, Skin Disease Edn. Found., 2004. Fellow: Am. Acad. Dermatology (mem. com. coding and reimbursement 2005); mem.: AMA, Soc. for Investigative Dermatology.

WEISS, STEPHEN J., lawyer; b. NYC, Sept. 12, 1938; s. Morris and Frances (Dinkin) Weiss; m. Madeline Adler, Aug. 12, 1962; children: Lowell Andrew, Valerie Elizabeth, Bradley Lawrence. BS, Queens Coll., 1959; LLB, Cornell U., 1962; LLM, Georgetown U., 1966. Bar: NY 1963, DC 1966, US Supreme Ct. 1975. Atty. SEC, Washington, 1962-65; assoc. firm Arent Fox Kintner Plotkin & Kahn, Washington, 1965-70, ptnr., 1971-94, Holland & Knight LLP, Washington, 1994—. Lectr. securities corp. law, dirs. and officers liability and ins. Am. Law Inst., ABA, Fed. Bar Assn., Practicing Law Inst., Bur. Nat. Affairs, Exec. Enterprises, Aspen Law & Bus. Orgn. Mgmt., Inc., Inst. Internat. Rsch., Profl. Liability Underwriting Soc.; mem. adv. bd. Securities Regulation and Law Report Bur. Nat. Affairs, 1980—. Author: Regulation D-A Practical Guide, 1994, Navigating the D&O Maze: A Handbook for Purchasers of Employment Practices Liability Insurance, 1998; dirs. and officers liability ins. columnist: Dirs. & Bds. mag., 1998—; contbr. articles to profl. jours. Named to Best Lawyers in Am., 2003—. Mem.: ABA (fed. regulation securities com. 1970—, chmn. com. fgn. corrupt practices legislation 1976—77, chmn. Rule 10b-5 subcom. 1976—78, chmn. civil liabilities subcom. 1978—81, mem. devels. bus. financing com. 1982—, mem. Guiding Principles Task Force bus. ins. com. 1994—95), Fed. Bar Assn. (chmn. securities law comm. 1968—70, mem. coun. securities law com. 1971—, chmn. coun. financing and taxation 1971—72, chmn. publs. bd. 1977—78, mem. nat. coun. 1972—80, Leadership commendation 1973, Disting. Svc. award), Cornell Law Club Washington (pres. 1971—79). Office: Holland & Knight LLP 2099 Pennsylvania Ave NW Washington DC 20006 Office Phone: 202-457-5920. Business E-Mail: steve.weiss@hklaw.com.

WEISS, STEVEN ALLAN, lawyer; b. NYC; BA cum laude, Cornell U., 1977; JD cum laude, U. Mich., 1980. Bar: Ill. 1980, U.S. Dist. Ct. (no. dist.) Ill. 1980, U.S. Ct. Appeals (7th cir.) 1982. Assoc. Reuben & Proctor, Chgo., 1980-87; ptnr. Schopf & Weiss, Chgo., 1987—. Contbr. article to profl. publs. Mem. ABA. Office: Schopf & Weiss Ste 2800 One So Wacker Dr Chicago IL 60606

WEISS, STEVEN GARY, physician; b. Gary, Ind., June 28, 1949; s. Morris Eugene and Edith (Wolinsky) W.; m. Irene Cohn, May 14, 1977; children: Leah Rose, Julia Inger, Mara Emily, Max martin. BA, Ind. U., 1971, MD, 1974. Intern Highland Gen. Hosp., Oakland, Calif., 1974; resident Mt. Zion Hosp. and Med. Ctr., San Francisco, 1977; fellow U. Chgo., 1982; Assoc. prof. U. South Fla. Coll. Medicine, Tampa, 1984—; physician pvt. practice, Clearwater, Fla., 1984—. Chief of med. staff Mease Hosps., Dunedin, Fla., 1991-92. Trustee Mease Health Care, 1991-94. Fellow Am. Acad. Allergy/Immunology, Am. Coll. Allergy.

WEISS, TERRI LYNN, lawyer; b. Oct. 9, 1957; AB, Georgetown U., 1978, JD, 1981. Bar: N.Y. 1982, U.S. Dist. Ct. (so. and ea. dists.) N.Y. 1982, U.S. Ct. Appeals (2nd cir.), 1982. Assoc. Morgan, Lewis & Bockius, NYC, 1981-86, Rosenman & Colin, NYC, 1986-90; ptnr. Marino & Weiss P.C., White Plains, N.Y., 1990—. Mem. editl. bd., Jour. Am. Acad. Matrimonial Lawyers, 1999-04; mem. editl. bd., Matrimonial Strategist, 1996-2005; contbr. articles to profl. jours.; lectr. profl. orgns. Neutral evaluator Matrimonial Alt. Dispute Resolution Program, N.Y. County, N.Y.C., 1997—; arbitrator Domestic Rels. Fee Dispute Resolution Program, White Plains, N.Y., 1996—, Nat. Assn. Securities Dealers, N.Y.C., 1989—; bd. of profl. med. conduct N.Y. State Office Profl. Med. Conduct, N.Y. State Bd. Health, N.Y.C., 1988-98. Fellow Am. Acad. Matrimonial Lawyers (amicus com. N.Y. chpt. 1994—), Internat. Acad. Matrimonial Lawyers; mem. ABA (litigation and family law sects.), N.Y. State Bar Assn. (exec. com. family law sect. 1996—), Westchester County Bar Assn. (family law sect.), Westchester Women's Bar Assn. Office: Marino & Weiss PC 162 Grand St White Plains NY 10601-4803

WEISS, WALTER STANLEY, lawyer; b. Newark, Mar. 12, 1929; s. Jack and Mollie (Orkin) W.; m. Misty M. Moore; children from previous marriage: Jack Stephen, Andrew Scott. AB, Rutgers U., 1949, JD, 1952. Bar: D.C. 1952, N.J. 1956, Calif. 1961. Trial atty. IRS, Phila., Los Angeles, 1957-62; asst. U.S. atty., chief tax div. Los Angeles, 1962-63; ptnr. firm Goodson & Hannam, Los Angeles, 1963-67; mng. ptnr. firm Long & Levit, Los Angeles, 1967-79; ptnr. firm Greenberg & Glusker, Los Angeles, 1979-81, Rosenfeld, Meyer and Susman, Beverly Hills, Calif., 1981-93; prin. Law Office of Walter S. Weiss, LA, 1993—. Judge pro tem L.A. and Santa Monica (Calif.) Mcpl. Cts., 1994—. Contbr. articles to legal jours. Served to capt. JAGC USAF, 1953-56. Named Arbitrator Nat. Assn. Securities Dealers, 1974 Fellow Am. Coll. Trial Lawyers; mem. ABA, Los Angeles County Bar Assn., Beverly Hills Bar Assn. Home: 12349 Ridge Cir Los Angeles CA 90049-1183 Office: 12400 Wilshire Blvd Ste 1300 Los Angeles CA 90025-1055 Home Phone: 310-471-4320; Office Phone: 310-207-6679. E-mail: waltersweiss@yahoo.com.

WEISS, ZEV, corporate financial executive; s. Morry Weiss. BA, Yeshiva Univ.; MBA, Columbia Univ. With Am. Greetings Corp., Cleve., 1992—, exec. dir., Nat. Accounts, 1997—2000, v.p., Strategic Business Unit Division, 2000—01, sr. v.p. ventures, 2001, exec. v.p. ventures & enterprise mgmt., 2001—03, CEO, 2003—. Bd. mem. Yeshiva Univ. Office: American Greeting Corp 1 American Rd Cleveland OH 44144-2398 *

WEISSBACH, HERBERT, biochemist, researcher; b. NYC, Mar. 16, 1932; s. Louis and Vivian (Ruhalter) W.; m. Renee Kohl, Dec. 27, 1953; children— Lawrence, Nancy, Marjorie, Robert BS, CUNY, 1953; MS, George Washington U., 1955, PhD, 1957. Chemist Nat. Heart Inst., Bethesda, Md., 1953-68; acting chief NIH, Bethesda, 1968-69; assoc. dir. Roche Inst. Molecular Biology, Nutley, NJ, 1969-83, dir., 1983-96; v.p. Hoffmann-La Roche, Nutley, 1983-96; disting. rsch. prof., dir. ctr. for molecular biology and biotech. Fla. Atlantic U., Boca Raton, 1997—. Adj. prof. George Washington U., 1964-69, Columbia U., 1969-85, U. Medicine and Dentistry N.J., Newark, 1981-93, Princeton U., 1984-85. Editor: Molecular Mechanisms of Protein Biosynthesis, 1977, Archives of Biochemistry and Biophysics; contbr. articles to profl. jours. Recipient Superior Svc. award HEW, 1968, Enzyme award Am. Chem. Soc., 1970, Disting. Alumni award George Washington U., 1994. Mem. Am. Chem. Soc., Am. Soc. Biol. Chemists, Am. Soc. Pharmacology and Exptl. Therapeutics, Am. Soc. Microbiology, Nat. Acad. Scis., AAAS Home: 8008 Desmond Dr Boynton Beach FL 33437-5011 Office: Fla Atlantic U 777 Glades Rd Boca Raton FL 33431-6424 E-mail: herbweissbach@aol.com.

WEISSBARD, SAMUEL HELD, lawyer; b. NYC, Mar. 3, 1947; children: Andrew Joshua, David S. BA, Case Western Res. U., 1967; JD with highest honors, George Washington U., 1970. Bar: D.C. 1970, U.S. Supreme Ct. 1974, Calif. 1998. Assoc. Fried, Frank, Harris, Shriver & Kampelman, 1970-73, Arent, Fox, Kintner, Plotkin & Kahn, 1973-78; prin. Weissbard & Fields, P.C., 1978-83; shareholder, v.p. Wilkes, Artis, Hedrick & Lane, Washington, 1983-86; ptnr. Foley & Lardner, Washington, 1986-97, LA, 1997-98, co-chair creditors' rights workout and bankruptcy group Washington, 1992-95; sr. counsel Cox, Castle & Nicholson, L.L.P., Newport Beach, Calif., 1998—2001; exec. v.p., gen. counsel Makar Properties, LLC, Newport Beach, 2001—. Editor in chief George Washington U. Law Rev., 1969-70. Bd. dirs. Luther Rice Soc., George Washington U., 1985-87, Atlanta Coll. Art, 1993, Nat. Learning Ctr., 1993-96, Georgetown Arts Commn. and gen. counsel 1995-96; Chmn. steering com. of Lawyer's Alliance for Nat. Learning Ctr. and Capital Children's Mus., 1989-90; mem. steering com. DC/NLC Don't Drop Out Campaign, 1992,93, bd. dirs., 1994-96; devel. com. Shelter for the Homeless, 1998-99. Recipient John Bell Larner medal, 1970. Mem. ABA, D.C. Bar, Calif. Bar Assn., Orange County Bar Assn., Georgetown Bus. and Profl. Assn. (bd. dirs. 1993-96, sec., gen. counsel 1993-96), Orange County Bus. Assn. (legis. com. 1998-99), Order of Coif. Office: Makar Properties LLC 4100 MacArthur Blvd Ste 200 Newport Beach CA 92660-2063 E-mail: sweissbard@makarproperties.com.

WEISS-CORNWELL, AMY, interior designer; b. Mpls., Dec. 8, 1950; d. August Carl and Margaret Amelia (Wittman) Weiss; m. Dan Cornwell, July 31, 1995; 1 child, Emma Cornwell. AA in Home Econs., Cerritos Coll.; student, Long Beach State U., Santa Ana Jr. Coll. Asst. to interior designer Bobbi Hart at Pati Pfahler Designs, Canoga Pk., Calif., 1974-75; interior designer B.A. Interiors, Fullerton, Calif., 1976-78, Birns Co., Rancho Mirage, Calif., 1978-79; staff interior designer Assoc. Design Studios, Costa Mesa, Calif., 1979-81; interior designer Carole Eichen Interiors, Fullerton, 1981, Sears, Roebuck and Co., Alhambra, Calif., 1982-84; sr. corp. designer, mgr. design studio Barratt Am., Irvine, Calif., 1984-88; owner, retail designer Amy Weiss Designs, Coronado, Calif., 1988—; interior designer office, yacht, residential, 1997—. Designer in residence San Diego Design Ctr., 1990—92; participant Pacific Design Ctr.; Designer on Call program, 1994—95. Prin. works include interior designs for residences, yachts; comml. interiors including lobbies and offices. Mem. Am. Soc. Interior Designers (Globe-Guilders steering com. 1989-92, chmn. Christmas party, co-chmn. Christmas on Prado 1989, 89, designer for ASID showcase house 1992, 93), Bldg. Industry Assn. (sales and mktg. coun. awards com. 1993, mem. sales and mktg. coun. 1986-88, mem. home builders coun. 1994, 2d place M.A.M.E. award 1987, 1st place M.A.M.E. award 1986, 2d place S.A.M. award 1987), Building Industry Assn. Remodeler's Coun., Nat. Kitchen and Bath Assn., Coronado C. of C., Coronado Cays Yacht Club. Office: Amy Weiss Designs 1123 Marysville Ave Chula Vista CA 91913 Home Phone: 619-482-0634; Office Phone: 619-216-6002. Business E-Mail: amy@amyweissdesigns.com.

WEISSENBERGER, HARRY GEORGE, lawyer; b. Berlin, Aug. 20, 1928; s. Georg Wilhelm and Gabriele Anna (Hochberg) W.; m. Margaret Looper, Dec. 23, 1950 (dec.); children: Carol Weissenberger Schlicht, Harry George Jr., Bruce Lee. Student, Swiss Inst. Tech., 1946-47; BEE, Ga. Tech. Inst., 1950; JD, Emory U., 1952; LLM, George Washington U., 1956. Bar: Ga. 1952, U.S. Dist. Ct. (no. dist.) Ga. 1952, U.S. Ct. Appeals (4th cir.) 1952, U.S. Supreme Ct. 1956, U.S. Ct. Customs and Patent Appeals 1956, Mo. 1957, U.S. Dist. Ct. (ea. dist.) Mo. 1957, U.S. Ct. Appeals (8th cir.) 1957, Mich. 1961, U.S. Dist. Ct. (we. dist.) Mich. 1961, U.S. Ct. Appeals (7th cir.) 1961, Calif. 1964, U.S. Dist. Ct. (no. and cen. dists.) Calif. 1964, U.S. Ct. Appeals (9th cir.) 1964, U.S. Dist. Ct. (ea. dist.) Calif. 1974, U.S. Dist. Ct. (we. dist.) Tex. 1976, U.S. Dist. ct. (so. dist.) Calif. 1982, U.S. Ct. Appeals (Fed. cir.) 1982. Examiner U.S. Patent Office, Washington, 1955-56; assoc. Bruninga & Sutherland, St. Louis, 1956-58, Sutherland, Polster & Taylor, St. Louis, 1958-59, Price & Heneveld, Grand Rapids, Mich., 1959-61, ptnr., 1961-63, Mellin, Hanscom & Hursh, San Francisco, 1963-67, Mellin, Hursh, Moore & Weissenberger, 1967-74, Phillips, Moore, Weissenberger, Lempio & Strabala, San Francisco, 1974-76, Phillips, Moore, Weissenberger, Lempio & Majestic, San Francisco, 1976-78, Newport Beach, Calif., 1978-81, Weissenberger & Peterson, Newport Beach, 1982-86, Laguna Hills, Calif., 1986-90, Weissenberger, Peterson, Uxa & Myers, Laguna Hills, 1990-93; pvt. practice atty. Laguna Hills, 1993-99; of counsel Stout, Uxa, Buyan & Mullins, Irvine, Calif., 1999—2001; pvt. practice cons., 2001—. Dir., gen. counsel Ctr. for Sutton Movement Writing, Inc., Newport Beach, Calif., 1983-93. Active Indsl. League Orange County, 1982-93; divsn. staff officer US Coast Guard Aux., 2003-, vice-flotilla comdr. 2004, flotilla comdr. 2005-06. 1st lt. USAF, 1953—55. Recipient Honored Citizen award Orange County Bd. Suprs., 1992. Mem. Calif. Bar Assn., Am. Intellectual Property Law Assn., Orange County Patent Law Assn. (pres. 1985), Am. Arbitration Assn., Rotary (chpt. bd. dirs. 1988-94, 98, pres. 1991-92, Rotarian of the Yr. 1989). Republican. Presbyterian. Office: 2408-B S Grand Ave Ste 200 Carthage MO 64836 Home Phone: 417-359-5737. E-mail: weisspat@aol.com.

WEISSKOPF, BERNARD, pediatrician, child behavior, development and genetics specialist, educator; b. Berlin, Dec. 11, 1929; came to U.S., 1939, naturalized, 1944; s. Benjamin and Bertha (Loew) W.; m. Penelope Allderdice, Dec. 26, 1965; children: Matthew David, Stephen Daniel. BA, Syracuse U., 1951; MD, U. Leiden, Netherlands, 1958. Diplomate Am. Bd. Med. Mgmt. Intern Meadowbrook Hosp., East Meadow, N.Y., 1958-59, resident, 1959-60, Johns Hopkins Hosp., Balt., 1962-64; fellow child psychiatry Johns Hopkins U. Sch. Medicine, Balt., 1962-64; asst. prof. pediatrics U. Ill. Coll. Medicine, Chgo., 1964-66; faculty U. Louisville, 1966—, prof. pediatrics, 1970-2000, emeritus prof. pediat., 2000—, assoc. in psychiatry, pathology and ob-gyn., 1966-2000, dir. Child Evaluation Ctr., 1966-2000. Chmn. Gov.'s Adv. Com. Early Childhood, Gov.'s Council on Early Childhood, Ky., 1986-88. Contbr. articles to profl. jours. Trustee Jewish Hosp., Louisville, 1974-77. Served to capt. USAF, 1960-62. Fellow Am. Acad. Pediatrics, Am. Assn. Mental Deficiency; mem. Am. Soc. Human Genetics, So. Soc. Pediatric Rsch., Am. Soc. Law and Medicine, Am. Coll. Physician Execs. Home: 6409 Deep Creek Dr Prospect KY 40059-9422 Office: Weisskopf Ctr Evaluation Children 571 S Floyd St Ste 100 Louisville KY 40202-3828 E-mail: bernweisul@aol.com.

WEISSMAN, BARRY LEIGH, lawyer; b. LA, May 30, 1948; s. Sidney and Eleanor (Siegel) W.; m. Beverly Jean Blumenfeld, Sept. 12, 1982. BA, U. Calif.-Davis, 1970; JD, U. Santa Clara, 1973. Bar: Calif. Supreme Ct. 1973, US Dist. Ct. (cen. dist.) Calif. 1976, US Supreme Ct. 1977, US Ct. Appeals (D.C. cir.) 1978, NY Ct. Appeals 1992. Sole practice law, Beverly Hills, Calif., 1974-82; ptnr. Valentini, Fini, Ferraro, Gallavotti & Weissman, Brentwood, Calif., 1982-85; mng. ptnr. LA office Kroll & Tract, 1985-87; ptnr. Knapp, Petersen & Clarke, LA, 1989-93; ptnr. Graham &

James, LA, Calif., 1994-2000, ptnr. Squire Sanders & Dempsey, LA, Calif., 2000-03, ptnr. Alschuler Grossman Stein & Kahan, LLP, 2003-05, ptnr. Sonnenschein Nath & Rosenthal, LLP, 2005-; judge pro tem LA Mcpl. Ct., 1975-1979; arbitrator Am. Arbitration Assn.; examiner State Bar Calif., 1976-80; mem. adv. commn malpractice ins., Calif. State Senate. Named a 2005 Southern Calif. SuperLawyer, Law & Politics, named in Chambers, US, 2007. Mem. ABA (mem. spl. com. on prepaid legal services, co-chmn. editorial bd. gen. practice sect.'s publs.), Beverly Hills Bar Assn., Century City Bar Assn. (bd. govs., chmn., editor Century City Bar Jour.), Beverly Hills C. of C. (co-chmn. legal justice com.), Calif. State Bar (chmn. standing com. ins. law, Bus. Law Sect.), Colorado River Assn., Western Los Angeles Regional C. of C. (dir., chmn. com. on energy prodn. and conservation). Office: Sonnenschein Nath & Rosenthal LLP Ste 2500 601 S Figueroa St Los Angeles CA 90017 Office Phone: 213-892-5098. Office Fax: 213-623-9924. Business E-Mail: bweissman@sonnenschein.com.

WEISSMAN, DAVID L., lawyer; b. NYC, Jan. 12, 1965; BA with honors, George Washington U., 1987; JD, Hofstra U., 1990; LLM, NYU, 1993. Bar: NY 1991, US Dist. Ct. So. Dist. NY 1991, US Dist. Ct. Ea. Dist. NY 1991. With Richards & O'Neil LLP, Seyfarth Shaw Fairweather & Geraldson; ptnr. Reed Smith LLP, NYC, 1999—, practice group head employment law & labor law group, 1999—. Mem.: Indsl. Rels. Rsch. Assn. (LI chpt.). Office: Reed Smith LLP 599 Lexington Ave 29th Fl New York NY 10022 Office Phone: 212-521-5466. Office Fax: 212-521-5450. Business E-Mail: dweissman@reedsmith.com.

WEISSMAN, IRVING L., medical researcher; b. Great Falls, Mont., Oct. 21, 1939; married, 1961; 4 children. BS, Mont. State Coll., 1960, DSc (hon.), 1992; MD, Stanford U., 1965. NIH fellow dept. radiology Stanford U., 1965—67, rsch. assoc., 1967—68, from asst. prof. to assoc. prof. dept. pathology, 1969—81; prof. pathology Stanford U. Sch. Medicine, 1981—, Karel & Avice Beekhuis Prof. Cancer Biology, 1987—, prof. devel. biology, 1989—, dir., Inst. of Stem Cell Biology and Regenerative Medicine, 2003—, prof. by courtesy, neurosurgery, prof. by courtesy, biol. sciences. Sr. Dernham fellow Calif. divsn. Am. Cancer Soc., 1969—73; mem. immunobiology study sect. NIH, 1976—80; mem. founding scientific adv. bd. Amgen, 1981—89, DNAX, 1981—92; James McGinnis Meml. lectr. Duke U., 1982; mem. sci. rev. bd. Howard Hughes Med. Inst., 1986; George Feigen Meml. lectr. Stanford U., 1987; Albert Coons Meml. lectr. Harvard U., 1987; Jame Stahlman lectr. Vanderbilt U., 1987; mem. sci. adv. com. Irvington House Inst., 1987; 5th Ann. vis. prof. cancer biology U. Tex. Health Sci. Ctr., 1987; R. E. Smith lectr. U. Tex. Sys. Cancer Ctr., 1988; co-founder SyStemix, Inc., 1988, bd. dirs., 1988—97; mem. founding scientific adv. bd. T-Cell Scis. (now Avant, Inc.), 1988—92; Chauncey D. Leake lectr. U. Calif., 1989; Harvey lectr. Rockefeller U., 1989; Rose Litman lectr., 90; disting. lectr. Western Soc. Clin. Investment, 1990; chmn. U.S.-Japan Immunology Bd., 1992—94; chmn. sci. adv. com. McLaughlin Rsch. Inst., 1992—, trustee, 1992—; bd. govs. Project Inform, 1995—; co-founder StemCells, 1996—, mem. bd. dirs.; co-founder Celtrans (now Cellerant), 2001—; chair scientific adv. bd. Cellerant; spkr. in field. Contbr. articles to profl. publications. Named One of Top 100 Alumni, Mont. State U., 1993, Mont. Conservationist of Yr., Mont. Land Reliance, 1994; recipient Faculty Rsch. award, Nat. Am. Cancer Soc., 1974—78, Basic Cell Rsch. award, Am. Soc. Cytopathology, Pasarow Award for cancer rsch., 1989, Kaiser Award for Excellence in Preclinical Teaching, Outstanding Investigator Award, NIH, E. Donnall Thomas Award, Am. Soc. Hematology, deVillers Award for Outstanding Achievements in Leukemia Rsch., Leukemia Soc. Am., J. Allyn Taylor Internat. Prize in Medicine, Bass Award, Soc. Neurological Surgeons, Calif. Scientist of Yr., 2002, Elliott Proctor Joslin medal, Am. Diabetes Assn., 2003, Van Bekkum Stem Cell Award, 2003, Disting. Scientist Award, Am. Assn. Cancer Inst., 2003, Alan Cranston Awardee, Alliance for Aging Rsch., 2004, Rabbi Shai Shacknai Mem. Prize in Immunology and Cancer Rsch., Lautenberg Ctr. for Gen. and Tumor Immunology, 2004, medal for Disting. Contributions to Biomedical Rsch., NY Acad. Medicine, 2004; scholar, Josiah Macy Found., 1974—75. Fellow: AAAS; mem.: IOM, NAS (steering com. NIOM AIDS panel 1985—86, chair, Panel on Sci. & Med. Aspects of Human Reproductive Cloning, Jessie Stevenson Kovalenko Medal 2004), Inst. Immunology, Am. Assn. Cancer Rsch., Am. Soc. Microbiology, Am. Assn. Pathologists, Am. Assn. Univ. Pathologists, Am. Assn. Immunologists (pres. 1994—95), Am. Acad. Arts and Scis. Achievements include research in phylogeny and developmental biology of cells that make up blood-forming and immune systems; first to isolate, in mice and in man, the blood-forming stem cell; knowledge expected to lead to improved treatment of people with myeloma, lymphoma and breast cancer. Avocations: football, ballet, fly fishing. Office: Stanford U Sch Medicine Dept Pathology B257 Beckman Ctr Stanford CA 94305-5323 E-mail: irv@stanford.edu.

WEISSMAN, JACK (GEORGE ANDERSON), retired editor; b. Chgo., June 6, 1921; s. Ben and Ida (Meyerson) W.; m. Bernice Platt, Nov. 13, 1949; children: Bruce, David, Ellen Weissman Montgomery. BA in Edn., Northwestern U., Evanston, Ill., 1943, MS in Journalism, 1944. Asst. editor Bankers Monthly, Chgo., 1944-45; mng. editor Practical Knowledge, Chgo., 1945-50; with pub. relations dept. Roosevelt U., Chgo., 1947-50; editor Opportunity Mag., Chgo., 1950-89, ret. Author: Make Money at Home, 1963, How to Make Correct Decisions, 1964, Money Making Businesses You Can Start for $500 Or Less, 1965, Making It Big in Selling, 1987. Served to cpl. USAAF, 1945-46 Mem. Sigma Delta Chi, Phi Delta Kappa. Jewish. Personal E-mail: jacknbernice@access4less.net.

WEISSMAN, MICHAEL LEWIS, lawyer; b. Chgo., Sept. 11, 1934; s. Maurice and Sue (Goldberg) Weissman; m. Joanne Sherwin, Dec. 19, 1961; children: Mark Douglas, Greg Steven, Scott Adam, Brett Anthony. Student White scholar, U. Chgo., 1951-52; BS in Econs, Northwestern U., 1954; MBA in Acctg., U. Pa., 1956; JD, Harvard U., 1958; postgrad. Fulbright scholar, U. Sydney, Australia, 1958-59; postgrad., Hague Acad. Internat. Law, 1959. Bar: D.C. 1958, Ill. 1959. Asst. prof. bus. law Roosevelt U., Chgo., 1959-61; pvt. practice Chgo., 1959—; mem. firm Aaron, Aaron, Schimberg & Hess, 1969-78; sr. ptnr. Boorstein & Weissman, 1978-82, Weissman, Smolev & Solow, 1982-88, Foley & Lardner, 1988-92, McBride Baker & Coles, Chgo., 1992—2001; exec. v.p., gen. counsel Bridgeview Bank Group, Chgo., 2001—04; of counsel Holland & Knight LLC, 2001—. Asst. prof. Roosevelt U., 1960—62; lectr. Lake Forest (Ill.) Coll., 1979—80; chmn. Banking Group, Union League Club Chgo.; panelist Risk Mgmt. Assn., Banking Law Inst., Midwest Fin. Conf., Greater O'Hare Assn., Miss. Law Inst., Bank Lending Inst., Chgo. Assn. Commerce and Industry, State of Art Seminars, Infocast Inc., SBA, Fed. Res. Bank Chgo., Lenders Ednl. Inst., Bank Adminstrn. Inst. Found., Lender's Forum, Clarion Legal; Fulbright sr. specialist Sch. Bus. Adminstrn., Turiba, Latvia, 2006; adj. prof. law John Marshall Law Sch., 2001—02, 2006—. Author: (book) Lender Liability, 1988, Commercial Loan Documentation and Secured Lending, 1990, How to Avoid Career-Ending Mistakes in Commercial Lending, 1996, The Lender's Edge, 1997; mem. editl. bd.: Commercial Damages, 1985—; contbr. articles to profl. jours. Mem. adv. bd. Affective Disorders Clinic, U. Ill. Med. Sch., 1979—81; instr. mentor program Risk Mgmt. Assn. Scholar, Fulbright Found., 1958—59, 2006; White scholar, U. Chgo., 1951—52. Mem.: ABA, Robert Morris Assn., Comml. Fin. Assn. Ednl. Found. (adv. bd.), Turnaround Mgmt. Assn. (steering com. Chgo. chpt.), Harvard Law Soc. Ill., Assn. Comml. Fin. Attys. (bd. dirs. 1989—2000, chmn. 2001—02), Ill. Inst. CLE (bd. dirs. 1989—2000, chmn. 2001—02), Ill. Bankers Assn. (mem. com. bank counsel 1987—88, vice chmn. 1988—89), Chgo. Bar Assn., Ill. Bar Assn., Beta Alpha Psi. Home: 2067 Old Briar Rd Highland Park IL 60035-4245 Office: Holland & Knight LLP 131 S Dearborn St 30th Fl Chicago IL 60603-5506 Office Phone: 312-715-5767. Business E-Mail: michael.weissman@hklaw.com.

WEISSMAN, ROBERT ALLEN, lawyer, real estate broker; b. LA, May 26, 1950; s. Joseph Jonas and Shirley Rhoda (Solitare) Weissman; m. Susan Renee Bashner, Apr. 5, 1975; children: Evan Gregory, Russell Joseph, Dustin Raymond. Student, Chapman Coll., Orange, Calif., 1970—71, World Campus Afloat, 1970—71; BA, UCLA, 1972; JD, Southwestern U., LA, 1975. Bar: Calif. 1975, U.S. Dist. Ct. Calif. 1976, D.C. 1980, U.S. Ct. Appeals (9th cir.) 1982, U.S. Supreme Ct. 1982, U.S. Dist. Ct. (no. dist.) Calif. 1985. Ptnr. Weissman & Weissman, L.A., 1975—81, prin., 1981—. Spkr. to profl. and trade groups on constrn. and mechanics' lien law. Co-author: How to Use the Mechanics' Lien Law, 1995, For Contractors Only, 1996, For Suppliers Only, 1996; contbg. author: Calif. Real Property Jour., 1987, columnist on mechanics' lien law and creditors rights: L.A. Daily Jour.; contbr. articles to profl. jours. Pres.'s adv. coun. City of Hope, 1981—86. Named one of Outstanding Young Men of Am., U.S. Jaycees, 1980. Mem.: ABA, Ventura County Bar Assn., San Fernando Valley Bar Assn. (co-chair bus. law sect. 1989—91, trustee 1991—92, treas. 1992—93, sec. 1993—, pres.-elect 1994, pres. 1995—, exec. com. 1996—), L.A. County Bar Assn. (trustee 1994—95, LA county founding mem., constrn. law subsect., pre-judgment remedies sect.), State Bar Calif., Calif. Lawyers for Arts, Acad. Magical Arts, Inc. Club. Democrat. Jewish. Office: Weissman & Weissman 2660 Townsgate Rd Ste 350 Westlake Village CA 91361-2714 Office Phone: 805-371-0500 ext 16. Personal E-mail: raw4law@verizon.net.

WEISSMAN, WILLIAM R., lawyer; b. NYC, Aug. 16, 1940; s. Emanuel and Gertrude (Halpern) W.; m. Barbra Phylis Gershman; 1 child, Adam; stepchildren: Eric, Jace, Julie Greenman. BA, Columbia U., 1962, JD cum laude, 1965. Bar: N.Y. 1965, D.C. 1969, U.S. Dist Ct. (no. dist.) Tex. 1965, U.S. Dist. Ct. (so. and ea. dists.) N.Y. 1977, U.S. Ct. Appeals (D.C. dir.) 1969, U.S. Ct. Appeals (9th cir.) 1973, U.S. Ct. Apeals (2d and 3d cirs.) 1974, U.S. Ct. Appeals (10th cir.) 1979, U.S. Ct. Appeals (11th cir.) 1981, U.S. Supreme Ct. 1968. News dir., progrm dir. WKCR-FM, NYC, 1960-62; law clk. U.S. dist. judge, Dallas, 1965-66; trial atty. antitrust divsn. Dept. Justice, Washington, 1966-69; spl. asst. U.S. atty. Washington, 1967; assoc. Wald, Harkrader & Ross, Washington, 1969-72, ptnr., 1973-85, Piper & Marbury LLP, Washington, 1986-99, Piper Rudnick LLP, Washington, 2000—04, DLA Piper US LLP, Washington, 2005—07, Venable LLP, Washington, 2007—. Instr. D.C. Bar continuing legal edn. program Georgetown U. Law Sch., Washington, 1980-89; environ. regulation course Exec. Enterprises, Inc., 1985-95. Mem. editl. bd. Jour. Environ. Regulation, 1991-95, Environ. Regulation & Permitting, 1995-2000. Mem. Arlington (Va.) County Tenant-Landlord Commn., 1973—77, chmn., 1975—77; parliamentarian Arlington County Dem. Com., 1971—75. Mem.: ASTM (E-50 com. environ. assessment 1996—, rec. sec. 1998—99, vice chmn. 2000—), ABA, Columbia U. Club Washington (bd. dirs. 1987—93). Jewish. Home: 3802 Lakeview Ter Falls Church VA 22041-1313 Office: Venable LLP 575 7th St NW Washington DC 20004-1601 Home Phone: 703-354-2666; Office Phone: 202-344-4503. Business E-Mail: wweissman@venable.com.

WEISSMAN-BERMAN, DEBORAH, biostatistics and composites engineer, researcher; b. NYC, June 9, 1938; d. Raphael H. and Sarah S. (Schreiber) Weissman; m. Lewis H. Berman, Aug. 1, 1958 (div. Apr. 1966); 1 child, Michelle B. Marchildon. BFA, Columbia U., 1967, profl. degree Civil Engr., 1985; M of Engring. in Ocean Engring., Stevens Inst. Tech., Hoboken, NJ, 1980; ScD, Eurotech. Rsch. U., Hilo, Hawaii, 1989; Cert. in Epidemiology and Biostats., Drexel U.; MPH, Fla. Internat. U., 2005. Asst. prof. naval architecture U.S. Merchant Marine Acad., Kings Point, N.Y., 1980-81; asst. prof. engring. SUNY Maritime Coll., Ft. Schuyler, N.Y., 1981-82; sr. naval architect M. Rosenblatt & Son, NYC, 1982-83; composites cons. Weissman-Berman & Co., Inc., Conn., NY, and Fla., 1983-92; rsch. prof. engring. Webb Inst. Naval Architecture, Glen Cove, N.Y., 1986-89; assoc./courtesy scientist U. Fla., Gainesville, 1990—; rsch. scientist Nova Southeastern U., Dania, Fla., 1996-2000, prof. quantitative methods in health rsch., 1998-2000. Creator composites software, COREDES, PLATES; co-chair 2d Internat. Conf. Sandwich Composites, Gainsville, 1992; pres. dwbus Assocs. Inc. Author: Research Guidelines for Aluminum, 1993; contbr. sci. papers to Trans. SNAME, Procs. 2d Internat. Conf. Sandwich Composites; contbr. chpt. to SAMPE Internat. Ency. Composites, 1990; assoc. editor SAMPE Jour., 1992-95. Recipient grad. scholarship SNAME, Jersey City, N.Y., 1979. Mem. APHA, ASME (v.p. rsch. com. 1990-96), Soc. Naval Architects and Marine Engrs., Am. Statis. Assn. Democratic. Jewish. Achievements include derivation of sandwich beam and plate equations with core as elastic foundation, derivation of sandwich composites yield equations, derivation of the mechanics modulus of residual stiffness (alpha), definition of bi-geometrical structure of sandwich beams, on scaling laws of bi-geometrical sandwich structures, high strain-rate predictions, derivation of predictive method for survival and health outcomes in biostatistics. Home and Office: 2731 Blairstone Rd No 166 Tallahassee FL 32301 Office Phone: 850-878-3993. Personal E-mail: dwbstats@yahoo.com.

WEISSMANN, ANDREW, lawyer, former prosecutor; b. NYC, Mar. 17, 1958; BA in Hist., Princeton U., 1980; JD, Columbia U. Law Sch., 1984. Bar: NY 1985. Law clk. to Hon. Eugene Nickerson US Dist. Ct. (ea. dist. NY), 1984—85; atty. Cleary, Gottlieb, Steen & Hamilton, LLP, NYC; asst. US atty. (ea. dist. NY), chief criminal divsn. US Dept. Justice, Bklyn., 2000—03; ptnr. Jenner & Block, LLP, NYC, 2006—. Dep. dir. Enron Task Force, US Dept. Justice, 2002—04, dir., 2004—05. Mem.: Legal Aid Soc., Assn. of the Bar of the City of NY. Office: Jenner & Block LLP 919 Third Ave New York NY 10022 Office Phone: 212-891-1650. Office Fax: 212-891-1699. E-mail: aweissmann@jenner.com. *

WEISSMANN, CHARLES, molecular biologist, educator; b. 1931; MD, PhD, U. Zurich, Switzerland; D honoris causa, U. Verona, Italy, 1992, U. Ghent, Belgium, 1994, Swiss Fed. Inst. Tech., Zurich, 1998, U. Zurich, 2000, U. St. Andrews, 2000, Ecole Polytech. Fed. Lausanne, 2001. Prof., dir. Inst. Molecular Biology, U. Zurich, 1967-99; pres. Swiss Soc. for Cell and Molecular Biology; chmn. sci. bd. Biogen, 1984-86; pres. Ernst Hadorn-Stiftung, Zurich, 1986—; prof., chmn. dept. Scripps Rsch. Inst., Fla., 2004—. Bd. dirs. F. Hoffmann-LaRoche Ltd., Basel, 1988—2001; mem. sci. adv. bd. ZMB, Heidelberg, 1988—2001, Roche Inst. Molecular Biology, Nutley, NJ, 1993—95, Osaka Biosci. Inst., Japan, 1994—2000, Roche Molecular Sys., Alameda, Calif., 1994—98, Swiss Inst. for Cancer Rsch., Lausanne, 1994—98; mem. sci. coun. Swiss Nat. Fund, 1989—94, Internat. Human Frontiers Rsch. Program, 1994—98; mem. internat. sci. adv. bd. The Netherlands Cancer Inst., Amsterdam; bd. govs. Tel Aviv U., 1997—2004; chmn. European Com. Group on Bovine Spongiform Encephalopathy, 1996; Samuel Rudin disting. vis. prof. Columbia U., NYC, 1999; vis. prof. Imperial Coll., London, 2001—04. Assoc. editor Molecular Medicine, 1994-03; mem. editl. bd. Procs. Royal Soc. Decorated fgn. mem. Order for Merit for Sci. and Art (Germany); Hon. Sr. fellow Inst. Neurology, U. Coll., London; recipient Ruzicka prize in chemistry, 1996, Otto Warburg prize, 1980, H.P. Heineken prize, 1982, Sir. H. Krebs medal, 1974, Marcel Benoist prize, Bern, 1970, Scheele medal, Uppsala, 1982, Krebspreis Schweizerische Krebsliga, 1987, Jung prize for medicine, Hamburg, 1988, Gabor medal Royal Soc., London, 1993, Robert Koch medal, Bonn, 1995, Datta lectureship award FEBS, 1998, Charles Leopold Mayer prize French Acad. Sci., 1996, Royal Soc. Glaxo Wellcome prize, 1996, August Wilhelm von Hofmann Denkmünze, 1997, Klaus Joachim Zülch prize, 1997, Max Delbrück medal, Berlin, 1997, Wilhelm Exner medal, Vienna, 1997, Disting. Svc. award, Miami, 1998, Mendel medal Genetical Soc., London, 1998, Koetser prize, Zurich, 2001, Friedrich-Bauer prize for med. rsch., Munich, 2001, Warren Alpert Found. prize, Boston, 2004, Fifth Ann. Dart/NYU Biotech. award, NY, 2006. Fellow: Am. Acad. Microbiology; mem.: NAS (fgn. assoc.), Acad. Med. Scis. (London chpt.), Berlin-Brandenburgischen Acad. Sci. (extraordinary), Nordheim-Westfälischen Acad. Sci. (corr.), Human Genome Orgn., Academia Europaea, Weizmann Inst. Sci. (bd. govs. 1985—), Royal Soc. (fgn.), Deutsche Akademie Naturforscher Leopoldina, Swiss Acad. Med. Sci., Am. Acad. Arts and Scis., European Molecular Biology Orgn. Office: Scripps Fla 5353 Parkside Dr RF-2 Jupiter FL 33458 Office Phone: 561-799-8910, 561-799-8895. Office Fax: 561-799-8960. Business E-Mail: charlesw@scripps.edu.

WEISSMANN, GERALD, internist, researcher, educator, editor, writer; b. Vienna, Aug. 7, 1930; came to U.S., 1938; s. Adolf and Greta (Lustbader) W.; m. Ann Raphael, Apr. 1, 1953; children: Lisa, Andrew. BA with honors, Columbia U., NYC, 1950; MD, NYU, 1954. Diplomate Am. Bd. Internal Medicine. Intern Mt. Sinai Hosp., NYC, 1954-55, asst. resident medicine, 1957-58; chief resident medicine Bellevue Hosp., NYC, 1959-60; fellow depts. biochemistry and medicine Arthritis and Rheumatism Fedn., NYU, 1958-59; rsch. asst. dept. medicine NYU Sch. Medicine, 1959-60, instr. medicine, 1959-62, asst. prof., 1962-65, assoc. prof., 1966-70, prof., 1970—, dir. div. cell biology, 1969-73, dir. div. rheumatology of dept. medicine, 1973-2000; dir. Ctr. Biotech. Studies, 2000—. USPHS spl. rsch. fellow dept. biophysics Strangeways Lab., Cambridge, Eng., 1960-61; sr. investigator Arthritis and Rheumatism Found., N.Y.C., 1961-65; career rsch. scientist Health Rsch. Coun. N.Y.C., 1966-71; instr. physiology Marine Biol. Lab., Woods Hole, Mass., 1973-77, investigator, 1970—, trustee, 1993—; vis. investigator ARC Inst. Animal Physiology, Babraham, Eng., 1964-69, Centre de Physiologie et d'Immunologie Cellulaires, Hosp. St. Antoine, Paris, 1973-74, William Harvey Rsch. Inst., London, 1987; mem. postdoctoral fellowships rev. com. Pfizer Internat., N.Y.C., 1983-89; mem. scholarship selection com. Pew Scholars in Biomed. Scis., New Haven, 1984-94; lectr. Johns Hopkins U., 1976, 89, Med. Coll. Ga., Augusta, 1980, Med. Coll. Pa., 1988, William Harvey Rsch. Inst., London, 1987, others; nat. adv. bd. Ellison Med. Found, 1997—; chair Prix Galien USA award com. Author: The Woods Hole Cantata, 1995, They All Laughed at Christopher Columbus, 1987, The Doctor With Two Heads, 1990, The Doctor Dilemma, 1992, Democracy and DNA, 1996, Darwin's Audubon, 1998, The Year of the Genome, 2001, Galileo's Gout, 2007; editor-in-chief Inflammation, 1975-01, Advances in Inflammation Rsch., 1979—, MD Mag., 1989-94, The FASEB Jour., 2005-; mem. editl. bd. Clin. Immunology and Immunopathology, 1972-88, Advances in Prostaglandin, Thromboxane and Leukotriene Rsch., 1975—, Am. Jour. Medicine, 1976-88, Tissue Reactions, 1979, Immunopharmacology, 1982; contbr. over 300 articles to profl. jours. Capt. M.C., U.S. Army, 1955-57. Recipient Allesandro Robecchi prize Internat. League Against Rheumatism, 1972, Marine Biol. Lab. award, 1974, 1979, U. Bologna medal, Italy, 1978, Lila Gruber Cancer Rsch. award Am. Acad. Dermatology, 1979, Solomon A. Berson Med. Alumni Achievement award NYU, 1980, Merit award NIH, 1987, Centennial award Marine Biol. Lab., 1988, others; Guggenheim Found. fellow, N.Y.C., 1973-74. Fellow AAAS; mem. Am. Coll. Rheumatology (pres. 1982-83, Disting. Investigator award 1992, Presdl. Gold medal 2005, master 1996), Am. Fedn. Clin. Rsch., Soc. Exptl. Biology and Medicine, Am. Soc. Pharmacology and Exptl. Therapeutics, Am. Soc. Exptl. Pathology, Assn. Am. Immunologists, Am. Soc. Cell Biology, Am. Soc. Clin. Investigation, Am. Soc. Biol. Chemistry and Molecular Biology, Assn. Am. Physicians, Harvey Soc. of N.Y. (pres. 1981-82), Interurban Clin. Club, PEN Am. Ctr., Cosmos Club, Phi Beta Kappa, Alpha Omega Alpha, fgn. mem. Accademia Nazionale dei Lincei (Rome) Avocation: tennis. Office: NYU Med Ctr Dept Medicine BCD686 550 1st Ave New York NY 10016-6402

WEISSMANN, HEIDI SEITELBLUM, radiologist, educator; b. NYC, Feb. 4, 1951; d. Louis and June (Joseph) Seitel Bloom; m. Murray H. Weissmann, June 16, 1973; 1 dau., Lauren Erica BS in Chemistry magna cum laude, Bklyn. Coll., CUNY, 1970; MD, Mt. Sinai Sch. Medicine, NYC, 1974. Diplomate Nat. Bd. Med. Examiners. Intern Montefiore Med. Ctr. Bronx, N.Y., 1974-75, resident in diagnostic radiology N.Y., 1975-78; fellow in computerized transaxial tomography and ultrasonography N.Y. Hosp.-Cornell U. Med. Ctr., NYC, N.Y., 1978-79; instr. in radiology and nuclear medicine Albert Einstein Coll. Medicine, Montefiore Med. Ctr., Bronx, N.Y., 1979-80; asst. prof. radiology and nuclear medicine Albert Einstein Coll. Medicine and Montefiore Med. Ctr., Bronx, N.Y., 1980-84, assoc. prof. nuclear medicine, 1984-94, assoc. prof. radiology, 1986-94; dir. Ctr. for Women, Medicine and Healthcare, Washington, 1994—. Adj. attending physician Montefiore Med. Ctr., 1979-87; chmn. Nuclear Medicine Grand Rounds: Greater N.Y., 1980-87; physician coord. Nuclear Medicine Technologist In-Service Tng. Program, 1982-86; cons. NIH, 1984-86, NIH Diagnostic Radiology, 1985-86 Assoc. editor Nuclear Medicine Ann., 5 vols., 1979-84, editor, 5 vols., 1985—; contbr. chpts. to books, articles to jours.; editor Jour. Sci. and Engring. Ethics, 1994—; reviewer Jour. of Radiology, 1981—, mem. editl. adv. bd., 1985-86, assoc. editor, 1986—; reviewer. Jour. of Nuclear Medicine, 1981—, Am. Jour. of Roentgenology, 1986—, Gastroenterology, 1986—, Western Jour. of Medicine, 1985—; contbr. audiovisual programs and films Recipient Saul Horowitz, Jr., Meml. award (Disting. Alumnus award), Mt. Sinai Sch. Medicine, 1980, Pres.' award, Am. Roentgen Ray Soc., 1979, Berta Rubinstein, M.D., Resident award, 1978, Cavallo award for moral courage, 1993, others. Mem. Radiol. Soc. N.Am. (mem. subcom. for nuclear medicine of program com., 1981, 82, 83, chmn. 1984, 85, 86), Soc. Nuclear Medicine (trustee 1983-87, 88—, sec.-treas. Correlative Imaging Council 1979-82, exec. bd. 1982-84, pres. 1984-86, exec. bd. 1986—, mem. acad. council 1980—, task force on interrelationship between nuclear medicine and nuclear magnetic resonance 1983-85, gov. Greater N.Y. chpt. 1983-85, treas., 1985-86, 86-87, 2d ann. Tetalman award of Edn. and Research Found. 1982, mem., vice chmn. coms. and subcoms.), Soc. Gastrointestinal Radiologists, Am. Inst. Ultrasound in Medicine, N.Y. Acad. Scis., Assoc. Alumni Mt. Sinai Med. Ctr., Nuclear Radiology Club (chmn. 1983—). Phi Beta Kappa. Home and Office: 14 Powder Hill Rd Saddle River NJ 07458-3215

WEISS NEWTON, JOANNE MARION, writer; b. Wayne, NJ, Mar. 16, 1960; d. Henry Daniel and Florence Frances (Zaratkiewicz) W.; 1 child, David. BA, Bennington Coll., 1982; MA, U. Cambridge, Eng., 1988. Prodn. mgr. The Suburban News, N.J., 1982-83; gardener Artistic Landscaping, N.J., 1983; case mgr. Mid-Bergan Mental Health Ctr., N.J., 1985-86. Founder Isis Farm Writers, 1995—, Cambridge Actors, 1988—. Author, dir. play The Gift, 1987, 88; author: (plays) Catherine the Queen, 1997, Mother America, 1998; contbr. 4 poems to Tears in the Fence, 2002. Translator Solidarity, Poland, 1983; co-leader Vols. for Peace, 1986; mem., worker Pregnancy Adv. Svc., Cambridge, 1991-92. Recipient scholarship Inst. for Brit. and Irish Studies, Trinity Coll., Dublin, 1985, Chancellor's medal for poetry U. Cambridge, Eng., 1988, grants for Edinburgh, Sir John Gielgud, 1988, grant Judith Wilson Fund, U. Cambridge, Eng., 1988. Mem. N.H. Carriage Horse Assn., Dramatists Guild, Am. Horse Show Assn. Avocations: horse training, organic farming.

WEISSTEIN, ULRICH WERNER, English literature educator; b. Breslau, Germany, Nov. 14, 1925; came to U.S., 1950, naturalized, 1959; s. Rudolf and Berta (Wende) W.; m. Elisabeth Rieckh; children: Cristina, Cecily, Eric Wolfgang, Anton Edward. Student, Goethe-Universität, Frankfurt, 1947-50, 51-52, U. Iowa, 1950-51; MA, Ind. U., 1953, PhD, 1954; Doctorate (hon.), U. Lund, Sweden, 1993. Instr. Lehigh U., Bethlehem, Pa., 1954—58, asst. prof., 1958; asst. prof. English and comparative lit. Ind. U., Bloomington, 1959-62, assoc. prof., 1962-66, prof. German and comparative lit., 1986—90, chmn. comparative lit. program, 1985-89; dir. Ind. U.-Purdue U. Studienprogramm U. Hamburg, 1981-82. Vis. prof. U. Wis., summer 1966, Middlebury Sch. German, summer 1970, U. Hamburg (Germany), spring 1971, spring 1982, U. Vienna, 1976, Stanford U., 1979,

Graz U., Austria, 1985, 95, 96, U. Bologna, Italy, 1991, U. Antwerp, Belgium, 1992, U. Salzburg, 1997; external examiner comparative lit. U. Hong Kong, 1974-76. Author: Heinrich Mann, 1962, The Essence of Opera, 1964, Max Frisch, 1967, Einführung in die Vergleichende Literaturwissenschaft, 1968, English version: Comparative Literature and Literary Theory, 1973; Spanish version: Introduccion a la Literatura Comparada, 1975, Chinese version, 1987, Japanese version, 1976, Korean version, 1979; Forschungsbericht zur Vergleichenden Literaturwissenschaft, 1968-1977, 1981, Links und links gesellt sich nicht: Gesammelte Aufsätze zum Werk Heinrich Manns und Bertolt Brechts, 1985; editor: Literatur und Bildende Kunst: Ein Handbuch zur Theorie und Praxis eines komparatistischen Grenzgebiets, 1992, Selected Essays on Opera 1960-1996, 2006; editor German sect. Twayne World Authors series, 1964-86, Yearbook of Comparative and General Literature, 1960-90, Oper Im Brennpunkt, 2001-, Expressionism as an International Literary Phenomenon, 1973; co-editor: Literature and the Other Arts, 1981, Texte und Kontexte: Festschrift für Norbert Fuerst, 1973, Intertextuality: German Literature and Visual Art from the Renaissance to the Twentieth Century, 1993, Musico-Poetics Today: Calvin S. Brown in Memoriam, 2000; translator: The Grotesque in Art and Literature (W. Kayser), 1963 Recipient Grosses goldenes Ehrenzeichen des Landes Steiermark, 1996; Guggenheim fellow, 1974-75; MLA grantee, 1958-59. Mem.: Gesellschaft der Freunde der Oper in Graz (pres. 1991—97, hon. pres. 2003—), Coun. Internat. Exchange Scholars (area com. for West Germany and Austria 1983—85), Internat. Comparative Lit. Assn. (exec. coun. 1979—85, sec. 1985—89). Home: Baierstrasse 54/IV 8020 Graz Austria

WEISWASSER, STEPHEN, electronics executive; b. Detroit, Nov. 21, 1940; BA, Wayne State U.; postgrad., Johns Hopkins U.; JD magna cum laude, Harvard U. Ptnr. Wilmer, Cutler & Pickering; sr. v.p. Capital Cities/ABC, Inc.; pres., CEO Americast, 1995-98; ptnr. Covington & Burling, Washington, 1998-99; exec. v.p., gen. counsel Gemstar Internat. Group Ltd., Pasadena, Calif., 1999—, also bd. dirs. Woodrow Wilson Nat. fellow Johns Hopkins U. Office Fax: 626-792-0257.

WEISZ, PAUL B(URG), physicist, researcher, chemical engineer; b. Pilsen, Czechoslovakia, July 2, 1919; naturalized, 1946; s. Alexander and Amalia (Sulc) Weisz; m. Rhoda A.M. Burg, Sept. 4, 1943; children: Ingrid B., P. Randall. Student, Tech. U. Berlin, 1937—39; BS, Auburn U., 1940; PhD, Swiss Fed. Inst. Tech., Zurich, 1966, ScD (hon.), 1980. Rsch. physicist Bartol Rsch. Found., Swarthmore, Pa., 1940—46; from rsch. assoc. to sr. scientist Mobil Oil Corp., 1946—61, mgr., corp. ctrl. rsch. lab. Princeton, NJ, 1969—84; disting. prof. chem. and bio-engring. sci. U. Pa., 1984—91, prof. emeritus, 1991—. Instr. elec. engring. Swarthmore Coll., 1942—43; with radiation lab. MIT, 1944—45; vis. prof. Princeton U., 1974—76, mem. adv. coun., dept. chem. engring., 1975—76, mem. adv. com., Sch. Engring., 1977—80, Pa. State U., 1996—99; chmn. ctr. policy bd. Ctr. for Catalytic Sci. and Tech., U. Del., 1977—81; cons. natural energy needs Pres. Coun. Sci. and Indsl. Rsch., South Africa, 1989; mem. energy rsch. adv. bd. U.S. Secretaries of Energy, 1985—90; cons. Ciba-Geigy Pharm. Ltd., Basel, Switzerland, 1990—92; adj. prof. Pa. State U., 1993—; mem. adv. com., future direction chem. related scis. Pres. Swiss Fed. Inst. Tech., 1992; cons. rsch. and tech. strategy. Editor: (ann. rev.) Advances in Catalysis, 1956—93; mem. editl. bd.:, 1985—, Jour. Catalysis, 1962—84; mem. editl. bd. Chem. Engring. Comms., 1972—78, Heterogeneous Chem. Revs., 1993—96; asst. editor: Semiconductor Surface Physics, 1957; editor: Kinetics and Catalysis, Chem. Engring. Progress Symposium Series, 1967, (book) Angiogenesis-Science, Technology, Medicine, 1992; author, column editor: Sci. of the Possible, Chemtech, 1980—81; contbr. (183 articles to sci. jours.). Recipient ann. award, Catalysis Club Phila., 1973, Lavoisier medal, Chem. Soc. France, 1983, Perkin medal, Internat. Soc. Chem. Industry, 1985, Nat. medal of Tech., Pres. U.S., 1992. Fellow: NAE (elected mem. 1977), AIChE (R.H. Wilhelm award 1978), Am. Inst. Chemistry (Chem. Pioneer award 1974), Am. Phys. Soc.; mem.: N.Y. Acad. Scis., Am. Chem. Soc. (sci. award South Jersey sect. 1963, E.V. Murphree award 1972, 1977, Chemistry of Contemporary Tech. Problems award 1986, Carothers award 1987), Nassau Club (Princeton). Mem. Soc. Of Friends. Achievements include 95 patents in field; research in radiation; electronics; solid state, energy, physics in all operating systems; angiogenesis; cell proliferation; R & D strategy, cross-disciplinary science, technology. Fax: 814-237-3202. Personal E-mail: pweisz@verizon.net. Business E-Mail: pbw5@psu.edu.

WEISZ, RACHEL, actress; b. London, Mar. 7, 1971; 1 child. BA, U. Cambridge, England. Motion picture and T.V. actress. Actor (films) Death Machine, 1995, Stealing Beauty, 1996, Chain Reaction, 1996, Going All the Way, 1997, Amy Foster, 1997, Land Girls, 1998, I Want You, 1998, Swept From the Sea, 1998, The Mummy, 1999, Sunshine, 1999, Beautiful Creatures, 2001, Enemy at the Gates, 2001, The Mummy Returns, 2001, About a Boy, 2002, The Shape of Things, 2003 (also prodr.), Confidence, 2003, Runaway Jury, 2003, She Died on Canvas, 2003, Envy, 2004, Constantine, 2005, The Constant Gardener, 2005 (Best Performance by an Actress in a Supporting Role in a Motion Picture, Hollywood Fgn. Press Assn., Golden Globe award, 2006, Outstanding Performance by a Female Actor in a Supporting Role, Screen Actors Guild award, 2006, Performance by an Actress in a Supporting Role, Acad. Motion Picture Arts & Sciences, 2006), The Fountain, 2006, Eragon, 2006; (TV films) Scarlet and Black, 1993, My Summer with Des, 1998; (plays) Design For Living, 1994, Last Summer, 1999, The Shape of Things, 2001. Office: c/o Creative Artists Agency 9830 Wilshire Blvd Beverly Hills CA 90212 *

WEITBERG, ALAN BARRY, physician, researcher; b. Phila., Mar. 2, 1950; s. Sidney and Esther Weitberg; m. Katherine Raphaela Bick, Sept. 6, 1975 (div. Apr. 1993); children: Allison Ross, Seth Raphael. AB, Cornell U., Ithaca, NY, 1972; MD, Univ. Medicine and Dentistry NJ, Newark, 1976; MEd (hon.), Brown U., Providence, 1992. Lic. MD RI, 1978, Mass., 1982, cert. Nat. Bd. Med. Examiners, 1977, Internal Medicine, 1980, Med. Oncology, 1987, Hematology, 1988. Resident and chief resident in medicine Roger Williams Med. Ctr. and Brown Med. Sch., Providence, 1976—80; hematology fellow Mass. Gen. Hosp. and Harvard U., Boston, 1980—82; instr. med. sch. Harvard Med. Sch., Boston, 1982—85; chief divsn. hematology, oncology Brown Med. Sch. and Roger Williams Med. Ctr., Providence, 1985—91; prof. and chmn., dept. medicine Roger Williams Med. Ctr. and Boston U. Sch. Medicine, Providence, 1991—. Dir. divsn. med. oncology Brown U., 1988—; prof. medicine Boston U. Sch. Medicine, 1988—; bd. trustees Roger Williams Med. Ctr., 2002—04. Author: Cancer of the Lung, 2002; contbr. more than 75 sci. papers to profl. jours., chapters to books, articles to over 60 profl. jours. Critical care, med. appraisal, med. audit, med. rec. Roger Williams Hosp., 1979—80, infection control, nutritional support, patient care/greivence, 1979—80, intern selection, clin. competence com., 1985—, chmn. cancer com., 1986—99, chmn. credentials com., 1987—91, transfusion com., 1988—92, physician's adv. com., 1989—, exec. com., 1991—, strategic planning com., 1992—, joint conf. com., 1992—, quality improvement steering coun., 1992—, oncology task force, 1995—, pres., med. assoc., 1996—, bd. trustees, 2002—, Univ. Med. Group, 1999—, exec. com. bd., 2001—; chmn. admissions com. for an integrated med. residency program Brown U., 1990—; com. sectional chiefs Boston U., 1997—. Nominee Ernesta Nuti Internat. prize for Cancer Rsch., Rome, 1992; named to Mu Eplison Delta Hon. Soc., Cornell U., 1971, Watts Scholarship Soc., Cornell Univ., 1971; recipient Dean Charles L. Brown award, Univ. Medicine and Dentistry NJ, 1976, Tchr. of Yr. award, Brown U. Sch. Medicine, 1992, Eminent Scientist award, Internat. Rsch. Promotion Coun., Physician's Recognition award with commendation, AMA, 2005; Arts and Sci. Dean's scholar, Cornell U., 1969, over 30 rsch. grants from various colls. and univs. Fellow: ACP (exec. coun. RI chpt. 1992—); mem.: AMA (Physicians Recognition award 2005—), AAAS, Cancer Trials Support Unit, Assn. Acad. Med. Ctr., Clin. Oncology Group, Am. Soc. Hematology, Assn. Am. Med. Coll., Leukemia Soc. Am. (bd. dirs. 1989—), Am. Bd. Internal Medicine (recertification com. 1993—), Am. Soc. Cancer Rsch. (chmn. carcinogeneses sect. 1987—, state legis. com. 1992—), Am. Soc. Clin. Oncology (chmn. lung cancer sect. 1987—), Am. Cancer Soc. (chmn. nominating com. 1992, instl. rsch. grant rev. study sect. 1992—), Am. Fedn. for Clin. Rsch. (chmn. hematology sect. 1993—), Internat. Soc. Free Radical Rsch., Sigma Xi. Avocations: painting, opera, running, reading. Office: Roger Williams Med Ctr Dept Medicine 825 Chalkstone Ave Providence RI 02908 Office Phone: 401-456-2070.

WEITHORN, STANLEY STEPHEN, lawyer; b. NYC, Aug. 28, 1924; s. Louis W. and Florence O. (Mandel) W.; m. Corinne J. Breslow, Dec. 26, 1949 (dec. 1987); children: Lois Ann, Michael J.; m. Muriel Casper, Sept. 9, 1990; 1 stepchild, Corey Casper. BSBA, Hofstra U., 1947; JD, NYU Law Sch., 1954, LLM in Taxation, 1956. Bar: N.Y. 1955. Assoc. firm Olwine, Connelly, Chase O'Donnell & Weyher, NYC, 1956—61; ptnr. firm Lewis, McDonald & Varian, NYC, 1961—62; pvt. practice NYC, 1962—63, 1967—68; ptnr. firm Wormser, Koch, Keily & Alessandroni, NYC, 1963—66; sr. ptnr. firm Baer, Marks & Upham (successor to Upham, Meeker & Weithorn), NYC, 1968—88, Epstein, Becker & Green, NYC, 1988—89; sr. counsel Reid & Priest, NYC, 1989—94, Morrison & Foerster, Palo Alto, Calif., 1994—96, Fennemore Craig, Phoenix, 1996—2000, Roberts & Holland, NYC & Scottsdale, 1996—. Spl. prof. law Hofstra U., 1974-78; adj. prof. law U. Miami, Fla., 1975-79; mem. adv. com. U. Miami Law Ctr. Ann. Inst. Estate Planning, 1974-80; coordinator fed. budget and tax policy course nat. policy studies program New Sch. Social Rsch., N.Y.C., 1975; mem. fund raising mgmt. adv. com. Grad. Sch. Mgmt. and Urban professions, New Sch. for Social Rsch., N.Y.C., 1977-84; mem. adv. com. N.Y. U. Inst. on Fed. Taxation, 1980-90; program chmn. Practicing Law Inst. confs., N.Y.C., 1962-78, N.Y. Law Jour. confs., 1980, NYU Inst. on Fed. Taxation confs., 1955-88; tax cons. Pres's Coun. on Environ. Quality, 1970; lectr. fed. taxation to univ. insts., non-profit org. confs., profl. bus. meetings. Author: Penalty Taxes on Accumulated Earnings and Personal Holding Companies, 1963, Tax Techniques for Foundations and Other Exempt Organizations, 7 vols, 1964, The Accumulated Earnings Tax, 1966; Contbg. editor, mem. adv. bd.: Tax Mgmt, 1959-68; feature columnist: Nat. Law Jour, 1978-79; Contbr. articles to profl. jours. Co-chmn. Port Washington-Manhasset (N.Y.) unit New Dem. Coalition, 1968-69; tax adviser nat. fin. com. McGovern for Pres., 1971-72, mem. N.Y. fin. com., 1971-72; bd. dirs., exec. com. Equal Employment Coun. Inc., N.Y.C., 1968-71; bd. dirs., sec. New Priorities Edn. Fund, 1969-70; bd. dirs., exec. com., sec., co-chmn., pres. Fund for New Priorities in Am., 1969-2004; bd. dirs., treas. Cow Bay Manpower Devel. Corp., Port Washington, 1969-71; bd. dirs., chmn. exec. com., pres. L.I. Pub. Affairs Coun., 1973-78; bd. dirs., pres. Mental Health Assn. Nassau County, N.Y., 1980-85, Herman and Amelia Ehrmann Found., 1977-95; pres. Weithorn and Ehrmann Families Found., 1995—, Am. Soc. Technion, 1992-2000, Social Venture Ptnrs. Ariz., 2003—; bd. dirs. Jewish Family and Children's Svcs., San Francisco; mem. legacy com. United Cerebral Palsy, N.Y.C., 1975-90; bd. dirs. Cmty. Action for Legal Svcs., 1976-78, Frederick and Amelia Schimper Found., 1977-94, Florence Weithorn Warner Found., N.Y.C., 1967-72, N.Y. Fedn. Reform Synagogues, 1973-78, Nat. Coalition for Children's Justice, 1980-90, Am. Inst. for Philanthropic Studies, L.A. and N.Y.C., 1981-92, Nat. Health Coun., 1984-92, Laurent and Alberta Gerschel Found., 1986-96, Interns for Peace, Am.-Israeli Civil Liberties Coalition, 1987-95, Inst. Am. Values, 1987-91; Fund for Human Dignity, 1989-90, Found. Fund, 1986-92, L.I. Cmty. Found., 1989-93, Cancer Prevention Rsch. Inst., 1989-96, Green Seal, 1989-92, New Israel Fund, 1996-2002, Albert L. Schultz Jewish Cmty. Ctr., 1996-2000, Nat. Ctr. Law & Social Justice, 1996-, Am. Jewish World Svc., 2001-, Internat. Edn. and Rsch. Network, 2002-, Heller Family Found., 1994-, Rouhana Family Found., 1990-, Scottsdale Cultural Coun., 2000-, Ariz. State U. Found., 1996-2004, Am. Com. for Weizmann Inst. Sci., 2000-, Piper Fund Proteus Found, 2000-; mem. Emergency Task Force on Juvenile Delinquency Prevention, 1976-79; mem. adv. panel N.Y. chpt. Am. Jewish Com., 1978-80; mem. com. on deferred giving Fedn. Jewish Philanthropies N.Y., 1978-86; mem. legal and tax panel United Jewish Appeal/Fedn. Jewish Philanthropies, N.Y., 1986-91; nat. chair Planned Giving Program, Am. Assocs. Ben-Gurion U. Negev, 1992-2000, mem. exec. com. N.W. region; mem. com. tax policy Nat. Assembly Vol. Health, Social Welfare Orgns. Inc., N.Y.C., 1961-73; mem. com. bequests and legacies Nat. Jewish Hosp., Denver, 1965-78; mem. estate planning com. ARC of Greater N.Y., 1970-98; mem. leadership coun. United Jewish Appeal, N.Y.C., 1966-70; mem. adv. com., project on ch., state and taxation NCCJ, 1980-85; mem. legacy adv. coun. Am. Jewish Congress, N.Y.C., 1968-72; mem. Internat. Coun. on Environ. Law, 1982-92; mem. Pres.'s adv. com. ACLU Found., 1983-2000; chmn. Uptown Tax Discussion Group, 1957-69, Exempt Orgns. Discussion Group, 1973-79, Fresh Meadows Civic Assn., 1961-63; mem. legal activities policy bd. Tax Analysts, 1974—. Served with AUS, 1943-46, ETO. Recipient Allard K. Lowenstein Meml. award Am. Jewish Congress, 1988; honoree Mental Health Assn. Nassau County, N.Y., 1991, Ariz. Citizen Action, 2000, Am. Com. for Weizmann Inst. Sci., 2002, Nat. Gay and Lesbian Task Force, 2003 Fellow Am. Coll. Tax Counsel, Am. Coll. Trust and Estate Counsel; mem. ABA (chmn. subcom. exempt orgns. 1965-69, subcom. charitable contbns. 1971-75), N.Y. State Bar Assn. (exec. com. 1967-69), Assn. of Bar of City of N.Y., Internat. Acad. Estate and Trust Law (exec. coun. 1974-78, 90-96), Univ. Club, Knickerbocker Yacht Club (bd. dirs. 1986-88). Jewish (trustee synagogue l970-74). Home (Winter): 10040 E Happy Valley Rd Lot 435 Scottsdale AZ 85255 Office: Roberts & Holland LLP 825 8th Ave 37th Fl New York NY 10019 also: 8655 E Via de Ventura G200 Scottsdale AZ 85258 Home (Summer): 150 Central Park S Apt 1610 New York NY 10019 Personal E-mail: sweithorn@rhtax.com. *No one truly is an altruist. We all attempt to do what most fulfills us. For some this motivates apparently selfish behavior; for others it is quite the opposite. However, why we act as we do affects only the actor whereas what we do affects society. Look to the deed, not to the doer; good deeds make for a better world.*

WEITZ, BRETT, broadcast executive; b. Feb. 16, 1974; s. Barry Weitz. Prodn. asst. for TV movies; mem. mailroom staff United Talent Agy.; dir. drama devel. Columbia TriStar TV, 2001; with drama dept. 20th Century Fox TV; v.p. creative affairs Fox 21, LA, 2004—. Achievements include working on the TV show North Shore. Office: Fox 21 10201 W Pico Blvd Bldg 88 Los Angeles CA 90035 *

WEITZ, HARVEY, lawyer, educator; b. Bklyn., Aug. 16, 1933; AB, Bklyn. Coll.; JD, Bklyn. Law Sch. Bar: N.Y. 1954, U.S. Dist. Ct. (ea. and so. dists.) N.Y. 1956. Diplomate Am. Bd. Profl. Liability Attys. Ptnr. Weitz & Assoc., P.C. (formerly known as Schneider, Kleinick, Weitz, Damashek & Shoot), NYC, 1966—; dean N.Y. State Trial Lawyers Inst.; adj. prof. Bklyn. Law Sch.; spl. master Supreme Ct., 1980-84. Author: A Compendium of the Art of Summation, Weitz on Automobile Litigation: The No-Fault Handbook, Vols. I & II; editor in chief Trial Lawyers Quar., 1972-80. Served with U.S. Army. Fellow Internat. Acad. Trial Lawyers, Internat. Soc. Barristers, Roscoe Pound Found.; mem. N.Y. State Trial Lawyers Assn. (bd. dirs.), Trial Lawyers for Pub. Justice (bd. dirs.), Am. Bd. Trial Advocates (nat. bd. mem.), ATLA (bd. govs. 1981-93, nat. sec. 1986-87), N.Y. State Trial Lawyers Assn. (pres. 1980-82), Bklyn. Law Sch. Alumni Assn. (bd. dirs.), Inner Circle of Advocates, Nat. Forensic Ctr. (mem. adv. panel), N.Y. State Bar (lectr.), Nat. Practice Inst. (lectr.), Assn. of the Bar, N.Y. County Lawyers Assn. (lectr.), N.Y.C. Trial Lawyers Assn. Office: Weitz & Assoc PC 233 Broadway Fl 5 New York NY 10279 Office Phone: 212-553-9300. Business E-Mail: hweitz@weitzlaw.com.

WEITZ, HOWARD HY, cardiologist, educator; b. Phila., July 6, 1952; s. Thelma and Arnold Weitz; m. Barbara Malett, May 3, 1987; children: Aaron Richard, Benjamin Isaac, Hannah Sarah. BS, Muhlenberg Coll., Pa., 1974, DS (hon.), 2003; MD, Jefferson Med. Coll., Phila., 1978. Diplomate Am. Bd. Internal Medicine, 1981, cert. Cardiovascular Diseases Am. Bd. Internal Medicine, 1985. Dir. divsn. cardiology Jefferson Med. Coll., Phila., 1995—98, prof. medicine, 2005—, sr. vice-chmn., dept. of medicine, 2005—; co-dir. Jefferson Heart Inst., Phila., 1998—; commr. Fed. Medicaid Commn., Washington, 2005—06. Author: Medical Management of the Surgical Patient, 1992 (NBI Healthcare Found. Humanism in Medicine Faculty award, 1998), 2d edit., 1998, Peripheral Vascular Disorders, 2004. Fellow: Am. Coll. of Cardiology, ACP. Office: Jefferson Heart Inst 925 Chestnut St Philadelphia PA 19027 Office Phone: 215-955-4194. Business E-Mail: howard.weitz@jefferson.edu.

WEITZ, JOHN JEROME, JR., city planner; b. Mobile, Ala., Aug. 19, 1961; s. John J. and Marcheta (Knight) W.; m. Patricia L. Weitz, Oct. 20, 1990 (div.); 1 child, John Jerome III. AA, Oxford Coll. of Emory Univ., 1981; BA, Emory U., Atlanta, 1983; M City Planning, Ga. Inst. Tech., Atlanta, 1985; D Philosophy Urban Studies, Portland State U., Oreg., 1998. Cert. planner. Planner technician City of Roswell, Ga., 1985-87; planner II Fulton County Dept. Planning and Econ. Devel., Atlanta, 1987-88; zoning adminstr. Albany-Dougherty Planning Commn., Albany, Ga., 1988-89; sr. planner Ga. Mountains Regional Devel. Ctr., Gainesville, 1989-94; urban growth mgmt. specialist State of Oreg., Salem, 1994-97; cons. Benkendorf Assocs., Portland, 1994-96; planning divsn. mgr. Cowlitz Coun, Kelso, Wash., 1997-99; planning dir. City of Roswell, 1999-2000; pres. Jerry Weitz & Assocs., Inc., Alpharetta, 2001—; adj. asst. prof. pub. adminstrn. Kennesaw (Ga.) State U., 2001; asst. prof. pub. adminstrn. Troy U., Atlanta, 2001—04. Exec. com. Ga. Planning Assn., Atlanta, 1993—94, v.p. legislative affairs, 2000—03, pres. -elect, 2002—03, pres., 2003—05; adj. faculty city and regional planning program Ga. Inst. of Tech., 2003—04. Author: Sprawl Busting: State Programs to Guide Growth, 1999, Jobs-Housing Balance, 2003; co-author: Smart Growth Audits, 2002. Coun. mem. City of Gillsville, Ga., 1994; mem. design rev. bd. City of Beaverton, Oreg., 1997-99. Recipient Outstanding Achievement award Alpharetta Jaycees, 1986. Mem. Am. Planning Assn., Urban Affairs Assn., Internat. City/County Mgmt. Assn., Assn. Collegiate Schs. Planning, Ga. Planning Assn. (disting. profl. achievement in planning award 2000), ASPA, Am. Inst. for Cert. Planners. Avocations: fishing, camping, golf. Home: 1225 Rucker Rd Alpharetta GA 30004 Personal E-mail: jweitz@bellsouth.net.

WEITZ, PERRY, lawyer; b. Bklyn., Aug. 5, 1959; BA, George Washington U., 1981; JD, Hofstra U., 1983. Bar: N.Y. 1985, U.S. Dist. Ct., Ea. and So. Dist. N.Y. 1986. Founding mem. Weitz & Luxenberg, New York, NY, 1986—. Faculty mem. Nat. Inst. for Trial Advocacy; liaison coun. N.Y. State Ct., Breast Implant Litig. Com., Ea. and So. Dist. Ct. on Asbestos Litig. Mem. bd. trustees North Shore U. Hosp.; mem. Dean's Counsel Hofstra U. Law Sch.; mem. exec. com. men's divsn. Children's Med. Fund, Schneider Children's Hosp. Named one of The 45 Under 45, The Am. Lawyer, 2003. Mem.: Jewish Lawyers Guild (bd. govs.), Trial Lawyers Pub. Justice, N.Y. State Trial Lawyers Assn., Assn. Trial Lawyers of Am., N.Y. County Lawyers Assn. (chairperson). Office: Weitz & Luxenberg 180 Maiden Lane New York NY 10038 Office Phone: 212-558-5500. *

WEITZEL, AMY RAGAN, not-for-profit developer; b. Houston, Mar. 31, 1963; d. Dee and Sally Ragan. BA in Modern European Studies, Vanderbilt U., Nashville, 1985. Dir. devel. Sheltering Arms, Houston, 1992—94, Casa de Esperanza, Houston, 2000—02, End Hunger Network, Houston, 2004—; asst. dir. devel. Kinkaid Sch., Houston, 1994—95; v.p. devel. Family Svcs. Greater Houston, 1995—2000. Pres. Eventful Times, Inc., Houston, 2000—07. Nominating com. Assn. Jr. Leagues Internat., NYC, 2003—05; leadership roles Jr. League Houston, 1988—2003; bd. mem. Vanderbilt U. Nat. Alumni Assn., Nashville, 1998—2002. Mem.: Assn. Fundraising Profls. (assoc.). Office: End Hunger Network 2445 N Freeway Houston TX 77009 Office Fax: 713-532-6587. Business E-Mail: aweitzel@endhungernetwork.org.

WEITZEL, GINGER M., entrepreneur, critical care nurse; b. Richland, Wash., Dec. 28, 1952; d. Carl Benton and Margaret Allee White; m. Gregory L. Weitzel, Aug. 28, 1978; children: Skylar Benjamin, Spencer Cameron. AA, Pima CC, Tucson, 1976; student, U. Ariz., 1971—73, U. Denver, 1995—98. RN, cert. ACLS. Nat. sales support mgr. Valleyrab, Boulder, Colo., 1984—90; exec. sales mgr. 3M, St. Paul, 1990—96; sales mgr. Am. Telecare, St. Paul, 1998—99; nurse emergency dept. Exempla Health Care, Wheat Ridge, Colo., 2000—02; pvt. practice Arvada, Colo., 2002—. Nat. acct. mgr. Sims-Deltec, St. Paul, 1994—96. Mem.: Legal Nurse Cons., Emergency Nurses Assn. Democrat. Methodist. Avocations: gardening, walking, reading, politics. Home: 5975 Braun Way Arvada CO 80004 Office: Weitzel and Assoc 5975 Braun Way Arvada CO 80004

WEITZEL, JOHN PATTERSON, lawyer; b. Pitts., Aug. 24, 1923; s. Albert Philip and Elizabeth (Patterson) W.; m. Elisabeth Swan, Mar. 20, 1965; children: Mary Middleton, Paul Patterson. AB, Yale U., 1946; LL.B., Harvard U., 1949. Bar: Mass. 1949, U.S. Supreme Ct. 1960. Asso. Herrick, Smith, Donald, Farley & Ketchum (now Herrick & Smith), Boston, 1949-53, ptnr., 1961-86, Palmer & Dodge, Boston, 1986-93, of counsel, 1993—2005; spl. asst. to asst. sec. treasury, 1953-55; asst. to under sec. treas, 1955-56; asst. gen. counsel Treasury Dept., 1956-59, dep. to sec. treasury, 1959-60, asst. sec. treasury, 1960-61; U.S. exec. dir. World Bank, 1960-61; of counsel Edwards, Angell, Palmer & Dodge, 2005—. Mem. planning bd. NSC, 1959-61; cons. to sec. def., 1973. Mem. Mass. Council Arts and Humanities, 1966-71; overseer, dir. sec. Boys and Girls Clubs, Boston; mem. corp. Mass. Gen. Hosp., Boston Mus. Sci.; trustee Roxbury Latin Sch. Served with USAAF, 1943-45. Mem. Am., Boston bar assns., Am. Law Inst. Clubs: Harvard (Boston), Union Boat (Boston). Home: 45 Devon Rd Chestnut Hill MA 02467-1851 Office: Edwards Angell Palmer & Dodge 111 Huntington Ave Boston MA 02199-7613

WEITZEL, JOHN QUINN, bishop; b. Chgo., May 10, 1928; s. Carl Joseph and Patricia (Quinn) W. BA, Maryknoll Sem., NY, 1951, M of Religious Edn., 1953; PMD, Harvard U. Ordained priest Roman Cath. Ch., 1955. With ednl. devel. Cath. Fgn. Mission Soc. of Am., Maryknoll, 1955—63, nat. dir. vocations for Maryknoll, dir. devel. dept. and info. services, 1963—72, mem. gen. coun., 1972—78; asst. parish priest Cath. Ch., Western Samoa, 1979—81, pastor, vicar gen., 1981—86; consecrated bishop, 1986; bishop Diocese of Samoa-Pago Pago, 1986—. Roman Catholic. Office: Diocese Samoa-Pago Pago PO Box 596 Pago Pago AS 96799-3594 E-mail: QUINN@samoatelco.com.

WEITZEL, MARK P., lawyer; b. 1954; AB with distinction, Stanford U., 1976; MBA, JD, UCLA, 1980. Bar: Calif. 1980, lic.: US Tax Ct., registered: Law Soc. of Eng. & Wales (fng. lawyer). Ptnr. Thelen Reid & Priest LLP, San Francisco, mem. partnership coun. Mem. UCLA Law Rev., 1979—80. Mem.: Order of Coif, Beta Gamma Sigma. Office: Thelen Reid & Priest LLP 101 Second St Ste 1800 San Francisco CA 94105-3601 Office Phone: 415-369-7007. Office Fax: 415-371-1211. Business E-Mail: mweitzel@thelenreid.com.

WEITZEL, WILLIAM CONRAD, JR., lawyer; b. Washington, Feb. 6, 1935; s. William Conrad and Pauline Lillian (Keeton) W.; m. Loretta LeVeck, Mar. 10, 1978; children: William Conrad III, Richard S., Sarah L., Andrew K. AB, Harvard U., 1956, LLB, 1959; postgrad., MIT, 1974. Bar: D.C. 1961. Law clk., chief judge U.S. Cts. Md., Balt., 1959-60; asst. U.S. atty., Washington, 1961-66; atty. Texaco, Inc., White Plains, N.Y., 1966-73, assoc. gen. counsel, 1973-76, gen. counsel, 1977-82, v.p., gen. counsel, 1982-84, sr. v.p., gen. counsel, 1984-90; pres. Texaco Philanthropic Found., Inc., 1980-90; ptnr. Cummings & Lockwood, Stamford, Conn., 1991—, chmn. bus. clients dept., 1991-94. Trustee Ctr. Am. Internat. Law Trustee Southwestern Legal Found., Forman Sch., 1998-2004. With USN, 1960-61. Mem. ABA, Am. Law Inst., Conn. Bar Assn., D.C. Bar Assn., Assn. Gen. Counsel (v.p., bd. dirs. 1988-90), Westchester-Fairfield Corp. Counsel Assn. (pres. 1981, chmn., chief legal officers com. 1982-90), Am. Petroleum Inst. (gen. com. on law, chmn. 1983-84), Harvard Club (dir. Harvard Alumni Assn. for Conn. 1990-93, pres. Fairfield County club 1987—2003). Republican. Episcopalian. Office: Cummings & Lockwood 6 Landmark Sq Stamford CT 06901

WEITZEL, WILLIAM DAVID, psychiatrist; b. Detroit, Sept. 16, 1942; s. William Howard and Mary Ann (Buscanics) Weitzel; m. Joan Carol Heiser, June 8, 1968; children: Erica Marie, Jennifer Joan, Sarah Elizabeth. BS cum laude, Xavier U., 1964; MD, St. Louis U., 1968; postgrad. alcohol studies, Rutgers U., 1970; tng. family therapy, The Washington Sch. Psychiatry, 1971—72. Diplomate Am. Bd. Psychiatry and Neurology, Am. Bd. Forensic Psychiatry. Intern William Beaumont Gen. Hosp., El Paso, Tex., 1968—69; psychiat. resident Walter Reed Gen. Hosp., 1969—72; chief dept. psychiatry and neurology Moncrief Army Hosp., Columbia, SC, 1972—74; asst. prof. psychiatry and dir. Hosp. Inpatient Psychiatry Svc. Coll. Medicine, U. Ky., Lexington, 1974—78, assoc. prof. psychiatry, 1979, assoc. clin. prof. psychiatry, 1980—88, clin. prof. psychiatry, 1988—. Lectr. Coll. Law, 1977—82; supervising and cons. psychiatrist William S. Hall Psychiat. Inst., Columbia, 1973—74; psychiat. cons. Commn. on Ministry Episcopal Diocese of Lexington, 1975—87, Clin. Rsch. Ctr. Project, Ky. Bur. Health Svcs., Homestead Nursing Ctr., Lexington, 1978—88. Contbr. numerous articles to profl. jours. Mem. Ky. Gov.'s Task Force on Welfare Reform, 1978—79, Ky. Commn. on Corrections and Cmty. Svc., 1992—96. Maj. MC AUS, 1968—74. Fellow: AAAS, Am. Psychiat. Assn. (disting. life) (pres. Ky. dist. br. 1979—80, co-author task force report on involuntary outpatient commitment 1987), Am. Coll. Psychiatrists; mem.: Am. Acad. Psychiatry and the Law, Group for Advancement of Psychiatry. Office: Ste 128 1725 Harrodsburg Rd Lexington KY 40504-3628 Home Phone: 859-269-5744; Office Phone: 859-277-5419. Personal E-mail: wweitzel@pol.net.

WEITZMAN, ARTHUR JOSHUA, language educator; b. Newark, Sept. 13, 1933; s. Louis I. and Cecele W.; m. Catherine Ezell, Aug. 8, 1982; children: Peter A., Anne E. BA, U. Chgo., 1956, MA, 1957; PhD, NYU, 1964. Instr. English, Bklyn. Coll., 1960-63; asst. prof. Temple U., Phila., 1963-69; assoc. prof. Northeastern U., Boston, 1969-72, prof., 1972—2002, prof. emeritus, 2002—; mem. faculty Brookline Adult and Cmty. Edn., Mass., 2003—, Cambridge Ctr. Adult Edn., Mass., 2003—; lectr. Sarasota Inst. of Lifetime Learning, 2006—. Editor: Letters Writ by a Turkish Spy (G.P. Marana), 1970; founder, co-editor: The Scriblerian, 1968—2004; co-editor: Milton and the Romantics, 1980-81; contbr.: revs. and articles to profl. jours. and newspapers including Los Angeles Times, Boston Globe, Miami Herald NEH fellow, 1972-73, Mellon fellow, 1976; Rsch. grantee Temple U., Northeastern U. Mem.: MLA, Na. Assn. Scholars, Am. Soc. 18th Century Studies. Jewish. Home: 4 Bellis Ct Cambridge MA 02140-3240 Personal E-mail: ajwajwajw@hotmail.com.

WEITZMAN, HOWARD L., lawyer, former film company executive; b. LA, Sept. 21, 1939; BS, U. So. Calif., 1962, JD, 1965. Bar: Calif. 1966, U.S. Dist. Ct. (ctrl., ea. and so. dists.) Calif., U.S. Ct. Appeals (9th cir.), U.S. Supreme Ct. 1976, U.S. Ct. Appeals (6th cir.) 1983. Pvt. practice, 1965—86; mng. ptnr. Wyman Bautzer LLP, 1986—91; ptnr., chmn. exec. com. Katten Muchin Zavis & Weitzman, LA, 1991—2001; exec. v.p. corp. ops. Universal Studios (formerly MCA), 1995—98; ptnr. Proskauer Rose LLP, LA, 2001—04, Kinsella Weitzman Iser Kump & Aldisert LLP, Santa Monica, Calif., 2005—. Lectr. U. So. Calif., 1973-83. Recipient Jerry Gielser Memorial award, 1979, 1984. Mem. ABA, L.A. County Bar Assn., Beverly Hill Bar Assn., Founders Cir. of the Fulfillment Fund Office: Kinsella Weitzman Iser Kump & Aldisert LLP 808 Wilshire Blvd 3rd Fl Santa Monica CA 90401 E-mail: hweitzman@kwikalaw.com.

WEITZMAN, MARC HERSCHEL, lawyer; b. Milw., Feb. 1, 1950; s. J. Leonard and Esther (Charne) W.; m. Natalyn Ann Gipstein, Oct. 5, 1980; children: Benjamin, Marissa, Laura, Emily. BA, U. Calif., Santa Barbara, 1972; JD, Western State U., Fullerton, Calif., 1976. Bar: Calif. 1978, U.S. Dist. Ct. (cen. dist.) Calif. 1979, U.S. Ct. Appeals (9th cir.) 1981, U.S. Supreme Ct. 1987. Atty. State Compensation Ins. Fund, Long Beach, Calif., 1979-82, State Farm Ins. Co., Costa Mesa, 1982—85; assoc. Grancell, Grancell & Marshall, Santa Ana, 1985—88; ptnr. Hertz & Weitzman, Huntington Beach, 1988—89; pvt. practice Marc H. Weitzman, LLP, Seal Beach, 1989—2006; ptnr. Weitzman & Estes, Seal Beach, 2006—. Judge pro tem State of Calif. Divsn. Indsl. Rels.-Divsn. Indsl. Accidents, Norwalk, 1986—, Long Beach, 1984—, Santa Ana, 1995—; cert. workers' compensation specialist Calif. Bd. Legal Specialization-State Bar Calif., 1988—; arbitrator State of Calif. Divsns. Indsl. Rels. and Indsl. Accident, 1991; asst. scoutmaster troop 319, Boy Scouts Am.; past mem. membership chmn. Pacifica Dist., Orange County Coun.; mem. Huntington Beach Cmty. Emer. Response Team. Mem. L.A. County Bar Assn., Orange County Bar Assn., Orange County Workers' Compensation Def. Assn., So. Calif. Rehab. Exch., Long Beach Bar Assn. Office: 3010 Old Ranch Pkwy Ste 200 Seal Beach CA 90740-2750

WEITZNER, HAROLD, mathematics professor; b. Boston, May 19, 1933; s. Morris and Alice Savitz W.; m. Lois S. Friedlander, June 12, 1962; children: Daniel J., Henry D. AB, U. Calif., Berkeley, 1954; AM, Harvard U., 1955, PhD, 1958. Assoc. rsch. scientist Courant Inst. NYU, NYC, 1959-60, rsch. scientist, 1960-62, asst. prof., 1962-65, assoc. prof., 1965-69, prof., 1969—; assoc. dir. Magneto-Fluids div. Courant Inst. NYU, NYC, 1988—, dir., 1973-79, 84-88; chmn. Math. Dept. Courant Inst. NYU, NYC, 1989-91. Cons. Oak Ridge Nat. Labs., Oak Ridge, Tenn., 1980—, mem. fusion energy divsn. adv. com., 2005-; mem. magnetic fusion adv. com. U.S. Dept. Energy, 1986-89, fusion energy adv. com., 1991-93; mem. adv. com. Gen. Atomics Corp., 1994-96. Contbr. articles to sci. jours. Fellow Am. Phys. Soc.; mem. Univ. Fusion Assn. (exec. com. 1993-96). Home: 10 Cedar Ave Larchmont NY 10538-4121 Office: NYU Courant Inst 251 Mercer St New York NY 10012-1110 Business E-Mail: weitzner@cims.nyu.edu.

WEITZNER, RONALD PHILIP, special education educator; b. Clev., Oct. 1, 1941; s. Herman Michael and Irene Weitzner; m. Carolyn; children: Rochelle Dayan, Ross David, Robert Louis. BS in Edn., Ohio State U., Columbus, 1965; MEd, Xavier U., Cin., 1969; cert. edn. specialist, John Carroll U., Cleve., 1975. Permanent tchg. Ohio State Bd. Edn., 1975, permanent supr. Ohio State Bd. Edn., 1975, permanent adminstr. Ohio State Bd. Edn., 1977. Tchr. SouthWestern City Sch., Grove City, Ohio, 1965—69; tchr., supr., asst. prin. to prin. Bellefaire Sch., Cleve. Heights, U. Bd. Edn., University Heights, Ohio, 1969—99; cons. Supplemental Sch. Dir., Cleve., 1999—2004; asst. prof. Cleve. State U., 2004—. Reading, learning specialist Ednl. Clinic, Columbus, Ohio, 1966—69; founder, dir. Weitzner Reading Clinic, Cleve., 1969—; cons., Cleve., 1972—; dir. reading svcs. Avvy Katz Found., Cleve., 1995—97; presentor in field. Reviewer: Introduction to Special Education, consultant: movie A Class of Kids. Pres. Beachwood Fraternal Order of Police Assoc., Ohio, 1990—96; dir. youth svcs. Suburban Temple, Beachwood, 1969—85, prin., dir. religious edn. Mandel Religious Sch., 1999—2004; bd. dirs. Temple Israel Ner Tamid, Mayfield Heights, Ohio, 1990—92. Recipient Pres. of Bd. Achievement award, Bellefaire/Jewish Children's Bur., 1969—89, 30 Years of Dedicated Svc. to Children, Cleve. Heights, U. Heights Bd. Edn. Mem.: Nat. Assn. Temple Educators (assoc.), Coun. Exceptional Children (assoc.), Harley Owner's Group (assoc.), Lake County Yacht Club (assoc.). Avocations: motorcycling, boating, auto restoration, fishing. Office: Cleve State Univ 2121 Euclid Ave RT1319 Cleveland OH 44115-2214 Home Phone: 216-409-4955; Office Phone: 216-523-7244. Office Fax: 216-687-5379. Personal E-mail: ronweitzner@adelphia.net. Business E-Mail: r.weitzner@csuohio.edu.

WEITZNER, STEVE, publishing executive; BA, York Coll., CUNY; MA, SUNY, Stony Brook. With Hearst Bus. Communications, CMP Tech. (formerly CMP Media, LLC), Manhasset, NY, 1984—, various positions, editor to pres., electronics group, exec. v.p., COO, 2002—05, pres., CEO, 2005—. Office: CMP Tech 600 Community Drive Manhasset NY 11030 Office Phone: 516-562-5000. *

WEIXELMAN, JOSEPH OWEN, history professor; b. Manhattan, Kans., Dec. 11, 1957; s. Donald Bernard and Diane Gayle Weixelman; m. Jessica Ryan Burke, Jan. 1, 1979 (div. Aug. 19, 1983); 1 child, Shawn Thomas; m. Cathy Fisher, Oct. 8, 1983 (div. July 17, 1989); children: Christopher George, James Husayn; m. Chris Tee Kuhlmann, Sept. 2, 1990; 1 child, Kai Anthony. BA in Anthropology, U. Colo., 1981; MA in History, Mont. State U., 1992; PhD in History, U. N.Mex, 2004. Tchr. social studies Sept. Sch., Boulder, Colo., 1982—88; tchr. social studies and english Western Wyo. H.S., Jackson, Wyo., 1989—90; tchr. social studies Durango (Colo.) H.S., 1992—96; guest lectr. Ea. Mich. U., Ypsilanti, 2000—01; instr. U. N.Mex, Albuquerque, 2002—07; asst. prof. history Wane State Coll., Nebr., 2007—; assoc. prof. Wayne State Coll., Nebr., 2007—. Interpretive ranger Mesa Verde (Colo.) Nat. Pk., 1993—, Yellowstone (Wyo.) Nat. Pk., 1999—2000, cultural resource asst., 1998—98; interpretive ranger Petroglyph Nat. Monument, Albuquerque, 1997. John F. Kennedy History fellowship, U. N.Mex., 2000, Senator Joseph M. Montoya History fellowship, 2001. Mem.: Colo. Hist. Soc., Nat. Coun. Pub. History, Am. Hist. Assn., We. History Assn. Bahá'Í. Avocations: travel, photography, hiking, backpacking. Home: 1002 W 2nd Ave Wayne NE 68787 Office: Dept History Politics Geography Wayne State Coll Connell Hall Rm 209 Wayne NE 68787 Home Phone: 402-833-5202; Office Phone: 402-375-7135. Personal E-mail: jweix@aol.com. Business E-Mail: jowixe1@wsc.edu.

WEIXLMANN, JOSEPH NORMAN, JR., language educator, academic administrator; b. Buffalo, Dec. 16, 1946; s. Joseph Norman and Mary C. (Degenhart) W.; m. Sharron Pollack, Mar. 14, 1982; children: Seth Jacob, Adira Jenna, Benjamin Ari. AB, Canisius Coll., 1968; MA, Kans. State U., 1970, PhD, 1973. Instr. U. Okla., Norman, 1973-74; asst. prof. Tex. Tech U., Lubbock, 1974-76; from asst. prof. to prof. Ind. State U., Terre Haute, 1976—2001, assoc. dean, 1987-92, acting dean, 1992-94, dean, 1994—2001; prof. St. Louis U., 2001—, dean, 2001—02, provost, 2002—. Author: John Barth, 1976, American Short-Fiction Criticism, 1982; co-editor: Black American Prose Theory, 1984, Belief vs. Theory in Black American Literary Criticism, 1986, Black Feminist Criticism, 1988, Studies in Black Am. Lit. Ann., 1984-88; editor African Am. Rev. jour., 1976-2004; contbg. editor High Plains Lit. Rev., 1987-2002; adv. editor Langston Hughes Rev., 1982—. Fellow NDEA, 1970-72, NEH, 1980; Nat. Endowment for Arts grantee, 1988-95; Disting. Editor award, Conf. Editors of Learned Jours., 2005. Mem. Coll. Lang. Assn., Langston Hughes Soc., Zora Neale Hurston Soc. Office: Saint Louis U DuBourg Hall #106 Saint Louis MO 63103 Home: 6344 Wydown Blvd Saint Louis MO 63105-2213 Home Phone: 314-721-8814; Office Phone: 314-977-3718. Business E-Mail: weixlmj@slu.edu.

WEIZMANN, HOWARD CHARLES, federal official; b. Akron, Ohio, June 12, 1948; s. Soloman and Ida Doris (Berkel) Bernson; m. Jane Kathleen Tice, Dec. 9, 1970; children: Brooke Suzanne, Haley Kathleen. AB Summa cum laude, Ohio U., 1970; MA, U. Mich., 1971, postgrad., 1973; JD, Georgetown Law Ctr., 1977. Bar: Pa. Assoc. atty Cohen, Shapiro et al., Phila., 1977-78, Dankner, Biddle & Reath LLP, Phila., 1978-81; sr. tax atty. Sun Co. Inc., Radnor, Pa., 1981-84, mgr., benefits planning & design, 1984-88; exec. dir. Assn. Pvt. Pension and Welfare Plans, Washington; v.p. pension & health benefits Aetna Life Insurance; mng. cons. Watson Wyatt Worldwide, Washington, 1994—2000; v.p. human resources Digex, Inc., 2000—01, sr. v.p. human resources, 2001—02, sr. v.p. human resources & comm., 2002—05; pres. Pvt. Sector Coun. (PSC), 2005—07; dep. dir. US Office Pers. Mgmt., Washington, 2007—. Contbr. articles to profl. jours. Tchr. Temple Beth Shalom, Annapolis, Md., 1989-91. Columbia Downing Knight Found. scholar, 1967-70; Denforth Found. Grad. fellow, 1970-73. Mem. City Club Washington; co-author: Rewards and Business Strategy: People, Pay, and Performance Democrat. Jewish. Avocations: tennis, biking, reading. Office: US Office Personnel Management 1900 E St Washington DC 20415 *

WEK, ALEK, model; b. Wau, Sudan, 1977; Attended, London Coll. of Fashion. Model Models One agy., London, Ford Agy., Paris, 1996, D Mgmt. Grp., Milan, IMG Models, NYC. Panel mem. Internat. Black Caucus Fgn. Affairs; mem. adv. bd. US Com. for Refugees; designer Wek1933 handbags, 2001—. Actor: (films) Four Feathers, 2002; author: Alek: From Sudanese Refugee to International Supermodel, 2007. Involved with Bracelet of Life Campaign, Doctors Without Borders, NYC Spl. Olympics, UNICEF, London Refugee Week, Design Industries Found. Fighting AIDS; spokesperson World Vision; founder W.E.K. (Working to Educate Kids). Named Best New Model, Venus de la Mode Fashion awards, 1997 MTV model of yr., Model of Decade, i-D mag.; named one of 50 Most Beautiful People, People mag., 1999, 50 Most Influential Faces in Fashion, i-D mag. Office: IMG Models 304 Park Ave S 12th Fl New York NY 10010 Office Phone: 212-253-8884. Office Fax: 212-253-8883. *

WELBORN, CARYL BARTELMAN, lawyer; b. Phila., Jan. 29, 1951; d. Raymond C. and Helen Ann Bartelman; m. Lucien Ruby, Apr. 11, 1987. AB, Stanford U., 1972; JD, UCLA, 1976. Bar: Ill. 1976, Calif. 1978. Assoc. Isham Lincoln & Beale, Chgo., 1976—78; from assoc. to ptnr. Morrison & Foerster, San Francisco and L.A., 1978—95; prin. Law Office of Caryl Welborn, 1995—2004; ptnr. DLA Piper US LLP, San Francisco, 2004—. Lectr. real property law. Named Best Lawyers in America. Mem. ABA (chmn. com. on partnerships, real property sect. 1989-93), Am. Coll. Real Estate Lawyers (bd. govs. 1994-2002, pres. 2001), Anglo-Am. Real Property Inst. Office: DLA Piper US LLP 153 Townsend St Ste 800 San Francisco CA 94105-2150 Business E-Mail: caryl.welborn@dlapiper.com.

WELBORN, REICH LEE, lawyer; b. Winston-Salem, NC, Nov. 1, 1945; s. Bishop M. and Hazel (Weatherman) W.; m. Martha Huffstetler, Aug. 27, 1966; children: Judson Allen, Spencer Brooks. AB, U. N.C., 1968, JD with honors, 1971. Bar: N.C. 1971. Assoc. Moore & Van Allen, PLLC and predecessor Powe Porter & Alphin, P.A., Durham, NC, 1971-76; ptnr. Moore & Van Allen and predecessor Powe Porter & Alphin, P.A., Durham, NC, 1976—. V.p. Family Counseling Svc., Durham, 1978-79; bd. trustees N.C. Sch. Sci. & Math., 2002—. Recipient Order of Long Leaf Pine award Gov. of N.C., 1981, Spl. Citation, 1983. Mem. ABA, N.C. Bar Assn., Durham County Bar Assn. (pres. 1989-90), N.C. State Bar, Croasdaile Club (pres. 1989-90), Sertoma (pres. Durham chpt. 1987-88), N.C. Jaycees (pres. 1981-82), Durham C. of C. (bd. dirs. 1992-93). Home: 4422 Myers Park Dr Durham NC 27705 Office: Moore & Van Allen PLLC PO Box 13706 Research Triangle Park NC 27709-4658 Office Phone: 919-286-8000. Business E-Mail: welbornr@mvalaw.com.

WELBURN, BRENDA LILIENTHAL, educational association administrator; Grad., Howard U.; postgraduate student, U. Pa. Social worker, Phila.; rsch. analyst US Ho. Reps. Select Com. on Assassinations; legis. asst. to Senator Paul Tsongas of Mass.; dir. govtl. affairs Nat. Assn. State Bds. Edn., Alexandria, Va., 1984—88, dep. exec. dir., 1988—93, exec. dir., 1993—. Presenter in field. Author: The American Tapestry: Educating a Nation; contbr. articles to profl. jours. Office: Nat Assn State Bds Edn 277 S Washington St Ste 100 Alexandria VA 22314 Office Phone: 703-684-4000. Office Fax: 703-836-2313. E-mail: brendaw@nasbe.org. *

WELBURN, EDWARD T., automotive executive; b. Phila., Dec. 14, 1950; BA, Howard U., 1972. Assoc. designer GM Advanced Design Studios, 1972, Buick Exterior Studio, 1973, Oldsmobile Exterior Studio, 1975—85, chief designer, 1989—98; with Saturn global design GM, Rüsselsheim, Germany, 1996—98, exec. dir. design body-on-frame architectures, 2002, v.p. design N. Am., 2003—05, v.p. global design, 2005—; dir. GM Corp. Brand Ctr., Warren, Mich., 1998—2001. Designer Indianapolis 500 Pace Car, 1985. Recipient The Best Concept Truck, N. Am. Internat. Auto Show, 2003, Best Concept Car, Autoweek, 1995, Award of Design Excellence, Indsl. Designers Soc. Am., 1988.

WELCH, ASHLEY JAMES, engineering educator; b. Ft. Worth, May 3, 1933; married, 1952; 3 children. BS, Tex. Tech U., 1955; MS, So. Meth. U., 1959; PhD in Elec. Engring., Rice U., 1964. Cert. profl. engr., Tex. Aerophys. engr. Gen. Dynamics, Ft. Worth, 1957-60; instr. elec. engring. Rice U., 1960-64; asst. prof. elec. engr. U. Tex., Austin, 1964—70, dir. engring. computer facility, 1964—68, 1995—96, assoc. prof. elec. engr., 1970—75, prof. elec. engr. and biomedical engr., 1971—, Marion E. Forsman Centennial prof. engring., 1985—, faculty advisor undergraduate biomedical engring. students, 2002—03. Chmn. Gordon Conf. in Lasers in Medicine and Biology, Am. Soc. Lasers in Med. Surgery Annual Meeting; bd. dirs. Am. Soc. Lasers in Med. Surgery, 1989—92, 1999—2002. Editor, author Optical-Thermal Response of Laser-Irradiated Tissue; contbr. more than 500 articles to profl. jours. Lt. US Army, 1955—56. Recipient Best Dissertation award, Rice U., 1964, Hocott award, U. Tex., 2004, Human Effectiveness Directorate Ann. Excellence award, USAF, 2006, Rsch. Excellence award, 2006. Fellow: IEEE, Am. Inst. for Med. and Biol. Engring., Am. Soc. Lasers in Surgery and Medicine (W.B. Mark award 2002); mem.: Internat. Soc. Optical Engring. (chmn. sessions, Pioneers in Biomed. Optics award 2006, Biomed. Optics Lifetime Achievement award 2007). Achievements include research in laser-tissue interaction, application of lasers in medicine; patents in field; pioneer in optics. Office: U Tex at Austin Dept Biomedical Engring Austin TX 78712 Home: 10821 Pointe View Austin TX 78738 Office Phone: 512-471-1453. Business E-Mail: welch@mail.utexas.edu.

WELCH, BILLY E., retired government agency administrator, retired management consultant; b. West, Tex., Sept. 16, 1929; s. Perry S. and Elizabeth D. Welch; m. Dorothy J. Poling, Mar. 10, 1956; children: Susan Glaeser children: William, Rebecca Royse, Janet Dillard. BS, Abilene Christian U., Tex., 1950; MS, Tex. A&M U., College Station, 1951, PhD, 1954. Sr. engr. Northrop Aircraft Corp., Hawthorne, Calif., 1957—59; dir. environ. scis. USAF Sch. Aerospace Medicine, San Antonio, 1959—72, dep. dir., 1977—81; spl. asst. for environ. quality Office of Sec. of Air Force, Washington, 1972—77; chief scientist Human Systems Ctr., San Antonio, 1981—89, program dir., 1989—90; dir. Armstrong Lab. Air Force Rsch. Lab., San Antonio, 1990—94; ret. Chair civilian exec. adv bd Air Force Material Command, Dayton, Ohio, 1988—94; Air Force sci. and engring. policy coun. Office of Sec. of Air Force, Washington, 1989—94; vice-chair adv. com. on rsch. Tex. Higher Edn. Coordinating Bd, Austin, 1994—; affiliate Los Alamos Nat. Lab., N.Mex., 1996—2004, Carlsbad Field Office US Dept. Energy, 2001—02. Various positions including mem., sec., v.p., pres. NE Ind. Sch. Dist., San Antonio, 1979—88; mem., pres. NE Ednl. Found., San Antonio, 1987—97; mem., chair Brooks Heritage Found., San Antonio, 1987—, Brooks Aerospace Found., San Antonio, 1997—; bd. mem. San Antonio New Schs. Found., 1991—95. Recipient Meritorious Exec. award, Pres. of US, 1988, Meritorious Civilian Svc. award, USAF, 1994. Fellow: Aerospace Med. Assn.; mem.: Internat. Acad. Astronautics, Am. Physiol. Soc., Sigma Xi. Avocations: golf, gardening, reading. Home: 122 Encino Blanco San Antonio TX 78232 Home Phone: 210-494-9198. Personal E-mail: billywelch@aol.com.

WELCH, C. DAVID, assistant secretary of state, former ambassador; b. Munich, 1953; m. Gretchen Gerwe; children: Emma, Molly, Hannah. BA, Georgetown U., 1975; MA, Tufts U., 1977; student, London Sch. Econs., 1973—74. With Office of Under Sec. for Security Assistance, Sci. and Tech., 1977—79; polit. officer US Embassy, Islamabad, Pakistan, 1979—81, officer responsible for Syria Washington, 1981—82, officer responsible for Lebanon, 1982—83, chief polit. sect. Damascus, Syria, 1984—86, polit. officer Amman, Jordan, 1986—88; mem. staff Nat. Security Coun. at White House, Washington, 1989—91; exec. asst. to under sec. polit. affairs US Dept. State, Washington, 1991—92; charge d'affaires US Embassy, Riyadh, Saudi Arabia, 1992—94, dep. chief of mission, 1992—95; prin. dep. asst. sec. of state Bur. Near Ea. Affairs US Dept. State, Washington, 1996—97, asst. sec. for internat. orgn. affairs, 1998—2001, U.S. amb. to Egypt Cairo, 2001—05, asst. sec. Bur. Near Eastern Affairs Washington, 2005—. Mem.: Am. Fgn. Svc. Assn., Coun. Fgn. Rels. Office: US Dept State Harry S Truman Bldg 2201 C St NW Rm 6242 Washington DC 20520 Office Phone: 202-647-7209.

WELCH, CHERIE LYNN, healthcare educator; b. Detroit, Feb. 5, 1966; d. Charles and Judith Welch. BS, Western Mich. U., 1990, MS, 1998. Secondary phys. edn. instr. Dept. Edn., Agana, Guam, 1992—93; secondary health, phys. edn. tchr. Hackett Cath. Ctrl. H.S., Kalamazoo, 1994—96; secondary phys. edn. tchr. Our Lady of Mercy H.S., Farmington Hills, Mich., 1996—97; phys. edn. instr. Western Mich. U., Kalamazoo, 1997—98; elem. and mid. sch. phys. edn. tchr. Grand Rapids Pub. Schs., Mich., 1998—2000; aquatic instr. Oakland CC, Farmington Hills, Mich., 2004—06; wellness instr. Rochester Cmty. Schs., Mich., 2000—06. Home: 3721 Barberry Cir Wixom MI 48393 Office Phone: 248-726-4000, 248-726-6696. Business E-Mail: cwelch@rochester.k12.mi.us.

WELCH, CLAUDE (RAYMOND), theology studies educator; b. Genoa City, Wis., Mar. 10, 1922; s. Virgil Cleon and Deone West (Grenelle) W.; m. Eloise Janette Turner, May 31, 1942 (div. 1970); children— Eric, Thomas, Claudia; m. Theodosia Montigel Blewett, Oct. 5, 1970 (dec. 1978); m. Joy Neuman, Oct. 30, 1982 (dec. 2005). BA summa cum laude, Upper Iowa U., 1942; postgrad., Garrett Theol. Sem., 1942-43; BD cum laude, Yale U., 1945, PhD, 1950; DD (hon.), Ch. Div. Sch. of Pacific, 1972, Jesuit Sch. Theology, 1982; LHD (hon.), U. Judaism, 1976. Ordained to ministry Meth. Ch., 1947. Instr. religion Princeton (N.J.) U., 1947-50, asst. prof., 1950-51, vis. prof., 1962; asst. prof. theology Yale U. Div. Sch., New Haven, 1951-54, assoc. prof., 1954-60; Berg prof. religious thought, chmn. dept. U. Pa., Phila., 1960-71, assoc. dean Coll. Arts and Scis., 1964-68, acting chmn. dept. philosophy, 1965-66; prof. hist. theology Grad. Theol. Union, Berkeley, Calif., 1971—, dean, 1971-87, pres., 1972-82. Vis. prof. Garrett Theol. Sem., 1951, Pacific Sch. Religion, 1958, Hartford Sem. Found., 1958-59, Princeton Theol. Sem., 1962-63, U. Va., 1987; Fulbright sr. lectr. U. Mainz, Germany, 1968; Sprunt lectr. Union Theol. Sem., Richmond, Va., 1958; Willson lectr. Southwestern U., Georgetown, Tex., 1994; dir. study of grad. edn. in religion Am. Coun. Learned Socs., 1969-71; del. World Conf. on Faith and Order, 1963. Author: In This Name: the Doctrine of the Trinity in Contemporary Theology, 1952, (with John Dillenberger) Protestant Christianity, interpreted through its Development, 1954, 2d rev. edit., 1988, The Reality of the Church, 1958, Graduate Education in Religion: A Critical Appraisal, 1971, Religion in the

Undergraduate Curriculum, 1972, Protestant Thought in the 19th Century, vol. 1, 1799-1870, 1972, vol. 2, 1870-1914, 1985; Editor, translator: God and Incarnation in Mid-19th Century German Theology (Thomasius, Dorner and Biedermann), 1965; Contbr. to publs. in field. Recipient decennial prize Bross Found., 1970; Guggenheim fellow, 1976; NEH research fellow, 1984, Fulbright research fellow, 1956-57. Mem. Am. Acad. Religion (pres. 1969-70), Coun. of Socs. for Study of Religion (chmn. 1969-74, 85-90), Soc. for Values in Higher Edn. (pres. 1967-71), Am. Soc. Ch. History, Am. Theol. Soc., Phi Beta Kappa. Methodist. Home: 123 Fairlawn Dr Berkeley CA 94708-2107 E-mail: claudew2@juno.com.

WELCH, CODY M., transportation and warehousing executive; s. Gary E. and Nancy Welch; m. Erin Welch, Aug. 16, 1997; children: Sterling K., Jackson R. BBA in Bus. Mgmt., Tex. Tech U., Lubbock, 1994. Wholesale/agt. account exec. SBC Wireless, Dallas, 1994—2002; wholesale account exec. Sebring Capital Corp., Dallas, 2003—05, Indpls.; v.p. sales CLM Pallet Recycling, Inc., Indpls., 2005—. Office: CLM Pallet Recycling Inc PO Box 19184 Indianapolis IN 46219 Office Phone: 317-437-9898. Business E-Mail: cwelch@clmfreightlines.com.

WELCH, DAVID WILLIAM, lawyer; b. St. Louis, Feb. 26, 1941; s. Claude LeRoy Welch and Mary Eleanor (Peggs) Welch; m. Candace Lee Capages, June 5, 1971; children: Joseph Peggs, Heather Elizabeth, Katherine Laura. BSBA, Washington U., St. Louis, 1963; JD, U. Tulsa, 1971. Bar: Okla. 1972, Mo. 1973, U.S. Dist. Ct. (we. dist.) Mo. 1973, U.S. Dist. Ct. (ea. dist.) Mo. 1974, U.S. Ct. Appeals (8th cir.) 1977, U.S. Ct. Appeals (7th cir.) 1991. Contract adminstr. McDonnell Aircraft Corp., St. Louis, 1965-66; bus. analyst Dun & Bradstreet Inc., Los Angeles, 1967-68; atty. U.S. Dept. Labor, Washington, 1972-73; ptnr. Moller Talent, Kuelthau & Welch, St. Louis, 1973-88, Lashly & Baer, St. Louis, 1988-96, Armstrong Teasdale LLP, St. Louis, 1996—. Author: (handbook) Missouri Employment Law, 1988; contbr. book chpts. Missouri Bar Employer-Employee Law, 1985, 87, 89, 92, 94, Missouri Discrimination Law, 1999; co-editor: Occupational Safety and Health Law, 1996. Mem. City of Creve Coeur Ethics Commn., 1987-88, Planning and Zoning Commn., 1988-96; bd. dirs. Camp Wyman, Eureka, Mo., 1982—, sec., 1987-88, 2nd v.p. 1988-89, 1st v.p. 1990-92, pres., 1992-94. Mem. ABA, Fed. Bar Assn., Mo. Bar Assn., Okla. Bar Assn., St. Louis Bar Assn., Kiwanis (bd. dirs. St. Louis 1979—, sec. 1982-83, 93-94, 2003-04, v.p. 1983-84, 88-90, 92-93, 2003-04, Man of Yr. award 1985). Democrat. Mem. Christian Ch. (Disciples Of Christ). Avocations: travel, music. Office: Armstrong Teasdale 1 Metropolitan Sq Ste 2600 Saint Louis MO 63102-2740

WELCH, DENNIS E., electric power industry executive; B in Environ., Health and Safety Mgmt., Ind. State U., Terre Haute; M in Bus. and Human Resource Mgmt., Rensselaer Poly. Inst., Troy, NY; grad. Environ. Leadership Program, Yale U. Sch. Forestry and Environ. Studies. Various positions Stone & Webster Engring.; positions including dir. environ. health and safety, mgr. occupational safety NE Utilities, v.p. environ., safety & ethics, pres., COO Yankee Energy Sys. subs., 2001; sr. v.p. environment, safety and health Am. Electric Power Svc. Corp., 2005—. Office: Am Electric Power Svc Corp 1 Riverside Plz Columbus OH 43215-2373 Office Phone: 614-716-1000. *

WELCH, FRANK D., architect; b. 1927; m. Katherine Welch. Grad. in Architecture, Tex. A&M U., College Station, 1951. With O'Neil Ford, Houston; prin. Frank Welch & Assocs., Inc., Dallas. Contbr. articles to profl. publs.; author: Philip Johnson & Texas, 2000; prin. works include West Lawther Dr., 1997, White Rock Lake Home, 1997, The Birthday, Sterling County, Tex. (25-Yr. award, Tex. Soc. Archs., 1997). Served in US Army. Recipient Award for Excellence in the Promotion of Architecture through the Media, Tex. Soc. Archs., 2003, Lifetime Achievement medal, 2006. Fellow: AIA. Office: Frank Welch & Assocs Inc 703 McKinney Ave Dallas TX 75202 Office Phone: 214-954-0072. *

WELCH, GERALD THOMAS, lawyer, electrical engineer; b. Detroit, Aug. 2, 1949; s. Gerald John and Mary Eileen (Metty) W.; m. Lucia Ann Urso, Sept. 10, 1972; children: Gerald J., Anthony M., David T., Lucia M. BEE, U. Notre Dame, 1971; MBA magna cum laude, U. Utah, 1974; JD, U. Toledo, 1979. Bar: Ohio 1980, Tex. 1981, NY 1990, U.S. Patent Office 1981, US Dist. Ct. (Tex. dist.), U.S. Ct. Appeals (Fed. cir.) 1982. Assoc. John C. Purdue Co., L.P.A., Toledo, 1978-80; atty. Exxon Prodn. Research, Houston, 1980-81; legal counsel Owens-Ill., Toledo, 1981-85; v.p., gen. counsel, sec. M&SD Corp., Lyndhurst, NJ, 1985—88; dir., licensing & tech. devel. Eastman Kodak Co., 1988—93; ptnr., Intellectual Property, Telecom. & Emerging Tech., Tech. Law practices Patton Boggs LLP, Dallas, dep. chmn., Intellectual Property dept., mem. mgmt. com., office mng. ptnr. V.p. Welmet Inc., Flemington, NJ. Served to capt. USAF, avionics engring. & JAG, 1971-77. Life fellow, Dallas Bar Found.; mem. ABA, Tex. Bar Assn., NY State Bar Assn., Dallas Bar Assn., Am. Intellectual Property Law Assn. (chmn. Mgmt. of IP Assets com. 2001-03), Am. Corp. Counsel Assn., Licensing Exec. Soc. Roman Catholic. Avocations: golf, tennis. Office: Patton Boggs LLP Suite 3000 2001 Ross Ave Dallas TX 75201-8001 Office Phone: 214-758-6610. Office Fax: 214-758-1550. Business E-Mail: gwelch@pattonboggs.com.

WELCH, JANET MARTIN, librarian; b. Chgo., Jan. 12, 1945; d. Lowell Arthur and Bella S. Martin; m. H. William Welch, Dec. 30, 1967; children: Scott Martin, Dana Michelle. BA magna cum laude, Bucknell U., 1967; MLS, Rutgers U., 1968. Project intern State Librs., Pa., N.J., Ill., 1966-67; dir. Rsch. Lab./NL Industries, Highstown, N.J., 1967-69; sci. libr. SUNY, Albany, 1969-71; dir. Resource Ctr. Ft. Ann (N.Y.) Ctrl. Sch., 1971-72; joint author, sr. rsch. assoc. Tucson Pub. Libr., 1973-74; editl./network cons. Pahlavi Nat. Libr., East Norwich, N.Y., 1974-76; learning resource cons. North Country C.C., Elizabethtown, N.Y., 1976-77; exec. dir. Rochester (N.Y.) Regional Libr. Coun., 1977-97; state libr., asst. commr. N.Y. State Edn. Dept., Albany, 1997—. Adj. prof. SUNY. Buffalo, 1986—; cons. N.Y. State Regions, 1986—. Editor NYLA semi-ann. publ. PR Alert, 1992; mem. editl. bd. The Bottom Line: Mng. Libr. Fins., 1986, others. Mem. governing bd. Greater Rochester Project, 1995—; del. White House Conf. Librs. and Info. Svcs., 1991, NY State Gov.'s Conf. Librs., Albany, 1990-91; bd. dirs. NY State Coun. Humanities, NYC, 1988-93. Recipient Ann. award for Legis. Success, ALA, 1996; Pres.'s award for pub. awareness of Librs., N.Y. Libr. Assn., 1995, also Spirit of Librarianship award, 1993, Outstanding Svc. to Librs. award, 1986. Office: NY State Libr 10 C 34 Cultural Ctr Albany NY 12234-0001 Office Phone: 518-474-5930. Business E-Mail: jwelch2@mail.nysed.gov.

WELCH, JASPER ARTHUR, JR., security company executive, consultant; b. Baton Rouge, Jan. 5, 1931; s. Jasper Arthur and Oramay Ballinger (Young) W.; m. Frances Carroll Wright, Mar. 28, 1953 (div. Nov. 1984); children: Jasper Arthur III, Carroll Welch Pawlikowski, Brent Ballinger; m. Jane Ann Alford Tudor, Dec. 31, 1985. BS in Physics, La. State U., 1952; MA in Physics, U. Calif., Berkeley, 1954, PhD in Physics, 1958. Commd. officer 2d lt. USAF, 1952, advanced through grades to maj. gen., 1975; chief analyst Hdqs. USAF, Washington, 1969—71; chief strategic analysis Office Sec. Def., Washington, 1971—74; chief strategic concepts Hdqs. USAF, 1974—75, asst. chief staff for analysis, 1975—79; coord. def. policy NSC, 1979—81; asst. dept. chief staff Hdqs. USAF, 1981—83; ret., 1983. Mem. tech. adv. coun. Sikorsky Aircraft, Stratford, Conn., 1984-2005; tech. cons. Jasper Welch Assocs., Santa Fe, 1984—; mem. adv. coun. NASA, Washington, 1985-89; chmn. mil. adv. panel to dir. CIA, Washington, 1986-98; mem. nat. security panel U. Calif., 2000-07. Author: Atomic Theory of Gas Dynamics, 1965; contbr. articles to sci. jours., including Phys. Rev., Strategic Rev. Youth dir. St. Matthews Epis. Ch., Pacific Palisades, Calif., 1969-74, St. Andrews Epis. Ch., Arlington, 1965-68; mem. found. bd. Santa Fe Chamber Music Festival, 1998—2004. Decorated D.S.M. with oak leaf cluster, Legion of merit with two oak leaf clusters. Mem. NAE (found. bd. 1999—2005), Am. Geophys. Union, Am. Phys. Soc., Coun. on Fgn. Rels. Avocations: music, theater, gardening, hiking, racing sailboats. Office: 2129 Foothills Rd Santa Fe NM 87505

WELCH, JOHN KIRTLAND, nuclear energy industry executive; b. Waltham, Mass., Mar. 8, 1950; s. Raymond Vencent and Justine Louise (Fairbank) W.; m. Michele Anne Mules, June 10, 1972; children: Nicole Kristen, Alison Corrinne. BA in Aero. Engring., U.S. Nav. Acad., 1972; MS in Aeronautics, Naval Postgrad. Sch., 1973; MBA in Fin., Loyola Coll., Balt., 1984. Registered profl. engr., Md. Commd. ens. USN, 1972, advanced through grades to lt., resigned, 1979; systems engr. Gen. Electric Co., Evendale, Ohio, 1979-80; div. dir. Gen. Physics Corp., Columbia, Md., 1980-84; ops. ctr. mgr. Advanced Tech., Inc., Reston, Va., 1984; various positions to exec. v.p. marine sys. group Gen. Dynamics Corp., 1989—2005; pres., CEO USEC Inc., 2005—. Lt. USNR, 1979—. Mem. ASME (chmn. plant engring. com. 1980—), Am. Soc. Naval Engrs. Avocations: swimming, photography, sailing. Office: USEC Inc 6903 Rockledge Dr Bethesda MD 20817 *

WELCH, JOSEPH DANIEL, lawyer; b. University City, Mo., Feb. 1, 1952; s. Robert Joseph and Mary Virginia (Church) W.; m. Sharon Susan Filipek, Mar. 16, 1973; children: Eric Ryan, Christopher Joseph, Colin Andrew, Maria Nicole, Theresa Katherine. BA cum laude, St. Louis U., 1974, JD, 1977. Bar: Mo. 1977, U.S. Dist. Ct. (ea. and we. dists.) Mo. 1977, U.S. Ct. Appeals (8th cir.) 1984, U.S. Supreme Ct. 1994. Assoc. Ely & Cary, Hannibal, Mo., 1977-79; ptnr. Ely, Cary & Welch, Hannibal, Mo., 1979-82, Ely, Cary, Welch & Hickman, Hannibal, Mo., 1982-99, Cary, Welch & Hickman, L.L.P., Hannibal, Mo., 1999—. Mem. Nat. Network of Estate Planning Attys., 2000—04, Mississippi River Pkwy. Commn., St. Paul, 1988—95; head Mo. del., 1988; prof. bus. law Hannibal-LaGrange Coll., 1993—98; mem. Nat. Heritage Corridor Commn., Washington, 1990—96; spkr. in field. Editor: Year in Review-Bankruptcy, 1991-94, co-author, 1988-90; spkr. various profl. orgns.; contbr. articles to profl. jours. Bd. dirs. Hannibal Pks. and Recreation Dept., 2000-03, Mark Twain Area Physician's Recruitment Assn., Hannibal, 1984-85, Hannibal Free Pub. Libr., 1980-82, Hannibal C. of C., 1978-80, pres. Hannibal Ctrl. Bus. Devel., Inc., 1982-85; mem. Mo. Right-to-Life, 1977—; cmty. adv. bd. St. Elizabeth Hosp., 1985-86; Birthright of Hannibal, Inc., 1980—, Holy Family Sch. Bd., 1990-95. Acad. scholar St. Louis U., 1970-74; recognition for Significant Contribution to Bush Administrn., Dept. Interior, 1993. Mem. Mark Twain Astron. Soc. (co-founder). Roman Catholic. Avocations: parenting, basketball, tennis, boating, creative writing. Home: 601 Country Club Dr Hannibal MO 63401-3033 Office: Cary Welch & Hickman 1000 Center St Hannibal MO 63401-3449 Office Phone: 573-221-0080.

WELCH, LLOYD RICHARD, electrical and communications engineer, educator, consultant; b. Detroit, Sept. 28, 1927; s. Richard C. and Helen (Felt) W.; m. Irene Althea Main, Sept. 12, 1953; children: Pamela Irene Towery, Melinda Ann, Diana Lia Worthington. BS in Math., U. Ill., 1951; PhD in Math., Calif. Inst. Tech., 1958. Mathematician NASA-Jet Propulsion Lab., Pasadena, Calif., 1956-59; staff mathematician Inst. Def. Analyses, Princeton, NJ, 1959-65; prof. elec. engring. U. So. Calif., LA, 1965-99, prof. emeritus, 1999—. Cons. in field of elec. comms Contbr. articles to profl. jours. Served with USN, 1945-49, 51-52 Fellow IEEE (Shannon award Info. Theory Soc. of IEEE 2003); mem. Nat. Acad. Engring., Am. Math. Soc., Math. Assn. Am., Phi Beta Kappa, Sigma Xi, Phi Kappa Phi, Pi Mu Epsilon, Eta Kappa Nu Office: U So Calif Elec Engring Bldg 500A Los Angeles CA 90089-0001 Business E-Mail: welch@usc.edu.

WELCH, LYMAN W., lawyer; BA cum laude, Knox Coll., 1964; JD, Harvard Law Sch., 1967. Bar: US Tax Ct. 1976, Fla. 1978, Ill. 1968. Ptnr. Sidley Austin, LLP, Chgo. Adv. to restatement of the law of trusts project Am. Law Inst. Contbr. articles to profl. publs. Named one of Top 2 Trust and Estate Lawyers in Chgo., Town and Country mag., 1998, Best Trusts and Estates Lawyers in Am., Bloomberg Personal Fin., 1999, Top 100 Attys., Worth mag., 2005—06. Fellow: Am. Coll. Trust and Estate Counsel (mem. fiduciary litig. and estate and gift tax coms.); mem.: ABA (mem. fed. tax sect. com. on fiduciary income tax and partnerships com.). Office: Sidley Austin LLP 1 S Dearborn Chicago IL 60603 Office Phone: 312-853-4165. Office Fax: 312-853-7036. E-mail: lwelch@Sidley.com. *

WELCH, LYNNE G., language and music educator; b. Long Beach, Calif., Dec. 13; d. Wallace M. Welch and Beth May Gardiner; children: Samuel Meadd, Thaddeus Cates. BA, Calif. State U., 1964, MA, 1970. ESL tchr. State of Calif., 2003—04; English tchr. Garden Grove Unit, Calif.; journalist Mass Media Sch. Dist.; English tchr. Compton Unit Sch. Dist. Recreational asst. Long Beach, Calif., 1997—99. Named Outstanding Tchr., Compton Unified Sch. Dist., 1995, 1996; named to Wall of Tolerance (signed by Rosa Parks); recipient Outstanding Tchr., Compton Unified Sch. Dist., 1996. Mem.: Coda Internat., Emotions Anonymous, Alanon Internat. Meth. Home: PO Box 1704 Lomita CA 90717

WELCH, MARTHA GRACE, physician, researcher; b. Buffalo, June 21, 1944; d. Thomas Harris and Jane Elizabeth (Todd) W.; m. Anthony H. Horan, July 11, 1970 (div. May 1985); 1 child, Thomas Bramwell Welch Horan. BA, N.Y.U., 1966; MD, Columbia U., 1971. Diplomate Am. Bd. Psychiatry and Neurology. Intern Greenwich (Conn.) Hosp. Assn., 1971-72; resident Albert Einstein Coll. Med., Bronx, N.Y., 1972-74, fellow, 1974-77, instr., 1977-79; dir., founder The Mothering Ctr., Greenwich, 1978—; asst. prof. clin. psychiatry Columbia U., NYC, 1997. Adj. asst. prof. NYU Sch. Medicine, 2007—. Author: Holding Time, 1989, (with others) Autistic Children, 1983; contbr. articles to profl. jours. Pres. alumni coun. Columbia U. Coll. Physicians and Surgeons, 2001-2002 Recipient Alumni Achievement award Middlebury (Vt.) Coll., 1995. Mem. Am. Psychiat. Assn., Internat. Soc. for Devel. Psychobiology, Soc. for Neuroscience. Avocations: reading, skiing, tennis, sewing, biking, music. Office: 15 E 91st St New York NY 10128-0648 Office Phone: 212-369-8566.

WELCH, MARTHA LYNN, environmentalist, educator; d. Margaret Melvina Sandifer and Richard Charles O'Connell; m. John Tyler Welch II, Aug. 28, 1987. BA in Environ. Studies, U. N.C., Wilmington, NC, 1983; MS in Edn., Old Dominion U., 1996; EdD, Fla. Internat. U., 2004. Asst. edn., exhibits coord. N.C. Aquarium, Ft. Fisher, 1984—86; owner, operator Manatee Tours, Inc., Islamorada, Fla., 1990—93; marine edn. specialist Coll. William and Mary, Va. Inst. Marine Sci., Gloucester Point, 1996—97; field leader, instr. Audubon Fla., Miami, 1999—2003; dir. edn. Fla. Flora and Fauna, Inc., Hutchinson island, 1999—. Cons. Sch. Dist. Palm Beach County, Fla., 2002—. Author: Mandy the Manatee Saves the Day; contbr. articles to profl. jours. Mem.: ASCD, NSTA (assoc.), Fla. Assn. Sci. Tchrs., Nat. Marine Edn. Assn. (assoc.), Nat. Audubon Soc., Fla. Marine Sci. Edn. Assn., Phi Kappa Phi. Avocations: travel, snorkeling, boating. Home and Office: 137 Queens Rd Hutchinson Island FL 34949 Office Phone: 561-951-9313. Personal E-mail: jwelch261@sprintpcs.com.

WELCH, MARTIN E., III, investor, retail executive; b. Detroit, June 25, 1948; m. Anne Welch; children: Michele, James, Mary Beth, Brian. BS in Acctg., U. Detroit Mercy, 1970, MBA, 1973. Audit mgr. Arthur Young & Co., Detroit, 1970-77; dir. mktg. acctg. Fruehauf divsn. Fruehauf Corp., Detroit, 1977-82; mgr. corp. acctg. Chrysler Corp., Highland Park, Mich., 1982-83, asst. contr., 1983-86, gen. auditor, 1987-88, asst. treas., 1988-91; CFO Chrysler Can., Windsor, Ont., 1986-87; sr. v.p., CFO Federal-Mogul corp., Southfield, Mich., 1991-95; exec. v.p., CFO Kmart Corp, Troy, Mich., 1995—2001; bus. advisor, dir. York Mgmt. Svcs., Somerset, NJ, 2002—; exec. v.p., CFO Oxford Automotive, Inc., Troy, Mich., 2003—04, United Rentals, Inc., Greenwich, Conn., 2005—. Mem. nat. adv. bd. JP Morgan Bank, 1997—2000; bd. dirs. No. Group Retail, Ltd., Delphi Corp. Bd. dirs. U. Detroit-Mercy. Mem.: Fin. Execs. Internat. Personal E-mail: martywelch@yahoo.com.

WELCH, MICHAEL JOHN, chemistry educator, researcher; b. Stoke-on-Trent, Staffordshire, Eng., June 28, 1939; came to U.S., 1965; s. Arthur John W. and Mary (Welch); m. Teresa Jean Conocchiolli, Apr. 22, 1967 (div. 1979); children: Colin, Lesley. BA, Cambridge U., Eng., 1961; MA, Cambridge U., 1964; PhD, London U., 1965. Asst. prof. radiation chemistry in radiology Washington U. Sch. Medicine, St. Louis, 1967-70, assoc. prof., 1970-74, assoc. prof. dept. chemistry, 1971-75, prof. dept. chemistry, 1978—, prof. radiology, 1991—, prof. molecular biology and pharmacology, 1993—; prof. biomed. engring. program Washington U., St. Louis, 1996; co-dir. Mallinckrodt Inst. Dir. radiol. scis. dept. Washington U., 1990—; mem. diagnostic radiology study sect. NIH, 1986-89, chmn., 1989-91; mem. sci. adv. com. Whitaker Found., 1995-2003. Author: Introduction to the Tracer Methods, 1972; editor: Radiopharmaceuticals and Other Compounds Labeled with Shortlived Radionuclides, 1977; assoc. editor Jour. Nuclear Medicine, 1989—2003; contbr. chpts. to books, more than 400 articles to profl. jours. Recipient Georg Charles de Hevesy Nuclear Medicine Pioneer award, 1992; scholar St. Catharine Coll. Cambridge U., 1958-61. Mem. Soc. Nuclear Medicine (trustee, pres. 1984, Paul C. Aebersold award 1980, de Hevesy Nuclear Pioneer award 1992), Radiopharm. Sci. Coun. (pres. 1980-81), Am. Chem. Soc. (St. Louis award 1988, award for nuclear chemistry 1990, Mid-West award 1991), Chem. Soc. London, Radiation Rsch. Soc., Inst. of Medicine, Sigma Xi Office: Washington U Sch Medicine Edward Mallinckrodt Inst Radiology 510 S Kingshighway Blvd Box 8225 Saint Louis MO 63110-1016 E-mail: welchm@mir.wustl.edu.

WELCH, MICHAEL R., sociologist, educator; b. Ogdensburg, NY, Feb. 8, 1947; s. Carlton Curtis Welch and Eleanor (Clary) Caruso; m. Helena Rose Kleist, Jan. 29, 1966; children: Kristen Reynolds, Michael Jr., Scott, Brian. BA, LeMoyne Coll., 1972; MA, U. N.C., 1975, PhD, 1980. Asst. prof. Fla. Atlantic U., Boca Raton, 1976—80, U. Cin., 1980—81; full prof. U. Notre Dame, 2006—. Contbr. articles to profl. jours. Mem.: Am. Soc. Criminology, Am. Sociol. Assn., Alpha Kappa Delta, Pi Gamma Mu. Roman Catholic. Office: Univ Notre Dame Sociology Dept 810 Flanner Hall Notre Dame IN 46556

WELCH, MORGAN E., lawyer; b. Joplin, Mo., May 25, 1950; s. Morgan and Virginia Welch; m. Cheryl Welch, Oct. 23, 1982; children: Rick Martin, Ashley. BS, Westminster Coll., 1972; JD, U. Ark., 1975. Bar: Ark. 1975, U.S. Dist. Ct. (ea. dist. Ark.) 1975, U.S. Dist. Ct. (we. dist. Ark.) 1975, U.S. Ct. Appeals (8th cir.) 1984, U.S. Supreme Ct. 1990, U.S. Air Force Ct. Mil. Rev., U.S. Army Ct. Mil. Rev., Armed Forces Ct. Appeals. Jr. ptnr. Patterson and Welch, North Little Rock, Ark., 1976—80; owner Morgan Welch PA, North Little Rock, 1980—89; ptnr. Hurley Whitwell Shephard & Welch, North Little Rock, 1989—90, Welch & Adcock, Little Rock, 1990—95; owner Morgan Welch PA, Little Rock, 1995—2000; ptnr. Eubanks, Welch, Baker, Schulze, Little Rock, 2000—03; sr. ptnr. Welch and Kitchens LLC, Little Rock, 2003—. Counsel Ark. Legis., Little Rock, 1975—76. Pres. North Little Rock Jaycees, 1978—79; sec. North Pulaski County Bar Assn., North Little Rock, 1979—80; mem. 8th cir. Ark. Ho. Dels., 1994—96. Recipient Roxanne Wilson Trial Adv. award, 1997. Mem.: ATLA (bd. govs.), ABA, Am. Inns Ct. Found. (Master of Bench), Ark. Trial Lawyers Assn. (pres. 1991, Outstanding Trial Lawyer award 1990, President's award 2005). Democrat. Methodist. Office: One Riverfront Pl Ste 413 North Little Rock AR 72114 Office Phone: 501-978-3030.

WELCH, OLIVER WENDELL, retired pharmaceutical executive; b. Jacksonville, Tex., Jan. 9, 1930; s. Jackson Andrew and Annie Laura (Trapp) W.; m. Wanda Virginia Urrey, Nov. 14, 1948. BA, Tex. Tech U., 1952; MA, Columbia U., 1958. Pharm. rep., supr. mktg. rsch., manpower devel. Warner Lambert Co., Morris Plains, N.J., 1962-72; mgr. corp. devel. Boehringer Mannheim Corp., NYC, 1972-75; v.p. Biomed. Data Co., NYC, 1975-77; assoc. dir., dep. dir. regulatory affairs Sterling Winthrop Inc., NYC, 1977-94; ret., 1994. Cons. Sanofi Winthrop, Inc., N.Y.C., 1995. Mem. Regulatory Affairs Profls. Soc., Drug Info. Assn., Order St. John of Jerusalem. Republican. Episcopalian. Avocations: music, travel, theater. *Pursue excellence. Pay attention to detail. Expect a positive result.*

WELCH, PETER F., congressman, former state legislator; b. Springfield, Mass., May 2, 1947; s. Edward and Mart (Tracy) Welch; m. Joan Smith, Dec. 10, 1975 (dec. 2004); 5 children. AB, Holy Cross Coll., 1969; LLB, U. Calif., Berkeley, 1973. Bar: Vt. Pvt. practice law; mem. Vt. State Senate, 1981—89, 2002—07, minority leader, 1982—84, pres. pro tempre, 1985—89, 2003—07; mem.-at-large US Congress from Vt., 2007—, mem. oversight & govt. reform com., rules com., 2007—. Democrat. Roman Catholic. Office: 1404 Longworth House Office Bldg Washington DC 20515 also: 30 Main St Ste 350 Burlington VT 05401 *

WELCH, PHILIP BURLAND, electronics and office products company executive; b. Portland, Maine, Nov. 15, 1931; s. Philip Gerald Welch and Clara Jenny (Berry) Hawxwell; m. Sheila Mae Preston, May 19, 1960 (dec.); children: Jahna Holly Welch Roth, Victoria Preston Welch Rothlubber; m. Aloma Gale Orr, Sept. 14, 2005. Student, Berklee Coll., 1955—58. Profl. trumpeter, arranger, composer, NYC, 1958—65; dist. sales mgr. Rheem Mfg. Co., Phila., 1965—66, regional sales mgr., 1966—70; nat. sales mgr. Akai Am. Ltd., Anaheim, Calif., 1970-73, BSR, USA, Blauvelt, NY, 1973-76; nat. sales and mktg. mgr. Philips High Fidelity Labs., Ft. Wayne, Ind., 1976-79; dir. mktg. Pioneer Electronics, Moonachie, NJ, 1979-82; pres. Schneider N.Am. Ltd., Dayton, NJ, 1982-83; v.p. Lyons & Assocs., Indpls., 1986-88; pres. Nat. Electric Mktg. Co., Jacksonville, Fla., 1975-88, Hemisphere Enterprises Corp., Jacksonville, 1988-91, Phil Welch Enterprises, Jacksonville, 1989-99, ret., 1999. Cons. ContraTech Corp., Portland, Oreg., 1986-87, Kukje Internat., NYC, 1986, FCI Inc., NJ, 1985, Multiform Products, Inc., Jacksonville, 1989-90, gen. mgr., v.p., 1990-96; pres. Atlantic Office Sources, Inc., Jacksonville, 1996-99, comdr. Am. Legion Post 372, Jacksonville, 2003, 04. Contbr. articles to profl. jours. With USAF, 1950—54. Named Man of Decade Audio/Video Cons. USA, 1982, Man of Yr. Soc. Audio Cons., 1974. Republican. Avocations: flying, golf. Home and Office: 12821 Julington Forest Dr W Jacksonville FL 32258-3454 Office Phone: 904-608-6073. E-mail: p_b_welch@yahoo.com.

WELCH, RICHARD L., priest, lawyer; b. Naples, Italy, Dec. 22, 1953; s. Richard and Alice (Nevin) W. BA, St. Alphonsus Sem., Suffield, Conn., 1977; MRE, Mt. St. Alphonsus, Esopus, NY, 1979, MDiv, 1981; JCL, U. St. Thomas Aquinas, Rome, 1995, JCD, 1998. Parish priest, PR, 1981-87; rector Catholic cathedral Caguas, PR, 1987-93; rector Notre Dame Sch., 1987-93; pres. Human Life Internat., 1997—2000; judge, promoter of justice Archdiocese of NY, 2001—. Author: (books) Blood of the Martyrs, 1994, Culture of Death Vs. Culture of Life, 1995, The Manifestation of Consciencr, 1998. Bd. dirs. For Human Life Internat, U.S., Can., Ireland, Australia, New Zealand, 1997, pres., 1997— Named Eagle Scout Boy Scouts of Am., 1968. Roman Catholic.

WELCH, RICHARD LEROY, personal improvement company executive; b. Lincoln, Nebr., Oct. 15, 1939; s. Raymond Nathanial and Helen Lila (Ludwig) W.; m. Donna Lee Gysegem, Nov. 3, 1991; children: Terri L. Flowerday, Julie A. Kuhl; 1 stepchild, Shannon Panzo. Student, U.

Nebr.; PhD (hon.), Devonshire U., Eng., 2000. Agt. Gurantee Mut. Life, Lincoln, Nebr., 1960-61; agt., mgr. Mut. of Omaha, 1962-68; gen. agt. Loyal Protective Life, Omaha, 1969-70; mgr. Mut. Benefit Life, Dallas, 1971-73; br. mgr. Great West Life, San Jose, Calif., 1973-74; pres. Internat. Speedreading Inst., Phoenix, 1975-80; CEO, founder Educom, Inc./Subliminal Dynamics, Dynamic Brain Mgmt., Centennial, Colo., 1980—. Mem. adv. bd. Great West Life, San Jose, 1973; pres. bd. dirs. Internat. Speedreading Inst., Phoenix, 1975-80, Subliminal Dynamics, Inc., San Jose, 1980-93, Educom, Inc., Aurora, 1993—; scientist, spkr., author, educator in field. Author: Brain Management, 1996. Inductee Lincoln H.S. Athletic Hall of Fame, 2000. Mem. Shriners, Masons (32d degree). Democrat. Avocations: sports, music, travel. Office: DBA Subliminal Dynamics Brain Mgmt 2553 North Carson St Ste 5885 Carson City NV 89706 Fax: 775-883-2384. E-mail: subdyn@subdyn.com.

WELCH, ROBERT BENNETT, retired music educator, retired conductor; b. Fleming, Ky., Feb. 20, 1935; s. Thomas Earl and Malinda Welch; m. Joyce Ann Broome, June 3, 1958; children: Robert Keith, David Bennett. BA, Morehead State U., Ky., 1963, MA, 1967; D in Musical Arts, U. Ky., Lexington, 1984. Cert. tchr. Ky., Va. Band dir. Letcher County Schs., Neon, Ky., 1957—58, Norton Schs., Va., 1958—63; band dir., orch. dir. Ea. HS, Louisville, 1963—67; condr. Louisville Youth Orch., 1964—68; band dir. We. Carolina U., NC, 1968—79; condr., artistic dir. Asheville Symphony Orch., NC, 1977—81; head divsn. fine arts Limestine Coll., Gaffney, SC, 1979—84; dean Coll. Arts Valdosta State Coll., Ga., 1984—2000. Dir. Jekyll Island Musical Theater, Jekyll Island, Ga., 1987—95, Artsouth, Valdosta, 1989—95; condr., founder Valdosta Symphony Orch., 1989—93; guest condr. over 300 occasions in US & Europe. Mgr. Arts Exch.Programs in Europe & US, 1980—84; mem. Arts Com., Cullowhee, NC, 1970—74; pres. Arts Assn., Gaffney, 1980—84; v.p. Lowndes Valdosta Arts Soc., 1985—95. Home: 1060 Arbor Creek Dr Roswell GA 30076 Personal E-mail: robertbwelch@bellsouth.com.

WELCH, ROBERT BOND, ophthalmologist, educator; b. Balt., May 24, 1927; s. Robert S.G. and Sally (Bond) W.; m. Elizabeth Truslow, May 30, 1953. AB, Princeton U., NJ, 1949; MD, Johns Hopkins U., Balt., 1953. Diplomate: Am. Bd. Ophthalmology. Intern in internal medicine Duke U. Hosp., 1953-54; resident in ophthalmology Wilmer Inst., Johns Hopkins U., 1954-57, chief resident in ophthalmology, 1959, co-dir. retina service, 1959-84, dir. retina service, 1984-85; retinal cons. in ophthalmology Walter Reed Army Hosp., 1961—2003, Bethesda Naval Hosp, 1976-99; assoc. prof. ophthalmology Johns Hopkins U.; chmn. dept. ophthalmology Greater Balt. Med. Ctr., 1985-91. Author: (with others) The Wilmer Institute 1925-1975, 1976; author: The Wilmer Opthalmological Institute 1925-2000, 2000; editor Transactions Am. Ophthal. Soc., 1984-91; mem. editorial staff Retina mag., 1980-86. Served with USNR, 1945-47. Recipient Disting. Alumnus award, Johns Hopkins U., 2001, Superior Civilian Svc. award, U.S. Army, 2004, Robert Bond Welch professorship in opthalmology, Johns Hopkins Medicine and Wilmer Eye Inst., 2006. Mem. Am. Ophthal. Soc. (v.p. 1992-93, pres. 1993-94, editor 1984-90), Retina Soc. (pres. 1981-83), Pan. Pacific Surg. Assn. (v.p. 1972-80), Md. Soc. Eye Physicians and Surgeons (pres. 1963-64), Md. Club., Elkridge Club, South River Club. Democrat. Episcopalian. Home: 4409 Atwick Rd Baltimore MD 21210-2811 Office: 86 State Cir Annapolis MD 21401-1906 Office Phone: 410-263-3492.

WELCH, ROSS MAYNARD, plant physiologist, educator; b. Lancaster, Calif., May 8, 1943; s. Lloyd C. and Theda W. (Slane) W.; m. Jill Susanne Varley, Aug. 22, 1965; children: Renell Cherie, Brent Ross BS, Calif. Poly. U., 1966; MS, U. Calif., Davis, 1969, PhD, 1971. Plant physiologist Agrl. Rsch. Svc. USDA, Ithaca, NY, 1971—; rsch. assoc. Cornell U., Ithaca, 1971—75, asst. prof. plant nutrition, 1975—81, assoc. prof. plant nutrition, 1981—87, prof., 1987—, co-organizer food sys. for improved health program Coll. Agr. and Life Scis., 1994—2000. Disting. vis. scientist Murdoch U., Perth, Australia, 1980-81; vis. disting. scholar and lectr. U. Adelaide, Australia, 1991—. Editor: Crops as Sources of Nutrients for Humans, 1984; co-editor: Micronutrients in Agriculture, 2d edit., 1989; contbr. over 185 rsch. articles and 55 rev. articles to profl. jours. Recipient Outstanding Scientist of Yr. award, USDA Agrl. Rsch. Svc., 2003. Fellow: Soil Sci. Soc. Am., Am. Soc. Agronomy (rsch. award N.E. br. 1992); mem.: AAAS, Am. Soc. Agronomy, Corp. Sci. Soc. Am., Am. Soc. Assn., Am. Soc. Plant Physiologists, Masons (master 1984—85), Sigma Xi. Republican. Mem. United Ch. of Christ. Achievements include discovery that nickel is an essential element for all higher plants; discovery that zinc plays a role in maintaining the integrity of root-cell plasma membranes. E-mial. Home: 24 Hickory Cir Ithaca NY 14850-9673 Office: US Plant Soil & Nutrition Lab Tower Rd Ithaca NY 14853 Business E-Mail: rmw1@cornell.edu.

WELCH, STANTON, performing company executive; b. Melbourne, Australia, Oct. 15, 1969; s. Garth Welch and Marilyn Jones. Studied at, San Francisco Ballet Sch. Dancer to soloist Australian Ballet, 1989, resident choreographer, 1995—2003; artistic dir. Houston Ballet, 2003—. Artistic assoc. Ballet Met, Columbus, Ohio. Choreographer (ballets) Maninyas, San Francisco Ballet, 1996, Taiko, 1999, Tutu, 2003, Falling, 2005, Powder, Birmingham Royal Ballet, 1998, Ønsket, Royal Danish Ballet, 1998, Ander, 1999, Indigo, Houston Ballet, 1999, Bruiser, 2000, Tales of Texas, 2004, Blindness, 2004, Bolero, 2004, Nosotros, 2005, Clear, Am. Ballet Theatre, 2001, Evolution, BalletMet, Don Quixote, A Dance in the Garden of Mirth, 2000, Green, Moscow Dance Theatre, 2000, OPUS X, 2001; created commissions for many of the world's best companies including American Ballet Theater, Houston Ballet, San Francisco Ballet, Royal Danish Ballet, Australian Ballet et al. Avocations: country music, country and western dancing. Office: Houston Ballet 1921 W Bell St Houston TX 77019 *

WELCH, W(ALTER) SCOTT, III, lawyer; b. Jackson, Miss., Sept. 7, 1939; s. Walter Scott Jr. and Velma Lou (Hines) W.; m. Hermine McBee Copeland, Nov. 5, 1960 (div. Sept. 1981); children: Hermine, Walt; m. Mary Anne Kendrick, Dec. 6, 1981; children: Dennis, Kasi. BA cum laude, U. of South, 1961; LLB with distinction, U. Miss., 1964. Bar: Miss. 1964, U.S. Dist. Ct. (no. dist.) Miss. 1964, U.S. Dist. Ct. (so. dist.) Miss. 1967, U.S. Ct. Appeals 1968, U.S. Supreme Ct., 1970. Assoc. Welch, Gibbes & Graves, Attys., Laurel, Miss., 1964; chmn. litigation dept. Butler, Snow, O'Mara, Stevens & Cannada, Jackson, 2002—05, ptnr., 1967—2006; shareholder Baker, Donelson, Bearman, Caldwell & Berkowitz, PC, 2006—. Mem. Miss. Supreme Ct. Commn. on Impaired Lawyers, 2005—; bd. dir. Harbor House Recovery Ctr., Jackson, Miss., 2004—. Capt. USAF, 1964—67. Fellow Am. Coll. Trial Lawyers, Am. Bar Found., Found. Am. Bd. Trial Advs. (trustee 1999-02, pres. 2001), Miss. Bar Found.; mem. ABA (ho. of del. 1994—, standing com. on public edn. 1998-00, 03-06, state del., nominating com. 2000-06, faculty tort and ins. practice sectin trial acad. 2003, bd. govs. 2006—), Am. Bd. Trial Advs. (nat. dir. 1992—, local pres. 1987, v.p. 1999, pres.-elect 2000, nat. pres. 2001), Internat. Assn. Def. Counsel (faculty def. counsel trial acad. 1997), Trial Attys. Am., Trucking Industry Def. Assn., Miss. Def. Lawyers (past bd. dirs.), Miss. State Bar Assn. (commr. 1989-95, exec. com. 1991-92, pres.-elect 1993-94, pres. 1994-95, Disting. Svc. award 2004), Hinds County Bar Assn. (pres. 1979-80), Chambers Ptnrs. Am.'s Leading Attys. Republican. Episcopalian. Home: 6223 Waterford Dr Jackson MS 39211-2910 Office: PO Box 14167 Jackson MS 39236-4167 Home Phone: 601-957-1016; Office Phone: 601-351-2440. Business E-Mail: swelch@bakerdonelson.com.

WELCOME, RICHARD MARK, radiologist; b. Mpls., Feb. 5, 1959; s. Dennis Palmer and Mary Kathleen Welcome; m. Mary Ann Huber; children: Andrew Colin, Brandon Mitchell. BS in Chemistry, UCLA, 1980; MD, U. Calif., Irvine, 1984. Diplomate Am. Bd. Radiology, 1989. Intern in internal medicine Kaiser Hosp., Oakland, Calif., 1984—85; resident in radiology Harbor-UCLA Med. Ctr., Torrance, Calif., 1985—89; fellow in interventional radiology Valley Med. Ctr., San Jose, Calif., 1989—90; mem. radiology staff Bakersfield Meml. Hosp., Calif., 1992—97; ptnr. radiologist Santa Monica Hosp., Calif., 1992—97, St. Mary's Regional Med. Ctr., Reno, 2000—; faculty radiologist Santa Monica/UCLA Hosp., 1997—2000. Den leader Cub Scouts, Reno, 2004—05. Mem.: AMA, Soc. Interventional Radiology, Am. Coll. Radiology. Avocations: skiing, golf, tennis, hiking, mountain biking. Office: St Mary's Regional Med Ctr 645 N Arlington Ste 245A Reno NV 89503

WELD, JONATHAN MINOT, lawyer; b. Greenwich, Conn., Feb. 25, 1941; s. Alfred White and Sally Weld; m. Jane Paige, June 19, 1965; children: Elizabeth, Eric. AB in History cum laude, Harvard U., 1963; JD, Cornell U., 1967. Bar: NY 1967, U.S. Ct. Appeals (2d cir.) 1969, U.S. Dist. Ct. (ea. and so. dists.) NY 1970. Assoc. Shearman & Sterling, NYC, 1967-75, ptnr., 1976—2004, London, 1982-85, of counsel, 2005—. Bd. dirs. Bank of N.S. Internat.; chmn., bd. dirs. The Evergreens, Bklyn. Hosp. Bd. dirs. St. Ann's Sch., Bklyn. Bot. Garden, NY Presbyn. Healthcare Sys.; former bd. dirs. Bklyn. Home for Children, Harvard Coll. Fund, Winant and Clayton Vols. Mem.: ABA, NY State Bar Assn. Office: 599 Lexington Ave Fl C2 New York NY 10022-6030 Office Phone: 212-848-8075. Business E-Mail: jweld@shearman.com.

WELD, WILLIAM F., former governor; b. Smithtown, NY, July 31, 1945; s. David and Mary Blake (Nichols) W.; m. Susan Roosevelt (div. 2002), June 7, 1975; children: David Minot, Ethel Derby, Mary Blake, Quentin Roosevelt, Frances Wylie; m. Leslie Marshall, June 14, 2003. AB summa cum laude, Harvard U., 1966, JD cum laude, 1970; diploma with distinction, Oxford U., Eng., 1967. Bar: Mass. 1970. Law clk. to Hon. R.A. Cutter, Supreme Jud. Ct. Mass., 1970-71; ptnr. Hill & Barlow, Boston, 1971-81; assoc. minority counsel US Ho. of Reps. Judiciary Com. Impeachment Inquiry, Washington, 1973-74; US atty. (Dist. Mass.) US Dept. Justice, Boston, 1981-86, asst. atty. gen., criminal divsn. Washington, 1986-88; sr. ptnr. Hale & Dorr, Boston, Washington, 1988-90; gov. Commonwealth of Mass., Boston, 1991—97; ptnr. McDermott, Will & Emery LLP, NYC and Boston, 1997—; prin. Leeds Weld & Co., NYC, 2001—06. Author: Mackerel by Moonlight, 1998, Big Ugly, 1999, Stillwater, 2002; actor: (films) Traffic, 2000. Republican nominee for atty. gen., Mass., 1978, US Senate, Mass., 1996. Republican. Office: McDermott Will & Emery LLP 340 Madison Ave New York NY 10173 Business E-Mail: bweld@mwe.com.

WELDER, RACHAEL MAE, mathematician, educator; d. Larry and Mary Hatzenbuhler; m. Sean Welder, May 26, 2001. MS in Math., U. ND, 2003; PhD in Math., Mont. State U., 2007. Cert. secondary edn. tchr. ND. Grad. tchg. asst. U. ND, Grand Forks, 2001—03; grad. tchg. asst., instr. Mont. State U., Bozeman, 2003—07; asst. prof. Hunter Coll. CUNY, NYC, 2007—. Activist People for the Ethical Treatment of Animals, Bozeman, 2000—06. Scholar, ND U. Sys., 1997—2001, US Achievement Acad., 2000, AAUW. Mem.: Nat. Coun. Tchrs. Math., Nat. Coun. Tchrs. Math., Am. Math. Soc. Democrat. Achievements include research in prerequisite knowledge for learning algebra and mathematical content knowledge needed for effective teaching; preservice elementary teacher's mathematical content knowledge. Avocations: volunteering at local animal shelter, travel, reading. Office: Hunter College Dept Curriculum and Tchg 695 Park Ave New York NY 10021

WELDON, CHARLES JAUVERNI, actor; b. Wetumka, Okla., June 1, 1940; s. Roosevelt and Beatrice (Jennings) W.; m. Debbi Morgan, 1979 (div.) 1984; children: Charles Jr., Barbara Rae, Nick Alonzo. Actor, dir. Negro Ensemble Co., NYC, 1970-94, now artistic dir.; pres. Alumni of Negro Ensemble Co., NYC, 1995-97. Featured in films Malcolm X, Stir Crazy, 1981, Fast Walking, A Woman Called Moses, 1978, The River Niger, Serpico, Rooster Cogburn, Drop Squad, Love Bazarr; (TVappearances) NY Undercover, Another World, LA Law, Law and Order, The Atlanta Child Murders, Hill St. Blues, Roots: The Next Generation, 1979, Another Woman's Child, All My Children, Sanford and Son, Kojak, Police Story, Streets of San Francisco, DA's Investigator, Wishing Tree; (Broadway/NY theatre) The River Niger, 1972, Big Time Buck White, Salaam Huey Salaam, Little Tommy Parker, Jonquil, Raisin in the Sun, Colored Peoples Time, The Great Macdaddy, The Brownsville Raid, Perry's Mission, Pillhill, Fences, Birdie Blue, 2005, Seven Guitars, 2006; (regional theatre) King Lear, Canterbury Tales, Fences, Two Trains Running, Ma Rainey's Black Bottom, Coming of the Hurricane, Much Ado About Nothing, King Henry VI Part 1, Saint Joan, Born a Unicorn, Are You Now...Or Have You Ever Been?, Soldier's Play, The Secret Place, Hair, Taming of the Shrew.

WELDON, CURT (WAYNE CURTIS WELDON), former congressman; b. Marcus Hook, Pa., July 22, 1947; m. Mary Gallagher; children: Karen, Kristin, Kimberly, Curt, Andrew. BA in Humanities, West Chester U., 1969; AAS in Fire Sci., Del. County CC, Media, Pa., 1972; state instrn. cert., Cheyney State Coll.; postgraduate student, Cabrini Coll., Temple U., St. Joseph's U. Lic. tchr. Pa. Tchr. to head tchr. Walnut St. Sch., Darby-Colwyn-William Penn Sch. Dist., Pa., 1972-76; dir. tng. and manpower devel. CIGNA (INA Corp.), Del. County, 1976-87; mayor Town of Marcus Hook, Pa., 1977—82; mem. county coun. Del. County, Pa., 1981-87, vice-chmn. to chmn. Pa., 1984-87; mem. US Congress from 7th Pa. dist., 1987—2007, mem. sci. com., vice chmn. armed svcs. com., chmn. tactical air and land forces subcommittee. Asst. dir. Elem. Secondary Edn. Act Title I Prog., 1972-76; environ. specialist Project KARE, 1972-76; chmn. R&D Ho. Nat. Security Com. Readiness; mem. Com. on Sci. Energy and Environ. Tech.; co-chmn. Congl. Fire Svcs. Caucus, Globe Ocean Protection Task Force, Congl. Missile Def. Caucus, US-FSU Energy Caucus. Named Man of Yr. Chester Bus. and Profl. Assn., Most Effective Freshman Legislator Am. Security Coun., Citizen of Yr. Del. County C. of C., Clean Air Champion Sierra Club, Man of Yr. Internat. Soc. Fire Protection Engrs., 1988, Taxpayers Hero Citizen's Against Government Waste; recipient Outstanding Govt. Leadership award Nat. Recycling Coalition, Fed. Legis. award Pa. Dirs. Assn. Cmty. Action Agencies, Spirit of Enterprise award US C. of C., Golden Bulldog Watchdogs of Treasury award. Republican. *

WELDON, DAVID JOSEPH, JR., congressman, physician; b. Amityville, NY, Aug. 31, 1953; s. David Joseph and Anna Weldon; m. Nancy Sourbeck, Aug. 18, 1979; children: Kathryn, David. BS, SUNY, Stony Brook, 1978; MD, SUNY, Buffalo, 1981. Intern Letterman Army Med. Ctr., 1981-82, resident in internal medicine, 1982-84; pvt. practice, Melbourne Internal Medical Assoc, 1987—94; mem. U.S. Congress from 15th Fla. dist., Washington, 1995—; mem. appropriations com. Fellow ACP; mem. AMA, Fla. Med. Assn Republican. Office: US Ho of Reps 2347 Rayburn Ho Office Bldg Washington DC 20515-0915 *

WELDON, JEFFREY ALAN, lawyer; b. Billings, Mont., May 6, 1963; s. Richard Allen and Monica (Michaud) Weldon; m. Leslie Helen Boileau, July 7, 1990; 2 children. BA, U. Mont., 1986, MPA, 1994, JD, 1996. Assoc. atty. Moulton Bellingham, Longo & Mather, P.C., Billings, Mont., 1997-2000; chief legal counsel Office of Pub. Instrn., State of Mont., Helena, 2000—03; legal counsel, human resources dir. Billings Pub. Schs., 2003—04; assoc. atty. Felt, Martin, Frazier & Jacobs PC, Billings, 2005—. State Senator, Mont., 1993—97. Office Phone: 406-248-7646.

WELDON, THEODORE TEFFT, JR., marketing executive; b. Evanston, Ill., July 19, 1932; s. Theodore Tefft and Dorothe Galbraith (Stover) Weldon; m. Barbara Ann Eskilson, Aug. 17, 1957; children: Lisa Courtney Weldon LeFevre, Theodore Tefft III, Margaret Helen Weldon Franklin. BA, Dartmouth Coll., 1954. Retail store salesman Sears Roebuck & Co., Gary, Ind., 1954-58, retail advt. mgr. Kankakee, Ill., 1958-62, sales mgr. Craftsman Chgo., 1962-69, advt. mgr. Craftsman, 1969-70, mktg. mgr. tires, 1970-81, sr. buyer sporting goods, 1981-82, nat. gen. catalog mgr., 1982-86; dir. home TV shopping Sears/QVC, Chgo., 1986-92; pres. Weldon & Weldon, Winnetka, 1992—, Weldon et Fille, 1996—, Weldon & Son, Ill., 1998—. Cons. Drake, Beam, Morin, Inc., Chgo., 1992-94, Focus Media, Inc., L.A., 1993-96, Std. Mktg. Corp., Naperville, Ill., 1993-98, King World Direct, L.A., 1993-97, Guthy-Renker, Las Vegas, 1997-98, Sears Roebuck and Co., 1997-2000, Ovation Group, Atlanta, 1997-2003, Home Depot, 1997-98, Kmart, 1997-98, Walmart, 1997-98, Pearle Vision, 1998, 3M, 1998, Tyee, Portland, Oreg., 1998-2000, Target Stores, 1998, Panasonic 1997-2000; v.p. mktg. Link Tools Internat., USA, 1998-2006, Content = Commerce Inc., 2001-03. Mem. Jr. Achievement, Chgo., 1966-68; rep. Winnetka (Ill.) Village Caucus, 1972-74; advisor Children's Theatre of Winnetka, 1972—; pres. Sunset Improvement Assn., Winnetka, 1975—. Avocations: travel, theater, swimming, bicycling, golf. Home and Office: 426 Sunset Rd Winnetka IL 60093-4232

WELDON, VIRGINIA V., retired food products executive, retired pediatrician; b. Toronto, Sept. 8, 1935; arrived in US, 1937; d. John Edward and Carolyn Edith (Swift) Verral; children: Ann Weldon Doyle, Susan Weldon Erlinger. AB cum laude, Smith Coll., 1957; MD, SUNY-Buffalo, 1962; LHD (hon.), Rush U., 1985. Diplomate Am. Bd. Pediatrics, Am. Bd. Pediatric Endocrinology and Metabolism, Nat. Bd. Med. Examiners (bd. dirs. 1987-89). Intern Johns Hopkins Hosp., Balt., 1962-63, resident in pediatrics, 1963-64; fellow pediatric endocrinology Johns Hopkins U., Balt., 1964-67, instr. pediatrics, 1967-68; from instr. to assoc. prof. Washington U., St. Louis, 1968—79, prof., 1979-89, v.p. Med. Ctr., 1980-89, dep. vice chancellor med. affairs, 1983-89, dir. Ctr. Study Am. Bus., 1998-99; v.p. sci. affairs Monsanto Co., St. Louis, 1989, v.p. pub. policy, 1989-93, sr. v.p. pub. policy, 1993-98. Mem. gen. clin. rsch. ctrs. adv. com. NIH, Bethesda, Md., 1976—80, mem. rsch. resources adv. coun., 1980—84; advisor, dir. Monsanto Co., 1989—98. Contbr. articles to sci. jours. Mem. risk assessment mgmt. commn. EPA, 1992—97; commr. St. Louis Zool. Pk., 1983—92; mem. Pres.'s Com. Advisors Sci. and Tech., 1994—2000; trustee Calif. Inst. Tech., 1996—, Whitaker Found., 1997—99, St. Louis Sci. Ctr.; bd. dirs., vice chmn., chmn. St. Louis Symphony Orch., 1993—2005, hon. trustee, 2005—; bd. dirs. United Way Greater St. Louis, 1978—90, St. Louis Regional Health Care Corp., 1985—91; mem. adv. com. on agrl. biotech. USDA, 2000—01. Fellow: AAAS, Am. Acad. Pediat.; mem.: St. Louis Med. Soc., Soc. Pediat. Rsch., Endocrine Soc., Am. Pediat. Soc., Assn. Am. Med. Colls. (disting. svc. mem., del., chmn. coun. acad. socs. 1984—85, chmn. assembly 1985—86), Nat. Acads. (nat. assoc.), Inst. Medicine, Alpha Omega Alpha, Sigma Xi. Roman Catholic. Home: 242 Carlyle Lake Dr Saint Louis MO 63141-7544

WELDON, WILLIAM C., pharmaceutical executive; b. Bklyn., Nov. 26, 1948; m. Barbara Weldon; 2 children. BS in biology, Quinnipiac U., 1971. With sales and mktg. McNeil Pharm. Johnson & Johnson, 1971—82; mgr. ICOM Regional Develop. Ctr., 1982—84; v.p. mng. dir. Korea Mcneal Ltd., 1984—86; mng. dir. Orthro-Cilag Pharm., 1986—89; v.p. sales mktg. Janssen Pharm., 1989—92; pres. Ethicon Endo-Surgery, 1992, group chmn., 1995, chmn., pharm. group, 1998; vice-chmn., bd. dirs. Johnson & Johnson, New Brunswick, NJ, 2001—02, chmn., CEO, 2002—. Mem. Bus. Coun., Bus. Roundtable; bd. dirs., exec. com. mem., chmn. Pharm. Rsch. and Manufacturers of Am.; bd. mem. JP Morgan Chase; chmn. Pharm. Rsch. and Mfr., 2005—. Serves Liberty Sci. Center Chmn.'s Adv. Coun.; mem. Sullivan Commn. on Diversity in the Healthcare Workforce; trustee Quinnipiac Univ. Avocation: basketball. Office: Johnson & Johnson 1 Johnson & Johnson Plaza New Brunswick NJ 08933 *

WELDON, WILLIAM FORREST, electrical and mechanical engineer, educator; b. San Marcos, Tex., Jan. 12, 1945; s. Forrest Jackson and Rubie Mae (Wilson) W.; m. Morey Shepard McGonigle, July 28, 1968; children: William Embree, Seth Forrest. BS in Engring. Sci., Trinity U., San Antonio, 1967; MME, U. Tex., Austin, 1970. Registered profl. engr., Tex. Engr. Cameron Iron Works, Houston, 1967-68; project engr. Glastron Boat Co., Austin, Tex., 1970-72; chief engr. Nalle Plastics Co., Austin, 1972-73; rsch. engr. U. Tex., Austin, 1973-77, tech. dir. Ctr. Electromechanics, 1977-85, dir. Ctr. Electromechanics, 1985-93, prof., 1985-2000, Josey Centennial prof. in energy resources, 1992-2000, Josey Centennial prof. emeritus, 2000—. Mem. permanent com. Symposium on Electromagnetic Launch Tech., Naval Rsch. Adv. Com., 1992-97, 2001-05, vice-chmn. 1995-98; cons. numerous cos. and govts., 1973—; chief scientist Office Naval Rsch.-Europe, 1998-99; tech. dir. Office Naval Rsch. Internat. Field Office, 1998-99. Contbr. articles to profl. jours. Bd. dirs Water Control and Improvement Dist. No. 10, Travis County, Tex., 1984—97. Recipient Peter Mark medal Electromagnetic Launch Symposium, 1986, IR 100 award Indsl. Rsch. mag., 1983, Navy Superior Pub. Svc. award, 1998, 99. Fellow ASME; mem. IEEE (sr.), NSPE. Achievements include patents in field. Personal E-mail: weldon@ctesc.net.

WELFARE, FREDERICK GEORGE, secondary school educator; b. Beloit, Wis., Sept. 19, 1956; s. Frederick George Welfare and Margaret Mary Grant. BA, Loyola U., Chgo., 1981; MA, Comumbia U., NYC, 1983; MS, CUNY, 1991, MS, 1999. Spl. edn. tchr. Albert Einstein Jr. H.S., Bronx, NY, 1988—99; sci. tchr. Humanities and Arts H.S., Queens, NY, 1994—. Testing dir. SAT, ACT Campus Magnet H.S., Queens, 1997—2003. Sgt. USAR, 1975—78, sgt. USAR, 1985—92. Mem.: Sci. Tchrs. Assn. NY. Avocations: racquetball, sports, bowling. Office: Humanities and Arts High Sch 207-01 116th Ave Cambria Heights NY 11411

WELGE, DONALD EDWARD, food manufacturing executive; b. St. Louis, July 11, 1935; s. William H. and Rudelle (Fritze) W.; m. Mary Alice Childers, Aug. 4, 1962; children: Robert, Tom. BS, La. State U., 1957. With Gilster-Mary Lee Corp., Chester, Ill., 1957—, pres., gen. mgr., 1965—. Dir. Buena Vista Bank of Chester; pres. Buena Vista Bankcorp. Former chmn. St. John's Luth. Bd. Edn. 1st lt. Transp. Corp, U.S. Army, 1958-63. Named So. Ill. Bus. Leader of Yr. So. Ill. U., 1988. Mem. Perryville C. of C. (pres. 1989), Chester, Ill. C. of C. (past pres.), Alpha Zeta, Phi Kappa Phi. Republican. Lutheran. Home: 5 Knollwood Dr Chester IL 62233-1416 Office: Gilster Mary Lee Co PO Box 227 Chester IL 62233-0227 Business E-Mail: dwelge@gilstermarylee.com.

WELGE, JACK HERMAN, JR., lawyer; b. Austin, Tex., Sept. 12, 1951; s. Jack Herman and Regina Victoria (Hunger) W.; m. Frances Ava Roddy Avent, Dec. 23, 1977; children: Kirsten Frances Page Welge, Kathleen Ava Regina Welge. BA, U. Tex., 1974; JD, St. Mary's U., 1977. Bar: Tex. 1977, U.S. Dist. Ct. (ea. dist.) Tex. 1979, U.S. Dist. Ct. (no. dist.) Tex. 1982, U.S. Ct. Appeals (5th cir.) 1983, U.S. Supreme Ct., 1984; cert. family law Tex. Bd. Legal Specialization 1984. Asst. dist. atty. Gregg County Criminal Dist. Atty., Longview, Tex., 1978-79; assoc. Law Office of G. Brockett Irwin, Longview, 1979-81; judge Mcpl. Ct. of Record, Longview, 1979-81; ptnr. Adams & Sheppard, Longview, 1981-83; pvt. practice, 1983—; mediation practice, 2005—. Of counsel East Tex. Assn. for Abused Families, Longview, 1985-90. Co-chair profl. divsn. Gregg County United Way, 1996—97; mem. bail bond bd. Gregg County, Tex., 2006—; mem. vestry Trinity Episcopal Ch., Longview, 1993—96, 2001—04; bd. directors Longview Cmty. Theater, 1979—82, East Tex. Coun. on Alcoholism and Drug Abuse, Longview, 1981—83, East Tex. Assn. for Abused Families, Longview, 1983—85, Longview Mus. and Arts Ctr., 1991—94;

bd. directors adv. com. Salvation Army, 1994—, chmn., 1997; mem. sch. bd. Trinity Sch. of Tex., 2001—04. Mem.: Tex. Acad. Family Law Specialists, Gregg County Bar Assn. (pres. 1983), N.E. Tex. Bar Assn., State Bar of Tex. (pro bono coll., contested custody case panel, protective case panel, Gregg County lawyers pro bono project, Outstanding Contbn. award 1990, Disting. Svc. award 1993, Outstanding Pro Bono Atty. 1994, Disting. Svc. award 1995, Outstanding Pro Bono Atty. 1997), East Tex. Knife and Fork Club (pres. 1983—84), Rotary (pres. Longview Club 1987—88, Paul Harris fellow 1982, 28 Yrs. Perfect Attendance 2006, IFFR fellowship 2006—), Shriners, Scottish Rite (25 yr. pin), Mason, Delta Upsilon (Tex. chpt. found. bd. 1974—78), Delta Theta Phi (dean 1977, Bickett Senate). Office: 413-415 S Green St PO Box 3624 Longview TX 75606-3624 Office Phone: 903-753-5683. Business E-Mail: welgelaw@sbcglobal.net.

WELIKSON, JEFFREY ALAN, lawyer; b. Bklyn., Jan. 8, 1957; s. Bennet Joseph and Cynthia Ann Welikson; m. Laura Sanders, Aug. 19, 1979; children: Gregory Andrew, Joshua Stuart. BS, U. Pa., 1976, MBA, 1977; JD, Harvard U., 1980. Bar: N.Y. 1981; CPA, N.Y. Assoc. Shearman & Sterling, NYC, 1980-83; staff counsel Reliance Group Holdings Inc., NYC, 1983-84, dir. legal dept., 1984-85, asst. v.p., corp. counsel, 1985-88, v.p., asst. gen. counsel, asst. sec., 1988-94; exec. v.p., gen. counsel, sec. Reliance Nat. Ins. Co., NYC, 1994-2000; sr. v.p., corp. sec., head corp. law Lehman Bros., NYC, 2000—04, mng. dir., 2004—, corp. sec., 2004—, head corp. law, 2004—. Contbg. editor Harvard U. Internat. Law Jour., 1979-80. Mem.: Am. Soc. Corp. Secs. and Governance Profls., Am. Corp. Counsel Assn. Office: Lehman Brothers Holdings Inc 1301 Ave of the Americas New York NY 10019

WELK, RICHARD ANDREW, plastic surgeon; b. Aug. 9, 1956; BS, U. Mich., 1977, MD, 1981. Diplomate Am. Bd. Surgery, Am. Bd. Plastic Surgery. Resident gen. surgery, Grand Rapids, Mich., 1981-86; resident plastic surgery U. Calif., Irvine, 1986-88; plastic surgeon pvt. practice, Kirkland, Wash., 1988-91, Polyclinic, Seattle, 1991—. Mem. Am. Soc. Plastic & Reconstructive Surgery, Am. Soc. Aesthetic Plastic Surgery, Wash. State Med. Assn., Wash. Soc. Plastic Surgeons (pres. 1995-96). Office: Polyclinic 1145 Broadway Seattle WA 98122-4299 Office Phone: 206-860-2317.

WELK, THOMAS JOHN, lawyer; b. Hoven, SD, Aug. 12, 1950; s. Al John and Monica Rose (Coyle) W.; m. Genevieve T. Welk, 1975; children: Colleen, David, Kathleen. BS in Econs. with honors, U. S.D., 1972, MBA, JD, 1975. Bar: S.D. 1975, U.S. Dist. Ct. S.D. 1967, U.S. Ct. Appeals (8th cir.) 1977, U.S. Ct. Appeals (9th cir.) 1987, U.S. Tax Ct. 1981, U.S. Supreme Ct. 1981; bd. cert. civil advocacy Nat. Bd. Trial Advocacy 1995. Asst. atty. gen. State of S.D., Pierre, 1975-79, dep. atty. gen., 1979; ptnr. Boyce, Greenfield, Pashby & Welk, LLP (formerly Boyce, Murphy, McDowell & Greenfield), Sioux Falls, SD, 1979—. Mem. ABA (adminstrv. law, antitrust sect.), SD Bar Assn. (chmn., com. mem., pres. 2004-05), Am. Bd. Trial Advs., Internat. Assn. Def. Counsel, Fedn. Def. and Corp. Counsel, SD Def. Lawyers Assn. (past pres., leadership award Def. Rsch. Inst.), Westward House Country Club (pres.). Republican. Roman Catholic. Avocations: golf, hunting, travel. Office: Boyce, Greenfield, Pashby & Welk LLP 101 N Phillips Ave Ste 600 PO Box 5015 Sioux Falls SD 57117-5015 Office Phone: 605-336-2424. Office Fax: 605-334-0618. Business E-Mail: tjwelk@bgpw.com.

WELKE, ELTON GRINNELL, JR., publisher, writer; b. Berkeley, Calif., June 15, 1941; s. Elton Grinnell and Elsie Maud (Shattuck) W.; m. Anna Lange, July 28, 1963 (div. 1980); children: Allison Espy, Erik Grinnell; m. Bonnie Jean Lum, Jan. 24, 1981; 1 child, Erin Irene. BA in Zoology, U. Calif., Berkeley, 1962. Staff writer Sunset mag., Menlo Pk., Calif., 1962-65, assoc. editor, 1965-69, sr. editor, 1978-80; travel editor Better Homes & Gardens, Des Moines, 1969-71; mng. editor Apt. Life mag., Des Moines, 1971-72; exec. editor Sunset Spl. Interest mags., Menlo Pk., 1972-78; freelance editorial cons. San Francisco and Seattle, 1981-84; v.p., dir. Livingston & Co., Seattle, 1984-89; publisher Microsoft Press, 1989-98; chmn. North Wave Comms., Inc., Alaska, 1996—. Bd. dirs. Smart Starters Corp., Seattle; vice chmn. Ibex Corp., Beijing, 1998—. Author: How to Survive Being Alive, 1977, Place's to go With Children Around Puget Sound, 1987. Bd. dirs. Olympic Nat. Pk. Assocs., Washington, 1965-69, March of Dimes, Western Washington, 1987-92, chmn. campaign com., 1989-92. Recipient 1st Pl. award Washington Press Assn., 1985, 86, 88, WPA award, 1987. Mem. Soc. Am. Travel Writers, PRSA, Internat. Assn. Bus. Communicators (Golden Quill award 1985), Safari Club, Alpha Delta Phi. Republican. Avocations: gardening, plant collecting, fly fishing, cattle ranching, asian art. Home and Office: 11329 NE 103d St Kirkland WA 98033-5178

WELKER, JAMES ANTHONY, physician; b. Pitts., Oct. 27, 1969; s. James Edward and Janet Rachael Welker. BS, Ohio No. U., 1991; DO, Phila. Coll. Osteo. Medicine, 1995. Diplomate Am. Bd. Internal Medicine, cert. physician investigator. Intern U. Medicine and Dentistry N.J., Stafford, 1995-96; resident in internal medicine Washington Hosp., 1996-99; dir. hospitalist sect. Harbor Hosp. Ctr., Balt., 1999—2004; dir. hospitalist residency Franklin Square Hosp., Balt., 2004—, dir. Clin. Trial Rsch. Ctr., 2004—; asst. prof. medicine U. Md. Sch. Medicine. Cons., software developer Med. Info. Sys.; founding ptnr. real estate investment co.; prin. investigator multi-instnl. clin. trials; mem. faculty Med. Sch., U. Md., 2005—; expert witness in med. malpractice; spkr. in field. Contbr. articles to profl. jours. Vol. physician Mobile Med. Care, Rockville, 1997-99; ref. for peer-reviewed jours. Recipient numerous honors and awards. Roman Catholic. Avocations: exercising, outdoors. Office: Franklin Sq Hosp 9000 Franklin Sq Dr Baltimore MD 21237 Office Phone: 443-777-7706. Personal E-mail: jimwelker@hotmail.com.

WELKER, JENNIFER CAROL MARIE, artist; b. Conroe, Tex., May 9, 1977; d. Pamela Diane and Ronald Vaughn Welker. AA in Fashion Design, Fashion Inst. Tech., NYC, 1999. Co-founder, designer IC3D, NYC, 1999—2002; mens designer Garren Inc., NYC, 2002; artist Briefly Stated Inc., NYC, 2003—. Co-founder D-Jeans, NYC, 2003—; founder War Angels, NYC, 2003—. Dir.: (documentary) Beyond The Ribbon. Mem. UNA-USA, NYC, 2005—06; rev. World Christianship Ministries, Fresno, Calif., 2006—06; sponsor, mentor Save the Children, NYC, 2005—06. Recipient Wall of Tolerance award, So. Poverty Law Ctr., 2005. Mem.: UN High Commn. for Refugees (life), Human Rights Watch (assoc.), Witness Orgn. (assoc.), Nat. Art Honor Soc. Achievements include design of digital custom clothing. Avocations: philanthropy, screen writing, human rights activist, sign language, actor. Home: 409 W 39th St Apt2A New York NY 10018 Home Phone: 212-594-7495. Personal E-mail: welker@beyondtheribbon.com.

WELKER, KARA, agent; b. Mar. 26, 1972; m. Steven Maloney, Apr. 23, 2004. Grad. in Creative Writing, U. Calif., Irvine. With booking dept. Irvine Improv, Calif.; asst. to mgr. Messina/Baker Entertainment Corp., 1994; mgr. 3 Arts Entertainment; ptnr., mgr. Rath-Welker Mgmt.; cofounder Generate, Santa Monica, Calif., 2006—. Exec. prodr.: (TV series) Slice o' Life, 2003, The Barenaked Ladies Variety Show, 2005, The Comedians of Comedy, 2005, Wonder Showzen, 2005; prodr.: Deal, 2005, The Andy Milonakis Show, 2005. Co-founder South Toward Home, Santa Monica, Calif. Office: Generate 1545 26th St Ste 200 Santa Monica CA 90404 E-mail: Kara@generatela.com. *

WELKER, KRISTINA DIANE, psychologist; b. July 9, 1960; BA, U. Ctrl. Okla., Edmond, 1989; MA, Ottawa U., Phoenix, 2000; D of Psychology, So. Calif. U. of Profl. Studies, 2006. Nat. cert. counselor 2003, lic. profl. counselor 2006. Pharm. sales rep. Mead Johnson Labs., Phoenix, 1992—94; profl. counselor, 2001—06; psychologist Well Within, LLC, 2006—. Contbr. articles to Ahwailukee Foothills News. Mem.: Nat. Bd. Cert. Counselors, Am. Counseling Assn., Am. Soc. Bariatric Physicians. Office: 12020 S Warner Elliot Loop Ste 104 Phoenix AZ 85044

WELKOWITZ, WALTER, biomedical engineer, educator; b. Bklyn., Aug. 3, 1926; s. Samuel and Shirley (Rosenblum) W.; m. Joan Horowitz, June 17, 1951; children: David, Lawrence, Julie. BS, The Cooper Union, NYC, 1948; MS, U. Ill., 1949, PhD, 1954. Profl. engr., N.J. Rsch. assoc. U. Ill., Urbana, 1948-54, Columbia U., NYC, 1954-55; asst. to pres., gen. mgr. Gulton Industries, Inc., Metuchen, NJ, 1955-64; prof., chmn. elec. engring. Rutgers U., Piscataway, NJ, 1964-86, prof. biomed. engring., 1986—, chmn. biomedical engring., 1986-90. Cons. Gulton Industries, Metuchen, N.J., 1964-74. Author: Engineering Hemodynamics: Application to Cardiac Assist Devices, 1977, 2d edit., 1987; co-author: Biomedical Instruments: Theory and Design, 1976, 2d edit., 1992; author numerous chpts. in books; contbr. more than 100 articles to profl. jours. With U.S. Navy, 1944-46. Rutgers U. Rsch. Coun. fellow, 1974-75; recipient Centennial medal IEEE, 1984, Excellence in Rsch. award Rutgers Bd. Trustees, 1985, IEEE Career Achievement award Soc. Engring. Med. Biology, 1991; Llewellyn Thomas vis. prof. U. Toronto, Can., 1989. Fellow IEEE (engring. in medicine and biol. soc. career achievement award 1991), N.Y. Acad. Medicine, Am. Inst. of Medicine and Biol. Engring. Achievements include 26 patents for Electron Tube, Ultrasonic Flowmeter, Ultrasonic Transducer, Piezoelectric Heart Assist Apparatus, Method and Apparatus for Non-Invasive Monitoring Dynamic Cardiac Performance, and others. Home: PO Box 2289 Lenox MA 01240-5289 Office: Rutgers U Biomed Engring PO Box 909 Piscataway NJ 08855-0909 Office Phone: 413-637-8267. Personal E-mail: wwelkowitz@msn.com.

WELLBERG, EDWARD LOUIS, JR., insurance company executive; b. Eagle Pass, Tex., June 5, 1945; s. Edward L. Wellberg and Nell L. (Kownslar) Walker; children: Elizabeth, Ashley, Jennifer; m. Yvonne Hill, Feb. 4, 1989. Student, St. Mary's U., San Antonio, 1978. CLU, Life Underwriters Tng. Coun. Fellow. Sales agt. Washington Nat. Ins. Co., San Antonio, 1969-82; ptnr. Mazur Bennett Wellberg Assocs., San Antonio, 1982-91; mktg. exec. Wellberg Assocs., San Antonio, 1991—. Bd. dirs. Tex. State Ins. Bd. Adv. Coun., Austin, 1988-94. Contbr. articles to profl. jours. Mem. Am. Soc. CLU's, Tex. Assn. Ins. and Fin. Advisors (bd. dirs. 1983-86, 92-93, pres. 1996, state nat. com. 1997-2000), Tex. Life Underwriters Polit. Action Com. (vice chmn. 1981-83, 88-90, chmn. 1990-92, state nat. committeeman 1997-2000), San Antonio Assn. Ins. and Fin. Advisors (pres. 1982). Home: 1746 Santa Fe Trail San Antonio TX 78232 Office: 14400 Northbrook Dr Ste 200 San Antonio TX 78232-5038 Office Phone: 210-490-1188. Personal E-mail: ed@wellberg.net.

WELLBORN, CHARLES IVEY, strategic planning consultant; b. Houston, Dec. 9, 1941; s. Fred W. and Emily R. (Gladu) W.; m. JD McCausland, Aug. 14, 1965; children: Westly O., Kerry W. Phillips. BA in Econs., U. N.Mex., 1963, JD, 1966; LLM, NYU, 1972. Bar: N.Mex. 1966, U.S. Dist. Ct. N.Mex. 1966. Assoc. Neal & Matkins, Carlsbad, N.Mex., 1966-68, Robinson & Stevens, Albuquerque, 1969-71; ptnr. Schlenker, Parker, Payne & Wellborn, Albuquerque, 1971-76, Parker & Wellborn, Albuquerque, 1976-82, Modrall, Sperling, Roehl, Harris & Sisk, Albuquerque, 1982-95; pres., CEO Sci. & Tech. Corp. at U. N.Mex., Albuquerque, 1995-2000; pres. Wellborn Strategies LLC, Albuquerque, 2000—06. Chmn. N.Mex. Tax Rsch. Inst., 2002—06, N.Mex. Small Bus. Investment Corp., 2003—06. Vice chair U. N.Mex. Found., Inc., 1990—94; mem. Econ. Forum, 1986—2002, chmn., 1995—96; mem. City-County Unification Charter Commn., 2002—03; bd. dirs. N.Mex. Assn. Commerce and Industry, 2003—, N.Mex. Cmty. Capital, 2005—, N.Mex. Symphony Orch., 1988—91, U. N.Mex. Anderson Schs. Mgmt. Found., 1989—94, N.Mex. First, 1989—93, 2000—04, Accion N.Mex., 1995—97, Outpost Performance Space, 2000—04; State N. Mex. Private Equity Investment adv. com., 1991—98; mem. Govs. Prayer Breakfast Com., 1991—2002, chair, 2000—02; bd. dirs. Next Generation Economy Inc., 2002—05, Sci. and Tech. Corp. U. N.Mex., 2000—. Sgt. USAF, 1968—69, Korea. Mem.: ABA (ho. of dels. 1984—91), State Bar N.Mex. (pres. 1982—83), N.Mex. Bar Found. (pres. 1980—82), Albuquerque Bar Assn. (pres. 1977—78). Democrat. Roman Catholic. Office: Wellborn Strategies LLC 3819 La Hacienda Dr NE Albuquerque NM 87110-6115 Office Phone: 505-238-7890.

WELLEIN, MARSHA DIANE AKAU, military educator, director; d. George Herbert and Trude (Michelson) Akau; m. Daniel Navarro Atoigue; 1 child, Daniet Hokule'a; m. Lawrence Theodore Wellein (dec.); children: Geoffrey Michael, Nicholas Patrick. BA, U. Hawaii, 1966, tchg. cert., 1971; MEd, U. Guam, 1974; postgrad. in ednl. leadership, Argosy U., 2005. Instr. Hawaii Job Corps Ctr., 1969—71; tchr. spl. edn., reading, lang. arts, adults, pre-kindergarten to HS, U. Guam, 1972—80; reading specialist Waipahu Intermediate; instr. (full and part time) Leeward CC, U. Hawaii, 1981—85, instr. reading, 1983—85; full time guidance counselor US Army, Ft. Shafter Edn. Ctr., 1983—85, Larson Barracks, Germany, 1985—86; edn. svcs. officer, dir. Multinat. Force and Observers, North Camp, El Gorah, Sinai, Egypt, 1987—90; full time guidance counselor Dept. Army, Schofield Barracks, 1990; edn. svcs. officer Dept. Army, Soto Cano Air Base, Honduras, 1991—93, Ft. Kobbe, Panama, 1991—93; edn. svcs. specialist Dept. Army, Kuwait and Saudi Arabia (Desert Storm), 1993, Schofield Barracks Edn. Ctr. 25th Infantry, Hawaii, 1994—96, Camp Zama Edn. Ctr., Japan, 1996—98, 8th Army, Republic of Korea, 1998—99; dir. edn. and libr. svcs. US Army South, PR, 1999—2000; edn. svcs. specialist Dept. Army, Ft. Shafter, 2000—01; regional dir. end. USAR, Honolulu, 2001—. Author: (juvenile hardback novel) The Endless Summer, An Adventure Story of Guam, 1976; editor: Kalihi Kids Can Communicate, 1976. Bd. mem. Internat. Reading Assn., 1972—80, pres., 1980; mem. Oahu Com. Children and Youth, Honolulu, 1969. Named Outstanding Edn. Svcs. Officer, Dir. Edn., USAR, 2003; recipient Multinat. Force and Observers medal, US State Dept, 1987—89, Achievement medal civilian svc., Kuwait, 1993, Japan, 1997, Comdr.'s award civilian svc., 1986, 1987, 1988, 1998, Cold War cert., Dept. Def., 1998, Equal Opportunity award, Camp Zama, Japan, 1998, Unsung Heroes award, Dir. Army Edn., Hdqrs., Washington, 2005, Lamp Lighters award, USAR, 2005. Mem.: Coun. Coll. and Mil. Educators, Am. Assn. Adult and Continuing Edn. Avocations: travel, reading, theater. Home: 95-086 Waihonu Pl Mililani HI 96789 Office: HQ G1 US Army Res 9RRC 1557 Pass St Honolulu HI 96819-2135 Office Fax: 808-438-1379. Personal E-mail: welleinmd@hotmail.com.

WELLEMS, THOMAS E., federal agency administrator; b. Anaconda, Mont., Aug. 2, 1951; PhD, U. Chgo., 1980; MD, U. Chgo. Pritzker Sch. Medicine, 1981. Cert. Internal Medicine. Intern, internal medicine Hosp. U. Pa., Phila., 1981—82, resident, tropical medicine, 1982—84; fellow NIH, Bethesda, Md., 1984—86; sr. staff fellow Nat. Inst. Allergy and Infectious Diseases/NIH, Bethesda, Md., 1987—91, head, GPS/LMR, 1991—95, chief, lab. malaria genetics sect. and vector rsch., 1995—. Frequent lectr., cons. and reviewer; serves on a number of adv. com. for founds. and pub.-private partnerships, including Medicines for Malaria Venture. Mem.: NAS. Address: NIAID Office of Communications and Pub Liaison 6610 Rockledge Dr MSC 6612 Bethesda MD 20892-6612 Office: NIAID Office Malaria and Vector Rsch Lab Twinbrook II 12441 Parklawn D 3E10A Bethesda MD 20892-0001 Office Phone: 301-496-2487. Business E-Mail: twellems@niais.nih.gov. *

WELLEN, ROBERT HOWARD, lawyer; b. Jersey City, Aug. 19, 1946; s. Abraham Louis and Helen Rose (Krieger) W.; m. Anita Fass, June 16, 1968; children: Elizabeth, Judith Maria. BA, Yale Coll., 1968; JD, Yale U., 1971; LLM in Taxation, Georgetown U., 1975. Bar: Conn. 1971, D.C. 1972, Colo. 1982. Assoc. Fulbright & Jaworski, Washington, 1975-76, participating assoc., 1976-79, ptnr., 1979-93, Ivins, Phillips & Barker, Washington, 1993—. Adj. prof. law Georgetown U. Law Ctr., 1982-85. Contbr. articles to legal publs. Served to lt. JAGC, USNR, 1971-75. Mem. ABA (past asst. sec., past chmn. com. on corp. tax, sect. taxation, past supr. editor sect. taxation newsletter, vice chair law devel. com. on corp. tax), Fed. Bar Assn. (coun. taxation), Phi Beta Kappa. Jewish. Office: Ivins Phillips & Barker 1700 Pennsylvania Ave NW Ste 600 Washington DC 20006-4723 Office Phone: 202-662-3401. E-mail: rwellen@ipbtax.com.

WELLER, ELIZABETH BOGHOSSIAN, child and adolescent psychiatrist; b. Aug. 7, 1949; m. Ronald A. Weller, Feb. 18, 1978; children: Andrew, Christine. BS, Am. U., Beirut, Lebanon, 1971, MD, 1975. Lic. psychiatrist, Lebanon, Mo., Ohio, Pa. Intern Am. U. of Beirut, 1974-75; resident Renard Hosp./Washington U., St. Louis, 1975-78; fellow U. Kans. Med. Ctr., Kansas City, 1978-79; asst. prof. psychiatry U. Kans. Med. Sch., Kansas City, 1979-85; chief child/adolescent psychiatry Ohio State U., Columbus, 1985-94, assoc. chair dept. psychiatry, 1994-96; prof. psychiatry and pediat. U. Pa., 1996—, chmn. dept. psychiatry child and adolescent psychiatry, 1996-99, vice chmn. dept. psychiatry, prof. psychiatry/pediatrics, 1996—. Fred Allen chair dept. psychiatry Children's Hosp. of Phila., med. dir. Child Guidance Ctr., 1996-99; pres. Am. Bd. Psychiatry and Neurology, 2004. Co-author: Psychiatric Disorders in Child/Adolescent, 1990, Current Perspectives on Major Depressive Disorders in Children, 1984, Children's Interview for Psychiatric Syndromes, 1999. Fellow APA, Am. Acad. Child/Adolescent Psychiatry; mem. AMA, ACP, World Fedn. for Mental Health, Soc. Biol. Psychiatry, Am. Bd. Psychiatry and Neurology (pres. 2004). Office: 3440 Market St Philadelphia PA 19104-4399 Home Phone: 610-617-3166; Office Phone: 215-590-7573. Business E-Mail: weller@email.chop.edu.

WELLER, GERALD C., congressman; b. Streator, Ill., July 7, 1957; s. LaVern and Marilyn Weller; m. Zury Rios Sosa. Degree in Agriculture, U. Ill., 1979. Aide to U.S. Congerssman Tom Corcoran, 1977-78; aide to U.S. Sec. of Agriculture John R. Block, 1981-85; active family farm, 1985-88; mem. Ill. Ho. of Reps., 1987—93, U.S. Congress from 11th Ill. dist., 1995—; asst. majority whip; mem. ways and means com., 1996—; mem. Internat. Relations Com., 2003—. Rep. House Republican steering com.; mem. Newt Gingrich's policy com.; exec. com. NRCC, House Banking Com., House Veterans Affairs Com., House Transp. and Infrastructure Com. Mem. 1st Christian Ch. of Morris, Ill. Mem. Nat. Republican Legis. Assn. (nominated Legislator of Yr.). Republican. Office: US Ho Reps 1210 Longworth Ho Office Bldg Washington DC 20515-1311 *

WELLER, MARTHA RIHERD, physics and astronomy professor, consultant; b. Charleston, SC, Oct. 20, 1952; d. Paul Markey and Martha Carroll Riherd; m. Robert Allen Weller, June 21, 1975; children: Rachel Weller Deaton, Robert Samuel, Rebecca Shelley. BA in Physics, Rice U., 1973; PhD in Physics, Calif. Inst. Tech., 1979. Rsch. physicist Naval Rsch. Lab., Washington, 1979—80; rsch. staff physicist, rsch. assoc. Yale U., New Haven, 1980—87; asst. prof. physics Mid. Tenn. State U., Murfreesboro, Tenn., 1988—93, assoc. prof. physics, astronomy, 1993—98, prof. of physics, astronomy, 1998—. Com. mem. Brentwood 2020, Tenn., 1998—98; pres. Edmondson Elem. PTO, Brentwood, Tenn., 1995—96, Centennial H.S. Parent Tchr. Student Orgn., Franklin, Tenn., 1998—99; sch. bd. rep. Williamson County Bd. of Edn., Franklin, Tenn., 2002—06. Mem.: Tenn. Acad. of Sci. (physics and astronomy editl. bd. 1991—, exec. bd. mem. 1995—97), Sigma Xi, Am. Assn. of Physics Tchrs., Am. Phys. Soc. Office: Mid Tenn State Univ PO Box 403 Murfreesboro TN 37132 Home Phone: 615-371-1164; Office Phone: 615-898-2792. Office Fax: 615-898-5303. E-mail: mweller@mtsu.edu.

WELLER, MILTON WEBSTER, wetland ecologist, educator; b. St. Louis, May 23, 1929; m. Doris Laverne Leach; 1 child, Mitchel Wayne. AA, Harris Jr. Coll., 1949; BA, U. Mo., 1951, MS, 1954, PhD, 1956. Instr. dept zoology U. Mo., Columbia, 1956-57; asst. prof. zoology Iowa State U., Ames, 1957-61, assoc. prof., 1961-67, prof.-in-charge wildlife and fish, 1967-74; prof., head fish and wildlife U. Minn., St. Paul, 1974-82; prof., Kleberg chair wildlife Tex. A&M U., College Station, 1982-94, prof. emeritus, 1995—. Dir. Nat. Audubon Soc., N.Y.C., 1987-92; mem. Environ. Steering Com., Tex. Utilities, Dallas, 1990-99; assoc. editor Wetlands, Ann Arbor, Mich., 1988-92. Editor: Waterfowl in Winter, 1988; author: Wetland Birds, 1999; Freshwater Marshes, 1994, 3rd edit.; contbr. chpts. to Wetland Creation & Restoration, 1989, Habitat Use By Breeding Waterfowl, 1992; contbr. articles to profl. jours. Recipient Lifetime Achievement award Soc. Wetland Sci., 1996, Aldo Leopold Meml. award The Wildlife Soc., 1997. Fellow AAAS, Am. Ornithologist Union. Achievements include rsch. in wetland dynamics in relation to wildlife populations and regional biodiversity, wetland restoration and creation, waterbird ecology and management.

WELLER, PETER, actor; b. Stevens Point, Wis., June 24, 1947; s. Frederick and Dorothy Weller. BA, North Tex. State U., 1970; cert., Am. Acad. Dramatic Arts, NYC, 1972; studies with Uta Hagen, H.B. Studios, NYC, 1974-77; Master's Degree in Roman and Renaissance art. Teaches a lit. and fine arts class Syracuse Univ. Appeared in various plays including Sticks and Bones, Streamers, The Woods, Daddy Wolf, Rebel Women, The Woolgatherer, Cat on a Hot Tin Roof; TV films The Man Without a Country, 1973, The Silence, 1975, The Dancing Princesses, 1978, Kentucky Woman, 1983, Two Kinds of Love, 1983, Apology, 1986, Women and Men: Stories of Seduction, 1990, Rainbow Drive, 1990, The Substitute Wife, 1994, Lakota Women: Siege at Wounded Knee, 1994, Present Tense, Past Perfect, 1995, End of Summer, 1997, Tower of the Firstborn, 1998, Dark Prince: The True Story of Dracula, 2000, Odyssey 2002-2003 (also dir. 2 episodes), The Poseidon Adventure, 2005; TV mini series Mourning Becomes Electra, 1978; films include Butch and Sundance: The Early Years, 1979, Just Tell Me What You Want, 1980, Shoot the Moon, 1982, Of Unknown Origin, 1983, Adventures of Buckaroo Bonzai Across the 8th Dimension, 1984, Firstborn, 1984, A Killing Affair, 1986, The Tunnel, 1987, Robocop, 1987, Shakedown, 1988, Leviathan, 1989, Cat Chaser, 1989, Robocop II, 1990, Naked Lunch, 1991, Fifty-Fifty, 1992, Sunset Grill, 1993, The New Age, 1994, Decoy, 1995, Beyond the Clunds, 1995, Screamers, 1995, Mighty Aphrodite, 1995, Top of the World, 1997, Diplomatic Siege, 1999, Shadow Hours, 2000, Falling Through, 2000, The Contaminated Man, 2000, Ivansxtc, 2000, Styx, 2001, The Order, 2003, The Hard Easy, 2005, Man of God, 2005, Undiscovered, 2005; cable film My Sister's Keeper; dir.: Michael Hayes (TV series), 1997; dir., prodr. (TV) Gold Coast, 1997, actor, writer, dir. (TV) Partners, 1993; guest appearances The Handler, 2003, Enterprise, 2005, 24, 2006, Monk, 2006 (also dir., 1 episode). Mem. Actor's Studio, 1979. Avocation: jazz. *

WELLER, ROBERT N(ORMAN), hotel executive; b. Harrisburg, Pa., Feb. 1, 1939; s. Charles Walter and Martha Ann (MacPherson) W.; m. Nancy M. Wood, June 21, 1975; children— Wendi Elizabeth, Terrie Lynn, Nikki Ann. BS, Cornell U., 1969. Mgr. Hall's Motor Transit Co., Harrisburg, 1961-65; market rsch. analyst Carrolls Devel. Corp., Syracuse, NY, 1970-72; asst. to pres. Econo-Travel Motor Hotel Corp., Norfolk, Va., 1972-74, dir. franchise sales, 1975, pres., dir., 1976-84, Econo-Travel Devel. Corp., Norfolk, 1977-84; pres. Internat. Data Bank Ltd., 1985-86; pres., dir. Econo Lodges of Am., 1986-90; group pres., exec. v.p. Choice Hotels Internat., Silver Spring, Md., 1990-91; with Hospitality Ventures, Virginia Beach, Va., 1991—93; pres. Super 8 Motels, Inc. divsn. Hospitality Franchise Systems, Parsippany, NJ, 1993—2001; group pres. hotel divsn. Cendant Corp., Parsippany, 2001—. Served in USMC, 1957-60. Home: 3027 Lynndale Rd Virginia Beach VA 23452-6233 Office: Cendant Hotel Group Inc One Sylvan Way Parsippany NJ 07054 Business E-Mail: bob.weller@cendant.com.

WELLER, ROBERT STEPHEN, anesthesiologist; b. Syracuse, NY, Feb. 1, 1955; s. Elizabeth W Stein and Ralph N Weller; m. Elizabeth A McGowan, Nov. 30, 1991; children: Erin E Power, Jeffrey M McGowan, Kevin P McGowan. MD summa cum laude, Northwestern U., Chgo., 1979. Asst. prof. of anesthesiology U. of Conn. Sch. of Medicine, Farmington, Conn., 1984—91, assoc. prof. of anesthesiology, 1991—97, Wake Forest U. Sch. of Medicine, Winston-Salem, NC, 1997—. Residency program dir. U. of Conn. Anesthesiology Dept., Farmington, Conn., 1986—96; cons. in anesthesiology Am. Bd. Anesthesiologists, 1984. Named Outstanding Tchr., Residents in Anesthesiology, 2001; recipient LB Arey award, Northwestern U. Sch. of Medicine, 1977, FK Rawson award, 1979, David Little award, Hartford Hosp. Anesthesiology Program, 1983. Mem.: Internat. Anesthesia Rsch. Soc., Am. Soc. of Regional Anesthesia and Pain Medicine, Am. Soc. of Anesthesiologists. Office: Wake Forest University School of Med Medical Center Blvd Winston Salem NC 27157 Home Phone: 336-924-0524; Office Phone: 336-716-7150. Personal E-mail: rweller@triad.rr.com. E-mail: rweller@wfubmc.edu.

WELLER, SOL WILLIAM, chemical engineering professor; b. Detroit, July 27, 1918; s. Ira and Bessie (Wieselthier) W.; m. Miriam Damick, June 11, 1943; children: Judith, Susan, Robert, Ira BS, Wayne State U., Detroit, 1938; PhD, U. Chgo., 1941. Asst. chief coal hydrogenation U.S. Bur. Mines, Pitts., 1945-50; head fundamental rsch. Houdry Process Corp., Linwood, Pa., 1950-58; mgr. propulsion rsch. Ford Aeronutronic Co., Newport Beach, Calif., 1958-61; dir. chem. lab. and materials rsch. lab. Philco-Ford Co., Newport Beach, 1961-65; prof. chem. engring. SUNY-Buffalo, 1965—; emeritus, 1989; C.C. Furnas prof. SUNY-Buffalo, 1983—. Vis. fellow Oxford U., 1989. Author numerous sci. papers, book chpts., ency. entries Fulbright lectr. Madrid, 1975, Istanbul, 1980; recipient Chancellor's Tchg. award SUNY, 1973. Mem. ASTM (founder com. D32 on catalysts), Am. Chem. Soc. (chmn. Orange County sect. 1964, H.H. Storch award 1981, E.V. Murphree award 1982, Schoellkopf medal 1984). Achievements include patents in field.

WELLER, STEPHEN G., botanist, educator; BS in Botany with high honors, U. Mich., Ann Arbor, 1971; PhD in Botany, U. Calif., Berkeley, 1975. Asst. prof. U. Ill., Chgo., 1975—81, assoc. prof., 1981—87, U. Calif., Irvine, 1987—92, prof. ecology and evolutionary biology, 1992—. Summer faculty U. Wash., 1975, U. Mich. Biol. Sta., 1981; vis. colleague dept. botany U. Hawaii, 1987; sr. Mellon fellow Smithsonian Instn., 1993—94; McBryde chair Hawaiian plant scis. Nat. Tropical Bot. Garden, 1995—98. Contbr. articles to sci. jours.; assoc. editor: Evolution, 1981—85. Mem.: Soc. Study of Evolution, Soc. Conservation Biology, Am. Soc. Plant Taxonomists, Bot. Soc. Am. (sec. 2006—). Office: Dept Ecology and Evolutionary Biology U Calif Irvine Irvine CA 92697-2525 Office Phone: 949-824-6581. Office Fax: 949-824-2181. E-mail: sgweller@uci.edu. *

WELLER, THERESE MARIE, not-for-profit fundraiser; b. Idaho Falls, Idaho, Jan. 16, 1969; d. Gary Thomas and Virginia Susan Weller. BS, Ft. Lewis Coll., Durango, Colo., 1990. Dir. devel. U. Colo. Found., Boulder, 1992—97, Holy Family HS, Broomfield, Colo., 1998—2000, Mont. State U. Big Sky Inst. Sci. and Natural History, Bozeman, 2002—04, Heart of the Valley Animal Shelter, Bozeman, 2004—05; maj. gifts officer office instl. advancement Colo. Sch. Mines, Golden, 2000—02, dir. corp. and found. rels. Mont. State U. Found., Bozeman, 2005—. Contbr. poetry to lit. publ. Bd. dirs. Heart of Valley Animal Shelter, Bozeman, 2007—. Mem.: Am. Assn. Grant Profls., Coun. Advancement and Support Edn., Assn. Fundraising Profls. (cert.), Rotary (bd. dirs. Bozeman Noon Club 2006—07). Home: 15 Prospector Tr Bozeman MT 59718 Office: Montana State U Found 1501 South 11th Ave Bozeman MT 59718 Office Fax: 406-994-6081. Business E-Mail: tweller@montana.edu.

WELLER, THOMAS HUCKLE, physician, retired medical educator; b. Ann Arbor, Mich., June 15, 1915; s. Carl V. and Elsie A. (Huckle) Weller; m. Kathleen R. Fahey, Aug. 18, 1945; children: Peter Fahey, Nancy Kathleen, Robert Andrew, Janet Louise. AB, U. Mich., 1936; MS, 1937, LL.D. (hon.), 1956; MD, Harvard, 1940; Sc.D., Gustavus Adolphus U., 1975, U. Mass., 1985; L.H.D., Lowell U., 1977. Diplomate Am. Bd. Pediatrics. Teaching fellow bacteriology Harvard Med. Sch., 1940—41, research fellow tropical medicine, pediatrics, 1947—48, instr. comparative pathology, tropical medicine, 1948—49, asst. prof. tropical pub. health Sch. Pub. Health, 1949—50, assoc. prof., 1950—54, Richard Pearson Strong prof. tropical pub. health, 1954—85, prof. emeritus, 1985—, head dept., 1954—81; intern bacteriology and pathology Children's Hosp., Boston, 1941, intern medicine, 1942, asst. resident medicine, 1946, asst. dir. research div. infectious diseases, 1949—55; mem. commn. parasitic diseases Armed Forces Epidemiol. Bd., 1953—72, dir., 1953—59. Contbr. articles to sci. jours. Maj. M.C. US Army, 1942—46. Named Stern Symposium honoree, 1972; recipient Mead Johnson award for devel. tissue culture procedures in study virus diseases, Am. Acad. Pediats., 1953, Kimble Methodology award, 1954, Nobel Prize in physiology and medicine, 1954, George Ledlie prize, 1963, Weinstein Cerebral Palsy award, 1973, Bristol award, Infectious Diseases Soc. Am., 1980, Gold medal and diploma of honor, U. Costa Rica, 1984, First Sci. Achievement award, VZV Rsch. Found., 1993, Walter Reed medal, Am. Soc. Tropical Medicine, 1996. Fellow: Am. Acad. Arts and Scis., Royal Soc. Tropical Medicine and Hygiene (hon.); mem.: NAS Inst. Medicine, Am. Soc. Tropical Medicine and Hygiene, Assn. Am. Physicians, Am. Pediat. Soc., Am. Epidemiol. Soc., Harvey Soc., NAS, AMA, Alpha Omega Alpha, Sigma Xi, Phi Beta Kappa.

WELLFORD, HILL B., JR., lawyer; b. Tulsa, Apr. 30, 1942; BA, Davidson Coll., 1964; JD, U. N.C., 1967. Bar: Va., 1968. Ptnr., adminstrv. head, litig., labor group Hunton and Williams LLP, Richmond, Va., 1990—. Lectr. in law. Fellow Am. Bar Found., Va. Law Found.; mem. ABA, Va. Bar Assn. (chmn. com. labor rels. and employment law 1977-87), Richmond Bar Assn., Phi Delta Phi. Office: Hunton & Williams Riverfront Plz East Tower 951 E Byrd St Richmond VA 23219-1535 Office Phone: 804-788-8518. Business E-Mail: hwellford@hunton.com.

WELLIN, KEITH SEARS, investment banker; b. Grand Rapids, Mich., Aug. 13, 1926; s. Elmer G. and Ruth (Chamberlin) W.; m. Carol D. Woodhouse, Sept. 5, 1951 (dec. 1970), m. Wendy C.H. Lane, Nov. 15, 2002; children: Cynthia Wellin Plum, Peter, Marjorie Wellin King. BA, Hamilton Coll., 1950; MBA, Harvard U., 1952. With E.F. Hutton & Co., Inc., Chgo., 1952-71, regional v.p., dir., 1962-66, pres. NYC, 1967-71, vice chmn., 1970-71; sr. v.p., treas., dir. Reynolds Securities Inc., 1971-74, pres., dir., 1974-78; exec. v.p., dir. Dean Witter Reynolds Orgn., from 1978; chmn. Dean Witter Reynolds Inter-Capital, from 1978; former vice chmn. Dean Witter Reynolds Inc. Chmn. bd. Moorco Internat., Houston; former gov., mem. exec. com. Assn. Stock Exchange Firms; mem. governing council Securities Industry Assn. Mem. investment com., trustee Hamilton Coll. Served to 2d lt., inf. AUS, 1945-47. Mem.: Knickerbocker (N.Y.C.); Clove Valley Rod and Gun (La Grangeville, N.Y.); Round Hill (Greenwich, Conn.); River Club. Home (Summer): Seaside Farm PO Box 335 Friendship ME 04547-0335 Office: c/o Dean Witter Reynolds 1345 Avenue Of The Americas New York NY 10105-0302 Home: John's Island 161 Coquille Way Vero Beach FL 32963

WELLING, KATHRYN MARIE, editor; b. Ft. Wayne, Ind., Feb. 4, 1952; d. Arthur Russell Sr. and Genevieve (Disser) W.; m. Donald Robert Boyle, Oct. 21, 1978; children: Brian Joseph, Thomas Arthur. BS in Journalism, Northwestern U., 1974. Copy reader Dow Jones News Retrieval, NYC, 1974-75; copy reader, reporter AP-Dow Jones, NYC, 1975-76; copy editor Wall Street Jour., NYC, 1976; reporter Barron's, NYC, 1976-81, asst. to editor, 1981, mng. editor, 1982-92, assoc. editor, 1992—99; ltd. ptnr. Weeden & Co. L.P., Greenwich, Conn., 1999—; prin. Welling@Weeden, Greenwich, 1999—. Columnist Welling's Acute Observations, Traders Mag. Online. Charter mem. Northwestern U. Coun. of One Hundred. Avocations: sailing, skiing. Office: Weeden & Co LP 145 Mason St Greenwich CT 06830 Home Phone: 973-763-6320; Office Phone: 203-861-7643. Business E-Mail: welling@weedenco.com.

WELLINGHOFF, JON, commissioner; BS, U. Nev., 1971; MS, Howard U., 1972; JD, Antioch Coll., 1975. Dep. dist. atty. consumer fraud divisn., Washoe County, Nev., 1976—77; asst. majority staff counsel consumer com., commerce com. U.S. Senate, 1978; staff atty. energy and product info. divisn. FTC, 1978—79; adimstrv. asst. Pub. Utilities Commn., Nev., consumer advocate Nev., staff counsel Nev.; mng. prin. and regulatory atty. Efficiency Engergy Systems, Inc.; commr. Fed. Energy Regulatory Commn, Washington, 2006—. Ptnr. Beckley Singleton. Office: Fed Energy Regulatory Commn 888 First St NE Washington DC 20426 Office Phone: 702-474-2629. Office Fax: 202-208-0064.

WELLINGS, TOM, chef; Degree in Culinary Arts, New Eng. Culinary Inst.; pastry degree, French Culinary Inst., 2004. Garde mange Hugo's, Portland, Maine, pastry cook; stage wd-50; pastry chef Ritz-Carlton, Tysons Corner, Va.; head pastry chef Restaurant Eve, Maestro, Ritz-Carlton, Tysons Corner. Named one of Washington DC's Rising Stars, StarChefs.com, 2006. Office: Maestro 1700 Tysons Blvd Mc Lean VA 22102 Office Phone: 703-821-1515. *

WELLINGTON, CAROL STRONG, law librarian; b. Altadena, Calif., Jan. 30, 1948; d. Edward Walters and Elizabeth (Leonards) Strong; m. David Heath Wellington, May 27, 1978; one child, Edward Heath BA, Lake Forest Coll., Ill., 1969; MLS, Simmons Coll., Boston, 1973. Libr. Hill & Barlow, Boston, 1973—88, Peabody and Arnold, LLP, Boston, 1988—2002, Day Pitney LLP (formerly Day, Berry, and Howard, LLP), Boston, 2002—. Mem.: Soc. of Competitive Intelligence Profls., Law Librs. of New England, Spl. Librs. Assn., Assn. Boston Law Librs. (v.p. 1979—80, pres. 1980—81), Am. Assn. Law Librs. Office: Day Pitney LLP One International Pl Boston MA 02110 Office Phone: 617-345-4807. Business E-Mail: cswellington@daypitney.com.

WELLINGTON, HARRY HILLEL, lawyer, educator; b. New Haven, Aug. 13, 1926; s. Alex M. and Jean (Ripps) W.; m. Sheila Wacks, June 22, 1952; children: John, Thomas. AB, U. Pa., 1947; LLB, Harvard U., 1952; MA (hon.), Yale U., 1960; LLD, N.Y. Law Sch. Bar: D.C. 1952. Law clk. to U.S. Judge Magruder, 1953-54, Supreme Ct. Justice Frankfurter, 1955-56; asst. prof. law Stanford U., 1954-56; mem. faculty Yale U., 1956—, prof. law, 1960—, Edward J. Phelps prof. law, 1967-83, dean Law Sch., 1975-85, Sterling prof. law, 1983-92, Sterling prof. emeritus law, 1992—, Harry H. Wellington prof. lectr., 1995—; pres., dean, prof. law N.Y. Law Sch., NYC, 1992-2000, dean emeritus, prof., 2000—. Ford fellow London Sch. Econs., 1965; Guggenheim fellow; sr. fellow Brookings Instn., 1968-71; Rockefeller Found. fellow Bellagio Study and Conf. Ctr., 1984; faculty mem. Salzburg Seminar in Am. Studies, 1985; John M. Harlan disting. vis. prof. N.Y. Law Sch., 1985-86; review person ITT-SEC; moderator Asbestos-Wellington Group; cons. domestic and fgn. govtl. agys.; trustee N.Y. Law Sch.; bd. govs. Yale U. Press; mem. jud. panel, exec. com. Ctr. Public Resources Legal Program; Harry H. Wellington lectr., 1995—. Author: with Harold Shepherd) Contracts and Contract Remedies, 1957, Labor and the Legal Process, 1968, (with Clyde Summers) Labor Law, 1968, 2d edit., 1983, (with Ralph Winter) The Unions and the Cities, 1971, Interpreting the Constitution, 1990; contbr. articles to profl. jours. Mem. ABA, Bar Assn. Conn., Am. Law Inst., Am. Arbitration Assn., Am. Acad. Arts and Scis., Common Cause (nat governing bd.). Office: NY Law Sch 57 Worth St New York NY 10013-2959 also: Yale U Sch Law New Haven CT 06520

WELLINGTON, RALPH GLENN, lawyer; b. Three Rivers, Mich., June 18, 1946; s. Cleon G. and Gladys M. (Cole) W.; m. Margaret Brennan; children: Ralph Glenn II, Jeffrey Scott, Tyler Cahill. BA, Kalamazoo Coll., 1968; JD, U. Mich., 1970. Bar: Pa. 1971, U.S. Dist. Ct. (ea. dist.) Pa. 1971, U.S. Dist. Ct. (mid. dist.) Pa. 1976, U.S. Ct. Appeals (3d cir.) 1978, U.S. Ct. Appeals (6th cir.) 1985, U.S. Supreme Ct. 1987. Atty. Schnader Harrison Segal & Lewis, Phila., chmn., 1998—. Frequent lectr. on litigation and ethics in U.S.A. and abroad. Contbr. articles to profl. jours. Trustee Kalamazoo Coll., 1992-2006; vice-chmn. bd. dir. Mann Ctr. Performing Arts; bd. dir. Phila. C. of C. and CEO Coun. Fellow Am. Coll. Trial Lawyers, Internat. Acad. Trial Lawyers; mem. ABA, Nat. Assn. R.R. Trial Counsel, Aviation Ins. Assn., Phila. Bar Assn. (chair profl. responsibility com. 1988), Phila. Cricket Club. Lutheran. Avocations: squash, golf, jazz piano. Home: 604 W Hartwell Ln Philadelphia PA 19118-4114 Office: Schnader Harrison Segal & Lewis 1600 Market St Ste 3600 Philadelphia PA 19103-7287 Office Phone: 215-751-2488. E-mail: rwellington@schnader.com.

WELLINGTON, WILLIAM GEORGE, entomologist, ecologist, educator; b. Vancouver, BC, Can., Aug. 16, 1920; s. George and Lilly (Rae) W.; m. Margret Ellen Reiss, Sept. 22, 1959; children: Katherine Jean, Stephen Ross. BA, U. B.C., 1941; MA, U. Toronto, 1945, PhD, 1947. Meteorol. officer Can. Meteorol. Svc., Toronto, 1942-45; rsch. entomologist Can. Dept. Agr., Sault Sainte Marie, Ont., 1946-51; head bioclimatology sect. Can. Dept. Forestry, Sault Sainte Marie, Ont., Victoria, B.C., 1951-67, prin. scientist Victoria, 1964-68; prof. ecology U. Toronto, Toronto, 1968-70; dir. Inst. Animal Resource Ecology, U. B.C., Vancouver, 1973-79, prof. plant sci. and resource ecology, 1970-86, hon. prof. dept. plant sci., 1986—, prof. emeritus, 1986—; Killam sr. rsch. fellow U. B.C., 1980-81. Inaugural lectr. C.E. Atwood Meml. Seminar Series, Dept. Zoology, U. Toronto, 1993; vis. prof. NC State U., 1972, 75, 81, San Diego State U., 1975, Laval U., 1981, U. Calgary, 1983, Simon Fraser U., 1987. Contbr. articles to profl. jours. Fellow Entomol. Soc. Can. (pres. 1976-78, Gold medal 1968), Royal Soc. Can., Explorers Club; mem. Am. Meteorol. Soc. (award 1969), Entomol. Soc. Am. (C. J. Woodworth award 1979), Japanese Soc. Population Ecology, Entomol. Soc. Ont., Am. Philatelic Soc. Club. Anglican. Home: 1010 W 42d Ave # 305 Vancouver BC Canada V6M 2A8 Office: U BC Faculty Land and Food Sys Vancouver BC Canada V6T 1W5

WELLISZ, STANISLAW, economics professor; b. Warsaw, Mar. 28, 1925; came to U.S., 1941; s. Leopold and Jadwiga (Landau) W.; children: Tadeusz, Krzysztof. BA magna cum laude, Harvard Coll., 1946, MA, 1949; postgrad., U. Cambridge, England, 1949-52; PhD, Harvard U., 1953; D (hon.), Warsaw U., 1998. Asst. prof. U. Chgo., 1957-60, assoc. prof., 1960-63; prof. Columbia U., NYC, 1964-94, Kathryn and Shelby Cullom Davis prof. econs. and internat. affairs, 1994—2006, prof. emeritus, 2006—. Vis. prof. Warsaw U., 1989-97; adv. Polish Ministry Fin., 1989-91. Author: The Economics of the Soviet Bloc, 1964; co-author: The Political Economy of Growth, 1993; co-editor: Stabilization in Poland, 1993. NSF fellow, 1975, 82; named officer Polish Order Merit, Govt. Poland, 1997. Business E-Mail: sw11@columbia.edu.

WELLIVER, WARREN DEE, lawyer, retired judge; b. Butler, Mo., Feb. 24, 1920; s. Carl Winfield and Burdee Marie (Wolfe) W.; m. Ruth Rose Galey, Dec. 25, 1942; children: Gale Dee (Mrs. William B. Stone), Carla Camile (Mrs. Dayton Stone), Christy Marie. BA, U. Mo., 1945; JD, U. Mo., 1948. Bar: Mo. 1948. Asst. pros. atty. Boone County, Columbia, 1948-54; sr. ptnr. Welliver, Atkinson and Eng, Columbia, 1960-79; tchr. law Law Sch. U. Mo., 1948-49; mem. Mo. Senate, 1977-79; justice Supreme Ct. Mo., Jefferson City, 1979-89. Mem. Gov. Mo. Adv. Coun. Alcoholism and Drug Abuse, chmn. drug coun., 1970-72; chmn. Task Force Revision Mo. Drug Laws, 1970-71; liaison mem. coun. Nat. Inst. Alcoholism and Alcohol Abuse, 1973-76; mem. Cen. Regional Adv. Coun. Comprehensive Psychiat. Svcs., 1990-92. Bd. dirs. Nat. Assn. Mental Health, 1970-76, regional v.p., 1973-76; pres. Mo. Assn. Mental Health, 1968-69, Stephens Coll. Assocs., 1965-79; pres. Friends of Libr., U. Mo., 1976, bd. dirs., 1979-92; chmn. Dem. Com., 1954-64; hon. fellow Harry S. Truman Libr. Inst., 1979—; bd. dirs. Supreme Ct. Hist. Soc., 1982—; vice chair adv. bd. U. Mo. Multiple Sclerosis Inst., 1992—; bd. curators Stephen's Coll., 1980-92. With USNR, 1941-45. Recipient Disting. Alumni medal and award U. Mo., 1994. Fellow Am. Coll. Trial Lawyers, Am. Bar Found., Mo. Bar Found.; mem. ABA, Mo. Bar Assn. (pres. 1967-68), Boone County Bar Assn. (pres. 1970), Am. Judicature Soc., Am. Legion (past post comdr.), Multiple Sclerosis Soc. (Gateway chpt. bd. dirs. 1986-92), Order of Coif, Country Club of Mo., Columbia Country Club (past pres.). Home: 3430 Woodrail Ter Columbia MO 65203-0926

WELLMAN, CARL PIERCE, philosophy educator; b. Lynn, Mass., Sept. 3, 1926; s. Frank and Carolyn (Heath) Wellman; m. Farnell Parsons, June 20, 1953; children: Timothy, Philip, Lesley, Christopher. BA, U. Ariz., 1949; MA, Harvard U., 1951, PhD, 1954; postgrad., U. Cambridge, Eng., 1951-52. Instr. Lawrence U., Appleton, Wis., 1953-57, asst. prof., 1957-62, assoc. prof., 1962-66, prof., chmn. dept. philosophy, 1966-68; prof. philosophy Washington U., St. Louis, 1968-88, Hortense and Tobias Lewin Disting. prof. humanities, 1988-99, Hortense and Tobias Lewin Disting. prof. emeritus, 1999—. Mem. rev. panel rsch. grants NEH, 1968—71. Author: The Language of Ethics, 1961, Challenge and Response: Justification in Ethics, 1971, Morals and Ethics, 1975, Welfare Rights, 1982, A Theory of Rights, 1985, Real Rights, 1995, An Approach to Rights, 1997, The Proliferation of Rights, 1999, Medical Law and Moral Rights, 2005. Recipient Uhrig Distinguished Teaching award Lawrence U., 1968; Am. Council Learned Socs. fellow, 1965-66; NEH sr. fellow, 1972-73; Nat. Humanities Center fellow, 1982-83 Mem.: Internat. Assn. for Philosophy Law and Social Philosophy (hon. pres.), Am. Philos. Assn. Home: 625 S Skinker Blvd # 902 Saint Louis MO 63105-2340 E-mail: cpwellma@artsci.wustl.edu.

WELLMAN, ROBERT JONATHAN, psychologist, educator; b. Riverside, Calif., Mar. 1, 1945; s. Harvey Wellman and Ethel Feinstein; m. Mary Margaret Haunss, Aug. 17, 1969. BA with honors, UCLA, 1965; MS, LI U., 1973; PhD, U. Conn., Storrs, 1982. Cert. psychologist, health service provider Mass., 1974, addictions specialist Am. Acad. Healthcare Providers in the Addictive Disorders, 1990. Ednl. rsch. cons. Brentwood Pub. Schs., NY, 1968—69, sch. psychologist, 1969—70, Bd. Coop. Ednl. Svcs., Riverhead, NY, 1968—69, Smithtown Pub. Schs., NY, 1970—72; counselor, adj. asst. prof. counseling LI U. - C. W. Post Campus, Brookville, NY, 1972—74; psychologist Pvt. Practice, Charlton, Mass., 1974—92; sr. psychologist Hubbard Human Svcs. Ctr., Webster, Mass., 1974—82; dir. adolescent & family svcs. Marathon of RI, Providence, 1988—89; clin. dir., dir. outpatient svcs. Attleboro Area Youth & Family Svcs., Mass., 1989—92; asst. prof. psychology Framingham State Coll., Mass., 1993—95; asst. prof. behavioral scis. Fitchburg State Coll., Mass., 1995—2000, assoc. prof. behavioral scis., 2000—05, prof. behavioral scis., 2005—, adj. assoc. prof. family medicine and cmty. health U. Mass. Med. Sch., Worcester, Mass., 2004—05, adj. prof. family medicine and cmty. health, 2005—. Founding editor, family psychologist APA Divsn. Family Psychology, Washington, 1984—89, member-at-large, bd. dirs., 1988—91, president-elect, 1992—93, pres., 1993—94, past pres., 1994—95. Contbr. articles various profl. jours. Recipient Faculty award for Rsch., Fitchburg State Coll. Found., 2006. Mem.: APA, Am. Acad. Healthcare Providers in the Addictive Disorders, Ea. Psychol. Assn., Assn. Psychol. Sci., Soc. Rsch. on Nicotine & Tobacco. Office: Fitchburg State Coll 160 Pearl St Fitchburg MA 01420-2697 Home Phone: 508-278-6600; Office Phone: 978-665-3708. Business E-Mail: rwellman@fsc.edu.

WELLNER, MARCEL NAHUM, research scientist, educator; b. Antwerp, Belgium, Feb. 8, 1930; came to U.S., 1949; s. Jules and Lucie (Rapoport) W.; m. Magdeleine Misselyn, Apr. 7, 1961; children: Pierre, Lucie. BS, MIT, 1952; PhD, Princeton U., 1958. Instr. Brandeis U., Waltham, Mass., 1957-59; mem. Inst. Advanced Study, Princeton, NJ, 1959-60; rsch. assoc. Ind. U., Bloomington, 1960-63; vis. scientist Atomic Energy Rsch. Establishment, Harwell, England, 1963-64; from asst. prof. to prof. Syracuse (N.Y.) U., 1964-95, prof. emeritus, 1995—; sr. rsch. scientist SUNY, Syracuse, 1995—. Author gen. physics textbook; contbr. numerous articles on quantum field theory, fractals and excitable media to profl. jours. Mem. Am. Phys. Soc. Office Phone: 315-464-8018.

WELLNITZ, CRAIG OTTO, lawyer, English language educator; b. Elwood, Ind., Dec. 5, 1946; s. Frank Otto and Jeanne (Albright) W.; m. Karen Sue Thomas, Apr. 13, 1974 (div. Sept. 1987); children: Jennifer Suzanne, Anne Katherine; m. Carol L. Hinesley, Jan. 23, 1988. BA, Purdue U., 1969; MA, Ind. U., 1972; JD, Ind. U.-Indpls., 1978. Bar: Ind. 1978, U.S. Dist. Ct. (so. dist.) Ind. 1978, U.S. Supreme Ct. 1983, U.S. Ct. Appeals (7th and Fed. cirs.) 1984, U.S. Dist. Ct. (no. dist.) 1990; registered mediator, Ind. Instr. Danville Jr. Coll., Ill., 1972-74, S.W. Mo. State U., Springfield, Mo., 1974-75; ptnr. Coates, Hatfield, Calkins & Wellnitz, Indpls., 1978-98; pub. defender criminal divsn. Marion Superior Ct., Marion County, 1979-88, master commr. criminal divsn., 1988-96, registered mediator, 1998—; ptnr. Coates, Hatfield & Wellnitz, Indpls., 1999—2002; pvt. practice Indpls., 2002—. Instr. U. Indpls., 1981-82; mem. adj. faculty dept. English Butler U., Indpls., 1982—; instr. English Ind. U.-Purdue U., Indpls., 1987-90; mem. U. Phoenix Online, 2003—; pres. Ind. Account Mgmt., Mpls., 1985-94; v.p. Carol Craig Assocs., Indpls., 1987—; lectr. in field. Co-author: Successful Judgment Collection in Indiana, 1996, Emerging Trends in Indiana Commercial Collections, 2001; columnist A Jury of Your Peers, 1984-86. Vice committeeman Indpls. Rep. precinct, 1978; chmn. fin. com. St. Luke's United Meth. Ch., 1985-87; sponsor Christian Children's Fund, 1990—; active Am. Mus. Natural History, Indpls. Zoo, Children's Mus. Indpls., The Royal Oak Found. Postgrad. study grantee S.W. Mo. State U., Springfield, 1975. Mem.: MLA, AAUP, Broad Ripple Village Assn., Internat. Spkrs. Network., Spkrs. U.S.A., Smithsonian Assocs., Internat. Assn. Comml. Collectors, ACA Internat., Rivera Club Indpls., Columbia Club, Elks. Office: 2575 B East 55 Pl Indianapolis IN 46220 Personal E-mail: craig@craig-wellnitz.com.

WELLON, ROBERT G., lawyer; b. Port Jervis, NY, Apr. 18, 1948; s. Frank Lewis and Alice (Stevens) W.; m. Jan Montgomery, Aug. 12, 1972; children: Robert F., Alice Wynn. AB, Emory U., 1970; JD, Stetson Coll. Law, 1974. Assoc. Turner, Turner & Turner, Atlanta, 1974-78; ptnr. Ridley, Wellon, Schwieger & Brazier, Atlanta, 1978-86; of counsel Wilson, Strickland & Benson, Atlanta, 1987—2000; pvt. practice Atlanta, 2000—. Adj. prof. Atlanta Law Sch., 1981—94; adj. prof. law Emory U. Sch. of Law, 1995—. Gov.'s task force chmn. Atlanta 2000, 1978; exec. com., treas., 2nd v.p. Atlanta Easter Seals Soc., 1983-88; rep. Neighborhood Planning Unit, 1981-83; adminstrv. bd. Northside United Meth. Ch., 1996-99, Stephen min.; active Atlanta Sports Coun. With USAR, 1970-76. Named Super Lawyer, Atlanta Mag., 2004, 05, 06. Master: Charles Longstreet Weltner Family Law Inn of Ct. (founding pres. 1997—2000);

fellow: Am. Bar Found.; mem.: Lawyers Found. of Ga., Atlanta Bar Found. (bd. dirs. 1996—), Am. Judicature Soc., Atlanta Bar Assn. (bd. dirs. 1978—88, pres. 1986—87, Atlanta continuing legal edn. bd. trustees 1994—97, del. to ho. of dels. 1999—2005, Charles E. Watkins Svc. award 1995, Disting. Svc. award 2005), State Bar. of Ga. (professionalism com. 1994—), Fla. Bar, Atlanta Found. for Psychoanalysis, Inc. (bd. dirs. 1994—, exec. com. 1997—), Old War Horse Lawyers Club, Lawyers Club Atlanta. Methodist. Office: Ste 1900 Promenade II 1230 Peachtree St NE Atlanta GA 30309 Home Phone: 404-355-4350; Office Phone: 404-942-3505. E-mail: rgwlaw@earthlink.net.

WELLS, ANNIE, photographer; b. 1954; B in Sci. Writing, U. Calif., Santa Cruz; postgrad., San Francisco State U. Past photographer Herald Jour., Logan, Utah, Greeley (Colo.) Tribune, Associated Press, San Francisco; photographer Press Dem., Santa Rosa, Calif., 1989—97, L.A. Times, 1997—. Photographer (permanent collections) Nat. Mus. Women Arts, Washington. Recipient Pulitzer Prize spot news photography, 1997. Office: LA Times 202 West First St Los Angeles CA 90012 E-mail: annie.wells@latimes.com.

WELLS, APRIL, language educator; b. Elgin, Ill., Sept. 24, 1976; d. Donnie Johnson and Delores Sharpe; m. Charles Wells, Dec. 31, 2004; 1 child, Wells Jene Kennedy. BA in Psychology, DePaul U., Chgo., 1999; MA in Tchg., Nat.-Louis U., Wheeling, Ill., 2006. English tchr. Ill. Sch. Dist. U-46, Elgin, 2002—. Edn. lab facilitator Living Daylight Corp., Elgin, 2002—. Youth leader Living Gospel Ch., Elgin, 2005—. Mem.: Nat. Coun. Tchrs. English. Home: 4165 Brookstone Ln Belvidere IL 61008 Home Phone: 847-594-5218. Personal E-mail: aprilwells@u-46.org.

WELLS, ARTHUR STANTON, retired manufacturing executive; b. Kingsport, Tenn., Jan. 8, 1931; s. Arthur Stanton and Blanche Welch (Duncan) W.; m. Ellen N. Blackburn, June 15, 1957; children: Arthur S., Thomas B., Emily B., Richard R. BS, Yale U., 1953; MBA, Harvard U., 1957. Fin. analyst Eastman Kodak Co., Kingsport, Tenn., 1957-65; mgr. profit analysis Xerox Corp., Rochester, NY, 1966-68, asst. treas. Stamford, Conn., 1969-76, treas., 1976-79; v.p. fin. Barnes Group Inc., Bristol, Conn., 1979-86, exec. v.p. fin., 1987-93, pres., CEO, 1994-96, also dir., 1994-96. Bd. dirs. Nash Engrng. Co., Trumbull, Conn., 1995—98. Trustee, treas. Wilton (Conn.) Libr. Assn., 1972-78; trustee Lincoln Acad., Newcastle, Maine, 2002—; bd. dirs. New Eng. Opera Assn., 1972-78; assoc. bd. dirs. Conn. Bank and Trust Co., Hartford, 1984-90; chmn. bd. trustees, exec. com. Conn. Pub. Expenditure Coun., Inc., 1990-93. With AUS, 1953-55. Mem. Fin. Execs. Inst. Democrat. Home: 4 CCIA Rd South Bristol ME 04568-4710 E-mail: wellses@midcoast.com.

WELLS, BARRY L., federal official; b. 1942; BA in Psych., MA in Social Work; attended, Fed. Exec. Inst.; attended exec. seminar, Aspen Inst. Country dir. US Peace Corps, Belize, Jamaica; joined Fgn. Svc. Inst., US Dept. State, 1988—, assoc. dean, Sch. Profl. & Area Studies, assoc. dean Sr. Seminar & Leadership & Mgmt. Sch., dep. dir., 2001—05, acting dir., 2005—06; dir. Office Civil Rights US Dept. State, 2006—, chief diversity officer, 2007—. Former assoc. dean and asst. dean Howard U. Grad. Sch. of Social Work; former lecturer U. Pitts., Youngstown State U., U. West Indies; mem. Thursday Luncheon Group; bd. dirs. Nat. MultiCultural Inst. Office: US Dept State 2201 C St NW Washington DC 20520 *

WELLS, BRADLEY W., foundation administrator; BA in polit. sci., Calif. State U., Long Beach, 1983. Positions at Calif. State U., Fullerton, 1983—86, dir. budget planning and adminstrn., 1986—89; joined Chancellor's Office Calif. State U. System, Long Beach, 1989, sr. fin. analyst, dir. info. and analysis, 1993—95, named exec. asst. to vice chancellor, CFO, 1995, asst. vice chancellor fin. services; assoc. dir. program analysis and planning J. Paul Getty Trust, LA, 1998—99, named v.p. fin., 2001, now v.p. fin. and adminstrn. Office: J Paul Getty Trust 1200 Getty Ctr Dr Los Angeles CA 90049-1679 Office Phone: 310-440-7300.

WELLS, CAROL MCCONNELL, genealogist, retired archivist; b. Phila., Feb. 21, 1918; d. William Hugh McConnell and Edith Mary Lower; m. Tom Henderson Wells, Dec. 31, 1943; children: Lucy, Sarah, Tom, Christopher, Julia, Peter. BA, Pa. State Coll., State College, 1939; MA, Northwestern State U., Natchitoches, La., 1973. Archivist Northwestern State U., Natchitoches, La., 1974-88; editor So. Studies, Natchitoches, 1982-88. Spkr. in field. Author: Williamson County, Tennessee: A Genealogical Abstract of the County Court Minutes, 1800-1804, 1987, 88, Davidson County, Tennessee, County Court Minutes 1783-1792, 1990, Davidson County, Tennessee, County Court Minutes, 1792-1799, 1991, Davidson County, Tennessee, County Court Minutes 1799-1803, 1991, Genealogical Abstracts of Edgefield, SC, Equity Court Records, 2002, Edgefield County, South Carolina, Probate Records, Boxes 1-3, 2004, Edgefield County, South Caroline Deed Books 39-41, 2007, many others. Mem. Natchitoches Hist. Found., 1994—. Lt. (j.g.) USNR, 1944. Named Woman of Yr. C. of C., 1975; recipient Clio award Phi Alpha Theta, 1988. Mem. DAR, Phi Mu, Phi Beta Kappa, Phi Kappa Phi. Republican. Anglican Catholic. Avocation: gardening. Home: 607 Williams Ave Natchitoches LA 71457 Personal E-mail: carolwells@cp-tel.net.

WELLS, CHARLES RAYBURN, retired insurance company executive; b. Norton, Va., Sept. 26, 1936; s. Richard Wells and Maude Minnix; m. Anna Ruth Breeding, July 9, 1994; m. Shirley Anne Amburgey, Apr. 3, 1956 (dec. Jan. 11, 1994); children: Rocky Vincent, Vicki Renea Barnick, Richard Shane, Robyn Cheryl Dunn. Bachelor, Brevard C.C., Melbourne, 1973; Masters in Ins., Ga., 1981. Ins. adjuster Allstate Ins. Co., St. Petersburg, Fla., 1963—75, property unit mgr. Ft. Lauderdale, 1975—79, property claim mgr. Atlanta, 1979—84. Ind. ins. adjuster Self Employed, Norton, Va., 1985—98; substitue tchr. Wise County Sch. Sys., Wise, Va., 1999—2007. Actor: (outdoor drama) Uncle Billy Beam (Outstanding Actor Award, 1997). Sch. bd. Dawson County, Ga., 1987—90. Staff sgt, inf. US Army, 1953—56, Ft. Bragg, Ft. Jackson and Korea. Decorated Cold War Cert. of Recognition Sec. of Def., Freedom Team Salute Gen. US Army Chief of Staff & Sect of Army, Army Overseas Svc. Ribbon, Korean Presdl. Citation, Cold War Ribbon, Expert Inf. Badge Dept. of Def. US Army, Good Conduct, Nat. Def. Svc. medal, Korean Svc. medal, Korean Def. Svc. medal, UN Svc. medal, Army Svc. Ribbon, Dept. Def. US Army; recipient Expdn. Reclaim, Allstate Regional Claims, St. Petersburg, FL, 1969, Outstanding Performance award, Allstate Ins. Co. Zone-Home Officce, 1970, Apollo Forty 1971 Victory, Allstate Ins. Co. So. Zone, 1971, Support, Participation and Accomplishments, So. Brevard Midget Football Assn., Melbourne, FL., 1974, Cmty. Svc. award, Greater West Melbourne Atheletic Asso, Melbourne, FL, 1975, Dedicated Svc. Dawson County Sch., Ga. Sch. Bd., 1987—90, Pres. award, Optimist Internat. Dawson County, GA, 1987, Top Gun award, Nat. Group Mktg., 1988, Svc. award, Optimist Internat. Dawson County, GA, 1988, Hon. Svc. 1987-1990, Dawson County Sch. Bd., 1990, Silver Star award, Charles B. Thacker Korea War Veterans, 2002, Nat. VFW Recruiting award, VFW, Kans. City, MO, 2005—06, Neas Read Across Am., NEA, 2005—06, Disting. All State Post Quartermaster, VFW Dept. of Va., 2005—07, Bronze and Silver Star awards, DAV, Nat. Hdqs., Cin. OH, 2006—07, Nat. Adc, Nat. VFW, Kans. City, MO, 2006—07, All Am. Dist. Comdr. award, VFW Dept. of Va., 2006—07. Mem.: DAV (life; chpt. comdr. 2003—04, Silver Star Pin 2006), VFW (life; dist. 12 comdr. 2004—07, All Am. Dist. Comdr. 2007), Korean War Vet. Assn. (life; past chpt. comdr. 2001—03), Masonic Lodge (jr. warden 2005—06), Son of Confederate Vet. (life). R-Consevative. Achievements include founded, and organized and first Commander of the first Korean War Veterans Chapter # 250 in Southwest Virginia; first to Organize and develop the present sports complex located in West Melbourne, Florida, 1967. Avocations: camping, travel, genealogy. Home: 6228 Josephine Rd Norton VA 24273 Office: A-Vet Emblem Uniform Co 6228 Josephine Rd Norton VA 24273 Home Phone: 276-679-2096; Office Phone: 276-679-2096. Business E-Mail: raywellsavet@aol.com.

WELLS, CHARLES TALLEY, state supreme court justice; b. Orlando, Fla., Mar. 4, 1939; BA, U. of Florida, 1961, JD, 1964. Bar: Fla. 1965, U.S. Dist. Ct. (mid. dist.) Fla., U.S. Ct. Appeals (5th and 11th cirs.) 1966, U.S. Supreme Ct. 1969, U.S. Dist. Ct., U.S. Dist. Ct. (so. dist.) Fla. 1976, U.S. Ct. of Claims 1990. Trial atty. U.S. dept justice, Washington, 1969; pvt. practice Maguire, Voohris and Wells, PA, Orlando, Fla., 1965—68, 1970—75, Wells, Gattis, Hollowes & Carpenter, PA, Orlando, Fla., 1976—94; justice Fla. Supreme Ct., Tallahassee, 1994—, chief justice, 2000—02. Active in Orange County Legal Aid Soc., 1968—94, mem. bd. trustees, 1988—89; bd. directors Conference of Chief Justices; mem. Federal Judicial Conference Standing Com. on Rules of Practice & Procedure. Former mem. bd. directors Orlando Area Chamber of Commerce, Orlando Jaycees, Orange County YMCA. Served in US Army. Fellow: Am. Bar Foundation; mem.: Tallahassee Bar Assn., ABA, Fla. Bar (bd. governors), Orange County Bar Assn. (pres. 1989—90). Methodist. Office: Fla Supreme Ct 500 S Duval St Tallahassee FL 32399-1925 *

WELLS, CHRISTOPHER M., lawyer; b. Honiton, England, Oct. 21, 1957; BA, Kalamazoo Coll., 1978; JD, Univ. Mich., 1981. Bar: NY 1982. Ptnr., head Global Investment Funds practice Coudert Bros. LLP, NYC. Contbr. articles to profl. jours. Mem.: Phi Beta Kappa. Office: Coudert Bros LLP 1114 Ave of the Americas New York NY 10036 Office Phone: 212-626-4925. Office Fax: 212-626-4120. Business E-Mail: wellsc@coudert.com.

WELLS, DAMON, investment company executive; b. Houston, May 20, 1937; s. Damon and Margaret Corinne W. BA magna cum laude, Yale U., 1958; BA, Oxford U., 1964, MA, 1968; PhD, Rice U., 1968. Owner, CEO Damon Wells Interests, Houston, 1958—; pres. Damon Wells Found., Houston, 1993—. Author: Stephen Douglas: The Last Years, 1857-61, 1971 (Tex. Writer's Roundup prize, 1971), paperback edit., 1990. Bd. dirs. Child Guidance Ctr. of Houston, 1970-73; trustee Christ Ch. Cathedral Endowment Fund, 1970-73, 84-88, chmn., 1987-88; trustee Kinkaid Sch., 1972-86, Camp Allen retreat of Episc. Diocese of Tex., 1976-78, Kinkaid Sch. Endowment Fund, 1981-86, Churchill Grave Trust, 2002—, Winston Churchill Found. U.S., 2003-; hon. friend of Somerville Coll., Oxford U., 1988—, mem. sr. common rm. Pembroke Coll., Oxford U., 1972-; founding bd. dirs. Brit. Inst. US, 1979-80; pres.'s coun. Tex. A&M U., 1983-89; hon. dir. Stephen A. Douglas Assn., 1975—; mem. Chancellors Ct. Benefactors, Oxford U., 2006—. Named Hon. Comdr. Most Excellent Order of Brit. Empire by Her Majesty Queen Elizabeth II, 1991, Outstanding Alumnus Yr. by Kinkaid Sch., 1994; fellow Jonathan Edwards Coll. (assoc.), Yale U., 1982—, Sterling fellow Yale U., 2000—, hon. fellow Pembroke Coll., Oxford U., 1984—. Mem. English-Speaking Union (nat. dir. 1970-72, v.p. Houston br. 1966-73), Coun. Fgn. Rels., Houston Country Club, Houston Club, Yale Club (NYC), United Oxford and Cambridge U. Club (London), Cosmos Club (Washington), Buck's Club (London), Coronado Club (Houston), Little Ship Club (London). Phi Beta Kappa, Pi Sigma Alpha. Anglican. Home: 5555 Del Monte Dr Houston TX 77056-4100 Office: 2001 Kirby Dr Ste 806 Houston TX 77019-6088

WELLS, DAVID LEE, professional baseball player; b. Torrance, Calif., May 20, 1963; Grad. high sch., San Diego. Pitcher Toronto Blue Jays, 1987—92, 1999—2001, Detroit Tigers, 1993-95, Cin. Reds, 1995, Balt. Orioles, 1996, NY Yankees, 1997-98, 2002—03, Chgo. White Sox, 2001, Boston Red Sox, 2005—06, San Diego Padres, 2004—05, 2006—07, LA Dodgers, 2007—. Named Am. League All-Star Team, 1995, 98, 2000; Perfect game thrown May 17th, 1999; mem. World Series champion Toronto Blue Jays, 1992, N.Y. Yankees, 1998. Office: Dodger Stadium 1000 Elysian Pk Ave Los Angeles CA 90012-1199 Office Phone: 323-224-1500. *

WELLS, DON, artist; b. Grand Haven, Mich., July 19, 1950; s. Doyle Anderson and Betty Jane Wells. Student, West Valley Jr. Coll., Campbel and Saratoga, Calif., 1970—72; studies privately with various acomplished artists, Calif. Self employed ind. artist, Campbell, 1970—80, Granite Falls, Wash., 1980—. Pvt. art tchr., Granite Falls, 1980—. Recipient Achievment award, Bank of America, 1970, Art award, Coats and Clark, Wash., 1983. Democrat. Avocations: reading, travel.

WELLS, GLADYSANN, library director; BA in English, Greensboro Coll., NC, 1970; MLS, SUNY, Albany, 1972. Libr. Empire State Coll., 1972—73; legis. reference libr. N.Y. State Libr., Albany, 1973—78; with Senate Rsch. Svc., 1975—80; libr. Senate Libr., 1978—80; adminstr. N.Y. State Libr., 1980—95; interim dir. N.Y. State Libr. Rsch. Libr., 1995—97; state libr. Ariz. State Libr., 1997—. Editor several books on the economy of the northeast; contbr. articles to profl. jours. Avocations: horseback riding, cross country skiing, hiking, snow shoeing. Office: Ariz State Libr 1700 W Washington Ste 200 Phoenix AZ 85007-2896

WELLS, H. GREELEY, JR., prosecutor; b. Knoxville, Tenn., Feb. 20, 1945; s. Horace G. and Dorris V. Wells; m. Sue Knight, Apr. 8, 1966; children: John K., Laura Wells Singley. BS, U. Tenn., Knoxville, 1967, JD, 1969. Bar: Tenn. 1970. Spl. agt. FBI, Washington, 1969—76; asst. dist. atty. gen. 2d Jud. Dist., Blountville, Tenn., 1976—93, dist. atty. gen., 1993—. Elder, deacon Presbyn. Ch. Mem.: Tenn. Dist. Atty. Gens. Conf. (Patrick H. McCutcheon award 2006), Tenn. Bar Assn. (bd. govs.), Rotary Club (charter mem. Downtown Kingsport club). Democrat. Office: Dist Atty Gen's Office 2d Jud Dist Po Box 526 Blountville TN 37617

WELLS, HUEY THOMAS, JR., lawyer; b. Gadsden, Ala., Mar. 22, 1950; s. Huey Thomas Sr. and Ruth (Allison) W.; m. Jan McKenzie, Dec. 29, 1972; children: Lynlee, Trey. BA with honors, U. Ala., Tuscaloosa, 1972, JD, 1975. Bar: Ala. 1975, US dist. Ct. (no. dist.) Ala. 1975, US Ct. Appeals (DC and 5th cirs.) 1977, US Supreme Ct. 1981, US Ct. Appeals (11th cir.) 1982. Assoc. Cabaniss, Johnston, Gardner, Dumas & O'Neal, Birmingham, Ala., 1977-82, ptnr., 1983-84, Maynard, Cooper & Gale P.C., 1984—. Chmn. adv. com. on civil justice reform US Dist. (no. dist.) Ala., 1991-95. Legal co-chmn. championship Profl. Golf Assn., Birmingham, 1984, legal chmn., 1990; legal chmn. US Amateur Golf Championship, Birmingham, 1986. Served to capt. USAF, 1975-77. Mem. ABA (standing com. profl. disciple 1985-88, standing com. on environ. law 1988-94, chmn. environ. litigation com. of litigation sect. 1988-91, chmn. ho. of dels. 2002-04, Ala. state del. 1992-2001—, mem. coun. litigation sect. 1992-95, chair litigation sect. 1999-2000, pres.-elect nominee 2007), Birmingham Bar Assn. (law day com., grievance com., divsn. dir. litigation sect. 1991-92), Ala. Bar Assn. (jud. liaison). Roman Catholic. Avocations: golf, softball, reading. Office: Maynard Cooper & Gale PC 2400 AmSouth/Harbart Plz 1901 6th Ave N Ste 2400 Birmingham AL 35203-4604 Home Phone: 205-595-2095; Office Phone: 205-254-1062. Business E-Mail: twells@maynardcooper.com.

WELLS, JAMES M., III, bank executive; b. 1946; AB in English, U. NC, Chapel Hill, 1968; student, Rutgers U. Stonier Grad. Sch. Banking. Mgmt. trainee United Va. Bankshares, 1968-71, corp. adminstrv. officer, sec., 1971; br. officer, mgr. United Va. Bankshares/State-Planters, 1971-74; v.p., treas. United Va. Mortgage Corp., 1974-79; pres., CEO United Va. Leasing Corp., 1974-79; exec. v.p. United Va. Bank, Norfolk, Va., 1979-83, pres. Ea. region, 1983-85, exec. v.p. corp. banking, 1985-86, exec. v.p. banking group, 1986-88; pres. Crestar Fin. Corp, Richmond, Va., 1988—2000, CEO, 2000; vice chmn. SunTrust Banks Inc., Atlanta, 2000—04, pres., COO, 2004—06, pres., CEO, 2007—. Bd. dirs. Visa USA. Mailing: SunTrust Banks Inc PO Box 4418 Atlanta GA 30308-4418 Office Phone: 404-588-7711. Office Fax: 404-827-6173. *

WELLS, JAMES WAYNE, retired secondary school educator; b. Birmingham, Ala., Feb. 13, 1941; s. William Edward and Margaret Louise (Wainwright) W.; m. Jan. 30, 1965; children: Erin Elizabeth,Risa Kathryne. BS, U. Ala., 1963; postgrad., No. Ariz. U., 1975, U. Ala., 1987, Calif. State U., San Bernadino, 1994. Sci. tchr. Rockdale County HS, Conyers, Ga., 1964-67; Spanish tchr. Charlotte Country Day Sch., NC, 1967-69; tchr. math. Charles Hard Sch., Bessemer, Ala., 1970-72; sci. tchr. Hayes HS, Birmingham, Ala., 1973-74; biology tchr. Chinle HS, Ariz., 1974-87, Jess Lahier HS, Bessemer, 1987-88; dir. Scouting Report of Ariz., Phoenix, 1988-89; ESL tchr. Calif. Dept. Corrections, Blythe, Calif., 1990—2002; ret. Mem. Calif. Prof. Educator Assn., Scottsdale C. of C. (com. mem. pub. affairs 1988). Democrat. Lutheran. Avocations: basketball, golf, franklin mint collector. Home: 195 Eunice Cir Blythe CA 92225-1333 Office: Chuckawalla Valley State Prison PO Box 2289 Blythe CA 92226-2289 Office Phone: 602-692-9131. Personal E-mail: jwells9820@aol.com.

WELLS, JOHN CALHOUN, retired physics professor; b. Tampa, Fla., May 12, 1941; s. John Calhoun and Ethel Bernice (Hitchcock) W.; m. Marilee Winifred Mays, Dec. 21, 1963; children: Sarah Kathleen, John Bryan. BS in Physics and Math. cum laude, Fla. State U., 1961; PhD in Nuc. Physics, Johns Hopkins U., 1968. Postdoctoral researcher U.S. Naval Ordnance Lab., Silver Spring, Md., 1968-70; asst. prof. Tenn. Tech. U., Cookeville, 1970-75, assoc. prof., 1975-80, prof. physics, 1980—2006; ret., 2006. Adj. rsch. scientist nuclear physics Oak Ridge (Tenn.) Nat. Lab., 1976—2001. Mem.: Tenn. Acad. Scis., Am. Phys. Soc., Sigma Xi. Avocation: music. Home Phone: 931-526-8802; Office Phone: 931-526-8802. Personal E-mail: jwells@tntech.edu.

WELLS, JOHN MARCUM, producer, writer; b. Alexandria, Va., May 28, 1956; s. Llewellyn Wallace Jr and Marjorie Elizabeth (Risberg) Wells; m. Belinda Casas, Dec. 30, 1978 (div.); m. Marilyn Wells; 2 children. BFA in Drama, Carnegie-Mellon U., 1979; MFA in Cinema, U. So. Calif., 1982. Founder, artistic dir. Pitts. New Playwrights Festival, 1978-79; asst. to v.p. mktg. Paramount Pictures Corp., 1981-82; theatrical producer various plays, Los Angeles, 1982-85; producer, writer Warner Bros. TV, Los Angeles, 1987, co-exec. producer, writer, 1988, 89, 90; producer New World Pictures, Los Angeles, 1986-87; suprg. producer, creater Roughhouse, Los Angeles, 1988. Prodr.(writer): (plays) Balm In Gilead, She Also Dances, Battery, Judgement, Ground Zero, Steaming, Femme Fatale, Tanzi, (writer, dir.): (TV series) China Beach (George Foster Peabody award, 3 Writers Guild of Am. Nominations, 6 Emmy nominations); exec. prodr.: Angel Street, 1992, Jonny Zero, 2005, The Evidence, 2006—, (writer, dir.) ER, 1994—2006, (writer) Trinity, 1998—99, The West Wing, 1999—2006, Third Watch, 1999—2005, Citizen Baines, 2001; exec. prodr. (writer): (TV series) Presidio Med, 2002—03; exec. prodr.(writer): (TV series) Smith, 2006; prodr.(writer): (films) Nice Girls Don't Explode, Interview With A Vampire, A Time To Kill, Wired, White Oleander, 2002, The Good Thief, 2002, A Home at the End of the World, 2004, Duma, 2005, Doom, 2005; exec. prodr.: The Grey Zone, 2001, One Hour Photo, 2002, Far from Heaven, 2002, Party Monster, 2003, The Company, 2003, A Dirty Shame, 2004, The Notorious Bettie Page, 2005, Infamous, 2006. Assoc. producer nat. Dem. fundraising events, LA, 1984, Carnegie-Mellon U. Endowment Drive, Pitts., 1986; mem. exed. adv. coun. U. So. Calif. Sch. Cinema and TV. Recipient Los Angeles Drama Critics Circle award, 1982, Los Angeles Weekly award, Drama-Logue mag. award, 1985, Writers Guild Am. award, 1989, Humanitas award, 1989, Peabody award, 1990, Golden Globe award, 1990, Paddy Chayefsky Laurel award, Writers Guild Am., West, 2007; grantee Triseme Corp., 1982. Mem.: NATAS, Carnegie-Mellon U. West Coast Alumni Assn. (bd. dirs. 1982—, pres. 1986—90), Writers Guild Am. (pres. Writers Guild Am. West 1999). Democrat. Episcopalian. Office: 4000 Warner Blvd # 2 Burbank CA 91522-0001 *

WELLS, JULIA ELIZABETH See DAME ANDREWS, JULIE

WELLS, KENNETH BROOKS, medical educator, researcher; Prof. psychiatry & biobehavioral scis. UCLA Semel Inst. & Hosp. and Sch. of Medicine; sr. scientist RAND; prin. investigator UCLA/RAND Ctr. for Rsch. Quality in Managed Care. Co-author: Caring for Depression, 1996, Beating Depression: The Journey to Hope, 2002. Recipient Young Investigator Award, Disting. Investigator Award, Acad. Health. Mem.: Am. Psychiatric Assn. (Sr. Health Svc. Rsch. Award), NAS, Inst. Medicine (chair Neuroscience and Behavioral Health Bd.). Address: 1776 Main St Santa Monica CA 90401-3208 Office: UCLA Health Svcs Rsch Ctr 10920 Wilshire Blvd, Ste 300 Los Angeles CA 90024-6505 Office Phone: 310-794-3725. E-mail: kenneth_wells@rand.org.

WELLS, KITTY (ELLEN MURIEL DEASON), musician; b. Nashville, Aug. 30, 1919; d. Charles Cary and Myrtle Bell (Street) Deason; m. Johnnie Robert Wright, Oct. 30, 1937; children: Ruby Jean Wright Taylor, Bobby Wright, Carol Sue Wright-Sturdivant. Grad. high sch. Country music singer; sang gospel in chs. as a child; formed group Deacon Sisters, performed on radio, early 30's; with Johnny and Jack and the Tenn. Mountain Boys, late 1930's-early 1940's, regular on Grand Ole Opry, from 1952, had own family TV show, late 1960's-early 1970's, now with Johnny Wright, Bobby Wright and the Tennessee Mountain Boys; songs include: Gathering Flowers for the Master's Bouquet, How Far is Heaven, Release Me, It Wasn't God Who Made Honky Tonk Angels, Making Believe, Thank You For the Roses; albums include Kitty Wells & Roy Drusky, Vol. 1 & 2, Back to Back Patsy Kline, 1995, (with Red Foley, Webb Pierce, others) Duets, 1995; author: Kitty Wells Cookbook. Bd. dirs. Nashville Meml. Hosp. Recipient award as number 1 female singer Cashbox Mag., 1953-62, Billboard 1954-65, award of yr. for top female country vocalist Record World mag. 1965, award for highest artistic achievement in rec. arts 1964, various awards Downbeat Mag., award as all-time queen of country music Music Bus. Mag. 1964, Woman of Yr. award 1974, Pioneer award Acad. Country Music 1985, Living Legend award Music City news 1991, voted nation's number one Country Female Artist for 14 consecutive years; named Top Female Artist of Decade, Record World Mag. 1974; named to Country Music Hall of Fame 1976. Mem. Country Music Assn., Nat. Assn. Rec. Arts and Scis. (Govs. award for Outstanding Achievement in Recording Industry, 1981, Grammy Lifetime Achievement award, 1991). Mem. Ch. of Christ. Achievements include being the first woman to hit No. 1 on the country charts with "It Wasn't God Who Made Honky Tonk Angels.".

WELLS, LESLEY, federal judge; b. Muskegon, Mich., Oct. 6, 1937; d. James Franklin and Inez Simpson Wells; m. Charles F. Clarke, Nov. 13, 1998; children: Lauren Elizabeth, Caryn Alison, Anne Kristin, Thomas Eliot. BA, Chatham Coll., 1959; JD cum laude, Cleve. State U., 1974. Bar: Ohio 1975, US Dist. Ct. (no. dist.) Ohio 1975, US Supreme Ct. 1989. Pvt. practice, Cleve., 1975; ptnr. Brooks & Moffet, Cleve., 1975—78; dir., atty. ABAR Litig. Ctr., Cleve., 1979—80; assoc. Schneider, Smeltz, Huston & Ranney, Cleve., 1980—83; judge Ct. Common Pleas, Cleve., 1983—94, US Dist. Ct. (no. dist.) Ohio, Cleve., 1994—2006, sr. judge, 2006—. Adj. prof. law and urban policy Cleve. State U., 1980-83, 90-93. Editor, author: Litigation Manual, 1980. Past pres. Cleve. Legal Aid Soc.; legal chmn. Nat. Women's Polit. Caucus, 1981-82; chmn. Gov.'s Task Force on Family Violence, Ohio, 1983-87; mem. biomed. ethics com. Case Western Res. U. Med. Sch., 1985-94; mem. NW Ordinance US Constn. Commn., Ohio, 1986-88; master William K. Thomas Inn of Ct., 1989—, counselor, 1993, pres., 1998-99; trustee Rosemary Ctr., 1986-92, Miami U., 1988-92, Urban

League Cleve., 1989-90, Chatham Coll., 1989-94. Recipient Superior Jud. award Supreme Ct. Ohio, 1983, J. Irwin award Womenspace, Ohio, 1984, award Womens City Club, 1985, Disting. Alumna award Chatham Coll., 1988, Alumni Civic Achievement award Cleve. State U., 1992, Golden Gavel award Ohio Judges Assn., 1994, Outstanding Alumni award Cleve. Marshall Law Alumni Assn., 1994, Greater Cleve. Achievement award YWCA, 1995. Mem. ABA (coun. litigation sect. 1996-99), Am. Law Inst., Ohio Bar Assn., Ohio Womens Bar Assn., Cleve. Bar Assn. (Merit Svc. award 1983), Cuyahoga County Bar Assn., Nat. Assn. Women Judges, Philos. Club Cleve. Office: 328 US Court House 201 Superior Ave Cleveland OH 44114-1234 Office Phone: 216-615-4480. Business E-Mail: lesley_wells@ohnd.uscourts.gov.

WELLS, LINTON, II, federal agency administrator; b. Luanda, Angola, Apr. 7, 1946; s. Linton and Helen Fay (Gillis) W.; m. Linda Marie Motta; children: Linton III, Frank. BS in Physics and Oceanography, U.S. Naval Acad., 1967; MSE in Math. Scis., PhD in Internat. Rels., Johns Hopkins U., 1975; student, Boueikeushusho (Japanese Nat. Def. Coll.), Tokyo. Commd. ensign USN, 1967; commdr. USS Joseph Strauss, 1984-86, Destroyer Squadron 21, 1989-91; advanced through grades to capt. USN, 1994, ret., 1994; asst. to under sec. for policy US Dept. Def., Washington, 1991-93, dep. to under sec. def. policy, 1993-98, dep. under sec. def. policy support, 1998, prin. dep. asst. sec. def. networks & info. integration, 1998—, acting asst. sec. def. networks & info. integration, chief info. officer, 2004—05. Co-author: Japanese Cruisers of the Pacific War, 1997. Decorated Def. Superior Svc. medal, Legion of Merit (2), others; recipient Def. Disting. Pub. Svc. medal, C.N.G. Hendrix award for excellence in oceanography, 1967, Arleigh Burke Leadership award, 1975, Silver medal prize essay contest Naval Inst., 1985. Mem. Army and Navy Club, U.S. Naval Inst., Soc. Physics Students, Explorers Club, Tau Beta Pi (hon.). Avocations: flying, scuba diving, reading, travel. Office: Prin Dep Asst Sec Def N11 6000 The Pentagon Rm 3e172 Washington DC 20301-6000

WELLS, LYNTON ALFRED, artist; b. Balt., Oct. 21, 1940; s. Alfred Rufus and Augusta Margurie Wells; m. Margaret Elizabeth Baur, May 25, 1964. BFA, RI Sch. Design, Providence, 1962; MFA, Cranbrook Acad. Art, Bloomfield Hills, Mich., 1965. One-man shows include Jonathan Shock Gallery, NYC, 2006, Rebecca Ible Gallery, Columbus, Ohio, 2007, Represented in permanent collections Mus. Modern Art, Walker Art Ctr., San Francisco Mus. Art, Dallas Mus. Art. Grantee, NY Coun. on Arts, 1975, Nat. Endowment of Arts, 1975, NY Coun. Arts, 1977.

WELLS, MARY ELIZABETH THOMPSON, deacon, chaplain, spiritual director, iconographer; b. Dallas, Oct. 9, 1936; d. Owen Perry and Ruth Marie Thompson; children: Tadd Whitney, Britony Ruth. BA in Sociology, Syracuse U., 1958; MA in Child Devel., Tufts U., 1964, MEd in Counseling Psychology, 1974; MA in Theology, St. Vincent de Paul Regional Sem., 2005. Ordained min. Diocese of Southeast Fla., 2002. Asst. dir. pub. rels. Inst. Crippled and Disabled, NYC, 1958-59; head tchr. Eliot-Pearson Children's Sch., Tufts U., Medford, Mass., 1964-66; psychotherapist Mental Health Ctr. Greater Cape Ann, Gloucester, Mass., 1974-89; deacon, chaplain, spiritual dir. St. Paul's Episcopal Ch., Delray Beach, Fla., 1999—2007, dir./dean Diocesan Sch. S.E. Fla., 2003—07. Mem.: APA, Spiritual Dirs. Internat., Assn. Profl. Chaplains, Assn. Clin. Pastoral Educators, Am. Orthopsychiatric Assn. Home: 231 Spring Hill Dr Gordonsville VA 22942

WELLS, MARY JULIA, psychologist; b. Arlington, Va., Nov. 23, 1958; d. John Murrell and Rollene Sumner Wells. BS, Va. Commonwealth U., 1980; MPhil, George Wash. U., 1988, PhD, 1990. Lic. clin. psychologist Va., 1991. Psychology assoc. Wash. Pain and Rehab Ctr., Wash., DC, 1988—90; asst. prof. Med. Coll. Va., Richmond, Va., 1990—93; clin. psychologist Inst. Chronic Pain Mgmt., Richmond, 1993—96, pvt. practice, Richmond, 1996—2000, Sheltering Arm Hosp., Richmond, 2000—. Contbr. chapters to books. Pres. Richmond Acad. Clin. Psychologists, Richmond, Va., 1995—96, mem. chair, 2002—04, pres., 2005; anti racism trainer Unitarian, Universalist Assn., Richmond, Va., 1999. Mem.: Am. Psychological Assn., Va. Psychological Assn., Richmond Acad. Clin. Psychologists. Democrat. Unitarian. Avocations: music, dogs. Office: Sheltering Arms Physical Rehab Hosp 8254 Atlee Rd Mechanicsville VA 23116 Office Phone: 804-723-3275. Business E-Mail: mwells@shelteringarms.com.

WELLS, MELISSA FOELSCH, retired ambassador; b. Tallinn, Estonia, Nov. 18, 1932; emigrated to U.S., 1936, naturalized, 1941; d. Kuno Georg and Miliza (Korjus) Foelsch; m. Alfred Washburn Wells, 1960; children: Christopher, Gregory. BS in Fgn. Service, Georgetown U., 1956. Fgn. svc. officer Dept. State, Washington, 1958-61, consular officer Trinidad, 1961-64; econ. officer mission OECD, Paris, 1964-66; econ. officer London, 1966-71; internat. economist, 1971-73; dep. dir. maj. export projects Dept. Commerce, 1973-75; comml. counselor Brazil, 1975-76; amb. to Guinea-Bissau and Cape Verde Dept. of State, 1976-77; U.S. rep. ECOSOC, UN, NYC, 1977-79; resident rep. UNDP, Kampala, Uganda, 1979-81, dir. IMPACT program Geneva, 1982-86; amb. to Mozambique, 1987-90; amb. to Zaire, Kinshasa, 1991-93; under-sec. gen. for adminstrn. and mgmt. UN, NYC, 1993-94; consul gen. Sao Paulo, Brazil, 1995-97; amb. to Republic of Estonia, 1998—2001; ret., 2001. Bd. dirs. U.S.-Baltic Found. Mem. Am. Fgn. Service Assn., Am. Acad. Diplomacy. Office: Casa Wells Plz Leoncio Bento 7 38830 Agulo Gomera Canary Islands Spain

WELLS, NINA MITCHELL, state official; b. 1950; m. Theodore V. Wells; 2 children. BA, Newton Coll. of Sacred Heart, 1973; JD, Suffolk U. Atty. Bell Comms. Rsch., 1985; dir. div. rate counsel NJ Pub. Advocate; dir. minority student program and fin. aid Rutgers U. Sch. Law, asst. dean, 1996—97; v.p. pub. affairs Schering-Plough Corp., Kenilworth, NJ, 1998—2004; sec. state State of NJ, Trenton, 2006—. Pres. Schering-Plough Found. Recipient Garden State Bar Assn. award, 2005. Democrat. Office: Office Sec of State PO Box 300 Trenton NJ 08625 Office Phone: 609-984-1900. Office Fax: 609-292-9897. E-mail: feedback@sos.state.nj.us. *

WELLS, PETER NATHANIEL, judge, lawyer; b. Ogdensburg, NY, May 13, 1938; s. John Harris and Mary Theresa (Houlihan) W.; m. Diana Barry Wells, Apr. 8, 1967; childen: Mary, Sarah, Matthew. BS in Polit. Sci., Manhattan Coll., 1960; LLB, Boston Coll., 1963. Bar: N.Y. 1964, U.S. Dist. Ct. (no. dist.) N.Y. 1967, U.S. Dist. Ct. (we. dist.) N.Y. 1971, U.S. Ct. Appeals (d cir.) 1974, U.S. Ct. Appeals (3d cir.) 1978, U.S. Supreme Ct. 1974. Asst. atty. gen. State of N.Y., 1964-68; assoc. Costello, Cooney & Fearon, Syracuse, N.Y., 1968-70, ptnr., 1970-76, Williams, Micale & Wells, Syracuse, 1976-88, Mackenzie Smith Lewis, Michell & Hughes, Syracuse, 1988; surrogate ct. judge Onondaga County, 1989—. Mem. EPTL-SCPA Legis. adv. com. of N.Y. State. Editl. bd. Warren's Heaton on Surrogate Ct.; mem. surrogate's adv. com. Office of Ct. Adminstrn. Chmn. Dewitt Republican Com., 1976-87; town justice Dewitt, N.Y., 1987-88. Served with USAR, 1963-69. Mem. Onondaga County Bar Assn., Def. Rsch. Inst., Upstate Trial Lawyers Assn., N.Y. State Surrogates Assn. (pres. 1999-2001), Cavalry Club, Manlius (N.Y.). Roman Catholic. Home: 100 Downing Rd De Witt NY 13214-1503 Office: Surrogate Ct Chambers Onondaga County Courth Syracuse NY 13202 Business E-Mail: pwells@courts.state.ny.us.

WELLS, PETER SCOVILLE, retired marketing professional; b. NYC, Apr. 25, 1938; s. Jonathan Godfrey and Eleanore Shannon (Scoville) Wells; m. Patricia Ann Trent, Dec. 8, 1973; 1 child from previous marriage, Peter Scoville. BA, 1961. Asst. to contr. Laird & Co., NYC, 1961-63; asst. to ptnr. charge ops. Goldman Sachs, NYC, 1963-64; mgr. new bus. dept. B.J. Herkimer Co., NYC, 1964-67; divisional policy and procedures adminstr. Paine, Webber, Jackson & Curtis, Inc., NYC, 1967-70, asst. to exec. cashier, 1970-73, asst. v.p., mgr. employment svcs., adminstr. equal employment opportunity, 1973-80; pers. officer, exec. recruiter N.Y. Stock Exch., NYC, 1980-86, mgr. employment; sr. v.p. Wesley Brown & Bartle, 1986-87; sr. v.p., dir. Alliance Mktg., Inc., 1987; ptnr. Richards & Wells, 1988-90, Brookman Assocs., Inc., 1990—2000; ret., 2000. With US Army, 1958—66. Mem.: SAR, Vet. Corps Arty., L'Ordre Militaire, KT, Order of Lafayette, Mil. Order Loyal Legion, Knights of Malta (knight comdr.), Phi Kappa Psi.

WELLS, RAYMOND O'NEIL, JR., mathematics professor, researcher; b. Dallas, June 12, 1940; s. Raymond O. and Hazel (Rand) W.; m. Rena Schwarze, Aug. 1, 1963; children: Richard Andrew, René Michael. BA, Rice U., 1962; MS, NYU, 1964, PhD, 1965. Asst. prof. math. Rice U., Houston, 1965-69, assoc. prof., 1969-74, prof. math., 1974-2000, prof. edn., 1993-2000; chmn. dept. math., 1976-79; chmn. dept. edn. Rice U., Houston, 1994-98, dir. sch. math. project, 1987-2000, dir. computational math. lab., 1990-2000, prof. math emeritus, 2000—, asst. to pres., 2000-01; v.p. external affairs, prof. math. Internat. U., Bremen, 2001—05, disting. prof. math., 2005—06, Jacobs U., Bremen, 2007—. Vis. asst. prof. Brandeis U., Waltham, Mass., 1967-68; vis. prof. U. Göttingen, Germany, 1974-75, U. Colo., Boulder, 1983-84, U. Bremen, Germany, 1995-96, Internat. U. Bremen, 1998-2001; adj. prof. cmty. medicine Baylor Coll. Medicine, 1994-2000; active Inst. for Advanced Study, Princeton, N.J., 1970-71, 79-80; exch. visitor NAS, Sofia, Bulgaria, 1984; planning com. Internat. U., Bremen, 1997-99. Author: Differential Analysis on Complex Manifolds, 1973, Mathematics in Civilization, 1973, Twister Geometry and Field Theory, 1990, Wavelet Analysis: The Scaleable Structure of Information, 1998; editor: Mathematical Heritage of Herman Weyl, 1989, (book series) Expositions in Mathematics, 1988—2003, The Founding of International University Bremen: Perspectives for the Twenty First Century, 2003; contbr. numerous articles to sci. jours. Pres. Stages Repertory Theater, Houston, 1989-90; sec. bd. dirs. IUB Found. Am., Inc., 2004—. Recipient Alexander von Humboldt Sr. U.S. Scientist award U. Göttingen, 1974-75; Fulbright fellow, 1968, Guggenheim fellow, 1974. Fellow AAAS (coun. 1989—); mem. Am. Math. Soc. (coun., editor 1978-88), Cosmos Club Washington, Carl Schurz Deutsch Am. Club (pres.). Home: Lüder-von-Bentheim Str 12 28209 Bremen Germany Office: Jacobs U Bremen PO Box 750561 28725 Bremen Germany Home Phone: 49 421 6520669; Office Phone: 49 421 200 4321. Business E-Mail: wells@jacobs-university.de.

WELLS, RICHARD A., manufacturing executive; BSBA, U. Wis., Madison, 1960; cert. in data processing, U. Wis., Milw. CPA, Wis. With Kohler (Wis.) Co., sr. v.p. fin., CFO, 1979-1999, also mem. exec. com., pension investment com., bd. dirs. Office: Kohler Co 444 Highland Dr Kohler WI 53044-1500

WELLS, ROBERT ALFRED, lawyer; b. Louisiana, Mo., Dec. 1, 1942; s. Harry Armstrong and Irene Jacobson W.; m. Binney Kitchel, Dec. 21, 1968; children: Hylah, Theodore. BA with honors, DePauw U., 1964; JD cum laude, U. Mich., 1967. Bar: N.Y. 1968, N.H. 1971, Mo. 1981, U.S. Tax Ct. 1973, U.S. Supreme Ct. 1976, U.S. Mil. Ct. Appeals 1978. Assoc. Dewey, Ballantine, Bushby, Palmer & Wood, NYC, 1967-68, McLane, Graf, Raulerson & Middleton, Manchester, N.H., 1971—. Trustee Heritage Heights/Homewood, 1994—2001, Soc. for Protection of N.H. Forests, 1988—96, sec., 1995—96; trustee, treas. Children's Trust Fund; dir., pres. Office Pub. Guardian; dir., v.p. Concord Cmty. Music Sch., 1995—2001; advance studies program chair adv. com. St. Paul's Sch.; active St. Andrew's Episc. Ch., Hopkinton, NH, 1971—, vestry mem., 1974—77, warden, 1979—85, trustee Protestant Episc. Ch. of N.H., 1985—; bd. dirs. Am. Lung Assn. of N.H., pres., 1980—81, sec., 1990—2002; bd. dirs. Am. Lung Assn., 1982—94, exec. com., 1987—2002, v.p., 1990; mem. Town of Hopkinton Planning Bd., 1977—79, Town of Hopkinton Budget Com., 1992—2005; co-chmn. Hopkinton Master Plan Revision Com., 1986—88; chmn. State Adv. Com. to the U.S. Civil Rights Commn., 1985—89; bd. dirs. Pat's Peak Ednl. Found., Inc., 1982—87, Youth Soccer Assn. Lt. USN, 1968—70. Mem. Am Coll. Trust and Estate Counsel, N.H. Bar Assn. (chmn. elderly legal devel. Program 1978-81, continuing legal edn. program 1981—, fee dispute resolution com. 1986-88), Internat. Assn. Fin. Planners (edn. com. 1985—90), Phi Beta Kappa. Episcopalian. Office: PO Box 326 Manchester NH 03105-0326

WELLS, ROGER STANLEY, software engineer; b. Seattle, Apr. 13, 1949; s. Stanley A. and Margaret W. BA, Whitman Coll., 1971; postgrad., U. Tex., Austin, 1973—74; BS, Oreg. State U., 1977. Software evaluation engr. Tektronix, Beaverton, Oreg., 1979—83; computer engr. Aramco, Dhahran, Saudi Arabia, 1983—84; software engr. Conrac Corp., Clackamas, Oreg., 1984—85, Duarte, Calif., 1985; software analyst Lundy Fin. Systems, San Dimas, Calif., 1986—89; pvt. practice Seattle, 1989—92; sr. project engr. Illuminet, Olympia, Wash., 1993—2000; mgr. configuration New Edge Networks, Vancouver, Wash., 2000; sr. product engr. Wind River Systems, Beaverton, 2000—01; tech. advisor E-corps Wash. Svc. Corps, 2002—04; software builder Volt Tech. Resources, 2004—05; computer process specialist Boeing, 2005—. Adv. to chair Cascadia N.Am. Sci. Fiction Conf., 2003—05; mem. Exec. of Yr. com. Illuminet, Olympia, 1998—99. Bd. dirs. Lydia Whitney Found., Collinsville, Conn., Found. for Preservation Sci. Fiction and Fantasy Memorabilia, Salem, Oreg.; co-founder, bd. dirs., pres. Oreg. Sci. Fiction Conv., 1979-81; vol. Americorps, Yakima, Wash., 2002-03, Pasco, Wash., 2003-04, ARC, 2004-06; Boeing vol. disaster responder, 2006-. Recipient R. L. Fanthorpe grand prize, Write-Alike Contest, 2006. Mem. IEEE, Am. Philatelic Soc., Nat. Assn. Parliamentarians, Am. Inst. Parliamentarians (chpt. v.p. 1996-97, pres. 1997-98), Fantasy Amateur Press Assn., N.W. Sci. Fiction Soc., Mensa, Assn. Computing Machinery, L.A. Sci. Fantasy Soc., Melbourne (Australia) Sci. Fiction Club, Toastmasters Internat. (club pres. 1980, v.p. edn. 1994-95, area gov. 1994-95, dist. 32 parliamentarian 1996-99), Internat. Platform Assn. (2d place Monologue contest 1997, conv. com. 1998-99, bd. govs. 1999-00, Grand prize R. L. Fanthorpe write-alike contest 2006). Achievements include design of software program to transfer billing records for regional telephone companies. Avocations: travel, public speaking, science fiction, stamp collecting/philately. Home: PO Box 69254 Seatac WA 98168-9254 Office: PMB 178 15031 Military Rd S Ste B Seatac WA 98188 Personal E-mail: rswells@acm.org.

WELLS, ROGER W., lawyer; b. Sioux Falls, SD, May 7, 1957; BSBA summa cum laude, Creighton U., 1979, JD summa cum laude, 1981. Bar: Nebr. 1981, U.S. Dist. Ct. Nebr. 1981, U.S. Tax Ct. 1981. Gen. counsel ConAgra Foods Inc., Omaha, 2002; head, mergers and acquisitions McGrath, North, Mullin & Kratz, Omaha, 1981—. Mem. editl. staff: Creighton U. Law Rev., 1980—81. Mem.: ABA (mem. corp., banking and bus. sect., mem. taxation sect., mem. internat. law sect.), Omaha Bar Assn., Nebr. Bar Assn., Beta Gamma Sigma. Office: McGrath North Mullin and Kratz PC Ste 3700 1st Nat Tower 1601 Dodge St Omaha NE 68102 Home Phone: 402-498-0941; Office Phone: 402-341-3070. Business E-Mail: rwells@mnmk.com. *

WELLS, SAMUEL ALONZO, JR., surgeon, educator; b. Cuthbert, Ga., Mar. 16, 1936; s. Samuel Alonzo and Martha Steele W.; m. Barbara Anne Atwood, Feb. 13, 1964; children: Sarah, Susan. Student, Emory U., 1954—57, MD, 1961. Intern Johns Hopkins Hosp., Balt., 1961—62, resident in internal medicine, 1962—63; asst. resident in surgery Barnes Hosp., St. Louis, 1963—64; resident in surgery Duke U., Durham, NC, 1966—70; guest investigator dept. tumor biology Karolinska Inst., Stockholm, 1967—68; asst. prof. surgery Duke U., Durham, NC, 1970—72, assoc. prof., 1972—76, prof., 1976—81; clin. assoc. surgery br. Nat. Cancer Inst., NIH, Bethesda, Md., 1964—66, sr. investigator surgery br., 1970—72, cons. surgery br., 1975—; prof., chmn. dept. surgery Washington U., St. Louis, 1981—98; dir. ACS, Chgo., 1998—99, group chair, prin. investigator, oncology group, 1998—2005, exec. dir. internat. thyroid cancer study group, 2005—. Dir. Duke U. Clin. Rsch. Ctr., 1978—81; mem. Residency Rev. Com. Surgery, 1987—93, chmn., 1991—93; mem. bd. regents ACS, 1989—98, vice chmn. bd. regents, 1998—; prof. surgery Duke U. Sch. Medicine, 2001—07. Mem. editl. bd.: Annals of Surgery, 1975—93, Surgery, 1975—93, Jour. Surg. Rsch., 1981—93, editor in chief: World Jour. Surgery, 1983—92, Current Problems in Surgery, 1989—. Pres. GM Cancer Rsch. Found., 1996—2006. Lt. comdr. USPHS, 1964—66. Fellow: AAAS; mem.: ACS, Soc. Internationale de Chirurgie (pres. 2001), Soc. Surg. Oncology (pres. 1993—94), Halsted Soc. (pres. 1987), Nat. Cancer Adv. Bd., Inst. Medicine of NAS, Am. Soc. Clin. Investigation, Soc. Clin. Surgery (treas. 1980—86, v.p. 1986—88, pres. 1988—90), Soc. Univ. Surgeons (exec. coun. 1976—78), Am. Surg. Assn. (mem. coun. 1986—91, pres. 1995—96, recorder, Sci. Achievement medallion 2004), Am. Bd. Surgery (exec. com. 1986—89, vice chmn. 1987—88, chmn. 1988—89), Alpha Omega Alpha. Office: Dept Surgery Wash Univ Sch Medicine 660 S Euclid Ave Campus Box 8109 Saint Louis MO 63110 Office Phone: 919-201-0310. Business E-Mail: wellss@wudosis.wustl.edu.

WELLS, SAMUEL FOGLE, JR., research center administrator; b. Mullins, SC, Sept. 13, 1935; s. Samuel Fogle and Mildred Inez (Meeks) W.; m. Novella R. Cloninger, June 15, 1957 (div. 1969); children: Lauren, Anthony (dec.), Jeffrey (dec.); m. Sherrill Perkins Brown, June 7, 1969; 1 child, Christopher Wentworth. AB, U. NC, 1957; MA, Harvard U., 1961, PhD, 1967. Instr. Wellesley (Mass.) Coll., 1963-65; asst. prof. U. NC, Chapel Hill, 1965-70, assoc. prof., 1970-78; dir. internat. security studies program Woodrow Wilson Ctr., Washington, 1977-87, assoc. dir., 1985-88, 99—, dep. dir., 1988-98. Cons. Office Sec. of Def., Washington, 1974-77; trustee Z. Smith Reynolds Found., Winston-Salem, NC, 1977-83. Author: The Challenges of Power: American Diplomacy, 1900-1921, 1990; editor and contbr. to books: Economics and World Power: An Assessment of American Diplomacy Since 1789, 1984, Limiting Nuclear Proliferation, 1985, Strategic Defenses and Soviet-American Relations, 1987, Security in the Middle East: Regional Change and Great Power Strategies, 1987, Superpower Competition and Security in the Third World, 1988, The Helsinki Process and the Future of Europe, 1990, New European Orders, 1919 and 1991, 1996, The Quest for Sustained Growth: Southeast Asian and Southeast European Cases, 1999, The Strategic Triangle: France, Germany, and the United States in the Shaping of the New Europe, 2006; contbr. articles to profl. jours. Capt. USMC, 1957-60. Woodrow Wilson fellow, 1957, Danforth Found. fellow, 1957, Peace fellow Hoover Instn., 1972-73, Woodrow Wilson Internat. Ctr. for Scholars fellow, 1976-77. Mem. Am. Hist. Assn., Internat. Inst. Strategic Studies, Orgn. Am. Historians, Soc. for Historians of Am. Fgn. Rels., Internat. Studies Assn., Coun. on Fgn. Rels. Avocations: hiking, soccer. Home: 1509 Woodacre Dr Mc Lean VA 22101-2538 Office: Woodrow Wilson Internat Ctr 1300 Pennsylvania Ave NW Washington DC 20004-3027 Office Phone: 202-691-4208. Business E-Mail: samuel.wells@wilsoncenter.org.

WELLS, THEODORE V., JR., (TED), lawyer; b. Washington, Apr. 28, 1950; m. Nina Mitchell, 1972; 2 children. BA, Coll. Holy Cross, 1972; MBA, Harvard U., 1976; JD, Harvard Law Sch., 1976. Bar: NJ 1977, DC 2001, NY 2001, US Supreme Ct., US Ct. Appeals (3rd and 9th cirs.), DC Ct. Appeals, US Dist. Ct. (dist. NJ and so. dist. NY). Law clk. to Hon. John J. Gibbons US Ct. Appeals (3rd cir.), 1976-77; ptnr. Lowenstein, Sandler, Kohl, Fisher & Boylan, P.C., Roseland, NJ, 1977—2000; ptnr., co-chair litig. dept. Paul, Weiss, Rifkind, Wharton & Garrison, LLP, NYC, 2000—. Mem. adj. faculty trade regulation Sch. Law, Seton Hall U., 1980-81; mem. faculty trial advocacy Practicing Law Inst., 1982—; mem. lawyers adv. com. US Ct. Appeals (3rd cir.), 1982-85, 88—; former mem. bd. dirs. CIT Corp.; co-chair White Collar Criminal Sect. Nat. Assn. Criminal Def. Lawyers; gen. counsel NJ Dem. Party; tchg. team mem. Harvard Law Sch. Trial Advocacy Workshop. Bd. trustees Coll. Holy Cross, 1977—, Newark Mus., 1979-82, NJ Performing Arts Ctr., NAACP Legal Def. Fund; bd. dirs. Essex County Urban League, 1979-88; NJ co-chairperson United Negro Coll. Fund; gen. counsel, NJ NAACP; fin. chmn. Bill Bradley's presdl. campaign, 2000. Named Lawyer of Yr., Nat. Law Jour., 2006; named one of 75 Best Lawyers in Washington, Washingtonian survey mag., 2002, Am.'s Top Black Lawyers, Black Enterprise mag., 2003, 100 Most Influential Lawyers, Nat. Law Jour., 2006. Fellow Am. Trial Lawyers Assn.; mem. ABA (antitrust law sect., state antitrust law subcommittee 1980—), Assn. Criminal Def. Lawyers (trustee 1984—), NJ State Bar Assn. (antitrust law com. 1980—) Office: Paul Weiss Rifkind Wharton & Garrison LLP 1285 Ave of the Americas New York NY 10019-6064 Office Phone: 212-373-3089. Office Fax: 212-373-2217. E-mail: twells@paulweiss.com. *

WELLS, THOMAS B., federal judge; b. Akron, Ohio, July 2, 1945; BS, Miami U., 1967; JD, Emory U., 1973; LLM, NYU, 1978. Atty. Graham & Wells, Vidalia, Ga., 1973—77; city atty. City of Vidalia, Ga., 1975—77; county atty. Toombs County, Ga., 1975—77; atty. Hurt, Richardson, Garner, Todd & Cadenhead, Atlanta, 1978—81, Shearer & Wells, Atlanta, 1981—86; judge US Tax Ct., Washington, 1986—, chief judge, 1997, 2000—04. With USNR, 1967—70. Recipient Disting. Alumnus award, Emory Law Alumni, 2001. Mem. ABA. Office: US Tax Ct 400 2nd St NW Washington DC 20217-0002 Office Phone: 202-521-0790.

WELLS, TULLOS, lawyer; b. Urbana, Ill., Apr. 11, 1949; m. Carri Baker Wells; 1 child, McKensie Lynd. BA, U. Tex., Austin, 1971; JD, U. Tex. Sch. Law, 1974. Bar: Tex. 1974, admitted to practice: US Ct. Appeals (DC Cir.), US Ct. Appeals (5th Cir.) 1981, US Ct. Appeals (11th Cir.) 1981, US Dist. Ct. (No. Dist.) Tex. 1980, US Dist. Ct. (So. Dist.) Tex. 1980, US Dist. Ct. (We. Dist.) Tex. 1980, cert.: Tex. Bd. Legal Specialization (in labor and employment law). Ptnr. Wells, Pinckney & McHugh; mng. ptnr. Bracewell & Giuliani, San Antonio, 1999—; outside gen. counsel San Antonio Spurs, 1995—. Hon. consul Can. in San Antonio, 2005—; spkr. in field. Bd. dir. Spurs Found.; bd. trustees, exec. com. United Way of San Antonio; bd. dir. Greater Kelly Devel. Corp., 1995—2000; chmn. bd. Greater San Antonio C. of C., 1995, former chmn., govt. affairs coun., former chmn., mil. affairs coun.; dir. Tex. Assn. of Atlantic Coun. of US, San Antonio Econ. Devel. Found.; bd. dir. Tex. Bus. Hall of Fame; bd. gov. Cancer Therapy & Rsch. Ctr.; chmn. bd. Austin-San Antonio Inter-Municipal Commuter Rail Dist. Named one of Top 50 Lawyers Ctrl. and West Tex. Region Super Lawyers, Tex. Super Lawyer, 2003, 2004, 2005, 2006. Mem.: State Bar Tex. Avocation: sailing. Office: Bracewell & Giuliani 800 One Alamo Ctr 106 S St Mary's St San Antonio TX 78205-3603 Office Phone: 210-299-3525. Office Fax: 210-299-0126. Business E-Mail: tullos.wells@bracewellgiuliani.com, tullos.wells@bgllp.com.

WELLS, VERNON, III, professional baseball player; b. Shreveport, La., Dec. 8, 1978; s. Vernon Wells Jr. and Dianne Wells; m. Charlene Valenti, Nov. 10, 2001; 2 children. Ctr. fielder Toronto Blue Jays, 2002—. Named to Futures Game, 1999, 2000, Am. League All-Star Game, 2006; recipient Rawlings Gold Glove, 2004, 2005. Achievements include being the youngest Blue Jay ever to have 100 RBIs, 2002; setting a Blue Jays franchise record with 215 hits in a single season, 2003. Mailing: Rogers Ctr 1 Blue Jays Way Ste 3200 Toronto M5V1J1 Canada Office Phone: 416-341-1000. *

WELLS, WILLIAM, criminal justice educator; s. Charles and Kathleen Wells; m. Amy Suhr, Sept. 5, 1999; children: Benjamin, Margaret, Ellen. BA, Ohio U., Athens, 1993; MA, Ind. U., Bloomington, 1995; PhD, U. Nebr., Omaha, 1999. Asst. prof. So. Ill. U., Carbondale, 1999—2005, assoc. prof., 2005—07, Sam Houston State U., Huntsville, Tex., 2007—. Grad. program dir. Ctr. for Study of Crime, Carbondale, 2005—06, interim dir., 2006—07. Contbr. articles to profl. jours. Active Ill. Acad. Criminology, Chgo., 2006—. Rsch. grantee, Nat. Inst. Justice, 2000—02, Nat. Alliance Mentally Ill-West Ctrl. Ind., 2003—05, George Mason U., 2007—. Mem.: Acad. Criminal Justice Scis., Am. Soc. Criminology (chair Gene Carte Student Paper Competition com. 2005—06), Midwestern Criminal Justice Assn. (v.p. 2007—). Achievements include clarification of the relationship between the presence of firearms in conflict situations and the likelihood of violent outcomes; identification of the results of an innovative police training program aimed at improving police responses to persons with a mental illness; documentation of the manner in which policing agencies were implementing community policing in the United States in the late 1990's; estimation of the effects of the availability of federally funded shelters for abused women on rates of intimate partner homicide in California. Office: Sam Houston State U Coll Criminal Justice Box 2296 Huntsville TX 77341 Office Phone: 936-294-1634. Business E-Mail: w_wells@yahoo.com.

WELLS-HENDERSON, RONALD JOHN, investment counselor; b. Jan. 28, 1934; s. William Noel and Sylvia Mary (Gowen) W.-H.; m. Kathleen Louise McDonnell, Sept. 14, 1957; children: Anne, John. BA, U. Wash., 1955; MBA, Northwestern U., 1957; grad., US Army Command & Gen. Staff Coll., 1969. CFA Chartered Fin. Analysts Inst., 1978. Security analyst Continental Bank, Chgo., 1957—59; fin. analyst Boeing Co., Seattle; trust investment mgr. Seattle Trust, 1970—80; prin. KAS Investment Cons., Seattle, 1980—. Contbr. articles to profl. jours. Mem. Seattle Art Mus., Bellevue Art Mus., 1957—; treas. Civil Affairs Assn., 1975—79; curator-treas. Seattle King County Mil. History Soc., 1978—80. Lt. col. USAR, 1955—83. Named Gazzam Found. scholar, 1952—55. Mem.: CFA Soc. Seattle, Washington Water Trails Assn., CFA Inst. (charter holder). Episcopalian. Home: 13005 SE 46th St Bellevue WA 98006-2042 Office: KAS Investment Cons PO Box 5617 Bellevue WA 98006-0117 Office Phone: 425-641-7645. Personal E-mail: ronw-h@prodigy.net.

WELMAKER, FORREST NOLAN, lawyer; b. McKinney, Tex., Aug. 13, 1925; s. Felix E. and Forrest Love (Baker) W.; div.; children: Forrest Nolan Jr., Mary Elizabeth Welmaker Young, Byron Skillin. BBA, U. Tex., 1950, LLD, 1953. Bar: Tex. 1953, U.S. Dist. Ct. (so. and we. dists.) Tex. 1956, U.S. Ct. Appeals (5th cir.) 1956, U.S. Tax Ct. 1959, U.S. Supreme Ct. 1956. Pvt. practice, San Antonio, 1953—. Past bd. dirs., officer United Fund San Antonio, San Antonio chpt. ARC, Children Welfare Bur. San Antonio, San Antonio YMCA. Capt. USNR, 1943-46, PTO, 1950-52, Korea. Fellow Tex. Bar Found., San Antonio Bar Found.; mem. San Antonio Bar Assn. (past bd. dirs., v.p., pres.), Tex. Assn. Def. Counsel, San Antonio Res. Officer Assn., Tex. Bar Assn. (past bd. dirs.), San Antonio German Club. Episcopalian. Avocations: handball, boating. Home: 114 W Brandon Dr San Antonio TX 78209-6404 Office Phone: 210-828-6033. Business E-Mail: forrestwelmaker@welmakerlawfirm.com.

WELNA, CECILIA, retired mathematics professor, dean; b. New Britain, Conn., July 15, 1927; d. Joseph and Sophie (Roman) Welna. BS, St. Joseph Coll., 1949; MA, U. Conn., 1952, PhD, 1960. Instr. Mt. St. Joseph Acad., 1949-50; asst. instr. U. Conn., 1950-55; instr. U. Mass., Amherst, 1955-56; prof., chmn. dept. math. and physics U. Hartford, 1956—82, dean Coll. Edn., Nursing and Health Professions, 1982—93, prof. math., 1993—. Mem.: Math. Assn. Am., Nat. Council Tchrs. Math., Assn. Tchrs. Math. Conn., Sigma Xi. Personal E-mail: seawell31@aol.com.

WELNAK, LLOWELL A., retired lawyer; b. Milw., July 19, 1926; s. Albert George Welnak and Wilhelmina Helena Struck; children: Ann Harvey, Peter. BA, Marquette U., 1948, LLB, 1950. Claim mgr. Md. Casualty Co., Phila., 1950—63, Ctrl. Mut., Van Wert, Ohio, 1963—73; v.p., claims and gen. counsel Peerless Ins. Co., Keene, NH, 1973—88; ret., 1988. Active YMCA. Mem.: Lions.

WELSCH, ROY ELMER, statistician, educator; b. Kansas City, Mo., July 31, 1943; AB, Princeton U., 1965; MS, Stanford U., 1966, PhD in math., 1969. Asst. prof. ops. rsch. Sloan Sch. Mgmt. MIT, Cambridge, Mass., 1969-73, assoc. prof., 1973-79, prof. mgmt. sci. and stats. & engrng. systems, 1979—, dir. statistics ctr., 1981—89. Sr. rsch. assoc. Nat. Bur. Econ. Rsch., 1973—79. Assoc. editor: Jour. Am. Statist. Assn. Fellow AAAS, Am. Statis. Assn., Inst. Math. Stats. Office: MIT Dept Mgmt & Stats Bldg E53-383 77 Massachusetts Ave Cambridge MA 02139-4307 Office Phone: 617-253-6601. Office Fax: 617-258-7579. E-mail: rwelsch@mit.edu.

WELSER-MÖST, FRANZ, conductor, music director; b. Linz, Austria, Aug. 16, 1960; LHD (hon.), Case Western Reserve U., 2003. Chief condr. Sinfonieorkester Norrköping, Sweden, 1986-91, Stadtorchester Winterthur, Switzerland, 1987-90; condr. St. Louis Symphony Orch., 1989; music dir. London Philharm., 1990—96, Zurich Opera, 1995—2002, prin. condr., 2002—05, gen. music dir., 2005—; music dir. The Cleve. Orch., 2002—. Guest condr. Berlin Philharmonic, Cleveland Orch. Youth Orch., Vienna Philharm., Bavarian Radio Symphony Orch., Gustav Mahler Youth Orch. Conducting debut Salzburg Festival, Austria, 1985; Am. debut St. Louis, 1989; appearances include Vienna biennial, Lucerne Festical, Carnegie Hall. Recipient Outstanding Achievement award, Western Law Ctr. for Disability Rights, 1995, Gramophone award, 1996, Condr. of Yr. award, Musical Am. Internat. Directory of Performing Arts, 2003, Silver medal of Region of Upper Austria, 2003. Mem.: Vienna Singverein (hon.). Office: Cleve Orch Severance Hall 11001 Euclid Ave Cleveland OH 44106 *

WELSH, SIR ALFRED JOHN, lawyer, investment advisor; b. Louisville, May 10, 1947; s. Elvin Alfred and Carol (Kleymeyer) W.; m. Lee Mitchell, Aug. 1, 1970; children: Charles Kleymeyer, Kathryn Thomas. BA, Centre Coll., 1969; JD, U. Ky., 1972; LLM in Internat. Law cum laude, U. Brussels, 1973. Bar: Ky. 1972, U.S. Dist. Ct. (we. and ea. dists.) Ky. 1972, U.S. Ct. Appeals (6th cir.) 1972, U.S. Supreme Ct. Asst. atty. Ky. Atty. Gen. Office, Frankfort, 1973-74; legis. counsel to congressman Ho. of Reps., Washington, 1974-77; mng. ptnr. Adams, Hayward and Welsh, Louisville, 1977—, Boone Welsh and Hayward Internat. Law. Hon. counsel of Belgium, 1983—; econ. devel. advisor Kingdom of Belgium; mem. Ky. Econ. Adv. Coun., 1991-94; pres. Transcontinental Trading Cons., Ltd.; del. North African Mideast Econ. Summit Conf., Morocco, 1994; bd. dirs. Intervention Resources Ctr., Inc.; presenter in field. Bd. dirs. Greater Louisville Swim Found., 1983-94, exec. com., 1994—; bd. dirs. Melody Lake Ranch Inc.; bd. dirs. Louisville com. Coun. Fgn. Rels., 1981—, also pres.; chmn. Louisville Com. on Fgn. Rels.; bd. dirs. Am. Com. on Fgn. Rels.; bd. dirs. Jefferson County Alcohol and Drug Abuse Found., Louisville, 1986-98, Internat. Resolve, Louisville Internat. Cultural Ctr.; mem. econ. task force of Ky. Legis. Agts.; mem. Louisville Meml. Auditorium Commn.; bd. dirs. Am. Com. Fgn. Rels.; mem. Union Internat des Avocats. Decorated knight Order of the Crown (Belgium). Mem. ABA (internat. law sect., commn. on impairment, com. on substance abuse), ATLA, Va. Bar Assn., Ky. Bar Assn. (bd. dirs. 1981-82, pres. young lawyers divsn. 1981-82), Ky. Acad. Trial Lawyers, Am. Judicature Soc., Louisville C. of C., Am. Ctr. Fgn. Rels. (chmn. Louisville com. on fgn. rels.), Am. Com. on Fgn. Rels. (exec. com.). Democrat. Presbyterian. Avocations: swimming, water polo, soccer. Office: Barristers Hall 1009 S 4th St Louisville KY 40203-3207 Home Phone: 502-459-3648; Office Phone: 502-584-8583. Personal E-mail: bwbh@earthlink.net.

WELSH, CAROLINE MASTIN, museum director, curator, art historian; b. St. Louis, Nov. 30, 1948; d. Charles O'Fallon and Georgann Logsdon Mastin; m. Peter Corbett Welsh, Sept. 8, 1970; 1 child, James Munson Corbett. Degree cum laude, Kent Sch., 1966; AB in Art History, Wellesley Coll., Mass., 1970. Editl. asst. Smithsonian Jour. History, 1969; coord. exhibits Travelling Exbn. Svc. Smithsonian Instn., 1971—72; guest curator Albany Inst. History and Art, NY, 1975—76; dir. exhibits Marketechs Exhibit Design and Prodn., Inc., York, Pa., 1976—86; prin., owner The Welsh Group, Camp Hill, Pa., 1984—88; from cons. curator to chief curator The Adirondack Mus., Blue Mountain Lake, NY, 1986—92, chief curator, 1992—2007, dir. ops., 1994—2006, acting dir. pubs., 2002—07, dir., 2007—. Adv. bd. Adirondack Pk. Centennial Project WCFE Pub. TV, 1991—92; advisor film WMHT Ednl. Telecomms., 1993—95; mem. com. visual arts Hamilton Coll., 2002—; bd. dirs. Lake Placid Winter Olympic Mus., Lake Placid Ctr. Arts. Contbr. articles to profl. jours. Fellow, Smithsonian Instn., 1970—71. Mem.: Am. Assn. Mus. (peer reviewer mus. assessment program 2002—), The Soc. Preservation Am. Modernists (bd. dirs. 1994—), The Century Assn. Home: 34 Second St Tupper Lake NY 12986 Office: The Adirondack Museum Rte 28/30 Blue Mountain Lake NY 12812 Office Phone: 518-352-7311.

WELSH, DIANE M., federal judge; BA in Polit. Sci. magna cum laude, Villanova U., 1976, JD, 1979. Bar: Pa. 1979, U.S. Dist. Ct. (ea. dist.) Pa. 1981, U.S. Ct. Appeals (3rd cir.) 1984, U.S. Supreme Ct. 1985. Legal counsel Pa. Senate Judiciary Com., 1980-81; dep. dist. atty. Bucks County Dist. Atty.'s Office, Pa., 1981-84; ptnr. Gold-Bikin Welsh & Assocs., 1984-94; magistrate judge U.S. Dist. Ct. (ea. dist.) Pa., Phila., 1994—. Spkr. in field. Contbr. articles to legal jours. Trustee Manor Jr. Coll., 1981-83, Norristown State Hosp., 1987-90. Mem. ABA, Fed. Bar Assn., Fed. Magistrate Judge Assn., Nat. Assn. Women Judges, Pa. Bar Assn., Montgomery County Bar Assn., Phila. Bar Assn., Brehon Law Soc. Office: US Courthouse 3029 US Courthouse 601 Market St Philadelphia PA 19106-1713

WELSH, DONALD EMORY, publisher; b. Youngstown, Ohio, Oct. 6, 1943; s. Edward Francis and Clevelle Rose W.; m. Elizabeth Bourne Floyd, June 25, 1966; children: Leah Bourne, Emory Philip. AB, Columbia U., 1965; JD, Cleveland Marshall Sch. Law, 1969. Bar: Ohio 1969. Trust devel. officer Cleve. Trust Co., 1968-70; advt. sales rep. Fortune mag., Time, Inc., NYC, 1970-75; advt. dir. Rolling Stone mag., NYC, 1975-77, v.p., assoc. pub., 1977-78; pub. Muppet mag. and pres. Lorimar Pub. Group (formerly Telepictures Publs., Inc.), 1982-87; pres. Welsh Pub. Group, Inc., 1987-94; exec. v.p. Marvel Comics Group, NYC, 1994-96; chmn. Group XXVII Comms., NYC, 1997-2000; pres. pub. group Digital Convergence Inc., NYC, 2000-2001; chmn. Budget Living Commn., NYC, 2001—05; pub. Outside's Go Mag., NYC, 2005—; bus. chmn. DEW LLC, Millerson, NY. Global advisor Outward Bound, U.S.A.; bd. dirs. Cousteau Soc.; former bd. dirs. Big Apple Circus, B.P.A. Consumer Mags. Mem. ABA, Mag. Pubs. Assn. (past bd. dirs.), Century Assn., Sharon Country Club (Conn.), Ocean Reef Club (Fla.), Brook Club (N.Y.C.). Home: 415 Undermountain Rd Millerton NY 12546-5162 E-mail: DonaldEWelsh@aol.com.

WELSH, DORIS MCNEIL, early childhood education specialist; b. Kansas City, Mo. d. Zelbert Melbourne and Anna May (Main) McNeil; children: J. Randall, Valerie M. BA, U. Calif., Berkeley, 1950, MA, 1952; postgrad., U. San Francisco, 1980-82. Cert. tchr., counselor, supr., Calif. Asst. dir. Bing Sch., Stanford, Calif., 1966-76; family devel. specialist Children's Hosp., Stanford, 1976-78; rsch. cons. Stanford U. Med. Ctr., 1970-87; dir. One Fifty Parker Sch., San Francisco, 1978-99; assoc. Lawrence Hall of Sci., U. Calif., Berkeley, 1996—. Citizen amb. del. edn. and childcare People to People Internat., St. Petersburg, Russia, Vilnius, Lithuania, Budapest, Hungary, 1993; pres. bd. dirs. Support for Parents of Spl. Children, San Francisco, 1986-87; bd. dirs. Family Svc. Assn. Mid-Peninsula, Palo Alto, Calif., 1970-80; leader Summer Camp for Pre-Schoolers, East Palo Alto, 1970-73; leader parenthood discussion groups U. Chgo., 1963-64; lectr. in field; cons., 1999—. Vol. Irving Mental Hosp., Chgo., 1963. Mem. Nat. Assn. Edn. Young Children, Assn. Childhood Edn. Internat., World Affairs Coun., Audubon Soc., Sierra Club. Avocations: natural sciences, hiking, horseback riding, gardening. Office: 26630 Ascension Dr Los Altos CA 94022-2001 E-mail: Kharis6@cs.com.

WELSH, DOROTHY DELL, columnist, writer; d. Roland Fields and Martha Gladys (Sheppard) Butler; m. James Robert Welsh, June 26, 1965; children: Pamela Jeanne(dec.), James Michael, Julie Marie. BA, U. Okla., 1957, MA, 1964; postgrad., U. Tex., Austin, 1983-84, U. Tex., San Antonio, 1984. Newspaper reporter summer intern Pryor Jeffersonian, Okla., 1952—55; tchr. English and journalism Classen HS, Oklahoma City, 1957-61, Henderson Jr. HS, Nev., 1961-62, Desert HS, Edwards, Calif., 1965-66; dir. publs. Amarillo (Tex.) HS, 1962-64; tchr. English Palmdale HS, Calif., 1964-65; lectr. English San Antonio Coll., 1979-88; tchg. assoc. U. Tex., San Antonio, 1986-91; reporter Swimming World mag., Sedona, Ariz., 1980—2000; freelance writer, 1992—. Lectr. journalism John Brown U., 1992. Author: The Butlers of Oklahoma, 1957, A Good Man is Hard to Find, 1961, To Seattle for a Bone Marrow Transplant, 1982, Fact, Fiction and Poetic License, 1995, The Butlers: A Newspaper Family, 2003; editor: Crescent News, 1974—80, 1983—86, The Swimmer's Ear, 1983—84, Off the Blocks, 1985—86; contbr. articles to profl. jours. Bd. dirs., publicity chmn. S. Tex. Swimming Assn., Austin, 1982—84; mem. info. com. Tex. Swimming Assn., Dallas, 1983—84; v.p. Mayes County Geneal. Soc., Okla., 2002; mem. Mayes County Hist. Soc., Okla., Rogers County Hist. Soc., Okla., Okla. Hist. Soc. Recipient citation superior work journalism, U. Interscholastic League, Austin, 1964, Svc. award, San Antonio Aquatic Club, 1983, Outstanding Svc. award, U.S. Swimming/Phillips 66, 1989, Pres.'s award, Okla. Press Assn., 2003. Mem.: DAR, MLA, Clan Grant Soc. U.S., Okla. Anthrop. Soc., Journalism Edn. Assn., Soc. Profl. Journalists, Okla. Hist. Soc., Tulsa Archeol. Soc., U. Okla. Assn., Okla. Geneal. Soc., Indian Women's Pochohontas Club, Elks, Pryor (Okla.) Red Hat Soc., First Families Okla., Gamma Phi Beta (internat. officer 1992—94, pres. San Antonio 1972—73, 1987—88, v.p. 1973—74, Svc. award 1977, Internat. Merit Roll 1986). Baptist. Office Phone: 405-872-7172. Business E-Mail: jrwddw39@okplus.net.

WELSH, GEORGE FRANKLIN, plastic surgeon, educator; b. Charles City, Iowa, Oct. 13, 1940; s. George S. Welsh and Aldeen (Paris) Welsh Taylor; m. Rosemary Dahlen, June 23, 1973; children: Christopher Franklin, Penelope Cosette, Bradford Alexander. BA, Carleton Coll., 1962; BS, U. N.D., 1964; MD, Harvard U., 1966; M in Hosp. Adminstrn., Xavier U., 1994; cert. in Horticulture, U. Cin., 2002. Diplomate Am. Bd. Surgery, Am. Bd. Plastic Surgery; cert. physician exec; Health Care Garden Design, Chgo., 2004. Commd. officer USAF, 1966, advanced through grades to lt. col., 1974; intern USAF Hosp., San Antonio, 1966—67; resident in surgery Mayo Clinic, Rochester, Minn., 1969—73; resident in plastic surgery U. Okla. Health Sci. Ctr., Oklahoma City, 1973—75; Maytag Fellow in plastic surgery U. Miami, Fla., 1976; plastic surgeon USAF, Dayton, Ohio, 1975—78, flight surgeon, dir. base med. svcs. United Arab Emirates, 1991; ret. USAFR, 1996; pvt. practice Cin., 1978—. Cons. on healthcare adminstrn., Cin., 1994—; asst. clin. prof. surgery Wright State U. Sch. Medicine, Dayton, 1975-78; vol. asst. prof. surgery U. Cin. Sch. Medicine, 1978-2002; vol. assoc. prof. surgery U. Cin. Sch. Medicine, 2007—. Contbr. chpt. to book; contbr. articles to profl. jours. including Surg. Clinics N.Am., Jour. Thoracic and Cardiovasc. Surgery, So. Med. Jour., Plastic and Reconstructive Surgery, Aesthetic Plastic Surgery, Brit. Jour. Plastic Surgery. Mem. Leadership Cin., 1981; citizen amb. People to People Internat., Albania, Russia, 1994, Cuba, 2000, Egypt, 2003. Fellow ACS, Am. Coll. Physician Execs.; mem. Am. Soc. Plastic Surgeons, Am. Soc. for Aesthetic Plastic Surgery, Millard Plastic Surg. Soc. (treas.), English Spkg. Union (past pres. Cin. br.), Gen. Soc. Colonial Wars (chmn. grants and contbns.) Ohio Soc., (programs), Cin. Hort. Soc. (trustee), Harvard Alumni Assn. Avocations: medical missions, landscape design, fishing. Office: Aesthetic Plastic Surgery Ctr 6200 Pfeiffer Rd Ste 320 Cincinnati OH 45242-5861 Office Phone: 513-793-0302. Personal E-mail: aestheticps@aol.com.

WELSH, H. RONALD, lawyer; b. Orange, NJ, Jan. 9, 1950; s. Harry A. and Faye L. (Neal) W.; children: Austin, Ben. BS, Northwestern U., 1972; JD, U. Tex., 1975. Bar: Tex. 1975, U.S. Dist. Ct. (so. dist.) Tex. 1989, U.S. Ct. Appeals (5th and 11th cirs.) 1981; cert. in civil trial law and personal injury trial law Tex. Bd. Legal Specialization. Ptnr. Vinson & Elkins, Houston, 1982—2003, Cunningham, Welsh, Darlow, Zook & Chapoton, LLP, Houston, 2004—. Fellow Am. Coll. Trial Lawyers, Am. Bd. Trial Advs., Tex. Bar Found., Houston Bar Found. Office: Cunningham Welsh Darlow Zook & Chapoton LLP Ste 1700 600 Travis St Houston TX 77002 Home Phone: 713-850-1504; Office Phone: 713-255-5500. Business E-Mail: rwelsh@cdzc.com.

WELSH, JACK DARYL, retired medical educator, writer; b. Grand Island, Nebr., Nov. 29, 1928; s. Robert Edward and Avis L. Welsh; children: Deborah Ann Frazier, Jack R., James J. BS, U. Nebr., Lincoln, 1951; MD, U. Nebr., Omaha, 1954. Diplomate Am. Bd. Internal Medicine, Am. Bd. Gastroenterology. From instr. to prof. Okla. Med. Sch., Oklahoma City, 1959—90, David Ross Boyd prof. medicine emeritus, 1990. Author: Medical Histories of Confederate Generals, 1995, Medical Histories of Union Generals, 1996, Two Confederate Hospitals and Their Patients, 2005. Sgt. US Army, 1946—47. Home: 610 Greenlea Chase West Oklahoma City OK 73170

WELSH, JOHN BERESFORD, JR., retired lawyer; b. Seattle, Feb. 16, 1940; s. John B. and Rowena Morgan Welsh. Student, U. Hawaii, 1960, Georgetown U., Washington, DC, 1960; BA, U. Wash., Seattle, 1962; LLB, 1965. Bar: Wash. 1965. Staff counsel Joint Com. on Govtl. Cooperation, 1965-66; asst. atty gen. Dept. Labor and Industries, 1966-67; atty. Washington State Legis. Coun., 1967—73; acting as counsel Pub. Health Com., Labor Com., Pub. Employees Collective Bargaining Com., Com. on State Instns. and Youth Devel., State of Wash., 1967-73; sr. counsel Wash. Ho. of Reps., Ho. Com. on Social and Health Svcs., Olympia, WA, 1973-86; atty., parliamentarian, spkr. Ho. of Reps., 1973; counsel Ho. Com. Human Svcs., 1987-91, 93-95, Ho. Com. on Health Care, 1987—2003, ret., 2003. Counsel Ho. Com. Trade and Econ. Devel., 1995—98, Joint Select Com. Nurse Del., 1995—98, Joint Select Com. Oral Health, 1996; legal cons. Gov.'s Planning Commn. Vocat. Rehab., 1968, Gov.'s Commn. Youth Involvement, 1969; envoy from Gov. Wash. to investiture Prince of Wales, London, 69; fac. Nat. Conf. State Legislatures, Denver, 1977, New Orleans, 77, Coun. Licensure, Enforcement and Regulation, San Francisco, 1984, Orlando, Fla., 85, Denver, 86, Kansas City, Mo., 87, Washington, 88, Indpls., 89, Seattle, 90, Ft. Lauderdale, Fla., 91, Albuquerque, 92, Boston, 94, San Antonio, 95, Norfolk, 97; mem. suggested state legis. com. Coun. State Govts., 1988—95, mem. steering com., 1986—90, mem. legis. issues com., 1986—88. Vol. Hampton Rds. US Naval Mus., mem. gov.'s state medal merit com., 1986—2003. Recipient Gov.'s award for excellence in state health care policy, 2002, Spkr. of House award for dedicated pub. svc., 2002, Sec. of State award for pub. svc. to state legislature and people of state of Wash., 2003, Sec. of Health award for creating meaningful health policy change, 2003. Mem.: Wash. Bar Assn., Assn. Washington Gens., Washington Rochambeau Hist. Revolutionary Rte. Program, N.W. Hist. Assn. (pres. 2003), Friends Willie and Joe, Colonial Williamsburg Found., Napoleonic Hist. Soc. (exec. v.p. 2007), English Speaking Union, Soc. des Amis du Musee de l'Armee, Alliance Francaise, Soc. Napoleonienne (pres.), Custer Battlefield Hist. and Mus. Assn., Friends Old Ft. Stevens (bd. dirs.), Sons Union Vets. Civil War, Nat. Soc. SAR, French Soc. SAR. Personal E-mail: jbwelsh@comcast.net.

WELSH, JOHN FRANCIS, retired advertising executive; b. New Haven, May 19, 1916; s. Pierce Jerome and Irene (Kennedy) W.; m. Margaret Burke, Sept. 18, 1947; children: Peter Burke, Diana Margaret. BA, Yale U., 1937. With Warwick & Legler, Inc., NYC, 1946-81; exec. v.p., mgmt. supr., mem. mgmt. com.; vice chmn. Warwick, Welsh & Miller, Inc., 1973-81. Served with AUS, 1941-45. Decorated Bronze Star, Croix de Guerre France). Mem.: Tokeneke (Darien). Home: 3372 Meadow Ridge Redding CT 06896

WELSH, JOHN JOSEPH (JAY), lawyer; m. Rae Terry Welsh; 5 children. B, Hamilton Coll., Clinton, NY, 1962; JD, U. Calif., Berkeley, 1965. Atty. pvt. firms, 1965—91; gen. counsel Jud. Arbitration and Mediation Svcs. (JAMS), Irvine, Calif., 1991—94, mediator, 1995, exec. v.p., gen. counsel. Adj. prof. law U. So. Calif., U. San Francisco; founder JAMS_Found., JAMS Inst. Mem.: Internat. Mediation Svcs. Alliance Europe (MEDAL). Avocation: travel. Office: JAMS 1920 Main St at Gillette Ave Ste 300 Irvine CA 92614 Office Phone: 949-224-1810. Office Fax: 949-224-1818. E-mail: jwelsh@jamsadr.com.

WELSH, KELLY RAYMOND, lawyer, investment company executive; b. Chgo., July 6, 1952; s. Raymond J. and Mary Jane (Kelly) W.; m. Ellen S. Alberding, June 28, 1985; children: Katherine A., Julia S. AB cum laude, Harvard U., 1974; MA, Sussex U., Eng., 1975; JD magna cum laude, Harvard U., 1978. Assoc. Mayer, Brown & Platt, Chgo., 1979-85, ptnr., 1985-89; corp. counsel City of Chgo., 1989-93; v.p., assoc. gen. counsel Ameritech Corp., Chgo., 1993-96, exec. v.p., gen. counsel, 1996—2001, Northern Trust Corp., Chgo., 2001—. Chmn. Met. Pier and Exposition Authority, Chgo., 1994—. Mem. ABA, Chgo. Bar Assn., Chgo. Coun. Lawyers, Chgo. Coun. Fgn. Rels. (mem. Chgo. com.), Legal Club Chgo. Office: Northern Trust Corp 50 S LaSalle Chicago IL 60675 Office Phone: 312-630-6000. *

WELSH, LOUIS WARD, otolaryngologist; b. Phila., Nov. 17, 1930; s. Louis R. and Roslyn A. Welsh; m. Janet B. MacCausland, July 13, 1957; children: David A., Suzanne M., Sheryl D., Stephen A. BS, St. Joseph U., Phila., 1952; MD, Hahnemann Med. Coll., Phila., 1956; MS, U. Iowa, Iowa City, 1961. Lic. Am. Bd. Otolaryngology, 1961, Pa., 1956, Calif., 1961. Intern Jefferson Med. Coll., Phila., 1956—57, resident, 1956—57; resident physician U. Iowa, Iowa City, 1958—60; post resident fellow NIH, Oxford, England, 1960—61; pvt. practice Jenkintown, Pa., 1963—2000. Asst. prof. La. State U., Shreveport, 1980—95; adj. prof. Temple U., Phila., 2001—04; cons. Wordsworth Acad., Ft. Washington, Pa., 1970—95; otolaryngologist emeritus Nazareth Hosp., Phila., 2000—, sr. attending physician emeritus; chief otolaryngology emeritus Abington Meml. Hosp., Pa., 2000—. Contbr. articles to profl. jours. Lt. comdr. USN, 1961—63. Recipient Excellence award, Am. Acad. Otolaryngology and Ophthalmology, 1961. Mem.: Neurotology Soc., Am. Acad. Otolaryngology Head and Neck Surgery, Sr. Physicians Assn. (adminstr. 2004—07), Am. Triologic Soc. (v.p. 1972—2007). Republican. Roman Catholic. Achievements include research in cancer of head and neck; lymph study of tumors; laryngeal lymphatics; irradiation effects on lymph node function; hearing-central auditory phenomena brain stem audiometry; vascular disorgers-cerebral and cervical. Avocations: horticulture, travel, photography, singing.

WELSH, MICHAEL JAMES, medical educator, biophysicist, educator; b. Marshalltown, Iowa, Dec. 22, 1948; Student, Loras Coll., 1967-69; BS, U. Iowa, 1970, MD, 1974. Intern and resident internal medicine U. Iowa Coll. Medicine, Iowa City, 1974-77; clin. fellow internal medicine U. Calif.

San Francisco, 1977-78; rsch. fellow cardiovasc. rsch. unit U. Calif., San Francisco, 1978-79; rsch. fellow physiology and cell biology U. Tex., Houston, 1979-80; asst. prof. medicine U. Iowa Coll. Medicine, Iowa City, 1981-84, assoc. prof. medicine, 1984-87, prof. medicine, 1987—, prof. physiology and biophysics, 1989—. Cons. VA Hosp., Iowa City, 1981—; investigator Howard Hughes Med. Inst., U. Iowa., Iowa City, 1989—. Contbr. chpts. to books and numerous articles to profl. jours. Recipient Doris F. Tulcin Cystic Fibrosis Rsch. award, 1992, Paul di Sant-Agnese Disting. Sci. Achievement award, 1993. Mem. Am. Fedn. for Clin. Rsch., Am. Physiol. Soc., Am. Thoracic Soc. (J. Burns Amberson award 1994), Iowa Thoracic Soc. Office: Howard Hughes Med Inst 500 EMRB Univ Iowa Coll Medicine Iowa City IA 52242

WELSH, PETER CORBETT, museum director, historian; b. Washington, Aug. 28, 1926; s. Arthur Brinkley and Susan Jane (Putney) W.; m. Catherine Beatrice Allen, Nov. 27, 1951 (div. 1969); children— Susan Jane, Peter Corbett; m. Caroline Levert Mastin, Sept. 8, 1970; 1 child, James Munson Corbett. BA, Mt. Union Coll., Alliance, Ohio, 1950; postgrad., U. Va., 1950-51; MA (Hagley fellow), U. Del., 1956. Research asst., fellowship coordinator Eleutherian Mills-Hagley Found., Wilmington, Del., 1956-59; assoc. curator dept. civil history Mus. History and Tech., Smithsonian Instn., 1959-61; curator Growth U.S., 1962-64, curator dept. civil history, 1964-69, asst. dir. gen. mus. of instn., 1969-70, dir. Office Mus. Programs, 1970-71; dir. N.Y. State Hist. Assn., Cooperstown, 1971-74; vis. prof. Cooperstown Grad. Program, N.Y. State Hist. Assn.; dir. Cooperstown Grad. Programs, 1971-74; dir. spl. projects N.Y. State Mus., Albany, 1975-76; dir. Bur. Mus., Pa. Hist. and Mus. Commn., 1976-84; pres. The Welsh Group, 1984-86; curator The Adirondack Mus., Blue Mountain Lake, N.Y., 1986-88, sr. historian, 1988-89; mus. cons., lectr., 1989—. Adj. prof. SUNY; cons. FDR Mus. and Little White House, Warm Springs, Ga., 1968-72; trustee Landon Sch., Bethesda, Md., 1964-70; bd. dirs., mem. exec. com. Ctr. for Conservation of Hist. Art and Artifacts, 1979-83; bd. dirs. Lake Placid Ctr. for the Arts, 1992-96; mem. publs. adv. com. The Adirondack Mus., 2002--. Author: Tanning in the United States: A Brief History, 1964, American Folk Art: The Art and Spirit of the People, 1967, Track and Road: The American Trotting Horse, 1820-1990, 1968, The Art of Enterprise: A Pennsylvania Tradition, 1983, Jacks, Jobbers and Kings: Logging the Adirondacks, 1850-1950, 1996; contbr. articles to profl. publs.; editor Smithsonian Jour. History, 1967-70. Served to 1st lt. AUS, 1951-54. Mem. Am. Hist. Assn., Am. Studies Assn., Am. Assn. Mus., N.Y. State Assn. Mus. (council 1971-75), Am. Assn. State and Local History (publ. com.), Soc. History of Tech., Sigma Nu. Clubs: Country of Harrisburg. Democrat. Roman Catholic. Office: 34 Second St Tupper Lake NY 12986-2011

WELSH, WILLIAM DANIEL, geriatric medicine family practice physician; b. Balt., May 18, 1950; s. Joseph Leo and Bessie Mary (Tangires) W.; m. Loraine Lynn Barkhaus, July 11, 1985; children: Sean William, Ryan Daniel. Student, Johns Hopkins U., 1971; BS in Biology cum laude, Fairleigh Dickinson U., 1972; DO, Coll. Osteo. Medicine-Surgery, Des Moines, 1975. Diplomate Nat. Bd. Osteo. Physicians; cert. ATLS; approved supr. physician assts. Osteopathic Med. Bd. Calif.; radiography and fluoroscopy x-ray supr., operator Calif. Intern Martin Place Hosp., Madison Heights, Mich., 1975-76, resident in internal medicine, 1976-77; pvt. practice Detroit, 1977-79; pvt. practice, Whittier, Calif., 1979—. Instr. ACLS, L.A., 1980-92; bd. dirs. Whittier Hosp. Med. Ctr., 1981, vice chief staff, 1982-84, med. dir. family asthma forum, 1979-88, med. dir. Summit Place alcohol treatment program, 1983-88; med. dir. Mirada Hills Rehab. Hosp., La Mirada, Calif., 1980-88; former clin. preceptor Coll. Osteo. Med. Pacific, Pomona, Calif., clin. assoc. prof. internal medicine; mem. dept. family practice, physician rev. com. Friendly Hills Regional Med. Ctr., La Habra, Calif., 1994-97; mem. staff Presbyn. Intercmty. Hosp., Whittier, Whittier Hosp. Med. Ctr., chmn. by laws com. 1999-2001, mem. exec. com. 1999-2001; med. dir. Royal Ct. Convalescent Hosp.; med. dir. First Choice Home Health Agy.; spkr. in field. Participant Calif. Beach Clean Up Day, 1996, Med. Mission, Mex. Recipient Physician Recognition award AMA, 1991, 95, 96, Commn. of Merit Rep. Nat. Com., 1995, Physician of Yr. award, Rep. Nat. Com., 2006. Mem. Am. Osteo. Assn., Am. Coll. Osteo. Family Physicians, Osteo. Physicians and Surgeons Calif., Am. Coll. Osteopathic Family Practitioners (bd. cert. family practice 1991, geriatrics 2000), Cancer Prevention award, Am. Cancer Soc. Republican. Roman Catholic. Avocations: boating, skiing, reading, tennis. Home: 16871 Marina Bay Dr Huntington Beach CA 92649-2913 Office Phone: 562-945-9333. Home Fax: 562-592-2259. Personal E-mail: wdwelsh@socal.rr.com.

WELSHANS, MERLE TALMADGE, retired management consultant; b. Murphysboro, Ill., June 17, 1918; s. Arthur Isaac and Martha Ellen (Blair) W.; m. Mary Katherine Whitenbaugh, June 2, 1942; children: Elizabeth Margaret Van Steenbergh, Arthur Edmund, Janice Ann. BEd, So. Ill. U., 1940; MA, Washington U., St. Louis, 1947, PhD, 1951. Asst. v.p. Merc. Mortgage Co., Olney, Ill., 1940; exec. officer, dept. bus. adminstrn. George Washington U., 1950-54; prof. fin. Grad. Sch. Bus. Adminstrn., Washington U., 1954-69; v.p. fin. Union Electric Co., St. Louis, 1969-83; mgmt. cons., 1983—; ret. Dir. Hotchkis & Wiley Funds, Deaconess Found. Author: (with R.W. Melicher) Finance, 9th edit., 1992; editor Fin. Newsletter, 1965-69. Capt. U.S. Army, 1942-45. Decorated Bronze Star medal. Mem. Fin. Mgmt. Assn. (dir.), Am. Econ. Assn., Am. Fin. Assn., Fin. Analysts Assn. St. Louis (trustee), Beta Gamma Sigma, others. Methodist. Address: 14360 Ladue Rd Chesterfield MO 63017-2524 Office Phone: 314-469-6066. Personal E-mail: mwelshans@worldnet.att.net.

WELSHIMER, MARK J., lawyer; b. Canton, Ohio, 1951; AB, Harvard U., 1973, JD, 1976. Bar: NY 1977. Assoc. Sullivan & Cromwell, NYC, ptnr., 1983—, and coord. asset-based fin. practice area. Mem.: ABA. Office: Sullivan & Cromwell 125 Broad St Fl 28 New York NY 10004-2489 Office Phone: 212-558-4000. Office Fax: 212-558-3588. Business E-Mail: welshimerm@sullcrom.com.

WELSOME, EILEEN, journalist, writer; b. NYC, Mar. 12, 1951; d. Richard H. and Jane M. (Garity) Welsome; m. James R. Martin, Aug. 3, 1983. BJ with honors, U. Tex., 1980. Reporter Beaumont (Tex.) Enterprise, 1980—82, San Antonio Light, 1982—83, San Antonio Express-News, 1983—86, Albuquerque Tribune, 1987—94, Westword Newspaper, Denver, 2000—01. Author: The Plutonium Files, 1999 (PEN/Martha Albrand award for first nonfiction, 2000). Recipient Clarion award, 1989, News Reporting award, Nat. Headliners, 1989, John Hancock award, 1991, Mng. Editors Pub. Svc. award, AP, 1991, 1994, Roy Howard award, 1994, James Aronson award, 1994, Gold Medal award, Investigative Reporters and Editors, 1994, Sigma Delta Chi award, 1994, Investigative Reporting award, Nat. Headliners, 1994, Selden Ring award, 1994, Heywood Broun award, 1994, George Polk award, 1994, Sidney Hillman Found. award, 1994, Pulitzer Prize for nat. reporting, 1994, PEN/West Lit. award for rsch. nonfiction, PEN, 2000; John S. Knight fellow, Stanford U., 1991—92.

WELT, PHILIP STANLEY, lawyer, consultant; b. Freeport, NY, July 5, 1959; s. Morris and Rose (Offenberg) W.; m. Karen Teresa Gault, May 22, 1994. BBA summa cum laude, Hofstra U., 1983; MBA, Columbia U., 1988; JD cum laude, NYU, 1995. Bar: NJ 1995, NY 1995; US Dist. Ct. NJ 1995, US Dist. Ct. (so. and ea. dists.) NY 1996, US Ct. Appeals (2d cir.) 1997, US Ct. Appeals Armed Forces 2000, US Supreme Ct. 1999; CPA, NY. Sr. mgr. Deloitte & Touche, NYC, 1983-92; assoc. Reboul MacMurray Hewitt Maynard & Kristol, NYC, 1993, Davis Polk & Wardwell, NYC, 1994, 1996-2001; jud. clk. U.S. Dist. Ct. N.J., Newark, 1995-96; spl. asst. dist. atty. Kings Co., NY, 1999—2001; asst. gen. counsel Am. Internat. Group, Inc., 2001—04; v.p., sr. counsel W.R. Berkley Corp., Greenwich, Conn., 2004—. Bd. dirs., treas. Pub. Interest Law Found., N.Y.C., 1993-94; guest spkr. Boy Scouts Am., Nassau County, 1984-91, Nat. Assn. Accts., N.Y./N.J., 1988-92, others. Sr. editor Columbia Jour. World Bus., 1986-88; sr. exec. editor Ann. Survey Am. Law, 1993-95; contbr. articles to profl. jours. Vol. income tax asst. Dept. Treasury, IRS, N.Y.C., 1981-87; vol. Variety-The Children's Charity, N.Y.C., 1985-87; advisor Friends of Jon Kaiman, Nassau County, 1995. Provost's scholar Hofstra U., 1981-83, Deloitt & Touche fellow Columbia U., 1986-88; recipient Appreciation cert. Dept. Treasury, IRS, 1981-87, Variety, 1985-87, Bovenaan Outstanding Cmty. Svc. award Hofstra U., 1983, Orison S. Marden Moot Ct. Advocacy award NYU Sch. Law, 1993, Seymore A. Levy meml. award, 1995. Mem. ABA, AICPA, N.Y. State Bar Assn., N.Y. State Soc. CPAs, Beta Alpha Psi, Beta Gamma Sigma. Avocations: golf, rock climbing, photography, stamp collecting/philately, amateur radio. Home: 157 Mountain Wood Rd Stamford CT 06903-2107 Office: W R Berkley Corp 475 Steamboat Rd Greenwich CT 06830 Office Phone: 212-629-3000. Business E-Mail: pwelt@wrberkley.com.

WELTCHEK, ROBERT JAY, lawyer; b. Elizabeth, NJ, July 28, 1955; s. Leslie Mayer and Patricia Marjorie (Schoenhaut) W.; m. Holly Prager; children: Nolan Joseph, Emily Rachel. BA, Rutgers U., 1977; JD with honors, U. Md., 1980. Bar: Md. 1980, US Dist. Ct. (dist. Md.) 1980, US Ct. Appeals (4th cir.) 1981, US Ct. Appeals (4th cir.) 1997, US Dist. Ct. (dist. DC). Assoc. Bertram M. Goldstein, P.A., Balt., 1980-82; ptnr. Goldstein, Weltchek & Assocs., Balt., 1983-89, Gebhardt & Smith, Balt., 1989-93, Snyder, Weltchek & Vogelstein, P.A., Balt., 1993-97, Snyder, Weiner, Weltchek, Vogelstein & Brown, Balt., 1997—2001, Weiner & Weltchek, Balt., 2001—06. Named one of Top 20 Lawyers of the Next Generation, Balt. Mag., 2003. Fellow Am. Coll. Trial Lawyers; mem. ABA, Md. State Bar Assn., Fed. Bar Assn., Balt. City Bar Assn., Assn. Trial Lawyers Am., Md. Trial Lawyers Assn. Democrat. Jewish. Avocations: tennis, racquetball. *Notable cases include: Maynard vs. George Washington U. Med. Ctr., Superior Ct. D.C., 1990, which involved $5 million jury verdict for the plaintiff in med. malpractice action.* *

WELTE, A. THEODORE, chamber of commerce executive; b. Mankato, Minn., Feb. 11, 1944; s. Arthur William and Bernice (Town) M.; m. Kathleen P. Browne, May 3, 1969; 1 child, Jason N. BA in Sociology, Psychology, Mankato State U., 1966, MA in Econs., 1972; cert., U. Notre Dame, 1987; cert. mgmt., Stonehill Coll., 1990. Cert. chamber exec. Program officer, br. officer Peace Corp, Washington, 1968-69; rsch. dir. Tech. Found., W.Va. Tech., Montgomery, 1969-70; project dir. Self-Help, Inc., Brockton, Mass., 1972-73; regional planner, planning supr. Old Colony Planning Coun., Brockton, 1974-81; pres., CEO Metro South C. of C., Brockton, 1981-90, MetroWest C. of C., Framingham, Mass., 1990—. Trustee Brockton Regional Econ. Devel. Corp., 1982-90; treas. Brockton Area Pvt. Industry Coun., 1987-89. Cubmaster pack 68 Boy Scouts Am., Easton, Mass., 1989-90, com. chair troop 86, 1991-94, bd. dirs. Algonquin/Knox Trail coun., 1991—, v.p. exploring, 1996-99. Mem. New Eng. Assn. C. of C. Execs. (sec. 1990-91, 2d v.p. 1991-92, 1st v.p. 1992-93, pres. 1993-94), Mass. Assn. C. of C. Execs. (pres. 1988-89), Rotary (sec. Brockton 1988-90, v.p. Framingham 1990-92, pres. 1993-94). Presbyterian. Office: MetroWest C of C 1671 Worcester Rd Ste 201 Framingham MA 01701-5400 E-mail: ted@metrowest.org.

WELTER, WILLIAM MICHAEL, marketing and advertising executive; b. Evanston, Ill., Nov. 18, 1946; s. Roy Michael and Frances (DeShields) W.; m. Pamela Bassett, June 11, 1971; children: Barclay, Robert Michael. BS, Mo. Valley Coll., 1966. Account exec. Leo Burnett Co., Inc., Chgo., 1966-74; v.p., account supr. Needham Harper Worldwide, Chgo., 1974-80; v.p. mktg. Wendy's Internat., Inc., Dublin, Ohio, 1981, sr. v.p. mktg., 1981-84, exec. v.p., 1984-87; owner, chief exec. officer Haunty & Welter Advt. Agy., Worthington, Ohio, 1987-91; sr. exec. v.p. mktg. Rax Restaurants Inc., Dublin, 1992; exec. v.p. mktg. Metromedia Steakhouses, Inc., Dayton, 1992-93; sr. v.p. mktg. Metromedia Co., Dayton, 1993-95; exec. v.p., chief mktg. officer Heartland Foods Inc., Dublin, Ohio, 1995-96; exec. v.p. brand mgmt. Late Nite Magic, Inc., Las Vegas, Nev., 1996—99; pres., CEO W.M. Welter & Assocs., Las Vegas, 1996—; pres. Wings West LLC, Las Vegas, 1999—, Buffalo Wild Wings, Inc., Las Vegas, 2001—. Founder Santa's Silent Helpers, Columbus, Ohio, 1985 Mem. Advt. Fedn. Las Vegas, Spanish Trail Country Club. Avocations: golf, fishing. Home: 1517 Angelberry Rd Las Vegas NV 89117-1372 Office: Ste 103 8064 W Sahara Las Vegas NV 89117 Office Phone: 702-304-9292. Fax: 702 360-8379. E-mail: buffalodad@hotmail.com.

WELTERS, ANTHONY, health services executive; BA in Econs., Manhattanville Coll.; JD, NYU. Atty. SEC; exec. asst. to Sen. Jacob Javits; sr.-level positions Amtrak and US Dept. Transp.; chmn. bd., pres., CEO Americhoice (subs. of UnitedHealth Grp.), 1989—; exec. v.p. UnitedHealth Group, Mpls., 2006—. Bd. trustees Healthcare Leadership Coun.; vice chmn. bd. Morehouse Sch. Medicine; mem. bd. NYU Law Sch., Wolf Trap Found. Recipient Horatio Alger award, 1998. Mailing: UnitedHealth Group PO Box 1459 Minneapolis MN 55440-1459 *

WELTMAN, EDWARD S., lawyer; AB cum laude, Brandeis U., 1972; JD, Washington U., 1975. Bar: NY 1976. Sr. ptnr. Schneck Weltman & Hashmall LLP, NYC; ptnr., litig. dept. Goodwin Procter LLP, NYC, chair, products liability group, mem., exec. com. Comment topics editor Wash. Univ. Law Quarterly. Mem.: Nat. Judicial Coll., Internat. Assn. Def. Counsel. Office: Goodwin Procter LLP 599 Lexington Ave New York NY 10022 Office Phone: 212-459-7420. Office Fax: 212-355-3333. Business E-Mail: eweltman@goodwinprocter.com.

WELTON, CHARLES EPHRAIM, lawyer; b. Cloquet, Minn., June 23, 1947; s. Eugene Frances and Evelyn Esther Welton; children: Spencer, Marshall. BA, Macalester Coll., 1969; postgrad., U. Minn., 1969-70; JD, U. Denver, 1974. Bar: Colo. 1974, US Dist. Ct. Colo. 1974, US Supreme Ct. 1979, US Ct. Appeals (10th cir.) 1980, cert.: Nat. Bd. Trial Advocacy (civil trial adv.) 2001. Assoc. Davidovich & Wanifuchi, Denver, 1974-77, Charles Welton and Assocs. and successor firms, Denver, 1978-86; ptnr. OSM Properties, Denver, 1982-97; prin. Brock House, LLC, Denver, 1997—. Prin. Charles Welton, P.C., 1986—; adj. prof. Inst. Advanced Legal Studies U. Denver, 1991—98; polit. and social commentator; lectr. in field; instr. Nat. Inst. Trial Advocacy, 1998—2001, Lorman Ednl. Svcs., 1999—2002. Author: instrnl. materials; editor: profl. publs.; contbr. articles to profl. jours. Sch. pres. PTSA, Denver, 1983—84; coach Colo. Jr. Soccer League, 1980—85, Odessey of Mind (formerly Olympics of Mind), 1986—88; bd. dirs. Virginia Vale Swim Club, officer, 1989—91; bd. dirs. Pioneer Jr. Hockey Assn., 1990—92. Served alt. mil. duty, 1970—72, Denver Gen. Hosp. Mem.: Colo. Trial Lawyers Assn. (bd. dirs. 1985—90, chmn. seminar com. 1986—88, mem. exec. com. 1987—88, mem. legis. com. 1988—94, keyperson 1997—), Colo. Bar Assn. (legal arbitration com.), Denver Bar Assn. (facilitator bench/bar retreat 1995, 1996, chmn. legal fee arbitration com. 2002—05), Exec. Ventures Group of Am. Leadership Forum (founding adv. bd. 1987—90), Am. Bldg. a Lasting Earth (founder). Democrat. Home: 680 Vista Ln Lakewood CO 80215-6037 Office: The Brock House 1800 Gaylord St Denver CO 80206-1211 Home Phone: 303-232-4358; Office Phone: 303-333-9800. E-mail: welton@charleswelton.com.

WELTON, SHARON MARIE, food service executive; b. Waterbury, Conn., Nov. 18, 1943; d. George Galvin Touponse and Catherine Marie Coon; m. Allen Richard Welton (div.); children: Catherine Welton-Pando, Douglas Allen Sr. AAS, Mattatuck Cmty. Coll., 1988; BS, U. Conn., 1996. Cert. dietary mgr. Nat. Dietary Managers Assn., 1992, instr. for Serv-Safe Course Nat. Restaurant Assn., 2002, food protection profl. 1996. Legal sec. Membrino/Fitzgerald, Waterbury, Conn., 1963—64; asst. mgr. Judy's Deli, Southbury, Conn., 1980—84; prin./mgr. Feasts by Sharon, Conn., 1981—2001; intern- affirmative action office Southbury Training Sch., Conn., 1995, supvr. food svc. Conn., 1984—. Cons./trainer State of Conn., 1990—, State of Conn. Nutritional Work Group, 1999—2003, Southbury Training Sch., 1992—. Polit. action com. mem. Dietary Managers Assn., 1993—95; mem./leader Girl Scouts, Watertown, Conn., 1951—61, 1977—81; com. mem. Christmas Town Festival, Bethlehem, 1999. Recipient State Achievement award, Dietary Managers Assn., 1994—95. Mem.: Dietary Managers Assn. (legis. coord. 1992—98, 2003—, pres. 1994—95). Republican. Avocations: clothing, jewlry design, sewing, swimming, wine tasting, water aerobics. Home: 143 Pine Hill Rd 22B Thomaston CT 06787 Office: Southbury Training Sch Rte 172 Southbury CT 06488 Office Phone: 203-586-2193.

WELTS, RICK, professional sports team executive; Student, U. Wash. Dir. pub. rels. Seattle SuperSonics; v.p. Bob Walsh & Assocs., 1979; dir. nat. promotions NBA Properties NBA, NYC, 1982—83, v.p. mktg. NBA Properties, 1983—84, v.p. mktg. and comm. NYC, 1984—88, pres. NBA Properties, 1988—99, exec. v.p., chief mktg. officer, 1996—99; pres. Fox Sports Enterprises, 1999, First In Line; ptnr. ONSPORT, 2001; pres., COO Phoenix Suns, 2002—. Named Co-Marketer of Yr., Brandweek, 1998. Office: Phoenix Suns 201 E Jefferson St Phoenix AZ 85004 *

WELTY, JOHN DONALD, academic administrator; b. Amboy, Ill., Aug. 24, 1944; s. John Donald and Doris (Donnelly) W.; m. Sharon Welty; children: Anne, Elisabeth, Bryan, Darren, Heather. BS, Western Ill. U., 1965; MA, Mich. State U., 1967; Ed.D., Ind. U., 1974. Asst. v.p. for student affairs SW State U., Marshall, Minn., 1973-74; dir. residences SUNY-Albany, 1974-77, assoc. dean for student affairs, 1977-80; v.p. for student and univ. affairs Indiana U. of Pa., 1980-84, pres., 1984-91, Calif. State U., Fresno, 1991—. Lectr. in field. Contbr. articles to profl. jours. Chair Am. Assn. State Colls. and Univs., Western Assn. Schs. and Colls. Recipient Chancellor's award SUNY, 1977, Chief Exec. Leadership award Coun. for Advancement and Support of Edn., 1999, John Templeton Found. award for leadership in student character devel., 1999. Mem. Fresno Bus. Coun., Fresno Econ. Devel. Commn., Sunnyside Country Club. Lodges: Rotary. Roman Catholic. Office: Calif State U 5241 S Maple Ave Fresno CA 93725-9739 Business E-Mail: johnw@csufresno.edu.

WELU, JAMES A., art museum director; b. Dubuque, Iowa, Dec. 15, 1943; s. Andrew L. and Anna E. (Riley) W. BA, Loras Coll., 1966; MA, U. Notre Dame, 1967, MFA, 1968; PhD, Boston U., 1977. Instr. St. Mary-of-the-Woods (Ind.) Coll., 1968-70; asst. curator Worcester Art Mus., Mass., 1974-76, assoc. curator Mass., 1976-80, instr. Mass., 1977-78, 80-81, chief curator Mass., 1980-86, dir. Mass., 1986—. Instr. Clark U., Worcester, 1980. Panelist Mass. Coun. on Arts and Humanities, Boston, 1981-82, 90, Utilization of Mus. Resources Nat. Endowment for the Arts, 1988; trustee Williamstown Regional Art Conservation Lab., Inc., Mass., 1981-86; mem. panel Utilization Mus. Resources, NEA, 1988. Boston U. grantee, 1973, NEA Mus.' Profl. grantee, 1976-81; Samuel H. Kress Found. fellow, 1973; recipient Netherland-Am. Found. award Netherland Found., 1973, Disting. Alumni award Boston U. Grad. Sch., 1986. Mem.: Historians Netherlandish Art, New Eng. Mus. Assn., Am. Assn. Mus. (accreditation commr. 2000—), Coll. Art Assn. Am., Am. Fedn. Arts, Assn. Art Mus. Dirs. (v.p. 1998—99, pres. 1999—2000, trustee 2000—01). Home: 10 Massachusetts Ave Worcester MA 01609-1649 Office: Worcester Art Mus 55 Salisbury St Worcester MA 01609-3196

WELZ, REBECCA BEALL, sculptor, educator; d. Carl John Welz and Jerry Beall Hatcher; m. Toshitada Sakai, July 10, 1999. BA, Empire State Coll., NYC, 1995. Adj. prof. with cert. of continuing employment Pratt Inst., Bklyn., 1988—; vis. instr. Parsons Sch. of Design, NYC, 1997—98; vis. artist Vt. Studio Ctr., Johnson, 2001. One-woman shows include Landmark Gallery, NYC, 1979, Bernice Steunbaum Gallery, 1985, Grace Borgenicht Gallery, 1989, 1991, 1994, June Kelly Gallery, 1997, 2000, 2002, 2005, Butters Gallery, 2001, 2003, Oakland Mus.-Gallery 555, Calif., 2004, exhibited in group shows at Boston City Hall, 1973, Auction 393, NYC, 1976, Landmark Gallery, 1982, Grace Borgenicht Gallery, 1987, World Trade Ctr., 1989, Coll. New Rochelle, NY, 1992, Rosa Esman Gallery, NYC, 1992, Rockville Arts Pl., Md., 1993, Va. Ctr. Craft Arts, Richmond, 1993, Adam Baumgold Gallery, NYC, 1995, Sotheby's, 1996, Pratt Inst., Bklyn., 1998, Rutgers U., NJ, 2001, Delaware Valley Arts Ctr., Narrowsburg, NY, 2003, Sculpturesite Gallery, San Francisco, 2005, Butters Gallery, Portland, Oreg., 2006, others, Represented in permanent collections Goldman Sachs, NYC, Merck, NJ, Prudential Life Ins. Corp., NYC, Cortec Corp., Sidney Lewis, Richmond, Va., William Kaufman Orgn., NYC, Credit Lyonnais, Warburg Pincus, Mound, Cotton, Wollan, Windmueller Fine Arts, Scarsdale, NY, Cleary, Gottlieg, Steen & Hamilton, NYC, AXA Corp., Pfizer. Recipient Faculty Devel. award, Pratt Inst., 2002, 2006; fellow, N.Y. Exptl. Glass Workshop (now Urban Glass), 1992; grantee, Pollock-Krasner Found., 1987, 1992, E.D. Found., 1990, 1995. Mem.: Assn. Women Indsl. Designers (founder 1991, pres. 1991—). Home Phone: 212-677-2396.

WEMPLE, ERIK C., editor-in-chief; b. Schenectady, NY, 1965; Washington corr. Inside.com, CableWorld mag.; sr. editor & polit. columnist Washington City Paper, Washington, editor-in-chief, 2002—. Office: Village Voice 36 Cooper Sq New York NY 10003

WEMPNER, GERALD ARTHUR, engineering educator; b. Waupun, Wis. s. Paul Christian and Thekla Nelda (Jung) W.; m. Lorraine Bischel, Sept. 6, 1952 (div. Apr. 1983); children: Susan K., Paul J. BS, U. Wis., 1952, MS, 1953; PhD, U. Ill., 1957. Instr. U. Ill., Urbana, 1953-57, asst. prof., 1957-59; assoc. prof. U. Ariz., Tucson, 1959-62; prof. U. Ala., Huntsville, 1964-73, Ga. Inst. Tech., Atlanta, 1973-91, prof. emeritus, 1991—. Vis. prof. U. Calif., Berkeley, 1962-63. Author: Mechanics of Solids, 1973; co-author: Mechanics of Deformable Bodies, 1961, Mechanics of Solids, 1995, Mechanics of Solids and Shells, 2003; contbr. articles to profl. jours. With US Army, 1946—48. NSF fellow, Stanford (Calif.) U., 1963-64, Sr. fellow Alexander von Humboldt Found., Germany, 1973, Killam fellow U. Calgary, Can., 1983. Fellow ASME (asssoc. editor 1976-83), Am. Acad. Mechanics. Avocations: art, sculpture, photography, woodwork. Home and Office: 3397 Hidden Acres Dr Doraville GA 30340-4445

WEN, LEANA S., epidemiologist; b. Shanghai; d. Ying Sandy Zhang, Xiaolu Wen. BS in Biochemistry, Calif. State Univ., LA; MD, Calif. State Univ., 2007; MSc. student in Global Health, Oxford Univ., 2007—. Appt. mem. Coun. on Grad. Med. Edn. by US Sec. of Health and Human Services. Rhodes Scholar. Mem.: Am. Med. Student Assn. (pres. 2005—06). Achievements include entering college at age 13; Global Health Fellow at WHO, Geneva, Switzerland; DOD David L. Boren Fellow in Rwanda to devel. treatment programs for women who are HIV-positive as the result of genocide-related rape; recipient NIH Fogarty Minority Internat. Rsch. Training Fellowship; an Arnold and Mabel Beckman Found. Rsch. Fellowship; and a Howard Hughes Med. Inst. Biomed. Professional Devel. Scholarship. *

WEN, SHEREE, computer company executive; BS in Physics, Natural Tsiug Hua U, Taiwan; PhD, U. Calif., Berkeley, 1979. Rsch. divsn. staff IBM, 1979-81, dept. mgr. Materials, Characterization and Analysis, 1981-84, program mgr. Tech., 1984-86, sr. mgr of Optics 1986, prog. mgr., tech. asst. to sr. v.p.; pres. WenLab USA Inc., NYC. Patentee in field; Contbr. articles to profl. jours. Recipient John E. Dom Achievement award Am.

Soc. for Metal, 1978, Outstanding tech. Achievement award, IBM, 1986, invention Achievement award, IBM, 1987; The Robert Lansing Hardy gold Metal The Metals, Materials & Minerals Soc. (TMS-AIME); the AIME as the most promising young Materials Scientist in Am., 1979 Mem. TMS-AIME's Process Monitor & Control Com. (chmn.), Materials Design & Mfg. Divsn. Award Com.; Indsl. Liaison for U. Calif. at Berkeley's ctr. for Materials. Office: Wen Technology Corp 22 Saw Mill River Rd Ste 5 Hawthorne NY 10532-1549

WEN, SHIH-LIANG, mathematics professor; came to U.S., 1959; s. S.W. and C.F. (Hsiao) W.; m. Liang Tao; children: Dennis, Andy, Jue, Nannan. BS, Nat. Taiwan U., Taipei, 1956; MS, U. Utah, 1961; PhD, Purdue U., 1968. Assoc. research engr. The Boeing Co., Seattle, 1961-63; with dept. math. Ohio U., Athens, 1968—, successively asst. prof., assoc. prof. and prof., chmn. dept. math., 1985-93. Rsch. analyst Applied Math Rsch. Lab. USAF, Wright-Patterson AFB, Ohio, summer, 1972; vis. rsch. scientist Courant Inst. Math. Scis. NYU, 1978-79; hon. prof. Jiangxi U., People's Republic of China, 1985; disting. vis. prof. Lanzhou U., People's Republic of China, 1989. Mem. Am. Math. Soc., Soc. for Indsl. and Applied Math., Math. Assn. Am. Avocations: fishing, bridge, music. Office: Ohio Univ Dept Math Athens OH 45701 Business E-Mail: wen@math.ohiou.edu.

WEN, SHIXING, school librarian; MA, Hangzhou U., China, 1984; MLS, Ind. U., Blooming, 1993. Asst. cataloging libr. So. Ill. U. Libraries, Carbondale, 1994—97; tech. svcs. team leader Fla. Gulf Coast U. Libr., Ft. Myers, 1997—99; tech. svcs. coord. Rensselaer Poly. Inst. Libraries, Troy, NY, 2000; head exch. and gifts U. Mich. Libr., Ann Arbor, 2000—06; head tech. svcs. U. Minn. Libr., Duluth, 2006—. Master: Chinese Am. Librairans Assn. (life; pres. 2004—05, policy making com. 1999—2006, Pres.'s Recognition award 2005); mem.: ALA (coun. mem. 2006—). Office: Univ Minn Duluth Libr 416 Library Dr Duluth MN 55812 Office Phone: 218-726-8498. Business E-Mail: swen@d.umn.edu.

WEN, XIAO-GANG, physics professor; b. Beijing, Nov. 26, 1961; came to US, 1982; s. Shi-Fu and Wan-Qin (Xue) W.; m. Xiao-Li Li, June 4, 1984; children: David Yi-Bo, Kevin Ruo-Song. BS in Physics, U. Sci. and Tech., Hefei, China, 1982; MA in Physics, Princeton U., NJ, 1983, PhD in Physics, 1987. Mem. Inst. Theoretical Physics U. Calif., Santa Barbara, 1987-89; mem. Inst. Advanced Study, Princeton, 1989—91; asst. prof. dept. physics. MIT, Cambridge, 1991-95, assoc. prof., 1995—2000, prof., 2000—, Cecil and Ida Green prof. physics, 2004—; Changjiang prof. Tsinghua U. Ctr. Advanced Study, China, 2000—. Contbr. articles to sci. jours.; author: Quantum Field Theory of Many-body Systems: From the Origin of Sound to an Origin of Light and Electrons, 2004. A.P. Sloan Found. fellow, 1992, Disting. Moore scholar Calif. Inst. Tech., 2006, 07; recipient Outstanding Young Rschr. award Overseas Chinese Physics Assn., 1994. Fellow: Am. Phys. Soc. Office: MIT Dept Physics Rm 12 106 77 Massachusetts Ave Cambridge MA 02139-4307 Office Phone: 617-253-5016. Fax: 617-253-2562. E-mail: wen@dao.mit.edu. *

WEN, XUEJUN, biomedical engineer, educator; s. Chunlin and Meiqin (Dong) Wen; m. Ning Zhang, 1972. MD, Henan Med. U., Zhengzhou, China, 1994; MS in Materials Sci. & Engring., Zhejiang U., Hangzhou, China, 1997, U. Cin., 2000; PhD in Bioengineering, U. Utah, Salt Lake City, 2003. Asst. prof. bioengineering, cell biology and orthop. surgery Clemson U., SC, 2003—; adj. asst. prof. cell biology and anatomy Med. U. SC, Charleston, 2003, adj. asst. prof. orthop. surgery, 2005—. Contbr. articles to sci. jours. Recipient Human Stem Cell Rsch. award, Michael J. Fox Found. Parkinson Rsch., 2005, Wallace H. Coulter Early Career Translational Rsch. award in Biomedical Engring., 2005. Mem.: Soc. Neuroscience, Tissue Engring. and Regenerative Medicine Internat. Soc., Am. Physiology Soc., Soc. Biomaterials. Office: Clemson U Med U SC Joint Bioengineering Prog 173 Ashley Ave BSB# 323 Charleston SC 29425 Office Phone: 843-792-5875. E-mail: wenxj@hotmail.com, xjwen@clemson.edu. *

WEN, YUNFEI, research scientist; d. Lili Zhang-Wen and J-B Wen. PhD (hon.), U. Nebr. Med. Ctr., Omaha, 2004. Assoc. Burnham Inst. Med. Rsch., La Jolla, Calif., 2005—. Active Entertainment Found. Colon Cancer Benefit, West Hollywood, Calif., 2002—. Fellow, Burnham Inst. Med. Rsch., 2004—05. Mem.: Am. Assn. Cancer Rsch. (assoc. Brigid G. Leventhal award 2007). Independent. Office Phone: 858-646-3100.

WENDEBORN, RICHARD DONALD, retired manufacturing executive; b. Winnipeg, Man., Can. came to U.S., 1976; naturalized, 1988; s. Curtis and Rose (Lysecki) W.; m. Dorothy Ann Munn, Aug. 24, 1957; children: Margaret Gayle, Beverley Jane, Stephen Richard, Peter Donald, Ann Elizabeth. Diploma, Colo. Sch. Mines, 1952; grad. advanced mgmt. program, Harvard U., 1974. With Can. Ingersoll-Rand Co., Montreal, 1952—, gen. mgr., v.p., dir., 1968, pres., 1969-74, chmn. bd., 1976—; exec. v.p. Ingersoll-Rand Co., Woodcliff Lake, NJ, 1976-89; ret., 1989. Mem. Can Govt. Oil and Gas Tech. Exch. Program with former USSR, 1972—. Minerals and Metals Mission to China, 1972—. Mem. Resource Fund Colo. Sch. Mines; past pres., dir. Town and River Civic Assn. Recipient Disting. Achievement medal, Colo. Sch. Mines, 1973. Mem. Machinery and Equipment Mfrs. Assn. Can. (bd. dirs. 1974—, past chmn.), Royal Palm Yacht Club (commodore 1994), Internat. Order of Blue Gavel (past Commodore's Club, past pres. Royal Palm br. dist. 8), Tau Beta Pi. Home: 12998 Beacon Cove Ln Fort Myers FL 33919-8203 Personal E-mail: dickandda@aol.com.

WENDEL, JOAN AUDREY, music educator; b. NYC, Dec. 1, 1931; d. Adam and Edna Sophia Wohlfart; m. Ralph Aurel Wendel, July 21, 1962 (dec. May 1998); 1 child, Tracy Lynn. BA summa cum laude, Dowling Coll., 1969; MA, Adelphi U., 1971. Cert. elem. tchr., N.Y. Sec. A.C. Edwards Inc., Sayville, NY, 1950-53; office mgr. John V. Potter Ins., East Islip, NY, 1953-59, Pilger Agy., Patchogue, NY, 1959-66; tchr. Connetquot CSD of Islip, Bohemia, NY, 1969-91; music dir. Christ Luth. Ch., Cape Coral, Fla., 1996—2006, Sounds of Fla., Cape Coral, 1999—2003; pvt. music tchr. Bohemia and Cape Coral, 1979—. Mem. Music Tchrs. Nat. Assn., Music Educators Nat. Conf., Assn. Luth. Ch. Musicians, Ft. Myers Music Tchrs. Assn. (v.p. 1999, 2007), Order Eastern Star (worthy matron 1964, assoc. grand marshal 1973, grand musician 1987). Republican. Lutheran. Avocations: walking, golf, music, reading. Home: 2218 SE 10th Ter Cape Coral FL 33990-6217

WENDEL, RICHARD FREDERICK, economist, educator, consultant; b. Chgo., Apr. 29, 1930; s. Elmer Carl and Victoria Matilda (Jeffrey) W.; m. Leslie Jane Travis, June 15, 1957; children: John Travis, Andrew Stewart. AB, Augustana Coll., 1951; MBA, U. Pa., 1957, PhD (fellow 1962-64), 1966. Asst. to pres. Flexonics Corp., Maywood, Ill., 1957-59; sales rep., product mgr. Kordite div. Nat. Distillers Corp., Macedon, N.Y., 1959-62; instr. Wharton Sch., U. Pa., 1964-65; asst. prof. mktg. Grad. Sch. Bus. Adminstrn., Washington U., St. Louis, 1965-69; asso. prof. U. Conn., 1969-74, prof., 1974-90, prof. emeritus, 1990. Mem. U.S. Census Field Adv. Commn., 1967-69; mem. acad. adv. commn. Bur. Labor Stats., U.S. Bur. Census Survey of Consumer Expenditures, 1971-76; mem. Conn. Export Devel. Council, Dept. Commerce, 1972-76; dir. Neon Software Inc. Author: (with M.L. Bell) Economic Importance of Highway Advertising, 1966; (with W. Gorman) Selling: Preparation. Persuasion. Strategy., 1983, 88; editor: Readings in Marketing, 1973-74, 75-76, 77-78, 78-79, 79-80, 80-81, (with C.L. Lapp) Add to Your Selling Know-How, 1968; editorial staff: jour. Mktg., 1965-74. Bd. dirs. Roper Center. Served with USAF, 1951-55. Center for Real Estate and Urban Econs. grantee, 1969-70 Mem. Am. Mktg. Assn., N.Y. Acad. Scis. Republican. Episcopalian. Home: 106 S Queen St Chestertown MD 21620-1522 Office Phone: 410-778-7185.

WENDER, IRA TENSARD, lawyer; b. Pitts., Jan. 5, 1927; s. Louis and Luba (Kibrick) W.; m. Phyllis M.Bellows, June 24, 1966; children: Justin B., Sarah T; children by previous marriage: Theodore M., Abigail A., John B. Swarthmore Coll., 1942-45; JD, U. Chgo., 1948; LLM, NYU, 1951. Atty. Lord, Day and Lord, NYC, 1950-52, 54-59; asst. dir. internat. program in tax. Harvard U. Law Sch., 1952-54; lectr. N.Y. U. Sch. Law, NYC, 1954-59; ptnr. Baker and McKenzie, Chgo., 1959-61; founding ptnr. N.Y.C. office, 1961-71; sr. ptnr. Wender, Murase & White, 1971-82; of counsel, 1982-86; chmn. C. Brewer and Co., Ltd., Honolulu, 1969-75; pres., CEO A. G. Becker Paribas Inc., 1978-82; chmn., CEO Sussex Securities Inc., 1983-85; of counsel Patterson, Belknap, Webb & Tyler, NYC, 1986-87, ptnr., 1988-93; of counsel, 1994—. Chmn. Perry Ellis Internat., Inc., N.Y.C., 1994; bd. dirs. REFAC Corp., N.Y.C., Dime Bancorp, N.Y.C.; bd. mgrs. Swarthmore Coll, 1978-89; pres., bd. mgrs. PARC Vendome Condominium, 1990-94; trustee Putnet (Vt.) Sch., 1985-92, 93—, vice chmn., 1998—; trustee Brearley Sch., N.Y.C., 1980-85. Author: (with E.R. Barlow) Foreign Investment and Taxation, 1995. Dir., treas. Fountain House, Inc., N.Y., 1998—; dir. Am. Near East Refuge Aid, Washington; mem. Coun. on Fgn. Rels. Mem. ABA, N.Y. State Bar Assn., Assn. of Bar of City of N.Y. Home: 115 E 67th St New York NY 10021-5951 Office: Patterson Belknap Webb & Tyler LLP Ste 2200 1133 Avenue Of The Americas New York NY 10036-6731

WENDER, PAUL ANTHONY, chemistry professor; BS, Wilkes Coll., 1969; PhD, Yale U., 1973; PhD (hon.), Wilkes U., 1993. Asst. prof., assoc. prof. Harvard U., 1974-81; prof. chemistry Stanford U., 1981—; Bergstrom prof. chemistry, 1994—. Cons. Eli Lilly & Co., 1980—, lectr. Am. Chem. Soc. Recipient ICI Am. Chem. award Stuart Pharm., merit award NIH, Pfizer rsch. award, 1995. Fellow AAAS; mem. Am. Chem. Soc. (Arthur C. Cope Sholan award 1990, Guenther award, award for creative work in synthetic organic chemistry 1998). Office: Stanford U Mudd Bldg Rm 390 Mail Code 5080 Stanford CA 94305

WENDER, PHYLLIS BELLOWS, literary agent; m. Ira Tensard Wender; children: Justin Bellows, Sarah Tensard. BA, Wells Coll., 1956. Publicity dir. Grove Press, NYC, 1958—60, Dell Pub. Co., NYC, 1960—63; theatrical agt. Artists Agy. Inc., NYC, 1963—66; prin. agt. Wender & Assocs., NYC, 1966—81; prin., agt., ptnr. Rosenstone/Wender, NYC, 1981—2007. Trustee Wells Coll., Aurora, N.Y., 1981-90. Mem. Women's Media Group (dir. 1988-90), Cosmopolitan Club. Office: The Gersh Agy 41 Madison Ave 33nd Fl New York NY 10010 Personal E-mail: pbwender@aol.com.

WENDLANDT, DOROTHEA SCHNEPF, artist, writer; b. Trenton, NJ, Aug. 17, 1927; d. Emil Ludwig Schnepf and Helen Dorothea Bruker, Cleveland A. Mulligan (Stepfather); m. Robert Jack Wendlandt, Aug. 14, 1974; children: Lynn Mioduszewski, Robert Jack Wendlandt, Jr., Leigh, Steven Daniel. Pictorial Illustration diploma, Newark Sch. of Fine and Indsl. Art, 1949. Artist Harold Pearson Advt., Edison, NJ, 1955—56; illustrator Joseph P. Schneider, NYC, 1957—58; asst. art dir. Batista Advt., NYC, 1959—60; ednl. exhibit designer/illustrator Binney and Smith, NYC, 1960—68; corp. dir. of advt. art Fedders Corp., Edison, NJ, 1968—74; artist, co-owner Bob's Art Ctr., Old Bridge, NJ/Sarasota, Fla., 1974—. Mem. N.J. Art Dirs. Club, 1971—74; art tchr. Middlesex Jr. Coll., Edison, NJ, 1972—73; owner DS and W Creative Art Svc., Old Bridge, NJ, 1974—78. One-woman shows include Beaux Art Gallery, St. Petersburg, Fla., 1982, exhibitions include Phila. Mus. of Art Craft, 1966, Represented in permanent collections Fedders Exec. Offices, Edison, N.J., acrylic painting, Out of Gas (Meml. Award Nat. Soc. of Painters in Acrylics and Casein, 1983), Tools (Meml. Award Nat. Soc. of Painters in Acrylics and Casien, 1987), Birds in a Window (first prize Manatee Art League, 1983), acrylic and watercolor paintings, Four Artists, Bodies Of Work (Parade of Prize Winners, 1984), watercolor, Cactus Collection 1989 (Best of State Nat. League of Am. Penwomen State Show, 1989), Cactus Collection Two (Venice Art League Best of Show, 1990); author: An Artist's Life: A Tale of Love & Woe, 2006. Treas. Metuchen Arts Coun., NJ, 1970—74; pres. Art Uptown, Sarasota, Fla., 1982—83; bd. dirs. Sarasota Art Assn., Fla., 1981—88; dir. St. Boniface Conservatory of Visual Arts, Sarasota, Fla., 1984—86. N/a N/A. Recipient Grumbacher award, Grumbacher Inc./ Sarasota Art Assn., 1983. Mem.: Nat. Soc. of Painters in Acrylics and Casein (life), Nat. League of Am. Penwomen (life; v.p. 1984—86). Democrat-Npl. Christian. Avocations: opera management, singing, writing, reading. Home: 5577 Burnt Branch Cir Sarasota FL 34232 Home Phone: 941-378-3724; Office Phone: 941-378-3724. Personal E-mail: lowerball243@aol.com.

WENDLANDT, GARY E., insurance company executive; married; 3 children. BS in applied math., computer sci., Wash. U., Mo. Various positions Mass. Mutual Life Ins. Co., 1972—92, exec. v.p., chief investment officer, 1992—99; exec. v.p., exec. mgmt. com. New York Life Ins. Co., NYC, 1999—2006, sr. exec. v.p., chief investment officer, 2006—. Fellow: Soc. of Actuaries; mem.: Am. Acad. of Actuaries. Office: NY Life Ins Co 51 Madison Ave New York NY 10010 *

WENDLINGER, ROBERT MATTHEW, communications and memory consultant; b. NYC, 1922; s. Harry and Rose (Pollock) W.; m. Dalis Peralta, 1955 (div. 1973); children: David, Marcella, Marta; m. Joan Hays Cole, June 23, 1984. Student, U. Calif., Berkeley, 1942—43, Columbia U., 1947—52. Editor script Radio Free Europe, NYC, 1950—52; assoc. editor Ind. Film Jour., NYC, 1953—57; gen. mgr. Kermit Rolland and Assocs., Princeton, NJ, 1957—59; exec. asst. in charge editl. svcs. United Hosp. Fund of N.Y., NYC, 1959—60; editl. assoc. in pub. rels. N.Y. Life Ins. Co., NYC, 1960—65; mgr. info. sect. Com. for Air and Water Conservation Am. Petroleum Inst., NYC, 1965—66; with Bank of Am. NT & SA, San Francisco, 1967—78, adminstrv. officer, 1967—70, asst. v.p. comm., 1970—78; pres. Comm. Cons. and Svcs., Berkeley, Calif., 1978—82; pub. rels. Nestle Corp., White Plains, NY, 1983—84; pres. Proust Press, Oakland, Calif., 1994—. Mem. grad. faculty St. Mary's Coll., Moraga, Calif., 1975-78; mem. Astron Corp. Author: (with James M. Reid, Jr.) Effective Letters: A Program in Self-Instruction, 1964, 3d edit., 1978, Japanese edit., 1996, The Memory Triggering Book: Using Your Memories to Enhance Your Life and Your Relationships, 1995; contbr.: Everybody Wins: TA Applied to Organizations, 1973, Affirmative Action for Women, 1973, McGraw-Hill Ency. Professional Management, 1978. Fellow Am. Bus. Comm. Assn.; mem. Indsl. Comm. Coun. (past pres.). Office Phone: 510-845-5551.

WENDORF, RICHARD HAROLD, library director, educator; b. Cedar Rapids, Iowa, Mar. 17, 1948; s. Harold Albert and Jeanne Ellen (Hamblin) Wendorf; m. Barbara Hilderman, 1970 (div. 1983); m. Diana Thanet French, 1984 (div. 1995); children: Reed Thanet Wendorf-French, Carolyn Thanet Wendorf-French; m. Elizabeth Morse, 1997. BA, Williams Coll., 1970; PhB, U. Oxford, Eng., 1972; MA, Princeton U., 1974, PhD, 1976. From asst. prof. English to assoc. prof. English Northwestern U., Evanston, Ill., 1976-86, assoc. dean, 1984-88, prof. English and art history, 1986-89; libr. dir. Houghton Libr., Harvard U., Cambridge, Mass., 1989-97; Stanford Calderwood dir. and libr. Boston Athenaeum, 1997—. Sr. lectr. fine arts Harvard U., 1990—97, acting libr. Fine Arts Libr., 1991—92, dir. NEH summer seminars coll. tchrs., 1990, 92, 96; lectr. Phi Beta Kappa Assocs., 1992—96; dir. NEH summer seminars coll. tchrs. Northwestern U., 1987, Boston Anthenaeum, 2002, 04; Robert Sterling Clark vis. prof. art history Williams Coll., 1993; bd. mgrs. Lewis Walpole Libr., 2005—. Author: William Collins and Eighteenth-Century English Poetry, 1981, The Elements of Life: Biography and Portrait Painting in Stuart and Georgian England, 1990, paperback edit., 1991, Sir Joshua Reynolds: The Painter in Society, 1996, The Scholar-Librarian, 2005, After Sir Joshua, 2005; editor: Articulate Images: The Sister Arts from Hogarth to Tennyson, 1983, Rare Book and Manuscript Libraries in the Twenty-First Century, 1993; editor: (with Charles Ryskamp) The Works of William Collins, 1979; contbr. essays in field; mem. editl. bd. Studies in 18th Century Culture, 1985—89, Word and Image, 1992—2000, Yale edit. Writings of Samuel Johnson, Old-Time New Eng., 1996—99. Trustee Mus. Fine Arts, Boston. Fellow, John Simon Guggenheim Meml. Found., 1989—90; grantee, NEH, 1979; Rsch. grantee, Folger Shakespeare Libr., Washington, 1976, Am. Philos. Soc., Phila., 1977, 1982, henry E. Hungtinton Libr., 1979, 2003, Yale Ctr. Brit. Art, 1983, Brit. Acad., 2003, Jr. Rsch. fellow, Am. Coun. Learned Socs., 1978—79, Sr. Rsch. fellow, 1981—82, Rsch. fellow, NEH, 1988—89. Mem.: Soc. Antiquaries London, Mass. Hist. Soc, The Johnsonians (chmn. 1994—95, 1997—98, 2007—08), Nat. Com. Stds. Arts, Colonial Soc. Mass., Soc. Brit. Art Historians, Coll. Art Assn., Am. Soc. 18th Century Studies (pres. Midwest regional soc. 1986, Annibel Jenkins Biography prize 1998), Am. Antiquarian Soc., Keats-Shelley Assn. Am. (bd. dirs. 1993—98), Signet Soc. (assoc.), U. Club (NY), Union Club Boston, Saturday Club, Cambridge Sci. Club, Grolier Club, Phi Beta Kappa (exec. bd. Chgo. 1984—87, nominating com. 1998—2002). Office: Boston Athenaeum 10 1/2 Beacon St Boston MA 02108-3777

WENDT, CHARLES WILLIAM, soil scientist, educator; b. Plainview, Tex., July 12, 1931; s. Charles Gottlieb and Winnie Mae (Bean) W.; m. Clara Anne Diller, Oct. 15, 1955; children: Charles Diller, John William, Elaine Anne, Cynthia Lynne. BS in Agronomy, Tex. A&M U., 1951, PhD in Soil Physics, 1966; MS in Agronomy, Tex. Tech U., 1957. Research asst. Tex. Tech Coll., 1953-55, instr. agronomy, 1957-61, asst. prof., 1961-63; research asst. soil physics Tex. A&M U., 1963-65, research assoc., 1965-66; asst. prof. Tex. A&M U. (Agrl. Research and Extension Center), Lubbock, 1966-69, assoc. prof., 1969-74, prof., 1974-91, prof. emeritus, 1991—. Cons. cotton prodn. Ministry of Agr. Sudan, summer 1960; cons. Irrigation Assn., 1977-81, Office of Tech. and Assessment, 1982, S.E. Consortium for Internat. Devel., 1989, Rhone Poulenc Agrl. Co., 1992-93; prin. backstop scientist U.S. AID West African Rsch. Program on Soil-Plant0Water Mgmt., 1982-91; chmn. agrl. sect. Southwestern and Rocky Mountain divsn. AAAS, 1982-83. Contbr. articles to profl. jours., chpt. to book. Del. Lubbock County Rep. Conv., 1978; elder Westminster Presbyn. Ch.; Tex. rep. to Great Plains Coun. 1 com. on evapotranspiration; bd. dirs. Presbyn. Ctr., Inc., 1999—, The South Plains Food Bank, 1999—, bd. dirs. farm, orchard and garden divsn., 2002- . 1st lt. U.S. Army, 1951-53. Named Outstanding Researcher High Plains Research Found., 1982; recipient Superior Achievement award for rsch., soil and crop scis. dept. Tex. A&M Univ., 1987, Vice Chancellors award in excellence as mem. TROPSOILS Rsch. team Tex. A&M U., 1996; grantee industry and water dists. Dept. Interior, U.S. AID, EPA. Mem. Soil Sci. Soc. Am., Am. Soc. Agronomy, Optimist Club (1st v.p., bd. dirs. 2001-2004). Home: 4518 22nd St Lubbock TX 79407-2515 Office: Texas Agrl Expt Station RR 3 Lubbock TX 79403-9803 Personal E-mail: absendt@aol.com.

WENDT, E. ALLAN, international affairs consultant; b. Chgo., Nov. 8, 1935; s. John Arthur Frederic and Dorothy S. BA magna cum laude, Yale U., 1957; Cert. in Politics, Inst. d'Etudes Politques, 1958; MPA, Harvard U., 1967. Econ. comml. officer Am. Embassy, Saigon, Vietnam, 1967-71; fin. officer U.S. Mission to European Cmtys., Brussels, 1971-74; State Dept. fellow Coun. on Fgn. Rels., NYC, 1974-75; dir. Office Internat. Commodities Dept. State, Washington, 1975-79; counselor for econ. and comml. affairs Am. Embassy, Cairo, 1979-81; dep. asst. sec. of state for internat. energy and resources policy Dept. State, 1981-86, sr. rep. for strategic tech. policy, 1987-92, with rank of amb., 1988-92, U.S. amb. to Republic of Slovenia Ljubljana, 1993-95, spl. rep. Internat. Donor Activities in Kosovo, 1998-2000; internat. affairs cons., 2000—. Councillor Atlantic Coun. of U.S.; mem. Coun. Fgn. Rels. Washington Inst. Fgn. Affairs.; mem. adv. bd Nat Youth Leadership Forum; bd. dir Assn. Dip Tng. and Studies. Contbr. articles to profl. jours., radio stas. and newspapers. Recipient award for heroism Dept. State, 1968, Presdl. Meritorious Svc. award, 1986, Superior Honor award Dept. State, 1992. Episcopalian.

WENDT, GEORGE ROBERT, actor; b. Chgo., Oct. 17, 1948; m. Bernadette Birkette; children: Joshua, Andrew, Hilary, Joe, Daniel. BA in Econs., Rockhurst Coll., 1971. Mem. Second City comedy troupe, Chgo., 1974-81. Actor: (feature films) My Bodyguard, 1980, Somewhere in Time, 1980, Airplane II: The Sequel, 1982, Jeckyl & Hyde: Together Again, 1982, The Women in Red, 1984, Thief of Hearts, 1984, No Small Affair, 1983, Fletch, 1985, House, 1986, Plain Clothes, 1988, Guilt by Suspicion, 1991, Forever Young, 1992, Man of the House, 1995, The Lovemaster, 1997, Rupert's Land, 1998, Outside Providence, 1999, Pooch and the Pauper, 1999, Lakeboat, 2000, Teddy Bears' Picnic, 2002, My Dinner with Jimi, 2003, King of the Ants, 2003, The Life Coach, 2005, Kids in America, 2005, (TV films) Alien Avengers, 1996, Star Truckers, 1997, Price of Heaven, 1997, Alice in Wonderland, 1999, My Beautiful Son, 2001, Robertson's Greatest Hits, 2001, (TV series) Cheers, 1982-1993, The George Wendt Show, 1995, The Naked Truth, 1995, Sabrina, the Teenage Witch, 2001-02, House of Dreams, 2004-; appeared in various commls.; guest-star: (TV series) Alice, Soap, Taxi, Hart to Hart, The American Dream, Seinfeld, Wings, St. Elsewhere, Spin City, The Simpsons, The Larry Sanders Show, Madigan Men, 2000, Becker, 2002, Frasier, 2002, The Jamie Kennedy Experiment, 2002; appeared on stage with the Second City comedy troupe, also Wild Men, 1993.

WENDT, RICHARD L., manufacturing executive; b. 1931; From mgr. frame factory to mgr. ops. Caradco; CEO Jeld-Wen Inc., Klamath Falls, Oreg., 1960—2003, chmn., 2003—. Address: Jeld Wen Inc PO Box 1329 Klamath Falls OR 97601-0268 Office: Jen Weld Inc 401 Harbor Isles Blvd Klamath Falls OR 97601

WENDT, THOMAS, finance company executive; CPA, Wis. Auditor Coopers & Lybrand, Milw., 1973-75; supr. Conley, McDonald, Sprague & Co., Milw., 1975-80; CFO E. Cen./Select Sires, Waupun, Wis., 1981—, also rec. sec., bd. dirs. Bd. dirs. Moravian Homes Inc., Mueller Apts., Inc., Marquardt Meml. Manor, Inc., Watertown, Wis., sec., treas. bd. dirs., 1986—; bd. dirs. Hus Apts., Inc., sec.-treas., 1993—. Mem. Marquardt Found., 1988—; bd. dirs. Zinsendorf Hall, 1989—, sec., treas., 1989—, forward campaign chmn., 1988; pres. bd. trustees Watertown Moravian Ch., 1981-84, bd. elders, 1990-93, ch. sec., 2000-03; adv. del. Western Dist. Synod, Wis., 1982, 86, 90, 96; bd. dirs. Moravian Homes of Sturgeon Bay, 1991—; bd. dirs. Hus Apts., Inc., 1993—, sec., treas., 1993—. Mem. AICPA, Wis. Inst. CPAs, Milw. Art Mus., Beaver Dam Lions Club (bd. dirs. 2005—). Office: E Central/Select Sires PO Box 191 Waupun WI 53963-0191

WENDT, VERNON EARL, internist, cardiologist; b. Cleve., Mar. 26, 1931; s. Raymond C. and Esther L. (Naujoks) Wendt; m. Hildegarde Caroline Moeller, Aug. 14, 1953; children: David, Frederick, Kathryn, Elizabeth, Doralyn, James, Vernon Earl Jr. BS in Zoology and Chemistry cum laude, Baldwin-Wallace Coll., 1952; MD, Columbia U., 1956. Diplomate Am. Bd. Internal Medicine. Intern Detroit Receiving Hosp., 1956—57, resident, 1959—62; USPHS postdoctoral fellow in cardiology Wayne State U. Sch. of Medicine, Detroit, 1962—65, from instr. to asst. prof. medicine, 1961—65; dir. rsch. Blodgett Meml. Med. Ctr., Grand Rapids, Mich., 1965—67; pvt. practice Grand Rapids, 1967—2000. Capt. M.C. USAF, 1957—59. Fellow: ACP, Coun. Geriatric Cardiology, Am. Coll. Angiology, Am. Coll. Cardiology; mem.: AMA, Mich. State Med.

Soc., Mich. Health Coun. (trustee 1998—), Am. Acad. Anti-Aging Medicine, Kent County Med. Soc., Mich. Soc. Internal Medicine (pres. 1991—92), Am. Lung Assn. Mich. (pres. 1978—80), Am. Heart Assn. Mich. (trustee 1973—93, pres. 1987—88). Lutheran. Avocations: golf, gardening, walking. Home and Office: 1620 Andover Rd SE Grand Rapids MI 49506 Office Phone: 616-949-6735. Personal E-mail: vhwendt@comcast.net.

WENDZEL, ROBERT LEROY, political science professor; b. May 28, 1938; married; 3 children. BA in Polit. Sci. magna cum laude, Kalamazoo Coll., 1960; PhD in Polit. Sci., U. Fla., 1965. Assoc. prof. polit. sci. U. Maine, Orono, 1977-81, 82-83; prof. internat. affairs U.S. Air War Coll., Maxwell AFB, Ala., 1981-82, prof. internat. politics, 1986-87, ednl. advisor to the Commandant, 1987-2000, prof. internat. security studies, 2002—06; asst. dean arts and scis., prof. polit. sci., coord. internat. affairs program U. Maine, 1984-86; Paschal P. Vacca prof. liberal arts U. Montevallo, Ala., 2001; Merrill prof. polit. sci. Utah State U., Logan, 2001. Internat. affairs com., U. Maine, 1970-86, budget adv. com., 1983-86, coord. internat. affairs program, 1984-86. Author: International Relations: A Policymaker Focus, Thai edit., 1989, Relacoes Internacionais, 1985, International Politics: Policymakers and Policymaking, 1981, International Relations: A Policymaker Focus, 1977, 2d edit., 1980; co-author: America's Foreign Policy in a Changing World, 1994, Defending America's Security, 1988, 2d edit., 1990, To Preserve the Republic: The Foreign Policy of the United States, 1985, Games Nations Play, 9th edit., 1996; contbr. articles to profl. jours. Mem. Phi Beta Kappa. Home: 160 Old Field Dr Montgomery AL 36117-3938 Personal E-mail: blw052838@aol.com.

WENEGRAT, SAUL S., art association administrator, educator; b. Jersey City, Mar. 28, 1933; s. John and Tillie (Freeman) W. BA, Rutgers U., 1960; PhD, Harvard U., 1965; cert., London U., 1975. Dir. art program Port Authority of N.Y. & N.J., NYC, 1962-95; prof. grad. divsn. Fashion Inst. Tech., NYC, 1987-95; v.p. Forums Internat., 1995—; cons. arts advisor Voorsanger and Assocs., Archs., 2001—04. Pub. art panelist N.J. State Com. Arts, Trenton, 1985-95, Conn. State Com. Arts, Hartford, 1988, N.Y.C. Cultural Affairs, 1980-88, Met. Transit Authority, N.Y.C., 1994-95. Editor: Art for the Public, 1985. Capt. USAF, 1953-57. Recipient Doris Freedman award Mayor of N.Y.C., 1984, Merit cert. Mcpl. Art Soc., 1980, 85; Carnegie fellow, 1960, Fels fellow, 1960. Mem. Nat. Assn. Corp. Art Adminstrn. (chmn. bd. 1985-95), Internat. Assn. Art Advisors, Am. Assn. Museums, Harvard Club. Avocations: bridge, walking, museums. Home: 2 Beekman Pl New York NY 10022-8058

WENER, BRIAN D., psychologist; s. Martin M. and Rachel Wener; 1 child, Sara. BA in Psychology with honors, Carleton U., 1971; MA in Psychology, SUNY, Plattsburgh, 1975; D of Psychology, Ctrl. Mich. U., 1982. Lic. psychologist NH, 1983, Mass., 1995, cert. sch. psychologist NH, 1981. Clin. psychologist Riverbend Counseling, Concord, NH, 1983—87; psychologist II Philbrook Ctr., 1975—78; clin. psychologist pvt. practice, Portsmouth, 1987—; sch. psychologist Hampton Schs., 2000—06. Cons., evaluator NH Medicaid Disability Unit, Concord, 1993—. Fellow: NH Psychol. Assn. (bd. dirs. 1992—94); mem.: APA, Nat. Assn. Sch. Psychologists. Avocations: photography, guitar. Office: 118 Maplewood Ave Portsmouth NH 03801 Office Phone: 603-431-1294. Personal E-mail: shaman426@comcast.net.

WENETSCHLAEGER, PATTY STRADER, lawyer; married; 2 children. MS in Clin. Psych., Abilene Christian U.; M of Dispute Resolution, Pepperdine U. Strauss Inst.; JD, Pepperdine U. Sch. Law, Malibu, Calif. Bar: Tex. Assoc. Brewer, Anthony & Middlebrook, P.C., Irving, Tex. Adj. grad. prof. family mediation Abilene Christian U. Named a Rising Star, Tex. Super Lawyers mag., 2006. Mem.: Am. Inn of Ct., ABA, Denton County Bar Assn., Tarrant County Family Law Bar Assn., Dallas Bar Assn. (mem. family law sect.). Office: Brewer Anthony & Middlebrook PC 5201 N O'Connor Blvd Ste 500 Irving TX 75039 Office Phone: 972-870-9898. E-mail: pwenetschlaeger@bamlawyers.net. *

WENG, GEORGE JUENG-CIOUS, engineering educator; b. Oct. 8, 1944; s. Wan-Chung and Kuang-chieh (Hsieh) Weng; m. Jackie Li; children: Shawn, Cidney, Zoe;children from previous marriage: Bruce, Joyce. BS, Taiwan U., 1967; MPhil, Yale U., 1971, PhD, 1974. Rsch. fellow Delft U. Tech., Netherlands, 1973—74; postdoctoral fellow Yale U., UCLA, 1974—76; sr. rsch. engr. GM Rsch. Lab., Warren, Mich., 1976—77; asst. prof. mech. and aerospace engring. Rutgers U., New Brunswick, NJ, 1977—80, assoc. prof., 1980—84, prof., 1984—92, disting. prof., 1992—, grad. dir., 1995—98. Editor Acta Mechanica, 1985—, tech. editor Jour. Engring. Materials and Tech., trans. ASME, 1992—97, mem. editl. bd. Internat. Jour. Plasticity, 1985—, Acta Mechanica Solida Sinica, 1997—, JSME Internat. Jour., 1997—2002, Mechanics and Materials in Design, 2004—, Mechanics of Advanced Materials and Structures, 2004—, Mechanics of Materials, 2007—, Open Mech. Engring. Jour., 2007—, Open Mechanics Jour., 2007—; contbr. more than 160 articles to profl. jours. NSF grantee, 1978—. Fellow ASME, Am. Acad. Mechanics. Achievements include research in mechanics of materials, micromechanics of composite materials, shape-memory alloys, ferroelectric ceramics, nanocrystalline materials. Home: 65 Sycamore Way Warren NJ 07059 Office: Sch Engring Rutgers U New Brunswick NJ 08903 Home Phone: 908-822-8828; Office Phone: 732-445-2223. Business E-Mail: weng@jove.rutgers.edu.

WENGER, JAMES L., education educator; b. Horton, Kans., Aug. 4, 1944; s. Donald and Edith Wenger; m. Phyllis C. Newton, June 2, 1973; children: Scott, Stacy. BSE, Emporia State U., Kans., 1967, MS, 1972. Cert. DP/CIS vocat. Kans. State Bd. Edn., 2006. Dir. data processing North Ctrl. Kans. Tech. Coll., Beloit, Kans., 1970—76; instr. Emporia State U., 1976—79, asst. prof., 1979—2004, assoc. prof., 2005—07, mem. emeritus faculty, 2007—. Contbr. articles pub. to profl. jour. Recipient Svc. award, Emporia State U., 1989, Pres. Equity award, 1997, 2003, Instrn. award, 2005, Disting. Rsch. award, Allied Academies, 2003; grantee Microsoft grant, Microsoft, 1997. Mem.: NEA, Kans. Nat. Edn. Assn., Assn. Info. Sys., Assn. Info. Tech. Profls., Mid Am. Assn. for Computers in Edn. (pres. 1982—83, bd. dirs. 1983—85, sec. 1985—), Beta Gamma Sigma. Lutheran. Avocations: golf, fishing.

WENGER, LARRY BRUCE, law librarian, educator; b. Everett, Wash., Dec. 21, 1941; s. Lester Edwin Wenger and Selma Marie (Norberg) W. Saterstrom; m. Marilyn Diane Watt, June 26, 1965; children: Bruce Daniel, Kathleen Marie. BA, U. Wash., 1964, JD, 1967; MLS, Simmons Coll., 1969. Reference libr. Sch. Law Harvard U., Cambridge, Mass., 1967-69; asst. law libr. SUNY, Buffalo, 1969-71, law libr., assoc. prof. law, 1971-76; law libr., prof. law U. Va., Charlottesville, 1976—. Cons. to law librs.; bd. dirs. Nat. Ctr. for Preservation Law. Editor: Marine Affairs Bibliography. Mem. Am. Assn. Law Librs., Internat. Assn. Law Librs. (pres. 1995-2001), Bibliog. Soc., Bibliog. Soc. Am. Home: 2630 Meriwether Dr Charlottesville VA 22901-9513 Office: U Va Law Libr 580 Massie Rd Charlottesville VA 22903-1739

WENGER, NANETTE KASS, cardiologist, researcher, educator; b. NYC, Sept. 3, 1930; d. Aaron Zelig and Edith (Malkin) Kass; m. Julius Wenger; children: Deborah, Judith, Beth. BA summa cum laude, Hunter Coll., 1951; MD, Harvard U., 1954. Intern Mt. Sinai Hosp., NYC, 1954—55, chief resident in cardiology, 1956—57; sr. resident in medicine Grady Meml. Hosp., Atlanta, 1958; fellow in cardiology Sch. Medicine, Emory U., 1958—59; instr. medicine Schs. Medicine and Dentistry, Emory U., Atlanta, 1959—62, assoc. in medicine, 1962—64, asst. prof. cardiology, 1964—68, assoc. prof., 1968—71, prof. medicine, 1971—; mem. med. staff Crawford W. Long Hosp., Atlanta, 1977—. Dir. cardiac clinics Grady Meml. Hosp., 1960—, chief cardiology, 1998—; cons. cardiology VA Med. Ctr., Atlanta, 1988—; participant numerous profl. symposiums and confs.; mem. cardiovas. and renal drugs adv. com. U.S. FDA, 1978-82; co-chair nat. plan for cardiac rehab. com. Div. Vocat. Rehab., Social and Rehab. Svcs., HEW, 1973-90; mem. Internat. Task Force for Prevention of Coronary Heart Disease, 1989—; founding fellow Soc. Geriatric Cardiology, 1986, bd. dirs., 1987—, pres., 1994-95; former chair, US Nat. Heart, Lung, and Blood Inst. Conf. on Cardiovascular Health and Disease in Women; cons. Emory Heart Ctr.; heads the Emory U. component of the Heart and Estrogen-Progestin Replacement Study (HERS). Mem. editl. bd. various profl. publs. including Cardiac Rehab. Quar., 1974-79, Primary Care, 1975-79, Internat. Jour. Sports Cardiology, 1983—, Med. Month, 1983-84, Jour. Cardiovasc. and Pulmonary Medicine, 1983—, Geriatric Cardiology, 1986—, Nutrition, Metabolism and Cardiovasc. Disease, 1989—; reviewer publs. including Am. Jour. Medicine, 1972—, Am. Jour. Cardiology, 1979—, Am. Heart Jour., 1975—, European Heart Jour., 1983—; editor Am. Jour. Geriatric Cardiology, editor-in-chief; assoc. editor The Heart; co-editor (with Peter Collins) Women and Heart Disease, 2005; contbr. articles to profl. jours.; contbr. book chpts. Chair Heart Sunday program, 1968-69, program chair Fulton County Heart Unit, 1969-71, bd. dirs., 1969-79, 80-82, pres., 1977-78; fellow coun. clin. cardiology, Am. Heart Assn., 1970, chair rehab. com., 1972-75, chair artherosclerosis task force, 1973-74, program v.p., 1975-76, pres., 1977-78, bd. dirs., 1975-79, mem./past mem. numerous other coms.; mem. med. adv. and cardiovasc. health coms. Butler St. YMCA, 1980-82; chair, WHO Expert Com. on Rehabilitation after Cardiovascular Disease; co-chair, Guideline Panel on Cardiac Rehabilitation, US Agy. for Healthcare Policy and Rsch. Recipient Myrtle Wreath award Atlanta Hadassah, 1967, award of Achievement, Nat. Ctr. for Vol. Action, 1978, Outstanding Profl. Achievement award, Hunter Coll., 1993, President's Women in Sci. award, Am. Med. Women's Assn., 1993, Citation, Am. Coll. Sports Medicine, 1994, Jan J. Kellermann Meml. award for Cardiovascular Prevention and Rehabilitation, Internat. Soc. Heart Failure, 1995, Juha P. Kokko award for Excellence in Cardiovascular Lecturing and Edu., Dept. Med. Housestaff, Emory Univ. Sch. Med., 1999-2000, Emory Williams Disting. Tchg. award, 2004, Evangeline Papageorge Alumni Tchg. award, 2004, Shining Star award Atlanta Women in Law and Medicine, 2000, Atlanta Bus. Chronicle Health-Care Heroes Lifetime Achievement award, 2005; Disting. Fellow Soc. Geriatric Cardiology, 2002; honoree Women of Yr. issue Time Mag., 1976; named Joseph B. Wolff Meml. Lectr., Am. Coll. Sports Medicine, 2001; named one of the 10 Most Important Women in Medicine, Ladies Home Jour., 1994; named to Best Doctors in Am.; recognized by McCall's Mag. for rsch. into causes and treatments for heart disease in women. Fellow Am. Heart Assn.(active Ga. affiliate 1960-, first woman president Ga. affiliate, fellow coun. clin. cardiology, 1970, chair rehab. com., 1972-75, chair artherosclerosis task force, 1973-74, program v.p., 1975-76, pres., 1977-78, bd. dirs., 1975-79, mem./past mem. numerous other coms., Bronze Disting. Svc. medallion Ga. affiliate Am. Heart Assn., 1970-71, Silver Disting. Svc. medallion, 1978, Gold Disting. Svc. medallion, 1979, named Physician of Yr., 1998, Disting. Achievement award, Sci. Coun., Women in Cardiol. Mentoring award, 1999, R. Bruce Logue award for Excellence in Medicine, 2001, Gold Heart award, 2004), Am. Coll. Cardiology (gov. for Ga. 1983-86, trustee 1987-89, various coms.), Am. Coll. Chest Physicians; master ACP (James D. Bruce Meml. award 2000); mem. AMA, WHO (expert adv. panel on cardiovasc. disease 1989—), Am. Assn. Cardiovasc. and Pulmonary Rehab. (trustee 1985-88, chairperson ethics com. 1985—, 2nd Ann. Lecture award 1987), Nat. Heart, Lung and Blood Inst., Internat. Soc. and Fedn. Cardiology (pres. sci. coun. on rehab. of cardiac patients 1984-88), Soc. Geriatric Cardiologists (officer, pres. 1994-95), Med. Assn. Ga., Med. Assn. Atlanta, Atlanta Clin. Soc.(emeritus), Soc. for Prevention of Heart Disease and Rehab. (hon.), Soc. Women's Health (bd. dirs. 2000—, vice chair 2002—), Philippine Heart Assn. (hon.), Philippine Coll. Cardiology (hon.), Omicron Delta Kappa. Office: Emory Univ Sch Medicine Grady Meml Hosp Glenn Bldg E278 49 Jesse Hill Jr Dr SE Atlanta GA 30303 Home Phone: 404-237-4802; Office Phone: 404-616-4420. Business E-Mail: nwenger@emory.edu.

WENGER, SCOTT ANDREW, orthopedist, surgeon; b. Winter Park, Fla., Nov. 25, 1971; s. Thomas James and Katherine Wenger; m. Virginia Elliott, June 22, 1996; children: Luke Andrew, Adam Scott. BA in Bus. Adminstrn., So. Meth. U., 1994, BSc in Biology, 1994; MD, U. Tex. Southwestern Med. Sch., 1998. Lic. physician Tex. State Bd. of Med. Examiners, 2003, Med. Bd. Calif., 2003. Intern gen. surgery U. Tex. Southwestern Med. Ctr., Dallas, 1998—99, resident orthop. surgery, 1999—2003; sports medicine fellow Kerlan-Jobe Orthop. Clinic, LA, 2003—04; orthopaedic surgeon Coll. Sta. (Tex.) Orthopaedics, 2004—. Mem.: AMA, Tex. Orthop. Assn., Tex. Med. Assn., Brazos-Robertson County Med. Soc., Am. Orthop. Soc. Sports Medicine, Am. Acad. Orthop. Surgeons, Arthroscopy Assn. N.Am. (assoc.), Alpha Omega Alpha. Office: College Station Orthopaedics 1602 Rock Prairie Road STE #460 College Station TX 77845 Office Phone: 979-696-3344.

WENGER, SHARON LOUISE, cytogeneticist, researcher, educator; b. Washington, Sept. 25, 1949; d. William Fred and Lois Helen (Compton) W.; m. George E. Fromlak Jr., Jan. 10, 1976; children: Nicholas Edward, Holly Louise, Andrea Lee. BA in Biology, Thiel Coll., 1971; MS in Human Genetics, U. Pitts., 1973, PhD in Human Genetics, 1976. Cert. in clin. cytogenetics Am. Bd. Med. Genetics. Asst. prof. U. Pitts. Sch. Med., 1980-89, assoc. prof., 1989—97; prof. pathology W. Va. U., 1997—. Contbr. articles to profl. jours. Mem. Am. Soc. Human Genetics, Am. Coll. Med. Genetics, Assn. Genetic Technologists, Assn. Molecular Pathology, Am. Soc. Hematology. Achievements include research of sister chromatid exchange and fragile sites, chromosome syndromes and mechanism of tissue limited mosaicism. Home: 50 Crescent Heights Morgantown WV 26505 Office: W Va U Dept Pathology PO Box 9203 Morgantown WV 26506-9203 Home Phone: 304-598-3872; Office Phone: 304-293-3212.

WENGLER, MARGUERITE MARIE, counseling administrator; b. Kokomo, Ind., Nov. 18, 1943; d. Eugene Ferdinand and Flavia Marie (Marullo) Scalzo; m. James Burton Wengler, Oct. 4,1969; children: James Eugene, Dale Douglas, Lauren Christine. BS in Edn., Hofstra U., 1964; MA in Moderate Spl. Needs Edn., Assumption Coll., 1991. Cert. elem. tchr. N.Y., Mass., spl. needs tchr. Mass. Spl. needs dir. Montessori Primary and Upper Schs., Lexington, Mass.; spl. edn. tchr. Lincoln-Sudbury Pub. Schs., Sudbury, Mass., 1987-88; from assoc. lectr. to sr. lectr. Program Advanced Lng. Curry Coll., Milton, Mass., 1993—, outreach dir., 1997-98. Dir. Learning Success Helpline, Acton, Mass., 1984—; profl. devel. provider towards tchr. cert. Dept. of Edn. state of Mass. Author: 60 Minutes to Much Higher Grades, coll. edit., 1995, 60 Minutes to Much Higher Grades, H.S. edit., 1997; contbg. author A Closer Look, 1995; mng. editor Shared Visions of Teaching and Learning, 1997-2001. Del. People to People/Citizen Amb., China, 1994; dir., founder A Friend in Need, Acton, Mass., 1990-96, bd. dirs. Recipient Grant to Friend in Need, United Way, 1991—94, Cmty. Chest, 1993. Mem. AAUP, Learning Disabilities Network. Office: Program Advancement Lng Curry Coll Blue Hill Ave Milton MA 02186-2302 Personal E-mail: learningsuccess@yahoo.com.

WENGLOWSKI, GARY MARTIN, economist; b. Rochester, NY, Sept. 2, 1942; s. Henry Bernard and Isabelle (Franc) W.; m. Joyce Richards, Oct. 3, 1964; children: Gary Martin, Catherine Jean. BS in Econs., U. Pa., 1964, MA, 1965, PhD in Econs., 1967. With Goldman Sachs & Co., NYC, 1967—, v.p., dir. econ. rsch., 1972-78, ptnr., 1978-86, ltd. ptnr., 1986-99; ret. ptnr., 1999—. Chmn. vis. com. econ. dept. U. Pa., 1985-98; adj. prof. Baruch Coll., 1998-02. Author: Industry Profit Forecasting, 1972, Industry Profit Forecasting— Progress Report, 1975. Trustee CARE Found., 1991—, Haystack Mountain Sch., 1993-2002. Named Best Economist on Wall St., Ann. Instnl. Investor Mag. Polls, 1976-86; NDEA fellow, 1965, 67. Fellow Nat. Assn. Bus. Economists; mem. Am. Econ. Assn., Deer Isle Yacht Club (vice commodore 1993-94, commodore 1994-2000). Home: 32 Partridge Ridge Rd Katonah NY 10536-3500

WENIG, CINDY L., lawyer; b. Queens, NY, Mar. 26, 1966; AB summa cum laude, Princeton U., 1988; JD, Columbia U., 1991. Bar: NY 1992. Ptnr., Real Estate Practice Group Chadbourne & Parke LLP, NYC. Adv. bd. Stewart Title Guaranty Co., Profl. Women's Alliance of NYC. Harlan Fiske Stone Scholar. Mem.: Real Estate Bd. NY, Women Exec. in Real Estate (WX) (sec.), Nat. Assn. Women Bus. Owners. Office: Chadbourne & Parke LLP 30 Rockefeller Plz New York NY 10112 Office Phone: 202-408-1188. Office Fax: 212-541-5369. Business E-Mail: cwenig@chadbourne.com.

WENIG, DEVIN NORSE, communications executive; b. Brooklyn, Oct. 20, 1966; BA, Union Coll., 1988; JD, Columbia U. Sch. Law. Mergers and acquisitions atty. Cravath, Swaine and Moore; corp. counsel Reuters N. Am. Reuters, 1993, various sr. mgmt. roles, including mng. dir. mktg. Reuters Info., sr. v.p. bus. devel., exec. v.p. mktg., Reuters Am., pres., Investment Banking Services London, 2001—03, pres. Reuters Info., 2001, pres. customer segments, 2003—06, COO, 2006—. Chmn. Nastech Pharmaceutical Co., 1991—99, bd. dirs., 1999—, Instinet. Named a Forty Under Forty, Crain's NY Bus., 2005. Office: Reuters 3 Times Sq New York NY 10036

WENK, EDWARD, JR., civil engineer, educator, writer, policy analyst; b. Balt., Jan. 24, 1920; s. Edward and Lillie (Heller) Wenk; m. Carolyn Frances Lyford, Dec. 27, 1941 (dec.); children: Lawrence Shelley, Robin Edward Alexander, Terry Allan(dec.). BE, Johns Hopkins U., 1940, DEng, 1950; MSc, Harvard U., 1947; DSc (hon.), U. R.I., 1968; LHD (hon.), Johns Hopkins U., 1989. Registered profl. engr. Head structures div. USN David Taylor Model Basin, Washington, 1942-56; chmn. dept. engring. mechanics S.W. Research Inst., San Antonio, 1956-59; sr. specialist sci. and tech. Legis. Reference Service, Library of Congress, Washington, 1959-61, chief sci. policy research div., 1964-66; tech. asst. to U.S. President's sci. adviser and exec. sec. Fed. Council for Sci. and Tech., White House, Washington, 1961-64; exec. sec. Nat. Council on Marine Resources and Engring. Devel., Exec. Office of Pres., Washington, 1966-70; prof. engring. and pub. affairs U. Wash., Seattle, 1970-83, prof. emeritus, 1983—, dir. program in social mgmt. tech., 1973-79; tech. advisor to gov. State of Wash., 1993-96. Nat. Adv. Com. on Oceans and Atmosphere, 1972-73; vice chmn. U.S. Congress Tech. Assessment Adv. Coun., 1973-79; adviser Congress, GAO, NSF, EPA, NOAA, White House, UN Secretariat, Wash. State, Alaska, U.K., Australia, Sweden, The Philippines, Alaska Oil Spill Commn., 1989, Wash. State Marine Oversight Bd., 1992, pub. interest groups, 1997, US Dept. Transportation; vis. scholar Woodrow Wilson Internat. Ctr. for Scholars, 1970-72, Harvard U., 1976, Woods Hole Oceanographic Instn., 1976, U. Sussex, 1977, Bellagio Ctr., Rockefeller Found., 1977, 90; lectr., cons. in field. Author: The Politics of the Oceans, 1972, Margins for Survival, 1979, Tradeoffs-Imperatives of Choice in a High-Tech World, 1986, Making Waves—Engineering, Politics and the Social Management of Technology, 1995, The Double Helix: Technology and Democracy in the American Future, 1999, How Safe is Safe? Coping with Mother Nature, Human Nature and Technology's Unintended Consequences, 2006; editor Exptl. Mechs. Jour., 1954-56, Engring. Mechs. Jour., 1958-60; mem. editl. bd. Tech. Forecasting, Tech. in Soc.; contbr. articles to profl. jours.; designer Aluminaut submarine. Bd. dir. Human Interaction Rsch. Inst., 1980-90, Smithsonian Sci. Info. Exch., 1977-82, URS Corp., 1973-88; mem. Interfaith Alliance. Ensign USNR, 1944-45. Recipient Navy Meritorious Civilian Svc. award, 1946, authors prize Gov. Wash., 1974, ann. prize Edn. Press Assn., 1997; named Disting. Alumnus Johns Hopkins U., 1979, Tchr. of Yr., Wash. State Engrs., 1980, Tchr. of Yr., Students in Pub. Adminstrn., 1986, Disting. Alumnus, Balt. Poly. Inst., 1991; Ford Found. grantee, 1970; Rockefeller Found. Bellagio fellow, 1976, 90; 1st Stuckenburg lectr. Wash. U., 1988; Regents lectr. U. Calif., Berkeley, 1989, Woodrow Wilson award Johns Hopkins U., 2004. Fellow ASME (exec., Ralph Coats Roe medal 1999), AAAS; mem. ASCE, NSPE, LWV, Soc. Exptl. Stress Analysis (past pres. and William M. Murray lectr.), Internat. Assn. Impact Assessment (pres. 1981-82), NAE (chmn. com. on pub. policy 1970-75), Nat. Acad. Pub. Adminstrn., Am. Soc. Pub. Adminstrn. (chmn. com. on sci. and tech. in govt. 1974-78), Assembly Engring. and Marine Bd. NRC, Nat. Oceanography Assn. (v.p. pub. affairs 1970-72), Cousteau Soc. (chmn. adv. bd. 1975-97), USA Club Rome (bd. dir. 1997-98), Explorers Club, Sigma Xi, Tau Beta Pi, Chi Epsilon. Home: 900 University St # 13G Seattle WA 98101 Business E-Mail: future@u.washington.edu. *Each of us has the opportunity, indeed responsibility, to contribute to the human experience and to enrich the lives of future generations. In a world of change, cultural diversity and uncertainty, we must be ourselves and not merely slaves of conventional thought. We must act on the basis of what we believe to be right rather than only from the desire to be loved.*

WENK, MICHAEL SCOTT, environmental services administrator; b. Livingston, NJ, Jan. 16, 1973; s. Robert Theodore and Georgia Irene Wenk; m. Cynde Lynn Hisel, Oct. 27, 1999; children: Andrew, Lauren. BS in Human Ecology, Rutgers U., New Brunswick, NJ, 1995; MS in Environ. Sci., NJ Inst. Tech., Newark, 2003; MBA, U. Md., College Park, 2006. Mgr. regulatory affairs Selig Industries, Atlanta, 1997—99, Eka Chems. Inc., Marietta, Ga., 1999—. Spkr. in field. The European Union's Eco-Management and Audit Scheme, 2005; contbr. articles to profl. jours. Mem.: Nat. Registry Environ. Profls. Office: Eka Chems Inc 1775 West Oak Commons Ct Marietta GA 30062

WENNER, CHARLES RODERICK, lawyer; b. New Haven, Jan. 10, 1947; s. Charles Bellew and Joan Rhoda (Morrison) Wenner; m. Jovita C. Vergara, June 11, 1999; children: Abigail Jessica, Charles Roderick Jr. BS, Coll. Charleston, 1969; JD, U. Conn., 1973. Bar: Conn. 1974, DC 1977. Law clk. Conn. Superior Ct., Hartford, 1973—74; staff atty. SEC, Washington, 1974—76, spl. counsel to chmn., 1976—77; assoc. Fulbright & Jaworski, 1977—81, ptnr., 1981—2005; of counsel Arnold & Porter LLP, 2005—. Lectr. law U. Conn. Sch. Law, 1973—74. Trustee United Meth. Ch., Arlington, Va., 1993—95, 1997—98; counselor Gospel Mission Washington, 1991—. Recipient Am. Hist. award, DAR, 1969. Mem.: ABA, DC Bar Assn. Methodist. Avocation: running. Home: 1808 South Lynn St Arlington VA 22202 Office: Arnold & Porter LLP 555 Twelfth St Washington DC 20004 Home Phone: 703-979-1684; Office Phone: 202-942-6974. Office Fax: 202-942-5999. Business E-Mail: charles.wenner@aporter.com.

WENNER, GENE CHARLES, arts management executive; b. Catasauqua, Pa., Dec. 21, 1931; s. Clinton G. and Bertha (Taggert) W.; m. Carole Brunner, Aug. 15, 1953; children: Robert Larren, Laurel E. Wenner Carsell BS in Music, West Chester StateColl., Pa., 1953; M.Ed. in Music, Pa. State U., 1954. Tchr. music Phila. pub. schs., 1945-55, 56-60; assoc. prof. Kutztown (Pa.) State Coll., 1960-66, dir. coll. choir, 1960-66; fine arts adv. Pa. Dept. Edn., 1966-69, U.S. Office Edn., 1969-71; asst. dir. arts in edn. program John D. Rockefeller 3d Fund, 1971-78; arts edn. coordinator Office Commr., U.S. Office Edn., 1978-79; pres. Am. Music Conf., Wilmette, Ill., 1979-81; v.p. for programs Nat. Found. Advancement in Arts, Miami, Fla., 1983-87; pres. Arts and Edn. Cons., Inc., Reston, Va., 1987-91; sr. cons. Bus. & Industry for Arts Edn., 1990-91; exec. dir. Charlotte (N.C.) Community Sch. for the Arts, 1991-96; pres. Arts & Edn. Cons., Inc., Pittsfield, Mass., 1996—. Fund raising cons. Nat. Pub. Radio, Nat. Music Found., Mohawk Theater Capital Campaign, Goldman Meml.

Band, Jacob's Pillow, Berkshire C.C. Non-Profit mgmt. Counsel, Mass. Coll. Liberal Arts; mus. dir. Allentown (Pa.) Mcpl. Oper, 1962-63, Allentown Civic Little Theatre, 1964, Little Theatre Alexandria, Va., 1971; dir. Hershey (Pa.) Little Theatre, 1967-68, Hershey Community Chorus, 1967-69 Composer: I'll Never Forget You, 1968, Chorale of Dedication, 1974, Great Things God Hath Done, 1986, In My Father's House, 1986; original music and script Adventures in the Arts, Hershey, 1968; also original TV music, I Am the Way, 1985, When You Remember, 1985; author papers, reports in field. Served with AUS, 1955-56. Named Best Mus. Dir. Little Theatre Alexandria Mem. Music Educators Nat. Conf., Network Performing and Visual Arts Schs. Clubs: Masons. Home and Office: 112 Doreen St Pittsfield MA 01201 Office Phone: 413-499-5311. Personal E-mail: gwenner@berkshire.rr.com.

WENNER, JANN SIMON, editor, publisher; b. NYC, Jan. 7, 1946; s. Edward and Ruth N. (Simmons) Wenner; m. Jane Ellen Schindelhiem, July 1, 1968 (separated 1995); children: Alexander Jann, Theodore Simon, Edward Augustus. Student, U. Calif.-Berkeley, 1964—66. Co-founding editor, pub. Rolling Stone mag., NYC, 1967—; editor, pub. Record, NYC, 1981—86, Look mag., NYC, 1979, Men's Jour., 1992—; editor in chief Outside Mag., San Francisco, 1977—79, US Mag., NYC, 1985—, Men's Jour., 1992—; pub. Family Life, 1993—95; editor in chief Wenner Media Inc., 1993—; founder Cease Fire Inc., 1995—. Vice chmn. Rock & Roll Hall of Fame. Author: Lennon Remembers, 1971, Garcia, 1972; actor: (films) Perfect, 1985, Jerry Maguire, 1996, Almost Famous, 2000, Breakfast with Hunter, 2003. Bd. dirs. Robinhood Found. Recipient Disting. Achievement award, U. So. Calif. Sch. Journalism and Alumni Assn., 1976, Nat. Mag. award, 1970, 1977, 1986, 1987, 1988, 1989, 2007, Lifetime Achievement award, Rock and Roll Hall of Fame, 2004. Mem.: Am. Soc. Mag. Editors. Achievements include youngest editor to be inducted into the American Society of Mag. Editors Hall of Fame, 1997. Office: Rolling Stone Wenner Media Inc 1290 Avenue Of The Americas Fl 2 New York NY 10104-0295 *

WENNERSTROM, ARTHUR JOHN, aeronautical engineer; b. NYC, Jan. 11, 1935; s. Albert Eugene and Adele (Trebus) W.; m. Bonita Gay Westenberg, Sept. 6, 1969 (div. Jan. 1989); children: Bjorn Erik, Erika Lindsay; m. Vicki Lynn Merrick, Feb. 17, 1990. BS in Mech. Engring., Duke U., 1956; MS in Aero. Engring., MIT, 1958; DSc of Tech., Swiss Fedn. Inst. Tech., Zurich, 1965. Sr. engr. Aircraft Armaments, Inc., Cockeysville, Md., 1958-59; rsch. engr. Sulzer Bros., Ltd., Winterthur, Switzerland, 1960-62; project engr. No. Rsch. and Engring. Corp., Cambridge, Mass., 1965-67; rsch. leader Air Force Aerospace Rsch. Lab., Dayton, Ohio, 1967-75, Air Force Aero Propulsion Lab., Dayton, 1975-91; dir. NATO Adv. Group for Aerospace R & D, Paris, 1991-94; engring. cons. Hillsborough, NC, 1994-95, Hot Springs Village, Ark., 1995—2003, Henderson, Nev., 2003—. Mem. tech. adv. com., von Karman Inst. for Fluid Dynamics, Rhode-St-Genese, Belgium, 1988-94, bd. dirs.; lectr. in field. Contbr. articles to profl. jours. 1st lt., USAF, 1962-65. Recipient Cliff Garrett Turbo Machinery award Soc. Automotive Engrs., 1986; named Fed. Profl. Employee of Yr. Dayton C. of C., 1975; fellow Air Force Wright Aeronautical Labs., 1987; named Hon. Prof., Inst. Engring. Thermophysics, Chinese Acad. Scis. and Beijing U. Aeronautics and Astronautics, 1994. Fellow AIAA (assoc. editor 1980-82, Air Breathing Propulsion award 1979), ASME (chmn. turbomachinery com. gas turbine divsn. 1973-75, mem. exec. com. 1977-82, chmn. 1980-81, program chmn. internat. gas turbine conf. 1976, Beijing internat. gas turbine symposium 1985, mem. nat. nominating com. 1985-87, mem. TOPC bd. on rsch. 1985-88, mem.-at-large energy conversion group 1986-88, mem. bd. comm. 1989-91, editor Jour. Engring. for Gas Turbines and Power 1983-88, chmn. bd. editors 1989-91, founder, editor Jour. Turbomachinery 1986-88, mem. internat. adv. com. 1995-96, R. Tom Sawyer award 1993). Achievements include introduction of wide-chord integrally-bladed fan, introduction of swept blading into mil. aircraft turbine engines; 5 patents in field. Home and Office: 363 Marlin Cove Rd Henderson NV 89012-4829 Home Phone: 702-837-1344; Office Phone: 702-837-1344. E-mail: wennco1@cox.net.

WENRICH, JOHN WILLIAM, college president; b. York, Pa., June 8, 1937; s. Ralph Chester and Helen Louise (McCollam) W.; m. Linda Larsen, June 23, 1961 (dec. Sept. 1966); 1 child, Thomas Allen; m. Martha Gail Lofberg, Sept. 1, 1967; 1 child, Margaret Ann AB, Princeton U., 1959; MA, U. Mich., 1961, PhD, 1968. Fgn. service officer Dept. State, Washington, 1962-65; rep. Internat. Devel. Found., NYC, 1965-66; project dir. U. Mich., Ann Arbor, 1966-69; asst. to pres. Coll. San Mateo, Calif., 1969-71; v.p. Ferris State U., Big Rapids, Mich., 1971-75, pres., 1984-88, Canada Coll., Redwood City, Calif., 1975-79, Santa Ana Coll., Calif., 1979-84; chancellor San Diego C.C. Dist., 1988-90, Dallas (Tex.) C.C., 1990—2003, chancellor emeritus, 2003—. Co-author: Leadership in Administration of Technical and Vocational Education, 1974, Administration of Vocational Education. Recipient Meritorious Service medal Dept. State, 1966; Hinsdale scholar Sch. Edn. U. Mich., 1968 Avocations: bridge, tennis, travel. Home: 3504 Springbrook St Dallas TX 75205-4337 Office: 4343 North Hwy 67 Mesquite TX 75150-2095 Home Phone: 214-521-9038; Office Phone: 972-860-7494. E-mail: bwenrich@dcccd.edu.

WENSINGER, ARTHUR STEVENS, literature and language professor, writer, translator; b. Grosse Pointe, Mich., Mar. 9, 1926; s. Carl Franklin and Suzanne (Stevens) W. Grad., Phillips Acad. Andover, 1944; BA, Dartmouth Coll., 1948; MA, U. Mich., 1951, PhD, 1958; postgrad., U. Munich, 1948, postgrad., 1950—51, U. Innsbruck, 1953—54. Instr., asst. prof., assoc. prof. Wesleyan U., Middletown, Conn., 1955-68, prof. German and humanities, 1968-93, Marcus Taft prof. German and humanities, 1977-93, prof. emeritus, 1994—, chmn. dept. German lang. and lit., 1971-93, also sr. tutor Coll. Letters; pres. Friends of Davison Art Ctr.; co-editor Higganum Hill Books, 2003—. Mem. selection com. German Acad. Exch. Svc., 1980-92. Author: Hogarth on High Life, 1970, 2d edit., 2007, Plays by Arthur Schnitzler, 1982-1983, 1995; translator, editor (with W. Gropius): The Theater of the Bauhaus, 1961, rev. edit., 1996, translator, editor: The Letters and Journals of Paula Modersohn-Becker, 1983, 2d edit., 1990, Querelle: The Film Book, 1983, Franz Kafka: Pictures of a Life, 1984; translator: Marlene Dietrich: Portraits, 1984, Shabbat (Peter Stefan Jungk), 1985, Hanna Schygulla and R.W. Fassbinder, 1986, Kaethe Kollwitz: The Work in Color, 1988, Niklas Frank, In the Shadow of the Reich, 1991, (plays) Arthur Schnitzler; co-translator: Kafka: The Sons, 1989, Günter Grass, Two States-One Nation?, 1990; editor: Stone Island (Peter S. Boynton), 1973; co-editor: Hesse's Siddhartha, 1962; continuing editor: Correspondence of Norman Douglas, 1868-1952, continuing translator: plays of Schnitzler, contbr.: Columbia U. Database CD-ROM for quotations, aphorisms, 1995—, contbr. (DVD): Munich 1948/2005, 2007; contbr. articles to profl. jours., exhbn. and symposium catalog articles; author: (exhbn. and symposium catalog articles) Norman Douglas, 2000, 2004, 2007. Wesleyan Ctr. for Humanities fellow, 1974, Reynolds fellow, 1950-51, Fulbright fellow, 1954-55, Danforth fellow, 1959, Ford Found. fellow, 1970-71; Inter Nations grantee, 1978, 82, NEH rsch. grantee, 1993. Mem. MLA, Am. Assn. Tchrs. German, Heinrich von Kleist Gesellschaft, Internat. Brecht Soc., Kafka Soc. Am., Auden Soc., Soc. Preservation New Eng. Antiquities, Conn. Acad. Arts and Scis., Yale Libr. Assocs., Haddam, Conn. Land Trust, Grosse Ile Nature and Land Conservancy, Phi Beta Kappa, Phi Kappa Phi, Delta Tau Delta. Home: Candlewood Farm 95 Jacoby Rd Higganum CT 06441-4225 Office: Wesleyan U Fisk Hall Middletown CT 06459-6082 Office Phone: 860-685-3357. Business E-Mail: awensinger@wesleyan.edu.

WENSITS, DAVID L., aerospace transportation executive; b. Sept. 19, 1947; AAS in Aviation Maintenance, Purdue U., 1968, BS in Indsl. Supervision, 1970. Mgr. F136 reliabilioty, maintainability and safety Rolls-Royce Corp., Indpls., 1970—. With U.S. Army, 1971-73. Recipient Aerospace Maintenance award AIAA, 1996. Office: Rolls-Royce Corp SPEED Code 020 PO Box 420 Indianapolis IN 46206-0420 Home Phone: 317-486-0586; Office Phone: 317-230-4949. E-mail: david.l.wensits@rolls-royce.com, davewensits@comcast.net.

WENSKI, THOMAS GERARD, bishop; b. West Palm Beach, Fla., Oct. 18, 1950; s. Chester Stephen and Louise Mary (Zawacki) W. AA, St. John Vianney Sem., Miami, Fla., 1970; BA, St. Vincent De Paul Sem., Boynton Beach, Fla., 1972, MDiv, 1975; MA, Fordham U. Ordained priest Roman Cath. Ch., 1976. Assoc. pastor Corpus Christi Cath. Ch., Miami, 1976-79; assoc. dir. Haitian Cath. Ctr., Miami, 1979-84, dir., 1984-98; pastor Notre Dame d'Haiti Roman Cath. Ch., Miami, 1984-98, aux. bishop, 1997—2004; bishop Diocese of Orlando, Fla., 2004—. Episcopal vicar to cultural groups, Miami, 1990-2003; dir. Cath. Charities Archdiocese Miami, 1996-2003; former chmn. migration com. US Conf. Cath. Bishops, chair Devel. and World Peace Internat. Policy Com., 2005. Office: Diocese of Orlando PO Box 1800 Orlando FL 32802 Office Phone: 407-246-4815.

WENTWORTH, DENNIS LADD, historic sites and parks administrator; b. Rochester, NH, Jan. 14, 1950; s. Arnold Harry Wentworth and Cora Rachel Downs; m. Ann Elizabeth Kennedy, Dec. 24, 1973; children: Rachel Ann, Margaret Kennedy, Trevor Downs. BA in Anthropology, Beloit Coll., 1972; MA in Anthropology, SUNY, Albany, 1988. Historic site asst. NY State Parks Bur. Hist. Sites, Waterford, 1975—96, archaeologist, 1976—87, collection mgr., 1988—90; regional hist. reservation supr. NY State Parks Saratoga Coastal Region, Saratoga Springs, 1987, NY State Parks Taconic Region, Staatsburg, 1992—95, 2005—, dir. regional ops., 1995—2005. Contbr. articles to profl. jours. Elder Pleasant Plains Presbyn. Ch., Staatsburg, 1990—92; mem. Hist. Hyde Park Corridor Commn., NY, 2000—; bd. dirs. Lyndhurst Property Coun., 2005—; bd. trustees Quitman Resource Ctr., Rhinebeck, NY; elder, deacon 1st United Presbyn. Ch., Troy, NY, 1982—90; elder 1st Presbyn. Ch., Poughkeepsie, NY, 1992—. Recipient Black Belt, World Tae Kwon Do Assn., 1998. Mem.: Hudson River Heritage (pres. 1994—95), Mid-Atlantic Assn. Museums. Avocations: gardening, music, hiking, walking, antiques. Home: 137 E Market St Rhinebeck NY 12572 Office: NY State Parks Staatsburg NY 12580 Personal E-mail: dennislw@frontiernet.net. Business E-Mail: dennis.wentworth@oprhp.state.ny.us.

WENTWORTH, DIANA VON WELANETZ, author; b. LA, Mar. 4, 1941; d. Eugene and Marguerite (Rufi) Webb; m. Frederic Paul von Welanetz, Nov. 2, 1963 (dec. Mar. 19, 1989); 1 child, Lexi Welanetz Bursin; m. Theodore S. Wentworth, Dec. 9, 1989; stepchildren: Christina-Wentworth Coyne, Kathryn Allison Wentworth Purdy. Student, UCLA, 1958-60. Ptnr. von Welanetz Cooking Workshop, LA, 1968-85; host TV series New Way Gourmet, 1983-86; founder Inside Edge Found. Edn., Calif., 1985-93. Spkr. in field. Author: The Pleasure of Your Company, 1976 (Cookbook of Yr.), With Love from Your Kitchen, 1976, The Art of Buffet Entertaining, 1978, The Von Welanetz Guide to Ethnic Ingredients, 1983, L.A. Cuisine, 1985, Celebrations, 1985, Chicken Soup for the Soul Cookbook, 1995, Send Me Someone, 2001, Chicken Soup to Inspire The Body and Soul, 2003. Treas. Louise L. Hay Found., Carson, Calif., 1988—; advisor Women of Vision, Calif., 1995—. Mem. Internat. Food, Wine & Travel Writers Assn., Angels of Arts/Orange County Performing Arts Ctr., Ctr. Club, Confrérie de La Chaîne des Rôtisseurs, N. Am. Travel Journalists Assn. Avocations: painting, art, travel, design. Office: 4631 Teller Ave Ste 100 Newport Beach CA 92660-8105 E-mail: diana@dianawentworth.com.

WENTWORTH, EARL JEFFREY, lawyer, realtor, state legislator; b. San Antonio, Nov. 20, 1940; s. Earl and Margaret Wentworth; m. Karla Whitsitt; children: Jason, Matthew. BA, Tex. A&M U., 1962; JD, Tex. Tech. U., 1972. Bar: Tex. 1971, DC. 1972. Staff mem. U.S. Congressman Bob Price; pvt. practice law San Antonio; mem. Tex. Ho. of Reps., 1988-92, Tex. Senate, 1993—. County commr. Bexar County, 1977-82; bd. regents Tex. State U. Sys., 1987-88. Spl. agt. U.S. Army Counterintelligence Corps, 1962—65. Republican. Office: PO Box 12068 Austin TX 78711-2068 also: Ste 925 1250 NE Loop 410 San Antonio TX 78209-1500 Office Phone: 210-826-7800. Personal E-mail: ejeffrey@swbell.net. Business E-Mail: jeff.wentworth@senate.state.tx.us.

WENTWORTH, JACK ROBERTS, business educator, consultant; b. Elgin, Ill., June 11, 1928; s. William Franklin and Elizabeth (Roberts) W.; m. Rosemary Ann Pawlak, May 30, 1956 (dec. April 29, 2006); children: William, Barbara. Student, Carleton Coll., 1946-48; BS, Ind. U., 1950, MBA, 1954, DBA, 1959. Coord. displays Cadillac divsn., Gen. Motors Corp., Detroit, 1954-56; asst. prof. bus., assoc. dir. research Sch. of Bus. Ind. U., Bloomington, 1957-60, assoc. prof., dir. rsch., 1960-70, prof., 1970-93, chmn. MBA program, 1970-76, chmn. dept., faculty rep. NCAA, 1978-85, dean Sch. of Bus., 1984-93, Arthur M. Weimer prof., 1993-97, Arthur M. Weimer prof. emeritus, 1997—. Mktg. cons., Bloomington, 1960—; bd. dirs. Kimball Internat., Jasper, Ind. Editor: (monograph) Marketing Horizons, 1965; exec. editor Bus. Horizons, 1960-70 Served to 1st lt. USAF, 1950-53. Recipient Teaching award MBA Assn., 1973, 78, 81, 84, 85, Svc. award Assn. for Bus. and Econ. Rsch., 1983; Disting. Alumni Svc. award Ind. U., 1999. Mem. Am. Mktg. Assn. (v.p. 1971-73), Grad. Mgmt. Admissions Coun. (chmn. bd. trustees 1977-78), Univ. Club, Masons, Beta Gamma Sigma (pres. Alpha of Ind. chpt. 1971-72, bd. govs. 1986-98, nat. pres. 1994-96). Republican. Methodist. Avocations: travel, bicycling, magic, model railroading, sports. Office: Indiana Univ Kelley Sch Bus Bloomington IN 47405 Personal E-mail: lurojack@yahoo.com.

WENTWORTH, LAVERNE WELLBORN, curriculum consultant; b. Bryan, Tex., July 26, 1929; d. Charles Floyd and Ethel Berneice (Swanzy) Wellborn; m. Thomas Richard Wentworth, 1951 (wid. 1986); children: Jason Charles, Rance Richard, Paige Lynn Wentworth Honkerkamp. BA, Baylor U., Waco, Tex., 1949, MA in Am. Civilization, 1954; postgrad., State Tchrs. U. N.J., Southwestern State Tchrs. U., San Marcus, Tex., U. Ky., Lexington. Sch. tchr. Tex. and NJ, 1949—58; mem. JFK White House Paper on Youth, 1963; comm. edn. instr. Georgetown Coll., Ky., 1988—90; coord. Elderhostel program U. Ky., Lexington, 1992—2001; Boyce Sch. instr. So. Bapt. Theol. Seminary, Lexington, 1990; pers. dept. Cardinel Hill Rehab. Hosp., Lexington, 1987-93. Tchg. cons. US Steel Co., Trenton, NJ, 1957; cons., instr. Interdenominational Young People Confs., Pocono Plateau, Pa., 1958-87; field supr. US Dept. Commerce, Bur. of Census, Washington, 1970-88; guest lectr. Georgetown (Ky.) Coll. Author: (books) Manifest Destiny in Walt Whitman's Prose, 1954, Tryst, 1959 Pres. Princeton Theol. Sem. Wives, 1956-57, Rotary Anne, W.Va., 1982-83; mem. Scott County Women's Club, Georgetown, 1987-93; mem. by-laws com. Ky. Bapt. Fellowship, 2004—10; resident counsel Windsor Gardens, Georgetown. Recipient Ship of State award W.Va. State of Sec., 1983. Mem. AAUW (pres. 1987-90), Scott County Hist. Soc., Georgetown Coll. Woman's Assn. (life), Faith Bapt. Ch. of Georgetown (tchr., chmn. by-laws 1998—2006).

WENTWORTH, LYNN A., housing products company executive, former telecommunications industry executive; b. Aug. 16, 1958; BSBA, Babson Coll.; MS in Taxation, Bentley Coll.; MBA Ga. State U. Various positions with numerous depts. including handling tax, strategic planning, investor rels. and finl. planning Bellsouth Corp., 1985—2003, v.p., treas., Comm. Group Atlanta, 2003—06; sr. v.p., CFO, treas. BlueLinx Holdings Inc., Atlanta, 2007—. Tutor C.W. Hill Elem. Sch., Atlanta. Mem.: AICPA, Ga. Soc. CPA's. Office: BlueLinx Holdings Inc 4300 Wildwood Pkwy Atlanta GA 30339 *

WENTWORTH, MURRAY JACKSON, artist, educator; b. Boston, Jan. 18, 1927; s. Harold Squires and Mary Louise (Murray) W.; m. Elaine Magnuson, June 16, 1953; 1 child, Janet Louise. Diploma, Art Inst. Boston, 1950. Advt. artist Agy. Art Svcs., Boston, 1950-58; instr. Art Inst. Boston, 1958-78; artist, instr. Norwell, Mass., 1968—. Group shows, Allied Artists Am., 1980, 82 (Silver medal 1980), Allied Art Am., 1982 (Obrig prize 1982), Am. Watercolor Soc., 1980 (Dolphin fellow 1980), Rocky Mount Nat. Exhibition, 1982 (Grumbacher award 1982). Cpl. U.S. Army, 1945-47. Recipient Hudson Valley Art Assn. award, 1991, Whitney Meml. award, 1996, Guild Boston Artists award, 1992, Watercolor award Acad. Artists' Assn., 1997, Daler Rowney award, 1998, Hudson Valley Art Assn. Watercolor award, 1998. Mem. NAD (Pike Meml. award 1986, award of merit 1997), Allied Artists Am. (Mina Mora Meml. award for watercolor 1997), Am. Watercolor Soc., New Eng. Watercolor Soc. (Grumbacher gold medal 1989). Home Phone: 607-432-6322; Office Phone: 607-432-6322.

WENTWORTH, THEODORE SUMNER, lawyer; b. Bklyn., July 18, 1938; s. Theodore Sumner and Alice Ruth (Wortmann) W.; m. Sharon Linelle Arkush, 1965 (dec. 1987); children: Christina Linn, Kathryn Allison; m. Diana Webb von Welanetz, 1989; 1 stepchild, Lexi von Welanetz. AA, Am. River Coll., 1958; JD, U. Calif., Hastings, 1962. Bar: Calif. 1963, U.S. Dist. Ct. (no. and ctrl. dists.) Calif., U.S. Ct. Appeals (9th cir.), U.S. Supreme Ct.; diplomate Nat. Bd. Trial Advocacy; cert. trial lawyer Calif. State Bar. Assoc. Adams, Hunt & Martin, Santa Ana, Calif., 1963-66; ptnr. Hunt, Liljestrom & Wentworth, Santa Ana, 1967-77; pres. Solabs Corp.; chmn. bd., exec. v.p. Plant Warehouse, Inc., Hawaii, 1974-82; ptnr. Law Offices of Wentworth, Paoli & Purdy, Newport Beach & Temecula, Calif.; judge pro tem Superior Ct. Attys. Panel Harbor Mcpl. Ct.; owner, CEO Home Guardens, Inc., Murrietta, Calif., 2000—05. Owner Eagles Ridge Ranch, Temecula, 1977-2003. Author: Build a Better Spouse Trap, 2002. Pres., bd. dirs. Santa Ana-Tustin Cmty. Chest, 1972; v.p., trustee South Orange County United Way, 1973-75; pres. Orange County Fedn. Funds, 1972-73; bd. dirs. Orange County Mental Health Assn. Mem. ABA, Am. Bd. Trial Advs., State Bar Calif., Orange County Bar Assn. (dir. 1972-76), Calif. Trial Lawyers Assn. (bd. govs. 1968-70), Orange County Trial Lawyers Assn. (pres. 1967-68), Bahia Corinthian Yacht Club (founder). Achievements include research in vaidika principles, natural law, quantum physics and mechanics. Office: 4631 Teller Ave Ste 100 Newport Beach CA 92660-8105 also: 41530 Enterprise Cir S Temecula CA 92590-4816 Home Phone: 949-212-7000; Office Phone: 949-752-7711. Personal E-mail: oclawfirm@aol.com.

WENTZ, JEFFREY LEE, information systems executive; b. Philippi, W.Va., Nov. 29, 1956; s. William Henry and Edith Marie (McBee) W.; m. Phuong Thi Thanh, Nov. 17, 2001. AS in Data Processing, Fairmont State Coll., W.Va., 1978, BS in Acctg., 1978. Programmer/analyst U.S. Dept. Energy, Morgantown, W.Va., 1978-79; analyst Middle South Svcs., New Orleans, 1979-81; sr. analyst Bank of Am., San Francisco, 1981-83; pres., info. sys. cons. Wentz Cons. Inc., San Francisco, 1983-2000; dir. tech. solutions Charles Schwab & Co., San Francisco, 2000—. E-mail: wentzcon@earthlink.net.

WENTZ, PETER (PETER LEWIS KINGSTON WENTZ III), musician; b. Wilmette, Ill., June 5, 1979; Student, DePaul U. Bassist, vocalist & lyricist Fall Out Boy, 2001—; owner Clandestine Industries, Decaydence Records. Author: The Boy With the Thorn in His Side, 2005; musician: (albums) Fall Out Boy's Evening Out With Your Girl, 2002, Take This to Your Grave, 2003, From Under the Cork Tree, 2005, Infinity on High, 2007, (songs) Sugar, We're Going Down, 2003 (MTV2 award, MTV Video Music Awards, 2005), Dance, Dance, 2005 (Choice Music Single, Choice Rock Track, Teen Choice Awards, 2006, Viewer's Choice award, MTV Video Music Awards, 2006); actor: (films) Bedussey, 2005. Recipient Choice Music Rock Group award, Teen Choice Awards, 2006. Office: Fall Out Boy Inc Box 219 1187 Wilmette Ave Wilmette IL 60091

WENTZ, SIDNEY FREDERICK, insurance company executive, foundation administrator; b. Dallas, Mar. 27, 1932; s. Howard Beck and Emmy Lou (Cawthon) W.; m. Barbara Strait, Sept. 9, 1961; children: Eric, Jennifer, Robin. AB, Princeton U., 1954; LLB, Harvard U., 1960. Bar: N.Y. 1961. Atty. White & Case, NYC, 1960-65, Western Electric Co., 1965-66, AT&T Corp., 1966-67; with Crum & Forster Inc., Morristown, N.J., 1967—, v.p., gen. counsel, 1967-71, sr. v.p., gen. counsel, 1971-72, exec. v.p., 1972, pres., 1972-87, chmn. bd., 1987-88, chmn. exec. com., 1988-90, also bd. dirs.; chmn. bd. Robert Wood Johnson Found., Princeton, N.J., 1989-99. Trustee Morristown Meml. Hosp., 1974-96, Drew U., 1991—. Served to lt. (j.g.) USNR, 1954-57. Mem. Morris County Golf Club, Sakonnet (R.I.) Golf Club, Baltusrol Golf Club, Jupiter Hills (Fla.) Golf Club, Loblolly Pines (Fla.) Golf Club, Carnegie Abby Golf Club (R.I.).

WENTZ, WILLIAM HENRY, JR., aerospace engineer, educator; b. Wichita, Kans., Dec. 18, 1933; BS in Mech. Engring. cum laude, Wichita State U., 1955, MS in Aeronautical Engring., 1961; PhD in Engring. Mechanics, U. Kans., 1969. Lic. profl. engr., Kans. Liaison engr. Beech Aircraft, 1952-53; propulsion engr. Boeing Co., Wichita, Kans., 1955; instr. mech. engring. Wichita State U., 1957-58; aerodynamicist Boeing Co., Wichita, 1958-63; from asst. prof. to assoc. prof. aeronautical engring. Wichita State U., 1963-75, prof. aeronautical engring., 1975-83, Gates-Learjet prof. aeronautical engring., 1983-86, disting. prof. aerospace engring., 1986-98, dir. Ctr. Basic and Applied Rsch. Inst. Aviation Rsch., 1986-89, exec. dir. Nat. Inst. Aviation Rsch., 1988-97; sr. fellow Nat. Inst. Aviation Rsch., 1997-98; disting. prof. emeritus aerospace engring., exec. dir. emer. Nat. Inst. Aviation Rsch., 1999; ret. Dir. rsch. projects Boeing Co., 1960, 61, NASA, 1964-66, 66-68, 70-71, 71-83, 86-87, 86-88, 82-87, Dept. of Def., 1986-88, Kans. Tech. Enterprise Corp., 1988-96, FAA, 1986-96. Contbr. articles to profl. jours. With USAF, 1955-57. Recipient Disting. Engr. Svc. award Wichita State U., 1999, Kans. Aviation Honors award Gov. Bill Graves, 1999; Sci. Faculty fellow NSF, 1967-68. Fellow AIAA (assoc., past chmn. Wichita sect., Outstanding advisor student chpt. 1964, 65, 70, Gen. Aviation award 1981, Engr. of Yr. award Wichita sect. 1992, Engr. of Yr. award Region V 1991-92; mem. Soc. Automotive Engrs. (Ralph R. Teeter award 1973), Sigma Gamma Tau, Tau Beta Pi. Personal E-mail: william.wentz@cox.net.

WENTZEL, PAUL H., JR., state agency administrator; b. 1949; m. Kathy Wentzel; 1 child, Sally. BA in polit. sci., MA in polit. sci., East Stroudsburg U. Rsch. analyst House Bus. and Commerce Com.; exec. asst. Pa. Dept. Banking, 1981—. Office: 333 Market St 16th fl Harrisburg PA 17101-2290 Office Phone: 717-787-2112.

WENZEL, LOREN ALVIN, finance educator; b. Dec. 12, 1945; s. Alvin Karl Gustav and Lois LaVonne (Kuechenmeister) W.; children: Lisa Anne (Wenzel) Szumilas, Karl Louis, Sara Kirsten Wenzel; m. Nylah Onalee. DBA, U. Memphis, 1990. Asst. prof. acctg. Wichita (Kans.) State U., 1987-88; prof. acctg. Mankato (Minn.) State U., 1988-98, U. Md. European Divsn., Heidelberg, Germany, 1996-97, Buena Vista U., Storm Lake, Iowa, 1998-99, Austin Peay State U., Clarksville, Tenn., 1999-2000; prof. and head divsn. accountancy and legal environment Marshall U., 2000—, Elizabeth McDowell Lewis endowed chair Lewis Coll. Bus., 2000—05, prof., 2005—, Bharatiya Vidya Bhavan, Bangalore, India, 2005—. Founder, pres. W.Va. Coun. Educators, 2003—05. Contbr. articles to profl.

publs. Named W.Va. Outstanding Acctg. Educator of Yr., W.Va. Soc. CPAs, 2004. Office: Marshall U Lewis Coll Bus Div Acctancy/Legal Environ One John Marshall Dr Huntington WV 25545 Office Phone: 304-696-2660. Business E-Mail: wenzel@marshall.edu.

WERBA, GABRIEL, public relations consultant; b. Paris, Feb. 28, 1930; came to U.S., 1941; s. Aron and Dina (Lewin) W.; m. Barrie Celia Sakolsky, June 1, 1952; children: Dean Steffen, Annmarie Alexandra Bragdon. BA in Journalism, U. Tex., 1948; postgrad., NYU Grad. Sch. Bus., 1948-49, NYU Sch. Law, 1961-62. Account exec. Harold C. Meyers & Co., NYC, 1959-61; dir. pub. rels. and advt. Yardney Electric Corp., NYC, 1961-63, 57-59; sr. assoc. Shiefman & Assocs., Detroit, 1963-66; account exec. Merrill Lynch, Detroit, 1966-70; exec. v.p. Shiefman Werba & Assocs., Detroit, 1970-73; sr. v.p., exec. v.p., pres., chief oper. officer Anthony M. Franco, Inc., Detroit, 1973-88; pres., chief exec. officer The Werba Group, Inc. and Gabriel Werba and Assocs., Inc., Detroit, 1988-94; prin. Durocher, Dixson, Werba, L.L.C., Detroit, 1994—2003; pres. Gabriel Werba & Assoc. LLC, Farmington Hills, Mich., 2004—05, Gabriel Werba & Assocs., Farmington Hills, 2005—. Bd. dirs. Intrepid Corp., Detroit. Contbr. articles to profl. jours. Bd. dirs. Oakland Citizens League, Detroit, 1970-93, Detroit Symphony Orch. Hall, 1985—, Detroit Chamber Winds, 1985-91, The Common Ground Sanctuary, Mich., 1989-2007, vice chmn., Bloomfield Hills, 2000-06, adv. bd., 2007—; bd. dirs. The Attic Theatre, Detroit, 1989-93, The Children's Ctr., Detroit; mem. strategic planning com., chmn. comm. com., bd. dirs., 1989-95, 1996-2002, 03-05, adv. bd., 1995-96, 2002-03; bd. dirs. NATAS, Detroit, 1993-98, The Jewish Cmty. Coun. Met. Detroit, 1989-95, 2004-2007, co-chair commn. com., 2006-2007, Margaret W. Montgomery Hosp., 1993-95, adv. bd. 1988-93; bd. dirs. Lawrence P. Doss Found., 2002—, 1st vice-chmn., 2002—; mem. comm. com. Detroit Inst. Arts, 1986-92, exhibits com., 1990-2001. Named to, PRSA-Detroit Hall of Fame, 2001. Mem. Nat. Investor Rels. Inst. (past dir., pres. Detroit chpt., spkr., panelist), Pub. Rels. Soc. Am. (bd. dirs. Detroit chpt. 1988-94, pres. 1992-93, past treas. Detroit Counselors' sect., past co-chair sr. coun., past co-chair, nat. sect. coun., past nat. chmn. fin. sect., mem. bd. ethics and profl. stds. 2003-06, chair audit com. 2005-07, spkr., panelist), Fin. Analysts Soc. Detroit (past chmn. pub. info. com.), Am. Mensa (bd. dirs. 1975-91, 2003-05, nat. chmn. 1979-83), Internat. Mensa (bd. dirs. 1979-83, 85-93). Avocations: art collecting, concerts, theater. Home: 21920 River Ridge Tr Farmington Hills MI 48335 Office: Gabriel Werba & Assoc 21920 River Ridge Tr Farmington MI 48335 Office Phone: 248-478-1281. Personal E-mail: gabewerba@sbcglobal.net.

WERBITT, WARREN, gastroenterologist, educator; b. Phila., Jan. 29, 1939; s. Saull Boris and Pearl (Weiner) W.; m. Drue Natalie Engman Werbitt, Aug. 30, 1964; children: Julie Michele, Jeffrey Brian. BS in Pharmacy, Temple U., 1960; D in Osteopathy, U. Osteo. Med. and Health Sci., Des Moines, 1966; MD, Drexel U. Coll. Med., 1973. Diplomate Am. Osteo. Bd. Internal Medicine, also sub-splty. bd. Gastroenterology; diplomate Am. Bd. Internal Medicine, also sub-splty. bd. Gastroenterology. Intern Doctor's Hosp., Columbus, Ohio, 1966-67, resident in internal medicine, 1967-68, Kennedy Meml. Hosps., Cherry Hill, NJ 1968-69, Mercy Cath. Med. Ctr., Phila., 1969-70, Drexel U. Coll. Medicine, Phila., 1971—72, fellow in gastroenterology, 1970-71, 72-74, instr., 1973—, attending physician and cons. in gastroenterology, 1977-94; instr. Phila. Coll. Osteo. Medicine, Phila., 1973-75, chmn. divsn. gastroenterology, 1975-77; clin. assoc. prof. medicine U. Medicine and Dentistry, NJ, 1977—; attending physician and cons. in gastroenterology Vet. Adminstrn. Hosp., Phila., 1972-75; chmn. Div. Gastroenterology, Dept. Medicine Phila. Coll. Osteopathic Medicine, 1975-77; chmn. Dept. Medicine Kennedy Meml. Hosp. U. Med. Ctr., Cherry Hill, 1979-81, chmn. subsect. Gastroenterology, 1979-87. Contbg. editor NJ Jour. for Osteo. Physicians and Surgeons, 1980—; mem. scientific adv. com. Phila. chpt. Nat. Found. Ileitis and Colitis, Inc., 1982—; contbr. articles to profl. jours. Recipient Profl. Svc. award Med. Soc. N.J., 1991. Fellow Am. Coll. Physicians, Am. Coll. Gastroenterology, Am. Gastroenterol. Assn., Acad. Med. N.J.; mem. AMA, Am. Soc. Gastrointestinal Endoscopy, Am. Soc. Parenteral and Enteric Nutrition, Am. Inst. Ultrasound in Medicine, Am. Assn. Gynecologic Laparoscopists, Phila. Gastrointestinal Rsch. Forum, State Med. Soc. N.J., Camden County Med. Soc., N.J. Endoscopic Soc., Del. Valley Soc. for Gastrointestinal Endoscopy, South Jersey Gastroenterol. Soc., Am. Osteo. Assn., N.J. Soc. Osteo. Physicians and Surgeons, Am. Coll. Osteopathic Internists, Camden County Osteo. Assn., Am. Cancer Soc. (bd. dirs. N.J. chpt.), Crohn's and Colitis Found. Am. Inc. (Phila. and Del.), Pres.'s Circle Am. U., N.Y. Acad. Scis., John Sherman Myers Soc., Med. Club Phila., Lambda Omicron Gamma. Avocations: golf, running, music, reading, american history. Office: Profl Gastroenterology Assn 1939 Route 70 E Ste 250 Cherry Hill NJ 08003-4507 Office Phone: 856-429-4433. Business E-Mail: progastro@comcast.net.

WERBNER, MARK S., lawyer; b. San Antonio, Oct. 8, 1954; BA with high honors, U. Tex., Austin, 1975; JD cum laude, So. Meth. U., Dallas, 1978. Bar: Tex. 1978, US Dist. Ct. (all dists. Tex.) 1978, US Ct. Appeals (5th cir.) 1978, US Supreme Ct. Atty. Carrington, Coleman, Sloman & Blumenthal, Dallas; founder, ptnr. Sayles Werbner, P.C., Dallas, 1994—. Named one of Best Lawyers in Dallas, D Mag., 2001, 2003, 2005, 2007. Master: Patrick E. Higginbotham Inn Ct.; fellow: Internat. Soc. Barristers, Am. Coll. Trial Lawyers; mem.: Dallas Bar Assn. (bd. dir. 2003), Am. Bd. Trial Lawyers. Office: Sayles Werbner PC 4400 Renaissance Tower 1201 Elm Street Dallas TX 75270 Office Phone: 214-939-8711. Office Fax: 214-939-8787. E-mail: mwerbner@swtriallaw.com.

WERDEGAR, KATHRYN MICKLE, state supreme court justice; b. San Francisco; d. Benjamin Christie and Kathryn Marie (Clark) Mickle; m. David Werdegar; children: Maurice Clark, Matthew Mickle. Student, Wellesley Coll., 1954—55; AB with honors, U. Calif., Berkeley, 1957; JD with highest distinction, George Washington U., 1962; JD, U. Calif., Berkeley, 1990. Bar: Calif. 1964, U.S. Dist. Ct. (no. dist.) Calif. 1964, U.S. Ct. Appeals (9th cir.) 1964, Calif. Supreme Ct. 1964. Legal asst. civil rights divsn. U.S. Dept. Justice, Washington, 1962—63; rsch. atty., author Calif. State Study Commn. on Mental Retardation, 1963—64; assoc. U. Calif. Ctr. for Study of Law and Soc., Berkeley, 1965—67; spl. cons. State Dept. Mental Health, 1967—68; cons., author Calif. Coll. Trial Judges, 1968—71; dir. criminal law divsn. Calif. Continuing Edn. of Bar, 1971—78; assoc. dean acad. and student affairs, assoc. prof. Sch. Law, U. San Francisco, 1978—81; sr. staff atty. Calif. 1st Dist. Ct. Appeal, 1981—85, Calif. Supreme Ct., 1985—91; assoc. justice Calif. 1st Dist. Ct. Appeal, 1991—94, Calif. Supreme Ct., San Francisco, 1994—. Regents' lectr. U. Calif., Berkeley, 2000. Author: Benchbook: Misdemeanor Procedure, 1971, Misdemeanor Procedure Benchbook rev., 1975, Misdemeanor Procedure Benchbook, 1983; contbr. California Continuing Education of the Bar books; editor: California Criminal Law Practice series, Discovery, 1975, California Uninsured Motorist Practice, 1973, I California Civil Procedure Before Trial, 1977. Recipient 5 Am. Jurisprudence awards, 1960—62, Charles Glover award, George Washington U., 1962, J. William Fulbright award for disting. pub. svc., George Washington U. Law Sch. Alumni Assn., 1996, Excellence in Achievement award, Calif. Alumni Assn., 1996, Roger J. Traynor Appellate Justice of Yr. award, 1996, Justice of Yr. award, Consumer Attys. of Calif., 1998, Citation award, Boalt Hall Sch. Law U. Calif., Berkeley, 2002. Mem.: Am. Law Inst., Nev./Calif. Women Judges Assn., Calif. Judges Assn., Nat. Assn. Women Judges, Calif. Supreme Ct. Hist. Soc. (bd. dir.), Order of the Coif. Office: Calif Supreme Court 350 McAllister St San Francisco CA 94102-4797 Office Phone: 415-865-7032.

WERDER, RICHARD I., JR., lawyer; b. White Plains, NY, 1957; BA magna cum laude, Canisius Coll., 1979; JD magna cum laude, U. Mich., 1982. Bar: Ohio 1984, NY 2003. Law clk. to Hon. Harry T. Edwards US Ct. Appeals (DC cir.), 1982; law clk. to Justice Byron White US Supreme Ct., 1983; assoc. Jones Day, NYC, 1984—89, ptnr., co-chmn. tech. issues practice; ptnr. Quinn, Emanuel, Urquhart, Oliver & Hedges, LLP, NYC, 2006—. Editor-in-chief Law Rev., 1982. Mem.: ABA, NY State Bar Assn., Cleve. Bar Assn., Ohio State Bar Assn., Prod. Liability Adv. Coun., Order of Coif. Office: Quinn Emanuel Urquhart Oliver & Hedges LLP 51 Madison Ave 22nd Fl New York NY 10010 Office Phone: 212-849-7231. E-mail: rickwerder@quinnemanuel.com. *

WERESH, MATTHEW JOHN, orthopedic surgeon; b. Oct. 8, 1964; BA, Wake Forest U., Winston-Salem, NC, 1987; MD, U. Iowa, Iowa City, 1991. Cert. Am. Bd. Orthop. Surgery, 1999. Orthop. resident Akron Gen. Med. Ctr., Ohio, 1989—94; orthop. trauma fellow Carolinas Med. Ctr., Charlotte, NC, 1996—97; staff mem. Des Moines Orthop. Surgeons, P.C., 1997—. Named one of Golf Digest 2006 Top Golf Doctors in Am. Fellow: Am. Assn. Orthop. Surgery; mem.: Iowa Orthop. Soc., Orthop. Trauma Assn. Office: Des Moines Orthop Surgeons 6001 Westown Pky West Des Moines IA 50266 Office Phone: 515-224-5216. Office Fax: 515-224-5140.

WERFELMAN, WILLIAM HERMAN, JR., public relations executive; b. Bridgeport, Conn., July 11, 1953; s. William H. and Helen D. (Rainier) W.; m. Patricia Aileen Maytrott, Aug. 28, 1977; children: Lauren Aileen, Juliana Aileen. BA in English, St. Bonaventure U., 1975; postgrad., Georgetown U., 1975—76. Staff writer Post-Telegram newspapers, Bridgeport, 1976—79; product publicity specialist Dictaphone Corp., Rye, NY, 1979—81; supr. press rels. GE, Fairfield, Conn., 1981—84; mgr. corp. pub. rels. Olin Corp., Stamford, Conn., 1984—90, dir. pub. rels./comm., 1990—94; v.p. external comms. Home Ins. Co., NYC, 1994—95; v.p. media rels. N.Y. Life Ins. Co., NYC, 1995—2003; first v.p. N.Y Life Ins. Co., NYC, 2003—. Mem., chmn. Zoning Bd. Appeals, Redding, Conn., 1977-89, 92-99; party recruitment chmn. Rep. Town Com., Redding, 1976-90. Recipient Fin. World Bronze award for ann. report, 1992. Mem. Internat. Assn. Bus. Communicators (Best Pub. Rels. results 1982), Pub. Rels. Soc. Am., Nat. Assn. Investors (Best Ann Report 1988, 90). Republican. Roman Catholic. Avocations: writing, investments. Home: 195 Gallows Hill Rd Redding CT 06896-1423 Office: NY Life Ins Co Rm 516 51 Madison Ave New York NY 10010-1603

WERKING, RICHARD HUME, librarian, historian, academic administrator; b. Charleston, SC, Sept. 29, 1943; s. F. Woody and Mary S. (Prissinger) W. BA, U. Evansville, 1966; MA in Am. History, U. Wis., 1967, PhD in Am. History, 1973; MA in Librarianship, U. Chgo., 1975. Instr. history Northland Coll., Ashland, Wis., 1967-68; pers. staffing specialist U.S. Civil Svc. Commn., Indpls., 1968-69; reference libr. Lawrence U., Appleton, Wis., 1975-77; head reference dept., asst./acting libr. dir. U. Miss., Oxford, 1977-81, asst. prof. history, 1977-81; assoc. libr. dir., asst. prof. history Trinity U., San Antonio, Tex., 1981-83, libr. dir., assoc. prof. history, 1983-91; libr. dir., assoc. dean, prof. history U.S. Naval Acad., Annapolis, Md., 1991—. Author: The Master Architects: Building the U.S. Foreign Service, 1977. With Ind. Nat. Guard, 1961—65, with US Army, 1962. Sparks fellow Phi Kappa Phi, 1966, postdoctoral fellow Coun. on Libr. Resources, 1974. Mem. ALA (chmn. coll. librs. sect. 1987-88), Soc. Historians of Am. Fgn. Rels. Office: US Naval Acad Nimitz Libr 589 Mcnair Rd Annapolis MD 21402-1323 Business E-Mail: rwerking@usna.edu.

WERKMAN, SIDNEY LEE, psychiatrist, educator; b. Washington, May 3, 1927; AB, Williams Coll., 1948; MD, Cornell U., 1952. Diplomate Am. Bd. Psychiatry and Neurology, Am. Bd. Child Psychiatry. Intern U. Va. Hosp., Charlottesville; resident in psychiatry Yale U., 1953-55, St. Elizabeth's Hosp., Washington, 1955-56; assoc. prof. psychiatry George Washington U., Washington, 1960-69; prof. U. Colo. Sch. Medicine, Denver, 1969-87; dir. div. adolescent psychiatry Children's Hosp. of Washington, 1965-69; clin. prof. Georgetown U. Sch. Medicine, Washington, 1989—; psychiatrist Capital Area Permanente Med. Group, Washington, 1990—. Cons. grants NIMH, Washington, 1982—, guest rschr., 1984—85. Author: The Role of Psychiatry in Medical Education, 1966, Only a Little Time: A Chronicle of Dying, 1972, Bringing Up Children Overseas, 1977 Bd. dirs. Med. U. So. Africa, Performing Arts Soc., Nat. Mus. Arts, Young Concert Artists Assn., Washington Concert Operas. Master sgt. U.S. Army. Fellow, Commonwealth Fund, Florence, Italy, 1963—64, NEH, 1979. Mem. Am. Psychiat. Assn., Am. Acad. Child Psychiatry, Group for Advancement Psychiatry, Am. Orthopsychiat. Assn. (bd. dirs. 1970-73), Colo. Psychiat. Soc. Office: 3636 16th St NW Ste AG29 Washington DC 20010-8138 Office Phone: 202-483-4637.

WERLIN, LAWRENCE B., obstetrician, gynecologist, endocrinologist; b. Albany, NY, 1948; s. Esther (Caplan) W.; m. Sally Rosso, Dec. 24, 1970; children: Rachel, Evan, Emma. BA, Boston U., 1970; MD, Mt. Sinai Sch. Medicine, NYC, 1976. Diplomate Am. Bd. Ob-Gyn. Intern Harbor Gen. Hosp., Torrance, Calif., 1976-77, resident in ob-gyn., 1977-80; fellow in reproductive endocrinology NIH, Bethesda, Md., 1980-82; mem. staff Hoag Meml. Hosp., Newport Beach, Calif. Nat. Reproductive Medicine fellow, 1980-82. Mem. AAAS, Am. Soc. Reproductive Medicine, Soc. for Assisted Reproductive Tech., Pacific Coast Fertility Soc. Office: Coastal Fertility Med Ctr 4900 Barranca Pky Ste 103 Irvine CA 92604-8603 E-mail: werlmd@coastalfertility.com.

WERMAN, DAVID SANFORD, psychiatrist, psychoanalyst; b. NYC, Jan. 1, 1922; s. Morris and Blanche (Heftel) W.; m. Marjolijn R. de Jager, Oct. 25, 1958 (div. 1975); children: Marco W., Claudia J. BA, Queens Coll., 1942; postgrad., Columbia U., 1946-47; MD, Cert. d'Etudes Medicales, U. Lausanne, Switzerland, 1952. Diplomate Am. Bd. Obstetrics and Gynecology, Am. Bd. Psychiatry and Neurology. Intern Beth Israel Hosp., NYC, 1953-54, resident, 1954-57, Montefiore Hosp., Bronx, NY, 1964-67; pvt. practice specializing in ob-gyn. NYC, 1957-64; faculty acad. psychiatry U. NC, Chapel Hill, 1967-76, assoc. prof., instr. psychoanalytic tng. program, 1974—; prof. psychiatry Duke U. Med. Ctr., Durham, NC, 1976—, supervising and tng. analyst psychoanalytic tng. program, 1981-97, Honored prof. psychiatry, 1990—, prof. emeritus, 1992—, supervising and tng. analyst emeritus, 1997—. Cons. Durham VA Hosp. Author: The Practice of Supportive Psychotherapy, 1984. Contbr. chpts. to books, articles to profl. jours. With AUS, 1943-45 Named Outstanding Tchr. psychiatry U. N.C., 1975, honored tchr. psychiatry Duke U., 1978, hon. prof., 1990. Fellow ACS, Am. Psychiat. Assn., Am. Coll. Psychoanalysts, others Home and Office: 111 E 85th St 23G New York NY 10028 Home Phone: 212-722-0744; Office Phone: 212-722-0744. Home Fax: 212-722-0744. Personal E-mail: davidwerman@aol.com.

WERMAN, THOMAS EHRLICH, record producer; b. Newton, Mass., Mar. 2, 1945; s. Lester and Ruth (Ehrlich) W.; m. Susan Lynne Gould, Aug. 25, 1968; children: Julia Gould, Nina Eve, Daniel Lester. BA, Columbia U., 1967, MBA, 1969. Asst. account exec. Grey Advt., NYC, 1969-70; asst. to dir. Epic Records Artistes and Repertoire, 1970-73; dir. talent acquisition Epic Records, 1973-76, staff producer, 1976-80; v.p., exec. producer CBS Records, Inc., LA, 1980-81; sr. v.p. Elektra Records, 1981-82; pres. Julia's Music Inc., LA, 1981—; v.p. artists and repertoire EMI-Capitol Entertainment Properties, LA, 1997-98; owner, operator Stonover Farm Bed and Breakfast, Lenox, Mass., 2001—. Bd. trustees Berkshire Music Sch. Recipient N.Y.C. Civilian Commendation award for heroism, 1968, 14 platinum records awards Rec. Industry Assn. Am., 1977—, 10 Gold Record awards, 1977—. Mem.: Lenox C. of C. (bd. dirs. 2005), Country Club of Pittsfield. Democrat. Jewish. E-mail: werm1000@aol.com.

WERMUTH, PAUL CHARLES, retired language educator; b. Phila., Oct. 28, 1925; s. Paul C. and Susan (Manga) W.; m. Barbara Ethel Braun, Aug. 26, 1951; children— Geoffrey Paul, Paul Charles, Alan John, Stephen Mark. AB, MA, Boston U., 1951; PhD, Pa. State U., 1955. Instr. Clarkson Coll., Potsdam, N.Y., 1951-52; part-time instr., grad. asst. Pa. State U., 1952-55; asst. prof. Coll. William and Mary, 1955-57; mem. faculty Central Conn. State Coll., New Britain, 1957-68, asso. prof. English, 1966-68; prof. English Northeastern U., 1968-90, prof. emeritus, 1990—, chmn. dept., 1968-75. Vis. prof. Middlebury Coll., 1963-64 Author: Modern Essays on Writing and Style, 2d edit, 1969, Essays in English, 1967, Bayard Taylor, 1974, Selected Letters of Bayard Taylor, 1997, also articles. Served with USAAF, 1943-46. Danforth summer study grantee, 1961 Mem. Modern Lang. Assn., AAUP, Mensa. Home: 73 Mostyn St Swampscott MA 01907-1616 Office: English Dept Northeastern Univ Boston MA 02115 Personal E-mail: pwermuth@comcast.net.

WERNER, CLARENCE L., transportation executive; b. 1937; Asst. mgr. Larson Grain Co., Omaha, 1958-61; with Bus. Motor Express, Inc., Omaha, 1961-62; founder Werner Enterprises, Inc., Omaha, 1956-82, pres., 1982-84, chmn., CEO, 1984—2007, chmn., 2007—. Office: Werner Enterprises Inc 14507 Frontier Rd PO Box 45308 Omaha NE 68145-0308 *

WERNER, DAVID A., paper company executive; BS, MBA, U. So. Calif. CPA. With Peat, Marwick, Mitchell & Co., 1974-78; various mgmt. positions Lear Siegler's Telecomms. divsns./subsidiaries, Anaheim, Calif., 1978-86, v.p. fin. and adminstrn., 1986-90; v.p., CFO Microdot Components Group, 1990-94; exec. v.p., dir. Kaynar Technologies Inc. (formerly Microdot Components), Orange, Calif., 1994-99; exec. v.p., CFO Day Runner, Irvine, 1999—. Office: 101 Oneil RD Sidney NY 13838-1055

WERNER, DAWN HETERICK, elementary school educator; b. Va. BA in Office Adminstrn., Va. Intermont Coll; MA in Edn., E. Tenn. State Univ., PhD in Edn., 2005. Worked in banking; Title I tchr., parent involvement coord., corrective reading dir. Fairmount Elem. Sch., Bristol, Tenn. Named Tenn. Tchr. of Yr., 2006; recipient E. Tenn. E. Grand Divsn. Tchr. of Yr., 2005. Office: Fairmount Elem Sch 500 Cypress St Bristol TN 37620 Business E-Mail: wernerd@btcs.org. *

WERNER, GREGORY L., transportation executive; Treas. Werner Enterprises, Omaha, 1982—86, v.p., 1984—96, exec. v.p., 1996—97, pres., 1997—99, pres., COO, 1999—2007, pres., CEO, 2007—. Office: Werner Enterprises 14507 Frontier Rd PO Box 45308 Omaha NE 68145-0308 *

WERNER, MARK J., healthcare executive, pediatrician; b. Evanston, Ill., Oct. 5, 1958; s. Robert J. and Sharon L. Werner; m. Deborah J. Van Horn, June 26, 1983; children: Elisa, Kristen. BA, Rice U., 1980; MD, Vanderbilt U., 1984. Cert. pediats., adolescent medicine, med. mgmt. Asst. prof. Vanderbilt U., 1990—95, assoc. prof., 1995—97, dir. divsn. adolescent medicine, 1995—97; v.p. med. affairs Medstar Health, 1997—2003; sr. v.p. med. affairs Carilion Health, 2003—06; chief med. officer Carilion Clinic, Roanoke, Va., 2006—. Cons. Va. Health Rsch. Bd., 2005—. Contbr. articles to profl. jours. on adolescent medicine and health policies. Dir. Child Health Investment Project, Roanoke, 2006—. Recipient Young Investigator award, Amersa, 1994. Fellow: Soc. Adolescent Medicine (Young Investigator award 1992, 1993, 1994), Am. Acad. Pediats., Am. Coll. Physician Execs.; mem.: Nat. Assn. Children Alcoholics (dir. 1998—2004), Am. Acad. Pediats. (cons. 2000—06), Assn. Med. Edn. and Rsch. Substance Abuse (pres. 2002—03). Avocations: running, tennis, landscaping. Office: Carilion Clinic PO Box 13367 Roanoke VA 24033

WERNER, PATRICE (PATRICIA ANN WERNER), academic administrator; b. Jersey City, May 31, 1937; d. Louis and Ella Blanche (Smith) W. BA in French, Caldwell Coll., 1966; MA in French, McGill U., 1970; PhD in French, NYU, 1976; postgrad. Inst. Ednl. Mgmt., Harvard U., 1991. Joined Dominican Sisters of Caldwell, 1954. Sch. tchr. Archdiocesan Sch. Systems, N.J., Ala., 1954-62; tchr. French, Latin Jersey City, Caldwell, NJ, 1962-72; instr. French Caldwell (NJ) Coll., 1973-76, dir. continuing edn., 1976-79, chair dept. fgn. langs., assoc. prof. French, 1979-85, acad. dean, prof. French, 1985-94, pres., 1994—. Trustee Caldwell Coll.; mem. corp., trustee Providence Coll.; mem. Dominican Higher Edn. Coun.; mem. NJ Pres.' Coun. accountability com., liaison com. to NJ Higher Edn. Partnership for Sustainability. Named Salute to Policy Makers award, Exec. Women NJ, 2006, Outstanding Woman in Am. History, DAR Maj. Joseph Bloomfield Chpt.; recipient Woman of Achievement award, N. N.J. Coun. of Boy Scouts of Am., 1999, The Archbishop T.E. McCarrick award for Disting. Svc. to the Ch., 2000, Cmty. Woman of Achievement, West Caldwell Hist. Soc. and West Essex Women's Club, 2000, Caldwell Cup, Excellence in Edn. award, N. Essex C. of C. Found., 2003; scholar AATF Summer Grant. Mem.: Assn. Gov. Bds. of Univs. and Colls., N.J. C. of C., Assn. Cath. Colls. and Univs., Nat. Assn. Ind. Colls. and Univs. (bd. dirs., sec. bd. dirs., com. policy analysis and pub. rels.), Coun. Ind. Colls. (bd. dirs., pub. info. com.), Ind. Coll. Fund. N.J. (trustee, vice chmn. exec. com.), Assn. Ind. Colls. and Univs. in N.J. (chmn. bd. dirs.). Avocations: tennis, reading, avid sports fan, travel. Office: Caldwell Coll 9 Ryerson Ave Caldwell NJ 07006-6195 Home Phone: 973-618-3283; Office Phone: 973-618-3217. Business E-Mail: spwerner@caldwell.edu.

WERNER, RAYMOND J., lawyer; b. Chgo., Aug. 25, 1944; s. Raymond and Marie (Vurpillat) W.; m. Lenore C. Werner, July 8, 1967; 1 child, Beth Anne. BS in Sci. and Commerce, DePaul U., 1967; JD, Ill. Inst. Tech., 1971. V.p., assoc. gen. counsel Chgo. Title Ins. Co., 1985; ptnr. Portes, Sharp, Herbst & Kravets Ltd., Chgo., 1985; now mng. ptnr. Arnstein & Lehr LLP, Chgo. Author: Modern Marketing Law and Practice, 1981, Real Estate Law 9th Edition, 1988, Real Estate Closings, 1988. Mem. ABA (real property sect., editor probate and trust law sect., bd. govs., 2006-), Am. Coll. Real Estate Lawyers, Chgo. Bar Assn. (exec. council, real estate law com. 1985—). Clubs: Park Ridge (Ill.) Country. Office: Arnstein & Lehr LLP Ste 1200 120 S Riverside Plz Chicago IL 60606-3910 Office Phone: 312-876-7152. Business E-Mail: rjwerner@arnstein.com.

WERNER, ROBERT L., lawyer, consultant; b. NYC, Feb. 28, 1913; s. Abraham L. and Elsa (Ludwig) W.; m. Raye Davies, Oct. 13, 1945; children: William, John. AB, Yale U., 1933; LLB, Harvard U., 1936. Bar: N.Y. 1936, U.S. Supreme Ct. 1936, also various fed. cts. and adminstrv. agys. 1936. Spl. asst. to U.S. atty. So. Dist. N.Y., 1936, asst. U.S. atty, 1937-40, confidential asst., 1940-42; dep. asst. atty. gen. U.S. Dept. Justice, Washington, 1946-47; spl. asst. to atty. gen. U.S., 1946-47; mem. law dept. RCA, NYC, 1947, v.p., gen. atty., 1951-62, exec. v.p., gen. atty., 1962-66, exec. v.p., gen. counsel, 1966-78, dir., 1963-79, cons., 1978-83. Mem. adv. bd. Internat. and Comparative Law Ctr. Southwestern Legal Found., Dallas, 1966—, treas., 1970-72, vice chmn., 1972-73, chmn. advisory bd., 1974-76, found. trustee 1976-88, hon. trustee 1988—; lectr. Conf. Bd., Practicing Law Inst., others; mem. nat. adv. council corp. law depts. Practising Law Inst., 1974-78; com. on restrictive bus. practices U.S. council Internat. C. of C., 1973-78; N.Y. Lawyers' Com. for Civil Rights under Law, 1972-78. Trustee Ithaca Coll., N.Y., 1968-88, hon. trustee, 1988—, chmn. bd., 1976-78; trustee Salisbury (Conn.) Sch., 1975-77, N.Y. Chiropractic Coll., 1986-89; bd. dirs. Midtown Arts Common at St. Peter's Ch., 1983-89. Capt. U.S. Army, 1942-44; to lt. col. USAAF, 1944-46, ETO. Recipient Disting. Service award Ithaca Coll., 1988. Fellow Am. Bar Found.; mem. Internat., Fed., Am., N.Y. State, City N.Y., FCC bar assns., IEEE (sr.), Am. Legion, Harvard Law Sch. Assn., Assn. Gen. Counsel (emeritus), U.S. Naval Inst., Internat. Law Assn. (Am. br.), Nat. Legal Aid and Defender Assn. (dir. 1974-79), Am. Judicature Soc., Newcomen Soc.,

N.Y. County Lawyers' Assn., Am. Soc. Internat. Law, Yale Club, Harvard Club N.Y., Army and Navy Club (Washington), Coral Beach Club (Bermuda). Home: 116 E 68th St New York NY 10021-5955

WERNER, ROBERT WILLIAM, federal agency administrator; b. Feb. 20, 1959; married; 3 children. Bachelor's degree, Amherst Coll.; master's degree, Columbia U.; JD, NYU. Law clk. to assoc. justices Lewis F. Powell, Jr. and Anthony M. Kennedy; officer Phoenix Home Life Mutual Ins. Co. (now The Phoenix Cos.); ptnr. Bingham Dana LLP (now Bingham McCutchen); assoc. atty. gen. State of Conn.; fed. prosecutor U.S. Atty.'s Office; head gaming regulatory agy.; with office legal counsel US Dept. Justice, Washington; asst. gen. counsel for enforcement and intelligence US Dept. Treasury, Washington, counselor to gen. counsel, dir. Office Fgn. Assets Control, 2004—06, dir. Fin. Crimes Enforcement Network, 2006—. Office: US Dept Treasury Fin Crimes Enforcement Network 1500 Pennsylvania Ave NW Washington DC 20220

WERNER, RYAN, film company executive; b. Jan. 23, 1974; Student, Boston U. Prodn. asst.; with Ind. Feature Project; v.p. acquisitions and distbn. Shooting Gallery; with Sundance Channel; v.p. acquisitions and distbn. Magnolia Pictures; head theatrical distbn. Palm Pictures, 2003, Wellspring; v.p. mktg. IFC Films, NYC, 2005—. Mem. spirit awards com. Someone to Watch Award, 2003; programmer Woodstock Film Festival, Phat Shorts. Exec. prodr.: (films) Tarnation, 2003, Unknown White Male, 2005. Office: IFC Films 323 6th Ave New York NY 10014 *

WERNER, SAMUEL ALFRED, physicist, educator; b. Elgin, Ill., Jan. 5, 1937; s. Charles August and Frances Agnes (Tasch) W.; m. Laura Louise Reed, Sept. 1, 1961; 1 dau., Catherine Louise. AB, Dartmouth Coll., 1959, MS, 1961; PhD, U. Mich., 1965. Staff scientist physics dept. Ford Motor Co., Dearborn, Mich., 1964-75; adj. prof. nuclear engring. U. Mich., Ann Arbor, 1968-75; prof. physics U. Mo., Columbia, 1975-2000, chmn. physics dept., 1981-83, Millsap Disting. prof., 1986—, Curator's prof., 1992—, prof. emeritus, 2000—; scientific cons.physics lab. Nat. Inst. Standards Tech., Gaithersburg, Md., 2000—. Vis. scientist A.B. Atomenergi, Studsvik, Sweden, 1970, Institut Laue-Langevin, Grenoble, France, 1977, Argonne Nat. Lab., Oak Ridge Nat. Lab., Brookhaven Nat. Lab.; cons. Argonne Nat. Lab., 1968—, mem. solid scis. div. rev. com., 1972-77, chmn. spl. com. Intense Pulsed Neutron Source, 1978-82; cons. Nat. Acad. Scis., 1977, 83; vis. scientist Nat. Bur. Stds, 1983-84; vis. scientist Nat. Inst. Stds. and Tech., 1996—, chmn. com. on assessment of physics lab., 1992-95. Contbr. numerous articles to profl. jours. Grantee NSF; fellow Swedish Rsch. Coun.; recipient outstanding alumni award U. Mich., 1980, Chancellor's award for Outstanding Rsch. U. Mo., 1980, Presdl. Rsch. award U. Mo., 1973. Fellow Am. Phys. Soc.; mem. Sigma Xi Home: 7620 Augustine Way Gaithersburg MD 20879-4587 Office: Reactor Bldg 235 NIST Mail Stop 8461 Gaithersburg MD 20899 Office Fax: 301-926-1604. Personal E-mail: slwerner@starpower.net.

WERNER, STUART LLOYD, computer services company executive; b. NYC, June 2, 1932; s. Leroy Louis and Frances Werner; m. Davideen Price, Jan. 6, 1990; children by previous marriage: Joan Leslie, Susan Lyn, Richard Wayne. BArch, Rensselaer Poly. Inst., 1954. Ptnr. in charge architecture Werner-Dyer & Assocs., Washington, 1959-68; v.p. Rentex Corp., Phila., 1968-70, ARA Svcs., Inc., 1981—83; pres. Werner & Assocs., Inc., Washington, 1970-81, Werner & Monk, Inc., 1983-90, STN, Inc., 1981-99, chmn. Falls Church, Va., 2000—04, chmn. emeritus, 2005—. Author: FilePro Developer's Reference, 4th edit., 2002; contbr. articles to tech. jours. Bd. dirs. Watergate South, 1984-90, Washington Opera Soc., Friends of the Corcoran Gallery, Washington, Hampton West Condo, 2001—, Fla. Grand Opera Guild; mem. Econ. Devel. Coun., City of Aventura, Fla., 2002. With AUS, 1955-57. Mem. AIA, Inst. Indsl. Engrs., Marinette Yacht Club, Masons, Tau Beta Pi. Democrat. Office Fax: 305-931-7028.

WERNER, TOM, television producer, professional baseball team executive; b. NJ, Apr. 12, 1950; m. Jill Werner; children: Teddy, Carolyn, Amanda. BA, Harvard Univ., 1971. With ABC Television, Inc., 1972-82; co-owner Carsey-Werner Co., Studio City, Calif., 1982—; chmn. San Diego Padres, 1991-94; co-owner Boston Red Sox baseball club, 2002—. Mem. bd. dirs. Old Globe Theatre, Sharp Hospital. Prodr.(co-exec): (TV series) Oh, Madeline, 1983—84, A Different World, 1987—93, Chicken Soup, 1989, Grand, 1990, Davis Rules, 1991, You Bet Your Life, 1992, Frannie's Turn, 1992, Grace Under Fire, 1993—98, She TV, 1994, Cosby, 1996—2000; exec. prodr.: The Cosby Show, 1984 (Emmy awd. Outstanding Comedy Series, 1985), Roseanne, 1988—97, Cybill, 1995—98, 3rd Rock from the Sun, Cosby, 1996—2001, Townies, 1996, Damon, 1998, God, the Devil and Bob, 2000, Normal, Ohio, 2000—01, Grounded for Life, 2001—05, You Don't Know Jack, 2001, The Downer Channel, 2001, That '80s Show, 2002, Whoopi, 2003—04, The Tracy Morgan Show, 2003—04, Game Over, 2004, Good Girls Don't..., 2004; exec. prodr.: (TV series) The Scholar, 2005—; exec. prodr.: (TV films) The Cosby Show: A Look Back, 2002, These Guys, 2003, Grand Union, 2006, Happy Hour, 2006; prodr.: (TV films) The Mayor of Oyster Bay, 2002; exec. prodr.: (films) Let's Go to Prison, 2006. Office: Carsey Werner Prodns 4024 Radford Ave Bldg 3 Studio City CA 91604-2101

WERNER-JACOBSEN, EMMY ELISABETH, developmental psychologist; b. Eltville, Germany, May 26, 1929; came to U.S., 1952, naturalized, 1962; d. Peter Josef and Liesel (Kunz) W. BS, Johannes Gutenberg U., Germany, 1950; MA, U. Nebr., 1952, PhD, 1955; postgrad., U. Calif., Berkeley, 1953-54. Research asso. Inst. Child Welfare, U. Minn., 1956-59; vis. scientist NIH, 1959-62; asst. prof. to prof. human devel., rsch. child psychologist U. Calif., Davis, 1962-94, rsch. prof., 1995—. Sr. author: The Children of Kauai, 1971, Kauai's Children Come of Age, 1977; author: Cross-Cultural Child Development: A View from the Planet Earth, 1979, Vulnerable, but Invincible, 1982, 3d edit., 1998, Child Care: Kith, Kin and Hired Hands, 1984, Overcoming the Odds, 1992, Pioneer Children on the Journey West, 1995, Reluctant Witnesses: Children's Voices From the Civil War, 1998, Through the Eyes of Innocents: Children Witness World War II, 2000, Unschuldige Zeugen, 2001, Journeys From Childhood to Mid Life: Risk, Resilience and Recovery, 2001, A Conspiracy of Decency: The Rescue of the Danish Jews in World War II, 2002, In Pursuit of Liberty, 2006; contbr. articles to profl. jours. Recipient Disting. Sci. Contbn. to Child Devel. award, Soc. Rsch. Child Devel., 1999, Dolly Madison Presdl. award for outstanding lifelong contbns. to devel. and wellbeing of children and families, Zero to Three, 1999, Arnold Gesell award, German Soc. Pediat., 2001, award for disting. career contbns. to sci. study of lifespan devel., Soc. for Study of Human Devel., 2005. Fellow: Assn. Psychol. Scis., Soc. Rsch. Child Devel., German Acad. Social Pediats. (hon.). Business E-Mail: eewerner@ucdavis.edu.

WERNICK, EDWARD RAYMOND, information technology executive; b. Irvington, NJ, Mar. 11, 1955; s. Edward Joseph and Ann (Czech) W.; m. Ione Sharon Greenbaum, Nov. 2, 1984; 1 child, Elissa Ann. BS in Computer Sci., Kean Coll., 1977. Computer analyst NY Life Ins., 1978—81; computer cons. Horizons, NYC, 1981—84; data base adminstr. oracle Std. & Poors, NYC, 1984—88; tchr. Sybase, NYC, 1988—89; data base adminstr. sybase Merrill Lynch, NYC, 1989—91, Paramount Comm., Old Tappan, NJ, 1991—95; v.p. Crossmar, Parsippany, NJ, 1995—2003; acting chief tech. officer Misys, Pearl River, NY, 2003—07, IT hosting head, 2007—. Computer, fin. cons., pvt. practice, Oradell, NJ, 1981—. Designer stage lighting for more than 80 plays, 1978-84; writer relational scripts for Australian govt., 1994; exhibited sculpture in India, 1991, Brazil, 1992, Oslo, Norway, 1994. Mem. Rep. Nat. Com.; sec. Stockton Rifle Club, NJ, 1974; pres. Irvington Masquers, 1978. Named Outstanding Young Rep. Union, NJ, Rep. Com., 1976; Best of Show sculpture Art Assoc., Irvington, 1979; 100 yd. standing rifle champion Stockton (NJ) Rifle Club, 1974. Mem. Assn. for Computing Machinery, Sybase Internat. Users Group, Relational Database Users Group, Oradell Arts Com., Internet Users Group. Roman Catholic. Avocations: lighting design, theater, logic. Home: 920 Oradell Ave Oradell NJ 07649-1925 Office: Crossmar 111 Sylvan Ave Englewood Cliffs NJ 07632 Personal E-mail: ednnj42@aol.com. Business E-Mail: edward.wernick@misys.com.

WERNICK, JOEL, health facility administrator; BBA, U. Ark, Fayetteville; MHA, Xavier U., Cin. V.p. ops. Baptist Reg. Health Svcs., Pensacola, Fla., 1982—88; pres., CEO Phoebe Putney Meml. Hosp., Albany, Ga., 1988—. Bd. dir. Voluntary Hosp. Am. (VHA) Health Found., Inc., Ga., 2003—, Ga. Alliance Cmty. Hosp.; chmn. Med. Resource Network. Mem. S.W. Ga. Alliance for Progress. Recipient Discovery Health Channel Med. Honors, 2004. Fellow: Am. Coll. Healthcare Exec. Office: Phoebe Putney Meml Hosp 417 Third Ave Albany GA 31701 Office Phone: 229-312-1000. Business E-Mail: jwernick@ppmh.org.

WERNICK, RICHARD FRANK, composer, conductor, educator; b. Boston, Jan. 16, 1934; s. Louis and Irene (Prince) W.; m. Beatrice Messina, July 15, 1956; children: Lewis, Adam, Peter (dec.). BA, Brandeis U., 1955; MA, Mills Coll., 1957. Instr. music U. Buffalo, 1964-65; asst. prof. music, dir. univ. symphony U. Chgo., 1965-68; conductor Pa. Contemporary Players, 1968-93; prof. music U. Pa., 1968-96, prof. emeritus, 1996—. Co-founder Community Youth Orch. of Delaware County; cons. Contemporary Music, The Phil. Orch., 1983-89, spl. cons. to the music dir., 1989-93; bd. dirs. Theodore Presser Co. Music dir. Royal Winnipeg Ballet Can., 1957-58; composer: Haiku of Basho, 1967, A Prayer for Jerusalem, 1971 (Naumburg award 1975), Moonsongs from the Japanese, 1972, Kaddish Requiem, 1973, String Quartet 2, 1973, Songs of Remembrance, 1974, Visions of Terror and Wonder, 1976 (Pulitzer prize 1977), Contemplations of the Tenth Muse, Book I, 1976, Book II, 1978, Introits and Canons, 1977, A Poison Tree, 1979, Concerto for Cello and Ten Players, 1980, In Praise of Zephyrus, 1981, Piano Sonata: Reflections of a Dark Light, 1982, Sonata for cello and piano: Portraits of Antiquity, 1982, The Oracle of Shimon bar Yochai, 1983, Concerto for Violin and Orch., 1983-84 (Friedheim 1st prize 1986); Oracle II for soprano, oboe and piano, 1985, Concerto for Viola and Orch., 1985-86, Musica Ptolemeica brass quintet, 1987, Symphony #1, 1988, String Quartet #3, 1988, Concerto for Piano and Orch. (Friedheim award 1992), 1989-90, Fragments of Prophecy, 1990, String Quartet #4, 1991 (Friedheim 1st prize 1991), Concerto for Saxophone Quartet and Orch., 1991, Cello Concerto #2, 1992, Symphony #2, 1993, ...and a time for peace, 1994, String Quartet #5, 1995, Cassation-Music Tom Jefferson Knew, 1995, Trio for violin, cello, piano, 1996, Da'ase for solo guitar, 1996, Games of Menoretti for solo bassoon, 1997, Sonata for violin and piano, 1997, Duettino for violin and oboe, 1997, String Quartet 6, 1998, Musica da Camerata, 1999, Telino's Acrobats, (for solo bass clarinet), 1999, Piano Sonata # 2, 2000, The Name of the Game, 2000, Duo for cello and piano, 2001, Quintet for Horn & String Quartet, 2002, Suite #1 for Unaccompanied Cello, 2003, Sextet (for string quartet, double bass, piano), 2003, Double Duo for 2 pianos, 2 cellos, 2004, A Song for Phil, 2004, Woodwind Quintet, 2005, Tristam Redux for guitar and percussion, 2006, String Quartet #7, 2007, Suite #2 for Unaccompanied Cello, 2007. Recipient music award Nat. Inst. Arts and Letters, 1976, Nat. Endowment Arts grantee, 1975, 79, 82; Fellow Ford Found., 1962-64, Guggenheim Found., 1976. Mem. ASCAP. Personal E-mail: rfwernick@aol.com.

WERNICK, SANDRA MARGOT, advertising and public relations executive; b. Tampa, Fla., Sept. 13, 1944; d. Nathan and Sylvia (Bienstock) Rothstein. BA in English, U. Fla., 1966. Tchr. English Miami Beach (Fla.) Sr. H.S., 1967; adminstrv. asst. pub. rels. Bozell & Jacobs, Inc., NYC, 1968-69; asst. to dir. pub. rels. Waldorf-Astoria, NYC, 1969-70; dir. advt. and pub. rels. Hyatt on Union Sq., San Francisco, 1974-82; pres. Wernick Mktg. Group, San Francisco, 1982—; exec. dir. Sales and Mktg. Execs. of the Bay Area, 1995-2000; mng. ptnr. The Stanford Group, 1998-99; pres. Auction Magic, San Francisco, 2003—. Bd. dirs. Nat. Kidney Assn., San Francisco, 1985-87; advisor Swords to Plowshares, San Francisco, 1988-89; mem. mktg. com. to bd. Boy Scouts of Greater East Bay, 1995-2000. Recipient Award of Merit, San Francisco Advt. and Cable Car Awards, 1979, Award of Excellence, San Francisco Art Dirs. 1978, Disting. Mktg. award Sales and Mktg. Internat., 1997, awards Am. Hotel and Motel Assn., 1981, 82. Mem. NAFE, Women in Comms. (bd. dirs. 1987-89), Am. Women in Radio and TV (bd. dirs. 1989-90), Pub. Rels. Soc. Am., San Francisco Publicity Club (pres. 1989, awards of excellence 1990, 94, 95-98), Variety Club, Profl. Bus. Women's Assn., Calif. Pacific Med. Ctr. (aux. 1988-95). Democrat. Jewish. Office: 1690 Broadway Ste 705 San Francisco CA 94109-2107 E-mail: sandie@wernickmarketinggroup.com.

WERONSKI, PAWEL, physicist, researcher; MSc in Physics, A. Mickiewicz U., Poznan, Poland, 1989; PhD in Chemistry, Polish Acad. Scis., Krakow, Poland, 2000. Asst. prof. Inst. Catalysis and Surface Chemistry, Polish Acad. Scis., 2000; postdoctoral assoc. dept. chem. engring. Yale U., New Haven, 2001—03; postdoctoral assoc. Los Alamos Nat. Lab., N.Mex., 2005—. Recipient Disting. Ph.D. Thesis award, Inst. Catalysis and Surface Chemistry, Polish Acad. Scis., 2000, Outstanding Oral Presentation in Bioscis. award, Los Alamos Nat. Lab., 2005; grantee, Polish Ministry Sci. Rsch. and Info. Tech., 2004. Achievements include research in Monte Carlo and molecular dynamics computer simulations in chemical physics, colloid and protein adsorption, self-assembling nanostructures, cellular membranes and nucleic acids, artificial life. Office: Los Alamos Nat Lab Ms-B284 Los Alamos NM 87544 Office Phone: 505-667-9956. Business E-Mail: pawel@lanl.gov.

WERT, JONATHAN MAXWELL, II, management consultant; b. Port Royal, Pa., Nov. 8, 1939; s. Jonathan Maxwell and Helen Leona (Leonard) Wert; m. Wendy J. Mast; children: Jonathan Maxwell III, Kimberly Dee, Jon Adam, Justin Tyler, Amanda Elizabeth, Gabriel Chadwick, Emily Lauren. BS in Biology, Austin Peay State U., 1966, MS in Biology, 1968; PhD in Adminstrn., U. Ala., 1974. Park supt., chief interpretive services Bur. State Parks Pa. Dept. Environ. Resources, Harrisburg, 1968-69; chief naturalist Bays Mountain Park Environ. Edn. Ctr., Kingsport, Tenn., 1969-71; environ. and energy edn. specialist TVA, Knoxville, 1971-75; cons. energy, environment, conservation U. Tenn., Knoxville, 1975; sr. assoc.-energy Energy Extension Svc., Coop. Extension Svc., Pa. State U., 1977-80; pres. Energy-Environ. Consultants, Port Royal, Pa., 1981-85, Mgmt. Diagnostics, Inc., Port Royal, 1985—. Author: Writing Environmental Education Grant Proposals, 1974, Environmental Education Study Projects for High School Students, 1974, Environmental Education Study Projects for College Students, 1974, Developing Environmental Study Areas, 1974, Developing Environmental Education Curriculum Material, 1974, Finding Solutions to Environmental Problems...A Process Guide, 1975, Assessing an Issue in Relation to Environmental, Economic, and Social Impact...A Process Guide, 1976, Energy Conservation Measures for Mobile Home Dwellers, 1978, Selected Energy Conservation Options for the Home, 1978, Selected Energy Management Options for Small Business and Local Government, 1978, Life Lines: A Book of Poetry, Prose, and Axioms, 1983, Survivorship and Growth in Employment: A Question and Answer Guide, 1983; mem. adv. bd.: Environ. Edn. Report, 1974—; cons. editor: Jour. Environ. Edn, 1975; contbr. articles to profl. jours. Counselor Boy Scouts Am., 1975. Served with USMC, 1958-61. Recipient Conservation award Am. Motors Co., 1976 Mem. U.S. Energy Assn., Inst. Mgmt. Cons., Orgn. Devel. Inst., Inst. of Mgmt. Cons. (cert. mgmt. cons.), The Cons. Bur. (profl. mgmt. cons.). Lutheran. Home: RR 5 Box 250 Mifflintown PA 17059-9576 Office: Mgmt Diagnostics Inc PO Box 240 Port Royal PA 17082-0240 Home Phone: 717-527-2622; Office Phone: 717-527-4399. Business E-Mail: jwert@mdi-wert.com.

WERTHAMER, NATHAN RICHARD, physicist; b. Milw., Feb. 9, 1935; BA, Harvard Coll., 1956; PhD in physics, U. Calif., 1961. Rsch. assoc. U. Calif., San Diego, 1961-62; mem. tech. staff Bell Labs, 1962-75; mem. corp. planning dept. AT&T, 1975-76; chmn. N.Y. State Energy Rsch. and Devel. Authority, 1976-78; sr. advisor sci. and tech. dept. Exxon Corp., 1978-83; exec. dir. Becton Dickinson Devel. Corp., 1983-89; exec. officer Am. Phys. Soc., 1990-93; mgmt. cons. Chelsea Technols, NYC, 1993—. Fellow AAAS, Am. Phys. Soc. Office: Chelsea Techs 43 W 16th St Apt 7D New York NY 10011-6321 Business E-Mail: chelseatechnologies@nyc.rr.com.

WERTHAN, JEFFREY MICHAEL, lawyer; b. NYC, Sept. 28, 1954; s. Fred and Evelyn (Rabinowitz) W.; m. Susan Elizabeth Miller, Aug. 27, 1978; children: David E., Benjamin J. Student, The Juilliard Sch., NYC, 1972-74; BA, Tufts U., 1976; JD, Boston U., 1979. Bar: D.C. 1979, N.Y. 1980, U.S. Ct. Appeals (1st, 6th and 9th cirs.). Staff atty. Fed. Home Loan Bank Bd./FSLIC, Washington, 1979—80, spl. asst. US atty., 1981, sr. atty., 1981-83; assoc. Silver, Freedman & Taff, L.L.P., Washington, 1983-85, ptnr., 1986—2001, Katten Muchin Rosenman LLP, Washington, 2001—. Mem. ABA (banking com. 1990—), Metro Baseball Umpires Assn. Avocations: music, baseball, golf. Office Phone: 202-625-3500. Office Fax: 202-339-8281. Business E-Mail: jeff.werthan@kattenlaw.com.

WERTHEIM, MARY DANIELLE, educational coordinator; b. NYC; d. Daniel Leo and Helen Loretta (Sudimick) Conroy; m. Stanley Claude Wertheim, Mar. 9, 1963. BA in English with honors, CCNY, 1960, MA in Psychology, 1979. Coord. English and lang. arts Horace Mann Lower Sch., Riverdale, NY, 1969—. Pvt. investor Wertheim Trust, N.Y.C., 1985—; pres. winner's cir. Horace Mann Investment Club, Riverdale, 1989—. Founder, advisor Horace Mann Lower Sch. Cmty. Svc. Group, Riverdale, 1980—; active Rep. nat. Com., 1980—. Mem.: ASCD, Nat. Assn. Investors Corp., The Internat. Netsuke Soc. (sec. N.Y. chapter), Priory Scholars, Am. Firm, Mensa, The Grolier Club. Avocations: desk top publishing, manuscript collecting. Home: 180 Cabrini Blvd # 57 New York NY 10033-1138 Office: Horace Mann Lower Sch 4440 Tibbett Ave Bronx NY 10471-3416 Office Phone: 646-286-3592. Personal E-mail: herbieboo@aol.com.

WERTHEIM, MITZI MALLINA, information technology executive; b. NYC; d. Rudolf and Myrtle B. (McGraw) Mallina; m. Ronald P. Wertheim, Feb. 25, 1965 (div. July 1988); children: Carter, Tiana. BA, U. Mich., 1960. Asst. dir. div. research Peace Corps, Washington, 1961-66; sr. program officer Cafritz Found., Washington, 1970-76; dep. undersec. navy, 1977-81; with Fed. Sector Div. IBM, 1981-94; v.p. enterprise solutions SRA Corp., 1994-98, CNA Corp., 1998—. Woodrow Wilson vis. fellow, 1979, 80; founder, dir. The Energy Consensus, 2005—. Founder, pres. The Energy Consensus, 2005; bd. dirs. Nat. Coalition Sci. and Tech., 1983—86; mem. vis. com. MIT, 1983—89; bd. dirs. Youth Policy Inst., 1986—91, VITA, 1989—2001, Cebrowski Inst., 2001, Naval Post Grad. Sch., 2001; founder MIT Seminar XXI, 1985—. Recipient Federally Employed Women award Def. Dept., 1980; Disting. Pub. Svc. medal Navy Dept., 1981; fellow Maxwell Sch. Syracuse U., 1996-97. Mem.: Naval Studies Bd., Coun. on Fgn. Rels. Episcopalian. Home: 3113 38th St NW Washington DC 20016-3726

WERTHEIM, RAM D., lawyer; b. Tel Aviv, May 15, 1954; BA cum laude, City U., 1979; JD magna cum laude, Georgetown U., 1982. Bar: NY 1983. Atty. Simpson, Thacher & Bartlett, NYC; gen. counsel, chief adminstrn. officer CapMAC Holdings, Inc.; co-head structured fin. divsn. MBIA, Inc., Armonk, NY, 1998—2000, v.p., gen. counsel, sec., 2000—. Alt. mem. legal, regulatory, acctg., and tax. com. Am. Securitization Forum. Editor: Georgetown Law Jour., 1981—82. Office: MBIA Inc 113 King St Armonk NY 10504 Office Phone: 914-765-3945. Office Fax: 914-765-3163. E-mail: ram.wertheim@mbia.com. *

WERTHEIM, ROBERT HALLEY, national security consultant; b. Carlsbad, N.Mex., Nov. 9, 1922; s. Joseph and Emma (Vorenberg) W.; m. Barbara Louise Selig, Dec. 26, 1946; children: Joseph Howard, David Andrew. Student, N.Mex. Mil. Inst., 1940-42; BS, U.S. Naval Acad., 1945; MS in Physics, M.I.T., 1954; postgrad., Harvard U., 1969. Commd. ensign U.S. Navy, 1945, advanced through grades to rear adm., 1972; assigned Spl. Projects Office, Washington, 1956-61, Naval Ordnance Test Sta., China Lake, 1961-62, Office Sec. Def., Washington, 1962-65; head Missile br. Strategic Systems Project Office, Washington, 1965-67, dep. tech. dir., 1967-68, tech. dir., 1968-77, dir., 1977-80; sr. v.p. Lockheed Corp., 1981-88; cons. nat. def., 1988—. Emeritus mem. Draper Lab., Inc.; pres. adv. coun. U. Calif.; sci. adv. group Dept. Def., Dept. Energy, U.S. Strategic Command; nat. security adv. Lawrence Livermore Nat. Lab. Decorated DSM with cluster, Legion of Merit, Navy Commendation medal, Joint Svc. Commendation medal; recipient Rear Adm. William S. Parsons award Navy League U.S., 1971, Chmn. Joint Chiefs of Staff Disting. Pub. Svc. award, 1996, Sec. of Def. medal, 1996, Disting. Grad. award U.S. Naval Acad., 2005; named Disting. Submariner, Naval Submarine League, 2006; named to Hall of Fame NMMI, 1987. Fellow AIAA, Calif. Coun. Sci. Tech.; mem. Am. Soc. Naval Engrs. (hon. mem., Gold medal 1972), Nat. Acad. Engring., U.S. Naval Inst., Bernardo Heights Country Club, Sigma Xi, Tau Beta Pi. Home: 17705 Devereux Rd San Diego CA 92128-2084 Office: Sci Applications Internat Corp 16701 W Berardo Dr MS RB-2 San Diego CA 92127-3608 E-mail: rhwertheim@aol.com.

WERTHEIM, SALLY HARRIS, director, academic administrator, dean, education educator, consultant; b. Cleve., Nov. 1, 1931; d. Arthur I. and Anne (Manheim) Harris; m. Stanley E. Wertheim, Aug. 6, 1950; children: Kathryn, Susan B., Carole J. BS, Flora Stone Mather Coll., 1953; MA, Case Western Res. U., 1967, PhD, 1970. Cert. elem. and secondary edn. tchr. Ohio. Social worker U. Hosps., Cleve., 1953-54; tchr. Fairmount Temple Religious Sch., Cleve., 1957-72; mem. faculty John Carroll U., Cleve., 1969—, chair dept. edn., 1969—86, dean Grad. Sch., 1986—99, dir. planning and assessment, 1999—2004, interim dean Coll. Arts and Scis., 2004—05, cons. Office of Acad. V.P., 2005—, interim dir. Career Ctr., 2005—06, interim dean Grad. Sch., 2007—. Cons. in field; cons. Jennings Found., Cleve.; chmn. sch. com. Cleve. Commn. on Higher Edn., 1987-99. Contbr. articles to profl. jours. Sec. Cuyahoga County Mental Health Bd., Cleve., 1978—82; pres. Montefiore Home, Cleve., 1987—90; bd. dir. Mt. Sinai Med. Ctr., Cleve., 1984—93; v.p. Mt. Sinai Health Care Found.; bd. dirs. Cleve. Edn. Fund, 1992—94, v.p., 2007; chair edn. com. Cleve. Found. Commn. on Poverty, 1988—93, Cleve. Cmty. Bldg. Initiative, 1993—95, United Way Svcs., 1994—2001; trustee Mt. Sinai Health Care Found., 1998, Gerson Found., 1998, Miller Found., 1998, Begun Found., 2001, Mandel Found., 2001; pres. Jewish Family Svc. Assn., Cleve., 1974—77; v.p. Jewish Cmty. Fedn., 1988—91, pres., 1994—97, life trustee, 1997—. Named One of 100 Most Influential Women, Cleve. mag., 1983, One of 29 Most Influential Women, Cleve. Mag., 1997; recipient award John Carroll U., Curtis Miles award for cmty. svc., 1997; grantee Jennings Found., 1984-87, Cleve. and Gund Found., 1987-90, Lilly Found., 1988; S.H. Wertheim scholarship and edn. excellence award established John Carroll U., 1997. Mem. Am. Assn. Colls. for Tchrs. Edn. (bd. dirs. 1982-85), Ohio Assn. Colls. for Tchrs. Edn. (pres. 1981-83), Coun. of Grad. Schs. Avocations: flower arranging, travel, antiques. Office: John Carroll Univ Grad Sch Cleveland OH 44118 Business E-Mail: wertheim@jcu.edu.

WERTHEIMER, ESTHER, sculptor; b. Poland; Student, Montreal Mus. Fine Arts, 1958-63, Internat. Acad., Austria, 1966, Acad. Belle Arte, Florence, Italy, 1967-68; BA, Loyola of Montreal, 1973; MA, Goddard Coll., 1975. Sculptures installed at Maimonides Hosp., Montreal, Can., Recreation Ctr., Pt. St. Lucie, Fla., Itami City Cultural Hall, Hyogo Prefecture, Japan, Okaloosa-Walton C.C., Niceville, Fla., Upper Iowa U., Fayette, Okayama Mcpl. Ctr., Japan, Health Care Ctr., Kyoto, Japan, Royal Palm Plaza, Boca Raton, Fla., Hikifune Cultural Ctr., Sumida-ku, Tokyo, 21st Century forest Park, Fukushima, Japan, Yumeji Mus. Okayama, Katsushika Performing Art Ctr., Tokyo, City of Hamura, Tokyo, Fukuoka City Hall, Japan, Hakone Open-Air Mus., Kanagawa-ken, Sun Bank, Palm Springs, Calif., North Miami Beach, Fla., Atrium of Alcan Aluminum Ltd., Montreal, Glouster City Hall for Carling Park of Commerce, East Ottawa, Joliette Mus., Que., Carling Exec. Pk., Ottawa, Cote St-Luc City Hall and Libr., Montreal, Conf. Bd. of Can., Ottawa, Douglas Hosp., Montreal, Gordon Gramm, Boulder, Colo., Livermore (Calif.) Pub. Libr., City of Palm Desert, Calif., The Palm Beach Internat. Sculpture Bienale, Wellington, Fla., others. Recipient awards Montreal Mus. Fine Arts, 1956-63, Borsa di Studio, Italian Govt., 1967-68, Govt. Que. Bource de l'Enseignement Superieur, 1974, Gold medal INT Tourismo, Rome, EUR Europa Premio, Rome, B'nai B'rith Internat. Arts award, 1997, others; Travel grant Can. Coun., 1967, Elizabeth T. Greenshields Meml. grant, 1969, Govt. Can., 1989-2007. Home: 6507 Brava Way Boca Raton FL 33433-8239 also: 145 Radcliffe Montreal PQ H4X 1C1 Canada Office Phone: 561-392-3503. Fax: 561-392-0065. E-mail: ewertheimer@ewertheimer.com.

WERTHEIMER, FREDRIC MICHAEL, public policy advocate; b. Bklyn., Jan. 9, 1939; s. Irving Wertheimer and Mildred (Klein) Van Brink; m. Linda Cozby, June 15, 1969. BA, U. Mich., 1959; LL.B., Harvard U., 1962. Bar: N.Y. bar 1963, D.C. bar 1971. Atty. SEC, 1963-66; legis. counsel Congressman Silvio Conte, 1967-68; counsel House Small Bus. Com., 1969-70; lobbyist, legis. dir., v.p. Common Cause, Washington, 1971-81, pres., 1981-95; news polit. analyst CBS News, Washington, 1996; pres. Democracy 21, 1997—. Fellow Press Politics and Policy Ctr. Harvard U., 1996; J. Skelly Wright fellow, vis. lectr. Yale Law Sch., 1997; polit. analyst ABC News, 1999-2000. Author: Common Cause Manual on Money and Politics. With U.S. Army, 1962-63. Fellow Inst. Politics Harvard U., 1972. Jewish. Home: 3502 Macomb St NW Washington DC 20016-3162

WERTHEIMER, MARILYN LOU, librarian, educator; b. Pueblo, Colo., Dec. 1, 1928; d. Louis Robert and Alice Erdine Schuman; m. Y. Ernest Satow, Jan. 4, 1953 (div. Oct. 1958); m. Michael M. Wertheimer, Sept. 12, 1970; stepchildren: Karen Anne, Mark David, John Benjamin. BA, Stanford U., Calif., 1950; MA and cert., Russian Inst. Columbia U., NYC, 1953; postgrad., U. Calif., Berkeley, 1961—62; MLS, U. Calif., LA, 1967. Sec., proofreader various publ. firms, NYC, 1953—56; sec. Rockefeller Bros. Fund, 1956—57; personal staff, sec. Nelson A. Rockefeller, 1957—58; sec. Gen. Dynamics Corp., San Diego, 1959—64; catalogue U. Calif., 1965—68; reference libr. U. Colo., Boulder, 1968—93, prof. honors sem., 1972—91, prof. emeritus, 1993—. Mem. libr. del. U.S. Exch. China, 1985, U.S. Exch. U.S.S.R., 1988; cons. Archives of History Am. Psychology, Akron, Ohio, 1980. Co-author: Sources of Information in the Social Sciences, 1986; co-editor: History of Psychology: A Guide, 1979; one-woman shows include Boulder (Colo.) Pub. Libr., 2004, Sun Microsystems, Broomfield, Colo., 2004, Norlin Libr. U. Colo., Boulder, 2005, Classical Acad., Colorado Springs, Colo., 2005. Mem. del. vis. Tibet, Boulder-Lhasa Sister Cities Program, 1988; vol. Christian Sci. Ch., 1986—; bd. dirs. U. Club, U. Colo., Boulder, 1976—79. Recipient First prize, Internat. Libr. Photography, Owings Mills, Md., 1999—2000. Mem.: ALA. Democrat. Home: 546 Geneva Ave Boulder CO 80302 Office: Norlin Libr U Colo Campus Box 184 Boulder CO 80309-0184 Business E-Mail: wertheim@colorado.edu.

WERTIME, TIMOTHY RAY, music educator; b. Chambersburg, Pa., Apr. 10, 1954; s. Rudolf Milton and Phyllis Jane (Carrington) Wertime. BA, Wittenberg U., 1976, M of Sacred Music, 1985. Cert. music/elem. tchr. Ohio Dept. Edn., water safety instr. Red Cross, 1990. Dir. youth choir Covenant Presbyn. Ch., 1975—76; substitute tchr. Springfield City Schs., Ohio, 1977—92, Clark County Schs., Springfield, 1977—92; organist Northminster Presbyn. Ch., Springfield, 1977—92; tchr. Wertime's Keyboard Studio, Greencastle, Pa., 1995—; organist/choirmaster St. John's Evang. Luth. Ch., Mercersburg, Pa., 1995—. Author: (rsch. project) English Liturgical Music of the Sixteenth Century, 1984; composer: (music anthem) Magnificat-Song of Mary, 1984. Singer Mercersburg Area Cmty. Chorus; deacon Northminster Presbyn. Ch., 1990. Fellowship of Christian Athletes, Wittenberg U., 1975—76. Mem.: Am. Guild Organists, Royal Sch. Ch. Music Eng., Music Educators Nat. Conf., Phi Delta Kappa. Republican. Presbyterian. Avocations: walking, hiking, music, camping, recitals. Home: 441 Leitersburg Rd Greencastle PA 17225 Studio: 207 Leitersburg St Greencastle PA 17225 Office Phone: 717-597-2213.

WERTS, MERRILL HARMON, retired management consultant; b. Smith County, Kans., Nov. 17, 1922; s. Mack Allen and Ruth Martha (Badger) Werts; m. Dorothy Wilson, Mar. 22, 1946 (dec. Jan. 15, 2003); children: Stephen M., Riley J., Todd J., Kelly M. BS, Kans. State U., 1947; MS, Cornell U., 1948. Beef sales mgr. John Morrell & Co., Topeka, Memphis, 1948-53; dir. mktg. Kans. Dept. Agr., Topeka, 1953-55; sec.-treas. Falley's Markets, Inc., Topeka, 1955-58; v.p. S.W. State Bank, Topeka, 1958-65; pres. First Nat. Bank, Junction City, Kans., 1965-78; pvt. practice mgmt. cons. Junction City, 1978-98; ret., 1998. Pres. Junction City CC, 1975—76. Mem. adv. com. U.S. Comptroller Currency, 1971—72; mem. Topeka Bd. Edn., 1957—61, Kans. Bank Mgmt. Commn., 1967—71, Kans. Pub. Employees Rels. Bd., 1989—94, Kans. Commn. Future Health Care, 1991—94; trustee Kans. State U. Found., 1958—2001, Kans. Synod Presbyn. Westminster Found., 1965—72, Kans. Pub. Policy Inst., 1995—99; pres. Junction City Indsl. Devel., Inc., 1966—72, Junction City-Geary County United Fund, 1967—68; chmn. Kans. WWII Commemoration Com., 1995—96, Kans. Commn. Vets. Affairs, 1995—98, Geary County Pub. Bldg. Commn., 1996—99; civillian aide Sec. Army for Kans., 1991—95; pres., bd. govs. Ft. Riley Ctrl. Kansas chpt. AUSA, 1994—95; mem. Kans. Senate, 1978—88; bd. dirs. Kans. Hist. Soc., 1989—97. 1st lt. inf. US Army, 1943—46. Decorated Bronze Star, Purple Heart; named Outstanding State legis., Am. Legis. Exch. Coun., 1988; named to Inf. Officer Candidate Hall of Fame, 1981. Mem.: DAV, VFW, Kans. Livestock Assn., Kans. Farm Bur., Kans. Bankers Assn., Assn. U.S. Army (bd. govs., Gen. Creighton W. Abrams medal 1997), Kans. State U. Alumni Assn. (pres. 1957), Junction City Country Club (past pres.), Rotary (dist. gov. 1973—74), Am. Legion, Masons, Jesters, Shriners, Sigma Phi Epsilon. Republican. Presbyterian. Address: 1228 Miller Dr Junction City KS 66441-3312

WERTSMAN, VLADIMIR FILIP, librarian, writer, library and information scientist, translator; b. Secureni, Romania, Apr. 6, 1929; came to U.S., 1967; s. Filip and Anna Wertsman. LLM summa cum laude, U. A.I. Cuza, Romania, 1953; MLS, Columbia U., 1969. Judge lower and appellate cts., Romania, 1953-67; examiner stock certs. 1st Nat. City Bank, NYC, 1967-68; reference libr. sci. div. Bklyn. Pub. Libr., NYC, 1969-74, sr. libr. Canarsie br., 1974-77, sr. libr. Greenpoint br., 1977-80, sr. libr. Leonard br., 1980-82; sr. libr., Slavic and Romanian specialist Donnell Libr. Ctr. N.Y. Pub. Libr., 1982-86; sr. libr. Learner's Adv. and Job Info. Ctr., 1987-93. Author, editor: The Romanians in America, 1748-1974, 1974, The Ukrainians in America, 1608-1975, 1976, The Russians in America, 1727-1970, 1977, The Armenians in America, 1618-1976, 1978, The Romanians in America and Canada, 1980, Librarian's Companion: A Handbook of Thousands of Facts and Figures on Libraries/Librarians, 1987, 2d edit., 1996, Career Opportunities for Bilinguals and Multilinguals: A Directory of Resources in Education, Employment and Business, 1991, 2d eidt., 1994, What's Cooking in Multicultural America, 1996, New York: The City in Over 500 Memorable Quotations From American & Foriegn Sources, 1996, paperback edit., 1999, Romanians in the United States and Canada: A Guide to Ancestry and Heritage Research, 2002, Directory of Ethnic and Multicultural Publishers, Distributors and Resource Organizations, 3d edit., 1995, 4th edit., 1999, 5th edit., 2003; co-author: Ukrainains in Canada and United States, 1981, Free Voices in Russian Literature, 1950s-1980s, 1986; editl. cons. Harvard Ency. Am. Ethnic Groups, 1980; contbr. Books, Libraries and Information in Slavic and East European Studies, 1986, Immigrant Labor Press in North America, 1840s-1970s, 1987, Through American Eyes, 1989, Ency. of N.Y.C., 1995; mem. adv. bd., contbr.: Gale Ency. Multicultural Am., 1995, 99; contbr. articles, book revs. to profl. jours. Recipient Disting. Lit. Achievement award Am. Soc. Writers, 1977, Cert. of Merit, Yeshiva U., 1981, Spl. Recognition award Pub. Libr. Assn. Am., 1990. Mem. ALA (chair multilingual libr. materials and svcs. com. 1976-88, chair pub. and multicultural material com. of Emie Round Table Ala. 1989—, ethnic and multicultural info. exchange roundtable, spl. merit award 1988, David Cohen Emiert Multicultural award 2003), Am. Assn. Advancement of Slavic Studies, Am. Romanian Acad. Arts and Scis., Delta Tau Kappa. Avocations: chess playing, travel, stamp collecting/philately, dance. Personal E-mail: vvladimirw@aol.com. *America is by its very nature of historical formation and development a multiethnic, multicultural and multilingual society. And if variety is the spice of life then American ethno-linguistic and cultural mosaique is the spice of our society. America's pluralism is also a microcosm of the entire world its citizens representing virtually all continents.*

WERTZ, JOHN ALAN, retired secondary school educator; b. Mpls., May 28, 1945; s. John Edward and Florence (Carlson) Wertz; m. Margaret M. Schlangen, 1993. BS, Hamline U., 1967; MS, St. Cloud State Coll., 1973; postgrad., George Washington U., 1985. Cert. St. Cloud Area Leadership Program. Tchr. social sci. St. Cloud Cmty. Schs., St. Cloud, Minn., 1967—2002; ret., 2002. Trainer, field rep. New Games Found., San Francisco, 1980—83; tchr., coach mock trial team Apollo HS, 1987—2000. Mem. affirmative action com. St. Cloud Cmty. Schs., 1975—78; mem. site coun. Apollo HS, 1994—96, co-chair site coun., 1995—96; chair St. Cloud Human Rights Commn., 1979—83; advisor Ctrl. Minn. Sexual Assault Ctr., 1981—83; bd. dirs. St. Cloud Area Tenants Assn., 1975—77, St. Cloud Area Spl. Olympics, 1982—83, United Way St. Cloud Area, 1996—2001, Minn. Edn. Assn., Great River Roundtable, 1997—2003, sec., 1997—98; mem. Edn. Minn. Transition Bd., 1998—99, Edn. Minn. Governing Bd., 1999—2002, St. Cloud Area Disabilities Coun., 1995—, pres., 2002—04; bd. dirs. St. Cloud Area Family YMCA, 2001—, bd. sec., 2002—03, 2007—, pres., 2003—05; counselor Sr. Corps Ret. Execs., 2002—; chpt. chmn., 2003—06, asst. dist. dir., 2006—; mem. Ctr. Svc. Learning and Social Change, 2004—07, treas., 2004—05; candidate Minn. State Legislature, 2000, 2002; mem. com. social action Minn. Synod Luth. Ch., 1971—74; chair social action com. Salem Luth. Ch. Coun., St. Cloud, 1974—76; mem. steering com. Create Cmty., 2004—. Recipient Merit award, St. Cloud Area Coun. Handicapped, 1976, Disting. Vol. award, YMCA USA, Minn. Alliance, 2004. Mem.: NEA, Am. Hist. Soc. Germans from Russia, St. Cloud Edn. Assn. (chair govtl. rels. coun. 1978—83, 1988—96), Edn. Minn., St. Cloud Area C. of C. (edn. divsn. 1992—97, vice-chmn. Pre K-12 com. 1993—94, chair edn. recognition com. 1994—96, mem. Thayer Youth Leadership steering com. 1995—97). Avocations: theater, travel. Home: 816 Rilla Rd Saint Cloud MN 56303-1037

WERTZ, KENNETH DEAN, real estate company officer; b. Okla. City, July 14, 1946; s. Walter K. and Kathryn L. (Moore) W.; children: Adam Troy, Kirsten Paige. BS in Acctg., Okla. State U., 1968, MS in Acctg. and Econs., 1969; JD, U. San Francisco, 1978. CPA, Okla., Calif; lic. real estate broker, Okla. Sr. acct. Deloitte, Haskins & Sells, San Francisco, 1969-70, 71-75; v.p. acquisitions, mng. dir. Landsing Corp., Menlo Park, Calif., 1975-86; pres. Detrick Salsberry Mgmt. Inc., Tulsa, 1987-88; v.p. asset mgmt. Corporex Co., Cin., 1989-90; exec. v.p. real estate Brunner Cos., Dayton, Ohio, 1990-92; pres. Pillar Real Estate Advisors, Dayton, 1992—. Lt. col. Med. Svc. corps U.S. Army, 1968-98. Decorated Army Commendation medal with three oak leaf clusters, Meritorious Svc. medal. Mem. AICPA, Okla. Soc. CPAs, Calif. Soc. CPAs, Nat. Assn. Securities Dealers (fin. prin., registered sales rep.). Republican. Methodist. Avocations: bicycling, snow and water skiing, racquetball, camping, fishing. Home: 835 Huntersknoll Ln Cincinnati OH 45230-4343 Office: Pillar Real Estate Advisors 5335 Far Hills Ave Ste 318 Dayton OH 45429-2317 Home Phone: 513-232-1513; Office Phone: 937-434-4250. Personal E-mail: dw@okclighthouse.com.

WERTZ, VIRGINIA LORYMA, retired librarian; b. Washington, Aug. 21, 1933; d. Melvin Moore and Ruth Belle (Johnson) W. AA, Am. U., Washington, 1958; BA, Am. U., 1961; MSLS, Cath. U., Washington, 1983. Clk. C and P Telephone Co., Washington, 1951—62; libr. Washington D.C. Pub. Libr. Sys., 1962—93; ret., 1993. Mem.: Order Ea. Star. Democrat. Episcopalian. Avocations: writing, theater, films. Home: 5332 41st St NW Washington DC 20015-1904

WESBERRY, JAMES PICKETT, JR., retired anti-corruption specialist, management consultant, speaker, author; b. Columbia, SC, Sept. 22, 1934; s. James P. and Ruby L. (Perry) W.; m. Lea Esdras Casteneda, June 13, 1975; children: Jonathan Jesse, Perry Latimer, Ruby Lee Nilda; children by previous marriage: James Pickett III, Elisa Marie, Lillian Sue, Paul Armand. BBA, Ga. State U., 1955; LLD (hon.), Atlanta Law Sch., 1967; MPA, Am. U., 1983. CPA, Ga.; cert. internal auditor, fraud examiner, govt. fin. mgr., fin. svcs. auditor. Page U.S. Ho. Reps., 1949-51; acct., mgmt. cons. Atlanta, 1956-67; v.p. fin. and adminstrn. Computer Tech. South, Atlanta, 1969-70; sr. cons. Inst. Pub. Adminstrn., NYC, 1967-69, 70-76; cons. to comptr. gen. Peru, 1970-74, Ecuador, 1974-78; adv., prof. Latin Am. Inst. Auditing Scis. Peruvian and Ecuadorean Sch. Govtl. Auditing, 1971-78; dir. sys., stds. and procedures Days of Inns Am., Inc., 1979-80; chief auditor OAS, Washington, 1980-82; cons. World Bank, 1982-83; prin. advisor acctg. and auditing pub. sector Latin Am. and Caribean Region, 1994-97; dir. America's accountability/anti-corruption project Casals & Assocs., Alexandria, Va., 1997—2001, dir. accountability audit, anti-corruption project Project -ATLATL-Mex., 2001—03; dir. Si Se Puede anti-corruption project Mgmt. Sys. Internat., Quito, Ecuador, 2003—06; ret., 2006. Founder, pres. Accountability 21, 1998—2003; advisor to pres. of Latin Am. Orgn. of Supreme Audit Instn., 1993—2000; sr. adv. to comptr. gen. U.S., 1983—85; dir. internat. ops. Price Waterhouse, 1985—88; sr. fin. advisor U.S.AID, 1988—93; pres., CEO Inst. Pub. Adminstrn., 1993—94, trustee; dir. N.Y. Bur. Mcpl. Rsch., 1993—94; mem. panel of experts in acctg. and auditing UN, 1972—82; adj. prof. Am. U., Washington, 1981—85; founding dir. Internat. Consortium Govtl. Fin. Mgmt., 1977—88, 1994—97, pres., 1984—87; cons., tchr. all Spanish-speaking We. Hemisphere nations Brazil, Haiti, Jamaica, The Netherlands Antilles, Guyana, Peoples Republic China, The Philippines, Can., U.S. Co-author: UN Handbook on Government Auditing for Developing Countries; editor: Latin American Manual of Professional Auditing in the Public Sector, Spanish Lang. newsletter Pistas de Auditoria, 1985-92; mem. editl. bd. Pub. Budgeting and Fin. Mgmt., 1982-92, The Govt. Accts. Jour.; contbr. articles to profl. jours. Mem. Ga. Senate, 1962-67, Fulton County Dem. Exec. Com., 1962-66. Decorated Order of Merit (Peru), 1972, Comptr. Gen. Venezuela, 1998; recipient Outstanding Career Achievement award USAID, 1993, Most Meritorious Accountant of the Americas award Interamerican Accounting Assn., 2003. Mem. AICPA (hon. life, chmn. interam. com. 1988-95), Interam. Acctg. Assn. (cert. assoc., bd. dirs. 1989-95, chmn. pub. sector com. 1989-91, 2000-2001, exec. com. 1994-95, Vet. Acct. Am. award 1987, Lifetime Acct. of Am. 1995, Most Meritorious Acct. 2003), Am. Acctg. Assn., Assn. Govt. Accts. (Authors award 1981-82, 89-90, chmn. internat. affairs com. 1981-82, 89-91), Inst. Internal Auditors (v.p. Latin Am. 1978-79, internat. rels. com. 1977-82, 84-88, regional dir. Latin Am. 1986-88, chpt. bd. govs. 1981-87, v.p. 1982-84, pres. 1984-85, vice chmn. internat. membership com. 1989-90, chpt. Disting. Svc. award 1987, Bradford Cadmus Meml. award internat. orgn. 1989, Outstanding Author's award 1990), Honduras CPA Soc. (Hon. award 1990), Jr. Chamber Internat. (life senator), Quito (Ecuador) Inst. Internal Auditors (life bd. dirs.), Lima Coll. Pub. Accts. (hon.), Lima Jr. C. of C. (hon.), Pinchicha (Ecuador) Coll. Pub. Accts. (hon.), Ecuador Fedn. Pub. Accts. (hon.). Baptist. Home: PO Box 17-22-20297 Cumbaya Quito Ecuador Personal E-mail: jwesberry@aol.com.

WESBURY, STUART ARNOLD, JR., health science association administrator, educator; b. Phila., Dec. 13, 1933; s. Stuart Arnold and Jennie (Glazewska) W.; m. June Carol Davis, Feb. 23, 1957; children: Brian, Brent, Bruce, Bradford. BS, Temple U., 1955; MHA, U. Mich., 1960; PhD, U. Fla., 1972. Capt. USPHS, 1955, served as adminstrv. officer, hosp. and clinic pharmacist, resigned, 1958; adminstrv. asst. Del. Hosp., 1960-61; asst. adminstr. Bronson Meth. Hosp., 1961-66; assoc. dir., asst. prof. U. Fla. Tchg. Hosp., 1966-67, dir., assoc. prof., 1967-69; v.p. Computer Mgmt. Corp., Gainesville, Fla., 1969-72; dir., prof. grad. studies in health svcs. mgmt. U. Mo., Columbia, 1972-78; pres. Am. Coll. Healthcare Execs., Chgo., 1979-91; sr. v.p. TriBrook Group, Inc., Westmont, Ill., 1992-94; prof. Sch. of Health Adminstrn. and Policy Ariz. State U., Tempe, 1994-2000, dir., exec. edn. programs Coll. Bus., 1996-2000, prof. emeritus, 2000—. Chmn. bd. trustees, trustee emeritus Blood Sys., Inc., Scottsdale, Ariz. Co-author: Why We Spend Too Much on Health Care; contbr. articles to profl. jours. Bd. dirs. Health Task, Inc., Atlanta, Boys Clubs, Gainesville, Heartland Inst.; chmn. bd. dirs. Mid-Am. chpt. ARC, 1988-91, DuPage County Dist., 1984-87; active Boy Scouts Am.; chmn. adminstrv. bd. Meth. Ch.; trustee Nat. Blood Found.; Rep. Congl. candidate Dist. 13, Ill. Named to Health Care Hall of Fame, 2005, Gallery of Success, Temple U.; recipient Award of Honor. Fellow Am. Coll. Health Care Adminstrs. (hon.), Am. Coll. Healthcare Execs. (Silver Medal award 1991); mem. APHA, Am. Hosp. Assn., Hosp. Mgmt. Sys. Soc., Assn. Univ. Programs in Health Adminstrn. (chmn. 1977-78), Am. Assn. Healthcare Cons. (hon.), Rotary (past pres.). Home and Office: 950 Willow Valley Lakes Dr H-312 Willow Street PA 17584 Home Phone: 717-464-4560. Business E-Mail: stu.wesbury@asu.edu.

WESCH, ANGELIA DEAN, lawyer; b. Dallas, Feb. 18, 1964; d. Calvin W. and Judy D. Wesch; children: Austin, Travis. BA with honors, U. Tex., 1986; JD, Tex. Tech U., 1989. Bar: Tex. 1989, U.S. Dist. Ct. (so. dist.) Tex. 1991, U.S. Ct. Appeals (5th cir.) 1991, Wash. 1993, U.S. Dist. Ct. (we. dist.) Wash. 1993, Alaska 1996. Atty. Andrews & Kurth, Houston, 1989-93, Stanislaw Ashbaugh LLP, Seattle, 1993-97, Eisenhower & Carlson PLLC, Tacoma, 1997—. Pres., bd. dirs. Crew Network. Mem. Wash. State Bar Assn. (environ. and land use sect.), Master Builders Assn. Pierce County. Office: Eisenhower & Carlson PLLC 1201 Pacific Ave Ste 1200 Tacoma WA 98402-4395

WESCH, MICHAEL, anthropology educator, cultural anthropologist, media ecologist; Grad. summa cum laude in Anthropology, Kansas State U., 1997; PhD in Anthropology, U. Va., 2004. Rsch. on social and cultural change in Melanesia in the Mountain Ok region of Papua New Guinea, 1999—2003; asst. prof. cultural anthropology, 2004—. Responsible for launching Digital Ethnography Working Group Kansas State U., coord., Peer Review of Tchg. Project; working with Educause Ctr. for Applied Rsch. on "The Tower and the Cloud" project; spkr. in field. Creator (short video) Web 2.0 ...The Machine is Us/ing Us, released on YouTube, 2007 (most popular video in the blogosphere and has been viewed over 3 million times, Rave award-video, WIRED Mag., 2007, #1 featured YouTube video, 2007), (digital ethnography) Nekalimin.net, (on-line resource) Virtual Snow; contbr. articles to profl. publications; guest editor Spl. issue, Visual Anthropology Review, Beyond e-Text. NSF Grad. Rsch. Fellowship, Jacob K. Javits Fellowship, Explorer's Club Grant, Fulbright-Hays Internat. Dissertation Rsch. Fellowship. Achievements include being active in the development of innovative teaching techniques, World Stimulation. Office: Kansas State U SASW 206 Waters Hall Manhattan KS 66506 Office Phone: 785-532-6866. Office Fax: 785-532-6978. Business E-Mail: mwesch@ksu.edu. *

WESCHCKE, CARL LLEWELLYN, publishing executive; BS, Babson Coll., 1951. Pres., publisher Llewellyn Worldwide Ltd., St. Paul, 1957—. Mem. Pub. Roundtable Minn. Office: Llewellyn Worldwide 2143 Wooddale Dr Saint Paul MN 55125-2989

WESCHLER, LAWRENCE MICHAEL, writer, journalist; b. Van Nuys, Calif., Feb. 13, 1952; s. Irving R. and Franzi (Toch) W.; m. Joanna S. Wegrzynowicz, Feb. 22, 1984; 1 child, Sara Alice. BA in Philosophy and Cultural History, U. Calif., Santa Cruz, 1974. Interviewer, editor Oral History Program UCLA, 1974-78; freelance writer LA, 1978-80; staff writer The New Yorker mag., NYC, 1981—. Author: Seeing is Forgetting the Name of the Thing One Sees: A Life of Contemporary Artist Robert Irwin, 1982, The Passion of Poland, 1984, David Hockney's Cameraworks, 1986 (Kodakpreis, 1986), Shapinsky's Karma, Boggs's Bills and Other True-Life Tales, 1988 (George Polk award, 1988), A Miracle, A Universe: Settling Accounts with Torturers, 1990, Mr. Wilson's Cabinet of Wonder, 1995, A Wanderer in the Perfect City: Selected Passion Pieces, 1998, Calamities of Exile: Three Nonfiction Novellas, 1998, Boggs: A Comedy of Values, 1999, Vermeer in Bosnia, 2004, Everything That Rises: A Book of Convergences, 2006 (Nat. Book Critics Circle award for Criticism, 2006); contbr. to Village Voice, L.A. Times, Internat. Herald Tribune, L.A. Weekly, Rolling Stone, N.Y. Times, Artforum, ArtNews, The Nation, others. Co-dir. Ernst Toch Archive & Soc., L.A., 1972—. Recipient Hemingway prize Overseas Press Club, 1982, Sidney Hillman award, 1989, George Polk award for best mag. reporting, 1992; Pointer fellow Yale U., 1982, Guggenheim fellow, 1986-87, N.Y. Inst. for Humanities fellow, 1991, Bard Ctr. fellow, 1992. Mem. PEN, Nat. Writers Union. Jewish. Office: The New Yorker 4 Times Sq New York NY 10036-6561 *

WESCOTT, JOSEPH WARREN, II, academic administrator, education educator; b. Wilmington, NC, July 19, 1959; s. James Warren and Delores (Pridgen) Wescott; m. Lisa Ann Blanton (div. Oct. 2002); children: Rachael, Joseph, Rose. BA, Wake Forest U., 1981, MA, 2000; MS, N.C. State U., 1998, EdD, 2005. Dir. alt. learning ctr. Beulaville Mid. Sch., NC, 1988; bus. mgr. Associated Ins. Agy., Wallace, NC, 1989—96; dir. grants and spl. projects Duplin County Hist. Assn., Rose Hill, NC, 1998—2000; coll. instr. James Sprunt C.C., Kenansville, NC, 1999—2001; fed. rels. analyst Duke U., Durham, NC, 2001—05; program specialist, grant approving agy., gen. admission U. NC, 2005—. Assoc. AAU Coun. on Fed. Rels., Washington, 2002—03; U. rep. The Sci. Coalition, Washington, 2001—03; com. mem. Edn. Adv. Com. and Ind. Agts., Raleigh, NC, 1998—2002. Editor: 1870 Fed. Census: The African Am. Population in Duplin County, 2000; author (contbr.): Ency. of N.C., 2005. Lay pastor Town Creek Christian Ch., Winabow, NC, 1990—; bd. dirs. Duplin County 250th Celebration, Kenansville, NC, 2000; bd. dirs., v.p. Duplin County Hist. Found., 2005—07. Capt. US Army, 1984—87. Rsch. grant, N.C. State U., 1998—2000, full fellowship, Wake Forest U., Winston-Salem, N.C., 1982—84. Mem.: Phi Alpha Theta, Phi Kappa Phi. Pentecostal. Avocations: reading, gardening, travel, public speaking. Home: 676 Wescott Rd SE Bolivia NC 28422-8562 Office: U NC Office of Pres Chapel Hill NC 27515 Office Phone: 919-733-7535. Business E-Mail: nceducation@earthlink.net.

WESCOTT, SETH, Olympic athlete; b. Durham, NC, June 28, 1976; US Olympian Snowboarder Winter Olympics, 2006; owner The Rack Restaurant, Kingfield, Maine. Achievements include Winning Snowboard Cross World Championships, 2004-2005; finishing second X Games Snowboard Cross Championship, 2005; Gold Medal in Snowboard Cross, Winter Olympics, 2006. Office: The Rack Restaurant Sugarloaf Mountain A Kingfield ME 04947

WESCOTT, WILLIAM BURNHAM, oral maxillofacial pathologist, educator; b. Pendleton, Oreg., Nov. 10, 1922; s. Merton Girard and Josephine (Creasey) W.; m. Barbara L., Dec. 31, 1944 (dec. June 12, 1969); children: William Douglas, Diane Elizabeth; m. Gloria Greer-Collins, Aug. 28, 1989. DMD, U. Oreg., Portland, 1951, MS, 1962. Asst. prof. to assoc. dean admin. U. Oreg. Dental Sch., Portland, 1953-72; co-dir. oral disease rsch. VA, Houston, 1972-75, dir. dental edn. ctr. LA, 1980-85; acting dir. Reg. Med. Edn. Ctr., Birmingham, Ala., 1978-80; chief dental svc. Dept. of Veteran's Affairs, San Francisco, 1985-94; clin. prof. U. Calif., San Francisco, 1994—; cons. Northern System of Clinics Dept. Vets. Affairs, 1994—. Dental surgeon, Oreg. Air N.G., Portland, 1954-68; cons. Madigan Army Med. Ctr., Ft. Lewis, W. Va., 1971-74, VA Med. Ctrs., No. Calif., 1985—, prof. pathology Duke U. Med. Sch., 1977-79; cons. U. Med. Ctr., Fresno, 1998—2006; mem. Enloe Hosp. Head and Neck Malignancy Tumor Bd. Contbr. 80 articles to profl. jours. and several chpts. to profl. books; 4 chtps. to books. Dist. chmn. Boys Scouts Am., Portland, 1965-67; bd. dirs. Am. Cancer Soc., Portland, 1964-67; comdr. Veterans Foreign Wars Post 5731, Gridley, Calif., 1994-95, comdr., 1996-98; chmn. Mil. Vets Ct. of Honor Meml., No. Calif., 1997—. With Oreg. N.G., 1938-40; with U.S. Army, 1940-42; lt. col. USAF, 1942-68. Decorated DFC with oak leaf cluster USAF, Oreg. N.G. Merit Svc. Medal, Portland, Fedn. des Anciens Combattants Français medal. Fellow Am. Acad. Oral and Maxillofacial Pathology, Mil. Officers Assn. Am. (sec. 2000—05), Omicron Kappa Upsilon, Sigma Xi. Avocations: woodworking, fishing. Home: 437 Justeson Ave Gridley CA 95948-9434 Office: U Calif Sch Dentistry S 512 San Francisco 3rd & Parnassus San Francisco CA 94143-0424 Office Phone: 415-476-4866. Business E-Mail: wesco83@sbcglobal.net.

WESELAK, ANNA MARIE SCHMIDT, educational association administrator, media consultant; b. Aurora, Ill., Oct. 28, 1949; d. John Joseph and Anna Florence (Sandor) Schmidt; m. Kevin John Weselak, May 20, 1972; children: Timothy Charles, Thomas John, Kristin Marie. BS, No. Ill. U., 1971, MS, 1974. Cert. early childhood edn. tchr., elem. edn. tchr. First grade tchr. Sch. Dist. 131, Aurora, 1971-75; kindergarten tchr. Pioneer Child Care Ctr., Lombard, Ill., 1987-92; sales and mktg. mgr. Minuteman Press, Addison, Ill.; owner, cons. Weselak & Assocs., 1994—; cons. Pearson Skylight, 1996—; sch. collaborative design team cons. The Ball Found., 1999—2000. Graphic media cons. Minuteman Press, Addison, Ill., 1991—; bd. dirs. DuPage regional unit Chgo. Assn. for Edn. Young Children; chmn. parent-child fair for Wk. of Young Child, 1988-89; program chmn., 1989-91, fall conf. chmn., 1991-92. Pres. Lombard PTA Coun., 1987-89, 5th dist. Gen. Fedn. Women's Clubs Ill., 1988-90, Lombard Newcomers, 1976-77, Lombard Svc. League, 1981-83; grand marshall Lombard Lilac Parade, 1993. Recipient 10 Yr. Svc. award No. Ill. U. Alumni Assn., 1980, Ill. State Bd. Edn. Those Who Excel award of merit, 1992-93; named gift AAUW, 1985, one of Outstanding Young Women Am., 1983, Lombard Woman Yr., 1989. Mem. Ill. PTA (bd. mgrs., dist. 32 dir. 1988-91, chair leadership tng. 1991-93, v.p. dist. dirs. 1993—, state conv. chmn. 1992, 93, Book of Recognition award 1990, hon. life mem.), Nat. PTA (hon. life mem., pres. elect 2003-05, pres. 2005-07), Ill. Fedn. Women's Clubs (chair budget and fin. 1990-92, editor Ill. Clubwoman mag. 1991—), Sigma Lambda Sigma (pres. 1970). Roman Catholic. Avocations: crafts, needlecrafts, sewing.

WESELY, EDWIN JOSEPH, lawyer; b. NYC, May 16, 1929; s. Joseph and Elizabeth (Bellas) W.; children: Marissa Celeste, Adrienne Lee; m. Marcy Brownson, Sept. 23, 1992. Ed., Deep Springs Coll., 1945-47; AB, Cornell U., 1949; JD, Columbia U., 1954. Bar: NY 1954, DC 1985, US Supreme Ct. 1960, others. Law clk. to judge US Dist. Ct. (so. dist.) NY, 1954-55; asst. US atty. So. Dist. NY, 1955-57; assoc. Winthrop, Stimson, Putnam & Roberts, NYC, 1957-63, ptnr., 1964-2000; sr. counsel Pillsbury Winthrop LLP, NYC, 2001—05, Pillsbury Winthrop Shaw Pittman LLP, NYC, 2005—. Spl. master numerous cases; chmn. spl. com. on effective discovery in civil cases US Dist. Ct. (ea. dist.) NY, 1982-84, com. on civil caseflow, 1985-88, com. on civil litigation, 1988-2002, chmn. emeritus, 2002—, civil justice reform adv. group, 1990-95; com. on pretrial phase civil cases Jud. Coun. 2d Cir., 1984-86, standing com. on improvement civil litigation, 1986-89; ex-officio Civil Justice Reform Act adv. group US Dist. Ct. (so. dist.) NY; pres. CARE, 1986-89, chmn., 1978-86, 89-90, internat. bd. dirs., 1981-90, pres., 1987-90; former bd. dirs. Internat. Rescue Com., bd. overseers, 2005—; bd. dirs., exec. com. Internat. Ctr. in NY, 1990—, chmn., 1998-2003, chmn. emeritus, 2003-. Trustee Deep Springs Coll., 1991-2000; vice-chair, 1998-2000. Decorated Order of Civil Merit (Republic of Korea); recipient World Humanitarian award Fgn. Press Assn., 1988, Commendation Bd. Judges US Dist. Ct. (ea. dist.) NY, 1993, Deep Springs Medal, Deep Springs Coll., 2003. Fellow Am. Coll. Trial Lawyers; mem. ABA (spl. adv. com. on internat. activities 1990-93, litigation sect. chmn. com. on discovery 1977-78, spl. com. study discovery abuse 1977-82, chmn. task force on liaison with internat. profl. assns. on matters of mutual concern 1989-93, Civil Justice Reform Act task force 1991-93, task force on the state of the justice sys. 1993-95, fed. initiatives task force 1995-98, co-chmn. task force on fed. and local rules 1997-98), UN Assn. USA (bd. dirs. 1991-2004), Assn. of Bar of City of NY (com. chmn., organized demonstration observation panel), Coun. on Fgn. Rels. Office: Pillsbury Winthrop Shaw Pittman LLP 1540 Broadway New York NY 10036-4039 Office Phone: 212-858-1712. Business E-Mail: edwin.wesely@pillsburylaw.com.

WESELY, MARISSA CELESTE, lawyer; b. NYC, Apr. 25, 1955; d. Edwin Joseph and Yolanda Teresa (Pyles) W.; m. Frederick Hameman; 1 child, Emma Elizabeth Wesely Allen. BA magna cum laude, Williams Coll., 1976; JD cum laude, Harvard U., 1980. Bar: N.Y. 1981. Assoc. Simpson Thacher & Bartlett, NYC, 1980-82, 84-88, London, 1982-84, ptnr., 1989—. Lectr., cons. Harvard Inst. Internat. Devel., Beijing, 1981, Jakarta, Indonesia, 1982; guest lectr. Yale Law Sch., New Haven, 1991; spkr. Am. Conf. Inst., Practicing Law Inst., Bankers Assn. for Fgn. Trade, N.Y. State Bar Assn. confs., 1993—. Bd. legal adv. Legal Momentum. Mem.: ABA, Internat. Bar Assn., N.Y. State Bar Assn., N.Y.C. Bar Assn., Phi Beta Kappa. Office: Simpson Thacher & Bartlett LLP 425 Lexington Ave Fl 20 New York NY 10017-3954 Office Phone: 212-455-7173. Office Fax: 212-455-2502. Business E-Mail: mwesely@stblaw.com.

WESLER, KEN, performing arts company executive; b. Phila., Apr. 3, 1964; s. Irwin Harvey and Marcia Elaine (Trilling) W.; m. Deborah Lee Rader, Nov. 2, 1986; children: Alexander, Samantha. BA, Temple U., 1994. Prodn. mgr. The Wilma Theatre, Phila., 1983-89; gen. mgr. Gretna Prodns., Inc., Mt. Gretna, Pa., 1989, 90, Walnut St. Theatre, Phila., 1989-95; CEO The Grand Opera House, Wilmington, 1995—. Guest lectr. Cabrini Coll., Phila., 1988, Temple U., Phila., 1988—1995, Springfield Coll. Bd. dirs. Downtown Visions. Office: The Grand Opera House 818 N Market St Wilmington DE 19801-3011 Home Phone: 610-361-0667; Office Phone: 302-658-7897. Personal E-mail: kwesler2000@yahoo.com.

WESLEY, GLEN, professional hockey player; b. Red Deer, Alta., Can., Oct. 2, 1968; m. Barb Wesley; children: Amanda, Josh, Matthew. Defenseman Boston Bruins, 1987—94, Hartford Whalers, 1994—97, Carolina Hurricanes, 1997—2003, 2003—, Toronto Maple Leafs, 2003. Player NHL All-Star Game, 1989. Achievements include being a member of Stanley Cup Champion Carolina Hurricanes, 2006. Office: Carolina Hurricanes RBC Ctr 1400 Edwards Mill Rd Raleigh NC 27607

WESLEY, JOHN MERCER, artist; b. LA, Nov. 25, 1928; s. Ner Wesley and Elsa Marie (Patzwaldt) W.; m. Hannah Allen Green, Dec. 18, 1971; children: Christine Alice, Ner. Student, Los Angeles City Coll., UCLA, 1947-50. One-man shows include, Robert Elkon Gallery, N.Y.C., 1963-80, 84, Premio Internat., Instituto Torcuato di Tella, Buenos Aires, 1967, Documenta 5, Kassel, 1972, Carl Solway Gallery, Cin., 1972, 85, 89, Galerie Rudolf Zwirner, Cologne, 1973, Rush Rhees Gallery, U. Rochester, 1974, PS 1, N.Y.C., 1978, Reinhard Onnasch Ausstellungen, Berlin, 1982-83, 101 Spring St. Gallery, N.Y.C., 1987, fiction/non fiction, N.Y.C., 1990, 91, Chinati Found., Marfa, Tex., 1990, 98, Daniel Weinberg Gallery, Santa Monica, Calif., 1992, 98, Portikus, Frankfurt, 1993, Stedelijk Mus., Amsterdam, 1993, Kunstverein, Ludwigsburg, Germany, 1993, daad-Galerie, Berlin, 1993, Galerie Rolf Ricke, Cologne, 1994, José Freire Gallery, N.Y.C., 1994, Jessica Fredericks Gallery, N.Y.C., 1996, 98, 99, 2000, 01, 02, 03, Galerie Haus Schneider, Karlsruhe, Germany, 1996, Danese Gallery, N.Y.C., 1998, P.S.1 Contemporary Art Ctr., N.Y.C., 2000-01, Sert Gallery, Harvard U., 2001, Gagosian Gallery, London, 2001, Daniel Weinberg Gallery, L.A., 2002, 04; group exhbns. include, Whitney Mus., 1968, 69, 76, Indpls. Mus., 1976, Royal Academy, London, 1991, Mus. Contemporary Art, L.A., 1992-93, Mus. Beaux Arts, Montreal, 1992-93, Deichtorhallen, Hamburg, 1997, Kunsthaus, Zürich, 1997; represented in permanent collections Albright-Knox Mus., Buffalo, Mus. Modern Art, N.Y.C., U. Tex., Austin, Mpls. Soc. Fine Arts., Chinati Found., Marfa, Tex., Rose Art Gallery, Brandeis U., Waltham, Mass., U. Kentucky, Lexington, Kunstmuseum, Basel, Switzerland, Dayton (Ohio) Mus. Art, Portland (Oreg.) Art Mus., Whitney Mus., Stedelijk Mus., Speed Mus., Louisville, Ky. Guggenheim fellow, 1976; grantee Nat. Endowment Arts, 1989. Address: 27 Washington Sq N New York NY 10011

WESLEY, NORMAN H., consumer products company executive; b. 1949; BA, MBA, U. Utah, 1973. With Crown Zellerbach Corp., San Francisco, 1973—83; pres., CEO, Fortune Brands Home & Office ACCO World Corp., Wheeling, Ill., 1983—99; pres. & COO Fortune Brands, Inc., Lincolnshire, Ill., 1999, chmn & CEO, 1999—. *

WESLEY, RICHARD C., federal judge; b. Canandaigua, NY, Aug. 1, 1949; s. Charles and Beatrice W.; m. Kathryn Rice; 2 children. BA summa cum laude, SUNY, Albany, 1971; JD, Cornell U., 1974. Bar: NY 1975. Assoc. Harris, Beach & Wilcox, 1974-76, Welch, Streb & Porter, 1976-77; ptnr. Streb, Porter, Meyer & Wesley, 1977—87; asst. counsel to minority NY State Assembly, 1979—82; justice Supreme Ct. 7th Jud. Dist., 1987—94; supervising judge Criminal Cts. 7th Jud. Dist., 1991; judge appellate div. Supreme Ct. 4th Dept., 1994—96; assoc. judge NY Ct. Appeals, Albany, 1997—2003; judge US Ct. Appeals (2nd cir.), New York, NY, 2003—. Creator Felony Screening Program, 1993; lectr. in field; bd. trustees Ctr. Dispute Resolution, Pre-Trial Svcs. Corp. Editor: Cornell Law Rev. Asst. counsel to Assembly Rep. leader James L. Emery, 1979-1982; assemblyman NY State 136th Assembly Dist., 1982-84, 84-86; chair Livingston County Alcohol and Drug Abuse Prevention Coun.; bd. trustees United Ch. Livonia, Chances and Changes, Charles Settlement House; bd. dirs. Myers' Found.; driver Livonia Vol. Ambulance. Named Legislator of Yr., Livingston-Wyoming Assn. Retarded Citizens, 1988; recipient Disting. SUNY Alumni award SUNY Alumni Assn., 1997. Fellow NY State Bar Found.; mem. Livingston County Bar Assn. (sec.), Supreme Ct. Justices Assn. (pres. 7th jud. dist.). Office: 1702 US Courthouse 40 Centre St New York NY 10007-1561 *

WESLIN, ANNA THERESE, clinical nurse specialist, dance consultant; d. Norman Uno and Mary Lou Weslin. AA, El Paso CC, Colorado Springs, 1977; BA, Dance Minor, St. Mary's Coll., Kans., 1981; BS in Nursing, Beth-El Coll. of Nursing, Colorado Springs, 1995; MSN, U. Colo., Colorado Springs, 2004. RN Colo. State Bd. of Nursing, Colo., 1995, cert. Clinical Nurse Specialist, Colo. State Bd. of Nursing, Colo., 2006. Assoc. dir., sec. treas. Colo. Springs Ballet Acad., 1981—2005; RN, charge nurse Health South Rehab. Hosp., Colorado Springs, 1996—2000; pres., CEO, tchr. La Sante et la Danse, Inc., Colorado Springs, 2003—; RN Pikes Peak Hospice & Palliative Care, Colorado Springs, 2006—; rn cardiology staff nurse Parkview Episcopal Hosp., Pueblo, Colo.; R&D plant mgr. Brown Disc Mfg., Colorado Springs. Recipient Best of Springs award (Best Pl. for Dancer's with a Broken Pointe), Gazette Newspaper, 2005. Mem.: Colo. Springs BBB, Colo. Springs C. of C., Performing Arts Medicine Assn., Internat. Assn. Dance Medicine and Scis., Sigma Theta Tau Internat. Achievements include development of 1st nursing based dance medicine clinic in the State of Colo; research in common injuries of adolescent dance students. Office: La Sante et la Danse Inc 2935 N Prospect St Ste 200 Colorado Springs CO 80907 Home Phone: 719-226-1022; Office Phone: 719-329-0714. Business E-Mail: lasante@comcast.net.

WESLING, DONALD TRUMAN, English literature educator; b. Buffalo, May 6, 1939; s. Truman Albert and Helene Marguerite (Bullinger) W.; m. Judith Elaine Dulinawka, July 28, 1961; children: Benjamin, Molly, Natasha. BA, Harvard U., 1960, PhD, 1965; BA, Cambridge U., Eng., 1962. Asst. prof. U. Calif. at San Diego, La Jolla, 1965-67, assoc. prof., 1970-80, prof., 1981—. Lectr. U. Essex, Colchester, Eng., 1967-70. Author: Wordsworth and Landscape, 1970, Chances of Rhyme, 1981, The New Poetries, 1985, The Scissors of Meter, 1996, (with T. Slawek) Literary Voice, 1995, Bakhtin and the Social Moorings of Poetry, 2003, On Literary Emotions, 2007. Office: U Calif Lit # 0410 La Jolla CA 92093 Business E-Mail: dwesling@ucsd.edu.

WESLOH, STEVEN M., lawyer; b. St. Louis, Mar. 22, 1971; BA, Ind. U., 1993; JD, U. Cin. Coll. Law, 1996. Bar: Ohio 1996. Sr. assoc. Frost Brown Todd LLC, Cin. Named one of Ohio's Rising Stars, Super Lawyers, 2006. Mem.: ABA (mem., Environment, Energy and Resources Sect.), Ohio State Bar Assn. (mem., Environ. Law Com.), Cin. Bar Assn. (mem., Environ. Law Com.). Office: Frost Brown Todd LLC 2200 PNC Ctr 201 E Fifth St Cincinnati OH 45202-4182 Office Phone: 513-651-6800. Office Fax: 513-651-6981.

WESSE, DAVID JOSEPH, higher education administrator, consultant; b. Chgo., May 5, 1951; s. Herman Theodore and Lorraine Joan (Holland) W.; m. Deborah Lynn Smith, Oct. 11, 1975; children: Jason David, Eric Joseph. AA, South Suburban Coll., 1971; postgrad., Purdue U., 1971-72; BEd, Ill. State U., 1973; MS, Loyola U., Chgo., 1983. Cert. mgr. adminstrn. Adminstr. Reuben H. Donnelley Corp., Chgo., 1974-76; adminstrv. mgr. Loyola U., Chgo., 1976-79, Joint Commn. on Accreditation of Healthcare Orgns., Oakbrook Terrace, Ill., 1979-81; adminstrv. dir., asst. sec. Northwestern U., Evanston, Ill., 1981-97; higher edn. cons. KPMG Peat Marwick, LLP, Chgo., 1997-2000; exec. dir. U. Houston, 2000; prin. Joslyn Assocs., Alexandria, La., 2000—; asst. v.p. U. North Fla., 2000—03; vice chancellor fin. and adminstrv. svcs. La. State U., Alexandria, 2003—. Seminar leader Nat. Assn. Coll. Aux. Svcs., 1998. Contbr. numerous articles to profl. publs. Pres., bd. dirs. Riverdale (Ill.) Libr. Dist., 1975, Riverdale Youth Commn., 1975; bd. dirs. Better Bus. Bur. Chgo. and No. Ill., 1991-97, Adminstrv. Mgmt. Soc. Found., 1998—, Ctrl. La. Bus. Incubator, 2006—; elder Redeemer Luth. Ch., 2006—. Recipient Svc. Recognition award Riverdale Libr. Dist., 1975, Excellence in Journalism award Nat. Assn. Coll. Aux. Svcs., 1989. Mem. Adminstrv. Mgmt. Soc. (bd. dirs. Chgo. chpt. 1983-88, pres. 1986-87, bd. regents 1986-88), Acad. Adminstrv. Mgmt. (bd. regents 1992-94), Profl. Office Mgmt. Assn. Chgo. (bd. dirs. 1992-93, sec. 1993-95, pres. 1995), Nat. Mgmt. Assn. (chpt. pres. 1995), Nat. Assn. Coll. and Univ. Bus. Officers (com. mem. 1986-87, 89-90, cost reduction awards 1986-88, 90, 92), Midwest Higher Edn. Commn. (com. mem. 1996-97), Assn. Coll. Adminstrn. Profls. (seminar leader 1995, 98, 99), Chgo. Area Bus. and Support Svc. Adminstrs. (founder 1988), Big Ten Bus. and Support Svc. Adminstrs. (founder 1992), Kiwanis Internat.(v.p. 2005-06, pres. 2006—), Ctrl. La. C. of C., U. North Fla. Adminstrv. and Profl. Assn. (pres. 2002-03), Phi Theta Kappa, Lambda Epsilon. Lutheran. Office: 8216 Tom Bowman Dr N Alexandria LA 71302-9307 Home Phone: 318-473-6490; Office Phone: 318-473-6409. Business E-Mail: dwesse@lsua.edu.

WESSEL, HENRY, photographer; b. Teaneck, NJ, July 28, 1942; s. Henry and Jennie (Cincotta) W.; children by previous marriage: Nicholas, Rider. BA, Pa. State U., 1966; M.F.A., SUNY, Buffalo, 1972. Propr., mgr. comml. photog. studio, State Coll., Pa., 1966-68; cinematographer for documentary film Dept. HEW, 1967; instr. dept. art Pa. State U., Phila., 1967-69; prof. dept. photography San Francisco Art Inst., 1973-98, chmn. grad. program photography, 1977-78, chmn. dept. photography, 1987-93; asst. prof. San Francisco State U., 1974-75; vis. lectr. photography various colls. and art schs., 1967-81; propr., dir. Photographic Resources, Point Richmond, Calif., 1977—. Vis. artist Mills Coll., 1987-88; resident faculty, San Francisco Art Inst. One-man show at Mus. Modern Art, NYC, 1973, Visual Studies Workshop, Rochester, NY, 1977, Fraenkel Gallery, San Francisco, 1981, 89, 92, Gallery Min, Tokyo, 1987, Gallery Ram, Santa Monica, Calif., 1996, Mus. Contemporary Art, LA, 1998, Rena Bransten Gallery, San Francisco, 2000, 02, Gallery Luisotti, Santa Monica, Calif., 2002, Palm Springs Art Mus., Calif., 2005, others; represented in permanent collections, Mus. Modern Art, NYC, Phila. Mus. Art, Boston Mus. Fine Arts, Library of Congress, Am. Arts Documentation Center, Exeter, Eng., Nat. Gallery of Can., Ottawa, Tokyo Met. Mus. Photography, Japan, Seattle Art Mus., Wash., Oakland Mus., Calif., Met. Mus. Art, NYC, Denver Art Mus., Colo., Australian Nat. Gallery, Canberra, Art Inst. Chgo., Ill., Charles Cowles Gallery, NYC, Robert Mann Gallery, NYC, others; author: Henry Wessel, 1987, House Pictures, 1992, Night Walk, 2000, Odd Photos, 2002, Five Books, 2006 Guggenheim fellow, 1971, 78; Nat. Endowment Arts fellow, 1975, 77, 78 Home: PO Box 70475 Richmond CA 94807-0475

WESSEL, MORRIS ARTHUR, retired pediatrician; b. Providence, Nov. 1, 1917; s. Morris Jacob and Bessie (Bloom) Wessel; m. Irmgard Rosenzweig, June 1, 1952; children: David, Bruce, Paul, Lois. BA, Johns Hopkins U., 1939; MD, Yale U., 1943. Diplomate Am. Bd. Pediat. Intern Babies Hosp., NYC, 1943-44; fellow in pediat. Mayo Found., Rochester, Minn., 1947-48; rooming-in fellow in pediat. Yale U. Sch. Medicine, 1948-51; asst. dir. pediatric outpatient clinic Yale-New Haven Hosp., 1951-52, dir. pediatric outpatient clinic, 1952-57; staff pediatrician, collaboration project Yale U. Sch. Medicine, 1957-62, instr. pediat., 1950-53, clin. asst. prof., 1963—71, clin. assoc. prof., 1961-75, clin. prof., 1975-97; ret., 2005. Bd. dirs. Clifford Beers Child Guidance Clinic, New Haven, 1950—55, cons. pediatrician, 1967—2005; bd. dirs. Women's Health Svc., New Haven, 1992—97, Child Welfare League, NYC, 1979—91. Author: Parents Book on Raising a Healthy Child, 1987. Maj. US Army, 1944—47, ETO. Mem.: New Haven County Med. Soc., Conn. Med. Soc., Soc. Adolescent Medicine, Am. Acad. Pediatrics (Practitioner Rsch. award 1994, C. Anderson Aldrich award 1997). Fax: 203-387-1927. E-mail: morriswessel@comcast.net.

WESSEL, PETER, lawyer; b. NYC, Feb. 2, 1952; s. Harry Nathan Jr. and Charlene (Freimuth) W.; married Vicki Brodsky Scheck; children: Daniel, Elizabeth, Justin Scheck, Matthew Scheck. BS, Syracuse U., NY, 1974, MPA, JD, 1980. Bar: NY 1981, US Dist. Ct. (no., so., ea. and we. dists.) NY 1981, Fla. 1984, US Ct. Mil. Appeals, 1988, U.S. Ct. Appeals (2d cir.) 1988, US Supreme Ct. 1988. Confidential law clk. to Hon. David F. Lee Jr. N.Y. Supreme Ct., 1980-82; sr. atty. criminal def. div. The Legal Aid Soc., NYC, 1982-87; pvt. practice NYC, 1987—. Notes and comments editor Syracuse Law Rev., 1979-80; contbr. articles to profl. jours. Robert M. Anderson award for Writing and Legal Scholarship, 1980, Neal Brewster scholar, 1977-78, Syracuse U. Coll. Law scholar 1978-79, Louis Waters Meml. scholar, 1979-80, Hiscock, Cowie, Bruce & Lee scholar, 1979-80; Martindale-Hubbell a-v rated. Mem. ABA, NY State Bar Assn., Assn. of Bar of City of NY, Fla. Bar Assn., Nat. Assn. Criminal Def. Lawyers, NY State Assn. Criminal Def. Lawyers, NY State Defender Assn., NY State Trial Lawyers Assn., NY County Lawyers Assn., NY Criminal Bar Assn. Office Phone: 212-421-0101. Business E-Mail: peterwessel@wessellaw.com.

WESSELINK, DAVID DUWAYNE, finance company executive; b. Webster City, Iowa, Sept. 5, 1942; s. William David and Lavina C. (Haahr) W.; m. Linda R. DeWitt, Dec. 27, 1971; children: Catherine, Bill. BA in Bus., Ctrl. Coll., 1964; MBA, Mich. State U., 1970. Tchr. Peace Corps, Turkey, 1964-66, Karabuk Koleji, Turkey, 1967-68, Robert Koleji, Turkey, 1969-70; rsch. analyst Household Fin. Corp., Chgo., 1971-73, asst. dir. rsch., 1973-77, asst. treas. Prospect Heights, Ill., 1977, v.p., dir. rsch., 1977-82, group v.p., CFO, 1982-86, sr. v.p., CFO, 1986—; v.p., treas. Household Internat., Prospect Heights, 1988-93; sr. v.p., CFO Advanta Corp., 1993-98; exec. v.p., CFO Metris Cos., Saint Louis Park, Minn., 1998-2000, vice chmn., 2000—02, chmn., CEO, 2002—05. Bd. dirs. Flex Fund Fin. Svcs., Irvine, Calif. Bd. dirs. Ctrl. Coll., Pella, Iowa, 1990—. Mem.: Fin. Execs. Inst., Econ. Club Chgo. E-mail: lrddw@juno.com.

WESSELKAMPER, SUE, academic administrator; m. Tom Wesselkamper; 2 children. BA History, Govt., Edgecliff Coll.; M Social Work, U. Mich.; PhD Social Welfare, CUNY. Head cmty., social svs. program New River Cmty. Coll.; dir. social work field instrn. program Radford U., Va.; dean sch. arts and scis., assoc. prof. social work Coll. New Rochelle, NY; pres. Chaminade U. Honolulu, 1995—. Author: Enhancing Ethnic Identity Through Cross-Cultural Interaction, An Intercultural Approach to Contemporary Ethnicity, Issues in Implementing Cultural Diversity Content, Role of the Social Worker in Health Planning. Chmn. bd. dirs. Family Svcs. Westchester County, NY; mem. adv. com. Pew Charitable Trust 3d Black Colls. Project on Student Retention; mem. Hawaii Cath. Conf., Hawaii State Network of Am. Coun. on Edn.'s Women Leaders in Higher Edn. Avocations: reading, movies, hiking, travel. Office: Chaminade U of Honolulu 3140 Waialae Ave Honolulu HI 96816 *

WESSELMANN, GLENN ALLEN, retired health facility administrator; b. Cleve., Mar. 21, 1932; s. Roy Arthur and Dorothy (Oakes) W.; m. Genevieve De Witt, Sept. 6, 1958; children: Debbie, Scott, Janet. AB, Dartmouth, 1954; MBA with distinction, Cornell U., 1959. Research aide Cornell U., Ithaca, NY, 1958-59; adminstrv. resident Meml. Hosp., NYC, 1957-58, adminstrv. asst., 1959-61, asst. adminstr., 1961-65, asst. v.p., 1965-68; v.p. for adminstrn. Meml. Hosp. for Cancer and Allied Diseases, NYC, 1968-79; exec. v.p., chief operating officer St. John Hosp., Detroit, 1979-84; pres., CEO St. John Health System, 1984-95, vice chmn., 1995-97; chmn., pres., CEO St. John Hosp. & Med. Ctr., 1984-94, ret., 1995. Mem. bus. adv. bd. City of Detroit, 1991-95, chmn., 1993-94; mem. exec. com. Greater Detroit Area Health Coun.; bd. dirs. Caymich Ins. Co. Ltd., Mich. Health Care Alliance, SelectCare, Detroit Econ. Growth Corp. Trustee Sisters of St. Joseph Health System 1981-94, Sisters of St. Joseph Health Svc., 1983-95, St. John Hosp. and Med. Ctr., 1979-95, St. John Health System, 1984-95, The Oxford Inst., 1984-95, Eastwood Clinics, 1992-95; pres. Providence Ch. Corp., Hilton Head Island, S.C., chmn. ch. fin. ocm., corp. pres. session; mem. bus. adv. bd.! City of Detroit, 1991-95, chmn. 1993-94. Served with MC AUS, 1955-57. Fellow ACHE; mem. Am.

Hosp. Assn., Internat. Hosp. Fedn., Mich. Hosp. Assn. (trustee, chmn. 1994-95, mem. exec. com.), Assn. Am. Med. Colls. (Coth rep.), Am. Cancer Soc. (regional adv. bd. 1994-95), Med. Group Mgmt. Assn., Soc. Health Service Adminstrs., Sigma Phi Epsilon. Home: 63 Big Woods Dr Hilton Head Island SC 29926-2604 Personal E-mail: glengen@hargray.com.

WESSELS, BRUCE W., materials scientist, educator, department chairman; b. NYC, Oct. 18, 1946; m. Beverly T. Wessels; children: David, Kirsten. BS in Metallurgy and Materials Sci., U. Pa., 1968; PhD in Materials Sci., MIT, 1973. Tech. staff GE R&D Ctr., 1972-77, acting br. mgr., 1976; from asst. prof. to assoc. prof. Northwestern U., Evanston, Ill., 1977-83, prof. materials sci. and engring., 1984—, prof. elec. and computer engring., 1987—, Walter P. Murphy prof., 1998—, dept. chair elec. engring. and computer sci., 2005—. Vis. sci. Argonne Nat. Lab., 1978; mem. program com. Internat. Conf. Superlattices, Microdevices and Microstructures, 1987. Editor 5 books including (with G.Y. Chin) Advances in Electronic Materials, 1986; mem. editl. bd. Jour. Electronic Materials, 1982-88, 98—, Hour. Electroceramics, 2006—; contbr. articles to profl. jours.; patentee in field. Fellow ASM, Am. Phys. Soc., AIME (bd. trustees 1996-97); mem. TMS, The Minerals, Metals and Materials Soc. (chmn. electronic materials com. 1987-89, conf. program chmn. 1986-87, key reader Trans. of AIME 1985-92, bd. dirs. 1993-98, vice-chmn. exec. coun. electronic, magnetic and photonic materials divsn. 1991-92, chmn. 1993-95, v.p. 1995, pres. 1996), Electrochem. Soc. Materials Rsch. Soc. (symposium organizer 1993, 95), Optical Soc. Am., Electroceramics (internat. program com. 2000-05), Sigma Xi, Tau Beta Pi. Office: Materials Science-Engring Northwestern U 2220 Campus Dr Evanston IL 60208-3108 E-mail: b-wessels@northwestern.edu.

WESSELS, DANIEL L., lawyer; b. Sewickley, Pa., Feb. 21, 1953; BA summa cum laude, U. Pa., 1976; JD, Harvard U., 1980. Bar: Pa. 1980. Assoc. Reed Smith Shaw & McClay; atty. Cohen & Grigsby, Pitts.; ptnr. Reed Smith LLP, Pitts., 2006—. Adj. prof. Duquesne U., John F. Donahue Grad. Sch. of Bus. Contbr. articles to profl. jours. Mem.: Phi Beta Kappa. Office: Reed Smith LLP 435 6th Ave Pittsburgh PA 15219 Office Phone: 412-288-5992. Office Fax: 412-288-3063. E-mail: dwessels@reedsmith.com.

WESSELS-MCCOY, DENISE WENDY, pre-school administrator, consultant; b. Windsor, NY, Aug. 18, 1955; d. Bess Marie Urbani and David Wilfred Wessels; children: Joseph J. McCoy, Ryan D. McCoy. BA in Child Devel., San Jose State U., 1977; MS, Nova Southeastern U., 1990, postgrad., 2002—. Owner Learning Tree Pre Sch., Santa Cruz, Calif., 1980—89; instr. U. Calif., Santa Cruz, 1989—91; child devel. program supr. Child Devel. Inc., Campbell, Calif., 1992—99; instr. Monterey Peninsula Coll., Monterey, Calif., 1996—2002, Cabrillo Coll., Aptos, Calif., 1999—2002, Ctrl. Sierra ROP, Placerville, Calif., 2002—05, Calif. State U., Sacramento, 2005—. Cons. Pathways Cons., Placerville, Calif., 2002—; county coord. ACT Against Violence, Santa Cruz, Calif., 2000—02; presenter in field. Active Human Rights Roundtable, Placerville, Calif., 2004—05; bd. dirs. Calif. Assn. for the Edn. of Young Children, Sacramento, 2000—04. Recipient Cert. of Appreciation, Santa Cruz County Children and Families Commn., 2002, Cabrillo Coll. ECE and Ctrl. Coast Assn. Edn. Young Children, 2002. Mem.: Nat. Assn. for the Edn. Young Children (sect. pres. 2002—04, acad. validator 1994—2005). Avocation: travel. Home: 1640 Pheasant Run Placerville CA 95667 Home Phone: 530-295-5574. Personal E-mail: travelerdenise@comcast.net.

WESSEN, DOUGLAS JOHN, psychologist; b. Rapid City, SD, Aug. 9, 1956; s. Donald Everett and Cynthia (Phillips) Wessen; life ptnr. Shelly Eidsness. BS, James Madison U., 1978, MEd, 1986, EdS, 1987. Tchr. spl. edn. We. State Hosp., Staunton, Va., 1979, Grafton Sch., Berryville, Va., 1979—81; tchr., spl. edn., group leader Dooley Sch., Richmond, Va., 1981—83; grad. asst. James Madison U., Harrisonburg, Va., 1983—85, tchg. asst., 1985—87; intern sch. psychologist Harrisonburg City Schs., 1987—88; sch. psychologist Southeast Regional Resources Ctr., Juneau, Alaska, 1988—89. Elem. counselor Juneau Sch. Dist., 1989—94, sch. psychologist, 1994—; glacier guide Northstar Trekking, 1998—. Pres. Alaska Sch. Psychologist Assn., 2000—01; exec. officer Juneau Mountain Rescue; team leader spl. teams Capital City Fire/Rescue Dept., Juneau, 1997—; coach Harborview Hoppers, Juneau, 1999—2002; asst. coach Juneau Jumpers, World Champion Jump Rope Team, 1996—97; bd. dirs. Critical Incident Stress Mgmt. Team, Juneau, Southeast Alaska Guidance Assn., Juneau, 1994—99. Recipient Cert. of Appreciation, Nat. Assn. Sch. Psychologist, 2003, Meritorious Pub. Svc. award, U.S. Coast Guard, 1999. Mem.: Mountain Rescue Assn., Critical Incidence Stress Found., Nat. Assn. Sch. Psychologists, Am. Alpine Club. Independent. Avocations: photography, softball, mountianering, sea kayaking. Home: 300 W 9th St Juneau AK 99801 Office: Juneau Sch Dist 10014 Crazy Horse Dr Juneau AK 99801 Office Phone: 907-523-1760. Office Fax: 907-523-1769. Business E-Mail: douglas_wessen@jsd.k12.ak.us.

WESSLER, MELVIN DEAN, farmer, rancher; b. Dodge City, Kans., Feb. 11, 1932; s. Oscar Lewis and Clara (Reiss) W.; m. Laura Ethel Arbuthnot, Aug. 23, 1951; children: Monty Dean, Charla Cay, Virgil Lewis. Grad. high sch. Farmer, rancher, Springfield, Colo., 1950—. Dir., sec. bd. Springfield Co-op. Sales Co., 1964-80, pres. bd., 1980—; pres. Arkansas Valley Co-op Coun., SE Colo. Area, 1965-87, Colo. Co-op Coun., 1969-72, v.p. 1974, sec. 1980-86; cmty. com. chmn. Baca County, Agr. Stablzn. and Conservation Svc., Springfield, 1961-73, 79—, vice chmn. Baca County Com., 1980-90; mem. spl. com. on grain mktg. Far-Mar-Co; mem. com. for PROMARK, Hutchinson, Kans., 1978. Mem. adv. bd. Denver Bapt. Bible Coll., 1984-89; chmn. bd. dirs. Springfield Cemetery Bd., 1985—; apptd. spl. com. Farmland Industries spl. project Tomorrow, 1987—. Recipient The Colo. Cooperator award Colo. Coop. Coun., 1990. Mem. Colo. Cattlemen's Assn., Colo. Wheat Growers Assn., Southeast Farm Bus. Assn. (bd. dirs. 1991-95), Big Rock Grange (treas. 1964-76, master 1976-82), Southwest Kans. Farm Bus. Assn. (dir. 1996—, pres. 1999-2001). Address: 18363 County Road Pp Springfield CO 81073 Personal E-mail: wesslerfarms@lcommic.com.

WESSLER, SUSAN R., biologist, educator; b. NYC, 1953; BS in Biology, SUNY, Stony Brook, 1974; PhD, Cornell U., 1980. Postdoctoral fellow Am. Cancer Soc. Carnegie Inst. Dept. Embryology, Washington, 1980—82; asst. prof. botany U. Ga., Athens, 1983, Regents prof. botany and genetics, 1992—, disting. rsch. prof., 1994—. Editl. bd. Current Opinions in Plant Biology, Proceedings of NAS, assoc. editor Genetics; co-author (with M. Gerald Neuffer and Edward H. Coe): The Mutants of Maize. Fellow: Am. Acad. Arts & Scis.; mem.: NAS (coun. mem.). Office: The Wessler Lab Univ Ga Dept Plant Biology 4505 Miller Plant Sciences Bldg Athens GA 30609 Office Phone: 706-542-1857. Office Fax: 706-542-1805. E-mail: sue@plantbio.uga.edu. *

WESSLING, GREGORY JAY, retail executive; b. Chgo., Dec. 11, 1951; s. Robert J. and Doris (Tosch) W.; m. Mary Anne Richmond, Nov. 16, 1974; children: Douglas A., James R., Robert E. BBA, U. N.C., 1974; postgrad., Wake Forest U. Sch. Bus., 1974-76, MBA, 1987. Store mgr. Lowe's Co., Inc., Winston-Salem, NC, 1973-76, mktg. mgr. North Wilkesboro, NC, 1976—, dir. merchandising, 1978-80, v.p. merchandising, 1980-96, sr. v.p., gen. merchandise mgr., 1996—99, sr. v.p. store ops., so. divsn., 1999—2004; prin. A&G Assocs. & Ptnrs., LLC, 2005—; chmn., CEO HouseRaising, Inc., 2005. Bd. dirs. DJR Corp., Winston-Salem; mem. alumni coun., bd. visitors Babcock Grad. Sch. Mgmt., Wake Forest U. Mem. Home Ctr. Leadership Council. Republican. Methodist. Avocations: skiing, water-skiing. Personal E-mail: team1agw@hotmail.com.

WESSLING, ROBERT BRUCE, retired lawyer; b. Chgo., Oct. 8, 1937; s. Robert Euans and Marguerite (Rickert) W.; m. Judith Ann Hanson, Aug. 26, 1961; children: Katherine, Jennifer, Carolyn. BA, DePauw U., 1959; JD, U. Mich., 1962. Bar: U.S. Ct. Appeals (9th cir.) 1965. Assoc. Latham & Watkins, LA, 1962-70, ptnr., 1970-94; ret., 1995. Bd. govs. Fin. Lawyers Conf., Los Angeles, 1974-2000. Mem. World Affairs Coun., L.A.; trustee DePauw U. Mem. ABA, Los Angeles Bar Assn., Phi Beta Kappa, Phi Delta Phi, Phi Eta Sigma, Order of Coif. Democrat. Methodist. Avocations: tennis, travel. Personal E-mail: bbwessling@aol.com.

WESSON, KENNETH ALAN, educational consultant; b. Oakland, Calif., Aug. 5, 1948; s. Oliver and Dorothy Mae Wesson; m. Victoria Vilay Lim, Sept. 29, 2000; children: Tyler Keanly, Adam Shai, Aaron Kenneth. MA, San Jose State U., 1972. Cert. tchr. Calif., 1972. Ind. ednl. cons. in neurosci., spkr. in field, San Jose, Calif. Spkr. in field. Author: What All Educators Should Know About the Human Brain, Where is God in the Brain, Memory and the Brain, Early Brain Development and Learning, Brain Basics, What Recent Brain Research Tells Us About Learning, The Neuropsychology of Prejudice. Mem.: AAAS, NSTA (Shell Sci. scholar 2002), ASCD, Am. Assn. Coll. Adminstrs., United Profs. Calif., Western Psychol. Assn., Nat. Kindergarten Alliance (founding mem.), Nat. Assn. Black Psychologists (founding mem.), Soc. Neurosci., Orgn. Human Brain Mapping, Nat. Coun. Tchrs. Math., Am. Math. Assn., Internat. Soc. Infant Studies, Tobacco Edn. and Rsch. Oversight Com., Justice Sys. Bd. Santa Clara County, Mental Health Bd. Santa Clara County, Tchr. Credentialing Task Force, Nat. Sch. Bds. Assn. D-Conservative. Achievements include research in cognitive neuroscience. Avocation: travel. Home: 1497 Elsman Ct San Jose CA 95120 Home Phone: 408-323-1497; Office Phone: 408-323-1498, 408-323-1498. Personal E-mail: kenawesson@aol.com.

WEST, ALFRED PAUL, JR., financial services executive; b. Brooksville, Fla., Dec. 7, 1942; s. Alfred Paul Sr. and Jane (Coogler) W.; m. Loralee Smith, June 16, 1964; children: Angela Paige, Alfred Paul III, Andrew Palmer. B in Aerospace Engring., Ga. Inst. Tech., 1964; MBA, U. Pa., 1967, postgrad., 1967-68. Chmn., chief exec. officer SEI Investments, Wayne, Pa., 1968—, pres., 1978. Bd. dirs. All-Star Forum, Phila., 1983—, Paoli Meml. Hosp., 1990—, grad. exec. bd. Wharton Sch. of Bus., 1983—; chmn. bd. dirs. Wharton's SEI Ctr. for Advanced Studies in Mgmt., 1989—; bd. dirs. World Affairs Council, Phila., 1985-89, mem. exec. com., 1989, chmn. adv. com., 1989—. Named one of Forbes' Richest Americans, 2006. Republican. Presbyterian. Avocations: skiing, golf, photography. Office: SEI Corp PO Box 1100 Oaks PA 19456-1100

WEST, ALISHA NICOLE, otolaryngologist, surgeon; b. San Francisco, Nov. 8, 1977; d. Robert Walker West Jr. and Pamela Leslie West. BS cum laude, U. Calif., San Diego, 1999, MS, 2001, MD, 2005. Dance instr. Calif. Acad. Performing Arts, Moraga, Calif., 1990—95; tchrs. asst. biology and chemistry U. Calif., San Diego, 1996—99, lab. technician, 1996—2001, rsch. scientist, neurosci., 1999—2001; gen. surgery intern U. NC, Chapel Hill, 2005—06, resident head and neck surgery, 2005—. Student coun. U. Calif., San Diego, 2001—02. Physician adv. Washington Advocacy Com., 2007; physician vol. Operation Smile, Mexico, 2000—05; vol. Habitat for Humanity, Mexico, 2001—05; med. student vol. Free Health Clinic, San Diego, 2004—05. Recipient Nat. Top Dancing Champion award, USA Dance, 1994, Selagi Rschr. Yr., U. Calif., LaJolla, 1999. Mem.: Am. Acad. Otolanyngic Allergy (scholar 2006—07), Am. acad. Otolaryngology Head and Neck Surgery, Am. Coll. Surgeons. Republican. Achievements include two-tim iron man finisher. Avocations: reading, skiing, surfing, flying, triathlon. Office: Univ NC 101 Manning Dr #7070 Chapel Hill NC 27515

WEST, A(RNOLD) SUMNER, chemical engineer; b. Phila., Jan. 12, 1922; s. Arnold and Mary (Sumner) W.; m. Beverly Helen Lehman, Oct. 5, 1946; children: Barbara Ann, Richard Sumner. BSChemE, U. Pa., 1943; MS, Pa. State U., 1946. With Rohm and Haas Co., Phila., 1946—87, rsch. engr., 1946—62, rsch. supr., 1962—72, mgr. rsch. dept., 1972—77, sr. tech. specialist govt. and regulatory affairs, 1978—87; owner, prin. A.S. West Assocs., Huntingdon Valley, Pa., 1987—. Cons. dept. chem. engring. U. Pa., 1952-72; mem. indsl. and profl. adv. com. Coll. Engring., Pa. State U., 1978-84, chmn. chem. engring. divsn., 1980-81, chmn. com., 1982-83. Editor: AIChE Safety and Health News, 1996—. Mem. Lower Moreland Twp. (Montgomery County) Authority, 1970, sec., 1971—; vice-chmn. bd. dirs. Chemical Heritage Found., 1984-92; pres. United Engring. Trustees, 1986-87. Fellow Am. Inst. Chem. Engrs. (dir. 1964-66, treas. 1973-75, v.p. 1976, pres. 1977); mem. Engrs. Joint Council (dir. 1976-79), Am. Assn. Engring. Socs. (vice chmn. public affairs council 1981, chmn. council 1982-83), Am. Chem. Soc., Nat. Soc. Profl. Engrs., Soc. Automotive Engrs., Water Environ. Fedn. Clubs: The Valley (Huntingdon Valley). Home and Office: 3896 Sidney Rd Huntingdon Valley PA 19006-2347 Office Phone: 215-938-7181. Personal E-mail: aswest@worldnet.att.net.

WEST, BARRY J., telecommunications industry executive; With British Telecom, dir., value-added svcs.; dir., corp. mktg. Cellnet (subsidiary of British Telecom); exec. v.p. Nextel Comm., Inc., Reston, Va., 1996—, chief tech. officer, 2005—. Office: Nextel Comm Inc 2001 Edmund Halley Dr Reston VA 20191 Office Phone: 703-433-4000.

WEST, BOB, pharmaceutical executive; b. Ellenville, NY, Mar. 7, 1931; s. Harry and Elsie May Wicentowsky; m. Betty Parker, May 9, 1957 (div.); children: Debra Ellen, Elizabeth Ann, Sharon Lynn; m. Jacqueline Cutler, Jan. 3, 1982. BS, Union U., 1952; MS, Purdue U., 1954, PhD, 1956; postgrad. mgmt. seminar, U. Chgo., 1972. Pres., dir. research Food, Drug Chem. Svcs., Stamford, Conn., 1975—; pres., dir. research Bob West Assocs., Inc., Stamford, 1975—. Pres. Drug Info. Assn., Phila., 1974-75; sci. adv. bd. Fountain Pharms., Inc., Largo, Fla., 1993—, Dovetail Techs., Inc., College Park, Md., 1996—, Phytopede, Inc., Sarasota, Fla., 1999—. Mem. editl. bd. Drug Info. Assn. Jour., Phila., 1977-85; contbr. articles to profl. jours. Mem. ASPET, Soc. Toxicology, Acad. Pharm. Scis., Assn. Rsch. Dirs., Drug Info. Assn., Assn. Univ. Tech. Mgrs. Home and Office: Food Drug Chem Svcs 7925 Meadow Rush Loop Sarasota FL 34238-4319 Home Phone: 941-925-8325; Office Phone: 941-925-8958. Personal E-mail: bjwest22@verizon.net.

WEST, CAROL CATHERINE, law educator; b. Phila., May 23, 1944; d. Scott G. and Helen (Young) West. BA, Miss. U. for Women, 1966; MLS, U. So. Miss., 1984; JD, U. Miss., 1970. Pub. svcs. law libr. U. Va., Charlottesville, 1966-67; catalog law libr. U. Miss., Oxford, 1967-70; legis. reference libr. Miss. Legislature, Jackson, 1970-75; law libr. Miss. Coll., Jackson, 1975-94, prof. law, 1975—. Del. White House Conf. Libr. and Info. Svcs., 1991; cons. to Parliament of Armenia, 1995, Parliament of Tanzania, 1997; mem. bd. commrs. Miss. Libr. Commn., 1993—98; mem., sec. Miss. Task Force on Gender Fairness in the Cts. Fellow: Miss. Bar Found.; mem.: AAUW (Miss. Woman of Yr. 2006), ABA, Miss. Women's Polit. Network (bd. dirs. 1998—2000), Miss. Libr. Assn., Miss. Women Lawyers Assn. (bd. dirs. 1991—93), Hinds County Bar (bd. dirs. 1995—96), Miss. Bar Assn. (Susie Blue Buchanan award 2001). Methodist. Office: Miss Coll Law Sch 151 E Griffith St Jackson MS 39201-1302

WEST, CATHERINE G., former retail executive; b. Sept. 6, 1959; BA, Lynchburg Coll., 1982. With People's Express Airline, 1981—85; v.p. credit card ops. Chevy Chase Bank FSB, 1985—91; sr. v.p. card mem. svcs. to exec. v.p. mktg. svcs. First USA Bank, 1991—2000; sr. v.p. U.S. consumer risk ops. Capital One, 2000—04, pres. U.S. card bus., 2004—06; exec. v.p., COO JC Penney Co., Inc., 2006. Named one of 50 Most Powerful Women in Business, Fortune mag., 2006.

WEST, CHARLES CONVERSE, retired theologian; b. Plainfield, NJ, Feb. 3, 1921; s. George Parsons and Florence (Farish) West; m. Ruth Floy Carson, Sept. 6, 1944; children: Russell Arthur, Walter Lawrence, Glenn Andrew. BA, Columbia U., 1942; B.D., Union Theol. Sem., NYC, 1945; PhD, Yale U., 1955. Ordained to ministry Presbyn. Ch. USA, 1946. Missionary, fraternal worker Bd. Fgn. Missions Presbyn. Ch. U.S.A., 1946-56; instr., chaplain Cheeloo U., Hangchow, China, 1948-49; instr. Nanking Theol. Sem., 1949-50; indsl. mission work Gossner Mission, Mainz-Kastel, Germany, 1950-51; lectr. Kirchliche Hochschule, Berlin, 1951-53; Lectr. Hartford Sem. Found., 1955-56; asso. dir. Ecumenical Inst., Bossey, Switzerland under World Council Chs., 1956-61; chargé de cours U. Geneva, 1956-61; instr. Peking Nat. U., 1948; assoc. prof. Christian ethics Princeton Theol. Sem., 1961-63, Stephen Colwell prof. Christian ethics, 1963-91, prof. emeritus, 1991—, acad. dean, 1979-84. Mem. commn. to form statement faith U. P. Ch. USA, 1961—67, chmn. internat. affairs adv. com., 1963—66; chmn. US Com. Christian Peace Conf., 1963—72; chmn. working com. dept. studies mission Evangelism World Coun. Chs., 1967—68; mem. commn. internat. affairs Nat. Coun. Chs., 1968—73. Author: Communism and the Theologians, 1958, Outside the Camp, 1959, Ethics, Violence and Revolution, 1969, The Power to be Human, 1971, Perspective on South Africa, 1985, Power, Truth and Community in Modern Culture, 1999, Storm Front, 2003; translator: J. Hamel - A Christian in East Germany, 1960; editor: The Sufficiency of God, Essays in Honor of Dr. W. A. Visser't Hooft, 1963; assoc. editor: Religion in Eastern Europe, 1985—2005. Mem.: Presbytery NYC, Am. Theol. Soc. (v.p. 1982—83, pres. 1983—84), Am. Soc. Christian Ethics (v.p. 1972—73, pres. 1973—74), Christian Associated Rels. with Eastern Europe (pres. 1988—92), Ams. Dem. Action. Presbyterian. Home: 9 Hedge Row Rd Princeton NJ 08540-5047 Office: Princeton Theological Seminary CN821 Princeton NJ 08542

WEST, CLARK DARWIN, pediatric nephrologist, educator; b. Jamestown, NY, July 4, 1918; s. Clark Darwin and Frances Isabel (Blanchard) W.; m. Ruthann Asbury, Apr. 12, 1944 (div.); children: Charles Michael, John Clark, Lucy Frances; m. Dolores Lachenman, Mar. 1, 1986. AB, Coll. of Wooster, 1940; MD, U. Mich., 1943. Intern Univ. Hosp., Ann Arbor, Mich., 1943-44, resident in pediatrics, 1944-46; fellow in pediatrics Children's Hosp. Research Found., Cin., 1948-49, research asso., 1951-89, asso. dir., 1963-89, dir. div. immunology and nephrology, 1958-89; with cardiopulmonary lab. chest service Bellevue Hosp., NYC, 1949-51; attending pediatrician Children's Hosp., 1951-89; asst. prof. pediatrics U. Cin., 1951-55, asso. prof., 1955-62, prof., 1962-89. Mem. coms. NIH, 1965-69, 1972-73 Mem. editorial bd.: Jour. Pediatrics, 1960-79, Kidney Internat., 1977-89, Clin. Nephrology, 1989-96; contbr. articles to profl. jours. Served to capt. M.C., AUS, 1946-47. Decorated Army commendation medal; recipient recognition award Cin. Pediat. Soc., 1980, Mitchell Rubin award, 1986, Henry L. Barnett award, 1995, Daniel Drake medal, 1996, John P. Peters award, 1996. Mem. Soc. Pediatric Research (sec.-treas. 1958-62, pres. 1963-64), Am. Pediatric Soc., Am. Soc. Pediatric Nephrologists (pres. 1973-74), Am. Physiol. Soc., Am. Assn. Immunologists, Am. Soc. Nephrology, Internat. Pediatric Nephrology Assn., Sigma Xi, Alpha Omega Alpha. Achievements include research on immunopathogenesis and treatment of glomerulonephritides and in the complement system. Home: 11688 Aristocrat Dr Harrison OH 45030-9753 Office: Children's Hosp Med Ctr Cincinnati OH 45229 Office Phone: 513-636-4531. Personal E-mail: CWest_2865@fuse.net.

WEST, CORNEL RONALD, humanities educator, writer; b. Tulsa, Okla., June 2, 1953; s. Clifton L. W.; 1 child from previous marriage, Clifton; m. Elleni Gebre Amlak. BA, Harvard U., 1973; PhD, Princeton U., 1977. Prof. religion Union Theol. Sem., NY, 1977-84, 87-88, Yale U. Divinity Sch., New Haven, 1984-87; prof. religion, dir. dept. Afro-Am. Studies Princeton U., 1988-94, Class of 1943 Univ. prof. of religion, 2002—; prof. Afro-Am. studies, philosophy of religion Harvard U., Cambridge, Mass., 1994—99, Alphonse Fletcher jr. prof., 1999—2002. Am. corr. Le Monde Diplomatique; vis. prof. U. Paris; DuBois fellow Harvard U., 1994-99. Author: Black Theology and Marxist Thought, 1979, Prophesy Deliverance! An Afro-American Revolutionary Christianity, 1982, Prophetic Fragments, 1988, The American Evasion of Philosophy: A Genealogy of Pragmatism, 1989, Breaking Bread: Insurgent Black Intellectual Life, 1991, The Ethical Dimensions of Marxist Thought, 1991, Race Matters, 1993, Beyond Eurocentrism and Multiculturalism, Vol. I: Prophetic Thought in Postmodern Times. Vol. II: Prophetic Reflections: Notes on Race and Power in America, 1993, Keeping Faith: Philosophy and Race in America, 1994, (with Paula Giddings) Regarding Malcolm X, 1994, (with Michael Lerner) Jews and Blacks: Let the Healing Begin, 1995, (with Michael Lerner) Jews and Blacks: A Dialogue on Race, religion, and Culture in America, 1996, (with Henry Louis Gates Jr.) The Future of the Race, 1996, Restoring Hope: Conversations on the Future of Black America, 1998, (with Roberto Unger) The Future of American Progressivism, 1998, (with Sylvia Ann Hewlett) The War Against Parents, 1998, The Cornel West Reader, 1999, (with Henry Louis Gates Jr.) The African American Century: How Black Americans Have Shaped Our Century, 2000, Democracy Matters: Winning the Fight Against Imperialism, 2004; co-prodr. (with Derek "D.O.A." Allen, Clifton West & Mike Daily) album, Sketches of my Culture, 2001, (with Andre Benjamin, Jill Scott, Talib Kweli, et. al.) album, Never Forget: A Journey of Revelations, 2007. Named one of 100 Most Influential Black Ams., Ebony mag., 2006; named to The Ebony Power 150, 2007; recipient Literary Lion award, NY Pub. Libr., 1993. Office: Princeton U Dept Religion Hall 208 Marx Hall Princeton NJ 08544-1066 Office Phone: 609-258-0021. E-mail: cwest@princeton.edu. *

WEST, DANIEL CHARLES, dentist; b. Trenton, NJ, July 23, 1955; s. Harry E. and Alma R. (Washburn) W.; m. Deborah L. Scott, May 28, 1977; children: Lauren Elizabeth, Colin Jeffrey, Aaron Samuel. BS, Ea. Nazarene Coll., 1977; DMD, U. Pitts., 1982; M, Acad. Gen. Dentistry, 2003. Min. youth music South Hills Ch. of the Nazarene, Bethel Park, Pa., 1977-82; pvt. practice Terre Hill, Pa., 1982-95; prin., owner New Holland (Pa.) Dental Care, 1995—. Mem. Internat. Gen. Bd. Ch. of Nazarene, Kansas City, Mo., 1989—2002, lay mem. dist. adv. bd. Phila. dist., Frazer, Pa., 1985—2007, coord. work and witness program, 1988—90, dir. compassionate ministries, 1990—; bd. dirs. Mission Am.; dir. Phila. Dist. IMPACT, 1982—89, 2001—05; trustee Ea. Nazarene Coll., Wollaston, Mass., 1984—, mem. exec. com., chmn. dept. fin., chmn. bd. dirs., 2002—06; mem. clin. faculty U. Pa. Sch. Dental Medicine, Med. U. Ukraine, Kiev, Pediat. Med. U., Moscow; mem. Mission Am. Bd., 1997—; mng. ptnr. Ctrl Am. Partnership, 2007—. Contbr. articles to jours. Bd. dirs. Garden Spot Village Retirement Cmty., 1996—97; interim min. music Fairview Village Ch. of Nazarene, 2001—02; mng. ptnr. CIS Partnership for Ministry, 1998—2002; chmn. bd. trustees Eastern Nazarene Coll., 2002—06, mem. found. bd., 2004—06. Lt. USPHS, 1982—85. Named Bus. Woman of Yr., Pa., 2007; recipient Alumni Achievement award, Eastern Nazarene Coll., 1996, Citation for Exceptional Achievement, Pa. Ho. Reps., 2004. Master Am. Acad. Gen. Dentistry; mem. ADA (Cert. Recognition for Internat. Svc. in a Fgn. County 1996), Am. Acad. Cosmetic Dentistry, Pa. Dental Assn., Lancaster County Dental Soc. Republican. Home: 1442 Hay Field Dr East Earl PA 17519-9685 Office: 650 E Main St New Holland PA 17557-1410 Office Phone: 717-354-3200. Business E-Mail: info@drdanwest.com. *The greatest joy I have is in serving others through ministry in the church, my dental practice, and especially in my home.*

WEST, DANIEL JONES, JR., health care consultant, educator; b. Coaldale, Pa., Sept. 19, 1949; s. Daniel J. and Mildred Elizabeth (Kreiger) West; m. Linda Jean Werdt, Sep. 18, 1971; children: Jeffrey Bryan,

Christopher Jones, Danielle K. BS cum laude, Pa. State U., 1971, EdM summa cum laude, 1972; postgraduate studies, Montgomery County Cmty. Coll., 1973, Rutgers U., 1974; PhD summa cum laude in Counseling Psych., Pa. State U., 1982. Adminstr. Good Samaritan Hosp., Pottsville, Pa., 1975-78, asst. v.p. ambulatory svcs., 1978-83; adminstr. MEDIQ, Inc. Scranton State Hosp., Pa., 1983-85; pres., CEO HTC Consulting Grp., Inc., Gouldsboro, Pa., 1986—; adj. prof. to asst. prof. Grad. Sch. Health Adminstrn. U. Scranton, 1983-93, chmn., assoc. prof., 1990, chmn., prof. Instr. Pa. State U., Schuylkill Haven, 1973-83, Univ. Park, 1974-75; adj. bd. dirs. Healthcare Mgmt. Forum of Northeastern Pa., 1997—; vice chmn. ABHM cert. com., 1997—; adv. bd., NRCI Hereditary Cancer Prog., 1997—; mem. Cmty. Med. Ctr. CPS planning com., 2000—; bd. mem., Behavioral Health Rsch. Inst., 1998—; mem. N.E. Regional Cancer Inst., edn. and support com., ann. workplan, 2001—; adv. panel, Pa. Med. Soc., 2002—; prof. Wilkes Coll., 1986; CEO Medi-Group, Inc., Penn Health Care, Inc., A.I.R., Inc., Med. Sci. Lab., Inc., Lackawanna Med. Grp., P.C., Scranton, 1986-91; stockholder, ptnr. Penn Health Care, Inc., 1987-1990, Health Care Support Svcs., Scranton, 1983-1990; stockholder, bd. dirs. N.E. Women's Diagnostic Ctr., Scranton, 1989-1990; regional dir. ops. HCP Consulting Grp., Inc., Willow Grove, Pa., 1990-95; moderator First Ann. Conf. on Drug and Alcohol Abuse, Bedford, Pa., 1977; mem. adv. com. to rehab. counseling progs. Pa. State U., 1983-93; numerous positions State Bd. of Medicine, Commonwealth of Pa., 1991-95; mem. departmental rev. bd. for rsch. U. Scranton, 1991—; me. Scranton Temple residency prog. instnl. rev. bd. Mercy Hosp., 1991—; mem. Fedn. of State Med. Bd. of US, Inc., 1994-96, mem. editl. adv. bd., 1984-85, voting del. from Pa. for osteopathic bd.; bd. dirs. comm. com. Midwest Regional Med. Bd., 1994-95; mem. task force on health care Econ. Devel. Coun. N.E. Pa., 1994-95; vis. prof. Trnava U., Slovakia, 1997—, assoc. prof., 1998-1999, full prof., 1999—; vis. prof. U. Matej Bel, Slovakia, 1997-1998; bd. dirs. Robert Charles Zaloga Found.; spkr. in field. Author manuals on mgmt. and health care; contbr. articles to profl. jours. Chmn. planning and implementation coun. Schuylkill County Gov.'s Coun. on Drug and Alcohol Abuse, State of Pa., 1973-74; mem. Drug Adv. Task Force, 1973-74, Task Force Child and Family Resource Devel. Prog., Schuylkill County, 1973-74, Criminal Justice Sys. Task Force, Schuylkill County, 1975-76; mem. adv. bd. Holy Family Home Health Care Agy., Schuylkill County, 1977-78, chmn. bd. edn. com., 1977-78; bd. dirs. St. David's Soc. Schuylkill and Carbon Counties, 1976-79, Health Sys. Agy., N.E. Pa., 1977-80; mem. instnl. rev. bd. Cmty. Med. Ctr., 1986-96; bd. dirs. Scranton Counseling Ctr., 1990—, mem. long range planning com. and pers. com.; bd. dirs. Telespond Sr. Svcs., Inc., 1991-1996; mem. Diocesan health care com. Diocese of Scranton, 1992-93; mem. steering com. Citizen Advocacy Ctr., AARP Health Advocacy Svcs., 1992-95; bd. dirs., v.p. Citizen Advocacy Ctr., Arlington, Va., 1994-95; mem. ad hoc com. on children health United Way, 1995-96. Recipient Rsch. award Am. Ednl. Rsch. Assn., 1983, Svc. and Leadership award Schuylkill County Drug and Alcohol Exec. Commn., 1982, Dedication and Leadership award Gov.'s Coun. Drug and Alcohol Abuse Drug Adv. Task Force, 1978; Fellow Accreditating Commn. Edn. for Health Svcs. Adminstrn., 1994-95, Regents award, 1997. Fellow Am. Acad. Med. Adminstrs. (editl. com. 1993—, diplomate award 1995), Internat. Acad. Behavioral Medicine, Counseling and Psychotherapy, Inc., Am. Coll. Healthcare Execs. (regents adv. bd. Pa. Area B 1995—, regents award 1997), Fedn. State Med. Bds. US, Inc. (editl. com. 1994-95), Coll. Osteo. Healthcare Execs. (editl. com. 1991-1998), Am. Coll. Med. Practice Execs., Am. Coll. Health Care Adminstr., Assn. Mental Health Adminstrs. (cert., editl. com. 1992—, mem. fellowship rev. com.); mem. APHA, AAAS, AAUP, Nat. Rehab. Assn., Nat. Rehab. Adminstrn. Assn., Am. Hosp. Assn., Med. Grp. Mgmt. Assn., Acad. Memg., Assn. Univ. Progs. in Health Adminstrn., NY Acad. Scis., Nat. Assn. Healthcare Consultants, Am. Soc. Tng. and Devel., Acad. Health Svcs. Rsch. and Health Policy, Strategic Mgmt. Soc., Nat. Coun. Cmty. Behavioral Healthcare, Cmty. Hosp. Med. Edn. Alliance, Hosp. Assn. Pa., Pa. Rehab. Assn., Pa. Med. Grp. Mgmt. Assn., Phi Kappa Phi, Iota Alpha Delta. Office: Dept Health Adminstrn and Human Resources U Scranton 415 McGurrin Hall Scranton PA 18510-4523 E-mail: westd1@scranton.edu.

WEST, DOYLE THOMAS, retired music educator; b. Smithfield, Utah, May 10, 1932; s. Preston Dangerfield West and Eliza Genevieve Mecham; m. Ardyth Mae Hansen, July 13, 1962; children: MaryLynne Pope, Barbara Ann Livacich, David Hansen, Roger Hansen, Paul Hansen. BS, Utah State U., 1954. Cert. tchr. Utah, Calif. Jr. HS choral music tchr. Tooele Sch. Dist., Utah, 1954—58; asst. Brigham Young U., Provo, Utah, 1961—62; HS choral music tchr. San Lorenzo Unified Sch. Dist., Calif., 1962—92, dist. music chmn., supr.; ret., 1992. Pvt. voice tchr., 1958—2006. Prodr., music dir.: Temple Hill Pageant, 1964—2004, music dir.: annual Handel's Messiah, 1977—2006. Missionary to Cape Town, South Africa LDS Ch., 1958—60. Named Outstanding Tchr. of Yr., San Lorenzo H.S., 1963, Dist. Tchr. of Month, San Lorenzo Unified Sch. Dist., 1992. Mem.: NEA (life), Am. Choral Dirs. Assn. (life), Calif. Music Educator Assn. (life), Choral Music Nat. Assn. (life), Music Educators Nat. Conf. (life). Republican. Mem. Lds Ch. Home: 19535 Eagle St Castro Valley CA 94546 Home Phone: 510-538-4806.

WEST, GAIL BERRY, lawyer; b. Cin. d. Theodore Moody and Johnnie Mae (Newton) B.; m. Togo D. West, Jr., June 18, 1966; children: Tiffany Berry, Hilary Carter. BA magna cum laude, Fisk U., 1964; MA, U. Cin., 1965; JD, Howard U., 1968. Bar: D.C. 1969, U.S. Supreme Ct. 1978. Staff atty. IBM, 1969-76; spl. asst. to sec. HUD, 1977-78; staff asst. to spl. asst. to Pres., Washington, 1978-80; dep. asst. sec. for manpower res. affairs installations Dept. Air Force, 1980-81; atty. AT&T, Washington, 1983-84; exec. dir. govt. affairs Bell Comm. Rsch. Inc., Washington, 1984-95; dir. govt. rels. Armstrong World Industries, Inc., Washington, 1995—2003, cons., 2003—06. Mem. exec. com. ARC, Washington, 1974-85; bd. dirs. Family and Child Svcs., Washington, 1974-87; trustee Corcoran Gallery Art, 1983-00, Arena Stage, 1992-99, Decatur House, 1994-, WETA, 1995-01, Fisher House Found., Inc.; bd. dirs. Meridian House, 1994-00; mem. DC Commn. Fine Arts, 2003-; mem. cathedral chpt. Nat. Cathedral, 1997-06; bd. dirs. Nat. Mus. Am. History, Smithsonian, 2005-. Ford Found. fellow, 1965-68. Mem. ABA, D.C. Bar Assn., Unified Bar D.C. Democrat. Episcopalian. Home: 4934 Rockwood Pkwy NW Washington DC 20016-3211

WEST, GEOFFREY B., theoretical physicist, physics professor; b. England; BA in Physics, Cambridge U., 1961; PhD in Physics, Stanford U., 1966. Faculty Stanford U., 1970; high energy particle physics grp. leader Los Alamos Nat. Lab., N.Mex., 1974, high energy physicist, 1982—; prof. biology U. N.Mex, Albuquerque, 1999—; disting. prof. Santa Fe Inst., 2003—, pres., 2005—. Sr. lab. fellow Los Alamos Nat. Lab., 2003. Named one of 100 Most Influential People, Time Mag., 2006. Fellow: Am. Phys. Soc. Office: Santa Fe Inst 1399 Hyde Pk Rd Santa Fe NM 87501 Office Phone: 505-946-2701.

WEST, JAMES C., JR., lawyer; b. White Sulphur Springs, W.Va., Mar. 15, 1932; LLB, W.Va. U., 1959. Bar: W.Va. 1959. Law clk. to Hon. Herbert S. Boreman, Judge of 4th Cir. Ct. Appeals, 1958—59; atty. Clifford, Jones & Williams, Clarksburg, W.Va., 1960—89, West & Jones (formerly Clifford, Jones & Williams), Clarksburg, W.Va., 1989—. Fellow: Am. Bd. Trial Advs., Am. Coll. Trial Lawyers; mem.: ABA, W. Va. Bar Assn. (pres. 2003), Assn. Trial Lawyers Am., W.Va. Trial Lawyers Assn. (pres. 1971), Harrison County Bar Assn., W.Va. State Bar (bd. govs. 1975 1978), Phi Delta Phi. Office: West and Jones PO Box 2348 360 Washington Ave Clarksburg WV 26301

WEST, JAMES EDWARD (JAMES EDWARD MACEO WEST), acoustical engineer, educator; b. Prince Edward County, Va., Feb. 10, 1931; s. Samuel Edward and Matilda West. Attended, Hampton U., Va.; BS in Physics, Temple U., 1957; DSc (hon.), NJ Inst. Tech., 1995. Summer intern, acoustics rsch. dept. Bell Lab., Murray Hill, NJ; acoustical scientist specializing in electroacoustics, physical and archtl. acoustics, disting. fellow AT&T Bell Labs., now Lucent Technologies, Bell Labs, Murray Hill, NJ, 1957—2001, ret., 2001; rsch. prof., dept. electrical and computer engring. John Hopkins U. Whiting Sch. Engring., Balt., 2003—. Headed numerous programs Bell Labs; founding mem. Assn. Black Labs Employees; chmn. John Hopkins Whiting Sch. Engring. Coun. on Diversity; mem. scientific adv. com. Internat. Symposium on Electrets. Contbr. articles to profl. jours. Bd. dir. Nat. Inventors Hall of Fame. Recipient Callinan award, Electrochemical Soc. Am., 1970, Senior award, IEEE Group on Acoustics, 1970, Lewis Howard Latimer Light Switch and Socket award, Nat. Patent Law Assn., 1989, George R. Stibitz Trophy Third Annual AT&T Patent Award, 1993, Golden Torch award, Nat. Soc. Black Engineers, 1998, Indsl. Rsch. Inst. 1998 Achievement award, Ronald H. Brown Am. Innovator award, 1999, Lewis Howard Latimer 2003 achievement award, John William Strutt, 3rd Baron of Rayleigh 2003 award, Mexican Inst. Acoustics; named to Nat. Inventors Hall of Fame, Akron, Ohio, 1999; named NJ Inventor of the Year for 1995, Audio Engring. Soc. Richard C. Heyser Meml. Lectr., 2002, 2006 Nat. Medal Tech. Laureate. Fellow IEEE, Acoustical Soc. Am. (pres. 1998, mem. exec. coun. 1998-2001, Silver medal in Engring. Acoustics, 1995); mem. NAE (mem. com. on diversity in the engring. workforce) Achievements include being co-inventor with Gerhard Sessler of Electret Microphone in 1962, concept used in everyday items such as telephones, hearing aids, camcorders and multimedia computers; Several US and Foreign patents. Office: John Hopkins U Whiting Sch Engring Dept Electrical & Computer Engring 3400 N Charles St Barton Hall 214 Baltimore MD 21218-2608 Office Phone: 410-516-8546. Business E-Mail: jimwest@jhu.edu.

WEST, JAMES HAROLD, finance company executive; b. San Diego, Oct. 11, 1926; s. Robert Reed and Clara Leona (Moses) W.; m. Norma Jean, 1953 (div.); 1 son, Timothy James; m. Jerel Lynn Smith, Nov. 16, 1976; 1 child, James Nelson. BS, U. So. Calif., 1949. CPA, Calif. Ptnr. McCracken & Co., San Diego, 1950-61; mgr. Ernst & Ernst, San Diego, 1961-64; ptnr. West Turnquist & Schmitt, San Diego, 1964—97, West, Rhode & Roberts, 1997—. Bd. govs. ARC, Washington, 1981-87; pres., bd. dirs. Combined Arts and Edn. Coun., San Diego, 1980-83; pres. Francis Parker Sch., 1988-90; bd. dirs. San Diego Hosp. Assn., 1981-95, 97—, San Diegans INc., 1989-92, Mus. Photographic Arts, 1990-92; trustee Calif. Western Sch. Law, 1985-2004; mem. bd. advisors U. So. Calif. Sch. Acctg., 1985-97; treas. San Diego Nat. Sports Tng. Found., 1988-92; mem. acctg. exec. bd. U. San Diego, 1992—. With AUS, 1945-46, PTO. Mem. AICPAs, Calif. Soc. CPAs (bd. dirs. 1963-64), Univ. Club (San Diego), Capital Hill Club (Washington), Masons. Republican. Home: 3311 Lucinda St San Diego CA 92106-2931 also: 3104 4th Ave San Diego CA 92163-5803 Business E-Mail: jhwest@wrr-cpa.com.

WEST, JAMES JOSEPH, lawyer; b. Tarentum, Pa., Nov. 26, 1945; s. Samuel Elwood and Rose (McIntyre) W.; m. Kathleen Geslak, Aug. 19, 1967; children: Joseph Allen, Yvonne Michelle, KaiLynn Ann. BS in Econs., St. Vincent Coll., 1967; JD, Duquesne U., 1970. Bar: Pa. 1971, U.S. Dist. Ct. (we. dist.) Pa. 1971, U.S. Ct. Appeals (3d cir.) 1971, U.S. Dist. Ct. (mid. dist.) Pa., 1980. Law clk. to presiding justice U.S. Dist. Ct., Pa., 1970-74; asst. U.S. atty. chief appellate sect. U.S. Atty.'s Office, Pitts., 1974-79; dep. dir. criminal law Pa. Atty. Gen.'s Office, Harrisburg, 1979-82; 1st asst. U.S. atty. U.S. Dist. Ct. (mid. dist.) Pa., Harrisburg, 1982-84, U.S. atty., 1984-93; assoc. Sprague & Sprague, Phila., 1993-95; pvt. practice Harrisburg, Pa., 1995—. Mem. Nat. Environ. Enforcement Coun. Recipient Outstanding Performance award U.S. Dept. Justice, 1974-78, Commendation Gov. of Pa., 1981. Mem. Pa. Bar Assn., Allegheny County Bar Assn., Dauphin County Bar Assn. Republican. Roman Catholic. Home: 1222 Cardinal Way Rd Hummelstown PA 17036-8548 Office: James West 105 N Front St Harrisburg PA 17101-1483 Office Phone: 717-233-5051. Personal E-mail: jwest@aol.com. Business E-Mail: jwest@jwestlaw.com.

WEST, JERRY ALAN, former professional sports team executive, retired professional basketball player; b. Chelyan, W.Va., May 28, 1938; s. Howard Stewart and Cecil Sue (Creasey) West; m. Martha Jane Kane, May 1960 (div. 1977); children: David, Michael, Mark; m. Karen Christine Bua, May 28, 1978; 1 child, Ryan. BS, W.Va. U., 1960; LHD (hon.), W.Va. Wesleyan Coll., W.Va. U., 2006. Player LA Lakers, 1960—74, head coach, 1976—79, spl. cons., 1979—82, gen. mgr., 1982—94, exec. v.p. basketball ops., 1994—2000; pres. basketball ops. Memphis Grizzlies, 2002—07. Author (with William Libby): Mr. Clutch: The Jerry West Story, 1969. Named NBA Finals MVP, 1969, NBA All-Star Game MVP, 1972, NBA Exec. of Yr., Sporting News, 1994—95, 1995, 2004; named to NBA All-Star Team, 1961—73, Naismith Meml. Basketball Hall of Fame, 1980, NBA 35th Anniversary All-Time Team, 1980. Achievements include winning the 1972 NBA Championship as a member of the Lakers. *

WEST, JESSAMYN CHARITY, librarian, blogger; b. Sept. 5, 1968; d. Tom West. MLS, U. Washington. Cmty. tech. person Randolph Technical Career Ctr., Vt.; moderator MetaFilter. Editor: Digital Versus Non-Digital Reference: Ask a Librarian Online and Offline, 2004; co-editor: Revolting Librarians Redux: Radical Librarians Speak Out, 2003. Named one of Movers and Shakers, Library Journal, 2002. Mem.: ALA (former coun. mem.). Mailing: PO Box 81 Bethel VT 05032 Home Phone: 802-234-6801. E-mail: jessamyn@gmail.com.

WEST, JESSE MICHAEL, pediatric neuropsychologist; b. Anderson, SC, Nov. 30, 1961; s. Ernest Calvin and Patricia (Byrd) West. BA, Clemson U., 1984; PhD, U. Oslo, Norway, 1994. Neuropsychologist Sunnaus Hosp., Oslo, 1994—96, Carolinas Hosp. Sys., Florence, SC, 1996—2000, U. SC, Florence, 2000—02; neuropsychologist, clin. instr. Med. U. of SC, Florence, 2002—05; neuropsychologist Carolina Neurobehavioral Assn., Florence, 2000—05. Medicaid adv. bd. Dept. of Health, State of SC, Columbia, SC, 2002—03; psychological cons. Lighthouse Care Ctrs., Conway, SC, 2002—05. Contbr. articles European Jour. of Pediat.Surgery. Mem. City Coun., Hoyre Party, Oslo, 1996. Mem.: SC Psychological Assn., Am. Psychological Assn. Office: Carolina Neurobehavioral Assoc 1504 Heritage Ln Florence SC 29505 Office Phone: 843-413-0303. Office Fax: 843-413-0340. E-mail: westbyrd@aol.com.

WEST, JOHN BURNARD, physiologist, educator; b. Adelaide, Australia, Dec. 27, 1928; came to U.S., 1969; s. Esmond Frank and Meta Pauline (Spehr) W.; m. Penelope Hall Banks, Oct. 28, 1967; children: Robert Burnard, Joanna Ruth. MB, BChir, Adelaide U., 1951, MD, 1958, DSc, 1980; PhD, London U., 1960; DSc (hon.), U. Barcelona, Spain, 1987, U. Ferrara, Italy, 2004, U. Athens, 2006. Resident Royal Adelaide Hosp., 1952, Hammersmith Hosp., London, 1953-55; physiologist Sir Edmund Hillary's Himalayan Expdn., 1960-61; dir. respiratory rsch. group Post-grad. Med. Sch., London, 1962-67, reader medicine, 1968; prof. medicine and physiology U. Calif., San Diego, 1969—. Leader Am. Med. Rsch. Expdn. to Mt. Everest, 1981; U.S. organizer China-U.S. Conf. on respiratory failure, Nanjing, 1986; mem. life scis. adv. com. NASA, 1985-88, task force sci. uses of space sta., 1984-87, aerospace med. adv. com., 1988-89, chmn. sci. verification com. Spacelab SLS-1, 1983-92, commn. on respiratory physiol. Internat. Union Physiol. Scis., 1985—, commn. on clin. physiol., 1991—, commn. gravitation physiol., 1986—, study sect. NIH, chmn., 1973-75; prin. investigator Spacelabs SLS 1, 2, LMS, Neurolab, 1983—; co-investigator European Spacelabs, D2, Euromir, 1987—; external examiner Nat. U. Singpore, 1995; Wiltshire lectr., London, 1971, Schwidetzky lectr., 1975, Fleischner lectr., 1977, Robertson lectr. Adelaide U., 1978, I.J. Flance lectr. Washington U., 1978, W.A. Smith lectr. Med. Coll. SC, 1982, S. Kronheim lectr. Undersea Med. Soc., 1984, McClement lectr. NYU, 1996. Author: Ventilation/Blood Flow and Gas Exchange, 1965, Respiratory Physiology-The Essentials, 1974, Translations in Respiratory Physiology, 1975, Pulmonary Pathophysiology-The Essentials, 1977, Translations in Respiratory Physiology, 1977, Bioengineering Aspects of the Lung, 1977, Regional Differences in the Lung, 1977, Pulmonary Gas Exchange (2 vols.), 1980, High Altitude Physiology, 1981, High Altitude and Man, 1984, Everest-The Testing Place, 1985, Best and Taylor's Physiological Basis of Medical Practice, 1985, 91, Study Guide for Best and Taylor, 1985, High Altitude Medicine and Physiology, 1989, The Lung: Scientific Foundations, 1991, 2d edit., 1997, Lung Injury, 1992, Respiratory Physiology: People and Ideas, 1996, High Life: A History of High Altitude Physiology and Medicine, 1998; founder, editor-in-chief High Altitude Medicine and Biology, 2000-. Recipient Ernest Jung prize for medicine, Hamburg, 1977, Presdl. citation Am. Coll. Chest Physicians, 1977, Kaiser Tchg. award 1980; scholar Macy Found., 1974; Jeffries Med. Rsch. award AIAA, 1992. Fellow Royal Coll. Physicians (London), Royal Australasian Coll. Physicians, Royal Geog. Soc. (London), AAAS (med. sci. nominating com. 1987-93, coun. del. sect. med. scis.), Am. Inst. for Med. and Biol. Engring. (founding fellow 1992), Am. Heart Assn. (G.C. Griffith lectr. 1978, D.W. Richards lectr. 1980), Internat. Soc. for Mountain Medicine (pres. 1991-94), Am. Acad. Arts and Scis.; mem. NAS (com. space biology and medicine 1986-90, subcom. on space biology 1984-85, com. advanced space tech. 1992-94, panel on small spacecraft tech. 1994), Am. Assn. Thoracic Surgery (hon.), Nat. Bd. Med. Examiners (physiology test com. 1973-76), Am. Physiol. Soc. (pres. 1984-85, coun. 1981-86, chmn. sect. on history of physiology 1984-92, hist. pubs. adv. com., Reynolds prize for history 1987, Ray Daggs award 1998, Guyton Tchg. award 2002, Julius H. Comroe lectr. 2003), Inst. of Medicine of NAS, Am. Soc. Clin. Investigation, Physiol. Soc. Gt. Britain, Am. Thoracic Soc. (Edward Livingston Trudeau medal 2002), Assn. Am. Physicians, Western Assn. Physicians, Russian Acad. Sci. (elected fgn. mem.), Explorers Club, Fleischner Soc. (pres. 1985), Harveian Soc. (London), Royal Instn. Gt. Britain, Royal Soc. Medicine (London), Hurlingham Club (London), La Jolla Beach & Tennis Club. Home: 9626 Blackgold Rd La Jolla CA 92037-1110 Office: U Calif San Diego Sch Medicine 0623 Dept Medicine La Jolla CA 92093 Home Phone: 858-587-9840. Business E-Mail: jwest@ucsd.edu.

WEST, JOHN THOMAS, retired surgeon; b. Live Oak, Fla., June 23, 1924; s. James Whitaker and Lelah Eulalia (Moore) W.; m. Ruth Marita Blakely, June 18, 1948; children: Phyllis Ann, Rebecca Ruth, James Carl, Jeffrey Moore, Paul Blakely. BS, U. Mich., 1946; MD, Vanderbilt U., 1951. Diplomate Am. Bd. Surgery. Commd. officer USPHS, 1951, advanced through grades to capt., 1963; rotating intern USPHS Hosp., Seattle, 1951—52; chief surgery USPHS Alaska Native Hosp., Anchorage, 1957—60, resident gen. surgery, 1954—57; chief surgery USPHS Hosp., Seattle, 1963—69, USPHS Indian Hosp., Phoenix, 1969—71; sr. investigator surg. br. Nat. Cancer Inst. USPHS, Bethesda, Md., 1960—63, ret. Nat. Cancer Inst., 1971; clin. asst. prof. U. Wash., Seattle, 1964—68; clin. assoc. prof. Tex. Tech U., Lubbock, 1974—77; pvt. practice La Grange, Ga., 1971—74, 1977—94; ret., 1994. Mem. active staff West Ga. Med. Ctr., La Grange, 1971-74, 77-94. Bd. dirs. Ga. divsn. Am. Cancer Soc., 1972-77, 77-92. Recipient Meritorious Svc. medal USPHS, 1968. Fellow ACS, Soc. Surg. Oncology. Presbyterian. Achievements include report of facilitation of major hepatic resection by an innovation in the surgical exposure of the liver. Home: 134 Hickory Ln Lagrange GA 30240-8622 Personal E-mail: rutom@mindspring.com.

WEST, KANYE, rap artist; b. Atlanta, June 8, 1977; s. Ray and Donda West. Founder G.O.O.D. (Getting Out Our Dreams) Music, 2004—. Prodr.: songs for various artists including Jay Z, Ludacris and Alicia Keyes; singer: (albums) The College Dropout, 2004 (Grammy award for Best Rap Album, 2005), Late Registration, 2005 (Grammy award for Best Rap Album, 2006), Graduation, 2007, (songs) Jesus Walks, 2004 (Best Male Video, MTV Video Music awards, 2005, Grammy award for Best Rap Song, 2005), Diamonds from Sierra Leone, 2005 (Grammy award for Best Rap Song, 2006), Gold Digger, 2005 (Grammy award for Best Rap Solo Performance, 2006, Soul Train Music award for Best Rap Video, 2006, 2 BET awards for Best Duet & Video of Yr., 2006); composer (for Alicia Keys) You Don't Know My Name, 2003 (Grammy award for Best R&B Song, 2005). Named Male New Artist of Yr., Billboard Music Awards, 2004, Best New R&B/Hip-Hop Artist of Yr., 2004, R&B/Hip-Hop Prodr. of Yr., 2004, Rap Artist of Yr., 2004; named one of Time Mag. 100 Most Influential People, 2005, The 10 Most Fascinating People of 2005, Barbara Walters Special; recipient Artist Achievement award, Billboard Music Awards, 2005, Vibe award, best rapper, 2005, 3 Grammy Awards, 2005, Image award for Outstanding New Artist, NAACP, 2005, 3 Grammy Awards, 2006, Best Hip Hop Entertainer, Internat. Reggae & World Music Awards, 2006, World's Best Rap/Hip Hop Artist, World Music Awards, 2007. Office: Roc A Fella Records 825 8th Ave 19th Floor New York NY 10019-7416 also: GOOD Records 2100 Colorado Ave Santa Monica CA 90404 also: c/o William Morris Agy 1 William Morris Pl Beverly Hills CA 90212 *

WEST, KAZUKO ITO, mathematics educator, department chairman; d. Hiroshi and Reiko Mori; m. Christopher Drane West, Sept. 5, 1998; 1 child, Shunsuke Ito. BS in Math., Waseda U., Tokyo, 1976, MS in Math., 1978; MEd, Harvard U., Cambridge, Mass., 1998; PhD in Math. Edn., Columbia U., NYC, 2005. Cert. tchr. math. high sch. Ministry of Edn., Japan, 1976. Math. tchr. Yokohama Tateno H.S., Japan, 1978—81, Ikuta H.S., Kawasaki, Japan, 1981—96; spl. edn. tchr. Takatsu HS, Kawasaki, 1996—97; math. tchr. Keio Acad., Purchase, NY, 1999—, math. dept. chairperson, 2002—. Contbr. articles to profl. jours. Mem. Riverside Ch., NYC. Named Dewey Scholar, Columbia U. Tchrs. Coll. Mem.: Math. and Edn. Reform Forum, Internat. Cmty. Tchrs. Math. Modelling and Applications, Japan Soc. Math. Edn., Math. Assn. Am., Am. Math. Soc. Achievements include research in Japanese High School Mathematics Teacher Competence. Home: 2900 Purchase St Purchase NY 10577 Office: Keio Academy of NY 3 College Rd Purchase NY 10577 Home Phone: 914-694-4353; Office Phone: 914-694-4825. Business E-Mail: westc-k@post.harvard.edu.

WEST, LEE ROY, federal judge; b. Clayton, Okla., Nov. 26, 1929; s. Calvin and Nicie (Hill) W.; m. MaryAnn Ellis, Aug. 29, 1952; children: Kimberly Ellis, Jennifer Lee. BA, U. Okla., 1952, JD, 1956; LL.M. (Ford Found. fellow), Harvard U., 1963. Bar: Okla. 1956. Individual practice law, Ada, Okla., 1956-61, 63-65; faculty U. Okla. Coll. Law, 1961-62; Ford Found. fellow in law teaching Harvard U., Cambridge, Mass., 1962-63; judge 22d Jud. Dist. Okla., Ada, 1965-73; mem. CAB, Washington, 1973-78, acting chmn., 1977; practice law Tulsa, 1978-79; spl. justice Okla. Supreme Ct., 1965; judge U.S. Dist Ct. (we. dist.) Okla., 1979-94; sr. judge U.S. Dist. Ct. (we. dist.), Okla., 1994—. Editor: Okla. Law Rev. Served to capt. USMC, 1952-54. Named to Field Trial Hall of Fame, 2005; recipient Humanitarian award Nat. Conf. Cmty. and Justice, 2000, Jud. Excellence award Okla. Bar Assn., 2000, E.T. Dunlap medal and Lectureship award, 2006, Constn. Day award Rogers State U., 2006. Mem. U. Okla. Alumni Assn. (dir.), Phi Delta Phi (pres. 1956), Phi Eta Sigma, Order of Coif. Home: 6500 E Danforth Rd Edmond OK 73034-7601 Office: US Dist Ct 3001 US Courthouse 200 NW 4th St Oklahoma City OK 73102-3027 Office Phone: 405-609-5140.

WEST, MACDONALD, real estate executive; b. Bournemouth, Eng., July 15, 1943; arrived in U.S., 1968; s. Joseph Stanley and Maisie Siswick W.; m. Charlotte Denise Duvall, Nov. 1, 1980. Diploma, London U. Coll. Estate Mgmt., 1968; MBA, Columbia U., NYC, 1970. Trainee surveyor Navy Works Dept., Admiralty, London, 1960—64; assoc. Finlay, Mather & Ptnrs., London, 1964—65; sr. assoc. Robinson & Roods, London, 1965—68; dir. cost control Nat. Liberty Corp., Valley Forge, Pa., 1970—71; v.p., dir. Philipsborn Cos., Coral Gables, Fla., 1972—76, Allen Morris Co., Miami, Fla., 1976—89; sr. v.p., COO Allen Morris Constrn. Co., 1978—89, also sr. v.p. asset mgmt. divsn.; pres. Miami Lakes Devel., Inc., Fla., 1989—91; exec. v.p. Graham Cos., Miami Lakes, 1989—91; pres., CEO Macdonald West Co., Miami, 1991—; mng. dir. Allen Morris Co., 2000—02. Deacon U. Bapt. Ch., Coral Gables, 1977—; chair Fla. chpt. RICS America, 2006-; bd. mem. RICS USA, 2006-. Fellow Royal Instn. Chartered Surveyors; mem. Counselors Real Estate (pres. 1995), Nat. Assn. Realtors, Am. Arbitration Assn., Realtors Comml. Alliance (chair 2000, 2004-2007), Nat. Assn. Indsl. and Office Parks, Indsl. Assn. Dade County, Realtors Comml. Alliance Greater Miami (pres. 2000), Builders Assn. South Fla. (pres. 1996), Nat. Assn. Home Builders, Ocean Reef Club, Rotary (Miami). Republican. Home: 5325 Orduna Dr Coral Gables FL 33146-2640 Office: 1172 S Dixie Hwy Ste 600 Miami FL 33146-2918 Office Phone: 305-667-2100.

WEST, MARC, information technology executive; B in Computer ci., U. Md.; M in Human Resource Mgmt., Golden State U., San Francisco. Various positions Quick & Reilly, Move.com, Oracle and Mobil Oil; sr. v.p. and global chief info. officer Electronic Arts, Redwood City, Calif., 2000—04; sr. v.p. & chief info. officer H&R Block, Kansas City, Mo., 2004—. Named one of Premier 100 IT Leaders, Computerworld, 2006. Office: SVP & CIO H&R Block Inc One H&R Block Way Kansas City MO 64105

WEST, MICHAEL ALAN, retired hospital administrator; b. Waseca, Minn., Aug. 4, 1938; s. Ralph Leland and Elizabeth Mary (Brann) W.; m. Mary Thissen, Jan. 21, 1961; children— Anne, Nancy, Douglas. BA, U. Minn., 1961, MHA, 1963. Sales corr. Physicians and Hosps. Supply Co., Mpls., 1959-60; adminstrv. resident R.I. Hosp., Providence, 1962-63, adminstrv. asst., 1963-65, asst. dir., 1965-68; exec. asst. dir. Med. Center U. Mo., Columbia, 1968-70, assoc. dir., 1970-74, asst. prof. community health and med. practice, 1968-74; v.p. for adminstrn. Luth. Gen. Hosp., Park Ridge, Ill., 1974-80, exec. v.p., 1980-84; pres., CEO Akron Gen. Med. Ctr., Ohio, 1984-97, Akron Gen. Health Sys., 1997—2002. Bd. dirs. Vol. Hosps. Am. Inc.; chair VHA-Ctrl., Inc. Bd. dirs. Great Trails Coun. Boy Scouts Am. Mem. Am. Coll. Healthcare Execs., Akron Regional Hosp. Assn. (chmn.), Portage Country Club, Akron City Club, Catawba Island Club, Noreaster Club. Home: 495 Woodbury Dr Akron OH 44333-2780

WEST, MICHAEL D., cloning and stem cell research company executive; BS, Rensselaer Polytechnic Inst., 1976; MS in Biology, Andrew U., 1982; PhD, Baylor Coll. Medicine, 1989. Organized and managed rsch. between Geron and academic collaborators James Thomson and John Gearhart that led to the first isolation of human embryonic stem and human embryonic germ cells, 1995—98; founder, dir., v.p. Gernon Corp., Menlo Park, Calif., 1990—98; CEO Advanced Cell Tech., Inc., Worcester, Mass., 1998—2005, chmn., 1998—, pres., chief scientific officer, 2005—. Adj. prof., bioengineering U. Calif. Berkeley. Extensive academic and business experience in age-related degenerative disease, telomerse molecular biology, and human embryonic stem cells research and development. Office: Advanced Cell Technology Inc 381 Plantation St Biotech V Worcester MA 01605 also: Advanced Cell Technology Inc 1201 Harbor Bay Pkwy Ste 120 Alameda CA 94502 Office Phone: 508-756-1212. Office Fax: 508-756-4468.

WEST, MICHAEL G., electric power industry executive; BS in Electronic Engring.; BS in Math., Oreg. State U.; MSEE, U. Ill. Integrated cir. designer Floating Point Sys., 1982—86; integrated cir. design engr. Bipolar Integrated Tech., 1986—87; chief scientist, sr. engr. In Focus Sys., 1988—96; co-founder, v.p. tech. Pixelworks, Inc., Tualatin, Oreg., 1997—, fellow, 2003—. Office: Pixelworks Inc Ste 300 8100 SW Nyberg Rd Tualatin OR 97062

WEST, NORMAN ELLSWORTH, artist; b. Exeter, NH, May 16, 1952; s. Norman Ellsworth and Alice Marie West. BS, Plymouth State Coll., 1976; BFA, Maine Coll. of Art, 1980. Leader color workshops regional schs., York County, 1981—; artist in residence Holderness Acad., Plymouth, N.H., 1989-91; set designer Shenanigans Prodns., Portland, Boston, 1993-96; tchr. Heartwood Coll. of Art, Kennebunk, Maine, 1994—. Dir. Heartwood Coll. Art Gallery, 2002. One person shows include West Kuhn Gallery, Cape Neddick, Maine, 1988, Van Ward Gallery, Ogunquit, Maine, 1994, 98; group shows include Currier Gallery, Manchester, N.H., 1988, 89, Barn Gallery, Ogunquit, 1988, Mast Core Galleries, Kennebunkport, Maine, 1988, 89, Ogunquit Art Assn., 1988—, Maine Coast Artists, Rockport, Maine, 1989, 90. Bd. dirs. Shellfish Commn., Ogunquit, Maine, 1996—; clam warden Town of Ogunquit, 1997-99. Mem. Ogunquit Art Assn. (curator invited sculptor's exhibit 1996—), Ogunquit Arts Collaborative (v.p. 2000—), Ogunquit Rotary Club. Home: PO Box 1560 Ogunquit ME 03907

WEST, PAUL NODEN, writer, playwright; b. Eckington, Derbyshire, Eng., Feb. 23, 1930; arrived in US, 1961, naturalized, 1971; s. Alfred Massick and Mildred (Noden) W. Student, Oxford U., 1950-53; MA, Columbia U., 1953. Asst. prof. English Meml. U. Nfld., Canada, 1957-58, assoc. prof., 1958-60; faculty Pa. State U., Pa., 1962-95, prof. English and comparative lit. Pa., 1968-95; prof. emeritus, 1995—. Crawshaw prof. Colgate U., 1972; Melvin Hill disting. vis. prof. Hobart and William Smith Coll., 1973; vis. English prof. Cornell U., 1986; disting. writer in residence Wichita State U., 1982; vis. prof. English Brown U., 1992; fiction judge Creative Artists Pub. Svc. Program, NYC, 1974, 81; writer-in-residence U. Ariz., 1984; judge Katherine Ann Porter Prize for Fiction, 1984, Artists Found. Author: Byron and the Spoiler's Art, 1960, rev. edit., 1990, I Said the Sparrow, 1963, The Snow Leopard, 1965, Tenement of Clay, 1965, The Wine of Absurdity, 1966, Alley Jaggers, 1967, libretta for opera, 1968, I'm Expecting to Live Quite Soon, 1970, Words for a Deaf Daughter, 1970, Caliban's Filibuster, 1972, Colonel Mint, 1973, Gala, 1976, The Very Rich Hours of Count von Stauffenberg, 1980, Out of My Depths: A Swimmer in the Universe, 1983, Rat Man of Paris, 1986, theatrical version, 1987, Sheer Fiction, 1987, The Universe and Other Fictions, 1988, The Place in Flowers Where Pollen Rests, 1988, Lord Byron's Doctor, 1989, Portable People, The Women of Whitechapel and Jack the Ripper, 1991, Sheer Fiction: II, 1991, James Ensor, 1991, Love's Mansion, 1992, Tenement of Clay, 2d edit., 1993, Sheer Fiction, III, 1994, A Stroke of Genius, 1995, The Tent of Orange Mist, 1995 (memoir) My Mother's Music, 1996, My Father's War, 2005; (novel) Sporting with Amaryllis, 1996, Terrestrials, 1997, Life With Swan, 1999, O.K.: The Corral, The Earps, and Doc Holliday, 2000, The Dry Danube: A Hitler Forgery, 2000, The Secret Lives of Words, 2000, A Fifth of November, 2001, Master Class, 2001, Oxford Days, 2002, Cheops: A Cupboard for the Sun, 2002, (play) Any Old How, 2002, (radio play) The Sacrifice, 1955, The Immensity of the Here and Now, 2003, Sheer Fiction IV, 2004, Samuel Beckett: Born Astride A Grave, 2004, My Father's War, 2005, Tea with Osiris, 2005, (TV) Sheer Fiction, 2007; contbr. Washington Post and NY Times, 1962—, Harper's Mag., Paris Rev., Yale Rev., Parnassus, Agni, Conjunctions, War, Literature and the Arts, First Intensity, Tin Roof; translator Les Romanesques by Rostand, 1954 fiction judge NY Found. for the Arts, Nat. Book award, 1990. Served RAF, 1954—57. Decorated chevalier de l'Ordre des Arts et des Lettres (France); recipient Aga Khan Fiction prize, 1973, Hazlett Meml. award for Excellence in Arts (lit.), 1981, Lit. award Am. Acad. and Inst. Arts and Letters, 1985, Pushcart prize 1987, 91, 2003, The Best Am. Essays award, 1990, Outstanding Achievement medal Pa. State U., 1991, Grand Prix Halpérine Kaminsky award, 1992, Lannan Fiction award, 1993, Tchg. award Northeastern Assn. Grad. Sch., 1994, Art of Fact prize SUNY, 2000; named Lit. Lion NY Pub. Libr., 1987; Guggenheim fellow, 1963; NEA Creative Writing fellow, 1979, 84; nominated for Médicis, Femina and Meilleur Livre Étranger prizes, France, 1991, Lannan Lit. Videos 35, Nat. Book Critics award for fiction, 1996; named to Honor Roll The Yr. in Fiction, DLB Yearbook, 1996, Conf. on works of West, U. of Tours, France, 2003; manuscript collection at Pattee Libr., Pa. State U. Office: Elaine Markson Agy 44 Greenwich Ave Fl 3 New York NY 10011-8389 *The unexamined life may not be worth having, but the examined life is endurable only to an open mind, through which life holistically flows, keeping that mind as incomplete as our knowledge of the universe itself.*

WEST, R. LELAND, veterinarian; b. Grand Rapids, Minn., Apr. 23, 1915; s. Ralph Leland and Elsie (Wardall) W.; m. Mary Elizabeth Brann, June 14, 1937; children: Michael Alan, Janet Lee West Friedrich, Thomas James. DVM, Iowa State U., 1936; MS, Purdue U., 1972. Pvt. practice, Waseca, Minn., 1936-42, 46-70; grad. asst. Sch. Vet. Medicine Purdue U., West Lafayette, Ind., 1970-72; asst. dir. sci. activities Am. Vet. Med. Assn., Schaumburg, Ill., 1972-77, dir. sci. activities, 1977-87. Contbr. articles to jours. in field. Mem. Pk. Bd., Waseca, 1948-50, Youth Commn., 1948-52; mem., chmn. Waseca Hosp. Bd., 1954-64; trustee Sunny Acres Village Inc., Denver, 1988-95. Maj. U.S. Army, 1942-46, ETO. Recipient Stange award Iowa State U., 1983. Mem. AMVA (award 1990), Am. Assn. Ret. Vets. (dir. 1987-90), Am. Vet. History Soc., Colo. Vet. Med. Assn., Minn. Vet. Med. Assn., Iowa State U. Vet. Alumni Assn., Phi Zeta. Republican. Avocations: reading, tv sports, stock market. Home: 1719 E Bijou St Apt 611 Colorado Springs CO 80909-5751 Personal E-mail: Wdrwest1@aol.com.

WEST, REXFORD LEON, retired bank executive; b. Syracuse, NY, Feb. 18, 1938; s. Rexford A. and Nina (Crysler) W.; children: Lisa, Julie, Gregory, Kristen AAS, Auburn C.C., NYC, 1957; BS magna cum laude, Syracuse U., NYC, 1972; Advanced Mgmt. Program, Harvard Bus. Sch., Boston, 1984. Accountant Marine Midland Bank, Syracuse, NY, 1959-67, v.p., asst. treas., 1967-72; v.p., contr. Marine Midland Services Corp., Buffalo, 1972-76; v.p. ops. divsn. Marine Midland Bank, N.A., Buffalo, 1976-77, sr. v.p., sr. ops. officer, 1977-79, exec. v.p., sr. ops. officer, 1979-85, divsn. exec. ops., 1985-87, sector exec. ops. and fin. mgmt., 1987-90, sr. exec. v.p. corp. engring., 1990-92; exec. v.p. adminstrv. svc. Fleet Bank, Melville, NY, 1992-94; exec. v.p. loan servicing Fleet Mortgage Group, Columbia, SC, 1994-96; ret., 1996. Served with U.S. Army, 1957-61

WEST, ROBERT GRADY, lawyer; b. Dallas, Aug. 13, 1947; s. Robert Sorrells and Thelma Grady W.; m. Marsha Lee Riegert, June 5, 1971; children: Kathryn Lee, Laura Elaine. BA, Midwestern State U., 1969; JD, U. Tex., 1972. Bar: Tex. 1972, U.S. Dist. Ct. (no. dist.) Tex. 1975, U.S. Ct. Appeals (5th cir.) 1976, U.S. Dist. Ct. (ea. dist.) Tex. 1992. Assoc. McGown, Godfrey, Decker, McMackin, Shipman & McClane, Ft. Worth, 1972-77, ptnr., 1977-88, Decker, McMackin & McClane, Ft. Worth, 1988-90, Decker, Jones, McMackin, McClane, Hall & Bates, Ft. Worth, 1990-93; assoc. Michener, Larimore, Swindle, Whitaker, et al, Ft. Worth, 1993-98, ptnr., 1999-2000, Whitaker, Chalk, Swindle & Sawyer, 2000—. Contbr. articles to profl. jours. Bd. regents Midwestern State U., Wichita Falls, Tex., 1992-98; dir. Grace Found., Dallas, 1990-92, Hist. Camp Bowie, Inc., Ft. Worth, 2002-; mem. Tex. Ctr. Legal Ethics and Professionalism, 1994—, Leadership Ft. Worth, 1984; elder, trustee Presbyn. Ch. Mem. ABA, Am. Assn. Profl. Landmen, State Bar Tex., Tarrant County Bar Assn. (chmn. real estate sect. 2001-02, 04-, spkr. CLE seminars). Avocations: travel, musical theatre, walking, volunteering. Office: Whitaker Chalk Swindle & Sawyer 3500 City Ctr Tower II 301 Commerce St Fort Worth TX 76102-4186 E-mail: rwest@whitakerchalk.com.

WEST, ROBERT MACLELLAN, science educator, consultant; b. Appleton, Wis., Sept. 1, 1942; s. Clarence John and Elizabeth Ophelia (Moore) West; m. Jean Sydow, June 19, 1965; 1 child, Christopher. BA, Lawrence Coll., 1963; SM, U. Chgo., 1964, PhD, 1968. Rsch. assoc. Princeton (N.J.) U., 1968-69; asst. prof. Adelphi U., Garden City, NY, 1969-74; curator geology Milw. Pub. Mus., 1974-83; dir. Carnegie Mus. Natural History, Pitts., 1983-87, Cranbrook Inst. Sci., Bloomfield Hills, Mich., 1987-91; prin. RMW Sci. Action, Washington, 1992-95; pres. Informal Sci., Inc., Washington, 1993-98, Informal Learning Experiences, Inc., Washington, 1999—. Adj. prof. U. Wis., Milw., 1974—83. Contbr. articles to profl. jours. Bd. dirs. Friends New Zoo, Pitts., 1984—87; treas. E. Mich. Environ. Action Coun., Birmingham, 1987—92. Named Man of the Yr. in Sci., Vectors Pitts., 1988; recipient Arnold Guyot prize, Nat. Geographic Soc., 1982; NSF fellow, 1965—68, NSF Rsch. grantee, 1970—82, Nat. Geographic Soc. Rsch. grantee, 1973, 1976, 1977, 1979, 1980, 1982. Mem.: Visitor Study Assn. (bd. dirs. 2005—), Am. Assn. Mus., Mus. Group, Paleontology Soc., Geol. Soc. Am., Soc. Vertebrate Paleontology, Nat. Ctr. Sci. Edn. (bd. dirs. 1984—88, 1992—), Rotary. Avocations: nature, history, sports. Office: Informal Learning Experiences Inc PO Box 42328 Washington DC 20015-0928 Home Phone: 202-686-1696; Office Phone: 202-362-5823. Business E-Mail: ile@informallearning.com.

WEST, ROYCE, lawyer, state legislator; b. Sept. 26, 1952; BA, MA, U. Tex., Arlington; JD, U. Houston. Sr. ptnr. Law Firm of West & Gooden, P.C.; mem. Tex. Senate, 1993—, mem. com. of the whole on legis. and congl. redistricting; mem. com. fin., health and human svs., jurisprudence; chmn. subcom. higher edn.; vice chmn. edn. Named one of 25 Most Powerful People in Tex. Politics, Tex. Monthly Mag., Ten Best Legislators in Tex., two-time hon. mention, Key Players of 2005 Legislature, Movers and Shakers list, AP. Democrat. Address: 5787 S Hampton Rd Ste 385 Dallas TX 75232-6331 Office: PO Box 12068 Austin TX 78711-2068 Office Phone: 214-467-0123.

WEST, STACY KATHLENA, athletic trainer; b. Flint, Mich., Sept. 22, 1979; d. Jay Robert and Sonia Kathleen Kelso; m. Aaron Michael West, May 3, 2003. BS, Cen. Mich. U., Mt. Pleasant, Mich., 2002. Cert. atletic trainer Nat. Athletic Trainers Assn. Cert. athletic trainer Mclaren Sports Medicine, Davison H.S., Mich., 2003—. Mem.: Nat. Athletic Trainers Assn. (assoc.). Home: 3106 Reid Rd Swartz Creek MI 48473 Office: Mclaren Sports Medicine 1240 Fairway Dr Davison MI 48423 Home Phone: 810-655-5912; Office Phone: 810-653-3962. Personal E-mail: kelso1sk@yahoo.com.

WEST, STEPHEN ALLAN, lawyer; b. Salt Lake City, Mar. 23, 1935; s. Allan Morrell and Ferne (Page) W.; m. Martha Sears, Mar. 21, 1960; children: Stephen Allan, Jr., Page, Adam. JD, U. Utah, Salt Lake City, 1961, BS in Philosophy, 1962. Law clk. to judge US Dist. Ct., Utah, 1961-62; assoc. Marr, Wilkins & Cannon, Salt Lake City, 1962-65, ptnr., 1965-67; atty. Jennings, Strouss, Salmon & Trask, Washington, 1967-68, Marriott Corp., Washington, 1968-71, asst. gen. counsel, 1971-74, v.p. and assoc. gen. counsel, 1974-87, v.p. and dep. gen. counsel, 1987-93; sr. v.p., gen. counsel Marriott Internat., Inc., Washington, 1993-94; pres. Tex. San Antonio Mission Ch. of Jesus Christ of Latter-day Saints, 1995-98, Gen. Authority, 1998—2004. Mem. exec. bd. Interfaith Conf. Met. Washington, 1989-93, vice chmn., 1992-93; mem. exec. bd. Christa McAuliffe Inst. Task Force of Nat. Found. for Improvement Edn. Mem. ABA (exec. coun. young lawyers sect. 1964-65), Utah Bar Assn. (exec. com. young lawyers sect. 1962-67), DC Bar Assn., Utah Profl. Rels. Com., U. Utah Alumni Assn. (Disting. Alumni award 1971), Skull and Bones, Owl and Key, Phi Delta Phi, Sigma Chi. Office: 1117 Fox Farm Rd Logan UT 84321

WEST, STEPHEN KINGSBURY, lawyer, director; b. Pittsfield, Mass., Sept. 28, 1928; s. William Bradford and Ruth (Osteyee) W.; m. Ann Wick, Apr. 30, 1955; children: Timothy Wick, Lucy West Engebretson, Todd Kingsbury, Daniel Wick. BA, Yale U., 1950; LL.B., Harvard U., 1953. Assoc. Sullivan & Cromwell, NYC, 1957-64, ptnr., 1964-97, sr. counsel, 1997—. Bd. dirs. Pioneer Mut. Fund, Boston, Swiss Helvetin Fund, Inc. Trustee Morven Mus. and Garden, Princeton, NJ, Hancock (Mass.) Shaker Village; dir. Atlantic Salmon Fedn. Served to lst lt. inf. US Army, 1953—53. Mem.: N.Y. State Bar Assn., Assn. Bar City N.Y. Office: Sullivan & Cromwell 125 Broad St Fl 28 New York NY 10004-2489

WEST, SYLVIA WANDELL, small business owner, director, educator, researcher; b. Harrisburg, Pa., Dec. 26, 1937; d. John George Wient and Kathleen Hill Wandell; m. Henry Earl Seidmeyer, Sept. 18, 1994; m. Jack Dennis West, Aug. 30, 1958 (div. June 15, 1971); children: Todd Conner, Jill Conner, Gary Conner, Susan Conner, Blake Conner. BFA, Tex. Christian U., 1961, MLA, 1988, MS, 1991, PhD, 1993. Tutor The Tutoring Rm., Ft. Worth, 1962—2005; founding dir. Lollypop Sch., 1964—67, Hill Sch., 1974—84; owner, dir. West Acad., 1984—. Rschr., presenter in field. Mem. Hill Sch., Ft. Worth, 1982—83. Achievements include research in Academic Achievement with Failure Avoidant Students. Avocations: swimming, reading, writing curriculum, cooking, interior remodeling. Home: 3821Arundel Ave Fort Worth TX 76109 Office: West Acad 3825 McCart Fort Worth TX 76110 Home Phone: 817-926-0286; Office Phone: 817-924-3535. Office Fax: 817-926-3399; Home Fax: 817-926-3399. E-mail: drsylviawest@yahoo.com.

WEST, TERESA L. (TERRI WEST), electronics executive; BA in Journalism, U. North Tex., 1982. Student intern Tex. Instruments, Inc., 1978, mgr. media rels., v.p., mgr. strategic comm., sr. v.p. comm. and investor rels. Dallas. Dir. Dallas Pub. Broadcasting Sys. affiliate, KERA-TV; mem. Nat. Investor Rels. Inst. and Conf. Bd.; founding mem. Women of Tex. Instruments Fund; v.p. Tex. Instruments Found.; chair comm. com. (during renewal of US-Japan Semiconductor Trade Arrangement) Semiconductor Industry Assn., 1992, 96. Mem. chancellor's leadership coun. U. North Tex. Office: Tex Instruments Inc PO Box 660199 Dallas TX 75266-0199 Office Phone: 972-995-2011, 972-995-4360. *

WEST, TOGO DENNIS, JR., lawyer, former secretary of veterans affairs; b. Winston-Salem, NC, June 21, 1942; s. Togo Dennis and Evelyn (Carter) W.; m. Gail Estelle Berry, June 18, 1966; children: Tiffany Berry, Hilary Carter. BSEE, Howard U., 1965, JD cum laude, 1968; LLD (hon.), Winston-Salem U., 1996, Gannon U., 1998. Bar: D.C. 1968, N.Y. 1969, U.S. Ct. Mil. Appeals 1969, U.S. Supreme Ct. 1978, U.S. Ct. Claims 1981. Elec. engr. Duquesne Light and Power Co., 1965; patent researcher Sughrue, Rothwell, Mion, Zinn and McPeak, 1966-67; legal intern U.S. EEOC, 1967; law clk. firm Covington & Burling LLP, Washington, 1967-68, summer assoc., 1968, assoc., 1973-75, 76-77, 2000—05; law clk. to Hon. Harold R. Tyler Jr. US Dist. Ct. (So. Dist.) NY, 1968-69; assoc. dep. atty. gen. US Dept. Justice, Washington, 1975-76; gen. counsel Dept. Navy, Washington, 1977-79; spl. asst. to sec. & dep. sec. US Dept. Def., Washington, 1979-80, gen. counsel, 1980-81; mng. ptnr. Patterson, Belknap, Webb & Tyler LLP, Washington, 1981-90; sr. v.p. govt. rels. Northrop Corp., Washington, 1990-93; sec. Dept. Army, US Dept. Def., Washington, 1993-98; chair Panama Canal Com., 1997; sec. US Dept. Veterans Affairs, Washington, 1998—2000; of coun. Covington & Burling, 2000—04; pres., CEO Joint Ctr. Polit. & Econ. Studies, 2004—06; with TLI Leadership Group, Washington, 2006—. Adj. prof. Duke U. Sch. Law, 1980-81; bd. cons. Riggs Nat. Bank, Washington, 1990-93; bd. dirs. Krispy Kreme Doughnuts, Inc., Bowater, Inc., Washington Hosp. Ctr.; mem. coun. trustees AUSA; chmn. bd. trustees Mitretek Sys., Inc., 2001—. Mng. editor: Howard Law Jour, 1968. Commr. D.C. Law Rev. Comm., 1982-89, chmn., 1985-89; mem. Nat. Council of Friends of John F. Kennedy Ctr. for Performing Arts, 1984-91, treas., 1987-91; bd. govs. Antioch U. Sch. Law, 1983-87, vice chmn., 1986-87; bd. visitors Wake Forest U. Sch. Law, 1991-94; chmn. Greater Washington Bd. Trade, legis. bur., 1987-89, bd. dirs., 1987-93, mem. exec. com. 1987-92; mem. fed. legis. com., 1990-93; chmn. Kennedy Ctr. Community and Friends Bd., 1991-2001; mem. Washington Lawyers' Com. Civil Rights Under Law, 1987-93, D.C. Com. on Pub. Edn., 1988-93, chmn., 1990-91; trustee The Aerospace Corp., 1983-90, Ctr. for Strategic and Internat. Studies, 1987-90, Nat. Lawyers Com. for Civil Rights Under Law, 1987-93, Inst. for Def. Analyses, 1989-91, Protestant Episcopal Cathedral Found., 1989-95, Shakespeare Theatre at The Folger, 1990-93, N.C. Sch. Arts, 1990-2002, Aerospace Edn. Found. of Air Force Assn., 1991-93; bd. dirs. D.C. Law Students in Ct. Program, 1986-92, World Affairs Coun., 1991-93, 2000—, Atlantic Coun., 1991-93, 2000—; mem. fin. com. Episcopal Diocese of Washington, 1989—90, mem. standing com., 1990-92; sr. warden St. John's Ch., Lafayette Sq.; mem. Coun. Fgn. Rels., 1996—; chmn. trustee coun. YMCA Metro. Wash., 1990-92; mem. nat. adv. com. UN Assn. USA, 1991-93; D.C. Ct. Appeals Admissions Com., 1990-93; pres. Nat. Capital Area Coun. Boy Scouts Am.; chmn. Greater Washington Bd. of Trade; bd. trustees Assn. of U.S. Army, 2001—. Served to capt. Judge Adv. Gen. Corps U.S. Army, 1969-73. Decorated Legion of Merit, Meritorious Svc. medal; recipient Disting. Pub. Svc. medal Dept. Def., 1981, 88, Disting. Eagle Scout award Boy Scouts Am., 1995, Svc. to Howard U. award, 1965, Medal of Merit, Brazil, Disting. Civil Svc. medal, 1998, Dept. Vet. Affairs, 2000, Silver Buffalo award, 2000, Silver Beaver award, 2003; named one of Most Influential Black Americans, Ebony mag., 2006. Mem. ABA, Nat. Bar Assn., Washington Coun. Lawyers (dir. 1973-75), Sigma Pi Phi, Phi Alpha Delta, Omega Psi Psi, Alpha Phi Omega. Clubs: Metropolitan, University (Washington). Office: TLI Leadership Group 888 17th St NW Ste 302 Washington DC 20006 Business E-Mail: twest@tlileaders.com.

WEST, W. RICHARD, museum director; b. San Bernardino, Calif., Jan. 6, 1943; s. W. Richard Sr. and Maribelle (McCrea) W.; m. Mary Beth Braden, June 29, 1968; children: Amy Elizabeth, Benjamin Braden. BA magna cum laude in Am. History, U. Redlands, 1965; AM in Am. History, Harvard U., 1968; JD, Stanford U., 1971; LHD (hon.), Bacone Coll., 1992, Ottawa U., 1994, U. Okla., 1995. Bar: Calif., DC, US Ct. Appeals (8th cir.), US Supreme Ct. Clk. to Hon. Benjamin C. Duniway U.S. Ct. Appeals (9th cir.), 1971-72; assoc. Fried, Frank, Harris, Shriver & Jacobson, Washington, 1973-79, ptnr., 1979-88; dir. direct support component Am. Indian Lawyer Tng. Program, Inc., 1976-77; ptnr. Gover, Stetson Williams & West P.C., Albuquerque, 1988-90; founding dir. Smithsonian Inst. Nat. Mus. Am. Indian, Washington, 1990—. Treas. Am. Indian Lawyer Tng. Program, Inc., 1973—; adj. prof. Indian law Stanford U., 1977. Mem. edit. bd. Am. Indian Historian, 1969-71; note editor Stanford Law Review, 1970-71; contbr. articles to profl. jours. Coord., treas. Native Am. Coun. Regents Inst. Am. Indian Arts, 1975-80; bd. visitors Stanford Law Sch., 1978-81; trustee Phelps Stokes Fund, 1981-87, Bush Found., 1991—, Bacone Coll., 1986-89, chmn., 1988-89, Morning Star Found., 1987-93, U. Redlands, 1991—, alumni bd., 1987-89, Ednl. Found. Am., 1993-96; bd. dirs. Amerindian Circle, Inc., 1981-88, Nat. Indian Justice Ctr., 1982-89; cultural edn. com. Smithsonian Inst., 1987-90; nat. support com. Native Am. Rights Fund, 1990—; adv. com. Winslow Found., 1991—; hon. coun. Wings Am., 1993—; mem. Environ. Def. Fund, bd. trustees, 1986—. Recipient Career Achievement award U. Redlands, 1987, Disting. Svc. award, 1992, award Appreciation and Recognition, Cheyenne and Arapaho Tribes Okla., 1990, Spirit of the People award Okla. Inst. Indian Heritage, 1990; named (with another) Amb. of Yr. Red Earth Indian Ctr. Okla., 1993; named to Centennial Honor Roll, Am. Assn. Museums, 2006. Mem. Am. Indian Bar Assn. (charter pres. 1976-77). Mem. Cheyenne and Arapaho Tribes Okla. *

WESTBERRY, ANITA PARRISH, education educator; b. Clewiston, Fla., Oct. 5, 1946; d. Virgil Ennis and Onetta Armour Parrish; m. Lawrence Ray Westberry, Sr., Nov. 5, 1966; children: Danita Westberry Thomas, Lawrence Ray Jr. AA, Edison Cmty., Fort Myers, Fla., 1978; BS, Nova S.E. U., Fort Lauderdale, Fla., 1988; MEd, Tenn. State U., Nashville, 1999. Elem. tchr. Glades County Schs., Moore Haven, Fla., 1988—89, Hendry County Schs., LaBelle, Fla., 1989—97; ESL tchr. Franklin County Schs., Winchester, Tenn., 1997—98, Rutherford County Schs., Murfreesboro, Tenn., 1998—2004; instr. U. Phoenix, Nashville, 2002—, online instr.; instr. Western Internat. U., Phoenix, 2004—, U. Phoenix, Nashville, Franklin, Chattanooga; online instr. Axia Coll., Western Internat. U. Rep. S.W. Fla. Tchr. Edn. Ctr., Fort Myers, 1995—97. Named Leader of Yr., 4-H, 1980. Church Of Christ. Avocations: reading, travel. Home: 256 White Oak Dr Manchester TN 37355 Office Phone: 931-570-5167. Personal E-mail: awestberry@charter.net. Business E-Mail: westberry03@email.phoenix.edu.

WESTBERRY, PAULA I., nursing administrator; b. Worcester, Mass., Aug. 7, 1954; d. Richard R. and Patricia I. (Gilbert) Wood; m. Chuck Westberry, 2005; children: Laura, Andrew, Brian, Paul. Diploma summa cum laude, David Hale Fanning Sch., 1974; BS in Computer Sci. summa cum laude, Clark U., 1986; AAS summa cum laude, SUNY, Albany, 1988; BSN, Barry U., Miami Shores, Fla., 1996, MSN summa cum laude, 1998, PhD in Nursing, 2006; PhD summa cum laude, Columbus U., 1999. Cert. nursing adminstrn. advanced. ANA, dir. nurses Nat. Assn. Dirs. Nursing Adminstrn./Long Term Care, nursing adminstrn. cert. legal nurse cons. Head nurse Seven Hills Adolescent Program, Worcester, 1985-88; coord. utilization rev. Worcester County Hosp., 1988-90, 45th St. Mental Health Ctr., West Palm Beach, Fla.; nurse mgr. N.Medico Neurol. Rehab. Ctr. of Palm Beach (Fla.), 1990-91; dir. nurses Edgewater Pointe Estates, Boca Raton, Fla., 1991-93; DON Empathy Care, Boca Raton, 1993-96; owner Traditional Home Health Svcs., Inc., Lake Worth, Fla., 1996-99; nurse mgr. Genesis Eldercare Network, Laconia, N.H., 1998-99; DON Hollywood Hills Nursing Home, 1999-2001; adminstr. Physician's Choice Home Health Svcs., 2001—03; v.p. clin. ops. Home Care Solutions Group, Ft. Lauderdale, 2003—06; adminstr. Total Home Health Inc., Sebring, Fla., 2006—. Mem. content expert panel ANCC Nurse Adminstrn., 2002—. Trustee Fla. Nurse Found., 2003—06, v.p., 2003—06. Mem.: ANA, Nat. Assn. Dir. Nursing Adminstrn. (chairperson home health coun., cert.), Fla. Nurses Assn. (Quality and Unity in Nursing coun. mem., dist. XI bd. mem.), Fla. Orgn. Nursing Execs., Sigma Theta Tau. Republican. Office: Total Home Health Inc 126 E Center Ave Sebring FL 33870 Office Phone: 863-385-8349. Personal E-mail: docpaula54@yahoo.com.

WESTBERRY, ROBERT KENT, lawyer; b. Marion, Ky., July 21, 1955; s. B.M. and Nancy Elizabeth (Kent) W.; m. Leslie Gail Fifield, Sept. 24, 1988. AB, Centre Coll., 1977; JD, Salmon P. Chase Coll., 1981. Bar: Ky. 1981, US Dist. Ct. (We. Dist. Ky) 1982, US Ct. Appeals (6th Cir.) 1982, US Supreme Ct. Assoc. Westberry and Roberts, Marion, 1981; asst. US atty. US Dist. Ct. (We. Dist. Ky.), Louisville, 1981-87; assoc. Greenebaum, Doll & McDonald, Louisville, 1987-89; spl. justice Ky. Supreme Ct., 1994; assoc. Landrum and Shouse, Louisville, 1989, ptnr. Moderator, lectr. Comprehensive Crime Criminal Act Seminar, 1985, Prosecution of Criminal RICO Action, 1986. Vice chmn. Jefferson County Rep. Party, Louisville, 1988; chmn. Civil Justice Reform Act Com., US Dist. Ct. (We. Dist. Ky.), 1991-95. Mem. Ky. Bar Assn. (chmn. younger lawyers sect., v.p. 2002-03, pres.-elect 2003-04, pres. 2004-05), ABA, Wong Sun Soc., Nat. Assn. Criminal Def. Atty. Episcopalian. Office: Landrum and Shouse Ste 1900 220 W Main St Louisville KY 40202 Office Phone: 502-589-7616. Office Fax: 502-589-2119. E-mail: kwestberry@landrumshouse.com. *

WESTBROCK, LEON E., energy and food products executive; B, St. Cloud State U., Minn. With Cenex, 1976, mgr. three local coops., with merchandising dept., mgr. lubricants dept., dir. retailing, v.p., exec. v.p. petroleum divsn., 1987; COO, exec. v.p. inputs CHS Inc. (merger of Cenex and Harvest States), Inver Grove Heights, Minn., 2000, exec. v.p., COO energy. Chmn. Nat. Coop. Refinery Assn. Vice chmn. Inver Grove Heights HS; mem. comml. devel. task force City of Inver Grove Heights. Served in US Army. Recipient Outstanding Alumni award, St. Cloud State U. Office: CHS Inc PO Box 64089 Saint Paul MN 55164-0089 Office Phone: 651-355-6000. *

WESTBROOK, BRIAN, professional football player; b. Washington, DC, Sept. 2, 1979; s. Ronald and Zelda Westbrook. BS in Mgmt. Info Sys., Villanova U., 2001, studied towards MBA, 2002. RB Phila. Eagles, 2002—. Appeared in: Campbell Chunky Soup Commls. with Donovan McNabb and other Phila. Eagle teammates, 2004, 2005. Organizer Variety Club, Phila.; host of Charity and Celebrity Weekend Police Athletic League Phila. Named to Pro-Bowl, NFL, 2004. Achievements include having jersey retired by Villanova U., Oct. 22, 2005. Avocations: golf, pool. Office: CSMG Sports c/o Fletcher Smith 20 W Kinzie St Ste 1000 Chicago IL 60610 *

WESTBROOK, CLINTON HOWARD, retired military petty officer, retired protective services official; b. Bklyn., Mar. 1, 1919; s. Alfred and Daisy (Gamble) Westbrook; m. Catherine Veronica Wetzel, Dec. 13, 1942 (dec. June 24, 2006); children: James Howard, Cathy Ann, John Alfred-(dec.), Clinton Howard Jr., Robert Vincent(dec.). Enlisted USN, 1940, served on USS Maddox and USS Arizona, 1940—41, served on 23 campaigns in Atlantic and Pacific, 1941—45, served on USS Taylor, 1942—46, recalled to active duty, 1950—52, ret. chief petty officer, 1967; discharged to active reserve USNR, 1946; security patrol So. Pacific Railroad, San Francisco, 1946; with Parcel Post, NYC, 1947; X-ray svc. engr.; field engr., 1952—56; dir. emergency/civil def. County of Seminole, Fla., 1967—74; vet. svcs. officer Seminole County, 1967—84; ret., 1984. Hon. chmn. Golden Age Games, Sanford, 2003; vol. county resource lectr. Seminole County Schs., Meml. Day Parade, Sanford, Fla., 2003, 2004, 2005, 2006, parade marshall, 2004, VIP guest, 2007. Decorated Purple Heart; named State Vet. Svc. Officer of Yr. outstanding svc., Seminole County Commr., 1967—84; recipient Order of the Eagle Feather plaque, numerous unit awards and citations, Presdl. Unit award. Mem.: DAV (life), Pearl Harbor Survivors Assn. (life), Tin Can Sailor Assn. (life), USS Ariz. Reunion Assn. (life; bd. dirs. 1999—2002, v.p. 2003, 2005, 2006—07). Democrat. Roman Catholic. Achievements include being a survivor of the USS Arizona during the Pearl Harbor attack in 1941; led USS Missouri into Tokyo Bay for Japanese surrender while on board USS Taylor. Avocations: stamp collecting/philately, coin collecting/numismatics, photography, volunteering. Home: Lakeview Ter Blgd C Unit 2 283 Raintree Dr Altoona FL 32702-9604

WESTBROOK, JACK HALL, metallurgist, consultant; b. Troy, NY, Aug. 19, 1924; s. Russell Tippett and Grace Hall (Wager) W.; m. Elizabeth Kirkland, Sept. 20, 1947 (dec.); children: Nicholas, Kathryn, Melissa, Kirkland, Daniel; m. Jeanette (Sylvain) Hughson, July 26, 2003. B in Metall. Engring., Rensselaer Poly. Inst., 1944, M in Metall. Engring., 1947; ScD, MIT, 1949. Registered profl. engr., N.Y. Mem. staff Gen. Electric Corp., Schenectady, NY, 1949—85, mgr. materials info. svcs., 1971-82, cons. engring. and mfg., 1982-85; pres., prin., cons. Sci-Tech Knowledge Sys., Scotia, NY, 1985-91, Brookline Techs., Ballston Spa, NY, 1991—. Trustee Engring. Info. Inc., N.Y.C., 1977-80, chmn. indsl. data comm., mem. exec. com. Codata, 1988-94; cons. in field. Editor: Intermetallic Compounds, 1967, various other books; co-editor: Intermetallic Compounds: Principles and Practice, Vols. 1 and 2, 1994, Vol. 3, 2002; editl. adv. bd. CRC Handbook of Chemistry and Physics, 1994-97; author publs. and book reviews. Mem. zoning bd. Town of Ballston, N.Y., 1966-72; bd. edn. Ballston Spa Sch. Dist., 1970-76. With USN, 1944-46. Recipient Turner award Electrochem. Soc., 1957, Hofmann prize Lead Devel. Assn., 1971, Rensselaer Poly. Inst. Outstanding Career award, 1988; NAS traveling fellow to USSR, 1971. Fellow AAAS, Am. Ceramic Soc., Am. Soc. Metals (Campbell lectr. 1976, Jeffries lectr. 1979, Sauveur award 2001), Am. Inst. Chemists, Inst. Physics U.K.; mem. ASTM (Templin award 1959), AIME (New Eng. Regional Conf. award 1963), Inst. Materials (U.K.), Nat. Acad. Engring. Achievements include 6 patents in field. Avocations: old house restoration, history of science and technology. Home and Office: 5 Brookline Rd Ballston Spa NY 12020-3523 Office Phone: 518-309-4359. Personal E-mail: westbrookjh@earthlink.net.

WESTBROOK, JAMES EDWIN, law educator; b. Camden, Ark., Sept. 7, 1934; s. Loy Edwin and Helen Lucille (Bethea) W.; m. Elizabeth Kay Farris, Dec. 23, 1956; children: William Michael, Robert Bruce, Matthew David. BA with high honors, Hendrix Coll., 1956; JD with distinction, Duke U., 1959; LLM, Georgetown U., 1965. Bar: Ark. 1959, Okla. 1977, Mo. 1982. Assoc. Mehaffy, Smith & Williams, Little Rock, 1959-62; asst. counsel, subcom. of U.S. Senate Jud. Com., Washington, 1963; legis. asst. U.S. Senate, Washington, 1963-65; asst. prof. law U. Mo., Columbia, 1965-68, asst. dean, 1966-68, assoc. prof., 1968-70, prof., 1970-76, 80—, James S. Rollins prof. law, 1974-76, 80—, Earl F. Nelson prof. law, 1982-99, emeritus prof., 1999—, interim dean, 1981-82; dean U. Okla. Coll. Law, Norman, 1976-80. George Allen vis. prof. law, U. Richmond, 1987; vis. prof. law Duke U., 1988, Washington U., St. Louis, 1996, 2001; reporter Mid-Am. Assembly on Role of State in Urban Crisis, 1970; dir. Summer Internship Program in Local Govt., 1968; cons. various Mo. cities on drafting home-rule charters; mem. Gov.'s Adv. Coun. on Local Govt. Law, 1967-68, Fed. Practice Com. U.S. Dist. Ct. (we. dist.) Mo., 1986-90; chmn. Columbia Charter Revision Commn., 1973-74; mem. spl. com. labor relations Mo. Dept. Labor and Indsl. Rels., 1975; mem., chmn. subcom. on domestic violence Task Force on Gender and Justice, Mo. Jud. Conf., 1990-93; mem. com. to rev. govtl. structure of Boone County, Mo., 1991. Author: (with L. Riskin) Dispute Resolution and Lawyers, 1987, supplement, 1993, 3d edit., 2005, (with L. Riskin, C. Guthrie, T. Heintz, J. Robbennolt and R. Reuben); contbr. articles to profl. jours. Chair search com. for chancellor U. Mo., Columbia, 1992, chair search com. for provost, 1998; mem. fin. com. Roman Cath. Diocese of Jefferson City, 2003—. Mem. ABA, Nat. Acad. Arbitrators, Assn. Am. Law Schs. (chmn. local govt. law round table coun. 1972), Ctrl. States Law Sch. Assn. (pres. 1982-83), Mo. Bar Assn. (vice chmn. labor law com. 1986-87, chmn. 1987-88, Spurgeon Smithton award 1995), Order of Coif, Blue Key, Alpha Chi. Roman Catholic. Home: 3609 S Woods Edge Rd Columbia MO 65203-6606 Office: U Mo Sch Law Columbia MO 65211-0001 Office Phone: 573-882-6540.

WESTBROOK, JAY LAWRENCE, law educator; b. Morristown, NJ, Dec. 11, 1943; s. Joel W. and Elaine Frances (Summers) W.; m. Pauline June Travis, Feb. 15, 1969; 1 child, Joel Mastin. BA in Polit. Sci./Philosophy, U. Tex., 1965, JD, 1968. Bar: Tex. 1968, D.C. 1969, U.S. Ct. Appeals (D.C. cir.) 1969, U.S. Supreme Ct. 1976, U.S. Ct. Appeals (4th cir.) 1978, U.S. Ct. Appeals (2d cir.) 1979. Assoc. Surrey & Morse (now Jones, Day, Reavis & Pogue), Washington, 1969-74; ptnr. Surrey & Morse (now Jones, Day & Reavis), Washington, 1974-80; mem. law faculty U. Tex., Austin, 1980—, Benno C. Schmidt Chair Bus. Law, 1991—. Vis. prof. U. London, 1990, Harvard Law Sch., 1991-92; advisor Tex. Internat. Law Jour., 1985-91; reporter Am. Law Inst. Transnat. Insolvency Project, 1994-2000; co-leader U.S. delegation to UN Commn. on Internat. Trade Law Working Group on Model Law Internat. Insolvency, 1995-97, 99; sr. advisor Nat. Bankruptcy Rev. Com., 1997; mem. State Dept. Adv. Com. on Pvt. Internat. Law, 1997-2000; vis. scholar Humboldt U., Berlin, 2002. Co-author: As We Forgive Our Debtors: Bankruptcy and Consumer Credit in America, 1989 (Silver Gavel award ABA 1989), The Law of Debtors and Creditors: Text, Cases and Problems, 5th edit., 2005, Teacher's Manual, The Law of Debtors and Creditors, 5th edit., 2005, The Fragile Middle Class: Americans in Debt(Ann. Writing award Am. Coll. Consumer Fin. Svcs. Lawyers), 2000; contbr. articles to profl. jours. Grantee U. Tex. Law Sch. Found., 1982, U. Rsch. Inst., 1982-83, NSF, 1983-86, Policy Rsch. Inst., Lyndon Johnson Sch. Pub. Affairs, 1984, Tex. Bar Found., 1985, Nat. Inst. Child Health and Human Devel., 1986, Nat. Conf. Bankruptcy Judges, 1991, 93, Am. Coll. Banker, 2004. Mem. ABA (bus. bankruptcy com., vice chair internat. bankruptcy subcom. 1999—, Meyer rsch. grant 1986), Am. Law Inst., Am. Coll. Bankruptcy, Nat. Bankruptcy Conf., State Bar Tex. (governing coun. internat. sect. 1987-89), Internat. Insolvency Inst. (bd. dirs. 2000—), Internat. Acad. Comml. and Consumer Law (pres.-elect 2006—), Order of Coif (pres.-elect 2006—). Office: U Tex Sch Law 727 E Dean Keeton St Austin TX 78705-3224

WESTBROOK, LYNDA A., financial consultant; b. Jersey City, July 27, 1960; d. Nicholas and Mildred Lucarelli; m. Kevin J. Westbrook, Apr. 28, 2001; m. Erik Vikjaer, Apr. 7, 1984 (div. Mar. 30, 1991); children: Amanda Vikjaer, Andrew Vikjaer. Grad., Cliffside Park H.S., NJ, 1978. Asst. v.p. Fifth Third Bank, Cin., 2000—. Diversity bd. mem. Fifth Third Bank, Cin., 2006—. Office: Fifth Third Bank 38 Fountain Square Plz MD10907E Cincinnati OH 45263 Office Phone: 513-534-0256. E-mail: lynda.westbrook@53.com.

WESTBY, TIMOTHY SCOTT, lawyer, researcher; b. Fargo, ND, Apr. 16, 1957; s. Joseph Arlo and Dorothy Mae (Nye) W.; m. Ann Amoroso Westby, June 16, 2001. SBChemE, MIT, 1979; PhDChemE, U. Tex., 1984; JD, U. Houston, 1994. Bar: Tex., U.S. Dist. Ct. (so. dist.) Tex., U.S. Patent and Trademark Office, U.S. Ct. Appeals (fed. cir., 5th cir.). Researcher Energy Lab., MIT, Cambridge, 1976-79; rsch. asst. U. Tex., Austin, 1979-84, teaching asst., 1981-83; assoc. rsch. engr. Shell Devel. Co., Houston, 1984-87, rsch. engr., 1987-91, sr. rsch. engr., 1991-94; assoc. Conley, Rose & Tayon, P.C., Houston, 1994—2002; shareholder, dir. Conley Rose, PC, Houston, 2002—. Mem. adv. com. Ohio Combustion Rsch., Columbus, 1985-90, Pa. Coal Rsch. Coop., University Station, 1986-89; adj. prof. chemistry Rice U., 1998—; spl. asst. atty. gen. State of ND, 2005-. Contbr. articles to profl. jours.; patentee method for in situ coal drilling, patentee coal blends having improved ash viscosity. Campaigner United Way, Houston, 1989-91. Scholar MIT, 1975-79; fellow U.S. dept. Energy, 1979-82, Getty Oil Co., 1983-84. Mem. ABA, AIChE, ASTM (com. D-5 1989-94), ASME (advisor rsch. com. on corrosion and deposits from flue gases 1988—), N.Am. Catalysis Soc., Southwestern Catalysis Soc., Am. Intellectual Property Law Assn., Fed. Cir. Bar Assn., Bar Assn. 5th Fed. Cir., State Bar of Tex., Houston Bar Assn., Houston Intellectual Property Law Assn., Coll. of State Bar of Tex., Porsche Club Am. (bd. dirs., treas. 2001—). Avocations: golf, sailing, skiing, auto racing. Office: Conley Rose 600 Travis Ste 7100 Houston TX 77002-2912 Office Phone: 713-238-8000. Business E-Mail: twestby@conleyrose.com.

WESTCOTT, BRIAN JOHN, manufacturing executive; b. Rexford, NY, June 19, 1957; s. John Campbell and Norma (Cornell) W.; children: Sarah Katharine, Paul Brian. BS, Lehigh U., 1979; MS, Stanford U., 1980, PhD, 1987. Engr. Combustion Engring., Windsor, Conn., 1980-81; rsch. engr. Gen. Electric Corp. Rsch., Niskayuna, NY, 1981-83; rsch. fellow Stanford (Calif.) Grad. Sch. Bus., 1987-88; mgr. Gen. Electric Corp. Mgmt., Bridgeport, Conn., 1988-89; prin. A.T. Kearney Tech. Inc., Redwood City, Calif., 1989—2005; CEO Westt, Inc., Menlo Park, Calif., 1990—2005, eInnovate, Menlo Park, Calif., 1999—2005, TTOC, Inc., 2005—. Author: (with others) Paradox and Transformation, 1988; contbr. articles to profl. jours.; inventor, patentee in field. Mem. Menlo Park Vitality Task Force, 1993-94; mem. Lehigh U. Leadership Coun., 2002—. Recipient Tech 500 award Westt, Inc., 1996, 97, 98, Inc. 500 award, 1997, Silicon Valley Tech fast 50 award, 1997, 98, San Francisco and San Jose award for top 100 fastest growing pvt. cos.; co. named among Top 50 Fastest Growing Pvt. Cos. in San Francisco and San Jose, 2001; postdoctoral rsch. fellow Stanford U. Grad. Sch. Bus., 1987, 88; rsch. fellow Electric Power Rsch., Stanford, 1983-87. Mem. ASME. Avocations: sports, politics. Office: eInnovate 325 Sharon Park Dr # 321 Menlo Park CA 94025 Personal E-mail: westcottbj@yahoo.com.

WESTCOTT, JOHN MCMAHON, JR., lawyer; b. NYC, Aug. 1, 1944; s. John M. Sr. and Mary Sabin (Pitkin) W.; m. Suzanne Hillard Laporte, June 27, 1970; children: Valerie, John M. III, Jeffrey. BA cum laude, Yale U., 1966; JD, Harvard U., 1969. Bar: Mass. 1969. Assoc. Hale and Dorr, Boston, 1969-75, jr. ptnr., 1975-79, sr. ptnr., 1979—2004, asst. mng. ptnr., 1980—2004; asst. mng. ptnr. & mem. Corp. dept. Wilmer Cutler Pickering Hale & Dorr, Boston, 2004—. Gen. ptnr. Hale and Dorr Capital Mgmt. LLC, Boston, 1988—. Mem. corp. Winsor Sch., Boston, 1986—, clk., trustee, 1989—. Served with USAR, 1969-75. Named a Mass. Super Lawyer, Boston Mag., 2004. Mem. Brookline Country Club, Union Boat Club, Somerset Club. Republican. Episcopal. Office: Wilmer Cutler Pickering Hale and Dorr 60 State St Boston MA 02109-1816 Office Phone: 617-526-6061. Office Fax: 617-526-5000. Business E-Mail: john.westcott@wilmerhale.com.

WESTEN, BRODIE CURTIS, JR., (CURT), lawyer; b. Champaign, Ill., Nov. 10, 1960; s. Brodie Curtis and Sarah Jane (Mullen) W.; m. Sue Lynn Heubner, Nov. 21, 1987. BS, Western Ill. U., 1982, MBA, 1983; JD, U. Calif., Berkeley, 1986. Bar: Ill. 1986. Fin. analyst Nat. Credit Union Adminstrn., Washington, 1983; atty. Lord, Bissell & Brook, Chgo., 1986—92; asst. gen. counsel, asst. sec. QualMed (merged with Health Net to form Health Systems Internat. Inc. in 1994), 1992—93, v.p. adminstrn., 1993—94, sr. v.p., gen. counsel, sec., 1994—95, Health Systems Internat. Inc. (merged with Found. Health Corp. to become Found. Health Sytems Inc. in 1997), 1995—97, Found. Health Systems Inc. (changed named to Health Net Inc. in 2000), 1997—2000, Health Net, Inc., Woodland Hills, Calif., 2000—07, sr. v.p., spl. counsel, 2007—. Mem. Colo. Commn. on Coop. Health Care Agreements, 1994—96. Bd. trustees The Children's Burn Found., Sherman Oaks, Calif. Mem. ABA, Ill. Bar Assn., Chgo. Bar Assn. Avocation: golf. Office: Health Net Inc 21650 Oxnard St Woodland Hills CA 91367-4901 *

WESTERBERG, ARTHUR WILLIAM, retired chemical engineering professor; b. St. Paul, Oct. 9, 1938; s. Kenneth Waldorf and Marjorie Claire (Darling) W.; m. Barbara Ann Dyson, July 14, 1963; children: Kenneth (dec.), Karl. BS, U. Minn., 1960; MS, Princeton U., 1961; PhD, Imperial Coll., London, 1964. Pres. Farm Engring. Sales Inc., Savage, Minn., 1964-65; sr. analyst Control Data Corp., San Diego, 1965-67; asst. prof., assoc. prof., prof. U. Fla., Gainesville, Fla., 1967-76; prof. chem. engring. Carnegie-Mellon U., Pitts., 1976—2004, chmn. dept., 1980-83, Swearingen prof., 1982—2004, dir. Design Research Ctr., 1978-80, univ. prof., 1992—; dir. Engring. Design Rsch. Ctr., 1986-89. Co-author: Process Flowsheeting, 1979, Systematic Methods of Chemical Process Design, 1997. Recipient Murphree award Am. Chem. Soc., 1997, Steven J. Fenves Sys. Engring. award Carnegie Mellon, 1998, Engring. Disting. Prof. award, 2002, Robert E. Doherty Edn. award, 2003. Fellow AIChE (lectr. 1989, Computers and Sys. Tech. divsn. award 1983, Walker award 1987, McAfee award 1990, Founders Outstanding Contbns. Chem. Engring. award 1995); mem. NAE, Am. Soc. Engring. Edn. (chem. engring. divsn. lectr. 1981, GE Sr. Rsch. award 1999, Computer Aides Chem. Engring. and Edn. Excellence in Chem. Engring. Edn. award 2003). Home: 5564 Beacon St Pittsburgh PA 15217-1972 Business E-Mail: a.westerberg@cmu.edu.

WESTERBERG, GARY W., lawyer; b. Fergus Falls, Minn., Jan. 1, 1945; BA, Cornell U., 1968; JD, So. Meth. U., 1971. Bar: Ill. 1971, US Dist. Ct. (no. dist. Ill.) 1973, US Dist. Ct. (dist. Ariz.) 1997, US Ct. Appeals (3rd cir.) 1982, US Ct. Appeals (7th cir.) 1972, US Ct. Appeals (10th cir.) 1982, US Surpeme Ct. 2007. Ptnr. Lord, Bissell & Brook, Chgo. Editor: Jour. Air Law & Commerce, 1970—71. Mem.: NTSB Bar Assn., ABA, Lawyer-Pilots Bar Assn., Internat. Assn. Def. Counsel, Internat. Bar Assn., Order of the Coif. Office: Lord Bissell & Brook LLP 111 S Wacker Dr Chicago IL 60606 Office Phone: 312-443-0245. Office Fax: 312-896-6245. E-mail: gwesterberg@lordbissell.com.

WESTERFIELD, CAROLYN ELIZABETH HESS, urban planner; b. New Haven, May 3, 1933; d. Orvan Walter and Carol Woodruff (Maurer) Hess; m. Holt Bradford Westerfield, Dec. 17, 1960; children: Pamela Bradford Bingham, Leland Avery. BA, Wellesley Coll., 1954; postgrad., Yale U., 1954-55, M of City Planning, 1959. Planner, office mgr. Tech. Planning Assocs., New Haven, 1955-57, 61-62; assoc. planner City Plan Dept., New Haven, Conn., 1956-59; planner, editor State of Conn. Devel. Commn., 1959-61; cons., 1962—; prin. planner South Cen. Conn. Planning Region, 1979-87; asst. plan dir. Town of Fairfield (Conn.), 1987; planning and zoning adminstr. Town of North Branford (Conn.), 1987-89. Devel. pvt. programs New Haven Hosp.-Boston City Hosp., 1952-54; lectr. city planning U. New Haven, 1988-2003. Mem. alumni bd. Yale U. Sch. Architecture, 1964-76, 85-96, pres., 1993-95; bd. dirs. alumni orgns. Prospect Hill Sch., New Haven, St. Thomas Day Sch.; class officer Wellesley Coll.; mem. Econ. Devel. Commn. Consortium, Hamden, Conn., mem. design rev. com.; clk. Ethics Commn. Mem. Am. Planning Assn., Am. Inst. Cert. Planners, Conn. Women in Planning and Devel., Alliance for Architecture (steering com. 1995-2007), New Haven Colony Hist. Soc., Jr. League New Haven (various exec. position), Watch Hill Improvement Soc. (pres. 1971-73), Conn. Child Welfare Assn., Yale U. Women's Orgn. (pres. 1979-81). Avocations: music, arts, sports, cultural exchange. Home and Office: 29 Old Orchard Rd North Haven CT 06473

WESTERFIELD, HOLT BRADFORD, retired political scientist; b. Rome, Mar. 7, 1928; s. Ray Bert and Mary Beatrice (Putney) W.; m. Carolyn Elizabeth Hess, Dec. 17, 1960; children: Pamela Bradford, Leland Avery. Grad., Choate Sch., 1944; BA, Yale U., 1947; MA, Harvard U., 1951, PhD, 1952. Instr. govt. Harvard U., 1952-56; asst. prof. polit. sci. U. Chgo., 1956-57; mem. faculty Yale U., 1957—, prof. polit. sci., 1965-2000, chmn. dept., 1970-72, Damon Wells prof. internat. studies, 1985-2000; prof. emeritus, 2000—; rsch. assoc. Washington Center Fgn. Policy Research, Johns Hopkins Sch. Advanced Internat. Studies, 1965-66. Vis. prof. Wesleyan U., Middletown, Conn., 1967, 71; bd. visitors U.S. Joint Mil. Intelligence Coll., Washington, 1998—. Author: Foreign Policy and Party Politics: Pearl Harbor to Korea, 1955, The Instruments of America's Foreign Policy, 1963; editor: Inside CIA's Private World: Declassified Articles from the Agency's Internal Journal, 1955-92, 1995. Sheldon traveling fellow Harvard, 1951-52; Henry L. Stimson fellow Yale, 1962, 73; sr. Fulbright-Hays scholar, 1973; hon. vis. fellow Australian Nat. U., 1973. Mem. Am. Polit. Sci. Assn. (Congl. fellow 1953-54), Internat. Polit. Sci. Assn., Internat. Studies Assn.

WESTERFIELD, PUTNEY, management consulting executive; b. New Haven, Feb. 9, 1930; s. Ray Bert and Mary Beatrice (Putney) W.; m. Anne Montgomery, Apr. 17, 1954; children: Bradford, Geoffrey, Clare. Grad., Choate Sch., 1942-47; BA, Yale, 1951. Co-founder, v.p. Careers, Inc., NYC, 1950-52; mgr. S.E. Asia Swen Publs., Inc., Manila, Philippines, 1952; mem. joint adv. commn. Korea, 1953-54; polit. officer Am. embassy, Saigon, Vietnam, 1955-57; asst. to pub. Time mag., NYC, 1957-59, asst. circulation dir., 1959-61, circulation dir., 1961-66, asst. pub., 1966-68, Life mag., NYC, 1968; pub. Fortune mag., NYC, 1969-73; pres. Chase World Info. Corp., NYC, 1973-75; v.p. Boyden Assocs. Internat., San Francisco, 1976-80, sr. v.p., western mgr., 1980-84, pres., chief exec. officer NYC, 1984-90, San Francisco, 1984—90, mng. dir. NYC, San Francisco, 1990—2005. Bd. dirs. Urban League, N.Y.C., 1969-71, Children's Village, 1968-71, Mediterranean Sch. Found., 1969-71, Nat. Boys Club, 1970-73,

U.S. -S. Africa Leaders Exch. Program, 1971-03, Bus. Coun. Internat. Understanding, 1974-76, Yale-China Assn., 1975-78, East Meets West Found., 1991—; trustee Choate Sch., Wallingford, Conn., 1967-76, Westover Sch., Middlebury, Conn., 1975-79, Watch Hill Chapel Soc., 1963-77; Assn. Yale Alumni, 1972-75, 80-83. Mem. Burlingame Country Club, Pacific Union Club, Bohemian Club. Home and Office: 10 Greenview Ln Hillsborough CA 94010-6424 E-mail: putneyw@pacbell.net.

WESTERFIELD, RANDOLPH W., finance educator, former dean; BA in Econs., UCLA, 1963, MA in Econs., 1965, PhD in Fin., 1968. Asst. prof. fin. The Wharton Sch., U. Pa., Phila., 1968-73, assoc. prof. fin., 1973-81, sr. rsch. assoc., Rodney L. White Ctr. Fin. Rsch., 1977-88, prof. fin., 1981-88, chair fin. dept., 1986-88; Charles B. Thornton prof. fin., bus. econs. chair U. So. Calif. Sch. Bus. Adminstrn., LA, 1988-93; dean, Robert R. Dockson chair in bus. adminstrn. Marshall Sch. Bus., U. So. Calif., LA, 1993—2004. Bd. dirs. William Lyon Homes, 2000-, Health Mgmt. Assocs. Inc., 2000-, Nicholas Applegate Growth Equity Fund; vis. prof. fin. U. Nova de Lisbon, Portugal, 1981, Stanford U., Palo Alto, Calif., 1981-82, Claremont (Calif.) Grad. Sch., 1983; mem. trust com. Continental Bank, Phila., 1979-88; mem. pension rsch. coun., The Wharton Sch., 1979-88; mem. editl. adv. bd. John Wiley & Sons (Asia) Pte Ltd., 1996; mem. authors adv. coun., Times Mirror-Irwin Co., 1987-97; chmn. Consortium for Grad. Study in Mgmt., 1997; past cons. AT&T, Mobil Oil, UN, U.S. Depts. Labor and Justice. Co-author: (with Stephen A. Ross, Jeffrey Jaffe) Corporate Finance, 1988, 90, 93, 96 (including Can., Australian and internat. edits.), (with Stephen A. Ross, Bradford D. Jordan) Fundamentals of Corporate Finance, 1992, 93, 95, 97 (including South African, Can., Australian, Chinese, Dutch and Spanish edits.), (with Stephen A. Ross, Bradford D. Jordan) Essentials of Corporate Finance, 1996; author monographs; contbr. chpts. to books, numerous articles to profl. jours. and conf. procs.; assoc. editor Fin. Rev., 1985-92. Mem. Nat. Assn. Corp. Bds. (mem. bd. L.A. chpt. 1996). Office: Marshall Sch Bus Adminstrn U So Calif Hoffman Hall 800 701 Exposition Blvd Los Angeles CA 90089-0001

WESTERGAARD, GEORGE HENRY, secondary school educator; b. Sumas, Wash., Aug. 4, 1942; s. Henry C. and Mary T. Westergaard; m. Donna M. Westergaard, June 20, 1964; 1 child, Kristen. BA in Edn., Ctrl. Wash. State Coll., 1964; MS in Interdisciplinary Studies, U. Oreg., Eugene, 1969; DA in History, Carnegie Mellon U., Pitts., 1976. Cert. secondary edn. tchr., Wash. Tchr. social studies and English Woodrow Wilson Jr. H.S., Yakima, Wash., 1964-67, Cal Young Jr. H.S., Eugene, 1967-73; mem. staff, asst. rsch. historian Carnegie Mellon U., Pitts., 1971-73; tchr. social studies, counselor Thomas Jefferson Jr. H.S., Eugene, 1973-83; tchr. govt., econs., global studies, and psychology South Eugene H.S., 1983-88, tchr. social scis., chair social studies dept., 1988-94, tchr. advanced placement govt. and politics, 1994-99; tchr. advanced placement psychology, comp. govt., politics, US history Sammamish H.S., Bellevue, Wash., 1999—. Cons. AP Govt. and Politics workshops, 1990—; adj. prof. edn. U. Oreg., summer 1991; mem. social studies task force State of Oreg., 1997-99; nat. reader, question leader AP Gov. and Politics; adj. prof. Pacific Luth. U., 2001-05; editor, writer govt. and politics curricula and texts; chmn. program devel. Sammamish H.S., 2002-05 Mem. budget rev. com. Bellevue Sch. Dist. Fellow Ind. Study in the Humanities, 1986. Avocations: photography, fishing, hiking, boating. Home: 2323 167th Ave NE Bellevue WA 98008 Office: Sammamish HS 100 140th Ave Rm 823 Bellevue WA 98005 Office Phone: 425-456-7701. Personal E-mail: westergg@comcast.net.

WESTERGARD, BILLIE, project engineer; b. Birgham City, Utah, Oct. 7, 1939; s. Orlee A. and Roma A. Westergaard; m. Sylvia Ann Devenney, July 25, 1942; children: Shelly Rene, Holly Lynn, William Lorin, Lara Lea. Design engr. DuPont Co., Wilmington, Del., 1962—80, project engr., 1980—93; cons. design engr. pvt. practice, 1994—2007, Bechtel Co., Richland, Wash., 2007—. Author: Hotson/Westergard Universe; contbr. scientific papers on particle spin and mass transfer. Trustee, sec. Mt. Cuba Astron. Obs., 1990—2007. Flight engr. USAF, 1960—80. Mem.: Del. Astron. Soc. (pres.), Nat. Philosophy Alliance. Avocations: astronomy, fishing, travel. Home: 32831 Almwick Ln Lewes DE 19958 Office: Bechtel Co 2435 Stevens Ctr Pl Richland WA 99354-1874 Business E-Mail: westerb@udel.edu.

WESTERGARD, SUE BENZEL, elementary education educator; b. Apr. 17, 1954; BA, Whitworth Coll., 1976; M in Curriculum & Instrn., Nazarene Coll., 1993. Learning specialist Walla Walla (Wash.) Sch. Dist., 1976—. Office Phone: 509-527-3077. E-mail: swestergard@wwps.org.

WESTERGREN, TIM, music company executive; BA in computer acoustics and recording tech., Stanford, 1988. CEO Nightfly Studios; founder, now chief strategy officer Pandora, 2000—; co-founder Savage Beast. Composer: (films) The Last Best Sunday, 1999, (ballets) Defying Gravity, 1999, (films) Now & Then: From Frosh to Seniors, 1999. Office: Pandora 360 22nd St Ste 440 Oakland CA 94612 Office Phone: 510-451-4100. Office Fax: 510-451-4286. *

WESTERHOFF, JOHN HENRY, III, priest, theologian, educator; b. Paterson, NJ, June 28, 1933; s. John Henry and Nona Celia (Walsh) W.; m. Alberta Louise Barnhart, Dec. 27, 1955 (div. 1991); children: Jill Louise, John Jeffrey, Beth Anne; m. Caroline Askew Hughes, Oct. 27, 1991. BS, Ursinus Coll., 1955; STB, Harvard U., 1958; EdD, Columbia U., 1974; DD, Ursinus Coll., 1990. Ordained to ministry United Ch. of Christ, 1958, Episcopal Ch., 1978; pastor Congl. Ch., Presque Isle, Maine, 1958-60, assoc. pastor Needham, Mass., 1960-64; pastor 1st Congl. Ch., Williamstown, Mass., 1964-66; edn. sec., editor Colloquy (United Ch. Bd. for Homeland Ministries), NYC, 1966-73; Lentz lectr. Harvard U. Div. Sch., 1973-74; prof. Duke U. Div. Sch., Durham, NC, 1974-94; dir. Inst. Pastoral Studies, Atlanta, 1992—2003; interim rector St. Bartholomew Episcopal Ch., Atlanta, 1993-94; theologian in residence St. Lukes Episcopal Ch., Atlanta, 1994—2004; vis. prof. Gen. Theol. Sem., NYC, 2004—05; priest assoc., resident theologian St. Anne's Episc. Ch., Atlanta, 2005—. Author: Values for Tomorrows Children, 1970, A Colloquy on Christian Education, 1972, Generation to Generation, 1974, Tomorrow's Church, 1976, Will Our Children Have Faith?, 1976, McGuffey and His Readers, 1978, Who Are We?, 1978, Learning Through Liturgy, 1978, Inner Growth-Outer Change, 1979, The Church's Ministry in Higher Education, 1979, Liturgy and Learning Through the Life Cycle, 1980, Christian Believing, 1980, Bringing Up Children in The Christian Church, 1980, A Faithful Church, 1981, The Spiritual Life: Learning East and West, 1981, Building God's People, 1983, A Pilgrim People, 1984, Living the Faith Community, 1985, On the Threshold of God's Future, 1986, Living Into Our Baptism, 1990, Schooling Christians, 1992, The Spiritual Life: Foundation for Preaching and Teaching, 1994; A People Called Episcopalians, 1995, Holy Baptism: A Guide for Parents and Godparents, 1996, Grateful and Generous Hearts, 1997, To Love and to Cherich Till Death Do Us Part, 1998, Sensing Beauty, 1998, A Pilgrim People, 1999, Will Our Children Have Faith?, 2000, Living Faithfully as a Prayer Book People, 2005; editor: Religious Edn, 1979-89. Mem. Assn. Profs. and Researchers in Religious Edn., Religious Edn. Assn. Democrat. Episcopalian. Personal E-mail: johnwest33@bellsouth.net.

WESTERHOLD, RUTH ELIZABETH, psychologist, educator; b. Youngstown, Ohio, Aug. 4, 1926; d. Samuel Gordon and Grace Elizabeth (Green) Meadows; m. Walter Charles Westerhold, June 1, 1949; children: Marsha L., Carl E. BS, Youngstown U., 1946; postgrad., Ohio U., 1947, U. Ill., 1947-49; PhD, So. Ill. U., 1978. Cert. sch. psychologist, Mo., Ill. Chief clin. psychologist Alton (Ill.) State Hosp., 1952-55; psychologist St. Louis County (Mo.) Spl. Sch. Dist., 1963-68; chief psychologist Kaskaskia Spl. Edn. Dist., Centralia, Ill., 1968-78; dir. learing comms. East Miss. Jr. Coll., Scooba, 1978-83, coord. instructional techniques, 1987—, coord. devel. edn., 1987-88. Cons. psychologist div. vocat. rehab. State of Ill., Alton, 1954-55. Counselor, lectr., writer ethics-morality, health and nutrition, body-mind relationships, child rearing, family, learning. USPHS fellow U. Ill., 1947-49. Mem. Soc. Sci. Exploration, Psi Chi. Home: 1887 Summertree Rd Starkville MS 39759-9761 Office Phone: 662-323-3465.

WESTERHOUT, GART, retired astronomer; b. The Hague, The Netherlands, June 15, 1927; arrived in U.S., 1962, naturalized, 1969; s. Gerrit and Magdalena (Foppe) W.; m. Judith Mary Monaghan, Nov. 14, 1956; children: Magda C., Gart T., Brigit M., Julian C. Drs., Leiden U., Netherlands, 1954, PhD, 1958. Asst. Leiden U. Observatory, 1952-56, sci. officer, 1956-59, chief sci. officer, 1959-62; prof., dir. astronomy U. Md., 1962-73, chmn. div. math. and phys. scis. and engring., 1972-73, prof. astronomy, 1973-77; sci. dir. U.S. Naval Observatory, Washington, 1977-93; vis. astronomer Max Planck Inst. Radio Astronomy, Bonn, Germany, 1973-74, mem. adv. bd., 1976-79. Mem. astronomy adv. bd. NSF, 1963-67; vice chmn. divsn. phys. sci. NRC, 1969-73; mem. com. on radio frequencies, 1971-92; trustee Assoc. Univs. Inc., 1971-74; mem. Inter Union Commn. on Allocation of Frequencies, 1974-82; mem. sci. coun. Stellar Data Ctr., Strasbourg, France, 1978-84, chmn., 1981; chmn. working group on astrometry, astronomy survey com. NAS, 1979-81; mem. adv. bd. Haystack-N.E. Radio Obs. Consortium, 1974-77; mem. Arecibo adv. bd. Nat. Astronomy and Ionosphere Ctr., 1977-80, chmn., 1979-80; mem. U.S. nat. com. CODATA, 1985-91. Contbr. on radio astronomy, spiral structure of our Galaxy and astrometry to profl. jours. Recipient citation for teaching excellence Washington Acad. Scis., 1972; U.S. Sr. Scientist award Alexander von Humboldt Stiftung, Ger., 1973; NATO fellow, 1959. Mem. Internat. Astron. Union (chmn. working group on astron. data 1985-91), Internat. Sci. Radio Union (pres. commn. on radio astronomy 1975-78), Am. Astron. Soc. (councillor 1975-78, v.p. 1985-87), Royal Astron. Soc. Roman Catholic.

WESTERMAN, LIANE MARIE, research scientist executive; b. Long Branch, NJ, June 20, 1949; d. Charles Wilson and Edith Doris (Johnson) Case; m. S. Thomas Westerman; children: David Aaron, Charles Paul. BA in Psychology, Monmouth U., West Long Branch, NJ, 1972; MA in Teaching, Coll. of N.J., 1979. Cert. tchr. of handicapped, N.J. Tchr. spl. edn., dir. afternoon program S.E.A.R.C.H., Ocean, NJ, 1972-74; tchr. spl. edn. Jackson (N.J.) Twp. Sch. System, 1974-79; exec. dir. Otologic Edn., Inc., Shrewsbury, NJ, 1980-88; dir. clin. rsch. Nat. Patent Analytical Systems, Inc., Roslyn Heights, NY, 1983-86, v.p. rsch., 1986-88; pres. Westerman Rsch. Assocs., Inc., Shrewsbury, NJ, 1988—. Participant numerous convs., profl. organs. and spl. interest groups, U.S.A., Israel and The Netherlands, 1974—; software devel. expert to knowledge engr. for Visual Perceptual System, 1984—; v.p. Otologic Edn., Inc., Shrewsbury, 1988—. Co-contbr. articles and chpts. to profl. publs.; U.S. and Can. patentee computer-aided drug-abuse detection. Fundraiser Am. Heart Assn., 1991; bd. dirs. Women's Coun. for Leon Hess Cancer Ctr. at Monmouth Med. Ctr., 2003—; active MADD; activist Nat. Audubon Soc. Mem. Am. Acad. Otolaryngology, Head and Neck Surgery (assoc.), Internat. Regulatory Affairs Profls. Soc., Nat. Graphic Soc., Assn. Clin. Pharmacologists, Regulatory Affairs Profls. Soc., Monmouth County Assn. Children with Learning Disabilities, Psi Chi, Sigma Xi. Avocations: travel, classical music, creative writing. Office: Westerman Rsch Assocs Inc 170 Ave at the Common Ste 6 Shrewsbury NJ 07702-4003

WESTERMANN, EDWARD BURTON, military officer, analyst, educator; b. Temple, Tex., Nov. 18, 1961; s. Francis X. and Suzann Westermann; m. Brigitte Angelika Engel, Dec. 16, 1991; children: Sarah E, Marie-Louise. BS, USAF Acad., 1984; MA in European History, Fla. State U., 1992; MA, Sch. Advanced Airpower Studies, Maxwell AFB, 1997; PhD in European History, U. N.C., 2000. Helicopter Pilot USAF, 1985. Commd. 2d lt. USAF, 1984, advanced through grades to col.; exch. instr. pilot with German air force Hubschraubertransportgeschwader 64, Ahlhorn, Germany, 1988—91; asst. prof. history U.S. Air Force Acad., Colorado Springs, 1992—95; strategy devel. officer Hdqs. European Command, Stuttgart, Germany, 2000—02; prof. comparative mil. theory Sch. Advance Air and Space Studies, Maxwell AFB, Ala., 2002—; sr. mil. prof. USAF Acad., 2006—. Selected mem. internat. adv. panel Royal Air force Ctr. for Air Power Studies, 2007. Author: (historical work) Hitler's Police Battalions: Enforcing Racial War in the East, Flak: German Anti-Aircraft Defenses, 1918-1945. Decorated Ehrenkreuz der Bundeswehr in Bronze Fed. Rep. Germany; recipient John L. Snell prize, 1998, League of WWI Aviation Historians Nat. award, 1999; fellow, German Academic Exch. Svc., U. Calif. Berkeley, 1993, Fulbright fellow, U.S. Govt., 1994—95, U.S. Holocaust Meml. Mus., 1999, German Academic Exch. Svc., 1999, 2003—04. Mem.: Soc. Mil. History (Mancado prize 2002), Am. Hist. Assn., German Studies Assn., Daedalians (life), Phi Alpha Theta. Independent. Roman Catholic. Office: Dept Mil Strategic Studies USAF Acad U S A F Academy CO 80840 Home: 4158 Douglass Way U S A F Academy CO 80840 Office Phone: 719-333-9402. Personal E-mail: bawebw4@aol.com. Business E-Mail: edward.westermann@usafa.af.mil.

WESTERMEIER, JOHN THOMAS, JR., lawyer, educator; b. West Point, NY, Sept. 14, 1941; s. John Thomas and Louise (Melick) W.; m. Joddie Lynn Stephens, Feb. 8, 1964 (div. Dec. 1966); 1 child, Blake Lynn; m. Cynthia Ann Heins, Aug. 23, 1980. BS, U.S. Mil. Acad., 1963; MBA, George Washington U., 1969, LLM, 1978; JD, Am. U., 1974; cert. in data processing, Inst. for Cert. of Computer Profls., 1978. Bar: Va. 1974, D.C. 1975, U.S. Supreme Ct. 1978, Md. 1982, U.S. Dist. Ct. D.C. 1982, U.S. Dist. Ct. (ea. dist.) Va. 1983, U.S. Dist. Ct., Md. 1987, U. S. Claims Ct. 1990. Commd. 2d lt. U.S. Army, 1963, advanced through grades to maj. Vietnam, 1966, 70, resigned, 1974; assoc. Arent, Fox, Kintner, Plotkin & Kahn, Washington, 1974-79; ptnr. Abrams, Westermeier & Goldberg P.C., Washington, 1980-89, Fenwick & West, Washington, 1989—98, DLA Piper, 1998—. Adj. prof. law Am. U., Washington, 1985-86; instr. continuing legal edn. Georgetown U. Law Ctr., Washington, 1987-95; mem. bd. advisors Computer Negotiations, Orlando, Fla., 1982-87, Computer Law Strategist, N.Y.C., 1985—. Computer Law Reporter, Washington, 1990—; mem. Va. Gov.'s Coun. Info. Mgmt., 1987-91. Author and editor: Data Processing and the Law, 1981, Computer Law Case Materials, 1986; articles editor Am. U. Law Rev., 1973; legal editor Information Strategy: The Executive's Jour., 1984—, bd. advisors, 1984—; contbr. over 180 articles to profl. jours. Bd. advisors No. Va. Hotline, Arlington, 1975-78; del. Va. Rep. Conv., Virginia Beach, 1985, Richmond, 1993. Col. USAR, ret. 1993. Decorated 2 Bronze Stars, 2 Meritorious Svc. medals, Joint Svc. Commendation medal, Army Commendation medal, Vietnamese Cross of Gallantry; recipient Disting. Information Scis. award Data Processing Mgmt. Assn., Chgo., 1987 Fellow Am. Bar Found. (life); mem. ABA (chmn. com. of professionalism and malpractice of computer specialists computer law divsn. 1978-87), D.C. Bar Assn. (instr. continuing legal edn., steering com. computer law sect. 1986-92, co-chmn. 1989), Data Processing Mgmt. Assn. Washington (chpt. pres. 1982), D.C. Computer Law Forum (bd. dirs. 1984), Phi Alpha Delta. Clubs: West Point Soc. (Washington) (bd. govs., sec. 1974-82). Republican. Episcopalian. Avocations: tennis, golf, swimming, writing. Office: DLA Piper 1775 Wiehle Ave Suite 400 Reston VA 20190-5159 Home Phone: 703-437-1010; Office Phone: 703-773-4216.

WESTERMEYER, JOSEPH JOHN, psychiatrist; b. Chgo., Apr. 8, 1937; m. Rachel Moga; children: Michelle, Joseph; 5 foster children. Student, U. Notre Dame and St. Thomas Coll., 1955-57; BS in Biology and Chemistry, U. Minn., 1959, MD, 1961, MA in Anthropology, 1969, MPH, PhD, 1970. Diplomate Am. Bd. Psychiatry and Neurology, Am. Bd. Family Practice. Rotating intern St. Paul-Ramsey Hosp., 1961-62; gen. practice medicine Payne Ave. Med. Clinic, St. Paul, 1962-65; dep. chief divsn. pub. health AID, Laos, 1965-67; resident in psychiatry U. Minn., Mpls., 1967-70, instr., 1970-71, asst. prof., 1971-74, assoc. prof., 1974-78, prof. psychiatry, 1978—, prof., chair, 1989, adj. prof. anthropology, 1979—89, 1993—, adj. prof. psychology, 1979—89, dir. med. student edn. dept. psychiatry, 1976-82; mem. psychiatry staff, outpatient psychiat. practice U. Minn. Hosps. and Clinics, Mpls., 1970-89; prof., chmn. dept. psychiatry and behavioral sci. Okla. U. Med. Ctr., Oklahoma City, 1989—92; founder, dir. acute in-patient service U. Minn. Hosps. and Clinics, Mpls., 1970-72, founder, dir. day hosp., 1971-73, cons. primary care clinic, 1970-83, founder, dir. outpatient clinic for refugees from S.E. Asia, 1977—89, founder, dir. program for alcohol and drug dependence, 1982—89, founder, dir. internat. clinic dept. psychiatry, 1984—89; chief psychiatry, dir. mental health Mpls. VA Med. Ctr., 1993—. Mem. ad hoc com. on Indochinese refugees Minn. Dept. Pub. Welfare, 1980-82; cons. methadone program Minn. VA Hosp., 1977-84, dept. psychiatry Mpls. VA Hosp., 1978-85; mem. case devel. com. for computer-based exam. Nat. Bd. Med. Examiners, 1983-88; mem. com. on mental and behavioral assessment and disorder in pilots FAA and AMA, 1984-85; chmn., co-editor devel. of a teaching manual on drug/alcohol dependence WHO, 1982-85, chmn., co-editor task force and report on methadone treatment in opiate dependence, 1982-85, research cons. internat. collaborative study of drug dependence intervention and treatment in primary health care, 1982-85; sec. Group for Advancement of psychiatry, 1999-2005, co-chair addiction psychiatry cert. Am. Bd. Psychiatry and Neurology, 2003-, Spl. Polulation Com. Health Svc Rsch VA, 2005-; cons. in field; vis. prof. various colls.; lectr. in field. Author: A Primer on Chemical Dependency: A Clinical Guide to Alcohol and Drug Problems, 1976, Poppies, Pipes and People: A Study of Opium and Its Use in Laos, 1983, (with C. Williams) Refugees Mental Health Issues in Resettlement Countries, 1986, A Clinical Guide to Drug and Alcohol Problems, 1986; (with A. Arif) A Manual for Substance Abuse Education, 1988, An Update on Methadone, 1988; The Psychiatric Care of Migrants, 1989; editor: Anthropology and Mental Health, 1976; co-editor: (with E. Foulks, R. Wintrob and A. Favazza) Transcultural Psychiatry, 1977, (with R. weiss and D. Ziedonis) Comorbid Affective Disorder and Substance Abuse, Johns Hopkins Press, 2003; contbr. revs. and articles to profl. jours., chpts. to books; mem. editorial bd. Am. Jour. Drug and Alcohol Abuse, 1973—, Jour. Operational Psychiatry, 1977-86, Am. Jour. Pub. Health, 1980-83, 83-87, Advances in Alcohol and Substance Abuse, 1980—, Alcoholism: Clin. and Exptl. Research, 1980-86, Alcohol and Research World, 1981—; social sci. editor Substance Abuse Newsletter, 1979-83; rev. reader Am. Jour. Psychiatry, 1978—, Transcultural Psychiat. Revs., 1980-84, Archives Gen. Psychiatry, 1981—, White Cloud Jour., 1981—, Jour. Nervous and Mental Disease, 1977—, Current Anthropology, 1979, 83, 85, Culture, Medicine and Psychiatry, 1979-80, various others. Recipient Meritorious Service award U.S. AID, 1967; Ginzburg fellow Group for Advancement of Psychiatry, 1969-70, NIH summer fellow Grad. Session in Epidemiology, U. Minn. Continuation Ctr., 1970, 72, 78; research grantee Office Internat. Programs, U. Minn., 1974-75, 78, 81, NIMH, 1973-74, 80-81, 82-84, Nat. Inst. Alcohol Abuse and Alcoholism, 1974-77, 78-79, Grad. Sch. U. Minn., 1977-78, Office Drug Abuse Prevention, U. Minn., 1977-78, Minn. Med. Found., 1974-75, 81, 82-83, Nat. Inst. Drug Abuse, 1977-78, 83-85, State Minn., 1979-80, Ctr. Urban and Regional Affairs, U. Minn., 1982-83, career tchr. grantee Alcohol, Drug Abuse and Mental Health Adminstrn., HEW, 1973-75, Biomed. research support grantee U. Minn. Med. Sch., 1977-78, Minn. Med. Found., 1977, tng. grantee Office Alcohol and Other Drug Abuse Programming, U. Minn., 1979-83, Indochinese Health Professionals, 1979-81, Archie; recipient neumerous other research grants. Fellow Am. Anthropol. Assn., Am. Assn. Family Practice, Am. Psychiat. Assn. (com. on drug abuse 1985—); mem. World Psychiat. Assn. (transcultural sect.), Am. Soc. Social Psychiatry, Soc. Med. Anthropology, Assn. Med. Educators and Researchers in Substance Abuse (award for disting. contributions to the field 1987), AAAS, Assn. Behavioral Sci. and Med. Edn., Assn. Acad. Psychiatrists, Am. Pub. Health Assn., Research Soc. on Alcoholism, World Psychiat. Assn. (sect. on transcultural psychiatry), Soc. for Study of Psychiatry and Culture (steering com. 1979—, secretariat 1984-85), Am. Med. Soc. on Alcoholism (state chmn. 1979—), Am. Acad. Psychiatrists in Alcoholism and Addictions, Soc. Traumatic Stress Studies, Minn. Psychiat. Assn. (mem. chem. dependency subcom. 1979—85, mem. Minn. mental health interdisciplinary interest group rep. 1980-85, pres. 1984-86), Minn. State Med. Assn. (resource group on alcoholism and other chem. dependencies 1976-81), Alpha Omega Alpha. Home: 1935 Summit Ave Saint Paul MN 55105-1430 Office Phone: 612-725-2037. Business E-Mail: joseph.westermeyer@med.va.gov, weste010@umn.edu.

WESTERN, BRUCE, sociologist, educator; BA with first class honors in Govt., Univ. Queensland, Australia, 1987; MA, UCLA, 1990, PhD, 1993. Asst. prof., sociology Princeton Univ., 1994—98, assoc. prof., 1998—2000, faculty assoc., Office Population Rsch., 1993—, prof., sociology, 2000—. Editl. bd. Political Analysis, 2001—, Sociological Methodology, 2001—, Socio-Economic Review, 2002—. Fellow: Am. Arts. & Scis.; mem.: Sociological Rsch. Assn., Soc. Advancement of Socio-Economics (exec. coun. 2002—05), Soc. Comparative Rsch. (exec. dir. 2002—05), Population Assn. Am., Australian Sociological Assn., Am. Statistical Assn., Am. Sociological Assn. Office: Dept Sociology Wallace Hall Princeton Univ Princeton NJ 08544 Office Phone: 609-258-2445. Office Fax: 609-258-2180. Business E-Mail: western@princeton.edu. *

WESTERN, KARL AUGUST, physician, epidemiologist; b. Trenton, NJ, July 6, 1940; s. August Earl and Lillian Theresa (Murphy) W.; m. Aileen Martin Worthington, May 2, 1964; children: Ann Western Bittman, Mark August. AB, Georgetown U., 1961, MD, 1965; diploma of tropical pub. health, London Sch. Tropical Medicine & Hygiene, 1972. Intern Bellevue Hosp.-Cornell Meml.-Sloan Kettering Joint Program, NYC, 1965-66, resident, 1966-67; medical epidemiologist Ctr. Disease Control, Atlanta, 1967-70; resident supr. infectious diseases L.A. County-USC Med. Ctr., 1971-72; med. epidemiologist Va. State Health Dept., Richmond, 1972-74; dept. head Pan Am. Health Orgn., Washington, 1975-79; asst. dir., dir. Office of Global Affairs, NIAID, Bethesda, Md., 1979—2006, sr. internat. rsch. advisor, 2006—. Med. dir. USPHS, 1967-97. Recipient Okeke award U. London, 1972, Meritorious Service award, 1970, Commendation award, 1983, Outstand. Service award, 1987, USPHS. Mem. AMA, Am. Soc. Tropical Medicine and Hygiene (editor Tropical Med. news, 1987-99), Am. Pub. Health Assn. (sec. epidemiology sect. 1973-78), Nat. Coun. Internat. Health (chair annual meeting 1986). Republican. Roman Catholic. Home: 6436 31st St NW Washington DC 20015-2342 Office: Nat Inst Allergy Infectious Diseases/NIH 9000 Rockville Pike Bethesda MD 20892-6613

WESTERNOFF, TRENT H., surgeon; s. Philip H. and Dorothy A. Westernoff; m. Nazly Mehdizadeh, Aug. 29, 2003. BA with honors, U. Calif., Santa Barbara, 1994; MD, U. Calif., San Francisco, 2001; DMD cum laude, Harvard U., Boston, 1998. General Surgery Internship U. of Calif., 2002; Oral and Maxillofacial Surgery Univeristy of Calif., 2004. Oral and maxillofacial surgery resident U. Calif., San Francisco, 1998—2004, gen. surgery intern, 2001—02; commd. 2d lt. US Army, advanced through grades to maj., 2004, oral and maxillofacial surgeon El Paso, Tex., 2004—05, 2006—, combat maxillofacial surgeon Mosul, Iraq, 2005; credentialling com. mem., drug audit officer US Army Dentac, El Paso, 2006—. Mem. pharmacy and therapeutics com. William Beaumont Army Med. Ctr., El Paso, 2006—07. Steering com. mem. United Way Found., Santa Barbara, Calif., 1992—93; mem. big brother/big sister program Harvard Med./Dental Sch., Boston, 1994—97; participant Cambridge Children's Oral Health Program, Mass., 1997. Decorated Meritorious Svc. medal US Army, Order of the Combat Spur; recipient Student

Scholarship award, Sigma Chi Found., 1993, Oral Biology award, Am. Assn. Oral Biologists, 1998; scholar, US Army, 1995—98. Fellow: Am. Dental Soc. Anesthesiology, Am. Assn. Oral and Maxillofacial Surgery, Nat. Dental Bd. Anesthesiology, Am. Bd. Oral and Maxillofacial Surgeons; mem.: Calif. Assn. Oral and Maxillofacial Surgeons (assoc.), Am. Coll. Oral and Maxillofacial Surgeons (assoc.), Am. Acad. Cosmetic Surgery (assoc.), Am. Legion, Thomas Barnes Hitchcock Soc., Golden Key Nat. Honor Soc. (life; sec. 1992—93), Sigma Chi Frat. (treas. 1992—93). Avocations: bicycling, running, skiing, travel. Home Phone: 415-218-2342.

WESTERVELT, GAYLE GAETANO, physical education educator; b. Utica, NY, Mar. 26, 1950; d. Felix Louis and Jeanne LaQuay Gaetano; m. Terry E. Westervelt, Aug. 3, 1975; 1 child, Marisa G. BS in Edn., SUNY, Cortland, 1973; postgrad., SUNY, Oneonta, 1976, St. Rose, Albany, NY, 1977—78. Cert. phys. edn. N.Y. Lifeguard and instr. swimming Town of Boonville, NY, 1967—73, Adirondack Ctrl. Sch., 1971—72; recreation instr. Cortland Dept. Pks. and Recreation, 1972—73; encore team facilitator Cobleskill-Richmondville Ctrl. Sch., Cobleskill, NY, 1993, phys. educator, 1973—, asst. athletic dir., 2001—, dist. health coord., 2004—. Chmn. health adv. com. Cobleskill-Richmondville Ctrl. Sch. Sch. and Cmty., Cobleskill, 2004—, coord. sch. health index, 2004—; mem. fit before 5 com. Bassett Hosp., Cobleskill, 2004—05; advisor Gymnastics Club, 1973—2002; coach girls basketball, girls tennis. Recipient N.Y. State Sportsmanship awards, 2002—05; Fitness grantee, BOCES, 1996, 1997, Health and Fitness grantee, BOCO and NYSPHERD, 2006. Mem.: Am. Assn. Health, Phys. Edn., Recreation and Dance, N.Y. Assn. Health, Phys. Edn., Recreation and Dance. Avocations: painting, swimming, gardening, interior decorating. Home: 244 Philip Schuyler Rd Cobleskill NY 12043 Office Phone: 518-234-8368 2030. Fax: 518-234-3950. E-mail: catboy@telenet.net.

WESTFALL, CONSTANCE COURTNEY, lawyer; b. Plainview, Tex., Nov. 29, 1960; d. M.H. and Carolyn Courtney; m. Monte Jay Westfall, Jan. 3, 1998; children: William, John. BS, U. Tex., 1982, JD, 1985. Bar: Tex., US Dist. Ct. (we. and no. dists.) Tex., US Dist. Ct. (we. and ea. dists.) Ark., US Dist. Ct. (we. dist.) Okla., US Ct. Appeals (5th and 8th cirs.) Tex. Com. clk. Natural Resources Com., Tex. Ho. of Rep., 1979; legis. staff to hon. Buck Florence Tex. Ho. of Rep., 1980-82; law clk. to hon. Jerre Williams U.S. Ct. Appeals (5th cir.), 1985-86; assoc. Thompson & Knight, Dallas, 1986-92, Brown McCarroll, Dallas, 1992-94; ptnr. Hutcheson & Grundy, Dallas, 1994-98, Strasburger & Price, Dallas, 1998—. Contbr. articles to profl. jours. Moderator So. Meth. U. Sch. Law Environ. Career Seminar, 1989-2000; pres. Monticello Estates Homeowners Assn., 2006-. Mem.: ABA, State Bar Coll., State Bar Tex. (mem. law sch. com. 1988—97, chmn. outreach com. environ. sect. 1989—92, chmn. law sch. com. 1997—2003, chmn. environ. and natural resources sect. 2003—04, mem. sect. coord. com. 2004—06). Office: Strasburger & Price 901 Main St Ste 4300 Dallas TX 75202-3724

WESTFALL, DAVID, lawyer, educator; b. Columbia, Mo., Apr. 16, 1927; s. Wilhelmus David A. and Ruth (Rollins) W.; children: Elizabeth Stewart, William Beatty, Thomas Curwen, Katharine Putnam. AB, U. Mo., 1947; LLB magna cum laude, Harvard U., 1950. Bar: Ill. 1950, Mass. 1956. Assoc. Bell, Boyd, Marshall & Lloyd, Chgo., 1950-55; asst. prof. law Harvard Law Sch., 1955-58, prof., 1958—, John H. Watson Jr. prof. law, 1980—83, John L. Gray prof., 1983—, Carl F. Schipper Jr. prof., 1996—. Author: Estate Planning Cases and Text, 1985, Every Woman's Guide to Financial Planning, 1984, Family Law, 1993; co-author: Estate Planning Law and Taxation, 4th edit., 2001; co-editor: Readings in Federal Taxation, 1983. Served as 1st lt. JAGC, AUS, 1951-53. Fellow Am. Coll. Trust and Estate Counsel (acad.); mem. ABA, Mass. Bar Assn., Am. Law Inst., Phi Beta Kappa, Phi Delta Theta.

WESTFALL, LYNN D., oil industry executive; B in Chem. Engring., U. Tex.; MBA, U. Houston. Process engr. Amoco Chems. Corp., 1975; v.p. strategy and strategic issues Ultramar Diamond Shamrock, San Antonio; v.p. devel. and bus. analysis Tesoro Corp., San Antonio, 2002—05, v.p., chief economist, 2005—06, sr. v.p. external affairs, chief economist, 2006—. Office: Tesoro Corp 300 Concord Plz San Antonio TX 78216-6999 Office Phone: 210-283-2000.

WESTFIELD, FRED MEINHARD, economics professor; b. Essen, Germany, Nov. 7, 1926; came to U.S., 1940; s. Dietrich and Grete (Stern) W.; m. Joyce A. Horwitz Nochlin, Nov. 15, 1968; stepchildren: Steven Nochlin, Keith Nochlin. BA magna cum laude, Vanderbilt U., 1950; PhD in Indsl. Econs., MIT, 1957. Teaching asst., instr. MIT, Cambridge, 1952-53; lectr. Northwestern U., Evanston, Ill., 1953-57, asst. prof., 1957-60, assoc. prof., 1960-65; prof. econs. Vanderbilt U., Nashville, 1965-98, mem. faculty coun. Coll. Arts and Scis., 1974-76, mem. faculty senate, 1979-82, 94-95, dir. undergrad. studies dept. econs. and bus. adminstrn., 1984-87, mem. grad. faculty coun., 1991, prof. econs. emeritus, 1998—. Vis. prof. U. Colo., summers 1973-74; condr. seminars, lectr., participant univs. and rsch. orgns.; Fulbright sr. lectr. U. Nac. del Sur, Argentina, 1986; cons. Coun. Econ. Advisers, Exec. Office Pres., 1968, World Bank and Water and Power Devel. Authority, Pakistan, 1970-72, World Bank and East African Power and Light Co., Kenya, 1975, NSF, 1975, FTC, 1976-78, World Bank, UN Devel. Program and Econ. Planning Bd. South Korea, 1975-76; expert witness Tenn. Pub. Svc. Commn., 1980-89, Consumer Advocate Tenn. Atty. Gen., 1994; also others. Mem. editl. bd. Utilities Policy, 1990—2002, mem. bd. editors So. Econ. Jour., 1973—75, editl. referee Am. Econ. Rev., Jour. Polit. Economy, Econometrica, So. Econ. Jour., Econ. Inquiry; contbr. articles and book revs. to profl. jours. With US Army, 1945—46. Fellow Gen. Edn. Bd., MIT, Ford Found., 1958-59. Mem. Am. Econ. Assn., Econometric Soc. (program com. 1967, chmn. conf. sessions), So. Econ. Assn. (v.p. 1976-77, chmn. conf. sessions), Phi Beta Kappa. Home: 1097 Lynnwood Blvd Nashville TN 37215-4540

WESTHAUSER, KARL E., historian; b. NYC, July 27, 1961; s. Karl Edwin and Margaret Marie Westhauser. BA, Cornell U., 1983; MA, Brown U., 1985, PhD, 1994. Prof. history Ala. State U., Montgomery, Ala., 1993—. Cons. Montgomery City-County Pub. Schs., Ala., 2006. Editor: Creating Community, 2005; mem. editl. bd.: Griot: Jour. African.-Am. Studies, 2005—. Docent Montgomery (Ala.) Mus. Fine Arts, 1996—2001. Mem.: So. Conf. African-American Studies, Am. Hist. Assn., Montgomery (Ala.) County Hist. Soc. Office: Campus Box 25 Alabama State U 915 S Jackson St Montgomery AL 36101 Home Phone: 334-265-9954; Office Phone: 334-229-4365.

WESTHEAD, PAUL, professional basketball coach; b. Phila., Feb. 21, 1939; m. Catherine Westhead; children: Monica, Patrice, Paul Jr., Julie. Grad., St. Joseph's Coll., Phila., 1961; MA, Villanova U. Head coach La Salle Coll., Phila., 1970-79; asst. coach NBA LA Lakers, 1979, head coach, 1979—82, NBA Chgo. Bulls, 1982-83, Loyola Marymount U., 1985-90, NBA Denver Nuggets, 1990—92, George Mason U., 1993—97, Am. Basketball Assn., 2000—01, Japanese Pro League, 2001—03; asst. coach NBA Orlando Magic, 2003—05; head coach WNBA Phoenix Mercury, 2005—. Achievements include leading the Lakers to the NBA Championship as head coach, 1980. Office: Phoenix Mercury 201 E Jefferson St Phoenix AZ 85004 *

WESTHEIMER, GERALD, optometrist, educator; b. Berlin, May 13, 1924; naturalized, 1944, came to U.S., 1951; s. Isaak and Ilse (Cohn) W. Optometry diploma, Sydney Tech. Coll., Australia, 1943, fellowship diploma, 1950; BSc, U. Sydney, 1947; PhD, Ohio State U., 1953; DSc (hon.), U. NSW, Australia, 1988; ScD (hon.), SUNY, 1990; MD (hon.), U. Tubingen, 2005. Practice optometry, Sydney, 1945-51; research fellow Ohio State U., 1951-53; prof. physiol. optics U. Houston, 1953-54; asst. prof., then assoc. prof. physiol. optics Ohio State U., 1954-60; postdoctoral fellow neurophysiology Marine Biol. Lab., Woods Hole, Mass., 1957; vis. researcher Physiol. Lab., U. Cambridge, Eng., 1958-59; mem. faculty U. Calif. at Berkeley, 1960—, prof. physiol. optics, 1963-68, chmn. group physiol. optics, 1964-67, prof. physiology, 1968-89, prof. neurobiology, 1989—, head div. neurobiology, 1987-92; adj. prof. Rockefeller U., N.Y., 1992—. Sackler lectr. Tel Aviv U. Med. Sch., 1988, D.O. Hebb lectr. McGill U., 1991, Grass Found. lectr. U. Ill., 1991, Wertheimer lectr. U. Frankfort on the Main, 1998; mem. com. vision NRC, 1957-72; mem. visual scis. study sect. NIH, 1966-70, chmn. visual scis. B study sect., 1977-79; mem. vision, research and tng. com. Nat. Eye Inst., NIH, 1970-74, chmn. bd. sci. counselors, 1981-83; mem. exec. council com. vision NAS-NRC, 1969-72; mem. communicative scis. cluster Pres.'s Biomed. Rsch. Panel, 1975. Author rsch. papers; editor: Vision Rsch., 1972-79; editl. bd. Investigative Ophthalmology, 1973-77, Exptl. Brain Rsch., 1973-89, Optics Letters, 1977-78, Spatial Vision, 1985—, Ophthalmic and Physiological Optics, 1985—, Vision Rsch., 1985-92, Jour. of Physiology, 1987-94. Recipient Von Sallman prize Columbia U., 1986; Prentice medal Am. Acad. Optometry, 1986, Bicentennial medal Australian Optometric Assn., 1988. Fellow AAAS, Royal Soc. London (Ferrier lectr. 1992, editl. bd. procs. 1990-96, 2000—), Am. Acad. Arts and Scis., Optical Soc. Am. (Tillyer medal 1978, assoc. editor jour. 1980-83), Am. Acad. Optometry; mem. Royal Soc. New So. Wales, Soc. Neurosci., Assn. Rsch. in Vision and Ophthalmology (Proctor medal 1979), Internat. Brain Rsch. Orgn., Physiol. Soc. Gt. Britain, Sigma Xi. Home: 582 Santa Barbara Rd Berkeley CA 94707-1746 Business E-Mail: gwestheimer@berkeley.edu.

WESTIN, DAVID LAWRENCE, broadcast executive, lawyer; b. Flint, Mich., July 29, 1952; s. Lawrence Rae and Mary Louise (Holman) W.; m. Victoria Peters; children: Victoria, Elizabeth, Matthew. BA, U. Mich., 1974, JD, 1977. Bar: D.C. 1979. Law clk. U.S. Ct. Appeals (2d cir.), NYC, 1977-78, U.S. Supreme Ct., Washington, 1979; assoc. Wilmer, Cutler & Pickering, Washington, 1979-84, ptnr., 1985-91; sr. v.p., gen. counsel Capital Cities/ABC, Inc., NYC, 1991-93; pres. of prodn. ABC TV Network, NYC, 1993-94, pres., 1994-97, pres. of news, 1997—. Lectr. Harvard U. Law Sch., Cambridge, Mass., 1986; adj. prof. Georgetown U. Law Ctr., Washington, 1989-91. Bd. dirs. Lincoln Ctr. Film. Soc., 1994—, Am. Arbitration Assn., 1991—. Mem.: Chevy Chase (Md.). Democrat. Presbyterian. Office: ABC TV Network 47 W 66th St Fl 5 New York NY 10023-6201

WESTLAKE, DONALD EDWIN (TUCKER COE, RICHARD STARK), writer; b. NYC, July 12, 1933; s. Albert Joseph and Lillian Marguerite (Bounds) W.; m. Nedra Henderson, Aug. 10, 1957 (div. 1966); m. Sandra Foley, Apr. 9, 1967 (div. 1975); m. Abigail Adams, May 18, 1979; children: Sean, Steven, Tod, Paul; stepchildren: Adrienne Adams, Patrick Adams, Katharine Adams. Student, SUNY, Plattsburgh and Binghamton. Author 50 novels including The Mercenaries, 1960, Killing Time, 1961, 361, 1962, Killy, 1963, Pity Him Afterwards, 1964, The Fugitive Pigeon, 1965, The Busy Body, 1966, The Spy in the Ointment, 1966, God Save the Mark, 1967 (Edgar Allen Poe award Mystery Writers Am. 1967), Philip, 1967, The Curious Facts Preceding My Execution, and Other Fictions, 1968, Who Stole Sassi Manoon, 1968?, Somebody Owes Me Money, 1969, Up Your Banners, 1969, The Hot Rock, 1970, Adios, Scheherezade, 1970, I Gave at The Office, 1971, Under An English Heaven, 1971, Bank Shot, 1972, Cops and Robbers, 1972, (with Brian Garfield) Gangway, 1972, Help I Am Being Held Prisoner, 1974, Jimmy The Kid, 1974, Two Much, 1975, A Travesty, 1975, Brothers Keepers, 1975, Dancing Aztecs, 1976, Enough!, 1977, Nobody's Perfect, 1977, Castle in the Air, 1980, Kahawa, 1982, Why Me?, 1983, Levine, 1984, A Likely Story, 1984, High Adventure, 1985, Good Behavior, 1986, (with Abby Westlake) High Jinx, 1987, (with A. Westlake) Transylvania Station, 1987, Trust Me On This, 1988, Sacred Monster, 1989, Tomorrow's Crimes, 1989, Drowned Hopes, 1990, Humans, 1992, Don't Ask, 1993, Baby, Would I Lie?, 1994, Smoke, 1995, The Ax, 1997, Put a Lid on It, 2003, Thieves Dozen, 2004, The Road to Ruin, 2004, Watch Your Back!, 2005, What's So Funny?, 2006; (as John B. Allan) Elizabeth Taylor: A Fascinating Story of America's Most Talented Actress and the World's Most Beautiful Woman, 1961; (as Tucker Coe) Kinds of Love, Kinds of Death, 1966, Murder among Children, 1968, Wax Apple, 1970, A Jade in Aries, 1971, Don't Lie to Me, 1972; (as Richard Stark) The Hunter, 1963 (pub. as Point Blank, 1973), The Man with the Getaway Face, 1963 (pub. as The Steel Hit, 1971), The Outfit, 1963, The Mourner, 1963, The Score, 1964, The Jugger, 1965, The Seventh, 1966, The Handle, 1966 (pub. as Run Lethal, 1966), The Damsel, 1967, The Dame, 1967, The Rare Coin Score, 1967, The Green Eagle Score, 1967, The Black Ice Score, 1968, The Sour Lemon Score, 1969, The Blackbird, 1969, Deadly Edge, 1971, Slayground, 1971, Lemons Never Lie, 1971, Plunder Squad, 1972, Butcher's Moon, 1974, Stark Mysteries, 1981, Ask the Parrot; screenwriter: Cops and Robbers, 1973, (with Michael Kane) Hot Stuff, 1979, The Stepfather, 1986, Why Me?, 1990, The Grifters, 1990 (Academy award nomination best adapted screenplay 1990), (TV movies) Supertrain, 1979, Jimmy the Kid, 1985, Fatal Confession: A Father Dowling Mystery, 1987. Served with USAF, 1954-56. Recipient Edgar Allen Poe Grand Master award Mystery Writers Am., 1992. Mailing: Mysterious Press Author Mail c/o Warner Books 1271 Ave of the Americas New York NY 10020 *

WESTLEY, JOHN RICHARD, economist; b. Fairmont, Minn., Feb. 25, 1939; s. Richard and Margaret (Kindschi) W.; m. Sidney Kathryn Bohanna, Mar. 26, 1966(div. Sept. 1977); children: Elizabeth Laura, Karen Margaret, Marian Bohanna; m. Joan Nancy Ehrlich, Apr. 12, 1980; 1 child, Katherine Matthea. BA in Philosophy, Yale U., 1961; MA in Econs., Columbia U., 1966; PhD in Econs., Am. Univ., 1983. Internat. economist U.S. Dept. Treasury, Washington, 1966-69; loan officer U.S. AID, Addis Ababa, Ethiopia, 1970-72, economist Nairobi, Kenya, 1973-75, Washington, 1976-78, program officer New Delhi, 1979-84, dir. mission to Bangladesh Dhaka, 1985-87, assoc. asst. adminstr. bur. Africa Washington, 1987-90, dir. mission to Kenya Nairobi, 1990-94; dir. Mission to Egypt US AID, Cairo, 1994-98; v.p. Internat. Fund Agrl. Devel., Rome, 1998—2002; adj. assoc. prof. econs. John Cabot U., Rome, 2002—. Author: Agriculture and Equitable Growth, 1986. With U.S. Army, 1961-64. Mem. Am. Econ. Assn., Phi Beta Kappa. Presbyterian. Office: John Cabot Univ Via Della Lungara 233 00165 Rome Italy E-mail: jwestle@tin.it.

WESTMAN, CARL EDWARD, lawyer; b. Youngstown, Ohio, Dec. 12, 1943; s. Carl H. and Mary Lillis (Powell) W.; m. Carolyn J., July 17, 1965; children: C. Forrest, Stephanie A. BBA, Sam Houston State U., 1966; JD, U. Miami, 1969, LLM in Taxation, 1972. Bar: Fla. 1969. Ptnr. Frost & Jacobs, 1983-93, Roetzel & Andress, 1993-98; adminstrv. ptnr. Steel, Hector & Davis, Naples, Fla., 1999—2004, Cohen & Grigsby, 2004—. Active S.W. Fla. coun. Boy Scouts Am. Eagle Bd. of Rev., 1987—; trustee David Lawrence Found. for Mental Health, Inc., 1976-86, chmn., 1985-86; trustee Pikeville Coll., 1993-2005; trustee, 1991, chmn. NCH Healthcare Sys. Inc., 2005—, chmn. profl. capabilities com. physician credentialing, 1998—; trustee, chmn. Naples Cmty. Hosp., 2001; past pres. bd. trustees, elder Moorings Presbyn. Ch. Master lic. capt. USCG. Mem. Fla. Bar Assn., Collier County Bar Assn., Estate Planning Coun., Marco Island Marina Assn. (pres.). Home: 1952 Crayton Rd Naples FL 34102-5070 Office: Cohent Grigsby 1100 Fifth Ave S Naples FL 34102 Office Phone: 239-430-1800. Business E-Mail: cwestman@cohenlaw.com.

WESTMAN, CRAIG ELLERY, academic administrator; s. Franklin A. and Virginia Westman Vickers; m. Lee Ann Elliott Westman, Aug. 14, 1993; children: Madeleine Lee, Erica Grace, Jillian Grace, Paige Martha. BA, Fla. Atlantic U., 1988, MA, 1990; PhD, Fla. State U., 1997. Asst. registrar Fla. State U., Tallahassee, 1993—98; registrar Ferris State U., Big Rapids, Mich., 1998—2000, assoc. dean enrollment svcs., 2000—. Cons. enrollment mgmt. Ferris State U., Big Rapids, Mich., 2003—06. Author: AACRAO's Guide to Basic Enrollment Management, 2005, Gamers Go To College, 2006. V.p.bd. trustees Woodbridge Group, Big Rapids, Mich., 2000—06. Recipient Distinguished Staff award, Ferris State U., 2004. Office: Ferris State U 1201 South State St Ste 201 Big Rapids MI 49307 Home Phone: 231-592-0421; Office Phone: 231-591-2797. Business E-Mail: westmanc@ferris.edu.

WESTMAN, JACK CONRAD, child psychiatrist, educator; b. Cadillac, Mich., Oct. 28, 1927; s. Conrad A. and Alice (Pedersen) W.; m. Nancy K. Baehre, July 17, 1953; children— Daniel P., John C., Eric C. MD, U. Mich., 1952. Diplomate Am. Bd. Psychiatry and Neurology. Intern Duke Hosp., Durham, NC, 1952-53; resident U. Mich. Med. Ctr., 1955-59; dir. outpatient svcs. Children's Psychiat. Hosp., Ann Arbor, Mich., 1961-65; assoc. prof. U. Mich. Med. Sch., 1964-65; coord. diagnostic and treatment unit Waisman Ctr., U. Wis., Madison, 1966-74, prof. psychiatry, 1965-96, prof. emeritus, 1997—. Cons. Joint Commn. on Mental Health of Children, 1967-69, Madison Pub. Schs., 1965-74, Children's Treatment Ctr., Mendota Mental Health Inst., 1965-69 Author: Individual Differences in Children, 1973, Child Advocacy, 1979, Handbook of Learning Disabilities, 1990, Who Speaks for the Children?, 1991, Licensing Parents, 1994, Born to Belong, 1997, Parenthood in America, 2001; editor Child Psychiatry and Human Devel., 1984-99; contbr. articles to profl. jours. Vice-pres. Big Bros. of Dane County, 1970-73; v.p. Wis. Assn. Mental Health, 1968-72; co-chmn. Project Understanding, 1968-75; pres. Wis. Cares, 1998—. With USNR, 1953-55. Fellow Am. Psychiat. Assn., Am. Coll. Psychiatrists, Am. Acad. Child and Adolescent Psychiatry, Am. Orthopsychiat. Assn. (bd. dirs. 1973-76); mem. Am. Assn. Psychiat. Svcs. for Children (pres. 1978-80), Multidisciplinary Acad. Clin. Edn. (pres. 1992-98). Home: 1234 Dartmouth Rd Madison WI 53705-2214 E-mail: jwestman@facstaff.wisc.edu.

WESTMAN, JUDITH ANN, clinical geneticist, dean; b. Columbus, Ohio, Nov. 7, 1957; d. Paul Marshall and Anna Marie (Stahly) Whetstone; m. David Arthur Westman, Apr. 12, 1980; children: Matthew, Joel, Rachel, Deborah. BA, Ohio No. U., 1978; MD, Ohio State U., 1981, MS, 1987. Diplomate Am. Bd. Pediatrics, Am. Bd. Med. Genetics. Resident in pediatrics Children's Hosp. Ohio State U., Columbus, 1981-84, chief resident, 1984-85, fellow clin. genetics, 1985-87, clin. asst. prof., 1987-95, clin. assoc. prof., 1995—, assoc. dean admissions and student affairs, 1996-99, assoc. dean student and med. edn., 1999—2005, assoc. dean med. edn. adminstrn., 2005—. Chair admissions com. Ohio State U. Coll. Medicine, 1990-96. Author: Medical Genetics for the Modern Clinician, 2005; contbr. articles to profl. jours. Mem. adv. bd. Coll. Arts and Scis., Ohio No. U., Ada, 1988-97, trustee, 1997—; trustee Malone Coll., Canton, Ohio, 1988-94. Grantee FDA, 1987, NCI, 2001. Fellow Am. Acad. Pediatrics, Am. Soc. Human Genetics. Republican. Mem. Ch. of God (Anderson). Avocations: music, church activities. Office: 155 Meiling Hall 370 W 9th Ave Columbus OH 43210-1238

WESTMAN, STEVEN RONALD, rabbi; b. Chgo., Sept. 16, 1945; s. Kurt S. and Hilda (Schmoller) W.; m. Sherri, Nov. 30, 1980; children: Rachel Dara, Emily Nicole, Molly Sarah Levin. BA, U. Ill., 1967; B of Hebrew Letters, Hebrew Union Coll., 1969, MA in Hebrew Letters, 1972, DDiv., 1997. Ordained rabbi, 1972. Asst. rabbi Congregation Rodeph Shalom, Phila., 1972-75; rabbi Temple Israel, Stroudsburg, Pa., 1975-83, Temple Beth Torah, Wellington, Fla., 1983-95, Temple Beth El Israel, Ft. Pierce, Fla., 1995-00, Temple Beth El, West Palm Beach, 2000—. Mem. Commn. for Jewish Edn., West Palm Beach, Fla., 1990-94; bd. dirs. Jewish Cmty. Day Sch., West Palm Beach, 1988-91, Jewish Cmty. Ctr., 1987-89; pres. Palm BEach County Bd. Rabbis, 1989-92. Bd. dirs. Palms West Hosp., Loxahatchee, Fla., 1986-91, Pocono Hosp., East Stroudsburg, Pa., 1979-83; found. bd. dirs. Hospice of Monroe County, East Stroudsburg, 1978-83; bd. dirs. Palm Beach Liturgical Culture Soc., West Palm Beach, 1986-95. Recipient Tower of David award State of Israel Bonds, 1988, Leadership award Jewish Fedn. of Palm Beach County, 1985. Mem. Cen. Conf. of Am. Rabbis, Rotary. Home: 5170 Foxhall Dr S West Palm Beach FL 33417 Office: Temple Beth El 2815 N Flagler Dr West Palm Beach FL 33407 Office Phone: 561-833-0339. Business E-Mail: rabbiwestman@bellsouth.net. *The theme and spirit of my rabbinate are found in the words of Pirkey Avot, the ethics of the Fathers: "Be of the disciples of Aaron, loving peace and pursuing peace, loving your fellow creatures and bringing them close to the Torah." (Avot 1:12).*

WESTMORE, MICHAEL GEORGE, make-up artist, writer; b. Hollywood, Calif., Mar. 22, 1938; s. Montague George and Edith Adeline Westmore; m. Marion Christine Bergeson, Dec. 4, 1965; children: Michael George, Michele, McKenzie. BA, U. Calif., Santa Barbara, 1961. Apprentice make-up artist Universal City Studios, Universal City, Calif., 1961-63, staff make-up artist, 1964, asst. head dept. make-up lab., 1965-71; freelance make-up artist various studios, Hollywood, Calif., 1971-87; make-up supr. and designer Paramount Studios, Hollywood, 1987—2005. Instr. theatre arts dept. Los Angeles Valley Coll., 1966—71; pres. Cosmetic Control Ctrs., Inc., 1971—76, Hollywood Magic Cosmetics, 1985—87; rsch. cons., lectr. therapeutic cosmetics for med. assns. Author: The Art of Theatrical Make-Up for Stage and Screen, 1971; contbr. chapters to books; co-author: Star Trek Makeup FX Journal, Star Trek-Aliens & Artifacts; make-up artist TV spls. Eleanor and Franklin (Emmy award NATAS, 1976), Why Me? (Emmy award, 1984), Three Wishes of Billy Grier (Emmy award, 1985), Star Trek (Emmy award, 1988, 1992, 1993, 1995, 1996, Emmy nomination, 2005), Amazing Stories (Emmy award, 1987), make-up artist films 2010 (Acad. award nomination, 1985), Mask (Acad. award, 1986), Clan of the Cave Bear (Acad. award nomination, 1987), Star Trek First Contact (Acad. award nomination, 1996); contbr. articles to Make-Up Artists mag. Served with AUS, 1956. Nominee Emmy, 1973, 1976; recipient Best Spl. Effects Make-up on TV for Geppetto award, Hollywood Make-up Artists Guild, 2001, Emmy, 1977, 1985, 1987, 1990, 1992, 1993, 1995, 1996, 1997, 1998, 1999, 2001, 2002, 2003, 2004, 2005, Three Emmys, 1978, Two Emmys, 1986, 1988, 1989, 1991, 1994, 2000, Spl. Achievement award, Canadian Space Channel, 2007. Mem.: Archive of Am. TV, Internat. Alliance Theatrical Stage Employees, Knights of the Vine, Soc. Make-up Artists, Vikings of Scandia, Lambda Chi Alpha (life Order of Achievement award). Address: 4616 Balboa Blvd Encino CA 91316-4105

WESTMORELAND, ANDREW, academic administrator; m. Jeanna Westmoreland; 1 child, Riely. Grad., Ouachita Baptist U., 1979; MA in Polit. Sci., U. Ark., Fayetteville; PhD in Higher Edn. Adminstrn., U. Ark., Little Rock. With Ouachita Baptist U., 1979—2006, prof. polit. sci. and edn., exec. v.p., v.p. devel., pres., 1998—2006, Samford U., Birmingham, Ala., 2006—. Cons., evaluator Higher Learning Commn. Author: Leading by Design, 2005. Office: Samford U 800 Lakeshore Dr Birmingham AL 35229 *

WESTMORELAND, JESSIE ALLRED, literature educator; b. Lovelock, Nev., July 25, 1953; d. Meade Walton and Patricia Jeanette Allred; children: Quinn Colin, Kelly Meade, Hayley Hiibel, Summer Warden. BS in Elem. Edn., U. Nev., Reno, 1984, MS in Literacy Studies, 2004. Literacy specialist Sonoma Heights Elem. Sch., Winnemucca, Nev., 2002—06; regional coord. early literacy Northeastern Nev. Regional Profl. Devel.

Program, Elko, Nev., 2006—. Tchr. reading recovery Sonoma Heights Elem. Sch., 2000—06. Mem.: ASCD, Internat. Reading Assn., Nat. Staff Devel. Assn. Office: 1500 Melarky St Winnemucca NV 89445 Home Phone: 775-623-4623.

WESTMORELAND, LYNN A., congressman; b. Atlanta, Apr. 2, 1950; m. Joan Eskew; children: Heather Smith, Marcy, Trae. Attended, Ga. State Univ. Mem. Ga. Ho. Reps., Atlanta, 1992—2004, US Congress from 8th Ga. dist., 2005—07, mem. Govt. Reform com., Small Bus. com., transp. and Infrastructure com.; mem. US Congress from 3rd Ga. dist., 2007—. Mem. Fayette (Ga.) Bd. Realtors, Nat. Bd. Realtors. Mem.: Midwest Ga. Homebuilders Assn. Republican. Baptist. Office: US Ho Reps 1118 Longworth Ho Office Bldg Washington DC 20515-1008 also: 1601-B E Highway 34 Newnan GA 30265 Office Phone: 202-225-5901. Office Fax: 202-225-2515. *

WESTOFF, CHARLES FRANCIS, demographer, educator; b. NYC, July 23, 1927; s. Frank Barnett and Evelyn (Bales) Westoff; m. Joan P. Uszynski, Sept. 11, 1948 (div. Jan. 1969); children: David, Carol; m. Leslie Aldridge, Aug. 1969 (div. Feb. 1993); m. Jane DeLung, May 1997. AB, Syracuse U., NY, 1949, MA, 1950; PhD, U. Pa., Phila., 1953. Instr. sociology U. Pa., 1950—52; rsch. assoc. Milbank Meml. Fund, NYC, 1952—55; rsch. assoc. Office Population Rsch. Princeton U., NJ, 1955—62, Maurice P. During '22 prof. demographic studies and sociology, 1962—99, prof. emeritus, 1999—, sr. rsch. demographer, 1999—, chmn. dept. sociology, 1965—70, assoc. dir. Office Population Rsch., 1962—75, dir., 1975—92; assoc. prof. sociology NYU, also chmn. dept. sociology Washington Sq. Coll., 1959—62; vis. sr. fellow East-West Population Inst., Honolulu, 1979—81; Disting. vis. prof. Am. U., Cairo, 1979; mem. vis. com. Harvard-MIT Joint Ctr. for Urban Studies, 1980—83. Exec. dir. Commn. Population Growth and Am. Future, 1970—72; mem. adv. com. on population stats. US Bur. Census, 1973—79; chmn. Nat. Com. for Rsch. on 1980 Census, 1981—88; bd. dirs. Alan Guttmacher Inst., 1977—88, 1989—; sr. tech. advisor Demographic Health Surveys, 1984—; bd. dirs. Population Resource Ctr., 1985—; Population Ref. Bur., 1988—94, Population Commns. Internat., 1992—98; com. on population NAS, 1983—88. Co-author: Family Growth in Metropolitan America, 1961, The Third Child, 1963, College Women and Fertility Values, 1967, The Later Years of Childbearing, 1970, From Now to Zero, 1971, Reproduction in the United States, 1965, 1971, Toward the End of Growth: Population in America, 1973, The Contraceptive Revolution, 1976, Demographic Dynamics in America, 1977, Mass Media and Reproductive Behavior in Africa, 1997, Unmet Need at the End of the Century, 2002, Reproductive Preferences in Developing Countries at the Turn of the Century, 2002, Trends in Marriage and Early Childbearing in Developing Countries, 2006, Recent Trends in Contraception and Abortion in Twelve Countries, 2005, The Stall in the Fertility Transition in Kenya, 2006; contbr. articles on demography and sociology to profl. jours. Recipient Irene Taeuber award for Outstanding Rsch. Contbns., 1995. Fellow: Am. Acad. Arts and Scis.; mem.: Internat. Union Sci. Study Population (Laureate award 2007), Population Assn. Am. (bd. dirs. 1960—62, 1968—70, 1st v.p. 1972—73, pres. 1974—75), Planned Parenthood Fedn. Am. (dir. 1978—81), Inst. Medicine-NAS. Home: 1 Highland Rd Princeton NJ 08540 Office: Princeton U Wallace Hall Princeton NJ 08544 Business E-Mail: westoff@princeton.edu.

WESTON, ARTHUR WALTER, chemist, consultant, retired chemicals executive; b. Smith Falls, Ont., Can., Feb. 13, 1914; came to U.S., 1935, naturalized, 1952; s. Herbert W. and Alice M. (Houghton) W.; m. V. Dawn Thompson, Sept. 10, 1940; children: Roger L., Randall K., Cynthia B. BA, Queen's U., Kingston, Ont., 1934, MA, 1935; PhD, Northwestern U., 1938. Postdoctoral fellow Northwestern U., Evanston, Ill., 1938-40; with Abbott Labs., North Chgo., Ill., 1940-79, dir. rsch. and devel., 1959-61, v.p. rsch. and devel., 1961-68, dir. company, 1959-68, v.p. sci. affairs, 1968-77, v.p. corp. licensing, 1977-79; v.p., dir. San-Abbott, Japan, 1976-79; cons. Abbott Labs., North Chgo., Ill., 1979-85; pres. Arthur W. Weston & Assocs., Lake Forest, Ill., 1979—. Contbr. chapters to books, articles to profl. jours. Mem. Office Sci. Rsch. and Devel., War Manpower Commn., 1942-45; mem. exec. com. indsl. chemistry, div. chemistry and chem. tech. NRC, 1961-65; mem. indsl. panel on sci. and tech. NSF, 1974-80; mem. ad hoc com. chem. agts. Dept. Def., 1961-65. Mem. Rsch. Dirs. Assn. Chgo. (pres. 1965-66), Am. Chem. Soc. (trustee Chgo. 1965-2004, dir. Chgo. sect. 1952-59, nat. com. corp. assocs. 1967-72), Dirs. Indsl. Rsch., Indsl. Rsch. Inst. (bd. dirs. 1970-73), Phi Beta Kappa, Sigma Xi, Phi Lambda Upsilon. Achievements include patents in field. Home and Office: 349 Hilldale Pl Lake Forest IL 60045-3031 Personal E-mail: awweston@aol.com.

WESTON, DAWN THOMPSON, artist, researcher; b. Joliet, Ill., Apr. 15, 1919; d. Cyril C. and Vivian Grace Thompson; m. Arthur Walter Weston, Sept. 10, 1940; children: Roger Lance, Randall Kent, Cynthia Brooke. Student, Penn Hall Jr. Coll., Chambersburg, Pa., 1937—38; BS, Northwestern U., 1942; student, Art Inst. Chgo., 1954, Pestalozzi-Froebel, Chgo., 1955; postgrad., Northwestern U., 1960—61; student, Phila. Inst. for Achievement Human Potential, 1963; postgrad., U. Ill., 1964; MA in Ednl. Adminstrn., Northwestern U., 1970. Cert. tchr./adminstr. Ill. Therapist USN Hosp., Great Lakes, Ill., 1940—45; tchr. Holy Child and Waukegan (Ill.) High Schs., 1946—54, Lake Forest (Ill.) H.S., 1966—69; elem. and jr. high art dir. Lake Bluff (Ill.) Schs., 1954—58; pioneer ednl. dir. Grove Sch. for Brain-Injured, Lake Forest, 1958—66, life mem., treas. corp., chmn. bd., 1982—. Ind. rschr., lectr. on shifting visual imagery due to trauma, 1982—99; rschr. on uneven growth, 1969—. One-woman shows include Evanston Woman's Club, Northwestern U., Deerpath Gallery, Lake Forest, The Hein Co., Waukegan, numerous group shows, 1939—76, Represented in permanent collections ARC, Victory Meml. Hosp., Waukegan, Sierra Assocs., Chgo., numerous pvt. collections U.S., Can., Japan, Africa, works include:, Poisonous Plants of Midwest set of etchings for Country Gentleman mag., 1956, Clouds mural, 1981. Mem. 1st found. bd. for srs. in Lake Forest, 1999; chair Grove Sch. Inc., 1996—; chmn. July 4th parade 100th Anniversary Child-Serve Greater Chgo., 1994; mem. Presdl. Gold Chain, Trinity Coll., 1979; mem. alumni bd. leadership com. Northwestern U., 2003—07; del. ann. conf. Meth. Ch., 1982—90; lay leader Grace United Meth. Ch., Lake Bluff, 1990—93. Named Citizen of Yr., Grove Sch., 1978, rm. at sch. named in her honor, 1982; scholar, Penn Hall Jr. Coll., 1937—38. Mem.: Deerpath Art League (bd. dirs.), Penn Hall Alumni Assn. (Chgo. pres. 1938—40), Art Inst. Chgo., Pi Lambda Theta. Home and Office: 349 E Hilldale Pl Lake Forest IL 60045-3031

WESTON, FRANCINE EVANS, secondary school educator; b. Mt. Vernon, NY, Oct. 8, 1946; d. John Joseph and Frances (Fantino) Pisaniello. BA, Hunter Coll., NYC, 1968; MA, Lehman Coll., Bronx, NY, 1973; cert., Am. Acad. Dramatic Arts, NYC, 1976; PhD, NYU, 1991. Cert. elem., secondary tchr., NY; profl. devel. series completion cert. of achievement, Fed. Emergency Mgmt. Inst., US Dept. Homeland Security, 2006. Tchr. Yonkers Bd. Edn., NY, 1968—; aquatic dir. Woodlane Day Camp, Irvington-on-Hudson, NY, 1967-70, Yonkers Jewish Community Ctr., NY, 1971-75. Creative drama tchr. John Burroughs Jr. HS, Yonkers, 1971-77; stage lighting designer Iona Summer Theatre Festival, New Rochelle, NY, 1980-81, Yonkers Male Glee Club, 1981-89, Roosevelt HS, 1980-97; freelance, 1998—; rsch. specialist Scholarship Locating Svc., 1992-94, Yonkers Civil Def. Police Aux., 1994—; master electrician NYU Summer Mus. Theatre, 1979-80; appointed program developer for Cadet Acad. of Police & Fire Scis., Pub. Safety Magnet, Roosevelt HS, 2001, program dir., 2004-. Actress in numerous comty. theater plays including A Touch of the Poet, 1979; dir. stage prodns. including I Remember Mama, 1973, The Man Who Came to Dinner, 1975; author: A Descriptive Comparison of Computerized Stage Lighting Memory Systems With Non-Computerized Systems, 1991, (short stories) A Hat for Louise, 1984, Old Memories: Beautiful and Otherwise, 1984; lit. editor: (story and poetry collection) Beautifully Old, 1984; editor: Command Post Dispatch quar., 1997—. Mem. Yonkers Civil Def. Police Aux., 1994—, adminstrv. asst. to comdg. officer, 1996—2004, capt. adminstrn., 2002—, capt., 2004—; steering com. chairperson Roosevelt H.S.-Middle States Assn. of Schs. and Colls. Self-Evaluation, 1985—88. Named Tchr. of Excellence, NY State English Coun., 1990, 95, 2000; recipient Monetary award for Tchg. Excellence, Carter-Wallace Products, 1992; President's Call to Svc. award, Lifetime award, USA Freedom Corps, 2005; named to Arrid Tchrs. Honor Roll, 1992. Republican. Roman Catholic. Avocations: swimming, theater. Office: Roosevelt High Sch Tuckahoe Rd Yonkers NY 10710

WESTON, SIR JOHN (SIR PHILIP JOHN WESTON), retired diplomat; b. Apr. 13, 1938; s. Philip George and Edith Alice Bray (Ansell) W.; m. Margaret Sally Ehlers, 1967; 3 children. Grad. with 1st class honors, Worchester Coll., Eng.; student Chinese lang., Hong Kong, 1964-66, Peking, China, 1967-68. Joined diplomatic svc. Govt. of Gt. Britain, 1962, served Fgn. Office, 1962-63, 69-71, with Treasure Ctr. for Adminstrv. Studies, 1964, permanent rep. to EEC Brussels, 1972-74, asst. pvt. sec. to sec. state fgn. affairs and commonwealth affairs, 1974-76, counsellor, head EEC presidency secretariat Fgn. and Commonwealth Office, 1976-77, counsellor Brit. Embassy Washington, 1978-81, head def. dept. Fgn. and Commonwealth Office, 1981-84, asst. under-sec. state Fgn. and Commonwealth Office, 1984-85, min. Brit. Embassy Paris, 1985-88, dep. sec. to cabinet Cabinet Office, 1988-89, dep. under-sec. state def. Fgn. and Commonwealth Office, 1989-90, polit. dir. Fgn. and Commonwealth Office, 1990-92, amb., permanent rep. to NATO, also accredited to Western European Union Brussels, 1992-95; U.K. amb. to UN, U.K. permanent rep. UN Security Coun., NYC, 1995-98. Vis. fellow Old Souls Coll., Oxford (Eng.) U., 1977-78; hon. fellow Worcester Coll., Oxford, 2003. Chmn. governing body Sherborne Sch., 2001-07; trustee Nat. Portrait Gallery; Am. assoc. Royal Acad., 1999-2004; bd. govs. Ditchley Found., 2000-04; mem. coun. Internat. Inst. Strategic Studies, 2001-04; hon. pres. Cmty. Found. Network, 1999—. Served Royal Marines, 1956-58. Decorated knight comdr. St. Michael and St. George (Eng.); Order of Merit with star (Fed. Republic Germany). Address: 13 Denbigh Gardens Richmond Surrey TW10 6EN England

WESTON, JOHN FREDERICK, business educator, consultant; b. Ft. Wayne, Ind., Feb. 6, 1916; s. David Thomas and Bertha W.; children: Kenneth F., Byron L., Ellen J. BA, U. Chgo., 1937, MBA, 1943, PhD, 1948. Instr. U. Chgo. Sch. Bus., 1940-42, asst. prof., 1947-48; prof. The Anderson Sch. UCLA, 1949—, Cordner prof. The Anderson Sch., 1981-94, prof. emeritus recalled The Anderson Sch., 1986—, dir. rsch. program in competition and bus. policy, 1969—, dir. Ctr. for Managerial Econs. and Pub. Policy, 1983-86. Econ. cons. to pres. Am. Bankers Assn., 1945-46; disting. lecture series U. Okla., 1967, U. Utah, 1972, Miss. State U., 1972, Miami State U., 1975. Author: Scope and Methodology of Finance, 1966, International Managerial Finance, 1972, Impact of Large Firms on U.S. Economy, 1973, Financial Theory and Corporate Policy, 1979, 2d edit., 1983, 3d edit., 1988, Mergers, Restructuring and Corporate Control, 1990, Takeovers, Restructuring and Corporate Governance, 3d edit., 2000, Managerial Finance, 9th edit, 1992; assoc. editor: Jour. of Finance, 1948-55; mem. editorial bd., 1957-59; editorial bd. Bus. Econs., Jour. Fin. Rsch., Managerial and Decision Econs.; manuscript referee Am. Econ. Rev., Rev. of Econs. and Statistics, Engring. Economist, Bus. Econs., Fin. Mgmt. Bd. dirs. Bunker Hill Fund. Served with Ordnance Dept. AUS, 1943-45. Recipient Abramson Scroll award Bus. Econs., 1989-94; McKinsey Found. grantee, 1965-68; GE grantee, 1967; Ford Found. Faculty Rsch. fellow, 1961-62. Fellow Nat. Assn. Bus. Economists; mem. Am. Finance Assn. (pres. 1966, adv. bd. 1967-71), Am. Econ. Assn., Western Econ. Assn. (pres. 1962), Econometric Soc., Am. Statis. Assn., Royal Econ. Soc., Fin. Analysts Soc., Fin. Mgmt. Assn. (pres. 1979-80) Home and Office: UCLA 258 Tavistock Ave Los Angeles CA 90049-3229 Office Phone: 310-472-5110. Business E-Mail: jweston@anderson.ucla.edu.

WESTON, MICHAEL C., retired lawyer; b. Asheville, NC, Aug. 13, 1938; m. Mary Ann Damme; two children. AB in English, Brown U., 1960; JD, U. Mich., 1963. Bar: Mich. 1964, Ill. 1973. Assoc. Clark Hill, Detroit, 1963-68; from sec. to pres. corp. and indsl. consortium Econ. Devel. Corp. of Greater Detroit, 1969-73; chief staff atty. Northwestern U., Evanston, Ill., 1973-81, v.p. legal affairs, 1981-89; v.p. and gen. counsel, 1990-2001; sr. cons. Acad. Search, Inc., 2004—. Lectr. minority bus. devel. Inst. Continuing Legal Edn., conflicts of interest Nat. Coun. Univ. Rsch. Adminstrs. Contbr. articles to profl. jours. Chmn. Univ. Gallery Com., 1982-85; bd. dirs. Northwestern U. Press. Mem. ABA (sec. taxation, com. on exempt orgns., ho. of dels., lectr. Inst. on Minority Bus. Devel.), Chgo. Coun. Lawyers, Nat. Assn. Coll. and Univ. Attys. (lectr. fed. tax matters, outside activities faculty mems. univ.-cmty. rels., med. risk mgmt., bd. dirs. 1985-88, 92-97, pres. 1995-96). E-mail: m-weston@northwestern.edu.

WESTON, R. TIMOTHY, lawyer, government administrator; b. Los Angeles, Oct. 9, 1947; s. Robert Freidell and Thelma U. (Prince) W.; m. Mary T. Webber, May 3, 1986. BA cum laude in math., U. Calif., Santa Barbara, 1969; JD cum laude, Harvard U., 1972. Bar: Pa., US Dist. Ct. (ea. & mid. dist.) Pa., US Ct. Appeals (3rd & 4th cir.), US Supreme Ct. Asst. atty. gen. Pa. Dept. Environ. Resources, Harrisburg, 1972-79; assoc. dep. sec. Dept. Environ. Resources, 1979-87; ptnr. Kirkpatrick & Lockhart Preston Gates Ellis LLP. Bd. dirs. Interstate Conf. on Water Policy, Washington, chmn. 1984-85. Author: Public Rights in Pa. Waters, 1976, Ground Water Law in Pa., 1976; contbr. articles to profl. jours. Commr. Del. River Basin Commn., Trenton, NJ, 1979-87, Susquehanna River Basin Commn., Harrisburg, Pa., 1980-87, Ohio River Basin Commn., Lexington, Ky., 1979-87, Great Lakes Commn., Ann Arbor, Mich., 1987-88; mem. Am. Soc. of Civil Engrs; bd. dir. Cmty. Life Team; bd. trustee Harrisburg U. for Sci. & Tech. Recipient Samuel Baxter Memorial award, by Water Resources Assn. of Delaware River Basin, 2001. Mem. ABA (sect. environ., energy & resources), ASCE, Am. Water Resources Assn., Phi Beta Kappa, Dauphin County Bar Assn., Pa. Bar Assn. Democrat. Editor-in-Chief, Harvard Civil Rights-Civil Liberties Law Review. Office: Kirkpatrick & Lockhart Preston Gates Ellis LLP 17 N 2nd St 18th Fl Harrisburg PA 17101-1507 Office Phone: 717-231-4504. Office Fax: 717-231-4501. Business E-Mail: tim.weston@klgates.com.

WESTON, ROGER LANCE, banker; b. Waukegan, Ill., Mar. 2, 1943; s. Arthur Walter and Vivian Dawn Weston; children: Cynthia Page, Kent Andrew, Arthur Eladio, Rebecca Dawn, Alice Sinclair, Elliot Churchill, Evan Walter, Spencer Lance. BS, MacMurray Coll., 1965; MBA, Washington U., St. Louis, 1967. Investment adviser Harris Trust & Savs. Bank, Chgo., 1967-69; sr. investment counselor Security Suprs., Chgo., 1969-70; gen. ptnr. Sierra Capital Group, Chgo., 1970-85; exec. v.p., treas., chief fin. officer Telemed Corp., Hoffman Estates, Ill., 1971-79; vice chmn. Bank Lincolnwood, Ill., 1979-85; pres., CEO, GSC Enterprises, Lincolnwood, 1979-85; chmn. bd. dirs., pres., CEO, GreatBanc, Inc., Chgo., 1986—. Mem. Barrington Hills (Ill.) Zoning Bd. Appeals, 1987-2003, com. Asian art Art Inst. Chgo., 1987; mem. nat. coun. John M. Olin Sch. Bus., Washington U. Mem. Washington U. Eliot Soc. (Chgo. nat. com., chmn. membership com. 1996-92), Univ. Club. Republican. Presbyterian. Office: Great Banc Inc 1 N Wacker Dr Ste 4075 Chicago IL 60606

WESTON, W. GALEN, SR., (GALEN WESTON), diversified financial services company executive; b. Eng., Oct. 29, 1940; s. Willard Garfield Weston and Reta L. Howard; m. Hilary Frayne, 1966; 2 children. BA, U. Western Ont., LLD (hon.). Pres. George Weston Ltd., 1974—96, CEO, 1978—, chmn. bd., 1978—, Wittington Investments, Ltd., George Weston Ltd., Toronto, Ont., Can., Holt, Renfrew & Co. Ltd., Loblaw Cos. Ltd., Selfridges & Co., Weston Foods Ltd. Bd. dirs. Fortnum and Mason PLC (U.K.); bd. dirs. Assoc. Brit. Foods PLC (U.K.), Brown Thomas Group Ltd. (Ireland). Hon. trustee The Upper Can. Coll. Found.; mem. internat. adv. bd. Columbia U. Named Officer of Order of Can., 1990; named one of World's Richest People, Forbes Mag., 1999—2007; recipient Order of Ontario, 2005. Mem. Windsor Club (Fla.), Deepdale Golf Club (NY). Office: George Weston Limited 22 St Clair Ave E Ste 2001 Toronto ON Canada M4T 2S3 Office Phone: 416-922-2500.

WESTPHAL, CAROL JEAN, media specialist; d. John Gerald and Florine Theresa Sapienza; m. Robert Michael Westphal, Aug. 11, 1979; 1 child, Christina Marie. BA in English, Iona Coll., 1976; MS in Spl. Edn., Coll. of New Rochelle, NY, 1979; MS in Libr. and Info. Sci., LI U., 2000. Montessori lic. St. Nicholas Tng. Ctr. Montessori tchr. New Rochelle Acad., 1976—87; 2d grade tchr. Christ the King, Yonkers, NY, 1987—88, computer tchr., 1988—96; libr. media specialist Ralph Waldo Emerson Mid. Sch., Yonkers, 1996—. Coun. mem. Yonkers Sch. Libr. Sys., 2003—. Grantee, Laura Bush Found., 2004. Mem.: ALA, Westchester Libr. Assn., Sch. Libr. Media Specialists of Southea. NY. Home: 2 E High St Valhalla NY 10595 Office: Ralph Waldo Emerson Mid Sch 160 Bolmer Ave Yonkers NY 10703 Office Phone: 914-376-8300 ext 254. Fax: 914-421-1825. E-mail: cwestphal@emerson.ypschools.org.

WESTRA, JAMES R., lawyer; b. Cleve., June 3, 1951; m. Jean Westra; children: Christian, Alexander, Nicholas. AB, Harvard Coll., 1973; JD, Boston U. Law Sch., 1977. Bar: Mass. 1978. With Hutchins, Wheeler & Dittmar, 1977—2002; ptnr. Weil, Gotshal & Manges, LLP, Boston, 2002—. Overseer Boston Symphony Orchestra; bd. chmn. CAST, Inc.; bd. dir. Rescue Mission; chmn. bd. appeals Wenham, Mass. Mem.: ABA. Office: Weil Gotshal & Manges 100 Federal St Fl 34 Boston MA 02110 Office Phone: 617-772-8377. Office Fax: 617-772-8333. Business E-Mail: james.westra@weil.com.

WESTRA, MITZI SUE, music educator; b. Sioux Falls, SD, Apr. 16, 1964; d. Marlin Duane Westra and Myrna Rae Hughes; m. Frank Felice, Nov. 12, 1993. BA, Augustana Coll., 1986; MusM, U. Minn., 1992, D of Mus. Arts, 1995. Adj. faculty Lamar U., Beaumont, Tex., 1996—98; pvt. voice tchr. Indpls., 1998—; adj. faculty Wabash Coll., Crawfordsville, Ind., 1998—2004; assoc. faculty U. Indpls., 1998—. Performing artist: CD For the Family, 2004. Choir dir. St. Andrew's Presbyn. Ch., Beaumont, Tex., 1996—98; contract singer 2d Presbyn. Ch., Indpls., 1998—. Mem.: Nat. Assn. Tchrs. of Singing, Coll. Music Soc. Avocations: hiking, reading, horseback riding. Home: 2040 Landmark Dr # 809 Indianapolis IN 46260 Office: Univ Indpls 1400 E Hanna Indianapolis IN 46227 Office Phone: 317-409-7654. E-mail: mitziwestra@yahoo.com.

WESTREICH, BENZION JOSEPH, lawyer; b. NYC, June 2, 1952; s. Osias and Gerda (Gerwitz) W.; m. Joyce M. Mayer, Sept. 13, 1978; children: Jonathan Michael, Daniel Stephan, Zachary Mark. BS summa cum laude, CUNY, 1974, postgrad., 1974-75; JD, Columbia U., 1978. Bar: N.Y. 1979, U.S. Dist. Ct. (ea. and so. dists.) N.Y., Calif. 1988. Assoc. Shearman & Sterling, NYC, 1978-86, ptnr., 1987-88, LA, 1988—, Katten Muchin Zavis Rosenman, LA. Stone scholar Columbia U., 1977, 78. Mem. Phi Beta Kappa. Office: Katten Muchin Zavis Rosenman Ste 2600 2029 Century Park E Los Angeles CA 90067 Office Phone: 310-788-4409, 310-712-8228. E-mail: benny.westreich@kmzr.com.

WESTREICH, NEIL P., lawyer; b. NYC, Mar. 7, 1950; BA with honors, Cambridge Univ., 1974; JD magna cum laude, Harvard Univ., 1977. Bar: England and Wales 1975, NY 1979. Atty., London, 1978—79; assoc. Cravath Swaine & Moore LLP, NYC, 1979—85, ptnr., corp., 1985—. Mem.: Bar Assn. City NY, NY State Bar Assn., ABA. Office: Cravath Swaine & Moore LLP Worldwide Plz 825 Eighth Ave New York NY 10019-7475 Office Phone: 212-474-1518. Office Fax: 212-474-3700. Business E-Mail: nwestreich@cravath.com.

WESTRICH, GEOFFREY HOWARD, orthopaedic surgery; b. South Orange, NJ, May 26, 1964; BS in Engring. (with honors), Tufts U., 1986; MD, Tufts U. Sch. Medicine, 1990. Cert. Orthopaedic Surgery, NY. Intern, gen. surgery North Shore-Cornell U. Program, Manhasset, NY, 1990—91; resident, orthop. surgery Hosp. for Spl. Surgery-NY Hosp. Cornell Med. Ctr., NY, 1991—95; orthop. trauma fellowship AO fellowship Inselpital, Bern, Switzerland, 1995; hip/knee fellowship, adult reconstruction Hosp. Spl. Surgery, NY, asst. scientist NY, 1996—, asst. attending, orthop. surgery NY, 1996—2002, assoc. attending, orthop. suregery NY, 2002—; asst. attending, orthop. surgery NY Presbyterian Weill Cornell Med. Ctr., NY, 2001—02, assoc. attending, orthop. surgery NY, 2002—; asst. prof., orthop. surgery Weill Med. Coll. Cornell U., 1999, assoc. prof. clin. orthop. surgery. Mem. Orthop. Trauma Svc. Contbr. articles to profl. jours. Named one of Medical Marvels, New York Mag., 2006; recipient Resident's award, NY Acad. Medicine, 1994, Resident award paper, Smith & Nephew Richards, Inc., 1995, Fellow award paper, Eastern Orthop. Assn., 1996, Hip Soc. Recipient, Orthop. Rsch. and Edn. Found., 1998. Mem.: NY County Med. Soc., Am. Acad. Orthop. Surgeons, AMA, Alpha Omega Alpha. Avocations: boating, fishing, skiing, tennis, calligraphy. Office: Hosp for Spl Surgery 535 E 70th St New York NY 10021-4872 also: Affiliated Physician Offices 176-60 Union Turnpike Fresh Meadows NY 11366 Address: NY Presbyterian Weill Cornell Med Ctr 525 E 68th St Starr 2 New York NY 10021 Office Phone: 212-606-1510. Office Fax: 212-639-9266. *

WESTROPE, MARTHA RANDOLPH, psychologist, consultant; b. Gaffney, SC, May 19, 1922; d. Gordon Robert and Hannah (Brown) Westrope; 1 adopted child, Ashley Randolph. BS, Winthrop Coll., Rock Hill, SC, 1942; MA, U. NC, Chapel Hill, 1944; PhD, U. Iowa, Iowa City, 1952. Lic. psychologist SC. Pvt. practice, Greenville, S.C., 1960—; part-time pvt. practice, 1987-96; part-time staff mem. Spartanburg Mental Health Clinic, SC, 1971-73, Greenville Mental Health Ctr., 1974-85, Patrick B. Harris Psychiat. Hosp., Anderson, S.C., 1985-87; med. cons. SC Vocat. Rehab. Dept., Greenville, 1987-91, part-time med. cons., 1993-99. Cons. SC Parole Bd. Psychol. Evaluation SC Dept. Corrections, 1983—87. Mem.: Coun. Nat. Register Health Svc. Providers Psychology, Am. Group Psychotherapy Assn., Greenville County Mental Health Assn., Am. Assn. Advancement Psychology, SC Psychol. Assn., Southeastern Psychol. Assn., Am. Psychol. Assn. Democrat. Presbyterian. Avocations: wildlife preservation, fine arts. Home: 11 Darien Way Greenville SC 29615-3236

WESTWOOD, ALBERT RONALD CLIFTON, management consultant, researcher; b. Birmingham, Eng., June 9, 1932; came to US, 1958, naturalized, 1974; s. Albert Sydney and Ena Emily (Clifton) W.; m. Jean Mavis Bullock, 1956; children: Abigail, Andrea. BSc with honors, U. Birmingham, 1953, PhD in Phys. Metallurgy, 1956, DSc in Materials Sci., 1968. Chartered engr. and physicist, UK. Tech. officer research dept., metals div. Imperial Chem. Industries, Birmingham, 1956—58, successively scientist, sr. scientist, assoc. dir., head materials sci. dept., dep. dir., 1958—74; dir. Martin Marietta Labs., Balt., 1974—84, corp. dir. R & D, 1984—87; v.p. R & D Martin Marietta Corp., Bethesda, Md., 1987—90, v.p. sci., 1990, v.p. rsch. and tech., 1990—93; v.p. rsch. and exploratory tech. Sandia Nat. Labs. divsn. Lockheed Martin Corp., Albuquerque, 1993—96; v.p. emeritus Sandia Nat. Labs., 2002—; chmn., chief exec. Ctrl. Lab. of Rsch. Couns., England, 1998—2000; internat. cons. R. and D. Mgmt. Mem. numerous govt. and univ. adv. coms. including Office Sci. and Tech. Policy, NASA, NRC, NAS, NAE, NSF, Nat. Inst. Stds. and Tech., U. Md., U. Fla., MIT, Ga. Inst. Tech., Coun. on Competetiveness; bd. dir. Martin Marietta Energy Systems, Assn. Ind. Rsch. and Tech. Orgns.

U.K., U.S. Civilian R&D Found.; mem. European rsch. coun. informatics and math. resources bd. Brit. Nat. Space Sci. Ctr.; mem. R&D coun. European Spallation Source; mem. coun. Found. Tech. Innovation and Soc. U.K.; lectr. in field. Contbr. over 120 articles to profl. jours. Chmn. Md. Humanities Coun., N.Mex. Humanities Coun., N.Mex. Symphony Orch.; bd. dirs. Santa Fe Opera; adv. com. Sci. and Tech. Corp., U. N.Mex., interim pres. Recipient Disting. Young Scientist award Md. Acad. Scis., 1966, Centennial award U. Md., 1994, Beilby gold medal Royal Inst. Chemistry, 1970, J. Herbert Holloman award Acta Metallurgica, 1996, Tewksbury lectr. U. Melbourne, 1974, Wenk lectr. Johns Hopkins U., 1995. Fellow AAAS (chmn. indsl. sci. sect.), Am. Soc. Metals Internat. (Burgess lectr. 1984, Campbell meml. lectr. 1987, disting. lectr. materials and soc. 1995, medal for advancement sci. 2006), Inst. of Physics, Inst. of Materials, The Minerals, Metals and Materials Soc. (dir., fin. officer, pres. 1990, Krumb lectr. 1988, leadership award 1992); mem. NRC (chmn. com. engrng. and tech. sys. 1992-97), ASME (disting. lectr. 1989), NAE (elected), Royal Swedish Acad. Engrng. Scis. (elected), Russian Acad. Engrng. (elected), Royal Acad. Engrng. (elected, UK), Md. Acad. Scis. (coun.), Md. Inst. Metals (pres.), Indsl. Rsch. Inst. (bd. dirs., pres. 1989-90). Avocations: theater, travel, music, piano. Home: 13539 Canada Del Oso Pl NE Albuquerque NM 87111-8045 Personal E-mail: arwestwood@aol.com.

WESTWOOD, JAMES NICHOLSON, lawyer; b. Portland, Oreg., Dec. 3, 1944; s. Frederick Alton and Catherine (Nicholson) W.; m. Janet Sue Butler, Feb. 23, 1980; children: Laura, David. BA, Portland State U., 1967; JD, Columbia U., 1974. Bar: Oreg. 1974, U.S. Dist. Ct. Oreg. 1974, U.S. Ct. Appeals (9th cir.) 1978, U.S. Ct. Appeals (10th cir.), 2003, U.S. Ct. Appeals (fed. cir.) 1984, U.S. Ct. Appeals (D.C. cir.) 1997, U.S. Supreme Ct. 1981. Assoc. Miller, Anderson, Nash, Yerke & Wiener, Portland, 1974-76, 78-81; asst. to pres. Portland State U., 1976-78; ptnr. Miller, Nash, Wiener, Hager & Carlsen, Portland, 1981-99, Stoel Rives LLP, Portland, 1999—. Recipient Disting. Svc. award Portland State U. Found., 1984, Outstanding Alumni award Portland State U., 1992. Mem. ABA (chmn. forest resources com. 1987-89), Oreg. Bar Assn. (chmn. appellate practice sect. 1996-97, chmn. constnl. law sect. 2006), Am. Acad. Appellate Lawyers, Univ. Club (bd. govs. 1994), Park Blocks Found. (pres. 1999—), CASA for Children (bd. mem. 2006-), City Club (pres. 1991-92). Republican. Unitarian Universalist. Home: 3121 NE Thompson St Portland OR 97212-4908 Office: Stoel Rives LLP 900 SW 5th Ave Ste 2600 Portland OR 97204-1268 Office Phone: 503-294-9187. Business E-Mail: jnwestwood@stoel.com.

WESTWOOD, MELVIN NEIL, horticulturist, pomologist; b. Hiawatha, Utah, Mar. 25, 1923; s. Neil and Ida (Blake) Westwood; m. Wanda Mae Shields, Oct. 12, 1946; children: Rose Dawn, Nancy Gwen, Robert Melvin, Kathryn Mae. Student, U. Utah, 1948-50; BS in Pomology, Utah State U., 1952; PhD in Pomology, Wash. State U., 1956. Field botanist Utah State U., Logan, 1951-52, supt. Howell Field Sta., 1952-53; rsch. asst. State Coll. Wash., 1953-55; rsch. horticulturist Agrl. Rsch. Svc. USDA, Wenatchee, Wash., 1955-60; assoc. prof. Oreg. State U., Corvallis, 1960-67, prof., 1967-80, prof. emeritus, 1986—; rsch. dir. Nat. Clonal Germplasm Repository, Corvallis, 1980-83, nat. tech. advisor, 1984-86. Author: Deciduous Fruit and Nut Production, 1976, Temperate-Zone Pomology: Physiology and Culture, 1978, 3d edit., 1993, Contract Military Air Transport: From the Ground Up, 1995, Pear Varieties and Species, 1996, The Foods of Lewis and Clark, 2005; author: (with others) Cherry Nutrition, 1966, Pear Rootstocks, 1987, Management and Utilization of Plant Germplasm, 1988, Maintenance and Storage: Clonal Germplasm, 1989, Genetic Resources of Malus, 1991; contbr. articles to profl. jours. With US Air Transport Command, 1943—45, with USAAF, 1946—47. Recipient Hartman Cup award, Oreg. Hort. Soc., 1989, Earl Price Excellence in Rsch. award, Oreg. State U., 1989; grantee, NSF, 1966. Fellow: Am. Soc. Hort. Sci. (mem. pomology sect. 1967—74, chmn. com. environ. quality 1971, mem. publs. com. 1971—74, pres. Western region 1974, bd. dirs. 1974—75, adv. coun. 1974—79, Joseph Harvey Gourley award for Pomology 1958, Stark award for Pomology 1969, Joseph Harvey Gourley award for Pomology 1977, Stark award for Pomology 1977, Outstanding Rschr. award 1986); mem.: AAAS, Am. Pomological Soc. (mem. adbv. bd. 1970—75, mem. exec. bd. 1980—84, Paul Howe Shepard award 1968, 1982, Wilder medal 1980), Am. Soc. Plant Physiologists, Amnesty Internat., UN Assn. USA, Ams. United Separation of Ch. and State, Gamma Sigma Delta, Phi Kappa Phi. Baptist. Achievements include patents for Autumn Blaze ornamental pear; research in Pyrus (pear), Malus (apple) and Prunus (plum, cherry, peach); physiology of rootstock genera. Office: Oreg State U Dept Horticulture Corvallis OR 97331

WETCHER-HENDRICKS, DEBRA ELIZABETH, social sciences educator; b. Allentown, Pa., Oct. 19, 1970; d. Neil Steven and Judith Ann Wetcher; m. Glenn Thomas Hendricks, June 7, 1997; children: Mitchell Jack Hendricks, Joel Spencer Hendricks. BA, Glassboro State Coll., NJ, 1991; MA, PhD, Lehigh U., Bethlehem, Pa., 1998. Vis. prof. Northampton CC, Bethlehem, 1998—99, Moravian Coll., Bethlehem, 1999—2001, asst. prof., 2001—. Contbr. articles to profl. jours. Mem. adv. bd. Dept. of Children Youth and Families, Northampton County, Pa., 2005—. Mem.: Americana, Internat. Chinese Statis. Assn., Alpha Kappa Delta. Achievements include research in corrections for attenuation that do not assume independent error scores and applicable to partial and part correlation coefficients were derived; an error in Bohrnstedt's (1969) derivation of formulas to compute for partial and part coefficients implicitly corrected for attenuation was discovered and corrected. Office: Moravian College 1200 Main St Bethlehem PA 18018 Office Phone: 610-861-1415. Office Fax: 610-625-7811. Business E-Mail: medwh02@moravian.edu.

WETENHALL, JOHN, museum director; b. June 1, 1957; s. Jack Wetenhall and Jane (Rinaud) Keating; m. Tanya Williams, Aug. 28, 2004. AB cum laude, Dartmouth Coll., 1979; MA, Williams Coll., Williamstown, Mass., 1982, Stanford U., 1985, PhD, 1988; MBA, Vanderbilt U., 1999. Fellow Smithsonian Instn., Washington, 1986-87, 88-89; lectr. Santa Clara (Calif.) U., 1985, U. Minn., Mpls., 1988; curator painting and sculpture Birmingham (Ala.) Mus. Art, 1989-95; dir. Checkwood Mus. Art, Nashville, 1995-2001; exec. dir. John and Mable Ringling Mus. Art, Sarasota, Fla., 2001—. Founder Thomas Art Projects, Birmingham, 1992-95, Carell Woodland Sculpture Trail, Nashville, 1996-99; cons. Vietnam Women's Meml. Project, Washington, 1988-89, U. So. Calif. Pub. Art Program, 1991. Author: (with Karal Ann Marling) Iwo Jima: Monuments, Memories and the American Hero, 1991, (with David Cass) (catalogue) Italian Paintings, 1850-1910, 1982; editor: (catalogue) Splendors of the American West, 1990; contbr. articles to profl. jours.; appearance in Am. Masters: Alexander Calder, PBS, 1998. Chair Livelier City Ctr. com. Ops. New Birmingham, 1994—95, chair cultural dist. forum, 1992—94; nat. register peers, design excellence program Gen. Svcs. Adminstrn., 1998—; chair Nashville Rotary Adopt-A House Program; mem. Leadership Manatee, 2002, Leadership Fla., 2003; bd. Sarasota Conv. and Visitors Bur., 2006—. Recipient Award of Excellence Tenn. Assn. Mus., 1996, 2001, Gold and Silver medals for ednl. programming Southeastern Mus. Conf., 1999; B. Gerald Cantor fellow, 1986, Nat. Endowment for the Arts grantee, 1991, Lyndon Baines Johnson Found. Moody Travel grantee, 1986, John F. Kennedy Libr. Found. grantee, 1986, Inst. Mus. and Libr. Svcs. grantee. Mem. Am. Tchrs. Assn. of the Martial Arts (sensei), Rotary (Paul Harris fellow), Kiwanis, Sarasota C. of C. (bd. dirs. 2005—06), Beta Gamma Sigma, Assn. Art Mus. Dirs., Am. Assn. Mus. (bd. dirs. 2007-). Avocations: white water kayaking, flying, aiki ju jitsu (blackbelt). Office: Ringling Mus of Art 5401 Bay Shore Rd Sarasota FL 34243 Business E-Mail: jwetenhall@ringling.org.

WETHERALL, ROBERT SHAW, librarian; b. Jesup, Ga., Aug. 18, 1944; s. Robert and Elizabeth (Shaw) W; m. Cynthia Jane Campbell, July 31, 1976; children— Robert G., Gerritt C. B.A. in History, U. Del., 1966, M.A. in History, 1968; M.L.S., Drexel U., 1973. Cert. profl. libr., N.J. Libr. Cumberland County Libr., Bridgeton, N.J., 1973-76; asst. dir., 1976-80, dir., 1981-89; dir. Dover (Del.) Pub. Libr., 1989—; mem. Cumberland County Audio-Visual Aids Commn., Bridgeton, 1981-89; pres. South Jersey Regional Libr. Coop., Inc., 1986-88, treas., 1988-89. Served with USAF, 1968-72. Mem. ALA, Del. Libr. Assn. (pres. 1992-93, action implementation com.). Office: Dover Pub Libr 45 S State St Dover DE 19901-7311

WETHERBE, HERBERT JOHN, pharmacist; b. Montague, Mass., Sept. 18, 1943; s. John Bond Wetherbe, Dorothy Mildred Wetherbe; m. Linda Ann Stines. MDiv, Trinity Evang. Div. Sch., 1979; PharmD, U. Ill., 1992. Registered pharmacist Ill., N.Y. Chemist Inmont Corp., Detroit, 1969—71; chief pharmacist Walgreens Drug Co., Deerfield, Ill., 1979—83; staff pharmacist VA Hosp., Danville, 1983—87, King Khaled Eye Specialist Hosp., Riyadh, Saudi Arabia, 1987—89; clin. pharmacist Northwestern Meml. Hosp., Chgo., 1992—93, Security Forces Hosp., Riyadh, 1993—96; pharmacist Kinney Drugs, Gouveneur, NY, 1996; clin. cons. hosp. info. sys. Nat. Consulting Bur. Huff Barrington Owens Alan Cooper, Inc., Safat, Kuwait, 1996—97, Integrated Solutions for Bus., Riyadh, 1998—2002, Nat. Consulting Bur. Huff Barrington Owens Alan Cooper, Inc., Safat, 2002—03, Kinney Drugs, Gouveneur, 2003—, supervising pharmacist, 2003—. Mem.: Northern NY Pharmacists Soc., Saudi Pharm. Soc., Intravenous Nurses Soc., Pharmacists Soc. State N.Y., Am. Soc. Health Sys. Pharmacists, Am. Pharm. Assn., Am Inst. Chemists, Am. Chem. Soc., Gen. Soc. Mayflower Descs., N.Y. State Coun. Health Sys. Pharmacists. Republican. Avocation: travel. Personal E-mail: hjwetherbe@yahoo.com.

WETHERBY, IVOR LOIS, retired librarian; b. Louisville, May 22, 1924; d. Luther Silas and Clara Morris (Hite) Wetherby; m. Herbert Charles Howard, July 4, 1947; children: Ivor Jane Howard, Elizabeth Wetherby Howard, John Allen Howard, Luther Hite Howard, Ann Dell Howard. AB, Ky. Wesleyan Coll., 1944; MLS, Fla. State U., 1965; SEd, Fla. Atlantic U., 1984; EdD, Fla. Internat. U., 1992. Various clerical and secretarial positions, 1944—50; tchr. Our Lady of Mercy Acad., Louisville, 1963—64; libr. Palm Beach Jr. Coll., Lake Worth, Fla., 1966—78; head libr. Sebring Pub. Libr., Fla., 1978; health scis. reference libr. Med. Ctr. Campus Miami Dade CC, Fla., 1978—87; libr. Moncrief Army Cmty. Hosp., Ft. Jackson, SC, 1987—89; reference libr. Fla. Internat. U., 1992; ret., 1992. Active First Alliance Ch., Hendersonville, NC, Pleasant Grove Bapt. Ch., Louisville. Mem.: DAR, Palm Beach County Geneal. Soc., Nat. Soc. Daus. Union 1861-65, Huguenot Soc., Holland Soc., Nat. Soc. Colonial Dames XVII Century, Daus. Founders and Patriots Am. Home: 615 Laurel Lake Dr Apt A224 Columbus NC 28722

WETHERELL, ALBERT A., secondary school educator; b. Queens, NY; s. Albert M. and Hedwig D. Wetherell. BA, St. John's U., Queens, 1965, PhD, 1979; MA, Fordham U., 1967. Tchr. NYC Bd. Edn., 1967—2004. Recipient Bunzel award, United Fed. Tchrs., 1992, Achievement award, Am. Fedn. Tchrs., 2005. Mem.: Polish Inst. Arts and Sci., Am. Hist. Assn., Queens Hist. Soc., Equestrian Order of the Holy Sepulchre Jerusalem (eastern lieutenancy), Phi Alpha Theta, Phi Delta Kappa. Avocation: historical research.

WETHERELL, THOMAS KENT, academic administrator; b. Daytona Beach, Fla., Dec. 22, 1945; m. Virginia B. Wetherell; children: Kent, Blakely, Page. BS in Social Studies, Fla. State U., 1967, MS in Social Studies, 1968, PhD in Adminstrn., 1974. Pres. Wetherell Enterprises, Inc.; dir. housing and adminstrn., asst. v.p., asst. dean housing U. Ctrl. Fla.; assoc. prof. Bethune-Cookman Coll.; exec. asst. to pres. to dean of instrn. Daytona Beach CC, v.p., provost acad. and univ. transfer programs, dist. v.p., planning and devel.; pres. First Am. Mortgage and Investments, Inc., Tallahassee CC, 1975, Fla. State U., Tallahassee, 2003—. Mem. Fla. Ho. of Reps., 1980-92, spkr. 1990-92, chair appropriations com., 1989-90, chair appropriations edn. com., 1986-88, chair higher edn. com., 1984-86, majority fl. leader, 1982-84, chair Volusia county legis. delegation, 1981-83, 86-87. Bd. dirs. Econ. Devel. Coun., ARC, Canaveral Nat. Seashore Park, Southern Scholarship Found., United Way. Mem. Tallahassee C. of C. (bd. dirs.), Lions, Kiwanis, Blue Lodge, Shriners, Bahia Temple. Office: Office of Pres Fla State U 211 Westcott Bldg Tallahassee FL 32306-1470 Office Phone: 850-644-1085. E-mail: wetherell@mailer.fsu.edu. *

WETHERILL, EIKINS, lawyer, investment company executive; b. Phila., Oct. 3, 1919; s. A. Heckscher and Edwina (Brunner) W. LL.B., U. Pa., 1948. Practiced in, Phila., 1948-55, Norristown, 1955-98; assoc. firm Evans, Bayard & Frick, 1948-50; ptnr. Reilly, Hepburn, Earle & Wetherill, 1950-55; firm Henderson, Wetherill, O'Hey & Horsey, 1955-98; pres. Phila. Stock Exchange, Inc., 1965-81. Bd. dirs. Germantown Savs. Bank; fin. commentator CBS-TV News, 1966-68; chmn. bd. Sta. WHYY-TV, 1970-76, dir., 1976-90; dir. 1st Pa. Corp., 1st Pa. Bank, solicitor to lt. gov. Pa., 1951-55, asst. U.S. atty. gen., 1953-55, treas., Montgomery County, 1956-59; pres. Montgomery County Bd. Commrs., 1960-63; chmn. Pa. Securities Commn., 1963-65; commr. Delaware Valley Regional Planning Commn., 1965—, chmn., 1968-69, 70-71, 78-79. Former bd. dirs. Greater Phila. Partnership; chmn. Phila. Drama Guild, 1975-80, dir., 1980-87; trustee Davis and Elkins Coll., 1973-91, G.H. Montgomery County Open Space, 1994—. Served to capt., cav. Signal Corps, OSS, AUS, 1941-45. Mem. ABA, Phila. Bar Assn., Phila. Club, Racquet Club (Phila.), Sunnybrook Golf Club, Delta Psi. Episcopalian.

WETHERILL-SMITH, LINDA MARIE, musician, educator, performing arts association administrator; b. Milw., Mar. 2, 1950; d. Albert Edward Christensen and Elsa Dorothea Etterman; m. Joseph David Smith, July 7, 2000. MusB, U. Rochester, 1972, performers cert., 1971; MusM, SUNY, Stony Brook, 1991. 1st flutist solo and ensemble Chamber Artists Garbarino of La Scala, Milan, 1973—76; solo and 1st flutist Frankfurt Radio Symphony Orch., 1975—76, IRCAM, Ensemble Intercontemporain, Paris, 1976—80; internat. soloist freelance, U.S.I.S. and McCann Artists, Ltd., London, 1973—; prof. music major Turkish univs., Istanbul, 1987—90; cultural amb. U.S. Info. Svc., Washington, 1985—; prof. music Adelphi U., Garden City, NY, 1994—; solo flutist Aspekte, 2006—, Salzburg Mozarteam, 2006—, Orch. of Our Time, NYC, 2006—, exec. dir., 2006—. Judge Internat. Competition, Salzburg, Austria, 2004—; solo performer, lectr. Internat. Soc. Cont. Music, Miami, 2004; performances and master classes in Argentina and Brazil; cons. various internat. programs, 1973—. Editor: LI Flute Notes, 1994—; editor, performer (solo CD) Sound and Repercussion, Far Amazon, 2000 (Amazon award, 2003), (book, CD) International Anthology of Solos for Alto and Bass Flutes, 2005, (concert, CD recording) George Rochterg Meml. Concert, 2006; contbr. articles and interviews to profl. jours. Pres., founder Muzarte, Phila., NYC, 1980—. Grantee, NY State Coun. for the Arts, 1997—2005. Mem.: LI Flute Club (bd. dirs., adv. bd. 1994—2005), Sigma Alpha Iota. Achievements include first woman to perform publicly for mixed audiences in Saudi Arabia in 1986; first American flute soloist to perform and teach in Hunan province of China in 2002. Avocations: travel, political diplomacy, world cultures. Home: 38 W 74th Ave Apt 3C New York NY 10023 Office: Adelphi U South Ave Garden City NY 11530 Personal E-mail: muzarte@msn.com. Business E-Mail: muzarte@lindawetherill.com.

WETLE, TERRIE FOX, gerontologist, educator, dean; b. Bremerton, Wash., Nov. 7, 1946; d. Gerald Lee and Elinor Myrle (Martindale) Todd; m. Richard W. Besdine, July 2, 1981; children: Sarah, Molly. BS in Psychology, Portland State U., 1968, MS in Psychology, 1971, PhD of Urban Studies, 1976; doctorate (hon.), U. Geneva Sch. Medicine, 2005. Asst. prof. Portland (Oreg.) State U., 1976-78; social policy analyst Dept. Health, Edn. and Welfare, Washington, 1978-79; asst. prof. Yale U., New Haven, 1979-81, Harvard U., Boston, 1981-88; dir. Braceland Ctr., Hartford, Conn., 1988-95; assoc. prof. U. Conn. Health Ctr., Farmington, 1989—95; dep. dir. Nat. Inst. Aging, NIH, Bethesda, Md., 1995-2000; assoc. dean medicine, prof. cmty. health Brown U. Med. Sch., Providence, 2000—. Bd. dirs. Armed Forces Retirement Home, Washington. Editor: Handbook of Geriatric Care, 1982, Older Veterans, 1984, Medicare Coming of Age: A Proposal for Reform, 1986, The Patient Self Determination Act and Advance Directives: A Curriculum for Nursing Home Staff, 1995, Public and Private Responsibilities in Long-Term Care: Finding the Balance, 1998, End of Life In Nursing Homes: Experiences and Policy Recommendations, 2004, Improving Aging and Public Health Research: Qualitative and Mixed Methods, 2006; contbr. articles to profl. jours. Pres. Alzheimer's Assn. Greater Hartford, 1993-95; bd. trustees Perishable Theater, 2002-, Ctr. Advancement of Health; bd. dirs., Internat. Assn. Gerontology Recipient Pres. award, Am. Coll. Health Care Adminstrs., DHHS Sex. Disting. Svc. award. Fellow: Gerontol. Soc. Am. (pres. 2003—04, chair com.); mem.: APHA (del., governing coun., Key award Outstanding Contbns. in Public Health and Aging), Am. Soc. Aging (pres. 2007—, Pres. award). Office: Brown Program in Public Health 121 S Main St G S121 Providence RI 02912

WETMORE, KEITH CHIDESTER, lawyer; b. Valparaiso, Ind., Oct. 17, 1956; s. Leonard Leander and Dorisann (Chidester) W. BA, Northwestern U., 1977; JD magna cum laude, U. Mich., 1980. Bar: Calif. 1981, U.S. Dist. Ct. (no. dist.) Calif. 1981. Law clk. to Hon. J. Edward Lumbard U.S. Ct. Appeals (2d cir.), 1980-81; assoc. Steinhart & Falconer, San Francisco, 1981-82, Morrison & Foerster LLP, San Francisco, 1982-86, ptnr., 1986—, chmn. NYC, 2000—. Articles editor U. Mich. Law Rev. 1980-81. Mem. ABA, Calif. Bar Assn., Bay Area Lawyers for Individual Freedom, San Francisco Bar Assn. Methodist. Office: Morrison & Foerster LLP 1290 Ave Americas New York NY 10104 Business E-Mail: kwetmore@mofo.com.

WETSCH, JOHN ROBERT, information scientist; b. Dickinson, ND, Aug. 27, 1959; s. Joseph John (dec.) and Florence Mae (Edwards) W.; m. Laura Jean Johnson, Aug. 29, 1981; children: Julie Elizabeth, Katherine Anne, John Michael, Joseph Harold. BS, Excelsior Coll., Albany, 1984; MA, Antioch U., 1989; PhD, Nova Southeastern U., 1994; BS, U. ND, 2001; M in Astronomy, U. Western Sydney, 2002; grad. in Theology, Australian Cath. U. Cert. project mgmt. profl. Project Mgmt. Inst. Radiation physics instr. Grand Forks Clinic, ND, 1983-85; sr. programmer PRC, Inc., Cavalier Air Force Sta., ND, 1987-91, PARCS project-SAFEGUARD sys.; pres. Dakota Sci. Inc., Langdon, ND, 1988-95; instr. U. N.D.-Lake Region, Devils Lake, 1988-91; systems adminstr. U.S. Courts Nat. Fine Ctr., Raleigh, NC, 1991-94; project leader U.S. Postal Svc., Raleigh Integrated Bus. Sys. Solution Ctr., 1994—2001, program mgmt. info. tech. enabling portfolio, 2001—03; sr. tech. fellow Litton/PRC, 1997—2002; tech. fellow Northrop Grumman Info. Tech., 2002—06, sys. engr., 2004—06; program dir. NC Window of Info. on Student Edn. NC Dept. Pub. Instrn., 2006—. Cons. on Wave Obs./ND Proposal, Gov.'s Office, Bismarck, 1991; founder, developer Dakota Sci., Inc., Langdon, 1988-95; instr. divsn. continuing edn. Wake Tech. CC, 1993-99; adj. faculty computer info. systems NC Wesleyan Coll., 1997—; adj. faculty NC State U., 1999-2000, Capella U., Mpls., 2000-02, U. Phoenix, 1998-2001. Author: Distributed UNIX System Administration, 1998; (with others) COMPUTE!'s 2nd Book of Amiga, 1988; contbr. articles to COMPUTE! Jour. of Progressive Computing, 1987, other profl. jours. Program coord. Lake Region Outreach, U. ND, Cavalier Air Force Sta., 1988—91; mem. bd. alumni trustees USNY-Regents Coll., Albany, 1995—2000, v.p., 1996—97, pres., 1997—2000, ex-officio mem. bd. overseers, 1997; pres. Zeta Rho chpt. Pi Kappa Alpha, Grand Forks, 1981; pres. Alumni Assn. Excelsior Coll., 1999—2001; ex-officio voting Excelsior Coll. Bd. Trustees, 1999—2001, bd. trustees, 2001—. Decorated knight comdr. Order of St. Gregory the Great (Vatican); named Larimore-Mathews scholar, U. ND, Grand Forks, 1978, ND Acad. Sci. scholar, 1978, SMITS scholar, ND Acad. Sci., 1990; named to Hon. Order of Ky. Cols., 2007; recipient Westinghouse Sci. Talent Search award, 1978, Nova Southeastern U. Leadership award, Internat. Alumni Assn., 1998, Excelsior Coll. Founder's award, 2001. Mem.: Project Mgmt. Inst., Dakota Astron. Soc. (pres. 1987—91, co-founder). Roman Catholic. Achievements include research in missile simulation; microcomputer short range weather forecasting algorithm, study in astronomy and culture, astronomy information systems, large scale system integration to government information systems. Office: 301 N Wilmington St Raleigh NC 27601 Personal E-mail: drwetsch@msn.com.

WETSCH, LAURA JOHNSON, lawyer; b. Fargo, ND, Nov. 18, 1959; d. Ronald Lee Johnson and Jacqualene Lee (Goudie) Johnson Trefz; m. John Robert Wetsch, Aug. 29, 1981; children: Julie Elizabeth, Katherine Anne, John Michael, Joseph Harold. AA, Bismarck State Coll., ND, 1980; BA, U. N.D., 1982, JD, 1985. Bar: N.D. 1985, N.C. 1992. Law clk. to Hon. Patrick A. Conmy US Dist. Ct. ND, Bismarck, 1985-88; pvt. practice Langdon, ND, 1988-91; assoc. Jordan Price Wall Gray Jones & Carlton, PLLC, Raleigh, NC, 1992-99; dir., v.p. legal affairs Hytec Cons., Inc., Cary, NC, 1999—2003; of counsel Joyce L. Davis & Assocs., Raleigh, 1999—2006; ptnr. Winslow Wetsch, PLLP, Raleigh, 2006—. Instr. bus. and criminal law U. N.D.-Lake Region, Cavalier, 1990-91; instr. paralegal studies Ctrl. Carolina C.C., Sanford, N.C., 1991-92; instr. bus. law Wake Tech. C.C., Raleigh, 1992-93. Author, editor (pamphlet) Crime Survivors Handbook, 1996; editor N.D. Women Lawyers Assn. Newsletter, 1990-91; contbr. articles to profl. jours. Vol. mediator and arbitrator Burleigh County Housing Authority, Bismarck, 1986-88; concessions co-chmn. Sanderson H.S. Band Boosters, 1996-2000; curbside cons. in employment law, N.C. Ctr. for Nonprofits, 1998. Mem. Nat. Employment Lawyers Assn., NC Bar Assn. (citizen edn. com. young lawyers divsn. 1994-96, chmn. membership svcs. com. young lawyers divsn. 1996-97), NC Acad. Trial Lawyers (chair employment law sect. 2007-), Wake County Bar Assn. (fee arbitration com. 2001—). Democrat. Roman Catholic. Office: 416 Morson St Raleigh NC 27601 Office Phone: 919-834-6534. E-mail: lwetsch@winslow-wetsch.com.

WETSEL, WILLIAM DAVID, literature educator; b. Sweetwater, Tex., May 28, 1949; s. W.B. Wetsel and Elizabeth Heriot Evans. BA with highest honors, U. Tex., 1971; MDiv, U. Chgo., 1989; PhD, Brandeis U., 1978. Vis. prof. U. Stuttgart (Germany), 2005, U. Paris IV, Sorbonne, 2006. Author: Scripture and the Rest: Pascal's Pensées in the Exegetical Tradition of Port-Royal, 1983, Pascal and Disbelief: Catechesis and Conversion in the Pensées, 1995; editor: N.Am. Soc. Seventeenth Century French Literature Tempe Acta, 6. vol., 2003, Pascal Translation Project. Faculty co-ordinator Gay and Lesbian Student Caucus Ariz. State U. Recipient Acad. Palms award, French Govt., 2005; fellow, Fulbright Found., 1971—72, Woodrow Wilson Found., 1972; grantee, Am. Coun. of Learned Societies, 1979; Andrew Mellon fellow, U. Pitts., 1980—81, Fulbright scholar, U. Paris, 1982—83. Mem.: N.Am. Soc. for Seventeenth-Century French Lit. (pres. 2000—02), Phi Beta Kappa. Democrat. Episcopalian. Achievements include research in French 17th century studies, Cajun French language, opera and literature, gay studies in France. Avocations: religious art, minority languages, opera, literature. Home: 3508 N Pueblo Way Scottsdale AZ 85251 Office: Arizona State U Dept Langs Tempe AZ 85287-0202 Office Phone: 480-994-8942. Personal E-mail: wdwetsel@aol.com.

WETTER, VIRGINIA FORWOOD PATE, broadcast executive; b. Havre De Grace, Md., Aug. 10, 1919; BA, Coll. William and Mary, 1940, PhD (hon.) in Pub. Svc., 2006. Pub. rels. Std. Oil Co. of Pa., 1940, Irwin and Leighton Contractor, 1941; pres., gen. mgr. WASA and WHDG radio Havre de Grace, MD, 1960—85; pres. Multiview Cable Co. (later Comcast), 1966—82; chmn. bd. Chesapeake Broadcasting Corp., 1985—. Trustee Harford CC Bd. of Trustees, 1959—69, chmn., 1966—69; pres. Md. Assn. Bds. of Edn., 1963—64, Md. Dist. of Columbia Del. Broadcaster's Assn., 1965—66; mem. Harford County Bd. Edn., 1959—69, pres., 1966—69; mem. radio code bd. Nat. Assn. of Broadcasters, 1966—71; libr. bd. Broadcast Pioneers, 1980—2004. Dir. Harford County Heart Assn. and Cancer Soc., Susquehanna Coun. of Girl Scouts; county chmn. Pres.'s Com. to Promote Employment of Physically Handicapped; plans bd. United Way; dir. Blood Bank of Md.; vol. Harford Meml. Hosp. Aux.; chmn. ann. fund drive Coll. William and Mary, 1985, endowment assn. trustee, pres.'s coun.; vestry St. John's Episcopal Ch., chair 150th anniversary celebration, co-chair bldg. com. Recipient Alumni Medallion award, Coll. William and Mary, 1969, Am. Broadcast Pioneer award, Broadcasters' Found., 2001, Disting. Svc. to Broadcasting award, Broadcast Pioneers of Washington Area, 2001. Mem.: Am. Women in Radio and Television (life; nat. pres. 1970—71, Bd. Dirs. award 1991, Radio Leadership award 2000), Md. Congress of Parents and Tchrs. (life), Delta Kappa Gamma (hon.). Home: 1000 Chesapeake Dr Havre De Grace MD 21078 Personal E-mail: vwetter@aol.com.

WETTERAU, MARK S., food products/distributor executive; m. Virginia Wetterau; children: Stephen, Elizabeth, Olivia. BA, Westminster Coll. With Wetterau Inc., 1980—92; pres., CEO Shop 'n Stop Warehouse Foods, 1988—90; pres. retail & ind. group Wetterau Inc., 1990—91, pres., COO, 1991—92; co-founder, ptnr. Wetterau Assoc., 1992—; pres., CEO Quality Beverage, 1992—98; chmn., CEO, pres. Golden State Foods (of Wetterau Assoc.), Irvine, Calif., 1998—. Chmn. GSF found.; bd. mem. Second Harvest Food Bank of Orange County. Office: Golden State Foods Ste 1100 18301 Von Karman Ave Irvine CA 92612

WETZEL, AMANDA GRACE, secondary school educator; b. Pitts., Pa., June 22, 1980; d. Richard James and Jacqueline Ann Wetzel. BA in History, John Carroll U., U. Heights, Ohio, 2002; MA in Liberal Studies, Duquesne U., Pitts., Pa. Cert. tchr. 7-12 social studies Dept. Edn., Ohio, 2002, tchr. 7-12 English Dept. Edn., Pa., 2006, tchr. 7-12 social studies Dept. Edn., Pa., 2004. Tchr. history Horizon Sci. Acad., Cleve., 2002—04; tchr. econs. and history Shaler Area Sch. Dist., Pitts., 2004—. Coach girls lacrosse Shaler Area Sch. Dist., 2006—. Event organizer ONE; vol. Big Bros. Big Sisters, Pitts., GLSEN, Pitts.; advisor MPowerment Young Women's Group, Pitts. Mem.: Nat. Coun. Tchrs. English, Nat. Coun. Social Studies. Roman Catholic. Avocations: running, politics, reading, writing. Office: Shaler Area Sch Dist 381 Wible Run Rd Pittsburgh PA 15209 Home Phone: 412-716-5712; Office Phone: 412-492-1200 x1667.

WETZEL, BETTY PREAT, writer; b. Roundup, Mont., Nov. 7, 1915; d. Alfred William and Rachel Preat (Johnston) Eiselein; m. Winston Warren Wetzel, June 5, 1940; children: Susan Hinman, Kurt, Gretchen Grafin von Rittberg, Rebecca. BA in Journalism, U. Mont., 1937. Columnist, reporter Roundup (Mont.) Rec.-Tribume, 1938-46; sec. SEATO Cholera Rsch. Lab. and Hosp., Dacca, Bangladesh, 1965-67; adminstrv. asst. to v.p. Wellesley (Mass.) U., 1969-73; dir. pub. rels. Oxfam-Am., Boston, 1973-77; book rev. editor Mont. Mag., Helena, 1989-91. Author: The Making of a Montanan, 1986, Missoula, The Town and The People, 1988, After You, Mark Twain, 1990; co-author: Older Women in the Outdoors, 1996. Bd. dirs. Flathead Lake Biol. Sta., Bigfork, Mont., 1980-86. Democrat. Avocations: mountain hiking, tennis, reading, politics. Home: 189 Pierce Ln PO Box 693 Bigfork MT 59911-0693 Personal E-mail: bwetzel@digisys.net.

WEVERS, JOHN WILLIAM, retired Semitic languages educator; b. Baldwin, Wis., June 4, 1919; emigrated to Can., 1951; s. Bernard and Wilemina (Te Grootenhuis) W.; m. Grace Della Brondsema, May 22, 1942; children: Robert Dick, John William, Harold George, James Merritt. AB, Calvin Coll., Grand Rapids, Mich., 1940; ThB, Calvin Sem., 1943; ThD, Princeton Theol. Sem., 1945; DD (hon.), Knox Coll., Toronto, 1973; DHC (hon.), Leiden U., 1985. Lectr., then asst. prof. O.T. and Semitic langs. Princeton Theol. Sem., 1946-51; mem. faculty U. Toronto, Ont., Canada, 1951—, prof. Near Eastern studies Ont., 1963—, prof. emeritus Ont., 1984—, grad. chmn. Ont., 1972-75, chmn. dept. Ont., 1975-80. Chmn. adminstrv. council Presbyn. Ch. Can., 1960-65 Author: Commentary on the Book of Ezekiel, 1969, Septuaginta Vetus Testamentum Graecum: Genesis, 1974, Deuteronomium, 1977, Numeri, 1981, Leviticus, 1986, Exodus, 1991; also text histories, 1974, 78, 83, 86, 92, Notes on the Greek Text of Exodus, 1990, Genesis, 1993, Deuteronomy, 1995, Leviticus, 1997, Numbers, 1998. Bd. govs. Ctrl. Hosp., Toronto, 1963-96, chmn., 1967-80; chmn. Hosp. Coun. Met. Toronto, 1974-75; bd. govs. Ont. Hosp. Assn., 1974-84, pres., 1978-79. Recipient Queen's Jubilee medal, 1978. Fellow Royal Soc. Can.; mem. Oriental Club Toronto, Internat. Orgn. Septuagint and Cognate Studies (pres. 1972-80, hon. pres. 1989—), Can. Bibl. Studies (hon. life), Akademie Wissenschaften Goettingen (corr.), Arts and Letters Club (Toronto). Home: 116 Briar Hill Ave Toronto ON Canada M4R 1H9 E-mail: j.wevers@utoronto.ca.

WEXELBAUM, MICHAEL, lawyer; b. Bklyn., Aug. 12, 1946; s. Joseph and Beatrice (Skurnick) W.; m. Cynthia Debra Schorr, Apr. 15, 1973 (dec. 1984); children: Joshua David, Stephanie Faye; m. Joan Brenda Math, Aug. 21, 1994; stepchildren: Jonathan David Kaye, Matthew Lawrence Kaye, Julie Dana Kaye. BA in Econs., Bucknell U., 1968; JD, NYU, 1971. Bar: N.Y. 1972, U.S. Dist. Ct. (so. and ea. dists.) N.Y. 1973, U.S. Dist. Ct. (ea. dist.) Wis. 1998. Assoc. Sherman, Citron & Karasik, P.C., NYC, 1972-80, ptnr., head litigation dept., 1980-2001; ptnr. litigation dept. Snow Becker Krauss P.C., NYC, 2001—, co-chair litigation dept., 2003—. Arbitrator Nat. Arbitration Forum, 1999—. Arbitrator Am. Arbitration Assn. and Gen. Arbitration Coun. of Textile and Apparel Industries, N.Y.C., 1982—. Named a N.Y. Super Lawyer, 2006. Mem. Bankruptcy Lawyers Bar Assn., Lawyers Assn. Textile and Apparel Industries (bd. govs.), Am. Arbitration Assn. (arbitrator), Nat. Arbitration Forum (arbitrator), Assn. Comml. Fin. Attys. Democratic. Jewish. Avocations: tennis, skiing, biking, theater. Home: 85 Norrans Ridge Dr Ridgefield CT 06877-4237 Office: Snow Becker Krauss PC 605 Third Ave New York NY 10158-0125 Office Phone: 212-455-0486. Office Fax: 212-455-0455. Personal E-mail: jmwex@hotmail.com. Business E-Mail: mwexelbaum@sbklaw.com.

WEXLER, ALLAN, architect, educator; BFA, R.I. Sch. Design, 1971, BArch, 1972; MArch, Pratt Inst, 1976. Asst. prof. Sch. Arch. N.J. Inst. Tech., 1974—83; mem. faculty environ. design Parsons Sch. Design, 1983—94; assoc. adjunct prof. Sch. Arch. Pratt Inst., 1994—; arch., designer Ronald Feldman Fine Arts, NYC. Mem. faculty Brown U. Sch. Art, 1986, Temple U. Tyler Coll. Art, 1989, Cooper Union Sch. Fine Arts, 1989; artist-in-residency U. Calif., San Diego, 1991; vis. prof. R.I. Sch. Design, Sch. Arch., 1992, Hochschule der Kunste, Berlin, 1994; vis. critic in sculpture SUNY, Purchase, 1993. One-man shows include Albright Coll., Freedman Gallery, Reading, Pa., 1985, Brown U., List Art Ctr., Providence, 1985, Ronald Feldman Fine Arts, N.Y.C., 1985, 1988, 1990, 1992, 1994, 1998, Temple U. Gallery, Phila., 1986, McIntosh/Drysdale Gallery, Washington, 1986, The Jewish Mus., N.Y.C., 1988, Univ. Gallery, U. Mass., Amherst, 1989, Inst. Contemporary Art, U. Pa., 1989, Horace Richter Gallery, Old Jaffa, Israel, 1990, San Diego Mus. Contemporary Art, La Jolla, Calif., 1991, U. Gallery, U. Mass., Amherst, 1991, The Forum Gallery, St. Louis, 1991, De Cordova Mus. and Sculpture Park, Lincoln, Mass., 1992, Karl Ernst Osthaus Mus., Hagen, Germany, 1993, Hochschule der Kunste, Berlin, 1994, Three Rivers Art Festival, Pitts., 1995, Md. Inst. Coll. Art, Balt., 1996, Parsons Sch. Design, Dept. Arch. and Environ. Design, 1997, Stadtgalerie Saarbricken, Germany, 1997, Gallery Joe, Phila., 1997, Atlanta Coll. Art Gallery and City Gallery at Chastain, Atlanta, 1999, Stephen Wirtz Gallery, San Francisco, 2000, Forum for Contemporary Art, St. Louis, 2000, San Francisco Mus. Modern Art, 2001, Ronald Feldman Fine Arts, NYU, 2002, Parrish Art Mus., Southampton, N.Y., 2002, exhibited in group shows at Arlene Bujese Gallery, East Hampton, N.Y., 1995, N.J. Ctr. Arts, Summit, 1995, Davis Mus. and Cultural Ctr., Wellesley (Mass.) Coll., 1996, Calif. Ctr. Arts. Mus., Escondido, 1996, Gallery Joe, Chgo., 1997, Union Brauerei/Dortmunder U., Germany, 1998, White Box, N.Y., 1999, Aldrich Mus. Contemporary Art, Ridgefield, Conn., 2000, 2002, Wave Hill Glyndor Gallery, Bronx, N.Y., 2000, Apex Art, N.Y.C., 2001, Westfalischen Landesmuseum, Munster, Germany, 2001, Hallwalls Contemporary Arts Ctr., Buffalo, N.Y., 2001, Yeshiva U., N.Y.C., 2002, Wilhelm-Hack Mus. and Kunstverein Ludwigshafen, Germany, 2002, Denver Art Mus., 2002, Karl Ernst Osthaus-Mus., Hagen, Germany, 2002, Ronald Feldman Fine Arts, N.Y.C., 2002, Mus. Contemporary Arts, Chgo., 2002, numerous others, commns. include, Vera List, Greenwich, Conn., 1990, Parson's Sch. Design, 1993, ARTWALK, 1995, others, NYC Bd. Edn., 1999, Schneider Vineyard, 2000—, Expo 2000, Hannover, Germany, 2000, Met. Transp. Authority, NYC, 2001—, Hudson River Park, 2002—. Recipient First prize The City as a Significant Environment Competition, Milan and Casabella Mag., 1972, First prize Birch Burdette Long Competition, Archtl. League, 1975, Bessie award 40 Under 40, Interiors Mag., 1986, Sponsored Project award N.Y. State Coun. on Arts, 1989, Chrysler award for design innovation, 1997, George Nelson Design award, Interiors mag., 1999; fellow, N.Y. Found. Arts, 1985, 1990; grantee, Archtl. League, 1975. Office: 305 W 20th St New York NY 10011

WEXLER, ANNE, government relations and public affairs consultant; b. NYC, Feb. 10, 1930; d. Leon R. and Edith R. (Rau) Levy; m. Joseph Duffey, Sept. 17, 1974; children by previous marriage: David Wexler, Daniel Wexler. BA, Skidmore Coll., 1951, LLD (hon.), 1978; DSc in Bus. (hon.), Bryant Coll., 1978. Assoc. pub. Rolling Stone mag., 1974-76; personnel adviser Carter-Mondale transition planning group, 1976-77; dep. undersec. regional affairs Dept. Commerce, 1977-78; asst. to Pres. of U.S., Washington, 1978-81; pres. Wexler and Assocs., Washington, 1981-82; govt. relations and pub. affairs cons., chmn. Wexler, Reynolds, Harrison & Schule, Inc., Washington, 1981-90; vice chmn. Hill and Knowlton PA Worldwide, Washington, 1990-92; chmn. The Wexler Group, 1992—. Bd. dirs. Methanex, Dreyfus Index Funds, Wilshire Mut. Funds, Dreyfus Family of Funds. Bd. dirs. Washington Econ. Club, WETA. Decorated officer Order of Australia; named Outstanding Alumna Skidmore Coll., 1972, recipient most disting. alumni award, 1984, Bryce Harlow award, 1989. Mem. Coun. on Fgn. Rels., Nat. Women's Forum. Jewish. Office: Wexler Group 1317 F St NW Ste 600 Washington DC 20004-1157

WEXLER, DAVID B., law educator; b. NYC, Apr. 4, 1941; s. Irving Wexler and Lillian Heiden; m. Ghislaine Laraque, Nov. 13, 2004; children: Nancy, Douglas. BA, Binghamton U., NY, 1961; JD, NYU, NY, 1964. Atty., criminal divsn. US Dept. Justice, Washington, 1965—67; Lyons prof. law and psychology U. Ariz., Tucson, 1967—. Dir. Internat. Network Therapeutic Jurisprudence, San Juan, 1997—; prof. law U. PR, San Juan, 1997—; cons. in field. Author: Mental Health Law: Major Issues, 1981, Essays in Therapeutic Jurisprudence, 1991; editor (author): Therapeutic Jurisprudence: The Law as a Therapeutic Agent, 1990, Law in a Therapeutic Key, 1996, Practicing Therapeutic Jurisprudence: Law as a Helping Profession, 2000, Judging in a Therapeutic Key: Therapeutic Jurisprudence and the Courts, 2003. Mem. legal task panel Pres.'s Commn. Mental Health, Washington, 1977—88; mem. rsch. network mental health and law MacArthur Found., Chco., 1987—97. Recipient Guttmacher Forensic Psychiatry award, Am. Psychiat. Assn., 1972, Outstanding Svc. award, Nat. Assn. for Mental Health, 1974, Creative Tchg. award, U. Ariz. Pres.'s Club, 1975, Disting. Tchg. Scholarship award, NYU Sch. Law, 1989, Disting. Svc. award, Nat. Ctr. State Cts., 2000; fellow, Fulbright Found., Australia, 2002. Mem.: Am. Psychology-Law Soc. (disting.). Achievements include development of the field of therapeutic jurisprudence. Office: PO Box 23349 San Juan PR 00931-3349 Personal E-mail: davidbwexler@yahoo.com.

WEXLER, HASKELL, film producer; b. Chgo., 1922; s. Simon Wexler; m. Nancy Ashenhurst (div.); two children; m. Marian Witt (div.); 1 son, Mark; m. Rita Taggart. Ednl. documentaries, Chgo., for eleven years; cinematographer films: The Hoodlum Priest, The Best Man, America America, The Loved One, In the Heat of the Night, Who's Afraid of Virginia Woolf? (Acad. award), The Thomas Crown Affair, American Graffiti, One Flew Over the Cuckoo's Nest, Introduction to the Enemy, Bound for Glory (Acad. award), Coming Home, Colors, Three Fugitives, 1988, Blaze, 1989, Lookin' to Get Out, Matewan, Other People's Money, The Babe, Mulholland Falls, 1995, Rich Man's Wife, 1995, (with others) Days of Heaven, (with others) Rolling Stones-IMAX, The Secret of Roan Inish, Canadian Bacon, Limbo, 1999, HBO 61—, 2001, Silver City, 2004; writer, dir., photographer: Medium Cool, 1969; wrote and directed Latino, 1985; feature documentary Bus Riders Union, Five Days in March, From Wharf Rats to Lords of the Docks, Who Needs Sleep?. Received star on Hollywood's Walk of Fame, 1996. Mem. Acad. Motion Picture Arts and Scis. (bd. govs. cinematographers br.). Personal E-mail: perigol@aol.com.

WEXLER, HERBERT IRA, retail company executive; b. Newark, Sept. 6, 1916; s. Irving and Jeanette (Lesser) W.; m. Elaine L. Ellis, Oct. 10, 1948; children: Susan, Peter, Toni. Student, Rutgers U., 1939-41; student Advanced Mgmt. Program, Harvard U., 1956. From stock boy to asst. buyer L. Bamberger & Co., 1935-47; from buyer appliances to sr. v.p., exec. com., dir. R.H. Macy & Co., NYC, 1947-73; pres., CEO, chmn. bd. dirs. Marcade Group Inc., NYC, 1973-86, cons., bd. dirs., 1987-97. Vice chmn. Greater N.Y. coun. Boy Scouts Am.; organizer, fundraiser Yale Grace New Haven Hosp.; mem. Gov. Harriman's Com. to Investigate Fraud and Misrepresentation in Consumer Products; mem. adv. coun. to bd. trustees Greens Farms Acad., Westport, Conn.; gen. chmn. State of Israel Bond Drive, 1980, testimonial, 1978; gen. chmn. N.Y. Cmty. Svc. Soc.; chmn. N.Y. sect. for fundraising Denver Jewish Hosp; dir. Children's Blood Found. N.Y. Hosp. Capt. US Army, 1941—46. Named Key Man of Yr. Am. Jewish Com. and B'nai B'rith, 1957; named B'nai B'rith Man of Yr., 1976; recipient Disting. Service award Am. Jewish Com. and Anti-Defamation League, 1960, Award of Honor Fedn. Jewish Philanthropies of N.Y., 1961, Scroll of Honor United Jewish Appeal of Greater N.Y., 1964, Man of Yr. award Conn. Digestive Disease Soc., 1973 Mem.: Birchwood Country Club, Harvard Club. Home: Greenfield Hunt 49 Palmer Brg Fairfield CT 06430-7830

WEXLER, JOAN G., dean, law educator; b. NYC, Nov. 25, 1946; m. Marvin Wexler, June 16, 1968 (div.); children: Matthew Eric, Laura Page. BS (hons. and distinction), Cornell U., 1968; MA in tchg., Harvard U., 1970; JD, Yale, 1974. Bar: N.Y. 1976. Jud. law clk. for Judge Jack B. Weinstein U.S. Dist. Ct. (ea. dist.), NY, 1974-75; assoc. Debevoise & Plimpton, NYC, 1975-77; asst. prof. law NYU Sch. Law, 1978-81, assoc. prof. law, 1981-85; prof. law Bklyn. Law Sch., 1985—87, assoc. dean acad. affairs, prof. law, 1987-94, acting dean, prof. law, 1994, dean, pres. and prof. law, 1994—. Spkr. in field; evaluator trust adminstrn. and estate adminstrn. courses N.Y. State Banking Assn., 1993; mem. planning com. Bench and Bar Conf. Fed. Bar Coun., 1995, 2003, chair Winter Bench and Bar Conf., Feb. 2002, bd. dirs. Fed. Bar Coun. Found.; mem. planning com. Workshop on Family and Juvenile Law Am. Assn. Law Schs., Washington, 1993; atty. mem. Jud. Conf. of State of N.Y., 2000—; with Bklyn. Legal Svcs. Corp. (mem. adv. com. 1994-). Contbr. articles to profl. jours. Bd. dirs. Downtown Bklyn. Devel. Assn., 1992-96, Fund for Modern Cts., 1994—, Assn. of the Bar of the City of N.Y. Fund, 1994-96; active Commn. on Alcohol and Substance abuse in the Profession, 1999—; mem. Commn. on Univ. Relations, Cornell U., 2001—. Recipient Spl. Recognition award, N.Y. Women's Bar Assn., 1996, Pres. Spl. award, 2002, award, Greater Boy Scout Soc. N.Y., 1999, William Schoenfeld award, Soc. Adolescent Psychiatry, 1999. Fellow Am. Bar Found.; mem. ABA (mem. continuing legal edn. com. 1997-98, 99-2001, ind. law schs. com. 1996-97, 2000-, sect. legal edn. and admissions to bar, new deans seminar planning com. 2001—), Am. Law Inst. (mem. mem's. consultative group-law family dissolution, spl. com. inst. size 1998-2000), Fed. Bar Coun. (pres.-elect 2002-, v.p. 2001-2002, chair Winter Bench and Bar Conf. 2001-2002, planning com. 2002-2003, pres. Fed. Bar Found. 1998-99, chair, Fed. Bar Coun. and Found. nominating com. 1998), N.Y. State Bar Assn. (mem. com. on children and law 1993-97, com. legal edn. and admission 1994—), N.Y. Women's Bar Assn. (v.p. 1987-88, 92-93, bd. dirs. 1998-91, Pres.'s Spl award 2002, Spl. Recognition award 1996), Greater Boy Scouts Coun. N.Y. (William Schoenfeld award 1999), Soc. Adolescent Psychiatry (William Schoenfeld award 1999), Jud. Conf. State N.Y. (atty. 2000-2002), Downtown Bklyn. Coun. (mem. exec. com. 2000-), State N.Y. Office of Ct. Adminstrn. (commn. on alcohol and substance abuse in profession 1999-), Practicing Law Inst. (mem. com. on programs and pubs. 1998, alt. mem., exec. com. 2001-), Fund Moderate Cts. (mem. bd. dirs., task force ct. facilities 2001), Downtown Bklyn. Devel. Assn., Assn. Bar City N.Y. Fund Inc. (v.p. 1996-97, mem. nominating com. 92-93, 1999, chair com. on honors 1997-2000, mem. com. on honors 1994-97, com. matrimonial law 1985-89, 92-95, long range planning com. 1992-95, com. on family ct. and family law, 1989-92, ad hoc com. on AIDS 1987-88, ad hoc com. surrogate parenting 1986-88), Pres.'s Coun. of Cornell Women (com. on univ. rels. 2001-), Com. to Restore Thurgood Marshall Landmark Courthouse, Bklyn. Legal Svs. Corp. A (mem adv. com. 1994-), Cornell U. (mem. Cornell Coun. 2002-, pres.'s coun. Cornell Women 1995-, mem. com. on u. rels. 2001), Second Cir. Task Force on Gender, Racial and Ethnic Fairness in Cts., N.Y. State Supreme Ct.(adv. com. 18-B family ct. panel, appellate divsn. first dept.), Jud. Conf. Second Cir. (planning and programming com. 1999-2002), Am. Assn. Law Schs. Workshop on Family and Juvenile Law, Downtown Bklyn. Coun. Exec. Com.; trustee Practising Law Inst. (mem. com. on programs and pubs., 1998-, alt. mem. exec. com., 2001-). Home: 1045 Nine Acres Ln Mamaroneck NY 10543-4706 Office: Bklyn Law Sch 250 Joralemon St Brooklyn NY 11201-3700 Business E-Mail: joan.wexler@brooklaw.edu.

WEXLER, LEONARD HOWARD, pediatric oncologist; b. Bklyn., Nov. 21, 1961; s. Theodore and Florence Wexler; m. Beth Sue Brown, Sept. 1999. BA, Boston U.; MD, Boston U. Sch. Medicine, 1985. Cert. Pediatrics, Pediatric Hematology-Oncology. Intern, pediatrics Albert Einstein/Montefiore, Bronx, NY, 1985—88, resident, pediatrics, 1985—88; fellow, pediatric hematology and oncology NIH-Nat. Cancer Inst., Bethesda, Md., 1988—92, sr. clin. investigator, pediatric branch, 1992—96; dir. clin. services Babies & Children's Hosp., NYC, 1996—99; assoc. mem. dept. pediatrics Meml. Sloan-Kettering Cancer Ctr., NY, 1999—; asst. prof. pediatrics Uniformed Services Univ. of the Health Sciences; assoc. prof. pediatrics, divsn. pediatric oncology Columbia U., NY, 1996—99; assoc. prof. pediatrics Weill Med. Coll.-Cornell U., NY, 1999. Co-chair of internat. study to evaluate the effectiveness of chemotherapy for the treatment of children with osteosarcoma; co-investigator clin. trial that evaluates a novel combination of chemotherapy agents & radiotherapy techniques for the treatment of children with rhabdomyosarcoma, Meml. Sloan-Kettering. Med. editl. adv. bd. Libby Shriver Sarcoma Initiative. Named one of Medical Marvels, New York Mag., 2006. Office: Dept Pediatrics #210 Meml Sloan Kettering Cancer Ctr 1275 York Ave New York NY 10021 Office Phone: 212-639-7990. Business E-Mail: wexlerl@mskcc.org. *

WEXLER, PATRICIA SUSAN, dermatologist, surgeon; b. 1951; MD, U. Libre de Bruxelles, Belgium, 1979. Diplomate Am. Bd. Internal Medicine 1983, Am. Bd. Dermatology 1986. Intern Beth Israel Med. Ctr., N.Y.C., 1979—80, resident in internal medicine, 1980—82, fellow in infectious disease, 1982—83, attending physician, Mt. Sinai Hosp., N.Y.C.; private practice Wexler Dermatology, N.Y.C. Assoc. clin. prof. dept. dermatology Mt. Sinai Med. Ctr., N.Y.C.; cons. in devel. of several skin care and make-up lines. Author medical rsch. publs. Recipient Am. Acad. Cosmetic Surgery award for Excellence in Cosmetic Surgery. Fellow: Am. Soc. Dermatologic Surgery. Office: 145 E 32nd St 7th Fl New York NY 10016-6055 Office Phone: 212-684-2626. E-mail: crespi666@aol.com.

WEXLER, PETER JOHN, artist, photographer, theatre designer, producer, director; b. NYC, 1936; s. S. David and Berda (Sarnoff) W.; m. Constance Ann Ross, Nov. 30, 1962. BS in Design, U. Mich., 1958; student, Yale Sch. Drama, 1958. Designs include White House stage, 1961, War and Peace, 1964, The White Devil, 1965, A Joyful Noise, 1966, The Happy Time, 1967, In the Matter of J. Robert Oppenheimer, 1968, Merv Griffin TV show, 1965, Terra Nova, 1979 (L.A. Dramalogue Critics award); prin. designer, Mark Taper Forum, Ctr. Theatre Group, L.A., 1967-70, designer, N.Y. Philharm. Promenades, 1965-78; play and film The Trial of the Catonsville 9, 1971-72; Leonard Bernstein's Mass, L.A., 1973, N.Y. Philharm. Rug Concerts, 1973-77, Les Troyens, Met. Opera Co., 1973, Le Prophète, Met. Opera Co., 1977, Un Ballo in Maschera, Met. Opera Co., 1980, Theatre Space, Prodns., Pitts. Pub. Theatre, 1975-81; mem. design team for Frank O. Gehry & Assocs., redesign Hollywood Bowl; designer: Albert Herring, Savonlinna Opera Festival, Finland, 1981; centennial prodn. Les Troyens, Met. Opera, 1983; directed: Cold Storage, Ariz. Theatre Co., 1978, Terra Nova, Pitts. Public Theatre, 1981; producer, Dallas Symphony Orch.'s Star Fest 80; producer Rocky Mountain Music Festival, Denver Symphony Orch., 1983-84, Star Spangled Banner, Permanent Exhbn. U.S. Nat. Emblem, Smithsonian Instn., Washington, 1982; prodr., design exhbn. Am. Anthem, LTV Ctr., Dallas/Smithsonian Instn., 1985; designer, broker exhbn. Liberties with Liberty, Trammell Crow Co./Mus. Am. Folk Art, 1985; designer Horizons '86, N.Y. Philharm., 1986; co-prodr., designer video, exhbn. and space Albany Urban Cultural Park, Albany, N.Y., 1986; prodr., dir. Pletka, multimedia theatre piece for orch., Dallas Symphony Orch., 1987; programmer, interior designer Trans-Hudson Ferry for the Port Authority of N.Y. and N.J., 1987-88; prodr. The Search for Life, Smithsonian Inst., 1987; prodr. Mstislav Rostropovich 60th Anniv. Gala Concert, Nat. Symphony Orch., Kennedy Ctr., Washington, 1987, Navy 87, Navy 89, USN multi-media orchestral prodn., Washington, 1987; founder, prodr., artistic dir. Spring Creek Music Festival, Garland, Tex. Dallas Ft. Worth Metroplex, 1992-94; dir. Lost in the Stars, A.C.O., Carnegie Hall, 1989; visual cons. Lifetime Med. (cable TV), 1989-90; design cons. Reebok River Stage - Radio City Music Hall Prodns, 1989; program designer Mega-Mall, Oxford Devel. Co., Pitts., 1990; designer Unfinished Stories, 1994; prodr. A Salute to Slava, Kennedy Ctr., Washington, 1994; cons. (TV project) Music in America Nat. Symphony Orch., Kennedy Ctr., Washington, 1997; creator Boston Pops Environment, 1995-97; cons. Boston Symphony Hall Sys. Update Plan, 1995-98; design cons. ABC News-Good Morning Am., 20/20, World News Tonight, 1997-98; cons., devel. new material Nextstage Entertainment Corp., 1999-2000; cons. concert environment, hall update and lighting, Midland Ctr. Arts, 2001-02; author, designer, photographer "The Remarkable Adventures of Texas and Bubba in Venice", 2003; designer scenery and projections The Talking Cure, Mark Taper Forum, 2004; con. design tent graphics, Big Apple Circus, 2005; one-man exhbn. Chgo. Cultural Ctr., US Equities; author, photographer (book) Reflections-Riflessioni, 2007. Project leader, design, planning, Outdoor Performance Facility, Met. Opera Co., N.Y. Philharm. Orch., Dept. Cultural Affairs City of N.Y., 1980-2004; cons. Temp. Quarters Project San Francisco Ballet, 1994. Recipient Internat. Theatre Inst. competition award ANTA, 1965, most imaginative use of scene design award Saturday Rev., 1965, Drama Desk-Joseph

Maharam award for The Happy Time as best designer of mus., 1968, L.A. Drama Critics Circle award, 1971, Bard award for Excellence in Architecture & Urban Design, 1996. Address: 277 W End Ave New York NY 10023-2604 Office Phone: 212-877-9494. Business E-Mail: peterwexler@mindspring.com.

WEXLER, ROBERT, academic administrator; m. Hannah Wexler. BA summa cum laude, UCLA, MA, PhD, UCLA; MBA, Baruch Coll. Ordained rabbi Jewish Theol. Seminary. Lectr. Near Eastern Studies Princeton U.; prof. U. Judaism, LA, 1978—, Colen Disting. Lectr. in Bible, pres., 1992—. Named one of The Top 50 Rabbis in America, Newsweek Mag., 2007. Mem.: Israel Democracy Inst. (exec. com. bd. mem.), World Coun.of Synagogues (exec. com. mem.), Am. Jewish Com. (exec. com. mem.). Office: U Judaism 15600 Mulholland Dr Los Angeles CA 90077-1599 E-mail: rwexler@uj.edu. *

WEXLER, ROBERT, congressman; b. Queens, Jan. 2, 1961; m. Laurie Wexler; children: Rachel, Zachary, Hannah. BA in Polit. Scis., U. Fla., 1982; JD, George Washington U. Law Sch., 1985. Mem. Fla. State Senate, 1990-96, U.S. Congress from 19th Fla. dist., 1997—; mem. internat. rels. com., judiciary com. Recipient Senatorial Leadership award Fla. Prosecutor's Assn.; named Legis. of the Year Palm Beach Police Benevolent Assn., Top Environ. Senator Fla. Leagues Conservation Voters, 1996. Democrat. Office: Ho Rep 213 Cannon Ho Office Bldg Washington DC 20515-0919 *

WEXLER, SANDRA M., artist, medical illustrator; b. NYC, Dec. 17, 1945; d. Irving and Sophie Engel; children: Jason, David. AA, Fashion Inst. Tech., 1965. Cert. medical asst. Balt., 1996. CMA Johns Hopkins Hosp., Lutherville, Md., 1996—97; CMA, clin. coord. Drs. Stanley Klatsky & Adam Basner, Balt., 1997—2000; CMA Dr. Eve Bruce, Lutherville, 2001—03, Dr. Seth Goldberg, Rockville, Md., 2004—06, Dr. Maria Lundquist, Rockville, 2006—. Exhibitions include Am. Inst. Architects Gallery, Sch. 33, Katzenstein Gallery, Slayton House Gallery, Women's Resource Ctr, Greater Balt. Med. Ctr., Gormley Gallery, Coll. Notre Dame, one-woman shows include Shainberg Gallery, Gallerie Elan, 2005, Represented in permanent collections The Art Resource, Balt., limited edit. greeting cards, Balt. Mus. Art Shop, corporate collections, Bloomingdales, NYC, Hyatt Regency, Balt., The Hammers Co., Greenbelt, Md., Wharton, Levin, Ehrmantraut, Klein & Nash, Bethesda, Md., Edward Friedman, CPA, Balt., Signature Mgmt., Balt., Levindale Hebrew Geriatric Ctr. & Hosp., Balt., Ampersand Inc., Reiserstown, Md., Penan & Scott, P.A., Rockville, Md., Martin, Junghans, Snyder & Bernstein, Balt., TCAG, Rockville, Potts & Potts, P.A., Balt., Royal Ins. Co., Balt., Cooper Wingard, Balt., Wiley, Rein & Fielding LLC, DC, Art Forms Gallery, Red Bank, NJ, A. Lee Dellon, MD, Balt., Arles Mgmt., Inc., NY, Gallerie Elan, Bethesda, Ellicott City, Md., Maslow Media Group, Inc. Vol. surg. holding area Sinai Hosp., Balt., 1993—2000. Fellow, Vt. Studio Colony, 1990. Jewish. Avocations: art, reading, travel, cooking, photography.

WEXNER, ABIGAIL, apparel executive; m. Leslie H. Wexner. Dir. Ltd. Brands, Inc., Columbus, Ohio, 1997—. Past chair governing com. Columbus Found.; chair Ctr. for Child and Family Advocacy; mem. bd. trustees Children's Hosp., Inc, The Columbus Acad., The Wexner Ctr. Found.; founder, chair Columbus Coalition Against Family Violence. Named one of Top 200 Collectors, ARTnews Mag., 2004. Avocation: Collector of Modern and Contemporary Art; British Sporting Pictures. Office: Ltd Brands Inc Three Limited Pky PO Box 16000 Columbus OH 43216

WEXNER, LESLIE HERBERT, retail executive; b. Dayton, Ohio, 1937; m. Abigail Wexner; 4 children. BSBA, Ohio State U., 1959, HHD (hon.), 1986; LLD (hon.), Hofstra U., 1987; LHD (hon.), Brandeis U., 1990; PhD (hon.), Jewish Theol. Sem. Founder, pres., chmn. bd. The Limited, Inc., fashion chain, Columbus, 1963—. Dir., mem. exec. com. Banc One Corp., Sotheby's Holdings Inc., vis. com. Grad. Sch. Design Harvard U.; mem. bus. adminstrn. adv. coun. Ohio State U.; chmn. Retail Industry Trade Action Coalition. Bd. dirs. Columbus Urban League, 1982-84, Hebrew Immigrant Aid Soc., NYC, 1982—; co-chmn. Internat. United Jewish Appeal Com.; nat. vice chmn., treas. United Jewish Appeal; bd. dirs., mem. exec. com. Am. Jewish Joint Distbn. Com., Inc.; trustee Columbus Jewish Fedn., 1972, Columbus Jewish Found., Aspen Inst., Ohio State U., Columbus Capital Corp. for Civic Improvement; former trustee Columbus Mus. Art, Columbus Symphony Orch., Whitney Mus. Am. Art, Capitol South Community Urban Redevel. Corp.; former mem. Governing Com. Columbus Found.; founding mem., first chair The Ohio State U. Found; exec. com. Am. Israel Pub. Affairs Com. Decorated cavaliere Republic of Italy; named Man of Yr., Am. Mktg. Assn., 1974; named one of Top 200 Collectors, ARTnews Mag., 2004, Forbes' Richest Americans, 1999—, Forbes' Exec. Pay, 1999—, World's Richest People, Forbes mag., 2001—. Mem. Young Presidents Orgn., Sigma Alpha Mu. Clubs: B'nai B'rith; fellow Am. Acad. Arts & Sciences Jewish. Avocation: Collector of Modern and Contemporary Art; British Sporting Pictures. Office: Limited Inc PO Box 16000 3 Limited Pkwy Columbus OH 43230-1450 *

WEYAND, CORNELIA MARITTA, medical educator; Prof., medicine and immunology Mayo Med. and Grad. Sch., Rochester, Minn., 1990—2003; prof., medicine Emory U., Atlanta, 2004—. Office: Emory Univ 101 Woodruff Cir #1003 Atlanta GA 30322 Office Phone: 404-727-7310.

WEYANDT, DANIEL SCOTT, retired naval officer, engineer, physicist; b. Altoona, Pa., Dec. 26, 1962; s. Blair Sherwood and Madolyn Rae (Dunmire) W.; m. Laura Anne Weatherington, Oct. 27, 2001; 1 child: Jacqueline Kateri; 2 children from previous marriage: Alexander James Collins, Jeremy Auden Collins. BS, Juniata Coll., Huntingdon, Pa., 1984; MS in Physics, Pa. State U., 1992; MBA, U. R.I., 1995. Commd. USN, 1984, advanced through grades to lt. comdr., 1996; divsn. officer USS John C. Calhoun, Charleston, SC, 1987, USS Simon Bolivar, Charleston, 1986-89; rsch. officer Naval Undersea Warfare Ctr. Divsn., Newport, RI, 1992-95; sr. engr., countermeasures mgr. Electronic Sensors and Sys. divsn. Northrop Grumman Corp., Balt., 1995-99; fellow engr., leading engr. torpedo def. oceanic and naval sys. divsn. Northrop Grumman Electronic Sys., Annapolis, Md., 1999—2005; res. duty, tng. officer, adminstrv. officer COMSUBRON 8 Det 1106, 1995-98; asst. dep. comdr. COMSUBRON 8, 1995-98; ops. specialist, tng. officer COMSUBEASTLANT DET 1005, 1998—2003; tng. officer Battle Group ASW specialist COMSUBLANT BGO DET 506, 2003—04, ret.; adv. engr. Northrop Grumman Electronic Sys., Linthicum, Md., 2005—. Decorated Navy achievement medal (2), Navy commendation medal (2). Mem. Am. Soc. Naval Engrs., Am. Phys. Soc., Altoona Horseshoe Chorus (assoc. dir. 1978—), Chorus of the Chesapeake, Sigma Pi Sigma. Republican. Roman Catholic. Avocations: music, water sports, exercise. Office: Northrop Grumman Corp PO Box 1693 Baltimore MD 21203-1693 Home Phone: 814-932-4833; Office Phone: 410-765-1162. E-mail: daniel.weyandt@ngc.com.

WEYERHAEUSER, GEORGE H., JR., paper manufacturing company executive; b. w; B in Philosophy/Maths., Yale U., 1976; MS, MIT, 1986. Tech. forester, contract logger adminstr., sawmill supr. Weyerhaeuser Co., Dierks, Ark., 1978-80, v.p., mill mgr. Containerboard Valliant, Okla., 1981-90, v.p. mfg. pulp & paper bus. Federal Way, 1990-93, pres., CEO Can. divsn., 1993-98, sr. v.p. technology, 1998—. Office: Weyerhaeuser Co 33663 Weyerhaeuser Way S PO Box 9777 Federal Way WA 98063-9777

WEYERS, LARRY LEE, energy executive; b. Nebr. BA, Doane Coll., 1967; MS, Columbia U., 1971; MBA, Harvard U., 1975. Registered profl. engr. With Babcock & Wilcox, 1971—73, Commonwealth Edison, 1975—84; mgmt. cons. Towers Perrin, 1984—85; dir. fuel svc. WPS Resources Corp., Green Bay, 1985—89, asst. v.p. energy supply, 1989—92, v.p. energy supply, 1992—94, v.p. power supply & engring., 1994—95, sr. v.p. power supply & engring., 1995, pres., COO, 1995—97, bd. dir., 1996—, pres., CEO, 1997, chmn., pres., CEO, 1998—2007; pres., CEO Integrys Energy Group (merger of WPS Resources & Peoples Energy), 2007—. Bd. dir. WS Packaging Corp., Wis. Pub. Svc. Corp., 1996—; bd. mem. Edison Elec. Inst., Am. Gas Assn., 2004, Assn. Edison Illuminating Cos., 2003. Bd. mem. Bellin Health, Green Bay Packers, Wis. Manufacturers & Comm., Competitive Wis., UTECH Ventures, Utility Bus. Edn. Coalition. Office: Integrys Energy Group PO Box 19001 Green Bay WI 54307-9001 *

WEYHRAUCH, BRUCE BUTLER, lawyer, former state legislator; b. Sacramento, Calif., Feb. 14, 1953; s. William Roger and Martha Janet (Crabbe) W.; m. LuAnn Elaine Bailey, June 30, 1990; Benjamin Butler, Maria and Barclay. BS in Natural Resource Planning, Calif. State U., 1979; JD, Lewis and Clark Coll., 1986. Bar: Alaska 1987, D.C. 1988, U.S. Ct. Appeals (9th cir.) 1988, U.S. Supreme Ct. 1990. Heavy equipment operator Burlington No. Railroad, Lincoln, Nebr., 1972-74; aquaculture technician Sheldon Jackson Coll, Sitka, Alaska, 1974-76; builder McGraw Constrn., Sitka, 1976-78; comml. fisherman Angoon, Alaska, 1978-79; environ. and econ. cons. Centaur Assocs., Washington, 1979-81; legis. aide State of Alaska Legis., Juneau, 1982; law clk. to Justice Pegues Superior Ct., Juneau, 1987-88; atty. Faulkner Banfield Doogan & Holmes, Juneau, 1989; mem. Alaska Ho. of Reps, 2003—06; atty. Law Offices of Bruce B. Weyhrauch LLC, Juneau, Alaska. Contbr. articles to profl. jours. Bd. dirs. AWARE Women's Shelter, Juneau, 1988-90, Big Bros./Big Sisters, Juneau, 1988-89; Juneau Econ. Devel. Coun., 1992; Juneau Port Authority Com., 1995. Recipient Sole Practitioner of Yr. award, ABA. Mem. (Juneau Bar Assn. (treas. 1988-89, sec. 1989-90, v.p. 1990-91, pres. 1994, 1996), Alaska State Bar Assn. (bd. govs. 2000-01), Alaska Comml. Fisherman's Meml., Juneau; Rotary. Republican. Avocations: classic films, camping, fishing, sports. Office: Law Office of Bruce Weyhrauch Ste 200 114 S Franklin St Juneau AK 99801 Office Phone: 907-463-5566. Office Fax: 907-463-5858. E-mail: whyrock@gci.net.

WEYMAN, JERZY MARIA, mathematics professor; b. Torun, Poland, Apr. 29, 1955; s. Andrzej and Elzbieta Weyman; m. Katarzyna Maria Paprocka; children: Andrzej Maria, Zuzanna Maria, Klementyna Maria, Elzbieta Maria. PhD, Brandeis U., Waltham, Mass., 1980. Asst. prof. Polish Acad. Sci., Torun, 1977—85, Northeastern U., Boston, 1985—90, assoc. prof., 1990—95, prof., 1995—. Author: (book) Cohomology of Vector Bundles and Syzygies. Recipient Kuratowski prize, Polish Math. Soc., 1983. Office: Northeastern Univ 360 Huntington Ave Boston MA 02115 Business E-Mail: j.weyman@neu.edu.

WEYMAN, STEVEN ALOYSIUS, retired military officer; b. Fort Thomas, Ky., May 31, 1957; s. Edward Joseph Weyman and Carol Jean (Steffen) Jackson; m. Kathleen Anne Bradford, June 2, 1990; 1 child, Jennifer Elizabeth. BS in Math., No. Ky. U., 1978; MS in Comm. Sys. Tech., Naval Postgrad. Sch., 1988. Commd. 2d lt. U.S. Army, 1978, advanced through grades to lt. col., 1995; bn. signal officer 8th Engr. Bn., 1st Cav. Divsn., Ft. Hood, Tex., 1979-81, 2nd M.I. Bn., Pirmasens, Germany, 1982-85; co. comdr. B Co., 307th M.I. Bn., Ludwigsburg, Germany, 1985-86; signal combat devel. project officer Combined Arms Command, Ft. Leavenworth, Kans., 1988-91; student U.S. Army Command Gen. Staff Coll., Ft. Leavenworth, 1991-92; bn. exec. officer 123rd Signal Bn., 3rd Inf. Divsn., Kitzingen, Germany, 1992-94; asst. divsn. signal officer 3rd Inf. Divsn., Wuerzburg, Germany, 1994-95; operational readiness evaluation team chief 5th U.S. Army (West), Ft. Lewis, Wash., 1995-97; def. info. sys. network deployed program mgmt. chief Def. Info. Sys. Agy., Arlington, Va., 1997-2000, ret., 2000; student Armed Forces Staff Coll., Norfolk, Va., 1998; tech. acct. mgr. Intel Online Svcs., 2000—01; teleport installation program mgr., prin. engr. Arrowhead Global Solutions Inc., 2001—03; project leader, network sys. lead engr. Mitre Corp., 2003—. Decorated Legion of Merit. Mem. U.S. Signal Corps Assn. (Bronze Order of Mercury 1995), Armed Forces Comm. Electronics Assn. Avocations: computers, travel, reading, sports. E-mail: steve@weyman.net, sweyman@mitre.org.

WEYMAN, TODD D., art appraiser; BA, Conn. Coll.; MA in Art Hist., Williams Coll. Curatorial asst. British Arts Ctr., Yale Univ., New Haven; head, acquisitions Johnson Art Mus., Cornell Univ., Ithaca, NY; now v.p., dir., print, drawings dept. Swann Gallery, NYC. Appraiser Antiques Roadshow, WGBH-PBS, 1997—. Office: Swann Galleries 104 E 25th St New York NY 10010 Office Phone: 212-254-4710 Ext. 32. Office Fax: 212-979-1017. Business E-Mail: tweyman@swanngalleries.com.

WEYMOUTH, ELIZABETH (LALLY) GRAHAM, editor, columnist; children: Katharine, Pamela Bass. BA in Am. History and Lit. with honors, Harvard U. Reporter The Boston Globe, 1965—66, freelance writer, reporter, 1966—76; with Bedford Stuyvesant Restoration Corp. Senator Robert Kennedy, 1968—69; freelance journalist, contbg. editor numerous publs. including NY Times Mag., Esquire, Atlantic Monthly, Parade, LA Times, New York, 1977—83; contbg. editor LA Times, 1983—86, Washington Post, 1987—92; sr. editor, spl. diplomatic corr. Newsweek Mag., 1992—. Interviewer Washington Post, 1986—; mem. Coun. Fgn. Rels. Author: America in 1876: The Way We Were, 1976; editor, compiler Thomas Jefferson: The Man, His World, His Influence, 1973. Mem. Coun. Foreign Relations; mem. adv. com. Ctr. Strategic and Internat. Studies.

WEYMOUTH, ELIZABETH K., bank executive; b. New Orleans, 1968; d. Henry Carter and Karen M. Kirk; m. Philip Blackburn Weymouth, Apr. 19, 1997; 3 children. BA, MBA, U. Va. Global investment specialist J.P. Morgan Pvt. Bank, NYC. Named one of 40 Under 40, Crain's NY Bus., 2007. Office: JP Morgan Chase & Co 270 Park Ave New York NY 10017-2070 Office Phone: 212-270-6000. *

WEYRAUCH, WALTER OTTO, law educator; b. Lindau, Germany, Aug. 27, 1919; came to U.S., 1952; s. Hans Ernst Winand and Meta Margarete (Lönholdt) W.; m. Jill Carolyn White, Mar. 17, 1973; children from previous marriages: Kurt Roman (dec.), Corinne Harriet Irene, Bettina Elaine (dec.). Student, U. Freiburg, 1937, U. Frankfurt Main, Germany, 1940-43, Dr. iur, 1951; LL.B., Georgetown U., 1955; LL.M., Harvard, 1956; J.S.D., Yale, 1962; Golden Dr. diploma (hon.), U. Frankfurt Main, 2001. Referendar, Frankfurt, Germany, 1943-48; atty. German cts. U.S. Ct. Appeals, Allied High Commn., Frankfurt, 1949-52; expert on trade regulations, visit in U.S. under auspices Dept. State, 1950; Harvard U. Dumbarton Oaks Library and Collection, Washington, 1953-55; asst. in instrn. Law Sch., Yale, 1956-57; assoc. prof. law U. Fla., Gainesville, 1957-60, prof., 1960-89, Clarence J. TeSelle prof. law, 1989-94, Stephen C. O'Connell chair, 1994—, disting. prof. law, 1998—; hon. prof. law Johann Wolfgang Goethe U., Frankfurt Main, 1980—. Vis. cons. U. Calif. Space Scis. Lab., Berkeley, 1965-66; vis. prof. law Rutgers U., 1968; vis. prof. polit. sci. U. Calif., Berkeley, 1968-69; vis. prof. law U. Frankfurt, 1975; cons. Commn. of Experts on Problems of Succession of the Hague Conf. on Pvt. Internat. Law, U.S. Dept. State, 1968-71; Rockefeller Found. fellow, Europe, 1958-59; Weyrauch disting. ann. lectr. in family law U. Fla., Gainesville, 2006—; lectr. in field. Author: The Personality of Lawyers, 1964, Zum Gesellschaftsbild des Juristen, 1970, Hierarchie der Ausbildungsstätten, Rechtsstudium und Recht in den Vereinigten Staaten, 1976, Gestapo V-Leute: Tatsachen und Theorie des Geheimdienstes, 1989, 2d edit., 1992; author: (with Sanford N. Katz) American Family Law in Transition, 1983; author: (with Katz and Frances E. Olsen) Cases and Materials on Family Law: Legal Concepts and Changing Human Relationships, 1994; author: Das Recht der Roma und Sinti: Ein Beispiel autonomer Rechtsschöpfung, 2002; author, editor: Gypsy Law: Romani Legal Traditions and Culture, 2001; contbr. chapters to books. Mem. Law and Soc. Assn., Internat. Soc. on Family Law, Assn. Am. Law Schs. (chmn. com. studies beyond 1st degree in law 1965-67), Order of Coif. Home: 2713 SW 5th Pl Gainesville FL 32607-3113 Office: U Fla Coll Law Gainesville FL 32611 Office Phone: 352-273-0662. Business E-Mail: weyrauch@law.ufl.edu.

WEYRICH, PAUL MICHAEL, think-tank executive; b. Racine, Wis., Oct. 7, 1942; s. Ignatius A. and Virginia M. (Wickstrom) W.; m. Joyce Anne Smigun, July 6, 1963; children: Dawn, Peter, Diana, Stephen, Andrew. AA, U. Wis., 1962. Ordained deacon Melkite Greek Eparchy, 1990. News dir., announcer, program dir. WLIP, WAXO-FM, Kenosha, Wis., 1960-63; reporter Milw. Sentinel, 1963-64; polit. reporter, newscaster CBS, Milw., 1964-65; news dir. Sta. KQXI, Denver, 1966; press sec. to Sen. Gordon Allott US Senate, Washington, 1967-73, spl. asst. to Sen. Carl T. Curtis, 1973-77; founder, pres. Heritage Found., 1973-74; nat. chmn. Free Congress PAC, Coalitions for Am., 1987—, BOD, Amtrak, 1987-93; pres. Free Congress Rsch. & Ednl. Found., 1977—2002, chmn., CEO, 2002—; pres. Krieble Inst., 1989—96. Nat. editor Transport Central, 1968-71; treas. Coun. Nat. Policy, 1981-92, pres. America's Voice, 1991-97; bd. dirs. All News Radio WEEI, Boston, 1984-90, Krieble Inst. Russia; nat. chmn. Com. for Effective State Govt.; chmn. bd. Yorktownuniversity.com, 1999—. Author: The Role of Rails series, 1964; pub. Polit. Report, 1975-89, The New Electric Rwy. Jour., 1988-96, Spotlight on Congress, 1989-93; host (daily talk show) Direct Line, 1993-98; co-host The New Electric Rwy. Jour., 1994-96, Ways & Means, 1994—. Recipient Youth of Yr. award Racine Optimist Club, 1960, Excellence in Reporting citation Milw. Common Council, 1964, Documentary of Yr. award for Wis. TV, 1965, Crystal Ball award for predicting outcome 1996 presdl. election Washington Post, 1996, Thomas Jefferson award for servant leadership Coun. Nat. Policy, 1997. Mem. Ctrl. Electric Railroaders Assn., Internat. Policy Forum (chmn. 1983-84); former mem. HUD Adv. Commn. on Regulatory Barriers to Affordable Housing. Greek Catholic. Home: 12615 Lake Normandy Ln Fairfax VA 22030-7262 Office: Free Congress Found 717 2nd St NE Washington DC 20002-4368 Office Phone: 703-815-1086. Business E-Mail: paulwey@freecongress.org.

WHALE, ARTHUR RICHARD, retired lawyer; b. Detroit, Oct. 28, 1923; s. Arthur B. and Orpha Louella (Doak) W.; m. Roberta Lou Donaldson, Oct. 29, 1949; children: Richard Donaldson, Linda Jean. BSChemE, Northwestern U., 1945; LLB, George Washington U., 1956. Bar: D.C. 1957, Mich. 1957, Ind. 1977, U.S. Patent and Trademark Office 1957. Chem. engr. Ansul Chem. Co., Marinette, Wis., 1946-47, Parke, Davis & Co., Detroit, 1947-50, writer med. lit., 1950-52; chem. engr. Bur. Ships, U.S. Dept. Navy, Washington, 1952-55, dep. sect. head, indsl. gas sect., 1954-55; patent engr. Swift & Co., Washington, 1955-56; patent atty. Upjohn Co., Kalamazoo, 1956-65; asst. mgr. organic chems. sect. patent dept. Dow Chem. Co., Midland, Mich., 1965-66, mgr., 1967-73, mng. counsel, 1973-75; asst. sec., gen. patent counsel Eli Lilly & Co., Indpls., 1975-86; of counsel Miller, Morriss, & Pappas, Lansing, Mich., 1986-89, Baker & Daniels, Indpls., 1987—2003; ret., 2003. Bd. dirs. Wyckoff Chem. Co., South Haven, Mich., 1985-99; lectr. Practicing Law Inst., John Marshall Law Sch. Contbr. articles to profl. jours. Pres. Nat. Inventors Hall of Fame Found., 1978-79; bd. dirs. Holcomb Rsch. Inst., Indpls., 1982-86. Served to lt. (j.g.) USNR, 1943-46. Mem. State Bar Mich. (chmn. patent trademark copyright sect. 1967-69), D.C. Bar Assn., Midland County Bar Assn. (pres. 1974-75), Am. Bar Assn, (mem. patent trademark copyright sect.), Assn. Corp. Patent Counsel, Nat. Coun. Patent Law Assns. (chmn. 1979-80), Am. Intellectual Property Law Assn. (pres. 1974-75), Ashlar Lodge, Masons, Shriners. Republican. Presbyterian. Avocation: golf. Office: Baker & Daniels Ste 2700 300 N Meridian St Indianapolis IN 46204-1782 Office Phone: 239-262-8561. Business E-Mail: arwhale@bakerd.com.

WHALEN, CHARLES WILLIAM, JR., writer, retail executive, congressman, educator; b. Dayton, Ohio, July 31, 1920; s. Charles William and Colette (Kelleher) W.; m. Mary Barbara Gleason, Dec. 27, 1958; children— Charles E., Daniel D., Edward J., Joseph M., Anne E., Mary B. BS, U. Dayton, 1942, HHD (hon.), 1980; MBA, Harvard U., 1946; postgrad., Ohio State U., 1959-60; LLD, Central State U., Ohio, 1966. Vice pres. Dayton Dress Co., 1946-52; faculty U. Dayton, 1952-66; mem. 90th-95th Congresses 3d Dist. Ohio; pres. New Directions, Washington, 1978-79; fellow Woodrow Wilson Internat. Center for Scholars, 1980; adj. prof. Sch. Internat. Service, Am. U., 1981. Mem. Ohio Ho. of Reps., 1954-60, Ohio Senate, 1960-66; mem. Internat. Vol. Svcs., Inc., 1985-95; v.p. Washington Inst. Fgn. Affairs, 1982-98; mem. U. Dayton adv. bd. Ctr. for Internat. Studies, 1990-96; bd. dirs. Harvard Bus. Sch., Washington, 1982-84, 91-94. 1st lt. AUS, 1943-46. Recipient Disting. Alumnus award U. Dayton Alumni Assn., 1975, Alumni Lifetime Achievement award U. Dayton Sch. Bus. Adminstrn., 2001. Mem.: Dayton Bicycle Club, Kenwood Country Club, Capitol Hill Club. Roman Catholic.

WHALEN, JOHN PHILIP, retired academic administrator, priest, lawyer; b. Troy, NY, Jan. 4, 1928; s. Philip Joseph and Mary Catherine (Doyle) W. BA summa cum laude, St. Mary's Sem. and Univ., Balt., 1949; STL, Cath. U., 1953, MA, 1954, STD summa cum laude, 1965; JD, George Washington U., 1976; postgrad., Johns Hopkins U., 1959-60, U. Md., College Park, 1958-59, Fordham U., 1953-54; LHD (hon.), Marymount U., 1987. Ordained priest Roman Cath. Ch., 1953. Instr. Mater Christi Sem., Albany, 1953-58; asst. prof. Mt. St. Mary's Coll., Emmitsburg, Md., 1959-61; assoc. prof. Cath. U. Am., Washington, 1961-67, acting pres., 1968-69; pastor St. Mary's Ch., Oneonta, NY, 1970-72; pres. Consortium of Univs. of Washington area, 1972-88; mng. editor New Cath. Ency., 1963-67; pres., editor-in-chief Corpus Publs., 1967-94, ret., 1994. Cons. 12 colls. and univs.; founder, chmn. Univ. Support Svcs., Inc., 1986—94, pres., CEO, founder; cons. student loans, capital access trust, capital loans to colls., 1999—2000; founder, prin. Power Systems, Inc.; founder prin. Full Measure, LLC, Whalen Holdings, LLC, JMJ Whalen Found., Inc., Vinegar Hill Assoc. LLC, 2005; founder, pres., dir. Mons Concept Found., Inc., 2007. Mem. editl. bd. Law and Edn.; weekly columnist Evangelist, Albany; contbr. to Nat. Geog. mag.; contbr. articles to ednl. and theol. jours. Pres. Univ. Ext. Ednl. Corp., 1974—94; mem. Fed. City Coun., 1982—, Coun. for Ct. Excellence, 1984—90; bd. dirs. Sta. WETA-TV, 1968—69, Washington Ctr. for Met. Studies, 1968—69, Cath. U. Am., 1968—69, Nat. Shrine of Immaculate Conception, 1968—69, Dumbarton Coll., 1970—72, Trinity Coll., 1969—72, St. Mary's Coll., South Bend, Ind., 1970—74, St. Anselm's, 1979—85, Mt. Vernon Coll., 1982—84, CBR Found., 2001—, Met. Bd. Trade, Washington, 1975—90, sec. bd. dirs., 1983—85; bd. dirs. US Fund for Improvement Postsecondary Edn., 1988—91. Named Man of the Yr., 1984; recipient Disting. Alumnus award George Washington U., 1988. Mem. Nat. Cath. Edn. Assn., Cath. Theol. Soc. Am. (dir. 1966-68), Fulbright Edn. Group Washington (pres. 1974-75), Tired Hands Club (pres. 1982-84), Cosmos Club (Washington), City Club, Rotary. Home and Office: 1614 Parham Rd Silver Spring MD 20903-2256 Personal E-mail: johnpwhalen@comcast.net.

WHALEN, JOHN SYDNEY, management consultant; b. Moncton, NB, Can., Sept. 26, 1934; s. Harry Edward and Sarah Maude (Bourgeois) W.; m. Margaret Joan Carruthers, May 3, 1958; children: Bradley Graham, Elizabeth Ann. Grad., Can. Inst. Chartered Accts., 1959. Chartered acct. Coopers & Lybrand (formerly McDonald, Currie & Co.), St. John, N.B.,

1954-63; with Kaiser Services, Oakland, Calif., 1963-75, telecommunications mgr., 1966-69, asst. controller, 1969-70, controller, 1970-74; mgr. corp. acctg. Kaiser Industries Corp., Oakland, 1975; controller Kaiser Engrs., Inc., Oakland, 1975-76, v.p. fin. and adminstrn., 1976-82; mgmt. cons., owner Whalen & Assocs., Inc., Alamo, Calif., 1983—. Pres. Round Hill Holdings, Inc., 1993-99. Mem. Commonwealth Club, Rancho Cañada Golf Club. Home: PO Box 709 Alamo CA 94507-0709 Office Phone: 925-820-3506. Personal E-mail: sydwhalen@aol.com.

WHALEN, LAURENCE J., federal judge; b. Pa., 1944; BA, Georgetown Coll., 1967; JD, Georgetown U., 1970, LLM in Taxation, 1971. Spl. asst. to asst. atty. gen. tax divsn. US Dept. Justice, Washington, 1971—72, trial atty tax divsn., 1971—75; atty. Hopkins, Sutter, Hamel and Park (formerly Hamel & Park), Washington, 1977—84, Crowe & Dunlevy, Oklahoma City, 1984—87; judge US Tax Ct., Washington, 1987—2002, sr. judge, 2002—. With USAR, 1971. Mem. ABA (taxation, litig. and bus. law sects.), Fed. Bar Assn. Office: US Tax Ct 400 2nd St NW Washington DC 20217-0002

WHALEN, LUCILLE, retired academic administrator; b. LA, July 26, 1925; d. Edward Cleveland and Mary Lucille (Perrault) W. BA in English, Immaculate Heart Coll., LA, 1949; MSLS, Catholic U. Am., 1955; DLS, Columbia U., 1965. Tchr. elem. and secondary parochial schs., LA, 1945—52; tchr., libr. Conaty Meml. HS, LA, 1950—52; reference/serials libr., instr. in libr. sci. Immaculate Heart Coll., 1955—58; dean Immaculate Heart Coll. (Sch. Libr. Sci.), 1958-60, 65-70; assoc. dean, prof. SUNY, Albany, 1971-78, 84-87, prof. Sch. Info. Sci. and Policy, 1979—84; dean grad. programs, libr. Immaculate Heart Coll. Ctr., LA, 1987—90; ref. libr. (part-time) Glendale CC, 1990—. Dir. US Office Edn. Instn. Author, editor (with others): Reference Services in Archives, 1986; author: Human Rights: A Reference Handbook, 1989; author: (with Nina Redman) Human Rights: A Reference Handbook, 2d edit., 1998. Mem. ACLU, Common Cause, Amnesty Internat. Democrat. Roman Catholic. Home: 320 S Gramercy Pl Apt 101 Los Angeles CA 90020-4542 Office: Glendale CC 1500 N Verdugo Rd Glendale CA 91208-2809 Personal E-mail: lucillew213@sbcglobal.net.

WHALEN, PAUL LEWELLIN, lawyer, educator, mediator; b. Lexington, Ky. s. Elza Boz Jr. and Barbara Jean (Lewellin) W.; m. Teena Gail Tanner, Jan. 26, 1985; children: Ashley, Lars, Lucy BA, U. Ky.; JD, Northern Ky. U.; cert., Bonn U., Fed. Republic Germany, 1981; student, U.S. Army J.A.G. Sch., 1988; diploma, USAF Squadron Officers Sch., 1998. Bar: W.Va. 1984, U.S. Ct. Appeals (6th cir.) 1984, Ky. 1985, U.S. Ct. Appeals (4th cir.) 1985, Ohio 1993. Assoc. Geary Walker, Parkersburg, W.Va., 1984-85; prin. Paul L. Whalen Sch., Ft. Thomas, Ky., 1985—; atty. Dept. of Air Force, Office of Chief Trial Atty. Contract Law Ctr., Wright Patterson AFB, 1988—99; prof. pub. contract law Air Force Inst. Tech., 1999—2000; prof. Def. Acquisition U., Wright Patterson AFB, 2000—04; of counsel EPA, Cin., 2004—05; chief counsel DOE-CBC, Cin., 2005—. Hearing officer, prosecutor Ky. Dept. Ednl. Profl. Stds. Bd., 1995—97; arbitration panel No. Ky., 1997—, Montgomery County, Ohio, 1998—; hearing officer IDEA, Ky., 1999—2000, Ky., 2004—; impartial due process hearing officer Ohio Dept. Edn., 2002—05; bd. dirs. No. Ky. Ency. Mem. Leadership No. Ky., Ft. Thomas Bd. Edn., 1987—99, chmn., 1990—94; mem. Ky. Bd. Edn., 2000—04, Ky. Commn. on Human Svcs.; mem. adv. bd. Ency. No. Ky.; pres. ch. coun. Highland United Meth. Ch., 2000—05; cert. lay spkr. United Meth. Ch.; pres. North Ky. Interfaith Commn.; mem. Campbell County Foster Care Rev. Bd., Newport, Ky., 1986, bd. pres., 2006—; bd. dirs. Ky. Coun. Child Abuse, Inc. Com. for Kids; dir. Ky. Sch. Bd. Assn., 1993—98; mem. Air Force Bicycle Team Ride Across Iowa, 1997—2005. Recipient Commendation No. Ky. Legal Aid, 1986-2006, Pres.'s Call to Vol. Svc. award, 2007. Fellow Commonwealth Inst. Leadership; mem. Fed. Bar Assn., No. Ky. Bar Assn., So. Assn. Schs. (mem. com.), Phi Alpha Delta. Democrat. Methodist. Avocations: freelance writing, stamp collecting/philately, politics, amateur radio, bicycling. Home: 113 Ridgeway Ave Fort Thomas KY 41075-1333 Office: PO Box 22 Fort Thomas KY 41075 Business E-Mail: paul.whalen@emcbc.doe.gov. E-mail: plewellinwhalen@aol.com. *Notable cases include: Givan vs. Ask Realty, Ky. App., 788 S.W. 2d 503, 1990, establishing that a real estate broker has a fiduciary relationship with seller even though he may be sub-agent; Oconto Electric, Inc., ASBCA No. 36789, 88-3 BCA, 21,188, regarding timeliness of appeals to bds. of contract appeals; Quintero v. Bell 256F.3d 409 (6th Cir. 2001), succesful writ of habeas corpus.*

WHALEN, THOMAS J., lawyer; b. Jersey City, July 29, 1938; s. Arthur and Mae (Cavannagh) Whalen; m. Anne Marie Donovan, Sept. 5, 1970; 1 child, Honore. BA, St. Peter's Coll., Jersey City; JD, Georgetown U., Washington, 1963. Bar: N.Y. 1974, U.S. Dist. Cts. (so. and ea. dists.) N.Y. 1975, U.S. Ct. Appeals (2d cir.) 1975, U.S. Ct. Appeals (3d. cir.) 1983, U.S. Supreme Ct. 1983, N.H. 1994, U.S. Dist. Ct. N.H. 1994, U.S. Ct. Appeals (1st cir.) 2001. Law sec. to judge U.S. Ct. Appeals (3d cir.), Newark, 1963—64; assoc. Condon & Forsyth, NYC and Washington, 1967—75, ptnr., 1975—. Author, spkr. on airline regulatory and liability law. Capt. JAGC US Army, 1964—67, Vietnam. Mem.: ABA, University Club (Washington), Fed. Bar Assn. Democrat. Roman Catholic. Office: Eckert Seamas Cherin & Mellott 1747 Pennsylvania Ave Washington DC 20006 Office Phone: 202-659-6621. Business E-Mail: twhalen@eckertseamans.com.

WHALEN, WAYNE W., lawyer; b. Savanna, Ill, Aug. 22, 1939; s. Leo R. and Esther M. (Yackley) W.; m. Paula Wolff, Apr. 22, 1970; children: Amanda, Clementine, Antonia, Nathaniel, Daniel. BS, U.S. Air Force Acad., 1961; JD, Northwestern U., 1967. Bar: Ill. 1967, US Ct. Appeals (7th cir.) 1968, US Supreme Ct. 1972. Commd. 1st lt. USAF, 1961, ret., 1964; assoc. Mayer, Brown & Platt, Chgo., 1967-74, ptnr., 1974, Skadden, Arps, Slate, Meagher & Flom LLP, Chgo., 1984—. Bd. dir. Van Kampen Funds, Oak Brook, Ill, Abraham Lincoln Pres. Libr., Springfield, Ill. Author: Annotated Illinois Constitution, 1972. Del. 6th Ill. Constitutional Conv., 1969-70, chmn. style drafting and submission com. Named Outstanding Young Lawyer, Chgo. Bar Found., 1970. Mem. Chgo. Club. Office: Skadden Arps 2 N La Salle St Ste 2200 Chicago IL 60602-3963

WHALEY, CHARLES HENRY, IV, communications company executive; b. Elmhurst, NY, Jan. 15, 1958; s. Charles Henry III and Edna Mae (Squires) W.; m. Jeanette Marie Smith, Sept. 26, 1987. AAS in Electrical Tech., Queensborough Community Coll., Bayside, NY, 1979. Testing engr. GTE/Telenet, Mount Laurel, NJ, 1979-81; field service engr. Gen. Dynamics Communications Co., St. Louis, 1981-82; ops. engr. United Techs. Communications Co., Pine Brook, NJ, 1982-84, sr. ops. engr. NYC, 1984-85, ops. supr., 1985-86; project mgr. Telex Computer Products, NYC, 1986; pres. Pertel Comms. of N.E., Hartford, Conn., 1990—, Metrocom Tech. Svcs., NYC, 1997—. Democrat. Presbyn. Avocations: computers, classic automobiles, music, US history. Office: 350 Fifth Ave New York NY 10018 also: Pertel Comm of NE Inc 14th Fl 100 Pearl St Hartford CT 06103 Home Phone: 917-553-5205; Office Phone: 212-760-1339. Business E-Mail: cwhaley@pertelne.com.

WHALEY, FRANK, actor; b. Syracuse, NY, July 20, 1963; m. Heather Bucha. Grad., State U. NY. Film appearances include: Ironweed, 1987, Field of Dreams, 1989, Little Monsters, 1989, Born on the Fourth of July, 1989, The Freshman, 1990, JFK, 1991, The Doors, 1991, Career Opportunities, 1991, Back in the U.S.S.R., 1992, A Midnight Clear, 1992, Hoffa, 1992, Swing Kids, 1993, Pulp Fiction, 1994, Swimming With Sharks, 1995, Homage, 1995, Cafe Society, 1995, The Winner, 1996, Broken Arrow, 1996, Retroactive, 1997, Went to Coney Island on a Mission from God: Be Back by Five, 1998, Curtain Call, 1999, Glam, 2001, Pursuit of Happiness, 2001, Chelsea Walls, 2001, A Good Night to Die, 2003, World Trade Center, 2006, The Hottest State, 2006, Crazy Eights, 2006, Vacancy, 2007; TV films include: Unconquered, 1989, Flying Blind, 1990, To Dance with the White Dog, 1993, Fatal Deception: Mrs. Lee Harvey Oswald, 1993, Dead Man's Gun, 1997, The Wall, 1998, When Trumpets Fade, 1998, Shake, Rattle and Roll: An American Love Story, 1999, Bad News Mr. Swanson, 2001, Sun Gods, 2002, Detective, 2005, Mrs. Harris, 2005, Where There's a Will, 2006; stage appearances include: Tigers Wild, 1986, The Years, 1993. Office: ICM 8942 Wilshire Blvd Beverly Hills CA 90211-1934 *

WHALEY, GARWOOD, music company executive; Diploma, Juilliard Sch., 1965; Mus M, Cath. U. Am., 1971, D of Musical Arts, 1977. Pres., founder Meredith Music Pub., 1979—. Condr. emeritus Bishop Ireton Symphonic Wind Ensemble, Alexadria, Va.; adj. prof. music Catholic Univ. of Am.; curriculum coord. instrumental music Diocese of Arlington SCh., Va. Editor (chief): Music for Percussion, Inc., author 22 method books; contbr. articles pub. to profl. jour. Recipient Outstanding Secondary Educators of Am. award, Nat. Band's Assn., Outstanding Nat. Cath. Bandmaster, Citation of Excellence, Nat. Fedn. Interscholastic Music Assn., Outstanding Music Educator award, John Philip Sousa Found., Legion of Honor. Mem.: Am. Bandmasters Assn. (assoc.), Kappa Delta Pi. Mailing: PO Box 344 Galesville MD 20765 Home Phone: 410-867-0410; Office Phone: 410-867-0074. E-mail: garwoodw@comcast.net.

WHALEY, ROGER GLENN, music educator; s. R. Glenn and Joan K. Whaley; m. Melanie J. Seela, July 19, 1986; children: Erika children: Mark. BS, ND State U., 1982; MS, So. Oreg. U., 1994. Cert. K-12 music tchr. Minn., ND, SD. Band dir. Beach (ND) Pub. Schs., 1982—87, Williams Mid. Sch., Sturgis, SD, 1987—89, Larimore (ND) Pub. Schs., 1989—93, Grandview Mid. Sch., Mound, Minn., 1993—. Cons. MakeMusic!, Eden Prairie, Minn., 2005—. Named Exceptional Tchr., Tech. Info. Edn. Svcs., 2004. Mem.: Edn. Minn., Music Educators Nat. Conf. Lutheran. Avocations: computers, photography, running, golf. Office: Westonka Pub Schs 1881 Commerce Blvd Mound MN 55364 Home Phone: 952-472-2441; Office Phone: 952-491-8338. Personal E-mail: roger@rogerwhaley.com.

WHALEY, ROSS SAMUEL, environmentalist, educator; b. Detroit, Nov. 7, 1937; s. Lyle John and Margaret Nielson (Semple) W.; m. Beverly Mae Heemstra, June 14, 1958; children: Heather Jean, Susan Lesli, Lindsay John. BS, U. Mich., 1959, PhD, 1969; MS, Colo. State U., 1961. Asst. prof., assoc. prof., prof. Utah State U., Logan, 1965—70, dept. head, 1967—70; assoc. dean Colo. State U., Ft. Collins, 1970—73; dept. head U. Mass., Amherst, 1973—76, dean, 1976—78; dir. econ. research USDA Forest Service, Washington, 1978—84; pres. SUNY Coll. Environ. Scis. and Forestry, Syracuse, 1984—2000, prof., 2000—03; chair Adirondack Park Agy., 2003—. Cons. UN FAO, Rome, 1983-84, UN, Budapest, Hungary, 1974, U.S. Peace Corps., South Am., 1972, Geddes, Brecher, Qualls & Cunningham, Denver, 1971-72. Contbr. articles to profl. jours. Bd. dirs. Glynwood Ctr.; trustee Paul Smiths Coll. Fellow Soc. Am. Foresters (pres. 1991). Mem. Christian Ref. Ch. Avocations: reading, swimming, hiking, fly fishing, cross country skiing.

WHALEY, STORM HAMMOND, retired federal agency administrator; b. Sulphur Springs, Ark., Mar. 15, 1916; s. Storm Onus and Mabel Etta (Prater) W.; m. Jane Florence Bucy, Oct. 6, 1935; children: Carroll Jean Whaley Anderson, Ann Marie Whaley Adams, Rebecca Glenn Whaley Dyess. BA, John Brown U., 1935; LL.D. (hon.), 1959; postgrad., Am. U. Law Sch., 1954; D.Sc. hon., U. Ark. for Med. Scis., 1983. Mgr. Sta. KUOA, Siloam Springs, Ark., 1935-53, Sta. KGER, Long Beach, 1948-53, KOME, Tulsa, 1951-53; asst. to Congressman J.W. Trimble, 1953-54; asst. to pres. U. Ark., 1954-59, acting pres., 1959-60, v.p. health scis., 1960-70; assoc. dir. communications NIH, Bethesda, Md., 1970-92; ret., 1992. Mem. U.S. del. World Health Assembly, 1962-64; nat. adv. health coun. USPHS, 1963-66; chmn. ad hoc com. Report to Pres. and Congress Regional Med. Programs, 1967; mem. U.S. Sr. Exec. Service, 1979 Author: They Call It, 1951. Del. Democratic Nat. Conv., 1940, 44, 48, 52. Recipient Superior Service award HEW, 1974, SES Performance award, 1982, Superior Service award USPHS, 1987; named Outstanding Alumnus, John Brown U., 2001. Fellow AAAS; mem. Broadcast Pioneers, Ark. Broadcasters Assn. (life), Masons (33d deg.), Omicron Delta Kappa, Lambda Chi Alpha. Home and Office: 849 Coast Blvd CN105 La Jolla CA 92037 E-mail: swhaley2@san.rr.com.

WHAM, DAVID BUFFINGTON, secondary school educator; b. Evanston, Ill., May 25, 1937; s. Benjamin and Virginia (Buffington) W.; m. Joan Field Wilber, Mar. 9, 1968 (div. May, 1972); children: Benjamin, Rachel. AB cum laude, Harvard U., 1959; MA, So. Ill. U., Carbondale, 1967. Instr. U. Wyo., Powell, 1963-65, So. Ill. U., Carbondale, 1965-67; legis. asst. U.S. Congress, Washington, 1969-78; freelance writer Chgo., 1980-89; tchr. Chgo. Pub. Schs., 1994—. Speechwriter Adlai Stevenson for Gov. campaign, 1986, Dawn Netsch for Gov. campaign, 1994. Author: My Farewell to Bohemia, 1968, The Comic Genuflection, 1984, A Wave of Bright Boys, 1994. With U.S. Army, 1959-62. Recipient fiction award Columbia Pacific U., 1994. Mem. Harvard Club Chgo. (interviewer 1984—), Spee Club Harvard, Hasty Pudding Club Harvard. Democrat. Episcopalian. Office: 125 S Clark St Chicago IL 60603-5200 Home: 625 E Fourth St Centralia IL 62801

WHANG, MATTHEW IHN SEONG, urologist; b. Seoul, Republic of Korea, June 28, 1960; s. Mike Dae Yun and Ok Joo Whang; m. Margaret K. Nam, June 18, 1988; children: Dana Youngha, Nicole Yoonha, Michael Joonha. BA in Biochemistry, Duke U., 1983; MD, Columbia U., NYC, 1987. Diplomate Am. Bd. Urology, 1995. Surgery resident Columbia Presbyn. Med. Ctr., 1987—89, urology resident, 1989—93; physician Physicians in Urology, Livingston, NJ, 1993—99; pres. Modern Urology, West Orange, NJ, 2000—. Dir. transplant urology St. Barnabas Med. Ctr., Livingston, NJ, 1999—. Contbr. articles to profl. jours., chapters to books. Fellow: ACS; mem.: Assn. Korean Am. Med. Graduates (v.p. 1997—99, pres. 1999—2001), Korean AMA (chmn. membership com. 1998—99, chmn. sci. and edn. com. 1999—2000, sec. gen. 2000—02, exec. v.p. 2002—04). Roman Catholic. Avocation: golf. Office: Modern Urology 1001 Pleasant Valley Way West Orange NJ 07052 Home Phone: 973-994-7341; Office Phone: 973-669-8448. Personal E-mail: matthewmd@msn.com.

WHANG, SUKOO JACK, pathologist, microbiologist; b. Seoul, South Korea, Feb. 3, 1934; arrived in U.S., 1963, naturalized; m. Chung A. Park, Nov. 30, 1963; children: Selena, Stephanie, John. BS, Oreg. State U., 1957; MS, UCLA, 1960, PhD, 1963; MD, Korea U., Seoul, 1972. Diplomate Am. Bd. Tropical Medicine, Am. Bd. Forensic Medicine, Am. Bd. Pathology, Am. Bd. Med. Microbiology. Intern Good Samaritan Hosp., Dayton, Ohio, 1973—74; resident White Meml. Med. Ctr., LA, 1974—77, clin. pathologist, 1977—90, chmn. infection control com., 1977—87, dir. Sch. Med. Tech., 1977—87; dep. med. examiner L.A. County Coroner's Dept., LA, 1991—2000. Recipient Physician's Recognition award, AMA, 1980—. Fellow: ACP, Coll. Am. Pathologists (Pathology Continuing Med. Edn. award 1984—), Am. Coll. Forensic Medicine, Am. Coll. Tropical Medicine, Am. Soc. Clin. Pathologists. Republican. Seventh Day Adventist. Avocations: swimming, reading. Home: 1325 Via Del Rey South Pasadena CA 91030

WHARTON, BERNARD MAPES, architect; Grad., RISD, 1978; student, U. Pa., Phila. With Romaldo Giurgola; founding mem., sr. ptnr. Shope Reno Wharton Architecture, Greenwich, Conn., 1981—. Prin. works include Twynn River Farms, NJ. Bd. trustees Marlboro Coll., Vt. Office: Shope Reno Wharton Architecture 18 W Putnam Ave Greenwich CT 06830 Office Phone: 203-869-7250. Office Fax: 203-869-2804. *

WHARTON, LENNARD, engineering company executive; b. Boston, Dec. 10, 1933; s. Nathaniel Philip and Deeda (Levine) W.; m. Judith R. Gordon, Dec. 26, 1957; children: Ruth, Rebecca, Nathaniel. BS in Chem. Engring, MIT, 1955; BA, MA, Cambridge U., 1957; A.M., Harvard U.; A.M. (NSF fellow 1957-60), 1960, PhD (Jr. fellow Soc. of Fellows 1960-63), 1963. Registered profl. engr., N.J., Ill. Prof. dept. chemistry U. Chgo., 1963-80; v.p. engring. ITE Imperial Corp., 1972-73; v.p. tech. Studebaker-Worthington, Barrington, Ill., 1978-79, McGraw Edison Co., Rolling Meadows, Ill., 1979-80, v.p. engring. and tech. Worthington group Mountainside, NJ, 1980-85; corp. v.p. tech. Material Research Corp., Pearl River, NY, 1985-87; v.p. Packer Engring. Inc., Naperville, Ill., 1987-95, chmn. bd., 1994-95; pres. Evidentia Engring. Inc., Short Hills, NJ, 1995—. Sloan fellow, 1964-66; named Outstanding Young Man of Chgo. Chgo. Jr. Assn. Commerce and Industry, 1968 Mem. IEEE (sr.), Nat. Fire Protection Assn., Am. Inst. Chem. Engrs. Office: 10 Park Pl Short Hills NJ 07078-2826

WHARTON, LESLIE, lawyer; b. Phila., July 7, 1951; BA summa cum laude, Boston U., 1973; PhD, Princeton U., 1979; JD cum laude, Harvard U., 1984. Bar: Tex. 1984, U.S. Dist. Ct. (we. dist.) Tex. 1986, D.C. 1990. Teaching asst. Princeton U., N.J., 1978; editor Lafayette Papers Project, Ithaca, N.Y., 1978-79; instr. Suffolk U., Boston, 1979-80; asst. to v.p. acad. affairs R.I. Sch. Design, Providence, 1980-81, assoc. faculty, 1982-83; assoc. Matthews and Branscomb, San Antonio, 1984-87, Arnold & Porter, Washington, 1988-93, ptnr., 1993—. Lctr. computer law, 1985-86. Author: Polity and the Good Public, 1980, Lafayette in the Age of American Revolution, Vol. 5, 1980; contbr. articles on protection of privilege claims in litig. in profl. jours. Mem. ABA, Phi Beta Kappa, co-chairs Legal Ethics subcom. ABA (litig. sect. com. corp. counsel), chairs subsection Ethics & Professionalism Com. Office: Arnold & Porter 555 12th St NW Washington DC 20004-1206 Office Phone: 202-942-5000. Office Fax: 202-942-5999. Business E-Mail: leslie.wharton@aporter.com.

WHARTON, RALPH NATHANIEL, psychiatrist, educator; b. Boston, June 15, 1932; s. Nathaniel Philip and Deeda (Levine) W.; children: Naida, Philip, Laura. AB cum laude, Harvard U., 1953; MD, Columbia U., 1957, degree in psychoanalysis, 1970. Cert. Neurology and Psychiatry 1969. Intern Cornell divsn. Bellevue Hosp., NYC, 1957—58; resident Columbia-Presbyn. Med. Ctr., 1961—64; pvt. practice psychiatry/pharm., 1964—; assoc. psychiatry Coll. Physicians and Surgeons, 1964—69, asst. prof. clin. psychiatry, 1969—72, assoc. prof., 1972—83, prof., 1984—; sr. rsch. psychiatrist N.Y. State Psychiat. Inst., 1964—70; assoc. attending psychiatry Columbia-Presbyn. Hosp., 1970—80, attending psychiatrist, 1980—; sr. cons. supr. psychiatric svc. NY Presbyteriuan Hosp. Ex-officio mem. bd. trustees Columbia-Presbyn. Med. Ctr., pres. soc. practitioners, 1980—82, attending, 1984—; exec. dir. Wharton Fund for Brain Rsch.; med. dir. Black Sea project Macalester Coll., 1994—98; co-dir. Reiner for Behaviour and Psychosomatic Rsch. and Tchg. Columbia U. Med. Ctr., 2004—; exec. dir. Wharton Fund Brain Rsch., 1993—. Author: Landmark Papers, Lithium Carbonate for Affective Disorders, 1966; contbr. Mood Anxiety chapters, Merritt's Textbook of Neurology, 2005, AARP chapter, Art of Aging, 2006, numerous papers, publs. in profl. jours. and chpts. to books. Mem. alumni coun. Coll. Physicians and Surgeons, Columbia U., 2001—. Served to Capt. M.C., U.S. Army, 1958-60, US Army Hosp. Orleans, France, 1960-61 Capt. med. corp US Army, 1958—60. Named one of Best Drs., NY Mag. Fellow: Am. Coll. Psychoanalysts (pres. 1996, bd. dirs. 1996—), N.Y. Acad. Medicine, Am. Psychiat. Assn. (life Hon. Life fellow 2002); mem.: AMA, Group for Advancement Psychiatry, Internat. Assn. Study of Pain (founding mem.), Royal Soc. Medicine, Soc. Practitioners (exec. com. 1990—), Harmonie Club, Harvard Club (class agent 1953—), Salon de Virtuosi (founding bd. mem. 1991—, treas. 1991—), Lotos Club. Avocations: skiing, sailing, literature. Office: Columbia-Presbyn Med Ctr Atchley Pavilion Ste 209 161 Ft Washington Ave New York NY 10032-3713 also: 1070 Park Ave Ste 1D New York NY 10128-1000 Office Phone: 212-860-2666. Business E-Mail: rnw1@columbia.edu.

WHATLEY, JACQUELINE BELTRAM, lawyer; b. West Orange, NJ, Sept. 26, 1944; d. Quirino and Eliane (Gruet) Beltram; m. John W. Whatley, June 25, 1966 (dec. July 1998). BA, U. Tampa, 1966; JD, Stetson U., 1969. Bar: Fla. 1969, Alaska 1971, cert.: (real estate law specialist). Assoc. Tucker, McEwen, Smith & Cofer, Tampa, Fla., 1969-71; pvt. practice Anchorage, Alaska, 1971-73; ptnr. Gibbons, Tucker, Miller, Whatley & Stein, P.A., Tampa, 1973—; pres., 1981—. Bd. dirs. Travelers Aid Soc., 1982-94; trustee Humana Women's Hosp., Tampa, 1987-93, Keystone United Meth. Ch., 1986-89, 99—. Mem. ABA, Fla. Bar Assn. (real estate cert. com. 1993-95), Alaska Bar Assn., Tenn. Walking Horse Breeders and Exhibitors Assn. (v.p. 1984-87, dir. Fla. 1981-87, 90-93, 97-99, adv. com. Tenn. Walking Horse Celebrateion 1994-97), Fla. Walking and Racking Horse Assn. (bd. dirs. 1988-89, pres. 1980-82), Athena Soc. Republican. Methodist. Home: PO Box 17595 Tampa FL 33682-7595 Office: 101 E Kennedy Blvd Ste 2190 Tampa FL 33602-5146 Office Phone: 813-228-7841. Business E-Mail: whatley@gte.net.

WHATLEY, JOE RAMON, JR., lawyer; b. Selma, Ala., June 14, 1953; AB cum laude, Harvard U., 1975; JD, U. Ala. Sch. Law, Tuscaloosa, 1978. Bar: Ala. 1978, Tex. 1997. Law clk. to Hon. Frank H. McFadden No. Dist. Ct. Ala., 1978—79; previously ptnr. with Cooper, Mitch, Crawford, Kukendall & Whatley, Birmingham, Ala.; ptnr. Whatley Drake LLC, Birmingham, Ala., 1998—. Mem.: Assn. Trial Lawyers of Am., Ala. Trial Lawyers Assn., Ala. State Bar (labor & employment sect. 1990—91, past pres.), ABA (labor & employment sect., litig. sect.). Office: Whatley Drake LLC 2323 2nd Ave N Birmingham AL 35203-2605 Office Phone: 205-328-9576. Office Fax: 205-328-9669. E-mail: jwhatley@whatleydrake.com.

WHATMORE, GEORGE BERNARD, research scientist, writer, internist; b. Seattle, Aug. 31, 1917; s. Harry Joseph and Delia (Frolich) Whatmore; m. Frances Maxwell Beatty, May 28, 1942; children: Pamela Frances, David Blake, Nancy Janice. BS, U. Wash., 1940, MS, 1941; PhD, U. Chgo., 1946, MD, 1948. Intern King County Hosp., Seattle, 1948—49, resident, 1949—50, Lab. Clin. Physiology, Chgo., 1950—51; pvt. practice and rsch. in internal medicine, clin. neurophysiology, functional disorders Seattle, 1951—. Mem. staff Virginia Mason Hosp., Seattle, 1951—, Swedish Hosp., Seattle, 1951—, Med.-Dental Bldg. Hosp., Seattle, 1951—, Eastern State Hosp., Medical Lake, Wash., 1955—58; prin. investigator Pacific N.W. Rsch. Found. and Inst., Seattle, 1966—. Author (with Daniel R. Kohli): Dysponesis: A Neurophysiologic Factor in Functional Disorders, 1968, The Physiopathology and Treatment of Functional Disorders, 1974; author: A Scientist Looks at Christianity, A Probability Analysis, 1992, 2d edit., 1995, A Scientist Looks at Religion, Based on Evidence Plus Logic, 2002, 3d edit., 2003, De-contaminating The New Testament, Based on Lessons Learned from The Galileo Scandal, 2004; contbr. articles to profl. jours. Recipient Ginsburg award, U. Chgo., 1946; Univ. fellow, 1941—45, Rawson fellow, 1945—46, Sheldon fellow, 1945—46. Mem.: AMA, AAAS (life), Western Acad. Beaux Arts, King County Med. Soc., Wash. State Med. Assn., Assn. for Applied Psychophysiology and Biofeedback, Acad. Psychosomatic Medicine, Behavior Therapy and Rsch. Soc., Biofeedback Rsch. Soc., Internat. Stress and

Tension Control Assn., Am. Physicians Soc. for Physiologic Tension Control, N.Y. Acad. Sci., Sigma Xi. Home and Office: 10524 SE 27th St Bellevue WA 98004-7231 Office Phone: 425-454-7273.

WHAYNE, THOMAS FRENCH, JR., cardiologist, educator; b. Ft. Leavenworth, Kans., Aug. 25, 1937; s. Thomas French and Mary Lutenia (Porter) W.; m. Eugenia McDonald Ingram, June 22, 1963; children: Thomas French III, James Givens, Katherine Ingram. AB in Chemistry, U. Pa., 1959, MD, 1963; PhD in Biochemistry, U. Calif., San Francisco, 1970. Intern in medicine The N.Y. Hosp., 1963-64, resident in medicine, 1964-66; fellow in cardiovascular disease Cardiovascular Rsch. Inst., San Francisco, 1966-69, U. Toronto, Ontario, Can., 1969-70; asst. prof. medicine Ohio State U., Columbus, 1970-72; assoc. prof. medicine U. Okla., Oklahoma City, 1972-77; clin. prof. medicine U. Ky., Lexington, 1977-98, prof. medicine cardiovascular medicine, 1998—. Assoc. mem. Okla. Med. Rsch. Found., 1972-77; staff cardiologist Lexington Clinic, 1977-98; presenter in field. Contbr. abstracts, chapters to books, articles to profl. jours. Named Man of Yr., Okla. Heart Assn., 1975—76. Fellow: ACP, Internat. Coll. Angiology, Coll. Physicians of Phila., Am. Heart Assn., Am. Coll. Cardiology. Presbyterian. Avocations: Spanish language, golf, scuba diving, photography. Office: Divsn Cardiovascular Medicine 326 Wethington Bldg 900 S Limestone Lexington KY 40536-0200 Office Phone: 859-257-1566. Business E-Mail: twhayn0@uky.edu.

WHEALEY, LOIS DEIMEL, humanities scholar; b. NYC, June 20, 1932; d. Edgar Bertram Deimel and Lois Elizabeth (Hatch) Washburn; m. Robert Howard Whealey, July 2, 1954; children: Richard William, David John, Alice Ann. BA in History, Stanford U., 1951; MA in Edn., U. Mich., 1955; MA in Polit. Sci., Ohio U., 1975, M in Social Sci., 2007. Tchr. 5th grade Swayne Sch., Owyhee, Nev., 1952-53; tchr. 7th grade Ft. Knox (Ky.) Dependent's Sch., 1955-56; tchr. adult basic edn. USAF, Oxford, 1956-57; tchr. 6th grade Amerman Sch., Northville, Mich., 1957-58; tchr. 8th grade English, social studies Slauson Jr. High Sch., Ann Arbor, Mich., 1958-59; adminstrv. asst. humanities conf. Ohio U., Athens, 1974-76, 83. Part-time instr. Ohio U., Athens, 1966—68, Athens, 1975, VISTA with Rural Action, 1996—99. Contbr. articles to profl. jours. Mem. Athens County Regional Planning Commn., 1974—78, treas., 1976—78; mem. Ohio coord. com. Internat. Women's Yr., 1977; v.p. Black Diamond Girl Scout Coun., 1980—86; chair New Day for Equal Rights Amendment, 1982; mem. Athens City Bd. Edn., 1984—90, v.p., 1984, pres., 1985; mem. Tri-County Vocat. Sch. Bd., Nelsonville, Ohio, 1984—90, v.p., 1988—89; mem. adv. com. Ohio River Valley Water Sanitation Commn., 1986—95; Ohio outreach liaison Nat. Town Meeting for Sustainable Am., 1999; bd. dirs. Ohio Environ. Coun., 1984—90, sec., 1986—90; bd. dirs. Ohio Alliance for Environ., 1994—98, v.p., 1998; bd. dirs. Organize Ohio, 1999—2007, bd. pres., 2001—07; bd. dirs. Ohio Women, Inc., 1995—, sec., 1997—; bd. dirs. Unitarian Universalist Svc. Com., 2001—03, Ohio Meadville Dist. Unitarian-Universalist Assn., 1975—81; co-chair nat. vol. network Unitarian Universalist Svc. Com., 2003—05. Named Woman of Achievement, Black Diamond Girl Scout Coun., 1987, Peacemaker, Appalachian Peace and Justice Network, 1998, Outstanding Feminist, Athens Herstory Celebration, 2002; recipient Unsung Unitarian Universalist award, Ohio-Meadville Dist. Unitarian Universalist Assn., 1984, How-to award, Ednl. Press Assn. Am., 1990, Donna Chen Women's Equity award, Ohio U., 1994, Cmty. Svc. award, Athens County Cmty. Svcs. Coun., 1998, award for individual contbn. over a lifetime, Ohio Alliance Environment, 2002, Thanks badge, Black Diamond Girl Scout Coun., 1986. Mem.: LWV (pres. 1975—77), AAUW (pres.Athens br. 1969—70, 1989—90, 1993—2001, AAUW/Ohio bd. 1995—2004), Phi Kappa Phi, Phi Lambda Theta. Democrat. Avocations: classical music, genealogy. Home: 14 Oak St Athens OH 45701-2605

WHEAT, BILL W., construction executive; BBA in Acctg. and Fin., Baylor U., Waco, Tex. CPA. Auditor Price Waterhouse LLP (now PricewaterhouseCoopers LLP); various positions including fin. planning mgr. and asst. contr. The Bombay Co., 1991—98; acctg. mgr. D.R. Horton, Inc., Fort Worth, 1998—2000, sr. v.p., contr., 2000—03, exec. v.p., CFO, bd. dirs., 2003—. Office: DR Horton Inc DR Horton Tower 301 Commerce St Ste 500 Fort Worth TX 76102 *

WHEAT, MYRON WILLIAM, JR., cardiothoracic surgeon; b. Sapulpa, Okla., Mar. 24, 1924; s. Myron William and Mary Lee (Hudiburg) W.; m. Erlene Adele Plank, June 12, 1949 (div. June 1970); children: Penelope Louise, Myron William III, Pamela Lynn, Douglas Plank; m. Carol Ann Karmgard, June 18, 1970 (div. Apr. 1996); 1 child, Christopher West. AB, Washington U., St. Louis, 1949; MD cum laude, Washington U., 1951. Diplomate Am. Bd. Surgery, Am. Bd. Thoracic Surgery. Instr., clin. fellow Washington U., St. Louis, 1956—58; asst. prof. surgery U. Fla., Gainesville, 1958—65, prof. surgery, 1965—72; dir. profl. svcs., chief clin. physician U. Fla. Shands Tchg. Hosp., Gainesville, 1968—72; prof. surgery, dir. thoracic and cardiothoracic surgery U. Louisville Sch. Medicine, 1972—75, clin. prof. surgery, 1975—; cardiothoracic surgeon Cardiac Surg. Assocs., P.A., St. Petersburg, Fla., 1975—91; cons., thoracic surgery Bay Pine VA Hosp., St. Petersburg, 1994—; clin. prof. surgery U. So. Fla. Sch. Medicine, Tampa, 1995—; cardiothoracic surgeon Cardiac Surg. Assocs., P.A., Clearwater, Fla., 1991—. Clin. prof. surgery U. South Fla., 1995—; cons. Bay Pines VA Hosp., St. Petersburg, 1991—; mem. Am. Bd. Thoracic Surgery, 1969-75 Author (with others) 18 books; mem. editl. bd. Am. Heart Jour., 1971; contbr. over 100 articles to profl. jours.; developed drug therapy for acute dissecting aneurysms of the aorta 1st lt. USAF, 1943-46, ETO Decorated DFC Air medal (4), Presdl. Citation; named First Howard W. Lillenthal Meml. lectr. Mt. Sinai Hosp., 1963. Fellow ACS (gov.), Am. Coll. Cardiology (chmn. bd. govs. 1968-69); mem. Am. Surg. Assn., Am. Assn. Thoracic Surgery (sec. 1972-78), So. Surg. Assn., So. Thoracic Surg. Assn., Soc. Thoracic Surgeons, Soc. Thoracic Surgeons Gr. Britain and Ireland, Alpha Omega Alpha Republican. Home and Office: PO Box 136 Largo FL 33779-0136 Office Phone: 727-446-4637. Personal E-mail: myronwheat@msn.com.

WHEATLAND, RICHARD, II, fiduciary services executive, museum executive; b. Boston, Nov. 25, 1923; s. Stephen and Dorothy (Parker) W.; m. Cynthia McAdoo, Feb. 13, 1954; 1 child, Sarah Wheatland Fisher. AB, Harvard U., 1944, postgrad., 1946-47; JD, Columbia U., 1949. Various positions with Marshall Plan adminstrn. Office Spl. Rep. in Europe, Dept. State, Paris, 1950-53; v.p. N.Y. Airways, NYC, 1953-68; pres. Acadia Mgmt. Co., Inc., Boston, 1968-93, chmn., 1993—. Bd. dirs., v.p. Pingree Assocs., Bangor, Maine. Mem. Mayor's Com. Insl. Leaders for Youth, N.Y.C., 1963-66; mem. corp. New Eng. Forestry Found.; mem., former chmn. Fund for Preservation of Wild Life and Natural Areas, Boston, 1980-92, bd. dirs. 1980-91; trustee Penobscot Marine Mus., Searsport, Maine, 1968-90, hon. trustee, 1990—,; bd. dirs. Friends of Pub. Garden, Boston, 1972-89, 90-96, 97—, Beacon Hill Civic Assn., Boston, 1985-89, Boston Natural Areas Fund, 1987—, asst. treas., 1993-94, treas. 1994-96, bd. dirs. 1997, acting chair, 1997—; treas. Frank Hatch for Gov. com., Boston, 1977-78; chmn., bd. trustees & overseers Peabody Essex Mus. (formerly Peabody Mus. of Salem), Salem, Mass., 1992—, trustee, 1972-92, pres., 1983-92. Lt. (j.g.) USN, 1943-46, PTO. Mem. Am. Assn. Mus. (bd. dirs. trustee com. 1976-86, govt. affairs com. 1985-89), Mus. Trustee Assn. (founder, bd. dirs. 1986—, sec. 1986-92), City Club Corp. (former bd. mgrs., former treas.). Avocations: jogging, sailing, travel.

WHEATLEY, CHRISTINE S., lawyer; b. Pitts., Feb. 27, 1971; BA, U. Notre Dame, 1993; JD, Ohio State U., 1996. Bar: Ohio 1996. Ptnr. Porter Wright Morris & Arthur LLP, Cin. Mem., Bd. Trustees Mercy Connections Cmty. Outreach Ctr. Named one of Ohio's Rising Stars, Super Lawyers, 2006. Mem.: Ohio State Bar Assn., ABA, Cin. Bar Assn. Office: Porter Wright Morris & Arthur LLP 250 E Fifth St Ste 2200 Cincinnati OH 45202-5117 Office Phone: 513-369-4229. Office Fax: 513-421-0991.

WHEATLEY, DEBORAH A., music educator; b. Mt. Clemens, Mich., Oct. 28, 1954; d. Ernest William Wheatley and Joanne Smith. AA with honors, Miami-Dade CC, 1975; BA magna cum laude, U. Ctrl. Fla., 1978; grad., US Army Element Sch. Music, 1984. Music tchr. Lecanto Primary, Fla., 1978—81; band dir. Lecanto Mid. Sch., 1981—83, fine arts tchr., 1986—96, band dir., 1996—; with signal corps band U.S. Army Elem. Sch. Music, Ft. Gordon, Ga., 1984; summer duty U.S. Army, 1986—92. With Signal Corps Band US Army, 1984—86. Recipient U.S. Army Commendation medal, 1986. Republican. Avocations: running, promoting healthy lifestyle to middle school students. Home: 1801 Silverwood St Inverness FL 34453 Office: Lecanto Mid Sch 3800 W Educational Path Lecanto FL 34461 Office Phone: 352-746-2050. E-mail: debwheat@mailstation.com.

WHEATLEY, MELVIN ERNEST, JR., retired bishop; b. Lewisville, Pa., May 7, 1915; s. Melvin Ernest and Gertrude Elizabeth (Mitchell) W.; m. Lucile Elizabeth Maris, June 15, 1939; children: Paul Melvin, James Maris, John Sherwood (dec.). AB magna cum laude, Am. U., 1936, DD, 1958; BD summa cum laude, Drew U., 1939; DD, U. of Pacific, 1948. Ordained to ministry Meth. Ch., 1939. Pastor area Meth. ch., Lincoln, Del., 1939-41; assoc. pastor First Meth. Ch., Fresno, Calif., 1941-43; pastor Centenary Meth. Ch., Modesto, Calif., 1943-46, Cen. Meth. Ch., Stockton, Calif., 1946-54, Westwood Meth. Ch., LA, 1954-72; bishop Denver Area, 1972-84; ret., 1984. Instr. philosophy Modesto Jr. Coll., 1944; summer session instr. Hebrew-Christian heritage U. of Pacific; instr. Homiletics U. So. Calif., So. Calif. Sch. Theology, Claremont; lectr. St. Luke's Lectures, Houston, 1966; mem. Bd. of Ch. and Soc., Commn. on Status and Role of Women, United Meth. Ch., 1976-84; condr. European Christian Heritage tour, 1961, Alaska and Hawaii Missions, 1952, 54, Israel in behalf of Stockton Jewish Congregation, 1951. Author: Going His Way, 1957, Our Man and the Church, 1968, The Power of Worship, 1970, Family Ministries Manual, 1970, Christmas Is for Celebrating, 1977; contbr. articles to profl. jours. Chmn. Community Rels. Conf. So. Calif., 1966-69; pres. So. Calif.-Ariz. Conf. Bd. Edn., 1960-68; hon. trustee Iliff Sch. Theology; hon. dir., active mem. Parents and Friends of Lesbians and Gays, 1980—. Recipient Disting. Alumnus award Am. U., 1979, Ball award Meth. Fedn. Social Action, 1984, Prophetic Leadership award The Consultation on Homosexuality, Tolerance and Roman Cath. Theology, 1985, Human Rights award Universal Fellowship of Met. Community Congregations, 1985, award for social justice Calif.-Pacific Meth. Fedn. for Social Action, 2000, Lifetime Achievement award Denver Parents, Families and Friends of Lesbians and Gays, 2000, Outstanding Svc. award Parents Reconciling Network, 2000, Hilton award Nat. Pa. Reconciling Network, 2004. Home: 859 Ronda Mendoza Unit A Laguna Woods CA 92637-5940

WHEATLEY, SEAGAL V., lawyer, legal association administrator; b. Houston, May 24, 1935; s. Seagal V.and Hilda (Guess) W.; m. Wanda Jean Wheatley, Dec. 15, 1978; children: Jill Wilder, Julie. BA in Govt., North Tex. U., 1957; JD, U. Tex., 1960. Bar: Tex. 1960. Ptnr. Beckman, Standard, Wood & Vance, San Antonio, 1960-69; atty. U.S. Dept. of Justice, Tex., 1969-71; pres. Oppenheimer, Rosenberg, Kelleher & Wheatley Inc., San Antonio, 1971—97; ptnr., litig. practice Jenkens & Gilchrist, San Antonio, 1997—. Adj. prof. U. Tex. Sch. of Law, Austin, 1985, 86, 89. Contbr. articles to profl. jours. Del. Rep. Nat. Conv., Miami, Fla., 1968; chmn. Bexar City Reps., San Antonio, 1968. Fellow Tex. Bar Found.; mem. ABA, Assn. Trial Lawyers Am., Tex. Bar Assn., San Antonio Bar Assn., Fed. Bar Assn., 5th Cir. Bar Assn. (past pres.), Internat. Soc. of Barristers. Avocations: golf, tennis. Office: Jenkens & Gilchrist Ste 900 Weston Ctr 112 E Pecan St San Antonio TX 78205-1533 Office Phone: 210-246-5635. Office Fax: 210-246-5999. Business E-Mail: swheatley@jenkens.com.

WHEATLEY, WILLIAM ARTHUR, consulting firm executive; b. Knoxville, Tenn., Sept. 23, 1944; s. Arthur Cornwallis and Inda Mary (Benway) W.; m. Celeste Ann George, Mar. 25, 1970 (div.); children: Charles Arthur, James Harris Giddings; m. Rosaria Giovanna Cilia, June 10, 1995. Student, Rice U., 1962-66; BA, U. St. Thomas, 1972. Registered architect, Pa. Design draftsman W.W. Alexander, Houston, 1966-70; chief prodn. W.W. Scarborough, Houston, 1970—72; project arch. Ronald H. Waldie & Assocs., Houston, 1972-74; pres. Wheatley & Assocs., Inc., Houston, 1974-81; project arch. Brooks Assn., Houston, 1977—79; mgr. design Stone Bldg. Systems, Inc., Houston, 1979-81; project arch. Bechtel, Houston, 1981—84; prin. Wheatley & Assocs., Houston, 1984-87; project mgr. STV/Sanders & Thomas, Pottstown, Pa., 1987-88, MDC Sys. Divsn. Day & Zimmermann Internat., Inc., Phila., 1988-97; prin., exec. v.p. MDC Sys., Inc., 1997-2000; chmn. MDC Sys. UK Ltd., Aberdeen, Scotland, 1999—2001; pres. Wheatley US Ltd., Bala Cynwyd, Pa., 2000—; chmn. Wheatley UK Ltd., London, 2002—. Composer piano solos, chorales, oratorio and cantata, 1961—; contbr. articles to profl. jours. Del. Tex. Rep. Convs., 1980, 82, 84, committeeman Rep. Com. Lower Merion Twp. and Narberth, Pa., 2005—. Mem. ABA (assoc.), Am. Arbitration Assn., Internat. Code Coun. Anglican. Avocations: writing music, poetry and fiction, drawing, painting, sculpture. Office: Wheatley US Ltd 2 Bala Plz Ste 300 Bala Cynwyd PA 19004-1501 also: Wheatley UK Ltd 1 Grosvenor Crescent London SW1X 7EF England Office Phone: 610-660-7819. Business E-Mail: w.wheatley@wheatleyus.com.

WHEATON, DOUGLAS B., city manager, lawyer; b. Milw., July 21, 1972; s. Frank and Doreen Wheaton. BS in criminal justice, Carroll Coll., 1994; JD, Marquette U. Law Sch., 1998; MA in polit. sci., Marquette U. Grad. Sch., 1999; attended program of inst. for law, Harvard Law Sch., 2000. Bar: Wis. 1998, US Ct. of Appeals, 7th Circuit, US Dist. Ct., Ea. Dist. Wis., US Dist. Ct., Western Dist. Wis. Legis. asst. Wis. State Legis., Madison, 1999—2002; govt. affairs dir. Wis. Realtors Assn., Madison, 2002—05; dir. city devel. City of Franklin, Wis., 2005—. Recipient CALI Excellence for the Future award, Ctr. for Computer Assisted Legal Instr., 1997, Outstanding Svc. award, Kenosha Realtors Assn., 2003, 2004. Mem.: Internat. Econ. Devel. Coun., Milw. Bar Assn., Am. Polit. Sci. Assn. Avocations: travel, reading. Office: Franklin City Hall 9229 W Loomis Rd Franklin WI 53132 Office Phone: 414-425-4024. Business E-Mail: dwheaton@franklinwi.gov.

WHEATON, M. GENE, investigator, consultant; b. Pawnee, Okla., May 19, 1935; s. Bert Albert Wheaton and Ruth Savannah Bartlett; m. Theresa Joyce Bryant, Nov. 23, 1956 (dec. June 2004); children: Gary B., Denise M., Anita L. BS in Law Enforcement, U. Nebr., Omaha, 1969; MA in Pub. Adminstrn., Webster U., 1975. Cert. polygraph examiner U.S. Army Polygraph Sch., Farsi linguist Def. Lang. Inst., bd. cert. police comdr. Internat. Assn. Chiefs of Police. Police officer Tulsa (Okla.) Police Dept., 1957—58; spl. agt. Office Spl. Investigations USAF, 1958—66; spl. agt. Criminal Investigations Divsn. U.S. Army, 1966—75; dep. dir. Pub. Safety Dept., Kish Island, Iran, 1976—77; exec. asst. to v.p. Rockwell Internat., Tehran, Iran, 1977—79; v.p. Nat. Airlines, Calif., 1985—86. Police/counter-terrorism advisor to Shah of Iran, 1971—73, 1975—79; mem. adv. bd. Nat. Security Inst., Framingham, Mass., 1986—93; cons. in field, 1986—. Mem. exec. bd. Homeowners Assn., Winchester, Calif., 2000. Sgt. USMC, 1953—56, chief warrant officer US Army, 1966—75. Decorated Bronze star U.S. Army, Vietnam, Legion of Merit U.S. Army, Iran, Meritorious Svc. medal U.S. Army. Mem.: VFW (life; former vice comdr.), CID Agts. Assn., Alpha Kappa Delta. Avocations: swimming, shooting, exercising.

WHEATON, MARILYN, musician; b. Warren, Ohio, Feb. 1, 1933; d. Russell and Donabelle Irene Donehue; m. Warren Randall Wheaton, June 20, 1953; 1 child, Janean Renee Vaupel-Wilson. BS in Music Edn. cum laude, Kent State U., 1955. Cert. Yamaha music instr. Pvt. piano and organ tchr., Ohio and Ariz., 1950—; profl. pianist, organist, accompanist, 1946—; elem. music supr. Austintown Pub. Schs., Youngstown, Ohio, 1955-61. Founder, dir. Potter's Clay Christian singing group, Phoenix, 1981-85; choir dir., organist, pianist at various chs., Ohio and Ariz., 1942—; rep. for elem. music texts and programs Mahoning County Schs., Youngstown, 1959-60; tchr., organizer student trips to numerous concerts; tchr., dir. choirs and soloists for dist. and state competitions, 1955—. Composer (poems to music) Seven Last Words of Christ, also anthems, introits, reponses; arranges music for beginning and handicapped students. Dir., accompanist Terry's Variety Show, Austintown, 1951, Potter's Clay, 1980-85; pianist at various sr. citizens' groups Kent State U. and Youngstown U. scholar, 1951-55. Mem. Music Tchrs. Nat. Assn., Delta Omicron (life, charter mem., pres. Delta Upsilon chpt.). Avocations: travel, camping, reading, walking, piano recitals. Home and Office: 3245 W Yucca St Phoenix AZ 85029-4133

WHEDON, RALPH GIBBS, manufacturing executive; b. Elizabeth, NJ, Aug. 10, 1949; s. Ralph Gibbs and Jane (MacMaster) W.; m. Lorna Jean Neebe, June 3, 1972; children: Deborah, David. Student, Clarkson Coll., 1968-70; BS, St. Lawrence U., 1972; student, Rensselaer Polytech. Inst., 1978; MBA, De Paul U., 1985. CPA, Ohio. Credit rep. Internat. Harvester Credit Corp., Albany, NY, 1972-75, ops. supr., 1975-79; mgr. export ops. Internat. Harvester Co., Chgo., 1979-86; treas. Pettibone Corp., Des Plaines, Ill., 1986-91; mgr. cash resources Bailey Controls Co., Wickliffe, Ohio, 1991-95, acting dir. treas., 1992-95, mgr. adminstrn., 1993-95; dir. MIS HMI Industries, Cleve., 1995-97; project mgr. Unum Am., Portland, Maine, 1997-98; mgr. Unum Provident, 1998—2003; CFO ProActivHealth, 2002—; info. sys. audit mgr. U. Maine System, 2004—. Sec. Tube Form, 1995-97; sec. Bliss Mgg., 1995-97; sec. Newton Falls Holding Co., 1995-97. Bd. dirs. Naperville (Ill.) Cmty. Chorus, 1985-87; trop leader Boy scouts Am., Naperville, 1985-91; mem. adv. coun. United Way, 1993-95; mem. adv. coun. Cleve. Treas. Club, 1992-97, bd. dirs., 1994-96; pres. Brightwood Lakes Assn., 1996-97; treas. S.J.E.C. Found., 1996-97. Episcopalian. Avocations: sailing, flying. Home (Summer): 7 Fairwind Way Ellsworth ME 04605-2935 Home: 15 S Spring St Box 137 Stillwater ME 04489-0137

WHEELAN, BELLE S., educational association administrator; 1 child, Reginald. BA in Psychology and Sociology, Trinity U., San Antonio, 1972; MA in Devel./Ednl. Psychology, La. State U., Baton Rouge, 1974; D in Ednl. Adminstrn., U. Tex., Austin, 1984. Asst. prof. psychology, dir. devel. edn., dir. acad. support svcs. San Antonio Coll., 1974—87; dean student svcs. Thomas Nelson C.C., Hampton, Va., 1987—89; provost Tidewater C.C., Portsmouth, Va., 1989—92; pres. Ctrl. Va. C.C., 1992—97, No. Va. C.C., 1998—2001; sec. of edn. Commonwealth of Va., Richmond, 2002—05; pres. Commn. on Colls. So. Assn. for Colls. and Schs., Decatur, Ga., 2005—. Mem. Am. Coll. Testing Bd., Nat. Commn. on NAEP 12th Grade Assessment and Reporting, 2003—. Recipient Disting. Grad. award, U. Tex., 1992, Outstanding Alumnus award, Trinity U., 2002, Strong Men and Women award, 2003. Mem.: Nat. Coun. on Black Am. Affairs (pres. roundtable). Roman Catholic. Office: Commn on Colls So Assn Colls and Schs 1866 Southern Lane Decatur GA 30033 Office Phone: 404-679-4512. Business E-Mail: belle.wheelan@sacscoc.org.

WHEELAN, R(ICHELIEU) E(DWARD), lawyer; b. NYC, July 10, 1945; s. Richard Fairfax and Margaret (Murray) Wheelan. BS, Springfield Coll., Mass., 1967; MS, Iona Coll., 1977; JD, Pace U., 1981. Bar: N.Y. 1982, Minn. 1983, Colo. 1989, Tex. 1990, U.S. Dist. Ct. (no dist.) Calif. 1982, (so. dist.) Tex. 1991, U.S. Internat. Trade 1982, U.S. Ct. Appeals (2d cir.) 1982, (9th cir.) 1983, (5th cir.) 1993, U.S. Supreme Ct. 1994, U.S. Tax Ct. 1998, U.S. Dist. Ct. (no. dist.) Tex. 2003, U.S. Dist. Ct. (ea. dist.) Tex. 2004; bd. cert. in criminal law. Lt. of detectives White Plains (N.Y.) Police Dept., 1969-81; area counsel IBM, Armonk, NY, 1981-89; gen. counsel Kroll Assocs. (Asia), Hong Kong, 1989-91; pvt. practice, Houston, 1991—. Abogado consultor Mex. Consulate. Mem.: ABA (mem. sentencing guidelines com.), Tex. Assn. Criminal Def. Lawyers, Pro Bono Coll. State Bar Tex., New York County Lawyers Assn., N.Y. State Bar Assn., Coll. of State Bar Tex., Nat. Assn. Criminal Def. Lawyers (life; mem. death penalty com., Champion adv. bd.). Office: 440 Louisiana St Houston TX 77002-1639 Home Phone: 281-286-9999; Office Phone: 713-225-1300. E-mail: defensecounsel@houston.rr.com.

WHEELDON, CHRISTOPHER, dancer, choreographer; b. Yeovil, Somerset, England, 1973; s. Peter and Judy Wheeldon. Student, West Coker Ballet Sch., Somerset, Royal Ballet Sch., London, 1981-89, student higher sch., 1989-91. Dancer Royal Ballet, 1991-93; dancer-corps de ballet NYC Ballet, 1993—98, soloist, 1998—2001, resident choreographer, 2001—; founder Morphoses the Wheeldon Co., 2007—. Early roles include Fritz in The Nutcracker, Royal Ballet, Covent Garden, 1984; choreographer The Syncopated Clock, Royal Ballet Sch., 1984, more recently Le Voyage, Royal Ballet, 1995, Danses Bohémiennes, NYC Ballet, 1995 (Mae L. Wien award for Young Choregrapher 1995), Souvenir, Royal Ballet, 1996, A Midsummer Night's Dream, Colo. Ballet, 1996, Diversions, Royal Ballet Sch., 1996; choreographer Ctr. Stage (film), 2000, Variations Serieuses, 2001, Polyphonia, 2001, Sweet Smell of Success, 2002, Tryst, 2002, Morphoses, 2002, Carousel, 2002, Carnival of the Animals, 2003, Liturgy, 2003. Named one of 40 Under 40, Crain's NY Bus., 2006; recipient Gold Medal for dance (original choreography), Prix de Lausanne, 1991, Nat. Dance award, best choreography (classical), London Critics' Cir., 2004, Dance Mag. award, 2005, Martin E. Segal award, Lincoln Ctr., Am. Choreography award, Olivier award. Office: c/o NYC Ballet 20 Lincoln Center Plz New York NY 10023-6913 *

WHEELER, ALBIN GRAY, retired military officer, retail executive, educator; b. Huntington, W.Va., Mar. 16, 1935; s. Harvey Gray and Hattie Benson (Weddle) W.; m. Beatrice Thomas, May 17, 1958; children: Dianne, Michelle, Patrice. BA, Marshall U., 1958; MBA, Pepperdine U., 1975; student, Army War Coll., 1976, Harvard U., 1990; DHL (hon.), Marshall U., 2004. Enlisted U.S. Army, 1952, commd. 2d lt., 1959, advanced through grades to maj. gen., 1982; comdr. divsn. spt. command, chief of staff 1st Inf. Divsn., Ft. Riley, Kans., 1978-80; CEO Army AF Exch. Svc.-Europe/Middle East, Munich, 1981-83; comdr. 2d Spt. Command, VII U.S. Corps, Germany, 1983-85; pres. Indsl. Coll. Armed Forces, Washington, 1985-89; CEO Army and Air Force Exch. Svc., Dallas, 1991-93; ret. U.S. Army, 1993; exec. dir. Arent Fox, Washington, 1993-96. Exec. com. Soc. Yeager Scholars, Marshall U. Decorated Def. and Army D.S.M., Bronze Star with two oak leaf clusters, Legion of Merit with two oak leaf clusters; inducted into Army Quartermaster Hall of Fame, 1999. Mem. Marshall U. Alumni Assn. (disting. alumnus 1983). Personal E-mail: albin10@verizon.net.

WHEELER, ANDREW R., lawyer; b. Hamilton, Ohio; BA, Case Western Reserve Univ., 1987; JD, Washington Univ., 1990; MBA, George Mason Univ., 1997. Bar: D.C. 1991. Spl. asst. EPA, Washington, 1991—95; legis. fellow U.S. Senator James Inhofe, 1995, gen. counsel, 1995—97; counsel Com. Environ. & Public Works, U.S. Senate, 1997—2000, chief counsel & staff dir., 2000—. Republican. Presbyterian. Office: Committee on Environment & Public Works Room 410 Senate Dirksen Office Building Washington DC 20510-6175

WHEELER, BURTON M., language educator, dean; b. Mullins, SC, Mar. 12, 1927; s. Paul and Elizabeth (Cleveland) W.; m. Jacquelyn Mulkey, Aug. 20, 1950; children— Paul, Geoffrey, Kristin AB, U. S.C., 1948, MA, 1951; PhD, Harvard U., 1961. Teaching fellow Harvard U., Cambridge, Mass.,

1953-56; mem. faculty Washington U., St. Louis, 1956-96, prof., 1974-96; prof. emeritus, 1996—; dean Coll. Arts and Scis. Washington U., St. Louis, 1966-78, interim dean univ. librs., 1988-89. Cons., panelist Danforth Found., St. Louis, 1958-82; mem. GPEP panel Assn. Am. Med. Colls., Washington, 1981-84; cons.-evaluator North Cen. Assn., Chgo. Author: Close to Me, But Far Away, 2001; contbr. articles to profl. jours. Mem. spkrs. bur. Alzheimers Assn. Eli Lilly Found. fellow, 1965-66 Mem. Alzheimer's Assn., Phi Beta Kappa (senator 1992-2004, chmn. qualifications com., chmn. com. on chpts.). Business E-Mail: bwheeler@artsci.wustl.edu.

WHEELER, CATHY JO, federal agency administrator; b. Birmingham, Ala., Feb. 14, 1954; d. Charles Edwin and Hazel Josephine Wheeler; m. David Arthur Tate, 1994. BA, U. Montevallo, 1975; postgrad., U. Ala., 1982—84. With Social Security Adminstrn., Birmingham, 1975—, sr. employment devel. specialist, 1983-85, mgr. tech. tng. dept., 1985-91, mgmt. analyst, 1991—2000, staff advisor to asst. regional commr. Process Ctr. Ops., 2000-01, fin mgmt specialist, 2001—. V.p. Fed. Women's Program, Birmingham, 1984—85; treas., charter mem. Federally Employed Women, Birmingham, 1984—88. Mem. Art Alumni Adv. Bd., 1997—2001, v.p., 1998—2000; bd. dirs. U. Montevallo Found., 2002—, sec. found. bd., 2005—. Mem.: ASTD (treas. 1987—88, pres. elect 1989, pres. 1990, asst. regional dir. 1991—92), Ala. Designer-Craftsmen, Soc. Govt. Meeting Planners (v.p. 1989—90, sec. 1990—91), Bluff Park Art Assn. (bd. dirs. 2007—), U. Montevallo Nat. Alumni Assn. (bd. dirs. 1991—94, v.p. fin. 1994—98, pres.-elect 1998—2000, pres. 2000—02, parliamentarian 2002—04), Riverchase Women's Club, Jaycees (v.p. mgmt. devel. Hoover Ala. chpt. 1988—89), Chi Omega Alumni Assn. (treas. 1991, advisor 1991—2000). Avocations: photography, reading, travel. Home: 4001 Fairchase Ln Birmingham AL 35244-1300 Office: Social Security Adminstrn 2001 12th Ave N Birmingham AL 35285 Personal E-mail: cathyjowheeler@bellsouth.net.

WHEELER, CHRIS D., investment company executive; Degree in Applied Physics with honors, Calif. Inst. Tech., 1978; MBA, Harvard U., 1980. Various positions including group mng. ptnr. Trammell Crow Residential, 1982-98; sr. v.p. strategic initiatives Gables Residential Trust, Atlanta, 1998-99, pres., CEO, 1999—. Office: Gables Residential Trust 2859 Paces Ferry Rd SE Ste 1450 Atlanta GA 30339-5716

WHEELER, DANIEL HARDING, architect, educator; BArch, RISD, 1981. Registered arch., Ill., Ind., Wis., SC, Mich. With Machado-Silvetti Archs., Boston; project arch. Skidmore, Owings & Merrill, Chgo., 1981—85, assoc., studio head, 1985; founder Daniel Wheeler Archs., 1987—90; prin., project arch. Wheeler Kearns Archs., Chgo., 1990—. Assoc. prof. architecture, chair bldg. sci./design integration curriculum U. Ill., Chgo., 2000—. Prin. works include Camp Madron, Chgo. Children's Mus., North Ave. Beach House, Marwen, Green Homes for Chgo. Bd. trustees to pres. bd. Graham Found. Advanced Studies in the Fine Arts, 1999—. Fellow: AIA (Young Architect award, Chgo. chpt. 1985). Office: Wheeler Kearns Archs 343 S Dearborn St Chicago IL 60604 Office Phone: 312-939-7787. Office Fax: 312-939-5108. E-mail: dan@wkarch.com. *

WHEELER, DAVID LAURIE, university dean; b. Saginaw, Mich., July 30, 1934; s. Clayton Final and Blanche Beatrice (Hunt) W.; m. Jane Louise Manchester, Sept. 6, 1958; children: Elizabeth, Anne. AB, U. Mich., 1956, AM, 1958, PhD, 1962. Asst. dean student service Ill. State U., Normal, 1967-68, assoc. dean, 1968-69, assoc. dean grad. sch., 1969-72; dean grad. sch. West Tex. State U., Canyon, 1972-79, Ball State U., Muncie, Ind., 1979-96, dean emeritus, 1996—. Cons. McGraw-Hill Pub. Co., N.Y.C., Van Nostrand Reinhold Pub. Co., N.Y.C. Editor: The Human Habitat: Contemporary Readings, 1971. Woodrow Wilson fellow, 1961; recipient Commdrs. Pub. Svc. award Dept. of Army, 1996. Mem. Assn. Am. Geographers, Nat. Coun. Univ. Rsch. Adminstrs., Western History Assn., Tex. State Hist. Assn., U.S. Army War Coll. Found., Rotary (Paul Harris fellow), Sigma Xi, Phi Kappa Phi, Kappa Sigma. Republican. Presbyterian. Personal E-mail: wheeler2@onlinecol.com.

WHEELER, DOUGLAS PAUL, conservationist, state agency administrator, lawyer; b. Bklyn., Jan. 10, 1942; s. Robert S. and Lottie (Neubauer) W.; m. Heather A. Campbell, Aug. 28, 1965; children— Clay Campbell, Christopher Campbell. AB in Govt. with honors, Hamilton Coll., Clinton, NY, 1963; LLB, Duke U., 1966. Bar: N.C. 1966, D.C. 1999. Assoc. Levine, Goodman & Murchison, Charlotte, NC, 1966-69; legis. atty. to asst. legis. counsel U.S. Dept. Interior, Washington, 1969-72, dep. asst. sec. Fish and Wildlife and Pks., 1972-77; exec. v.p. Nat. Trust for Hist. Preservation, Washington, 1977-80; pres. Am. Farmland Trust, Washington, 1980-85, now life mem.; exec. dir. Sierra Club, San Francisco, 1985-86; v.p. Conservation Found., Washington, 1986-88, exec. v.p., 1989-91; sec. resources State of Calif., Sacramento, 1991—99; ptnr. Hogan & Hartson LLP, Washington, 1999—. Bd. mem. Lincoln Inst. Land Use Policy, Am. Farmland Trust. Contbr. chapters to books. Hon. life mem. bd. visitors Duke U. Sch. of Law; mem. adv. coun. The Conservation Fund; mem. biodiversity conservation working group N.Am. Commn. Environ. Cooperation; trustee Colo. Conservation Trust; mem. coun. Yosemite Fund; candidate N.C. Ho. of Reps., 1968; mem. D.C. Rep. Ctrl. Com., 1984-85; chmn. adv. bd. Nat. Park Sys. Lt. JAGC, USNR, 1969-75. Recipient commendation U.S. Dept. Interior, 1976, Achievement award, 1980, Conservation award Gulf Oil Corp., 1985, Charles S. Murphy award for pub. svc, 1995, Presdl. award for sustainable devel., 1996, Nat. Conservation Leadership award The Conservation Fund, 1997. Mem. ABA, D.C. Bar Assn., N.C. Bar Assn., Sierra Club (life), Am. Farmland Trust (life). Episcopalian. Home: 4541 45th St NW Washington DC 20016-4473 Business E-Mail: dpwheeler@hhlaw.com.

WHEELER, EDWARD, engineering educator; b. Milan, Tenn., Feb. 16, 1959; s. Wylie and Marie Wheeler; m. Ellen Glassco, June 26, 1982; 1 child, Abigail. BS in Engrng. Tech., U. Tenn., Martin, 1980; MBA, U. Tenn., 1982; MS in Indsl. and Sys. Engrng., U. Memphis, 1987. Assoc. prof. dept. engrng. U. Tenn., Martin, 1980—. Editor: (textbook supplement) Study Guide for Engineering Economic Analysis, 2004. Named an Oustanding Outline Tchr., U. Tenn., Martin, 2006—07. Mem.: Am. Soc. Engrng. Edn. (chmn. engrng. economy divsn. 2002—03). Home: 2019 Chickadee Dr Milan TN 38358 Office: U Tenn Martin 101 Johnson EPS Bldg Martin TN 38238

WHEELER, GEORGE CHARLES, JR., materials engineer, process engineer; b. Balt., Oct. 9, 1923; s. George Charles and Julia Elizabeth (Atrous) Wheeler; m. Dorothy W. Whittemore, Sept. 13, 1947; children: Scott, Craig, Mark, Matthew, Tracy, Bruce; m. Clara Frances Weiner, Jan. 21, 1978. BS in Metall. Engrng., Lehigh U., 1944. Various engrng. and supervisory positions GE, Mass. and N.Y., 1944-62; mgr. materials, welding and nondestructive test engrng. Knolls Atomic Power Lab., G.E., Schenectady, NY, 1962-68; mgr. nondestructive testing G.E. Power Sys., Schenectady, NY, 1968-85; pres., CEO Wheeler Nondestructive Testing, Inc., Schenectady, 1985-95, Materials and Processes Cons., Schenectady, 1995—; mgr. tech. svcs. Am. Soc. for Nondestructive Testing, Columbus, Ohio, 1993-94. Cons. UN, NYC, 1985—98, IAEA, Vienna, 1985—98, ASNT, 1997—, others; guest lectr. Rennsselaer Poly. Inst., Troy, NY, Union Coll., Schenectady, 1978—87; mem. math. sci. and tech. com. Schenectady County CC, 1978—85, adj. prof., 1987—97; US del. Internat. Stds. Orgn., mem. com. TC 135/SC7 NDT Pers. Qualification, 1987—97, convenor working group #2 ISO-9712; mem. ASNT Cert. Mgmt. Bd., 1994—98, chmn., 1976—80, 1986—89. Author: Guide to Personnel Certification, 1990, rev. edit., 2003, Guide to Developing Certification Exams, 1992; co-author: rev. edit., 2005, Level II Study Guide: Radiographic Testing, 1998, Level II Study Guide: Ultrasonic Testing, 1999; contbg. editor: JMaterials Evaluation Jour. ASNT, tech. editor: Nondestructive Testing Handbook, 3d edit., vol. 3. Fellow: Am. Soc. Nondestructive Tsting (hon.; bd. dirs. 1976—85, pres. 1983—84, chmn. 1984—85, chmn. cert. com. 1976—80, 1986—89, Gold medal); mem.: ASTM (mem. com. internat. stds., mem. com. nondestructive testing), NRA (life), Nature Conservancy (life), Am. Soc. Metals (life), Trout Unlimited (life), Adirondack Mountain Club, Adirondack Forty-Sixers. Achievements include pioneering personnel certifications for nondestructive testing work worldwide for ASTM, ISO and ASNT. Avocations: mountain climbing, flying, firearms, photography, cross country skiing, golf, fishing.

WHEELER, GERALD, church musician, educator; b. Richmond, Surrey, Eng., Mar. 26, 1929; arrived in US, 1996; s. William George and Rosina Musgrave (Hall) Wheeler; m. Elizabeth Jennifer Taylor (div.); children: Gillian, Andrew, Sarah, Jane; m. Jean Borntraeger Wheeler, Apr. 23, 1990; children: Christian, Justin, Henry, Katherine. Student, Royal Coll. Music, London, 1949—52; ThD in Religious Studies (hon.), McGill U., Montreal, Can., 1996. Dir. music St. Olane's Sch., Tower Bridge, London, 1956—56, St. Mathew's Ch., Ottawa, 1956—65, Christ Ch. Cathedral, Montreal, 1965—96; prof. music Marianopolis Coll., Montreal, 1965—95; dir. music Blue Hill Congl. Ch., Maine, 2005—. Organist Montreal Symphony Orch., 1965—96; harpischordist, organist McGill Chamber Orch., Montreal, 1965—96. Recipient Arts award, Can. Coun., 1968. Fellow: Royal Coll. Organists; mem.: Club Atwater. Episcopalian. Avocations: skiing, walking. Home: 77 Old Ferry Rd Deer Isle ME 04627

WHEELER, GERALD F., educational association administrator; BS in Sci. Edn., Boston U.; M in Physics, SUNY, Stony Brook, PhD in Exptl. Nuc. Physics. HS tchr. physics, chemistry and phys. sci.; dir. sci./math resource ctr., prof. physics Mont. State U.; exec. dir. Nat. Sci. Tchrs. Assn., Arlington, Va. Mem. adv. bd. Voyage of the Mimi, CRO; co-dir. Nat. Tchrs. Enhancement Network; mem. nat. adv. com. Keystone Sci. Network. Contbr. articles to profl. pubis.; creator, host: (TV series) Sidewalk Science. Fellow: W. K. Kellogg Found., AAAS (head Pub. Understanding of Sci. and Tech. divsn.); mem.: Am. Assn. Physics Tchrs. (former pres., Milliken award). Office: Nat Sci Tchrs Assn 1840 Wilson Blvd Arlington VA 22201 Office Phone: 703-243-7100. E-mail: gwheeler@nsta.org. *

WHEELER, GERALDINE HARTSHORN, historian, writer; b. Pomona, Calif., Feb. 5, 1919; d. Albion True and Beatrice Osa (Barnes) Hartshorn; m. Lloyd Franklyn Wheeler, Dec. 2, 1938 (dec. Mar. 1996); children: Russell Lloyd, Robert Gerald. *Her intense interest in history led Geraldine Hartshorn Wheeler into researching her family roots and the social life of earlier times. Her love of the flow of words has led to writing essays for local newspapers, giving lectures, and now into transcribing old family diaries. She also has a special interest in the historical side of earthquakes, where and when they happened, and how people reacted under the stress of the events. She also enjoys doing volunteer activities she which started at the age of seven and in which she is still involved.* AA, Santa Ana CC, Calif., 1950s. Co-owner Atheling's, Santa Barbara, Calif., 1971-76, Pomona, 1976-90; chmn. bd. trustees Atheling Heritage Trust, Claremont, Calif., 1994—. Pub., editor: mag. Atheling's, 1974—75, newsletter Grand Priory of America Order of St. Lazarus, 1974—86; editor: St. Margaret's Jour., 1975—; author: (essays) A World Full in 1891, 1975—, President John Adams-A Profile, 1975—, Ralph Waldo Emerson-A Profile, 1975, The Many Masks of Communism, 1975, A Tale of St. Nicholas, 1995, Post Cards and Postal Cards, 1996, Pocahontas Kinships, 1996. Vol. PTA, Fontana and Santa Barbara, 1945-60; mem. various coms. and choir First Congl. Ch., Santa Barbara, 1952-72; leader Cub Scouts Am., Santa Barbara, 1953-56; grey lady unit chmn. Santa Barbara chpt.-ARC, 1958-62; women's project bd. v.p., activities chmn., active various coms. Santa Barbara Hist. Soc., 1960-74; exec. sec. 1960 Nixon for Pres. Campaign, Santa Barbara, 1960; mem. spkrs. bur. Nixon for Gov. Campaign, Santa Barbara, 1962; mem. Rep. state ctrl. com. State of Calif., 1962-64; blitz chmn. Rockefeller for Pres. Campaign, Santa Barbara, 1964; coord. vol. svcs. Office of Civil Def., City of Santa Barbara, 1965-76; coord. tv series on earthquakes Sta. KEYT, Office of Civil Def., Santa Barbara, 1968; bd. dirs. Calif. Ctrl. Coast Area, U.S.O., 1968-76, treas. bd., 1970-76; supporter Vis. Nurses and Hospice Assn., 1994—; others. Decorated Dame of Grace, Mil. and Hospitaller Order of St. Lazarus of Jerusalem, Cert. of Merit, 1973, The Alan Weaver Hazelton award; recipient Cert. of Merit, Santa Barbara Jr. Coll., 1954-55, Medal of Appreciation SAR, 1972, Cert. of Award Nat. Soc. Daus. of Founders and Patriots of Am., 1977. Mem. Acad. Polit. Sci., Calif. Hist. Soc., New Eng. Hist. and Geneal. Soc., The Pomona Ebell (pres. 1998-2000), Wilson Ctr. Assocs., Smithsonian Assocs., Nat. Trust for Hist. Preservation, Am. Farmland Trust, Nat. Woman's History Mus., Nat. Arbor Day Found., Pomona Valley Hist. Soc., La Verne Hist. Soc., La Salle County Hist. Soc., Nat. Wildlife Fedn., Colonial Williamsburg Found., The Postcard Soc. (founder), Musicians Club Pomona Valley, Shakespeare Club Pomona Valley, Nat. Soc. DAR (past regent chpts.), Calif. Huguenot Soc., Nat. Soc. Daus. Founders and Patriots (past nat. officer, orgn. pres. So. Calif. chpt.), Colonial Dames Am. (orgn. pres. chpt. XX), Nat. Soc. Daus. Colonial Wars (state officer), Nat. Soc. Women Desc. Ancient and Honorable Artillery Co. (past nat. chaplain and state officer), Soc. Mayflower Desc. (past colony gov.), Nat. Soc. Dames of the Ct. of Honor, Nat. Soc. New Eng. Women, Hereditary Order Desc. Colonial Govs. (past nat. officer), Soc. Desc. Most Noble Order of the Garter, Ams. Armorial Ancestry, Ams. Royal Descent, Colonial Order of the Crown, The Plantagenet Soc., Nat. Soc. Magna Charta Dames, Order of the Crown of Charlemagne in USA, Nat. Soc. Ams. Royal Descent, Nat. Soc. Desc. Early Quakers (founding nat. clk.), Nat. Guild St. Margaret of Scotland (founder), Nat. Gavel Club, Mt. Vernon Ladies' Assn., Order of the Merovingian Dynasty. Republican. Avocations: book collecting, reading, genealogy, classical music, needlecrafts. Home: 1047 E Baseline Rd Claremont CA 91711-1577

WHEELER, HEWITT BROWNELL, surgeon, educator; b. Louisville, July 21, 1929; s. Arville and Lois (Vance) W.; m. Elizabeth Jane Maxwell, July 21, 1956; children: Stephen, Elizabeth, Jane, Mary. Student, Vanderbilt U., 1945-48; MD, Harvard U., 1952. Diplomate Am. Bd. Surgery (bd. dirs. 1984-90). Cushing fellow Harvard Med. Sch., Boston, 1953, Peters fellow, 1956, research fellow, 1959-60, instr. surgery, 1961-64, clin. assoc. surgery, 1964-67, asst. clin. prof. surgery, 1967-70, assoc. prof. surgery, 1970-71; asst. in surgery Peter Bent Brigham Hosp., Boston, 1959-60, jr. assoc. surgery, 1961-64, assoc. surgery, 1964-69, sr. assoc. surgery, 1969-71; asst. chief surgery Roxbury VA Hosp., Boston, 1961-62, chief surgery, 1962-71, chief of staff, 1968-71; cons. surgery U. Mass. Med. Sch., Worcester, 1966-71; prof., chmn. dept. surgery U. Mass. Med. Sch. at Worcester, 1971-96, Harry M. Haidak disting. prof. surgery, 1985-98, prof. emeritus, 1998—; chief staff U. Mass. Hosp., 1974-76, surgeon-in-chief, 1976-96; exec. dir. Ctr. for Advanced Clin. Tech., 1995—; affiliate prof. biomed. engrng. Worcester Poly. Inst., 1974—; lectr. surgery Harvard Med. Sch., 1974-96; chief surgery St. Vincent Hosp., Worcester, 1971-75. Cons. Meml. Hosp., Worcester City Hosp., 1970-96, Worcester Hahnemann Hosp., 1974-94, Peter Bent Brigham Hosp., 1973-96; chmn. surg. research program com. VA, Washington, 1965-67, nat. participant surg. cons., 1965-69, chmn. ad hoc adv. com. surgery, 1969-71. Pres. Mass. Compassionate Care Coalition, 2000—04; trustee Ctrl. Mass. Health Care Found., 1975—77, Worcester Found. for Biomed. Rsch., 1996—2004, Hospice Ctrl. Mass. Inc., 1997—2000, U. Mass. Meml. Found., 1998—2005, Boston Med. Libr., 1996—2002. 1st lt. M.C. AUS, 1953—55. Mem. ACS (bd. govs. 1984-90, coun. Mass. chpt. 1973-76, pres. 1980), AAAS, AMA, Am. Surg. Assn., Soc. Univ. Surgeons, Internat. Cardiovascular Soc., New Eng. Surg. Soc. (treas. 1977-84, v.p. 1986-87, pres. 1989-91), Boston Surg. Soc. (pres. 1995-96), Worcester Surg. Soc. (pres. 1973-75), Transplantation Soc., Mass. Med. Soc. (100th Shattuck lectr. 1990; lifetime achievement award 2005), Worcester Dist. Med. Soc. (sec. 1996-99, v.p. 1999-00, pres. 2000-01), New Eng. Vascular Soc. (v.p. 1985-86, pres. 1988-89). Achievements include rsch. in exptl. transplantation, blood vessel surgery, method to detect blood clots, improving end-of-life care. Home: 52 Cloyster Rd South Portland ME 04106-5110 E-mail: bwheele1@maine.rr.com.

WHEELER, JANE, investment banker; Grad., U. Va. Various positions to mng. dir. Morgan Stanley, NYC, 1993—2005; sr. mng. dir. Evercore Ptnrs. Inc., NYC, 2005—. Bd. trustees Brearley Sch. Named to Online Fin. 40, Instl. Investor, 2005, 2006; recipient Rainmaker prize, Dealmaker mag., 2006. Mem.: Phi Beta Kappa. Office: Evercore Ptnrs 43rd Fl 55 East 52nd St New York NY 10055 Office Phone: 212-857-3100. Office Fax: 212-857-3101. *

WHEELER, JANE FRANCES, protective services official; b. McAlester, Okla. Dir. Consumer Protection, Oklahoma City, 1984—. Office: Consumer Protection Atty Gen 313 NE 21st St Oklahoma City OK 73105

WHEELER, JOHN ARCHIBALD, physicist, educator; b. Jacksonville, Fla., July 9, 1911; s. Joseph Lewis and Mabel (Archibald) Wheeler; m. Janette Hegner, June 10, 1935; children: Isabel Letitia Wheeler Ufford, James English, Alison Christie Wheeler Lahnston. PhD, Johns Hopkins U., 1933; ScD (hon.), Western Res. U., 1958, U. N.C., 1959, U. Pa., 1968, Middlebury Coll., 1969, Rutgers U., 1969, Yeshiva U., 1973, Yale U., 1974; PhD (hon.), U. Uppsala, 1975; ScD (hon.), U. Md., 1977, Gustavus Adolphus U., 1981, Cath. U. Am., 1982, U. Newcastle-upon-Tyne, 1983, Princeton U., 1986, U. Conn., 1989, U. Maine, 1992, Tufts U., 1992; LLD (hon.), Johns Hopkins U., 1977; LittD (hon.), Drexel U., 1987. NRC fellow, NY and Copenhagen, 1933—35; from asst. prof. to assoc. prof. physics U. N.C., 1935—38; asst. prof. physics Princeton U., 1938—42, assoc. prof., 1945—47, prof., 1947—76, Joseph Henry prof. physics, 1966—76, Joseph Henry prof. physics emeritus, 1976—; prof. physics and dir. Ctr. for Theoretical Physics, U. Tex., Austin, 1976—86; Ashbel Smith prof. U. Tex., Austin, 1979—86, Blumberg prof., 1981—86, Smith and Blumberg prof. emeritus, 1986—. Cons. and physicist on atomic energy projects Princeton U., 1939—42, U. Chgo., 1942, E.I. duPont de Nemours & C, Wilmington, Del., Richland, Wash., 1943—45, Los Alamos, 1950—53; dir. Project Matterhorn (H-bomb) Princeton U., 1951—53; Guggenheim fellow, Paris and Copenhagen, 1949—50; summer lectr. U. Mich., U. Chgo., Columbia U; Lorentz prof. U. Leiden, 1956; Fulbright prof. Kyoto U., 1962; vis. fellow Clare Coll., Cambridge U., 1964; Ritchie lectr. Edinburgh, 1958; vis. prof. U. Calif.-Berkeley, 1960; Battelle prof. U. Wash., 1975; I.I. Rabi vis. prof. Columbia U., 1983; sci. advisor U.S. Senate del. to 3d ann. conf. NATO Parliamentarians, Paris, 1957; mem. adv. com. Oak Ridge Nat. Lab., 1957—65, U. Calif., Los Alamos and Livermore, 1972—77; v.p. Internat. Union Physics, 1951—54; chmn. joint com. on history of theoretical physics in 20th century Am. Phys. Soc. and Am. Philos. Soc., 1960—72; sci. adv. bd. USAF, 1961—62; chmn. Dept. Def. Advanced Rsch. Projects Agy. Project 137 (now Project Jason), 1958; mem. U.S. Gen. Adv. Com. Arms Control and Disarmament, 1969—72, 1974—77. Author: Geometrodynamics, 1962; author: (with others) Gravitation Theory and Gravitational Collapse, 1965; author: Spacetime Physics, 1966; author: (with E. Taylor) Spacetime Physics, 2d edit., 1992; author: (in German) Einstein's Vision, 1968; author: (with C.W. Misner and K.S. Thorne) Gravitation, 1973; author: (with M. Rees and R. Ruffini) Black Holes, Gravitation Waves and Cosmology, 1974; author: Frontiers of Time, 1979, A Journey into Gravity and Spacetime, 1990, At Home in the Universe, 1994; author: (with I. Ciufolini) Gravitation and Inertia, 1995; author: also translations, 1991—92; author: (with Kenneth Ford) Geons, Black Holes and Quantum Foam: A Life in Physics, 1998; editor (with W. Zurek): Quantum Theory and Measurement, 1983; contbr. 375 articles to profl. jours. Trustee Battelle Meml. Inst., 1959—89, S.W. Rsch. Inst., San Antonio, 1977—92, Unitarian Ch., 1965. Recipient A. Cressy Morrison prize for work on nuc. physics, N.Y. Acad. Scis., 1947, Albert Einstein prize, Strauss Found., 1965, Enrico Fermi award, AEC, 1968, Franklin medal, Franklin Inst., 1969, Nat. medal of Sci., 1971, Herzfeld award, 1975, Outstanding Grad. Tchg. award, U. Tex., 1981, Niels Bohr Internat. Gold medal, 1982, Oersted medal, Am. Assn. Physics Tchrs., 1983, J. Robert Oppenheimer Meml. prize, 1984, Matteucci medal, Nat. Acad. Sci. Rome, Soc. of the Forty, 1994, Wolf prize in physics, Wolf Found., Israel, 1997. Fellow: AAAS (dir. 1965—68), Am. Phys. Soc. (pres. 1966, Einstein prize 2003); mem.: NAS, Royal Danish Acad. Scis., Royal Soc. (London), Accademia Nazionale dei Lincei, Internat. Union Physics (v.p. 1951—54), L'Academie Internationale de Philosophie des Sciences (v.p. 1987—90), Tex. Philos. Soc., Royal Acad. Sci. (Uppsala, Sweden), Philos. Soc. of Tex., Am. Philos. Soc. (councillor 1963—66, v.p. 1971—73, councillor 1976—79, Franklin medal 1989), Am. Acad. Arts and Scis., Internat. Astron. Union, Am. Math. Soc., Princeton Club (N.Y.C.), Century Assn. (N.Y.C.), Sigma Xi, Phi Beta Kappa. Unitarian Universalist. Office: Princeton U Dept Physics Princeton NJ 08544-0001 Business E-Mail: jawheeler@pupgg.princeton.edu. *We will first understand how simple the universe is when we recognize how strange it is.*

WHEELER, JOHN CRAIG, astrophysicist, writer; b. Glendale, Calif., Apr. 5, 1943; s. G. L. and Peggy Wheeler; m. Hsueh Lie, Oct. 29, 1967; children: Diek Winters, J. Robinson. BS in Physics, MIT, 1965; PhD in Physics, U. Colo., 1969. Asst. prof. astronomy Harvard U., Cambridge, Mass., 1971-74; assoc. prof. U. Tex., Austin, 1974-80, prof., 1980—, Samuel T. and Fern Yanagisawa Regents prof. astronomy, 1985—, chmn. astronomy dept., 1986-90. Vis. fellow Joint Inst. Lab. Astrophysics, Boulder, 1978—79, Japan Soc. Promotion Sci., 1983; 1st vis. prof. Assn. Univs. Rsch. Astronomy, 1990; vis. sr. scientist Inst. Theoretical Physics U. Calif., Santa Barbara, 1997; gen. mem. Aspen (Colo.) Ctr. Physics; mem. exec. com. Tex. Symposium Relativistic Astrophysics; mem. com. origin and evolution life NRC Space Studies Bd., 2002—05, mem., 2002—06. Author: The Krone Experiment, 1986, Cosmic Catastrophes, 2000; editor: Accretion Disks in Compact Stellar Systems, 1993, Supernovae, 1990, Disk Instabilities in Close Binary Systems, 1999, Proceedings of the 20th Texas Symposium on Relativistic Astrophysics, Cosmic Explosions in Three Dimensions. Recipient award, U. Tex., 1984, 1986, 1999, Pres.'s Assocs. Tchg. Excellence award, 1999; Fulbright fellow, Italy, 1991, Dads Assn. Centennial Tchg. fellow, U. Tex., 1999. Mem.: Am. Phys. Soc., Acad. Disting. Tchrs., Internat. Astron. Union, Am. Astron. Soc. (v.p. 1999—2002, pres. 2006—), Sigma Xi. Avocations: running, writing, reading. Office: U Tex Dept Astronomy Austin TX 78712

WHEELER, JOHN OLIVER, retired geologist; b. Mussoorie, India, Dec. 19, 1924; s. Edward Oliver and Dorothea Sophie (Danielsen) W.; m. Nora Jean Hughes, May 17, 1952; children: Kathleen Anna Wheeler Hunter, Jennifer Margaret Wheeler Crompton. BASc in Geol. Engrng., U. BC, 1947, DSc (hon.), 2000; PhD in Geology, Columbia U., NYC, 1956. Geologist Geol. Survey Can., Ottawa, Ont., 1951-61, Vancouver, BC, 1961-65, rsch. scientist, 1965-70, rsch. mgr. Ottawa, 1970—, chief regional and econ. geology divsn., 1970-73, dep. dir. gen., 1973-79; rsch. scientist Geol. Survey Can. (Cordilleran divsn.), 1979-90, rsch. scientist emeritus, 1990—2006. Gen. editor: Geology of Canada, 8 vols., 1989-2006; compiler of regional geol. maps of we. Can., Can. and no. N.Am. and Greenland; contbr. articles to profl. jours.; chpts. to books. Recipient Queen's Silver Jubilee medal, 1977, Can. 125 medal, 1994, Earth Sci. Sector and Dept. awards Nat. Resources Can., 1996, Spl. award of BC-Yukon Chamber of Mines for outstanding contbn. to Can. Cordilleran geology, 2000, Massey medal Royal Can. Geog. Soc., 2002, hon. fellow 2003. Fellow Royal Soc. Can., Geol. Assn. Can. (pres. 1970-71, Logan medal 1983, Disting. fellow 1996), Geol. Soc. Am. (councillor 1971-74), Can. Geosci. Coun. (pres. 1981); mem. Can. Inst. Mining and Metallurgy, Can. Geol. Found. (pres. 1974-79), Can. Alpine Club (hon.), Am. Alpine Club. Anglican.

WHEELER, JOHN S., JR., urologist; s. John S. Wheeler Sr. and Virginia S. Wheeler; m. Michele A. Marganski, June 4, 1977; children: Nicholas, Anne. BA, Dartmouth Coll., 1972; MD, Georgetown U., 1977. Lic. physician Ill., cert. Mass. Resident gen. surgery Boston Med. Ctr., 1977—79, resident urology, 1979—82, urodynamics fellowship, 1983; faculty Loyola U. Med. Ctr., Maywood, Ill., 1983—; staff urologist Hines VA Hosp., 1983—, RML Hosp., Hinsdale, 2003—. Cons. in field. Contbr. articles to profl. jours., chapters to books. Fellow, Boston U. Med. Ctr., 1982—83. Mem.: Am. Paraplegia Soc. (rsch. com. 1984—), Am. Coll. Surgeons, Am. Urological Assn., Alpha Omega Alpha. Roman Catholic. Avocations: golf, skiing. Office: Loyola U Med Ctr Dept Urology 2160 S First Ave Maywood IL 60153 Office Phone: 708-216-4076. Business E-Mail: jwheeler@lumc.edu.

WHEELER, JOHN WATSON, lawyer; b. Murfreesboro, Tenn., Sept. 11, 1938; s. James William and Grace (Fann) W.; m. Dorothy Anita Pressgrove, Aug. 5, 1959; children: Jeffrey William, John Harold. BS in Journalism, U. Tenn., 1960, JD, 1968. Bar: Tenn. 1968, U.S. Dist. Ct. (ea. dist.) Tenn. 1968, U.S. Dist. Ct. (mid. dist.) Tenn., U.S. Dist. Ct. (we. dist.) Tenn., U.S. Supreme Ct. 1974, U.S. Ct. Appeals (6th cir.) 1975. Editor The Covington (Tenn.) Leader, 1963-65; adminstrv. asst. to lab. dir. UT-AEC Rsch. Lab., Oak Ridge, Tenn., 1965-68; assoc. Hodges, Doughty & Carson, Knoxville, Tenn., 1968-72, ptnr., 1972—2005, of counsel, 2005—. Mem. commn. to study Appellate Cts. in Tenn.; chair U.S. magistrate merit selection panel, U.S. Dist. Ct. (ea. dist.) Tenn., 1991, 2002, 03, mem. bankruptcy judge merit selection panel, 1992-94; chmn. hist. soc., U.S. Dist. Ct. (ea. dist.) Tenn., 1993-2004. Mem. organizing com. Tenn. Supreme Ct. Hist. Soc. Lt. U.S. Army, 1961-63, capt. Res. Fellow Am. Bar Found. (life, Tenn. chair 1999—), Tenn. Bar Found. (life); mem. ABA (ho. of dels. 1986-2000), Tenn. Bar Assn. (pres. 1989-90, bd. govs. 1981-91), Nat. Conf. Bar Pres., Am. Inns. of Ct. (master of bench, emeritus), Internat. Assn. Def. Counsel, So. Conf. Bar Pres., 6th Cir. Jud. Conf. (life), Fox Den Country Club (bd. dirs. 2001-04). Republican. Lutheran. Avocations: golf, travel. Home: 12009 N Fox Den Dr Knoxville TN 37934 Office: Hodges Doughty & Carson PO Box 869 Knoxville TN 37901-0869 Home Phone: 865-966-5323; Office Phone: 865-546-9611. Business E-Mail: jwheeler@hdclaw.com.

WHEELER, KARLA, education educator; d. Kristine and George Blogechl; m. Robert Wheeler, May 11, 1996. BA in Art History, U. Wis., Milw., 1998, MA in Pub. History, 2001; postgrad., U. Wis., Madison, 2006—. Curatorial asst. Waukesha County Mus., Wis., 1998—2000, dir. of pub. edn., 2000—02; curator of edn. Logan Mus. of Anthropology, Beloit, Wis., 2002—; asst. prof. Beloit Coll., Wis., 2002—. Grad. student rep. UW-Milw., Dept. of History, 2001. Mem.: Nat. Coun. for History Edn., Mus. Edn. Roundtable, Nat. Coun. on Pub. History, Assn. of Midwest Museums, Am. Assn. of Museums, Nat. Vocat. and Tech. Honor Soc. (life). Avocation: travel. Office: Beloit College 700 College St Beloit WI 53511 Office Phone: 608-363-2678. E-mail: wheelerk@beloit.edu.

WHEELER, KATHERINE WELLS, retired state legislator; b. St. Louis, Feb. 8, 1940; d. Benjamin Harris and Katherine (Gladney) Wells; m. Douglas Lanphier Wheeler, June 13, 1964; children: Katherine Gladney, Lucille Lanphier BA, Smith Coll., 1961; MA, Washington U., St. Louis, 1966. Founder auction N.H. Pub. TV, Durham, 1973-76; pub. mem. N.H. Pub. Broadcasting Coun., Durham, 1975-80; founding mem. bd. govs. N.H. Pub. TV, 1980-88; elected N.H. Ho. of Reps., Concord, 1988, 90, 92,94; mem. N.H. Senate, 1996—98, 1998—2000, 2000—02, chmn. health & human svcs. com. Coord. internat. visitors program N.J. Coun. World Affairs, 1981-95. Bd. dirs. Planned Parenthood No. New England, 1989-95, Gt. Bay Svcs., Newington, N.H., 1989-97, Behavioral Health and Devel. Svcs. Strafford County, Inc., 1991—; vice chairperson Strafford County Legis. Del., 1993-94; active Commn. on Health, Human Svcs. and Elderly Affairs N.H. Ho. of Reps., Concord, 1988-96; bd. dirs. N.H. Pub. Health Assn., 1996—, pres., 2003--; bd. dirs. NAMI N.H., 2002--, NARAL N.H. Found., 1998-- Named Woman of Yr., Union Leader Newspaper, 1984, Citizen of Yr., Homemakers of Strafford County, 1990, N.H. sect. NASW, 1993, Legislator of Yr., N.H. Nurses Assn., 1996, N.H. Acad. Pediat., 1996; recipient Elizabeth Campbell Outstanding Pub. TV Vol. award Nat. Friends Pub. Broadcasting, 1984, Meritorious Svc. award N.H. Women's Lobby, 1992, Dist. Contbn. award N.H. Psychol. Orgn., Inc., 1994, Cert. of Achievement for Outstanding Legis. Leadership N.H. Citizen Action, 1994; Fleming fellow Leadership Inst., Ctr. for Policy Alternatives, Washington, 1997-98. Mem. AAUW, LWV, Am. Assn. Ret. Persons, Order of Women Legislators, N.H. Smith Coll. Club (v.p. 1974-76, pres. 1976-78, v.p. class of 1961, 1991-96), N.H. Assn. Social Workers (Legislator of Yr. 1993), N.H. Psychol. Orgn. Inc. (Disting. Contbn. award 1994). Democrat. Mem. United Ch. of Christ. Home and Office: 27 Mill Rd Durham NH 03824-3006

WHEELER, M. CASS, health science association administrator; b. Tex. BA in Advertising, U. Texas, Austin, 1963. Stockbroker NY Stock Exch. firm, Dallas, 1969—73; with Am. Heart Assn., Austin, Tex., 1973—82, COO Dallas, 1982, sr. v.p., field ops., 1996, CEO, 1997—. Guest lecturer Harvard U. Sch. of Bus. & Pub. Health, U. Texas Sch. of Mgmt., Dallas, U. Texas Lyndon B. Johnson Sch. of Pub. Affairs, Austin; former bd. chmn. Nat. Health Coun.; bd. mem. Partnership for Prevention, Research! Am., Nat. Ctr. for Tobacco-Free Kids, Nat. Assembly of Health and Human Service Organizations; advisory bd. mem. Discovery Health Media, Inc.; mem. Citizens Advisory Council for the Campaign for Med. Rsch.; former mem. President's Commn. on Improving Econ. Opportunity in Communities Dependent on Tobacco Production While Protecting Pub. Health. Avocations: running, skiing, bicycling. Office: Am Heart Assn 7272 Greenville Ave Dallas TX 75231-5129

WHEELER, MALCOLM EDWARD, lawyer, educator; b. Berkeley, Calif., Nov. 29, 1944; s. Malcolm Ross and Frances Dolores (Kane) W.; m. Donna Marie Stambaugh, July 25, 1981; children: Jessica Ross, M. Connor. SB, MIT, 1966; JD, Stanford U., 1969. Bar: Calif. 1970, Colo. 1992, U.S. Dist. Ct (cen. dist.) Calif. 1970, U.S. Ct. Appeals (9th cir.) 1970, U.S. Ct. Appeals (10th cir.) 1973, U.S. Dist. Ct. (no., so., ea. and cen. dists.) Calif. 1975, U.S. Ct. Appeals (11th cir.) 1987, U.S. Ct. Appeals (D.C. cir.) 1987, U.S. Supreme Ct. 1976, U.S. Ct. Appeals (3d cir.) 1989, (4th cir.) 1992, (8th cir.) 1993, (5th cir.) 1995, (Fed. cir.) 1998. Assoc. Howard, Prim, Smith, Rice & Downs, San Francisco, 1969-71; assoc. prof. law U. Kans., Lawrence, 1971-74; assoc. Hughes Hubbard & Reed, Los Angeles, 1974-77, ptnr., 1977-81, 83-85, cons., 1981-83; ptnr. Skadden, Arps, Slate, Meagher & Flom, Los Angeles, 1985-91; dir. Parcel, Mauro, Hultin & Spaanstra P.C., Denver, 1991-98, Wheeler Trigg & Kennedy, P.C., Denver, 1998—. Vis. prof. U. Iowa, 1978, prof., 1979; prof. U. Kans., Lawrence, 1981-83; chief counsel U.S. Senate Select Com. to Study Law Enforcement Undercover Activities, Washington, 1982-83. Mem. editl. bd. Jour. Products Liability, 1984-90, Fed. Litigation Guide Reporter, 1986-90; contbr. articles to profl. jours. Fellow Am. Coll. Trial Lawyers; mem. ABA, Calif. Bar Assn., Colo. Bar Assn., Am. Law Inst. Home: 100 Humboldt St Denver CO 80218-3932 Office Phone: 303-292-2525. Business E-Mail: wheeler@wtklaw.com.

WHEELER, MARGARET JANE, actress, soprano, voice educator; b. Apr. 16, 1925; d. William Henry and Ruth Bond Wheeler. BA in Voice, George Peabody Coll. (now Vanderrbilt U.), Nashville, 1947; grad. study in voice and opera with L. Vaida, St. Louis Inst. Music, 1950; grad. study with Oren Brown, 1976—77; studied voice, Franco Iglesias, Aida Favia Artsay, Thomas Houser, Thomas Cultice, Willard Young, Julia Drobner, Anthony Frisell, 1960—90; acting study, Stella Adler Studio, 1964—65, David LeGrant Sudio, 1965—69; MA in Voice Performance, Hunter Coll., NYC, 1976. Louis Nicholas voice tchr. Peabody Coll., 1943—47; tchr. Army Dependents Sch., La Rochelle, France, 1955—56; tchr. music Rockland County Pub. Schs., NY, Westchester County Pub. Schs.; tchr.music L.I. Pub. Schs., St. Louis Pub. Schs.; asst. prof. music dept. Millersville State Coll., Pa. Dir. adult choir Asbury Meth. Ch., Croton-on-Hudson, NY; dir. Cmty. Chorus, Croton-on-Hudson, NY; dir. choirs Evang. Ch., Overland, Mo.; voice tchr. Bronx Conservatory of Music, NY, 1990—; tchr. sr. citizen singing classes Co-op City, 2001—04; voice tchr. Bronx Music Ho., Bennett Conservatory of Music, Croton-on-Hudson; tchr. continuing edn. opera appreciation Briarcliff Manor, NYC, White Plains. Performer: (classical and light opera) Brunswick Summer Playhouse, 1961, Lake George Opera Co., 1965, Pitts. Civic Light Opera Co., 1967, Phila. Grand Opera Co., 1971, Assoc. Concert Artists, 1972, 1973, Sycamore Performing Arts Festival, 1973, (classical and light opera conducted by Thomas Cultice) The Medium, 1975, (classical and light opera) Staten Island Opera Co., 1976, (sacred music) Peabody Coll., 1947, Park Ave. Meth. Ch., 1960, St. Matthew's Luth. Ch., 1980, North Yonkers Cmty. Ch., 1985—94; soloist: sacred music Park Ave. Meth. Ch., 1961—67, Christian Sci. Ch., 1968—72, 1974—75, Cmty. Synagogue, 1968—72, soloist: First Westminster Presbyn. Ch., 1976, St. Paul's Episcopal Ch., 1976—77; performer: (showcases) Gunda Morden, 1960, Opera Club of Am., 1960, Messina Opera Co., 1960; soloist and recitalist: Bronx Conservatory of Music, 1970—90, Grad. Recital Hunter Coll. Playhouse, 1976, Westchester Conservatory Music, 1977, Faculty Recitals Millersville (Pa.) Coll., 1977—78, Stewart Smith Singers Concert, 1985, North Yonkers Cmty. Ch., 1985—94, Warner Libr., 1986, Bennett Conservatory, 1986, Westchester CC, 1991; soloist and recitalist Westchester CC, 1994; soloist and recitalist: Sigma Alpha Iota Am. Musicales, 1999—2002; performer: Met. Opera Extra Chorus, 1962, Schola Cantorum NY, 1962—70, Camerata Singers, 1970; dir.: Children's Wing Croton Shakespeare Festival; performer: (musical theater) The Sound of Music, 1971, (multimedia) A Weapon Most Unusual!, 2005, (caberet show) Entertainment Express, 2006. Mem. delegation music tchrs. People to People, China, 1988, Hong Kong, 1988. Mem.: Nat. Assn. Tchrs Singing, Am. Guild Musical Artists, Actor's Equity, Sigma Alpha Iota. Home: 786 Sleepy Hollow Rd Briarcliff Manor NY 10510-2525 E-mail: peggyjanewhe@juno.com.

WHEELER, MICHAEL THOMAS, pain medicine specialist, director; b. Lansing, Mich., June 10, 1969; s. Dennis Leon and Phyllis Loray Wheeler; m. Cammy Ann Regan, Nov. 28, 1997; children: Annie Shea, Jack Michael. BS with high honors, Mich. State U., E.Lansing, 1990—92, MD in Osteo. Medicine, 1995—99. Cert. athletic trainer Nat. Bd. Athletic Trainers, 1992, diplomate Am. Bd. Phys. Medicine & Rehab., 2006, with subspecialty in pain medicine Am. Bd. Phys. Medicine & Rehab., 2006. Indsl. rehab. & corp. fitness Occupl. Med. Assocs., Lansing, 1992—95; med. intern Am. Osteo. Assn., Lansing, 1999—2000; resident physician phys. medicine & rehab. Mich. State U., 2000—02, chief resident phys. medicine & rehab., 2002—03; fellowship in interventional pain mgmt. Spine Tech. & Rehab., Ft. Wayne, Ind., 2003—04, attending physician in interventional pain mgmt., 2004—06; med. dir. pain mgmt. & rehab. svcs. Gt. Lakes Spine Ctr., Flint, Mich., 2006—. Contbr. articles to profl. jours. Fellow: Am. Acad. Phys. Medicine & Rehab.; mem.: Am. Soc. Interventional Pain Physicians (assoc.), Am. Assn. Neuromuscular & Electrodiagnostic Medicine (assoc.), N.Am. Spine Soc. (assoc.), Am. Osteo. Assn. (assoc.). D-Conservative. Cath. Avocations: sports, art. Office: Great Lakes Spine Ctr G-3239 Beecher Rd Flint MI 48532 Home Phone: 517-575-0173. Office Fax: 810-733-2880. Business E-Mail: wheele23@msu.edu.

WHEELER, OTIS BULLARD, retired language educator, retired director; b. Mansfield, Ark., Feb. 1, 1921; s. Clarence Charles and Georgia Elizabeth (Bullard) W.; m. Doris Louise Alexander, Jan. 17, 1943; children: Ann Carolyn, Ross Charles; m. Anne Carol Loveland, Mar. 23, 1991. BA, U. Okla., 1942; MA, U. Tex., 1947; PhD, U. Minn., 1951. Mem. faculty La. State U., Baton Rouge, 1952—, prof. English, 1965-81, prof. emeritus, 1981—, chmn. dept., 1974, asst. dean grad. sch., 1962-67, vice chancellor for acad. affairs, 1974-80, acting chancellor, 1981. Fulbright-Hayes lectr. U. Innsbruck, Austria, 1968-69 Author: The Literary Career of Maurice Thompson, 1965; photographer: (with R.W. Heck) Religious Architecture in Louisiana, 1995, (with Anne C. Loveland) From Meetinghouse to Megachurch, 2003. Served with U.S. Army, 1942-46, 51-52. Decorated Bronze Star medal. Mem. Phi Kappa Phi, Omicron Delta Kappa. Democrat. Methodist. Home: 657 Highland Oaks Dr Baton Rouge LA 70810-5348

WHEELER, RAYMOND LOUIS, lawyer; b. Ft. Sill, Okla., Feb. 10, 1945; s. Raymond Louis and Dorothy Marie (Hutcherson) W.; m. Priscilla Wheeler, July 1, 1966 (div. 1982); children: Jennifer, Hilary; m. Cynthia Lee Jackson, July 14, 1984 (div. 1994); children: Matthew Raymond, Madeline Elizabeth; m. Freddie Kay Park, June 10, 1995. BA, U. Tex., 1967; JD, Harvard U., 1970. Bar: Calif. 1972, U.S. Dist. Ct. (no., cen., ea., so. dists.) Calif., U.S. Ct. Appeals (9th cir., 7th cir.), U.S. Ct. Appeals (7th cir.), U.S. Supreme Ct. Law clk. to hon. Irving L. Goldberg U.S. Ct. Appeals 5th cir., 1970-71; assoc. Morrison & Foerster, San Francisco, 1971-76, ptnr., 1976-90, Palo Alto, Calif., 1990—, labor & employment dept. coord. Chmn. labor and employment law dept. Morrison & Foerster, San Francisco, 1984-88, 92—; lectr. labor and EEO law. Exec. editor Harvard Law Rev., 1969-70; editor in chief The Developing Labor Law; mem. nat. adv. bd. Berkeley Jour. Employment and Labor Law, 1980—; contbr. articles to law jours. Fellow Coll. Labor and Employment Lawyers; mem. ABA (chmn. com. on law devel. under labor rels. act 1990-93, coun. mem. sect. labor and employment 1994-02). Republican. Office: Morrison & Foerster LLP 755 Page Mill Rd Palo Alto CA 94304-1018 Office Phone: 650-813-5656. Office Fax: 650-494-0792. Business E-Mail: rwheeler@mofo.com.

WHEELER, R(ICHARD) KENNETH, lawyer, educator; b. Washington, July 25, 1934; s. Nathaniel Dudley and Ruth Lee (Matthews) W.; m. Christine Kandris, Jan. 11, 1990; children by previous marriage: Jennifer L., Ruth E. BA, Emory and Henry Coll., U. Richmond, 1957; LLB, U. Richmond, 1964. Bar: Va. 1963, D.C. 1977, U.S. Tax Ct. 1978. Assoc., then ptnr. Hunton, Williams, Gay, Powell & Gibson and successor firms, Richmond, 1963-88; sr. ptnr. Kane, Wheeler, Fenderson & Jeffries, Richmond, 1988-90; counsel Durrette, Irvin, Lemons & Fenderson, P.C., Richmond, 1990-94; sr. ptnr. Wallace, Harris & Wheeler, Richmond, 1994-95. Adj. prof. law T.C. Williams Sch. Law, U. Richmond, 1966, 83, bd. dirs., 1977-79; adj. prof. law Va. Commonwealth U., 1970; lectr. trial practice U. Va., 1981-82, 85, 87; arbitrator Am. Arbitration Assn. Served to capt. USMCR, 1957-61. Williams scholar U. Richmond, 1961-63. Mem. Am. Law Inst., Va. State Bar (chmn. com. liaison with law schs. 1977-78, chmn. com. legal edn. and admission to bar 1978-80, spcl. com. on professionalism 1987-88), Web Soc., McNeill Law Soc., Marine Corps League (life), Rector's Club (U. Richmond, life), Pi Sigma Alpha, Phi Delta Phi, Omicron Delta Kappa (hon.).

WHEELER, ROBERT TREIDE, microbiologist, researcher; b. Phila., May 9, 1971; s. James English and Jenette Harvey Wheeler; m. Nives Dal Bo-Wheeler, July 7, 2000; children: Thomas Dal Bo, James Harvey. BA, Harvard U., Cambridge, Mass., 1993; PhD, Stanford U., Calif., 2000. Post-doctoral fellow Whitehead Inst., Cambridge, 2000—. Fellow, Life Sci. Rsch. Found., 2001—04; scholar, NSF, 1994—97; Adah and Bushrod Campbell fellowship, Charles A. King Trust, 2004—06. Mem.: AAAS. Achievements include invention of use of beta-glucan as diagnostic and drug development tool. Office: Whitehead Inst 9 Cambridge Ctr Cambridge MA 02142 Office Phone: 617-258-5214.

WHEELER, RURIC E., mathematics professor; b. Clarkson, Ky., Nov. 30, 1923; s. Mark H. and Mary (Sullivan) Wheeler; m. Joyce Ray, May 31, 1946; children: Eddy Ray, Paul Warren. AB, We. Ky. U., 1947; MS, U. Ky., 1948, PhD, 1952. Instr. math. U. Ky., Lexington, 1948—52; asst. prof. stats. Fla. State U., 1952—53; assoc. prof. math. Samford U., 1953—55, prof., head math. dept., 1955—65, chmn. natural scis. divsn., 1965—67, asst. to dean, 1967—68; dean Howard Coll. Arts and Scis., 1968—70, v.p. acad. affairs, 1970—87, univ. prof., 1987—94, rsch. prof., 1994—. Cons. in field; dir. NSF Inst., 1961, Ala. Vis. Scientist Program, 1962—67. Author: Modern Math., 1966, 12th edit., 2005, Fundamental Concepts of Math, 1968, 2d edit., 1976, Modern Math for Business, 1969, 4th edit., 1986, A Programmed Study of Number Systems, 1972, Finite Mathematics, 1974, 3d edit., 1985, Intuitive Geometry, 1975, Introduccion a los Conjuntos Numericos, 1976, Mathematics, an Everyday Language, 1979, Student Activities Manual, Elementary Mathematics, 1984, Mathematicas un Lenguaje Cotidiano, 1982, Activities Manual for Elementary School Teachers, 1988, Modern Mathematics for Elementary School Teachers, 1994, Finite Mathematics (A Problem Solving Approach), 1991, College Mathematics (a Graphing Calculator Approach), 1996, Brief Calculus (a Graphing Calculator Approach), 1996, Chinese Translation of Brief Calculus, 1997, (novels) All Because of Polly, 2002, Modern Mathematics: Fundamentals and Concepts, 2005, Modern Mathematics for Elementary Educators, 2005. Mem. Birmingham Manpower Area Planning Coun., 1972—75; trustee Gorgas Found., 1968—94, chmn., 1988—92; mem. Jefferson County Ednl. Consortium, 1981—93, pres., 1986—90; mem. Com. to Upgrade Jefferson County Schs., 1982—86; deacon Bapt. Ch. Lt. USAAF, 1943—46. Mem.: Conf. Acad. Deans So. States (pres. 1985—86), So. Conf. Deans Faculties and Acad. V.P. (pres. 1982), Am. Conf. Acad. Deans, Am. Assn. Univ. Adminstrs. (exec. com. Ala. sect. 1972—74, v.p. 1974—76, pres. 1976—77), Assn. Ala. Coll. Adminstrs. (exec. com. 1976—80, pres. 1978—79), Am. Assn. Higher Edn., Ala. Acad. Sci. (pres. 1967—69), Assn. So. Bapt. Colls. and Schs. (sec. 1973, v.p. 1974, pres. 1975, deans sect.), Assn. Math. Tchrs. Ala. (pres. 1963), Nat. Coun. Tchrs. Math., Am. Math. Assn. (chmn. SE sect. 1966—67, vis. lecture program 1989—93), Am. Math. Soc., Am. Edn. Assn., Rotary (pres. of Vestavia rotary club 1983—84). Home: 1347 Badham Dr Birmingham AL 35216-2939 Office Phone: 205-726-2389. Business E-Mail: rewheele@samford.edu.

WHEELER, STEPHEN FREDERICK, legal administrator; BA in Polit. Sci., Mt. Union Coll., Alliance, Ohio, 1968; MS in Adminstrn. of Justice, Am. U., 1974. Probation officer 19th Dist. Juvenile and Domestic Rels. Ct. Prince William County, Manassas, Va., 1972-75; ct. systems planner Office of Jud. Planning Ky. Jud. Coun., Frankfort, 1975-76; co-dir. Ky. pretrial svcs. Adminstrv. Office of Cts. Ky. Ct. of Justice, Frankfort, 1976-81; ct. adminstr. Jud. Dist. 27A, Gastonia, N.C., 1982-87, Colorado Springs (Colo.) Mcpl. Ct., 1987—2005; ret. Ct. systems cons. Nat. Criminal Justice Collaborative, Sea Island, Ga., 1981-85. E-mail: stvwhlr@cs.com.

WHEELER, STEVE DEREAL, neurologist; b. Chgo., Sept. 15, 1951; s. Clarence and Tommie L. (Andrews) W.; m. Debra B. Buckingham; children: Winter N., Ryan S., Gabrielle S. Student, Mich. State U., 1970-73; MD, Dartmouth Coll., 1976. Diplomate Am. Bd. Psychiatry and Neurology, Nat. Bd. Med. Examiners; lic. Mich., Ohio, Fla. Intern Thomas Jefferson U., Phila., 1976-77; emergency physician River Dist. Hosp. Emergency Cons., Inc., St. Clair, Mich., 1977-78; fellow Dartmouth Med. Sch., 1978; resident U. Miami, Fla., 1978-81; fellow Washington U., St. Louis, 1981-82; instr. in neurology Med. Coll. Pa., Phila., 1982-83; electroencephalograph reader, attending neurologist VA Med. Ctr., Phila., 1982-83; asst. neurologist, attending neurologist Muscle Clinic U. Hosps. Cleve., 1983-86; electromyographer Rainbow Babies and Children's Hosp., U. Hosps. Cleve., 1983-86; chief neuromuscular diseases divsn., asst. prof. neurology Case Western Res. U., Cleve., 1983-86, co-dir. muscle disease ctr. and lab., 1985-86; clin. assoc. prof. of neurology U. Miami, 1987-89; pvt. practice Miami, 1987—; dir., co-founder Ryan Wheeler Headache Treatment Ctr., Miami, 2001—. Lectr. Myasthenia Gravis Found., Vermillion, Ohio, 1984, Cleve., 1983—86; vol. assoc. prof. U. Miami Sch., 1992—97, 2004—, vis. lectr., 1993—2001; chief headache divsn. Neurologic Ctr. for South Fla.; neurology cons. Low Back Pain Team U. Hosps. Cleve., 1984—86; mem. quality assurance com. Coral Reef Hosp., Miami, 1987—88; cons. dir. planning Bapt. Headache Clinic Bapt. Hosp., Miami, 1993—95; mem. adminstrv. com. Deering Hosp. Pain Mgmt. Ctr., Miami, 1993—94; mem. sleep diagnostic ctr. com. Bapt. Hosp., 1990—92, 1994—98, advisor to headache support group, 1995—; lectr. in field; co-founder, dir. Ryan Wheeler Headache Treatment Ctr. Author: (chpt.) Intensive Care For Neurological Trauma and Disease, 1982, (chpt.) Migraine and the Primary Headaches, 2002; mem. editl. bd.: Headache, 2001—02, ad hoc reviewer:, 2000—02, Cephalalgia, 1999—, Jour. Nat. Med. Assn., 2001—, contbr. chpt.: Miscellaneous Primary Headache, 2004. Named Internat. Man Yr., 1991-92; recipient Celebration Excellence Black Achiever award Family Christian Assn. Am., 1992. Fellow Royal Soc. Medicine, Am. Acad. Neurology; mem. ACP, Am. Headache Soc., So. Med. Assn. (chmn. psychiatry and neurology sect. 2000-02), Nat. Headache Found., Internat. Headache Soc., Fla. Med. Assn., Fla. Soc. Neurology, Fla. Soc. Internal Medicine, N.Y. Acad. Scis., Muscular Disease Soc. Northeastern Ohio (trustee 1984-86), Dade County Med. Assn., So. Pain Soc., Internat. Assn. Study of Pain, Dartmouth Club Greater Miami, Am. Coun. for Headache Edn. Achievements include research in plasmaphereses in treatment of acute Guillain-Barre Syndrome; repeat neuroimaging in headache when first study normal, migraine with cluster features, hemicrania continua, migraine-associated gluten sensitivity, secondary headaches, novel phenotype-driven strategies for headache and migraine prevention. Office: Ryan Wheeler Headache Treatment Ctr 5975 Sunset Drive Ste 501 Miami FL 33143 Office Phone: 305-661-2022. Office Fax: 305-661-2133.

WHEELER, SUSIE WEEMS, retired school system administrator; b. Cassville, Ga., Feb. 24, 1917; d. Percy Weems and Cora (Smith) Weems-Canty; m. Dan W. Wheeler Sr., June 7, 1941; 1 child, Dan Jr. BS, Fort Valley State U., Ga., 1945; MEd, Atlanta U., 1947, EdD, 1978; postgrad., U. Ky., 1959-60; EdS, U. Ga., 1977. Tchr. Bartow County Schs., Cartersville (Ga.) City Schs., 1938-44, Jeanes supr., 1946-58; supr., curriculum dir. Paulding Sch. Sys.-Stephens Sch., Calhoun City, 1958-64; summer sch. tchr. Atlanta U., 1961-63; curriculum dir. Bartow County Schs., 1963-79; ret., 1979. Former co-owner Wheeler-Morris Svc. Ctr., 1990—; mem. Ga. Commn. on Student Fin., 1985-95. Coord. Noble Hill-Wheeler Meml. Ctr. Project, 1983—. Recipient Oscar W. Canty Cmty. Svc. award, 1991, Woman in History award Fedn. Bus. and Profl. Women, 1995, New Frontiers Cmty. Svc. award, 1997, Outstanding Achievement for Preserving Georgia Hist., 2000, Life Achievement award Etowah Valley Hist. Soc., 2005; recognized for dedicated svc. on behalf of Bartow County Citizens Comm. Clarence Brown, 2003; named one of Women of Excellence, Star of the Past Bartow Women at Work, 2003. Mem. AAUW (v.p. membership 1989-91, Ga. Achievement award 1993, Edn. Found. award Cartersville-Bartow br.), Ga. Assn. Curriculum and Supervision (pres.-elect 1973-74, pres. 1974-75, Johnnye V. Cox award 1975), Delta Sigma Theta (pres. Rome alumnae chpt. 1978-80, mem. nat. bd. 1984, planning com. 1988—, Dynamic Delta award 1967, 78, Grand Chpt. cert. recognition 2002, recognition 50 plus years, Cartersville Rotary Club (Jean Harris award, 2004), Delta Sigma Theta Sorority, Inc., 2002), Ga. Jeanes Assn. (pres. 1968-70), Delta Kappa Gamma. Home: 477 Hillandell Dr Birmingham AL 35244

WHEELER, THOMAS CRAIG, federal judge; b. Chgo., Mar. 18, 1948; married; 2 children. BA, Gettysburg Coll., 1970; JD, Georgetown U., 1973. Bar: DC, US Dist. Ct. DC, US Ct. Appeals 4th, 10th, DC, and Fed. Cirs., US Ct. Fed. Claims, US Supreme Ct. Ptnr. DLA Piper Rudnick Gray Cary (formerly Piper & Marbury), Washington, 1995—2005; judge US Ct. Fed. Claims, Washington, 2005—. Mem.: DC Bar Assn., Nat. Def. Indsl. Assn., Boards of Contract Appeals Bar Assn., ABA (pub. contract law sect., litig. sect.). Avocations: skiing, photography, writing, softball, hiking. Office: US Ct Fed Claims 717 Madison Pl NW Washington DC 20005 *

WHEELER, THOMAS EDGAR, private equity executive; b. Redlands, Calif., Apr. 5, 1946; s. Charles Taylor and Martha (Edgar) W.; married; children: Nicole Fraser, Maxwell. BS, Ohio State U., 1968. Asst. dir. Ohio State U. Alumni Assn., Columbus, 1968-69; v.p. Grocery Mfrs. Am., Inc., Washington, 1969-76; exec. v.p. Nat. Cable TV Assn., Washington, 1976-79, pres., CEO, 1979-85, NABU: The Home Computer Network, 1985-86; chmn., CEO, NuCable Resources Corp., Washington, 1986-94; pres., CEO, Cellular Telecom. Industry Assn., Washington, 1992—2003; pres. Shiloh Group, LLC, 2003—; ptnr. Core Capital Ptnrs., 2004—. Author: Leadership Lessons from the Civil War, 1999, Mr. Lincoln's T-Mails, 2006. Bd. dirs. Earthlink; pres. Found. for Nat. Archives; chmn. Very Spl. Arts. Democrat. Office: Core Capital 1401 I St NW Ste 1000 Washington DC 20005

WHEELER, WILLIAM J., insurance company executive; AB, Wabash Coll., 1983; MBA, Harvard Univ. Sr. v.p. Donaldson Lufkin Jenrette, MetLife, Inc., NYC, 1997—2003, exec. v.p., CFO, 2003—. Bd. dir. LIMRA. Trustee Wabash Coll. Mem.: Phi Beta Kappa. Office: MetLife Inc 200 Park Ave New York NY 10166 *

WHEELER, W(ILLIAM) SCOTT, composer, conductor, music educator; b. Washington, Feb. 24, 1952; s. Malcolm Frederick and Aurora Dorothy (Anas) W.; m. Christen Struthers Frothingham, Jan. 5, 1985; children: Margaret Lee, Catherine Elizabeth. BA, Amherst Coll., 1973; MFA, Brandeis U., 1978, PhD, 1984. Artistic dir. Dinosaur Annex Music Ensemble, Boston, 1975—; dir. Cambridge (Mass.) Chorale, 1976-78; tchr. music, condr. Emerson Coll., Boston, 1978—. Composer (choral) A Babe is Born, 1979, (chamber) Winter Hills, 1987 (Somerville Arts Coun. Commn.), (symphony) Northern Lights, 1987 (Koussevitzky commn.), (operas) The Construction of Boston (libretto by Kenneth Koch), 1989, Democracy, 2004, (choral) The Angle of the Sun, 1994 (Nat. Endowment for the Arts). Guggenheim fellow, 1988-89. Mem. Am. Music Ctr., ASCAP. Episcopalian. Home: 6 Sunset Ave North Reading MA 01864-1427 Office: Emerson Coll Div Performing Arts 120 Boylston St Boston MA 02116-4624 Office Phone: 617-824-8385. Business E-Mail: scott_wheeler@emerson.edu.

WHEELER, WILMOT FITCH, JR., diversified manufacturing company executive; b. Southport, Conn., June 5, 1923; s. Wilmot Fitch and Hulda Day (Chapman) W.; m. Barbara Rutherfurd, Sept. 30, 1944 (dec. Sept. 1971); children: Wilmot Fitch III, James Alexander, John R. (dec.), Susan; m. Nonnye Landers, Dec. 20, 1973; children: Tracy Lynne, Alexa Margaret. BA, Yale U., 1945; postgrad., NYU, 1947-48; LLD honoris causa, Sacred Heart U., 1999. Staff engr. Stevenson, Jordan & Harrison, Inc. (mgmt. cons.), 1946-51; with Am. Chain & Cable Co., Inc., NYC, 1951-76, pres., chmn., CEO, 1966-76; chmn., dir. Jelliff Corp., Southport, Conn., 1976—; prin. Case & Co. Inc. (mgmt. cons.), 1977-82; trustee Dollar Savs. Bank, 1974-83, chmn., CEO, 1982-83; chmn., trustee, CEO Dollar Dry Dock Savs. Bank, 1983-84. Vice chmn., chmn., bd. dirs., CEO Manhattan Nat. Corp., 1986-90; v.p. William T. Morris Found., 1976—; bd. dirs. Am. Mut. Liability Ins. Co., 1969-89, Am. Policyholders Ins. Co., 1969-89, Am. Dist. Telegraph Co., 1968-88, Bristol Co. of Can. Ltd., 1955-76, Brit. Wire Products Ltd. (Eng.), 1955-76, Cables Automotrices S.A. (Mexico), 1955-76, Dominion Chain Co. Ltd., 1955-76, FATA, SpA (Italy), 1975-76, Hersey Products Corp., 1976-86, Instrumentos Bristol, S.A. (Mexico), 1955-76, Manhattan Life Ins. Co., 1972-93, Arthur G. McKee & Co., 1972-79, Parsons Controls Ltd., 1955-76, People's Bank, 1988-98, People's Mut. Holdings, 1975-98, Pratt-Read Corp., 1978-85, Pujol y Tarrago S.A. (Spain), 1969-85, Sormir Petroleum, Inc., 1994-98, Union Ctrl. Life Ins. Co., 1990-93, Wilmot F. Wheeler Found., 1944—. Trustee Am. Farm Sch., 1981-93, Bridgeport Hosp., 1977-94, U. Bridgeport, 1978-88. With AUS, 1943-46. Decorated Bronze Star. Mem. Yale Club (N.Y.C.), Country Club Fairfield. Episcopalian. Home: PO Box 429 Southport CT 06490-0429 Office: Jelliff Corp PO Box 758 354 Pequot Ave Southport CT 06490-1369

WHEELESS, CHARLOTTE ANN, science educator; d. Fred Simmons and Kathleen B Hattenhauer; m. Gene Wheeless, May 12, 1990; children: Patrick, Nicholas, Jessica. BS in Edn. summa cum laude, Williams Bapt. Coll., Walnut Ridge, Ark., 1994; MEd, Grand Canyon U., Phoenix, 2006. Sci. tchr. Walnut Ridge Mid. Sch., Ark., 1996—. Tchr. tng. workshop facilitator Interactive Tng. Media, Orlando, Fla., 2003—05; tchr. adv. bd. mem. Williams Bapt. Coll., Walnut Ridge, 2000—01. Adult leader 4-H Western Wranglers Horse & Pony Club, Black Rock, Ark., 2001—07, Ark. 4-H State Tech. Team, Little Rock, 2005—07; bd. mem. Lawrence County Hist. Soc., Powhatan, 2000—07. Recipient Tchr. Yr., Walnut Ridge Pub. Sch., 1999, Wal-Mart Tchr. Yr., Wal-Mart Corp., 1999, Young Achievement award, Williams Bapt. Coll., 1999—2000; grantee, Ark. Sci. and Tech. Authority, 2002—06, 2003; scholar, Walnut Ridge Bus. & Profl. Women Assn., 2005; Japan Fulbright tchr. participant, 2006. Mem.: Ark. Sci. Tchrs. Assn., Nat. Sci. Tchrs. Assn., Bus. & Profl. Women Assn. Avocations: travel, reading. Office: Walnut Ridge Public School 508 East Free Street Walnut Ridge AR 72476 Office Phone: 870-886-6697.

WHEELOCK, DOUGLAS H., astronaut, military officer; b. Binghamton, NY, May 5, 1960; s. Olin and Margaret Wheelock; m. Cathleen Hollen; 1 child. BS in Applied Sciences and Engring., U.S. Mil. Acad., West Point, NY, 1983; MS in Aerospace Engring, Ga. Inst. Tech., 1992. Commd 2d lt. U.S. Army, West Point, NY, 1983; student Army Aviation Sch., Ft. Rucker, Ala., 1983—84; from combat sect. leader, platoon leader, co. exec. officer, battalion ops. officer and comdr. officer Pacific Theater, Air Cavalry Troop. 9th U.S. Cavalry; advanced weapons rsch. and devel. engr. Aviation Directorate of Combat Developments, Fort Rucker, Ala.; mem. class 104 U.S. Naval Test Pilot Sch.; from exptl. test pilot to divsn. chief for fixed wing testing of airborne signal and imagery intelligence systems. U.S. Army Aviation Tech. Test Ctr., 1997—98; astronaut NASA Johnson Space Ctr., Houston, 1998—; support engr. for 5 space missions, lead engr, for 2 NASA, 2000—. Crew support astronaut Internat. Space Station Expedition 2, 2001, Internat. Space Station Expedition 4, 2001—02; spacecraft communicator (CAPCOM) Mission Control Ctr., Houston, 2002; lead CAPCOM Internat. Space Station Expedition 8; NASA's dir. ops. Gagarin Cosmonaut Tng. Ctr., Star City, Russia, 2005; mission specialist STS-120 Mission to Internat. Space Station, 2006. Named Outstanding Spokesman for Freedom, VFW, 1990, Disting. Grad., U.S. Army Initial Entry Flight Tng. Course, 1984; recipient Gamble award, U.S. Naval Test Pilot Sch., 1995, Group Acheivement award, NASA, 1997, NASA Group Achievement awards: Global Positioning System, 1997, Russian Liaison Support Team, 2001, NASA Superior Accomplishment award, 2002, 2004. Mem.: Army Aviation Assn. Am., Assn. U.S. Army, Soc. Am. Military Engineers, Soc. Exptl. Test Pilots. Avocations: baseball, flying, coaching youth sports, hiking, sports. Office: Astronaut Office/CB Johnson Space Ctr Houston TX 77058

WHEELON, ALBERT DEWELL, physicist; b. Moline, Ill., Jan. 18, 1929; s. Orville Albert and Alice Geltz (Dewell) W.; m. Nancy Helen Hermanson, Feb. 28, 1953 (dec. May 1980); children: Elizabeth Anne (dec. Mar. 2006), Cynthia Helen; m. Cicely J. Evans, Feb. 4, 1984. BSc, Stanford U., 1949; PhD, MIT, 1952. Tchg. fellow, then rsch. assoc. physics MIT, Boston, 1949-52; with Douglas Aircraft Co., 1952-53, Ramo-Wooldridge Corp., 1953-62; dep. dir. sci. and tech. CIA, Washington, 1962-66; with Hughes Aircraft Co., LA, 1966-88, chmn., CEO, 1987-88. Vis. prof. MIT, 1989; mem. Def. Sci. Bd., 1968-76; mem. Pres.'s Fgn. Intelligence, 1983-88; mem. Presdl. Commn. on Space Shuttle Challenger Accident, 1986; trustee Aerospace Corp., 1990-93, Calif. Inst. Tech., 1985-, Rand Corp., 1993-2001. Author Electromagnetic Scintillation: Vol. 1 and 2, 2001, 03; contbr. 36 papers on radiowave propagation and guidance systems. Recipient R.V. Jones Intelligence award, 1994. Fellow IEEE, AIAA (Von Karman medal 1986, Goddard Astronautics award 1997), Am. Phys. Soc.; mem. NAE, Sigma Chi. Episcopalian. Independent. Address: 181 Sheffield Dr Montecito CA 93108-2242

WHELAN, COLM T., physicist, researcher; b. Dublin, Sept. 28, 1955; s. James and Sarah Whelan; m. Agnieszka Kroman, Mar. 28, 1980; children: Eoin, Edward. BSc, U. Coll. Dublin, 1977, MSc, 1979; PhD, Cambridge U., 1985, ScD, 2003. Rschr. U. London, 1982—88; fellow Royal Soc. Rsch., Frankfurt am Main, Germany, 1989; sr. rsch. assoc. SERC Rutherford Appleton Lab., 1990—91; advanced rsch. fellow Cambridge U., 1991—96, asst. dir. rsch. dept. applied math. and theoretical physics, 1996—2001; prof. physics Old Dominion U., Norfolk, Va., 2001—, chmn. physics dept., 2001—05. Editor: (e.2e) and Related Processes, 1993, Coincidence Studies of Electron and Photon Impact Ionization, 1997, New Directions in Atomic Physics, 1999, From the Atomic to the Nanoscale, 2003, Electron Scattering from Atoms, Molecules, Nuclei and Bulk Matter, 2003; contbr. over 150 articles to sci. jours. Fellow, Magdalene Coll., Cambridge U., 1991—2001. Fellow Am. Phys. Soc., Inst. Physics. E-mail: cwhelan@odu.edu.

WHELAN, DAVID A., engineering executive; b. Oct. 7, 1954; BA in Physics, U. Calif., San Diego, 1977; MA in Physics, UCLA, 1978, PhD in Physics, 1983. Engring. specialist Northrop Corp., 1983—85; rsch. physicist Lawrence Livermore Nat. Lab., 1985—88; prog. mgr. GM-Hughes Electronics, 1988—94; dir. tactical tech. office Def. Advanced Rsch. Projects Agy., 1995—2001; v.p., chief tech. officer Space and Comm. Boeing Co., 2001—02, v.p. enterprise strategic growth Phantom Works Seal Beach, Calif., 2002—. Mem. sci. adv. bd. USAF. Recipient Sec. of Def. medal, Outstanding Pub. Svc., 1998, Sec. of Def. medal, Outstanding Civil Svc., 2001. Mem.: AIAA, IEEE, Am. Phys. Soc., NAE. Achievements include patents in field. Office: Boeing Phantom Works PO Box 2515 Seal Beach CA 90740 Office Phone: 562-797-2020. *

WHELAN, JAMES ROBERT, investor, mining company executive; b. Buffalo, July 27, 1933; s. Robert and Margaret (Southard) Whelan; children from previous marriage: Robert J., Heather Elizabeth. Student, U. Buffalo, 1951-53, U. RI, 1955-57; BA, Fla. Internat. U., 1974. Staff corr. UPI, Buffalo, 1952—53, bur. mgr. Providence, 1955—57, divsn. news editor Boston, 1957—58, fgn. corr. Buenos Aires, 1958—61, country mgr. Caracas, Venezuela, 1961—66, divsn. mgr San Juan, 1966, divsn. mgr., 1968; regional dir. corp. rels., then v.p. ops. ITT World Directories, San Juan, 1968—70; Latin Am. corr. Scripps-Howard Newspaper Alliance, Washington, 1970-71; mng. editor Miami News, Fla., 1971-73; free-lance writer, 1973-74; pres., editor, pub. Hialeah Pub. Co., Fla., 1975-77; v.p., editl. dir. Panax Corp., Washington, 1977-80; v.p., editor Sacramento Union, 1980-82; editor, pub. Washington Times, 1982-84; mng. dir. CBN News, 1985-86; pres. Capital Comm. Internat., 1986—; editor-in-chief Conservative Digest, 1988-89; vice chmn. Inter-Am. Found., Arlington, Va., 1991-94; external affairs advisor Inter-Am. Investment Corp., 1992-93; dir. strategic planning Cocetel Holding, Santiago, Chile, 1993-94; pres. Minera Silver Standard S.A., 1994—. Silver Std. Resources, Mexico, 1995—2000, advisor to bd., 2001—04, advisor to pres., 2004—. Freelance writer; guest lectr. Boston U., U. Miami, Ctrl. U., Venezuela, Cath. U., Washington, Andrès Bello U., Chile, U. Chile, U. Tex., Austin, U. Concepcion, Chile, U. Santiago; guest prof. U. Fla., 1973; adj. prof. U. Md., 1992—93; vis. prof. Polit. Sci. Inst. U. Chile, 1993—95; assoc. prof. Finis Terrae U., 1993—; scholar World Assn. Internat. Studies Stanford U., 1999—; adj. scholar Inst. World Politics, Washington, 2003—. Author: Through the American Looking Glass; Central America's Crisis, 1980, Allende: Death of a Marxist Dream, 1981, Catastrophe in the Caribbean: The Failure of America's Human Rights Policy in Central America, 1984, The Soviet Assault on America's Southern Flank, 1988, Out of the Ashes: Life, Death and Transfiguration of Democracy in Chile, 1833-1988, 1989, Hunters in the Sky, 1991, Desde las Cenizas: Vida, Muerte y Transfiguracion de la Democracia en Chile, 1833-1988, 1993, 2nd edit., 1995. Bd. dir. Christian Cmty. Svc. Agy., Miami, 1973, Hialeah-Miami Springs C. of C., 1976-77, Wolf Trap Found., 1984-87; bd. dirs. Nat. Coun. for Better Edn.; chmn. print media div. United Way campaign, Sacramento, 1981; bd. govs. Council on Nat. Policy, Washington, 1981-87; del. Commn. of Californias, 1981; chmn. Coun. for Inter-Am. Security Ednl. Inst., 1986-90; mem. spl. task force on pub. safety Greater Washington Bd. Trade; mem. Nat. Commn. on Free and Responsible Media, 1983-84; bd. dir. Nat. Bus. Consortium for Gifted and Talented Children, 1985-87; bd. govs. Internat. Policy Forum, 1985—; mem. Presdl. Bd. Fgn. Scholarships (Fulbright Commn.), 1986-92, exec. planning com., 1987-92. With Signal Corps U.S. Army, 1953-55. Nieman fellow Harvard U., 1966-67; recipient citation of excellence Overseas Press Club, 1971, Unity award Lincoln U., 1976, Golden Press award Am. Legion Aux., 1977, Freedom award Valley Forge Found., 1981, Bernardo O'Higgins award Chilean Govt., 1990, presented at Chilean Embassy by Amb. Octavio Errazuriz. Mem.: Instituto O'Higginiano de Chile, Harvard Club (NYC), Cosmos Club, Georgetown Club. Personal E-mail: jamesrwhelan@hotmail.com.

WHELAN, JOHN JOSEPH, education educator; b. Cleve., May 2, 1942; s. Thomas Patrick and Margaret Mary (Geddes) W; children: Sean Joseph, Thomas Gordon. BA, John Carroll U., 1965; MS, Case Western Res. U., 1970. Cert. K-8 tchr., elem. prin., Ohio. Tchr. 7th, 8th and 12th grades St. Francis Sch., Cleve., 1965-67; tchr. 6th grade Prospect Elem. Sch., East Cleveland, Ohio, 1967-69; prin. Chambers Elem. Sch., East Cleveland, 1969-90; fellow in urban edn., asst. prof. edn. John Carroll U., University Heights, Ohio, 1991—. Instr. John Carroll U., 1987, 88; apptd. peer reviewer and adv. Office Ednl. Rsch. and Improvement, 1988; panelist Chpt. 1 Nat. Program Unusually Successful Programs the Serve Disadvantaged Youth, 1988; mem. review panel Am. Educators since a Nation at Risk, 1988; mem. Whitman Award panel 1989-90, urban concersn com. Ohio Assn. Elem. Sch. Adminstrs., 1990; adv. bd. John Carroll Profl. Devel. Ctr. for Adminstrs. and Tchrs., 1990, Greater Clevel. Mental Devel. Ctr., 1991; ednl. cons. Scholarship-in-Escrow, Cleve., 1990-91; mem. parental involvement task force Cleve. Summit on Edn., 1990; spk, numerous confs. and events including Goshen (Ind.) H.S., IRA Plains Conf., S.D., Ontario Sch. Dist., Oreg. NAESD, San Francisco, Minn. Sch. Bds. Assn., 1990, Parent Tng. Inst., 1990, Pa. Sch. Bds. Assn., 1990, Met. Sch. Dist., 1990, Warrick County Sch. Corp., 1991, Minn. Elem. Prin. Assn., 1991, Ill. Renewal Inst., Saratoga Springs, N.Y., 1991, Ednl. Commn. States Nat. Forum, Denver, 1991, U. Calif., Santa Cruz., 1991, Big Springs Sch. Dist., Pa., 1991, Nat. Assn. Elem. Sch. Prins., 1992, Nat. Prins. Meeting, San Diego, 1994, Archdiocese of Denver, N.D. Reading Assn., Reading Assn. of Ireland,Dublin, Bottineau Pub. Schs. in N.D., Baldwin Coll., Cleve., NAESP, Orlando, San Diego; sr. cons. Natl. Sch. Conf. Inst./Learning 24/7, Phoenix, 2003. Bd. trustees John Carroll U.; life mem. Ohio PTA. Named Nat. Disting. Prin. Ohio, U.S. Dept. Edn., 1988-89; recipient Educator's award United Black Fund, Cleve., 1987, Ednl. Excellence award Urban League Greater Cleve., 1987, Recognition award Rotary Club Cleve., 1987. Mem. NAESP (Nat. Disting. Prin. award 1988), ASCD, Nat. Assn. for Schs. Excellence, John Carroll U. Alumni Assn. (pres. Cleve. 1992, recipient Alumni medal 1986), Phi Delta Kappa (v.p. 1986-87). Roman Catholic. Avocations: skiing, golf, jogging. Home: 344 E 276th St Euclid OH 44132-1304 Office: John Carroll U Dept Edn 20700 N Park Blvd Dept Edn University Heights OH 44118-4581

WHELAN, JOSEPH L., neurologist; b. Chisholm, Minn., Aug. 13, 1917; s. James Gorman and Johanna (Quilty) W.; m. Gloria Ann Rewoldt, June 12, 1948; children: Joe, Jennifer. Student, Hibbing Jr. Coll., 1935-38; BS, U. Minn., 1940, MB, 1942, MD, 1943. Diplomate Am. Bd. Psychiatry and Neurology. Intern Detroit Receiving Hosp., 1942-43; fellow neurology U. Pa. Hosp., Phila., 1946-47; resident neurology U. Minn. Hosps., Mpls., 1947-49; chief neurology svc. VA Hosp., Mpls., 1949; spl. fellow electroencephalography Mayo Clinic, Rochester, Minn., 1951; practice medicine specializing in neurology Detroit, 1949-73, Petoskey and Gaylord, Mich., 1973-87; asst. prof. Wayne State U., 1957-63. Chief neurology svcs. Grace Hosp., St. John's Hosp., Bon Secour Hosp., Detroit; cons. neurologist No. Mich. Hosps., Charlevoix Area Hosp.; instr. Med. Sch. U. Minn., 1949; cons. USPHS, Detroit Bd. Edn. Contbr. articles to profl. jours. Founder, mem. ad hoc Com. to Force Lawyers Out of Govt. Fellow Am. Acad. Neurology (treas. 1955-57), Am. Electroencephalography Soc.; mem. AMA, AAAS, Assn. Rsch. Nervous and Mental Diseases, Soc. Clin. Neurologists, Mich. Neurol. Assn. (sec.-treas. 1967-76, Disting. Physician award 1988), Mich. Med. Soc., No. Mich. Med. Soc., Grosse Pointe (Mich.) Club.

WHELAN, ROGER MICHAEL, lawyer, educator; b. Montclair, NJ, Nov. 12, 1936; s. John Leslie and Helen Louise (Callahan) W.; m. Rosemary Bogdan, Aug. 26, 1961; children: Helen, Theresa, John, James, Kathleen (dec.), Julie, Jennifer. AB cum laude, Georgetown U., Washington, DC, 1959, JD, 1962. Bar: DC 1962, US Dist. Ct. DC 1962, US Ct. Appeals (DC cir.) 1962, US Supreme Ct. 1968. Assoc. Fried, Rogers & Ritz, Washington, 1961—66; ptnr. Doctor & Whelan, Washington, 1967—72; judge US Bankruptcy Ct., Washington, 1972—83; sr. mem. Verner, Liipfert, Bernhard, McPherson & Hand, Chartered, Washington, 1984—89; ptnr., sr. counsel Shaw, Pittman, Potts & Trowbridge, Washington, 1989—2000; outside counsel to several Washington & Md. law firms, 2000—; resident scholar Am. Bankruptcy Inst., 2004. Dir. Lincoln Ctr. for Legal Studies, Arlington, Va., 1974-84; disting. lectr. Columbus Sch. Law, Cath. U. Am., Washington, 1975—; bd. govs. Conf. on Consumer Fin. Law, 1995-2005; resident scholar Am. Bankruptcy Inst., 2004. Sec. local campaign com., Alexandria, Va., 1964; trustee YMCAA, Silver Spring, Md., 1972-74. Recipient award DC Cir. Jud. Conf., 1984. Fellow: Am. Coll. Bankruptcy (bd. regents 1989—95, bd. dirs. 1995—2002); mem.: FBA (chmn. bankruptcy subcom. 1988, exec. com. 1993—96, pres. 1999—2000), Assn. Former Bankruptcy Judges (sec.-treas. 1996—), Am. Bankruptcy Inst. (bd. dirs. 1991—97, chmn. legis. com. 1991—99, exec. com. 1993—95, apptd. resident scholar 2004), Walter Chandler Inn of Ct. (master emeritus 1990—). Republican. Roman Catholic. Avocations: fishing, hunting, boating. Home: 17908 Ednor View Ter Ashton MD 20861-9757 Office Phone: 301-260-7707. Personal E-mail: rmwhelan@verizon.net.

WHELAN, STEPHEN THOMAS, JR., lawyer; b. Phila., July 28, 1947; s. Stephen Thomas and Virginia King (Ball) W.; m. Elizabeth Ann Murphy, Apr. 3, 1971; children: Christine B. Whelan. BA magna cum laude, Princeton U., 1968; JD, Harvard U., 1971. Bar: N.Y. 1972, U.S. Dist. Ct. (so. dist.) N.Y. 1975. Assoc. Mudge Rose Guthrie & Alexander, NYC, 1971-75, Thacher Proffitt & Wood, NYC, 1975-77; ptnr. Thacher Proffitt & Wood LLP, NYC, 1978—, exec. com., 1982—88, 2003—05, chmn. corp. dept., 1992-97; lectr. politics dept. Princeton U., 1999—. Chmn. Witherspoon Inst., Princeton, NJ, 2006—. Author: New York's Uniform Commercial Code Article 2A, 1994, The ABCs of the UCC: Article 2A (Leases), 1997, The ABCs of the UCC: Amended Article 2A, 2005; contbr. articles to profl. jours. Bd. dir. Atlantic Legal Found., 1997—; active N.Y. County Rep. Com., 1985—; active Princeton U. Alumni Coun., 1993—; trustee The Cloister Inn of Princeton U., 1996—, mem. adv. coun. James Madison program, 2000-. Fellow Am. Coll. Investment Counsel; mem. ABA (chmn. subcom. on leasing 1994-04), N.Y. State Bar Assn., Equipment Leasing Assn. Am. (fed. govt. rels. com. 1992-97, legal com. 1995-97), S.R. (bd. dir. NY 1979—). Roman Catholic. Avocations: road racing, golf. Office Phone: 212-912-7654. Business E-Mail: SWhelan@tpw.com.

WHELAN, WILLIAM J., III, lawyer; b. NYC, Apr. 29, 1959; BA with distinction, Univ. Va., 1980; JD cum laude, Fordham Univ., 1983. Bar: NY 1984. Law clk., Hon. William H. Timbers US Ct. of Appeals, 2nd Cir.; assoc. Cravath Swaine & Moore LLP, NYC, 1984—90, sr. atty., 1990—98, ptnr., corp., 1998—. Mng. editor Fordham Law Rev. Mem.: ABA, Assn. Bar City NY (securities regulation com.). Office: Cravath Swaine & Moore LLP Worldwide Plz 825 Eighth Ave New York NY 10019-7475 Office Phone: 212-474-1644. Office Fax: 212-474-3700. Business E-Mail: wwhelan@cravath.com.

WHELCHEL, SANDRA JANE, writer; b. Denver, May 31, 1944; d. Ralph Earl and Janette Isabelle (March) Everitt; m. Andrew Jackson Whelchel, June 27, 1965; children: Andrew Jackson, Anita Earlyn. BA in Elem. Edn., U. No. Colo., 1966; postgrad., Pepperdine Coll., 1971, UCLA, 1971. Elem. tchr. Douglas County Schs., Castle Rock, Colo., 1966-68, El Monte (Calif.) schs., 1968-72; br. libr. Douglas County Librs., Parker, Colo., 1973-78; zone writer Denver Post, 1979-81; reporter The Express newspapers, Castle Rock, 1979-81; history columnist Parker Trail newspapers, 1985-93; columnist Authorship Mag., 1991—, Gothic Jour., 1994; writing tchr. Aurora Parks and Recreation, 1985-91; writing instr. Arapahoe C.C., 1991-2000; exec. dir. Nat. Writers Assn., 1991—. Lectr. writing and history Durango Writer's Workshop, 1996-97, Estes Park Writer's Retreat, 1996-97, Pikes Peak Writer's Workshop, 1997, Sinipee Writer's Workshop, 1998, Oasis for Seniors, 2000, Denver Women's Press Club, 1999, Rocky Mountain Gold Conf., 1999, Colo. Writers Fellowship, 2000, Colo. Ind. Publishers, 2000; spkr. in field. Editor Authorship mag., 1992-98; lit. agent NWLA, 1996-99; contbr. short stories and articles to various publs. including: The Writer, Writer's Open Forum, Writer's Jour., Reunions, Fresno Bee, Ancestry Newsletter, Calif. Horse Rev., Jack and Jill, Child Life, Children's Digest, Peak to Peak mag.; author: (non-fiction) Your Air Force Academy, 1982, A Guide to the U.S. Air Force Acad., 1990, Parker, Colorado: A Folk History, 1990, The Beginning Writer's Writing Book, 1996, A Folk History of Parker and Hilltop, 1996; co-author: The Writer's Office, 1998, Writing for Beginners, 2006, The Register, 1989, (coloring books) A Day at the Cave, 1985, A Day in Blue, 1984, Pro Rodeo Hall of Champions and Museum of the American Cowboy, 1985, Pikes Peak Country, 1986, Mile High Denver, 1987, (novel) Hide & Seek, 2006, Check & Mate, 2007; contbr. chpts. to books. Mem.: Nat. Writers Assn. (pres. 1990, 1991, 2003—04), Colo. Author's League (awards com. 1999—2000, who's who com. 2001), Parker Area Hist. Soc. (pres. 1987—89), Nat. Writer's Club (treas. Denver Metro chpt. 1985—86, v.p. membership 1987, sec. 1990, bd. dirs., pres. 1990—91, v.p. programs 1992, v.p. membership 2002, bd. dirs., pres. 2003). Office Phone: 303-841-0246. *Personal philosophy: Tenacity and perseverance are keys to success. Optimism and self-belief open the door. The goals achieved through these elements are the most thrilling and savory.*

WHELDEN, CRAIG B., retired army officer; b. Ind., Oct. 8, 1951; m. Karen Lusk; children: Scott, Holly. BA, Purdue U.; MA, Webster U. Commd. 2d lt. U.S. Army, 1973, advanced through grades to maj. gen.; comdr. 98th area Support Group, Wuerzburg, Germany, 1994-95; chief of staff 3d Inf. Divsn., 1995-96; dep. dir. for ops. Nat. Mil. Command Ctr., Pentagon, Washington, 1996-98; comdg. gen. Cmty. and Family Support

Ctr., Alexandria, Va., 1998—2000; dep. comdr. U.S. Army Pacific, Ft. Shafter, Hawaii, 2000—04; ret.; ind. sales assoc. Pre-Paid Legal Svcs., Inc., Celebration, Fla. Bd. mem. World Trade Ctr.-Orlando, Army's Morale, Welfare and Recreation Exec. Com. Decorated Legion of Merit, Army Commendation medal, others. Home and Office: 1250 Celebration Ave Celebration FL 34747

WHELESS, ALBERT EUGENE, lawyer; b. Timmonsville, S.C., Feb. 15, 1935; s. Arthur B. and Marie (Martin) W.; m. Celeste Graham, Sept. 6, 1958; children— Al, Art, Ann Marie. BA, Wofford Coll., Spartansburg, SC, 1959; JD, U. SC, 1969. Bar: SC 1969. Assoc. John W. Jenrette, North Myrtle Beach, SC, 1969, ptnr. Jenrette & Wheless, North Myrtle Beach, 1970-75, Jenrette, Wheless, McInnis & Breeden, North Myrtle Beach, 1976-79, Wheless & McInnis, North Myrtle Beach, 1980—; city recorder North Myrtle Beach, 1970-71, city atty., 1972-79. Mem. ABA, SC Bar Assn., Horry County Bar Assn. (pres. 1982-84), ATLA, SC Trial Lawyers Assn., SC Def. Attys. Assn. Office: 457 Main St North Myrtle Beach SC 29582-3023 Personal E-mail: albertwheless@msn.com.

WHELESS, JAMES WARREN, neurologist; b. Glens Falls, NY, Apr. 18, 1956; s. True and Adelphine Ada (Bump) Wheless; m. Annette Carolyn Hyland, Apr. 7, 1984; children: Catherine Elizabeth, Margaret Caroline. BS, U. Okla., Oklahoma City, 1978, MD, 1982. Diplomate Am. Bd. Pediatrics, Am. Bd. Psychiatry and Neurology, Am. Bd. Clin. Neurophysiology. Intern, then pediatric resident U. Okla.-Tulsa Med. Coll., 1982-85; fellow in child neurology Northwestern U., Chgo., 1985-88; fellow in clin. neurophysiology/epilepsy Med. Coll. Ga., Augusta, 1988-89; asst. prof. neurology and pediatrics U. Tex., Houston, 1989-95, dir. epilepsy monitoring unit, 1989—2005, assoc. prof. neurology and pediatrics, 1995-2000, prof. neurology and pediats., 2000—05; dir. pediat. epilepsy sect., head clin. EEG, dir., co-founder Tex. Comprehensive Epilepsy Program, 1998—2005; prof. neurology and pediat., chief pediat. neurology, LeBonheur chair in pediatric neurology U. Tenn. Health Sci. Ctr., 2005—. Dir. LeBonheur Comprehensive Epilepsy Program; dir. Neurosci. Inst. LeBonheur Children's Med. Ctr.; clin. chief,dir. pediat. neurology St. Jude Children's Rsch. Hosp., Memphis. Contbr. articles to profl. jours., chapters to books; mem. editl. bd. Jour. Child Neurology, Formulary. Camp physician Kamp Kleidoscope, Livingston, Tex., 1995—2005; exec. bd. internat. epilepsy consortium Nat. Tuberous Sclerosis Assn., mem. profl. bd., Citizens United Rsch. Epilepsy. Pres.'s Fund grantee, U. Tex., Houston, 1990, Children's Miracle Network Telethon grantee, Hermann Children's Hosp., Rsch. grantee, NIH. Fellow: Child Neurology Soc., Am. Acad. Neurology; mem.: AMA, Epilepsy Assn. Houston/Gulf Coast (chmn. profl. adv. bd. 1992—94), Am. Acad. Pediat., Am. Epilepsy Soc. Avocations: running, camping, hiking, travel, reading. Office: UTHSC Pediatric Neurology 777 Washington Ave P335 Memphis TN 38105 Office Phone: 901-287-5207. Business E-Mail: jwheless@utmem.edu.

WHELIHAN, ALAN STUART, real estate developer, automotive executive; b. Phila., Sept. 17, 1932; s. John Franklin and Dorothy Dodge W.; m. Joan Murrell, June 20, 1959; children: Pamela, Deborah, Linda, Jacqueline. BS in Engring., Princeton U., 1954; MBA, U. Pa., 1960. Elect. engr. Philco Corp., Phila., 1954-55; product line mgr. govt. and indsl. divsn. RCA, Camden, NJ, 1959-65; gen. mgr. Chem. Micromilling Co., Pensauken, NJ, 1965-66; mgmt. cons. Peat Marwick Mitchell & Co., Washington, NJ, 1966-72; asst. commr. Fed. Supply Svc., Arlington, Va., 1973-79; dir. planning and coordination U.S. Metric Bd., Arlington, Va., 1979-82; dir. metric program U.S. Dept. Commerce, Washington, 1983-94; pres. VAW, LLC, Frederick, Md., 1994—, W Properties, L.L.C., Frederick, 1994. Dir. Am. Nat. Stds. Inst., 1973-75, Am. Nat. Metric Coun., Washington, 1990-92; consumer adv. coun. Underwriters Labs., 1974—. Lt. Comdr. USNR, 1955-57. Mem. IEEE (life), Congl. Country Club. Republican. Avocation: collecting antique automobiles. Office: W Properties LLC Stanford Indsl Park 4975 Winchester Blvd Frederick MD 21703-7400 Home: PO Box 221 Adamstown MD 21710-0221

WHELPLEY, DENNIS PORTER, lawyer; b. Mpls., Feb. 16, 1951; s. John Olsen and Harriet Marie (Porter) W.; m. Patricia Jan Adamy, Nov. 27, 1976; children: Heather Nicolle, Christopher Eric. BA, U. Minn., 1973, JD magna cum laude, 1976. Bar: Minn. 1976. Assoc. Oppenheimer Wolff & Donnelly, St. Paul, 1976-83, ptnr., 1983—. Mem. Order of Coif (Minn. chpt.), Phi Beta Kappa (Alpha of Minn. chpt.), Psi Upsilon (Mu chpt.), Dellwood Hills Golf & Country Club. Avocations: golf, tennis, squash, bridge. Home: 49 Locust St Mahtomedi MN 55115-1542 Office: Oppenheimer Wolff & Donnelly 45 S 7th St Ste 3300 Minneapolis MN 55402-1614 Home Phone: 651-426-0949; Office Phone: 612-607-7397. Business E-Mail: dwhelpley@oppenheimer.com.

WHERRY, ROBERT ALLEN, JR., federal judge, lawyer; b. Langley Field, Va., Apr. 7, 1944; s. Robert Allen and Lorene Fletcher (Ivy) W.; m. Leslie Anne Ross, June 23, 1943; children: Richard Washburn, Marsha Ivy. Student, Ohio State U., 1962-63; BS, U. Colo., 1966, JD, 1969; LLM in Taxation, NYU, 1972. Bar: Colo. 1969, US Dist. ct. (fed. dist.) 1969, US Tax Ct. 1973, US Ct. Appeals (10th cir.) 1976, US Ct. Claims, 1978, US Ct. Appeals (fed. cir.) 1991, US Supreme Ct. 1992. Constrn. laborer EBY Constrn. Co., Denver, 1965; acct. CF&I Steele, Pueblo, Colo., 1966; jr. acct. Ernst & Ernst, Denver, 1967-69; tax analyst Colo. Atty. Gen. Office (Inheritance Tax Divsn.), Denver, 1972; atty. Lentz, Evans & King P.C., Denver, 1973—; judge US Tax Ct., Washington, 2003—. Spkr. continuing edn. U. Denver, Tulane U. Tax Inst., Colo. Soc. CPA's, Englewood, 1984—; corr. State Tax Notes, Tax Analysts, Arlington, Va., 1991—. Tax coun. Colo. Assn. Commerce & Industry, 1978—; mem. Colo. Dept. Revenue Adv. Com., 1989-82, 89-90, Denver Mayor's Tax Com., Denver, 1992-93. Served in US Army, 1970—71. Fellow Am. Coll. Tax Counsel (regent); mem. ABA (former chmn. adminstrv. practice com. tax sect.), Colo. Bar Assn. (tax sect., chmn. 1981-82), Greater Denver Tax Counsel (chmn. 1986). Republican. Methodist. Avocations: bridge, chess. Office: US Tax Ct 400 2nd St NW Washington DC 20217 *

WHETSEL, ROGER GIRTON, retired aerospace engineer; b. Alexandria, Ind., Sept. 4, 1938; s. Woodrow Wilson and Milderd Lucille Whetsel; m. Sharon Ruth Bagley, June 26, 1963; children: Rhonda Beth Schmitt, Kirby Roy, John David, Angela Leigh Bohanan. BS in Elec. Engring., U. Cin, Ohio, 1961; MS in Indsl. Engring., Purdue U., Indiana, 1963; MS in Elec. Engring., U. Tenn., Tullahoma, 1967. Engr. in tng., Ohio, 1961, profl. engr., Tenn., 1968. Engring. coop student Excello Corp., Detroit, 1956—61; engr. Hazeltine, Indpls., 1962—63, ARO Inc., Tullahoma, Tenn., 1963—80, Calspan Corp., Tullahoma, 1980—95, Microcraft Corp., Tullahoma, 1995—96, Jacobs Sverdrup Tech., Tullahoma, 1996—2003, Aerospace Testing Alliance, Tullahoma, 2004—. Contbr. articles various profl. jours. Foster parent Tenn. Dept Human Svcs., Winchester, Tenn., 1974—80; missionary churches of Christ, Winchester, 2004. Named to Hall of Fame, Tenn. Waterski Fedn., 1996; recipient Kappa Kappa Psi Music Honor, U. Cin., 1960, Eta Kappa Nu Engring. Honor, 1961; Grad. fellowship, Purdue U., 1962. Mem.: USA Waterski (sr. judge 1987—2007). Avocations: philosophic theology, water-skiing. Home: 3363 Morris Ferry Bridge Winchester TN 37398 Home Phone: 931-976-6514.

WHETSELL, PAUL W., hotel executive; Grad., Davidson Coll. Various positions to v.p. Quality Inns; v.p. devel. Lincoln Hotels, Dallas; founder, chmn., pres., CEO CapStar Hotel Co., Washington, 1987—; chmn. & CEO MeriStar Hotels & Resorts, Inc., MeriStar Hospitality Corp, Washington, D.C. Bd. dirs. Cystic Fibrosis Found. of Nat. Capitol Area; bd. govs. Marriott Hospitality H.S. NAREIT. Office: Meristar Hospitality Corp #800 4501 Fairfax DR Arlington VA 22203-1656 Fax: 202-295-2230.

WHETSTONE, JONI LEE, music educator; b. Cumberland, Md., July 25, 1955; d. John Moyer and Eleanor Mae Shambach; 1 child, Leanna Lynn. MusB in Edn., Lee U., 1977; MusM, Ind. U. Pa., 1982. Instr. vocal music Everett (Pa.) Area Jr. Sr. H.S., 1983—. Lectr. music Pa. State U., Altoona, Pa., 1986—; instr. vocal music Everett (Pa.) Christian Academy, 1977—78, 1980—83; dir. music First Evang. Luth. Ch., Altoona, 1987—89. Named Claes Nobel Educator Distinction, Nat. Soc. H.S. Scholars, 2004; named one of Outstanding Am. Tchrs., Nat. Honor Roll, 2006, 2007. Mem.: NEA, Pa. State Educators Assn., Am. Choral Dirs. Assn., Pa. Music Educators Assn., Music Educators Nat. Conf. Republican. Home: PO Box 1495 Altoona PA 16603 Office: Everett Area Jr Sr High Sch 1 Renaissance Cir Everett PA 15537-1406 Office Phone: 814-652-9114 1302. Business E-Mail: jwhetstone@everett.k12.pa.us.

WHETTEN, JOHN D., food products executive; b. Chgo., June 8, 1940; s. Lester and Kate (Allred) Whetten; m. Becky Pearse; children: Carma, Rebecca, Mary Coza. BS, Brigham Young U., 1965; MBA, U. Calif., Berkeley, 1967. Advt. and mktg. mgr. The Clorox Corp., Oakland, Calif., 1967-79; pres., CEO Challenge Dairy Products, Inc., Dublin, Calif., 1982—; CEO DairyAmerica, Inc., Dublin, Calif., 1995-98. U.S. rep. Internat. Dairy Mktg. and Promotion Ann. Meeting, 1996. Co-chair U.S. Butter Task Force, 1990—97; bd. dirs. Epidermolysis Bullosa Med. Rsch. Found., 1991—, U.S. Dairy Export Coun., 1995—98; mem. nat. steering com. Brigham Young U. Sch. Mgmt., 1992—95; mem. nat. adv. coun. Utah Valley State Coll., 2001—. Recipient Disting. Svc. award, Brigham Young U. Sch. Mgmt., 2005. Mem.: Western Assn. Milk Mktg. Coop. (bd. dirs. 1992—2002, sec. 1994—2002), Barbecue Industry Assn. (dir. 1974—79, pres. 1977—78), Dairy Mktg. Coop. Fedn. (pres. 1992—), Dairy Export Incentive Program Coalition (pres. 1994—), Am. Dairy Products Inst. (bd. dirs. 1982—98, hon. life dir. 1999—), Am. Butter Inst. (bd. dirs. 1982—, v.p. 1995—99, pres. 1999—2001, Pres.'s Disting. Svc. award 1991). Office: Challenge Dairy Products Inc 11875 Dublin Blvd Ste B230 Dublin CA 94568-2818 E-mail: john@challengedairy.com.

WHETZEL, ROBERT WILLIAM, lawyer; b. Pitts., Jan. 17, 1960; BSChemE, U. Del., 1981; JD, Villanova U., 1984. Dir. Richards, Layton & Finger, Wilmington, Del., 1984—. Mem. adv. com. U.S. Dist. Ct. for Dist. of Del., 1994—. Co-author: Environmental Law Practice Guide, 1992. Mem. Del. Hazardous Substance Cleanup Act Advisory Group, 1990—; dir. Del. State C. of C., 2003—. Mem. ABA, Del. Bar Assn. (chair, sect. environ. law 1994-96). Office: Richards Layton & Finger One Rodney Sq Wilmington DE 19899 Office Phone: 302-651-7700.

WHICHARD, WILLIS PADGETT, lawyer, retired educator, judge; b. Durham, NC, May 24, 1940; s. Willis Guilford and Beulah (Padgett) W.; m. Leona Irene Paschal, June 4, 1961; children: Jennifer Diane, Ida Gilbert. AB, U. N.C., 1962, JD, 1965; LLM, U. Va., 1984, SJD, 1994. Bar: N.C. 1965. Law clk. NC Supreme Ct., Raleigh, 1965-66, assoc. justice, 1986-98; assoc. judge NC Ct. Appeals, Raleigh, 1980-86; ptnr. Powe, Porter, Alphin & Whichard, Durham, 1966-80; dean, prof. law Campbell U., 1999—2006. Instr. grad. sch. bus. adminstrn. Duke U., 1978; vis. lectr. U. N.C. Sch. Law, 1986-98. Contbr. articles to profl. jours. Rep. N.C. Ho. of Reps., Raleigh, 1970-74; senator N.C. Senate, 1974-80, chair numerous coms. and commns.; N.C. legis. rsch. commn., 1971-73, 75-77, land policy coun., 1975-79; bd. dirs. Sr. Citizens Coordinating Coun., 1972-74; chair local crusade Am. Cancer Soc., 1977, state crusade chair, 1980, chair pub. issues com., 1980-84; pres., bd. chmn. Downtown Durham Devel. Corp., 1980-84; bd. dirs. Durham County chpt. ARC, 1971-79; Durham county campaign dir. March of Dimes, 1968, 69, chmn., 1969-74, bd. dirs. Triangle chpt., 1974-79; bd. advisors Duke Hosp., 1982-85, U. N.C. Sch. Pub. Health, 1985-96, U. N.C. Sch. Social Work, 1989—; bd. visitors N.C. Ctrl. U. Sch. Law, 1987—; mem. law sch. dean search com. U. N.C., 1978-79, 88-89, self-study com., 1985-86; pres. N.C. Inst. Justice, 1984-94; bd. dirs. N.C. Ctr. Crime and Punishment, 1984-94. Staff sgt. N.C. Army NG, 1966-72. Recipient Disting. Service award Durham Jaycees, 1971, Outstanding Legis. award N.C. Acad. Trial Lawyers, 1975, Outstanding Youth Svc. award N.C. Juvenile Correctional Assn., 1975, named Citizen of Yr. Eno Valley Civitan Club, Durham, 1982, Faith Active in Pub. Life award N.C. Coun. of Churches, 1983, Outstanding Appellate Judge award N.C. Acad. Trial Lawyers, 1983; named to Durham H.S. Hall of Fame, 1987. Mem. ABA, N.C. Bar Assn. (v.p. 1983-84, 2001-02), Durham County Bar Assn., U. N.C. Law Alumni Assn. (pres. 1978-79, bd. dirs. 1979-82), Nat. Guard Assn. (judge adv. 1972-73, legis. com. 1974-76), Order of Golden Fleece, Order of Grail, Order of Old Well, Amphoterothen Soc., Order of Coif, Phi Alpha Theta, Phi Kappa Alpha, Durham-Chapel Hill Torch Club (pres. 1984-85), Watauga Club (Raleigh, pres. 1994-95). Democrat. Baptist. Home: 84402 Winslow Chapel Hill NC 27517 Office: Moore and Van Allen Attys PO Box 13076 Research Triangle Park NC 27709 Office Phone: 919-286-8054. Business E-Mail: williswhichard@mvalaw.com.

WHIFFEN, JAMES DOUGLASS, surgeon, educator; b. NYC, Jan. 16, 1931; s. John Phillips and Lorna Elizabeth (Douglass) W.; child from a previous marriage, Gregory James; m. Sally Vilas Runge, Aug. 21, 1993. BS, U. Wis., 1952, MD, 1955. Diplomate: Am. Bd. Surgery. Intern Ohio State U. Hosp., 1955-56; resident U. Wis. Hosp., 1956-57, 59-61; instr. dept. surgery U. Wis. Med. Sch., 1962-64, asst. prof., 1964-67, asso. prof., 1967-71, prof., 1971-96, vice chmn. dept., 1970-72, acting chmn., 1972-74; asst. dean Med. Sch., 1975-96; prof. emeritus U. Wis. Med. Sch., 1996—; mem. exam. council State of Wis. Emergency Med. Services, 1974-77. Bd. dirs. Wis. Heart Assn. Served to lt. comdr. USNR, 1957-59. John and Mary R. Markle scholar in acad. medicine, also; Research Career Devel. award NIH, 1965-75 Fellow A.C.S., Am. Soc. Artificial Internal Organs. Clubs: Maple Bluff Country. Achievements include research publs. on biomaterials, thrombo-resistant surfaces and the physiology of heart-lung bypass procedures. Home: 17 Cambridge Ct Madison WI 53704-5906 Office: 600 Highland Ave Madison WI 53792-0001 E-mail: jwhiffen@wisc.edu.

WHIGHAM, MARK ANTHONY, computer scientist; b. Mobile, Ala., Jan. 14, 1959; s. Tommie Lee Sr. and Callie Mae (Molette) W. BS in Computer Sci., Ala. A&M U., 1983, MS in Computer Sci., 1990; postgrad., Ala. A&M Univ., 1995; student in Religious Edn., Andersonville Theological Sem., Camilla, GA, 2003—; cert., Am. C.C. Leadership Acad., U. Ala., 2005. Cert. Microsoft cert. profl., A+ cert CompTIA, i-Net+ cert. profl. CompTIA, network + cert. profl. CompTIA, Microsoft Office specialist cert. 2003, others. Computer programmer U.S. Army Corps of Engrs., Huntsville, Ala., 1985-88; programmer analyst, coord. acad. computing Ala. A&M U., Normal, Ala., 1988-89, programmer analyst II, DEC systems coord., instr. part-time computer sci. dept., 1989-91; systems engr. Advanced Bus. Cons. Inc.-La. div. Dow Chem. Co., 1991-93; owner Whigham's Computer Cons., 1990—; sys. engr. DOW Chem. Co.-USA La. Divsn., Plaquemine, La., 1991-93; instr. computer info. system Calhoun C.C., Decatur, Ala., 1993-97; network specialist/cons. Ala. A&M U., Normal, 1994—; computer info. sys. instr. Calhoun C.C., Decatur, Ala., 1994—; mgmt. info. sys. dir., CIO J.F. Drake Tech. Coll., Huntsville, Ala., 1997-98; software engr. Colsa Corp., Huntsville, Ala., 1998—99; dir. info. tech. Lane Coll., 1999—2000; instr. computer sci. Lawson State CC, 2000—. Instr. computer sci. dept. Ala. A&M U., 1989-91; network specialist, cons. Ala. A&M U., Normal, 1994—. Active Huntsville Interdenominational Ministerial Fellowship, Huntsville, 1984. Mem. Nat. Assn. Sys. Programmers, Computer Sci. Tchrs. Assn., Ala. Info. Tech. Assn. (adv.com.), Ala. Coun. for Computer Edn., Assn. for Computing Machinery, Huntsville Jaycees, Nat. Soc. Black Engrs., Assn. Info. Tech. Profls., So. Poetry Assn., Nat. Arts Soc., Internat. Black Writers and Artists Assn., Optimists, U.S. Chess Fedn. (cert. chess coach), Future Bus. Leaders of Am.-Phi Beta Lambda, Sigma Tau Epsilon, Alpha Phi Omega. Democrat. Baptist. Avocations: chess, skating, reading, playing piano. Office: Lawson State CC 3060 Wilson Rd ACATT Ste 250 Birmingham AL 35209-1542 Home: Apt 202 917 Valley Ridge Dr Birmingham AL 35209-1542 Office Phone: 205-929-2023. Business E-Mail: mark_whigham@msn.com, mwhigham@lawsonstate.edu.

WHILDEN, ROBERT HARRAL, JR., lawyer; b. Houston, May 20, 1935; s. Robert Harral and Elizabeth (Hoyt) W.; m. Mary Preston, Aug. 24, 1957; children: Elizabeth, Margaret, Robert III. BA, U. Tex., 1957, LL.B., 1960. Bar: Tex. Ptnr. Vinson & Elkins, Houston, 1960—2000, mem. mgmt. com.; sr. v.p., gen. counsel, sec. BMC Software Inc., 2000—05. Bd. dir. W-H Energy Svcs., Inc., 1989—. Mem. Tex. Bar Assn., Houston Bar Assn. Office: BMC Software 2101 City W Blvd Houston TX 77042 Office Phone: 713-918-8800. E-mail: bob_whilden@bmc.com.

WHINERY, MICHAEL ALBERT, physician; b. Watsford, Eng., June 30, 1951; s. Leo Howard and Doris Eileene W. and Alma Piper; m. Tatijana Dunnebier, 1976 (dec. Jan. 1981); m. Judy Renee Wright, Apr. 30, 1982; children: Rhiannon Daire Eileene, Terron Rae Lee. BS, Okla. U., 1976; D of Osteopathy, Okla. State U., 1980. Diplomate Am. Bd. Family Practice. Intern Hillcrest Health Ctr., Oklahoma City, 1980-81; with McLoud Clinic, McLoud, Okla., 1981-98; staff physician Okla. Vets. Ctr., Claremore, 2000—. House physician McLoud Nursing Ctr., 1988—; med. examiner Pottawatomie County Health, McLoud, 1983--. Author: Poetic Voices of America, 1991; composer lyrics and music at Stella Gospel Rec. Studio, 2000, A Soldier Last Prayer. Mem. Presdl. Order Merit Nat. Repub. Senatorial Com., Washington, 1991, Presdl. Task Force, 1983—, Senatorial Commn. Repub. Senatorial Inner Circle, Washington, 1991; mem. U.S. Congrl. Adv. Bd., 1993. Served with USMC, Vietnam era. Recipient Acknowledgement of Outstanding Contbn. in Clin. Rsch. award SANDOZ Labs., 1992, Rep. Presdl. Legion of Merit, 1994, Rep. Majority medal, U.S. Senate, 1997, Rep. Task Force medal of merit, 1997. Mem. Am. Legion, C. of C., Jr. C. of C., U.S. Senatorial Club (preferred mem.), U.S. Congressional Act Bd. (state advisor 1990-91). Baptist. Avocations: fishing, music, composing songs, poetry and writing lyrics. Office: PO Box 2745 3001 W Bluestarr Claremore OK 74018-2745 Office Phone: 918-342-5432. Business E-Mail: mwhinery@odva.state.ok.us.

WHINSTON, ARTHUR LEWIS, lawyer; b. NYC, Feb. 5, 1925; s. Charles Nathaniel and Charlotte (Nalen) W.; m. Melicent Ames Kingsbury, Mar. 19, 1949; children: Ann Kingsbury, James Pierce, Melicent Ames, Louise Ellen, Patricia Kingsbury. B.C.E., Cornell U., 1945; MSE., Princeton U., 1947; JD, N.Y. U., 1957. Bar: N.Y. 1957, Oreg. 1964, U.S. Supreme Ct 1966, U.S. Patent Office 1958, U.S. Ct. Appeals (fed. cir.) 1959; registered profl. engr., N.Y., Oreg. Engr. Chas. N. & Selig Whinston, NYC, 1947-50; lectr. Coll. City N.Y., 1950-51; structures engr. Republic Aviation Corp., Farmingdale, NY, 1951-57; patent lawyer Arthur, Dry & Kalish, 1957-64, Klarquist Sparkman, LLP, 1964—; chmn. Oreg. Bar com. on patent, trademark and copyright law, 1968-69, 77-78, mem. com. unauthorized practice law, 1970-73, chmn., 1972-73, com. on profl. responsibility, 1973-75. Served as ensign, C.E.C., USNR, 1945-46. Recipient Fuertes medal Cornell U. Sch. Civil Engring., 1945 Mem. ABA, Oreg. Bar Assn., N.Y. Bar Assn., Multnomah County Bar Assn., Am. Intellectual Property Law Assn., N.Y. Intellectual Property Law Assn., Oreg. Patent Law Assn. (pres. 1977-78), Profl. Engrs. Oreg. (past state legis. chmn.), Sigma Xi, Chi Epsilon, Phi Kappa Phi. Clubs: Multnomah Athletic. Republican. Home: 3824 SW 50th Ave Portland OR 97221-2112 Office: One World Trade Ctr Ste 1600 Portland OR 97204 Personal E-mail: artmeli@comcast.net.

WHINSTON, STEPHEN ALAN, lawyer; b. Stamford, Conn., Mar. 27, 1948; s. Alfred Leonard and Rose (Eisgrau) W.; m. Joan Lenett, June 4, 1978; children: Stephanie Portnoy, Brian Arasim, Joshua. BA, Colgate U., 1970; JD, Case Western Res. U., 1973. Bar: Pa. 1973, U.S. Dist. Ct. (ea. dist.) Pa. 1973, U.S. Ct. Appeals (3d cir.) 1973, U.S. Ct. Appeals (8th cir.) 1995, U.S. Ct. Appeals (2d cir.) 2000, U.S. Supreme Ct. 2001. Trial atty. U.S. Dept. Justice, Washington, 1974-79, sr. trial atty., 1979-83; atty. Berger & Montague, P.C., Phila., 1983-85, shareholder, 1986—. Bd. dirs. Jewish Fedn. Housing, Inc., Cherry Hill, NJ, 1994-96. Mem. Pa. Prison Soc. (bd. dirs.). Avocation: music. Office: Berger & Montague PC 1622 Locust St Philadelphia PA 19103-6305 Business E-Mail: swhinston@bm.net.

WHIPPLE, DEAN, federal judge; b. 1938; BS, Drury Coll., 1961; postgrad., U. Tulsa, 1961-62; JD, postgrad., U. Mo., Kansas City, 1965. Pvt. practice, Lebanon, Mo., 1965-75; cir. judge div. II 26th Jud. Cir. Mo., 1975-87; judge US Dist. Ct. (we. dist.) Mo., Kansas City, 1987-2000, chief judge, 2000—07. Prosecuting atty. Laclede County, Mo., 1967-71. With Mo. N.G., 1956-61; USAR, 1961-66. Mem. Mo. Bar Assn. (mem. bd. govs. 1975-87, mem. exec. com. 1983-84, 86-87), Mo. Trial Judges Assn., 26th Jud. Bar Assn., Laclede County Bar Assn. (pres. 1968-69, 72-73), Kansas City Met. Bar Assn., Kansas City Inn of Ct. (instr. 1988-93), Mo. Hist. Soc., Phi Delta Phi. Office: US Courthouse 400 E 9th St Kansas City MO 64106-2607

WHIPPLE, JACQUELINE CONANT, writer, media specialist; b. Columbus, Ohio, Mar. 31, 1921; d. William Horace and Gertrude Virginia (Bryant) Conant; AB magna cum laude, Mt. Holyoke Coll., 1943; postgrad. Art. Inst. Boston, 1974-79; MA Lesley Coll., 1991; m. David Collins Whipple, Sept. 6, 1944; children: Nancy, Roger, Leah, Benjamin. Reporter, Scarsdale Inquirer, NY, 1939-43; scriptwriter radio dept. J. Walter Thompson Co., NY, 1943-45; reporter Washington Daily News, 1945-47; broadcast journalist, chief editorial writer Sta. WCRB-AM-FM, Waltham, Mass. and Boston, 1960-67; with sch. divsn. Houghton Mifflin Co., Boston, 1967-86; freelance all media; jury chmn. excellence in pub. writing/support of edn. Council for Advancement and Support of Edn., Washington, 1981. Chmn. Know Your Town-Waltham LWV, 1951, v.p., 1953; pres. Cohasset (Mass.) PTA, 1963. Recipient Tom Phillips award, UPI Broadcasters of Mass., 1963; cert. of merit Art Inst. Boston, 1976, Cohasset Yacht Club. Democrat. Unitarian. Contbr. articles to popular mags. Home and Office: 119 N Main St Cohasset MA 02025-1317

WHIPPLE, JUDITH ROY, retired editor; b. NYC, May 14, 1935; d. Edwin Paul and Elizabeth (Levis) Roy; m. William Whipple, Oct. 26, 1963. AB, Mount Holyoke Coll., 1957. Head libr. Am. Sch. Lima (Peru), S.A., 1957-59; asst. editor children's books G.P. Putnam's Sons, NYC, 1959-62; assoc. editor W.W. Norton & Co., Inc., NYC, 1962-68; editor Four Winds Press, 1968-75; editor-in-chief Scholastic Gen. Book Divsn., 1975-77; pub. Four Winds Press subs. Scholastic Inc., NYC, 1977-82; pub., v.p. Macmillan Pub. Co., NYC, 1982-89, exec. editor, 1989-94; editl. dir. Cavendish Children's Books, Tarrytown, NY, 1994—2002, ret., 2002. Mem.: PEN, Children's Book Coun. (pres. 1977, bd. dirs. 1970—79), Women's Nat. Book Assn., Soc. Children's Book Writers and Illustrators. Avocations: gardening, swimming, piano, travel. Personal E-mail: jrwhipple@stny.rr.com.

WHIPPLE, KENNETH, utilities executive; b. 1934; BS, MIT, 1958. With Ford Motor Co., Dearborn, Mich., 1958—, systems mgr. Ford Credit, 1966-69, mgr. mgmt. svcs. dept. fin. staff, 1969-71, systems analysis mgr. fin. staff, 1971-74, asst. contr. internat. fin. staff, 1974-75, v.p. fin. Ford Credit, 1975-77, exec. v.p. Ford Credit, 1977-80, pres. Ford Credit, 1980-84, v.p. corp. strategy, 1984-86; v.p. chmn. Ford of Europe, 1986-88;

exec. v.p., pres. Ford Fin. Svcs. Group, Dearborn, 1988—99; chmn., CEO CMS Energy, Dearborn, Mich., 2002—04, chmn., 2004—. Office: CMS Energy 1 Energy Plaza Drive Jackson MI 49201 *

WHIPPLE, MATTHEW ROBERT, secondary school educator; m. Deborah L. Whipple. BS in Comm. Studies, Northwestern U., Evanston, Ill., 1988; MA in Ednl. Adminstrn., Roosevelt U., Chgo., 1996. Tchr., debate coach Winston Churchill HS, San Antonio, 1988—92, Glenbrook South HS, Glenview, Ill., 1992—. Named Gold Key Coach, Emory U., Atlanta, 1998, Triple Diamond Coach, Nat. Forensic League, 2004; named to Hall of Fame, Nat. Debate Tournament of Champions, 2002; recipient Outstanding Tchr. award, Dartmouth Coll., 1991, U. Chgo., 1998, Outstanding Leadership award, Congrl. Youth Leadership Coun., 2001. Mem.: World History Assn., Nat. Coun. for the Social Studies, Ill. Coun. for the Social Studies. Avocations: music, Russian literature, travel, basketball. Office: Glennrook South High Sch 4000 W Lake Ave Glenview IL 60026

WHIPPLE, WILLIAM, JR., government policy consultant, writer; b. Cinclare, La., Feb. 4, 1909; s. William and Genevieve (Randolph) W.; m. Dixie Ancrum, Mar. 30, 1935 (dec. Oct. 1955); children: Anne Calhoun, William III, Claire Randolph; m. Renée Pauline Exiga, July 21, 1956 (div. May 1974); 1 child, Philip; m. Frances Edith Cheek, June 1, 1974 (dec. July 1983); m. Alice Terry Goodloe, Dec. 1, 1984. BS, U.S. Mil. Acad., 1930; BA, Oxford U., Eng., 1933, MA, 1937; Civil Engr., Princeton U., 1936. Registered profl. engr., N.J. Commd. 2d lt. Corps Engrs., U.S. Army, 1930, advanced through grades to brig. gen., ret., 1960; chief engr. N.Y. World's Fair Corp., Flushing Meadow, N.Y., 1960-64; pvt. practice cons. engr. NYC, 1964-65; dir. Water Resources Rsch. Inst. Rutgers U., New Brunswick, N.J., 1965-79, rsch. prof. Coastal and Environ. Inst., 1979-81; asst. dir. divsn. water resources Dept. Environ. Protection, Trenton, N.J., 1981-89, coord. nonpoint cource control program divsn. water resource, 1989-90; prin. Greeley Polhemus Group, Chester, Pa., 1990-2000; pvt. practice cons. Princeton, N.J., 1999—. Author: New Perspectives on Water Supply, 1994, Comprehensive Water Planning and Regulation, 1996, Water Resource: A New Era for Coordination, 1998; contbr. articles to publs. on water resources. Chmn. Flood Control Com., Princeton, N.J., 1975-81; adv. coun., Revision of N.J.'s Water Supply Master Plan, 2001. Recipient Trustees award N.J. inst. Tech., 1985, govt. award Water Resource Assn. of Delaware River Basin, 1987, Toulmin award for best articles Mil. Engr., 1975, Formal Commendation from Pres. of U.S., 1971. Fellow AAAS, ASCE (life, chmn. urban water resources rsch. coun. 1973-75, Lifetime Achievement award Inst. Environment and Water Resources 2001), Soc. Am. Mil. Engrs. (life), Am. Water Resources Assn. (pres. 1993, Icko Iben award 1978, William Ackerman medal 1989, Boggess award; mem. Am. Acad. Environ. Engrs. (diplomate), Univs. Coun. on Water Resources (chmn. 1976-78), Sigma Xi. Avocation: history and biography. Home and Office: 2 Hedge Row Rd Princeton NJ 08540-5055 Office Phone: 609-514-2713.

WHIPPLE, WILLIAM PERRY, foundation administrator; b. Cedar Rapids, Iowa, Nov. 1, 1913; s. Robert Milo and Jeanette (Fry) W.; m. Gayle Schroeder, Sept. 18, 1937; children: John William, Robert Milo. BA, Coe Coll., 1935, PhD (hon.), 1996. Prin. Whipple Ins. Agy., Cedar Rapids, 1935-57; pres. Whipple and Winterberg, Cedar Rapids, 1957-71; chmn. Frank B. Hall of Iowa, Inc., Cedar Rapids, 1971-74; pres. Hall Found., Inc., Cedar Rapids, 1974-95, also bd. dirs.; chair Hall-Perrine Found., Cedar Rapids, 1995—. Exec. in residence Colo. State U., Fort Collins, 1973; bd. dirs. Fire Mark Cir. of Ams., Chamblee, Ga., Interocean Reins. Corp., Cedar Rapids, 1st Fed. Savs. and Loan, Cedar Rapids, Nissen Corp., Cedar Rapids, 1966-72, Banks of Iowa, Inc., Des Moines, 1982-85. Trustee Cedar Rapids Pub. Library, Coe Coll., chmn.; hon. bd. dirs. Methwick Manor, Cedar Rapids, Linn County ARC, Greater Cedar Rapids Found. Recipient Outstanding Layman award YMCA, Cedar Rapids, 1986, Alumni Achievement award, Coe Coll., 1990, Founders Day award Coe Coll., 2001, First Community Svc. award, Cedar Rapids Rotary, 1993. Mem. Rotary (Paul Harris fellow 1987), Elks. Presbyterian. Avocations: signevierist, stamp collecting/philately. Home: 1224 13th St NW Cedar Rapids IA 52405-2404 Office: Hall-Perrine Found 115 3d St SE Cedar Rapids IA 52401-1222

WHIPPLE, WOODROW THOMAS, artist, educator; b. Brattleboro, Vt., June 5, 1944; s. Howard Woodrow Whipple and Anna Mastelar; m. Tina Sue Huggins, Dec. 31, 1992 (div. Apr. 24, 1996); m. Evelyn Crowley, May 9, 1967 (div. June 29, 1988); 1 child, Lori Michelle Pate. Student, Columbus Sch. of Art, Ga., 1963—65. Graphic artist Dept. of Def., Ft. Benning, Ga., 1971—74; gallery owner, art instr. Le Gallerie, Columbus, Ga., 1974—78; visual info. specialist Dept. of Def., Ft. Benning, Ga., 1978—95; art instr., graphic designer, cons. Visual Imagery Prodns., Columbus, Ga., 1995—99; instr. graphic arts Ga. Dept. of Corrections, Pulaski State Prison, Hawkinsville, 1999—; owner, founder BackYard Woodys Grill-N-Sauces, Bonaire, Ga., 2000—. Mem. Macon Art Coun., 2007—. Author (illustrator): Wing Ding Party Book; painting, Gunboat Chattahoochee (Purchase award for Ga. Bicentenial Top 10 Ga. Artist, 1975), Savannah Pier (Purchase award for permanet exhbn. collection in the Bradley Mus. of Art, 1975), exhibit, CISM XXIV Internation Shooting Championships Norway (Outstanding Contibution, 1985). Mem.: Ga. Correctional Edn. Assn., Lower Chattahoochee Archaeol. Soc. (pres. 1985—86), Middle Ga. Culinary Assn., Am. Culinary Fedn. (sgt. at arms 2005—06), Sports Car Club of Am. (regional exec. 1966—67), US Power Squadron (comdr. 1987—88), Columbus Artist Guild. Republican. Episcopalian. Avocations: fine art, photography, cooking, travel. Home: 110 Chipper St Bonaire GA 31005 Office: Ga Dept of Corrections PSP Rte 2 Upper River Rd Hawkinsville GA 31036 Personal E-mail: gdcwhip@cox.net.

WHIPPO, SCOTT DEAN, consultant; s. Harold Eugene and Peggy Frances (Connelly) Whippo; m. Constance Louise Taylor, Nov. 11, 1978 (div. Oct. 20, 1988); 1 child, Ross Douglas Byron; m. Olga Olegovna Kholmogorova, Jan. 14, 1994; 1 child, Nicholai Alexi. BA in Comm., U. Wash., Seattle, 1978. Cert. creative writing in poetry U. Wash., 1992, video & film prodn. mgmt. U. Wash., 1996. Head ships med. dept. US Coast Guard, Detroit, 1972—74; indsl. engr. Boeing Airplane & Aerospace, Seattle, 1978—95; prodn. mgr. Video Internat. Prodns., Seattle, 1995—99; ops. comdr. Bosnia, 2000; sr. intelligence officer Def. Intelligence Agy., 2000—02, Joint Staff, DC, 2002; team leader spl. ops. forces Kosovo, 2003—04; counterterrorism expert Office Spl. Investigations, Afghanistan, 2004—06. Chmn. long range planning com. NW Chamber Orch., Seattle, 1994—97. Maj. US Army, 2000—04. Decorated Achievement award for counterterrorism US Army, Commendation award for spl. ops. in the Balkans. Mem.: Am. Anti-Slavery Group., Nat. Acad. TV Arts and Scis. (Emmy awards judge 1997—98), Eureka #20 Free and Accepted Masons. Episcopalian. Achievements include having poem selected by Artist Stewart Wavell-Smith as an adendum to his painting, The Bucket Brigade, currently hanging in the Pentagon. Personal E-mail: sdwhippo@comcast.net.

WHIPPS, EDWARD FRANKLIN, lawyer; b. Columbus, Ohio, Dec. 17, 1936; s. Rusk Henry and Agnes Lucille (Green) W.; children: Edward Scott, Rusk Huot, Sylvia Louise, Rodyard Christian. BA, Ohio Wesleyan U., 1958; JD, Ohio State U., 1961. Bar: Ohio 1961, U.S. Dist. Ct. (so. dist.) Ohio 1962, U.S. Dist. Ct. (no. dist.) Ohio 1964, U.S. Ct. Claims 1963, U.S. Supreme Ct. 1963, Miss. 1965, U.S. Ct. Appeals (6th cir.) 1980. Assoc. George, Greek, King & McMahon, Columbus, 1961-66; ptnr. George, Greek, King, McMahon & McConnaughey, Columbus, 1966-79, McConnaughey, Stradley, Mone & Moul, Columbus, 1979-81, Thompson, Hine & Flory, Columbus, 1981-93; prin. Edward F. Whipps & Assocs., Columbus, 1993-94, 2000—; ptnr. Whipps & Wistner, Columbus, 1995-99. Founder, trustee Creative Living, Inc., 1969—; trustee, v.p. Unverferth House, Inc., 1989; trustee Eagle Scholarship Trust. Host: (TV) Upper Arlington Plain Talk, 1979-82, Bridging Disability, 1981-82, Lawyers on Call, 1982—, U.A. Today, 1982-86, The Ohio Wesleyan Experience, 1984—. Mem. Ohio Bd. Psychology, 1992-02, pres. 2001-02; active Upper Arlington (Ohio) Bd. Edn., 1971-80, pres., 1978-79; bd. alumni dirs. Ohio Wesleyan U., 1975-79; trustee Walden Ravines Assn., 1992-96, pres. 1993-96. Mem. ABA, Columbus Bar Assn., Ohio State Bar Assn., Assn. Trial Lawyers Am., Ohio Acad. Trial Lawyers, Franklin County Trial Lawyers Assn., Columbus Bar Found., Columbus C. of C., Upper Arlington Area C. of C. (trustee 1978-80), Lawyers Club, Barrister Club, Columbus Athletic Club, Nat. Football Found. & Hall of Fame, Columbus Touchdown Club, Downtown Quarterback Club, Ohio State U. Faculty (Columbus) Club, Ohio State U. Golf Club, Highlands Golf Club (dir. 2001—, v.p. 2005—), Delta Tau Delta (nat. v.p. 1976-78). Republican. Home: 51 Highland Ct Pataskala OH 43062-8910 Office: Edward F Whipps & Assocs 500 S Front St Columbus OH 43215-7619 Office Phone: 614-461-6006. Personal E-mail: efwhipp@aol.com. *Personal philosophy: Commitment to personal growth, the development of interpersonal relationships, the rule of law and a firm belief in the unique value of every individual in a holographic universe are the primary factors seen in my approach to life.*

WHISENHUNT, DONALD WAYNE, historian, educator, dean; b. Meadow, Tex., May 16, 1938; s. William Alexander Whisenhunt and Beulah (Johnson) King; m. Betsy Ann Baker, Aug. 27, 1960; children: Donald Wayne Jr., William Benton. BA, McMurry Coll., 1960; MA, Tex. Tech U., 1962, PhD, 1966. Tchr. Elida (N.Mex.) High Sch., 1961-63; from asst. to assoc. prof. history Murray (Ky.) State U., 1966-69; assoc. prof., chmn. dept. Thiel Coll., Greenville, Pa., 1969-73; Dean Sch. Liberal Arts and Scis., Ea. N.Mex. U., Portales, 1973-77; v.p. acad. affairs U. Tex., Tyler, 1977-83; v.p., provost Wayne (Nebr.) State Coll., 1983-91, interim pres., 1985; prof. history, chmn. dept. Western Wash. U., Bellingham, 1991—. Fulbright lectr. Peoples Republic of China, 1995, Republic of Korea, 1994, Belarus, 2004. Author: Environment and American Experience, 1974, Depression in the Southwest, 1979, Chronological History of Texas, Vol. 1, 1982, Vol.2, 1987, Texas: Sesquicentennial Celebration, 1984; editor: Encyclopedia USA, 1988—, Poetry of the People: Poems to the President, 1929-1945, 1996, Tent Show: Arthur Names and His Famous Players, 2000, It Seems to Me: Selected Letters of Eleanor Roosevelt, 2001. Democrat. Methodist. Home: 1139 Martin St Sycamore IL 60178 Business E-Mail: donw@wwu.edu.

WHISENHUNT, KEN, professional football coach; b. Atlanta, Feb. 28, 1962; m. Alice Whisenhunt; children: Kenneth Jr., Mary Ashley. BS in Civil Engring., Ga. Tech. U., 1990. Tight end Atlanta Falcons, 1985—88, Washington Redskins, 1990, NY Jets, 1991—92; spl. teams, half backs, & tight ends coach Vanderbilt U., 1995—96; tight ends coach Balt. Ravens, 1997—98; spl. teams coach Cleve. Browns, 1999; tight ends coach NY Jets, 2000, Pitts. Steelers, 2001—03, offensive coord., 2004—06; head coach Ariz. Cardinals, 2007—. Office: Ariz Cardinals 8701 S Hardy Dr Tempe AZ 85284 *

WHISLER, JAMES STEVEN, retired mining executive, lawyer, rancher; b. Centerville, Iowa, Nov. 23, 1954; s. James Thomas and Betty Lou (Clark) W.; m. Ardyce Dawn Christensen, Jan. 20, 1979; children: James Kyle, Kristen Elyse. BS, U. Colo., Boulder, 1975; JD, U. Denver, 1978; MS, Colo. Sch. Mines, 1984, DSc (hon.), 2001; AMP, Harvard Bus. Sch., 1998. Bar: Colo. 1978; CPA, Ariz. Assoc. gen. counsel, sec. We. Nuc., Inc., Denver, 1979—81; exploration counsel Phelps Dodge Corp., NYC, 1981—85, legal and adminstrv. mgr. Phoenix, 1985—87, v.p., gen. counsel, 1987—88, sr. v.p., gen. counsel, 1988—91; pres. Phelps Dodge Mining Co., 1991—98; pres., COO Phelps Dodge Corp., Phoenix, 1997—99, chmn., pres., CEO, 2000—03, chmn., CEO, 2003—07. Bd. dirs. Am. West Holdings Corp., 2001—05, Phelps Dodge Corp., Burlington No. Santa Fe Corp., U.S. Airways Group, Inc., Copper Devel. Assn., Internat. Copper Assn., Nat. Mining Assn.; mem. Bus. Coun. Mem.: AIME, AICPA, Nat. Cowboy and Western Heritage Mus., Mining and Metall. Soc. Am., Colo. Bar Assn., Soc. Mining Engrs., Mont. Cattlemen's Assn. E-mail: jswhisler@phelpsdodge.com.

WHISLER, JOE B., lawyer; b. Nevada, Mo., May 31, 1947; BA, Ctrl. Meth. Coll., 1969; JD, So. Meth. Univ., Dallas, 1972. Bar: Mo. 1972, US Ct. Appeals (8th Cir.) 1980, US Ct. Appeals (10th Cir.). Mem., atty. Cooling & Herbers PC, Kans. City, Mo. Bd. of editors: Jour. of Air Law and Commerce, 1971—72. Mem.: ABA, Lawyers Assn. of Kans. City (pres., jr. sect. 1977—78), Kans. City Met. Bar Assn., Bar Assn. of Met. St. Louis (chmn. aviatin law com. 1998, mem. planning commn. City Westwood, Kans. 1998), Barristers, Mo. Bar (bd. gov. 1979—83, 1996—, pres.-elect 2003, pres. 2004), Phi Alpha Delta. Office: Cooling & Herbers PC 2400 City Center Sq 1100 Main St Kansas City MO 64105 *

WHISNAND, REX JAMES, association housing executive; b. Van Nuys, Calif., Jan. 2, 1948; s. Harold Theodore Whisnand and Laura Fay Brigham Whisnand; m. Cathy Ladeane Bennett, Apr. 1, 1978; 1 child, Bryce James. BS in Agrl. Bus. Mgmt., Calif. Poly State U., 1970; BSBA, Calif. State U., Sacramento, 1976; MPA in Housing Adminstrn., U. San Francisco, 1985; grad., U.S. Naval Submarine Sch., 1972; postgrad., Inst. for Orgn. Mgmt.; EdD in Orgn. and Leadership, U. San Francisco, 2000. Generalist W & W Hardware Store, Orcutt, Calif., 1964—70; state park ranger Calif. Dept. Parks and Recreation, Lompoc and Sacramento, 1969—75; exec. asst. Constrn. Industry Legis. Coun., Sacramento, 1974—75; dir. assn. svcs. Bldg. Industry Assn. Superior Calif., Sacramento, 1976—79; exec. v.p. West Bay divsn. Bldg. Industry Assn. No. Calif., Redwood City, 1980—84; exec. v.p. Bldg. Industry Assn., Tacoma/Pierce County, 1984—86; supr. Lumberjack Store, Lodi, Calif., 1988—90; exec. v.p. Rental Housing Owners Assn. of So. Alameda County, Hayward, Calif., 1990—96; field ops. supv., crew leader census 2000, Am. Housing Survey, 1997—98, crew leader, 2000; field rep. Westat survey U.S. Pub. Health Svc., 2000—02; exec. dir. Housing Conservation and Devel. Corp., San Francisco, 2002—05; exec. v.p. Calaveras County Assn. Realtors, Angels Camp, Calif., 2005—07. Com. mem. Calif. Bldg. Industry Assn., Sacramento, 1976-84; mem. exec. officers coun., local govt. com. Calif. Apt. Assn., 1991-96; mem. Alameda County Housing Rsch. Adv. Bd., Hayward, 1990-93; adj. faculty U. San Francisco; guest svc. rep. Oakland Athletics, 1997-05; columnist Calaveras Enterprise, 2006. Editor Pierce County Builder, 1984-86 (Assn. Achievement award Nat. Assn. Home Builders 1984-85), Superior California Builder Mag., 1978-80. Active 20-30 Club Internat. #1, Sacramento, 1976-80, officer, 1981-82; mem. South Sacramento Area Cmty. Planning Adv. Bd., 1978-79; grad. Pleasanton Leadership, 1995; chmn. Coastside Coalition for Safe Hwys., Half Moon Bay, 1983-84; bd. congregations Family Emergency Shelter Coalition Alameda County, 1995-96; active Pleasanton Gen. Plan Econ./Fiscal Growth Com., 1994-96, Bay Area Indsl. Edn. Coun., 1995-96, Hayward Coalition for Youth, 1995-96, San Francisco Coun. Cmty. Housing Orgns., 2002-05; mem. San Francisco Planning and Urban Rsch. Assn.-Homeless Taskforce, Housing Com., 2002-04, Non-Profit Housing Assn. No. Calif., 2002-05, Pleasanton Housing Commn., 2003-06, Pleasanton Housing Authority, 2003-06; officer Half Moon Bay C. of C., 1982-84; cert. basketball coach Nat. Youth Sports Assn., 1994-97. With USNR, 1970-76, U.S. Army, N.G., 1990-92. Named Outstanding Young Man. in Am., Jr. C. of C., Foster City, Calif., 1983. Mem. Internat. Assn. Bus. Communicators (pres. Sacramento chpt. 1979, pres. Peninsula chpt. 1981), Am. Soc. Assn. Execs. (cert.), No. Calif. Soc. Assn. Execs. (bd. dirs. 1994-97, com. chmn. 1993-95), Pleasanton C. of C. (econ. devel. com. 1990-96), Wash. State Home Builders Assn. (pres. exec. officers coun. 1985), We. Conf. Assn. Execs. (com. 1995-96), Hayward C. of C. (govt. rels. coun. 1990-95), Calif. Vocat. Indsl. Clubs Am. (bd. dirs. 1977-80), Calif. Polytech. Alumni Assn., San Francisco Comprehensive House (affordable strategy com. 2002-04), Calif. Assn. Realtors (exec. officer coun. 2006—07, govt. affairs dir. 2006—07, land use and environ. com., rural forum com.), Alpha Gamma Rho (charter, com. chair 1969-99). Episcopalian. Avocations: dog breeding, genealogy. Home: 2410 Buffalo Way Copperopolis CA 95228-9572

WHISNANT, JACK PAGE, neurologist; b. Little Rock, Oct. 26, 1924; s. John Clifton and Zula I. (Page) W.; m. Patricia Anne Rimmey, May 12, 1944; children: Elizabeth Anne, John David, James Michael. BS, U. Ark., 1948, MD, 1951; MS, U. Minn., 1955; MD (hon.), U. Edinburgh, Scotland, 1996. Intern Balt. City Hosp., 1951-52; resident in medicine and neurology Mayo Grad. Sch. Medicine, Rochester, Minn., 1952-55, instr. neurology, 1956-60, asst. prof., 1960-64, asso. prof., 1964-69, prof., 1969—; Meyer prof. neurosci. Mayo Med. Sch.; chmn. dept. neurology Mayo Clinic, Mayo Med. Sch., Mayo Grad. Sch. Medicine, 1971-81; chmn. dept. health scis. research Mayo Clinic and Mayo Med. Sch., 1987-93. Cons. neurology Mayo Clinic, 1955-96, head sect. neurology, 1963-71; dir. Mayo Cerebrovascular Clin. Rsch. Ctr., 1975-96. Contbr. articles on neurology and cerebrovascular disease to med. jours. Trustee YMCA, Rochester, pres., 1977. With USAAF, 1942-45. Decorated Air medal. NIH grantee, 1959-96. Fellow Am. Heart Assn., Am. Acad. Neurology (pres. 1993-95); mem. AMA, Am. Neurol. Assn. (pres. 1981-82), Am. Bd. Psychiatry and Neurology (bd. dirs. 1983-90, pres. 1989), Zumbro Valley Med. Soc., Minn. Med. Assn., Minn. Soc. Neurol. Scis., Ctrl. Soc. Neurol. Rsch. (pres. 1964), Alumni Assn. Mayo Found. (Disting. Alumnus award 2003). Presbyterian. Office: Mayo Clinic Dept Health Scis Rsch 200 1st St SW Rochester MN 55905-0001 Home: 211 2nd St NW Apt 716 Rochester MN 55901-2813 Personal E-mail: whisnant24@charter.net. Business E-Mail: whisnant@mayo.edu.

WHITACRE, EDWARD E., JR., retired telecommunications industry executive; b. Ennis, Tex., Nov. 4, 1941; m. Linda Whitacre; 2 children. BS in Indsl. Engring., Tex. Tech U., 1964. With Southwestern Bell Tel. Co., 1963-85, various positions in ops. dept., pres. Kans. divsn. Topeka, 1982-85; group pres. Southwestern Bell Corp., 1985-86, v.p. revenues and pub. affairs, vice-chmn., CFO St. Louis, 1986-88, pres., COO, 1988-89; chmn., CEO SBC Communications (now AT&T, Inc.), San Antonio, 1990—2007. Mem. adv. coun. Nat. Security Telecomm.; bd. dirs. Anheuser Busch, Inc., May Dept. Stores, 1989—2004, Burlington No. Santa Fe, Inc., Emerson Electric Co., 1990—2004. Pres. Boy Scouts Am., 1999—2000; campaign chmn. United Way, San Antonio, 1998; mem. gov. bus. coun. State of Tex.; chmn. bd. regents Tex. Tech U. Health Sci., Lubbock, Tex., 1992—98; bd. govs. S.W. Found. Bio Med. Rsch. Recipient Internat. Citizen of Yr. award World Affairs Coun. San Antonio, 1997, Spirit of Achievement award Nat. Jewish Med. and Rsch. Ctr., 1998, Freeman award San Antonio C. of C., 1997; named to Tex. Bus. Hall of Fame, 1997; named one of 50 Who Matter Now, CNNMoney.com Bus. 2.0, 2006. Presbyterian. Avocations: golf, hunting, cooking, reading. Office: AT&T Inc 175 E Houston St San Antonio TX 78205-2255 *

WHITAKER, BRUCE EZELL, college president; b. Cleveland County, NC, June 27, 1921; s. Oveda E. and Fay A. Whitaker; m. Esther Adams, Aug. 22, 1947; children: Barry Eugene, Garry Bruce. BA, Wake Forest U., 1944; BD, So. Bapt. Theol. Sem., 1947, ThM, 1948, PhD, 1950; postgrad., George Peabody Coll., 1952; DL, Wake Forest U., 1987. Ordained to ministry Bapt. Ch., 1945; pastor Smithfield, Ky., 1945-49; instr. sociology and philosophy Ind. U., 1947-50; prof. religion Cumberland U., Lebanon, Tenn., 1950-51, Belmont Coll., Nashville, 1951-52; prof. sociology, asst. to pres. Shorter Coll., Rome, Ga., 1952-53; assoc. pastor, min. edn. Atlanta, 1953-54; state sec., student dept. Bapt. State Conv., NC, 1954-57; pres. Chowan Coll., Murfreesboro, NC, 1957-69, pres. emeritus, 1969—. Mem. adv. com. to Nd. Higher Edn., 1962-66; to NC Commn. Higher Edn. Facilities, 1964—; pres. NC Conf. Social Svc., 1965-67, Assn. Governing Bds., 1973-82, Assn. So. Baptist Colls. and Schs., 1967-68, Assn. Eastern NC Colls., 1968-69; bd. dirs. Regional Edn. Lab. for Carolinas and Va. Pres. bd. trustees NC Found. Church-Related Colls., 1970-74; bd. dirs., v.p. Nat. Coun. Ind. Jr. Colls., 1974-75, pres., 1975-76; mem. adv. coun. presidents Assn. Governing Bds., from 1973; mem. NC Bd. Mental Health, from 1966; bd. dirs. Am. Assn. Cmty. and Jr. Colls., 1976-82; pres. NC Assn. Colls. and Univs., 1977-78; chmn. NC Commn. Mental Health/Mental Retardation Sers., 1978-81; mem. NC Commn. on Mental Health, Developmental Disabilities, and Alcohol and Drug Svcs., 1995—. Author: From Ploughboy to College President, 2008. V.p. Bapt. State Conv. NC, 1989-91. Named Tarheel of Week Raleigh News and Observer, 1962, Boss of Year NC Jaycees, 1972; named to Hall of Fame, Cmty. Action Assn., 2005; tribute paid in Congl. Record, 1962, 89, NC Com. Action Assn. Hall of Fame, 2005; Whitaker Libr. at Chowan Coll. named for him; Whitaker Sch. at Butner, NC named for him; selected one of nation's 18 most effective coll. pres. in 1985, funded study Exxon Found.; featured in We the People of North Carolina, 1989. Mem. NC Lit. and Hist. Assn. (pres. 1970-71), Am. Acad. Polit. and Social Scis., NEA, Am. Assn. Community and Jr. Colls. (dir. 1976-82, Leadership Recognition award 1989), Nat. Assn. Ind. Colls. and Univs. (dir. 1977-78, 81-85), Am. Assn. Higher Edn., Am. Coun. Edn. (bd. dirs. 1985-89), Internat. Platform Assn., Omicron Delta Kappa. Clubs: Capital City (Raleigh, NC), Rotary (chmn. dist. student exchange com. 1969-72, Paul Harris fellow); Optimist; Beechwood Country (Ahoskie, NC); Harbor (Norfolk, Va.). Home Phone: 918-848-7430; Office Phone: 918-848-7430. Personal E-mail: bwhitaker10@nc.rr.com.

WHITAKER, DARLA, electronics executive; BSEE, So. Meth. U., 1989; MBA, U. Dallas, 1997. With Tex. Instruments, Inc., 1984—, compensation mgr. Asia region Taipei and Singapore, human resources mgr. ASIC orgn., dir. human resources for application specific products bus. unit, v.p., mgr. compensation and human resource systems and svcs., sr. v.p., dir. worldwide human resources, mem. strategy leadership team. Office: Tex Instruments Inc PO Box 660199 Dallas TX 75266-0199 Office Phone: 972-995-2011. Office Fax: 972-995-4360. *

WHITAKER, ELIZABETH D., lawyer; b. Washington, Feb. 20, 1953; BA in Anthropology magna cum laude, Wheaton Coll., 1979; JD cum laude, So. Meth. U., Dallas, 1980. Bar: Tex. 1980. Co-mng. ptnr. Bracewell & Giuliani, LLP, Dallas. With Carrington, Coleman, Sloman & Blumenthal LLP, 1980—81, 1982—99, Dallas County Dist. Atty. Office, 1981—82; exec. com., bd. dirs. Com. for Qualified Judiciary, 2000, 01; exec. com. So. Meth. U. Sch. Law, 1998—, Inst. Tech. Law; barrister Patrick Higginbotham Inns of Ct., 2004—; trustee Ctr. Am Internat. Law; spkr. in field. Contbr. articles to profl. law jours. Commr. State of Tex. Lottery Commn., 2000—03; mem. United Way, Women's Initiative, 2002; bd. dirs. Cmtys. in Schs., 2004—, Grammen Chiapas Initiative, 2004—. Recipient The Innovator award, Profiles in Leadership, 2004. Fellow: Am. Bar Found. (founder), Dallas Bar Found., Tex. Bar Found.; mem.: Am. Law Inst., Order of Coif, Coll. of State Bar Tex., State Bar Tex. (chair continuing legal edn. com. 1996—97, bd. dirs. 1996—99, chair bd. dirs. 1998—99, pres.-elect 2002—03, pres. 2003—04). Republican. Office: Bracewell & Patterson LLP 500 N Akard St Ste 4000 Dallas TX 75201-3387 Home Phone: 214-363-2349; Office Phone: 214-758-1000. Business E-Mail: betsywhitaker@hotmail.com. E-mail: betsy.whitaker@bracewellgiuliani.com.

WHITAKER, FOREST, actor; b. Longview, Tex., July 15, 1961; m. Keisha Nash, May 4, 1996; children: Sonnet, True Isabella 1 stepchild, Autumn; 1 child, Ocean Alexander. Attended, U. So. Calif. Pres. Spirit Dance Entertainment; exec. dir. Nodance Film Festival, 2003—. Stage appearances (London) Swan, Romeo and Juliet, Hamlet, Ring Around the

Moon, Craig's Wife, Whose Life Is It Anyway?, The Greeks, Patchwork Shakespeare, Beggar's Opera, Jesus Christ Superstar; actor: (films) TAG: The Assassination Game, 1982, Fast Times at Ridgemont High, 1982, Vision Quest, 1985, The Color of Money, 1986, Platoon, 1986, Stakeout, 1987, Good Morning, Vietnam, 1987, Bloodsport, 1988, Bird, 1988 (Best Actor Cannes Film Festival 1988), Johnny Handsome, 1989, Downtown, 1990, Rage in Harlem, 1991, Article 99, 1992, Diary of a Hit Man, 1992, Consenting Adults, 1992, Body Snatchers, 1993, The Crying Game, 1993, Bank Robber, 1993, Blown Away, 1994, Jason's Lyric, 1994, Prêt-à-Porter, 1994, Species, 1995, Smoke, 1995, Phenomenon, 1996, Body Count, 1998, Ghost Dog: The Way of the Samuai, 1999, Light It Up, 1999, Battlefield Earth, 2000, Four Dogs Playing Poker, 2000, Green Dragon, 2001, The Follow, 2001, The Fourth Angel, 2001, Panic Room, 2002, Phone Booth, 2002, Jiminy Glick in La La Wood, 2004, Mary, 2005, A Little Trip to Heaven, 2005, Even Money, 2006, The Marsh, 2006, The Last King of Scotland (Hollywood Actor of the Yr. award, Hollywood Awards, 2006, Best Actor award, LA Film Critics Assn.(Tie) & NY Film Critics Circle awards, 2006, Best Actor, Nat. Bd. Review, 2006, African-American Film Critics Assn., 2006, Nat. Soc. Film Critics, 2007, 2006 Critics Choice award, Broadcast Film Critics Assn., 2007, Best Performance by an Actor in a Motion Picture-Drama, Golden Globe award, Hollywood Fgn. Press Assn., 2007, Outstanding Performance by a Female Actor in a Leading Role, SAG, 2007, Actor in a Leading Role, British Acad. Film and TV Arts, 2007, Acad. award best actor in a leading role, 2007, Actor in a Motion Picture, NAACP Image Awards, 2007), 2006, (voice only) Everyone's Hero, 2006; (TV movies) Grand Baby, 1985, Hands of a Stranger, 1987, Criminal Justice, 1990, Last Light, 1993, Lush Life, 1993, The Enemy Within, 1994, Rebound: The Legend of Earl "The Great" Manigault, 1996, The Split, 1998, Witness Protection, 1999, Deacons for Defense, 2003; (TV mini-series) North & South, 1985, North and South Book II, 1986; (TV series) The Shield, 2006-; (TV appearances) Making the Grade, 1982, Cagney & Lacey, 1983, Trapper John, M.D., 1984, Hill Street Blues, 1984, The Fall Guy, 1985, Diff'rent Strokes, 1985, Amazing Stories, 1986, Feast of All Saints, 2001, The Twilight Zone, 2003, ER, 2006; actor, dir., exec. prodr.: (films) First Daughter, 2004; actor, exec. prodr.: (films) Green Dragon, 2001, American Gun, 2005; (TV movies) Feast of All Saints, 2001; dir.: (films) Waiting to Exhale, 1995, Hope Floats, 1998; (TV films) Strapped (Toronto Film Festival award for best new dir.), 1993, Black Jaq, 1998; prodr. (films) Chasing Papi, 2003; co-exec. prodr. (TV films) Door to Door, 2002 Named Best Actor, Black Entertainment TV (BET) Awards, 2007; recipient of a star on the Hollywood Walk of Fame, 2007. Office: care DGA 7920 W Sunset Blvd Los Angeles CA 90046-3300 *

WHITAKER, G(EORGE) WARREN, lawyer; b. NYC, Oct. 13, 1950; s. George Warren Jr. and Stella S. (Stann) W.; m. Marian Kramer, Sept. 15, 1982; children: Alexander Stuart, Emily Kate. BA, Rutgers U., 1972; JD, Columbia U., 1976. Bar: NJ 1976, NY 1977, US Tax Ct. 1991. Assoc. Davidson, Dawson, NYC, 1977-80, Curtis, Mallet, NYC, 1980-83; sr. atty. Breed, Abbott, NYC, 1983-91; assoc. Chadbourne & Parke, NYC, 1991-94; sr. atty. Jones, Day, Reavis & Pogue, NYC, 1994-96; ptnr. Law Offices James E. Hughes Jr., NYC, 1996-98, Hughes and Whitaker, NYC, 1998—2001, Day, Berry & Howard, LLP, NYC, 2002—06, Day Pitney LLP, NYC, 2007—. Counsel Pelham Art Ctr., NY, 1995-2001; bd. dirs. Shakespeare's Globe, USA; mem. banker lawyer adv. com. NY Philharmonic, 2003-; counsel, bd. dirs. Picture Ho. Regional Theater, 2005—. Named one of Top 100 Attys., Worth mag., 2005—06. Fellow NY Bar Found.; mem. ABA (vice chair internat. estate planning com. 1996—), Soc. Trust and Estate Practioners (chmn. NY chpt. 1998-06, US chmn. 2005-), NY State Bar Assn. (chair internat. estate planning com. 1996-98, 1st dist. rep. 1999-01, treas. 2001-02, sec. 2002-03, chair-elect 2003—04, chair 2004-05), NYC Bar Assn. (estate tax com. 1996—). Republican. Avocations: bicycling, book collecting. Home: 514 Esplanade Pelham NY 10803-2400 Office: Day Pitney 7 Times Sq Fl 20 New York NY 10036 Office Phone: 212-297-2468. Business E-Mail: gwwhitaker@daypitney.com.

WHITAKER, JOEL, publishing executive, public official; b. Indpls., May 27, 1942; s. Quincy Myers and Sigur Elizabeth (Moore) W.; m. Donna Kay, Apr. 27, 1986. BS in Bus. Journalism, Ind. U., 1964, MA in Journalism, 1971; JD, Temple U., 1979. Reporter St. Petersburg (Fla.) Times, 1964, copy editor, 1966-68, Wall St. Journal, NYC, 1968-73; bus. news editor Phila. Evening and Sunday Bull., 1973-78; law clk. Fellheimer, Krakower & Eiclen, Phila., 1978—79; mng. editor Bank Letter, NYC, 1979-80; editor, pres. Whitaker Newsletters Inc., Silver Spring, Md., 1980—. Chmn. Fanwood Planning Bd., 1981-85; trustee Fanwood cmty. Found. 1998-2004; mem. Downtown Redevel. Commn., Fanwood, 1983-85; mem. Union County (N.J.) local adv. commn. on alcoholism and drug abuse, 1993-97, chmn., 1994-95, vice chmn. 1997; councilman Borough of Fanwood, 1998-2003, coun. pres., 2000-03. Mem. Newsletter Publishers Assn. (bd. dirs. 1983-92, found. trustee 1986—, treas. 1989-93, found. treas. 2005-06), Soc. Profl. Journalists (treas. N.J. profl. chpt. 1997-2005), Nat. Press Club (Washington), Rotary (bd. dirs. Fanwood-Scotch Plains club 1996-98), Army and Navy Club (Washington). Republican. Roman Catholic. Office: Whitaker Newsletters Inc 14305 Shoreham Dr Silver Spring MD 20905-4481 Home Phone: 301-879-8802; Office Phone: 301-384-1573. Personal E-mail: joelwhitaker@verizon.net.

WHITAKER, JOHN KING, retired economics professor; b. Burnley, Lancashire, Eng., Jan. 30, 1933; arrived in US, 1967; s. Ben and Mary Whitaker; m. Sally Bell Cross, Aug. 24, 1957; children: Ann Elizabeth, Jane Claire, David John. BA in Econs., U. Manchester, 1956; AM, Johns Hopkins U., 1957; PhD, Cambridge U., 1962. Lectr. U. Bristol, England, 1960-66, prof., 1966-69; vis. prof. U. Va., Charlottesville, 1967-68, prof. econs., 1969-86, chmn. dept. econs., 1979-82, Paul Goodloe McIntire prof. econs., 1986-92, Georgia Bankard prof. econs., 1992—2003, Georgia Bankard prof. econs. emeritus, 2003—. Author: The Early Economic Writings of Alfred Marshall, 1867-1890, 2 vols., 1975, The Correspondence of Alfred Marshall, Economist, 3 vols., 1996. Fellow: History Econs. Soc. (disting.). Home: 1615 Yorktown Dr Charlottesville VA 22901-3046

WHITAKER, LINTON ANDIN, plastic surgeon; b. Navasota, Tex., Nov. 16, 1936; s. Ira Andin and Lena Rivers (Stedman) W.; m. Renata Grasmanis, Dec. 20, 1963; children: Derek Andin (dec.), Ingrid Marlena, Brandon Andrew. BA, U. Tex., 1958; MD, Tulane U., 1962. Diplomate Am. Bd. Surgery, Am. Bd. Plastic Surgery. Founder, dir. ctr. human appearance U. Pa. Med. Ctr., Phila., 1988—; resident in gen. surgery Dartmouth Affiliated Hosps., Hanover, NH, 1965-69; resident in plastic surgery U. Pa. Hosp., Phila., 1969-71; chief plastic surgery Grad. Hosp., 1971-77, U. Pa. Hosp., Phila., 1987—2005, attending surgeon, 1971—; chief plastic surgery Children's Hosp. Phila., 1981—2001, attending surgeon, 1971—; v.p. med. staff Children's Hosp., Phila., 1992-94, pres. med. staff, 1994-96; attending physician VA Hosp., 1971—, Phila. Gen. Hosp., 1971-77; assoc. in plastic surgery Sch. Medicine, U. Pa., Phila., 1971-73, asst. prof. in plastic surgery, 1973-76, assoc. prof., 1976-81, prof., 1981—; founder, dir. ctr. human appearance U. Pa. Med. Ctr., Phila., 1988—. Vis. prof. South Australia Craniofacial Unit, Adelaide, Australia and New Zealand, 1981, U. Hawaii, 1983, Brown U., Providence, 1983, Mass. Gen. Hosp., Boston, 1984, U. Utah, Salt Lake City, 1984, U. B.C., Vancouver, 1986, U. Pitts., 1988, U. Calif., San Diego, 1992, Ohio Valley Soc. for Plastic and Reconstructive Surgery, 1992, N.Y. U., 1994; Curts vis. prof. Dartmouth U. Med. Ctr., Hanover, N.H., 1990, Kazanjian vis. prof. Mass. Gen. Hosp., Boston, 1990; First Seiichi Ohmori Meml. lectr. All Asiatic Congress on Aesthetic Surgery, Tokyo, 1988; vis. speaker Inst. Cosmotology and Inst. Stomatology, Moskow, Russia, 1985, vis. prof. Seoul Nat. U. and vis. speaker Korean Soc. for Plastic Surgeons, 1994; hon. vis. spkr. Chinese Plastic Surgery Soc., Beijing, 1996; lectr., speaker at univs., assns. in field. Co-author: Atlas of Cranio-maxillofacial Surgery, 1982, Aesthetic Surgery of the Facial Skelton, 1992; editor (with P. Randall): Symposium on the Reconstruction of Jaw Deformity, Clinics in Plastic Surgery, 1987, 1991; co-editor: Yearbook of Plastic and Reconstructive Surgery, 1980—97; assoc. editor: Seminars in Complementary Medicine, 2001—, mem. editl. bd.: Jour. Cutaneous Aging and Cosmetic Dermatology, 1988—; contbr. articles to profl. jours. Capt. M.C., U.S. Army, 1963-65. Foederer fellow Foederer Fund for Excellence, 1985-88; NIH grantee, 1976-79, 81-87, 82-85, 89, Plastic Surgery Edn. Found. Rsch. grantee, 1980-82; recipient James IV Surg. Traveller award, 1979. Fellow ACS, Am. Soc. Ophthalmic Plastic and Reconstructive Surgery (hon.); mem. AMA, Am. Assn. Plastic Surgeons (mem. program com. 1988, chmn. 1989, Rsch. grantee 1984-85), Am. Surg. Assn., Am. Alpine Workshop in Plastic Surgery (founding mem.), Am. Cleft Palate Assn. (chmn. com. classification craniofacial anomalies 1976-80, mem. program com. for 1978 mtg. 1977, mem. long-range planning com. 1980, mem. coun. 1981-84, chmn. internat. rels. com. 1981-83), Am. Cleft Palate Ednl. Found. (bd. dirs. 1975-84, chmn. rsch. com. 1975-78, chmn. instrl. courses 1980-81), Am. Soc. Aesthetic Plastic Surgery, Am. Soc. Craniofacial Surgery (mem. coun. 1992—), Am. Soc. Maxillofacial Surgeons (Spl. Honors 2003, bd. dirs. 2003—), Am. Soc. Plastic and Reconstructive Surgeons, mem. plastic surgery speakers bur. 1977—), Am. Soc. Plastic and Reconstructive Surgeons Ednl. Found. (chmn. ednl. assessment com., maxillofacial trauma and craniofacial anomalies 1975-78, mem. clin. symposia com. 1978-82, chmn. clin. symposia com. 1981-82), Internat. Cleft Palate and Related Craniofacial Anomalies Soc., Internat. Soc. Aesthetic Surgery, Internat. Soc. Craniofacial Surgeons (founding mem., organizer, mem. exec. com. 1987—, sec and treas. 1993-95, pres. 1995-97), Phila. Med. Soc., Phila. Acad. Surgery, Coll. Physicians Phila., Assn. Acad. Surgery, Northeastern Soc. Plastic Surgeons N.Y. (chmn. program com. 1987, mem. programcom. 1988), Plastic Surgery Rsch. Coun., John Morgan Soc., Robert H. Ivy Soc., The Columbian Soc. Plastic, Maxillofacial and Hand Surgery (hon.), Academia Medica Lombarda (Italy, hon.), Sociedad Jamie Planas de Cirugia Plastica (Spain, hon.), Mt. Kenya Safari Club (hon.), Japan Soc. Craniomaxillofacial Surgeons (hon.), Asian Pacific Cranofacial Assn., Japan Soc. Plastic and Reconstructive Surgery (hon.), Phila. Club, Merion Cricket Club, Confrerie des chevaliers du Tastevin, Grand Senechat. Avocations: mountain climbing, skiing, wines. Office: U Pa Med Ctr 10 Penn Tower 3400 Spruce St Philadelphia PA 19104-4206 Office Phone: 215-662-2048. Business E-Mail: linton.whitaker@uphs.upenn.edu.

WHITAKER, MARK THEIS, broadcast executive, editor; b. Lower Merion, Pa., Sept. 7, 1957; s. Cleophus Sylvester and Jeanne (Theis) W.; m. Alexis Lynn Gelber, May 5, 1985; children: Rachel Eva, Matthew Edward. BA summa cum laude, Harvard U., 1979; postgrad., Oxford U., Eng., 1979-81; LLD (hon.), Wheaton Coll. Assoc. editor Newsweek mag., NYC, 1981-83, gen. editor, 1983, sr. writer, 1984-86, sr. editor, bus. editor, 1987-91, asst. mng. editor, 1991-95, mng. editor, 1996-98, corp. editor, editor NYC, 1998—2006; v.p., editor in chief new ventures Washingtonpost Newsweek Interactive Co., LLC Washington Post Co., 2006—07; sr. v.p. TV programming & web content NBC News, 2007—. Featured in Ebony mag., 2007. Bd. dir. Literacy Partners, NYC. Marshall scholar Brit. Marshall Fund, Oxford U., 1979-81. Mem. Nat. Assn. Black Journalists, Am. Soc. Mag. Editors (bd. dirs., 1999-, pres., 2004-2006), Coun. on Fgn. Rels., Century Assn., Phi Beta Kappa. Achievements include first African-American editor of a newsweekly; Newsweek won two National Magazine Awards for General Excellence during his tenure as editor. Office: NBC 30 Rockefeller Plz New York NY 10112 *

WHITAKER, MARY FERNAN, lawyer; b. Kansas City, Mo., May 29, 1958; d. James Paul and Mildred Louise (Connor) Fernan; m. Mark Dwight Whitaker, May 28, 1983; children: Paul Connor, James Sullivan, Helen Foster. BSN, George Mason U., 1982, JD, 1987, MEd, 2004. Bar: Va. 1987, Pa. 1995; cert. swim coach, Md. cert. swim judge. Nurse George Washington Med. Ctr., Washington, 1980-82, Mt. Vernon Hosp., Alexandria, Va., 1982-84; atty. Legal Svcs. No. Va., Arlington, 1987, Office Rev. and Appeals, EEOC, Falls Church, Va., 1987-88; pvt. practice Annadale, Va., 1988-93, Pottsville, Pa., 1993-95, Coopersburg, Pa., 1995-96, Solomons, Md., 1996—2000; faculty St. Mary's Ryken High Sch., 1999—2000; lawyer pvt. law practice, 2001—. Adj. faculty paralegal program No. Va. C.C., 1992; counselor, mem. legal com. My Sister's Pl., Washington, 1987-93; mem. pro bono panel Legal Svcs. No. Va., Falls Church, 1997—. Vol. ARC, Alexandria, 1987; vol. atty. Women's Legal Def. Fund, Washington, 1989-91, Legal Svcs. No. Va., 1997—; mem. Shelter Outreach Program, 1990-93; v.p. Ravensworth Bristow Civic assn., 1990-93; head makeup design for cmty. theatre troupe Camelot Players, 1990-91; tchr. 3d grade religious edn. St. Michael's Ch. Choir, 1991-92, tchr. 8th grade religious edn., 1992-93, choir, 1992-93; tchr. 7th grade religious edn. St. Joseph Ch., 1995-96; swimmer U.S. Masters, 1997, 98; cert. stroke and turn judge Md. Swimming, 1998—2001. U.S. Master Swimmer, 1997-98. Mem. Am. Trial Lawyers Assn., Abrandria City Bar Assn., Va. State Bar Assn., Phi Delta Phi. Roman Catholic. Avocations: bicycling, swimming. Home: 7104 Marlan Dr Alexandria VA 22307 Office: 1010 Cameron St Alexandria VA 22314 Office Phone: 703-300-3533. Business E-Mail: mwhitaker@medlawservices.com.

WHITAKER, MATTHEW GEORGE, prosecutor; JD, MBA, U. Iowa, 1995. Corp. counsel Supervalu; atty. Briggs & Morgan, Finley Alt Smith, Des Moines; US atty. (so. dist.) Iowa US Dept. Justice, Des Moines, 2004—. Office: US Courthouse Annex Ste 286 110 E Ct Ave Des Moines IA 50309 *

WHITAKER, PERNELL (SWEET PEA WHITAKER), retired boxer; b. Norfolk, Va., Jan. 2, 1964; Profl. boxer, 1984—2001; lightweight champion North Am. Boxing Fedn., 1987, US Boxing Assn., 1987, Internat. Boxing Fedn., 1989, light welterweight champion, 1992; lightweight champion World Boxing Coun., 1989, welterweight champion, 1993—97; lightweight champion World Boxing Assn., 1990, light middleweight champion, 1995. Named Fighter of Yr., 1989, pound for pound best boxer in the world, Ring mag., 1995; named to Internat. Boxing Hall of Fame, 2007; recipient Gold medal, Lightweight Divsn., Olympics, 1984. Achievements include winning 6 world championship titles in 4 weight classes; career record of 201-14 with 91 knock-outs. *

WHITAKER, SCOTT, former federal agency administrator, lobbyist; m. Michelle Whitaker; 2 children. B in Polit. Sci., Palm Beach Atlantic Coll.; M in Govt., Johns Hopkins U. Legis. asst. Senate Asst. Majority Leader Don Nickles, 1994—97, policy adviser, 1997—2001; asst. sec. for legislation US Dept. HHS, Washington, 2001—03, chief of staff, 2003—05; exec. v.p. Biotechnology Industry Org., Wash., DC, 2005—. Republican. Office: Biotech Industry Org 1225 Eye St NW Suite 400 Washington DC 20005

WHITAKER, SUSANNE KANIS, veterinary medical librarian; b. Clinton, Mass., Sept. 10, 1947; AB in Biology, Clark U., 1969; MS in Library Sci., Case Western Res. U., 1970. Regional reference libr. Yale Med. Libr., New Haven, 1970-72; med. libr. Hartford Hosp., Conn., 1972-77; asst. libr. Cornell U., Ithaca, NY, 1977-78; vet. med. libr. Coll. Vet. Medicine, Cornell U., 1978-98, vet. pub. svcs. libr., 1998—. Mem. Med. Libr. Assn. (vet. med. librs. sect. 1983-84, chmn. 1984-85, chmn. pub. rels. com. 2000—), Med. Libr. Assn. (Upstate NY and Ont. chpt.), Acad. Health Info. Profls. (disting. mem.), Am. Vet. Med. History Soc. (sec.-treas. 2004—). Home: 23 Wedgewood Dr Ithaca NY 14850-1064 Office: Cornell U Coll Vet Medicine Flower-Sprecher Libr Ithaca NY 14853-6401 Home Phone: 607-257-9248; Office Phone: 607-253-3499. Business E-Mail: skw2@cornell.edu.

WHITAKER, THOMAS O'HARA, theater educator, theater director; s. Thomas Russell and Dorothy Whitaker. BA, Oberlin Coll., Ohio, 1975; MFA, Carnegie-Mellon U., Pitts., 1983. Instr. acting Carnegie-Mellon U., Coll. Fine Arts, 1982—83; instr. SW Mo. State U., Springfield, 1983—84; asst. prof. Ind. State U., Terre Haute, 1984—87, U. Tex., Austin, 1987—92, U. Calif., Santa Barbara, 1992—96, assoc. prof., 1996—. Cons. dir., tchr. Conn. Humanities Coun., Hartford, 1980—81; cons. Ctr. Theatre Techniques Edn., Stratford, 1980—81, Comprehensive Arts Program, New Haven, 1980—81; guest artist Oberlin Theater Inst., 1987; tenured dir. Tex. Shakespeare Festival, Kilgore, 1989—; cons. Beijing Inst. World Theater and Film, 2005—; guest prof. Nanjing U., China, 2006—. Actor(musician): (theater/puppet) Young Woman's Sorrow, Man is Man, Loot, The Misanthrope, Advice to the Players, Love's Labor's Lost; actor: King Lear; dir.: Tartuffe, Taming of the Shrew; actor: Heartbreak House, (theatre/puppet) Grey Lady Cantata; dir.: (theater) The Bourgeois Gentleman, Two Gentlement of Verona; dir., dir.: As You Like It; actor: Henry IV, part 1; dir.: Big Love, Arms and the Man, The Merchant of Venice, Life's a Dream, Cyrano de Bergerac, bobrauschenbergamerica; actor: (film) The Meadow's Green; dir.: (theater) Revel's World of Shakespeare; actor: The Marilyn Project, The Forced Marriage; dir.: Time Play, Misalliance, Fool for Love, Buried Child, Man of La Mancha, 2007. Recipient Boettcher award Directing, Carnegie-Mellon U., 1983; grantee, Conn. Humanities Coun., 1980; scholar, Carnegie-Mellon U., 1982—83. Mem.: Phi Beta Kappa.

WHITAKER, THOMAS PATRICK, lawyer; b. Washington, Sept. 22, 1944; s. Thomas J. and Mary K. (Finn) W.; m. Donna Mae Brenish, Feb. 16, 1974; children: Laura, Kevin. BA, George Washington U., 1966, MPA, 1973, JD, 1979; postgrad., Naval War Coll., 1984, Nat. Def. U., 2005. Bar: Va. 1979. Staff asst. Adminstrn. Office of U.S. Cts., Washington, 1972-73, analyst, 1975-77; cons. Planning Research Corp., McLean, Va., 1973-75; program analyst Social Security Adminstrn., Falls Church, Va., 1982—; congrl. aide Rep. Abercrombie, 2005. Served to lt. (j.g.) USNR, 1966-71, Vietnam, capt. with Res. 1983-97. Asst. U.S. Naval Attache, Egypt, 1988, Malaysia, 1992. Home: 9817 Days Farm Dr Vienna VA 22182-7306 Office Phone: 703-605-8292. Personal E-mail: twhitake@hotmail.com.

WHITAKER, THOMAS RUSSELL, English literature educator; b. Marquette, Mich., Aug. 7, 1925; s. Joe Russell and Sarah Genevieve (Houk) W.; m. Dorothy Vera Barnes, June 17, 1950 (dec. Dec. 1995); children: Thomas O'Hara, Sarah Mae, Mary Beth, Gwendolyn Anne; m. Joan Bower Horwitt, Oct. 4, 1997 (div. Sept. 2002); m. Lillian Ann Traub, Jul. 26, 2003. BA summa cum laude, Oberlin Coll., 1949; MA, Yale U., 1950, PhD, 1953. Instr. English Oberlin (Ohio) Coll., 1952-55, asst. prof., 1955-59, assoc. prof., 1959-63, prof., 1963-64; tchr. lit. Goddard Coll., Plainfield, Vt., 1964-66; prof. English U. Iowa, Iowa City, 1966-75, Yale U., New Haven, Conn., 1975-95, prof. theater studies, 1986-95, chmn. dept. English, 1979-85, Frederick W. Hilles prof. English, 1989-95; Frederick W. Hilles prof. emeritus English, 1995—. Author: Swan and Shadow: Yeats's Dialogue with History, 1964, 2d edit. with new preface, 1989, William Carlos Williams, 1968, rev. edit., 1989, Fields of Play in Modern Drama, 1977, Tom Stoppard, 1983, augmented edit., 1984, Mirrors of Our Playing: Paradigms and Presences in Modern Drama, 1999; editor: Twentieth Century Interpretations of the Playboy of the Western World, 1969, Teaching in New Haven: The Common Challenge, 1991; editor Iowa Rev., 1974-77; chmn. editorial bd. On Common Ground, 1993—; author, narrator video script: Excellence in Teaching: Agenda for Partnership, 1997; writer, advisor Yale-New Haven Tchrs. Inst. Nat. Demonstration Project, 1998-02, Yale Nat. Initiative, 2002—. Served with C.E. U.S. Army, 1944-46. Recipient Harbison award for gifted teaching Danforth Found., 1972, Seton Elm and Ivy award, City of New Haven and Yale U., 2005; fellow, Am. Council Learned Socs., 1969—70, NEH-Huntington, 1981. Mem. MLA. Home: 38 Wilford Rd Branford CT 06405-5321

WHITBREAD, THOMAS BACON, language educator, writer; b. Bronxville, NY, Aug. 22, 1931; s. Thomas Francis and Caroline Nancy (Bacon) W. BA, Amherst Coll., 1952; A.M., Harvard U., 1953, PhD, 1959. Instr. English, U. Tex. at Austin, 1959-62, asst. prof., 1962-65, asso. prof., 1965-71, prof., 1971—. Vis. asso. prof. Rice U., 1969-70; mem. lit. adv. panel Tex. Commn. on Arts and Humanities, 1972-76 Author (poetry): Four Infinitives, 1964, Whomp and Moonshiver, 1982, The Structures Minds Erect, 2007; co-author: Prize Stories, 1962, The O. Henry Awards, 1962; editor: Seven Contemporary Authors, 1966. Recipient third Aga Khan prize for fiction Paris Rev., 1960, Lit. Anthology Program award Nat. Endowment for Arts, 1968, Outstanding Freshman Tchr. award Phi Eta Sigma, 1972-73 Mem. AAUP, Tex. Inst. Letters (Poetry award 1965, 83), Nat., Am. amateur press assns., Phi Beta Kappa. Democrat. Home: 1014 E 38th St Austin TX 78705-1835 Office: U Tex Dept English 1 Univ Station B5000 Austin TX 78712 Business E-Mail: whitbread@mail.utexas.edu.

WHITBURN, MERRILL DUANE, English literature educator; b. Mpls., Apr. 29, 1938; s. George and Marie Ellen (Carlstedt) W.; m. Diane Robertson, June 15, 1960; children: Stephen, Mark, Elizabeth. AB, U. Mich., 1960, AM, 1968; PhD, U. Iowa, 1973. With Western Electric Co., NYC and Indpls., 1965-67; asst. prof. Tex. A&M U., College Station, 1973-77, assoc. prof., 1977-79; assoc. prof. Rensselaer Poly. Inst., Troy, NY, 1979-83, prof., 1983-89, Louis Ellsworth Laflin prof., 1989—, chmn. dept., 1979-85, 88-95; rsch. fellow Yale U. Divinity Sch., New Haven, 2003; Rensselaer Poly. Inst. Exch. prof. humanities and social sci. SUNY-Albany U., 2005. Co-owner Pride and Prejudice Books, Ballston Lake, N.Y., 1985—. Author: Rhetorical Scope and Performance: The Example of Technical Communication, 2000; co-author: (booklet) Guide for Departments of English, 1985; contbr. articles to profl. publs. Recipient Disting. Svc. award Tex. A&M U., 1976, Disting. Teaching award, 1979, Jay R. Gould award for excellence in tchg. tech. comm. Soc. Tech. Comm., 1995, Trustee's Outstanding Tchr. award Rensselaer Poly. Inst., 2002; grantee Fund for the Improvement of Postsecondary Edn., 1983. Mem. Nat. Coun. Tchrs. English (best article in tech. writing award 1981), Coun. for Programs in Tech. and Sci. Communication.

WHITCOMB, BRIAN, sports association executive; m. Stefanie Whitcomb; 2 children. BPE, Ariz. State U., 1978. Bd. dirs. PGA S.W. sect., 1989—91, sec., 1991—93, v.p., 1993—95, pres., 1995—97, hon. pres., 1997—99, tournament chairperson, edn. chairperson, golf pass chairperson; designer, co-operator The 500 Club, Phoenix, 1989—; designer Club West, Phoenix, 1992; designer, owner Lost Tracks Golf Club, Bend, Oreg., 1995—; co-owner The Golf Club at Beardance, Castle Rock, Colo.; bd. dirs. from Dist. 14 PGA, 1998—2001, mem. Properties Bd., 1999—, sec., 2002—04, v.p., 2004—06, pres., 2006—. Mem. PGA, 1984—. Bd. mem., fin. contbr. Crystal Peaks Youth Ranch, Bend, Oreg. Office: Lost Tracks Golf Club 60205 Sunset View Dr Bend OR 97702 Mailing: PGA 100 Ave of Champions Box 109601 Palm Beach Gardens FL 33410-9601 *

WHITCOMB, JAMES HALL, geophysicist, foundation administrator; b. Sterling, Colo., Dec. 10, 1940; s. Clay Thane and Julia Melvina Whitcomb; m. Sandra Lynn McMurdo, July 13, 1965 (div. 1978); m. Teresa R. Idoni, Feb. 3, 1989; children: Lisa Michelle, Marisa Giulia, Sabina Maria. Geophysics engring. degree, Colo. Sch. of Mines, 1962; MS in Oceanography, Geophysics, Oreg. State U., 1964; PhD in Geophysics, Calif. Inst. Tech., 1973. Grad. rsch. asst. dept. oceanography Oreg. State U., Corvallis, 1962-64; geophysicist Ctr. Astrogeology U.S. Geol. Survey, Flagstaff, Ariz., 1964-66; Fulbright-Hayes program rsch. fellow Seismol. Inst. U.

Uppsala, Sweden, 1966-67; grad. rsch. asst. seismol. lab. Calif. Inst. Tech., Pasadena, 1967-73, sr. rsch. fellow seismol. lab., 1973-79; assoc. prof. attendant rank dept. geol. scis. U. Colo., Boulder, 1979-82, fellow Coop. Inst. Rsch. in Environ. Scis., 1979-84; v.p. technical applications and mktg. ISTAC, Inc., Pasadena, 1984-88; program dir. seismology NSF, Washington, 1989-99, acting dep. divsn. dir., 1999—2002, sect. head, 2002—. Expert witness U.S. Ho. Reps. Com. on Sci. and Tech., 1977; mem. geodynamics rev. bd. Jet Propulsion Lab., 1980-82, com. on geodesy Nat. Acad. Scis., 1982-85; pres. Boulder Systems, Inc., Pasadena, 1987-88. Recipient Outstanding Achievement award U.S. Geol. Survey, 1964, Dir.'s award for mgmt. excellence NSF, 1995, 2003; scholar State of Colo., 1958-62, Mobil Oil Co., 1960; fellow Sweden-Am. Found., 1966. Mem. AAAS, Am. Geophysical Union, Seismol. Soc. Am., Soc. Exploration Geophysicists (scholar 1963), Tau Beta Pi, Phi Kappa Phi, Sigma Xi. Office: Nat Sci Found Geosciences 4201 Wilson Blvd Arlington VA 22230-0002

WHITCOMB, JAMES HOWARD, JR., investment banker; b. Bryn Mawr, Pa., Nov. 15, 1954; s. James Howard, Sr. and Eleanor (Keady) Whitcomb; m. Havilande Bayard Brown, Oct. 11, 1986; children: James Howard III, Ashton Bayard, Christiana Prescott. BA with honors, Williams Coll., 1976; MBA, U. Va., 1981. Sr. v.p. Lehman Bros., NYC, London, 1981-93; mng. dir. Chem. Securities, NYC, 1995-97; sr. v.p. NatWest Markets, NYC, 1997-98; prin. Shattuck Hammond Ptnr. LLC, NYC, 1998—2003; mng. dir. The Chart Group, NYC, 2003—. Trustee Southport Conservancy, 2000—, pres., 2006—; trustee Southport Conglist. Ch., 1998—2000. Fellow: Fgn. Policy Assn.; mem.: Williams Club (NYC), Yale Club (NYC), Fairfield County Hunt Club, Pequot Yacht Club. Avocations: foreign relations, sailing, skiing, travel. Office: 75 Rockefeller Plz New York NY 10019

WHITCOMB, JAMES STUART, videographer, photographer, production company executive; b. Buffalo, May 7, 1957; s. C. Stuart and Helen Nancy (O'Reilly) W. BA in Journalism/Broadcasting, SUNY, Buffalo, 1983. Cert. master herbalist, iridologist. Pres., owner Ad Astra Prodns., Williamsville, NY, 1987—; co-owner, videographer, photographer STB Prodns., Williamsville, 1989—; owner legal books and computer software co. JSW Pub., Williamsville, 1997—. Videographer, editor nature/stress reduction Videos A Celebration of the Four Seasons, 1991, Autumn on Cape Code and Martha's Vineyard, 1993, Gardens, Blossoms & Blooms, 1994, A Walk Through St. Francis Woods, 1994, Nantucket Noel: Christmas on Nantucket, 1994, Reflections: Nature's Watercolors, 1995, Autumn in Vermont, 1995, A Day On the Farm, 1995, Window Shopping, 1995, Singalong with your Old Favorites, 1997, A Celebration of the Four Seasons II: Seasons of the Seashore, 1997, Kids and Animals, 1998; videographer, writer promotion video Internat. Modeling and Talent Assn., 1990; videographer numerous prodns. for modelling, fashion, and spl. interest, owner, Jim's Project's Inc. Supporter St. Joseph's Indian Sch., Chamberlain, S.D, supporter Interlink Resources, Taraz, Kazakhstan. Mem. People for Ethical Treatment of Animals, Wilderness Soc., Am. Hiking Soc., Nat. Audubon Soc., Farm Sanctuary, Best Friends Animal Sanctuary, Assn. for Rsch. and Enlightenment, Adirondack Mountain Club. Achievements include started a small non-profit organization called Jim's Project's Inc. to help the children in Kazakhstan, and in China, and to bring a better life to the orphan children. Avocations: skiing, hiking. Home: 71 Rinewalt St Williamsville NY 14221-5736 Office: Ad Astra and STB Prodns PO Box 1725 Williamsville NY 14231-1725 Office Phone: 716-626-5319.

WHITCOMB, RICHARD TRAVIS, aeronautical consultant; b. Evanston, Ill., Feb. 21, 1921; s. Kenneth Frederick and Gladys (Travis) Whitcomb. BS in Aero. Engring., Worcester Poly. Inst., 1943, DEng (hon.), 1956; DSc (hon.), Old Dominion U., 1985. Aero. rsch. scientist Langley Rsch. Ctr. NASA, Hampton, Va., 1943—58, head transonic aerodynamics br., 1958—80, disting. rsch. assoc., 1980—85; pvt. practice aero. cons. Hampton, 1980—90. Patentee aero. equipment. Named to Nat. Inventors Hall of Fame, 2003; recipient Collier Trophy, Nat. Aero. Assn., 1955, Nat. Medal for Sci., Office of the Pres. U.S., 1973, Wright Bros. trophy, Nat. Aero. Assn., 1974, award in Aero. Engring., NAS, 2000. Fellow: AIAA (hon. Reed award 1969, Daniel Guggenheim medal 2002); mem.: NAE. Avocations: music, reading, exercise.

WHITE, ALAN FREDERICK, academic administrator; b. Evansville, Ind., Dec. 17, 1937; s. Hubert Ruben and Nota Lizzee (Culver) W.; m. Patricia Lynn Townsend, Nov. 7, 1959; children: Gregory Townsend, Samuel Townsend. AB, Miami U., Oxford, Ohio, 1963; MS, MIT, 1971. Dir. U. Hawaii Ctr. Crosscultural Tng. and Rsch., Hilo, 1967-70, exec. asst. to pres. Honolulu, 1971-73; Alfred P. Sloan fellow MIT, Cambridge, 1970-71, assoc. dir. exec. edn., 1973-78, dir. exec. edn., 1978-85, assoc. dean for exec. edn., 1985-95, sr. assoc. dean, COO, sr. lectr., 1991; vis. prof. Hong Kong U. Cons. AT&T, Brit. Petroleum, Alcoa Young Pres. Orgn.; bd. dirs. Ceridian Corp., Internat. Consortium for Exec. Edn. Rsch.; bd. advisors Toffler Assoc., Lingnan U., China; mem. Internat. Mgmt. Devel., 1985—; vis. prof. Hong Kong U., 2006. Contbr. articles to profl. jours. Recipient Gordon Y. Billard award for Disting. Svc. to MIT, 2005. Mem. Consortium of Univ. Dirs. of Exec. Edn., Mgmt. Scis. for Health (bd. dirs.). Avocations: painting, tennis, swimming, golf, gardening. Home: 13 Pickman Dr Bedford MA 01730-1009 Office Phone: 617-253-7189.

WHITE, ALICE VIRGINIA, academic administrator; b. Wichita, Kans., June 30, 1946; d. Harry Houston White and Margaret V. Milligan. BA in Spanish with distinction and with honors in Russian, U. Kans., 1967; MS in Counseling, Ft. Hays State U., 1973; PhD in Journalism, U. Tex., 1991. Tchr. Russian and Spanish Ingalls Sch. Dist., Kansas City, Mo., 1967-72; instr. Dodge City (Kans.) C.C., 1972-73, 84; tchr. Arrowhead West, Inc., 1984-85; asst. dir. Ctr. for Bus. & Industry Dodge City C.C., Kans., 1984-85, dir. community rels. and resource devel., 1985-87; co-founder, treas. Breitenbach Farms, Inc., Dodge City, Kans., 1970-79, pres., 1979-85; asst. to dean for devel. Coll. Comm., U. Tex., Austin, 1990-93, asst. instr. journalism, 1988-90, lectr. pub. rels., 1992; asst. coord. Shots Across Tex. coord. Tex. Dept. Health, Austin, 1993-95, coord. spl. health initiatives, 1995-96; mgr. Tex. Vol. Health Corps, 1996—2002; liaison Tex. Alliance for Healthy Communities, 1999—2002; program dir., interim campaign dir. Coll. for Texans Campaign, 2004; dir. pub. rels. Tex. Tech U. System, 2005—06; liaison, cmty. coll. rels. Tex. Tech. U., 2006—. Media judge Headliners Found., Austin, 1989, Tex. Hosp. Assn., 1990, 91; dir. job placement Kans. Elks Tng. Ctr. for Handicapped, 1984-85; mgr. dental office, 1973-83; bd. dirs. Dispute Resolution Ctr., 1992-93; adv. bd. N.E. Caregivers of Austin, 2002-04; mem. chancellor's coun. Tex. Tech. U. Sys., 2005—; founder Tex. Tech. U. Coun. Endowed Scholarship, 2005, 06. Treas. Ford County Hist. Soc., 1972—77, Ofcl. Bicentennial Com. Ford County, 1975—77; active Leadership Austin, 1990—91, Leadership Tex., 1999; co-founder Leadership Dodge, 1987, Tex. Leadership Inst. Lower Colo. River Authority, 1999—2004; active Leadership Lubbock, 2006—07; founder Walk-a-Dog project Williamson County SPCA, Austin State Sch., 1991—92; media judge Tex. PTA, 1992, Tex. Med. Assn., 1993; mem. chancellors coun. U. Tex. Sys.; mem. endowment com. United Way Capital Area, 1994; mem. Ready Teddy, the Emergency Med. Svcs. Bear-A-Medic Mascot, 1994—2001, Wiley the Crab mascot Coll. for Texans Campaign, 2005, Gov.'s Blue Ribbon Selection Com. for Tex. Vol. awards, 1998, 1999; mem. Vols. of Yr. selection com. Tex. Commn. on Volunteerism and Cmty. Svcs., 2000—03; mem. Gov.'s Unified State Planning/Cmty. Svc. Com., 1997, 1998; 2d v.p. Pub. Health Mus. of Tex., 1999—2002, bd. dirs., 2003—04; treas. Pet Helpers, Inc., 2000—04; mem. Animal Trustees of Austin's Vol. Spotlight, 2000; mem. selection com. for Tex. vol. awards Tex. Dept. Human Svcs., 2001; hon. life. laboratorian Tex. Dept. Health, 2000—; 5th grade mentor Gullett Elem. Sch., 2001—03; mem. founding adv. bd. Women's Giving Network, 2003—04; Goodwill Amb. to Turkey, Interfaith Dialog, 2006; mem. adv. coun. Tex. Tech. U. Coll. Edn., South Plains Coll. Tech. Prep.; founder Lubbock Animal Svcs. endowment Lubbock Area Found., 2007; founder Dog & Cat Welfare endowment Wichita Cmty. Found., 2006; founder endowment South Flains Tech., Tex. Tech. U. Coll. Edn. Recipient Most Creative Vol. Project award Tex. Mental Health and Mental Retardation, 1992, Athena winner Women's C. of C., 1987, Kans. PRIDE honoree, 1988; U. Tex. fellow, 1987-89; named of one of 100 Best-Managed Farms in U.S., Farm Futures Mag., 1983; named endowments at Austin Cmty. Found., Arthur E. and Cornelia Scroggins Found., Dodge City; Paul Harris fellow Rotary Internat., 2007. Fellow: Tex. Pub. Health Assn.; mem.: AAUW (treas. 1977—78, pres. Kans. 1979—81, gift honoree 1973, 1981, 1991), Austin C. of C., Women in Comm. (liaison to student chpt. 1989—91), Tex. Health Found. (life), Nat. Assn. Individual Investors (life), Tex. Pub. Rels. Soc. (bd. dirs. 1993), Pub. Rels. Soc. Am. (mentor, profl. advisor U. Tex. 1987—93), Tex. Tech. Alumni Assn., Austin-Travis County Humane Soc. (life), Phi Beta Kappa Alumni Assn. Greater Austin (life), Phi Beta Kappa Alumni Assn. West Tex. and Ea. N.Mex. (life), Leadership Kans. Alumni (life), U. Kans. Alumni Assn. (nat. bd. dirs. 1977—82), U. Tex. Pres.'s Assocs., U. Tex. Littlefield Soc., Waterloo Benevolent Soc. of United Way Capital Area, Leave a Legacy Tex. Style, Tex. Exes Alumni Assn. (life), Lone Star Cir. (State Employee Charitable Campaign 2001—02, 2004—05, 2005—), KLRU Pub. TV Prodrs. Cir., Lubbock Rotary (Paul Harris fellow 2007), U. Kans. Chancellor's Club, Phi Kappa Phi, Phi Beta Kappa (treas. Austin Alumni Assn. 2001—02, founding mem. Tex. chpt.), Chi Omega Alumnae Austin (life). Home: 403 Topeka Lubbock TX 79416-4906 Office: Tex Tech U Box 45005 Lubbock TX 79409 Home Phone: 806-785-2331; Office Phone: 806-742-1480 Ext. 261. Business E-Mail: alice.white@ttu.edu.

WHITE, ANN MARIE, medical educator; d. Domenick and Beatrice H. White; m. David Robert Mowry; 2 children. BS with honors, Cornell U., 1992; MA, Columbia U. Tchrs. Coll., 1993; EdD, Harvard U., 2002. Rsch. asst. Cornell U., Ithaca, NY, 1991—92, Tchrs. Coll., Columbia U., NYC, 1992—93, Harvard U., Cambridge, Mass., 1993—95; data analyst Wellesley Coll., 1993—99; rsch. assoc. Harvard Grad. Sch. Edn., 1998—2001; sr. instr., dir. dept. psychiatry U. Rochester Med. Ctr., NY, 2004—. Rsch. cons. in field. Fellow, U.S. Senate, Washington, 2002—03, NIH, Bethesda, Md., 2003—04. Mem.: Soc. Rsch. Child Devel. (student rep. to policy com. 1997—99). Roman Catholic. Office: U Rochester Med Ctr 300 Crittenden Blvd Rochester NY

WHITE, AUGUSTUS AARON, III, orthopaedic surgeon; b. Memphis, June 4, 1936; s. Augustus Aaron and Vivian (Dandridge) White; m. Anita Ottemo; children: Alissa Alexandra, Atina Andrea, Annica Akila. BA cum laude in Psychology, Brown U., Providence, 1957, DMS (hon.), 1997; MD, Stanford U., Calif., 1961; PhD, Karolinska Inst., Sweden, 1969; degree in Mgmt., Harvard U., Cambridge, Mass., 1984; DHL (hon.), U. New Haven, Conn., 1987; DS (hon.), So. Conn. State U., New Haven, 2000. Diplomate Nat. Bd. Examiners, Am. Bd. Orthopaedic Surgery. Intern U. Mich. Hosp., Ann Arbor, 1961-62; asst. resident in gen. surgery Presbyn. Med. Center, San Francisco, 1962-63; asst. resident in orthopaedic surgery Yale Med. Center, New Haven, 1963-65, sr. instr., resident orthopaedic surgery, 1965-66; asst. prof. orthopaedic surgery Yale Med. Sch., 1969-72, assoc. prof., 1972-76, prof., 1977-78, dir. biomech. rsch. dept. orthopaedics, 1970-78; prof. orthopaedic surgery Harvard Med. Sch., 1978—; orthopaedic surgeon-in-chief Beth Israel Deaconess Med. Ctr., Boston, 1978-92, orthopaedic surgeon-in-chief emeritus, 1996—; sr. assoc. orthopaedic surgery Children's Hosp. Med. Ctr., Boston, 1979-89; assoc. in orthopaedic surgery Brigham & Women's Hosp., Boston, 1980-89; cons. div. surgery Sidney Farber Cancer Inst., Boston, 1980—; Disting. Ellen and Melvin Gordon prof. of med. edn., prof. orthopaedic surgery Harvard Med. Sch., 2002—07. Rschr. biomechanics lab. Beth Israel Deaconess Med. Ctr.; chair sci. adv. bd., dir. OrthoLogic, Inc., Phoenix; sci. adv. bd. Am. Shared Hosp. Svcs., San Francisco; chair sci. adv. bd., bd. dirs. Zimmer Holding, Inc.; cons. orthop. surgery West Haven VA Hosp., Conn., 1970—78, Hill Health Ctr., New Haven, 1970—78; chief orthop. surgery Conn. Health Care Plan, 1976—78; adv. coun. Nat. Inst. Arthritis, Metabolism and Digestive Disease, NIH, 1979—82; mem. admissions com. Yale Med. Sch., 1970—72; presenter, moderator Symposium on Cervical Myelopathy, San Francisco, 1987; chmn. grant rev. com. NIH, 1985; founding mem., bd. overseers Brown U. Sch. Medicine, 1996—99; bd. overseers WGBH Radio/TV, Boston, 1996—98, trustee, 1998—2007, bd. overseers, 2007—; Alfred R. Shands Jr. lectr. Am. Orthop. Assn., 2001; pres. guest lectr. Scoliosis Rsch. Soc., 2001; chair com. culturally competence care Harvard Med. Sch., 2002—06; hon. staff orthopaedics Beth Israel Deaconess Med. Ctr., 2005; mem. adv. coun. biology and medicine Brown U., 2005; mem. adv. coun. Nat. Ctr. for Minority Health and Health Disparities, NIH, 2001—06. Author: Clinical Biomechanics of the Spine, 1978, 2d edit., 1990, (with M. Panjabi) Biomechanics in the Musculoskeletal System, 2001, Symposium on Idiopathic Low Back Pain, 1982, Your Aching Back-A Doctor's Guide to Relief, 1983, rev. edit., 1990, translated in German, 1992; guest editor Clin. Orthop. and Related Rsch., 1999; contbr. articles to profl. jours., chpts. to books. Trustee Brown U., Providence, 1971-76, bd. fellows, 1981-92, fellow emeritus, 1992—, chmn. corp. com. on minority affairs, 1981-86, chmn. corp. com. on med. edn., 1989-96, chmn. vis. com. on diversity; trustee Northfield Mt. Hermon Sch., Northfield, Mass., 1976-81; bd. dirs. The Partnership, Boston, 1984—. Capt. AUS, 1966-68. Decorated Bronze Star medal; named one of 10 Outstanding Young Men US Jr. C. of C., 1969, Selected for Exceptional Black Scientist poster series CIBA-GEIGY Corp., 1982; recipient Martin Luther King, Jr. Med. Achievement award, 1972, Kappa Delta award, nat. prize for outstanding rsch. in orthopaedics field, 1975; nat. award for spinal rsch. Eastern Orthopaedic Assn., 1980, Disting. Svc. award Northfield Mt. Hermon Sch. Alumni Assn., 1983; William Rogers award Associated Alumni Brown U., 1984, Outstanding Achievement award Delta Upsilon, 1986, Brown Bear award Brown Alumni Assn., Lifetime Achievement award Beth Israel Deaconess Med. Ctr., 2005, Candle in the Dark in Medicine award Morehouse Coll., 2006, J.E. Wallace Sterling Lifetime Achievement award Stanford Med. Sch., 2006, Smith and Nephew Disting. Clin. Educator award Am. Orthop. Assn., 2006; Am.-Brit.-Canadian Travelling fellow Am. Orthopedic Assn., 1975, Disting. Clin. Educator award, 2006; Ann. Spine Symposium named in his honor Beth Israel Deaconess Med. Ctr., 2004. Fellow Am. Acad. Orthopaedic Surgeons (chmn. diversity com. 1997—, Diversity award 2006), Scoliosis Rsch. Soc.; mem. The Acad. Harvard Med. Sch., Orthopaedic Rsch. Soc., Cervical Spine Rsch. Soc., Internat. Soc. for Study Lumbar Spine, Internat. Soc. Orthopaedic Surgery and Traumatology, Nat. Med. Assn. (Orthopaedic Scholar award 1994), Cervical Spine Rsch. Soc. (pres. 1988), N.Am. Spine Soc., Acad. Orthopaedic Soc. (co-chmn. com. on diversity), Clin. Orthopedic Soc. (Nix Ethics award 2002), J. Robert Gladden Orthopaedic Soc. (founding pres. 2000-03), Fedn. of Spine Assns. (pres. 1998), Sigma Xi, Sigma Pi Phi, Delta Upsilon (pres. Brown U. chpt. 1956, Charles Evan Hughes award for advancement of justice 2006, Augustus White award for excellence in medicine established 2006). Office: HMS Landmark East 401 Park Dr Boston MA 02215 Office Phone: 617-998-8802. Business E-Mail: augustus_white@hms.harvard.edu.

WHITE, BARRY BENNETT, lawyer; b. Boston, Feb. 13, 1943; s. Harold and Rosalyn (Schneider) W.; m. Eleanor Greenberg; children: Joshua S., Adam J., Benjamin D. AB magna cum laude, Harvard U., 1964, JD magna cum laude, 1967. Bar: Mass. 1967, U.S. Dist. Ct. Mass. 1967, U.S. Ct. Appeals (1st cir.) 1967. Assoc. Foley Hoag & Eliot, Boston, 1969—74, chmn. exec. com., 1987—91, mng. ptnr., 1991—92, 1993—2001, ptnr., 1975—. Chmn. Lex Mundi, 1994; bd. dirs. Edgewater Tech., Inc., 2005—. Editor Harvard Law Rev., 1965-67. Sec., gen. counsel, exec. com. Greater Boston C. of C., 1998—, Initiative for Competitive Inner City, 1995—; bd. dirs., exec. com. Mass. Assn. Mental Health, 1985—, pres., 1993-95; bd. dirs., exec. com. Boston Mcpl. Rsch. Bur., 2003—, Vol. Lawyers Project, 1987-93, Support Ctr. of Mass., 1988-95; active Jewish Family and Children's Svcs., Boston, 1979-87; bd. visitors Boston U. Grad. Sch. Dentistry, 1981—; bd. trustees Jewish Cmty. Rels. Coun., 1988-92; chmn. com. for Clinton/Gore New Eng. Lawyers, 1992-96; chmn. Tsongas for Pres. Com., 1991-98; co-chair Mass. Lawyers for Kerry for Pres., 2004. With USPHS, 1967-69. Mem. ABA, Mass. Bar Assn., Boston Bar Assn., Internat. Bar Assn., Am. Acad. Hosp. Attys., Am. Hosp. Assn. (adj. task force on health planning 1982-84, contbg. editor hosp. law manual 1981-84), Harvard Club Boston, Badminton and Tennis Club. Democrat. Office: Foley Hoag LLP 155 Seaport Blvd Boston MA 02210 Office Phone: 617-832-1254. Business E-Mail: bbwhite@foleyhoag.com.

WHITE, BENJAMIN, communications executive; b. 1970; Co-founder Tagworks, Platform Network, 1996; co-founder, editor-in-chief Complex mag., Bullseye mag., Target Corp.; v.p., Digital Media MTV Networks. Named one of 40 Executives Under 40, Multichannel News, 2006. Office: MTV Networks Co 1515 Broadway New York NY 10036 Office Phone: 212-258-8000. Office Fax: 212-258-6175.

WHITE, BENJAMIN TAYLOR, lawyer; b. Atlanta, Nov. 10, 1946; s. Edward Street and Jane Shannon (Taylor) W.; m. Ramona Taylor, Aug. 14, 1971; 1 child, Alexander Taylor. AB with honors, U. N.C., 1969; JD cum laude, Harvard U., 1973. Bar: Ga. 1973. Assoc. Alston & Bird LLP, Atlanta, 1973-79, ptnr., 1979—, and group leader, exempt orgns. group. Trustee The Taft Sch., Watertown, Conn., 1978-81, Woodruff Arts Ctr., Atlanta, 1983—; pres., founder Ga. Vol. Lawyers for the Arts, 1979-82; chmn. Lee Harper and Dancers, Atlanta, 1979-83; pres. Alliance Theatre Co., Atlanta, 1985—. Fellow Am. Coll. Probate Counselors; mem. ABA, State Bar of Ga. (chmn. fiduciary law sect. 1986—), Atlanta Bar Assn., Internat. Bar Assn., Atlanta Tax Forum, Atlanta Estate Planning Council, Harvard Law Sch. Assn. Ga. (pres. 1981-82). Home: 3315 Valley Rd NW Atlanta GA 30305-1150 Office: Alston & Bird 1 Atlantic Ctr 1201 W Peachtree St NW Atlanta GA 30309-3424 Office Phone: 404-881-7488. Office Fax: 404-881-7777. Business E-Mail: bwhite@alston.com.

WHITE, BERTRAM MILTON, chemicals executive; b. Boston, Nov. 17, 1923; s. Samuel Louis and Jennie Anne (Cohen) W.; m. Bernice Hannah Ginns; children: Mark Alan, Leland Jeffrey. BS, Lowell Inst. Tech., Cambridge, Mass., 1943. Product mgr. Philipps Bros. Chems. Inc., Holbrook, Mass., 1952-65, Sobin Chems. Inc., South Boston, 1965-69; pres. Solvent Chems. Co., Inc., Malden, Mass., 1969-73; v.p. I.C.C. Chems. Inc., NYC, 1973—80; sr. v.p. Asoma Chems. Inc., Boston, 1980-83, Laporte Chems. USA, Hackensack, N.J., 1983-84; pres. Gen. Plastics and Chems. Co., Natick, Mass., 1984-91, GFI Chems. Inc., Sudbury, Mass., 1991-93; vice chmn. E & F King & Co. Inc., Norwood, Mass., 1994—96; cons. Holtrachem Inc., 1997—2000. Bd. dirs. Sudexco N.V., Brussels, Recochem Inc., Montreal, Que., Can.; cons. Holtrachem Group, Natick, 1996-2000, Lithium Co., LLC, White Plains, NY, 1997-2000, BMW Chems. Inc., 1998—, Salvage.com, Houston, 2000-01; pres. BMW Chems., Inc., Natick, Mass. Served with Corps of Engring. U.S Army, 1943-46, ETO. Decorated Purple Heart. Mem. Drug Chem. and Allied Trades Assn., New Eng. Chemists Club, N.Y.C. Chemists Club, Salesmen's Assn. of Am. Chem. Industry. Jewish. Avocations: tennis, golf, boating. Office Phone: 508-650-5800. Office Fax: 508-651-0294. Personal E-mail: bmwchem@aol.com.

WHITE, BETTY, actress, comedienne; b. Oak Park, Ill., Jan. 17, 1922; m. Dick Barker 1945 (div. 1945), m. Lane Allen 1947 (div. 1949), m. Allen Ludden, 1963 (dec. 1981). Student pub. schs., Beverly Hills, Calif. Appearances on radio shows This Is Your FBI, Blondie, The Great Gildersleeve; actress: (TV series) including Hollywood on Television, The Betty White Show, 1954-58, Life With Elizabeth, 1953-55, A Date With The Angels, 1957-58, The Pet Set, 1971, Mary Tyler Moore Show, 1974-77, The Betty White Show, 1977, Mama's Family, 1983-86, The Golden Girls, 1985-92 (Emmy award for best actress 1986), Another World, 1988, The Golden Palace, 1992-93, Maybe This Time, 1995, (TV films) With This Ring, 1978, The Best Place to Be, 1979, Before and After, 1979, Eunice, 1982, Chance of a Lifetime, 1991, The Story of Santa Claus, 1996, A Weekend in the Country, 1996, The Retrievers, 2001, Annie's Point, 2005, (films) Advise and Consent, 1962, Dennis the Menace 2, 1998, Hard Rain, 1998, The Story of Us, 1999, Bringing Down the House, 2003, The Third Wish, 2004; guest appearances include Petticoat Junction, 1969, The Odd Couple, 1972, Fame, 1983, St. Elsewhere, 1985, Who's the Boss, 1985, Matlock, 1987, Empty Nest, 1989, 92, Carol & Company, 1990, Nurses, 1991, Diagnosis Murder, 1994, The Naked Truth, 1995, Suddenly Susan, 1996, (voice) King of the Hill, 1999, 2002, Ally McBeal, 1999, (voice) The Simpsons, 2000, Yes, Dear, 2002, Providence, 2002, That 70s Show, 2002, 03, Everwood, 2003, 04, The Practice, 2004, My Wife and Kids, 2004, Malcolm in the Middle, 2004, (voice) Father of the Pride, 2004, Boston Legal, 2005; frequent celebrity guest on numerous game shows including Hollywood Squares, Match Game; summer stock appearances Guys and Dolls, Take Me Along, The King and I, Who Was That Lady?, Critic's Choice, Bells are Ringing; author (book) Betty White's Pet-Lovers: How Pets Take Care of Us, 1987, Here We Go Again: My Life in Television, 1995; contbr. to forward(book) The Irrepressible Toy Dog, Dr. Fisher's Life on the Ark: Green Alligators, Bushman and Other "Hare Raising" Tales from America's Most Popular Zoo and Around the World, 2004, (preface) The Pets are Wonderful Family Album. Mem. Morris Animal Found., 1976—; zoo commr. Greater LA Zoo, 1998—. Recipient Emmy award NATAS, 1975, 76, 86; LA Area Emmy award, 1952, Living Legacy award, Women's Internat. Ctr., 1988, star on the Hollywood Walk of Fame; inducted into TV Hall of Fame, 1995; named Amb. to the Animals, Greater LA Zoo, 2006. Mem. AFTRA, Am. Humane Assn., Greater LA Zoo Assn. (dir.). Office: c/o William Morris Agy Betty Fanning 151 S El Camino Dr Beverly Hills CA 90212-2704

WHITE, BEVERLY JANE, cytogeneticist; b. Seattle, Oct. 9, 1938; Grad., U. Wash., 1959, MD, 1963. Diplomate Nat. Bd. Med. Examiners, Am. Bd. Pediatrics, Am. Bd. Med. Genetics; lic physician and surgeon, Wash., Calif. Rsch. trainee dept. anatomy Sch. Medicine U. Wash., Seattle, 1960-62, pediatric resident dept. pediatrics, 1967-69; rotating intern Phila. Gen. Hosp., 1963-64; rsch. fellow med. ob-gyn. unit Cardiovascular Rsch. Inst. U. Calif. Med. Ctr., San Francisco, 1964-65; staff fellow lab. biomed. scis. Nat. Inst. Child Health and Human Devel. NIH, Bethesda, Md., 1965-67, sr. staff fellow, attending physician lab. exptl. pathology Nat. Inst. Arthritis, Metabolism and Digestive Diseases, 1969-74, acting chief sect. cytogenetics, 1975-76, rsch. med. officer, attending physician sect. cytogenetics lab. cellular biology and genetics, 1974-86, dir. cytogenetics unit, interinstitute med. genetics program clin. ctr., 1987-95; dir. cytogenetics Corning Clin. Labs., Teterboro, NJ, 1995-96; assoc. med. dir. cytogenetics Nichols Inst.-Quest Diagnostics, San Juan Capistrano, Calif., 1996-97, med. dir. cytogenetics, 1998—2000, med. dir. genetics divsn., 2000—02, med. dir. cytogenetics, 2002—. Vis. scientist dept. pediat. divsn. genetics U. Wash. Sch. Medicine, 1983-84; intramural cons. NIH, 1975-95; cons. to assoc. editor Jour. Nat. Cancer Inst., 1976; cons. dept. ob-gyn. Naval Hosp., Bethesda, 1988-89; lectr., presenter in field. Recipient Mosby Book award, 1963, Women of Excellence award U. Wash. and Seattle Profl. chpt. Women in Comm., 1959, Reuben award Am. Soc. for Study Sterility, 1963. Fellow Am. Coll. Med. Genetics (founding), Am. Acad. Pediatrics; mem. AMA. Am. Soc. Human Genetics, Assn. Genetic Technologists (program com. 1989). Office: Nichols Inst Quest Diagnostics Inc Dept Cytogenetics San Juan Capistrano CA 92690-6130 Office Phone: 425-836-4200. Business E-Mail: beverly.j.white@questdiagnostics.com.

WHITE, BILL (WILLIAM HOWARD WHITE), mayor; b. San Antonio, June 16, 1954; m. Andrea White; 3 children. BS in Econs. magna cum laude, Harvard U., 1976; JD, U. Tex., 1979. Atty. Susaman Godfrey LLP, Houston, 1979—93; instr. antitrust law and voting rights U. Tex., Austin; dep. sec., COO US Dept. Energy, Washington, 1993—95; chmn. Howe-Baker Internat., Tyler, Tex., 1997—2000; pres., CEO The Wedge Group, Houston, 1997—2003; mayor City of Houston, 2004—. Recipient Profile in Courage award, John F. Kennedy Libr. Found., 2007. Office: City Hall 901 Bagby St 3rd Fl Houston TX 77002 also: PO Box 1562 Houston TX 77251 Office Phone: 713-247-2200. E-mail: mayor@cityofhouston.net. *

WHITE, BRETT, real estate company executive; BA, U. Calif., Santa Barbara. Sales trainee, indsl. salesperson CB Richard Ellis, LA, 1984—91, sales mgr. San Diego, 1991—2001, mng. dir. Newport Beach LA, 1991—2001, regional mgr. L.A., 1991—2001, pres. brokerage, 1991—2001, chmn. The Ams., 1991—2001, pres., 2001—05, pres., CEO, 2005—, bd. dirs., 1998—, mem. exec. com., 1999—. Bd. dirs. Edison Internat., Southern Calif. Edison. Mem. LA Mus. Contemporary Art, Jr. Achievement. Named Brokerage Exec. of Yr., 2005, Real Estate Industry Exec. of Yr., 2006, Brokerage Exec. of Yr., Comml. Property News, 2006. Office: CB Richard Ellis 11150 Santa Monica Blvd Los Angeles CA 90025 Office Phone: 310-405-8919. Office Fax: 310-405-8950. Business E-Mail: brett.white@cbre.com. *

WHITE, BURTON LEONARD, retired educational psychologist, writer, consultant; b. Boston, June 27, 1929; s. Jack J. and Evelyn S. W.; m. Janet Hodgson-White; children— Laura, Emily, David, Daniel. BSM.E., Tufts Coll., 1949; BA, Boston U., 1956, MA, 1957; PhD, Brandeis U., 1960. Research assoc. Brandeis U., 1960-62, M.I.T., 1962-65; sr. research assoc. Harvard Grad. Sch. Edn., 1965-78; head Center Parent Edn., Newton, Mass., 1978-99, ret., 1999. Author: books including Human Infants, 1971, Experience and Environment, Vol. I, 1973, Vol. II, 1978, The First Three Years of Life, 1975, latest edit. 1995, The Origins of Competence, 1979, Educating the Infant and Toddler, 1988, Raising A Happy, Unspoiled Child, 1994, The New First Three Years of Life, 1995; contbr. articles to profl. jours. Served with AUS, 1951-53. Home: 115 Pine Ridge Rd Newton MA 02468-1616

WHITE, C. VANESSA, director; d. Robert Lee White and Doris Jean Redd White Foster, Herbert Randolph Foster (Stepfather). BS, No. Ill. U., DeKalb, 1978; M in Theol. Studies, Cath. Theol. Union, Chgo., 1990, D in Ministry, 2005. Cert. master catechist Xavier U. La., 1991. Child life specialist Michael Reese Hosp., Chgo., 1979—85; dir. Claretian vols. and lay missionaries Claretian Missionaries, Chgo., 1986—94; dir. retreat program and staff Christian Brother's LaSalle Manor Retreat Ctr., Plano, Ill., 1994—97; dir. Augustus Tolton scholar's program Cath. Theol. Union, Chgo., 1998—. Faculty Inst. for Black Cath. Studies Xavier U., New Orleans; bd. dirs. US Conf. Cath. Bishops Commn. on Certification and Accreditation, Washington; adv. bd. Fullerton Cenacle Retreat Ctr., Chgo. Editor: Songs of Our Hearts and Meditations of Our Souls; contbr. documentary film, articles to profl. jours. Active Secular Franciscan Order, Chgo., 1985—2006. Recipient Fr. Augustus Tolton Archdiocesan award, Archdiocese of Chgo., 1998. Mem.: Cath. Theol. Union Alumni Assn., Nat. Assn. for Lay Ministry, Knights of Peter Claver - Ladies Aux. (Sr. Thea Bowman award 1992, Adele Stadeker Svc. award 2003). Independent. Roman Catholic. Office: Catholic Theological Union 5401 S Cornell Chicago IL 60615 Home Phone: 708-481-0930; Office Phone: 773-753-7478. Business E-Mail: tolton@ctu.edu.

WHITE, CALVIN JOHN, zoo executive, zoological association executive, financial manager; b. Twillingate, Nfld., Can., Feb. 28, 1948; s. Harold and Meta Blanche (Abbott) W.; m. Lorna Joan Maclachlan; children: Chelsea Elizabeth, Evan Alexander. B in Commerce, U. Toronto, Ont., Can., 1971. Fin. analyst Can. GE Co. Ltd., Toronto, 1971-72, Ford Motor Co. Can., Oakville, Ont., 1972-74; sr. fin. analyst Municipality of Met. Toronto, 1974-77, asst. dir. budget and ops. analysis, 1977-81, dir. budget analysis and internal control, 1981-86; CEO Toronto Zoo, 1986—. Bd. dirs. Borealis Hydro Elec. Holdings Inc., Can. Assn. Zoos and Aquariums, Ctr. for Endangered Reptiles, 1989-91, Rouge Pk. Alliance, Toronto Chongqing Assn., Can. Mus. Assn., Textile Mus. Can. Pres. Tourism Toronto, 2005—. Fellow Am. Zoo and Aquarium Assn.; mem. Am. Assn. Zoo Keepers, Inst. Pub. Adminstrn. Can. (bd. dirs. 1989-91), Toronto Zoo Found. (bd. dirs. 1991—, CEO 1994—), World Conservation Union, World Zoo Orgn., Toronto Sportmen's Assn., Mensa. Office: Toronto Zoo 361A Old Finch Ave Scarborough ON Canada M1B 5K7 Office Phone: 416-392-5909. Business E-Mail: cwhite@torontozoo.ca.

WHITE, CECIL RAY, librarian, consultant; b. Hammond, Ind., Oct. 15, 1937; s. Cecil Valentine and Vesta Ivern (Bradley) W.; m. Frances Ann Gee, Dec. 23, 1960 (div. 1987); children: Timothy Wayne, Stephen Patrick. BS in Edn., So. Ill. U., 1959; postgrad., Syracuse U., 1961; MDiv, Southwestern Bapt. Sem., 1969; MLS, No. Tex. State U., 1970, PhD, 1984. Libr. Herrin (Ill.) H.S., 1964-66; acting reference libr. Southwestern Sem., Ft. Worth, 1968-70, asst. libr., 1970-80; head libr. Golden Gate Bapt. Sem., Mill Valley, Calif., 1980-88, West Oahu Coll., Pearl City, Hawaii, 1988-89; dir. spl. projects North State Coop. Libr. System, Yreka, Calif., 1989-90; dir. libr. St. Patrick's Sem., Menlo Park, Calif., 1990—. Library cons. Hist. Commn., So. Bapt. Conv., Nashville, 1983-84, Internat. Bapt. Sem., Prague, Czech Republic, 1996; mem. Thesaurus Com., 1974-84; adv. bd. Cath. Periodical and Lit. Index, 1995—, chair, 1999—. Bd. dirs. Hope and Help Ctr., 1986-88, vice chmn., 1987-88. With USAF, 1960-64. Lilly Found. grantee Am. theol. Assn., 1969. Mem. ALA, Am. Theol. Libr. Assn. (coord. cons. svc. 1973-78, program planning com. 1985-88, chmn. 1986-88), Nat. Assn. Profs. Hebrew (archivist 1985—), Assn. Coll. and Rsch. Librs., Cath. Libr. Assn. (mem. exec. bd. 1999-2005), Phi Kappa Phi, Beta Phi Mu. Democrat. Baptist. Home: 229 Rome Place Hayward CA 94544 Office: St Patricks Sem 320 Middlefield Rd Menlo Park CA 94025-3563 Home Phone: 510-429-1955; Office Phone: 650-321-5655. E-mail: cecilrwhite@hotmail.com, stpats@ix.netcom.com. *Personal philosophy: Except for the gift of life and faith, the best gift that has been given to me, and which I can give, is the unique gift of oneself in friendship. No one else can give it, and it cannot be bought at any price.*

WHITE, CHARLES OLDS, aeronautical engineer; b. Beirut, Apr. 2, 1931; s. Frank Laurence and Dorothy Alice (Olds) W.; m. Mary Carolyn Liechty, Sept. 3, 1955; children— Charles Cameron, Bruce Blair. B.S. in Aero. Engring., MIT, 1953, M.S., 1954. Aero. engr. Douglas Aircraft Long Beach, 1954-60, aero. engr. Ford Aerospace & Communication Corp., Calif., 1960-79, sr. engr. specialist, 1979-80, staff office of gen. mgr. DIVAD div., 1980-81, tech. mgr. DIVAD Fuzes, 1981-82, supr. design and analysis DIVAD div., 1982-85; tech. mgr. Advanced Ordnance Programs, 1985-87, PREDATOR Missile, 1987-90, cons. 1990-93; engring. tech. prin. Aerojet Corp., 1993-94; tech. prin. OCSW Ammunition Olin Ordinance, 1994-97, cons., 1997—. Mem. AIAA, AAAS, Nat. Mgmt. Assn., Am. Aviation Hist. Soc., Sigma Gamma Tau. Republican. Presbyterian. Clubs: Masters Swimming, Newport Beach Tennis. Contbr. articles to profl. jours.

WHITE, CHARLES R., former mayor; b. Boston; m. Maria White; 4 children. Grad., Riverside CC. Mayor City of Moreno Valley, 1997. Mem. Moreno Valley City Coun., 1996—; mem. So. Calif. Assn. Govt., Regional Coun., Transp. & Comm. Policy Com., Magnetic Levitation Task Force, Growth Visioning Com.; bd. Riverside Transit Agency; mem., chmn. March Joint Powers Commn., 1999, vice chmn., 2001, chmn., 02. Served Planning Commr., Redevelopment Project Area Com., Traffic Safety Adv. Com., Disaster Preparedness Com., Mayor's Drug Task Force; treasurer Friends Moreno Valley Sr. Ctr.; pres. Moreno Valley Elks Lodge; vice comdr. Moreno Valley VFW Post; jr. deacon Moreno Valley Masonic Lodge; pres. Sunnymead Little League; v.p. Sunnymead PTA; co-founder Moreno Valley Youth Fedn. Served USAR. Mem.: Idylwild Am. Legion Post (life). Office: 14177 Frederick St PO Box 88005 Moreno Valley CA 92552

WHITE, CHARLES SIDNEY JOHN, retired humanities educator; b. New Richmond, Wis., Sept. 25, 1929; s. Ferne Rosemary Holt. BA in English with honors, U. Wis., Madison, 1951; MA magna cum laude, U. de las Am. Mexico City Coll., Mexico City, 1957; MA, U. Chgo., 1962, PhD with distinction, 1964. Staff pub. rels. and advt. Wallace Supplies Mfg. Co., Chgo., 1957—61; asst. prof. Indian studies U. Wis., Madison, 1965—66; asst. prof. religious thought U. Pa., 1966—71; assoc. prof. philosophy and religion Am. U., Washington, 1971—78, prof. philosophy and religion, 1978—94, prof. emeritus philosophy and religion, 1995—, dir. Asia Ctr. Sch. Internat. Svc., 1976—78, chmn. dept. philosophy and religion, 1984—87, 1988—94. Vis. lectr. history of religions Princeton (N.J.) U., 1968; vis. prof. world religions Lakehead U., Thunder Bay, Ont., Canada, 1974—88; vis. prof. Wesley Seminary, 1985, 86; lectr. in field; vis. prof. Hindu studies faculty theology Oxford U., England, 2002; mem. program adv. com. diploma in Buddhist studies U. Hyderabad, 2006. Author: The Caurāsī Pad of Śrī Hit Harivaṃś, 1977, Ramakrishna's Americans, 1979, The Adyar Library, The Institute for Vaisnava Studies and The American University Microfilm Collection of Vaisnava Literature, 2001, Teaching Saranagati: A Dialogue with HH Sri Sathguru Swami Gnanananda Sarasvathi, 2002, Catalogue of Vaisnava Literature, 2004, The Garden of Loneliness, Jay Shankar Prasad's Tears, 2006, Roses from the Desert of my Heart, A Book of Poetry, 2007; co-author: The Religious Quest, 1983, 2d edit., 1985, Joseph Campbell: Transformations of Myth Through Time, 1990; contbr. chapters to books, articles to profl. jours. and encyclopedias. With USN, 1951—55. Fellow, Hindi-Urdu U., Chgo., 1961—64, Am. Inst. Indian Studies, India, 1964, 1968, 1974, 1978, 1995; grantee, Smithsonian Instn., India, 1982—83. Mem.: Am. Inst. Indian Studies (exec. com. 1988—90). Office Phone: 202-885-2925. Business E-Mail: philrel@american.edu.

WHITE, CHRISTOPHER TODD, language educator, anthropologist; b. Columbia, Mo., Dec. 7, 1965; s. Eric B. and Barbara K. White; life ptnr. Ryan C. Reiss. BA, U. Nebr., Lincoln, 1990; MA, U. Mo., Kansas City, 1994, U. Nev., Las Vegas, 1998; PhD, U. So. Calif., LA, 2005. Adj. lectr. Rockhurst Coll., Kansas City, Mo., 1994—95; editl. asst. BkMk Press, Kansas City, 1993—95; adj. lectr. English U. Mo., Kansas City, 1993—95; acad. advisor Ednl. Talent Search, Las Vegas, Nev., 1995—96; asst. prof./lectr. U. Nev., Las Vegas, 1996—98; instr. Glendale C.C., Calif., 1998—2003; tchr., rsch. asst. dept. anthropology U. So. Calif., LA, 1998—2005; asst. prof. anthropology SUNY, Brockport, NY, 2005—. Dir. Homosexual Info. Ctr., LA, 2001—, ONE Inst. and Archives, LA, 2001—02. Editor: U. Nev.-Las Vegas Jour. Anthropology, 1995—2005, San Dieguito and La Jolla: The Collected Works of Claude N. Warren on the Archaeology af Southern California, 2006; asst. editor Before Stonewell: Activists for Gay and Lesbian Rights in Historical Context, 2002, mem. editl. bd. Collegiate Press, 2002, referee Popular Culture Rev.; columnist: Orange County/Long Beach Blade Mag., 2006—07; author: Pre Gay L.A.: A Social History of the Movement for Homosexual Rights, 2007; contbr. articles to profl. jours. Recipient Patricia Roccio Award in Anthropology, U. Nev.-Las Vegas, 1997, Dissertation Fellowship award, U. So. Calif., 2005; scholar Hal Call Mattachine scholar, Inst. for Study of Human Resources, 2000—01. Mem.: Assn. for Psychol. Anthropology, Homosexual Info. Ctr. (sec.-treas. 2001—), Southwestern Anthropol. Assn., Soc. of Lesbian and Gay Anthropologists (sec.-treas. 1998—), Soc. of Linguistic Anthropology, Am. Anthropol. Assn., Am. Fedn. Tchrs. Democrat. Avocations: camping, book collecting, piano, running, bicycling. Office: SUNY Coll at Brockport Dept Anthropology 350 New Campus Dr Brockport NY 14420 Office Phone: 585-395-5707. Personal E-mail: ctgrant@mac.com.

WHITE, CINDY HAGEMEIER, adult education educator; b. San Antonio, Jan. 11, 1965; d. Garren Wayne Hagemeier and Margaret Lee Schultz; m. John Alan White, June 6, 1987. MA, Tex. Tech. U., 1989; PhD, U. Ariz., 1996. Acad. advisor, instr. Tex. Tech. U., Lubbock, 1989-91; grad. assoc. U. Ariz., Tucson, 1991-95; asst. prof. U. Colo., Boulder, 1995—. Active adv. bd. Restorative Justice Program, 1999. Grad. Coll. fellow U. Ariz., 1991, AASERT Rsch. fellow Army Rsch. Inst., 1994. Office: U Colo Dept Comm Boulder CO 80309 E-mail: Cindy.White@colorado.edu.

WHITE, CLARA JO, small business owner, consultant; b. County Cherokee, Tex., June 26; children: Anita, Jackie, Mona Lisa, Jeris, Gina. Diploma, Ft. Worth Bus. Coll., Tex., 1947; AA in Social Sci., Riverside City Coll., 1986. Cert. graphoanalyst 1977, master graphoanalyst Internat. Graphanalysis Soc., Inc., 1979, mus. docent 1977, diploma IGAS Congress Inst. Training, 1979, cert. mgmt. supr. devel. U. Calif., Riverside, 1986, counseling skills U. Riverside, 1990. Owner, pres. White Handwriting Analysis Svc., Riverside, Calif., 1982—. Instr. Internat. Congress and Resident Inst., Internat. Graphoanalysis Soc., 1989, discussion group leader, 88; analyzed handwriting Lady Margaret Beaufort, 1992, Mary Queen of Scots, 1994, Hillary Rodham Clinton, 1994, Pres. Bill Clinton, 1997, Georgia O'Keeffe, 1999, presidents George Washington, Abraham Lincoln, John F. Kennedy, 2000; presenter, cons., spkr. in field. Editor (asst. editor): Reflections, 1986; author: numerous poems. Mem. children's conf. planning com. Riverside Mental Health Assn., 1981—; v.p. Heritage Ho. Mus., Riverside, Calif., 1981—, co-pres., 1985—86, pres; historian Riverside Juvenile Hall Aux., 1984—, pres., 1987—; mem. U.S. Olympic Com., 1984; bd. dir. Riverside Mus. Assoc., 1985—87, vol., 1985—88, aux. historian, 1984—, pres., 1987—88; bd. mem. KCET TV PBS, LA, 2005—. Named Vol. of the Yr.; named to Hall of Fame, Riverside Juvenile Hall Aux., 1984; recipient cert. of Appreciation, Riverside County Probation Dept., 1986, County Riverside Suprs., 1988, Riverside Mental Health, 1990, Nat. Law enforcement Officers Meml. Fund, 1998, award, F. H. Butterfield Sch., 1980, Golden Post award, Homer Honor Soc., 1987, 1990, cert., Libr. of Congress, 1998, cmty. svc. cert., Riverside City Coll., 1982, 1st pl. writing-poetry, Am. Biog. Rsch. Assn., 1991, trophy Outstanding Svc. to Cmty., Sta. KQLH-FM, trophy, Vol. Ctr. Riverside, 1991, trophy and Individual Svc. award, Riverside County Juvenile Hall of Fame, 1990—91, cert. of Recognition, Riverside County Probation Dept., 1991, Calif. Legis.-State Assembly, 1991, So. Calif. chpt. IGAS, 1990—91, Riverside County Bd. Suprs. and Riverside County Probation Dept., 1993, 26th Children's Conf. Com., 1999, Internat. Gold medal of Honor for Disting. Participation, ABI/IBC 26th Congress Arts and Comm., 1999, Graphoanalysts of the Yr. award, So. Calif. chpt. Graphoanalysts, 2000, Disting. Svc. award, City of Riverside, 2004, Order of Ambs. Sovereign award, ABI/IBC Inaugural World Forum, 2006. Master: Internat. Graphoanalysis Soc. (life; 2d then 1st v.p. so. Calif. chpt. 1984, Merit cert. 1981, Pres. Excellence award 1982, 1983, 1984, Pres. Merit citation 1988, Achievement cert. 1995); mem.: NAFE, YWCA, AAUW, DAV Aux. (life), Nat. Mus. Women in Arts, KCET TV PBS, Calif. Probation, Parole, and Corrections Assn. (cert. of tng. 1995), Met. Mus. Assocs., Nat. Geographic Soc., Smithsonian Assocs., Riverside C. of C., World War II Meml. Soc. (charter mem.), Top Cops Nat. Assn. Police Orgns., Rsch. Coun. of Scripps Clinic and Rsch. Found., US Olympic Soc. (U.S. Olympic Team, U.S. Olympic Com. Sixth Ring charter mem. 2004, Replica Bronze medal 2004), Women's Networking Club (Riverside chpt.), Confederation of Chivalry (life; grand coun., dame officer). Avocations: sewing, music, collecting antiques, dance, exercise. Home and Office: 7965 Helena Ave Riverside CA 92504-3513

WHITE, DALE ANDREW, journalist; b. Jacksonville, Fla., Feb. 17, 1958; s. John Andrew and Jeannelle Corinne White. B in Journalism, U. Fla., 1983. Reporter UPI, Miami, Fla., 1980, Orlando (Fla.) Sentinel Star, 1981; corr. Fla. Times-Union, Gainesville, 1982; reporter, columnist, editl. writer, editor Sarasota Herald-Tribune, Fla., 1983—. Contbr. short stories to profl. publs. Recipient Chmn.'s award N.Y. Times, 1987, 2004, 3d place Editorial Writing award Fla. Soc. Newspaper Editors, 1993, 1st place Ind. Reporter Media award Fla. Sch. Bds. Assn., 1996. Office: PO Box 1695 Bradenton FL 34206-1695

WHITE, DANA, sports association executive; b. Manchester, Conn., 1971; Attended, U. Mass. Founder Dana White Enterprises, Las Vegas, 1992; boxing trainer, group exercise instr.; mgr. of boxers and mixed martial arfts fighters including Tito Ortiz and Chuck Liddell Ultimate Fighting Championship (UFC), 2000, pres., 2000—; co-owner Zuffa LLC. Prodr.: (TV series) The Ultimate Fighter, 2005—. Office: Zuffa LLC 2960 W Sahara Ste 200 Las Vegas NV 89102 *

WHITE, DANIEL BOWMAN, lawyer; b. Charlotte, NC, Apr. 12, 1948; s. William Garner and Elizabeth (Bowman) W.; m. Sarah de Saussure Peterson, May 29, 1976; children: Bentley Parker, Sarah de Saussure. AB, Davidson Coll., 1970; JD, U. S.C., 1976. Bar: S.C. 1976, U.S. Dist. Ct. S.C. 1976, U.S. Ct. Appeals (4th cir.) 1978, U.S. Ct. Appeals (fed. cir.) 1990. Ptnr. Gallivan, White & Boyd P.A., Greenville, SC, 1976—. Mem. Fed. Cir. Jud. Conf. Comments editor U. S.C. Law Rev., 1975-76. Commr. Greenville Zoning Commn., 1980-85; mem. Supreme Ct. Bd. Commrs. on Grievances and Discipline, 1988-91. 1st lt. U.S. Army, 1971-73. Decorated Bronze Star; Dana scholar Davidson Coll., N.C., 1966-70. Mem.: Assn. Def. Trial Attys., Internat. Assn. Def. Counsel, Nat. Assn. R.R. Trial Counsel, S.C. Bar (ho. dels. 1986—, chmn. ho. dels. 2000—02, bd. govs. 1992—95, 2000—, sec. 2002—03, treas. 2003—04, pres.-elect 2004—05, pres. 2005—06), Def. Rsch. Inst., Greenville Young Lawyers Club (pres. 1981). Episcopalian. Office: Gallivan White & Boyd PO Box 10589 Greenville SC 29603-2804 Office Phone: 864-271-5342. Business E-Mail: dwhite@gwblawfirm.com.

WHITE, DANIEL EUGENE, lawyer; b. Cheyenne, Wyo., Sept. 6, 1950; s. Philip and Rita Ann (Moran) W.; m. Diane Dreher McInerney, Oct. 4, 1986; children: Caroline M., Stephanie M. BA in Polit. Sci., U. Wyo., 1972, JD, 1976. Bar: Wyo. 1976. Asst. atty. gen. State of Wyo., Cheyenne, 1976-79; dep. county atty. Converse County, Wyo., 1979-80; exec. dir. Wyo. State Bar, Cheyenne, 1980-83; ptnr. Gusea, Pattno & White, P.C., Cheyenne, 1983—2006, Woodard & White, P.C., Cheyenne, 2006—. Chmn. appellate rules divsn., permanent rules adv. com. Wyo. Supreme Ct. Co-founder, organizer Wyo. High Sch. Mock Trial Tournament, 1985-95. Mem. ABA, Wyo. Bar Assn. Democrat. Roman Catholic. Avocations: swimming, gardening, biking, camping. Home: 304 Carriage Dr Cheyenne WY 82009-2008 Office: 1720 Carey Ave Ste 600 Cheyenne WY 82001 Office Phone: 307-634-2731. Personal E-mail: bwomail@qwest.net.

WHITE, DAVID C., archivist, historian; b. Flint, Mich., July 23, 1954; s. Charles B. and Patricia A. White. Assocs. in Bus., Mott C.C., Flint, 1974; BA in History, U. Mich., Flint, 1980; MA in Hist. Preservation, Ea. Mich. U., Ypsilanti, 1984. Curator of collections Sloan Mus., Flint, 1979—2001; dir. archives Kettering U., Flint, 2001—. Author: Flint 1890-1960, 2004, Genesee 1900-1960, 2006. Chmn. Flint Hist. Dist. Assn., 1980—88; pres. Genesee County Hist. Soc., Flint, 1982—86, 2005—06, Whaley Hist. House, Flint, 1982—86, 2000—06, Nash House Enterprises, Flint, 1984—96, Durant-Dort Found., Flint, 1985—, Greater Flint Arts Coun., 1996—98; chief steward Automobile Nat. Heritage Area, Detroit, 1998—2006; bd. mem. Flint Downtown Devel. Authority, 2002—06. Recipient Heritage award, Genesee County Hist. Soc., 1978, Preservation award, Mich. Hist. Soc., 1979, Vol. award, Gov. Mich., 2004. Mem.: Automotive Historians, Am. Archivist Assn., Mich. Archival Assn., Buick Club Am. Avocations: antiques, antique cars, home restoration. Home: 500 S Grand Traverse Flint MI 48502

WHITE, DAVID CALVIN, electrical engineer, educator, energy executive, consultant; b. Sunnyside, Wash., Feb. 18, 1922; s. David Calvin Sr. and Leafie Eloise (Scott) W.; m. Glorianna Guilii, July 30, 1949 (dec. Dec. 1965); 1 child, Julie Anne White Coman (dec.); m. Margot Ann Fuller, June 4, 1966; 1 child, Constance Anne. BS, Stanford U., 1946, MS, 1947, PhD, 1949. Registered profl. engr. Elec. engr. Kaiser Industries, Vancouver, Wash., 1941-42, 43-45; assoc. prof. elec. engring. U. Fla., Gainesville, 1949-52; asst. prof. elec. engring. MIT, Cambridge, 1952-54, assoc. prof., 1954-58, prof., 1958-62, Ford prof. engring., 1962-92, dir. energy lab., 1972-89, Ford prof. engring. emeritus, 1992—. Pres., dir. Energy Conversion, Inc., 1961-64; cons. Gulf Oil, 1976-84, Johnson Controls, 1980-98; sr. advisor and vis. prof. Birla Inst., India, 1968-70; mem. council U. Benin, Nigeria, 1972; trustee Lowell Tech. Inst., Mass., 1972-74; mem. corp. Woods Hole Oceanographic Inst., Mass., 1977-84; mem. research coordinating panel Gas Research Inst., Chgo., 1977-85; chmn. adv. council Electric Power Research Inst., Palo Alto, Calif., 1984-86, mem., 1980-87. Author: (with others) Electromechanical Energy Conversion, 1959 Commr. Electric Light Plant, Concord, Mass., 1959-64, Kalmia Woods Water Dist., Concord, 1960-63 Named hon. prof. Instituto Politecnico Nacional, Mex., 1961 Fellow IEEE; mem. Nat. Acad. Engring., Am. Acad. Arts and Scis., Am. Soc. Engring. Edn. (George Westinghouse award 1961), Country Club Boca Raton, Phi Beta Kappa, Sigma Xi, Tau Beta Pi, Eta Kappa Nu. Republican. Avocations: golf, boating. Home: 23401 Water Cir Boca Raton FL 33486 Office: MIT 77 Massachusetts Ave Rm E40-473 Cambridge MA 02139-4307 Personal E-mail: dcmfwhite@aol.com.

WHITE, DAVID HYWEL, physics professor, researcher; b. Cardiff, Wales, June 4, 1931; arrived in US, 1959, naturalized, 1966; s. William Richard and Bessie (Morgan) W.; m. Frances Mary Shearman, July 23, 1954; children: Richard Gerwyn, Christopher David. BS, U. Wales, 1953; PhD, Birmingham U., 1956. Asst. lectr. Birmingham U., 1958—59; asst. prof. U. Pa., 1961—64; asso. prof. Cornell U., Ithaca, NY, 1964—69, prof., 1969—78; sr. physicist, head exptl. facilities div. Isabelle Project, Brookhaven Nat. Lab., Upton, L.I., NY, 1978—86; group leader nuclear and particle physics rsch. P divsn. Los Alamos Nat. Lab., N.Mex., 1986—98, lab. fellow N.Mex., 1996—. Cons., 1967-69, 76-78, 99—. Author: Elementary Electronics, 1967; Editor: Scintillation Counters, 1966. NSF sr. postdoctoral fellow, 1970; JSPS fellow, 1981 Fellow Am. Phys. Soc. Home: 913 Calle Vistoso Santa Fe NM 87501-1031 Personal E-mail: hywelwhite@comcast.net.

WHITE, DAVID L., electronics executive; b. Kansas City, Mo., Apr. 20, 1955; s. Joseph D. and Barbara H. (Gosling) W.; m. Nicole J. Davis, Dec. 18, 1976; children: Christina L., Jennifer M., Trisha D. BS in Physics, Brigham Young U., 1977; MBA, U. Wash., 1979. Applications cons. Burroughs Corp., Seattle, 1978-79; mgr. fin. planning Digital Equipment Corp., Colo. Springs, Colo., 1979-84; corp. controller Zehntel Inc., Walnut Creek, Calif., 1984-89; v.p., corp. controller Conner Peripherals, Inc., San Jose, Calif., 1989; pres., CEO Candescent Tech.; sr. v.p., CFO Asyst Tech.; exec. v.p., CFO Sanmina-SCI Corp., San Jose, Calif., 2004—. Advisor Boy Scouts Am., 1979-92. Named to All Am. Swimming Team, NCAA, 1975.

Mem. Fin. Execs. Inst., Am. Prodn. and Inventory Control Soc. Republican. LDS ch. Avocations: swimming, racquetball. Office: Sanmina SCI Corp 2700 N First St San Jose CA 95134 *

WHITE, DAVID R., healthcare company executive; Grad., Univ. Tenn.; M healthcare adminstrn., Trinity Univ., San Antonio. Regional v.p. Republic Health Corp.; exec. v.p., COO Cmty. Health Systems Inc.; pres. Atlantic group HCA/Columbia, 1994—98; pres., CEO LifeTrust, 1998—2000; non-exec. chmn. IASIS Healthcare, Franklin, Tenn., 1999—2000, CEO, 2000—04, pres., 2001—04, chmn., CEO, 2004—. Bd. dir. Am. Fedn. Hospitals. Office: IASIS Healthcare Corp Bldg E 117 Seaboard Ln Franklin TN 37067 *

WHITE, DAWN MARIE, elementary school educator; b. Providence, Oct. 1, 1961; d. Edgar George and Linda Joan Hamel; m. Steven Ralph White, June 19, 1982; children: Brandon John Michael, Karlyca Lee-Anne, Steven Ralph Edgar George. BS in Edn magna cum laude, R.I. Coll., Providence, 2000. Profl. tchr. elem. edn. R.I. Dept. Elem. and Secondary Edn., 2000, advanced religious cert. Diocese of Providence, 2001. Dietary aide Zambarano Meml. Hosp., Wallum Lake, RI, 1981—84; waitress Levesques Restaurant, Pascoag, 1990—91; bus monitor Burrillville Sch. Dept., Harrisville, 1991—94; prop. Pennies Consignment Store, Pascoag, 1993—94; tchr. aide and substitute tchr. Father Holland Elem. Sch., 1994—2000; tchr. grade 3 Greater Woonsocket Cath. Regional Sch. Sys., 2000—. Mem. prin. search com. Wiliam Callahan Sch., Harrisville, 1992; sch. coord. CAT testing Diocese of Providence, 2001—; revisor sci. and social studies curriculum com. Greater Woonsocket Cath. Regional Sch. Sys., 2003—. Sr. vol. resource instr. U.S. Army Reserve Family Readiness Program, Washington, 2001—; vol. Operation Stand Down for Homeless Veterans, Woonsocket, 1993—94; asst. den leader Boy Scouts Am., Pascoag, 1990—92; master trainer family team bldg. U.S. Army Cmty. and Family Support Command, Alexandria, Va., 1995—; family support coord. U.S. Army Reserves 94th Regional Support Command, Devens, Mass., 1996—2000; catechist St. Joseph Roman Cath. Ch., Pascoag, RI, 1993—2000. Carr scholar, Feinstein Sch. of Edn. and Human Devel., 1999—2000, Gilda R. Martone 38 Endowment scholar, 1999—2000, Phyllis Moorman Salk scholar, 1999—2000. Mem.: Nat. Cath. Ednl. Assn., Pi Epsilon Rho, Kappa Delta (life). Roman Catholic. Avocations: camping, travel, boating, foreign currency collecting.

WHITE, DENNIS J., lawyer; b. Waterbury, Conn., Apr. 10, 1947; s. Alfred and Emily W.; m. Judith A. Biondi, June 30, 1973; children: Lindsey, Christopher. BA summa cum laude, Coll. of the Holy Cross, 1969; JD cum laude, Harvard U., 1975. Bar: Mass. 1975. Ptnr. Herrick & Smith, Boston, 1983-86, Sullivan & Worcester, Boston, 1986—, McDermott Will & Emery. Chmn. Capital Budgeting and Investment Com., Wellesley, Mass., 1987-90. Woodrow Wilson Found. fellow 1969, leading lawyer by Chambers USA 2006. Mem. ABA, Boston Bar Assn., Brit.-Am. Bus. Assn. New Eng., (negotiated acquisitions com.) ABA. Avocations: golf, reading. Office: McDermott Will & Emery 28 State St Boston MA 02109-1775 Office Phone: 617-535-4011. Office Fax: 617-535-3800. Business E-Mail: dwhite@mwe.com.

WHITE, DONALD D., finance educator, consultant; s. Donald and Evelyn Wil White; m. Marilyn Jean Hayes (dec.); children: D. Christopher, Gregory H. BSBA, Ctrl. Mo. State U., Warrensburg, 1966; MA, Ctrl. Mo. State U., 1968; PhD, U. Nebr., Lincoln, 1971. Instr. mgmt. Ctrl. Mo. State U., 1967—68; prof. mgmt. U. Ark., Fayettville, 1971—2006, chmn. mgmt. dept., 1986—95; prof. mgmt. CIMBA, Asolo, Italy, 1995—2006. Adj. prof. Kans. U., Lawrence, 2001—07, Clemson U., SC, 1995—2000; exec. dir. Ark. Exec. Forum, Fayetteville, 1986—2006. Author: Organizational Behavior. Pres. Friends of Youth, Fayetteville, 1979—80. Presbyterian. Avocations: reading, golf, hiking. Office: U Ark 402 WCOB Fayetteville AR 72701 Office Phone: 479-575-6229.

WHITE, DONALD HARVEY, retired physics professor; b. Berkeley, Calif., Apr. 30, 1931; s. Harvey Elliott and Adeline White; m. Beverly Evalina Jones, Aug. 8, 1953; children: Jeri, Brett, Holly, Scott, Erin. AB, U. Calif., Berkeley, 1953; PhD, Cornell U., 1960. Rsch. physicist Lawrence Livermore (Calif.) Nat. Lab., 1960-71, cons., 1971-90; prof. physics Western Oreg. U., Monmouth, 1971-95; ret. Vis. rsch. scientist Inst. Laue-Langevin, Grenoble, France, 1977-78, 84-85, 91-92. Author: (with others) Physics, an Experimental Science, 1968, Physics and Music, 1980. Pres. Monmouth-Independence Cmty. Arts, 1983. DuPont scholar, 1958; Minna-Heineman Found. fellow, Hannover, Germany, 1977. Mem. Am. Phys. Soc., Oreg. Acad. Sci. (pres. 1979-80), Phi Kappa Phi (pres. West Oreg. chpt. 1989-90) Democrat. Presbyterian. Home: PO Box 87 Monmouth OR 97361 Office Phone: 503-623-5470.

WHITE, DOUGLAS JAMES, JR., lawyer; b. NYC, Mar. 20, 1934; s. Douglas James and Margaret (Stillman) W.; m. Denise Beale, May 28, 1960; children: Brian Douglas, James Roderick. BA, U. Oreg., 1955; LLB, Willamette U., 1958. Bar: Oreg. 1958. Law clk. to assoc. justice Oreg. Supreme Ct., Salem, 1958-59; assoc. Schwabe, Williamson & Wyatt (formerly known as Mautz, Souther, Spaulding, Kinsey & Williamson), Portland, Oreg., 1959-69; shareholder, gen. ptnr. Schwabe, Williamson & Wyatt, P.C. (formerly known as Schwabe, Williamson, Wyatt, Moore & Roberts), Portland, Oreg., 1969-79, sr. ptnr., 1979-93; shareholder, 1994-98; of counsel, 1999—. Trustee Jesuit H.S., Beaverton, 1991-94; bd. dirs. St. Vincent de Paul Child Devel. Ctr., Portland, 1979-90, Portland Coun., Soc. St. Vincent de Paul, 1989-92, Portland House of Umoja, 1995—, Friends Sat. Acad., 2006—; bd. dirs., officer Maryville Nursing Home, Beaverton, 1993-99, St. Vincent de Paul Conf. of St. Thomas More, Portland, 1966—; adv. bd. Saturday Acad., Portland, 1982-2005. Mem.: Oreg. State Bar Assn. (real estate and land use sect. exec. com. 1984—85), Flyfisher Club Oreg., Multnomah Athletic Club. Republican. Roman Catholic. Avocations: fly fishing, bridge, walking, travel, hiking. Home: 6725 SW Preslynn Dr Portland OR 97225-2668 Office: Schwabe Williamson & Wyatt 1211 SW 5th Ave Ste 1800 Portland OR 97204-3713 Office Phone: 503-222-9981.

WHITE, DOUGLAS RICHIE, anthropology educator; b. Mpls., Mar. 13, 1942; s. Asher Abbott and Margaret McQuestin (Richie) W.; m. Jayne Chamberlain (div. Feb. 1971); m. Lilyan Amdur Brudner, Mar. 21, 1971; 1 child, Scott Douglas. BA, U. Minn., 1964, MA, 1967, PhD, 1969. Asst. prof. U. Pitts., 1967-72, assoc. prof., 1972-76, U. Calif., Irvine, 1976-79, prof., 1979—. Dep. dir. Lang. Attitudes Rsch. Project, Dublin, 1971—73; vis. prof. U. Tex., Austin, 1974—75, Ecole des Hautes Etudes en Sci. Sociales, Paris, 1999—2002, Inst. Nat. d'Etudes Démographique, 2000; chmn. Linkages: World Devel. Res. Coun., Md., 1986—, pres., Md., 1986—90. Co-editor: Research Methods in Social Networks, 1989, Anthropology of Urban Environments, 1972, Kinship, Networks and Exchange, 1998; founder, gen. editor World Cultures Jour., 1985-90; author sci. software packages; editor Structure and Dynamics Jour.; contbr. articles to profl. jours. Recipient Sr. Disting. U.S. Scientist award, Alexander von Humboldt Stiftung, Bonn, Germany, 1989—91, Bourse de Haute Niveau award, Ministry Rsch. and Tech., Paris, 1992; fellow, Ctr. for Advanced Studies, Western Behavioral Sci. Inst., La Jolla, Calif., 1981—84. Mem. Social Sci. Computing Assn. (pres. elect 1991, pres. 1992.), Santa Fe Inst. (mem. working groups 1999, 2000, 2001, external faculty 2004-). Democrat. Home: 8633 Via Mallorca Unit C La Jolla CA 92037 Office: U Calif School Social Sci Irvine CA 92697-0001 Office Phone: 949-824-5893.

WHITE, EDMUND WILLIAM, chemical engineer; b. Phila., July 8, 1920; s. Edmund Brittin and Grace Salome (Faunce) W.; m. Kathrine Nathalie Cadwallader, Apr. 24, 1948; children: Christine Louise, William Cadwallader, Thomas Edmund, James Christopher. BA, Columbia Coll., 1940; BS, Columbia Sch. Engring., 1941, MChemE, 1942; PhD, Lehigh U., 1952. Jr. chemist Westvaco Chlorine Products Corp., South Charleston, W.Va., 1942-44; chem. engr. C.L. Mantel, NYC, 1946-47, Diamond Alkali Co., Painesville, Ohio, 1947-49; grad. asst. Lehigh U., Bethlehem, Pa., 1949-51; sr. chemist Cities Svc. R & D Co., various cities, NJ, 1951-59, 1964—65, Athabasca Inc., Edmonton, Alberta, Canada, 1960-64; project mgr. U.S. Dept. Navy, Washington, 1965-66; rsch. chem. engr. Naval Surface Warfare Ctr., Annapolis, Md., 1966-95; ret., 1995. Cons. in field; mem. U.S. del. to ISO TC 28 mtgs. in Budapest, 1990, Phila., 1992, Paris, 1994; mem. Quadripartite Navies group on Fuels, Lubricants and Allied Products, mem. U.S. del., Ottawa, Can., 1989, Canberra, Australia, 1991; meeting co-chmn. Annapolis, Md., 1993, Windsor, UK, 1995; presenter in field. Contbr. articles to profl. jours. Treas., v.p., pres. sch. PTAs, Silver Spring, Md., 1968-79; den father, mem. troop com. Boy Scouts Am., Silver Spring, 1966-75. Ensign USN, 1944-46. Fellow ASTM (chair task force, sect. subcom., com. 1967—, mem. award of merit com. 1996-98, mem. coord. com. on Flash Point 1989-99, Award of Merit 1990, Scroll of Honor 1993, Award of Excellence 1999, Lowrie B. Sargent Jr. award 2003, George V. Dysoff award, 2005); mem. AIChE (50 Yr. award), Am. Chem. Soc. (50 Yr. award), Potomac Curling Club (bd. dirs., pres. 1982-84), Internat. Assn. for Stability and Handling of Liquid Fuels (hon. mem., mem. steering com. 1985-95, Hon. Membership award 1999), Sigma Xi. Republican. Achievements include 4 patents and 2 Canadian patents; research in consensus standardization, fuel stability testing, fuel stability, synthetic fuels, separation processes, wax oxidation, mixing and chlorine-caustic electrolytic cell. Home: 908 Crest Park Dr Silver Spring MD 20903-1307

WHITE, EDWARD ALFRED, lawyer; b. Elizabeth, NJ, Nov. 23, 1934; BS in Indsl. Engring., U. Mich., 1957, JD, 1963. Bar: Fla. 1963, U.S. Ct. Appeals (5th cir.) 1971, U.S. Ct. Appeals (11th cir.) 1981, U.S. Supreme Ct. 1976. Assoc. Jennings, Watts, Clarke & Hamilton, Jacksonville, Fla., 1963-66, ptnr., 1966-69, Wayman & White, Jacksonville, Fla., 1969-72; pvt. practice Jacksonville, Fla., 1972—. Mem. aviation law com. Fla. Bar, 1972-94, chmn., 1979-81, bd. govs., 1984-88, admiralty com., 1984—, chmn., 1990-91, chmn. pub. relations com., 1986-88, exec. coun. trial lawyers sect., 1986-91, chmn. admiralty cert. com., 1995-97. Fellow Am. Bar Found.; mem. ABA (vice chmn. admiralty law com. 1995—), Fla. Bar Assn. (bd. cert. civil trial lawyer, bd. cert. admiralty lawyer), Jacksonville Bar Assn. (chmn. legal ethics com. 1975-76, bd. govs. 1976-78, pres. 1979-80), Assn. Trial Lawyers Am. (sustaining mem. 1984—), Acad. Fla. Trial Lawyers (diplomate), Fla. Coun. Bar Assn. Pres.'s, Lawyer-Pilots Bar Assn., Am. Judicature Soc., Maritime Law Assn. (proctor in admiralty), Southeastern Admiralty Law Inst. (bd. dirs. 1982-84, chmn., pres. 1994), Am. Bd. Trial Advocates (city of Jacksonville Mpl. code enforcement bd., 2006—). Home: 1959 Largo Rd Jacksonville FL 32207-3926 Office: 901 Blackstone Bldg 233 E Bay St Jacksonville FL 32202-3452 Office Phone: 904-356-6500. Office Fax: 904-356-6508.

WHITE, EDWARD ALLEN, electronics executive; b. Jan. 1, 1928; s. Joseph and Bessie (Allen) W.; m. Joan Dixon, Dec. 22, 1949 (div. Aug. 1978); children: Leslie Ann Loclar; m. Nancy Rhoads, Oct. 6, 1979. BS, Tufts U., 1947. Vice chmn. White Electronic Designs Corp., Phoenix, 1951—. Pres. Ariz. Digital Corp., Phoenix, 1975—91, Interactive Digital Corp., Phoenix, 1992—. Patentee in field. Bd. dirs. Gov.'s Coun. Children, Youth and Families, Phoenix, 1982-84, Planned Parenthood Fedn. Am., 1984-88; pres., bd. dirs. Planned Parenthood Ctrl. and No. Ariz., 1984-88; trustee Internat. House, N.Y.C., 1973-75, Tufts U., 1973-83. Recipient Horatio Alger award, 1962. Mem.: World Pres.'s Orgn., Paradise Valley Country Club, Tau Beta Pi. Home: 5786 N Echo Canyon Cir Phoenix AZ 85018-1242 Office: White Electronic Designs Corp 3601 E University Dr Phoenix AZ 85034-7254 Home Phone: 602-840-0704; Office Phone: 602-437-1520 x111. Business E-Mail: ewhite@whiteedc.com.

WHITE, EDWARD GIBSON, II, lawyer; b. Lexington, Ky., Nov. 7, 1954; s. Russell Edwin White and Betty Lee White-Estabrook; children: Edward Gibson III, William Elliot, John Alexander, Albert Grahm. BA, U. Tenn., Chattanooga, 1980; JD, U. Tenn., Knoxville, 1983. Bar: Tenn. 1983, U.S. Dist. Ct. (ea. dist.) Tenn. 1984, U.S. Ct. Appeals (6th cir.) 1985. Assoc. Hodges, Doughty & Carson, Knoxville, 1983-87, ptnr., 1988—. Bd. dirs. Knoxville affiliate The Susan G. Komen Breast Cancer Found., Inc., Elizabeth R. Griffin Rsch. Found., West High Found., Inc. Named one of Best 150 Attys. in Tenn., Tenn. Bus. Mag., 2007. Fellow: Tenn. Bar Found., Knoxville Bar Found. (bd. dirs.); mem.: Hamilton Burnett Am. Inn of Ct. (Master of the Bench 2005—), Am. Bd. Trial Advocates, Def. Rsch. Inst. (med./legal com. 1985—), Tenn. Def. Lawyers Assn., Knoxville Bar Assn. (treas. 1995—96, continuing legal edn. com. 1985—86, 1988—91, chmn. 1992—94, naturalization com. 1985—87, bd. govs. 1993—94, pres.-elect 1996, pres. 1997, Pres.'s award 1992), Tenn. Bar Assn. (interprofl. code com. 1989—, med./legal com. 1991—), Knoxville Racquet Club, Cherokee Country Club, Univ. Club, U. Tenn. Pres.'s Club. Republican. Avocations: tennis, golf, boating, water sports, fishing. Office: Hodges Doughty & Carson 617 Main St # 869 Knoxville TN 37902-2602 Office Phone: 865-292-2307. Business E-Mail: twhite@hdclaw.com.

WHITE, EILEEN, science educator, researcher; BS, Rensselaer Polytechnic Inst.; PhD, SUNY, Stony Brook, NY, 1983. Postdoctoral fellow Cold Spring Harbor Lab., staff investigator; prof., dept. molecular biology and biochemistry Rutgers, The State U. NJ, assoc. investigator, Howard Hughes Med. Inst., 1998—2005, prin. investigator, White Lab., resident faculty mem., Ctr. for Advanced Biotechnology and Medicine; program leader, assoc. dir. basic sci. Cancer Inst. NJ. Adj. prof., dept. surgery U. Medicine Dentistry NJ-Robert Wood Johnson Med. Sch. Contbr. articles to profl. jours. Office: Ctr for Advanced Biotechnology and Medicine 679 Hoes Lane CABM Room 140 Piscataway NJ 08854-5638 Office Fax: 732-235-5329, 732-235-5795. Business E-Mail: ewhite@cabm.rutgers.edu. *

WHITE, EMMET, JR., retirement community administrator; b. Newark, Oct. 18, 1946; s. Emmet, Sr. and June (Howlett) White; m. Betty Orr, June 7, 1970; children: Benjamin, Suzanne, George. BA, Lafayette Coll., 1968; JD, Coll. William and Mary, 1971. Bar: Hawaii 1972; nursing home adminstr., Hawaii. Law ptnr. Mau and White, AAL, Honolulu, 1975-83, White and Tom, AAL, Honolulu, 1983-95; pres., CEO Arcadia Retirement Residence, Honolulu, 1996—. Trustee Ctrl. Union Ch., Honolulu, 1980-84, chmn. 1983-84, moderator, 1987, also deacon; mem. Health Planning Coun. Honolulu, Am. Oahu Workforce Investment Bd. Col. USAR, 1968-94. Mem.: Nat. Com. Employer Support of Guard and Res. (ombudsman), Hawaii Long Term Care Assn. (chmn. 2001—03, 2007—), Hawaii Bar Assn. Avocation: physical activities. Office: Arcadia Retirement Residence 1434 Punahou St Honolulu HI 96822-4754 Office Phone: 808-983-1823. E-mail: ewhite@arcadia-hi.org.

WHITE, EUGENE VADEN, retired pharmacist; b. Cape Charles, Va., Aug. 13, 1924; s. Paul Randolph and Louise (Townsend) W.; m. Laura Juanita LaFontaine, Aug. 28, 1948; children: Lynda Sue, Patricia Louise. BS in Pharmacy, Med. Coll. Va., 1950; PharM (hon.), Phila. Coll. Pharmacy and Sci., 1966; DSc (hon.), Shenandoah U., 2001. Pharmacist McKim & Huffman Drug Store, Luray, Va., 1950, Miller's Drug Store, Winchester, 1950-53; pharmacist, ptnr. Shiner's Drug Store, Front Royal, 1953-56; pharmacist, owner Eugene V. White, Pharmacist, P.C., Berryville, 1956-98; ret., 1998. Sturmer lectr. Phila. Coll. Pharmacy and Sci., 1979; Lubin vis. prof. U. Tenn. Sch. Pharmacy, Memphis, 1974; mem. bd. visitors Sch. Pharmacy, U. Pitts., 1969. Author: The Office-Based Family Pharmacist, 1978; created first office practice in community pharmacy, 1960, developed patient medication profile record, 1960. 2d lt. USAAC, 1943-45. Recipient Nat. Leadership award Phi Lambda Sigma, 1979, Outstanding Pharmacy Alumnus award Med. Coll. Va. Sch. Pharmacy Alumni Assn., 1989; Eugene V. White scholarship named in his honor Shenandoah U. Sch. Pharmacy, 1996, Eugene V. White Disting. Lecture Series established by Delta Xi chpt. Kappa Psi Pharm. Fraternity, Shenandoah U. Sch. Pharmacy, 1998. Fellow Am. Coll. Apothecaries (J. Leon Lascoff award 1973); mem. Am. Pharm Assn. (Daniel B. Smith award 1965, Remington Honor medal 1978), Va. Pharm. Assn. (Pharmacist of Yr. award 1966, Outstanding Pharmacist award 1992). Methodist. Avocations: reading, woodworking, computers. Personal E-mail: evwhite@visuallink.com.

WHITE, FLORENCE MAY, retired special education educator; b. Ottawa, Kans., Sept. 1, 1936; d. O.C. Robert and Effie Lynne (Walker) Arnold; m. Donald L. White, June 1, 1958 (dec. Jan. 1996); children: Tab Vincent, Jacque Sue, Michelle May. BA, Ottawa U., 1958; MS, Kans. U., 1974; postgrad., Kans. U. Med. Ctr., 1975—76. Cert. reading specialist, learning disabilities specialist; cert. elem. and mid. sch. edn.: lang. arts, social studies, elem. curriculum. Classroom tchr. 2d grade Wellsville Elem., Kans., 1958-59; learning disabilities tchr. Olatha Spl. Edn. Coop., Kans., 1971-74; learning disabilities specialist, tchr. 7-9 Ottawa Mid. Sch., 1974-77; learning disabilities specialist, tchr. Paola Spl. Edn. Coop., Richmond, Kans., 1980-95; tchr. learning disabilities class elem. level Ctrl. Heights Elem. Sch., Richmond, Kans., 2001—02. Pub. rep., speaker on learning disabilities to civic groups and local orgns., 1972-75. Den mother Boy Scouts Am. and Brownies, Ottawa, 1968-70; chair state GOP women's polit. activities Rep. State Party, Topeka, 1964-67; chair scholarship contest DAR, Ottawa dist., 1984-96; Sunday sch. tchr. Meth. Ch., Ottawa; crafts tchr. local 4-H, Ottawa; mem. Central Heights PTA (projects com. 1980-95); mem. Ottawa Arts Coun. State of Kans. scholar State Spl. Edn. Dept., 1976. Mem.: PEO, Kans. Assn. Ret. Sch. Employees, Franklin County Reading Coun. (pres.-elect 1989—91, pres. 1991—92, v.p.), Kans. Reading Assn., Internat. Reading Assn., Garden Club, Soroptimist, Ottawa Area C. of C., Alpha Delta Kappa. Roman Catholic. Avocations: oil painting, reading, travel, music, volunteer work.

WHITE, FRED B., III, lawyer; b. Somerville, NJ, 1947; BA, Wheaton Coll., 1969; JD with honors, George Washington U. Nat. Law Ctr., 1972. Bar: NJ 1972, DC 1972, Mass. 1976, Del. 1983, NY 1990. Co-head, banking/savings and loans mergers and acquisitions Skadden, Arps, Slate, Meagher & Flom LLP, NYC. Office: Skadden Arps Slate Meagher & Flom LLP 4 Times Sq New York NY 10036 Office Phone: 212-735-2144. Office Fax: 917-777-2144. Business E-Mail: fwhite@skadden.com.

WHITE, GARY RICHARD, electrical engineer; b. Detroit, Nov. 15, 1962; s. Thomas Richard and Davene (Reynolds) White. BSEE, Wayne State U., 1986; MBA, MS in Info. Systems, Hawaii Pacific U., 2006. Electronics engr. U.S. Army Info. Sys. Engring. Command, Ft. Belvoir, Va., 1987-88, Ft. Shafter, Hawaii, 1988-92; elec. worker U.S. Navy Pub. Works Ctr., Pearl Harbor, Hawaii, 1992-96, plant operator, 1996—. Mem. IEEE, NRA, NSPE, Assn. Computing Machinery, Am. Assn. Individual Investors, Am. Mgmt. Assn. Avocations: weightlifting, bicycling, computers, music, movies. Office: PO Box 19055 Honolulu HI 96817-8055 Office Phone: 808-474-2202. Personal E-mail: garywhite4me@yahoo.com.

WHITE, GAYLE CLAY, aerospace company executive; b. Wyandotte, Mich., Sept. 28, 1944; s. John Leonard and Irene Frances (Clay) W.; m. Sharon Wong, June 8, 1968; children: Lai Jean, Quinn Yee. BBA, Ea. Mich. U., 1967; MBA, Utah State U., 1971; MPA, Auburn U., 1976; postgrad., Nova U., 1985—99. Computer system analyst USAF Logistics Command, Odgen, Utah, 1967-71, U.S.-Can. Mil. Officer Exec., Ottawa, Ont., 1971-73; mgr. software devel. USAF Data System Design Ctr., Montgomery, Ala., 1973-77; data base adminstr. Supreme Hdqrs. Allied Powers Europe, Casteau, Belgium, 1977-81; mgr. software configuration System Integration Office, Colorado Springs, Colo., 1981-83; mgr. computer ops. N.Am. Aerospace Def. Command, Colorado Springs, 1983-84; dir. ops. 6 Missile Warning Squadron, Space Command, Cape Cod, Mass., 1984-86, comdr., 1986-87; mgr. program devel. Rockwell Internat., Colorado Springs, 1987-96; mgr. bus. devel. The Boeing Co., Colorado Springs, 1996-99; ret. Mem. faculty computer sci. and bus. Regis U., Colorado Springs, 1981—97; sr. mem. exec. staff Computer Scis. Corp., 1999—2006, dir. air, missile and nat. def. Colo. ops., 2006—. V.p. European Parents, Tchrs. and Students Assn., 1979—81; mem. Pikes Peak Regional Workforce Investment Bd., 2002—, vice chmn., 2004—05, chmn., 2005—06; treas. Christian Ctr. Ch., Colorado Springs, 1989—95. Recipient Mil.-Civilian Rels. award, Otis Civilian Adv. Coun., 1987, cert., Data Processing Mgmt. Assn., 1973. Mem.: C. of C. Mil. Affairs Com., Christian Businessmen's Assn., Nat. Security Indsl. Assn. (bd. dirs. Rocky Mountain chpt. 1990—97, bd. dirs. space divsn. 1993—2003, vice chmn. ctrl. region 1996—97, chpt. pres. 1997—99, exec. vice chmn. 1999—2000, chmn. nat. space com. 2000—02, sr. advisor 2003—04, Significant Svc. award 1998, Exceptional Svc. award 2001, Gold medal 2003), SHAPE Officers Assn., Air Force Assn. (v.p. membership Lance Sijan chpt. 2000—02, chmn. Space Symposium com. 2003, pres. Lance Sijan chpt. 2003—05, Chpt. Exceptional Svc. award 2001—02, chpt. Star award 2003), Global Positioning Sys. Internat. Assn., Inst. Nav. (treas. Rocky Mountain sect. 1996—97), Armed Forces Comm. Electronics Assn., Colo. Air Force Assn. (exec. v.p. 2005—07, pres. 2007—, Nat. Medal Merit 2001, State Exceptional Svc. award 2002, Colo. State Mem. of Yr. 2004, Nat. Medal Merit 2004, Nat. Exceptional Svc. award 2005, State Exceptional Svc. award 2006, 2007), Woodmoor Pines Golf Club, Alpha Kappa Psi. Republican. Avocations: hiking, camping, coin collecting/numismatics. Office: Computer Scis Corp 460 Wooten Rd Ste 144 Colorado Springs CO 80916 Personal E-mail: gwhite22@csc.com.

WHITE, GEORGE COOKE, theater director, foundation administrator; b. New London, Conn., Aug. 16, 1935; s. Nelson Cooke and Aida (Rovetti) W.; m. Elizabeth Conant Darling, July 5, 1958; children: George Conant, Caleb Ensign, Juliette Darling. Student, U. Paris, 1956; BA, Yale U., 1957, MFA, 1961; student, Shakespeare Inst., 1959; ArtsD (hon.), Conn. Coll., 1994. Stage mgr. Imperial Japanese Azumakabuki Co., 1955; asst. mgr. Internat. Ballet Festival, Nervi, Italy, 1955; prodn. coordinator Talent Assos., 1961-63; adminstrv. v.p. score prodns. Paramount Pictures, 1963-65; founder, pres. Eugene O'Neill Meml. Theatre Found., 1965—2000; adviser, dir. Theatre One, Conn. Coll. Women, 1967-70; exec. dir. The Johnny Mercer Found., 1999; regional theater cons. Nat. Ednl. TV Network; guest lectr. Wagner Coll., 1970; acting dir. Hunter Coll. Arts, 1972-73; chmn. Florence Acad. Art, 2004—. Adj. prof. U. NC; prof. theater adminstrn. program Yale U., 1978-91; co-chmn. Yale Drama Sch.; mem. exec. com. Theatre Libr. Assn., 1967; bd. govs. Am. Playwrights Theatre; mem. bd. ANTA, 1967-68; mem. Mayor NYC's. Theatre Adv. Com.; advisory bd. Internat. Theatre Inst.; panel mem. Exptl. Theatre; US State Dept. cultural exchange grantee to Australia; guest adminstr. Australian Nat. Playwrights Conf., 1973; US del. Internat. Theatre Inst. Congress, Moscow, 1973; mem. Conn. Commn. on Arts, 1978-93, mem. exec. com., 1979-83, vice chair, 1992-93; co-founder Caribbean-US Theatre Exchange; dir. Actors Theatre St. Paul, 1979, 80, 82, 83, 86, Hartman Repertory Theatre, 1980; guest dir. Chinese Theater Assn., Beijing, 1984, 87, Hedgerow Theatre, 1986; mem. nominating com. Antoinette Perry Awards, 1984-86, 88, 94-96, 98-2002, adminstrv. com. Am. Theater Wing, 1997; dir. Anna Christie Beijing Cen. Dramatic Theater, 1984, 87; bd. dirs. New London Day. Appeared in TV series Citizen Soldier, 1959-61; appeared in off-Broadway prodn. John Brown's Body. Trustee Goodspeed Opera House, 1966-68, Nat. Theatre Conf., 1973—, Eastern Conn. Symphony, Dance Arts Coun., Conn. Opera Assn., Conn. Pub. TV, 1973-83, Mitchell Coll., 1994—, Arts & Bus. Coun., 1994—, Arts Internat., 2001, 02, Boston Conservatory, 2000-; trustee Conn. Edn. Telecommunications Corp., 1973-83, chmn., 1982; mem. planning bd. Op. Rescue; bd. dirs. Rehearsal Club, Centre for Inter-Am. Rels., Theater of Latin Am., Manhattan Theatre Club, 1970-80, Met. Opera Guild; Performance mag.; exec. com. Yale Drama Alumni, 1963-73; mem. Yale Alumni Bd.; bd. overseers drama dept. Brandeis U.; adv. bd. Am. Musical Theatre Program, Hartford Conservatory, Bd. Arts & Bus. Coun., Brandeis Creative Arts Award Jury, Theater and New Music Theatre Works Panel, NEA; mem. Waterford (Conn.) Rep. Town Meeting, 1975-77, 2001—; presdl. appointment to Nat. Coun. NEA, 1992; mem. Nat. Coun. Arts, 1992-97; trustee Arts Internat.; bd. dirs. Day Pub. Co., RKO Pictures, American Acad. Dramatic Arts; bd. mem. Boston Conservatory; mem. Coast Guard Auxillary, watch q.m. US Coast Guard Barque Eagle. Served with AUS, 1957-59; Flotilla Cmdr., US Coast Auxillary, 1998-99. Named Officer first class, Royal Swedish Order of Polar Star; recipient spl. citation, New England Theatre Conf., 1968, 1998, Margo Jones award, 1968, Pub. Svc. award, New London County Bar Assn., 1975, Disting. Citizen's award, Town of Waterford, 1976, Distin. Svc. award, Conn. mag., 1981, Contbns. to State award, 1981, Lifetime Contbn. to Theatre award, Am. Theater Assn., 1989, Contbn. to Conn. Arts award, Quinnipiac Coll., 1989, Medal of Arts, Russian Federation, Chevalier des artes et des lettres (France), 1983, gold medal, Cairo Internat. Experimental Theater Festival, Cavalieri, Order of St. Maurice and Lazarus; grantee Internat. Communications Agy. cultural exch. grantee to People's Republic of China, 1980. Fellow Royal Soc. Arts, Coll. of Am. Theatre; mem. Chinese Theatre Assn. (hon.). Clubs: Century; Cosmos (Washington); Thames (New London); White's Point Yacht. Office: 234 W 44th St New York NY 10036 Office Phone: 212-382-2790, 860-439-0667. Personal E-mail: whitebg@att.net.

WHITE, GEORGE EDWARD, lawyer, educator; b. Northampton, Mass., Mar. 19, 1941; s. George LeRoy and Frances Dorothy (McCafferty) W.; m. Susan Valre Davis, Dec. 31, 1966; children: Alexandra V., Elisabeth McC. BA, Amherst Coll., Mass., 1963; MA, Yale U., New Haven, Conn., 1964, PhD, 1967; JD, Harvard U., Cambridge, Mass., 1970. Bar: DC 1970, Va. 1975, US Supreme Ct. 1973. Vis. scholar Am. Bar Found., 1970—71; law clk. to Chief Justice Warren US Supreme Ct., 1971—72; asst. prof. law U. Va., 1972—74, assoc. prof., 1974—77, prof., 1977—86, John B. Minor prof. law and history, 1987—2003, disting. univ. prof., John B. Minor prof. law and history, 1992—2003, David and Mary Harrison disting. prof. law, 2003—. Vis. prof. Marshall-Wythe Law Sch. spring 1988, NY Law Sch., fall 1988; acad. visitor London Sch. Econs. and Polit. Sci., 2005 Author: The American Judicial Tradition, 1976, 3d edit., 2007, Tort Law in America: An Intellectual History, 1980 (Gavel award ABA, 1981), 2nd edit., 2003, Earl Warren: A Public Life, 1982 (Gavel award ABA, 1983), The Marshall Court and Cultural Change, 1988, 2nd edit., 1991 (James Willard Hurst prize, 1990), Justice Oliver Wendell Holmes: Law and the Inner Self, 1993 (Gavel award ABA, 1994, Scribes award, 1994, Littleton-Griswold prize, 1994, Triennial Order of the Coif award, 1996), Intervention and Detachment: Essays in Legal History and Jurisprudence, 1994, Creating the National Pastime: Baseball Transforms Itself, 1903-1953, 1996, The Constitution and the New Deal, 2000, Alger Hiss's Looking-Glass Wars, 2004, History and the Constitution, 2007, others; editor: Studies in Legal History, 1980—86, Delegate in Law, 1986—97. Mem. AAAS, Am. Law Inst., Am. Soc. Legal History (bd. dirs. 1978-81), Soc. Am. Historians. Office: Law Sch U Va 580 Massie Rd Charlottesville VA 22903-1789 Office Phone: 434-924-3455. Business E-Mail: gew@virginia.edu.

WHITE, GORDON ELIOT, historian, writer; b. Glen Ridge, NJ, Oct. 25, 1933; s. Maurice Brewster and Sarah Fullilove (Gordon) W.; m. Nancy Johnson, 1955 (div. 1957); m. Mary Joan Briggs, Aug. 6, 1960 (dec. Nov. 1987); children: Sarah Elizabeth and Gordon O'Neal Brewster (twins), David McIntyre; m. Francis C. Barrineau, 1989 (div. 1996); m. Angela Tyler, Mar. 27, 1999. BA, Cornell U., 1955; MS in Journalism, Columbia U., 1957. Lic. master mariner USCG; lic. pilot FAA. Stringer Nassau Daily Rev.-Star, Rockville Centre, L.I., NY, 1948-50, Freeport (N.Y.) Leader, 1949-50; sports writer Morris County (N.J.) Citizen, 1950-51; stringer Ithaca (N.Y.) Evening News, 1951-55; photo editor, editl. writer Cornell Daily Sun, 1951-55; copy editor Am. Banker, NYC, 1958; Washington corr. Chgo. Am., 1958-61; chief Washington bur. Deseret News, Salt Lake City, 1961-88. Also corr. in Europe, U.S. and Antarctic for WJR, Detroit; KSL-KSL-TV, Salt Lake City, also KGMB, Honolulu; free lance writer with U.S. Navy, Army and Air Force, 1959; cons. Nat. Air and Space Mus.; auto racing, mil. aviation electronics historian. Author: Offenhauser, the Legendary American Racing Engine and the Men Who Built It, 1996, The Indianapolis Racing Cars of Frank Kurtis, 1940-1963, 2000, Kurtis-Kraft: Masterworks of Speed & Style, 2001, Lost Race Tracks, 2003, The Marvelous Mechanical Designs of Harry A. Miller, 2004, Ab and Marvin Jenkins and the Mormon Meteors, 2006. Advisor auto racing Nat. Mus. Am. History, Smithsonian Instn., 1989—; curator Miller-Offenhauser Archive of historic race engine blueprints. Recipient Raymond Clapper Meml. award White House Corrs. Assn., 1978; award for excellence in reporting Exec. Dept. and White House; Roy W. Howard award for outstanding pub. svc. by a newspaper corr., 1979; award for disting. investigative reporting Investigative Reporters and Editors, 1980, Reser-Tuthill award for writing on history of automobile racing, Indpls., 1985. Mem. Nat. Press Club (Washington, Excellence in Reporting award 1979), Sigma Delta Chi (1st prize for newsphoto, 1954, Nat. award 1979), Pi Kappa Phi, Pi Delta Epsilon Episcopalian. Home and Office: PO Box 129 Hardyville VA 23070 Office Phone: 804-776-7947. Personal E-mail: gewhite@crosslink.net.

WHITE, GREGORY A., prosecutor; b. Nov. 1949; BA in Criminal Justice and Police Adminstrn., Kent State U., 1973; JD magna cum laude, Cleveland Marshall Coll., 1976. Atty. Wilcox and White Law Firm, 1977—84; law dir. City of Elyria, 1979; prosecutor Lorain County, Ohio, 1981—2002; US atty. (no. dist.) Ohio US Dept. Justice, 2003—. With USMC, Vietnam. Office: US Attys Office 801 W Superior Ave Ste 400 Cleveland OH 44113-1852 *

WHITE, GRETCHEN NANCE, education educator, writer; d. Virginia Lee Nance; m. Ronald Craig White (dec.); children: Loronzo De'Warren, David Lee, Mark Du'Pree, Paul Keith, Anthony O'Lunte, Michelle Ja'Nesse Jefferson. Diploma in child daycare, ICS, Pa., 1995; diploma in mgmt. in health care, Calif. Coll. of Health Scis., 1998, diploma in bus. comm., 2001. Cert. ordination Tex., 2001, Tex. Notary Pub. Commn. Pvt. duty nurses asst. Meth. Hosp., Houston, 1984—87; vocat. coord. Richmond (Tex.) State Sch., 1988—. Founder, pres. White's Internat. Scholarship, Inc., Wharton, Tex., 2001—. Author: (book) It's Vision Time, 2000, The Four F''s/Faith, Fear, Failure, Forgiveness, 2000, A Nation on the Rise to Be Educated or Not to Be Educated, 2003. Host bible study chat group, vol. Read-A-Thon; sponsor free hot meal program for low-income housing project area, 2004—; pastor A Nation on the Rise Youth/Teen Ministry Explosion. Grantee, Wal-mart Super Ctr., 2004. Avocations: cooking, reading, health glider, sports. Office: Whites Internat Scholarship Inc PO Box 1283 Rosenberg TX 77471 Office Phone: 281-846-8558. Business E-Mail: gretchen.white@dads.state.tx.us.

WHITE, H. KATHERINE, lawyer; b. Salina, Kans., May 21, 1945; BS, MIT, 1967; JD, Rutgers U., 1975. Bar: Calif. 1975, NJ 1982. Joined Sealed Air Corp., Elmwood Park, NJ, 1982, v.p., gen. counsel, sec., 1998—. Mem.: ABA, Soc. Corp. Secretaries and Governance Profls., NJ Corp. Counsel Assn. (dir. 1994—96), Assn. Corp. Counsel, State Bar Calif., NJ State Bar Assn. Office: Sealed Air Corp 200 Riverfront Blvd Elmwood Park NJ 07407

WHITE, HAROLD JACK, pathologist; b. Bklyn., Jan. 4, 1920; s. Abraham and Jennie (Warshawsky) W.; m. Lucette Darby, July 19, 1962; children: Elizabeth, Darby, Matthew, Esther. BS, Harvard U., 1941; MD, U. Geneva, 1952. Diplomate Am. Bd. Pathology. Intern, resident in pathology Yale U. Sch. Medicine, New Haven, 1953-58, fellow, 1957-58; assoc. pathologist Brigham and Women's Hosp., Boston, 1962-66; chief lab. svc. VA Hosp., West Roxbury, Mass., 1962-66, Little Rock, 1966-80; sr. scientist, acting head biomed. sci. dept. GM Rsch. Labs., Warren, Mich., 1980-85, cons., 1985—. Prof. pathology, microbiology U. Ark. Med. Sch., Little Rock, 1966—; vis. scientist dept. comparative medicine, MIT, Cambridge, 1988—. Contbr. over 100 articles, abstracts in pathology, microbiology, immunology, toxicology, biomedicine to profl. jours. 1st lt. USAAF, 1942-46. Fellow Coll. Am. Pathologists, Internat. Coll. Pathology. Home: 24 Bass Rocks Rd Gloucester MA 01930-3276 Office: 35 Main St Gloucester MA 01930-5730 Office Phone: 978-281-3531. E-mail: hjwriverrun@aol.com.

WHITE, HARRY EDWARD, JR., lawyer; b. Menominee, Mich., Apr. 26, 1939; s. Harry Edward and Verena Charlotte (Leisen) W.; m. Mary P.A. Sheaffer, June 7, 1980. BS in Fgn. Svc., Georgetown U., Washington, 1961; LLB, Columbia U., 1964. Bar: N.Y. 1965, U.S. Supreme Ct. 1970, U.S. Dist. Ct. (so. dist.) N.Y. 1979, U.S. Tax Ct. 1980. Assoc. Milbank, Tweed, Hadley & McCloy, NYC, 1964-65, 67-73, ptnr., 1974—2004, cons. ptnr., 2004—. Contbr. chpts. to books, articles to legal jours. Served with M.I., U.S. Army, 1965-66, Vietnam. Decorated Bronze Star. Mem. ABA, Internat. Bar Assn., N.Y. State Bar Assn. (chmn. taxation com. internat. law practice sect. 1987-90, co-chmn. exempt orgns. com. tax sect. 1987-88), Internat. Law Assn., ssn. Bar City N.Y., Internat. Fiscal Assn., The Players. Republican. Roman Catholic. Home: 333 E 55th St New York NY 10022-8316 Office: Milbank Tweed Hadley & McCloy 1 Chase Manhattan Plz Fl 47 New York NY 10005-1413 Home Phone: 212-753-6603; Office Phone: 212-530-5092. E-mail: hwhite@milbank.com.

WHITE, HELENE NITA, federal judge; b. Jackson Heights, NY, Dec. 2, 1954; d. Frank William and Ruth (Gruber) White. AB, Columbia U., 1978; JD, U. Pa., 1978. Bar: Pa. 1979, Mich. 1979. Law clk. to justice Mich. Supreme Ct., Southfield, 1978—80; judge Common Pleas Ct., Detroit, 1981, 36th Dist Ct., Detroit, 1981—83, Wayne Cir. Ct., Detroit, 1983—92, Mich. Ct. Appeals, Detroit, 1992—. Bd. dirs., chmn. bylaws com. Met. Detroit YWCA, 1986—87, Coalition Temporary Shelter, 1986—, chmn. nominating com., 1988—; program com. bus. and profl. divsn. Jewish Welfare Fedn., 1987—; bd. advisors Sojourner Found., 1988, Detroit Women's Forum, 1988—. Mem.: ABA, Women Lawyers Assn. Mich., Nat. Assn. Women Judges (chmn. publicity 1984, membership com. 1985—), Detroit Bar Assn., Pa. Bar Assn. Jewish.

WHITE, HENRY F., JR., legal association administrator, retired military officer; b. NYC; BS, U.S. Naval Acad.; JD, Fordham U., 1976. Pres. Inst. Internat. Container Lessoers; mem. adv. com. on comml. ops. customs and border protection U.S. Dept. Homeland Security; mem. Hill, Betts & Nash, LLP; dep. commr. transp. NYC; counsel to Mayor; mng. mem. Barger & Wolen LLP; exec. dir., COO ABA, Chgo., 2006—. Rear admiral, vice comdr., U.S. Fleet Forces Command USNR. Office: ABA 321 N Clark St Chicago IL 60610-4714 Office Phone: 312-988-5000. Office Fax: 312-988-6281. *

WHITE, HENRY J., engineering educator, consultant; b. NYC, Nov. 20, 1965; s. Henry and Dolores White; m. Yuxie P. White, Dec. 26, 1998; children: Hillary X., Francis H. BS, Poly. U., Bklyn., 1987; MS, U. Tenn., 1992; PhD, Stony Brook U., 1999. Registered profl. engr., NY. Metall. technician Lucius Pitkin Inc., NYC, 1985—87, LI Testing Lab., North Babylon, NY, 1986—87; metallurgist ABB Lummus Global, Bloomfield, NJ, 1987—90; materials engr. Misonix Inc., Farmingdale, NY, 1993—94; mgr. heat treating ops. Skyo Industries Inc., Deer Park, NY, 1994—2000; prof. Stony Brook (NY) U., 2000—. Cons. NSF, Arlington, Va., 2000—, Air Force Office Sci. Rsch., Arlington, 2005—; ABET program evaluator Metall. Soc., Warrendale, Pa., 2002—, profl. registration com., 2003—, faculty fellow. Fellow, Am. Soc. for Engring. Edn./ NASA, 2001; grantee, NSF, 2004. Mem.: Assn. Iron and Steel Tech., Metall. Soc., Materials Rsch. Soc., Am. Soc. Engring. Edn., Am. Soc. Materials Internat. (chmn. LI chpt. 2002—03, bd. dirs. metro NY/NJ chpt. 2003—, vice chmn. metro NY/NJ chpt. 2006—, Quality Performance Program award 2002, 2003), Soc. Mfg. Engrs. Achievements include patents for densification of thermal spray coatings. Home: 6 Raspberry Ln Nesconset NY 11767 Office: Stony Brook Univ Dept Materials Sci Stony Brook NY 11794-2275 Home Phone: 631-360-3218. Personal E-mail: hwhite@notes.cc.sunysb.edu.

WHITE, HERBERT SPENCER, library and information scientist, educator, dean; b. Vienna, Sept. 5, 1927; came to U.S., 1938, naturalized, 1944; s. Leon and Ernestine (Lichteneger) Hochweis; m. Mary Virginia Dyer, Feb. 19, 1953 (dec.); 1 son, Jerome; m. Nancy J. Cornell, May 1, 2002. BS in Chemistry, CCNY, 1949; MSLS, Syracuse U., 1950; PhD in Humane Letters (hon.), Ind. U., 2003. Intern Libr. of Congress, Washington, 1950, mem. tech. info. divsn., 1950-53; tech. libr. AEC, Oak Ridge, Tenn., 1953-54; organizer, mgr. corp. libr. Chance Vought Aircraft, Dallas, 1954-59; mgr. engring. libr. IBM Corp., Kingston, N.Y., 1959-62, mgr. tech. info. ctr. Poughkeepsie, N.Y., 1962-64; exec. dir. NASA Sci. and Tech. Info. Facility, College Park, Md., 1964-68; v.p. info. mgmt. Leasco Systems & Rsch. Corp., Bethesda, Md., 1968-70; sr. v.p. Inst. Sci. Info., Phila., 1970-74, corp. dir., 1971-74; pres. Stechert-Macmillan, Inc., Pennsaucken, N.J., 1974-75; prof., dir. Rsch. Ctr. Grad. Libr. Sch. Ind. U., Bloomington, 1975-80, dean Sch. Libr. and Info. Scis., 1980-90, disting. prof., 1991-95; prof. emeritus, 1995—. Adj. prof. U. Ariz. Sch. Libr. Scis., 1995—; vis. prof. Alberta, San Jose State, Hawaii; cons., lectr. Author: Librarianship Quo Vadis?, 2000, others; contbr. articles to profl. publs.; columnist Libr. Jour. Mem. Pres.'s Adv. Com. for Adminstrn. Title II-B Higher Edn. Act, 1965-68, Libr. Rsch. Planning Com. for 1980s, U.S. Dept. Edn., v.p. Green Valley Cmty. Coordinating Coun., 1997—; grant reviewer Inst. Mus. and Librs., 1998—. Spl. honoree, U. of Essen (Germany) Conf., 1992. Fellow Spl. Libraries Assn. (pres. 1969-70, J.C. Dana award 1985, Hall of Fame 1994); mem. ALA (councillor 1988-92, planning com. 1989-91, Dewey medal 1987), Am. Soc. Info. Sci. (pres. 1973-74, W. Davis award 1977, award of merit 1981, named Pioneer, 1987), Assn. Libr. and Info. Sci. Edn. (chmn. govtl. rels. com. 1980-88), Am. Fedn. Info. Processing Socs. (dir. 1972-78), Federation Internationale de Documentation (Netherlands, bd. dir. 1976-78, treas. 1978-82), Soc. for Scholarly Pub. (bd. dirs. 1981-82), Assn. Rsch. Libraries (com. on libr. edn, 1983-85), Coun. Libr. Resources (rsch. priorities task force 1984-88, Ind. Libr. Lifetime Achievement award 1990), Beta Phi Mu (Svc. award 1995). Address: 5950 N Fountains Ave #7102 Tucson AZ 85704-7863

WHITE, HORACE COUNCIL, business manager; b. Phila., Apr. 8, 1972; s. Horace Council Turner and Vera Mae White. AA, U. Md., Tokyo, 1996, BS, 1998; postgrad. in Distance Edn., U. Md., 1999—. USN RADAR specialist cert. Sr. counselor City of Phila., 1987-89; data entry specialist H&R Block, Phila., 1988-89; asst. mgr. Transit Automotive/Sunoco, Phila., 1989-90; RADAR specialist Dept. of Navy, Japan, 1990-94; bus. mgr. U.S. State Dept., Japan, 1995—. With USN, 1990-94. Mem. Am. C. of C. in Japan, Kanto Plain African Am. Heritage Club. Democrat. Roman Catholic. Avocations: reading, movies, basketball, martial arts, photography. Home: 523 Essex Ave Gloucester MA 01930-2004

WHITE, HOWARD D., information science educator; b. 1936; PhD in Librarianship, U. Calif., Berkeley, 1974. With Coll. Info. Sci. and Tech. Drexel U., Phila., 1974—, prof. libr. sci., disting. prof., 1998—2002, prof. emeritus, 2002—. Contbr. articles to profl. publs.; co-author (with Marcia Bates and Patrick Wilson): For Information Specialists: Interpretations of Reference and Bibliographic Work, 1992; author: Brief Tests of Collection Strength, 1995. Recipient Rsch. award, Am. Soc. Info. Sci. and Tech., 1993, Award of Merit, 2004, Derek John de Solla Price Meml. medal, Internat. Soc. Scientometrics and Informetrics, 2005. Office: Drexel U Coll Info Sci & Tech Rush Bldg 421 33rd and Market St Philadelphia PA 19104 Office Phone: 215-895-2484. Office Fax: 215-895-2494. E-mail: whitehd@drexel.edu.

WHITE, IAN, information technology executive; m. Ellen White; 3 children. Grad. in Elec. Engring., U. Nottingham, Eng.; grad. in Electronic Engring., Derby Tech. Coll., Eng. With Rolls Royce; rsch. & devel. engr. telecom. co.; with Computervision, Sun Microsystems, Inc., 1989—, dir. UK customer svc. ops. & customer edn., dir. UK Installed Base Sales & Sales Support, v.p. Europe, Mid. East and Africa, v.p. Internat. Ams., v.p. Sun Svcs. Ams., sr. v.p. global customer svcs. Office: Sun Microsystems Inc 4150 Network Cir Santa Clara CA 95054 Office Phone: 650-960-1300. *

WHITE, JACK (JOHN ANTHONY GILLIS), musician, producer; b. Detroit, July 9, 1975; m. Meg White, Sept. 21, 1996 (div. Mar. 24, 2000); m. Karen Elson, June 1, 2005; children: Scarlett Teresa, Henry Lee. Former drummer Goober and the Peas, The Go, The Upholsterers, Jack White and The Bricks; singer, guitarist The White Stripes, 1997—. Singer (with The White Stripes): (albums) The White Stripes, 1999, De Stijl, 2000, Party of Special Things to Do, 2000, White Blood Cells, 2001, Maximum, 2002, Elephant, 2003 (Grammy award for best alt. music album, 2003, Grammy award for best rock song, 2003), Get Behind Me Satan, 2005, Icky Thump, 2007; actor, composer (films) Cold Mountain, 2003; actor: (films) Coffee and Cigarettes, 2003; prodr.: (albums) Lack of Communication, 2001, Do Rabbits Wonder?, 2003; prodr., guitarist, singer (Loretta Lynn album) Van Lear Rose, 2004 (Grammy award for best country album, 2004). Office: Press Here Publicity 138 W 25th St New York NY 10001

WHITE, JAMES ALFRED, lawyer; b. Bay City, Mich., Jan. 5, 1939; s. Gerald J. and Clara E. (Barnes) White; m. Barbara J. White, Feb. 14, 1980. BA cum laude, Alma Coll., 1961; JD, U. Mich., 1964. Bar: Mich. 1964. Assoc. Foster, Swift, Collins & Coey, Lansing, Mich., 1964—69, ptnr., 1969—88, White, Schneider, Young & Chiodini PC, Okemos, Mich., 1988—. Counsel Mich. Edn. Assn., 1966—; mem. labor arbitrator labor panel Am. Arbitration Assn. Bd. dirs. Big Bros. and Big Sisters of Greater Lansing, Inc., 1972—80, Girl Scouts Capital Coun., 2007—. Mem.: ABA, Ingham County Bar Assn., Mich. Bar Assn., Met. Flying Club (pres.). Home: 2410 Emerald Lake Dr East Lansing MI 48823 Office Phone: 517-347-7208. Business E-Mail: jwhite@wsbyc.com.

WHITE, JAMES BOYD, law educator; b. Boston, July 28, 1938; s. Benjamin Vroom and Charlotte Green (Conover) W.; m. Mary Louise Fitch, Jan. 1, 1978; children: Emma Lillian, Henry Alfred; children by previous marriage: Catherine Conover, John Southworth. AB, Amherst Coll., 1960; AM, Harvard U., 1961, LLB, 1964. Assoc. Foley, Hoag & Eliot, Boston, 1964-67; asst. prof. law U. Colo., 1967-69, assoc. prof., 1969-73, prof., 1973-75; prof. law U. Chgo., 1975-83; Hart Wright prof. law and English U. Mich., Ann Arbor, 1984—. Vis. assoc. prof. Stanford U., 1972 Author: The Legal Imagination, 1973, (with Scarboro) Constitutional Criminal Procedure, 1976, When Words Lose Their Meaning, 1981, Heracles' Bow, 1985, Justice as Translation, 1990, "This Book of Starres", 1994, Acts of Hope, 1994, From Expectation to Experience, 1999, How Should We Talk About Religion?, 2006, The Edge of Meaning, 2001, Living Speech, 2006. Sinclair Kennedy Traveling fellow, 1964-65; Nat. Endowment for Humanities fellow, 1979-80, 92; Guggenheim fellow, 1993; vis. scholar Phi Beta Kappa, 1997-98. Mem. AAAS, Am. Law Inst. Office: U Mich Law Sch 1035 Legal Research 625 S State St Ann Arbor MI 48109-1215 Office Phone: 743-936-2989. Business E-Mail: jbwhite@umich.edu.

WHITE, JAMES PATRICK, law educator; b. Iowa City, Sept. 29, 1931; s. Raymond Patrick and Besse (Kanak) W.; m. Anna R. Seim, July 2, 1964. BA, U. Iowa, 1953, JD, 1956; LLM, George Washington U., 1959; LLD (hon.), U. Pacific, 1984, John Marshall Law Sch., 1989, Weidner U., 1989, Campbell U., 1993; Jur D (hon.), Whittier Coll., 1992; LLD (hon.), Campbell U., 1993, Southwestern U., 1995, Quinnipiac U., 1995, Calif. Western Law Sch., 1997; LLD, Roger Williams U., 1999, New England Sch. of Law, 2001, Seattle U., 2001, We. New Eng. Coll., 2002; LHD (hon.), Barry U., 2005. Bar: Iowa 1956, D.C. 1959, U.S. Supreme Ct. 1959. Teaching fellow George Washington U. Law Sch., 1958-59; asst. prof. U. N.D. Law Sch., Grand Forks, 1959-62, asso. prof., acting dean, 1962-63, prof., asst. dean, 1963-67; dir. agrl. law rsch. program, prof. law Ind. U. Law Sch., Indpls., 1967—2002, also dir. urban legal studies program, 1971-74, prof. emeritus, 2002—; dean acad. devel. and planning, spl. asst. to chancellor Ind. U., Indpls., 1974-83. Mem. for N.D., Commn. on Uniform State Laws, 1961-66; cons. legal edn. ABA, 1974-2001, cons. emeritus, 2001—. Contbr. papers to tech. lit. Trustee Butler U., John Marshall Law Sch., Atlanta, Indpls. Mus. Art. Capt. JAGC, 1st lt. USAF, 1956—58. Recipient Thomas More award, St. Mary's U., 1965, Sagamore of the Wabash award, State of Ind.; Carnegie postdoctoral fellow, U. Mich. Ctr. for Study Higher Edn., 1964—65. Fellow: Soc. for Advanced Legal Studies (Eng.) (chair Fulbright com. awards in law 1989—92), Indpls. Bar Found. (disting. fellow), Am. Bar Found. (life); mem.: ABA (Kutak award medal 2001), Indpls. Bar Assn., Am. Law Inst. (life), Iowa Bar Assn., Ind. Bar Assn., Woodstock Club (Indpls.), Order of Coif. Roman Catholic. Home: 7707 N Meridian St Indianapolis IN 46260-3651 Office: Ind U 530 W New York St Indianapolis IN 46202-3225 Home Phone: 317-253-4066; Office Phone: 317-278-9690. Business E-Mail: jwhite@iupui.edu.

WHITE, JAMES RICHARD, lawyer; b. McKinney, Tex., Jan. 22, 1948; s. James Ray and Maxine (Brown) White; children: Nicole Olivia, Mandi Leigh, James Derek. BBA, So. Meth. U., 1969, MBA, 1970, JD, 1973, LLM, 1977. Bar: Tex. 1973, US Tax Ct. 1975, US Supreme Ct. 1989, US Ct. Appeals (5th cir.) 1989); cert. Comml. Real Estate Law Tex. Bd. Legal Specialization. Assoc. Elliot, Meer, Vetter, Denton & Bates, Dallas, 1973-74, Atwell, Cain & Davenport, Dallas, 1974-75; atty. Sabine Corp., Dallas, 1975-77; assoc. Brice & Barron, Dallas, 1977-79; ptnr. Millard & Olson, Dallas, 1979-82, Johnson & Swanson, Dallas, 1982-83, Winstead, Sechrest & Minick P.C., Dallas, 1983—, hiring ptnr., 1987-2001, exec. com., 2000-01. Mem. staff Southwestern Law Jour., Dallas, 1971-73; mem. So. Meth. U. Moot Ct. Bd., Order Barristers, Dallas, 1972-73; prof. North Lake Coll., Dallas, 1985; bd. dirs. Tex. Assn. Young Lawyers, Austin, 1980-82; sec. bd. dirs. Dallas Assn. Young Lawyers, 1976-80. Contbr. articles to profl. jours. Chmn. bd. dir. Tex. Lawyers Credit Union, Austin, 1980-82; pres. North Tex. Premier Soccer Assn., Dallas, 1979-81; v.p. Lake Highlands Soccer Assn., 1995-96, pres., 1996—; North Tex. State Soccer Assn., Volunteer of the Year, 2003; mem. regional mobility task force Real Estate Coun., City of Dallas, 1991-92, mem. downtown revitalization com., 1995-97; mem. Dallas Indsl. Devel. Bd., 1992-93, Dallas Higher Edn. Authority Bd., 1994-96; spkr.'s bur. and accreditation divsn. World Cup USA '94; mem. exec. coun. Recreational Interleague Assn. Dallas, 2002—;

pres. Storm Soccer Club, 2003-05; founding mem. Premiere Acad. League, 2004—; mem. outstanding sr. man selection com. dad's club So. Meth. U., 2007. Named a Texas Super Lawyer, 2003—; named Vol. of the Yr., North Tex. State Soccer Assn., 2003; named to Best Lawyers in Am., 2003—. Mem. ABA (mem. title ins. and survey, mortgage loan origination and structure com., mortgage financing and opinion, non-traditional comml. real estate fin. coms.), Tex. Bar Assn. (cert. 1973, mem. mortgage loan opinion com.), Tex. Coll. Real Estate Attys., Coll. State Bar Tex., Storm Soccer Club (pres. 2003-05). Methodist. Avocations: soccer, golf, skiing, racquetball. Home: 8003 Hundley Ct Dallas TX 75231-4728 Office: 901 Main St Ste 5500 Dallas TX 75202 Office Phone: 214-745-5126. Business E-Mail: jrwhite@winstead.com.

WHITE, JAN TUTTLE, information technology executive; b. Bridgeport, Conn., Nov. 5, 1943; d. Michael and Jennie Agnes (Leko) Soltis; m. David Dustin Tuttle, Oct. 7, 1972 (div. Apr. 1988); m. Benjamin Winthrop White, May 6, 1989. BS in Math., Bates Coll., Lewiston, Maine, 1965; MBA in Mktg. and Ops. Rsch., Columbia U., NYC, 1967. Cert. comml. real estate broker, Mass. With corp. staff IBM Corp., Armonk, NY, 1966, sys. engr. NYC, 1967—69, mktg. rep. to Harvard U., corp. staff, sys. engr., Harvard U. account mgr. Cambridge, Mass., 1969—72; asst. to dir. info. processing svcs. MIT, Cambridge, 1972—75; mng. dir. Tuttle Family Trust, Cambridge, 1975—81; VAX product mktg. mgr., then sr. product mgr. Digital Equipment Corp., Marlborough, Mass., 1981—86, multiprocessing programs mgr., 1986, artificial intelligence market devel. mgr., 1986—87, program mgr., Robots and Beyond: The Age of Intelligent Machines, collaboration with US Sci. Mus. Exhbn., 1986—87, fin. sys. group market devel. mgr., 1987—90, market devel. mgr. banking/investments group, 1990; program mgr. MIT Internat. Fin. Svc. Rsch. Ctr., Hudson; med. sys. mgr. Beth Israel Deaconess Med. Ctr., Boston, 1990—. Spkr. in field; sponsor Harvard Host Family Program; marshall US Sr. Golf Tournament, 1986-87; scorer US Open Tennis Tournament, 1968. Appeared in Disney channel documentary film Silver Men, 1987, Boston Mus. Sci. introductory film for opening of Mugar Omni Theatre, 1987; contbr. (books) An Olde Concord Christmas, 1980, Boston Symphony Orch. Cookbook, 1983, Boston Cooks, 1991; contbr. articles to profl. jours., chpts. to books. Chmn. Boston Concord Coun. Boston Symphony Orch., assoc. assn. vols., supporter Tanglewood scholarship programs, capt. Centennial Major Gifts campaign; active guild bd. Opera Co. Boston, co-chmn. auditions com.; patron Fledrmaus Ball; life mem., chmn. Emerson Hosp. Aux.; co-founder, Emerson Hosp. Golf Tournament, Concord, Mass., 1978; trustee, mem. mgmt. rev. com. Women's Ednl. and Indsl. Union; edn. com. chmn. Ladies Assn.; life mem., bd. Concord Antiquarian Mus., nominating com. edn. long-range planning com., chmn. edn. com., costumes and textiles com., exhibit designer An Old Concorde Christmas, established family meml. fund; bd. adv. Sci. Mus. Exhibit Collaborative, Garden Club Concord, Boston Mus. Sci.; life mem. Mus. Fine Arts, Boston, patron Friends Music; life mem. Nat. Trust for Scotland, Friends Loch Lomond, Friends Beth Israel Med. Ctr, Harvard Neighbors; mem. fin. com. Trinitarian Congl. Ch.; trustee, life mem. Women's Ednl. and Indsl. Union; bd. dirs., life mem. Hannah Duston Garrison House Assn.; life mem. Friends New Eng. Deaconess Hosp., Boston, Friends Beth Israel Deaconess Med. Ctr., Boston; mem. Isabella Stewart Gardner Mus.; invitational alumni Hurricane Island (Maine) Outward Bound Sch., Thompson Island Bound (Boston Harbour) Sch., mem. adv. bd., 1987-90, underwriter Silver Anniversary video 1987; water safety instr., sr. life saving instr., First Aid instr. Red Cross Nat. Aquatic Sch., 1964. Recipient numerous industry achievement awards, 10th Anniversary Cert. Appreciation VAX Sys. Spl. Interest Group U.S. chpt. Digital Equipment Corp. User Soc.; nominated White House fellow, 1971; honoree Nat. Women's Day, 1987 Mem. Am. Assn. Artificial Intelligence, Inst. for Mgmt. Scis., Ops. Rsch. Soc. Am., MIT Faculty Club, Harwich Hist. Assn. (life), Stratford Hist. Soc. (life), Cambridge Hist. Soc., Bates Coll. Class 1965 (sec., treas., reunion chmn., com. chmn. 25th reunion major gifts; charter mem. Ptnrs. of Pres.), Columbia U. Grad. Sch. Bus. Alumni Assn. (nat. chmn. membership, bd. dirs.), Mass. Hort. Soc., Conn. Soc. Genealogists, Nat. Assn. Underwater Instrs. (cert. scuba diver), Columbia Bus. Club Boston (founding dir., bd. dirs.), Columbia U. Club New Eng. (founding dir.), Columbia Club NY, Concord Country Club, Harvard Club (Boston, NYC), Harvard U. Art Mus., Harvard Faculty Club, Stone Horse Yacht Club, Women's City Club (com. membership), Royal Scottish Automobile Club, North Atlantic Yacht Racing Union, So. Mass. Yacht Racing Assn., Arnold Arboretum Harvard U., Housatonic Boat Club Republican. Avocations: the arts, sports, horticulture, environmental preservation, genealogy.

WHITE, JEFFREY D., federal agency administrator; BS in applied engring. and physics, Cornell U., 1979; MD, Howard U., 1984. Resident in internal medicine Washington Hosp. Ctr., Washington, fellow in oncology, fellow in hematology; joined Metabolism Br. Nat. Cancer Inst., 1990, dir. Clin. Trials and Clin. Care Program, Metabolism Br.; oncology cons. to NIH Nat. Ctr. for Complementary and Alternative Medicine, 1995—98; dir. Office of Cancer Complementary and Alternative Medicine Nat. Cancer Inst., 1998—. Office: Office Cancer Complementary and Alternative Medicine Nat Cancer Inst 6116 Executive Blvd Ste 609 MSC 8339 Bethesda MD 20892

WHITE, JEFFREY GEORGE, healthcare consultant; b. Lawrence, Mass., Apr. 16, 1944; s. Alfred James and Ruth Virginia (Maylum) W.; children: Jennifer L., Tracy E. AB in Econs., Bowdoin Coll., 1966; MBA, U. N.H., 1985. Asst. pers. dir., then asst. adminstr. Maine Med. Ctr., Portland, 1967-71; asst. adminstr. Regional Meml. Hosp., Brunswick, Maine, 1971, adminstr., 1971-74; assoc. dir. Elizabeth Ann Seton Hosp., Waterville, 1974-75; assoc. adminstr. Mid-Maine Med. Ctr., 1975-79, v.p. ops., 1979-83; asst. dir. Wentworth-Douglass Hosp., Dover, NH, 1983-85; exec. v.p. Frisbie Meml. Hosp., Rochester, NH, 1985-89, pres., 1989-92; sr. cons., prin. Helms & Co., Inc., Concord, NH, 1992—. Interim pres., CEO New London (NH) Hosp., 2002-03; preceptor dept. health mgmt. and policy U. NH, Durham, 1985-92, adj. asst. prof., 1991-93, asst. prof., 1993-97, dean's leadership coun. sch. health human svcs., 1998—; bd. dirs. Riverwoods at Exeter, 2000-2003. Vol. pub. TV sta.; bd. dirs. Greater Seacoast United Way, 1991-94, chmn. comty. campaign, 1993; pres. Greater Rochester C. of C., 1990. Fellow Am. Coll. Healthcare Execs. (past regent for N.H.); mem. N.H. Hosp. Assn. (trustee emeritus). Republican. Avocations: walking, skiing, reading, travel. Home: Rivermoor Landing 21 125 Main St Newmarket NH 03857 Office: Helms & Co Inc 1 Pillsbury St Concord NH 03301-3556 Home Phone: 603-868-6294; Office Phone: 603-225-6633. E-mail: jwhite@helmsco.com.

WHITE, JEFFREY MUNROE, lawyer; b. Lewiston, Maine, Jan. 16, 1948; BS in Applied Physics magna cum laude, Tufts U., Medford, Mass., 1970; JD, Boston Coll., 1975. Bar: Maine 1975, US Ct. Appeals (1st cir.) 1979. Semiconductor engr. Fairchild Semiconductor, 1970—72; ptnr., head litig. group and antitrust and trade regulation group Pierce Atwood, Portland, Maine, 1975—. Lectr., contbr. to profl. publs. on antitrust, litig., and intellectual property topics. Chmn. Cape Elizabeth Sch. Study Com., 1990-91, Corporator Hospice of So. Maine, 2004-; mem. IS Eng. adv. coun. U. Maine, 2006-. Mem. ABA (antitrust, intellectual property and litig. sects.), N.E. Bar Assn. (dir. 1982-85), Maine Bar Found., Maine State Bar Assn. (co-chmn. com. CLE 1981-83), Maine Trial Lawyers Assn., Cumberland County Bar Assn. Office: Pierce Atwood Monument Sq Portland ME 04101 Office Phone: 207-791-1100. Business E-Mail: jwhite@pierceatwood.com.

WHITE, JENNIFER ELIZABETH BELK, corporate training specialist; b. Houston, July 29, 1967; d. Joe Harvey and Joan Pardue Belk; m. Thomas Roger White, Apr. 28, 2007. BA, U. Tex., Austin, 1988; student, Am. Acad. Dramatic Arts, 1992; postgrad., U. Houston, Clear Lake, 1990—91, Am. Acad. Dramatic Arts, 1992, U. So. Calif., LA, 2001—. Admissions counselor U. Tex., Austin, 1988—90; coll. field rep. Prentice Hall, Houston, 1990—92; trainer Kaplan Test Prep and Admissions, NYC, 1993—97, master tchr. LA, 1997—2001, dir. of tng., 2001—04; mgr. internal communication and instrnl. design Pub. Storage, Glendale, Calif., 2004—07, corp. tng. mgr., 2007—. Vol. L.A. Chamber Orch., 2004—; mem. Angel City Chorale, LA, 2004—, mng. dir., 2005—; deacon St. Philip Presbyn. Ch., Houston, 1991—93. Named Tchr. of Yr., Kaplan Test Prep and Admissions, 1994; recipient People's Choice award, Pub. Storage, 2005, 2006. Mem.: ASTD, Internat. Soc. Performance Improvement, Mensa, Golden Key, Alpha Lambda Delta, Phi Eta Sigma. Office: Public Storage Inc 701 Western Avenue Glendale CA 91201 Home Phone: 818-244-8752; Office Phone: 818-244-8080 ext. 1577. Home Fax: 818-230-2540. Personal E-mail: jenbelk@yahoo.com.

WHITE, JESSE, state official; b. Alton, Ill., June 23, 1934; BS, Ala. State Coll., 1957. Profl. baseball player Chgo. Cubs; tchr., adminstr. Chgo. Pub. Sch. Sys.; mem. Ill. Gen. Assembly, Springfield, 1972—74, 1976—92, chmn. com. human svcs., mem. edn. com., mem. select com. children and aging; recorder of deeds Cook County, Chgo., 1992—98; sec. state State of Ill., Springfield, 1999—. Founder Jesse White Tumbling Team, 1959; Dem. committeeman 27th Ward, Chgo., 1996—; libr. State of Ill. State Libr.; archivist State of Ill. Served in Ill. Nat. Guard, paratrooper 101st Airborne Divsn. US Army. Recipient Archbishop Richard Chenevix Trench award, 1999; Inductee Southwestern Athletic Conf. Hall of Fame, 1995, Chgo. Pub. League Basketball Coaches Assn. Hall of Fame, 1995, Ala. State U. Sports Hall of Fame, 1999; named one of 100 Most Influential Black Americans, Ebony mag., 2006. Democrat. Office: Sec of State 213 State Capitol Springfield IL 62706 Office Phone: 217-782-2201. Office Fax: 217-785-0358. E-mail: jessewhite@ilsos.net.

WHITE, JILL CAROLYN, lawyer; b. Santa Barbara, Calif., Mar. 20, 1934; d. Douglas Cameron and Gladys Louise (Ashley) W.; m. Walter Otto Weyrauch, Mar. 17, 1973. BA, Occidental Coll., LA, 1955; JD, U. Calif., Berkeley, 1972. Bar: Fla. 1974, Calif. 1975, U.S. Supreme Ct. Staff mem. U.S. Dept. State, Am. Embassy, Rio de Janeiro, 1956-58; with psychol. rsch. units Inst. Human Devel., Inst. Personality Assessment and Rsch., U. Calif., Berkeley, 1961-68; adj. prof. criminal justice program U. Fla., Gainesville, Fla., 1976-78; pvt. practice immigration and nationality law, Gainesville, 1976—2002. Contbr. articles to profl. jours. Mem.: Fla. Bar (immigration and nationality law cert. com. 1994—99, chmn. cert. com. 1997—98, cert. in immigration and nationality law 1995—), Bar Assn. 8th Jud. Cir. Fla., Am. Immigration Lawyers Assn. (bd. dirs. Ctrl. Fla. chpt. 1985—94, 1995—96, 1997—2000, chmn. Ctrl. Fla. chpt. 1988—89, co-chmn. so. regional liaison com. 1990—92, nat. bd. dirs. 1988—89), Altrusa. Democrat. Home Phone: 352-375-6205; Office Phone: 352-380-9122. Personal E-mail: jwhite49@earthlink.net.

WHITE, JO LYNN, lawyer; Atty. environ. law, Buffalo and Kansas City, Mo.; environ. counsel Allied Waste Industries, Inc., Scottsdale, Ariz., 1997—99, asst. corp. sec., 1999—, dep. gen. counsel, 2003—, v.p., 2005—, acting gen. counsel. Office: Allied Waste Industries Inc Ste 100 15880 N Greenway-Hayden Loop Scottsdale AZ 85260 Office Phone: 480-627-2700. Office Fax: 480-627-2703. *

WHITE, JOHN, JR., lawyer; b. St. Louis, Oct. 20, 1943; s. John Aaron and Helen Inez (Stewart) W.; children: Dorian, Cameron, Lauren, John Aaron III. B.A., U. Nev., 1965; J.D., George Washington U., 1968. Bar: D.C. 1969, Nev. 1969, U.S. Dist. Ct. (D.C. dist.) 1969, U.S. Supreme Ct. 1979. Atty. City Atty.'s Office, Reno, 1969-74; sole practice Reno, 1974-78; ptnr. White Law Chartered, Reno, 1978—; adj. prof. in bankruptcy Old Coll. Nev. Sch. of Law, 1986-87; lectr. computers and law Nev. State Bar Conv., 1986. Co-author: Nevada Civil Practice Manual, 1986-88. Mem. Gov.'s Commn. on Status of People, 1975-78; founder Family Ch. Jesus. Served with USMCR, 1961-68. Mem. ABA, Nev. State Bar Assn., D.C. Bar Assn., Am. Bankruptcy Inst., Washoe County Bar Assn., Reno Host Lions (past pres.). Pioneer in litigating early cases against Dow Corning and Dow Chemical involving silicone breast implants. Republican. Office: White Law Chartered 335 W 1st St Reno NV 89503-5344 Office Fax: 775-322-1228. E-mail: john@whitelawchartered.com.

WHITE, JOHN ARNOLD, physics professor, research scientist; b. Chgo., Jan. 30, 1933; s. Maxwell Richard and Dorothy Edith (Arnold) W.; m. Rebecca Anne Cotten, June 20, 1964; children: Lauren, Thomas, Julia. BA, Oberlin Coll., 1954; MS, Yale U., 1955, PhD, 1959. Instr. physics Yale U., 1958-59, Harvard U., 1959-62; research assoc. Yale U., 1962-63; research physicist Nat. Bur. Standards, Washington, 1963-64; research assoc. U. Md., College Park, 1965-66; assoc. prof. Am. U., Washington, 1966-68, prof., 1968-97, prof. emeritus, 1997—. Cons. Nat. Bur. Standards, 1965-72; mem. tech. staff Bell Telephone Labs., summers 1954, 60-62; vis. scientist MIT, fall 1972, Nat. Bur. Standards, Washington, summer 1981; vis. prof. Inst. for Phys. Sci. and Tech., U. Md., College Park, fall 1993. Author sci. papers on atomic structure and fluorescence, magnetism, lasers, speed of light, thermodynamic fluctuations, critical point phenomena, extended renormalization group theory of fluids. Recipient (with Zoltan Bay) Boyden Premium Franklin Inst., Phila., 1980; honor scholar, 1950-54; Noyes Clark fellow, 1954-57; NSF fellow, 1957-58; grantee NSF, 1966, 67, 69, 71; grantee Office Naval Research, 1973, 74; Am. Soc. Engring. Edn. faculty fellow Naval Research Lab., Washington, summer 1985; Dept. Energy Office Basic Energy Scis. grantee, 1986, 88, 90. Fellow Am. Phys. Soc.; mem. AAUP, Washington Philos. Soc., Phi Beta Kappa, Sigma Xi. Home: 7107 Fairfax Rd Bethesda MD 20814-1234 Office: Am U Dept Physics Washington DC 20016-8058 E-mail: jwhite@american.edu.

WHITE, JOHN AUSTIN, JR., academic administrator, engineering educator; b. Portland, Ark., Dec. 5, 1939; s. John Austin and Ella Mae (McDermott) W.; m. Mary Elizabeth Quarles, Apr. 13, 1963; children: Kimberly Elizabeth White Brakmann, John Austin III. BS in Indsl. Engring., U. Ark., 1962; MS in Indsl. Engring., Va. Poly. Inst., 1966; PhD, Ohio State U., 1970; PhD (hon.), Cath. U. of Leuven, Belgium, 1985, George Washington U., 1991. Registered profl. engr., Va. Indsl. engr. Tenn. Eastman Co., Kingsport, 1961-63, Ethyl Corp., Baton Rouge, 1965; tchg. assoc. Ohio State U., Columbus, 1966-70; instr. Va. Poly. Inst. and State U., Blacksburg, 1963-66, asst. prof., 1970-72, assoc. prof., 1972-75, Ga. Inst. Tech., Atlanta, 1975-77, prof., 1977-84, Regents' prof., 1984-97, Gwaltney prof., 1988-97, dean engring., 1991-97; disting. prof. indsl. engring., chancellor U. Ark., Fayetteville, 1997—. Asst. dir. engring. NSF, 1988-90, acting dep. dir., 1990-91; founder, chmn. SysteCon Inc., Duluth, Ga., 1977-84; exec. cons. Coopers & Lybrand, N.Y.C., 1984-93; mem. mfg. studies bd. NRC, Washington, 1986-88; bd. dirs. Russell Corp., 1992-2006, Eastman Chem. Co., 1994-2004, Motorola Corp., 1995-, Logility Inc., 1997-, J.B. Hunt Transport Svcs., Inc., 1998-, Nat. Sci. Bd., 1995-2006, Malcolm Baldrige Nat Quality Award Found., 1999-; pres, Southeastern U. Rsch. Assn., 2003-04, chair coun. presidents 2004; pres. Nat. Consortium for Grad. Degrees for Minorities in Engring. and Sci., Inc., 1993-95; bd. dirs. Nat. Collegiate Athletic Assn.; mem. exec. com. NCAA, 2002—05; apptd. U.S. del. to the Internat. Steering Com. of the Intelligent Mfg. System, 1995-97; dir. Ark. Sci. and Tech. Authority, 2002-, chair, 2004-05; dir. Ark. Biosciences Inst. 2002-; pres. S.E. Conf., 2002—04, pres. NW Ark. Regional Airport Authority, 2005-; co-chair NW Ark. Coun., 2005-. Co-author: Facility Layout and Location: An Analytical Approach, 1974 (Book of Yr. award Inst. Indsl. Engrs. 1974), 2d edit., 1991, Analysis of Queueing Systems, 1975, Principles of Engineering Economic Analysis, 4th edit., 1998, Capital Investment Decision Analysis for Management and Engineering, 1980, 3d edit., 2005, Facilities Planning, 1984 (Book of Yr. award Inst. Indsl. Engrs. 1984), 2d edit., 1996; editor: Production Handbook, 1987; co-editor: Progress in Materials Handling and Logistics, Vol. 1, 1989; also numerous articles to profl. jours., chpts. to books and handbooks in field, conf. procs. Recipient Outstanding Tchr. award Ga. Inst. Tech., 1982, Disting. Alumnus award Ohio State U. Coll. Engring., 1984, Disting. Indsl. Engring. alumnus award Va. Polytech. Inst. and State U., 1993, Reed-Apple award Material Handling Edn. Found., 1985, Disting. Svc. award NSF, 1991, Rodney D. Chipp Meml. award Soc. Women Engrs., 1994, Disting. Alumnus award U. Ark. Alumni Assn., 2005, Humanitarian of Yr. award NW Ark. chpt. Nat. Coalition for Cmty. and Justice, 2005. Fellow Am. Inst. Indsl. Engrs. (pres. 1983-84, facilities planning and design award 1980, outstanding indsl. engr. award region III 1974, region IV 1984, Albert G. Holzman disting. educator award 1988, outstanding pub. award 1988, David F. Baker disting. rsch. award 1990, Frank and Lillian Gilbreth award 1994), Am. Assn. Engring. Socs. (bd. govs., chmn. 1986, Kenneth Andrew Roe award 1989); mem. Nat. Acad. Engring., Ark. Acad. Indsl. Engring. (John L. Imhoff Global Excellence award 2006), Am. Soc. Engring. Edn. (Donald E. Marlowe award 1994), Internat. Material Mgmt. Soc. (material mgr. of yr. 1989), Soc. Mfg. Engrs. (mfg. educator award 1990), Nat. Soc. Profl. Engrs. Inst. for Ops. Rsch. and the Mgmt. Scis. (hon.), Golden Key, Sigma Xi (Regent's medallion of Merit 2005), Alpha Pi Mu, Omicron Delta Kappa, Phi Kappa Phi, Tau Beta Pi, Omega Rho. Baptist. Avocations: reading, golf, writing. Office: Chancellor U Ark Office of the Chancellor 425 Administration Bldg Fayetteville AR 72701 Office Phone: 501-575-4140. E-mail: jawhite@uark.edu.

WHITE, JOHN DAVID, composer, musician; b. Rochester, Minn., Nov. 28, 1931; s. Leslie David and Millie (Solum) W.; m. Marjorie Manuel, Dec. 27, 1952; children: Jeffrey Alan, Michele Kay, David Eliot. BA magna cum laude, U. Minn., 1953; MA, U. Rochester, 1954, PhD, 1960, performance cert., 1960. Mem. faculty Kent (Ohio) State U., 1956-58, 60-63, 65-73, prof. music, assoc. dean Grad. Sch., 1967-73; asst. prof. U. Mich., 1963-65; dean Sch. Music, Ithaca (N.Y.) Coll., 1973-74; vis. prof. U. Wis., 1975-78; chmn. music dept. Whitman Coll., 1978-80; prof. U. Fla., 1980-97, prof. emeritus, 1997—; prof. U. Innsbruck, 1994; dist. chair U. Vienna, 2003—04. Prin. cellist Eastman Philharmonia, 1959, Akron Symphony Orch., 1969-73; cellist Fla. Baroque Ensemble, 1980-97, Fla. Arts Trio, 1986-93; dir. Fla. Musica Nova, 1991-97; author: (with A. Cohen) Anthology of Music for Analysis, 1965, Understanding and Enjoying Music, 1968 (pub. in Japanese 1978), Music in Western Culture, 1972, The Analysis of Music, 1976, 2d edit., 1984, Guidelines for College Teaching of Music Theory, 1981, 2d edit., 2002, Comprehensive Musical Analysis, 1994, Theories of Musical Texture in Western History, 1995, New Music of the Nordic Countries, 2002; editor: Music and Man; editl. bd. Jour. for Musicological Research, Jour. Music Theory Pedagogy; contbr. articles to profl. jours.; Composer: Symphony No. 2, 1960, Blake Songs, 1961; Divertimento for Flute, Violin and Viola, 1961; opera The Legend of Sleepy Hollow, 1962; Three Choruses From Goethe's Faust, 1965, Three Joyce Songs, 1966, Ode to Darkness, 1967, Cantos of the Year, 1969; (for clarinet and piano) Variations, 1971, Whitman Music, 1970, Three Madrigals, 1971, Russian Songs for Voices and Winds, 1972, Prayer (Solzhenytsin), 1973, String Quartet 1, 1975, Variations, 1976, Suite, 2001; Ode on the Morning of Christ's Nativity (Donne), 1977, Music for Oriana, 1978, Pied Beauty, 1980; (for cello and piano) Sonata, 1981, Zodiac, 1981, Music for violin and piano, 1982, The Soft Voice, 1983, Concerto for Flute and Wind Ensemble, 1983, Dialogues, 1984, Sonata, 2001, Symphony for Wind Band (3rd Symphony), 1985, Concerto da Camera, 1985, Symphony for a Saint (4th Symphony), 1986, Music for Cello and Percussion, 1988, Songs of the Shulamite, 1989, Mirrors, 1990, But God's Own Descent (5th Symphony), 1991, Music of the Open Road, 1993, Daylight and Moonlight, 1993, O Sing to the Lord a New Song, 1993, Illusions for Three, 1994, Tryptich, 1994, Ars Poetica, 1995, Colors of Earth and Sky (6th Symphony), 1995, Summer Storm Madrigals, 1996, Time and the Water, 1996, O Sing to the Lord a New Song, 1997, Maria Laudata, 1998, God's Own Descent, 1998, The Song of Ruth, 1999, Symbolic Interaction for Orchestra, 1999; Suite for for Harpsichord, 1999, The Heavens are Telling, 1999, Flower Songs, 2000, Concerto, 2000, Sonata da Camera for Piano, 2001, Music for 2 Cellos, 2002, Pindar Hymns for Choir and Orch., 2003, Olympiad for Chorus, Brass, Percussion and Piano, 2004, The Canonical Hours for Chorus, 2005, Music for Victims of our Earth, 2005, Echoes and Airs for Soprano, Viola and Piano, Mass for Chorus, 2006, Alone and not Alone, 2006, The Divine Image, 2007; recs. on Advent, Mark, Capstone, Cygnus and Opus One Labels. With AUS, 1954-56. Recipient Benjamin award, 1960, award Nat. Fedn. Music Clubs, 1962, internat. composition award U. Wis.-Oriana Trio, 1979, composition award Am. Choral Dirs. Assn., 1984; grantee NEA; Fulbright rsch. fellow, 1995-96; Fulbright Disting. Lectr., 2003-04. Fellow Am. Scandinavian Found., 1997; mem. ASCAP (awards 1965—), Soc. Composers, Inc. (nat. coun. 1987-89, 93-96), Soc. Music Theory, Pi Kappa Lambda, Delta Omicron (nat. patron), Phi Mu Alpha, Phi Beta Delta. Home: 10599 N Osceola Dr Westminster CO 80031 Personal E-mail: jwhite48@earthlink.net.

WHITE, JOHN JOSEPH, III, lawyer; b. Darby, Pa., Nov. 23, 1948; s. John J. Jr. and Mary (Lafferty) W.; m. Catherine M Staley, Dec. 9, 1983. BS, U. Scranton, 1970; MPA, Marywood U., 1977; JD, Loyola U., New Orleans, 1983. Bar: Pa. 1983, U.S. Dist. Ct. (ea. dist.) Pa. 1983, N.J. 1984, U.S. Ct. Appeals (3d cir.) 1983, U.S. Dist. Ct. N.J. 1984, U.S. Tax Ct. 1984, D.C. 1985, U.S. Supreme Ct. 1987. Exec. dir. Scranton Theatre Libre, Inc., Pa., 1973—77; pub. Libre Press Inc., Scranton, 1977—83; pvt. practice Phila., 1983—. Founder, publ. Metro Mag., 1977—83; pres. eMercury, Inc., Lansdowne, Pa., 1987—99; N.Am. agt. Palacky U. Med. Sch., Olomouc, Czech Republic, 1995—2001. Founder, Scranton Pub. Theatre, 1976; exec. dir. Scranton Theatre Libre, Inc., 1973. Capt. USAF, 1970—73, lt. col. Res., 1973—99, col. ANG, 1999—2000, ret., 2000. Mem.: ABA, N.G. Assn., Phila. Bar Assn., Nat. Acad. Elder Law Attys., Mil. Order of Fgn. Wars, Air Force Assn. (chpt. pres. 1975—), Phi Delta Phi Internat. Legal Frat. Democrat. Roman Catholic. Avocations: jogging, art collecting. Office Phone: 215-732-2000. Personal E-mail: lawfirmusa@aol.com.

WHITE, JOHN PATRICK, lawyer; b. Boston, Oct. 14, 1946; s. John Marion and Margaret Patricia (Gannon) W.; m. Gemma Mary Flattly, Feb. 9, 1980; 1 son, John Myles. BS in Chem. Engring., Columbia U., 1968, MA in Biochemistry, 1971, MPh in Molecular Biology, 1975; JD, Fordham U., 1977. Bar: NY 1978, US dist. ct. (ea. and so. dists.) NY 1978, US Ct. Customs and Patent Appeals 1979, US Ct. Appeals (Fed. cir.) 1982, US Supreme Ct. 2006. Legis. dir. Cmty. Coun. Greater N.Y., 1971-77; assoc. Cooper, Dunham, Clark, Griffin & Moran, NYC, 1977-81, ptnr., 1981-88, Cooper & Dunham, LLP, NYC, 1988—. Owner Shallow Brook Farm, Stillwater, N.J.; breeder Reg Angus Cattle, Ringneck Pheasants and Carriage Horses; dir. OSI Pharm., Inc., BioTech. Gen. Corp.; instr. Practicing Law Inst. Contbr. articles to sci. and legal jours. Democratic dist. leader, 1975-81; vice chmn. Dem. Com. N.Y. County, 1977-81; jud. del. 1st jud. dept., 1975, 76, 77, 79; adminstr. screening panel 2d Mcpl. Ct. Dist.; pub. mem. Columbia U. Recombinant DNA Biosafety Com. Columbia U. faculty fellow, 1969-71; NIH grantee, 1969-71. Mem. ABA, Am. Chem. Soc., Am. Intellectual Property Law Assn., NY Intellectual Property Law Assn., Assn. Bar City NY, Fed. Bar Coun. (com. patents), Club: Columbia of NYC, Four In Hand Club, Newton (NJ) Country Club, NY Coaching Club. Office: Cooper & Dunham LLP Ste 2200 1185 Avenue Of The Americas New York NY 10036-2615 Office Phone: 212-278-0421. Business E-Mail: jwhite@cooperdunham.com.

WHITE, JOHN VINCENT, surgeon, consultant; b. Chgo., May 7, 1952; BS, Northwestern U., 1974; MD, Columbia U., 1978. Diplomate Am. Bd. Surgery. Instr. surgery Columbia U., NYC, 1982-83; asst. prof. surgery Temple U., Phila., 1984-88, assoc. prof. surgery, 1988-94, prof. surgery, 1994-99; chmn. dept. surgery Luth. Gen. Hosp., Park Ridge, Ill., 1999—. Adj. sr. fellow Sch. Health Econs. U. Pa., Phila., 1994—; tech. cons. Boston Scientific Corp., Natick, Mass., 1995—; surg. cons. Dept. of Health N.Y. State, 1993; surg. tech. cons. Congl. Office of Tech. Assessment, Washington, 1995; laser tech. cons. Office of Naval Rsch., Washington, 1993-97. Editor: Hemodilution in Patient Care, 1989, Alternatives to Open Vascular Surgery, 1995, Surgical Clinics of North America, 1998; founding editor: Jour. Laparoendoscopic Surgery, 1990. Recipient Samuel D. Gross award Phila. Acad. Surgery, 1992. Mem. Am. Soc. Laser Medicine and Surgery, Soc. Univ. Surgeons (mem. found. bd. dirs. 1994-98), Del. Valley Vascular Soc. (pres. 1995—), Soc. Vascular Surgery (mem. com. outcomes analysis 1994—), Alpha Omega Alpha. Office: Lutheran Gen Hosp 1775 Dempster St Park Ridge IL 60068-1173 Office Phone: 847-723-7200. Office Fax: 847-696-3394. Business E-Mail: john.white-md@advocatehealth.com.

WHITE, JOHN W., federal agency administrator, lawyer; b. Washington, Dec. 2, 1947; BS cum laude, U. Va., 1970; JD magna cum laude, NYU, 1973. Bar: NY 1974. Law clk. to Hon. John J. Gibbons US Ct. Appeals, (3rd cir.); assoc. Cravath Swaine & Moore LLP, NYC, 1975—80, ptnr., corp. fin., governance, 1980—2006; dir. divsn. corp. fin. SEC, Washington, 2006—. Mem. NYSE Legal Adv. Com.; vice chmn. Securities Regulation Inst.; mem. advisory group Pub. Co. Acctg. Oversight Bd., 2006. Mng. editor NYU Law Rev. Office: SEC 100 F St NE Washington DC 20549

WHITE, JOHN WESLEY, JR., retired academic administrator; b. Nashville, Oct. 20, 1933; s. John W. and Ernestine (Engle) W.; m. Martha Ellen Bragg, June 24, 1956; children: Marcus Wesley, Michelle Suzanne. Student, Martin Jr. Coll., 1952-54; BA, Vanderbilt U., 1956, BD, 1959; MA, George Peabody Coll., 1966, PhD, 1968; LHD, U. Nebr., 1983; LLD, Kwansai Gakuin U., Japan, 1991. Dean admissions, dir. student affairs Martin Coll., 1960-65; asst. to acad. v.p. George Peabody Coll., 1965-67; assoc. dean for humanities Oklahoma City U., 1968-70, dean Coll. Arts and Scis., 1970-77, assoc. prof. English, 1968-73, prof., 1973-77; pres. Nebr. Wesleyan U., 1977-97, chancellor, 1997-98, pres. emeritus, 1998—. Cons., spkr. in field; chmn. Nebr. Ednl. Temecom. Commn., 1996-97. Past pres. U. Senate, United Meth. Ch.; bd. dirs. Cooper Found. Eli Lilly Sr. scholar Vanderbilt U., 1959. Mem. Nat. Assn. Ind. Colls. and Univs. (bd. dirs. 1989-93, 95-97), Lincoln C. of C. (bd. dirs. 1990-93), Rotary (pres. West Oklahoma City 1976), Kappa Delta Pi, Phi Kappa Phi, Alpha Mu Gamma, Blue Key. *Two principles have been paramount in my life: One, related to the attitude toward myself, is that we can help to shape life, not simply endure it. We are "creative" creatures, not just "surviving" creatures. The second principle, related to the attitude toward others, is that communication is essential to coexistence; and only as we make a real effort to hear what is meant, rather than simply what is said or written, are we able to communicate effectively.*

WHITE, JOSEPH CHARLES, manufacturing and retailing company executive; b. Toronto, Aug. 14, 1922; s. Joseph Cleveland and Edith Parker (Johnson) W.; m. G. Evelyn Vipond, July 15, 1944; children— Ronald, Richard, JoAnne. Chartered acct., Queens U., Kingston, Ont.; B.Commerce, U. Toronto. Vice-pres., dir. Agnew-Surpass, Inc., Brantford, Ont., Can., 1964-78; v.p., dir. Genesco Can., Inc., Cambridge, Ont., Can., 1978-82, exec. v.p., dir., 1982-87, pres., gen. mgr. retail op., 1986-87. Dir., v.p. Genesco Group Inc.; dir. Genesco Fin. Ltd.; pres. Brantford Art Gallery, 1994-95, Brantford Probus Club, 1995-96. Chmn. Ross MacDonald Found., Brantford, Ont., 1983-86; pres. YMCA, Brantford, 1968-69; chmn. Brant County Post-Secondary Edn. Corp., Brantford, 1973-76. Served with Royal Can. Air Force, 1943-45 Mem. Ont. Inst. Chartered Accts., Can. Council Distbn. (pres. 1972-73), Brant County C. of C. (treas. 1966-68) Mem. United Ch. of Can. Avocations: skiing, tennis. Office: Genesco Can Inc 401 Fountain St Cambridge ON Canada N3H 4V5 Home: 40 Museum Drive Unit 420 Orillia ON L3V 7T9 Canada

WHITE, JOY MIEKO, retired communications executive; b. Yokohama, Japan, May 1, 1951; came to U.S., 1951; d. Frank Deforest and Wanda Mieko Mellen; m. George William White, June 5, 1948; 1 child, Karen. BA in Comm., Calif. State U., Fullerton, 1974, student, 1977, Orange Coast CC, Costa Mesa, Calif., 1981, Golden West CC, Westminster, Calif., 1990. Cert. secondary tchr., Calif.; cert. tchr. Coast C.C.s Dist. Secondary tchr. Anaheim Union H.S. Dist., Calif., 1977—80; tech. writer Pertec Computer Corp., Irvine, Calif., 1980—81; supr. large sys. disvn. Burroughs, Mission Viejo, Calif., 1981—83; mgr. Lockheed divsn. CalComp, Anaheim, 1983—86; owner, pres. Communicator's Connection, Irvine, 1986—90; pres. Info Team, Inc., 1989—2004; ret., 2004. Adj. faculty, coord. tech. comm. program Golden West Coll., Huntington Beach, Calif., 1987-90; instr. U. Calif., Irvine, 1987-89, Calif. State U., Fullerton, 1988-91; sec. Santa Ana Dist. chpt. US SBA Assn. for Minority-Owned Bus., 1991-96; presenter in field. Active Performing Arts, Costa Mesa, 1986— Fellow Soc. Tech. Comm. (assoc., internat. assoc., sr., Orange County chpt. 1987, Mem. of Yr.); mem. NAFE, Soc. Profl. Journalists, Women in Comm. (pres. Orange County Profl. chpt. 1989-90), Nat. Assn. Women Bus. Owners, Rembrandts Wine Club (Yorba Linda), Girl Scouts U.S. (life, active 1994—, troop leader 1995-2003) Republican. Avocations: writing short stories, needlecrafts, camping, fishing. Home: 3531 Brentridge Dr Corona CA 92881-8445 Office Phone: 951-818-3891. Personal E-mail: joywhitemk@ca.rr.com. Business E-Mail: infoteam@ca.rr.com.

WHITE, JOYCE LOUISE, librarian; b. Phila., June 7, 1927; d. George William and Louisa (Adams) W. BA, U. Pa., 1949; MLS, Drexel U., 1963; MA in Religion, Episc. Sem. S.W., 1978. Head libr. Penniman Libr. Edn. U. Pa., Phila., 1960-76; archivist St. Francis Boys' Home, Salina, Kans., 1982-84; libr. Brown Mackie Coll., Salina, 1983-86; libr., dir. St. Thomas Theol. Sem., Denver, 1986-95; libr., dir. Archbishop Vehr Theol. Libr. Archdiocese of Denver, 1995-96. Author: Biographical and Historial Yarnall Library, 1979, Colorado Episcopal Clergy in the 19th Century: A Biographical Register, 2003; asst. editor: Women Religious History Sources, 1983; contbr. articles to profl. jours. and chpts. to books. Vol. libr. St. John's Cath., Denver, 1993—. Mem. Ch. and Synagogue Libr. Assn. (life, founding, pres. 1969-70, exec. sec. 1970-72, exec. bd. 1967-76, ann. conf. chair 1996). Avocations: gardening, cats, church libraries. Office: 1350 Washington St Denver CO 80203-2008

WHITE, JULIE, actress; b. San Diego, June 4, 1962; d. Edwin and Sue Jane W.; m. Carl Pandel, 1984 (div.); 1 child, Alexandra. Student, Fordham U., Tex. State U. Actress Carsey-Werner Co., CBS-MTM Studios, Studio City, Calif. TV appearances: Grace Under Fire, 1993-97, Six Feet Under, 2001-03; stage appearances: Dark of the Moon, 1984-85, The Geography of Yearning, 1985-86, Lucky Stiff, 1988, Early One Evening at the Rainbow Bar, Grille, 1989, Largo Desolato, 1990-91, Marathon '91, 1991, The Stick Wife, 1991, Spike Heels, 1992, Money and Friends, 1992-93, Absurd Person Singular, 1992-93, The Heidi Chronicles, 1995, Over Texas, The Family of Mann, Just Say No, Dinner With Friends, 1999, Barbra's Wedding, Bad Dates, Fiction, Marvin's Room, The Little Dog Laughed, 2005 (OBIE award Village Voice 2006, Tony award best performance by a leading actress in a play, 2007); film appearances: Take Down, 1978, Flypaper, 1997, Say It Isn't So, 2001, Slap Her...She's French, 2002, War of the Worlds, 2005, The Astronaut Farmer, 2007. *

WHITE, JUNE MILLER, mathematics professor, educational consultant; b. East Bernstadt, Ky., June 13, 1938; d. James Fulton and Ida Mae (Hansel) Miller; m. Richard Allen White, Aug. 27, 1960; children: Jennifer Lynn, Richard Allen Jr. BS with high honors, Denison U., 1960; MA, U. Rochester, 1969; PhD, Bryn Mawr Coll., 1980. Engring. asst. AT&T, Kansas City, Mo., 1960-61; math. tchr. William Chrisman H.S., Independence Pub. Schs., Independence, Mo., 1961-62, Brighton (N.Y.) H.S., 1962-69, Conestoga H.S., Tredyffrin-Easttown Pub. Schs., Berwyn, Pa., 1970-72; chair math. dept. Hill Top Prep. Sch., Rosemont, Pa., 1972-76, curriculum coord., 1976-81; instr. math. St. Petersburg Jr. Coll., Clearwater, Fla., 1982-84, dir. math. program, 1984—2002, prof. math. edn., 2002—. Presenter in field. Author: A Collection of Mathematics Applications for College Students, 1989; editor SPECTRUM, 1983-95; contbr. articles to profl. jours. Elder Northwood Presbyn. Ch., Clearwater, 1986-90; chmn. blood drive ARC, King of Prussia, Pa., 1973-74; chmn. citizens adv. com. Upper Merion Pub. Schs., King of Prussia, 1975-76. Mem. Am. Math. Assn. of Two Yr. Colls., Math. Assn. Am. (v.p. Fla. and Caribbean sect. 1988-91, sec. 1994-99, pres.-elect 1999, pres. 2000), Nat. Coun. Tchrs. Math., Fla. Assn. Cmty. Colls., Rsch. Coun. for Diagnostic and Prescriptive Math., Pinellas County Assn. for Children and Adults with Learning Disabilities (bd. dirs. 1987-88), Phi Beta Kappa. Avocations: camping, sailing, travel. Home: 4951 Bacopa Ln S Unit 103 Saint Petersburg FL 33715-2617 Business E-Mail: white.june@spcollege.edu.

WHITE, KAREN RUTH JONES, information systems executive; b. Ft. Meade, Md., Oct. 8, 1953; d. Frank L. Jones and Inge H. Lesser; m. M. Timothy Heath, Apr. 23, 1973 (div. Aug. 1976); m. Carl W. White, May 30, 1993 AS Electronic Data Processing, N.H. Tech. Inst., Concord, 1977; BS MIS high honors, Northeastern U., Boston, 1984, MS Info. Sys., 1997. Prof. Project Mgmt. Inst., 2001. Programmer Chubb Life Ins. Co., Concord, NH, 1977—79, Retailers Electronics Account Processing, Woburn, Mass., 1979—82; sr. programmer, analyst N.H. Ins. Group, Manchester, 1982—84; prin. sys. analyst Wang Labs., Inc., Lowell, Mass., 1984—89; project mgr. TASC, Inc., Reading, Mass., 1989—2000; sr. dir. consulting svcs. PM Solutions, Havertown, Pa., 2000—. Bd. dirs. Brandywne Common Assn., Derry, N.H., 1991-94; mem. St. Paul's Sch. Advanced Studies Program Alumni Assn., Concord With U.S. Army Res., 1974-84 Decorated Army Commendation medal, 1980 Mem.: NAFE, IEEE (program chair 5th reengring. forum 1996, exec. adv. bd. 1996—99, dep. conf. chair 6th reengring. forum 1998, computer soc., tech. com. in software engring.), Project Mgmt. Inst. (Mass. Bay chpt. program dir. 1992—93, project chair 1994—96, dir. seminars/symposium 1996—98, adv. group 1999—2000, ethics rev. com. 2000—02, awards rev. com. 2001—03, chair ethics rev. com. 2003—06, ethics stds. rev. com. 2004—06, chairperson ethics stds. implementation planning com. 2006, bd. dirs. Edn. Found.), Sigma Epsilon Rho. Home: 50 Merrill Rd Weare NH 03281-4708 Office: PM Solutions 50 Merrill Rd Weare NH 03281-4708 Business E-Mail: kwhite@pmsolutions.com.

WHITE, KATE, editor-in-chief; m. Brad Holbrooke; 2 children. BA, Union Coll. Editor Child mag., 1988—89; editor-in-chief Working Woman mag., NYC, 1989—91, McCall's mag., NYC, 1991—94, Redbook, NYC, 1994—98, Cosmopolitan mag., NYC, 1998—. Author: Why Good Girls Don't Get Ahead and Gutsy Girls Do, 1995, (novels) If Looks Could Kill, 2002, A Body to Die For, 2003, 'Til Death Do Us Part, 2004, Over Her Dead Body, 2005. Recipient Matrix award, Women in Comms., 2003. Office: Cosmopolitan Hearst Magazines 300 W 57th St New York NY 10019-3299 also: Sandra Dijkstra Lit Agy 1237 Camino Del Mar Del Mar CA 92014 Office Phone: 212-649-3561. Office Fax: 212-397-7581. *

WHITE, KATHERINE PATRICIA, lawyer; b. NYC, Feb. 1, 1948; d. Edward Christopher and Catherine Elizabeth (Walsh) W. BA in English, Molloy Coll., 1969; JD, St. John's U., 1971. Bar: N.Y. 1972, U.S. Dist. Ct. (ea. and so. dists.) N.Y., 1973, U.S. Supreme Ct. 1976. Atty. Western Electric Co., Inc., NYC, 1971-79; sr. atty. AT&T Corp., NYC, 1979-96, chief regulatory counsel-New Eng., 1996-97, law and govt. affairs v.p., gen. atty.-New Eng., 1997—2002. Adj. prof. law N.Y. Law Sch., N.Y.C., 1987-88, Fordham U. Sch. Law, 1988-91, 2002—; bd. dirs. First Security Benefit Life Ins. Co. N.Y. Vol. Sloan Kettering Inst., 1973, North Shore U. Hosp., 1975, various fed., state and local polit. campaigns; judge N.Y. State Bicentennial Writing Competition, N.Y.C., 1977-78; chmn. Com. to Elect Supreme Ct. Judge, N.Y.C., 1982; bd. dirs. The Flea Theatre Co., N.Y.C., 2000—. Mem. Am. Corp. Counsel Assn., N.Y. State Bar Assn. (corp. counsel sect.), Assn. Bar City N.Y. (adminstrv. law com. 1982-85, young lawyers com. 1976-79, judge nat. moot ct. competition 1979-91, 2002—), Cath. Lawyers Guild for Diocese of Rockville Centre (pres. 1980-81), St. John's U. Sch. Law Alumni Assn. (pres. L.I. chpt. 1986-88), Women's Nat. Rep. Club (bd. govs. 1988-91), Met. Club Avocations: racing sailboats, figure skating, golf, tennis. Home: 1035 5th Ave Apt 14D New York NY 10028-0135 Personal E-mail: kpwhite@nyc.rr.com.

WHITE, KATHLEEN ANN, elementary school educator; d. Fay H. and Anna Faye Harper; m. William D. White; 1 child, Amanda K. B, Glenville State Coll., Glenville, W.Va., 1979; M, W.Va. U., Morgantown, 2001. Tchr. elem. sch. Ritchie County Schs., Harrisville, W.Va., 1980—. Tchr., adv. bd. mem. Time For Kids/Time, Inc., NYC, 1998—2006; team mem., profl. devel. sch. W.Va. U., Parkersburg; exec. com. and team capt. Am. Cancer Soc.-Relay For Life, Harrisville, W.Va., 2004—06. Grantee, Edn. Alliance, 2002, 2004. Mem.: Harrisville Elem. PTO, Nat. Fedn. Tchrs., W.Va. Fedn. Tchrs., Delta Kappa Gamma. Avocations: travel, handweaving. Office: Harrisville Elementary School 1201 E Main St Harrisville WV 26362 Home Phone: 304-643-2220; Office Phone: 304-643-2220.

WHITE, KENDRED ALAN, lawyer; b. Madisonville, Tenn., Oct. 2, 1938; s. Leonard A. and Nora (Clyde) W.; m. Peggy Ann Cowling, Aug. 24, 1963; children: Jonathan C., Erik K., Lauren A. BS, U. Tenn., 1961, JD, 1964. Bar: Tenn. 1964, U.S. Dist. Ct. (ea. dist.) Tenn. 1966, U.S. Supreme Ct. 1971. Pvt. practice law, Madisonville, 1964—. Hearing com. Bd. of Profl. Responsibility, Tenn. Supreme Ct., 1982-85; bd. dirs. Vol. Fed. S&L, Madisonville. With USAF, 1958-64. Fellow Tenn. Bar Found.; mem. ABA, Tenn. Bar Assn., Phi Delta Phi (province pres. 1996-2004). Republican. Baptist. Avocation: travel.

WHITE, KERR LACHLAN, retired physician, foundation administrator; b. Winnipeg, Man., Can., Jan. 23, 1917; s. John Alexander and Ruth Cecelia (Preston) Stevenson; m. Isabel Anne Pennefather, Nov. 26, 1943; children: Susan Isabel, Margot Edith. BA with honors (Oliver Gold medal), McGill U., 1940, MD, CM, 1949; DM (hon.), U. Leuven, 1978; postgrad., London Sch. Hygiene and Tropical Medicine, 1960; DSc (hon.), McMaster U., 1983. Intern, resident in medicine Mary Hitchcock Meml. Hosp., Hanover, NH, 1949—52; Hosmer fellow McGill U. and Royal Victoria Hosp., Montreal, Que., Canada, 1952—53; asst. prof. medicine U. N.C. Sch. Medicine, Chapel Hill, 1953—57, assoc. prof. medicine and preventive medicine, 1957—62; Commonwealth advanced fellow Med. Rsch. Coun., Social Medicine Rsch. unit London Hosp., 1959—60; chmn., prof. epidemiology and community medicine U. Vt., Burlington, 1962—64; prof. Sch. Hygiene and Pub. Health Johns Hopkins U., Balt., 1965—76, chmn. dept. health care orgn., 1965—72; dir. Inst. Health Care Studies United Hosp. Fund N.Y., 1977—78; dep. dir. health scis. Rockefeller Found., NYC, 1978—97, ret., 1997. Chmn. U.S. Nat. Com. Vital and Health Stats., 1975—79; mem. health adv. panel Office of Tech. Assessment, U.S. Congress, 1975—82; cons. Nat. Ctr. Health Stats., 1967—83, WHO, 1967—. Editor: Manual for Examination of Patients, 1960, Medical Care Research, 1965, Health Care: An International Study, 1976, Epidemiology as a Fundamental Science, 1976, Task of Medicine, 1988, Healing the Schism, 1991; mem. editl. bd.: Med. Care, 1962—73, Inquiry, 1967—79, Internat. Jour. Epidemiology, 1971—81, Internat. Jour. Health Svcs., 1971—; contbr. chapters to books, articles to profl. jours. Trustee Case-Western Res. U., 1974—79; bd. dirs. Found. for Child Devel., 1969—80. With Can. Army, 1942—45. Recipient Pew Primary Care Achievement award, 1995, Baxter Found. award, 1996, Wood award for lifetime contbns. to primary care rsch., 1999. Fellow: APHA (gov. coun. 1964—68, 1971—73, coun. med. care sect. 1962—65), NAS (Inst. Medicine coun. 1974—76, chmn. membership com. 1975—77), ACP, AAAS, Am. Heart Assn., Am. Acad. Preventive Medicine, Royal Soc. Medicine (hon.); mem.: AMA, Kerr L. White Inst. Health Svcs. Rsch. (hon. dir. 1995—), Internat. Epidemiol. Assn. (hon.; life, pres. 1974—77, treas., exec. com. 1964—71, 1974—77, coun. 1971—81), Am. Hosp. Assn. (adv. coun. ednl. and rsch. trust 1965—68), Assn. Tchrs. Preventive Medicine (coun. 1963—68), Century Club (N.Y.C.), Cosmos Club (Washington), Alpha Omega Alpha, Sigma Xi. Office Phone: 434-972-2499. Business E-Mail: klw2j@virginia.edu.

WHITE, LARRY NASH, library and information scientist; BA, Univ. Fla., 1988; MLS, Fla. State Univ., 1995, PhD, 2002. Asst. prof. libr. sci. & instr. tech., MLS prog. dir. Ea. Carolina Univ., Greenville, NC. Contbr. chapters to books, articles to profl. jours. Named one of the Movers & Shakers, Libr. Jour., 2007. Mem.: ALA, Internat. Fedn. Libr. Assn., NC Libr. Assn., Pub. Libr. Assn. Office: Coll Edn 1804 Joyner Libr E Carolina Univ Greenville NC 27858 Office Phone: 252-353-2315. Office Fax: 252-328-4368. Business E-Mail: whitel@ecu.edu.

WHITE, LAWRENCE EDWARD, finance executive; b. Pitts., Mar. 5, 1950; s. Edward A. and Dolores C. (Cole) W.; children: Matthew E., Christopher L. BS in Chem. Engring., Carnegie-Mellon U., 1972, MS in Indsl. Adminstrn. with distinction, 1976. Product devel. engr. Eastman Kodak Co., Rochester, 1972-74; fin. analyst, supr. Ford Motor Co., Dearborn, Mich., 1976-82; mgr. fin. analysis Lone Star Techs., Dallas, 1982-85, mgr. corp. acctg., 1985-87; dir. fin. analysis and planning, corp. treas. TGI Friday's Inc., Dallas, 1987-89; v.p., treas. Metromedia Steakhouses, Inc., Dayton, Ohio, 1989—92; exec. v.p., CFO, El Chico Restaurants, Inc., Dallas, 1992—98, Boston Chicken, Inc., Golden, Colo., 1998—99; sr. v.p., CFO, CBRL Group, Inc., Lebanon, Tenn., 1999—. Active YMCA Youth Orgns., local ch. fin. com.; trustee BUMC Found. Mem. Assn. for Corp. Growth., Fin. Execs. Inst., Carnegie-Mellon Univ. Alumni Assn. Republican. Methodist. Home: 6 Sugarloaf Ln Brentwood TN 37027 Office: CBRL Group Inc PO Box 787 Lebanon TN 37088

WHITE, LAWRENCE J., economics professor; b. NYC, June 1, 1943; s. Martin H. and Florence M. (Meiman) W. AB, Harvard U., 1964, PhD, 1969; MS in Econs., London Sch. Econs., 1965. Econ. adviser Harvard Devel. Adv. Svc., Pakistan and Indonesia, 1969-70; asst. prof. econs. Princeton U., NJ, 1970-76; mem. faculty Stern Sch. Bus., NYU, 1976—, prof. econs., 1979—, chmn. dept., 1990-95, dep. chmn. dept., 2005—; sr. staff economist U.S. Coun. Econ. Advisers, 1978-79; dir. econ. policy office, antitrust div. Dept. Justice, Washington, 1982-83. Mem. Fed. Home Loan Bank Bd., 1986-89; cons. in field. Author: The Automobile Industry Since 1945, 1971, Industrial Concentration and Economic Power in Pakistan, 1974, Reforming Regulation: Processes and Problems, 1981, The Regulation: Processes and Problems, 1981, The Regulation of Air Pollutant Emissions from Motor Vehicles, 1982, The Public Library in the 1980s: The Problems of Choice, 1983, International Trade in Ocean Shipping Services: The U.S. and the World, 1988, The S&L Debacle: Public Policy Lessons for Bank and Thrift Regulation, 1991; editor or co-editor: The Deregulation of the Banking and Securities Industries, 1979, Mergers and Acquisitions: Current Problems in Perspective, 1982, Technology and the Regulation of Financial Markets: Securities, Futures and Banking, 1986, Private Antitrust Litigation: New Evidence, New Learning, 1988, The Antitrust Revolution, 1989, Bank Management and Regulation, 1992, Structural Change in Banking, 1993, The Antitrust Revolution: The Role of Economics, 2d edit., 1994, The Antitrust Revolution: Economics, Competition, and Policy, 3d edit., 1999, 4th edit., 2004; N.Am. editor Jour. Indsl. Econs., 1984-87, 90-95; co-editor Rev. of Indsl. Orgn., 2003-04, gen. editor, 2004-. NSF fellow, 1965—69. Mem. Am. Econ. Assn., Western Econ. Assn. Internat. (bd. mem., treas. 2006—), Phi Beta Kappa. Office: NYU Stern Sch Bus 44 W 4th St New York NY 10012-1126 Office Phone: 212-998-0880. Business E-Mail: lwhite@stern.nyu.edu.

WHITE, LILLIAS, actress; Appeared in Broadway plays Titanic, Cats, Once on This Island, Dreamgirls, Rock 'n' Roll: The First 5000 Years, Barnum, How to Succeed in Business..., The Life (Tony award 1997), Chicago, 2006; (off-Broadway) Waiting for Godot, The Princess and The Black-eyed Pea, Antigone Africanus, Romance in Hard Times (Obie award); (nat. and internat. tour) Ain't Misbehavin', The Wiz, Tintypes, Dreamgirls (Drama-Logue award), Purlie, 2005, South Pacific, 2005; (TV series) Sesame Street (Emmy award), Law & Order, NYPD Blue; (film) (voice) Hercules; concert appearance include Carnegie Hall, Lincoln Ctr., The White House. Office: Don Buchwald & Assocs 10 E 44th St Fl 2 New York NY 10017-3654

WHITE, LINDA DIANE, lawyer; b. NYC, Apr. 1, 1952; d. Bernard and Elaine (Simons) Schwartz; m. Thomas M. White, Aug. 16, 1975; 1 child, Alexandra Nicole. AB, U. Pa., Phila., 1973; JD, Northwestern U., Evanston, Ill., 1976. Bar: Ill. 1976. Assoc. Walsh, Case, Coale & Brown, Chgo., 1976-77, Greenberger & Kaufmann (merged into Katten, Muchin), Chgo., 1977-82, ptnr., 1982—85, Sonnenschein Nath & Rosenthal LLP, 1985—, chair fin. com., 2007—. Mem. law bd. Northwestern U. Sch. Law; mem. trustees coun. Penn Women; mem. Samuel Zell and Robert Lurie Real Estate Ctr., Wharton Sch., U. Pa. Fellow: Am. Bar. Found.; mem.: ABA (mem. real property fin. com., mem. comml. leasing com., mem. real property, probate and trust law sect. 1987—), Practicing Law Inst. (chmn. program negotiating comml. leases 1995—99, mem. real estate law adv. com.), Chgo. Bar Assn., Ill. Bar Assn. Office: Sonnenschein Nath & Rosenthal LLP 7800 Sears Tower 233 S Wacker Dr Ste 7800 Chicago IL 60606-6491 Home Phone: 312-943-5108; Office Phone: 312-876-8950. Business E-Mail: lwhite@sonnenschein.com.

WHITE, LONNIE JOE, retired history educator; b. Knox City, Tex., Feb. 12, 1931; s. John Alexander and Fannie Coates White; m. Nancy Louella Evans, June 23, 1951; children: John Evans, Brenda Jo White Holman. BA in History, W. Tex. State Coll., 1950; MA in History, Tex. Tech. Coll., 1955; PhD in History, U. Tex., Austin, 1961. Tchg. asst. history U. Tex., Austin, 1957—61; prof. history Memphis State Univ. (now U. Memphis), 1961—89; prof. emeritus U. Memphis, 1989—. Editl. adv. bd. Jour. of the West, Manhattan, Kans., 1963—88; assoc. edit. Military History of Texas and the Southwest, Austin, Tex., 1977—88. Author: Politics on the Southwestern Frontier: Arkansas Territory, 1819-1836, 1964, Panthers to Arrowheads: The 36th (Texas-Oklahoma) Division in World War I, 1984, The 90th Division in World War I: The Texas-Oklahoma Draft Division in the Great War, 1996; co-author: Hostiles and Horse Soldiers: Indian Battles and Campaigns In the West, 1972; co-editor: By Sea to San Francisco, 1849-50: The Journal of Dr. James Morison, 1977, 2nd edit., 2000; editor: Old Mobeetie, 1877-1885: Texas Panhandle News Items from the Dodge City Times, 1967, The Miles Expedition of 1874-1875: An Eyewitness Account of the Red River War, 1971, Chronicle of a Congressional Journey: The Doolittle Committee in the Southwest, 1865, 1975; contbr. more than 45 articles to profl. jour., book reviews over 97 pub. to profl. jour. Sgt. US Army, 1951—53. Grantee Rsch. Grant, Am. Philos. Soc., 1963. Mem.: So. Hist. Assn., Am. Hist. Assn. Republican. Baptist. Avocations: history, writing, travel, flying, genealogy.

WHITE, LORAY BETTY, TV talk show host, writer, television producer, director, vocalist, actress; b. Houston, Nov. 27, 1934; d. Harold White and Joyce Mae (Jenkins) Mills; m. Sammy Davis Jr., 1957 (div. 1958); 1 child,

Deborah R. DeHart. Student, UCLA extension, 1948-50, 90-91, Nichiren Shoshu Acad., 1988-92; AA in Bus., Sawyer Bus. Sch., 1970; study divsn. mem. dept. L.A., Calif. Study Group of Japan, 1970-86. Editor, entertainment writer L.A. Community New, 1970-81; exec. sec. guest rels. KNBC Prodns., Burbank, Calif., 1969-75; security specialist Xerox X10 Think Tank, LA, 1975-80; exec. asst. Ralph Powell & Assocs., LA, 1980-82; pres., owner, producer LBW & Assocs. Pub. Rels., LA, 1980—; owner, producer, writer, host TV prodn. co. Pub. Pub. Rels., LA, 1987—. Dir., producer L.B.W. Prodn. "Yesterday, Today, Tomorrow, L.A., 1981-2005; with CBS news dept./Bogey's Corner, The Vol. Brigade Corps, KCBS News, 1999. Actor: (films) Ten Commandments, 1956; singer: (films) The Jazz Review, 1960—65; headline singer Radio City Music Hall, N.Y.C., 1961, Can Can Cafe Concert in Mex., 1967—75, feature singer Hilton Hotel Mex., featured singer Hotel Maria Isabel, Acapulco, Disneyland, Calif.; singer: TV, 1981, (Broadway plays) Joy Ride; entertainment editor (newspaper) L.A. Community News, 1970—73, writer (column) Balance News, 1980—82; talk show host: Yesterday, Today, Tomorrow, 1981—2005; performer: (commercials including) Budweiser Beer, Old Gold Cigarettes, Salem Cigarettes, Cheer, Puffs Tissue, Coca Cola, Bufferin. Vol. ARC, 1995, L.B.W. & Assocs., Ltd. Ann. Prodn. of Mother and Daughter of the Yr. Tribute, 1999, United Peace and Cultural Exch. Dinner and Awards Show, 1999; exec. prodr. The Fifth L.B.W. and Assocs. Internat. Ann. Achievement Awards Show, 1999. The Sixth L.B.W. and Assocs. Internat. Ann. Achievement Awards Show, 2000; mem. Habitat for Humanity Internat, Nat. Com. Preserve Soc. Sec. and Medicare, 1998-99, Nat. Black Network Assn., AARP, So. Calif. Com. Sr. Citizens, re-elect Scott Wildmen Rep. campaign; judge J. Von Shay Nat. Face of Glamor, 2007, J.Von Shay Internat. Top 10 Models, 2007; mem. resident adv. bd. Burbank Housing Authority, HUD, 2000—, spkr., 2007; mem. Com. to Reelect Ted McConkey to Burbank City Coun., 1999; bd. dir. Chamblee Found. of Calif., 1998-; apptd. area coord. San Fernando Valley area, Myohoji Temple of Nichiren Shoshu, West Hollywood, Calif., 2004-. Recipient Cert. of Honor, ARC, 1984, Internat. Orgn. Soka Gakkai Internat. of Japan, Cmty. Vols. of Am. award, 1994, Mother and Daughter of Yr. Tribune, 2000-01, 6th Internat. Achievement award L.B.W. and Assoc.; named Performer of Yr. Cardella Demillo, 1976-77. Mem. ARC (planning, mktg., prodn. event com. 1995), UCLA Alumni Assn., Lupus Found. Am. (So. Calif. chpt.), Nat. Fedn. Blind, Myohoji-Hokkeko Internat. (USA chpt., 2002, attendee Tozon Internat., participant 750th Anniv. of Nichiren Shoshu Head Temple Taisekiji, Japan), Libr. of Congress Assoc. (charter). Buddhist. Avocations: singing, acting, tv writing and producing. Office Phone: 818-955-7728. Personal E-mail: lbwbootsietwo@peoplepc.com. *Accepting challenges in life is a choice. The choice is always yours. I've chosen never to give up-to always give my best. To constantly keep a growing and open mind. To remember to strengthen and reinforce the quality of my integrity no matter what. Be a winner to yourself.*

WHITE, LOWELL ELMOND, JR., retired medical educator; b. Tacoma, Wash., Jan. 16, 1928; s. Lowell E. and Hazel (Conley) W.; m. Margie Mae Lamb, June 21, 1947; children: Henry, Leanna White Maynes, Inger-Britt White Peterson. BS in Pharm., U. Wash., 1951, MD, 1953. Diplomate Am. Bd. Neurol. Surgery. Intern N.C. Meml. Hosp., Chapel Hill, 1953-54; resident neurosurgery, asst. to instr. U. Wash., 1954-60, asst. prof., 1960-64, assoc. prof., 1964-70; asso. dean U. Wash. Sch. Medicine, 1965-68; prof., chief divsn. neurol. surgery U. Fla., 1970-72; prof. U. South Ala., 1972-94, chmn. divsn. neurosci., 1972-77, ret., 1994. Adj. prof. Ala. Sch. Math. and Sci., 1993-94; chmn. nat. adv. com. Animal Resources NIH, 1966-70; cons. rsch. facilities and resources NIH; cons. divsn. hosp. and med. facilities USPHS; cons. grants adminstrn. policy U.S. Dept. HEW. Contbr. articles profl. jours. Bd. dirs. Mobile County Emergency Med. Svcs. Coun., 1973-82, Epilepsy chpt. Mobile, 1973-89, Mobile cpt. Myasthenia Gravis Found. Am., 1974-90, Mobile, Ala. Mental Health Assn., 1979-89, Spl. Edn. Action Com., 1985-97, pres. 1996; vol. Homeland Security Med. Res.Corps and ARC, 2005. With USN, 1946—47, with USNR, 1948—66. Guggenheim fellow, 1958-59 Mem. AMA, Am. Assn. Neurol. Surgeons, Am. Assn. Neuropathologists, Am. Acad. Neurol. Surgeons, Soc. for Neurosci., Assn. Am. Med. Colls., Am. Assn. Anatomists, Rsch. Soc. Neurol. Surgeons, Neurosurg. Soc. Ala. (pres. 1975), Am. Physicians Poetry Assn., Odyssey U. South Ala., Soc. for Arts in Healthcare, Snohomish County Med. Soc., Sigma Xi. Home: 11009 E Villa Monte Dr Mukilteo WA 98275-4881

WHITE, LUCETTE DARBY, painter, sculptor; b. Sprinfield, Ill., Nov. 22, 1931; d. William Edson and Maurine McVicar Darby; married, July 19, 1962; children: Elizabeth, Darby, Matthew, Esther. At, Newcomb Coll., New Orleans, La., 1950—51, U. Ark., Fayetteville, 1951—53, Sarasota Sch. Art, Fla., Inst. Contemporary Art, Boston, Ark. Arts Ctr., Little Rock; studied with, Helen Terry Marshall, Russellville, Ark., Edwin Brewer, Little Rock, James Valone, Ark. Arts Ctr., Hilton Leech, Sarasota, Fla., George Demetrios, Boston. Bd. trustees Ark. Arts Ctr., Little Rock, 1972—76; mem. acquisition com. Cape Ann Mus., Gloucester, Mass., 1988—90; bd. trustees Montserrat Sch. Art, Beverly, Mass., 2000. Prin. works include Black Light, Storm Fantasy, one-woman shows include U. Ark. Med. Sch., Little Rock, 1959, Lakewood Ho. Gallery, North Little Rock, 1966, ML Gallery Fine Arts, N.Y.C., 1976, La. Tech. U., Ruston, 1976, Judi Rotenberg Gallery, Boston, 1990, Endicott Coll., Beverly, Mass.1990, Turnbridge (Vt.) Pub. Libr., 1995, Mercury Gallery, Boston, 1996, 1998, Rockport, Mass, 2002, Hill Country Arts Found., Ingram, Tex., 1997, Granite Shore Gallery, Rockport, 2000, 2001, exhibitions include 62d Ann. Exhibit Allied Artists in Am., N.Y.C., 1975, 63d Ann. Exhibit Allied Artists in Am., 1976, Nat. Acad. Design 153d Ann. Exhbn., 1978, Judi Rotenberg Gallery, Boston, 1987, 1991, 1992, DeCordova & Dana Mus., Lincoln, Mass., 1988—90, Boston - "90, 1990, West End Gallery, Gloucester, Mass., 1997, Acacia Gallerey, 1998, 2000, Cape Ann Hist. Mus., 1999, Mercury Gallery, Boston, 2000, 2002, 2003, 2004, U.S. Artist Am. Fine Art Exhibit, Phila., 2002, Represented in permanent collections Bank Am., Little Rock, First Nat. Bank, Harrison, Ark., Nat. Old Line Ins. Co., Little Rock, St. Vincent Infirmary, William J. Clinton Presdl. Libr. Mem.: Nat. Acad. Design (assoc.), Allied Artists Am. (assoc.). Democrat. Avocations: swimming, hiking, outdoor painting. Home: 24 Bass Rocks Rd Gloucester MA 01930

WHITE, MARGIT TRISKA, financial advisor; b. Greenport, NY; d. Joseph A. and Esther M. (Olstad) Triska; m. Robert Lamar Cannon (div. 1971); children: Catherine Margit, Sandra Leigh, Robert Milchrist II. BA, Duke U. CFP. Adminstr. Washington Opportunities for Women, 1971-80; account exec. Merrill Lynch, Bethesda, Md., 1980-82; v.p. investments, fin. planner Prudential Securities, Washington, 1982-94, Morgan Stanley Dean Witter, Washington, 1994—. Mem. fin. adv. bd. Bus. Women Internat., Women of Washington. Mem. Internat. Assn. Fin. Planning, Inst. Cert. Fin. Planners, Women in Housing and Fin., Fin. Women's Assn., The Internat. Alliance, Zeta Tau Alpha.

WHITE, MARILYN DOMAS, information science educator; b. Franklin, La., Aug. 16, 1940; d. George Julian and Norma Domas; m. Roger Stuart White, Aug. 31, 1968; 1 child, Joshua Stuart. BA, Our Lady of the Lake Coll., San Antonio, 1962; MS, U. Wis., 1963; PhD, U. Ill., 1971. Dir. Commerce Libr. U. Wis., Madison, 1963-65; head Social Sci./Bus. Libr. So. Ill. U., Edwardsville, 1965-67; cons. So. Ill. U./U.S. AID Adv. Team, South Vietnam, 1967; asst. prof. SUNY, Buffalo, 1972-74; lectr., vis. asst. prof. U. Md., College Park, 1976-77, asst. prof. info sci., 1977-82, assoc. prof. info. sci., 1982—2006, prof. emerita, 2006—. Cons. USIA, Washington and abroad, 1977—83, Inst. for Def. Analyses, Bowie, Md., Supercomputing Rsch. Ctr., 1990—91, Am. Health Care Assn., Washington, 1990—92, Am. Coun. on Edn., 1995, U.S. Bur. of Census, 2003—04. Contbr. articles to profl. jours. including Libr. Quar., Libr. & Info. Sci. Rsch., Jour. Documentation, Jour. Am. Soc. for Info. Sci. James Lyman Whitney grantee ALA, 1983, Spl. Libr. Assn. rsch. grantee, 1993-94, Coun. Libr. Resources grantee, 1995-96, Info. Sci. Abstracts grantee, 1997-98. Mem. Am. Soc. for Info. Sci., Spl. Libr. Assn. Office: U Md Coll Info Studies Hornbake 4117E South Wing College Park MD 20742-0001 Office Phone: 301-405-2058. Business E-Mail: whitemd@umd.edu.

WHITE, MARTHA VETTER, allergist, immunologist; b. Richmond, Va., Oct. 23, 1951; d. Robert Joseph and Miriam Ernestine (Thomas) Vetter; m. Frederick Joseph Kozub, Oct. 11, 1975 (div. June 1982); m. John Irving White, Feb. 18, 1984; children: Josh, Christie. Student, Vanderbilt U., Nashville, 1969-71; BA, U. Richmond, 1973; MD, Va. Commonwealth U., Richmond, 1978. Cert. m. Bd. Pediatrics, Am. Bd. Allergy and Immunology. Pediatric intern and resident Va. Commonwealth U., Richmond, 1978-81; locum tenens Pub. Health, Richmond, Va., 1981-82; fellow Allergy and Immunology U. Southern Calif., LA, 1983-84, Georgetown U., 1983-84; sr. staff fellow Food and Drug Adminstrn., Bethesda, Md., 1984-85; NSRA fellow Nat. Inst. Allergy and Infectious Diseases, Bethesda, Md., 1985-88; sr. staff fellow, 1988-93; rsch. dir. Inst. for Asthma and Allergy, Wheaton, Md., 1993—. Cons. Sandoz Pharms., Marion Merrell Dow, Glaxo, Boehringer Ingleheim, Ciba-Geigy, Miles Genentech; rschr. Glaxo, Abbott, Pfizer, Marion Merrell Dow, Miles, Rhône Poulenc Rhoen, Sanofi, Adams, Astra, Merck, Neurbiol. Techs., 3M, Zeneca, Wyeth, Smith-Kline Beecham; bd. dirs. Allery & Asthma Network/Mothers of Asthmatics, 1987—; med. editor MA Report, 1986—; assoc. editor Allergy, Asthma and Immunology Guide, 1989-90. Contbr. numerous scientific papers, abstracts, chpts. and reviews in field. Recipient Norwich Eaton Rsch. award, 1987; Merrell Dow scholar in allergy, 1989; Geigy fellow, 1984. Mem.: Soc. Prin. Investigators (pres. 2002—03), Am. Thoracic Soc., Am. Coll. Allergy and Immunology, Adm. Acad. Allergy and Immunology, Am. Acad. Pediat., Am. Assn. Immunologists, Gamma Sigma Epsilon, Psi Chi, Beta Beta Beta. Office: Inst Asthma and Allergy 11002 Veirs Mill Rd # 414 Wheaton MD 20902 Home Phone: 301-962-1600; Office Phone: 301-962-5800.

WHITE, MARTIN CHRISTOPHER, academic administrator; b. Anderson, SC, Oct. 16, 1943; s. Jesse Martin and Christine Freida (Powell) W.; m. Linda Ann Fleming, July 31, 1965; children: Martin Lynn, Andrew Christopher. AB, Mercer U., 1965; MDiv, So. Bapt. Theol. Sem., 1968; PhD, Emory U., 1972. Prof. Elon Coll. (N.C.), 1972-76, dean acad. affairs, 1976-82, v.p. for acad. and student affairs, 1982-86; pres. Gardner-Webb U., Boiling Springs, NC, 1986—2002, Chowan U., Murfreesboro, NC, 2002—. Cons. So. Assn. Colls. and Schs., Atlanta, 1982—. Contbr. articles in field. Bd. dirs. United Way, Shelby, N.C., 1987. Woodrow Wilson fellow, 1971. Mem. Soc. Bibl. Lit., Nat. Assn. Bapt. Profs. of Religion, N.C. Ind. Coll. Assn., Alpha Chi, Omicron Delta Kappa. Lodges: Rotary (bd. dirs. Burlington, N.C. chpt. 1986). Democrat. Baptist. Avocations: golf, tennis, music, travel. Home: 100 Jones Dr Murfreesboro NC 27855-1800 Office: One University Dr Murfreesboro NC 27855 Home Phone: 252-398-5266; Office Phone: 252-398-6221. E-mail: whitec@chowan.edu.

WHITE, MARY JO, lawyer, former prosecutor; b. Kansas City, Mo., Dec. 27, 1947; d. Carl and Ruth King Monk; m. John W. White, Jan. 24, 1970. BA, Coll. William and Mary, 1970; MA in Psychology, New Sch. for Social Rsch., 1971; JD, Columbia U., 1974. Bar: NY 1975. Law clk. to Hon. Marvin E. Frankel US Dist. Ct. (So. dist.) NY, 1975—76; assoc. Debevoise & Plimpton LLP, 1976—78, litig. ptnr., 1983—90, ptnr., chair of litig., 2002—; asst. U.S. atty., chief appellate atty. criminal divsn. (So. dist.) NY US Dept. Justice, 1978—81; instr. in profl. responsibility and ethics Columbia Law Sch., 1981—; chief asst., acting U.S. Atty. (ea. dist.) NY US Dept. Justice, Bklyn., 1990—93, U.S. atty. (So. dist.) NY Manhattan, 1993—2002. Chair Atty. Gen. Janet Reno's Adv. Com. of U.S. Attys., 1993—94; dir. mem. Exec., Audit, and Policy Committees Nasdaq Stock Exchange, 2002—06. Named one of 100 Most Influential Lawyers, Nat. Law Jour., 2006, The 50 Most Influential Women Lawyers in Am., 2007; recipient "Magnificent 7" award, Bus. & Profl. Women USA, Law Enforcement Person of the Year award, Soc. of Profl. Investigators, Human Relations Award, Anti-Defamation League Lawyer's Div., 1996, Edward Weinfeld award for disting. contbn. to Admin. of Justice, N.Y. County Lawyers' Assn., 1998, Nat. Law Jour. 2002 list of Top Women Litigators, John P. O'Neill Pillar of Justice award, Respect for Law Alliance, 2002, Sandra Day O'Connor award for Distinction in Public Svc., 2002, dir. of FBI's Jefferson Cup award for contbn. to Rule of Law in the fight against terrorism and crime, 2002, George H. W. Bush award for excellence in counter-terrorism and the Agency Seal Medallion, CIA, 2002, Women of Power and Influence award, NOW. Fellow: Am. Coll. Trial Lawyers; mem.: ABA (Vice-Chair Comm. on Discretionary Justice, Adminstrv. Law Sect. 1980—81), N.Y. State Bar Assn., Assn. Bar City of N.Y., Phi Beta Kappa. Achievements include being first women to serve as US Attorney for Southern District of NY. Office: Debevoise & Plimpton LLP 919 Third Ave 46t Fl New York NY 10022 Business E-Mail: mjwhite@debevoise.com. *

WHITE, MEG(AN) (MARTHA), musician, vocalist; b. Grosse Pointe, Mich., Dec. 10, 1974; m. John Gillis, 1996 (div. 2000). Drummer, vocalist The White Stripes, 1997—; toured with Pavement and Sleater-Kinney, 1999, 2000. Performer: (albums) The White Stripes, 1999, De Stijl, 2000, White Blood Cells, 2001, Maximum, 2002, Elephant, 2003, Get Behind Me Satan, 2005, Icky Thump, 2007; actor: (films) Coffee and Cigarettes, 2003, Cold Mountain, 2003. Office: Monotone Inc 150 S Rodeo Dr # 200 Beverly Hills CA 90212-2408

WHITE, MELVIN, lawyer; BA, Morehouse Coll., 1984; JD, U. Va., 1987. Bar: DC, Ark. Judicial clk. to Hon. G. Thomas Eisele US Dist. Ct. (Ea. Dist. Ark.), chief law clk.; ptnr. Trial Dept. McDermott Will & Emery, Washington. Dir. and co-chmn. Washington Lawyers' Com. for Civil Rights and Urban Affairs. Eastern region fundraising chmn. Dr. Martin Luther King Nat. Meml. Found., 1998—2001; bd. dirs. Dance Inst. Washington. Served with USAF. Fellow: Am. Bar Found.; mem.: Edward Bennett Williams Inn of Ct., GAYLAW, Women's Bar Assn. DC, Nat. Bar Assn., ABA (mem. Commn. on Minorities in the Legal Profession), DC Bar (pres.-elect 2006—07, bd. gov.), Alpha Phi Alpha (pres. mu lambda chpt. 1996—98). Office: McDermott Will & Emery 60013th St NW Washington DC 20005-3096 Office Phone: 202-756-8031. Office Fax: 202-756-8087. E-mail: mwhite@mme.com.

WHITE, MICHAEL DENNIS, food products executive; b. Norwood, Mass., Jan. 11, 1952; s. Thomas Michael and Sally (Davenport) W.; m. Susan Lee Burns, June 30, 1972; children: Larissa, Paul, Jennifer. BA, Boston Coll., Newton, Mass., 1974; cert. of proficiency, Leningrad U., Russia, 1974; MA in Internat. Rels., Johns Hopkins U., 1976. CPA, Mass. Cons. Arthur Andersen & Co., Mgmt. Info. Cons. Div., Washington, Boston, 1976-80, mgr., 1980-81; cons. Bain & Co., Boston, 1981-84, mgr., 1984-86; v.p. planning, devel. Avon Products, NYC, 1986-87, v.p. retail devel., 1987-88; sr. v.p., gen. mgr. internat. Parfums Stern Inc. (subs. Avon Products), NYC, 1988-90; v.p. planning Frito-Lay Inc., Plano, Tex., 1990—91, sr. v.p. fin., CFO; exec. v.p., CFO PepsiCo, Intern. Snack div.; sr. v.p., CFO Pepsi-Cola Co., 1996—98, PepsiCo, Inc., 1998—2000; pres., CEO Frito-Lay, Europe/Africa/Middle East division, 2000—03; chmn., CEO PepsiCo International, 2003—; vice chmn. PepsiCo, Inc., 2006—. Active Tri-State United Way, N.Y.C.; v.p. Westport (Conn.)-Weston United Way, 1988-90. Office: PepsiCo Inc 700 Anderson Hill Rd Purchase NY 10577 *

WHITE, MILES D., pharmaceutical executive; b. Minneapolis, MN; BS in Mech. Engring., Stanford U., MBA. Mgmt. cons. McKinsey & Co.; with Abbott Labs., 1984—, v.p. diagnostic sys. and ops., 1993-94, sr. v.p. diagnostic ops., 1994-98, exec. v.p., dir., 1998-99, chmn., CEO, 1999—. Bd. trustee Field Mus., Chicago, Northwestern U., Joffrey Ballet, Chicago, Culver Ednl. Found.; dep. chmn. Fed. Reserve Bank of Chgo.; mem. Stanford Grad. Sch. of Bus. Adv. Coun., Stanford Adv. Coun. on Interdisciplinary Biosciences. Mem.: Econ. Club of Chgo., Executives' Club of Chgo. (chmn.). Office: Abbott Labs 100 Abbott Park Rd Abbott Park IL 60064-6400 *

WHITE, MORTON GABRIEL, philosopher, writer, historian, retired educator; b. NYC, Apr. 29, 1917; s. Robert and Esther (Levine) Weisberger; m. Lucia Perry, Aug. 29, 1940 (dec.); children: Nicholas Perry, Stephen Daniel; m. Helen Starobin, June 30, 1997. BS, CCNY, 1936; L.H.D., CUNY, 1975; A.M., Columbia U., 1938, PhD, 1942. Instr. philosophy Columbia U., 1942—46; instr. physics CCNY, 1942—43; asst. prof. philosophy U. Pa., 1946—48, Harvard U., 1948—50, assoc. prof., 1950—53, prof., 1953—70, chmn. dept., 1954—57, acting chmn. dept., 1967—69; prof. Inst. Advanced Study, 1970—87; prof. emeritus, 1987—; ret., 1987. Guggenheim research fellow, 1950-51; vis. prof. Tokyo U., 1952, 60, 66, U. Oslo, 1977-78; Neesima lectr. Doshisha U., Kyoto, 1985, CUNY, 1968-69, Rutgers U., 1987-88, 88-89 Keio U., Tokyo, 2002-03; mem. Inst. Advanced Study, 1953-54, 62-63, 67-68, 68-69. Author: The Origin of Dewey's Instrumentalism, 1943, Social Thought in America, 1949, The Age of Analysis, 1955, Toward Reunion in Philosophy, 1956, Religion, Politics, and the Higher Learning, 1959; (with Lucia White) The Intellectual Versus the City, 1962; Editor: (with Arthur M. Schlesinger, Jr.) Paths of American Thought, 1963, Foundations of Historical Knowledge, 1965, Science and Sentiment in America, 1972, Documents in the History of American Philosophy, 1972, Pragmatism and the American Mind, 1973, The Philosophy of the American Revolution, 1978, What Is and What Ought to Be Done, 1981; (with Lucia White) Journeys to the Japanese, 1952-79, 1986, Philosophy, The Federalist and the Constitution, 1987, The Question of Free Will, 1993, A Philosopher's Story, 1999, A Philosophy of Culture, 2002, From a Philosophical Point of View, 2005. Fellow Center Advanced Study Behavioral Scis., 1959-60; fellow Am. Council Learned Socs., 1962-63 Mem. Am. Acad. Arts and Scis., Am. Antiquarian Soc., Am. Philos. Soc. Office: Inst for Advanced Study Princeton NJ 08540

WHITE, NICHOLAS JOHN, musician, director, composer; b. London, Aug. 9, 1967; arrived in USA, 1990, permanent resident, 1991; s. Ronald John and Andre Bernice White; 1 child, Samuel Dempsey. MA, Cambridge U., 1986—89. Organ scholar Clare Coll., Cambridge, England, 1986—89; dir. of choral music McMurry U., Abilene, Tex., 1992—94; asst. organist and choirmaster Wash. Nat. Cathedral, Washington, 1994—98; music dir. Woodley Ensemble, Washington, 1997—2000; dir. of music St. Michael's Ch., NYC, 1998—2005; music dir. Tiffany Consort, NYC, 2003. Composer: (choral work) Magnificat, 1997, Full Freedom, 2002, Alleluia! Puer Natus Est Nobis, 2003, In Sure and Certain Hope, 2007; musician: (cd recording) The Amsterdam Bach, 1999, O Magnum Mysterium, 2004 (Grammy nominee, 2006). Bd. mem. St. Wilfrid's Club, NYC, 2001—04. Mem.: Am. Guild of Organists (advtg. dir. 1998—2005, exec. bd. mem. 1998—2003), Assn. of Anglican Musicians, Royal Coll. of Organists (assoc.), St. Wilfrid's Club. Anglican. Avocations: theater, travel, cooking. Home: 4701 Pine St D-12 Philadelphia PA 19143 Home Phone: 954-471-2442. Personal E-mail: nicholaswhite@earthlink.net.

WHITE, NICHOLAS L., law educator; b. 1925; AB, Ohio Wesleyan U., 1950; JD, U. Cin., 1956. Bar: Ohio 1956, Ind. 1971, Tenn. 1978. Assoc. Taft, Stettinius & Hollister, Cin., 1956-65, ptnr., 1965-70; asst. dean adminstrn. Ind. U., Bloomington, 1970-73, prof. law, 1970-77, assoc. dean, 1974-77; dean, prof. law Memphis State U., 1977-84; prof. law Humphreys Law Sch. U. Memphis, 1985—. Vis. prof. McGeorge Sch. of Law, Sacramento, Calif., 1984-85; cons. EPA Water Planning Divsn., 1974-77, Nat. Commn. Water Quality, 1975. Served with USMC, 1943-46. Mem. Phi Beta Kappa, Order of Coif, Omicron Delta Kappa. Office: Rm 227 Humphreys Law Sch U Memphis Memphis TN 38152 Office Phone: 901-678-4259. Business E-Mail: nlwhite@memphis.edu.

WHITE, NORVAL CRAWFORD, architect; b. NYC, June 12, 1926; s. William Crawford and Caroline Ruth (Taylor) W.; m. Joyce Leslie Lee, May 24, 1958 (div.); children: William Crawford, Thomas Taylor, Gordon Crawford, Alistair David; m. Camilla Cecilia Crowe, June 7, 1992. BS, Mass. Inst. Tech., 1949; student, Sch. Fine Arts, Fontainbleau, 1954; M.F.A., Princeton, 1955. Designer, assoc. Lathrop Douglass (Architect), 1955-59; prin. Norval C. White (Architect), NYC, 1959-62, 66-67; partner Rowan & White (Architects), NYC, 1962-66, Gruzen & Partners, NYC, 1967-70; prin. Norval C. White & Assos., NYC, 1970-74; ptnr. Levien, Deliso & White, 1974-80, Levien Deliso White Songer, 1980-86. Asst. prof. architecture Cooper Union, 1961-67; prof. architecture City Coll., CUNY, 1970-95, prof. emeritus, 1995—, chmn. dept. 1970-77. Author (with E. Willensky): AIA Guide to New York City, 1968, AIA Guide to New York City, 4th edit., 2000; author: The Architecture Book, 1976, New York: A Physical HIstory, 1987, The Guide to the Architecture of Paris, 1991; prin. works include Seiden House, Tenafly, N.J., 1960, Essex Terrace (housing), Bklyn., 1970, N.Y.C. Police Hdqrs., 1973, Brookhaven Parks (L.I.) Sanitary Landfill, 1971, Forsgate Indsl. Park, South Brunswick, N.J., 1978—86, Del Vista Condominiums, Miami, 1981, 61 Christopher Street, Greenwich Village, 1987, White House, Salisbury, Conn., 1998, Goodman House, Oyster Bay Cove, NY, 2003, White House, Mouchan, France, 2004. Trustee Bklyn. Inst. Arts and Scis., 1973-82, Bklyn. Pub. Libr., 1993-96; gov. Bklyn. Mus., 1973-82, adv. com., 1982-2006; mem. NYC Art Commn., 1975-86, sec., 1975-77, v.p., 1978-80. With USNR, 1944—46. Fellow AIA; mem. Soc. Archtl. Historians, N.Y. State Assn. Architects. Clubs: Century Assn. (N.Y.C.). Democrat. Home and Office: Village 32310 Roques France E-mail: norval.white@wanadoo.fr.

WHITE, PAMELA JANICE, lawyer; b. Elizabeth, NJ, July 13, 1952; d. Emmet Talmadge and June (Howlett) W. BA, Mary Washington Coll., 1974; JD, Washington and Lee U., 1977. Bar: Md. 1977, U.S. Supreme Ct. 1981. Assoc. Ober, Grimes & Shriver, Balt., 1977-84; prin. Ober, Kaler, Grimes & Shriver PC, Balt., 1985—2007; assoc. judge Cir. Ct. Balt. City, 2007—. Chair Employment Group, 1994—2007; mem. bd. law examiners, 1986-94, select com. on Gender Equality, 1989-2000, chair, 1997-99, judiciary pub. trust and confidence com., 2001-05, spl. com. on ethics 2002-04, jud. campaign conduct com., 2005—07; mem. fed. dist. ct. adv. group Civil Justice Reform Act, 1990; exec. com. Md. Inst. Continuing Profl. Edn. Lawyers, 2000-02, vol. faculty; adv. bd. Md. Mediation and Conflict Resolution Ctr., 2001-02; equal justice coun. Legal Aid Bur., 2000-06; mem. Md. Conf. Cir. Judges. Note and comment editor Washington and Lee Law Rev. 1976-77, Washington and Lee Law Council 1983-87, pres. 1991-92. Mem. Fed. Ct. Bicentennial Com., 1988-90; vol. Profl. Gov.'s Drug-Free Workplace Initiative, 1990-93; trustee Washington and Lee U., 1995-2004, Balt. Hist. Soc., 2002—07. Recipient Leadership in Law award Md. Daily Record, 2001, Exemplary Svc. award Legal Aid Bur. 2002, Outstanding Pro Bono Cert., 2004; named Disting. Alumna, Washington and Lee U., 1994, Mary Washington Coll., 2001, Cir. Excellence, 2007. Fellow Am. Bar Found., Md. Bar Found. (award for excellence 1996, bd. dirs. 2000-07); mem. ABA (chair tort and ins. practice employer/employee rels. com. 1999-2000, del. 2000-02), Am. Arbitration Assn. (arbitrator, mediator employment and comml., large complex case panels), Nat. Assn. Women Judges, Balt. Bar Found. (bd. dirs. 2003—), Fed. Bar Assn., Md. State Bar Assn. (coun. legal edn. sect. 1987-96, chmn. 1992-93, labor sect. coun. 1992-96, professionalism com. 1991—, chmn. 1994-97, bd. govs. 1993-95, 1998-2003, exec. com. 1994-95, 99-01, pres. 2001-02, immediate past pres. 2002-03, task force on professionalism chair 1996-97), D.C. Bar Assn., Balt. City Bar Assn. (exec. coun. 1995-96,

1997-98), Md. Legal Svcs. Corp. (bd. mem. 2006-), U. Mary Washington Alumni Assn. (bd. dirs. 2006—), Women's Bar Assn. Md. (treas. 1986-87, v.p. 1987-88, pres.-elect 1988-89, pres. 1989-90, bd. dirs. 1984-86, Rita C. Davidson award 2000), Pro Bono Resource Ctr. (exec. com. 2000-02, trustee 2002-03, Leaders of Equal Justice award 2002), Order of Coif, Phi Beta Kappa (hon. alumni), Omicron Delta Kappa (hon. alumni). Presbyterian. Avocation: baseball. Office: Circuit Ct Balt City 111 N Calvert St Baltimore MD 21202

WHITE, PAMELA JO, elementary school educator; b. Lynchburg, Va., June 20, 1943; d. Robert E. and Josephine T. (Patterson) W. BA in Art and Elem. Edn., Lynchburg Coll., 1968, MA in Teaching, 1969; postgrad., U. Va., Kent State U. Elem. tchr. Baltimore County Pub. Schs., Towson, Md., Bedford County Pub. Schs., Bedford, Va., Appomattox County Pub. Schs., Appomattox, Va.; ret., 1990. Recipient Outstanding Vol. award 4-H Club, Cystic Fibrosis Found. Mem. Am. Fedn. Tchrs., Nat. Trust for Hist. Preservation, Smithsonian Assocs., Kappa Delta Pi, Delta Kappa Gamma, Beta Sigma Phi.

WHITE, PATRICIA DENISE, dean, law educator; b. Syracuse, NY, July 8, 1949; d. Theodore C. and Kathleen (Cowles) Denise; m. Nicholas P. White, Feb. 20, 1971 (div. 1997); children: Olivia Lawrence, Alexander Cowles; m. James W. Nickel, Sept. 15, 2005. BA, U. Mich., 1971, MA, 1974, JD cum laude, 1974. Bar: D.C. 1975, Mich. 1988, Utah 1995. Assoc. Steptoe & Johnson, Washington, 1975-76; vis. asst. prof. Coll. of Law U. Toledo, 1976-77; assoc. Caplin & Drysdale, Washington, 1977-79; vis. assoc. prof. Law Ctr. Georgetown U., 1979—80, asst. prof., 1980—84, assoc. prof. Law Ctr., 1985-88; vis. prof. Law Sch. U. Mich., Ann Arbor, 1988-94; prof. U. Utah, Salt Lake City, 1994-98; counsel Parsons, Behle and Latimer, Salt Lake City, 1995—98; dean, prof. Sandra Day O'Connor Coll. Law Ariz. State U., 1999—. Counsel Bodman, Longley and Dahling, Detroit, Ann Arbor, 1990-95. Contbr. articles to profl. jours. Fellow: Am. Coll. Tax Coun.; mem.: Law Sch. Admission Coun. (fin. and legal affairs com. 2001—03, chair audit com. 2003—04, chair test devel. and rsch. com. 2005—07), Am. Law Deans Assn. (bd. dirs. 2001—), Gruter Inst. Law and Behavioral Rsch. (adv. bd. 2001—), Assn. Am. Law Schools, AAUP Tax Com., Assn. Am. Law Schools, Ariz. State Bar. Office: Ariz State Sandra Day O'Connor Coll Law McAllister & Orange Sts PO Box 877906 Tempe AZ 85287-7906 Home Phone: 480-838-6550; Office Phone: 480-965-6188. Office Fax: 480-965-6125. Business E-Mail: patricia.white@asu.edu.

WHITE, PATRICIA MARIE, psychology professor, researcher; d. Robert Amos and Margaret Agnes White; m. William Tate Troyer, Aug. 17, 1997; 1 child, Dylan Jon Troyer. BA, Stanford U., 1981, BS, 1986; PhD, UCLA, 2001. Asst. prof. U. Oreg., Eugene, 2001—. Recipient Michael Goldstein Disting. Dissertation award, UCLA, 2001. Mem.: APA, Assn. Behavioral and Cognitive Therapies, Soc. Psychophysiological Rsch. Achievements include research in ERP, P50 suppression. Office: U Oregon 1227 University of Oregon Eugene OR 97403-1227 Home Phone: 541-344-6214; Office Phone: 541-346-3942. Office Fax: 541-346-4911; Home Fax: 541-346-4911. Personal E-mail: troyer@uoregon.edu. Business E-Mail: pmwhite@uoregon.edu.

WHITE, PATRICK E., academic administrator; m. Chris White; children: Katie, Molly, Paddy. Grad. with honors, U. Chgo., 1971; MA in English and Am. Lit., PhD in English and Am. Lit., U. Iowa. Tchr. Westmar Coll., 1976—85; chair Dept. Language and Lit. Pfieffer Coll., 1985—88; assoc. dean faculty St. Mary's Coll., Notre Dame, Ind., 1988—2002, v.p., dean faculty, 2002—06, co-founder Ctr. for Academic Innovation; pres. Wabash Coll., Crawfordsville, Ind., 2006—. Office: Wabash Coll Office of Pres PO Box 352 Crawfordsville IN 47933 Office Phone: 765-361-6221. Office Fax: 765-361-6461. E-mail: president@wabash.edu.

WHITE, PETER C., lawyer; b. NYC, 1957; BA, Aldelphi U., 1980; JD, St. John's U., 1984. Bar: NY 1985, Fla., NJ 1987. Ptnr. sports fin. practice Nixon Peabody LLP, Garden City, NY. Named a Dealmaker of Yr., Am. Lawyer mag., 2007. Mem.: Fla. Bar Assn., Nat. Assn. Bond Lawyers and Govt. Fin. Officers Assn. Office: Nixon Peabody LLP 437 Madison Ave New York NY 10022 Office Phone: 212-940-3148. Office Fax: 866-947-2131. E-mail: pwhite@nixonpeabody.com. *

WHITE, RALPH PAUL, automotive executive, consultant; b. Watertown, Mass., Aug. 1, 1926; s. Irving William and Margaret Sarah (McGowan) W.; m. Shirley Irene Christie, Nov. 22, 1947; children: Karin Ann, Eric John. BS in Indsl. Engring., Columbia U., 1951; postgrad., Yale U., 1958-59. Instr. engring. mechanics U. Conn., Torrington, 1956-57; mgr. data processing. B.F. Goodrich Co., Shelton, Conn., 1956—61; ptnr., mgmt. cons. Bavier, Bulger & Goodyear, New Haven, 1961-66; v.p. Davidson Rubber Co., Dover, NH, 1966-69, pres., 1969-80; group v.p. parent co. Ex-Cell-O, Troy, Mich., 1980-83; pres. Troy (N.H.) Mills Inc., 1983-86, chief exec. officer, 1983-89, chmn., 1987-89. Bd. dirs. J.A. Wright Co., Keene, NH, J.D. Cahill Co., Hampton, NH, Exeter Trust Co., D.G. O'Brien Co., Seabrook, NH. Mem. N.H. Indsl. Devel. Authority, 1972-80, 85-88, Pease Devel. Authority, State of N.H., 1990-93, N.H. Bus. Fin. Authority, 1992-2004; exec. bd. Whittemore Sch. Bus., U. N.H., Durham, 1984-2002. Mem. Am. Inst. Indsl. Engrs., Soc. Automotive Engrs., N.H. Bus. and Industry Assn. (bd. dirs. 1970-80, pres. 1972-73, vice chmn. 1984-86), Abenaqui Country Club, Rye Beach Club. Republican. Roman Catholic. Avocations: skiing, golf. Home Phone: 603-964-5271. Personal E-mail: rpw99@aol.com.

WHITE, RAYMOND LESLIE, geneticist; b. Orlando, Fla., Oct. 23, 1943; s. Lawrence and Marjorie White; m. Joan Palmer Distin, June 1, 1968; children: Juliette, Jeremy. BS in Microbiology, U. Oreg., 1965; PhD in Microbiology, MIT, 1971; postdoctoral studies, Stanford. Rsch. assoc., instr. MIT, Cambridge, 1971-72; postdoctoral fellow Sch. Medicine Stanford (Calif.) U., 1972-75; asst. prof. Dept. Microbiology U. Mass. Sch. Medicine, Worcester, 1975-78, assoc. prof. Dept. Microbiology, 1978-80; investigator Howard Hughes Med. Inst. U. Utah Med. Ctr., 1980-94; assoc. prof. Dept. Cellular, Viral and Molecular Biology U. Utah Sch. Medicine, 1980-84, co-chmn. Dept. Human Genetics, 1984-94, prof. Dept. Oncological Scis., 1985—; prof. Dept. of Human Genetics U. Utah Sch. of Medicine, 1985—; chmn. Dept. Oncological Scis. U. Utah Sch. Medicine, 1994—, dir. Huntsman Cancer Inst., 1994—2000; chief sci. officer DNA Scis., Inc., Fremont, Calif., 2000—02; dir. Ernest Gallo Clinic & Rsch. Ctr. U. Calif. San Francisco (UCSF), Emeryville, Calif., 2002—, vice chair, prof. neurology, 2002—. Ad hoc mem. NIH Gen. Med. Sci. Inst. Coun., 1984, mem. NIH study sect., 1979-83. Consulting editor Jour. Clin. Investigation; subject area editor Genomics, 1987-90; contbr. articles to profl. jours. Woodrow Wilson fellow, 1965-66, NIH grad. fellow, 1966-71, Jane Coffins Childs Found. fellow, 1971-75; Nat. Cancer Inst. Cancer Ctr. Support grantee, 1995—; recipient Sword Hope award Am. Cancer Soc., 1995, Lewis S. Rosenstiel award Disting. Work Basic Med. Scis., Brandeis U., 1992, Rosenblatt award for excellence, 1993, Nat. Med. Rsch. award Nat. Health Coun., 1991, Friedrich von Recklinghausen award Nat. Neurofibromatosis Found., 1990, Charles S. Mott prize Gen. Motors Cancer Rsch. Found., 1990, Raymond Bourfine award, Paris, 2002. Mem. NAS, Am. Soc. Human Genetics (Allen Cancer Rsch. award 1989, assoc. editor Cancer Rsch.), Utah Acad. Scis., Inst. Medicine. Achievements include the development of a new technology for mapping and ultimately identifying human genes causing disease and the discovery of fundamental genes and genetic mechanisms important in the inherited and cellular pathways to cancer. Office: Ernest Gallo Clinic & Rsch Ctr Ste 200 5858 Horton St Emeryville CA 94608 Office Phone: 510-985-3102. Office Fax: 510-985-3101. E-mail: rayw@egcrc.net.

WHITE, RAYMOND PETRIE, JR., dentist, educator, dean; b. NYC, Feb. 13, 1937; s. Raymond Petrie and Mabel Sarah (Shutze) White; m. Betty Pritchett, Dec. 27, 1961; children: Karen Elizabeth, Michael Wood. Student, Washington and Lee U., 1955—58; DDS, Med. Coll. Va., 1962, PhD, 1967. Diplomate Am. Bd. Oral and Maxillofacial Surgery. Postdoctoral fellow anatomy Med. Coll. Va., Richmond, 1962—67, resident in oral surgery, 1964—67; asst. prof. U. Ky., Lexington, 1967—70, assoc. prof., 1970—71, chmn. dept. oral surgery, 1969—71; prof., asst. dean adminstrn. Va. Commonwealth U., Richmond, 1971—74; prof. Sch. Dentistry U. N.C., Chapel Hill, 1974—, Dalton L. McMichael disting. prof., 1993—, dean Sch. Dentistry, 1974—81, assoc. dean Sch. Medicine, Sch. Dentistry, 1981—92. Mem. staff U. N.C. Hosps., mem. exec. com., 1974—98, sec., 1977—78, assoc. chief staff, 1981—92; mem. adv. panel on dentistry U.S. Pharmacopial Conv., 1985—; sr. program cons. The Robert Wood Johnson Found., 1982—90. Author (with E.R. Costich): Fundamentals of Oral Surgery, 1971; author: (with Bell and Proffit) Surgical Correction of Dentofacial Deformities, 1980; author: (with W.R. Proffit) Surgical Orthodontic Treatment, 1990; author: (with M.R. Tucker, B.C. Terry, J.E. Van Sickels) Rigid Fixations for Maxillofacial Surgery, 1991; co-editor: Internat. Jour. Adult Orthodontics and Orthodontic Surgery, 1985—2002; asst. editor: Jour. Oral and Maxillofacial Surgery, 1993—; author (with W.R. Profit, R.P. Jr., and D. Sarver): Contemporary Treatment of Dentofacial Deformity, 2002; contbr. sci. articles to profl. jours. Bd. dirs. Am. Fund for Dental Health, 1978—86, v.p., 1982—85. Recipient Disting. Svc. award, Am. Fund Dental Health, 1987, Dental Found. N.C., 1981, John C. Brauer award for acad. distinction, U. N.C. Alumni Assn., 2000, Daniel M. Laskin award, 2002, Rsch. Excellence award, Oral and Maxillofacial Surgery Found., 2003. Mem.: AAAS, ADA, N.C. Assn. Oral and Maxillofacial Surgeons, Am. Assn. Oral and Maxillofacial Surgeons (gen. chmn. sci. sessions com. 1974—76, chmn. strategic planning com. 1990—96, Outstanding Svc. award as committeeman 1976, William Gies award 2000, Disting. Svc. award 2003), Chalmers J. Lyons Acad. Oral Surgery, Inst. Medicine of NAS, Internat. Assn. Dental Rsch. (pres. Ky. sect. 1970), N.C. Dental Soc., Sigma Xi, Omicron Kappa Upsilon, Sigma Zeta, Alpha Sigma Chi, Delta Tau Delta, Psi Omega. Roman Catholic. Home: 1506 Velma Rd Chapel Hill NC 27514-7601 Office: U NC Sch Dentistry Dept Oral/Maxillofacial Surgery Chapel Hill NC 27599-7450 Office Phone: 919-966-1126. Business E-Mail: ray_white@dentistry.unc.edu.

WHITE, REBECCA E., advocate; b. Washington, Nov. 17, 1945; d. Edward and Anna Pendleton White. BS, D.C. Tchrs. Coll., 1971; postgrad., Pepperdine U., Malibu, Calif., 1993, Calif. State U., LA, 2003—04. Cert. tchr., D.C., Calif. Tchr. English D.C. Pub. Schs., Washington, 1971-73; paralegal specialist U.S. Dept. Justice, Washington, 1973-81; adminstr. U.S. Dept. Vet. Affairs VA Med. Ctr., LA, 1982-89, 94-96, Sepulveda, Calif., 1992-94; patient/employee advocate U.S. Dept. Vet. Affairs, LA, 1982-89, 92-96; tchr. English L.A. Unified Sch. Dist., 1989-91, children's advocate, 1989—2005; tchr. English Inglewood (Calif.) Unified Sch. Dist., 1996-97, children's advocate, 1996—98; tchr. spl. edn. Gladstone St. Elem. Sch., Azusa, Calif., 2003—04; freelance writer, 2005—; tchr. English Mpls. Pub. Schs., 2005—. Cmty. advocate Baldwin Hills Cmty., L.A., 1983—2004; children's advocate L.A. County Schs., 2005—; mem. L.A. World Affairs Coun., 1999-2004; mem. Nat. Campaign For Tolerance, 2006-. Mem. NEA, Calif. Tchrs. Assn. Avocations: writing, hiking, entertaining, reading. Business E-Mail: rebecca.white@mpls.k12.mn.us.

WHITE, REBECCA HANNER, dean, law educator; BA, Ea. Ky. U.; JD, U. Ky. Judicial law clerk to Chief Judge George C. Edwards Sixth Cir. U.S. Ct. Appeals; atty. Dinsmore & Shohl, Cincinnati; prof. U. Ga. Sch. Law, 1989—, assoc. provost and assoc. v.p. academic affairs, interim dean, 2003—04, dean, 2004—, J. Alton Hosch Prof. Law. Co-author: Employment Discrimination, 2002, Cases and Materials on Employment Discrimination, 2003; editl. bd. The Labor Law Jour. Recipient Josiah Meigs Award, 2000, John C. O'Byrne Award, Woman of Distinction award, State Bar Ga. Younger Lawyers Div., 2004, Faculty Book Award for Excellence in Teaching. Fellow: Foundation Fellows, U. Ga. (sr.); mem.: Teaching Acad., U. Ga. Office: University of Georgia Law School Office of the Dean Athens GA 30602 Office Phone: 706-542-7140. Office Fax: 706-542-5556. E-mail: rhwhite@uga.edu. *

WHITE, RICHARD EDMUND, human resources specialist; b. Reading, Pa., June 8, 1944; s. Carl Marshall and Miriam Elizabeth (Curry) W.; m. Kristen Margaret Lloyd, June 17, 1967; children: Ross, Peter, Andrew. BS in Econs., U. Pa., 1967; MBA with distinction, U. Mich., 1968. Gen. mgr. mktg. H. J. Heinz Co., Pitts., 1970-81; dir. mktg. Seven Up Co., St. Louis, 1981-83; v.p. mktg. & sales Herr Foods, Inc., Nottingham, Pa., 1984—2006, sr. v.p. human resources, 2006—. Bd. dirs. Conard-Pyle Co. Chmn. fin. com. Sewickley Borough Coun., Pa., 1977—81; pres. So. Chester County Devel. Found., Jennersville, Pa., 1988—94, So. Chester County YMCA, West Grove, Pa., 1988—93, bd. mgrs., 1988—93, Avon Grove United Way, 1988—93, pres., 1988—93; chmn. Health and Welfare Found. So. Chester County, 2001—, So. Chester County Med. Ctr., 1988—2001, bd. dirs., 1988—2001, Brandywine YMCA Assn.; chmn. bd. dirs. Jenners Pond, 2001—03. Mem. Am. Mgmt. Assn. (mktg. coun.), Soc. Human Resource Mgrs. Republican. Avocations: physical fitness, reading. Home: 7 Sullivan Chase Dr Avondale PA 19311-9347 Office: Herr Foods Inc PO Box 300 Nottingham PA 19362-0300 Business E-Mail: richard.white@herrs.com.

WHITE, RICHARD THOMAS, radiologist; b. Binghamton, NY, May 10, 1941; s. William Joseph and Winifred (Murphy) W.; 1 child by previous marriage, Kevin Michael; m. Rory Lynn Leyman. BS, SUNY, Binghamton, 1967; DO, Chgo. Coll. Osteo. Medicine, 1972. Intern Bi County Hosp., Warren, Mich.; staff radiologist Bi-County Hosp., 1977-79; resident Detroit Hosp., Children's Hosp., Detroit, 1973-76; fellow Johns Hopkins Hosp., Balt., 1976; asst. prof. radiology Mich. State U., East Lansing, 1980-84, cons. ultra-sound rsch., 1980-83, cons. nuclear magnetic rsch., 1982-83; asst. prof. radiology U. Tex., Houston, 1984-85, U. Ill., Chgo., 1985-88; chief radiology VA Med. Ctr., Bath, NY, 1988—; clin. prof. radiology U. Rochester (N.Y.) Sch. Medicine and Dentistry, 1989—. Cons. varsity sports, 1980-84, handicapped athletes Spl. Olympics, Washington, 1978-84, Detroit Red Wings hockey team, 1977-84; cons. in radiology St. James Hosp., Hornell, N.Y., 1989—. Med. dir. Mich. Spl. Olympics Ctrl. Mich. U., Mt. Pleasant, 1977-84; bd. dirs. Spl. Olympics, Mich., 1980-84, N.Y. Spl. Olympics, 1996-2000; med. advisor Amateur Hockey Assn. USA, Colorado Springs, Colo., 1980-84. With U.S. Army, 1960-66; lt. col. USAR, 1990-96, ret. Recipient Outstanding Contbn. award Spl. Olympics, 1980; named Team Physician U.S. Nat. Hockey Team, Mich. Amateur Hockey Assn., 1979, 81, 83. Mem. AMA, Am. Osteo. Assn., Am. Osteo. Coll. Radiology, Assn. Mil. Physicians and Surgeons, Am. Osteopath Assn., Radiol. Soc. N.Am., Am. Coll. Radiology, Am. Inst. Ultrasound in Medicine, Am. Acad. Sci., Soc. Med. Cons. to U.S. Armed Forces, Kiwanis, Am. Legion. Office Phone: 607-664-4408.

WHITE, RICK, lawyer, former congressman; b. Nov. 6, 1953; BA in Govt. and French, Dartmouth Coll., 1975; postgrad., Pantheon-Sorbonne; JD, Georgetown U., 1980. Mem. 104th to 105th Congresses from 1st Wash. dist., 1995—98; mem. house commerce com.; ptnr. Perkins Coie LLP, Seattle, 1999—2001; pres., CEO TechNet, Palo Alto, Calif., 2001—05. Bd. dir. Motricity. Founder Congl. Internet Caucus, Books for Kids. Republican. Mailing: TechNet 2600 E Bayshore Rd Palo Alto CA 94303

WHITE, ROBERT BROWN, medical educator; b. Ennis, Tex., Jan. 5, 1921; s. Robert Brown and Willia Elizabeth (Latimer) W.; m. Jimmie Estelle Sims, Oct. 18, 1942; children: Robert B., Canelia White Layton, Margaret White Gilbert. BS, Tex. A & M Coll., 1941; MD, U. Tex., 1944; cert., Western New Eng. Psychoanalytic Inst., 1959. Intern Phila. Gen. Hosp., 1944-45; psychiat. residency John Sealy Hosp., Galveston, Tex., 1945-46, 48-49; psychiatry fellow Austen Riggs Ctr., Stockbridge, Mass., 1949-51, staff psychiatrist, 1951-62; assoc. prof. U. Tex. Med. Br., Galveston, 1962-67, prof., 1967—, Marie Gale prof. of psychiatry, 1981-93; prof. emeritus, 1993—; tng. analyst New Orleans Psychoanalytic Inst., 1966-76. Tng. analyst Houston-Galveston Psychoanalytic Inst., 1974-94; analyst emeritus, 1994—. Author: Elements of Psychopathology, 1975; contbr. chpts. to books and articles to profl. jours. Capt. US Army, 1946-48. Recipient David Rapaport prize Western New Eng. Psychoanalytic Inst., New Haven, 1959; Ohio State award Ohio State U., 1976. Fellow Am. Psychiat. Assn., Am. Coll. Psychiatrists, Am. Coll. Psychoanalysts (bd. regents 1988-91); mem. Am. Psychoanalytic Assn., Alpha Omega Alpha. Democrat. Avocations: photography, carpentry. Home: 8523 Thackery St apt 7008 Dallas TX 75225-3960 Office: Univ Tex Med Br Galveston TX 77550

WHITE, ROBERT EDWARD, think-tank executive; b. Melrose, Mass., Sept. 21, 1926; s. Edward V. and Emily G. (McGuire) W.; m. MaryAnne Cahill, June 4, 1955; children: Christopher, Kevin, Claire, MaryLouise, Laura. BA, St. Michael's Coll., Winooski, Vt., 1952, DHL (hon.), 1978; MA, Tufts U., 1954; DHL (hon.), Simmons Coll., 1985. Joined Fgn. Svc., Dept. State; dir. Latin Am. Peace Corps, Washington, 1968-70; dep. chief mission Am. Embassy, Managua, Nicaragua, 1970-72, Bogota, Colombia, 1972-75; dep. rep. Orgn. Am. States, Washington, 1975-77; US amb. to Paraguay US Dept. State, Asuncion, 1977-79, US amb. to El Salvador San Salvador, 1979-81; sr. assoc. Carnegie Endowment for Internat. Peace, Washington, 1981-83; prof. internat. rels. Simmons Coll., Boston, 1983-85; pres. Ctr. for Internat. Policy, Washington, 1985—. Pres.'s spl. rep. Inter-Am. Conf. on Edn., Sci. and Culture, 1977-79. Contbr. numerous articles to Commonweal, Atlantic, N.Y. Times. With USN, 1944-46; PTO. Fulbright scholar U. Bristol, Eng., 1953. Mem. Fgn. Svc. Assn., Fund for Constl. Govt. (bd. dirs.), Cosmos Club. Office: Ctr for Internat Policy 1717 Massachusetts Ave NW Washington DC 20036-2102

WHITE, ROBERT I., lawyer; b. Ventnor City, NJ, 1951; BA with honors, Haverford U., 1974; JD with honors, George Washington U., 1977. Bar: DC 1977, registered: US Ct. Appeals (5th cir.), US Ct. Appeals (8th cir.), US Ct. Appeals (10th cir.), US Ct. Appeals, (DC cir.). Atty., Office of Gen. Counsel Fed. Trade Commn., 1977—80; ptnr. Squire, Sanders & Dempsey LLP, Washington, chmn., Energy Practice Group. Mem.: Fed. Energy Bar Assn., ABA. Office: Squire Sanders & Dempsey LLP 1201 Pennsylvania Ave NW PO Box 407 Washington DC 20044-0407 Office Phone: 202-626-6285. Office Fax: 202-626-6780. Business E-Mail: rwhite@ssd.com.

WHITE, ROBERT JAMES, retired columnist; b. Mpls., Nov. 6, 1927; s. Robert Howard and Claire Lillian (Horner) W.; m. Adrienne Hoffman, Sept. 24, 1955; children: Claire, Pamela, Sarah. BS, U.S. Naval Acad., 1950. V.p. White Investment Co., Mpls., 1957-67; editl. writer Mpls. Tribune, 1967-73, assoc. editor, 1973-82; editor editl. pages Mpls. Star Tribune, 1982-93, columnist, 1993-95, contbg. columnist, 1996—. Trustee Refugee Policy Group, Washington, 1985—95. Destroyer officer, fighter pilot, flight instr., aide and flag lt. to cmdr. Fleet Air Jacksonville USN, 1946—58. Recipient cert. of excellence Overseas Press Club, 1981. Mem. Coun. Fgn. Rels., Mpls. Club. Congregationalist. Home: Summit House 400 Groveland Ave #2212 Minneapolis MN 55403 Personal E-mail: rjw823@aol.com.

WHITE, ROBERT JOEL, lawyer; b. Chgo., Nov. 1, 1946; s. Melvin and Margaret (Hoffman) W.; m. Gail Janet Edenson, June 29, 1969 (div. Dec. 1982); m. Penelope K. Bloch, Dec. 22, 1985. BS in Accountancy, U. Ill., 1968; JD, U. Mich., 1972. Bar: Calif. 1972, N.Y. 1985, U.S. Dist. Ct. (ctrl., ea., so. dists.) Calif. 1972, U.S. Ct. Appeals (9th cir.) 1978, U.S. Ct. Appeals (5th cir.) 1983, U.S. Ct. Appeals (6th cir.) 1984, U.S. Supreme Ct. 1977. Staff auditor Haskin & Sells, Chgo., 1968-69; assoc. O'Melveny & Myers, LA, 1972-79, ptnr., 1980—2007, chair reorgn. and restructuring dept., 1986—2001; CEO O'Melvey Cons. LLC, 2001—03. Vis. lectr. U. Mich. Law Sch., Ann Arbor, 1986; lectr. Profl. Edn. Sys., Inc., Dallas, 1987, L.A., 1987, 89, Phoenix, 1990, Practicing Law Inst., San Francisco and N.Y.C., 1989-93, 2001-, Southwestern Legal Found., Dallas, 1991, UCLA Bankruptcy Inst., 1993, UCLA, 1993; mem. L.A. Productivity Commn., 1993-96. Contbr. articles to profl. jours. Active Constl. Rights Found., 1980—; active Am. Cancer Soc., 1989—, mem. L.A. bd. dirs., 1995—, vice chair, partnership com., 2003-; chair chpt. 11 com. Nat. Bankruptcy Conf., 2004-. Fellow Am. Coll. Bankruptcy; mem. ABA (litig. sect., mem. comml. law and bankruptcy com. 1972—), L.A. County Bar Assn. (comml. law and bankruptcy sect., chmn. fed. cts. com. 1981-82, exec. com. 1982—), Assn. Bus. Trial Lawyers (bd. govs. 1983-85), Fin. Lawyers Conf. (bd. govs. 1986—, pres. 1990-91), Am. Bankruptcy Inst. Avocations: skiing, running, history. Office: O'Melveny & Myers 1999 Ave of Stars Los Angeles CA 90067-6035 Office Phone: 310-246-8485. Business E-Mail: rwhite@omm.com.

WHITE, ROBERT LEE, electrical engineer, educator; b. Plainfield, NJ, Feb. 14, 1927; s. Claude and Ruby Hemsworth Emerson (Levick) W.; m. Phyllis Lillian Arlt, June 14, 1952; children: Lauren A., Kimberly A., Christopher L., Matthew P. BA in Physics, Columbia U., 1949, MA, 1951, PhD, 1954. Assoc. head atomic physics dept. Hughes Rsch. Labs., Malibu, Calif., 1954-61; head magnetics dept. Gen. Tel. and Electronics Rsch. Lab., Palo Alto, Calif., 1961-63; prof. elec. engring., materials sci. and engring. Stanford U., Palo Alto, 1963, chmn. elec. engring. dept., 1981-86, William E. Ayer prof. elec. engring., 1985-88, prof. emeritus, 1988—; exec. dir. The Exploratorium, San Francisco, 1987-89; dir. Inst. Electronics in Medicine, San Francisco, 1973—87, Stanford Ctr. Rsch. on Info. Storage Materials, 1991—2003; initial ltd. ptnr. Mayfield Fund, Mayfield II and Alpha II Fund, Rainbow Co-Investment Ptnrs., Halo Ptnrs.; pres. MacArray, Inc., 2005—. Vis. prof. Tokyo U., 1975, Nat. U. Singapore, 2002; Sony sabbatical chair, 1994; cons. in field. Author: (with K.A. Wickersheim) Magnetism and Magnetic Materials, 1965, Basic Quantum Mechanics, 1967; contbr. numerous articles to profl. jours. With USN, 1945-46. Fellow Guggenheim Oxford U., 1969-70, Canton Hosp., Swiss Fed. Inst. Tech., Zurich, 1977-78, Christensen fellow Oxford U., 1986, IEEE Magnetics Soc. Disting. lectr., 1998. Fellow IEEE, Am. Phys. Soc.; mem. Sigma Xi, Phi Beta Kappa. Home: 450 El Escarpado Stanford CA 94305-8431 Office: Stanford U Dept Material Sci Engr Stanford CA 94305 Office Phone: 650-799-4650. Business E-Mail: rlwhite450@sbcglobal.net.

WHITE, ROBERT LESLIE GORDON, JR., aerospace transportation executive; b. Orange, NJ, Dec. 20, 1941; s. Robert L.G. and Gertrude Marie (Wilson) W.; m. Joan Adam, May 9, 1970; children: Robert L.G. III, Sonya Lynn. BS in Metallurgical Engring., Lafayette Coll., 1964. Sr. engr. Crucible Steel Co., 1964-68; various positions Curtiss-Wright Corp., Woodridge, NJ, 1968-76, plant mgr. nuclear facility, 1976-80, dir. gas turbine overhaul, 1980-83; v.p., gen. mgr. Curtiss-Wright/Marquette, Inc., Fountain Inn, SC, 1983-87; pres. GEC-Marconi Aerospace Inc., Whippany, NJ, 1987-94, Breeze-Eastern, Union, NJ, 1994—98; pres. aerospace products group Transtechnology Corp., Union, NJ, 1998—2003, pres., CEO, 2003—; CEO Breeze-Eastmen Corp., Union, 2006—. Office: Breeze-Eastern Corp 700 Liberty Ave Union NJ 07083-8198

WHITE, ROBERT MARSHALL, retired physicist, educator, government official, consultant; b. Reading, Pa., Oct. 2, 1938; s. Carl M. and Miriam E. White; m. Sara Tolles; children: Victoria, Jonathan. BS in Physics, MIT, 1960; PhD, Stanford U., 1964. Vis. scientist Osaka (Japan) U., 1963; NSF postdoctoral fellow U. Calif., Berkeley, 1965-66; asst. prof. physics Stanford U., Palo Alto, Calif., 1966-70; NSF sr. postdoctoral fellow

Cambridge U., England, 1970-71; mgr. solid state rsch. area XEROX PARC, 1971-78, mgr. storage tech., 1978-83, prin. scientist, 1983-84; v.p. rsch. and tech. Control Data Corp. Data Storage Products Group, Mpls., 1984-86; chief tech. officer, v.p. rsch. and engring. Control Data Corp., Mpls., 1986-89; v.p., dir. advanced computer techs. Microelectronics & Computer Tech. Corp., Austin, Tex., 1989-90; undersec. of commerce for tech. Dept. Commerce, Washington, 1990-93; prof., head dept. elec.l and computer engring. Carnegie Mellon U., Pitts., 1993-99, prof., dir. Data Storage Sys. Ctr., 1999—2004, prof. emeritus, 2004—; cons. prof. materials sci. & engring. Stanford U., 2004—. Vis. scientist Ecole Polytechnique, Paris, 1976-78, U. Pernambuco, Brazil, 1978, Max Planck Inst., Stuttgart, 1981; cons. prof. applied physics Stanford U., 1982-93; adj. prof. dept. physics U. Minn., 1987-89; bd. dirs. Found. Nat. Medals Sci. and Tech., Silicon Graphics, STMicroelectronics, ENSCO; mem. sci. adv. bd. Data Storage Inst., Singapore, 2002—; mem. adv. bd. Pacific Enterprise Capital, LLC; mem. Nat. Adv. Com. on Semicondrs., 1990-92, Mfg. Forum, 1991, Nat. Critical Techs. Panel, 1990-91. Author: Quantum Theory of Magnetism, 1970 (Russian transl., 1972, Polish transl., 1979); Long Range Order in Solids, 1979 (Russian transl., 1982); Quantum Theory of Magnetism, 1983, 3d edit., 2007; Introduction to Magnetic Recording, 1985. Contbr. articles to profl. jours. Recipient Alexander von Humboldt prize, Fed. Republic of Germany, 1981. Fellow AAAS, IEEE (disting. lectr. Magnetics Soc., mem. editl. bd. SPECTRUM, IEEE Disting. Pub. Svc. award 1993), Am. Phys. Soc. (George E. Pake prize 2004); mem. NAE, NRC (mem. nat. materials adv. bd., chmn. com. magnetic materials 1984, material sci. and engring., vice chmn. IUPAP commn. on magnetism), Conf. Magnetism and Magnetic Materials (adv. com. 1976-78, 80-95, program com. 1973-75, chmn. 1981, chmn. Intermag. Conf. 1991), Internat. Conf. Magnetism (program chmn. 1985). Office: Carnegie Mellon U Elec & Computer Engring Dep Pittsburgh PA 15213-3890 Business E-Mail: white@ece.cmu.edu.

WHITE, ROBERT MAYER, meteorologist; b. Boston, Feb. 13, 1923; s. David and Mary (Winkeller) W.; m. Mavis Seagle, Apr. 18, 1948; children: Richard Harry, Edwina Janet. BA, Harvard, 1944; MS, Mass. Inst. Tech., 1949, Sc.D., 1950; D.Sc., L.I. U., 1976; D.Sc. (hon.), Rensselaer Poly. Inst., 1977, U. Wis., Milw., 1978; ScD (hon.), U. Bridgeport, 1984, U. R.I., 1986, Clarkson U.; PhD (hon.), Johns Hopkins U., 1982, Drexel U., 1985, Ill. Inst. Tech., 1994. Project scientist Air Force Cambridge Research Center, 1950-58, chief meteorol. devel. lab., 1958-59; asso. dir. research dept. Travelers Ins. Co., 1959-60; pres. Travelers Research Center, Inc., 1960-63; chief U.S. Weather Bur., 1963-65; adminstr. Environ. Sci. Services Adminstrn., 1965-70, NOAA, 1970-77; pres. Joint Oceanographic Inst., Inc., 1977-79; chmn. Climate Research Bd., exec. officer Nat. Acad. Scis., 1977-79; Washington; adminstr. Nat. Research Council, 1979-80; pres. Univ. Corp. Atmospheric Research, 1980-83, Nat. Acad. Eng., 1983-95; Karl T. Compton lectr. MIT, Cambridge, 1995-96; sr. fellow Univ. Corp. Atmospheric Rsch., 1995—. Sr. fellow H. John Heinz III Ctr. for Sci., Econs. and Environment, 1996—2000; pres. Wash. Adv. Group, 1996—. Author: articles in field; mem. editl. bd.: Am. Soc. Engring. Edn. Jour. Bd. overseers Harvard U., 1977—79; mem. vis. com. Kennedy Sch. Govt., Harvard U.; bd. dirs. Resources for the Future, 1980—. Capt. USAF, World War II. Decorated Legion of Honor France; recipient Godfrey L. Cabot award, Aero Club Boston, 1966, Cleveland Abbe award, Am. Meteorol. Soc., 1969, Jesse L. Rosenberger medal, U. Chgo., 1971, Rockefeller Pub. Svc. award, 1974, David B. Stone award, New Eng. Aquarium, 1975, Neptune award, Am. Oceanic Orgn., 1977, Matthew Fontaine Maury award, Smithsonian Instn., 1976, Internat. Conservation award, Nat. Wildlife Fedn., 1976, Internat. Meteorol. Orgn. prize, 1980, Tyler prize for Environ. Achievement, U. Calif., 1992, Vannevar Bush award, Nat. Sci. Bd., 1998, Centenary medal, Australia, 2003, Milennium award, Australian Acad. Engring., 2003. Fellow: Am. Acad. Arts and Scis., Australian Acad. Tech. Scis. and Engring., Am. Geophys. Union, World Acad. Art and Scis., AAAS, UCAR (sr.), Am. Meteorol. Soc. (coun. 1965—67, 1977—, pres. 1980, Charles Franklin Brooks award1978); mem.: Royal Acad. Engring. (U.K.), Russian Acad. Engring., Royal Acad. Engring. (hon.), Engring. Acad. Japan (fgn. assoc.), Am. Philos. Soc., Finnish Acad. Tech. (fgn.), Nat. Action Coun. Minorities in Engring. Inc., Coun. Fgn. Rels., Marine Tech. Soc., NAE (coun. 1977, pres. 1983—95), Cosmos Club (Washington). Home: Somerset House II 5610 Wisconsin Ave Apt 1506 Bethesda MD 20815-4439 Office: 1275 K St NW Ste 1025 Washington DC 20005-4089 Business E-Mail: rmw@theadvisorygroup.com.

WHITE, ROBERT STEPHEN, retired physics professor; b. Ellsworth, Kans., Dec. 28, 1920; s. Byron F. and Sebina (Leighty) White; m. Freda Marie Bridgewater, Aug. 30, 1942; children: Nancy Lynn, Margaret Diane, John Stephen, David Bruce. AB, Southwestern Coll., 1942, DSc (hon.), 1971; MS, U. Ill., 1943; PhD, U. Calif., Berkeley, 1951. Physicist Lawrence Radiation Lab., Berkeley, Livermore, Calif., 1948-61; head dept. particles and fields Space Physics Lab. Aerospace Corp., El Segundo, Calif., 1962-67; physics prof. U. Calif., Riverside, 1967-92, prof. emeritus physics dept., rsch. physicist, 1992—, dir. Inst. Geophysics and Planetary Physics, 1967-92, chmn. dept. physics, 1970-73. Lectr. U. Calif., Berkeley, 1953—54, Berkeley, 1957—59. Author: Space Physics, 1970, Why Science?, 1998, Energy for the Public: The Case for Increased Nuclear Fission Energy, 2006; contbr. articles to profl. jours. Officer USNR, 1944—46. Grantee, NASA, NSF, USAF, numerous others; Sr. Postdoctoral fellow, NSF, 1961—62. Fellow: AAAS, Am. Phys. Soc. (mem. exec. com. 1972—74); mem.: Am. Astron. Soc., Am. Geophys. Union. Home: 5225 Austin Rd Santa Barbara CA 93111-2905 Personal E-mail: stevewhite2@cox.net.

WHITE, ROBERTA LEE, financial analyst; b. Denver, Sept. 18, 1946; d. Harold Tindall and Araminta (Campbell) Bangs; m. Lewis Paul White, Jr., Jan. 23, 1973 (div. Sept. 1974). BA cum laude, Linfield Coll., 1976; postgrad., Lewis and Clark Coll. Lic. tax preparer, Oreg. Office mgr. Multnomah County Auditor, Portland, Oreg., 1977-81; rsch. asst. Dan Goldy and Assocs., Portland, 1981-83; regional asst. Vocat. Rehab., Eugene, Oreg., 1983-85; internal auditor Multnomah County, Portland, 1985-89; cons. Portland, 1989-91; fin. analyst City of Portland, 1991-93; comptr. Wordsmith Svc., Portland, 1993-97; fin. analyst City of Portland, 1997—. Mem. Com. for Implementation of the ADA, Portland, 1991—93. Treas. Mary Wendy Roberts for Sec. of State, Portland, 1992, Re-Elect Mary Wendy Roberts, Portland, 1990, Elect Hank Miggins Com., 1994; mem. Oreg. Women's Polit. Caucus, Portland, 1982-85, City Club, Portland, 1978-81. Democrat. Mem. Disciples Of Christ. Avocations: reading, hiking, opera, symphony, ballet. Home: 6685 W Burnside # 336 Portland OR 97210 Office: City of Portland Office of Mgmt/Fin Facil Svc Divsn Rm 1204 1120 SW 5th Ave Portland OR 97204-1912 Home Phone: 503-292-9377.

WHITE, RONALD JOSEPH, biomedical researcher, physiologist, educator; b. Opelousas, La., Dec. 4, 1940; s. John Wesley and Alma Louise (LaSalle) White; m. Margaret Helen Launey, June 8, 1963; children: Joseph LaSalle, Angela Alma, Margaret Leslie. BS in Chemistry, U. S.W. La., 1963; PhD in Phys. Chemistry, U. Wis., 1968. NSF postdoctoral fellow in theoretical chemistry U. Oxford, England, 1967-68; rsch. assoc. Bell Tel. Labs., Murray Hill, NJ, 1968-70; from asst. prof. to assoc. prof. math. U. S.W. La., Lafayette, 1970—76, prof. math., dir. Univ. Honors Program, 1976—80; rsch. assoc. dept. physiology and biophysics U. Miss. Med. Ctr., Jackson, 1973-75; sr. scientist GE Co./Mgmt. and Tech. Svcs. Co., Washington and Houston, 1980-85; chief scientist Life/Biomed. Scis. and Applications Divsn. NASA, Washington, 1985—96; rsch. prof. physiology Uniformed Svcs. U. Health Scis., Bethesda, Md., 1985—96; prof. dept. otorhinolaryngology Baylor Coll. Medicine, Houston, 1996—2003; assoc. dir. Nat. Space Biomed. Rsch. Inst., 1997—2003; sr. fellow Univs. Space Rsch. Assn., Houston, 2003—. V.p. Assn. Gifted and Talented Students, La., 1977—80; pres. La. Collegiate Honors Coun., 1978—79. Editor (assoc. life scis.): Simulation, 1974—75; editor: (spl.) Medicine and Sci. in Sports and Exercise, 1996; contbr. chpts. to books, papers to profl. jours. Recipient NASA traineeship, 1963—66, Am. Inst. Chemists award, 1963, Disting. Prof. award, 1978, Med. Info. Processing Best Paper award, 15th ann. Hawaii Internat. Conf. on Systems Sci., 1982, Hon. Mem. award, Soc. NASA Flight Surgeons, 1992, Exceptional Achievement medal, NASA, 1992; fellow, Woodrow Wilson Found., 1963. Mem.: Internat. Soc. Computational Biology, Internat. Acad. Astronautics (bd. trustees 1997—, chair life scis. 2001—, commr. space life scis. 2001—03, Luigi Napolitano Lit. award 1996), Am. Soc. Gravitational and Space Biology (charter mem.), Am. Phys. Soc., Aerospace Med. Assn., Sigma Xi (rsch. award 1976), Phi Kappa Phi. Home: 1303 Primrose Ln Seabrook TX 77586-4718 Office: USRA Divsn Space Life Scis 3600 Bay Area Blvd Houston TX 77058 Home Phone: 281-291-9419; Office Phone: 281-244-2025. Business E-Mail: white@dsls.usra.edu.

WHITE, RONALD LEON, retired business executive; b. West York, Pa., July 14, 1930; s. Clarence William and Grace Elizabeth (Gingerich) W.; m. Estheranne Wieder, June 16, 1951; children: Bradford William, Clifford Allen, Erick David. BS in Econs, U. Pa., 1952, MBA, 1957. Cost analysis supr. Air Products & Chem. Corp., Allentown, Pa., 1957-60; cost control mgr. Mack Trucks, Inc., Allentown, 1960-64; mgmt. cons. Peat, Marwick, Mitchell & Co., Phila., 1964-66; mgr. profit planning Monroe, The Calculator Co. (divsn. Litton Industries), Orange, NJ, 1966-67, contr., 1967-68; v.p. fin. Bus. Sys. Group of Litton Industries, Beverly Hills, Calif., 1968-70; pres. Royal Typewriter Co. (divsn. Litton Industries), Hartford, Conn., 1970-73; exec. v.p., COO, treas., dir. Tenna Corp., Cleve., 1973-75, pres., dir., 1975-77; v.p. fin. Arby's, Inc., Youngstown, Ohio, 1978-79; exec. v.p., dir. Roxbury Am., Inc., 1979-81; v.p. fin., treas. Royal Crown Cos., Inc., Atlanta and Miami Beach, Fla., 1981-86, TDS Healthcare Sys. Corp., Atlanta, 1987-88; v.p. Corp. Fin. Assocs., Atlanta, 1988-90; prin. The Janelle Co., Atlanta, 1991—2006; ret., 2006. Vice chmn. Ga. Mental Health, Mental Retardation, Substance Abuse Regional Bd. #6, 1994-2002, chmn. leadership coun., 1999-2000; v.p. and dir. Ga. Alliance for Mentally Ill, 1997-2003; instr. acctg. Wharton Sch. U. Pa., 1952-53, instr. industry, 1953-54. Deacon United Ch. of Christ. Lt. USNR, 1954-57. Mem. Am. Mgmt. Assn., Inst. Mgmt. Accts., Nat. Assn. Corp. Dirs., Fin. Execs. Internat., Acacia, Masons, Rotary. Personal E-mail: rlwea@comcast.net.

WHITE, RONNIE L., retired state supreme court justice; b. St. Louis, Mo., May 31, 1953; m. Sylvia White. AA, St. Louis C.C., 1977; BA, St. Louis U., 1979; JD, U. Mo., Kansas City, 1983. Bar: Mo. Law intern Jackson County Prosecutors Office; legal asst. U.S. Def. Mapping Agy.; trial atty. Office of Pub. Defender; mem. Mo. Ho. of Reps., 1989-93; judge Mo. Ct. Appeals, 1994; spl. judge Mo. Supreme Ct., 1994-95, justice, 1994-95, assoc. justice, 1995—2007, chief justice, 2003—05. Adj. faculty Washington U. Sch. Law, 1997—. first African-Am. Supreme Ct. justice of Mo. Office: PO Box 150 Jefferson City MO 65102-0150 *

WHITE, ROY BERNARD, performing arts association administrator; b. Cin. s. Maurice and Anna (Rudin) W.; m. Sally White, June 17, 1951; children: Maurice, Barbara Dee, Daniel Robert. BA, U. Cin., 1949. Sales staff Twentieth Century Fox Films, Cin.; pres. Mid-States Theatres; dir. Nat. Assn. Theatre Owners, nat. pres., exec. com., chmn. bd. Mem. film adv. panel Ohio Arts Coun.; bd. dirs. Will Rogers Meml. Fund, Found. Motion Picture Pioneers, Inc.; mem. media arts panel Nat. Endowment for Arts. Served with USAAF, 1944-45. Named Exhibitor of Year Internat. Film Importers and Distbrs. Am. Mem. Nat. Assn. Theater Owners (pres.), Am. Film Inst. (trustee 1972-75, exec. com. 1972-75, trustee emeritus), Fedn. Motion Picture Pioneers (v.p.), Masons, Queen City Racquet, Amberley Village (Ohio) Tennis Club (pres. 1972-73), Bankers Club, Quail Creek Country Club, Bay Colony Country Club, Bay Colony Golf Club, Morrings Country Club. Home: 1274 Waggle Way Naples FL 34108-1994 Personal E-mail: royb3140@aol.com.

WHITE, SHARMAN LYNELL, lawyer; b. Albany, Ga., Aug. 19, 1968; d. Frank Irvin and Annette Jones White; 1 child, Andrew Franklin White Cleary. BA in Govt. cum laude, Harvard Coll., Cambridge, Mass., 1990; JD, U. Tex., Austin, 1995. Bar: NY 1996. Assoc. Beveridge & Diamond, PC, Washington, 1995—97; atty., adviser U.S. Dept. Agr., 1997—. Mem. unexploded ordnance panel US Dept. Interior, Conf. Environment, Albuquerque, 2001; spkr. pub. lands and natural resources seminar US Dept. Justice, Nat. Advocacy Ctr., Columbia, SC, 2000; appointee Fed. Natural Resource Damage Assessment and Restoration Adv. Com.; mem. legal rsch. bd. U. Tex. Law Sch. Lead articles editor: Tex. Environ. Law Jour., 1994—95. Sponsor Christian Children's Fund. Recipient Performance awards, USDA Office Gen. Counsel, 1998—2004, On the Spot award, 1999, Extra Effort award, 2000, Departmental awards, USDA Hazardous Materials Mgmt. Group, 2001, 2005. Mem.: ACLU, Harvard Crimson, Harvard Club Washington, Potomac Pedalers Touring Club, MENSA. Avocations: travel, writing, bicycling, movies, boating. Office: US Department of Agriculture 1400 Independence Avenue SW Washington DC 20250 Home Phone: 703-590-1515; Office Phone: 202-720-6716. Personal E-mail: sharmian.white@post.harvard.edu. E-mail: sharmian.white@usda.gov.

WHITE, SHAUN ROGER, Olympic athlete, professional snowboarder, professional skateboarder; b. San Diego, Sept. 3, 1986; s. Kathy and Roger White. Profl. snowboarder Burton Snowboarding team, 1999—; skateboarder Tony Hawk Gigantic Skatepark Tour, 2002; profl. Skateboarder, 2003—; designer The White Collection. Snowboarder US Olympic Team, Torino, Italy, 2006. Actor: (films) The White Album, 2004. Named Sports-Choice Action Sports, Teen Choice Awards, 2006; recipient ESPY Award Best Action Sports Athlete, 2003, 2006, ESPY award Best US Olympian, 2006. Achievements include being the youngest snowboarder to win the US Open Slopestyle Championship, 2004; being the first athlete to compete in both Winter and Summer X Games, 2003; winning the gold medal at Winter X Games, Slopestyle, 2003-2006, Halfpipe, 2003, 2006; winning the gold metal at Summer X Games, Vert, 2005; winning all 5 Grand Prix Superpipes, 2005-2006; winning a gold metal at Torino Olympic Games, Men's Halfpipe, 2006. Office: c/o USSA Box 100 1500 Kearns Blvd Park City UT 84060

WHITE, SHELBY, art association administrator; m. Leon Levy (dec. 2003). BA, Mount Holyoke Coll; MA, Columbia U. Chmn. Shelby White-Leon Levy Prog. for Archaeol. Publs., 1997—. Mem. Cultural Property Adv. Com., 2000; bd. dirs. Alliance Capital Money Market Funds. Bd. dirs. Met. Mus. Art, NYC; cofounder New Initiative Program Inst. Advanced Studies, Princeton, NJ; cofounder Leon Levy Biogenetics Ctr. Rockefeller U.; chair White-Levy Program for Archaeological Publications. Named one of Top 200 Collectors, ARTnews Mag., 2004, 2006. Avocation: Collector of Antiquities. Office: Semitic Mus Harvard U 6 Divinity Ave Cambridge MA 02138 Office Phone: 617-495-9317. E-mail: info@whitelevy.org. *

WHITE, STANLEY ARCHIBALD, electrical engineer, researcher; b. Providence, Sept. 25, 1931; s. Clarence Archibald White and Lou Ella (Givens) Arford; m. Edda María Castaño-Benítez, June 6, 1956; children: Dianne, Stanley Jr., Paul, John. BSEE, Purdue U., 1957, MSEE, 1959, PhD in Elec. Engring. and Aero. and Engring. Scis., 1965. Registered profl. engr., Ind., Calif. Engr. Rockwell Internat., Anaheim, Calif., 1959-68, mgr., 1968-84, sr. scientist, 1984-90; pres. Signal Processing and Controls Engring. Corp., 1990—2000; pvt. practice San Clemente, Calif., 2000—. Lectr. in elec. engring. U. Calif., 1959-84, adj. prof., 1984-97; cons. and lectr. in field; bd. dirs. Asilomar Signals, Systems and Computers Conf. Corp., 1988-02. Contbr. chpts. to books; contbr. articles to encys. and profl. jours. With USAF, 1951-55. N.Am. Aviation Sci. Engring. fellow, 1963-65; recipient Disting. Lectr. award Nat. Electronics Conf., Chgo., 1973, Engr. of Yr. award Orange County (Calif.) Engring. Coun., 1984, Engr. of Yr. award Rockwell Internat., 1985, Leonardo da Vinci Medallion, 1986, Sci. Achievement award, 1987, Disting. Engring. Alumnus award Purdue U., 1988, Meritorious Inventor's award Rockwell Internat. Corp., 1989, Outstanding Elec. Engr. award Purdue U., 1992, Boeing N.Am. Aviation Top Inventor award, 1998. Fellow AAAS (life), AIAA, IEEE (life; Centennial medal, Millenium medal, chair of ICASSP and ISCAS, Signal Processing Soc. disting. lect. and founding chmn. L.A. coun. chpt., Circuits and Sys. Soc. Tech. Achievement award 1996, Golden Jubilee medal 1999), Inst. for Advancement Engring., N.Y. Acad. Scis. (life); mem. VFW (life), Air Force Assn. (life), Am. Legion (life), Sigma Xi (life; founding pres. Orange County chpt., pres. 1988-00, 05—), Eta Kappa Nu (Paul K. Hudson disting. fellow, internat. dir. emeritus, Vladimir Karapetoff award 2005), Tau Beta Pi. Achievements include 82 US patents in field. Avocation: choral music. Office Phone: 949-498-5519. Business E-Mail: stan.white@ieee.org.

WHITE, STEPHEN HALLEY, biophysicist, educator; b. Wewoka, Okla., May 14, 1940; s. James Halley and Gertrude June (Wyatt) W.; m. Buff Ertl, Aug. 20, 1961 (div. 1982); children: Saill, Shell, Storn, Sharr, Skye, Sunde; m. Jackie Marie Dooley, Apr. 14, 1984. BS in Physics, U. Colo., 1963; MS in Physics, U. Wash., 1965, PhD in Physiology and Biophysics, 1969. USPHS postdoctoral fellow biochemistry U. Va., Charlottesville, 1971-72; asst. prof. physiology and biophysics U. Calif., Irvine, 1972-75, assoc. prof. physiology and biophysics, 1975-78, prof. physiology and biophysics, 1978—, vice chmn. physiology and biophysics, 1974-75, chmn. physiology and biophysics, 1977-89. Guest biophysicist Brookhaven Nat. Lab., Upton, L.I., N.Y., 1977-99; mem. NIH BBM study sect., 2005—. Contbr. numerous articles to profl. jours. Served to capt. USAR, 1969-71. Recipient Research Career Devel. award USPHS, 1975-80, Kaiser-Permanente Tchg. award, 1975, 92; fellow Biophysical Soc., 2002; grantee NIH, 1971—, NSF, 1971—. Mem. NSF (adv. panel for molecular biology 1982-85, mem. nat. steering com. advanced neutron source 1992-95), Internat. Union Pure and Applied Biophysics (U.S. nat. com. 1997—2004, chmn. 2000-04), Fedn. Am. Soc. for Exptl. Biology (bd. dirs. 1998-2002), Biophys. Soc. (chmn. membrane biophysics subgroup 1977-78, acting sec., treas. 1979-80, coun. 1981-84, exec. bd. 1981-83, program chmn. 1985, ann. meeting, sec. 1987-95, pres. 1996-97, Disting. Svc. award 1999), Am. Physiol. Soc. (editl. bd. 1981-93, membership com. 1985-86, publ. com. 1987-91), Assn. Chmn. Depts. Physiology (rep. to coun. acad. socs. 1981-82, councilor 1982-83, pres. 1986-87), Soc. Gen. Physiologists (treas. 1985-88), The Protein Soc. (electronic pub. coord. 1993—, NIH BBM study section 2005—). Avocations: skiing, cooking, travel. Office: U Calif Dept Physiology & Biophysics Med Sci I-D346 Irvine CA 92697-4560

WHITE, TERESA LYNNE, insurance company executive; married; 2 children. BBA, U. Tex., Arlington; M in Mgmt., Troy U., Ala. Second v.p. policy/payroll account svcs. AFLAC Inc., Columbus, Ga., 1998—2000, v.p. client svcs., 2000—04, sr. v.p. sales support and adminstrn., 2004—07, sr. v.p., dep. chief adminstrv. officer, 2007—. Bd. dirs. Communicorp, Columbus. Bd. mem. Columbus Housing Initiative; mem. bd. pensions South Ga. Conf. of United Meth. Ch. Named one of Top 77 Women in Exec. Leadership Worth Watching in 2006, Profiles in Diversity Jour.; named to 2006 Divas List, Bus.-to-Bus. mag. Fellow: Life Mgmt. Inst. Office: AFLAC Inc 1932 Wynnton Rd Columbus GA 31999 Office Phone: 706-323-3431. *

WHITE, TERRENCE HAROLD, academic administrator, sociologist; b. Ottawa, Ont., Can., Mar. 31, 1943; s. William Harold and Shirley Margaret (Ballantine) W.; m. Susan Elizabeth Hornaday; children: Christine Susan, Julie Pamela. PhD, U. Toronto, 1972. Head dept. sociology and anthropology U. Windsor, Ont., Canada, 1973-75; prof., chmn. dept. sociology U. Alta., Edmonton, Canada, 1975-80, dean faculty of arts, 1980-88; pres. T.H. White Orgn. Rsch. Svcs. Ltd., Edmonton, 1975—2000, Brock U., St. Catharines, Ont., 1988-96, U. Calgary, Alta., 1996—2001, pres. emeritus, prof. bus., 2001—06; dir. corp. affairs and communication Husky Energy, 2006—. Author: Power or Pawns: Boards of Directors, 1978, Human Resource Management, 1979; editor: Introduction to Work Science, 1981, QWL in Canada: Case Studies, 1983. Bd. dirs. Progressive Conservative Assn., Edmonton South, 1976-81, 1st v.p., 1981-85, pres., 1985-87; bd. dirs. Tri-Bach Festival Found., Edmonton, 1981-88, Alta. Ballet Co., 1985-88, Edmonton Conv. and Tourism Authority, Arch Enterprises, 1984-88, Niagara Symphony Soc., YMCA, St. Catharines, 1988-92; chair United Way Campaign St. Catharines, 1992, Fox Found., 1990-96, Can. Summer Games 2001 Bid Com.; bd. dirs. Edmonton Symphony Soc., v.p., 1986-88; bd. govs. U. Alta., 1984-88, Brock U., 1988-96, Ridley Coll., 1990—, Alta. Heritage Found. for Med. Rsch.; active Calgary R & D Authority, 1997; divsn. chair Calgary United Way Campaign, Calgary Econ. Devel. Authority, 1997-2000, McMahon Stadium Soc., Calgary Children's Initiative, Ctr. for Affordable Water and Sanitation; nat. bd. gov.'s Scouts Can., 2003- Recipient Can. 125 Commemorative medal Govt. of Can., Queen's Golden Jubilee medal. Mem. Calgary Petroleum Club, Ranchmen's Club, Rotary (pres. Edmonton South 1981-82), Delta Tau Kappa, Alpha Kappa Delta. Home: Box 68028 28 Crowfoot Terr NW Calgary AB Canada T3G 3N8 Office: U Calgary 2500 University Dr NW Calgary AB Canada T2N 1N4

WHITE, TERRY EDWARD, physician; b. Springfield, Mo., May 30, 1954; s. Roy Edward and Eselean (Moffis) W.; m. Susan Marie Peters, Aug. 16, 1981. BA, Drury Coll., 1976; MD, U. Mo., 1980. Diplomate Am. Bd. Physical Medicine and Rehab. Physician Lakeshore Hosp., Birmingham, Ala., 1983-86; clin. instr. U. Ala., Birmingham, 1984-86; physician Thomas Rehab., Asheville, NC, 1986-97, chief staff, 1994-97, vice-chief staff, 1992-94; physician Rehab. Solutions Western N.C., Asheville, 1998—; attending physician Mission Hosp., 1986—. Alternate Medicare State Carrier adv. com., Greensboro, N.C., 1993; bd. dirs. Nationwide Post Polio Support Group, Dallas, N.C., 1992-94; vice chmn. Western N.C. Health Care Provider Coun., 1995-96, chmn., 1996-97; mem. editl. adv. com. Stroke Rehabilitation. Author: A Patient's and Physician Guide to Late Effects of Polio, 1995; mem. editl. staff Stroke Rehabilitation-Patient Education Guide, 1995. Named Rehab. Physician Yr., N.C. Med. Soc., 1993. Fellow Am. Acad. Phys. Medicine and Rehab.; mem. N.C. Soc. Phys. Medicine and Rehab. (v.p. 1989-91, pres. 1991-93). Republican. Mem. Christian Ch. Avocations: gardening, woodwork, metal work, reading, music. Office: Rehab Solutions Western NC 4 Doctors Park Ste C Asheville NC 28801-4523 Home Phone: 828-299-7406; Office Phone: 828-283-9795. Personal E-mail: terrywhite@aol.com.

WHITE, THOMAS EDWARD, lawyer; b. NYC, July 11, 1933; s. Thomas Aubrey and Gladys Mary (Piper) W.; m. Joan Carolyn Olsen, Dec. 2, 1967 (dec.); children: Charles Garret, Nancy Carolyn, Linda Marie, Penelope Lindsay, Elizabeth Ann. AB, Princeton U., 1955; LLB, Columbia U., 1960; BA summa cum laude, SUNY-Purchase Coll., 2002; student in Fine Arts, NYU, 2002—04. Bar: N.Y. 1961. Atty. Seward & Kissel, NYC, 1960-69; gen. counsel Howmet Corp., NYC, 1969-70; v.p., gen. counsel, sec. Howmedica, Inc., NYC, 1970-74, sr. v.p., dir., 1974-83; pvt. practice NYC, 1983-97. Ptnr. Westmed Venture Ptnrs. (formerly Integrated Med. Venture Ptnrs.), N.Y.C., 1987-99; chmn. Shoreside Cons. Ltd., Miami, Fla., 1987-98. Mem. Mamaroneck Town Coun., 1971-75; mem. vestry Episcopalian Ch., 1987-90; mem. diocesan coun. Episcopal Ch. N.Y., 2001--. Served to 1st lt. U.S. Army, 1955-57. Mem.: Larchmont (N.Y.) Yacht; Princeton (N.Y.C.). Republican. Home: 260 Barnard Rd Larchmont NY 10538-1941

WHITE, TIMOTHY DOUGLAS, biology professor, educator; b. LA, Aug. 24, 1950; s. Robert Julian and Georgia Johnston (McDougall) W. BS in Biology, U. Calif., Riverside, 1972, BS in Anthropology, 1972; MA, U. Mich., 1974, PhD, 1977. Paleontologist East Rudolf Research Project, N. Kenya, 1974-77, Laetolil Expdn., N. Tanzania, 1978, 88, Middle Awash Valley, Ethiopia, 1981—, Olduvai Gorge, 1985-86, Paleoanthropological Inventory of Ethiopia, 1988—; prof. U. Calif., Berkeley, 1977-95, prof. integrative biology, 1995—, co-dir. lab. for human evolutionary studies, 1995—. Contbr. articles to profl. jours. Grantee NSF, Nat. Geog. Soc.; Recipient David S. Ingalls Jr. Award, Cleveland Mus. of Natural History Fellow Calif. Acad. Sci.; mem. Soc. Vertebrate Paleontology, AAAS. An excavator earliest human ancestor footprints, Tanzania, 1978; co-discoverer earliest human ancestors A. afarensis "Lucy" 1978-79; A. ramidus 1994. Office: U Calif Berkeley Dept of Integrative Biology 3060 Valley Life Sciences Bldg 3140 Berkeley CA 94720-3140 Office Phone: 510-642-2889. E-mail: timwhite@berkeley.edu. *

WHITE, TIMOTHY PAUL, brokerage house executive; b. Ft. Sill, Okla., Jan. 9, 1963; s. Paul R. and Lucille (Mattison) White; m. Susan Gertrude Foreman, Dec. 29, 1984; children: Jessica Lynn, Rebecca Anne, Kathleen Marie. BS in Fin., Pa. State U., 1985. Cert. fin. planner Colo. Assoc. planner, agt. Pa. Fin. Group, Harrisburg, Pa., 1988-92; mgr. mktg. and sales Meridian Securities, Inc., Reading, Pa., 1992-96; v.p. products and sales mgr. Core States Securities Corp., Reading, 1996-98; regional sales mgr. First Union Brokerage Svcs. Inc., 1998-2001; fin. advisor, sr. v.p. First Union Securities Inc., 2001—02; pres. Investors Ctrl. Comm. Inc.; mng. dir. Guidon, LLC, 2001—; fin. advisor Wachovia Securities LLC, 2002—. Spkr. Nat. Mut. Fund Conf., 1995, Cmty. Bank Investment Program Symposium, 1996, Nat. Investment Products Conf., 1996. Author: Money Smart Records, 2002; contbg. editor: Bank Securities Jour.; contbr. articles to profl. jours. Program cons. Jr. Achievement, Lancaster, Pa., 1990—91; pres. Adamstown Recreation Bd., 1996; bd. dirs. Dollars for Scholars, Lancaster, Pa. 1st lt. US Army, 1985—88, capt. USAR, 1989—92. Decorated Commendation medal, Achievement medal; recipient George C. Marshal award, U.S. Army, 1985; scholar ROTC, 1981—85. Mem.: Fin. Planning Assn., Ctrl. Pa. Soc. Inst. CFP (bd. dirs. 1996—, pres.-elect 1998, pres. 1999), U.S. Cav. Assn. (fundraising com. 1994—96), Inst. CFP. Republican. Lutheran. Avocations: military and political history, reading, gardening, woodworking. Office: Wachovia Securities LLC 12 E Market St York PA 17401 Home Phone: 717-336-5663; Office Phone: 717-852-5214. Business E-Mail: tim.white@wachovia.com.

WHITE, TIMOTHY PETER, academic administrator, physical education educator; b. Buenos Aires, July 9, 1949; came to U.S., 1957; s. Anthony Robert and Mary (Weston) W.; m. Nina Marie Kasper, Oct. 11, 1981; children: Randall Patrick, Timothy Anthony, Alexander John. Student, Diablo Valley Community Coll., 1966-67; BA magna cum laude, Fresno State U., 1970; MS, Calif. State U., Hayward, 1972; PhD, U. Calif., Berkeley, 1977. Asst. prof. phys. edn. U. Mich., Ann Arbor, 1978-82, assoc. prof., 1982-84, assoc. prof., chmn. dept. kinesiology, 1985-89; rsch. scientist Inst. Gerontology, 1986-91; prof., chmn. U. Mich., Ann Arbor, 1989-91; dept. chmn., prof. dept. human dynamics U. Calif., Berkeley, 1991—2000; provost, exec. v.p. Oreg. State Univ., 2000—04, interim pres., 2002—03; pres. Univ. Idaho, 2004—. Editor: (with others) Frontiers of Exercise Biology, 1983; contbr. articles to profl. jours. and chpts. to books on exercise and muscle. Fellow Am. Coll. Sports Medicine (trustee, v.p. 1991—, New Investigator award 1981), Am. Acad. Phys. Edn.; mem. AAAS, AAHPERD, Gerontol. Soc. Am., Am. Physiol. Soc., Sigma Xi, Phi Kappa Phi. Avocations: woodworking, nordic skiing, sailing, swimming, running. Office: University of Idaho Office of the President PO Box 443151 Moscow ID 83844-3151 *

WHITE, TODD WILLIAM, lawyer, educator; s. William Robert and Patricia Ann White; m. Tisa Lynn Lovett, Aug. 18, 1990; children: Mary Elizabeth, Abigail Ann. BA, U. Tex., 1987; JD, Tex. Tech U. Sch. Law, 1987—90. Bar: Tex. 1990, US Dist. Ct.: (no. dist.) Tex. 1991, (ea. dist.) Tex. 1996, US Ct. Appeals: (5th cir.) 1992, US Supreme Ct.: 1997. Assoc. Jones, Day, Reavis & Pogue, Dallas, 1990—95; pvt. practice Rockwall, Tex., 1995—. Assoc. prof. Collin County C.C., Plano, Tex., 2000—. Mem. Goals Rev. Com., Rockwall, Tex., 1991, North Ctrl. Tex. Regional Rev. Com., Arlington, Tex., 1996; mem., vice-chmn. Zoning Bd. of Adjustment, Rockwall, Tex., 1991—93; vice-chmn. Econ. Devel. Planning Com., Rockwall, Tex., 1992—93; chmn. Corridor Planning Taskforce, Rockwall, Tex., 1991—92, Rockwall County Reps., Rockwall, 1991—92, vol. legal coun., 1999—2004; coun. mem. City of Rockwall, 1993—98, mayor pro tem, 1996—97; chmn. Rockwall Housing Authority, Rockwall, Tex., 1999. Scholar, Helen Hodges Charitable Trust, 1989. Mem.: Tex. Tech U. Law Rev., Rockwall County Bar Assn., State Bar of Tex., KC, Order of the Coif, Phi Kappa Phi. Office: The White Law Firm 301 N San Jacinto Rockwall TX 75087 Home Phone: 972-722-3316; Office Phone: 972-771-8011. Office Fax: 972-771-8081. Business E-Mail: twhite@thewhitelawfirm.com.

WHITE, TONY L., health and medical products executive; BA, We. Carolina U., 1969. Sales rep. Baxter Internat. Inc., 1970-74, dist. mgr., 1974-76, export mgr. Latin Am., 1976-82, v.p. AMPAC, pres. Travenol-Can., 1982-85, pres. Fenwal divsn., 1985-86, pres. scientific products, biomedical divsn., 1986, v.p. diagnostics Deerfield, Ill., 1986-92, exec. vp, 1992-95; chmn., pres., CEO Applera Corp., Norwalk, Conn., 1995—. With USAR, 1968-74. Office: Applera Corp 301 Merritt 7 PO Box 5435 Norwalk CT 06856-5435 Office Phone: 203-840-2000. *

WHITE, TYLER GOODRICH, composer, conductor; b. Atlanta, Nov. 9, 1961; s. Edwin Chappell and Barbara Tyler White; m. Laura Garrigues Mooneyham, May 27, 1994; children: Caroline Barbara, Nicholas Garrick Chappell. AB Music, Univ. N.C., Chapel Hill, NC, 1983; MFA Musical Composition, Cornell Univ., Ithaca, NY, 1986; guest student, Kobenhavns Univ., Copenhagen, Denmark, 1986—87; DMA, Cornell Univ., Ithaca, NY, 1991. Dir. orchestral activities, asst. prof. music Trinity Univ., San Antonio, 1989—94, Univ. Nebr., Lincoln, 1994—2000, dir. orchestral activities, assoc. prof. music, 2000—. Resident condr. Lincoln Symphony Orch., Nebr., 2000—; guest faculty (conducting) Ctrl. Conservatory of Music, Beijing, 2004. Composer: (symphony) Mystic Trumpeter (symphony no. 2), (opera) O Pioneers!, 1999, (concerto) Threnos for Cello and Orchestra, 1993. Recipient Best Prodn. award, Nat. Opera Assn., 1999, 2001, Prix Maurice Ravel, Conservatoire Am. De Fontainebleau and Mply. of Avon, France, 1988; Individual Artist fellowship, Nebr. Arts Coun., 2005. Mem.: Conductors Guild, Am. Music Ctr., Am. Soc. Composers, Authors, and Pub., Phi Beta Kappa. Episcopalian. Home: 6540 Rexford Dr Lincoln NE 68506 Office: Univ Nebr Lincoln Sch Music Westbrook Music Bldg 0100 Lincoln NE 68588 Office Phone: 402-472-7698.

WHITE, W. CHRISTOPHER, lawyer; b. Boston, Dec. 30, 1951; s. William George and Patricia Elizabeth (Brophy) W.; m. Anne Marie Cosgriff, Aug. 19, 1972; children: Jennifer, Andrew, Meghan. BA, U. Notre Dame, 1973; postgrad., London Sch. Econs., 1974; JD, U. Mich., 1977. Bar: N.Y. 1981, Mass 1978. Atty. Ryan & White, Springfield, Mass., 1977—78, Fred F. French Co., NYC, 1978—80, Breed Abbot & Morgan, NYC, 1980—87; ptnr. Breed, Abbott & Morgan, NYC, 1984-87, Cadwalader Wickersham & Taft, NYC, 1987—, chmn. Real Estate Dept. & mem. exec. com. Mem. Univ. Club. Office: Cadwalader Wickersham & Taft LLP 1 World Fin Ctr New York NY 10281 Office Phone: 212-504-6633. Office Fax: 212-504-6666. Business E-Mail: christopher.white@cwt.com.

WHITE, W. ROBIN, writer; b. Kodaikanal, Madras, India, July 12, 1928; arrived in US, 1944; s. Emmons Eaton and Ruth Esther (Parker) W.; m. Marian Lucille Biesterfield, Feb. 3, 1948 (dec. Mar. 1983); children: Christopher, Parker, Shelley. BA, Yale U., 1950; MA, Calif. State Poly. U., 1991. Instr. writers program UCLA, 1985-93; lectr. Calif. State Poly. U., Pomona, 1985-93. Exec. officer Calif. State Regional Ctrs., Ukiah, Calif., 1973-79. Author: Elephant Hill, 1959 (Harper prize), House of Many Rooms, 1958, Men and Angels, 1961, Foreign Soil, 1962, All in Favor Say No, 1964, His Own Kind, 1967, Be Not Afraid, 1972, The Special Child, 1978, The Troll of Crazy Mule Camp, 1979, Moses the Man, 1981, The Winning Writer: Studies in the Art of Self-Expression, 1997; anthologies include: Best American Stories, O. Henry Prize Stories, Best Modern Short Stories, Seventeen's Stories, others; contbr. numerous mags. including Harper's, The New Yorker, New York Times, L.A. Times, Harper's Bazaar, Saturday Evening Post, Ladies' Home Jour., Seventeen, Nat. Wildlife, Mademoiselle, The Reporter; author poetry (Poetry award 1993, 94, 95); editor-in-chief Per/Se Internat. Quar., 1965-69; fiction editor UCLA West/Word, 1989-90. Class rep. Kodai-Woodstock Found., 1986-2000; elder Presbyn. Session, Claremont, Calif., 1988-91; mem. libr. commn. Pasadena Presbyn. Ch., 1996-99. Recipient Disting. Achievement award Ednl. Press Assn., 1974, North Coast Regional Ctr., Ukiah, 1978, Harper prize Harper & Bros., 1959, O. Henry award Doubleday, 1960, New Century Writers award, 2000; Bread Loaf fellow Middlebury Coll., 1956, Stegner fellow Stanford U., 1956-57. Mem. Calif. State Poetry Soc., Authors Guild, Am. Acad. Poets. Democrat. Presbyterian. Avocations: backpacking, gardening, photography, birds. Personal E-mail: romarwrite@aol.com.

WHITE, WILL WALTER, III, public relations consultant, writer; b. Glen Ridge, NJ, July 3, 1930; s. Will Walter and Miriam Chandler (Milburn) W.; m. Phyllis Marcia DuFlocq, Dec. 28, 1951 (div. 1971); children: Will Walter IV, Scott, Alan; m. Anne Elizabeth Levenson, Nov. 21, 1971 (div. 1992); children: Duncan, Christopher; stepchildren: Michael, Susan; m. Catherine Laur, Aug. 26, 1992. BA, Cornell U., 1952. Supr. Union Carbide Corp., NYC, 1954-59; account exec. Ketchum, MacLeod & Grove, NYC, 1959-62; sr. v.p. Wilson, Haight & Welch, Hartford, Conn., 1962-72; chmn., chief exec. officer Lowengard & Brotherhood, Hartford, 1972-83; pres., chief exec. officer Harland & Tine & White, Hartford, 1983-87; chmn. Donahue Inc., Hartford, 1987-89; ptnr. Laur White & White, Heathsville, Va., 1992—2000; owner Omega Cubed Press, 1996—. Exec. com. Conn. Dist. Export Council, 1979-88. Author: The Sunfish Book, 1983, 96; contbg. editor Mid-Gulf Sailing mag., 1994-95. Mem. exec. com. Hartford Stage Co., 1982-86; pres. Vis. Nurse Assn., Hartford, 1979; fin. chmn. Vis. Nurse and Home Care, Inc., Hartford and Waterbury, 1982-91; mem. pub. rels. com. Fairfield County Rep. Com., 1961; chmn. S.W. Fla. Regional Harbor Bd., 1995-2000. 1st lt. U.S. Army, 1952-54. Nat. champion Sunfish Racing Class, 1966, 68 Mem. Pub. Rels. Soc. Am. (accredited, chmn. investor rels. sect. 1983, charter mem. Hall of Fame 1990), Bus. Profl. Advt. Assn. (cert. bus. communicator), Nat. Investor Rels. Inst., U.S. Sunfish Class Assn. (pres. 1985-88, charter mem. Hall of Fame 1991), Boaters Action and Info. League (exec. v.p. 1992-2000), Hist. Soc. Sarasota County (bd. dirs. 1995-2000). Address: 3220 S E Hansel Ave Arcadia FL 34266-3143

WHITE, WILLIAM BLAINE, geochemist, researcher; b. Huntingdon, Pa., Jan. 5, 1934; s. William Bruce and Eleanor Mae (Barr) W.; m. Elizabeth Loczi, Mar. 27, 1959; children: Nikki Elizabeth White Vezendi, William Brion (dec.). BS, Juniata Coll., 1954; PhD, Pa. State U., 1962. Rsch. assoc. Mellon Inst., Pitts., 1954-58; asst. prof. Pa. State U., University Park, 1963-67, assoc. prof., 1967-72, prof. geochemistry, 1972—2002, emeritus prof., 2002—, chmn. grad. program in materials, 1990-93. Assoc. editor Am. Mineralogist, 1972-75, Materials Rsch. Bull., 1979-93, Jour. Am. Ceramic Soc., 1985-93, Water Resources Bull., 1992-93; editor earth scis. Nat. Speleological Soc. Bull., 1964-94; author: Geomorphology and Hydrology of Karst Terrains, 1988; (with Elizabeth L. White) Karst Hydrology: Concepts from the Mammoth Cave Area, 1989; (with Susan Barger) Daguerreotype: Nineteenth-Century Technology and Modern Science, 1991; (with David C. Culver) Encyclopedia of Caves, 2004, Benchmark Papers in Karst Science, 2007; contbr. articles to profl. jours. Home: 4538 Miller Rd Petersburg PA 16669-2711 Office: Pa State U Materials Rsch Lab University Park PA 16802 Home Phone: 814-667-2709; Office Phone: 814-865-1152. Business E-Mail: wbw2@psu.edu.

WHITE, WILLIAM DUDLEY, safety engineer; b. Birmingham, Mich., June 11, 1958; s. Paul Richard and Annetta Carole (Manhart) W.; m. Tamara Jean Wishon, Mar. 13, 1992; 1 child, Stacy Michelle; 1 stepchild, Royce Edward Vorel. BS cum laude, U. Ctrl. Okla., 1994. Chief maintenance engr. First Union Mgmt., Oklahoma City, 1984-89; safety rep., chmn. safety and suggestion coms. E-Systems, Inc., Greenville, Tex., 1994—. Creator curriculum for various safety programs, 1994, 96. Pack master Boy Scouts Am., Edmond, Okla., 1991-92; CPR instr., std. first aid instr. ARC, Hunt County, Tex., 1993—. Mem. Am. Soc. Safety Engrs., Alpha Chi. Roman Catholic. Achievements include development of safety certification/O-J-T checklist tng. program to meet OSHA, Air Force Occupational Safety and Health and Department of Defense standards regarding task proficiency for aircraft servicing, maintenance and daily ops. powered aircraft ground and mobile equipment; restructured indsl. hygiene program in accordance with American Conference of Governmental Industrial Hygienists guidelines.

WHITE, WILLIAM FREDRICK, lawyer; b. Elmhurst, Ill., Sept. 30, 1948; s. William Daniel and Carol Ruth (Laier) W.; m. Kathie Jean Nichols, May 27, 1979; children: Nicholas Roland, Andrew William. BA, U. Ill., 1970; JD, Antioch Sch. of Law, 1976. Bar: U.S. Ct. Appeals (D.C. cir.) 1976, Wis. 1982, U.S. Dist. Ct. (we. dist.) Wis. 1982, U.S. Dist. Ct. D.C. 1976, U.S. Ct. Claims 1978, U.S. Ct. Appeals (7th and 10th cirs.) 1982. With U.S. Dept. Labor, Washington, 1976; interim exec. dir. Common Cause, Washington, 1977; asst. counsel Nat. Treasury Employees Union, Washington, 1977-79, assoc. gen. counsel, 1979-81, dir. litigation, 1981-82; assoc. Michael, Best & Friedrich LLP, Madison, Wis., 1982-88, ptnr., chmn. assoc. devel. com., 1988-96, ptnr., 1988—, chair land and resources legal practice area, 1999—2002, mng. ptnr. Madison (Wis.) Office, 2002—06. Bd. dirs. Med. Physics Publ. Co.; dir. Med. Physics Found., 1988—, sec., 1994—. Chmn. Pub. Health Commn., Madison, 1983-89; bd. dirs. exec. com. Dane County Mediation Program, Madison, 1983-90, Perinatal Found., Madison, 1984-96, Arthritis Found., Madison, 1984-92, Arthritis Found., Madison, 1986-92, chmn., 1991-92; bd. dirs. Dane County Natural Heritage Found., 1988-91, Veridian Found., 2005-07; mem. Dane County Regional Airport Commn., 1991—, chmn. 1994—; chancellor Wis. Ann. Conf. United Meth. Ch., 1992—, gen. coun. Fin. and Adminstrn., 1991-2000, chmn. Legal Svcs. Com., 1992-96; bd. dirs. Downtown Madison Inc., sec. 1995-2001, chair transp. com.; mem. Dane County Transferrable Devel. Rights Task Force, Team Terrace Transp. Com., 1996-97, chair; bd. trustees Madison Mus. Contemporary Art, 1998—, dir., 2000—; co-chair Friends of Hudson Park, 1999—; Madison program chair Dane County Pub. Affairs Coun., 2000-02; dir. Capital Region Econ. Devel. Entity, Apt. Assn. South Ctrl. Wis. Mem. ABA, D.C. Bar Assn., Med. Physics Found. (bd. dirs. 1987—), Dane County Bar Assn., State Bar Assn. (sec. Health Law sect.), Transp. Devel. Assn. (dir. 1999-2003, exec. com. 1999-2003). Democrat. United Methodist. Avocations: bicycling, skiing. Office: Michael Best & Friedrich LLP Ste 700 1 S Pinckney St Madison WI 53703-2892

WHITE, WILLIAM NELSON, lawyer; b. Balt., Sept. 8, 1938; s. Nelson Cardwell and Ellen Atwell (Zoller) W.; m. Mary Kathleen Bitzel, Sept. 2, 1960 (div. 1971); children: Craig William, Jeffrey Alan, Colin Christopher; m. Christine Lewin Hanna, July 8, 1978. LLB, U. Md., 1968, JD, 1969. Bar: Md. 1972, US Ct. Appeals (4th cir.) 1975, US Dist. Ct. Md. 1976, US Supreme Ct. 1976. Asst. state's atty., Balt., 1972; assoc. Brooks & Turnbull, Balt., 1973—76; pvt. practice Balt., 1977—. Former counsel St. Andrews Soc. Balt., 1989—; former counsel, bd. dirs. St. George's Soc. Former elder, pres. deacons, trustee Roland Park Presbyn. Ch.; former mem. worship, music and sacrament coun., former elder Second Presbyn. Ch. Mem.: SAR (chancellor Md. soc., former 3d v.p., 2d v.p., chpt. pres.), Md. Bar Assn., U. Md. Alumni Assn. for Greater Balt. (pres. 1977). Avocations: history, philosophy, classical music, tennis, sailing.

WHITE, WILLIAM NORTH, retired chemistry professor; b. Walton, NY, Sept. 16, 1925; s. George Fitch and Frances (Peck) W.; m. Hilda R. Sauter, Sept. 8, 1951; children: Carla Ann, Eric Jeffrey. AB, Cornell U., 1950; MA, Harvard U., 1951, PhD, 1953. NRC postdoctoral fellow Calif. Inst. Tech., Pasadena, 1953-54; asst. prof. Ohio State U., Columbus, 1954-59, asso. prof., 1959-63; prof. chemistry U. Vt., Burlington, 1963-76, 77-95, prof. emeritus, 1995—, chmn. dept., 1963-70, acting chmn. dept., 1975-76; prof. chemistry U. Tex. at Arlington, 1976-77, chmn. dept., 1976-77; ret., 1995. NSF sr. postdoctoral fellow Brookhaven Nat. Lab., Upton, N.Y., 1963-64, Harvard U., 1965; vis. scholar Brandeis U., 1974-75; chmn. arrangements com. Nat. Organic Chemistry Symposium, 1965-67 Contbr. articles on organic chemistry profl. jours. Selectman Town of Shelburne, Vt., 1968-74, water commr., 1973-74, justice of the peace, 1981-, sewer commr., 1991-93, Natural Resources and Conservation com., 1970-74, 2004-; mem. Chittenden County Regional Planning Commn., 1983-91; mem. bd. suprs. Winooski (Vt.) Natural Resources Conservation Dist., 1999-2004. With AUS, 1943-46. Recipient Outstanding Forest Stewardship award Winooski Conservation Dist., 1997. Mem. Am. Chem. Soc. (chmn. Western Vt. sect. 1966-67), Royal Soc. Chemistry, New Eng. Assn. Chemistry Tchrs., AAAS, N.Y. Acad. Scis., Phi Beta Kappa, Sigma Xi, Phi Kappa Phi, Phi Lambda Upsilon. Home: 226 Pierson Dr Shelburne VT 05482 Business E-Mail: wnwhite@uvm.edu.

WHITE, WILLIAM SAMUEL, foundation executive; b. Cin., May 8, 1937; s. Nathaniel Ridgway and Mary White; m. Claire Mott, July 1, 1961; children: Tiffany, Ridgway Harding. BA, Dartmouth Coll., 1959, MBA, 1960; degree (hon.), GMI Engring. and Mgmt. Inst., 1996; LLD (hon.), Eastern Mich. U., 1975, U. Mich., 2006. With Barrett & Williams, NYC, 1961-62; sr. assoc. Bruce Payne & Assos., NYC, 1962-71; v.p. C. S. Mott Found., Flint, Mich., 1971-75, pres., 1976—, trustee, 1971—, also chmn. bd. dirs. Chmn. bd. dirs. U.S. Sugar Corp.; bd. dirs. Am. Water Works, 1999—2003. Mem. exec. com. Daycroft Sch., Greenwich, Conn., 1966-70; bd. dirs. Flint Area Conf., 1971-84, Coun. on Founds., 1985-90, Independent Sector, 1994-99, 2004—, Am. Friends Czech Republic, 1999-2004, European Found. Centre, 1994—, Civicus, 1995-2001; citizens adv. task force U. Mich., Flint, 1974-79; chmn. Coun. of Mich. Founds., 1979-81, Flint Area Focus Coun., 1988—, Afterschool Allstars, 2004-; mem. Pres.'s Task Force on Pvt. Sector Initiatives, 1982; trustee GMI Engring. and Mgmt. Inst., 1982-86, Network European Founds., 2000—, Madriaga Found., 2004—. With U.S. Army, 1960-62. Office: C S Mott Foundation 1200 Mott Foundation Bldg Flint MI 48502-1807

WHITE, YONSENIA S., artist, educator; BA, Va. Tech, Blacksburg, 1996, BFA, 1997; MFA, Rutgers U., New Brunswick, NJ, 1999. Instr. dept. art and art history Va. Tech., Blacksburg, 1999—2000, asst. prof. dept. art and art history, 2000—06, assoc. prof., 2006—. Manna from the Marquis: Spiritual Guidance from the Side of the Road, visual art exhibitions, Stereotypes & Catharsis, Hard to Ingest, Race (Enter Personal Politics), As I Am, 3rd Annual Women's Art Show. Prayer team leader St. Paul AME Ch., Blacksburg, Va., 2003—05. Recipient Minority Blueprint award, Rutgers U., Dept. Art, Mason Gross Sch. Arts, 1999; grantee, Peninsula Fine Arts Ctr., 1999, Va. Tech., U. Writing Program, 2003. Mem.: Women's Caucus Art, Nat. Mus.Women Arts, Southeastern Coll. Art Conf., Founds. Art Theory and Edn., Coll. Art Assn. Liberal. Avocations: fine and performing arts, poetry, sports, travel, jazz. Home Phone: 540-239-4396; Office Phone: 540-231-3807. Personal E-mail: yonsenia@yahoo.com.

WHITED, MARY ELIZABETH, marketing professional; Marketing N.Y. Times Syndication Sales Corp. Office: NY Times Syndication Sales Corp 609 Greenwich St 6th Fl New York NY 10014 Office Phone: 212-499-3417. Office Fax: 212-499-3382. E-mail: whiteme@nytimes.com.

WHITE-HAMMOND, GLORIA E., pastor, pediatrician, human rights advocate; m. Ray A. Hammond, 1973; children: Mariama, Adiya. BA in Biology, Boston U.; MD, Tufts U., 1976; MDiv, Harvard Divinity Sch., 1997; LHD (hon.), Tufts U., 2006. Pediatrician South End Cmty. Health Ctr., 1981—; co-pastor (with husband Rev. Ray A. Hammond, M.D.) Bethel AME Ch., Boston, 1997—. Medical missionary in several African countries including Botswana, Cote D'Ivoire and South Africa. Co-founder My Sister's Keeper, Sudan, 2002—; chair Million Voices for Darfur campaign; founder, cons. Do the Write Thing, 1994—; co-convener The Red Tent Group; co-chair Mass. Coalition to Save Darfur; trustee Brigham and Women's Hosp.; bd. overseers Tufts U. Coll. Cmty. and Public Svc.; bd. dirs. Am. Anti Slavery Group, Boston, Christian Solidarity Internat., Zurich. Recipient Humanitarian award, Boston Theological Inst., 2004, Liberating Vision award, Greater Boston Sect. Nat. Coun. Negro Women, 2004, Impact award, Am. Assn. Retired Persons, 2004, Exceptional Women award, Magic 106.7, 2006. Achievements include being involved in obtaining the freedom of 10,000 women and children in Southern Sudan who were enslaved during the two decades long civil war. Office: Bethel AME Church 215 forest Hills St Jamaica Plain MA 02130-3302

WHITEHEAD, DAVID BARRY, lawyer; b. San Francisco, Oct. 14, 1946; s. Barry and Fritzi-Beth (Bowman) W.; m. René Dayan, May 26, 1970. AB in History, Stanford U., 1968, JD, 1971. Bar: Calif. 1972, U.S. Dist. Ct. (no. dist.) Calif. 1972, U.S. Ct. Appeals (9th cir.) 1972, U.S. Dist. Ct. (cen. dist.) Calif. 1974. Assoc. Cullinan Hancock Rothert & Burns, San Francisco, 1972-74, Cullinan Burns & Helmer, San Francisco, 1975-77, ptnr., 1977-78, Burns & Whitehead, San Francisco, 1979-85, Whitehead & Porter, San Francisco, 1986-97, Whitehead, Porter & Gordon LLP, San Francisco, 1998—. Bd. dirs. Rainbow Music, Inc., San Francisco, ITP, Inc., Sunnyvale, Calif.; founding dir. A. Lincoln High Sch. San Francisco, 1989—. Mem. San Francisco Rep. Steering Com., 1984—89; bd. dirs. Enterprise for High Sch. Students, San Francisco, 1982—86; bd. dirs. San Francisco chpt. Easter Seal Soc., 1986—90; bd. dirs. Opera West Found., San Francisco, 1986, Traveler's Aid Soc., San Francisco, 1989—90, Hosp. de la Familia, 1995—2000, Gold Rush Trail Found., 1998, Calif. Hist. Soc. Found., 1998. Mem. ABA, Calif. Bar Assn., San Francisco Bar Assn., Calif. Scholarship Fedn. (life) Family Club San Francisco (bd. dirs. 1986-89, 93-95), World Trade Club, Abraham Lincoln High Sch. San Francisco Alumni Assn. (founding dir.). Roman Catholic. Avocations: writing, art, directing, singing. Office: Whitehead Porter LLP 220 Montgomery St Fl 18 San Francisco CA 94104-3402 Mailing: 81 San Andreas Way San Francisco CA 94127-2027

WHITEHEAD, EDGAR DOUGLAS, urology educator; b. Galashiels, Scotland, Aug. 24, 1939; 1 child, Robin Stacey. BA, Vanderbilt U., 1961; MD, Ind. U., 1965; postgrad., U. London, 1972. Diplomate Am. Bd. Urology; med. lic. Ind., Ill., N.Y., Calif., N.J. Surgery intern Mount Sinai Hosp., NYC, 1965-66; resident in surgery Presbyn.-St. Luke's Hosp., Chgo., 1966-67; resident in urology N.Y.U. Med. Ctr., 1969-73; clin. assoc. urology Mount Sinai Sch. Medicine, NYC, 1973-77, sr. clin. instr. urology,

1977-80, asst. clin. prof. urology, 1980-92; pvt. practice, NYC, 1973—; assoc. clin. prof. urology Mount Sinai Sch. Medicine, 1992-94, Albert Einstein Coll. of Medicine, 1994—; attending NYU Downtown Hosp. Assoc. attending Beth Israel Med. Ctr., N.Y.C.; advisor Impotence Anonymous & Jr., Diabetes Self-Mgmt., 1983-85, Jour. Urol. Nursing; med. adv. bd. Colostomy Soc., N.Y., Inc.; investigator Protocol 2560 (alfus) Alfuzosin study, 1998; cons. and speaker in field. Author: Viagra--The Wonder Drug for Peak Performance; editor: Current Operative Urology, 1975, 2d rev. edit., 1984, ann. edits., 1989-92, Mgmt. Impotence and Infertility, 1994, Sex Over Forty, 1990-2000, Atlas Surgical Techniques in Urology, 1997; mem. editl. bd. Female Patient, Med. Aspects of Human Sexuality; memcontbr. articles to profl. jours. Grantee U.S.P.H., Clin. Research Ctr. Fellow ACS, Clin. Soc. Am. Diabetes Assn., N.Y. Diabetes Affiliate; mem. AMA, AAAS, Am. Urol. Assn., Soc. Internat. Urology (diplomate), Sexual Medicine Soc. N.Am., Am. Assn. Clin. Urologists, N.Y. State Urol. Assn., Am. Acad. of Phalloplasty Surgeons (pres., bd. dirs.), Internat. Soc. for Artificial Organs, Am. So. Nephrology, Am. Assn. Sex Educators, Counselors and Therapists, Soc. for the Sci. Study of Sex, Soc. for Sex Therapy and Rsch., Sex Info. and Edn. Coun. of the U.S. Coalition on Sexuality and Disability, Am. Cancer Soc., Nat. Kidney Found., Am. Geriatric Soc., N.Y. Acad. Sci., N.Y. Acad. Medicine, N.Y. Urodynamic Soc., Internat. Continence Soc., Soc. Genitourinary Reconstructive Surgeons, Assn. Male Sexual Dysfunction (dir.), N.Y. Phalloplasty (dir.). Achievements include patents in field.

WHITEHEAD, J. RENNIE, science administrator, consultant; s. William and Beatrice Cora (Fenning) W.; m. Nesta Doone James, Nov. 1, 1944; children— Valerie Lesley (dec.), Michael James Rennie. B.Sc. in Physics, Manchester U., Lancashire, Eng., 1939; PhD in Phys. Chemistry, Cambridge U., Eng., 1949. Cert. profl. engr., Ont.; chartered engr., U.K. Sci. officer TRE (UK Radar), England, 1939-51; assoc. prof. McGill U., Montreal, P.Q., Canada, 1951-55; dir. research RCA Victor Co Ltd., Montreal, 1955-65; prin. sci. adviser Govt. of Can., Ottawa, Ont., 1965-75; sr. v.p. Philip A. Lapp Ltd., Ottawa, 1975-82; pvt. practice sci. cons. Ottawa, 1982-86. Author: Superregenerative Receivers, 1949. Bd. dirs. Found. for Internat. Tng., Toronto, 1976—86. Fellow Royal Soc. Can., Inst. Physics, Instn. Elec. Engrs., Can. Aeronautics and Space Inst., Can. Assn. for Club of Rome (chmn. 1976-81, editor and pub. newsletter and procs. 1987-99). Anglican. Avocations: automobiles, stamp collecting/philately, carpentry, computers. Home and Office: 1368 Chattaway Ave Ottawa ON Canada K1H 7S3 E-mail: drrennie@sympatico.ca.

WHITEHEAD, JOHN CUNNINGHAM, former bank executive; b. Evanston, Ill., Apr. 2, 1922; s. Eugene C. and Winifred W.; m. Helene E. Shannon, Sept. 28, 1946 (div. Dec. 1971); children: Anne Elizabeth, John Gregory; m. Jaan W. Chartener, Oct. 22, 1972 (div. 1986); 1 child, Sarah; m. Nancy Dickerson, 1989 (dec. 1997); m. Cynthia Matthea, Feb. 7, 2007. BA, Haverford Coll., 1943; MBA, Harvard U., 1947; LLD (hon.), Pace. U., Rutgers U., Haverford Coll., Harvard U., Amherst Coll., Seton Hall U.; LLD, Bates Coll., 2004; Gen. Theological Seminary, Berea Coll. With Goldman, Sachs & Co., NYC, 1947-84, ptnr., 1956-76, sr. ptnr., co-chmn., 1976-84; dep. sec. US Dept. State, Washington, 1985-89; chmn. Fed. Res. Bank NY, NYC, 1996—2000, Lower Manhattan Devel. Corp., NYC, 2001—06. Trustee Haverford Coll.; past pres. bd. overseers Harvard U.; co-chmn. greater N.Y. coun. Boy Scouts Am.; past chmn. Internat. Rescue Com., UN Assn. U.S.A.; Andrew Mellon Found; chmn. Goldman Sachs Found., 1999—; founding chmn. World Trade Ctr. Meml. Found., 2005—, emeritus; chmn. Brookings Instn., Internat. House, Nat. Gallery of Art; dir. Nature Conservatory, East West Inst., Eisenhower Exch. Fellowship. With USNR, 1943—46. Mem. Coun. on Fgn. Rels., Links Club, Univ. Club.

WHITEHEAD, JOHN WAYNE, lawyer, educator, writer; b. Pulaski, Tenn., July 14, 1946; s. John M. and Alatha (Wiser) W.; m. Virginia Carolyn Nichols, Aug. 26, 1967; children: Jayson Reau, Jonathan Mathew, Elisabeth Anne, Joel Christofer, Joshua Benjamen. BA, U. Ark., 1969, JD, 1974. Bar: Ark. 1974, U.S. Dist. Ct. (ea. and we. dists.) Ark. 1974, U.S. Supreme Ct. 1977, U.S. Ct. Appeals (9th cir.) 1980, Va. 1981, U.S. Ct. Appeals (7th cir.) 1981, U.S. Ct Appeals (4th and 5th cirs.). Spl. counsel Christian Legal Soc., Oak Park, Ill., 1977-78; assoc. Gibbs & Craze, Cleve., 1978-79; sole practice law Manassas, Va., 1979-82; pres. The Rutherford Inst., Charlottesville, Va., 1982—, also bd. dirs. Frequent lectr. colls., law schs.; past adj. prof. O.W. Coburn Sch. Law. Author: Schools on Fire, 1980, The New Tyranny, 1982, The Second American Revolution, 1982, The Stealing of America, 1983, The Freedom of Religious Expression in Public High Schools, 1983, The End of Man, 1986, An American Dream, 1987, The Rights of Religious Persons in Public Education, 1991, Home Education: Rights and Reasons, 1993, Religious Apartheid, 1994, Slaying Dragons, 1999, Grasping For the Wind, 2001, others; writer, dir.: (video series) Grasping for the Wind (Silver World medal N.Y. Film Festival), 1998-99; contbr. articles to profl. jours., chpts. to books. 1st lt. U.S. Army, 1969-71. Named Christian Leader of Yr. Christian World Affairs Conf., Washington, 1986; recipient Bus. and Profl. award Religious Heritage Am., 1990, Hungarian Freedom medal, Budapest, 1991. Mem. ABA, Ark. Bar Assn., Va. Bar Assn. Office: The Rutherford Inst PO Box 7482 Charlottesville VA 22906-7482 Office Phone: 434-978-3888. Business E-Mail: johnw@rutherford.org.

WHITEHEAD, KENNETH DEAN, writer, translator, retired federal agency administrator; b. Rupert, Idaho, Dec. 14, 1930; s. Clarence Christian and May Bell (Allen) W.; m. Margaret Mary O'Donohue, Aug. 2, 1958; children: Paul Daniel, Steven Francis, Matthew Patrick, David Joseph. BA in French, U. Utah, 1955; postgrad., U. Paris, 1956-57; cert. in Arabic and Middle East studies, Fgn. Service Inst., Beirut, 1962; LittD (hon.), Franciscan U., Steubenville, Oho, 2003. Instr. English U. Utah, Salt Lake City, 1955-56; fgn. service officer Dept. State, Rome, Beirut and Tripoli, Libya, 1957-65; chief Arabic service Voice of Am., Washington, 1965-67; dep. dir. fgn. currency program Smithsonian Instn., Washington, 1967-72; exec. v.p. Caths. United for Faith Inc., New Rochelle, NY, 1972-81; dir. Ctr. for Internat. Edn. U.S. Dept. Edn., Washington, 1982-86, dep. asst. sec. for higher edn. programs, 1986-88, asst. sec. for postsecondary edn., 1988-89. Author: Respectable Killing: The New Abortion Imperative, 1972, Agenda for the Sexual Revolution, 1981, Catholic Colleges and Federal Funding, 1988, DOA: The Ambush of the Universal Catechism, 1993, Political Orphan? The Prolife Cause after 25 Years of Roe v. Wade, 1998, One, Holy, Catholic, and Apostolic: The Early Church Was the Catholic Church, 2000; co-author: The Pope, The Council and the Mass, 1981, rev. edit., 2006, Flawed Expectations: The Reception of the Catechism of the Catholic Church, 1996; sr. editor: World Almanac Book of Dates, 1982, Macmillan Concise Dictionary of World History, 1983; editor: Marriage and the Common Good, 2001, Pope John Paul II--Witness to Truth, 2001, The Catholic Imagination, 2003, Voices of the New Springtime, 2004, The Catholic Citizen: Debating the Issues of Justice, 2004, The Church, Marriage, and the Family, 2007; co-editor: The Battle for the Catholic Mind, 2001; translator 20 books from French, German, Italian, 1980—. Bd. dir. Notre Dame Inst. for Advanced Study, Arlington, Va., 1986-95, Philosophy Edn. Soc., 1995—, Christas Magister Found., 1997-2001. Fulbright scholar U.S. Dept. State, 1956-57. Mem. Fellowship Cath. Scholars (bd. dir. 1990-2000, 04—), Brent Soc. Cath. Profls. (bd. dir. 1992-98), Cath. League for Religious and Civil Rights (bd. dir. 1992—), KC. Republican. Home: 809 Ridge Pl Falls Church VA 22046-3631 Office Phone: 703-538-5085. Fax: (703) 534-3015. E-mail: whiteheadz@msn.com.

WHITEHEAD, LINDA SUE, literature and language educator, history educator, special education educator; b. Riverton, Wyo., May 22, 1953; d. Wayne Edmund Gotfredson and Julia Ann Davidson; m. Dan Frank Whitehead, Nov. 6, 1975; children: Rachel Ann Brooks, Jesse Linn, Jared Pierce, John Paul, Naomi Marie. BA, Brigham Young U., Provo, Utah, 1975; MA, Adams State Coll., Alamosa, Colo., 1998. Instr. Mancos Sch. Dist., Colo., 1994—. Chair accountability com. Mancos Re-6 Sch. Dist., 1992—93; pres. local women's orgn. LDS Ch., 1990—94. Mem.: Writer's Club (cofounder 1999—2006). Mem. Lds Ch. Achievements include design of Lesson Plan chosen for Summer History Institute. Avocations: writing, reading, gardening, fishing, hiking. Office: Mancos School District 355 W Grand Mancos CO 81328 Home Phone: 970-533-7948; Office Phone: 970-533-7746. Business E-Mail: lwhitehead@mancosre6.edu.

WHITEHEAD, MICHAEL ANTHONY, chemistry professor; b. London, June 30, 1935; arrived in Can., 1962, naturalized, 2003; s. Francis Henry and Edith Downes (Rotherham) W.; 1 son, Christopher Mark. B.Sc. in Chemistry with honors, Queen Mary Coll., U. London, 1956, PhD, 1960, D.Sc., 1974. Asst. lectr. Queen Mary Coll., U. London, 1958-60; postdoctoral fellow U. Cin., 1960, asst. prof., 1961; asst. prof. theoretical chemistry McGill U., Montreal, Que., Canada, 1962-66, asso. prof., 1966-74, prof., 1974-99, prof. emeritus, 1999—. Vis. prof. U. Cambridge, Eng., 1971-72, U. Oxford, Eng., 1972-74; vis. professorial fellow Univ. Coll. Wales, Aberystwyth, 1980, U. Oxford, 1990-91; invited prof. U. Geneva, 1983-84; life guest prof. Nat. U. Def. Tech., Changsha, People's Republic of China; vis. Erskine fellow chemistry dept. U. Canterbury, Christchurch, N.Z., 2000, co-chair history and advanced in quantum chemistry 84th conf., Montreal, 2001; mem. Internat. Com. on Nuclear Quadrupole Resonance.; co-chmn. 7th Internat. Symposium on Nuclear Quadrapole Resonance, Kingston, Ont., Can., 1983; convenor Can. and Internat. N.E. Symposium of Montreal, 2004; mem. Ctr. for Molecular Modelling, Concordia U., Montreal, 2005—; joint chmn. 1st Applied Pulp and Paper Molecular Modelling Symposium, 2005. Contbr. articles to profl. jours. Mem. parish coun. St. John the Evangelist; exec. coun. Can. Sci. and Christian Affiliation; chmn. Montreal Sch. Theology; mem. Planned Giving Com. Montreal Anglican Diocese. Fellow Royal Chem. Soc., Chem. Inst. Can., Royal Soc. Arts; mem. Am. Chem. Soc., Am. Phys. Soc., James McGill Soc. (pres. 1993-95), Sigma Xi (pres. McGill chpt. 1971-72, 81-82, 92-95, 97-99, dir. Can. and internat. constituency group 2000—06, chair awards com. 2001—06, ad hoc mem. internat. com. 2001-05), McGill Savoy Soc. (founder, life), Phi Lambda Upsilon. Anglican. Office: McGill U Dept Chemistry 801 Sherbrooke St W Montreal PQ Canada H3A 2K6 Home Phone: 514-286-1378; Office Phone: 514-398-6239. Business E-Mail: tony.whitehead@mcgill.ca. *My faith in God and belief in Christ.*

WHITEHEAD, PAUL, lawyer, labor union administrator; b. 1951; BA, U. Wis.; JD, Harvard U. Bar: Pa. 1980. Asst. gen. counsel United Steelworkers Am., Pitts., 1999—2001, gen. counsel, 2001—. Adj. prof. Carnegie Mellon U.; chmn. bd. CC Allegheny County, 1994—. Office: General Counsel United Steelworkers Am 5 Gateway Ctr Pittsburgh PA 15222 Office Phone: 412-562-2400. Office Fax: 412-562-2484. *

WHITEHEAD, TANYA DIANNE GRUBBS, psychologist, educator, researcher; b. Scottsbuff, Nebr., June 23, 1953; d. William Elliott Grubbs and Esther Mary Cooper Grubbs; m. William Downing Whitehead, Aug. 12, 1971; children: Shana Alexandra, Thomas William, Bethany Rose. B in Psychology summa cum laude, Ottawa U., 1990; M in Clin. Psychology, Avila U., 1992; D in Psychology, U. Mo., 2001. Cert. specialist, developmental and handicapping conditions U. Kans. Sch. Medicine, 1993. Clin. instr. U. Kans. Sch. Medicine, Kansas City, 1987—96; rsch. prof. U. Mo., Kansas City, 1996—. Psychol. consulting burn unit, craniofacial team, spina bifida clinic, pediatric gastroenterology Sch. Medicine, U. Kans., Kansas City, 1987—96; state, regional and nat. advisor People First Self Advocacy Tng. Adults With Devel. Disabilities, 1997—2001; peer grant rev. facilitator and chair US Depts Health and Human Svcs., Corp. for Nat. Svc., Washington, 1999—; program evaluator, impact of asset bldg. on youth from disadvantaged circumstances Office of Cmty. Svc., US Dept. Health and Human Svs.; program evaluation: promoting higher edn. partnerships for global devel. US AID, Assn. Liaison Office for U. Cooperation in Devel., Cape Town, South Africa; dir. AmeriCorps VISTA Project in Self Advocacy, Statewide, Mo., 1998—2000; cons.: cmty. movement for urban progress cmty. devel. corp. Urban Core Cmty. Devel. Project, Kansas City, 2002—04; sr. program evaluator; assets for independence demonstration project, us hhs, office cmty. svcs. PeopleWorks, Inc., Washington, 2000—01. Author: (Self Determination Workshops) New Media Workshops for Adults with DD, (book) Exploring Self Advocacy from a Social Power Perspective, (film) Enslaved Minds: Final Barrier to Freedom and Justice; contbr. new media toolkit (Crystal Communicator Award, 2001); author: (disability accommodation guide) Exchange City Accommodation Guide. Fellow Ctr. for the City, U. Mo., 2004-2005; fellow, Studies in Cmty. Change, 2000. Mem.: ANA (mem. commn. accreditation), AAUP, AAUW, LWV, APA, Assn. for the Advancement Ednl. Rsch. (bd. mem.), Am. Nurses Credentialing Ctr. (bd. Commn. on Accreditation). Home Phone: 913-488-7722; Office Phone: 913-488-7722. Business E-Mail: whiteheadt@umkc.edu.

WHITEHILL, ANGELA ELIZABETH, artistic director; b. Leeds, Yorkshire, Eng., Oct. 21, 1938; arrived in US, 1963, naturalized, 1995; d. Donald Paul and Audrey May (Clayforth) Warner; m. Norman James Whitehill, Jr., Dec. 23, 1959; children: Norman James III, Pamela Elizabeth; m. William Parker Noble, Dec. 27, 1998. Student, Arts Ednl. Sch., London, 1955-59. With corps de ballet Ballet Paris, 1958-59; dir. London Sch. Ballet, St. Thomas, V.I., 1960-63; asst. dir. Ocean County Ballet Co., Toms River, NJ, 1965-68; founder, dir. Shore Ballet Sch., Toms River, 1968-76; artistic dir. Shore Ballet Co., Toms River, 1971-76; artist in residence Castleton State Coll., Rutland, Vt., 1977-79; founder, artistic dir. Burklyn Ballet Theatre, Johnson, Vt., 1977—2003, founding artistic dir., 2003—; dir. Ballet Umbrella, Dance Coun., Burklyn Designs, 2003—; artistic dir. Paradise Ballet Theatre, Key West, Fla., 2005—07. Vis. prof. Colby Sawyer Coll., New London, N.H., 1978-80; resident designer Atlanta Ballet Co., 1981-83; designer, pub. relations N.J. Ballet Co., Orange, 1983-85; artistic dir. Vt. Ballet Theatre, Burlington, 1985-94; master tchr. 1st Congress Internat. de Ballet Classico Contemporaneo, Mex., 2000, Ft. Wayne Ballet, 2005, Regional Dance Am. SW Festival, 2006; interim artistic dir. Huntington Ballet Theatre, 2006, artistic dir., 2006-07. Choreographer Arensky Dances, 1983, A Deux, 1984, 4 Plus 2, 1986, Twins From A Time Gone By, 1987, Heart of the Island, 2002; co-author: Parent's Book of Ballet, 1988, 2d edit., 2003, The Young Professional's Book of Ballet, 1990, The Dancer's Book of Ballet, 2000, Ballet Magic, The Burklyn Story, 2001, Nutcracker Backstage, 2004; dir. artistic advisor Paradise Ballet Theatre, Nutcracker Key West, 2005; costumer designer Grand Rapids Ballet Swan Lake Act III, 1984, Scottish Am. Ballet, La Sylphide, 1984, Legend of Ench. Bird, 1994, Burklyn Youth Ballet, 1999-05, Hansel & Gretel, Alice in Wonderland, Cinderella & The Flower Fairies, Little Mermaid, Beauty and the Beast, Aladdin, Huntington Ballet Theatre, Cinderella, 2005, Nutcracker Key West ACT II, 2005, Burklyn Youth Ballet, 2006, Sleeping Beauty, 2007. Dir. Vt. Ballet Theatre Found., Calledonia County, 1986-96. Recipient Francis Hopkins award Ocean County, N.J., 1976, Woman of Achievement award Vt. Woman, 1989, Author's award N.J. Inst. Tech., 1989. Mem. Vt. Council on the Arts, Regional Dance Am. Mem. Soc. Of Friends. Home: 218 Ocean Ave Island Heights NJ 08732 Home (Winter): PO Box 907 Island Heights NJ 08732-0907 Office: Dance Counsel PO Box 493 Johnson VT 05656-0493 Home Phone: 723-288-2660; Office Phone: 732-288-2660. Personal E-mail: awhitehill@aol.com. E-mail: awhitehill@comcast.net.

WHITEHORN, CLARK ALLAN, retired urologist; b. Chgo., Jan. 1, 1926; s. Rex Whitehorn and Pearl May Pollock; m. Virginia Brandt (dec.); m. Virginia Ida Gunn; children: Clark A.(dec.), Robert Brandt(dec.). Student, Johns Hopkins U., Balt., 1943—44; MD, U. Md., Balt., 1948. Lic. physician Fla., diplomate Am. Bd. Urology, Nat. Bd. Med. Examiners. Intern Detroit Receiving Hosp., 1948—49; asst. resident gen. surgery Md. Gen. Hosp., Balt., 1949—50; urology intern Johns Hopskins Hosp., Balt., 1950—51; urology resident Duke Hosp., Durham, NC, 1953—55; founder, chief of urology Gulf Coast Medl. Ctr./Hosp., Panama City, Fla.; chief of staff, chief of surgery Bay Med.l Ctr. Hosp., Panama City; ret. Chmn. allocation com. Cmty. Svc. Found., 2006; comdr. U.S. Power Sqdn., Dist. 15, 1984; elder 1st Presbyn. Ch., 1984—2005; dir. Cmty. Svc. Found., 1990—. Capt. M.C. USAF, 1950—53. Fellow: Am. Coll. Urol. Surgeons; mem.: AMA, Internat. Soc. Urology, Fla. State Urol. Soc. (pres.), Bay Med. Soc. (pres.), Yacht Club. Avocations: gardening, golf, travel, reading.

WHITEHORTON, THELMA, educational administrator; b. Blyesville, Ark., Feb. 7, 1949; d. William Soloman and Corrine (Carrigans) White; m. Charles D. Horton, May 20, 1970 (div. 1991); children: Corrine Daniel Horton, Tiffany Louise, Charles William. Student, Fla. Internat. U.; BSW, Boise State U., 1975; D (hon.), World U.; student, St. Thomas U., 2006—. Team tchr. Dade County Pub. Schs., Parks and Recreation Coll., North Miami, 1979—80; lead tchr. gifted edn. Dade County Elem. Schs., Miami Dade C.C., Miami, 1980—; owner, dir. Hi School Day Care and Learning Ctr., Cutler Ridge, Fla., 1981—; reading tchr. Miami Dade CC, 1981—83. Lead tchr. gifted Naranja Elem. Sch.; owner Charisma, Fla.; tutor English, Perrine, Fla., 1982—; with Comet Lab, 1996-97; cons. WESTAT Rsch., Barr Industries, Perrine, 1981—, The Rand Co., Student Travel Svc. student placement; temp. Dade County Pub. Schs.; alternative edn. tchr. 5th grade Peskoe Elem. Sch.; advocate African-Am. voices; tchr. liberal arts Wardstone Coll.; adminstr. R.E.S.S. program for implementation of the Met. Test/Archdiocese of Miami; creator of The Horton Chart for Math; pvt. tchr. tap dance. Author: Have Your Cake and Eat it Too, The Black C, Reciprocal Reading, African Curriculum Integration for Intermediate Education in the Classroom, Reciprocal Reading 1996-97, Epinions.com., Ms. T. Tuttle's 2nd Grade Class T.E.A.M., The Reading Quagmire: ERIC, Lessonpro, The Dream Catcher, 2004; contbr. papers to profl. jours. Active Boy Scouts Am., PTSA, ARC; mem. usher bd. Martin Meml. Meth. Ch.; st. capt. Neighborhood Crime Watch; advocate for Nat. Tchr. Cert., 1995-96; vol. The Horton Chart Eisenhower Nat. Clearinghouse; advocate African Am. Voices; children's adv. Idaho Gov.'s ADvocacy Program, Boise, 1974-76. Named Comet Lab. Tchr. of Yr., 1996; recipient Equity and Excellence award, Magnet Innovative Programs, Cmty. Svc. award, JESCA orgn. Mem. ACLU, The Exec. Female, Children's Advocates (pres. 1975-83), United Tchrs. Dade County, Alumni Assn. Boise State U., Inst. Children's Lit., Miami C. of C., Fla. Assn. for the Gifted, Kappa Delta Pi. Office: 13990 SW 264th St Homestead FL 33032-7402 Home Phone: 305-378-0412. Personal E-mail: pug@bellso.net. E-mail: chinatown48@yahoo.com.

WHITEHOUSE, DAVID BRYN, museum director; b. Workson, Nottinghamshire, Eng., Oct. 15, 1941; came to U.S., 1984; s. Brindley Charles and Alice Margaret (Dobson) W.; m. Ruth Delamain Ainger, 1963; children: Sarah, Susan, Peter; m. Elizabeth-Anne Ollemans, 1975; children: Julia, Simon, Nicola. BA, Cambridge U., 1963, MA, 1965, PhD, 1967. Dir. Brit. Inst. Afghan Studies, Kabul, Afghanistan, 1973-74, Brit. Sch., Rome, 1974-84; chief curator Corning Mus. Glass, NY, 1984-87, dep. dir., 1988-92, dir., 1992-99, exec. dir., 1999—. Dir. Siraf expdn. Brit. Inst. Persian Studies, Tehran, Iran, 1966-73. Author: (with Ruth Whitehouse) Archaeological Atlas of the World, 1975, (with David Andrews and John Osborne) Aspects of Medieval Lazio, 1982, (with Donald B. Harden and others) Glass of the Caesars, 1987, Glass of the Roman Empire, 1988, (with Richard Hodges) Mohammed, Charlemagne and the Origins of Europe, 1983, Glass: A Pocket Dictionary, 1993, English Cameo Glass, 1994, Roman Glass in The Corning Museum of Glass, Vol. 1, 1997, Vol. 2, 2001, Vol. 3, 2003, Excavations at ed-Dur (Umm al-Qaiwan, UAE), Vol. 1, The Glass Vessels, 1998, The Corning Museum of Glass, A Decade of Glass Collecting, 1990-1999, 2000, (with Stefano Carboni) Glass of the Sultans, 2001, Sasanian and Post-Sasanian Glass in the Corning Museum of Glass, 2005 (with Susan Rossi-Wilcox) Drawing upon Nature: Studies for the Blaschkas Glass Models, 2007, Reflecting Antiquity, 2007; contbr. numerous articles and revs. to profl. jours. Wainwright fellow, Oxford U., 1966—73. Fellow Soc. Antiquaries (London), Royal Geog. Soc., Pontificia Accademia Romana di Archeologia; mem. Accademia Fiorentina delle Arti del Disegno, Accademia di Archeologia, Lettere e Belle Arti di Napoli, Deutsches Archaologisches Inst., Internat. Assn. for the History of Glass (pres. 1991-95), Athenaeum Club (London). Office: Corning Mus of Glass 1 Mus Way Corning NY 14830-2253 Office Phone: 607-974-8424. Business E-Mail: whitehoudb@cmog.org.

WHITEHOUSE, FRED WAITE, endocrinologist, researcher; b. Chgo., May 6, 1926; s. Fred Trafton Waite and Grace Caroline (Peters) W.; m. Iris Jean Dawson, June 6, 1953; children: Martha, Amy, Sarah. Student, Northwestern U., 1943-45; BS, U. Ill., Chgo., 1947, MD, 1949. Diplomate Am. Bd. Internal Medicine; cert. endocrinology and metabolism. Intern, then resident Henry Ford Hosp., Detroit, 1949-53, staff physician, 1955—, chief divsn. metabolism, 1962-88, chief divsn. endocrinology and metabolism, 1988-95; divsn. head emeritus, 1995—; fellow Joslin Clinic, Boston, 1954-55. Cons. FDA, Washington, 1980—; mem. Coalition on Diabetes Edn. and Minority Health, 1989-91. Contbr. articles to profl. jours. Bd. dirs. Wheat Ridge Found., 1984-93. Lt. USNR, 1951-53. Master ACP; mem. NIH (nat. diabetes adv. bd. 1984-88), Am. Diabetes Assn. (pres. 1978-79, Banting medal 1979, Outstanding Clinician award 1989, Outstanding Physician Educators award 1994, Best award 1994), Detroit Med. Club (pres. 1976), Detroit Acad. Medicine (pres. 1991-92). Lutheran. Avocations: bicycling, gardening. Home: 1265 Blairmoor Ct Grosse Pointe Woods MI 48236-1230 Office: Henry Ford Med Group 3031 W Grand Blvd Ste 800 Detroit MI 48202 Home Phone: 313-884-1324; Office Phone: 313-916-2131. Office Fax: 313-916-8343. Business E-Mail: fwhiteh1@hfhs.org.

WHITEHOUSE, JOHN HARLAN, JR., systems software consultant, diagnostician; b. Lakewood, Ohio, Sept. 12, 1951; s. John Harlan and Frances Elizabeth (Nation) W.; divorced; 1 child, John Harlan III. BA magma cum laude, Ohio Wesleyan U., 1973; postgrad., U. Chgo., 1974; MBA, Cleve. State U., 1976; PhD, Columbia Pacific U., San Rafael, Calif., 1988; postgrad., Vedic U. of Am., 1996—. Cert. computing profl.; cert. info. sys. auditor; cert. in Visual Basic. Programmer San Antonio Express-News, 1977; programming mgr. S.W. Info. Mgmt. Sys., San Antonio, 1977, Utility Data Corp., Houston, 1978; sr. data sys. auditor Nat. City Corp., Cleve., 1978-81; sys. programmer Std. Oil Co., Cleve., 1981-84; adv. sys. engr. IBM, Cleve., 1984-92; pres. Semiotica Corp., 1992—. Mem. exams. editl. coun. Inst. for Cert. Computer Profls., Des Plaines, 1990—, test deployment mgr., 1996-2001, dir. certification, 1999—. Author: CICS Problem Determination Workshop, 1990; co-author: ICCP Guidelines for Recertification, 1990, ICCP Official Study Guide, 1991-95; editor Clifton-Gaston Allen Light, 1994-2004; also numerous articles, columnist. Mem. Assn. for Computing Machinery (chmn. Greater Cleve. chpt. 1982-83, Svc. Recognition award 1984), Assn. of Inst. for Cert. Computer Profls. (regional dir. 1989-93, nominating com. 1991), Masons (dist. edn. officer 2001-02, dist. dep. Grand Master 2002-05), Philalethes Soc. (pres. Western Res. chpt. 2005-06), Phi Beta Kappa. Unitarian Universalist. Home: 22291 Berry Dr Rocky River OH 44116-2013 Office: Semiotica Corp Software Ohio PMB 241 25935 Detroit Rd Westlake OH 44145-2449 Office Phone: 440-356-8738. Business E-Mail: sales@softwareohio.com.

WHITEHOUSE, SHELDON, senator, former state attorney general; b. NYC, Oct. 20, 1955; s. Charles Sheldon and Mary (Rand) Whitehouse; m. Sandra Christine Thornton, Sept. 20, 1986; 2 children. BA, Yale U., 1978;

JD, U. Va., 1982. Bar: W.Va. 1982, RI 1983, US Dist. Ct. RI 1984, US Supreme Ct. 1986, US Ct. Appeals (1st cir.) 1984. Atty. State of RI, Providence, 1983—84, spl. asst. atty. gen., 1985—90, chief regulatory unit, 1988—90, asst. atty. gen., 1989—90, exec. counsel to Gov., 1991, dir. gov. policy office, 1991—92, dir., Dept. Bus. Regulation, 1992—94; US atty. Dist. RI US Dept. Justice, Providence, 1994—98; atty. gen. State of RI, Providence, 1999—2003; US Senator-elect from RI, 2007—. Recipient Robert M. Goodrich award for Outstanding Pub. Employee, RI Pub. Expenditure Coun., 1993, Secret Svc. Honor award, US Dept. Treasury, 1998, Pub. Achievement award, Common Cause, 1999. Democrat. Office: US Senate B-40D Dirksen Senate Office Bldg Washington DC 20510 *

WHITEHURST, BROOKS MORRIS, chemical engineer; b. Apr. 9, 1930; s. David Brooks and Bessie Ann (Lowry) W.; m. Carolyn Sue Boyer, July 4, 1951; children: Garnett, Anita, Robert. BS, Va. Poly. Inst. and State U., 1951. Registered profl. engr., NC. Sr. process asst. Am. Enka Corp., Lowland, Tenn., 1951-56; sr. process devel. engr. Va.-Carolina Chem. Corp., Richmond, Va., 1956-63; project engr. Texaco Inc., Richmond, 1963-66; mgr. engring. svcs. Texasgulf, Inc., Aurora, NC, 1967-80, mgr. spl. projects, long range planning, 1980-81; pres. Whitehurst Assocs., Inc., New Bern, NC, 1981—. Instr., lectr., cons. alt. sources of energy comty. colls. and univs.; presenter paper Solar World Forum, Brighton, Eng., 1981. Co-chmn. NC state supt. task force on secondary edn., 1974—; mem. NC state adv. com. on trade and indsl. edn, 1971-77; chmn. Gov.'s Task Force Vols. in Workplace, 1981; chmn. State Adv. Coun. Career Edn., 1977—; gov.'s liaison for edn. and bus., 1978-79. Recipient commendation Pres. US, 1981 Mem. AIChE, Am. Inst. Chemists (cert., bd. dirs. 1980-84), NC Inst. Chemists (pres. 1975-77), Nat. Soc. Profl. Engrs., NC Soc. Profl. Engrs., Royal Soc. Chemistry. Achievements include patents and current work on biodegradable chelate systems, municipal yard waste disposal, micronutrients for agriculture, waste rubber recycling, conversion of industrial by-products containing manganese and phosphorous to useful non-toxic materials for use in agriculture for environmental clean-up; development of environmentally friendly products for forest fertilization and chelates for organic agriculture, and a process for purification of impure phosphoric acid, patent for the development of products and processes to minimize ammonia volatilization from urea. Home: 1983 Hoods Creek Rd New Bern NC 28562-9103 Office: PO Box 3335 New Bern NC 28564-3335

WHITEHURST, GROVER JAY, federal agency administrator, psychologist, educator; b. Washington, NC, Sept. 28, 1944; s. Grover J. and Dixie (Daniel) W.; m. Janet E. Fischel, June 7, 1981; children: Owen E., Adam E. BA, East Carolina U., Greenville, 1966; MA, U. Ill., 1968, PhD, 1970. Lic. psychologist, N.Y. Asst. prof. SUNY, Stony Brook, 1970—74, assoc. prof., 1975—79, prof. psychology, 1981—2002, chair dept. psychology, 1998—2002; sr. lectr. U. N.S.W., Sydney, Australia, 1974—75; acad. v.p. Merrill-Palmer Inst., Detroit, 1979—81; dir. Inst. of Edn. Sciences, 2002—. Author: Child Behavior, 1977; editor Developmental Rev., 1981-2000; contbr. over 100 articles to profl. jours. Grantee NIH, 1985, Smith Richardson Found., 1990, Pew Charitable Trusts, 1992, U.S. Adminstrn. Children and Families, 1996, 2000. Fellow APA, Am. Assn. Profl. and Applied Psychology; Nat. Rsch. Coun. (commn. early childhood); Head Start, Nat. Adv. Bd. on Rsch. Avocation: sailing. Mailing: Dir Inst Educ Sciences US Dept Edu 555 New Jersey Ave NW Rm 600-D Washington DC 20208-5500 Office Phone: 202-219-1385. E-mail: grover.whitehurst@ed.gov. *

WHITEHURST, JIM (JAMES M. WHITEHURST), former air transportation executive; b. Columbus, Ga., 1967; m. Lauren N.; 2 children. BS in Computer Sci. and Econs., Rice U., Houston, 1989; student, Friedrich-Alexander U., Erlangen, Germany, London Sch. Econs.; MBA, Harvard Bus. Sch. V.p., dir. Boston Consulting Group, 2001; sr. v.p. fin., treasury & bus. devel. Delta Air Lines, Inc., Atlanta, 2002—04, sr. v.p., chief network and planning officer, 2004—05, COO, 2005—07. *

WHITEHURST, LUCINDA SNYDER, school librarian; d. Wilma Jones and William Franklin Snyder; m. Mark Alexander Whitehurst, May 20, 1989; children: Megan Macye, Alexander William. BA, Coll. William and Mary, 1986; MS, U. Ill., 1987. Children's libr. DC Pub. Libr., 1987—89; young adult libr. County of Henrico Pub. Libr., Richmond, Va., 1989—92; lower sch. libr. St. Christopher's Sch., Richmond, 1992—. Adj. instr. continuing edn. U. Va., Richmond, 2001—. Contbr. articles and reviews to profl. jours.; editor: (newsletter) The Open Book. Mem. Friends of the Richmond Pub. Libr., 2000—02, State Networking Users Adv. Bd., Richmond, 2000—02; pres. Garfield F. Childs Meml. Fund, Richmond, 2003—04. Lois Wells Irwin fellow, U. Ill. Grad. Sch. Libr. and Info. Sci., 1986. Mem.: Va. Ednl. Media Assn., ALA (com. chair 2004—05). Office: St Christopher's Sch 711 St Christopher's Rd Richmond VA 23226 Home Phone: 804-360-7313.

WHITEHURST, WILLIAM WILFRED, JR., management consultant; b. Balt., Mar. 4, 1937; s. William Wilfred and Elizabeth (Hogg) Whitehurst; m. Linda Joan Potter, July 1, 1961; children: Catherine Elizabeth, William Wilfred III. BA, Princeton U., 1958; MS with distinction, Carnegie Inst. Tech., 1963. Mathematician Nat. Security Agy., Fort George G. Meade, Md., 1961—63; mgmt. cons. McKinsey & Co., Inc., Washington, 1963—66; ptnr. L.E. Peabody & Assocs., Washington, 1966—69, exec. v.p., dir. Lanham, Md., 1969—82, pres., dir., 1983—86; pres. W.W. Whitehurst & Assoc., Inc., Cockeysville, Md., 1986—. Contbr. Code of Fed. Regulations 49 C.F.R. Sect. 1157. Comdr. USNR, 1958—65. Recipient Diploma De Honor 14th Pan Am. Rwy. Congress. Mem.: CFA Inst., Washington Soc. Investment Analysts, Am. Rwy. Engring. Assn. Home and Office: 12421 Happy Hollow Rd Cockeysville Hunt Valley MD 21030-1711

WHITEKER, ROY ARCHIE, retired chemistry professor; b. Long Beach, Calif., Aug. 22, 1927; s. Ewing Harris and Mabel Mary (Williams) W.; m. Jean Fiske MacLean, June 3, 1960; 1 son, Scott MacLean. BS, UCLA, 1950, MS, 1952; PhD, Calif. Inst. Tech., 1956. Instr. chemistry M.I.T., 1955-57; asst. prof. Harvey Mudd Coll., Claremont, Calif., 1957-61, assoc. prof., 1961-67, prof. chemistry, 1967-73; assoc. dir. fellowships Nat. Acad. Scis., Washington, 1967-68; dep. exec. sec. Com. on Internat. Exch. of Persons, Washington, 1971—72, exec. sec., 1972—75; dir. Coun. Internat. Exchange Scholar, 1975-76; prof. chemistry U. Pacific, Stockton, Calif., 1976-92, dean Coll. Pacific, 1976-89; ret., 1992. Bd. dirs. Stockton Symphony Assn., 1978-80; dir. cmty. adv. bd. Sta. KUOP, 1981-89; bd. dirs. Stockton Chorale, 1989-97; pres. U. of the Pacific Emeriti Soc., 1992-94, 2000-02. With USNR, 1945-46. Dow Chem. Co. fellow, 1953-54, DuPont Tchg. fellow, 1954-55, NSF Sci. Faculty fellow Royal Inst. Tech., Stockholm, Sweden, 1963-64 Mem. Am. Chem. Soc., Alpha Chi Sigma, Phi Beta Kappa, Phi Kappa Phi, Sigma Xi. Home: 3400 Wagner Hts Rd # 30 Stockton CA 95209 Office Phone: 209-946-2606. Business E-Mail: rwhiteker@pacific.edu.

WHITELEY, BENJAMIN ROBERT, retired insurance company executive; b. Des Moines, July 13, 1929; s. Hiram Everett and Martha Jane (Walker) W.; m. Elaine Marie Yunker, June 14, 1953; children— Stephen Robert, Benjamin Walker BS, Oreg. State U., 1951; MS, U. Mich., 1952; postgrad. advanced mgmt. program, Harvard U.; DHL (hon.), Pacific U., 2001. Clk. group dept. Standard Ins. Co., Portland, Oreg., 1956-59, asst. actuary group dept. then asst. actuary actuarial dept., 1959-63, asst. v.p., asst. actuary, 1963-64, asst. v.p., assoc. actuary, 1964-70, v.p. group ins. adminstrn., 1970-72, v.p. group ins. div., 1972-80, exec. v.p. group ins., 1980-81, exec. v.p., 1981-83, pres., CEO, 1983-92, chmn. bd. dirs., CEO, 1993-94, chmn. bd. dirs., 1994—98; ret., 2000. Bd. dir. The Greenbriar Cos., chmn. bd., 2004—. Past pres. Columbia Pacific coun. Boy Scouts Am.; past chmn. bd., trustee Pacific U., Forest Grove, Oreg.; past chmn. Oreg. Health Scis. Found., Oreg. Trail Coordinating Coun., Portland Opera Assn.; trustee Oreg. Cmty. Found., 1998—2006, chmn., 2004-06; campaign chair, bd. dir. United Way Portland, 1994. 1st. lt. USAF, 1952—55. Recipient Silver Beaver award Cascade Pacific coun. Boy Scouts Am., 1993, Harvey and Emiline Clark medal Pacific U., 1991, Alumni fellow award Oreg. State U., 1991, Aubrey R. Watzek award Lewis and Clark Coll., 1994, Lifetime Achievement award Bus. Youth Exch., Portland, Oreg., 1995. Fellow Soc. Actuaries; mem. Arlington Club (pres. 1991), Waverley Country Club, Multnomah Athletic Club. Republican. Methodist. Personal E-mail: eorbwhiteley@earthlink.net.

WHITELEY, HENRY HOWARD, religious studies educator, minister; b. Roswell, N.Mex., Oct. 31, 1928; s. Alford and Ruth Henrich Whiteley; m. Yvonna Margaret Cornell, Feb. 28, 1953; children: Emma Lachelle Whiteley Yoder, Lynn Howard. BS in Music Edn., John Brown U., Siloam Springs, Ark., 1961; postgrad., West Tex. State U., 1963. Tchr., band dir. K-12 Gravette Pub. Schs., Ark., 1960—62, Balko Pub. Schs., Okla., 1962—63; minister Big Spring, Tex., Galena, Kans., Hardesty, Okla., Logan, Okla., Baxter Springs, Kans.; prof. music, bibl. studies Apostolic Faith Bible Coll., Baxter Springs, 1965—68, 1984—88, 1995—, supt., 1977—78; pastor Pampa Chapel of Apostolic Faith, Tex., 1988—95. Founder, dir. Cantatas cmty. choir, 1965—70. Editor: Apostolic Faith Report, 1964—72. Dir. Ann. Nat. Ch. Camp, Laverne, Okla., 1973; pres. Ministerial Alliance, Pampa, 1990, sec. Baxter Springs, Kans., 1999—2000; dir. Ann. Youth Camp, Baxter Springs, 1965—69, 1996—2002, Ann. Nat. Ch. Camp, Baxter Springs, 1965—69, Ann. Youth Camp, Laverne, Okla., 1973—75; adv. bd. Salvation Army, Pampa, 1993—95; bd. dirs. Apostolic Faith Bible Coll., 1977—79. Cpl. US Army, 1948—51. Trinity Apostolic Faith. Avocations: reading, music, travel. Mailing: 2353 Washington Baxter Springs KS 66713 Office Phone: 620-856-3283.

WHITELEY, ROSE MARIE, city clerk, treasurer; b. Benkelman, Nebr., Mar. 26, 1942; d. Alvin James and Grace Rebecca (Alsbury) W. BS, Nebr. State U., Kearney, 1963; MS, Colo. State U., 1968. Cert. home cons./bus. secondary tchr. Home econs. instr. Deuel County H.S., Chappell, Nebr., 1963-66; adult ednl. cons. McCalls Patterns, NYC, 1967-70; exec. dir. Nebr./Iowa chpt. Nat. Multiple Sclerosis Soc., Omaha, 1971-78; grant writer, fundraising dir. Omaha Theatre, 1978-94; city clk., treas. City of Benkelman, 1994—. Cons. Fundraising/Grantwriting, Omaha, 1982-94, 94—. Contbr.: The Harvest Gardener, 1992. Treas. Prevention Policy Bd., 1994—, Dundy County Resource Ctr., 1994-2001, pres., 2001--; mem. Benkelman Tree Bd., 1994—. Mem. S.W. Clks. Assn. (pres.), Nebr. Mcpl. Clks. Assn., Internat. Inst. of Mcpl. Clks., Kappa Omicron Phi. Avocations: gardening, gourmet cooking. Home: HC 64 Box 58 Benkelman NE 69021-9156 Office: City of Benkelman PO Box 347 Benkelman NE 69021-0347

WHITE-LIEF, DAVID WESTCOTT, lawyer; b. Boston, Mar. 5, 1955; s. David Westcott and Mona Thea (Smith) W.; m. Janice Amy, July 20, 1980; 1 child, Amanda Elizabeth. BS, U. Vt., 1978; JD, Northeastern U., 1984. Bar: Mass., U.S. Dist. Ct. Mass., U.S. Ct. Appeals (1st cir.). Assoc. dir. Vt. Pub. Interest & Research Group, Montpelier, Vt., 1979-81; law clk. to presiding justice Mass. Superior Ct., Boston, 1984-85; assoc. Sugarman & Sugarman P.C., Boston, 1985; prin. Breakstone, White-Lief & Gluck, Boston. Justice of Peace, Montpelier, 1980—; mem. Vt. Health Policy Council, Montpelier, 1985—. Mem. Assn. Trial Lawyers Am., Mass. Bar Assn. (chmn. civil litig. sect., chmn. law mgmt. sect., pres.-elect, 2006-07), Mass. Lawyers Guild. Democrat. Home: 181 Wachusett St Jamaica Plain MA 02130-4233 Office: Sugarman & Sugarman PC 141 Tremont St Boston MA 02111-1209

WHITEMAN, DAVID BRUCE, librarian, poet; b. Brampton, Ont., Can., June 18, 1952; s. Ralph David and Marguerite June Whiteman; m. Deborah Emily Scharbach, Aug. 31, 1973 (div.); children: Thera Emily, Jesse David; life ptnr. Kelly Jo Maynard. BA with honors, Trent U., Peterborough, Ont., Can., 1975; MA, U. Toronto, Ont., Can., 1977, MLS, 1979. Rsch. collections libr. McMaster U. Libr., Hamilton, Ont., Canada, 1979—88; head dept. rare books and spl. collections McGill U. Librs., Montreal, Que., Canada, 1988—96; head libr. William Andrews Clark Meml. Libr., UCLA, 1996—. Author: (poetry) The Invisible World Is in Decline, Books I-VI, Visible Stars: New and Selected Poems; author, editor: exhbn. catalogue The World From Here: Treasures of the Great Libraries of Los Angeles (Am. Assn. Museums Design award, 2003). Grantee, U. Calif., LA Librs. Assn., 1999, 2002—03. Mem.: ALA, Soc. for History of Authorship, Reading, and Pub., Bibliog. Soc. Am. (grantee 1997), Am. Musicological Soc., Zamorano Club, Grolier Club. Avocations: piano, book collecting. Office: William Andrews Clark Meml Libr 2520 Cimarron St Los Angeles CA 90018-2098 Home Phone: 310-384-8041; Office Phone: 323-731-8529. Office Fax: 323-731-8617. Personal E-mail: whiteman@humnet.ucla.edu.

WHITEMAN, DOUGLAS E., publisher; b. Emporia, Kans., Mar. 4, 1961; s. Floyd E. and Phyllis E. (Troyer) W.; m. Susan R. Anderson, Sept. 14, 1985; 1 child, Aaron Anderson Douglas. BSBA, U. Kans., 1983. With Putnam Pub. Group, Denver and NYC, 1983—, dir. trade sales and mktg., internat. sales mgr. NYC, 1987—89, v.p. sales and mktg., 1989—94; sr. v.p., pub. Putnam and Grosset Book Group, NYC, 1994—95, pres., pub., 1995—97; pres. Penguin Group (USA) Books for Young Readers, NYC, 1997—; exec. v.p. Penguin Group, 1998—. Vice chmn., bd. dirs. Eric Carle Mus. of Picture Book Art, 2001—07; bd. dirs. Children's Book Coun., 2004—, Acelero Learning, Monmouth County, NJ, 2007—. Mem.: Pub.'s Lunch Club N.Y.C. (pres. 2004—05). Methodist. Avocations: literature, tennis, fantasy baseball. Office: Penguin Group USA 345 Hudson St Fl 14 New York NY 10014-4592 Business E-Mail: doug.whiteman@us.penguingroup.com.

WHITEMAN, JOSEPH DAVID, retired lawyer, manufacturing company executive; b. Sioux Falls, SD, Sept. 12, 1933; s. Samuel D. and Margaret (Wallace) W.; m. Mary Kelly, Dec. 29, 1962; children: Anne Margaret, Mary Ellen, Joseph David, Sarah Kelly, Jane. BA, U. Mich., 1955, JD, 1960. Bar: D.C. 1960, Ohio 1976. Assoc. Cox, Langford, Stoddard & Cutler, Washington, 1959-64; sec., gen. counsel Studebaker group Studebaker Worthington, Inc., NYC, 1964-71; asst. gen. counsel. United Telecommunications, Inc., Kansas City, Mo., 1971-74; v.p., gen. counsel, sec. Weatherhead Co., Cleve., 1974-77, Parker Hannifin Corp., Cleve., 1977-98; ret., 1998. Immediate past chmn. bd. dirs. St. Lukes Med. Ctr. Served as lt. USNR, 1955-57. Mem. ABA, Beta Theta Pi, Phi Delta Phi. Republican. Roman Catholic. Home and Office: 2508 Robinson Springs Rd Stowe VT 05672

WHITEMAN, RICHARD FRANK, architect; b. Mankato, Minn., Mar. 24, 1925; s. Lester Raymond and Mary Grace (Dawald) W.; m. Jean Frances Waite, June 20, 1948 (dec. May 1980); children: David, Sarah, Lynn, Ann, Carol, Frank, Marie, Steven; m. Mavis Patricia Knutsen, May 30, 1982. BArch, U. Minn., 1945; MArch, Harvard U., 1948. Registered architect, Minn. Designer Ellerbe Co., St. Paul, Minn., 1946; architect Thorshov and Cerny, Mpls., 1948-53; ptnr. Jyring and Whiteman, Hibbing, Minn., 1953-62; pres. AJWM Inc., Hibbing and Duluth, Minn., 1963-72, Architects Four, Duluth, 1972-83; owner Richard Whiteman, Duluth, 1983-95; sr. architect U. Minn., Duluth. Chmn. Architect Sect. Registration Bd., Minn., 1972-80. Prin. works include Washington Sch., Hibbing, 1957 (Minn. Soc. Architects Design award 1957), Whiteman Summer Home, Pengilly, Minn. (Minn. Soc. Architects Design award 1959), Bemidji State Coll. Phys. Edn. Bldg. (Minn. Soc. Architects Design award 1960), Whiteman Residence, Griggs Hall UMD, 1990. Pres. U. for Srs., 1993-94, 2000-01; chair Duluth Housing Authority, 2001-06, vice chair, 2006—07. With USNR, 1943—45. Mem. Minn. Soc. Architects (pres. 1972), Northeast Minn. Architects (pres. 1962), Minn. Designer Selection Bd. (chmn. 1990). Clubs: Kitchi Gammi (Duluth). Lodges: Kiwanis. Democrat. Roman Catholic. Avocations: photography, fishing, cross country skiing, travel. Home: 3500 E 3rd St Duluth MN 55804-1812 E-mail: arch032425@aol.com.

WHITEMAN, RICHARD MARK, lawyer; b. Detroit; s. Wayne Donald and Margaret Rose (Marshick) Whiteman; m. Ellen Beth Rosenthal, Aug. 30, 1986; 1 child, Andrew. BA, Colgate U., 1970; JD, Wayne State U., 1982. Bar: Mich. Labor mgmt. relations examiner Nat. Labor Relations Bd., Detroit, 1973—84, atty., 1984—93, supr. atty., 1993—2002, dep. regional atty., 2002—. Mem.: State Bar Mich., Labor and Employment Law Section. Avocations: golf, jogging, tennis, travel, reading. Office: Nat Labor Relations Bd 477 Mich Ave Detroit MI 48226

WHITENER, CAROLYN RAYE, artist; b. Corpus Christi, Texas, Feb. 2, 1941; d. Rayburn N. and Alice G. Hamilton; children: Mark Dwain, Rynn Rayna. Student, Okla. State U., 1970, U. Sci. and Arts Okla., 1981-85. Co-owner Honk'n'Holler's, Stillwater, Okla., 1962-75; owner Clynn's Designs, Okla. City, 1969—; co-owner W&W Cattle Ranch, Okla., 1973—; comml. artist, co-owner Colorvision, Inc., Okla. and Tex., 1979—. Cons. Tele-Weight, Buena Vista, Colo., 1985-92, Craig Versus Boren, 1972-76; comml. design cons. for one and two dimensional rendering drawings Rynn's Lawncare & Landscaping, Oklahoma City, 1997—; dir. staging and backdrops, N.Y., Stillwater, Okla., 1973-74; mem. adv. coun. Status of Okla. Woman, 2001—. Active Grady County Environ. Coalition, 1991—92; adv. mem. Gov.'s Okla. Commn. on Status of Women, 2000—. Recipient Outstanding Cmty. Svc. award, Ninnekah, Oka., 1992, One Person Who Made a Difference LWVOK, 1997, Pres. Prestigious award Okla. State U., 1996, First Adv. award Okla. Commn. on Status of Women, 2001, Gov. Commendation award Gov. Frank Keating, 2001, State of Okla. Citation award Rep. Richard Phillips and Sen. Mike Fair, 2001; named Woman of Yr. Okla. City Coun. of Beta Sigma Phi, 1997-98. Mem. Okla. Assn. Family Cmty. and Edn., Grady County Ext. Homemakers, Oklahoma City Newcomer's Club, Beta Sigma Phi (Woman of Yr. award 1997-98, Outstanding Svc. award 1992, Evening Lions Homecoming Window Design awards, 1966-68), All 50's and 60's Chickesha Okla. HS Alumni Class (decorations com. 1989—). Democrat. Methodist. Avocations: art, sewing, cooking, travel. E-mail: CrWhitener@aol.com.

WHITENER, MARTHA SARRATT, retired history educator; b. Union, SC, June 8, 1929; d. Sidney Gilbert and Rose Cox Sarratt; m. William Jackson Whitener, June 28, 1952. BA, Winthrop U., Rock Hill, SC, 1950. Tchr. Gastonia HS, NC, 1950—52, Jordan HS, Columbus, Ga., 1952—53, Union HS, SC, 1953—54, US Mil. Acad. Elem. Sch., West Point, NY, 1956—60. Mem. State Coll. Bd. Trustees, 1985—88; chair presdl. search com. Lander U., Greenwood, SC, 2001. Trustee Lander U., 1988—2002, chair, 1997—2001; pres. Union County Hist. Soc., 1981—82; bd. trustees Union Carnegie Libr., SC. Recipient Mary Mildred Sullivan award, Winthrop U., 1950, Cmty. Svc. award, Union County C. of C., 1994—95. Mem.: DAR (vice regent 1991), Union Music Club, Women's Study Club (v.p. 2004—06). Avocations: travel, antiques, reading, music. Home: 203 Thomson Blvd Union SC 29379

WHITENER, WILLIAM GARNETT, dancer, choreographer; b. Seattle, Aug. 17, 1951; s. Warren G. and Virginia Louise (Garnett) Whitener. Student, Cornish Sch. Allied Arts, Seattle, 1958-69. Dancer NYC Opera, 1969, Joffrey Ballet, NYC, 1969-77, Twyla Tharp Dance, NYC, 1978-87; asst. to choreographer Jerome Robbins for Robbins' Broadway, NYC, 1988; artistic dir. Les Ballets Jazz de Montréal, 1991-93, Royal Winnipeg Ballet, 1993-95, Kansas City Ballet, 1996—. Coord. dance dept. Concord Acad., Mass., 1988; vis. artist U. Wash., 1989—91; dance faculty mem. Harvard U. Summer Dance, 1989—90, NYU, 1985. Dancer (Broadway plays) Dancin', 1978, choreographer Princeton Ballet, Joffrey II, John Curry Ice Theatre, Ballet Hispanico of NY, Boston Ballet Internat. Choreography Competition, Tommy Tune, Martine van Hamel/Kevin McKenzie, Ann Reinking, Seattle Repertory Theatre, Am. Ballroom Theatre, NYC, Hartford Ballet, Conn., On the Boards with Bill Irwin, PBS-TV Alive From Off Center, (Operas) A Little Night Music, Pacific Northwest Ballet, Rusalka, Seattle Opera, (Operas) Aida, Kansas City Repartory Theatre, The Pearlfishers Eugene Oreg., Lyric Opera Kans. City, dancer (films) Amadeus, Zelig, (TV films) The Catherine Wheel, Dance in America; performer: Garden of Earthly Delights, 1988. Bd. trustees DanceUSA, 2000—. Ford Found. scholar, 1963—64. Mem.: Am. Guild Musical Artists, Actor's Equity. Office: Kansas City Ballet 1616 Broadway Kansas City MO 64108-1207 *

WHITENER, WILLIAM JACKSON, retired military officer, retired dean; b. Mount Holly, NC, Apr. 21, 1922; s. David Henry and Elizabeth Jane (Barrett) Whitener; m. Martha Pacolette Sarratt, June 28, 1952; 1 child, Martha Sarratt Whitener Walker. BSc, US Mil. Acad., West Point, NY, 1946; MA, Columbia U., NYC, 1966; MSc, George Washington U., DC, 1967; HHD (hon.), Lander U., Greenwood, SC, 1992. Col. US Army, USA, Germany, Korea, Vietnam, 1946—75, brigade comdr. Aschaffenburg, Germany, 1969—70, with G-3 ctrl. army group Mannhein, Germany, 1970—72, army advisor, Air U. Maxwell AFB, Ala., 1972—75; dean U. SC, Union, SC, 1977—84, interim chancellor Spartanburg, 1993—94; chief of staff US Mil. Acad., West Point, 1967—69; ret., 1995. Chmn. SC Commn. Higher Edn., Columbia, SC, 1989—93. Editor: Some Reminiscences For My Nieces and Nephews, 2005. Pres. Union County Hist. Soc., 2003—06; chmn. Union Cmty. Found., 2006. Republican. Methodist. Avocation: historic preservation. Home: 203 Thomson Blvd Union SC 29379 Personal E-mail: wjwhit@bellsouth.net.

WHITESCARVER, JACK EDWARD, federal agency administrator; b. Palestine, Tex., May 16, 1937; s. A.B. and Elizabeth Lorraine (Kimball) W. BS, Sam Houston State U., 1959, MS, 1965; PhD, U. Medicine Dentistry NJ, 1974. Rsch. assoc. Harvard U. Sch. Pub. Health, Boston, 1976-77; grants assoc. NIH, Bethesda, Md., 1977-78; spl. asst. to dir. NIH/NIAID, Bethesda, 1978-84; asst. dean R&D Emory U. Sch. Medicine, Atlanta, 1984-86, asst. prof. pathology, 1985-88, assoc. dean, 1986-88; dep. dir. Office AIDS Rsch., NIH, Bethesda, 1988—99, acting dir., 1999—2002, dir., 2002—. Contbr. articles to Jour. Infectious Diseases, Jour. Investigative Dermatology, Tex. Reports Biol. Medicine. Fellow Albert Soiland Cancer Found., 1967-70; recipient Alumnus of Yr. Award U. Medicine and Dentistry NJ, 1991. Mem. Am. Acad. Allergy and Immunology, Am. Soc. for Microbiology, Infectious Diseases Soc. Am., Internat. AIDS Soc., Royal Soc. Medicine. Office: Office AIDS Rsch NIH 5635 Fishers Ln Rockville MD 20892 Office Phone: 301-496-0357. Office Fax: 301-496-3119.

WHITESELL, JOHN EDWIN, retired motion picture company executive; b. DuBois, Pa., Feb. 23, 1938; s. Guy Roosevelt and Grace Ethlyn (Brisbin) W.; m. Amy H. Jacobs, June 12, 1960; 1 child, Scott Howard; m. Martha Kathlyn Hall, Sept. 3, 1975; m. Phyllis Doyle, May 8, 1993. BA, Pa. State U., 1962. Asst. mgr. non-theatrical div. Columbia Pictures Corp., NYC, 1963-66; with Warner Bros., Inc., 1966—2003, nat. sales mgr. non-theatrical div. Burbank, Calif., 1968-75, v.p., 1975-76; v.p. internat. sales adminstrn. Warner Bros. Internat. TV Distbn., 1976-2001, cons., 2001—03, ret., 2003. Bd. dirs. Mastermedia Internat. Inc.; past bd. dirs. Found. for Entertainment Programming in Higher Edn.; mem. self-study com. Nat. Entertainment Conf., 1974-75. Served with USNR, 1956-58. Recipient Alumni Fellow award Pa. State U., 2001, Outstanding Alumnus award Pa. State U. DuBois Campus, 1995, Founders award Nat. Entertainment Conf., 1975. Mem. Nat. Audio-Visual Assn. (motion picture coun. 1973-76, exec. com. film coun. 1969-76, ednl. materials producers coun. 1970-76), Acad. TV Arts and Scis. 1976-80, Nat. Assn. Media Educators (adv. com. 1973-76)

WHITESELL, STEPHEN ERNEST, parks director; BS in Environ. Resources, Calif. State U., Sacramento, 1973; M in Landscape Architecture, Harvard U., 1977. Landscape architect, planner Denver Svc. Ctr., Lakewood, Colo., 1977-80, Ind. Dunes Nat. Lakeshore, Porter, Ind., 1980-83; chief maintenance Apostle Islands Nat. Seashore, Bayfield, Wis., 1983-84; supt. Longfellow, John F. Kennedy, Frederick Law Olmsted Nat. Hist. Sites, Cambridge, Mass., 1984-87; supt. Sandy Hook Unit Gateway Nat. Recreation Area, Highlands, NJ, 1987—91; supt. Petroglyph Nat. Monument, San Antonio, 1991-95, San Antonio Missions Nat. Hist. Park, 1995—. Bd. dirs. Cultural Alliance of San Antonio Area Tourism Coun., City Year San Antonio. Recipient Award of Merit Boston Soc. Landscape Architects, 1985, U.S. Dept. Interior Superior Svc. Honor award, 1998. Mem. Rotary Club San Antonio, Los Compadres de San Antonio Missions (adv. bd.), San Antonio Tourism Coun. (bd. dirs.), Cultural Alliance San Antonio (City of Yr. San Antonio). Avocations: golf, fishing, gardening. Office: San Antonio Missions Nat Hist Park 2202 Roosevelt Ave San Antonio TX 78210-4919 Home Phone: 210-699-1817; Office Phone: 210-534-8833. Office Fax: 210-534-1106. Business E-Mail: steve_whitesell@nps.gov.

WHITESELL, WILLIAM MAYBERRY, III, legal association administrator; Cert. credit consumer counselor 1985. Sr. acct. mgr. Dun & Bratstreet, Freehold, NJ, 1970—79; office mgr. Law Office William M. Whitesell Jr., W. Long Branch, NJ, 1980—89; legal supr. Calif. Fissat, Stuart, Fla., 1994—98. Mem.: Am. Mensa (life; north area coord. 1974). Home: 3182 SW Crenshaw St Port Saint Lucie FL 34953

WHITESIDE, ANN BAIRD, library director; BA in Art History, Boston Coll.; MLS, Simmons Coll., Boston, MA. Asst. libr. Rotch Libr., Mass. Inst. Tech., Boston, 1983—95, head libr., 2006—; visual resources libr. Harvard Grad. Sch. of Design, Frances Loeb Libr.; libr., depts. Architecture, Landscape, Architectural History, Urban and Environ. Planning U. Va. Contbr. articles to numerous profl. jours. Mem.: Art Libr. Soc. No. Am. (pres. elect 2006). Office: Rotch Libr MIT Sch Architecture and Planning 77 Massachusetts Ave 7-231 Cambridge MA 02139

WHITESIDE, CAROL GORDON, foundation executive; b. Chgo., Dec. 15, 1942; d. Paul George and Helen Louise G.; m. John Gregory Whiteside, Aug. 15, 1964; children: Brian Paul, Derek James. BA, U. Calif., Davis, 1964. Pers. mgr. Emporium Capwell Co., Santa Rosa, 1964-67; pers. asst. Levi Strauss & Co., San Francisco, 1967-69; project leader Interdatum, San Francisco, 1983-88; with City Coun. Modesto, 1983-87; mayor City of Modesto, 1987-91; asst. sec. for intergovtl. rels. The Resources Agy., State of Calif., Sacramento, 1991-93; dir. intergovtl. affairs Gov.'s Office, Sacramento, 1993-97; pres. Great Valley Ctr., Modesto, Calif., 1997—. Bd. dirs. Lincoln Inst. Land Policy. Trustee Modesto City Schs., 1979-83; nat. pres. Rep. Mayors and Local Ofcls., 1990; mem. Sierra Nev. Conservancy Bd., 2005—; chmn. bd. Sierra Health Found. Recipient Lifetime Achievement award League of Calif. Cities, 2002, Excellence in Pub. Svc. award, Fresno Bus. Coun., 2004, Olmstead medal Am. Soc. Landscape Archs., 2007; named Outstanding Woman of Yr. Women's Commn., Stanislaus County, Calif., 1988, Woman of Yr., 27th Assembly Dist., 1991; Toll fellow Coun. of State Govts., 1996, Champion of Am. Dream, Calif. State U., Stanislaus, 2002. Republican. Lutheran. Office: Great Valley Ctr 201 Needham St Modesto CA 95354-0903 Home Phone: 209-521-0485. E-mail: carol@greatvalley.org.

WHITESIDE, CHARLES B., III, investment company executive; b. Ft. Smith, Ark., Mar. 17, 1941; s. Charles B. Jr. and R. Evelyn cindy Whiteside; m. Catherine Ware, Jan. 29, 1966; children: Carrie H., Charles B. IV. BSBA, U. Ark., Fayetteville, 1963. 1st v.p. Merrill Lynch & Co., Little Rock, 1965—. Trustee Ark. Children's Hosp., 1974—, chmn., treas., 1983—88; vice chmn. bd. dirs. Ark. Children's Hosp. Found., 1983—; trustee Ark. Children's Rsch. Inst., 1989—2000, chmn., 1990—; trustee, treas. Lyon Coll., Batesville, Ark., 1992—; bd. advisors U. Ark., Fayettville, 2006. 1st lt. US Army, 1963—65. Recipient Outstanding Vol. Fundraising award for State of Ark., Nat. Soc. Fund Raising Execs., 2000; Sr. Paul Harris fellow, Rotary. Mem.: Kappa Sigma Alumni Assn. (pres. bd. dirs. 1974—). Episcopalian. Avocations: hunting, fishing. Office: Merrill Lynch 2200 Rodney Parham Ste 300 Little Rock AR 72212 Office Phone: 501-312-7285.

WHITESIDE, WILLIAM ANTHONY, JR., retired lawyer; b. Phila., Feb. 23, 1929; s. William Anthony and Ellen T. (Hensler) Whiteside; m. Eileen Ann Ferrick, Feb. 27, 1954; children: William Anthony III, Michael P., Eileen A., Richard F., Christopher J., Mary P. BS, Notre Dame U., 1951; LLB, U. Pa., 1954. Bar: Pa. 1955. Assoc. Speiser, Satinsky, Gilliland & Packel, Phila., 1956—58, ptnr., 1958—61, Fox, Rothschild, O'Brien & Frankel, Phila., 1961—2001; ret., 2001. Past chmn. Police Athletic League, Phila.; trustee LaSalle Coll. HS, Phila., Am. Coll. Mgmt. and Tech., Dubrovnik, Croatia; chmn. emeritus bd. trustees, emeritus trustee Rochester Inst. Tech.; emeritus trustee CC Phila. Found.; pres. adv. coun. U. Notre Dame; emeritus trustee Germantown Acad., past pres. 1st lt. USAF, 1954—56. Named Man of Yr., Notre Dame Club Phila., 1967. Mem.: ABA, Pa. Soc., Phila. Bar Assn., Pa. Bar Assn., Wissahickon Skating Club, Union League Club Phila. Republican. Roman Catholic. Home: 7808 Cobden Rd Glenside PA 19038-7256 also: 901 Gardens Plz Ocean City NJ 08226-4719 Office: Fox Rothschild LLP 2000 Market St Ste 10 Philadelphia PA 19103-3231 Office Phone: 215-299-2032.

WHITESIDES, GEORGE MCCLELLAND, chemistry professor; b. Louisville, Aug. 3, 1939; m. Barbara Breasted; children: George Thomas, Benjamin Haile. AB, Harvard U., 1960; PhD, Calif. Inst. Tech., 1964; D Honoris Causa (hon.), U. Twente, The Netherlands, 2001. Asst. prof. dept. chemistry MIT, Cambridge, 1963—69, assoc. prof., 1969—71, prof., 1971—75, Arthur C. Cope prof., 1975—80, Haslam and Dewey prof., 1980—82; prof. dept. chemistry Harvard U., Cambridge, 1982—86, Mallinckrodt prof., 1986—2004, Woodford L. and Ann A. Flowers U. prof., 2004—. Adv. position NRC, NSF, Dept. Def. Advanced Rsch. Projects Agy. Recipient Pure Chemistry award, Am. Chem. Soc., 1975, Harrison Howe award, Rochester sect., 1979, Disting. Alumni award, Calif. Inst. Tech., 1980, Remsen award, 1983, Arthur C. Cope Scholar award, 1989, James Flack Norris award, 1994, Arthur C. Cope award, 1995, Def. Advanced Rsch. Projects Agy. award for Significant Technical Achievement, 1996, Madison Marshall award, Am. Chem. Soc., 1996, Nat. Medal of Sci., 1998, Disting. Chemist award, Sierra Nev. sect. Am. Chem. Soc., 1999, Wallac Oy Innovation award, Soc. Biomolecular Screening, 1999, Excellence award in Surface Sci., Surfaces Biomaterials Found., 1999, Von Hippel award, Material Rsch. Soc., 2000, World Tech. award for materials, World Tech. Network, 2001, Rschr. of Yr. award, Small Times Mag., 2002, Pitts. Analytical Chemistry award, Soc. Analytical Chemists of Pitts., 2003, Kyoto prize for advanced tech., Inamori Found., 2003, Paracelsus prize, Swiss Chem. Soc., 2004, Ralph and Helen Oesper award, Cin. sect. Am. Chem. Soc., 2004, Jacob Heskel Gabbay award in biotech. and medicine, 2004, Dickson Prize in Sci., 2005, Dan David Found. prize, 2005, Emanuel Merk Lect. prize, 2005, Linus Pauling medal, 2005, Welch award in Chemistry, 2005, Emanuel Merck Lecture prize, 2005, Linus Pauling Medal award, 2005, Welch award, 2005; Alfred P. Sloan fellow, 1968. Fellow: AAAS, Indian Nat. Sci. Acad., World Tech. Network, Chem. Rsch. Soc. India (hon.); mem.: NAE, NAS, Academia Sinica (chmn. internat. sci. adv. bd. Genomics Rsch. Ctr. 2006—), Royal Netherlands Acad. Arts and Scis., Materials Rsch. Soc. India (hon.), Am. Philos. Soc., Am. Acad. Arts and Scis. Office: Harvard U Dept of Chemistry 12 Oxford St Cambridge MA 02138-2902 Business E-Mail: gwhites.des@gmwgroup.harvard.edu.

WHITESIDES, JOHN LINDSEY, JR., aerospace engineering educator, researcher; b. San Antonio, Feb. 27, 1943; s. John Lindsey and Florene Lyndelle (Wheelis) W.; m. Sheila LaVerne Beadle, May 30, 1964 (div. 1975); children: Lisa Diane, John Gregory; m. Andrea Martina Chavez Lewis, Mar. 26, 1994. BS in Aerospace Engring., U. Tex., 1965, PhD, 1968. Asst. prof. George Washington U., Hampton, Va., 1968-74, assoc. prof., 1974-80, prof., 1980—2005, prof. emeritus, 2006—; assoc. dir. Joint Inst. for Advancement of Flight Scis., Hampton, 1986—2005. Contbr. articles to profl. jours. Mem. Sigma Series Lectures, Hampton, 1990-2000. Recipient disting. pub. svc. medal NASA, 1993, Malina medal Internat. Astronautical Fedn., 1995. Fellow AIAA (dir. 1987-93, nat. faculty advisor 1989, v.p. mem. svcs. 1999-2002, v.p. publs. 2006—); mem. Am. Soc. Engring. Edn., Soc. Engring. Sci. (organizing com. 1975, 76, 77), Tau Beta Pi, Phi Eta Sigma, Sigma Gamma Tau. Avocations: sports, art. Home: 670 Anns Way Blanco TX 78606 Office: George Washington U MAE Dept Washington DC 20052 Home Phone: 830-833-0516. Business E-Mail: jlw@gwu.edu.

WHITE-THOMSON, IAN LEONARD, retired mining executive; b. Halstead, Eng., May 3, 1936; came to U.S., 1969; s. Walter Norman and Leonore (Turney) W-T.; m. Barbara Montgomery, Nov. 24, 1971. BA with 1st class honors, New Coll., Oxford U., 1960, MA, 1969. Mgmt. trainee Borax Consol. Ltd., London, 1960-61, asst. to sales mgr., 1961-64, asst. to sales dir., 1964; comml. dir. Hardman & Holden Ltd., Manchester, Eng., 1965-67, joint mng. dir., 1967-69; v.p. mktg. dept. U.S. Borax Inc., Los Angeles, 1969-73, exec. v.p. mktg., 1973-88, pres., 1988-98, also dir., chmn., 1996-99; group exec. Pa. Glass Sand Corp., Ottawa Silica Co., U.S. Silica Co., 1985-87; exec. dir. L.A. Opera, 2000—01. Bd. dirs. Canpotex Ltd., chmn. bd., 1974-76. Bd. dirs. L.A. Master Chorale, Colburn Sch.; bd. dirs. Thornton Sch. U. So. Calif. With Brit. Army, 1954—56. Named Mfr. of Yr., Calif. Mfrs. Assn., 1997. Mem. Can. Potash Prodrs. Assn. (v.p. 1976-77, dir. 1972-77), Chem. Industry Coun. of Calif. (bd. dirs. 1982-85, chmn. 1984), Am. Mining Congress (bd. dirs. 1989), RTZ Borax and Minerals (bd. dirs. 1992, chief exec. 1995-99), Kerr-McGee Corp. (bd. dirs. 1999-2006), Calif. Club, Valley Hunt Club. Home: 1897 Braemar Rd Pasadena CA 91103-3712 Personal E-mail: iwhitethom@aol.com.

WHITE-WHITFIELD, LISA DENISE, social worker; b. LA, June 11, 1968; d. Charles L. White and Martha Staten; m. Ervin L. Whitfield, Apr. 25, 1992 (div. Oct. 1, 1995); 1 child, Alexis Ximara. BS in Bus. Adminstrn., Calif. State U., Long Beach, 1992; MPA, Calif. State U., Carson, 2006. Tchg. credential Calif. Bank teller Wells Fargo Bank, Lakewood, Calif., 1987—88; proof operator Bank of Am., Long Beach, 1988—89; spl. edn. tchrs. asst. Inglewood (Calif.) Unifield Sch. Dist., 1989—91; adminstrv. asst. Remax Realtors, Carson, 1991—92; substitute tchr. Compton (Calif.) Unified Sch. Dist., 1992—93; acctg. clk. United Airlines, El Segundo, Calif., 1993—94; social worker LA County Dept. Pub. Social Svcs., 1994—. Mentor Welfare-to-Work Career Mentor Program, El Monte, Calif., 2002—. Vol. March of Dimes, LA, 1994—2000; vol., bd. mem. The Dance Connection Dance Acad., LA, 2002; vol. Redeemer Christian Acad., LA, 1999, West Angeles Ch. of God in Christ, LA, 1996—2002. Scholar, Calif. Regional Purchasing Com., 1986. Mem.: ASPA, Dominguez Pub. Adminstrn. Assn., Assn. County Administrs., Calif. State U. Long Beach Alumni Assn., Phi Kappa Phi, Phi Alpha Alpha. Avocations: running, social research, volunteering, hiking, travel. Office: LA County DPSS Mangemental Rsch Svcs Section 3220 Rosemead Blvd El Monte CA 91731 Personal E-mail: ldwmarathoner@yahoo.com

WHITFIELD, EDWARD (WAYNE), congressman; b. Hopkinsville, Ky., May 25, 1943; m. Constance Harriman; 1 child, Kate. BS in Bus., U. Ky., 1965; JD, U. Ky. Coll. of Law, 1969. Mem. Ky. Ho. of Reps., 1974-75; pvt. practice law, 1970-79; govt. affairs counsel Seaboard Sys. R.R. subs. CSX Corp., 1979-83, counsel to pres., 1983-85; v.p. state rels. CSX Corp., 1986-88, v.p. fed. r.r. affairs, 1988-91; legal counsel to chmn. Interstate Commerce Commn., 1991-93; mem. US Congress from 1st Ky. dist., 1995—; mem. energy and commerce com. 1st lt. USAR. Republican. Office: US Ho Reps 2411 Rayburn House Office Bldg Washington DC 20515 also: 1403 S Main St Hopkinsville KY 42240 Office Phone: 202-225-3115. *

WHITFIELD, ERICA SHARON, director, career planning administrator; b. Roanoke, Va., July 5, 1980; d. Edith Cookie (Peirce) and David James Whitfield. BS with honors, Lynchburg Coll., Va., 2001, MEd, 2004. Hall dir., grad. asst. residence life Lynchburg Coll., 2002—04, career counseling intern, 2003; counselor intern New Land Jobs, Lynchburg, 2003, Ctrl. Va. CC, Lynchburg, 2003—04; counselor Region 2000 Workforce Ctr., Lynchburg, 2003—04; dir. career devel. svcs. Mary Baldwin Coll., Staunton, Va., 2004—06; event planner, edn. coord. Alpha Sigma Alpha Sorority, Indpls., 2006—. Conf. chair Consortium of Va. Women's Coll. and Univ., Staunton, Va., 2005. Scholar, Mary Baldwin Coll., 2006. Mem.: ACA, Va. Found. for Ind. Coll., Va. Assn. Colleges and Employers, Nat. Assn. Colleges and Employers, Am. Coll. and Pers. Assn., Nat. Career Devel. Assn. (field editor for career convergence 2005—06), Alpha Psi Omega, Psi Chi, Kappa Delta Pi, Omicron Delta Kappa, Alpha Sigma Alpha (chpt. advisor 2004—06). Home: 3030 Bentwood Cir S Dr 1B Indianapolis IN 46268 Office: Alpha Sigma Alpha Sorority 9550 Zionsville Rd Ste 160 Indianapolis IN 46268 Home Phone: 434-258-2456; Office Phone: 317-871-2920. Personal E-mail: eryielle@yahoo.com. Business E-Mail: ewhitfield@alphasigmaalpha.org.

WHITFIELD, FRED, JR., professional sports team executive; s. Fred Whitfield; m. Mary Whitfield. BBA in Econs., Campbell U., Buies Creek, NC, 1980, MBA in Mktg.; JD, NC Ctrl. U., Durham. Pvt. practice lawyer, Greensboro, NC; dir. Carolinas region Falk Assocs. Mgmt. Enterprises; dir. player devel. basketball divsn. Nike, dir. bus. and legal affairs Brand Jordan divsn., 2003—06; dir. player pers., asst. legal counsel Washington Wizards, 2000—03; pres., COO Bobcats Sports & Entertainment, Charlotte, NC, 2006—. Founder, dir. Achievements Unlimited Basketball Sch., Greensboro, NC, 1985—. Named to Campbell U. Sports Hall of Fame, 1995. Office: Charlotte Bobcats 333 E Trade St Charlotte NC 28202 *

WHITFIELD, GRAHAM FRANK, orthopedic surgeon; b. Eng., 1942; arrived in U.S., 1969, naturalized, 1975; s. Reginald Frank and Marjorie Joyce W. BSc, King's Coll., U. London, 1963; PhD, Queen Mary Coll., U. London, 1969; MD, NY Med. Coll., 1976. Rsch. scientist Unilever Rsch. Lab., England, 1963-66; postdoctoral fellow dept. chemistry Temple U., 1969-71, instr., 1971-72, asst. prof., 1972-73; resident in surgery NY Med. Coll. Affiliated Hosps., NYC, 1976-78, resident in orthopedics, 1978-79, sr. resident in orthop. surgery, 1979-80, chief resident, 1980-81; attending orthop. surgeon Good Samaritan Hosp., West Palm Beach, Fla., 1981-87, JFK Med. Ctr., Lake Worth, Fla., 1981—, Palms Wellington Surg. Ctr., West Palm Beach, 1994-96, Wellington Regional Med. Ctr., West Palm Beach, 1996—, Bethesda Health City, Boynton Beach, Fla., 1996—, Palms West Hosp., Loxahatchee, Fla., 1997—2004, Columbia Hosp., West Palm Beach, 1997—2002. Instr. health professions divsn. Nova Southeastern U., North Miami, Fla., 1994-95, clin. asst. prof. dept. surgery, Coll. Osteo. Medicine, Nova Southeastern U., Ft. Lauderdale, Fla., 1995—. Author: (with Joseph Cohn and Louis Del Guercio) Critical Care Readings, 1981; editl. bd., contbg. editor Hosp. Physician, 1978-82; cons. editor Physician Asst. and Health Practitioner, 1979-82; orthop. cons. Conv. Reporter, 1980-82; assoc. editor-in-chief Critical Care Monitor, 1980-82; editl. bd. Complications in Orthopedics, 1986-96; practice panel cons. in orthop. surgery Complications in Surgery, 1982-96. Recipient N.Y. Med. Coll. Surg. Soc. award, 1976. Fellow: Internat. Coll. Surgeons; mem.: AMA, Fla. Orthop. Soc., So. Orthop. Assn., Royal Inst. Chemistry (Eng.), Palm Beach County Med. Soc., Fla. Med. Assn., Soc. the Four Arts, Rotary, Explorer's Club (N.Y.C.), Brit. Schs. and Univs. Club, Soc. Sons of St. George (N.Y.C.), Venerable Order Hospitalers of St. John of Jerusalem, Sigma Xi. Office: 2150 S Congress Ave West Palm Beach FL 33406-7604 Home Phone: 561-863-7780. Personal E-mail: gfw2150@aol.com.

WHITFIELD, MARGARET DENNY, retired music educator; b. Richmond, Va., Apr. 18, 1936; d. Theodore Marshall and Elizabeth Denny (Dixon) Whitfield; children: David Yong Kim, Susanne Elisabeth Nelson. MusB cum laude, Western Md. Coll., 1958; MusM, Eastman Sch. Music, 1964; student, Cornell U., Western Md. U., U. Tenn. Tchr. Meth. Bd. Missions, Okadayama, Japan, 1958—61; instr. piano Hochstein Sch. Music, Rochester, NY, 1963—64; instr. piano Dept. Prep. Peabody Conservatory, Balt., 1964—65; orch. dir. Hanover (Pa.) Pub. Schs., 1968—70; dir. orch. Fairfax County (Va.) Pub. Schs., 1970—98. Ch. organist, 1957—58, 1963—; guest dir. orch. clinic James Madison U., Harrisonburg, Va., 1984; dir. H.S. orch. Carnegie Hall, NYC, 1996. Piano concert soloist Western Md. Coll., 1957, Ithaca Coll. Orch., 1965; musician: Hanover (Pa.) Hall Nursing Home, 2003—04, various chs., 1960—61, Am. Cancer Soc., 2005. Vol. Eng. tchr., Japan, 1958—61; vol. driver Am. Cancer Soc., Falls Ch., 1999—; founder clothing shop Westminster (Md.) Meth. Ch., 1952; vol. Christian Witness Mission, Paducah, Ky., 1950, Christian Work Camp, Pharr, Tex., 1956, Seoul, Republic of Korea, 1959; missionary Meth. Bd. Missions and English Tchrs. Recipient Outstanding Intermediate Orch. award, Fairfax (Va.) Music Educators Assn., 1990, Citation award, Gov.'s Sch. of the Arts, 1993; scholar, Eastman Sch. Music, 1962—64. Mem.: Am. Guild Handbell Rings, Am. Guild Organists, Fairfax County (Va.) Ret. Educators Assn. Avocations: gardening, knitting, volunteering. Home: 7402 Monticello Blvd Springfield VA 22150 Office: Westover Baptist Ch 1125 N Patrick Henry Dr Arlington VA 22205

WHITFIELD, SIMON, Olympic athlete; b. Kingston, Ont., Can., May 16, 1975; Can. Triathlon champion, Winnipeg, 1998—99, 2001; 1st place winner ITU World Cup, 2001; Bronze medallist Pan Am. Game, Winnipeg, 1999; competed and placed 10th (jr.) World Championships, Cancun, Mexico, 1995, competed and placed 9th Perth, Australia, 1997, competed and placed 7th Montreal, 1999, competed and placed 6th Edmonton, 2001; Gold medallist, flag bearer Can. Olympic Team Olympic Games, Sydney, Australia, 2000; Gold medallist Commonwealth Games, 2002. Spokesperson Multiple Sclerosis Soc., 2001. Named Triathlete of Yr., Triathlon Can., 2000, 11th Pl. Canadian Olympian, Athens, 2004; named to B.C. Sports Hall of Fame, 2001; recipient David Foster Olympic Achievement award. Office: c/o Michelle Comeau IMG Canada 175 Bloor St E Ste 400 S Tower Toronto ON Canada M4W 3RB

WHITFORD, BRADLEY, actor; b. Madison, Wis., Oct. 10, 1959; m. Jane Kaczmarek, Aug. 15, 1992; children: Frances, George, Mary. BA, Wesleyan U., 1981. Actor: (plays) Curse of the Starving Class, Three Days of Rain, Measure for Measure, Corionlanus; (Broadway plays) A Few Good Men, 1989—91; (films) Dead as a Doorman, 1986, Adventures in Babysitting, 1987, Revenge of the Nerds II, 1987, Vital Signs, 1990, Presumed Innocent, 1990, Young Guns II, 1990, Awakenings, 1990, Scent of a Woman, 1992, The Silent Alarm, 1993, RoboCop 3, 1993, My Life, 1993, A Perfect World, 1993, Philadelphia, 1993, The Client, 1994, Cobb, 1994, Billy Madison, 1995, My Fellow Americans, 1996, The Spittin' Image, 1997, The People, 1997, Masterminds, 1997, Red Corner, 1997, Wildly Available, 1999, The Muse, 1999, Bicentennial Man, 1999, Kate & Leopold, 2001, The Sisterhood of the Traveling Pants, 2005, Little Manhattan, 2005; (TV films) C.A.T. Squad, 1986, The Betty Ford Story, 1987, Web of Deception, 1994, Nothing But the Truth, 1995, The Desperate Trail, 1995, In the Line of Duty: Blaze of Glory, 1997, Cloned, 1997, The Sky's on Fire, 1998, Behind the Mask, 1999, Fathers & Sons, 2005; (TV series) NYPD Blue, 1994, The West Wing, 1999—2006, Studio 60 on the Sunset Strip, 2006—07. Co-founder Clothes Off Our Back Found. Office: Endeavor Agy 10th Fl 9601 Wilshire Blvd Beverly Hills CA 90212

WHITING, ALBERT NATHANIEL, former university chancellor; b. Jersey City, July 3, 1917; s. Hezekiah Oliver and Hildegarde Freida (Lyons) W.; m. Charlotte Luck, June 10, 1950; 1 dau., Brooke Elizabeth. AB, Amherst Coll., 1938; student, Columbia, summer 1938, U. Pitts., 1938-39; MA in Sociology, Fisk U., 1941, L.H.D. (hon.), 1980; PhD in Sociology, Am. U., 1952; LL.D., Amherst Coll., 1968, Western Mich. U., 1974, Duke, 1974, Kyung Hee U., Seoul, Korea, 1981; L.H.D. (hon.), N.C. Central U., 1983. Research and teaching asst. Fisk U., 1939-41; instr. sociology, dir. rural community study Bennett Coll., Greensboro, NC, 1941-43, 46-47; asst. prof. sociology Atlanta U., 1948-53; dean coll., prof. sociology Morris Brown Coll., Atlanta, 1953-57; asst. dean coll. Morgan State Coll., Balt., 1957-59, dean of college, 1960-67; pres. N.C. Central U., Durham, 1967-72, chancellor, 1972-83. Mem. bd. regents U. Md. Sys., 1988-95. Contbr. articles profl. jours. Bd. dirs. Am. Coun. Edn., Ednl. Testing Svc.; bd. dirs., past pres. Assn. State Colls. and Univs.; v.p. Internat. Assn. Univ. Pres.; bd. dirs. Research Triangle (N.C.) Inst.; mem. Md. Higher Edn. Commn., 1995-98. 1st lt. AUS, 1943-46. Episcopalian. Home: 11253B Slalom Ln Columbia MD 21044-2810

WHITING, ANTHONY, executive search consultant; b. Saigon, Indochina, Nov. 6, 1951; s. Dinty Warmington and Lorraine (Yarborough) W. BA summa cum laude, Tulane U., 1973; MA with honors, Columbia U., 1974, MPhil, 1977, PhD, 1984. V.p. Columbia Consulting Group, NYC, 1987-92; partner Johnson, Smith, and Knisely, NYC, 1993-99; mng. dir. Illsley Bourbonnais, NYC, 1999-2000; mng. ptnr. The Waterman Group, NYC, 2000—. Vis. scholar Columbia U., 2001—03, Union Theol. Sem., 2006—07. Author: The Never Resting Mind: Wallace Stevens' Romantic Irony, 1996, Edward Thomas, 1996; contbg. author: Wallace Stevens: Comprehensive Research and Study Guide, 2003. Mem. SAR, Soc. of Mayflower Descendants, Order of Crown of Charlemagne, Baronial Order of Magna Carta, Soc. of the Cinn., Hereditary Order of Descendants of Colonial Govs., Soc. of Order of Founders and Patriots of Am., Soc. of Descendants of Colonial Clergy, Phi Beta Kappa. Office: 267 Fifth Ave New York NY 10016

WHITING, BRIAN CHRISTOPHER, hospitality consultant; b. Bronxville, NY, Aug. 14, 1969; s. William Gordon Whiting and Doris Edna (Chubb) Whiting Simmons. BA, U. R.I., 1990. Dir. The Ams. and Asia Pacific Commonweath of Mass./Dept. Econ. Devel./Office Travel & Tourism, Boston, 1996—99; mgr./dir. internat. mktg. Europe and Mid. East Travel Industry Assn. Am., London, 1999—2000; travel and tourism practice leader, mgr. sports conv. and tourism PricewaterhouseCoopers LLP, NYC, 2000—03; pres. & CEO Providence Warwick Conv. & Visitors Bur., Providence, 2003—. Chmn. bd. dirs. RI Festival of Trees; mem. RI Sports Commn., RI Transit and Urban Transp. Subcom.; mem. dean's adv. coun. U. R.I. Coll. Arts and Scis. Mem.: Destination Orgn. (bd. dirs. nat. coun.), Nat. Coun. Destination Orgns. (bd. dirs.), NY Soc. Assn. Execs., Internat. Assn. Conv. and Visitors Burs. Edn. Com. (mem. visitors bur. edn. com.), Am. Soc. Assn. Execs., Profl. Conv. Mgmt. Assn., Travel Industry Assn. Am., Skal Club Internat., Assn. Travel Mgmt. Execs., New Eng. Soc., The Downtown Assn., Bronxville Field Club, Racquet and Tennis Club, The Boston Athenaeum, Masons, Sigma Alpha Epsilon (pledge class pres. 1987—88). Republican. Avocations: travel, shooting, racquet sports.

WHITING, GORDON JAMES, investment banker; b. Bronxville, NY, Nov. 17, 1965; s. William Gordon Whiting and Doris (Chubb) Whiting Simmons; m. Cornelia Conway Cabot, Aug. 30, 2003. BS, Cornell U., 1988; MBA, Columbia U., 1994. Sales and mktg. mgr. Epcot Ltd., Tsim Sha Tsui, Kowloon, Hong Kong, 1989-90; mng. dir. Stapenhurst Ltd., Victoria, Hong Kong, 1990-92; acquisitions assoc. W. P. Carey & Co. LLC, NYC, 1993-94, 2d v.p., 1994-95, v.p., 1995-97, 1st v.p., 1997-98, sr. v.p., 1998-2000, dep. dir. of acquistions, 1999—2003, exec. dir., 2000—; exec. v.p. and portfolio mgr. Corp. Property Assocs.: 14 Inc., NYC, 1998-2000, pres. and portfolio mgr., 2000—. Bd. dir. Fed. Ret. Thrift Investment Bd.; mem. coun. Cornell U., 2002—. Local bd. mem. Selective Svc. Sys., Eagle Scout. Mem. Profl. Assn. Diving Instrs., Bronxville Field Club, Constant Spring Golf Club (Jamaica), Holland Lodge No. 8 F&AM, Leander Club (U.K.), The Camp Fire Club Am., Mashomack Preserve Club (Pine Plains, N.Y.), The Order of St. John, The Pilgrims, Hon. Order Ky. Cols., Racquet and Tennis Club, Royal Hong Kong Yacht Club, Sigma Chi. Republican. Episcopalian. Avocations: fly fishing, golf, scuba diving, skiing, squash. Home: 70 E 96th St Apt 11b New York NY 10128-0752 E-mail: gwhiting@angelogordon.com.

WHITING, HUGH RICHARD, lawyer; b. East Chgo., Ind., Dec. 8, 1945; s. Harold C. and Nina (Hofstetter) W.; m. Sherry Ballast, July 2, 1965; 1 child, Kristin Anne. BA, U. Mich., 1967; JD, Ohio State U., 1974. Bar: Ohio 1974, Tex. 1981. Salesman, adminstr. Procter & Gamble, Cin., 1967-71; law clk. to Judge George Edwards U.S. Ct. Appeals (6th cir.) Ohio, Cin., 1974-75; assoc. Jones, Day, Reavis & Pogue, Cleve., 1975-81, ptnr., 1982—; mng. ptnr. Houston office Jones Day. Chmn. Firmwide Profl. Svcs. Com.; mem. civil justice reform act adv. com. No. Dist. Ohio Adv. Com., Cleve., 1990—; mem. Ohio State U. Coll. Law Nat. Coun., Columbus, 1984—; speaker, presenter on legal practice and practice mgmt. various confs. and seminars. Co-chmn. Gen. Bus. Campaign Cleve. Orch., 1992. Mem. ABA (litigation sect., sect. bus. law), Tex. Bar Assn., Cleve. Bar Assn., Mayfield Country Club, Order of Coif. Avocations: golf, travel, reading. Office: Jones Day Ste 3300 717 Texas Houston TX 77002-2712 Office Fax: 832-239-3600. Business E-Mail: hrwhiting@jonesday.com.

WHITING, MARTHA COUNTEE, retired secondary school educator; b. Marshall, Tex., Mar. 24, 1912; d. Thomas and Nannie Selena (Yates) Countee; m. Samuel Whiting, June 8, 1937; children: Jacqueline Bostic, Sammie Ellis, Nan Broussard, Tommye Casey, Martha Goddard. BA in Sci., Bishop Coll., 1934; M of Secondary Edn., Tex. So. U., 1959, postgraduate, 1962; postgrad., U. Colo., 1963. Tchr., sci., math. Houston Ind. Sch. Dist., 1942-73; researcher, local history Houston, 1973—. Lectr. in field. Mem. exec. com. (life mem.) Houston YWCA, 1977; advisor Preservation 4th Ward, Houston, 1991—; trustee Antioch Missionary Bapt. Ch., Houston, 1977; instrumental in getting the Antioch Missionary Bapt. Ch. in Christ Inc. on the Nat. Register of Hist. Places, 1976; presented Queen Elizabeth II with miniature history of Antioch Missionary Bapt. Ch. in Christ, 1991; author nomination form for Tex. hist. marker Antioch Missionary Bapt. Ch. in Christ, 1994; presenter to Harris County Heritage Soc. of Jack Yates House, the only house built by a former slave to be maintain ed by a U.S. city, and chmn. Pathfinder presentation of achievements of 64 Negro pioneers in Harris County, 1966-1986. Named Woman Courage, Houston Radcliffe Club, 1985, Black Womens Hall Fame Mus. Africal Am. Life, Dallas, 1986; recipient Friend of the Soc. award Harris County Heritage Soc., 1994. Mem. Tex. Ret. Tchrs. Assn., Houston Mus. Fine Arts, Harris County Heritage Soc. (exec. com. 1984), Bluebonnet Garden Club (pres. 1968), Jack & Jill Am. (pres. Houston chpt. 1955-57), Smithsonian, Nationwide Trust for Historic Preservation. Avocations: writing, gardening, travel, sewing, singing. Home: 3446 Southmore Blvd Houston TX 77004-6349

WHITING, ORAN F., lawyer; b. Chgo., 1961; BS in Econs., U. Pa., 1983, BA in Internat. Bus., 1983; postgraduate student, Centro de Estudios Hispanicos, Madrid, 1984; JD, Georgetown U., 1986. Bar: Ill. 1987, US Dist. Ct. (no. dist. Ill.) 1987, US Dist. Ct. (ctrl. dist. Ill.) 1995, US Ct. Appeals (10th cir.) 1992, US Ct. Appeals (7th cir.). Counsel to Spkr. Ill. Ho. Reps., 1995—97; spl. counsel Sedgwick, Detert, Moran & Arnold, Chgo.; ptnr. Holland & Knight, LLP, Chgo., 2006—. Commr. Ill. Ct. Claims, 1997—2006; interim gen. counsel Mercy Hosp., Chgo., 2001—02. Contbr. articles to law jours. Bd. mem. Sargent Shriver Nat. Ctr. Poverty Law, Evanston Symphony Orch. Mem.: Leading Lawyers Network, Ill., ABA (assoc. editor Litig. News 1996—2003, co-chmn. Electronic Pub. com., Litig. sect.), Cook County Bar Assn., Chgo. Bar Assn. Office: Holland & Knight LLP 30th Fl 131 Dearborn St Chicago IL 60603 Office Phone: 312-715-5774. E-mail: oran.whiting@hklaw.com. *

WHITING, RICHARD ALBERT, lawyer; b. Cambridge, Mass., Dec. 2, 1922; s. Albert S. and Jessie (Coleman) W.; m. Marvelene Nash, Feb. 22, 1948 (div. 1984); children— Richard A. Jr., Stephen C., Jeffrey D., Gary S., Kimberly G.; m. Joanne Sherry, Oct. 14, 1984 AB, Dartmouth Coll., 1944; JD, Yale U., 1949. Bar: D.C. 1949. Assoc. Steptoe & Johnson, Washington, 1949-55, ptnr., 1956-86, of counsel, 1987—. Adj. prof. Vt. Law Sch., South Royalton, 1985-90; mem. exec. com. Yale Law Sch. Assn., New Haven, 1985-88; mem. adv. bd. The Antitrust Bull., N.Y.C., 1975-99. Contbr. articles to profl. jours. Trustee Colby-Sawyer Coll., 1987-97. 1st lt. U.S. Army, 1945-46. Mem. ABA (council mem. Antitrust Law sect. 1977-85, del. to Ho. Dels. 1982-83, chmn. 1984-85) Presbyterian. Office: 1330 Connecticut Ave NW Washington DC 20036-1704 Office Phone: 202-429-8080.

WHITING, S. CAROL, music educator; b. Bryan, Tex., Sept. 1, 1948; d. Robert Louis and Helen Sharon Whiting. MusB, U. Tex., Austin, 1970. Strings instr. Houston Ind. Sch. Dist., 1976—85, Spring Branch Ind. Sch. Dist., Houston, 1985—93, 2006—07, Arlington Ind. Sch. Dist., Tex., 1993—95; orch. instr. Bryan Ind. Sch. Dist., 1995—99, Richardson Ind. Sch. Dist., Tex., 1999—2000, Garland Ind. Sch. Dist., Tex., 2000—01. Mem.: Suzuki Assn. Ams., Am. String Tchr. Assn., Tex. Music Educator Assn. Avocations: crafts, gardening. Home: 207 Fireside College Station TX 77840 Office: 625 Balitmore Houston TX 77079

WHITING, STEPHEN CLYDE, lawyer; b. Arlington, Va., Mar. 20, 1952; s. Richard A. Whiting; m. Patrice Quinn, May 24, 1980; children: Kelsey, Daniel, Seth, Samuel. BA magna cum laude, Dartmouth Coll., 1974; JD, U. Va., 1978. Bar: Maine 1978, U.S. Dist. Ct. Maine 1978, U.S. Ct. Appeals (1st cir.) 1999. Ptnr. Douglas, Whiting, Denham & Rogers, Portland, Maine, 1978-98; founder The Whiting Law Firm, P.A., Portland, 1998—. Maine state dir. Am. Ctr. Law and Justice, 1998—. Co-author: Trying the Automobile Injury Case in Maine, 1993, Premises Liability: Preparation and Trial of a Difficult Case in Maine, 1994, Trying Soft Tissue Injury Cases in Maine, 1995, How to Litigate Your First Civil Trial in Maine, 2001, How to Successfully Resolve Automobile Injury Cases, 2006, Depositions A-Z, 2007. Mem. ATLA, Maine Bar Assn., Maine Trial Lawyers Assn., Phi Beta Kappa. Office: The Whiting Law Firm PA 75 Pearl St Ste 207 Portland ME 04101 Home Phone: 207-883-3403; Office Phone: 207-780-0681. E-mail: mail@whitinglawfirm.com.

WHITING, SUSAN DICKINSON, media research company executive; b. Chgo., Aug. 1, 1956; d. Lawrence H. Whiting Jr.; BA in Econs. cum laude, Denison U., 1978. Mgmt. devel. program Nielsen Media Rsch., Dunedin, Fla., 1979-86, v.p. Nielsen Homevideo Index, 1986-87, mktg. mgr., 1987-93, sr. v.p., dir. mktg., 1993-97, gen. mgr. nat. svcs. & emerging markets, 1997—2001, pres., COO NYC, 2001—02, pres., CEO, 2002—; also exec. v.p., Media Measurement & Info. Group VNU Bus. Media, 2005—. Named an Outstanding Female Role Model, NBA Wives Awards Luncheon, 2005; named one of 50 Women to Watch, Wall St. Jour., 2006. Mem. Cable TV Adminstrv. and Mktg. Assn., Women in Cable & Telecomm., Conn. Women's Forum (v.p.), NY Radio and TV Rsch. Coun. (past pres.). Office: Nielsen Media Rsch Inc 770 Broadway New York NY 10003 *

WHITINGTON, PETER FRANK, pediatric hepatologist, educator; b. Memphis, May 8, 1947; s. Frank Everett and Mary Lena (Hollingsworth) Whitington; m. Susan Maurine Hoagland, June 6, 1967; children: Helen Frances Josephic, Mary Louise, Katherine Daphne, Patrick M. BA in Econs., Tulane U., 1968; MD, U. Tenn., Memphis, 1971. Diplomate Am. Bd. Pediat., Am. Bd. Pediatric Gastroenterology. Resident in pediat., then chief resident U. Tenn. Ctr. for Health Scis., 1972—74, instr., 1975, asst. prof., 1978—81, assoc. prof., 1981—84, chief divsn. pediatric gastroenterology, 1978—84; rsch. fellow in gastroenterology Johns Hopkins Hosp., Balt., 1975—77; rsch. fellow in gastroenterology dept. pediatrics U. Wis., Madison, 1977—78; assoc. prof. dept. pediat. U. Chgo. Pritzker Sch. Medicine, 1984—87, assoc. prof. depts. pediat. and medicine, 1987—92, prof., 1992—97; prof. pediat. Northwestern U. Med. Sch., 1997—, Sally Burnett Searle prof. pediat. and transplantation; dir. divsn. gastroenterology, hepatology & nutrition Children's Meml. Hosp., Chgo., 1997—, dir. organ transplantation, Siragusa Transplantation Ctr., 1997—; co-dir. Northwestern U. Affiliated Transplant Ctrs., 1997—. Chief gastroenterology LeBonheur Children's Med. Ctr., Memphis, 1978—84; numerous invited lectures and guest spkr. at profl. meetings, workshops, symposia, hosps., confs.; mem. pediatric transplantation com. United Network for Organ Sharing, Nat. Organ Procurement and Transplantation Network, 1992—94; reviewer numerous med. jours. including New Eng. Jour. Medicine, Gastroenterology, Hepatology, Jour. Pediat., Digestive Diseases and Scis., Pediat., Transplant. Editl. bd. Jour. Pediatric Gastroenterology and Nutrition, 1991—96, Liver Transplantation, 1994—, Pediatric Transplantation, 1997—, sect. editor Birth Defects Compendium, 1987—90, contbr. numerous articles and abstracts to med. jours. Mem. sci. adv. bd. Mid-South chpt. Nat. Found. for Ileitis and Colitis, Memphis, 1983—84; chmn. med. adv. com. Ill. chpt. Am. Liver Found., 1996—, mem., med. adv. on bd. dirs., 1993—; med. dir. The Johnny Genna Found., Chgo., 1987—; bd. dirs. Parents for Ctrl. H.S., Memphis, 1983—84, Liver/Organ Transplant Fund, Memphis, 1983—84. Recipient Cmty. Svc. award, NCCJ, Memphis, 1983; fellow postdoctoral rsch. NIH, 1977. Mem.: Am. Assn. Transplantation, N.A.m Soc. for Pediatric Gastroenterology and Nutrition, Soc. for Pediatric Rsch., Am. Gastroenterol. Assn., Gastroenterology Rsch. Group, Am. Assn. for Study of Liver Diseases. Avocations: making furniture, fly fishing. Home: 5490 S South Shore Dr Apt 8 Chicago IL 60615-5984 Office: Childrens Meml Hosp Box 57 2300 Childrens Plaza Chicago IL 60614-3394 Business E-Mail: p-whitington@northwestern.edu.

WHITLEY, JOSEPH D(ALLY) (JOSEPH DALLY WHITLEY), lawyer; b. Atlanta, Nov. 12, 1950; s. Thomas Youngie and Mary Jo (Dally) W.; m. Kathleen Pinion, Sept. 27, 1975; children: Lauren Jacqueline, Thomas McMillan. BA, U. Ga., 1972, JD, 1975. Bar: Ga. 1975, DC, 1990, US Supreme Ct. 1989. Assoc. Kelly, Denney, Pease & Allison, Columbus, Ga., 1975-78; asst. dist. atty. Chattahoochee Jud. Cir., Columbus, 1978-79; assoc. Hirsch, Beil & Partin, P.C., Columbus, 1979-81; US atty. (mid. dist.) GA US Dept. Justice, Macon, 1981-87, dep. asst. atty. gen., criminal divsn. Washington, 1987-88, dep. assoc. atty. gen., 1988-89, acting assoc. atty. gen., 1989; ptnr. Smith, Gambrell & Russell, Atlanta, 1989-90; US atty. (no. dist.) GA US Dept. Justice, Atlanta, 1990-93; ptnr. Kilpatrick Stockton, Atlanta, 1993-97, Alston & Bird, Atlanta, 1997—2003, 2005—; gen. counsel US Dept. Homeland Security, Washington, 2003—05. Mem. Atty. Gen.'s adv. com. dept. justice, Washington, 1982-85; chmn. organized crime and violent crime subcom. Atty. Gen.'s adv. com., 1990-93; mem. investigative subcom.; chmn. white collar crime subcom., 1993-99; program chmn. Ga. Inst. of Continuing Legal Edn. Programs; lectr. in field. Treas. Muscogee County Young Reps., Columbus, 1979-80. Mem. ABA (mem. criminal justice dect. voun., vice-chmn. govt. affairs 2002-03), Ga. Bar Assn., Macon Bar Assn., Young Lawyers Club (pres. Columbus chpt. 1980-81), Lawyers Club of Atlanta. Republican. Presbyterian. Office: Alston & Bird LLP The Atlantic Bldg 950 F St NW Washington DC 20004 also: One Atlantic Ctr 1201 W Peachtree St Atlanta GA 30309 Office Phone: 202-756-3300. Business E-Mail: joe.whitley@alston.com.

WHITLEY, LENA FRANCES, French educator; b. LaGrange, Ga., Oct. 27, 1962; d. John Hamilton and Lena Knight Whitley. BA in French, Psychology, Agnes Scott Coll., Decatur, Ga., 1984; MAT in French, Emory U., Atlanta, 1988. Cert. tchr. French Ga. French tchr. LaGrange Acad. Edn., LaGrange, 1986—87, Chambers County Bd. Edn., Valley, Ala., 1988—91; French, lang. arts tchr. Springwood Pub. Schs., Lanett, Ala., 1992—93; French tchr. The O'Neal Sch., Pinehurst, NC, 1993—94, Fulton County Bd. Edn., Atlanta, 1994—. Mem. Atlanta Hist. Soc.; vol. Margaret Mitchell House, Atlanta; mem. Thoreau Soc., Concord, Mass.; mem., vol. John F. Kennedy Mus., Boston. Mem.: NEA, PAGE, Am. Coun. on Tchg. Fgn. Langs., Ga. Edn. Assn., Am. Assn. Tchrs. French, Phi Beta Kappa. Democrat. Methodist. Avocations: reading, writing, theater, concerts. Office: Autrey Mill Middle School 4110 Old Alabama Rd Alpharetta GA 30022

WHITLEY, ROB, medical educator, sociologist, researcher; b. Jersey, England, Aug. 3, 1972; arrived in US, 2005; BSc, U. Coll. London, 1995; MSc, London Sch. Hygiene and Tropical Medicine, 1998; PhD, King's Coll. London, 2003. Rsch. fellow McGill U., Montreal, Canada, 2003—05; asst. prof. Dartmouth Med. Sch., Hanover, NH, 2005—. Cons. U. W.I., Mona, Jamaica, 2005—, U. Addis Ababa, Ethiopia, 2004—. Office: Dartmouth Psychiatric Rsch Ctr Ste 202 2 Whipple Pl Lebanon NH 03766 Home Phone: 603-643-2375; Office Phone: 603-448-0263. Business E-Mail: rob.whitley@dartmouth.edu.

WHITLOCK, CHARLES PRESTON, former university dean; b. Highland Park, NJ, June 19, 1919; s. Frank Boudinot and Rosena Craig (Foster) W.; m. Patricia Hamilton Hoey, Mar. 10, 1960; children: Carol Foster, Adam Hoey, Susan Boudinot, Matthew Fitzsimmons, Beth Brewer. BA, Rutgers U., 1941; MA, Harvard U., 1947. Assoc. dir. Bur. Study Counsel Harvard U., 1948-52, Allston Burr sr. tutor, 1952-58, lectr. social psychology, 1955-72, asst. to pres., 1958-70, assoc. dean of coll., 1970-72, dean of coll., 1972-76, assoc. dean faculty, 1976-82, master Dudley House, 1976-82. Dir. Cambridgeport Savs. Bank.; Mem. Mass. Higher Edn. Facilities Commn. Co-author: Harvard University Reading Films. Trustee Charity of Edward Hopkins, Lesley Coll.; bd. corporators New Eng. Deaconess Hosp.; treas. Annisquam Village Ch. Col. USAF. Decorated Silver Star, D.F.C., Air medal. Mem. Phi Beta Kappa. Home: 9 Barberry Heights Rd Gloucester MA 01930-1201 Office: Harvard U Cambridge MA 02138

WHITLOCK, GARY L., energy executive; b. Houston, 1950; B in Bus. Adminstrn. Acctg., Sam Houston State U., 1972. CPA. Joined Dow Chem. Co., 1972, responsible for worldwide fin. consolidation and mgmt. reporting, 1981, fin. dir. UK and Ireland, 1984; v.p. fin., CFO Dow AgroScis. subs. Dow Chem. Co., 1998—2001; exec. v.p., CFO delivery group Reliant Energy, 2001—02; exec. v.p., CFO CenterPoint Energy, Houston, 2002—. Mem.: AICPA, Tex. Soc. CPAs, Inst. Mgmt. Accts. Office: CenterPoint Energy PO Box 1700 Houston TX 77251-1700 *

WHITLOCK, JOHN JOSEPH, museum director; b. South Bend, Ind., Jan. 7, 1935; s. Joseph Mark and Helen Marcella (Cramer) Whitlock; m. Sue Ann Kirkman, June 10, 1956; children: Kelly Ann, Michele Lynn, Mark. BS in Art, Ball State U., 1957, MA in Art, 1963; EdD, Ind. U., 1971. Tchr. art Union City (Ind.) Pub. Schs., 1957-59; tchr. art, art dir. Madison (Ind.) City Schs., 1959-64; prof. art, dir. gallery Hanover (Ind.) Coll., 1964-69; dir. Burpee Art Mus., Rockford, Ill., 1970-72; prof. arts and humanities Elgin (Ill.) Community Coll., 1970-72; dir. Brooks Meml. Art Gallery, Memphis, 1972-78; prof. mus. studies Southwestern Coll., Memphis, 1973-78; adj. asst. prof. art and museology Memphis State U., 1976-78; dir. Univ. Mus., mem. grad. faculty So. Ill. U., Carbondale, 1978-2000, emeritus dir., 2000—, also dir. mus. studies, 1978-2000, adj. assoc. prof. anthropology, 1978-2000, adj. assoc. prof. polit. sci., 1988—, adj. assoc. prof. history, 1994—, dir. mus. studies, 1989—, mem. ROTC acad. avc. coun., 1988—, mem. president's coun., 1988-93, adj. assoc. prof. art Univ. Mus., 1978-99, vis. emeritus prof., 2000—; instr. art John A. Logan Coll., 2001—. Chmn. bd. Nat. Coal Mus., 1983-85; mem. Newsfront adv. bd. NC Broadcast News, Washington, 1982-85; sr. cons. Marine Mil. Acad. Mus., 1988—, mem. bd. advisors, 1991-97. Mem. Rockford Human Rels. Commn., 1971-72; mem. pres.'s coun. Southwestern Coll., 1973-78; vol. Carbondale Police Dept., 2000—, com. resources, forensics records and acad.; bd. dirs. Carbondale Crime Stoppers, 2000—, pres., 2006—; bd. dirs. DARE, 2000—, pres., 2006—; bd. dirs. Carbondale Fire and Police Commn., 2003—; univ. club bd. So. Ill. U., 2000—, univ. mus. amb., 2000—. Mem. Am. Assn. Mus., Internat. Coun. Mus., Midwest Assn. Mus., Assn. Art Mus. Dirs., Marine Corps League (commandant Shawnee detachment 1994-96, 99-2001, comdr. USCG Aux. 1994-95), Dept. Ill. Marine Corps League (trustee rank and file 1994-99, judge advocate 1999-2005), Semper Fi Soc. (faculty adviser So. Ill. U. 1995—). Office: So Ill U 605 W Walnut St Carbondale IL 62901-2615

WHITLOCK, JOHN L., lawyer; b. New Orleans, Oct. 24, 1946; s. John Bert and Virginia Katherine (Marzolf) W.; m. Dorothy Florence Oeste, Sept. 13, 1969; children: Sarah Katherine, Thomas John. AB, Harvard U., 1968, JD, 1973. Bar: Mass. 1973, U.S. Dist. Ct. Mass. 1974, U.S. Ct. Appeals (1st cir.) 1975. Assoc. Herrick & Smith, Boston, 1973—80, ptnr., 1981—86, Edwards Angell Palmer & Dodge LLP, Boston, 1986—. Mem. ethics rules adv. com. Mass. Supreme Jud. Ct., 1996—, chair, 2006—. Bd. dirs., sec. Harvard-Radcliffe Collegiate Mus. Found., Inc., 1978—; treas. The Boston Cecilia, Inc., 1974-85, 98—, bd. dirs., 1974-86, 94—, pres., 1994-98. With U.S. Army, 1968-70. Mem. Boston Bar Assn. (coun. 1996-97). Lutheran. Avocation: singing. Office: Edwards Angell Palmer & Dodge LLP 111 Huntington Ave Boston MA 02199-7613 Office Phone: 617-239-0100. Business E-Mail: jwhitlock@eapdlaw.com.

WHITLOW, MARY ANN, retired elementary school educator; b. Lawton, Okla., Feb. 11, 1942; d. Cleon C. and Oletta S. Howell; m. Samuel Whitlow, Sept. 27, 1963. BS in Edn., South Ark. U., Magnolia, 1970. Elem. tchr. El Dorado Sch. Dist., Ark., 1970—74, Anna schs., Ill., 1974—75, Pulaski County Sch. Dist., Little Rock, 1975—81, El Dorado Sch. Dist., Little Rock, 1981—96; jr. HS tchr. Little Rock Sch. Dist., 1996—2004; ret. Named Tchr. of Yr., Henderson Jr. HS, Little Rock, 2003; grantee, Murphy Oil, El Dorado, 1991. Mem.: Delta Kappa Gamma. Home: 36 Eagles Nest Ct Little Rock AR 72210

WHITMAN, BURKE WILLIAM, health services executive; b. Newport, RI, Feb. 26, 1956; s. Homer William and Anne (Sarran) W. BA cum laude, Dartmouth Coll., 1978; MBA, Harvard U., 1984. Project mgr. HCB Contractors/Barker Interests Ltd., Atlanta, Houston, 1979-85; investment banker Morgan Stanley & Co. Inc., NYC, 1988-92; v.p. fin./devel. Almost Family Inc., Balt., 1992-94; pres., CFO Deerfield Healthcare Corp., Balt., 1994-99; CFO Triad Hosps., Inc., Plano, Tex., 1999—2005; pres., COO Health Mgmt. Assocs., Inc., Naples, Fla., 2005—07, pres., CEO, 2007—. Bd. dirs. Fedn. Am. Hosps., chmn. audit com., 2005—06. Former bd. dirs. Outward Bound, Police Athletic League; bd. advisors Marine Corps U.; mem. Founders Group, Nat. Mus. Marine Corps. With USMC, 1985—2005, lt. col. USMCR, 1988—. Mem.: Fedn. Am. Hosps. (bd. dirs.), Piedmont Driving Club. Episcopalian. Avocations: hiking, bicycling, outdoor sports. Office: Health Mgmt Assocs Inc 5811 Pelican Bay Blvd Ste 500 Naples FL 34108 *

WHITMAN, CHRISTINE TODD, former federal agency administrator, governor; b. NYC, Sept. 26, 1946; d. Webster Bray and Eleanor Schley Todd; m. John Whitman, 1974; children: Kate, Taylor. BA in Govt., Wheaton Coll., 1968. Freeholder Somerset County, 1982—87; pres. NJ State Bd. Pub. Utilities, 1988—90; host radio talk show Sta. WKXW, Trenton, N.J.; gov. State of N.J., 1994-2001; adminstr. EPA, Washington, 2001—03. Chmn. Com. for an Affordable N.J.; bd. dirs. Texas Instruments Inc., 2003-, Millennium Challenge Corp., S.C. Johnson and Son, Inc., United Tech. Corp., 2003-, Chgo. Climate Exchange, Inc.; mem. steering com. Cancer Inst. NJ Leadership Coun.; co-chair Nat. Smart Growth Coun., Smart Growth Am.; mem. leadership coun. Rep. Pro-Choice Coalition, gov.'s bd. Oquirrh Inst., S&T presdl. and fed. adv. com. Appointments of Nat. Acads. Author: It's My Party Too: The Battle for the Heart of the GOP and the Future of America, 2005. Columnist newspapers. Bd. freeholders Somerset County, N.J., 1982-87; bd. pub. utilities, 1988-89; Rep. candidate for senator State of N.J., 1990.; mem. Ctr. Civic Engagement and Volunteerism adv. bd. Raritan Cmty. Coll., UN sec-gen. adv. bd. Water and Sanitation. Republican. Achievements include first female governor in N.J.; delivered Republican response to President Clinton's 1995 State of the Union address.

WHITMAN, DALE ALAN, lawyer, educator; b. Charleston, W. Va., Feb. 18, 1939; m. Marjorie Miller: 8 children. Student, Ohio State U., 1956-59; BES, Brigham Young U., 1963; LLB, Duke U., 1966. Bar: Calif. 1967, Utah 1971. Assoc. O'Melveny & Myers, Los Angeles, 1966-67; asst prof., then assoc prof. sch. law U. N.C., Chapel Hill, 1967-70; vis. prof. law UCLA, 1970-71; dep. dir. Office Housing and Urban Affairs Fed. Home Loan Bank Bd., Washington, 1971-72; sr. program analyst FHA, HUD, Washington, 1972-73; prof. law Brigham Young U., 1973—78, 1992—98, U. Wash., 1978—82; vis. prof. law U. Mo., Columbia, 1976; prof. law, dean U. Mo. Sch. Law, Columbia, 1982-88, prof., 1988—91, 1998—. Cons., lectr. in field; reporter Am. law Inst. Co-author: Cases and Materials on Real Estate Finance and Development, 1976, Real Estate Finance Law, 1979, 5th edit., 2007, Cases and Materials on Real Estate Transfer, Finance and Development. 1981, 7th edit., 2006, Land Transactions and Finance, 1983, 4d edit., 2004, The Law of Property, 1984, 3d edit., 2000, Contemporary Property, 1996, 2d edit., 2002, Restatement of Property (Mortgages), 1997; contbr. articles to profl. jours. Fellow Am. Bar Found.; mem. Am. Law Inst., Am. Coll. Real Estate Lawyers, Am. Coll. Mortgage Attys., Assn. Am. Law Schs. (pres. 2002). Avocations: piano, flying. Office: Univ Mo 216 Hulston Hall Columbia MO 65211 Office Phone: 573-884-0946. Business E-Mail: whitmand@missouri.edu.

WHITMAN, GREGORY THEODORE, neurologist; b. Lansdale, Pa., Oct. 16, 1966; s. Steven and Sheila Whitman. BA, Cornell Univ., Ithaca, NY, 1985—89; MD, Univ. of Conn., Farmington, 1990—94. Cert. in Neurology Am. Bd. of Psychiatry and Neurology, 2000. Intern medicine Boston City Hosp., Boston U., 1994—95, resident neurology, 1995—97, Tufts U., Boston, 1997—98; clin. instr. neurology U. Calif., LA, 1998—2000, asst. prof. neurology Irvine, 2000—. Dir. neurology residency program U. Calif., Irvine, 2002—05; asst. clin. prof. neurology UCLA, 2006—. Co-author: (journal articles) Neurology, Archives of Neurology, Jour. of Neuroimaging, Stroke, Neurobiology of Aging. Mem.: Am. Acad. of Neurology. Office Phone: 714-456-2324.

WHITMAN, JEFFREY, ophthalmologist; b. Dallas, Jan. 18, 1956; s. Jack and Augusta Whitman; m. Bonnie H. Gerson, June 15, 1980; children: Andrea Lauren, Allison Leigh. MD, Southwestern Med. Sch., Dallas, 1980. Diplomate Am. Bd. Ophthalmology, 1986, Am. Bd. Eye Surgery, 2000, lic. ophthalmologist Fla., 2000. Pres. Key-Whitman Eye Ctr., Dallas, 1995—, chief surgery, 1995—. Chmn. Ret. Sr. Vol. Program Greater Dallas.,

1988—90; bd. dirs. Tiferet Israel Synagogue, Dallas, 2000—07. Named Best Ophthalmologist in Dallas, D Mag., 2002—06. Fellow: Am. Acad. Ophthalmology (assoc.); mem.: Am. Coll. Eye Surgeons (pres. 2007—), Dallas Acad. Ophthalmology (assoc.; pres. 2002—03), Am. Soc. Cataract and Refractive Surgery (assoc.), Tex. Ophthal. Assn. (assoc.). Office: Key-Whitman Eye Ctr 2801 Lemmon Ave Ste 400 Dallas TX 75204 Office Phone: 214-754-0000.

WHITMAN, KATHY VELMA ROSE (ELK WOMAN WHITMAN), artist, painter; b. Bismarck, ND, Aug. 12, 1952; d. Carl Jr. and Edith Geneva (Lykken) W.; m. Robert Paul Luger, Feb. 21, 1971 (div. Jan. 1982); children: Shannon, Lakota, Cannupa, Palani; m. Dean P. Fox (div. 1985); 1 child, Otgadahe. Student, Standing Rock C.C., Ft. Yates, ND, 1973-74, Sinte Gleska Coll., Rosebud, SD, 1975-77, U. S.D., 1977, Ariz. State U., 1992-93. Instr. art Sinte Gleska Coll., 1975-77, Standing Rock C.C., 1977-78; co-mgr. Four Bears Motor Lodge, New Town, ND, 1981-82; store owner Nux-Baga Lodge, New Town, 1982-85; jeweler, painter Phoenix. Artist-in-residence N.D. Coun. on Arts, Bismarck, 1983-84, bd. dirs., 1985; artist-in-residence Evanston Twp. H.S., Ill., 1996; cultural cons. movie prodn., Phoenix, Ariz., 1994. One woman shows include Mus. of Am. Indian, N.Y.C., 1983, Charleroi Internat. Fair, Belgium, 1984, Heard Mus., Phoenix, 1987-92, Phoenix Gallery, Nurnburg, Germany, 1990-96, Lovena Ohl Gallery, Phoenix, 1990-94, Phoenix Gallery, Coeur d'Alene, Idaho, 1992, Silver Sun Gallery, Santa Fe, N.Mex., 1992-96, Tribal Expessions Gallery, Arlington Heights, Ill., 1994-96, others; represented in permanent collections at Mus. of the Am. Indian, N.Y.C., Mesa (Ariz.) C.C. Bd. dirs. Ft. Berthold C.C., New Town, 1983-85; pres. Cannonball (N.D.) Pow-Wow Com., 1978; parent rep. Head Start, Ft. Yates, 1974. Recipient mentor for First Peoples Fund, 2001, 02, best craftsman spl. award Bullock's Indian Arts and Crafts, 1986, best of fine arts award No. Plains Tribal Arts, Sioux Falls, S.D., 1988, best of show award Pasadena Western Relic and Native Am. Show, 1991, 2 1st place awards Santa Fe Indian Market, 1993, 2 2nd place awards, 1994, 2 3rd place awards, 1994, 74th Ann. SWAIA Santa Fe Indian Mkt. 1st place award, 1995, 2d place award, 1995, 97, 2 3rd place awards, 1995, 2 Honorable Mentions in sculpture N.Mex. State Fair, 1996, Best of Show/Fine Arts, N.M. State Fair, 1999, 01. Mem. Indian Arts and Crafts Assn., S.W. Assn. on Indian Affairs (life, 1st and 2nd place awards Santa Fe Indian Market 1995, 2 3rd place awards 1995, 1st place and 2nd place awards Santa Fe Indian Market 1996). Avocations: native american crafts, furniture building, running and hiking, dance, singing. Office Phone: 602-377-4452. E-mail: elkwomn39@aol.com.

WHITMAN, MARINA VON NEUMANN, economist, educator; b. NYC, Mar. 6, 1935; d. John and Mariette (Kovesi) von Neumann; m. Robert Freeman Whitman, June 23, 1956; children: Malcolm Russell, Laura Mariette. BA summa cum laude, Harvard U., 1956; MA, Columbia U., 1959, PhD, 1962; DHL (hon.), U. Mass., 1975; LittD (hon.), Williams Coll., 1980; LLD (hon.), Mount Holyoke Coll., 1980, Lehigh U., 1981; LHD (hon.), Clemson U., 1984; LLD (hon.), U. Notre Dame, 1984, Ea. Mich. U., 1992. Mem. faculty U. Pitts., 1962-79, prof. econs., 1971-73, disting. pub. svc. prof. econs., 1973-79; v.p., chief economist Gen. Motors Corp., NYC, 1979-85, group v.p. pub. affairs, 1985-92; disting. vis. prof. bus. adminstrn., pub. policy U. Mich., Ann Arbor, 1992-94, prof. bus. adminstrn., pub. policy, 1994—. Mem. Trilateral Commn., 1973-84, 88-95; mem. Pres. Adv. Com. on Trade Policy and Negotiations, 1987-93; mem. tech. assessment adv. coun. U.S. Congress Office of Tech. Assessment, 1990-95; mem. Consultative Group on Internat. Econs. and Monetary Affairs, 1979—; mem. U.S. Price Commn., 1971-72, Coun. Econ. Advisers, Exec. Office of Pres., 1972-73. Author: Government Risk-Sharing in Foreign Investment, 1965, International and Interregional Payments Adjustment, 1967, Economic Goals and Policy Instruments, 1970, Reflections of Interdependence: Issues for Economic Theory and U.S. Policy, 1979, New World, New Rules: The Changing Role of the American Corporation, 1999, American Capitalism and Global Convergence, 2003; bd. editors: Am. Econ. Rev., 1974-77; mem. editl. bd. Fgn. Policy; contbr. articles to profl. jours. Trustee Nat. Bur. Econ. Rsch., 1993—, Princeton U., 1980-90, Inst. Advanced Study, 1999—; bd. dirs. Peterson Inst. for Internat. Econs., 1986—, Salzburg Seminar, 1994—, Eurasia Found., 1992-95; bd. overseers Harvard U., 1972-78, mem. vis. com. Kennedy Sch., 1992-98. Fellow Earhart Found., 1959-60, AAUW, 1960-61, NSF, 1968-70, Social Security Rsch. Coun.; recipient Columbia medal for excellence, 1973, George Washington award Am. Hungarian Found., 1975. Mem. Am. Econ. Assn. (exec. com. 1977-80), Am. Acad. Arts and Scis., Coun. Fgn. Rels. (dir. 1977-87), Phi Beta Kappa. Office: U Mich Gerald Ford Sch Pub Policy Joan and Sanford Weill Hall Rm 3228 Ann Arbor MI 48109-3091 Office Phone: 734-763-4173. Business E-Mail: marinaw@umich.edu.

WHITMAN, MARLAND HAMILTON, JR., lawyer; b. Balt., Oct. 13, 1947; s. M. Hamilton and Josephine Lee (Chatard) W.; m. Susan Zimmerman, Mar. 21, 1976; children: Elizabeth Miles, Hannah Minor. AB, Princeton U., 1969; JD, U. Va., 1976. Bar: Md. 1976, U.S. Supreme Ct. 1982, U.S. Ct. Appeals (3d cir.) 1986, (4th cir.) 1979, U. S. Ct. Internat. Trade 1985, U.S. Dist. Ct. Md. 1977. From assoc. to ptnr. Ober, Kaler, Grimes & Shriver, Balt., 1976-98, shareholder, 1998—. Contbr. chpt. (book) Construction Litigation: Strategies and Techniques, 1990. Lt. USN, 1969-73. Mem. ABA, Maritime Law Assn. of U.S. (proctor 1977—), Md. State Bar Assn., Bar Assn. of Balt. City, Propeller Club of U.S. Pt. of Balt. Office: Ober Kaler Grimes & Shriver 120 E Baltimore St Baltimore MD 21202-1643 Office Phone: 410-347-7354.

WHITMAN, MARTIN J., portfolio manager; b. NYC, Sept. 30, 1924; s. Irving and Dora (Cukier) W.; m. Lois M. Quick, Mar. 10, 1956; children: James Q., Barbara E., Thomas I. Chartered fin. analyst. Rsch. analyst, buyer Shearson Hammill & Co., NYC, 1950—56; analyst William Rosenwald Co., NYC, 1956—58; head rsch. Ladenburg, Thalmann & Co., NYC, 1958—60; gen. ptnr. Gerstley Sunstein & Co., Phila., 1960—67; v.p., dir. Blair & Co., Inc., NYC, 1967—68; pres., founder M.J. Whitman & Co. (now Inc.), NYC, 1969—84; pres., CEO Equity Strategies Fund, Inc., NYC, 1984—90; founder, chmn. Third Ave. Value Fund, Inc. (now Third Ave. Mgmt. LLC), NYC, 1990—. CEO, Third Ave. Mgmt. LLC, 1990—95; dir. Nabors Industries, Inc.; past chmn. bd. Danielson Holding Corp.; Disting. Mgmt. Fellow in Fin. Yale U., New Haven, 1972—; mem. adv. bd. Yale Sch. Mgmt., New Haven, 1994—95; cons. disclosure study SEC, 1968; cons. Pres.'s Commn. on Accident at Three Mile Island, 1979; adj. prof. Sch. Bus. Columbia U., NYC, 2001—; adj. prof. Whitman Sch., Syracuse U. Author: Value Investing: A Balanced Approach, 1999; coauthor: The Agressive Conservative Investor, 1979. new edit., 2005; contbr. articles to profl. publs. Chmn. 3d Ave. Fund, 1991. Served with USNR, 1942-46. Named in his hon. Martin J. Whitman Sch. of Mgmt., Syracuse Univ. named its bus. sch., 2003. Mem. N.Y. Soc. Security Analysts, Phila. Econ. Soc. Jewish. Home: 285 Central Park W New York NY 10024-3006 Office Phone: 212-888-5222. Business E-Mail: mwhitman@thirdave.com.

WHITMAN, MEG (MARGARET C. WHITMAN), Internet company executive; b. LI, NY, Aug. 4, 1956; m. Griffith R. Harsh IV; children: Griff, Will. BA in Econs., Princeton U., 1977; MBA, Harvard U., 1979. Brand asst. Procter & Gamble, 1979—81; v.p. Bain & Co., 1982—89; sr. v.p. mktg. & consumer products divsn. Walt Disney Co, Burbank, Calif., 1989—92; corp. v.p. strategic planning Stride Rite Corp., 1992—93, exec. v.p. Keds divsn., 1993—94, pres. Stride Rite Divsn., 1994—95; pres., CEO Florists' Transworld Delivery (FTD), 1995—97; gen. mgr. preschool divsn. Hasbro Inc., 1997—98; pres., CEO eBay, Inc., San Jose, Calif., 1998—. Bd. dirs. eBay, Inc., 1998—, Staples Inc., 1999, The Goldman Sachs Group Inc., 2001—02, Procter & Gamble Co., 2003—, The Gap Inc., 2003—06, DreamWorks Animation SKG, Inc. Bd. trustees Princeton U. Named Number One on List of Best CEO's, Worth, 2002; named one of 25 Most Powerful Business Mgrs. (annually since 2000), Business Week, 25 Most Powerful People in Business, Fortune, 2004, Most Powerful Women in American Business, World's 100 Most Influential People, Time Mag., 2004, 2005, 100 Most Powerful Women, Forbes mag., 2005—06, 2006, 50 Women to Watch, Wall St. Jour., 2005, 2006, 50 Most Powerful Women in Bus., Fortune mag., 2006; recipient Webby Lifetime Achievement (eBay), 2007. Avocation: fly fishing. Office: eBay Inc 2145 Hamilton Ave San Jose CA 95125 *

WHITMAN, ROBERT VAN DUYNE, civil engineer, educator; b. Pitts., Feb. 2, 1928; s. Edwin A. and Elsie (Van Duyne) W.; m. Elizabeth Cushman, June 19, 1954; children: Jill Martyne Whitman Marsee, Martha Allerton (dec.), Gweneth Giles Whitman Kaebnick. BS, Swarthmore Coll., 1948, DSc (hon.), 1990; SM, MIT, 1949, ScD, 1951. Faculty MIT, 1953—, prof. civil engring., 1963-93, head structural engring., 1970-74, head soil mechanics divsn., 1970-72; prof. emeritus, 1993—. Vis. scholar U. Cambridge, Eng., 1976-77; cons. to govt. and industry, 1953—; mem. adv. com. for nat. earthquake hazard reduction program Fed. Emergency Mgmt. Agy., 1991-94, mem. commn. engring. and tech. systems NRC, 1992-97. Author: (with T. W. Lambe) Soil Mechanics. Mem. Town Meeting Lexington, Mass., 1962-76, 85—, mem. permanent bldg. com., 1968-75, mem. bd. appeals, 1979-81, 84-2000. Lt. (j.g.) USNR, 1954-56. Recipient U.S. Scientist award Humboldt Found., 1984-90; Norwegian Geotech. Inst. Rsch. fellow, 1984. Mem. NAE, ASCE (Rsch. award 1962, Terzaghi Lecture 1981, Terzaghi award 1987, C. Martin Duke Lifeline Earthquake Engring. award 1992, James Croes medal 1994, H. Bolton Seed medal, 2006), Boston Soc. Civil Engrs. (Structural Sect. prize 1963, Desmond Fitzgerald medal 1973, Ralph W. Horne Fund award 1977), Internat. Soc. Soil Mechanics and Found. Engrs., Mex. Soc. Soil Mechanics (hon., Nabor Carrillo lectr. 2000), Earthquake Engring. Rsch. Inst. (dir. 1978-81, 84-88, v.p. 1979-81, pres. 1985-87, Disting. lectr. 1994, hon. 1997—). Achievements include research in soil mechanics, soil dynamics, earthquake engineering and earthquake loss estimation. Home: 1010 Waltham St 346 Lexington MA 02421 Office: MIT Dept Civil and Environ Engring Cambridge MA 02139

WHITMER, FREDERICK LEE, lawyer; b. Terre Haute, Ind., Nov. 5, 1947; s. Lee Arthur and Ella (Diekhoff) W.; m. Valeri Cade; children: Caitlin Margaret, Meghan Connors, Christian Frederick. BA, Wabash Coll., 1969; JD, Columbia U., 1973. Bar: N.Y. 1975, U.S. Dist. Ct. (so. dist.) N.Y. 1975, N.J. 1976, U.S. Dist. Ct. N.J. 1976, U.S. Ct. Appeals (3d cir.) 1977, U.S. Ct. Appeals (fed. cir.) 1983, U.S. Ct. Appeals (2d cir.) 1987, U.S. Supreme Ct. 1988, U.S. Ct. Appeals (7th cir.) 1994. Assoc. Kaye, Scholer, Fierman, Hays & Handler, NYC, 1973-76, Pitney Hardin and Kipp, Morristown, NJ, 1976—78; ptnr. Pitney Hardin LLP, Morristown, 1979—2004, Brown, Raysman, Millstein, Felder & Steiner, NYC, 2004—06, Thelen Reid Brown Raysman & Steiner, LLP, NYC, 2006—. Mem. ABA, N.J. Bar Assn., Phi Beta Kappa. Republican. Episcopalian. Home: 190 Hurlbutt St Wilton CT 06897-2706 Office: Thelen Reid Brown Raysman & Steiner LLP 875 3d Ave New York NY 10022 Office Phone: 212-603-2074. Business E-Mail: fwhitmer@thelen.com.

WHITMER, RICHARD E., insurance company executive; BS in Political Science, W. Mich. U., 1963; JD, U. Mich. Law School, 1965. Legislative counsel Gov. of Mich.; dir. Mich. Dept. of Commerce; sr. v.p., gen. counsel Blue Cross Blue Shield Mich., Detroit, 1977—87, pres., CEO, 1987—. Bd. mem. Greater Detroit Chamber of Commerce, Detroit Renaissance, United Way of Southeastern Mich., Detroit Economic Growth Corp.; chmn. New Detroit, 1991—93. Office: Blue Cross Blue Shield Mich 600 E Lafayette Blvd Detroit MI 48226-2927 Office Phone: 313-225-9000.

WHITMORE, BRUCE G., lawyer; BA, Tufts U., 1966; JD, Harvard U., 1969. Bar: N.Y. 1970, Calif. 1973, Pa. 1979. Gen. atty. ARCO Transp. Co., 1985-86; assoc. gen. counsel corp. fin. ARCO, 1986-90; v.p., gen. counsel ARCO Chem. Co., 1990-94; sr. v.p., gen. counsel, corp. sec. Atlantic Richfield Co., LA, 1995-2000. Mem. ABA.

WHITMORE, DONALD CLARK, retired engineer; b. Seattle, Sept. 15, 1932; s. Floyd Robinson and Lois Mildred (Clark) W.; m. Alice Elinor Winter, Jan. 8, 1955; children: Catherine Ruth, William Owen, Matthew Clark, Nancy Lynn, Peggy Ann, Stuart John. BS, U. Wash., 1955. Prin. engr. The Boeing Co., Seattle, 1955-87, ret., 1987. Developer, owner mobile home pk., Auburn, Wash., 1979—; vis. scholar Henry M. Jackson Sch. Internat. Studies, U. Wash., 2005—. Author: Towards Security, 1983, Characterization of the Nuclear Proliferation Threat, 1993, Rationale for Nuclear Disarmament, 1995. Activist for arms control, Auburn, Wash., 1962—; chmn. Seattle Coun. Orgns. for Internat. Affairs, 1973, Auburn Citizens for Schs., 1975; v.p. Boeing Employees Good Neighbor Fund, Seattle, 1977, Spl. Svc. award, 1977; pres. Abe Keller Peace Edn. Fund, 1998—, v.p., 2000—; pres., founder Third Millennium Found., 1993—; founder abolishnukes.com. Recipient Human Rights award, Seattle chpt. UN Assn., 2001. Avocations: hiking, travel, collecting. Home and Office: 16202 SE Lake Moneysmith Rd Auburn WA 98092-5274 Personal E-mail: 3rdm@gte.net.

WHITMORE, DOUGLAS MICHAEL, physician; b. Cambridge, Mass., Oct. 30, 1947; s. Donald Herbert and Marcela (Klein) W.; m. Ana Maria Lopez. BS, MS in Physics, U. Ill., Champaign-Urbana, 1969; MS in Physics, Stanford U., 1970, PhD in Physics, 1975; MD, U. Miami, 1978. Diplomate Am. Bd. Internal Medicine, Am. Bd. Pulmonary Disease, Am. Bd. Critical Care Medicine, Am. Bd. Geriatric Medicine. Physician Holy Cross Hosp., Ft. Lauderdale, Fla., 1983—. Pres. med. staff Holy Cross Hosp., 1996-97, chief of medicine, 1995-98. Trustee Holy Cross Hosp., 1995-98. Fellow ACP, Am. Coll. Chest Physicians; mem. Caducean Med. Soc. (pres. 1996-97), Am. Thoracic Soc., Royal Soc. Medicine. Office: Med Complex West 1930 NE 47th St Ste 205 Fort Lauderdale FL 33308-7728

WHITMORE, FRANK CLIFFORD, JR., retired geologist; b. Cambridge, Mass., Nov. 17, 1915; s. Frank Clifford and Marion Gertrude (Mason) W.; m. Martha Burling Kremers, June 24, 1939; children: Geoffrey, John, Katherine, Susan. BA, Amherst Coll., 1938; MS, Pa. State U., 1939; MA, Harvard U., 1941, PhD, 1942. Instr. geology R.I. State Coll., Kingston, 1942-44; geologist U.S. Geol. Survey, Washington, 1944-84, chief mil. geology br., 1946—59, rsch. paleontologist, 1959—84, scientist emeritus, 1984—; mem. com. rsch. and exploration Nat. Geog. Soc., 1970-96, vice chmn., 1990-96, emeritus, 1997—; rsch. assoc. dept. palebiology Smithsonian Instn., Washington, 1967—97; ret., 1997. Sci. cons. U.S. Army, Philippines, Japan, Korea, 1945-46; mem. adv. bd. Ctr. for Study of Early Man, U. Maine, Orono, 1985-90. Editor: Resources for 21st Century, 1982; contbr. articles to profl. jours. Bd. dirs. Prince Georges County Boys Clubs, Md., 1954-56; mem. program com. Nat. Capital coun. Girl Scouts U.S.A., Washington, 1967-69; pres. Thornton Soc., Washington, 1977-84. Recipient medal of Freedom U.S. Army, 1946, spl. achievement award U.S. Geol. Survey, 1980, Meritorious Svc. award U.S. Dept. Interior, 1981, Arnold Guyot Meml. award Nat. Geog. Soc., 1993, Thomas Jefferson medal Va. Mus. Natural History, 2002; Tchg. fellow Harvard U., Cambridge, 1940-42. Fellow AAAS, Geol. Soc. Am.; mem. Soc. Vertebrate Paleontology (hon. life, exec. com. 1960-62), Midriver Club, Harvard Club. Democrat. Avocation: architectural history. Home: 20 Woodmoor Dr Silver Spring MD 20901-2447

WHITMORE, JON SCOTT, academic administrator, play director; b. Seattle, Mar. 22, 1945; s. Walter James and Eurma (Thody) W.; m. Jennifer Gean Gross, Aug. 17, 1985; children: Ian Scott, Amy Lee. BA in Speech and Theatre, Wash. State U., 1967, MA in Speech and Theatre, 1968; PhD in Dramatic Arts, U. Calif., Santa Barbara, 1974. Instr. theatre Highline Coll., Seattle, 1968-71; grad. asst. U. Calif., Santa Barbara, 1971-74; asst. prof. theatre W.Va. U., Morgantown, 1974-78, assoc. prof., 1978-82, prof., 1979-85, chmn. dept., 1979-84, interim dean, 1984-85; prof., dean faculty arts and letters SUNY, Buffalo, 1985-90; dean Coll. Fine Arts, U. Tex., Austin, 1990-96; provost, prof. theater arts U. Iowa, Iowa City, 1996—2003; pres. Tex. Tech U., Lubbock, 2003—. Mem. exec. com. Big XII Athletic Conf., 2006—07. Dir. plays including Suddenly Last Summer, The Miracle Worker, Equus, Romeo and Juliet, Long Days Journey Into Night, The Sea Gull, The Comedy of Errors, The Glass Menagerie, Blithe Spirit, The Tavern, Black Comedy, You're a Good Man Charlie Brown, Vanities, The Effect of Gamma Rays on Man-In-The-Moon Marigolds, Epiphany, Endgame, The Miser, J.B., The Mousetrap, Knapp's Last Tape, Miss Julie, Servant of Two Masters, Before We Were; actor various classical, modern and contemporary plays, and performance pieces; author: Directing Postmodern Theater, 1994, William Saroyan, 1994. Mem. Erie County (N.Y.) Cultural Resources Adv. Bd., 1986-89, long range planning com. Studio Arena Theatre, Buffalo, 1986-90, trustee, 1987-90; mem. coun. fellows Am. Coun. Edn., 1984—; pres. W.Va. Theater Conf., 1978-80, pres.-elect, 1977-78, founding mem., bd. dirs., 1975-81. Recipient ACE Fellow award Am. Council Edn., 1983-84; fellow U. Calif., Santa Barbara, 1973-74, Lilly Found., 1976-77; Maynard Lee Daggy scholar Wash. State U., 1967. Mem. Internat. Coun. Fine Arts Deans, Am. Coun. Arts, Assn. Theatre in Higher Edn. (v.p. adminstrn. 1991—, chmn. nat. conf. planning com. chief adminstrs. program, 1987), Assn. Comm. Adminstrn. (elected to exec. com. 1982-85, chmn. task force theatre adminstrn., 1982-84), Speech Comm. Assn., Coun. Colls. Arts and Scis., Assn. Coll., Univ. and Cmty. Arts Adminstrs., Nat. Assn. State Univs. and Land-Grant Colls. (chair elect commn. arts, 1990-92, chair 1992-93, chair coun. on acad. affairs 2001—). Home: 4606 7th St Lubbock TX 79416-4715 Office: Tex Tech U Office of Pres 2500 Broadway Lubbock TX 79409 Office Phone: 806-742-2011. E-mail: tech.president@ttu.edu. *

WHITNEY, BENSON K., ambassador; m. Mary Whitney; 4 children. BA magna cum laude, Vassar Coll.; JD, U. Minn. Atty. Popham, Halk, Schnobrich, Kaufman and Doty. Ltd.; mng. gen. ptnr. Gideon Hixon Fund; pres. Minn. Venture Capital Assn.; CEO Whitney Mgmt. Co.; U.S. amb. to Norway US Dept. State, Oslo, 2005—. Exec. dir., fin. chair Bush-Cheney '04 Rep. Nat. Com., Minn. Former trustee, dir., chmn., advisor numerous nonprofit orgns. including Guthrie Theater, Wilderness Inquiry, Minnesotans for Term Limits, Mpls. Acad., Persephone Fund, Headwaters Fund. Office: Am Embassy 5460 Oslo Pl Washington DC 20521

WHITNEY, CRAIG RICHARD, journalist; b. Milford, Mass., Oct. 12, 1943; s. A. Gordon and Carol Alma (Kennison) W.; m. Heidi Witt, May 11, 1974; children: Alexandra Kennison, Stefan Robert. AB, Harvard, 1965. Reporter New York Times, Washington, 1965-66, NYC, 1969-70, Saigon, Vietnam, 1971-72, Bonn, West Germany, 1973-77, Moscow, USSR, 1977-80, dep. fgn. editor, 1980-82, fgn. editor, 1982-83, asst. mng. editor, 1983-86, Washington Bur. chief, 1986-88, London bur. chief, 1988-92, European diplomatic corr., 1992-2000, asst. mng. editor, 2000—. Author: Spy Trader, 1993, All the Stops, 2003, The WMD Mirage, 2005. Served with USNR, 1966-69. Mem. Coun. Fgn. Rels., Harvard Club (N.Y.C.). Home: 1 Pierrepont St Brooklyn NY 11201-3302 Office: NY Times 620 Eigth Ave New York NY 10018 Office Phone: 212-556-3909. E-mail: whitney@nytimes.com.

WHITNEY, DANIEL LAWRENCE See LARRY THE CABLE GUY

WHITNEY, DAVID See MALICK, TERRENCE

WHITNEY, EDWARD BONNER, retired investment banker; b. Glen Cove, NY, June 6, 1945; s. Edward Farley and Millicent Bonner (Bowring) W.; m. Martha Congleton Howell, Aug. 17, 1974; children: William Howell, John Howell. BA, Harvard U., 1966, MBA, 1969. Systems engr. IBM, Cambridge, Mass., 1966-67; assoc. Dillon, Read & Co. Inc., NYC, 1969-74, v.p., 1975-79, sr. v.p., 1980-83, mng. dir., 1984-97, also bd. dirs.; mng. dir. UBS Warburg, London, 1997—2002. Bd. dirs., IRRC Inst.; bd. dirs., chmn. Am. Rivers. Trustee Butler Fund for the Environment; pres. coun. Wilderness Soc. Mem. Harvard Club NYC E-mail: Nedwhitney@aol.com.

WHITNEY, FRANK DEARMON, federal judge, former prosecutor; b. Charlotte, NC, Nov. 22, 1959; s. A. Grant and Lillian (DeArmon) Whitney; m. Catherine Whitney; children: Anne Stone, Frances Hunter. BA, Wake Forest U., 1982; MBA, JD, U. NC, 1987. Bar: NC 1987, DC 1988. Assoc. McKenna Conner Cuneo, Washington, 1987—90; law clk. to Hon. David B. Sentelle US Ct. Appeals (DC Cir.), 1988—89; asst. US atty. (we. dist.) NC US Dept. Justice, Charlotte, 1990—2001, US atty. (ea. dist.) NC Raleigh, 2002—06; counsel Kilpatrick Stockton LLP, Charlotte, 2001—02; judge US Dist. Ct. (we. dist.) NC, 2006—. Serves in USAR, 1982—. Presbyterian. Office: US Dist Ct Charles R Jonas Bldg 401 W Trade St Charlotte NC 28202 Office Phone: 704-350-7480.

WHITNEY, JONATHAN B., lawyer; b. July 12, 1954; BA, Skidmore Coll., 1977; JD, Fordham Univ., 1981. Bar: NY 1982. Ptnr., leader NY Fin. dept. Pillsbury Winthrop Shaw Pittman, NYC. Mem.: ABA, Assn. Bar City of NY, Phi Beta Kappa. Office: Pillsbury Winthrop Shaw Pittman 1540 Broadway New York NY 10036 Office Phone: 212-858-1405. Office Fax: 212-858-1500. Business E-Mail: jonathan.whitney@pillsburylaw.com.

WHITNEY, KENT R.E., securities trader; b. Chgo., Feb. 7, 1979; s. Kent R.N. and Arlene M. Whitney; m. Kiva R. Cosson, Mar. 21, 2004 (div. Apr. 18, 2006); 1 child, Kent E.E. Options market maker Chgo. Bd. Options Exchage, 1997—2000, COMEX, NYC, 1999—2000; mem. Chgo. Bd. Trade, 2000—. Named Entrepreneur of Yr., Ernst & Young, 1997. Mem.: Plz. Club (life). Home: 233 East Wacker Dr Chicago IL 60601 Office: 141W Jackson Blvd Chicago IL Home Phone: 312-203-2361; Office Phone: 312-789-8172. Personal E-mail: krwoptions@yahoo.com.

WHITNEY, PATRICK FOSTER, design educator; b. Edmonton, Alta., Can., Sept. 5, 1951; came to US, 1974; s. Gordon and Geraldine (Walker) W.; m. Cheryl Kent. BFA in Design with distinction, U. Alta., 1974; MFA in Design, Cranbrook Acad. Art, Bloomfield Hills, Mich., 1976. Designer RVI Corp., Chgo., 1976-79; chmn. Div. of Design Mpls. Coll. Art and Design, 1979-83; chmn. Inst. of Design, Ill. Inst. Tech., Chgo., 1983-87, dir., 1987—, Steelcase/Robert C. Pew Prof. Design. Lectr. in the field; mem., disting. advisor bd. Assn. Computing Machinery's Special Interest Group in Computer Human Interaction; chmn. US Conf. of Internat. Coun. on Graphic Design Assns., 1978; juror Presdl. Design Awards, 1995; mem. White House Council on Design; pres. Am. Ctr. for Design (ACD); principal investigator for a rsch. project called Global Companies in Local Markets. Editor Design in the Information Environment, 1984, Design Journal; author numerous published articles on design and communications. Mem. Am. Ctr. for Design (bd. dirs. 1984-86, v.p. 1986-90, pres. 1992-94), Arts Club. Office: Ill Inst Tech Inst Design 350 N LaSalle St Chicago IL 60610 Office Phone: 312-595-4900. Business E-Mail: whitney@id.iit.edu.

WHITNEY, RALPH ROYAL, JR., financial executive; b. Phila., Dec. 10, 1934; s. Ralph Royal and Florence Elizabeth (Whitney) W.; m. Fay Wadsworth, Apr. 4, 1959; children: Lynn Marie, Paula Sue, Brian Ralph. BA, U. Rochester, 1957, MBA, 1972. Spl. agt. Prudential Ins. Co., Rochester, NY, 1958-59, divsn. mgr., 1959-63; gen. agt. Nat. Life Vt., Syracuse, 1963-64; contr. Wadsworth Mfg. Assocs. Inc., Syracuse, 1964-65, v.p., 1965-68, pres., 1968-71, Warren Components Corp., Pa., 1968—72; chmn. Hammond Kennedy Whitney & Co., NYC, 1972—. Chmn., CEO Grobet File Co.; bd. dirs. Baldwin Tech. Corp.., MedTek Inc., 1st Internet Bank, Seneca Printing, Inc., Dura Automobile Sys. Inc.,Cheyenne Capital Trustee U. Rochester; past chmn., dir. U. Wyo Found. Mem. NY Yacht Club, Lotus Club (NYC), Century Club (Syracuse), Naple Yacht & Sailing Club, Princeton Club. Episcopalian. Office Phone: 212-867-1010. Business E-Mail: rrw@hkwinc.com.

WHITNEY, RAY, professional hockey player; b. Saskatchewan, Alta., Can., May 8, 1972; s. Floyd and Wendy Whitney Stick boy Edmonton Oilers, 1986-87, 87-88, player, 1997, Spokane Chiefs, 1988-91, 90-91, San Jose Sharks, 1991—97, Edmonton Oilers, 1997—98, Fla. Panthers, 1998—2001, Columbus Blue Jackets, 2001—03, Detroit Red Wings, 2003—04, Carolina Hurricanes, 2005—. Named most valuable player WHL, 1988-91, 90-91, Most Valuable Player All-Star Game IHL, 1992. Achievements include being a member of Stanley Cup Champion Carolina Hurricanes, 2006. Avocation: golf. Office: Carolina Hurricanes RBC Ctr 1400 Edwards Mill Rd Raleigh NC 27607-3624

WHITNEY, RICHARD BUCKNER, lawyer; b. Corpus Christi, Tex., Mar. 1, 1948; s. Franklyn Loren and Betty Wolcott (Fish) Whitney; m. Chantal Marie Gindt, Aug. 18, 1972; children: Jennifer L, James R, Katherine E. BA in Polit. Sci., Union Coll., 1970; JD, Case Western Res. U., 1973. Bar: Ohio 1973, N.Y. 1998, US Ct Appeals (6th cir) 1974, US Ct Appeals (3d cir) 1987, US Dist Ct (so dist) NY 2000, U.S. Dist. Ct. (no. dist.) Ohio 1974. From assoc. to ptnr. Jones Day, Cleve., 1973—. Trustee Hospice of the We. Res. Mem.: Am Inns of Ct., Cleve. Bar Assn., Order of Coif. Home: 2750 Southington Rd Shaker Heights OH 44120-1603 Office: Jones Day 901 Lakeside Ave Cleveland OH 44114-1190 Business E-Mail: rbwhitney@jonesday.com.

WHITNEY, RODGER FRANKLIN, academic administrator; b. Dallas, Feb. 2, 1948; s. Roger Albert and Genevieve Mae (Mohr) W. Cert. higher studies, U. Lausanne, Switzerland, 1970; BA, So. Meth. U., 1971, M Liberal Arts, 1973; EdD, Harvard U., 1978. Dir. upperclass residences So. Meth. U., Dallas, 1971-73, mem. faculty, 1973-75; dir. Mohr Edn. Found., Dallas, 1975-77; dir. North Park East, Raymond D. Nasher Co., Dallas, 1977-79; dir. Stanford Housing Ctr., asst. dean student affairs Stanford (Calif.) U., 1979-91, exec. dir. housing, 1991—. Dir. Camp Grady Spruce, YMCA, Dallas, 1971-76, bd. dirs., 1976-80. Bd. dirs. Kentfield Commons, Redwood City, Calif., 1989-91. Mem. Assn. Coll. and Univ. Housing Officers, Harvard Club San Francisco, Phi Beta Kappa. Avocations: swimming, travel, history, reading, music. Home: 861 Whitehall Ln Redwood City CA 94061-3685 Office: Stanford U Housing 565 Cowell Ln Stanford CA 94305-8512

WHITNEY, SHARRY JAN, science educator; b. Houston, Tex., Aug. 6, 1960; d. Lonie Gene and Elizabeth Janet Cook; m. Michael William Whitney, Nov. 15, 1997; children: Jennifer, Stephanie, Richard; children: David, Allie, Carson. BS, Baylor U., Waco, Tex., 1982. Cert. Tchr. grades 1-8 (sci. emphasis) Tex. Dept. Edn. 2d grade tchr. Hurst-Euless-Bedford Ind. Sch. Dist., Hurst, Tex., 1982—83, Gravette Pub. Schs., Ark., 1984—86; 5th grade tchr. Nashville Pub. Schs., Tenn., 1990—99; 7th grade sci. tchr. Lewisville Ind. Sch. Dist., Tex., 1999—2006, AIS instrnl. specialist, 2006—. Recipient Tchr. of Yr., Rosepark Mid. Sch., Nashville, 1998, Tchr. Who Makes a Difference award, Griffin Mid. Sch., The Colony, Tex., 2004, 2005. Mem.: ASCD. Avocations: mountain biking, reading, skiing, hiking. Office: Delay Middle Sch Lewisville TX 75057

WHITNEY, WILLIAM ELLIOT, JR., advertising agency executive; b. Albany, NY, Feb. 22, 1933; s. William Elliot and Louise E. (Goldsmith) W.; m. Nancy B. Bivings, Mar. 1, 1958; children— Susan, James, Douglas. BA cum laude, Amherst Coll., 1954; MBA, Harvard U., 1956. Account exec. McCann-Erickson, NYC, 1956-58, Marschalk Co., NYC, 1958-60; v.p., then sr. v.p. Ogilvy & Mather, NYC, 1960-80, sr. v.p., mng. dir. Chgo., 1980-85, exec. v.p., 1985-87, pres., 1987-89, chmn., 1990-91; cons. ptnr. Redirections, Inc., 1991-98. Lectr. U. Chgo. Grad. Sch. Bus., 1991-98. Bd. dirs., v.p. Chgo. Coun. Boy Scouts Am., 1978-81, 88—, Off-the-St. Club, Chgo., 1979—, pres., 1988-89; bd. dirs. Hinsdale (Ill.) Cmty. House, 1981, King-Bruwaert House, 1988-2004; v.p. civic adv. bd. Hinsdale Hosp., 1989-93; bd. dirs. Exec. Svc. Corps of Chgo., 1996-2004, life dir., 2005-; trustee Village of Hinsdale, 1993-97, pres., 1997-2001; bd. dirs. Hinsdale Area United Way, 2001-04. Mem. Econs. Club, Hinsdale Golf Club. Home: 736 S Park Ave Hinsdale IL 60521-4646

WHITSEL, RICHARD HARRY, retired biologist, entomologist; b. Denver, Feb. 23, 1931; s. Richard Elstun and Edith Muriel (Harry) W.; m. Laurie Pearson, May 25, 1997; children by previous marriages: Russell David, Robert Alan, Michael Dale, Steven Deane. BA, U. Calif., Berkeley, 1954; MA, San Jose State Coll., 1962. Sr. rsch. biologist San Mateo County Mosquito Abatement Dist., Burlingame, Calif., 1959—72; mgr. environ. program, chief watershed mgmt., chief planning, chief wetlands planning office Calif. Regional Water Quality Control Bd., Oakland, 1972—2000; ret., 2000. Trustee Alameda County Mosquito Abatement Dist., 1999-2001; mem. grad. faculty water resource mgmt. U. San Francisco, 1987-89. Served with Med. Svc. Corps, U.S. Army, 1954-56. Mem. Soc. Wetland Scientists, Entomol. Soc. Am., Calif. Alumni Assn., The Benjamin Ide Wheeler Soc., Nat. Parks and Conservation Assn. (life), Sierra Club. Democrat. Episcopalian. Home: 17901 Minnow Way Penn Valley CA 95946 Personal E-mail: lauriewhitsel@comcast.net.

WHITSELL, JOHN CRAWFORD, II, general surgeon; b. St. Joseph, Mo., Dec. 21, 1929; s. Ora Earl and Lorena (Spratt) W. AB, Grinnell Coll., Iowa, 1950; MD, Washington U., St. Louis, 1954. Diplomate Am. Bd. Surgery, Am. Bd. Thoracic Surgery. From instr. to clin. prof. surgery Cornell U. Med. Ctr., NYC, 1963—70; from asst. attending to attending in surgery NY Hosp., NYC, 1964—70; surg. dir. Rogosin Kidney Ctr. NY Hosp.-Cornell Med. Ctr., NYC, 1973—75; attending in surgery NY Hosp., 1970—98, hon. attending surgeon, 2001—; clin. prof. surgery Cornell Med. Coll., 1970—98, clin. prof. surgery emeritus, 1998—. Surg. cons. Rogosin Kidney Ctr., 1975—, Sharon Hosp., Conn., 1976-2001. Contbr. articles to profl. jours. Capt. USAF, 1961-63. Eng. Fellow ACS; mem. Transplantation Soc., NY Surg. Soc., Am. Soc. Transplant Surgeons, NY Soc. for Thoracic Surgery, Soc. Thoracic Surgeons, NY Acad. Medicine, NY Soc. Cardiovasc. Surgery, Union Club of NY, Phi Beta Kappa. Avocations: golf, fishing, auto racing, antique cars. Personal E-mail: rmwhitsell@aol.com.

WHITSETT, JEFFREY ALLEN, pediatric educator; b. Cleve., May 19, 1947; s. William F. and Kathryn A. (Gilletly) W.; m. Dorinda Dew, May 3, 1975; children: Sarah, Anna, Margaret, David. BA, Colgate U., 1969; MD, Columbia U., 1973. Diplomate Am. Bd. Pediatrics, Am. Bd. Neonatology. Intern and resident Mt. Sinai Hosp., NYC, 1973-76; fellow U. Cin. Children's Hosp., 1976-78, prof. pediatrics, pharmacology, cell biophysics, 1978—, dir. pulmonary biology, 1988—, chief neonatology, perinatal & pulmonary biol. sect. Contbr. articles to sci. publs.; patentee in field. Recipient E. Mead Johnson award Bristol-Meyers Co., 1988, NIH Merit award, William Cooper Procter award, Cin. Children's Hosp., Amerson Lecture award, Am. Thoracic Soc., Daniel Drake medal, U. Cin. Coll. Med.; Human Embryololgy Devel. and Study Sect. grantee NIH, 1987-91. Mem. Soc. for Pediatric Rsch. (coun. 1989-91), Am. Soc. Cell Biology, Am. Soc. Clin. Investigation, Inst. Medicine of NAS. Office: U Cin Childrens Hosp 231 Bethesda Ave Cincinnati OH 45229-2827 Office Phone: 513-636-4830. Office Fax: 513-636-7868. E-mail: jeff.whitsett@cchmc.org.

WHITSITT, BOB (ROBERT JAMES WHITSITT), former professional football team executive; b. Madison, Wis., Jan. 10, 1956; s. Raymond Earl and Dolores June (Smith) W.; m. Jan Leslie Sundberg; children: Lillian Ashley, Sean James. BS, U. Wis., Stevens Point, 1977; MA, Ohio State U., 1978. Intern Ind. Pacers, Inpls., 1978, bus. tickets mgr., 1979, dir. bus. affairs and promotions, 1980, asst. gen. mgr., 1981-82; v.p. mktg. Kansas City Kings, 1982-84, v.p., asst. gen. mgr., 1984-85, Sacramento Kings, 1985-86; pres. Seattle Supersonics, 1986-97, Portland Trail Blazers, 1997—2003; pres. football ops. Seattle Seahawks, 1996—2005. Recipient Exec. of the Year, NBA, 1994. Mem. Nat. Basketball Assn. (alternate gov., mem. competition and rules com.). Lodges: Rotary. Republican. Lutheran. Avocations: skiing, jogging, reading, music.

WHITSON, ELIZABETH TEMPLE, graphics designer; b. Washington, Oct. 1, 1959; d. Norman Burkey Musselman, Elizabeth Temple (Henry) Musselman; m. William Stuart Whitson, Dec. 21, 1985; 1 child, Ian Alexander. BA, Va. Tech. U., 1982. Artist, office asst. Artisan Graphics, Alexandria, Va., 1983—84; graphic artist, office asst. Gestalt Assocs., Alexandria, 1984—86; graphic artist, sales rep., prodn. mgr. Gestalt Prodns., Herndon, Va., 1986—89, ImageMatrix, Inc., Falls Church, Va., 1989—91; graphic designer, publ. dept. head CompuSlides, Vienna, Va., 1991—94, New Media Comms., Vienna, 1994—95; graphic designer, owner Port City Prodns., Inc., Alexandria, 1993—. Newsletter chmn.: Meeting House Coop. Pre-sch., 2000—03; editor (illustrator): Highlights of the Alexandria Com., 1988. Mem. Brookville/Seminary Valley Civic Assn., Alexandria, 1988—2002; vol. Torpedo Factory Art Ctr.; active mem. The Alexandria Libr. Co.; com. vol., tchr., mem. Old Presbyn. Meeting House. Mem.: DAR (corr. sec. 1995—98, chmn. two coms. Mt. Vernon chpt.), The Old Presbyterian Meeting House (worship com. 1995—97, childcare com. 2000—03, childhood edn. com. 2003—04, Godly Play tchr. 2003—), Friends of Gunston Hall, The Alexandria Assembly, Nat. Soc. Colonial Dames of Am. (rec. sec. 1999—2002, directory chmn. 2002—, vice chmn. 2004—, Alexandria com.). Presbyterian. Avocations: remodeling, gardening, painting, illustration, piano. Home and Office: 1701 Sherwood Hall Ln Alexandria VA 22306 Office Phone: 703-718-0105. E-mail: portcity23@verizon.net.

WHITSON, JERRY E., lawyer; b. Alexandria, Va., June 15, 1955; BA in English cum laude, SUNY, Stony Brook, 1977; JD cum laude, Boston Univ., 1980. Bar: Va. 1980, NY 1991. Assoc. Hunton & Williams LLP, NYC, 1980—88, ptnr., global capital mkts, mergers, acquistions, 1988—. Exec. editor Boston Univ. Law Rev., 1980. Mem.: ABA. Office: Hunton & Williams 53rd Fl 200 Park Ave New York NY 10166-0136 Office Phone: 212-309-1060. Office Fax: 212-309-1100. Business E-Mail: jwhitson@hunton.com.

WHITT, GREGORY SIDNEY, evolution educator; b. Detroit, June 13, 1938; s. Sidney Abram and Millicent (Ward) W.; m. Dixie Lee Dailey, Aug. 25, 1963. BS, Colo. State U., 1962, MS, 1965; PhD, Yale U., 1970. Asst. prof. zoology U. Ill., Urbana, 1969-72, asso. prof. genetics and devel., 1972-77, prof., 1977-87, prof. ecology, ethology and evolution, 1987-2000, prof. animal biology, 2000—. Affiliate Ill. Natural History Survey, 1981—; mem. NIH study sect., 1975-76 Co-editor: Isozymes: Current Topics in Biological and Medical Research, 1977-87; editor: Isozyme Bull., 1978-81; mem. editl. bd. Biochem. Genetics, 1975—, Devel. Genetics, 1978-83, Jour. Molecular Evolution, 1979-2000, Molecular Biology and Evolution, 1983-93, Molecular Phylogenetics and Evolution, 1992-2000; contbr. articles to profl. jours. Fellow AAAS; mem. Am. Soc. Microbiology, Soc. Protection Old Fishes, Archaeol. Inst. Am. Office: U Ill Dept Animal Biology 515 Morrill Hall 505 S Goodwin Ave Urbana IL 61801-3707 Home: 3108 Earle Ct Urbana IL 61802-7091

WHITT, RICHARD ERNEST, reporter; b. Greenup County, Ky., Dec. 15, 1944; s. Walter Charles and Irene (Hayes) W.; m. Terri Bellizzi; children: Hayes Chadwick, Emily Catherine, Christen Leigh McCollough. Student, Ashland Community Coll., Ky., 1966-68; BA in Journalism, U. Ky., 1970. Reporter Middlesboro (Ky.) Daily News, 1970-71; asst. state editor Waterloo (Iowa) Courier, 1971-72; city editor Kingsport (Tenn.) Times, 1972-76; No. Ky. bur. chief Courier-Jour., Louisville, 1977, Frankfort bur. chief, 1977-80, spl. projects reporter, 1980-89; investigative reporter Atlanta Jour. & Constn., 1989—. Served with USN, 1962-66. Decorated Air medal; recipient Pulitzer prize for coverage of Beverly Hills Supper Club fire, 1978; named Outstanding Ky. Journalist, 1978; recipient John Hancock award for excellence, 1983; named to U. Ky. Journalism Hall of Fame, 1995. Democrat. Office: Atlanta Jour & Constn 72 Marietta St NW Atlanta GA 30303-2804 Office Phone: 770-509-4079. E-mail: rwhitt@ajc.com, rewhitt@yahoo.com.

WHITTAKER, BILL DOUGLAS, minister; b. Bowling Green, Ky., June 14, 1943; s. Ewing A. and Lois (Jenkins) W.; m. Rebecca Kaye Howard, June 18, 1966; children: John, Karen, Mary. BA, Western Ky. U., 1965; MDiv, So. Bapt. Theol. Sem., Louisville, 1969, D of Ministry, 1974; MA, Union Coll., 2004. Ordained to ministry So. Bapt. Conv., 1964. Pastor 1st Bapt. Ch., Sturgis, Ky., 1969-76, Murray, Ky., 1976-82; missionary Internat. Mission Bd., So. Bapt. Conv., The Philippines, 1983-86; pastor Downtown Bapt. Ch., Orlando, Fla., 1986-88; pres. Clear Creek Bapt. Bible Coll., Pineville, Ky., 1988—2007; pastor Glasgow Bapt. Ch., Ky., 2007—. Author: Preparing to Preach, 1999, Korean edit. 2002; columnist Western Recorder newspaper, 1988—07; editor: Ky. Bapt. Heritage, 2001—. Bd. dirs. Coalition for the Homeless, Cen. Fla. YMCA, Orlando, 1986-88; mem. Ky. Bapt. Archives Adv. Bd. Mem. Assn. Bible Colls. (accredited, del. 1988—07), Assn. So. Bapt. Colls. and Schs. (del. 1988—07), So. Assn. Coll. and Schs. (del. 1999—), Kiwanis (pres. Pineville chpt. 1994-95, dist. 6 lt. gov. 1997-98), Ky. Bapt. Conv. (pres. 1980). Baptist. Home: 105 Terrace Manor Glasgow KY 42141 Office Phone: 270-651-2186. Business E-Mail: bill@glasgowbaptist.org.

WHITTAKER, JAMES KEVIN, retired social sciences educator; b. Newton, Mass., Mar. 30, 1942; s. Brendan Joseph and Julia Okren Whittaker; m. Kathleen Mary Fontaine, Dec. 2, 1967; children: Matthew, Patrick, Abby. AB, Boston Coll., 1964; MA, U. Mich., Ann Arbor, 1964; PhD, U. Minn., Mpls., 1970. LICSW Wash., 2001, ACSW Nat. Assn. Social Work, 1968. Asst. dir. Walker Home Children, Needham, Mass., 1966—68; assoc. prof. social work U. Wash., Seattle, 1970—76, prof. social work, 1976—2004; Charles O. Cressey endowed prof. U. Wash., Sch. Social Work, Seattle, 2004—07, Charles O. Cressey endowed prof. emeritus, 2007—. Vis. scholar Nat. Inst. Social Work, London, 1978—79; fellow U. NC Bush Inst. Child & Family Policy, Chapel Hill, 1983—84; nat. rsch. advisor Holy Cross Svcs., Clinton, Mich., 1985—2001. Contbr. articles to profl. jours. Mem. ARC Trust Wash., Seattle, 1994. Fellow: Am. Orthopsychiat. Assn. (life). Avocations: camping, fishing. Office: Univ Wash Sch Social Work 4101 15th Ave NE Seattle WA 98105-6299 Office Phone: 206-543-5731. Business E-Mail: jimw@u.washington.edu.

WHITTAKER, JEANNE EVANS, retired journalist; b. Detroit, Jan. 1, 1934; d. Alfred Heacock and Margaret (Evans) W.; m. Charles Martin Hines Jr., Sept. 29, 1962 (div. Feb. 1970); children: Charles M. Hines III, Margaret Helen Whittaker Zimmerman. Student, Northwestern U., Evanston, Ill., 1952-53; BS in History, U. Mich., 1956. Clubmobile worker UN forces ARC, Republic of Korea, 1956—58; staff programmer ARC France, Chaumont, Evreux, 1958—61; dir. Bexar County chpt. youth ARC, San Antonio, 1961—62; staff writer/columnist Detroit Free Press, 1970—75; editor Mich. Social Register, 1975—77; Lifestyle editor Observer and Eccentric newspapers, Birmingham, Mich., 1977—87; staff writer, columnist Detroit News, 1987—91; cons. in field, 1992—. Mem. adv. com. Wayne State U. Press, 2000—. Contbr. articles to mags. Bd. dirs. Detroit chpt. ARC, 1989-92; Mem. Univ.-Liggett Sch. Aumni Bd., 2003—; mem. adv. bd. Greenfield Village Antiques Show, 2000-05. Recipient Penney-Mo. award U. Mo., 1984; 1st place lifestyles/Family award Mich. Press Assn., 1982, 84, Gen. Excellence award 1982, 86; Gen. Excellence award Suburban Newspaper Assn., 1979. Mem. Detroit Hist. Soc. (bd. dirs. 1986-91), Detroit Inst. Arts Women's Assn. Episcopalian. Avocations: writing, reading, travel. Home: 552 Cadieux Rd Grosse Pointe MI 48230-1508 Personal E-mail: jeannewhittaker@aol.com.

WHITTAKER, JUDITH ANN CAMERON, lawyer; b. NYC, June 12, 1938; d. Thomas Macdonald and Mindel Cameron; m. Kent E. Whittaker, Jan. 30, 1960; children: Charles Evans II, Catherine Cameron. BA, Brown U., 1959; JD, U. Mo., 1963. Bar: Mo. 1963, U.S. Dist. Ct. (we. dist.) Mo. 1963, U.S. Ct. Appeals (8th cir.) 1965, U.S. Supreme Ct. 1980, D.C. 1987. Assoc. and ptnr. Sheffrey, Ryder & Skeer, Kansas City, Mo., 1963-72; asst. and assoc. gen. coun., exec. v.p. gen. coun. Hallmark Cards, Inc., Kansas City, 1972—2004; dir., v.p., gen. coun. Univision Holdings, Inc., Kansas City, 1988-92; sec., bd. dirs. Crown Media Holdings, Inc., 2000—04; of counsel Shook, Hardy & Bacon, Kansas City, Mo., 2004—. Bd. dirs. Am. Arbitration Assn., 1997-2003. Trustee Brown U. Providence, 1977-83, U. Mo. Law Found., Kansas City, 1977-90; dir. Kansas City (Mo.) Indsl. Devel. Authority, 1981-84, Legal Aid Kansas City, 1971-77, De La Salle Sch. Episcopalian. Avocations: reading, skiing, hiking, piano, golf. Office: Shook Hardy & Bacon 2555 Grand Blvd Kansas City MO 64198-2613

WHITTAKER, WILLIAM L. (RED WHITTAKER), engineering educator, research scientist; b. Holidaysburg, Pa., 1958; m. Kathleen M. Whittaker. BS, Princeton U., 1973; MS, Carnegie Mellon U., 1975, PhD, 1979. Chief sci. RedZone Robotics, Homestead, Pa.; chief sci., founder Robotics Engrng. Consortium Carnegie Mellon U.; prin. rsch. sci. Robotics Inst. Carnegie Mellon U., 1986—96, founder, dir. field robotics ctr., 1986—, Fredkin Prof. Robotics. Mem. com. to provide interim oversight of U.S. Dept. Energy nuc. weapons complex NAS, 1988—89, mem. peer rev. com. on U.S. Dept. Energy environ. mgmt. technologies, 1994—95; mem. commn. on engrng. and tech. systems, com. on advanced space techonologies Nat. Rsch. Coun. Contbr. articles to profl. jours. Named Man of Yr. in Tech., Pitts., 1994; named one of Top 100 U.S. Innovators, Sci. Digest mag., 1987; recipient Smithsonian award, Computerworld, 1992, Teare award for Tchg. Excellence, Carnegie Mellon U. Fellow: Am. Assoc. Artificial Intelligence; mem.: Am. Nuc. Soc. Robotics and Remote Systems Divisn., Ctr. Comml. Devel. of Space Studies Inst. Office: Carnegie Mellon U Robotics Inst 5000 Forbes Ave Pittsburgh PA 15213 E-mail: red@ri.cmu.edu.

WHITTELL, POLLY (MARY KAYE WHITTELL), editor, journalist; b. Washington, Oct. 20; d. Alfred Whittell Jr. and Mary Halsey (Patchin) Hopper. BA in English, U. Calif., Berkeley; postgrad., Radcliffe Coll.; postgrad. in journalism, Columbia U. Rschr. Nat. Rev. Mag., NYC, 1970-71; asst. to presdl. speech writer The White House, Washington, 1971-72; asst. editor TravelAge East Mag., Dun & Bradstreet Publs., NYC, 1973-75; copy editor Ski Mag. Skier's Guides, Times Mirror Mags. and Am. Express, NYC, 1975-76; asst. editor to sr. editor Hearst Mags., Motor Boating & Sailing Mag., NYC, 1977-2000; contbg. editor Powerboat Mag., 2000—01, Hearst Mags., 2002—. Contbg. author: (anthology) Against the Sea, 1998; contbr. articles to other nat. and internat. consumer mags. Mem. charity benefit com. Youth Counseling League, N.Y.C., 1975-85, Am. Cancer Soc., 1998-99, and others; v.p. Knickerbocker Rep. Club, N.Y.C., 1979-80; elected mem. N.Y. Rep. County Com., N.Y.C., 1980-84. Mem. Boating Writers Internat. (award for environ. article 1995), Soc. Profl. Journalists, Princeton Club (N.Y.), SandBar Beach Club (v.p. membership 1980-82). Episcopalian. Avocations: photography, travel, boating, skiing. Personal E-mail: pollywhitt@aol.com.

WHITTEMORE, ALICE, biostatistician; b. NYC, July 5, 1936; BS, Marymount Manhattan Coll., 1958; MA, Hunter Coll., 1964; PhD in Mathematics, CUNY, 1967. From asst. prof. to assoc. prof. math. Hunter Coll., NYC, 1967-74; adj. assoc. prof. environ. med. N.Y.U., 1974-76, mem. faculty dept. statistics, 1976-87; prof. epidemiology dept. health rsch. and policy Stanford U., Palo Alto, Calif., 1987—. Recipient Sloan Found. rsch. grant, Soc. Ind. and Applied Math. Inst. Math and Soc., 1974-76, Rockefeller Found rsch. grant 1976-77. Mem. NAS Inst. Medicine, AAAS, Soc. Indsl. and Applied Math, Am. Math Soc., Math Assn. Am., Sigma Xi Office: Stanford U Sch Medicine Dept Health Rsch and Policy HBP Redwood Bldg Stanford CA 94305-5092

WHITTEMORE, ANNE MARIE, lawyer; b. Southampton, Eng., Mar. 19, 1946; (parents Am. citizens); d. Rober R. and Vera (McMullen) Grimes; m. F. Case Whittemore, June 22, 1968; 1 child, Robert Pendleton. AB, Vassar Coll., 1967; LLB, Yale U., 1970. Bar: Va. 1970. Law clk. to presiding judge U.S. Ct. Appeals (4th cir.), Alexandria, Va., 1970-71; assoc. McGuire, Woods, Battle & Boothe, Richmond, Va., 1971-77; ptnr. McGuire, Woods, Battle & Boothe (now McGuireWoods LLP), Richmond, Va., 1977—. Bd. dirs. Fed. Res. Bank of Richmond. Bd. of govs. Greater Richmond Community Found., 1978—; bd. advisors Va. Commonwealth U., Richmond, 1981—; trustee Confederate Meml. Library Soc., Richmond, 1988—. Named one of Best Lawyers in Am., Woodward/White, Inc., The 50 Most Influential Women Lawyers in Am., Nat. Law Jour., 2007; named to Leading Lawyers in Am. list, Lawdragon 3000, 2006. Mem. Richmond Bar Assn. (exec. com. 1986—), Va. Law Found. (bd. of govs. 1986—), Downtown Club (bd. dirs.). Republican. Roman Catholic. Home: 1 Huntley Rd Richmond VA 23226-3305 Office: McGuireWoods LLP 1 James Ctr 6th Fl 901 E Cary St Richmond VA 23219 Office Fax: 804-698-2206. Business E-Mail: awhittemore@mcguirewoods.com. *

WHITTEMORE, ANTHONY DUNSTER, vascular surgeon; b. Boston, Nov. 5, 1944; s. Anthony Rogers Whittemore and Kathrine Gansevoort Binnian Howe; m. Rhoda Belknap Stetson, June 18, 1966; children: Anthony Rogers, Joshua Stetson, Sarah Belknap. BS, Trinity Coll., 1966; MD, Columbia U., 1970. Resident in surgery Columbia Presbyn. Med. Ctr., 1970-76; research assoc. Columbia U., N.Y.C., 1972-73, NIH trainee, 1975-76; vascular fellow Peter Bent Brigham Hosp., Boston, 1976-77; chief vascular surgery Naval Regional Med. Ctr., Portsmouth, Va., 1977-79; instr. surgery Harvard Med. Sch/Peter Bent Brigham Hosp., Boston, 1979-80; asst. prof. surgery Harvard U., Boston, 1981-87, assoc. prof. surgery, 1987-93, prof. surgery Harvard Med. Sch., 1993—; dir. surg. tng. program Harvard Med. Sch./Brigham and Women's Hosp., 1979; mem. med. staff Brigham and Women's Hosp., 1979—, chief divsn. vascular surgery, 1990-1999, apptd. dir. Vascular Ctr., 1991, chief medical officer, 1999—; cons. Bard CardioSurgery, Billerica, Mass., 1982—, Meadox Medicals, Oakland, N.J., 1983—, instrumentation Labs., North Andover, Mass., 1980—; investigator grants NIH, 1979, 83. Contbr. Articles to profl. publs. Served to lt. comdr. USN, 1977-79. Recipient Commendation USN, 1979. Fellow ACS; mem. Assn. Acad. Surgery, Am. Surg. Assn., Am. Soc. for Artificial Internal Organs (program com. 1982—), Am. Surg. Soc., Soc. U. Surgeons, Boston Surg. Soc., Internat. Cardiovascular Soc., Soc. Vascular Surgery, New Eng. Surg. Soc., New Eng. Soc. Vascular Surgery,

Soc. Internat. de Chirurgie, The Country Club; patents in field. Home: 148 Farm Rd Sherborn MA 01770-1622 Office: Brigham & Women's Hosp 75 Francis St Boston MA 02115-6106 Office Phone: 617-732-8515.

WHITTEMORE, BRIAN, media consultant, advertising executive; Anchor morning news, dir. news Sta. WGY-AM, Albany, NY, 1983—86; anchor morning news WHDH Radio, Boston, 1987—90; dir. news and program WBZ Radio, Boston, 1990—95; v.p., gen. mgr. Sta. KDKA-AM, Pitts., 1996—98, Sta. WCCO-AM, Mpls., 1999—2003; pres. Best/Whittemore Prodns., LLC, Prior Lake, Minn., 2003—.

WHITTEMORE, EDWARD REED, II, poet, retired educator; b. New Haven, Sept. 11, 1919; s. Edward Reed and Margaret Eleanor (Carr) W.; m. Helen Lundeen, Oct. 3, 1952; children: Catherine Carr, Edward Reed III, John Lundeen (dec.), Margaret Goodhue. AB, Yale U., New Haven, Conn., 1941; postgrad., Princeton U., NJ, 1945-46; Litt.D., Carleton Coll., Northfield, Minn., 1971. Mem. faculty Carleton Coll., 1947-67, prof. English, 1962-67, chmn. dept., 1962-64; program assoc. Nat. Inst. Pub. Affairs, 1966-68; cons. in poetry Libr. of Congress, 1964-65, 84-85; Bain-Swiggett lectr. Princeton, 1967; prof. U. Md., 1968-84, prof. emeritus, 1984—; poet laureate State of Md., 1985-88. Lit. editor New Republic, 1969-74. Author: Heroes and Heroines, 1947, An American Takes a Walk, 1956, The Self-Made Man, 1959, The Boy From Iowa, 1962, The Fascination of the Abomination, 1963, Poems, New and Selected, 1967, From Zero to the Absolute, 1967, 50 Poems 50, 1970, The Mother's Breast and the Father's House, 1974, William Carlos Williams: Poet from Jersey, 1975, The Poet as Journalist, 1976, The Feel of Rock, 1982, Pure Lives, 1988, Whole Lives, 1989, The Past, the Future, the Present, 1990, Six Literary Lives, 1993, A Literary Life Against the Grain, 2007; editor: Furioso, 1939-53, Browning, 1960, Carleton Miscellany, 1960-64, Delos mag., 1988-91. Capt. USAAF, 1941-45. Decorated Bronze star, 1945. Home: 4526 Albion Rd College Park MD 20740-3610

WHITTEMORE, LAURENCE FREDERICK, bank executive; b. Bangor, Maine, Mar. 7, 1929; s. John Cambridge and Elizabeth Payson (Prentiss) Whittemore; m. Sarah Lee Arnold, Aug. 9, 1958; children: Arianna, Gioia, Lia, Nike. BA, Yale U., 1951; MBA, Harvard U., 1953; student, Balliol Coll., Oxford U., Eng., 1950. Account mgr. Brown Bros. Harriman, NYC, 1956-72, gen. mgr., 1972-74; ptnr. Brown Bros. Harriman & Co., NYC, 1974—2003, ltd. ptnr., 2004—. Dir. Manhattan Life Ins. Co., NYC, Albany Ins. Co., NYC; mem. investment adv. com. Union Investment GmbH, Frankfurt, Germany, 1973—2002; mem. Chgo. Stock Exch., 1975—2003. Trustee Sarah Lawrence Coll., 1988-2000, hon. trustee, 2001—; trustee Am. Inst. Contemporary German Studies, 1994—2002, Asia Soc., 1998-2006, trustee emeritus, 2007—; mem. Nat. Com. on U.S. China Rels., N.Y.C., 1982—, Chgo. Coun. on Fgn. Rels., 1980—; del. Assn. Yale Alumni, New Haven, 1982-86; chmn. Yale 35th Reunion Gift Drive, 1983-86; gov. Opportunity Internat., 1996—; dir. New Eng. Air Mus., 1999—. Fellow Sterling fellow, Yale U., 2001—. Mem.: Chgo. Club, Yale Club, Links Club. Republican. Episcopalian. Office: Brown Bros Harriman & Co 140 Broadway New York NY 10005-1101

WHITTEMORE, PAUL BAXTER, psychologist; s. Harry Ballou and Margaret B. Whittemore; m. Jane Moore, Apr. 22, 1995. BA in Religion, Ea. Nazarene Coll., 1970; MDiv., Nazarene Theol. Sem., 1973; MA in Theology, Vanderbilt U., 1975, PhD in Theology, 1978; PhD in Clin. Psychology, U. Tenn., 1987. Cert. in clin. psychology Am. Bd. Profl. Psychology, lic. psychologist Calif. Asst. prof. philosophy Trevecca Nazarene Coll., Nashville, 1973—76; asst. prof. philosophy and religion Point Loma Coll., San Diego, 1976—80; asst. prof. philosophy Mid. Tenn. State U., Murfreesboro, 1980—83; clin. psychology intern LA County/U. So. Calif. Med. Ctr., LA, 1986—87; coord. behavior health ctr. Calif. Med. Ctr., LA, 1987—88; clin. asst. prof. family medicine U. So. Calif. Sch. Medicine, LA, 1988—; pvt. practice Newport Beach, Calif., 1991—. Mem. behavioral sci. faculty Glendale Adventist Family Practice Residency Program, Glendale, Calif., 1989—90; inpatient group therapist Ingleside Hosp., Rosemead, Calif., 1990—92; founder, pres. Date Coach, 1992—2000. Contbr. articles to profl. jours. Recipient Andrew W. Mellon Postdoctoral Faculty Devel. award, Vanderbilt U., 1981. Mem.: AAUP (chpt. v.p. 1982—83), APA, Orange County Psychol. Assn. (bd. dirs. 1996—2001), Calif. Psychol. Assn. (media divsn. sec.-treas. 1997—98), Am. Philos. Assn., Am. Acad. Religion. Achievements include discovery of link between phenylthiocarbamide tasting and depression. Office: 1001 Dove St Ste 145 Newport Beach CA 92660-2123

WHITTEN, CHARLES ALEXANDER, JR., physics professor; b. Harrisburg, Pa., Jan. 20, 1940; s. Charles Alexander and Helen (Shoop) W.; m. Joan Emann, Nov. 20, 1965; 1 son, Charles Alexander III. BS summa cum laude, Yale U., 1961; PhD in Physics, Princeton U., 1966. Rsch. assoc. A.W. Wright Nuclear Structure Lab., Yale U., 1966-68; asst. prof. physics UCLA, 1968-74, assoc. prof., 1974-80, prof., 1980—, vice chmn. physics dept., 1982-86. Vis. scientist Centre d'Etudes Nucléaires de Saclay-Moyenne Energie, France, 1980—81, 1986—87; Vis. prof. U. Sci. and Tech., Hefei, China, 2007. Contbr. articles to profl. jours. Mem. Am. Phys. Soc., Sigma Pi Sigma, Phi Beta Kappa. Home: 9844 Vicar St Los Angeles CA 90034-2719 Office: U Calif Dept Physics Los Angeles CA 90024 Office Phone: 310-825-1691. Business E-Mail: whitten@physics.ucla.edu.

WHITTEN, JERRY LYNN, chemistry professor; b. Bartow, Fla., Aug. 13, 1937; s. John Graves and Dorothy Iola (Jordan) W.; m. Mary Hill (div. Sept. 1977); 1 child, Jerrard John; m. Adela Chrzeszczyk, June 21, 1980; 1 child, Christina. BS in Chemistry, Ga. Inst. Tech., 1960, PhD, 1964. Cert. chemist. Rsch. assoc. to instr. Princeton (N.J.) U., 1963-65; asst. prof. chemistry Mich. State U., East Lansing, 1965-67, SUNY, Stony Brook, 1967-68, assoc. prof., 1968-73, prof., 1973-89, chmn. chemistry dept., 1985-89; prof. chemistry, dean Coll. Phys. and Math. Scis. N.C. State U., Raleigh, 1989-99. Vis. prof. Centre Europèen de Calcul Atomique et Molèculaire, Orsay, France, 1974-75, Univ. Bonn and Wuppertal, Fed. Republic Germany, 1979-80, Eidgenossische Technische Hochschule, Zurich, Switzerland, 1984, U. Wuppertel, 2005 Contbr. more than 190 articles to profl. jours. Bd. dirs. N.C. Sch. Sci. and Math Found., chair; bd. dirs. Burroughs Wellcome Fund. Recipient Alexander von Humboldt U.S. Sr. Scientist award, 1979; grantee Petroleum Rsch. Fund, 1966-67, 74-76, 77-81, NSF, 1967-72, U.S. Dept. Energy, 1977—; SDIO/ONR grantee, 1991-92; Alfred P. Sloan fellow, 1969-71. Mem. AAAS, Am. Phys. Soc., Am. Chem. Soc., N.Y. Acad. Scis., Sigma Xi (pres. N.C. chpt.), Phi Beta Kappa, Phi Kappa Phi. Democrat. Episcopalian. Avocations: boating, tennis, skiing. Office: NC State U Coll Dept Chemistry PO Box 8204 Raleigh NC 27695-0001 Office Phone: 919-515-7960. E-mail: j_whitten@ncsu.edu.

WHITTEN, LESLIE HUNTER, JR., writer, poet, reporter; b. Jacksonville, Fla., Feb. 21, 1928; s. Leslie Hunter and Linnora (Harvey) W.; m. Phyllis Webber, Nov. 11, 1951; children: Leslie Hunter III, Andrew, Daniel, Deborah Wilson Engle. BA in Journalism/English magna cum laude, Lehigh U., 1950, LHD, 1989. Journalist Radio Free Europe, 1952-57, I.N.S., 1957-58, U.P.I., 1958, Washington Post, 1958-63; with Hearst Newspapers, 1963-66, asst. bur. chief Washington, 1966-69; sr. investigator Jack Anderson's Washington Merry-Go-Round, 1969-92; pres. Athanor Inc., 1977-93. Vis. assoc. prof. Lehigh U., 1967-69; adj. prof. So. Ill. U., 1984. Author: Progeny of the Adder, 1965, Moon of the Wolf, 1967, Pinion the Golden Eagle, 1968, The Abyss, 1970, F. Lee Bailey, 1971, The Alchemist, 1973, Conflict of Interest, 1976, Washington Cycle, 1979, Sometimes a Hero, 1979, A Killing Pace, 1983, A Day Without Sunshine, 1985, The Lost Disciple, 1989, The Fangs of Morning, 1994, Sad Madrigals, 1997, Moses, the Lost Book of the Bible, 1999, The Rebel, 2005; contbr. numerous poems to anthologies and other publs. Vol. Hospice, 1987-2003. Served with AUS, 1946-48. Recipient hon. mention pub. service Washington Newspaper Guild, 1963, Edgerton award ACLU, 1974 Home and Office: 114 Eastmoor Dr Silver Spring MD 20901-1507 Home Phone: 301-593-5943. Personal E-mail: lhwhitjr@aol.com.

WHITTEN, MARY LOU, nursing educator; b. Vandalia, Ill., Apr. 8, 1946; d. Otto M. and Lucille (Mattes) Elam; m. Dennis L. Whitten, Aug. 27, 1966; children: Michael, Christopher, Andrew. BSN, Baylor U., 1968; MS in Nursing, So. Ill. U., 1990. RN, Ill. Instr. health occupations Okaw Vocat. Sch., Vandalia, Ill.; head nurse med.-surg. Fayette County Hosp., Vandalia; DON Kaskaskia Coll., Centralia, Ill. CPR instr. Am. Heart Assn. Vol. ARC. Mem. Am. Assn. of Women in C.C. Ill., Ill. Coun. Dirs. of Nursing, Phi Kappa Phi. Home: RR 3 Box 848 Vandalia IL 62471-9204 Office: Kaskaskia Coll 27210 College Rd Centralia IL 62801-7800 Office Phone: 618-545-3331. Business E-Mail: mwhitten@kaskaskia.edu.

WHITTEN, SHANNON NICOLE, education educator; b. West Palm Beach, Fla., July 20, 1974; d. Michael Edward and Nocha Jean Whitten. PhD, U. Memphis, 2003. Instr. U. Ctrl. Fla., Orlando-Palm Bay, 2003—. Contbr. articles to profl. jours. Mem.: Soc. Text and Discourse. Office: 250 College Pkwy Palm Bay FL 32909 Home Phone: 321-373-4886; Office Phone: 321-433-7981. Office Fax: 321-433-7977. Business E-Mail: swhitten@mail.ucf.edu.

WHITTENBERG, IRA ORVILLE, lawyer; b. Ft. Worth; s. Ira Orville and Thyra Finch Whittenberg; m. Emma Jo Noland, Apr. 14, 1962; children: Ira Grant, Cheryl Lynn, Wendy Ann. BS in Indsl. Enging., So. Meth. U., 1957, LLB, 1961, LLM, 1977. Bar: Tex. 73. Contract mgr., corp. counsel Bell Helicopter Textron, Ft. Worth, 1961—89; dir. contracts, corp. counsel Murdock Engring., Irving, Tex., 1989—91; pvt. practice cons., mediator Colleyville, Tex., 1991—. Capt. USAF, 1955—57. Fellow: Nat. Contract Mgmt. Assn. (pres. 1962—); mem.: State Bar Tex. (award 2002), Toastmasters Internat. (chpt. pres. 1982—). Republican. Presbyterian. Avocations: sailing, bicycling. Home and Office: 3607 Cliffwood Dr Colleyville TX 76034 Office Phone: 817-498-8141. E-mail: docwh@tx.rr.com.

WHITTERS, JAMES PAYTON, III, lawyer, educator; b. Boston, Oct. 23, 1939; s. James P. Jr. and Norene (Jones) W.; m. Elizabeth Robertson, July 19, 1969; children: James P. IV, Catharine A. BA in History, Trinity Coll., Hartford, Conn., 1962; JD, Boston Coll., 1969; MA in Am. studies, U. Mass., Boston, 2002. Bar: Mass. 1969, US Dist. Ct. Mass. 1970, US Ct. Appeals (1st cir.) 1972. Assoc. Ely, Bartlett, Brown & Proctor, Boston, 1969-74, Gaston Snow & Ely Bartlett, Boston, 1974-79, ptnr., 1979-88, Gaston & Snow, Boston, 1988-91; of counsel Peabody & Brown, Boston, 1991-95; dir. Office Career Devel., Suffolk U. Law Sch., Boston, 1995—2004, adj. prof. Am. legal history, 1997—. Bd. dirs., sec. Robertson Factories, Inc., Taunton, Mass., 1979-04; v.p. The Alkalol Co., Boston, 1976-97, sr. v.p., 1997-05, pres., treas., gen. counsel, 2005—; vis. tchr. Groton Sch., Mass., 1993-94; mem. Mass. Conflict Intervention Mediation Team, 1995—. Bd. dirs. New Eng. com. NAACP Legal Def. Fund, 1982-2006, Beacon Hill Nursery Sch., 1976-78, Mass. Appleseed Ctr. Law and Justice, 1997—, The Esplanade Assn., 2005-, New Workplace Inst., 2006-; chmn. Mass. Outdoor Advt. Bd., Boston, 1975-81; vice chmn. Mass. Jud. Nominating Coun., Boston, 1983-87; trustee Trinity Coll., 1984-95; trustee, sec. Hurricane Island Outward Bound Sch., 1977-87; bd. dirs. Mass. affiliate Am. Heart Assn., 1979-98, chmn., 1989-91; bd. dirs. Greater Boston Legal Svcs., 1982-84, 93-99, Mass. Assn. Mediation Programs and Practitioners, 1993-98; founder Beacon Hill Seminars, 2000-2001, bd. dirs., 2001-02; facilitator Boston City Wide Dialogues on Racial and Ethnic Diversity, 2003-. Lt. (j.g.) USN, 1962-65. Recipient Alumni Excellence award Trinity Coll., 1987, Touchdown Club award Trinity Coll., 2006. Mem.: ABA, Boston Bar Assn. (standing com. on work-life balance, children's outreach task force, pub. svc. and criminal justice task force, Pres.'s award 2007), The Country Club (Brookline, Mass.). Democrat. Episcopalian. Avocations: mountain climbing, jogging, yoga, reading. Home: 44 Mount Vernon St Boston MA 02108-1302 Office Phone: 617-248-8822. Personal E-mail: jpwhit3@aol.com.

WHITTIER, BARBARA J (BOBBIE), retired biology educator, retired chemistry educator; b. New Rochelle, NY, July 13, 1943; d. Gordon F. and Elinor E. Whittier. BS, Cornell U., Ithaca, NY, 1965; MAT, Harvard U., Cambridge, Mass., 1966. Postgraduate Professional License Va. State Bd. of Edn., 1968, Collegiate Professional Va. State Bd. of Edn., 1966. Sci. educator Wakefield HS, Arlington, Va., 1966—98, sci. dept. chair, 1990—95; ret., 1998. Cons. Arlington Pub. Schools, 1998—2003; project asst. Biotechnology Inst., Arlington, Va., 2003—; softball coach Wakefield H.S., 1983—90. Mem., elder, clk. of session, meals on wheels Arlington Presbyn. Ch., 1980—2006; pnc liaison and mem., com. on ministry Nat. Capital Presbytery, Washington, 2000—06; com. mem. Va. Jr. Acad. Sci., Richmond, 1982—2006, sponsor, 1982—2006; mem. Wakefield Alumni Assn., Arlington, 2003—06. Named to Wakefield HS Hall of Fame, 2005; recipient Presdl. award for Excellence in Sci. and Math. Tchg. (PAESMT), NSF, 1986, Outstanding Educator award, Joint Bd. on Sci. and Engring. Edn. and the Wash. Acad. of Sci., 1984, Nat. Sci. Week award, NSF, 1958, Disting. Svc. award, Va. Jr. Acad. Sci., 2006. Mem.: Va. Assn. of Sci. Teachers (Va. Jr. Acad. Sci. rep. 2005—06), Nat. Assn. of Biology Teachers (life), Delta Delta Delta. Presbyn. Avocation: sports. Home: 2424B S Walter Reed Dr Arlington VA 22206-4086 Personal E-mail: bwhittier@aol.com.

WHITTINGHAM, CHARLES ARTHUR, library director, publishing executive; b. Chgo., Feb. 11, 1930; s. Charles Arthur and Virginia (Hartke) W.; m. Jean Bragger Whittingham, June 4, 1955; children: Mary Elizabeth, Charles Arthur III, Philip Alexander, Leigh Ann. BS in English Lit. cum laude, Loyola U., Chgo., 1951. With McCall Corp., Chgo., 1956-59, Time, Inc., Chgo., 1959-62; pub.'s rep. Fortune mag., Time, Inc., NYC, 1962-65, mgr. San Francisco, 1965-69; asst. to pub. Fortune, NYC, 1969-70, asst. pub., 1970-78; pub. Life mag., NYC, 1978-88; sr. v.p. N.Y. Pub. Libr., 1989-92; exec. prodr. Kunhardt Prodns., Inc., 1995—. Lt. j.g. USNR, 1951—55. Named to Athletic Hall of Fame Loyola U., Loyola Acad. Mem.: Century Assn., The Pilgrims, Brook Club. Home and Office: 800 Fifth Ave 8C New York NY 10021

WHITTINGHAM, HARRY EDWARD, JR., retired banker; b. Albany, NY, Dec. 25, 1918; s. Harry E. and Mary (Baer) Whittingham; m. Gladys D. Willstaedt, Sept. 2, 1942; children: Jeffrey A., Neal E. Grad., Stonier Grad. Sch. Banking, 1961. With Schenectady Trust Co., 1947-84, pres., chief exec. officer, 1974-82, chmn., chief exec. officer, 1982-84. Author (with Purdy, Schneider, Aldom): Automation in Banking, 1962. Vestryman Episcopal Ch. With AUS, 1941—46. Home: 2025 Cockrell Pt NW Kennesaw GA 30152

WHITTINGHAM, KENNETH, television director; Dir.: (TV series) The Amanda Show, 2000—01, Girlfriends, 2001—03, Mano a Mano, 2005, The Bernie Mac Show, 2002—06, The King of Queens, 2003—06, One on One, 2001—06, Everybody Hates Chris, 2005—07, My Name is Earl, 2006—07, The Office, 2005—07 (NAACP Image award best dir. of comedy series, 2007), Scrubs, 2002—07. *

WHITTINGHAM, M(ICHAEL) STANLEY, chemist; b. Nottingham, Eng., Dec. 22, 1941; came to U.S., 1968, naturalized, 1980; s. William Stanley and Dorothy Mary (Findlay) W.; m. Georgina Judith Andai, Mar. 23, 1969; children: Jenniffer Judith, Michael Stanley. BA in Chemistry, Oxford U., 1964, MA, DPhil, 1968. Rsch. assoc., head solid state electrochemistry group Materials Ctr., Stanford U., 1968-72; mem. staff Exxon Rsch. Co., Linden, N.J., 1972—; group head solid state chem. physics, 1975-78; dir. solid state scis., 1978-80; mgr. chem. engring. tech., 1980-84; dir. phys. scis. Schlumberger Co., Ridgefield, Conn., 1984-88; prof. chemistry and materials sci. and engring., dir. The Inst. for Materials Rsch., SUNY, 1988—; vice provost for rsch. SUNY, 1994-2000; vice-chair bd. dirs. Rsch. Found., 1995-2001. Cons., lectr. in field; JSPS fellow U. Tokyo. Author, editor papers in field; author 5 books. Recipient Gas Coun. scholarship, Oxford U., 1964-67. Mem. Electrochem. Soc. (Young Author award 1971, N.Y. chmn. 1980-81, Battery Rsch. award 2002, fellow 2004), Am. Chem. Soc. (chmn. solid state sect. 1987, chmn. Binghamton sect. 1991), Am. Phys. Soc., Materials Rsch. Soc. Achievements include patents in field; reversible (rechargeable) lithium batteries and methods for making intercalation batteries; method for making TiS_2 mixed material cathodes, high briteness luminescent displays. Home: 396 Meeker Rd Vestal NY 13850-3230 Office: SUNY Dept Chemistry Binghamton NY 13902 Office Phone: 607-777-4623. E-mail: stanwhit@binghamton.edu.

WHITTINGTON, ANNE ELIZABETH, diabetes educator; b. Berea, Ohio, Apr. 4, 1957; d. Richard Murphy and Eleen Elizabeth (Cooney) Whittington. ADN, Sante Fe Coll., 1979; BSN, U. N.C., 1983; MSN, Med. Coll. Ga., 1990; MBA, Brenau U., 1997. Tchr. Nat. Cert. Bd. for Diabetes Educators; cert. water aerobics instr. Staff nurse U. Fla. Teaching Hosp., Gainesville, 1979-80, New Hanover Meml. Hosp., Wilmington, N.C., 1980-81, Cape Fear Meml. Hosp., Wilmington, 1983-84; home health nurse New Hanover Home Health Agy., Wilmington, 1984-85, Comprehensive Home Health Care, Augusta, Ga., 1985; coord. outreach edn. for Ga. Dept. of Human Resources Grant, Augusta, 1990—2000; dir. diabetes programs Naval Med. Ctr., San Diego, 2001—, dir. Paws That Heal program, 2005—. Docent Augusta Richmond County Mus., 1987-91; dir. Our Lady of Peace Choir, North Augusta, 1990—; co-founder Cen. Savannah River Area Arthritis Support Group, Augusta, 1991—; Cath. chaplaincy Augusta Correctional Instn., 1991—. Recipient Woman of Excellence award Cen. Savannah River Area, 1992; named Outstanding Diabetes Educator, GADE, 1992, Outstanding Alumnus, Med. Coll. Ga. Sch. Nursing, 1992, Outstanding Diabetes Educator, Am. Assn. Diabetes Edn., 1993; torchbearer Atlanta Olympics, 1996. Mem.: Arthritis Health Profl. Assn., Ga. Nurses Assn., U. N.C. Sch. Nursing Alumni Assn. (bd. dirs. 1989—93), Am. Diabetes Assn., Am. Assn. Diabetes Educator (sec. visual impaired preson speciality practice group 1994—97, chair visual impaired person speciality group 1997—2000, bd.dirs. 1999—2002, treas. 2002—), Greater Augusta Diabetes Educators (chmn. profl. edn. 1991—2000, pres. 1995—97), ANA, Sigma Theta Tau (Grad. Student of Yr. 1991). Democrat. Roman Catholic. Avocations: music, water aerobics. Mailing: Attn: Health Promotion Dept 34800 Bob Wilson Dr San Diego CA 92134-1301

WHITTINGTON, JOHN P., lawyer; b. Kannapolis, NC, Apr. 17, 1947; BA, Guilford Coll., 1969; JD, Samford U., 1972. Bar: Ala. 1972. Ptnr. Bradley, Arant, Rose & White LLP, Birmingham, chair Restructuring and Reorganization Practice Group, 1990—2005; interim gen. counsel, corp. sec. HealthSouth Corp., Birmingham, 2006, exec. v.p., gen. counsel, corp. sec., 2006—. Adj. prof. Cumberland Sch. Law, Samford U., Birmingham, Ala., 1990—. Mem. ABA (mem. bankruptcy law sect.), Comml. Law League of Am. (mem. bankruptcy and insolvency sect.), Am. Bankruptcy Inst., Am. Coll. of Bankruptcy, Birmingham Bar Assn., Ala. State Bar. Office: HealthSouth Corp One Healthsouth Parkway Birmingham AL 35243 *

WHITTINGTON, RALPH EDWARD, retired curator, librarian; b. Washington, Jan. 13, 1945; s. Ralph John and Mildred May Whittington; m. Jennifer Kay Rutland, June 7, 1969 (div.); 1 child, Amanda Anne. Grad., Surrattsville HS, Clinton, Md., 1963. Deck attendant Libr. of Congress, Washington, 1963—76, searcher libr. materials locator, 1976—85, curator main reading rm., 1985—2000; cons. Mus. Sex, NYC, 2001—; ret. Avocation: vinyl record collector. Home: 9204 Greenfield Ln Clinton MD 20735

WHITTINGTON, REBECCA ANN, lawyer; d. W. Carl and Eva Bennett Whittington. JD, Washington U., St. Louis, 1983. Law clk. US Dist. Ct. (so. dist.) Ill., Benton, 1983—85; assoc. Mitchell, Brandon and Schmidt, Carbondale, Ill., 1985—88; ptnr. Feirich, Schoen, Mager, Green, Carbondale, 1988—97; pvt. practice Carbondale, 1997—; trial atty., counselor City of Benton, 1997—; atty. Coal Valley Water Dist., Marion, Ill., 2000—; gen. counsel City of Zeigler, Ill., 2003—. Mem. com. character and fitness Ill. Supreme Ct., Springfield, 2006—. Pres. C. of C., Carbondale, 1996; mem. Hist. Preservation Soc.-Cert. Local Govt., Benton, 1997—2007, So. Ill. Symphony, Carbondale, 2001—07; bd. dirs. Sta. WSIU-PBS, Carbondale, 2003—07; co-chair fundraising Am. Heart Assn. so. Ill. chpt., Marion; musician, music dir. First United Meth. Ch.; musician, music coord. Franklin Bapt. Assn.; musician, pianist, organist Immanuel Bapt. Ch.; bd. visitors So. Ill. U. Law Sch., Carbondale, 2004—. Master: So. Ill. Am. Inn Ct. (officer 1999—2007); mem.: ATLA, Ill. State Bar Assn. (held various sect. coun. positions 1985—2001). Office: 930 W Walnut St Carbondale IL 62901 Home Phone: 618-435-3649; Office Phone: 618-549-8999. Office Fax: 618-529-5125. Business E-Mail: rwhittington1@aol.com.

WHITTINGTON, STEPHEN LUNN, museum director; b. Washington, Jan. 31, 1956; s. Charles Lunn and Alice Marie (Doyle) W.; m. Christine Ann Carlson, Aug. 18, 1979; children: Daniel, Joseph. AB in Anthropology, U. Chgo., 1977; MA, Pa. State U., 1981, PhD, 1989. Dir. Proyecto Arqueologico Ostuman, Copan, Honduras, 1989, U. Maine Hudson Mus., 1991—2002, Teozacoalco Archaeol. Project, 2002—; asst. curator collections Wyo. Hist. and Geol. Soc., Wilkes-Barre, Pa., 1989-90; cooperating assoc. prof. dept. anthropology U. Maine, 1991—2002. Dir. Iximche Osteological Project, 1992—95; adj. assoc. prof. dept. anthropology Wake Forest U., dir. Mus. Anthropology, 2002—. Author: Archaeology and Ethnohistory of Iximche, 2003; editor: Bones of the Maya, 1997; contbr. articles to profl. jours. Active Maine State Mus. Commn., 1998—2002; mem. Southeastern Mus. Conf. Coun., 2005—; chair Hispanic Arts Initiative Steering Com., 2005. Grantee Wenner-Gren Found. for Anthrop. Rsch., 1992-93, NSF, 1989, Inst. Internat. Edn., 1988, Found. for the Advancement of Mesoamerican Studies, 1995, 99, 2002, NEH, 1997, 2005. Mem. Am. Assn. Mus., N.C. Mus. Coun., Soc. for Am. Archaeology, Southeastern Mus. Conf. Avocations: jogging, fencing, bicycling. Home: 1307 Brookwood Dr Winston Salem NC 27106 Office: Wake Forest Univ Mus Anthropology PO Box 7267 Winston Salem NC 27109 Office Phone: 336-758-5827. E-mail: whittisl@wfu.edu.

WHITTINGTON, THOMAS LEE, lawyer; b. Waukesha, Wis., July 14, 1943; s. Floyd Leon and Winifred Carol (McDonald) W.; m. Ashley J. Whittington; children: Erin, Hilary, Eric Cartner, Ryan Cartner, Kyle Sanders. BA, Coll. of Wooster, 1965; JD, U. Mich., 1967. Bar: Trust Terr. of Pacific Islands 1967, Mich. 1969, Wash. 1974, U.S. Dist. Ct. (we. dist.) Wash. 1974. Vol. Peace Corps, Micronesia, 1967-69; staff asst. legis. office Dept. Interior, Washington, 1969-74; ptnr. Thomas, Whittington, Anderson, Bergan & Studebaker, Issaquah, Wash., 1974—2000, Scottsdale, Ariz., 2000—05, Carefree, Ariz., 2005—. Mailing: PO Box 5827 Carefree AZ 85377

WHITTINGTON-BROWN, VANESSA ELIZABETH, secondary school educator; b. Boston, Apr. 15, 1960; d. Samuel Wall and Ernestine (Brazand Hundley) Whittington; m. Alphonso Brown, July 25, 1992. BS, Bridgewater State U., 1978; postgrad., Cambridge Coll., 1992—. Elem. tchr. Boston (Mass.) Pub. Schs., 1983—, Pauline A. Shaw, Dorchester,

Mass., 1987-92; tchr. The Josiah Quincy Sch., Boston, 1992—. Adult edn. sec. Boston Pub. Schs., 1982, 83, mem. graphic learning com., 1983, impact II tchr. adaptor; musician cable TV program Gospel Expressions Prodns.; tutor Metco (after sch. program); mem. Primary Summer Source Inst., 1991; local pres. Sunshine Band, 1986, state pres., 1989-92. Composer: Lord I'm Coming Home, 1986. Mem. Children's Mus. and the Mus. Sci., Women's Heritage Trail, 3 Regent St. Young Adult Choir, Women's Choir, Boston Writing Project, Professional Dev. Program; co-dir. Specially Trained Youth Leadership in Excellence (STYLE), 1997; church musician Church of God in Christ Church, 1976-92. With USAR, 1979-91. Mem. Assn. Supervision and Curriculum Devel., Greater Boston Reading Coun., Boston Tchrs. Union, Black Educators Alliance of Mass., Nat. Coun. Tchrs. English, Women's Heritage Trail, African Meeting House. Democrat. Avocations: music, bowling, racquetball, basketball, poetry. Home Phone: 617-510-1269; Office Phone: 617-635-8497. E-mail: vewb@myway.com.

WHITTLESEY, JUDITH HOLLOWAY, public relations executive; b. Bartlesville, Okla., Dec. 28, 1942; d. Harry Haynes and Suzanne (Arnote) Holloway; m. Dennis Jeffrey Whittlesey, Aug. 3, 1968; children: Kristin Arnote, Kevin Jeffrey. BA, U. Okla., 1964; postgrad., Tulsa U., 1965, U. Va., 1971-72. Staff aide Office of the V.P. of U.S., Washington, 1979-81, Com. for Future of Am., Washington, 1981-82; dep. dir. scheduling and advance Mondale-Ferraro Campaign, Washington, 1982-84; dir. media rels. Susan Davis Internat., Washington, 1986-87, v.p., 1987-88, exec. v.p., 1988—. Bd. dirs. Cultural Alliance of Greater Washington, 1983-93, Washington Project for the Arts, 1987-93, Levine Sch. Music, 1993-98, Food Rsch. and Action Ctr., 1993—; bd. dirs. Decatur House, Suited For Change, Leadership Washington, 2004. Avocation: contemporary art. Office: Susan Davis Internat 1350 I St NW Washington DC 20005 Office Phone: 202-408-0808. Business E-Mail: judy@susandavis.com.

WHITWORTH, HALL BAKER, forest products company executive; b. St. Paul, NC, Feb. 15, 1919; s. A. Frederick and Maude Ethel (Baker) W.; m. Mary Margaret Mease, May 18, 1946; children: Hall Baker, Laura Ellen, David Allen. Student, Miss. So. Coll., 1942, U. N.C., 1957. With Champion Internat., Canton, NC, 1936-62, mgr. materials, 1956-62, dir. materials packages div. Chgo., 1962-65, dir. purchase U.S. Plywood-Champion Papers, Inc. (now champion Internat. Corp.) Hamilton, Ohio, 1965-68, dep. dir. corporate materials services, 1966, v.p., dir. purchase, 1968-75, v.p. materials Stamford, Conn., 1975—, dir., 1975—, now ret.; v.p., dir. So. Agrl. Co., 1985—; pres., dir. H. Whitworth Enterprises, Cin., 1985—. Bd. dirs. Pathfork-Harlan Coal Co., Elmac Corp. Served with U.S. Army, 1942-46. Recipient Thomas award Carolina-Va. Purchasing Agts. Assn., 1963 Mem. Am. Paper Inst. (chmn. energy subcom.), Am. Mgmt. Assn. (v.p. purchasing, transp. and phys. distbn. div. council) Clubs: Canton Toastmakers (founder, 1st pres.). Lodges: Elks; Lions. Methodist. Home and Office: 1111 S Lakemont Ave Apt 442 Winter Park FL 32792-5473 Office Phone: 407-306-9412. Personal E-mail: hall_whitworth@msn.com.

WHITWORTH, HORACE ALGERNON, mechanical engineer; b. Kingston, Jamaica, W.I., Mar. 24, 1953; came to U.S., 1967; s. Egbert Leopold and Violet Cecilia (Trouth) W. BSME, U. Mass., 1975; MS, George Washington U., 1977, DSc, 1983. Asst. prof. Howard U., Washington, 1983-89, dir. grad. studies dept. mech. engring., 1988-96, assoc. prof. mech. engring., 1989-99, prof. mech. engring., 1999—, chmn. dept. mech. engring., 2004—. Contbr. articles to profl. jours. Bd. dirs. Jamaica Support Found., Washington, 1991-95. Recipient Sr. Fellows Found. award Pacific Telesis Found., 1988, Prof. Acad. award Honeywell Corp., 1992; rsch. grantee in field. Mem. ASME (bd. dirs. Washington chpt. 1994—, Instr. of Yr. student chpt. 1985-86, 87-89), Am. Soc. Metals, Soc. for Exptl. Mechanics. Democrat. Methodist. Achievements include development of mathematical models to evaluate fatigue damage development in fibrous composite materials. Office: Howard U 2300 6th St NW Washington DC 20059-2323 Home Phone: 301-871-2711; Office Phone: 202-806-6600. Business E-Mail: hwhitworth@howard.edu.

WHITWORTH, KATHRYNNE ANN, professional golfer; b. Monahans, Tex., Sept. 27, 1939; d. Morris Clark and Dama Ann (Robinson) W. Student, Odessa Jr. Coll., tex., 1958. Joined tour Ladies Profl. Golf Assn., 1959—. Named to Hall of Fame Ladies Profl. Golf Assn., Tex. Sports Hall of Fame, Tex. Golf Hall of Fame, World Golf Hall of Fame; Capt. of Solhiem Cup, 1990-92. Mem. Ladies Profl. Golf Assn. (sec. 1962-63, v.p. 1965, 73, 88, pres. 1967, 68, 71, 89, 1st mem. to win over $1,000,000). Office: care Ladies Profl Golf Assn 2570 Volusia Ave Daytona Beach FL 32114-8144

WHITWORTH, WILLIAM A., magazine editor; b. Hot Springs, Ark., Feb. 13, 1937; s. William C. and Lois Virginia (McNabb) W.; m. Carolyn Hubbard, Dec. 27, 1969; children— Matthew, Katherine. BA, U. Okla., 1960. Reporter Ark. Gazette, Little Rock, 1960—63; reporter N.Y. Herald Tribune, 1963—65; staff writer The New Yorker, 1966—72, assoc. editor, 1973—80; editor-in-chief The Atlantic Monthly, Boston, 1981—99, editor emeritus, 1999—; editor-at-large The American Scholar, Washington, 2002—04. Office: 600 New Hampshire Ave NW Washington DC 20037 Personal E-mail: ww131@comcast.net.

WHOLLEY, MICHAEL CHRISTOPHER, retired military officer, lawyer; b. Lawrence, Mass., Oct. 7, 1944; m. Kathleen S. Sheehy, Sept. 3, 1966; children: Griffin, Clayton. BA in History and Lit., Harvard U., Cambridge, Mass., 1966; JD, U. Va. Law Sch., 1977; LLM in Environ. Law and Land Use, George Washington U., 1985; MA in Nat. Security and Strategic studies, Naval War Coll., 1989. Naval aviator, 1968; commd. USMC, 1966, advanced through grades to brig. gen., 1993; officer Chu Lai, Vietnam, 1969-70; with 54th Squadron, Coningsby, England, 1972-74; various legal billets/assignments 2nd Marine Divsn., Camp Lejeune, NC, 1977-81; mil. judge, chief judge Navy & Marine Corps Judiciary, 1981, 92-93; staff judge advocate to comdt., dir. judge advocate divsn., Hdqs. USMC, Washington, 1993-96; gen. coun. NASA, Washington, 2004—. Dir. Cherry Point Fed. Credit Union, Havelock, N.C., 1986-88; chmn. supervisory com. Navy Fed. Credit Union, Vienna, Va., 1993—. Mem. FBA, Va. Bar Assn., Judge Advocates Assn., Marine Corps Assn., Marine Corps Aviation Assn. Avocation: sailing. Office: NASA 300 E St SW Washington DC 20546-0005 Office Phone: 202-358-2450. Office Fax: 202-358-2741.

WHORISKEY, ROBERT DONALD, lawyer; b. Cambridge, Mass., May 9, 1929; s. John Joseph and Katherine Euphemia (MacDonald) W.; m. Martha Beebe Poutas, Apr. 16, 1966; children: Alexandra, Jonathan, Eliza. AB, Harvard U., 1952; JD, Boston Coll., 1958; LLM, NYU, 1960. Bar: Mass. 1958, NY 1963, U.S. Tax Ct. 1961, U.S. Claims Ct. 1969, U.S. Dist. Ct. (so. dist.) NY 1969, U.S. Ct. Customs 1971, U.S. Ct. Appeals (2d cir.) 1972, U.S. Supreme Ct. 1974, U.S. Ct. Appeals (3d cir.) 1983, U.S. Ct. Appeals (DC cir.) 1991. Sr. trial atty. Office Chief Counsel, IRS, NYC, 1960-67; assoc. Curtis, Mallet-Prevost, Colt & Mosle, NYC, 1967-70, ptnr., 1970-2000, of counsel, 2001—, exec. com., 1978-82, chmn. tax dept., 1982-87. Bd. dirs. InterNat. Tax Inst., v.p., lectr., 1980-84, chmn. bd., pres., lectr., 1985-87; lectr. Practicing Law Inst., World Trade Inst., Tax Execs. Inst., Am. Mgmt. Assn., Coun. for Internat. Tax Edn.; bd. dirs. Life Ins. Co. of Boston and NY, Inc. Author: Foreign Trusts, 1977, Annual Institute on International Taxation, 1966, 80, 81, (with Sidney Pine, Ralph Seligman) Tax and Business Benefits of the Bahamas, 1986; contbg. author: International Boycotts, CCH Federal Tax Service, 1988, CCH Smart Tax CD-ROM: Third Party Information, John Wiley and Sons, Inc.'s Transfer Pricing, 1993, Transfer Pricing Under IRC & 482: Overview and Planning, Part I, 1996, Accuracy Related Penalty Regulations for Transfer Pricing, Part II, 1997, Third Party Information, Part III, 1997, U.S. Taxation of International Operations, Warren, Gorham Lamont, 1998; mem. editl. adv. bd. Corp. Bus. Taxation Monthly, 2000—. Trustee, treas. Montessori Sch. Westchester, 1974-77; mem. bd. ethics Village of Larchmont, NY, 1988—. With U.S. Army, 1952-54. Mem. ABA (com. on alternative tax sys. tax sect. 1994-2004, com. on ct. procedure tax sec. 1997-2004), NY State Bar Assn. (com. on practice and procedure tax sect. 1990—), Harvard Club, Larchmont Yacht Club. Democrat. Roman Catholic. Office: Curtis Mallet-Prevost Colt & Mosle 101 Park Ave 35th Fl New York NY 10178-0061 Home Phone: 914-834-8151; Office Phone: 212-696-6031. Personal E-mail: rwhoriskey@aol.com. Business E-Mail: rwhoriskey@cm-p.com.

WHORTON, JAMES CLIFTON, history professor; b. Bayboro, NC, Oct. 31, 1942; s. Charlie Clifton Whorton and Lucy Margaret Brite; m. Jacquelyn S. Sims, Oct. 30, 1993; 1 child, Adrian Meade; m. Sue V. Moseley, Dec. 21, 1663 (dec. June 1989). BS, Duke U., Durham, NC, 1964; PhD, U. Wis., Madison, 1969. Prof. U. Wash., Seattle, 1970—. Author hist. monographs. Office: Univ Wash Box 357120 Seattle WA 98195 Office Phone: 206-616-1817. Office Fax: 206-685-7515. Business E-Mail: jwhorton@u.washington.edu.

WHORTON, M. DONALD, physician, epidemiologist; b. Las Vegas, N.Mex., Jan. 25, 1943; s. R. H. and Rachel (Siegal) Whorton; m. Diana L. Obrinsky, Apr. 9, 1972; children: Matthew Richard, Laura Elizabeth, Julie Hannah. Student, U.S. Naval Acad., 1961—62; B of Biology, N.Mex. Highlands U., 1964; MD, U. N.Mex., 1968; MPH, Johns Hopkins U., 1973. Intern Boston City Hosp., 1968—69; resident in pathology U. N.Mex., Albuquerque, 1969—71; instr., resident in medicine Balt. City Hosp., 1972—74; instr. Johns Hopkins U., Balt.; assoc. dir. divsn. emergency medicine Balt. City Hosps., 1974—75; clin. asst. prof. divsn. ambulatory and cmty. medicine U. Calif. Sch. Medicine, San Francisco, 1975—77; lectr. U. Calif. Sch. Pub. Health, San Francisco, 1975—79; med. dir. labor occup. health program Inst. Indsl. Rels., Ctr. for Labor Rsch. and Edn., 1975—79, assoc. clin. prof. occup. medicine, 1979—87; prin. Environ. Health Assocs., Inc., Oakland, 1978—88; v.p. ENSR Health Scis., 1988—94; pvt. practice Alameda, Calif., 1994—2001; with WorkCare, 2001—. Chmn. adv. com. for hazard evaluation svc. and info. system Indsl. Relations Dept., State of Calif., 1979—84; cons. in field; chmn. statewide adv. com. on occupl. and environ. health U. Calif. Ctrs., 1996—. Contbr. articles to profl. jours. Recipient Upjohn Achievement award, 1968; scholar, Robert Wood Johnson Found., 1972—74. Fellow: Am. Coll. Occupl. and Environ. Medicine, Am. Coll. Epidemiology; mem.: APHA, Inst. Medicine NAS, Calif. Med. Assn. (adv. panel on occupl. and environ. medicine), Soc. for Occupl. and Environ. Health, Alpha Omega Alpha. Office: WorkCare 1320 Harbor Bay Pkwy # 115 Alameda CA 94502-6556 Office Phone: 510-748-6900 ext. 201. Personal E-mail: whobrin@lmi.net. Business E-Mail: dwhorton@workcare.com.

WHOULEY, KATE, writer, consultant; b. Key West, Fla., Oct. 10, 1958; d. Paul Francis and Anne Marie (Ford) W BA magna cum laude in Philosophy, Lit. and Music, Baldwin Wallace Coll., Berea, Ohio, 1980. Bookseller, asst. mgr., store mgr. Waldenbooks, Newport, RI, 1980—83, Needham, Mass., 1980—83; book buyer, mgr. gen. books Boston U. Bookstore, 1983—86; dir. mdse. and mktg. Garland & Grace/dba Booksmith Musicsmith, West Barnstable, Mass., 1986—88; founder, owner, cons. Books in Common, Centerville, Mass., 1988—. Author: Customers and Service, 1997, Cottage for Sale, Must Be Moved, 2004; co-author (editor): Manual on Bookselling, 5th edit., 1996; contbg. author: The Practical Writer: From Inspiration to Publication, 2004; editor: Open Learning Study Series, 1997—2000; tech. editor Bookselling for Dummies, 2003. Prin. flute Cape Cod Conservatory Concert Band, 1993— Recipient Grover award Baldwin Wallace Coll., 1980 Mem. Am. Booksellers Assn. (v.p. Booksellers Pub. Inc. subs., Tarrytown, N.Y. 1994-98), New Eng. Booksellers Assn., AAUW, Coop. Am Avocations: music, gardening, reading, holistic studies, middle eastern dance.

WHYATT, ROBIN M., healthcare educator; d. Robert C. Murphy and Nathalie H. Osborn; m. Thomas E. Whyatt, May 12, 1974; children: Erin E. Cercena, Matthew D. BA, Earlham Coll., 1966; MPH, Columbia U., 1985, DrPH, 1995. Exec. dir. Scenic Hudson Inc., Poughkeepsie, NY, 1977—81; sr. project scientist Natural Resources Def. Coun., NYC, 1984—90; sr. staff assoc. Columbia U., NYC, 1990—97, assoc. rsch. scientist, 1997—2000; dep. dir. Columbia Ctr. for Children's Environ. Health, 1998—; asst. prof. dept. pub. health Columbia U., 2000—04, assoc. prof., 2004—06, prof., 2007—. Condr. workshops in field; mem. sci. adv. bd. Cin. Children's Envion. Health Ctr., 2000—; co-chair chem. exposure workgroup Nat. Children's Longitudinal Cohort Study, 2002—; mem. sci. adv. bd. Trichlorethylene Health Risk Assessment, U.S.EPA, 2002; mem. com. human biomonitoring for environ. toxicants NAS. Contbr. numerous articles and abstracts to profl. jours. Founding mem. Citizens Against Aerial Spraying, 1981; mem. PCB citizen's adv. com. EPA, Region II, 1980—81; bd. dirs. Alice Desmond and Hamilton Fish Libr., Garrison, NY, 1991—93; coach Odyssey of the Mind, Garrison Union Free Sch., 1992—96. Grantee, NIEHS/EPS, 1997—, EPA, 2000—03, NYC Coun. Spkrs. Fund for Biomed. Rsch., 2002—04, NIEHS, 2003—06, 2004—. Mem.: APHA, Internat. Soc. for Exposure Analysis. Avocations: canoeing, hiking. Office: Dept Environmental Health Sci Columbia Univ Mailman Sch Pub Health 60 Haven Ave New York NY 10032

WHYBARK, DAVID CLAY, business educator, researcher; b. Tacoma, Sept. 18, 1935; s. Clay Alfred and Irene (Stanton) W.; m. Neva Jo Richardson, July 6, 1957; children: Michael David, Suzanne Marie (dec.). BS, U. Wash., 1957; MBA, Cornell U., 1960; PhD, Stanford U., 1967. Rsch. assoc. Stanford (Calif.) U., 1962-67; asst. prof. Ariz. State U., Tempe, 1965-66; assoc. prof. Purdue U., West Lafayette, Ind., 1967-76; prof. Ind. U., Bloomington, 1976—90; Macon G. Patton disting. prof. U. NC, Chapel Hill, 1990—. Vis. prof. Shanghai Inst. Mech. Engring., 1986-87, Chinese U. of Hong Kong, 1996, Victoria U., New Zealand, 1996, Canterbury U., New Zealand, 1996; adj. prof. Inst. for Mgmt. Devel., Lausanne, Switzerland, 1981-82, 85-90; dir., founder Global Mfg. Rsch. Group, 1990—; cons. in field. Author: Master Production Scheduling: Theory and Practice, 1979, Manufacturing Planning Control Systems, 1984, International Operations Management, 1989, Integrated Production and Inventory Management, 1993, Why ERP?, 2000, Manufacturing Planning and Control Systems for Supply Chain Management, 2004; editor: Internat. Jour. Prodn. Econs., 1991-95, Global Manufacturing Practices, 1993. Recipient Lilly Alumni MBA Tchg. Excellence award, 1990, Disting. Rsch. award, Kenan-Flagler Sch., 1998. Fellow: Pan Pacific Bus. Assn. (mem. coun., Disting. Global Leadership award 2007), Internat. Soc. Inventory Rsch. (mem. coun., pres. 2000—02), Decision Scis. Inst. (past pres., Disting. Svc. award 1984); mem.: Ops. Mgmt. Assn. (pres. 1992—93), Am. Prodn. Inventory Control Soc. Avocations: travel, winemaking. Office: U NC Kenan-Flagler Sch Chapel Hill NC 27599-3490 Business E-Mail: clay_whybark@unc.edu.

WHYBROW, PETER CHARLES, psychiatrist, educator, director, author; b. Hertfordshire, Eng., June 13, 1939; U.S. citizenship, 1975; s. Charles Ernest and Doris Beatrice (Abbott) W.; children: Katherine, Helen Student, U. Coll., London, 1956—59; MB BS, U. Coll., 1962; diploma psychol. medicine, Conjoint Bd., London, 1968; MA (hon.), Dartmouth Coll., 1974, U. Pa., 1994. House officer endocrinology U. Coll. Hosp., 1962, sr. house physician psychiatry, 1963—64; house surgeon St. Helier Hosp., Surrey, England, 1963; house officer pediat. Prince of Wales Hosp., London, 1964; resident psychiatry U. N.C. Hosp., 1965—67, instr., rsch. fellow, 1967—68; mem. sci. staff neuropsychiat. rsch. unit Charshalton, Surrey, 1968—69; dir. residency tng. psychiatry Dartmouth Med. Sch., Hanover, NH, 1969—71, prof. psychiatry, 1970—84, chmn. dept., 1970—78, exec. dean, 1980—83; prof., chmn. dept. psychiatry U. Pa., Phila., 1984—86, Ruth Meltzer prof. psychiatry, 1992; chief psychiatrist Hosp. U. Pa., 1984—96; prof. psychiatry and biobehavioral scis., chmn. dept. psychiatry Sch. Medicine UCLA, 1996—, dir. Semel Inst. for Neurosci. and Human Behavior, 1996—, physician-in-chief Neuropsychiat. Hosp., 1996—99, Judson Braun disting. prof. psychiatry, 1999—. Dir. psychiatry Dartmouth Hitchock Affiliated Hosp., 1970-78; vis. scientist NIMH, 1978-79; cons. VA, 1970—, NIMH, 1972—; chmn. test com. Nat. Bd. Med. Examiners, 1977-84; rschr. psychoendrocrinology Author: Mood Disorders: Toward a New Psychobiology, 1984, The Hibernation Response, 1988, A Mood Apart, 1997, American Mania: When More Is Not Enough, 2005 (Gradiva Book award, Nat. Assn. Advancement Psychoanalysis, 2006); editor: Psychosomatic Medicine, 1977 (Ann. Book award NIH 2005); mem. editl. bd. Cmty. Psychiatry, Psychiat. Times, Directions in Psychiatry, Neuropsychopharmacology, Depression; contbr. articles to profl. jours Recipient Anclote Manor award psychiat. rsch. U. N.C., 1967, Sr. Investigator award Nat. Alliance for Rsch. into Schizophrenia and Depression, 1989; scholar Josiah Macy Jr. Found., 1978-79; fellow Ctr. Advanced Studies in Behavioral Sci., Stanford, 1993-94; recipient Lifetime Investigator award NDMDA, 1996; decorated Knight of Merit, Sovereign Order of St. John of Jerusalem, 1993; Disting. Prof. U. Calif., 2004 Fellow AAAS, Am. Psychiat. Assn., Royal Coll. Psychiatrists (founder), Am. Coll. Psychiatrists, Ctr. Advanced Study of Behavioral Scis. (hon.), Soc. Psychosomatic Rsch. London (hon.); mem. Am. Assn. Chmn. Depts. Psychiatry (pres. 1977-78), Royal Soc. Medicine, Am. Psychopath Assn., Am. Coll. Neuropsychopharmacology, Soc. Biol. Psychiatry, N.Y. Acad. Scis., Soc. Neurosci., Sigma Xi, Alpha Omega Alpha Office: UCLA Semel Inst Neuroscience & Human Behavior 760 Westwood Plz Los Angeles CA 90095-8353 Office Phone: 310-206-1233. Fax: 310-825-3942. Business E-Mail: pwhybrow@mednet.ucla.edu.

WHYTE, ALISON ANNE, conservator; b. Oct. 9, 1971; BA in Anthropology, U. BC, Vancouver, Can., 1993; MA in Art History, U. Toronto, Ontario, Can., 1997; M in Art Conservation, Queen's U., Kingston, Ontario, Can., 2001. Asst. conservator Kerkenes Dag Excavations, Turkey, 2005; conservator Archeol. Exploration of Sordis, Turkey, 2006, Oriental Inst. Mus., Chgo., 2001—. Contbr. articles to profl. jours. Office: Oriental Inst Mus 1155 E 58th St Chicago IL 60637 Office Phone: 773-702-9519. Business E-Mail: aawhyte@uchicago.edu.

WHYTE, GEORGE KENNETH, JR., lawyer; b. Waukegan, Ill., Oct. 10, 1936; s. George K. and Ella Margaret (Osgood) W.; m. Ann B. Challoner, June 20, 1964; children: Mary, Douglas. AB in Polit. Sci., Duke U., 1958; LLB, U. Wis., 1965. Bar: Wis. 1965. Law clk. to chief justice Wis. Supreme Ct., Madison, 1965-66; assoc. Quarles & Brady, Milw., 1966-73, ptnr., 1973—2004; ret., 2004. Lt. USN, 1958—62. Mem. ABA (employment law sect.), Wis. Bar Assn. (former chmn. labor and employment law sect.), Rotary (pres. 2002-03), The Town Club, Milw. Country Club. Congregationalist. Home: 1026 W Shaker Cir Mequon WI 53092-6034 E-mail: gkw@quarles.com.

WHYTE, MICHAEL P., genetics educator, researcher, director; b. NYC, Dec. 19, 1946; s. Michael Paul and Sophie (Dziuk) W.; m. Gloria Frances Golenda, Oct. 26, 1974; 1 child, Catherine Alexandra. BA in Chemistry, NYU, 1968; MD, SUNY, Bklyn., 1972. Diplomate Am. Bd. Internal Medicine, Nat. Bd. Med. Examiners. Intern, 1st yr. resident dept. medicine NYU Sch. Medicine Bellevue Hosp., NYC, 1972-74; clin. assoc. devel. and metabolic neurology br. Nat. Inst. Neurol. and Communicative Disorders and Stroke NIH, Bethesda, Md., 1974-76; fellow divsn. bone and mineral metabolism dept. medicine Washington U. Sch. Medicine, 1976-79, instr. dept. medicine, 1979-80, asst. sci. dir. Clin. Rsch. Ctr., 1979—; asst. physician Barnes Hosp., 1979—; staff physician St. Louis Children's Hosp., 1979—; NIH clin. assoc. physician Clin. Rsch. Ctr. Washington U. Sch. Medicine, 1980-82, asst. prof. medicine dept. medicine, 1980-86, assoc. prof. medicine dept. medicine, 1986-91, asst. prof. pediat. Edward Mallinckrodt dept. pediat., 1982-89, assoc. prof. pediat. Edward Mallinckrodt dept. pediat., 1989-92, prof. medicine dept. medicine, 1991—, prof. pediat. Edward Mallinckrodt dept. pediat., 1992—, prof. genetics James S. McDonell dept. genetics, 1997—; med. dir. Metabolic Rsch. Unit Shriners Hosp. for Children, St. Louis, 1982-2000, mem. staff, 1983—; assoc. attending physician Jewish Hosp., 1983—. Mem. editl. bd. Calcified Tissue Internat., 1995-2000, Jour. Bone and Mineral Rsch., 1994—; med. adv. bd. Osteogenesis Imperfecta Found., 1986—, med. adv. panel Paget's Disease Found., 1986—; chmn. med. adv. com., bd. dirs. Osteogenesis Found., 1995—; med.-sci. dir. Ctr. for Metabolic Bone Disease and Molecular Rsch. Shriners Hosp. for Children, St. Louis, 2000—. Assoc. editor: Primer on Metabolic Bone Diseases and Disorders of Mineral Metabolism, 1990, 93, 96, 99, 2003, 06; assoc. editor Calcified Tissue Internat., 1989-2000; contbr. chpts. to books, articles to profl. jours. Lt. comdr. USPHS, 1974-76. Fellow Am. Coll. Endocrinology; mem. ACP (assoc.), Assn. Am. Physicians, Am. Soc. Cell Biology, Am. Soc. Clin. Investigation, Am. Fedn. Clin. Rsch., Am. Soc. Advancement Sci., Am. Soc. Bone and Mineral Rsch. (ednl. com. 1987—, Fuller Albright award 1987, Young Investigator award 1983, Dr. Boy Frame award 1997, Frederic C. Bartter award, 2007), Am. Soc. Human Genetics, Endocrine Soc., Soc. Exptl. Biology and Medicine, Japanese Soc. Inherited Metabolic Disease (hon.), NY Acad. Scis. Office: Barnes-Jewish Hosp 216 S Kingshighway Blvd Saint Louis MO 63110-1026 Office Phone: 314-872-8305. Business E-Mail: mwhyte@shrinenet.org.

WHYTE, NANCY MARIE, performing arts educator; b. Myrtlepoint, Oreg., Mar. 12, 1948; d. Lawrence Edward and Carol Elizabeth (Johnson) Guderian; m. Anthony John Whyte, Aug. 7, 1967 (div. Sept. 1968); 1 child, Charles Lawrence; m. Douglas Brian Graff, June 27, 1971 (div. Oct. 1974); m. Lawrence Hanson, Mar. 12, 1976 (div. Aug. 1984); m. Joseph Paul Deacon, Aug. 10, 1985; 1 child, Nina Alexandra. Student, U. Wash., 1969-72, Am. Sch. Dance, 1972; BA, Evergreen State Coll., 1987. Owner, dir. Nancy Whyte Sch. Ballet, Bellingham, Wash., 1969—; artistic dir. Garden Street Dance Players, Bellingham, 1969-72, MT Baker Ballet, Bellingham, 1975—, Alpha and Omega Worship Dancers, 2003—; co-dir. Exptl. Performance Workshop, Bellingham, 1975-77; instr. creative dance St. Paul's Primary Sch., Bellingham, 1993-97; facilitator dance workshop Allied Arts/Whatcom Co., Bellingham, 1995—. Guest lectr. Western Wash. U., Bellingham, 1976—83, 1996—2003; guest faculty Dance Theatre N.W., Tacoma, 1995—2001; liturgical dance cons. Assumption Cath. Sch., 2001—05; artistic dir. Alpha and Omega Worship Dancers, 2003—. Author: Memoirs of a Child of Theatre Street, 1993; soloist Raduga Folk Ballet/N.Y. Character Ballet, N.Y.C., 1978-79; choreographer numerous ballets, 1972—. Mem. Nat. Dance Assn., Dancers Over 40, Sacred Dance Guild, Vancouver Ballet Soc. Democrat. Avocations: voice, writing. Office: MT Baker Ballet 1412 Cornwall Ave PO Box 2393 Bellingham WA 98227-2393 Home Phone: 360-671-6790; Office Phone: 360-734-9141. Personal E-mail: isadorables@msn.com.

WHYTE, RONALD M., judge; b. 1942; BA in Math., Wesleyan U., 1964; JD, U. So. Calif., 1967. Bar: Calif. 1967, U.S. Dist. Ct. (no. dist.) Calif. 1967, U.S. Dist. Ct. (cen. dist.) Calif. 1968, U.S. Ct. Appeals (9th cir.) 1986. Assoc. Hoge, Fenton Jones & Appel, Inc., San Jose, Calif., 1971-77, mem., 1977-89; judge Superior Ct. State of Calif., 1989-92, U.S. Dist. Ct. (no. dist.) Calif., San Jose, 1992—. Judge pro-tempore Superior Ct. Calif., 1977-89; lectr. Calif. Continuing Edn. of Bar, Rutter Group, Santa Clara Bar Assn., State Bar Calif.; legal counsel Santa CLara County Bar Assn.,

1986-89; mem. county select com. Criminal Conflicts Program, 1988. Bd. trustees Santa Clara County Bar Assn., 1978-79, 84-85. Lt. Judge Advocate Gen.'s Corps, USNR, 1968-71. Recipient Judge of Yr. award Santa Clara County Trial Lawyers Assn., 1992, Disting. Svc. award Berkeley Ctr. Law and Tech., 2001; nmaed Fed. Judge of Yr., Santa Clara (Calif.) County Trial Lawyers Assn., 2003. Mem. Calif. Judges Assn., Assn. Bus. Trial Lawyers (bd. govs. 1991-93), Santa Clara Inn of Ct. (exec. com. 1993—), San Francisco Bay area Intellectual Property Inn of Ct. (exec. com. 1994—). Office: US Courthouse 280 S 1st St Rm 2112 San Jose CA 95113-3002

WIACEK, RAYMOND J., lawyer; b. Detroit, Dec. 5, 1950; BA, Yale U., 1973; JD, Harvard U., 1976. Bar: Mich. 1976, D.C. 1977. Lawyer Jones, Day, Reavis & Pogue, Washington; ptnr. fin. affairs and tax group coord. Jones Day, Washington. Adj. prof. taxation Georgetown Univ. Law Ctr. Mem. Phi Beta Kappa. Office: Jones Day 51 Louisiana Ave NW Washington DC 20001-2113 Office Phone: 202-879-3908. Office Fax: 202-626-1700. Business E-Mail: rjwiacek@jonesday.com.

WIANT, SARAH KIRSTEN, law librarian, educator, director; b. Waverly, Iowa, Nov. 20, 1946; d. James Allen and Eva (Jorgensen) Wiant; m. Robert E. Akins (dec.). BA, Western State Coll., 1968; MLS, U. North Tex., 1970; JD, Washington & Lee U., 1978. Asst. law libr. Tex. Tech. U., 1970—72, Washington & Lee U., Lexington, Va., 1972—78, dir. Law Libr., 1978—, asst. prof. law, 1978-83, assoc. prof. law, 1984-92, prof. law, 1993—. Participant Conf. on Fair Use, NII, 1995—98; visitor U. Melbourne, Monash U., 2001. Co-author: Copyright Handbook, 1984, Libraries and Copyright: A Guide to Copyright Law in the 1990s, 1994, UCITA Encyclopedia of Lib. and Information Science, 2005; co-author: (Va. sect.) Legal Research in the District of Columbia, Maryland and Virginia, 2005; co-author: (admiralty chpt.) Specialized Legal Research, 2005; co-author: Developments on Copyright Law, 2005; mem. adv. bd. Westlaw, 1988—93, 2003—; contbr. chapters to books. Mem.: ABA (com. on librs. 1987—93), U.S. Trademark Assn., Maritime Law Assn., Spl. Librs. Assn. (chair copyright com. 1990—96, John Cotton Dana award 1997), Am. Assn. Law Schs. (chmn. sec. on librs. 1990—92, accreditation com. 1991—94), Am. Assn. Law Librs. (mem. exec. bd. 1981—84, mem. copyright com. 1990—94, chmn. 2003—04, copyright office rep., Pres.' award 2001, Spl. Dist. Svc. award Southeastern chpt. 1997). Office: Washington & Lee U Law Libr Lewis Hall Lexington VA 24450 Home Phone: 540-463-2402; Office Phone: 540-458-8540. Business E-Mail: wiants@wlu.edu.

WIATER, RICHARD M., manufacturing executive; b. Green Bay, Wis., Jan. 21, 1936; s. Adam Frank and Evelyn Catherine (Griakowski) W.; m. Eleanor G. Wiater, Mar. 17, 1987. Acctg. degree, Xavier U., 1961. Acct. P&G, Cin., 1957-62, various, 1963-66; mgr. auditing Aircraft Engine Group-GE, Cin., 1967-70, mgr. mfg. fin. analysis resource planning, 1971-78, mgr. fin. analysis overseas mfg., 1978-85; dir. Tusas Engine Industries, Aircraft Engine-GE, Turkey, 1986-89; mgr. GE90 fin. and bus. planning Aircraft Engine Group-GE, Cin., 1990-95; bus. cons. Cin., 1996-98; pres. Tactical Vehicle Sys. divsn. Stewart & Stevenson Svc., Inc., Sealy, Tex., 1999-2000, COO Specialty Wheeled Vehicle divsn. Houston, 2001—. Mem. AUSA, NDIA. Avocations: history, woodworking. Home: 1640 E T C Jester Blvd Apt 1017 Houston TX 77008-2578

WIATT, JAMES ANTHONY, theatrical agency executive; b. LA, Oct. 18, 1946; s. Norman and Catherine (Sonners) W.; m. Randie Laine. BA, U. So. Calif., 1969. Campaign coord. Tunney for Senate, LA, 1969-71; adminstrv. asst. Senator John V. Tunney, LA, 1972-75; agt. FCA, LA, 1976-78; lit. agt. Internat. Creative Mgmt., LA, 1978-81, motion picture agt., 1981-83, head of motion picture dept., 1983-85, pres., COO, from 1985, co-chmn., co-CEO Beverly Hills, Calif., to 1999; pres., co-CEO William Morris Agy., Beverly Hills, 1999—. Mem. bd. councilors USC Sch. Cinema-TV; mem. bd. govs. Music Ctr. L.A., Am. Film Inst.; mem. exec. bd. med. scis. UCLA; exec. coun. The Quills. Named one of 50 Most Powerful People in Hollywood, Premiere mag., 2004—06. Office: William Morris Agy 151 S El Camino Dr Beverly Hills CA 90212-2775 E-mail: jwiatt@wma.com.

WIBERG, DONALD MARTIN, electrical engineering educator, consultant; b. Battle Creek, Mich., Sept. 20, 1936; s. Martin and Lina (Havstein) W.; children: Erik M., Kristin A., Kenneth C. BS, Calif. Inst. Tech., 1959, MS, 1960, PhD, 1965. Registered profl. engr., Calif. Sr. design engr. Convair, San Diego, 1964-65; asst. prof. elec. engring. UCLA, 1965-71, assoc. prof., 1971-77, prof., 1977-94, prof. anesthesiology, 1979-94, vice chmn. dept. elec. engring., 1985-86, prof. emeritus, 1994-2001; prof. emeritus dept. elec. engring. U. Calif., Santa Cruz, 2001—, rsch. prof. Ctr. for Adaptive Optics, 2002—. Cons. in field; vis. prof. German Rsch. Orgn. for Air and Space Flight, Munich, 1969-70, dept. elec. engring. and computer sci. U. Newcastle, Australia, 1989-90, Inst. for Systems Rsch., U. Md., College Park, 1994, Ajon U., Suwon, Korea, 2006. Author: State Space and Linear Systems, 1971; co-editor: Regulation of Breathing, 1983. Mem. adv. bd. Parthenia Sch., Los Angeles, 1971-74. Sr. NATO research fellow KFZ Karlsruhe, W.Ger., 1973; sr. Fulbright fellow, Copenhagen, 1976-77, Trondheim, Norway, 1983-84 Fellow IEEE (applications assoc. editor Trans. on Automatic Control 1983, assoc. editor-at-large 1987-89, 92-94, named Congl. fellow legis. asst. office Senator Tom Harkin, D-IA 1995), Am. Physiol. Soc. (assoc. editor Modelling Methodology Forum 1980-91), Sigma Xi. Home: 2395 Delaware Ave #153 Santa Cruz CA 95060-5716

WIBERG, LARS-ERIK, occupational compatibility consultant; b. Wakefield, Mass., June 1, 1928; s. Sverker Claesson and Ingrid (Heurlin) W.; m. Elizabeth Margaret (Allenbrook), Oct. 18, 1957; children: Kirsten, Margaret, Brenda. BS in Geology, MIT, 1950; MAT, Harvard U., 1952. From engr. to dir. corp. comm. EG and G Inc., Boston and Bedford, Mass., 1956—69; from asst. v.p. to v.p. compensation, orgnl. planning and ombudsman for officers First Nat. Bank of Boston, 1969—81; cons. Rockport, Mass., 1981—. Lectr. human resources mgmt. Boston U., 1988—92; lectr. job search and career planning U. Karlstad, Sweden, 1992; corporator Granite Savs. Bank, 1981—. Author: It's Your Move, 1991; inventor in the field of Occupl. Compatibility; interviewed in Rockport Recollected. Mem. Gov. John A. Volpe's Mgmt. Engring. Task Force, 1965; mem. planning bd., Rockport, 1965-72, chmn., 1969-72; pres. ch. coun. Swedenborg Chapel, Cambridge, Mass., 1984-2004; dir. Mass. New Ch. Union, 1990-2004; mem. zoning bd. appeals, Rockport, 1986-2006, chmn., 2006-07, mem. site rev. com., 1999-2001; v.p., founder The Uses Trust, Ltd., 2005. 1st lt., USAF, 1953-55. Mem. Affiliated New Eng. Cons. (founding mem. Lexington, Mass. 1985), Life Ext. Found., Heritage Found., Swedenborg Sci. Assn. Avocations: home repair, music, cooking, reading. Home and Office: 90 South St Rockport MA 01966-1916 Business E-Mail: bjara@gis.net.

WICH, DONALD ANTHONY, JR., lawyer; b. Apr. 13, 1947; s. Donald Anthony and Margaret Louise (Blatz) W. BA with honors, Notre Dame U., Ind., 1969; JD, Notre Dame U., 1972. Bar: Fla. 1972, U.S. Dist. Ct. (so. dist.) Fla. 1972, U.S. Ct. Appeals (5th and 11th cirs.) 1982, U.S. Supreme Ct. 1976; cert. civil trial lawyer, 1983. Assoc. VISTA, Miami, Fla., 1972-74; atty. Legal Svcs., Miami, 1973-75; adj. prof. law U. Miami, 1974-75; ptnr. Wich, Wich & wich, P.A., Ft. Lauderdale, Fla., 1992—. Pres., dir. Legal Aid of Broward, Ft. Lauderdale, 1976-82; mem. 17th Cir. Jud. Nominating Commn., 1998-02; spl. prosecutor, grievance chmn. The Fla Bar, 1982-90; chmn. UPL Standing Com., 2001-2004 Bd. dirs. St. Thomas More of So. Fla., 1989-. Mem. ATLA, Am. Arbitration Assn., North Broward Bar Assn. (pres. 1983-84), Acad. Fla. Trial Lawyers Assn. (sustaining mem.), Broward County Trial Lawyers Assn. (pres. 1988-89, sustaining mem.), Broward Bar Assn. (chmn. legis. com. 1984-85, exec. com. 1986-92, 94-98, chmn. bench-bar com. 1993-94, chmn. clk.-bar com. 1993-95, mem. 1998-99, pres. 1997-98), Tex. Trial Lawyers Assn., N.Y. Trial Lawyers Assn., Pompano Beach C. of C. (pres. 1989-90, dir. 1984-87, 92-95, govtl. affairs chmn. 1983-84, art show chmn. 1984-85, seafood festival chmn. 1986-90), Notre Dame Frederick Sorin Soc., Rotary (bd. dirs. 1987-91), Woodhouse (bd. dirs. 1990-91). Office: Wich Wich & Wich PA # 620 2400 E Commercial Blvd Fort Lauderdale FL 33308-4030 Office Phone: 954-776-1600. E-mail: wich3@msn.com.

WICHERN, DEAN WILLIAM, business educator; b. Medford, Wis., Apr. 29, 1942; s. Arthur William and Rebecca Ann (Ambler) W.; m. Dorothy Jean Rutkowski, Dec. 7, 1968; children: Michael, Andrew. BS in Math., U. Wis., 1964, MS in Stats., 1965, PhD in Stats., 1969. Instr. Sch. Bus. U. Wis., Madison, 1967-69, asst. prof., 1969-72, assoc. prof., 1972-76, prof., 1976-84, chmn. quantitative analysis dept., 1975-78; prof. Mays Bus. Sch. Tex. A&M U., 1984—2006, head info. and ops. mgmt. dept., 1984—88, 1997—98, 2004—06, assoc. dean, 1988-95, John E. Pearson prof. bus. adminstrn., 1985—2006, prof. emeritus, 2006—. Vis. prof. Math. Rsch. Ctr., 1978-79. Co-author: Intermediate Business Statistics, 1977, Applied Multivariate Statistical Analysis, 6th edit., 2007, Business Statistics: Decision Making With Data, 1997, Business Forecasting, 8th edit., 2005; mem. editl. bd. Jour. Bus. and Econ. Stats., 1983—91. Mem. Royal Statis. Soc., Am. Statis. Assn., Inst. Oper. Rsch. and Mgmt. Sci., Internat. Inst. of Forecasters, Beta Gamma Sigma, Phi Kappa Phi. Home: 9217 Riverstone Ct College Station TX 77845-8333 Office: Tex A&M U Mays Bus Sch 4217 TAMU College Station TX 77843-4217 Business E-Mail: d-wichern@tamu.edu.

WICHMAN, KAREN LIN, medical transcriptionist; b. Mt. Pleasant, Mich., Nov. 7, 1969; d. Patrick Dale Mahoney and Elaine Marie Geweniger, Diana Mahoney (Stepmother); m. Dustin Michael Wichman, Sept. 12, 1998; children: Brandon Michael, Brianna Marie. Cert., Gt. Lakes Jr. Coll. of Bus., Saginaw, Mich., 1989. Med. transcriptionist St. Mary's Med. Ctr., Saginaw, Mich., 1994—2000, Spheris, Inc., Franklin, Tenn., 2000—. Mem.: Am. Assn. Med. Transcription (assoc.). Home Phone: 989-642-8836.

WICHMANN, DAVID S., health care services executive; Ptnr. Arthur Andersen; sr. v.p. corp. develop. UnitedHealth Group, Minnetonka, Minn., 1998—2004, pres., COO specialized care services, 2001—03, CEO specialized care services, 2003—04, pres., COO, 2004—. Office: United-Health Group PO Box 1459 Minneapolis MN 55440-1459 *

WICK, DOUGLAS, producer; m. Lucy Fisher; 3 children. Grad. cum laude, Yale U. Owner Red Wagon Prodns., Culver City, Calif. Assoc. prodr. Starting Over 1979; prodr. Wolf, 1994, The Craft, 1996, Hush, 1998, Working Girl (six Acad. Award Nomiations, five Golden Globes including Best Picture), 1988, Stuart Little, 1999, Girl, Interrupted, 1999, Gladiator, 2000, The Hollow Man, 2000, Stuart Little 2, 2002, Peter Pan, 2003, Win A Date With Tad Hamilton, 2004, Bewitched, 2005, Memoirs Of A Geisha, 2005, Jarhead, 2005. Recipient David O. Selznick Achievement award in Theatrical Motion Pictures, Producers Guild Am., 2007. Office: Red Wagon Prodns Hepburn West Bldg 10202 W Washington Blvd Culver City CA 90232 Fax: 310-244-1480. *

WICK, MITCHELL A., physician; b. NYC, July 15, 1954; s. Edwin and Doris Wick. BA in Chemistry, U. South Fla., 1976; postgrad., U. Miami, Coral Gables, Fla., 1972—73; D.O., Kirksville Coll. Osteo. Medicine, Mo., 1980. Diplomate Am. Osteo. Bd. Family Physicians, Am. Acad. Pain Mgmt., Am. Assn. Integrative Medicine. Intern Southeastern Med. Ctr., N. Miami, Fla., 1980—81; resident Parkview Hosp., Toledo, 1981—83; staff physician Walk-in Family Medicine Ctr., Boynton Beach, Fla., 1983—86; physician Davie-Dania Med. Ctr., Fla., 1986—96; staff physician Meml. Pembroke Hosp., Pembroke Pines, Fla., 1991—. Author: Megaphysics, A New Look at the Universe, 2003. Mem.: Fla. Osteo. Med. Assn., Am. Osteo. Assn. Achievements include research and copywrite on physics theory regarding the fractal nature of spacetime manifolds and how matter and energy interact with thereof utilizing string theory. Avocations: physics, tensor calculus. Home: 914 S Chippewa Cir Boynton Beach FL 33436 Office Phone: 561-736-2000. Personal E-mail: mitchell598@comcast.net, wickmitchell@gmail.com.

WICK, ROBERT THOMAS, retired supermarket executive; b. St. Louis, Nov. 26, 1927; s. Robert Berninger and Katherine (Burke) W.; m. Virginia Rose Allen, Sept. 6, 1952; children: Susan, Patrick, Nancy, Robert J. BS, St. Louis U., 1955; cert. in food distbn., Mich. State U., 1956. Sales mgr. Nat. Tea Co., St. Louis, 1966-68, asst. div. mgr., 1968-69, div. mgr. Sioux City, Iowa, 1969-71, Milw., 1971-73, Chgo., 1973-74; v.p., gen. mgr. A&P Food Stores, Indpls., 1975-77; div. v.p. Colonial Food Stores- Grand Union, Norfolk, Va., 1977-79; pres., chief exec. officer Bonnie Be-Lo Markets, Inc., Norfolk, 1979-90, ret., 1990. Bd. dirs. Virginia Beach (Va.) Community Svcs. Bd., 1985-89; mem. adv. bd. Straight, Inc., Chesapeake, Va., 1987-91; dir. Community Alternatives, Inc., Virginia Beach, 1991-92. Tech. cpl. U.S. Army, 1946-48. Recipient Citizen of Yr. award St. Louis Argus Newspaper, 1968. Mem. Food Mktg. Inst. (bd. dirs. 1982-89), Va. Food Dealers Assn. (bd. dirs. 1981-87), Tidewater Retail Mchts. Assn. (pres., bd. dirs. 1981-91). Conservative. Roman Catholic. Avocations: travel, golf. Home: 801 Winthrope Dr Virginia Beach VA 23452-3940 Personal E-mail: rwick@cox.net.

WICK, TAMARA, photographer, artist, writer; b. July 15, 1966; d. James Alan and Maxine Evelyn (Tankersley) W.; m. John E. Kulukundis, 1986. BA in Comm./Broadcasting, Ariz. State U., 1984; grad., Am. Acad. Dramatic Arts, NYC. Asst. to exec. prodr. video devel. Columbia Pictures Industries, NYC, 1986-87; pub. rels. coord., asst. to Estée Lauder Estée Lauder Cos., NYC, 1987-90; founder, creative dir. Imagination Enterprises, Inc., NYC, 1993—; founder, photographer Santa Paws, NYC, 1993—. Active Met. Mus. Art, N.Y.C. Merit scholar U. Ariz., 1976. Mem. NAFE, U.S. Equestrian Team, N.Y. Women in Comm., N.Y. Zool. Soc., N.Y. Young Reps. Club, Ariz. State U. Alumni, Kappa Kappa Gamma Alumnae. Episcopalian. Avocations: showed horses on english circuit, tennis, skiing, watercolor painting, photography. Home: 150 W 56th St Apt 3010 New York NY 10019-3842

WICK, WILLIAM SHINN, clergyman, chaplain, pastor; b. West Chester, Pa. s. William R. and Barbara (Shinn) W.; m. Debra R. Smith, Apr. 1, 1989; 1 child, Christopher R. BA, Trinity Internat. U., Deerfield, Ill., 1975; MDiv, Trinity Evang. Div. Sch., Deerfield, 1978. Ordained to ministry Evang. Free Ch. Am., 1978. Pastor Bradford (Vt.) Evang. Free Ch., 1978-85, Cornerstone Evangelical Fee Ch., Vt., 1985-89, Grace Evang. Free Ch., Northfield, Vt., 1989-96; chaplain Norwich U., Northfield, 1989—; interim pastor First Bapt. Ch., Barre, Vt., 2001—03, Resurrection Bapt. Ch., Montpelier, Vt., 2003—04, Orange Christian and Missionary Alliance Ch., 2004—05, Websterville Baptist Ch., 2006. Mem. bd. govs. Trinity Western U., Langley, B.C., Can., 1999—; mem. Evangelical Free Ch. Am. Chaplain's Commn., 2006—. Capt. CAP, 2005—. Mem.: Profl. Ski Instrs. Am. Avocations: alpine skiing, racquetball, tennis, scuba diving, sailing, astronomy. Home: 763 S Main St Northfield VT 05663-5601 Office: White Chapel Norwich U 158 Harmon Dr Northfield VT 05663-1000 Office Phone: 802-485-2128. Personal E-mail: theskiingrev@hotmail.com. Business E-Mail: chaplain@norwich.edu.

WICKER, DOROTHY BALDWIN, physicist; b. Buffalo, Jan. 27, 1943; d. August A. and Dorothy (Smith) Cenkner; m. Frank J. Baldwin, Feb. 10, 1973 (dec. 1994); m. James E. Wicker, Aug. 9, 1996. BA in Physics (magna cum laude), Hartwick Coll., 1965; MA in Physics, Kent State U., 1968; PhD in Applied Mgmt. Decision Scis., Walden U., 1999. Cert. physics educator, N.J., Fla; cert. modeling and simulation profl. Nat. Tng. Sys. Assn./Nat. Def. Indsl. Assn., 2003. Physics instr. Kent (Ohio) State U., 1968-70; physics tchr. Watchung Hills (N.J.) High Sch., 1970-73, Edgewater High Sch., Orlando, Fla., 1973-77; adj. physics instr. Valencia Community Coll., Orlando, 1977, Fla. Tech. U., Orlando, 1975, 73; physicist Naval Tng. Equipment Ctr., Orlando, 1977-84; sr. engring. specialist Gen. Dynamics Corp. (now Lockheed Martin), Fort Worth, 1984-90; engring. project mgr. Gen. Dynamics Corp., Fort Worth, 1990-96, staff specialist, mgr., 1997—2001, prin. sys. engr., 2001—. Tech. program com. Inter Svc. Industry Tng. System Conf., 1987, 91, 92, 93. Contbr. articles to profl. jours. Co-founder Friendship Force Ft. Worth Metroplex, 1985, pres., 1990-93. Recipient Cost Savs. award Gen. Dynamics, 1986. Mem. NAFE, Nat. Def. Indsl. Assn. (life mem.), Nat. Mgmt. Assn., Women in Defense, Mensa, Friendship Force Internat., Sigma Xi. Achievements include patents in field. Home: 3436 Clayton Rd E Fort Worth TX 76116-7342 Office: Lockheed Martin Tactical Aircraft Sys MZ 8848 PO Box 748 Fort Worth TX 76101-0748 Office Phone: 817-935-4543. Business E-Mail: dorothy.b.wicker@lmco.com.

WICKER, ROGER F., congressman, lawyer; b. Pontotoc, Miss., July 5, 1951; s. Fred and Wordna Wicker; m. Gayle Long; 3 children. BA in Polit. Sci. and Journalism, U. Miss., 1973; JD, Ole Miss Law Sch., 1975. Judge adv. USAF, 1976—80; mem. staff rules com. Staff of US Rep. Trent Lott, Miss., 1980-82; pvt. practice, 1982—; pub. defender Lee County, Miss., 1984—87; mem. Miss. State Senate, 1987—94, US Congress from 1st Miss. dist., 1995—, dep. majority whip; mem. House appropriations com., 1995—, House Task Force for a Drug Free America, Rep. Policy Com., 2001—, subcommittee on labor, health and human svcs. and edn., subcommittee on def., subcommittee on energy and water devel., subcommittee on fgn. ops., budget com., 2003—; former chmn. Tenn. Valley Authority Congl. Caucus. Mem. Cmty. Devel. Found., Lions Club, Tupelo First Baptist Church, Miss. With USAF, 1976—80, positions up to lt. col. USAFR, 1980—2004. Recipient Nat. Pub. Svc. award, Am. Heart Assn., 1998, Capitol Dome award, Am. Cancer Soc., 2003, Award, Mfg. Excellence, NAM, 2003. Republican. Office: US House Reps 2350 Rayburn House Office Bldg Washington DC 20515 Office Phone: 202-225-4306. Office Fax: 202-225-3549. *

WICKER, THOMAS CAREY, JR., retired judge; b. New Orleans, Aug. 1, 1923; s. Thomas Carey and Mary (Taylor) Wicker; m. Jane Anne Trepanier, Dec. 29, 1995; children: Thomas Carey III, Catherine Anne. BBA, Tulane U., 1944, LLB, 1949, JD, 1969. Bar: La. 1949. Law clk. La. Supreme Ct., New Orleans, 1949—50; asst. U.S. Atty., New Orleans, 1950—53; ptnr. Simon, Wicker & Wiedemann, New Orleans, 1953—67, Wicker, Wiedemann & Fransen, 1967—72; dist. judge Jefferson Parish, La., 1972—85; judge La. Ct. Appeal 5th cir., 1985—98. Mem. faculty Nat. Jud. Coll., 1979—93, Tulane U. Sch. Law, 1978—83. Co-author (with others): Judicial Ethics, 1982, Modern Judicial Ethics, 1992; editor: Tulane Law Rev., 1949. Past bd. visitors Tulane U.; bd. dirs. La. Jud. Coll.; past pres. Sugar Bowl. Lt. (j.g.) USNR, 1944—46. Mem.: ABA (jud. divsn. coun.), La. Dist. Judges Assn. (past. pres.), Am. Judicature Soc., Jefferson Parish Bar Assn., La. Bar Assn. (chmn. jr. bar sect. 1958—59, gov. 1958, ho. of dels. 1960—72), Tulane U. Alumni Assn. (past pres.), Order of Coif, Metairie Country Club, Rotary (pres. 1971—72), Pi Kappa Alpha, Beta Gamma Sigma. Episcopalian. Avocations: golf, photography, military history.

WICKERT, JONATHAN ADAM, engineering educator; b. El Paso, Tex. BS, U. Calif.-Berkeley, 1985, MS, 1987, PhD, 1989. Rsch. fellow U. Cambridge, England, 1989—90; prof. mech. engring. Carnegie Mellon U., Pitts., 1990—2007; prof. Iowa State U., Ames, 2007—, mech. engring. dept. chair, 2007—. Mem. Wickert Consulting Svcs. LLC, Allison Park, Pa., 2003—. Author: (textbook) An Introduction to Mechanical Engineering, (articles) Applied Mechanics Revs., Internat. Jour. Nonlinear Mechanics, Jour. Acoustical Soc. Am., Shock and Vibration Digest, Jour. Vibration and Acoustics, Jour. Manufacturing Sci. and Enging., Jour. Tribology, Jour. Micromechanics and Microengring.; associate editor Jour. Info. Storage Systems. Recipient George Tallman Ladd Rsch. award, Carnegie Mellon U., 1993, Ralph Teetor Ednl. award, Soc. Automotive Engrs., 1996, Marsha and Philip Dowd Faculty Fellowship, Carnegie Mellon U., 1998, Benjamin Teare Ednl. award, 2000, Curtis McGraw Rsch. award, Am. Soc. for Enging. Edn., 2002, Tech. Achievement award, Info. Storage Industry Consortium, 2003, Curriculum Innovation award, ASME, 2005; fellow, NSF/NATO, 1989—90; grantee rsch. in dynamics, applied mechanics, and vibration, NSF, 1991—2006. Fellow: ASME; mem.: AAUP, Soc. Automotive Engrs., Am. Soc. Engring. Edn. Achievements include patents for damper for brake noise reduction; research in high-density computer data storage; machine dynamics; manufacture of sheet metal, fiberglass, polymer materials; design of automotive disk brakes. Avocations: long distance running, woodworking. Office: Iowa State U Dept Mech Engring 2025 Black Engring Bldg Ames IA 50011

WICKES, GEORGE, English literature educator, writer; b. Antwerp, Belgium, Jan. 6, 1923; came to U.S., 1923; s. Francis Cogswell and Germaine (Attout) W.; m. Louise Westling, Nov. 8, 1975; children by previous marriage: Gregory, Geoffrey, Madeleine (dec.), Thomas, Jonathan. BA, U. Toronto, Ont., Can., 1944; MA, Columbia U., 1949; PhD, U. Calif., Berkeley, 1954. Asst. sec. Belgian Am. Ednl. Found., NYC, 1947-49; exec. dir. U.S. Ednl. Found. in Belgium, 1952-54; instr. Duke U., Durham, N.C., 1954-57; from asst. prof. to prof. Harvey Mudd Coll. and Claremont Grad. Sch., Calif., 1957-70; prof. English and comparative lit. U. Oreg., Eugene, 1970—, dir. comparative lit., 1974-77, head English dept., 1976-83. Lectr. USIS, Europe, 1969, Africa, 1978, 79; vis. prof. U. Rouen, France, 1970, U. Tübingen, Germany, 1981, U. Heidelberg, Germany, 1996. Editor: Lawrence Durrell and Henry Miller Correspondence, 1963, Henry Miller, Letters to Emil, 1989, Henry Miller and James Laughlin: Selected Letters, 1995; Author: Henry Miller, 1966, Americans in Paris, 1969, The Amazon of Letters, 1976, Memories, 2006: translator: The Memoirs of Frederic Mistral, 1986. With US Army, 1943—46. Fulbright lectr. France, 1962-63, 66, 78; sr. fellow Ctr. for Twentieth Century Studies, U. Wis.-Milw., Milwaukee, 1971, Creative Writing fellow Nat. Endowment Arts, 1973, Camargo fellow, 1991. Mem.: PEN. Office: U Oreg English Dept Eugene OR 97403 Office Phone: 541-346-3938. Business E-Mail: wickes@uoregon.edu.

WICKES, R(ICHARD) PAUL, lawyer; b. Camden, NJ, June 11, 1948; s. Richard Gordon and Nancy Elizabeth (Roy) W.; m. Jane Avis Hunter, June 8, 1970, (div. Feb. 1978); m. Gail Thain Parker, Apr. 9, 1978. BA cum laude, Williams Coll., 1970; JD, Harvard U., 1973. Bar: Vt. 1973, U.S. Supreme Ct. 1976, Okla. 1982, Tex. 1985, NY 1991, US Ct. Appeals (2nd, 3rd, 5th and 9th cir.), various US Dists. and Bankruptcy Cts. Ptnr. Williams & Wickes, Bennington, Vt., 1973-77; commr. Vt. Dept. Taxes, Montpelier, 1977-78; assoc. Gravel, Shea & Wright, Burlington, Vt., 1978-80; counsel to Gov. State of Vt., Montpelier, 1980-82; ptnr. Watson & McKenzie, Oklahoma City, 1982-84, Thompson & Knight, Dallas, 1984-90, Shearman & Sterling, NYC, 1990—2003, Linklaters, NYC, 2003—04, mng. ptnr., 2004—. Mem.: NY Bar Assn. Office: Linklaters 1345 Ave of America New York NY 10105 Office Phone: 212-903-9038. Business E-Mail: paul.wickes@linklaters.com.

WICKESBERG, ALBERT KLUMB, retired management consultant; b. Neenah, Wis., Apr. 2, 1921; s. Albert Henry and Lydia (Klumb) W.; m. Dorothy Louise Ahrensfeld, Oct. 28, 1944; children— Robert, William, James. BA, Lawrence Coll., 1943; MBA, Stanford U., 1948; PhD, Ohio State U., 1955. Staff accountant S.C. Johnson & Son, Inc., Racine, Wis., 1948-50; asst. prof. Sacramento State Coll., 1950-51; prof. U. Minn., Mpls., 1953-86, prof. emeritus, 1987—, chmn. dept. bus. adminstrn., 1959-62, dir. grad. studies, 1963-66, chmn. dept. mgmt. and transp., 1971-77. Author: Management Organization, 1966. Served with AUS, 1943-46, 51-52. Soc. Advancement Mgmt. fellow, 1972 Mem. Acad. Mgmt., Soc. Advancement Mgmt. (pres. Twin Cities chpt. 1961-62). Congregationalist. Home: 4501 Roanoke Rd Minneapolis MN 55422-5268

WICKFIELD, ERIC NELSON, investment company executive; b. Bryn Mawr, Pa., Feb. 14, 1953; s. Paul Gilbert Jacobs and Patricia Ruth (Nelson) Davies; m. Kristine Margaret Erikson, June 21, 1974 (div. 1976); m. Sara Lou Datt, July 23, 1977 (div. 1990); 1 child, Eric N. Jr.; m. Leslie Walsh Willingham, June 8, 1990; 1 child, Douglas N. BS, Rochester Inst. Tech., NY, 1974; MBA, Boston U., 1990. Project mgr. Flight Safety Internat., Wichita, Kans., 1976-82; v.p. Aufleger-Garrett, Stillwater, Okla., 1982-86; demonstration pilot citation div. Gen. Dynamics, Wichita, 1986-87; pres. Prompt Fin. Inc., Concord, Mass., 1987—, bd. dirs.; adj. faculty Boston U. Grad. Sch. Mgmt., 1997—. Co-author: Sustaining High Performance, 1990; editor: 421 Pilot's Training Manual, 1981; author: Financial Users Network User's manual, 1997, Losing Situational awareness, 2001, Communicating the Loss of SA, 2004. Bd. dirs. Groton Ctr. for The Arts. Mem. Internat. Operator's Coun., Aircraft Owner's & Pilot's Assn., Aero Club New Eng. (bd. dirs.). Republican. Methodist. Avocation: skiing. Office: Prompt Fin Inc 30 Monument Sq Concord MA 01742-1858

WICKHAM, JOHN ADAMS, JR., retired army officer; b. Dobbs Ferry, NY, June 25, 1928; s. John Adams and Jean Gordon (Koch) W.; m. Ann Lindsley Prior, June 18, 1955; children: Lindsley, John Adams, Matthew. BS, U.S. Mil. Acad., 1950; MA, Harvard U., 1955, M.P.A., 1956; grad., Nat. War Coll., 1967. Commd. 2d lt. U.S. Army, 1950, advanced through grades to gen., 1979; asst. prof. social scis. U.S. Mil. Acad., 1956-60; bn. comdr. 1st Cavalry Div., Republic of Vietnam, 1967; brigade comdr., chief of staff 3d Inf. Div., Fed. Republic of Germany, 1969-70; army mem. chmn.'s staff group Office of Chmn. Joint Chiefs of Staff, Washington, 1970-71; dep. chief of staff for econ. affairs Mil. Assistance Command, Republic of Vietnam, 1971-73; dep. chief, negotiator U.S. del. Four Party Joint Mil. Commn., Republic of Vietnam, 1973; sr. mil. asst. to Sec. Def. Washington, 1973-76; comdr. 101st Airborne Div. (Air Assault), Ft. Campbell, Ky., 1976-78; dir. Joint Staff Orgn. Washington, 1978-79; comdr. in chief UN Command, Republic of Korea-U.S. Combined Forces Command, Korea, 1979-82; vice chief of staff U.S. Army, Washington, 1982-83, chief of staff, 1983-87, ret., 1987; pres., chief exec. officer Armed Forces Communications and Electronics Assn., Fairfax, Va., 1987-92. Bd. dirs. Cooper Inst. for Aerobic Rsch., Xsirius, Inc., Honeywell Fed. Sys., Advanced Photonics, Nortel Inc. Author: Korea on the Brink, 2000. Pres. Sun City Town Coun., 1996—99, Sun City Found., 2001—03; elder St. Andrews Presbyn. Ch., 2001—. Decorated D.S.M. (8), Silver Star (2), Legion of Merit (4), Bronze Star with V device, Air medal (11), Purple Heart, Legion of Honor (France), Order of Mil. Merit (Rep. of Korea), Royal Order of Polar Star (Sweden); recipient Disting. Grad. award West Point, 2005, Infanry Doughboy award, 2006. Mem. Assn. U.S. Army, 101st Airborne Assn., Retired Officers Assn. Home: 13500 N Rancho Vistoso Blvd No 519 Tucson AZ 85755-5801 Personal E-mail: j55wick@comcast.net.

WICKLEIN, JOHN FREDERICK, journalist, educator; b. Reading, Pa., July 20, 1924; s. Raymond Roland and Parmilla Catherine (Miller) W.; m. Myra Jane Winchester, July 31, 1948 (dec. 2002); children: Elizabeth, Peter, Joanna. LittB, Rutgers U., 1947; MS in Journalism, Columbia, 1948. Reporter Newark (N.J.) Evening News, 1947-51; news mng. editor Elec. World (McGraw-Hill weekly), NYC, 1951-54; reporter, editor N.Y. Times, 1954-62; news dir. Sta. WNET-TV, NYC, 1962-64; exec. producer news Sta. WABC-TV, NYC, 1964-67; exec. producer Washington Bur. chief Pub. Broadcast Lab. (Nat. Ednl. TV), 1967-70; mng. news and pub. affairs broadcasts Sta. WCBS-TV, NYC, 1970-71; gen. mgr. Sta. WRVR, NYC, 1971-74; prof. journalism and broadcasting Boston U., 1974-80; dean Sch. Public Communication Boston U., 1974-78; vis. prof. communication Meth. U., São Paulo, Brazil, 1979; program officer for news and pub. affairs programs Corp. for Pub. Broadcasting, 1980-84; Willard M. Kiplinger chair in pub. affairs reporting, dir. Kiplinger mid-career program for journalists Ohio State U., 1984-89, mem. adv. bd. Kiplinger program, 2004—; Fulbright rsch. scholar Charles Sturt Univ., Bathurst, NSW, Australia, 1990. Lectr., cons. Rutgers U. Media Resources Ctr., Cracow, Poland, 1992, 94; Ayers vis. prof. journalism Jacksonville (Ala.) State U., 1992-93; prodr. news documentaries for pub. and comml. TV; ind. writing, reporting and editing coach for newspapers including Washington Post, Buffalo News, Memphis Comml. Appeal, 1994—; coord. Working Group for Pub. Broadcasting, 1987-89; spl. com. on regulation of media ACLU, 1988-92; adj. faculty Poynter Inst. for Media Studies, 1988; adj. prof. journalism for rsch. Ohio State U., 1991-93; media ethics com. Nat. Coun. Chs., 1975-92; fellow Inst. Dem. Comm. Boston U., 1975-78; newsroom trainers group Poynter Inst., 1995—; lectr., cons. in field. Author: (with Monroe Price) Cable Television: A Guide for Citizen Action, 1972, Electronic Nightmare: The New Communications and Freedom, 1981; editor: Investigative Reporting: The Lessons of Watergate, 1975; contgb. editor The Washington Monthly, 1969-72; contbr. to Am. Journalism Review, The Progressive, TV Quar., Atlantic Monthly, Columbia Journalism Rev., Archeology, Quill, Australian Journalism Rev., others. Recipient George Polk award, 1963, documentary award, Venice Film Festival, 1968, DuPont award, 1973, Brechner Freedom Info. prize, 1987. Mem.: ACLU, Soc. Profl. Journalists, Amnesty Internat. USA, Phi Beta Kappa. Democrat. Home and Office: 7 Riverwoods Dr C116 Exeter NH 03833 Office Phone: 603-772-4032. Personal E-mail: jfwicklein@comcast.net.

WICKLUND, DAVID WAYNE, lawyer; b. St. Paul, Aug. 7, 1949; s. Wayne Glenwood and Elna Katherine (Buresh) W.; m. Susan Marie Bubenko, Nov. 17, 1973; children: David Jr., Kurt, Edward. BA cum laude, Williams Coll., 1971; JD cum laude, U. Toledo, 1974. Bar: Ohio 1974. Assoc. Shumaker, Loop & Kendrick, Toledo, 1974-80, ptnr., 1981—. Adj. instr. law, U. Toledo, 1988. Editor-in-chief U. Toledo Law Rev. 1973-74. Mem.: ABA, Toledo Bar Assn., Ohio State Bar Assn. (bd. govs. antitrust sect. 1994—2001), U. Toledo Coll. Law Alumni Assn. (pres. 1999—2000), Inverness Club. Office: Shumaker Loop & Kendrick N Courthouse Sq 1000 Jackson St Toledo OH 43624-1573 Office Phone: 419-321-1213. Business E-Mail: dwicklund@slk-law.com.

WICKLUND, LEE ARTHUR, retired school system administrator; b. Fort Atkinson, Wis., Aug. 10, 1938; s. Verner F. and Ellen V. (Anderson) W.; m. Georganne Emilie Trumbull, June 27, 1964; children: Eric Trumbull, Lance Frederick. BE, Chgo. Teachers Coll., 1961; MEd, Loyola U., Chgo., 1964; EdD, U. Oreg., Eugene, 1969. Cert. std. adminstr., supt., prin., Oreg. Elem., secondary tchr., asst. prin. Chgo. Bd. Edn., 1961—67; rsch. asst. Bur. Ednl. Rsch. and Svc., U. Oreg. Coll. Edn., 1967—69; dir. lab. sch., asst. prof. edn. Idaho State U. Grad. Faculty, Pocatello, 1969—71; R&D specialist NW Regional Edn. Lab., Portland, Oreg., 1971—72, supt. in residence, 1994—95; assoc. prof. ednl. adminstrn. U. Wis. Grad. Faculty, Superior, 1972—75; dir. curriculum and instrnl. svcs. North Bend Sch. Dist., Oreg., 1975—89; assoc. supt. Mercer Island Sch. Dist., Wash., 1989—92; supt., prin. Riverdale Sch. Dist., Portland, 1992—94; asst. supt. instrn. Racine Unified Sch. Dist., Wis., 1995—2003. Pres. Idaho ASCD, 1971; sr. fellow Inst. for Devel. of Edn. Activities, Kettering, Ohio, 1977-2000; chmn. Oreg. State Textbook Commn., Salem, 1981-87; mem. instrnl edn. com. Am. Assn. Sch. Adminstrs., 1985-88, chmn. internat. edn. com., 1990-93; rep. alumni bd. Alumni Soc. Coll. Edn. U. Oreg., 1987-88, 1994-95; past chair Inter-Luth. Commn. for Continuing Edn., Tacoma, 1982-89; adj. prof. U. Oreg. Coll. Edn., 1984-88; alumni pres. coll. edn., U. Oreg., 1986-87, 1993-94; adj. instr. U. Wash. Coll. Edn., 1991. Chmn. budget com. North Bay Rural Fire Dist., North Bend, 1984-89; mem. adv. com. South Slough Natural Estuarine Res., Coos Bay, Oreg., 1984-89; sec. exec. com. United Way of S.W. Oreg., Coos Bay, 1978-83; mem. exec. com. Music Enrichment Assn., Coos Bay, 1977-81; trustee Lake Oswego (Oreg.) Libr. Bd., 1993-95; bd. dirs. Slingerland Inst., vice chmn., Bellevue, Washington, 1989-94; bd. dirs., U.S. dir.-at-large alumni bd. U. Oreg., 1998-2004; exec. com., area dir., planning com. mem. Palisades Neighborhood Assn., Lake Oswego, Oreg., 2004-07; v.p., treas. Greentree Swimming Pool Assn., Lake Oswego, 2004-; mem. budget com. Lake Oswego Sch. Dist., 2004-, mem. reconfiguration com., respectful culture com., 2005-. Staff sgt. Hdqs. Ill. Air NG, 1956—65. Recipient Honor Recognition Svc. award, Oreg. State Bd. Edn., 1988, Svc. award, Oreg. Supt. Pub. Instrn., 1988, Presdl. citation, Nat. Assn. Equal Opportunity in Higher Edn., 1998; rsch. asst., U. Oreg., 1967—69. Fellow, Paul Harris; mem. ASCD, Am. Ednl. Rsch. Assn., Am. Assn. Sch. Adminstrs., U. Oreg. Alumni Assn. (charter, life), Arnold Bennett Hall Soc. Pres. Assoc. Oreg., Club of Portland, Lake Oswego Rotary, Phil Delta Kappa. Lutheran. Achievements include co-author of over $3 million of funded proposals. Avocations: travel, boating, reading. Home: 16860 Lakeridge Dr Lake Oswego OR 97034-6819 Home Phone: 503-636-1985.

WICKMAN, JOHN EDWARD, librarian, historian; b. Villa Park, Ill., May 24, 1929; s. John Edward and Elsie (Voss) W.; m. Shirley Jean Swanson, Mar. 17, 1951; children— Lisa Annette, Eric John. AB, Elmhurst Coll., Ill., 1953; A.M., Ind. U., 1958, PhD, 1964; LLD, Lincoln Coll., Ill., 1973. Instr. history Hanover Coll., Ind., 1959-62, Southeast Campus, Ind. U., Jeffersonville, 1962; asst. prof. history Northwest Mo. State Coll., Maryville, 1962-64; asst. to Gov. William H. Avery of Kans., Topeka, 1964-65; asst. prof. history Regional Campus, Purdue U., Fort Wayne, Ind., 1965-66; dir. Dwight D. Eisenhower Libr., Abilene, Kans., 1966-89; ret., 1989. Contbr. articles on Am. West, archival mgmt., adminstrv. history, oral history to profl. publs. Served with US Army, 1953-55. Nat. Ctr. for Edn. in Politics faculty fellow, 1964-65; Am. Polit. Sci. Assn. Congl. fellow, 1975-76 Mem. Oral History Assn. (v.p. 1971-72, pres. 1972-73), Western History Assn. (coun. 1972-75), Kans. Hist. Soc. (2d v.p. 1974-75, pres. 1976-77, dir.). Home: 411 W 4th St PO Box 325 Enterprise KS 67441-0325

WICKMAN, LANCE B., lawyer; b. Seattle, Nov. 11, 1940; s. Alton C. and Irene Marilyn (Carlson) Wickman; m. Patricia Farr; 5 children. AB, U. Calif., Berkeley, 1964; JD, Stanford U., 1972. Bar: Calif. 1972. With Latham & Watkins, San Diego; gen. counsel Church of Latter-Day Saints. Capt. USAR, 1964—69. Mem.: San Diego Bar Assn. Mailing: c/o Church of Latter-Day Saints 10 E S Temple St Salt Lake City UT 84133

WICKMAN, LESLIE, research scientist, science administrator; b. Wash. d. Walter and Joan Wickman. BA, Willamette U., 1980; MS, Stanford U., 1983, PhD, 1994. Cert. tchr. Calif., 1998. Faculty mem., dir. Ctr. Rsch. in Sci. Azusa Pacific U., Calif., 1999—; rsch. scientist The RAND Corp., Santa Monica, Calif., 1999—; mem. faculty AuSable Inst., Grand Rapids, Mich., 2004—; campus pastor Parkcrest Christian Ch., Long Beach, Calif., 2005—. Cons. Wickman Enterprises, Long Beach, Calif., 1997—; Celebration of Roses guest spkr. Azusa Pacific U., 2003; NSF guest lectr. Whitworth Coll., 2003. Primary author (tech. paper) Lunar Life Support System Study: Metabolic Energy and Water Considerations, Load-Carrying in Reduced Gravities-Operational Considerations, Locomotion while Load-Carrying in Reduced Gravities; author: (tech. paper) Zero-Gravity Induced Osteoporosis, The Effects of Automation on Work in Space, Hubble Space Telescope - Dawn of the Era of Serviceable Spacecraft, Space-Based Servicing, (science article) Mars: Mission Possible?, (doctoral dissertation) The Influence of Reduced Gravity on Human Load-Carrying and Preferred Load Placement; co-author: (book) Absorbing Air Force Fighter Pilots: Parameters, Problems, and Policy Options, (tech. report) Crew Volume Estimating, (rsch. report) Comparing Animal and Robot Capabilities for Military Missions; prodr.: (exhbn.) Space Technology Transfer to Earth Health and Medical Applications; singer: (Christian music CD) Prepare the Way. Volleyball player CBVA, FIVB, Athletes in Action, 1982—2006; football player Calif. Quake Women's Football Team, Long Beach, 2001—06; adv. com. Acad. Evang. Scientists and Ethicists, Madison, Wis., 2005—; rev. panel mem. Jet Propulsion Lab Mars Sci. Lander; vis. faculty mem. Internat. Space U., Strausburg, France. Nominee Tech. Adv. Com. US Sec. of Def., Aerospace Industry, 1990; recipient award, AAUW, 1980, Mark O. Hatfield prize in polit. sci., Willamette U., 1980, Space Sta. Program commendations, Lockheed Missiles and Space Co., 1986, Commendations space sta. EVA simulations, McDonnell Douglas Corp., 1986, Lockheed Corp. Astronaut tng. and designation, Lockheed Missiles and Space Co., 1986—96, Commendations Hubble Space Telescope Program, NASA and Lockheed, 1990, Disting. Alumni award, Willamette U., 2000, Transformational Scholarship Champion award, Azusa Pacific U. Provost's Office, 2004; Stanford Honors Coop. Grad. Program scholarship, SRI Internat. and Lockheed, 1981—83, 1988—90, Rsch. grant, NASA and Stanford U., 1990—94, Tchg. Learning Tech. Roundtable grant, Azusa Pacific U., 2001, Rsch. grant, Christian Scholars Found., 2003—06, Azusa Pacific U. Faculty Rsch. Coun., 2004—05, inducted into, Seaside H.S. Hall of Fame, 2003. Mem.: AIAA, Azusa Pacific U. Faculty Rsch. Coun., Human Factors and Ergonomics Soc., Soc. Automotive Engrs. (Arch T. Colwell Merit award 1997), Aerospace Med. Assn. (Presentation award 1995), Cornerstone Soc., Stanford U. Alumni Assn., Sigma Rho Phi. Achievements include Willamette University Pentathlon All-Time Record Holder; member Women's Football World Bowl Championship Team member and Conference All-Star. Avocations: football, volleyball, surfing, skiing, music. Home Phone: 310-403-3282.

WICKNER, SUE HENGREN, biochemist; BS, American U., 1967; MS, Georgetown U., 1970; PhD, Albert Einstein Coll. Med., 1973. Rsch. chemist lab molecular biology Nat. Cancer Inst., NIH, 1977—94, chief molecular biology, lab. molecular biology, 1994—. Recipient Merit award, NIH, 1995; Postdoctoral Rsch. fellow, 1974—76, Staff fellow, 1976—77. Mem.: Nat. Acad. Scis. Office: Nat Cancer Inst NIH Lab Molecular Biology Bldg 37 Rm 2D19 37 Convent Dr MSC 4255 Bethesda MD 20892-4255

WICKRAMASINGHE, HEMANTHA KUMAR, electrical engineer, physicist; b. Colombo, Sri Lanka, May 31, 1949; naturalized U.S. citizen, 1996; s. Percival Herbert and Therese Elizabeth (Soysa) W.; m. Sophie Marie de La Porte, Nov. 17, 1973; children: Lucille Samantha, Anita Elizabeth. BSc in Electronic Engring., U. London, 1970, PhD in Electronic and Elec. Engring., 1974. Assoc. rsch. asst. dept. electronic and elec. engring. U. Coll. London, 1974-75, lectr. dept. electronic and elec. engring., 1978-83; rsch. assoc. E.L. Ginzton Lab. Stanford (Calif.) U., 1975-78; from mgr. phys. measurements T.J. Watson Rsch. Ctr. to fellow IBM, Yorktown Heights, NY, 1984—2000, fellow T.J. Watson Rsch. Ctr., 2000—, sr. mgr. nanoscale and quantum studies Almaden Rsch. Ctr. San Jose, Calif., 2002—03, sr. mgr. nanoscale sci. and tech., 2003—05, chief tech. officer sci. and tech., 2005—07; Henry Samueli endowed chair, dept. elec. engring. and comuter sci. U. Calif., Irvine, 2007—. Cons. Hirst Rsch. Ctr. GE Co., London, 1980-83, U.K. Atomic Energy Authority, Harwell, Eng., 1980-82; adj. prof. Poly. Inst. N.Y., Bklyn., 1985-87; mem. editl. bds. Nanotech., 1991-96, Advances in Nanoscale Physics, electonics and Engring., 1991—, Rev. of Sci. Instruments, 1996—; prof. Editor: Scanned Probe Microscopy, 1992; co-editor: Determining Nanoscale Properties of Materials by Microscopy and Spectroscopy, 1994; contbr. over 150 articles to profl. jours.; holder numerous patents in field. Recipient V.K. Zworykin premium, Inst. Elec. Engrs., 1983, Disting. Corp. Inventor award, Nat. Inventors Hall of Fame, 1998, Morris E. Leeds award, IEEE, 1992, Joseph F. Keithley award, Am. Phys. Soc., 2000; Emeritus fellow, IBM, 2007—. Fellow: IBM, Royal Microscopical Soc., Inst. of Physics, IEEE, Am. Phys. Soc. (centennial spkr. 1999); mem.: Nat. Acad. Engring. Achievements include first introduction of vibrating mode atomic force microscopes, atomic force microscopes into manufacturing lines, first deployment of a magnetic force microscope capable of imaging nanometer scale magnetic properties, work in areas of optics, acoustics, photoacoustics, metrology and scanning probe microscopy. Office: Univ Calif Henry Samueli Sch Engring Dept Elec Engring and Computer Sci 616F Engring Tower Irvine CA 92697

WICKS, DAVID O., JR., communications executive; b. Boston, May 17, 1941; s. David O. and Elizabeth L. Wicks; m. Joan Gagnebin, Sept. 7, 1963; children: Perrin, Sara. BA, Trinity Coll., Hartford, Conn., 1963; MBA, U. Va., 1968. With nat. divsn. Chem. Bank, 1963—66; specialist in venture capital and cable TV Warburg Paribas Becker, NYC, 1968—83, mng. dir., 1979—83; gen. ptnr. Becker Venture Assoc., Becker Comms. Assoc. II; sr. ptnr. Criterion Venture Ptnr., Houston, 1983—88. Mng. dir. Criterion Investments, Inc., 1983-88; pres. Criterion Investments, Inc., 1985-88; v.p. Cablevision Sys. Corp., Bethpage, NY, 1996-2002; pres. Devonshire Comms. Assocs., cons., 2002-; ptnr. The Alwyn Group, LLC, 2002—; exec. NASA Mid Continent Tech. Transfer Ctr., 1992-95; adj. prof. Columbia U., N.Y.C., 2004—; mem. NY Mayor's Broadband Com., 2007—; expert witness on cable TV, US Congress and state regulatory bodies. Contbr. articles to profl. jour. Chmn. Cable Positive, Inc., 2003—05; elected pioneer CATV, 2000; bd. dirs. Vis. Nurse Assn. NY, Union Chapel Shelter Island, Friends of Cath. Univ. in Chile. Recipient Vanguard award Nat. Cable TV Assn., 1978. Mem.: Shelter Island Yacht Club, Univ. Club. Office Phone: 516-695-2951. Personal E-mail: dwicksjr@aol.com.

WICKS, JOHN R., lawyer; b. Ottumwa, Iowa, Dec. 8, 1937; m. Nedra Morgan, Mar. 27, 1940; children: Catherine, John. BSC, U. Iowa, 1959, JD, 1964. Bar: Iowa 1964, Minn. 1966. Assoc. Dorsey & Whitney LLP, Mpls., 1966-71, ptnr. Rochester, Minn., 1972-2000, of counsel Mpls., 2001—. Fellow: Am. Coll. Trusts and Estates Counsel; mem.: Minn. State Bar Assn. (probate and trusts law coun. 1989—92). Office: Dorsey & Whitney LLP 50 S 6th St Minneapolis MN 55402-1498 Office Phone: 612-340-8898. E-mail: wicks.john@dorsey.com.

WICKS, WILLIAM WITHINGTON, retired public relations executive; b. Chgo., Dec. 20, 1923; s. William and Alice (Withington) W.; m. Frances M. Horner, Nov. 29, 1947; children: Barbara Anne, Christine Frances. BNS, U. Notre Dame, Ind., 1944, AB in Journalism magna cum laude, 1947. Staff corr. United Press Assn., Milw., 1947; pub. rels. mgr. Internat. Harvester Co., Louisville, 1948-58; mgr. field svcs. pub. rels. Std. Oil Co. (Ind.), Chgo., 1959—60; v.p. pub. rels. Griswold-Eshleman Co., Chgo., 1961-68; dir. pub. rels. G. D. Searle & Co., Chgo., 1968-74; from dir. pub. rels./investor rels. to v.p. Kimberly-Clark Corp., Neenah, Wis., 1974—89, v.p. Dallas, 1989-92, asst. to CEO, 1989—92, ret., 1992. Chmn. pub. relations sect. Pharm. Mfrs. Assn., Washington, 1974. Pres. Jr. Achievement Neenah-Menasha, 1978-81; bd. mem. Friends of the Irving Pub. Libr., 1997-99. Served to lt. (j.g.) USNR, 1942-46, PTO. Recipient Silver Anvil award Pub. Rels. Soc. Am., 1963, 79, J. Sinnott Meyers Burse for Journalism award, U. Notre Dame, 1946-47. Mem. PRSA (founder, pres. Bluegrass chpt. 1957-58), Optimist (pres. South End Club in Louisville 1957), Publicity Club of Chgo. (pres. 1967-68), Las Colinas Sports Club (Irving), USN Meml. Found. (plank owner), Navy League U.S., Patrol Craft Sailors Assn. Republican. Roman Catholic. Home: 1312 Travis Cir S Irving TX 75038-6243

WICKSTROM, ERIC, biophysical chemist, educator; b. Chgo., Dec. 21, 1946; s. Eric Lester and Lillian (Partnoy) W.; m. Lois June Sinsheimer, July 1, 1967; children: Erica Lorraine, Eileen Anitra. BS in Biology with honors, Calif. Inst. Tech., 1968; PhD in Chemistry, U. Calif., Berkeley, 1972. Research assoc. U. Colo., Boulder, 1973-74; asst. prof. U. Denver, 1974-81; sr. research scientist So. Biotech, Tampa, Fla., 1981-82; vis. assoc. prof. U. South Fla., Tampa, 1982-83, asst. prof., 1983-87, assoc. prof., 1987-91, prof., 1991-92, Thomas Jefferson U., Phila., 1992—. Mem. Inst. Biomolecular Sci., Tampa, 1984-92, Kimmel Cancer Ctr., 1992—; guest rschr. Nat. Cancer Inst., Bethesda, Md., 1986, Max Planck Inst. Molecular Genetics, Berlin, 1986; co-founder Panagenic, Smart Implant, Gene Seen. Editor: Prospects for Antisense Nucleic Acid Therapy for Cancer and AIDS, 1991, Clinical Trials of Genetic Therapy with Antisense DNA and DNA Vectors, 1998; mem. editl. bd. Biotech. Healthcare, Bioconj. Chem., Oligonucleotides. Grantee, NSF, 1976—81, Nat. Inst. Gen. Med. Sci., 1976—89, Leukemia Soc. Am., 1986—87, U.S. Army, 1986—88, Nat. Cancer Inst., 1987—, Am. Found. AIDS Rsch., 1989—90, Fla. High Tech. Indsl. Coun., 1988—91, Genta, Inc., 1989, Am. Cancer Soc., 1990—96, Dept. of Energy, 2000—06. Mem.: Oligonucleotide Therapeatics Soc., Internat. Soc. Nuclsds, Nucltds and Nucleic Acids, Am. Assn. Cancer Rsch., Am. Soc. Biochem and Molecular Biology, Am. Chem. Soc. Office: Thomas Jefferson U Dept Biochemistry/Molecular Biol 233 S 10th St Rm 219 Philadelphia PA 19107-5541

WICKSTROM, JON ALAN, telecommunications executive, consultant; b. San Antonio, Apr. 17, 1949; s. Stanley Alan and Louise W.; m. Mary Carmen Sparkman, Jan. 25, 1969 (div. Jan. 1978); children: Dana Marie, Jon Alan Jr.; m. Jane Bielbey Slawson, June 19, 1988. BS, Tex. Tech. U., 1975; MS, U. Tex., 1998. Ptnr. Hensley & Assocs., Albuquerque, 1976—78; mgr. dealer svcs. Gulf States Toyota, Houston, 1978—80; mgr. comms. Hughes Tool Co., Houston, 1980—85; mgr. network svcs. Tenneco Oil Co., Houston, 1986—89; mgr. comms. Clarke Am., San Antonio, 1989—94; info/tech. planner USAA, San Antonio, 1994—96; sr. mgr. MMC Ernst & Young LLP, San Antonio, 1996—2000, Cap Gemini Ernst & Young, 2000—02; prin. Comm. Tech. Cons., Houston, 1980—96, 2002—. Author: (reference) 1976 Population Estimates for Bernallio County, New Mex., 1976. Rep. precinct chmn. Bexar County, Tex., 1992-94; cons. Houston Symphony Orch., 1988. Mem. Alamo Area Telecomms. Assn. (bd. dirs 1990-94, pres., 1992-93), S.W. Comms. Assn. (bd. dirs. 1981-85, pres. 1982-84), Tex. Telecomms. Conf. (bd. dirs. 1982-84, chmn. 1983), Am. Mensa. Avocations: sailing, golf, music, investing.

WICKWIRE, PATRICIA JOANNE NELLOR, psychologist, educator; d. William McKinley and Clara Rose (Pautsch) Nellor; m. Robert James Wickwire, Sept. 7, 1957; 1 child, William James. BA cum laude, U. No. Iowa, Cedar Falls, 1951; MA, U. Iowa, Iowa City, 1959; PhD, U. Tex., Austin, 1971; postgrad., U. So. Calif., LA, UCLA, Calif. State U., Long Beach. Lic. ednl. psychologist, marriage and family therapist, Calif. Tchr. Ricketts Ind. Schs., Iowa, 1946-48; tchr., counselor Waverly-Shell Rock Ind. Schs., Iowa, 1951-55; reading cons., head dormitory counselor U. Iowa, Iowa City, 1955-57; tchr., sch. psychologist, adminstr. S. Bay Union H.S. Dist., Redondo Beach, Calif., 1962-82, dir. student svcs. and spl. edn. Cons. mgmt. and edn.; pres. Nellor Wickwire Group, 1981—; mem. exec. bd. Calif. Interagy. Mental Health Coun., 1968-72, Beach Cities Symphony Assn., 1970-82; chmn. Friends of Dominguez Hills, Calif., 1981-85. Contbr. articles in field to profl. jours. Pres. Calif. Women's Caucus, 1993-95, 2003-06. Mem. APA, AAUW (exec. bd., chpt. pres. 1962-72), Nat. Career Devel. Assn. (media chair 1992-98), Am. Assn. Career Edn. (pres. 1991—), LA County Dirs. Pupil Svcs. (chmn. 1974-79), LA County

Pers. and Guidance Assn. (pres. 1977-78), Assn. Calif. Sch. Adminstrs. (dir. 1977-81), LA County SW Bd. Dist. Adminstrs. for Spl. Edn. (chmn. 1976-81), Calif. Assn. Sch. Psychologists (bd. dirs. 1981-83), Am. Assn. Sch. Adminstrs., Calif. Assn. for Measurement and Evaluation in Guidance (dir. 1981, pres. 1984-85, 98-2000, 04-05), ACA (chmn. Coun. Newsletter Editors 1989-91, mem. com. on women 1989-92, mem. com. on rsch. and knowledge 1994-97, chmn. 1995-97, mem. and chmn. bylaws com. 1998-2001, rep. to joint com. on testing practices 2001—), Assn. Measurement and Eval. in Guidance (Western regional editor 1985-87, conv. chair 1986, editor 1987-90, exec. bd. dirs. 1987-91), Calif. Assn. Counseling and Devel. (exec. bd. 1984—, pres. 1988-89, jour. editor 1990-2002), Nat. Assn. for Ind.-Edn. Coop. (bd. dirs. 2002-05), Internat. Career Assn. Network (chair 1985—), Pi Lambda Theta, Alpha Phi Gamma, Psi Chi, Kappa Delta Pi, Sigma Alpha Iota, Phi Delta Kappa. Office: The Nellor Wickwire Group 2900 Amby Pl Hermosa Beach CA 90254-2216 Office Phone: 310-376-7378.

WIDDEL, JOHN EARL, JR., lawyer; b. Minot, ND, Nov. 17, 1936; s. John Earl Sr. and Angela Victoria W.; m. Yvonne J. Haugen, Dec. 21, 1973; children: John P., James M., Susan N., Andrea K. PhB, U. ND, 1966, BSBA, 1966, JD, 1971. Bar: ND 1971, US Dist. Ct. ND, 1971, US Ct. Appeals (8th cir.) 1989, Minn. 2004. Ptnr. Thorsen & Widdel, Grand Forks, ND, 1971-97; shareholder Law Offices ND, PC. Mcpl. judge City of Grand Forks, 1972—; ct. magistrate Grand Forks County, 1975. Mem. N.D. Foster Parent Program, 1974-87, Nat. Conf. of Bar Pres.; mem. bd. dirs. YMCA, Grand Forks, 1982; dist. chmn. Boy Scouts Am., 1987-88; corp. mem. ALTRU Hosp. With U.S. Army, 1960-62. Mem.: ND Mcpl. Judges Assn. (dir. 1993—), Nat. Assn. Estate Planning Coun. (accredited estate planner 1994—), Grand Forks Jaycees, Grand Forks Hist. Soc. (pres. 1983), Grand Forks Cemetery Assn. (bd. dirs. 1984—96, pres. 1989—94), NE Ctrl. Jud. Dist. (pres. 1983), Greater Grand Forks County Bar Assn. (pres. 1982), State Bar Assn. ND (bd. govs. 1983—88, pres. 1986—87), Minn. State Bar Assn., Antique Automobile Club Am. (pres. ND region 1977—78, 1983—84, nat. bd. dirs. 1984—2000, v.p. 1985—89, sec.-treas. 1989), Sertoma Grand Forks (bd. dirs. 1994—99, pres. 1997—98, ND dist. gov. 2001—05, Sertoma Internat.), Am. Legion (comdr. ND Post 201 2006—07), Masons (Kem Temple Potentate 1995), Elks (exalted ruler 1985—86). Office: Law Offices North Dakota PC PO Box 5624 Grand Forks ND 58206-5624 Home: 215A S 4th St Grand Forks ND 58201 Office Phone: 701-746-7485.

WIDDER, EDITH ANNE, biologist; b. Boston, June 11, 1951; d. David Vernon and Vera Adela (Ames) Widder; m. David Charles Smith, Feb. 9, 1972. BS magna cum laude in Biology, Tufts U., Medford, Mass., 1973; MS in Biochemistry, U. Calif., Santa Barbara, 1977, PhD in Neurobiology, 1982. Cert. sci. rsch. pilot for atmospheric diving sys. submersibles 1984. Lab. asst. phycology U. Mass. Field Sta. Environ. Scis., 1968—69; rsch. assoc. NIH Resource Lab. Electron Probe Microanalysis Harvard U. Med. Sch., Boston, 1973-75; assoc. rschr. ONR bioluminescence prog. U. Calif., Santa Barbara, 1977-83, postdoctoral rsch. biologist, 1983-85, asst. rsch. biologist, co-prin. investigator Marine Sci. Inst. and Neuroscience Rsch. Inst., 1985-89; asst. scientist, prin. investigator Harbor Br. Oceanog. Instn., Ft. Pierce, Fla., 1989-91, assoc. scientist, prin. investigator, 1991—93, acting divsn. dir., 1993—94, sr. scientist, prin. investigator, 1993—2005; prof. biol. scis. Fla. Inst. Tech., 1991—; pres., sr. scientist Ocean Rsch. & Conservation Assn., 2005—. Sci. cons. Dynamics Tech., Inc., LA, 1987—89; disting. scientist adj. Monterey Bay Aquarium Rsch. Inst., 1998—; adj. rsch. prof. earth and planetary scis. dept. Johns Hopkins U., 2000—; affiliate prof. dept. biol. sci. Fla. Atlantic U., 2000—; adj. sr. rsch. scientist Bigelow Lab. Ocean Scis., 2005—. Contbr. articles to profl. jours.; mem. editl. bd.: Marine Tech. Soc. Named Earle C. Anthony fellow, 1978; recipient Women of Discovery award, Sea, Wings WorldQuest, 2006; grantee, NSF, 1986—88, 1990—91, 1991—, MacArthur Fellow, John D. and Catherine T. MacArthur Found., 2006. Mem. AAAS, Am. Soc. Limnology and Oceanography, Am. Soc. Zoologists, Soc. Neuroscience, Soc. Photo-Optical and Instrumentation Engrs., Internat. Soc. Bioluminescence and Chemiluminescence (councilor), Am. Acad. Underwater Scis., Explorers Club. Achievements include patents in field; first to make video recordings of bioluminescence in the ocean, 1985. Office: Ocean Rsch & Conservation Assn 1420 Seaway Dr Fort Pierce FL 34949 Office Phone: 772-467-1600. Business E-Mail: ewidder@oceanrecon.org.

WIDDER, KENNETH JON, pathologist, educator; b. Chgo., Jan. 14, 1953; s. Alan A. and Edith Widder. BS, Carleton Coll., 1974; MD, Northwestern U., Evanston, Ill., 1979. Intern Duke U., Durham, N.C., 1979-80, resident in pathology, 1980-81; asst. clin. prof. pathology U. Calif., San Diego, 1981-84, assoc. clin. prof., 1984—; chmn., chief exec. officer Molecular Biosystems, Inc., San Diego, 1981—. Cons. Eli Lilly & Co., Indpls., 1978-83; mem. adv. com. Congl. Sci. and Tech. Com., Washington, 1986-88. Editor: Methods in Enzymology: Drug and Enzyme Targeting, 1985; patentee in field. Recipient Wiley J. Forbus award N.C. Sco. Pathology, 1981. Mem. AAAS, Am. Soc. Clin. Pathologists, Young Pres. Orgn., Sigma Xi. Office: Santarus Inc 10590 W Ocean Air Dr Ste 200 San Diego CA 92130

WIDDICOMBE, RICHARD PALMER, librarian; b. Paterson, NJ, Apr. 12, 1941; s. Robert Lord and Elvira Barbara (Guttilla) W.; m. Martha Elizabeth Bruyn, Feb. 26, 1972 BA, Alfred U., 1963; MS L.S., Syracuse U., 1964. Asst. librarian Yonkers Pub. Library, NY, 1964-65; asst. librarian Cooper Union, NYC, 1965-66, Stevens Inst., Hoboken, NJ, 1966-72, dir. library, 1973—2006; curator Frederick Winslow Taylor Collection, 2007—. Trustee Alfred U., NY, The Sagamore Inst., 2006—; trustee, chmn. bd. Hoboken Hist. Mus., 2002—. Episcopalian. Office: SC Williams Libr Stevens Inst Hoboken NJ 07030 Home: 1711 Sherman Dr Utica NY 13501-5839 Home Phone: 315-749-8528; Office Phone: 201-216-5421. Business E-Mail: richard.widdicombe@gmail.com.

WIDEMAN, IDA DEVLIN, science educator; d. John Cole and Lillie Alma Devlin; m. Leroy Wideman, May 12, 1945; children: Michael Andre, Leroy Maurice. BS, SC State U., 1964—68; MAT, U. of SC, 1976—77. Sci. tchr. West Side H.S., Newark, 1971—73, Hopkins Jr. H.S., Hopkins, SC, 1976—83, St. Andrews Mid. Sch., Columbia, SC, 1983—. Co-dir. NSF grant Ctr. for Sci. Edn., U. S.C.; master tchr. sci. U. S.C., Columbia, Aiken; presenter in field. Mem. Nat. Assn. of U. Women, Columbia, SC, 1990. Named Tchr. of Yr., St. Andrews Middle Sch., state winner, Presdl. Awards for Excellence in Math. and Sci. Tchg. Mem.: Richland County Edn. Assn., SC Edn. Assn., NEA, SC Earth Sci. Teachers Assn. (past pres., v.p. 1988—90), SC Sci. Coun., NSTA, Delta Sigma Theta Sorority (life). United Methodist. Avocations: walking, reading. Home: 446 Koon Store Rd Columbia SC 29203 Office: St Andrews Middle Sch 1231 Bluefield Rd Columbia SC 29210 Home Phone: 803-735-0963; Office Phone: 803-731-8910. Office Fax: 803-731-8913; Home Fax: 803-333-0542. Personal E-mail: lwideman@sc.rr.com. E-mail: iwideman@richlandone.org.

WIDEMAN, JOHN EDGAR, English literature educator, novelist; b. Washington, June 14, 1941; married; 3 children. BA, U. Pa., 1963; BPhil, Oxford U., Eng., 1966; postgrad., U. Iowa Writers Workshop, 1967; DLitt (hon.), U. Pa., 1985, Rutgers U. Mem. faculty U. Wyo., Laramie, prof. English, 1974—85, U. Mass., Amherst, Mass., 1986—2001, disting. prof. English, 2001—; prof. dept. African studies Brown U, Providence. USIS lectr. in Ea. Europe. Author: A Glance Away, 1967, Hurry Home, 1969, The Lynchers, 1973, Hiding Place, 1981, Damballah, 1981, Sent for You Yesterday, 1983 (PEN Faulkner award for fiction, 84), Brothers and Keepers, 1984, Reuben, 1987, Fever, 1989, Philadelphia Fire, 1990 (PEN Faulkner award for fiction, 91), The Homewood Books, 1992, The Stories of John Edgar Wideman, 1992, All Stories Are True, 1993, Fatheralong, 1994, The Cattle Killing, 1996, Two Cities, 1998, Hoop Roots, 2001, God's Gym, 2005; co-author (with Mumia Abu-Jamal): Live from Death Row, 1995; author: (short stories) Weight, 2000 (O. Henry award, 2000); contbr. numerous articles and revs. to profl. jours., mags. Recipient Lannan award, 1991; fellow Kent fellow, MacArthur fellow, 1993; grantee, Nat. Endowment for Humanities; scholar Ben Franklin scholar, Rhodes scholar. Mem.: MLA, Am. Acad. Arts Scis., Am. Studies Assn. (mem. coun. 1980—81), Am. Assn. Rhodes Scholars (dir.). Office: Brown U Dept African Studies Providence RI 02912

WIDENER, CHARLENE, theater director, educator; d. Richard Widener and Helen Chism; m. Patrick Reading, Oct. 30, 1993. AA, Hutchinson C.C., Kans.; BSc, M, Kans. State U., Manhattan; PhD, U. Mo., Columbia. Dir. theatre Hutchinson C.C., Kans., 2002—. Dir.: (theatrical prodn.) Death of A Salesman, Macbeth, How I Learned to Drive, A Moon for the Misbegotten. Bd. mem. Hutchinson Theatre Guild, 2004—. Recipient Horizon award, Phi Theta Kappa, 2004, Paragon Advisor award, 2005. Mem.: NEA (membership chairperson 2003—06), Hutchinson C.C. Faculty Senate (pres. 2006—). Office: Hutchinson Community Coll 1300 N Plum Hutchinson KS 67501 Office Phone: 620-665-3544.

WIDENER, HIRAM EMORY, JR., judge; b. Abingdon, Va., Apr. 30, 1923; s. Hiram Emory and Nita Douglas (Peck) Widener; children: Molly Berentd, Hiram Emory III. Student, Va. Poly. Inst., 1940—41; BS, U.S. Naval Acad., 1944; LLB, Washington and Lee U., 1953, LLD, 1977. Bar: Va. 1951. Pvt. practice, Bristol, Va., 1953—69; judge US Dist. Ct. (we. dist.) Va., Abingdon, 1969—71, chief judge, 1971—72; judge US Ct. Appeals (4th cir.), Abingdon, 1972—2007, sr. judge, 2007—. US commr. Western Dist. Va., 1963—66; mem. Va. Election Laws Study Commn., 1968—69. Chmn. Rep. 9th Dist., Va., 1966—69; state exec. com. Va. Rep. State Ctrl. Com., 1966—69. Lt. (j.g.) USN, 1944—49, lt. USNR, 1951—52. Decorated Bronze Star with combat V. Mem.: Va. State Bar, Va. Bar Assn., Am. Law Inst., Phi Alpha Delta. Republican. Presbyterian. *

WIDENER, MARY LEE, non-profit financial executive; b. Schaal, Alaska, July 6, 1938; d. Mert and Johnnie (Newton) Thomas; children: Warren Jr., Michael, Stephen. Diploma, Heald Bus. Coll., 1956; Pub. Adminstrn. Program, U. San Francisco Sch. Profl. Studies, 1978; LLD (hon.), John F. Kennedy U., 1979. Adminstrv. asst. to exec. v.p. U. Calif., Berkeley, 1959-69, office mgr. gifts and endowments, 1959-69; urban program coord. Fed. Home Loan Bank Bd., Washington, 1972-73; housing cons. Ford Found., NYC, 1973-74; exec. dir. Oakland Neighborhood Housing Svcs., Oakland, 1973-76; program cons. Urban Reinvestment Task Force, Washington, 1974-76; pres., CEO Neighborhood Housing Svcs. of Am., Inc., Oakland, 1974—. Chmn., Fed. Home Loan Bank, San Francisco, 1994-2003, Social Compact, 2004-06; bd. dirs. The PMI Group, S.H. Cowell Found., The First Am. Corp.; bd. trustees Nat. Housing Conf., 2000—. Author: (with others) Housing America, 1993. Trustee, San Francisco Found., 1988-98, chair, 1996-98; trustee Ptnrs. for Livable Cmtys.; adv. bd. PEW Charitable Trusts Partnership for Civic Change, Phila.; former dir. KQED, San Francisco, United Way Bay Area, Univ. YWCA, BRIDGE Housing Corp., John F. Kennedy U., program adv. coun. Inst. Nonprofit Orgn. Mgmt., U. San Francisco; former state chair Calif. Dem. Ctrl. Com., San Francisco; former mem. U.S. Senate Housing Task Force, Washington, Commn. on Homelessness, Oakland; former chair affordable housing adv. coun. Fed. Home Loan Bank, San Francisco; former mem. Fannie Mae's Adv. Coun.; former participant Internat. Exch. Housing Profls. Recipient award Nat. Coalition of 100 Black Women, N.Y., 1989, San Francisco LWV Women who could be Pres. award, 1996; named Housing Person of Yr., Nat. Housing Conf., Washington, 2000. Democratic. Methodist. Avocations: tennis, travel, golf. Office: Neighborhood Housing Svc Am 1970 Broadway Fl 4 Oakland CA 94612-2212 Office Phone: 510-287-4201.

WIDERA, GEORG ERNST OTTO, mechanical engineering educator, consultant; b. Dortmund, Germany, Feb. 16, 1938; arrived in U.S., 1950; s. Otto and Gertrude (Yzermann) Widera; m. Kristel Kornas, June 21, 1974; children: Erika, Nicholas. BS, U. Wis., 1960, MS, 1962, PhD, 1965. Asst. prof. then prof. dept. materials engring. U. Ill., Chgo., 1965-82, prof. mech. engring., 1982-91, head dept., 1983-91, acting head indsl. sys. engring. dept., 1985-86, dir off-campus engring. programs, 1987-88; prof., chmn. mech. and indsl. engring. dept. Marquette U., Milw., 1991—2002, co-dir. Ctr. Joining and Mfg. Assembly, 2002—, dir. Discovery Learning Ctr., 2000—07, sr. assoc. dean Coll. Engring., 1999—2007, interim dean Coll. Engring., 1998—99, 2003. Gastdozent U. Stuttgart, Germany, 1968; vis. prof. U. Wis.-Milw., 1973—74, Marquette U., Milw., 1979—80; cons. Ladish Co., Cudahy, Wis., 1967—76, Howmedica, Inc., Chgo., 1972—75, Sargent & Lundy, 1970—88, Nat. Bur. Stds., 1980; bd. dirs. Engrs. and Scientists Milw., 1996—98; vis. scientist Argonne Nat. Lab., Ill., 1968. Editor: Procs. Innovations in Structural Engring., 1974, Pressure Vessel Design, 1982, Jour. Pressure Vessel Tech., 1982—93, 2005—; co-editor: SME Handbook of Metalforming, 1985, 1994, Design and Analysis of Plates and Shells, 1986; assoc. editor: Pressure Vessel Tech., 1977—81, 2003—05, Applied Mechanics Revs., 1987—94, Mfg. Rev., 1991—95, mem. editl. adv. bd.: Acta Mechanica Sinica, 1990—98, mem. editl. bd.: Pressure Vessels and Piping Design Technology, 1982. Fellow Std. Oil Co. Calif., 1961—63, NASA, 1966, von Humboldt, Fed. Republic Germany, 1968—69. Fellow: WRC (chmn. subcom. design procedures for shell intersections 1983—87, chmn. com. reinforced openings and external loads 1987—91, vice chmn. com. polymer pressure components 1991—99, chmn. com. shells and ligaments 1994—97, pressure vessel rsch. coun.), ASCE (sec.-treas. structural divsn. Ill. sect. 1972—73, chmn. divsn. 1976—77, chmn. peer rev. com., tech. coun. rsch. 1984, coun. structural plastics), ASME (chmn. machine design div. Chgo. sect. 1967—68, exec. com. Chgo. sect. 1970—73, editor newsletter Chgo. sect. 1971—73, chmn. jr. awards com. applied mechanics divsn. 1973—76, chmn. design and analysis com. pressure vessel and piping divsn. 1980—83, chmn. pressure vessel rsch. com. 1982—87, bd. editors 1983—93, mem. exec. com. and program chmn. pressure vessel and piping divsn. 1985—89, vice-chmn., sec. pressure vessel and piping divsn. 1989—90, mem. bd. pressure tech. codes and stds. 1989—94, chmn. 1990—91, mem. materials and structures group 1990—91, historian, senate pressure vessel and piping divsn. 1992—93, honors and awards chmn. Milw. sect. 1992—95, mem. coun. engring. 1992—96, v.p., chair materials and structures group 1993—96, mem. tech. execs. com. 1993—96, bd. editors 2005—, Pressure Vessel and Piping medalist 1995), Wis. Mfg. Curriculum Com. (vice-chmn. exec. com. 1998—2002), 2d China Nat. Stds. Com. Pressure Vessels (hon. cons. 1989—94), Internat. Coun. Pressure Vessel Tech. (chmn. Am. regional com. 1988—, internat. chmn. 1992—96, 2003—06), Am. Soc. Engring. Edn., Soc. Mfg. Engrs. (sr.), French Pressure Vessel Assn.; mem.: Wis. Assn. Rsch. Mgmt. (v.p. 2003—04, pres. 2004—05), Tau Beta Pi. Achievements include research in mechanics of composite materials, plate and shell structures, stress analysis, pressure vessels, mechanics of deformation processing. Office: Marquette U Coll Engring PO Box 1881 Milwaukee WI 53201-1881 Home Phone: 262-789-8387; Office Phone: 414-288-4427. Business E-Mail: jpvt@marquette.edu.

WIDING, ERIC P., auction specialist; BA in Art History, Williams Coll. Head, american paintings dept. Christie's, NYC, sr. v.p. Contbr. articles to art jours. Mem.: Phi Beta Kappa. Office: Christie's NY 20 Rockefeller Plz New York NY 10020 Home Phone: 724-238-7784; Office Phone: 212-636-2140. Office Fax: 212-636-4924. Business E-Mail: ewiding@christies.com.

WIDLUND, OLOF BERTIL, computer science educator, mathematician; b. Stockholm, Feb. 11, 1938; s. Sten O. and Dagmar W.; m. Nadine H. Taub, June 13, 1972. MS in Engring., Royal Inst. Tech., Stockholm, 1960, PhD, 1964; habilitation, Uppsala U., Sweden, 1966. Asst. prof. NYU, NYC, 1968-72, assoc. prof., 1972-75, prof. computer sci., 1975—, chmn. dept. computer sci., 1980-86. Contbr. articles to profl. jours. and a rsch. monograph. Achievements include research in numerical solutions of partial differential equations. Office: NYU Courant Inst 251 Mercer St New York NY 10012-1110 Business E-Mail: widlund@cims.nyu.edu.

WIDMAN, GARY LEE, lawyer; b. Fremont, Nebr., June 1, 1936; s. Benjamin H. and Alice C. (Negley) W.; m. Mary Margaret Donnelly, Mar. 5, 1972(div. 1988); children: Andrew Scott, Natalie Claire. BS, U. Nebr., 1957; JD, Hastings Coll. Law U. Calif., 1962; LLM, U. Mich., 1966. Bar: Calif. 1962, D.C. 1982. Assoc. Thelen, Marrin, Johnson & Bridges, San Francisco, 1962-65; assoc. prof. law U. Denver, 1966-69; prof., dir. resource and environ. law program Hastings Coll. Law, U. Calif., San Francisco, 1969-80; gen. counsel Coun. Environ. Quality, Exec. Office Pres., Washington, 1974-76; lectr. U. Calif. at Davis, 1978, Boalt Hall, 1977-79; assoc. solicitor Dept. Interior, Washington, 1980-81; of counsel Fulbright & Jaworski, 1981-85; dir. staff attys. U.S. Ct. of Appeals (9th cir.), San Francisco, 1985-87; atty. Bronson, Bronson & McKinnon, San Francisco, 1988-95; chief counsel State Dept. Parks and Recreation, Sacramento, 1995-96; prof. law Santa Clara (Calif.) U. Law Sch., 1998-99; sr. mediator Concur Inc., Berkeley, Calif., 2001—04. Trustee Rocky Mountain Mineral Law Found., 1969-74, 77-80; apptd. by gov. P. Wilson to Bay-Delta Oversight Coun., 1993-95. Author and project dir.: Legal Study of Oil Shale on Public Lands, 1969. Bd. dir. Sustainable Bus. Inst., Achenbach Graphic Arts Coun., Fine Arts Mus. San Francisco, 2004—. Served with U.S. Army, 1957-59. Mem. ABA (coun. sect. natural resources 1975-77, spl. com. energy law 1977-82, coun. lawyers and scientists 1984-90), Fed. Bar Assn. (chmn. com. natural resources 1977), Calif. Bar Assn., Trout Unltd. Calif. (pres. 1986-90), Calif. Heritage Coun. (pres. 2004-06), Presidio Hist. Assn (v.p 2004-06, pres. 2006—, bd. chair 2006—). Home: 28 Marinero Cir Apt 31 Tiburon CA 94920-1644 Office Phone: 415-435-0360. Personal E-mail: gwidman@mindspring.com.

WIDNALL, SHEILA EVANS, aeronautical educator, former secretary of air force, university official; b. Tacoma, July 13, 1938; d. Rolland John and Genievieve Alice (Krause) Evans; m. William Soule Widnall, June 11, 1960; children: William, Ann. BS in Aero. and Astronautics, MIT, 1960, MS in Aero. and Astronautics, 1961, DSc, 1964; PhD (hon.), New Eng. Coll., 1975, Lawrence U., 1987, Cedar Crest Coll., 1988, Smith Coll., 1990, Mt. Holyoke Coll., 1991, Ill. Inst. Tech., 1991, Columbia U., 1994, Simmons Coll., 1994, Suffolk U., 1994, Princeton U., 1994. Asst. prof. aeros. and astronautics MIT, Cambridge, 1964-70, assoc. prof., 1970-74, prof., 1974-93, head divsn. fluid mechanics, 1975-79; dir. Fluid Dynamics Rsch. Lab., MIT, Cambridge, 1979-90; chmn. faculty MIT, Cambridge, 1979-80, chair com. on acad. responsibility, 1991-92, assoc. provost, 1992-93; sec. USAF, 1993-97; Inst. prof. MIT, Cambridge, 1997—. Bd. dirs. Gen. Corp., Chemfab Inc., Bennington, Vt., Aerospace Corp., L.A., Draper Labs., Cambridge, Gencorp; past trustee Carnegie Corp., 1984-92, Charles Stark Draper Lab. Inc.; mem. Carnegie Commn. Sci., Tech. and Govt, mem. Columbia Accident Investigation Bd, 2003-. Co-author: Lean Enterprise Value: Insights from MIT's Lean Aerospace Initiative, 2002 (Engrng. Sci. Book award Internat. Acad. Astronautics 2003); contbr. articles to profl. jours.; patentee in field; assoc. editor AIAA Jour. Aircraft, 1972-75, Physics of Fluids, 1981-88, Jour. Applied Mechanics, 1983-87; mem. editorial bd. Sci., 1984-86. Bd. visitors USAF Acad., Colorado Springs, Colo., 1978-84, bd. chair, 1980-82; trustee Boston Mus. Sci., 1989-93, Sloan Found., 1998-. Named to Nat. Women's Hall of Fame, 2003; recipient Washburn award, Boston Mus. Sci., 1987. Fellow AAAS (bd. dirs. 1982-89, pres. 1987-88, chmn. 1988-89), AIAA (bd. dirs. 1975-77, Lawrence Sperry award 1972, Durand Lectureship for Pub. Svc. award 1996, pres. 2000-01), Am. Phys. Soc. (exec. com. 1979-82); mem. ASME (Applied Mechs. award 1995, Pres. award 1999), NAE (coun. 1992-93, v.p. 1998—), NAS (panel on sci. responsibility), Am. Acad. Arts and Scis., Soc. Women Engrs. (Outstanding Achievement award 1975), Internat. Acad. Astronautics, Seattle Mountaineers. Office: MIT Bldg 33-411 77 Massachussetts Ave Cambridge MA 02139 Office Phone: 617-253-3595. E-mail: sheila@mit.edu.

WIDNER, RALPH RANDOLPH, retired public administrator; b. Phila., Oct. 21, 1930; s. Ralph Litteer and Viola (Cunningham) W.; m. Joan Sundelius Ziegler, July 9, 1955; children: Jennifer Anne, Wendy Widner Ducharme. BA, Duke U., 1952; postgrad., NYU, 1957, Georgetown U., 1958; DHL (hon.), Union Coll., Ky., 1970, Capital U., Columbus, Ohio, 1971. Journalist Paterson (N.J.) Evening News, 1955-56, N.Y. Times, 1956-58; Congressional fellow Am. Polit. Sci. Assn., 1958; dir. pub. affairs Pa. Dept. Forests and Waters, 1959-60; asst. dir. Pa. Planning Bd., 1960-62; legis. asst. to U.S. Senator Clark, 1962-65; exec. dir. Appalachian Regional Commn., 1965-71; pres. Acad. for contemporary problems, 1971-82; adj. prof. pub. adminstrn. and city planning Ohio State U., 1971-82; pres. Nat. Tng. and Devel. Service for State and Local Govt., 1979-81; staff v.p. Urban Land Inst., 1982-83; exec. dir. Greater Phila. First Corp., 1983-88; chmn. emeritus Fairfax House Internat. Author: Forests and Forestry in the American States, Regional Development in the United States; co-author: Revitalizing the Industrial City. Bd. dir. Am. Forestry Assn., Landscape Architecture Found., Am. Soc. Public Administrn., Nature Conservancy, Va., Northeast-Midwest Inst. Lt. jr. grade USN, 1952—55. Rsch. fellow, Urban Land Inst., 1975. Fellow Nat. Acad. Pub. Adminstrn. (sr.). Democrat. Office Phone: 609-924-9184. Personal E-mail: rwidner@patmedia.net.

WIDNER, ROBERTA ANN, accountant, artist; b. El Paso, Tex., Sept. 27, 1940; d. Wilburn Alton and Frances (Martin) Leavelle; m. Jerry Wesley Widner, Jan. 21, 1959; children: Kim, Mark. Attended, Fechin Inst., 1986. Civil svc. Fed. Govt., 1958, cert. state merit system State of N.Mex, 1958. Stenographer Employment Security Commn. Legal Dept., Albuquerque, 1958, Cannon AFB Comdr.'s Office, Clovis, 1958; sec. to pres. Walker Wholesale Hardware, Jacksonville, 1959; stenographer Household Fin. Corp., San Diego, 1960—61; temp. clk. U.S. Post Office, Clovis, 1974; sec./acctg. Coop. Ext. Svc./Dir. - 4-H - NMSU Rodeo Dept., Las Cruces, 1977—. Sec. N.Mex Employment Security Commn., Albuquerque, 1958; state triticale sec. N.Mex Triticale Assn., Clovis; profl. improvement com. Coop. Ext. Svc., Las Cruces, 1983—84. Oils, pastels, watercolors. Planning com. fashion fund raisers Am. Cancer Soc., Las Cruces, 1991—92; planning com. ann. renaissance fair Dona Ana Arts Coun., Las Cruces, 1985—85; planning com. nat. maid of cotton fashion show Cotton Inc., Las Cruces. Recipient Pres.'s Star Performer award, NMSU, 2002. Mem.: Border Book Festival, Dona Arts Coun., Mesilla Valley Arts Guild (treas. 1985). Achievements include juried Exhibit - El Paso Museum of Art, 1987; juried - Internat. Penwomens' Mex./U.S. Exhibit; juried Art - Cinco Pintores - Linda Lundeen Gallery/Las Cruces; juried - Southern New Mexico Arts Profls., 1999; juried - Rio Grande Arts Invitational, 1998. Avocations: painting, Mexican/European travel, ballooning, sewing, waterskiing. Home Phone: 505-522-0391. Business E-Mail: rwidner@nmsu.edu.

WIDOM, BENJAMIN, chemistry professor; b. Newark, Oct. 13, 1927; s. Morris and Rebecca (Hertz) W.; m. Joanne McCurdy, Dec. 21, 1953; children: Jonathan, Michael, Elisabeth. AB, Columbia U., NYC, 1949; PhD, Cornell U., Ithaca, NY, 1953; DSc (hon.), U. Chgo., 1991; Dr. honoris causa, U. Utrecht, 1999. Rsch. assoc. U. N.C., Chapel Hill, 1952-54; instr. chemistry Cornell U., Ithaca, NY, 1954-55, asst. prof., 1955-59, assoc. prof., 1959-63, prof., 1963-83, Goldwin Smith prof., 1983—2007, prof. emeritus, 2007—; van der Waals prof. U. Amsterdam, Netherlands, 1972;

vis. prof. Harvard U., Cambridge, Mass., 1975; IBM vis. prof. Oxford U., England, 1978. Lorentz prof. U. Leiden, The Netherlands, 1985; vis. prof. Kath. U. Leuven, Belgium, 1988, U. Aix Marseille, France, 1995; Kramers/Debye prof. U. Utrecht, 1999. Co-author: (with J.S. Rowlinson) Molecular Theory of Capillarity, 1982; author: Statistical Mechanics, 2002. With US Army, 1946-47. Recipient Clark disting. tchg. award Cornell U., 1973, Dickson prize for sci. Carnegie-Mellon U., 1986, Hirschfelder Prize in Theoretical Chemistry U. Wis., 1991, Bakhuis Roozeboom medal Royal Netherlands Acad. Arts & Scis., 1994, Onsager medal U. Trondheim, Norway, 1994, Boltzmann medal Internat. Union of Pure and Applied Physics, Commn. on Statis. Physics, 1998. Fellow Am. Phys. Soc., Am. Acad. Arts and Scis., NY Acad. Scis. (Boris Pregel award for chem. physics rsch. 1976); mem. NAS, Am. Philos. Soc., Am. Chem. Soc. (Langmuir award in chem. physics 1982, Hildebrand award in theoretical and exptl. chemistry of liquids 1992, Theoretical Chemistry award 1999). Home: 204 The Parkway Ithaca NY 14850-2247 Office: Cornell U Chemistry Dept Ithaca NY 14853 Office Phone: 607-255-3363. Business E-Mail: bw24@cornell.edu.

WIDOM, HAROLD, mathematician, educator; b. Newark, Sept. 23, 1932; s. Morris and Rebecca (Hertz) W.; m. Lois Sanow, Mar. 20, 1955 (div. Sept. 1976); children: Barbara, Jennifer, Steven; m. Linda Novick, May 26, 1985. Attended, CUNY, 1951; MS, U. Chgo., 1952, PhD, 1955. From instr. to prof. Cornell U., Ithaca, NY, 1955-68; with U. Calif., Santa Cruz, 1968—, prof. emeritus. Author: (book) Lectures on Measure and Integration, 1969, Lectures on Integral Equations, 1969; assoc. editor Jour. Integral Equations Operator Theory, Asymptotic Analysis, Mathematical Physics, Analysis and Geometry; hon. editor Integral Equations and Operator Theory; contbr. over 130 articles to profl. jours. NSF postdoctoral fellow, 1959-60, Alfred P. Sloan Found. fellow, 1964-65, J.S. Guggenheim Found. fellow, 1967-68, 72-73; NSF grantee, 1970—; co-recipient with Craig Tracy, George Polya prize, Soc. Indsl. and Applied Math., 2002 Fellow: Am. Acad. Arts and Sciences; mem.: Am. Math. Soc. (and the Soc. for Indsl. and Applied Math., Norbert Wiener prize in Applied Math. with Craig Tracy 2007). Office: Professor Emeritus Math Dept 133B Kerr Hall 353B Baskin Engineering Santa Cruz CA 95064 Office Phone: 831-459-2652. Office Fax: 831-459-3260. E-mail: widom@math.ucsc.edu.

WIDOM, JENNIFER, computer science and electrical engineering educator; m. Alex Aiken; children: Tim, Emily. BA, Ind. U., 1982; PhD in Computer Sci., Cornell U., 1987. Rsch. staff mem. IBM Almaden Rsch. Ctr.; joined faculty Stanford U., 1993, prof. computer sci. and elec. engrng. Contbr. articles to profl. jours. Guggenheim Fellow. Fellow: ACM; mem.: NAE. Office: Dept Computer Sci Gates Bldg 4A Stanford U Stanford CA 94305-9040 Office Phone: 650-723-6790. Office Fax: 650-725-2588. E-mail: widom@cs.stanford.edu.

WIDOM, JONATHAN, biology professor; b. Ithaca, NY, Oct. 25, 1955; BA in Chemistry, Cornell U., 1973—77; PhD in Biochemistry, Stanford U. Sch. Medicine, 1977—82. Rsch. collaborator biology dept. Brookhaven Nat. Lab., 1982—83; Jane Coffin Childs Meml. Fund postdoctoral fellowship Med. Rsch. Coun. Lab. Molecular Biology, Cambridge, England, 1983—85; asst. prof. dept. chemistry U. Ill. Urbana-Champaign, 1985—91, asst. prof. biochemistry, 1985—91, asst. prof. Beckman Inst. Advanced Sci. and Tech., 1989—91, asst. prof. biophysics, 1989—91; assoc. prof. dept. biochemistry, molecular biology and cell biology Northwestern U., 1991—98, assoc. prof. dept. chemistry, 1991—98, prof., 1998—, Cook prof. biochemistry, molecular biology and cell biology, 2001—. Dir. NIH Molecular Biophysics Tng. Prog., 1992—98; dir. Ctr. Structural Biology Northwestern U., 1994—2000, chmn. dept. biochemistry, molecular biology and cell biology, 1998—2004; vis. prof. Rockefeller U., 2003—04. Contbr. articles to profl. jours.; mem. editl. bd.: Current Opinion in Microbiol., 1998—2001, Gene, 1999—. Recipient Presdl. Young Investigator award, 1988—93. Office: Dept Biochemistry Molecular Biology and Cell Biology Northwestern U 2153 Sheridan Rd Evanston IL 60208-3500 E-mail: j-widom@northwestern.edu.

WIDRAN, JERROLD JOSEPH, urologist; b. Chgo., Dec. 1, 1926; s. Louis Widran and Bess Lanoff; m. Lita June Soible, June 12, 1951; children: Susan, Deborah, Sanford. MD, U. Ill., Chgo., 1950. Diplomate Am. Bd. Urology. Surg. urologist, Ill. Pres. surg. staff Skokie Valley Hosp., 1983—85; pres. Grant Hosp., 1985—88; v.p. staff Our Lady of Resurrection, 2000—01. Contbr. articles to profl. jours. With USN, 1943—46. Fellow: ACS; mem.: Am. Urol. Assn., Chgo. Urol. Soc., Ill. Urol. Soc. Achievements include patents in field. Avocations: tennis, golf, bridge. Home: 939 Mesa Grande Dr Palm Desert CA 92211 Fax: 760-345-5167. Personal E-mail: widran12@verizon.net.

WIDYOLAR, SHEILA GAYLE, dermatologist; b. Vancouver, BC, Can., June 11, 1939; d. Walter Herbert and Olive Louise (O'Neal) Roberts; Kithi K. Widyolar, 1960 (div. 1979); 1 child, Keith. BS, Loma Linda U., 1962; MD, Howard U., 1972. Resident U. Calif., Irvine, 1973-76; dermatologist pvt. practice, Laguna Hills, Calif., 1976—. Clin. instr. U. Calif. Sch. Medicine, 1978—86. Chmn. bd. dirs. Opera Pacific, Costa Mesa, Calif., 1996-97. Fellow Am. Acad. Dermatology, Am. Soc. Dermatopathology; mem. AMA, Calif. Med. Assn., Dermatol. Soc. Orange County (pres. 1983), Alpha Omega Alpha. Avocations: music, travel. Office: Ste 403 23911 Calle de Mag Dalena Laguna Hills CA 92653 Office Phone: 949-452-3814.

WIE, MICHELLE SUNG, professional golfer; b. Honolulu, Oct. 11, 1989; d. Byung-Wook and Hyun-Kyong Sung Wie. Played in major LPGA Tournaments US Women's Open, 2003, Kraft Nabisco Championship, 2003, 2004; winner Jennie K. Wilson Invitational, 2001, Hawaii State Women's Stroke Play Championship, 2001, USGA Women's Amateur Pub. Links Championship, 2003; profl. golfer, 2005—. Named one of 100 Most Influential People, Time Mag., 2006. Mem.: Hawaii State Jr. Golf Assn. Achievements include youngest player to win Hawaii State Women's Stroke Play Championship, Jennie K. Wilson Internat., and US Amateur Pub. Links Championship; youngest player to make an LPGA cut, playing in the Kraft Nabisco Championship; youngest player to ever compete and win the Curtis Cup, 2004. Avocations: reading, drawing, computers. Office: c/o LPGA 100 Internat Golf Dr Daytona Beach FL 32124-1092

WIEBE, RICHARD HERBERT, reproductive endocrinologist, educator; b. Herbert, Sask., Can., Dec. 28, 1937; came to U.S., 1971; s. Herbert and Olga Maragratha (Jahnke) W.; m. Jacquelyn Dee Yancy, Aug. 30, 1975; 1 child, Richard Herbert, Jr. MD, U. Sask., 1962. Resident Queen's Univ., Kingston, Ont., Canada, 1970; asst. to assoc. prof. Duke U., Durham, NC, 1972-81; assoc. prof. to prof. U. So. Ala., Mobile, 1981-88; chmn. and prof. Dept. Ob-Gyn. U. S.D., Sioux Falls, 1988-95; chmn., prof. dept. ob-gyn. East Tenn. State U., Johnson City, 1996-98. Editorial cons., Fertility/Sterility, Birmingham, Ala., 1978—; sec., Univ. Physicians, Sioux Falls, 1991-93. Contbr. numerous articles to profl. jours. Recipient, Rsch. Grant, NIH, Ala., 1981-89, Edn./Svc. Grant, USPHS, S.D., 1989-95. Mem. ACOG, Assn. Profs. of Ob-Gyn., Am. Soc. Primatologists, Soc. for Gynecol. Investigation, Soc. for Study of Reproduction, Am. Soc. Reproductive Medicine, Endocrine Soc. Home: 316 Settler Ln Kure Beach NC 28449-4835 E-mail: rhwiebe@bellsouth.net.

WIEBENSON, DORA LOUISE, architectural historian, editor, writer; b. Cleve., July 29, 1926; d. Edward Ralph and Jeannette (Rodier) W. BA, Vassar Coll., 1946; MArch, Harvard U., 1951; MA, NYU, 1958, PhD, 1964. Architect, N.Y., 1951-66; lectr. Columbia U., 1966-68; assoc. prof. U. Md., 1968-72, prof., 1972-77; vis. prof. Cornell U., 1974; prof. U. Va., Charlottesville, 1977-92, prof. emeritus, 1992—, chmn. div. archtl. history, 1977-79, assoc. fellow U. Va. Ctr. Advanced Studies, 1982-83; pres. Archtl. Publs., NYC, 1982—; editor-in-chief Centropa, 2000—. Editor: Marsyas XI: 1962-64, 1965, Essays in Honor of Walter Friedlaender, 1965; Architectural Theory and Practice from Alberti to Ledoux, 1982, rev., 1983, Spanish transl., 1988; Guide to Graduate Degree Programs in Architectural History, 1982, rev., 1984, 86, 88, 90; co-editor: The Architecture of Historic Hungary, 1998, Hungarian transl., 1998; author: Sources of Greek Revival Architecture, 1969, Tony Garnier: The Cité Industrielle, 1969, Japanese transl., 1983, The Picturesque Garden in France, 1978, Mark J. Millard Architectural Collection, Vol. I: French Books: Sixteenth through Nineteenth Centuries, 1993; contbr. articles to profl. jours. Student fellow Inst. Fine Arts, 1961-62, 62-63; grantee Am. Philos. Soc., 1964-65, 70, Samuel H. Kress Found., 1966, 72-73, 98, Gen. Rsch. Fund, U. Md., 1969, 74, 76, NEH, 1972-73, Am. Coun. Learned Socs., 1976, 81, 85, Ctr. Advanced Studies, U. Va., 1980, 81, 97, Graham Found. Advanced Studies Fine Arts, 1982, 93, Archtl. History Found., 1996; fellow Yale Ctr. Brit. Art, 1983; sr. rsch. fellow NEH, 1986-87. Mem. Soc. Archtl. Historians (bd. dirs. 1974-77, 80-83, chair edn. com. 1976-90), Coll. Art Assn., Am. Assn. Advancement Slavic Studies, Am. Soc. Eighteenth Century (mem. exec. bd. 1991-94). Business E-Mail: centropa@rcn.com.

WIEBERS, DAVID OWEN, physician; b. Mar. 26, 1951; MD, U. Nebr., 1975. Diplomate Am. Bd. Psychiatry and Neurology. Intern in medicine U. Minn., Mpls., 1975-76; resident in neurology Mayo Clinic, Rochester, Minn., 1976-80, chair divsn. cerebrovasc. diseases, 1994—2002, head sect. neurology, 1987-96, dir. Mayo Stroke Ctr., 1994—; prof. neurology Mayo Med. Sch., Rochester, Minn., 1991—. Vis. prof. more than 77 acad. med. ctrs. Author: 7 books, 5 med. textbooks; co-author: 1 med. textbook; contbr. more than 340 articles to profl. jours. Chair, bd. dirs. Humane Soc. U.S., Washington, 1999—, Human Soc. Internat. (bd. dirs. 1994—), Earth Voice Internat. (bd. dirs. 1995-2005). Recipient 19 internat. and 51 U.S. awards for sci. and med. achievement. Mem.: Doris Day Animal League (bd. dirs. 2005—), Fund for Animals (bd. dirs. 2005—), Humane Soc. Legis. Fund (chair bd. dirs. 2005—06), World Soc. Protection of Animals (bd. dirs. 1997—, London). Office: Mayo Clinic Dept Neurology 200 1st St SW Rochester MN 55905-0002 Office Phone: 507-284-9735. Business E-Mail: wiebers.david@mayo.edu.

WIECHA, JOSEPH AUGUSTINE, language educator; b. Chorzów II, Poland, Sept. 20, 1926; came to U.S., 1955, naturalized, 1958; s. Karol and Gertruda (Rudzki) W.; m. Mary Ruth Moore, 1953; children: Joseph Damian, Charles Francis, John Moore. BA with first class honors, Nat. U. Ireland, 1950; PhD with distinction, NYU, 1963. Instr. fgn. langs. U.S. Third Air Force, London, 1951-55; instr. German and Spanish U. Md., London, 1951-55; tchr. Spanish and math. Bklyn. Friends Sch., 1955-56; instr. German NYU, NYC, summer, 1958; lectr. German and humanities Harvard U., Boston, 1959-63; lectr. German lit. Colby Coll., summer 1963; prof. German SUNY, Oswego, 1963-69, chmn. dept. fgn. langs. and lit., 1963-69, chmn. dept. Germanic and Slavic langs. and lit., 1969-72, disting. teaching prof., 1973-92, disting. tchg. prof. emeritus, 1992—; chmn. SUNY Fgn. Studies Ctr., 1972-73. Lectr. and cons. methodology of tchg. fgn. langs., 1959—; condr. seminars tchg. methodology fgn. langs. Nat. U. Pedro Enriquez Ureña, Santo Domingo, 1973, U. Pisa, Italy, 1974, Moscow State Pedagogical Inst.; Fgn. Langs., USSR, 1976; vis. prof. U. Wroctaw, Poland, 1977. Served as officer 2d Polish Corps Brit. VIII Army, 1944-47. Decorated Bronze medal Polish Army, Brit. Def. medal; French Star; Star of Italy; recipient diploma of spl. recognition U. Nat. Pedro Enriquez Ureña, 1973; Galileo medal U. Pisa, 1974; Ogden Butler fellow, 1958-59, Fels fellow, 1956-59, Kosciuszko Found. fellow, 1959. Mem. MLA, N.Y. State Assn. Fgn. Lang. Tchrs. (dir. 1975-78, Disting. Tchr. award 1975, Disting. Bd. Dirs. award 1978, Spl. Contbn. to Teaching Fgn. Langs. award 1979), Am. Assn. Tchrs. of German, Polish Inst. Arts and Scis. in Am., Nat. Spanish Honors Soc. (hon.), Am. Coun. on Edn. (nat. honor roll), Delta Phi Alpha (hon.), Dobro Slovo (hon.) Achievements include development of Wiecha Progressive-Reflex method of teaching fgn. langs. Home: 710 Copa De Oro Marathon FL 33050-5406 also: 45 Tall Oaks Dr Northport ME 04849-4435 Personal E-mail: joemarywiecha@bellsouth.net.

WIECHERT, ALLEN LEROY, educational association administrator; b. Independence, Kans., Oct. 25, 1938; s. Norman Henry and Serena Johanna (Steinke) W.; m. Sandra Swanson, Aug. 19, 1961; children: Kristin Nan, Brendan Swanson, Megan Ann. BArch, Kans. State U., 1962. Lic. Lic. arch., Kans., cert. Nat. Coun. Archtl. Registration Bds. Arch. in tng. McVey, Peddie, Schmidt & Allen, Wichita, Kans., 1962-63; arch. Kivett & Myers, Kansas City, Mo., 1963-68; asst. to vice chancellor plant planning and devel. U. Kans., Lawrence, 1968-74, assoc. dir. facilities planning, 1974-78, univ. dir. facilities planning, 1978-92, univ. arch., 1993-95; campus planner Gould Evans Assocs., Lawrence, 1995-96; code enforcement officer City of Prairie Village, Kans., 1997-2001; ret.; project mgr. subs. corp. Kans. Bd. Regents, 2003—04; architect Kans. State Hist. Preservation Office, 2004—05; long range phys. planning cons., 2005—; audience svcs. coord. Lied Performing Arts Ctr., 2006—. Mem. long range phys. planning com. Kans. Bd. Regents, 1971-95; designer, archtl. programmer ednl. facilities; bd. dirs. Kans. U. Fed. Credit Union, 1972-81, pres. bd., 1974. Editor, contbr.: Physical Development Planning Work Book, 1973. Chmn. horizons com. Lawrence Bicentennial Commn.; designer Kaw River Trail, 1976; mem. Action 80 Com., 1980-81, Lawrence-Douglas County Horizon 2020 Task Group, 1993-95; mem. standing com. Kans. Episcopal Diocese, 1976-80, pres. com., 1981, mem. diocesan coun., 1982-84, chmn. coll. work com., 1982-84, commn. on ch. arch. and allied arts, 1986-99, long range planning com., 1988; sr. warden Trinity Episc. Ch., Lawrence, 1978-80, 2001-02, mem. vestry, 1997-99; trustee Kans. Sch. Religion, 1973-80, 82-95, v.p., 1984-85, pres., 1986-92, trustee friends of the dept. of religious studies, 1995-2005; mem. adv. bd. Salvation Army, 1990-2005; bd. dirs. Trinity Group Care Home, 1973-79; advancement chmn. troop com. Boy Scouts Am., 1981-87, dist. com. Pelathe dist., 1984—, vice chmn., 1984, chmn., 1985-87; exec. bd. Heart of Am. Coun., 1985-87; bd. dirs. Lawrence Habitat for Humanity, 2006—07; appointed mem. Lawrence Hist. Resources Commn., 2007-. 1st lt. Kans. Air NG, 1961—67. Recipient Dist. Award of Merit, Boy Scouts Am., 1988, Silver Beaver award, 1991, Follow Me Boys award, 2002. Mem. AIA, Assn. Univ. Archs. (sec.-treas. 1986-87, v.p. 1987-88, pres. 1988-89), Nat. Hist. Trust, Kans. U. Endowment Assn. (sec. 1981-85, founder, exec. bd. Hist. Mt. Oread Fund divsn.), Nat. Cathedral Assn. (regional co-chairperson 1993-2005). Home: 813 Highland Dr Lawrence KS 66044-2431

WIECHMANN, ERIC WATT, lawyer; b. Schenectady, NY, June 12, 1948; s. Richard Jerdone and Ann (Watt) W.; m. Merrill Metzger, May 22, 1971. BA, Hamilton Coll., Clinton, NY, 1970; JD, Cornell U., Ithaca, NY, 1974. Bar: Conn. 1974, US Dist. Ct. (so. and ea. dists.) NY 1975, US Dist. Ct. Conn. 1975, US Dist. Ct. D.C. 1981, US Ct. Appeals (2nd cir.) 1975, US Ct. Appeals (9th cir.) 1980, US Ct. Appeals DC 1982, US Ct. Appeals (5th cir.) 1986, US Ct. Appeals (10th cir.) 1989, US Supreme Ct. 1978. Assoc. Cummings & Lockwood LLC, Stamford, Conn., 1974—82, ptnr., 1982—2003, mng. ptnr. Hartford office, bd. dirs., 1996—2003, bus. clients exec. com., 2003; ptnr. McCarter & English LLP, Hartford, Conn., 2003—, mng. ptnr., Hartford office, 2003—04, mem. exec. com., 2003—, mem. compensation com., 2004—, firm mng. ptnr., 2007—. Spl. pretrial master US Dist. Ct. Conn., 1984—; state atty. trial referee, 1986—, mem. evidence code oversight com., 2002—; civil task force, 1995—, civil jury instrn. com. Conn. Superior Ct., 1996-2000, docket control com., 2001—; comml. arbitrator Am. Arbitration Assn. Contbr. articles to profl. jours. Mem. Zoning Bd. Appeals, New Canaan, Conn., 1984-85; bd. dirs. Conn. Rivers coun. Boy Scouts Am., trustee; bd. dirs. Internat. Assn. Def. Counsel Found., pres., 2005—. Mem. ABA (vice-chmn. toxics and hazardous law com. TIPS sect.), Def. Rsch. Inst., Internat. Assn. Def. Counsel (faculty Def. Trial Acad. 1996, chmn. toxic and hazardous substance com. 1998-99, chmn. CLE bd. 2000-02, bd. dirs. 2006-), Internat. Soc. Barristers, Conn. Bar Assn. (life fellow; exec. com. antitrust sect. 1982—, ct. rules adv. com, chmn. 1991-93), Conn. Bar Found. Republican. Episcopalian. Home: 10 Langley Park Farmington CT 06032-1541 Office Phone: 860-275-6731. Personal E-mail: ewiech@yahoo.com. Business E-Mail: ewiechmann@mccarter.com.

WIECZOREK, DENNIS E., lawyer; b. June 4, 1952; AB magna cum laude, Washington Univ., St. Louis, 1974; JD, Duke Univ., 1977. Bar: Ill. 1977, US Dist. Ct. (no. dist.) Ill. Ptnr., co-chair Franchise & Distribution practice group DLA Piper Rudnick Gray Cary, Chgo. Lectr.; contbr. articles to profl. jours.; co-author: Annual Franchise & Distribution Law Delelopments, 2002, Franchising: A Planning & Sales Compliance Guide; author (contributing): Fundamentals of Franchising. Mem.: ABA, Chgo. Bar Assn., Ill. Bar Assn. Office: DLA Piper Rudnick Gray Cary Ste 1900 203 N LaSalle St Chicago IL 60601-1293 Office Phone: 312-368-4087. Office Fax: 312-236-7516. Business E-Mail: dennis.wieczorek@dlapiper.com.

WIECZOREK, JOHN RICHARD, application developer, systems analyst; b. River Falls, Wis., Mar. 8, 1963; s. John Richard Vichorek and Sara Ellen Wieczorek; life ptnr. Eileen Anne Lacey. AB in Physics, Cornell U., 1984. Programmer, analyst Mus. of Vertebrate Zoology, U. Calif., Berkeley, 1997—. Mem. sci. subcom. data access and database interoperability Global Biodiversity Info. Facility, Copenhagen, 2004—; co-convenor of geospatial interest group Taxonomic Databases Working Group, 2004—. Co-developer (distributed database protocol) Distributed Generic Information Retrieval. Recipient Ebbe Nielsen prize, Global Biodiversity Info. Facility, 2006. Avocations: volleyball, travel. Office: U Calif Mus Vertebrate Zoology 3101 VLSB Berkeley CA 94720 Office Phone: 510-642-5409. Office Fax: 510-643-8238. Business E-Mail: tuco@berkeley.edu.

WIED, GEORGE LUDWIG, physician; b. Carlsbad, Czechoslovakia, Feb. 7, 1921; came to U.S., 1953, naturalized, 1960; s. Ernst George and Anna (Travnicek) W.; m. Kayoko Y. Yamauchi, 1980; 1 child, George. MD, Charles U., Prague, 1945, Hon. Med. Degree, 1995. Intern County Hosp., Carlsbad, Czechoslovakia, 1945; intern U. Chgo. Hosps., 1955; resident in ob-gyn U. Munich, Fed. Republic Germany, 1946-48; practice medicine specializing in ob-gyn West Berlin, 1948-53; asst. ob-gyn Free U., West Berlin, 1948-52; assoc. chmn. dept. ob-gyn Moabit Hosp., Free U., West Berlin, 1953; asst. prof., dir. cytology U. Chgo., 1954-59, assoc. prof., 1959-65, prof., 1965-91, mem. bd. adult edn., 1964-68, prof. pathology, 1967-91, Blum-Riese prof. ob-gyn, 1968-91, acting chmn. dept. ob-gyn, 1974-75. Editor-in-chief Jour. Reproductive Medicine, Acta Cytologica, Analytical and Quantitative Cytology, Clinical Cytology; editor: Introduction to Quantitative Cytochemistry, Automated Cell Identification and Cell Sorting, Compendium on Clinical Cytology, Compendium on the Computerized Cytology and Histology Laboratory, Compendium on Quality Assurance in Clinical Cytology; sr. editor Gen. and Diagnostic Pathology. Hon. dir. Chgo. Cancer Prevention Ctr., 1959-83; chmn. jury Maurice Goldblatt Cytology award, 1963-92. Recipient Cert. of Merit, U.S. Surgeon Gen., 1952, Maurice Goldblatt Cytology award, 1961, George N. Papanicolaou Cytology award, 1970, Masubuchi Gold Medal award 13th Internat. Cytology Congress, 1998, Kazumsa Masubuchi Lifetime Achievement award, 1998. Mem. Am. Soc. Cytology (pres. 1965-66), Mex. Soc. Cytology (hon.), Spanish Soc. Cytology (hon.), Brazilian Soc. Cytology (fgn. corr.), Indian Acad. Cytology (hon., Lifetime Achievement award 1998), Latin-Am. Soc. Cytology (hon.), Japanese Soc. Cytology (hon.), Internat. Acad. Cytology (pres. 1977-80), German Soc. Cytology (hon.), Ctrl. Soc. Clin. Rsch., Chgo. Path. Soc., Chgo. Gynecol. Soc. (hon.), Am. Soc. Cell Biology, German Soc. Ob-Gyn, Bavarian Soc. Ob-Gyn, German Soc. Endocrinology, Russian Assn. Cytologists (hon.), Swedish Soc. Medicine (hon.), Austrian Soc. Clin. Cytology (hon.), Sigma Xi. Home and Office: 1640 E 50th St Chicago IL 60615-3161 E-mail: wied@cytology.

WIEDEBUSCH, MARY KATHRYNE, dance educator; b. Clarksburg, W.Va. d. Danton Leon and Mary Margaret (Dixon) Caussin; m. Charles Edward Wiedebusch, July 12, 1952 (dec.); children: Carole Jean, Charles Edward II. BS, W.Va. U., 1951, MA, 1974; postgrad., Radford Coll., 1975, Am. U., 1979, Duke U., 1980. Tchr., choreographer Morgantown (W.Va.) H.S., 1951; asst. prof., choreographer Orchesis Modern Dance Ensemble W.Va. U., Morgantown, 1955-90, assoc. prof., dir., choreographer, 1990-93, prof. dance, coord. dance program, 1993—, dir. Orchesis Dance Ensemble, 1993—. Mem. faculty fine arts music camp W.Va. U., 1976, dir. fund raiser project/residency program, 1978—, founder, dir. dance artist-in-residence program, 1978—; mem. faculty Governors Honor Acad., Morgantown, 1997; bd. dir. Metro. Theatre Found., mem. commn. bd., 2003. Choreographer gala performances W.Va. State Dance Festivals, 1975-95; choreographer, dir. theatrical dance prodns. W.Va. U. Creative ARts Ctr., 1976—. Chair Golf Classic, 1993-95. Named to Hall of Fame, Sch. of Phys. Edn., W.Va. U., 1994. Mem. Am. Coll. Dance Festival Assn. (founding bd. dirs. 1973-87, nat. awards 1990-91). Avocations: golf, boating. Office: WVA U Coll Creative Arts PO Box 6111 Morgantown WV 26506-6111 Office Phone: 304-293-8623. Personal E-mail: cgwiehe@aol.com.

WIEDEMANN, CHARLES LOUIS, dentist; b. Belvidere, NJ, May 6, 1936; s. Charles and Clothilde Paulina (Fischer) W.; m. Jacqueline Burdzy, June 11, 1960; children: Lorraine Carol, Julie Patricia. BA in Biol. Sci., Rutgers U., 1957; DDS with honors, Fairleigh Dickinson U., 1962; grad., U.S. Army Med. Field Svc. Sch., 1962; postgrad. student, Inst. for Grad. Dentists, 1968-69, St. Clare's Hosp. Continuing Edn., NJ, 1972—, U. Pa., 1974-75, Boston U. Sch. Grad. Dentistry, 1991. Pvt. practice dentistry, Hackettstown, N.J., 1966—. Founder dental sect. staff dept. surgery Hackettstown Regional Med. Ctr., chief dentistry, 1973-75, 77-78, chief of staff dental sect. dept. surgery, 1974, 80, 85; dental health dir. Clarence W. Sickles Med. Ctr., Hackettstown, 1970-90; co-dir. Stargazer, Bd. of Ed, Online Mag. telecomm. sys., 1985-86; pres. Rexxcom Sys. Electronic Pub. and Computer Software, Co., 1990—; lectr. in field. Author: The Now Philosophy for Dentistry, 1972, Fantastic Facts About Dental Health, 1975, (computer software) The Format Machine, 1987, Autofont, 1990, The Magic Font Machine (Magifont, Magivue, Magishow), 1990, News 1, 1991, Digipad, 1993, The Autofont Titler, 1994; co-author: Autodoc, 1990, rev. edit., 1993, Font Mania, 1991;: rev. edit., 1996, XL1000, 1993, XL2000, 1993, XL2001; 1994, rev. edit., 1995, E-Z Book, 1995, Autofont Titler, 1995; editl. adv. panel: Dental Econs. Jour., 1979—80; editor: DPA News, 1993—95; contbr. articles to profl. jours. and mags.; columnist: Hackettstown Gazette, 1983—85. Chmn. Bd. of Health, Washington Twp., Morris County, N.J., 1975-78; co-dir. telecomm. sys. Hunterdon Ctrl. Regional H.S., 1989-98; presentations to Morris, Warren, and Sussex Counties, N.J. elem. schs. ann., 1966-93. Capt. Dental Corps., U.S. Army, 1962-65. Recipient cert. Stuart L. Isler Found. for Preventive Dentistry, 1986. Fellow Acad. Gen. Dentistry, Am. Endodontic Soc. (Harold Katz Meml. award 1983); mem. ADA (panel on quar. survey of pvt. practitioners 1990-93), Digital Pub. Assn. (founder, bd. dirs.), Am. Analgesia Soc., Internat. Analgesia Soc., N.J. Dental Assn., Warren-Sussex Dental Soc., Tri-County Dental Soc. (tchr. dental practice adminstrn. 1970-71), Hackettstown Dental Study Group (co-founder 1974-2006), Found. for Motivation in Dentistry (founder, chmn., bd. dirs.), Hosp. Assn. Neighborhood Dentists. Republican. Achievements include design of computer fonts, modules, graphics simulations; giant talking toothbrush, talking molar;

development of painless dental injections; improved nerve-block anesthesia technique; first to develop electronic publishing software; invention of Rexxcom character set. Office: 110 Mill St Hackettstown NJ 07840-2343 Office Phone: 908-852-0880.

WIEDEN, DAN G., advertising executive; b. 1945; m. Bonnie Wieden. BS journalism, Univ Oreg., 1967. With Georgia-Pacific Corp., Portland, Oreg., 1967-72; free-lance writer, 1972-78; with McCann-Erickson, Portland, 1978-80, William Cain, Portland, 1980-82; pres., exec. creative dir. Wieden & Kennedy Internat., Portland, 1982—. Named to Hall of Achievement, Sch. Journalism and Comm., Univ. Oreg., 2000. Office: Wieden & Kennedy Internat LLC 224 NW 13th Ave Portland OR 97209-2953

WIEDER, BRIAN H., neurosurgeon; b. LA, Oct. 22, 1963; MD, U. So. Calif., LA, 1991. Diplomate Am. Bd. of Neurol. Surgery, 2002. Ptnr. Rocky Mt. Neurosurgical Alliance, Denver, 1998—2006, Wyo. Brain and Spine Associates, Casper, 2006—. Co-director, acute spinal cord injury program Colo. Neurologic Inst., Englewoos, Colo., 1998—2005. Fellowship, U. Miami, Jackson Meml. Hosp., 1998. Mem.: Am. Assn. Neurol. Surgery. Office: Wyoming Brain and Spine Assoc 419 S Wahington St Casper WY 82601 Office Phone: 307-266-2222. Office Fax: 307-233-0266. Business E-Mail: wyo@brainandspine.com.

WIEDER, BRUCE TERRILL, lawyer, electrical engineer; b. Cleve., Dec. 9, 1955; s. Ira J. and Judith M.W. BSEE, Cornell U., 1978; MBA, U. Tex., 1980, JD with honors, 1988. Bar: Tex. 1988, U.S. Dist. Ct. (we. dist.) Tex. 1989, U.S. Patent and Trademark Office 1989, U.S. Ct. Appeals (fed. cir.) 1990, D.C. 1991, U.S. Supreme Ct. 1992, U.S. Dist. Ct. (no. dist.) Tex. 1995, Va. 1997, U.S. Dist. Ct. (ea. dist.) Va. 1997. Engr. Motorola, Inc., Austin, Tex., 1979-85; assoc. Arnold, White & Durkee, Austin, 1988-90; law clk. U.S. Ct. Appeals (Fed. cir.), Washington, 1990-91; assoc. Burns, Doane, Swecker & Mathis, Alexandria, Va., 1991-97, ptnr., 1998—2005; mem. Dow Lohnes, Washington, 2006—. Adj. prof. Georgetown U. Law Ctr., 1998—. Mem. IEEE, ABA, Am. Intellectual Property Law Assn., Giles S. Rich Am. Inn of Ct., Alpha Phi Omega, Beta Gamma Sigma. Office: Dow Lohnes 1200 New Hampshire Ave NW Washington DC 20036-6802 Office Phone: 202-776-2000. Business E-Mail: bwieder@dowlohnes.com.

WIEDERHORN, SHELDON MARTIN, materials scientist engineer; b. NYC, May 4, 1933; s. Joseph and Estha (Wasinsky) W.; m. Nancy Irene Wanderman, Feb. 18, 1961; children: Jonathan David, Miriam Ruth. BSChemE, Columbia U., 1956; MSChemE, U. Ill., 1958, PhDChemE, 1960. Rsch. engr. E.I. duPont de Nemours & Co., Wilmington, Del., 1960-63; phys. chemist Nat. Bur. Standards, Gaithersburg, Md., 1963-66, rsch. chemist, 1966-68, supervisory rsch. chemist, 1968-78, chief div., 1978-81, group leader, 1981-88; sr. fellow Materials Sci. and Engring. Lab. Nat. Inst. Standards and Tech. (NIST), Gaithersburg, 1988—. Contbr. numerous articles to profl. jours. Recipient Silver medal Dept. Commerce, 1970, Gold medal, 1982. Fellow Am. Ceramic Soc. (disting. lifetime mem. 1998, chmn. basic sci. div. 1974-75, Morey award 1977, John Jeppson award 1994, editor jour. 1991-94); mem. NAE. Home: 2700 Calvert St NW Washington DC 20008-1135 Office: Nat Inst Stds and Tech Materials 223 Rm A357 100 Bureau Dr Stop 8500 Gaithersburg MD 20899-8500 Office Phone: 301-975-5772. Business E-Mail: sheldon.wiederhorn@nist.gov.

WIEGAND, ELIZABETH GRIEGER, musician, educator; b. Michigan City, Ind., Sept. 25, 1931; d. Leo Theodore and Ella Martha Grieger; m. Lee Paul Wiegand, June 17, 1950; children: David Lee, Elaine Martha Johnson, Susan Elizabeth, Christine Mary. Cert. music tchr., Valparaiso U. Cert. Nat. Cert. Music Tchrs., permanent cert. Music Tchrs. Nat. Assn. Organist Queen All Sts. Ch., Michigan City, 1954—92; organist, choir dir. St. Stanislaus Kostka Consolation Choir, Michigan City, 1992—, spl. Eucharistic min., 1998—; chapel organist St. Anthony Meml. Hosp., Michigan City, 1998—. Competition judge Nat. Tchrs. Music Conf., Nat. Assn. Organ Tchrs. Musician: Tex. Women's U. Repository, 1999, Cath. of Antwerp, 1998, St. Williams Ch. Music dir., organist St. Peter's Ch., LaPorte, Ind. Named Music Educator of the Yr., Am. Music Conf., 1995—2005. Fellow: Nat. Fedn. Music Clubs; mem.: ASCAP (Popularity award 1980—2006), Am. Coll. Musicians (1st Pl. gold medal Internat. Rec. Competition), Sigma Alpha Iota. Roman Catholic. Avocations: embroidery, art, photography. Home: 7421 W Johnson Rd Michigan City IN 46360 Office Phone: 219-878-9511.

WIEGAND, PENELOPE TARLETON, elementary school educator; arrived in US, 1946; d. John and Jean Mills; m. John Wiegand, July 30, 1988; m. Donald P. Eilmes, Dec. 26, 1968 (div. June 1975); children: John Eilmes, Judy Eilmes, Velma Eilmes. BA in Edn., Calif. State U., LA, 1964, M in Urban Edn., 1980; PhD in Spl. Edn., U. Calif., Riverside, 2003. Cert. tchr. Calif. Bank reconciler Security Pacific, LA, 1960—64; tchr. La Seda Sch., Rowland Heights, Calif., 1964—68, Rowland Unified Sch. Dist., 1975—87; resource specialist Shelyn Sch., Rowland Heights, 1987—2004. Recipient Ada Mae Warner award, Shelyn PTA, 1996, Hon. Svc. award, 2004; grantee, Dist. Grant Pools, 1993, San Gabriel Valley Pub. Schs. Credit Union, 1996—97. Mem.: Calif. Assn. Spl. Edn. Adminstrn., Nat. Assn. Sch. Psych., Calif. Reading Assn., Internat. Reading Assn. Democrat. Baptist. Home: 6345 Yale St Chino CA 91710 Personal E-mail: onehungryhungarian@verizon.net.

WIEGAND, ROBERT C., lawyer; b. Hayward, Calif., Sept. 5, 1969; BA, U. Ark., 1991; JD cum laude, So. Meth. U. Dedman Sch. Law, 1994. Bar: Tex. 1994, US Dist. Ct. (no. dist. Tex.) 1998, US Ct. Appeals (5th cir.) 2000. Ptnr. Godwin, Pappas, Langley & Ronquillo, L.L.P., Dallas. Assoc. editor: So. Meth. U. Law Rev., 1993—94. Named a Rising Star, Tex. Super Lawyers mag., 2006. Mem.: Dallas Bar Assn. Office: Godwin Pappas Langley Ronquillo LLP Renaissance Tower Ste 1700 1201 Elm St Dallas TX 75270 Office Phone: 214-939-4831. E-mail: rwiegand@godwinpappas.com. *

WIEGAND, WAYNE AUGUST, library and information science educator; b. Manitowoc, Wis., Apr. 15, 1946; s. Edward and Germaine Ann (Leider) W.; m. Shirley Ann Abitz, June 15, 1965; children: Corinna Faye, Scott Edward, Andrew Wayne. BA, U. Wis., Oshkosh, 1968; MA, U. Wis., Milw., 1970; MLS, Western Mich. U., 1974; PhD, So. Ill. U., 1974. Instr. Northwestern Acad., Lake Geneva, Wis., 1969-70; coll. libr. Urbana (Ohio) Coll., 1974-76; asst. prof. libr. and info. sci. U. Ky., Lexington, 1976-82, assoc. prof. library and info. sci., 1982-86, U. Wis., Madison, 1987-89, prof., 1989—2002; F. William Summers prof. library and info. studies, prof. Am. Studies Fla. State U., 2003—. Dir. Fla. Book Awards, 2006—. Author: History of a Hoax, 1979, Politics of an Emerging Profession, 1986, Patrician in Progressive Era, 1988, An Active Instrument for Propaganda, 1989, Irrepressible Reformer: A Biography of Melvil Dewey, 1996, (with Shirley A. Wiegand) Books on Trial: Red Scare in the Heartland, 2007; editor Leaders in Am. Acad. Librarianship, 1983, Supplement to Dictionary of American Library Biography, 1990; co-editor: Libraries as Agencies of Culture, 2003, Genreflecting, 2006, Wienen in Print, 2006. Mem. ALA (Herbert Putnam award 1975, Libr. Rsch. Round Table award 1979, Justin Winsor award 1982, William B. Hesseltine award 1990, G.K. Hall award 1988, 91), Am. Hist. Assn., Am. Studies Assn., Orgn. Am. Historians, Assn. Libr. and Info. Sci. Educators (rsch. paper awards 1983, 87). Office: Fla State U Sch Info Studies 254 Louis Shores Bldg Tallahassee FL 32306-2100 Office Phone: 850-644-8123. Office Fax: 850-644-9763. Business E-Mail: wwiegand@ci.fsu.edu.

WIEGEL, ROBERT LOUIS, consulting engineering executive; b. San Francisco, Oct. 17, 1922; s. Louis Henry and Antionette L. (Decker) W.; m. Anne Pearce, Dec. 10, 1948; children: John M., Carol E., Diana L. BS, U. Calif., Berkeley, 1943, MS, 1949. Mem. faculty U. Calif. at Berkeley, 1946—, prof. civil engring., 1963-87, prof. emeritus, 1987—, asst. dean Coll. Engring., 1963-72, acting dean, 1972-73; dir. state tech. svcs. program for Calif. U. Calif., 1965-68, sec. acad. senate, 1988-89; vis. prof. Nat. U. Mex., summer 1965, Polish Acad. Sci., 1976, 88, U. Cairo, 1978; sr. Queen's fellow in marine sci. Australia, 1977; cons. to govt. and industry, 1946—. Chmn. U.S. com. for internat. com. oceanic resources, mem. marine bd. Nat. Acad. Engring., 1975-81; pres. Internat. Engring. Com. on Oceanic Resources, 1972-75, hon. mem., 1988; mem. coastal engring. research bd. Dept. Army, 1974-85; mem. IDOE adv. panel NSF, 1974-77, Gov. Calif. Adv. Commn. Ocean Resources, 1967, Calif. Adv. Commn. on Marine and Coastal Resources, 1967-73, Tsunami Tech. Adv. Council, Hawaii, 1964-66; U.S. del. U.S.-Japan coop. sci. programs, 1964, 65 Author publs. in field; editor Shore and Beach jour., 1988-96; patentee in field. V.p., bd. dirs. Am. Shore and Beach Preservation Assn., 1988-95, dir. emeritus, 1995—; mem. Nat. Rsch. Coun. com. on Beach Nourishment and Protection, 1992-95. 1st lt. U.S. Army, 1942-46. Recipient Outstanding Civilian Svc. medal Dept. Army, 1985, Berkeley citation U. Calif., 1987, Joe W. Johnson Outstanding Beach Preservation award Calif. Shore and Beach Preservation Assn., 1993, Coastal Zone Found. award, 1993, Morrough P. O'Brien award Am. Shore and Beach Preservation Assn., 1995, Oral History award Bancroft Libr., U. Calif., 1997; Robert L. Wiegel scholar, 2001—. Fellow AAAS; mem. NAE, ASCE (hon., chmn. exec. com. waterways, harbors, coastal engring. div. 1974-75, vice chmn. coastal engring. rsch. coun. 1964-78, chmn. 1978-92, chmn. task com. wave forces on structures 1960-67, chmn. com. on coastal engring. 1970-71, Rsch. prize 1962, Moffatt-Nichol Coastal Engring. award 1978, Internat. Coastal Engring. award 1985), Japan Soc. Civil Engrs. (hon.), Sigma Xi. Home: 1030 Keeler Ave Berkeley CA 94708-1404 Office Phone: 510-642-7340.

WIEGLEY, ROGER DOUGLAS, lawyer; b. Buffalo, Dec. 8, 1948; s. Richard John and Georgianna (Eggleston) W. BA, SUNY, Buffalo, 1970; JD magna cum laude, U. Wis., 1977. Bar: Wis. 1977, Hawaii 1978, N.Y. 1982, D.C. 1982, Calif. 1986. Spl. asst. U.S. atty. U.S. Justice Dept., Honolulu, 1978-81; spl. asst. to gen. counsel Dept. of the Navy, Washington, 1981-82; assoc. Sullivan & Cromwell, Washington, 1982-88; ptnr. Sidley & Austin, Washington, 1988-94, Winthrop, Stimson, Putnam & Roberts, Washington, 1994-98; dir. Credit Suisse First Boston, NYC, 1999—2001, Winterthur Ins. Group, NYC, 2001—. Arbitrator nat. panel Am. Arbitration Assn., 1988—98. Co-author: Trade and Export Finance, 2d edit., 2000; contbr. numerous articles to profl. jours. Served with USN, 1973-82. Mem. Assn. of Bar City of N.Y. (chmn. banking law com. 2000-03). Address: 50 Old South Salem Rd Ridgefield CT 06877 Home Phone: 203-438-4147. Personal E-mail: roger.wiegley@srsmail.com.

WIEGMAN, EUGENE WILLIAM, minister, academic administrator; b. Fort Wayne, Ind., Oct. 27, 1929; s. A. Henry and E. Catherine (McDonald) W.; m. Kathleen Wyatt, Apr. 26, 1952; children: Kathryn, Rose Marie, Mark, Jeanine, Gretchen, Matthew. BS, Concordia Coll., 1953; MS, U. Kans., Lawrence, 1956, EdD, 1962; grad., Pacific Luth. Theol. Sem., 1985. Tchr., coach Trinity Luth. Sch., Atchison, Kans., 1954-58; prin. tchr. St. John's Coll., Winfield, Kans., 1958-61; prof. Concordia Coll., Seward, Nebr., 1961-65; adminstrv. asst. to Rep. Clair Callan, Lincoln, Nebr., 1965-66; asst. to adminstr. fed. extension service Dept. Agr., Washington, 1966-67; dean community edn. Fed. City Coll., Washington, 1967-69; pres. Pacific Luth. U., Tacoma, 1969-75, Independent Colls. Wash., 1975-76; dir. Wash. Office Community Devel., 1977-78; commr. Dept. of Employment Security, 1978-81; exec. dir., pres., CEO emeritus Family Counseling Service of Tacoma and Pierce County, Wash., 1987-97; assoc. pastor Luther Meml. Ch., Tacoma, 1987-90; pastor Gethsemane Luth. Ch., Tacoma, 1990-98, Luther Meml. Ch., Tacoma, 1998—2002; dean clin. pastoral edn. Grad. Sch. of Korea, 1992—. Mem. Wash. State Employment and Tng. Council; mem. cabinet Gov. of Wash., 1977-81. Candidate for U.S. Congress from 6th dist. Wash., 1976; mem. Council on Washington's Future; exec. bd. dirs. Pacific Harbors Coun. Boy Scouts Am.; bd. dirs. Tacoma Area Urban Coalition; past chmn. Wash. Friends Higher Edn.; bd. dirs. Tacoma Urban League, Bellarmine Prep. Sch., Tacoma, Camp Brotherhood, Nativity House; trustee Tacoma Gen. Hosp., Pacific Sci. Center; mem. Commn. on Children, Youth and Families for Tacoma and Pierce County; mem. com. Faith Homes for Young Women; pres. Second City chamber of Tacoma. Recipient Disting. Teaching award City Winfield, Kans., 1960, Freedom Found. Teaching award, 1961, Disting. Eagle Scout award, 1982, Pres. award St. Martins Coll., 1980. Mem. Kiwanis, Phi Delta Kappa. Home: 405 N Stadium Way Tacoma WA 98403-3228 Personal E-mail: eugenewiegman@msn.com.

WIEGNER, EDWARD ALEX, financial and energy executive; b. Waukesha, Wis., Dec. 13, 1939; s. Roy Edward and Margaret (Kuehnlein) Wiegner; m. Cathryn J. Mullens, Oct. 16, 1970; children: Carlin, Ryan; 1 child from previous marriage, Christine. BBA, U. Wis., Madison, 1961, MS in Econs., 1965, PhD in Econs., 1969. Asst. prof. bus. adminstrn. Marquette U., Milw., 1965-71; assoc. prof U. Wis., Madison, 1972-73; sec. Wis. Dept. Revenue, Madison, 1971-74; sr. v.p. fin., bd. dirs. Wis. Power and Light Co., Madison, 1974-76, sr. v.p. consumer, pub. and fin. affairs, dir., 1976-80, exec. v.p., bd. dirs., 1980-82; sr. v.p., CFO, bd. dirs. Am. Natural Resources Co., 1982-85, exec. v.p., chief adminstrv. officer, bd. dirs., 1985-86; sr. v.p. Coastal Corp., 1985-86; sr. v.p., chief fin. officer Household Internat., Inc., 1986-88; exec. v.p., CFO Progressive Corp., Mayfield Heights, Ohio, 1988-91, pres. fin. svcs. div., 1989-93; gen. ptnr. Aurora Ptnrs., 1994-96; vice chmn. 1st Am. Ins. Co., Kansas City, Mo., 1994-97; chmn., CEO First Am. Fin. Corp., 1997-98; chmn. Geologix, Inc., Placerville, Calif., 1998—, Ins. Distbn. Solutions, LLC, Jacksonville, Fla., 1999—. Contbr. articles to profl. jours. Mem.: Grand Harbor Country Club. Home and Office: 151 Shores Dr Indian River Shores FL 32963 Personal E-mail: edward@wiegner.com.

WIEHL, LIS W., legal analyst, educator; b. Seattle, Aug. 9, 1961; d. Richard Lloyd and Inga (Wolfsberg) W.; children: Jacob, Danielle. JD, Harvard U., 1987; MA, U. Queensland, Brisbane, Australia, 1985; BA, Columbia U, 1983, U. Helsinki, Helsinki, Finland, 1978-79. Bar: Wash., US Dist. Ct. Wash., US Ct. Appeals (9th cir.). Assoc. Perkins Coie Law Firm, Seattle, 1987-90; fed. prosecutor U.S. Attys. Office, Seattle, 1990-95; assoc. prof. Law Sch., dir. of trial advocacy program U. Washington, Seattle, 1995. Counsel Perkins Coie Law Firm, Seattle; exec. asst. U.S. atty., Seattle, summer 1998; prin. dep. chief investigative counsel to U.S. Ho. of Reps. Com. on Judiciary, 1998-99; legal commentator Nat. Pub. Radio, NBC News, 2000-01, Sta. KIRO (CBS) News, 2001-02, legal analyst Fox-TV News Channel, 2001-; vis. prof., law and journalism dir. NY Law Sch. Contbr. to law rev, U. Wash., 1987, U. Mich., 1998; contbr. articles to New York Times, ABA Jour., Jour. Trial Advocacy, Harvard Blackletter Law Jour. Treas. Lawyers Students Engaged in Resolution, Seattle, 1995-99. Recipient Distinction in Teaching award Harvard U., 1987, Emil Gumpert award A. Coll. Trial Lawyers, Richardson S. Jacobson award for Excellence in Tchg. Trial Advocacy Roscoe Pound Inst., 2001. Mem. Fed. Bar Assn., Order of the Coif, Phi Beta Kappa. Business E-Mail: lis.wiehl@foxnews.com.

WIEHOFF, JOHN P., trucking executive; With Arthur Anderson, 1984—92; contr., treas. C.H. Robinson Worldwide, 1992—98, sr. v.p., CFO, 1998—99, pres., 1999—2006, CEO, 2002—06, chmn., CEO, 2006—. Office: 8100 Mitchell Rd Eden Prairie MN 55344 *

WIELAND, GILBERT DARRYL, medical researcher, anthropologist, gerontologist; b. Hagerstown, Md., Oct. 31, 1951; s. Gilbert Hugh and Joan Kanaga Wieland; m. Manhal A. Wieland, Apr. 26, 1980; 1 child, Christopher. BA cum laude in Anthropology, Am. U., Washington, DC, 1972; PhD in Anthropology, U. Rochester, NY, 1982; MPH in Health Svcs., UCLA, 1983. Sr. rsch. scientist VA Geriatric Rsch., Edn. and Clin. Ctr., Sepulveda, Calif., 1982—96; rsch. dir. Beverly Found., Pasadena, Calif., 1987—90; assoc. rsch. prof. divsn. geriat. UCLA, 1991—96; prof. U. S.C. Sch. Medicine, Columbia, 1996—; rsch. dir. geriat. Palmetto Health Richland, Columbia, 1998—. Dep. editor Journal of Gerontology: Medical Sciences, 2005—, assoc. editor Aging: Clinical and Experimental Research, 2005—, mem. editl. bd., reviewer 30 med. and sci. jours., —. Fellow: Soc. Applied Anthropology, Gerontol. Soc. Am. (chair pub. policy com. 2000—02, chair rsch. task force), Am. Geriatrics Soc. (mem. rsch. com. 2000—05). Office Phone: 803-434-4330. Office Fax: 803-434-4331. Business E-Mail: darryl.wieland@palmettohealth.org.

WIELAND, JOHN, real estate executive; m. Sue Wieland; 2 children. BA magna cum laude, Amherst Coll., 1958; MBA with high distinction, Harvard Bus. Sch., 1964; LHD (hon.), Amherst Coll., 1993. Chmn. John Wieland Homes and Neighborhoods, Inc., Atlanta, 1970—. Bd. dirs. Fed. Res. Bank Atlanta. Internat. bd. dirs. Habitat for Humanity; bd. dirs. Piedmont Hosp. Found., Atlanta Neighborhood Devel. Partnership; former chmn. High Mus. Art; former vice chmn. Woodruff Arts Ctr.; chmn. Adv. Coun., Emory U. Ctr. Ethics. Mem. Nat. Assn. Home Builders (life bd. dirs.), Atlanta (Ga.) C. of C. (mem. exec. com), Phi Beta Kappa. Office: 1950 Sullivan Rd Atlanta GA 30337-5706 Business E-Mail: john.wieland@jwhomes.com.

WIELAND, PAUL OTTO, environmental control systems engineer; b. Louisville, Apr. 9, 1954; s. Otto George and Flora Carolyn (Wolf) W. BS in Botany, U. Louisville, 1982, BS in Applied Sci., 1985, M. in Engring., 1987. Lic. profl. engr., Ala., Va.; cert. indoor air quality profl. Assn. of Energy Engrs. Paper carrier Courier-Jour., Louisville, 1976-77; youth program dir. UNICORN, Louisville, 1978; recreation worker Met. Parks Dept., Louisville, 1978-80; retail sales clk. Lose Bros. Lawn and Garden, Louisville, 1980-82; trainee engr. Sealand Svc., Inc., Elizabeth, NJ, 1982; engr. NASA Marshall Space Flight Ctr., Huntsville, Ala., 1983—2005; pres. Wiseland Svcs., Huntsville, 1996—. Author: Designing for Human Presence in Space: An Introduction to Environmental Control and Life Support Systems, 1994, Living Together in Space: The Design and Operation of the Life Support Systems on the International Space Station, 1996, rev. edit., 1998, A Guidebook to a Healthier House, 1999, Living Together in Space: The International Space Station Internal Active Thermal Control System Issues and Solutions - Sustaining Engineering Activities at the Marshall Space Flight Center from 1998 to 2005, 2007; contbg. author: Space Launch and Transportation Systems, 2005; contbr. articles to profl. jours. Vol. advocate R.A.P.E. Relief Ctr., Louisville, 1977-80; vol. tutor Adult Basic Edn. Program, Huntsville, 1988-89; vol. projectionist Film Co-op., Huntsville, 1990-91; vol. tech. advisor Am. Lung Assn. Health House '96, Huntsville. Mem. ASME, ASHRAE, AIAA (chmn. student chpt. 1984-85), NSPE (mathcounts vol. 1990-91), Inst. for Advanced Studies in Life Support (treas. 1990-92). Avocations: nature, art, dance. Home and Office: 4212 9th Ave SW Huntsville AL 35805-3408 Office Phone: 256-426-4325.

WIELAND, WILLIAM DEAN, healthcare consulting executive; b. Peoria, Ill., Feb. 15, 1948; s. George William and Virginia Lee (Delicath) W.; m. Joyce Lumia; 1 child, William Michael. BBA, Bradley U., 1971. Asst. adminstr. Galesburg (Ill.) Cottage Hosp., 1973-74; v.p. Anton & Damian, Iowa City, 1975-76; mgr. Clifton, Gunderson & Co., Peoria, 1977-80; v.p. OHMS Health Mgmt. Services, Columbus, 1980-84, dir., cons. VHA Cons. Svcs., Tampa, Fla., 1984-88; divsn. mgr. VHA, Inc., Tampa, Fla., 1988-95; sr. cons. mgr. Cost Sys. Group, Inc., Tampa, Fla., 1995-96; prin. Medifax Assocs., Tampa, Fla., 1997-98; project mgr. U. Cmty. Health, Tampa, Fla., 1998—. Small bus. cons. Clifton, Gunderson & Co., 1977-80; cons. OHMS Health Mgmt. Svcs., Columbus, 1980-84. Mem.: Healthcare Info. and Mgmt. Sys. Soc., Am. Bus. Club, Sigma Nu (Zeta Phi chpt.). Office Phone: 813-615-7200 ext. 51174. Personal E-mail: fl_bill_23u@msn.com.

WIEMAN, CARL E., physics professor; b. Corvallis, Oreg., Mar. 26, 1951; m. Sarah Gilbert. BS, MIT, 1973; PhD, Stanford U., 1977; DS (hon.), U. Chgo., 1997. Asst. rsch. physicist dept. physics U. Mich., Ann Arbor, 1977—79, asst. prof. physics, 1979—84; assoc. prof. physics U. Colo., Boulder, 1984—87, prof., 1987—97, disting. rsch. prof., 1997—; fellow Joint Inst. for Lab. Astrophysics, Boulder, 1985—; prof. Physics and Astronomy Dept. U. BC, Vancouver, 2007—, dir. Carl Wieman Sci. Edn. Initiative (CWSEI), 2007—. Loeb lectr. Harvard U., 1990—91; Rosenthal Meml. lectr. Yale U., 1988, Columbia U., 1988; Cherwell-Simon Meml. lectr. Oxford U., 1999; vis. scholar Phi Beta Kappa, 1999—2000. Recipient Ernest Orlando Lawrence Meml. award, U.S. Dept. Energy, 1993, Einstein medal for laser sci., Soc. Optical and Quantum Electronics, 1995, Fritz London prize for low temperature physics, 1996, Newcomb Cleveland prize, AAAS, 1996, King Faisal Internat. prize for Sci., 1997, Sci. award, Bonfils Stanton Found., 1998, Lorentz medal, Netherlands Royal Acad. Sci., 1998, Benjamin Franklin Medal in Physics, 2000, The Nobel Prize in Physics, 2001, Nat. Sci. Found. Dir. Award for Dist. Teaching Scholars, 2001, U.S. Outstanding Doctoral and Rsch. Univ. Prof., Coun. for Advancement and Support of Edn. & Carnegie Found. for Advancement of Tchg., 2004, Nat. Prof. of the Year, Carnegie Found. for the Advancement of Teaching & the Council for Advancement & Support of Edn., 2005. Fellow: Guggenheim, 1990-1991, Hertz Found., 1973-1977, Am. Phys. Soc. (Davisson-Germer prize 1994, Schawlow prize in laser sci. 1998); mem.: NAS, 1995, Am. Physical Soc. (fellow, 1990), Am. Acad. Arts and Sci., 1998, Am. Assn. Physics Tchrs. (Richtmyer lectr. award 1996), Optical Soc. Am. (R.W. Wood prize 1999). Achievements include first to achieve Bose-Einstein condensation, 1995. Office: Dept Physics and JILA CB440 Univ Colo Boulder CO 80309-0440 also: U BC 2146 Health Sciences Mall Vancouver BC Canada V6T 1Z3 Office Phone: 604-822-1732. E-mail: carl.wieman@phas.ubc.ca. *

WIEMER, ROBERT ERNEST, film and television producer, writer, director; b. Highland Park, Mich., Jan. 30, 1938; s. Carl Ernest and Marion (Israelian) W.; m. Rhea Dale McGeath, June 14, 1958; children: Robert Marshall, Rhea Whitney. BA, Ohio Wesleyan U., 1959. Ind. producer, 1956-60; dir. documentary ops. WCBS-TV, NYC, 1964-67; ind. producer of television, theatrical and bus. films NYC, 1967-72; exec. producer motion pictures and TV, ITT, NYC, 1973-84, pres. subs. Blue Marble Co., Inc., Telemontage, Inc., Alphaventure Music, Inc., Betaventure Music, Inc., 1973-84; founder, chmn., chief exec. officer Tigerfilm, Inc., 1984—; chmn., bd. dirs. Golden Tiger Pictures, Hollywood, Calif., 1988—; pres, CEO Tuxedo Pictures Corp., Hollywood, Calif., 1993—. Bd. dirs., v.p. prodn. Las Vegas Internat. Film Festival; v.p. prodn. Cinevegas. Writer, prodr., dir.: (feature films) My Seventeenth Summer, Witch's Sister, Do Me a Favor, Anna to the Infinite Power, Somewhere, Tomorrow, Night Train to Kathmandu; exec. prodr.: (children's TV series) Big Blue Marble (Emmy and Peabody awards); dir. (TV episodes) New York Undercover, seaQuest DSV, Star Trek: The Next Generation, Deep Space Nine, The Adventures of Superboy; composer (country-western ballad) Tell Me What To Do. Capt. USAF, 1960-64. Recipient CINE award, 1974, 76, 77, 79, 81, Emmy award, 1978. Mem. NATAS, ASCAP, Info. Film Producers Assn. (Outstanding Producer award), Nat. Assn. TV Programming Execs., Am. Women in Radio and TV, N.J. Broadcasters Assn., Dirs. Guild Am., v.p., bd. mem. CineVegas The Las Vegas Internat. Film Festival. Office: Golden Tiger Pictures 3896 Ruskin St Las Vegas NV 89147-1097

WIENECKE, NATHANIEL FREDERICK, federal agency administrator; b. Jan. 10, 1972; s. Paul and Jean Wienecke; m. Chantal Wienecke; 1 child, Kendall. BA, SUNY, Oneonta, 1995. Dep. asst. sec. for external affairs & comm., Econ. Devel. Adminstrn. US Dept. Commerce, Washington, dep. asst. sec. for legis. and intergovernmental. affairs, 2005—06, acting asst. sec. for legis. and intergovernmental affairs, 2006, asst. sec. for legis. and intergovernmental affairs, 2006—. Office: US Dept Commerce 1401 Constitution Ave NW Washington DC 20230

WIENEKE, DARIN SCOTT, lawyer; BA cum laude in Bus. Mgmt. and Polit. Sci., Hamline U., 1996; JD cum laude, U. Minn. Law Sch., Mpls., 2000. Bar: Minn. 2001, US Dist. Ct. (dist. Minn.) 2003. Assoc. Tewksbury, Kerfeld & Zimmer, P.A., Mpls. Named a Rising Star, Minn. Super Lawyers mag., 2006. Mem.: Minn. Trial Lawyers Assn. (co-chair new lawyers sect.), Hennepin County Bar Assn., Minn. State Bar Assn. Office: Tewksbury Kerfeld & Zimmer PA 88 S 10th St Ste 300 Minneapolis MN 55403 Office Phone: 612-334-3399. E-mail: dwieneke@tkz.com. *

WIENER, HESH (HAROLD FREDERIC WIENER), publishing executive, consultant; b. Bklyn., July 20, 1946; s. Jesse Leonard and Regina (Rappaport) W. BS in Polit. Sci., MIT, 1969; LLB with honors, Open U., London, 2002. Mem. staff systems devel. Data Gen. Corp., Southboro, Mass., 1969-70; dir. computer edn. project U. Calif., Berkeley, 1970-72; editor Computer Decisions Mag., Rochelle Park, NJ, 1973-78; editor, pub. Tech. News Am., NYC, 1976-88; pres. Tech. News of Am. Co., Inc., NYC, 1982—; mng. dir. Tech. News Ltd., London, 1992—. Pub. Computer and Comms. Buyer Newsletter, 1979-95, Mainstream Newsletter, 1980-82, Infoperspectives Newsletter, 1982—, Storage Tech. Monitor, 1984-87, Infoperspectives Internat., UK, 1989—, Mid. East, 1991—, The Four Hundred Newsletter, UK, 1990-97, The Four Hundred Newsletter, US, 1990-97; editor Infoperspectives Internat., Italy, 1991-98, The Four Hundred Newsletter, Italy, 1995—; pub. US edit. Computergram Internat. Newsletter, 1985-90; corr. Processeurs mag., 1989-99; cons. Hewlett-Packard Co., Paris, 1971-72, Xerox Corp., 1972-73; advisor NSF, 1975; columnist 451.com, 2000—06. Author: Big Blue and You, The IBM Atlas, The Mainframe; corr. Computer Weekly, UK, 1975-81, Computable, Amsterdam, 1976-87, Computing Can., 1977-78, Ordinateurs, Paris, 1977-89, Data News, Brussels, 1979-86, Informatics, UK, 1981-85, Datanytt, Copenhagen, 1982-89, Mgmt. Tech. mag., 1983-85; editor BusinessWeek Newsletter for Info. Execs., 1987-90, Datamation Mag., 1983-90, Infoperspectives Internat., Milan, 1991—; contbg. editor Bus. and Soc. Rev., 1978-85; contbr. NY Times Syndicate, Los Angeles Times Syndicate, N.Am. Newspaper Alliance Wireservice, Newsday, Manhattan, Inc., Rom Mag., Informatique, Paris, The Economist, London, Dun's Bus. Month, Software News, Intermedia, Digital News, Data Communications, Bus. Week Newsletter for Info. Execs., Bus. Strategy Internat., Nikkei Watcher on IBM, Tokyo, 1989-96; contbg. editor Midrange Svc. Pubs., 2002-05, IT Jungle Publs., 2003—; contbg. editor Big Iron News, 2005—; webmaster tech-news.com, 1995—, PrimroseHill.com, 1997—, luminum.com, 1999—, SongLakeBooks.com, 2000-, The Guild Cos., 2005-, Thinks Rsch., 2007-, Schlamstone.com, 2007-. Mem.: Overseas Press. Home: 246 6th Ave Brooklyn NY 11215-2103 Office: Tech News Am 123 7th Ave Brooklyn NY 11215-1383

WIENER, JACQUES LOEB, JR., federal judge; b. Shreveport, La., Oct. 2, 1934; s. Jacques L. and Betty (Eichenbaum) Wiener; m. Sandra Mills Feingerts; children: Patricia Wiener Shifke, Jacques L. III, Betty Ellen Wiener Spomer, Donald B. BA, Tulane U., 1956, JD, 1961. Bar: La. 1961, US Dist. Ct. (we. dist.) La. 1961. Ptnr. Wiener, Weiss & Madison, Shreveport, 1961—90; judge US Ct. Appeals (5th cir.), New Orleans, 1990—. Mem. coun. La. State Law Inst., 1963—; master of the bench Am. Inn of Ct., 1990—98. Pres. United Way N.W. La., 1975, Shreveport Jewish Fedn., 1969—70. Fellow: La. Bar Found., Am. Bar Found., Am. Coll. Trust and Estates Counsel; mem.: ABA, Am. Law Inst., Shreveport Bar Assn. (pres. 1982), La. Bar Assn., Internat. Acad. Estate and Trust Law (academician). Avocations: fly fishing, upland game bird hunting, photography, travel. Office: Court of Appeals Building 600 Camp St Rm 244 New Orleans LA 70130-3425 *

WIENER, JOEL HOWARD, historian, educator; b. NYC, Aug. 23, 1937; s. Philip Wiener and Elizabeth Weissman; m. Suzanne Wolff Wiener, Sept. 4, 1961; children: Paul, Deborah, Jane. BA, NYU, 1959; postgrad., U. Glasgow, Scotland, 1961—63; PhD, Cornell U., Ithaca, NY, 1965. Asst. prof. history Skidmore Coll., Saratoga Springs, NY, 1964—67, CUNY, 1967—71, assoc. prof. history, 1972—78, prof. history, 1978—2000, emeritus prof. history, 2000—. Dir. study abroad program in Eng. CUNY, 1971—73, prof. history doctoral program, 1980—2000, chmn. dept. history, 1981—85; cons., advisor Cornell U. Press, U. NC Press, Victorian Studies, NEH, English Lit. in Transition, 1880-1920, Princeton U. Press, Greenwood Press, UK Social Sci. Rsch. Coun., Ill. U. Press, Victorian Periodicals Rev., Am. Journalism, Albion, Jour. Brit. Studies, Rutgers U. Press, PSC-CUNY, Dictionary Labour Biography, Harvester Press; mem. editl. bd. Media History. Author: The War of the Unstamped, 1969, A Descriptive Finding List of Unstamped British Periodicals, 1830-1836, 1970, William Lovett, 1989, Radicalism and Freethought in Nineteenth-Century Britain, 1983; editor: Great Britain: Foreign Policy and the Span of Empire, 4 vols., 1972, Great Britain: The Lion at Home, 4 vols., 1974, Innovators and Preachers, 1985, Papers for the Millions, 1988; co-editor (with Mark Hampton): Anglo-American Media Interactions, 1850-2000, 2007; assoc. editor Dictionary of National Biography, 1999—2004; mem. adv. bd.: Dictionary of Nineteenth-Century Journalism; contbr. articles to profl. jours. Grantee, Oxford Bibliog. Soc., 1971—72, Am. Philos. Soc., 1971—72. Fellow: Royal Hist. Soc.; mem.: Am. Journalism Historians Assn. (rsch. com. 1998—), Rsch. Soc. for Victorian Periodicals (v.p., pres. 1981—85). Avocations: travel, theater, cinema. Home: 267 Glen Ct Teaneck NJ 07666 Office Phone: 201-837-5452. Home Fax: 201-837-8658. Personal E-mail: jwiener267@aol.com.

WIENER, JON, history professor; b. St. Paul, Minn., May 16, 1944; s. Daniel N. and Gladys (Aronsohn) Spratt. BA, Princeton U., 1966; PhD, Harvard U., 1971. Acting asst. prof. UCLA, 1973-74; asst. prof. history U. Calif.-Irvine, 1974-83, prof., 1984—. Plaintiff Freedom of Info. Lawsuit against FBI for John Lennon Files, 1983—. Author: Social Origins of the New South, 1979; Come Together: John Lennon in His Time, 1984, Professors, Politics, and Pop, 1991, Gimme Some Truth: The John Lennon FBI File, 2000, Historians in Trouble, 2005; contbg. editor The Nation mag.; contbr. articles to profl. jours. including The New Republic and New York Times Book Rev. Mem. Am. Hist. Assn., Nat. Book Critics Circle, Orgn. Am. Historians, Liberty Hill Found. (bd. dirs.). E-mail: wiener@uci.edu.

WIENER, JOSEPH, pathologist, educator; b. Toronto, Can., Sept. 21, 1927; arrived in U.S., 1949, naturalized, 1960; s. Louis and Minnie (Salem) W.; m. Judith Hesta Ross, June 20, 1954; children: Carolyn L., Adam L. MD, U. Toronto, 1953. Intern Detroit Receiving Hosp., 1953-54; resident to chief resident pathology Mallory Inst. Pathology, 1954-55, 57-60; from asst. to assoc. prof. pathology Columbia U., NYC, 1960-68; prof. pathology N.Y. Med. Coll., NYC, 1968-78, Wayne State U., Detroit, 1978—, chmn. dept., 1978-90. Cons. NIH, 1970— Served to capt. M.C. U.S. Army, 1955-57. Grantee Heart, Lung and Blood Inst., 1971-93; fellow Coun. for High Blood Pressure Rsch., 1982. Fellow Am. Heart Assn., Am. Stroke Assn., Coll. Am. Pathologists; mem. AAAS, Am. Soc. Investigative Pathology, Am. Soc. Cell Biology, Mich. Path. Soc., Internat. Acad. Pathology, Am. Heart Assn., U.S./Can. Acad. Pathology, Mich. Heart Assn. (dir.), Internat. Soc. Hypertension. Achievements include rsch. on cellular/molecular biology of experimental hypertension. Office: 540 E Canfield St Detroit MI 48201-1928 Office Phone: 313-577-1157. Business E-Mail: j.wiener@wayne.med.edu.

WIENER, MALCOLM HEWITT, historian, writer; b. Tsingtao, China, July 3, 1935; (parents Am. citizens); s. Myron and Ethel (Zimmerman) W.; m. Carolyn Talbot Seely, June 8, 1990; children: Kate, Elizabeth, Thomas, Jonathan. BA, Harvard U., 1957, JD, 1963; LittD (hon.), U. Sheffield, 1997; PhD (hon.), Eberhard-Karl U., Tübingen, Germany, 1998; Doctorate (hon.), U. Athens, Greece, 1998. Bar: N.Y. 1964. Atty., NYC, 1963-71; pvt. practice investing, 1971-98; chmn. Millburn Corp., NYC, 1977-98; chmn. bd. trustees Malcolm Hewitt Wiener Found., NYC, 1984—. Columnist Newsday. Co-dir. Aegean Bronze Age Colloquium, NYU Inst. Fine Arts, 1975—; founder, exec. dir. Inst. Aegean Prehistory, 1982-89, pres., 1990—; trustee Am. Sch. Classical Studies in Athens, Metro. Mus. Art; mem. adv. bd. Malcolm Wiener Ctr. for Social Policy, Kennedy Sch. Govt. Harvard U.; mem. Coun. Fgn. Rels., chmn. Indep. Task Force Non-lethal Tech. Mil. Implications and Options, 1995. With USN, 1957-60. Fellow: AAAS, Soc. Antiquaries London, Archaeol. Inst. Am. (life); mem.: ABA, Chevalier de l'Ordre des Arts et des Lettres, Osterreichische Akademie Wissenschaften (corr.), Royal Swedish Acad. Letters, History and Antiquities (corr.), Austrian Archaeol. Inst. (corr.). Office: Villa Cardia 66 Vista Dr Greenwich CT 06830 Office Phone: 203-862-9334. Business E-Mail: cpadgett@instap.org.

WIENER, MARVIN S., rabbi, editor, executive; b. NYC, Mar. 16, 1925; s. Max and Rebecca (Dodell) W.; m. Sylvia Bodek, Mar. 2, 1952; children: David Hillel, Judith Rachel. BS, CCNY, 1944, MS, 1945; BHL, Jewish Theol. Sem. Am., 1947, MHL, Rabbi, 1951, DD (hon.), 1977. Registrar, sec. faculty Rabbinical Sch., Jewish Theol. Sem. Am., 1951-57; cons. Frontiers of Faith TV Series, NBC, 1951-57; dir., instr. liturgy Cantors Inst.-Sem. Coll. Jewish Music, Jewish Theol. Sem. Am., 1954-58; faculty coord. Sem. Sch. and Women's Inst., 1958-64; dir. Nat. Acad. for Adult Jewish Studies, United Synagogue Am., NYC, 1958-78; editor Burning Bush Press, 1958-78, United Synagogue Rev., 1978-86; dir. com. congrl. stds. United Synagogue Am., 1976-86, cons. cmty. rels. and social action, 1981-82, editor, exec. joint retirement bd., 1986—. Mem. Joint Commn. on Rabbinic Placement, 1951-57, Joint Prayer Book Commn., 1957-62; mem. exec. coun. Rabbinical Assembly, 1958-86, summer Rabbi, Forest Hills Jewish Ctr., 1961-64; editl. cons. N.Y. Bd. Rabbi, 1987-89; trustee joint retirement bd. Jewish Theol. Sem. Am. Rabbinical Assembly and United Synagogue Am., 1959-86, sec. 1968-76, 84-85, vice chmn., 1976-82, 85-86, chmn. 1982, treas., 1983-84; co-chmn. Jewish Bible Assn., 1960-64; chmn. bd. rev. Nat. Coun. Jewish Audio-Visual Materials, 1968-69; mem. exec. com. Nat. Coun. Adult Jewish Edn., 1966—; mem. exec. bd., editl. adv. bd., v.p. Jewish Book Couns., 1976-96; chmn. Internat. Conf. Adult Jewish Edn., Jerusalem, 1972. Editor: Nat. Acad. Adult Jewish Studies Bull., 1958-78, The High Holy Days, Book I (Herman Kieval), 1959, The Jewish Dietary Laws (Samuel H. Dresner and Seymour Siegel), 1959, Past and Present: Selected Essays (Israel Friedlaender), 1961, Heart of Wisdom, Book I (Bernard S. Raskas), 1962, Book II, 1979, Judaism: Profile of a Faith (Ben Zion Bokser), 1963, The Wisdom of Solomon Schechter (Bernard Mandelbaum), 1963, Jewish Tract Series, 1964-78 (15 titles), Foundations of A Faith (Simon Greenberg), 1967, Judaism and the Christian Predicament (Ben Zion Bokser), 1967, The Maturing of the Conservative Movement (Bernard Mandelbaum), 1968, The Sabbath (Samuel L. Dresner), 1970, Adult Jewish Edn., 1958-78, Talmudic Law and the Modern State (Moshe Silberg), 1973, Self-Incrimination in Jewish Law (Aaron Kirschenbaum), 1970, Sex and the Family in the Jewish Tradition (Robert Gordis), 1970; contbr. articles to numerous periodicals. Mem. Am. Acad. Jewish Rsch., Assn. Jewish Studies, N.Y. Bd. Rabbis, Rabbinical Assembly. Home: 67-66 108th St Apt D-46 Forest Hills NY 11375-2974 Office: Joint Retirement Bd Ste 1515 One Penn Plaza New York NY 10119 Office Phone: 212-947-2400.

WIENER, MORRIS JAY, air transportation executive; b. Phila., Aug. 23, 1941; s. William V. and Sylvia B. Wiener; m. Diane Q. Quick, June 18, 1966; children: Ann Elizabeth, Michael Jay, Jennifer Beth. BFA, Phila. Coll. Art Design, 1967; MEd, Temple U., Phila., 1973, PhD, 1975. Cert. aircraft accident investigator, US FAA, 2003; air transport pilot B-737, B-757, B-767 US FAA, 1992. Comml. diver Aquarama, Phila., 1960—62; photographer Cherry Hill, NJ, 1964—; tchr. Woodbury Pub. Sch., Woodbury, NJ, 1967—72; asst. prof. Temple U., Phila, 1972—84; firefighter Cherry Hill Fire Dept., 1970—; pilot Franklin Realty Group, Blue Bell, Pa., 1984—87, Presdl., Herndon, Va., 1987—89, United Airlines, Chgo., 1989—2001; investigator FAA, Washington, 2001—; owner Images Ltd., Cherry Hill, 2003—. Dir. instrnl. design Woodhaven Ctr., Phila., 1974—84; fire commr. Cherry Hill Fire Dept., 1979—82. Recipient Bronze medal, Carnegie Hero Fund, 1966, Lifesaving Merit award, ARC, 1966, Firefighter Yr., Schlitz Brewing Co., 1977, Heroism award, Cherry Hill Fire Dept., 1987. Avocations: photography, graphic design. Home: 306 Pleasant Dr Cherry Hill NJ 08003 Office: US Dept Transp FAA 2 International Plz Philadelphia PA 19113 Home Phone: 856-795-2005; Office Phone: 610-595-1500.

WIENER, RONALD MARTIN, lawyer; b. Phila., June 1, 1939; s. William V. and Sylvia Wiener; children: Carol Jan, Alan Mark. AB, U. Pa., 1961; JD magna cum laude, Harvard U., 1964. Bar: DC 1965, Pa. 1966. Law clk. U.S. Tax Ct., 1964-66; assoc. Wolf, Block, Schorr and Solis-Cohen, LLP, Phila., 1966-72, ptnr., 1972—. Mem. commr.'s adv. group IRS, 1992—93. Fellow: Am. Coll. Tax Counsel (regent 3d cir. 1996—2003); mem.: ABA, Phila. Bar Assn. (chair tax sect. 1989—90), Pa. Bar Assn. Office: Wolf Block Schorr and Solis-Cohen LLP 1650 Arch St 22d fl Philadelphia PA 19103-2678 Office Phone: 215-977-2266. Business E-Mail: rwiener@wolfblock.com.

WIENER, THOMAS ELI, lawyer; b. Dallas, Nov. 29, 1940; s. Samson and Fan (Gardner) W.; m. Felice Gloria Goodwin, Jan. 24, 1970; children: Gary Allen, Debra Roslyn, Allison Beth, Todd David. BA, U. Tex., 1962, JD with honors, 1968. Bar: Tex. 1968, D.C. 1969, Pa. 1972, U.S. Supreme Ct. 1972. Atty.-advisor office chief counsel IRS, Washington, 1968-72; assoc. Pepper Hamilton & Scheetz, Phila., 1972-74, Abrahams & Loewenstein, Phila., 1974-76, Goodis, Greenfield, Henry & Edelstein, Phila., 1976-77, Mesirov, Gelman, Jaffe, Cramer & Jamieson, Phila., 1977-78; prin. Franklin, Margulies & Huntington, 1978-91, Riley & DeFalice, P.C., Phila., 1991-92, Wiener & Caplan, P.C., Phila., 1992-95; pvt. practice Bala Cynwyd, Pa., 1995—. Bd dirs. Lufkin (Tex.) Industries, Inc. Author: (with others) Tax Problems of Fiduciaries, 1977. Trustee Golden Slipper Club; pres. Main Line Reform Temple, 1992-94, pres. brotherhood 1981-83; pres. Rotary Gundaker Found., 1986-87; 1st v.p. N. Am. Fedn. Temple Brotherhoods, 1999-01; v.p. Phila. Fedn. Reform Synagogues, 1993-98; pres. Rotary Club of Phila., 1994-97; trustee Union Am. chmn. Synagogue Fedn. Coun. of Phila., 1994-97; trustee Union Am. Hebrew Congregations, 1995—, exec. com., 2001-05, ARZA/World Union N.Am. Mem. D.C. Bar Assn., Pa. Bar Assn., Tex. Bar Assn., Phila. Bar Assn., Am. Law Inst. (life), Order of Coif, Masons (32 degree K.C.C.H., past master), Rotary (pres. chpt. 1985-86). Home: 1233 Remington Rd Wynnewood PA 19096-2329 Office: One Belmont Ave Ste 605 Bala Cynwyd PA 19004-1609 Office Phone: 610-667-8999. Personal E-mail: twiener@aol.com.

WIENER, VALERIE, state senator, writer, communications executive; BJ, U. Mo., 1971, MA, 1972, U. Ill., Springfield, 1974; postgrad., McGeorge Sch. Law, 1976—79. Prodr. Checkpoint Sta. KOMU-TV, Columbia, Mo., 1972-73; v.p., owner Broadcast Assocs., Inc., Las Vegas, 1972-86; pub. affairs dir. First Ill. Cable TV, Springfield, 1973-74; editor Ill. State Register, Springfield, 1973-74; prodr. and talent Nev. Realities Sta. KLVX-TV, Las Vegas, 1974-75; account exec. Sta. KBMI (now KFMS), Las Vegas, 1975-79; nat. traffic dir. six radio stas., Las Vegas, Albuquerque and El Paso, Tex., 1979-80; exec. v.p., gen. mgr. Stas. KXKS and KKJY, Albuquerque, 1980-81; exec. adminstr. Stas. KSET AM/FM, KVEG, KFMS and KKJY, 1981-83; press sec. U.S. Congressman Harry Reid, Washington, 1983-87; adminstrv. asst Friends for Harry Reid, Nev., 1986; press sec. U.S. Senator Harry Reid, Washington, 1987-88; owner Wiener Comm. Group, Las Vegas, 1988—; mem. Dist. 3 Clark County Nev. State Senate, Carson City, 1996—; owner PowerMark Pub., Las Vegas, 1998—. Mem. Nev. Drug Commn., 1997—2000, Nev. Commn. on Aging, 1997—; chair Commn. on Sch. Safety and Jevenile Violence, 1999—2000; mem. Nev. Technol. Crimes Task Force, 2001—03, Nev. Anti-Bullying Task Force, 2001—03, Gov.'s Task Force on Corrections, 2002; chair legis. com. on obesity Nev. State Senate, 2003—06, minority whip, 2001—. Author: Power Communications: Positioning Yourself for High Visibility (Fortune Book Club main selection 1994, Money Book Club selection 1995, Communicator award of distinction 2000), Gang Free: Friendship Choices for Today's Youth, 1995, 2d edit., 1996, The Nesting Syndrome: Grown Children Living at Home, 1997, Winning the War Against Youth Gangs, 1999, Power Positioning: Advancing Yourself as The Expert, 2000 (Nat. awards), PowerMaster HandBook Series, 2000— (eight nat. awards); contbg. writer The Pacesetter, ASAE's Comm. News. Sponsor Futures for Children, Las Vegas, Albuquerque, El Paso, 1979—83; mem. El Paso Exec. Women's Coun., 1981—83, Clark Coun. Sch. Dist. and Bus. Cmty. PAYBAC Spkrs. and Partnership Programs, 1989—, chair legis. com. on juvenile justice, 1999—2000; steering com. Youth Recovery Network, 2001—02; founding mem. Nev. team Action Healthy Kids; media chmn. Gov.'s Coun. Small Bus., 1989—93; vice chmn. Congl. Awards Coun., 1989—93; med. dir. Gov.'s Conf. on Women, 1990; vice chmn. Gov.'s Commn. on Postsecondary Edn., 1992—96; mem. VIP bd. Easter Seals, El Paso, 1982; bd. dirs. BBB So. Nev., 1994—, Pub. Edn. Found., 1997—. Named Outstanding Vol., United Way, El Paso, 1983, SBA Nev. Small Bus. Media Adv. of Yr., 1992, Nev.'s Disting. Sr. Athlete, 2000, So. Nev. Health Care Policy Hero, 2003, Nev. Legislator of Yr., Soc. Pub. Health Educators, 2004; named one of 27 Healthy Sch. Heroes in U.S., 2002; named to Hall Fame, Leadership Las Vegas, 2006; recipient 175 Comm. awards, 1989—, Outstanding Achievement award, Nat. Fedn. Press Women, 1991, Disting. Leader award, Nat. Assn. Cmty. Leadership, 1993, Gold medals in fitness and weightlifting, Nev. Sr. Olympics, 1998—2003, Gold medals in swimming, 2002—03, Gold medals in fitness and weightlifting, 2005, Gold medals in swimming, 2005, Walking Silver medal, 2005, Gold medals in fitness and weightlifting, 2006, Gold medals in swimming, 2006, Outstanding Women Adv. for Edn. award, Va. Commonwealth U., 2000, Internat. Cmty. Svc. award, Internat. New Thought Alliance, 2001, Winner Nev. 100 Fitness Challenge, Nev. State Legis. Session, 2005, Special Svc. award, Nev. Athletic Trainers Assn., 2007. Mem. Nat. Assn. Women Bus. Owners (media chmn., nat. rep. So. Nev. 1990-91, Nev. Adv. of Yr. award 1992), Nev. Press Women, Nat. Spkrs. Assn., Small Pubs. Assn. N.Am., Dem. Press Secs. Assn., El Paso Assn. Radio Stas., U.S. Senate Staff Club, Las Vegas C. of C. (Circle of Excellence award 1993), Soc. Profl. Journalists. Democrat. Avocations: reading, writing, fitness and weighlifting training and competition, public speaking, community involvement. Office: 1500 Foremaster Ln Ste 2 Las Vegas NV 89101-1150

WIENS, ARTHUR NICHOLAI, psychology professor; b. McPherson, Kans., Sept. 7, 1926; s. Jacob T. and Helen E. (Kroeker) W.; m. Ruth Helen Avery, June 11, 1949; children: Barbara, Bradley, Donald. BA, U. Kans., 1948, MA, 1952; PhD, U. Portland, 1956. Diplomate: Am. Bd. Examiners Profl. Psychology. Clin. psychologist Topeka State Hosp., 1949-53; sr. psychologist outpatient dept. Oreg. State Hosp., Salem, 1954-58, chief psychologist, 1958-61, dir. clin. psychology internship program, 1958-61; clin. instr. U. Oreg. Med. Sch., Portland, 1958-61, asst. prof., 1961-65, assoc. prof., 1965-66; prof. med. psychology, 1966—96; prof. emeritus med. psychology, 1997—. Field assessment officer Peace Corps, 1965; cons. psychologist Portland Ctr. for Hearing and Speech, 1964—67, Dammasch State Hosp., 1967—69, Raleigh Hills Hosp., 1968—84, Oreg. Vocat. Rehab. Divsn., 1973—2001, mem. state adv. com., 1976—93; cons. William Temple Rehab. House, Episcopal Laymen's Mission Soc., 1968—88; chmn. State Oreg. Bd. Social Protection, 1971—84, State of Oreg. Bd. Psychologist Examiners, 1963—66, 1974—77; v.p. bd. dirs. Raleigh Hills Rsch. Found., 1974—80. Contbr. articles to profl. jour. Fellow AAAS, APA (chmn. com. on vis. psychologist program 1972-76, chmn. accreditation com. 1978, mem. task force edn. and credentialing 1979-84); mem. Am. Assn. State Psychology Bd. (pres. 1978-79), Nat. Register Health Svc. Providers in Psychology (bd. dirs. 1985-92, chmn. 1989-92), Profl. Exam. Svc. (bd. dirs. 1982-88, 90-96, chmn. 1986-88), Sigma Xi. Home: 74 Condolea Way Lake Oswego OR 97035-1010 Office: Oreg Health Scis U Portland OR 97201

WIENS, BEVERLY JO, psychology professor; b. Oildale, Calif., Oct. 2, 1947; d. Ernest and Irene Josephine (Klassen) Bartel; m. Gary D. Wiens, Aug. 19, 1967; children: Nicole Marie Wiens Cook, Katie Lyn Wiens. BA, San Jose State U., 1969, MA, 1971, Santa Clara U., 1992; PhD, No. Calif. Grad. U., 2001. Lic. counselor, Calif. Tchr. West Valley Coll., Saratoga, Calif., 1971-76, San Jose (Calif.) City Coll., 1974-75, San Jose State U., 1978; marriage, family therapist Coalition of Counseling Centers, Los Gatos, Calif., 1982-86; assoc. prof. San Jose Bible Coll., 1982-87; prof., dept. chair, counseling psychology San Jose Christian Coll., 1988—2004; dept. chair counseling psychology William Jessup U., Rocklin, Calif., 2004—. Lectr. in field. Mem. Am. Assn. Christian Counselors, Am. Counseling Assn., Calif. Assn. Marital Family Therapists. Republican. Mem. Mennonite Brethren. Office: William Jessup U 333 Sunset Blvd Rocklin CA 95765 Office Phone: 916-577-2261. Business E-Mail: bwiens@jessup.edu.

WIENS, ROBERT NIESSEN, retired financial analyst; b. Aberdeen, Sask., Can., Apr. 11, 1938; arrived in US, 1938; s. Henry Gerhardt and Marguerite Wiens; m. Jacqueline Yvonne Good, Sept. 20, 1957; 1 child, Robin Dawn McDuffie. BA, Chapman U., Orange, Calif., 1969. Mgr. Far West Svcs., Newport Beach, Calif., 1958—66; mgmt. analyst Dept. Fin. State of Calif., Sacramento, 1971—75, fin. analyst Dept. Fin., 1983—97, chief Bur. Automotive Repair, 1975—83; ret., 1997. Cons. Little Hoover Commn., Sacramento, 1974. Bd. mem. River City Recovery, Sacramento, 1995. Recipient award, Wall Street Jour., 1969, Grey Key award, Chapman U., 1969; grantee, Waltmar Found., 1968. Mem.: Am. Mensa. Independent. Avocations: boating, reading, volunteering in literacy and childrens' home. Home: 2948 26th St Sacramento CA 95818-3512

WIER, LEANNE M., life sciences educator; b. San Antonio, Aug. 29, 1977; adopted d. Glen W. and Shirley Diane Latimer Wier. BS in Agrl. Devel., Tex. A&M U., College Station, 2000; MS Animal Sci., Okla. State U., Stillwater, 2004. Lab. technician Okla. State U., Stillwater, 2001—05; lab. tech. Ultimate Genetics, Franklin, Tex., 2000—01; prof. Rose State Coll., Midwest City, Okla., 2005—. Lab. tech. OvaGenix, Bryan, Tex., 2001—05. Co-chair food ct. RSC Global Okla., Midwest City, Okla., 2006. Tchg. in Cmty. grantee, Rose State Coll., 2006—. Mem.: Okla. Microscopy Soc., Nat. Sci. Tchrs. Assn., Classic Motorcycle and Scooter Riders Okla., Phi Kappa Phi. Achievements include research in evaluation of gene expression during development of the neonatal porcine uterus using suppression subtractive hybridization. Home: 9712 S Bryant Terrace Oklahoma City OK 73160 Office: Rose State College 6420 SE 15th Street Midwest City OK 73110 Office Phone: 405-733-7553. Business E-Mail: lwier@rose.edu.

WIER, PATRICIA ANN, publishing executive, consultant; b. Coal Hill, Ark., Nov. 10, 1937; d. Horace L. and Bridget B. (McMahon) Norton; m. Richard A. Wier, Feb. 24, 1962; 1 child, Rebecca Ann. BA, U. Mo., Kansas City, 1964; MBA, U. Chgo., 1978. Computer programmer AT&T, 1960-62; lead programmer City of Kansas City, Mo., 1963-65; with Playboy Enterprises, Chgo., 1965-71, mgr. systems and programming, 1971; with Ency. Britannica, Inc., Chgo., 1971—; v.p. mgmt. svcs. Ency. Britannica USA, 1975-83, exec. v.p. adminstrn., 1983-84; v.p. planning and devel. Ency. Britannica, Inc., 1985, pres. Compton's Learning Co. divsn., 1985; pres. Ency. Britannica (USA), 1986-91, Ency. Britannica N.A., 1986—94; exec. v.p. Ency. Britannica, Inc., 1986-94; pres. Ency. Britannica N.Am., 1986—94; mgmt. cons. pvt. practice, Chgo., 1994—. Cons. pvt. practice, Chgo., 1994—; bd. dirs. Alcas Corp., Mannatech Inc. Life mem. coun. Grad. Sch. Bus., U. Chgo.; mem. bd. regents Lewis U. Mem. Direct Selling Assn. (bd. dirs. 1984-93, chmn. 1987-88, named to Hall of Fame 1991), Women's Coun. U. Mo. Kansas City (hon. life) Com. 200, The Chgo. Network. Roman Catholic. Office: Patricia A Wier Inc 175 E Delaware Pl Ste 8305 Chicago IL 60611-7748 Office Phone: 312-787-4151. Personal E-mail: wier@prodigy.net.

WIER, RICHARD ROYAL, JR., lawyer; b. Wilmington, Del., May 19, 1941; s. Richard Royal and Anne (Kurtz) W.; m. Anne E. Edwards, Nov. 25, 1978; children— Melissa Royal, Emma Kurtz; children from previous marriage: Richard Royal, III, Mimi Poole. BA in English, Hamilton Coll., 1963; LLB, U. Pa., 1966; postgrad., Temple U., 1981-82. Bar: D.C. 1967, Del. 1967, Pa. 1980, U.S. Dist. Ct. Del., U.S. Ct. Appeals (3d cir.), U.S. Supreme Ct. Assoc. Connolly, Bove & Lodge, Wilmington, 1966-68; dep. atty. gen. State of Del., Wilmington, 1968-70; state prosecutor Del. Dept. Justice, Wilmington, 1970-74; atty. gen. State of Del., Wilmington, 1975-79; ptnr. Prickett, Jones, Elliott, Kristol & Schnee, Wilmington, 1979-92; pvt. practice Wilmington, 1993—. Lectr. criminal and labor law various instns. Active United Way campaign, 1976-77; supervisory bd. Gov.'s Commn. on Criminal Justice; bd. dirs. Del. Coun. Crime and Justice, 1982-89; adv. coun. Diabetes Control, 1990-92; dir. Project Assist, 1992-95, Commn. on Outreach, 1994—. Recipient Law Enforcement award Newark Police Dept., 1974; Law Enforcement Commendation medal Nat. Soc. SAR, 1976; Ideal Citizen award Am. Found. for Sci. Creative Intelligence, 1976; Commendation Del. Gen. Assembly Senate, 1976-77, 80; named one of Top Labor/Employment Attys. in Del., Del. Today, 1999—. Mem. ABA, Nat. Dist. Attys. Assn. (state dir.), Del. Bar Assn. (chmn. criminal law sect. 1987-91, co-chmn. on drug crisis 1993—, vice chmn. labor law sect. 1987-88, chmn. 1989-90), Pa. Bar Assn., D.C. Bar Assn., Nat. Assn. Attys. Gen. (hon. life, exec. com.), Soc. Attys. Gen. Execs. (emeritus), Am. Judicature Soc., Am. Del. Trial Lawyers Assn., Nat. Assn. Extradition Ofcls. (hon. life, regional v.p., exec. dir.), Italian Radio/TV Assn. (hon., Outstanding Achievement award), Internat. Platform Assn., Pi Delta Epsilon. Achievements include inventor in field. Office: Two Mill Rd Ste 200 Wilmington DE 19806 Office Phone: 302-888-3222. Business E-Mail: rwier@wierlaw.com.

WIERMAN, JOHN CHARLES, mathematician, educator; b. Prosser, Wash., June 30, 1949; s. John Nathaniel and Edith Elizabeth (Ashley) W.; m. Susan Shelley Graupmann, Aug. 13, 1971; 1 child, Adam Christopher. BS in Math., U. Wash., 1971, PhD in Math., 1976. Asst. prof. math. U. Minn., Mpls., 1976-81; asst. prof. Johns Hopkins U., Balt., 1981-82, assoc. prof., 1982-87, prof., 1987—, chmn. math. scis. dept., 1988-2000, dir. entrepreneurship and mgmt. program, 1996—, dir. Ctr. for Leadership Edn., 2004—. Sr. rsch. fellow Inst. Math. and Its Applications, Mpls., 1987—88; Navy ASEE fellow Naval Surface Warfare Ctr., 2001—02. Co-author: First-Passage Percolation on the Square Lattice, 1978; contbr. articles to profl. jours. Grad. fellow, NSF, 1971—74, NSF rsch. grantee, 1976—93, sabbatical fellow, Navy-ASEE, 2001—02. Fellow Inst. Math. Stats. (organizer spl. session on percolation theory 1982, organizer spl. session on probability and math. stats. 1986), Inst. of Combinatorics and its Applications; mem. Am. Soc. Quality, Inst. Math. Stats., Am. Math. Soc., Am. Statis. Assn., Math. Assn. Am., Sigma Xi, Phi Beta Kappa. Office: Johns Hopkins U Dept Applied Math and Stats 34th & Charles Sts Baltimore MD 21218 Office Phone: 410-516-7211. Business E-Mail: wierman@jhu.edu.

WIERNIK, PETER HARRIS, oncologist, educator; b. Crocket, Tex., June 16, 1939; s. Harris and Molly (Emmerman) W.; m. Roberta Joan Fuller, Sept. 6, 1961; children: Julie Anne, Lisa Britt, Peter Harrison. BA with distinction, U. Va., 1961, MD, 1965; Dr. honoris causa, U. Republic, Montevideo, Uruguay, 1982. Diplomate Am. Bd. Internal Medicine, Am. Bd. Med. Oncology (mem. writing com. 1981-87). Intern Cleve. Met. Gen. Hosp., 1965—66, resident, 1969—70; resident Osler Svc. Johns Hopkins Hosp., Balt., 1970—71; sr. asst. surgeon USPHS, 1966, advanced through grades to med. dir., 1976; sr. staff assoc. Balt. Cancer Rsch. Ctr., 1966—71, chief med. oncology sect., 1971—76, chief clin. oncology br., 1976—82, dir., 1976—82; assoc. dir. cancer treatment divsn. Nat. Cancer Inst., 1976—82; assoc. dir. Albert Einstein Cancer Ctr., Bronx, 1982—98, prof. medicine, 1983—98, prof. radiation oncology, 1996—98, head med. oncology divsn. Asst. prof. medicine U. Md. Sch. Medicine, Balt., 1971-74, assoc. prof., 1974-76, prof., 1976-82; prof. medicine radiation oncology NY Med. Coll., 1998—; cons. hematology med. oncology Union Meml. Hosp., Greater Balt. Med. Ctr., Franklin Sq. Hosp.; bd. dirs. Balt. City unit Am. Cancer Soc., 1971-78; chmn. patient care com., 1972-75, profl. edn. grants com., NYC divsn., 1983-90, nat. clin. fellowship com., 1984-96; med. adv. com. Nat. Leukemia Assn., 1976-88, chmn. med. adv. com., 1989—; chmn. adult leukemia com. Cancer Leukemia Group B, 1976-83; prin. investigator Ea. Coop. Oncology Group, 1982-94, 96—; chmn. gynecol. oncology com., 1986-88, chmn. leukemia com., 1988-94; sci. cons. Vt. Regional Cancer Ctr., 1987—; dir. OLM Comprehensive Cancer Ctr., NY Med. Coll., 1998—. Editor: Controversies in Oncology, 1982, Supportive Care of the Cancer Patient, 1983, Neoplastic Diseases of the Blood, 1985, 4th edit., 2003, Adult Leukemias, 2001; editor: (assoc.) Medical Oncology and Tumor Pharmacotherapy, 1987—91; editor: (sr.), 1991—; editor: (assoc.) Am. Jour. Therapeutics, 1994—; co-editor: Year Book of Hematology, 1986—98, Handbook of Hematologic and Oncologic Emergencies, 1988—98, Bone Marrow Transplantation (textbook), 1995, Am. Jour. Medical Scis., 1976—81; editor: Jour. of Cancer Rsch. and Clin/Oncology, 1986—89, Jour. Clin. Pharmacology, 1985—; mem. editl. bd. Cancer Treatment Reports, 1972—76, Leukemia Rsch., 1977—86, 1991—2005, Leukemia, 1986—2003, Cancer Clin. Trials, 1977—, Jour. of Therapeutic Rsch., 1994—, Hospital Practice, 1979—, Jour. of Clin. Oncology, 1989—91, Leukemia and Lymphoma, 1989—, PDQ National Cancer Inst., 1987—94, Cancer Investigation, 1998—2007, Serbian Archives Medicine, 2005—; contbr. articles to profl. jours., chapters to books. Recipient Z Soc. award U. Va., 1961, Byrd S. Leavell Hematology award U. Va. Sch. Medicine, 1965, Gold medal 1st Polish Congress Oncology, 2002. Fellow AAAS, ACP, Am. Coll. Clin. Pharmacology (awards com. 1999—), Internat. Soc. Hematology, Royal Soc. Medicine (London), NY Acad. Medicine; mem. Am. Soc. Clin. Investigation (instl. rep. 1997—), Am. Soc. Clin. Oncology (chmn. edn. tng. com. 1976-79, 84, subcom. clin. investigation 1980-82, program com. 1990, pub. issues com., 1990-95, com. rsch. awards 1996-2000, com. health svcs. rsch. 2000-2003), Am. Assn. Cancer Rsch. (clin. cancer rsch. com. 2002—), Am. Soc. Hematology, Am. Fedn. Clin. Rsch., Am. Acad. Clin. Toxicology, Internat. Soc. Exptl. Hematology, NY Acad. Sci., Am. Soc. Hosp. Pharmacy, Am. Soc. Clin. Pharmacology Therapeutics, Am. Radium Soc. (program com. 1987-93, exec. com. 1988-95, publ. com. 1988-92, sec. 1990-91, pres.-elect, 1992-93; pres. 1993-94, Janeway medalist, 1996), Polish Oncology Soc. (hon., finalist Gold medal), Harvey Soc., Uruguayan Hematology Soc. (hon.), Acad. Medicine Uruguay (corr.), European Assn. Cancer Rsch., European Soc. Hematology, Phi Beta Kappa (assoc.), Sigma Xi, Alpha Omega Alpha, Phi Sigma (award 1961). Office: Comprehensive Cancer Ctr Our Lady Mercy Med Ctr 600 E 233rd St Bronx NY 10466-2604 Office Phone: 718-304-7220. Personal E-mail: pwiernik@aol.com. Business E-Mail: wiernik@jimmy.harvard.edu, pwiernik@olmhs.org. *Always remember why you entered a profession in the first place. Leave the politics to those who have forgotten.*

WIERSBE, WARREN WENDELL, clergyman, writer, lecturer; b. East Chgo., May 16, 1929; s. Fred and Gladys Anna (Forsberg) W.; m. Betty Lorraine Warren, June 20, 1953; children: David, Carolyn, Robert, Judy. B.Th., No. Baptist Sem., 1953; D.D. (hon.), Temple Sem., Chattanooga, 1965, Trinity Ev-Div. Sch., 1986; LittD (hon.), Cedarville U., 1987. Ordained to ministry, Bapt. Ch., 1951. Pastor Central Bapt. Ch., East Chicago, 1951-57; editl. dir. Youth for Christ Internat., Wheaton, Ill., 1957-61; pastor Calvary Bapt. Ch., Covington, Ky., 1961-71; sr. min. Moody Ch., Chgo., 1971-78; bd. dirs. Slavic Gospel Assn., Wheaton, 1973-87; columnist Moody Monthly, Chgo., 1971-77; author, conf. minister, 1978-80; pres. ScripTex, Inc., Lincoln, Nebr., 1982—. Vis. instr. pastoral theology Trinity Div. Sch., Deerfield, Ill.; gen. dir. Back to the Bible Radio Ministries, Lincoln, Nebr., 1984-89; writer-in-residence Cornerstone Coll., Grand Rapids, Mich.; disting. prof. preaching Grand Rapids Bapt. Sem. Author: over 150 books including William Culbertson, A Man of God, 1974, Live Like a King, 1976, Walking with the Giants, 1976, Be Right, 1977, (with David Wiersbe) Making Sense of the Ministry, 1983, Why Us? Why Bad Things Happen to God's People, 1984, Real Worship: It Can Transform Your Life, 1986, The Integrity Crisis, 1988, Be What You Are, 1988, The New Pilgrim's Progress, 1989, Living With the Giants, 1993, Preaching and Teaching with Imagination, 1994, Be Myself, 1994, The Bible Exposition Commentary, 6 vols., 2004. Home and Office: 441 Lakewood Dr Lincoln NE 68510-2419

WIERSMA, G. BRUCE, dean, forester, educator; b. Paterson, NJ, Oct. 26, 1942; s. George and Marjorie (Zeedyk) W.; m. Ann Becker, Aug. 15, 1964; children: Heather, Robin, Jennifer, Joshua. BS, U. Maine, 1964; MF in Forestry, Yale U., 1965; PhD Coll. Environ. Sci. & Forestry, SUNY, 1968. Teaching asst., 1965-66; rsch. biologist Coll. Environ. Sci. and Forestry SUNY, 1968; combat devels. staff officer U.S. Army Inst. Land Combat, Alexandria, Va., 1968-70; head monitoring sect. EPA, Washington, 1970-72, chief ecol. monitoring branch, 1972-74, chief pollutant pathways br. Las Vegas, Nev., 1974-79, sr. ecologist, 1979-80; mgr. environ. earth scis. group, Idaho Nat. Engring. Lab. EG&G Idaho, Inc., 1980-87; instr. Idaho Falls Campus of Higher Edn. U. Idaho, 1981-90, affiliate grad. faculty Coll. Forestry Wildlife and Range Scis., 1988-90; mgr., dir. Ctr. Environ. Monitoring and Assesment Environ. Sci. and Tech. Group, 1989-90; dir. Ctr. Environ. Monitoring and Assesment Idaho Nat. Engring. Lab., EG&G Idaho, Inc., Idaho Falls, 1988-90; dean Coll. Forest Resources, assoc. dir. Maine Agrl. Experiment Sta., prof. Forest Resources U. Maine, Orono, 1991-93, dean Coll. Natural Scis., Forestry and Agr., dir. Maine Agrl. and Forest Exptl. Sta., 1993—2006, dir. Ctr. for Rsch. on Sustainable Forests, 2006—. Dir. Ctr. Environ. Monitoring and Assessment, Idaho Falls, Idaho, 1980-90; ad-hoc task force to plan global environ. monitoring sys., 1993-95; trustee Nature Conservancy, 1993-95; UN ad hoc task force to plan global terrestrial observing sys., 1993-95; bd. dirs. Maine Forest Products Coun., 1993—; U.S. Nat. Com. on Data for Sci. and Tech., 1990-92; chmn. com. on databased NRC, 1990-94, com. on marine monitoring, 1986-90; forest resources adv. com. U.S. Sec. Agr., 1998-2005; mem. Gov. Maine's Com. on Sawmill Biomass Conversion, 1999. Contbr. chpts. to books, articles to profl. jours; editor, founder Jour. Environ. Monitoring and Assesment. Pilot, Maine wing CAP. Capt. U.S. Army, 1968-70. Recipient numerous rsch. grants from various orgns. Mem. NRC (chair com. on databases, 1990-94, com. on marine monitoring, 1986-90, Nat. Assn. Profl. Forestry Schs. (exec. com. 1993-98), Assn. Expt. Sta. Dirs. (exec. com. N.E. region 1996-2000, chmn. 1998-99, com. on policy 1997-2000). Avocations: jogging, swimming, cross country skiing, backpacking. Home: 103 Wildwood Estates Dr Holden ME 04429-7344 Office: U Maine Ctr Rsch on Sustainable Forests 5755 Nutting Hall Orono ME 04473 Home Phone: 207-843-5885; Office Phone: 207-581-3794. Business E-Mail: wiersma@maine.edu.

WIERSMA, KEVIN, lab administrator; Various positions, fin. and opers. mgmt. Medtox Scientific, Inc., St. Paul, 1992—98, v.p., 1998—, COO, lab. divsn., 2000—, CFO, 2002—. Office: Medtox Scientific Inc 402 W County Rd D Saint Paul MN 55112

WIERZCHOLSKI, WUNSCHIK CHRISTOPH, mechanical engineer, mathematician, information scientist; b. Znin, Poland, Mar. 18, 1939; s. Henryk and Kanarkowska Maria Wunschik; m. Anna Poznanska, Apr. 27, 1974; 1 child, Michalina. M of Engring., Tech. U., Poznań, Poland, 1967, ScD, PhD, 1970; MSc in Math., U. Poznań, 1967. Asst. prof. Tech. U., Lublin, Poland, 1983-85, Szczecin, Poland, 1985-90, prof., 1990—, Maritime U. Gdynia, 2000, Gdansk U. Tech., 2003—. Head dept. applied math. U. Szczecin, 1986-88; head dept. tech. mechanics Agrl. Acad. Szczecin, 1990-94; lectr., Tech. U. Hannover, Germany, 1992, guest prof. mech. engr., Tech. U. Essen, Germany DFG, German Rsch. Found., 1997; coord. European Union Grantee Transfer of Knowledge, 2004—. Contbr. over 350 articles to profl. sci. jours. in field of tech. mechanics tribology. Coord. EU Grant Transfer of Knowledge, 2004—. Polish grant, 1990, 94, 97, 99, 2001, 2003, German grantee DLR-Berlin-POL, 1980-96; recipient Sci. State award in topic hydrodynamic lubrication, 1981. Mem. Polish Math. Soc., Polish Acad. Scis. (sect. of biomechanics 1999—), Polish Tribological Soc. (mem. mgmt. 1997—), Scientific Soc. of Szczecin, N.Y. Acad. Roman Catholic. Avocation: numerical and analytical applications in biomechanics. Office: Seledynowa st 9/7 PL70-781 Szczecin Poland Address: Stettin Seledynowastr 9/7 PL70781 Szczecin Poland

WIES, BARBARA, publishing executive, editor; b. Dec. 5, 1939; BA, U. Conn., 1961; student, New Sch. for Social Rsch., 1961-62. Product devel. Fearn Soya, Melrose Park, Ill., 1973-75; product devel. Modern Products, Milw., 1973-75; editor, pub. Bestways Mag., Carson City, Nev., 1977-89; pub. The Healthy Gourmet Newsletter, 1989-91, Fine Wine-Good Food Newsletter, 1991—; publicity dir. Nev. Artists Assn., 1994—; owner Gualala (Calif.) Galleries, 1989-90; assoc. pub., mgr. Edn. Range Mag., 1998—2005. Owner, operator cooking sch. Greensboro N.C. 1969-73; instr. Very Spl. Arts Nev., 1997. Author: Natural Cooking, 1968, Wok and Tempura, 1969, Japanese Home Cooking, 1970, The Wok, 1971, Super Soy, 1973, The Health Gourmet, 1981, International Healthy Gourmet, 1982; editor: Desert News, 2004—; one-woman shows include paintings Dolphin Gallery, Gualala, Calif., 1990, River Gallery, Reno, 1994—, 2-woman shows, 1992, 1994, 1996, Dolphin Gallery, Calif., 1994, solo exhbn., Nev. Artists Assn. Gallery, 1993, 1995, 1996, 1997, featured artist, Nev. State Libr., 1996, Silver State Gallery, Reno, 1998, West Nev. CC, 1996, art show judge, 1997; restaurant critic Reno Gazette Jour., 1995—2001, editor, designer Nev. Episcopal Diocesan newsletter Desert Spirit, 2004—, Bishop's Staff, Episcopal Diocese of Nev., 2005—06, The Vineyard, St. James Episcopal Ch., Wilmington, NC, 2007—. Staff assoc. Wilmington Children's Mus., 2006—; del. Nev. Episcopal Diocese Conv., 2002; vestry St. Peter's Episcopal Ch., 2003—, sr. warden, 2005; performer Nev. Arts sponsored Tumblewords, 2000—. Grantee Nev. Arts Coun., 2002; recipient First Place adult fiction Nev. State Lit. Co., 1995, First Place fiction State Lit. Comp., 1998, 2d Place fiction Writers Block; Nev. Arts Coun. fellow, 1999-2000. Mem. Nat. League Am. Pen Women (chair 1st and 2d ann. lit. competition Reno br., chairperson 1st Nat. Lit. award), Inst. Food Technologists, Pastel Soc. of the West Coast, Inst. Am. Culinary Profls.

WIESCHAUS, ERIC F., molecular biologist, educator; b. South Bend, Ind., June 8, 1947; BS, U. Notre Dame, 1969; PhD in Biology, Yale U., 1974. Rsch. fellow Zool. Inst., U. Zurich, Switzerland, 1975-78; group leader European Molecular Biol. Lab., Germany, 1978-81; from asst. prof. to assoc. prof. Princeton U., 1981-87; prof. molecular biology Princeton U., 1987—. Fellow Lab. de Genetique Moleculaire, France, 1976; vis. rschr. Ctr. Pathobiology, U. Calif., Irvine, 1977; mem. sci. adv. coun. Damon Runyon-Walter Winchell Cancer Fund, 1987-92. Contbr. articles to numerous profl. jours. Recipient Nobel prize in physiology or medicine, 1995. Fellow Am. Acad. Arts and Scis.; mem. NAS. Office: Princeton U MOF 435 Dept Molecular Biology Washington Rd Princeton NJ 08544-0001

WIESE, DANIEL EDWARD, marketing and communications researcher; b. Cedar Rapids, Iowa, June 16, 1936; s. Erwin Edward and Bernice Virginia (Cristy) W.; m. Mary Virginia Smith, Nov. 3, 1958 (div. 1982); children: Anne, John, Amy; m. JoBeth Kuehl, Aug. 6, 1982; children: Jamie, Jill, Eric. BS, Iowa State U., 1958. Agy. assoc. ConnGen Life Ins., Hartford, Conn., 1959—61; rsch. assoc. Meredith Pub. Co., Des Moines, 1961—65; rsch. dir. Popular Sci. Pub. Co., NYC, 1965—66; assoc. rsch. dir. Reader Digest Assn., NYC, 1966—67; rsch. dir. Successful Farming divsn. Meredith Corp., Des Moines, 1967—77; mgr. Agtrack divsn. Chilton Rsch. Svcs., Radnor, Pa., 1977—80; v.p., dir. rsch. svcs. Creswell, Munsell, Fulta & Zirbel, Inc., Cedar Rapids, Iowa, 1980—86; pres. Dan Wiese Mktg. Rsch., Cedar Rapids, Iowa, 1986—. Mem. editl. adv. bd. Agrimarketing mag., 1989. Bd. dirs. Plymouth Congl. Nursery Sch., Des Moines, 1975; mktg. com. Cedar Rapids Symphony, 1984; mem. adv. bd. Cedar Rapids Better Bus. Bur., Area Mktg. Task Force, Linn County I-Club Bd., 1991-92; bd. dirs., chmn. mktg. com. Witwer Sr. Ctr., 2001—; mem. Celebration of Agr. Com., 1999—; mem. Linn County 15 in 5 Early Childhood Comms. Com., 2006—. Capt. U.S. Army, 1959. Mem. Nat. Agri-Mktg. Assn. (chmn. mktg. rsch. com. 1982-83, Cornbelt chpt. bd. 1995-2001), Advt. Fedn. Cedar Rapids (1st v.p. 1988-89, pres. 1989-90, bd. dirs. 1987-90, mem. adv. bd. 2002—, inducted Hall of Fame 2003), Cedar Rapids C. of C. (agr.-bus. com.), Ag-Maizing Cedar Rapids (exec. com. 1998-99), Rotary. Home and Office: 2108 Greenwood Dr SE Cedar Rapids IA 52403-2727 Home Phone: 319-364-2866; Office Phone: 319-364-2866. Business E-Mail: danwiese@mchsi.com.

WIESE, JOHN PAUL, federal judge; b. Bklyn., Apr. 19, 1934; s. Gustav and Margaret W.; m. Alice Mary Donoghue, June 1961; 1 child, John Patrick. BA cum laude, Hobart College, Geneva, NY, 1962; LLB, U. Va., Charlottesville, 1965. With Cox, Langford & Brown, Washington, 1967-1969, Hudson & Creyke, 1969-74; trial commr. US Claims Ct., Washington, 1974-1986; judge US Ct. Fed. Claims, Washington, 1986—2001, sr. judge, 2001—. Mem. Phi Beta Kappa, Bar Assn. DC. Office: US Ct of Federal Claims 717 Madison Pl NW Washington DC 20439-0002 *

WIESE, WOLFGANG LOTHAR, physicist, researcher; b. Tilsit, Germany, Apr. 21, 1931; came to U.S., 1957; naturalized, 1965; s. Werner Max and Charlotte (Donath) W.; m. Gesa Ladehoff, Oct. 12, 1957; children: Margrit, Cosima. BS, U. Kiel, Fed. Republic Germany, 1954, PhD, 1957, PhD (hon.), 1993. Rsch. assoc. U. Md., College Park, 1958-59; rsch. physicist Nat. Bur. Standards, Gaithersburg, Md., 1960-62, chief plasma spectrosc. sect., 1962-77, chief atomic and plasma radiation div., 1978-91, chief atomic physics div., 1991—2004; ret., 2004; NIST rsch. assoc., 2005—. Lectr. U. Calif., 1963, 64. Author: Atomic Transition Probabilities, Vol. I., 1966, Vol. II, 1969, Vol. III, 1988, Vol. IV, 1988, Atomic Transition Probabilities for C, N, and O, 1996, Spectral Data for Highly Ionized Atoms, 2000. Recipient Silver Medal award Dept. Commerce, 1962, Gold Medal award, 1971, Humboldt award, 1986, A.S. Fleming award U.S. C. of C., 1971, Disting. Career in Sci. award Wash. Acad. Sci., 1992, Disting. Postdoctoral award U. Md., 2003, Guggenheim fellow, 1966. Fellow Am. Phys. Soc., Optical Soc. Am., Wash. Acad. Sci.; mem. Internat. Astron. Union. Lutheran. Home: 8229 Stone Trail Dr Bethesda MD 20817-4555 Home Phone: 301-365-2863; Office Phone: 301-975-3201. Business E-Mail: wiese@nist.gov.

WIESEL, ELIE, writer, educator; b. Sighet, Romania, Sept. 30, 1928; arrived in Paris, 1945; came to US, 1956, naturalized, 1963; s. Shlomo and Sarah (Feig) W.; m. Marion Erster, 1969; 1 son, Shlomo Elisha; 1 stepchild, Jennifer. Student, The Sorbonne, Paris, 1948-51; LittD (hon.), Jewish Theol. Sem., NYC, 1967; LHD (hon.), Hebrew Union Coll., 1968, Manhattanville Coll., Purchase, NY, 1972, Yeshiva U., NYC, 1973; D of Hebrew Letters (hon.), Spertus Coll. Judaica, 1973; PhD (hon.), Bar-Ilan U., 1973; LHD (hon.), Boston U., 1974; LLD (hon.), Hofstra U., Hempstead, NY, 1975; LittD (hon.), Marquette U., Wis., 1975, Simmons Coll., Boston, 1976; LHD (hon.), Coll. St. Scholastica, 1978; LLD (hon.), Talmudic U. Fla., 1979; LHD (hon.), Wesleyan U., 1979; LLD (hon.), U. Notre Dame, Ind., 1980; LHD (hon.), Brandeis U., Waltham, Mass., 1980; LittD (hon.), Anna Maria Coll., 1980, Yale U., New Haven, Conn., 1981; LHD (hon.), Kenyon Coll., 1982, Hobart/William Smith Coll., 1982, Emory U., Atlanta, 1983, Siena Heights Coll., 1983, Fla. Internat. U., Miami, 1983, Fairfield U., Conn., 1983, Dropsie Coll., 1983, Moravian Coll., Bethlehem, Pa., 1983, Colgate U., Hamilton, NY, 1984; LittD (hon.), Wake Forest U., Chgo., 1985; LHD (hon.), SUNY, Binghamton, 1985, Lehigh U., Pa., 1985; LittD (hon.), Haverford Coll., Pa., 1985; HHD (hon.), U. Hartford, 1985; LHD (hon.), Coll. New Rochelle, 1986, Tufts U., Medford, Mass., 1986, Georgetown U., Washington, DC, 1986; LittD (hon.), Capital U., 1986; LHD (hon.), Hamilton Coll., 1986, Rockford Coll., 1986; PhD (hon.), U. Haifa, 1986; LittD (hon.), LI U., 1986; LHD (hon.), Villanova U., Pa., 1987, Coll. St. Thomas, 1987, U. Denver, 1987, Walsh Coll., Troy, Mich., 1987, Loyola Coll., Balt., 1987; LittD (hon.), U. Paris, Sorbonne, 1987; HHD (hon.), Lycoming Coll., Williamsport, Pa., 1987; LittD (hon.), U. Conn., Storrs, 1988; PhD (hon.), Ben Gurion U., 1988; LittD (hon.), U. Ctrl. Fla., Orlando, 1988; LLD (hon.), La Salle U., 1988; LHD (hon.), Ohio U., 1988; HHD (hon.), U. Miami, 1988; LittD (hon.), Wheeling Jesuit Coll., 1989, Wittenberg U., Springfield, Ohio, 1989; HHD (hon.), Brigham Young U., Provo, Utah, 1989; DSc (hon.), U. Health Scis./Chgo. Med. Sch., 1989; LHD (hon.), Concordia Coll., 1990, NYU, 1990, Fordham U., Bronx, NY, 1990, Conn. Coll., New London, 1990; ThD (hon.), U. Åbo Akadem, 1990; LHD (hon.), Upsala Coll., 1991, Duquesne U., Pitts., 1991, Roosevelt U., 1991, Hunter Coll., NYC, 1992, Susquehanna U., Selinsgrove, Pa., 1992, Am. U., 1992; LittD (hon.), Fairleigh Dickinson U., Teaneck, NJ, 1993; LHD (hon.), Millersville U., Pa., 1993; degree (hon.), U. Dayton, 1993, U. Mich., 1993, U. Bordeaux, 1993; LHD (hon.), Gustavus Adolphus Coll., 1994, McGill U., Montreal, 1994, Mt. Sinai Med. Sch., 1994, Spelman Coll., Atlanta, 1995; Doctorat (hon.), U. Catholique de Louvain, 1995; LLD (hon.), Bates Coll., Lewiston, Maine, 1995; LHD (hon.), Sacred Heart U., Fairfield, Conn., 1995; D (hon.), U. Buenos Aires, 1995; Docteur (hon.), U. de Picardie Jules Verne, Amiens, France, 1996; LHD (hon.), Briar Cliff Coll., Sioux City, Iowa, 1996, Clark U., Worcester, Mass., 1996, Phila. Coll. Textiles, 1996, U. Mass., Dartmouth, 1997, U. South Fla., Tampa, 1997, Fla. Atlantic U., Boca Raton, 1997, U. RI, Kingston, 1997, U. Mass., Lowell, 1997; LLD (hon.), U. Guelph, 1997; LHD (hon.), De Paul U., Chgo., 1997, Seton Hall U., South Orange, NJ, 1998; LittD (hon.), St. John's U., 1998; LHD (hon.), Eckerd Coll., St. Petersburg, Fla., 1998, Appalachian State U., Boone, NC, 1998, Merrimack U., 1998; D. (hon.), Cedar Crest Coll., Allentown, Pa., 1998; LHD (hon.), Gettysburg Coll., Pa., 1998, Loyola U., Chgo., 1999; HHD (hon.), Mich. State U., East Lansing, 1999; Doutor (hon.), U. do Estado do Rio de Janeiro, 1999; Docteur (hon.), U. Montreal, 1999; LHD (hon.), St. Norbert Coll., De Pere, Wis., 1999, St. Joseph's U., 2000, U. Fla., Gainesville, 2000; PhD (hon.), Hebrew U., Israel, 2000, U. Bologna, 2000; EdD (hon.), Regis U., 2001; Docteur (hon.), U. Paris, Sorbonne, 2001; LHD (hon.), Hebrew Coll., 2001; EdD (hon.), Stockton Coll., 2003, Meredith Coll., Raleigh, NC, 2003, Old Dominion U., Norfolk, Va., 2003,

Elon U., 2004, Case Western Reserve U., Cleve., 2004; LHD (hon.), Chapman U., Orange, Calif., 2005, Israel Inst. Tech., 2005, Snow Coll., Ephraim, Utah, 2006, Dartmouth Coll., Hanover, NH, 2006; HHD (hon.), McDaniel Coll., 2005; DHL (hon.), Cabrini Coll., Radnor, Pa., 2006, U. Vt., 2007. Disting. prof. Judaic studies CCNY, 1972-76; Andrew W. Mellon prof. in the humanities Boston U., 1976—, prof. religious studies and univ. prof., 1976—, prof. philosophy, 1988—. Disting. vis. prof. Henry Luce, 1982-83, Yale U.; lectr. Andrew W. Mellon Ann. Lecture Series Boston U., 92d St. YMHA, YWHA Ann. Lectr. Series, ann. radio broadcast series, 1966-86, advisory bd. Rena Costa Ctr. for Yiddish Studies at Bar-Ilan U., 1994, advisory coun. Carnegie Commn. on Preventing Deadly Conflict, 1994; chmn. US Pres.'s Commn. on the Holocaust, 1979-80, US Holocaust Meml. Coun., 1980-86; hon. chmn. Holocaust Studies Ctr. of Bronx HS Sci., Nat. Jewish Resource Ctr., NYC; hon. coun. Vancouver Holocaust Ctr. Soc., 1992—, Ctr. Christian-Jewish Understanding, Sacred Heart U., Am. Friends of Ghetto Fighter's House; co-chmn. Children of Chernobyl/Children at Heart, 1995—; steering com. The Balkan Inst., 1996—; mem. Nat. hon. com. Darius Milhaud Soc.; mem. coun. Ethic Accord Project on Ethic Rels., (hon.) Am. Friends of Neve Shalom/Wahat al-Salam, 1996—; leadership coun. Tanenbsum Ctr. Interreligious Understanding, 1997—; founder Elie Wiesel Found. for Humanity, 1987; founding pres. Paris-based Universal Acad. Cultures, 1993; pres. Comité Français Pour "Yad Vashem." Am. Gathering of Jewish Holocaust Survivors, 1985, Am. Kurdish Info. Network, 1997, adv. bd., 1997; v.p. Internat. Rescue Com., 1985—; adv. bd. The Raoul Wallenberg Commn. of US, 1981—, Friends of LeChambon, 1982, Boston U. Inst. for Philosophy & Religion, 1986, Boston U. Students for a Free Tibet, Nat. Inst. Against Prejudice & Violence, Internat. Ctr. in NY, 1986—, Friends of Akim USA, 1991, Sholom Aleichem Meml. Found., Nat. Jewish Law Students Assn., 1995—, AmeriCares, 1995, React Take Action Awards, 1996—, No Greater Love, 1996—, Inst. Study of Violence, 1996—, Global Lawyers and Physicians: Working Together for Human Rights, 1997; internat. adv. bd. Elmhurst Coll. Holocaust Edn. Project, 1996—; Am. bd. adv. The Moscow Ctr.; adv. coun. US Com. Refugees, 1996—, Nat. Endowmet for Democracy, 1996—; Helsinki adv. com. Human Rights Watch; bd. govs. Haifa U., (mem. emeritus) Tel Aviv U. 1976—, Massuah - Inst. Study of Holocaust, Israel; bd. dirs. Nat. Com. on Am. Fgn. Policy, Elaine Kaufman Cultural Ctr., Humanitas, Am. Assocs. Ben-Gurion U. of the Negev, Mut. of Am., France Libertés; hon. dir. HIAS; bd. trustees Annenberg Rsch. Inst., 1983-89, Am. Jour. World Svc., 1985—, Haifa U., Tel-Aviv U., Yeshiva U., 1977—, Am. Jewish Heritage Ctr., Mus. Jewish Heritage, NY; patron Internat. Peace U., Berlin, 1995—; colleague Cathedral St. John the Divine, 1975—; mem. jury Neustadt Internat. Prize Lit., 1984; mem. Task Force Apprehending Indicted War Criminals, 1998—. Author: Night (Oprah's Book Club 2006), 1960, Dawn, 1961, The Accident, 1962, The Town Beyond the Wall, 1964, The Gates of the Forest, 1966, The Jews of Silence, 1966, Legends of Our Time, 1968, A Beggar in Jerusalem, 1970, One Generation After, 1970, Souls on Fire, 1972, The Oath, 1973, Ani Maamin, 1973, Zalmen, or the Madness of God, 1974, Messengers of God, 1976, A Jew Today, 1978, Four Hasidic Masters, 1978, The Trial of God, 1979, The Testament, 1980, Le Testament D'Un Poète Juif Assassiné (France's Prix Livre-Inter 1980, Bourse Goncourt, 1980, Prix des Bibliothécaires, 1981), 1985, Images from the Bible, 1980, Five Biblical Portraits, 1981, Somewhere A Master, 1982, Paroles d'Étranger, 1982, The Golem, 1983, The Fifth Son (Grand Prix de la Littérature, City of Paris), 1985, Signes d'Exode, 1985, Against Silence (3 vols., ed. Irving Abrahamson), 1985, Job ou Dieu dans la Tempête, 1986, A Song for Hope, 1987, The Nobel Address, 1987, Twilight, 1988, Un desir fou de danser, 2006; (essays) Silences et Mémoire d'hommes, 1989, L'Oublié, 1989, From the Kingdom of Memory, 1990, Célébration Talmudique, 1991, Sages and Dreamers, 1991, The Forgotten, 1992, (with John Cardinal O'Connor) A Journey of Faith, 1990, (with Albert Friedlander) The Six Days of Destruction, 1988, (with Kofi A. Annan) Confronting Anti-Semitism, 2006, (novel) Un désir fou de danser, 2006, (dialogues with Philippe-Michaël Saint-Cheron) Evil and Exile, 1990, commentaries to A Passover Haggadah, 1993, All Rivers Run To The Sea (a memoir), 1995, (with Jorge Semprun) Se taire est impossible, 1995, (with François Mitterand) Memoir in Two Voices, 1996, Et la Mer N'est Pas Remplie, Memoirs II, 1996, Célébration Prophétique, Portraits et Légendes, 1998, Les juges, 1999, King Solomon and His Magic Ring, 1999, And the Sea is Never Full (English transl. of Et la mer n'est pas remplie, Memoirs II 1999), The Judges, 2002, (dialogues with Michael de Saint Cheron) Le Mal et L'Exil/Dix ans après, 1999, (essays) D'où viens-tu? (pub. by Le Seuil), 2001, After the Darkness, 2002, Wise Men and Their Tales, 2003, The Time of the Uprooted, 2005, (essays) Et où vas-tu?, 2004, (essays) Confronting Anti-Semitism, 2006; mem. editl. and adv. bds. Midstream, Religion and Lit. (U. Notre Dame), Sh'ma: Jour. of Responsibility, Hadassah Mag., Acad. of the Air for Jewish Studies, Holocaust and Genocide Studies: An Internat. Jour., Passages, Religion and the Arts; subject of more than 55 books; journalist Israeli, French and Am. newspapers. Chmn. adv. bd. World Union Jewish Students, 1985—; comité d'Honneur Ligue Internationale Contre le Racisme et l'Antisemitisme, 1985—; founder Nat. Jewish Ctr. Learning and Leadership, 1974; mem. soc. fellows Ctr. Judaic Studies, U. Denver, 1980, bd. overseer Bar-Ilan U., 1970—. Recipient Prix Rivarol, 1963, Prix de l'Universite de la langue Francaise, 1963, Ingram Merrill award, 1964, Jewish Heritage award, Haifa U., 1975, Remembrance award, 1965, Prix du Souvenir, 1965, Nat. Jewish Book Council award, 1965, 1973, Prix Médicis, 1968, Prix Bordin, French Acad., 1972, Eleanor Roosevelt Meml. award, NY United Jewish Appeal, 1972, Am. Liberties medallion, Am. Jewish Com., 1972, Martin Luther King Jr. medallion, CCNY, 1973, Ann. award for Disting. Service to Am. Jewry, Nat. Fedn. of Jewish Men's Clubs, 1973, Faculty Disting. Scholar award, Hofstra U., 1974, Rambam award, Am. Mizrachi Women, 1974, Meml. award, NY Soc. Clin. Psychologists, 1975, First Spertus Internat. award, 1976, Myrtle Wreath award, Hadassah, 1977, King Solomon award, 1977, Liberty award, HIAS, 1977, Jewish Heritage award, B'nai B'rith, 1966, Avodah award, Jewish Tchrs. Assn., Jewish Tchrs. Assn., 1972, Humanitarian award, B'rith Sholom, 1978, Joseph Prize for Human Rights, Anti-Defamation League, 1978, Zalman Shazar award, State of Israel, 1979, Presdl. Citation, NYU, 1979, Inaugural award for Lit., Israel Bonds Prime Minister's Com., 1979, Jabotinsky medal, S.Y. Agnon medal, State of Israel, 1980, Rabbanit Sarah Herzog award, Emunah Women of Am., 1981, Le Grand Prix Littéraire du Festival Internat. Deauville, 1983, Internat. Lit. prize for Peace, Royal Acad. Belgium, 1983, Lit. Lions award, NY Pub. Libr., 1983, Jordan Davidson Humanitarian award, Fla. Internat. U., 1983, Anatoly Scharansky Humanitarian award, 1983, Grand Officer, Legion of Honor, France, Congl. gold medal, 1985, Voice of Conscience award, Am. Jewish Congress, 1985, Remembrance award, Israel Bonds, 1985, Anne Frank award, 1985, 4 Freedoms award, FDR 4 Freedoms Found., 1985, Medal of Liberty award, Statue of Liberty Presentation, 1986, Nobel Peace Prize, 1986, First Herzl Lit. award, First David Ben-Gurion award, Nat. UJA, Gov.'s award, Shaarei Tzedek, Internat. Kaplun Found. award, Hebrew U. Jerusalem, Scopus award, 1974, Am.-Israeli Friendship award, Disting. Writers award, Lincolnwood Library, 1984, First Chancellor Joseph H. Lookstein award, Bar-Ilan U., 1984, Sam Levenson Meml. award, Jewish Cmty. Rels. Coun., 1984, Comenius award, Moravian Coll., 1985, Henrietta Szold award, Hadassah, 1985, Disting. Cmty. Svc. award, Mut. Am., 1985, Covenant Peace award, Synagogue Coun. Am., 1985, Jacob Pat award, World Congress Jewish Culture, 1985, Humanitarian award, Internat. League Human Rights, 1985, Disting. Fgn.-Born Am. award, Internat. Ctr. NY, Inc., 1986, Freedom Cup award, Women's League Israel, 1986, First Jacob Javits Humanitarian award, UJA Young Leadership, 1986, Boston City Coun. Commendation, 1986, medal of Jerusalem, 1986, Freedom award, Internat. Rescue Com., 1987, Achievement award, Artist and Writers for Peace in the Mid. East, 1987, La Grande Médaille de Vermeil de la Ville de Paris, 1987, La Médaille de la Chancellerie de l'Université de Paris, 1987, La Médaille de l'Université de Paris, 1987, First Eitinger prize, U. Oslo, 1987, Lifetime Achievment award, Present Tense mag., 1987, Spl. Christopher award, The Christophers, 1987, Achievement award, State Israel, 1987, Sem. medal, Jewish Theol. Sem. Am., 1987, Metcalf Cup and Prize for Excellence in Teaching, Boston U., 1987, Spl. award, Nat. Com. on Am. Fgn. Policy, 1987, Grã-Cruz da Ordem Nacional do Cruzeiro do Sul, Brazil's highest distinction, 1987, Profiles in Courage award, B'nai B'rith, 1987, Centennial medal, U. Scranton, 1987, Citation from Religious Edn. Assn., 1987, Golda Meir Sr. Humanitarian award, 1987, Presdl. medal, Hofstra U., 1988, Bicentennial medal, Georgetown U., 1988, Human Rights Law award, Internat. Human Rights Law Group, 1988, Janus Korczak Humanitarian award, INTERPHIL, 1989, Count Sforza award in Philanthropy, Am. Hungarian Found., 1989, Lily Edelman award for Excellence in Continuing Jewish Edn., B'nai B'rith Internat., 1989, George Washington award, NAHE, Kent State U., 1989, Bicentennial medal, NYU, 1989, Humanitarian award, Human Rights Campaign Fund, 1989, Internat. Brotherhood award, C.O.R.E., 1990, Frank Weil award for Disting. Contbn. to Adv. of N.Am., Jewish Culture Jewish Cmty. Ctrs. Assn. N.Am., 1990—, 1st Raoul Wallenberg medal, U. Mich., 1990, Award of Highest Honor, Soka U., 1991, Facing History and Ourselves Humanity award, 1991, La Medaille de la Ville de Toulouse, 1991, 1st Internat. Primo Levi award, 1992, Lit. Arts award, Nat. Found. for Jewish Culture, 1992, Ellis Island Medal of Honor, 1992, Guardian of the Children award, AKIM USA, 1992, Bishop Francis J. Mugavero award for religious and racial harmony Cath. Newman Ctr. Queens Coll., 1994, Golden Slipper Humanitarian award, 1994, Interfaith Coun. on the Holocaust Humanitarian award, 1994, Crystal award Davos World Economic Forum, 1995, First Niebuhr award, Elmhurst Coll., 1995, Mathilde Schecter award Women's League Conservative Judaism, 2000, Manhattan award Nat. Arts Club, 2000, Benediction medal The Delbarton Sch., 2001, Humanitarian award Israel Cancer Rsch. Fund, 2004, Inaugural award Louise T. Blouin Found., 2005, Grifo d'Oro award Mayor of Genoa, Italy, 2005, Light of Truth award Internat. Campaign Tibet, 2005; named Humanitarian of the Century Coun. Jewish Orgns., Presdl. medal Freedom, 1992; Beth Hatefutsoth hon. fellow, 1988; honors established in his name: Elie Wiesel award for Holocaust Rsch., U. Haifa, Elie Wiesel Chair in Holocaust Studies, Bar-Ilan U., Elie Wiesel Endowment Fund for Jewish Culture, U. Denver, 1987, Elie Wiesel Disting. Svc. award, U. Fla., 1988, Elie Wiesel awards for Jewish Arts and Culture B'nai B'rith Hillel Founds., 1988, Elie Wiesel Chair in Judaic Studies Conn. Coll., 1990, Disting. Libery award NYC Refugee Employment Project, 1995, Freedom award Nat. Civil Rights Mus., 1995, Humanitarian award Queensborough Comty. Coll./Holocaust Resource Ctr. Archives, 1995, Socio Honorario de la Sociedad Hebrai ca Argentina, 1995, Pres. award Quinnipac Coll., 1996, Golden Plate award Am. Acad. Achievement, 1996, Lotos medal of Merit, The Lotos Club, 1996, Guardian of Zion award Ingeborg Rennert Ctr. Jerusalem Studies, Bar-Ilan U., 1997, Eisenhower Leadership prize Eisenhower World Affairs Inst. Gettysburg Coll., 1997, Canterbury medalist Becket Fund for Religious Liberty, 1998, ABA ann. award, 1998, Rabbi Marc H. Tanenbaum award for Advancement Interreligious Understanding, 1998, Yitzhak Rabin Peacemaker award Merrimack Coll., 1998, Aesop prize Children's Am. Folklore Soc. for King Solomon and His Magic Ring (Children's Folklore sect. 1999), Raoul Wallenberg Internat. Humanitarian award The Am. Jewish Joint Distbn. Com., 1999, Comdr.'s Cross, Order of Merit, Republic of Hungary, 2004, King Hussein award, Hashemite Kingdom of Jordan, 2005, Hon. Citizen City of Santa Margherita, Italy, 2005, Cosmos Club award, 2006, Literary Lions award NY Pub. Libr., 2006, Chubb Fellowship award Timothy Dwight Ho., Yale U., 2006, La Grande Médaille de la Ville de Paris, 2006; named Man of Year Tel Aviv Mus. Art, 2005, Hon. Citizen, City of Aix-en-Provence, France, 2006; named one of 100 Most Influential People, Time Mag., 2006; named Honorary Knight in the Most Excellent Order of the Brit. Empire, 2006. Fellow Jewish Acad. Arts and Scis., Am. Acad. Arts and Letters (dept. lit.), Am. Acad. Arts and Scis., Modern Lang. Assn. Am. (hon.), Timothy Dwight Coll., Yale U.; mem. Fgn. Press Assn. (hon. life), Amnesty Internat., PEN (New England coun. 1993—), Writers and Artists for Peace in Middle East, Writers Guild of Am. East, The Author's Guild, Royal Norwegian Soc. Scis. and Letters, Soc. des auteurs Paris, European Acad. of Arts, Sci. and Humanities, Albert Einstein Soc. (hon., Phila.), Phi Beta Kappa (Assocs. award 1994). Office: Boston U 147 Bay State Rd Boston MA 02215 Office Phone: 617-353-4561.

WIESEL, SAM W., medical educator, academic administrator; b. Birmingham, Ala., July 7, 1945; MD, U. Pa., 1971. Cert. Orthop. Surgery. Intern Hosp. U. Pa., 1971—72, fellow, orthop., 1972—73, resident, orthop., 1973—76; exec. v.p. health studies, exec. dean sch. medicine Georgetown U. Med. Ctr., Washington, 1996—2002, sr. v.p., dean clin. affairs, 2002—, chmn. dept. orthop. surgery sch. medicine, prof., dept. orthop. surgery. Mem. Ctr. for Neural Injury and Recovery. Author: The Aging Lumbar Spine, 1982, Neck Pain, 1992, Industrial Low Back Pain (Contemporary Litigation Series); co-editor: The Year Book of Orthopedics, 1995 (Year Book of Orthopedics), 1995, The Lumbar Spine, 1996, Essentials of Orthopedic Surgery, 2nd edit., 1997, Essentials of Orthopedic Surgery, 3rd edit., 2006; co-author: Emergency Orthopedic Radiology, 1985, Hip and Knee Pain, 1990, Essentials of Orthopedic Surgery, 1993, Low Back Pain: Medical Diagnosis and Comprehensive Management, 1995, Neck Pain: Medical Diagnosis and Comprehensive Management, 1996, Ortopedia-Fundamentos, 2000, Principles of Orthopaedic Medicine and Surgery, 2001, Low Back Pain, 1999, The Adult and Pediatric Spine: An Atlas of Differential Diagnosis, 2003, Hand and Wrist Pain. Achievements include being an expert in adult spine reconstruction; major research interests have been in the area of diagnosis and treatment of low back pain. Office: Georgetown Orthop 4445 Willard Ave Ste 202 Chase Tower Bldg Chevy Chase MD 20815 also: Georgetown U Med Ctr Dept Orthopedic Surgery 4000 Reservoir Rd NW Ste 120 Washington DC 20007 Office Phone: 240-235-2360. Business E-Mail: wiesels@georgetown.edu. *

WIESEL, TORSTEN NILS, neurobiologist, educator; b. Upsala, Sweden, June 3, 1924; arrived in U.S., 1955; s. Fritz Samuel and Anna-Lisa Elisabet (Bentzer) Wiesel; 1 child, Sara Elisabet. MD, Karolinska Inst., Stockholm, 1954; D Medicine (hon.), Karolinska Inst, Stockholm, 1989; AM (hon.), Harvard U., 1967; D Medicine (hon.), Linköping U., 1982; ScD (hon.), NYU, 1987, U. Bergen, 1987. Instr. physiology Karolinska Inst., 1954—55; asst. dept. child psychiatry Karolinska Hosp., 1954—55; fellow in ophthalmology Johns Hopkins U., 1955—58, asst. prof. ophthalmic physiology, 1958—59; assoc. in neurophysiology and neuropharmacology Harvard U. Med. Sch., Boston, 1959—60, asst. prof. neurophysiology and neuropharmacology, 1960—64, asst. prof. neurophysiology, dept. psychiatry, 1964—67, prof. physiology, 1967—68, prof. neurobiology, 1968—74, Robert Winthrop prof. neurobiology, 1974—83, chmn. dept. neurobiology, 1973—82; Vincent and Brooke Astor prof. neurobiology, head lab. Rockefeller U., NYC, 1982—98, pres., 1991—98, pres. emeritus, 1998—, dir. Shelby White and Leon Levy Ctr. for Mind, Brain & Behavior, 1998—; sec. gen. Human Frontier Sci. Program, 2000. Ferrier lectr. Royal Soc. London, 1972, NIH lectr., 75; Grass lectr. Soc. Neurosci., 1976; lectr. Coll. de France, 1977; Hitchcock prof. U. Calif.-Berkeley, 1980; Sharpey-Schafer lectr. Phys. Soc. London; George Cotzias lectr. Am. Acad. Neurology, 1983; chmn. bd. govs. NY Acad Scis., 2001—. Contbr. numerous articles to profl. jours. Recipient Jules Stein award, Trustees for Prevention of Blindness, 1971, Lewis S. Rosenstiel prize, Brandeis U., 1972, Friedenwald award, Assn. Rsch. in Vision and Ophthalmology, 1975, Karl Spencer Lashley prize, Am. Philos. Soc., 1977, Louisa Gross Horwitz prize, Columbia U., 1978, Dickson prize, U. Pitts., 1979, Nobel prize in physiology or medicine, 1981, W.H. Helmerich III award, 1989, 2005 Nat. Medal Sci., NSF, 2007. Mem.: AAAS, Inst. Medicine (chmn. com. on human rights 1994—2004, David Rall medal 2005), Royal Swedish Acad. Scis. (fgn.), Royal Soc. (fgn.), Soc. Neurosci. (pres. 1978—79), Swedish Physiol. Soc., Nat. Acad. Arts and Scis., Am. Acad. Arts and Scis., Am. Philos. Soc., Am. Physiol. Soc., Physiol. Soc. (Eng.) (hon.). Office: Rockefeller U 1230 York Ave New York NY 10021-6399 E-mail: wiesel@mail.rockefeller.edu. *

WIESEN, DONALD GUY, retired diversified manufacturing company executive; b. NYC, July 4, 1928; s. Benjamin and Grace (Heath) W.; m. Patricia Ann Elfers, Apr. 29, 1950; children: Mara, Caitlin, Elizabeth, Anne, Megan. BS, Columbia U., 1948, MS, 1954. C.P.A., N.Y. Sr. tax specialist Price Waterhouse & Co., NYC, 1950-58; with Chesebrough-Pond's Inc., Greenwich, Conn., 1958-87, gen. mgr. ops. Europe, 1965-70, treas., 1970-72, group v.p., chief fin. officer, 1972-77, group v.p., internat., 1977-82, sr. group v.p., 1982-84, vice chmn., chief fin. officer, 1984-87, also dir., ret., 1987. Bd. dirs. Skandia Am. Corp., 1985-91. Trustee Greenwich Libr., 1974-80; bd. govs. St. Bernard Coll., Cullman, Ala., 1973-75; rep. Columbia U. Alumni, Geneva, 1968; bd. dirs. Inner-City Found. for Charity and Edn., Bridgeport, Conn., 1992-93. Capt. USMC, 1951-54. Mem. AICPA, Indian Harbor Yacht Club, Univ. Club (N.Y.). Roman Catholic.

WIESENBERG, RUSSEL JOHN, statistician; b. Kaukauna, Wis., Apr. 9, 1924; s. Emil Martin and Josephine (Appelbaker) W.; m. Jacqueline Leonardi, Nov. 23; children: James Wynne, Deborann Donna. BS, U. Wis., 1951; postgrad. Cornell U., 1960-61, U. Mich., 1969, George Washington U., 1976. Analyst, GE, West Lynn, Mass., 1951-56; specialist Internat. GE, Rio de Janeiro, 1956-59; statistician Gen. Motors Corp., Lockport, NY, 1959-65, sr. statistician, Harrison Radiator divsn., 1965-78, sr. reliability engr., 1978-82, sr. reliability statistician, 1982-87. Auditor Cmty. Chest Fund, 1952-55; umpire Little League Baseball, 1962-65; committeeman Buffalo Area coun. Boy Scouts Am., 1962—, Cub Scout committeeman, 1962-64, Webelos cubmaster, 1963-64; mem. Nat. Congress Parents and Tchrs., 1963—; heart fund Vol. Heart Assn., 1968; tournament dir. Am. Legion Baseball, 1975; vol. United Way campaign, 1983, nat. telethon March of Dimes, 1983-84. Served with AUS, 1943-46. Decorated Bronze Star. Mem. AAAS, Am. Statis. Assn., Nat. Register Sci. and Tech. Pers., U. Wis. Alumni Assn., Artus, Internat. Platform Assn., Phi Kappa Phi. Lutheran. com.). Contbr. articles to profl. jours. Home: 14 Norman Pl Buffalo NY 14226-4233

WIESENFELD, KURT ARN, physicist, researcher; b. Roslyn Heights, NY, Feb. 12, 1958; s. David and Elaine Kaye (Dattner) W.; m. Karla Mari Jennings, Aug. 17, 1985; children: Alexis Elaine and Sophia Stella (twins). BS in Physics, MIT, 1979; MA in Physics, U. Calif., Berkeley, 1982, PhD in Physics, 1985. Lectr., rschr. physics U. Calif., Santa Cruz, 1984-85; rschr. Brookhaven Nat. Lab., Upton, NY, 1985-87; asst. prof. Ga. Inst. Tech., Atlanta, 1987-92, assoc. prof., 1992-97, prof., 1997—. Contbr. numerous articles to sci. jours. Fellow Am. Phys. Soc. Office: Ga Inst Tech Sch Physics 837 State St Atlanta GA 30332-0001 Business E-Mail: Kurt.wiesenfeld@physics.gatech.edu.

WIESER, HELMUT, metal products executive; b. Steyr, Austra, Oct. 11, 1953; M in Mech. Engring. and Econs., U. Graz, Austria, 1981. Various sr. mgmt. positions including pres. Voest Alpine Venezuela Voest Alpine; various mgmt. positions in rolled products unit up to mem. exec. bd., COO Austria Metal Group; v.p. ops. Flat-rolled products group Alcoa, Inc., Geneva, 2000—01, pres. Flat-rolled products group, 2001—04, pres. North Am. and European Mill Products, v.p., 2004—05, group pres. global mill products, rigid packaging and hard alloy extrusion businesses, exec. v.p. NYC, 2005—. Bd. govs. Internat. Grad. U., Washington. Achievements include representing Austria in the Modern Pentathlon event at the 1980 Summer Olympics in Moscow. Office: Alcoa Inc 390 Park Ave New York NY 10022 Office Phone: 212-836-2600. *

WIESLER, JAMES BALLARD, retired banker; b. San Diego, July 25, 1927; s. Harry J. and Della B. (Ballard) W.; m. Mary Jane Hall, Oct. 3, 1953; children: Tom, Ann, Larry. BS, U. Colo., 1949; postgrad., Rutgers U., 1962, Advanced Mgmt. Program, Harvard U., 1973. With Bank of Am., NT & SA, 1949-87; v.p., mgr. main office San Jose, Calif., 1964-69; regional v.p. Cen. Coast adminstrn., 1969-74; sr. v.p., head No. European Area office Frankfurt, Fed. Republic of Germany, 1974-78; exec. v.p., head Asia div. Tokyo, 1978-81; exec. v.p., head N.Am. div. Los Angeles, 1981-82; vice chmn., head retail banking San Francisco, 1982-87; ret., 1987. Bd. dirs. Visa USA, Visa Internat., Sci. Applications Internat. Corp.; bd. dirs., chmn. Bank Adminstrn. Inst., 1986-87. Pres. Santa Clara County United Fund, 1969, 70, San Jose C. of C., 1968; fin. chmn. Santa Clara County Reps., 1967-74; bd. dirs. San Diego Armed Svcs., YMCA, Sidney Kimmell Cancer Ctr.; trustee Borrego Cmty. Health Found., 2002-06; trustee, chmn. bd. dirs. Sharp Meml. Hosp.; hon. consul-gen. for Japan, 1990-95. With USN, 1945-46. Mem. San Diego Hosp. Assn. (bd. dirs., treas.), San Diego Zool. Soc., Greater San Diego C. of C. (pres., CEO 1998-99), Bohemian Club, DeAnza Country Club, San Diego Yacht Club. Presbyterian. Home: 605 San Fernando St San Diego CA 92106-3312 Office: Bank Am Nat Trust & Savs 450 B St San Diego CA 92101-8001 Office Phone: 619-515-5938.

WIESNER, DAVID, illustrator, children's writer; b. Bridgewater, NJ; m. Kim Khang; 2 children. BFA in Illustration, R.I. Sch. Design. Illustrator Houghton Mifflin, NYC. Author (illustrator): (books) Free Fall, 1988 (Caldecott Honor book), Hurricane, 1990, Tuesday, 1991 (Caldecott medal, 1992), June 29, 1999, 1991 (Reading Rainbow book), Sector 7, 1999, Three Pigs, 2001 (Caldecott medal, 2002, Prix Sorcières); illustrator (books) Kite Flier, 1986, The Sorcerer's Apprentice, 1989, The Rainbow People, 1989, Tongues of Jade, 1991, Man From the Sky, 1992, Night of the Gargoyles, 1994, Flotsam, 2006 (Caldecott medal, 2007), creator (CD-ROM) The Day the World Broke; one-man shows include Nat. Ctr. for Children's Illustrated Lit., Abilene, Tex., 1999. Office: Houghton Mifflin 222 Berkeley St Boston MA 02116 *

WIESNER, JOHN JOSEPH, retail chain store executive; b. Kansas City, Mo., Mar. 31, 1938; s. Vincent A. and Jane Ann (Hagerty) W.; m. Georgiana Schild, Oct. 15, 1960; children: Susan, John V., Gretchen. BS in Bus. Adminstrn., Rockhurst U., 1960. Vice pres., contr. Fisher Foods, Cleve., 1970-77; asst. corp. contr. Richardson Vicks, NYC, 1960-70; sr. exec. v.p. Pamida, Inc., Omaha, 1977-85, vice chmn., chief exec. officer, 1985-87; CEO C.R. Anthony Co., Oklahoma City, 1987-97, chmn., CEO, 1992-97; dir. Stage Stores, 1997—. Bd. dirs. Elder Beerman, Dayton, Lamonts, Inc., Kirkland, Wash. Bd. dirs. Omaha Area Council on Alcohol and Drug Abuse, 1983—; bd. dirs. Fontenelle Forest, Omaha, chmn., 1983, 84, A Chance to Change Fedn.; mem. bd. regents Rockhurst U, Okla. City Golf & Country Club, Oklahoma City, Kansas City, Mo. Named Bus. Assoc. of Yr., Am. Bus. Women's Assn., 1983. Mem. Nat. Assn. Accts. Republican. Roman Catholic. Home: 1476 S San Joaquin Dr Palm Springs CA 92264-8685

WIESNET, DONALD RICHARD, retired hydrologist; b. Buffalo, Feb. 7, 1927; s. Charles Anthony Wiesnet and Rose Elizabeth Nee Hildenbrand; m. Evelyn Elaine Jordan, Dec. 27, 1952; children: Peter Christopher, Ellen Elaine, Andrew John, Elizabeth Ann. AS, Syracuse U., 1947; BA in Geology, SUNY, Buffalo, 1950, MA in Geology, 1951. Teaching Certificate NY State Bd. Regents, 1952. Geologist US Geol. Survey, Washington, 1952—61, hydrogeological map editor, 1961—64; rsch. hydrologist US Naval Oceanog. Office, Suitland, Md., 1967—71; sr. rsch. hydrologist NOAA / Nat. Environ. Satellite Svc., Camp Springs, Md., 1971—80; chief, land sciences br. NOAA / Nat. Environ. Satellite Data & Info. Svc., Camp Springs, Md., 1980—82; CEO Satellite Hydrology, Inc., Vienna, Va.,

1982—90. Author: (book) Satellite Hydrology; contbr. (book) Manual of Remote Sensing, V. II, Manual of Photographic Interpretation, Facets of Hydrology. Del. White House Conf. on Aging, Washington, 1995; silver rep. Nat. Silver Haired Congress, Alexandria, Va., 1996—2004; advisor on sr. affairs Rep. Tom Davis III US Congress, 1993—2004. Capt. USNR - Ret., 1965—87. NY State Veterans' Scholarship, NY State, 1951, Govt. Employee Grad. Scholarship, US Geol. Survey, 1964, Monetary Grant - Antarctic Mapmaking, NSF, 1978. Fellow: Am. Soc. Photogrammetry & Remote Sensing, Geol. Soc. of Am.; mem.: Nat. Assn. Ret. Fed. Employees (chpt. pres. 1993—94). Roman Catholic. Achievements include pioneer in the application of remote-sensing techniques and satellite data to snow measurements, river basin parameters, flood mapping, ocean currents, and estuarine tidal flows. Avocation: ornithology. Home: 601 McKinley St NE Vienna VA 22180

WIESSLER, DAVID ALBERT, news correspondent; b. Cambridge, Mass., July 20, 1942; s. Albert Francis and Vivian Mary Wiessler; m. Mary Judith Burton, Dec. 28, 1968. AB, Princeton U., 1964; MA, U. Tex., 1968. Editor UPI, Dallas, NYC, Washington, 1966-82; assoc. editor U.S. News & World Report, Washington, 1982-84; Washington Bur. chief UPI, Washington, 1984-90, sr. polit. editor, 1990-93; news editor Bloomberg News Svc., 1994-95; editor nat. news Reuters, Washington, 1995-98, sr. Wash. corr., 1998—. Recipient Best Feature Writer award, Dallas Press Club, 1970. Mem.: Washington Gridiron Club. Avocations: reading, travel, cooking.

WIEST, ANDREW ALLEN, history professor, writer; b. Chicago Heights, Ill., Oct. 28, 1960; s. John Thomas Wiest and Wanda Jeanne Stegall; m. Jill Ann Guillory, Mar. 11, 2000; children: Abigail Georgia, Luke Jacob. BS, U. So. Miss., Hattiesburg, 1982, MA, 1984; PhD, U. Ill., Chgo., 1990. Vis. sr. lectr. Royal Mil. Acad., Sandhurst, Camberly, Surrey, England, 1996; prof. history U. So. Miss., Hattiesburg, 1988—. Vis. prof. USAF Air War Coll., Montgomery, Ala., 2006—; spkr. in field. Author numerous hist. monographs; contbr. articles to profl. jours., chapters to books. Vol. U. So. Miss. Vet. Adminstrn., Hattiesburg, 2000—06; cmty. tchr. Oschner Inst. Lifelong Learning, Hattiesburg, 2002—; newspaper cmty. columnist Hattiesburg Am., 2006—; mem. Sacred Heart Cath. Ch., Hattiesburg, 2002—. Recipient Excellence in Tchg. award, U. So. Miss., 1996, Excellence Tchg. award, 2002, Tchr. Yr.award, Miss. Humanities Coun., 2002, Disting. Program award, Assn. Continuing Higher Edn., 2002, Student Govt. Outstanding Prof. award, U. So. Miss. Student Govt. Assn., 2004, Outstanding Staff award, U. So. Miss. Office Disability Accommodations, 2004; grantee, US Govt., 2006—. Mem.: Commn. Brit. Mil. History, Soc. Mil. History, Phi Alpha Theta. Avocations: golf, reading, travel. Office: Univ So Miss 118 College Dr Box 5047 Hattiesburg MS 39406 Home Phone: 601-554-0609; Office Phone: 601-266-4333. Business E-Mail: andrew.wiest@usm.edu.

WIEST, DIANNE, actress; b. Kansas City, Mo., Mar. 28, 1948; Student, U. Md. Appeared in numerous plays including Ashes (off-Broadway), 1976, Leave It to Beaver is Dead, The Art of Dining (Obie award, 1979, Theatre World award 1983), Bonjour La Bonjour, Three Sisters, Serenading Louie (Obie award, 1983), Othello, After the Fall, Heartbreak House, Our Town, and Hunting Cockroaches, 1987, In the Summer House, 1993, Blue Light, 1994, Memory House, 2005, Third, 2005; appeared in films including It's My Turn, 1980, I'm Dancing as Fast as I Can, 1982, Independence Day, 1982, Footloose, 1984, Falling in Love, 1984, The Purple Rose of Cairo, 1985, Hannah and Her Sisters, 1986 (Acad. award for Best Supporting Actress 1987), Radio Days, 1987, Lost Boys, 1987, September, 1987, Bright Lights, Big City, 1988, Parenthood, 1989 (Acad. award nominee), Cookie, 1989, Edward Scissorhands, 1990, Little Man Tate, 1991, Cops and Robbersons, 1994, The Scout, 1994, Bullets Over Broadway, 1994 (Golden Globe award Best Supporting Actress-Drama 1995, Acad. award for Best Supporting Actress 1995), Drunks, 1995, The Birdcage, 1996, The Associate, 1996, Practical Magic, 1998, The Horse Whisperer, 1998, Portofino, 1999, I Am Sam, 2001, Dr. Rey!, 2002, (voice) Robots, 2005; TV appearances include The Wall, 1982, The Face of Rage, 1983, Simple Life of Noah Dearborn, 1999, The 10th Kingdom, 2000.

WIETING, GARY LEE, federal agency executive; b. Huron, SD, Apr. 24, 1937; s. LeRoy Charles and Edna Lorraine (Crawley) W.; m. Nancy Lou Clark, July 9, 1961 (div. 1991); children: Kevin Clark, Brian David; m. Julia Gladys Eli, Dec. 31, 1998 (div. 2005). BA, U. Ill., 1961; MBA, Lake Forest Sch. Mgmt., 1983; diploma in travel and tourism, Heritage Coll., Las Vegas, Nev., 1997. Logistics mgr. U.S. Army, Vietnam, 1967-68, NATO/Shape Support Group, Belgium, 1968-72, 8th U.S. Army, Korea, 1972-73, U.S. Army Readiness Region, Ft. Sheridan, Ill., 1973-77, U.S. Army Recruiting Command, Ft. Sheridan, Ill., 1977-83; rsch. and devel. logistics mgr. Belvoir Rsch. and Devel. Ctr., Ft. Belvoir, Va., 1983-85, 88-90; personal svcs. logistics mgr. Hdqrs. Dept. of Army, Washington, 1985-88; logistics mgr., assoc. program mgr. for adv. automation FAA, Washington, 1990-94; ret., 1994. Travel counselor, 1997; mem. So. Nev. Area Mil. Retiree Coun., 1998. Capt. U.S. Army, 1957-77, ret. lt. col., 1986. Decorated Army Commendation medal, Bronze Star medal; recipient Comdr. Award for Civilian Svc., U.S. Army, 1988. Mem.: Delta Sigma Phi. Avocations: travel, art. Home: 262 Patti Ann Woods Dr Henderson NV 89002 Personal E-mail: g_leew37@yahoo.com.

WIEU, ANDREW W. RIANG, government agency administrator; b. Malakal, Sudan, Jan. 1, 1928; arrived in US, 1976; s. Riak Wieu Riak and Abok Jok Radol; m. Teresa Nyagi Kuok (dec.); children: Helena, Bol, Abei; m. Nyanbeny Akom Deng (dec.); children: Ding, Anying; m. Mary Nyandeng Obuti; children: Jiel, Riak. Diploma, Khartoum U., Sudan, 1954; LLD, Wheaton Coll., Ill., 1977; MA in Polit. Sci., Am. U., Washington, 1978, postgrad., 1978. Mem. treasury staff Province Adminstrn., Malakal, 1951; police profl., adminstr. Province Police, Malakal, 1951; field adminstr. Western Nuer Dist., Bentiu, Sudan, 1952—53; adminstr. sch. law Khartoum U. Coll., 1954; adminstr. officer Bor Dist. Adminstrn., Sudan, 1954—55, Western Darfur Dist., Zelinge, Sudan, 1956; asst. dist. commr. Lakes Dist., Kumbek, Sudan, 1957—58, Dar Hamar Dist., Nahud, Sudan, 1959—61; asst. local govt. Kasala Province, Sudan, 1962; inspector local govt. No. Region Adminstrn., Marowe, Sudan, 1962; ret. Dep. spkr. Nat. Assembly, Khartoum, 1972—74, leader ho., 1994; min. state Rep. Palace, Khartoum, 1974—76; min. agrl. Sudan Govt., Khartoum, 1955; founder, pres. Devel. Ext. Consultancy Svcs. Internat. Co. Ltf., Trinity Ch. Sudan; Social Care and Humanitarian Agy. Mem.: Concerned Scientists, Americans for the Arts, Sierra Club, Oxford Investment Club (premier mem.). Democrat. Avocations: reading, history, politics, anthropology. Home: 300 Pond St Apt 218 Syracuse NY 13208 Office: Trinity United Ch Sudan Thora Jalaba Malakal Sudan

WIG, ROBERT CURTIS, retired music educator, conductor; b. Montevideo, Minn., Oct. 10, 1934; s. Emil Corneilius and Melda Dena Wig; m. Marilyn Ruth Berg, Oct. 16, 1960; children: Curtis, Karen, Kathleen. BS, St. Cloud State U., 1957, MS, 1963. Registered music educator Music Educators Nat. Conf., Washington, 1991. Music tchr. Dassel (Minn.) Pub. Sch., 1957—64, Milaca (Minn.) Pub. Sch., 1964—93, Pease (Minn.) Christian Sch., 1999—2000; ret. Mem., past condr. St. Cloud (Minn.) Mcpl. Band, 1957—; dir. Alleluia Singers, Milaca, 1993—. Recipient Commendation Mcpl. Band, City of St. Cloud, 1986. Mem.: NEA (life), Assn. Concert Bands, Ret. Edn. Assn. Minn. (life), Minn. Edn. Assn. (life), Windjammers Unlimited Inc., Lions Club (past pres.). Lutheran. Avocations: gardening, golf, bowling, music. Home: 525 2nd Ave SW Milaca MN 56353

WIGAN, GARETH, film company executive; b. London, Dec. 2, 1931; m. Patricia Wigan. Agent MCA, London, 1957—60, John Redway & Associates, 1960—61, Gregson & Wigan, 1961—68; co-founder London Internat., 1968—70; independent film prodr., 1970—75; v.p. creative affairs 20th Century Fox, Los Angeles, 1975—76, v.p. production, 1976—83; co-founder W.W. Productions, 1983—87; production consultant Columbia Pictures, 1987—93, exec. v.p., 1993—97; co-vice chair Sony Pictures Entertainment, 1997—98, Columbia Tristar Motion Picture Group, 1998—. Office: Columbia TriStar Motion Picture Group 10202 Washington Blvd Culver City CA 90232-3119

WIGAND, ROBERT CHARLES, JR., retired civil engineer, retired aerospace engineer; b. SI, NY, June 17, 1924; s. Robert Charles Wigand Sr. and Marion Carolyn (Waner) Wigand; m. Wanda Constance Beelick, Mar. 10, 1952; children: Gwendolyn Mary Bolling, James Robert, John Theodore. BS in Civil Engring., U. Colo., Boulder, 1944. Lic. profl. engr. and land surveyor. Miner Climax Molybdenum Co., Colo., 1943; supt. trainee Callan Builders Inc., Manhasset, NY, 1946; constrn. supt. Johns-Manville Corp., NY, 1947—50; real estate supr. N.E. region Household Fin. Corp., NYC, 1953—55; engr. Franki Found. Co., NYC, 1955, Worcester, Mass., 1956; engr., field supr. power plant constrn. Burns and Roe Inc., NYC, 1957—58, siting engr. project Mercury tracking stas., 1959—60, Indonesia, 1961, Europe, 1962; project mgr., engr. Alaska tracking sta. NASA Goddard Space Flight Ctr., Fairbanks, Alaska, 1963—64, project mgr. Apollo tracking antennas worldwide network, 1965—70, supr. tracking network facilities Greenbelt, 1971—95. Contbr. articles to profl. jours. Lt. col. USMCR, 1942—77. Recipient Project Team awards, NASA, 1967—95. Fellow: ASCE, Am. Congress Suveying and Mapping; mem.: NSPE, Res. Officers Assn., Am. Soc. Mil. Engrs., Goddard Retirees and Alumni Assn. (bd. dirs.), Am. Geophys. Union.

WIGELL, RAYMOND GEORGE, lawyer; b. Chgo., Apr. 18, 1949; s. Raymond Carl and Amanda D. (Santiago) W.; m. Barbara E. Buettner, June 28, 1980; children: Katherine, Elizabeth, Charles. BA, U. Ill., Chgo., 1971; JD, John Marshall Law Sch., 1975; LLM in Taxation, DePaul U., 1991. Bar: Ill. 1975, U.S. Dist. Ct. (no. dist.) Ill. 1975, U.S. Dist. Ct. (no. dist.) Ind. 2002, U.S. Ct. Appeals (7th cir.) 1978, U.S. Supreme Ct. 1979, U.S. Tax Ct. 1987. Pvt. practice law Raymond G. Wigell, Chgo., 1975-77; trial atty. Cook County Pub. Defender, Chgo., 1977-78; pres., owner, atty. Wigell & Assocs., Matteson, Ill., 1978—. Instr. MacCormac Jr. Coll., Chgo., 1976-77; lectr. in bus. law Oakton C.C., Des Plaines, Ill., 1976-84; adj. prof. Govs. State U., University Park, Ill., 1984-92. Commn. chair inquiry bd. Atty. Registration Disciplinary Commn. Supreme Ct. Ill., Chgo., 1985-90, commn. chair hearing bd., 1990-95. With USN, 1971-77. Mem. Ill. State Bar Assn., South Suburban Bar Assn. (bd. dirs.), Nat. Assn. Criminal Def. Lawyers, U. Ill. Alumni Assn. (life). Roman Catholic. Office: Wigell & Assocs Atty at Law 4749 Lincoln Mall Dr Ste 505 Matteson IL 60443 Office Phone: 708-481-4800. Business E-Mail: rwigell@waalaw.com.

WIGENTON, SUSAN DAVIS, federal judge; b. Neptune, NJ, Oct. 12, 1962; BA, Norfolk State U., 1984; JD, Coll. William & Mary, 1987. Bar: NJ 1987. Law clk. judge Lawrence M. Lawson, Superior Ct. NJ, 1987—88; ptnr. Giordano, Halleran & Ciesla, PC, Middletown, NJ, 1988—97; pvt. practice Middletown, 1997—2000; part-time magistrate judge US Dist. Ct. NJ, 1997—2000, magistrate judge, 2000—06, dist. judge, 2006—. Office: Martin Luther King Jr Fed Bldg & US Courthouse 50 Walnut St Newark NJ 07101 Office Phone: 973-645-5903. *

WIGFIELD, RITA L., elementary school educator; b. Mpls., Dec. 14, 1945; d. Willard Ernest and Bernice Eleanor (Peterson) Ahlquist; m. Vernon Carter Wigfield, Oct. 9, 1982. BS, U. Minn., 1967; grad., St. Thomas Coll.; postgrad., Hamlin U. Cert. elem. educator, Minn. Tchr. Alice Smith Sch., Hopkins, Minn., 1967-80, Meadowbrook Sch., Hopkins, 1980-86, Gatewood Sch., Hopkins, 1986—. Owner Swede Country, Minnetonka, Minn., 1983—; elem. team leader Prin.'s Adv. Bd.; chmn. bldg. tech. com. Hopkins Sch. Dist., past supr. bldg. sch. patrol; coop. tchrs. Gustavus Adolphus Coll.; cons. and presenter in field. Author: We Love Literature, 1991 (Grand Prize Scholastic Inc., 1991). Mem. Wooddale Choir Evang. Christian Ch., decorating com., Mission commn., organizer fellowship dinners; mem. Loaves and Fishes, Minn. Landscape Arboretum. Recipient Hon. Mention Learning Mag., 1990, Nat. Coun Econ. edn./Internat. Paper Col. Found., 1992, 2d pl. Minn. Coun. Econ. Edn., 1992, Ashland Oil award, 1994; named Minn. Tchr. of Yr., 1992. Mem. ASCD, Nat. Assn. Miniature Enthusiasts, Am. Quilting Soc., Internat. Reading Assn., Minn. Edn. Assn., Hopins Edn. Assn. (bldg. rep., treas.), Delta Kappa Gamma (pres. Beta Beta chpt.), Kappa Delta Pi. Avocations: miniatures, quilting, flowers, cross-stitch, antiques. Office: Gatewood Elem Sch 14900 Gatewood Dr Minnetonka MN 55345-6731 Home: 7610 Smetana Ln Apt 201 Eden Prairie MN 55344-4751

WIGGER, JARREL L., lawyer; b. Wiesbaden, Germany, May 12, 1963; s. Philip Lee and Ervinetta (Maxey) W.; m. Rose Marie Riley, Aug. 1, 1987; children: Amy Elizabeth, Jordan Lee. BA in English, The Citadel, 1985; JD, Wake Forest U., 1988. Bar: S.C. 1988, U.S. Dist. Ct. S.C. 1993, U.S. Ct. Mil. Appeals 1991, U.S. Supreme Ct. 1998. Student prosecutor Forsyth County Dist. Atty. Office, Winston-Salem, N.C., 1988; assoc. Drose, Davidson & Bennett, Charleston, S.C., 1992-94, jr. ptnr., 1995-98; ptnr. Davidson, Bennett & Wigger, Charleston, 1999—2005; pvt. practice, 2005—. Co-editor, author: U.S. Navy Mass Casualty Handbook, 1991; co-editor: Law School for Nonlawyers Handbook, 1995. Lt. USN, 1986-92. Mem. ABA, ATLA, S.C. Trial Lawyers Assn., S.C. Bar Assn., Charleston County Bar Assn., Claimant Assn. for Workers Compensation (bd. govs.), Assn. Citadel Men (life), Citadel Brigadier Found., Charleston Area Citadel Club, Citadel Old Timers Wrestling Club (pres. 1996—), Sigma Tau Delta. Avocations: running, guitar, wrestling, coaching. Office: 8086 Rivers Ave North Charleston SC 29406 Business E-Mail: jwigger@wiggerlawfirm.com.

WIGGIN, KENDALL FRENCH, state librarian; b. Manchester, NH, Aug. 21, 1951; s. Ralph M. Jr. and Frances (Miltimore) W.; m. Elaine M. Elliott, June 2, 1973 (div. Jan. 1989); children: Sara, Douglas; m. Laura A. Larson, May 26, 1990 (div. May 26, 1990); children: Lindsey, Tess; m. Patricia Copes, Sept. 5, 2004. BA, U. N.H., 1974; MS in LS, Simmons Coll., 1975. Libr. Litchfield (N.H.) Pub. Libr., 1975; dir. Merrimack (N.H.) Pub. Libr., 1975-83; coord. tech. svcs. Manchester City Libr., 1983-90; state libr. N.H. State Libr., Concord, 1990-99, Conn. State Library, Hartford, 1999—. Mem. mgmt. team Conn. History Online Project; mem. Online Computer Libr. Ctr. Mem. Coun.; chair Conn. Comm. on Ednl. Tech.; bd. dir. Am. for Libr. Coun.; bd. judges Sarah Josepha Hall award; mem. adv. bd. Webjunction. Mem. ALA, NH Libr. Assn., Chief Officers State Libr. Agys., Chief Officers State Libr. Agys. in NE, Am. Philatelic Soc. Republican. Presbyterian. Avocations: stamp collecting/philately, gardening. Office: 231 Capitol Ave Hartford CT 06106 Office Phone: 860-757-6510. Business E-Mail: kwiggin@cslib.org.

WIGGINS, BARBARA SUE, pharmacist, educator; b. St. Louis, Va., Mar. 5, 1969; d. Earl Leonard and Carrie Sue Pigg; m. John Wesley Wiggins, Nov. 4, 1962; children: Luke James, Lauren Grace. BS in Pharmacy, St. Louis Coll. Pharmacy, 1992; PharmD, Va. Commonwealth U./Med. Coll. Va., 1998. Bd. cert. pharmacotherapy specialist with added qualifications in cardiology. Clin. specialist - cardiology U. Wash. Med. Ctr., Seattle, 1999—2002; clin. instr. U. Wash. Sch. Pharmacy, Seattle, 1999—2002; ACLS instr. Am. Heart Assn., Seattle, 1999—2002; pharmacy clin. specialist- cardiology U. Va. Health Sys., Charlottesville, 2002—; clin. instr. Sch. Nursing U. Va., Charlottesville, 2002—; ACLS instr. Am. Heart Assn., Richmond, Va., 2002—; clin. instr. Sch. Medicine U. Va., 2003. Contbg. editor and reviewer Springhouse (Pa.) Pub., 1998. Contbr. chapters to books, articles to profl. jours. Chair profl. affairs Wash. Soc. Health Sys. Pharmacists, Seattle, 2002—02. Lt. USN, 1993—99. Recipient Merck Award for Clin. Rsch., 1998. Mem.: Am. Soc. Health Sys. Pharmacists, Va. Soc. Health Sys. Pharmacists (assoc.), Am. Heart Assn. (assoc.), Rho Chi. Achievements include 1996 United States Olympic Marathon Trials Qualifier. Avocations: running, tennis, bicycling, hiking. Office: Univ Va PO Box 800674 Charlottesville VA 22908-0674 E-mail: bsw4v@virginia.edu.

WIGGINS, CHARLES HENRY, JR., lawyer; b. Balt., July 15, 1939; s. Charles Henry and Kathryn Wilson (Walker) W.; m. Wendy Jane Horn, June 20, 1964 (div. 1996); children: Charles Hunter, Rebecca Rae, Melinda Marie; m. Karen Ann Kowal, Apr. 26, 1997 (div. 2002). BSEE, U. Ill., Urbana, 1962; JD with honors, U. Ill., 1965. Bar: Ill. 1965, U.S. Dist. (no. dist.) Ill. 1970, U.S. Tax Ct. 1974, U.S. Ct. Appeals (7th cir.) 1983. Assoc. Vedder, Price, Kaufman & Kammholz, Chgo., 1969-73, ptnr., 1974—. Mem. zoning bd. appeals Village of Indian Head Pk., Ill., 1984-91. Capt. U.S. Army, 1965-68. Mem. Chgo. Bar Assn., University Club (Chgo.), Edgewood Valley Country Club (LaGrange, Ill., bd. dirs. 1991-98), SAR. Avocations: golf, tennis, bridge. Office Phone: 312-609-7525. Business E-Mail: cwiggins@vedderprice.com.

WIGGINS, D. SCOTT, headmaster; m. Susan Wiggins. BA, Boston U.; JD, Ariz. State U. Coll. of Law. Former sci. & math teacher Fessenden Sch., West Newton, Mass., former dir. athletics; former dir. admissions Fountain Valley Sch., Colorado Springs, Colo.; various positions including dean of students, dir. of residential life, and mathematics chair Indian Mountain Sch., Lakeville, Conn.; former principal Metairie Park Country Day Sch., La.; headmaster Lawrence Acad., Groton, Mass., 2003—. Office: Lawrence Acad Powderhouse Rd PO Box 992 Groton MA 01450 E-mail: swiggins@lacademy.edu. *

WIGGINS, DAVID STEWART, state supreme court justice; b. Chgo., Oct. 19, 1951; s. Kalman G. and Joan (Feldman) W.; m. Marsha Wiggins, Dec. 23, 1973; children: Samantha, Sydney, Taylor. BA in Philosophy, U. Ill., Chgo., 1973; JD, Drake U., 1976. Bar: Iowa 1976, U.S. Dist. Ct. (no. and so. dists.) Iowa 1976, U.S. Ct. Appeals (8th cir.) 1976, U.S. Ct. Claims, 1979, D.C. Ct. Appeals, 1979, U.S. Supreme Ct. 1979. Assoc. to ptnr. Williams, Hart, Lavorato & Kirtley, 1976—79; ptnr. Wiggins & Anderson P.C. (now Anderson & Tully), West Des Moines, 1979—2003; justice Iowa Supreme Ct., 2003—. Mem. Iowa Jud. Com. Cost of Litig., 1988, Iowa Jud. Adv. Com. Rules of Civil Procedure, 1991—97; chair Iowa Jud. Qualifications Commn., 2000—03; mem. Iowa Jud. Redistricting Commn., 2002. Fellow C. Edwin Moore Am. Inn of Ct. (master emeritus). Home: 3604 Pommel Pl West Des Moines IA 50265-3168 Office: Jud Br Bldg 1111 East Ct Ave Des Moines IA 50319 Office Phone: 515-281-5175. Business E-Mail: david.wiggins@jb.state.ia.us.

WIGGINS, DEWAYNE LEE, financial executive; b. Stillwater, Okla., Jan. 6, 1949; s. Lloyd Lee Wiggins and Joyce Yvonne Blair; m. Susan Sochinski, Sept. 9, 1978. BS in Acctg., Okla. State U., 1972; MBA, Ind. U., 1984. Pilot Braniff Internat., Dallas, 1977-82; investment analyst Duff & Phelps, Inc., Chgo., 1984-86; portfolio mgr. Centerre Trust Co., St. Louis, 1986-88; pres. Lindbergh Capital Mgmt., Inc., St. Louis, 1988—; founder, pres. Lindbergh Signature Fund, St. Louis, 1999—2005. Capt. USAF, 1972-76. Mem. Ind. U. Alumni Assn., Beta Gamma Sigma. Roman Catholic. Avocations: reading, tennis, gardening. Office: Lindbergh Capital Mgmt Inc 5520 Telegraph Rd Ste 204 Saint Louis MO 63129-3570

WIGGINS, KIM DOUGLAS, artist, appraiser, dealer; b. Roswell, N.Mex., Apr. 8, 1959; s. Walton Wray Wiggins and Barbara Jo Chesser; m. Mary Allison Raney, Sept. 4, 1977 (div. May 1984); children: Rebekah, Mona; m. Maria C. Trujillo, June 17, 1995; children: Gianna Josiah, Elisha Douglas, Eden Renee. Student, Ea. N.Mex. U., Roswell, 1977, 83-84, San Antonio Coll., 1978-79, Ind. Bapt. Coll., Dallas, 1982-83, Santa Fe Inst. Fine Art, 1989. Dir. Clarke-Wiggins Fine Art, Palm Springs, Calif., 1986-89; owner, mgr. Wiggins Fine Art, Santa Fe, 1989-93, Wiggins Studio, Roswell, 1991—. Cons. Mus. N.Mex., Santa Fe, 1992—, Cline Fine Art, Santa Fe, 1993—98; lectr. SE Cowboy Symposium, Atlanta, 2004, Roswell Mus. and Art Ctr., 2006. One man shows include Altermann Morris Galleries, Houston, Dallas, Santa Fe, N.Y.C., 1992-07, Studio Gallery, Laguna Beach, San Diego, 1998, Roswell Mus. and Art Ctr., 2006; exhibited in group shows at Pa. Acad. Fine Art, Phila., 1992-96, M.H. DeYoung Mus., San Francisco, 1993-96, Autry Mus. Western Heritage, L.A., 1999-07, Desert Caballeros Western Mus., Wickenburg, Ariz., 2000, Denver Art Mus., 2000, The Corcoran Gallery of Art, 2001, Joslyn Art Mus., 2002, Art Inst. Chgo., 2003, Booth We. Art Mus., Atlanta, 2005, C.M. Russell Mus., 2006; represented in permanent collections Mus. N.Mex., Sante Fe, Anschutz Collection, Denver, Staples Ctr., L.A., Autry Mus. Western Heritage, L.A., Booth Western Art Mus., Atlanta; editor: K. Douglas Wiggins: Sense of Spirit, 1993; pub., contbr.: Art of the American West, 1999, Painters and the American West, 2000, The Trail of Painted Ponies, 2001, Gathered by Grace, 2002, Grace for the Moment, 2005, Enchanted Lands, 2006. Mem. NRA, HOG, CMA, Internat. Platform Assn., Soc. Am. Impressionists, Coun. for Art of West, Gladney Ctr., Assurance Home, Other Side of the West. Republican. Avocations: printmaking, poetry, motorcycling, scuba diving, fencing. Home: 6 El Arco Iris Dr Roswell NM 88201-7711 Studio: Altermann Galleries 225 Canyon Rd Santa Fe NM 87501-2755

WIGGINS, MARY ANN WISE, small business owner, educator; b. Coushatta, La., Dec. 25, 1940; d. George Wilkinson and Maitland (Allums) Wise; m. Gerald D. Paul (div. Nov. 1977); children: John Barron, James Gordon, Brenda Michelle; m. Billy J. Wiggins, Oct. 3, 1981; children: Marshall Wade, Brian David, William Joshua, George Justin; stepchildren: Joseph James, Winona Gail. BA, Northwestern State U., Natchitoches, La., 1964, postgrad., 1994, Weatherford Coll., 1967, North Tex. State U., 1968; grad., La Tech. U., 2005. Lic. ins. agt., real estate agt., La., pvt. pilot. Tchr. U.S. Army Schs., Nuremberg, Germany, 1964—66, Mineral Wells Ind. Sch. Dist., 1967—70; bookkeeper Wise Dept. Store, Coushatta, La., 1966—67; amb. of good will Vietnam, 1971; owner, mgr. Mary Ann's Furniture & Hardware, Coushatta, 1977—97; tchr. Springville Mid. Sch., 1994—96, Red River Parish Alternative Sch., 1996—98, tchr. Ware Youth Ctr., 1998—. Com. mem. Instrn. and Profl. Devel. Com. La. Assn. Educators, 1998-2000, vice chmn. 1999-2002; v.p. La. Juvenile Detention Tchrs. Assn., 1999—; tchr. leader La. Tech., 2002-03. Columnist: Wise Old Owl Coushatta Citizen, 2004—. Chmn. Am. Cancer Soc., Conway, Ark., 1972, Red River Parish United Way, Coushatta, 1987-88; treas., bd. dirs. Hall Summit United Meth. Ch.; pres. Red River Parish Assn. Educators Polit. Action Com. Recipient German-Am. hospitality award Orgn. German-Am. Women, Nuremberg, 1965. Mem. NEA, La. Assn. Educators (chmn. legis. com. 2000-04), Red River Assn. Educators (v.p. 1994, pres. 1998-2001), U.S. C. of C., Coushatta-Red River C. of C. (charter, bd. dirs. 2007), Pi Kappa Sigma, Sigma Kappa. Democrat. Methodist. Avocations: gardening, swimming, horseback riding, computers, week-enders with family, landscaping. Home: 2217 E Carrol St Coushatta LA 71019-8567

WIGGINS, NORMAN ADRIAN, academic administrator, law educator; b. Burlington, NC, Feb. 6, 1924; s. Walter James and Margaret Ann (Chason) W.; m. Mildred Alice Harmon. AA, Campbell Coll., 1948; BA, Wake Forest Coll., 1950, LLB, 1952; LLM, Columbia U., 1956, JSD, 1964; Exec. Program, U. N.C., 1968-69; LLD, Gardner-Webb Coll., 1972. Deacon Wake Forest Baptist Ch., Winston-Salem, N.C., 1963-66, Buies Creek (N.C.) Bapt. Ch., 1973—; deacon, tchr. Sunday sch., 1952—; lay preacher, 1953—; pres. N.C. Found. of Ch.-Related Coll., 1969-70, Campbell U., Buies Creek, 1967—, prof. law, 1976—. Mem. Chief Justice Commn. on Professionalism, 2004—. Author: Wills and Administration of Estates in North Carolina, 1964—, (with Gilbert T. Stephenson) Estates and Trusts, 1973; Editor: N.C. Will Manual, 1958—, Trust Functions and Services, 1978; Contbr. articles to legal jours. Chmn. Gov.'s Task Force Com. on Adjudication of the Com. on Law and Order, 1969-71; mem. Com. on Drafting Intestate Succession Act for N.C., 1957-59; mem. Com. for Revision of the Laws Relating to the Adminstrn. of Descs.' Estates, 1959-67, chmn., 1964-67; trustee Sunday Sch. Bd., So. Bapt. Conv., 1975—, chmn. bd. trustees, 1978—, nominations com., 1988—; pres. Bapt. State Conv. N.C., 1983-85; bd. dirs. N.C. Cititzens for Bus. and Industry, 1982—. Recipient Outstanding Civilian Svc. award Dept. Army, 1985, Comdr.'s award for Pub. Svc., 1995, Internat. Freedom of Mobility award, 1995, Patriotic Civilian Svc. award U.S. Dept. Army, 1998, award longest tenure as univ. pres. Coalition Christian Colls. and Univs., 1998, The Order of the Long Leaf Pine award, 1998, John J. Parker award, 1999, NC Bapt. Heritage award, 2004, Bapt. State Conv., 2005, The Charles D. Johnson Outstanding Educator award, 2005, James Iredell award, 2006; Campbell Law Sch. renamed in his honor the Norman Adrian Wiggins Sch. of Law, 1989; recognized for outstanding svc. to high edn. and legal edn. Newcomen Soc. U.S., 1993; named to List of 100 Influential Bapt. Leaders in 20th Century, 2000. Mem. ABA, Nat. Assn. Coll. and Univ. Attys. (pres. 1972-73, Disting. Svc. award 1991), Am. Assn. Presidents Ind. Colls. and Univs. (pres. 1981-83), N.C. Assn. Colls. and Univs. (exec. com. 1980—, pres. 1984-85), N.C. Assn. Ind. Colls. and Univs. (pres. 1970-72, exec. com. 1980-81), N.C. Bar Assn., Harnett County Bar Assn., Nat. Fellowship Baptist Men (pres. 1987-90), Jay Waugh Evang. Assn. (dir./pres. 1970-72), Dunn Area C. of C., Wake Forest Alumni Assn., Rotary (hon. mem. Dunn club), Phi Alpha Delta, Phi Kappa Phi, Omicron Delta Kappa. Office: Campbell U PO Box 280 Buies Creek NC 27506-0127 Business E-Mail: byrde@webster.campbell.edu.

WIGGINS, SAMUEL PAUL, education educator; b. Salisbury, NC, Sept. 20, 1919; s. James Andrew and Mollie (Wilhelm) W.; m. Linda Jean Bessent, June 29, 1947; children: Stanley, David, Timothy, Mark. BS, Ga. Tchrs. Coll., 1940; M.Ed., Duke U., 1942; PhD, Peabody Coll., 1952. Teaching prin., Alma, Ga., 1939-40; dir. lab. sch. Ga. Southwestern Coll., 1940-42; dir. student teaching Emory U., 1947-53; prof., adminstr. Peabody Coll., 1953-67; dean Coll. Edn., Cleve. State U., 1967-75, prof., 1975-85, Norfolk State U., 1985-96, co-dir. project nat. bd. profl. tchg. stds., 1995-96. Chief advisor ICA (AID), Korea Tchr. Edn. Project, 1961-62; Fulbright lectr., Colombia, S.Am., 1966, Lisbon, Portugal, 1978; pres. Am. Assn. Colls. Tchr. Edn., 1974-75; mem. forum of leaders Nat. Ednl. Orgns. USOE, 1975-77. Author: Successful High School Teaching, 1958, Student Teacher in Action, 1957, Southern High Schools and Jobless Youth, 1961, The Desegregation Era in Higher Education, 1966, Higher Education in the South, 1966, Battlefields in Teacher Education, 1964, Educating Personnel for Urban Schools, 1972, Improving Education for the Youth of Portugal, 1980, Revolution in Teacher Education: A Review of Reform Reports, 1985; co-author: Equity and Excellence for Minorities in T.Ed. (A.T.E.), 1988, Served with USNR, 1942-47, comdr. Res. ret.

WIGGINS, STEPHEN EDWARD, physician; b. Phila., May 7, 1951; s. Ralph Cannon and Bernice J. (Maslovitz) W.; m. Rebecca del Carmen, Oct. 3, 1992; children: Daniel Stephen, Elizabeth Rebekah. BA, Rutgers U., 1973; MD, Med. Coll. Va., 1977. Diplomate Am. Bd. Family Practice. Resident in family practice Riverside Hosp., Newport News, Va., 1977-80; staff emergency physician North Arundal Hosp., Glen Burnie, Md., 1980-81, So. Md. Hosp. Ctr., Clinton, 1982-84; med. dir. Convenient Health Care, Waldorf, Md., 1984—. Ptnr. Old Line Med. Partnership, Waldorf, 1990-97, Convenient Health Care Mgmt., Waldorf, 1989-97; instr. family practice Georgetown U. Sch. Medicine, Washington, 1995—2005; pres. 640 Old Line Ctr. L.P., 1997—; pres. Old Line Med. Svcs. P.C., 1997—. Vol. physician and citizen diplomat Gesundheit Inst., Russia, 1991; citizen diplomat U.S.-China Peoples Friendship Assn., China, 1988; vol. physician March of Dimes Walk-a-thon, Md., 1985-86. William Demarest scholar, Rutgers U., New Brunswick, N.J., 1969-73. Fellow Am. Acad. Family Physicians; mem. Med. and Chirurg. Faculty of the State of Md., Md. Acad. Family Physicians, Charles County Med. Soc. Avocation: scuba diving. Office: Convenient Health Care 12090 Old Line Ctr Waldorf MD 20602-2556

WIGGLESWORTH, MARGARET, real estate company executive; b. Potomac, Md. BA, U. Md. Staff for Senator Charles McC. Mathias Jr. US Senate, Washington; asst. dir. nat. affairs Nat. Pub. Radio; exec. dir. US Coalition of Svc. Industries, Inc., Washington; pres. Colliers Internat. USA, Boston, 1998—, CEO. Office: Colliers International USA 50 Milk St 20th Floor Boston MA 02109 Office Phone: 617-722-0221. Office Fax: 617-722-0224. E-mail: margaret@colliers.com, mwigglesworth@colliers.com. *

WIGHT, NATHAN, music educator; s. Schuyler B. and Patricia Wight. MusD, Ariz. State U., Tempe, 2003. Asst. prof. voice Jacksonville State U., Ala., 2003—. Mem.: Nat. Assn. Tchrs. Singing. Office: Jacksonville State University 700 Pelham Rd North Jacksonville AL 36265 Office Phone: 256-782-5876. Office Fax: 256-782-5896.

WIGHT, PATRICIA ANNE, neuroscience educator; b. Providence, June 10, 1955; d. Howard Morrison Jr. and Nancy Lee (Phillips) W.; m. Mark David Crew, Jan. 15, 1988; children: Joseph David, Kyle Douglas, Michael Patrick. BS, U. Calif., Irvine, 1978; PhD, U. Calif., Riverside, 1988. Rsch. asst., tchg. asst. U. Calif., Riverside, 1981—88; postdoctoral fellow UCLA, 1988—92; asst. prof. U. Ark. Med. Scis., Little Rock, 1992—99, assoc. prof., 1999—2006, prof., 2006—. Contbr. articles to profl. jours. Mem. AAAS, Am. Soc. Neurochemistry, Am. Physiol. Soc., Soc. for Neurosci., Sigma Xi. Roman Catholic. Avocations: hiking, skiing, swimming. Office: U Ark Med Scis 4301 W Markham St # 750 Little Rock AR 72205-7101 Home Phone: 501-228-7977; Office Phone: 501-686-5366. E-mail: pwight@uams.edu.

WIGHT, ROBERT JOSEPH, lawyer; b. Rome, Ga., Dec. 13, 1949; s. Arthur Arley and Maude T. (Lacey) W.; m. Donna Ruth Bishop, Feb. 18, 1972; children: Cynthia Ashley, Laura Christine. BA cum laude, Ga. State U., 1979; JD cum laude, U. Ga., 1983. Bar: Ga. 1983, U.S. Dist. Ct. (no. dist.) Ga. 1983, U.S. Dist. Ct. (mid. dist.) Ga. 1985. Assoc. Craig & Gainer, Covington, Ga., 1983-84, Heard, Leverett & Adams, Elberton, 1984-86; gen. counsel Group Underwriters, Inc., 1987—2002; legal cons. Health Plan Select, Athens, 2001—. Mem. editl. staff Ga. Jour. Internat. and Comparative Law, 1981-82. Mem. State Bar Ga. (sec. legal econs. sect. 1987-88, chmn. legal econs. sect. 1988-90), Order of Coif, Masons, Phi Alpha Delta. Baptist. Home: 1030 E Canyon Creek Ct Watkinsville GA 30677-1500 Personal E-mail: rjw30677@bellsouth.net.

WIGHTMAN, ALEC, lawyer; b. Cleve., Jan. 23, 1951; s. John and Betty Jane (Follis) W.; m. Kathleen A. Little, June 19, 1976; children: Nora, Emily. BA, Duke U., 1972; JD, Ohio State U., 1975. Bar: Ohio 1975, U.S. Tax Ct. 1982, U.S. Ct. Appeals (6th cir.) 1983. Assoc. Krupman, Fromson & Henson, Columbus, Ohio, 1975-77; ptnr. Krupman, Fromson, Bownas & Wightman, Columbus, 1978-82; assoc. Baker & Hostetler, Columbus, 1982-83, ptnr., 1984—, exec. ptnr., 2004—. Bd. trustees The Arthur G. James Cancer Hosp., Richard J. Solove Rsch. Inst.; bd. dirs. Cleve. Rock & Roll., Inc. Mem. ABA, Ohio Bar Assn., Columbus Bar Assn., Ohio Oil and Gas Assn. Avocation: tennis. Office: Baker & Hostetler 65 E State St Ste 2100 Columbus OH 43215-4260 Home Phone: 614-222-0999; Office Phone: 614-462-2636. Business E-Mail: awightman@bakerlaw.com.

WIGHTMAN, ARTHUR STRONG, physicist, researcher; b. Rochester, NY, Mar. 30, 1922; s. Eugene Pinckney and Edith Victoria (Stephenson) W.; m. Anna-Greta Larsson, Apr. 28, 1945 (dec. Feb. 11, 1976); 1 child, Robin Letitia (dec. Mar. 2, 2001); m. Ludmilla Popova, Jan. 14, 1977. BA, Yale U., 1942; PhD, Princeton U., 1949; DSc, Swiss Fed. Inst. Tech., Zurich, 1969, Göttingen U., 1987. Instr. physics Yale, 1943-44; from instr. to asso. prof. physics Princeton, 1949-60, prof. math. physics, 1960-92; prof. emeritus, 1992—; Thomas D. Jones prof. math. physics Princeton, 1971-92. Vis. prof. Sorbonne, 1957, École Polytechnique, 1977-78. Served to lt. (j.g.) USNR, 1944-46. NRC postdoctoral fellow Inst. Teoretisk Fysik, Copenhagen, Denmark, 1951-52; NSF sr. postdoctoral fellow, 1956-57; recipient Dannie Heineman prize math. physics, 1969, Poincaré prize Internat. Assn. Math. Physics, 1997. Fellow NAS, Am. Acad. Arts and Scis., Royal Acad. Arts, Am. Phys. Soc.; mem. AAAS, Am. Math. Soc. Office: Princeton U 350 Jadwin Hl Princeton NJ 08544-0001 Office Phone: 609-258-5835. Business E-Mail: wightman@princeton.edu.

WIGHTMAN, SHARON LEILANI, librarian; d. Frank Bacon and Hazel Elizabeth Drake; m. James Ernest Wightman, Oct. 9, 1965; children: Wendy Joy, Kim Diane, Dawn Lyn, Robin Gail. BS in Liberal Arts, Cazenovia Coll., 1995; MLS, Syracuse U., 1999. Cert. pub. libr. N.Y. State. Tailor, owner Wightman Tailoring, Cazenovia, NY, 1982—88; admissions rep. Cazenovia Coll., 1988—95; sales lead coord. Inchcape Testing, Cortland, NY, 1995—97; children's libr. Fayetteville (N.Y.) Free Libr., 1999—2001; libr. ITT Tech. Inst., Liverpool, 2001—. Bd. trustees CLRC NY Libr. Resources Coun., 2006—. Bd. dirs. 4-H Found., Madison County, 2001—04. Named Employee of the Quar., ITT Tech. Inst., 2002, Employee of the Yr., 2002; recipient Achievement in Profl. Devel., Reference Adult Svc. Sect., N.Y. Libr. Assn., 2004. Mem.: ALA, AAUW, Am. Soc. Notaries, NY Libr. Assn., Librn. Unltd. (v.p. 2004—05, pres. 2005—06). Republican. Avocations: travel, reading, gardening, surf fishing. Office: ITT Tech Inst 235 Greenfield Pkwy Liverpool NY 13088 Office Phone: 315-461-8000. Personal E-mail: swightman@hotmail.com.

WIGINGTON, RONALD LEE, retired chemical information services executive; b. Topeka, May 11, 1932; s. Oscar and Virginia C. (Ritchie) W.; m. Margaret E. Willey, Aug. 17, 1951; children: Linda (dec.), Carol, David, Brian. BS in Engring. Physics, U. Kans., 1953; MEE, U. Md., 1959; PhD in Elec. Engring., U. Kans., 1964; postgrad. in Advanced Mgmt., Harvard Bus. Sch., 1976-77. Tech. staff Bell Telephone Labs., Murray Hill, NJ, 1953-54; divsn. chief Dept. Def., Washington, 1956-68; dir. R & D Chem. Abstracts Svc., Am. Chem. Soc., Columbus, Ohio, 1968-84; dir. Washington ops. Am. Chem. Soc., 1984-86; CEO, dir. Chem. Abstracts Svc., Am. Chem. Soc., Columbus, 1986-91; dir. info. tech. Am. Chem. Soc., Columbus, 1991-94. Chmn. bd. Online Computer Libr. Ctr., Dublin, Ohio, 1985-87, trustee, 1978-92; lectr. Am. U., Washington, 1967-68; adj. assoc. prof. Ohio State U., 1969-78. Contbr. chpts. to books; contbr. articles to profl. jours. Pres., various positions PTA Prince George's County, Md., 1966-68; moderator, treas. Cmty. Assn. Upper Arlington (Ohio) Schs.; 1970-74; mem. Upper Arlington Civic Orch., 1970-84, pres., 1973-76; bd. dirs. Material Property Data Network, 1987-94, Ohio Ctr. of Sci. and Industry, 1988-93; trustee Health Coalition of Ctrl. Ohio, Columbus, 1991-99, treas., 1994-99, vice-chmn., 1996-99. With US Army, 1954—56. Named Honor Man of U. Kans, 1953; named to, Topeka H.S. Hall of Fame, 2001; recipient Nat. Capital award, D.C. Coun. Engring. and Archtl. Socs., 1967, Meritorious Civilian Svc. award, Dept. Def., 1967; Summerfield scholar, U. Kans., 1949. Fellow: Am. Inst. Chemists, Coun. Sci. and Tech. Info. (exec. bd. and treas. 1992—94, fellow 1995—), Nat. Fedn. Abstracting and Info. Svcs. (bd. dirs. 1979—84, pres. 1982—83, hon. fellow 1995—); mem.: IEEE (sr.), Am. Chem. Soc., Sigma Xi. Avocations: gardening, music, genealogy. Home: 2470 Wimbledon Rd Columbus OH 43220-4212 Personal E-mail: rwigingt@columbus.rr.com.

WIGLESWORTH, MICHAEL BLAND, advertising executive; b. Balt., Apr. 13, 1949; s. Reginal A. and Janice (Peppler) W.; m. Barbara Atkinson, Aug. 5, 1972 (div. Apr. 1980); m. Shari Kulik, Dec. 7, 1997. BS, Va. Commonwealth U., 1975. Account exec. Richmond Newspapers, Va., 1973—75; v.p. mktg. Bunch & Laughon Advt., Richmond, 1975—76; pres. Collier & Wiglesworth, Inc., Richmond, 1976—80; v.p. account svcs. Brand Edmonds Bolio, Richmond, 1980—82; v.p. sales promotion Eisner & Assocs., Balt., 1983—85; dir. promotion J. Walter Thompson, LA, 1985—87; mgmt. supr. Einson Freeman, Paramus, NJ, 1987—89; sr. v.p., mgmt. supr. SAI/Earle Palmer Brown Promotions, Phila., 1989—94; sr. v.p. acct. svc. Hadley, NYC, 1994—96; ptnr. Allegis Mktg., 1996—2000; sr. v.p. acct. svcs. SAI Mktg., 1996—2000; v.p. promotional mktg. Marketsource, Cranbury, NJ, 2000—01; group dir., relationship mktg. Carlson Mktg. Group, Phila., 2001—03; sr. v.p. Mastermind Mktg., Phila., 2003—06; ptnr. Dreamscapes Builders, LP, Houston, 2004—. Pres. M & W Ventures, Richmond, 1977-83; ptnr. Recreation Unltd., Inc., Richmond, 1979-80. Recipient best in Show award Am. Newspaper Assn., N.Y.C., 1979, Maxi award Direct Mail Assn., 1992, Reggie award Promotional Marketers Assn. Am., 1993, Pro award Coun. of Sales Promotion Agencies, 1994. Mem. Am. Advt. Fedn. (Retail Advt. award 1979), Am. Mktg. Assn. (Effie award 1980, Spire award 1992), Phi Kappa Sigma. Republican. Avocations: jogging, skiing, scuba diving, travel, music. Home: 520 Station Ave Glenside PA 19038-1419 Office: 1814 B Binz Houston TX 77004 Office Phone: 713-529-2335. Personal E-mail: mwiglesworth@comcast.net.

WIGLEY, DIANA GAIL, respiratory therapist; d. Roland Eugene and Jewel Maxine Box; children: Trent Matthew, Kyle Brandon. Diploma, Ind. Voc. Tech Sch., 1984. Registered respiratory therapist Ind., 1997, EEG Tech & Evoked Potenial Tech Ind., 2003. Staff therapist Bedford Med. Ctr., Ind., 1980—90; staff therapist, lead therapist James W. Riley Children's Hosp., Indpls., 1990—92; area supr. Golden Care, 1993—96; staff therapist, EEG tech Wash. County Hosp., Washington, 1996—97; registered respiratory therapist Bloomington Hosp., 1997—, registered EEG tech, IOM tech, 2000—. Office: Bloomington Hosp 402 West 2nd St Bloomington IN 47402 Home Phone: 812-849-3450; Office Phone: 812-353-5222. Office Fax: 812-353-5220. Personal E-mail: blmgtneeg@verizon.net.

WIGMORE, STEVEN P., lawyer; s. Alfred A. and Patricia D. Wigmore; m. Christine A. Wigmore, June 1, 1994; children: C., W., E. JD, Cath. U. Am., Washington, 1998; BSME, U. Md., College Park, 1992. EIT Md.; bar: Ga. 2000, US Patent & Trademark Office 1997. Mech. engr. EG&G Wash. Analytical Svcs. Ctr., Alexandria, Va., 1993—93; patent examiner US Patent & Trademark Office, Alexandria, 1993—96; patent agt. Birch, Stewart, Kolasch, and Birch LLP, Falls Church, Va., 1996—99; counsel intellecual property lawyer King & Spalding LLP, Atlanta, 1999—. Sec. Atlanta Electronic Commerce Forum, 2004—; mem. licensing com. Ga. State Bar Intellectual Property Sect., 2003—04, chair licensing com., 2004—06, treas., 2006—07. Mem.: ABA, ASME (sec., newsletter editor Atlanta sect. 2004—07, Atlanta Sect. Mem. of Yr. 2004—05), Atlanta Bar Orgn., Am. Intellectual Property Law Assn. Avocation: tennis. Office: King & Spalding LLP 1180 Peachtree St NE Atlanta GA 30309-3521 Office Phone: 404-572-2884. Office Fax: 404-572-5134. Business E-Mail: swigmore@kslaw.com.

WIGNER, PRESTON DOUGLAS, lawyer; BA, James Madison U.; JD cum laude, U. Richmond. Assoc. Hunton & Williams; assoc. Capital Formation Sect. and Corp. and Securities Law Groups Williams, Mullen, Clark & Dobbins, PC, 2000—03; counsel Universal Leaf, 2003—04, sr. counsel, 2004—05; gen. counsel, sec. Universal Corp., Richmond, Va., 2005—. Former atty., bd. mem. Richmond Recreation and Parks Found. Office: Universal Corp 1501 N Hamilton St Richmond VA 23230 Office Phone: 804-359-9311. *

WIGSMOEN, SUSAN CATANIA, elementary school educator; b. Chgo., Sept. 13, 1964; d. Anthony Edward and Susan Catherine (Kmetty) Catania; m. David Andrew Wigsmoen, July 10, 1993. BA, St. Xavier Coll., 1986; MA, St. Xavier U., 1995. Tchr. kindergarten Bridgeport Cath. Acad., Chgo., 1986—99; tchr. Luther Burbank Elem. Dist. 111, Ill., 2004—, reading specialist dist. III, 1999—2004. Mem. pub. rels. com. Epilepsy Found. of Greater Chgo. 1994. Mem. Ill. Assn. for Supervision and Curriculum Devel. Republican. Roman Catholic. Avocation: piano. Home: 8745 S Utica Ave Evergreen Park IL 60805-1034 Home Phone: 708-499-2320; Office Phone: 312-376-6223, 708-499-0838. Personal E-mail: schwigs@msn.com.

WIGSTON, DAVID LAWRENCE, biologist, dean; b. London, Dec. 12, 1943; came to U.S., 1993; s. Frederic Roland Wigston and Joan Mavin; m. Patricia Anne Werner, May 25, 1991; 1 child, Alexa Joan Dobinson. BSc with 1st class honors, U. Exeter, Eng., 1965; PhD in Forest Ecology, U. Exeter, 1972. Lectr. in biology Exeter Coll., 1967-69; sr. lectr. biology Coventry (Eng.) U., 1970-74; reader environ. sci. Plymouth (Eng.) U., 1974-82; prof., chair dept. forestry Papua New Guinea U. Tech., Lae, 1982-86; prof. environ. sci. No. Territory U., Darwin, Australia, 1986-93, dean faculty of sci., 1986-92; rsch. prof. U. Fla., Gainesville, 1993-96; rsch. assoc. dean U. Mich., Flint, 1996—. Vis. fellow St. Cross Coll. Oxford (Eng.) U., 1980; cons. Swedish Biomass Energy Program, 1981-82; chief wildlife scientist No. Territory (Australia) Govt., 1992-93. Narrator (symphonic works) Peter & The Wolf, Jungle Book, Hassan, 1961—. Cons. Internat. Convention Biodiversity, Australia, 1992-93; pres., bd. dirs. Gainesville Symphony Orch., 1994-96. Fellow Australian Inst. Biology (sec. No. Territory br. 1987-93); mem. Ecol. Soc. Am., Soc. Human Ecology, Soc. Econ. Botany. Avocations: music, theater, art, literature. Office: U Mich 303 Kearsley St Flint MI 48502

WIGTON, CHESTER MAHLON, physician; b. Pueblo, Colo., Jan. 12, 1928; s. Washington Irving and Bessie Marie (Ramsey) W.; m. Marjorie Chanak, Aug. 29, 1953 (dec. Jan. 1981); children: Robin, Renee, Kent, Lance, Bruce, Scott; m. Anita Kay Nelson, July 4, 1993; children: Sallie Michelle Short, Sadie Kay Short. BS cum laude, Colo. Coll., Colorado Springs, 1950; MD, U. Colo., Denver, 1954. Diplomate Am. Bd. Family Practice. Intern Swedish Hosp., Seattle, 1954-55; pvt. practice family medicine, Durango, Colo., 1957—; emeritus active Med. Mercy Hosp., Durango, 1990—, v.p. staff, 1970-73. Med. dir. Hacienda Nursing Home, Bloomfield, N.Mex., 1992-95. Pres. CAMP Inc., Durango, 1970, CEOW Inc., Durango, 1964; treas. Tamarron Owners Assn. Bd., Durango, 1986-95; sec. Durango Sch. Bd., 1969-73; dir. San Juan Devel., Durango, 1971. Lt. (j.g.) USPHS, 1955-57; sec. Cmty. Hosp. Bd., Durango, 1986-92. Fellow Am. Acad. Family Practice; mem. Durango C. of C. (pres. 1965-66), Durango Rotary Club (pres. 1968), Electra Lake Sporting Club (pres. 1982-85), Delta Epsilon, Sigma Nu, Nu Sigma Nu. Republican. Presbyterian. Avocations: skiing, tennis, golf, fishing, hunting. Home and Office: 151 Riverview Dr Durango CO 81301-4349 Personal E-mail: cwigton@frontier.net.

WIIG, KARL MARTIN, knowledge management expert and consultant; b. Karasjok, Norway, Feb. 8, 1934; came to U.S., 1957; s. Alf Kristian and Margarethe (Soylann) W.; Elisabeth Hemmersam Nielsen, June 10, 1958; children: Charlotte Elisabeth, Erik Daniel (dec.) BS, Case Inst. Tech., 1959, MS, 1964. Rschr. Chr. Michelsen Inst., Bergen, Norway, 1960—64; sys. engr. GE, Cleve., 1964—66; mgr. sys. engring. Dundee Cement Co., Mich., 1966—70; chmn. bd. Abacus Alpha, Inc., Newton, Mass., 1980—81; mgr. sys. and policy analysis Arthur D. Little, Inc., Cambridge, Mass., 1970—80, dir. artificial intelligence, 1981—87; ptnr. Coopers & Lybrand, Dallas, 1987—89; mng. ptnr. Wiig Group, Arlington, Tex., 1989—95; chmn. bd., CEO Knowledge Rsch. Inst., Inc., Arlington, 1995—. Adj. prof. Hong Kong Polytechnic U., 2004—; co-founder Internat. Knowledge Mgmt. Network; lectr. in field; cons. in field; presenter in field. Author: The Economics of Offshore Oil and Gas Supplies, 1977, Expert Systems: A Manager's Guide, 1990, Knowledge Management Foundations: Thinking About Thinking--How People and Organizations Create, Represent and Use Knowledge, 1993, Knowledge Management: The Central Management Focus for Intelligent-Acting Organizations, 1994, Knowledge Management Methods: Practical Approaches to Manage Knowledge, 1995, Approaching Knowledge Management in Practice, 1996, Leveraging Knowledge for Business Performance, 1997, People-Focused Knowledge Management, 2004; (publs.) Managing Knowledge: Executive Perspectives, 1989, Knowledge-Based Systems and Issues of Integration, 1988, Management of Knowledge: A New Opportunity, 1988, Knowledge Management Goals at Different Levels of Society and the Enterprise, 1996, Knowledge Management: Where Did It Come From--and Where Will it Go?, 1997, Knowledge Management: An Introductory Perspective, 1998, What Future Knowledge Management Users May Expect, 1999, (with Elisabeth H. Wiig) On Conceptual Learning, 1999, Introducting Knowledge Management into the Enterprise, 1999, What Future Knowledge Management Users May Expect, 1999, Knowledge Management in Innovation and R&D, 2000, Application of Knowledge Management in Public Administration, 2000, Exploiting Knowledge for Productivity Gains, 2001, Knowledge Management: The Major Enabler of Enterprise Performance, 2002, People-Focused Knowledge Management: How effective decision making leads to corporate success, 2004; contbr. chpts. to books, articles to profl. publs With Norwegian Army, 1953-54 Achievements include patent in variable ratio power steering. Home and Office: 7101 Lake Powell Dr Arlington TX 76016-3517 Office Phone: 817-572-6254. Personal E-mail: kmwiig@krii.com.

WIJNBERG, SANDRA S., investment company executive; b. Aug. 1, 1956; BA English, UCLA; MBA, U. So. Calif., LA. With Morgan Stanley & Co. Inc.; joined PepsiCo as v.p., treas., 1994; sr. v.p., CFO KFC Corp. Divsn.; sr. v.p., treas. Tricon Global Restaurants Inc, 1997—2000; sr. v.p., CFO Marsh & McLennan Cos., NYC, 2000—06; chief adminstrv. officer Aquiline Holdings LLC, 2007—. Bd. dirs. Pvt. Sector Coun., 2001—, Tyco Internat. Ltd., 2003—. Corp. adv. bd. N.Y.C. Ballet. Office: Aquiline Holdings LLC 535 Madison Ave 27th Fl New York NY 10022 *

WIKMAN, MICHAEL RAYMOND, advertising executive; b. Mpls., Dec. 28, 1950; s. Charles Pierce and Jeanne Elizabeth W.; m. Carrie Brandt, Feb. 7, 1981; children: Caroline Celeste, Charles Michael. B in Elected Studies, U. Minn., 1973. Analyst, supr. media services Campbell-Mithun Advt., Mpls., 1973-77, account mgr., 1977-80; pres. MWA Direct, Mpls., 1980—. Mem. Direct Mktg. Assn. (Echo award 1987), Midwest Direct Mktg. Assn. (Art, Response and Copy award 1987). Avocations: art collecting, downhill skiing, tennis, sailing. Home: 5404 Richmond Ln Minneapolis MN 55436-2437

WIKSTROM, FRANCIS M., lawyer; b. Missoula, Mont., Aug. 20, 1949; BS, Weber State Univ., 1971; JD, Yale U., 1974. Bar: Utah 1974, US Dist. Ct. Utah 1974, US Ct. Appeals (10th cir.) 1979, US Ct. Appeals (fed. cir.) 2002, US Supreme Ct. 1980. Asst. U.S. atty. U.S. Dist. Ct. Utah, 1979-80, U.S. atty., 1981; mem. Parsons Behle & Latimer, Salt Lake City, 1982—. Mem. Utah State Bar Commn.; former chmn. Utah Judicial Conduct Commn.; chmn. adv. com. on rules civil procedure Utah Supreme Ct.; mem. 10th Cir. Adv. Com.; adj. prof. trial advocacy, U. Utah Coll. Law, 1986-89. Recipient Best Lawyers in Am., Outstanding Lawyer award, Fed. Bar Assn. of Utah, 2002. Fellow Am. Bar Found., Am. Coll. Trial Lawyers; mem. ABA, Salt Lake County Bar Assn. (pres. 1993-94), Am. Inns Ct. II (master bench), Internat. Assn. Def. Counsel. Office: Parsons Behle & Latimer 201 S Main St 1 Utah center Ste 1800 PO Box 45898 Salt Lake City UT 84111-2218 Office Phone: 801-532-1234. Office Fax: 801-536-6111. Business E-Mail: fwikstrom@parsonsbehle.com.

WILANSKY, HEYWOOD, retail executive; Graduate, Canaan Coll. With May Dept. Stores Co., 1976—95, pres., CEO Filene's div., 1991—92, pres., CEO Foley's div., 1992—95; pres., CEO Bon-Ton Stores Inc., 1995—2000; prof. of mktg. Univ. Md., 2000—03; pres., CEO Filene's Basement Inc., 2003—04, Retail Ventures Inc., Columbus, Ohio, 2004—. Office: Retail Ventures Inc 3241 Westerville Rd Columbus OH 43224 *

WILBANKS, DONNIE JO, healthcare educator; b. Oklahoma City, Okla., Feb. 21, 1950; s. James Henry and Laura Aneice (Henderson) Wilbanks; m. Sandra Kay Smith, Aug. 6, 1977; children: Kimberly Lynn, Eric Leslie. BA, Mo. Bapt. Coll., St. Louis, 1976; MA in Tchg., Webster U., St. Louis, 1991. Vocat. instr. State of Mo. and State of Ill. Assoc. pastor Fourth Bapt. Ch., St. Louis, 1972—76; alcoholism counselor Project Promised Land, St. Louis, 1972—75; bus. agt. Svc. Employees Internat. Union, St. Louis, 1985—86; children's svc. worker Mo. Family Svcs., 1986—93; in-home family therapist Mo., 1993—98; instr. psychology, anatomy, physiology St. Louis Coll. Health Careers, 1998—. Author: (textbook) Applied Psychology for Health Care, 2007. Vol. fund raising ARC, St. Louis, 2006. Cpl. USMC, 1968—71. Named Instr. of the Quarter, St. Louis Coll. of Health Careers, 2004, Instr. of the Yr., 2005; recipient Outstanding Svc. award, 2004. Mem.: MENSA, Am. Assn. of Profl. Hypnotherapists. Office: St Louis Coll of Health Careers 909 S Taylor Saint Louis MO 63110 Home Phone: 314-352-0225; Office Phone: 314-652-0300 2502.

WILBANKS, JAN JOSEPH, retired philosopher; b. Lynchburg, Ohio, Dec. 17, 1928; s. James Odell and Bernice Elizabeth (Daugherty) W.; m. Alice Ramona Pacheco, Nov. 14, 1953; children— Elise, Anita, Jennifer. BS, Cin. Coll. Pharmacy, 1951; PhD in Philosophy, Ohio State U., 1964. Instr. philosophy Purdue U., 1961-64; mem. faculty Marietta (Ohio) Coll., 1964-89, prof. philosophy, 1973-89. Author: Hume's Theory of Imagination, 1968, also articles. With AUS, 1951-53. Home: 122 High St Marietta OH 45750-2636

WILBER, ROGER ALAN, library supervisor, writer; b. Ravena, NY, Sept. 14, 1946; s. John Henry Wilber, Jr. and Sarah Frances (Krom) Wilber; m. Cyndy Michele Borowski, July 21, 1969; children: Roger Alan Wilber, Jr., Ami Leah (Wilber) Mosher. Diploma, A.P. Bible Sch., 1975, Moody Bible Inst. Corr. Sch., 1975; tchg. cert., Albany Bible Inst., 1978—79. Cert. C.P.R. Instr. ARC, 1982. Supr. libr. clk. III N.Y.S. Edn. Dept., Albany, 1981—. Deacon Apostolic Pentecostal Ch., Glenmont, NY, 1976—77; head deacon U.C.C. Ch., Ravena, NY, 1991—92; co-sec., treas. Capital Dist. Friends of Jung, Albany, 1994—96; facilitator Parallel Orgn. N.Y.S. Libr., Albany, 2000—04; N.Y.S. libr. rep. Collections Stewardship Team Cultural Edn. Ctr., Albany, 2000—, floor marshal for Tenant Safety Orgn., 2001—05; guest lectr. Ravena-Coeymans Hist. Soc., 2004, 05. Author: (historical book) Teacher, Soldier, Doctor - The Life of John H. Wilber, M.D. (Copyrighted, 2003), William W. Wilber & the 113th Regiment - N.Y. Volunteers - 7th Heavy Artillery, NY in the Civil War (Copyright, 2004), Call To Duty - The Town of Coeymans in The Civil War (Copyright, 2004); editl. bd. and contbg. author: newsletter NYS Library Staff Information Bulletin, 1997—2000, NYS Library Information Bulletin, 2000—06; contbg. author Schoharie County Hist. Review, 2003; contbr. articles to profl. jours. Book repair instr. Ravena Free Libr., NY, 1992—92; guest lectr. Ravena-Coeymans Hist. Soc., 2004, 2005; adult bible study tchr. Ravena, Glenmont, & Albany, NY, 1970—2004. CTA 2 USN, 1966—68. Decorated Nat. Def. Svc. Medal U.S. Navy; recipient NYS Merit awards, 1974, 1977, 1983, 1984, 20 Yrs. Svc. award, N.Y.S. Edn. Dept., 1990, 25 Yrs. Svc. award, 1995, 30 Yrs. Svc. award, 2000, 35 Yr. Svc. award, 2005, Commr. Richard P. Mills Supr. Cert., 2003. Mem.: editorial bd. NYS Library Info. Bulletin. Independent. Avocations: coin collecting/numismatics, paper clip collecting, writing, historical research, fishing. Home: 3 Jefferson Avenue Ravena NY 12143-1120 Office: New York State Rsch Libr Cultural Education Center Albany NY 12230

WILBERG, MACK J., conductor, composer; b. Price, Utah, Feb. 20, 1955; s. LaMar Joseph and Helen McNeil Wilberg; m. Rebecca Susan Wilcox, Dec. 8, 1984; children: Kirstin, Jeffrey, James, Cara. MusB, Brigham Young U., 1979; MusM, U. So. Calif., LA, 1981, D in Musical Arts, 1985. Prof. music Brigham Young U., Provo, Utah, 1984—99; assoc. music dir. Mormon Tabernacle Choir, Salt Lake City, 1999—. Mem.: Am. Choral Dirs. Assn. (life). Office: Mormon Tabernacle Choir 50 E North Temple St Salt Lake City UT 84150 Office Phone: 801-240-4150.

WILBUR, COLBURN SLOAN, foundation consultant, trustee, former executive; b. Palo Alto, Calif., Jan. 20, 1935; s. Blake Colburn and Mary (Sloan) W.; m. Maria Grace Verburg, Sept. 1, 1961; children: Marguerite Louise, Anne Noelle. BA in Polit. Sci., Stanford U., 1956, MBA, 1960. Asst. cashier United Calif. Bank, San Francisco, 1960-65; v.p. Standata, San Francisco, 1965-68; adminstrv. mgr. Tab Products, San Francisco, 1968-69; exec. dir. Sierra Club Found., San Francisco, 1969-76, David and Lucile Packard Found., Los Altos, Calif., 1976—99, CEO, trustee, 1999—; sr. fellow Council on Found., 1999—2000, interim pres., CEO, 2005. Bd. dirs. Colo. Coll., Colorado Springs. Bd. dirs. Philanthropic Ventures Found.; former bd. dirs., mem. adv bd. Global Fund Women, Palo Alto, Calif.; past bd. dirs. Big Bros. San Francisco, Calif. Confederation Arts, Peninsula Grantmakers, Women's Fund Santa Clara; former bd. dirs., pres. Big Bros. Peninsula, North Fork Assn., Peninsula Conservation Ctr.; past bd. dirs., chmn. No. Calif. Grantmakers; bd. dirs., mem. adv. bd. Sierra Club Found., Stanford Theater Found., Palo Alto, U. San Francisco/Inst. Nonprofit Orgn. Mgmt. With U.S. Army, 1957-58. Mem. Commonwealth Club (bd. advisors). Office: David & Lucile Packard Found 300 2nd St Los Altos CA 94022-3694 E-mail: C.Wilbur@packard.org.

WILBUR, E. PACKER, investment company executive; b. Bridgeport, Conn., Sept. 9, 1936; s. E. Packer and Elizabeth (Wells) Wilbur; m. Laura Mary Ferrier, Sept. 17, 1965; children: Alison Mary Thompson, Andrew Packer, Gillian Elizabeth Stratmann. BA, Yale U., New Haven, Conn., 1959; MBA, Harvard U., Cambridge, Mass., 1965. Cons. McKinsey & Co. Inc., NYC, 1964-67; dir. corp. planning Am. Express Co., NYC, 1967-69; v.p. Van Alstyne Noel & Co., NYC, 1969-70; exec. v.p., dir., mem. exec. com. Newburger Loeb & Co. Inc., NYC, 1970-73; pres. E. P. Wilbur & Co., Inc., Southport, Conn., 1973—, Southport Fin. Corp., 1986—. Chmn. bd. dirs. Criterion Mgmt., Inc., Trend Mgmt., Inc., Fairfield Advisors, Inc., EPW Securities, Inc.; gen. ptnr. Embankment Properties Ltd., London, others; former allied mem. N.Y. Stock Exch., NYC. Contbr. articles to fin. jours. Bd. dirs. Discovery Mus., Bridgeport, Wakeman Meml. Boys/Girls Club, Southport, Greater Bridgeport Jr. Hockey League, Pequot Libr., Southport, Northfield-Mt. Hermon Sch., Mass., Charter Revision Commn., Harbor Mgmt. Commn., Fairfield, Conn.; mem. dean's coun. John F. Kennedy Sch. Govt Harvard U., mem. bd. Inst. Social and Econ. Policy in Mid. East; mem. dean's internat. coun. Harris Sch. Pub. Policy Studies U. Chgo. With US Army, 1959—60. Mem.: Royal Victorian Aero. Club, Royal No. Yacht Club (Scotland), Yale Club (NYC), Country Club Fairfield, Pequot Running Club (Southport, founder), Pequot Yacht Club (Southport). Office: 2507 Post Rd Southport CT 06890-1259 Home: PO Box 669 227 Main St Southport CT 06890

WILBUR, MARCIA KAORU, writer; d. Willard Leroy and Masayo Wilbur; children: Tina, Zack, Cordell, Alex Emmett Marian. AAS, Three Rivers, Norwich, CT, 1999—2000; BS, Ariz. State U., 1998—2002. Intern Free Software Found., Cambridge, Mass., 2002; ind. contractor/writer Aries Tech., Tempe, 2003—04; contract tech. writer NCS Pearson, Mesa, Ariz., 2004. Author: (book) Digital Millennium Copyright Act; author: (subject matter expert) (computer based curriculum) Linux Essentials; editor: (online directory) DMCA editor, (online journal) Computing Life; author: Binary Freedom/ System Toolbox. Com. mem. Digital Speech Project - FSF, Cambridge, Mass., 2002—03. Home Phone: 602-743-1061. Personal E-mail: aicra@well.com.

WILBUR, RICHARD PURDY, writer, educator; b. NYC, Mar. 1, 1921; s. Lawrence L. and Helen (Purdy) W.; m. Mary Charlotte Hayes Ward, June 20, 1942; children: Ellen Dickinson, Christopher Hayes, Nathan Lord, Aaron Hammond. AB, Amherst Coll., 1942, AM, 1952, DLitt (hon.), 1967; AM, Harvard U., 1947; LHD (hon.), Lawrence Coll., Washington U., Williams Coll., U. Rochester, SUNY, Potsdam, 1986, Skidmore Coll., 1987, U. Lowell, 1990; LHD (hon.), Mass. Coll. Liberal Arts, 2002; DLitt (hon.), Clark U., Am. Internat. Coll., Marquette U., Wesleyan U., Carnegie-Mellon U.; DLitt. (hon.), Lake Forest Coll., 1982, Smith Coll., 1996, Sewanee U., 1996; DD (hon.), St. Mary's Sem. and U., 2001. Jr. fellow Harvard U., Cambridge, Mass., 1947-50, Asst. prof. English, 1950-54; assoc. prof. Wellesley Coll., 1955-57; prof. Wesleyan U., 1957-77; writer in residence Smith Coll., 1977-86. Author: The Beautiful Changes, 1947, Ceremony, 1950, A Bestiary, 1955, 2d edit., 1993, Things of This World, 1956, Poems 1943-56, 1957, Advice to a Prophet, 1961, Poems of Richard Wilbur, 1963, Walking to Sleep, 1969, The Mind-Reader, 1976, Seven Poems, 1981, The Whale, 1982, New and Collected Poems, 1988 (Pulitzer prize for poetry, 1989), Bone Key and Other Poems, 1998, Mayflies: New Poems and Translations, 2000, Collected Poems 1943-2004, 2004, (children's books) Loudmouse, 1963, Opposites, 1973, More Opposites, 1991, A Game of Catch, 1994, Runaway Opposites, 1995, The Disappearing Alphabet, 1998, Opposites, More Opposites and Some Differences, 2000, The Pig in the Spigot, 2000, (criticism) Responses, 1976, expanded edit., 2000, (prose pieces) The Catbird's Song, 1997; co-author (with Lillian Hellman): (comic opera) Candide, 1957; co-author: (with William Schuman) (cantata) On Freedom's Ground, 1986; translator (Moliere): The Misanthrope, 1955, Tartuffe, 1963 (co-recipient Bollingen Translation prize, 1963), The School for Wives, 1971, The Learned Ladies, 1978, Four Comedies, 1982, Lovers' Quarrels, 2006; translator: (Racine) Andromache, 1982, Phaedra, 1986, The Suitors, 2001; translator: Moliere's The School for Husbands, 1992, Imaginary Cuckold, 1993, Molière's Amphitryon, 1995, Don Juan, 1998, Molière's The Bungler, 2000, Pierre Corneille's Theatre of Illusion, 2007; editor: Complete Poems of Poe, 1959, Poems of Shakespeare, 1966, Selected Poems of Witter Bynner, 1978, Edgar Allan Poe: Poems and Poetics, 2003. Decorated chevalier Ordre des Palmes Academiques; recipient Harriet Monroe prize Poetry mag., 1948, Oscar Blumenthal prize, 1950, Prix de Rome, Am. Acad. Arts and Letters, 1954, Edna St. Vincent Millay Meml. award, 1957, Nat. Book award, 1957, Pulitzer prize, 1957, Sarah Josepha Hale award, 1968, Bollingen prize, 1971, Brandeis U. Creative Arts award, 1971, Prix Henri Desfeuilles, 1971, Shelley Meml. award, 1973, Harriet Monroe Poetry award, 1978, St. Botolph's Club Found. award, 1983, Drama Desk award, 1983, Aiken-Taylor award, 1988, Bunn award, 1988, Washington Coll. Lit. award, 1988, St. Louis Lit. award, 1989, Grand Master award Birmingham-So. Coll., 1989, Gold Medal for Poetry, Am. Acad. Inst. Arts and Letters, 1991, Edward MacDowell medal, 1992, Nat. Arts Club Medal of Honor for Lit., 1994, PEN/Manheim Medal for Translation, 1994, Milton Ctr. prize, 1995, Acad. Am. Achievement award, 1995, Robert Frost medal Poetry Soc. Am., 1996, T.S. Eliot award, 1996, Wallace Stevens award, 2003, Ruth Lilly prize, 2006; Guggenheim fellow, 1952-53, 63, Ford fellow, 1960-61, Camargo Found. fellow, 1985; named U.S. Poet Laureate, Libr. Congress, 1987, Nat. Medal of the Arts, 1994; named to Theater Hall of Fame, 2003. Fellow: MLA (hon.); mem.: PEN (Transl. award 1983), ASCAP, AAAL (pres. 1974—76, chancellor 1976—78, 1980—81), Dramatists Guild, Acad. Am. Poets (chancellor emeritus), Am. Acad. Arts and Scis. Home: 87 Dodwells Rd Cummington MA 01026-9705

WILBUR, RICHARD SLOAN, medical association administrator, physician; s. Blake Colburn and Mary Caldwell (Sloan) Wilbur; m. Betty Lou Fannin, Jan. 20, 1951; children: Andrew, Peter, Thomas. BA, Stanford U., 1943, MD, 1946; JD, John Marshall, 1990. Cert. ABIM (Gastroenterology Am. Bd. Internal Medicine, 1954. Intern San Francisco County Hosp., 1946—47; resident Stanford Hosp., 1949—51, U. Pa. Hosp., 1951—52; postgrad. tng. U. Mich. Hosp., 1957, Karolinska Sjukhuset, Stockholm, 1960; staff Palo Alto (Calif.) Med. Clinic, 1952—69; dep. exec. v.p. AMA, Chgo., 1969—71, 1973—74; asst. sec. for health and environment dept. def., 1971—73; sr. v.p. Baxter Labs., Inc., Deerfield, Ill., 1974—76; exec. v.p. Council Med. Splty. Socs., 1976—91, sec. accreditation coun. for continuing med. edn., 1979—91; assoc. prof. medicine Georgetown U. Med. Sch., 1971—77, Stanford Med. Sch., 1952—69; pres. Nat. Resident Matching Plan, 1991—92. Chmn. bd., CEO Inst. Clin. Info., 1994—99; sr. v.p. healthcare Buckeye Corp. Pte, Ltd., Singapore, 1997—2000; CEO Medic Alert, 1992—94; pres. Am. Bd. Med. Mgmt., 1992; mem. Am. Bd. Electrodiagnostic Medicine, 1993—98; chmn. med. adv. bd. Med. City, Bangalore, India, 1997—2000; bd. visitors Drew U. Postgrad. Med. Sch. Contbr. articles to profl. jours. Bd. govs. ARC; chmn. Mid-Am. Blood Svcs. Bd., Lifesource Blood Bank, 1996—98; vice-chmn. Rep. Cen. Com. Santa Clara County, Calif., 1966—89; bd. dir. Nat. Adv. Cancer Coun., Nat. Health Coun., 1993—95; chmn. bd. dir. Medic Alert Found.; chmn. bd. Calif. Med. Assn., 1968—69, Calif. Blue Shield, 1966—68, Am. Med. Found., 1987—; pres. Royal Soc. Medicine Found., 1998—2004. With USNR, 1942—58. Recipient Disting. Svc. medal, Dept. Def., 1973, Scroll of merit, Nat. Med. Assn., 1971. Fellow: ACP, Am. Coll. Physician Execs. (bd. regents 1985—89, pres. 1988—89, 2006—07), Am. Coll. Legal Medicine, Internat. Coll. Dentistry (hon.); mem.: Am. Soc. Internal Medicine, Am. Gastroent. Assn., Santa Clara County Med. Soc. (hon.), Lake County Med. Soc., Ill. Med. Assn., Inst. Medicine, Union League Phila., Cedars Club, Pacific Interurban Clin. Club, Alpha Omega Alpha, Phi Beta Kappa. Home: 985 Hawthorne Pl Lake Forest IL 60045-2217 Office: APT Management Inc 736 N Western Ave #222 Lake Forest IL 60045 E-mail: aptmgmnt@aol.com.

WILBURN, DONALD LEE, military officer, retail executive; b. Portsmouth, Ohio, Jan. 28, 1930; s. Morton and Nona Wilburn; m. Lorraine Ann Minshull, Feb. 12, 1950; children: Donald Lee Jr., Derrick Lawrence, David Louis. Student, George Washington U., DC, 1969—71. V.p. Mitchell's Formal Wear, Inc., Atlanta, 1972—81. Pres. Winmill Manor Residents Assn., Bradenton, Fla., 2000—02. Mem.: Mil. Officers Assn. (life). Independent. Avocations: stamp collecting/philately, electronics, photography. Home and Office: 5320 53rd Ave E #T-11 Bradenton FL 34203-5646 E-mail: donops@verizon.net.

WILBURN, JOHN, editor; B in Govt., Coll. William and Mary; M in History, George Mason U. Fact checker Reader's Digest; joined Houston City Mag., 1979; founder San Antonio Light's Viva Mag., 1983; editor Dallas Morning News' Sunday mag. Dallas Life, 1985, Houston Press, 1989—93; assoc. prodr. David Frost's PBS TV Interview Program, 1993—97; exec. prodr. The Houston Sidewalk website, 1997—2000; news and ops. mgr. KHOU-TV website, 2000—02; asst. mng. editor Houston Chronicle, 2002—03, interim mng. editor, 2003—04, mng. editor, 2004—. Office: Houston Chronicle 801 Texas St Houston TX 77002

WILBURN, MARY NELSON, lawyer, writer, poet, translator; b. Balt., Feb. 18, 1932; d. David Alfred and Phoebe Blanche (Novotny) Nelson; m. Adolph Yarbrough Wilburn, Mar. 5, 1957; children: Adolph II, Jason David. AB cum laude, Howard U., 1952; MA, U. Wis., 1955, JD, 1975; cert. in translation, Georgetown U., 1997. Bar: Wis. 1975, U.S. Supreme Ct. 1981. Commr. Nat. Coun. of Negro Women Commn. on Edn., 1986—2000; English lang. officer U.S Dept. of State, Washington, 1999—. Vol. One Ch. One Family, 1995—, bd. dirs., 1997—; mem. bd. Office Employee Appeals, D.C., 1997—2001; vol. Black Revolutionary War Patriots' Found., 1998—, Leadership Am., 1991—; bd. dirs. U. Wis. Law Sch.; mem. bd. edn. Cath. Archdiocese of Washington, 1995—2000. Mem. Internat. Fedn. Women Lawyers (exec. coun. 1996—, UN rep. 2000-02, internat. sec. 2002-05), Am. Translators Assn, Links, Inc., Leadership Greater Washington (bd. dirs. 1992-94, v.p. 1995-96), Zonta Internat., Friends of Remington Ctr. Endowment, Law Sch., U. of Wis. (bd. dirs.). Office Phone: 202-277-3557. E-mail: mnwilburn@juno.com.

WILCHER, LARRY K., lawyer; b. Lebanon, Ky., July 19, 1950; s. Dwain LaRue and Juanita (Tungate) W.; m. Mary Jo Hayden, Aug. 21, 1971; children: Emily Jane, Joseph Keith. BS in Pharmacy, St. Louis Coll. Pharmacy, 1973; JD, No. Ky. U., 1984; program of instrn. for lawyers, Harvard U., 1987, 91, 94. Dir. real estate SuperX Drugs Corp., Cin., 1975-84; dir. real estate, real estate counsel Dollar Gen. Corp., Goodlettsville, Tenn., 1984-85, gen. counsel, corp. sec., 1985—2002; pres. Nations Title Co., Inc., 1999—2002; ptnr. Wyatt, Tarrant & Combs LLP, 2002—. Dir. Ky. Auth. for Ednl. TV, chmn. fin. com. Contbg. author: Kentucky Business Organizations, 1989, Corporate Governance and Compliance Strategies, 2007; presenter in field. Sec., dir. Scottsville-Allen County Indsl. Devel. Authority, Inc., 1991—2006; dir. Leadership Ky., 1994—2000, mem. exec. com., 1997—2000; dir. Bowling Green-We. Ky. U. Symphony Orch., 1998—2000; chmn. Warren County Young Reps, Bowling Green, Ky., 1979, Scottsville-Allen County Planning Commn., 1997—. Named to Hon. Order Ky. Cols., 1968, One of Outstanding Young Men of Am., U.S. Jaycees, 1978; recipient Johnson & Johnson award St. Louis Coll. Pharmacy, 1973, Thurston B. Morton Leadership award Ky. Young Rep. Fedn., 1979. Mem. ABA, Nat. Assn. Corp. Dirs., Ky. Bar Assn. (recognition award 1987), Def. Rsch. Inst. Republican. Baptist. Office: Wyatt Tarrant & Combs LLP 918 State St Bowling Green KY 42101 Office Phone: 270-842-1050. Business E-Mail: lwilcher@wyattfirm.com.

WILCHINS, HOWARD MARTIN, lawyer; b. Paterson, NJ, Mar. 6, 1945; s. Philip Aaron and Esther (Blake) Wilchins; m. Margaret Mandon, Sept. 6, 1970 (dec. July 2001); children: Julie, Daniel; m. Sue Renay Rubinstein, Mar. 21, 2004. AB, Mich. State U., 1966; JD, U. Chgo., 1969. BAR: DC 1969, US Supreme Ct. 1975. Trial atty. FPC, Washington, 1969-70; spl. asst. to N.Y. Public Service Commn., Albany, 1970-72; dep. sect. chief AEC, Washington, 1972-75; dep. gen. counsel-litigation U.S. Ry. Assn., Washington, 1975-81, gen. counsel, 1981-84; dep. chief enforcement div. FCC Common Carrier Bur., Washington, 1984-90; v.p. Arnold S. Tesh Advisors, Washington, 1990-92; sr. litigation atty. Office Nuclear Safety Enforcement, U.S. Dept. Energy, Washington, 1992—2007; exec. cons. Epsilon Sys. Solutions Inc., 2007—. Mem. faculty Trial Practice Inst., US CSC, 1977-79 Bd. dirs. United Jewish Appeal Greater Washington, 1984-90, 92-96; bd. dirs. Charles E. Smith Jewish Day Sch., 1983—, v.p., 1986-88, pres., 1988-90; mem. Hillel of Greater Washington, 1990-2006, v.p., 1992-94, pres., 1994-96; bd. dirs., mem. Capital Camps, 1990-96; bd. dir. Jewish Edn. Svc. N.Am., 1996—, asst. treas., 2000-02, treas., 2003-05, v.p., 2005—; bd. dirs. Tikvat Israel Congregation, Rockville, Md., 2000-04, Gesher Jewish Day Sch., 2005-. Mem. ABA, DC Bar Assn., Fed. Comm. Bar Assn. (co-chmn. com. on arbitration and mediation 1991-94). Home: 10308 Snowpine Way Potomac MD 20854-3940 Office: Epsilon Sys Solutions Inc 1660 Internat Dr Ste 400 Mc Lean VA 22102 Business E-Mail: hwilchins@epsilonsystems.com.

WILCHINS, STEPHEN N., lawyer; b. Mount Vernon, NY, Sept. 15, 1954; BS, Fairlaigh Dickinson U., 1975; JD, Suffolk U., 1982. CPA; bar: Mass. 1982. Ptnr. Seegel, Lipshutz & Wilchins, P.C., Wellesley, Mass. Mem. bd. trustees Boston U. Hosp.; mem. bd. visitors Boston Ctr. of Arts. Named Mass. SuperLawyer, 2004; named one of Top 100 Lawyers, Worth mag., 2005. Mem.: Mass. Bar Assn., ABA, U. Club (mem. fin. com.), Kernwood Country Club (sr. v.p.). Office: Seegel Lipshutz & Wilchins PC Wellesley Office Park 20 William St Ste 130 Wellesley MA 02481 *

WILCHINSKY, MARK E., orthopaedic surgeon; b. Bridgeport, Conn., Mar. 18, 1952; s. William and Rita Wilchinsky; children: Jenna, Mark. BS, Fairfield U., 1974; MD, Tulane U., 1975. Diplomate Am. Bd. Orthop. Surgery. Resident in orthopedic surgery U. Mass. Med. Ctr., Worcester; pvt. practice Merritt Orthop. Assocs., Bridgeport, Conn.; asst. prof. orthop. surgery U. Mass. Med. Ctr., Worcester, 1984—. Exec. bd. Goodwill Industries, Bridgeport, 1994—, Burroughs Cmty. Ctr., Bridgeport, 1995—. Fellow Am. Acad. Orthop. Surgeons, Am. Arthroscopy Assn.; mem. New Eng. Orthop. Assn., Ea. Orthop. Assn. Roman Catholic. Avocations: golf, skiing, piano. Office: Merritt Orthopedic Assocs 3909 Main St Bridgeport CT 06606-2846 *

WILCOX, ALLEN JAMES, epidemiologist; b. Columbus, Ohio, Sept. 30, 1946; s. Alfred Thomas and Virginia Wilcox; m. Claire Berteel Wilcox; children: Lauren, Joseph. BA, U. Mich., 1969, MD, 1973; MPH, U. N.C., Chapel Hill, 1976, PhD, 1979. Diplomate Am. Bd. Preventive Medicine. Sr. investigator Nat. Inst. Environ. Health Sci./NIH, Durham, NC, 1979—, chief epidemiology br., 1991—2001. Editor-in-chief: Epidemiology, 2001—. Co-founder Durham Ctrl. Park, Inc., Durham, NC, 1995—. Recipient Outstanding Svc. medal, U.S. Pub. Health Svc., 1990, DSM, Pub. Health Svc., 2002, Herman Tyroler Dist. Alumni award, U. N.C., 2000, Dir.'s award, NIH, 2001. Fellow: Am. Coll. Epidemiology; mem.: Am. Epidemiol. Soc. (President 2002—03), Soc. Epidemiol. Rsch. (President 1997—98), Soc. Perinatal Epidemiol. Rsch. (President 1995—96). Office: Nat Inst Environ Health Sci 111 S Alexander Dr Durham NC 27709 Office Phone: 919-541-4660.

WILCOX, BENSON REID, cardiothoracic surgeon, educator; b. Charlotte, NC, May 26, 1932; s. James Simpson and Louisa (Reid) W.; m. Lucinda Holderness, July 25, 1959 (div. June 2003); children: Adelaide, Alexandra, Melissa, Reid; m. Harriet H. Davis, Aug. 15, 2005. BA, U. N.C., 1953, MD, 1957. Diplomate Am. Bd. Surgery, Am. Bd. Thoracic Surgery (chmn. 1991-93). Resident Barnes Hosp., St. Louis, 1958—59, N.C. Meml. Hosp., Chapel Hill, 1959—60, 1962—64; clin. assoc. Nat. Heart Inst., Bethesda, Md., 1960—62; instr. U. N.C., Chapel Hill, 1963—65, asst. prof., 1965—68, assoc. prof., 1968—71, chief cardiothoracic surgery divsn., 1969—98, chief emeritus, 1998—, prof. surgery, 1971—. Cons. NIH Grant Com., Bethesda, 1986—89; pres. Atlantic Coast Conf., Greensboro, NC, 1980—81; dir. Am. Bd. Thoracic Surgery, 1983—93, chmn., 1991—93; mem. coun. for grad. edn., 1993—96; bd. dirs. Nat. Residency Matching Program, 1998—, 2007, vice chmn. res. rev. com. for thoracic surgery, 2001—03, pres., 2001—02, sec., treas., 2003—06, rsch. rev. com. thoracic surgery, 2000—06, vice chmn.rsch. rev. com. thoracic surgery, 2004—06. Author (with others): Atlas of the Heart, 1988, Surgical Anatomy of the Heart, 1992, 3d edit., 2004 (BMA Med. Book award 2006); contbr. articles to profl. jours. Recipient Hadassah Myrtle Wreath award, 1979, Disting. Alumnus award Darlington Sch., Rome, Ga., 1997, Samaritan's Purse award, 1999; Markle scholar John and Mary Markle Found., 1967. Mem.: ACS (mem. adv. coun. cardiothoracic surgery 1992—, chmn. 1998—2002), Grad. Med. Edn. (coun. 1993—), Womack Soc. (pres. 1991—93), Thoracic Surgery Dirs. Assn. (pres. 1985—87), So. Surg. Assn., Soc. Univ. Surgeons, Soc. Thoracic Surgeons (treas. 1980—86, pres. 1994—95), Am. Surg. Assn., Am. Assn. Thoracic Surgery, CTS Net Corp. (bd. dirs. 1999—2005). Democrat. Presbyterian. Avocations: medical history, golf, hiking. Office: U NC Med Sch Womack Bldg CB 7065 3040 Burnett Chapel Hill NC 27599-0001 Office Phone: 919-966-3381. Personal E-mail: bensonreid@aol.com. Business E-Mail: benson@med.unc.edu.

WILCOX, DAVID ERIC, electrical engineering, educator, consultant, business owner; b. Cortland, NY, Sept. 4, 1939; s. James A. and Lucille (Fiske) C.; m. Phillipa Ann Wilcox, Jan. 23, 1977; children: Terri L., Cindy A., Jana L. 0postgrad., Syracuse U., 1965; BSEE, U. Buffalo, 1961;

0postgrad., Marist Coll., Rutgers U.; MS, U. Bridgeport, 1977. Registered profl. engr., N.Y. Rsch. engring. mgr. input/output devices Rome (NY) Air Devel. Ctr., 1966—70; dir. sales Mercom Inc., Winsooki, Vt., 1970-73; pres. Wilcox Tng. Sys., Newburgh, NY, 1973—98; pres., CEO Global Skills Exch., Alexandria, Va., 2003—. Exec. dep. dir., Nat. Skill Stds. Bd., 1998-2003, bd. dirs.; prin. Exec. Effectiveness, Inc., NYC; instr. Dale Carnegie courses. Author: Information System Sciences, 1965; contbr. articles to profl. jours.; patentee in field. Pres. N.Y. State Jaycees, 1972-73, chmn., 1973-74; dir. U.S. Jaycees, 1970-71; bd. dirs., v.p. N.Y. State Spl. Olympics, 1972-73; bd. dirs., treas. Family Counseling Svc., Inc.; mem. Orange County Pvt. Industry Coun., N.Y. State Excelsior Examiner, 1995. Lt. USAF, 1961-65. Mem. IEEE, Soc. Info. Display, N.Y. State Soc. Profl. Engrs., Internat. Transactional Analysis Assn., Internat. Platform Assn., Am. Soc. Quality Control. Methodist. also: 30 W 60th St New York NY 10023-7902 Office: Global Skills Exch 1410 King St Alexandria VA 22314 Home: 413 N Fairfax St Alexandria VA 22314-2321 Office Phone: 703-684-5067. Business E-Mail: dwilcox@gskillsxchange.com.

WILCOX, HARRY HAMMOND, retired anatomist; b. Canton, Ohio, May 31, 1918; s. Harry Hammond and Hattie Estelle (Richner) W.; m. D. June Freed., June 21, 1941; children: Joyce L. Wilcox Graff, Margaret J. (Mrs. Grayson S. Smith), James Hammond. BS, U. Mich., 1939, MS, 1940, PhD, 1948. Asso. prof. biology Morningside Coll., Sioux City, Iowa, 1947-48; asso. in anatomy U. Pa., 1948-52; mem. faculty U. Tenn. Center for Health Scis., 1952-83, Goodman prof. anatomy, 1966-83, emeritus prof. anatomy, 1983—. Assoc. editor: Anat. Record, 1968-83. Docent Memphis Zoo, 1983—, emeritus, 2005. With US Army, 1945—46. Mem.: AAAS, Soc. for Integrative and Comparative Biology, Am.Assn. Anatomists, Sigma Xi. Home: 1031 Marcia Rd Memphis TN 38117-5513

WILCOX, HARRY WILBUR, JR., retired manufacturing executive; b. Phila., Feb. 13, 1925; s. Harry Wilbur and Justine Elizabeth (Doolittle) Wilcox; m. Colleen Ann Cerra, Apr. 6, 1946 (dec. 2004); children: Justine, Harry Wilbur III; m. Elizabeth W. Crowther, 2006. BS, Yale U., New Haven, Conn., 1949. With GE Co., NYC, 1949-50; mfg. supt. Sylvania Electric Products, 1951-67; v.p., gen. mgr. Granger Assocs., Palo Alto, Calif., 1967-70; gen. mgr. ITT-Cannon Electric Co., Phoenix, 1970-72; pres. Hills McCanna Co., Carpentersville, Ill., 1972-75, VSI, and group v.p. IU Internat. Corp., 1975-78; exec. v.p. ITT-Grinnell, 1978-85; pres. ITT Indsl. and Constrn. Divsn., Lancaster, Pa., 1985-88; ret., 1988. Bd. dirs. Meyer Industries, Nat. Temperature Control Ctrs., Paul N. Howard Co.; former chmn. VSI, VSI-UK. Mem. adv. com. Town of Sherborn, Mass. With US Army, 1943—46. Decorated Bronze Star. Mem.: Madison Beach Club (Conn.), Grand Harbor Golf and Beach Club (Vero Beach), Yale Club of Treasure Coast. Achievements include patents in field. Home: 1135 Harbor Links Cir Vero Beach FL 32967 also: 47 Middle Beach Rd Madison CT 06443 Personal E-mail: harcon13@comcast.net.

WILCOX, HARVEY JOHN, lawyer; b. Elyria, Ohio, Nov. 1, 1937; s. Hubbard Clyde and Sylvia (Wahter) W.; m. Leslie Louise Coleman, Apr. 11, 1970. BA cum laude, Amherst Coll., 1959; LLB, Yale U., 1962. Bar: Ohio 1962, Va. 1994. Mem. firm Wilcox & Wilcox, 1962-78; with office gen. counsel Dept. Navy, Washington, 1966-94, asst. to gen. counsel, 1969-72, counsel Naval Air Systems Command, 1972-76, Navy dep. gen. counsel, 1976-94, cons. atty., arbitrator, 1994—. Guest lectr. US Army Logistics Mgmt. Ctr.; mem. Navy Contract Adjustment Bd., 1968-72 Designed Arlington County (Va.) flag, 1983. Bd. dirs. Navy Fed. Credit Union, 1974-77, sec.-treas., 1974-75, 2d v.p., 1975-77; mem. Def. Adv. Panel on Streamlining Acquisition Laws, 1991-92. Lt. USNR, 1963-66. Recipient Meritorious Exec. rank 1980, Disting Exec. rank, 1981, 89, Navy Disting. Civilian Svc. award, 1989, Defense Disting. Civilian Svc. award, 1994. Mem. Ohio Bar Assn., Va. State Bar, Charlottesville-Albemarle Bar Assn., Nat. Trust Hist. Preservation, Nature Conservancy, Piedmont Environ. Coun. Home: PO Box 338 Turner Mountain Rd Ivy VA 22945-0338 Personal E-mail: wilcoxivy@earthlink.net.

WILCOX, HELENA MARGUERITA (HELENA RITA WILCOX), music educator; b. Manhattan, Kans., Feb. 16, 1930; d. Virgil Otis Jones and Helena Mary Viers-Jones; children: Charles E., Marguerita E., Patricia A. MusB, State U. Iowa, 1952, MA, 1959. Cert. music tchr. Ariz., 1959, Calif., 1967, Jr. Coll. Calif., 1972. Pvt. kindergarten, Springerville, Ariz., 1959—60; art supr. Yuma (Ariz.) Elem. Sch. Dist., 1960—67; violin tchr. Ariz. Western Cmty. Coll., Yuma, 1965—67; string instrument tchr. Stockton (Calif.) Unified Sch. Dist., 1967—2002; Suzuki violin tchr. San Joaquin Delta Coll., Stockton, 1972—; musician Stockton (Calif.) Symphony, 1967—; tchr. summer arts Stockton (Calif.) Arts Commn.; organ. Symphony Orch., Yuma, 1962—67. Recipient Start Edn. award, Stockton Arts Commn., 2007; Production grant, Stockton Unified Sch. Dist., 1980. Mem.: Nat. Music Educators, Calif. Tchrs. Assn., Suzuki Assn. of the Am., Music Tchrs. Assn. of Calif., Stockton Br. (pres. 2003—), Am. String Tchrs. Assn. (pres. 1975). Democrat. Unitarian. Home: 2348 W Alpine Ave Stockton CA 95204 Home Phone: 209-464-2456. Personal E-mail: ritaviola@sbcglobal.net.

WILCOX, HUGH EDWARD, plant physiologist; b. Manchester, Calif., Sept. 2, 1916; s. Leroy Fremont and Lulu Abbie (Gaspar) W.; m. Elizabeth Irene Bufford, Aug. 21, 1938; children: Irene Wilcox Barmore, Janet Wilcox Ievins, Kenneth Hugh, Linda Wilcox Bitzer, Carol Wilcox Folsom. BS, U. Calif., Berkeley, 1938, PhD, 1950; MS, N.Y. State Coll. Forestry, 1940. Technician in forestry U. Calif., Berkeley, 1941-42, physicist Radiation Lab., 1942-45; physicist U.S. Naval Ordnance Test Sta., Inyokern, Calif., 1945-46; wood technologist, assoc. prof. Oreg. Forest Products Lab., Corvallis, 1946-51; rsch. assoc., project leader Rsch. Found. SUNY, Syracuse, 1951-54, assoc. prof. Coll. of Forestry, 1954-59, prof. Coll. Environ. Sci. and Forestry, 1959-86, prof. emeritus Coll. Environ. Sci. and Forestry, 1986—, acting dept. chmn. dept. forest botany & pathology, 1968-69. Fulbright lectr. Tel Aviv U., 1965-66; guest lectr. Helsinki (Finland) U., 1975; presenter in field. Contbr. articles to profl. publs., chpts. to books. Grantee NSF, 1954-57, 79-81, Rsch. Found. SUNY, 1954-75, McIntire-Stennis, 1965-91, Pinchot Consortium, 1980-82. Fellow AAAS; mem. Soc. Am. Foresters (program chmn. and organizer 1976, mem. forest biology workshops), Am. Inst. Biol. Scis., Botanical Soc. Am., Am. Soc. Plant Physiologists, Am. Mycorrhizal Confs. (charter mem.), Internat. Union Forestry Rsch. Orgns. (root physiology and symbiosis working group), Sigma Xi. Avocations: gardening, painting, photography, canoeing.

WILCOX, JAROSLAVA ZITKOVA, physicist; d. Antonin Zitek and Barbora Zitkova; children: Elizabeth, Marc. MS, Charles U., 1966; PhD in Physics, UCLA, 1972. Rsch. assoc. Czech Acad. Scis., Prague, Czech Republic, 1966—68; prof. Tufts U., Medford, Mass., 1972—74; sr. tech. staff TRW, Redondo Beach, Calif., 1974—90; sr. tech. staff Caltech JPL, Pasadena, Calif., 1990—. Cons. BW9 Inc., Calif., 1998—2000; presenter in field. Contbr. over 100 publs. in field; art and painting exhibits include, Czech Consulate, Lee Strasberg Theater, JPL. Recipient Tech. Achievement Roll Hon., TRW, 1983; fellow, Czech Acad. Scis., 1966—68, Tufts U., 1973; grantee, TRW, 1980—90, NASA, 1998, 2001, 2003, 2005. Mem.: West L.A. Artists (organizer 2000—). Achievements include invention of the AEXS instrument, vibrational microgyroscope, several diode laser concepts, SAW devices; patents in field. Avocations: travel, photography, drawing, painting. Home: 235 N Kenter Ave Los Angeles CA 90049 Office: Jet Propulsion Lab - Caltech Pasadena CA 91109 Home Phone: 310-476-8941; Office Phone: 818-354-3556. Business E-Mail: jzw@jpl.nasa.gov.

WILCOX, JOHN CAVEN, lawyer, financial executive; b. NYC, Nov. 12, 1942; s. Daniel A. and Jessie Alexandra (Caven) W.; m. Vanessa Guerrini-Maraldi, Sept. 30, 1983; children Daniel D.G., William G.M., Julia G.M. BA magna cum laude, Harvard U., 1964; MA, U. Calif., Berkeley, 1965; JD, Harvard U., 1968; LLM, NYU, 1981. Bar: N.Y. 1973. Account exec. Georgeson & Co. Inc., NYC, 1973-79, mng. dir., 1979-90, chmn., 1990—2005; sr. v.p. head corp. governance TIAA-CREF, 2005—. Dir. GSC Proxitalia, 1999-05; bd. govs. Internat. Corp. Governance Network, 2002- 05; chair ICGN com. on cross-border voting practices. Trustee Woodrow Wilson Nat. Fellowship Found., 1996, vice chmn., 1996—; trustee Family Dynamics, Inc., NYC, 1979-96, Bennington Coll., 1998—. With US Army, 1968-70, Vietnam. Woodrow Wilson fellow. Mem. ABA (com. corp. laws), NYSE (shareholders comm. com. 1989-95), Am. Soc. Corp. Secs., Nat. Assn. Security Dealers (issuer affairs com 1990-05), Nat. Assn. Corp. Dirs. (adv. bd. NY chpt.), The Brook, Harvard Club (NYC), Phi Beta Kappa. Democrat. Home: 580 West End Ave New York NY 10024-1723 Office: TIAA-CREF 730 Third Ave New York NY 10017 Home Phone: 212-877-3413; Office Phone: 212-916-5404. Business E-Mail: jwilcox@tiaa-cref.org.

WILCOX, JON P., state supreme court justice; b. Berlin, Wis., Sept. 5, 1936; m. Jane Ann; children: Jeffrey, Jennifer. AB in Polit. Sci., Ripon Coll., 1958; JD, U. Wis., 1965. Pvt. practice Steele, Smyth, Klos and Flynn, LaCrosse, Wis., 1965-66, Hacker and Wilcox, Wautoma, Wis., 1966-69, Wilcox, Rudolph, Kubasta & Rathjen, Wautoma, 1969-79; mem. Wis. State Legislature, 1969—75; judge Waushara County Cir. Ct., 1979-92; justice Wis. Supreme Ct., 1992—. Commr. Family Ct., Waushara County, 1977-79; del. Wis. Conservation Congress, 1975-80; vice chmn., chmn. Wis. Sentencing Commn., 1987-92; chief judge 6th Jud. Dist., 1985-92; mem. State-Fed. Jud. Coun., 1992-99, Jud. Coun. Wis., 1993-98; mem. Prison Overcrowding Task Force, 1988-90; mem. numerous coms. Wis. Judiciary; mem. faculty Wis. Jud. Coll., 1985-96; chmn. Wis. Chief Judges Com., 1990-92; co-chair comm. on judiciary as co-equal br. of govt. Wis. State Bar, 1995-97; lectr. in field. Contbr. (with others): Wisconsin News Reporters Legal Handbook: Wisconsin Courts and Court Procedures, 1987. Bd. visitors U. Wis. Law Sch., 1970—76. Lt. US Army, 1959—61. Named Outstanding Jaycee Wautoma, 1974; recipient Disting. Alumni award Ripon Coll., 1993. Fellow Am. Bar Found.; mem. ABA (com. on continuing appellate edn.), Wis. Bar Assn. (bench bar com., state bar and media law rels. com.), Wis. Law Found. (bd. dirs.), Tri-County Bar Assn., Dane County Bar Assn., Trout Unltd., Ducks Unltd., Rotary, Phi Alpha Delta. Office: Supreme Court State Capitol PO Box 1688 Madison WI 53701-1688 *

WILCOX, MARK DEAN, lawyer; b. May 25, 1952; s. Fabian Joseph and Zeryle Lucille (Tase) W.; m. Catherine J. Wertjes, Mar. 12, 1983; children: Glenna Lynn, Joanna Tessie, Andrew Fabian Joseph. BBA, U. Notre Dame, 1973; JD, Northwestern U., 1976; CLU, Am. Coll., 1979, ChFC, 1992. Bar: Ill. 1976, U.S. Dist. Ct. (no. dist.) Ill. 1976, Trial Bar 1982, U.S. Ct. Appeals (7th cir.) 1987, U.S. Supreme Ct. 1989. Staff asst. Nat. Dist. Attys. Assn., Chgo., 1974-75; trial asst. Cook County States Atty., Chgo., 1975; intern U.S. Atty. No. Dist. Ill., Chgo., 1975-76; assoc. Lord, Bissell & Brook, LLP, Chgo., 1976-85, ptnr., 1986—2005; founding ptnr. Walker Wilcox Matousek, LLP, Chgo., 2005—. Venue ofcl. Internat. Spl. Olympics; bd. mgrs. YMCA Met. Chgo., exec. com.; active No Bats Baseball Club Hall of Fame; past trustee Trinity United Meth. Ch.; bd. dirs., past chair Irving Park YMCA. Fellow Am. Bar Found.; mem. ABA (tort and ins. practice sect.), Am. Soc. CLU and ChFC, Chgo. Bar Assn. (ins. law com.), Am. Health Lawyers Assn., Nat. Assn. Ins. and Fin. Advisors, Def. Rsch. Inst., Soc. Fin. Svc. Profls., Trial Lawyers Club Chgo., Notre Dame Nat. Monogram Club, Union League Club, Chgo. Lions Rugby Football Club, Beta Gamma Sigma. Office Phone: 312-244-6722.

WILCOX, MARY MARKS, retired Christian education consultant, educator; b. Madison, Wis., Apr. 23, 1921; d. Roy and Mary Celia (Leary) Marks; m. Ray Everett Wilcox, Nov. 28, 1942; children: Peter, Anne, Susan, Steven. BA, U. Wis., 1942; MRE, Iliff Sch. Theology, Denver, 1968. Cert. Christian educator. Cons. local chs., Lakewood, Littleton, Wheat Ridge, Colo., 1963-74; instr., leader numerous seminars throughout U.S. and Can., 1963—; interim parish cons. 1st Presbyn. Ch., Lakewood, 1988-90, profl. assoc. for faith devel., 1993-97; adj. prof. Iliff Sch. Theology, 1970—; ret., 2002. Author: Developmental Journey, 1979; co-author: Viewpoints, 1998; contbr. articles to various publs., chpts. to books. Trustee, mem. exec. bd. Nat. Ghost Ranch Found., Abiquiu, N. Mex., 1983-93. Recipient award Iliff Alumni Assn., 1989. Mem.: Assn. Presbyn. Christian Educators (past mem. exec. bd.). Democrat. Presbyterian. Home: 3590 Estes St Wheat Ridge CO 80033-5933

WILCOX, MAUD, editor; b. NYC, Feb. 14, 1923; d. Thor Fredrik and Gerda (Ysberg) Eckert; m. Edward T. Wilcox, Feb. 9, 1944 (dec. 1998); children: Thor(dec.), Bruce, Eric, Karen. AB summa cum laude, Smith Coll., 1944; A.M., Harvard U., 1945. Teaching fellow Harvard U., 1945-46, 48-51; instr. English Smith Coll., Northampton, Mass., 1947-48, Wellesley Coll., Mass., 1951-52; exec. editor Harvard U. Press, 1958-66, humanities editor, 1966-73, editor-in-chief, 1973—89; freelance editorial cons. Cambridge, 1989—; ret. Cons., panelist NEH, Washington, 1974-76, 82-84; cons. Radcliffe Pub. Course, 1991. Mem. MLA (com. scholarly edits. 1982-86), Assn. Am. Univ. Presses (chair com. admissions and standards 1976-77, v.p. 1978-79, chair program com. 1981-82), Phi Beta Kappa. Democrat. Episcopalian. Home and Office: 63 Francis Ave Cambridge MA 02138-1911 Home Phone: 617-864-3625. Personal E-mail: maudwilcox@post.harvard.edu.

WILCOX, RAYMOND I., oil industry executive; b. Mar. 19; BSME cum laude, U. Mich., 1968; postgrad., London Bus. Sch., 1994. Design and constrn. engr. Chevron, 1968—81, mem. fgn. ops. staff, 1981—86, ops. supt. Lafayette, La., 1986—90; mng. dir. Chevron Asiatic, Melbourne, Australia, 1990—96; v.p., gen. mgr. marine transp. Chevron Shipping Co., San Ramon, Calif., 1996—99; gen. mgr. asset mgmt. Chevron Nigeria Ltd., 1999—2000, chmn., mng. dir., 2000—01; mng. dir. Nigeria/Mid-Africa strategic bus. unit ChevronTexaco Corp., 2001—02; pres. ChevronTexaco Exploration and Prodn. Co., 2002—06; v.p. ChevronTexaco Corp., Houston; pres., CEO Chevron Phillips Chem. Co. LLC, 2006—. Bd. dirs. Dynergy Inc., 2003—. Bd. dirs. Spindletop Charities, Greater Houston Partnership; chmn. Century divsn. United Way of Tex. Gulf Coast, 2003. Mem.: Am. Petroleum Inst. (mem. upstream com.). Office: Chevron Phillips Chem Co 10001 Six Pines Dr The Woodlands TX 77380

WILCOX, SHIRLEY JEAN LANGDON, genealogist; b. Arcata, Calif., Dec. 10, 1942; d. Elmore Harold and Alberta May (Starkey) Langdon; m. Wayne Kent Wilcox, June 22, 1963; 1 child, Harold Bonner. BS, U. Md., 1964. Cert. Bd. for Certification of Genealogists. Tchr. Prince George's County (Md.) Sch. System, 1964-67, substitute tchr., 1968-73; profl. genealogist Lanham, Md., Arlington, Va., 1973—; genealogy tchr. Fairfax County Pub. Schs., 1995-99. Level II coord. Mid-Atlantic Genealogy and History Inst., George Mason U., Fairfax, Va., 1986; trustee Bd. for Certification of Genealogists, 2000—. Editor: A Bibliography of Published Genealogical Source Records, Prince George's County, Maryland, 1975, Prince George's County Land Records, Vol. A, 1696-1702, 1976, 1850 Census Prince George's County, Maryland, 1978, 1828 Tax List Prince George's County, Maryland, 1985; author: The National Genealogical Society: A Look at Its First One Hundred Years, 2003. Elder Presbyn. Ch., 1970-73, 95-98. Fellow: Nat. Geneal. Soc. (chmn. conf. program subcom. 1990, 2d v.p. 1990—94, councilor 1994—96, pres. 1996—2000); mem.: DAR (libr. Belle Air chpt. 1985—, Outstanding Jr. Mem. award 1979), Fairfax Geneal. Soc. (pres. 1989—89), Prince George's County Geneal. Soc. (pres. 1973, 1975—76, book rev. editor 1976—96, Jane Roush McCafferty award of excellence 1985), Va. Geneal. Soc. (gov. 2001—), Assn. Profl. Genealogists (pres. 1991—93, pres. Nat. Capital area chpt. 1994—96, dir. region 3 2004—06, Grahame Thomas Smallwood Jr. award of merit 1995), Clay Family Soc. (dir. 2002—06), Soc. Mayflower Descs. in DC (bd. assts. 2007—), Paperweight Collectors Assn. (pres. Md.-DC-Va. chpt. 1988—90), numerous others. Avocation: collecting paperweights. Home: 1500 23rd St S Arlington VA 22202-1523

WILCOX, STEVEN ALAN, lawyer; b. RI, Mar. 1955; s. Donald W. and Edna Wilcox; m. Nancy Wilcox, Aug., 1980. BA summa cum laude, Boston Coll., 1977, JD cum laude, 1980. Bar: Mass. 1980. Assoc. Ropes & Gray, Boston, 1980-89, ptnr. corp. dept., 1989—, head life sci. practice group. Mem. ABA, Mass. Bar Assn., Boston Bar Assn. Office: Ropes & Gray 1 International Pl Boston MA 02110-2624 Office Phone: 617-951-7319. Office Fax: 617-951-7050. Business E-Mail: swilcox@ropesgray.com.

WILCOX, TRE, chef; Corp. trainer Eatzi's; chef Toscana; grill cook Abacus Restaurant, Dallas, 1999, sous chef, exec. sous chef, 2003, chef de cuisine. Menu cons. KRLD Restaurant Week, Dallas, 2003. Guest appearances include Tex. Cable News Network, Good Morning Tex., ABC, Good Day Dallas, Metro, Fox News. Named one of Top Young Guns in Dallas, D Mag., Dallas' Rising Stars, StarChefs.com, 2007; recipient Best Food & Wine Pairings award, KRLD Restaurant Week, 2003, First Place, Rising Star Chef contest, Dallas Morning News, 2004. Office: Abacus 4511 McKinney Ave Dallas TX 75205 *

WILCOXSON, ROY DELL, plant pathologist, researcher, educator; b. Columbia, Utah, Jan. 12, 1926; m. Iva Wall, 1949; children: Bonnie, Paul, Karren, John. BS, Utah State U., 1953; MS, U. Minn., 1955, PhD in Plant Pathlogy, 1957. Asst. prof., 1957-66; prof. plant pathology U. Minn., St. Paul, 1966-91, prof. emeritus, 1991—. Spl. staff mem. Rockefeller Found.; vis. prof. Indian Agrl. Rsch. Inst., New Delhi; dir. Morocco project U. Minn., 1983-87; adj. prof. Inst. Agronomy and Vet. Medicine, Hassan II, Rabat, Morocco, 1985—. Fellow Am. Phytopath Soc., Indian NAS, Indian Phytopath Soc., AAAS. Achievements include research in diseases of forage crops and cereal crops; cereal rust diseases. Office: 1669 County Road 8230 West Plains MO 65775-5766 Address: Dept Plant Path U Minn Saint Paul MN 55101

WILCZEK, FRANK ANTHONY, physics professor; b. Mineola, NY, May 15, 1951; s. Frank John and Mary Rose (Cona) W.; m. Elizabeth Jordan Devine, July 3, 1973; children: Amity, Mira. BS in Math., U. Chgo., 1970; MA in Math., Princeton U., 1972, PhD in Physics, 1974; Doctorate degree (hon.), Universitè de Montrèal, 2001; Doctorate degree, Clark U., 2007, Ohio State U., 2007. Instr. Princeton U., NJ, 1974, asst. prof. NJ, 1974-76, Princeton, NJ, 1977—78, assoc. prof., 1978—80, prof., 1980-81; prof., Sch. of Natural Scis. Inst. for Advanced Study, Princeton, NJ, 1989—2000; prof. U. Calif., Santa Barbara, Calif., 1980—88, Inst. for Theoretical Physics, Santa Barbara, Calif., 1981-88; Herman Feshbach Prof. Physics MIT, Cambridge, Mass., 2000—. Vis. fellow Inst. Advanced Study, Princeton, 1976-77; Chancellor Robert Huttenback prof. of physics U. Calif., Santa Barbara, 1984-90; vis. prof. Harvard U., 1987-88; J. Robert Oppenheimer prof. Inst. for Advanced Study, 1997-2000; adj. prof. Centros Estudios Cientificos, 2002-; vis. Schrodinger-prof. City of Vienna, Austria, 2002; Leland J. Haworth Disting. Scientist, Brookhaven Nat. Lab., 1994-97; lectr. several univs. and socs.; serves several adv. bds. Author: Longing for the Harmonies, 1988, Geometric Phases in Physics, 1989, Fractional Statistics and Anyon Superconductivity, 1990, Fantastic Realities, 2006; editor-in-chief Annals of Physics, 2001-; editl. advisor, Daedalus, 2002-; contbr. articles to profl. jours. Trustee U. Chgo., 1998—2004. Recipient J.J. Sakurai prize Am. Phys. Soc., 1986, Dirac medal UNESCO, 1994, Michelson-Morley prize Case Western Res. U., 2002, Lorentz medal, 2002, Lilienfield prize Am. Physics Soc., 2003, Europhysics prize, 2003; named A.P. Sloan fellow, 1975-77, MacArthur fellow, 1982-87, Regent's Fellow, Smithsonian Astrophysical Observatory, 1986-88; co-recipient High Energy and Particle Physics prize, European Physical Soc., 2003, Nobel Prize in Physics, 2004, King Faisal prize (Sci.), King Faisal Found., 2005. Fellow: AAAS, Am. Philos. Soc., Am. Philos. Soc.; fgn. mem. Royal Netherlands Acad. Arts and Sci.; mem. NAS, Am. Acad. Arts and Scis. Achievements include discovery of asymptotic freedom in the theory of the strong interaction. Avocations: chess, music, logic puzzles. Office: MIT-NE25-4010 Ctr for Theoretical Physics 6-301 5 Cambridge Center Cambridge MA 02142 Business E-Mail: wilczek@mit.edu.

WILCZYNSKI, JANUSZ S., manufacturing executive, retired physicist; b. Warsaw, May 12, 1929; came to US, 1962; m. Brahna Lauger. Diploma in Indsl. Mechanics, Mining Acad., Cracow, Poland, 1954; MSc in Physics, Jagellonian U., Cracow, Poland, 1957; PhD in Physics and Optics, Imperial Coll. U. London, 1961. Physicist Watson, Ltd., London, 1961-62; rsch. staff mem. T.J. Watson Rsch. Ctr., IBM, Yorktown Heights, NY, 1962-63, mgr. tech. optics, 1963-83, 2d level mgr., 1983-84, sr. mgr., 1984-86, dir., 1986-93; gen. ptnr. Wilc Instruments LLP, 1995. Contbr. over 60 articles to profl. jours. Recipient 13 Invention awards, 1966-98, 7 Outstanding Innovation awards IBM, 1968-91; IBM fellow, 1981. Fellow Optical Soc. Am. (Richardson medal 1988); mem. NAE. Avocation: astronomical optics. Home: PO Box 790 Sandia Park NM 87047-0790 Office Phone: 505-286-8285. Office Fax: 505-286-8272. Personal E-mail: wilczyn@swcp.com.

WILD, EARL, musician, composer; b. Pitts., Nov. 26, 1915; Grad., Pitts. Carnegie Tech. (now Carnegie Mellon U.), 1937; DFA, 2007. Performer KDKA Radio, Pitts., 1927—35; pianist Pitts. Symphony Orch., 1924—34; staff pianist NBC Network, 1937—44; staff pianist, conductor, composer ABC Network, 1944—68; composer The Caesar Hour, 1952—56. Musician US Navy; tchr. Ctrl. Conservatory of Music, Beijing, Toho-Gakuen Sch. Music, Tokyo, SunWah Sch., Seoul, Manhattan Sch. Music, Ohio State U.; disting. vis. artist Carnegie Mellon U., Pitts.; founder, artist dir. & pianist Concert Soloists of Wolf Trap, Vienna, 1978—82. With USN, 1942—44. Named Instrumentalist of Yr., Musical Am., 2005; recipient Alumni Merit award, Carnegie Mellon U., 1996, Disting. Achievement award, 2000, Grammy award, 1997. Achievements include becoming first artist to perform a piano recital on US television, 1939; being youngest American piano soloist ever engaged by NBC Symphony; performing for 6 consecutive presidents (Herbert Hoover to Lyndon Johnson). Mailing: c/o Michael Rolland Davis Prodn 2233 Fernleaf Ln Columbus OH 43235 Office Phone: 614-761-8709.

WILD, JAMES ROBERT, biochemistry and genetics professor; b. Sedalia, Mo., Nov. 24, 1945; s. Robert Lee and Frances Elleta (Wheeler) W.; m. Ann Lynn Brenner, Aug. 1, 1973; 1 child, Kalli Ann. BA in Zoology, U. Calif., Davis, 1967; PhD in Cell Biology, U. Calif., Riverside, 1971, post doctoral fellow, 1972. From asst. to assoc. prof. genetics and biochemistry Tex. A&M U., Coll. Sta., Tex., 1975-84, prof., chair genetics faculty, 1984—, prof. biochemistry & genetics, 1984—2000, head biochemistry and biophysics dept., 1986-90, exec. assoc. dean Coll. Agr. and Life Scis., 1987—92, prof., head dept. biochemistry and biophysics Coll. Agr. and Life Scis., 1994—2000, chmn. faculty genetics. Fellow faculty Tex. Agrl. Experiment Sta., 1999. With USN, 1972-75. Recipient So. Regional award for excellence in coll. anduniv. tchg. in food and agrl. scis., Higher Edn. program USDA, 1992. Fellow AAAS. Methodist. Office: Tex A&M U 2128 Biochemistry Bldg Rm 332 College Station TX 77843-2128 Office Phone: 979-845-6539. Business E-Mail: j-wild@tamu.edu.

WILD, JOHN JULIAN, surgeon, researcher, medical educator; b. Sydenham, Kent, Eng., Aug. 11, 1914; came to U.S., 1946; s. Ovid Frederick and Ellen Louise (Cuttance) W.; m. Nancy Wallace, Nov. 14, 1949 (div. 1966); children: John O., Douglas J.; m. Valerie Claudia Grosenick, Aug. 9, 1968; 1 child, Ellen Louise. BA, U. Cambridge, Eng., 1936, MA, 1940, MD, 1942, PhD, 1971. Intern, resident U. Coll. Hosp., London, 1938-42; intern U. College Hosp., London, 1938-42; staff surgeon Miller Gen., St. Charles and North Middlesex Hosps., London, 1942-44; venereologist Royal Army Med. Corps, 1944-45; rsch. fellow, instr. depts. surgery and elec. engring., prin. investigator U. Minn., Mpls., 1946-51; dir. rsch. Medico.-Technol. Rsch. Dept. St. Barnabas Hosp., Mpls., 1953-60; dir. Medico-Technol. Rsch. Unit Minn. Found., St. Paul, 1960-63; pvt. practice Mpls., 1966—90; dir. Medico-Technol. Rsch. Inst. Mpls., St. Louis Park, Minn., 1965—2006. Lectr. in field of medical instruments, ultrasound. Contbr. articles to profl. jours. Recipient Japan prize in Medical Imaging, Sci. and Tech. Found. Japan, 1991, 1st Frank Annunzio award Christopher Columbus Fellowship Found., 1998, lifetime achievement award U. Minn. Med. Sch., 2000, Ian Donald Tech. Achievement aard ISUOG, 2000. Fellow Am. Inst. Ultrasound in Medicine (Pioneer award 1978); mem. AMA, World Fedn. Ultrasound in Medicine and Biology, Minn. State Med. Assn., Hennepin County Med. Soc., N.Am. Alvis Owners Club; hon. mem. Brit. Inst. Radiology, Japan Soc. of Ultrasound in Medicine. Achievements include patents in field; origination of ultrasonic medical imaging instruments and diagnostic techniques; origination of the field of pulse-echo ultrasonic diagnostic medicine. Home and Office: Medico-Technol Rsch Inst 4262 Alabama Ave S Minneapolis MN 55416-3105

WILD, NELSON HOPKINS, lawyer; b. Milw., July 16, 1933; s. Henry Goetseels and Virginia Douglas (Weller) W.; m. Joan Ruth Miles, Apr. 12, 1969; children: Mark, Eric; m. Diana Morris, Sept. 7, 2002. AB, Princeton U., 1955; LL.B., U. Wis., 1961. Bar: Wis. 1962, Calif. 1967; cert. specialist in probate, estate planning and trust law State Bar of Calif. Research assoc. Wis. Legis. Council, Madison, 1955-56; assoc. Whyte, Hirschboeck, Minahan, Harding & Harland, Milw., 1961-67, Thelen, Marin, Johnson & Bridges, San Francisco, 1967-70; sole practice law San Francisco, 1970—. Mem. State Bar Calif. Client Trust Fund Commn., 1983, mem. exec. com. conf. dels., 1985-88. Contbr. articles to legal jours. Bd. dirs. Neighborhood Legal Assistance Found., San Francisco, 1974-85, chmn. bd., 1978-81. Served with USAF, 1956-58. Mem. ABA, Calif. Bar Assn., San Francisco Bar Assn., Am. Bar Found., Lawyers of San Francisco Club (gov. 1975, treas. 1981, v.p. 1982, pres.-elect 1983, pres. 1984), Calif. Tennis Club (bd. dirs. 1995-97, pres. 1997). Office: 332 Pine St Ste 710 San Francisco CA 94104-3230 Personal E-mail: nwildlaw@aol.com.

WILD, RICHARD, music educator, musician; b. Santa Monica, Calif., Dec. 15, 1954; s. Caryll Harris and Marguerite Grunseth Wild; m. Julie Marie Ahern, Sept. 19, 1981; children: Eve Noel, Benjamin Caryll. BA in Music, UCLA, 1976; BA in Elem. Edn., Coll. Santa Fe, 1995. Nat. bd. cert. tchr. 2005. Gen. organ builder Abbott and Sieker Organ Builders, LA, 1977—79; proprietor Rick Wild Organbuilder, Albuquerque, 1984—; organist 1st Prebyn. Ch., Albuquerque, 1988—2001; tchr. Sandia Prep. Sch., Albuquerque, 1988—89, Manzano Boys Sch., Albuquerque, 1988—94; music specialist Albuquerque Pub. Schs., 1998—; organist Ctrl. United Meth. Ch., Albuquerque, 2001—. Composer: How Can I Deny God's Grace, 2003. Mem. fine arts adv. bd. Albuquerque Arts Alliance, 2004—07; bd. dirs. University Heights Assn., Albuquerque, 1992—93. Mem.: Am. Orff-Schuler Assn., N.Mex. Music Educators Assn. (John Batchellor award for excellence in tchg. elem. music 2005), Am. Guild Organists (post dean 2003—04, N.Mex. dist. convenor 2001—07), PI Lambda Theta. Methodist. Avocations: amateur radio, sailing, bicycling. Home: 205 Cornell SE Albuquerque NM 87106 E-mail: wild@aps.edu.

WILD, RICHARD P., lawyer; b. NYC, Aug. 13, 1947; s. Alfred P. and Harriet C. (Hoffman) W.; m. Deirdre L. Felbin, June 15, 1969; children: Nicholas B., Daniel M. AB, Columbia U., 1968; JD, Yale U., 1971. Bar: Pa. 1971, U.S. Dist. Ct. (ea. dist.) Pa. 1971, U.S. Tax Ct. 1973, U.S. Claims Ct. 1977. Assoc. Dechert LLP, Phila., 1971-78, ptnr., 1978—. Mem. Phila. Bar Assn. (tax sect.). Office: Dechert LLP Cira Ctr 2929 Arch St Philadelphia PA 19104-2808

WILD, ROBERT ANTHONY, academic administrator; b. Chgo., Mar. 30, 1940; s. John Hopkins and Mary Dorothy (Colnon) Wild. BA in Latin, Loyola U., Chgo., 1962, MA in Classical Lang., 1967; STL, Jesuit Sch. Theology, Chgo., 1970; PhD in Study of Religion, Harvard U., 1977. Ordained priest 1970. From asst. to assoc. prof. Marquette U., Milw., 1975—83; vis. prof. Pont. Istituto Biblico, Rome, 1983—84; dir. Jesuit philosophate program Loyola U., Chgo., 1984—85, assoc. prof. theology, 1985—92; provincial superior Chgo. Province S.J., 1985—91; pres. Weston Jesuit Sch. Theology, Cambridge, Mass., 1992—96, Marquette U., Milw., 1996—. Trustee Jesuit Sch. Theology, Berkeley, 1985—90, Weston Sch. Theology, Cambridge, Mass., 1985—96, Marquette U., 1990—, St. Louis U., 1994—2002, Milw. Rsch. Park, 2002—05, Greater Milw. Commn., 2002—, Wis. Assn. Ind. Colls. and Univs., 1996—, chmn., 2001—07, St. Joseph's U., Pa., 2004—. Author: Water in the Cultic Worship of Isis and Sarapis, 1981; co-editor: Sentences of Sextus, 1981; contbr. articles to profl. jours. Mem.: Cath. Bibl. Soc., Soc. Bibl. Lit. Office: Marquette Univ O'Hara Hall PO Box 1881 Milwaukee WI 53201-1881 Home Phone: 414-288-5000; Office Phone: 414-288-7223. Business E-Mail: robert.wild@marquette.edu.

WILD, ROBERT WARREN, lawyer; b. Syracuse, NY, Mar. 25, 1942; s. Robert Sumner and Evelyn I. (Yorman) W.; m. Elizabeth Trowbridge, Sept. 5, 1965; children: Robert Mason, Alexander Lewis, Elizabeth Anne. BS, MIT, 1964; JD, Cornell U., 1970. Bar: N.Y. 1971, D.C. 1973. Engr. Smithsonian Astrophysical Obs., Cambridge, Mass., 1965-67; atty., advisor U.S. Dept. Justice, Washington, 1970-72; law clk. to Hon. Justice William H. Rehnquist U.S. Supreme Ct., Washington, 1972-73; ptnr. Nixon Peabody LLP, Rochester, NY, 1973—. Mem. Monroe County Bar Assn. (trustee 1990-91, 92-94, treas. 1992-94, counsel 1994—). Office: Nixon Peabody LLP Clinton Sq PO Box 31051 Rochester NY 14603-1051 Home Phone: 585-248-8751; Office Phone: 585-263-1302. Business E-Mail: rwild@nixonpeabody.com.

WILDASIN, DAVID E(ARL), economics professor; b. Willimantic, Conn., Dec. 2, 1950; m. Kathleen Ann Preslin, Aug. 10, 1973. BA in Econs., U. Va., Charlottesville, 1972; PhD Econs., U. Iowa, Iowa City, 1976. Asst. prof. U. Ill., Chgo., 1976—79, Ind. U., Bloomington, 1979—82, assoc. prof., 1982—86, prof. econs., 1986—93, prof. West European studies, 1993; prof. econs. Vanderbilt U., Nashville, 1993—2000; endowed prof. pub. fin. Martin Sch. Pub. Policy and Adminstrn., prof. econs. U. Ky., Lexington, 2000—, dir. Inst. Federalism and Intergovtl. Rels., 2005—. Cons. World Bank, 1992—2002, long-term cons. policy rsch. dept. pub. econs. divsn., 1995—96; vis. assoc. prof. Queen's U., Kingston, Ont., Canada, 1982—83; vis. prof. U. Cath. Louvain, Louvain-la-Neuve, Belgium, 1986—87, Sch. of Higher Studies in Social Scis., Marseille, France, 1995; summer fellow U. Bonn, Germany, 1990; vis. scholar Interuniv. Ctr. for Econ. Studies, Gadjah Mada U., Indonesia, 1990, Ctr. for Econ. Studies U. Munich, 1991, U. B.C., Canada, 1992; econ. policy rsch. unit Copenhagen Bus. Inst., 1996; cons. Ky. C. of C., 2002—03; cons. consensus forecast group Commonwealth of Ky., 2007—; internat. rsch. fellow Oxford U. Ctr. for Bus. Taxation, 2007—; lectr. in field; cons. in field. Author: Urban Public Finance, 1986; co-author: Public Sector Economics, 1984; editor: Fiscal Aspects of Evolving Federations, 1997; assoc. editor: Regional Sci. and Urban Econs., 1987—2004, Jour. Regional Sci., 1989—, Jour. Urban Econs., 1991—, Internat. Tax and Pub. Fin., 1993—, Rev. Internat. Econs., 1994—, Nat. Tax Jour., 1998—, Jour. Pub. Econ. Theory, 1999—, Jour. Pub. Econs., 1999—2003, Papers in Regional Sci., 1999—2001, German Econ. Rev., 2000—, Finanzarchiv, 2000—, CESifo Econ. Studies, 2003—, Contbns. to Econ. Analysis, 2004—, Founds. and Trends in Microecons., 2005—06, referee: profl. jours.; contbr. over 90 articles to Am. Econ. Rev., Econ. Jour., others. Fellow, Ctr. Ops. Rsch. and Econometrics, U. Cath. de Louvain, Belgium, 1986—87; grantee, NSF, 1978—81, Inst. Study of Labor, U. Bonn, Germany, 2000—; Ameritech fellow, Ind. U., 1988—89, U. Bonn, Germany, 1990. Mem. Am. Econ. Assn., Econometric Soc, Nat. Tax Assn., Tax Inst. Am. Office: U Ky Martin Sch Pub Policy Lexington KY 40506-0027 Office Phone: 859-257-2456. Business E-Mail: dew@davidwildasin.us.

WILDE, DANIEL UNDERWOOD, computer engineering educator; b. Wilmington, Ohio, Dec. 27, 1937; s. Arthur John and Ruby Dale (Underwood) Wilde. BSEE, U. Ill., 1960; MS, M.I.T., 1962, PhD, 1966. Rsch. instr. medicine Boston U. Med. Sch., 1964-66; asst. prof. info. adminstrn. U. Conn., 1966-69, assoc. prof., 1970-75, prof., 1976-85; assoc. dir. New Eng. Rsch. Application Ctr., Storrs, Conn., 1966-72, dir., 1973-85, NASA Indsl. Application Ctr., 1972-91; pres. NERAC, Inc., Tolland, Conn., 1985-99. Cons. NERAC Inc., 1999-2004; trustee Engring. Index, Inc.; cons. Am. Soc. Metals, 1973-76; bd. dirs. Internat. Coun. Sci. Info. Author: Author: Introduction to Computing: Problem Solving, Algorithms and Data Structures, 1973; contbr. articles to profl. jours. With USAF. Recipient NASA Public Service award, 1975 Fellow Nat. Fedn. Abstracting and Indexing Svcs. (hon.), Internat. Coun. Sci. Info. (hon.); mem. IEEE, Am. Soc. Info. Sci., Assn. Computing Machinery, Assn. Info. and Dissemination Centers (sec.-treas. 1976-79, pres. 1979-81).

WILDE, EDWIN FREDERICK, retired mathematics professor; b. Lombard, Ill., Jan. 14, 1931; s. Edwin Frederick and Carrie Belle (Hammond) W.; m. Connie Mae Rawlings, Aug. 23, 1952 (dec. July 2002); children— Brad Alan, Bruce Ramon, Elizabeth Lynn; m. Kathleen Wright, Sept. 25, 2004. BS, Ill. State U., Normal, 1952, MS, 1953; MA, U. Ill., Champaign-Urbana, 1955, PhD, 1959; postgrad., U. Wis., Madison, part time, 1955-58, Stanford U., Calif., 1964-65. With Beloit Coll., Wis., 1955-76, prof. math., dean faculty Wis., 1969-71, v.p. for planning Wis., 1971-75; dean Roger Williams Coll., Bristol, RI, 1976-80; provost, dean of faculty U. Tampa, Fla., 1980-86; vice chancellor U. S.C., Spartanburg, 1986-91, prof. math., 1991-99; ret., 1999. Cons. AID insts., India, 1964, Insts. Internat. Edn., East Pakistan, 1969 NSF Sr. Sci. Faculty fellow, 1964-65 Mem. Math. Assn. Am. (bd. govs. 1968-69, 72-75). Home: 275 James Rd Gaffney SC 29341-4013 E-mail: efw1931@yahoo.com.

WILDE, HAROLD RICHARD, college president; b. Wauwatosa, Wis., May 14, 1945; s. Harold Richard and Winifred (Wiley) W.; m. Benna Brecher, Feb. 4, 1970; children: Anna, Henry, Elizabeth Ty. BA, Amherst Coll., 1967; MA, PhD, Harvard U., Cambridge, Mass., 1973. Spl. asst. to gov. Office of Gov., State of Wis., Madison, 1972-75; ins. commr. Office of Commr. of Ins., State of Wis., Madison, 1975-79; spl. asst. to pres. U. Wis. System, Madison, 1979-81; v.p. for external affairs Beloit (Wis.) Coll., 1981-91; pres. North Ctrl. Coll., Naperville, Ill., 1991—. Bd. dirs. Ctr. for Pub. Representation, Inc., Madison, 1981-87, Beloit Community Found., 1988-91, Budget Funding Corp., 1993-99, Naperville Devel. Partnership, 1996—. Mem.: Phi Beta Kappa. Home: 329 S Brainard St Naperville IL 60540-5401 Office: North Ctrl Coll 30 N Brainard St Naperville IL 60540-4607 Office Phone: 630-637-5454. Business E-Mail: hrwilde@noctrl.edu.

WILDE, NORMAN TAYLOR, JR., investment banking company executive; b. Phila., Sept. 13, 1930; s. Norman Taylor and Elizabeth (Duthie) W.; m. Ruth Nancy Osterndorf, Sept. 26, 1959 (dec.); children: Karen, Suzanne, Norman Taylor III. BS, U. Pa., 1953. Vice pres. Janney, Montgomery, Scott, Inc., Phila., 1966-69; pres. Janney, Montgomery, Soctt, Inc., Phila., 1969-99, co-chmn., 2000—. Chmn. NASDAQ Stock Market, 1984. Bd. dirs. Abington Meml. Hosp. Served to lt. USN, 1953-55. Mem.: Securities Industries Assn. (gov. 1979—82), Nat. Assn. Security Dealers (chmn. 1983—), Phila. C. of C. (bd. dirs. 1998—), Sunnybrook Golf Club, Phila. Cricket Club, Pine Valley Golf Club. Office: Janney Montgomery Scott Inc 1801 Market St Lbby 11 Philadelphia PA 19103-1602

WILDE, WILLIAM RICHARD, lawyer; b. Markesan, Wis., Mar. 1, 1953; s. Leslie Maurice and Elaine Margaret (Schweder) W.; 1 child, Leah Marie; m. Barbara Joan Rohlf, Jan. 6, 1990. BA, U. Wis., Milw., 1975; JD, Marquette U., 1980. Bar: Wis. 1980, U.S. Dist. Ct. (ea. and we. dists.) Wis. 1980. Dist. atty. Green Lake County, Green Lake, Wis., 1980—83, corp. counsel, 1981; ptnr. Curtis, Wilde and Neal, Oshkosh, Wis., 1983—97; ptnr. pvt. practice Oshkosh, 1997—. Mem. ATLA, Wis. Bar Assn., Wis. Acad. Trial Lawyers (Amicus Curiae Brief com. 1987-92, bd. dirs., assoc. editor The Verdict, treas. 1993, sec. 1994, v.p. 1995, pres.-elect 1996, pres. 1997), Winnebago County Bar Assn., Green Lake County Bar Assn. Office: Wilde Law Offices LLC 600 S Main St 2d Fl PO Box 3422 Oshkosh WI 54903-3422 Address: 10 E Water St Markesan WI 53946 Office Phone: 920-235-0748. Business E-Mail: wwilde@wildelawoffice.com.

WILDE, WILSON, insurance company executive; b. Hartford, Conn., Sept. 24, 1927; s. Philip Alden and Alice Augusta (Wilson) W.; m. Joanne Gerta Menzel, June 19, 1953; children— Stephen W., David W., Elisabeth L., Richard A. Student, Swarthmore Coll., 1945-46; BA, Williams Coll., 1949. Sales agt. Conn. Gen. Life Ins. Co., Hartford, 1949-53; with Hartford Steam Boiler Inspection & Ins. Co., 1953-70, exec. v.p., 1970-71, pres., CEO, 1971—, from chmn., CEO to chmn. emeritus, 1993-98, chmn. emeritus, 1998—. Corporator Inst. Living, Hartford; hon. bd. dirs. Hartford Stage Co., 1973—, Jr. Achievement, Old State House Assn., 1976—; trustee Loomis-Chaffee Sch., 1974—, chmn. bd., 1988-98. With USNR, 1945-47, 51-53. Office: PO Box 5024 Hartford CT 06102-5024

WILDENTHAL, C(LAUD) KERN, physician, educator; b. San Marcos, Tex., July 1, 1941; s. Bryan and Doris (Kellam) W.; m. Margaret Dehlinger, Oct. 15, 1964; children: Pamela, Catharine. BA, Sul Ross Coll., 1960; MD, U. Tex. Southwestern Med. Ctr., Dallas, 1964; PhD, U. Cambridge, Eng., 1970. Intern Bellevue Hosp., NYC, 1964-65; resident in medicine, fellow cardiology Parkland Hosp., Dallas, 1965-67; rsch. fellow Nat. Heart Inst., Bethesda, Md., 1967-68; vis. rsch. fellow Strangeways Rsch. Lab., Cambridge, 1968-70; asst. prof. to prof. internal medicine and physiology U. Tex. Southwestern Med. Ctr., Dallas, 1970-76, prof., dean grad. sch., 1976-80, prof., dean Southwestern Med. Sch., 1980-86, prof., pres., 1986—. Hon. fellow Hughes Hall, U. Cambridge, 1994—. Author: Regulation of Cardiac Metabolism, 1976, Degradative Processes in Heart and Skeletal Muscle, 1980; contbr. articles to profl. jours. Bd. dirs. Lasker Found., Dallas Ctr. Performing Arts, Dallas Symphony, Dallas Opera, Dallas Mus. Art, Dallas Citizen's Coun., Greater Dallas C. of C., Cambridge in Am., Hoblitzelle Found., Reves Found. Recipient rsch. career devel. award NIH, 1972; spl. rsch. fellow USPHS, 1968-70; Guggenheim fellow, 1975-76. Mem. AMA, Inst. Medicine/NAS, Am. Soc. Clin. Investigation, Am. Coll. Cardiology, Royal Soc. Medicine Gt. Britain, Am. Physiol. Soc., Internat. Soc. Heart Rsch. (past pres. Am. sect.), Am. Fedn. Clin. Rsch., Assn. Am. Med Colls., Assn. Am. Physicians, Am. Heart Assn. (past chmn. sci. policy com.), Assn. Acad. Health Ctrs. (past chmn. sci. policy com.), Brit. N.Am. Com. Home: 4001 Hanover Ave Dallas TX 75225-7010 Office: U Tex Southwestern Med Ctr 5323 Harry Hines Blvd Dallas TX 75390-7208 Office Phone: 214-648-2508.

WILDER, C. JOHN (JOHN WILDER), energy executive; b. Mo. m. Susan Burford; 3 children. BS magna cum laude in Bus. Adminstrn., S.E. Mo. State U., 1980; MBA, U. Tex., Austin, 1994. With Royal Dutch/Shell Group of Cos., asst. treas.; dir. econs. and fin. Shell Exploration and Prodn. Co.; asst. treas. Shell Oil Co.; CEO Shell Capital, 1998; exec. v.p., CFO Entergy Corp., New Orleans, 1998—2004; pres., CEO TXU Corp., Dallas, 2004—05, chmn., pres., CEO, 2005—. Mem. adv. bd. McCombs Sch. Bus., U. Tex., Austin, Global Energy Mgmt. Inst., U. Houston, A.B. Freeman Sch. Bus., Tulane U. Named Best CFO in Am., Institutional Investor, 2003. Mem.: Nat. Petroleum Coun., Edison Elec. Inst. Methodist. Office: TXU Corp Energy Plz 1601 Bryan St Dallas TX 75201-3411

WILDER, CHARLES DAVID, lawyer; b. Orlando, Fla., Aug. 6, 1948; s. Thomas Vaughn and Virginia (McKinney) W. BA, U. South Fla., 1970; JD cum laude, Nova southeastern U. Ctr. for Study of Law, 1980; LLM in Taxation, U. Fla., 1981. Bar: Fla. 1980, US Dist. Ct. (mid. dist. Fla.) 1980; cert. Fla. Bar (wills, trusts and estates). Mgr. So. Bell Tel. Co., Miami, Fla., 1970-77; assoc. Broad & Cassel, Orlando, Fla., 1981-84; pvt. practice Orlando, 1984-85; ptnr. Johnson & Wilder, Orlando, 1985-88, Dittmer & Wilder, Maitland, Fla., 1988-92, Wilder & Culton, Maitland, Fla., 1992-94, Wilder & Assocs., Winter Park, Fla., 1994-95, Wilder & Berkson, Winter Park, Fla., 1995; founder, sr. atty. Estate Planning & Legacy Law Ctr., Maitland, Fla. Named one of Top 100 Attys., Worth mag., 2005. Mem. Fla. Bar Assn. (exec. coun. real property probate & trust law sect. 1994), Orange County Bar Assn. (estate planning com. 1984), Ctrl. Fla. Estate Planning Coun., Estate Planning Discussion Grp. (chmn. 1985). Republican. Avocations: water sports, photography, dance. Office: Estate Planning and Legacy Law Ctr PLC 159 Lookout Pl Ste 101 Maitland FL 32751 Office Phone: 407-647-7526. Office Fax: 407-644-2194. Business E-Mail: cwilder@epllc-plc.com.

WILDER, DAVID RANDOLPH, retired materials engineer; b. Lorimor, Iowa, June 11, 1929; s. Rex Marshall and Ethel Marie (Busch) W.; m. Donna Jean Moore, June 17, 1951; children: Susan, Michael, Margaret, Bruce. BS, Iowa State U., 1951, MS, 1952, PhD, 1958. Registered profl. engr., Iowa (inactive). Engr. Ames Lab., 1951-81; faculty mem. dept. materials sci. and engring. Iowa State U., Ames, 1955—, prof. engring., chmn. dept., 1961-89, prof. engring., 1989-91, prof. emeritus, 1991—; cons. to various industries, fed. agys, 1955—. Contbr. numerous tech. paper to profl. lit.; patentee in field. Fellow Am. Ceramic Soc., Accreditation Bd. for Engring. and Tech.; mem. Nat. Inst. Ceramic Engrs., Am. Soc. for Engring. Edn., Keramos. Home: 1214 Ridgewood Ave Ames IA 50010-5208

WILDER, GENE, actor, film director, writer; b. Milw., June 11, 1935; s. William J. and Jeanne (Baer) Silberman; m. Mary Joan Schutz, Oct. 27, 1967 (div. 1974); 1 child, Katharine Anastasia; m. Gilda Radner, 1984 (dec.); m. Karen Boyer, Sept. 8, 1991. BA, U. Iowa, 1955; postgrad., Bristol Old Vic Theatre Sch., 1955-56. Appeared in Broadway play: The Complaisant Lover, 1962 (Clarence Derwent award); appeared in London production of Laughter on the 23rd Floor, 1996; appeared in motion pictures: Bonnie and Clyde, 1966, The Producers, 1967 (Acad. award nom. best supporting actor), Start the Revolution Without Me, 1968, Quackser Fortune Has a Cousin in the Bronx, 1969, Willy Wonka and the Chocolate Factory, 1970, Everything You Always Wanted to Know About Sex, 1971, Rhinoceros, 1972, Blazing Saddles, 1973, The Little Prince, 1974, Silver Streak, 1976, The Frisco Kid, 1979, Stir Crazy, 1980; Hanky Panky, 1982, See No Evil, Hear No Evil, 1989, Funny About Love, 1990, Another You, 1991; (TV films) Murder in a Small Town, 1999, Alice in Wonderland, 1999, The Lady in Question, 1999; dir., writer, actor film: The Adventures of Sherlock Holmes' Smarter Brother, 1975, The World's Greatest Lover, 1977, Sunday Lovers, 1980, The Woman in Red, 1984, Haunted Honeymoon, 1986; actor, co-writer film: Young Frankenstein, 1974 (Acad. award nomination); TV appearances include: The Trouble With People, 1973, Marlo Thomas Spl., 1973, The Scarecrow, 1972, Thursday's Games, 1973, (series) Something Wilder, 1994-95; guest appearances TV series The Defenders, 1962, The DuPont Show of the Week, 1962-63, The Frank Skinner Show, 1997, Will & Grace, 2002-03 (Emmy award best guest actor 2003); author: Kiss Me Like a Stranger: My Search for Love and Art, 2005, My Frnech Whore, 2006. Campaigned with Elaine May and Rene Taylor for Eugene McCarthy, Allard Lowenstein and Paul O'Dwyer, 1968. Served with U.S. Army, 1956-58. Actors Equity Assn., Am. Federation of Television & Radio Artists, DGA, WGA. *

WILDER, JAMES EDWARD, resident manager; b. Washington, Dec. 28, 1948; s. Nathaniel Everett and Marie Inez Wilder; m. Barbara Anne Tracey, Aug. 13, 1973; 1 child, Huan. B of Ministry magna cum laude with high honors, Andersonville Bapt. Sem., Camilla, Ga., 1999. Cert. resident mgr. RM801484, D.C. Dept. Consumer and Regulatory Affairs, Occupl. and Profl. Licensing Adminstrn., Real Estate Commn.; lic. minister, 1994. Mgr. hardware dept. Gaylord's Dept. Store, New Castle, Pa., 1970-72; sales rep. Gumpert Printing Co., Silver Spring, Md., 1980-82; shipping/receiving mgr. Bradlees, Annandale, VA., 1982-84; warehouse mgr. Juhl Pacific Corp., Landover, Md., 1984-86; resident mgr. William C. Smith Co., Washington, 1989—. Pres. Altar of Ed Ministry, Washington, 1994—. Editor: (newsletter) Breach Repairer News, 1997—; creator: (Web site) Altar of Ed Ministry, 1999; host (radio program) Sta. KYTX, Beeville, Tex., 2001. Bd. dirs. Cmty. Coun. for the Homeless at Friendship Pl., Washington, 1994-96; pres. Student Govt. Assn., Prince George's C.C., 1981-82; advisor Triple C Jaycees, 1979-80; founder, pres. Centennial Slammer Jaycees, 1977-78, advisor, past pres., 1978-79. Specialist 4/E4 U.S. Army, 1966-69, Vietnam. Recipient Keyman award Centennial Slammer Jaycees, 1978-79, Keyman award Triple C Jaycees, 1979-80; named one of 25 Outstanding Jaycees Pres. in U.S., 1977-78. Mem. VFW (life), DAV (life), Internat. Critical Incident Stress Found., Am. Numismatic Assn., Am. Assn. Christian Counselors (charter), Baptist. Avocations: post-prison ministry, eagle collectibles, collecting coins. Office: Altar of Ed Ministry Ste 506 2800 Ontario Rd NW Apt 506 Washington DC 20009-2227 Fax: (202) 319-7704. E-mail: altaredmin@aol.com.

WILDER, JAMES SAMPSON, III, lawyer, judge; b. Knoxville, Tenn., Mar. 15, 1949; s. James Sampson and Florence Louise (Summers) W. BS, Lambuth Coll., Jackson, Tenn., 1971; JD, Memphis State U., 1974. Bar: Tenn. 1974, U.S. Dist. Ct. (we. dist.) Tenn. 1975, U.S. Supreme Ct. 1981, U.S. Ct. Appeals (6th cir.) 1982. Assoc. Lt. Gov. John S. Wilder, Somerville, Tenn., 1974-75, ptnr., 1975-76, Wilder, Wilder & Johnson, Somerville, 1976-83; pvt. practice James S. Wilder III, Somerville, 1983-95; gen. sessions judge Fayette County, Somerville, 1985-90; assoc. Petkoff and Lancaster, Memphis, 1995—2000; pvt. practice Somerville, 2000—02; atty. Law Office of John M. Lannom, Dyersburg, Tenn., 2002—. Scoutmaster troop 95 Boy Scouts Am., Somerville, 1975-77, com. person, 1977—. Paul Harris fellow Rotary, Somerville, 1977. Mem. ABA, Assn. Trial Lawyers Am., Tenn. Bar Assn., Tenn. Trial Lawyers Assn. (dir. 1983-86), Fayette County C. of C. (dir. 1979—), Somerville Rotary (dir. 1976—, charter pres. 1976-78). Methodist. Avocations: hunting, fishing. Home: PO Box 342 Dyersburg TN 38025 Office: 422 McGaughey St PO Box 1729 Dyersburg TN 38024 Home Phone: 731-538-2883; Office Phone: 731-285-0374.

WILDER, JANET MARY, performing company executive; d. Robert and Jean; m. Ward Wilder; children: Suzanne, Robert. BS, U. Colo., 1966. Cecchetti tchr. cert. Cecchetti Coun. Am., tchr. cert. Chgo. Nat. Dance Masters Assn., tchg. cert. Calif. Tchr. Santa Venetia Mid. Sch., San Rafael, Calif., 1967—68; fitness/dance instr. Am. Wives' Club, Ghedi, Brescia, Italy, 1969—71; instr. Julie Ward Sch. Dance, Rapid City, SD, 1972—77, Spokane Ballet, Wash., 1981—83, Capitol City Ballet, Sacramento,

1985—87, Marguerite Phares Sch. Dance, Sacramento, 1985—87; artistic dir. Dakota Repertory Dance Co., Rapid City, 1975—77, San Antonio Dance Theatre, 1983—85, Dance Theatre NW, Spokane, 1994—2004, Ballet Spokane, 2003—; instr., co-dir. Entenman Sch. Dance, Bellvue, Nebr., 1978—81; dancer Omaha Ballet, 1979—81; dir. Ballet Arts, San Antonio, 1983—85; co-dir. Ballet Arts Acad., Spokane, 1987—94; co-founder, dir. Theatre Ballet Spokane, 1987—94; choreographer/prodr./dir. Coeur d'Alene (Idaho) Summer Theatre, 1991—96; resident choreographer Spokane/Coeur d'Alene Opera, 1987—; owner, dir. Acad. Dance, Spokane Valley, Wash., 1994—. Founder/mem. Inland NW Dance Assn., Spokane, 1989—; ballet adv. bd. mem. Greater Spokane Music & Allied Arts Festival, 1988—2000, MusicFest NW, Spokane, 2000—; dance edn. del. to China People to People, Bejing, 1996. Author: (book) Terms Every Dancer Should Know; writer, prodr., dir.: (ballets) The Toy Shelf; choreographer (over 150 ballets, operas & musicals). Mem. Rapid City Svc. League, 1975—77; mem./officer PTA, Rapid City, 1975—77; com. mem. First Night Spokane, 2003; mem. entertainment com. Diamonds & Divas, Spokane, 2000—05. Recipient Outstanding Mem., Ghedi Air Force Wives' Club, 1971, Ellsworth Officer's Wives' Club, 1977, Outstanding Young Women of Am., Outstanding Young Women of Am. program, 1973, Wash. State Dance Sch. Dir., Dance Excellence Internat. Festival for Young Dancers, 1992—95, Bowl Games of Am./CocaCola Olympic City, 1996, Jim Chase Asset builder, Chase Youth Commn., 1997, Dir. in charge - Teen Group Creativity Award, 2000, Dir. in charge - Teen Group Cmty. Svc. Hon. Mention, 2001. Mem.: Nat. Dance Edn. Orgn., Nat. Dance Assn., MusicFest NW, Inland NW Dance Assn. (v.p. 2002—04). Avocations: writing, scuba diving, skiing, boating. Home Phone: 509-244-2710; Office Phone: 509-922-3023. Personal E-mail: janetwilder123@aol.com.

WILDER, JANOS, chef; b. Redwood City, Calif., Feb. 5, 1954; Attended, U. Colo.; BA in Polit. Sci., U. Calif. Berkeley, 1976. Chef Gold Hill Inn, La Reserve, Le Duberne; owner, exec. chef Janos, Barrio Viejo, Ariz., 1983—98, Tucson, 1998—, J Bar, Tucson, 1999—, KAI Restaurant, Phoenix, 2002—; cons. Gila River Cmty. Author: Janos: Recipes and Tales from a Southwest Restaurant, 1990. Nominee Top Chef Southwest, James Beard Found., 1992—99; named Best Chef: Southwest, 2000; recipient Silver Spoon award, Tucson Citizen, Hall of Fame award, Scottsdale Culinary Festival, People's Choice award, award of Excellence, Wine Spectator, 1993—99, Best award of Excellence, 2000—07. Achievements include being named Ariz. Highest Rated Restaurant and Tucson's Favorite Restaurant by Zagat. Office: Janos 3770 E Sunrise Dr Tucson AZ 85718 Office Phone: 520-615-6100. Business E-Mail: janosrest@aol.com. *

WILDER, JOHN SHELTON, state senator, former lieutenant governor; b. Fayette City, Tenn., June 3, 1921; s. John Chamblee and Martha (Shelton) W.; m. Marcelle Morton, Dec. 31, 1941; children: John Shelton Wilder, II, David Morton. Student, U. Tenn.; LLB, U. Memphis, 1957. Bar: Tenn. 1957. Engaged in farming, Longtown, Tenn., 1943—; supr. mgmt. Longtown Supply Co.; judge Fayette County Ct.; mem. Tenn. Senate, 1959—60, 1966—; lt. gov., spkr. senate State of Tenn., 1971—. Past pres. Nat. Assn. Soil Conservation Dists., Tenn. Soil Conservation Assn., Tenn. Agrl. Council; exec. com. So. Legis. Conf., Conf. Lt. Govs.; dir. Bank Tenn., Cumberland Bank; chmn. Cumberland BanCorp, Inc. Served with U.S. Army, 1942-43. Mem. Tenn. Cotton Ginners Assn. (past pres.), Shriner, Scottish Rite, Mason, Delta Theta Phi. Clubs: Shriners. Democrat. Methodist. Office: Tenn State Senate 4020 Highway 59 Mason TN 38049 *

WILDER, KSENIA A., systems analyst; b. Yoshkar-Ola, Mari El, Russia, Oct. 5, 1978; d. Alexander G. Kosov and Nataliya M. Kosova; m. Christopher Marc Wilder, Oct. 10, 2003. BS, BA, Keene State Coll., NH, 2002. Computer operator Chittenden Bank and Trust, Brattleboro, Vt., 2003—06; bus. systems analyst Liberty Mut. Ins., Keene, 2006—. Recipient Bravo award, Liberty Mut., 2006. Mem.: Am. Mensa, French Honor Soc., Computer Sci. Honor Soc. Avocation: badminton. Home Phone: 603-358-3966. Personal E-mail: ksusha33@hotmail.com.

WILDER, L(AWRENCE) DOUGLAS, mayor, former governor; b. Richmond, Va., Jan. 17, 1931; children: Lynn, Larry, Loren. BS, Va. Union U., 1951; JD, Howard U., 1959. Bar: Va. Mem. Va. Senate, 1969-85; lt. gov. State of Va., 1986-89, gov., 1989-93; Al Douglas Wilder Disting. prof. Va. Commonwealth U., 1988—; mayor Richmond, Va., 2005—. Del. Democratic Nat. Conv., 1980; agt. NAACP Legal Def. Fund. Bd. dirs. United Givers Fund; chmn. bd. Red Shield Boys' Club. Served with U.S. Army, 1952-53 Decorated Bronze Star; named one of 100 Most Influential Black Americans, Ebony mag., 2006; recipient Spingarn Medal, NAACP, Anna Eleanor Roosevelt Medallion of Honor, Thurgood Marshall Award of Excellence. Mem. ABA, Va. Bar Assn., Nat. Bar Assn., Am. Judicature Soc., C. of C., Urban League (bd. dirs. Richmond), Omega Psi Phi. Clubs: Masons; Shriners. Democrat. Office: Virginia Commonwealth Univ 919 W Franklin St PO Box 842028 Richmond VA 23284-2028 also: Mayor's Office Rm 201 900 E Broad St Richmond VA 23219 Office Phone: 804-828-4971, 804-646-7970. Office Fax: 804-646-7987.

WILDER, MICHAEL STEPHEN, former insurance company executive; b. New Haven, Sept. 8, 1941; BA, Yale U., 1963; JD, Harvard U., 1966. Bar: Conn. 1966. Atty. Hartford (Conn.) Fire Ins. Co., 1967-69, asst. gen. counsel, 1969-71, assoc. gen. counsel, 1971-75, gen. coun., sec., 1975-87, sr. v.p., gen. counsel, sec., 1987-95; sr. v.p., gen. counsel The Hartford Fin. Svcs. Group, Inc., 1995—2001; ret., 2001. Mem. ABA, Conn. Bar Assn. Home: 85 Emily Way West Hartford CT 06107-3136

WILDER, ROLAND PERCIVAL, JR., lawyer; b. Malden, Mass., June 21, 1940; s. Roland Percival and Clarissa (Hunting) W.; m. Susan McAra Randell, Sept. 3, 1965 (dec. Jan. 1996); children: Roland Percival III, William Randell; m. Carolyn Sue Whisenhunt, Nov. 26, 2004. BA, Washington and Jefferson Coll., 1963; JD, Vanderbilt U., 1966. Bar: D.C. 1967, U.S. Dist. Ct. D.C. 1967, U.S. Dist. Ct. Md. 1994, U.S. Dist. Ct. Colo. 1997, U.S. Dist. Ct. (ea. dist.) Mich. 1999, U.S. Ct. Appeals (D.C. cir.) 1967, U.S. Ct. Appeals (4th, 5th and 6th cirs.) 1976, U.S. Ct. Appeals (8th and 9th cirs.) 1977, U.S. Ct. Appeals (2d cir.) 1978, U.S. Ct. Appeals (11th cir.) 1981, U.S. Ct. Appeals (3d cir.) 1997, U.S. Ct. Appeals (7th cir.) 2002, U.S. Supreme Ct. 1972. Atty. Office of Solicitor U.S. Dept. Labor, Washington, 1967-69; asst. counsel civil rights office of solicitor U.S. Dept. Labor, Washington, 1969-70, counsel civil rights office of solicitor, 1970-71; supr. atty. office gen. counsel NLRB, Washington, 1972-74; assoc. gen. counsel Internat. Brotherhood Teamsters, Washington, 1974-85; sr. mem. Baptiste & Wilder P.C., Washington, 1985—. Lectr. in field. Mng. editor Vanderbilt U. Law Rev., 1965-66; contbr. articles to profl. jours. V.p. Arlington (Va.) Cubs Youth Club, Inc., 1975-81; coach Fairfax (Va.) Hockey Club, 1979-83. Mem. ABA, DC Bar Assn., Phi Delta Phi, Pi Sigma Alpha, Phi Alpha Theta, Roosevelt Soc., Joint Coun. Flight Attendant Unions (hon. flight attendant 1985). Democrat. Avocations: history, tennis, skiing. Office: Baptiste & Wilder PC 1150 Connecticut Ave NW Ste 500 Washington DC 20036-4194 Home Phone: 703-837-0475; Office Phone: 202-223-0723. Business E-Mail: rpwilderjr@bapwild.com.

WILDER, RONALD PARKER, economics professor; b. Freeport, Tex., Jan. 15, 1941; s. J. Barton and Lois (Parker) W.; m. Charlotte D. Pearson, Sept. 4, 1965; children: Erika, Rachel, David. BA, Rice U., 1963, MA, 1964; PhD, Vanderbilt U., 1969. Asst. prof. econs. U. S.C., Columbia, 1970-75, assoc. prof., 1975-80, prof., 1980—2006, prof. emeritus, 2006—, chmn. dept. econs., 1987—2002. Co-author: Stock Life Insurance Profitability, 1986; mem. editorial bd. So. Econ. J., 1978-80; contbr. articles to profl. jours. Capt. U.S. Army, 1968-70. Fellow Ford Found., Vanderbilt U., 1964-65. Mem. Am. Econ. Assn., So. Econ. Assn., Omicron Delta Epsilon. United Methodist. Avocations: hiking, canoeing. Office: U of SC Dept Of Econs Columbia SC 29208-0001

WILDERMUTH, BRUCE R., lawyer; b. Bklyn., Feb. 19, 1952; BA in History, George Washington U., 1974; JD, St. John's U., 1979. Bar: NY 1980, US Dist. Ct. Ea. Dist. NY, US Dist. Ct. So. Dist. NY, US Dist. Ct. No. Dist. NY. Ptnr. Wilson, Elser, Moskowitz, Edelman & Dicker LLP, NYC. Mem.: NY State Bar Assn. Office: Wilson Elser Moskowitz Edelman & Dicker LLP 150 E 42nd St 3rd Fl New York NY 10017-5639 Office Phone: 212-490-3000 ext. 2142. Office Fax: 212-490-3038. Business E-Mail: wildermuthb@wemed.com.

WILDEROTTER, JAMES ARTHUR, lawyer; b. Newark, July 25, 1944; s. Arthur Walter and Dorothy Theresa (King) W.; children: James, Kristin, Kathryn. BA, Georgetown U., 1966; JD, U. Ill., 1969. Bar: D.C. 1969, U.S. Supreme Ct. 1974. Assoc. Covington & Burling, Washington, 1969-71; spl. asst. to Under Sec. Commerce, Washington, 1971-73; exec. asst. to Sec. HUD, Washington, 1973-74; assoc. dept. atty. gen. U.S. Washington, 1974-75; assoc. counsel to Pres. U.S., 1975-76; gen. counsel U.S. Energy Research and Devel. Adminstrn., Washington, 1976-77; of counsel Morgan, Lewis & Bockius, Washington, 1977-78; ptnr. Jones, Day, Reavis & Pogue, Washington, 1978—91, 1995—2006; v.p., gen. counsel Internat. Paper Co., Purchase, NY, 1991-94; gen. counsel U. S. Trade and Devel. Agy., Washington, 2006—. Editor in chief: U. Ill. Law Rev., 1968-69. Gen. counsel rules com. Rep. Nat. Conv., 1980; sec. James S. Brady Presdl. Found., 1982-88; gen. counsel Nat. Sudden Infant Death Syndrome Found., 1986-90, sec. Sudden Infant Death Syndrome Alliance, 1990-93. With USN, 1962-68. Mem. ABA Republican. Roman Catholic. Home: 5903 Mount Eagle Dr Alexandria VA 22303 Office: US Trade and Devel Agy 1000 Wilson Blvd Ste 1600 Arlington VA 22209 Office Phone: 202-879-3832. Personal E-mail: jawilder@yahoo.com. Business E-Mail: jwilderotter@ustda.gov.

WILDEROTTER, MAGGIE (MARY AGNES WILDEROTTER), software company executive, former cable television executive; b. Neptune, NJ, Feb. 9, 1955; d. Denis James and Constance Rosemary (Shields) Sullivan; m. Philip Jay Wilderotter; children: Christopher, Daniel. BA in Economics and Bus. Adminstrn., Holy Cross Coll., 1977. Accts. receivable supr. CableData, Sacramento, 1979-80, mgr. acctg. svcs., 1980-82, mgr. reg. support, 1982, mktg. mgr., 1982-83, dir. mktg., 1983, dir. nat. accts., 1983-85, v.p., 1985—87, sr. v.p., sales & mktg., 1987—91; sr. v.p. McCaw Cellular Communications, 1991—95; exec. v.p., nat. ops. & CEO, Aviation Communications div. AT&T Wireless Svcs., Inc., 1995—97; pres., CEO Wink Communications, 1997—2002; sr. v.p., worldwide pub. sector Microsoft Corp., 2002—04; pres., CEO Citizens Communications Co., 2004—06, chmn., CEO, 2006—. Bd. dirs. McClatchy Co., Phoenix Cable Ptnrs., San Rafael, Calif., 1988-, Satellite Video Ctr., Rancho Cordova, Calif., 1988-, CableData Europe Ltd., Leeds, Eng., 1989-, Citizens Communications Co., 2004-, Xerox Corp., 2006-, Yahoo! Inc., 2007-. Recipient Top 10 Women in Cable & Telecommunications award, Women in Cable and Telecommunications Found., 1989, Outstanding Mentor award, 1999, Vanguard award for Disting. Leadership, Nat. Cable TV Assn., 1989, 2000 (one of only 20 individuals to have received two of these awards since its inception). Mem. Nat. Cable TV Assn. (bd. dirs. 1987-), Women in Cable (exec. mem.), Cable TV Adminstrn. & Mktg. Soc., Calif. Cable TV Assn., Nat. Acad. Cable Programming. Republican. Roman Catholic. Office: Citizens Communications 3 High Ridge Park Stamford CT 06905-1390 *

WILDHACK, WILLIAM AUGUST, JR., lawyer; b. Takoma Park, Md., Nov. 28, 1935; s. William August and Martha Elizabeth (Parks) W.; m. Martha Moore Allston, Aug. 1, 1959; children: William A. III, Elizabeth L. BS, Miami U., Oxford, Ohio, 1957; JD, George Washington U., 1963. Bar: Va. 1963, D.C. 1965, Md. 1983, U.S. Supreme Ct. 1967. Agt. IRS, Va., 1957-65; pvt. prac. Washington, 1965—69; v.p., corp. counsel B.F. Saul Co. and affiliates, Chevy Chase, Md., 1969-87, Chevy Chase Bank, F.S.B. and affiliates, 1987-90; atty. pvt. practice, Arlington, Va., 1990—. Sec. B.F. Saul Real Estate Investment Trust, Chevy Chase, 1972-87. Mem. ABA, Md. Bar Assn., D.C. Bar, Va. Bar, Arlington County Bar Assn. (chmn. trusts and estates sect. 2002—), Nat. Acad. Elder Law Attys., Soc. Corp. Secretaries and Governance Profls. Business E-Mail: waw@wildhacklaw.com.

WILDING, DIANE, computer scientist, consultant; b. Chicago Heights, Ill., Nov. 7, 1942; d. Michael Edward and Katherine Surian; m. Manfred Georg Wilding, May 7, 1975 (div. 1980). BSBA in Acctg. magna cum laude, No. Ill. U., DeKalb, 1963; postgrad., U. Chgo., 1972—74; cert. in German lang., Goethe Inst., Rothenburg, Germany, 1984; cert. in internat. bus. German, Goethe Inst., Atlanta, 1994; cert. in Web page design, Kennesaw State U., Ga., 2000. Lic. cosmetologist. Sys. engr. IBM, Chgo., 1963-68, SAP cons. Atlanta, 1993—; data processing mgr. Am. Res. Corp., Chgo., 1969-72; system R & D project mgr. Continental Bank, Chgo., 1972-75; fin. industry mktg. rep. IBM Can., Ltd., Toronto, Ont., 1976-79; regional telecom. mktg. exec. Control Data Corp., Atlanta, 1980-84; gen. mgr. The Plant Plant, Atlanta, 1985-92. Pioneer installer on-line automatic teller machines Pos Equipment. Author: The Canadian Payment System: An International Perspective, 1977. Mem. Chgo. Coun. Fgn. Rels.; bd. dirs. Easter House Adoption Agy., Chgo., 1974—76. Mem.: Internat. Brass Soc., Mensa, Goethe Inst., Libertyville Racquet Club, Royal Ont. Yacht Club, Ponte Verde Club (Fla.). Avocations: travel, gourmet cooking, languages, antiques. Home and Office: PO Box 723055 Atlanta GA 31139-0055 Office: IBM 1600 Riveredge Pkwy NW Atlanta GA 30328-4697 Personal E-mail: diane.wilding@gmail.com.

WILDING, RICHARD J., library director; Bus. mgr. Mid-Continent Pub. Libr., Independence, Mo., asst. dir., 1998—2006, dir. librs., 2006—. Treas. officer's coun. Kans. City Met. Libr. & Info. Network. Office: Mid-Continent Pub Libr 15616 E 24 Hwy Independence MO 64050-2057 Office Phone: 816-836-5200. Office Fax: 816-521-7253. E-mail: dwilding@mcpl.lib.mo.us. *

WILDMAN, IRIS J., retired law librarian; b. Chgo., May 10, 1930; d. Isadore and Stella (Stark) W. BS, Northwestern U., Evanston, Ill., 1952; MLS, Case Western Res. U., 1954; JD, Santa Clara U., 1978. Asst. cataloger U. Chgo. Law Libr., 1952-53; cataloger Copyright Office/Libr. of Congress, 1954; law cataloger U.S. Army Libr./Pentagon, 1954-56; cataloger U.S. Dept. of Justice Libr., Washington, 1956-57; head tech. svcs. Ohio State U. Law Libr., Columbus, 1957-59, Skokie (Ill.) Pub. Libr., 1959-60; head cataloging and classification Northwestern U. Law Libr., Chgo., 1961-64; chief acquisitions and binding Yale Law Libr., New Haven, 1965-74; pub. svcs. libr. Stanford U. Law Libr., 1976-85; sr. reference and spl. projects libr. Robert Crown Law Libr. Stanford (Calif.) U., 1985-95; ret. Cons. Corp. Counsel, Govt., Washington D.C. Libr., 1957, U. P.R. Law Libr., 1968; faculty/dir. AALL Institutes on Cataloging, Classification and Acquisitions, 1966, 70, 73; libr./lectr. Stanford Law Sch., 1978-82, 85-93. Compiler: Federal Judges and Justices, 1987-2001; editor: Law Libraries in the U.S. and Can., 1958, Directory of Law Librs., 1964, 66; indexer: Index to Foreign Legal Periodicals, 1983-2000; contbr. articles to profl. jours. Mem. No. Calif. Assn. Law Librs. (v.p., pres. elect 1980-82), Am. Assn. Law Librs. Avocations: writing, reading, photography, gardening. Home: 1757 Pilgrim Ave Mountain View CA 94040-2363 Business E-Mail: iwildman@stanford.edu.

WILDMAN, MAX EDWARD, lawyer, director; b. Terre Haute, Ind., Dec. 4, 1919; s. Roscoe Ellsworth and Lena (Shaw) W.; m. Joyce Lenore Smith, Sept. 25, 1948; children: Leslie, William. BS, Butler U., 1941; JD, U. Mich., 1947; MBA, U. Chgo., 1952. Bar: Ill., Ind. Ptnr. Kirkland & Ellis, Chgo., 1947-67; mng. ptnr. Wildman, Harrold, Allen & Dixon, Chgo., 1967-89. Dir. Colt Industries, N.Y., Nat. Blvd. Bank, Ill. Contbr. articles to profl. jours. Trustee Butler U., Indpls., Lake Forest Hosp., Ill., Lake Bluff Library Bd., Ill.; chmn. Lake Bluff Zoning Bd. Served to lt. col. USAF, 1943-46; PTO Fellow Am. Coll. Trial Lawyers; mem. Soc. Trial Lawyers, Law Club, Legal Club, Trial Lawyers Club of Chgo. Clubs: Anglers (Chgo.), Pere Marquette Rod and Gun (Baldwin, Mich.), Shoreacres (Lake Bluff), Univ. of Chgo. Presbyterian. Office: Wildman Harrold Allen & Dixon 225 W Wacker Dr Chicago IL 60606-1224 Office Phone: 312-201-2627.

WILDMAN, PETER ROBERTS, mathematics professor; b. Glendale, Calif., Aug. 18, 1959; s. Neol Roberts and Maria Anna Wildman; m. Karen Louise Muehl, June 15, 1985; children: Daniel, Andrew, Matthew. BA, Occidental Coll., 1981; MS, N.Mex. State U., 1992. Instr. Murlborough Sch., LA, 1982—90; asst. N.Mex. State U., Las Cruces, N.Mex., 1990—92; instr. math. Casper (Wyo.) Coll., 1992—. Co-dir. Wyo. Math and Sci. Coalition, Casper, 1995—2003. Bd. dirs., fundraiser Sci. Zone Mus., Casper, 2004—; cubmaster, den leader Boy Scouts Am., Casper, 1997—. Mem.: Nat. Coun. Tchrs. Math., Math. Assn. Am., Wyo. Math. Assn. Two Yr. Colls. (pres. 2000—02), Am. Math. Tchrs. Two Yr. Coll. (v.p. ctrl. region 2004—, Tchr. Excellence award 2001), Phi Theta Kappa (Tchg. award 2004). Democrat. Baptist. Home: 4920 E 18th Casper WY 82609 Office: Casper Coll 125 College Dr Casper WY 82601 Office Phone: 307-268-2506.

WILDNAUER, RICHARD HARRY, pharmaceutical executive; b. New Kensington, Pa., Feb. 14, 1940; s. Richard Michael and Rosemary Elizabeth (Moore) Wildnauer; m. Sharon Ann Novick, Jan. 22, 1966; 1 child, Tara Lynne. BS in Chemistry, St. Vincent Coll., 1962; PhD in BioChemistry, W.Va. U., 1966; MBA in Mgmt., Rider U., 1974. NIH trainee W.Va. U., 1963—66; sr. rsch. assoc. in skin biology, exploratory rsch. divsn. Johnson & Johnson Domestic Operating Co., New Brunswick, NJ, 1967—75, assoc. mgr. tech. planning, exploratory rsch. divsn., 1975—77; sr. project coord. new products, pharm. divsn. McNeil Labs., Ft. Washington, Pa., 1977—79; dir. new product devel. Janssen Pharmaceutica Inc., New Brunswick, 1979—82, v.p. R&D, 1982—88; v.p. tech. and bus. devel. Johnson & Johnson Corp., New Brunswick, 1988—92; pres. Baker Cummins Dermatologicals, Inc., Lakewood, NJ, 1992—95; pres., CEO NeoStrata Co., Inc., Princeton, NJ, 1995—2007; founder RHW Assoc. LLC, East Brunswick, NJ, 2007—. Contbr. articles to profl. jours. Trustee, bd. dirs. United Way Ctrl. N.J., 1988—95, pres., 1991—93. Mem.: Nat. Assn. Corp. Dirs., Soc. Co. Chemists, NY Acad. Scis., Soc. Investigative Dermatology, Am. Acad. Dermatology (life), Sigma Xi. Roman Catholic. Office: RHW Assoc LLC 6 Pilgrim Run East Brunswick NJ 08816 Business E-Mail: rhwildnauer@aol.com.

WILDONER, NANCY SCHAMU, music educator, fine arts department chairman; b. Syracuse, NY, June 8, 1957; d. Frederick William and Marlyn Meyer Schamu; m. Robert Sterling Wildoner, Aug. 15, 1987; children: Melody June, Robert Sterling III. BA in Music Edn., Fredonia State U., 1979; MusM, Binghamton U., 1983; studied organ with M. Searle Wright and Paul Jordan. Tchng. Cert. NY. Music tchr. Norwich Sch. Dist., NY, 1979—81; grad. asst. Binghamton U., NY, 1981—83; substitute tchr. Broome County, Binghamton, NY, 1983—85; K-12 music tchr., chair fine arts dept. Chenango Forks Sch., Binghamton, NY, 1984—; choir dir., organist First Congregational Ch., Binghamton, NY, 2002—. Church organist various chs., 1977—2005; pvt. piano and organ tchr., Binghamton, NY, 2001—. Womens aux. mem. Sanitaria Springs Fire Dept., NY, 1989—2005. Mem.: Broome County Music Educators Assn. (mem. exec. coun. 2000—), NY Sch. Music Assn., Music Educators Nat. Conf., Am. Guild of Organists. Protestant. Avocations: theater, travel. Home: 778 Brotzman Rd Binghamton NY 13901 Office: Chenango Forks elem Sch 6 Patch Rd Binghamton NY 13901 Business E-Mail: wildonern@cforks.org.

WILDS, BONNIE, writer, volunteer; b. Phila. m. Walter Warren Wilds; children: Stephanie Wilds Shea Blackhurst, Eugenia Wilds Ardrey, Vanessa Wilds Cunningham Wassenar, Pamela Wilds Cole. BA, Sarah Lawrence Coll.; MA, PhD, U. Pitts. Desk officer Dept. State, Washington, economist. Author: A Critical Edition of El Animal Profeta by Antonio Mira de Amescua, 1979. Women's com. Carnegie Mus. Art, Pitts.; social svc. bd. Shadyside Hosp., Pitts.; pres. women's aux. bd. Magee Women's Hosp., Pitts; v.p. Bethany Lenox Hill Day Care Ctr., NYC; bd. dirs., v.p. Mary Walton Children's Ctr., NYC; bd. dirs. Musicians Emergency Fund., pres.; bd. dirs., pres., past pres. Hospitality Com. for UN Dels.; resource coordinator Inst. of Internat. Edn.; past v.p. Hospitality Com. for UN Dels. Recipient Pub. Svc. citation, City of Pitts. Fellow: Frick Collection, Pierpont Morgan Libr.; mem.: MLA, UN Assn., USA Fgn. Policy Assn., The New Eng. Soc., Preservation Soc. Newport County, St. George's Soc., Church Club, Union Club, The Pilgrims, Colony Club (N.Y.). Republican. Episcopalian. Avocations: community service, travel, reading. Home: 20 E 68th St New York NY 10065-5837

WILDS, DANIEL O., health products executive; BA, Calif. State U., LA; MBA, Northwestern U., Evanston, Ill. With Baxter Internat., 1968—92, pres. chemotherapy svc. divsn., pres., COO diagnostic joint venture with Genentech, gen. mgr. Mexico City ops., gen. mgr. Container Devel. Bus. Ctr., dir. strategy devel., v.p. corp. alliances; pres., CEO Medisense, Inc., Adeza Biomed. Corp., 1992—96, Shiloov Biotechnologies (USA) Inc., 1997—98; pres., CEO, dir. Northwest Biotherapeutics, Inc., Boethell, Wash., 1998—.

WILE, JOAN, composer, lyricist, singer; b. Rochester, NY, July 17, 1931; d. Louis and Janet Louise (Wile) Meltzer; children: Ron Wasserman, Diana Wasserman McCloskey. BA, U. Chgo., 1952. Freelance composer, lyricist, singer, mus. book writer. Rec. artist Vanguard Records, 1954; singer Storyville, 1954, The Crystal Palace, 1957; mem. vocal-revue act The Neighbors performances include The Village Vanguard, Le Ruban Bleu, The Bon Soir and The Living Room; singer, lyricist feature film The Happy Hooker, 1974; singer radio and TV jingles, movie sound tracks, supper clubs, hotels, TV music spls. and variety shows; lyricist, composer mus. Tobacco Road, 1974, Seven Ages of Woman, 1987 (named most promising new musical); writer, producer When They Turned on the Tap at the Watergate, The Truth Come Pourin' Out; lyricist songs for Romper Room, 1983; lyricist, composer, writer People is People, 1983; lyricist, composer script for children's albums for Golden and Peter Pan Records, others; lyricist, composer material in Julius Monk's Upstairs at the Downstairs, 1958; lyricist, composer, performer Nancy's Economic Plan, 1980; lyricist, composer Mothers and Daughters, 1984; lyricist, composer, author The Symposium, 1987; lyricist, composer From There to Here, 1987; writer Rhyme, Women and Song; lyricist, librettist, composer Museum of Natural Sex History, 1992; composer Women Walking, 1997, composer-lyricist What A Woman (Homage to Peggy Lee), 2003; founder, singer The NY Granny Chicks, 2005. Organizer Women in Def. Eleanor Roosevelt, NYC, 1989—; founder, dir. Grandmothers Against the War, 2003; founder, organizer Revolt Against the Tax Refund, 2001; founder Granny Peace Brigade, 2005; treas. bd. dirs. Soc. Singers, 2002. Runner-up Am. Song Festival, 1976 Mem.: ASCAP (Popular award 1970—2005), AFTRA, SAG, Theatre Artists Workshop, Dramatists Guild, Soc. of Singers (bd. dirs.). Avocations: politics, music. Home and Office: 263 West End Ave Apt 4B New York NY 10023-2613 E-mail: joanwile@grandmothersagainstthewar.org.

WILEMAN, GEORGE ROBERT, retired lawyer; b. Ironton, Ohio, June 1, 1938; s. George Merchant and Marguerite (McCormick) W.; children: John Chandler, Julie Jo. AB, Duke U., Durham, NC, 1960; JD, Georgetown U., Washington, DC, 1963. Bar: Ohio 1968, Tex. 1977, US Supreme Ct. 1993. Pvt. practice, Dallas, 1977—. Democrat. Personal E-mail: bobwilemon@sbcglobal.net.

WILENS, MICHAEL ENGBER, information technology executive, researcher, educator; b. Chgo., Aug. 23, 1953; s. Charles E. and Norma J. (Myers) W. S.B. in Elec. and Computer Engring., MIT, 1975, S.M. in Elec. and Computer Engring., 1976; M.S. in Computer Sci., U. Mich., Ann Arbor, 1979, Ph.D. in Computer Sci., 1984, M.B.A., 1980. Sr. systems analyst Digital Equipment Corp., 1972-73; computer scientist Naval Surface Weapons Ctr., White Oak, Md., 1973-74; teaching asst. elec. engring. MIT, 1975, project mgr. Sloan Sch. Ctr. for Info. Systems Research, 1975-76; teaching fellow computer sci. U. Mich., Ann Arbor, 1976-80, project mgr. Info. Systems Research Group, 1976-80, research asst. Grad. Sch. Bus., 1981, instr. software engring, elec. engring., 1981-82; staff cons. Infosystems Mgmt., Ann Arbor, 1981; pres., CEO Computerized Office Services, Inc., Ann Arbor, 1982; sr. mgmt. positions Groupe Lagardere, Lawyers Coop. Publishing and HCIA; pres., CEO legal & regulatory group, Thomson Corp.; exec. v.p., CTO West Group, 1996-2000; pres., CEO N. Am. Legal, Thomson Legal and Regulatory 2000; exec. v.p., CTO Thomson Corp. 2006-. Cons. mil. services. Instr. fin. planning and control Midwest Assn. of Housing Coops., Ann Arbor. Named for Teaching Excellence U. Mich., 1979. Mem. Assn. of Computing Machinery (reviewer Computing Revs. jour.), IEEE, Ann Arbor Computer Bus. Assn. (pres. 1983), AAAS, Sigma Xi. Office: Thomson Corp Metro Ctr One Station Pl Stamford CT 06902

WILENSKY, GAIL ROGGIN, economist, researcher; b. Detroit, June 14, 1943; d. Albert Alan and Sophia (Blitz) Roggin; m. Robert Joel Wilensky, Aug. 4, 1963; children: Peter Benjamin, Sara Elizabeth. AB (hon.), U. Mich., 1964, MA in Econs., 1965, PhD in Econs., 1968; degree (hon.), Hahnemann U., 1993, Rush U., 1997, U. Scis., Phila., 2002. Economist President's Commn. on Income Maintenance Programs; exec. dir. Md. Coun. of Econ. Advs., 1969-71; sr. rschr. Urban Inst., Washington, 1971-73; assoc. rsch. scientist, pub. policy and pub. health U. Mich., Ann Arbor, 1973-75, vis. asst. prof. econs., 1973-75; sr. rsch. mgr. Nat Ctr. for Health Svcs. Rsch., Hyattsville, Md., 1975-83; assoc. profl. lectr. George Washington U., 1976-78; v.p. div. health affairs Project HOPE, Millwood, Va., 1983-90; adminstr. Health Care Fin. Adminstrn., Washington, 1990-92; dep. asst. to the pres. for policy devel. White House, 1992-93; sr. fellow Project HOPE, Bethesda, Md., 1993—, chair phys. payment rev. com., 1995-97; chmn. Medicare Payment Adv. Commn., 1997—2001; co-chair Pres.'s Task Force to Improve Healthcare Delivery for Vets., 2001—03, Dept. Def. Task Force on Future of Mental Health Care, 2006—07. Contbr. 100 articles in field to profl. jours. Dir. Am. Heart Assn., 1980-85, bd. dirs., 2002—; mem. health adv. com. Compt. Gen. U.S., 1987-90; bd. dirs. United Healthcare Corp., Cephalon, ManorCare, Gentiva Health Svcs., Inc., Quest Diagnostics; mem. vis. com. med. sch. U. Mich., 1993-97; trustee United Mine Workers Am. Retirement Fund, 1993—; commr. WHO Commn. on the Social Determinants of Health, 2005-. Flinn Found. disting. scholar, 1985; recipient Dean Conley award Am. Coll. Healthcare Execs., 1989. Mem. NAS Inst. Medicine (coun. mem. 2006-), Am. Econ. Assn. (women's com. 1982-84), Fedn. Orgn. of Profl. Women (chmn. econ. task force 1981-83), Am. Statis. Assn., Nat. Tax Assn., Washington Women Economists, Assn. Health Svc. Rsch. (dir. 1984-87), Found. Health Svc. Rsch. (bd. dir. 1987-90), Acad. Health (chair bd. dir. 2000—, Cosmos Club (Washington). Home: 2807 Battery Pl NW Washington DC 20016-3439 Office Phone: 301-656-7401. Business E-Mail: gwilensky@projecthope.org.

WILENSKY, HAROLD L., political science professor, sociologist, researcher; b. New Rochelle, NY, Mar. 3, 1923; s. Joseph and Mary Jane (Wainsten) W.; children: Stephen David, Michael Alan, Daniel Lewis. Student, Goddard Coll., 1940-42; AB, Antioch Coll., 1947; MA, U. Chgo., 1949, PhD, 1955. Asst. prof. sociology U. Chgo., 1951-53, asst. prof. indsl. relations, 1953-54; asst. prof. sociology U. Mich., Ann Arbor, 1954-57, assoc. prof., 1957-61, prof., 1961-62, U. Calif., Berkeley, 1963-82, prof. polit. sci., 1982—, research sociologist Inst. Indsl. Relations, 1963—, project dir. Inst. Internat. Studies, 1970-90; project dir. Ctr. for German and European Studies, Berkeley, 1994-96, Inst. Govtl. Studies, 1996—. Mem. rsch. career awards com. Nat. Inst. Mental Health, 1964—67; cons. in field. Author: Industrial Relations: A Guide to Reading and Research, 1954, Intellectuals in Labor Unions: Organizational Pressures on Professional Roles, 1956, Organizational Intelligence: Knowledge and Policy in Government and Industry, 1967, The Welfare State and Equality: Structural and Ideological Roots of Public Expenditures, 1975, The New Corporatism, Centralization, and the Welfare State, 1976, Rich Democracies: Political Economy, Public Policy, and Performance, 2002, (with C.N. Lebeaux) Industrial Society and Social Welfare, 1965, (with others) Comparative Social Policy, 1985, (with L. Turner) Democratic Corporatism and Policy Linkages, 1987; editor: (with C. Arensberg and others) Research in Industrial Human Relations, 1957, (with P.F. Lazarsfeld and W. H. Sewell) The Uses of Sociology, 1967; contbr. articles to profl. jours. Pilot USAAF, 1943—45. Recipient aux. award Social Sci. Rsch. Coun., 1962, Book award McKinsey Found., 1967; fellow Ctr. for Advanced Study in Behavioral Scis., 1956-57, 62-63, German Marshall Fund, 1978-79; Harry A. Millis rsch. awardee U. Chgo., 1950-51. Fellow AAAS; mem. AAUP, Internat. Sociol. Assn., Internat. Polit. Sci. Assn., Indsl. Relations Research Assn. (exec. com. 1965-68), Soc. for Study Social Problems (chmn. editorial com.), Am. Polit. Sci. Assn., Am. Sociol. Assn. (exec. council 1969-72, chmn. com. on info. tech. and privacy 1970-72), Council European Studies (steering com. 1980-83). Democrat. Jewish. Avocations: music, trumpet, skiing. Office: U Calif Dept Polit Sci 1950-210 Barrows Hall Berkeley CA 94720-1902 E-mail: hwilensk@socrates.berkeley.edu.

WILENTZ, SEAN, historian, educator, writer; b. NYC, Feb. 20, 1951; s. Elias and Jeanne Marie (Campbell) W.; m. Christine Stansell, Jan. 30, 1980; children: James Thomas Farrell, Hannah Cady Rose. BA, Columbia Coll., 1972, U. Oxford, Eng., 1974; MA, Yale U., New Haven, Conn., 1975, MPhil, 1976, PhD, 1980. Asst. prof. Princeton U., NJ, 1979-85, assoc. prof., 1985-87, Dayton-Stockon prof., history, 1987—2004, dir. program in Am. studies, 1995—, prof. Am. history, 2004—06, Sidney and Ruth Lapidus prof. Am. revolutionary era, 2007—. Author: Chants Democratic, 1984, anniversary edition, 2004, The Rise of American Democracy, 2005 (Bancroft prize for history, Columbia Univ., 2006), Andrew Jackson: The Seventh President, 1829-1837, 2005; editor: Rites of Power: Symbolism, Ritual and Politics Since the Middle Ages, 1985; co-author: The Kingdom of Matthias, 1994; co-editor: The Key of Liberty, 1993, The Rose & the Briar: Death, Love and Liberty in the American Ballad, 2004; editl. bd. Dissent, NYC, 1992—; contbg. editor The New Republic, Washington, 1995—. Recipient Alfred Beveridge award Am. History Assn., 1984, Frederick Jackson Turner award Orgn. Am. Historians, 1985; Guggenheim fellow John Simon Guggenheim Meml. Found., 1990-91. Fellow Soc. Am. Historians (exec. bd. 1986-96). Democrat. Avocations: baseball, jazz. Office: Dept History Princeton U Princeton NJ 08544-0001

WILES, ANDREW J., mathematician, educator; b. England, Apr. 11, 1953; married. BS in Math., Oxford U., England; PhD in Math., Cambridge U., England; DSc (hon.), Yale Univ., 2005. Lectr. Inst. Advanced Studies, Princeton, NJ; asst., assoc. prof. math. Harvard U., Cambridge, Mass.; prof. math. Princeton U., 1982—88, 1990—. Recipient Wolf prize in math., Wolf Found., Israel, 1995, NAS award in Math., 1996, Royal medal, Royal Soc., 1996, Frank Nelson Cole prize in algebra, Am. Math. Soc., 1996, Frank Nelson Cole prize in number theory, 1997; fellow John D. and Catherine T. MacArthur Found. fellow, 1997. Achievements include solving (with Richard Taylor) Pierre de Fermat's last theory of 1637. Office: Princeton U Dept Math, 602 Fine Hall Princeton NJ 08544-0001

WILES, BETTY JANE, accountant; b. Scott County, Ark., Dec. 21, 1940; d. Edd and Nellie Margaret (Richey) Staggs; m. Ralph A. Wiles, July 18, 1959; children: Ralph A. Jr., Penny Margaret. BBA magna cum laude, Henderson State Coll., 1983. CPA Ark. Sec. Royalty Holding Co., Oklahoma City, 1959-65, Rector & Eubanks, Mena, Ark., 1966-69; paralegal Shaw & Shaw Attys., Mena, Ark., 1969-83; pvt. practice acctg. Mena, Ark., 1984—. Cons. adv. bd. Mena H.S., 1985-86; cons. adv. bd. St. John Libr., Rich Mountain C.C., 1987-90, mem. svc. adv. com., 1988-90; trustee Mena Hosp. Com., 1991-2005. Mem. AAUW (pres. Mena br. 1993-95), Ark. Soc. CPAs (emergency assistance com., govt. acct. and auditing com. 1993-95), Ouachita Chpt. CPAs (v.p. 1996-97, pres. 1997-98, 2004), Quachita Writer's Guild. Baptist. Avocation: poetry. Home: PO Box 522 Mena AR 71953-0522 Office: 601TB Hwy 71 N Mena AR 71953-3337

WILES, CHARLES PRESTON, minister; b. Frederick, Md., Aug. 5, 1918; s. Charles Wesley and Nellie (Burgess) W.; m. Mary McCallum; children: Mary Margaret, Charles Preston, Wade Burgess. AB, Washington Coll., Chestertown, Md., 1939; postgrad., U. Va., Charlottesville, 1940; MA, Duke U., Durham, NC, 1945, PhD (Univ. fellow 1947-51, Kearns Honor fellow 1949-50), 1951; B.D., Va. Theol. Sem., Alexandria, 1947. Ordained to ministry Episc. Ch., 1947. Priest-in-charge St. Joseph's Ch., Durham, NC, 1947-51; rector St. Mary's Episcopal Ch., Burlington, NJ, 1951-64; pres., trustee Burlington Coll., 1951-64, faculty cons., 1956-64; mem. faculty Phila. Div. Sch., 1959-62, lectr. ch. history, 1960-62; dean St. Matthew's Episcopal Cathedral, Dallas, 1964-87, dean emeritus, 1989; assoc. priest St. Luke's, Dallas, 1987—. Faculty US Army War Coll., Carlisle, Pa., 1964; dep. gen. Conv. from Diocese Dallas, 1967, 69, 70, 73, 76, 79; del. Provincial Synod from Diocese Dallas, 1966, 69, 72, 75, 78; mem. exec. coun. Diocese Dallas, 1967—77, 1984—86, pres. mem. standing com., 1970—73, pres., 1971—73, bd. missions, 1967—69, chmn. dept. coll. work, 1965—71, bd. examining chaplains, 1965—71, mem. standing liturgical commn.; dean, warden Cathedral Ctr. for Continuing Edn. and Pastoral Concern, 1971—87, Commn. Ministry, 1971—76; dean Dallas Deanery, 1965—69, 1984—86, Bicentennial preacher, 1975; pres. convocation and clericus Diocese of NJ, 1961—64, examining chaplain, bd. missions,bd. Christian edn., dean Burlington-Trenton convocation; instr., dean Drew Conf. for Adults in NJ, 1952—56; retreat condr. St. Martin's Ho., Bernardsville, NJ, St. John Bapt. Convent, Mendham, NJ; dean Diocesan Sch. Religion, NJ, 1962—63; founding dean Anglican Sch. Theology, 1971—75; parish life lab. and weekend condr. Nat. Dept. Christian Edn., 1962; co-founder, dean Princeton Conf., NJ, 1956—64; mem. Goals for Dallas Com.; co-chmn. N.Am. Cathedral Deans' Conf., 1980—81. Author: Sacrament and Sacrifice, 2d edit., 1973, Lancelot Andrews, Caroline Divine, 1951, Lift Up Your Hearts, 1956, A Manual of Prayers, 1975, The Holy Eucharist: Word and Sacrament, 1993, The Gate of Heaven, 1993, A Centennial Narrative History of the Episcopal Diocese of Dallas, 1995, Troubadours of God, 1998, Windows for Faith, 2000. Trustee Gen. Theol. Sem., 1968-80; bd. dirs. Evergreen Home for Aging, St. Philip's Community Center, Overseas Mission Soc. Named Priest of Yr., 1969. Mem.: Ch. Hist. Soc. (dir. 1960—68), Navy League, Burlington County Country Club, Vesper Club (Phila.), Dallas Athletic Club, Kiwanian Club (Disting. Svc. award 1951, Disting. Citizen award Brunswick, Md. 1986). Home: 7023 Northwood Rd Dallas TX 75225-2439 Personal E-mail: dr.cpwiles@dallastexas.com.

WILES, DAVID MCKEEN, chemist; b. Springhill, NS, Can., Dec. 28, 1932; s. Roy McKeen and Olwen Gertrude (Jones) W.; m. Valerie Joan Rowlands, June 8, 1957; children: Gordon Stuart, Sandra Lorraine. BSc with honors, McMaster U., 1954, MSc, 1955; PhD in Chemistry, McGill U., 1957. Rsch. officer chemistry divsn. NRC Can., Ottawa, 1959-66, head textile chemistry sect. chemistry divsn., 1966-75, dir. chemistry divsn., 1975-90; pres. Plastichem Cons., Victoria, B.C., Canada, 1990—. Chmn. Can. High Polymer Forum, 1967—69; v.p. N.Am. Chem. Congress, Mexico City, 1975. Contbr. articles to profl. jours.; mem. editl. adv. bd. numerous profl. jours.; patentee in field. Can. Ramsay Meml. fellow, 1957-59. Fellow Chem. Inst. Can. (chmn. bd. dirs. 1972-74, pres. 1975-76, Dunlop Lectr. award 1981), Royal Soc. Chem. London, Royal Soc. Can.; mem. Am. Chem. Soc. (Polymer Chem. divsn.). Home and Office: 3965 Juan Fuca Terr Victoria BC Canada V8N 5W9 Home Phone: 250-731-0732; Office Phone: 250-721-0732. Personal E-mail: dmwiles@telus.net.

WILES, LESSLEY DECKER, foundation administrator, preservationist; b. Pitts., Apr. 19, 1939; d. John Ellsworth and Irma Evelyn Decker; m. William Wharton Wiles, Aug. 20, 1961; 1 child, Kenneth William. BA, U. Ky., 1960. Statistician Wis. State Employment Svc., Madison, 1962—65, U.S. Dept. Labor, Wash., 1965—67; project mgr. HUD, Wash., 1967—72, new cmty. program officer, 1972—83, sr. program specialist, 1983—91, dir., coinsurance mgmt. divsn., 1991—92, sr. program officer, 1992—95; self-employed housing cons. York, Pa., 1996—. Mem., FHA commr.'s asset mgmt. strategy working team HUD, Wash., 1993—94. Mem. and com. chair Arlington/Tyson's Civitan Clubs, Fairfax County, Va., 1985—2005; ch. counsel sec. Walker Chapel United Meth. Ch., Arlington, 1988—97, flower com. chair, 1995—2002; mem. Arlington Cmty. Residences, Inc., 1982—88. Recipient Civitan of Yr., Arlington Civitan Club, 1991, 1992. Mem.: Pa.-Del. AHMA. Liberal. United Methodist. Avocations: crafts, gardening, volunteering. Home: 2635 Twin Lane York PA 17402-8248 Home Phone: 717-741-6854.

WILES, MICHAEL E., lawyer; b. July 23, 1953; AB, Georgetown U., 1975; JD, Yale U., 1978. Bar: NY 1979. Assoc. Debevoise & Plimpton LLP, NYC, 1978—87, litig. ptnr., 1987—. Mem.: ABA, Assn Bar of City NY. Office: Debevoise & Plimpton LLP 919 Third Ave New York NY 10022 Office Phone: 212-909-6653. Office Fax: 212-909-6836. E-mail: mewiles@debevoise.com.

WILES, WILLIAM WHARTON, retired federal government official; b. Knoxville, Tenn., June 9, 1931; s. James H. and Sally May (Wharton) W.; m. Lessley K. Decker, Aug., 1961; 1 child, Kenneth W. BA, Murray State U., 1953; MBA, U. Ky., 1959; PhD, U. Wis., 1973. Instr. U. Ky., 1959-61; with Fed. Res. Sys., Washington, 1964-98, sec. of bd., 1981-98. With U.S. Army, 1954-56. Home: 2635 Twin Ln York PA 17402 E-mail: Lessleyva@aol.com.

WILETS, LAWRENCE, physicist, educator; b. Oconomowoc, Wis., Jan. 4, 1927; s. Edward and Sophia (Finger) W.; m. Dulcy Elaine Margoles, Dec. 21, 1947; children: Ileen Sue, Edward E., James D.; m. Vivian C. Wolf, Feb. 8, 1976. BS, U. Wis., 1948; MA, Princeton U., 1950, PhD, 1952. Rsch. assoc. Project Matterhorn, Princeton, NJ, 1951-53, U. Calif. Radiation Lab., Livermore, 1953; NSF postdoctoral fellow Inst. Theoretical Physics, Copenhagen, 1953-55; staff mem. Los Alamos (N.Mex.) Sci. Lab., 1955-58; mem. Inst. Advanced Study, Princeton, 1957-58; mem. faculty U. Wash., Seattle, 1958—, prof. physics, 1962-95, prof. emeritus, 1995—. Cons. to pvt. and govt. labs.; vis. prof. Princeton U., 1969, Calif. Inst. Tech., 1971. Author: Theories of Nuclear Fission, 1964, Nontopological Solitons, 1989; contbr. over 180 articles to profl. jours. Del. Dem. Nat. Conv., 1968. NSF sr. fellow Weizmann Inst. Sci., Rehovot, Israel, 1961-62; Nordita prof. and Guggenheim fellow Lund (Sweden) U., Weizmann Inst., 1976—; Sir Thomas Lyle rsch. fellow U. Melbourne, Australia, 1989; recipient Alexander von Humboldt sr. U.S. scientist award, 1983. Fellow Am. Phys. Soc., AAAS; mem. Fedn. Am. Scientists, AAUP (pres. chpt. 1969-70, 73-75, pres. state conf. 1975-76), Explorers Club, Phi Beta Kappa (chpt. pres. 1996-97), Sigma Xi. Achievements include research on theory of nuclear structure and reactions, nuclear fission, atomic structure, atomic collisions, many body problems, subnuclear structure and elementary particles. Office: U Wash Dept Physics PO Box 351560 Seattle WA 98195-1560 Personal E-mail: wilets@comcast.net. Business E-Mail: wilets@u.washington.edu.

WILEY, C. MARK, lawyer, department chairman; b. High Point, NC, Oct. 9, 1963; BS cum laude, Wake Forest U., 1985, JD cum laude, 1988; LLM in Taxation, NYU, 1989. CPA 1988; bar: NC 1988, admitted to practice: US Dist. Ct. (Mid. Dist. NC) 1988, US Tax Ct. 1989, US Fed. Ct. of Claims 1990. Clk. Carruthers & Roth, P.A., Greensboro, NC, 1987; mem. Womble Carlyle Sandridge & Rice PLLC, Winston-Salem, NC, leader, tax practice group, 1998—2002, mem. mgmt. com., 2002—05, mem. ops. com.; chmn. Firmlogic, LLC. Mem. Wake Forest Law Review, 1988. Former mem. Forsyth County Estate Planning Coun. Recipient Wake Forest Law Faculty Scholar, I. Beverly Lake award. Mem.: Northwest Piedmont Chpt. CPA, NC Assn. CPA, ABA, NC Bar Assn., Forsyth County Bar Assn. Office: Womble Carlyle Sandridge & Rice PLLC One W 4th St Winston Salem NC 27101 Mailing: Womble Carlyle Sandridge & Rice PLLC PO Box 84 Winston Salem NC 27102 Office Phone: 336-721-3605. Office Fax: 336-733-8406. Business E-Mail: mwiley@wcsr.com.

WILEY, CARL ROSS, timber company executive; b. Astoria, Oreg., Apr. 17, 1930; s. Hamilton Ross and Ada Ellen (Smith) W.; m. Dolores Eileen Brice, Dec. 19, 1953; children: Susan, Steven, Kenneth. BS in Indsl. Engring., Oreg. State U., 1958; grad. exec. tng. program, MIT, 1974. Quality control engr. Oreg. Metall. Corp., 1958-59; indsl. engr. Osborne Electronics Corp., Portland, Oreg., 1959-62; v.p. timber and mfg. Boise Cascade Corp., Idaho, 1962-80; exec. v.p. Roseburg (Oreg.) Lumber Co., 1980-85; chief exec. officer Puget Sound Plywood, Tacoma, 1986-93; pres., CEO Lane Plywood, Eugene, Oreg., 1993-96; retired, 1996. Bd. dirs. Boise YMCA, 1975-78. With AUS, 1951-53. Mem. Am. Plywood Assn. (trustee), Western Wood Products Assn. (bd. dirs., chmn. econ. svcs. 1974-80). Lutheran. E-mail: wileycd@juno.com.

WILEY, EDWIN PACKARD, retired lawyer; b. Chgo., Dec. 10, 1929; s. Edwin Garnet and Marjorie Chastina (Packard) W.; m. Barbara Jean Miller, May 21, 1949; children: Edwin Miller, Clayton Alexander, Stephen Packard. BA, U. Chgo., 1949, JD, 1952. Bar: Wis. 1952, Ill. 1952, U.S. Dist. Ct. (ea. dist.) Wis. 1953, U.S. Supreme Ct. 1978. Assoc. Foley & Lardner, Milw., 1952-60, ptnr., 1960-98; ret. Bd. dirs. Genetic Testing Inst., Inc., other corps. and founds. Co-author: Bank Holding Companies: A Practical Guide to Bank Acquisitions and Mergers, 1988, Wisconsin Uniform Commercial Code Handbook, 1971; author: Promotional Arrangements: Discrimination in Advertising and Promotional Allowances, 1976; editor in chief U. Chgo. Law Rev., 1952. Bd. dirs. Blood Ctr. Southeastern Wis., pres., 1978-82; pres. Blood Ctr. Rsch. Found., Inc., 1983-87; v.p. Friends of Schlitz Audubon Ctr., Inc., 1975-87; pres. Wis. Conservatory ofMusic, 1968-73; pres. First Unitarian Soc. Milw., 1961-63; v.p. Mid-Am. Ballet Co., 1971-73, Milw. Ballet Co., 1973-74; pres. Florentine Opera Co., 1983-86; bd. dirs. Milw. Symphony Orch., pres., 1993-95; bd. dirs. Milw. Pub. Mus., Inc., sec., 1992-2005; bd. dirs. Wis. History Found., v.p., 1998-2005; bd. dirs. Preserve Our Parks, Inc., 1999—; mem. Wis. Gov.'s Commn. on Historic Sites, 2002-2003. Mem. ABA, State Bar of Wis., Milw. Bar Assn., Am. Law Inst., Order of Coif, Univ. Club, Phi Beta Kappa (pres. Greater Milw. assn. 1962-63). Home: 929 N Astor St Unit 2101 Milwaukee WI 53202-3488 Office Phone: 414-297-5780. Personal E-mail: ewilev@mac.com. Business E-Mail: ewiley@foley.com.

WILEY, GREGORY ROBERT, publisher; b. Sept. 21, 1951; s. William Joseph and Terese (Kunz) W.; children: Kathleen, Mary Glennon. BA in Pers. Adminstrn., U. Kans., 1974. Dist. sales mgr. Reader's Digest, St. Loius, 1976-80, regional sales dir. Chgo., 1980-82; nat. sales mgr. retail divsn. Rand McNally & Co., Chgo., 1982-83, nat. sales mgr. premium incentive divsn., 1983-86, nat. sales mgr. bookstore and mass market sales, 1986-88; book pub. The Sporting News, St. Louis, 1988-90; v.p. mktg. Marketmakers Internat., St. Louis, 1990-93, Sofsource Inc., St. Louis, 1993—96; eastern regional v.p. Handleman Co., St. Louis, 1996—2002; dir. sales and marketing, books The Sporting News, St. Louis, 2002—. Mem. Nat. Premium Sales Execs., Promotional Mktg. Assn. Am. Roman Catholic. Avocations: private pilot, historic restoration, golf. Home: 4245 Maryland Ave Saint Louis MO 63108-2905

WILEY, JAMES DEE, retired history and biology educator, national park service ranger; b. Douglas, Ariz., May 14, 1950; s. James David Wiley and Harriett D. Rattliff. BS in Edn., No. Ariz. U., 1972; MS in Edn., Corpus Christi State U., 1990; PhD, Kensington U., London, 1998. Cert. instr. Ariz. Assn. Cmty. Colls., 2000. Tchr./coach Douglas Pub. Schs., Ariz., 1985—2001; instr. Cochise C.C., Douglas, 1991—2001; pk. ranger Nat. Pk. Svc.-Independence NHP, Phila., 2003—07. Cons. Douglas Wild Life Zoo, 1990—2001. Contbr. articles to profl. jours. and pubs. Lobbyist Douglas Edn. Assn., 1991—2001, Douglas Pub. Schools, 1991—2001, Ariz. Edn. Assn., Phoenix, 1991—99. Mem.: NSTA (assoc.), NEA (life; polit. action com. 1991—95, Reach for the Stars award 1994), SW Herpalogical Assn. (assoc.), Ariz. Herpalogical Assn. (assoc.), Nat. Biology Teachers Assn. (assoc.), Douglas Edn. Assn. (life; pres. 1994—98), Ariz. Edn. Assn. (life; polit. action com. 1991—99), SCV (assoc.). Avocations: travel, reading, carving, photography. Home: PO Box 775 Reserve NM 87830 Personal E-mail: dr_jim_wiley@excite.com.

WILEY, JASON LARUE, JR., neurosurgeon; b. Canandaigua, NY, Dec. 2, 1917; s. Jason LaRue and Eva Althea (Moore) W.; m. Alma Williams, Jan. 4, 1944 (div. Feb. 1956); children: Robert W., Richard L.; m. Ann Valentine Gerrish, Apr. 14, 1956 (div. July 1979); children: Martha V., Pamela M., Catherine A. Student, Antioch Coll., 1934-37; MD, Harvard U., 1941. Diplomate Am. Bd. Surgery, Am. Bd. Neurol. Surgery. Intern Kings County Hosp., Bklyn., 1941-42; asst. resident surgery Ellis Hosp., Schenectady, NY, 1948-49; from asst. to assoc. resident surgery Rochester (N.Y.) Gen. Hosp., 1949-51; from asst. to assoc. to chief resident neurosurgery Yale U. and Hartford Hosp., New Haven and Hartford, Conn., 1951-54; practice medicine specializing in neurosurgery Kansas City, Mo., 1954—56, Rochester, NY, 1956—89. Chief neurosurgery Rochester Gen. Hosp., 1959-71, emeritus neurosurgeon, 1989—; clin. asst. prof. neurosurgery U. Rochester, 1961-88. Mem. Bd. for Profl. Med. Conduct, N.Y. State Dept. Health, Troy, N.Y., 1985-2004. Served to lt. comdr. USN, 1942-47, PTO. Mem. Med. Soc. County Monroe, Med. Soc. State N.Y., N.Y. State Neurosurg. Soc., Congress Neurol. Surgeons, Am. Assn. Neurol. Surgeons. Republican. Episcopalian. Avocations: fishing, genealogy. Office: 1445 Portland Ave Rochester NY 14621-3036

WILEY, JOHN D., academic administrator; BS in Physics, Ind. U., 1964; MS in Physics, U. Wis., Madison, 1965, PhD in Physics, 1968. Tech. staff Bell Telephone Labs., Murray Hill, NJ, 1968—74; Alexander von Humboldt rsch. and tng. fellow Max Planck Inst., Stuttgart, Germany, 1974—75; mem. elec. and computer engring. faculty U. Wis., Madison, 1975—, co-founder Ctr. for X-Ray Lithography and Engring. Rsch. Ctr. for Plasma-Aided Mfg., chair Materials Sci. program, 1982—86, assoc. dean for rsch., Coll. Engring., 1986—89, dean, Grad. Sch., and sr. rsch. officer, 1989—94, provost & vice chancellor for acad. affairs, 1994—2000, chancellor, 2001—. Office: U Wis 161 Bascom Hall 500 Lincoln Dr Madison WI 53706 *

WILEY, JOHN EDWIN, cytogeneticist; b. Roanoke, Va., Mar. 2, 1951; s. James Edwin and Marie Rita (Cassell) W. BA, U. N.C., Greensboro, 1973, MA, 1976; PhD, N.C. State U., 1981. Diplomate Am. Bd. Med. Genetics-Clin. Cytogenetics. Biomed. rschr. St. Paul's Coll., Lawrenceville, Va., 1981-82; postdoctoral trainee U. Wis., Madison, 1982-84; mem. faculty East Carolina U. Sch. Medicine, Greenville, NC, 1984—. Contbr. articles to profl. jours. Biomed. rsch. support grantee United Way, Greenville, 1986-87, USPHS, Washington, 1987-90. Mem. AAAS, Am. Soc. Human Genetics, Am. Soc. Zoologists, Am. Soc. Ichthyologists and Herpetologists. Democrat. Achievements include observation that certain genes on frog chromosomes seem to move frequently around, that chromosome constitution in many breast cancer tumors seems normal, that in some patients with ring X chromosomes the ring may not be turned off, that the addition of tumor promoting agents helps white blood cells in many vertebrates to divide, and that DNA sequences on ends of frog chromosomes are the same as those on the ends of human chromosomes. Office: East Carolina U Brody Sch Medicine 600 Moye Blvd Greenville NC 27834-4300 Home: 206 Ravenwood Dr Greenville NC 27834-6737 Home Phone: 252-758-0621; Office Phone: 252-744-2525. E-mail: wileyj@ecu.edu.

WILEY, LAKESHA M., pharmacist, educator; d. Ezekiel and Bessie Wiley. PhD in Pharmacy with honors, Mercer U., Atlanta, 2005. Cert. immunization APhA, 2003, diabetes Mercer U., 2005, advanced life support Am. Heart Assn., 2005. Pharmacy internship St. Joseph Hosp. Atlanta, 2001—05, Walgreens Pharmacy, Stone Mountain, Ga., 2002—05; pharmacy practice resident U. Ill., Chgo., 2005—06; clin. asst. prof. So. Ill. U., Edwardsville, Ill., 2006—; clin. pharmacist St. Joseph Health Ctr., St. Charles, Mo., 2006—. Vol. Am. Diabetes Assn., Atlanta, 2001—06, Am. Cancer Soc., Ga., 2000—03, Am. Heart Assn., Atlanta, 2001—06, Good Samaritan, Atlanta, 2004. Recipient Pharmacy Communication award, Roche Pharms., 2005. Mem.: Ga. Soc. Hosp. Pharmacists (assoc.; treas. 2003—04), Am. Pharmacists Assn. (assoc.; com. chair 2003—04). Office: So Univ Ill Edwardsville 200 University Park Dr Ste 200 Edwardsville IL 62026-2000 Office Fax: 618-650-5163. Business E-Mail: lwiley@siue.edu.

WILEY, MICHAEL E., oil industry executive; BS in Petroleum Engring., U. Tulsa; MBA, U. Dallas. Various engring. and operational positions ARCO Gas and Oil Co., various locations, 1972, sr. and exec. v.p., pres., 1993—2000, COO, 1998—2000; pres. Vastar, 1993—94, CEO, 1994—96, chmn. bd. dirs.; chmn., pres., CEO Baker Hughes Inc., Houston, 2000—. Office: Baker Hughes Inc 3900 Essex Ln Ste 1200 Houston TX 77027-5177

WILEY, RICHARD ARTHUR, lawyer; b. Bklyn., July 18, 1928; s. Arthur Ross and Anna Thorsen (Holder) W.; m. Carole Jean Smith, Aug. 13, 1955; children: Kendra Elizabeth, Stewart Alan, Garett Smith. AB, Bowdoin Coll., Brunswick, Maine, 1948, LLD, 1994; BCL, Oxford U., Eng., 1951; LLM, Harvard U., 1959. Bar: Mass. 1954, U.S. Ct. Mil. Appeals 1954, U.S. Dist. Ct. Mass. 1962, U. S. Supreme Ct. 1985. Atty. John Hancock Mut. Life Ins. Co., Boston, 1956-58; from atty. to mng. ptnr. Bingham, Dana & Gould, Boston, 1959-76; gen. counsel, asst. sec. Dept. Def., 1976-77; v.p., counsel First Nat. Bank Boston, 1977-78, exec. v.p., 1978-85, Bank of Boston Corp., 1985; ptnr. Csaplar & Bok, Boston, 1986-90, mem. exec. com., 1987-90, chmn., 1989-90, of counsel, 1990, Gaston & Snow, Boston, 1990-91; dir. Powers and Hall P.C., Boston, 1991-94, of counsel, 1994-95, Hill & Barlow, Boston, 1995—2002, Foley & Hoag LLP, Boston, 2002—. Bd. dirs., chmn. Mass. Higher Edn. Assistance Corp.; bd. dirs. Nomadic Structures, Inc., NP Med., Inc., Nypro, Inc., Carlo Gavazzi Mupac, Inc.; lectr. Boston U. Law Sch., 1961-64; past vice chmn. New Eng. Conf. on Doing Bus. Abroad; trustee New Eng. Legal Found., chmn., 1980-83; adj. prof. govt. and legal studies Bowdoin Coll., 1995-2002; adj. prof. law Boston Coll. Law Sch., 1998— Author: Cases and Materials on Law of International Trade and Investment, 1961; contbr. articles to profl. jours. Bd. overseers Bowdoin Coll., 1966-81, pres., 1977-80, trustee, 1981-93, trustee emeritus, 1993—; mem. Mass. Edn. Financing Authority, 1986-91, chmn., 1987-91; mem. Wellesley (Mass.) Town Meeting, 1971-75, mem. fin. adv. com., 1973-74; chmn. Mass. Bd. Regents of Higher Edn., 1991; bd. regents Task Force on Student Fin. Aid, 1987; mem. Mass. Higher Edn. Coord. Coun., 1991-95, vice chmn., 1991-93, chmn., 1993-95; chmn. lawyers divsn. United Way Mass. Bay, 1975; mem. devel. com., trustees of donations Episcopal Diocese Mass., 1971-75; trustee, exec. com. North Conway Inst., mem., 1980-92, chmn., 1988-92; bd. trustees Internat. Coun. Trust, Boston; trustee, mem. exec. com., chmn. Mass. Taxpayers Found., 1989-92; chmn. bd. trustees World Peace Found., Boston, 1983-95; corporator Schepens Eye Rsch. Inst., 1991-95; dep. chmn. planning Mass. rep. state com., 1971, vice chmn. fin. com., 1971-72. Officer USAF, 1953-56. Decorated Air Force Commendation medal; recipient Dep. Def. Disting. Pub. Svc. medal, 1977; Rhodes scholar, 1949. Mem.: ABA (vice chmn. fgn. and internat. bus. law com. 1967—69), Boston Bar Assn. (exec. com., antitrust com. 1965—68), Boston Com. on Fgn. Rels. (chmn. 1980—83), Coun. on Fgn. Rels., Phi Beta Kappa.

WILEY, RICHARD EMERSON, lawyer; b. Peoria, Ill., July 20, 1934; s. Joseph Henry and Jean W. (Farrell) W.; m. Elizabeth J. Edwards, Aug. 6, 1960; children: Douglas S., Pamela L. BS with distinction, Northwestern U., 1955, JD, 1958; LLM, Georgetown U., 1962; LLD (hon.), Cath. U. of Am., 1998. Bar: Ill. 1958, DC 1972. Pvt. practice, Chgo., 1962—70; gen. counsel FCC, Washington, 1970—72, mem., 1972—74, chmn., 1974—77, chmn. FCC's adv. com. on advanced TV svc., 1987—96; mng. ptnr. Wiley Rein, LLC, Washington, 1983—; Nat. co-chmn. lawyers Bush-Quayle campaign, 1992, Bush-Cheney campaign, 2000. Prof. law John Marshall Law Sch., U. Chgo., 1963-70. Chmn. bd. Media Inst., 1999-, Inst. for Tele-Info., Columbia U., 1997—. Capt. AUS, 1959-62. Recipient Medal of Honor, Electronic Industries Am., 1996, Emmy award Nat. Acad. TV Arts & Sci. 1997, Disting. Svc. award Nat. Assn. Broadcasters, 2002, named one of 75 Best Lawyers, Washingtonian mag., 2002, Internat. Achievement award N.Am. Broadcasters Assn., 2004; named to Most Influential Lawyers in Am. six times, and recognized as an enduring influence in 2003, by Nat. Law Jour., named Rep. Lawyer of Yr. by Rep. Nat. Lawyers Assn. 2004, named one of 100 Most Influential Lawyers, Nat. Law Jour., 2006. Fellow: Am. Bar Found.; mem.: ABA (chmn. Forum com. on comm. 1985—87, ho. of dels. 1969—71, 1977—84, chmn. young lawyers sect. 1977—84, chmn. bd. editors ABA Jour. 1984—89, chmn. com. on scope and correlation of work 1989, chmn. adminstrv. law & regulatory practice 1993—94, chmn. nat. law day 2003), Rep. Nat. Lawyers Assn. (bd. mem., co-chmn. judicial advocacy panel), Adminstrv. Conf. U.S. (coun., sr. fellow), Chgo. Bar Assn., Ill. Bar Assn., Fed. Comm. Bar Assn. (pres. 1987), Fed. Bar Assn. (pres. 1977), Phi Delta Kappa, Phi Delta Phi. Methodist. Office: Wiley Rein LLC 1776 K St NW Ste 1100 Washington DC 20006-2332 Office Phone: 202-719-7010. Business E-Mail: rwiley@wileyrein.com.

WILEY-HART, DEBRA, musician, educator; d. Nathaniel D. Duberstein and Miriam Scott Levine; m. Michael Andrew Hart, Apr. 17, 1994. BA, Hunter Coll., 1978; MA, NYU, 1988. Tchr., coach to singers and actors, NYC, 1982—; acting and voice tchr. Henry St. Settlement, NYC, 1988—92; acting tchr. Harlem Sch. for Arts, NYC, 1989, Marymount Manhattan, NYC, 2004—05, Lee Strasberg Theater and Film Inst., NYC, 1995—2005; voice specialist Montclair (NJ) State U., 2004—; head voice and acting divsn. ABC Film and Video, LLC, NYC, 2005—. Dir., coach Mannes Coll. Music, NYC, 1998; acting tchr. for musical theater Disney Theatrical Prodns., NYC, 2001; guest artist Dalcroze Inst., Juilliard Sch., NYC, 2002—03. Singer, actor: Songs and Sonnets of Edna St. Vincent Millay, 2001; singer: NY Singing Tchrs. Assn. Vocal Pedagogy Seminar, 2004. Stage dir. New Triad Collaborative Arts, NYC, 2006, Juilliard Chamberfest, NYC, 2006, Chamber Music Am., NYC, 2006, NYU Steinhardt, NYC, 2006. Mem.: AFTRA, SAG, Nat. Assn. Tchrs. of Singing, Am. Guild Variety Artists, Am. Guild Mus. Artists, NY Singing Tchrs. Assn., Actors Equity Assn. Office: ABC Film & Video LLC 303 5th Ave New York NY 10016 Office Phone: 212-686-3490. Personal E-mail: debra@abcfilmvideo.com.

WILFERT, CATHERINE M., medical association administrator, pediatrician, epidemiologist, educator; b. LA, July 26, 1936; m. Samuel L. Katz; children: Rachel, Catherine stepchildren: John, David, William, Deborah, Susan, Penelope. BA with distinction, Stanford Coll., 1958; MD cum laude, Harvard U., 1962. Med. intern Boston City Hosp., 1962—63; resident in pediat. Children's Hosp., Boston, 1964—66, fellow in infectious diseases, 1966—68; asst. prof. pediat. and virology Duke U., 1969—73, assoc. prof. pediat., 1974—79, prof. pediat. and microbiology, chief pediatric infectious diseases, 1980—96, prof. emeritus; sci. dir. Elizabeth Glaser Pediat. AIDS Found., Santa Monica, Calif., 1997—. Chair Adv. Com. on Immunization Practices, 1980, Perinatal Working Group of Prevention Trials Network, NIH; mem. adv. com. Office of AIDS Rsch., 1999—2005. Mem.: NIH AIDS Coms., Inst. Medicine, Infectious Diseases Soc. Am. (pres. 2000). Office: Elizabeth Glaser Pediatric AIDS Found 1917 Wildcat Creek Rd Chapel Hill NC 27516-9786 Office Phone: 919-968-0008. Home Fax: 919-968-0447. Personal E-mail: wilfert@mindspring.com.

WILFORD, JOHN NOBLE, JR., science news correspondent; b. Murray, Ky., Oct. 4, 1933; s. John Noble and Pauline (Hendricks) W.; m. Nancy Everett Watts, Dec. 25, 1966; 1 child, Nona. Student, Lambuth Coll., 1951-52; BS, U. Tenn., 1955; MA, Syracuse U., 1956; Internat. Reporting fellow, Columbia, 1961-62; DHL (hon.), R.I. Coll., 1987; DSc (hon.), Middlebury Coll., 1991. Reporter Comml. Appeal, Memphis, summers 1954-55; reporter Wall St. Jour., NYC, 1956, 59-61; contbg. editor Time mag., NYC, 1962-65; sci. reporter N.Y. Times, 1965-73, asst. nat. editor, 1973-75, dir. sci. news, 1975-79, sci. corr., 1979—. Vis. journalist Duke U., 1984; McGraw lectr. Princeton U., 1985; Disting. prof. journalism, U. Tenn., Knoxville, 1989-90; mem. Am. Mus.-Mongolian Gobi Expdn., 1991, Dir.'s Visitor, Inst. for Advanced Study, 1995. Author: We Reach The Moon, 1969, The Mapmakers, 1981, The Riddle of the Dinosaur, 1985, Mars Beckons, 1990, The Mysterious History of Columbus, 1991; co-author: The New York Times Guide to the Return of Halley's Comet, 1985, (with William Stockton) Spaceliner, 1981, Israel: The Historical Atlas, 1997; editor: Scientists at Work, 1979, Cosmic Dispatches, 2000. With CIC AUS, 1957-59. Recipient Book award Aviation/Space Writers, 1970, Writing award Aviation/Space Writers, 1983, G.M. Loeb Achievement award U. Conn, 1972, Press award Nat. Space Club, 1974, AAAS-Westinghouse Sci. Writing award, 1983, Ralph Coats Roe medal ASME, 1995, Pulitzer prize, 1984, N.Y. Times Pulitzer Prize Winning Team, 1987, N.Y.C. Mayor's award, 2001, Am. Geol. Inst. award, 2001, Sagan award Coun. Sci. Soc. Pres., 2001. Mem. Nat. Assn. Sci. Writers, Authors Guild, Soc. Profl. Journalists, Am. Geog. Soc. (councilor 1994—, sec. 2000—), Am. Acad. Arts and Scis., Century Assn., Sigma Chi, Phi Beta Kappa. Home: 232 W 10th St New York NY 10014-2976 Office: 620 Eigth Ave New York NY 10018-1405 Office Phone: 212-556-7485. Business E-Mail: wilford@nytimes.com.

WILHELM, CATHY S., elementary school educator; m. Larry Joseph Wilhelm, July 30, 1988; 1 child, Melanie Elaine; 1 child, Michael Eric Kyle. M, U. Akron, Ohio, 1979. Permanent Tchg. Cert. State of Ohio, 1979. Instr. English and Reading Highland Local Schs., Medina, Ohio, 1976—. Treas. Highland Edn. Assn., Medina, 1989—; mem. Strategic Planning Com. Highland Local Schs., Medina, 2005—06; mem. scholarship com. Highland Edn. Assn., Medina, past pres., 1979—88; mem. text com. Medina County Bd. Edn., 1979—98. Dir.(drama performance): Thespis Awards (Life Time Achievement Award, 2001). Chair exec. com. Highland Cmty. Support Network, Medina, 2004—06. Named Who's Who Among Am. Tchrs.; recipient Tchrs. Golden Apple award, Ashland Oil; fellow, Martha Holden Jennings Assn., 1983—84. Mem.: NOW, ACLU, LWV, AAUW, NEA (life), Ohio Edn. Assn., Nat. Campaign for Tolerance, Highland Found. for Ednl. Excellence, Phi Delta Kappa. Democrat-Npl. Office: Highland Local Schools 3880 Ridge Rd Wadsworth OH 44281 Office Fax: 330-239-7388.

WILHELM, DAVID C., investment company executive; m. Degee Dodds; children: Luke, Logan. BA, Ohio U., 1977; MPP, Harvard U., 1990; Doctorate (hon.), U. Charleston. Rsch. dir. pub. employee dept. AFL-CIO, 1981-83; campaign mgr. Senator Paul Simon, 1984, Senator Joseph Biden for Pres., Iowa, 1985-87, Richard M. Daley for Mayor, Chgo., 1989, 91, Gov. Bill Clinton for Pres., 1991-92; exec. dir. Citizens for Tax Justice, Washington, 1985-87; pres. The Strategy Group, Chgo., 1988-91; chmn. Nat. Dem. Com., 1993-94; sr. mng. dir. investment banking Kemper Securities, Inc. (now First Union), Chgo., 1995-97; founder, sr. v.p. Wilhelm & Conlon, Inc., Chgo., 1998—2004; founder, pres. Woodland Venture Mgmt., Chgo., 2002—; founder, ptnr. Adena Ventures, 2002—, Hopewell Ventures, 2004—; founder, pres. The Strategy Group. Lectr. U. Chgo.; bd. dirs. Christian Century Mag., League of Chgo. Treasures, Children's Meml. Hosp., Chgo., Ill. Venture Capital Assocs., Chicagoland Entrepreneurial Ctr., Ill. Ventures. Bd. dirs. Chgo. Project for Violence Prevention, Ctr. for Tax and Budget Accountability. Fellow Inst. of Politics, Harvard U., 1996, recipient hon. Dr. of Public Service, Ohio Univ. Office: Woodland Venture Mgmt 20 N Wacker Dr Ste 2200 Chicago IL 60606 E-mail: wilhelm@woodlandvc.com.

WILHELM, EDWARD W., corporate financial executive; Grad., U. of Detroit. With PricewaterhouseCoopers, 1981—91; contr., v.p./contr. Kmart Corp., 1991—94; v.p. fin. Borders Group, Ann Arbor, Mich., 1994—97, v.p. planning, reporting and treasury, 1997—2000, sr. v.p., CFO, 2000—. Office: Borders Group 100 Phoenix Dr Ann Arbor MI 48108-2202

WILHELM, GARY BRETZ, physician; s. Norman E. and Madeleine Bretz Wilhelm; m. Katherine Jean Kuhlman; 1 child, John Hunter. BA in Biology, Capital U., Columbus, Ohio, 1974; PhD in Human Anatomy and Neurosci., U. Tex., Galveston, 1980; MD, U. Tex., San Antonio, 1986. Postdoctoral fellow dept. pathology U. Tex. Health Sci. Ctr., San Antonio, 1980—81, instr. in human anatomy, 1980—82; intern Brooke Army Med. Ctr., Fort Sam Houston, Tex., 1987; resident in orthop. William Beaumont Army Med. Ctr., Fort Bliss, Tex., 1991—96; commd. 2d lt. US Army, 1986, advanced through grades to maj.; physician extender staff US Army Acad. Health Scis., San Antonio, 1990—91, resident physician Fort Bliss, 1991—96; chief, phys. exams clinics and aerospace medicine Munson Army Health Ctr., Ft. Leavenworth, Kans., 1996—; flight surgeon Mo. Army Nat. Guard, Jefferson City, 1996—. Chief, phys. exams clinics and aerospace medicine Munson Army Health Ctr., Fort Leavenworth, Kans., 1996—; orthopedic tech. course dir. Acad. Scis., Fort Sam Houston, 1990—91. Contbr. articles to profl. publs. Co-dir. Nat. Student Rsch. Forum, Galveston, 1978—79. Col., flight surgeon Mo. Army NG. Decorated Meritourious Svc. medal US Army, Civilian Achievement award; named Flight Surgeon of Yr., Soc. Army Flight Surgeons, 1988. Episcopalian. Avocations: flying, fox hunting, reading. Office: Munson Army Health Center 550 Pope Avenue Fort Leavenworth KS 66048 Office Phone: 913-684-6000.

WILHELM, JENNIFER ANNE, mathematics and science professor; d. Maryellen Regina and Edward Sundberg; m. Ronald Joseph Wilhelm, June 10, 1989; children: Olivia Danielle, Samuel Joseph. MS, Mich. State, Lansing, 1991; PhD, U. Tex., Austin, 2001. Cert. tchr. Austin, Tex., 1998. Grad. rsch. asst. U. Tex., Austin, 1998—2001; asst. prof. Tex. Tech U., Lubbock, 2002—. Prin. investigator NASA grant Tex. Tech. U., 2006—. Grantee, Space Telescope Sci. Inst., 2006—. Mem.: Am. Edn. Rsch. Assn. (corr. grantee 2003—05). Office: Texas Tech U Coll Edn PO Box 41071 Lubbock TX 79409 Office Phone: 806-742-1997 ext. 229. Office Fax: 806-742-2179. Business E-Mail: jennifer.wilhelm@ttu.edu.

WILHELM, JOHN L., health facility administrator; b. Chgo., 1943; MPH, U. Ill., Chgo., 1979; MD, Loyola U. Stritch Sch. Medicine. Internist Mercy Hosp., Chgo., 1969—71; resident, ob-gyn. Northwestern-Wesley Hosp., Chgo., 1971—73; resident, gyn. endocrinology Michael Reese Hosp., Chgo., 1974—75; chief, bur. pub. health Chgo. Health Dept., 1990; dep. commr. Chgo. Dept. Pub. Health, commr., 2000—05; exec. dir. Infant Welfare Soc. Chgo., 2005—. Office: Infant Welfare Soc Chgo 3600 W Fullerton Chicago IL 60647

WILHELM, JOHN W., labor union administrator; m. Elizabeth B. Gilbertson, 1969; 2 children. B with high honors, Yale Coll., 1967. Org. & bus. agent Local 217 Conn./R.I. Hotel and Restaurant Employees Internat. Union, 1969—71, sec., treas., 1971—83, bus. mgr., 1978—86; internat. v.p. Hotel Employees and Restaurant Employees Internat. Union (HERE), 1982-1996, gen. sec.-treas., 1996-98, gen. pres., 1998—2004; pres. hospitality industry UNITE HERE, Washington, 2004—06. Trustee Welfare/Pension Funds Hotel and Restaurant Employees Internat. Union, 1988—; trustee S. Nevada Culinary and Bartenders Pension Fund, 1995—; commr. Nat. Gambling Impact Study Commn., 1997—99. Mem.: Phi Beta Kappa. Office: UNITE HERE 1775 K St NW Ste 620 Washington DC 20006 Office Phone: 202-393-4373.

WILHELM, KATE (KATY GERTRUDE), author; b. Toledo, June 8, 1928; d. Jesse Thomas and Ann (McDowell) Meredith; m. Joseph B. Wilhelm, May 24, 1947 (div. 1962); children: Douglas, Richard; m. Damon Knight, Feb. 23, 1963; 1 child, Jonathan. PhD in Humanities (hon.), Mich. State U., 1996. Writer, 1956—. Co-dir. Milford Sci. Fiction Writers Conf., 1963-76; lectr. Clarion Fantasy Workshop Mich. State U., 1968-94. Author: More Bitter Than Death, 1962; (with Theodore L. Thomas) The Clone, 1965, The Nevermore Affair, 1966, The Killer Thing, 1967, Let the Fire Fall, 1969, The Year of the Cloud, 1970, Abyss: Two Novellas, 1971, Margaret and I, 1971, City of Cain, 1971, The Clewiston Test, 1976, Where Late the Sweet Birds Sang, 1976, Fault Lines, 1976, Somerset Dreams and Other Fictions, 1978, Juniper Time, 1979; (with Damon Knight) Better Than One, 1980, A Sense of Shadow, 1981, Listen, Listen, 1981, Oh! Susannah, 1982, Welcome Chaos, 1983, Huysman's Pets, 1986; (with R. Wilhelm) The Hills Are Dancing, 1986, The Hamlet Trap, 1987, Crazy Time, 1988, Dark Door, 1988, Smart House, 1989, Children of the Wind: Five Novellas, 1989, Cambio Bay, 1990, Sweet, Sweet Poison, 1990, Death Qualified, 1991, And the Angels Sing, 1992, Seven Kinds of Death, 1992, Naming the Flowers, 1992, Justice for Some, 1993, The Best Defense, 1994, A Flush of Shadows, 1995, Malice Prepense, 1996, The Good Children, 1998, Defense for the Devil, 1999, No Defense, 2000, The Deepest Water, 2000, Desperate Measures, 2001, Skeletons, 2002, Clear and Convincing Proof, 2003, The Unhidden Truth, 2004, Storyteller, 2005, The Price of Silence, 2005, Sleight of Hand, 2006; (multimedia space fantasy) Axoltl, U. Oreg. Art Mus., 1979, (radio play) The Hindenburg Effect, 1985; editor: Nebula Award Stories #9, 1974, Clarion SF, 1976; contbr. articles to popular mags., profl. jours. Mem. Nat. Writers Union, Mystery Writers Am., Authors Guild. Address: 1645 Horn Ln Eugene OR 97404-2957 E-mail: kate@katewilhelm.com.

WILHELM, ROBERT OSCAR, lawyer, civil engineer; b. Balt., July 7, 1918; s. Clarence Oscar and Agnes Virginia (Grimm) W.; m. Grace Sanborn Luckie, Apr. 4, 1959. BSCE, Ga. Tech. Inst., 1947, MSIM, 1948; JD, Stanford U., 1951. Bar: Calif. 1952, U.S. Supreme Ct. Mem. Wilhelm, Thompson, Redwood City, Calif., 1952—92; gen. counsel Bay Counties Gen. Contractors; pvt. practice civil engring., Redwood City, 1952—. Pres. Bay Counties Builders Escrow, Inc., 1972-88. Author: The Manual of Procedures for the Construction Industry, 1971, Manual of Procedures and Form Book for Construction Industry, 9th edit., 1995, Construction Law for Contractors, Architects and Engineers; columnist Law and You in Daily Pacific Builder, 1955-2001. With C.E., AUS, 1942-46. Named to Wisdom Hall of Fame, 1999. Mem. Bay Counties Civil Engrs. (pres. 1957), Peninsula Builders Exch. (pres. 1958-71, dir.), Calif. State Builders Exch. (treas. 1971), Del Mesa Carmel Cmty. Assn. (bd. dirs. 1997-99), Masons, Odd Fellows, Eagles, Elks. Home: 134 Del Mesa Carmel Carmel CA 93923-7950 Office: 600 Allerton St Ste 202 Redwood City CA 94083 Home Phone: 831-625-5291.

WILHELM, WILLIAM JEAN, civil engineering educator; b. St. Louis, Oct. 5, 1935; s. Maurice Ferdinand and Winifred Eileen (McClintock) W.; m. Patricia Jane Zietz, Aug. 17, 1957; children: William, Robert, Andrew, Mary, David. BME, Auburn U., 1958, MS, 1963; PhD, N.C. State U., 1968. Lic. profl. engr., Kans. Structural engr. Palmer & Baker Engrs., Mobile, Ala., 1958-60; instr. engring. graphics Auburn U., 1960-64; asst. prof. civil engring. W.Va. U., Morgantown, 1967-72, assoc. prof., 1972-76, prof., 1976-79, chmn., 1974-79; dean engring., prof. Wichita State U., 1979-2000, dean, prof., emeritus, 2000—, dir. Ctr. for Productivity Enhancement, 1984-86, exec. dir. Ctr. for Tech. Application, 1988-91. Bd. dirs. Kans. Tech. Enterprise Corp., Orthopaedic Rsch. Inst. Via Christi Regional Med. Sys.; chair bd. dirs. Envision. Found.; mem. bldg. commn. Cath. Diocese of Wichita. Contbr. articles to profl. jours. Officer C.E. U.S. Army, 1959, 62. Recipient Recognition award Wichita State U. Alumni Assn., 1993, Engr. Svc. award Wichita Coun. Engring. Socs., 2000. Fellow NSPE, ASCE, Am. Soc. Engring. Edn. (George K. Wadlin award 1998, MidWest sect. Spl. Appreciation award 2001), Am. Concrete Inst. (Joe W. Kelley award 1986, Henry L. Kennedy award 1994); mem. Soc. Women Engrs. (sr., Rodney D. Chipp Meml. award 2000), Kans. Soc. Profl. Engrs. (pres. 1994-95, Outstanding Engr. of Yr. award 1989, Career Recognition award 2000), W.Va. Acad. Civil Engrs. (hon.), Order of the Engr., Sigma Xi, Phi Kappa Phi, Tau Beta Pi, Pi Tau Sigma, Chi Epsilon (chpt. hon. W.Va. U. 1979), Golden Key (hon.). Roman Catholic. Home: 7014 E 25th St N Wichita KS 67226-1734 Personal E-mail: billwilhelm1@cox.net.

WILHELMI, CYNTHIA JOY, information technology manager, information scientist, consultant; Student, Iowa State U., Ames, 1964—66; BA in Art and Edn., U. Iowa, 1966; MA in Comm., U. Nebr., Omaha, 1996. Master Artist-in-Residence Nebr. Arts Coun., Omaha, 1985—91; grad. tchg. asst., tchg. fellow U. Nebr., Omaha, 1993—95; Family Friends of Eastern Nebr. program coord. Vis. Nurse Assn., Omaha, 1996—97; instr. Midland Luth. Coll., Fremont, Nebr., 1997—99; info. tech. cons., project mgr., test engr., bus. analyst Bass & Assocs., Omaha, 1999—2000; info. tech. cons. Robert Half Internat. Cons., 2000, Maxim Group/TEKSystems, 2000—02, Client Resources Inc., 2003; data mgr. TEKsystems, 2003; govt. bid proposal coord. NuGenSof cons. co., 2003—04; bus. sys. analyst Wells Fargo; data mgr. Raytheon, 2003, proposal coord., 2003—04; bus. sys. analyst Praxis Tech. Group, 2005; sr. quality assurance, testing engr. Acacia Tech. Svcs. Inc., 2006; sr. project mgr. and coord. Profl. Project Ptnrs., Inc., 2006; project mgr. MSI Solutions Integrators, 2006—. Sr. project mgr., bus. analyst Alegent Health, Ameritrade, Omnium Worldwide, Lincoln Benefit Life, Raytheon, Wells Fargo, Praxis Tech. Group; IT data mgr., govt. info. tech. proposal coord.; sr. test engr. Ameritrade, Lincoln Benefit Life, Ameritas, Alegent Health, Nationwide Ins., 2006; project mgr. Alegent Health, Ameritrade, Lincoln Benefit Life, Wells Fargo; data mgr. Omnium Worldwide, Raytheon, Northrop Grumman Mission Sys., Ameritrade; 3d-party vendor mgr. Alegent Health, Lincoln Benefit Life; CD installation tester Lincoln Benefit Life; tech. documentor Alegent Health, Omnium Worldwide, Ameritrade, PerClick-dot-com, Ameritas, Raytheon Sys., Inacom; data mgr. Northrop Grumman Mission Sys.; bus. sys. cons. Wells Fargo, Nationwide Agribusiness Ins., Nationwide Insurance Agile Tech.; project mgr., enterprise field ops. release coord. Wells Fargo Corp. Offices; project mgr. MSI Sys. Integrators, Inc.; farmer, 2001—. Editor, pub., contbg. author Salaam mag., 1985-86. Mem. adv. coun. Foster Grandparents, Omaha, 1999-2005; bd. dirs., pub. rels./publicity chair U. Nebr. Friends of Art, Omaha, 1997-99; bd. dirs. Nebr. SIDS Found., 2002—03 Named Outstanding Grad. Tchg. Asst., U. Nebr., Omaha, 1995, Adm. in the Gt. Navy of Nebr., 1990 Mem.: AAUW, Nebr. Adms. Assn., Soc. for Tech. Comm. (bd. dirs., chair pub. rels. 1999), Am. Meteor. Soc., Soc. for Collegiate Journalists (hon.), Mensa (Nebr., Western Iowa exec. com. 2003—05, SIGHT coord. 2003—05, nat. nominating com. Nebr.-Western Iowa 2004—05, nat. nominating com. Ctrl. Iowa 2006—), Ctrl. Hawkeye Gas Engine and Tractor Assn., Phi Delta Gamma. Republican. Personal E-mail: cwi813@earthlink.net.

WILHELMSEN, HAROLD JOHN, accountant; b. Kansas City, Mo., July 13, 1928; s. Karl John and Cora Irene (Reynolds) W.; m. Audrey Loraine Woodard, Oct. 14, 1950. BBA, U. Wis., 1950. CPA, Wis. With S.C. Johnson & Son Inc., Racine, Wis., 1953-90, dir. fin. South Pacific, 1970-72, mgr. overseas fin. svcs., 1972-76, contr. U.S. ops., 1976-78, v.p., contr. internat. ops., 1978-90, ret., 1990. Pres. Racine Symphony Orch. Assn., 1957-60; trustee Carthage Coll., Kenosha, Wis., 1984-91, dir., sec. Pinnacle Peak Country Club Estates, 1992-95; dir., 1993-97, pres. Pinnacle Peak Country Club, 1996-97; treas. Christ the Lord Luth. Ch. Served with U.S. Army, 1950-52. Mem.: Ranch Village Health Club and Spa, Pinnacle Peak Country Club. Republican. Lutheran. Avocations: golf, squash, bridge, reading, music. Personal E-mail: hjw-az@cox.net.

WILHIDE, STEPHEN D., medical association administrator; BA in Social Scis., Frostburg State U., Md., 1965; MSW, U. Md., 1972; MPH, U. Pitts., 1976. Exec. dir. So. Ohio Health Svcs. Network, 1976—2002, Nat. Rural Health Assn., Alexandria, Va., 2002—. Vol. VISTA, NC. With US Army, Vietnam. Named one of Most Powerful People in Healthcare, Modern Healthcare mag., 2003. Office: National Rural Health Associ 1600 Prince St Ste 100 Alexandria VA 22314-2836 Office Phone: 703-519-7910. Business E-Mail: wilhide@nrharural.com.

WILHITE, STEVE, automotive executive; married; 1 child. BA, Stanford U., 1974; MBA, U. Calif., Berkeley. Mktg. exec. Ford Motor Co.; sr. mktg. exec. Volkswagen of Am., 1990—99; v.p. worldwide mktg. comms. Apple Computer, Inc., 1999—2001; v.p. mktg. Nissan N.Am., Inc., 2001—04; sr. v.p. global mktg. Nissan Motor Co., Ltd., Tokyo, 2004—06; COO Hyundai Motor Am., Fountain Valley, Calif., 2006—. Office: Hyundai Motor Am 10550 Talbert Ave Fountain Valley CA 92708-6031 Office Phone: 714-965-3000. Office Fax: 714-965-3149. *

WILHITE, TAMARA SUE, public health service officer; b. Long Beach, Calif., Aug. 14, 1958; d. Maurice Roscoe and Nema Maylee Harding; m. Jon Richard Knauss, Sept. 7, 1980 (div. Mar. 0, 1992); children: Ian Zachery Knauss, Rachel Erin Knauss; m. Robert Michael Wilhite Jr., June 14, 1997. BS in Food. Sci. and Tech., Oreg. State U., Corvallis, 1988. Lic. practical nurse, Colo., 1978, Oreg., 1978. Practical nurse Kaiser Permanente, Clackamas, Oreg., 1981—82; R&D tech. Oreg. Freeze Dry, Albany, 1988—93; sanitation, safety mgr. Chef Francisco, Eugene, Oreg., 1993—95; quality assurance supr. Foster Farms, Creswell, Oreg., 1995—98; health insp. Ln. County Environ. Health, Eugene, 1998—; bioterrorism sanitarian Ln. County Pub. Health, Eugene, 2002—. Site leader Jobs for Life, Eugene, 2005; pres., exec. dir. Ashes to Beauty Recovery Program, Eugene, 2006. With USAR, 1983—92. Decorated Army Superior Unit award US Army; grantee Jess Hanson scholarship, Oreg. State U., 1987; scholar, Cenex Found., 1987; scholar, Ralston Purina, 1986, jr., sr. scholar, Inst. Food Technologists, 1986—87, Raymond Powell scholar, 1987. Office: Lane County Environmental Health 125 E 8th Ave Eugene OR 97401 Home Phone: 541-688-4152; Office Phone: 541-682-3497. Office Fax: 541-682-7459. Business E-Mail: tamara.wilhite@co.lane.or.us.

WILHOIT, GENE, educational association administrator; m. Rebecca Campbell Wilhoit; children: Christopher, Kara, Jason. BA in Hist. and Econs., Georgetown Coll.; M in Tchg., Polit. Sci. and Econs., Ind. U.; student in Edn. Adminstrn., W.Va. Coll. Grad. Studies. Social studies tchr., Ohio, Ind.; prog. dir. Ind. Dept. Pub. Instrn.; adminstr. Kanawha County, W.Va.; spl. asst. US Dept. Edn., 1979—83; exec. dir. Nat. Assn. State Bds. Edn., 1986—93; chair edn. commn. State Adv. Commn., 1989—91; dir., chief state sch. officer Ark. Dept. Edn., 1994—97; dep. commr. bur. learning support svcs. Ky. Dept. Edn., 1997—2000, commr. edn., 2000—06; exec. dir. Coun. Chief State Sch. Officers, Washington, 2006—. Spkr. in field. Office: Coun Chief State Sch Officers One Massachusetts Ave NW Ste 700 Washington DC 20001-1431 Office Phone: 202-336-7000. Office Fax: 202-408-8072. *

WILHOUR, BRIAN EDWARD, composer, music director; b. Lewisburg, Pa., Nov. 7, 1969; s. Edward and Joanne Wilhour. MusB, Bucknell U., Lewisburg, Pa., 1991; MusM, Westminster Choir Coll., Princeton, NJ, 1994. Dir. of music Trinity Luth. Ch., Dover, NJ, 1992—94, First Presbyn. Ch., Idaho Falls, Idaho, 1994—98, Immanuel Presbyn. Ch., McLean, Va., 1998—. Lead tenor Idaho Falls Opera, 1996; condr. Idaho Falls Symphony Chorale, 1996—98; organist Washington Chamber Symphony, 2000—02; guest organist Washington Nat. Cathedral, 2003, organ solo recitalist, 07. Composer: (orchestral) Symphony No. 1, Symphony No. 2, (orchestral/choral) Mass in E Minor, (suite for orch.) The Passion of Christ, (orchestral/choral) Gloria in Excelsis - A Cantata for Christmas, Revelation - for Orchestra and Chorus, Hope of the World - Cantata, Magnificat, God Our Refuge, Requiem, (film score) Vacancy. Music fund raiser various local charities, McLean, Va., 1998—. Recipient Grad. Organ Competition award, Westminster Choir Coll., 1992, Ruth and Raymond Young Composition prize, 1993, Hoke Ch. Music Composition award, 1993, Donald E. Allured Handbell prize, 1993; McRae scholar, Bucknell U., 1987—91, Charlotte W. Newcombe scholar, Westminster Choir Coll., 1993. Mem.: Am. Choral Dirs. Assn., Condrs. Guild, Am. Guild English Handbell Ringing (area X state chair 1996—98), Am. Guild Organists (local bd. dirs. 1996—98), Am. Composers Forum. Avocations: swimming, bicycling, cooking, sailing. Home: 1400 S Joyce St Apt 132 Arlington VA 22202 Office: Immanuel Presbyterian Church 1125 Savile Ln Mc Lean VA 22101 Home Phone: 703-888-7735; Office Phone: 703-356-3042.

WILK, RONALD, physician; b. NYC, Nov. 27, 1944; BA, L.I. U., Bklyn., 1966; MD, U. Bologna, Italy, 1972. Diplomate Am. Acad. Neurology, 1980. Intern, resident Mt. Sinai Hosp., NYC, chief resident, 1977. Fellow: Royal Soc. Medicine, Am. Acad. Neurology.

WILK, STUART, publishing executive; Reporter, asst. city editor Milwaukee Sentinel; night city editor The Dallas Morning News, 1980, metro editor, asst. mng. editor, dep. mng. editor, mng. editor, 1996—2004, v.p., assoc. editor, 2004—, Belo Corp. (parent co. of The Dallas Morning News), 2004—. Discussion leader Am. Press Inst.; profl. in residence Marshall U. W. Page Sch. Journalism, 2001; faculty Cross-Media Journalism Pilot Program, Robert C. Maynard Inst. of Journalism Edn. Bd. dir. Freedom of Information Found. Tex. Mem.: Associated Press Mng. Editors (pres., mem. exec. com., chair, Mktg., Ethics and Diversity Com., supervised nationwide survey on diversity in the newsroom 1996). Office: Dallas Morning News 508 Young St Dallas TX 75202 Office Phone: 214-977-8222. Business E-Mail: swilk@dallasnews.com.

WILKE, CONSTANCE REGINA, elementary school educator; b. Camden, NJ, Mar. 20, 1944; d. Matthew Stanley Sr. and Regina Rita (Przeradzki) Wojtkowiak; m. Alvin Frank Wilke Jr., Apr. 20, 1968; children: Joseph Alvin, Suzanne Renee. BA in Elem. Edn., Glassboro State U., 1967, MA in Reading and Supervision, 1979. Cert. tchr. and reading speicalist, N.J. Tchr. 5th grade Bellmawr (N.J.) Bd. Edn., 1967-70; tchr. 2d grade Ethel M. Burke Sch., Bellmawr, NJ, 1970-97; tchr. 5th grade Bell Oaks Sch., Bellmawr, 1997—. Author: Wojtkowiak Family History, 1992. Vol. Gloucester (N.J.) City Libr., 1972-75, Vet.'s Standdown, Meals on Wheels, Cathedral Soup Kitchen; contact reassurance vol. Am. Heart Assn. Walk; sec. E.M. Burke Sch. PTA, Bellmawr, 1973-78, publicity person, 1980-85, pres., 1982-85, author and editor publicity book, 1980-83, rec. sec., 1995-97; advisor Cmty. Edn. Bd., Gloucester City, 1973-74; eucharistic minster St. Mary's Ch., Gloucester City, 1990—, 150 yr. Jubilee com., renew com., lector, parish coun.; dir., founder of Internat. Day at E.M. Burke Sch., dir. and founder Vet.'s Day Program, MS Read-a-thon, Jump Rope for Heart, Book It programs, Reading is the Ticket program. Named Citizen of Yr., Polish-Am. Congress, 1983, N.J. VFW Citizenship Tchr. of Yr., 2002. Mem. NEA, N.J. Epilepsy Found., N.J. Edn. Assn., West Jersey Reading Assn., Bellmawr Edn. Assn. (faculty rep.), Asthma Assn. Roman Catholic. Achievements include being instrumental in having Veteran Memorial built honoring Bellmawr veterans. Office: Bell Oaks Sch 256 Anderson Ave Bellmawr NJ 08031-1199

WILKE, LEROY, retired church administrator; m. Jane Wilke. Grad., Golden Valley Lutheran Coll.; MA, Minn. State U.; LittD (hon.), Concordia U., 1999. Chaplain's asst. US Army; adminstr., dir. Christian Edn., Mpls., 1969; prof. edn. Concordia Coll., St. Paul, 1976; exec. dir. dist. and congl. svcs. Luth. Ch.-Mo. Synod, St. Louis, 1985—2005. Sec. Karpenko Inst. for Nurturing and Developing Leadership Excellence, 2005—. Lutheran. Office: KINDLE c/o Emmauel Luth Ch 3120 Irving St Denver CO 80211-3632 Office Phone: 303-433-3303. Office Fax: 303-433-2280. E-mail: leroy.wilke@lcms.org.

WILKEN, JIMMY LOUIS, radio news director, radio station manager, professional photographer; b. Nacogdoches, Tex., Sept. 8, 1949; s. Albert Louis Wilken and Marie (Reese) Zipperian; m. Rachel Whitefield, Jan. 3, 1986; children: Robert, Leah, Jonathan, Matthew. Student, Del Mar Coll., 1970-85; grad., Cleve. Inst. Electronics, 1972, N.Y. Inst. Photography, 1983. Lic. radio and TV engr. Air personality Sta. KRYS Radio, Corpus Christi, Tex., 1966-72; music dir. Sta. KZFM Radio, Corpus Christi, 1972-74; news dir. Sta. KSPL Radio, Lufkin, Tex., 1974-75; ops. mgr. Sta. KIKN Radio, Corpus Christi, 1975-84; news dir. Sta. KOUL Radio/KCTA Radio, Corpus Christi, 1986-91; owner Wilken Photo Svc., Rockport, Tex., 1983-86, The Trinity Record Studio, Corpus Christi, 1989—; sta. mgr. Sta. KFGG Radio, Corpus Christi, 1991—; broadcast ops. mgr. Roloff Evangelistic Enterprises. Cons. Sta. KPCB Radio, Rockport, 1984-85; motivation trainer Total Communications, Corpus Christi, Tex., 1986—. Author newspaper column, 1974; writer comml. Boot Barn, 1976 (Addy award 1976); producer Miller Beer comml. Sta. KOUL, 1986 (Addy award 1986); producer record Shores of Icky Goey, 1984, The Old Stars and Stripes, Miracle Man, You Are Love, 1989, 90, Higher Love, 1997. Chmn. Seafare, Rockport, 1980-85; evangelist World Christian Ministries, Corpus Christi, 1987; mem. tech. adv. com. Miller H.S., 1996-97. Recipient Best on Scene award AP, Lufkin, 1972, Mark Twain award AP, Dallas, 1986, Best Photo of Show award Roundup Days, Ingelside, Tex., 1986. Mem. Tex. Profl. Photographers Assn., Rockport Profl. Phtographers Assn. (pres. 1984-85), Assoc. Photographers Internat., Am. Radio Relay League, Quarter Century Wireless Assn. Clubs: Corpus Christi Amateur Radio; South Tex. Amateur Repeater. Episcopalian. Avocations: photography, tennis. Office: 410 SPID PO Box 1177 Corpus Christi TX 78403-1177

WILKENING, LAUREL LYNN, academic administrator, aerospace scientist; b. Richland, Wash., Nov. 23, 1944; d. Marvin Hubert and Ruby Alma Wilkening; m. Godfrey Theodore Sill, May 18, 1974 BA, Reed Coll., Portland, Oreg., 1966; PhD, U. Calif., San Diego, 1970; DSc (hon.), U. Ariz., 1996. From asst. prof. to assoc. prof. U. Ariz., Tucson, 1973—80, dir. Lunar and Planetary Lab., head planetary scis., 1981—83, vice provost, prof. planetary scis., 1983—85, v.p. rsch., dean Grad. Coll., 1985—88; divsn. scientist NASA Hdqrs., Washington, 1980; prof. geol scis., adj. prof. astronomy, provost U. Washington, Seattle, 1988—93; prof. earth system sci., chancellor U. Calif., Irvine, 1993—98. Dir. Rsch. Corp., 1991-2003, Seagate Tech., Inc., 1993-2000, Empire Ranch Found., 1998-2003, 2005—; vice chmn. Nat. Commn. on Space, Washington, 1984-86, Adv. Com. on the Future of U.S. Space Program, 1990-91; chair Space Policy Adv. Bd., Nat. Space Coun., 1991-92; co-chmn. primitive bodies mission study team NASA/European Space Agy., 1984-85; chmn. com. rendezvous sci. working group NASA, 1983-85; mem. panel on internat. cooperation and competition in space Congl. Office Tech. Assessment, 1982-83; trustee NASULGC, 1994-97, UCAR, 1988-89, 97-98, Reed Coll., 1992-2002. Editor: Comets, 1982. Recipient trainee, NASA, 1967—70; grantee fellow, U. Calif Regents, 1966—67. Fellow Meteoritical Soc. (councilor 1976-80), Am. Assn. Advanced Sci.; mem. Am. Astron. Soc. (chmn. div. planetary scis. 1984-85), Am. Geophys. Union, AAAS, Planetary Soc. (dir. 1994-2000, v.p. 1997-2000), Phi Beta Kappa. Democrat. Avocations: gardening, camping, swimming.

WILKENS, LENNY (LEONARD RANDOLPH WILKENS JR.), sportscaster, former professional sports team executive, retired professional basketball player; b. Bklyn., Oct. 28, 1937; s. Leonard Randolph Sr. and Henrietta (Cross) W.; m. Marilyn J. Reed, July 28, 1962; children: Leesha Marie, Leonard Randolph III, Jamée McGregor. BS in Econs., Providence Coll., 1960, HHD (hon.), 1980. Profl. basketball player St. Louis Hawks, 1960—68, Seattle SuperSonics, 1968—69, Cleve. Cavaliers, 1972—74; player/coach Seattle SuperSonics, 1969—72, head coach, 1977—85, gen. mgr., 1985—86; head coach Cleve. Cavaliers, 1986—93; vice chmn. Seattle SuperSonics, 2006—07, pres. basketball ops., 2007; counselor Jewish Employment Vocat. Svcs., 1962—63; salesman packaging divsn. Monsanto Co., 1966; player/coach Portland Trail Blazers, 1974—76; head coach Atlanta Hawks, 1993—2000, Toronto Raptors, 2000—03, NY Knicks, 2004—05; color analyst Pac-10 men's basketball FSN, 2004—05, NBA analyst, 2005—06, Seattle SuperSonics color analyst, 2006—. Head coach 4 NBA All-Star Teams, World Champion Basketball Team, 1979, Olympic Basketball Team, 1996, asst. coach, 92. Author: The Lenny Wilkens Story, 1974. Bd. regents Gonzaga U., Spokane; bd. dirs. Seattle Ctr., Big Bros. Seattle, Bellevue Boys Club, Wash., Seattle Opportunities Industrialization Ctr., Seattle U.; co-chmn. UN Internat. Yr. of Child prog., 1979; organizer Lenny Wilkens Celebrity Golf Tournament for Spl. Olympics. 2nd lt. US Army, 1961—62. Named to NBA All-Star Game, 1963-65, 67-71, 73, NIT-NIKE Hall of Fame, 1988, Naismith Meml. Basketball Hall of Fame, 1989 (as a player), 1998 (as a coach); named NBA All-Star Game MVP, 1971, Man of Yr., Boys High Alumni chpt. LA, 1979, Sportsman of Yr., Seattle chpt. City of Hope, 1979, Congl. Black Caucus Coach of Yr., 1979, Continental Basketball Assn. Coach of Yr., 1979, Coach of Yr., Black Pubs. Assn., 1979, NBA Coach of Yr., 1994; named one of NBA's 50 Greatest Players, NBA's Top Ten Coaches, 1997; recipient Whitney Young Jr. award NY Urban League, 1979, Disting. Citizens award Boy Scouts Am., 1980. Achievements include holding record for most career NBA wins. *

WILKERSON, EDWARD, apparel designer; Grad., Parsons Sch. Design. Designer Anne Klein & Co., 1984, Calvin Klein, Donna Karan; design dir. Lafayette 148 NY, NYC, 1998—. Mem. bd. dirs. Fashion Outreach. Featured in Ebony mag., 2007. Mem.: Coun. Fashion Designers Am. Office: Lafayette 148 Inc 148 Lafayette St Fl 2 New York NY 10013-3115 *

WILKERSON, LUANN, dean, medical educator; BA magna cum laude, Baylor U., 1969; MA in English, U. Tex., 1972; EdD, U. Mass., 1977. Tchg. asst. dept. English U. Tex., Austin, 1970-72; tchr. grade 8 lang. arts Quabbin Regional H.S., Barre, Mass., 1974-75; rsch. asst. Clinic to Improve Univ. Tchg. U. Mass., Amherst, 1974-76, staff assoc., 1976-77; dir. tchg. and media resource ctr., asst. prof. speech and theatre Murray State U., Ky., 1977-80; acting dir., coord. faculty devel. office ednl. devel. and resources Coll. Osteopathic Medicine Ohio U., Athens, 1980-81; assoc. dir. office curricular affairs, asst. prof. family medicine Med. Coll. Wis., Milw., 1981-83; ednl. specialist ednl. devel. unit Michael Reese Hosp. and Med. Ctr., Chgo., 1983-84; dir. faculty devel. office ednl. devel. Harvard Med. Sch., Boston, 1984-91, lectr. in med. edn., 1988-91; dir. Ctr. for Ednl. Devel. and Rsch. UCLA Sch. Medicine, 1992-99, asst. dean med. edn., 1992-94, assoc. prof. medicine, 1992-95, prof. medicine, 1996—, assoc. dean med. edn., 1995-97, sr. assoc. dean med. edn., 1998—. Mem. editl. bd. Advances in Health Scis. Edn., 1995—, Med. Edn., 1995—, Acad. Medicine, 2001—; reviewer: Acad. Medicine, 1989—, Tchg. and Learning in Medicine, 1990—, Jour. Gen. Internal Medicine, 1988—, Am. Ednl. Rsch. Assn., 1987—, Rsch. Med.Edn. Ann. Conf., 1988—; contbr. articles to profl. jours. and chpts. to books; lectr. in field. Recipient Clinician Tchr. award Calif. Regional Soc. Gen. Internal Medicine, 1995, Excellence in Edn. award UCLA Sch. Medicine, 1998. Mem. Am. Assn. Med. Colls. (mem. rsch. med. edn. com. 1990-93, western chair group on ednl. affairs 1995-97, co-dir. fellowship in med. edn. rsch. 1995-97, convenor spl. interest group on faculty devel. 1997-98, chair group on ednl. affairs 1997—), Am. Ednl. Rsch. Assn., Profl. and Orgnl. Devel. Network (mem. nat. core com. 1977-80, 84-86, exec. dir. 1984-85), Phi Beta Kappa. Office: UCLA Sch Medicine Ctr Ednl Devel & Rsch PO Box 951722 Los Angeles CA 90095-1722 Office Phone: 310-794-7018. E-mail: lwilkerson@mednet.ucla.edu.

WILKERSON, MATHA ANN, retired oil company executive; b. Mill Creek, Okla., Sept. 1, 1937; d. Frank and Lottie Evelyn (Cordell) Stie; m. Ronald Gene Wilkerson, Dec. 22, 1956; 1 child, Mitchell Linn. BS in Edn., East Ctrl. U., Ada, Okla., 1966. Elem. sch. tchr. Moore (Okla.) Pub. Schs., 1966—74; office mgr. S. S. Sanbar, M.D., Oklahoma City, 1974—78; ops. mgr., acct. John A. Taylor Oil Co., Oklahoma City, 1978—84; office mgr., controller Lance Ruffel Oil & Gas Corp., Oklahoma City, 1984—2005; ret. Mem. Coun. of Petroleum Accounts Soc. (com. mem. 1979—). Baptist. Avocations: crafts, reading, theater, cooking.

WILKERSON, WILLIAM HOLTON, banker; b. Greenville, NC, Feb. 16, 1947; s. Edwin Cisco and Agnes Holton (Gaskins) W.; m. Ellen Logan Tomskey, Oct. 27, 1973; 1 child, William Holton Jr. AB in Econs., U. N.C., 1970. Asst. v.p. 1st Union Nat. Bank, Greensboro, NC, 1972-77; v.p. Peoples Bank & Trust Co., Rocky Mount, NC, 1977-79, exec. v.p., 1987-89, pres., 1989-90; sr. v.p. Hibernia Nat. Bank, New Orleans, 1979-86; group exec. officer, vice chmn. bd. dirs. Centura Banks, Inc., Rocky Mount, 1990-97, pres., 1998—2001, Wilkerson Co., Inc., Greenville, NC, 2001—. Bd. visitors U. N.C., Chapel Hill, 1999-2003; investment adv. com. City of Greenville. Mem. Greenville-Pitt Assn. Realtors, Rocky Mount C. of C. (bd. dirs. 1989-96, vice chmn. 1992-94, chmn. 1995), Omicron Delta Epsilon, Chi Beta Phi, Phi Sigma Pi. Republican. Home: 407 Rutledge Rd Greenville NC 27858 Office: PO Box 2095 Greenville NC 27836-0095

WILKES, BRENT AMES, management consultant; b. Melrose, Mass., Sept. 30, 1952; s. Gordon Borthwick and Frances (Ames) W.; 1 child, Erin; m. Linda Dadourian, Oct. 18, 1998. Bachelor, U. Mass., 1974; M of Pub. Affairs, U. Conn., 1977. Cert. assn. exec., 1998, assoc. risk mgmt., 1998, ins. cons., 2004. Adminstrv. asst. Town of Tolland, Conn., 1975-76; mgmt. specialist Mass. Dept. Community Affairs, Boston, 1976-79; adminstrv. asst. to mayor City of Gloucester, Mass., 1979-80; assoc. dir., dir. of field svcs. Mass. Mcpl. Assn., Boston, 1980-89; v.p., treas. Mass. Interlocal Ins. Assn., Boston, 1984-89; pres. MMA Consulting Group, Inc., Boston, 1989-94, MMA Mgmt. Svcs. Inc., Boston, 1995-98, N.E. Pub. Risk, Inc., Boston, 1998, Northeast Assn. Mgmt., Inc., Boston, 1999—; v.p., treas. Pub. Employer Risk Mgmt. Assn., Albany, NY, 1989—97, pres., 1997—; bd. dirs. NLC Mut. Ins. Co., 1994—2000. Bd. dirs. Assn. Govt. Risk Pools, 2000—, pres., 2003—05; adj. prof. Suffolk U. Grad. Sch. Mgmt., Boston, 1980—82; lectr. numerous regional and nat. trade assns. Author and editor: Managing Small Towns, 1986; contbr. articles to profl. jours. Mem. fin. com. Town of Acton, Mass., 1977-79; mem. town meeting Town of Reading, Mass., 1987-89; pres. Unitarian Universalist Ch. of Reading, 1990-93. Mem. Am. Soc. Assn. Execs., Internat. City Mgmt. Assn. (cert. in mgmt.), NYC County Mgmt. Assn. Democrat. Unitarian Universalist. Avocations: golf, tennis, volleyball, reading, boating. Office: 9 Cornell Rd Latham NY 12110 Office Phone: 518-220-9815. Business E-Mail: bwilkes@neami.com.

WILKES, DELANO ANGUS, architect; b. Panama City, Fla., Jan. 25, 1935; s. Burnice Angus and Flora Mae (Scott) W.; m. Dona Jean Murren, June 25, 1960 (dec. Nov. 26, 2006). BArch, U. Fla., 1958. Cert. Nat. Coun. Archtl.; registration bds. cert. personal trainer, older adult specialty cert. Am. Coun. on Exercise. Designer Perkins & Will Partnership, Chgo., 1960-63; designer, job capt. Harry Weese, Ltd., Chgo., 1963-66; project arch. Fitch Larocca Carrington, Chgo., 1967-69; arch. Mittelbusher & Tourtelot, Chgo., 1970-71; assoc. Bank Bldg. Corp., Chgo., 1972-75; sr. assoc. Charles Edward Stade & Assocs., Park Ridge, Ill., 1975-77; sr. arch. Consoer Morgan Arch., Chgo., 1977-83, mktg. coord., 1980-83; design cons. Chamlin & Assocs., Peru and Morris, Ill., 1969-82, dir. arch., 1983-86, v.p. arch., 1986-2000. Archtl. cons. Sweet's divsn. McGraw Hill, Inc., Chgo., 1984-90; ptnr. Deri Wilkes Assocs., 1990-95; trainer Fitness Barn, 1995-96, Q Sports Club, 1997-98, Alpha Fitness, 1999-2001; ptnr. River Town Properties, Comml. Devel., Palatka, Fla., 2004; owner Angus Asian Antiques, 2006—. Author: Colonel Ebenezer Folsom, 1778-1789, North Carolina Patriot and Tory Scourge, 1975, Shrangri-La's New Face, 2006; editor Folsom Bull., 1977-80; prodr. documentary film The Angry Minority, Menninger Found., 1978. Mem. coord. com. Dune Acres Plan Commn. (Ind.), 1983-91; bldg. commr. City of Dune Acres, 1984-89; chmn. Ind. party Dune Acres, 1987; elected trustee Dune Acres Town Bd., 1988-91, pres., 1988-89; mem. Dune Acres Civic Improvement Found., 1988-91 (leadership recognition for drive to restore Dune Acres Clubhouse); cons. Inst. of Crippled and Disabled, N.Y.C., 1978-83; guest lectr. field trip guide Coll. DuPage, Glen Ellyn, Ill., 1968-76; guest arch. med. adv. com. to Pres.'s Com. for Handicapped, 1977, 78; vice chmn. Westchester County Dem. Precinct, Porter County, Ind., 1986; chmn. selection com. Dem. Hdqrs., Porter County, 1986; treas. Com. to Elect Kovach to Coun., Porter County, 1986; vice chmn. Duneland Dems., 1988-92; pres. Ocean House Condominium Assn., St. Augustine, Fla., 1993-94; mem. EMMA Concert Assn., 1000—. Mem.: AIA, Putnam County Hist. Soc., New Eng. Hist. Geneal. Soc. (adv. coun. 2007), Am. Soc. Interior Design (coord. info. fair 1979), Chgo. Assn. Commerce and Industry (display dir. 1979 mtg.), Art Inst. Chgo., Chgo. AIA (chmn. design awards display com. 1978-79, prodr. New Mem. Show 1979, chmn. pub. rels. com. 1980), Folsom Family Assn. Am. (pres. 1978-82, v.p. 1982-, nominating chmn. 1983, host ann. meeting, Chgo. 1981), Businessmen for Pub. Interest, Wilkes Family Rsch. Assn., Gargoyle, Soc. Colonial Wars, Chgo. Lyric Opera Guild, Cook County Hist. Soc., German Shorthaired Pointer Club North Fla., Marsh Creek Country Club (mem. archtl. rev. bd. 1999—, chmn. Fla. landscape com. 2003). Democrat. Unitarian Universalist. Home: 332 Marsh Point Cir Saint Augustine FL 32080-5858 Office Phone: 904-471-6956. Personal E-mail: dawilkes@bellsouth.net.

WILKES, JOHN MICHAEL, military officer, auditor; b. Pitts., Dec. 16, 1950; s. John Joseph Wukits and Anne Lebanik. BA in Econs. and Polit. Sci., U. Pitts., 1972; student, La Roche Coll., 1984—88, BS in Acctg. magna cum laude, 1991, MS in Human Resources Mgmt., 1995; AS in Math. and Physics with honors, C.C. Allegheny County, 1998; BS in Natural Scis., U. Pitts., 2004. Spl. accounts mgr. Dell Fastener Corp., Pitts., 1974—78; commd. ens. USN, 1980, advanced through grades to lt. comdr., 1990; auditor Office of Insp. Gen. US Dept. Agr., Hyattsville, Md., 1988—90; sales Sun Book Co., Pitts., 2000—04; asst. engring. dept. Destroyer squadron 10, USS STUMP, 1980—81; lt. missile sys. Destroyer Squadron 22, USS FAHRION, 1983—84, surface combatant with Task Group 60.4 Beirut, 1983—84; asst. tng. officer, staff duty officer Commander Naval Surface Group Mediterranean, 1985—89; pers. officer Naval Embarked Adv. Team, 1996—97. Asst. So Others Might Eat, Wash., DC, 1989—90. Decorated Naval Expeditionary Medal, Nat. Def. Svc. Medal, Sea Svc. Deployment Ribbon. Republican. Cath. Achievements include invention of Decorative Door Guard system; Illuminated Decorative Door Guard System. Avocations: golf, jogging. Home: 208 Lucille St Glenshaw PA 15116

WILKEY, ELMIRA SMITH, illustrator, artist, writer, educator; b. Kankakee, Ill., Dec. 13, 1936; d. Edmond Anthony and Dorothy Agnes (Schilling) Smith; m. Lowell Gene Wilkey; children: Anthony, Eric, Martin, Barry, Tad, Jeremy. BA cum laude, Loretto Heights Coll. (now Regis U.), Denver, 1958. Mgr. Duncan Assocs., Champaign, Ill., 1960-61; English/drama speech tchr. Kankakee Sch. Dist., 1958-60; substitute tchr. Kankakee County, 1965-80; art instr. Kankakee C.C., 1988, 2000; behavior couns. Nutri-Sys., Bourbonnais, Ill., 1987-91; English tchr. Bishop McNamara H.S., Kankakee, 1994-2000; founder, co-owner, printer Studio Sans Serif Divsn., Bronte Press Ltd. Edits., Manteno, Kankakee, Bourbonnais, 1977—. Textbook art cons. DSP, Boston, 1965—74; art adj. Olivet Coll., Bourbonnais, 1993—94; writer, art presenter W.C. Workshops Olivet Coll., Kankakee Art League, 1980—90; design cons. for histories Sisters, Servants of the Holy Heart of Mary, 2002—04; editl. cons. Hoofbeats, 2001; lectr. in field. Illustrator: Come Spring, History of Rockville, with Children's Book Program, cable TV, 1996—99, 11 books including classic, historical prose, poetry, folklore, herbal subjects, and 2 children's books, columnist: Pat's Meanders, 1992—; one-woman shows include Galesburg Civic Art Ctr., 1984, ONU Brandenberg Gallery, 1994—, exhibitions include Prairie State Coll., 1980—, Western Mich. U., exhibited in group shows at Ill. Women in the Arts Invitation, —, Prairie State Coll., 1980, Copley Soc., Boston, 1986, Tall Grass Art Assn., 2001, 2005, 2006, 2007—, Xavier U., 2004, 2005, Vanderpoel, Chgo., 2004—05, Sanctuary Gallery, Ill., 2005, 2006, 2007. Cmty. arts. coun. Kankakee; cmty. art adv. bd. Kankakee C.C.; donates artwork annually to Hospice, Catholic Charities, United Way. Recipient numerous awards in art; Straw Series Signature art technique, V.I.P. Mem. Nat. League Am. Penwomen (Ill. state pres, Chgo. br. v.p. 1979, treas. 2002—04), Ill. State Poetry Soc. (charter), Transparent Watercolor Soc. Am., Nat. Mus. Women in Arts, Great Books (charter, pres. 1980-85), Miniature Book Soc., Christians in Visual Arts. Republican. Roman Catholic. Avocations: walking, herb/plant identification, singing, piano, camping. Home and Office: Studio Sans Serif Divsn The Bronte Press 4136 W 6940N Rd Bourbonnais IL 60914-4208 Office Fax: 815-936-9913. Personal E-mail: miraswilkey@yahoo.com.

WILKEY, MALCOLM RICHARD, retired ambassador, retired judge; b. Murfreesboro, Tenn., Dec. 6, 1918; s. Malcolm Newton and Elizabeth (Gilbert) W.; m. Emma Secul Depolo, Dec. 21, 1959. AB magna cum laude, Harvard U., 1940, LLB, 1948; LLD (hon.), Rose-Hulman Inst. Tech., 1984. Bar: Tex. 1948, NY 1963, US Supreme Ct. 1952, DC 1970. US atty. So. Dist. Tex., 1954-58; asst. atty. gen. US, 1958-61; ptnr. Butler Binion Rice & Cook, 1961-63; gen. counsel, sec. Kennecott Copper Corp., 1963-70; judge US Ct. Appeals DC Cir., 1970-85; US amb. to Uruguay, 1985-90. Ofcl. in charge fed. forces at Little Rock Sch. Crisis, Dept. Justice, 1958; mem. US-Chile Arbitration Commn., 1991-97; lectr. internat. constl. and adminstrv. law London Poly., 1979, 80; lectr. Tulane U. Law Summer Sch., Grenoble, France, 1981, 83, San Diego Law Summer Sch., Oxford, Eng., 1983, Brigham Young Law Sch., 1984, 93; vis. fellow Wolfson Coll., Cambridge U., 1985; chmn. Pres.'s Commn. on Revision Fed. Ethics Laws, 1989; spl. counsel to Atty. Gen. for inquiry into the House Banking Facility, 1992. Author: Is It Time For A Second Constitutional Convention, 1995, As the Twig is Bent, 2003. Del. Rep. Nat. Conv., 1960. Served from 2d lt. to lt. col. AUS, 1941-45. Named Am. mem., Fulbright Commn., 2002—; hon. fellow, Wolfson Coll., Cambridge. Fellow Am. Bar Found.; mem. Am. Law Inst. (adv. com. restatement fgn. rels. law of US), Jud. Conf. US (com. on standards for admission to fed. cts. 1976-79), Phi Beta Kappa, Delta Sigma Rho, Phi Delta Phi (hon.). Republican. Address: Av El Bosque 379 Providencia Santiago Chile E-mail: mrw@wilkey.us.

WILKIE, DONALD WALTER, retired biologist, aquarium administrator; b. Vancouver, BC, Can., June 20, 1931; s. Otway James Henry and Jessie Margaret (McLeod) W.; m. Patricia Ann Archer, May 18, 1980; children: Linda, Douglas, Susanne. BA, U. B.C., 1960, M.Sc., 1966. Curator Vancouver Pub. Aquarium, 1961-63, Phila. Aquarama, 1963-65; exec. dir. aquarium-mus. Scripps Instn. Oceanography, La Jolla, Calif., 1965-93, exec. dir. emeritus, 1993—; founding dir. Birch Aquarium of Scripps, 1992. Cons. aquarium design, rschg. exhibit content; sci. writer and editor naturalist-marine edn. programs. coach, Scholastic Clay Targets Prog. Author books on aquaria and marine ednl. materials; contbr. numerous articles to profl. jours. Bd. mem. San Diego Shotgun Sports Assn.; pres. UCSD Retirement Assn. 1999-02. Mem. San Diego (Calif.) Zool. Soc. Home: 4548 Cather Ave San Diego CA 92122-2632 Office: U Calif San Diego Scripps Instn Oceanography Libr 9500 Gilman Dr La Jolla CA 92093-0219 E-mail: dwilkie@ucsd.edu, donwilkie1@mac.com. *As a biologist and teacher my major goal has been to increase public interest in learning about our environment and promoting proper use of the earth's resources.*

WILKIE, ROBERT LEON, JR., federal agency administrator; b. Frankfort, Germany, Aug. 6, 1962; s. Robert Leon and Joy Ann (Somerville) W.; m. Julia Cameron Bullard, May 19, 1990; children: Adam, Megan BA cum laude, Wake Forest U., 1985; JD, Loyola of the South, 1988; LLM in Internat. Law & Legis., Georgetown U., 1992; M in Strategic Studies, US Army War coll., 2002. Legis. counsel U.S. Senator Jesse Helms, Washington, 1988-95; legis. dir. U.S. Rep. David Funderburk, 1995; dir. N.C. Republican Party, 1996-97; counsel & adv. to Senate Majority Leader Trent Lott US Senate, 1997—2003; sr. dir. NSC, Washington, 2003—05; spl. asst. to Pres. for nat. security affairs The White House, Washington, 2003—05; prin. dep. asst. sec for legis. affairs US Dept. Def., Washington, 2005—06, acting asst. sec. for legis. affairs, 2006, asst. sec. for legis. affairs, 2006—. Mem. Loyola Moot Ct. Bd., 1988. Author newspaper polit. editorials, 1990-93. Staff mem. Rep. Nat. Conv., 1992. Intelligence officer USNR. Recipient Bustamonte award for outstanding achievement in internat. law The Soc. Jesus, New Orleans, 1987, Am. Jurisprudence awards for excellence in Latin Am. law Internat. Law and Legislation, 1987-88; named Jr. Intelligemce Officer (Res.) of the Yr., Office Naval Intelligence Mem. ABA, Rep. Nat. Lawyers Assn., The Federalist Soc. Republican. Roman Catholic. Avocations: English history, mil. history, So. history and lit., distance running. Office: US Dept Def 1300 Def Pentagon Rm 3D747 Washington DC 20301 *

WILKIE, VALLEAU, JR., foundation executive; b. Summit, NJ, July 3, 1923; s. Valleau and Amelia (Parry); children: Janice, Robert. AB, Yale U., 1948; MA, Harvard U., 1954. Instr. history Phillips Acad., 1948-59; headmaster Gov. Dummer Acad., Byfield, Mass., 1959-72, mem. bd. trustees, 1960-72, dir. devel., 1972-73; exec. v.p. Sid W. Richardson Found., Ft. Worth, 1973—. Bd. dirs. Nat. Charities Info. Bureau Bd. dirs. S.W. Ednl. Devel. Lab., 1976-82, pres. 1981-82; mem. Council on Founds., Inc., 1980—, bd. dirs., 1981-87, chmn. bd., 1985-87; bd. dirs. Conf. of S.W. Founds., 1977-82, pres., 1981-82; bd. dirs. Found. Ctr., 1982-91, Nat. Charities Info. Bur., 1991—. Served to 1st lt. USAAF, 1942-45. Mem. Headmasters Assn., N.E. Assn. Schs. and Colls. (chmn. commn. on ind. secondary schs. 1967-70, pres. 1972-73), Delta Kappa Epsilon. Episcopalian. Office: Sid Richardson Museum 201 Main St Ste 180 Fort Worth TX 76102-3142

WILKIN, ALANA ZIMMER, elementary school educator; b. Danville, Pa., June 3, 1961; d. Albert Arthur and Alma Clara Zimmer; m. Timothy Vail Wilkin; children: Brandon Zimmer Madura, Albert Peyton Madura. BA, Thiel Coll., Greenville, Pa., 1983; MS, U. South Ala., Mobile, 1998. Cert. med. technologist Am. Soc. Clin. Pathologists, 1984, specialist in blood banking Am. Soc. Clin. Pathologists, 1984. Med. technologist Montefiore Hosp., Pitts., 1984—85, St. Elizabeth Hosp., West Lafayette, Ind., 1985—86; blood bank specialist St. Lukes Episcopal Hosp., Houston, 1986—87; quality control technologist Gamma Biologicals, Houston, 1987—90; med. technologist - tng. specialist ARC, Mobile, 1990—97; quality control mgr./trainer Gamma Biologicals, Houston, 1997—2001; tchr. lang. arts Cypress-Fairbanks Ind. Sch. Dist., Houston, 2001—. Recipient Spotlight Tchr., Cypress-Fairbanks Ind. Sch. Dist., 2006. Mem.: Assn. Tex. Profl. Educators, Pi Lambda Theta, Kappa Delta Pi. Home: 13311 Blackbird Dr Cypress TX 77429 Office: Lowery Elem 15950 Ridge Park Houston TX 77095 Home Phone: 281-970-7143; Office Phone: 281-463-5900. Business E-Mail: alana.wilkin@cfisd.net.

WILKIN, LINDA D., sports medicine physician, educator; b. Columbus, Ohio, June 7, 1947; d. Guy S. and Hilda L. Sargent; 1 child, Jason N. PhD, Ohio State U., Columbus, 2002. Asst. prof. Calif. State U., San Bernardino, 2002—. Mem.: Nat. Strength and Conditioning Assn., Am. Coll. Sports Medicine. Office: Calif State Univ San Bernardino 5500 University Pky San Bernardino CA 92407 Home Phone: 909-534-0617; Office Phone: 909-537-7236. Office Fax: 909-537-7085. Business E-Mail: lwilkin@csusb.edu.

WILKIN, RICHARD EDWIN, clergyman, religious organization administrator; b. nr. Paulding, Ohio, Nov. 3, 1930; s. Gaylord D. and Beulah E. (Tarlton) W.; m. Barbara A. Zehender, Aug. 10, 1952; children— Richard Edward, James Lee, Deborah Ann. Student, Giffin Jr. Coll., 1948-49; BS, Findlay Coll., 1952, D.D., 1975; postgrad., Ind. U., 1959-60. Ordained to ministry Churches of God Gen. Conf., 1953; pastor Neptune Ch. of God, Celina, Ohio, 1952-59, Wharton (Ohio) Ch. of God, 1959-64, Anthony Wayne Ch. of God, Ft. Wayne, Ind., 1964-70; adminstr., chief exec. Chs. of God Gen. Conf., Findlay, Ohio, 1970-87; supr. mission work India, Bangladesh, Haiti, 1970-85; dir. field edn. and Inst. for Biblical Studies, faculty mem. Winebrenner Theol. Sem., Findlay, 1987-92, adj. facult O.T., 1993-97; interim sr. pastor Coll. 1st Ch. of God, Findlay, 1992-93. Dir. summer youth camps, sec., mem. exec. com. Ohio Conf., 1952-59, state clk., pres., 1959-64; chmn. Commn. on Edn., mem. exec. com. Ind. Conf., 1964-70; adv. com. Am. Bible Soc.; steering com. U.S. Ch. Leaders, 1979; pres. Ft. Wayne Ministerial Assn.; bd. dirs. Associated Chs. of Ft. Wayne and Allen County, 1966-70; tchr. Center Twp. Jr. High Sch., Celina, Mendon (Ohio) Union High Sch., Van Del High Sch., Van Wert, Ohio, 1954-59; interim pastor Shawnee First Ch. of God, Lima, Ohio, 1987-88, ch. cons., 1987-98. Vice pres. bd. trustees Winebrenner Haven, mem. adv. com. in race rels. regarding sch. reorgn. and busing, Ft. Wayne, 1967-69; trustee Winebrenner Theol. Sem., 1980-87, sec. bd. trustees; trustee U. Findlay, 1985—, chmn. com. trustees; sec. bd. of pensions Gen. Conf., Ch. of God, 1986-99; bd. dirs. Found. Great Lakes, Conf. Chs. of God, 1998-2006, chmn. adminstr.'s adv. com., 1998-2003. Recipient Outstanding Tchr. award, 1958; Disting. Alumnus award Findlay Coll., 1973, Outstanding Leadership award Ohio Conf. Chs. of God, 1986, Disting. Assoc. award U. Findlay, 1992; named Hon. Alumnus Winebrenner Theol. Sem., 1978.

WILKINS, ADDI L., retired lay worker; b. Gleason, Tenn., June 9, 1933; d. Roy Thomas and Sendy Estelle Wilkins; children from previous marriage: Raybarn, Regina, Theresa, Roscoe, Anthony. At, Stowe Coll., St. Louis, 1953—55, St. Louis U., 1987, Valparaiso U., Ind., 1988. Consecrated Luth. Deaconess Assn., 1989. Adminstrv. asst. All Nation and Transfiguration Luth. Ch., St. Louis, coord. social ministry. Sec. no. zone women's group Luth. Women's Missionary League, St. Louis; sec. dist. bd. social ministry Luth. Family Svc. Luth. Ch. Mo. Synod; spkr. to ch. and youth groups. Chmn. bd. Pruitt Igo Devel. Housing Corp., St. Louis; bd. dir. United Ch. Christ Neighbor Houses, Friends of Moms; bd. mem. Luth. Family and Children Svcs. Named Mother of Yr., Sigma Gamma Rho (St. Louis chpt.), 1989; recipient Cmty. Svc. award, Nat. Coun. Negro Women, 2004, Star Bethel Bapt. Ch., 2004. Mem.: Luth. Deaconess Assn. Democrat. Lutheran. Avocations: gardening, reading, crafts, quilting. Home: 1905 E Warne Ave Saint Louis MO 63107-1017 Office Phone: 314-385-2653.

WILKINS, AMY P., publishing executive; BA, Holy Cross Coll. Assoc. pub., advt. dir. Health Mag., 1994—95, pub., 1995—97; pres. Petersen Youth Group1, 1997—98; pub. Biography Mag., 1998—2000, Smithsonian, Smithsonian Air & Space Mag., 2000, Better Homes and Gardens Mag., Country Home, 2006—. Office: Country Home Mag Meredith Publ 375 Lexington Ave New York NY 10017-5514 *

WILKINS, BARRATT (GEORGE WILKINS), librarian; b. Atlanta, Nov. 6, 1943; s. George Barratt and Mabel Blanche (Brooks) W. BA, Emory U., 1965; MA, Ga. State U., 1968, U. Wis., 1969. Reference libr. SC State Libr., Columbia, 1969-71; instl. libr. cons. Mo. State Libr., Jefferson City, 1971-73; asst. state libr. State Libr. Fla., Tallahassee, 1973-77, state libr., 1977—2003; dir. div. Libr. and Info. Svcs. State Fla., Tallahassee, 1986—2003; acting asst. sec. state Fla. Dept. of State, 1987. Abstractor Hist. Abstracts, 1967—71; dir. survey project Nat. Ctr. Edn. Stats., 1976—77, chmn. state libr. agys. survey steering coun., 2003—; bd. dirs. S.E. Libr. Network, Inc., 1979—82, treas., 1980—81, vice chmn., 1981—82; mem. adv. coun. US Pub. Printer, 1983—86, S.E. Atlantic Regional Med. Libr. Svcs., 1986—89; mem. planning com. Fla. Automated Edn. Commn., 1989—94; del The White House Conf., Libr., Info Svcs., 1991; mem. steering com. pub., state libr. surveys Nat. Ctr. Edn. Stats., 1992—; mem. adv. coun. Fla. State Bd. Ind. Colleges, Universities, 1995—98, Fla. State U. Sch. Info. Studies, 1999—2000; mem. pub. libr. surveys Nat. Ctr. Ednl. Stats., 1997—2003; mem. privacy, tech. task force State Fla., 2000—01; mem. Speakers Legis. Hist. Preservation Com., 2000—03; mem. libr. stats. revision com. Nat. Info. Stds. Orgn., 2001—03; del The White House Conf. Sch. Librs., 2002; bd. dirs. First Am. Found., Inc., Fla. Distance Learning Network, Inc.; mem. planning com. Fla. Gov.'s Conf. Libraries, Info. svcs.; cons. in field. Contbr. articles profl. jours. Mem. adv. com. statewide jail project Mo. Assn. Social Welfare, 1971-73, bd. dirs. ctrl. divsn., 1971-73; mem. State Univ. System Interinstl. Lib. Com., 1977-2003; bd. dirs. Fla. Ctr. Libr. Automation, 1984-2003, Fla. Ctr. for the Book, 1984—, Fla. Coll. Ctr. for Libr. Automation, 1990-2003, Coun. for Fla. Librs., 1981—; pres. Rose Hollow Homeowners Assn., 2004-; patron Atlanta Hist. Soc., Hist. Oakland Found. Recipient Leadership Achievement award Assn. Specialized and Coop. Libr. Agys., 1991, Outstanding Pub. Svc. award Gov. of Fla., 1991, Keppel award and Lorenz award Nat. Ctr. Edn. Stats., 1995—, Profl. Achievement award Assn. Specialized and Coop. Libr. Agencies, 2003, Disting. Alumni award U. Wis. Sch. Libr. and Info. Studies, 2003; U. Wis. fellow, 1969. Mem.: ALA (coun. 1981-85, legis. com. 1982-86, com. on orgn. 1988-90, planning com., 1993-95, standards, 1996-98, legis. honor roll 1996), Assn. State Libr. Agys. (pres. 1976-77), Assn. Hosp. Instl. Librs. (bd. dirs. 1973-74), Am. Correctional Assn. (chair instn. libr. com. 1975-80), Southeastern Libr. Assn. (pres. 1982-84), Assn. Specialized and Coop. Libr. Agys. (bd. dirs. 1981-85, 87-89, stds. rev. 1997—2003, chair awards com., 2003-05, chair legis. com., 2005-), Fla. Libr. Assn. (hon. life mem.), Libr. Adminstrn. and Mgmt. Assn. (chair govt. affair com. 1984-86), Chief Officers of State Libr. Agys. (bd. dirs. 1980-82, pres. 1990-92, chair legis. com. 1992-96, chair rsch. & stats. com. 1998-2003), Univ. Club, Gov.'s Club, Beta Phi Mu, Phi Alpha Theta. Episcopalian. E-mail: barratt.wilkins@mac.com.

WILKINS, BURLEIGH TAYLOR, philosophy educator; b. Bridgetown, Va., July 1, 1932; s. Burleigh and Helen Marie (Taylor) W.; children: Brita Taylor, Carla Cowgill, Burleigh William. BA summa cum laude, Duke U., 1952; MA, Harvard U., 1954, Princeton U., 1963, PhD, 1965. Instr. MIT, Cambridge, 1957-60, Princeton U., 1960-61, 63; asst. prof. Rice U., Houston, 1965-66, assoc. prof., 1966-67, U. Calif., Santa Barbara, 1967-68, prof., 1968—. Author: Carl Becker, 1961, The Problem of Burke's Political Philosophy, 1967, Hegel's Philosophy of History, 1974, Has History Any Meaning?, 1978, Terrorism and Collective Responsibility, 1992. Mem.: Phi Beta Kappa. Office: U Calif Dept Philosophy Santa Barbara CA 93106

WILKINS, CAROLINE HANKE, advocate, political organization worker; b. Corpus Christi, Tex., May 12, 1937; d. Louis Allen and Jean Guckian Hanke; m. B. Hughel Wilkins, 1957; 1 child, Brian Hughel. Student, Tex. Coll. Arts and Industries, 1956—57, Tex. Tech. U., 1957—58; BA, U. Tex., 1961; MA magna cum laude, U. Ams., 1964. Instr. history Oreg. State U., 1967-68; adminstr. Consumer Svcs. divsn. State of Oreg., 1977-80, Wilkins Assoc., 1980—. Mem. PFMC Salmon Adv. subpanel, 1982-86. Author: (with B. H. Wilkins) Implications of the U.S.-Mexican Water Treaty for Interregional Water Transfer, 1968. Mem. Kerr Libr. Bd., Oreg. State U., 1989—95, pres., 1994—95; mem. Corvallis-Benton County Libr. Found., 1991—2001, sec., 1993, v.p., 1994, pres., 1995, mission and goals com. chair, 2000—01; pres. Oreg. State-Corvallis chpt. UNIFEM, 1998—2002; mem. Women and Philanthropy, Oreg. State U. Giving Cir., 2003—, Oreg. Jud. Fitness and Disability Commn., 2004—, vice chair, 2006, chair, 2007; Dem. precinct committeewoman Benton County, Oreg., 1964—90; publicity chmn. Benton County Gen. Election, 1964; chmn. Get-Out-the-Vote Com., Benton County, 1966; vice chmn. Benton County Dem. Ctrl. Com., 1966—70, 1st Congl. Dist., Oreg., 1966—67, chmn., 1967—68; vice chmn. Dem. Party of Oreg., 1968—69, chmn., 1969—74; mem. exec. com. Western States Dem. Conf., 1970—72; vice chmn. Dem. Nat. Com., 1972—77, mem. arrangements com., 1972, 1976, mem. Dem. Charter Commn., 1973—74, mem., 1972—77, 1985—89, mem. size and composition com., 1987—89, mem. rules com., 1988; mem. ethics commn. Oreg. Govt., 1974—76; del., mem. rules com. Dem. Nat. Conv., 1988; 1st v.p. Nat. Fedn. Dem. Women, 1983—85, pres., 1985—87, parliamentarian, 1993—95, 1999—2001, chair Pres.'s coun., 2001—03, chair by-laws com., 2003—05, parliamentarian, 2005—, western regional dir., 2005—; pres. Oreg. Fedn. Dem. Women, 1997—2001; bd. dirs. Oreg. chpt. US Lighthouse Soc., pres., 1997—98; bd. dirs. Oreg. State U.-Corvallis Symphony, 1998—2001, v.p., 1999—2000, resources com., mem. endowment task force, 2007; bd. dirs. Oreg. State U. Acad. Lifelong Learning, 2003—. Named Outstanding Mem. Nat. Fedn. Dem. Women, 1992, Woman of Achievement, Oreg. State U. Women's Ctr., 1998. Mem.: Soc. Consumer Affairs Profls., Nat. Assn. Consumer Agy. Adminstrs., Oreg. State U. Folk Club (pres. faculty wives 1989—90, scholarship chair 2000—01, grants com. 2002—03), Zonta Internat. (vice area bd. dirs. dist. 8 1992—94, bd. dist. 8 1994—96, by laws and resolutions chair 1997—98, internat. rels. coord. dist. 8 2000—02, chair dist. 8 nominating com. 2003—06, chair 2005—06, parliamentarian 2006—, Zonta Internat. Found. bd. dirs. 2007—, chair devel. com. 2007—). Office: 3311 NW Roosevelt Dr Corvallis OR 97330-1169

WILKINS, CHARLES L., chemist, educator; b. LA, Aug. 14, 1938; s. Richard and Lenore M. Wilkins; m. Ingrid Fritsch, 1997; children: Mark R., Connor W. Fritsch, Eric. BS, Chapman Coll., 1961; PhD, U. Oreg., 1966. Prof. chemistry U. Nebr., Lincoln, 1967-81; prof. U. Calif., Riverside, 1981-98; disting. prof. U. Ark., Fayetteville, 1998—. Recipient Frank H. Field and Joe L. Franklin award for Outstanding Achievement in mass spectrometry, Am. Chem. Soc., 1997, Eastern Analytical Symposium award in the fields of Analytical Chemistry, 2002, Alumni Disting. Achievement award, Ark. U., 2003, Alumni Achievement award, U. Oreg. Dept. Chemistry, 2004—05, Fulbright Coll. Master Rschr.; award, 2006. Fellow: Soc. Applied Spectroscopy (life). Office: U Ark Dept Chem & Biochem Fayetteville AR 72701 E-mail: cwilkins@uark.edu.

WILKINS, CHRISTOPHER PUTNAM, conductor; b. Boston, May 28, 1957; s. Herbert Putnam and Angela (Middleton) W. BA, Harvard U., 1978; MusM, Yale U., 1981. Condr.-in-residence SUNY, Purchase, 1981-82; asst. condr. Oreg. Symphony, Portland, 1982-83, Cleve. Orch., 1983-86; assoc. condr. Utah Symphony, Salt Lake City, from 1986; condr. Colo. Springs Symphony Orch., 1989-96, artistic advisor, 1998—; music dir. San Antonio Symphony, 1992—. Condr. Exxon Arts Endowment, 1982-86. Office: San Antonio Symphony Po Box 658 San Antonio TX 78293-0658 Home: 11 Edmonds Rd Concord MA 01742-2649

WILKINS, DAVID BRIAN, law educator, director; b. Chgo., Jan. 22, 1956; BA in Govt., Harvard U., 1977, JD, 1980. Bar: DC 1982. Law clk. to Hon. Wilfred Feinberg US Ct. Appeals 2nd Cir., NY, 1980—81; law clk. to Justice Thurgood Marshall US Supreme Ct., 1981—82; assoc. Nussbaum, Owen & Webster, Washington, 1982—86; asst. prof. law Harvard Law Sch., Cambridge, Mass., 1986—92, dir. program on the legal profession, 1991—, prof., 1992—, Kirkland and Ellis prof. law, 1996—, dir. Ctr. Lawyers and the Profl. Svcs. Industry, 2006—. Dir. Ctr. Lawyers and Profl. Svcs. Industry, 2004—. Office: Harvard Law Sch Ctr Lawyers and the Profl Svcs Industry 23 Everett St Cambridge MA 02138 Office Phone: 617-495-0958. Office Fax: 617-496-8489. Business E-Mail: dwilkins@law.harvard.edu.

WILKINS, DAVID GEORGE, fine arts educator; b. Battle Creek, Mich., Sept. 12, 1939; s. George Henry and Marjorie Ewing (Pierce) Wilkins; m. Ann Thomas, June 25, 1966; children: Rebecca Louise, Katherine May. BA, Oberlin Coll., 1961; MA, U. Mich., 1963, PhD, 1969. Instr. U. N.H., Durham, 1963—64; prof. dept. history of art and arch. U. Pitts., 1967—, chair, 1989—92, 1998—2004, dir. univ. art gallery, 1976—92. Faculty mem summer sessions Sarah Lawrence Col-Univ Mich, Florence, Italy, 1975—81, Duguesne U., Rome, 2004, Rome, 07. Author (with Bernard Schultz and Katheryn M Linduff): Art Past/Art Present, 2004; author: (with Bonnie Bennett) Donatello, 1984, Maso di Banco, 1985; author: (with K J Arbitman) The Illustrated Bartsch, Vol 53, Pre-Rembrandt Etchers, 1985, The Art of the Duquesne Club, 2002; author: (with Mark M Brown and Lu Donnelly) The History of the Duquesne Club, 1989; author: (with F. Hartt) History of Italian Renaissance Art, 6th edit., 2006; editor (with Rebecca L Wilkins): The Search for a Patron in the Middle Ages and the Renaissance, 1996; editor: (with Sheryl Reiss) Beyond Isabella: Secular Women Patrons of Art in the Italian Renaissance, 2001; editor: The Collins Big Book of Art, 2005, A Reflection of Faith: St. Paul Cathedral, Pittsburgh, 1906-2006, 2007. Mem Humanities Coun, 1984—88; mus adv panel Pa Coun Arts, 1985—87; bd dirs Pittsburgh Ctr Arts, 1979—98; Mendelssohn Choir Pittsburgh, 1979—84. Recipient Chancellor's Disting. Tchg. award, U. Pitts., 1987; fellow William E. Suida, Kress Found, Kunsthistorisches Inst, Florence, 1966—67. Mem.: Renaissance Soc. Am., Italian Art Soc., Coll. Art Assn. (Disting. Tchg. Art History award 2005). Democrat. Home: 1217 Shady Ave Pittsburgh PA 15232-2811 E-mail: dgw2@pitt.edu.

WILKINS, DAVID HORTON, ambassador, former state legislator; b. Greenville, SC, Oct. 12, 1946; m. Susan Clary; children: James, Robert. BA (hon.), Clemson U., 1968; JD, U. SC, 1971; degree (hon.), Med. U. SC, Citadel. Bar: SC. Mem. SC House Reps., 1980—2005, chmn. judiciary com., 1986—92, spkr. pro tempore, 1992-95, spkr., 1995—2005; US amb. to Can. US Dept. State, Ottawa, 2005—. Adj. prof. Greenville Tech. Coll., 1972—94; chmn. Greenville County Legis. Del., 1985—86; pres. Nat. Spkrs. Assn., 1998—2005; fellow Am. Acad. Matrimonial Lawyers. Served in US Army, 1971, served in USAR, 1973—76. Recipient Friend of the Taxpayer award SC Assn. Taxpayers, others; named Outstanding Legislator of Yr. by SC C. of C., Dept. Probation of Parole, SC Sch. Bds. Assn., SC Troopers Assn., others, Nat. Rep. Legislator of Yr. Nat. Rep. Legis. Assn. Republican. Baptist. Office: DOS Amb 5480 Ottawa Pl Washington DC 20521-5480 *

WILKINS, DOMINIQUE (JACQUES DOMINIQUE WILKINS), professional sports team executive, retired professional basketball player; b. Orléans, France, Jan. 12, 1960; came to US, 1964; s. John and Geraldine Wilkins; m. Nicole Berry, Sept. 26, 1992 (div.); children: Iyisha, Chloe; m. Robin Wilkins; 2 children. BBA, U. Ga., 1982. Player Atlanta Hawks, 1982—94, LA Clippers, 1994, Boston Celtics, 1994—95, Panathinaikos-Athens, Greece, 1995—96, San Antonio Spurs, 1996—97, Teamsystem, Bologna, Italy, 1997—98, Orlando Magic, 1998—99, Anaheim Roadrunners, 2000; spl. asst. to the exec. v.p., player devel. asst. to v.p. basketball Atlanta Spirit, LLC (parent co. of NBA Atlanta Hawks, NHL Atlanta Thrashers and Philips Arena). Named to NBA All-Rookie Team, 1983, NBA All-Star Team, 1986-94, All-NBA First Team, 1986, Ga. Sports Hall of Fame, 2004, Atlanta Sports Hall of Fame, 2005, Naismith Basketball Hall of Fame, 2006 Achievements include holding a single game record for most free throws without a miss (23), 1992; 9th all-time leading scorer in NBA history; NBA scoring leader, 1986; NBA slam dunk champion NBA, 1985, 90; won European Championship as a member of Panathinaikos-Athens, 1996. Office: Atlanta Spirit LLC 101 Marietta St NW Ste 1900 Atlanta GA 30303 Office Phone: 404-878-3800. *

WILKINS, EARLE WAYNE, JR., retired surgery educator; b. Albany, NY, Aug. 17, 1919; s. Earle Wayne and Mildred Anna (Dana) W.; m. Suzanne Porter, Aug. 26, 1944; children: Clinton Porter, Wendy Dana Wilkins Hopkins, Wayne Lawrence. AB, Williams Coll., 1941; MD, Harvard U., 1944. Diplomate Am. Bd. Surgery, Am. Bd. Thoracic Surgery. Surg. resident Mass. Gen. Hosp., Boston, 1944-46, 48-51, mem. staff, 1952-59, vis. surgeon, 1968-78; mem. staff Harvard Med. Sch., Boston, 1953—, clin. prof. surgery, 1979-89, prof. emeritus, 1989—. Fulbright vis. prof. Allgemeines Krankenhaus, Vienna, Austria, 1964-65; vis. prof. Nat. Def. Med. Ctr., Taipei, Taiwan, 1989; surgeon Boston Bruins Hockey Club, 1969-85; physician tech. advisor Divsn. Emergency Med. Svcs., Washington, 1977-81, med. dir. Mass. Region IV, Boston, 1980-82; chmn. bd. Boston Med. Flight, 1985-87; Earle W. Wilkins, Jr. vis. prof. MGH, 1998. Editor: Current Therapy in Cardiothoracic Surgery, 1989, Esophageal Cancer, 1988, Emergency Medicine: Scientific Foundations and Current Practice, 1989; contbr. numerous articles to profl. jours. Trustee Williams Coll., Williamstown, Mass., 1971-89, pres. Soc. of Alumni, 1967-69. Lt. (j.g.) USNR, 1946-48. Recipient Sports Illustrated Silver Anniversary All-Am. award Time Inc., N.Y.C., 1965, Commonwealth award Commonwealth of Mass., 1986, Disting. Alumnus award Albany Acad., 1988, Rogerson Cup Williams Coll., 1991, Bicentennial medal Williams Coll., 1993. Fellow ACS, Am. Surg. Assn.; mem. AMA, Mass. Med. Soc., Boston Surg. Soc., Am. Assn. Thoracic Surgery (councillor 1984-88), Soc. Thoracic Surgeons, New England Surg. Soc. (pres. 1980-81), Gen. Thoracic Surg. Club, Taconic Golf Club (pres. 1990-95). Republican. Achievements include Emergency Dept. No. Adams Regional Hosp., 2004, named in honor of. Avocations: golf, tennis, skiing, travel, stamps. Home: 240 South St Williamstown MA 01267-2822

WILKINS, FLOYD, JR., retired lawyer; b. Fowler, Calif., Sept. 8, 1925; s. Floyd and Kathryn (Springborg) W.; m. Holly Blee, June 18, 1949 (div. Jan. 1964); children: Douglas B., Janet H., Steven B., Kevin D.; m. Sybil Ann Perrault, Feb. 22, 1964. BS, U. Calif., Berkeley, 1946; LLB, Harvard U., 1952. Bar: N.Y. 1953, Calif. 1959. Assoc. Dwight, Royall, Harris, Koegel & Caskey, NYC, 1952-58; v.p., trust officer San Diego Trust & Savs. Bank, 1958-63; assoc., then ptnr., prin. Seltzer Caplan Wilkins & McMahon, P.C. and predecessors, San Diego, 1963-91. Lectr. U. So. Calif. Tax Inst., L.A., 1975, Title Ins. and Trust Co., L.A. and Santa Ana, Calif., 1973, 78, 83, Trust Svcs. of Am. Tax Forum, San Diego, U. Calif. Continuing Edn. of Bar, San Diego, 1977-91. Bd. dirs., pres. San Diego County Citizens Scholarship Found. Served with USNR, 1944-46. Mem. ABA, State Bar Calif., San Diego County Bar Assn. Republican. Avocations: travel, photography, wine, gardening. Home: 2005 Soledad Ave La Jolla CA 92037-3904 Personal E-mail: fwilkins@san.rr.com.

WILKINS, FRED CLAYTON, physician, educator, engineer; b. Barnwell, SC, Aug. 18, 1958; s. Fred C. Wilkins and Mary Josephine Erskine; m. Sharon Rawls Wilkins, Dec. 1, 1990 (dec. June 26, 2004); 1 child, Marshall Clayton. BS in Applied Sciences and Engring., US Mil. Acad., West Point, 1980; MS in Systems Mgmt., U. So. Calif., 1988; MD, U. Miss. Med. Ctr., 1997; M in Biomedical Sci., U. Miss., Jackson, 2004. Cert. flight instr. FAA, 1991. Airborne inf. officer Inf. Ctr., Fort Benning, Ga., 1980—81; flight instr. Army Aviation Ctr., Fort Rucker, Ala., 1982—84; aviation platoon leader Fourth Squadron, Seventh US Cav., Uijongbu, Republic of Korea, 1984—85; aviation maintenance co. comdr. Fifth Squadron, Seventeenth Air Cav., Fort Hood, Tex., 1986—88; sr. test program engr. USAF, Eglin, Fla., 1989—90; state aviation standardization officer Miss. Army N.G., Jackson, 1990—91; family practice resident Naval Hosp. Pensacola, Fla., 1997—98; dir. clin. services, sr. med. officer Naval Air Sta. Whiting Field, Pensacola, 1999—2002; naval aviator, flight surgeon dual designator Chief Naval Air Tng., Pensacola, 2003—. Adj. prof. Pensacola Jr. Coll., Fla., 2003—. Editor: (aviation textbook) Naval Helicopter Aerodynamics. Maj. US Army, 1980—93, Republic of Korea, lt. comdr. USN, 1997—2007. Recipient Proctor and Gamble Profl. Opportunity award, Am. Physiology Soc., 1993, Outstanding Student award, Miss. State Legislature and Bd. Higher Edn., 1997; fellow, Glaxo Rsch. Inst., 1993-1995; Hearin-Hess Scholarship, U. Miss., 1991-1992, Dean's Scholarship, 1992-1995, Health Profession Scholarship, USN, 1993-1997. Mem.: Am. Bd. Utilization Rev. and Quality Assurance (assoc.), US Naval Inst. (life), Army Aviation Assn. Am. (life; treas. 1982—83), Assn. Mil. Surgeons of the US (life). Christian. Avocations: flying, travel, sailing, scuba diving, tennis. Home Phone: 850-981-0822. Personal E-mail: clay.wilkins@navy.mil.

WILKINS, JEFFREY M., computer company executive; Co-founder CompuServe, 1969; founder Discovery Sys., 1985-91; pres., CEO Metatec Corp., Dublin, Ohio, 1991—, chmn. bd. dirs. Office: Metatec Internat Inc 7001 Metatec Blvd Dublin OH 43017-3219

WILKINS, JOHN P., university librarian; BA, Antioch Coll., 1979; MA in English, U. Va., 1980; MLS, U. Tenn., 1986. Rsch. libr. resident U. Mich., Ann Arbor, 1986—88, data svcs. libr., English selector, 1988—92, head Humanities Text Initiative, 1994—96, head Digital Libr. Production Svc., 1996—, interim assoc. dir. Digital Libr. Svcs., 2002, assoc. univ. libr. Libr. Info. Tech., 2003—, interim co-univ. libr., 2006—07; sys. libr. info. svcs. U. Va., Charlottesville, 1992—94. Contbr. articles to profl. jours. Office: Libr Adminstrn U Mich 818 Hatcher S Ann Arbor MI 48109-1205 Office Phone: 734-764-9356. Office Fax: 734-763-5080. E-mail: jpwilkin@umich.edu.

WILKINS, JOHN WARREN, physics professor; b. Des Moines, Mar. 11, 1936; s. Carl Daniel and Ruth Elizabeth (Warren) W. BS in Engring, Northwestern U., 1959; MS, U. Ill., 1960, PhD, 1963; DTech (hon.), Chalmers Tekniska Hogskola, Göteborg, 1990. NSF fellow U. Cambridge, Eng., 1963-64; asst. prof. physics Cornell U., 1964-68, assoc. prof., 1968-74, prof., 1974-88; eminent scholar, prof. physics Ohio State U., 1988—. Vis. prof. H.C. Ørsted Inst., Copenhagen, 1968, Nordita, Copenhagen, 1972-73, 75-76, 79-81; cons. Los Alamos Nat. Lab., 1984—, Lawrence Livermore Nat. Lab., 1997—; adv. com. U. Chgo. Sci. and Tech., 1990—. Assoc. editor Physica Scripta, 1977-85, Phys. Rev. Letters, 1982-85, Rev. Modern Physics, 1983-95; mem. editorial bd. Phys. Rev. B, 1991-94; coord. Comments on Condensed Matter Physics, 1985-90. Sloan fellow, 1966; Guggenheim fellow, 1985. Fellow AAAS, Am. Phys. Soc. (publs. oversight com. 1995-97, chmn. 1995-96, councillor divsn. condensed matter physics 1989-93, exec. com. divsn. biol. physics 1973-77, vice-chair through past chair divsn. condensed matter physics 2001—); mem. European Phys. Soc. Office: OSU Physics 191 W Woodruff Ave Columbus OH 43210 E-mail: wilkins@mps.ohio-state.edu.

WILKINS, LUCIEN SANDERS, gastroenterologist; b. Sanford, NC, Mar. 30, 1942; s. Alexander Betts and Olive Elizabeth (Pittman) Wilkins; m. Freda Barry Hartness, July 16, 1966; children: Lucien Sanders Wilkins Jr., Elise Perryman. BA, Duke U., 1963; MD, Med. Coll. Va., 1967. Diplomate Am. Bd. Internal Medicine. Intern Medical Coll. Va., Richmond, 1967-68, resident in internal medicine, 1970-72, gastroenterology fellow, 1972-73; clin. gastroenterologist Wilmington Health Assoc., NC, 1973—99; pres. Lucien Wilkins Cons., 2000—; pres., med. dir. Am. Physician Ptnrs. Assn., 1992—; pres. Strategic Med. Planning and Design, 1992—, DeWitt Healthcare, 2003—06, mng. dir., 2003—06; pres. pvt. consulting firm, 2007—. Vis. physician Hopital St. Croix, Leogane, Haiti, 1979—84, founder Divsn. Gastrointestinal Endoscopy, 1984; 1st Endoscopic Ambulatory Surgery Facility State of N.C., 1990; chmn. dept. medicine New Hanover Regional Med. Ctr., Wilmington, NC, 1990—92; asst. prof. clin. medicine U. N.C., Chapel Hill, 1974—; bd. dirs. Br. Banking and Trust, Wilmington; physician adv. Nat. Found. Ileitis and Colitis, 1976—78. Author: Progeny, 1994. Bd. dirs. Cape Fear Coun. for Arts, Wilmington, 1976—77, New Hanover Regional Med. Ctr. Found., Wilmington, 1993—95, exec. com., 1994—95; bd. dirs. Com. of 100, Wilmington, 1992—95. Lt. comdr. M.C.1970 USN, 1968. Recipient winner GTP-L Holbert Meml. Race, Sebring, Fla., 1995; fellow A. D. Williams rsch. fellow, 1965, Paul Harris fellow, Rotary, 1986. Mem.: ACP, New Hanover-Pender County Med. Soc. (pres. 1980), Wrightsville Beach Ocean Racing Assn. (commodore), Figure Eight Island Yacht Club (charter), Surf Club, Cape Fear Country Club. Presbyterian. Avocation: sports car racing. Home: 2215 Lynnwood Dr Wilmington NC 28403-8026 Office: 3317 Masonboro Loop Rd Ste 150 Wilmington NC 28409 Office Phone: 910-332-3680. Business E-Mail: lucien@lwilkinsconsulting.com. *Being a true physician means continually learning from your patients, about your patients, and on behalf of your patients.*

WILKINS, MICHAEL JON, state supreme court justice; b. Murray, Utah, May 13, 1948; s. Jack L. and Mary June (Phillips) W.; m. Diane W. Wilkins, Nov. 9, 1967; children: Jennifer, Stephanie, Bradley J. BS, U. Utah, 1975, JD, 1976; LLM, U. Va., 2001. Bar: Utah 1977, U.S. Dist. Ct. Utah 1977, U.S. Ct. Appeals (10th cir.) 1987, U.S. Supreme Ct. 1986. Mng. ptnr. Wilkins, Oritt & Headman, Salt Lake City, 1989-94; judge Utah Ct. Appeals, 1994—2000; justice Utah Supreme Ct. 2000—03, assoc. chief justice, 2003—, mem. jud. coun., 2000—. Mem. Gov.'s Adv. Com. on Corp., Salt Lake City, 1989-94; mem. Utah Supreme Ct. Complex Steering Com., 1993-94; mem. Judiciary Standing Com. on Tech., 1995-2000, chmn., 1995-2000; mem. Legis. Compensation Commn., 1994-95. Trustee Utah Law Related Edn. Project, Inc., Salt Lake City, 1991-95, chmn., 1992-94. 1st lt. U.S. Army, 1968-72. Mem. Lds Ch. Office: Utah Supreme Ct 450 S State St PO Box 140210 Salt Lake City UT 84114-0210 *

WILKINS, RAYFORD, JR., telecommunications industry executive; b. Waco, Tex. m. Lorena Wilkins; 1 child. BBA, U. Tex., Austin, 1974. Comml. asst. Southwestern Bell Tel., Houston, 1974; with SBC Comm., 1983—2005, pres. Kans. & western Mo. area, pres. Pacific Bell Bus. Comm. Svcs., 1997, pres. SBC Comm. Svc., 1997—99, pres. CEO Southwestern Bell Tel., pres. SBC bus. comm. svcs., 1999—2000, pres., CEO Pacific Bell, 2000, grp. pres. SBC mktg. & sales, 2000, grp. pres., CEO SBC enterprise bus. svcs.; group pres., diversified businesses AT&T Inc. (merger of SBC Comm. with AT&T Corp.), San Antonio, 2005—. Chmn. bd. Cingular Wireless; bd. mem. H&R Block, Telefonos de Mexico, Am. Movil. Bd. mem. AT&T Found., Tiger Woods Found., Tiger Woods Learning Ctr.; mem. adv. coun. U. Tex. McCombs Sch. Bus., Austin. Named CEO of Yr., Minority Supplier Coun., 1997; named one of Top 50 African Ams., Black Enterprise mag., 1999, Nation's 50 Most Powerful Black Execs., Fortune mag., 2002, 50 Most Important African Ams. in Tech., eAccess Corp., 2002, 2005, 75 Most Powerful African Ams. in Corp. Am., Black Enterprise mag., 2005, 100 Most Important Blacks in Tech., US Black Engr. & Info. Tech. mag., 2006, Top 100 Blacks in Corp. Am., Black Profl. mag., 2006; recipient Eagle award, Nat. Eagles Leadership Inst., 1997. Mailing: AT&T Inc 175 E Houston St PO Box 2933 San Antonio TX 78299-2933 *

WILKINS, ROBERT HENRY, neurosurgeon, educator, editor; b. Pitts., Aug. 18, 1934; s. George H. and Mary M. (Lemon) W.; m. Gloria A. Kohl, Dec. 28, 1957; children: Michael I., Jeffrey K., Elizabeth A. BS, U. Pitts., 1955, MD, 1959. Diplomate Am. Bd. Neurol. Surgery. Intern, resident gen. surgery Duke U. Med. Ctr., Durham, NC, 1959-61, resident in neurosurgery, 1963-68, asst. prof. neurosurgery, 1968-72, prof. neurosurgery, 1976—2004, chief divsn. neurosurgery, 1976-96, emeritus prof. neurosurgery, 2005—; clin. assoc. surgery br. Nat. Cancer Inst., Bethesda, Md., 1961-63; chmn. dept. neurosurgery Scott and White Clinic, Temple, Tex., 1972-75; assoc. prof. neurosurgery U. Pitts., 1975-76. Lectr. Cook County Grad. Sch. Medicine, Chgo., 1976-96; attending neurosurgeon Durham VA Hosp., 1968-72, 78-98; mem. Nat. Adv. Coun. Nat. Inst. Neurol. Disorders and Stroke, 1989-92. Co-editor: Neurosurgery, 2d edit., 3 vols., 1996, Neurosurgery Updates I and II, 1990, 91, Neurosurgical Operative Atlas, 1991-2000, Principles of Neurosurgery, 1994; editor Clin. Neurosurgery, 1972-75; assoc. editor Surg. Neurology, 1975-76; founding editor Neurosurgery, 1977-82, mem. editl. rev. bd., 1997-2001; mem. editl. bd. Jour. Neurosurgery, 1987-96, chmn., 1996-97, mem. adv. bd., 1997—; neurosurgery editor Key Neurology and Neurosurgery, 1993-96, Yr. Book of Neurology and Neurosurgery, 1994-97. Recipient Travel award Copenhagen, Nat. Inst. Neurol. Diseases and Blindness, 1965, Royal Australasian Coll. Surgeons, Found. lectr. Adelaide 1986. Fellow ACS (gov. 1996); mem. Congress Neurol. Surgeons (pres. 1979-80), Am. Assn. Neurol. Surgeons (treas. 1989-92), So. Neurosurg. Soc. (sec. 1988-91, pres. 1992-93), Soc. Neurol. Surgeons (v.p. 1995-96), Am. Bd. Neurol. Surgery (dir. 1991-97, chmn. 1996-97), Phi Beta Kappa, Alpha Omega Alpha. Democrat. Avocation: medical writing and editing. Office: Duke U Med Ctr PO Box 3807 Durham NC 27710-0001 Personal E-mail: rhwilkins@aol.com.

WILKINS, ROBERT PEARCE, writer, lawyer; b. Jesup, Ga., Sept. 10, 1933; s. Ransom Little and Sarah (Pearce) W.; m. Rose Truesdale, Jan. 7, 1956; children: Robert Pearce, Chisolm Wallace (dec.), Sarah Ruth Weiss, Rose Anne Brooks. BA, U. S.C., 1953, JD, 1954; LL.M., Georgetown U., 1957. Bar: S.C. 1954; cert. mediator and arbitrator, S.C. Atty. Office Gen. Counsel, Sec. Army, Washington, 1956; trust officer First Nat. Bank S.C., Columbia, 1957-60; practice law Columbia, 1960-64; ptnr. McLain, Sherrill & Wilkins, Columbia, 1964-68, McKay, Sherrill, Walker, Townsend & Wilkins, Columbia, 1969-75; sole practice law Columbia and Lexington, S.C., 1975-88; of counsel Nelson, Mullins, Riley & Scarborough, Lexington, 1988—. Pres. Sandlapper Press, Inc., 1967-72, pub. Sandlapper Mag. S.C., 1968-72; editor Sandlapper Mag. S.C., 1968-69, 89—; editor, pub. S.C. History Illustrated, 1970; pres. R.P.W. Pub. Corp.; mem., chmn. S.C. Splty. Adv. Bd. Estate Planning and Probate, 1982-85; lectr. in law U. S.C., 1971-78. Author: Draftin Wills and Trust Agreements in South Carolina, 1971, Drafting Wills and Trust Agreements in Michigan, 1978, Wills and Trust System (Arkansas), 1978, Drafting Wills and Trust Agreements: A Systems Approach, 1998, 3d edit., 1999, software edit., 50 Things to Do with the Rest of Your Life, 2003; (with others) Word Processing for a Law Office, 1979, also articles; editor: The Lawyer's Microcomputer, 1982-85, The Lawyer's PC, 1983-97, What a Lawyer Needs to Know to Buy and Use a Computer, 1984, The Perfect Lawyer, 1990-97, The Lawyers' Word, 1991, Shepard's Elder Care/Law Newsletter, 1991-95, Hot docs Toolbox, 1996-97, Drafting Wills and Trust Agreements Newsletter, 1997. Del., Spl. Liaison Tax Com. Southeastern Region, 1967-70; exec. com. Richland County Rep. Com., 1960-64; sec.-treas. Richland County Rep. Club, 1960; bd. dirs. Ctrl. Tb-RD Assn.; trustee Sch. Dist. 1, Lexington County, S.C., 1971-78, sec., 1972-75, chmn., 1975-78; mem. S.C. Commn. on Higher Edn., 1978-80, S.C. Commn. on Lawyer Competence, 1980-82; bd. dirs. Crime Stoppers of the Midlands, 1983-85, RPW Learning Ctr., 1987-94, Mt. Hope Cemetary, 1991—, also v.p., 1992—; v.p. 11th cir. Alumni Coun. U. S.C., 1993-95, mem. awards com., 1995-97; mem. commn. Riverbanks Zoo, 1986—, sec., 1991-95, chmn., 1995-96, 97—, vice-chmn., 1996-97. With AUS, 1954-55. Recipient Compleat Lawyer award Law Sch. U. S.C., 1997, Diamond Circle award U. S.C. Coll. Journalism and Mass Comms., 1998. Fellow Am. Bar Found., Am. Coll. Trust and Estate Counsel (publs. com. 1984-87, bd. regents 1986-87, mem. tech. com. 1989-98), Am. Coll. Tax Counsel, Coll. Law Practice Mgmt. (charter, trustee 1994-98), S.C. Bar (tax coordinating com. 1968-70, chmn. legal econs. com. 1973-75, ho. of dels. 1978-80, editor S.C. Lawyer 1989-91, mem. alternative dispute resolution sect. 1993—), S.C. Bar Found. (life, bd. dirs. 1984-88, v.p. 1986-87, pres. 1987-88); mem. ABA (ho. of dels. 1986-87, chmn. valuation subcom., estate and gift tax com., taxation sect. 1967-73, vice chmn. svc. and assistance to law student div. com. gen. practice sect. 1971-72, vice chmn. corp. counsel com. gen. practice sect. 1972-74, editor econs. of law practice sect. legal econs. 1974-78, sec. 1977-78, vice chmn. 1978-79, chmn. 1980-81, mem. standing com. assn. comm. 1981-84, real property, probate and trust law, mem. publs. com. 1985-89, editor Probate and Property, 1986-89), Richland County Bar Assn. (chmn. probate sect. 1973-74, unauthorized practice of law com. 1976), Lexington County Bar (chmn. mediation com. 1994—), Columbia Jaycees (sec.-treas. 1958-59), Columbia Estate Planning Coun. (pres. 1964-65), Am. Y-Flyer Yacht Racing Assn. (area v.p. 1971, internat. dir. 1972-73), Omicron Delta Kappa, Sigma Chi Clubs: Columbia Sailing (dir. 1968-71), Columbia Tip Off (dir. 1968-73), Columbia (pres. 1971-72). Home: 124 Lake Murray Ct Lexington SC 29072-9104 also: PO Box 729 Lexington SC 29071-0729 E-mail: rpw@50thingstodo.com.

WILKINS, WILLIAM WALTER, federal judge; b. Anderson, SC, Mar. 29, 1942; s. W. Walter Wilkins and Evelyn Louise (Horton); m. Debra Ann Dill, Aug. 19, 1999; children: Lauren, Lyn, Walt. BA, Davidson Coll., 1964; JD, U. SC, 1967. Bar: SC 1967, US Dist. Ct. SC 1967, US Ct. Appeals (4th cir.) 1969, US Supreme Ct. 1970. Law clk. to Hon. Clement F. Haynsworth Jr. US Ct. Appeals (4th cir.), 1969—70; legal asst. to US Senator Strom Thurmond, 1970—71; ptnr. Wilkins & Wilkins, Greenville, SC, 1971—78; solicitor 13th Jud. Cir., 1974—81; judge US Dist. Ct., Greenville, 1981—86, US Ct. Appeals (4th cir.), 1986—2003, chief judge, 2003—. Lectr. Greenville Tech. Coll., 1973—97, Taft Seminar, Clemson Univ., SC, 1973—97; chmn. US Sentencing Commn., 1985—94; chmn. com. on criminal law Jud. Conf. US, 2000—03; disting. prof. Charleston Sch. Law, 2004—. Editor-in-chief: SC Law Rev., 1967; contbr. articles to profl. jours. With US Army, 1967—69, with USAR, 1969—83, with SC Army Nat. Guard, 1983—94. Mem.: SC Bar Assn., Wig and Robe. Republican. Baptist. Office: US Ct Appeals 4th Cir PO Box 10857 Greenville SC 29601-0857 *

WILKINSON, ALAN HERBERT, nephrologist, educator; b. Johannesburg, July 11, 1948; came to U.S., 1985; s. Raymond C. and Nonie (Levick) W.; m. Angelika A. E. Adami, Dec. 22, 1973; one child: Rebecca Kate Adami. BS in Physiology, Biochemistry, Philosophy, U. Witwatersrand, South Africa, 1969, BS in Biochemistry with honors, 1970, MB, BCh, 1975; cert. health care mgmt., U. Calif., Irvine, 1998. Fellow Royal Coll. Physicians (U.K.), specialist in clin. hypertension. Vis. assoc. Dept. Internal Medicine U. Iowa, Iowa City, 1987-88; assoc. prof. of medicine UCLA Sch. Med., 1988-95, prof. med., 1995—; dir. clin. nephrology UCLA Dept. Med., 1988-93, dir. kidney and pancreas transplantation, 1993—. Contbr. articles to profl. jours. Mem. steering com. Nat. Kidney Found.; mem. U.S. Transplant Games, L.A., 1992; bd. dirs. So. Calif. Renal Disease Coun., 2002-04, med. adv., 2004—. Recipient Exceptional Svc. award Nat. Kidney Found., 1992; Nat. Kidney Found. fellow. Mem. Am. Soc. Transplantation, Internat. Nephrology Soc., Am. Soc. Nephrology. Avocations: ornithology, gardening. Office: UCLA Dept Med 200 Medical Plz Box 951693 Los Angeles CA 90095-1693

WILKINSON, ALBERT MIMS, JR., lawyer; b. Nashville, June 29, 1925; s. Albert Mims and Mary Nelle (Derryberry) W.; m. Edythe Bush, Mar. 27, 1953 (div.); children: William Terry, Elizabeth Ann, David Bush; m. Dolores Jean Attard, Oct. 22, 1971 (div.); 1 child, Mary Dolores. Student, Emory U., 1942-43; JD, U. Ga., 1949. Bar: Ga. 1948. Pvt. practice law, Atlanta, 1950-85; gen. counsel GEC-Marconi Avionics Inc., Atlanta, 1985-98; hon. legal adviser to Brit. Consul Gen. at Atlanta. Author: The Winning of the Revolutionary War in the South, 1976, The Rights of Unsecured Creditors-The Law in Ga., 1979; editor: Chronicles of the Old Guard of the Gate City Guard of Atlanta, 1858-2001 (3 vols.), 2002. Mem. DeKalb County Bd. Elections, 1966-72; chmn. 4th Congl. Dist. Republican Exec. Com., 1968-70, Ga. State Rep. Exec. Com., 1968-74; 1st vice chmn. Ga. Rep. Party, 1972-74, asst. gen. counsel, 1974-75; vice chmn., trustee Atlanta Counseling Center, Inc., 1960-83. Served with USCGR, 1943-46. Decorated Order Brit. Empire. Fellow Comml. Law Found.; mem. BA, Ga. Bar Assn., Atlanta Bar Assn., Ga. Soc. (pres. 1962-63), SAR, Southeastern Mem.'s Assn. (pres. 1960-61), Comml. Law League Am., Ga. Soc. Colonial Wars, Old Guard of Gate City Guard (comdt. 1986), N.C. Soc. of Cincinnati, Sphinx Club, Gridiron Club, Commerce Club, Civitan, Masons, Blue Key, Omicron Delta Kappa. Baptist. Home and Office: 66 Demorest Ln # 333 Sky Valley GA 30537-2581 Office Phone: 706-746-2374. Personal E-mail: amims@alltel.net. *By precept and example my parents pointed out the upward way in life, on a foundation of religious faith. "To do justly, to love mercy, to walk humbly with thy God." Later a beloved teacher taught the lines from Ulysses as he prepared to set sail, "To strive, to seek, to find and never yield." Their inspiration has continued throughout my life.*

WILKINSON, BETH A., lawyer, finance company executive; BA cum laude, Princeton U., 1984; JD, U. Va., 1987. Bar: DC 1999, NY 1988. Capt., asst. to Army Gen. Counsel for intelligence, spl. ops., and nat. security matters, 1987—91; asst. US atty. Eastern Dist. NY, 1991; ptnr., litig. dept. Latham and Watkins, Litigation Dept., 1998—2006; exec. v.p., corp. sec., gen. counsel Fannie Mae, Washington, 2006—. Co-chair Latham and Watkins' White Collar Crime Practice Group. Author: "When Talk is Not Cheap: Communications With The Media, The Government, And Other Parties in High Profile White Collar Criminal Cases", Am. Criminal Law Review, 2002; featured on news programs such as NBC "Today" show, Nightline, NewsHour with Jim Lehrer, Face the Nation & Good Morning America, featured in National Law Journal, American Lawyer & Legal Times. Trustee Nat. Youth Leadership Forum; co-chmn.

Constn. Project's Death Penalty Initiative. Named one of 75 Best Lawyers in Washington, Washingtonian Mag., 2002. Achievements include received the Exceptional Svc. award twice, Atty. Gen. highest commendation; prosecutor in Okla. City Bombings case; lead trial counsel for Gen. Electric; represented Ford Motor Co. during Firestone investigation. Office: Fannie Mae 3900 Wisconsin Ave, NW Washington DC 20016-2892

WILKINSON, BRUCE W., construction executive; b. Dallas, 1944; married. BA, U. Okla., 1966, JD, 1969; LLM, U. London, 1970. Gen. counsel Dresser Industries, Inc., Dallas, 1970-78; v.p., treas. CRS Sirrine, Inc. (now CRSS Inc.), Houston, 1978-79, sr. v.p., treas., 1979-82, pres., CEO, 1982—96, chmn. bd. dirs., CEO, 1989—96; interim pres., CEO Proler Internat., Inc., 1996; pres., CEO Tyler Corp., 1997; chmn., CEO Chem. Logistics Corp., 1998—99; prin. Pinnacle Equity Ptnrs., LLC, 1999—2000; pres., COO McDermott Internat., Inc., Houston, 2000, chmn. bd., CEO, 2000—, pres., COO J. Ray McDermott, S.A., 2002—03. Bd. dirs. Cameron Internat. Corp., 2002—. Office: McDermott Internat Inc 777 N Eldridge Pky Houston TX 77079-4425 Office Phone: 281-870-5901. *

WILKINSON, CHARLES P., ophthalmologist; b. Syracuse, 1940; MD, Johns Hopkins U. Sch. Medicine, 1966. Intern Johns Hopkins Hosp., 1966—67; resident Wilmer Inst., Balt., 1967—70; fellow U. Miami, 1970—71; chmn. dept., prof. ophthalmology Johns Hopkins U. Sch. Medicine. Co-author: Michels Retinal Detachment, 1996. Mem.: Am. Bd. Ophthalmology (vice chmn. 2003, chmn. 2004). Avocation: golf. Office: Greater Balt Med Ctr 6569 N Charles St #505 Towson MD 21204-5809 Office Phone: 443-849-2196.

WILKINSON, CLAUDE HENRY, writer, artist, English literature educator; b. Memphis, Dec. 17, 1959; s. Henry Bridgforth and Lula (Moncrief) W. BSc, U. Miss., 1981; cert. d'excellence, Alliance Française, Memphis, 1991; MA, U. Memphis, 1992. Instr. English McNeese State U., Lake Charles, La., 1990-91, U. Memphis, 1991-92, Lane Coll., Jackson, Tenn., 1992-94, LeMoyne-Owen Coll., Memphis, 1998-99; owner Claude Wilkinson Fine Art Studio, Nesbit, Miss., 1984—. Editor River City Mag., Memphis, 1991; John and Renée Grisham So. writer in residence U. Miss., 2000-01, provost scholar, 2006. Author: Reading the Earth, 1998 (Naomi Long Madgett Poetry award, 1998), Joy in the Morning, 2004; author poetry; contbr. articles to profl. jours. Recipient New Poets award, Ursus Press, 1984, Grand prize, Miss. Poetry Soc., 1985, W.M. Whittington Jr. Purchase award, Cottonlandia Mus. Juried Exhbn., 1993, 1st prize in painting, Carnegie Ctr. for Arts and History, 1994, Pioneer Br. Poetry award, Ark. Writers' Conf., 1995, Kenneth Beaudoin Meml. award, Mid-South Poetry Festival, 1995, Paul Laurence Dunbar Poetry award, Detroit Black Writers Guild, 1998, Whiting Writer's award, Mrs. Giles Whiting Found., 2000; Provost Scholar, U. Miss., 2006, Walter E. Dakin fellow, Sewanee Writers' Conf., 1999. Avocations: music, mythology, nature study. Office Phone: 662-429-4935.

WILKINSON, DANIEL MELVIN, music educator; b. San Miguel de Tucuman, Argentina, Feb. 14, 1959; arrived in U.S., 1967; s. Melvin Leon and Carol Evangeline Wilkinson. BS in Music Edn., Trevecca Nazarene U., Nashville, 1983; MM in Performance, Western Ky. U., 1984. Instr. Madisonville CC, Ky., 1990—98; assoc. prof. Hopkinsville CC, Ky., 1998—. Contbr. poetry and photography to The Round Table; vocalist, accompanist: Town and Gown Chorale, 1998—2005, musician piano and organ recitals, performance in master class before Madame Marie-Louise Langlais. Mem.: Am. Guild Organists (sub-dean Evansville chpt. 2002—04), Hopkinsville Art Guild. Republican. Avocations: reading, composition, travel, movies, photography. Home: 622 Foxfield Rd Hopkinsville KY 42240 Office: Hopkinsville C C PO Box 2100 North Dr Hopkinsville KY 42240 Office Phone: 270-707-3864. Business E-Mail: dwilkins@hopkinsville.net, daniel.wilkinson@kcts.edu.

WILKINSON, DAVID STANLEY, pathologist, consultant, researcher, educator; b. Richmond, Va., Feb. 2, 1945; s. Herbert Carroll and Hattie Mae (Vaughan) Wilkinson; m. Judith Farish Pace, June 16, 1967; children: Jill Marie, Julie Lynne, Virginia Ann. BS in Chemistry, Va. Mil. Inst., Lexington, 1967; PhD in Exptl. Oncology and Pathology, U. Wis.-Madison, 1971; MD, U. Miami, 1978. Diplomate Am. Bd. Pathology. Fellow McArdie Lab. Cancer Rsch. U. Wis., 1967—71; asst. prof. biochemistry U. South Fla., Tampa, 1972—76; resident in pathology Walter Reed Army Med. Ctr., Washington, 1978—82; instr. pathology Uniformed Svc. U. Health Sci., Bethesda, 1979—82; chief clin. pathology Eisenhower Army Med. Ctr., Ft. Gordon, Ga., 1982—84; instr. pathology Med. Coll. Ga., Augusta, 1982—84; assoc. prof. pathology George Washington U. Med. Ctr., 1984—89, dir. clin. pathology div., 1984—92, prof. pathology, 1989—93; med. dir. George Washington U. Hosp., 1992—93; prof. pathology, chmn. dept. pathology Va. Commonwealth U., 1993—. Lectr. in field. Editor: (other) Clinical Laboratory Management Review, 1989—2004; contbr. articles to profl. jours. Commd. 2nd lt. US Army, 1967, advanced through grades to maj. US Army, 1982. Fellow: Coll. Am. Pathologists, Am. Soc. Clin. Pathology; mem.: AMA, Assn. Pathology Chairs (pres. 2004—06), Med. Soc. Va. (del.), Richmond Acad. Medicine (trustee), U.S. and Canadian Acad. Pathology, Am. Soc. Investigative Pathology, Am. Assn. Blood Banks, Clin. Lab. Mgmt. Assn., Am. Assn. Clin. Chemistry, Soc. Exptl. Biology and Medicine, Am. Assn. Cancer Rsch., VMI Keydet (Lexington, Va.). Republican. Office: Va Commonwealth Univ Dept Pathology PO Box 980662 Richmond VA 23298-0662

WILKINSON, DENISE V., psychologist; b. Coral Gable, Fla., Apr. 17, 1953; d. John Edward Van Diver and Doris Helen Sandner; m. Michael Bert Wilkinson; children: Melissa Brittany, Justin Bert. BA, Univ. S. Fla., Tampa, Fla., 1979, MA, 1981, Edn. Specialist, 1988. Cert. sch. psychologist 1987; lic. 1988. Mental health tech. Upper Pinellas Assn. for Retarded Citizens, Clearwater, Fla., 1974—76; psychometrist pvt. practice, Tampa, Fla., 1976—79, Devel. Ctr., Tampa, Fla., 1979; sch. psychologist Pasco County Sch. Bd., Land O'Lakes, Fla., 1982—. Sch. psychologist pvt. practice, Land O'Lakes, Fla., 1989—. Contbr. articles pub. to profl. jour. Recipient Student Svcs. Tchr. of the Yr., Pasco County Sch. Bd., 1996. Mem.: Nat. Assn. of Sch. Psychologist, Fla. Assn. of Sch. Psychologist. Independent. Unitarian Universalist. Avocations: photography, travel, beach, seashell collecting, collecting postcards. Office: Pasco County Sch Bd 7227 US Hwy 41 N Land O Lakes FL 34639 Home: 22846 Chesterview Loop Apt 101 Land O Lakes FL 34639-5343

WILKINSON, DORIS, medical sociology educator; b. Lexington, Ky., June 13, 1936; d. Howard Thomas and Regina Wilkinson. BA, U. Ky., 1958; MA, Case Western Res. U., 1960, PhD, 1968; MPH, Johns Hopkins U., 1985; postgrad., Harvard U., summer 1991. Asst. prof. U. Ky., Lexington, 1968-70; assoc. prof., then prof. Macalester Coll., St. Paul, 1970-77; exec. assoc. Am. Sociol. Assn., Washington, 1977-80; prof. med. sociology Howard U., Washington, 1980-84; vis. prof. U. Va., 1984-85; prof. sociology U. Ky., Lexington, 1985—. Chmn. panel women in sci. program NSF, Washington, 1976; rev. panelist Nat. Inst. Drug Abuse, Washington, 1978—79; mem. bd. sci. counselors Nat. Cancer Inst., Bethesda, Md., 1980—84; vis. scholar Harvard U., Cambridge, Mass., 1989—90, vis. prof. (summers), 1992, 93, 94, 97; Rapoport vis. prof. social theory (summers) Smith Coll., 1995, 96; bd. dirs. Nat. Conf. for Cmty. Justice, 1992—96; dir. Heritage Project, 2000—. Author: Workbook for Introductory Sociology, 1968; editor: Black Revolt: Strategies of Protest, 1969; co-editor: The Black Male in America, 1977, Alternative Health Maintenance and Healing Systems, 1987, Race, Gender and the Life Cycle, 1991, Race, Class and Gender, 1996; social history photographic exhbn. "The African American Presence in Medicine" Harvard Med. Libr., 1991, Pearson Mus.- So. Ill. U. Med. Sch., 1992, N.J. Coll. Medicine and Dentistry, 1993, Louisville Mus. History and Sci., 1994, U. Cin. Med. Sch. Libr., 1994, Albert Einstein Coll. of Medicine, 1995, Midway Coll., 1996; contbr. articles to profl. jours. Bd. overseers Case Western Res. U., Cleve., 1982-87; apptd. Ky. Commn. on Women, 1993-96. Named to Hall of Disting. Alumni, U. Ky.,1989; recipient Pub. Humanities award U. Ky., 1990, Midway Coll. Women's History Month award, 1991, Gt. Tchr. award Nat. Alumni Assn. U. Ky., 1992, Disting. Scholar award Assn. Black Sociologists, 1993, Cmty. Svc. award Frankfort-Lexington Links, Inc., 2005-, Cmty. Svc. award Girl Scout Wilderness Road Coun., Lexington, Ky., 2005, Ida Lee Willis Mem. award Ky. Heritage Found., 2006 Coretta Scott King award Alpha Kappa Alpha, 2007; fellow Woodrow Wilson Found., 1959-61, Ford Found., 1989-90; grantee Social Sci. Rsch. Coun., 1975, Nat. Inst. Edn., 1978-80, Nat. Cancer Inst., 1986-88, Ky. Humanities Coun., 1988, 01, Am. Coun. Learned Soc., 1989-90, NEH, 1991; Disting. Prof. in Coll. Arts and Scis., U. Ky., 1992-93, Coll. of Social Work Hall of Fame, U. Ky., 1999; Disting. Lectureship named in her honor African Am. Studies Rsch. Program, 2000. Mem.: Ea. Sociol. Soc. (v.p. 1983—84, pres. 1992—93, I. Peter Gellman award 1987), Soc. Study Social Problems (v.p. 1984—85, pres. 1987—88), DC Sociol. Soc. (pres. 1982—83), So. Sociol. Soc. (honors com. 1993—94), Am. Sociol. Assn. (exec. assoc. 1977—80, budget com. 1985—88, v.p. 1991—92, mem. coun. 1994—97, elected History of Sociology sect. 2003, Dubois-Johnson-Frazier award 1988), Phi Beta Kappa.

WILKINSON, EDWARD ANDERSON, JR., retired military officer, manufacturing executive; b. Selma, Ala., Sept. 21, 1933; s. Edward Anderson and Alice Margaret (Moorer) W.; m. Barbara Anne Parker, June 4, 1955 (dec. June 1991); children: Daryl Edward, Daniel Bryan, Edward Anderson III, David Park; m. Sondra Marie Moore, Oct. 2, 1994. BS, U.S. Naval Acad., 1955; MS in Mech. Engring., 1964; grad., Nat. War Coll., 1972. Commd. ensign U.S. Navy, 1955, advanced through grades to rear adm., 1979; dir. Anti-Submarine Warfare Systems Program Office, Washington, 1978-79; dep. dir. Def. Mapping Agy., Washington, 1979-81; cmdr. Patrol Wings, U.S. Atlanta Fleet, Brunswick, Maine, 1981-83; dir. Def. Mapping Agy., Washington, 1983-85; ret., 1985; exec. v.p. Internat. Fed. Systems Intergraph Corp., Reston, Va. Recipient Decorated Legion of Merit, Dept. Def., Disting. Svc. medal. Methodist. Home and Office: 9680 Perdido Vista Dr Elberta AL 36530-6028 Home Phone: 251-961-1314; Office Phone: 251-213-3733. Business E-Mail: andy.wilkinson@intergraph.com.

WILKINSON, EUGENE PARKS, nuclear engineer, director; b. Long Beach, Calif., Aug. 10, 1918; s. Dennis William and Daisy Amelia (Parks) W.; m. Janice Edith Thuli, Mar. 28, 1942; children: Dennis Eugene, Stephen James, Marian Lynn, Rodney David. AB in Chemistry, San Diego State U., 1938. Instr. chemistry San Diego State U., 1938-39; commd. ensign U.S. Navy, 1940, advanced through grades to vice adm., 1970; served various locations including 1st comdg. officer USS Nautilus (1st nuclear-powered submarine), 1953-57; 1st comdg. officer USS Long Beach, 1959-63, 1st nuclear-powered surface ship; ret., 1974; exec. v.p. Data Design Labs., Cucamonga, Calif., 1977-80; pres., chief exec. officer Inst. Nuclear Power Ops., Atlanta, 1980-84, pres. emeritus, 1984—. Chmn. bd. dirs. MDM Svcs. Corp., Laguna Niguel, Calif. Decorated Legion of Merit, Silver Star, D.S.M. with three oak leaf clusters, others, Second Order Sacred Treasure Japan; recipient George Westinghouse Gold medal ASME, 1983, Oliver Townsend medal Atomic Indsl. Forum, 1984, Gold medal Uranium Inst., 1989. Mem. Am. Soc. Naval Engrs., Am. Nuclear Soc. (Henry DeWolf Smyth Nuclear Statesman medal 1994, Walter Zinn award 1998), Navy League, Submarine League, Nat. Acad. Engring. Avocations: tennis, bridge. Home: 1449 Crest Rd Del Mar CA 92014-2530

WILKINSON, FRANCES CATHERINE, librarian, educator; b. Lake Charles, La., July 20, 1955; d. Derrell Fred and Catherine Frances (O'Toole) W.; div.; 1 child, Katrina Frances. BA in Comm. with distinction, U. N.Mex., 1982, MPA, 1987; MLS, U. Ariz., 1990. Mktg. rsch. auditor Mktg. Rsch. N.Mex., Albuquerque, 1973—78; freelance photographer, 1974—75; from libr. supr. gen. libr. to assoc. dean libr. svcs. U. N.Mex., Albuquerque, 1978—2001, interim dean, 2001—02, 2006—07, assoc. dean librs., 2007—. Cons., trainer ergonomics univs. and govt. agys. across U.S., 1986—; bd. dirs. Friends of U. N.Mex. Librs., Albuquerque, 1991-94; mediator Mediation Alliance, 1991-94, U. N.Mex. Faculty Dispute Resolution, 1999—; mediation coach U. N.Mex., 1999-2000. Contbr. articles to profl. jours. Counselor, advocate Albuquerque Rape Crisis Ctr., 1981-84. Recipient James Fulton Zimmerman award for adminstrv. excellence, Friends of U. N.Mex. Librs., Inc. Mem.: ALA (com. 1990—2000, 2003—, Leadership in Libr. Acquisitions award 2000), N.Mex. Assn. Rsch. Librs., N.Mex. Preservation Alliance (vice chair 1995—96), N.Mex. Libr. Assn., N.Am. Serials Interest Group (com. 1994—97, exec. bd. 1997—2001, com. 2001—03), Pi Alpha Alpha, Phi Kappa Phi (chpt. treas. 1991—92, chpt. pres. 1992—94). Home: PO Box 8102 Albuquerque NM 87198-8102 Office: U N Mex Univ Librs MSC 05 3020 1 University of New Mex Albuquerque NM 87131-0001 Office Phone: 505-277-4241. Business E-Mail: fwilkins@unm.edu.

WILKINSON, HARRY EDWARD, management educator, consultant; b. Richmond Heights, Mo., June 30, 1930; s. Harry Edward and Virginia Flo (Shelton) W.; m. Sara Beth Kikendall, Aug. 30, 1958; children: Linda Beth, Cheryl Susan. BA in Physics, Princeton U., 1952; MBA, Washington U., St. Louis, 1957; DBA, Harvard U., 1960. Lic. psychologist, Mass. Staff engr. Southwestern Bell Tel. Co., St. Louis, 1954-57; traffic engr. New Eng. Tel. & Telegraph Co., Boston, 1957-60; sr. mgmt. cons. Harbridge House Inc., Boston, 1961-65; dean bus. adminstrn., dir. Mgmt. Inst., Northeastern U., Boston, 1965-67; pres., chmn. bd. Univ. Affiliates Inc., North Port, Fla., 1967-2000; vis. prof. mgmt. Rice U., Houston, 1990-94, 97-2000, dir. office of exec. devel., 1993-97. Cons. to various industries and govt., 1961—. Author: Influencing People in Organizations, 1993; contbr. articles to mgmt. jours. Lt. (j.g.) USNR, 1952-54, Korea. Mem. APA, Acad. Mgmt., N.Am. Case Rsch. Assn., Harvard Bus. Sch. Assn. Personal E-mail: hewilkinson@sbcglobal.net.

WILKINSON, JAMES ALLAN, lawyer, healthcare executive; b. Cumberland, Md., Feb. 10, 1945; s. John Robinson and Dorothy Jane (Kelley) W.; m. Elizabeth Susanne Quinlan, Apr. 14, 1973; 1 child, Kathryn Barrett. BS in Fgn. Svc., Georgetown U., Washington, DC, 1967; JD, Duquesne U., Pitts., 1978; MA, U Pitts., 2001. Bar: Pa., US Dist. Ct. (we. dist.) Pa. Legis. analyst Office of Mgmt. and Budget, Washington, 1972-73; dep. exec. sec. Cost of Living Coun., Washington, 1973-74; sr. fin. analyst US Steel Corp., Pitts., 1974-82; ptnr. Buchanan Ingersoll, Pitts., 1982-88; exec. v.p., gen. counsel Meritcare, Pitts., 1988—2006; sr. v.p. Culwell Health Inc., 1991—2001; exec. dir. Soc. for Contemporary Craft, 2007—. Adj. prof. U. Pitts. Sch. Law, 1988-91. Author: Financing and Refinancing Under Prospective Payment, 1985, Family Caregivers' Guide Planning and Decision Making for the Elderly, 1998; contbr. articles to profl. jours. Chmn. Oversight Com. on Organ Transplantation, Pitts., 1986—; sec.-treas. bd. dirs. Pitts. Symphony Soc., 1986-98, exec. com. bd. dirs., 1999-2002, 03—, vice-chmn., 2003—; bd. dirs. We. Pa. Com. Prevention of Child Abuse, 1987-90, Comprehensive Safety Compliance, 1988-91, Buchanan Ingersoll Profl. Corp., 1988-90, Parental Stress Ctr., 1990-94; sec. Ross Mountain Club, 1995-98, 1999-2003, 05—, v.p., 1999-2001, pres., 2001-03; exec. com. bd. dirs. Carnegie Inst., 1997-2003, 05—, sec., 2005—, life trustee, 2002—; exec. com. bd. dirs. Carnegie Mus. Natural History, 1997-2003, Andy Warhol Mus., 1998—, vice chair, 2004-06, co-chair, 2006—; exec. com. bd. dirs. Soc. for Contemporary Craft, 1999-05, treas., 2000-01, v.p., 2001-02, pres., 2002-04; bd. dirs. Craft Emergency Relief Fund, 2003—, treas., 2003-05, vice chair, 2006—. Mem. Audubon Soc. Southwestern Pa. (treas. 1996-2000), Duquesne Club. Republican. Episcopalian. Home: 1005 Elmhurst Rd Pittsburgh PA 15215-1819

WILKINSON, J(AMES) HARVIE, III, federal judge; b. NYC, Sept. 29, 1944; s. James Harvie and Letitia (Nelson) W.; m. Lossie Grist Noell, June 30, 1973; children: James Nelson, Porter Noell. BA, Yale U., 1963-67; JD, U. Va., 1972; JD (hon.), U. Richmond, 1997, U. SC, 1998; LLD (hon.), Christopher Newport U., 2003. Bar: Va. 1972. Law clk. to Hon. Lewis F. Powell, Jr. US Supreme Ct., Washington, 1972-73; asst. prof. law U. Va., 1973-75, assoc. prof., 1975-78; editor Norfolk Virginian-Pilot, Va., 1978-81; prof. law U. Va., 1981-82, 83-84; dep. asst. atty. gen. Civil Rights divsn. US Dept. Justice, 1982-83; judge US Ct. Appeals (4th Cir.), 1984—, chief judge, 1996—2003. Author: Harry Byrd and the Changing Face of Virginia Politics, 1968, Serving Justice: A Supreme Court Clerk's View, 1974, From Brown to Bakke: The Supreme Court and School Integration, 1979, One Nation Indivisible: How Ethnic Separatism Threatens America, 1997. Bd. Visitors U. Va., 1970-73; Republican candidate for Congress from 3d Dist. Va., 1970; bd. dirs. Fed. Jud. Ctr., 1992-96, James Madison Meml. Found, 2003-. Served with US Army, 1968-69. Recipient Thomas Jefferson Found. medal Law, U. Va., 2004. Mem. Va. State Bar, Va. Bar Assn., Am. Law Inst. Episcopalian. Office: US Ct Appeals 255 W Main St Ste 230 Charlottesville VA 22902-5058 Home Phone: 434-979-3528; Office Phone: 434-296-7063. *

WILKINSON, JEFFERY ALAN, animal scientist; b. Ogden, Utah, Jan. 20, 1958; s. Donald Huband Wilkinson and Bonnie Joy Walter; m. Misao Fujiwara, Mar. 13, 1982; children: David Hiroshi, Jennifer Ai. BS, Brigham Young U., Provo, Utah, 1985, MS, 1989; PhD, Tex. Tech U., Lubbock, 1997. Rsch. assoc. Calif. Acad. Scis., San Francisco, 1999—, coord. Gaoligongshan biodiversity survey project, 2002—. Herpetologist H.T. Harvey & Assocs., San Jose, Calif., 2000—06. Grantee, Nat. Geog. Soc., 1991, 2002, NSF, 1994, John D. and Catherine T. MacArthur Found., 2005; scholar, Japanese Ministry Edn., Sci., and Culture, 1990—92; Tilton Postdoctoral fellow, Calif. Acad. Scis., 1997—98. Mem.: Am. Soc. Ichthyologists and Herpetologists, Herpetologists League. Achievements include research in phylogenetic systematics; discovery of new species. Avocations: sports, Shorinji Kempo. Office: Calif Acad Scis 875 Howard St San Francisco CA 94103 Office Phone: 415-321-8282. E-mail: jwilkinson@calacademy.org.

WILKINSON, JOHN HART, lawyer; b. Newton, Mass., Dec. 31, 1940; s. Roger Melvin and Margaret (Carter) Wilkinson; children: Heather, Carter. BA, Williams Coll., 1962; LLB, Fordham U., 1965. Bar: NY 1965, US Dist. Ct. (so. and ea. dists.) NY 1968, US Ct. Appeals (2d cir.) 1981, US Ct. Appeals (11th cir.) 1982, US Ct. Appeals (3d cir.) 1984, US Ct. Appeals (5th cir.) 1987. Assoc. Donovan, Leisure, Newton & Irvine, NYC, 1965, 67-73, ptnr., 1973-98, editor, contbg. author firm's ADR Practice Book, 1990; law clk. presiding justice US Dist. Ct. (so. dist.) NY, 1967-68; of counsel Fulton, Rowe & Hart, NYC, 1998—. Spkr. field. Contbr. articles to profl. jours. Bd. dirs., pres. Childfind Am., Inc., 1993—94; vol. learning disabled children Chelsea Neighborhood, NYC, 1965—67; v.p. bd. dirs. Pelham (NY) Family Svc., 1982—85; bd. dirs. Catskill Ctr. Conservation Devel., 1993—. Recipient Am. Jurisprudence award, Fordham U. Mem.: ABA (alt. dispute resolution com. 1989—93), Assn. Bar City NY (profl. responsibility com. 1987—89, pub. assistance com. 1991—94), NY State Bar Assn. (alt. dispute resolution com. 1989—93). Avocations: woodworking, fly fishing, bicycling, camping. Office: Fulton Rowe & Hart One Rockefeller Plz New York NY 10020 Office Phone: 212-586-0700. Personal E-mail: johnhwilkinson@msn.com.

WILKINSON, LOUISE CHERRY, psychology professor, dean; b. Phila., May 15, 1948; BA magna cum laude, Oberlin Coll., 1970; EdM, EdD, Harvard U., 1974. Prof., chmn. dept. ednl. psychology U. Wis., Madison, 1976-85; prof., exec. officer Grad. Sch. PhD Program CUNY, NYC, 1984-86; disting. prof., dean Grad. Sch. Edn. Rutgers U., 1986—2003; dean Sch. Edn. Syracuse (NY) U., 2003—05, disting. prof. edn., psychology and comm. scis., 2003—. Chair ednl. strategic planning Rutgers U.; mem. nat. rev. bd. Nat. Inst. Edn., 1977, 85, 87; cons. Nat. Ctr. for Bilingual Rsch., 1982, 84, US Dept. Edn., 1995—96; adv. bd. Nat. Reading Rsch. Ctr., 1992—98; co-chair commn. on literacy leadership Internat. Reading Assn.; vis. prof. U. London, 2006—, East China Normal U., 2006—; hon. guest prof. Beijing Normal U., 2001—05. Co-author: Communicating for Learning, 1991; editor: Communicating in Classroom, 1982, Social Context of Instruction, 1984, Gender Influences in the Classroom, 2002; co-editor: Literacy and Language Learning, 2004; contbr. articles to profl. jours.; mem. editl. bds. various publs.:. Fellow: APA, Am. Assn. for Applied and Preventive Psychology, Am. Psychol. Soc.; mem.: NJ Coun. Acad. Policy Advisors, Am. Ednl. Rsch. Assn. (v.p. 1990—92, program chair 1997). Home: 315 Riverside Dr #15A New York NY 10025

WILKINSON, MALCOLM DOYLE, retired pharmacist; b. Gloster, Miss., Aug. 27, 1922; s. Guy William and Elseba Lucille Wilkinson; m. Joyce Pearl Montgomery, Dec. 26, 1946; children: Elizabeth Anne Johnson, James Edward, Martha Sue. BS in Pharmacy, U. Tex., Austin, 1948. Registered pharmacist Tex., 1948. Med. svc. rep. Abbott Labs., Chgo., 1952—60; pharmacy owner City Drug Store, Raymondville, Tex., 1960—71; chief pharmacist Christus Spohn Hosp., Corpus Christi, Tex., 1972—88; pharmacy surveyor Tex. Dept. Health, Corpus Christi, 1988—91; ret., 1992. Sgt. US Army, 1942—45, European Theatre. Home: 625 Gregory Dr Apt 23 Corpus Christi TX 78412 Home Phone: 361-991-8666.

WILKINSON, RALPH RUSSELL, retired biochemistry educator, toxicologist; b. Portland, Oreg., Feb. 20, 1930; s. Tracy Chandler and Lavern (Russell) W.; m. Evelyn Marie Wickman, Aug. 5, 1956. BA, Reed Coll., 1953; PhD, U. Oreg., 1962; MBA, U. Mo., Kansas City, 1974. Rsch. chemist VA Hosp., Kansas City, Mo., 1973-74; sr. rsch. chemist Midwest Rsch. Inst., Kansas City, 1975-84; prof. Rockhurst Coll., Kansas City, 1985-86, Cleve. Chiropractic Coll., Kansas City, 1987-99, prof. emeritus, 1999—. Cons. in biochemistry, toxicology, environ. impact, tech. assessment, Kansas City, 1984—. Author: (book) Neurotoxins and Neurobiological Function, 1987; contbr. articles to profl. jours. Mem. Southtown Coun., Kansas City, Mo., 1989—, Spina Bifida Assn. Am., Kansas City, 1989—. NSF fellow, 1959-60. Mem. Am. Chem. Soc., Sigma Xi. Avocations: travel, history, biography, music, antiques. Home: 7911 Charlotte St Kansas City MO 64131-2175

WILKINSON, ROSEMARY REGINA CHALLONER, poet, writer; b. New Orleans, Feb. 21, 1924; d. William Lindsay Challoner Jr. and Julia Regina (Sellen) Challoner/Schillo; m. Henry Bertram Wilkinson, Oct. 15, 1949; children: Denis James, Marian Regina, Paul Francis, Richard Challoner. Lifetime credential to teach poetry, San Francisco State U., 1978; LHD (hon.), Livre U., Pakistan, 1975; DLitt (hon.), World Acad. Arts & Culture, Rep. of China, 1981. Lectr./reader of poetry. Author: (poetry) A Girl's Will, 1973, California Poet, 1976, Earth's Compromise, 1977, It Happened to Me, 1978, I Am Earth Woman, 1979, The Poet and the Painter, 1981, Poetry and Arte, 1982, Gems Within, 1984, Nature's Guest, 1984, In the Pines, 1985, Longing for You, 1986, Purify the Earth, 1988, Sacred in Nature, 1988, Earth's Children, 1990, New Seed, 1991, Angels and Poetry, 1992, Cambrian Zephyr, 1993, Collected Poems, 1994, Poetry: Nature, 1996, Poetry: Spiritual, 1997, Poetry Calendar 2000, 1999, A Song in the Wind with Love, 2001, My Plea, 2001, Selected Verses, 2001, Blessing of Poetry, 2002, Living Spring Water, 2005, 2006, others, (epic)

An Historical Epic, 1974, Epic of the Ships Captain, 1986. Founder Poetry-Fine Arts Divsn. of San Mateo (Calif.) County Fair, 1977, Dr. Williams Poetry Workshop, Burlingame H.S., 1985; sec.-gen. World Acad. Arts and Culture-USA, San Francisco, 1985—95, pres., 1994—2003. Mem.: Authors League Am., The Authors Guild, Acad. Am. Poets, Poetry Soc. of Am., Nat. League Am. Pen Women Inc. (Washington 4th and 5th v.p. 1986—90, Berkeley, Calif. pres. 1988—90, Lake Tahoe br. 1988—), World Acad. of Arts and Culture/World Congress of Poets, World Congress of Poets (Taipei, Taiwan bd. dirs. 1973—2003, San Francisco pres. 1981, sec.-gen. 1985—95, pres. 1994—2003), Soroptomist Internat. (hon.). Democrat. Roman Catholic. Avocations: reading, research, brush painting, lecturing. Home: 3146 Buckeye Ct Placerville CA 95667-8334

WILKINSON, SIGNE, cartoonist; b. Wichita Falls, Tex. married. BA in English, 1972; student, Pa. Acad. Fine Arts. Reporter West Chester (Pa.) Daily Local News, Academy of Natural Scis., Phila.; freelance cartoonist Phila. and N.Y. publs.; cartoonist San Jose (Calif.) Mercury News, 1982-85, Phila. Daily News, 1985—. Illustrator: Abortion Cartoons in Demand, 1992, You Bet Your Tomatoes, 2002, How to Grow the $735 Tomato, 1999; contbr. to Univ. Barge Club News, various mags. Bd. dirs. Fair Hill Burial Ground. Recipient Pulitzer Prize for editl. cartooning, 1992, Overseas Press Club award, 1997, 2001, 2007, Robert F. Kennedy award, 2002. Mem. Assn. Am. Editl. Cartoonists (pres. 1994-95). Avocations: gardening, rowing. Office: Phila Daily News PO Box 7788 400 N Broad St Philadelphia PA 19130-4015 Business E-Mail: wilkins@phillynewes.com.

WILKINSON, WARREN SCRIPPS, manufacturing executive; b. Detroit, Feb. 2, 1920; s. Almadus DeGrasse and Harriet Gertrude (Whitcomb) W.; m. Joan Todd, June 14, 1941; m. Mireille De Bary, Dec. 17, 1966. Grad., Hotchkiss Sch., Lakeville, Conn., 1937; BS in Math, Harvard U., 1941; student, Calif. Inst. Tech., 1941-42. With U.S. Rubber Co., Detroit, 1942-43, Hanson Van Winkle-Munning Co., Matawan, NJ, 1946-64, pres., 1961-64; v.p., gen. mgr. Hanson-Van Winkle-Munning div. M & Chems. Inc., 1964-66; chmn. RPI Designs, Marlette, Mich., 1966—. Overseer's com. on univ. resources Harvard U. With USN, 1943—46. John Harvard fellow, 1996. Home: 2 Woodland Pl Grosse Pointe MI 48230-1920

WILKINSON, WILLIAM SHERWOOD, lawyer; b. Williston, ND, Sept. 6, 1933; s. John Thomas and Evelyn (Landon) W.; m. Carol Ann Burns, Aug. 20, 1960; children— Leslie Ann, Richard Sherwood, Greta Diann. BS in Bus, U. Idaho, 1955; JD, U. Denver, 1960. Bar: Colo. 1960, Mich. 1966. Practiced in, Canon City, Colo., 1960-66; asst. dist. atty. 11th Jud. Dist., Colo., 1961-65; gen. counsel, sec. Mich. Farm Bur. Family Cos., Lansing, 1966-96. Lectr. Pre-Parole Release Center, Colo. State Penitentiary, 1961-65; instr. adult edn., Canon City, 1965; counsel Canon City Recreation Dist., 1964-65 Mem. lay adv. bd. St. Thomas More Hosp., Canon City, 1963-66; Del., county, dist. and congl. convs. Republican party, 1964. Served to capt. USAF, 1955-58. Recipient Cmty. Disting. Svc. award Canon City Jr. C. of C., 1964; named to Outstanding Young Men of Am., 1965. Mem. ABA, Colo. Bar Assn., Mich. Bar Assn., Am. Judicature Soc., Am. Corp. Counsel Assn., Nat. Coun. Farmer Coops. (legal, tax and acctg. com.), Phi Delta Phi, Tau Kappa Epsilon. Methodist (lay leader, mem. ch. ofcl. bd.). Home: 1707 Foxcroft Rd East Lansing MI 48823-2131 Personal E-mail: wwilca@aol.com.

WILKOW, BRIAN RICHARD, hospital administrator and clinician; b. Bklyn., June 3, 1964; s. Elliot and Marcia W. BS, Touro Coll., 1987. Lic. physician asst. Nat. Commn. on Cert. Physician Assts. Coord. physician assts. Luth. Med. Ctr., Bklyn., 1989—96; dir. physician asst. svcs. N.Y. Meth. Hosp., Bklyn., 1996—. Adj. lectr. Coll. Staten Is., N.Y., 1993—; EMT instr. coord. Staten Is. Emergency Med. Tng., 1993—, preceptor SUNY, Bklyn., 1996—. Pres. Shorefront Vol. Ambulance Corps, Bklyn., 1990-2000, Bklyn. Critical Incident Stress Mgmt. Team, 1999—; v.p. Temple Beth Ahavath Sholom, Bklyn., 1997-2001, pres. 2001—. Fellow Am. Acad. Physician Assts., Am. Assn. Surg. and Physician Assts., N.Y. State Soc. Physician Assts. Office: NY Meth Hosp 506 6th St Brooklyn NY 11215-3645 E-mail: brwpac@aol.com.

WILKOWSKI, E. TODD, lawyer; b. Phillippines, June 2, 1967; BS, USAF Acad., 1989; MA, Regent U. Sch. Pub. Policy, 1998; JD, Regent U. Sch. Law, 1998. Bar: Ohio 1998, US Dist. Ct. Southern Dist. Ohio 1999, US Ct. of Appeals Sixth Cir. 2006. Counternarcotics intelligence officer Pentagon, South Am. embassies; ptnr. Keating Muething & Klekamp PLL, Cin. Dir. St. Rita Sch. for Deaf, 2000—06; dir., Alumni Bd. Regent U. Law Sch., 2000—06; dir. Friars Club, Inc., 2001—04, Cin. Teen Challenge, Inc.; mem., Bd. Trustees Coun. on Child Abuse of Southern Ohio, Inc.; mentor Help One Student to Succeed Prog., Oyler Elem. Sch.; treasurer St. Thomas More Soc. Greater Cin.; dir. Catholic Men's Fellowship, Inc.; mem., Young Exec. Com. Catholic Inner-city Schools Edn. Named one of 40 Under 40, Cin. Bus. Courier, 2004, Ohio's Rising Stars, Super Lawyers, 2005, 2006; recipient Def. Meritorious Svc. award, 1994. Mem.: Cin. Acad. Leadership for Lawyers (Class X), USAF Acad. Assn. of Graduates, Ohio State Bar Assn., Cin. Bar Assn. (vice chmn., Constrn. Law Com.). Office: Keating Muething & Klekamp PLL One E Fourth St Ste 1400 Cincinnati OH 45202 Office Phone: 513-579-6498. Office Fax: 513-579-6457.

WILKS, DANA LYN, protective services official, writer; b. Long Beach, Calif., Dec. 27, 1964; d. Donald Lee and Helen Arlene Wilks; m. Kim Kreimeyer, Apr. 3, 2004. BA, Colo. State U., Fort Collins, 1988, MA, 1993. Ordained to ministry Universal Life Ch., Calif., 2004; cert. corrections mgr. Am. Correctional Assn., 2004. Cert. addicitons counselor New Beginnings, Fort Collins, Colo., 1988—91; grad. tchg. asst. Colo. State U., 1992—93; case mgr. supr. The Restitution Ctr., Greeley, 1993—96; free-lance rschr. Denver, 1995—2006; probation officer 19th Jud. Dist., Greeley, 1996—2001; probation supr. 18th Jud. Dist., Centennial, 2001—; instr. U. No. Colo., Greeley, 2004—05. Trainer Colo. Jud. Br., Denver, 1995—; presenter in field. Author short stories, of poems. Mem. So. Poverty Law Ctr., Montgomery, Ala., 2005—06; mem., vol. Human Rights Campaign, Washington, 2003—06; vol. Shambhala Meditation Centers, Colo., 2003—06; project dir. Trek for Hospice, 2006—. Recipient Outstanding Svc. award, Colo. Alcohol and Drug Driving Safety Program, 2004. Mem.: Colo. Probation Supr. Assn. (chairperson 2004—06), Am. Correctional Assn., Am. Probation and Parole Assn. Achievements include first to pass testing and be granted the American Correctional Association's Certified Corrections Manager certification in Colorado. Avocations: travel, writing. Office: 18th Judicial Probation Dept 7305 S Potomac St 201 Centennial CO 80112-4041 Home Phone: 303-975-2705; Office Phone: 303-662-5946. Office Fax: 303-662-5900. E-mail: dana.wilks@judicial.state.co.us.

WILKS, DAVID M., energy executive; BS in Mech. Engring., Tex. A&M U., College Station; MS in Bus. Fin. Mgmt., George Washington U. Various positions in engring. and ops. Southwestern Pub. Svc. Co.; pres. Mktg. and Svcs. New Century Energies, 1997—98, pres. Delivery; pres. Energy Supply Xcel Energy (merger of No. States Power Co. and New Century Energies). Mem. Greater Golden C. of C.; mem. adv. bd. Tex. A&M Coll. Engring.; bd. dirs., bd. trustees Denver Area Coun. Boy Scouts Am. Recipient Ally award, Women's Vision Found., 2003. Office: Xcel Energy 414 Nicollet Mall Minneapolis MN 55401-1993 *

WILKS, LARRY DEAN, lawyer; b. Columbia, SC, Jan. 8, 1955; s. Ray Dean and Jean (Garrett) W.; m. Jan Elizabeth McIllwain, May 2,1981; children: John Ray, Adam Garrett. BS, U. Tenn., 1977, JD, 1980. Bar: Tenn. 1981, U.S. Dist. Ct. (mid. dist.) Tenn. 1981, U.S. Supreme Ct. 1986, U.S. Ct. Appeals (6th cir.) 1993, U.S. Dist. Ct. (we. dist.) Tenn. 1996. Assoc. Mayo & Norris, Nashville, 1981-82; sole practice Springfield, Tenn., 1982-84; ptnr. Walton, Jones & Wilks, 1984, Jones & Wilks, 1984-89; pvt. practice Springfield, Tenn., 1989—. Chmn. Dem. Orgn. Robertson County Tenn., 1986-93. Fellow Tenn. Bar Found.; mem. ABA, ATLA, Tenn. Bar Assn. (assoc. gen. counsel 1991-94, gen. counsel 1994-99, bd. profl. responsibility 1993-98, bd. govs. 1991—, young lawyers divsn. lifetime fellow, asst. treas. 1999-2000, treas. 2000—03, co-chair leadership law 2003-04, v.p. 2004-2005, pres. elect 2005-06, pres. 2006-07, immediate past pres. 2007—), Tenn. Assn. Criminal Def. Lawyers, Tenn. Trial Lawyers Assn. (bd. govs. 2002—), Robertson County Bar Assn. (pres. 1993-96), Nat. Assn. Criminal Def. Laywers, Tenn. Young Lawyers Conf. (bd. dirs. 1987, editor quar. newsletter 1987-88, Mid. Tenn. v.p. 1988-89, v.p. 1989-90, pres.-elect 1990-91, pres. 1991-92), Robertson County U. Tenn. Alumni Assn. (pres. 2003-04) Methodist. Office: Atty at Law 509 W Court Sq Springfield TN 37172-2413 Office Phone: 615-384-8444.

WILL, ALFRED JOSEPH, lawyer, engineer; s. James George and Catherine Rose (Steinmuller) Will; m. Therese Catherine Will, Nov. 23, 1972; children: Peter Simon, Daniel Alfred, Meredith Marie, Eric James. BS in Engring., U.S. Merchant Marine Acad., 1972; JD, St. John's Law Sch., 1975. Bar: N.Y. 1976, U.S. Dist. Cts. (so. and ea. dists.) N.Y. 1976, U.S. Ct. Appeals (2d cir.) 1982, U.S. Supreme Ct. 1982. Assoc. Tabak, Ezratty & Mellusi, NYC, 1975—76; sr. assoc. Vincent, Berg, Russo, Marcigliano & Zawacki, NYC, 1976—81; sr. ptnr. Badiak & Will, NYC, 1981—. Past pres., founder Admiralty Law Sch. St. John's U., NYC, 1974—75. Served to lt. USNR, 1969—78. Named Athlete of Yr. (track), U.S. Merchant Marine Acad., 1972; recipient Gov.'s Scholastic award, N.Y. State, 1967—68. Mem.: Maritime Law Assn. of U.S., Average Adjusters Assn. of U.S., N.Y. County Bar Assn. Roman Catholic. Home: 23 Robbins Dr E Williston Williston Park NY 11596-2009 Also: Badiak Will & Kallen 17071 W Dixie Hwy North Miami Beach FL 33160-3765 Office: Badiak & Will LLP 106 Third St Mineola NY 11501 Office Phone: 516-877-2225. Personal E-mail: lawbwm@aol.com. Business E-Mail: awill@badiakwill.com.

WILL, CLARK BRADFORD, lawyer; b. Ft. Sam Houston, Tex., Sept. 17, 1955; s. Clement Herbert and Mary Louise (Cantu) W.; m. Donna Gail Fletcher, Oct. 14, 1978; children: Nathanael Aaron, Nicholas Andrew. BA with distinction, U. Tex., Austin, 1977; JD with distinction, St. Mary's U., San Antonio, 1980; diploma in Mil. Law, U. Va., Judge Advocate Gens. Sch., Charlottesville, 1981. Bar: Tex. 1980, U.S. Ct. Mil. Appeals 1981, U.S. Dist. Ct. (no., we., ea. dist.) Tex. 1986, U.S. Ct. Appeals (5th cir.) 1990, U.S. Ct. Fed. Claims, 2004. Legal asst. officer Ft. Sill, Okla., 1980-81, trial counsel Okla., 1981-84; assoc. Payne & Vendig, Dallas, 1986-88; mem. Payne & Vendig PC, Dallas, 1989-93, Brown, Herman, Scott Dean & Miles LLP, Ft. Worth, 1993—98; ptnr. Quilling, Selander, Cummiskey & Lownds, PC, 1998—. Elder Prince of Peace Luth. Ch., Carrollton, Tex., 1986-87, exec. elder, 1987-93; mem. Hillcrest Ch., Dallas, 1995-2004. Capt. U.S. Army, 1980-86. Army Commendation medal, 1984, Hon. Order Saint Barbara, 1984, Meritorious Svc. medal, 1986; Named one of Outstanding Young Men in Am., 1982. Mem. NRA, Dallas Bar Assn. (environ. law and litigation sect.), State Bar Tex. (litig. natural resources, and environ. law sect.), American Legion. Conservative. Lutheran. Avocations: golf, hunting, hockey, baseball. Home: 848 Aberdeen Ct Coppell TX 75019-2859 Office: Quilling Selander Cummiskey and Lownds PC 2001 Bryan St Ste 1800 Dallas TX 75201 Office Phone: 214-871-2100. Business E-Mail: cwill@qsclpc.com.

WILL, CLIFFORD MARTIN, physicist, researcher, educator; b. Hamilton, Ont., Can., Nov. 13, 1946; m. Leslie Saxe Moser, June 26, 1970; children: Elizabeth Sue Torop, Rosalie Will Boxt. BS, McMaster U., Hamilton, 1968; PhD, Calif. Inst. Tech., 1971. Enrico Fermi fellow U. Chgo., 1972-74; asst. prof. physics Stanford U., Palo Alto, Calif., 1974-81; assoc. prof. physics Washington U., St. Louis, 1981—85, prof. physics, 1985—2005, James S. McDonnell prof. physics dept. physics and McDonnell Ctr. Space Scis., 2005—, chmn. dept. physics, 1991—96, 1997—2002. Vis. assoc. physics Calif. Inst. Tech., 1976; chmn. com. on time transfer in satellite systems Air Force Studies Bd., Washington, 1984—86; rsch. assoc. Nat. Ctr. Sci. Rsch. Obs. Paris, Meudon, France, 1996; vis. prof. Hebrew U. Racah Inst. Physics, Jerusalem, 1997, U. Pierre and Marie Curie, Paris, 2006, Inst. Henri Poincare and U. Paris IX, 2006; chmn. sci. adv. com. NASA Gravity Probe B, 1998; rsch. assoc. Nat. Ctr. Sci. Rsch. Inst. Astrophysics, Paris, 2003—04, 2005, 06, 07. Assoc. editor Phys. Rev. Letters, 1989-92, Phys. Rev. D, 1999-2001; author: Theory and Experiment in Gravitational Physics, 1981, rev. edit., 1993, Was Einstein Right?, 1986, rev. edit., 1993. Alfred P. Sloan Found. fellow, 1975-79, J.S. Guggenheim Found. fellow, 1996-97, J.W. Fulbright fellow, 1996-97; recipient Sci. Writing award Am. Inst. Physics, 1987, Disting. Alumni award, McMaster U., 1996. Fellow Am. Phys. Soc. (exec. com. astrophysics divsn. 1988-90, vice chair, chair elect, chair topical group on gravitation 1997-2001), Am. Acad. Arts and Scis.; mem. NAS, Am. Astron. Soc., Am. Assn. Physics Tchrs. (Richtmyer Meml. Lectr. 1987), Internat. Soc. Gen. Relativity and Gravitation (pres. 2004—). Office: Washington U Dept Physics Campus Box 1105 1 Brookings Dr Saint Louis MO 63130-4899 Office Phone: 314-935-6244. Office Fax: 314-935-6219. E-mail: cmw@wuphys.wustl.edu. *

WILL, FREDERIC, academic administrator, educator, writer; b. New Haven, Dec. 4, 1928; s. Samuel F. and Constance B. Will; m. Julie Omotejohwo, July 27, 1995; children: Barbara, Alex, Jennifer, Chris, Carson, Kyle. BA, Ind. U., 1948; PhD, Yale U., 1954. Asst. prof. classics Dartmouth, Hanover, N.H., 1952-54, Pa. State U., University Park, 1955-60; prof. classics U. Tex., Austin, 1960-65; prof. comparative lit. U. Iowa, Iowa City, 1965-70, fellow Inst. Advanced Studies, 1985-92; prof. comparative lit. U. Mass., Amherst, 1971-84; pres. Mellen U., Mt. Vernon, Iowa, 1995—2000; prof. Am. studies U. Ivory Coast, 2000—02; vis. prof. classics Cornell Coll., Iowa, 2002; vis. prof. Hunan Normal U., China, 2003; prof. U. Robert de Boron, France, 2004—. Vis. prof. Deep Springs Coll., Calif., 2003—06. Author: Intelligible Beauty in Aesthetic Thought, 1958, Mosaic and Other Poems, 1959, A Wedge of Words, 1963, The Twelve Words of the Gypsy, (trans.) 1964, Metaphrasis, 1964, Flumen Historicum, 1965, Hereditas, 1965, Literature Inside Out, 1966, The King's Flute (trans.), 1966, From A Year in Greece, 1967, Planets, 1968, Archilochos, 1969, Herondas, 1972, Brandy in the Snow, 1972, The Fact of Literature, 1973, The Knife in the Stone, 1973, The Jargon of Authenticity, (trans.) 1973, Guatemala, 1973, Botulism, 1975, The Generic Demands of Greek Literature, 1976, Belphagor, 1977, Epics of America, 1977, Our Thousand Year Old Bodies: Selected Poems, 1980, Shamans in Turtlenecks, 1984, The Sliced Dog, 1984, The Fall and The Gods 3 vols., 1988-92, Entering the Open Hole, 1989, Big Rig Souls, 1992, Translation Theory and Practice, 1993, Literature as Sheltering the Human, 1993, Singing with Whitman's Thrush, 1993, Recoveries, 1993, Trips of the Psyche, 1993, Textures, Spaces, Wonders, 1993, Field Research in North American Agricultural Communities, 2002, Social Reflections on Work, 2002, Miroirs d'Eternité, 2002, Flesh and the Colour of Love, 2002, English for Success, 2002, Three Essays on Mellen University: Early Life and Times, 2004, The Male's Midlife Rite of Passage: Three Imagined Lives, 2006, China, a Modern History, 2006; founding editor Arion, 1962, Micromegas, 1965—; lit. papers archived in Humanities Rsch. Ctr., U. Tex., Austin. Recipient award, Tex. Inst. Letters, 1962, NY Quar. prize, 1962, awards, PEN Club/Writers' Union, 1962—67; fellow, Fulbright Found., Greece, 1952, Germany, 1957, Tunisia, 1976, Cote d'Ivoire, 2000—02, Chad, 2003, Bollingen Found., 1956, Am. Coun. Learned Socs., 1957, Nat. Endowment Arts, 1960; grantee, Coordinating Coun. Lit. Mags., 1962—67; tchg. intern, Ford Found., 1953. Buddhist. Home: 617 7th St NW Mount Vernon IA 52314 Office Phone: 319-895-6159. Personal E-mail: samuelw981@aol.com.

WILL, JAMES FREDRICK, academic administrator, former steel company executive; b. Pitts., Oct. 12, 1938; s. Fred F. and Mary Agnes (Ganter) W.; m. Mary Ellen Bowser, Dec. 19, 1964; children: Mary Beth, Kerry Ann. BSEE, Pa. State U., 1961; MBA, Duquesne U., 1972. Works mgr. Kaiser Steel Corp., Fontana, Calif., 1976-78, v.p. ops., 1978-80, v.p. planning, 1980-81, exec. v.p., 1981, pres., 1981-82; exec. v.p., pres. indsl. group Cyclops Corp., Pitts, 1982-86, pres., chief operating officer Pitts., 1986-88, pres., chief exec. officer, 1989-92; pres., chief oper. officer Armco Inc., Parsippany, NJ, 1992-93, pres., chief exec. officer Pitts., 1994-96, chmn., pres., CEO, 1996—2000; pres. Saint Vincent Coll., Latrobe, Pa., 2000—06, pres. emeritus, vice chancellor, 2006—. Vice-chmn. 1994, chmn. 1995, Specialty Steel Industry of N.Am. Office: Saint Vincent Coll 300 Fraser Purchase Rd Latrobe PA 15650-2690

WILL, KATHERINE HALEY, academic administrator; m. Oscar Henry Will, III; 4 children. Student, Carleton Coll., 1970-73; BA in English, Tufts U., 1974; MA in English, U. Ill., Urbana, 1975, PhD in English, 1986. Instr. English Augustana Coll., Sioux Falls, S.D., 1977-86, asst. prof. English, 1986-90, faculty dir. new student seminar program, 1987-91, assoc. prof. English, 1990-96, dean grad. study, dir. gen. edn., 1991—96; provost, prof. English Kenyon Coll., Gambier, Ohio, 1996-99; pres. Whittier Coll., Calif., 1999—2004, Gettysburg Coll., Pa., 2004—. Participant Mgmt. Devel. Seminar for Higher Edn. Adminstrs., Harvard U., summer 1992; cons. and presenter in field. Contbr. articles to profl. jours. Bd. dirs. United Way Great L.A. NEH fellow Summer Seminar in Romanticism and Gender, UCLA, 1989. Mem.: Annapolis Group (exec. com.), Coun. Ind. Colls. (bd. dirs.), Nat. Assn. Ind. Colls. and Univs. (bd. dirs.). Office: Gettysburg Coll Pennsylvania Hall, 3 Fl W 300 N Washington St Gettysburg PA 17325 Office Phone: 717-337-6011. Office Fax: 717-337-6008. E-mail: will@gettysburg.edu. *

WILL, ROLAND TRACY, II, writer, editor, journalist, publisher, television producer; b. Schenectady, NY, May 18, 1954; s. Albert Roland and Constance Mary (Headley) W.; m. Gay Adair Strandemo, July 1, 1989; children: Roland Leigh Leonard, Glenn Tracy. BA, U. Wis., 1988. Polit. sci. and comm. arts editor, pub., journalist Wis. Health Policy Report, Wis. Ind. News Svc., Madison, 1994—99. Author: (Compass Am. Guide) Wisconsin, 1994, 3d edit., 2001, History of Dane the Capital County, 2000; (plays) Packer Glory, 1984, Fatal Time to Final End, 1986; actor (plays) Bombs Away Enola Gay, 1983, Hans Brinker and Silver Skates: Rock Musical on Roller Skates, 1984, Light My Fire—Jim Morrison, 1985, The Cherry Orchard, 1985, The Hangwoman, 1986, The Phantom of Shopppko, 1987, Joe a Life: The Story of Joe McCarthy, 1988, Chain Reaction, 1996; series editor, contbr. Wisconsin: Buildings of America, 2006; writer, prodr. (TV spl.) Spanish Spoken Here, 2005 (named Best Documentary, Wis. Broadcasters Assn.). Bus. mem. Dane County Hist. Soc., Madison, 1995; sec. bd. dirs. Broom St. Theater, Madison, 1984-2005; curator photography exhibit Wis. Hist. Mus.; TV host/prodr. Wisconsin Stories, Wis. Pub. TV, 1999-2002; curriculum com. Wannakee Sch. Bd., 2005; vestry St. Dunstan's Episcopal Ch., Madison. Episcopalian. Avocations: history, architecture, travel. Personal E-mail: tracy.will@yahoo.com.

WILL, TREVOR JONATHAN, lawyer; b. Ashland, Wis., Aug. 11, 1953; s. William Taylor and Geraldine Sue (Trevor) W.; m. Margaret Ann Johnson, Aug. 28, 1976; children: Tyler William, Alexandra Marie, Jennifer Catherine. BA summa cum laude, Augustana Coll., 1975; JD cum laude, Harvard U., 1978. Bar: Wis. 1978, U.S. Dist. Ct. (ea. dist.) Wis. 1978, U.S. DIst. Ct. (we. dist.) Wis. 1980, U.S. Ct. Appeals (7th cir.) 1983, U.S. Supreme Ct. 1984, U.S. Dist. Ct. (ea. dist.) Mich. 1985. Assoc. Foley & Lardner LLP, Milw., 1978-87, ptnr., 1987—, chmn. product liability practice group. Adj. law prof. Marquette U. Law Sch., 1994-00. Mem. ABA, State Bar Wis., Milw. Bar Assn., Def. Rsch. Inst. Office: Foley & Lardner LLP 777 E Wisconsin Ave Ste 3800 Milwaukee WI 53202-5306 Office Phone: 414-297-5536. Office Fax: 414-297-4900. Business E-Mail: twill@foley.com.

WILLADSEN, MICHAEL CHRIS, marketing professional, sales executive; b. Cheboygan, Mich., Sept. 18, 1946; s. Chris Jens and Helen Margaret (Barr) W.; m. Kay Ann Brooks, Dec. 10, 1964, (div. Dec. 10, 1989); children: Michael Jr., Erik; m. Linda Sue Degroff, Apr. 4, 1992; children: Stephanie, Gretchen, Ross. Student, Delta Coll., 1964—66; A in Bus. Mgmt., Northwood Inst., 1968, BA in Bus. Mgmt., 1969. Mktg. rep. Detroit dist. Petemco, Inc., 1970-73, mktg. rep. Indpls. Dist., 1973-74; dist. mgr. Petemco Inc.-Ind. Ohio Mich., Ind., Ohio, Mich., 1974-76, Consolidated Stas. Marathon Oil, Oshkosh, Wis., 1976-79; sales mgr. Champaign (Ill.) Dist. Marathon Oil, 1981-82, supr. Credit Card Ctr. Findlay, Ohio, 1982-84; wholesale mktg. profl. Marathon Brand Mktg./Ohio, Mich., Ky., 1982-84; jobber sales Marathon Oil/Ohio, Pa., W.Va., Ohio, Pa., W. Va., 1984-92, Marathon Oil/Ill., Wisc., Chgo., Chgo., 1992-2000, Marathon Ashland Petroleum, Atlanta, 2000—, N.C., S.C., Ala.; real estate rep. Marathon Petroleum Co., Chgo., 2006—. Named to Nat. Assn. Intercollegiate Athletes Sml. Coll. All-State Football Team/Dist. 23, 1968; inducted into Mich. Touch Football Hall of Fame/Team Category, 2002. Mem. Cleve. Petroleum Club (v.p. 1988-91), Chgo. Oilmens. Republican. Presbyterian. Avocations: camping, softball, basketball, physical work out. Office: 8585 Broadway Ste 600 Merrillville IN 46410

WILLAM, KASPAR J., civil engineer, educator; b. Vienna, Dec. 20, 1940; came to U.S., 1981; s. Alphons and Margarete (Meusburger) W.; m. Veronica Collins, Dec. 28, 1971; children: Alison Katherine, Angela Lucinda. Dipl. Ing., Tech. U., Vienna, 1964; MS, Calif. State U.-San Jose, 1966; PhD, U. Calif.-Berkeley, 1969; Privatdozent, U. Stuttgart, Germany, 1980. Research assoc. U. Calif., Berkeley, 1967-70; sec. leader U. Stuttgart, 1970-81; prof. civil engring. U. Colo., Boulder, 1981-88; prof. mechanics U. Karslruhe, Germany, 1988-90; prof. civil engring. U. Colo., Boulder, 1990—. Vis. lectr. NTH Trondheim, Norway, 1975, Northwestern Polytechnical U., Xian, China, 1980; vis. prof. Nanjing Inst. Tech., China, 1985, Nagoya U., Japan, 1992, Politecnico di Milano, 1993, U. Stuttgart, 1995, 98, Vienna U. of Tech., 1997, Polytechnical U. of Catalonia, 1998. Adv. editor: Computer Methods in Applied Mechanics and Engring., 1981—; editorial bd.: Engring. Computations, 1983—. Mem. ASCE, ASME, NAE, Gesellschaft für Angewandte Methematik und Mechanik. Office: Univ Colo PO Box 428 Boulder CO 80303 Office Phone: 303-492-7011, 303-492-7317. E-mail: willam@colorado.edu.

WILLANS, JEAN STONE, bishop, religious organization administrator; b. Hillsboro, Ohio, Oct. 3, 1924; d. Homer and Ella (Keys) Hammond; m. Richard James Willans, Mar. 28, 1966; 1 dau., Suzanne Jeanne. Student, San Diego Jr. Coll.; DD (hon.), Am. Coll. Sems., 1996. Ordained archdeacon, 1996, ordained priest 1997, consecrated bishop 1998, Ch. of the East. Asst. to v.p. Family Loan Co., Miami, Fla., 1946-49; civilian supr. USAF, Washington, 1953-55; founder, dir. Blessed Trinity Soc.; editor Trinity mag., LA, 1960-66; co-founder, exec. v.p., dir. Soc. of Stephen, Altadena, Calif., 1967—; exec. dir. Hong Kong, 1975-81. Lectr. in field. Author: The Acts of the Green Apples, 1974, rev. edit. 1995, Chinese edit., 2003; co-editor: Charisma in Hong Kong, 1970, Spiritual Songs, 1970, The People Who Walked in Darkness, 1977, The People Who Walked in Darkness II, 1992, 2d edit., 2000; works archived at Fuller Theol. Sem., 2004. Recipient Achievement award Nat. Assn. Pentecostal Women, 1964;

monument erected in her honor Kowloon Walled City Park, Hong Kong Govt., 1996. Republican. Office: Soc of Stephen PO Box 6225 Altadena CA 91003-6225 Office Phone: 626-797-9667.

WILLANS, JOANNE JOY, music educator; b. Hackensack, NJ, July 5, 1969; d. Carol May and Daniel Gaetano Macaluso (Stepfather), Ignazio Salvatore Ciaravino; m. Steven Davey Willans, June 6, 1992; children: Benjamen Davey, Timothy Luke, Joshua Roswell, Samantha Joy. MusB in Music Edn., Rutgers U., 1992. Handbell choir dir. 1st Presbyn. Ch. of Whippany, NJ, 1991—, sr. high youth fellowship adviser, 1994—; music tchr. Hanover Twp. Bd. of Edn., Whippany, NJ, 1999—. Bassoonist Hanover Wind Symphony, Whippany, 1999—. Ch. sch. coord., youth adviser 1st Presbyn. Ch. of Whippany, Whippany. Mem.: NEA, N.J. Music Educators Assn., N.J. Edn. Assn. (life), Am. Guild of English Handbell Ringers, Rutgers U. Alumni Assn. (life). Presbyterian. Avocations: performing various instruments, writing Christian youth skits and sermons, sewing, poetry. Home: 11 Grove Pl Whippany NJ 07981 Home Phone: 973-599-0006.

WILLARD, ATOM (ADAM WILLARD), musician; b. San Diego, Aug. 15, 1973; Drummer Rocket from the Crypt, 1992—2000, Offspring, 2005—; co-founder & drummer Angels & Airwaves, 2005—. Musician: (albums) (with Rocket from the Crypt) Circa: Now!, 1992, Scream, Dracula, Scream!, 1995, RFTC, 1998, (with Angels & Airwaves) We Don't Need to Whisper, 2006. Co-recipient Woodie of Yr. award (with Angels & Airwaves), mtvU Woodie Awards, 2006. *

WILLARD, GARCIA LOU, artist; b. Huntington, W.Va., Apr. 15, 1943; d. Harry Lee and Laura Lillian (Riley) Hall; m. Victor Percy Young, Sept. 2, 1972 (dec. Mar. 1980); m. Roger Lee Willard, Aug. 22, 1988. Student, Marshall U., 1978—83, W.Va. U., 1993, U. N.D., 1994—95. Owner, pres. Young's Fine Art, Huntington, 1975-85, Dyna Line, Wheeling, W.Va., 1980-85; instr. pastel and drawing Oglebay Mus.'s Stifel Fine Art Ctr., Wheeling, 1984-87; instr. pastel and portraiture Ohio U., Athens, 1987; owner, operator Outlines, Phoenix, Ariz., 1988-91; contbg. artist Sonoran Gallery, Phoenix, 1993—. Mem. adv. bd. Profl. Art League, St. Clairsville, Ohio, 1984-85; lectr. and exhbn. juror various art orgns., Ohio, W.Va., Pa., 1987-88; art cons. Journey's End Designs, Wheeling, 1987. One woman shows include: Delf-Norona Mus., Moundsville, W. Va., Ariel Gallery, N.Y.C., Sonoran Gallery, Phoenix; Group shows include: Pen & Brush Club, N.Y.C., 1988, Hermitage Found. Mus., Va., 1988; contbr., illustrator: (book) Dr. Horton on African Art, 1985. Advisor Ariz. Fine Arts Commn., Phoenix, 1989-92. Recipient Best of Show award Delf-Norona Mus., 1985, Molly Guion award for graphics Catharine Lorillard Wolfe Art Club, 1988, Douglas Pickering Carnegie Mellon award, 1986. Fellow Am. Artists Profl. League (Pastel award 1988); mem. Pastel Soc. Am. (signature mem. artist mem., A & M design award, 1988), Acad. Artists Assn. (artist mem., award for pastel portrait 1989), Degas Pastel Soc. (artist mem., M. Grumbacher award for pastel excellence 1988), Nat. Drawing Assn., Art Assn. Harrisburg (artist mem.), Signature Mem. Pastel Soc. Am., N.Y.C. Republican. Avocations: archaeology, astronomy, paper-making, symphonies, travel. Office: Sonoran Gallery 8819 W Corrine Dr Peoria AZ 85381-8166 Home Phone: 623-594-1918; Office Phone: 623-773-1958. Personal E-mail: rrollo88@cox.net.

WILLARD, H(ARRISON) ROBERT, electrical engineer; b. Seattle, May 31, 1933; s. Harrison Eugene and Florence Linea (Chelquist) Willard. BSEE, U. Wash., 1955, MSEE, 1957, PhD, 1971. Lic. profl. engr., Wash. Staff assoc. Boeing Sci. Rsch. Labs., Seattle, 1959-64; rsch. assoc. U. Wash., 1968-72, sr. engr., rsch. prof. applied physics lab., 1972-81; sr. engr. Boeing Aerospace Co., Seattle, 1981-84; dir. instrumentation and engring. MetriCor Inc. (formerly Tech. Dynamics, Inc.), Redmond, Wash., 1984-92; sr. engr. B.E. Meyers & Co., Inc., Redmond, 1992—. Contbr. articles to profl. jours. With US Army, 1957—59. Mem.: IEEE, Am. Geophys. Union, Sigma Xi, Phi Beta Kappa, Tau Beta Pi. Achievements include patents in field. Office: 14540 NE 91st St Redmond WA 98052-4939

WILLARD, JOHN GERARD, communications executive, consultant, writer, educator; b. Pitts., Nov. 20, 1952; s. Cornelius Merle and May E. (Hinds) W.; m. Lorraine L. Franze, Sept. 2, 1978; children: Mary Elizabeth, Kristen Anne, Lisa Lorraine, Jessica Kathleen. BA in Journalism, Duquesne U., 1974. Producer, dir. air talent Sta. WDUQ-FM, Pitts., 1971-73; master control tech. dir. Sta. KDKA-TV, Pitts., 1973; cons. comms. Better Bus. Bur., Pitts., 1974; asst. account exec. Marc & Co. Advt., Pitts., 1975; adminstr., employee benefit adminstrn. Rockwell Internat. Corp., Pitts., 1975-80, adminstr. relocation and corp. personnel procedures, 1980-81, mgr. corp. policy, 1981-82; pres. John G. Willard Cons., 1982—. Contbr. articles to profl. jours. Office: 360 Middlegate Dr Bethel Park PA 15102-1438 Home Phone: 412-831-8650; Office Phone: 412-831-5650. E-mail: jgw7@telerama.com.

WILLARD, LOUIS CHARLES, librarian; b. Tallahassee, Sept. 28, 1937; s. Bert and Rose (De Milly) W.; m. Nancy Booth, June 22, 1963. BA, U. Fla., 1959; BD, Yale, 1965, MA, 1967, PhD, 1970. Tchr. Tripoli (Lebanon) Boys' Sch., 1959-62; ordained to ministry Presbyn. Ch., 1965; acting librarian Princeton Theol. Sem., 1968-69, librarian, 1969-86; librarian, mem. faculty Harvard Div. Sch., 1986-99; dir. accreditation and instnl. evaluation Assn. Theol. Schs., 1999—. Mem. A.L.A., Theol. Library Assn., Soc. Bibl. Lit., Am. Acad. Religion, Phi Beta Kappa, Chi Phi. Office: Assn Theol Schs 10 Summit Park Dr Pittsburgh PA 15275-1103 Home: 970 Villeroy Greens Dr PO Box 5040 Sun City Center FL 33573 Office Phone: 412-788-6505. Business E-Mail: charles@willard.com.

WILLARD, NANCY MARGARET, writer, educator; b. Ann Arbor, Mich. d. Hobart Hurd and Margaret (Sheppard) W.; m. Eric Lindbloom, Aug. 15, 1964; 1 child, James Anatole. BA, U. Mich., 1958, PhD, 1963; MA, Stanford U., 1960. Lectr. English Vassar Coll., Poughkeepsie, NY, 1965—. Author: (poems) In His Country: Poems, 1966; Skin of Grace, 1967; A New Herball: Poems, 1968, Testimony of the Invisible Man: William Carlos Williams, Francis Ponge, Rainer Maria Rilke, Pablo Neruda, 1970, Nineteen Masks for the Naked Poet: Poems, 1971, The Carpenter of the Sun: Poems, 1974, A Visit to William Blake's Inn: Poems for Innocent and Experienced Travelers, 1981 (Newbery Medal 1982), Household Tales of Moon and Water, 1983, Water Walker, 1989, The Ballad of Biddy Early, 1989; (short stories) The Lively Anatomy of God, 1968, Childhood of the Magician, 1973; (juveniles) Sailing to Cythera and Other Anatole Stories, 1974, All on a May Morning, 1975, The Snow Rabbit, 1975, Shoes Without Leather, 1976, T0e Well-Mannered Balloon, 1976, Night Story, 1986, Simple Pictures are Best, 1977, Stranger's Bread, 1977, The Highest Hit, 1978, Papa's Panda, 1979, The Island of the Grass King, 1979, The Marzipan Moon 1981, Uncle Terrible, 1982, (adult) Angel in the Parlor: Five Stories and Eight Essays, 1983, The Nightgown of the Sullen Moon, 1983, Night Story, 1986, The Voyage of the Ludgate Hill, 1987, The Mountains of Quilt, 1987, Firebrat, 1988; (novel) Things Invisible To See, 1984, Sister Water, 1993, The Flying Bed, 2007; (play) East of the Sun, West of the Moon, 1989, The High Rise Glorious Skittle Skat Roarious Sky Pie Angel Food Cake, 1991, A Nancy Willard Reader, 1991, Pish Posh said Hieronymus Bosch, 1991, Beauty and the Beast, 1992; illustrator: The Letter of John to James, Another Letter of John to James, 1982, The Octopus Who Wanted to Juggle (Robert Pack), 1990, (novel) Sister Water, 1993, (essays) Telling Time, 1993, (juvenile) A Starlit Somersault Downhill, 1993, (juvenile) The Sorcerer's Apprentice, 1993; author, illustrator: An Alphabet of Angels, 1994; (juvenile) Gutenberg's Gift, 1995, The Good Night Blessing Book, 1996, Cracked Corn and Snow Ice Cream, 1997, The Tortilla Cat, 1998; (poems, with Jane Yolen) Among Angels, 1995, Swimming Lessons, 1996, The Magic Cornfield, 1997; editor: (anthology of poems) Step Lightly: Poems for the Journey, 1998, The Tale I Told Sasha, 1999, (juvenile) Shadow Story, 1999, (juvenile) The Moon and Riddles Diner and the Sunny Side Cafe, 2001, (juvenile) The Mouse, the Cat and Grandmother's Hat, 2003, Cinderella's Dress, 2003, (young adult) Paradise Lost, 2004, Sweep Dreams, 2005. Recipient Hopwood award, 1958, Devins Meml. award, 1967, John Newbery award, 1981, Empire State award, 1996; Woodrow Wilson fellow, 1960; NEA grantee, 1987. Mem. The Lewis Carroll Soc. Office: Vassar Coll Dept English Raymond Ave Poughkeepsie NY 12604-0001

WILLARD, RALPH LAWRENCE, retired surgeon, physician, academic administrator, educator; b. Manchester, Iowa, Apr. 6, 1922; s. Hosea B. and Ruth A. (Hazelrigg) W.; m. Norma L. Hattel, Nov. 12, 1943 (div. 1968); children: Laurie, Jane, Ann, H. Thomas; m. Margaret Dyer Dennis, Sept. 26, 1969. Student, Cornell Coll., 1940-42, Coe Coll., 1945; D.O., Kirksville Coll. Osteo. Medicine, 1949; EdD (hon.), U. North Tex., 1985; ScD (hon.), W.Va. Sch. Osteo. Medicine, 1993. Intern Kirksville Osteo. Hosp., 1949-50, resident in surgery, 1954-57; chmn. dept. surgery Davenport Osteo. Hosp., 1957-68; dean, prof. surgery Kirksville Coll. Osteo. Medicine, 1969-73; asso. dean acad. affairs, prof. surgery Mich. State U. Coll. Osteo. Medicine, 1974-75; dean Tex. Coll. Osteopathic Medicine, 1975-76, pres., 1981-85, prof. surgery, 1985-87; v.p. med. affairs North Tex. State U., Denton, 1976-81; assoc. dean W.Va. Sch. Osteo. Medicine, Lewisburg, 1988-91. Mem. Nat. Adv. Council Edn. for Health Professions, 1971-73, Iowa Gov.'s Council Hosps. and Health Related Facilities, 1965-68; chmn. council deans Am. Assn. Colls. Osteo. Medicine, 1970-73, pres., 1979-80 Served with USAAF, 1942-45; Served with USAF, 1952-53; col. USAFR, ret. Decorated D.F.C., Air medal with 4 oak leaf clusters, Meritorious Svc. medal, Legion of Merit; recipient Robert A. Kistner Educator award Am. Assn. Colls. Osteo. Medicine, 1989; named Disting. scholar Acad. Osteo. Medicine Nat. Acads. Practice, 2000. Fellow Am. Coll. Physician Execs., Am. Coll. Osteo. Surgeons; mem. Am. Osteo. Assn. (Disting. Svc. cert. 1992), Tex. Osteo. Assn., W.Va. Soc. Osteo. Medicine, Am. Acad. Osteopathy, Acad. Osteo. Dirs. Med. Edn., Quiet Birdmen, Davis-Monthan Officers Club, Masons, Shriners, Rotary (Paul Harris fellow), Internat. Comanche Soc., Order of Daedalians. Democrat. Episcopalian. Address: PO Box 79267 Fort Worth TX 76179-0267 Personal E-mail: willardrl@aol.com. *The wise man has faith, the fool is he who betrays that faith.*

WILLARD, RICHARD KENNON, lawyer, former pharmaceutical company executive; b. Houston, Sept. 1, 1948; s. Fair McDaniel Willard and Elsbeth Rowe (Kennon) Willard Armistead; m. Leslie Harral Hopkins, July 10, 1976; children: Stephen Hopkins, Lauren Suzanne. BA, Emory U., 1969; JD, Harvard U., 1975. Bar: D.C. 1988, Tex. 1978, Ga. 1975. Law clk. US Ct. Appeals, San Francisco, 1975-76, US Supreme Ct., Washington, 1976-77; atty. Baker & Botts, Houston, 1977-81; counsel for intelligence policy US Dept. Justice, Washington, 1981-82, dep. asst. atty. gen. civil divsn., 1982-83, asst. atty. gen., 1983-88; ptnr. Steptoe & Johnson, Washington, 1988-99; sr. v.p., gen. counsel The Gillette Co., Boston, 1999—2005; sr. v.p. gen. counsel Bristol-Myers Squibb Co., NYC, 2005—06. Adj. prof. Georgetown U. Law Ctr., 1991-96, Boston U. Law Sch., 2002-05. Note editor: Harvard U. Law Rev., 1974-75. Gen. counsel Republican Party of Tex., Austin, 1980-81. Served to 1st lt. U.S. Army, 1969-72. Mem. Met. Club. Episcopalian.

WILLARD, ROBERT F., career military officer; b. L.A., 1950; m. Donna J. Willard. Grad., U.S. Naval Acad., 1973; M in Engring. Mgmt., Old Dominion U. Advanced through grades to adm., 2005; F-14 naval aviator; served with Fighter Squadrons Two (VF-2), Twenty Four (VF-24), and One Twenty Four (VF-124) NAS Miramar; ops. and exec. officer, instr. Navy Fighter Weapons Sch. (Top Gun); exec. and commdg. officer Screaming Eagles; commdr. USS Tripoli, 1994, USS Abraham Lincoln, 1995—98; commdr. Carrier Group 5 USS Kitty Hawk, 2000—01; dep. chief of staff, comdr. US Pacific Fleet, 2001; comdr. 7th Fleet, 2002—04; vice chief naval ops. USN, 2005—07, comdr. US Pacific Fleet Honolulu, 2007—. Aerial coord. (films) Top Gun, 1986. Decorated Def. Disting. Svc. Medal, DSM, Legion of Merit (4), others; named Pacific Fleet Tailhooker of Yr., 1982. Office: Commander US Pacific Fleet 250 Makalapa Dr Pearl Harbor HI 96860 E-mail: bob.willard@navy.mil.

WILLAUER, GEORGE JACOB, English literature educator; b. Oct. 30, 1935; s. George Jacob and Mary Catherine (Eshleman) W.; m. Cynthia Cameron Thun, June 11, 1966; children: George Jacob III, Elizabeth Christian. BA, Wesleyan U., 1957; MA, U. Pa., 1959, PhD, 1965. Asst. instr. U. Pa., Phila., 1958-62; instr. Conn. Coll., New London, 1962-66, asst. prof., 1966-72, assoc. prof., 1972-78, prof., 1978—2002, chair dept. English, 1972—77, 1991—94, 2000—02. Charles J. MacCurdy prof. of Am. Studies, 1993-02; coll. marshal, 1989-02, dean of acad. programs, 1997-00; instr. Williams Coll.-Mystic Seaport Program in Maritime Studies, 1986-88; vis. prof. lit. U. Dar es Salaam, Tanzania, 1995. Author: A Lyme Miscellany: 1776-1976, 1977; editor: Original Discontent: Commentaries on the Creation of Connecticut's Constitution of 1818; contbr. articles to profl. jours. Trustee Cmty. Found. Southeastern Conn., 1996-02, pres. 2000-02; trustee Florence Griswold Mus., 1978-, pres. 1983-88, Lymes Youth Svc. Bur., 1978-83, Lyme Land Conservation Trust, 1996-02, Lyme Pub. Libr., Inc., 1988—, pres., Lyman Allyn Art Mus., 1983-88, 96-04, Music Masterworks, 2001—, v.p., MacCurdy-Salisbury Ednl. Found., Conn. Humanities Coun., 2004—; deacon First Congl. Ch., Old Lyme. English-Speaking Union fellow, 1969, 72. Mem. MLA, Century Assn. Home: 55-1 Beaver Brook Rd Old Lyme CT 06371-3219

WILLAUER, WHITING RUSSELL, retired manufacturing executive, systems engineer; b. Boston, May 24, 1931; s. Whiting and Louise Knapp (Russell) Willauer-Jackson; m. Julie Mackie McConihe, Mar. 15, 2001 (div.); m. Julie Matheson Arnold, July 11, 1959 (div.); children: Whiting Russell, Jr., William Arnold. BS, Princeton U., 1955, MS, 1959; PhD, Georgetown U., 1964. Research assoc. joint research com. Dept. Def., 1951-52; ops. mgr. Civil Air Transport Airline Taiwan, 1952-53; scientist Analytic Services, Inc., 1958-61; asst. prof. astronomy Georgetown U., 1965-68; mgr. TRW Systems Group support to chief Naval ops., McLean, Va., 1968-73, TRW support to U.S. Navy Antisubmarine program, 1973-79, TRW Amphibious Ship Bldg. program, 1979-85; advanced systems mgr. TRW Systems Integration Group, 1985-90, cost estimating mgr., 1990-95, sr. cons., 1995-99; sr. v.p., chief strategist K12Nation.net, 1999-2000. Cons. Nat. Geog. Soc., 1961-65, U. Tex., 1962, NSF, 1963, Booz-Allen & Hamilton, 1966-67. Mng. editor: Jour. Astronautical Scis, 1969-71; Designer: Orrery Planetarium Nat. Geog. Soc. Asst. chief steward Alpine Venue XIII Olympic Winter Games, Lake Placid, 1980; mem. U.S. Olympic Com., bd. dirs., 1987-94, sec. nat. governing bodies, 1989-92, mem. membership svcs. com., 1988-92, mem. athletic devel. com., 1992-96; chef de mission Winter Pan Am. Games, Las Lenas, Argentina, 1990; asst. chief de mission XVI Winter Olympics, Albertville, France, 1992; U.S. Olympic Com. liaison to VI Paralympic Winter Games, Lillehammer, Norway, 1994. Research fellow Georgetown U., 1961-65. Fellow AAAS (coun.); mem. Am. Astronautical Soc. (v.p. fin.), Blue Ridge Ski Coun. (pres. 1976-78), U.S. Ski Assn. (pres. 1982-87, Julius Blegan award 1988, Mary and Bud Little award 1998), U.S. Ski and Snowboard Assn. (vice chmn. 1994-96, trustee emeritus 1997—), Internat. Ski Fedn. (chmn. U.S. del. 1983, 85, chmn. recreational skiing com. 1987-98, eligibility com. 1988-98), Ea. Ski Assn. (treas. 1980-82), Pan Am Sports Orgn. (winter games adv. com. 1988—), Sigma Xi, Chevy Chase Club (Md.), Nantucket Yacht Club (Mass.) (commodore 1981-83, bd. govs. 1957-59, 68—), Nantucket IOD Fleet Assn. (fleet capt. 2002-04), Arthur Knapp Prize 2003 IOD World Championship, USCG Aux. Flotilla 11-7 (sec. 2003—, Mem. of Yr. 2004), Nantucket Alliance Substance Abuse Prevention (pres. 2004-05, Nantucket Island Bd. Selectman 2005—, chmn. 2006—). Personal E-mail: whitey@willauer.com.

WILLBORN, STEVEN L., dean, law educator; BA magna cum laude, Northland Coll., 1974; MS in Counseling, U.Wis.-Madison, 1976; JD cum laude, U. Wis. Law Sch., 1976. Asst. prof. law U. Nebr.-Lincoln Coll. Law, 1979, assoc. prof., 1982, prof., 1985, Richard C. & Catherine Stuart Schmoker Prof. Law, 1999—, dean, 2001—. Pvt. practice, 1976—79; vis. prof. University Mich. Law Sch., 1992. Co-author: Employment Law: Cases and Materials, The Statistics of Discrimination: Using Statistical Evidence in Discrimination Cases, 2002; contbr. articles to law jours. Grantee Lincoln Coll., Oxford U., 1993; vis. scholar Australian Nat. U., Canberra, 1988, U. Toronto, 1991; Fulbright Scholar, Inst. Advanced Legal Studies, U. London, 1985—86. Office: U Nebr-Lincoln Coll Law Ross McCollum Hall PO Box 830902 Lincoln NE 68583 E-mail: willborn@unl.edu.

WILLE, LOIS JEAN, retired editor; b. Chgo., Sept. 19, 1931; d. Walter and Adele S. (Taege) Kroeber; m. Wayne M. Wille, June 6, 1954. BS, Northwestern U., 1953, MS, 1954; Litt.D. (hon.), Columbia Coll., Chgo., 1980, Northwestern U., 1990, Rosary Coll., 1990. Reporter Chgo. Daily News, 1958-74, nat. corr., 1975-76, assoc. editor charge editorial page, 1977; assoc. editor charge editorial and opinion pages Chgo. Sun-Times, 1978-83; assoc. editor editorial page Chgo. Tribune, 1984-87, editor editorial page, 1987-91, ret., 1991. Author: Forever Open, Clear and Free: the Historic Struggle for Chicago's Lakefront, 1972, At Home in the Loop: How Clout and Community Built Chicago's Dearborn Park, 1997. Recipient Pulitzer prize for public svc., 1963, Pulitzer prize for editorial writing, 1989, William Allen White Found. award for excellence in editorial writing, 1978, numerous awards Chgo. Newspaper Guild, numerous awards Chgo. Headline Club, numerous awards Nat. Assn. Edn. Writers, numerous awards Ill. AP, numerous awards Ill. UPI. Home: 1530 S State St Apt 1011 Chicago IL 60605 Personal E-mail: lowille@aol.com.

WILLE, ROSANNE LOUISE, educational consultant; b. Hackensack, NJ, Aug. 4, 1941; d. Albert Wille and Rose Marie (Rock) Eberhardt; m. George B. Jacobs, Mar. 12, 1980; children: Leigh, Steven, Alexander, Jeffrey. M Pub. Adminstrn., Rutgers U., 1976; PhD, N.Y.U., 1980. Dept. chair Rutgers U., Newark, 1978-84, Lehman Coll., Bronx, NY, 1984-87, dean, 1987-92, provost, sr. v.p., 1992—2002; cons. for higher edn., 2002—. Contbr. articles to profl. jours. Bd. dirs. Family Support Svcs., Bronx, N.Y., 1994-2002, bd. dirs. South Bronx Overall Economic Devel., Inc., Bronx, 1991-2002. Recipient Vision award Family Support Svcs., Bronx, 1996, Thousand Points of Light award Pres. George Bush, Washington, 1991. Mem. N.Y. Acad. Scis., N.Y. Acad. Medicine, Am. Assn. Higher Edn. Avocations: aviation, golf. Address: PO Box 799 Hampton Bays NY 11946 Personal E-mail: rlwille@earthlink.net.

WILLE, WAYNE MARTIN, retired editor; b. Des Plaines, Ill., Nov. 17, 1930; s. Clarence Louis and Lois Naomi (Martin) W.; m. Lois Jean Kroeber, June 6, 1954. BSJ, Northwestern U., 1952, MSJ, 1953. Reporter Chgo. Sun Times, 1956-57; dir. press info. WBBM-TV and CBS-TV, Chgo., 1957-58; feature editor Sci. and Mechanics mag., 1958-60, mng. editor, 1960-62; news editor Nat. Safety Council, Chgo., 1962-64, asst. dir. pub. info., 1964-67; mng. editor World Book Year Book, Chgo., 1967-69; exec. editor World Book Yr. Book, 1969-83; mng. editor World Book Yr. Book and Sci. Yr. and Health & Med. Ann., 1983-91. Served with AUS, 1953-55. Mem. Chgo. Headline Club (pres. 1967-68), Soc. Profl. Journalists, Art Inst. Chgo., Oriental Inst. Clubs: La Salle Street Rod and Gun.

WILLEBEEK-LEMAIR, MARC, information technology executive; BSEE, George Mason Univ.; PhD in Elec. Engring, Cornell Univ. With T.J. Watson Rsch. Ctr. IBM; founder NetPliance Inc. (became Tipping Point), Austin, Tex.; chief tech., strategy officer Tipping Point Tech. Inc. (acquired by 3Com), Austin, Tex.; chief tech. officer, sr. v.p., product ops. 3Com, Marlborough, Mass. Named one of Top 25 Chief Tech. Officers, Infoworld mag., 2007. Achievements include holding 10 patents. Office: 3Com 350 Campus Dr Marlborough MA 01752-3064 Office Phone: 508-233-5000. *

WILLENBECHER, JOHN, artist; b. Macungie, Pa., May 5, 1936; s. John George and Geneva (Bacon) W. BA, Brown U., 1958; postgrad., N.Y. U., Inst. Fine Arts, 1958-61. Sculptor-mem. N.Y.C. Art Commn., 1980-92; mem. commn. for plaza and pavillion, Mpls. Inst. Arts, 1991. Exhibited in one-person shows including Hamilton Gallery Contemporary Art, N.Y.C., 1977, 80, 82, U. Mass. Art Gallery, Amherst, 1977, Wright State U. Art Gallery, Dayton, Ohio, 1977, Jaffe-Friede Gallery, Dartmouth Coll., Hanover, N.H., 1977, Fine Arts Ctr. U. R.I., Kingston, 1978, Neuberger Mus., SUNY at Purchase, 1979, Allentown (Pa.) Art Mus., 1979, Mpls. Inst. Arts, 1991, U. N.Mex. Art Gallery, Albuquerque, 1996, 5 Myles Gallery, Bklyn., 2003, CUNY Grad. Ctr., N.Y.C, 2003; exhibited in numerous group shows including Albright-Knox Art Gallery, Buffalo, 1963, Whitney Mus. Am. Art, N.Y.C., 1964-68; represented in permanent collections including Solomon R. Guggenheim Mus., N.Y.C., Met. Mus., N.Y.C., Whitney Mus. Am. Art, Albright-Knox Art Gallery, Phila. Mus. Art, Centre d'Art et Culture Georges Pompidou, Paris, Hirshhorn Mus. and Sculpture Garden, Washington, Art Inst. Chgo. Nat. Endowment for Arts grantee, 1977, Esther and Adolph Gottlieb Found. grantee, 1994. Achievements include being subject of profl. articles and catalogues.

WILLENBRING, MARK LEON, psychiatrist; b. Virginia, Minn., Aug. 15, 1949; s. Raymond Hilary and Margaret Leona (Quaas) W.; m. Katherine Alice Meyers, Apr. 14, 1979; children: Jesse, Morgan. BS, U. Minn., 1970, MD, 1974. Cert. Am. Bd. Psychiatry and Neurology. Intern St. Paul Ramsey Med. Ctr., 1974-75; resident psychiatry U. Calif., Davis, 1977-80; med. dir. Dane Co. Detox Ctr., Madison, Wis., 1980-82; staff psychiatrist Dane County Mental Health Ctr., Madison, 1980-82; asst. prof. U. Minn. VA Med. Ctr., Mpls., 1982—2004; dir. alcohol problems clinics VA Med. Ctr., Mpls., 1987—2004; dir. treatment, recovery rsch. divsn. Nat. Inst. Alcohol Abuse, Alcoholism NIH, Bethesda, Md., 2004—. Rsch. dir. drug dependency treatment program U. Minn. VA Med. Ctr., Mpls., 1982—2004; co-chmn. med. students concerned about med. students U. Minn., Mpls., 1987—2004; clin. prof. psychiatry George Washington Sch. Medicine, Washington, 2004—; dir. alcohol and substance abuse clinic George Washington U., Washington, 2004—. Contbr. articles to profl. jours. Mem. Govs. task force CD in Elderly, St. Paul, 1983-85, Mpls. Adv. Com. Alcohol-Drug Problems, Mpls., 1982—. U. Minn. grantee, 1983, VA grantee, 1984-88, Nat. Inst. Alcohol Abuse and Alcoholism grantee, 1988-90; recipient GEICO Pub. Svc. award in alcoholism prevention and treatment, 1989. Mem.: Am. Acad. Addiction Psychiatry, Am. Soc. Addiction Medicine, Rsch. Soc. Alcoholism., Am. Med. Soc. Alcohol and Other Drug Abuse, Am. Psychiat. Assn. Avocations: blues music, bicycling. Office: Divsn Treatment and Recovery Rsch 5635 Fishers Ln MSC9304 Rm 2047 Bethesda MD 20892 also: Alcohol and Substance Abuse Clinic George Washington Univ 2150 Pa Ave NW 8th Fl Washington DC 20037-3201 Home: 1834 Hampshire Ave Saint Paul MN 55116 Office Phone: 301-443-1208, 202-741-2888. Business E-Mail: mlw@niaa.nih.gov.

WILLENBRINK, ROSE ANN, retired lawyer; b. Louisville, Ky., Apr. 20, 1950; d. J.L. Jr. and Mary Margaret (Williams) W.; m. William I. Cornett Jr. Student, U. Chgo., 1968-70; BA in Anthropology with highest honors, U. Louisville, 1973, JD, 1975. Bar: Ky. 1976, Ind. 1976, U.S. Dist. Ct. (we. dist.) Ky. 1976, Ohio 1999. Atty. Mapother & Mapother, Louisville, 1976-79; v.p., counsel Nat. City Bank, Louisville, 1980-99, v.p., sr. atty.

Cleve., 1999—2004, Louisville, 2004—05, ret., 2005. Mem. Ky. Bar Assn., Phi Kappa Phi. Home: 6803 Chadworth Pl Prospect KY 40059 Home Phone: 502-292-2857. Personal E-mail: willenbrink@yahoo.com.

WILLER, EDWARD HERMAN, real estate broker; b. Concord, NC, June 12, 1941; s. Emil Francis and Mary (McKinley) W.; m. Cornelia Campbell, Nov. 30, 1963; children: Laura Campbell, Edward Groves. AB, Davidson Coll., 1963. V.p., sales mgr. Bacon & Co., Realtors, Raleigh, N.C., 1971-84; pres. residential div. York Properties, Inc., Raleigh, 1984—2001. Treas. N.C. Real Estate Ednl. Found., Greensboro, 1984, pres., 1988; bd. dirs. Rex Hosp. Found., Raleigh, 1988-89, Relo, The Internat. Referral Network, Inc., Chgo., dir., 1988-92, treas., 1992. Author: Real Estate Exam Ready Book, 1984; contbr. articles to profl. jours. Bd. dirs. Ea. N.C. Multiple Sclerosis Soc., Raleigh, 1982-85; campaign chair United Way of Wake County, 1996, bd. dirs., 1994-2000, mem. exec. com., 1996-97, treas., 2001—. 1st lt. U.S. Army, 1963-66, Vietnam. Named Realtor of the Year, 1984. Mem. Nat. Assn. Realtors (cert.), N.C. Assn. Realtors (bd. dirs. 1978-82), N.C. Real Estate Ednl. Found. (pres.), Raleigh Bd. Realtors (pres. 1979), Greater Raleigh C. of C. (bd. dirs. 1991-94), Quite Birdmen Club. Democrat. Presbyterian. Avocations: teaching, flying, woodworking. Home: 1512 Saint Mary's St Raleigh NC 27608-2217 Office: York Simpson Underwood 311 Oberlin Rd Raleigh NC 27605-3125 Office Phone: 919-412-2602. E-mail: ed@edwiller.com.

WILLES, MARK HINCKLEY, media specialist; b. Salt Lake City, July 16, 1941; s. Joseph Simmons and Ruth (Hinckley) W.; m. Laura Fayone, June 7, 1961; children: Wendy Anne, Susan Kay, Keith Mark, Stephen Joseph, Matthew Bryant. AB, Columbia Coll., 1963, PhD, 1967. Staff banking and currency com. Ho. of Reps., Washington, 1966-67; asst. prof. fin. Wharton Sch. U. Pa., Phila., 1967-69; economist Fed. Res. Bank, Phila., 1967, sr. economist, 1969-70, dir. rsch., 1970-71, v.p., dir. rsch., 1971, 1st v.p., 1971-77; pres. Fed. Res. Bank of Mpls., 1977-80; exec. v.p., chief fin. officer Gen. Mills, Inc., Mpls., 1980-85, pres., COO, 1985-92, vice-chmn., 1992-95; chmn., pres., CEO Times Mirror Co., LA, 1995-2000; pub. L.A. Times, 1997-99; disting. prof. mgmt. Brigham Young U., Provo, Utah, 2000, 2004—; pres. Hawaii Honolulu Mission, Ch. of LDS, 2001—04. Office: Brigham Young Univ 3651 N 100 E Ste 300 Provo UT 84604 *My success is based on adherence to principles I learned in the home, which is the most basic and important organizational unit in the world. Three of those principles stand out in my mind: Be just, honest and moral—do things not only because they are required, but because they are right. Have mercy—care enough about others to be fair and kind. Be humble—you can get more done effectively with the help of others than you can do on your own.*

WILLET, E. CROSBY (EVERETT CROSBY WILLET), artist; b. Phila., Jan. 8, 1929; s. Henry Lee and Katharine Muriel (Crosby) W.; m. Augusta Winter, Nov. 27, 1954; children: William, Nancy Lee, Katharine Crosby, Henry Lee II. BA, Lafayette Coll., 1950; DFA (hon.), Orthodox Cath. Archdiocese, Phila., 1982. Apprentice Blenko Glass Co., Milton, W.Va., 1950; craftsman Willet Stained Glass Studio Inc., Phila., 1950-54, v.p., 1954-64, pres., 1964—. Works include: Portsmouth Priory, R.I., 1956, Folger Bay Washington Cathedral, 1973, Assocs. Dining Room, Smithsonian Instn., 1976, 2d Bapt. Ch., Houston, 1985-86, Gethsemane Cathedral, Fargo, N.D., 1992-95, Peachtree Road United Methodist Church, Atlanta, 2001, St. Martins Episcopal Ch., Houston, 2004. Recipient George Washington Kidd award Lafayette Coll., 1985, Elbert M. Conover award AIA/IFRAA, 2002. Fellow Stained Glass Assn. Am. (exec. bd. 1958-78, 81, pres. 1964-66); mem. InterFaith Forum, Religion, Art and Architecture (exec. bd. 1979-2001, Conover award, 2002), Am. Soc. Appraisers (sr. mem.), Appraisers Assn. Am., Nantucket Yacht Club, Moorings Club. Republican. Presbyn. Home and Office: Willet Hauser Archtl Glass 10 E Moreland Ave Philadelphia PA 19118-3539 Home Phone: 772-234-8824; Office Phone: 215-247-5721. E-mail: ecwillet@earthlink.net.

WILLET, JOHN, lawyer; BS, U. So. Miss., Hattiesburg, 1993; JD, U. Memphis, Tennessee, 1997. US Dist. Ct.: Tenn. 1997. Ptnr. Less, Getz & Lipman, Memphis, 2000—. Editor (found. mem.): Tenn. Jour. of Practice and Procedure, 1996—97; co-author: (treatise) Construction Law Handbook, Chapter 33. Mem., steering com., divsn. four; tech. com. Forum Com. for the Constrn. Industry, 2006; chair, tech. com. Tenn. Assn. of Constrn. Coun., 2006—. Mem.: Associated Gen. Contractors of Am., Tenn. Assn. Constrn. Counsel, ABA, Tenn. Bar Assn., Memphis Bar Assn. Achievements include U. Memphis Law Review, 1994-97. Office: Less Getz & Lipman 100 Peabody Place Ste 1150 Memphis TN 38103 Office Phone: 901-525-8700. Office Fax: 901-525-3569. E-mail: john.willet@lgllaw.com.

WILLETT, DON R., state supreme court justice; BBA, Baylor U.; JD, MA in Polit. Sci., Duke U. Former law clerk to Judge Jerre S. Williams U.S. Ct. of Appeals for Fifth Circuit, Tex.; atty. Haynes and Boone, L.L.P., 1993—96; legal adv. to gov. Tex., 1996—2000; dep. atty. gen. for legal counsel Tex., 2000—04; justice Tex. Supreme Ct., 2005—. Served on Bush-Cheney 2000 Presidential Campaign and Transition Team; supreme ct. liaison Tex. Ctr. for Legal Ethics and Professionalism. Former mem. Tex. Commn. on Volunteerism & Community Svc.; bd. mem. Nat. Fatherhood Initiative, Big Brothers Big Sisters of Central Tex., SafePlace, the Tex. Lyceum Assn. Recipient Austin Under 40 award for Govt./Polit. Affairs, 2006. Fellow: Tex. Bar Found.; mem.: Tex. Assn. for Ct. Administration (judicial adv. bd.), Am. Law Inst. Office: Tex Supreme Ct PO Box 12248 Austin TX 78711 Office Phone: 512-463-1312. Office Fax: 512-463-1365. *

WILLETT, JOHN A., lawyer; b. NYC, Aug. 4, 1946; BA, Bucknell U., 1968; MBA, JD, Stanford U., 1972; LLM, NYU, 1976. Bar: Calif. 1972, N.Y. 1973. Ptnr., N.Y.C. office mgr. Arnold & Porter LLP, NYC. Fellow Am. Coll. Investment Counsel; mem. ABA, State Bar Calif., Assn. Bar City of N.Y. Office: Arnold & Porter LLP 399 Park Ave Fl 35 New York NY 10022-4690 Office Phone: 212-715-1001. Office Fax: 212-715-1399. Business E-Mail: john.willett@aporter.com.

WILLETT, NIKKI, computer company executive; d. Donald and Monique Willett; m. Waclaw Jurczyk, Sept. 9, 1989. BA in Computer Sci., Boston U. Dir. mktg. Siperian, Foster City, Calif.; vp mktg. and regulatory products Pilgrim Software, Tampa, Fla., 2003—. Dir. products Eloquent, San Mateo, Calif. Office: Pilgrim Software 2807 W Busch Blvd Tampa FL 33618 Home Phone: 727-776-3522; Office Phone: 813-915-1663. Personal E-mail: nikki123willett@yahoo.com. Business E-Mail: willettn@pilgrimsoftware.com.

WILLETT, ROBERT E., lawyer; b. Glendale, Calif., June 21, 1943; BA, San Fernando Valley State Coll., 1971; JD, U. Calif., Berkeley, 1974. Bar: Calif. 1974, U.S. Supreme Ct. 1987, U.S. Tax Ct. 1988. Lawyer O'Melveny & Myers, LA. Mem. state bar com. for adminstrn. of justice, 1987-90. Assoc. editor Calif. Law Rev., 1972-73, notes and comments editor, 1973-74. Mem. ABA sections on antitrust and litigation, L.A. County Bar Assn. sections on antitrust and litigation (vice chair ct. improvements com. 1985-87), Order of Coif. Office: O'Melveny & Myers LLP 400 S Hope St Los Angeles CA 90071-2899 Office Phone: 213-430-6355. Office Fax: 213-430-6407. Business E-Mail: rwillett@omm.com.

WILLETT, ROSLYN LEONORE, public relations executive, food service consultant, writer, editor; d. Edward and Celia (Stickler) Sternberg; m. Edward Willett (div.); 1 child, Jonathan Stanley. BA, Hunter Coll., NYC; postgrad., Columbia U., CUNY, NYU, New Sch. Dietitian YWCA, NYC; tech. and patents libr., food technologist in charge tech. svcs. and devel. Stein Hall & Co., NYC; editor McGraw-Hill, Inc., NYC, Harcourt Brace Jovanovich, Inc., NYC; pub. rels. writer Farley Manning Assocs., NYC; cons. pub. rels. and food svc. Roslyn Willett Assocs., Inc., NYC, 1959—. Adj. prof. Hunter Coll., Poly U., Columbia U. Sch. Pub. Health; dir. West End Writers Workshop, 1998—2002; seminar presenter in field. Author: The Woman Executive in Woman in Sexist Society, 1971, also short stories and essays; assoc. editor Timber Creek Rev., Words of Wisdom, 2001—, Bulls Head Creek Rev., 2004—. V.p. North Shore Ams. for Dem. Action; ofcl. rapporteur Post-Assembly Tech. Sessions, WHO; juror Am. Film Festival, Arts and Scis., 1962—88; chmn. Women's Polit. Caucus, Inc. NY, NJ, Conn, 1971—73; v.p. Mid Hudson Arts and Sci. Ctr., Poughkeepsie, NY; apptd. to regional adv. coun. Fed. SBA, 1976—78; chmn. image of woman com. NOW; bd. dirs. Small Bus. Task Force, Assn. for Small Bus. and Professions, 1981—85, Rhinebeck Chamber Music Soc., 1985—86, Will Inst., New Paltz, 1980—2001, Women Studies Abstracts, 1971—81; pres. Hunns Lake Assn., 1999—2001. Mem. Pub. Rels. Soc. Am. (accredited), Food Svc. Cons. Soc. Internat. (bd. dirs. 1978-80), NY Acad. Scis., Inst. Food Technologists, Juilliard Assn., Assn. for Japanese Art in Am., Inc., Alliance Française, Paris Club, NY Print Club, Met. Mus. Art, Mus. Modern Art, Mus. Natural History. Avocations: writing, dance, art collecting, hiking, swimming. Home: 97 W Hunns Lake Rd Stanfordville NY 12581-5606 Office: 441 West End Ave New York NY 10024-5328

WILLETT, THOMAS EDWARD, lawyer; b. NYC, Nov. 8, 1947; s. Oscar Edward and Alice (Fleming) W.; m. Marilyn Kenney, Dec. 28, 1969; children: Thomas Justin, Christopher Joseph. BS, USAF Acad., Colo., 1969; JD with distinction, Cornell U., 1972. Bar: N.Y. 1973, U.S. Ct. Claims 1973, U.S. Supreme Ct. 1977. Judge advocate USAF, Syracuse, NY, 1973-75, Kincheloe AFB, Mich., 1975-77, USAF Hdqs., Washington, 1977-79; assoc. Harris Beach LLP, Rochester, NY, 1979-84, ptnr., 1985—. Pres. Monroe County Legal Assistance Corp., Rochester, 1983-89. Capt. USAF, 1969-79. Mem. ABA, N.Y. State Bar Assn., Monroe County Bar Assn., Order of Coif. Office: Harris Beach LLP 99 Garnsey Rd Pittsford NY 14534 Home Phone: 585-586-1384; Office Phone: 585-419-8646. E-mail: twillett@harrisbeach.com.

WILLEY, CHARLES WAYNE, lawyer; b. Dillon, Mont., Oct. 7, 1932; s. Asa Charles and Elizabeth Ellen Willey; m. Helene D., July 21, 1962 (div.); children: Stephen Charles, Heather Helene, Brent David, Scott D.; m. Alexis W. Grant, Jan. 26, 1986. BS with honors, Mont. State U., 1954; JD with high honors, U. Mont., 1959. Bar: Mont. 1959, Calif. 1960, U.S. Ct. Claims 1975, U.S. Tax Ct. 1975, U.S. Ct. Appeals (9th cir.) 1959, U.S. Ct. Appeals (Fed. cir.) 1983, U.S. Supreme Ct. 1972. Law clk. to presiding judge U.S. Ct. Appeals (9th cir.), 1959-60; ptnr. Price, Postel & Parma, Santa Barbara, Calif., 1960-77; pvt. practice Santa Barbara, 1977-97; shareholder Hollister & Brace, Santa Barbara, 1998-2001. Prof. law corp.; instr. Santa Barbara City Coll., 1961—63, U. Calif., Santa Barbara, 1963—64; lectr. Mont. Tax Inst., 1990, 92, Am. Agr. Law Assn., 1993, 96; adj. prof. law U. Mont., 2005. Chief editor Mont. Law Rev., 1958—59. Pres. Legal Aid Found. Santa Barbara, 1970; mem. Laguna Blanca Sch. Bd., pres. 1980-81; v.p. Phoenix of Santa Barbara. Served to capt. USAF, 1954-56. Mem.: State Bar of Mont. (chair sect. bus., estates, tax, trusts and real estate 2004—05), State Bar of Calif., Santa Barbara County Bar Assn. (pres. 1972—73), Rotary, Kiwanis, Phi Delta Phi, Phi Eta Sigma, Phi Kappa Phi. Republican. Episcopalian. Avocations: reading, writing, travel. Office: 806 Parkview Way Missoula MT 59803 Home Phone: 406-549-3852.

WILLHAM, LORANN ELLYN, assistant principal; d. Kenneth John and Doris (Reichman) Schultz; m. W. Michael Willham, June 13, 1970; children: John Edward Christopher, Douglas Michael Thomas, Polly Ellyn Reynolds. BA, Ind. State U., Terre Haute, 1966—70; MA, Ind. U., South Bend, 1974—76; EdS, Ind. U., Bloomington, 1987—89. Asst. prin. Met. Sch. Dist. Perry Twp., Indpls., 1996—97, Franklin Twp. Mid. Sch., Indpls., 1997—. Christmas giving tree Mid. Sch., Indpls., 2000—06; planning com. mem. Saints Francis & Claire Ch., Greenwood, Ind., 1998—2000. Roman Cath. Avocations: golf, scuba diving, reading, crafts, painting. Office: Franklin Twp Cmty Sch Corp 6141 S Franklin Rd Indianapolis IN 46259 Home Phone: 317-422-4249. Office Fax: 317-862-7271. Business E-Mail: lorrie.willham@ftcsc.k12.in.us.

WILLHAM, RICHARD LEWIS, zoology educator; b. Hutchinson, Kans., May 4, 1932; s. Oliver S. and Susan E. (Hurt) W.; m. Esther B. Burkhart, June 1, 1954; children: Karen Nell, Oliver Lee. BS, Okla. State U., 1954; MS, Iowa State U., 1955, PhD, 1960. Asst. prof. Iowa State U., Ames, 1959-63, assoc. prof., 1966-71, prof. dept. animal sci., 1971-78, Disting. prof., 1978—; assoc. prof. Okla. State U., Stillwater, 1963-66. Cons. in field; tchr. livestock history; guest curator exhbn. Art About Livestock, 1990. Author: A Heritage of Leadership - The First 100 Years of Animal Science at Iowa State University, 1996. Recipient Svc. award Beef Improvement Fedn., 1974, Edn. and Rsch. award Am. Polled Hereford Assn., 1979, Rsch. award Nat. Cattlemen's Assn., 1986, 91, Disting. Alumnus award Okla. State U., 1978, Regents Faculty Excellence award Iowa State U., 1993; named to Hall of Fame Am. Hereford Assn., 1982, Am. Angus Assn., 1988. Fellow Am. Soc. Animal Sci. (animal breeding and genetics award 1978, industry service award 1986). Home: 2316 Hamilton Dr Ames IA 50014-8201 Office: Iowa State U Dept Animal Sci Ames IA 50011-0001 Office Phone: 515-294-3533. E-mail: rwillham@iastate.edu.

WILLHITE, G. PAUL, chemical engineer, petroleum engineer, educator; BSChemE, Iowa State U., Ames, 1959; PhD in Chem. Engring., Northwestern U., 1962. Joined faculty U. Kans., 1969, co-founder, chair co-dir. Tertiary Oil Recovery Project, 1974, Ross H. Forney Disting. prof. Recipient John Franklin Carll Award, 2001, IOR Pioneer Award of Petroleum Engrs., 2004. Mem.: NAE, Am. Soc. Engring. Educators, Am. Inst. Chem. Engrs., Soc. Petroleum Engrs. Office: U Kans Sch Engring Eaton Hall 1520 W 15th St, Rm 1 Lawrence KS 66045 Office Phone: 785-864-2906. Office Fax: 785-864-4967. Business E-Mail: willhite@ku.edu.

WILLI, STEVEN MATTHEW, physician, educator, researcher; s. John Edward and Doris Mae (Smith) Willi; m. Maria Szpiech, July 27, 2002. BA cum laude, Johns Hopkins U., 1981, MD, 1985. Diplomate in pediatrics and pediatric endocrinology Am. Bd. Pediatrics. Resident in pediat. Children's Hosp. of Phila., 1985—88; fellow in pediatric endocrinology Children's Hosp. Phila., 1988—91; instr. pediat. U. Pa., Phila., 1991—92, assoc. prof. pediat., 2004—; asst. prof. pediat. Med. U. S.C., Charleston, 1992—98, assoc. prof., 1998—2004. Contbr. chpts. to books, articles to profl. jours. Med. dir. Camp Adam Fisher for Children with Diabetes, Summerton, S.C., 1995-2003; bd. dirs. Juvenile Diabetes Found., 1995-99; dir. Diabetes Ctr. for Children, Children's Hosp. of Phila., 2004—. Recipient Nat. Rsch. Svc. award NIH, 1990, Clin. Assoc. Physician award NIH, 1996; Healfman scholar, 1985. Fellow Am. Acad. Pediatrics; mem. Endocrine Soc., Lawson Wilkins Pediatric Endocrine Soc., Am. Diabetes Assn. (profl. sect., mem. youth svcs. com. 1993—), So. Med. Assn., Charleston County Med. Soc. Avocations: tennis, bicycling, photography, golf. Office: Childrens Hosp of Phila Divsn Endocrinology/Diabetes 34th St Civic Ctr Blvd Philadelphia PA 19104-0001

WILLIAM, DAVID, theater director, actor; b. London, Eng., June 24, 1926; arrived in Can., 1986; s. Eric Hugh and Olwen (Roose) W. BA, U. Coll., Oxford, Eng., 1950. Artistic dir. Glasgow Citizen's Theatre, The Nottingham Playhouse, The New Shakespeare Co., London, The National Theatre of Israel, Stratford Festival, Can., 1989-93. Vis. prof. theater dept. De Paul U., Chgo., 1985-88; founder, 1st artistic dir. Ludlow Festival. Profl. debut as Rosencrantz to Richard Burton's Hamlet, Old Vic Theatre, London, 1953; theatre directing credits include: Bacchae, The Importance of Being Earnest, The Tempest, Entertaining Mr. Sloane, Love Letters, Treasure Island, Hamlet, Love for Love, The Shoemaker's Holiday, Murder in the Cathedral, Troilus and Cressida, The Winter's Tale, She Stoops to Conquer, Antigone, Separate Tables, Romeo and Juliet, Othello, King Lear, Volpone, Albert Herring, The Merry Wives of Windsor, Twelfth Night; directing world premièrs of operas include: Therese, Royal Opera House Covent Garden, The Lighthouse, Edinburgh festival, Red Emma; other operas directed include Iphigenie en Tauride, The Fairy Queen, Lisbon, La Traviata, Scottish Opera, Il Re Pastore, Camden Festival, Albert Herring, Aldeburgh Festival, Cosl Fan Tutte, Opera St. Louis, Tosca, Can. Opera Co., Mrs. Mozart, Hartford Symphony Orch., 1999; appeared in Uncle Vanya as Serebryakov, As You Like It as Jaques, Twelfth Night as Malvolio; appeared in numerous TV prodns. most notably as Richard the Second in the BBC series An Age of Kings; compiled, directed and acted in My Shakespeare, Stratford Festival and CBC Radio; played A.E.H. in The Invention of Love, Guthrie Theatre, Mpls., 2000, Studio Theater, Washington, 2001, Boyet in Love's Labours Lost, Nat. Arts Ctr, Ottawa, 2005; played in Under Milk Wood, St. Mary's, Ont., 2004. Home: 194 Langarth St E London ON Canada N6C 1Z5 Personal E-mail: may.king@rogers.com.

WILL.I.AM, See ADAMS, WILLIAM JR.

WILLIAMES, LEE JOHN, academic administrator, history professor; b. Phila., July 4, 1942; m. Frances, Feb. 24, 1968; 3 children. BA in Pre-Law and Liberal Arts, LaSalle U., 1964; MA in European History, Niagara U., 1966, ACS in Soviet Studies, 1966; PhD in History, SUNY, Binghamton, 1981. Prof., honors dir. Coll. Misericordia, Dallas, Pa., 1966-86; asst. provost, prof. U. Scranton, Pa., 1987-92; v.p. acad. affairs, prof. history U. St. Thomas, 1992—2000, acting pres. summer, 1997, now prof. history and emeritus v.p. acad. affairs, 2000—; vis. prof. Mary Immaculate Coll., U. Limerick, Ireland, 2000. Frequent spkr. Russian univs.; sec. gen. internat. coun. U. St. Thomas, 1995-97. Author: Anton Chekov: Iconoclast, 1989; (curriculum exercises) Odyssey of the Mind, 1988-96, written over 20 articles on history and on teaching, Commr. Northeastern Pa. coun. Boy Scouts Am., 1988-92, v.p., 1984-88; mem. water safety bd. ARC, N.E. Pa., 1988-91; chair steering com. St. Thomas/Shell Oil/Helms Collaboration, 1997—. Recipient Silver Beaver medal Boy Scouts Am., 1984, St. George medal Cath. Com. on Scouting, 1986, Jubalarian medal La Salle U., Phila., Centennial medal U. Scranton. Fellow Am. Coun. on Edn. (exec. com. coun. fellows 1989-92); mem. Mid. Atlantic Hist. Assn. of Cath. Colls. and Univs. (editor jour. 1985-92), Am. Assn. for Advancement of Slavic Studies. Roman Catholic. Avocations: swimming, canoeing, martial arts, stained glass, antique restoration. Office: U St Thomas 3800 Montrose Blvd Houston TX 77006-4626 Office Phone: 713-525-3810. E-mail: williames@stthom.edu.

WILLIAMS, ALAN KEISER, management consultant; b. Harrisburg, Pa., Dec. 19, 1928; s. Paul Rupp and Margaret Helen (Keiser) W.; m. Barbara Elaine Hanson, Aug. 7, 1952 (div. Aug. 1975); children: Margaret Vivian Williams Westfall, Bryn Barbara Williams Stuart, Andrew Hanson Williams; m. Peggie Lucille Hall, May 29, 1988. BA, U. No. Colo., 1952. Sr. rsch. mgr. Dow Chem. Co., Golden, 1952-74; v.p. Allied-Gen. Nuclear Svc., Barnwell, S.C., 1974-83; prin. engr., project mgr. Bechtel Nat. Inc., San Francisco, 1983-91; sr. program analyst Sci. Applications Internat. Co., Germantown, Md., 1991-95; pvt. cons., 1995—. Contbr. articles to Jour. Electro Chem. Soc. Tech. co-chmn. ENC-3 Brussels, 1982. With U.S. Army, 1946-47. Fellow Am. Nuclear Soc. (chmn. Savannah River sect 1980, bd. dirs. 1982-85); mem. AAAS, Am. Chem. Soc. Achievements include research in processing and handling actinide elements, principally uranium, plutonium and americium. Home and Office: 39531 S Moonwood Dr Tucson AZ 85739 Personal E-mail: akwplw@wbhsi.net.

WILLIAMS, ALFRED B., retired management educator; b. Oakland City, Ind., Sept. 17, 1940; s. Ross Merl and Jesse Adell (Helsley) W. BS cum laude, Oakland City U., 1963; MS, Ind. U., 1964; PhD, Ga. State U., 1974. Tchr. Arlington H.S., Indpls., 1964-65, Oakland City (Ind.) U., 1965-69; editor Southwestern Pub. Co., Cin., 1969-72, cons., 1981-93; adj. prof. Ga. State U., Atlanta, 1972-74; prof. mgmt. and bus. comm. U. La., Lafayette, 1975—2002, chmn. dept., 1986-96; prof. emeritus, 2002. Adj. prof. U. La., Lafayette, 2004-05; cons. John Wiley Pub. Co., NY, 1988-89, Irwin Pub., 1989. Author study guides; editor Info. Systems Bus. Comm. Jour., 1983, 93. Help One Student to Succeed reading mentor North Lewis Elem. Sch., New Iberia, La., 2003-07. Mem. AAUP, Assn. Bus. Communicators (bd. dirs. 1986-90, Francis W. Weeks Merit award 1984), La. Assn. Higher Edn., Sierra Club, Phi Delta Kappa, Phi Kappa Phi, Delta Pi Epsilon, Beta Gamma Sigma. Methodist. Personal E-mail: abwilliams917@aol.com.

WILLIAMS, ALLEN W., JR., lawyer; b. Milw., Sept. 8, 1944; AB cum laude, Harvard U., 1966; JD cum laude, Columbia U., 1970, MBA, 1970. Bar: Wis. 1970. Legal counsel to Gov. Patrick J. Lucey State of Wis., 1971-72; ptnr. Foley & Lardner LLP, Milw. Chmn. legal com. Edison Electric Inst., 1981—. Mem. bd. editors Columbia Law Review, 1969-70. Bd. dirs. Planned Parenthood Wis., 1974-76; bd. dirs. Milw. Inst. Art and Design, 2005—, chmn., 2006. Mem. State Bar Wis., Milwaukee County Zool. Soc. (bd. dirs. 1977-89, pres. 1984-86), Med. Coll. Wis. (bd. dirs. 1977-97, chmn. 1984-1987). Office: Foley & Lardner LLP Firstar Ctr 777 E Wisc Ave Milwaukee WI 53202 Office Phone: 414-297-5808. Office Fax: 414-297-4900. Business E-Mail: awilliams@foley.com.

WILLIAMS, AMY MCDANIEL, lawyer; b. Birmingham, Ala., Sept. 7, 1962; BA cum laude, Duke U., 1985; JD magna cum laude, Cornell Univ., 1990. Bar: Va. 1990. Assoc. Hunton & Williams LLP, Richmond, Va., 1992—99, ptnr., bus. practice group, 1999—, chmn. ethics com., 2002—. Sr. note editor Cornell Law Rev., 1990. Mem.: ABA, Met. Richmond Women's Bar Assn., Nat. Assn. Women Lawyers. Office: Hunton & Williams LLP Riverfront Plz East Tower 951 E Byrd St Richmond VA 23219-4074 Office Phone: 804-788-7388. Office Fax: 804-788-8218. Business E-Mail: awilliams@hunton.com.

WILLIAMS, ANN CLAIRE, federal judge; b. Detroit, Aug. 16, 1949; m. David J. Stewart. BS, Wayne State U., 1970; MA, U. Mich., 1972; JD, U. Notre Dame, 1975; degree (hon.), Lake Forest Coll., 1987, U. Portland, 1993, U. Notre Dame, 1997. Law clk. to Hon. Robert A. Sprecher, 1975-76; asst. US atty. US Dist. Ct. (no. dist.) Ill., Chgo., 1976-85; faculty Nat. Inst. for Trial Advocacy, 1979—, also bd. dirs.; adj. prof., lectr. Northwestern U. Law Sch., 1979—, John Marshall Law Sch., 1979—; judge US Dist. Ct. (no. dist.) Ill., 1985-99, US Ct. Appeals (7th cir.), Chgo., 1999—. Chief Organized Crime Drug Enforcement Task Force for North Ctrl. Region, 1983-85; mem. ct. adminstrn. and case mgmt. com. Jud. Conf. US, 1990-97, chair, 1993-97. Sec. bd. trustees U. Notre Dame; founder Minority Legal Resources, Inc. Recipient Earl Burns Dickerson award, Chgo. Bar Assn., 1997, Tradition of Excellence award, Minority Legal Resources, Inc., 1997, Thurgood Marshall Jurist of Year, Legal Ministry of Second Baptist Church, 1997, Alumni of Year, Black Law Students Assn., U. Notre Dame, 1997, Morton A. Brody Disting. Jud. Svc. award, Colby Coll., 2002. Mem. FBA, Fed. Judges Assn., Ill. State Bar Assn., Ill. Jud. Coun., Cook County Bar Asn., Women's Bar Assn. Ill., Black Women's Lawyers Assn. Greater Chgo. Office: US Ct Appeals 7th Circuit 219 S Dearborn St Ste 2612 Chicago IL 60604-1803 *

WILLIAMS, ANNA LASSITER, psychologist, researcher; d. Charles L. William and Jane W. (Williams) Metcalfe. BS, Coll. Charleston, SC, 2001; MA, Columbia U., NYC, 2004; postgrad., NYU; postgrad. semester at sea, U. Pitts. Rsch. asst. Columbia U., 2002; counselor alcohol & substance abuse, coord. early intervention program LI Coll. Hosp., NYC, 2003; case mgr. Urban Pathways, NYC, 2004—05; vocat. case mgr. FEGS, NYC, 2005; assoc. psychologist Austin State Hosp., Tex., 2006—. Rsch. assoc. Austin Neurol. Clinic, 2006—; chair patient satisfaction com. Austin State Hosp., 2006—. Mem. Greenpeace, Planned Parenthood Fedn. Am. Recipient Commonwealth award, Roanoke Coll., 1998, Loyal and Valuable Vol. Svc. award, Med. U. SC, 2000—02; grantee, Roanoke Coll., 1998. Mem.: APA, Am. Psychol. Soc., Internat. Neurol. Soc., Inst. Neurosci. and Consciousness Studies, Coll. Charleston Psychology Club, Kappa Delta Pi. Home: 5000 A Evans Ave Austin TX 78751

WILLIAMS, ANTHONY, lawyer; b. NYC, Jan. 12, 1946; s. Patrick and Palma (Leone) W. AB in Govt. cum laude, Harvard U., 1968; JD, NYU, 1973. Bar: N.Y. 1974, Calif. 1977, US Supreme Ct. 1980. Assoc. Coudert Bros., NYC, 1973-75, San Francisco, 1976-79, ptnr. NYC, 1981—, adminstrv. ptnr., 1982-85, chmn., 1993—2001, head Global Life Sci. practice. Bd. chmn. Fenn, Wright & Manson, England; bd. vice chmn. Senetek PLC; mem. internat. adv. bd. Intelligent Engineering Ltd., Trautman Wasserman & Co.; dir. Brook Capital Corp., DBT America Inc., German Am. C. of C., Plymouth Holdings Ltd., British Virgin Islands, River Ventures Inc., Hong Kong. Editor (in chief): NYU Jour. Internat. Law; contbr. articles to profl. jours. Vice chmn. HELP USA Inc.; bd. mem. City Univ. of NY, Friends of Heidelberg Ctr. for Am. Studies, Harvard MIT Div. of Life Sci. & Tech., Metro Internat. NY, Robert F. Kennedy Mem. & Ctr. for Human Rights, Sheltering Arms Svc. Served US Army, 1968—70. Mem. ABA, N.Y. Bar Assn., Assn. Bar of City of N.Y., Calif. Bar Assn. Avocations: reading, baseball, golf. Office: Coudert Bros 1114 Avenue Of The Americas Fl 4 New York NY 10036-7710 Office Phone: 212-626-4418. Office Fax: 212-626-4120. Business E-Mail: williamsa@coudert.com.

WILLIAMS, ANTHONY ALLAN (TONY), former mayor; b. 1951; s. Lewis and Virginia W.; m. Diana Lynn Simmons; 1 child, Asantewa Foster. BA in Polit. Sci. magna cum laude, Yale U., 1982; JD, M of Pub. Policy, Harvard U., 1987. Law clk. to Hon. David Nelson US Dist. Ct., Boston, 1987-88; asst. dir. Boston Redevel. Authority, 1988-89; exec. dir. Cmty. Devel. Agy., St. Louis, 1989-91; dep. comptr. State of Conn., Boston, 1991-93; exec. dir. Cmty. Devel. Agy., St. Louis, 1989-91; dept. contr. State of Conn., 1991-93; CFO Dept. Agr., Washington, 1995—98; mayor Washington, DC, 1999—2007. Adj. prof. pub. affairs Columbia U., NYC, 1992-93. Pres. pro tempore, chmn. cmty. devel. com. Conn. Bd. Alderman, 1980-83; dir. comm. Conn. Spkr. House and Assembly Dem., 1983; second v.p., Washington, DC-based National League of Cities (NLC), 2002-. Named one of 100 Most Influential Black Americans, Ebony mag., 2006; Kellogg Found. Nat. fellow, 1991. Democrat.

WILLIAMS, ANTHONY ERVIN, music educator; b. Nashville, Aug. 25, 1960; s. Albert Osborne and Marion Ervin Williams. MusB in Organ Performance, U. Cin., 1982; MusM in Organ Performance, U. Mich., 1984; DMA in Organ Performance, Am. Conservatory Music, Hammond, Ind., 2006. Music dir., organist Good Shepherd United Meth. Ch., Dearborn, Mich., 1983—86; instr. music, univ. organist Fisk U., Nashville, 1986—90, assoc. prof. music, 2006—; asst. prof. music, univ. organist Dillard U., New Orleans, 1990—2005. Dir. Fisk Jubilee Singers Fisk U., Nashville, 1987—90, organist, 2006—; dir. music and arts First Presbyn. Ch., Hendersonville, Tenn., 2006—. Musician organ recitals. Bd. dirs. New Orleans Mission, 1992—2004, John Wesley Work III Meml. Found., Nashville, 2007—. Recipient Strader Organ scholarship, U. Cin., Coll. Conservatory of Music, 1978—82, Provost Extra Mile award, Dillard U. Mem.: Mus. Arts Soc. New Orleans (bd. dirs. 1992—2006), Am. Guild Organists (bd. dirs. New Orleans chpt. 1992—94, bd. dirs. Nashville chpt. 2006—). Avocations: cooking, travel, ballroom dancing. Home: 3603 Batavia St Nashville TN 37209-2530 Office: Fisk U 1000 17th Ave N Nashville TN 37208 Home Phone: 615-438-9933; Office Phone: 615-329-2033. Home Fax: 615-321-5645. Personal E-mail: awilli6034@aol.com.

WILLIAMS, ARTHUR COZAD, retired broadcasting executive; b. Forty Fort, Pa., Feb. 12, 1926; s. John Bedford and Emily Irene (Poyck) W.; m. Ann Cale Bragan, Oct. 1, 1955; children: Emily Williams Van Hoorickx, Douglas, Craig. Student, Bucknell U., 1943-44; BA cum laude, U. So. Calif., 1949. Trainee Kaiser Aluminum, 1949; sales Sta. KPMC, 1950-51; v.p., mgr. KFBK and KFBK-FM Radio Stas., Sacramento, 1951-80; with public relations dept. Sacramento Bee, McClatchy Newspapers, 1981-86; ret., 1986. Dir.-treas. Norkal Opportunities, Inc.; pres. Sacramento Bee Credit Union. Served with AUS, 1944-46. Mem. Sigma Delta Chi. Clubs: Rotary, Sutter, Valley Hi Country, Masons, Shriners. Home: 1209 Nevis Ct Sacramento CA 95822-2532 Personal E-mail: artcwilliams@sbcglobal.net.

WILLIAMS, B. JOHN, JR., retired federal agency administrator, lawyer; b. Lancaster, Pa., Dec. 13, 1949; s. Bernard John and Sarah Elizabeth (Sykes) W.; m. Martha Caroline Roberts, Aug. 6, 1977; children: Robert, Sarah, Anne, Bernard. BA, George Washington U., 1971, JD, 1974. Bar: D.C., Pa., U.S. Tax Ct., U.S. Ct. Appeals (3rd, 9th and fed. cirs.), U.S. Supreme Ct. Law clk. to judge U.S. Tax Ct., Washington, 1974-76; assoc. Ballard, Spahr, Andrews & Ingersoll, Phila., 1976-81; spl. asst. to chief counsel IRS, Washington, 1981-83; dep. asst. atty. gen. Tax Div. Dept. Justice, Washington, 1983-84; ptnr. Morgan, Lewis & Bockius, Washington, 1984-85; judge U.S. Tax Ct., Washington, 1985-90; ptnr. Morgan, Lewis & Bockius, Washington, 1990-2000, Shearman & Sterling, Washington, 2000—02; chief counsel, IRS U.S. Dept. Treasury, Washington, 2002—03. Mem. adv. com. U.S. Ct. Appeals, Fed. Cir. Fellow Am. Coll. Tax Counsel; mem. ABA, Am. Law Inst., Phi Beta Kappa, Omicron Delta Kappa. Republican.

WILLIAMS, BARBARA ANNE, retired academic administrator; b. Camden, NJ, Oct. 14, 1938; d. Frank and Laura Dorothy (Szweda) W. BA cum laude, Georgian Ct. U., 1963; MLS, Rutgers U., 1965; MA, Manhattan Coll., 1973; postgrad., NYU, 1976—81, postgrad., 1993—. Cert. English tchr., N.J.; joined Sisters of Mercy, 1957. Sec. Camden Cath. H.S., 1956-57; registrar Georgian Ct. U., Lakewood, NJ, 1960-66, dir. libr. svcs., 1966-74, dean acad. affairs, 1974-80, pres., 1980-2000, sci. and math. libr., 2000—04, pres. emerita, 2000—, archivist, 2003—. Mem. Mid-Atlantic Regional Archives Conf., 2003—. Mem. editl. bd. N.J. Woman mag. Bd. dir., mem. ednl. adv. coun. Diocese of Trenton, N.J., 1983-90, NJ Natural Gas Co., 1986-91; mem. adv. bd. Ocean County Ctr. Arts, Lakewood, NJ, 1983-91; mem. Ocean County Pvt. Industry Coun., 1983-92; bd. dir. Monmouth/Ocean Devel. Coun., 1981-84; mem. State NJ Student Assistance Bd., 1995-99; mem. Ocean County School-to-Career Com., 1996-2000; mem. art adv. coun. Nat. Mus. Cath. Art and History, 2000—; trustee Camden Cath. H.S., 2005—. Named Outstanding Woman N.J. Assn. Women Bus. Owners, 1983; recipient Humanitarian award Monmouth/Ocean Devel. Coun., 1985, Salute to Policymakers award Exec. Women N.J., 1986, Woman in Leadership award Monmouth Coun. Girl Scouts, 1987, Citizen of Yr. Alcoholism & Drug Abuse Coun. Ocean County, 1993, Brotherhood/Sisterhood award Monmouth/Ocean County chpts. NCCJ, 1994, Friend of Scouting award Boy Scouts Am. Jersey Shore Coun., 1999, Leadership award Mercy Higher Edn. Colloquium, 2000. Mem. Assn. Mercy Colls. (pres. 1981-83, sec. 1996-98), Mercy Higher Edn. Colloquium (mem. exec. com. 1980-87), Ocean County Bus. Assn. (trustee 1982-84), Nat. Assn. Inc. Colls. and Univs. (secretariat 1981-83, 87-91), NAIA (coun. of pres. 1997-2000), Soc. Am. Archivists. Home and Office: Georgian Ct Univ 900 Lakewood Ave Lakewood NJ 08701-2600 Home Phone: 732-987-2511; Office Phone: 732-987-2441. E-mail: williamssb@georgian.edu.

WILLIAMS, BARBARA IVORY, educational researcher; b. Detroit, Apr. 28, 1936; d. Henry Oliver and Willa Mae (Frazier) I.; m. Alney Elliott Whitener, Jan. 1, 1987 (dec.). BS, Wayne State U., 1957, MEd, 1960; PhD, U. Washington, 1973. Tchr. Detroit Pub. Schs., 1957-68; program assoc. Mich.-Ohio Regional Lab., Detroit, 1968-70; lectr. predoctoral U. Wash., Seattle, 1970-73; sr. program assoc. Far West Lab. for Ednl. Research and Devel., San Francisco, 1973-76; sr. cons. E.H. White & Co., San Francisco, 1976-77; sr. program assoc. Northwest Regional Lab., Portland, Oreg., 1977-84; area coord. Ednl. Testing Service, Washington, 1984-85; edn. group dir. Research and Evaluation Assocs., Washington, 1985-87; ind. cons. Washington, 1987-89; assoc. dir. edn. studies Westat, Rockville, Md., 1989—. Mem. Am. Ednl. Research Assn., Am. Psychol. Assn., Nat. Assn. Black Sch. Educators, Phi Delta Kappa, Alpha Kappa Alpha (pres. Portland chpt. 1980-84). Democrat. Baptist. Avocation: needlecrafts. Home: 13601 Belle Chasse Blvd Unit 414 Laurel MD 20707-9433 Office Phone: 301-251-4249. E-mail: barbaraji@mac.com.

WILLIAMS, BARBARA STAMBAUGH, editor; b. Jenkins, Ky., Nov. 22, 1937; d. James Cosby and Jessie Kate (Bise) Stambaugh; m. Manning Williams, Sept. 11, 1963. BS in Journalism, U. Tenn., 1959. Polit. reporter News and Courier, Charleston, S.C., 1961-63, 67-76, asst. mng. editor, 1976-81; city hall reporter Camden (N.J.) Courier Post, 1963-67; editor The Evening Post, Charleston, S.C., 1981-90, The Evening Post and News and Courier, Charleston, SC, 1990—91, The Post and Courier, Charleston, SC, 1991—. Pres. Nat. Conf. Editl. Writers, Rockville, Md., 1992. Bd. dirs. Charleston Sci. and Cultural Edn. Fund. Named Outstanding Newspaper Woman in S.C., S.C. Press Assn., 1962. Mem. Sigma Delta Chi (ByLiner award 1973). Achievements include first woman editor of a daily newspaper in SC; first woman reporter to cover legislature in SC. Office: The Post & Courier 134 Columbus St Charleston SC 29403-4800 Office Phone: 843-937-5526. Business E-Mail: barbara@postandcourier.com.

WILLIAMS, BART H., lawyer; b. Orleans, France, Oct. 24, 1962; BA, Yale U., 1984, JD, 1987. Bar: Calif. 1988, US Dist. Ct. (ctrl. dist. Calif.) 1988. Assoc. Munger, Tolles & Olson LLP, LA, 1987—91, ptnr., 1994—, co-mng. ptnr., 2004—; asst. US atty. criminal divsn., major frauds sect. Central Dist. Calif., 1991—94. Lawyer del. Ninth Circuit Judicial Conf., 1997—99; mem. bd. trustees Charles R. Drew U. Medicine and Sci.; mem. LA County Bar Assn. Task Force on Criminal Justice System; dep. gen. counsel LA Police Commn. Independent Review Panel; co-chair ABA Lit. Section's Expert Witness Com.; adj. prof. law Loyola Law Sch.; adj. prof. Nat. Inst. Trial Advocacy. Bd. dirs. Alliance Children's Rights. Named Prosecutor Yr., Internat. Assn. Credit Card Investigators, 1993; named one of Top 20 Lawyers in State of Calif. Under 40 Yrs. Age, Calif. Law Bus. Mag., 2002, 45 Under Forty-Five, Am. Lawyer Mag., 2003, Am. Top Black Lawyers, Black Enterprise Mag., 2003, Calif. Superlawyers, Law & Politics Mag., 2004; recipient Potter Stewart prize, Yale Moot Ct. Appeals. Mem.: ABA (mem. task force on ind. counsel act 1997—98, mem. litig. and criminal law sects., chair govt. litig. com. 2000—02), State Bar Calif. Office: Munger Tolles & Olson LLP 355 S Grand Ave 35th Fl Los Angeles CA 90071 Office Phone: 213-683-9295. Office Fax: 213-683-5195. E-mail: Bart.Williams@mto.com. *

WILLIAMS, BEN, editorial director online magazine; BA, Univ. Kent, Canterbury, Eng.; MA, NYU. Assoc./mng. editor CitySearch, NYC, 1996—99, editor-in-chief, 1999—2003; books, movies, music columnist Slate, NYC, 2003—04; sr. editor, Strategist sect. NY Mag., NYC, 2004—06; editl. dir., website editl. & prodn. NYMag.com, 2006—. Contbr. articles to Village Voice, Time Out NY, Artforum, Paper, and Urb. Recipient Nat. Mag. award for Interactive Feature, Am. Soc. Mag. Editors, 2007. Office: NY Magazine Website 444 Madison Ave New York NY 10022 *

WILLIAMS, BENJAMIN R., health facility administrator; CIO Horizon/CMS Healthcare Corp., Albuquerque; v.p., info. services & CIO St. Joseph Health Sys., Orange, Calif., 1998, now sr. v.p., strategic innovation & chief info. officer. Spkr. in field. Recipient Innovator of Yr. award., Coll. of Healthcare Info. Mgmt. Executives, 2004. Office: St Joseph Health Sys 500 S Main St Ste 1000 PO Box 14132 Orange CA 92863-1532

WILLIAMS, BENJAMIN V., IV, headmaster, history educator; m. Ginger Williams; children: Ben, Grace, Carson. BA in Am. Studies, Williams Coll.; MA in Am. Civilization, Brown U. With First Boston, NYC; history and English teacher, dir. of development St. Sebastian's Sch., Mass.; dean of middle and upper schools St. John's Sch., Houston, 1993—97; headmaster Cate Sch., Carpinteria, Calif., 1997—. Office: Cate Sch PO Box 5005 Carpinteria CA 93014-5005 Office Phone: 805-684-4127 ext. 200. *

WILLIAMS, BERNARD, film producer; Prodr., exec. prodr.: (films) A Clockwork Orange, 1971, Lady Caroline Lamb, 1973, Barry Lyndon, 1975, The Last Remake of Beau Geste, 1977, The Big Sleep, 1978, Flash Gordon, 1980, Ragtime, 1981, Amityville II: The Possession, 1982, The Bounty, 1984, Miracles, 1986, Manhunter, 1986, Wisdom, 1986, Who's That Girl, 1987, Dirty Rotten Scoundrels, 1988, War Party, 1989, What About Bob?, 1991, Housesitter, 1992, So I Married An Ax Murderer, 1993, Star Trek: Generations, 1994, The Indian in the Cupboard, 1995, Blood and Wine, 1996, Bowfinger, 1999, The Score, 2001, Daredevil, 2003, Charlotte's Web, 2006. *

WILLIAMS, BERNARD, Olympic athlete; b. Balt., Jan. 19, 1978; Student, Barton County C.C., Great Bend, Kans., U. Fla., 2000—. Co-winner Gold Medal 4X100 meter relay U.S.A. Track and Field Team, Sydney, 2000; gold medal 4x100m relay US World Outdoor Champions, 2001; bronze medal World Champion, 2001; gold medal 4x100m relay USA Champion, 2003; silver medal winner 200m Olympics, 2004. Office: USA Track and Field Team One RCA Dome Ste 140 Indianapolis IN 46225 Business E-Mail: olympic2@ufl.edu.

WILLIAMS, BERNIE (BERNABE FIGUEROA WILLIAMS), professional baseball player; b. San Juan, Sept. 13, 1968; Outfielder New York Yankees, 1991—2006. Named ALCS MVP, 1996; named to Am. League All-Star team, 1997—2001; recipient Am. League Gold Glove Award, 1997—2000. Achievements include being a member of World Series Champion New York Yankees, 1996, 1998-2000; led American League in batting average (.339), 1998. Office: New York Yankees Yankee Stadium E 161 St and River Ave Bronx NY 10451

WILLIAMS, BETHTINA QUBRÉ, minister; d. Cleophus Noble Marshall and Marilyn Etta Marshall-Pierce; m. Stanley Davis Williams, Feb. 28, 1986; children: Stanley II, Jonathan, Joshua. BA, Friends Internat. Christian U., Merced, Calif., 1990, MA, 1996, DMin, 2001. Ordained min. Living Word Christian Ctr., Inc., 1996. Adminstrv. asst. Tex. Tech. U., Lubbock, Tex., 1983—84; health and safety coord., tchr. Kinder Care Pre-Sch., Lubbock, 1985—87; assoc. mgr. Paul Harris Store, Lubbock, 1987—89; libr. asst. Torreion (Spain) AFB, 1990—91; co-founder, copastor, exec. adminstr. Lighthouse of Faith Cmty. Ch., Ft. Walton Beach, Fla., 1997—; network pastor Life Cmty. Fellowship, 2001—05. Adv. bd. West Navarre Elem. Sch., 2004—05. Author: Women of Character and Destiny, 2005. Dir. outreach in humanitarian svc. Landstuhl (Germany) Base Chapel, 1993. Recipient Appreciation cert., Wayland Bapt. U., 1986, Commdr.'s Commendation medal, USAF, Ramstein, Germany, 1995, Appreciation cert., USAF, 2000, Commdr.'s medal, Hurlbut Field AFB, Fla., 2000, cert. of honor, King of Shai State, Ghana, 2004. Avocations: writing, exercise, singing, travel, motivational speaking. Office: Lighthouse of Faith Church Inc 755 Lovejoy Rd NW Fort Walton Beach FL 32548

WILLIAMS, BETTY OUTHIER, lawyer; b. Woodward, Okla., Sept. 11, 1947; d. Robert E. and Ethel M. (Castiller) Outhier; children: Amanda J., Emily Rebecca. BA, Oklahoma City U., 1969; JD, Vanderbilt U., Nashville, 1972. Bar: Okla. 1972, U.S. Dist. Ct. (no. dist.) Okla. 1972, U.S. Dist. Ct. (ea. dist.) Okla. 1973, U.S. Dist. Ct. (we. dist.) Okla. 1988, U.S. Tax Ct. 2001, U.S. Ct. Appeals (10th cir.) 1973, U.S. Supreme Ct. 1980. Atty. Reginal Heber Smith Cmty. Lawyer Fellowship, Tulsa, 1972-73; asst. U.S. atty. Muskogee, Okla., 1973-81; U.S. atty., 1981-82; ptnr. Robinson, Locke, Gage, Fite & Williams, Muskogee, 1982-96, Robinson, Gage & Williams, Muskogee, 1996-97, Gage & Williams, Muskogee, 1997—2005; appellate judge Okla. Ct. on the Judiciary, 2003—; pvt. practice Muskogee, 2005—; adv. com. Tenth Cir., 2006—. Chair local rules com. U.S. Bankruptcy Ct. Ea. Dist., Okla., 1994, U.S. Dist. Ct. Dist. Okla., 1995; adj. settlement judge U.S. Dist. Ct. Ea. Dis. Okla., 1998-. Mem. editl. bd. Okla. Law Enforcement Ops. Bull., 1993-94; editor Okla. Bar Jour., 1996-2002. Pres. Bus. and Profl. Women, Muskogee, 1975-77, 83; pres., bd. dirs. YWCA, Muskogee, 1975-82; bd. dirs. Green County Mental Health, Muskogee, 1986-88, WISH, 1990—; trustee Frontier Heritage Found., 1990-98; chmn. bd. commrs. Muskogee Housing Authority; adminstrv. bd. chmn., St. Paul United Meth. Ch., Muskogee, 1999-2001; state exec. com. Internat. Order the Rainbow for Girls, 1999—. Named One of Outstanding Young Career Women, Bus. and Profl. Women, 1974. Fellow: Am. Bar Found. (fellow 2004—), Okla. Bar Found. (trustee 1989—, v.p. 1994, pres. 1996, gov. 2000—); mem.: Muskogee County Bar Assn. (pres. 1984—85), Okla. Bar Assn. (editl. bd. 1996—, bd. govs. 2000—), ABA, Soroptomists (pres. 1986—88), Order Eastern Star (Hope chpt., Worthy Matron 0203), Gamma Phi Beta (alumnae pres. 1993—). Republican. Methodist. Home: 4326 Oklahoma St Muskogee OK 74401-2351 Office: Betty Outhier Williams Law Office PO Box 87 Muskogee OK 74402-0087 Home Phone: 918-683-3318; Office Phone: 918-687-5425. Personal E-mail: bowlaw@sbcglobal.net.

WILLIAMS, BRADLEY BENNETT, historian; b. LA, Mar. 5, 1948; s. Robert E. and Helen L. Williams; m. Susan E. Poster, May 25, 1980. BA, U. So. Calif., 1972; MA, San Diego State U., 1977; PhD, U. Iowa, 1984. Cert. fundraising U. Calif., 1996. Dir. Heritage Mus., Coralville, Iowa, 1983—84; assoc. registrar LA County Mus. Art, 1984—85; registrar Skipball Mus., Hebrew Union Coll., LA, 1985—86; assoc. for alumni devel. Loyola Marymount U., LA, 1990—92; dir. Ninth Judicial Cir. Hist. Soc., Pasadena, 1992—. Editor: (scholarly jour.) Western Legal History, 1992—. Pres. Southwest Oral History Assn., 1997—98; mem. bd. dirs. Theodore Payne Found., LA, 1993; v.p. Pasadena Arts Council, 1987—90. Recipient Trustee's award, State Historical Soc. of Iowa, 1983, Svc. award, Southwest Oral History Assn., 1999; NEH Challenge Grant, Pasadena Hist. Soc., 1989. Mem.: Southwest Oral History Assn. (pres. 1997—98), Oral History Assn., Am. History Assn., Am. Assn. for State and Local History, Northwest Oral History Assn. (pres. 2005—). Home: 952 E Athens St Altadena CA 91001 Office: Ninth Judicial Cir Historical Soc 125 S Grand Ave Pasadena CA 91105 E-mail: historyconsultant@hotmail.com.

WILLIAMS, BRIAN, network news anchor; b. Middletown, NJ, May 5, 1959; m. Jane Stoddard; 2 children. Student, George Washington U., Cath. U. Am.; Doctorate (hon.), Elmira Coll., Providence Coll., Cath. U. Am., 2004; LLD (hon.), Villanova U., 2003; LHD (hon.), Bates Coll., 2005. Corr. various stas., Phila., Washington, Pittsburgh, Kans.; anchor, corr. Sta. WCBS-TV, NYC; anchor, mng. editor NBC Nightly News Sat., NYC, 1993—99; chief White House corr. NBC, Washington, 1994—96; anchor, mng. editor The News with Brian Williams MSNBC/CNBC, NYC, 1996—2004; anchor, mng. editor NBC Nightly News, NYC, 2004—. Fmr. vol. firefighter, NJ; mem. Coun. Fgn. Rels., NYC; bd. dirs. Congl. Medal of Honor Found. Named Father of Yr., Nat. Father's Day Com., 1996, Best Anchor, USA Today, Man of Yr., GQ Mag., 2001; recipient Emmy award, 1987, 1993, 2001, 2003, 2005, 4 Nat. Edward R. Murrow awards, 2005, George Foster Peabody award for Coverage of Hurricane Katrina, 2005, Sigma Delta Chi award, Soc. Profl. Journalists, 2006, Tulane President's Medal, Tulane U., 2006. Office: NBC News 30 Rockefeller Plz Fl 3 New York NY 10112

WILLIAMS, BROWN F, media specialist, consultant; b. Evanston, Ill., Dec. 22, 1940; s. Jack Kermit Williams and Virginia Helen (Benjamin) Likar; m. Linda Francee Ludt, Sept. 1961 (div. 1968); 1 child, Eden Carol Williams McCarthy; m. Martha Amidon Powers, Sept. 1970 (div. 1974); m. Sandra Ann Matkowski, Jan. 1984 (dec. May 2000); 1 child, Bronwyn Emily. AB in Math. and Physics, U. Calif., Riverside, 1962, MA in Physics, 1964, PhD in Physics, 1966. Mgr. Electro-Optics Lab., Princeton, NJ, 1969-75; dir. RCA Labs., Princeton, 1976-82, v.p., 1982-87; pres. Williams Cons. Group, Princeton, 1988-90. CEO, chmn. Princeton Video Image, 1990—2004; v.p. R&D Evergreen Solar, 2004- Fellow IEEE; mem. AAAS, Am. Phys. Soc., Sigma Xi. Avocations: skiing, sailing, horseback riding. Home: 1 Devonshire Pl Boston MA 02109 Office Phone: 609-648-2652. E-mail: bfwilliams1@comcast.net.

WILLIAMS, CARL CHANSON, insurance company executive; b. Cin., Oct. 16, 1937; s. Charles J. and Alcie (Brazile) W.; m. Claire Bathé, May 26, 1985; 1 child, Michelle. A.S., U. Cin., 1965; BS, SUNY-Brockport, 1974; MBA, U. Rochester, 1975. Mgr. fin. systems Xerox Corp., Rochester, N.Y., 1972-77; dir. info. mgmt. Am. Can Co., Greenwich, Conn., 1977-79, mng. dir. info. mgmt., 1979-80, mng. dir. ops. control, 1980-82; sr. v.p., dir. mgmt. info. systems DDB Needham Worldwide, NYC, 1982-91; pres. The Intertechnology Group, Inc., NYC, 1990-91; v.p. infosystems and tech. Macmillan Pub. Co., NYC, 1991-93; gen. mgr. info. tech. Amoco Corp., Chgo., 1993-94, v.p. info. tech., 1994-97; sr. v.p., chief info. officer Principal Fin. Group, Des Moines, Iowa, 1997—. Cons. Stamford (Conn.) Bd. Edn., 1981-82; lectr. U. Rochester, N.Y., 1975-77; adj. prof. Fordham U., 1991—. Exec. dir. Concerned Assn. Rochester, N.Y., 1971-75; bd. dirs. Stamford Cmty. Arts Coun., 1983-84; trustee Roosevelt U., 1995-97, U. Rochester, 1999—, Exec. Leadership Found., 2000—; mem. Exec. Leadership Coun. 1993—. Mem. Soc. Info. Mgmr. (exec. coun. 1980-83, pres. 1985, pres. coun. 1986—), Exec. Leadership Coun. (found. bd. trustees). Office: Principal Fin Group 711 High St Des Moines IA 50392-0002 Home: 2420 Vintage Hill Dr Durham NC 27712-9476 E-mail: williams.carl@principal.com.

WILLIAMS, CARLISLE M., JR., municipal official, insurance company executive; b. Painter, Va., June 27, 1937; s. Carlisle M. and Evelyn Hickman Williams; m. Barbara Belle Schuyler, July 11, 1987; m. Dolly Evans Taylor, June 15, 1958 (div. Mar. 19, 1987); children: Carlisle M. III, Valerie Taylor. AA, Goldey-Beacom Coll., Wilmington, Del., 1958; BA, East Carolina U., Greenville, 1960; DHL (hon.), Mary Washington Coll., 2003. County adminstr. County of Accomack, Va., 1966—83, County of Stafford, Va., 1984—2003; corp. officer, v.p. Silver Co., Fredericksburg, Va., 2005—; corp. officer, sec. Vaco Reins. Co. Ltd., Brit. Virgin Islands, 2006—. Adminstrv. officer & sec./treas. George Washington Boyhood Home Found., Stafford, 1992—99; chmn. Fredericksburg Area Met. Planning Orgn., Va., 2001—03, VACO Group Self Ins. Assn., Roanoke, Va., 2001—05; pres. Va. Local Govt. Mgmt. Assn., Richmond, Va., 1981—82; sec./treas. Cedar Island Bridge and Beach Authority, Accomac, 1975—83. Chmn. com. Stafford County Mus.; mem. adv. com. Stafford

County Cable Commn.; sec.-treas. Accomack County Indsl. Devel. Authority, Cedar Island Bridge and Beach Authority; mem. new bldg. com. Fredericksburg Area Mus. and Culture Ctr., 2004—; chmn. Fredericksburg Area Met. Planning Orgn., 2001—03; local govt. chmn. Rappahannock United Way, 2000—01; mem. adv. bd. Salvation Army; chmn. supervisory bd. Va. Assn. Counties Group Self-Ins. Assn., 2001—05; mem. supervisory bd. Va. Assn. Counties Risk Pool, 2001—05; pres. Ea. Shore Jaycees, Onancock, Va., 1967—68, Onancock Rotary Club, 1981—82; bd. dirs. Mary Washington Hosp. Found., 2003—, U. Mary Washington Found., 2006—, Rappahannock United Way, Rappahannock Regional Criminal Justice Acad., Rappahannock Regional C. of C. Recipient Jefferson Cup, Va. Assn. Counties, 2000, James Monroe Medal, Mary Washington Coll., 2003. Mem. Am. Soc. Pub. Adminstrn., Urban Land Inst., Nat. Assn. County Adminstrs., Nat. Civic League, Nat. Trust for Hist. Preservation, Internat. City/County Mgmt. Assn., Va. Emergency Mgmt. Assn., Va. Innovations Group, Stafford County Hist. Soc., No. Va. Mgrs. Assn., Va. Local Govt. Mgmt. Assn. Methodist. Avocation: sailing. Home: 12 Aiken Rd Fredericksburg VA 22405-3340 Office: County of Stafford 1300 Courthouse Rd PO Box 339 Stafford VA 22555-0339 E-mail: cmwjr@co.stafford.va.us.

WILLIAMS, CECILIA LEE PURSEL, optometrist; b. Lewisburg, Pa., Nov. 15, 1948; d. Lee LaVerne and Geraldine May (Steininger) Pursel; m. Richard Lee Williams, May 17, 1975; 1 son, Kent Lee. Student, Lycoming Coll., 1966—68; BS, Pa. Coll. Optometry, 1970, OD, 1972. Lic. and/or cert. optometrist, D.C., Pa., N.Y., N.J., Va. Rsch. optometrist in soft lens materials Gumpelmayer Optik, Vienna, Austria, 1973; optometrist Sterling Optical Co. Contact Lens Ctr., Washington, 1974-79; pvt. practice optometry Springfield, Va., 1980—. Recipient Clin. Efficiency award Pa. Coll. Optometry, 1972; Women's Aux. of Pa. Optometrists scholar, 1968-70, 70-72; Pa. State grantee, 1968-70, 70-72. Mem. Optometric Ctr. of Nation's Capital (dir. 1977-80), Am. Optometric Assn., Va. Optometric Assn., No. Va. Optometric Soc., Nat. Honor Soc. for Optometry, Omega Delta. Home: 3600 Wilton Hall Ct Alexandria VA 22310-2176 Office: 7241 Commerce St Springfield VA 22150-3411 Office Phone: 703-866-9364.

WILLIAMS, CHARLES JUDSON, lawyer, writer; b. San Mateo, Calif., Nov. 23, 1930; s. John Augustus and Edith (Babcock) W.; children: Patrick, Victoria, Apphia. AB, U. Calif., Berkeley, 1952, LLB, 1955. Bar: Calif. 1955, U.S. Supreme Ct., 1970. Assoc. Kirkbride, Wilson, Harzfeld and Wallace, San Mateo County, Calif., 1956-59; sole practice Solano County, Calif., 1959-64, Martinez, Calif., 1964—2002, Benicia, Calif., 1981-88; city atty. Pleasant Hill, 1962-80, Yountville, Calif., 1965-68, Benicia, 1968-76, 80-82, Lafayette, Calif., 1968—, Moraga, Calif., 1974-92, Danville, Calif., 1982-88, Pittsburg, Calif., 1984-93, Orinda, Calif., 1985-97; of counsel Best, Best and Krieger, 2002—04; atty. pvt. practice, Martinez, Calif., 2004—. Lectr. Calif. Continuing Edn. Bar 1964-65, U. Calif. Extension 1974-76, John F. Kennedy U. Sch. Law 1966-69; spl. counsel to various Calif. cities; legal advisor Alaska Legis. Council 1959-61; advisor Alaska sup. ct. 1960-61; advisor on revision Alaska statues 1960-62; atty. Pleasant Hill Redevel. Agy. 1978-82; sec., bd. dirs. Vintage Savs. & Loan Assn., Napa County, Calif., 1974-82; bd. dirs. 23d Agrl. Dist. Assn., Contra Costa County, 1968-70. Author: California Code Comments to West's Annotated California Codes, 3 vols., 1965, West' California Code Forms, Commercial, 2 vols., 1965, West's California Government Code Forms, 3 vols., 1971, Supplement to California Zoning Practice, 1978, 80, 82, 84, 85, 87, 89, 91, 94, 96, 98, 2000, 01; contbr. articles to legal jours. Mem. ABA, Calif. Bar Assn., Contra Costa County Bar Assn. Office: 1330 Arnold Dr Ste 149 Martinez CA 94553-6538 Office Phone: 925-228-3840. Personal E-mail: chaslaw@sbcglobal.net.

WILLIAMS, C(HARLES) K(ENNETH), poet, educator, literature educator; b. Newark, Nov. 4, 1936; s. Paul Bernard and Dossie (Kasdin) W.; m. Sarah Dean Jones, June, 1966 (div. 1975); 1 child, Jessica Anne; m. Catherine Justine Mauger, Apr. 15, 1975; 1 child, Jed Mauger. BA, U. Pa., 1958. Vis. prof. lit. Beaver Coll., Jenkintown, Pa., 1975, Drexel U., Phila., 1976, U. Calif., Irvine, 1978, Boston U., 1979-80, Bklyn. Coll., 1982-83; Mellon vis. prof. lit. Franklin and Marshall Coll., Lancaster, Pa., 1977; prof. writing Columbia U., NYC, 1981-85; prof. lit. George Mason U., Fairfax, Va., 1982-95. Halloway lectr. U. Calif., Berkeley, 1986, Princeton U., 1995—. Author: A Day for Anne Frank, 1968, Lies, 1969, I Am the Bitter Name, 1972, With Ignorance, 1977, The Lark, The Thrush, The Starling, 1983, Tar, 1983, Flesh and Blood, 1987, Poems, 1963-1983, 1988, The Bacchae of Euripides, 1990, Helen, 1991, A Dream of Mind: Poems, 1992, Selected Poems, 1994, The Vigil, 1997, Poetry and Consciousness, 1998, Repair, 1999, Misgivings, A Memoir, 2000, The Singing: Poems, 2003, Collected Poems, 2006; contbg. editor Am. Poetry Rev., 1972—; translator: Women of Trachis (Sophocles), 1978. Sponsor People's Fund, Phila., 1967—. Recipient Nat. Book Critics Circle award in poetry, 1987, Morton Dauwen Zabel prize, Am. Acad. of Arts and Letters, 1989, Lit. prize, 1999, Harriet Monroe prize, 1993, Berlin prize, Am. Acad. in Berlin, 1998, Pulitzer prize, 2000, Book award, L.A. Times, 2000, Weathertop prize, 2000, Pen Marth Albrand Memoir prize, 2001, Nat. Book award, 2003, Lifetime Achievement award, 5th Internat. Conf. on AIDS, India, 2005; fellow, Guggenheim Found., 1975, Nat. Endowment for Arts, 1985, 1993; grantee, Lila Wallace-Reader's Digest, 1993—95. Mem. PEN (Voelcker Career Achievement award 1998), Poetry Soc. Am., Am. Acad. Arts and Scis., Am. Acad. Arts and Letters. Avocations: piano, guitar, drawing.

WILLIAMS, CHARLES LAVAL, JR., retired preventive medicine physician; b. New Orleans, Jan. 19, 1916; s. Charles Laval and Lewise (McLaurine) W.; m. Ellen Clendenin Ustick, Dec. 14, 1946; children: Ellen Clendenin, Katherine McLaurine. Student, U. Va., 1933-35; MD, Tulane U., 1940; M.P.H., U. Mich., 1945. Diplomate: Am. Bd. Preventive Medicine and Pub. Health. Intern U.S. Marine Hosp., New Orleans, 1941; with USPHS, 1941-67; assigned N.C. State Health Dept., 1941-44, USPHS States Relations div., 1944, U. Mich., 1944-45, Am. Acad. Pediatrics Nat. Study Child Health Services, 1945-47; chief planning unit, asst. chief div. commd. officers, 1947-51; with US/AID Div. Pub. Health, 1951-62; chief pub. health adviser AID Mission to Peru, 1959-62; asso. dir. internat. relations Office Internat. Health, 1962-64; chief Office Internat. Research, NIH, Bethesda, Md., 1965-66; dep. dir., then dir. Office Internat. Health, Office Surgeon General, USPHS, Washington, 1966-67; dep. dir. Pan Am. Health Orgn., 1967-79; ret.; exec. v.p. Am. Assn. World Health, 1980-84. U.S. del./alt. or advisor to eight world health assemblies between 1955 and 1967, and to ten sessions of the Directing Coun. of the Pan Am. Health Orgn. between 1953 and 1966. Fellow Am. Pub. Health Assn.; mem. U.S.-Mexico Border Pub. Health Assn., Phi Kappa Phi, Delta Omega. Home: 5600 Wisconsin Ave Apt 1009 Chevy Chase MD 20815-4411

WILLIAMS, CHARLES WESLEY, retired engineering executive, consultant, researcher; b. Palestine, Ark. s. Fredrick Charles and Fannie Rochet (Southall) W.; m. Nancy Sue Rhea, Sept. 5, 1959; children: Brent L., Brian E. BSEE, U. Tenn., 1959, MS, 1963. Registered profl. engr., Ohio. Devel. engr. Mead Rsch. Lab., Chillicothe, Ohio, 1959-60, Oak Ridge (Tenn.) Nat. Lab., 1960-63; tech. mgr. EG & G Ortec, Oak Ridge, 1963-76, tech. dir. phys. and life sci., 1976-81, dir. positron emission tomograph sys., 1981—85; pvt. practice Oak Ridge, 1985—. Contbr. articles to profl. jours. Fellow: IEEE (life; v.p. NS 1979). Baptist. Personal E-mail: charles02@comcast.net.

WILLIAMS, CHRISTOPHER, investment company executive; BArch, Howard U.; MBA, Dartmouth Coll. Former sr. v.p. Lehman Brothers, NY; former pres. Williams Finl. Mkts.; CEO Williams Capital Group, LP, NYC; chmn. Williams Capital Mgmt., LLC, 2002—, CEO, 2002—; co-CEO EH Williams Capital Mgmt. Bd. dirs. Wal-Mart, Harrah's Entertainment. Bd. dirs. NYC Partnership, Nat. Dance Inst., Alvin Ailey Dance Found., WNYC Radio. Mem.: Century Assoc., Young President's Org., Nat. Assoc. Securities Professionals (bd. dirs.), Securities Industry Assn. (bd. dirs. N.Y. dist.), Econ. Club N.Y. (bd. dirs.). Office: Williams Capital Group LP 650 5th Ave 11th Flr New York NY 10019

WILLIAMS, CHRISTOPHER, photographer; b. LA, 1965; Exhibitions include Carnegie Museum, Pittsburgh, Pa., Museum Boijmans Van Beuningen, Rotterdam, Lenbachhaus, Munich, Mus. Contemporary Art, LA, The UBS Corp. Art Coll., exhibited in group shows at Whitney Biennial, Whitney Mus. Art, NYC, 2006, David Zwirner Gallery, NYC. Office: c/o David Zwirner Gallery 525 W 19th St New York NY 10002

WILLIAMS, CLARA A., sculptor; b. Nashville, Sept. 16, 1972; Attended, Sch. Visual Arts; MFA, Yale U. Exhibited in group shows at P.S. 1 Some Young New Yorkers, 1997, PPOW Gallery, 1999, Richard Tells Gallery, 1999, Friedrich Petzel Gallery, 1999, Mus. Contemporary Art, San Diego, 2000, Zobeide & Man With Bags, Nicole Klagsbrun Gallery, 2000, The Price, Pub. Art Fund, 2003, Man with Luggage, Pierogi Gallery, 2000. Fellow Conn. Commn. on Arts, 2001, Guggenheim Meml. Found., 2004. E-mail: williams_greaterny@hotmail.com.

WILLIAMS, CLAY C., energy executive; Engr. Shell Oil, 1985—92; assoc. SCF Partners, 1994—96; dir. corp. develop. Nat. Oilwell Varco, Houston, 1996—97, v.p. corp. develop., 1997—2000, 2001—02, v.p. pipeline services, 1999—2001, v.p. fin. & corp. develop., 2002—03, v.p., CFO, 2003—05, sr. v.p., CFO, 2005—. Office: Nat Oilwell Varco 10000 RIchmond Ave Houston TX 77042-4200 *

WILLIAMS, CLAY RULE, lawyer; b. Milw., Sept. 25, 1935; s. George Laverne and Marguerite Mae (Rule) W.; m. Jeanne Lee Huber, Jan. 18, 1986; children: Gwynne, Amy, Daniel, Sarah. BA, Lawrence U., 1957; LLB, U. Mich., 1960. Bar: Wis. 1960, U.S. Dist. Ct. (ea. and we. dists.) Wis. 1964, U.S. Ct. Appeals (7th cir.) 1965, U.S. Ct. Mil. Appeals 1963, U.S. Supreme Ct. 1963. Assoc. Gibbs, Roper & Fifield, Milw., 1963-67; sr. counsel Von Briesen & Roper, S.C., Milw., 1967-99, of counsel, 1999—. Mem. Gov.'s Task Force Creation Bus. Ct., 1994-99; instr. profl. seminars. Author: Berry, Davis, Deguire and Williams, Wisconsin Business Corporation Law, 1992; contbr. articles to profl. jours. Active Shorewood (Wis.) Sch. Bd., 1976-79. Capt. USAF, Judge Adv. Corps., 1960-63. Fellow Wis. Bar Found.; Fellow, ABA Found., mem. ABA (sect. antitrust law, corp. counseling com.), Wis. Bar Assn. (co-chmn. com. to revise corp. laws 1986-90, chmn. standing com. on bus. corp. law 1990-97, Pres.'s Award of Excellence 1990, 97), Am. Law Inst., Milw. Club, Univ. Club. Republican. Episcopalian. Avocations: hunting, fishing, skiing, reading. Office: von Briesen & Roper SC 411 E Wisconsin Ave Milwaukee WI 53202 Home Phone: 505-751-7521; Office Phone: 414-273-7000. Business E-Mail: cwilliam@vonbriesen.com.

WILLIAMS, CLORETTA MAE, retired elementary school educator; b. St. Johns County, Fla., Apr. 17, 1932; d. Daniel and Flossie Evelana Cohen, Paul and Susie Green; married, Dec. 10, 1952; children: Janice Edmond, Audrey Jackson, Renee, Curtis. BS, Fla. Meml./Indsl. Coll., 1952; post-grad., numerous univs. Music and 3d grade tchr. Flagler County H.S., Bunnell, Fla., 1951—53; 1st grade tchr. Coleman Elem. Sch., Pompano, Fla., 1956—58; head start, 1st, 3d, 4th and 5th grade tchr. Charles Drew Elem. Sch., Pompano, Fla., 1958—86, ret., 1986. Sch. rep. Broward County North Area Advisory, Pompano, Fla., 1997; mem. adv. bd. Am.'s Choices Networking, Pompano, Fla., 2005. Recipient Tchr. of Yr. award, Charles Drew Sch.-Broward County Sch. Bd., 1964, Honored Pioneer of Broward County award, Broward County Hist. Com., 1999. Mem.: AARP, So. Poverty Law Ctr. (Plaque on Wall 2005), Heart Found. Democrat. Baptist. Home: 2738 NW Fourth Ct Pompano Beach FL 33069 Office: Mitchell/Moore Srs Program 910 NW Tenth St Pompano Beach FL 33060 also: E Pat L'arkins Sr Program 520 Martin Luther King Jr Blvd Pompano Beach FL 33069

WILLIAMS, CONSTANCE, state senator; b. June 27, 1944; m. Sankey V. Williams; 2 children. BA, Barnard Coll., 1966; MBA, U. Pa., 1980. Mem. Pa. House of Reps., Harrisburg, 1996—2001, Pa. State Senate, Harrisburg, 2001—. Democrat. Jewish. Office: 352 Main Capital Senate Box 203017 Harrisburg PA 17120-3017 Business E-Mail: chwilliams@pasenate.com.

WILLIAMS, CRAIG STEWART, organist, music educator, director; b. Lynwood, Calif., Sept. 17, 1962; s. Barry Edward and Malvina Louise Williams; m. Lee Nielsen Williams, July 8, 1990; children: Abigail Leigh, Stewart Thomas. MusB, U. So. Calif., 1984; MusM, Juilliard Sch., 1986, Rider U., 1997. Organist Peace Luth. Ch., Tustin, Calif., 1981—84; organist, dir. music Covenant Ch. LI, Floral Park, NY, 1986—87, 1st Presbyn. Ch., Jamaica, NY, 1987—94; organist JFK Internat. Airport Protestant Chapel, Jamaica, NY, 1987—95; organist, dir. music Calvary Bapt. Ch., NYC, 1995—2000, Cadet Chapel, US Mil. Acad., West Point, NY, 2000—. Commr. NYC Presbytery, 1992—95; demonstrator, recitalist Baldwin Organ Co., Babylon, NY, 1993—97; adj. faculty Rider U., 1999—, Nyack Coll., 2003—; cons. pipe organ project Calvary Bapt. Ch., NYC, 2001—03. Worship and workshop music leader Kiwanis Club, Middletown, NY, 2001—02; participant Mohonk Mountain House, Shawangunk, NY, 2003; vis. lectr. U. Redlands, Calif., 2003. Mem.: Hymn Soc. Am., Am. Guild Organists (dean 1990—92), Pi Kappa Lambda. Avocations: gardening, poetry. Office: Cadet Chapel US Mil Acad Bldg 722 West Point NY 10996 Office Phone: 845-938-7352. Business E-Mail: craig.williams@usma.edu.

WILLIAMS, DANNA BETH, reading specialist, educator; b. Aurora, Ill., Apr. 13, 1956; d. Daniel Strango and Roberta Arlene Roberts; m. Norman Charles Williams, June 25, 1988; children: Scott, Samuel, Spencer. BSc, U. Nev., Reno, 1978; postgrad. in Curriculum and Instrn., Concordia U., Irvine, Calif., 2006—. Cert. TESOL Nev. Lic. of Edn., tchg.credential Calif. Reading specialist Job Corps, Stead, Nev., 1979; tchr. Churchill County Schools, Fallon, 1979—88; sub. tchr. Irvine Sch. Dist., Calif., 1988—90, Mission Viejo Sch. Dist., 1989—90; tchr. pvt. schools Orange County, 1990—96; tchr. Orange Unified Sch. Dist., 1996—2000, reading specialist, 2000—. Lang. arts mentor, tchr. Orange Unified Sch. Dist., 1999—2001, English lang. learner adv., 2005—, Consortium on Reading Excellence trainer fifth grade tchrs., 2003—04. Religious educator San Francisca Solano, 1988—91, 2002—04, Cath. Ch., 1983—88. Mem.: ASCD, Calif. Teachers Assn., Internat. Reading Assn. Roman Catholic. Home: 21022 Los Alisos Blvd Apt 614 Rancho Santa Margarita CA 92688 Office: Cambridge Elem Sch 425 N Cambridge Orange CA 92866 Office Phone: 714-997-6103. E-mail: dwilliam@orangeusd.k12.ca.us.

WILLIAMS, DARCEL PATRICE, writer, editor; b. Houston, Nov. 23, 1958; d. Leroy and Estelle Forch Williams; m. Jason LaRue Williams, Sr., May 26, 1979 (div. Sept. 0, 1985); 1 child, Jason LaRue II. Student, Tex. So. U., 1977—81, U. Houston, 1985—88. Lic. massage therapist City of Tulsa, 1993. Acctg. Taft Broadcasting, Houston, 1981—85; office mgr. DeColores Prodns., Houston, 1989—90; cmty. ctr. dir. Helping Hands - Riverview Pk., Tulsa, 1995; author Am. Book Pub. Group, Salt Lake City, 1999—, sr. editor, 1999—2003. Creative adviser/cons. Various Ind. Entrepreneurial Enterprises, Tulsa, 1989—2003. Author: (novel) Soaring On Clipped Wings (Book of Month, 2004), (screenplay) Fighting to Love; senior editor: novels Cryer's Valley, Have No Mercy, writer, dir.: Sadie's Soap Suds TV Show, 2004, author numerous poems. Named Humanitarian of Month, 2003; recipient Best New Writer of Yr. Disilgold Mag. award, Younity Reviewers Guild, 2004. Mem.: Younity Revs. Guild Worldwide, Disilgold Lit. Network Assn., Nat. Writers Union, Authors Den Forum (life). Achievements include design of safety product for use in vehicular transportation of children; product for walking in hazardous environmental conditions. Avocations: singing, music, sewing and design, swimming, reading. Office Phone: 918-499-8722. Personal E-mail: eagledfly@yahoo.com.

WILLIAMS, DARLENE F., federal agency administrator; BA, Howard U.; MBA, Chgo. U.; PhD, Stanford U. Mgr. mktg., planning and rsch. Ryder Systems, Inc.; corp. policy mgr. TXU; gen. dep. asst. sec. policy devel. and rsch. HUD, Washington, 2003—05, gen. dep. asst. sec., 2005, asst. sec., 2005—. Office: HUD 451 Seventh St SW Mail Code R Rm 8100 Washington DC 20410-6000 Office Phone: 202-708-1600. Office Fax: 202-619-8000.

WILLIAMS, DARRYL MARLOWE, medical educator; b. Denver, Apr. 3, 1938; s. Archie Malvin and Dorothy Merle (Grapes) W.; m. Susan Arlene Moore, June 24, 1966; children: Carol Ruth, Peter Todd, Sarah Elizabeth. Student, U. Colo., 1956—58; BS, Colo. State U., 1963; MD, MS in Anatomy, Baylor U., 1964; MPH, U. Tex., 2001. Diplomate Am. Bd. Internal Medicine, Am. Bd. Hematology. Intern and resident Baylor Affiliated Hosps., Houston, 1964-66, 67-68; resident U. Utah, Salt Lake City, 1966-67, fellow in hematology, 1968-73, asst. prof., 1973-77; assoc. prof. La. State U., Shreveport, 1977-81, prof., 1981-90, chief hematology sect., 1977-85, asst. dean/rsch., 1981-85, dean Sch. Medicine, 1985-90; prof. medicine, dean Sch. Medicine Tex. Tech U. Health Scis. Ctr., Lubbock, 1990-95; prof. medicine, exec. dir. office border health, project dir. Hispanic Ctr. of Excellence Tex. Tech. Health Scis. Ctr., El Paso, 1995—2006, prof. emeritus, 2006—, dir. curriculum planning office, 2002—07, also bd. dirs., 1995—2005, dir. med. edn. Cmty. Partnership, 1995—2001, dir. health careers opportunity program, 2005—06. Mem. hemophilia adv. com. La. Legislature, Baton Rouge, 1977-83; vice chair La. Lung and Cancer Bd., New Orleans, 1984-90; pres. N.W. La. AIDS Task Force, Shreveport, 1987. Mem. editl. bd. Tex. Jour. Rural Health, 1990—2004. Mem. Am. Heart Assn., Lubbock chpt., Shreveport Biracial Commn., 1988, Lubbock Indigent Health Care Coalition Task Force, 1991-92, Health Professions Edn. Adv. Com., Lubbock Friends of Pub. Radio; vice chair health profls. edn. adv. com. Tex. Coord. Bd. Higher Edn., 1992-95; sec. Health Edn. and Tng. Consortium of Tex., 1990-99, vice chmn., 1999-2002, chmn., 2002-04; mem. steering com. Border Vision Fronteriza, 1995-2000; bd. dirs. El Paso Cancer Consortium; project dir. Hispanic Ctr. of Excellence, 2001-2007; adv. com., Tex. State Dept. Health Cmty. Health Workers, 2003—05; exec. dir. Health Edn. Tng. Ctr. Alliance of Tex., 2003-2007; project dir. Tex. Tech. Regional Ctr. Pub. Health, Medicine Edn., 2003-06. Recipient award Nat. Ski Patrol Sys., Salt Lake City, 1975, Disting. Svc. award Multicultural Diversity, 2005, Disting. Svc. award Tex. Tech U. Sch. Medicine, 2005 Fellow ACP, Am. Coll. Nutrition; mem. Am. Soc. Hematology, Am. Inst. Nutrition, Am. Soc. Clin. Nutrition, Tex. Med. Assn. (physicians oncology edn. com.), Am. Cancer Soc. (bd. dirs. El Paso unit 1999-2004, pres. 2001-03), Alpha Omega Alpha. Office: Tex Tech Health Sci Ctr at El Paso 4800 Alberta Ave El Paso TX 79905-2709 Home Phone: 505-471-1775; Office Phone: 915-545-5742. Business E-Mail: darryl.williams@ttuhsc.edu.

WILLIAMS, DAVE HARRELL, investment company executive; b. Beaumont, Tex., Oct. 5, 1932; s. George Davis and Mary (Hardin) W.; m. Reba White, Mar. 15, 1975. BS in Chem. Engring, U. Tex., 1956; MBA (Baker scholar, Teagle fellow), Harvard U., 1961. Chartered fin. analyst. Chem. engr. Exxon Corp., Baton Rouge, 1959; security analyst deVegh & Co., NYC, 1961—64; dir. research Waddell & Reed, Kansas City, Mo., 1964—67; exec. v.p. Mitchell Hutchins, Inc., NYC, 1967—77; chmn. bd. Alliance Capital Mgmt. Corp., NYC, 1977—2001, chmn. emeritus, 2001—04. Contbr. articles to profl. jours. Trustee U.S.S. Intrepid Mus. Found. Served with USNR, 1956-59. Named one of Top 200 Collectors, ARTnews Mag., 2004, 2006. Mem. Fin. Analysts Fedn. (past officer, dir.), N.Y. Soc. Security Analysts (past pres.), Bond Club N.Y., Econ. Club N.Y., Knickerbocker Club, Grolier Club. Presbyterian. Avocation: Collector of Am. Prints. Office: White Williams Holdings 41 W 57th St New York NY 10019 Office Phone: 212-752-5480. Business E-Mail: dwilliams@white-williams.com.

WILLIAMS, DAVID ALEXANDER, retired chief pilot; b. Helena, Mont., May 29, 1939; s. Daniel samuel and Dorothy (Alexander) W.; m. Jacqueline anders, Feb. 14, 1964 (div. Mar. 1988); children: Daniel Alexander, Darryl Jackson. BA, U. So. Calif., LA, 1962. Lic. airline transport pilot, FAA. Commd. ensign USNR, 1963, advanced through grades to capt., 1985; tng. and test pilot McDonnel Douglas, Long Beach, Calif., 1980-87, chief pilot flight stds. and safety, 1987-97, Douglas Products divsn. Boeing, Long Beach, 1997-99; ret., 1999. Mem. internat. adv. com. Flight Safety Found., Washington, 1987-99; mem. windshear tng. aid task force FAA/industry, Washington, 1985-87; mem. CFIT tng. com. Flight Safety Found./FAA, 1992-96, joint safety analysis team FAA Industry, 1997-99. Author: Turbulence Education and Training Aid FAA/Industry, 1996-97. Mem.: Mil. Officers Assn. Am., Naval Res. Assn. Avocations: cycling, sailing, scuba diving. Home: 223 Mission Ln San Luis Obispo CA 93405 Personal E-mail: davew805@gmail.com.

WILLIAMS, DAVID ALFRED, elementary school educator; b. Jacksonville, Fla., May 24, 1961; s. Merle W. Long and John Alfred Williams, James Elbert Toby Long (Stepfather). A, Brewton Parker Coll., 1982; BFA in Music Edn., Tift Coll./Mercer U., Macon, Ga., 1984; M in Ednl. Adminstrn. and Leadership, Cambridge Coll., Mass., 2006, EdS in Ednl. Adminstrn. and Leadership, 2007. Profl. tchr. Ga., 2006, cert. Ga. Real Estate Bd., 2004. Music specialist Appling County Elem. Sch., Baxley, Ga., 1987—; owner, event cons. Seasonings, LLC; owner, artist, instr. The Studio. Musician (pianist/vocalist): (albums) Reflections & Memories; musician: Remember When. Mem. First Bapt. Ch., Baxley, Ga., 2000—05. Mem.: Ga. Music Educators Assn. (assoc.), Nat. Music Educators Assn. (assoc.), Friends of Johnny Mercer (assoc.), Waycross Heritage Soc. (assoc.). Baptist. Avocations: swimming, travel, cake decorating, music, cooking. Home: 556 Pineview Ave Baxley GA 31513 Office: Appling County Elem Sch 680 Blackshear Hwy Baxley GA 31513 Home Phone: 912-367-6655; Office Phone: 912-367-8640. Office Fax: 912-367-8649; Home Fax: 912-367-5992. Personal E-mail: david@thekeyboardkid.com. Business E-mail: dwilliams@appling.k12.ga.us.

WILLIAMS, DAVID HOWARD, lawyer; b. Las Vegas, Nev., Sept. 21, 1945; s. Howard Cummins and Alice Emma (Taufenbach) W.; m. Kathleen Graham, Sept. 2, 1967; children: David Howard Jr., Jonathan Graham. BA in History cum laude, Denison U., 1967; MA in Polit. Sci., Columbia U., 1969; JD cum laude, Ohio State U., 1973. Bar: Ohio 1973, Ga. 1980. Assoc. Vorys, Sater, Seymour & Pease, Columbus, Ohio, 1973-79; from assoc. to ptnr. Powell, Goldstein, Frazer & Murphy, Atlanta; ptnr. Hunton & Williams, Atlanta; now ptnr. Schiff Hardin LLP, Atlanta, co-leader Employee Benefits and Exec. Compensation Group. Adj. prof. U. Ga. Sch. Law, 1995-97; lectr. in field. Bd. dirs. Atlanta Ballet, 1991-92, Ga. Assn. for Primary Health Care; former trustee, co-pres. parents' assn. Trinity Sch., Atlanta; former trustee Northside Youth Orgn., Atlanta; former asst. gen. counsel Ga. Rep. Party; former mem. coun. legal advisors Rep. Nat. Com.; mem. Benefits Coun., ASPA, Atlanta, 1998-99, Midtown Leadership Program, Atlanta, 2001. Mem. ABA, State Bar Ga., Atlanta Bar Assn.; Am. Soc. Pension Actuaries, ASPA Benefits Coun. of Atlanta, ESOP Assn.

Office: Schiff Hardin LLP One Atlantic Ctr, Ste 2300 1201 W Peachtree St Atlanta GA 30309-3574 Office Phone: 404-437-7010. Office Fax: 404-437-7100. E-mail: dwilliams@schiffhardin.com.

WILLIAMS, DAVID JON, historian, artist; b. Muskegon, Mich., June 21, 1944; s. Donald John and Arlene Myrtle (Hegman) Williams; m. Andrea Rees, Aug. 31, 1968; children: Lisa, Sara, Matthew Rees, Anna. AA, Muskegon CC, Mich., 1964; BA, Mich. State U., East Lansing, 1966, MA, 1972. Cert. med. illustration practitioner Med. Arts Assn., Eng., 2000. Asst. prof. med. illustration Purdue U., West Lafayette, Ind., 1973—77, assoc. prof. med. illustration, 1977—96, prof. med. illustration, 1996—. Mem. grad. faculty Purdue U., West Lafayette, 1997—, assoc. dir. med. illustration and comm., sch. vet. medicine, 1973—96, dir. med. illustration and comm., sch. vet. medicine, 1996—; Charles Henry Hackley disting. lectr. humanities Hackley Pub. Libr., Ind., 2004; invited spkr. nat. and internat. lectures. Editor: Jour. Vet. Heritage, 2005—; co-author: (books) Veterinary Medicine: An Illustrated History, 1996—, Fundamental Techniques in Veterinary Surgery, 1987—; contbr. articles to profl. jours. Pres., chmn. bd. Montessori Sch. Greater Lafayette, West Lafayetter, 1982—83; mem. senate Purdue U., West Lafayetter, 1988—91, 1991—94, 2004—07, 2007—; mem. parish coun. Ch. Blessed Sacrament, West Lafayetter, 1995—98. Recipient Med. Illustration award, Ann. SAMA-Eaton Med. Art Awards Program, 1969. Fellow: Assn. Med. Illustrators (25 Yr. Outstanding Svc. award 1999); mem.: Soc. Phi Zeta, Assn. Med. Illustrators, Med. Artists Assn. Gt. Britain, Am. Vet. Med. History Soc., World Assn. for the History Vet. Medicine, Biol. Photography Assn. (Med. Illustration award 1984), Gamma Sigma Delta (pres. Purdue chpt. 2001—02). Liberal. Roman Catholic. Avocations: writing, gardening, antiques. Office: Purdue Univ Lynn Hall Rm G-226 625 Harrison St West Lafayette IN 47907-2026 Office Phone: 765-494-1156. Office Fax: 765-494-6197; Home Fax: 765-494-6197. Personal E-mail: djwilliams@insightbb.com.

WILLIAMS, DAVID R., sociologist, educator, senior research scientist; BTh hons., Carribean Union Coll.; MDiv cum laude, Andews U., 1979; MPH in Health Edn., Loma Linda U.; PhD; MA in Sociology, U. Mich., 1954, PhD in Sociology, 1986. Harold R. Cruse prof. sociology U. Mich, Ann Arbor; and dir. South Africa Initiatives Office U. Mich.; sr. scientist Survey Rsch. Ctr., U. Mich., Ann Arbor. Faculty assoc. African Am. Mental Health Rsch. Ctr., Ann Arbor, Mich.; mem. editl. bd: Contemporary Sociology, 1990—92, Social Psychology Quarterly, 1996—, Social Problems, 1996—; Mem. Nat. Acad. Scis. Panel on Needle Exchange and Bleach Distrbn. Programs, 1993—95, Nat. Sci. Found. Bd. Overseers for NORC's Gen. Social Survey, 1993—97; mem. rev. panel Nat. Inst. Mental Health Social and Group Processes Grants, 1996—99. Assoc. editor (sociological jour.) Ethnicity and Disease, 1993—; contbr. articles to profl. jours. Recipient Investigator award in Health Policy Rsch., Robert Wood Johnson found., 1995—96; fellow (Jr. faculty) in Social Scis., Yale U., 1990—91, (sr. faculty), 1992—93. Fellow: Am. Acad. Arts & Scis.; mem.: Internat. Soc. Hypertension in Blacks, Assn. Black Sociologists, Am. Psychol Assn., Am. Pub. Health Assn., Soc. Epedemiological Rsch., Am. Sociological Assn. (sec.-treas. med. sociology sect. 1995—97), Nat. Rsch. Coun., Nat. Acad Scis. Inst. Medicine. Office: Univ Mich Inst Social Rsch 426 Thompson St Rm 2230 Ann Arbor MI 48106-1248 E-mail: wildavid@umich.edu. *

WILLIAMS, DAVID R. (DAFYDD RHYS WILLIAMS), astronaut; b. Saskatoon, Saskatchewan, Can., May 16, 1954; s. William and Isobel Williams; m. Cathy Fraser; 2 children. BSc in Biology, McGill U., 1976, MSc in Physiology, 1983, MD, CM, McGill U., 1983; LLD (hon.), U. Saskatchewan, 2004. Resident in family practice U. Ottawa Faculty Medicine, Canada, 1983—85; resident in emergency medicine U. Toronto, Canada, 1985—88; fellow in emergency medicine Royal Coll. Physicians & Surgeons, Canada, 1988; emergency physician Sunnybrook Health Sci. Ctr., 1988—89, med. dir., Advanced Cardiac Life Support Program, coord. postgraduate tng. in emergency medicine, 1990—92, dir., dept. emergency svcs.; emergency physician Emergency Assocs. Kitchener. Waterloo, Canada, 1988—90; med. dir. Westmount Urgent Care Clinic, 1989—90; with Can. Space Agy., 1992—95; astronaut NASA, Houston, 1995—. Lectr. dept. surgery U. Toronto, Canada, 1988, asst. prof. surgery, Canada, 1989—90, adj. prof. surgery, Canada; course dir. Can. Heart & Stroke Found., Am. Coll. Surgeons; asst. prof. surgery McGill U., adj. prof. surgery; mem. staff St. Mary's Hosp., Montreal Gen. Hosp.; mission specialist Neurolab, 1998; dir. space & life sci. directorate (first non-Am. to hold sr. mgmt. position with NASA) NASA, 1998—2002; first dep. associated adminstr. for crew health and safety, Office Space Flight NASA Hdqs., 2001; aquanaut, NEEMO 1 Mission (first Canadian to have lived and worked in space and in the ocean) NASA-NOAA, 2001, crew comdr., NEEMO 9, 06; mission specialist 3 STS-90 Mission (Columbia), 1998; mission specialist, spacewalker STS-118 Mission (Endeavour) to Internat. Space Station, 2007. Named Patron of the Internat. Life Saving Fedn., 2002, Spokesperson for the Life Saving Soc. Cand. and Hon. Amb., SmartRisk Found.; recipient Commonwealth cert. Thanks, 1973, Commonwealth Recognition award, 1975, A.S. Hill bursary, McGill U., 1980, Walter Hoare bursary, 1981, J.W. McConnell award, 1981—83, Psychiatry prize, Wood Gold Medal award, NASA Space Flight medal, 1998, Melbourne W. Boynton award, Am. Astronautical Soc., 1999, Bronze medal for contbn. to neuroscience during Mission STS-90, Ramon y Cajal Inst. Neurobiology, Spanish Coun. for Scientific Rsch., 1999, Rotary Nat. award for Space Achievement, 2000, NASA Outstanding Leadership medal, 2002, NASA Johnson Space Ctr. Space & Life Scis. Directorate Spl. Profl. Achievement award for implementation of Automatic External Defibrillator Program, 2003. Fellow: Royal Coll. Physicians & Surgeons Can., Coll. Family Physicians Can.; mem.: Montreal Physiol. Soc., NY Acad. Sci., Soc. Neuroscience, Undersea and Hyperbaric Medicine Soc., Can. Aeronautics & Space Inst., Can. Soc. Aerospace Medicine, Aerospace Med. Assn., Can. Assn. Emergency Physicians, Ontario Med. Assn., Coll. Physicians & Surgeons Ontario. Avocations: flying, scuba diving, hiking, sailing, kayaking, canoeing, downhill and cross-country skiing. Office: Astronaut Office CB NASA Johnson Space Ctr Houston TX 77058 *

WILLIAMS, DAVID RUSSELL, retired music educator; b. Indpls., Oct. 21, 1932; s. H. Russell and Mary Dean (Whitmer) W.; m. Elsa Bühlmann, Jan. 30, 1960. AB, Columbia U., 1954, MA, 1956; PhD, U. Rochester, 1965. Dir. music Windham Coll., Putney, Vt., 1959-62; opera coach Eastman Sch. Music, Rochester, NY, 1962-65, assoc. prof. theory, adminstr. of MusM program, 1965-80; prof., chmn. dept. music U. Memphis (formerly Memphis State U.), 1980-87, prof. music, 1980-98, prof. emeritus, 1998—. Bd. dirs. Memphis Youth Symphony, Memphis Symphony, 1984-90; mem. exec. bd. Opera Memphis, 1980-87, Salute to Memphis Music, 1980-87. Author: Bibliography of the History of Music Theory, 1971, Conversations with Howard Hanson, 1988, Music Theory from Zarlino to Schenker: A Bibliography and Guide, 1990; producer: Highwater Records album 8201 featuring John Stover, classical guitar, 1983; composer Suite for Oboe, Clarinet and Piano, 1968, Five States of Mind, 1970. Bd. dirs., sec. Rochester Philharm. Orch., 1976-78; v.p., bd. dirs. Rochester Chamber Orch., 1974-78; pres., bd. dirs. Opera Theatre of Rochester, 1973-74; bd. dirs., chmn. Am. Ritual Theatre, 1979-80; bd. sponsors Met. Opera Mid. South Region, Memphis, 1983—. Served as cpl. U.S. Army, 1957-59. Recipient Eastman Sch. Music Pub. award, 1970. Mem. NARAS (treas. Memphis chpt. 1984-86), Coll. Music Soc. (sec. 1973-83), Music Tchrs. Nat. Assn. Sci. (state chmn. 1971-74), Nat. Assn. Schs. of Music (chmn. region 8 1989-92), Tenn. Assn. Music Execs. in Colls. and Univs. (pres. 1986-87), Rochester Club, Univ. Club, Summit Club, Pi Kappa Lambda (pres. U. Memphis chpt. 1988-90), Phi Beta Kappa, Phi Mu Alpha, Sigma Alpha Iota. Avocations: language study, word puzzles. Home: 273 W Central Park St Apt 1 Memphis TN 38111-4570

Having had a family background that was superior in so many ways has helped me to sharpen my purpose in life, in that it has made me realize to what an extent affirmative action is necessary in order to provide a milieu in which truly equal opportunity can exist. Many doors of opportunity have been held open for me; those of disadvantaged access are often not aware that these doors exist. The more individuals I can lead to these portals, the more I will have achieved in my lifetime.

WILLIAMS, DEBORAH LEE, foundation administrator; b. LA, Feb. 11, 1954; d. Eleazer Deming and Jeanne Sanford Williams; m. Charles (Skip) Robert Roy, Apr. 6, 1985; 1 child, Andrew Roy. BA, Pomona Coll., 1975; JD, Harvard U., 1978. Bar: Alaska 1979. Atty. solicitors honors program Dept. Interior, Washington, 1978—79, atty. Nat. Pk. Svc. and Nat. Fish and Wildlife Svc. Anchorage, 1979—81, spl. asst. to sec. for Alaska, 1994—98; exec. dir. Alaska Consumer Advocacy Program, Anchorage, 1981—82; atty. Hellen, Partnow and Condon, Anchorage, 1983—86, 1989—93; exec. dir. Am. Lung Assn. Alaska, Anchorage, 1986—89, Alaska Conservation Found., Anchorage, 1999—. Pres. bd. dirs. Trustees for Alaska, Anchorage, 1982—85; bd. dirs. TransAlaska Pipeline Liability Fund, Washington, 1994—98; adj. prof. Alaska Pacific U., Anchorage, 1993—94, U. Alaska, Anchorage, 1987—88; commr. Anchorage Mcpl. Health Commn., 1981—85. Founder, editor Harvard Environ. Law Rev., 1976; contbr. law rev. articles to profl. jours. Trustee Exxon Valdez Oil Spill Trustee Coun., Anchorage, 1994—98. Recipient Nat. Performance Rev. award, V.P. of U.S., 1997, 1998. Mem.: Green Star (bd. dirs. 2002—), Planned Parenthood of Alaska (bd. dirs., chair nominating com. 1997—2003), Rotary Internat., Phi Beta Kappa. Achievements include making appearances on 60 Minutes, 60 Minutes Australia, BBC, and many Alaskan TV shows; being the subject of cover stories in Alaska Business Monthly, We Alaskans and other publications. Avocations: backpacking, travel, building. Office: Alaska Conservation Found 441 W 5th Ave Ste 402 Anchorage AK 99501 Business E-Mail: dwilliams@akcf.org.

WILLIAMS, DENISE, academic administrator; b. Iowa, 1972; BBA, Detroit Coll. Bus.; M, Marygrove Coll. Assoc. dir. U. Detroit Mercy, 2001, dean of admissions, 2003—. Named one of 40 Under 40, Crain's Detroit Bus., 2006. Office: Univ Detroit Mercy FAC 100 4001 W McNichols Rd Detroit MI 48221 Office Phone: 313-993-1245. Office Fax: 313-993-3326.

WILLIAMS, DOCIA SCHULTZ, small business owner; b. St. Louis, Sept. 12, 1930; d. John Frederick and Statira Jim (Thornton) Schultz; m. Stanley Good Southworth Jr. (div. 1983); 1 child, Sarah Elizabeth Southworth; m. Roy Donald Williams, Dec. 1, 1984. BA, Tex. Womans U., 1951. Fashion coordinator Ike Clark of Dallas, Dallas, 1951—53, Harveys Dept. Store, Nashville, Tex., 1953—55; model, coordinator Freelance, San Antonio, 1968; owner, boutique shop San Antonio, 1973—79; tour mgr. numerous travel co., 1979—89; owner, operator Mission City Tours, San Antonio, 1989—. With S.A. Writers Guild, San Antonio; writer C.S. Journal, San Antonio Conservation Soc., San Antonio, 2003—. Author: Spirits of San Antonio, 1992, When Darkness Falls, 1994, Ghosts Along The Texas Coast, 1993, Phantoms of the Plains, 1995, Best Tales of Texas Ghosts, 1998, Exploring San Antonio with Children, 2000, History and Mystery of the Menger Hotel, 2000; speaker (various profl. conventions). Nat. pres. Tex. Woman's U. Assn. of Former Students, 1982—84. Named one of Ten Outstanding Women in San Antonio, Express News Pub. Co., 1973; recipient Spirit of San Antonio award, San Antonio Hotel and Lodgings Assn., 2003. Mem.: Nat. Assn. Women Bus. Owners (Entrepreneurial Spirit award 2004), Tour Guides Assn. of S.A. (charter mem., Disting. Svcs. award 2004), S.A. Coun. Presidents, San Antonio Hist. Soc., Nat. Soc. Arts and Letters. Methodist. Avocations: music, travel, creative writing, antiques. Home and Office: 1319 Vista Del Monte San Antonio TX 78216 Personal E-mail: dociasw@aol.com.

WILLIAMS, DONALD JOHN, physicist, researcher; b. Fitchburg, Mass., Dec. 25, 1933; s. Toiro John and Ina (Kokkinen) Williams; m. Priscilla Mary Gagnon, July 4, 1953; children: Steven John, Craig Mitchell, Eino Stenroos. BS, Yale U., 1955, MS, 1958, PhD, 1962. Sr. staff physicist Johns Hopkins U. Applied Physics Lab., 1961-65; head particle physics br. Goddard Space Flight Center, NASA, 1965-70; dir. Space Environ. Lab., NOAA, Boulder, Colo., 1970-82; prin. investigator Energetic Particles expt. NASA Galileo Mission, 1977—2003; prin. staff physicist Johns Hopkins U. Applied Physics Lab., 1982-89, dir. Milton S. Eisenhower Rsch. Ctr., 1990-96, chief scientist rsch. ctr., 1996-99, ret., 1999. Mem. nat. and internat. sci. planning coms.; chmn. com. solar-terrestrial rsch. NAS, 1989—93; sci. adv. bd. USAF, 1993—97. Assoc. editor: Jour. Geophys. Rsch., 1967—69, Revs. Geophysics and Space Rsch., 1984—86; editor (with G. D. Mead): Physics of the Magnetosphere, 1969, Physics of Solar-Planetary Environments, 1976; mem. editl. bd. Space Sci. Revs., 1975—85; author (with L. R. Lyons): Quantitative Aspects of Magnetospheric Physics, 1983; contbr. articles to profl. jours. Lt. USAF, 1955—57. Recipient Sci. Rsch. award, NOAA, 1974, Disting. Authorship award, NOAA and Johns Hopkins Applied Physics Lab., 1976, 1985, 1997. Fellow: Am. Geophys. Union; mem.: Internat. Acad. Astronautics, Internat. Assn. Geomagnetism and Aeronomy (pres. 1991—95), Am. Phys. Soc., Sigma Xi. Home: 117 Tivoli Trace Ct Poinciana FL 34759 Personal E-mail: donaldwfl@verizon.net.

WILLIAMS, DONALD R., social sciences educator; b. Hamilton, Ohio, Feb. 11, 1956; BBA, U. Wis., Milw., 1977; PhD, Northwestern U., Evanston, Ill., 1984. Asst. prof. econs. Kent State U., Ohio, 1983—88, assoc. prof. econs., 1988—94, prof. econs., 1994—, assoc. dean grad. sch. of mgmt., 2003—06, assoc. dean Coll. Bus. Adminstrn., 2006—. Sr. rsch. assoc. CEPS/INSTEAD, Differdange, Luxembourg, 2002—; vis. prof. KU Leuven, Belgium, 2003—. Mem.: European Assn. Labour Economists, Soc. Labor Economists, Am. Econ. Assn. Office: Kent State Univ Coll Bus Administration Kent OH 44242 Office Phone: 330-672-2772. Business E-Mail: dwilliam@kent.edu.

WILLIAMS, DOROTHY STANDRIDGE, retired food products manager, civic worker; b. Powder Springs, Ga. d. Robert Anderson and Bertie Mae Standridge; m. Harold Thomas Barfield (div.); 1 child, H. Gregory; m. J. Arden Williams (div.). Student, DeKalb Coll., Atlanta, 1982—83, U. Que., 1997, U. Laval, Que., 1998, U. Paris-Sorbonne, 2000. Assoc. promotion mgr., promotion coord. Coca-Cola USA, Atlanta, 1978-83, promotions mgr., 1983-86; mgr. internat. promotion svcs. The Coca-Cola Co., Atlanta, 1986-90, mgr. global promotion svcs., 1990-94. Cons., judge Point-of-Purchase Advt. Inst., 1995. Attaché Atlanta Conv. and Visitors Bur., 1992—; vol. Welcome South Ctr., Atlanta, 1995—; bd. advisors Life Coll. for Knowledge and Tng., 1995—; chmn. cmty. rels. com. Life Coll., 1995-96, vice chmn. bd. adv. Knowledge and Tng. program, 1997-98, chmn. bd. advisors Knowledge and Tng. program, 1998-99. Mem. Ga. Trust for Hist. Preservation, Atlanta High Mus. Art, Atlanta Bot. Garden, Alliance Francaise, Smyrna Hist. Soc. Avocations: travel, french language, interior design, hiking, bridge.

WILLIAMS, DOUGLAS LEONARD, lawyer; b. Cleve., Nov. 2, 1953; s. Douglas L. and Irene (Kennedy) W.; children: Nicole, Brian. BS, USAF Acad., Colorado Springs, 1975; MS, Ctrl. Mo. State U., 1977; JD with honors, Ohio State U., 1980. Bar: Ohio 1980, Calif. 1981. Atty. USAF Acad., 1980-84; asst. prof. law Ohio State U., Columbus, 1984-85; atty. Schwartz, Kelm, Warren & Rubenstein, Columbus, 1985-93, Vorys, Sater, Seymour and Pease, Columbus, 1993-98; v.p., sr. counsel The Limited, Inc., Columbus, 1998—2006, exec. v.p., gen. counsel, 2006—. Bd. dirs. Children Defense Fund, Ohio, 1997, United Way of Columbus, 1998—. Lt. col. USAFR, 1975—. Mem. ABA, Calif. Bar Assn., Ohio Bar Assn., Columbus Bar Assn., Order of Coif. Office: The Limited Inc PO Box 16000 Columbus OH 43216 Office Fax: 614-415-7188.

WILLIAMS, DOYLE Z., finance educator; b. Shreveport, La., Dec. 18, 1939; s. Nuell O. and Lurline (Isbell) Williams; m. Maynette Derr, Aug. 20, 1967; children: Zane Derr, Elizabeth Marie. BS, Northwestern State U., 1960; MS in Acctg., La. State U., 1962, PhD, 1965. CPA Tex. Mgr. spl. edn. projects AICPA, NYC, 1967—69; assoc. prof. Tex. Tech. U., Lubbock, 1969—71, prof. acctg., 1972—73, prof. area acctg., coord., 1973—78; prof. acctg. U. So. Calif., LA, 1976—93, dean Sch. Acctg., 1979—87, interim dean Sch. Bus., 1986—88; dean Walton Coll. Bus. U. Ark., Fayetteville, 1993—2005, dean emeritus, 2005—, prof., 2005—06; sr. scholar Kennesaw State U., 2006—. Vis. prof. U. Hawaii, Honolulu, 1971—72. Contbr. articles to profl. jours. Chmn. Acctg. Edn. Change Commn., 1989—93. Named Mem. of the Yr., N.Y. chpt. Nat. Assn. Accts., 1967, Outstanding Acctg. Educator, Beta Alpha Psi, 1982; named to Hall Distinction, La. State U. Coll. Bus., 2007; recipient Disting. Faculty award, Calif. CPA Found., 1983, Nat. Leadership award, Acad. Bus. Adminstrs., 1995, Lifetime Achievement award, Ark. Soc. CPA. Mem.: AICPA (coun. 1983—91, v.p. 1987—88, bd. dirs. 1987—91, Outstanding Educator award 1990, Gold medal 2002), Assn. Advance Coll. Schs. Bus. Internat. (chair acctg. accreditation com. 1995—97, bus. accreditation com. 1995—97, chair acctg. accreditation com. 1999—2000, bd. dirs., vice chair 2003—04, chair 2004—05), S.W. Bus. Deans Assn. (pres. 1998—99), Adminstrs. Acctg. Programs (pres. 1977—78), Fedn. Schs. Accountancy (pres. 1982, Faculty Merit award 1993), Am. Acctg. Assn. (dir. edn. 1973—75, pres. 1984—85, Outstanding Educator award 1996).

WILLIAMS, DREW DAVIS, surgeon; b. San Augustine, Tex., Jan. 18, 1935; s. Floyd Everett and Villamae (Morehead) W.; m. Marilyn Raus, June 27, 1958; children: Leslie, Cynthia, Matthew, Jennifer, Amelia. BS, Tex. A&M Coll., 1957; MD, U. Tex., 1960; grad., naval flight surgeon, U.S. Naval Sch. Aviation Medicine, 1963. Diplomate Am. Bd. Surgery, Am. Bd. Quality Assurance and Utilization Rev. Physicians. Intern USPHS Hosp., Seattle, 1960-61; resident in gen. surgery U. Tex. Med. Br., Galveston, 1961-62, 64-68; resident in pulmonary svc. M.D. Anderson Hosp., Houston, 1968; pvt. practice Baytown, Tex., 1968—. Active staff San Jacinto (Tex.) Meth. Hosp., 1968-95, chief of surgery, 1972, 73, pres. med. staff, 1976; mem. courtesy staff Bay Coast Hosp., Baytown, 1968-95; cons. staff Baytown Med. Ctr. Hosp., 1972-95; 1st chmn. dept. surgery in devel. of family practice residency program affiliated with Tex. Med. Sch., Houston, 1977; mem. Tex. State Bd. Med. Examiners, 1983-89, sec.-treas., 1984-88, pres., 1988-89; unit med. dir., clin. instr. dept. preventive medicine and cmty. health U. Tex. Med. Br., Galveston, 1995-99. Contbr. chpt. to book and articles to profl. jours. Flight surgeon USN, 1962-64; lt. comdr. USNR, ret., 1967. Clin. fellow, Am. Cancer Soc., 1966—67. Mem.: SAR (past pres. local chpt.), AMA (Physicians Recognition award), ACS, Ret. Physicians Orgn. (med. reserve com.), Houston Surg. Soc. (past pres.), Baytown Surg. Soc., East Harris County Med. Soc. (pres. 1982), Harris County Med. Soc. (exec. bd. 1994, chmn. coun. med. splty., co-chmn. disaster response com. of ret. physician orgn.), Singleton Surg. Soc. (past pres.), Tex. Surg. Soc., Tex. Med. Assn., Sovereign Colonial Soc.-Am. of Royal Descent, Colonial Order of the Crown, Soc. Descendents of Colonial Clergy, Sir William Osler Soc., Sons of Republic of Tex. (at large life), Magna Carta Barons, Am. Cancer Soc. (pres. Baytown chpt. 1970—71), Knights Templar, Shriners, Masons (32 degree). Democrat. Mem. Ch. of Christ. Avocations: hunting, fishing, genealogy, painting, gardening. Home and Office: 1217 Kilgore Rd Baytown TX 77520-3912 Office Phone: 281-422-7969. Business E-Mail: ddw@hal-pc.org.

WILLIAMS, EARL PATRICK, JR., retired editor, freelance writer; b. Washington, May 14, 1950; s. Earl Patrick Sr. and Charlie Mae (Wright) W.; m. Susan Miller Day, July 20, 1985 (div. 2005). BA, U. Md., 1973; postgrad., Cath. U., Washington, DC, 1974. Duplication machine operator Applied Physics Lab. Johns Hopkins U., Silver Spring, Md., 1968—74; substitute tchr. Fairfax County Va. Schs., 1974—75; clk. U.S. Govt. Printing Office, Washington, 1975—76; editor U.S. GAO, Washington, 1976—2005, ret., 2005. Freelance writer, Washington, 1974—. Author: Amtrak's Washington-New York Corridor, 1977, What You Should Know About the American Flag, 1987, What You Should Know About Flags of the Confederacy, 1993; contbr. articles to mags. and newspapers. Active in efforts to achieve recognition of Francis Hopkinson, the designer of first ofcl. US flag; lectr. to sch. groups and civic orgns. on history of US flag; discussed history of US flag on radio and TV broadcasts nationwide; mem. NJ Coun. for Social Studies. Recipient Cert. of Appreciation Mil. Order of World Wars, Bronze Good Citizenship medal Nat. Soc. SAR Mem.: N.Am. Vexillological Assn., Nat. Cathedral Assn., Star Spangled Banner Flag House Assn. Democrat. Methodist. Avocations: railroad buff, history, singing folk music. Home: 2323 40th Pl NW Apt 201 Washington DC 20007-1630

WILLIAMS, EDDIE NATHAN, retired think-tank executive; b. Memphis, Aug. 18, 1932; s. Ed and Georgia Lee (Barr) W.; m. Jearline F. Reddick, July 18, 1981; children: Traci Lynne, Edward Lawrence, Terence Reddick. BS, U. Ill., 1954; postgrad., Atlanta U., 1957, Howard U., 1960; LLD, U. D.C., 1986; DHL, Bowie State Coll., 1980, Chgo. State U., 1994, Dillard U., 2001; LLD, Benedict Coll., 2003, Clark-Atlanta U., 2005. Reporter Atlanta Daily World Newspaper, 1957-58; staff asst. U.S. Senate Com. on Fgn. Relations, Washington, 1959-60; fgn. service res. officer U.S. Dept. State, Washington, 1961-68; v.p. U. Chgo., 1968-72; pres., CEO Joint Ctr. for Polit. and Econ. Studies, Washington, 1972—2004, pres. emeritus, 2005—; pres., CEO Eddie Williams & Assocs., 2004—. Vis. pub. policy fellow Howard U., 2005—. Editorial columnist: Chgo. Sun Times, 1970-72; contbr. articles to profl. jours. Am. Polit. Sci. Assn. fellow, 1958, MacArthur Found. fellow, 1988, Nat. Acad. Pub. Adminstrn. fellow, 1993, Am. Acad. Arts and Scis. fellow, 1998; recipient Adam Clayton Powell Award Congl. Black Caucus, 1981, Washingtonian of Yr. award Washingtonian Mag., 1991, Alumni of Yr. award U. Ill. Alumni Club of Greater Washington, 1994, Outstanding Leadership award Korean Am. Alliance, 1994. Mem. Kappa Tau Alpha, Omega Psi Phi, Sigma Pi Phi. Office: Eddie Williams & Assocs 1250 Connecticut Ave NW Ste 200 Washington DC 20036 Office Phone: 202-558-3521. Business E-Mail: ewilliams@eddiewilliamsllc.com.

WILLIAMS, EDNA ALETA THEADORA JOHNSTON, journalist; b. Halifax, NS, Can., Sept. 19, 1923; d. Clarence Harvey and Edna May (Lewis) Johnston; m. Albert Murray Williams, Apr. 16, 1949 (dec.); children: Murleta, Norma, Martin, Charla, Kerrick, Renwick, Julia. Student, Maritime Bus. Coll., 1943. Typist Dept. Treas. (Navy), Halifax, 1944-49; with Bedford (N.S.) Mag., Halifax br., 1954-55, Presbyn. Office, New Glasgow, N.S., 1965-67, Thompson and Sutherland, New Glasgow, 1967-69; family editor, columnist, reporter New Glasgow Evening News, 1969-88, ret., 1988; soc. corr. Evening News, 1997—. Mem. coun. Halifax YMCA; founding mem. Pictou County YM-YWCA, 1966—; ref. person media and religion Black History Month; New Glasgow Bapt. rep. Pictou County Coun. of Chs., 1978—82, sec., 1980—82; pres. ch. aux. 2d United Bapt. Ch., 1979—83; chorus dir. Men's Choir, 1980—, hon. mem. ch. aux., v.p., 1993—; treas. Ch.'s Men's Brotherhood, 1995—; organist St. James Anglican Ch., 1983—85, provincial organist, 1994—; organist St. Bee's Anglican Ch., 1996—2003; provincial pres. Women's Inst. of African United Bapt. Assn., 1983—86; bd. dirs. Pictou County YM-YWCA, 1967—77, corr. sec., v.p., 1974—75, 1975—77; past pres., past provincial dir., Home and Sch. provincial sec. African United Bapt. Assn. of N.S., 1988—90; sec. area IV Atlantic United Bapt. Conv., 1989—93; past officer local interracial com.; bd. dirs. Big Bros./Big Sisters, 1984—86, Pictou

County United Way, 1983—96, Palliative Care Aberdeen Hosp., 1985—, Black United Front; chair Pictou County Srs. Festival, 1999—2001. Recipient Hon. award, United Way, 1993, Grot award, Black Cultural Ctr. N.S., 1999, honored by, Pictou County Music Festival, 1994, award, 2d United Bapt. Ch., 1997, Cultural Heritage award, Town of New Glasgow, 2004, Palliative Care Vol. award, 2005, Honored over 50 yr. mem. and 20 yr. organist, African United Bapt. Assn. Women's Inst., 2005. Mem. N.S. Sr. Secretate, Can. Press Assn., Black Journalists Assn. N.S., Can. Bible Soc. (pres. 2004—, Certificate, 1998), African United Baptist Assn. Women's Inst. Home: 230 Reservoir St New Glasgow NS Canada B2H 4K4 Office: Evening News 352 East River Rd Glasgow NS Canada B2H 5E2 Personal E-mail: karryw@ns.sympatico.ca.

WILLIAMS, EDWARD DAVID, information technology management consultant; b. Scranton, Pa., June 20, 1932; s. David Thomas and Mabel (Sims) W. m. Natalie Imnadze, Oct. 18, 1952; children: Denise, Claudia. BBA, Hofstra U., 1961; postgrad. in Bus. Adminstrn., Fairleigh Dickenson U., 1979. Cons. Cresap, McCormick and Paget, NYC, 1964—65; sr. mgmt. cons. Union Carbide Corp., NYC, 1965—67; asst. contr. data processing We. Union, NYC, 1967—69; v.p. mgmt. info. sys. ABC, Hackensack, NJ, 1970—86; v.p., chief info. officer Blue Cross Blue Shield of NJ, Newark, 1986—88; v.p. Chantico Pub. Co., Carrellton, Tex., 1989—90; pres. SMC-BIS Inc., Basking Ridge, NJ, 1990—93; pres., CEO Strategic Outsourcing Svcs. Inc., Mountain Lakes, NJ, 1993—97; sr. v.p. Computer Horizons Corp., Mountain Lakes, 1997—99; exec. v.p. PRT Group Inc., Windsor, Conn., 1999; pres. Ed. Williams Assoc. Ltd., Franklin Lakes, NJ, 1995—. Spkr. in field. With US Army, 1948-52. Decorated Silver Star with oak leaf cluster, Bronze Star with V; recipient Purple Heart with 2 oak leaf clusters, Combat Info. Badge. Mem. Soc. Mgmt. Info. Systems, NJ C. of C., Profit Oriented Systems Planning Bd. (bd. dirs.), Masons. Republican. Home and Office: Ed Williams Assoc Ltd 662 Cheyenne Dr Franklin Lakes NJ 07417 Office Phone: 201-847-9148. Personal E-mail: edward.d.williams@att.net.

WILLIAMS, EDWARD EARL, JR., entrepreneur, educator; b. Houston, Aug. 21, 1945; s. Edward Earl and Doris Jewel (Jones) W.; m. Susan M. Warren, June 28, 1983; children: Laura Michelle, David Brian. BS, U. Pa., 1966; PhD, U. Tex., 1968. Asst. prof. econs. Rutgers U., New Brunswick, NJ, 1968-70; assoc. prof. fin. McGill U., Montreal, Que., Canada, 1970-73; v.p. Svc. Corp. Internat., Houston, 1973-77; prof. adminstrv. sci. Rice U., Houston, 1978-82, Henry Gardiner Symonds prof., 1982—, prof. stats., 1995—. Chmn. bd. dirs. Edward E. Williams & Co., Houston, 1976-92; chmn. bd., pres. Tex. Capital Investment Co., 1979-95; chmn. bd. First Tex. Venture Capital Corp., 1983-92; mng. dir. First Tex. Venture Capital, LLC, 1992-2000, Svc. Corp. Internat., Simugram Sys., Inc.; adv. dir. Frost Nat. Bank Author: Prospects for the Savings and Loan Industry, 1968, An Integrated Analysis for Managerial Finance, 1970, Investment Analysis, 1974, Business Planning for the Entrepreneur, 1983, The Economics of Production and Productivity: A Modeling Approach, 1996, Entrepreneurship and Productivity, 1998, The N.Y. Times Pocket MBA Series: Business Planning, 1999, Models for Investors in Real World Markets, 2003, Preparing an Entrepreneurial Business Plan, 2004; contbr. articles to profl. jours. Benjamin Franklin scholar, Jesse Jones scholar U. Pa., 1966; fellow Tex. Savs. and Loan League, fellow NDEA U. Tex., 1968. Mem. Am. Statis. Assn., Coll. Innovation and Entrepreneurship, Fin. Mgmt. Assn., So. Pacific Hist. and Tech. Soc., Santa Fe Rlwy. Hist. and Modeling Soc., Soc. on Econs. and Mgmt. in China, Raveneaux Country Club, Jewish Comm. North, Beta Gamma Sigma, Alpha Kappa Psi. Republican. Home: 7602 Wilton Park Dr Spring TX 77379-4672 Office: Rice U Jesse H Jones Grad Sch Mgmt Houston TX 77251 Business E-Mail: jmkeynes@rice.edu.

WILLIAMS, EDWIN NEEL, newspaper editor; b. Rives, Mo., Jan. 14, 1942; s. Carl Edwin and Vina Marie (Edmonston) W.; m. Marylyn Lentine, 1973; 1 child, Jonathan Lentine. BA in History, U. Miss., 1965. Reporter Clarksdale (Miss) Press-Register, 1965; reporter, editor Delta Dem.-Times, Greenville, Miss., 1967-72; Nieman fellow Harvard U., Cambridge, Mass., 1972-73; writer, researcher Ford Found., NYC, 1973; editorial writer Charlotte (N.C.) Observer, 1973-76, editor of editorial pages, 1976-80, 87—. Chmn. KinderMourn, Charlotte, 1988, N.C. Harvest, 1993-94; bd. dirs. N.C. Ctr. for Pub. Policy Rsch., Raleigh, 1992-95. With U.S. Army, 1965-67. Baptist. Home: 916 Mount Vernon Ave Charlotte NC 28203-4845 Office: Charlotte Observer PO Box 30308 Charlotte NC 28230-0308 Office Phone: 704-358-5012. E-mail: ewilliams@charlotteobserver.com.

WILLIAMS, ELEANOR JOYCE, retired government air traffic control specialist; b. College Station, Tex., Dec. 21, 1936; d. Robert Ira and Viola (Ford) Toliver; m. Tollie Williams, Dec. 30, 1955 (div. July 1978); children: Rodrick, Viola Williams Smith, Darryl, Eric, Dana Williams Robinson, Sheila Williams Watkins, Kenneth. Student, Prairie View A&M Coll., 1955-56, Anchorage Community Coll., 1964-65, U. Alaska-Anchorage, 1976. Clk./stenographer FAA, Anchorage, 1965-66, adminstrv. clk., 1966-67, pers. staffing asst., 1967-68, air traffic control specialist, 1968-79, air traffic control supr. San Juan, P.R., 1979-80, Anchorage, 1983-85, airspace specialist Atlanta, 1980-83, with Washington, 1985-87; area mgr. Kansas City Air Rt. Traffic Control Ctr., Olathe, Kans., 1987-89, asst. mgr. Quality Assurance, 1989-91, supr. traffic mgmt., 1991, supr. system effectiveness section, 1991-93, asst. air traffic mgr., 1993-94; air traffic mgr. Cleve. Air Route Traffic Control Ctr., Oberlin, Ohio, 1994-97; acting mgr. sys. mgmt. br. Des Plains, Ill., 1995-96; mem. human resource reform team task force Washington, 1996—; acting regional exec. mgr. Great Lakes Region Des Plaines, Ill., 1996-97. Propr. Williams Apts., Anchorage. Sec. Fairview Neighborhood Coun., Anchorage, 1967-69; mem. Anchorage Bicentennial Commn., 1975-76; bd. dirs. Mt. Patmos Youth Dept., Decatur, Ga., 1981-82; mem. NAACP; del. to USSR Women in Mgmt., 1990; v.p. A&M Consol. Lincoln HS Alumni Assn., 2000—; citizens amb. program People to People Internat.; adv. bd. Lincoln Recreation Ctr. Recipient Mary K. Goddard award Anchorage Fed. Exec. Assn. and Fed. Women's Program, 1985, Sec.'s award Dept. Transp., 1985, Pres. VIP award, 1988, C. Alfred Anderson award, 1991, Disting. Svc. award Nat. Black Coalition of Fed. Aviation Employees, 1991, Paul K. Bohr award FAA, 1994, Nat. Performance Rev. Hammer award from V.P. Al Gore, 1996, Regional Adminstrs. award for meritorious svc. Gt. Lakes Regional Adminstrn., 1997, Top Flight award for outstanding svc. FAA, 1997; A salute to Her Name in the Congl. Record 104th Congress, 1995, Execs. in Profile award for exemplary career performance Region Ten Blacks in Govt., 1998, Pres.'s award for outstanding svc. Lincoln Former Students Assn.; named Disting. Alumnus Lincoln H.S., 2000; named Youth Advocate Cmty. Champion State of Tex., Tex. Commn. Alcohol and Drug Abuse, 2001; inducted into Black Aviation Hall fame, 2001, Woman of Yr. award North to the Future Bus. and Profl. Women's Club, Anchorage, 2006 Mem.: Women in Mgmt. (del. Soviet Union), Internat. Platform Assn., Fed. Mgrs. Assn., Air Traffic Contrs. Assn., Profl. Women Contrs. Orgn., Nat. Black Coalition of Fed. Aviation Employees (pres. cen. region chpt. 1987—92, Over Achievers award 1987, Disting. Svc. award 1988, Sojourner Truth award Great Lakes region 1997), Blacks in Govt., Nat. Assn. Negro Bus. and Profl. Women USA Inc. (North to the Future club, charter pres. 1975—76), Gamma Phi Delta. Democrat. Baptist. Avocations: singing, sewing. Home: 7931 Old Seward Hwy Apt 8 Anchorage AK 99518-3265 Personal E-mail: ejw4atc@aol.com, ejtwmsent@msn.com.

WILLIAMS, ELIZABETH, human services administrator; d. Sylvester and Lucinda Williams; m. Willie Alfred Oden (div.); 1 child, Robert Earl Oden (dec.). Student, Hammel Bus. Coll., Akron, Ohio, 1960—61, Washtenaw CC, Ann Arbor, Mich., 1962—63, Econ. Inst. Christian Edn., Stanford, Conn., 1968, Norwalk CC, Conn., 1969—70, Roosevelt U., Chgo., 1972, City Coll. NY, Manhattan, 1972—74. LCSW Mich., 1974. Founder, owner Al's Restaurant, Akron, 1964—68; head sports dept. Lord and Taylors, Stanford, 1968—70; supr., planner, bd. dirs. Washtenaw County Neighborhood Svcs., Ypsilanti, Mich., 1970—76; founder, exec. dir. New Bethel Cmty. Ctr., Ypsilanti, 1976—80, People's Choice Multi Purpose Ctr., Inc., Ypsilanti, 1976—80, founder, pres. LA, 1981—87; program dir. Watts Labor Com. Action, LA, 1980—81; founder, pres. EOW Enterprises, LA, 1987—94, SLW Fin. and Investment Corp., 1993—, EW Capital Sys. Enterprises, 2002—. Founder Sr. Citizens Edn. and Tutoring Program, 1970—76; program dir. campus svc. E. Mich. U., Ypsilanti, 1979—80; coord. youth tng. Mich. Tech. Inst., Ann Arbor, 1980; program coord. U. Mich. Dept. Continuing Edn. for Women. Founder Washtenaw County Lit. Coun., Ann Arbor, Mich., 1976—80; mem. Solid Front for Unity in Am., 1982—85, Nat. Orgn. Black Lawyers, Calif., Nat. Coun. Aging, Calif., Ypsilanti Orgn. Social Workers, Nat. and State Orgn. Social Workers, Calif., Ypsilanti area Coll. Life-Long Learning, Wayne State U., Detroit; rep. Bd. Licenses and Regulations, Mich.; spl. program dir. Mt. Zion Ch. of God in Christ, Ypsalanti, 1973—81; bd. mem. YWCA, Stanford, Conn.; state chair Conf. Black Women, Stanford; mem. Stanford Housing Project, MLK Birthday Commn., LA, 1982—85; program planner, program dir., recruiter, trustee Hong Kong Internat. Humanitarian Self Liquidating Loan Program, 1991—2005; mem., bd. dirs. Nat. Orgn. Social Workers; mem. exec. com. United Way, Calif.; mem. Mich. State Steering Com.; mem. bd. dirs. extended opportunity program Boy Scouts of Am., Ypsilanti. Named Exec. Adminstr. of Yr., Compton, Calif., 1983—84, Bus. Woman of Yr., CBS TV, 1984, Citizen of Week, KNX News, 1985, Bus. Woman of Yr., ACC News, 1986, Miss Christianity, ACC Churches and Cmty. News, 1987; recipient Pauline award, Ministers Alliance, LA, 1983—84, Entrepreneur award, Philanthropist Christian Club, LA, 1983—84, Agy. of Yr. award, Calif., 1983—84, Excellent Cmty. Svc. award, NAACP, 1984, Outstanding Svc. to LA Cmty. award, IRS, 1985, Humanitarian award, People's Choice bd. dirs., 1986, Keys to the City, Compton, 1987, Feeding the Hungry spl. award, 1987; Unique Partnership in Conservation award grant, So. Calif. Gas Co., 1986. Avocations: checkers, chess, cooking, dominoes, interior decorating.

WILLIAMS, ELLA, healthcare educator; b. Oct. 29, 1941; d. Gus and Velma Dukes Sr.; m. Charles B. Williams, Apr. 15, 1981; children: Beverly A. Jackson, Glynn D. Jackson, Donatus C. Mbaliri. BS in Edn., Southern U., Baton Rouge; postgrad., U. Houston. Unit mgr. Earl K. Long Hosp., Baton Rouge, 1963—72; tchr. Holy Child's Coll., Lagos, Nigeria, 1976—80; owner, mgr. Health Care Co., Houston, 1980—. Author: A Cultural Shock, 1984. Facility Home for Disabled and Mentally Challenger, Morgania, La., 2005—07. Grantee, U. Houston, 1980. Mem.: Houston Bd. Realtons. Avocations: travel, fishing, writing, history. Home: 5617 Bissonnet St #108B Houston TX 77081

WILLIAMS, ELLA MARILYN, mathematics educator; b. Raleigh, NC, Aug. 15, 1950; d. Thomas Harold and Ella W. BA, Bennett Coll., Greensboro, NC, 1972; MA, N.C. Ctrl. U., Durham, 1973. Cert. math. tchr., D.C. Tchr. D.C. Pub. Schs., Washington, 1973, Greensboro (N.C.) Pub. Schs., 1973-77; math. specialist U. D.C., Washington, 1977-80; tchr. DC Pub. Schs., Washington, 1980—. Participant in Honors Tchrs. Workshop, Mich. State U., East Lansing, 1987, St. John's Ins. Inst. for Educators, 2003, Nat. Security Agy. Summer Inst., 2005. Nominee for Presidential award, DC Pub. Schs. Math. Dept., Washington, 1987 Mem. Nat. Coun. Tchrs. of Math. (rep. standards implementation com., rep. 2000—, chmn. nominating com. 1989-2005, Rep., 1999—), D.C. Coun. Tchrs. of Math. (nominating com. 1989-2006). Home: 3715 Alabama Ave SE # B Washington DC 20020-2403 Office: DC Pub Schs Eastern High 1700 E Capitol St NE Washington DC 20003 Office Phone: 202-698-4500. Personal E-mail: emarilynw@aol.com.

WILLIAMS, ELLEN D., physics professor; BS in Chemistry, Mich. State U., 1976; PhD, Calif. Inst. Tech., 1981. Summer rschr. Miles Lab., Elkhart, Ind., 1974, Kodak Rsch. Lab., Rochester, NY, 1976; tchg. asst. Calif. Inst. Tech., 1976—79, grad. rsch. asst., 1977—81; rsch. assoc. Dept. Physics and Astronomy U. Md., 1981—83, asst. prof., 1983—87, assoc. prof., 1987—91, assoc. prof. Inst. Physical Sci. and Tech., 1990—91, dir. Chem. Physics Program, 1993—95, prof. Dept. Physics, Inst. Physical Sci. and Tech., 1991—, disting. prof., 2000—. Editl. bd. Nano Letters, 2003—. Named Outstanding Woman of Yr., U. Md., 1996; recipient E.W. Mueller award, U. Wis., 1996, David Turnbull award, Materials Rsch. Soc., 2003; Nat. Sci. Found. fellowship, 1976—79, IBM Grad. fellowship, 1979—80, Cottrell Rsch. Grant, 1983. Fellow: Japan Soc. for Promotion of Sci., Am. Vacuum Soc., Am. Physical Soc. (physics policy com. 2005—, David Adler Lectureship award 2001, Maria Goeppert-Mayer award 1990); mem.: Am. Acad. Arts & Sciences, NAS (bd. army svc. and tech. 2007—). Office: Dept Physics Univ Maryland John S Toll Physics Bldg College Park MD 20742-4111 Office Phone: 301-405-6156. E-mail: edw@physics.umd.edu.

WILLIAMS, ERVIN EUGENE, religious organization administrator; b. Corning, NY, Feb. 25, 1923; s. Douglas Lewis and Mina P. (Barnes) Williams; m. Ruth Evelyn Snyder, June 12, 1945; children: Roger Eugene, Virginia Ruth. Student, Toccoa Falls Coll., Ga., 1939, Cornell U., 1942; BA, Pa. State U., 1949; MA, Mich. State U., 1961, PhD in Communications, 1971. Ordained to ministry Ind. Bapt. Ch., 1950. Acad. dean Greensburg (Pa.) Bible Inst., 1949-51; min. Bapt. Ch., New Kensington, Pa., 1951-53; instr. Pa. State U., 1953-55; sr. min. East Lansing (Mich.) Trinity Ch., 1955-71; vis. prof. Trinity Evang. Div. Sch., Deerfield, Ill., 1968-71, prof. comm. and practical theology, 1971-77, dir. D Ministry program, 1975-76; gen. dir. Am. Missionary Fellowship, Villanova, Pa., 1977-92; exec. min. Ch. of the Apostles, Atlanta, 1993-95; ch. and instl. cons. Smyrna, Ga., 1995—; sr. pastor New Life Bible Ch., Man-O-War Cay, Abaco, The Bahamas, 1997—98; assoc. Mattocks & Assoc., Inc., Fairfax, Va., 2005—. Chaplain Mich. State U., East Lansing, 1955—71; cons. Haggai Inst. Advanced Leadership Tng., Atlanta, 1969—95; lectr. Calvary Bapt. Coll., Kansas City, Mo., 1962, Haggai Inst. Third World Leaders, Singapore, 1970—95; cons. to mission bds., 1967—76; assoc. dir. Camp of Woods, Speculator, NY, 1971—77; Staley lectr. Robert Wesleyan Coll., North Chill, NY, 1973, Judson Coll., Elgin, Ill., 1977—79. Author: What Say You?, 2007, Joy Where it Counts, 2007, Airplane Views of the Bible, 2007, A Second War on Terror, 2007, Divine Sovereignty and Human Responsibility, 2007; contbr. articles to profl. jours. Trustee Gospel Vols., Speculator, 1963—93, Dorothy H. Theis Meml. Found., Sierra Vista, Ariz., 1987—95; mem. bd. regents Owosso (Mich.) Coll., 1971—73. Pilot USAAF, 1942—45, prisoner of war, ETO. Decorated DFC, Air medal with 2 oak leaf clusters, POW medal, ETO Campaign medal with 6 clusters, Victory medal; recipient Presdl. citation. Mem.: Mich. Acad. Arts and Scis., Christian Assn. Psychol. Studies, Aircraft Owners and Pilots Assn., Nat. Sunday Sch. Assn., Phi Beta Kappa, Alpha Kappa Delta, Phi Kappa Phi, Pi Gamma Mu. Office Phone: 770-329-5054. E-mail: msupsu@bellsouth.net. *It is much more difficult to conceal ignorance and prejudice than it is to acquire knowledge and fairness.*

WILLIAMS, EVAN, Internet company executive; b. Nebr., 1972; Web application developer O'Reilly Media, Intel, Hewlett Packard; co-founder, CEO (and developer of Blogger) Pyra Labs (acquired by Google), 1999—2003; head, Blogger Google, 2003—04; co-founder Oden podcasting (acquired by Obvious); founder Twitter, 2006—. Named one of 50 Who Matter Now, Business 2.0, 2007. Office: Twitter Inc 164 South Park San Francisco CA 94107 Office Phone: 866-924-2008. *

WILLIAMS, FRANK J., state supreme court chief justice, historian, writer; b. Providence, Aug. 24, 1940; s. Frank and Natalie L. (Corelli) W.; m. Virginia E. Miller, Aug. 24, 1966. BA, Boston U., 1962, JD, 1970; MS in Taxation, Bryant Coll., Smithfield, RI, 1986, LHD (hon.), 2004, Lincoln Coll., Ill., 1987; LLD (hon.), So. New England Sch. Law, 2001; LHD (hon.), Johnson & Wales U., 2002; Lincoln diploma of honor, Lincoln Meml. U., Harrogate, Tenn., 2002; LLD (hon.), Roger Williams U., Bristol, RI, 2004, Mass. Sch. Law, 2004, U. RI, Kingston, 2006, Okla. State U., 2007. Bar: RI 1970, US Dist. Ct. RI 1970, US Supreme Ct. 1976. Assoc. Tillinghast, Collins & Graham, Providence, 1970-75, Leonard Decof Ltd., Providence, 1976-78; law clk. Graham, Reid, Ewing & Stapleton, Providence, 1969; law clk., adminstrv. asst. RI Atty. Gen., Providence, 1967-68; pres. Frank J. Williams Ltd., attys.-at-law, Providence, 1978-95; assoc. justice RI Superior Ct., 1995-2001; chief justice RI Supreme Ct., 2001—. Judge of probate Town of Hopkinton, RI, 1978-82, 84-90, solicitor, 1978-82, 84-87; judge of probate Town of West Greenwich, RI, 1984-86, 92-95, solicitor, 1984-92, asst. solicitor, 1992-95; dep. judge of probate, 1987-92; solicitor Town of Coventry, RI, 1972-74, 76-78, Town of Barrington, RI, 1993-95, Town of Bristol, RI, 1995, Town of South Kingstown, RI, 1995; past spl. counsel Towns of Westerly, Bristol, Hopkinton, South Kingstown, City of Providence; atty. Town of Smithfield Sewer Authority, 1974-90; legis. counsel RI Retail Fedn., 1975-93, Credit Info. Bur., RI Mortgage Bankers Assn., 1992-95; adj. prof. Roger Williams U. Sch. of Law, 1997—, US Naval War Coll., 2003—; lectr. bus. and legal practice RI Sch. Design, Providence, 1976-80; panel of arbitrators Am. Arbitration Assn., panel of mediators RI Superior Ct., 1993-95; mem. RI Bd. Bar Examiners, 1987-95, chair, 1995; chair RI Housing and Mortgage Fin. Corp., 1995, Lincoln Forum, 1996—; apptd. by pres. to Mil. Commns. Rev. Panel for mil. tribunals, Guantanamo Bay, Cuba, 2004—. Pres. Lincoln Group of Boston, 1976—88, Abraham Lincoln Assn., Springfield, Ill., 1986—95, Ulysses S. Grant Assn., 1990—; elected del. RI Constnl. Conv., 1986; elected town moderator Richmond, RI, 1992—95; dist. moderator Chariho Regional Sch. Dist., 1994; bd. dirs. John E. Fogarty Found. for Persons with Mental Retardation, 1975—, South County Hosp., 1995—2004, RI Coun. for the Humanities, 2001—07, Narragansett Coun. Boy Scouts Am., 1969—80, 1998—2001. Capt. US Army, 1962—67, Germany and Vietnam. Decorated Bronze Star, Combat Infantryman's badge, Army Commendation medal, Air medal with 2 oak leaf clusters, Republic of Vietnam Gallantry Cross with silver star; named Hon. Brigadier Gen., R.I. Militia, 2003; named to RI Heritage Hall of Fame, 2004; recipient Disting. Eagle Scout award, 2005. Fellow: ATLA (jud.); mem.: RI Bar Assn. (chmn. new lawyers adv. com. 1976—87, ho. of dels. 1986—93, chmn. mcpl. law com. 1993), Conf. Chief Justices (bd. dirs. 2004—06), Am. Law Inst., Nat. Assn. for Ct. Mgmt., Am. Judges Assn., Am. Antiquarian Soc., Phi Alpha Delta, Alpha Phi Sigma, Phi Sigma Alpha. Roman Catholic. Office: 250 Benefit St Providence RI 02903 Office Phone: 401-222-3290.

WILLIAMS, FRANKLIN CADMUS, JR., bibliographer; b. Palestine, Tex., July 30, 1941; s. Franklin Cadmus and Cathryn Lucille (Pessoney) W. BA, Baylor U., 1963; MA, Stephen F. Austin State U., 1965; PhD, U. Wis., 1975. Cert. in secondary edn. English and History. Teaching fellow Stephen F. Austin State U., Nacogdoches, Tex., 1964-65, U. Wis., Madison, 1965-68; instr. English Austin Peay State U., Clarksville, Tenn., 1970-71; adj. asst. prof. East Tex. State U., Commerce, 1975; asst. prof. English Jarvis Christian Coll., Hawkins, Tex., 1976-78, 79-81; ind. scholar Palestine, Tex., 1981—; owner, bibliographer Goldsmith Archive, Palestine, 1981—. Cons. Diocese of Galveston-Houston, 1977-84, Tex. State Hist. Assn., Austin, 1988; speaker, editor Jarvis Christian Coll., Hawkins, Tex., 1976-78, 79-81; nat. teaching fellow Office Edn., Washington, 1976-77; del. to Baylor U., U. Wis. System, Madison, 1981. Author: Lone Star Bishops: The Roman Catholic Hierarchy in Texas, 1997; contbr. articles to profl. jours. Mem. Modern Lang. Assn., Tex. State Hist. Assn., Tex. Cath. Hist. Soc., Baylor Alumni Assn. (life), Wis. Alumni Assn. (life), Sigma Tau Delta. Avocations: reading, record collecting, historical genealogy, tennis, swimming. Office: PO Box 96 Palestine TX 75802-0096

WILLIAMS, FREDA VIDELL, speech pathology/audiology services professional; d. Norman Freeman Williams and Coreen Videlle Davis; children: Shannon O'Neal Otwell, Michael Scott Otwell. MS in Speech-Pathology and Audiology, Fla. State U., Tallahassee. Speech-lang. pathologist Sunland Tng. Ctr., Marianna, Fla., 1979, Jackson County Schs., 1979—79, Houston County Schs., Dothan, Ala., 1980—80, Sunland Tng. Ctr., Marianna, 1980—80, Wash. County Schs., Chipley, Fla., 1981—83, pvt. practice, 1983—87, Leon County Schs., Tallahassee, 1987—88, Programs Infants and Children, Anchorage, 1988—89, Lauderdale County Schs., Meridian, Miss., 1989—90, Dothan City Schs., Ala., 1990—97, Programs Infants and Children, Anchorage, 1997—99, Bay Dist. Schs., Panama City, Fla., 1999—2002, coord. speech-lang. pathology, 2002—. Coord. Emerald Coast Speech-Lang. Pathology Consortium, Panama City, 2004—. Builder Habitat Humanity, Panama City, 2005—06; councilwoman Dem. Exec. Com., Marianna, 1981—82; builder United Meth. Ch., Oaxaca, Mexico, 1983—83. Mem.: Am. Speech-Lang.-Hearing Assn. (assoc.). Conservative. Avocations: painting, swimming, walking, travel. Home Phone: 850-747-5862.

WILLIAMS, FREDERICK TYRONE, entrepreneur, pastor; b. Monroe, La., Mar. 27, 1982; s. Felix Anthony and Alberta Joyce Williams; m. Rakiyyah Nitaka Hart, July 27, 2005; children: Taylor Jerome Hart, Madisson Tiana Hope, Kennedy Caleb Aaron, Phoebe Laken McKenzie. BS in Bus. Mgmt., Kaplan U., Ft. Lauderdale, Fla., 2006. Microsoft Office Certified Olive Harvey Coll., Chgo., 2004; Church Planter North Am. Mission Bd., Ga., 2004; Area Youth Development Chgo. AYD, 2005; Television and Video Production DeKalb H.S. of Tech., Ga., 2000. Youth pastor Light of the World, Chgo., 2001—05, Christian Worship Ctr., Chgo., 2005—; case mgr. Riviera Manor Nursing Home, Chgo., 2002—06; CEO, chmn. Fred T. Williams Ministries, Chgo., 2006, Impact to Empower Comm., LLC, Chgo., 2006; CEO Nu Wine Graphics and Design, Chgo., 2006—. Singer, praise and worship leader: gospel choir workshop Nat. Black Coll. Choir Gospel Workshop of Am.; actor, composer, editor: (short film for television) Youth With A Purpose Motion Picture; musical recording, Undivided Attention by Out-World. Bd. mem. Christian Worship Ctr., Chgo., 2005. Democrat. Avocations: writing poetry / musical composition, public speaking, musical performances, travel. Office: Fred T Williams Ministries 1308 W 103rd St Suite 2 Chicago IL 60643 Home Phone: 773-853-3348; Office Phone: 773-853-3348. Office Fax: 773-881-8675; Home Fax: 773-881-8675. Personal E-mail: pastorfredwilliams@yahoo.com. Business E-Mail: contact@fredtwilliams.com.

WILLIAMS, GARY MURRAY, pathologist, educator; b. Regina, Sask., Can., May 7, 1940; s. Murray Austin and Selma Ruby (Domstad) W.; m. Julia Christine Lundberg; children: Walter, Jeffrey, Ingrid. BA, Washington and Jefferson Coll., 1963; MD, U. Pitts, 1967. Diplomate Am. Bd. Pathology, Am. Bd. Toxicology. Assoc. prof. pathology Temple U., Phila., 1971-75; mem. Fels Rsch. Inst., Phila., 1971-75; rsch. prof. N.Y. Med. Coll., Valhalla, 1975-98, prof. pathology, environ. pathology and toxicology, dir., 1999—. Mem. working group Internat. Agy. Rsch. on Cancer, Lyon, France, 1976, 80, 1982—83, 1985—87, 1989, 91, 1996—99; mem. subcom. on upper reference levels of nutrients NRC, 1999—2003, com. health effects dioxin, 2004—06; advisor joint expert com. on food additives WHO, 2001—07. Founding editor Cell Biology and Toxicology, 1984—, mem. editl. bd. Archives of Toxicology, 1988—, European Jour. Cancer Prevention, 1991—, Drug and Chem. Toxicology, 1994—, Toxicologic Pathology, 2003—, assoc. editor, 2005—, Food and Chem. Toxicology, 2005—; contbr. more than 495 articles to profl. jours.; editor or co-editor 8 books, —. Lt. comdr. USPHS, 1969-71. Recipient Sheard-Sanford award Am. Soc. Clin. Pathologists U. Pitts., 1967, Dean's Disting. Rsch. award NY Med. Coll., 2006, 50th Anniversary 5 Yr. Svc. medal

WHO, 2006; named Disting. Scientist Am. Chem. Soc., 2005. Fellow Internat. Acad. Toxicol. Pathology (accreditation com. 2000), Royal Coll. Pathologists; mem. Soc. Toxicology (Arthur J. Lehman award 1982, Lectr. award 1996, Advancement Animal Welfare award 2002), Soc. Toxicol. Pathology, Phi Beta Kappa, Alpha Omega Alpha. Home: 8 Elm Rd Scarsdale NY 10583-1410 Office: Dept Pathology NY Med Coll Valhalla NY 10595-1549 Home Phone: 914-723-8739; Office Phone: 914-594-4146. Business E-Mail: gary_williams@nymc.edu.

WILLIAMS, GARY RANDALL, lawyer; b. Gainesville, Ga., Oct. 16, 1946; s. Ernest Eugene and Ruby Louise (Conner) W.; m. Linda (Meg) Eberhart, May 12, 1990. LLB, LaSalle U., 1969; AA, SUNY, Albany, 1973; JD, Woodrow Wilson Coll. Law, 1976; ThM, Global Ch. U., 2004; PhD, St. Luke Evangelical Sch. Bible Studies, 2004; ThB, Christian Life Sch. Theology, 2005. Bar: Ga. 1978, US Tax Ct. 1978, US Dist. Ct. (no. dist.) Ga. 1979, US Ct. Claims 1980, US Supreme Ct., 1997. Atty. IRS, Washington, 1977-80; lawyer ADP Pension Svcs., Inc., El Toro, Calif., 1981-82; pvt. practice Marietta, Ga., 1980—86; tax specialist Ga. Dept. Revenue, Atlanta, 1986-92; pvt. practice Hiram, Ga., 1992—2003, Dallas, Ga., 1994—2003; judge protem Paulding County Probate Ct., 1997—2003; assoc. juvenile judge Tallapoosa Jud. Cir., 1999—2003. Affiliate atty. Am. Ctr. for Law and Justice. With U.S. Army, 1966-73. Mem. State Bar Ga., Paulding County Bar Assn. (sec., treas. 1994, pres. 1998-99). Avocations: computers, automobiles. Office: 777 Cleveland Ave SW Ste 607 Atlanta GA 30315 Personal E-mail: grw2@bellsouth.net.

WILLIAMS, GEORGE CHRISTOPHER, biologist, ecology and evolution educator; b. Charlotte, NC, May 12, 1926; s. George Felix and Margaret (Steuart) W.; m. Doris Lee Calhoun, Jan. 25, 1951; children: Jacques, Sibyl, Judith, Phoebe. AB, U. Calif., Berkeley, 1949; PhD, UCLA, 1955; ScD (hon.), Queen's U., Kingston, Ont., Can., 1995, SUNY, Stony Brook, 2000. Instr. and asst. prof. Mich. State U., East Lansing, 1955-60; assoc. prof. dept. ecology and evolution SUNY, Stony Brook, 1960-66, prof., 1966-90. Adj. prof. Queens U., Kingston, Ont., Can., 1980-95. Author: Adaptation and Natural Selection, 1966, Sex and Evolution, 1975, Natural Selection: Domains, Levels and Challenges, 1992, The Pony Fish's Glow, 1997; co-author: (with R.M. Nesse) Why We Get Sick: The New Science of Darwinian Medicine, 1995; co-editor: (with James Paradis) Evolution and Ethics, 1989; editor Quar. Rev. Biology, SUNY, 1965-98. With U.S. Army, 1944-46. Recipient Eminent Ecologist award Ecol. Soc. Am., 1989, Daniel Giraud Elliot medal Nat. Acad. Sci., 1992, Royal Swedish Acad. Crafoord prize, 1999; fellow Ctr. Adv. Study Behavioral Sci., Stanford, 1981-82, Guggenheim Found., 1988-89. Fellow AAAS, Soc. Study Evolution (v.p. 1973, pres. 1989), Nat. Acad. Sci., Am. Soc. Ichthyologists and Herpetologists, Am. Soc. Naturalists (editor 1974-79), Icelandic Natural History Soc. Home Phone: 631-650-3122.

WILLIAMS, GEORGE LEO, historian, retired secondary school educator, landmark director; b. NYC, June 29, 1931; s. Leo Dominick and Cathryn Margaret (Schellderfer) W.; m. Adelia Gilda Musa, Feb. 26, 1958; children: Adelia, Marina, Gilda. BA, CUNY, 1953, MA, 1955; PhD, NYU, 1966. Tchr. Port Washington (N.Y.) Pub. Schs., 1953, chairperson integrated studies, 1960-65, coord. Amherst project, 1968-69, chairperson English dept., 1970-90; adminstrv. asst. secondary and higher edn. dept. NYU, NYC, 1965-66. Adj. prof. NYU, 1966-74, Adelphi U., Garden City, N.Y. 1967-69, Hofstra U., Hempstead, N.Y., 1967-74; chmn. profl. growth and devel. com. Port Washington Pub. Schs., 1973-90, chmn. bicentennial com. 1989-90, mem. policy bd. Port Washington Tchr. Ctr., 1987-90; mem. alumni bd. Queens Coll. History Dept., 1996-2000; dir. Sandminers Monument, Inc., 2004—. Co-author: (play) The Triumph of the Constitution, 1988, Secession: A Township Divided, 2005; author: Fascist Thought and Totalitarianism in Italy's Secondary Schools: Theory and Practice, 1922-1943, 1993, Port Washington in the Twentieth Century: Places and People, 1995, Papal Genealogy: The Families and Descendants of the Popes, 1998, (play) Remembrances of the First Colonial Settlement, 1993, A Family HIstory, Book I, 1990, Book II, 2006; contbg. author: Erziehungsstaaten, 1998; editor Port Arrow Community Newsletter, 1973-84, Cow Neck Peninsula Hist. Soc. Newsletter, 1974-77, Cow Neck Peninsula Hist. Soc. Jour., 2001—; contbg. editor L.I. Forum, 1985-2004; author, prodr. (video) Port Washington into the 21st Century, 1996. Chair landmarks com. Cow Neck Peninsula Hist. Soc., Port Washington, 1980—97, trustee, 1974—77, trustee emeritus, 2005—; commr. landmarks com. Village of Port Washington North, 1983—; pres. Hist. Soc. North Hempstead, 2001—04, pres. emeritus, 2005—; mem., chairperson Hist. Landmark Preservation Comm., North Hempstead, NY, 1984—, chmn., 1991—; chairperson 1701 Roslyn Grist Mil Com., 1997—; mem. Port Washington Continuing Edn. Adv. Coun., 1988—97; co-chair Roslyn Clock Tower Com., 1994—96; mem. Preservation League of N.Y., Bigelow Soc., N.Y. Pub. Libr., W.A.R. Goodwin Soc.; grant writer Dodge House Restoration Com.; mem. orgnl. com. Landmark on Main St., 1984—90; mem. Cow Neck Peninsula Hist. Soc. Dodge House Restoration Com.; adv. bd. records Town of North Hempstead, 1994—; mem. 1998 ann. com. L.I.R.R. to Port Washington; mem. Bay Walk Nautical Arts Com., 2006—. Recipient environ. award Residents for a More Beautiful Port Washington, 1994, numerous Certs. of Appreciation, Civic award for Outstanding Cmty. Svc., Port Washington Rotary, 2001, Cert. of Appreciation, Port Washington Police Dist., 2001, Exec. Citation, Nassau County, 2001, citation N.Y. State Assembly, 2001, 07, Legis. citation Nassau County, 2001, Queens Coll. Dept. History Cert. Appreciation, 2002, Town of North Hempstead's Proclamation, 2002, 07, Cmty. Leadership award Cow Neck Peninsula Hist. Soc., 2007, State NY Office of Comptr. Proclamation, 2007. Mem.: Friends of the Arts, Friends of Planting Fields, Nat. Trust Hist. Preservation, N.Y. State Mus. Assocs., Fulbright Assn., Am. Hist. Assn. (cert. recognition 1988), Port Washington Tchrs. Assn. (v.p. 1963—64, bd. dirs. 1966—74, newsletter editor 1990—92, founder and 1st pres. ret. tchrs. chpt. 1991), Soc. for Preservation L.I. Antiquities, Assn. Pub. Historicans of N.Y. State, N.Y. State Hist. Assn., N.Y. Geneal./Biog. Soc., Residents for a More Beautiful Port Washington (Environ. Quality Recognition award 2003), Roslyn Landmark Soc., Pi Sigma Alpha, Phi Alpha Theta, Phi Beta Kappa. Home: 84 Radcliff Ave Port Washington NY 11050-1600 E-mail: geoleowms@aol.com.

WILLIAMS, GEORGE WALTON, language educator; b. Charleston, SC, Oct. 10, 1922; s. Ellison Adger and Elizabeth Simonton (Dillingham) W.; m. Harriet Porcher Simons, Nov. 28, 1953; children: George Walton Jr., Ellison Adger II, Harriet Porcher Stoney. BA, Yale U., 1947; MA, U. Va., 1949, PhD, 1957. Asst. cashier Carolina Savs. Bank, Charleston, 1949-54; asst. prof. English, Duke U., 1957-63, asso. prof., 1963-67, prof., 1967, chmn. dept. English, 1982-86, prof. emeritus, 1993—. Dir. summer inst. Commn. on English, Coll. Entrance Exam. Bd., 1962; pres. Durham Savoyards, Ltd., 1966-68, 81-82; sr. fellow Coop. Program in Humanities, Duke-U. N.C., 1969; Historiographer, Diocese of S.C., 1960-78; vis. prof. U.S. Mil. Acad., 1982-83 Author: St. Michael's, Charleston, 1751-1951, 1951, rev. edit., 2001, Image and Symbol in the Sacred Poetry of Richard Crashaw, 1963, The Craft of Printing and the Publication of Shakespeare's Plays, 1985, 5 children's books; editor: Romeo and Juliet, 1964, Complete Poetry of Richard Crashaw, 1970, Jacob Eckhard's Choirmaster's Book, 1971, Shakespeare's Speech-Headings, 1997; contbg. editor Dramatic Works of Beaumont and Fletcher, 1966-96; assoc. gen. editor Arden Shakespeare, 1996—. With US Army, 1943—45, ETO. Decorated Combat Inf. badge; recipient Outstanding Civilian Service medal Dept. Army, 1983; Guggenheim Found. fellow, 1977-78; Huntington Library fellow, 1981 Mem. MLA (com. on new variorum 1980-92, chmn. Shakespeare divsn. 1990), South Atlantic MLA (pres. 1980-81, J.H. Fisher award 2001), Southeastern Renaissance Conf. (editor 1960-70, 91-95, pres. 1973, hon. life 2002), SC Hist. Soc., Malone, Carolina Yacht Club (Charleston), St. Cecilia Soc. (Charleston), Elizabethan Club Yale U., N.Am. Guild Change Ringers, Phi Beta Kappa, Phi Kappa Phi. Home: 1 Tradd St Charleston SC 29401 Office: Duke U Dept English PO Box 90015 Durham NC 27708-0015 Office Phone: 919-684-5827.

WILLIAMS, H. THOMAS (TOM WILLIAMS), academic administrator, physicist, educator; b. Hampton, Va. BS in Physics, U. Va., 1965, PhD in Physics, 1967. NSF post-doctoral rsch. fellow Nat. Bur. Stds., 1967—69; rschr. Inst. for Theoretical Physics, U. Erlangen-Nuernberg, Germany, 1970—71; staff scientist Kaman Scis. Corp., Colorado Springs, Colo., 1971—73; mem. faculty Washington and Lee U., Lexington, Va., 1974—, Edwin A. Morris prof. physics, 1994—, chair dept. physics, 1989—2000, assoc. dean, 1986—89, chief acad. officer, provost, 2003—. Cons. Nat. Bur. Stds., 1974—86, Los Alamos Sci. Lab., 1987—93. Office: Washington and Lee Univ Lexington VA 24450 Business E-Mail: williamsh@wlu.edu.

WILLIAMS, HANK, JR., (RANDALL HANK WILLIAMS), country music singer, songwriter; b. Shreveport, La., May 26, 1949; s. Hank and Audrey Williams; m. Gwen Yeargain (div.); 1 child, Hank III; m. Becky White (div.); children: Hilary, Holly; m. Mary Jane Thomas, July 1, 1990; children: Katharine Diane, Samuel. Performer throughout US; recorded song Ain't Misbehavin'; latest albums include: Montana Cafe, 1986, Hank Live, 1987, Born to Boogie, 1987, Wild Streak, 1988, Greatest Hits III, Lone Wolf, 1990, Pure Hank, 1991, (with Clink Black) Maverick, 1992, Out of Left Field, 1993, A Tribute to My Father, 1993, (with Waylon Jennings and Ray Charles) Greatest Hits, vol. 2, 1994, Hog Wild, 1995, High Notes: Original Classic Hits Vol. 8, 1995, American Legends: Best of The Early Years, 1995, 20 Hits Special Collection Vol. 1, 1995, A.K.A. Wham Bam Sam, 1996, The Hits, 1997, The Complete Hank Williams Jr., 1999, Stormy, 1999, I'm One of You, 2003; composer All My Roudy Friends, 1993, TV film Willa, 1979 (also actor); singer in films The Dangerous Days of Kiowa Jones, 1966, Kelly's Heroes, 1970, The Moonshine War, 1970, actor A Time to Sing, 1968, Roadie, 1980, (voice) Tom Sawyer, 2000, TV series (voice) The Simpsons; author Living Proof: An Autobiography, 1979. Recipient 18 Gold albums, 5 Platinum albums, 1 Double Platinum album, Entertainer of Yr. award, Country Music Assn., 1987, 1988, Music Video of Yr. award, 1987, Entertainer of Yr. award, Acad. Country Music., 1987—89, Video of Yr. award, 1987—89, Album of Yr., 1989, Grammy award, 1990, Johnny Cash Visionary award, Country Music TV, 2006. Office: c/o Ken Levitan and Ross Schilling Vector Mgmt PO Box 120479 Nashville TN 37212 also: Curb Records 48 Music Sq E Nashville TN 37203

WILLIAMS, HAROLD MARVIN, lawyer, retired foundation, academic and federal agency administrator; b. Phila., Jan. 5, 1928; s. Louis W. and Sophie (Fox) W.; m. Nancy Englander; children: Ralph A., Susan J., Derek M. AB, UCLA, 1946; JD, Harvard Law Sch., 1949; postgrad. in law, U. So. Calif., 1955-59; DHL (hon.), Johns Hopkins U., 1987, Occidental Coll., 1997, Calif. State U., 1998. Bar: Calif. 1950. Pvt. practice, LA, 1950, 1953—55; with Hunt Food and Industries Inc., 1955-68, v.p., 1958-60, exec. v.p., 1960-68; gen. mgr. Hunt-Wesson Foods, 1964-66, pres., 1966-68, Hunt Food and Industries Inc., 1968; chmn. bd., fin. com. Norton Simon, 1968—70; prof. mgmt. UCLA, 1970-77; chmn. SEC, Washington, 1977-81; pres., CEO J. Paul Getty Trust, 1981-98, pres. emeritus; of counsel Skadden Arps et al, 1998—. Pres., dir. Special Investments Securities, Inc., 1961—66. Pub. mem. Nat. Advt. Review Bd., 1971—75; trustee Nat. Humanities Ctr., 1987—93; mem. Coun. Fgn. Rels., Com. Econ. Devel., Pres.' Com. Arts, Humanities, 1993—2001, Comm. Econ. Devel. State Calif., 1973—77; energy coord. City of LA, 1973—74; regent U. Calif., 1983—94; commn. rev. master plan higher edn. State Calif., Calif., 1985—87; co chair Calif. Citizens Commn. Higher Edn.; dir. Ethics Resource Ctr.; mem. Commn. Acad. Presidency; co-chmn. Pub. Comm. LA County Govt.; dir. Pub. Policy Inst. Calif., 1995—2003, Calif. Endowment, 1995—2004, Alliance for Coll. Ready Schs., Alliance for Excellent Edn.; chair bd. visitors UCLA Sch. Arts and Arch. 1st lt. AUS, 1951—53, Korea. Decorated Bronze Star. Mem.: State Bar Calif. Office: J Paul Getty Trust 1200 Getty Center Dr Ste 1100 Los Angeles CA 90049-1668 also: Skadden Arps Slate Meagher Flom LLP 300 S Grand Ave Ste 3400 Los Angeles CA 90071 Office Phone: 310-440-6417, 213-687-5370. E-mail: hwilliams@getty.edu.

WILLIAMS, HAROLD ROGER, economist, educator; b. Arcade, NY, Aug. 22, 1935; s. Harry Alfred and Gertrude Anna (Scharf) W.; m. Lucia Dorothy Preuschoff, Apr. 23, 1955; children: Theresa Lynn, Mark Roger. BA, Harpur Coll., SUNY, Binghamton, 1961; MA, Pa. State U., 1963; PhD, U. Nebr., 1966; postgrad., Harvard U., 1969-70. Instr., Pa. State U., 1962-63; Instr. U. Nebr., 1965-66; mem. faculty Kent State U., Ohio, 1966—, prof. econs. and internat. bus., 1972—, chmn. dept., 1974-81, dir. Internat. Bus. Program, Grad. Sch. Mgmt., 1980-86, chmn. faculty senate, 1988-89, now prof. emeritus; assoc. dean Grad. Sch. Mgmt., 1994-96; program dir. Kent State-Geneva Program, Geneva, 1996-97. Econ. cons. and adv. to numerous govt., bus. and internat. orgns. Author over 100 books and articles in field. Served with AUS, 1954-57. Grantee NSF. Mem. Am. Econ. Assn., Internat. Econs. Assn., Acad. Internat. Bus., Midwest Econ. Assn. (v.p. 1969-70), So. Econ. Assn., Phi Gamma Mu, Omicron Delta Epsilon, Beta Gamma Sigma, Phi Beta Delta. Home: 415 Suzanne Dr Kent OH 44240-1933 Office: Rm 478 Dept Econs Kent State U Kent OH 44242-0001 Office Phone: 330-672-1085. Business E-Mail: Hwilliam@kent.edu.

WILLIAMS, HELENA E., rail transportation executive; b. 1955; BA with honors, SUNY, Oneonta; JD, St. John's U. Sch. Law, 1981. Bar: New York 1982. Labor counsel Met. Transp. Authority; assoc. counsel Office of Labor Rels., NYC; chief of staff Long Island Bus (formerly Met. Suburban Bus Authority), 1986—93, pres., 1993—98; atty. Schupbach, Williams & Pavone, 1999; dep. exec. Nassau County; sr. counsel Cablevision; pres. Long Island R.R., 2007—. Named to Hall of Fame, New York Pub. Transit Assn., 1999. Office: Met Transp Authority 2 Broadway 16th Fl New York NY 10004 *

WILLIAMS, HENRY WARD, JR., lawyer, writer; b. Rochester, NY, Jan. 12, 1930; s. Henry Ward and Margaret Elizabeth (Simpson) W.; m. Barbara Dimmick; children: Edith Williams Linares, Margaret Williams Warren, Sarah Williams Farrand, Ann Williams Treacy, Elizabeth DeLancey, Victoria Maureen AB, Dartmouth Coll., 1952; LLB, U.Va., 1958. Bar: N.Y. 1959, U.S. Dist. Ct. (we. dist.) N.Y. 1959, U.S. Dist. Ct. (so. dist.) Mich. 1982, U.S. Ct. Appeals (2d cir.) 1963, U.S. Tax Ct. 1960, U.S. Supreme Ct. 1968, D.C. 1978. Ptnr. Harris, Beach & Wilcox, Rochester, 1958—78, Robinson, Williams, Angeloff & Frank, Rochester, 1979—80, Weidman, Williams, Jordon, Angeloff & Frank, Rochester, 1980—82, The Williams Law Office, Rochester, 1982—. Exec. editor Va. Law Rev., 1957-58 Chmn. Genesee Finger/Lakes Regional Planning Coun., 1973-89; majority leader Monroe County Legislature, 1967-73; councilman Town of Wheatland, N.Y., 2002—; mem. alumni coun. Dartmouth Coll., 1995-99; mem. Nat. Ski Patrol Sys.; founding dir., chair Geva Theatre. Lt. (j.g.) USN, 1952-55. Mem. ABA, N.Y. State Bar Assn., Monroe County Bar Assn. (trustee 1982-85), Landmark Soc. Western NY, Rochester Yacht Club, Royal Can. Yacht Club, Lake Yacht Racing Assn. (pres. 1985-87, hon. pres. 1988-90), Royal Ocean Racing Club, Royal Nfld. Yacht Club, Raven Soc., Order of Coif, Omicron Delta Kappa. Office: The Williams Law Office PO Box 8 Scottsville NY 14546-0008 Office Phone: 585-889-3000.

WILLIAMS, HOWARD RUSSELL, law educator; b. Evansville, Ind., Sept. 26, 1915; s. Clyde Alfred and Grace (Preston) W.; m. Virginia Merle Thompson, Nov. 3, 1942 (dec. Dec. 2000); 1 son, Frederick S.T. AB, Washington U., St. Louis, 1937; LLB, Columbia U., 1940. Bar: N.Y. 1941. With firm Root, Clark, Buckner & Ballantine, NYC, 1940-41; prof. law, asst. dean U. Tex. Law Sch., Austin, 1946-51; prof. law Columbia U. Law Sch., NYC, 1951-63; Dwight prof. Columbia Law Sch., 1959-63; prof. law Stanford U., 1963-85, Stella W. and Ira S. Lillick prof., 1968-82, prof. emeritus, 1982, Robert E. Paradise prof. natural resources, 1983-85, prof. emeritus, 1985—. Oil and gas cons. President's Materials Policy Commn., 1951; mem. Calif. Law Revision Commn., 1971-79, vice chmn., 1976-77, chmn., 1978-79 Author or co-author: Cases on Property, 1954, Cases on Oil and Gas, 1956, 5th edit., 1987, Decedents' Estates and Trusts, 1968, Future Interests, 1970, Oil and Gas Law, 8 vols., 1959-64 (with ann. supplements/rev. 1964-95), abridged edit., 1973, Manual of Oil and Gas Terms, 1957, 11th edit., 2000. Bd. regents Berkeley Bapt. Divinity Sch., 1966-67; trustee Rocky Mountain Mineral Law Found., 1964-66, 68-85. Pvt., maj. US Army, 1941—46. Recipient Clyde O. Martz Tchg. award Rocky Mountain Mineral Law Found., 1994. Mem.: Phi Beta Kappa. Democrat. Home: 360 Everett Ave Apt 4B Palo Alto CA 94301-1422 Office: Stanford U Sch Law Nathan Abbott Way Stanford CA 94305 Office Phone: 650-725-5875.

WILLIAMS, HOWARD WALTER, aerospace engineer, engineering executive; b. Evansville, Ind., Oct. 18, 1937; s. Walter Charles and Marie Louise (Bollinger) W.; m. Phyllis Ann Scofield, May 4, 1956 (div. Sept. 1970); m. Marilee Sharon Mulvane, Oct. 30, 1970; children: Deborah, Steven, Kevin, Glenn, Lori, Michele. AA, Pasadena City Coll., 1956; BSME, Calif. State U., Los Angeles, 1967; BSBA, U. San Francisco, 1978; PhD in Comml. Sci. (hon.), London Inst. Rsch., 1992. Turbojet, rocket engr. Aerojet-Gen. Corp., Azusa, Calif., 1956-59, infrared sensor engr., 1959-60, rocket, torpedo engr., 1960-66, power, propulsion mgr. propulsion divsn. Sacramento, 1967-73, high speed ship systems mgr., 1974-78, combustion, power mgr., rocket engine and energy mktg. mgr., 1979-89, dir. strategic planning, 1989-94; strategic analyst, program mgr. Pratt & Whitney Space Propulsion, West Palm Beach, Fla., 1995—2003. Mgmt. cons., 2004—. Author: (with others) Heat Exchangers, 1980, Industrial Heat Exchangers, 1985, History of Liquid Rocket Engine Development in the U.S., 1992, Aerojet: The Creative Company, 1997; co-inventor Closed Cycle Power System, 1969. Recipient Energy Innovation award U.S. Dept. Energy, 1985. Mem. AIAA (sr., Best Paper 1966), Am. Soc. Metals (organizing dir. indsl. heat exch. confs. 1985). Avocation: bicycling. *Personal philosophy: I hope to be as good a parent and grandparent as mine have been.*

WILLIAMS, HUGH ALEXANDER, JR., retired mechanical engineer, consultant; b. Spencer, NC, Aug. 18, 1926; s. Hugh Alexander and Mattie Blanche (Megginson) W.; m. Ruth Ann Gray, Feb. 21, 1950; children: David Gray, Martha Blanche Williams Heidengren. BS in Mech. Engring., NC State U., Raleigh, 1948, MS in Diesel Engring., 1950; postgrad. Inst. Mgmt., Benedictine U., Lisle, Ill., 1977. Registered profl. engr., Ill. Jr. engr.-field svc. engr. Baldwin-Lima Hamilton Corp., Ohio, 1950-52, project engr. Ohio, 1953-55, Electro-Motive divsn. Gen. Motors Corp., La Grange, Ill., 1955-58, sr. project engr., 1958-63, supr. product devel. engine design sect., 1963-86, staff engr. advanced mech. tech., 1986-87. Editor So. Engr., 1947-48; contbr. articles to profl. jours. Trustee Downers Grove San. Dist., Ill., 1965-92, pres., 1974-91, v.p., 1991-92; pres. Ill. Assn. San. Dists., 1976-77, bd. dirs., 1977-89; mem. statewide policy adv. com. Ill. EPA, 1977-79; mem. DuPage County Intergovtl. Task Force Com., 1988-92; elder Presbyn. Ch. Served with USAAC, 1945. Recipient Trustee Svc. award Ill. Assn. San. Dists., 1986, Citizens award Downers Grove Evening chpt. Kiwanis, 1991; Norfolk So. R.R. fellow, 1950. Fellow ASME (chmn. honors and awards com. 1993-96, Diesel and Gas Engine Power Divsn. Spkr. awards 1968, 84, Divsn. citation 1977, 97, Internal Combustion Engine award 1987, exec. com. Internal Combustion Engine divsn. 1981-87, 88-92, chmn. 1985-86, sec. 1988-92); mem. Soc. Automotive Engrs. (life), ASME (chmn. Soichiro Honda medal com. 1987-92, chmn. Internal Combustion Engine Award com. 1993-98), Ill. Assn. Wastewater Agys. (Outstanding Mem. award 1990, hon. mem. 1992), Raleigh Host Lions Club (pres. 1996-97), SAR (pres. Raleigh chpt. 2000-01), St. Andrew's Soc. NC, Jamestowne Soc. (1st NC co. lt. gov. 2006-07), Masons (32 degree), Sigma Pi. Republican. Achievements include patentee in field. Home: 2108 Weybridge Dr Raleigh NC 27615-5562 Personal E-mail: Hector26@aol.com.

WILLIAMS, IAN GEORGE, writer; b. Liverpool, Eng., Sept. 21, 1949; s. Edward and Margaret (Cooper) W.; m. Anora Mahmudova, Nov. 30, 2002; children: Alexander James, Ian Anton Norbek. BA with honors, Liverpool U., 1973. Speechwriter for Neil Kinnock UK Labor Party, 1987; pres. UN Corr. Assn., 1995—96, v.p., 1997—98. Author: The Alms Trade, 1989, The UN For Beginners, 1995, Deserter: Bush's War on Military Families, Veterans and His Own Past, 2004, Rum: A Social and Sociable History of the Real Spirit of 1776, 2005; contbr. chapters to books, numerous articles to mags. and profl. publs. Mem. Royal Inst. Internat. Affairs, London Press Club, Overseas Press Club (N.Y.C.). Avocations: theater, reading, bicycling, sailing. Home Phone: 917-362-1477; Office Phone: 212-686-8884. E-mail: uswarreport@igc.org.

WILLIAMS, IDA JONES, consumer and home economics educator, writer; b. Coatesville, Pa., Dec. 1, 1911; d. William Oscar and Ida Ella (Ruth) Jones; m. Charles Nathaniel Williams, Mar. 17, 1940 (dec. July 1971). BS, Hampton Inst., 1935; MA, U. Conn., Storrs, 1965. Cert. high sch. tchr., English, sci., home econs., Va., Pa. Tchr. sci. and home econs. Richmond County H.S., Ivondale, Va., 1935—36; tchr. English and home econs. Northampton County H.S., Chesapeake, Va., 1936—40, tchr. consumer and home econs. Machipongo, Va., 1940—70, Northampton Jr. H.S., Machipongo, 1970—76. Author: Starting Anew After Seventy, 1980 (plaque 1980), News and Views of Northampton County High Principals and Alumni, 1981, Great Grandmother, Leah's Legacy-Remember You're Free, 2000, History of Education for African Americans During the Segregation Period 1886 Through 1970 in Northampton County Virginia, 2007; co-author: The History of Virginia State Federation of Colored Women's Clubs, Inc., 1996; editor: Fifty Year Book 1935-1985 - Hampton Institute Class, 1985, Favorite Recipes of Ruth Family & Friends, 1986. V.p. Ea. Lit. Coun., Melfa, Va., 1987-89; active Ea. Shore Coll. Found., Inc., Melfa, 1988-2000, Gov.'s Adv. Bd. on Aging, Richmond, Va., 1992-94; instr. Ladies Cmty. Bible Class, 1976-80 (Plaque 1980); sec., treas., v.p. Hospice Support of Ea. Shore, 1980-94; mem. Northampton/Accomack Adv. Coun., 1992-94; marshall 28th anniv. commencement Ea. Shore CC, 1996; bd. dirs. Ea. Shore CC Found., 1998-2000; com. mem. Va. State Legis., 1995-2002 Named Home Econs. Tchr. of Yr., Am. Home Econs. Assn. and Family Cir., 1975, Woman of Yr., Prog. Women of E.S., 1997, Ida J. Williams scholarship in her honor, Keller Ch. Christ, 1999; recipient Jefferson award, Am. Inst. Pub. Svc., Wavy-TV-Bell Atlantic and Mattress Discounters, 1991, Nat. Sojourner Truth Meritorious Svc. award, Negro Bus. and Profl. Women's Clubs, Gavel Ea. Shore Ret. Tchrs. Assn., 1994, Gov.'s award for vol. excellence, 1994, Contribution to Edn. award, Ea. Shore Coll. Found., 1997, plaque, Southeastern Assn. Colored Women's Clubs, Inc., 2001, Leadership award, 2001, Dedicated Svc. award, Nat. Assn. Colored Women's Club, 1998, Exemplary Svc. award, 2001, Svc. award, E.S. C.C. Found., Inc., 2000, plaque 1st Black Northampton County, Ea. Shore Va. C. of C., 2002, Black Achievement award, Ebenezer A.M.E. Ch., 2003, Achievement award, Chester County Hist. Soc. of Pa., 2003, Ednl. Achievement award, Northampton County H.S. Alumni Assn., 2003, Dedicated Svc. award, S.E. Assn. Colored Women's Clubs Inc., 2003—05, Honored as Oldest Living Mem. of Ruth Family, 2006; Honored at Ceremony for Mother Ida Ella Ruth Jones at hist. road marker on Route 82, Pa., 2004, Honored at Ceremony for Uncle William Chester Ruth at historical road marker ceremony on Route 30, Pa. Hist. Mus., Salisbury Hist. Soc., 2006. Mem. AARP (Citation award 1996,

Mem. of Yr. 1997, v.p. Northampton chpt. 1998-2000), Ida J. Williams Cultural Club (formerly Progressive Women of Ea. Shore. pres. 1985-93, Gold Necklace 1993, Woman of Yr. 1997), C. of C., Univ. Women (v.p. Portsmouth br. 1985-87), Ea. Shore Ret. Tchrs. (pres. 1977-84), Dist. L Ret. Tchrs. (pres. 1989-91, chmn. legis. com. 1998, 99, 2001, chmn. edn. and scholarship com. 2001-05, Dedicated and Outstanding Svc. award 2003), Va. State Fedn. Colored Women's Club (pres. 1990-94, editor history com. 1994-96) Mem. Ch. of Christ. Avocations: crafts, travel, writing, lecturing. Home and Office: PO Box 236 14213 Lankford Hwy Eastville VA 23347-0236

WILLIAMS, J. BRYAN, lawyer; b. Detroit, July 23, 1947; s. Walter J. and Maureen June (Kay) Williams; m. Jane Elizabeth Eisele, Aug. 24, 1974; children: Kyle Joseph, Ryan Patrick. AB, U. Notre Dame, 1969; JD, U. Mich., 1972. Bar: Mich. 1972, U.S. Dist. Ct. (ea. dist.) Mich. 1972. Atty. Dickinson, Wright, PLLC (and predecessor firm), Detroit, 1972—, CEO Bloomfield Hills, Mich., 1991-2000. Pres. U.S. Law Firm Group, Inc., 2002. Mem. City of Birmingham Planning Bd., Mich. Mem.: ABA, Detroit Legal News Co. (bd. dirs. 1997—2006), Econ. Club Detroit (bd. dirs. 1996—2001), Mich. Bar Assn., Detroit Regional C. of C. (bd. dirs. 1994—2002, vice chmn. 1998—2002), Nat. Club Assn. (bd. dirs. 1994—2006, sec. 1995—97, treas. 1997—98, v.p. 1998—2002, chmn. 2002—03), Oakland Hills Country Club, Notre Dame Club Detroit (pres. 1984). Roman Catholic. Home: 993 Suffield Ave Birmingham MI 48009-1242 Office: Dickinson Wright PLLC 38525 Woodward Ave Ste 2000 Bloomfield Hills MI 48304 Office Phone: 248-433-7289. Business E-Mail: jwilliams@dickinsonwright.com.

WILLIAMS, J. LINDA, librarian; b. Bethesda, Md., June 30, 1945; d. Joseph Gordon and Annie Louise (Whitfield) DiMisa. BS in Secondary Edn., English and History, Radford U., 1966; MLS, U. Md., 1977. Cert. tchr., librarian, adminstrn., supr. Bowie State U., Md., 1987. Tchr. English, history Prince William County Pub. Schs., Woodbridge, Va., 1967—73; tchr. English Charles County Pub. Schs., LaPlata, Md., 1973—76; library media specialist St. Mary County Pub. Schs., Leonardtown, Md., 1977—84; staff specialist Md. Dept. Edn., Balt., 1985—94; supr. media and instrnl. materials Prince George's County Pub. Schs., Landover, Md., 1994—99; dir. libr. media svcs. Anne Arundel County Pub. Schs., Annapolis, Md., 1999—. Named Alumnus of Yr., Coll. Library and Info. Svcs., 1988 U. Md.; profl. devel. grantee 3M, 1981. Mem. ALA (pres.-elect 2004-05), AASL (pres. 2005-06), Md. Libr. Assn., Md. Edn. Media Assn. (pres. 1998-99), Beta Phi Mu. Office: 1657 Crofton Centre Crofton MD 21114 Personal E-mail: jw177@aol.com. Business E-Mail: lwilliams@aacps.org.

WILLIAMS, J. VERNON, retired lawyer; b. Honolulu, Apr. 26, 1921; s. Urban and W. Amelia (Olson) W.; m. Malvina H. Hitchcock, Oct. 4, 1947 (dec. May 1970); children— Carl H., Karin, Frances E., Scott S.; m. Mary McLellan, Sept. 6, 1980. Student, Phillips Andover Acad., 1937-39; BA cum laude, Amherst Coll., 1943; LL.B., Yale, 1948. Bar: Wash. 1948. Assoc. Riddell, Riddell & Hemphill, 1948-50, ptnr., 1950-95; sr. prin. emeritus Riddell Williams, P.S., Seattle, 1996—. Sec., dir. Airborne Freight Corp., 1968-79, gen. counsel, 1968-96. Chmn. March of Dimes, Seattle, 1954-55; Mem. Mayor's City Charter Rev. Com., 1968-69; chmn. Seattle Bd. Park Commrs., 1966-68; co-chmn. parks and open space com. Forward Thrust, 1966-69; dir. bd. and commrs. br. Nat. Recreation and Parks Assn., 1968-69; chmn. Gov.'s adv. com. Social and Health Services, 1972-75; Bd. dirs. Seattle Met. YMCA, 1965—, pres., 1976-79; trustee Lakeside Sch., 1971-79; mem. alumni council Phillps Andover Acad., 1970-73, Yale Law Sch., 1969-77; chancellor St. Mark's Cathedral, Seattle, 1964-2000. Served with USAAF, 1943-45. Mem. Univ. Club, Seattle Tennis Club, Birnam Wood Golf Club. Home: 2061 43rd Ave E #201 Seattle WA 98112 Office: 4500 1001 4th Ave Plz Seattle WA 98154-1065

WILLIAMS, JACK MARVIN, research chemist; b. Delta, Colo., Sept. 26, 1938; s. John Davis and Ruth Emma (Gallup) W. BS with honors, Lewis and Clark Coll., 1960; MS, Wash. State U., 1964, PhD, 1966. Postdoctoral fellow Argonne (Ill.), Nat. Lab., 1966-68, asst. chemist, 1968-70, assoc. chemist, 1970-72, chemist, 1972-77, sr. chemist, group leader, 1977—; vis. guest prof. U. Mo., Columbia, 1980, 81, 82, U. Copenhagen, 1980, 83, 85. Chair Gordon Rsch. Conf. (Inorganic Chemistry), 1980. Bd. editors: Inorganic Chemistry, 1979-96, assoc. editor, 1982-93. Crown-Zellerbach scholar, 1959-60; NDEA fellow, 1960-63; recipient Disting. Performance at Argonne Nat. Labs. award U. Chgo., 1987, Centennial Disting. Alumni award Wash. State U., 1990. Mem. AAAS, Am. Crystallographic Assn., Am. Chem. Soc. (treas. inorganic div. 1982-84), Am. Phys. Soc., Phi Beta Kappa. Office: Chemistry Div 9700 S Cass Ave Lemont IL 60439-4803

WILLIAMS, JACK RAYMOND, civil engineer; b. Barberton, Ohio, Mar. 14, 1923; s. Charles Baird and Mary Williams; m. Mary Berneice Jones, Mar. 5, 1947 (dec.); children: Jacqueline Rae, Drew Alan; m. Betty Ruth Scholfield, Nov. 9, 1990 (dec.). Student, Colo. Sch. Mines, 1942—43, Purdue U., 1944—45; BS, U. Colo., 1946. Gravity and seismograph engr. Carter Oil Co., Western U.S. and Venezuela, 1946-50; with Rock Island R.R., Chgo., 1950-80, structural designer, asst. to engr. bridges, asst. engr., 1980-82, engr. bridges system, 1963-80; sr. bridge engr. thomas K. Dyer Inc., 1980-82; v.p. Alfred Benesch & Co., 1982-96. Served with USMCR, 1943-45. Fellow ASCE (life); mem. Am. Concrete Inst., Am. Ry. Bridge and Bldg. Assn. (past pres.), Am. Ry. Engring. Assn. (hon. mem., past chmn. com. 8, Concrete and Foundations, past chmn. com. 10 concrete ties). Home: 293 Minocqua St Park Forest IL 60466-1942

WILLIAMS, JAMES A., labor union administrator; b. 1951; m. Gerrie Williams; 4 children. Elected pres., bus. mgr. Glaziers, Archtl. Metal and Glass Workers' Local 252, Phila., 1975, former co-chmn. Pension, Annuity, Health & Welfare and Vacation Funds; region gen. v.p. Union of Painters and Allied Trade, 1994—95, sec. and treas., 1995—2002, pres., 2003—. Mem. exec. council AFL-CIO, 2004—. Contbr. articles to profl. jours. Served in US Army, 1969—71, Vietnam. Decorated 2 Bronze Stars, Army Accommodation medal, Air medal; recipient Labor Man of the Yr. award, Israeli Bond Assoc., 1990, Vietnam Veterans Labor Leader of the Yr. award, 1992. Office: Internat Union Painters & Allied Trade 1750 New York Ave NW Washington DC 20006 *

WILLIAMS, JAMES ARTHUR, retired military officer, information technology executive; b. Paterson, NJ, Mar. 29, 1932; s. Charles M. and Elsie (Kretszchmar) W.; m. Barbara Widnall, June 26, 1959; children: Steven, Karen. BS, U.S. Mil. Acad.; MA in Latin Am. Studies, U. N.Mex. Commd. 2d lt. U.S. Army, 1954, advanced through grades to lt. gen.; asst. army attache U.S. Def. Attache Office, Caracas, Venezuela, 1966-72; exch. officer State-Def. Exch. Program Office of Sec. Def., Washington, 1972-74; comdr. 650th MI Group, Shape, 1974-76; dep. dir. estimates Def. Intelligence Agy., Washington, 1977-80; dep. chief staff for intelligence U.S. Army, Europe, 1980-81; dir. Def. Intelligence Agy., Washington, 1981-85; ret., 1985; v.p. PSC Corp., 1986; pres. Direct Info. Access Corp., Annandale, Va., 1987—; chmn. bd. dirs. Info. Ops. Inc., 2000—04; pres. Info Assure, Inc., Arnold, Md., 2004—. Sr. fellow Joint Forces Staff Coll., 1998; intelligence advisor Dept. Homeland Security, 2004. Bd. visitors Joint Mil. Intelligence Coll., 1996. Decorated Legion of Merit, Bronze Star with oak leaf cluster, Air medals, D.S.M., Nat. Intelligence D.S.M.; Legion of Honor (France); named Disting. Mem. Mil. Intelligence Hall of Fame. Mem. Assn. U.S. Army, Nat. Mil. Intelligence Assn. (chmn. bd. 1986—). Methodist. Office: Info Assure Inc 1298 Bay Dale Dr Ste 207 Arnold MD 21012-2815

WILLIAMS, JAMES BRYAN, banker; b. Sewanee, Tenn., Mar. 21, 1933; s. Eugene G. and Ellen (Bryan) W.; m. Betty G. Williams, July 11, 1980; children: Ellen, Elizabeth, Bryan. AB, Emory U., 1955. Pres. Peachtree Bank & Trust Co., Chamblee, Ga.; chmn. bd. First Nat. Bank & Trust Co., Augusta, Ga.; pres. Sun Banks, Inc., Orlando, Fla., Trust Co. of Ga., Atlanta; chmn. exec. com. SunTrust Banks, Inc., Atlanta; retired, 1998. Bd. dirs. The Coca-Cola Co., Atlanta, 1979-, Genuine Parts Co., Atlanta, Rollins, Inc., Ga.-Pacific Corp., Atlanta, RPC, Inc., Atlanta, Genuine Parts Co., Atlanta. Trustee Emory U.; chmn. bd. trustees Robert W. Woodruff Health Scis. Ctr.; nat. trustee Boys & Girls Clubs Am.; trustee Robert W. Woodruff Found.; trustee emeritus Westminster Schs., Atlanta. Lt. USAF, 1955-57. Mem.: Bankers Roundtable, Ga. C. of C. (dir. emeritus), Peachtree Golf Club, Augusta Country Club, Commerce Club, Capital City Club, Ocean Forest Golf Club, Piedmont Driving Club, Phi Beta Kappa, Omicron Delta Kappa. Office: SunTrust Banks Inc PO Box 4418 25 Park Pl NE Atlanta GA 30303-2900

WILLIAMS, JAMES BUCHANAN, retired surgeon; b. El Paso, Tex., May 28, 1919; s. Jasper Buchanan and Clara Belle Williams; m. Willeen Agnes Brown, May 30, 1951; children: Brenda Joyce, James Buchanan II. BS, N.Mex. A&M, State College, 1947; MD, Creighton U. Sch. Medicine, Omaha, 1951; MS in Surgery, Creighton Med. Sch., Omaha, 1956. Cert. MD Nebr., 1956, Am. Bd. Surgery, 1957. Pres. Creighton U. Surg. Soc., Omaha, 1982—84, Cook County Physician, Chgo., 1982—84. Bd. dirs. N.Mex. State U., Las Cruces, 1985—90, Creighton Med. Planning Adv. Bd., Omaha, 1981—86. First lt. U.S. Air Corps, 1942—46. Recipient Alumni Merit award, N.Mex. A&M, 1961, Outstanding Alumni award, N.Mex. State U., 1967, Alumni Merit award, Creighton U. Sch. Medicine, 1999. Master: NAACP (life); fellow: Am. Coll. Surgeons; mem.: Alpha Omega Alpha Soc. Catholic. Achievements include establishing Clara B. Williams scholarship, N.Mex. A&M, 1985; street named in his honor (Williams Ave.), 1967. Avocations: fishing, hunting.

WILLIAMS, JAMES CASE, metallurgist; b. Salina, Kans., Dec. 7, 1938; s. Luther Owen and Clarice (Case) W.; m. Joanne Rufener, Sept. 17, 1960; children: Teresa A., Patrick J. BS in Metall. Engring, U. Wash., Seattle, 1962, MS, 1964, PhD, 1968. Rsch. engr., lead engr. Boeing Co., Seattle, 1961-67; tech. staff N.Am. Rockwell Corp., Thousand Oaks, Calif., 1968-74; mgr. interdivisional tech. program N.Am. Aerospace group, 1974, program devel. mgr. structural materials, 1974-75; prof. metallurgy, co-dir. Ctr. for Joining of Materials, Carnegie-Mellon U., Pitts., 1975-81; pres. Mellon Inst., Pitts., 1981-83; dean Carnegie Inst. Tech., Carnegie-Mellon U., Pitts., 1983-88; gen. mgr. materials dept. GE Aircraft Engines, 1988-99; prof., Honda chair Ohio State U., Columbus, 1999—, dean engring., 2001—04. Bd. dirs. com. on engring. and tech. systems NRC, 1996-2001; chmn. Nat. Materials Adv. Bd., 1988-95, materials and structures com. NASA Aero. Adv. Com. 1992-97; mem. NASA Propulsion Rsch. and Tech. Com., 1997-99; mem. Materials Sci. and Engring. Study, 1986-88; bd. govs. Inst. for Mechs. and Materials, U. Calif., San Diego, 1989-95; trustee Min. Math. Sci. and Engring., Cin., 1988-99; mem. sci. adv. bd. USAF, 1996-2001; mem. materials rsch. com. Def. Advanced Rsch. Projects Agy., 1981-2000; adv. com. Divsn. Engring. and Phys. Sci., NRC, 2001-04, chair Nanotechnology Assessment com., 2005-06. Co-author: Titanium, 2003, 2d edit., 2007; co-editor: Scientific and Technological Aspects of Titanium and Titanium Alloys, 1976; contbr. numerous articles to tech. jours. Trustee Oreg. Grad. Inst. Sci. and Tech., 1988-94; cons. Cubmaster Boy Scouts Am., 1976-77. Recipient Ladd award Carnegie Inst. Tech.; Adams award Am. Welding Soc.; Boeing doctoral fellow. Fellow: TMS-AIME, Am. Soc. Metals (Disting. lectr. on materials and soc. 1997, Campbell lectr. 1999, Gold medal 1992); mem.: AIME (Leadership award 1993, App to Pract award 2002), NAE, ASM, Internat. Ti Assn. (Achievement award 2003), Alpha Sigma Mu. Republican. Episcopalian. Home: 7711 Charlotte Hull Ct New Albany OH 43054-9680 Office: Ohio State U Dept Materials Sci and Engring 143 Fontana Labs 116 W 19th Ave Columbus OH 43210 Office Phone: 614-292-7251. Business E-Mail: williams.1726@osu.edu.

WILLIAMS, JAMES EUGENE, management consultant; b. Macon, Ga., June 23, 1927; m. Linda K. Magnuson, June 23, 1984; children: Paul David, Lisa Jane Williams Robertson, Philip Alan, Gail Ellen Williams Feeney, Amanda Allen Thompson, Jason Douglas Allen, Joel Winston Allen BS in Aero. Engring., Iowa State Coll., 1950. Engr., Robins AFB, Ga., 1950-54, Hdqrs. USAF, Washington, 1954-61; dep. asst. sec. Office Asst. Sec. Air Force, Washington, 1961-85; dir. govt. bus. policy Northrop Corp., Washington, 1986-88; pvt. practice mgmt. cons. Chandler, Ariz., 1988—. Co-founder The Williams Inst. for Ethics and Mgmt., Tempe, 1993—. Recipient Presdl. Meritorious Exec. award, 1981, Presdl. Disting. Exec. award, 1982. Home: 955 E Knox Rd Unit 129 Chandler AZ 85225 Personal E-mail: LJWMS@aol.com.

WILLIAMS, JAMES FRANCIS, JR., religious organization administrator; b. Coffeyville, Kans., June 20, 1938; s. James Francis and Sarah Kathryn (Tavenner) W.; m. Alice Carol Kinney, June 1, 1963; children: James F. III, Todd Alexander, Leslie. BA, So. Meth. U., 1960; ThM, Dallas Theol. Sem., 1964; HHD, U. Tex., 1988. Ordained min. N.W. Presbyn. Ch., 1967. Campus dir. Campus Crusade for Christ, Dallas, 1961-64, area dir. various North Tex. locations, 1964-68; dir. music campus Crusade for Christ, Arrowhead, Calif., 1967-71; regional dir. Campus Crusade for Christ, 1968-71, nat. dir. tng. U.S., 1971-72; founder, min. at large Probe Ministries, Internat., Dallas, 1973—, pres., 1973—98. Dir. music Campus Crusade for Christ, Arrowhead, Calif., 1967-71. Soloist, chorus Dallas Opera, 1982-84. Named one of Outstanding Young Men in Am. Dallas Jaycees, 1965. Mem. Evangelical Christian Ch. Office: Probe Ministries 1900 Firman Dr Ste 100 Richardson TX 75081-6796 Office Phone: 972-480-0240.

WILLIAMS, JAMES FRANKLIN, II, dean, librarian; b. Montgomery, Ala., Jan. 22, 1944; s. James Franklin and Anne (Wester) W.; m. Madeline McClellan, Jan. 1966 (div. May 1988); 1 child, Madeline Marie; m. Nancy Allen, Aug. 1989; 1 child, Audrey Grace. BA, Morehouse Coll., 1966; MLS, Atlanta U., 1967. Reference libr. Wayne State U. Sci. Libr., Detroit, 1968-69; document delivery libr. Wayne State U. Med. Libr., Detroit, 1969-70, head of reference, 1971-72, dir. med. libr. and regional med. libr. network, 1972-81, regional dir., 1975-82; assoc. dir. of librs. Wayne State U., 1981-88; dean librs. U. Colo., Boulder, 1988—. Bd. regents Nat. Libr. Medicine, Bethesda, Md., 1978-81; bd. dirs. Denver Art Mus., 1997—, pres. 1999—; bd. dirs. Ctr. Rsch. Librs., 1998—; pres. Big Twelve Plus Libr. Consortium, 2000; bd. dirs. Coun. on Librs. and Info. Resources. Mem. editl. bd. Portal: Libraries and the Academy; contbr. articles to profl. jours., chpts. to books; book editor and author. Bd. dirs. Educom, 1997-98, Boulder Cmty. Hosp., 2000—. Subject of feature interview in centennial issue Am. Librs. jour., 1976. Mem. ALA (Visionary Leader award 1988, Melvil Dewey medal 2002), Portal (editl. bd.), Assn. Rsch. Librs. (bd. dirs. 1994-96, 2000-03), Boulder C. of C. (bd. dirs.). Avocations: bicycling, travel, fishing. Office: U Colo Office Dean Librs PO Box 184 Boulder CO 80309-0184 Office Phone: 303-492-7511. Business E-Mail: james.williams@colorado.edu.

WILLIAMS, JAMES HENRY, JR., mechanical engineer, educator, consultant; b. Newport News, Va., Apr. 4, 1941; s. James H. Williams and Margaret L. (Holt) Mitchell; children: James Henry III, Mariella Louisa. Student, Newport News Apprentice Sch., 1965; BS, MIT, 1967, MS, 1968; PhD, Cambridge U., 1970. Sr. design engr. Newport News (Va.) Shipyard, 1960-70; asst. prof. mech. engring. MIT, 1970-74, assoc. prof., 1974-81, prof., 1981—2000, duPont prof., 1973, Edgarton prof., 1974-76, prof. writing and humanistic studies, 2000—. Cons. in field. Contbr. articles on stress analysis, materials and nondestructive testing to profl. jours. Named Prof. of Tchg. Excellence, Sch. Engring., 1991, C.F. Hopewell faculty fellow, 1993; recipient Charles F. Bailey Bronze medal, 1961, Silver medal, 1962, Gold medal, 1963, Baker award, 1976. Mem. ASME, Am. Soc. Nondestructive Testing, Nat. Tech. Assn. Office: MIT Room 3-360 77 Massachusetts Ave Rm 3-360 Cambridge MA 02139-4307 Office Phone: 617-253-2221. Business E-Mail: jhwill@mit.edu.

WILLIAMS, JAMES LEE, finance company executive; b. Tampa, Fla., Nov. 5, 1941; s. Donald Clark and Nell (Medlin) W.; m. Linda Taylor, Dec. 28, 1968; children: Donald Clark II, Taylor Lee. AA, St. Petersburg Jr. Coll., Fla., 1965; BS, Fla. State U., 1967. Mgmt. Ryder Truck Lines, Jacksonville, Fla., 1967—69; dist. mgr. underwriting divsn. U.S. Leasing Corp., Dallas, 1969—73; area v.p. Mfrs. Hanover Leasing Corp., Houston and London, 1973—79; v.p. corp. fin. Underwood Neuhause & Co. Inc., Houston, 1979—81; chmn., CEO 1st City Leasing Corp., Houston, 1981—85; mng. dir. capital markets 1st City Bancorp., Houston, 1985—89; mng. dir. fin. svcs. M.P.S.I. Sys. Inc., Dallas, 1989—90; pres., CEO Strategic Decisions Holdings Corp., Dallas, 1990—92; sr. mng. dir. Williams and Assocs., 1992; pres. Global Svcs. Capital Corp., Houston, 1993—96; v.p., dist. CFO Ikon Hou Adminstrv. Svc. Ctr., Houston, 1997—98; CFO Insync Internet Svcs., Houston, 1998—99, Walkabout Software, 1999—2001; pres. BancLeasing, Inc., 2001—03; mng. dir. Global Svcs., Houston, 2003—04; exec. dir. SIRE-Therapeutic Equestrian Ctrs., 2004—. Served with USN, 1959-62. Mem. Equipment Leasing Assn. (fed. govt. rels. com. 1984-88, 95—), Tex. Assn. Equipment Lessors (bd. dirs. 1985-89), Greater Houston Partnership (Arabian horse and Announcer's com., Houston Livestock Show and Rodeo), Houston Ctr. Club (bd. dirs. 1985-89), Lakeside Racquet Club (athletic com. 1986-89), Forum Club Houston. Republican. Presbyterian. Avocations: golf, jogging, swimming. Office: SIRE 24161 Spring Dr Hockley TX 77447

WILLIAMS, JAMES M., foundation administrator; BS in engring., U. Mich.; MBA in fin., U. Chgo. Mgr. pension asset mgmt. dept. Ford Motor Co.; pres. Harbor Capital Advisors, Harbor family of mutual funds; v.p., chief investment officer J. Paul Getty Trust, LA, 2002—. Office: J Paul Getty Trust 1200 Getty Ctr Dr Los Angeles CA 90049-1679 Office Phone: 310-440-7300.

WILLIAMS, JAMIE GAYE, medical transcriptionist; d. James Clayton and Becky Gaye Chambers; m. Dereck Chad Williams; children: Dylan Sloan Thomas, Montana Nicole. Degree in Med. Transcription, Internat. Bus. Coll., Lubbock, Tex., 2001. Registered birth registrar Tex. Atty. Gen., 2006. Technician Payne Family Pharmacy, Floydada, Tex., 1996—99; med. transcriptionist W. J. Mangold Meml. Hosp., Lockney, Tex., 2001—. Coord. fundraising Relay for Life, Tex., 2001—06, Am. Cancer Soc., Tex., 2007, Mar. of Dimes, Tex., 2006. Recipient Five Star award, State Tex., 2005. Mem.: Am. Acad. Med. Transcriptionists. Baptist. Avocations: going to the lake, golf, travel, livestock shows. Office: W J Mangold Meml Hosp 320 North Main St PO Box 37 Lockney TX 79241 Home Phone: 806-983-3553.

WILLIAMS, JANICE H., business executive; d. William Leroy and Mamie Louise Abernathy; m. Ruben J. Williams, Sr., 1966; children: Ruben J. Williams, Jr., Chauncey J., Anjalon D.K. Assoc. Degree, Davenport Bus. Sch., 1981; Degree, Grand Rapids Jr. Coll., 1981; Bachelor Degree, Davenport Bus. Sch., 1987; Divinity Cert., Oral Roberts U., 1998. Cert. personal ins. Inst. Cert., 1976, comml. ins. Inst. Cert., 1977. Exec. sec. Christman Constrn., Grand Rapids, Witmark Co., Grand Rapids; underwriter St. Paul Ins., Grand Rapids; asst. underwriter Aetna Ins., Grand Rapids; exec. sec. Spartan Stores, Grand Rapids; investigator Ford Motor Credit, Grand Rapids; pres., CEO Lakeside Orgn., Inc., Grand Rapids. Reporter St. Paul Ins., Grand Rapids, 1982—84; employment cons. Lakeside Orgn., Inc., 1994—2004; Power Point videographer Chrisman Constrn., Grand Rapids, 1999—2000. Amb., task force mem., vol. 4-H Mich. State U., 1990—2002; adult literacy trainer Kent County Lit. Coun., Mich., 1992—96; charter mem., fin. supporter Trail Blazer Girl Scouts, Grand Rapids, 1996—. Recipient Booker T. Washington Vol. Svc. to Children award, Kent County Child Abuse and Neglect, 1993, Vol. Svc. award, Nat. Assn. Negro Bus. Assn., 1994. Mem.: Cambridge England Adv. Coun. (hon.), Historic Mount Vernon Legacy (leader 2002—05), Girl Scouts of Am. (life). Avocations: poetry reading, golf, sewing, photography. Home: 2240 Delange Dr SE Grand Rapids MI 49506

WILLIAMS, JASON CHANDLER, professional basketball player; b. Belle, W.Va., Nov. 18, 1975; s. Terry Williams; m. Denika Williams; 2 children. Student, U. Fla. Guard Sacramento Kings NBA, 1998—2001, Memphis Grizzlies, 2001—05, Miami Heat, 2005—. Named Schick All-Rookie First Team, 1998—99. Mailing: The HEAT Group 601 Biscayne Blvd Miami FL 33132

WILLIAMS, JATIKA, social worker, educator; b. LA, Apr. 23, 1975; d. Byron Eugene and Macomie Williams. B of Social Work, Calif. State U., LA; MSW, Calif. State U., Long Beach. Tchr. LA Unified Sch. Dist., 2000—07; social worker Jasmine Ctrs., Inc., Inglewood, Calif., 2004—07, LA County Dept. Children and Family Svcs., 2007—. Mem.: Phi Delta Gamma, Golden Key Honor Soc.

WILLIAMS, JEFFERY LYNN, secondary school educator, consultant, writer; b. Zanesville, Ohio, Sept. 17, 1965; s. Barbara June and Glenn Eugene Harris (Stepfather), Jeffrey James Williams; life ptnr. William Don LaRiccia. BS in Edn., Ohio State U., 1990; Med, John Carroll U., Ohio, 2003. Cert. Tchr. Ohio Dept. of Edn., 2006. Tchr. Whitehall (Ohio) City Schools, 1990—93, Chagrin Falls (Ohio) Exempted Village Sch. Dist., 1993—2000; K-12 dist. literacy tchr. leader and reading recovery tchr. Solon (Ohio) City Schs., 2000—; adj. prof. Ashland (Ohio) U., 2001—. Ednl. cons. Solon (Ohio) City Schs., 1998—. Siri adv. com. Ohio Dept. Edn., Columbus, 2001—04. Sgt. US Army, 1984—86. Recipient Tchr. of Yr., Chagrin Falls Schs., 1998, Tchr. of Month, Cuyahoga County Edn. Svc. Ctr., 1998. Mem.: Internat. Reading Assn., Reading Recovery Coun. of N.Am., Golden Key Nat. Honor Soc., Pi Lambda Theta Nat. Honor Soc. (Outstanding Excellence award 2007), Phi Kappa Phi, Phi Delta Kappa. Liberal. Roman Catholic. Achievements include development of Literacy Learning. Avocations: travel, writing, genealogy, cross country skiing, cooking. Home: 18844 Rivers Edge Dr Chagrin Falls OH 44023 Office: Solon City Schs 6795 Solon Blvd Solon OH 44139 Home Phone: 440-543-0579; Office Phone: 440-349-7757 5721. Business E-Mail: jwilliams@solonboe.org.

WILLIAMS, JEROME DENEAN, advertising educator; b. Phila., Jan. 11, 1947; s. Jerome Jay and Gloria Elizabeth (Dixon) W.; m. Lillian Regina Harrison, June 21, 1969; children: Denean, Derek, Daniel, Dante, Dachia. BA, U. Pa., 1969; MS, Union Coll., 1975; PhD, U. Colo., 1986. Publicist Gen. Electric Co., Phila., 1969-70, Schenectady, NY, 1970-71, sr. publicist, 1971-75, supr., 1975-78; mgr. pub. info. Solar Energy Research Inst., Golder, Colo., 1978-80; v.p. Sierra Services, Arvada, Colo., 1980-87; asst. prof. Pa. State U., University Park, 1987. F.J. Heyne Centennial prof. comm. Dept. Advertising U. Tex., Austin, prof. Ctr. for African and African American Studies. Co-editor: Diversity in Advertising: Broadening the Scope of Research Directions. Mem. Acad. Mktg. Sci., Am. Acad. Advt., Am. Mktg. Assn. (mem. bd. trustees), Am. Psychol. Assn., Assn. for Consumer Research. Jehovah'S Witness. Avocation: running. Office: U Tex at Austin Advt Dept 1 University Station A1200 Austin TX 78712 Office Phone: 512-471-7302. E-mail: Jerome.williams@mail.utexas.edu. *

WILLIAMS, J.(JOHN) RODMAN, theologian, educator, clergyman; b. Clyde, NC, Aug. 21, 1918; s. John Rodman and Odessa Lee (Medford) W.; m. Johanna SerVaas, Aug. 6, 1949; children: John, Lucinda Lee, David Bert. AB, Davidson Coll., 1939; BD, Union Theol. Sem., 1943, ThM, 1944; PhD, Columbia U., 1954. Ordained to ministry Presbyn. Ch., 1943. Chaplain USNR, 1944—46; chaplain, assoc. prof. philosophy Beloit Coll., 1949—52; pastor First Presbyn. Ch., Rockford, Ill., 1952—59; prof. systematic theology and philosophy of religion Austin Presbyn. Theol. Sem., 1959—72; prof. Christian doctrine, pres. Melodyland Sch. Theology, Anaheim, Calif., 1972—82; prof. systematic theology Regent U.; Virginia Beach, Va., 1982—. Author: Contemporary Existentialism and Christian Faith, 1965, The Era of the Spirit, 1971, The Pentecostal Reality, 1972, Ten Teachings, 1974, The Gift of the Holy Spirit Today, 1980, Renewal Theology, Vol. 1, God, the World, and Redemption, Vol. 2, 1988, Salvation, the Holy Spirit and Christian Living, Vol. 3, 1990, The Church, the Kingdom, and Last Things, 1992, Renewal Theology, 3 vols. in one, 1996. Home: 608 Fleet Dr Virginia Beach VA 23454-7344 *There is only one ultimate "Who", Jesus of Nazareth, in whose light all the rest of us are but dimly burning candles.*

WILLIAMS, JOBETH, actress; b. Houston, Dec. 6, 1948; m. John Pasquin, Mar. 14, 1982; children: Nick, Will. Grad., Brown U. Appeared in plays A Coupla White Chicks Sitting Around Talking, 1980, Gardenia, 1982, Idiot's Delight, 1986, Cat on a Hot Tin Roof, 1993; films include Kramer vs. Kramer, 1979, The Dogs of War, 1980, Stir Crazy, 1980, Poltergeist, 1982, Endangered Species, 1982, The Big Chill, 1983, American Dreamer, 1984, Teachers, 1984, Desert Bloom, 1986, Poltergeist II, 1986, Memories of Me, 1988, Welcome Home, 1989, Switch, 1991, Dutch, 1991, Stop! Or My Mom Will Shoot, 1992, Me, Myself and I, 1993, Wyatt Earp, 1994, Parallel Lives, 1994, Little City, 1997, Just Write, 1997, Jungle 2 Jungle, 1997, When Danger Follows You Home, 1997, Justice, 1998, Repossessed, 2002, The Rose Technique, 2002, Into the Fire, 2004, Fever Pitch, 2005, Crazylove, 2005, In the Land of Women, 2007; TV films include Fun and Games, 1980, The Big Black Pill, 1981, Adam, 1983 (Emmy award nominee, Golden Globe award nominee), The Day After, 1983, Kids Don't Tell, 1985, Adam: His Song Continues, 1986, Murder Ordained, 1987, Baby M, 1988 (Emmy award nominee, Golden Globe award nominee), My Name is Bill W., 1989, Child in the Night, 1990, Victim of Love, 1991, Jonathan: The Boy Nobody Wanted, 1992, Sex, Love and Cold Hard Cash, 1993, Chantilly Lace, 1993, Voices from Within, 1994, Lemon Grove, 1994, Parallel Lives, 1994, Voices from Within, 1994, Season of Hope, 1994, Ruby Jean and Joe, 1996, Breaking Through, 1996, It Came From the Sky, 1998, A Chance of Snow, 1998, Justice, 1999, Jackie's Back!, 1999, Trapped in a Purple Haze, 2000, The Ponder Heart, 2001, Homeward Bound, 2002, 14 Hours, 2005, Into the Fire, 2005, Stroller Wars, 2006; TV series include The Guiding Light, 1977-81, Somerset, 1975-76, (voice) Fish Police, 1992, John Grisham's The Client, 1995-96, (voice) Stories from My Childhood, 1998, Payne, 1999; co-exec. prodr.: (TV movie) Bump in the Night, 1991; dir. (films): On Hope, 1994 (Acad. award nominee for Best Live Action Short Film 1995), Winona's Web, 2001. *

WILLIAMS, JODY, political organization administrator; b. Rutland, Vt., Oct. 9, 1950; BA, U. Vt.; MA, Sch. Internat. Tng.; MA in Internat. Studies, Johns Hopkins U.; PhD (hon.), Briar Cliff Coll., Marlboro Coll., U. Vt., Williams Coll., Pa. State U., Royal Mil. Coll. Canada, Wesleyan U., Franklin Pierce Coll., Regis U., Shensu U., Rockhurst U., Gustaus Adolphus Coll., Lehman Coll., Smith Coll. Former coord. Nicaragua-Honduras Edn. Project, Washington; assoc. dir. Children's Project Med. Aid El Salvador, L.A./El Salvador, 1986—92; founder Internat. Campaign to Ban Landmines Vietnam Vet. Found. Am., Washington, 1991—; amb. Internat. Campaign to Ban Landmines, Alexandria, Va., 1997—; founder Sponsor a Mine-Detection Dog program, 1998—. Patron Internat. Peace Found., Vienna, 1998—; adv. com., arms divsn. Human Rights Watch, 1998—; adv. com. Code of Conduct on the Arms Trade, Arias Found. for Peace and Human Progress, 1998—, Rep. Eddie Bernice Johnson's Women for World Peace Fund, 2003—; disting. vis. prof. social work and global justice Univ. Houston, Tex., 2004—. Contbr. articles to profl. jours, co-author: After the Guns Fall: The Enduring Legacy of Landmines, 1995. Founder Nobel Women's Initiative, 2006. Co-recipient Nobel Peace Prize, 1997; named one of 100 Most Powerful Women in World, Forbes Mag., 2004; recipient Distinguished Peace Leadership award, Nuclear Age Peace Found., 1998, Fiat Lux award, Clark U., Hollywood Humanitarian award, 2002. Address: ICBL 33 rue de Bruxelles 1470 Genappe Belgium E-mail: williams@icbl.org.

WILLIAMS, JOHN ANDREW, physiology researcher, educator; b. Des Moines, Aug. 3, 1941; s. Harold Southall and Marjorie (Larsen) W.; m. Christa A. Smith, Dec. 26, 1965; children: Rachel Jo, Matthew Dallas. BA, Cen. Wash. State Coll., 1963; MD, PhD, U. Wash., Seattle, 1968. Staff fellow NIH, Bethesda, Md., 1969-71; research fellow U. Cambridge, Eng., 1971-72; from asst. to prof. physiology U. Calif., San Francisco, 1973-87; prof. physiology, chair dept. physiology, prof. internal medicine U. Mich., Ann Arbor, 1987—. Mem. gen. medicine study sect. NIH, Bethesda, 1985-88, NIDDK, DDK-C study sect., 1991-95. Contbr. numerous articles to profl. jours.; editor Am. Jour. Physiology: Gastrointestinal Physiology, 1985-91; assoc. editor Jour. Clin. Investigation, 1997-01; sect. editor Ann. Rev. Physiology, 2001-05. Trustee Friends Sch. in Detroit, 1992—2000. Grantee, NIH, 1973—. Fellow Am. Assn. Advancement Sci.; mem. Am. Physiol. Soc. (Hoffman LaRoche prize 1985, mem. coun. 1996-99, pres. 2003-04), Am. Soc. Cell Biology, Am. Soc. Clin. Investigation, Am. Gastroenterology Assn., Am. Pancreatic Assn. (pres. 1985-86), Assn. Am. Physicians. Democrat. Home: 1115 Woodlawn Ave Ann Arbor MI 48104-3956 Office: Dept Molecular & Intergrative Physiology Univ of Mich Med Sch Ann Arbor MI 48109 Business E-Mail: jawillms@umich.edu.

WILLIAMS, JOHN EDWARD, lawyer; b. Atlanta, May 21, 1946; s. Edward Carl and Mary E. (Griffin) W.; m. Kristin Forsberg, May 22, 1976; children: Alexandra, Courtney, Charles. BA, Yale U., 1968; JD, U. Va., 1974; LLM in Taxation, Georgetown U., 1977. Bar: Va. 1974, D.C. 1975, U.S. Dist. Ct. D.C. 1975, U.S. Tax Ct. 1975, U.S. Ct. Appeals (D.C. cir.) 1975, U.S. Supreme Ct. 1977. Law clk. to Judge Charles R. Richey U.S. Dist. Ct. (D.C. dist.), 1974-75; assoc. Patton, Boggs & Blow, Washington, 1975-78, Cadwalader, Wickersham & Taft, Washington, 1978-81; asst. to the commr. IRS, Washington, 1981-84; tax counsel Ropes & Gray, Washington, 1984-86; ptnr. David & Hagner, P.C., Washington, 1986-90, Winston & Strawn, Washington, 1990-2000; atty. Law Offices of John E. Williams, 2000—. Editl. bd. U. Va. Law Review, 1972-74; mem. Jud. Conf. of D.C. Cir., 1978, 82, 85, 87, 92. With USAR, 1968—74. Recipient IRS Commissioner's award, 1984. Mem. ABA (tax sect., chmn. tech. subcom., adminstrv. practice com. 1986-88), Met. Club, Yale Club N.Y.C., Heritage Hunt Club. Office: 3213 Duke St Ste 601 Alexandria VA 22314 Office Phone: 703-838-2939. Business E-Mail: johnedwardwilliams@earthlink.net.

WILLIAMS, JOHN HORTER, civil engineer, energy industry executive; b. Havana, Cuba, Aug. 17, 1918; s. Charles P. and Alice Magruder (Dyer) W.; m. Emily Alice Ijams, June 6, 1942 (dec.); children: John H., Burch I., S. Miller; m. Joanne Harwell Simpson., Feb. 1, 1975. BS, Yale U., 1940. Registered profl. engr., Okla., Minn. With The Williams Cos. Inc., Tulsa, 1940-42, 46-50, pres., dir., 1950-70, chmn., chief exec. officer, 1971-78, now hon. dir. Bd. dirs. Apco Argentina, Inc., Unit Corp.; hon. bd. dirs. Willbros Group, Inc. Served with USNR, 1942-46. Decorated Order of Condor of Andes (Bolivia); named Okla. Hall of Fame, 1977; recipient Outstanding Okla. Oil Man awad Okla.-Kans. Oil and Gas Assn., 1982, Disting. Svc. award Nat. Petroleum Hall of Fame, 1985; inducted into Okla. Commerce and Industry Hall of Honor, 1986, Tulsa Hall of Fame, 1993. Mem. ASCE, Yale Engring. Assn. Office: The Williams Cos Inc Ste 4500 One Williams Ctr Tulsa OK 74172

WILLIAMS, JOHN JAMES, JR., architect; b. Denver, July 13, 1949; s. John James and Virginia Lee (Thompson) W.; m. Mary Serene Morck, July 29, 1972. BArch, U. Colo., 1974. Registered architect, Colo., Calif., Idaho, Va., Utah, N.Mex., Wyo., Ohio, Nebr., Mo., Ga., Ariz., Tex. Project architect Gensler Assoc. Architects, Denver, 1976, Heinzman Assoc. Architects, Boulder, Colo., 1977, EZTH Architects, Boulder, 1978-79; prin. Knudson/Williams PC, Boulder, 1980-82, Faber, Williams & Brown, Boulder, 1982-86, John Williams & Assocs., Denver, 1986-97; John Williams Architecture P.C., 1997—. Panel chmn. U. Colo. World Affairs Conf.; vis. faculty U. Colo. Sch. Architecture and Planning, Coll. Environ. Design, 1986-91; dean's adv. bd. Coll. Arch. and Planning, 2000-04. Author (with others) State of Colorado architect licensing law, 1986. Commr. Downtown Boulder Mall Commn., 1985-88; bd. dirs. U. Colo. Fairway Club, 1986-88; mem. Gov.'s. Natural Hazard Mitigation Coun., State of Colo., 1990. Recipient Tchg. Honorarium, U. Colo. Coll. Architecture and Planning, 1977-80, 88, Excellence in Design and Planning award City of Boulder, 1981-82, Citation for Excellenc, WOOD Inc., 1982, 93, Disting. Profl. Svc. award Coll. Environ. Design U. Colo., 1988, James Sudler Svc. award AIA, Denver, 1998 Mem. AIA (sec. 1988, bd. dirs. Colo. North chpt. 1985-86, chair Colo. govtl. affairs com. 1995-98, Design award 1993, 2001, pres. 1990, sec. Colo. chpt. 1988, ednl. fund Fisher I traveling scholar 1988, state design conf. chair 1991, North chpt. Design award 1993, treas. Denver chpt. 1998, v.p. 1999, pres. edn. Colo. chpt. 2001, Disting. Svc. award Colo. chpt. 2001, Pres. Svc. award, 2004), Architects and Planners of Boulder (v.p. 1982), Nat. Coun. Architect Registration Bd., Nat. Golf Found. (sponsor), Kappa Sigma (chpt. pres. 1970). Avocations: golf, political history, fitness and health. Home: 1031 Turnberry Cir Louisville CO 80027-9594 Office: John Williams Architecture PC 350 Interlocken Blvd Ste 340 Broomfield CO 80021 Office Phone: 303-295-6190. Business E-Mail: johnw@jwarchitecture.com.

WILLIAMS, JOHN LEE, lawyer; b. Nashville, Dec. 23, 1942; s. Leslie Elwood and Gladys Mae (Ridings) W.; m. Norma Jean Givens, May 27, 1967; 1 child, Jacob Andrew. BA, Tenn. Technol. U., 1964; JD, U. Tenn., 1967. Bar: Tenn 1967. Ptnr. Porch, Peeler & Williams, Waverly, Tenn., 1967-78, Porch, Peeler, Williams & Thomason, Waverly, 1978—; asst. dist. atty. 23d Jud. Cir. Ct. Tenn., 1972-74; judge Ct. Gen. Sessions of Humphreys County, Tenn., 1978-82. County atty. Humphreys County, 1968—72, 1982—86, 1994—; city atty. City of Waverly, 1978—, City of McEwen, Tenn., 1978—, City of Lobelville, Tenn., 1985—89; gen. counsel Meriwether Lewis Elec. Coop., Centerville, Tenn., 1980—. State legal counsel Tenn. Jaycees, 1970; treas., sec. Humphreys County Dem. Exec. Com., 1978-2001; chmn. Humphreys County Election Comm., 1968-72. Col. U.S. Army ret. Mem.: Humphreys County Bar Assn. (pres. 1978—), Tenn. Bar Assn. (ho. of dels.), Masons (master 1985, 1999, 2005). Home: 1739 Ogden Rd Mc Ewen TN 37101 Home Phone: 931-296-1369; Office Phone: 931-296-7741. Business E-Mail: john.williams@porchpeeler.com.

WILLIAMS, JOHN N., dean, dental educator; BA with honors, Transylvania U., Lexington, KY, 1974; DMD Dental-Gen. Practice, U. Louisville, 1980, MBA, 1987. Asst. u. provost U. Louisville, 1988—91; dean U. Louisville Sch. Dentistry, 1999—2005; assoc. dean for ednl. programs U. of Louisville Sch. of Dentistry, 1991—98; prof. dept. periodontics, endontics and dental hygiene U. Louisville Sch. Dentistry; dean U. N.C. Sch. Dentistry, Chapel Hill, NC, 2005—. Mem. editl. bd. Jour. Contemporary Dental Practice. Mem.: Am. Acad. Devel. Medicine and Dentistry. Avocations: boating, classical & choral singing. Office: Sch Dentistry NC Univ CB #7450 1090 Old Dental Bldg Chapel Hill NC 27599-7450 Office Phone: 919-966-2731. Business E-Mail: john_williams@dentistry.unc.edu.

WILLIAMS, JOHN TAYLOR, lawyer; b. Cambridge, Mass., June 19, 1938; s. Paul Merchant Taylor and Audrey Arlene Dowling; m. Leonora Hall; children: Caleb, Jared, Nathaniel. AB, Harvard U., 1960; LLB, U. Pa., 1965. Bar: Mass. 1965, U.S. Dist. Ct. Mass., U.S. Ct. Appeals (1st cir.), U.S. Supreme Ct. Corp. loan officer State St. Bank & Trust Co., Boston, 1960-62; from assoc. to ptnr. Haussermann, Davison & Shattuck, Boston, 1965-83; ptnr. Palmer & Dodge, Boston, 1983—2021, Hill & Barlow, Boston, 2001—02; prin. Fish & Richardson PC, Boston, 2003—. Lectr. on 1st amendment, copyright, pub. and intellectual property law for Practicing Law Inst., Mass. CLE/New Eng. Law Inst., Nat. Assn. Archivists, Boston Patent Lawyers Assn., others; apptd. mem. U.S. Courthouse Arts Comm., U.S. State Dept. Del. to China, 1993; mem. lit. panel Nat. Endowment for the Arts, 1990, 91, 94, mem. presentation and creation panel, 1996. Author: (screenplay) Rolf in the Woods, 1987, (screenplay) Toussaint L'Overture, 1989, (with E. Gabriel Perle) Perle and Williams on Publishing Law, 2 vols. (revised annually); contbg. author: Legal Problems in Book Publishing, 1981, 84, 86; contbg. editor: Small Voices and Great Trumpets: Minorities and the Media, 1980. Bd. dirs. City of Cambridge Arts Coun., 1973-83, chmn., 1981-83; bd. dirs. Ploughshares Inc., 1988-89; trustee Arthur Fiedler Meml. Inc., 1983—87, Boston Philharm. Orch., 1983-85, Petra Found., 1988—2003; trustee, gen. counsel Inst. Contemporary Art, 1970-92; mem. corp. Mass. Gen. Hosp., 1985—; mem. Patent and Tech Conflicts Coms., 1985-91; clk. John F. Kennedy Meml. Commn. Inc., 1986—; trustee, co-chair Provincetown Fine Arts Work Ctr., 1992—. Named one of Boston's top lawyers, Boston Mag., 2002, Mass. Super Lawyers, 2006, 2007; recipient Learned Hand award, Am. Jewish Com., 2005. Mem. ABA (sect. patent, trademark, copyright law, chmn. com. on authors 1978-81, comms. and entertainment law forum coms.), Boston Bar Assn. (former chmn. com. on delivery of legal svcs. to indigent), Lawyers' Com. for Civil Rights under Law (chmn. steering com. 1988-91), Nat. Lawyers' Com. for Civil Rights (bd. dirs. 1989—95), Tavern Club (Boston). Office: Fish & Richardson PC 225 Franklin St Boston MA 02110 Office Phone: 617-521-7820. Office Fax: 617-542-8906. Business E-Mail: jtwilliams@fr.com.

WILLIAMS, J(OHN) TILMAN, insurance company executive, real estate agent, municipal official; b. Detroit, Feb. 26, 1925; s. Aubrey and Martha (Lou) W.; m. Sally Jane Robinson, Aug. 22, 1947; children: Leslie Ann, Martha Lou. BS in Agr, Mich. State U., 1951. Pres. Satellite Ins. Brokerage, Garden Grove, Calif., 1959—. Pres. Satellite Real Estate, Satellite Mortgage & Loan Co. Mayor Garden Grove, 1976-78, re-elected, 1987, mem. coun., 1980-92, apptd. vice mayor, 1989—; mem. Ad Hoc Com. on Property Tax to Limit Govt. Spending with Spirit of 13 Initiative; elected to Orange County Dem. Cen. Com., 68th Assembly Dist., 1996; past pres. Garden Grove High Sch. Band Boosters; trustee Garden Grove Unified Sch. Dist., 2000—; Dem. candidate for Congress, 2004. With USAAF, World War II, PTO. Mem. Bd. Realtors, Ind. Ins. Agts. Assn., Orange County Esperanto Assn. (pres. 1985—), Am. Legion, VFW. Clubs: Toastmasters (Anaheim, Calif.); Fifty-Plus Sr. Citizens of Garden Grove (pres. 1986—). Lodges: Lions, Elks. Democrat. Home: 11241 Chapman Ave Garden Grove CA 92840-3301 Office: 12311 Harbor Blvd Garden Grove CA 92840-3809 Office Phone: 714-750-4333. *Service to one's fellowman and community is the greatest avocation and pleasure one can follow.*

WILLIAMS, JOHN TOWNER, composer, conductor; b. LI, NY, Feb. 8, 1932; s. John and Esther Williams; m. Barbara Ruike, 1956 (dec. 1974); children: Jennifer, Mark, Joseph; m. Samantha Winslow, 1980. Student UCLA; studied with Mario Castelnuovo-Tedesco, Los Angeles; student, Juilliard Sch.; studied with Madame Rosina Lhevinne, NYC; degree (hon.), Berklee Coll. Music, Boston, Northeastern U., Tufts U., U. So. Calif., Boston U., New Eng. Conservatory Music, Providence Coll. Pianist Columbia & Twentieth Century-Fox, 1956—; condr. Boston Pops Orch., 1980—93, laureate condr., 1993—; artist-in-residence Tanglewood Music Ctr., Boston, 1993—94. Guest condr. with orchestras including Cleveland Orch., Denver Symphony, Indianapolis Symphony, London Symphony Orch., Los Angeles Philharmonic, Montreal Orch., Philadelphia Orch., and Toronto Orch. Works include: composer (film scores) I Passed for White, 1960, Because They're Young, 1960, The Secret Ways, 1961, Bachelor Flat, 1962, Diamond Head, 1962, Gidget Goes to Rome, 1963, The Killers, 1964, John Goldfarb, Please Come Home, 1964, None But the Brave, 1965, How to Steal a Million, 1966, The Rare Breed, 1966, Not With My Wife, You Don't, 1966, The Plainsman, 1966, Penelope, 1966, A Guide for the Married Man, 1967, Valley of the Dolls, 1967 (Acad. award nominee), Fitzwilly, 1968, Sergeant Ryker, 1968, The Reivers, 1969 (Acad. award nominee), Daddy's Gone A-Hunting, 1969, Goodbye, Mr. Chips, 1969 (Acad. award nominee), The Story of A Woman, 1970, Fiddler on the Roof, 1971 (Acad. award for musical adaptation 1971), The Cowboys, 1972, The Poseidon Adventure, 1972 (Acad. award nominee), Images, 1972 (Acad. award nominee), Pete 'n' Tillie, 1972, The Paper Chase, 1973, The Long Goodbye, 1973, The Man Who Loved Cat Dancing, 1973, Cinderella Liberty, 1973 (Acad. award nominee), Tom Sawyer, 1973 (Acad. award nominee), Sugarland Express, 1974, Earthquake, 1974, The Towering Inferno, 1974 (Acad. award nominee), Conrack, 1974, Jaws, 1975 (Acad. award, Grammy award, Golden Globe award 1976), The Eiger Sanction, 1976, Family Plot, 1976, Midway, 1976, The Missouri Breaks, 1976, Raggedy Ann and Andy, 1977, Black Sunday, 1977, Star Wars, 1977 (Acad. award, 3 Grammy awards, Golden Globe award 1977), Close Encounters of the Third Kind, 1977 (2 Grammy awards, Acad. award nominee 1978), The Fury, 1978, Jaws II, 1978, Superman, 1978 (2 Grammy awards 1979), Meteor, 1979, Quintet, 1979, Dracula, 1979, "1941", 1979, The Empire Strikes Back, 1980 (2 Grammy awards, Acad. award nominee 1980), Raiders of the Lost Ark, 1981 (Grammy award, Acad. award nominee 1981), Heartbeeps, 1981, E.T., 1982 (Acad. award for best original score, 3 Grammy awards, Golden Globe award 1982), Monsignor, 1982, Yes, Giorgio, 1982 (Acad. award nominee), Superman III, 1983, Return of the Jedi, 1983 (Acad. award nominee), Indiana Jones and the Temple of Doom, 1984 (Acad. award nominee), The River, 1984 (Acad. award nominee), Space Camp, 1986, Emma's War, 1986, The Witches of Eastwick, 1987 (Acad. award nominee), Empire of the Sun, 1987 (Acad. award nominee), Jaws: The Revenge, 1987, Superman IV: The Quest for Peace, 1987, The Secret of My Success, 1987, The Accidental Tourist, 1988 (Acad. award nominee, Indiana Jones and the Last Crusade, 1989 (Acad. award nominee), Always, 1989, Born On The Fourth of July, 1989 (Acad. award nominee), Stanley and Iris, 1990, Presumed Innocent, 1990, Home Alone, 1990 (Acad. award nominee), Hook, 1991 (Acad. award nominee), JFK, 1991 (Acad. award nominee), Far and Away, 1992, Home Alone II, 1992, Jurassic Park, 1993, Schindler's List, 1993 (Acad. award 1993, Grammy award 1994), Sabrina, 1995 (Acad. award nominee for best original score 1996), Nixon, 1995 (Acad. award nominee 1996), Sleepers, 1996, Rosewood, 1997, The Lost World: Jurassic Park, 1997, Seven Years In Tibet, 1997 (Acad. award nominee), Amistad, 1997 (Acad. award nominee), Saving Private Ryan, 1998 (Acad. award nominee, Grammy award 1998), Stepmom, 1998, Star Wars Episode I: The Phantom Menace, 1999, Angela's Ashes, 1999 (Acad. award nominee, Grammy award 2000), The Patriot, 2000 (Acad. award nominee), Artificial Intelligence, 2001 (Acad. award nominee), Harry Potter and The Sorcerer's Stone, 2001 (Acad. award nominee), Minority Report, 2002, Star Wars Episode II: Attack Of The Clones, 2002, Harry Potter: The Chamber Of Secrets, 2002, Catch Me If You Can, 2002 (Acad. award nominee), Harry Potter: The Prisoner Of Azkaban, 2004, The Terminal, 2004, Star Wars Episode III: The Revenge of the Sith, 2005, War of the Worlds, 2005, Harry Potter and the Goblet of Fire, 2005, Memoirs of a Geisha, 2005 (Broadcast Film Assn. award, 2006, Best Original Score-Motion Picture, Hollywood Fgn. Press Assn., Golden Globe award) 2006, Grammy award, 2007), Munich, 2005 (Grammy award, 2007), Superman Returns, 2006; composer music for songs including:(from Sabrina, lyrics by Alan and Marilyn Bergman) Moonlight, 1995 (Acad. award nominee 1996); composer:(TV programs) Heidi, 1969 (Emmy award), Jane Eyre, 1971 (Emmyaward), Masterpiece Theatre, 1971, Malcolm in the Middle, 2000, Smallville, 2001, (main theme) Jack & Bobby, 2004, others; composer numerous concert pieces and symphonies including Jubilee 350 Fanfare for the Boston Pops, 1980, theme to the 1984 Summer OlympicGames, Liberty Fanfare, 1987; recorded numerous albums with Boston Pops Orch. including Pops in Space, That's Entertainment (Pops on Broadway), Pops on the March, Pops Aroundthe World (Digital Overtures), Aisle Seat, Pops Out of This World, Boston Pops on Stage, America, the Dream Goes On; collaborator: (with Jessye Norman) With A Song in My Heart, Swing, Swing, Swing, Unforgettable; guest condr. major orchs. including London Symphony Orch., Cleve. Orch., Phila. Orch., Toronto Orch., Montreal Orch. Served with USAF, 1952-54. Recipient several gold and platinum records Rec. Industry Assn. Am., Kennedy Ctr. Honors, John F. Kennedy Ctr. Performing Arts, 2004. Composer of over seventy-five film scores. Office: Boston Symphony Orch 301 Mass Ave Boston MA 02115 also: The Gorfaine Schwartz Agency Inc 4111 W Alameda Ave Ste 509 Burbank CA 91505-4171

WILLIAMS, JOSEPH DALTON, pharmaceutical executive; b. Washington, Pa., Aug. 15, 1926; s. Joseph Dalton and Jane (Day) W.; m. Mildred E. Bellaire, June 28, 1973; children: Terri, Daniel. BS in Pharmacy, U. Nebr., 1950; DSc (hon.), Union U., 1991, U. Nebr., 1989; LHD (hon.), Albany Coll. Pharmacy, Union U., 1980, Rutgers U., 1987, Long Island U., 1988; DSc (hon.), Phila. Coll. Pharmacy and Sci., 1988, Long Island U., 1988, Albany Coll. Pharmacy of Union U., 1991; D Human Svcs. (hon.), Caldwell Coll., 1989; LLD (hon.), Bethune-Cookman Coll., 1990, Coll. St. Elizabeth, 1990, Seton Hall U., 1990, U. Md., 1991, St. Augustine Coll., 1992. Pres. Parke-Davis Co., Detroit, 1973-76; pres. pharm. group Warner-Lambert Co., Morris Plains, NJ, 1976-77; pres. Internat. Group, 1977-79; pres., dir. Warner-Lambert Corp., 1979-80, pres., chief operating officer, 1980-84, chmn., CEO, 1985-91, chmn. exec. com., 1991-97; retired, 1997. Bd. dirs. AT&T, 1984-1997, J.C. Penny & Co., 1985-1998, Exxon Corp., 1985-1997, Rockefeller Fin. Svcs. Inc., Rockefeller and Co., Inc., 1992-1999, Eckerd Corp., 1997-2000. Trustee emeritus Columbia U. With USNR, 1943—46. Mem. Am. Pharm. Assn., Links Club, Pine Valley Golf Club, Baltusrol Golf Club, Mid Ocean Club. Office: Warner-Lambert Co 55 Madison Ave Morristown NJ 07960-7397 Office Phone: 973-285-3277.

WILLIAMS, JOYCE See BENNETT, VELMA

WILLIAMS, JUAN, news correspondent; BA in Philosophy, Haverford Coll., 1976. Editl. writer, op-ed columnist, White House corr. Washington Post, 1976—97; host, Talk of the Nation Nat. Public Radio (NPR), 2000—01, sr. nat. corr.; polit. contbr. FOX News Channel, 1997—, weekend anchor. Regular panelist, FOX News Sunday with Tony Snow FOX News Channel. Author: Eyes on the Prize: America's Civil Rights Years, 1954-1965, 1988, Thurgood Marshall: American Revolutionary, 2000, My Soul Looks Back in Wonder: Voices of the Civil Rights Experience, 2004; contbr. articles to Fortune, Atlantic Monthly, Ebony, GQ, New Republic; guest appearances Nightline, ABC, Washington Week in Review, PBS, Oprah. Office: FOX News Channel 400 N Capitol St NW Ste 550 Washington DC 20001

WILLIAMS, JUANITA ROSALIE, artist; b. Zanesville, Ohio, Aug. 7, 1933; d. Joseph Russell and Gladys Lucille (Worden) Somers; m. Roy George Williams, Feb. 16, 1952 (div. 2002); children: Karin Sue Williams Brandi, Kenneth Roy. Grad. high sch., Zanesville. Juror Bexley (Ohio) Art Guild, Capital U., 1984. One-woman shows include Collector's Gallery Columbus Mus. Fine Art, Ohio, 1972, Pomerene Fine Arts Ctr., 1991, McDonough Gallery, Marietta Coll., 1991, Blue Sky Gallery, Columbus,

1992, exhibited in group shows at Zanesville Art Ctr., 1981, 1990, Franklin U., Columbus, Ohio, 1985, Marietta (Ohio) Coll., 1991, Pomerene Fine Arts Ctr., Coshocton, Ohio, 1991, No. Ariz. U., 1992, French Art Colony, Gallipolis, Ohio, 1992, Soc. Layerists in Multi-Media, San Miguel Allende, Mex., 1996, Marlborough, Eng., 1997, Sirius Gallery, Santa Fe, 2001, Represented in permanent collections Zanesville Art Ctr., Ohio, Soc. Bank Cleve., Edward Cherry Corp., Columbus, Nat. WaterColor Soc. Bd. dirs. Zanesville Art Ctr., 1986-90. 92-95. Recipient 1st award Rocky Mountain Nat., 1984, Elsie and David Wu-Ject Key award Am. Watercolor Soc., 1989, 4th award San Diego Watercolor Soc., 1993. Mem. Nat. Watercolor Soc., Soc. Layerists in Multi-Media, Ohio Watercolor Soc. (silver Buckeye award 1986), Southeastern Ohio Watercolor Soc. (co-founder, 1st pres. 1978-79). Avocations: gardening, interior decorating, reading, metaphyics, travel. Mailing: 9908 Wild Turkey NW Albuquerque NM 87114 Office Phone: 505-792-7782. E-mail: juan1aran@aol.com.

WILLIAMS, JULIE LLOYD, federal agency administrator, lawyer; b. Washington, May 24, 1950; d. Walter Herbert and Jean (Grabill) W.; m. Don Scroggin, May 9, 1981; 1 child, Patrick Conner. BA, Goddard Coll., 1971; JD, Antioch Sch. Law, 1975. Bar: Va. 1975, D.C. 1976. Assoc. Fried, Frank, Harris, Shriver, Washington, 1975-83; assoc. gen. counsel Fed. Home Loan Bank Bd., Washington, 1983-86, dep. gen. counsel, 1986-89; dep. chief counsel Office of Thrift Supervision, Washington, 1989-91, sr. dep. chief counsel, 1991-93; dep. chief counsel Comptr. of Currency, Washington, 1993-94, chief counsel, 1994-98, acting comptr., 1998, 2004—05, first sr. dep. comptr., chief counsel, 1999—; bd. dir. FDIC, 2004—. Co-author: (handbook) How to Incorporate: A Handbook for Entrepreneurs & Professionals, 1987; author: Savings Institutions: Mergers, Acquisitions & Conversions, 1988, National Banks and the Dual Banking System, 2003. Mem. ABA (banking law com.), Women in Housing and Fin. Office: Office of Comptr of Currency Independence Sq 250 E St SW Washington DC 20219-0001 Office Phone: 202-874-5200. *

WILLIAMS, KAREN HASTIE, lawyer; b. Washington, Sept. 30, 1944; d. William Henry and Beryl (Lockhart) Hastie; m. Wesley S. Williams, Jr.; children: Amanda Pedersen, Wesley Hastie, Bailey Lockhart. Cert., U. Neuchatel, Switzerland, 1965; BA, Bates Coll., 1966; MA, Tufts U., 1967; JD, Cath. U. Am., 1973. Bar: D.C. 1973. Staff asst. internat. gov. relations dept. Mobil Oil Corp., NYC, 1967-69; staff asst. com. Dist. Columbia U.S. Senate, 1970, chief counsel com. on the budget, 1977-80; law clk. to judge Spottswood Robinson III U.S. Ct. Appeals (D.C. Cir.), Washington, 1973-74; law clk. to assoc. justice Thurgood Marshall U.S. Supreme Ct., Washington, 1974-75; assoc. Fried, Frank, Harris, Shriver & Kampelman, Washington, 1975-77, 1975-77; adminstr. Office Mgmt. and Budget, Washington, 1980-81; of counsel Crowell & Moring, Washington, 1982, ptnr., 1982—2004; ret., 2005. Bd. dirs. Chubb Corp., Gannett Co., Inc., Sun Trust Bank, Inc., Washington Gas Light Co., Continental Airlines. Trustee, past chair Greater Washington Rsch. Ctr. Mem. ABA (pub. contract law sect., past chair), Nat. Bar Assn., Washington Bar Assn., Nat. Contract Mgmt. Assn., NAACP (legal def. fund, bd. dirs.). Office: Crowell & Moring 1001 Pennsylvania Ave NW Ste 1100 Washington DC 20004-2595

WILLIAMS, KAREN JOHNSON, federal judge; b. Orangeburg, SC, Aug. 4, 1951; d. James G. Johnson and Marcia Johnson (Reynolds) Dantzler; m. Charles H. Williams, Dec. 27, 1968; children: Marian, Ashley, Charlie, David. BA, Columbia Coll., 1972; postgrad., U. SC, 1973, JD cum laude, 1980. Bar: SC 1980, US Dist. Ct. SC 1980, US Ct. Appeals (4th cir.) 1981. Tchr. Irmo (SC) Mid. Sch., 1972—74, O-W H.S., Orangeburg, 1974—76; assoc. Charles H. Williams PA, Orangeburg, 1980—92; judge US Ct. Appeals (4th cir.), 1992—. Exec. bd. grievance commn. SC Supreme Ct., Columbia, 1983—92. Child devel. bd. First Bapt. Ch., Orangeburg; bd. dirs. Orangeburg County Mental Retardation Bd., 1986—94, Orangeburg-Calhoun Hosp. Found., Columbia Coll., 1988—92, Reg. Med. Ctr. Hosp. Found., 1988—92; adv. bd. Orangeburg-Calhoun Tech. Coll., SC, 1987—92. Mem.: ABA, Nat. Assn. of Women Judges, Bus. and profl. Women Assn., SC Trial Lawyers Assn., Orangeburg County Bar Assn. (co-chair Law Day 1981), SC Bar Assn., Fed. Judges Assn., Am. Judicature Soc., Rotary, Order of Coif, Order of Wig and Robe. Home: 2503 Five Chop Rd Orangeburg SC 29115-8185 Office: Lewis F Powell Jr US Cthse Annex 1100 E Main St Ste 617 Richmond VA 23219-3517 *

WILLIAMS, KENNETH SCOTT, entertainment company executive; b. Tulsa, Okla., Dec. 31, 1955; s. David Vorhees Williams and Mary Louise (Newell) Rose; m. Jann Catherine Wolfe, May 20, 1989; children: Catherine Eloise, Michael Holbrook. BA, Harvard Coll., 1978; MS, Columbia U., 1985. Bank officer Chase Manhattan Bank, NYC, 1978-82; asst. treas. Columbia Pictures Entertainment, NYC, 1982-84, v.p., treas., 1984-89, sr. v.p. fin. and adminstrn. Burbank, Calif., 1990-91; sr. v.p. corp. ops. Sony Pictures Entertainment, Culver City, Calif., 1991-95, exec. v.p., 1995-96; pres. Digital Studio divsn. Sony Pictures Entertainment, 1996-2000, Technicolor Digital Cinema, Burbank, Calif., 2002; pres., CEO Stan Lee Media, Inc., Encino, Calif., 2000—02; COO Ascent Media Group, Santa Monica, Calif., 2002—03, pres., CEO, 2003—06. Past pres., bd. dirs. L.A. Conservancy; former chmn. Entertainment Tech. Ctr. U. So. Calif.; former trustee U. Calif., Riverside; bd. dirs. L.A. Music Ctr., L.A. Pub. Access TV Channel 36, L.A. Master Chorale; mem. Blue Hill Troupe, NYC, 1979—. Mem. N.Y. Soc. Securities Analysts, Acad. Television Arts and Scis., Fin. Execs. Inst. (v.p.), Acad. Motion Picture Arts & Scis., Digital Coast Roundtable (bd. dirs.), Harvard Club So. Calif. (exec. v.p., bd. dirs.), Beta Gamma Sigma. Home: 457 Cuesta Way Los Angeles CA 90077-3434 Personal E-mail: kenneth_s_williams@hotmail.com.

WILLIAMS, KIM ALLAN, cardiologist, educator; b. Chgo., Ill., Nov. 10, 1954; MD, U. Chgo.-Pritzker Sch. Medicine, 1979. Cert. Cardiology, Internal Medicine, Nuclear Medicine, Nuclear Cardiology. Intern, internal medicine Emory U., Atlanta, 1979—80, resident, cardiology, 1980—82; fellow, nuclear medicine U. Chgo., Ill., 1982—84; practicing, 1983—; assoc. prof. medicine U. Chgo Med. Ctr., Ill.; prof. medicine U. Chgo. Med. Ctr., Ill., dir., nuclear cardiology Ill. Contbr. articles to profl. jours. Named one of Chicago's Top Doctors, Chicago Mag., 1996, 2000, 2004. Fellow: Assn. Black Cardiologists, Am. Heart Assn., Am. Soc. Nuclear Cardiology (pres.), Am. Coll. Cardiology (bd. trustee); mem.: Soc. Nuclear Medicine, Nat. Med. Assn., Assn. U. Radiologists, Am. Soc. Echocardiography. Office: U Chgo Hosps Ctr for Advanced Medicine 5758 S Maryland Ave MC 9025 Chicago IL 60637 Office Phone: 773-702-6258. Office Fax: 773-702-3512. Business E-Mail: kwilliam@medicine.bsd.uchicago.edu. *

WILLIAMS, KIMBERLY ELIZABETH, history professor; b. Falls Church, Va., Nov. 3, 1971; d. Ronald David and Dea Antoinette Williams. MA, East Carolina U., Greenville, NC, 2000. Prof. history Hillsborough C.C., Tampa, Fla., 2002—07; faculty advisor Internatioanl Scholar Laureate Program, Vienna, Va., 2006—. Dir. Ybor City Mus. Soc., Tampa, 2006—. Author: (book) Alexandria and the Sea (Discovery Channel Book Club Selection, 2004). Vol. Habitat for Humanity, Tampa, 2004—06. Avocations: travel, scuba diving. Home: 1810 E Palm Ave Apt 5317 Tampa FL 33605 Office: Hillsborough C C 2112 N 15th St Tampa FL 33605 Home Phone: 813-253-7641; Office Phone: 813-253-7641. Office Fax: 813-253-7775; Home Fax: 813-253-7775. E-mail: kwilliams1@hccfl.edu.

WILLIAMS, LANCE, journalist; Sports staff writer San Francisco Chronicle. Contbr. articles to numerous profl. jours.; numerous appearances on sports radio and television shows; author: (Sports Book) Game of Shadows, 2006. Recipient Dick Schaap Excellence in Sports Journalism award, 2004, George Polk award, 2004, Edgar A. Poe, White House Correspondents' Assn., 2004. Office: San Francisco Chronicle 901 Mission St San Francisco CA 94103-2988

WILLIAMS, LAWRENCE SOPER, JR., photographer; b. Balt., July 8, 1917; s. Lawrence S. and Ida (Exall) W.; m. Avilda Leyshon Williams, Nov. 21, 1940; children: Jay Stephen, Wendy Lauren. Student, Md. Inst. Wirephoto operator AP, Balt., 1937—38; news photographer Balt. Sun Papers, 1938—40, Harris and Ewing News Photos, Washington, 1940—41; war corr., photographer Bur. Info. U.S. War Dept., Washington, 1941—45; picture editor Holiday mag., Phila., 1945—48; freelance photographer Havertown, Pa., 1949—59; pres. Lawrence S. Williams, Inc., Upper Darby, Pa., 1959—83, chmn., 1983—93. Pres. Archtl. Photographers Assn., N.Y.C., 1968-70, Paoli (Pa.) Woods Homeowner's Assn., 1985-86; chmn. archtl. landscape com. Robynwood Village, Hershey's Mill; vol., TV audio instr. West Chester Sch. Dist. Recipient Gold medal Artist Guild of Phila., 1965, Silver medal Artist Guild of Pa., 1964, George W. Berry trophy Soc. Comml. Photographers Del. Valley, 1961, 66, 78, 79, 82, Best of Show trophy Am. Mus. Photography, Phila., 1966, 71, 77, 79, 82, Best Comml. Print trophy Guild of Profl. Photographers Del. Valley, 1971, 70, Award of Excellence Am. Advtg. Assn. Pa., 1978, Pres.'s Cup Profl. Photographers Assn. Pa., 1971, Silver medal for Sixty Years World in Colour, Internat. Photo competition, Hague, Netherlands, 1973, numerous archtl., comml., indsl., pictorial awards. Fellow Am. Soc. Photographers; mem. Soc. Comml. Photographers Del. Valley (life), Profl. Photographers Assn. Pa. (life), Profl. Photographers Am., Inc. (life, master photography degree 1966, craftsman photography degree 1968), Shriners. Republican. Lutheran. Achievements include assembly of the largest collection of architectural photographs in U.S. consisting of over 250,000 negatives which are now in the archives of the Athenaeum of Philadelphia, Pa. Avocation: travel. Home: 14410 Shannondell Dr Audubon PA 19403-5609 Office: PO Box 694 Kimberton PA 19442-0694 E-mail: larryvil@sdlifestyle.com.

WILLIAMS, LENA, sportswriter; b. Washington, Mar. 2, 1950; BA cum laude in English, Howard U., 1972; MS in Journalism, Columbia U., 1973. Assoc. editor Black Sports Mag.; clk. NY Times, 1974—76, reporter, 1976—88, sports writer, 1988—. Author: It's the Little Things: The Everyday Interactions That Get Under the Skin of Blacks and Whites, 2000. Named one of Outstanding Women in Mktg. and Comms., Ebony Mag., 2001; recipient Excellence award, Nat. Assn. Black Journalism, 1997, Black Achievers award, Young Men's Christian Assn. Mem.: Newspaper Guild (chair of Times-Guild unit). Office: NY Times Sports Desk 229 W 43d St New York NY 10036 Office Phone: 212-556-7371. Office Fax: 212-556-5848.

WILLIAMS, LEONARD TODD, JR., hotel sales and marketing executive; b. Portchester, NY, Jan. 9, 1947; s. Leonard Todd and Elsie Pauline (Brasa) W.; m. Barbara Ellen Warsh, Jan. 20, 1982; 1 child, Stephanie. BS, U. Nev., Las Vegas, 1979. Asst. gen. mgr. Holiday Inn Fin. Ctr., San Francisco, 1978-79; resident gen. mgr. Holiday Inn Center Strip, Las Vegas, 1979-80; gen. mgr. Holiday Inn South, Las Vegas, 1980-81; dir. lodging and beverages Holiday Inn, Holiday Casino, Las Vegas, 1981-86, dir. sales promotion mktg., 1985-86; dir. tourist mktg. Tropicana Hotel, Las Vegas, 1986-87; regional dir. sales and mktg. Summitt Hotel Mgmt. Corp., Phoenix, 1987-89; dir. mktg. Guest Quaters Ste. Hotel, Troy, Mich., 1989—. Adj. prof. Golden Gate U., San Francisco, 1978-79, U. Nev., Las Vegas, 1979-84 Bd. dirs. Easter Seals Soc. Nev., 1976-83, Phoenix; area exec. coord. United Way So. Nev., 1982-83; mem. exec. coun. Phoenix Boys and Girls Club; mem. exec. com. Sands Branch Boys and Girls Club, 1988-89. Recipient Exec. of Yr. award Profl. Secs. Assn., Las Vegas, 1985, also appreciation awards Easter Seals, Muscular Dystrophy Assn., Boys Club. Mem. Hotel Sales and Mktg. Assn., Fedn. Hoteliers (pres. Las Vegas 1978-79), Kiwanis (pres. Las Vegas 1978-79). Democrat. Lutheran. Avocations: golf, snowmobiling, bicycling. Office: 850 Tower Dr Troy MI 48098-2868

WILLIAMS, LILLIAN SERECE, historian, social studies educator; BA, U. Buffalo, 1966, MA, 1973, PhD, 1979. Tchr. Buffalo Bd. Edn., 1966—69; asst. prof. U. Buffalo, 1972—76, vis. asst. prof., 1985—87, assoc. prof., dept. chair, 2002—; asst. prof. Howard U., Washington, 1976—85; from asst. to assoc. prof. U. Albany, NY, 1987—2002. Historian NAACP, Balt., 1992—93, Girl Scouts U.S.A., NYC, 1995—97, N.Y. State Mus., Albany, 1997—98; dir. Inst. for Rsch. on Women U. Albany, 1998—2002. Author: Strangers in the Land of Paradise, 1999; editor: (documentary) Records of the National Association of Colored Women, 1993, 1994; assoc. editor: Jour. African Am. History, Afro-Ams. in N.Y. Life and History. Mem. exec. bd. Assn. for Study African Am. Life and History. Named one of 8 Outstanding Citizens of Western NY, Buffalo News, 2006; recipient Nuala McGann Drescher award, United Univ. Profls., Lifetime Achievement award, Niagara County Black Achievers, Niagara Falls, N.Y., 2000, Augspurger award in local history, Buffalo and Erie County Hist. Soc., 2006; State Farm Ins. fellow, Nat. African Am. Women Leadership Inst., 2001. Mem.: Afro-Am. Hist. Assn.the Niagara Frontier, Orgn. Am. Historians, Delta Sigma Theta. Avocations: reading, art, interior decorating. Office: SUNY Buffalo African Amer Studies Dept 732 Clemens Hall Buffalo NY 14260 Office Phone: 716-645-2082.

WILLIAMS, LINDA C., lawyer; b. Portsmouth, Va., Apr. 4, 1956; BA with high honors, Univ. Va., 1978, JD, 1982. Bar: Calif. 1984. Law clk. Judge Albert Tate, Jr., US Ct. Appeals (5th cir.), New Orleans; ptnr., head Corp. Securities & Fin. Inst. group Pillsbury Winthrop Shaw Pittman, San Francisco. Instr. Univ. San Francisco Sch. Law. Mem.: Order of the Coif. Office: Pillsbury Winthrop Shaw Pittman 50 Fremont St San Francisco CA 94105 Office Phone: 415-983-7334. Office Fax: 415-983-1200. Business E-Mail: linda.williams@pillsburylaw.com.

WILLIAMS, LINDA STALLWORTH, literature and language professor; b. Atlanta, Dec. 13, 1951; d. James Owen Stallworth and Pearl Bell Willis; m. Max Virgil Williams, Sept. 29, 1972; children: Laura LeAnne, Max Brenton. BA, U. W.Ga., Carrollton, 1972; MA, U. Ctrl. Okla., Edmond, 1986; PhD, U. Okla., Norman, 1990. Vis. lectr. U. Okla., Norman, 1988—91; prof. English Rose State Coll., Midwest City, Okla., 1991—94; acad. coord. faculty devel. Bd. Regents, U. Sys. Ga., Atlanta, 1996—98; assoc. prof. English N.Ga. Coll. and State U., Dahlonega, 1997—. Recipient Dorothy Golden award for Excellence in Tchg. of Composition, Student Success in First-Year Composition Conf., 2001, Cert. of Appreciation for Patriotic Civilian Svc., Dept. of Army, 2005. Mem.: Conf. Coll. Composition and Comm., Assn. Bus. Comm., Nat. Coun. Tchrs. of English. Home: 11000 Big Canoe Big Canoe GA 30143 Office: North Georgia Coll and State Univ 100 College Cir Dahlonega GA 30597 Office Phone: 706-864-1681.

WILLIAMS, LISA A., special education educator; d. Ida M. Williams. B. Music Edn., Howard U., Washington, 2000, M. Music Edn., 2003; MEd in Spl. Edn., U. San Diego, Calif., 2002; EdS in Spl. Edn., Fla. State U., Tallassee, 2005. Cert. tchr. Music K-12 Calif., Va., Fla., 2000, tchr. spl. edn. Fla., 2004. Tchr. spl. edn San Diego City Schs., San Diego, 2000—02; tchr. music Fairfax County Schs., Fairfax, Va., 2002—03; tchr. spl. edn. Leon County Schs., Tallahassee, 2004—06, San Diego Unified Sch. Dist., 2006—. Acad. counselor Fla. State U., Tallahassee, 2003—04; site coord. Leon County Schs., Title I Program, Tallahassee, 2004; dir. children's choir Bethel AME Ch., San Diego, 2000—02. Named Riley Minority Educator of Yr., 2006; Spl. Edn. and Minority scholar, Howard U., Grad. asst., 2002—03, Doctoral fellow, Phi Delta Kappa Internat., 2003—04, Childhood Edn., Reading and Disability Svcs. fellow, Fla. State U., 2005—06. Mem.: Nat. Assn. Music Educators, Phi Delta Kappa Internat., Internat. Clarinet Assn., Nat. Assn. for Black Sch. Educators, NEA, Coun. for Exceptional Children, Tau Beta Sigma, Alpha Kappa Alpha (Ednl. Advancement Found. scholar 2005), Sigma Alpha Iota (life). Home Phone: 850-222-9210. Personal E-mail: pindrop26@aol.com.

WILLIAMS, LOUIS CLAIR, JR., public relations executive; b. Huntington, Ind., Nov. 7, 1940; s. Louis Clair and Marian Eileen W.; children—Terri Lynn, L. Bradley, Lisa C.; m. Mary Clare Moster. B.A., Eastern Mich. U., 1963. Copywriter, Rochester (N.Y.) Gas and Electric Co., 1963-65, editor RG&E News, 1965-66; employee info. specialist Gen. Ry. Signal Co., Rochester, 1966-67, supr. employment and employee rels., 1967-69; supr. pub. rels. Heublein, Inc., Hartford, Conn., 1969-70; dir. corp. communications Jewel Cos., Inc., Chgo., 1970-71; account exec. Ruder & Finn of Mid-Am., Chgo., 1971-73, v.p., 1973-76, sr. v.p., 1976-78; cons. Towers, Perrin, Forster & Crosby, Los Angeles, 1978-79; exec. v.p., gen. mgr. Harshe-Rotman & Druck, Inc., Chgo., 1979, pres. midwest region, 1979-80; v.p. Hill & Knowlton, Inc., Chgo., 1980-81, sr. v.p., 1981-83; pres. Savlin Williams Assocs., Evanston, Ill., 1983-85, L.C. Williams & Assocs., Chgo., 1985—. Mem. Internat. Assn. Bus. Communicators (chmn. found., pres., chmn. Chgo. chpt. 1979-80), Inst. Pub. Rels. (chmn. rsch. com. 2005), Pub. Rels. Soc. Am., Publicity Club Chgo. Personal E-mail: LCWA@att.net.

WILLIAMS, LOWELL CRAIG, lawyer, employee relations executive; b. Tehachapi, Calif., Dec. 3, 1947; s. Lyndon Williams and Gertrude (White) Sievert; m. Marsha Mendelssohn; children: John S., Jeffrey A. Bescheinigungeschichte, Georg August U., Germany, 1968; BA, U. Calif., Santa Barbara, 1969; JD, Columbia U., 1972. Bar: N.Y. 1973, U.S. Ct. Appeals (2nd cir.) 1974, U.S. Supreme Ct. 1974. Assoc. Sullivan & Cromwell, NYC, 1972-75; sr. v.p. Elf Aquitaine, Inc., NYC, 1976-95; v.p. Compagnie des Machines Bull, NYC, 1995—, exec. v.p. group human resources, 1998-99; exec. dir. Exult Inc., NYC, 1999—2001; sr. advisor TPI Sourcing Inc., The Woodlands, Tex., 2002—03; v.p. global human resource svcs., gen. counsel EquaTerra, Inc., Houston, 2003—. Past pres. Scarsdale Synagogue. Mem. Internat. Bar Assn., German Law Assn. (past bd. dirs.). Office: EquaTerra Inc Three Riverway No 1660 Houston TX 77056 Office Phone: 914-661-7904. Business E-Mail: williams.lowell@equaterra.com.

WILLIAMS, LUIDA K., retired elementary school educator; b. Valparaiso, Ind., May 15, 1942; d. Edgar Pricer and Velma (Cook) Williams. BS in Elem. Edn., Ind. U., Bloomington, 1965; MS in Elem. Edn., Butler U., Indpls., 1968. Cert. tchr. Tchr. William A. Bell Sch., 1965—2004; ret., 2004. Basketball coach William A. Bell Sch., 1968—90. Summer camp organizer for at-risk children, Englishton, Ind.; agent Jameson Camp, Indpls., 1966—2004, Englishton Camp, Lexington, Ind., 1970—2004. Recipient Tchr. of Yr. award, IPS Sch., 1991, Mary McClelland Vol. award, Jameson Camp, 1995, Tchr. of Yr. award, Soc. Intensified Edn. Mem.: NEA, Indpls. Edn. Assn. (rep. 1965—2004), Indpls. Edn. Assn., Ind. State Tchr. Assn. (lobbyest Ind. Gen. Assembly 1970—2000, ethics com. 1981—83). Avocation: tennis. Home: 7356 Mikesell Dr Indianapolis IN 46260

WILLIAMS, LUTHER STEWARD, research scientist; b. Sawyerville, Ala., Aug. 19, 1940; s. Roosevelt and Mattie B. (Wallace) W.; m. Constance Marie Marion, Aug. 23, 1963; children: Mark Steward, Monique Marie. BA magna cum laude, Miles Coll., 1961; MS, Atlanta U., 1963; PhD, Purdue U., 1968, DSc (hon.), 1987, U. Louisville, 1992, Capitol Coll., 1996, Bowie State U., 1996, Tuskegee U., 1997, U. DC, 1999. NSF lab. asst. Spelman Coll., 1961-62, Atlanta U., 1962-63, instr. biology, faculty rsch. grantee, 1963-64, asst. prof. biology, 1969-70, prof. biology, 1984-87, pres., 1984-87; grad. tchg. asst. Purdue U., West Lafayette, Ind., 1964-65, grad. rsch. asst., 1965-66, asst. prof. biology, 1970-73, assoc. prof., 1973-79, prof., 1979-80, NIH Career Devel. awardee, 1971-75, asst. provost, 1976-80; dean Grad. Sch., prof. biology Washington U., St. Louis, 1980-83; v.p. acad. affairs, dean Grad. Sch. U. Colo., Boulder, 1983-84; Am. Cancer Soc. postdoctoral fellow SUNY-Stony Brook, 1968-69; assoc. prof. biology MIT, 1973-74; spl. asst. to dir. Nat. Inst. Gen. Med. Scis., NIH, Bethesda, Md., 1987-88; dep. dir. Nat. Inst. Gen. Med. Scis. NIH, Bethesda, 1988-89; sr. sci. advisor to dir. NSF, Washington, 1989-90, asst. dir. for edn. and human resources, 1990-99; visiting scholar Payson Ctr. Internat. Devel./Tech., Arlington, Va., 1999-2000, edn. cons., 2000—; provost, v.p. for acad. affairs Tuskegee U., Ala., 2006—. Educator, cons., 2000—; dir. edn., sr. advisor to dir. Mo. Bot. Garden, St. Louis, 2001-05; chmn. rev. com. MARC Program, Nat. Inst. Gen. Med. Scis., NIH, 1972-76; grant reviewer NIH, 1971-73, 76, NSF, 1973, 76-80, Med. Rsch. Coun. of N.Z., 1976; mem. life scis. sreening com. recombinant DNA adv. com. HEW, 1979-81; mem. nat. adv. gen. med. sci. council NIH, 1980-85; mem. adv. com. Office Tech. Assessment, Washington, 1984-87; chmn. fellowship adv. com. NRC Ford Found., 1984-85; mem.-at-large Grad. Record Exam. Bd., 1981-85, chmn. minority grad. edn. com., 1983-85; mem. health, safety and environ. affairs. com. Nat. Labs., U. Calif., 1981-87; mem. adv. panel Office Tech. Assessment, US Congress, 1985-86; mem. fed. task force on women, minorities and the handicapped in sci. and tech., 1987-91; mem. adv. panel to dir. sci. and tech. ctrs. devel. NSF, 1987-88; mem. nat. adv. com. White House Initiative on Historically Black Colls. and Univs. on Sci. and Tech., 1986-89; numerous other adv. bds. and coms. Contbr. sci. articles to profl. jours. Vice-chmn. bd. advisors Atlanta Neighborhood Justice Ctr., 1984-87; bd. dirs. Met. Atlanta United Way, 1986-87, Butler St. YMCA, Atlanta, 1985-87; trustee Atlanta Zool. Assn., 1985-87, Miles Coll., 1984-87, Atlanta U., 1984-87, 90-96; mem. nominating com. Dana Found; mem. St. Louis CC Found. Bd., 2004-06. NIH predoctoral fellow Purdue U., 1966-68; recipient William A. Hinton Rsch. Trng. award, Am. Soc. Microbiology, 1998, trustee award Acad. Scis. St. Louis, 2004; named to Black Coll. Hall of Fame, 2002. Fellow Am. Acad. Microbiology, Acad. Sci. St. Louis; mem. Am. Soc. Microbiology, Am. Chem. Soc., Am. Soc. Biol. Chemists (mem. ednl. affairs com. 1979-82, com. on equal opportunities for minorities 1972-84). Home and Office: 15286 Brightfield Manor Dr Chesterfield MO 63017 Office Phone: 314-577-5139. Personal E-mail: lswilliams1960@sbcglobal.net. Business E-Mail: lswilliams1968@sbcglobal.net. E-mail: luther.williams@tuskegee.edu.

WILLIAMS, LYNELL R., educational association administrator; Peer tutor, spanish Content Area Tutoring Prog., Idaho State U., 1997; dir. CAT Prog., Idaho State U., 2003; coord., tutoring & learning ctr. U. NC at Wilmington, 2003—; dir. SMART Learning Commons, U. Minn. Mem.: Assn. for Tutoring Profession (pres. 2006—07). Office: SMART Learning Commons Magrath Library 6034 1984 Buford Ave Saint Paul MN 55108 *

WILLIAMS, MARCUS DOYLE, judge; b. Nashville, Oct. 24, 1952; s. John Freelander and Pansy (Doyle) W.; m. Carmen Myrie, May 21, 1983; children: Aaron Doyle, Adam Myrie. BA with honors, Fisk U., 1973; JD, Cath. U. of Am., 1977. Bar: Va. 1977, D.C. 1978. Asst. commonwealth's atty. County of Fairfax, Fairfax, Va., 1978-80; asst. county atty. Fairfax, Va., 1980-87; dist. ct. judge 19th Jud. Dist., Va., 1987-90; judge 19th Jud. Cir., Va., 1990—. Lectr. bus. legal studies George Mason U., Fairfax, 1980-95; instr. pvt. investigators North Va. Community Coll., Fairfax, 1979; mem. Fairfax Criminal Justice Adv. Bd., 1980-86; faculty advisor Nat. Jud. Coll., 1991, faculty, 1992—; Am. participant lectr. for USIA, 1990; lectr. George Mason U. Law Sch., 1987. Book reviewer for ABA Jour., 1981-84; contbr. articles to legal jours. Bd. visitors Cath. U. Law Sch., 1998—. Recipient cert. of appreciation for outstanding svc. Burke-Fairfax Jack & Jill, Cert. of Appreciation, Nat. Forum for Black Pub. Adminstrs. and Black Women

United for Action, 1995; Thomas J. Watson Found. fellow, 1977, Otis Smith award Black Law Students Assn. of Cath. U. Law Sch.; Outstanding Achievement and Svc. award Black Law Students Assn., 2001. Mem. ABA (chair subcom. Victims of Crimes 1996-2000), Fairfax Bar Assn. (CLE com., vice chmn. 1986-87), Am. Bus. Law Assn., Am. Judges Assn., Phi Alpha Delta, Beta Kappa Chi, Omega Psi Phi. Methodist. Office: Cir Ct 4110 Chain Bridge Rd Fairfax VA 22030-4009

WILLIAMS, MARIO, professional football player; b. Richlands, NC, Jan. 31, 1985; Studied Pro Sports Mgmt., NC St. Univ., 2004—06. Defensive end Houston Texans, 2006—. Named Nat. Preseason Defensive Player Yr., Blue Ribbon Coll. Football, 2005; named to NC Shrine Bowl Team, 2002, first team All-ACC, 2006; recipient Bob Warren award for Integrity and Sportsmanship. Achievements include being the the first overall selection in the 2006 NFL Draft. Office: Houston Texans Two Reliant Park Houston TX 77054

WILLIAMS, MARSHA C., travel company executive; b. 1951; B in Econs., Wellesley Coll.; Masters, U. Chgo. Various positions Amoco Corp., 1989—93, treas., 1993—98, v.p., treas., 1997—98; chief adminstrv. officer Crate & Barrel, 1998—2002; exec. v.p., CFO Equity Office Properties, Chgo., 2002—07; sr. v.p., CFO Orbitz Worldwide, Inc., Chgo., 2007—. Office: Orbitz Worldwide Inc 500 W Madison Ave Ste 1000 Chicago IL 60661 *

WILLIAMS, MARSHA E., broadcast executive; BA, Conn. Coll.; MA, Washington U. With The Psychological Corp., Cleve., San Antonio, Children's TV Workshop (now Sesame Workshop), 1991—95, MTV Networks Co., NYC, 1996—, v.p. rsch. and planning Nickelodeon Networks, sr. v.p. rsch. and planning Nickelodeon Networks, 2006—. Office: MTV Networks Co Nickelodeon Networks 1515 Broadway 42d Fl New York NY 10036

WILLIAMS, MARSHA RHEA, computer scientist, educator, researcher, consultant; b. Memphis, Aug. 4, 1948; d. James Edward and Velma Lee W. Cert., Schiller Coll., West Berlin, Germany, 1968; BS in Physics, Beloit Coll., 1969; MS in Physics, U. Mich., 1971; MS in Sys. and Info. Sci., Vanderbilt U., 1976, PhD in Computer Sci., 1982. Cert. data processor. Engring. coop. student Lockheed Missiles & Space Co., Sunnyvale, Calif., 1967-68; asst. transmission engr. Ind. Bell Tel. Co., Indpls., 1971-72; sys. analyst, instr. physics Memphis State U., 1972-74; computer-assisted instrn. project programmer Fisk U., 1974-76; mem. tech. staff Hughes Rsch. Labs., Malibu, Calif., 1976-78; assoc. sys. engr. IBM, Nashville, 1978-80; rsch. and tchg. asst. Vanderbilt U., Nashville, 1980-82, spl. asst. to dean Grad. Sch., spring 1981, minority engr. advisor, 1975-76; cons. computer-assisted instrn. project Meharry Med. Coll., Nashville, summer 1982; assoc. prof. computer sci. Tenn. State U., Nashville, 1982-83, 84-90, full tenured prof., 1990—, univ. marshal, 1992-97. Assoc. prof. U. Miss., Oxford, 1983-84, faculty senator; assoc. program dir. Applications of Advanced Techs. Sci. and Engring. Edn., NSF, 1987-88, apptd. USRA Sci. and Engring. Edn. Coun., Advanced Design Program, 1992-94; cons. on minority scientists and engrs. Univ. Space Rsch. Assn., Washington, 1988; vis. scientist CSNET-Minority Instn. Networking Project Bolt, Beranek & Newman, Cambridge, Mass., 1989; mem. tech. staff Bell Comm. Rsch., Red Bank, N.J., 1990; prin. investigator NSF Computer Sci., Engring. & Math. Scholarships Project, 2002-03; presenter papers profl. meetings. Editor-in-chief newspaper Pilgrim Emanuel Bapt. Ch., 1975-76. Advisr Chi Rho Youth Fellowship, Temple Bapt. Ch., 1975-81, adv. com. Golden Outreach Sr. Citizens Fellowship, 1979-80, 86-87, 89-93, Women's Day spkr., 1979-81, Ebenezer Missionary Bapt. Ch., 1993; adviser Nat. Soc. Black Engring. Students, 1983-84; founder, coord. Tenn. State U. Assn. for Excellence in Computer Sci., Math. and Physics (AE-COMP), 1986-87, coord. Tech. Opportunities Fair, 1986, 87; dir. Tenn. State U. Minorities in Sci., Engring. and Tech. Rsch. Project-MISET, 1989—; child sponsor World Vision, 1981—; mem., newsletter staff Lake Providence Missionary Bapt. Ch. Recipient Disting. Instr. award, 1984, Disting. Svc. citation Beloit Coll. Alumni Assn., 1994; grantee Digital Equipment Corp., 1989-92; rsch. grantee Tenn. State U., 1993, 94, NSF, 2002-03. Mem. AAUP, NAACP (nat. judge ACT-SO sci. olympics 1992), Assn. Computing Machinery, Assn. Info. Tech. Profls. (edn. chmn., bd. dirs. 1986), Tenn. Acad. Sci., Phi Kappa Phi. Home: PO Box 281946 Nashville TN 37228 Office: Tenn State U Dept Computer Sci PO Box 9604 Nashville TN 37209

WILLIAMS, MARTHA ETHELYN, information science educator; b. Chgo., Sept. 21, 1934; d. Harold Milton and Alice Rosemond (Fox) Williams. BA, Barat Coll., 1955; MA, Loyola U., 1957. With IIT Rsch. Inst., Chgo., 1957-72, mgr. info. scis., 1962-72, mgr. computer search ctr., 1968-72; adj. assoc. prof. sci. info. Ill. Inst. Tech., Chgo., 1965-73, lectr. chemistry dept., 1968-70; rsch. prof. info. sci., coordinated sci. lab. Coll. Engring. U. Ill., Urbana, also dir. info. retrieval rsch. lab., 1972—, prof. info. sci. grad. sch. of libr. info. sci., 1974—, affiliate, computer sci. dept., 1979—. Chair large data base conf. Nat. Acad. Sci./NRC, 1974, mem. ad hoc panel on info. storage and retrieval, 1977, numerical data adv. bd., 1979-82, computer sci. and tech. bd., nat. rsch. network rev. com., 1987-88, chair utility subcom., 1987-88, subcom. promoting access to sci. and tech. data for pub. interest; task force on sci. info. activities NSF, 1977; U.S. rep. review com. for project on broad system of ordering, UNESCO, Hague, Netherlands, 1974; vice-chair Gordon Rshc. Conf. on Sci. Info. Problems in Rsch., 1978, chair, 1980; mem. panel on intellectual property rights in age of electronics and info. U.S. Congress, Office of Tech. Assessment; program chmn. Nat. Online Meeting, 1980-2001; founder, pres. Info. Market Indicators, Inc., 1982-; cons. in field; invited lectr. Commn. European Communities, Industrial R&D adv. com., Brussels, 1992. Editor-in-chief: Computer-Readable Databases Directory and Data Sourcebook, 1976—89, founding editor;, 1989—; editor: Ann. Rev. Info. Sci. and Tech., 1976—2001, Online Rev., 1979—92, Online and CD-ROM Rev., 1993—2000; mem. editl. adv. bd.: Database, 1978—88, mem. editl. bd.: Info. Processing and Mgmt., 1982—89, The Reference Libr., founding editor: Online Info. Rev., 2000—; contbr. articles to profl. jours. Trustee Engring. Info., Inc., 1974-87, bd. dirs., 1976-91, chmn. bd. dirs., 1982-91, v.p., 1978-79, pres., 1980-81; regent Nat. Libr. Medicine, 1978-82, chmn. bd. regents, 1981; mem. task force on sci. info. activities NSF, 1977-78; mem. nat. adv. com. ACCESS ERIC, 1989-91. Recipient best paper of year award H. W. Wilson Co., 1975; Travel grantee NSF, Luxembourg, 1972, Honolulu, 1973, Tokyo, 1973, Mexico City, 1975, Scotland, 1976 Fellow: AAAS (mem. nominating com. 1983, 1985), Nat. Fedn. Abstracting and Info. Svcs. (hon.), Inst. Info. Scis. (hon.); mem.: NAS (mem. joint com. with NRC on chem. info. 1971—73), Internat. Fedn. for Documentation (U.S. nat. com.), Assn. Sci. Info. Dissemination Ctrs. (v.p. 1971—73, pres. 1975—77), Assn. Computing Machinery (pub. bd. 1972—76), Am. Soc. Info. Sci. (councilor 1971—72, mem. publs. com. 1974—, pres. 1987—88, councilor 1987—89, contbg. editor bull. column 1974—78, Award of Merit 1984, Pioneer Info. Sci. award 1987, Watson Davis award 1995), Am. Chem. Soc. Home: 2134 Sandra Ln Monticello IL 61856-8036 Office: U Ill 1308 W Main St Urbana IL 61801-2307 E-mail: m-will13@uiuc.edu.

WILLIAMS, MARY ALICE BALDWIN, retired home economist, volunteer; b. St. Louis, Mar. 24, 1928; d. Ulysses Grant and Irene (Jenkins) Gray; m. Earl Randolph Baldwin, June 28, 1952 (div. 1973); 1 child, Arlene Denise; m. Robert Williams Jr., Dec. 21, 1985. BS, Lincoln U., 1952; MA, Webster U., 1971; postgrad., Harris Stowe Tchrs. Coll., 1976-78, Cen. Mo. State U., 1979-80, U. Mo., 1981-82. Cert. home economist, Mo. Tchr. home econs. Cen. H.S., Hayti, Mo., 1952-53, Cleve. Pub. Schs., 1953-56; tchr. elem. sch. St. Louis Pub. Schs., 1958-67, tchr. home econs., 1968-83, curriculum supr. home econs., 1984-93, cons. home econs. and character edn., 1993; ret., 1993; vol. cons. Family & Consumer Sci. Fiber Art, 1993—. Presenter in field. Author curriculum materials in home econs. and character edn. Fund raising com. Annie Malone Children's Home, St. Louis, 1987-90; 75th anniversary com. YYWCA Phyllis Wheatley, St. Louis, 1988. Mem. Nat. Assn. Univ. Women (del. 1992, Woman of Yr. 2001, N. Ctrl. sectional lay mem. 1999-2003), Am. Home Econs. Assn. (ethics com. 1989-90, population com. 1990-91), Mo. Home Econs. Assn. (tchr. rep. 1988-90), Am. Vocat. Assn., Mo. Vocat. Assn. (legis. com.), St. Louis Home Econs. Tchrs. Assn. (founder, adviser), Lincoln Univ. Alumni Assn. (chair founders day), Delta Sigma Theta. Avocations: sewing, clothing design, music, reading, tennis, designer and quilter African Am. history and story quilts. Home: 4910 Maffitt Pl Saint Louis MO 63113-1727

WILLIAMS, MARY ELLEN COSTER, federal judge; b. Flushing, NY, 1953; married; 2 children. BA summa cum laude in Latin and Greek, Cath. U., 1974, MA in Latin, 1974; JD, Duke U., 1977. Assoc. Fulbright and Jaworski, Washington, 1977—79, Schnader, Harrison, Segal and Lewis, Washington, 1979—83; asst. US atty. civil divsn. US Dept. Justice, Washington, 1983—87; ptnr. Janis, Schuelke and Weschler Law Firm, Washington, 1987—89; adminstrv. judge GSA Bd. Contract Appeals, Washington, 1989—2003; judge US Ct. Fed. Claims, Washington, 2003—. Mem. editl. bd. Duke Law Jour. Fellow: Am. Bar Found. (life); mem.: DC Bar (sec.), DC Young Lawyers Sect. (chair), Bar Assn. of DC (found. pres., trustee, bd. dirs.), ABA (sect. rep. com. of ethics and professionalism 1998—2000, commn. on evaluation of rules of profl. conduct 1998—2000, presdl. task force on govt. lawyers 2000—01, chair sect. pub. contract law 2002—, chair elect, vice chair, sec., sect. rep. ho. delegates 2004—). Office: US Ct Fed Claims 717 Madison Pl NW Washington DC 20005 *

WILLIAMS, MARY IRENE, business education educator; b. Hugo, Okla., June 30, 1944; d. Primer and Hylar B. (Tarkington) Jackson; m. Lee A. Williams (div. June 1981); 1 child, Monica Ariane. BS in Bus. Edn., Langston U., 1967; MS in Bus., Emporia State U., Kans., 1973; EdS, U. Nev., Las Vegas, 1977; DBA in Internat. Bus., Alliant U., 1992. Instr. Spokane (Wash.) C.C., 1967-70; tchr. bus. Topeka Pub. Schs., 1970-73; prof. C.C. So. Nev., Las Vegas, 1973—, assoc. dean of bus., 1978—93, dean acad. support svcs., 1993—95, prof. bus./mgmt., 1997—, chmn. bus. adminstrn. dept., 2006—; prof. bus./mgmt., asst. to assoc. v.p., asst. coord. bus. Langston U., Tulsa, 1995—97. Adj. prof. So. Nazarene U., 1996-97; adj. prof. Tulsa Jr. Coll., 1997. Author: A Journey Upward, 2004. Named Educator of Yr. Nucleus Plaza Assn., 1985, New Visions, Inc., 1986. Mem. AAUW, Nat. Bus. Edn. Assn., Alpha Kappa Alpha Avocations: exercising, studying languages, reading. Office: CCSN 6375 W Charleston Blvd W2C Las Vegas NV 89146-1164 Personal E-mail: marywmslvnv@aol.com.

WILLIAMS, MARY PEARL, judge; b. Brownsville, Tex., Jan. 12, 1928; d. Marvin Redman and Theo Mae (Kethley) Hall; m. Jerre Stockton Williams, May 28, 1950; children: Jerre Stockton, Shelley Wiliams Austin, Stephanie Williams Laden. BA, U. Tex., 1948, JD, 1949. Bar: Tex. 1949, U.S. Supreme Ct. 1955, U.S. Dist. Ct. (we. dist.) Tex. 1987. Asst. atty. gen. State of Tex., Austin, 1949-50; relief judge Mcpl. Ct., Austin, 1964; asst. instr. dept. govt. U. Tex., Austin, 1966-67; atty. Office of Emergency Preparedness, Exec. Office of Pres., Washington, 1968-70; labor arbitrator, mem. arbitration panel Am. Arbitration Assn., 1972-73; judge County Ct. Law 2, Travis County, Tex., 1973-80, 53d Jud. Dist. Ct., Austin, 1981-2000, sr. judge, 2000—. Cons. HEW, 1966—67. Mem. adv. com. Juvenile Bd. Travis County, 1964—67; trustee United Way, 1974—78. Named Outstanding Woman, Austin Am.-Statesman, 1974, Austin Citizen, 1978, Woman of the Yr., Austin Dist. Bus. and Profl. Women, 1977; named to Austin HS Hall of Fame, 1996. Fellow: ABA, Am. Bar Found.; mem.: Inst. Jud. Adminstrn., Am. Judicature Soc., Am. Law Inst., Travis County Bar Assn., Coll. State Bar Tex., State Bar Tex., Jr. League Austin, Kappa Alpha Theta, Delta Kappa Gamma (hon.). Democrat. Methodist. Home: Apt 137 4100 Jackson Ave Austin TX 78731-6034 Office: Travis County Courthouse PO Box 1748 Austin TX 78767-1748 E-mail: greatimpy@aol.com.

WILLIAMS, MELVIN DONALD, anthropologist, educator; b. Pitts., Feb. 3, 1933; s. Aaron and Gladys Virginia (Barnes) W.; m. Faye Wanda Strawder, June 20, 1958; children: Aaron Ellsworth, Steven Rodney, Craig Haywood. AB, U. Pitts., 1955, MA, 1969, PhD, 1973. Cert. in secondary edn., social sci. Pa. Dept. Edn., 1974. Owner, operator Wholesale Periodical Distbn. Co., Pitts., 1955-66; instr. dept. sociology and anthropology Carlow Coll., 1969-71, asst. prof., 1971-75, chmn. dept. sociology and anthropology, 1973-75; assoc. prof. anthropology U. Pitts., 1976-79, adj. prof., 1979-82; prof. anthropology Purdue U., 1979-83, U. Md., College Park, 1983-88, U. Mich., Ann Arbor, 1988—. Olie B. O'Connor prof. Am. instns. Colgate U., 1976-77 Author: On the Street Where I Lived, Community in a Black Pentecostal Church, The Human Dilemma, The Black Middle Class, An Academic Village, Race for Theory; editor: Selected Readings in Afro-American Anthropology; contbr. articles to profl. publs. Co-chmn. project area com. Urban Redevel. Authority, Pitts., 1972—; co-dir. interdisciplinary family community project Western Psychiat. Inst. and Clinic, 1973-76; bd. dirs. Cath. Social Svc. of Allegheny County, Pa., 1973-76; coll. ombudsman, 1991-93, faculty senate, 1993-96. Career Svc. award U. Mich., 2004; fellow NSF, 1967, NDEA, 1969; grantee NSF, 1969-72, Cmty. Action Pitts., 1969-71, Social Sci. Rsch. Coun., 1974-75, Lilly Endowment, 1980-83, 85-86, Career Achievement award U. Mich., 2004, Lifetime Svc. award U. Mich., 2004. Fellow Am. Anthrop. Assn. (long range planning com. 2005—); mem. African Studies Assn., AAAS, AAUP, Am. Sociol. Assn., Assn. Study Afro-Am. Life and History, Soc. for Psychol. Anthropology, Am. Authors Assn. (long-range planning commn. 2005—). Home: 520 W Washington St Ann Arbor MI 48103-4232 Office: University of Michigan Dept Anthropology 101 West Hall 108 S University Ave Ann Arbor MI 48109-1107 Office Phone: 734-764-7274. Business E-Mail: mddoublu@umich.edu. *Personal philosophy: An abiding interest in people has stimulated me to discover more and more about humankind and has been an ever-present motivation to develop, grow and experience.*

WILLIAMS, MICHAEL ANTHONY, lawyer; b. Mandan, ND, Sept. 14, 1932; s. Melvin Douglas and Lucille Ann (Gavin) Williams; m. Marjorie Ann Harrer, Aug. 25, 1962 (div. 1989); children: Ann Margaret, Douglas Raymond, David Michael; m. Dorothy Ruth Hand, 1989. BA, Coll. of St. Thomas, 1954; LLB, Harvard U., 1959. Bar: Colo. 1959, N.D. 1959, U.S. Dist. Ct. Colo. 1959, U.S. Ct. Appeals (10th cir.) 1959, U.S. Supreme Ct. 1967. Assoc. Sherman & Howard and predecessor Dawson, Nagel, Sherman & Howard, Denver, 1959—65, ptnr., 1965—91; pres. Williams, Youle & Koenigs, P.C., Denver, 1991—2002; prin. Michael A. Williams LLC, Denver, 2002—. Served as 1st lt. USAF, 1955—57. Mem.: ABA, Am. Coll. Comml. Arbitrators, Colo. Bar Assn., Am. Law Inst., Colo. Bar Found., Am. Bd. Trial Advs., Am. Coll. Trial Lawyers. Office: 950 17th St Ste 1800 Denver CO 80202-2811 Office Phone: 303-785-7999. Business E-Mail: mwilliams@wyk.com.

WILLIAMS, MICHAEL EDWARD, lawyer; b. Ft. Worth, Aug. 10, 1955; s. Jerrol Evans and Helen Louise (Hoffner) Williams; m. Jackie Ann Gordinier, Dec. 30, 1978; children: Margaret Eileen, James Andrew. BA, U. Calif., Riverside, 1977; JD, U. San Diego, 1980. Bar: Calif. 1980, U.S. Dist. Ct. (so. dist.) Calif. 1980, U.S. Tax Ct. 1981, U.S. Dist. Ct. (ea. and cen. dists.) Calif. 1982, U.S. Dist. Ct. (no. dist.) Calif. 1985. Assoc. Jamison & McFadden, Solana Beach, Calif., 1980-86, Dorazio, Barnhorst & Bonar, San Diego, 1986; sole practice Encinitas, Calif., 1987—. Pres. Casa de Amistad, Centro de Ensenaza, 2001—03. Vice moderator San Diego Presbytery, Presbyn. Ch. U.S.A., 1998, moderator, 1999; vice moderator Synod So. Calif. and Hawaii, Presbyn. Ch. U.S.A., 2003, moderator, 2004. Mem. Calif. State Bar Assn. (fee arbitrator 1992—), San Diego County Bar Assn. (client rels. com. 1990—, fee arbitration com. 1991—, ct. arbitrator). Democrat. Presbyterian. Office: 4405 Manchester Ave Ste 206 Encinitas CA 92024-7902 Office Phone: 760-436-0158. Business E-Mail: atty@michaelewilliams.com.

WILLIAMS, MICHAEL EDWARD, SR., dean; b. Mobile, Ala., July 30, 1960; s. Charles Edward and Ollie Jo (Hayes) Williams; m. Roberta Jean Norton, Nov. 28, 1987; children: Michael Edward Jr., Joshua Cody, Carey Alan. BS in Secondary Edn. Hist., Troy State U., 1982; MA in Hist., Auburn U., 1984; MDiv, Souwestern Bapt. Theological Sem., 1987, PhD in Ch. Hist., 1993. Grad. tchg. asst. Auburn (Ala.) U., 1982—84; pastor Trinity Hills Bapt. Ch., Benbrook, Tex., 1987—94; tchg. fellow ch. hist. Southwestern Bapt. Theological Sem., Fort Worth, Tex., 1991, adj. prof. ch. hist., 1994; adj. prof. hist. Dallas (Tex.) Bapt. U., 1991—94, asst. prof. hist., 1995—96, prof. hist., 1996—, dean coll. humanities and social scis., 1996—. Edtl. bd. Bap. Hist. Heritage Jour., 1997—, Jour. Tex. Bapt. Hist., Dallas, 1998—; academic book review editor Bapt. Hist. Heritage Jour., Nashville, 2003—. Author: Isaac Taylor Tichenor: The Creation of the Baptist New South, 2005, To God Be The Glory: The Centennial History of BBU, 1998 (Tex. Bapt. Hist. Soc. Ch. Hist. award, 1998), Victory Thru Faith: A History of the Rosen Heights Baptist Church, 1996 (Tex. Bapt. Hist. Soc. Ch. Hist. award, 1996); contbr. articles various profl. jours. Named Prof. of Yr., Dallas Bapt. U., 1999—2000; recipient Hon. Alumnus award, Decatur Bapt. Coll., 1999. Mem.: So. Hist. Assn., Fellowship Bapt. Historians (sec.), Bapt. Hist. and Heritage Soc. (v.p. 2007—). Independent. Bapt. Avocations: sports, jogging, bicycling, swimming, movies. Home: 169 Deer Creek Dr Aledo TX 76008 Office: Dallas Bapt U 3000 Mt Crest Pkwy Dallas TX 75211

WILLIAMS, MICHAEL G., publishing executive; b. NY, Aug. 1956; married. With Aetna Life and Casulaty Co., Emery Air Freight Corp.; chief info. officer Seagram Asia-Pacific; v.p., info. tech., chief tech. officer spirits and wine group Seagram Co., 1992—98; v.p., chief info. officer NY Times, 1998—, NY Times Co., 2000—04. Working coun. for chief info. officers Corp. Adv. Bd. Co. Office: New York Times Co 229 W 43rd St New York NY 10036-3959

WILLIAMS, MICHAEL J., philosopher, educator; b. July 7, 1947; m. Meredith Williams. BA, Oxford Univ.; PhD, Princeton Univ. Faculty Yale Univ., Univ. Md., Northwestern Univ.; Krieger-Eisenhower prof., chair of philosophy Johns Hopkins Univ., Balt. Author: Groundless Belief, 1977, Unnatural Doubts, 1992, Problems of Knowledge, 2001. Fellow: Am. Acad. Arts & Scis. Office: Dept Philosophy Gilman Hall 347 3400 N Charles St Baltimore MD 21218 Office Phone: 410-516-7030. Office Fax: 410-516-6848 410-516-6848. Business E-Mail: mwilliams@jhu.edu. *

WILLIAMS, MICHAEL JAMES, lawyer; b. July 13, 1954; s. Robert L. and Carol J. (Edenborg) W.; m. Sherry L. Schnieder, Oct. 27, 1984; children: Taylor Michael, Tory Lyn. AA, N.D. State Coll. Sci., 1974; Bachelor's, U. N.D., Grand Forks, 1976, JD, 1979. Bar: N.D. 1979, U.S. Dist. Ct. N.D., 1982, U.S. Dist. Ct. Minn. 1982, U.S. Ct. Appeals (8th cir.) 1982, Minn. 1985. Atty. Kapsner & Kapsner, Bismarck, N.D., 1979-82; ptnr. Miller Norman Kenney & Williams, Moorhead, Minn., 1983-89; atty. Hagen Law Office, Fargo, N.D., 1989-92; ptnr. Maring Williams Law Office, Fargo, 1992—. Mem. N.D. Bar Assn. (pres. 2005), N.D. Trial Lawyers Assn. (prers. 2004), Minn. Trial Lawyers Assn., Minn. Bar Assn. Avocation: sports. Office: Maring Williams Law Office PC 1220 Main Ave Ste 105 Fargo ND 58107-2103 *

WILLIAMS, MICHAEL RICHARD, protective services official; b. Ypsilanti, Mich, Aug. 29, 1955; s. Jodie and Charlene (Walker) Williams; m. Karen Gayles Williams, Sept. 16, 1989. BBA, Western Mich. U., Kalamazoo, 1978; MDiv, Va. Union U., Richmond, Va., 2001. Auditor US Dept. Labor, Chgo., 1980—81, Mich. Dept. Treasury, Lansing, Mich., 1978—80; asst. mgr. corp. income tax Maccabess Mutual Life Ins. Co., Southfield, Mich., 1981—83; auditor US Dept. Labor OIG, Chgo., 1983—86; spl. agt. US Dept. Treasury IRS, Merrillville, Ind., 1986—90, US Dept Treasury OIG, Washington, 1990—. Pres. v.p. Genesis II Housing, Chgo., 1981—89. Author: (book poetry) Proverbs For The Heart, 1997, Mystseries In Human Nature, 1987. Vol. Detroit 300, 2003, Jamestown 400, Va., 2007; assoc. min. First Bapt. Ch., 1994—. Recipient Spl. Achievement award, Inspector Gen. Labor, 1983, Spl. award, Inspector Gen. Treas., 1993, Spl. Recognition award, Sec. Treasury, 2007. Independent. Baptist. Avocations: photography, music, writing, poetry.

WILLIAMS, MICHELLE, actress; b. Kalispell, Mont., Sept. 9, 1980; d. Larry and Carla; 1 child, Matilda Rose. Actor: (films) Lassie, 1994, Species, 1995, Timemaster, 1995, A Thousand Acres, 1997, Halloween H20: 20 Years Later, 1998, Dick, 1999, But I'm a Cheerleader, 1999, Perfume, 2001, Prozac Nation, 2001, Me Without You, 2001, The United States of Leland, 2003, The Station Agent, 2003, A Hole in One, 2004, Imaginary Heroes, 2004, Land of Plenty, 2004, The Baxter, 2005, Brokeback Mountain, 2005 (Critics Choice award, best supporting actress, Broadcast Film Critics Assn., 2006), The Hawk is Dying, 2006; (TV series) Raising Caines, 1995, Dawson's Creek, 1998—2003; (TV films) My Son Is Innocent, 1996, Killing Mr. Griffin, 1997, If These Walls Could Talk 2, 2000. Named one of 21 Hottest Stars Under 21, Teen People mag., 1999. Avocations: reading, boxing. Office: Creative Artists Agy 9830 Wilshire Blvd Beverly Hills CA 90212

WILLIAMS, MICHELLE (TENITRA MICHELLE WILLIAMS), singer; b. Rockford, Ill., July 23, 1980; Mem. Destiny's Child, 2000—05. Singer: (albums) Heart to Yours, 2002, Do You Know, 2004; singer: (with Destiny's Child) (songs) Say My Name, 2000 (MTV Video Music award, 2000, Grammy Award for best group R&B performance, best R&B song, 2001), (albums) Survivor, 2001 (MTV Video Music award, 2001, Am. Music award, Favorite Pop Album, 2002, Grammy award for best group R&B vocal performance, 2002), 8 Days of Christmas, 2001, Destiny Fulfilled, 2004 (Am. Music award, Favorite R&B Album, 2005); actor: (Broadway plays) Aida, 2002. Recipient Best Female Group, BET, 2001, Favorite R&B Group, Am. Music Awards, 2001, 2002, 2005, Image award for Outstanding Duo or Group, NAACP, 2001, 2005, 2006, Brit award, Best Internat. Group, 2002, World's Best-Selling Group, World Music Awards, 2002, World's Best-Selling Pop Group, 2002, 2006, World's Best-Selling R&B Group, 2002, 2006, Best-Selling Female Group of All Time, 2006. Address: 1505 Hadley Houston TX 77002 Office Phone: 212-833-3000. Office Fax: 713-772-5175.

WILLIAMS, MILLER, retired poet, writer, translator; b. Hoxie, Ark., Apr. 8, 1930; s. Ernest Burdette and Ann Jeanette (Miller) W.; m. Lucille Day, Dec. 29, 1951 (div.); m. Rebecca Jordan Hall, Apr. 11, 1969; children: Lucinda, Robert, Karyn. BS, Ark. State Coll., 1951; MS, U. Ark., 1952; postgrad., La. State U., 1951, U. Miss., 1957; HHD (hon.), Lander Coll., 1983; DHL, Hendrix Coll., 1995. Instr. in English La. State U., 1962-63, asst. prof., 1964-66; vis. prof. U. Chile, Santiago, 1963-64; assoc. prof. Loyola U., New Orleans, 1966-70; Fulbright prof. Nat. U. Mex., Mexico City, 1970; co-dir. grad. program in creative writing U. Ark., 1970-84, assoc. prof., 1971-73, prof. English and fgn. langs., dir. program in transl., 1973-87, univ. prof., 1987—2004, dir. poetry-in-the prisons programs div. continuing edn., 1974-79, chmn. program in comparative lit., 1978-80; ret., 2004. Fellow Am. Acad. in Rome, 1976—, mem. adv. coun. Sch. Classical Studies, 1985-91; first U.S. del. Pan Am. Conf. Univ. Artists and Writers, Concepcion, Chile, 1964; invited del. Internat. Assembly Univ. Press Dirs., Guadalajara, Mex., 1991; mem. poetry staff Bread Loaf Writers Conf., 1967-72; founder, exec. dir. Ark. Poetry Cir., 1975; founding dir. U. Ark.

Press, 1980-97; participant Assn. Am. Univ. Presses Soviet Mission, 1989. Author: (poems) A Circle of Stone, 1964, Recital, 1965, So Long At the Fair, 1968, The Only World There Is, 1971; (criticism) The Achievement of John Ciardi, 1968, The Poetry of John Crowe Ransom, 1971; (with John Ciardi) (criticism) How Does a Poem Mean?, 1974; (poems) Halfway From Hoxie: New & Selected Poems, 1973, Why God Permits Evil, 1977, Distractions, 1981, The Boys on Their Bony Mules, 1983; translator: (poems) Poems & Antipoems (Nicanor Parra), 1967, Emergency Poems (Nicanor Parra), 1972, Sonnets of Giuseppe Belli, 1981; editor: (poems) 19 Poetas de Hoy en Los Estados Unidos, 1966, (with John William Corrington) Southern Writing in the Sixties: Poetry, 1967, Southern Writing in the Sixties: Fiction, 1966, Chile: An Anthology of New Writing, 1968, Contemporary Poetry in America, 1972, (with James A. McPherson) Railroad: Trains and Train People in American Culture, 1976, A Roman Collection: An Anthology of Writing about Rome and Italy, 1980, Ozark, Ozark: A Hillside Reader, 1981, (criticism) Patterns of Poetry, 1986, (poetry) Imperfect Love, 1986, Living on the Surface: New and Selected Poems, 1989, Adjusting to the Light, 1992, Points of Departure, 1995, The Ways We Touch, 1997, Some Jazz A While: The Collected Poems, 1999, The Lives of Kevin Fletcher: Stories Mostly Short, 2002, Making a Poem: Some Throughts About Poetry and the People Who Write It, 2006; poetry editor La. State U. Press, 1966-68; contbr. articles to profl. publs. Named Bread Loaf fellow in poetry, 1963; recipient Henry Bellaman Poetry award, 1957, award in poetry, Arts Fund, 1973, Prix de Rome, Am. Acad. Arts and Letters, 1976, Nat. Poets prize, 1990, Charity Randall citation, Internat. Poetry Forum, 1993, John William Corrington award for excellence in lit., Centenary Coll., Shreveport, La., 1994, Acad. Lit. award, AAAL, 1995, Presdl. Inaugural Poet, 1997. Mem. MLA, PEN, AAUP, South Ctrl. MLA, Am. Lit. Translators Assn. (v.p. 1978-79, pres. 1979-81), Authors' Guild, Soc. Benemerito dell'Assn. Centro Romanesco Trilussa (Rome). Home: 1111 Valley View Dr Fayetteville AR 72701-1603

WILLIAMS, MONTEL, television talk show host; m. Rochele See (div.); children: Ashley, Maressa; m. Grace Morley, 1992 (div. 2000); children: Montel, Wyntergrace. Host The Montel Williams Show, 1990—. Actor(TV films): Perry Mason: The Case of the Telltale Talk Show Host, 1993, Educating Matt Waters, 1996, (TV series): A Different World, The New Adventures of Robin Hood, JAG; co-author: Bodychange, 2001; author: A Dozen Ways to Sunday, 2001, Mountain Get Out of My Way; co-author: Climbing Higher, 2004. Recipient Daytime Emmy Award for Outstanding Talk Show Host, 1996. Office: 433 W 53rd St New York NY 10019-5603

WILLIAMS, NANCY, lawyer; b. Kansas City, Mo., Jan. 2, 1945; BS in Journalism, Northwestern U., 1967; JD magna cum laude, U. Mich., 1980. Bar: Wash. 1981, US Ct. Appeals (9th Cir.), US Dist. Ct. (We. Dist.) Wash., US Dist. Ct. (Ea. Dist.) Wash. Volunteer PeaceCorp, 1967—69; pub. info. officer US Dept. Labor, 1973—78; ptnr. Perkins Coie LLP, Seattle, mem. exec. com., chmn. Labor & Employment Practice Area Seattle Office. Co-editor: Washington Employment Law Letter, 1994—; rev. asst. Equal Employment Law Update, 1996, 1997, 1998; contbg. editor: (rev. asst.) Equal Employment Law Update, 2003—, Employment Discrimination Law, 1996. Mem.: ABA (Labor & Litig. Sect.). Office: Perkins Coie LLP 1201 Third Ave Ste 4800 Seattle WA 98101-3099 Office Phone: 206-359-8473. Office Fax: 206-359-9000. Business E-Mail: nwilliams@perkinscoie.com.

WILLIAMS, NEIL, JR., retired lawyer; b. Charlotte, NC, Mar. 22, 1936; s. Lyman Neil and Thelma (Peterson) W.; m. Sue Sigmon, Aug. 23, 1958; children: Fred R., Susan S. AB, Duke U., 1958, JD, 1961. Bar: Ga. 1962, U.S. Dist. Ct. (no. dist.) Ga. 1977, U.S. Ct. Appeals (11th cir.) 1977. Assoc. Alston & Bird (and predecessor firm), Atlanta, 1961—65, ptnr., 1966—99, mng. ptnr., 1984-96; gen. counsel, global ptnr. Amvescap PLC, Atlanta, 1999—2002; ret., 2002. Bd. dir. Printpack, Inc., Atlanta, Acuity Brands, Inc., Atlanta. Chmn. bd. trustees Duke U., 1983—88, trustee, 1980—93; chmn. bd. trustees Vasser Woolley Found., Atlanta, 1975—, Leadership Atlanta, 1976—80; trustee Brevard Music Ctr., 1977—86, 1991—2001, Presbyn. Ch. USA Found., Jeffersonville, Ind., 1983—90, Research Triangle Inst., 1983—88, The Duke Endowment, Charlotte, NC, 1997—, Halle Found., Atlanta, 2005—; bd. dir. Atlanta Symphony Orch., 1970—76, 1984—93, 1995—98, pres., 1988—90; bd. dir. Woodruff Arts Ctr., 1987—98, 1999—, chmn., 2001—; bd. counsellors The Carter Ctr., Atlanta, 1987—96, Ctrl. Atlanta Progress, 1984—96; bd. dir. Am. Symphony Orch. League, Washington, 1990—2000, chmn., 1995—99. Recipient Disting. Alumni award Duke U., 1991, Rhyne award, 1996, Learned Hand award Am. Jewish Com., 2006. Mem. ABA, Am. Bar Found., State Bar Ga., Am. Law Inst., Atlanta C. of C. (bd. dirs. 1992-97, vice chmn. 1994-97), Piedmont Driving Club, Commerce Club (Atlanta), University Club (N.Y.C.), Phi Beta Kappa, Omicron Delta Kappa. Home: 3 Nacoochee Pl NW Atlanta GA 30305-4164 Office Phone: 404-881-7883. Business E-Mail: neil.williams@alston.com.

WILLIAMS, NEVILLE, solar power company executive; b. Muncie, Ind., Mar. 28, 1943; s. Donald Charles and Rose Eileen (Boughton) W. Student, U. Colo., 1964-66, U. Neuchatel, Switzerland, 1967. Freelance corr., Vietnam, 1968-69; freelance journalist Montreal, Que., Can., 1970-71, London, 1971-73; writer, prodr. Sta. WNBC-TV News, NYC, 1973-74; freelance writer Telluride, Colo., 1975-79; media liaison Office of Solar Energy U.S. Dept. Energy, Washington, 1979-80; dir. of mktg. Telluride Ski Resort, Inc., 1981-83; owner, operator Hist. Sheridan Opera House, Telluride, 1983-85; nat. media dir. Greenpeace USA, Washington, 1987-89; chmn. exec. dir., founder Solar Electric Light Fund, Washington, 1990—97. Chmn., CEO, founder Solar Electric Light Co., 1997-2003; chmn. SELCO-India, 1995-2005; founder, chmn. Standard Solar, Inc. Author: The New Exiles, 1971, Chasing the Sun, 2005; contbr. articles to NY Times mag., Outside, New Times, The Nation, The New Republic, Nature, Solar Today, others. Apptd. mem. Adv. Com. for Commerce and Devel., State of Colo., 1980-85, Gov.'s Motion Picture & TV Commn., 1981-85. Recipient Corp. Excellence award, U.S. Dept. of State, 2001. Fellow Internat. Solar Energy Soc. Business E-Mail: neville@standardsolar.com.

WILLIAMS, NOEL BROWN, information technology executive; CIO Am. Svc. Group, Tenn.; with HCA-Hosp. Corp. of Am. Info. Svcs., 1979—93; v.p. info. svcs. HCA Information Svcs., 1993—95; cons., 1995—96; chief info. officer Am. Svc. Group/ Prison Health Svcs., Inc., 1996—97; sr. v.p., chief info. officer HCA Inc., Nashville, 1997—. Office: HCA Inc One Park Pl Nashville TN 37203

WILLIAMS, NORMA JEAN, lawyer; b. NY, Sept. 19, 1952; d. Arthur Robert and Mildred (McDaniel) Williams; m. Bruce Ephraim Goldstein, Oct. 28, 1989. BA magna cum laude, Wesleyan U., Middletown, Conn., 1974; JD, U. Calif., Berkeley, 1977. Bar: Calif. 1977, US Dist. Ct. (no. dist. Calif.) 1977, US Dist. Ct. (so. dist. Calif.) 1991. Assoc. Crosby, Heafey, Roach & May, Oakland, Calif., 1977-81; assoc. counsel Crocker Nat. Bank, San Francisco, 1981-82; assoc. Berger, Kahn, Shafton & Moss, LA, 1983-84, Brown, Winfield & Canzoneri, LA, 1984-85; ptnr. Williams & Assocs., LA, 1985—. Mem. Urban Land Inst., LA; mem. faculty Practicing Law Inst., NYC. Contbr. articles to profl. jours. Recipient Cert. Appreciation City of LA, 1987. Mem. State Bar Calif. (mem. exec. com. real property law sect. 1990-93, chair real property sect. 1993-96, so. Calif. co-chair fin. sub-sect. real property law sect. 1988-90), LA County Bar Assn. (exec. com. 1993-, chair real property sect.), Fin. Lawyers Conf., Am. Coll. Real Estate Lawyers (hon.), Am. Coll. Mortgage Attys. (bd. regents 2004-). Office: Williams & Assocs 555 W 5th St Ste 3100 Los Angeles CA 90013 Office Phone: 213-996-8464. Office Fax: 213-947-1799. E-mail: njwilliams@willassoc.com. *

WILLIAMS, O'BANION, III, lawyer; b. Houston, 1956; BA, Tex. Tech. U., 1979; JD, St. Mary's U. Sch. Law, 1983. Bar: Tex. 1983. Ptnr., Energy Transactions, Real Estate Andrews Kurth LLP, Houston, treas., Lawyers for Am. Com. Sr. assoc. editor St. Mary's Law Jour. Mem.: Houston Bar Assn., State Bar Tex., ABA, Phi Delta Phi. Office: Andrews Kurth LLP 600 Travis St Ste 4200 Houston TX 77002-3090 Office Phone: 713-220-4340. Office Fax: 713-238-7147. Business E-Mail: owilliams@andrews-kurth.com.

WILLIAMS, OLIVER FRANKLIN, priest, educator; b. West Orange, NJ, Dec. 4, 1939; s. Justin James Williams and Ruth Amelda Flammer. BS in Chem. Engring., U. Notre Dame, 1961, MTh, 1969; PhD, Vanderbilt U., 1974. Prof. U. Notre Dame, Ind., 1973—, dir. MDiv program Ind., 1974—77, assoc. provost Ind., 1987—94, dir. Ctr. for Ethics and Religious Values in Bus. Ind., 1994—. Chmn. bd. Leadership Devel. Program U.S. - South Africa, Washington, 1995—2004; mem. adv. coun. U.S. Cos. in South Africa (Sullivan Principles), NYC, 1987—94; trustee St. Augustine's U., Johannesburg, 1996—; bd. dirs. UN Global Compact Learning Forum Academic Network, 2002—; vis. prof. U. Cape Town, Stellenbosch U., 2003—; bd. dirs. Found. for UN Global Compact, 2006—. Co-author: Economic Imperatives and Ethical Values, 2001; author: The Apartheid Crisis, 1986; editor, contbr.: Global Codes of Conduct: An Idea Whose Time Has Come, Business, Religion and Spirituality: A New Synthesis, 2003. Bd. dirs. Edn. Africa, Johannesburg, 1993, Catholic Charities, Diocese of Fort Wayne, South Bend, 1986—92, King's Coll., Pa., 2004—. Recipient Charles C. Slater Meml. award, Jour. Macromarketing, 1992. Mem.: Assn. for Practical and Profl. Ethics, Soc. for Bus. Ethics, Acad. Mgmt. (chair social issues divsn. 1990—91). Roman Catholic. Avocations: hiking, travel, writing. Home: 400 Siegfried Hall Notre Dame IN 46556 Office: U of Notre Dame 255 Mendoza Coll Bus Notre Dame IN 46556 Office Phone: 574-631-5761 x 6072. Business E-Mail: williams.80@nd.edu.

WILLIAMS, PAT, professional sports team executive; b. Phila., May 3, 1940; m. Ruth Williams; 19 children. B in Phys. Edn., Wake Forest U.; MS in Phys. Edn., Ind. U., 1964. Bus. mgr. Fla. State League Miami Marlins Class A Baseball Club, 1964—65; gen. mgr. West Carolina League Spartanburg Phillies, SC, 1965—67, pres., 1967—68, Orlando Double-A So. League Baseball Team, 1990—93; bus. mg
Phila. 76ers, 1968—69,
gen. mgr., v.p., 1974—86; gen. mgr. Chg
lls, 1969—73, Atlanta
Hawks, 1973—74; gen. mgr., COO Orla
c, 1986—96, sr. v.p.,
1996—. Author: Making Magic, Coach
to be Leaders: The
Keys to Unlocking Their Potential,
Be a Champion,
How to Be Like Coach Wooden.
ec. of Yr., The
Sporting News, 1967; named
2001, Wake
Forest Sports Hall of Fame.
s Office:
Orlando Magic 8701 M
0-5915
Office Phone: 407-9
nail:
pwilliams@patwillia

WILLIAMS,
May 26, 19
Coll.Wil
Philos
Vic
Sh
Chr
Hazar
Theology
(Jour.) Un
Quaker Unif
encys. Mem. A
Washington, 199
Montgomery. Fello
Quaker Universalist F
Soc. for History, Philos
chmn. 1992—93), Philoso
Assn. Higher Edn. Mem. So
PO Box 69 Covesvi
theologyauthor@aol.com.

WILLIAMS, PATRICIA BADIA,
Robert Murray Johnson and Orienta
Williams, July 6, 1989; children: Kristin
Harrison stepchildren: Celeste Anderson, L
Jody, Beth Thayden, Megan Clark. BA with
U.
Calif., San Jose, 1971; MA in Counseling Psyc
Clara,
Calif., 1976; postgrad., Kent State U., Ohio, U. Was
e Coll.,
U. N.Mex., U. Puget Sound, Youngstown State U.
Cert. clin.
criminal justice specialist (CCCJS) Nat. Assn. Forensic C
selors, master addictions counselor AODA Cert. Bd., nat. sch. counselor, nat. bd. counselor, lic. tchr., counselor Ohio, 2006, cert. tchr. Colo., lic. counselor Ariz., cert. secondary sch. tchr., tchr. Wash., lic. counselor Wash., cert. tchr. Calif. Jr. h.s. math.tchr., 1971—77; instr. math Olympic Coll., Bremerton, Wash., 1978—79, instr. prevention of child sexual abuse, 1985; adj. prof. Seattle Pacific U., 1986; jr. high counselor, math. tchr. South Kitsap Sch. Dist. 402, Port Orchard, Wash., 1977—79; mid. sch. counselor Bainbridge Island Sch. Dist., Bainbridge Island, Wash., 1979—89; jr. high counselor Marana Unified Sch. Dist., Marana, Ariz., 1989—93; mid. sch. counselor Fremont RE-1 Sch. Dist., Canon City, Colo., 1993—98; tchr. math. Canfield Village Sch. Dist., Canfield, Ohio, 1999—2000; ret., 2000; tchr. talented and gifted program Canfield Village Mid. Sch., 2007. Sch., cmty. trainer in prevention of child sexual abuse, 1985—87. Active numerous civic orgns./founds.; vol. tchr. Ceasar Chavez Farmer Worker Assn., 1970—71; charter bd. dirs. Storybook Mus.; bd. dirs. Mid. Sch. Alternative Program, Canon City, 1996—97; bd. mem. Salem Hist. Hope Cemetery, 2006; charter mem. Kitsap County Human Rights Commn., 1989; trustee Salem Preservation Soc. Named Outstanding Alumna of Yr., U. Santa Clara, 1999, Lifetime Hon. Rotarian Cmty. Svc., 1993, Mid. Sch. Counselor of Yr. hon. mention, Colo. Sch. Counselor Assn., 1997; recipient Recognition Svc. to Youth, Kiwanis, 1998. Mem.: Ohio Sch. Counselors Assn. (bd. dirs. 1999—2000, dist. 9 rep.), Nat. Assn. Forensic Counselors, Am. Sch. Counselors Assn., Am. Assn. Christian Counselors, Ohio Counselors Assn., Salem Preservation Soc. Achievements include initiated peer mediation programs in Colo. and Ariz. Office Phone: 330-332-5536. Personal E-mail: rwilliams4@neo.rr.com.

WILLIAMS, PATRICIA J., law educator; b. Boston, 1951; BA, Wellesley Coll, 1972; JD, Harvard Univ, 1975. Bar: Calif, US Ct Appeals, 9th cir. Dep. city atty. LA City Atty. Office, 1976—78; atty. Western Ctr. on Law & Poverty, LA, 1978—80; asst. prof. Golden Gate Coll., 1980—84, assoc. prof., 1984—85, CUNY, 1984—88; prof. Univ. Wis., Madison, 1988—93, Columbia U., NYC, 1991—, James L. Dohr prof. law. Trustee Wellesley Coll. Columnist The Nation; author: The Alchemy of Race & Rights, 1991, The Rooster's Egg: On the Persistence of Prejudice, 1995, Seeing a Color-Blind Future: The Paradox of Race, 1997. Grantee MacArthur Fellowship, 2000. Office: Columbia Law Sch 435 W 116th St New York NY 10027-7297 E-mail: williams@law.columbia.edu.

WILLIAMS, PATTERSON BOUIC, museum educator; b. Sandy Springs, Md., Dec. 7, 1941; d. William Viers and Doris (Patterson) Bouic; m. James M. Williams, May 11, 1968. B.F.A., Denison U., 1964; M.A. in Art History, U. Mich., 1966. Mus. tchr. Walters Art Gallery, Balt., 1966-68, Phila. Mus. of Art, 1968-74, adminstr. sch. programs, 1974-79; dir. edn. Denver Art Mus., 1979—, master tchr. asian art; adv. mus. edn. issues, Houston Mus. Art, Art Loan Prog.; adv. com. Getty Ctr. Arts Edn., 1984; cons., corr., speaker. Contbr. articles to profl. jours. Bd. dirs. Front Range Women in Arts, Denver, 1982; mem. program com. Denver 125th Anniversary Celebration, 1984. Mem. Colo. Assn. for Arts Edn. (treas. 1979-81), Assn. Am. Museums (v.p. edn. commn. 1981, councilor-at-large 1984, named to Centennial Honor Roll, 2006), Mountain Plains Mus. Conf. (edn. regional rep. 1981-82), Phi Beta Kappa. Democrat. Episcopalian. *

WILLIAMS, PAUL, retired federal agency administrator; b. Jacksonville, Ill., Aug. 6, 1929; s. Russell and Bernice (Wheeler) W.; m. Ora B. Mosby; 1 child, Reva Williams. BA, Ill. Coll., 1956, LHD, 1980. Dir. fin. City of Chgo., 1956-63; assoc. dir. fin. United Planning Orgn., Washington, 1964-65; internat. adminstrv. officer U.S. Dept. State, Washington, 1965-68; dir. office mgmt. U.S. HUD, Washington, 1968-93, gen. dep. dept. fair housing and equal opportunity, 1993-94, dep. ops. and mgmt., 1994-97, ret., 1997. Cons. S.E. Econ. Devel. Corp., Nat. Exec. Svc. Corp., 1998; Buzan learning instr. for mind mapping, 2000-2002. Author: Questionnaire on Execution of Urban Renewal Programs, 1959. Pres. Bel Pre Civic Assn., Wheaton, Md., 1978, bd. dirs., 1971, 79; pres. Bel Pre PTA, Wheaton, 1973, Rossmoor Kiwanis Club, 2002, Rossmore Kiwanis Found., 2004-05; bd. dirs. Rockville C. of C., African Am. C. of C. Sgt. U.S. Army, 1948-52. Recipient letter of recognition for 36 yrs. fed. svc. U.S. Pres., letter of recognition for 36 yrs. govt. svc. Senators of Md., citation for 36 yrs. dedicated govt. svc. Gov. of Md., cert. of recognition Nat. Assn. Black and Minority C. of C., 1987. Baptist. Avocations: reading, jogging, golf, tai chi. Home: Unit 306 2900 N LeisureWorld Blvd Silver Spring MD 20906-2321 Office Phone: 301-598-2899. Personal E-mail: owilli7738@aol.com.

WILLIAMS, PAUL ROBERT, lawyer, foreign policy analyst; b. Pasadena, Calif., June 3, 1965; s. Robert David and Janice Martha W.; m. Kathleen Elizabeth, June 3, 1965, July 24, 1964. AB in Polit. Sci., U. Calif. Davis, 1987; JD, Stanford U., 1990; PhD, U. Cambridge, 1997. Bar: Calif. 1990. Law clk. to Justice William H. Erickson Colo. Supreme Ct., Denver, 1990-91; atty., adviser U.S. State Dept. Office of Legal Adviser, Washington, 1991-93; Fulbright Rsch. scholar U. Cambridge, 1993-96; exec. dir. Pub. Internat. Law and Policy Group, 1994—; sr. assoc. Carnegie Endowment for Internat. Peace, 1996—. Author: Treatment of Detainees, 1990; contbr. articles to profl. jours. Nominee Nobel Peace Prize, 2005. Mem. ABA, Am. Soc. Internat. Law. Lutheran.

WILLIAMS, PAUL STRATTON, executive recruiter; b. San Francisco, Oct. 9, 1959; s. Henry Stratton and Frances (Spurlock) W.; m. Laura Dawn Coleman, Sept. 15, 1984; children: Scott Coleman, Ryan Stratton. AB, Harvard Coll., 1981; JD, Yale U., 1984. Bar: Calif. 1984, Ohio 1987. Assoc. Gibson, Dunn & Crutcher, LA, 1984-87, Vorys, Sater, Seymour & Pease, Columbus, Ohio, 1987-90; gen. counsel Info. Dimensions, Inc., Dublin, Ohio, 1994-95; v.p., asst. gen. counsel Cardinal Health, Inc., 1995—99, sr. v.p., dep. gen. counsel, 2000—01, exec. v.p., chief legal off. and sec., 2001—05; mng. dir. Major, Lindsey and Africa, 2005—. Bd. dir. State Auto Fin. Corp.; bd. dirs. Bob Evans Farms Restaurants. Mem. Harvard Club Central Ohio. Democrat. Avocations: running, tennis. Office Phone: 312-456-1848. Business E-Mail: pwilliams@mlaglobal.com.

IAMS, PEARL See GOOD, EDITH

MS, PEGGY RYAN, academic administrator; b. Montreal, Que.,
1947; d. Fred Smith and Carol (Kennedy) Ryan; m. David
30, 1970. BA psychology, U. Toronto, St. Michael's
d, U. Vt., 1976; EdD, Harvard U., 1983. Caseworker,
e County Dept. Social Svcs., Rochester, NY,
ker Med. Ctr. Hosp. of Vt., Burlington, 1972;
sor CC of Vt., Lamoille County, 1973—75,
, 1975—76, regional dir. Montpelier, 1976-82;
1978—85; asst. to the pres. Johnson (Vt.) State
chg. fellow Harvard U., 1981; dir. ednl. and pers.
cellor Vt. State Colleges, Waterbury, 1982-85; assoc.
., Burlington, 1985—89, chair, dept. bus & economics,
. acad. dean, 1988-89; pres. Lyndon State Coll., Lyndon-
89-97, Ithaca (N.Y.) Coll., 1997—; dir. Coun. Ind. Colls. Adj.
ohnson State Coll., 1984—86. Active The Ithaca Downtown
ship Cmty. Adv. Bd.; bd. mem. Sacred Heart Sch. Montreal, bd.
r, 1998—2001; bd. mem. Tompkins Trust Co., 1999—; com. mem.
ornell U. Johnson Mus. Art Cmty. Adv. Coun.; mem. adv. coun. Finger Lakes Land Trust, 2000—03. Recipient Jackie M. Gibbons Leadership award, Am. Coun. Edn./Nat. Identification Program, 1984, Margaret R. Williams Emerging Profl. award. Mem. Am. Assn. Higher Edn., 1973-, Am. Coun. on Edn., 1981- (bd. dirs., 2000-), Nat. Assn. Women in Edn., 1985-, Office: Ithaca Coll Job Hall Ithaca NY 14850

WILLIAMS, PETER MACLELLAN, nuclear engineer; b. NYC, Aug. 30, 1931; s. Gilbert Harris and Evelyn (Buss) W.; m. Lois Crane, Oct. 6, 1956; children: Jane, Gilbert, Katherine, Anne, Louise, Robert. BChemE, Cornell U., 1954; MS in Nuclear Engring., MIT, 1957; PhD in Nuclear Engring., U. Md., 1971. Engr. DuPont Savannah River, Aiken, SC, 1954-55; task engr. AGN, San Ramon, Calif., 1957-60; project mgr. Am. Machine & Fdry., Greenwich, Conn., 1960-62; research staff Princeton U., NJ, 1962-67; sr. project mgr., specialist in high temperature gas cooled reactors U.S. Nuclear Regulatory Commn., Washington, 1967-91; dir. div. high temperature gas cooled reactors U.S. Dept. of Energy, Washington, 1991-94; cons. Internat. Atomic Energy Agy., Vienna, 1994—; cons. nuclear engr., 1995—. Mem. Chernobyl Tracking Team, 1986; U.S. del. to gas-cooled reactors working group, Internat. Atomic Energy Agy., 1991; steering com. mem. U.S.-Japan Implementing Agreement on gas-cooled reactors, 1991 Contbr. articles to profl. jours.; author various reports. Scoutmaster Boy Scouts Am., Potomac, Md., 1972, cubmaster, 1983-86; pres. PTA Winston Churchill High Sch., Potomac, 1981. Assoc. fellow AIAA; mem. Am. Nuclear Soc. (instr. workshhop gas coolent reactor 2001, instr. profl. devel. workshop 2005), Sigma Xi Democrat. Unitarian Universalist. Achievements include patent for liquid core nuclear rocket; patent pending for advanced helium turbine reactor. Home and Office: 9418 Thrush Ln Potomac MD 20854-3991 Office Phone: 301-299-7236. Personal E-mail: peterwill@starpower.net.

WILLIAMS, PHILIP COPELAIN, gynecologist, obstetrician; b. Vicksburg, Miss., Dec. 9, 1917; s. John Oliver and Eva (Copelain) W.; B.S. magna cum laude, Morehouse Coll., 1937; M.D., U. Ill., 1941; m. Constance Shielda Rhetta, May 29, 1943; children— Philip, Susan Carol, Paul Rhetta. Intern, Cook County Hosp., Chgo., 1942-43, resident in ob-gyn, 1946-48; resident in gynecology U. Ill., 1948-49; practice medicine specializing in ob-gyn, Chgo., 1949—; mem. staff St. Joseph Hosp., Ill. Masonic Hosp., Cook County Hosp., McGaw Hosp.; clin. prof. Med. Sch. Northwestern U., Chgo. Bd. dirs. Am. Cancer Soc. Chgo. unit and Ill. div. Served with U.S. Army, 1943-45. Recipient Civic award Loyola U., 1970; Edwin S. Hamilton Interstate Teaching award, 1984; diplomate Am. Bd. Ob-Gyn, Fellow ACS, Internat. Coll. Surgeons; mem. AMA, Chgo., Ill. med. socs., AMA, Chgo. Gynecol. Soc. (treas. 1975-78, pres. 1980-81), Am. Fertility Soc., Inst. Medicine, N.Y. Acad. Scis., AAAS. Presbyn. Clubs: Barclay, Carlton, Plaza. Contbr. articles to profl. jours. E-mail: pwill2oo@aol.com. Home: 1040 N Lake Shore Dr Chicago IL 60611 E-mail: pwill200@sbcglobal.net.

WILLIAMS, PHYLLIS CUTFORTH, retired realtor; b. Moreland, Idaho, June 6, 1917; d. William Claude and Kathleen Jessie (Jenkins) Cutforth; m. Joseph Marsden Williams, Jan. 21, 1938 (dec. 1986); children:

Joseph Marlis, Bonnie Lou Williams Thompson, Nancy Kay Williams Stewart, Marjorie Williams Karren, Douglas Claude, Thomas Marsden, Wendy Kathleen Williams Clark, Shannon Irene Williams Ostler. Grad., Ricks Coll., 1935. Tchr. Grace (Idaho) Elem. Sch., 1935-38; realtor Williams Realty, Idaho Falls, Idaho, 1972-77; mem. Idaho Senate, Boise, 1977. Owner, mgr. river property. Compiler: Idaho Legisladies Cookbook, Cookin' Together, 1981. With MicroFilm Ctr., LDS Ch. Mission, Salt Lake City, 1989-90; former block chmn., vol. Cancer Drive; active Idaho State Legisladies Club, 1966-84, v.p., 1982-84; mem. Bonneville County (Idaho) Rep. Women. Avocations: genealogy, music, politics, cooking, attending grandchildren's special events.

WILLIAMS, QUINN PATRICK, lawyer; b. Evergreen Park, Ill., May 6, 1949; s. William Albert and Jeanne Marie (Quinlan) Williams; children: Michael Ryan, Mark Reed, Kelly Elizabeth. BBA, U. Wis., 1972; JD, U. Ariz., 1974. Bar: Ariz. 1975, US Dist. Ct. Ariz. 1976, NY 1984. V.p., sec., gen. counsel Combined Comm. Corp., Phoenix, 1975-80; sr. v.p. legal and adminstrn. Swensen's Inc., Phoenix, 1980-86; ptnr. Winston & Strawn, Phoenix, 1985—89, Snell & Wilmer, Phoenix, 1989—2002; shareholder Greenberg Traurig, 2002—; pres. Enterprise network, 2001. Bd. dirs. Ariz. Venture Capital Conf., 1993—2000, Ariz. Tech. Coun., 2001—; co-chmn. Gov.'s Small Bus. Adv. Exec. Coun., 1996—2000; vice-chair Gov. Regulatory Coun., 1995—97; sec. GSPED High Tech. Cluster, 1993—; chair, bd. dirs. Greater Phoenix Econ. Coun., 1996—2000; mem. exec. com. A2Tech Coun., 2002—; mem. Gov.'s Coun. Innovation and Tech., 2003—. With USAR, 1967—73. Mem.: ABA, NY Bar Assn., Maricopa County Bar Assn., State Bar Ariz., Internat. Franchise Assn., Scotsdale C. of C. (bd. dirs. 2003—), Paradise Valley Country Club, Scottsdale Charros. Office: Greenberg Traurig 2375 E Camelback Rd Ste 700 Phoenix AZ 85016-9000 Office Phone: 602-445-8344. Business E-Mail: williamsq@gtlaw.com.

WILLIAMS, R. NEIL, finance company executive; B in acctg., Univ. So. Miss. CPA. Acct. Touche Ross & Co.; sr. v.p. & controller Deposit Guaranty Nat. Bank; sr. mgmt. positions First Commerce Corp.; vice-chmn. Premier Bancorp., Premier Bank; exec. v.p., group mgr. nat. enterprise ops. Bank One Corp., 1995—2001; exec. v.p. fin. Visa USA, San Francisco, 2001—04, exec. v.p., CFO, 2004—. Mailing: Visa USA PO Box 194607 San Francisco CA 94119-4607 *

WILLIAMS, RALPH CHESTER, JR., physician, educator; b. Washington, Feb. 17, 1928; s. Ralph Chester and Annie (Perry) W.; m. Mary Elizabeth Adams, June 23, 1951; children: Cathy, Frederick (dec.), John (dec.), Michael, Ann AB with distinction, Cornell U., 1950, MD, 1954; MD (hon.), U. Lund, Sweden, 1991. Diplomate Am. Bd. Internal Medicine. Intern Mass. Gen. Hosp., Boston, 1954-55, asst. resident in internal medicine, 1955-56; resident in internal medicine N.Y. Hosp., 1956-57; chief resident Mass. Gen. Hosp., Boston, 1959-60; guest investigator Rockefeller Inst., NYC, 1961-63; physician in internal medicine and rheumatology, 1963—; assoc. prof. U. Minn., Mpls., 1963-68, prof., 1968-69; prof., chmn. dept. medicine U. N.Mex., Albuquerque, 1969-88; Schott prof. rheumatology and medicine U. Fla., Gainesville, 1988-98; with rheumatology dept. U. N.Mex. Sch. Medicine, Albuquerque, 1998, emeritus prof. medicine, 1998—. Assoc. editor: Jour. Lab. and Clin. Medicine, 1966-69; mem. editl. bd.: Arthritis and Rheumatism, 1968—; contbr. articles to profl. jours. Capt. USAF, 1957—59. Recipient Regents' Meritorious Svc. award, U. N.Mex., 2003. Master Am. Coll. Rheumatology (Gold medal 2004); fellow ACP; mem. Am. Assn. Immunology, Assn. Am. Physicians, Am. Fedn. Clin. Rsch., Am. Soc. Clin. Investigation, Ctrl. Soc. Clin. Rsch., Western Soc. Clin. Investigation, Phi Beta Kappa, Alpha Omega Alpha. Achievements include research in immunologic processes and connective tissue diseases. Home: 624 E Alameda St Apt 13 Santa Fe NM 87501-2293 Office: Ste A 1630 Hop Dr Santa Fe NM 87505 Personal E-mail: coolypatch22@aol.com.

WILLIAMS, RALPH WATSON, JR., retired security firm executive; b. Atlanta, July 2, 1933; s. Ralph Watson and Minnie Covington (Hicks) W.; m. Nancy Jo Morgan, Mar. 19, 1955 (dec. Dec. 1989); children: Ralph Watson III, Nancy Jane, John Martin Hicks; m. Almonese Brown Clifton, Nov. 24, 1990. Grad., Sewanee Mil. Acad., 1951; BBA, U. Ga., 1955. Trainee banking Trust Co. Ga., Atlanta, 1955; mcpl. sales staff Courts & Co., Atlanta, 1955-57; v.p., salesman securities First Southeastern Corp., Atlanta, 1957-60; br. mgr. Francis I. duPont & Co., 1960-69; spl. partner duPont Glore Forgan Inc., NYC, 1969-70, gen. partner, 1970, exec. v.p., 1971—, sr. v.p., bd. dirs., mem. exec. com., 1972—; sr. v.p., dir., mem. exec. com. duPont-Walston Inc., 1973-74; sr. v.p. E.F. Hutton & Co. Inc., 1974-81; exec. v.p., dir. E.F. Hutton & Co., Inc., 1981-88; exec. v.p. Shearson Lehman Hutton Inc., Atlanta, 1988-89; ret., 1989. Former bd. trustees, chmn. fin. com. St. Andrews Sewanee (Tenn.) Sch.; former exec. com. mem. U. Ga., Ga. Tech. Found. Mem. Nat. Assn. Security Dealers (chmn. dist. com. 7), Benedicts Atlanta, Phi Delta Theta. Clubs: Commerce (Atlanta), Capital City (Atlanta), Piedmont Driving (Atlanta). Presbyterian. Home: 3504 Dumbarton Rd NW Atlanta GA 30327-2614 Home Fax: 404-237-1812. Personal E-mail: ralphnesie@comcast.net.

WILLIAMS, REBA WHITE, corporate financial executive, writer, researcher; m. Dave H. Williams. BA in Enlgish, Duke U., Durham, NC; MBA, Harvard U., Cambridge, Mass.; MA in Art History, Hunter Coll., NYC; MA in Philosophy, CUNY, PhD in Art History. Former rschr. McKinsey & Co., Inc.; securities analyst Mitchell Hutchins, Inc. Dir. spl. projects, mem. bd. dir. Alliance Capital Mgmt.; vice chmn. White Williams Holdings, Ltd., 2001—. Mem. editl. bd. Print Quar.; contbr. articles to Am. Artist, Bus. and Soc., Instl. Investor Chgo. Daily News, Fin. Analysts Jour., others; author catalog essays. Mem. Manhattan Cmty. Bd. 8, 1999-2000; mem. Art Commn. City NY, 1995-98, pres., 1997-98; mem. NY State Coun. on the Arts, 1996-99, vice chmn., 1999; hon. keeper of Am. prints The Fitzwilliam Mus., Cambridge, Eng. Decorated Polish Order of Merit, cavalier of grand cross Order of Poland 1st class; recipient Pacesetter award NY City Coun., 1999, Disting. Cultural Leadership award NY Rep. County Com., 1999, Augustus Graham medal Bklyn. Mus., 1998; named one of Top 200 Collectors, ARTnews Mag., 2004, 2006, others. Mem. Cosmopolitan Club. Avocation: Collector of Am. Prints. Office: 258 Atlantic St Stamford CT 06901 Office Phone: 212-752-1705. Business E-Mail: reba@rebawhitewilliams.com.

WILLIAMS, REBECCA LYNN, lawyer, nurse; b. LaGrange, Ill., Jan. 24, 1959; d. Richard Fowler and Anita (Albro) W. BSN magna cum laude, Duke U., 1981; JD, Loyola U., 1986. Bar: Ill. 1986, U.S. Dist. Ct. (no. dist.) Ill. 1986. Nurse Children's Meml. Hosp., Chgo., 1981-84, St. Jude's Hosp., Vieux Fort, St. Lucia, 1983; assoc. McDermott, Will & Emery, Chgo., 1986-88, Winston & Strawn, Chgo., 1988-93; ptnr. Sonnenschein Nath & Rosenthal, Chgo., 1993-98, Davis Wright Tremaine LLP, Seattle, 1998—. Contbr. articles to profl. jours. Patron various civic, environ., charitable and polit. groups. Mem.: ANA, ABA, Workgroup for Electronic Data Interchange (chair preemption subwork group), Am. Health Lawyers Assn. Avocations: scuba diving, reading, hiking, photography. Office: Davis Wright Tremaine LLP 1201 Third Ave Ste 2200 Seattle WA 98101-3045 Business E-Mail: beckywilliams@dwt.com.

WILLIAMS, REDFORD BROWN, medical educator; b. Raleigh, NC, Dec. 14, 1940; s. Redford Brown Sr. and Annie Virginia (Betts) W.; m. Virginia Carter Parrott, August 9, 1940; children: Jennifer Betts, Lloyd Carter. AB, Harvard U., 1963; MD, Yale U., 1967. Diplomate Am. Bd. Internal Medicine. Intern, then resident Yale-New Haven Med. Ctr., 1967-70; sr. surgeon USPHS, Bethesda, Md., 1970-72; asst. prof. Duke U. Med. Ctr., Durham, NC, 1972, prof. psychiatry, 1977—, prof. psychology, 1990—, dir. behavioral medicine rsch. ctr., 1985—; CEO Williams LifeSkills, Inc., 1997—. Cons. NIH rev. coms., Bethesda, 1977—. Author: The Trusting Heart, 1989, Anger Kills, 1993, Lifeskills, 1998, In Control, 2006; contbr. articles to profl. jours. Dir. NC Heart Assn., Chapel Hill, 1980-83. Recipient Rsch. Scientist award NIMH, 1974—; NIH grantee, 1976—. Fellow Soc. Behavioral Medicine (pres. 1984-85, Upjohn Disting. Scientist award 1992), Acad. Behavioral Medicine Rsch. (pres. 1995—); mem. Am. Psychosomatic Soc. (bd. dirs. 1978-81, pres. 1992), Internat. Soc. Behavioral Medicine (pres.-elect 2004-06, pres. 2006-08). Unitarian Universalist. Avocation: tennis. Office: Duke U Med Ctr PO Box 3926 Durham NC 27710-0001 Home Phone: 919-383-2115; Office Phone: 919-684-3863. Business E-Mail: redfordw@duke.edu.

WILLIAMS, RICHARD DWAYNE, physician, educator, urologist; b. Wichita, Kans., Oct. 7, 1944; s. Errol Wayne and Roseanna Jane (Page) W.; m. Beverly Sue Ferguson, Aug. 29, 1964; 1 child, Wendy Elizabeth. BS, Abilene Christian U., 1966; MD, Kans. U., 1970. Diplomate Am. Bd. Urology, Nat. Bd. Med. Examiners. Intern, then resident in gen. surgery U. Minn., Mpls., 1970-72, resident in urology, 1972-76, asst. prof., 1976-79, U. Calif., San Francisco, 1979-84, assoc. prof., 1984; prof., chmn. dept. urology U. Iowa, Iowa City, 1984—. Chief urology VA Med. Ctr., San Francisco, 1979-84, VA Med. Ctr., Iowa City, 1984-88; mem. task force on bd. exams Am. Bd. Urology, 1981-85, guest examiner Oral exams, 1984-, trustee, 1994-2000; Rubin H. Flocks chair in urology U. Iowa, 1994; mem. nat. adv. coun. NIDDK, NIH. Author: (with others) Advances in Urologic Oncology, 1987, Genitourinary Cancer: Basic and Clinical Aspects, 1987, Adult and Pediatric Urology, 1987, General Urology, 1988, Textbook of Medicine, 1988, also others; editor: Advances in Urologic Oncology, 1987; guest editor Seminars in Urology, 1985, Problems in Urology: Prostate Cancer, 1989; bd. editors Jour. Urology, 1980-88; mem. editorial bd. Urology, Jour. Urology; also articles. Bd. dirs. Iowa chpt. Nat. Kidney Found., bd. sci. advisors 1989-92; pres. Am. Found. Urologic Diseases, 2003-05. Maj. USAR, 1971-77. Bordeau scholar Kans. U. Med. Ctr., 1968-69; NIH, VA, Am. Cancer Soc. grantee. Fellow ACS (chmn. urology sect. No. Calif. chpt. 1980-82, chmn. ann. meeting programs 1988, mem. residency rev. com. urology 1993-99, vice chair 1995, chair 1997); mem. AAAS, Iowa Med. Soc., Iowa Urologic Soc., Am. Urologic Assn. (dir. seminar on residency evaluation 1987, bd. editors alt. 1988-, rep. North Ctrl. sect., prodr. slide presentations 1988, recipient prizes 1982, 87, com. mem. 1987-, bd. dirs. 1994, pres.-elect 1997), Am. Assn. for Cancer Rsch., Am. Soc. Clin. Oncology, Am. Assn. GU Surgeons, Clin. Soc. Genitourinary Surgeons (sec.-treas. 1997-2000), Soc. Internat. D'Urologie (pres. US sect. 2003-06), Soc. Univ. Urologists (chmn. com. on residency evaluation 1986-88, councillor 1987-, pres. 1993), Soc. Surg. Oncology, Soc. Urologic Oncology (chmn. membership com. 1987-90, sec. 1990-94, pres.-elect 1995, pres. 1996), Johnson County Med. Soc., Flock's Soc., Western Urologic Forum, Alpha Omega Alpha. Republican. Office: U Iowa Dept Urology 200 Hawkins Dr Iowa City IA 52242-1009 Office Phone: 319-356-0760. Business E-Mail: richard-williams@uiowa.edu.

WILLIAMS, RICHARD LEROY, federal judge; b. Morrisville, Va., Apr. 6, 1923; s. Wilcie Edward and Minnie Mae (Brinkley) W.; m. Eugenia Kellogg, Sept. 11, 1948; children: Nancy Williams Davies, R. Gregory, Walter L., Gwendolyn Mason. LLB, U. Va., 1951. Bar: Va. 1951. Ptnr. McGuire, Woods & Battle and predecessor firms, 1951-72; judge Cir. Ct. City of Richmond, 1972-76; ptnr. McGuire, Woods & Battle, 1976-80; dist. judge U.S. Dist. Ct., Richmond, Va., 1980—, sr. judge, 1992—. 2d lt. Air Corps., U.S. Army, 1940-45. Fellow Am. Coll. Trial Lawyers; mem. Va. State Bar, Va. Bar Assn., Richmond Bar Assn. Office: US Dist Ct/Lewis F Powell Ste 305 1000 E Main St Richmond VA 23219-3525 Office Phone: 804-916-2240.

WILLIAMS, RICHARD LUCAS, III, electronics executive, director, lawyer; b. Evanston, Ill., Oct. 30, 1940; s. Richard Lucas Jr. and Ellen Gene (Munster) W.; m. Karen Louise Carmody, Nov. 11, 1967 AB, Princeton U., 1962; LLB, U. Va., 1965. Bar: Ill. 1965, D.C. 1968, U.S. Supreme Ct. 1968. Assoc. Winston & Strawn, Chgo., 1968-74, ptnr., 1974-79; sr. v.p., gen. counsel Gould Inc., Rolling Meadows, Ill., 1979-81, sr. v.p., adminstrn., gen. counsel, 1981-90, also bd. dir., 1985-88; ptnr. Smith Williams and Lodge, Chgo., 1990-95, Vedder, Price, Kaufman & Kammholz, Chgo., 1995—. Bd. dirs. GNB Batteries, Inc., 1984-86, ULINE Inc., Waukegan, Ill. Bd. dirs., 1990—, Internat. Tennis Hall of Fame, Newport, R.I., 1993-97; v.p. Chgo. Dist. Tennis Assn., 1968-70; vice chmn. Am. Cancer Soc., Chgo., 1984; bd. dirs., pres. Lake Shore Found. for Animals, Chgo., 1990-94. With JAGC USNR, 1965-68. Mem. ABA, Ill. Bar Assn., Chgo. Bar Assn., Execs. Club Chgo. (co-chmn. Western Europe internat. com. 1990-97, 2003—), The Lawyers Club (Chgo., 1997—), Meadow Club (Rolling Meadows, gov. 1979-90, chmn. 1985-90), Club Internat. Home: 1200 N Lake Shore Dr Chicago IL 60610-2370 Office: Vedder Price 222 N La Salle St Ste 2600 Chicago IL 60601-1104 Office Phone: 312-609-7588. Business E-Mail: rwilliams@vedderprice.com.

WILLIAMS, RICHARD THOMAS, lawyer; b. Evergreen Park, Ill., Jan. 14, 1945; s. Raymond Theodore and Elizabeth Dorothy (Williams) W. AB with honors, Stanford U., 1967, MBA, JD, Stanford U., 1972. Bar: Calif. 1972, U.S. Supreme Ct. 1977. Assoc.,then ptnr. Kadison Pfaelzer Woodard Quinn & Rossi, LA, 1972-87; ptnr. Whitman & Ransom, 1987-93, Whitman, Breed, Abbott & Morgan, LA, 1993-2000, Holland & Knight, LLP, LA, 2000—. Contbg. editor Oil and Gas Analyst, 1978-84. Mem. ABA, L.A. County Bar Assn. Office: Holland & Knight LLP 633 W 5th St Los Angeles CA 90071-2005 Office Phone: 213-896-2410. Business E-Mail: richard.williams@hklaw.com.

WILLIAMS, RICHMOND DEAN, library consultant and appraiser; b. Reading, Mass., Dec. 10, 1925; s. Theodore Ryder and Anabel Lee (Hutchison) W.; m. Eleanor Davidson Washbourne, Sept. 26, 1953; children— Richmond Lyttleton, Eleanor Davidson, Anne Ryder. AB cum laude, Williams Coll., 1950; MA, U. Pa., 1952, PhD, 1959. Instr., asst. dean Williams Coll., Williamstown, Mass., 1954-56; dir. Wyo. Hist. and Geol. Soc., Wilkes-Barre, Pa., 1956-60; asst. dir. Am. Assn. State and Local History, Madison, Wis., 1960-61; dir. libraries Eleutherian Mills-Hagley Found., Wilmington, Del., 1962-87. Instr. Acad. Lifelong Learning U. Del., 1996—; cons. archivist M.S. Hershey Found., Pa., 1981—, Md. Dept. Housing and Cmty. Devel., 1993—94; bd. dirs. Rhistoric Inc. Co-author: A Look at Ourselves, 1962; author: They Also Served, 1965; compiler: Directory of Historical Records in Delaware, 1995; (series) Writing Haiku—, 1997-06. Sec., U. Del. Library Assocs., Wilmington, 1972-86; mem. adv. bd. Del. Hist. Records, Dover, 1976-02; mem. Del. Humanities Forum, Wilmington, 1984-91; trustee Conservation Ctr. Phila., 1984-86. Served to 1st lt. AUS, 1943-47. Pennfield fellow U. Pa., 1953 Mem.: Am. Antiquarian Soc., Am. Assn. State and Local History (pres. 1974—76), Mid-Atlantic Regional Archives Com., Econ. History Assn. (sec.-treas. 1975—88), Phi Beta Kappa. Avocations: golf, book collecting. Home and Office: 202 Brecks Ln Wilmington DE 19807-3011 Office Phone: 302-654-0986. Business E-Mail: rdwms@udel.edu.

WILLIAMS, RICKY (ERRICK LYNNE WILLIAMS), professional football player; b. San Diego, May 21, 1977; s. Errick and Sandy Williams; children: Marley, Prince. Grad, U. Tex. Running back/receiver New Orleans Saints, 1999—2002; running back Miami Dolphins, 2002—04, 2005—06, Toronto Argonauts, 2006—. Actor: (films) Stuck On You, 2003. Founder Run Ricky Run Foundation. Recipient Heisman Trophy, 1998; named to Pro-Bowl, 2002 Achievements include led NFL in rushing yards, 2002. Office: Toronto Argonauts Ste 3300 One Blue Jays Way Toronto ON M53 1J3 Canada Office Fax: 416-341-2714.

WILLIAMS, RITA CARROLL, protective services official, language educator, poet, librarian; b. Norfolk, Va., Jan. 11, 1962; d. William Henry Carroll Jr. and Joyce Riddick Carroll; m. Stafford Clayton Williams Jr., Dec. 2, 1985; 1 child, Thaddeus Clayton. BA in English, BS in Geology, Elizabeth City State U., 1985; student in mid. grades lang. arts, 2002. Cert. English, lang. arts middle grades tchr. 2002. Libr. Rivers Correctional Instn. Author: (poetry) Daily Inspirations: Daily Living With God, 2002, Daily Inspirations: One More Day's Journey on the Way to Heaven, 2003, Book 2, 2003, (CD and cassette) The Sound of Poetry, numerous poems. Release preparation coord. Rivers Correctional Instn. Named Employee of Month, Rivers Correctional Instn., 2005; recipient Outstanding Achievement in Poetry award, Famous Poets Soc., 1999, Editor's Choice award, Internat. Libr. Poetry, 1999, 2003, Outstanding Poetry award, 2003, Spot award, Rivers Correctional Instn., 2004. Mem.: NEA, Internat. Soc. Poets, N.C. Assn. Educators, Alpha Kappa Mu (Cert. of Merit). Avocations: poetry, stamp collecting/philately, coin collecting/numismatics, sports card collecting. Home: 213 Linwood Dr Elizabeth City NC 27909-7022

WILLIAMS, RITA TUCKER, lawyer; b. Atlanta, Jan. 26, 1950; d. Claude Edward and Lillian Bernice (Barber) Tucker; m. Raymond Williams, Jr., Jan. 1, 1973; children: Monet Danielle, Brandon Raynard, Blake Hassan. BA, Spelman Coll., 1972; MA, U. Mich., 1976; JD, Emory U., 1987. Bar: Ga. 1987. Tchr. pub. schs., Suisun, Calif., 1977-82; assoc. Alston & Bird, Atlanta, 1987-89, Bernard & Assocs., Decatur, Ga., 1989-90; prin. Williams & Assocs., Decatur, Ga., 1990—. Instr. seminar Nat. Inst. Trial Advocacy, Emory U., Atlanta, spring 1992-95, tutor 1st yr. law students, 1996. Named Outstanding Alumna, Emory U. Law Sch., 1996. Mem. ABA, State Bar Ga. Assn., Ga. Trial Lawyers Assn., Omicron Delta Kappa. Democrat. Office: 220 Church St Decatur GA 30030-3328 Office Phone: 404-370-3783. Personal E-mail: ritw@atlonline.com. Business E-Mail: rtwilliams@williamsandassoc.com.

WILLIAMS, ROBERT CHADWELL, history professor; b. Boston, Oct. 14, 1938; s. Charles Reagan and Dorothy (Chadwell) W.; m. Ann Bennett Kingman, Aug. 27, 1960; children: Peter, Margaret, Katharine. BA, Wesleyan U., 1960; A.M., Harvard U., 1962, PhD, 1966. Asst. prof. history Williams Coll., Williamstown, Mass., 1965-70; prof. history Washington U., St. Louis, 1970-86; dean of faculty, prof. history Davidson Coll., NC, 1986-98, Vail prof. history, 2000—03. Pres. Central Slavic Conf., 1971-72; v.p. History Assocs. Inc., Gaithersburg, Md., 1980—; sr. research assoc. St. Antony's Coll., Oxford, 1985. Author: Culture in Exile, 1972, Artists in Revolution, 1976, Russian Art and American Money, 1980 (Pulitzer nominee), The Other Bolsheviks, 1986, Klaus Fuchs, Atom Spy, 1987, Russia Imagined, 1997, Ruling Russian Eurasia, 2000, The Historian's Toolbox, 2003, Horace Greeley, 2006; co-author: Crisis Contained, 1982; mem. editorial bd.: Slavic Rev., 1979-82. Trustee Wesleyan U., 1996-99, Agnes Scott Coll., 2003-. Fellow Kennan Inst., 1976-77; fellow Am. Council Learned Socs., 1973-74, W. Wilson Found., 1960-61 Mem. Am. Assn. for Advancement of Slavic Studies, Phi Beta Kappa, Sigma Xi Presbyterian. E-mail: bob03harmony@yahoo.com.

WILLIAMS, ROBERT E., lawyer; BA with highest honors, U. Calif., Santa Barbara, 1973; JD, Harvard U., 1976. Bar: Calif. 1976. Ptnr. Fin. and Bankruptcy Practice Group Sheppard, Mullin, Richter & Hampton LLP, LA. Mem.: Am. College of Real Estate Lawyers, Phi Beta Kappa. Office: Sheppard, Mullin, Richter & Hampton LLP 48th Fl 333 S Hope St Los Angeles CA 90071 Office Phone: 213-617-4169. Office Fax: 213-620-1398. Business E-Mail: rwilliams@sheppardmullin.com.

WILLIAMS, ROBERT HENRY, oil industry executive; b. El Paso, Jan. 12, 1946; s. William Frederick and Mary (Page) W.; m. Joanne Marie Mudd, Oct. 22, 1967; children: Lara, Michael, Suzanne, Jennifer. BS in Physics, U. Tex., El Paso, 1968; PhD in Physics, U. Tex., Austin, 1973; MS in Physics, Va. Poly. Inst., 1971. Dir. Gulf Oil R&D, Houston, 1978-81; tech. mgr. Gulf Oil Internat., Houston, 1981-83; exploration mgr. Gulf Oil Co., Houston, 1983-85; mgr. geophys. rsch. Tenneco Oil Co., Houston, 1985-87, mgr., chief geophysicist, 1987-88; founder, mng. dir. Dover Energy, Houston, 1988—; exec. v.p. Tatham Offshore Inc, Houston, 1989-95, also bd. dirs.; chmn., CEO Dover Tech. Inc., Houston, 1989—. Cons. Tenneco Inc., Houston, 1989—; DeepTech Internat., 1992-95; Ukraine Acad. Sci., 1993; bd. dirs., exec. v.p. DeepTech Inc., 1991-95; founder, pres. Westway tech. Assocs., 1986—; co-founder, chmn. CEO Castaway Graphite Rods, Inc., 1990—; owner, CEO Team Tex. Inc., 1993—; Bulldog Lures, Inc., 1994—; founder, CEO Houston Books Inc., 1994—; founder, CEO, chmn. Dover Energy Exploration, 1995—; pres. Westway Interests; chmn., CEO, bd. dirs. W.B. Oil & Gas Inc., 1997-2001, Dover (Belize), 1996-2002; bd. dirs. Tatham Offshore, Swep, Inc.; CEO Norman Lures, 1997—; founder, bd. dirs., CEO Win Leisure Products, 1997—; dir./founder William Found., 1998—; CEO, chmn. bd. dirs. Airrus Fishing Products, 2003-07. Contbr. articles to profl. jours. Coun. mem. Boy Scouts Am., Houston, 1989—; leader Girl Scouts U.S., Houston, 1989—. Mem. Soc. Exploration Geophysics, Am. Assn. Petroleum Geologists, Am. Geophys. Union. Republican. Avocations: scuba diving, book collecting, fishing. Office: Dover Tech 14420 Westway Ln Houston TX 77077

WILLIAMS, ROBERT JOSEPH, retired museum director, educator; b. Bennington, Vt., June 21, 1944; s. Joseph and Ruthe Allison (Moody) Williams. BS in Edn., U. Vt., 1970; MA in Interdisciplinary Social Sci., San Francisco State U., 1981. Tchr. adult edn. Mt. Anthony Union H.S., Bennington, Vt., 1972-74; columnist Bennington Banner, 1972-77; tchr. San Francisco State U., 1976-79; founder, dir. NORRAD Drug Rehab. Ctr., San Francisco, 1986-88; mus. curator Shaftsbury (Vt.) Hist. Soc., 1989—2005; ret., 2005. Founder, dir. Bennington Tutorial Ctr., 1971-74. Author: Toward Humanness in Education, 1981, Chalice of Leaves: Selected Essays and Poems, 1988, Modern Salvation: Guidelines from Cosmology, 1994, Superstring Displacement as a Common Factor in Gravity, Electromagnetic Radiation and Molecular Adhesion, 2004; author: (with others) Intimacy, 1985. Recipient Edmunds Essay medal Vt. Historical Soc., Montpelier, 1961, award League Vt. Writers, 1972, Golden Poet award World of Poetry, Sacramento, Calif., 1990. Democrat. Avocation: cosmology. Home: 102 Putnam St Bennington VT 05201-2348 *I sought the truth, and sought to live by it.*

WILLIAMS, ROBERT JOSEPH, behavioral health services executive, psychologist; b. Durango, Colo., Feb. 14, 1948; s. Owen C. and Florence K. Williams; m. Kay Lynn Williams, Mar. 24, 1973; children: Robin, Matthew, Nicholas. BA, U. Colo., 1970; MA, U. No. Colo., 1976; PhD, U. Minn., 1979. Diplomate Am. Bd. Psychol. Specialties. Tchr. math. Jefferson County Schs., Lakewood, Colo., 1970-76; psychologist Pikes Peak Mental Health Ctr., Colorado Springs, Colo., 1979-82, clin. dir., 1982-83; dir. Inst. for Family and Personal Devel., Colorado Springs, 1983-86; mng. ptnr. Marriage and Family Treatment Ctr., Colorado Springs, 1986-90; COO Quinco Behavioral Health Systems, Columbus, Ind., 1990-92, pres., CEO, 1992—. Feedback cons. Ctr. for Creative Leadership, Colorado Springs and San Diego, 1986-96; facilitator Franklin Covey Ctr., Columbus, 1994-99; cons. Trustee Leadership Tng. Program, Indpls., 1991-98; adj. faculty U. Denver, U. Colo., Colorado Springs, 1981-90. Contbr. articles to profl. jours. Trustee Bartholomew Consol. Sch. Corp., Columbus, 1996-2001, pres., 1999-2000; past pres., moderator Leadership Bartholomew County; mem. Healthy Communities Coun. 1995—, co-chmn. 2004-05; bd. dirs. Columbus Ind. Philharmonic, 2001—, pres. 2003-04; bd. mem. Rotary, 2004-05, Columbus Area C. of C., 2005—. Sgt. USMCR, 1970—76. Boettcher Found. scholar, 1966-70; Regents scholar, 1966.

Mem. Rotary Club, Masons. Democrat. Presbyn. Avocations: hiking, reading, motorcycling, weight training. Office: Quinco Behavioral Health Sys 720 North Marr Rd Columbus IN 47201 E-mail: rjwilliams@quincoinc.com.

WILLIAMS, ROBERT LEON, retired psychiatrist, neurologist, educator; b. Buffalo, July 22, 1922; s. Leon R. and L. Paulyne (Ingraham) W.; m. Shirley Glynn Miller, Feb. 5, 1949; Karen, Kevin BA, Alfred U., 1944; MD, Albany Med. Coll., Union U., 1946. Chief neurology and psychiatry Lackland AFB Hosp., USAF, San Antonio, 1952-55; cons. neurology and psychiatry to USAF Surgeon Gen., 1955-58; faculty Coll. Medicine, U. Fla., Gainesville, 1958-72, prof., chmn. dept. psychiatry, 1964-72; prof. psychiatry Baylor Coll. Medicine, Houston, 1972-92, chmn. dept., 1972-90, prof. neurology, 1976-92, acting chmn. dept., 1976-77, prof. emeritus psychiatry and neurology, 1992—; ret. Mem. faculty various univs., part time 1949-58 including Albany Med. Coll. at Union U., Columbia Coll. Physisicans and Surgeons, Boston U., U. Tex., Georgetown U. Author: (with W.B. Webb) Sleep Therapy: A. Bibliography and Commentary, 1966, (with others) EEG of Human Sleep: Clinical Applications, 1974; editor: (with Ismet Karacan and Carolyn J. Hursch) Psychopharmacology of Sleep, 1976, Sleep Disorders: Diagnosis and Treatment, 1978, 2d edit., 1988; (with others) Phenomenology and Treatment of Anxiety, 1979, of Alcoholism, 1980, of Psychophysiological Disorders, 1982, of Psychosexual Disorders, 1983, of Psychiatric Emergencies, 1984 Served from 1st lt. to lt. col. USAF, 1949-58; col. Res., ret. Recipient Cert. Profl. Achievement USAF Surgeon Gen., 1967 Mem. Am. Psychiat. Assn., Am. Electroencephalographic Soc., Am. Coll. Psychiatrists (pres. 1982-83), Am. Acad. Neurology, AMA, Group for Advancement of Psychiatry, Benjamin Rush Soc. (pres. 1986-88), Accreditation Coun. for grad. Med. Edn. (residency rev. com. for psychiatry 1985-93), Alpha Omega Alpha. Achievements include research in basic psychophysiology of human sleep.

WILLIAMS, ROBERT P., II, lawyer; b. Albuquerque, 1959; BA, Johns Hopkins Univ., 1981; JD, Univ. Ga., 1984. Bar: Ga. 1984. Assoc. Troutman Sanders LLP, Atlanta, 1984—92, ptnr., govt. law group, 1993—, and practice group leader, telecom. and electronic commerce. Staff mem. Ga. Jour. Internat. & Comparative Law, 1982—83; editor: Ga. Jour. Internat. & Comparative Law, 1983—84. Mem.: ABA, State Bar Ga. (secy, adminstrv. law sect. 1989—91, vice chmn., adminstrv. law sect. 1991—92, chmn., adminstrv. law sect. 1993—94), Phi Delta Phi. Office: Troutman Sanders LLP Ste 5200 600 Peachtree St NE Atlanta GA 30308-2216 Office Phone: 404-885-3438. Office Fax: 404-962-6721. Business E-Mail: robert.williams@troutmansanders.com.

WILLIAMS, ROBERT SANDERS (SANDY WILLIAMS), dean, academic administrator, educator, researcher; b. Athens, Ga. m. Jennifer Williams; children: Molly, Nicholas, Owen. Degree, Princeton U., 1970; MD, Duke U., 1974; internship and residency internal medicine, Mass. Gen. Hosp., 1974—76; fellowship in cardiology, Duke U. Med. Ctr., 1977—80. Asst. prof. medicine, physiology, cell biology Duke U. Sch. medicine, 1980—84; assoc. prof. medicine and microbiology Duke U. Sch. Medicine, 1986—90, dean, vice chancellor acad. affairs, 2001—07; chief cardiology, prof. internal medicine, biochemistry, and molecular biology, dir. Ryburn Ctr. for Molecular Cardiology U. Tex. Southwestern Med. Ctr., 1990—2001. Rschr. in field; vis. prof. dept. biochemistry Oxford U., 1984—85; vis. scientist Cold Spring Harbor Lab., NY, 1995—96; dir.'s adv. com. NIH; bd. external advisors Nat. Heart, Lung and Blood Inst. Contbr. more than 150 scholarly articles to biomed. jours., Proceedings of the Nat. Acad. Scis. Recipient Disting. Alumnus Award, Duke U. Sch. Medicine, 2000. Fellow: AAAS; mem.: NAS, Inst. of Medicine, Assn. Univ. Cardiologists, Am. Heart Assn. Achievements include being the leader of the Dallas Heart Disease Prevention Project, an innovative program of research in the genetic epidemiology of cardiovascular disease.

WILLIAMS, ROBERTON CAPELL, III, economics professor; b. Keflavik, Iceland, Dec. 2, 1972; s. Roberton Capell Williams, Jr. and Jane Carlile Hilder. AB, Harvard Coll., 1990—94; PhD, Stanford U., 1994—99. Asst. prof. U. Tex., Austin, 1999—2007, assoc. prof., 2007—. Faculty rsch. fellow Nat. Bur. Econ. Rsch., Cambridge, Mass., 2000—; Andrew W. Mellon fellow in econ. studies Brookings Instn., Washington, 2002—03; vis. rsch. scholar Stanford Inst. Econ. Policy Rsch., 2003—04. Co-editor: Jour. Environ. Econs. & Mgmt.; editor (assoc.): Jour. Pub. Econs.; mem. editl. coun.: Berkeley Electronic Jour. in Econ. Analysis & Policy; contbr. papers to profl. jours. and pubs. Grantee Grad. fellowship, NSF, 1994—97, STAR Grad. fellowship, EPA, 1997—99. Mem.: Assn. Environ. and Resource Economists, Nat. Tax Assn., Am. Econ. Assn., Austin Yacht Club. Avocations: sailboat racing, travel, landscape photography. Office: Dept Econs Univ Tex 1 University Sta #C3100 Austin TX 78712-0301 Office Phone: 512-475-8522. Business E-Mail: rwilliam@eco.utexas.edu.

WILLIAMS, ROBIN, actor, comedian; b. Chgo., July 21, 1951; s. Mr. and Mrs. Robert W.; m. Valerie Velardi, June 4, 1978 (div. 1988); 1 child, Zachary; m. Marsha Garces, Apr. 30, 1989; children: Zelda, Cody. Attended, Claremont Men's Coll., Marin Coll., Juilliard Sch., NYC. Started as stand-up comedian in San Francisco clubs, including Holy City Zoo, The Boardinghouse; appeared in TV series Laugh-In, The Richard Pryor Show, America 2-Night, Happy Days, Homicide: Life on the Streets, 1993 (Emmy nomination, Guest Actor - Drama Series, 1994); Mork and Mindy, 1978-82 (People's Choice award), (cable) Robin Williams: An Evening at the Met, 1986 (Grammy award), host of HBO's Shakespeare: The Animated Tales, 1993 (CableAce Award, Best Entertainment Host); film appearances include: Popeye, 1980, The World According to Garp, 1982, The Survivors, 1983, Moscow on the Hudson, 1984, The Best of Times, 1986, Club Paradise, 1986, Seize the Day, 1986, Good Morning Vietnam, 1987 (Golden Globe award 1988, Acad. Award nominee for best actor), The Adventures of Baron Munchausen, 1988, Dead Poets Society, 1989 (Best Actor nomination Golden Globe award, 1994, nominated best actor Acad. award), Cadillac Man, 1990, Awakenings, 1990, Dead Again, 1991, The Fisher King, 1991 (Golden Globe award, Acad. award nominee for best actor 1991), Dead Again, 1991, Hook, 1991, Aladdin (voice) (Spl. Achievement award Hollywood Fgn. Press, Nat. Bd. Rev. 1992), 1992, Toys, 1992, Mrs. Doubtfire, 1993 (Best Picture, Best Actor in a Musical or Comedy, Golden Globe, 1994, Best Picture, Best Actor, People's Choice award, also prodr.), Nine Months, 1995, Jumanji, 1995, The BirdCage, 1996, Jack, 1996, The Secret Agent, 1996, Hamlet, 1996, Deconstructing Harry, 1997, (TV series, voice) Great Minds Think for Themselves, 1997, Father's Day, 1997, Flubber, 1997, Good Will Hunting, 1997, What Dreams May Come, 1998, Patch Adams, 1998, Bicentennial Man, 1999, Jakob the Liar (also exec. prodr.), 1999, Artificial Intelligence (voice), 2001, One Hour Photo, 2002, Death to Smoochy, 2002, Insomnia, 2002, The Final Cut, 2004, The House of D, 2004, Noel, 2004, Robots (voice), 2005, RV, 2006, The Night Listener, 2006, Man of the Year, 2006, Happy Feet (voice), 2006, Night at the Museum, 2006, License to Wed, 2007; theatre: Waiting for Godot, 1988; recorded albums: Reality, What a Concept, 1979 (Grammy award), Throbbing Python of Love, A Night at the Met (Grammy award); host Comic Relief, 1986; appeared in TV variety programs, ABC Presents a Royal Gala, 1988 (Emmy award, 1988), Carol, Carl, Whoopi & Robin, 1987 (Emmy award), Robin Williams: Live at the Met, 1986, Robin Williams Live, 1986, Comic Relief, 1986, Young Comedians All Star Reunion, 1988, Robin Williams: Live on Broadway, 2002 (Emmy nomination, Grammy award, 2003) Recipient Golden Apple award Hollywood Women's Press Club, ACE award, Am. Comedy award, 1987, 88, Grammy award for best comedy rec., 1987, Man of Yr. award Hasty Pudding Theatricals, 1989, People's Choice award Favorite Comedy Motion Picture Actor, 1994, ShoWest Conv. award Male Star of Yr., 1994, Cecil B. DeMille award, Hollywood Fgn. Press, 2005, Hollywood Career Achievement award Hollywood Awards, 2006, Favorite Funny Male Star, People's Choice Award, 2007. *

WILLIAMS, ROGER (J. ROGER WILLIAMS), former state official; b. Evanston, Ill., Sept. 13, 1949; m. Patty Williams; children: Jaclyn, Sabrina. B, Tex Christian U., 1972. Pres. & CEO Jack Williams Automall, 1974—95; profl. basketball player Atlanta Braves farm team, 1971—74; owner & operator San Antonio Brewers profl basketball club, 1972—75; asst. head coach to head coach-basketball team Tex. Christian U.; sec state State of Tex., Austin, 2004—07; chmn. Tex. Rep. Victory 2008 Coordinated Campaign, 2007—. Chmn. bd. Roger Williams Automall, Weatherford, Vestry Fin. Corp. Republican. *

WILLIAMS, ROGER COURTLAND, lawyer, arbitrator, mediator; b. Atlanta, June 11, 1944; s. Ralph Roger and Beatrice (Hill) W.; m. Jo Ann Davenport, June 9, 1968; children: Melissa, Kimberly, Courtland. BS, U. Ala., 1966, JD, 1969. Bar: Ala. 1969, US Dist. Ct. (no. and mid. dists.) Ala. 1969, US Supreme Ct. 1972. V.p. Williams, Williams & Williams, P.C., Tuscaloosa, Ala., 1969-90, pres., 1990—. Adj. prof. U. Ala. Sch. Law, 1999—. Mem. bd. trustees Tuscaloosa Acad., 1987—, pres., 1990-94; bd. dirs. Children's Hands On Mus., Tuscaloosa, 1986-97. 1st lt. U.S. Army, 1969-71. Mem.: ABA, Am. Arbitration Assn., Nat. Acad. Arbitrators Assn., Am. Trial Lawyers Am., Ala. State Bar (vice chmn. ADR com. 1997—98), Indian Hills Country Club (bd. dirs. 1996—, v.p. 2003—05, pres. 2005—), Kiwanis Internat. (George F. Hixson fellow), Kiwanis of Ala. (dist. lt. gov. 2001—02), Kiwanis of Tuscaloosa (bd. dirs. 1974, 1990, v.p. 1995—99, pres. 1998—99), Tuscaloosa Toastmasters (pres. 1975), Toastmasters Internat., Jaycees (state pres. 1978—79, nat. assoc. legal counsel 1979—80, pres. Ala. Found. 1980—81, Internat. Senator). Methodist. Office: PO Box 2690 Tuscaloosa AL 35403-2690 Office Phone: 205-758-8332. Personal E-mail: rogercwilliams@bellsouth.com.

WILLIAMS, ROGER LAWRENCE, historian, educator; b. Boulder, Colo., June 22, 1923; s. Raymond Ustick and Mabel (Woolf) W. BA, Colo. Coll., 1947; MA, U. Mich., 1948, PhD, 1951. Asst. prof. Minn. State Coll., Mankato, 1950-52, MIT, Cambridge, 1952-55; vis. prof. Mich. State U., East Lansing, 1955-56; assoc. prof. Antioch Coll., Yellow Springs, Ohio, 1956-65; prof. U. Calif., Santa Barbara, 1965-71, U. Wyo., Laramie, 1971-78, Disting. prof., 1978-88. Author: French Revolution of 1870-71, 1969, The Mortal Napoleon III, 1971, The Horror of Life, 1980, Aven Nelson of Wyoming, 1984, Gérard and Jaume: Two Neglected Figures in the History of the Jussiaean Classification, 1988, Napoleon III and the Stoffel Affair, 1993, The Letters of Dominique Chaix, Botanist-Curé, 1997, Botanophilia in 18th Century France: The Spirit of the Enlightenment, 2001; co-author: How Modernity Came to a Provençal Town, 1988, Handbook of Rocky Mountain Plants, 1992, A Guide to Rocky Mountain Plants, 2002, French Botany in the Enlightenment: the Ill-fated Voyages of La Pérouse and His Rescuers, 2003, A Region of Astonishing Beauty, the Botanical Exploration of the Rocky Mountains, 2003, An Intellectual Biography of Elie-Abel Carrière, 2004, Revolution and Madness: Blanqui and Trelat, 2005, From Malesherbes to Tocqueville, The Legacy of Liberalism, 2006; mem. editl. bd.: Antioch Rev., 1958—64. Vol. Rocky Mountain Nat. Park, Estes Park, Colo., 1986-87. Mem. French Hist. Studies (life), History Sci. Soc. (life), Hist. Soc., Nat. Coun. for History Edn., N.Y. Bot. Soc., Denver Bot. Soc. Home: 1701 S 17th St Laramie WY 82070-5406

WILLIAMS, RONALD A., health insurance company executive; b. Chgo., Nov. 11, 1949; m. Cynthia Williams; 1 child. BA in Psychology, Roosevelt U., 1970; MS in Mgmt., MIT, 1984. Sr. v.p. mktg. and specialty products to exec. v.p. group and network svc. Blue Cross Calif., 1987—95, pres., 1995—99; sr. v.p. Vista Health Corp.; group mktg. exec. Control Data Corp.; pres., co-founder Integrative Sys.; pres. large group divsn. WellPoint Health Networks Inc., 1999—2001; exec. v.p., chief of health operations Aetna Inc., 2001—02, pres., 2002—06, chmn., pres., CEO, 2006—. Bd. dir. Aetna Inc., 1992—, Lucent Technologies, 2003—06, Am. Express, 2007—; trustee Conference Bd.; mem. dean's advisory coun. Mass. Inst. Tech., mem. corp. vis. com., mem. Alfred P. Sloan Mgmt. Soc. Avocations: jazz, movies. Office: Aetna Inc 151 Farmington Ave Hartford CT 06156 *

WILLIAMS, RONALD DAVID, telecommunications industry executive; b. Marshall, Ark., Mar. 15, 1944; s. Noble Kentucky and Elizabeth (Karns) W.; m. Beth L. Williams, Nov. 1977; children: Stephanie Noble, Keith Michael. BA, Columbia U., 1966, BS, 1967, MBA, 1973. Process engr. DuPont, Deepwater, NJ, 1966; design engr. Combustion Engring. Co., Hartford, 1971; cons. Arthur Andersen & Co., NYC, 1973-76; corp. planner Amax Inc., Greenwich, Conn., 1976-77, group planning adminstr., 1978-80, mgr. corp. planning and analysis, 1980-94, dir. fin. analysis, 1984-86; project mgr. Olin Corp., Stamford, Conn., 1977-78; mgr. ops. planning and analysis Savin Corp., Stamford, 1986-88; dir. fin. Bandgap Tech. Corp., Broomfield, Colo., 1988-90, v.p. fin. and adminstrn., 1990-93; v.p., gen. mgr. Bandgap Chem. Corp., 1992-94; contr. Heraeus PMR, Inc., Alden, NY, 1994-95, v.p. fin. and adminstrn., 1995-96; gen. mgr. Acoustiflo, Boulder, Colo., 1996-97; sr. fin. staff analyst Energy Corp., New Orleans, 1998-99; mgr. fin. planning Energy Tech. Co., 1999—. Mem. Fred's team Meml. Sloan Kettering Cancer Ctr. With USN, 1967-70, Vietnam. NASA trainee, 1971; S.W. Mudd scholar, 1971. Mem. AAAS, Am. Chem. Soc., Am. Mgmt. Assn., Utility Telecom. Coun., Ark. Hist. Assn., Westport Hist. Soc., Colo. Hist. Soc., Appalachian Mountain Club, Boulder Road Runners, Chalmette Track Club, New Orleans Track Club, Gulf Coast Running Club, Pine Belt Pacers, Mesa Monument Striders, West Bank Track Club, Fred's Team. Home: 7361 S Meadow Ct Boulder CO 80301-3951 Office: 639 Loyola Ave New Orleans LA 70113-3125 Office Phone: 504-576-4449. Business E-Mail: rwill16@entergy.com.

WILLIAMS, RONALD DEAN, minister, religious organization administrator; b. Decatur, Ill., Oct. 23, 1940; s. Henry Lawrence and Ella Loudica Williams; m. Carole Jeanette Lane, June 16, 1962; children: Scott Allan, Mark Lawrence, Derek James. BTh, LIFE Bible Coll., LA, 1965; DD, Internat. Ch. Foursquare Gospel, LA, 1992. Ordained to ministry Internat. Ch. Foursquare Gospel, 1966. Pastor Foursquare Gospel Ch., Surrey, Canada, 1965-69, missionary Hong Kong, China, 1969-85; prof. Life Bible Coll., 1985-95; mng. editor Foursquare World Advance, 1993—2002; comm. officer Internat. Ch. Foursquare Gospel, 1988-2000. Bd. dirs. Forsquare Gospel Ch., denominational historian, 2004—; pres. exec. bd. Internat. Pentecostal Press Assn., Oklahoma City, 1990—98; comm. officer Pentecostal/Charismatic Ch. N.Am., Memphis, 1994—2005; coord. E. Coun. Foursquare Miss., 1979—82. Editor: The Vine and The Branches, 1992; mng. editor: Foursquare World Advance mag., 1985—2002. Coord. 19th Pentecostal World Conf., 2001. With USAF, 1958—61. Avocations: writing, golf, reading, music. Office: Internat Ch Foursquare Gospel 1910 W Sunset Blvd Ste 200 Los Angeles CA 90026-3295 Business E-Mail: ron@foursquare.org.

WILLIAMS, RONALD DOHERTY, lawyer; b. New Haven, Apr. 6, 1927; s. Richard Hugh and Ethel W. (Nelson) w.; m. Laura Costarelli, Aug. 25, 1951; children: Craig F., Ronald D., Ellen A., Jane E. BA, U. Va., 1951, LLB, 1954. Bar: Conn. 1954. Assoc. Pullman, Comley, Bradley & Reeves, Bridgeport, Conn., 1954-60; ptnr., 1960-88, Williams, Cooney & Sheehy, 1989—. Mem. Fed. Jud. Com., 1988-91, com. unauthorized practice law, 1988-94, com. to study rules civil practice & procedure, 1984-86; atty. state trial referee, 1984-90. Selectman Town of Easton (Conn.), 1975-85, justice of the peace, 1977—, town atty., 1985-2000; mem. Bridgeport Area Found., 1971-90, emeritus dir., 1991—; adv. com. U. Bridgeport Law Sch., 1982-92; mem. statewide grievance com., 1985-91, chmn., 1989-91; mem. exec. bd. Sch. Law Quinnipiac Coll., 1994—. Served with US Army, 1945-46. Fellow Am. Coll. Trial Lawyers; mem. ABA, Conn. Bar Assn. (bd. govs. 1975-78), Bridgeport Bar Assn. (pres. 1975), Conn. Def. Lawyers Assn. (pres. 1984-85). Republican. Roman Catholic. Home: 14 Newman Dr Easton CT 06612-1915 Office: 799 Silver Ln Trumbull CT 06611-0753 Office Phone: 203-380-1741. E-mail: wilcooshee@aol.com.

WILLIAMS, RONALD OSCAR, mathematician; b. Denver, May 10, 1940; s. Oscar H. and Evelyn J. (Johnson) Williams. BS in Applied Math., U. Colo., Boulder, 1964; postgrad., U. Colo., 1968—70, U. Denver, 1975; postgrad. Advanced Tech. Edn. Program, Hughes Aircraft Co., 1980—89; postgrad., George Washington U., DC, 1985; postgrad. Spl. Electronics Course, Lowry AFB, Denver. Computer programmer Apollo Sys. dept. Missile and Space div. Gen. Electric Co., Kennedy Space Ctr., Fla., 1965-67; computer programmer Apollo Sys. dept. Missile and Space divsn. Manned Spacecraft Ctr. (now Johnson Space Ctr.), Houston, 1967—68; computer programmer Grad. Sch. Computing Ctr. and Lab. Atmospheric and Space Physics U. Colo., Boulder, 1968-73; computer programmer analyst Def. Sys. divsn. Sys. Devel. Corp. at Ent AFB, Colorado Springs, Colo., 1974—75, NORAD Cheyenne Mountain Complex, Colorado Springs, 1974—75; engr. def. sys. and command-and-info. sys. Martin Marietta Aerospace (now Lockheed Martin), Denver, 1976—80; sys. engr., def. info. sys. divsn. space and comm. group Hughes Aircraft Co. at Aerospace Data Facility, Buckley AFB, Colo., 1980—89; rsch. analyst Math. Rsch. Ctr., Littleton, Colo., 1990—, dir., sr. rsch. mathematician, 1996—. First chair trombonist Wash. Park Elem. Sch. Orch., All-City Elem. Sch. Orch., Merrill Jr. HS Concert Band, Merrill Jr. HS Concert Orch., Merrill Jr. HS German Band, Denver Jr. Police Band, Mile-High Boys' Band, Wells Music Dance Band. Vol. fireman Clear Lake City Fire Dept., Tex., 1968; officer Boulder Emergency Squad, 1969-76, rescue squad officer, 1969-76, liaison officer to cadets, 1971, pers. officer, 1971-76, exec. bd., 1971-76, EMT, 1973—; res. dispatcher A-1 Ambulance, Boulder, 1973-74; spl. police officer Boulder Police Dept., 1970-75; spl. dep. sheriff Boulder County Sheriff's Dept., 1970-71; nat. adv. bd. Am. Security Coun., 1979-91, Coalition of Peace Through Strength, 1979-91. Non-commd. officer USMCR, San Diego, Camp Matthews, Camp Elliott, Camp Wilson, Camp Pendleton (Camp San Onofre), Twentynine Palms, Camp Wilson, Denver Fed. Ctr., 1958—66. Decorated Organized Res. medal, Marine Corps League medal, M-1 Rifle Sharpshooter medal; recipient award of merit Boulder Emergency Squad, 1971-72, Dedicated Svc. award Boulder Emergency Squad, 1976, Cost Improvement Program award, Sys. Performance Improvement award, Top Cost Improvement Program award in Def. Sys. Divsn., Space and Comm. Group Hughes Aircraft Co., 1982. Mem. AAAS, AIAA (sr.), Math. Assn. Am., Am. Math Soc., Soc. Indsl. and Applied Math., Math. Study Unit of Am. Topical Assn., Armed Forces Comm. and Electronics Assn., Assn. Old Crows, Nat. Def. Indsl. Assn., Assn. For Intelligence Officers, Nat. Mil. Intelligence Assn., Nat. Cryptologic Mus. Found., US Naval Cryptologic Vet. Assn., Friends of Bletchley Pk., Marine Corps Assn., Marine Corps Heritage Found. (charter mem.), Marine Corps League, Nat. Mus. Marine Corps and Heritage Ctr. (campaign mem.), Air Force Assn., US Naval Inst., Nat. Geog. Soc., Smithsonian Inst., Nat. Space Soc., Soc. Amateur Radio Astronomers, Radio History Soc., Met. Opera Guild, Colo. Pub. Radio (classical music), Rocky Mountain PBS, Colo. Hist. Soc., Hist. Denver, Hist. Boulder, Colorado Railroad Hist. Found, Colorado Railroad Mus., Hawaiian Hist Soc., Denver Bot. Gardens, Denver Mus. Nature and Sci., Denver Zool. Found., Pacific Aviation Mus. Pearl Harbor (founding mem.), Wings Over the Rockies Air & Space Mus., Alumni Assn. U. Colo. Boulder, South High Alumni and Friends Denver, Am. Mensa Ltd., Denver Mile-Hi Mensa, Acoustic Neuroma Assn., Nat. Brain Tumor Found., Crystal Cathedral Ministries Sparrows Club, Eagles Club. Lutheran.

WILLIAMS, ROY, men's college basketball coach; b. Spruce Pine, NC, Aug. 1, 1950; m. Wanda; children: Scott, Kimberly. BA in Edn., U. NC, 1972, MAT, 1973. Asst. coach U. NC, 1978—88, head coach, 2003—, U. Kans., 1988—2003. Asst. coach U.S.A. Sr. Men's Nat. Basketball Team, 2003, US Olympic Men's Basketball Team, Athens, Greece, 2004. Named Nat. Rookie Coach of Yr., Basketball Times, 1989, Nat. Coach of Yr. 1990-92, 1997, 2006, Big 8 Coach of Yr. (7 times), Coach of Yr., AP, 1992, 2006, ACC Coach of Yr., 2006; recipient John R. Wooden Legends of Coaching award LA Athletic Club, 2003, Nat. Coach of Yr. award NY Athletic Club, 2005; named to Naismith Meml. Basketball Hall of Fame, 2007. Achievements include coaching the NCAA Nat. Champion U. NC Tarheels, 2005. Office: U NC Athletic Dept Men's Basketball PO Box 2126 Chapel Hill NC 27514 Office Phone: 919-962-6000. E-mail: williara@email.unc.edu. *

WILLIAMS, ROY, professional football player; b. Odessa, Tex., Dec. 20, 1981; Attended, Univ. Tex., 2004. Wide receiver Detroit Lions, 2004—. Vol. HAVEN domestic violence shelter, 2004—, Boys and Girls Club, Detroit, 2004—. Actor: (films) Friday Night Lights, 2002. Named to All-American Dream Team, NFL Draft Report, 2004. Office: Detroit Lions 222 Republic Dr Allen Park MI 48101

WILLIAMS, ROY L., fraternal organization administrator; m. Barbara Williams; 2 children. BA, U. Tex., Arlington, 1971. Dirt. exec. Longhorn Coun. Boy Scouts of Am., Fort Worth, Tex., 1972, dist. exec. Abilene, Tex., fin. dir. Little Rock, 1978, scout exec. Jayhawk Area Coun. Topeka, 1981, dir. Boy Scout Div., Nat. Coun., scout exec. Narragansett Coun. Providence, 1990, regional dir. Western Region Tempe, Ariz., chief scout exec. Irving, Tex., 2000—. Vet. USAF. Recipient Vigil Honor, Order of Arrow, Disting. Svc. Award. Mem.: Tribe of Mic-O-Say. Office: Boy Scouts of Am National Coun PO Box 152079 Irving TX 75015-2749

WILLIAMS, S. LINN, lawyer; b. St. Louis, July 1, 1946; s. Sidney Duane and Elizabeth Gertrude (Relfe) W.; m. Noriko Kurosawa, Sept. 13, 1975. BA, Princeton U., 1968; JD, Harvard U., 1971; postgrad., Cambridge U., 1972-74. Bar: Mass. 1971, D.C. 1972, Pa. 1987. Law clk. to Hon. I.L. Goldberg U.S. Ct. Appeals 5th Cir., Dallas, 1971-72; assoc. Blakemore & Mitsuki, Tokyo, 1974; assoc., then ptnr. Leva, Hawes, Symington, Martin & Oppenheimer, Washington, 1975-81; v.p., gen. counsel Overseas Pvt. Investment Corp., Washington, 1981-84, Sears World Trade, Inc., 1984-85; ptnr. Gibson Dunn and Crutcher, Washington, Tokyo, 1985-89, 92-93, Jones Day Reavis & Pogue, Washington, 1993-94; corp. sr. v.p., counsel, pres., mng. dir. European divsn. Edison Mission Energy, Irvine, Calif., 1994—98, CEO European Divsn., 1998—2000; internat. C. of C. arbitrator, overseas investment cons., 2001—05; exec. v.p., gen. counsel Mirant Corp., 2005—. Japanese fgn. legal cons. Tokyo Dainibengoshikai, 1987-89; dep. U.S. trade rep., amb., Washington, 1989-91; mem. bd. dirs. The Benham Cos., Benham Group, Oklahoma City; sr. fellow Ctr. Strategic and Internat. Studies, Washington; mem. bd. adv. European Inst., Washington. Author: Developing an Export Trading Business, 1989; contbr. chpts. in book, also numerous articles on trade and investments. Fulbright scholar, 1972, NEH fellow, 1972, McConnell fellow, 1967, Ford Found. fellow, 1972. Mem. United Oxford & Cambridge Club (London), Met. Club (Washington). Office: Mirant Corp 1155 Perimeter Ctr W Atlanta GA 30338 Office Phone: 678-579-5000. *

WILLIAMS, SANKEY VAUGHAN, health services researcher, internist; b. San Antonio, Apr. 15, 1944; s. James Sankey and Helen (Long) W.; m. Constance Hess, June 27, 1972; children: Elizabeth Helen, Jennifer Lee. AB, Princeton U., 1966; MD, Harvard U., 1970. Diplomate Am. Bd. Internal Medicine. Intern Hosp. of U. Pa., 1970-71, jr. resident, 1971-72, chief med. resident, 1974-75; assoc. dir. clin. rsch. Ctr. for Study of Aging,

U. Pa., 1982-86; assoc. dir. for med. affairs Leonard Davis Inst. for Health Econs., U. Pa., 1978-90; dir. clin. scholars program U. Pa., Phila., 1988-96; prof. health care systems Wharton Sch., U. Pa., Phila., 1989—; prof. medicine U. Pa., Phila., 1989—, chief div. gen. internal medicine, 1992—, Sol Katz prof. medicine, 1992—. Commr. Prospective Payment Assessment Commn., U.S. Congress, Washington, 1988-91; chairman health svcs. rsch. devel. grants study sect. Agy. for Health Care Policy and Rsch., 1991-94; counselor for med. affiars to the pres. U. Pa., 1990-92. Co-editor: The Physician's Practice, 1980; author 35 revs, chpt. or editorials; contbr. 62 articles to various sci. jour., assoc. editor, annals of Internal Medicine, 2003-. Lt. comdr. USPHS, 1972-74. Recipient Career Devel. award Henry S. Kaiser Family Found., 1981-86. Mem. ACP (master, chmn. clin. privileges com. 1989-93, Soc. for Med. Decision Making (pres. 1985-86), Soc. for Gen. Internal Medicine (coun. 1979-84, editor Jour. Gen. Internal Medicine 1994-99, pres. 2000-01). Office: Hosp Univ of Pa Divsn Gen Internal Medicine 1220 Blockley Hall 423 Guardian Dr Philadelphia PA 19104-6021

WILLIAMS, SERENA, professional tennis player, apparel designer; b. Saginaw, Mich., Sept. 26, 1981; d. Richard and Oracene Williams. Prof. tennis player WTA Tour, 1995—; designer Aneres clothing line. TV appearances include: My Wife and Kids, 2002; Law and Order: Special Victims Unit, 2004; The Division, 2004; (voice) The Simpsons, 2001. Named WTA Most Improved Player, 1999, Player of the Year, TENNIS Mag., 1999, Female Athlete in the World, AP, 2002, WTA Tour Player of the Year, 2002, #1 most marketable female athlete, Sports Business Daily, 2003, Best Female Athlete, Black Entertainment TV (BET) Awards, 2007; recipient Espy award for Best Female Athlete, ESPN, 2003, Espy award for Best Female Tennis Player, 2003, 2004. Achievements include winner of 28 career singles titles, 10 career doubles titles, and 2 mixed doubles titles, WTA tour; Grand Slam Championships: US Open, 1999, 2002, Wimbledon, 2002, 2003, Roland Garros, 2002, Austalian Open, 2003, 2005, 2007; winner of doubles titles (with Venus Williams) Australian Open 2001, 2003, Wimbledon, 2000, Roland Garros, 1999, US Open, 1999; Mixed Doubles (w/ Max Mirnyi), Wimbledon, 1998; winner of doubles gold medal (with Venus Williams), Sydney Olympic games, 2000; winning 4 Grand Slam tournaments in a row, 2002-2003; signing largest endorsement deal to date by a female athlete with Nike, 2003. Office: c/o USTA 70 W Red Oak Ln White Plains NY 10604-3602 *

WILLIAMS, SHANNON RENEE, mental health services professional; d. Joyce Bromley Wright; m. Anthony Markell Williams, July 5, 1997; children: JaHarold, Justin, Jamilla. BS, Bowie State U., 1990, MA, 1993; PhD, Howard U., 2004. Lic. clin. profl. counselor Md. Mental health assoc. Regional Inst. for Children and Adolescents, Rockville, Md., 1990—94; correctional psychologist assoc. Dept. Pub. Safety and Correctional Svcs., Jessup, Md., 1994—2005; therapist Wash. Assessment and Therapy Svc., Lanham, Md., 2005—06; psychotherapist Bowie Counseling Svcs., 2006—, All That's Therapeutic, 2006—; pvt. practice Upper Marlboro, 2007—. Coord. Diamonds in the Rough womanhood tng. program Paramount Bapt. Ch., Washington, 2000—. Mem.: APA. Avocations: reading, singing. Office Phone: 301-627-0568. Business E-Mail: docswilliams@verizon.net.

WILLIAMS, SOLOMON JOSEPH, III, military officer; b. Phila., July 27, 1974; s. Solomon Joseph Williams, Jr. and Almaree Williams; m. Michelle Cheryl-Ann Turner, May 25, 1999. BA in Polit. Sci., NC A&T State U., Greensboro, 1993—96; MS in Telecom. Mgmt., U. Md. U. Coll., Adelphi, 2003; MPA, George Mason U., Fairfax, Va., 2004. Ops. officer US Coast Guard Honor Guard, Alexandria, Va., 1996—98; damage control asst. US Coast Guard Cutter Vigorous, Cape May, NJ, 1998—99; equal opportunity cons. US Coast Guard Office Civil Rights, DC, 1999—2002; IT mgmt. postgraduate study US Coast Guard, Adelphi, Md., 2002—04; divsn. chief US Coast Guard Ops. Systems Ctr., Kearneysville, W.Va., 2004—. Vol. High Point Beepball Team, NC, 1987—2006. Lt. comdr. US Coast Guard, 1996—2006, Kearneysville. Decorated Commandant's Letter of Commendation award Commdg. Officer, US Coast Guard Cutter Vigorous, US Coast Guard Commendation medal Asst. Comdt. Civil Rights, Commandant's Letter of Commendation award Commdg. Officer, US Coast Guard Ops. Sys. Ctr. Mem.: Mensa (assoc.). Non-Partisan. Home: 269 Winslow Dr Martinsburg WV 25404 Office: US Coast Guard 408 Coast Guard Dr Kearneysville WV 25430 Home Phone: 304-267-4047. Office Fax: 304-264-3817. Personal E-mail: solw@adelphia.net. Business E-Mail: solomon.j.williams@uscg.mil.

WILLIAMS, SONIA KAY, retired secondary school educator; b. Duluth, Minn., Jan. 13, 1939; d. Allen Parke and Ruth Adelaide (Mitchell) Swayne; m. William Fedrick Williams, Mar. 26, 1960; children: Keith Douglass, Jennifer Gay. BMus, U. Tenn., Chattanooga, 1960; M in Secondary Tchg. of English, Statesboro U., 1975; edn. specialist, Valdosta State U., 1988. Tchr. North Chattanooga Jr. HS, 1960—61; music tchr. Savannah Country Day Sch., Ga., 1968—72; English tchr. Appling County Jr. HS, Baxley, Ga., 1972—74, Appling County Comprehensive HS, Baxley, 1974—2001; ret., 2001. Accompanist Appling Applause, Baxley, 1978-92; drama tchr. Appling County HS, 1990-92. Prodr. videotape Sonia's Signya's, 1991. Bd. dirs., Sunday sch. tchr. First United Meth. Ch., Baxley, 1980-94; pres. Friends of Libr., Baxley, 1990-92; charter mem. Appling Hist. Soc., Baxley, 1980—, bd. dirs., 1992-94; mem. Appling Heritage Com., Baxley, 1992-2007; vol. ARC, Am. Cancer Soc., Appling Co. Food Bank, 2003-07, CASA, 2002-07; ct.-apptd. spl. adv. for abused and neglected children. Named Star Tchr., Appling County C. of C., 1984, outstanding Retired Educator of Yr. Altamaha Tech. Coll., 2004; recipient Outstanding Educator award Ga. Retired Educators Assn., 2001, Cmty. Svc. award, 2003, Cmty. Svc. award AARP, 2007. Mem. Nat. Coun. Tchrs. English, Ga. Assn. Educators (instrnl. and profl. devel. com. 1992-97, Dist. Tchr. of Yr. 1997-98), Lions Internat. (pres. Baxley Lions Club 2007), Delta Kappa Gamma (pres. Alpha Pi chpt. 1997-99). Avocations: reading, writing, swimming, drama. Home: 177 Torrance Rd Baxley GA 31513-6726

WILLIAMS, STEPHEN, anthropologist, educator; b. Mpls., Aug. 28, 1926; s. Clyde Garfield and Lois (Simmons) Williams; m. Eunice Ford, Jan. 6, 1962; children: Stephen John, Timothy. BA, Yale U., 1949, PhD, 1954; MA, U. Mich., 1950; MA (hon.), Harvard U., 1962. Asst. anthropology dept. Peabody Mus., Yale U., 1950-52; mem. faculty Harvard U., Cambridge, Mass., 1958—, prof. anthropology, 1967-72, Peabody prof., 1972-93, prof. emeritus, 1993—, chmn. dept., 1967-69; rsch. fellow Peabody Mus., Harvard U., Cambridge, 1954-57, mem. staff, 1954—, dir. mus., 1967-77. Curator N.Am. Archaeology, 1962-93, hon. curator 1993—; dir. rsch. of Peabody Mus.'s Lower Miss. Survey, 1958-93. Author books and articles on N.Am. archaeology, "Fantastic" archaeology and the history of Am. anthropology. Home: 1017 Foothills Trail Santa Fe NM 87505-4537 Office: PO Box 22354 Santa Fe NM 87502-2354 Office Phone: 505-983-8836. Personal E-mail: williamsstephen@msn.com.

WILLIAMS, STEPHEN EDWARD, retired lawyer; b. Clarkesburg, Va., Dec. 8, 1948; AB, Harvard U., 1970; JD, W.Va. U., 1974. Bar: W.Va. 1974. Lawyer Consolidated Gas, 1974-78, sr. lawyer, 1978-82, gen. lawyer, 1982-84, asst. gen. counsel, 1984-87; sec., gen. counsel Consolidated Natural Gas, 1987-92, assoc. gen. counsel, 1992, sr. v.p., gen. counsel, 1992—2005. Mem. Am. Corp. Counsel Assn., Pa. Bar Assn., Fed. Energy Bar Assn., W.Va. State Bar, Pitts. Symphony Soc. (bd. dirs., exec. com.). *

WILLIAMS, STEPHEN FAIN, federal judge; b. NYC, Sept. 23, 1936; s. Charles Dickerman and Virginia (Fain) Williams; m. Faith Morrow, June 11, 1966; children: Susan, Geoffrey Fain, Sarah Margot Nu, Timothy Dwight, Nicholas Morrow. BA, Yale U., 1958; JD, Harvard U., 1961. Bar: NY 1962, Colo. 1977. Assoc. Debevoise, Plimpton, Lyons & Gates, NYC, 1962—66; asst. atty. US Dist. Ct. (so. dist.), NY, 1966—69; asst. prof. law U. Colo., Boulder, 1969—77, prof., 1977—86; judge US Ct. Appeals (DC cir.), Washington, 1986—2001, sr. judge, 2001—. Vis. prof. UCLA, 1975—76; vis. prof., fellow in law and econs. U. Chgo., 1979—80; vis. William L. Hutchison prof. energy law So. Meth. U., 1983—84; cons. Adminstrv. Conf. US, 1974—76, FTC, 1983—85; mem. Boulder Area Growth Study Commn., 1972—73. Contbr. articles to profl. jours. and mags.; author: Liberal Reform in an Illiberal Regime: The Creation of Private Property in Russia, 1906-1915, 2006. With US Army, 1961—62. Mem.: ABA, Fed. Energy Bar Assn., Am. Law Inst. Office: US Courthouse 333 Constitution Ave NW Washington DC 20001 E-mail: SFWilliams@cadc.uscourts.gov. *

WILLIAMS, STEVEN A., JR., environmental services administrator, former federal agency administrator; b. Bellows Falls, Vt. m. Beth Williams; 2 children. B in Environ. Resource Mgmt., Pa. State U., D in Forest Resources; MS, U. N.D. Grad. tchg. asst. U. N.D., 1979—81, Pa. State U., 1981—85; wildlife biologist Mass. Divsn. Fisheries and Wildlife, 1985—89, asst. dir. for wildlife, 1989—92; dep. exec. dir. Pa. Game Commn., 1992—95; sec. Kans. Dept. Wildlife and Parks, 1995—2002; dir. US Fish & Wildlife Svc., US Dept. Interior, Washington, 2002—05; pres. Wildlife Mgmt. Inst., Washington, 2005—. Mem.: Wildlife Soc., Internat. Assn. Fish and Wildlife Agys. Office: Wildlife Mgmt Inst 1146 19th St NW Ste 700 Washington DC 20036 E-mail: swilliams@wildlifemgt.org. *

WILLIAMS, STEVEN D., plastic surgeon; b. Mpls., Minn. m. Yvonne Christian William, June 1, 1991. BA, U. Chgo., 1979; MD, Loyola U., Maywood, Ill., 1985. Former cert. State Med. Bd. OH, Mich. Bd. Medicine, former lic. State Med. Bd. OH, Mich. Bd. Medicine, cert. State Ill. Med. Bd., Fed. Drug Enforcement Adminstrn., lic. State Ill. Med. Bd., Fed. Drug Enforcement Adminstrn., bd. cert. Nat. Bd. Med. Examiners, Am. Bd. Plastic Surgery, splty. bd. cert. Am. Bd. Plastic Surgery, 1998. Resident, intern, gen. surgery U. Ill., 1985—89, chief resident, gen. surgery, 1989—90; fellow, staff attending-burn fellowship, dir. ICU Cook County Hosp., 1990—91; resident, plastic and reconstructive surgery Med. Coll. OH, Toledo, 1991—92, adminstrv. chief resident, plastic and reconstructive surgery, 1992—93; attending physician, plastic surgeon, pvt. practice Ctr. Reconstructive Surgery, 1993—95, Cmty. Health Ctr. Bourbonnais, 1995—. Chmn., chief surgery Riverside Med. Ctr. & St. Mary's Hosp., 2005—, chmn. operating room coms.; mem. Med. Ctr. Trauma Com., Kankakee, Ill., Riverside Med. Ctr. Dept. Profl. Edn., Kankakee, Riverside Med. Ctr. Oper. Rm. Com., Kankakee, Riverside Med. Ctr. Physicians Adv. Bd., Kankakee, Provena St. Mary's Hosp. Oper. Rm. Com., Ill.; presenter, spkr. in field; med. dir. Riverside Ambulatory Surgery Ctr. Contbr. articles to profl. jours. Mem. Am. Breast Cancer Found., Am. Cancer Soc., Am. Diabetes Assn., Am. Found. for Blind, Am. Fedn. Police, Am. Heart Assn., Am. Inst. Cancer Rsch., Alzheimers Assn., Amnesty Internat., Arthritis Found., Cath. Charities, Covenant House, Cystic Fibrosis Found., Feed the Children, Hospice Edn. Inst., Internat. Humane Soc., Habitat for Humanity, Macular Degeneration Rsch. Found., Mercy Home Boys & Girls, Multiple Sclerosis Assn. Am., NAACP, Nat. Found. Cancer Rsch., Nat. Geog. Soc., Nat. Hort. Soc., Nat. Humane Soc., Nat. Osteoporosis Found., Nat. Parkinsons Found., Nat. Pub. & Chgo. Pub. Radio, Oblate Missions, Pub. TV, United Negro Coll. Found., USO, Sacred Heart League, World Conf. Religion & Peace; ptnr. Spl. Olympics; vol., vision and blood pressure screening test; mem. Big Bros./Big Sisters Met. Chgo., Chgo. Anti-Cruelty Soc., Harbor House Kankakee, Maryknoll Fathers and Bros., So. Poverty Law Ctr., St. Jude's Childrens Hosp. Assn., St. Labre Am. Indian Sch., LWV; ch. lector. Fellow: Am. Coll. Surgeons, ACS; mem.: AMA, Kankakee County Med. Soc., Phenylketonuria Action Group, Karl A. Meyer Surg. Soc. of Cook County Hosp., Kanakakee County Med. Soc. (v.p. 2005—, pres. 2006—), Chgo. Med. Soc., Ill. State Med. Soc., Am. Burn Assn., Chgo. Soc. Plastic Surgeons, Midwest Assn. Plastic Surgeons (treas.), Am. Soc. Plastic Surgeons, VFW, Am. Vets. Assn., Paralyzed Vets. Found., Consumers Union, U. Chgo. Varsity Athletic Letterman's Club, Phi Gamma Delta. Avocations: bicycling, hiking, guitar, photography, travel.

WILLIAMS, SUE DARDEN, library director; b. Miami, Fla., Aug. 13, 1943; d. Archie Yelverton and Bobbie (Jones) Eagles; m. Richard Williams, Sept. 30, 1989. BA, Barton Coll., Wilson, NC, 1965; M.L.S., U. Tex., Austin, 1970. Cert. librarian, N.C., Va. Instr. Chowan Coll., Murfreesboro, NC, 1966-68; libr.'s asst. Albemarle Regional Libr., Winston, NC, 1968-69; br. libr. Multnomah County Pub. Libr., Portland, Oreg., 1971-72; asst. dir. Stanly County Pub. Libr., Albemarle, NC, 1973-76, dir., 1976-80; asst. dir. Norfolk (Va.) Pub. Libr., 1980-83, dir., 1983-94, Rockingham County Pub. Libr., Eden, NC, 1996—2004, Albemarle Regional Libr., Winton, NC, 2004—. Mem. ALA (coun. 1987-91, orientation com. 1990-92, chair 1991), Libr. Adminstrv. and Mgmt. Assn. (pub. rels. sec. 1985-87bd. dirs. 2004—), Southeastern Libr. Assn. (staff devel. com. 1986-88, Rothrock award com. 1984-86, sec. pub. libr. sect. 1982-84), Va. Libr. Assn. (SELA rep. 1993-96, com. 1984, 88-91, 93-96, ad hoc conf. guidelines com. 1985-86, chmn. conf. program 1984, awards and recognition com. 1983, mem. SELA outstanding libr. program award com. 2002), Pub. Libr. Assn. (bd. dirs.-at-large Met. area 1986-89), Va. State Libr. (coop edn. com. 88-89), N.C. Libr. Assn. (scholarship com. 1999-2005, chair 2001-2005), LAMS. Home: 109 Chowan Rd Murfreesboro NC 27855 Office: Albermarle Regional Libr PO Box 68 303 W Tryon St Winton NC 27986 Office Phone: 252-358-7832. E-mail: swilliams_arl@yahoo.com.

WILLIAMS, SUE M., federal agency administrator, writer; b. Sumter, SC, Aug. 20, 1942; d. Perry Harrington and Ida (Sumter) Taylor; 2 children. Diploma, cert., Comms. Inst. Am., 1968; BA, U. Colo., 1974; R. Sc. F., Ernest Holmes Coll. Ch. of Religious Sci., 1979; M in Mgmt. Sci., Regis U., Denver, 1999. Ordained to ministry. Long distance operator Mountain Bell/Penn Bell, Phila. & Colorado Springs, Colo., 1964-69; comml. teller Exch. Nat. Bank, Colorado Springs, 1969-74; ops. trainee Cen. Bank of Denver, 1974-75; legal specialist USAFR, Lowry AFB, Colo., 1975-77; asst. mgr. Western Airlines, LA, 1974-87; supr. reservation sales Delta Air Lines, LA, 1987-88; sr. sec., office mgr. U. Colo., Denver, 1988-89; sales coord. Hewlett Packard Co., Englewood, Colo., 1989-90; supr. U.S. Sprint (United Telecom), Denver, 1990—2006; supr. distbn. ops. U.S. Postal Svc., sr. bus. svc. specialist, 2006—. Contbr. articles to profl. jours. Mem. Vets. Club, Colorado Springs, 1973-74; various offices L.A. Election Dept., 1983-85; appointed vet. com. Calif. Reps., L.a., 1985; participant Hands Across Am., L.A., 1985, The Bolder Boulder, various walking races for local charity; charter mem. Women in Mil. Meml. Found., Washington, 1990. With USAF, 1961-63. Mem. Am. Legion, Coll. Devine Metaphysics Alumni Assn. (area v.p. 1982—).

WILLIAMS, SUNITA L., astronaut; b. Euclid, Ohio, Sept. 19, 1965; d. Deepak N. and Ursaline B. Pandya; m. Michael J. Williams. BS in Physical Sci., U.S. Naval Acad., 1987; MS in Engring. Mgmt., Fla. Inst. Tech., 1995. Commn. ensign USN, 1987, advanced through grades to lt. comdr., various assignments, 1987—89, overseas combat, 1989—92; officer in charge Hurrican Andrew Relief Ops. USS Sylvania, 1992—93; various assignments USN, 1993—95; served on USS Saipan, Norfolk, Va., 1995—98; astronaut NASA, Houston, 1998—. Worked with Russian Space Agy. on Russian contbn. to Internat. Space Station (ISS) and with first Expedition Crew to ISS; worked withing Robotics branch of ISS Robotic Arm and the follow on Spl. Purpose Dexterous Manipulator; NEEM02 crewmember; flight engr. (after traveling to the International Space Station with the crew aboard STS-116) Expedition-14, 2006, will perform spacewalks, 06. Decorated Commendation medal USN, Achievement medal USN & USMC, Humanitarian Svc. medal USN. Mem.: Soc. Flight Test Engrs., Soc. Exptl. Test Pilots, Am. Helicopter Assn. Sets women's spacewalk record of 22 hours and 27 minutes on Expedition-14 mission (record includes the following spacewalks-one in December, 2006 & two in February, 2007). Spacewalks marked the first time three spacewalks have been conducted in such a short period without a space shuttle docked to it. Total time spent in space on Expedition-14 mission was 29 hours and 17 minutes of walking in space. Will run Boston Marathon aboard international space station using a treadmill and bungee cords to keep from floating away. On astronaut time, so start time will differ from Boston, Massachusetts race in 2007 (finished, unofficially, 4 hours, 23 minutes and 46 seconds). Set an endurance record for the longest single spaceflight by a woman at 195 days in 2007. Office: Astronaut Office CB NASA Johnson Space Center Houston TX 77058 *

WILLIAMS, SUSAN SHIDAL, language educator; b. Atlanta, Jan. 7, 1963; d. L. Neil and Sue (Sigmon) W. BA, Yale U., 1985, PhD, 1991. Asst. prof. English Ohio State U., Columbus, 1991-97, assoc. prof. English, 1997—2006, prof. English, 2006—. Author: Confounding Images: Photography and Portraiture in Antebellum American Fiction, 1997, Reclaiming Authorship: Literary Women in America 1850-1900, 2006; co-editor: Reciprocal Influences: Literary Production Distribution, and Consumption in America, 1999, American Periodicals; manuscript reviewer and contbr. articles to profl. jours. Mem. Columbus Symphony Orch. Chorus, 1992-98. Whiting fellow Yale Univ., New Haven, Conn., 1990-91, Steven Botein fellow Am. Antiquarian Soc., Worcester, Mass., 1997; Coca-Cola Crit. Difference for Women Rsch. grantee Ohio State U., 1996-97, Nat. Endowment for the Humanities, 2006. Mem. MLA, Am. Studies Assn., Soc. History of Authorship, Reading & Pub., Rsch. Soc. Am. Periodicals (mem. adv. bd. 1997-2005). Office: Ohio State Univ English Dpt 164 W 17th Ave Columbus OH 43210-1370 Office Phone: 614-688-3147. E-mail: williams.488@osu.edu.

WILLIAMS, SUZANNE, state senator; b. Oklahoma City, Feb. 3, 1945; m. Ed Williams; 2 children. BA in Edn., Baylor U.; MA in Spl. Edn., U. Colo. Educator; state sen. dist. 41 Colo. Senate, Denver, 1996—, mem. edn. and transp. and energy coms. Recipient Gov.'s award for curriculum innovation, 1985, Gov.'s Action Plan award, 2000, Insider award, Aurora Sentinel, 1994, Leadership award, Colo. Edn. Assn., 1999, Outstanding Leadership Legis. award, AIA, Colo., 2001, cert. appreciation, Denver Indian Family Resource Ctr., 2002. Mem.: AAUW, Colo. Soc. Sch. Psychologists, Assn. Sch. Nurses, Colo. Assn. Edn. Young Children, Women in Govt., Aurora Sister Cities Internat., Delta Kappa Gamma. Democrat. Avocations: reading, music, exercising. Office: State Capitol # 271 200 E Colfax Ave Denver CO 80203 Office Phone: 303-866-3432.

WILLIAMS, TED VAUGHNELL, physical education educator; b. Bronx, NY, Apr. 1, 1952; s. Joseph Alexander and Annie (Canady) W. BS, Springfield Coll., 1977. Cert. tchr., N.Y. Substitute tchr. Valhalla (N.Y.) High Sch., 1977; tchr. aide for handicapped children, tchr. spl. edn. Rye Lake Campus, Valhalla, 1978; supr. recreation activities Springfield (Mass.) Girl's Club Family Ctr., 1979; assoc. dir. boy's and men's phys. edn. dept. Trenton YMCA, 1979—; house supr. Cardinal McCloskey's Group Home, Tappan, N.Y., 1980-81; phys. edn. tchr. Our Lady of Refuge Sch., Bronx, N.Y., 1982-83; tchr. phys. edn. various Cath. elem. schs. Yonkers, N.Y., 1983—. With ops. dept. Hudson Valley Nat. Bank, 1990-92. Active Walk Am. for Healthier Babies, March of Dimes, 1990-93. Recipient Ed Steitz award Basketball Hall of Fame, 1975, Capitol award Nat. Leadership Coun., 1991; named to Wall of Tolerance, Civil Rights Meml. Ctr., Montgomery, Ala. Mem. ASCD, AAHPERD, Am. Assn. Leisure and Recreation, Hudson Valley Leisure Svcs. Assn. Democrat. Baptist. Home: 49 Bradford Ave White Plains NY 10603-2143 Office Phone: 914-965-2356. E-mail: tedww@aol.com.

WILLIAMS, TERRIE M., biology professor; MS, PhD, Rutgers U., New Brunswick, NJ. NIH postdoctoral fellow Scripps Instn. Oceanography, 1981—84; Kaiser environ. fellow San Diego Zool. Soc., 1984—86; prof. ecology and evolutionary biology U. Calif., Santa Cruz. Contbr. articles to sci. jours.; author: The Hunter's Breath: On Expedition with the Weddell Seals of the Antarctic. Recipient Women of Discovery, Sea award, Wings WorldQuest, 2007. Office: Ctr Ocean Health U Calif 100 Shaffer Rd Santa Cruz CA 95060 Office Phone: 831-459-5123. Office Fax: 831-459-3383. E-mail: williams@biology.ucsc.edu. *

WILLIAMS, TERRIE MICHELLE, public relations executive; b. Mt. Vernon, NY, May 12, 1954; MA, BA cum laude, Brandeis U., 1975; MS, Columbia U., 1977. Exec. dir. World Inst. of Black Community, NYC, 1982; dir. pub. rels. Essence Communications Inc., NYC, 1982-86, v.p., dir., 1986-88; pres. The Terrie Williams Agy., NYC, 1988—. Med. soc. worker N.Y. Hosp., NYC, 1977-80; program adminstr. Black Filmmaker Found., N.Y.C., 1980-81; exec. dir. Black Owned Communications Alliance, N.Y.C., 1981-82. Author: The Personal Touch, 1995. Recipient Entrepeneur of the Yr. award Nat. Assn. Market Developers, 1990, Flo Kennedy Media award, 1990, Matrix award N.Y. Women in Communications, 1991. Mem. Women in Communications, NOW, Brandeis U. Alumni Assn. (bd. dirs.), NY TV Acad. Arts and Scis., Pub. Rels. Soc. Am. (D. Parke Gibson award 1981). E-mail: tmwms@terriewilliams.com.

WILLIAMS, TERRY NEAL, secondary school educator; b. McComb, Miss., July 18, 1957; s. Aubrey Felder and Alice Anita Williams. BA, U. So. Miss., Hattiesburg, 1979; MA, U. Pitts., 1984; PhD, Fla. State U., Tallahassee, 1994. Nat. bd. cert. tchr. Ga., 2006. Tchr. Instituto La Inmaculada, Comayagua, Honduras, 1979—81, Chamberlain-Hunt Acad., Port Gibson, Miss., 1984—85; Fulbright jr. lectr. Selcuk U., Konya, Turkey, 1985—86; tchr. Parklane Acad., McComb, Miss., 1986—87; instr. Ga. Inst. Tech., Atlanta, 1990—94; pub. svc. assoc. U. Ga., Athens, 1994—2001; tchr. Meadowcreek H.S., Norcross, Ga., 2002—07; title III program specialist Gwinnett County Pub. Schs. Instrnl. Support Ctr., Suwanee, Ga., 2007—. Pres. Ga. Tchrs. of English to Speakers of Other Langs., Athens, 2000—01. Bd. mem. Reaching Every Adult Learner: The Athens-Clarke County Cert. Literate Cmty. Program, 1996—2001. Mem.: Toastmasters of Centerville. Unitarian-Universalist. Home: 3048 Jonathan Ct Snellville GA 30039 Office: Gwinnett County Pub Schs Instrnl Support Ctr 437 Old Peachtree Rd NW Suwanee GA 30024 Home Phone: 770-985-1177; Office Phone: 678-301-6814.

WILLIAMS, THELMA B., retired principal; d. Joseph and Floria Bush; m. McDonald Williams, Oct. 9, 1955; children: Donald J., Patricia A. Johnson. BS in Edn., Paine Coll., 1963; EdM, U. Ga., 1974, EdS, 1981. Tchr. Levi White Elem., Augusta, Ga., 1963—72; reading specialist Richmond County Schs., Augusta, 1972—76; asst. prin. Glenn Hills High, Augusta, 1976—81; prin. W.S. Hornsby Elem., Augusta, 1981—99. Edn. vol. Richmond County Schs., 1999—2002; founder after-sch. tutorial program, 2005—. Vice chair Richmond County Hist. Commn., 1995—; mem. Augusta Richmond County Hist. Preservation Commn., 1995—2003, vice chair, 2006—; mem. several ministries Macedonia Bapt. Ch., organizer after school tutorial program, 2004; mem. Augusta Classic, 1998—, Alzheimer's Assn., Augusta, 1983—2003. Recipient Meritorious Svc. award, Richmond County Prin. Assn., 1999, Pres.'s award, Paine Coll., 2001, Disting. award of edn., Nat. Assn. Equal Opportunity in Higher Edn., 2002, United Negro Coll. Fund award, Tom Joyner Found., 2003, Yough Svc. award, Ga. Rep. Quincy Murphy, 2004, Outstanding Educators award, W.S. Hornsby and East Augusta Cmty. Neighborhood Assn. and PCS Nitrogen, 1998. Mem.: Richmond County Ret. Tchrs. Assn., Art Factory for Creative Arts (sec. 1990—92), Loyal Christian Women Civic Group (v.p. 2006—, vice chair 2006—), Paine Coll. Alumni Assn. (chmn. ballot com. 1997—99, pres. Augusta chpt. 2001—), Paine Coll. Platinum

Club (pres. 1983—, lectr. Founder's Day 1994, nat. chairballots 1997—99, chmn. ballots com. 1997—99, local pres. 2001—03, pres. Augusta chpt. 2001—), Phi Delta Kappa, Zeta Phi Beta (Founder's Day Lectr. 1994). Avocations: travel, reading, baking, teaching. Personal E-mail: TBW51@comcast.net.

WILLIAMS, THEODORE JOSEPH, engineering educator; b. Black Lick, Pa., Sept. 2, 1923; s. Theodore Finley and Mary Ellen (Shields) W.; m. Isabel Annette McAnulty, July 18, 1946; children: Theodore Joseph, Mary Margaret, Charles Augustus, Elizabeth Ann. BSCh.E., Pa. State U., 1949, MSCh.E., 1950, PhD, 1955; MS in Elec. Engring., Ohio State U., 1956. Research fellow Pa. State U., University Park, 1947-51; asst. prof. Air Force Inst. Tech., 1953-56; technologist Monsanto Co., 1956-57, sr. engring. supr., 1957-65; prof. engring. Purdue U., Lafayette, Ind., 1965-94, prof. emeritus, 1995—, dir. control and info. systems lab., 1965-66; dir. Purdue Lab. Applied Indsl. Control, 1966-94, dir. emeritus, 1995—; cons., 1964—. Vis. prof. Washington U., St. Louis, 1962-65; hon. prof. Inst. Automation, Academia Sinica, Shenyang, China, 1992. Author: Systems Engineering for the Process Industries, 1961, Automatic Control of Chemical and Petroleum Processes, 1961, Progress in Direct Digital Control, 1969, Interfaces with the Process Control Computer, 1971, Modeling and Control of Kraft Production Systems, 1975, Modelling, Estimation and Control of the Soaking Pit, 1983, The Use of Digital Computers in Process Control, 1983, Analysis and Design of Hierarchical Control Systems - With Special Reference to Steel Plant Operations, 1985, A Reference Model for Computer Integrated Manufacturing (CIM) - A Description from the Viewpoint of Industrial Automation, 1989, The Purdue Enterprise Reference Architecture, 1992; editor: Computer Applications in Shipping and Shipbuilding, 6 vols., 1973-79, Proceedings Advanced Control Confs., 19 vols., 1974-93, Architectures for Enterprise Integration, 1996. Served to 1st lt. USAAF, 1942-45; to capt. USAF, 1951-56. Decorated Air medal with 2 oak leaf clusters. Fellow AAAS, AIChE, Instrument Soc. Am. (hon. mem., pres. 1968-69, Albert F. Sperry gold medal 1990, Lifetime Achievement award 1995), Am. Inst. Chemists, Inst. Measurement and Control (London, Sr. Harold Hartley silver medal 1975), Indsl. Computing Soc.; mem. IEEE (sr.), Internat. Fedn. for Info. Processing (Silver Core award 1978), Soc. for Computer Simulation (hon.), Am. Chem. Soc., Am. Automatic Control Coun. (pres. 1965-67), Am. Fedn. Info. Processing Socs. (pres. 1976-78), Sigma Xi, Tau Beta Pi, Phi Kappa Phi, Phi Lambda Upsilon. Home: 208 Chippewa St West Lafayette IN 47906-2123 Office: Purdue U Potter Rsch Ctr Inst Interdisciplinary Engring Studies West Lafayette IN 47907-1293 Office Phone: 765-463-7828. Business E-Mail: tjwil@ecn.purdue.edu.

WILLIAMS, THEODORE JOSEPH, JR., lawyer; b. Pitts., July 23, 1947; s. Theodore Joseph and Isabel (McAnulty) W.; m. Sherri Lynn Foust, July 4, 1970; children: Kelley Shields, Jonathan Stewart, Jordan Fuller. BA, Purdue U., West Lafayette, Ind., 1969; JD, U. Tulsa, Okla., 1974. Bar: Ill. 1975, Colo. 1996, US Ct. Appeals (7th cir.) 1975, US Dist. Ct. (no., so. and ctrl. dists.) Ill. 1975, Mo. 1978, US Ct. Appeals (8th cir.) 1978, US Dist. Ct. (ea. and we. dists.) Mo. 1978, US Supreme Ct. 1978, DC 1981, US Ct. Appeals (DC cir.) 1988, US Dist. Ct. DC 1988, US Ct. Mil. Appeals 1991, US Ct. Appeals (10 cir.) 1996, US Dist. Ct. (no. dist.) Ind. 2000, Kans. 2006, Okla. 2006, Wis. 2007. Asst. city prosecutor City of Tulsa, 1974; trial atty., law dept. Chgo. and North Western R.R., Chgo., 1975-78; assoc. Thompson and Mitchell, St. Louis, 1978-81, Shepherd, Sandberg & Phoenix, P.C., St. Louis, 1981-84, ptnr., 1984-88; ptnr., chmn. transp. law dept. Armstrong, Teasdale, Schlafly & Davis, St. Louis, 1988-2001, mem. mgmt. com., 1994—2000; ptnr. Williams, Venker & Sanders, LLC, St. Louis, 2001—, chmn., 2001—. State Counsel for Mo. and Ill., Chgo. and North Western Transp. Co., 1981-95. Assoc. editor Law. Jour., U. Tulsa, 1974. Treas. sch. bd. Mary Queen of Peace Sch., Webster Groves, Mo., 1986, v.p., 1987. Lt. Col. US Army. Mem. ABA (vice-chmn. rail and motor carrier law com., torts and ins. practice law sect. 1989-90, chair-elect 1990-91, chair 1991-92), Ill. Bar Assn., Mo. Bar Assn., Wis. Bar Assn., Def. Rsch. Inst. (chair, railroad law com. 1996), Nat. Assn. R.R. Trial Coun. (exec. com. 2002—), We. Conf. Ry. Coun., Assn. ICC Practitioners, Maritime Law Assn., Internat. Assn. Def. Coun., Transp. Lawyers Assn., Assn. Transp. Practitioners, Fedn. Def. and Corp. Counsel, DC Bar Assn., Colo. Bar Assn., Kans. Bar Assn., Okla. Bar Assn., Am. Bd. Trial Advs. (adv.). Republican. Roman Catholic. Office: Williams Venker Sanders LLC Ste 2100 100 N Broadway St Saint Louis MO 63102 Office Phone: 314-345-5000. Business E-Mail: Twilliams@wvslaw.com.

WILLIAMS, THOMAS ALAN, elementary school educator, small business owner; b. Kingston, Pa., Dec. 15, 1961; s. Thomas Elwin and Lois Jean (Vanderhoff) Williams; m. Jeanne Ann Sweinberg, July 10, 1993; children: Lindsay Nicole, Thomas Lee. BS in Edn., Bloomsburg U., Pa., 1983; MS in Counselor Edn., U. Scranton, Pa., 1987. Cert. secondary counselor, elem. counselor. Tchr. N.W. Sch. Dist., Shickshinny, Pa., 1983-84; tchr. grades 4-6 Lake-Lehman (Pa.) Sch. Dist., 1984-88, tchr. social studies grades 7-8, 1988-93, tchr. social studies grades 10-12, 1993-99, tchr. grades 4-6, 1999—, asst. athletic dir., 2001—04; pres. T&J Williams Enterprises Inc., 2001—; owner Curves, Lehman, 2001—, Plains, 2001—, Hanover, 2001—, Nanticoke, 2004—, Wilkes-Barre Twp., 2004—. Wrestling coach Lake-Lehman Sch. Dist., 1984—99; owner Curves for Women Exercise and Fitness Franchise, Plains, Pa., 2002—; pres. T&J Williams Enterprises, Inc., Dallas. Wrestling ofcl. Pa. Interscholastic Athletic Assn., Wilkes-Barre, 1981—. Named Pa. N.E. Regional Coach of the Yr., Regional Wrestling Com., 1991; recipient, 1995, Coach of the Yr., Times-Leader, 1990, 1991, 1992, 1994, 1995, 1996, 1997. Mem.: Wrestling Coaches Assn. (Coach of the Yr. 1992, 1995, Sportsmanship award 1995), Pa. Wrestling Coaches Assn., Pa. State Athletic Dirs. Assn., Nat. Wrestling Coaches Assn., Pa. Interscholastic Athletic Assn. (chmn. dist. wrestling rep. 2007—), Caldwell Consistory, Shriners, Masons. Republican. Methodist. Avocations: fishing, collectibles, photography, travel, gardening. Home: 1087 Mountain View Dr Dallas PA 18612-9539 Office: Lake-Lehman H S Lehman PA 18627 Personal E-mail: tnjwilly@aol.com.

WILLIAMS, THOMAS ARTHUR, biomedical computing consultant, psychiatrist; b. Racine, Wis., May 11, 1936; s. Robert Klinkert and Marion Anne (Wisneski) Williams; m. Christine Frances Fannon, July 3, 1970; children: Jennifer, Thomas, Hailey, Renate, Alexa. BA, Harvard Coll., 1958; MD, Columbia U., 1963; postgrad., NIH, 1967-68. Diplomate Nat. Bd. Med. Examiners, Am. Bd. Psychiatry and Neurology. Intern in surgery Columbia Presbyn. Med. Ctr., NYC, 1963-64; resident in psychiatry Columbia Presbyterian Med. Ctr., N.Y. State Psychiat. Inst., NYC, 1964-67; chief depression sect. NIMH, Bethesda, Rockville, Md., 1967-71; asst. prof. U. Pitts., 1969-70; assoc. prof. U. Utah, Salt Lake City, 1971-77; prof., chmn. dept. psychiatry Eastern Va. Med. Sch., Norfolk, Va., 1977-78; clin. dir. Sheppard & Enoch Pratt Hosp., Towson, Md., 1978-80; prof. U. South Fla., Tampa, 1980-83; practitioner psychiat. medicine, med. dir. St. Augustine (Fla.) Psychiat. Ctr., 1983-89, 89-90; prin. Williams & Assocs., Palm Harbor, Fla., 1990—. Treas., pres. Klinkert Realty Co., Inc., Racine, Wis., 1960—85. Chief editor: Psychobiology of Depression, 1972, Mental Health in the 21st Century, 1979; contbr. numerous articles to profl. jours. and chpts. to books. Mem. Gov.'s Adv. Com. on Mental Health, Salt Lake City, 1971-77, Gov.'s Adv. Com. on Penal Code, Richmond, Va., 1978, Dist. Mental Health Bd., Tampa, 1980-83; mem. U.S. Govt. Mission on Psychiatry to USSR, 1974; sponsor, coach Forest Hills Little League Baseball, Tampa, 1980-83. Sr. surgeon USPHS, 1958-67. Recipient Predoctoral fellowship NIMH, 1960-61, Alumni Rsch. award N.Y. State Psychiat. Inst., 1964, Rush Bronze Medal award Am. Psychiat. Assn., 1973, Rsch. grants VA, 1971-77. Mem. AMA, Fla. Med. Assn., Hillsborough County Med. Assn., Columbia U. Alumni Club (dir. 1995—), Harvard Club of the West Coast of Fla. Avocations: computers, classical music, opera, basketball. Home: 3844 Muirfield Ct Palm Harbor FL 34685 Personal E-mail: tawmd@verizon.net.

WILLIAMS, THOMAS EUGENE, pediatric hematologist, pediatric oncologist, pharmaceutical executive; b. Texarkana, Ark., May 13, 1936; s. Thomas Earle and Frankie Jo (Garner) W.; m. Peggy Jane O'Neill, May 31, 1958; children: Thomas Eugene, Elizabeth Anne, James David. BA, Yale U., 1958; MD, U. Tex. Southwestern Med. Sch., 1962. Diplomate Am. Bd. Pediat., Am. Bd. Pediat. Hematology and Oncology. Rotating intern Hermann Hosp., Houston, 1962-63; pediat. resident Children's Med. Ctr., Dallas, 1963-65; fellow pediat. hematology U. Va. Sch. Medicine, Charlottesville, 1967-68; rsch. assoc. Cancer Rsch. Lab., U. Va., Charlottesville, 1968-69; asst. prof. pediat. and pathology U. Tex. Health Sci. Ctr., San Antonio, 1969-72, assoc. prof. pediat., asst. prof. pathology, 1972-73, assoc. prof. pediat. and pathology, 1973-79, assoc. prof. pediat., 1985-94. Med. dir. Santa Rosa Children's Hosp. Cancer Rsch. and Treatment Ctr., 1974—79, South Tex. Comprehensive Hemophilia Ctr., 1977—79, dir. pediat. bone marrow transplantation program, 1986—93; sr. clin. rsch. scientist Burroughs Wellcome Co., 1979—85; dir. new drug devel. Orphan Med., Inc., 1994—96; dir. med. affairs Ilex Oncology Svcs., Inc., 1997—98, ILEX Oncology Products, Inc., 1998—2002; clin. assoc. prof. pediat. U. N.C. Sch. Medicine, 1979—85; clin. fellow bone marrow transplantation program Johns Hopkins U. Sch. Medicine, Balt., 1985; sr. dir. Divsn. Oncology ICON Clin. Rsch., Inc., 2002—. Contbr. articles to profl. jours. Exec. dir. Episcopal Med. Missions Found., 1997—. Lt. cmmdr. USNR, 1965—67. Recipient travel award Am. Soc. Pharmacology and Exptl. Therapeutics, 1968; Am. Cancer Soc. advanced clin. fellow, 1968-69, 70-72. Mem. Am. Soc. Clin. Oncology, Am. Soc. Hematology, Am. Assn. for Cancer Rsch. Episcopalian. Office: ICON Clin Rsch Inc 10999 W IH 10 Ste 255 San Antonio TX 78230-1355 Home Phone: 830-899-2855; Office Phone: 215-616-3250. Personal E-mail: drtommd@satx.rr.com. Business E-Mail: williamst@iconus.com.

WILLIAMS, THOMAS FRANKLIN, physician, educator; b. Belmont, NC, Nov. 26, 1921; s. T. F. and Mary L. (Deaton) Williams; m. Catharine Carter Catlett, Dec. 15, 1951; children: Mary Wright, Thomas Nelson. BS, U. N.C., 1942; MA, Columbia U., 1943; MD, Harvard U., 1950; DSc (hon.), Med. Coll. Ohio, 1987, U. N.C., 1992; DMS, Thomas Jefferson U., 2003. Intern Johns Hopkins, Balt., 1950—51, asst. resident physician, 1951—53; resident physician Boston VA Hosp., 1953—54; research fellow U. N.C., Chapel Hill, 1954—56, instr. dept. medicine and preventive medicine, 1956—57, asst. prof., 1957—61, assoc. prof., 1961—68, prof., 1968; attending physician Strong Meml. Hosp., Rochester, NY, 1968—; cons. physician Genesee Hosp., Rochester, NY, 1973—; prof. medicine, preventive medicine and cmty. health U. Rochester, 1968—92, prof. radiation biology and biophysics, 1968—91, on leave, 1983—91, prof. emeritus, 1992—; clin. prof. medicine U. Va., 1983—89; lectr. medicine Johns Hopkins U., 1983—89; clin. prof. depts. family medicine and medicine Georgetown U., 1983—89; dir. Nat. Inst. on Aging NIH, 1983—91; asst. surgeon gen. USPHS, 1983—91, ret., 1991; attending physician Monroe Cmty. Hosp., Rochester, 1991—, vice-chmn. cmty. coalition for long term care, 1991—; disting. physician VA Med. Ctr., Canandigua, NY, 1995—98. Adv. bd. U. Rochester Sch. Medicine and Dentistry, 1968—83; med. dir. Monroe Cmty. Hosp., Rochester, 1968—83; mem. rev. coms. Nat. Ctr. for Health Svcs. Rsch.; adv. bd. St. Ann's Home; mem. gov. bd. NRC, 1981—83; sci. dir. Am. Fedn. Aging Rsch., 1992—; cons. in field. Contbr. articles to profl. publs. With USNR, 1943—46. Recipient Civic award for health care, Rochester N.Y. C. of C., 1998; fellow, USPHS, 1966—67; scholar Markle scholar, 1957—61. Fellow: ACP, APHA; mem.: NAS (coun. 1980—83, governing bd. 1981—83, Gustav O. Lienhard award Inst. Medicine 1969), AAAS, Am. Clin. Climatol. Assn., N.C. Coun. for Human Rels. (chmn. 1963—66), Rochester Regional Diabetes Assn. (pres. 1977—79), Am. Gerontol. Soc., Am. Geriatrics Soc., Soc. Exptl. Biology and Medicine, Am. Fedn. Clin. Rsch., Am. Diabetes Assn. (bd. dirs. 1974—80), Monroe County Med. Soc., N.Y. State Med. Soc., Assn. Am. Physicians, Inst. Medicine. Episcopalian. Home: 287 Dartmouth St Rochester NY 14607-3202 Office: Monroe Cmty Hosp Office Med Dir Rochester NY 14620 Office Phone: 585-760-6357.

WILLIAMS, THOMAS W., electrical engineer; b. Rochester, NY, Aug. 3, 1943; s. Thomas Alfred and Mary Anne (Boryszewski) W.; m. Suzane Louise Sawyer, Dec. 26, 1964 (div. 1982); children: Megan Ren+245, David Thomas; m. Candace Merrill, Mar. 16, 1985. BSEE, Clarkson U., 1965; MA in Maths., Binghamton U., 1968; PhD in Elec. Engring., Colo. State U., 1971. From staff to sys. designer IBM, Endicott, NY, 1968-73, mem. ISI design rules and control group Boulder, Colo., 1973-77, from sr. engr., mgr. to sr. tech. staff, mgr. VLSI Design, 1977-1998; Synopsys fellow Test Technology, Synopsys, Inc. Guest prof., Robert Bosch fellow, U. Hannover, Germany, 1985, 1996-98; adj. prof. U. Calgary, Can. Contbr. articles to profl. jours. Grantee NSF. Fellow IEEE (W. Wallace McDowell award 1989); mem. IEEE (bd. govs. 1987-93, 95-, bd. dirs. 2001-02, 2007-), Phi Kappa Phi, Eta Kappa Nu. E-mail: t.williams@computer.org.

WILLIAMS, TOD CULPAN, architect, educator; b. Detroit, May 11, 1943; s. Richard Jamison and Bettina Joy (Culpan) Williams; m. Patricia Jones, June 21, 1966 (div. Mar. 1975); children: Rachel, Tod C.; m. Billie Tsien, Feb. 14, 1983; 1 child, Kai Tsien. BA, Princeton U., NJ, 1965; postgraduate student, U. Cambridge, Eng., 1966; MFA, Princeton U., NJ, 1967. Registered arch., NY, Conn., Mass., NJ, Mich., Tex. Assoc. Richard Meier & Assocs., NYC, 1967—74; owner, ptnr. Potters/Williams, NYC, 1975—78; prin. Tod Williams/Billie Tsien Archs., NYC, 1978—. Prof. architecture Coopen Union, NYC, 1974—89; advisor Princeton Sch. Architecture, 1983; Ruth Carter Stevenson chair U. Tex., Austin, 1995; Eliel Saarinen chair U. Mich., 2002; Louis I. Kahn chair Yale U., New Haven, 2003, New Haven, 05; Thomas Jefferson chair U. Va., 2004. Author, curator: book/exhbn. Window Room Furniture, 1982—83; contbr. articles to archtl. jours. Advanced fellow, Am. Acad. Rome (Graham Found.), 1983. Fellow: Am. Acad. Arts & Scis.; mem.: AIA (Disting. Architecture award 1982, 1986, 1987), Nat. Coll. Archs. Registration Bds. Office: Tod Williams/Billie Tsien 222 Central Park S New York NY 10019-1408 Office Phone: 212-582-2385. *

WILLIAMS, TONDA, entrepreneur, consultant; b. NYC, Nov. 21, 1949; d. William and Juanita (Rainey) W.; 1 child, Tywana. Student, Collegiate Inst., NYC, 1975—78, C.W. Post Coll., 1981—83; BA in Bus. Mgmt., Am. Nat. U., Phoenix, 1983; grad., LI Bus. Inst., 1996. Notary pub. NY. Asst. controller Acad. Ednl. Devel., NYC, 1971-81; mgr. office Chapman-Apex Constrn. Co., Bayshore, NY, 1982-84; specialist computer RGM Liquid Waste Removal, Deerpark, NY, 1985-87; contr. LaMar Lighting Co., Freeport, NY, 1987—; owner, pres. Omni-Star, Bklyn., 1981—; pres. Omni-Data Tech., Bayshore, NY, 1996—. Author: Tonda's Songs in Poetry, 1978, The Magic of Life, 1991; co-author: Computer Management of Liquid Waste Industry, 1986. Recipient Golden Poet award World of Poetry, 1992. Mem. Am. Mus. Natural History, Am. Soc. Notary Pubs. Avocations: bowling, chess, singing. Home: 74 Cedar Dr Bay Shore NY 11706-2419 Home Phone: 631-665-2152; Office Phone: 631-968-0016. Office Fax: 631-968-1016. Business E-Mail: tonda@omnidatatech.com.

WILLIAMS, TYLER JAMES, actor; b. Westchester County, NY, Oct. 9, 1992; Actor: (TV series) Sesame Street, 2002—05, Law & Order: Spl. Victims Unit, 2005, Everybody Hates Chris, 2005—06 (NAACP Image award best actor in a comedy series, 2007); (films) Unaccompanied Minors, 2006, (voice): (TV series) Little Bill, 2000; (films) The Ant Bully, 2006, Everyone's Hero, 2006; guest appearances on The Oprah Winfrey Show, 2005, The Ellen DeGeneres Show, 2005, Jimmy Kimmel Live, 2005, The Tonight Show with Jay Leno, 2005, Late Show with David Letterman, 2006, The Megan Mullally Show, 2006. Avocations: basketball, piano, history. Office: c/o Mollo Mgmt Inc 1143 W Broadway Hewlett NY 11557 *

WILLIAMS, UNA JOYCE, psychiatric social worker; b. Youngstown, Ohio, June 24, 1934; d. Samuel Wilfred and Frances Josephine (Woods) Ellis; children: Wendy Louise, Christopher Ellis, Sharon Elizabeth. BA, U. Ala., 1957; MSW, Adelphi U., 1963. Diplomate in profl. counseling Internat. Acad. Behavioral Medicine, Counseling and Psychotherapy. Dir. Huntington Program Sr. Citizens, 1963—67; psychiat. social worker-supr. N.Y. State Dept. Mental Hygiene, Suffolk Psychiat. Hosp., Central Islip, 1969—72; info.-referral counselor Mental Health Assn. Nassau County, Hempstead, NY, 1993—; therapist Madonna Heights Family Clinic, Dix Hills, NY, 1994—99; med. and psychiat. social worker Northport VA Med. Ctr., NY, 1994—2005, psychiat. social worker acute psychiat. treatment svcs., 2005—, med. social worker dialysis svcs., 2007—. Cons. on programs for aging Luth. Social Svcs. Met. N.Y., 1959, sr. citizens programs, Bd. Edn. Port Jefferson, N.Y., 1961-63. Chmn. Huntington Twp. Com. Human Rels., 1970; sec. bd. trustess Unitarian Universalist Fellowship Huntington, 1984. Mem. NASW (diplomate in social work), Am. Assn. Family Counselors and Mediators,Germany Philatelic Soc. (pres. chpt. 30, 1990, Mem. of Yr. 1987). Avocations: painting, stamp collecting/philately, music (voice & piano), genealogy. Home: 316 Lenox Rd Huntington Station NY 11746-2640

WILLIAMS, VANESSA (VANESSA LYNN WILLIAMS), recording artist, actress; b. Millwood, NY, Mar. 18, 1963; d. Milton and Helen; m. Ramon Hervey II, 1988 (div. 1997); children: Melanie, Jillian, Devin; m. Rick Fox, 1999 (div.); 1 child, Sasha Gabriella Fox. Recording artist, 1988—. Stage appearances include: (Broadway) Kiss of the Spider Woman, 1993-95 (Theatre World award, 1995), Into the Woods, 2002(nominee Drama Desk award for Outstanding Actress in a Musical, 2002, Tony award Best Actress in a Musical, 2002); film appearances include Pick-up Artist, 1987, Under the Gun, 1988, Another You, 1991, Harley Davidson and the Marlboro Man, 1991, Eraser, 1996, Hoodlum, 1997, Soul Food, 1997, Dance with Me, 1998, The Adventures of Elmo in Grouchland, 1999, Light It Up, 1999, Shaft, 2000, Johnson Family Vacation, 2004,(TV films) Full Exposure: The Sex Tapes Scandal, 1989, The Kid Who Loved Christmas, 1990, Perry Mason: The Case of the Silenced Singer, 1990, Stompin' at the Savoy, 1992, Jacksons: An American Dream, 1992, Nothing Lasts Forever, 1995, Bye Bye Birdie, 1995, The Odyssey, 1997, Futuresport, 1998, Courage to Love, 2000 (also exec. prodr.), Don Quixote, 2000, A Diva's Christmas Carol, 2000, WW3, 2001, Keep the Faith, Baby, 2002, (TV mini series) Nothing Lasts Forever, 1995, (TV series) Ugly Betty 2006-(Supporting Actress in a Comedy Series, NAACP Image Awards, 2007, Choice TV: Villain, Teen Choice Awards, 2007); guest appearances Partners in Crime, 1984, T.J. Hooker, 1986, The Love Boat, 1986, The Fresh Prince of Bel-Air, 1990, Between Brothers, 1997, Vanessa Williams and Friends: Christmas in N.Y., 1996, Star Trek: Deep Space Nine, 1996, L.A. Doctors, 1999, Ally McBeal, 2002, Boomtown, 2003, South Beach, 2006; albums: The Right Stuff, 1988, The Comfort Zone, 1991, The Sweetest Days, 1994, Star Bright, 1996, Next, 1997, Alfie, the Best of Vanessa, 1998; # 1 hit single Save the Best for Last; vocalist (soundtracks) Beverly Hills 90210, 1990, Harley Davidson and the Marlboro Man, 1991, Adventures of Priscilla, Queen of the Desert, 1994, The Mask, 1994, Pocahontas, 1995, Eraser, 1996, Dance with Me, 1998, The Adventures of Elmo in Grouchland, 1999, Isn't She Great, 2000; host Style World, 2000; spokesperson for Proactive Solution (Acne Medication); commercial appearances Radio Shack. Recipient 8 Grammy award nominations, received star on the Hollywood Walk of Fame, 2007; named one of 50 Most Beautiful People, People Mag. Achievements include being the first Black to be named Miss America, 1983 (resigned title 1983). Office: Mercury Records care Dawn Bridges 825 8th Ave New York NY 10019-7416 also: Mercury Records 11150 Santa Monica Blvd Los Angeles CA 90025-3380 Address: William Morris Agy 151 El Camino Dr Beverly Hills CA 90212 *

WILLIAMS, VAUGHN CHARLES, lawyer; b. LA, Mar. 2, 1945; s. David Welford and Ovida M. (White) W. AB, Harvard U., 1966; JD, Stanford U., 1967. Bar: Calif. 1969, D.C. 1971, N.Y. 1977, U.S. Ct. Appeals (2d cir.) 1977, U.S. Ct. Appeals (5th, 8th and 9th cirs.), U.S. Supreme Ct. 1981. Law clk. to Hon. Carl McGowan U.S. Ct. of Appeals (D.C. cir.), Washington, 1969-70; counsel U.S. Senate, Dist. Col. Comm., Washington, 1970-71; assoc. Wilmer Cutler & Pickering, Washington, 1971-74; gen. counsel U.S. Coun. on Wage-Price Stability, Washington, 1975-76; assoc. Skadden Arps Slate Meagher & Flom, NYC, 1977-79, ptnr., 1979—. Dir. N.Y.C. Campaign Fin. Bd., 1994—; mem. Merit Selection Panel So. Dist. of N.Y. Dir. Lincoln Ctr. for Performing Arts, N.Y.C., Bklyn. Acad. Music, God's Love We Deliver, Inc., Lawyers For Children, Inc.; vice chmn. Fund for the City of N.Y. Named to Am.'s Top Black Lawyers, Black Enterprise mag., 2003. Mem. Assn. Bar of City of N.Y. (Bainbridge-Smith com., com. for future, former mem. long range planning com.), University Club. Office: Skadden Arps Slate Meagher & Flom 4 Times Sq Fl 24 New York NY 10036-6595 E-mail: vwilliam@skadden.com.

WILLIAMS, VENUS, professional tennis player; b. Lynwood, Calif., June 17, 1980; d. Richard and Oracene Williams. Prof. tennis player WTA tour, 1994—; owner V Starr Interiors; designer Venus Williams Collection Wilson's Leather Co.; designer EleVen fashion label, 2007—. Recipient ESPY award for outstanding women's tennis player, 2001, Espy award for Best Female Tennis Player, 2001, 2006, Espy award for Best Female Athlete, 2002; named Most Impressive Network Newcomer award, 1997, TENNIS Mag. Most Improved Player, WTA Tour, 1998 Mem.: WTA Tour Players' Coun. Jehovah'S Witness. Achievements include winner 35 career singles titles, 9 career doubles titles, WTA; winner 1 career doubles title, ITF; Grand Slam Championships:(singles) US Open, 2000, 2001, Wimbledon, 2000, 2001, 2005, 2007, (doubles) French Open, 1999, US Open 1999, Wimbledon, 2000, 2002, Australian Open, 2001, 2003; singles and doubles gold winner, Sydney Olympics, 2000; mem. US Fed Cup Team, 1999, 2003-05, 2007, US Olympic Team, 2000, 2004. Avocations: interior decorating, fashion design. Office: US Tennis Assn 70 W Red Oak Ln White Plains NY 10604-3602

WILLIAMS, VERONICA MYRES, psychotherapist, social worker; b. Shreveport, La., May 11, 1947; d. McEura and Margie Virgina (Reagan) Myres; divorced; children: Nicole Leann, Jennifer Lyn, Erica Maria. BA, La. Tech. U., Ruston, 1969; MSW, U. Mich., Ann Arbor, 1977; PhD, So. Calif. U., 2001. Diplomate Am. Bd. Clin. Social Workers, Am. Psychotherapy Assn.; cert. social worker, Mich. Probation counselor Citizens Probation Authority, Flint, Mich., 1970-72; unit dir., therapist Svcs. to Overcome Drug Abuse Among Teenagers, Flint, 1972-74; psychiat. therapist Psycho-Therapeutic Treatment Clin., P.C., Flint, 1974-77; psychiat. social worker Hurley Med. Ctr., Flint, 1977-79; field instr. Sch. Social Work U. Mich., Ann Arbor, 1978-79, 86—; psychiat. social worker Inst. Mental Health, Flint, 1979-81, Psychotherapeutic Treatment Clinic, 1981-83; clin. social worker Flint Bd. Edn., 1979-83; pupil apprasal spl. edn. Caddo Parish Sch. Bd., Shreveport, La., 1983—85; psychiat. therapist Mott Children's Health Ctr., 1986—92, Oakland Psychol. Clinic, P.C., 1991—92; owner and dir. V. Williams, PhD, MSW, ACSW, BCD, PC, Flint, Mich., 1992—. Developer dropout prevention program Flint Bd. Edn., 1986-98; Beecher Sch. Dist., 1998-2006. Bd. dirs. Boys & Girls Club. Mem. NASW, ACSW, NEA, Mich. Edn. Assn. Democrat. Office: Ste 110 225 E 5th St Flint MI 48502 Home Phone: 810-695-5610; Office Phone: 810-232-0018. E-mail: drvmw@yahoo.com.

WILLIAMS, WALKER RICHARD, JR., social services administrator; b. Dayton, Ohio, July 11, 1928; s. Walker Richard Sr. and Addie Mary (Smith) W.; m. Eddora L. Saunders, Aug. 6, 1949 (dec. Sept. 1966); 1 child, Yvette R.; m. Emma Jean Griffin, Sept. 4, 1971; children: Timotny E., Walker R. III. Student, U. Dayton, 1946-48. Commd. 2d lt. U.S. Army, 1952; advanced through grades to capt. USAF, Wright Patterson AFB, Ohio, 1963, supply cataloger, supr., 1963, employee rels. specialist, pers. mgmt. specialist, 1966-71; EEO investigator and grievance examiner, chief EEO and affirmative action programs Army and Air N.G., Wright Patterson AFB, Ohio, 1971-88; retired USAR, 1988; program dir. Youth Svc. U.S.A.-Dayton, 1988-89; pvt. contractor Dayton, 1989—. Mem. Adjutant Gen. Ohio Minority Recruiting Adv. Com., 1988—; bd. dirs. Dayton Opportunities Industrialization Ctr., 1976—, Wright Patterson Domestic Action Programs, Inc., 1984—; pres. Jefferson Twp. Bd. Edn., 1980—; mem. Nat. Black Caucus of Black Sch. Bd. Mems., 1980—, Nat. Black Caucus Local Elected Officials, Gov.'s Com. to Preserve Statue of Liberty, 1987, Citywide Vocat. Ednl. Com., 1986—, adv. com. Dayton Bd. Edn., 1980—, Miami Valley Mil. Affairs Assn., Black Elected Democrats of Ohio. Recipient Air Force Civilian Svc. award, Dayton C. of C., Internat. Personnel Mgmt. Assn. Employee of the Yr., Blacks in Govt. Pres.'s award, Federally Employed Women's Supr. of the Yr. runner up, Hispanic Heritage Wk. Spl. award, NAACP Humanitarian award, Community Svc. award, Dayton Bd. Edn., James W. Cisco award, Ohio Vocat. Edn. award Wilberforce U., Urban League Humanitarian award, Svc. to Youth award Girl Scouts U.S., Spl. award United Negro Coll. Fund, Beautillion Militaire Legacy award, Jack & Jill, 7 Air Force Logistics Command Significant Achievement awards, AG of Ohio award, Ohio State U. award, Black Studies Group award, Russell Lyle award Wright Patterson AFB Quarter Century Club, Student Intervention Program Radcliff Sch., Blacks in Glvt. Mediation award, others; a day named in his honor, Dayton, 1987, 88, Svc. award Jefferson Township Bd. Edn. Mem. Miami Valley Pers. Assn., Internat. Pers. Mgmt. Assn., Retired Officers Assn., Air Force Assn., NAACP, Urban League, Blacks in Govt., Dayton Intergovt. EEO Coun. (chmn., historian 1967—), Miami Valley Mil. Affairs Assn., Wright Patterson Quarter Century Club (past pres.). Democrat. Avocations: reading, photography. Home: 5050 Fortman Dr Dayton OH 45418-2233

WILLIAMS, WALTER JOSEPH, lawyer; b. Detroit, Oct. 5, 1918; s. Joseph Louis and Emma Geraldine (Hewitt) W.; m. Maureen June Kay, Jan. 15, 1944; 1 child, John Bryan. Student, Bowling Green State U., 1935-36; BSBA, Ohio State U., 1940; JD, LL.B., U. Detroit, 1942. Bar: Mich. 1942. Title atty. Abstract & Title Guaranty Co., 1946-47; corp. atty. Ford Motor Co., 1947-51, Studebaker-Packard Corp., 1951-56; asst. sec., house counsel Am. Motors Corp., Am. Motors Sales Corp., Am. Motors Pan-Am. Corp., Evart Products Co., Ltd., 1956-65, corp. sec. house counsel, 1965-72; asst. corp. sec., dir. Am. Motors (Can.) Ltd.; dir. Evart Products Co., 1959-72; dir., corporate sec., house counsel Jeep Corp., Jeep Sales Corp., Jeep Internat. Corp., 1968-72; partner Gilman and Williams, Southfield, Mich., 1972-74; atty. Detroit Edison Co., 1974-75; asst. sec., sr. staff atty. Burroughs Corp. (and subsidiaries), 1975-84; pvt. practice, pres. Walter J. Williams P.C., Bloomfield Hills, Mich., 1984—. Charter commr. City of Dearborn Heights, Mich., 1960-63; dir. Detroit Met. Indsl. Devel. Corp., 1962-72, asst. sec. Capt. U.S. Army, 1942-46. Mem. ABA, Detroit Bar Assn. (chmn. corp. gen. counsel com. 1965-68), Fed. Bar Assn., State Bar Mich., Ohio State U. Alumni Assn. (pres. Detroit 1961-63), U. Detroit Law Alumni, Oakland Hills Country Club, Delta Theta Phi. Home and Office: 3644 Darcy Dr Bloomfield Hills MI 48301-2125

WILLIAMS, WALTER WAYLON, lawyer, agricultural products supplier; b. Gause, Tex., Nov. 12, 1933; s. Jesse Nathaniel and Lola Fay (Matthews) W.; m. Velmalene Von Gonten, Mar. 6, 1953; children— Diana Lee, Virginia Marie. BBA with honors, U. Tex., 1959, JD with honors, 1960. Bar: Tex. bar 1960. Since practiced in, Houston; mem. firm Fulbright, Crooker, Freeman, Bates & Jaworski, 1960-63, Bates & Brock, 1964-66, Brock, Williams & Boyd, 1966-79, Williams & Boyd, 1979-88; pres. Nat. Pecan Growers Coun., 1976-78, Tex. Pecan Growers Assn., 1976-78. Served with AUS, 1953-55. Named Outstanding Soldier of Second Army, 1955 Mem. ABA, Houston Bar Assn., State Bar Tex., Tex. Trial Lawyers Assn. (dir. 1972-76), Houston Trial Lawyers Assn. (dir. 1969), Assn. Trial Lawyers Am., Chancellors, Beta Gamma Sigma, Phi Delta Phi. Home: 545 Williams Rd Yoakum TX 77995-5320

WILLIAMS, WENDY, radio personality, writer; b. July 18, 1964; m. Kevin Hunter; 1 child, Kevin. BA, Northeastern U., 1986. Intern Matt Siegel morning show, Kiss 108, Boston; radio personality WVIS, St. Croix, WOL-AM, Washington, DC, WQHT, NYC, WPLJ, WRKS, WQHT-FM, 1995—98, WUSL-FM, Phila., 1998—2001, WBLS-FM, NYC, 2001—, host The Wendy Williams Experience, 2003—; host Wendy Williams Is on Fire VH1, 2003—. Co-author (with Karen Hunter): (memoirs) Wendy's Got the Heat, 2003, The Wendy Williams Experience: Queen of Radio, 2004, (novels) Drama Was Her Middle Name, 2006, Is the Bitch Dead or What?: The Ritz Harper Chronicles Book 2, 2007. Office: WBLS-FM 3 Park Ave # 41 New York NY 10016 *

WILLIAMS, WILLIAM COREY, theology educator, consultant; b. Wilkes-Barre, Pa., July 12, 1937; s. Edward Douglas and Elizabeth Irene (Schooley) W.; m. Alma Simmenroth Williams, June 27, 1959; 1 child, Linda. Diploma in Ministerial Studies, NE Bible Inst., 1962; BA in Bibl. Studies, Cen. Bible Coll., 1963, MA in Religion, 1964; MA in Hebrew and Near Ea. Studies, NYU, 1966, PhD in Hebrew Lang. and Lit., 1975; postgrad., Hebrew U., 1977-78, Inst. Holyland Studies, 1986. Ref. libr. Hebraic section Libr. Congress, Washington, 1967-69; prof. Old Testament So. Calif. Coll./Vanguard U., Costa Mesa, 1969—; adj. prof. Old Testament Melodyland Sch. Theology, Anaheim, Calif., 1975-77; vis. prof. Old Testament Fuller Theol. Sem., Pasadena, Calif., 1978-81, 84, Asian Theol. Ctr. Evangelism Missions, Singapore and Sabah, E. Malaysia, 1985, Continental Bible Coll., Saint Pieters-Leeuw, Belgium, 1985, 2000-01, Mattersey Bible Coll., England, 1985, Inst. Holy Land Studies, Jerusalem, 1986, Regent U., 1994. Transl. cons. reviser New Am. Std. Bible, 1969-94; transl. cons. New Internat. Version, 1975-76, New Century Version, 1991, The New Living Translation, 1992-95, New Internat. Version, Reader's Version, 1993-94; transl. cons. editor Internat. Children's Version, 1985-86. Author: (books, tapes) Hebrew I: A Study Guide, 1980, Hebrew II: A Study Guide, 1986, They Spoke From God, 2004; contbr. articles to International Standard Bible Encyclopedia, New International Dictionary of Old Testment Theology and Evangelical Dictionary of Biblical Theology; contbr. articles to profl. jours.; contbr. notes to Spirit Filled Life Study Bible; editor: They Spoke From God, 2004. Nat. Def. Fgn. Lang. fellow NYU, 1964-67; Alumni scholar N.E. Bible Inst., 1960-61; NEH fellow, summer 1992; recipient Disting. Educator's award Assemblies God, 1997. Mem. Soc. Bibl. Lit., Evang. Theol. Soc. (exec. office 1974-77), Inst. Bibl. Rsch., Lockman Found. (hon. mem. bd. dirs 1992-94, mem. editl. bd. 1974-94). Home: 1817 Peninsula Pl Costa Mesa CA 92627-4591 Office: Vanguard U 55 Fair Dr Costa Mesa CA 92626-6520 Office Phone: 714-556-3232. Business E-Mail: wwilliams@vanguard.edu.

WILLIAMS, WILLIAM EARLE, artist, educator, curator; b. Vicksburg, Miss., Apr. 19, 1950; s. Willie and Estella (Steele) W.; m. Mary Katherine Meermans, Aug. 19, 1978; children: Emily Katherine, Daniel Earle. BA, Hamilton Coll., Clinton, NY, 1973; MFA, Yale U., 1978. Prof. art, curator photography Haverford (Pa.) Coll. Author: Party Pictures, 1985; author, editor: Photographers of Sculpture, 1988, Paul Strands: Prints into Ink, 2007; editor: Japanese Wood Block Prints, 1987, Gettysburg: Journey in Time, 1997, Unsung Heroes: African American Soldiers in the Civil War, 2007; one-man shows include Cleve. Mus. of Art, 1990, South East Mus., 2001, Bryn Mawr Coll., 2002, Canton-Fitzgerald Gallery, 2007, exhibited in group shows at Allentown Mus. Art, 1995, Bardini Mus., Florence, Italy, 1990, Phila. Mus. Art, 2000, Princeton U. Mus., 2006, Represented in permanent collections Phila. Mus. Art, Met. Mus. Art, Cleve. Mus. Art, others. Fellow in photography, Pa. Coun. on the Arts, 1986, 1997, 2002, Pew fellow, 1997, Guggenheim fellow, 2003. Mem.: Soc. Photog. Edn. (bd. dirs. 1996—2003, vice chair 2000, treas. 2001), Phila. Athenaeum, Franklin Inn Club. Avocations: running, bicycling, walking. Home: 753 College Ave Haverford PA 19041-1301 Office: Haverford Coll 370 Lancaster Ave Haverford PA 19041-1336 Office Phone: 610-896-1259.

WILLIAMS, WILLIAM HARRISON, retired librarian; b. Seattle, Apr. 18, 1924; s. William E. and Letah M. (Hollenback) W.; m. Mary Helen Sims, Apr. 19, 1945; children: Linda Lee, Dee Ann. BS, Brigham Young U., 1969, M.L.S., 1970. Dir. Provo Pub. Library, Utah, 1969-70; Wyo. State Librarian, 1970-78; dir. Wyo. state Archives and Hist. dept., 1971-78; exec. sec. Wyo. Hist. Soc., 1971-78; sr. research analyst Wyo. Taxpayers Assn., 1978-84. Served to lt. col. USAAF, 1943-64. Decorated USAF commendation with oak leaf cluster. Mem. Masonic Order, Order of the Ea. Star, Order of the Amaranth, Beta Phi Mu, Phi Alpha Theta. Home: 18616 N 99th Ave Apt 1028 Sun City AZ 85373 E-mail: weewilli@juno.com.

WILLIAMS, WILLIAM JOHN, JR., lawyer; b. New Rochelle, NY, Feb. 6, 1937; s. William John and Jane (Gormley) W.; m. Barbara Reuter. BA, Holy Cross Coll., Worcester, Mass., 1958; LLB, NYU, 1961. Bar: N.Y. 1961. Assoc. Sullivan & Cromwell LLP, NYC, 1962—68, ptnr., 1969—2004, of counsel, 2005—. Mem. legal adv. bd. NASD, 1988—94; mem. legal adv. com. NYSE, 1997—2000, 2003—. Trustee NYU Law Sch. Found., 1977-2007, Holy Cross Coll., 1988-96; chmn. bd. Sofia Am. Sch. in Bulgaria; past gen. counsel, chmn. rules golf com., sec., v.p. and pres. US Golf Assn., 1974-88. Fellow Am. Bar Found.; mem. ABA, Am. Law Inst., N.Y. State Bar Assn., N.Y.C. Bar Assn. Democrat. Roman Catholic. Office: Sullivan & Cromwell LLP 125 Broad St Fl 32 New York NY 10004-2498

WILLIAMS, WILLIAM JOSEPH, retired hematologist, educator; b. Bridgeton, NJ, Dec. 8, 1926; s. Edward Carlaw and Mary Hood (English) W.; m. Margaret Myrick Lyman, Aug. 12, 1950 (dec. Aug., 1985); children: Susan Lyman, William Prescott, Sarah Robb; m. Karen A. Hughes, Feb. 18, 1989. Student, Bucknell U., 1943-45; MD, U. Pa., 1949. Diplomate: Am. Bd. Internal Medicine. (hematology com. 1976-80). From intern to assoc. prof. U. Pa., Phila., 1949—61, assoc. prof. to prof. medicine, chief hematology, 1961—69; sr. instr. microbiology Case We. Res. U., 1952; asst. prof. medicine Washington U., St. Louis, 1959—60; rsch. fellow Oxford U., England, 1960—61; mem. hematology tng. com. Nat. Inst. Arthritis and Metabolic Disease, 1964—68, mem. rsch. career program com., 1968—72; chmn. dept. medicine SUNY Health Sci. Ctr., Syracuse, 1969—92, prof. medicine, 1969—, interim dean Coll. Medicine, 1991—92, dean coll. medicine and v.p. biomed. scis., 2002—04, disting. svc. prof., 2002—, dean emeritus Coll. Medicine, 2004—06; ret., 2006—. Vis. scientist Walter and Eliza Hall Inst., Melbourne, Australia, 1980; vis. prof. Monash U., Melbourne, 1980; mem. thrombosis adv. com. Nat. Heart and Lung Inst., 1969-73, chmn., 1971-73; adv. coun. Nat. Arthritis, Metabolism and Digestive Diseases, 1975-79; mem. residency rev. com. internal medicine Accreditation Coun. Grad. Med. Edn., 1983-89, mem. bd. appeals panel for internal medicine, 1989-2000; mem. N.Y. State Coun. Grad. Med. Edn., 1987-89. Editor-in-chief: Hematology, 1972, 4th edit., 1989, Williams Hematology Companion Handbook, 1996; co-editor: Williams Manual of Hematology, 2003; contbr. articles to med. lit. Trustee Everson Mus. Art, 1975-81, 83-89. With USNR, 1944-46, 52-54. Recipient Research Career Devel. award Nat. Heart Inst., 1963-68; Daland fellow Am. Philos. Soc., 1955-57; Markle scholar, 1957-62 Mem. ACP (gov. Upstate N.Y. 1976-81), Am. Soc. Biochemistry and Molecular Biologists, Am. Soc. Clin. Investigation, Assn. Am. Physicians, Am. Clin. and Climatol. Assn., Am. Soc. Hematology, Interurban Clin. Club (sec. 1964-70), Alpha Omega Alpha. Mem. Soc. Friends. Home: 5160 Peck Hill Rd Jamesville NY 13078-9724 Office: 750 E Adams St Syracuse NY 13210-2306 Home Phone: 315-446-0546; Office Phone: 315-464-9788. Business E-Mail: williamw@upstate.edu.

WILLIAMS, WILLIAM LOUIS See AS-SALAAM, JAMAAL

WILLIAMS, WILLIAM MAGAVERN, headmaster; b. Niles, Mich., Dec. 22, 1931; s. Errol Edwin and Mary Elizabeth (Magavern) W.; m. Linda Carol Grush, June 15, 1958; children: Diana, William Jr., Sarah. BA, Williams Coll., 1953, LHD (hon.), 1984; postgrad. in Philosophy, Columbia U., 1954-58, MA in Ednl. Psychology, 1966. Tchr. elem. English, history, phys. edn. McTernan Sch., Waterbury, Conn., 1953-54; head guidance, boarding, and humanities depts., instr. English, coach varsity wrestling Riverdale Country Sch., Bronx, NY, 1955-66; headmaster Doane Acad., Burlington, NJ, 1966-70, Poly. Prep. Country Day Sch., Bklyn., 1970-00, headmaster emeritus, 2000—. Trustee Bklyn Inst. Arts and Scis., 1972-79, Bklyn. Ctrl. YMCA, 1974-78, Profl. Children's Sch., 1976-79, Bklyn. Children's Mus., 1979-82, Plymouth Ch. Pilgrims, 1979-86, NY State Assn. Ind. Schs., 1980-86, Northern Stage, 2003-; chmn. bd. dirs. Stafford Sch., Vt., 2002-03, United Ch. of Stafford, 2003-06. Mem. Headmasters' Assn., Country Day Sch. Headmasters' Assn. (v.p. 1998-99, pres. 1999-2000), Cum Laude Soc. (regent dist. III 1971-87, dep. pres. gen. 1981-87, pres. gen. 1987-96, regent-at-large 1996—), Guild Ind. Schs. N.Y. (pres. 1986-88). Avocations: sailing, skiing, chess, travel, civil war history. Home: 15 Beacon Hill Rd Strafford VT 05072 Personal E-mail: wmw232@aol.com.

WILLIAMS, WILLIAM PROCTOR, literature educator; b. Glade, Kans., Sept. 1, 1939; s. Joseph Earl and Mildred Bernice Williams; m. Antonia Forster, June 2, 1984; children: Elizabeth Anne Dewbray, William Proctor II. BA, Kans. State U., 1961, MA, 1964, PhD, 1968. Asst. prof. English No. Ill. U., DeKalb, 1967—70, assoc. prof. English, 1970—78, prof. English, 1978—99, assoc. dean rsch., grad. sch., 1982, dir. librs., 1982—83; vis. prof. English Mary Baldwin Coll., Staunton, 2004—04, 2007; sr. lectr. English U. of Akron, Ohio, 2000—. Editor Analytical and Enumerative Bibliography, DeKalb, 1976—2002. Author: An Introduction to Bibliographical and Textual Studies, 1985, A Bibliography of the Writings of Robert Graves, 1987; editor: Macbeth, 2006, Romeo and Juliet, 2007, Richard III, 2007; contbr. articles to profl. jours. Reader gen. ordination exam. Episcopal Ch., 1974—77. Fellow, Newberry Libr., 1974; sr. rsch. fellow, Fulbright Commn., 1983, Charlton Hinman fellow, Folger Shakespeare Libr., 2003—04, Rsch. grantee, Nat. Endowment for Humanities, 1978. Fellow: Bibliog. Soc. Am.; mem.: Malone Soc., Soc. Textual Scholarship, Midwest MLA (mem. exec. com. 1987—90), Shakespeare Assn. Am. Achievements include discovery of Castle Ashby manuscripts. Avocations: gardening, historic aircraft, cricket. Home: 2006 White Pond Dr Akron OH 44313 Office: U Akron Dept English Akron OH 44325 Home Phone: 330-835-1465. Business E-Mail: wpw@uakron.edu.

WILLIAMS, WILLIE, JR., physicist, researcher; b. Independence, La., Mar. 24, 1947; s. Willie Sr. and Lee Anner (Booker) W.; 1 child, Willie Williams III. BS, So. U., 1970; MS, Iowa State U., 1972, PhD, 1974. Mem. faculty Lincoln U., Lincoln University, Pa., 1974—, assoc. prof. physics, 1979-84, prof. physics, 1984—, chmn. dept., 1976-95, chmn. sci. and math. div., 1978-80, 83-88, founder, dir. Lincoln Advance Sci. and Engring. Reinforcement (LASER) Program, 1980-96, dir. pre-engring., 1976-96, dir., prin. investigator Early Alert-Young Scholars Program, 1992-96. Bd. dirs. women tech. program Lincoln U. Urban Ctr., Phila.; vis. prof. Ctr. for Teaching Innovation, Drexel U., 1975; liaison officer Nat. Assn. for Equal Opportunity in Higher Edn., Dept. Def. Program., 1987—; mem. steering com. NSF Comprehensive Ctr. for Minorities, Phila.; bd. dirs. Prime Inc., Phila. Contbr. articles to profl. jours. Chmn. Cheyney Lincoln Temple Cluster, 1974-78; pres. The Men Fedn., So. U., 1968-69. Recipient Lindback award for Outstanding Teaching, 1976, Outstanding Scientist award White House Initiative, 1988; named one of Outstanding Young Men of Am., 1979; fellow NASA, 1979, Mobil Oil Corp., 1977, Nat. Bur. Standards, 1979, Dept. Def., 1980-81, Navy fellow, 1982 Mem. AAAS, AAUP (pres. Lincoln U. chpt. 2001-03), Am. Assn. Physics, N.Y. Acad. Scis., Math. Assn. Am., Am. Phys. Soc., Nat. Soc. Black Physicists, Nat. Geog. Soc., Iowa State Alumna Assn., Sigma Xi, Sigma Pi Sigma. Baptist. Home: 448 W Baltimore Pike West Grove PA 19390-9201 Office: Lincoln U Dept Physics Lincoln University PA 19352 Home Phone: 703-742-0418; Office Phone: 610-932-8300 ext. 3474. E-mail: wwillie2@aol.com. *Throughout my life I have always striven to achieve the very best and have held on to the belief that wherever possible improve upon today, so that everyone might have a better tomorrow! I have been guided by the principle of being selective in my endeavors, having specific objectives, followed by detailed analysis, concise actions, and intense work with continous review.*

WILLIAMS, WILLIE ALVIN, retired literature educator; b. Windom, Tex., Oct. 16, 1919; s. Elie Williams and Louease Kimble-Williams; m. Trula Amanda Sloan, Sept. 23, 1943; 1 foster child, Jacqueline L. Maxwell. BA, Wiley Coll., 1948. Tchr. English Rhodes H.S., Daingerfield, Tex., 1948—49, Pemberton H.S., Marshall, Tex., 1950—77, Toyei Boarding Sch., Ganada, Ariz., 1977—83; ret., 1983. Water safety instr. ARC Gregg County, Longview, Tex., 1968—77. Author: Cousins, Unlimited, 2003, booklets. Mem. local chpt. NAACP, 1984—89; mem. Gregg County Hist. Com., 1990—; mem. disaster team ARC, Longview, 1986—89; tchr. Sunday Sch. Wesley/McCabe United Meth. Ch., Longview, 1967—; bd. dirs. Longview chpt. ARC, Longview, 1987—89; bd. dirs. Habitat for Humanity, Longview, 1984—87. Master sgt. US Army, 1940—45. Named Sunday Sch. Tchr. of Yr., Wesley/McCabe United Meth. Ch., 2001; recipient Martin Luther King Humanitarian award, Pan Hellenic Coun., Longview, 1987. Democrat. Avocations: swimming, fishing, woodworking. Home: 2102 Armond Dr Longview TX 75602 E-mail: kimsharwaw@aol.com.

WILLIAMS-DERRY, AMY, lawyer; b. NYC, Feb. 19, 1970; BA in Sociology with hon., Brown Univ., 1993; JD, Univ. Va., 1998. Bar: Wash. 1998, US Dist. Ct., Western and Eastern Dist. Wash. 1998, US Ct. Appeals Ninth Circuit 1999. Former litig. assoc. Hillis Clark Martin & Peterson, P.S., Seattle, 1998—2003; assoc. atty. Earth Justice, 2003—05, Keller Rohrback, L.L.P., Seattle, 2005—. Contbr. articles to numerous profl. jours. Named Wash. Rising Star, SuperLawyer Mag., 2006. Mem.: ABA, King Co. Bar Assn., Wash. Bar Assn. Office: Keller Rohrback LLP Ste 3200 1201 Third Ave Seattle WA 98101-3052

WILLIAMS-DE SILVA, LISA ANNETTE, small business owner, adult nurse practitioner; d. Joice Renee and Charles Braden (Stepfather); m. Lionel De Silva, June 12, 2003. BS in Bus., Ariz. State U., 1988, BSN, 2000, MSN, Nurse Practitioner, 2003. Cert. Achievement Cynosure Laser, Cert. Proficiency, Aesthetic Laser Sys. Sciton Aesthetic. Pres. Medical-Legal Support Svcs., Inc., Scottsdale, Ariz., 1998—. Owner and nurse practitioner Ultra Smooth Skin, Inc., Scottsdale, 2003—. Faculty Wives Club scholar, Ariz. State U., 1998—2000, STAR Program scholar, 1998—2000. Mem.: Dermatology Nurses Assn., Internat. Acad. of Laser Medicine and Surgery (assoc.), Am. Assn. of Legal Nurse Consultants (assoc.), Am. Coll. of Phlebology (assoc.), Am. Acad. of Nurse Practitioners (assoc.), Am. Soc. of Laser Medicine and Surgery (assoc.). Avocations: hiking, travel, scuba diving. Office: Med-Legal Support Svcs Inc 14891 N Northside Scottsdale AZ 85260 Home Phone: 480-699-1244; Office Phone: 480-699-1244.

WILLIAMSEN, DANNYE SUE, personal development educator, publisher; b. Memphis, Mar. 26, 1949; d. Roy Fauntly and Arliss Wyleen Goodroe; m. Jon Charles Beckum, Dec. 23, 1969 (div. Mar. 1972); m. John Dean Williamsen, Dec. 24, 1986. BA cum laude, U. Memphis, 1995. Adminstr. Security Investments, Inc., Memphis, 1972—75; nightclub owner, investor Memphis, 1976—78; internat. tech. analyst ContiCommodity, Inc., Memphis, 1977—80; owner, tech. analyst Commodity Cons., Inc., Memphis, 1981; project mgr. B&P Devel. Co., Austin, Tex., 1982—84; asst. to pres. Memphis C. of C., 1984—86; owner, dental technician Williamsen Dental Lab., Memphis and Prophetstown, Ill., 1986—; ptnr., editor Personal Edn. Network, Prophetstown, Ill., 2001—; owner/pub. Networx Pub., Prophetstown, 2002—05, MindSlap! (formerly Williamsen Pubs.), Kennesaw, Ga., 2006—; life coach Make Your Life Creative!, 2006—. Bd. dirs. Heartland Equine Assisted Therapeutic Ctr., Rock Falls, Ill., 2000—01; show host Tips & Techniques for the Creative Entrepreneur, 2007. Author: Illusions, 1998, IT'S YOUR MOVE! Transform Your Dreams from Wishful Thinking to Reality, 2004, Metaphysical Minute, 2006, MindSlap!, 2007, The Creative Matrix, vol. I, 2007; editor: Creative Living-an evolving approach to bus. life, 2001—, (e-newsletter) Metaphysical Minute, 2003—04; columnist: Penwomanship Mag, 2003—04, Penwomanship Mag., 2005; editor: (newsletter) MindSlap!; editor: Tips & Techniques for the Creative Entrepeneur, 2007, Just a Taste..., 2007; prodr.: (CD) Stop Wallowing & Start Winning, 2007; prodr.: (CD) Simplicity for the Soul, vol. I, 2007. Mem. AAUW (pres. 1998-99), APA, NOW, NAFE, Am. Bus. Women's Assn., Assn. for Humanistic Psychology, Nat. Assn. Women Writers, Small Pubs. Assn. N.Am., Pubs. Mktg. Assn., Psi Chi, Chi Beta Phi. Avocations: reading, counseling. Office: MindSlap PO Box 680924 Marietta GA 30068-0016 Office Phone: 770-438-0889. Business E-Mail: dannyew@mindslaponline.com.

WILLIAMSON, ALAN BACHER, literature educator, poet, writer; b. Chgo., Jan. 24, 1944; s. George and Jehanne (Bacher) W.; m. Anne Winters, Oct. 12, 1968 (div. Feb. 1988); 1 child, Elizabeth Kilner. BA, Haverford Coll., 1964; MA, Harvard U., 1965, PhD, 1969. Asst. prof. U. Va., Charlottesville, 1969-75; Briggs-Copeland lectr. Harvard U., Cambridge, Mass., 1977-80; Fannie Hurst lectr. Brandeis U., Waltham, Mass., 1980-82; prof. English, U. Calif., Davis, 1982—. Poetry panelist Nat. Endowment for Arts, 1989. Author: (criticism) Pity the Monsters, 1974, Introspection and Contemporary Poetry, 1984, Eloquence and Mere Life, 1994, Almost a Girl, 2001, Westerness: A Meditation, 2006, (poetry) Presence, 1983, The Muse of Distance, 1988, Love and the Soul, 1995, Res Publica, 1998, The Pattern More Complicated: New and Selected Poems, 2004. Poetry fellow Nat. Endowment for Arts, 1973; Guggenheim fellow, 1991. Mem. MLA (exec. com. div. on poetry 1987-91). Democrat. Buddhist. Office: U Calif Dept English Davis CA 95616 Business E-Mail: abwilliamson@ucdavis.edu.

WILLIAMSON, BARRY SCOTT, conductor, performing arts educator; b. Washburn, Wis., Dec. 13, 1955; s. Mortimer Leo and Esther Edna Williamson; 1 child, Caitlin Rose. MusB, Concordia Coll., Moorhead, Minn., 1978; MusM in Choral Conducting, U. of Ariz., 1982; Dr. of Mus. Arts in Choral Conducting, U. Tex., 1993. Vocal instr./coach Williamson Vocal Studio, Austin, Tex., 1986—; founding artistic dir. and condr. Tex. Choral Consort, Austin, 1997—; choir dir. and organist Koenig Ln. Christian Ch., Austin, 1998—. Dir. of music ministries St. John Neumann Cath. Ch., Austin, 1989—91; choir dir. Hyde Pk. Christian Ch., Austin, 1987—89; vocal music dir. Cholla H.S., Tucson, 1982—86; choirmaster and organist St. Alban's Episc. Ch., Tucson, 1984—86; condr., univ./cmty. chorus U. of Ariz., Tucson, 1981—82; asst. dir. Tucson Ariz. Boys Chorus, 1981—82; paid singer St. Phillip's On the Hill Episc. Ch., Tucson, 1981—82; vocal music dir. Rice Lake Sr. H.S., Rice Lake, Wis., 1980—81; choir dir. Bethany Luth. Ch., Rice Lake, 1980—81; vocal music dir., grades 7-12 Kasson-Mantorville Jr-Sr. H.S., Kasson, Minn., 1978—80; dir. of music ministries NW Hills United Meth. Ch., Austin, 1996—98; choir dir. St. John's Luth. Ch., Kasson, Minn., 1978—80; asst. dir.,Cconcordia choir Concordia Coll., Moorhead, Minn.; dir. of choral activities U. of Tex. at El Paso, 1993—96; choirmaster and organist St. Francis On the Hill Episc. Ch., El Paso, Tex., 1993—95; dir. of choral activities Trinity U., San Antonio, 1992—93; artistic dir. and condr. Austin Civic Chorus, Austin, 1987—91; condr. chorus U. of Tex. at Austin, 1986—88; asst. chorus dir., asst. to the condr. Austin Lyric Opera, Austin, 1986—88; dir. of music ministries Good Shepherd Episc. Ch., Austin, 1991—92. Mem.: Chorus Am., Tex. Choral Dirs. Assn., Am. Choral Dirs. Assn. Office: Texas Choral Consort PO Box 300597 Austin TX 78703-0010 Home Phone: 512-422-3022; Office Phone: 512-372-3233. E-mail: barry@txconsort.org.

WILLIAMSON, BRUCE A., gas industry executive; b. Great Falls, Mont. B in Fin., U. Mont., 1981; MBA, U. Houston. With Royal Dutch/Shell Group, 1981—95; sr. v.p. fin. bus. develop. and risk mgmt. PanEnergy Corp., v.p. fin., 1995—97; pres., CEO Duke Energy Internat., 1997—2001, Duke Energy Global Markets, 2001—02; bd. dir. Dynegy Inc., Houston, 2002—, CEO, 2002—, chmn., 2004—. Bd. dir. Questar Corp. Chancellor's nat. adv coun. U. Houston, Dean's adv. bd., C.T. Bauer Coll. Bus.; bd. dir. Greater Houston Partnership. Office: 1000 Louisiana Ste 5800 Houston TX 77002 Office Phone: 713-507-6400, 877-439-6349. Office Fax: 713-767-6652, 713-507-3871. *

WILLIAMSON, CAROLYN, research scientist; b. Milw., Mar. 30, 1974; d. William and Judy Wickert; m. Chane Williamson, Apr. 26, 2003; children: Kieran, Cameron. BS, Cath. U. Am., Washington, 1996; MBA, LeMoyne Coll., Syracuse, NY, 2001. Cert. Project Mgmt. Inst., 2007. Validation specialist Bristol Myers Squibb, East Syracuse, NY, 1997—2004, scientist. Dir., v.p., pres. YWCA Syracuse and Onondage County, NY, 1999—2006. Recipient Amber Reilly Outstanding Svc. award, YWCA Syracuse and Onondaga County, 2006. Mem.: PDA, ToastMasters (treas.). Home: 11 Damson Lane Liverpool NY 13090 Office: Bristol Myers Squibb 6000 Thompson Rd East Syracuse NY 13057 Home Phone: 315-883-2234; Office Phone: 315-432-2437. Business E-Mail: carolyn.williamson@bms.com.

WILLIAMSON, CHARLES HARVEY KAYE, mechanical and aerospace engineering educator; m. Chantal Champagne; children: Nicolas, Emilie, Philippe. BSc, Southampton U., Eng., 1978; PhD, Trinity Coll., U. Cambridge, Eng., 1982. Staff engr.; HS math. and physics. tchr. London; pvt. tutor to Prince Pavlos, son of King Constantine of Greece; prof. mech. and aerospace engring. Cornell U., Ithaca, NY. Contbr. articles to sci. jours.; editor: Jour. Fluids and Structures. Recipient Calder prize, Royal Instn. Naval Archs., 1979, Keck Found. award for Excellence in Tchg., 1994, US Prof. of Yr. award, Carnegie Found. for Advancement of Tchg. and Coun. for Advancement and Support of Edn., 2006. Fellow: Am. Phys. Soc. Achievements include winning the Gallery of Fluid Motion competition at the annual meeting of the American Physical Society six times, 1988-89, 93-96. Avocation: sailing. Office: Sch Mech and Aerospace Engring Cornell U 252 Upson Hall Ithaca NY 14853 Office Phone: 607-255-3838. Office Fax: 607-255-1222. E-mail: cw26@cornell.edu. *

WILLIAMSON, CHARLES R., retired energy company executive; PhD in Geology, U. Tex., Austin, 1978. Rsch. assoc. Sci. and Tech. Divsn. Unocal Corp., Brea, Calif., 1977-83, chief exploration geologist U.K., 1983-86; exploration mgr., dir. Unocal Netherlands, The Hague, 1986-89; v.p. exploration Unocal Thailand, Bangkok, 1989-92; v.p. Energy Resources Divsn. Unocal, 1992-94, v.p. planning and info. svcs., 1994-95, v.p. corp. planning and econs., 1995-96, group v.p. internat. opers., 1996-97, group v.p. Asia Opers., 1997-99, exec. v.p. internat. energy ops. Unocal Corp., El Segundo, Calif., 1999—2001; CEO, chmn. Unocal (acquired by Chevron Corp.), 2001—05; exec. v.p., mem. exec. com. Chevron Corp., 2005. Mem. adv. bd. earth scis. dept. Stanford U.; bd. dir. Weyerhaeuser Co., 2004—, Talisman Energy Inc., 2006—, PACCAR Inc., 2006—. Mem. Am. Soc. Petroleum Geologists, Soc. Econ. Paleontologists and Mineralogists, Soc. Petroleum Engrs., Internat. Assn. Sedimentologists. Mailing: PACCAR Inc Bd Directors PO Box 1518 Bellevue WA 98009

WILLIAMSON, CHARLES READY, III, lawyer; b. Boston, Jan. 2, 1944; s. Charles Ready and Anne Margaret (Livingstone) W.; m. Julie Anne Williamson, Nov. 6, 1971; 1 dau., Anne Lucinda. B.A., Colgate U., 1965; LL.B., Suffolk U., 1968. Bar: Mass. 1968, Oreg. 1970, U.S. Supreme Ct. 1977. Law clk. to Judge Joseph B. Silverio, Mass. land ct., Boston 1968-69; VISTA atty., dep. dir. Multnomah County Legal Aid Service, Portland, 1970-74; assoc. Kell, Alterman & Runstein, Portland, 1974-78, 88—; pvt. practice, Portland, 1978-88; pres. Oreg. Legal Service Corp., 1976-77; mem. Oreg. Bd. Psychologist Examiners, 1973-74; chmn. Oreg. Grad. Sch. Profl. Psychology, Pacific U. Pres. Oreg. Consumer League, 1972-74; councilor Met. Service Dist. 1978-84; treas. Democratic Bus. Forum 1982-84. Mem. ABA, Oreg. Bar Assn. (pres.-elect 2002-03, pres. 2003-04), Multnomah County Bar Assn. Club: Portland City. Contbr. in field. Office: Kell Alterman & Runstein 520 SW Yamhill Ste 600 Portland OR 97204-1329

WILLIAMSON, CLINT (JOHN CLINT WILLIAMSON), ambassador; b. 1961; Asst. dist. atty., New Orleans; trial atty. organized crime sect. U.S. Dept. Justice; trial atty. Internat. Criminal Tribunal for Yugoslavia (ICTY) The Hague, Netherlands, 1994—2001; dir. Dept. Justice UN Mission Kosovo, 2001—02; sr. adv. Iraqi Ministry Justice, 2003; dir. stability ops. NSC, 2003—06, acting spl. asst. to Pres., sr. dir. relief, stabilization, and devel., 2006; US amb.-at-large for war crimes issues US Dept. State, 2006—. Office: US Dept State Office War Crimes Issues 2201 C St NW Washington DC 20520 *

WILLIAMSON, DONALD ELLIS, public health service officer, state agency administrator; b. Louisville, Miss., June 17, 1955; m. Anita Hudspeth; 1 child, Jonathan Stuart. Student, East Miss. Jr. Coll., 1972-73, Miss. State U., 1973-75; MD cum laude, U. Miss., 1979. Diplomate Am. Bd. Internal Medicine. Intern, resident in internal medicine U. Va. Hosp., Charlottesville, 1979-82; with East Miss. State Hosp., Meridian, 1979; state tb control oficer Miss. State Dept. Health, 1982-86; dir. divsn. disease control Ala. Dept. Pub. Health, 1986-88, dir. bur. preventive health svcs., 1988-92, state health officer, 1992—. Faculty mem. Injury Control Rsch. Ctr. U. Ala., Birmingham; clin. assoc. prof. dept. internal medicine U. South Ala.; presenter in field. Contbr. articles to profl. jours. Chmn. Ala. Pub. Health Care Authority, Ala. Radiation Adv. Bd. Health; mem. Ala. Commn. Aging, State Bldg. Commn., Statewide Health Coordinating Coun., Ala. Youth Svcs. Bd., Ala. Child Abuse & Neglect Prevention Bd., Ala. Resource Devel. Com., Ala. Anat. Bd., Planning and Adv. Coun. Devel. Disabilities, Ala. Bd. Med. Scholarship Awards, Pesticides Adv. Com., Gov.'s Interagy. Coordinating Coun., Ala. Juvenile Justice Coordinating Coun., Emergency Med. Svcs. Adv. Coun., 1986-92, Legis. Adv. Com. AIDS, 1988-90, Atty. Gen.'s Task Force Med.Waste, 1989, Water Resources Adv. Coun., exec. coun. Ala. Children's Svcs. Facilitation Team, 1993—; mem. med. adv. com. ARC. Recipient Mosby Book award, 1979, Dr. Robert Ramsey award, 1993; Pub. Health Leadership Inst. scholar, 1996. Mem. APHA, Assn. State and Territorial Health Ofcls. (exec. com. 1995-2000, pres. 1997-98), Am. Acad. of Pediatrics (Child Health Advocate of the Yr. award 1999), Pub. Health Found. (Theodore R. Ervin award 1999), Med. Assn. State Ala., Ala. Pub. Health Assn. (bd. dirs. 1991—, chmn. disease control and epidemiology sect. 1991-92, D.G. Gill award 1997), Pub. Health Found. (bd. dirs. 1995-99, treas. 1997—), Phi Theta Kappa, Phi Kappa Phi, Alpha Omega Alpha. Home: 8113 Lichfield Ct Montgomery AL 36117-5124 Office: Ala Dept Pub Health PO Box 303017 201 Monroe St Montgomery AL 36104-3735

WILLIAMSON, DONALD RAY, retired career Army officer; b. Amarillo, Tex., Oct. 13, 1943; s. Floy Edwin and Dorothy Lorene (Orr) W.; m. Beverly Ann Howard, Aug. 31, 1963; children: Rebecca Ann, Catherine Paige. BS in Econs., W. Tex. State U., 1966; MA in Bus., Cen. Mich. U., 1977; degree, Dept. Def. Program Mgrs., 1982, U.S. Army Command and Gen. Staff Coll., 1980. Commd. 2d lt. U.S. Army, 1966, advanced through grades to lt. col., 1982, retired, 1986, comdg. officer combat support co. Ft. Hood, Tex., 1973-74, comdg. officer 2d aviation co., 1974-75, dep. insp. gen. Ft. Leavenworth, Kans., 1975-78, comdg. officer 213th aviation co. Rep. of Korea, 1978-79, asst. program mgr. advanced scout helicopter program, 1981-86; owner Witan Group, Chesterfield, Mo., 1986-88; pres., owner Sys. Test Evaluation Inc., Huntsville, Ala., 1988-99; gen. mgr. LESCO, Huntsville, Ala., 1999-2000. Contbr. articles to profl. jours. Decorated Bronze Star, 37 Air medals with "V" device, D.F.C. with oak leaf cluster, Legion of Merit. Mem. Army Aviation Assn. Am., Assn. U.S. Army, Lansing Jaycees (past pres.), Mensa. Avocations: flying, reading, tennis. Home: 2110 Greenslope Trl NE Huntsville AL 35811-2608

WILLIAMSON, DOUGLAS FRANKLIN, JR., lawyer; b. Anniston, Ala., Mar. 23, 1930; s. Douglas Franklin and Elizabeth Louise (Connor) W.; m. Barbara Tuerk, Dec. 28, 1957; children: Mary Leyden, Douglas Franklin III, Bruce Reynolds. AB summa cum laude, Amherst Coll., 1952; LLB, Yale U., 1955. Bar: NY 1958, Fla. 1976. Assoc. Breed, Abbott & Morgan, NYC, 1957-63, ptnr., 1963-72, Williamson & Hess and predecessor firm, NYC, 1972-79; of counsel Winthrop, Stimson, Putnam & Roberts, NYC, 1979-81, ptnr., 1982-95, sr. counsel, 1996-2000, Pillsbury Winthrop Shaw Pittman LLP and predessors, NYC, 2001—. Bd. dirs. World Wildlife Fund, Washington, 1979-88, treas., 1986-88, mem. nat. coun., 1988-2006; bd. dirs. Conservation Found., Washington, 1985-88, treas., 1986-88; bd. dirs. Ea. N.Y. chpt. Nature Conservancy, Mt. Kisco, N.Y., 1976-87, 93-97, sec., 1976-87, hon. dir., 1987—, chmn., 1993-94; bd. dirs. Oblong Land Conservancy, Pawling, N.Y., 1990-98, chmn. 1996-98; bd. dirs. Quaker Hill Civic Assn., Pawling, 1974-2000, past pres.; chmn. Pawling Assessment Rev. Bd., 1976-2001. With U.S. Army, 1955-57. Fellow: N.Y. State Bar Found.; mem.: Assn. Bar City N.Y. (life), English Speaking Union, Old Guard Soc. Palm Beach, Soc. Colonial Wars, Everglades Club, Quaker Hill Country Club (pres. 1980—81), Phi Beta Kappa, Phi Beta Kappa Soc. (sec. 1975—77, v.p. 1977—79). Office: Pillsbury Winthrop Shaw Pittman LLP 1540 Broadway New York NY 10036-4039 Office Phone: 212-858-1000.

WILLIAMSON, EDWIN DARGAN, lawyer, former federal official; b. Florence, SC, Sept. 23, 1939; s. Benjamin F. and Sara (Dargan) W.; m. Kathe Gates, July 12, 1969; children: Samuel Gates, Edwin Dargan Jr., Sara Elizabeth. BA cum laude, U. of the South, 1961, DCL (hon.), 1992; JD, NYU, 1964. Bar: NY 1965, DC 1988. Assoc. Sullivan & Cromwell LLP, NYC, 1964-70, ptnr., 1971-76, London, 1976-79, NYC, 1979-88, Washington, 1988-90, 93—, coord. internat. trade and investment practice area; legal adviser US Dept. State, Washington, 1990-93. Mem. Permanent Ct. Arbitration, 1991—2004; mem. U.S. adv. NTT DoCoMo, 2002—04. Regent U. of the South, Sewanee, Tenn., 1981-87, chmn., 1985-87, coun. fgn. rels., 1995—; bd. dirs. Nat. Dance Inst., NYC, 1984-88, Episcopal Ch. Found., NYC, 1986-90; vestryman St. James Episcopal Ch., NYC, 1984-88; bd. mem. SC Govs. Sch. for Sci. and Math. Found., 2003-04. Mem. US Coun. Internat. Bus., Bus. and Industry Adv. Com. to OECD (vice chmn. com. on multinat. enterprise and investments 1993—2004, chmn. BIAC expert group on multilat agt. on investment 1996-99, vice-chmn. 1998-2004, mem. exec. com. USCIB 1999—, chmn. task force corp. govt. 2002-04), Met. Club. Republican. Office: Sullivan & Cromwell LLP 1701 Pennsylvania Ave NW Washington DC 20006-5805 Office Fax: 202-293-6330. Personal E-mail: edwinwilliamsonsr@msn.com. Business E-Mail: williamsone@sullcrom.com.

WILLIAMSON, (EULAH) ELAINE, elementary school educator; b. NYC, July 27, 1945; d. Eddie Lee and Eulah Genola (Hardie) Riley; m. George Leslie Williamson, Feb. 17, 1973 (div. 1999); children: George Todd, Michelle Elaine, Heather Dawn BA, Hampton U., 1967; MA in Urban Edn., Jersey City State Coll., 1998; postgrad., St. Peter's Coll., Jersey City. Cert. elem. tchr. K-8, supr., N.J. Tchr. elem. Englewood (N.J.) Pub. Schs., 1967-78, Irvington (N.J.) Pub. Schs., 1988-97; tchr. math. Hackensack (N.J.) Pub. Schs., 1997—. Mem. NEA, Nat. Mid. Sch. Assn., Nat. Coun. Tchrs. Math., Nat. Black Child Devel. Inst., N.J. Edn. Assn., Hackensack Edn. Assn., Profl. and Bus. Women NAACP, Phi Delta Kappa Democrat. Bapt. Avocations: photography, football, horseback riding. Office: Hackensack Mid Sch 360 Union St Hackensack NJ 07601-4394 also: 5/6 Sch 320 State St Hackensack NJ 07601 Office Phone: 201-646-8170. E-mail: blackie727@aol.com.

WILLIAMSON, FLETCHER PHILLIPS, real estate broker; b. Cambridge, Md., Dec. 16, 1923; s. William Fletcher and Florence M. (Phillips) Williamson; m. Betty June Stoker, Apr. 6, 1943 (div. 1972); 1 child, Jeffrey Phillips; m. Helen M. Stumberg, Aug. 28, 1972 (dec. Jan. 2002). Student, U. Md., 1941—42. Test engr. engring. lab. Glen Martin Co., 1942-43; salesman Corkran Ice Cream Co., Cambridge, 1946-50; real estate broker, 1950—. Chmn. bd. Williamson Real Estate, Dorchester Indsl. Devel. Corp., 1963—72; dir. Dorchester indsl. Devel. Corp.; vice-chmn. bd., dir. Nat. Bank Cambridge, 1979—; dir. Cam-Storage, Inc., Delmarva Bank Data Processing Ctr.; co-receiver White & Nelson, Inc.; v.p. Delmarva Bank Shares. Bd. dirs. Delmarva coun. Boy Scouts Am., Dorchester County Pub. Libr.; past pres. Cambridge Hosp., United Fund Dorchester County; bd. dirs., v.p. Game Conservation Internat., Del. Mus. Natural History. Sgt. AUS, 1943—46, ETO. Methodist. Home: 310 E Wildwood Dr San Antonio TX 78212-1756 E-mail: fpworldtraveler@aol.com.

WILLIAMSON, JOEL RUDOLPH, humanities educator, writer; b. Anderson County, SC, Oct. 27, 1929; s. James Henry and Carrie Mae (Swaney) W.; m. Marie Ahearn, Nov. 17, 1953 (div. May 1983); children: Joelle, William, Alethea; m. Anna Woodson, Oct. 18, 1986. AB, U. S.C., 1948, MA, 1951; PhD, U. Calif., 1964. Instr. dept. history U. N.C., Chapel Hill, 1960-64, asst. prof., 1964-66, assoc. prof., 1966-69, prof., 1969-85, Lineberger prof. in humanities, 1985—. Resident fellow Rockefeller Ctr., Bellagio, Italy, 1988; Eudora Welty prof. in so. studies Millsaps Coll., 1984; disting. vis. prof. Rhodes Coll., 1984; vis. prof. dept. history, assoc. Lowell House Harvard U., 1981-82. Author: After Slavery: The Negro in South Carolina During Reconstruction, 1861-1877, 1965, The Origins of Segregation, 1968, New People: Miscegenation and Mulattoes in the United States, 1980, The Crucible of Race, 1984 (Francis Parkman prize Soc. Am. Historians, Ralph Waldo Emerson award Phi Beta Kappa, Mayflower Cup, Frank L. and Harriet C. Owsley award 1985, Robert Francis Kennedy Book award, Pulitzer prize in History nomination 1985), A Rage for Order, 1986, William Faulkner and Southern History, 1993 (Pulitzer prize in History nomination 1994, Mayflower Cup), also articles. Lt. USN, 1951-55. Fellow Guggenheim Found., 1970-71, NEH, 1987-88, Ctr. for Advanced Study in Behavioral Scis., Stanford, Calif., 1977-78, summer 1979, 80, 81, So. fellow, 1961-62, Charles Warren Ctr., 1981-82. Mem. Soc. Am. Historians, Orgn. Am. Historians, Am. Hist. Assn., So. Hist. Assn., So. Assn. for Women Historians. Achievements include having one of two books that were finalists for the Pulitzer Prize in History. Avocation: travel. Home: 211 Hillsborough St Chapel Hill NC 27514-3522 Personal E-mail: annaleoww@aol.com.

WILLIAMSON, JOHN PRITCHARD, retired utilities executive; b. Cleve., Feb. 22, 1922; s. John and Jane (Pritchard) W.; m. Helen Morgan, Aug. 3, 1945; children: John Morgan, James Russell, Wayne Arthur. BBA, Kent State U., 1945; postgrad., U. Toledo, 1953-56, U. Mich., 1956. CPA, Ohio, ret. Sr. acct. Arthur Andersen & Co., Detroit and Cleve., 1945-51; dir. methods and procs. Toledo Edison Co., 1951-59, asst. treas., 1959-60, sec., 1960-62, sec.-treas., 1962-65, v.p. finance, 1965-68, sr. v.p., 1968-72, pres., chief exec. officer, 1972-79, chmn., chief exec. officer, 1979-86; founding chmn. Centerior Energy Corp. (now First Energy Corp.), 1985—86. Chmn. emeritus Toledo Edison Co.; dir. emeritus, chmn. 1st Nat. Bank of Toledo, 1974-75; chmn. N.Am. Electric Reliability Coun., 1984-87; chmn. Nat. Electric Security Com., 1987-88; guest lectr. U. Toledo, 1976-. Pres. Ohio Electric Utility Inst., 1972; chmn. East Cen. Area Power Coordination Pool, 1971-72, mem. exec. com. Edison Electric Inst., 1981-85; mem. Ohio Devel. Adv. Coun., 1973-79; trustee Assn. Edison Illuminating Cos., 1982-84; pres. Toledo C. of C., 1970; chmn. Ohio C. of C., 1979-81, life dir.; pres. Toledo Symphony Orch., 1985-86; hon. trustee Toledo Mus. Art, Toledo Hosp., Toledo Symphony; trustee U. Toledo Found., 1980-87; hon. trustee Kent State U. Found.; vice chmn. Greater Toledo Corp., 1984-86; trustee, treas. Rio Verde Cmty. Ch., 1989-92; founding elder Covenant Presbyn. Ch., Stephen minister, 1996; pres. Toledo Cmty. Chest, 1972; chmn. Greater Toledo Area United Way, 1971, Epworth Meth. Ch. Found.; dir. Rio Verde Cmty. Assn., 1998-2003 Named Toledo Area's Outstanding Citizen, 1976; recipient Kent State U. medallion, 1992; Williamson Alumni Ctr. named in his honor, 1991. Mem. Fin. Analysts Soc. Toledo (pres. 1968-69), Sys. and Procs. Assn. (internat. treas. 1960), Inst. Pub. Utilities (chmn. exec. com. 1969-70), Toledo Boys Club (Echo award 1974), Kent State U. Alumni Assn. (pres. 1971-72, Outstanding Alumnus 1974), Belmont Country Club, Rio Verde Country Club, Inverness Club (gov., treas. 1967-76, com. chair 1979 U.S. Open, 1986 PGA Championship, winner 1965 Amateur Invitational), Rio Verde Saddle Club (past pres.), Kiwanis (past pres. Toledo chpt., Disting. Svc. award 1977, 02, past internat. pres. award 2002), Ky. Cols. (hon.), Blue Key, Delta Sigma Pi, Beta Alpha Psi (hon.), Beta Gamma Sigma (hon.), Delta Upsilon. Republican. Home: 10661 Cardiff Rd Perrysburg OH 43551-3404 also: 18524 E Poco Vista Rio Verde AZ 85263-7125

WILLIAMSON, JOHN THOMAS, SR., minerals company executive; b. Atlanta, Oct. 1, 1925; s. Walter Berry and Clare (Mathews) W.; m. Ava Gene Shealy, June 11, 1949; children: John Thomas, Ava Clare, Robin E., Leila Ann. Diploma, N. Ga. Coll., 1942-43; BS in Indsl. Engring., Ga. Inst. Tech., 1949. Registered profl. engr. and land surveyor, Ga. Chief engr. Thiele Kaolin Co., Sandersville, Ga., 1949-57; assoc. W.C. Davis and Assocs., Atlanta and Tallahassee, 1957-60; chief engr. So. Clays, Inc., Gordon, Ga., 1960-63; asst. gen. mgr. Freeport Kaolin Co., NYC, 1972-77, v.p., gen. mgr., 1977-78, pres., 1978-85; cons., gen. mgr. Gordon ops. Engelhard Corp., N.J., 1985-86; pres. IMPEX Corp., Milledgeville, Macon, Brunswick, Ga., 1987—. Bd. dirs. Freeport Export Corp., Freeport Overseas Sales Co., 1978-83. Patentee on processing kaolins; contbr. articles to profl. jours. Mem. adv. bd. Ga. Coll., 1979-82, found. bd., 1983-98, emeritus, 1998—, vice chmn. found. bd., 1988-89, chmn., 1989-90; mem. nat. adv. bd. Ga. Tech. Inst., 1979-85, emeritus; adv. bd. sch. mgmt. U. Ga., 1979-80; mem. Ga. Mil. Coll. Found. Bd., 1993—, exec. com., 1st v.p., 1995. With USNR, 1943-46. Recipient Robert Earll McConnell award AIME, 1996, GMC Hon. Alumni award, 2000. Mem. TAPPI, China Clay Prodrs., Ga. State Mining Assn., Ga. Soc. Profl. Engrs., Ga. Bus. and Industry Assn. (bd. dirs. 1978-83), Bus. Coun. Ga. (bd. dirs. 1983-88), Ga. Soc. Mining Engrs., Ga. C. of C., Jaycees, Lions (pres. 1957), Baldwin County Progressive Farmers Club, Alpha Tau Omega. Baptist (deacon). Home: 1810 Tanglewood Rd Milledgeville GA 31061-2461 Office: PO Box 1028 Milledgeville GA 31059-1028 also: IMPEX Corp 157 Darien Hwy Brunswick GA 31525-2423 also: IMPEX Corp 2474 Kingsley Dr Macon GA 31204-1757

WILLIAMSON, KEITH HARVEY, lawyer; b. St. Louis, May 16, 1952; s. Irving Alexander and Elizabeth Rebecca (Giddings) W.; m. Addie L. Perkins, Oct. 29, 1988.; 1 child. BA, Brown U., 1974; MBA, JD, Harvard U., 1978; LLM in Taxation, NYU, 1986. Bar: DC 1978, NY 1983. Assoc. Covington & Burling, Washington, 1978-81, Reavis & McGrath, NYC, 1981-88; dir. taxes Pitney Bowes Credit Corp., Shelton, Conn., 1988-94, asst. gen. counsel, 1993—94, v.p., sec., gen. counsel, 1994—98; sr. assoc. gen. counsel, mergers and acquisitions Pitney Bowes Inc., 1998—99, pres., capital svcs. divsn., 1999—2006; sr. v.p., sec., gen. counsel Centene Corp., St. Louis, 2006—. Bd. dirs. Clayton C.of C.; founder Minority Corp. Counsel Assn.; mem. Black Exec. Exch. Program, Urban League. Office: Centene Corp 7711 Carondelet Ave Saint Louis MO 63105 Personal E-mail: keithwmson@aol.com.

WILLIAMSON, KENNETH LEE, chemistry professor; b. Tarentum, Pa., Apr. 13, 1934; s. James D. and Mary June (Becker) W.; m. Mary Louise Hoerner, Sept. 15, 1956; children: Christopher Lee, Tania Louise, Kevin Keith. BA cum laude (Nat. scholar), Harvard, 1956; PhD (Allied Chem. and Dye Co. fellow), U. Wis., 1960. Mem. faculty Mt. Holyoke Coll., 1961—, prof. chemistry, 1969—, Mary E. Woolley prof. chemistry, 1984-99, Mary E. Woolley prof. chemistry emeritus, 1999—. Mem. Grad. faculty U. Mass., 1965—; vis. prof. Cornell U., 1966, Dartmouth Coll., 1986-87, Harvard U., 1989-90, U. Trondheim, Norway, 1991, U. Louis Pasteur, Strasbourg, France, 1991, U. Amsterdam, Basel U., Switzerland, 1992, U. Canterbury, New Zealand and U. Auckland, New Zealand, 1994; vis. prof. MIT, 1996, 97, Calif. Inst. Tech., 2000. Author papers and books in field; patentee in field. Mem. South Hadley Hist. Commn., 1983—, South Hadley Cultural Coun., 2000-03; chair, Sycamores Com., South Hadley Hist. Soc., 1992-. NIH postdoctoral fellow Stanford, 1960-61; NSF sci. faculty fellow U. Liverpool, Eng.; also fellow of univ., 1968-69; Guggenheim fellow, 1975-76; Oxford (Eng.) U. fellow of univ., 1976, 1983; research assoc., Calif. Inst. Tech., 1975, 82. Mem. Am. Chem. Soc., AAAS, Sigma Xi. Congregationalist. Avocations: sailing, cabinetry. Home: 43 Woodbridge St South Hadley MA 01075-1138 E-mail: williamson98@comcast.net.

WILLIAMSON, KENT D., educational association administrator; B in Acctg., U. Ill., Urbana-Champaign, 1980, M in Polit. Sci.; student, U. Ill. Coll. Law, Salzburg Coll., Austria. Dir. mktg. and membership Nat. Coun. Tchrs. English, Urbana, Ill., assoc. exec. dir. bus., exec. dir., Am. Dairy Sci. Assn., 1999. Trainee Peace Corps, Tonga. Office: Nat Coun Tchrs English 1111 W Kenyon Rd Urbana IL 61801-1096 Office Phone: 217-328-3870. Office Fax: 217-328-0977. E-mail: kwilliamson@ncte.org. *

WILLIAMSON, MARILYN, retired secondary school educator; b. St. Louis, Apr. 6, 1930; d. Herschel and Estella (Wolff) W. BA, Roosevelt U., Chgo., 1951; MEd, U. Ill., 1955; life reading spl. cert., Harris-Stowe State Coll., St. Louis, 1968; postgrad., Washington U., St. Louis. Cert. life elem. and secondary tchr., reading specialist, Mo. Elem. tchr. St. Louis Pub. Schs., tchr. verbal skills, head lang. arts dept., reading specialist. Historian met. St. Louis chpt. Coalition 100 Black Women; sec. St. Louis chpt. Top Ladies Distinction; active ch. orgns.; co-chair Lane Tabernacle Scholarship. Recipient Retirement award Top Ladies Distinction St. Louis chpt., 50 Yr. Membership plaque Lane Tabernacle C.M.E. Ch., Cmty. Svc. award Top Ladies Distinction, Inc., 2005; named Top Lady of Yr., top Ladies of Distinction Inc., 1994 Mem. NAACP, Internat. Reading Assn., Mo. Tchrs. Assn., Nat. Coalition of 100 Black Women, (Shero award, Cmty. Svc. award 2004), Nat. Coun. Negro Women, Phi Delta Kappa (past pres., chair founder's day, v.p. Alpha Nu chpt.), Iota Phi Lambda (Apple for Tchr. award 1984), Delta Sigma Theta. Home: 5236 Vernon Ave Saint Louis MO 63113-1522

WILLIAMSON, MARILYN LAMMERT, literature educator, academic administrator; b. Chgo., Sept. 6, 1927; d. Raymond Ferdinand and Edith Louise (Eisenbies) Lammert; m. Robert M. Williamson, Oct. 28, 1950 (div. Apr. 1973); 1 child, Timothy L.; m. James H. McKay, Aug. 15, 1974. BA, Vassar Coll., 1949; MA, U. Wis., 1950; PhD, Duke U., 1956. Lectr. Duke U., Durham, NC, 1955-56, 58-59, N.C. State U., Raleigh, 1957-58, 61-62; asst. prof. Oakland U., Rochester, Mich., 1965-68, assoc. prof., 1968-72; prof. English Wayne State U., Detroit, 1972-90, Disting. prof. English, 1990-97, Disting. prof. emerita, 1997—, chmn. dept. English, 1972-74, 81-83, assoc. dean Coll. Liberal Arts, 1974-79, dir. women's studies, 1976-87, dep. provost, 1987-91, sr. v.p. for acad. affairs, provost, 1991-95, 98-200. Pres. Assn. Depts. English, 1976-77. Author: Infinite Variety, 1974, Patriarchy of Shakespeare's Comedies, 1986, British Women Writers 1650-1750, 1990, Tales of Two Dogs, 2005; editor: Renaissance Studies, 1972, Female Poets of Great Britain, 1981, Shakespeare Studies: Middle Comedies, 2003; contbr. articles to profl. jours. Pres. LWV, Rochester, 1963-65. Recipient Detroit Disting. Svc. award, 1986, Faculty Recognition award Bd. Govs., Wayne State U., 1991, 30 Yr. award Mich. Humanities Coun., 2004; Bunting Inst. fellow, 1969-70, AAUW fellow, 1982-83, J.N. Keal fellow, 1985-86. Mem.: MLA (exec. coun. 1977—80, mem. editl. bd. 1992—94), Fed. State Humanities Coun. (bd. dirs. 1994—2001, chair 1997—99), Mich. Coun. Humanities (bd. dirs. 1988—2001, chair 1991—93), Mich. Acad. (pres. 1978—79). Democrat. Home: 2275 Oakway Dr West Bloomfield MI 48324-1855

WILLIAMSON, MARVEL, dean, nursing administrator, sexologist, educator; b. Holton, Kans., Nov. 4, 1953; d. Thomas Arthur and Lois M. (Ihrig) Ansley; m. Paul Williamson, May 12, 1973; children: Marcus W., Sean W. BS in Nursing, Wichita State U., 1976; MS in Nursing, U. Ky., 1978; PhD, U. Iowa, 1987. Cert. sex educator, nurse educator. Prof. U. Iowa, Iowa City, 1980-89; dir. patient svcs. Ransom Meml. Hosp., Ottawa, Kans., 1989-91; dir. schs. nursing at Rolla, Sikeston and Kansas City Park Coll., Parkville, Mo., 1991-97; prof. Albany (Ga.) State U., 1997-99; sexologist Silver Spring, Md., 1999—2001; dean Kramer Sch. Nursing, Oklahoma City U., 2001—. Contbr. articles to profl. jours. Mem. ANA, Am. Assn. Sex Educators, Counselors and Therapists, Sigma Theta Tau. Home and Office: 3141 NW 18th St Oklahoma City OK 73107 Office: Oklahoma City U 2501 N Blackwelder Oklahoma City OK 73106 Office Phone: 405-208-5900.

WILLIAMSON, OLIVER EATON, economics and law professor; b. Superior, Wis., Sept. 27, 1932; m. Dolores Jean (Celeni); children: Scott, Tamara, Karen, Oliver, Dean. BS, Mass. Inst. Tech., 1955; MBA, Stanford U., 1960; PhD, Carnegie Mellon U., 1963; PhD (hon.), Norwegian Sch. Econ. and Bus. Adminstrn., 1986; PhD in Econ. sci. (hon.), Hochschule St. Gallen, Switzerland, 1987, Groningen U., 1989, Turku Sch. Econ. and Bus. Admin, St. Petersburg, Russia, 1996, HEC, Paris, 1997, Copenhagen Bus. Sch., 2000, U. Chile, 2000, Valencia U., 2004, Nice U., 2005. Project. engr. U.S. Govt., 1955-58; asst. prof. econ. U. Calif., Berkeley, Calif., 1963-65; assoc. prof. Pa. State U., Phila., 1965-68, prof., 1968-83, Charles and William L. Day prof. econ. and social sci., 1977-83; Gordon B. Tweedy prof. econ. law and orgn. Yale U., 1983-88; Transam. prof. of bus., econ. and law U. Calif., Berkeley, Calif., 1988-94, Edgar F. Kaiser prof. bus. adminstrn., prof. econ. and law, 1994—. Spl. econ. asst. to asst. atty. gen. for antitrust Dept. Justice, 1966—67; dir. Ctr. for Study of Orgnl. Innovation, U. Pa., 1976—83; cons. in field. Author: The Economics of Discretionary Behavior, 1964; Corp. Control and Bus. Behavior, 1970; Markets and Hierarchies, 1975; The Econ. Instn. of Capitalism, 1985; Econ. Orgn., 1986, Antitrust Economics, 1987; The Mechanisms of Governance, 1996; assoc. editor, Bell. Jour. Econ., 1973-74; editor, 1975-82; co-editor Jour. Law, Econ. and Orgn., 1983—2003. Fellow Ctr. for Advanced Study in Behavioral Sci., 1977-78; Guggenheim fellow, 1977-78; Fulbright scholar, 1999; Am. Acad. Arts and Sci. fellow, 1983; recipient Alexander Henderson Award Carnegie-Mellon U., 1962, Alexander von Humboldt Rsch. prize, 1987, Irwin award Acad. Mgmt., 1988, John von Newmann lectr., 1999, H.C. Recktenwald prize in econs., 2004. Fellow Econometric Soc., Am. Acad. Polit. and Social Sci., Acad. Internat. Bus. (eminent scholar), Am. Econ. Assn. (disting., v.p. 2000-01); mem. NAS, Internat. Soc. for New Instnl. Econ. (pres. 1999-2001), Am. Law and Econ. Assn. (pres. 1997-98), Western Econ. Assn. (pres. 1999-2000), Internat. Indsl. Econ. Assn. Office: Univ Calif Dept Econ Berkeley CA 94720-0001

WILLIAMSON, PETER DAVID, lawyer; b. Houston, Oct. 13, 1944; s. Sam and Sophie Ann (Kaplan) W.; m. Patricia Golemon; children: Heather, Amber, Asia, Ginger. BA, U. Ill., 1966; JD, U. Tex., 1969. Bar: Tex. 1969, US Supreme Ct. 1974, US Ct. Appeals (4th, 5th, 6th, 8th, 9th, 10th, 11th and DC cirs.); lic. comml. pilot. Pvt. practice, Houston, 1971—. Founder IMMLAW, The Nat. Consortium of Immigration Law Firms. Mem. Am. Immigration Lawyers Assn. (pres. 1994-95). Home: 1522 Park St Houston TX 77019-5324 Office: Chamberlain Hrdlicka White Williams & Martin 2 Allen Ctr 1200 Smith St # 1400 Houston TX 77002 Office Phone: 713-658-2508. Business E-Mail: peter.williamson@chamberlainlaw.com. *I do not believe in the existence of national boundaries. The philosophy of my practice of the law is to help my clients achieve the ability to pass freely through such artificial political barriers.*

WILLIAMSON, PHILEMONA, artist; b. NYC; BA, Bennington Coll., 1973; MA, NYU, 1979. Various positions Harlem Sch. Arts, 1978—83; vis. artist Norfolk (Va.) State U., 1982; artist Met. Mus. Art, 1983; artist, tchr. workshops Arts Connection, 1986—89; vis. artist Ctr. D'Art, Port-Au-Prince, Haiti, 1987; artist-in-residence Vey Spl. Arts, 1987—88; supr. student tchrs. dept. post-baccalaureate edn. Sch. Visual Arts, 1988—89; adj. faculty R.I. Sch. Design, 1989—90; painting faculty Bard Coll. Milton Avery Grad. Sch. Arts, 1991; adj. faculty Parsons Sch. Design, 1991—92, vis. artist MFA program, 1994. Mem. adv. bd. Getty Ctr. Edn. in Arts, 1989—98; panelist in field; artist-in-residence Millay Colony for Arts, Austerlitz, NY, 1983. One-woman shows include The Queens (N.Y.) Mus. Art, 1988, Wenger Gallery, L.A., 1989, Fine Arts Gallery, Southampton (N.Y.) Coll. L.I. U., 1990, June Kelly Gallery, N.Y.C., 1990, 1992, 1995, 1998, African Am. Mus., Hempstead, N.Y., 1991, Powers Art Gallery, East Stroudsburg U., Pa., 1992, Pa. State U., University Park, 1993, Flushing Coun. on Culture and Arts, N.Y.C., 1993, John Michael Kohler Arts Str., Sheboygan, Wis., 1999, exhibited in group shows at The Mint Mus. Art, Charlotte, N.C., 1991, U. Wis. at Milw. Fine Arts Gallery, 1992, Lehman Coll. Art Gallery and Krasdale Foods Arts Gallery, Bronx, 1994, Anderson Gallery, Buffalo, 1994, Kingsborough C.C. Art Gallery of CUNY, Bklyn., 1996, Pratt Manhattan Gallery, N.Y.C., 1996, Rubelle and Norman Schafler Gallery, Pratt Inst., Bklyn., 1996, Spelman Coll. Mus. Fine Art, Atlanta, 1996, numerous others, Represented in permanent collections pub. and corp. collections. Recipient Arts in Transit Poster Commn., Union Sq. Sta., N.Y., 1992, Joan Mitchell Found. award in painting, 1997; fellow Fellow in painting, NEA, 1987—88, fellow in painting, N.Y. Found. Arts, 1991; grantee exhbn. grantee, Artist Space, 1988; Pollock-Krasner Found. grantee, 1989—90, Ludwig Vogelstein grantee, 1993—94. Office: 11 LaSalle Rd Montclair NJ 07043

WILLIAMSON, R. MARK, lawyer; b. Pensacola, Fla., Oct. 7, 1960; MusB, La. State U., 1981; MusM, U. North Tex., 1983; JD with highest honors, Fla. State U., 1991. Bar: Wis. 1991, Ga. 1996. Assoc. Foley & Lardner Law Firm, Milw.; ptnr., co-leader, wealth planning group Alston & Bird LLP, Atlanta. Adj. prof. law Univ. Wis., Madison, Wis. Exec. editor Fla. Law Rev. Recipient Best Young Author award, Estates and Trusts Mag., 1997. Fellow: Am. Coll. Tax and Estate Counsel; mem.: Order of Coif. Office: Alston & Bird LLP One Atlantic Ctr 1201 W Peachtree St NW Atlanta GA 30309-3424 Office Phone: 404-881-7993. Office Fax: 404-881-7777. Business E-Mail: mwilliamson@alston.com.

WILLIAMSON, RICHARD HALL, federal agency administrator; b. Canton, NC, July 29, 1940; s. James Eustace and Gwendolyn (Nevada) H.; m. Julia Draper Brown, Nov. 7, 1965 (div. Jan. 1981); children: Shawn Nicol, Kevin Carson; m. Janie E. Shaheen, Nov. 18, 1998. BS in Physics, N.C. State U., 1962, MS in Nuclear Engring., 1970, postgrad., 1972. Instr. N.C. State U., Raleigh, 1968-72; chief, energy systems analysis AEC, Washington, 1972-75; asst. dir., energy analysis U.S. Energy R & D Adminstrn., Washington, 1975-77; dir., program analysis U.S. Dept. Energy, Washington, 1977-80, dir., policy devel., 1980-84, dep. asst. sec. for internat. affairs, 1984-94; dep. exec. dir. U.S. Energy Assn., Washington, 1995-99. Bd. dirs. Houston World Energy Congress Inc., 1994-99; chmn. Worth Assocs. Inc., Flint Hill, Va., 1998—. Author: A Group Strategy for Energy Research, Development and Demonstration, 1980; contbr. articles to jours. in field. Football ofcl. Atlantic Coast Conf., Greensboro, N.C., 1980-2002, Rose Bowl, Pasadena, Calif., 1995; treas. Sigma Alpha Mu Endowment Fund, 1994—, Sigma Alpha Mu Found., 1989—; treas. St. Simons Island Newcomers Club, 2001—03. 1st lt. U.S. Army, 1962-64; col. USAR, 1964-93. NSF fellow, 1964-65; AEC fellow, 1965-68; recipient Outstanding alumnus award IFC, N.C. State U., 1971, Presdl. Rank award U.S. Dept. Energy, 1990, Atlantic Coast Conf. Svc. to Football Officiating award, 2000. Mem. Atlantic Coast Conf. Ret. Football Ofcls. Assn. (ret. 2003—), Sigma Alpha Mu (nat. pres. 1984-86), Tau Beta Pi, Phi Kappa Phi, Omicron Delta Kappa, Sigma Pi Sigma, Pi Mu Epsilon. Republican. Methodist. Avocations: stamp collecting/philately, tennis, golf, skiing. Home: 906 Champney Saint Simons Island GA 31522-5464 Office: Worth Assocs PO Box 456 820 Fodderstack Rd Flint Hill VA 22627 Office Phone: 540-675-1250.

WILLIAMSON, RICHARD SALISBURY, ambassador; b. Evanston, Ill., May 9, 1949; s. Donald G. and Marion (Salisbury) W.; m. Jane Thatcher, Aug. 25, 1973; children: Elizabeth Jean, Craig Salisbury, Richard Middleton. AB with honors, Princeton U., 1971; JD, U. Va., 1974. Bar: Ill., 1974, D.C., 1975. Legis. counsel, adminstrv. asst. to Congressman Philip M. Crane of Ill., 1974-76; assoc. firm Winston & Strawn, Washington, 1977-80, ptnr., 1980; asst. to Pres. for intergovernmental affairs President's Task Force on Regulatory Relief, 1981-83; perm. rep. to UN US Dept. State, Vienna, 1983-85; sr. v.p., corp. & internat. relations Beatrice Cos., Inc., Chgo., 1985-86; ptnr. Mayer, Brown & Platt, Chgo., 1986—2001; asst. sec. for internat. orgn. affairs US Dept. State, Washington, 1988-89, alt. rep. to U.N. for special polit. affairs, 2002—. Editor: Trade & Economic Growth, 1993, United States Foreign Policy and the United Nations System, 1996; co-editor: (with Paul Laxalt) A Changing America: Conservatives View the 80's From the United States Senate, 1980; author: Reagan's Federalism: His Efforts to Decentralize Government, 1990, The United Nations: A Place of Promise and of Mischief, 1991, Disorder in the New World, 1997, Seeking Firm Footing: America in the World in the New Century, 2001. Chmn. Ill. Rep. Party, 1999-2002. Republican. *

WILLIAMSON, SAMUEL RUTHVEN, JR., historian, educator; b. Bogalusa, La., Nov. 10, 1935; s. Samuel Ruthven and Frances Mitchell (Page) Williamson; m. Joan Chaffe Andress, Dec. 30, 1961; children: George Samuel, Treeby Andress, Thaddeus Miller. BA, Tulane U., 1958; AM, Harvard U., 1960, PhD, 1966, grad. in Advanced Mgmt., 1986; degree (hon.), Furman U., Va. Theol. Sem., Centre Coll., The U. of the South, 2006. Asst. prof. U.S. Mil. Acad., 1963—66; from instr. history to asst. dean Harvard U., 1966—69, asst. to dean of Harvard Coll., 1969—70; rsch. assoc. Inst. Politics, faculty assoc. Ctr. for Internat. Affairs, 1971—72; mem. faculty J.F. Kennedy Sch. Govt., 1971—72; from assoc. prof. history to provost U. N.C., Chapel Hill, 1972—84, provost univ., 1984—88; pres., vice chancellor U. of South, Sewanee, Tenn., 1988—2000, vice chancellor emeritus, prof. history, 2000—05, Robert M. Ayres Jr. disting. univ. prof., 2001—05. Cons. historian's office Office of Sec. Def., 1974—76; vis. fellow Churchill Coll., 1976—77; mem. vis. com. Harvard Coll., 1986—92; dir. Rsch. Triangle Inst., 1984—88; mem. bd. visitors Air U., 1994—2002. Author: The Politics of Grand Strategy: Britain and France Prepare for War 1904-1914, 1969, 1990; co-author: The Origins of U.S. Nuclear Strategy, 1945-53, 1993, July 1914: Soldiers, Statesmen, and the Coming of the Great War, 2003; editor: The Origins of a Tragedy, July 1914, 1981, War and Soc. Newsletter, 1973—88; co-editor: Essays on World War I: Origins and Prisoners of War, 1983, Austria-Hungary and the Origins of the First World War, 1991. Mem. cen. com. Morehead Found., 1978—93; vice chmn. bd. visitors Air U., 1996—98, chmn. bd. visitors, 1998—2000. Capt. US Army, 1963—66. Fellow, NEH, 1976—77, Nat. Humanities Ctr., 1983; grantee, Ford Found., 1976; Fulbright scholar, U. Edinburgh, 1958—59, Woodrow Wilson Ctr. scholar, Washington, 2002, Woodrow Wilson fellow, 1958—63, Danforth fellow, 1958—63. Mem.: Nat. Assn. Colls. and Univs. (vice chmn., chmn. bd. dirs. 1993—95), Internat. Inst. Strategic Studies, Am. Hist. Assn. (George Louis Beer prize 1970). Democrat. Episcopalian. Home: PO Box 837 Sewanee TN 37375-0837 Office: U of South duPont Libr Sewanee TN 37383-1000 Business E-Mail: swilliam@sewanee.edu.

WILLIAMSON, SUSAN, retired mathematician, educator; b. Boston, Dec. 29, 1936; d. Richard Phillip and Mary Elizabeth Williamson. AB, Radcliffe Coll., Cambridge, Mass., 1958; MA, PhD, Brandeis U., Waltham, Mass., 1963. Instr. Cardinal Cushing Coll., Brookline, Mass., 1962—63; asst. prof. Boston Coll., Chestnut Hill, Mass., 1963—64, Regis Coll., Weston, Mass., 1965—67, assoc. prof., 1967—71, acad. dean, 1973—75, prof., 1971—2002, prof. emerita, 2002—. Reviewer Math. Revs., Ann Arbor, Mich., 1968—. Contbr. articles to profl. jours. Overseer DeCordova Mus., 2004—. Mem.: AAUP, Assn. Harvard Coll. Class Secs. and Treas., History Edn. Soc., Math. Assn. Am., Am. Math. Soc. Avocation: drawing. Home: 37 Hagen Rd Newton Center MA 02459

WILLIAMSON, THOMAS ARNOLD, publishing executive; b. Sagamore, Pa., Oct. 4, 1939; s. Thomas and Mabel (Kennedy) Williamson; m. Kathryn Steiner White, Mar. 1, 1980; 1 child, Thomas J. Grad., Phillips Exeter Acad., 1957; AB, Harvard U., 1961. From sales person to sr. v.p. Harcourt Brace & Co., NYC, 1962—88, sr. v.p., 1988—95; pres. Psychol. Corp., San Antonio, 1982—88; v.p. Holt Rinehart & Winston Harcourt Brace, 1989—95; pres. Harcourt Sch. Publishers, 1989—93, Learning Initiative, Austin, Tex., 1994—, T. Williamson Assocs., Inc., Austin, 1995—2005, Focused Learning, Ltd., Austin, 1998—2005; exec. v.p. Kathryn Williamson Real Estate, Austin, 2003—. Bd. dirs. The Austin Project, 2000—. Co-chmn. vis. com. to psychology dept. U. Tex., Austin, 1986—89, 1995—98; vol., chair chpt. 249 SCORE, 2003—04. Mem.: Hills Country Club, Town and Gown Club, Harvard Club N.Y.C. Home: 5 Cheverly Ct Austin TX 78738-1511 Office: Keller Williams Realty 1927 Lohmans Crossing Ste 102 Austin TX 78734 Personal E-mail: tawilliamson@austin.rr.com.

WILLIAMSON, VIKKI LYN, university official, financial executive; b. Huntington, W.Va., June 30, 1956; d. Ernest E. and Wanda C. (Cole) W. BA in Secondary Edn., English, Temple U., 1978; postgrad. in Acctg. and Fin., U. Cin., 1984-86; MA in Mgmt., Antioch U., 2002. CPA, Ohio; cert. tchr., Tenn., Ohio. Tchr. Springfield Christian Acad., Tenn., 1978-79; acctg. asst. Children's Hosp. Med. Ctr., Cin., 1979-84; asst. dir. fin. svcs. U. Cin. Med. Ctr., 1984-85, dir. fin. svcs., 1985-88, dir. fin. and adminstrn., 1988-91, dep. dir., CFO, 1991-2000; chief fin. adminstrv. officer Antioch U McGregor, Yellow Springs, Ohio, 2000—02; dir. budget and fin. planning Ctrl. State U., 2002—05, asst. v.p. adminstrn. and fin., 2005—. Bd. dirs. Contemporary Dance Theatre, 1987-90; mem. fin. oversight com. Beavercreek City Schs., 2004—. Bd. dirs. Habitat for Humanity-Hamilton, 1991-94, v.p., 1991, pres., 1992; v.p. PTA, 1997-98, pres., 1989-99, treas. 1999-2001; treas., bd. dirs. Tawawa Cmty. Devel. Found., 2002—05. Mem. AICPA, Healthcare Fin. Mgmt. Assn., Am. Assn. Blood Banks, Ohio Assn. Blood Banks (fin. com. 1986-90, treas. 1991-97), Am.'s Blood Ctrs. (fin. com. 1991-2000, alt. trustee 1991-2000), Assn. Women Adminstrs. (fin. com. 1987-90), Assn. Mid-Level Adminstrs. (bd. dirs. 1987-90), Ohio Assn. Coll. and Univ. Bus. Officers (exec. com. 2004—, sec. 2005, v.p. 2005, pres. 2006—), Alpha Epsilon Theta, Beta Gamma Sigma, Delta Mu Delta. Office: Central State Univ PO Box 1004 Wilberforce OH 45384 Office Phone: 937-376-6632. Business E-Mail: vwilliamson@centralstate.edu.

WILLIAMSON, WALTER BLAND, lawyer; b. Selma, Ala., Apr. 6, 1938; s. Walter Bland and Tina (Matheny) W.; children: Michael Davis, Amy Caroline; m. Dana Leigh Freiburger, Jan. 2, 1999. BS, Stetson U., 1959; JD, Emory U., 1963. Bar: Okla. 1969, Ga. 1963, U.S. Ct. Mil. Appeals 1963, U.S. Supreme Ct. 1969. Atty. Office Gen. Counsel Fed. Deposit Ins. Corp., Washington, 1967; atty. Office Std. Policy U.S. Dept. Commerce, 1968-69; shareholder Pray, Walker, Jackman, Williamson & Marlar and predecessors, Tulsa, 1969—, pres., 1993-98. Steering com. conf. on nuclear power generation Nat. Energy Law and Policy Inst., 1981; adv. com. on natural gas allowables Okla. Corp. Commn., 1983, 88. Mem. Okla. Energy Resources Bd., 1992-95; trustee Grace and Franklin Bernsen Found., Philbrook Mus. Art; bd. dirs. Indian Nations Coun., Boy Scouts Am.; governing bd. Jasmine Moran Childrens Mus. Capt. U.S. Army, 1963-67. Mem. ABA (vice-chmn. natural gas mktg. and transp. com., natural resource sect. 1986-88, co-chmn. energy com. adminstrv. law and regulatory practice sect. 1998-2000), Okla. Bar Assn. (chmn. mineral law sect. 1982), Tulsa County Bar Assn. (chmn. mineral law sect. 1979), Ind. Petroleum Assn. Am. (regional v.p. 1991-95), Okla. Ind. Petroleum Assn. (chmn. legal com. 1979-83, gen. counsel 1983—, Mem. of Yr. 1987), Energy Advocates (coord. 1987-88, 91), Phi Delta Phi. Home: 1228 E 19th St Tulsa OK 74120-7419 Office: 900 Oneok Plz Tulsa OK 74103 Home Phone: 918-566-0664; Office Phone: 918-581-5504. E-mail: wbw@praywalker.com.

WILLIAMSON, WAYNE C., internist, geriatrician; b. Hammond, Ind., 1952; BA, Northwestern U., 1974; MD, U. Cin., 1978. Cert. Am. Bd. Internal Medicine, 1984, in Geriatric Medicine 1992. Intern Rush Presbyn., St. Luke's Med. Ctr., Chgo., 1978—79, resident, internal medicine, 1979—81, physician; asst. prof. Rush Med. Coll.; physician Northwestern Meml. Hosp., 1999—; mem. faculty Steinberg Sch. Medicine, 1999—. Office: Northwestern Meml Hosp Galter Pavillion 201 E Huron 11-105 Chicago IL 60660 Office Phone: 312-642-7493.

WILLIAMSON, WILLIAM PAUL, JR., journalist; b. Des Moines, Mar. 30, 1929; s. William Paul and Florence Alice (Dawson) W.; m. Vania Torres Nogueira, Nov. 27, 1959; children: Mary Liz, Jon Thadeus, Margaret Ann Student, Mexico City Coll., 1952, U. Havana, 1955; BA, U. No. Iowa, 1953; MA, U. Iowa, 1954. Editor Brazilian Bus., Rio de Janeiro, 1958-60; mng. ptnr. Editora Mory Ltd., Rio de Janeiro, 1960-79; editor Brazil Herald, Rio de Janeiro, 1960-80; exec. dir. Inter Am. Press Assn., Miami, Fla., 1981-94, hon. life mem., mem. adv. coun., 1994—, dir., 1966-80, chmn. awards com., 1975-80. Solo navigator 1st passage Madeira Island, Portugal-Madeira Island, Brazil, 1994-95. Editor for Brazil, Fodor's South America, 1970-79; contbr. articles to various newspapers and mags. Pres. Am. Soc., Rio de Janeiro, 1968; bd. dirs. Instituto Brasil-Estados Unidos, Rio de Janeiro, 1977-80, Am. C. of C. for Brazil, Rio de Janeiro, 1964-68; rear commodore Seven Seas Cruising Assn., 2000—. With USMC, 1946—48, with USMCR, 1948—51. Decorated Order of Rio Branco (Brazil); recipient Citizen of Rio de Janeiro award State Legislature, 1975; Hon. Carioca award O Globo Newspaper, Rio de Janeiro, 1972; Ralph Greenberg award Am. Soc. Rio de Janeiro, 1977; Outstanding Svc. to Freedom of Expression and Newspapers awards Internat. Fedn. of Newspaper Pubs. and Internat. Assn. of Broadcasting, 1994; Benemeritous Citizen award Mcpl. Legislature, Itaquai, Brazil, 1995. Mem. Am. Soc. Assn. Execs., South Fla. Soc. Assn. Execs. (pres. 1987), Soc. Profl. Journalists, Overseas Press Club Am., Brazil Fgn. Corr. Assn. (founder, mem. honor), Rio Yacht Club, Ilha da Madeira Yacht Club, Kappa Tau Alpha. Home: 3051 NE 47th Ct Apt 204 Fort Lauderdale FL 33308-5304 Personal E-mail: billvania@yahoo.com.

WILLIAMS-PAISLEY, KIMBERLY, actress; b. Rye, NY, Sept. 14, 1971; d. Gurney and Linda W.; m. Brad Paisley, Mar. 15, 2003. Grad., Northwestern U. Actress Creative Artists Agy., Beverly Hills, Calif. Actor: (films) Father of the Bride, 1991, Secret Games, 1992, Indian Summer, 1993, Samuel Beckett Is Coming Soon, 1993, Coldblooded, 1995, Father of the Bride Part II, 1995, The War At Home, 1996, Safe House, 1998, Elephant Juice, 1999, Simpatico, 1999, Ten Tiny Love Stories, 2001, How to Go Out on a Date in Queens, 2006, How to Eat Fried Worms, 2006, We Are Marshall, 2006, (TV films) Stood Up!, 1990, Jake's Women, 1996, Follow the Stars Home, 2001, The Christmas Shoes, 2002, (TV series) Relativity, 1996-97, According to Jim, 2001-06, (TV appearances) The MTV Movie Awards, 1992, Jake's Woman, 1996, The U.S. Olympic Open Golf Championship, 1986; stage appearances: The Last Night of Ballyhoo, 1997, The Vagina Monologues, Speed the Plow; actor, dir., prodr.: (films) Shade, 2006; actor, co-prodr.: (TV films) Lucky 7, 2003, Identity Theft: The Michelle Brown Story, 2004. Spokesperson Elizabeth Glazer Pediatric AIDS Found.; bd. dirs. Earth Comm. Office. Office: Creative Artists Agy 9830 Wilshire Blvd Beverly Hills CA 90212-1825 *

WILLIAMS-PERRY, BRENDA LEE, pre-school educator; b. Colorado Springs, Colo., July 24, 1960; d. Arthur Lee and Rebecca Beard; m. Carl Eugene Perry, Jan. 11, 1991; 1 child, Kenneth Earl Williams Jr. AA in Child Devel., Almeda U., Boise, Idaho, 2006; BA in Early Childhood Edn., Almeda U., 2006; MA in Ednl. Adminstrn., Almeda U., Boise, 2006. Child Development Associate's Credential Coun. for Profl. Recognition, 2004, Directorship Certification Tex. Dept. of Protective & Regulatory Services, 2006, G-Tube Feeding Certification Gateway Child Devel. Ctr., 2004, Instructor CPR & First Aid Certified ARC, 2006, Infant Modules USAF, 2004. Dir. San Antonio Urban Ministries, 1999—2001; lead infant tchr. Jewish Cmty. Child Devel. Ctr., San Antonio, 2001—03; child devel. program technician Gateway Child Devel. Ctr., San Antonio, 2003—06; dir. St. Philip's Coll. Child Devel. Ctr., San Antonio, 2006—. Mem.: Nat. Black Child Devel. Inst. (assoc.). Home: 8021 W Military Dr Apt#807 San Antonio TX 78227-1861 Office: St Philip's College Child Dev Center 2207 Wyoming St San Antonio TX 78203 Home Phone: 210-675-3308; Office Phone: 210-271-7033. Personal E-mail: brendawilliamsperry@msn.com. E-mail: bwilliam@accd.edu.

WILLIAMS-THOMAS, ELIZABETH A., financial planner, consultant; b. San Francisco, Jan. 16, 1948; d. John and Myrtle Mary (Thierry) W.; children: Brian, Jonathan. Degree, U. Calif., 1979, MBA. Manpower coord., fed. programs U.S. Govt., San Francisco; patient svc. rep. Health Care Svc., Oakland, Calif.; ins. and real estate cons.; pres. Investments Unlimited, Oakland, EWJ & Assocs. Mktg. Firm; planning commr. City of Pitts.; CEO Ultimate Vacations Inc. Human rels. commr. Contra Costa County. Recipient Pub. Speaking award; European Investment fellow. Mem. AAUW, NAFE, NAACP, Nat. Real Estate Owners Assn., Nat. Notary Assn., Order Ea. Star, Heroines Jericho, Daus. Isis, Soroptimist Inc., Toastmistress Club, Beta Phi Sigma. Home: PO Box 523 Pittsburg CA 94565-0052

WILLIE, CHARLES VERT, social sciences educator; b. Dallas, Oct. 8, 1927; s. Louis James and Carrie (Sykes) W.; m. Mary Susannah Conklin, Mar. 31, 1962; children: Sarah Susannah, Martin Charles, James Theodore.

BA, Morehouse Coll., 1948, DHL (hon.), 1983; MA, Atlanta U., 1949; PhD, Syracuse U., 1957, DHL (hon.), 1992, Berkley Divinity Sch., Yale U., 1972, RI Coll., 1983, Johnson C. Smith U., Charlotte, NC, 1991, Franklin Pierce Coll., Rindge, NH, 1996, Haverford Coll., 2000; DD (hon.), Gen. Sem., 1974, Episcopal Div. Sch., 2004; MA (hon.), Harvard U., 1974; DL (hon.), Framingham State Coll., Mass., 1992; D of Engring. Tech. (hon.), Wentworth Inst. Tech., 1996; D of Canon Law (hon.), Seabury-Western Theol. Sem., 2005. Instr. to asst. prof. sociology Syracuse U., 1952-63, assoc. prof., 1964-67, prof., 1968-74, chmn. dept. sociology, 1967-71, v.p., 1972-74; prof. edn. and urban studies Grad. Sch. Edn. Harvard U., Cambridge, Mass., 1974-98, Charles William Eliot prof. edn. Grad. Sch. Edn., 1998-99, prof. emeritus Grad. Sch. Edn., 1999—. Instr. dept. preventive medicine SUNY Upstate Med. Ctr., Syracuse, 1955-60; rsch. dir. Washington Action for Youth delinquency prevention project, Pres.' Com. on Juvenile Delinquency and Youth Crime, Washington, 1962-64; vis. lectr. dept. psychiatry Harvard U. Med. Sch., Boston, 1966-67; vis. lectr. Episcopal Divsn. Sch., Cambridge, Mass., 1966-67; commr. Pres.'s Commn. on Mental Health, 1977-78; mem. tech. adv. bd. Maurice Falk Med. Fund, 1968-99; bd. dirs. Social Sci. Rsch. Coun., 1969-75; master Boston Sch. Desegregation case, Fed. Dist. Ct., 1975; mem. nat. adv. com. Maxwell Sch. Syracuse U., 1992-2000, Hogg Found. Mental Health, 1998-02, Morehouse Rsch. Inst., 1997-02; bd. overseers Boston Sci. Mus., 1997-2001, overseer emeritus, 2002—; corporator Emerson Hosp., Concord, Mass., 1998-2006; chmn. bd. dirs. Judge Baker Children's Ctr., Boston, 2001-03; mem. nat. adv. com. The History-Makers, 2002-06. Author: Church Action in the World, 1969, The Family Life of Black People, 1970, (with A. McCord) Black Students at White Colleges, 1972, (with J. Beker)Race Mixing in the Public Schools, 1973, (with B. Brown and B. Kramer) Racism and Mental Health, 1973, Black/Brown/White Relations, 1977, Oreo, 1975, (with R. Edmonds) Black Colleges in America, 1978, (with R. Reddick) A New Look at Black Families, 1976, 5th edit., 2003, The Sociology of Urban Education, 1978, The Caste and Class Controversy on Race and Poverty, 1979, 2d edit., 1989, The Ivory and Ebony Towers, 1981, (with S. Greenblatt) Community Politics and Educational Change, 1981, Race, Ethnicity and Socioeconomic Status, 1983, School Desegregation Plans That Work, 1984, Black and White Families, 1985, Five Black Scholars, 1986, (with Michael Grady) Metropolitan School Desegregation, 1986, Effective Education, 1987, (with Inabeth Miller) Social Goals and Educational Reforms, 1988, (with Michael Grady and Richard Hope) African-Americans and the Doctoral Experience, 1991, (with A. Garibaldi and W. Reed), The Education of African-Americans, 1991, Theories of Human Social Action, 1994, (with P. Rieker, B. Kramer and B. Brown) Mental Health, Racism and Sexism, 1995, (with Michael Alves) Controlled Choice, 1996, (with Ralph Edwards) Black Power/White Power in Public Education, 1998, (with Edwards and Alves) Student Diversity, Choice and School Improvement, 2002, (with R. Reddick and R. Brown) The Black College Mystique, 2006. Hon. trustee Episcopal Div. Sch., Cambridge; invited mem. United Negro Coll. Fund, pres. assembly, 1983-90; chair bd. dirs. Dana McLean Greeley Found. for Peace and Justice, 1989-92; mem. nat. exec. coun. Episcopal ch., 1967-74, v.p. gen. conv. House of Deps., 1970-74; host Inner City Beat nat. pub. affairs weekly TV program, monitor channel, 1991-92. Recipient Faculty Svc. award Nat. Univ. Ext. Assn., 1969, 50th Anniversary Disting. Alumnus award Syracuse U. Maxwell Sch., 1974, Spirit of Pub. Svc. award, 1994, Lee-Founders award Soc. for Study Social Problems, 1983, Family Scholar award, 1986, Disting. Career Contbn. award com. on role and status of minorities in edn. Am. Ednl. Rsch. Assn., 1990, Benjamin E. Mays Svc. award Morehouse Coll., 1994, Father John LaFarge, S.J. award Fairfield U., 1995, Disting. Career award Assn. Black Sociologists, 1996, Outstanding Book award for mental health, racism and sexism Myers Ctr. for Study of Human Rights, 1996, Arents Alumni award Syracuse U., 2000, Outstanding Tchr. award, Harvard U., 2005, US Spkr. and Specialist Grant award, US State Dept., The Bahamas, 2007. Mem. Am. Ednl. Rsch. Assn., Am. Sociol. Assn. (coun. 1980-83, 95-98, v.p. 1996-97, DuBois-Johnson-Frazier award 1994, William Foote Whyte award 2004, Career Disting. Scholarship award 2005), Ea. Sociol. Soc. (past pres., Robin M. Williams Disting. Lectureship award, 1994, Outstanding Contbn. award 2006, Merit award, 2006, Sorokin lectr. 2006), Phi Beta Kappa, Alpha Phi Alpha. Episcopalian. Home: 41 Hillcrest Rd Concord MA 01742-4615 Office: Harvard U Grad Sch Edn 410 Gutman Libr 6 Appian Way Cambridge MA 02138-3704 Office Phone: 617-495-4678. Home Fax: 978-371-1529. Personal E-mail: cvmswillie@comcast.net.

WILLIFORD, DRURY FISHER, JR., retired historical researcher, writer, editor; b. Memphis, Nov. 27, 1929; s. Drury Fisher and Irene Frances (Dawson) Williford; m. Virginia Lucile Jackson, Dec. 1950 (div. Sept. 1971); children: Peggy Leigh, Virginia Fisher, Alan Lyle, Mark Edward; m. Shirley Ann Hagedom, Aug. 1981. BA, W.Va. U., 1986. Cert. police firearms instr. Fed. Law Enforcement Tng. Ctr. Audit clk. Nat. Bank of Commerce, Memphis, 1953-54; patrolman Memphis Police Dept., 1954-55; patrol insp. U.S. Border Patrol, El Paso, Tucson and Buffalo, 1955-57; from insp. to ops. officer U.S. Customs Svc., Toronto, Ont., 1957-63, Buffalo, 1963-72, Washington, 1972-81; ret., 1981. Freelance photographer. Contbr. articles to profl. jours. Boys hockey coach Amherst (NY) Hockey Assn., 1964—72, Wheaton (Md.) Hockey Club, 1972—73, Morgantown (W.Va.) Hockey Club, 1981—82; literacy vol. tutor, 1985—88. With USN, 1950—52. Named Marion County Tutor of the Yr., 1987; named to Hockey Hall of Fame, Amherst, 1984; recipient High Quality Performance award, Dept. of Treasury, 1975, 1976, 1979, Spl. Achievement award, 1981; Judith Hemdon fellow, W.Va. Legislature, 1984. Democrat. Avocations: animal protection, habitat conservation, ultralight aircraft builder and pilot. Home: PO Box 734 Reedsville WV 26547-0734

WILLIFORD, SANDRA SIMMONS, music educator; b. Anderson, SC, Nov. 6, 1972; d. Rocshell Simmons II; m. William Lamont Williford, June 22, 2006; children: Paris Monet, A'Lonzo Nygel. BA in Music, Ch., Charleston So. U., SC, 1995; B in Music Edn., Anderson U., SC, 1998; MEd, So. Wesleyan U., Central, SC, 2003. Cert. tchr. music S.C. Tchr. gen. music, choir dir. Parker Acad., Greenville, SC, 1998—99; tchr. gen. music, chorus Hughes Acad., Greenville, 1999—2000; tchr. gen. music, instr. performing arts, choir dir., coach step team Varennes Elem. Sch., Anderson, 2000—. Chairperson Parents and the Cmty. Varennes Elem. Sch., 2005—06. Vol. Adopt-A-Hwy., Anderson, 2004—. Recipient Golden Apple, Anderson Sch. Dist. #5, 2005—06; grantee, Donors Choose Grants, 2005—06. Mem.: Zeta Phi Beta. Avocations: singing, reading, movies. Home: 2504 McGaha Dr Anderson SC 29626 Office: Varennes Elem Sch 1820 Hwy 29 S Anderson SC 29626 Office Phone: 864-260-5215. E-mail: sandrawilliford@andersons.net.

WILLIFORD, VELMA JEAN, minister; b. Anderson, SC, May 15, 1947; d. Eugene and Zora Etrulia Hagood; m. Claude Riley Williford, Apr. 14, 1965; children: Claude Rodriques, Maximo Jermaine, William Lamont. DMin, Christian Life Sch. Theology, Columbus, Ga., 1994—2004. Pres. Tabernacle of Faith Min., Inc., Anderson, SC, 1991—2005. Mem.: Gold Reagents. Avocations: reading, cooking, camping. Office: Gospel Tabernacle Faith Ch 1613 S Main St Anderson SC 29624 Office Phone: 864-261-6107. Business E-Mail: gospeltfc@bellsouth.com.

WILLIG, BARBARA ADELE, music educator; b. Phila., Apr. 24, 1941; d. Paul and Jeanne Willig; 1 child, Julie Rose Braman. B Music Edn., Temple U., 1963, M Music Edn., 1976, supervision cert., 1982. Cert. music, vocal tchr., supr. Pa. Coord. music theater, accompanist Abington Mus. Theatre, Pa., 1984—87; co-dir. music theater workshop Bucks County CC, Richboro, Pa., 1990—98; mentor tchr. for student tchrs. Phila. Sch Dist.; supr. student tchrs. Drexel U., Phila.; cons., artist-in-residence Phila. Sch. Dist. Presenter, writer grants in field; leader arts groups, presenter Phila. Sch. Dist., 1988—96; devel. presch. music workshops Settlement Music Sch. Author curriculum materials; composer, condr.: sabbath svc. record and performance Chants for Peace, 1972; co-dir.: Pa. premier performance Alice in Wonderland. Vol. various election campaigns, 1990—; mem., sec., v.p. B'Nai B'Rith Educators Unit, Phila., 1992—. Recipient Svc. to Cmty. award, B'Nai B'Rith Educators Unit, 1993, Tchr. of Excellence award, Chapel of Four Chaplains. Mem.: LWV, Am. Choral Dirs. Assn., Nat. Orff Assn., Pa. Music Educators Assn., Music Educators Nat. Conf., Temple U. Boyer Coll. Music Alumni Assn. (pres.-elect 2005), Phi Delta Kappa. Avocations: fitness, tai chi, theater, travel, languages. Home: 813 Roslyn Ave Glenside PA 19038

WILLIG, KARL VICTOR, computer company executive; b. Idaho Falls, Idaho, June 4, 1944; s. Louis Victor and Ethel (McCarty) W.; m. Julianne Erickson, June 10, 1972; 1 son, Ray. BA magna cum laude, Coll. of Idaho, 1968; MBA (Dean Donald Kirk David fellow), Harvard U., 1970. Pres. Ariz. Beef, Inc., Phoenix, 1971-73; group v.p. Ariz.-Colo. Land & Cattle Co., Phoenix, 1973-76; v.p. Rufenacht, Bromagen & Hertz, Inc., Chgo., 1976-77; pres. Sambo's Restaurants, Inc., Santa Barbara, Calif., 1977-79; ptnr. Santa Barbara Capital, 1979-85; pres. EURUSA Equities Corp., 1985-86; pres., chief exec. officer InfoGenesis, 1986—2004; chmn. bd. Am. Commn., 2005—. Trustee Am. Bapt. Sem. of West, 1977-85; mem. Chgo. Merc. Exch., 1976-77, mem. audit com. and membership coms., 1976-77; chmn. bd. Gold Crest LLC, 2006—; bd. dirs. E2-Assocs., Inc. Bd. dirs. Santa Barbara Rescue Mission, 2002—, Los Padres coun. Boy Scouts Am., 2004—. Named one of Outstanding Young Men of Am., 1972; recipient Assn. of U.S. Army award, 1964; named Entrepeneur of Year, South Coast Bus. and Tech. awards, 2005 Baptist.

WILLIG, KENNETH C. H., lawyer; b. NYC, Mar. 3, 1949; BA cum laude, Bklyn. Coll., 1970; MA, Univ. Pa., 1971, PhD, 1975, JD, 1980; Mombusho vis. scholar, Univ. Osaka, Japan, 1972—75. Bar: NY 1981. Ptnr., joint global leader Comml. practice group, chmn. Project Fin. practice group DLA Piper Rudnick Gray Cary, NYC. Editor: Univ. Pa. Law Rev.; mem. adv. bd. Jour. of Internat. Econ. Law. Mem.: ABA, NY State Bar Assn., Assn. Bar City of NY. Office: DLA Piper Rudnick Gray Cary 1251 Ave of the Americas New York NY 10020-1104 Office Phone: 212-835-6240. Office Fax: 212-835-6001. Business E-Mail: kenneth.willig@dlapiper.com.

WILLIG, ROBERT DANIEL, economics professor; b. Bklyn., Jan. 16, 1947; s. Jack David and Meg W.; m. Virginia Mason, July 8, 1973; children: Jared Mason, Scott Mason, Brent Mason, Alexandra Mason. BA, Harvard U., 1967; MS in Ops. Rsch., Stanford U., 1968, PhD in Econs, 1973. Lectr. Stanford U., Palo Alto, Calif., 1971-73; tech. staff Bell Labs., Holmdel, NJ, 1973-77, supr. dept. econs. rsch., 1977-78; prof. econs. and pub. affairs Princeton U., 1978—; task force on future of postal svc. Aspen Inst., 1978-80; dep. asst. atty. gen. U.S. Dept. Justice, Washington, 1989-91. Cons. in field; rsch. fellow U. Warwick, Eng., 1977; organizing com. Telecom Policy Rsch. Conf., 1977-78; rsch. adv. bd. Am. Enterprise Inst., 1980-88; mem. N.J. Gov.'s Task Force on Market-Based Pricing of Electricity, 1987; bd. dirs. Consultants in Industry Econs., Inc., 1992-2005, Competition Policy Assocs., Inc.; 2002-2005, mem. Def. Sci. Bd. Task Force on Antitrust for the Def. Industry, 1993-94, Transp. Rsch. Bd. Task Force, 1995-96; advisor Inter-Am. Devel. Bank, 1997-00. Author: Welfare Analysis of Policies Affecting Prices and Products, 1973, Contestable Markets and the Theory of Industry Structure, 1982; editor: Handbook of Industrial Organization, 1986, Can Privatization Deliver: Infrastructure for Latin America, 1999, Second Generation Reforms in Infrastructure Services, 2002; contbr. articles to profl. jours.; mem. editl. bd. MIT Press Series on Govt. Regulation, 1978—, Am. Econ. Rev., 1980-83, Jour. Indsl. Econs., 1985-89, Utility Policy, 1989-2001. Adv. bd. B'nai B'rith Hillel Found., Princeton U., 1978-89. Grantee, NSF, 1979—85. Fellow Econometric Soc. (program com. 1978-81); mem. Am. Econ. Assn. (nominating com. 1980-81). Office: Princeton Univ Economics Dept Princeton NJ 08540

WILLINGHAM, CLARK SUTTLES, lawyer; b. Houston, Nov. 29, 1944; s. Paul Suttles and Elsie Dell (Clark) W.; m. Jane Joyce Hitch, Aug. 16, 1969; children: Meredith Moores, James Barrett. BBA, Tex. Tech U., 1967; JD, So. Meth. U., 1971, LLM, 1984. Bar: Tex. 1971. Ptnr. Kasmir, Willingham & Krage, Dallas, 1972—86, Finley, Kumble et al, Dallas, 1986—87, Brice & Mankoff, Dallas, 1988—98, Moseley Law PC, Dallas, 1999—. Contbr. articles to profl. jours. Bd. dirs. Dallas Summer Musicals, 1971—, exec. com., 1979-93, 97-2003, pres. 1994. Mem. ABA (chmn. agrl. com. tax sect. 1984-86), State Bar Tex. (chmn. agrl. tax com. 1985-87), Dallas Bar Assn., Am. Law Inst., Tex. Rangers Law Enforcement Assn.(bd. dirs.), Nat. Cattlemen's Beef Assn. (bd. dirs., pres. 1998), U.S. Meat Export Fedn. (exec. com. 1991-93), Beef Industry Coun. (exec. com. 1990-91, promotion chmn. 1992-94), Tex. Cattle Feeders Assn. (bd. dirs., pres. 1988), Tex. Bd. Vet. Med. Examiners (pres. 1994), Tex. Beef Coun. (bd. dirs., pres. 1989), Dallas Country Club. Republican. Episcopalian. Home: 3824 Shenandoah St Dallas TX 75205-1702 Office: Moseley Law PC 3878 Oak Lawn Ave Fl 4 Dallas TX 75219-4460 Home Phone: 214-526-7008; Office Phone: 214-525-3940. E-mail: clarkw@airmail.net.

WILLINGHAM, EDWARD BACON, JR., ecumenical minister, administrator; b. St. Louis, July 27, 1934; s. Edward and Harriet (Sharon) W.; m. Angeline Walton Pettit, June 14, 1957; children: Katie, Carol. BS in Physics, U. Richmond, 1956; postgrad., U. Rochester, 1958—59; MDiv., Colgate Rochester Div. Sch., 1960. Ordained to ministry Am. Bapt. Ch., 1960. Min. Christian edn. Delaware Ave. Bapt. Ch., Buffalo, 1960-62; dir. radio and TV Met. Detroit Coun. Chs., 1962-75; exec. dir. Christian Communication Coun. Met. Detroit Chs., 1976-98. Broadcast cons. Mich. Coun. Chs., 1965-75; guest cons. religious broadcasting Germany, 1968; coord. com. Mich. Ecumenical Forum, 1986, 90-92, chmn., 1991-92. Bd. mgrs. Broadcasting and Film Commn., Nat. Coun. Chs., 1965-73; mem. Muslim-Christian-Jewish Leadership Forum, 1987—; bd. deacons 1st Bapt. Ch. Birmingham, chmn., 1994-95. Recipient Gabriel award Cath. Broadcasting Assn., 1972, 1st Ann. Ecumenical award Am. Bapt. Chs. Mich., 1992, Race Rels. award Booker T. Washington Bus. Assn. Detroit, 1983, Brotherhood award Bethal AME Ch., Detroit, 2000 Mem. Assn. Regional Religious Communicators (pres. 1969-71), World Assn. Christian Comm. (cen. com. 1973-78, chmn. N.Am. Broadcast sect. 1970-71, bus. mgr., 1972-98, Pioneer in Religious Comm. award 2004), Phi Gamma Delta, Sigma Pi Sigma. Office: 21440 Lathrup St Southfield MI 48075-4218

WILLINGHAM, JEANNE MAGGART, performing arts educator and company executive; b. Fresno, Calif., May 8, 1923; d. Harold F. and Gladys (Ellis) Maggart. Student, Tex. Woman's U., 1942; student profl. dancing schs. worldwide. Tchr. dance Beaux Arts Dance Studio, Pampa, Tex., 1948—; artistic dir. Pampa Civic Ballet, 1972—. Mem. Tex. Arts and Humanities Coun., Tex. Arts Alliance, Pampa C. of C. (fine arts com.), Pampa Fine Arts Assn. Office: Pampa Civic Ballet Beaux Arts Dance Studio 315 N Nelson St Pampa TX 79065-6013 Office Phone: 806-669-6361.

WILLINGHAM, MARY MAXINE, fashion retailer; b. Childress, Tex., Sept. 12, 1928; d. Charles Bryan and Mary (Bohannon) McCollum; m. Welborn Kiefer Willingham, Aug. 14, 1950; children: Sharon, Douglas, Sheila. BA, Tex. Tech U., 1949. Interviewer Univ. Placement Svc., Tex. Tech U., Lubbock, 1964-69; owner, mgr. buyer Maxine's Accent, Lubbock, 1969—. Speaker in field. Leader Campfire Girls, Lubbock, 1964-65; sec. Cmty. Theatre, Lubbock, 1962-64. Recipient Golden Sun award Dallas Market, 1985, Woman of Excellence award in Bus., YWCA, 2001; named Outstanding Mcht., Fashion Retailer Mag., 1971, also Outstanding Retailer. Mem. Ranch and Heritage Ctr. Office Phone: 254-947-0933.

WILLINGHAM, WARREN WILLCOX, psychologist; b. Rome, Ga., Mar. 1, 1930; s. Calder Baynard and Eleanor (Willcox) W.; m. Anna Michal, Mar. 17, 1954; children: Sherry, Judith, Daniel. Student, Ga. Inst. Tech., 1952; PhD, U. Tenn., 1955. Rsch. assoc. World Book Co., NYC, 1959-60; dir. evaluation studies Ga. Inst. Tech., Atlanta, 1960-64; dir. rsch. Coll. Bd., NYC, 1964-68, dir. access rsch. office Palo Alto, Calif., 1968-72; asst. v.p., disting. rsch. scientist Ednl. Testing Svc., Princeton, NJ, 1972—. Vis. prof. U. Minn., 1988; mem. adv. bd. on ednl. requirements on Sec. Navy, 1968; leader Psychometric Seminar, Nat. Inst. Testing and Evaluation, Jerusalem, 1999; cons. to numerous schs., colls. U.S. Office Edn. Author: Free Access Higher Education, 1970, Source Book for Higher Education, 1973, College Placement and Exemption, 1974, Assessing Experimental Learning, 1977, Selective Admissions in Higher Education, 1977, Personal Qualities and College Admissions, 1982, Success in College, 1985, Testing Handicapped People, 1988, Predicting College Grades, 1990; Gender and Fair Assessment, 1997; editor: Measurement in Education, 1969-72; mem. editl. bd. Jour. Ednl. Measurement, 1971-75, Alternate Higher Edn., 1976-80, Am. Ednl. Rsch. Jour., 1968-71; contbr. articles, tech. reports to profl. jours. Served to lt. USNR, 1955-59. Recipient Ann. award So. Soc. Philosophy and Psychology, 1958 Fellow Am. Psychol. Assn., AAAS; mem. Nat. Council on Measurement in Edn. (dir.), Am. Ednl. Research Assn., Am. Psychol. Soc., CAEL (hon. life mem.), Sigma Xi. Mailing: 131 Bertrand Dr Princeton NJ 08540

WILLIS, ARTHUR WILLIAM, ophthalmologist; b. Englewood, NJ, June 8, 1941; m. Suzanne Willis. BA in Med. Sci., Ind. U., MD, 1966. Diplomate Am. Bd. Ophthalmology. Intern Wilmington Med. Ctr., Del., 1966—67; resident ophthalmology Med. Coll. Ga., 1969—72; fellow diseases and surgery retina Alice McPherson, M.D., Houston, 1972; clin. instr. dept. ophthalmology Baylor Coll. Medicine, Houston, 1973—85, clin. asst. prof. dept. ophthalmology, 1985—90, clin. assoc. prof. dept. ophthalmology, 1991—. Clin. assoc. prof Weill med. coll. Cornell U., Houston, 2006; mem. records com. Meth. Hosp., Houston, 1979—, utilization rev. officer ophthalmology, mem. operating rm. com. neurosensory ctr., 1987—92; trustee Retina Rsch. Found., 1974—76; oral examiner Am. Bd. Ophthalmology, 1996—; presenter in field. Contbr. articles to profl. jours. With USAF, 1967—69. Recipient First Prize Paper award, Med. Assn. Ga. Fellow: ACS; mem.: AMA, Tex. Soc. Ophthalmology Otolaryngology (sec. 1997—), Pan Am. Assn. Ophthalmology, Am. Soc. Retina Specialists, Tex. Soc. Prevention Blindness, Tex. Ophthal. Assn., Tex. Med. Assn., Harris County Med. Soc. (mem. pub. grievance com. 1977—79, sec. 1978, chmn. 1979), Am. Acad. Ophthalmology, West Coast Retina Study Club, So. Retina Study Club. Home: 1202 Bissonnet Houston TX 77005 Office: Retina and Vitreous of Tex 2727 Gramercy St Ste 200 Houston TX 77025

WILLIS, BEN, writer, artist; b. Racine, Wis., Dec. 4, 1930; s. Ben Sherlock Willis and Beryl Hester (Smith) Young; div. 1971. Attended, Phila. Coll. Art, 1953—54, Pa. Acad. Fine Arts, 1954—55, Academie Julian, Paris, 1955—57. Author: The Tao of Art, 1987, Internet reprint edit., 2001; collaborator: The Art of Oriental Embroidery, 1980; exhibited in group shows Salmagundi Club, N.Y.C., 1971-75, 1980, Am. Watercolor Soc., Nat. Acad. Design, N.Y.C., 1978, Cicchinelli Galleries, N.Y.C., 1980, Nat. Arts Club, N.Y.C., 1980, Manasquan Group Artists, 1981, Pastel Soc., N.Y.C., 1982, Allied Artists Am., N.Y.C., 1982, Am. Artists Profl. League, N.Y.C., 1984; represented in numerous pvt. collections. Seaman 1st class, USN, 1948-52, Korea. Recipient 1st prize N.Y.C. Ctr., 1960, Manasquan Outdoor Art Show, 1981, Best in Show award Manasquan Group Artists, 1981, others. Fellow Alumni Fellowship Pa. Acad. Fine Art, Author's Guild. Episcopalian. Avocations: languages, music, reading, Judo. Home: 10 C Bennington Ln Whiting NJ 08759-1621

WILLIS, BEVERLY ANN, architect; d. Ralph William and Margaret Amanda (Porter) W. BFA, U. Hawaii, 1954; PhD in Fine Arts (hon.), Mt. Holyoke Coll., 1983. Registered architect, Calif. Prin. Willis Atelier, Honolulu, 1954-58, Willis & Assocs., Inc., San Francisco, 1958-88. Pres. Beverly Willis Architecture Found., 2002—; pres., dir. Architecture Rsch. Inst., Inc., NYC, 1993—2005; co-chair Rebuild Downtown Our Town Coalition, 2002; prof. Internat. Women's U., Kassel, Germany, 2000. Author: Invisible Images: The Silent Language of Architecture, 1997; contbg. author: City and Gender-International Discourse on Gender, Urbanism and Architecture, 2003, Creating Sustainable Urban Environments: Future Forms and Design for Sustainable Cities, 2005; prin. works include Union St. Stores (merit award San Francisco AIA, award of distinction State of Calif.), Nob Hill Cts. (merit award AIA), 1970, Margaret Hayward Park (grand and merit awards Pacific Coast Bldg. Con., Honor award Design Internat.), 1983, San Francisco Ballet Bldg., 1984, Manhattan Village Acad. H.S., N.Y.C., 1995; contbr. articles to profl. jours., chpts. to books. Founding trustee Nat. Bldg. Mus., Washington, 1976—, mem. bd. infrastructure and the constructed environ., 1971-79, chair fed. facility coun., 1976-79; pres. Beverly Willis Arch. Found., NYC, 2002—, Mus. Modern Art Program, 2007. Recipient Phoebe Hearst Gold Medal award, 1969. Fellow AIA (v.p. Calif. coun. 1979, pres. 1980); mem. Achievement Rewards for Coll. Scientists, Internat. Women's Forum, Lambda Alpha (pres. San Francisco chpt. 1981-82), Villa Taverna and Nat. Arts Club. Avocations: poetry, sketching, tennis. Office Phone: 212-577-1200. Business E-Mail: bevwillis@architect.org.

WILLIS, BRUCE DONALD, judge; b. Mpls., Jan. 29, 1941; s. Donald Robert and Marie Evelyn (Edwards) W.; m. Elizabeth Ann Runsvold, July 17, 1971; children: Andrew John, Ellen Elizabeth. BA in English, Yale U., 1962; LLB, Harvard U., 1965. Bar: Minn., 1965, U.S. Dist. Ct. Minn. 1965, U.S. Ct. Fed. Claims 1989, U.S. Ct. Appeals (8th cir.) 1991, U.S. Supreme Ct. 1992. Assoc. Popham, Haik, Schnobrich & Kaufman, Ltd., Mpls., 1965-71, ptnr., 1971-95; judge Minn. Ct. Appeals, 1995—. Mem. jud. adv. bd. Law and Orgnl. Econs. Ctr., U. Kans., 1997—2001; adv. bd. Minn. Inst. Legal Edn., 1986—2003. Contbr. articles to profl. jours. Del. Rep. Nat. convs., 1976, 88; vice chmn. Ind.-Rep. Party Minn., 1979-81; mem. State Ethical Practices Bd., 1990-95, sec. 1990-91, vice chmn. 1991-92, chmn., 1992-93; mem. Minn. Commn. on Jud. Selection, 1991-94; mem. Minn. Bd. Jud. Stds., 1997—2005; mem. adv. com. on rules of civil appellate procedure Minn. Supreme Ct., 1997—. Named one of 1990's Lawyers of Yr., Minn. Jour. Law and Politics, 1991, one of Minn.'s Best Trial Lawyers, Minn. Lawyer, 1991. Mem.: ABA, Minn. Bar Assn. (professionalism com. 1998—). Mem. United Ch. of Christ. Home: 2940 Walnut Grove Ln N Plymouth MN 55447-1567 Office: Minn Jud Ctr 25 Rev Dr Martin Luther King Jr Blvd Saint Paul MN 55155-1500 E-mail: bruce.willis@courts.state.mn.us.

WILLIS, CLAYTON, broadcaster, former government official, educator, arts consultant; b. Washington, Aug. 11, 1933; s. William H. and Elizabeth Carl (Keferstein) W. Student, Sorbonne, Paris, 1953-54; BA, George Washington U., 1957; student, U. Oslo, 1953; grad., N.Y. Inst. Fin., 1966, Assn. Commodities Exch. Firms Inc., 1966. Spl. assignment Am. Embassy, London, 1957; writer NBC Network radio show Tex and Jinx, 1958; spl. corr. NBC News, La Paz, Bolivia, 1959; spl. Washington corr. Fin. News TV Network (now CNBC), NYC, 1988; contbr., anchor, TV prodr., corr. Saudi Arabian TV, Newsweek mag., Phillips News Svc. Hope (Ark.) Star; contbr., corr. Christian Sci. Monitor, L.A. Times-Mirror Syndicate, Palm Beach (Fla.) Post, Greenwich (Conn.) Time, Fin. News TV Network, New York, Mainichi, Tokyo, China Post, Taipei, Taiwan, Chattanooga Times, Nashville Tennesseean, Daily Nation of Kenya, Khartoum Echo, Sudan,

The Washington Daily News, Washington Post, Cape Argus of Capetown, South Africa, Bangkok Post, Irish Times, Dublin; reporter, movie, art critic Albuquerque Tribune, 1959-61; asst. editor Newsweek Mag., NYC, 1961-62; TV broadcaster-writer UPI Newsfilm, NYC, 1962; White House corr., chief bur., anchor World Radio News, Houston; White House, Washington corr. WAVA Radio Sta., Washington, 1963-65; editorial writer, corr. Hearst Newspapers, NYC, 1965; press officer UN, NYC, 1965-66; spl. assignment Am. Embassy, Reykjavik, Iceland, 1967; editorial writer, critic, corr. N.Y. Amsterdam News, NYC, 1967-68; cons. govt., law, and ethics programs Ford Found., NYC, 1968-69; dir. pub. affairs U.S. EEOC, Washington, 1969-70; cons. OEO, Washington, 1970, Pres.'s Nat. Coun. on Indian Opportunity, Washington, 1970-71, Cmty. Rels. Svc., U.S. Dept. Justice, Washington, 1970-73, Cabinet Com. on Opportunities for Spanish-Speaking People, 1971-72, Fed. Energy Adminstrn., Washington, 1973-74; dir. pub. affairs Office of Petroleum Allocation, U.S. Dept. Interior, 1973-74; dir. Congl. rels., dir. pub. affairs Pres.'s Nat. Commn. on Fire Prevention and Control, 1971-73; pub., editor, owner Four Corners Chieftain, Ignacio and Durango, Colo., 1972-73; lectr. Sch. of Bus., U. D.C., Washington, 1973-74; owner, White House corr., photojournalist Willis News Svc., Washington, 1974—; pub. affairs dir. Inaugural Vets. Com., 1976-77; White House corr.; anchor Channel 33, Arlington, Va., 1991—. Adviser to Fernando E.C. de Baca, spl. asst. to the Pres., White House, 1974-76; lectr. nat., internat. affairs, Haiti, art, communications, energy; corr.-broadcaster Sta. KTEN-TV, Ada, Okla., 1985; mem. staff presdl. transition office U.S. Pres. Bush, 1988-89, 90; dir. and curator L. Clayton Willis Art Collection, Palm Beach, Fla.; anchor, corr. Channel 33 Arlington, Va., 1991—; pres., White House corr., congressional corr., photojournalist, The Evening News Broadcasting Co., Willis News Service; prodr., anchor documentary programs Saudi Arabian TV, 1992—; exec. prodr., anchor Glimpses of the World documentaries, 1993; White House corr., photojournalist Hope (Ark.) Star, 1994—; dir., curator L. Clayton Willis Art Collection, Palm Beach; chmn. emeritus Haitian Art Mus., Delray Beach, Fla.; exec. prod., host, commentator The Clayton Willis Talk Show, WPBR, Palm Beach, Fla, 2000-. Co-author: Capital Fare, 1977, Lott-Willis Pictorial Digest of U.S. Presidential Elections and Inaugurations, 1997; host/exec. prodr., commentator The Clayton Willis Talk Show, WPBR, 1998-; pres.'s White House corr. Evening News Broadcasting Co., Washington, 2000; contbr. articles to Daily Mail, London, London Sunday Express, Umtali Post, Zimbabwe, Gwelo (Zimbabwe) Times, To the Point news mag., Johannesburg, The Citizen, Johannesburg, Hartford Courant, Sacramento Union, Chattanooga Times, UPI Radio Networks, Washington Post, The Hope (Ark.) Star, Phillips News Svc., also other mags. and newspapers. Broadcaster with Bush/Quayle Nat. Campaign Hdqrs., Washington, 1988; adviser Presdl. Transition Office of Pres. George Bush, 1988-89; loaned Haitian paintings for spl. exhbn. to Haitian Embassy, Washington, 1991, Milw. Art Mus., 1992, Hypoluxo Town Hall, Fla., 2005. Recipient Outstanding Svc. award Harlem Prep. Sch., Johannes Gutenberg medal (Mainz, Germany), 1984, Letters of Cert. Appreciation Pres. of U.S., 1989. Covered Vietnam, Congo, Mid. East, Rhodesian and South African wars; covered Clarence Thomas and Robert Gates U.S. Senate confirmation hearings, 1991; covered 2000 presdl. election and re-count, Palm Beach, Fla.; covered Haitian rebellion and fall of Pres. Aristide, Haiti, 2004; covered the 2004 Kerry-Bush Presidential Campaign. Office Phone: 561-688-1777. Personal E-mail: lclaytonwillis@aol.com.

WILLIS, CONNIE (CONSTANCE E. WILLIS), writer; b. Denver, Dec. 31, 1945; m. Courtney Willis; 1 child. Tchr. elem. and jr. H.S., Branford, Conn., 1967-69. Author: (short stories) Letter from the Clearys, 1982 (Nebula award, 1982, Hugo award, 1983), Even the Queen, 1992 (Nebula award, 1992, Hugo award, 1993), Death on the Nile, 1993 (Hugo award, 1994), The Soul Selects Her Own Society, 1996 (Hugo award, 1997), (novels) Water Witch, 1982, Fire Watch, 1985 (Nebula award, 1982, Hugo award, 1983), Lincoln's Dreams, 1987 (John W. Campbell Meml. award), Doomsday Book, 1992 (Nebula award, 1992, Hugo award, 1993), Impossible Things, 1993, Unchartered Territory, 1994, Uncharted Territory, 1994, Remake, 1995, Bellwether, 1996, To Say Nothing of the Dog, 1997 (Hugo award, 1999), Miracle, 1999, Promised Land, 1997, Miracle and other Christmas Stories, 1999, Passage, 2001 (Locus award, Hugo award nominee, 2002, Nebula award nominee, 2002), Inside Job, 2005, (novellas) The Last of the Winnebagos, 1989 (Nebula award, 1988, Hugo award, 1989), The Winds of Marble Arch, 2000 (Hugo best novella nominee, 2000). Named Best Sci. Fiction/Fantasy Author of Nineties Locus Mag. Address: 1716 13th Ave Greeley CO 80631-5418 E-mail: conniewillis@juno.com.

WILLIS, CRAIG DEAN, academic administrator; b. Cambridge, Ohio, Mar. 21, 1935; s. John Russell and Glenna (Stevens) W.; m. Marilyn Elaine Foster, June 9, 1956; Mark Craig, Bruce Dean, Todd Laine, Garth John. BA, Ohio Wesleyan U., Delaware, 1957; MA, Ohio State U., Columbus, 1960, PhD, 1969. Registrar Ohio Wesleyan U., 1964-69; dir. admissions Wright State U., 1970-72, dean, 1971-77; v.p. acad. affairs Concord Coll., 1977-82; pres. Lock Haven U. Pa., 1982—2004, Eastern Mich. U., Ypsilanti, 2004—. Chmn. internat. affairs com. Am. Assn. State Colls. and Univs.; A.C.E. pres.'s commn. on internat. edn.; vice chmn. Clinton region Mellon Bank Ctr., 1987, chmn., 88, also bd. dirs.; bd. dirs. Lock Haven U.; cons. Ellis Assocs., Princeton, W.Va., 1980—82. Chmn. bd. Kirkmont Preschool, Beavercreek, Ohio, 1974-77, Beavercreek Library, 1976-77, Regional Edn. Service Agy., Beckley, W.Va., 1978-82; mem. N.E.-Midwest leadership Coun., 1989—. Recipient Disting. Alumnus award dept. edn. Ohio Wesleyan U., 1991; scholar Sohio Oil, 1953, Govt. of France, Paris, 1964, Shell Oil Co, 1967. Mem. Commn. State Coll. and Univ. Pres., Assn. State Colls. annd Univs., Clinton County C. of C. (pres.), Rotary (v.p., pres. elect, Citizen of Yr. award Lock Haven 1989), Ohio Wesleyan U. Alumni Assn. (Disting. Sesquicentennial Alumnus of the Edn. 1992), Phi Kappa Phi, Kappa Kappa Psi, Phi Delta Kappa, Kappa Delta Pi. Presbyterian. Office: Eastern Mich U 202 Welch Hall Ypsilanti MI 48197 Business E-Mail: cwillis@lhup.edu.

WILLIS, DAWN LOUISE, legal assistant, small business owner; b. Johnstown, Pa., Sept. 11, 1959; d. Kenneth William and Dawn Louise (Joseph) Hagins; m. Marc Anthony Ross, Nov. 30, 1984 (div.); m. Jerry Wayne Willis, Dec. 16, 1989 (div.). Grad. high sch., Sacramento, Calif. Legal sec. Wilcoxen & Callahan, Sacramento, 1979-87, paralegal, 1987-88; legal adminstr. Law Office Jack Vetter, 1989-99; legal asst. Foley & Lardner, 1999-2001; case mgr. Larry Lockshin, Esq. Law Corp., 2001—02; legal asst. Hunter, Richey, Di Benedetto & Eisenbeis, 2002—03; legal sec. Downey Brand LLP, 2003—. Vol. ARC, 1985, Spl. Olympics, 1997—, Grace Found. No. Calif., 2006—. Mem.: Sacramento Legal Secs. Assn. (pres. 2004—05, parliamentarian 2005—06). Democrat. Avocations: water sports, camping, reading, cooking. Office: Downey Brand LLP 555 Capitol Mall Sacramento CA 95814 Personal E-mail: doe9121@yahoo.com.

WILLIS, DONTRELLE, professional baseball player; b. Oakland, Calif., Jan. 12, 1982; Pitcher Fla. Marlins, Miami, 2003—. Mem. Team USA, World Baseball Classic, 2006. Named Nat. League Rookie of the Yr., 2003, California High School Player of the Year, 2000; named to, Nat. League All-Star Team, 2003, 2005. Achievements include member of World Series Champion Florida Marlins, 2003. Office: c/o Florida Marlines Pro Player Stadium 2267 Dan Marino Blvd Miami FL 33056

WILLIS, EDWARD OLIVER, management consultant, state agency administrator; b. St. Louis, Apr. 6, 1948; s. George Washington and Mary (Fantroy) W.; m. Jennifer Linnea Johnson, June 17, 1972 (div. Dec. 1991); children: Edward, Linnea, Eric; m. Linda Diane Clark, Aug. 8, 1992. AA, Am. River Coll., Sacramento, 1972; BS in BA, Calif. State U., Sacramento, 1974; MBA in Mgmt., Golden Gate U., San Francisco, 1978. Divsn. ops. supr., casualty claims investigator Allstate Ins. Co., Menlo Park, Sacramento, 1974-75; budget analyst Dept. Fin., State of Calif., Sacramento, 1975-77; assoc. govtl. program analyst Dept. Health, Medi-Cal Procurement Project, State of Calif., Sacramento, 1977-78; chief fiscal br. solid waste mgmt. bd. State of Calif., Sacramento, 1978-79, mgr. adminstrv. svcs. state lands commn., 1979-80, asst. to assoc. supt. pub. instrn. dept. edn., 1980-82, dep. dir. adminstrn. dept. fish and game, 1982-90, acting adminstr. office of oil spill prevention and response, 1990-92, dep. dir. adminstrn. dept. developmental svcs., 1992-93, dep. dir. adminstrv. svcs. program dept. toxic substances, 1993-94, asst. sec. policy devel. Calif. Environ. Protection Agy., 1994-95, chief dep. dir. Calif. Conservation Corps, 1995—98; owner, prin. cons. WW Assocs., 1994—; chief adminstrv. officer Santa Clara Valley Water Dist., San Jose, Calif., 1998—2002; interim exec. dir. Calif. Coun. Developmental Disabilities, Sacramento, 2005; prin. cons. CPS Human Resource, Sacramento, 2006. Part-time instr. Cosumnes River Coll., Sacramento, 1980-83. Author: Business Employment Equity Plan, 1994. Vol. United Way Campaign, United Negro Coll. Fund, Sacramento Children's Home, YMCA; 1st v.p. Nat. Black Child Devel. Inst., Sacramento, 1981-82; chmn. Black Adv. Com. to State Pers. Bd., 1984-85; mem. St. Francis of Assisi Sch. Bd., Sacrammento, 1996—, pres., 1991-93; bd. trustees Black Advocates in State Svc., 1992; bd. dirs. Nat. Forum for Black Pub. Adminstrs., Washington, 1993-04, 2d v.p., 2003-04; Little League coach, 1996—. With USAF, 1966-70. Decorated Air medals (4). Mem. Nat. Forum for Black Pub. Adminstrs. (Sacramento chpt. bd. dirs. 1993—, 1st v.p. 1990-91, pres. 1991-93), Am. Soc. Pub. Adminstrn. (Pub. Adminstr. of Yr.). Avocations: golf, softball. Home: 27214 N Makena Pl Peoria AZ 85383 Office Phone: 602-574-1831. Personal E-mail: edwardowillis@msn.com.

WILLIS, FRANK EDWARD, retired air force officer; b. Clinton, Ill., June 19, 1939; s. William Edward and Bernardine (Saveley) W.; m. Clarice Marie Hull, June 7, 1961; children: Michael, Steven, William. BS in Engring., USAF Acad., Colorado Springs, Colo., 1961; MA in Bus. Mgmt., U. Nebr., Offutt AFB Ext. Campus, 1973. Commd. 2d lt. USAF, 1961, advanced through grades to maj. gen., 1989; dep. comdr. 314th Tactical Airlift Group, Little Rock AFB, 1978-79, comdr., 1979-80; vice comdr. 374th Tactical Airlift Wing, Clark Air Base, The Philippines, 1980-81, comdr., 1981-83, 317th Tactical Airlift Wing, Pope AFB, N.C., 1983-84; vice comdr. Air Force Manpower and Pers. Ctr., Randolph AFB, Tex., 1984-85; comdt. Air Command and Staff Coll., Maxwell AFB, Ala., 1985-88; vice comdr. 22d Air Force, Travis AFB, Calif., 1988-89; dir. and dep. chief of staff for requirements Air Mobility and Mil. Airlift Command, Scott AFB, Ill., 1989-93; ret., 1993; co-owner retail hobby shop Tinker Town, Inc, St. Louis, 1994—2006; ret. Decorated D.S.M. (2), Legion of Merit (2), Air medal (7), Meritorious Svc. medal (2). Presbyterian. Avocations: electronics, computers, model building. Home: 14673 Air Garden Ln Colorado Springs CO 80921 Home Phone: 719-487-1907.

WILLIS, FRANK ROY, historian, educator; b. Prescot, Lancashire, Eng., July 25, 1930; s. Harry and Gladys Reid (Birchall) W.; children from previous marriage, Jane, Clare, Geoffrey. BA, Cambridge U., Eng., 1952, cert. in edn., 1955, diploma in devel. econs., 1974; PhD, Stanford U., Calif., 1959. Instr. Stanford U., 1959-60; from instr. to assoc. prof. history U. Wash., Seattle, 1960-64; assoc. prof. then prof. U. Calif., Davis, 1964—. Author: The French in Germany, 1962, France, Germany and the New Europe, 1945-1967, 1968, Europe in the Global Age, 1968, Italy Chooses Europe, 1971, Western Civilization: An Urban Perspective, 1973, World Civilizations, 1982, The French Paradox, 1982, Western Civilization: A Brief Introduction, 1987. Fellow, Rockefeller Found., Paris, 1962—63, Guggenheim Found., Rome, 1966—67, Social Scis. Rsch. Coun., Cambridge, 1973—74. Avocation: travel. Office: U Calif Dept History Davis CA 95616

WILLIS, HAROLD WENDT, SR., real estate developer; b. Marion, Ala., Oct. 7, 1927; s. Robert James and Della (Wendt) W.; m. Patsy Gay Bacon, Aug. 2, 1947 (div. Jan. 1975); children: Harold Wendt II, Timothy Gay, April Ann, Brian Tad, Suzanne Gail; m. Vernette Jacobson Osborne, Mar. 30, 1980 (div. 1984); m. Ofelia Alvarez, Sept. 23, 1984; children: Ryan Robert, Samantha Ofelia. Student, Loma Linda U., 1950, San Bernardino Valley Coll. Ptnr. Victoria Guernsey, San Bernardino, Calif., 1950-63, co-pres., 1963-74, pres., 1974—. Pres. Energy Delivery Sys., Food and Fuel, Inc. San Bernardino City water commr., 1964-98, pres. bd. water commrs., 1964-98; bd. councillors Loma Linda U., Calif., 1968-85, pres., 1971-74; active So. Calif. Strider's Relay Team (set indoor Am. and World record in 4x800 1992, sec distance medley relay US and World record for 60 yr. old 1992); pres. So. Calif. Striders Track and Field Club, 2001-02. Ensign, US Mcht. Marine, 1945-46. Mem. Calif. Dairy Industries Assn. (pres. 1963, 64), Liga Internat. (2d v.p. 1978, pres. 1982, 83), Socal Striders Masters Track & Field Club (pres. 2001-02). Seventh-day Adventist (deacon 1950-67). Avocation: pvt. pilot. Office: PO Box 5607 San Bernardino CA 92412-5607 Office Phone: 909-889-0828 ext 303. Personal E-mail: foodnfuel@verizon.net.

WILLIS, JERRY WELDON, computer systems educator, writer; b. Tuscumbia, Ala., Jan. 27, 1943; s. Elbert Cartr and Lavice Mae (McAlpin) W.; m. Dee Anna Smith, Mar. 28, 1987 (div. 1997); 1 child, Amy Elizabeth. BA, Union U., 1966; MA, PhD, U. Ala., 1970. Asst prof. U. Guelph, Ong., Can., 1972-74, U. Westrn Ont., London, 1974-76, U. B.C., Vancouver, 1976-78; prof. edn. Tex. Tech. U., Lubbock, 1978-87; dean Edn. and Home Econs. Miss. U. for Women, 1987-88; prof., program coord. Instrnl. Tech.-Ednl. Computing, E. Carolina U. Sch. Edn., 1988-91; prof., dir. ctr. for info. tech. and tchr. edn. Coll. of Edn., U. Houston, 1991-98; prof. curriculum and tech. Iowa State U., 1998—, dir., Ctr. for Tech., Learning and Tchg., 1999—. Pres. Willis Pub. Group; adv. Pres's. Panel on Tech. in Edn., 1995. Author: Peanut Butter and Jelly Guide to Computers, 1978 (Outstandig Computer Book, Am. Libr. Jour.); Nailing Jelly to a Tree, 1981, Computers for Everybody, 1981 (Outstanding Computer Book, Am. Libr. Jour.), Computers for People, 1982, Computers, Teaching and Learning, 1983, The Essential Commodore 128 User's Guide, 1986, The Essential Atari ST User's Guide, 1986, Super Calc 3: Learning, Mastering and Using, 1986, Using Super Calc 4, 1987, Desktop Publishing with your IBM PC and Compatible, 1987, Educational Computing: An Introduction, 1986, 96, Computer Simulations: A Guide to Educational Applications, 1986, Teaching with Artificial Reality, 1990, Works Tutorial and Applications, 1990, Computers, Reading and Language Arts, 1996; assoc. editor: Computers in the Schools; contbg. editor Educational Technology; also 34 other books and transls. in 9 langs.; contbr. chpt. to book. Mem. Internat. Soc. for Tech. in Edn., Assn. for Computing Machinery, Assn. for Tchr. Educators, Soc. for Info. Tech. and Tchr. Edn. (founder, pres. 1991-95, jour. co-editor 1991—, Outstanding Contbns. award 1996). Office: Iowa State U CTLT Coll of Edn Ames IA 50010 Home: 4949 Tulane Dr Baton Rouge LA 70808-4764

WILLIS, JOHN ALEXANDER, lawyer; b. Queens, NY, Feb. 3, 1966; s. John Joseph Willis and Dorothy Elizabeth (Savides) White. BA, SUNY, Stony Brook, 1989; JD, Nova Southeastern Law Ctr., 1994. Bar: Fla. 1994, U.S. Ct. Appeals (11th cir.) 1994, N.Y. 1995, U.S. Dist. Ct. (so. dist.) Fla. 1995, U.S. Supreme Ct., 1999. Acct. coord. Met. Life Ins. Co., Hauppauge, NY, 1989—91; cert. legal intern Palm Beach County State's Atty Office, West Palm Beach, Fla., 1994; assoc. David & French, P.A., Boca Raton, Fla., 1994—2000, Baker & Zimmerman, P.A., Boca Raton, 2000—01; ptnr. Law Offices of John A. Willis, P.A., Boca Raton, 2001—. Mem.: ATLA, Palm Beach County Trial Lawyers Assn., Broward County Bar Assn., Palm Beach County Bar Assn., South Palm Beach County Bar Assn., Acad. Fla. Trial Lawyers, Million Dollar Advocates Forum. Avocations: golf, computers, softball. Office: Law Offices of John A Willis 5355 Town Center Rd #801 Boca Raton FL 33486 Office Phone: 561-417-7033. E-mail: jawillis@willislaw.com.

WILLIS, JOHN PATRICK, chemist; b. Albany, NY, Mar. 10, 1947; s. John James and Mary Catherine (Varden) W.; m. Tientje Jane Dirzuweit, July 22, 1972. BS, Iona Coll., 1969; MS, SUNY, Oswego, 1974; PhD, U. Conn., 1977. Assoc. prodn. chemist Winthrop Labs., Rensselaer, N.Y., 1970-72; rsch. chemist Uniroyal, Inc., Middlebury, Conn., 1977-79; postdoctoral rschr. U. Minn., Mpls., 1979-80; mgr. chem. rsch. Nova Biomed Corp., Newton, Mass., 1980-83; founder, chmn. Ilex Corp., Marlboro, Mass., 1983-87; med. cons., 1987-88; founder T.J. Assocs., Biomed. Cons., 1987-89; v.p., chief oper. officer Sharon Drive Corp., Westlake, Ohio, 1988-93; dir. rsch. Medisense, Inc., Waltham, Mass., 1993-97; pres., CEO Teknow Source Inc., Shirley, Mass., 1997—2002; chmn., CEO North Country Naturals, Inc., Shirley, Mass., 2000—05; tech. dir. biotech. Mohawk Innovative Tech, Inc., Albany, NY, 2001—04; rsch. prof. dept. chemistry and chem. biology Rensselaer Polytechnic Inst., Troy, NY, 2004—05; founder, chmn. Ultradian Diagnostics LLC, 2004—. Mem. adv. bd. Clin. Lab. Practice, Mass. Dept. Pub. Health, 1986-87, 128 Entrepreneurs' Ctr., Waltham, Mass., 1986-88; mem. tech. adv. coun. Edison Biotech. Ctr., Cleve., 1988-90. U. Conn. Rsch. Found. fellow, 1976. Fellow Am. Inst. Chemists; mem. Am. Chem. Soc., Electrochem. Soc., Am. Assn. Clin. Chemistry, N.Y. Acad. Scis., Sigma Xi, Phi Kappa Phi, Phi Lambda Upsilon. Achievements include research in bioelectrochemistry, organic electrochemistry and biosensors; patents in field. Office: Ultradian Diagnostics LLC 5 Univ Pl Ste A324 Rensselaer NY 12144 Office Phone: 518-618-0046. Personal E-mail: jwillis@tiac.net.

WILLIS, JOHN T., former secretary of state; b. Nov. 1, 1946; m. Kathy S. Mangan; children: Karen M., James T. BA in Econs. cum laude, Bucknell U., 1968; JD, Harvard Law Sch., 1971. Clk. Army Ct. of Mil. Rev., 1971-74; legal asstance officer Aberdeen Proving Grounds, 1974-75; pvt. practice atty. Westminster, Balt. City, Md., 1975-90; chief of staff County Exec. of Prince George's County, 1990-94; apptd. sec. of state State of Md., 1995—2003. Adj. prof. McDaniel Coll.(formerly Western Md. Coll.), 1979—; past chmn. Gov.'s Commn. on Md. Mil. Monuments; adv. bd. U. Balt.'s Schaefer Ctr. for Pub. Policy; adj. prof. govt. and pub. adminstrn. U. Balt. Author: Presidential Elections in Maryland, 1984; contbg. author: Western Maryland: A Profile, 1980, Justice and the Military, 1972; contbr. articles to profl. jours.; editor: The Advocate, 1973-74. Vice-chmn. Md. Dem. Party, 1987-89, mem. various coms. and del. to Dem. Nat. Convs., 1976-2000; former chair Dem. Secs. of State. Judge advocate gen. corps U.S. Army, 1968-75. Mem. Md. Bar Assn., Carroll County Bar Assn., Md. Hist. Soc., Carroll County Arts Coun. (past pres.). Democrat. Office: U Balt 1420 N Charles St Baltimore MD 21201 E-mail: jwillis@ubalt.edu.

WILLIS, JUDY ANN, lawyer; b. Hartford, Conn., July 7, 1949; d. Durward Joseph and Angeline Raphael (Riccardo) Willis. BA, Ctrl. Conn. State U., 1971; postgrad., U. Conn. Law Sch., 1976—77; JD, Boston Coll., 1979. Bar: Mass. 1979, U.S. Dist. Ct. Mass. 1980, Calif. 1990. Sr. atty. H.P. Hood Inc., Charleston, Mass., 1979-83; v.p. law Parker Bros., Beverly, Mass., 1983-89; sr. v.p. bus. affairs Mattel, Inc., El Segundo, Calif., 1989—. Office: Mattel Inc M1-1112 333 Continental Blvd El Segundo CA 90245-5012 E-mail: judy.willis@Mattel.com.

WILLIS, KEVIN, airport administrator; Mgr. Atlantic City Internat. Airport, until 1996; compliance specialist FAA, Washington, 1996—. Office: FAA Airport Safety and Compliance Branch AAS-310 800 Independence Ave SW Washington DC 20591-0001 Business E-Mail: kevin.willis@faa.gov.

WILLIS, NORMAN HUNT, author, writer, director, producer; b. Ft. Worth, Feb. 11, 1934; s. Ray Logan and Ima H. Willis; m. Andrea Marie Laurent, June 11, 1934 (div. Aug. 1981); children: Christi, Michelle, Leslie; m. Mary Theresa Ciociola, Feb. 19, 1945. Student, Tex. Christian U., 1951-52, San Diego State Coll., 1953, George Washington U., 1955-56. Audio-visual specialist The Asphalt Inst., College Park, Md., 1956-58; film specialist GE, Evendale, Ohio, 1958-60; scriptwriter Scripts by Oeveste Granducci, Washington, 1960-61; supr. med. films Wyeth Labs., Radnor, Pa., 1961-66; exec. prodr. H.G. Peters & Co., Primose, Pa., 1966-68; pres. Intermedica, Inc., Wayne, Pa., 1968-80, Intermedia Comms., Inc., Paoli, Pa., 1980-91; media cons. Paoli, 1991-96; sr. med. writer Otsuka Am., 1997-2000; mgr. Quintiles Inc., 1997-2000; dir. clin. comm. Pfizer La Jolla, 2000—03; dir. med. writing Ligand Pharms., Inc., 2003—07; med. writing cons. San Diego, 2007—. Author: (book) Basic Infant Nutrition, 1964; dir. (film) Drivin' and Drugs, 1968 (CINE Golden Eagle award); writer, dir., prodr. (video) Quinolones: Mechanisms of Action, 1986 (Silver medal N.Y. Internat. Film and TV Festival), (film) Sterilization Procedures for the Medical Office, 1963 (Golden Eagle award), Tracy, 1978 (Silver medal); dir. prodr. (film) Your Life and the Pill, 1975 (Silver medal, CINE Golden Eagle award). With USN, 1952-56, Korea. Mem. Internat. Interactive Comms. Soc., Am. Med. Writers Assn., Am. Mensa, Drug Info. Assn., Regulatory Affairs Profl. Soc. Avocations: tennis, noncommercial photography. Home: 11301 E San Raphael Dr San Diego CA 92130 E-mail: normanhw@aol.com.

WILLIS, PAUL ALLEN, retired librarian, retired dean; b. Floyd County, Ind., Oct. 1, 1941; s. Clarence Charles and Dorothy Jane (Harritt) Willis; m. Barbara Marcum, June 15, 1963; children: Mark, Sally. AB, U. Ky., 1963, JD, 1969; MLS, U. Md., 1966. Cataloger Libr. Congress, Washington, 1963; head descriptive cataloging br. Sci. and Tech. Info. Facility NASA, College Park, Md., 1963-66; law libr., prof. law U. Ky., Lexington, 1966-73, dir. librs., 1973—2002, acting dean Coll. Libr. Sci., 1975-76, 88; dean librs. U. SC, Columbia, 2002—07; ret. Exec. sec. Ky. Jud. Retirement and Removal Commn., 1977-81; adv. com. Ctr. Jud. Conduct Orgns., Am. Judicature Soc., Chgo., 1979-81; chmn. Southeastern Libr. Network, Atlanta, 1998-99; exec. com. Ky. Hist. Soc., 1984-88; mem. Ky. Adv. Coun. on Librs., 1985-2002, adv. com. Online Computer Libr. Ctr., 1986-90; cons. SE Consortium Internat. Devel., U. Sriwijaya, Palembang, Sumatera, Indonesia, 1987-88, Hanoi U. Tech., 1999, 2001, Vietnam Nat. U., Ho Chi Minh City, 1999 Sr. fellow, UCLA, 1982. Mem. Assn. Southeastern Rsch. Librs. (chair 1986-88, bd. dirs. 2002-), Assn. Rsch. Librs. (bd. dirs. 2002—05). Personal E-mail: willis@scoast.net.

WILLIS, RALPH HOUSTON, mathematics professor; b. McMinnville, Tenn., Dec. 26, 1942; s. Carl Houston and Carrie Lee (Hill) Willis; m. Gayle Catherine Celestin, June 29, 1973 (div. Apr. 1985); m. Velma Inez Church, Aug. 10, 1985; 1 stepchild, Bobbie Lynn White Buckner. BS in Math., Mid. Tenn. State U., 1964, MA in Math., 1966. Cert. secondary edn. tchr. Instr. depts. math. and computer sci. Western Carolina U., Cullowhee, NC, 1968-73, asst. prof., 1973-83, assoc. prof., 1983—. Co-founder State Math Contest Com., 1977—78, mem. western regional rep. exec. steering com., recording sec., 1978—; co-founder NC Math. League, 1981—82, mem. problem writing com., 1981—84. Editor: (newsletter) Abelian Grapevine-Secondary Math., 1970—88, The Child Math.-Elem.-Mid. Grade Math., 1972—78; mem. editl. bd. The Centroid, 1995—2000; contbr. articles to profl. jours. Coord. state road paving project Univ. Heights Cmty. Devel. Orgn., 1974—76, chmn. founder cmty. watch, 1978—79, coord. pub. water sys. upgrade project, 1980—84; founder, coord., bd. dirs., trustee Hunerwadle Cmty. Cemetery Assn., Beersheba, Tenn., 1983—; co-founder NC State Math. Contest and Contest Network, 1977—78; founder., dir., coord. HS Math. Contest, founder., coord. math. dept. student awards program Western Carolina U., 1970—, solicitor-coord. Math. Contest Scholarship Program, 1971—82, initiator-coord. math. dept.'s vis. spkr. program, 1974—77, founder., faculty sponsor NC Coun. Tchrs. Math. Student Affiliate. Recipient Hon. Mention NC Gov.'s award for Excellence, 1991, Exeplary Site award, State Math. Contest Com., 1990, Paul A. Reid Disting. Svc. award for Faculty, 1991, Coll. Arts and Scis. Disting. Career Svc. award, 2003. Mem.: NC Coun. Tchrs. Math. (state bd. dirs., historian 1993—98, mem. editl. bd. Centroid 1995—2000), Nat. Coun. Tchrs. Math. (W. W. Rankin award 2001), Kappa Mu Epsilon, Phi Kappa Phi. Avocations: genealogy, gardening, military history, model building, die cast model collector. Office: Western Carolina U Math Dept Stillwell Bldg Cullowhee NC 28723

WILLIS, RALPH WALKER, retired firefighter; b. Redondo Beach, Calif., Nov. 21, 1921; s. Achatius Walker and Elizabeth Margaret (Dehm) Willis; m. Helen Elizabeth Willis, May 18, 1946 (dec. June 2006). Grad. h.s., San Diego. Firefighter Richmond (Calif.) Fire Dept., 1946-67; pres. Firefighters Union IAFF AFL CIO, 1964—67. Author: Sansei Banzai, 1986, War and Rememberance Revisted, 1988, The Eternal Regiment, 1995, My Life as a Jarhead, 1999 (The Ernie Pyle WWII Roundtable award). Sgt. USMC, 1941-45. Mem.: VFW (life), American's for Historical Accuracy, Iwo Jima Survivors Assn. American Independent Party. Avocations: travel, painting, writing. Home: 579 Camino Mercado # 218 Arroyo Grande CA 93420 Personal E-mail: jarheadrw@charter.net.

WILLIS, RUTH, freelance/self-employed theater director, actress; b. Toledo, Nov. 7, 1932; d. Thomas LeRoy and Ruth Caroline (Ehmann) Ramsey; m. Charles Perrin Willis, Nov. 14, 1956; children: David, Laura. BE cum laude, U. Toledo, 1954. Grade sch. tchr. Toledo Pub. Schs., 1954—61; acting tchr. Cin. Children's Home, 1958—59, Contemporary Arts Mus., Houston, 1972, Jewish Cmty. Ctr., 1969—72; dir. Exptl. Wing Country Playhouse, 1968—72; mem. Actor's Studio Ariz. State U., Phoenix, 1980—81; dir. Plays for Living Family and Children's Svcs., Pitts., 1984—87; adult acting tchr. Point Park Coll. Conservatory, 1987—2001; artistic dir. Open Stage Theatre, 1991—. Dir.: (over 100 major prodns.); actor: (plays) The Women (named Best Actress, Assn. Cmty. Theatres, Cin.), The Sleeping Prince (named Best Actress, Country Playhouse, Houston), Sweet Bird of Youth (named Best Actress, Stagebrush Theatre, Scottsdale, Ariz.); dir.: Candida (named Best Dir.), Lucia Mad (Best Top Ten Evenings of Theatre, Pitts. Gazette, 1997). Gen. bd. mem. Mariemont Players, Cin., 1958—60, Phoenix Children's Theatre, 1978—81; exec. bd. mem., sec. Phoenix Theatre, 1978—79, exec. bd. mem., v.p., 1980—81; founder Open Stage Theatre, Pitts., 1991. Recipient Svc. award, Phoenix Little Theatre Bd. Dirs., 1981. Mem.: Charlevoix Garden Club, Nat. Soc. Arts and Letters, Pi Epsilon Delta. Avocations: piano, painting, yoga, gardening, decorating.

WILLIS, SELENE LOWE, electrical engineer, application developer, consultant, information technology manager; b. Birmingham, Ala., Mar. 4, 1958; d. Lewis Russell and Bernice (Wilson) Lowe; m. André Maurice Willis, June 12, 1987. BSEE, Tuskegee U., Ala., 1980; postgrad., UCLA, 1993—94, postgrad., 1996, postgrad., 1999. Component engr. Hughes Aircraft Corp., El Segundo, Calif., 1980—82; reliability and lead engr. Aero Jet Electro Sys. Corp., Azusa, Calif., 1982—84; sr. component engr. Rockwell Internat. Corp., Anaheim, Calif., 1984, Gen. Data Comm. Corp., Danbury, Conn., 1984—85; design engr. Lockheed Missile and Space Co., Sunnyvale, Calif., 1985—86; mgr. property Penmar Mgmt. Co., LA, 1987—88; aircraft mechanic McDonnell Douglas Corp., Long Beach, Calif., 1989—93; unix sys. adminstrn. Santa Cruz Ops., Calif., 1994; bus. ops. mgr., cons. New Start, Santa Monica, Calif., 1995; software developer Nat. Advancement Corp., Calif., 1996; entrepreneur Datatronics, Calif., 1996—; exec. v.p., owner LA Network Engr. Jet Propulsion Lab., 1996—2000; software engr., network engr., application engr., lead engr. Jet Propulsion Lab, Pasadena, Calif., 1996—2000, project mgr., 1999—2000, lead UNIX engr. LA, 1998—2000; mgmt. sys. engr. Tech. Jet Propulsion Lab., Pasadena, 1998—2000, mgr. project element, 1999—; cons., sr. project mgr. Amgen, Thousand Oaks, Calif., 1999—2000, sr. sys. engr., 2000—; mgr. project So. Calif. Edison, 2002—03, mgr., settlements, 2003—, mgr. energy supply and mgmt., 2003—05, mgr. structured contracts, 2005—. Cons., software designer Kern and Wooley, atty., Westwood, Calif., 1995; software developer Nat. Advancement Corp., Santa Ana, Calif., 1995—. Vol. Mercy Hosp. and Children's Hosp., Birmingham, Ala. 1972-74; mrm. LA Gospel Messengers, 1982-84, West Angeles Ch. of God and Christ, LA, 1990; cons., mgr. bus. ops. New Start, Santa Monica Bay Area Drug Abuse Coun., Calif., 1995; vol. Pres. Clinton's Going-To-Coll. Program through UCLA, 1997—; chair UCLA Transfer Coll. Scholarship Program, 1998-99. Scholar Bell Lab., 1976-80, UCLA, 1994, Gem Award, UTA, 1999, Outstanding Group Award, JPL, 1999. Mem. IEEE, ASME, Aerospace and Aircraft Engr., So. Calif. Profl. Engring. Assn., Tuskegee U. Alumni Assn., UCLA Alumni Assn. (scholarship and adv. com.), Eta Kappa Nu, Christian Ch. Avocations: piano, computers, softball, real estate.

WILLIS, SOLOMON LEE, mathematics educator; s. Eddie and Brenda Willis. BS in Math., Gardner Webb U., 1999; MA in Math. Edn., Appalachian State U., 2004. Cert. tchr. NC. HS math. tchr. Gaston Day Sch., Gastonia, NC, 2000—06; coll. math. tchr. Cleve. CC, Shelby, NC, 2002—. T-cubed regional instr. Tex. Instruments, Dallas, 2003—. Dir., organizer talent show Gaston Day Sch.; educator adv. bd. Discovery Pl., Charlotte, NC, 2003—04. MELT scholar, Appalachian State U., 2002—04, Te@ch Tech. grantee, Best Buy, 2004. Mem.: Math. Assn. Am. (assoc.), Nat. Coun. Tchrs. Math. (assoc. Trust Fund scholar 2002—03). Home Phone: 704-435-8337; Office Phone: 704-484-4016. Personal E-mail: solomon.willis@yahoo.com.

WILLIS, WALTER BRUCE (BRUCE WILLIS), actor, vocalist; b. Idar-Oberstein, Fed. Republic Germany, Mar. 19, 1955; came to U.S., 1957; s. David and Marlene Willis; m. Demi Moore, Nov. 21, 1987 (div. Oct. 18, 2000); children: Rumer Glenn, Scout Larue, Tallulah Belle. Student, Montclair State Coll.; studied with Stella Adler. Mem. First Amendment Comedy Theatre. Actor: (off-Broadway prodns.) Heaven and Earth, 1977, Fool for Love, 1984, The Bullpen, The Bayside Boys, The Ballad of Railroad William; (films) Prince of the City, 1981, The Verdict, 1982, Blind Date, 1987, Sunset, 1988, Die Hard, 1988, In Country, 1989, (voice only) Look Who's Talking, 1989, Die Hard 2: Die Harder, 1990, Bonfire of the Vanities, 1990, Mortal Thoughts, 1991, Hudson Hawk, 1991, Billy Bathgate, 1991, The Last Boy Scout, 1991, Death Becomes Her, 1992, Striking Distance, 1993, Color of Night, 1994, North, 1994, Pulp Fiction, 1994, Nobody's Fool, 1994, Die Hard With a Vengeance, 1995, 12 Monkeys, 1995, Four Rooms, 1995, Last Man Standing, 1996, The Jackal, 1997, The Fifth Element, 1997, Mercury Rising, 1998, Armageddon, 1998, The Siege, 1998, Breakfast of Champions, 1999, The Sixth Sense, 1999, The Story of Us, 1999, The Kid, 2000, Unbreakable, 2000, Bandits, 2001, Harts War, 2002, Grand Champion, 2002, True West, 2002, Tears of the Sun, 2003, (voice only) Rugrats Go Wild!, 2003, Charlie's Angels: Full Throttle, 2003, The Whole Ten Yards, 2004, Hostage, 2005, Sin City, 2005, Alpha Dog, 2006, Lucky Number Slevin, 2006, (voice only) Over the Hedge, 2006, Fast Food Nation, 2006, The Astronaut Farmer, 2007, Grindhouse (Planet Terror segment), 2007, Perfect Stranger, 2007, Live Free or Die Hard, 2007; actor, prodr. The Whole Nine Yards, 2000, 16 Blocks, 2006; exec. prodr.: Crocodile Hunter: The Collision Course, 2002; (TV movies) True West, 2002; (TV appearances) Miami Vice, The Twilight Zone; (TV series) Moonlighting, 1985-89 (People's Choice award 1986, Emmy award 1987, Golden Globe award 1987); singer (albums) The Return of Bruno, 1987, If It Don't Kill You, It Just Makes You Stronger, 1989; (TV spl.) The Return of Bruno, 1986 Named Internat. Broadcasting Man of Yr. Hollywood Radio and TV Soc.; recipient Star on Walk of Fame, 1998, People Choice award, 2000, Order of Arts & Letters, Govt. France, 2005 Office: Creative Artists Agency c/o Arnold Rifkin 9830 Wilshire Blvd Beverly Hills CA 90212 *

WILLIS, WILLIAM DARRELL, JR., neuroscientist, educator; b. Dallas, July 19, 1934; s. William Darrell and Dorcas (Chamberlain) W.; m. Jean Colette Schini, May 28, 1960 (dec. Jan. 1, 2006); 1 child, Thomas Darrell. BS, BA, Tex. A&M U., 1956; MD, U. Tex. Southwestern Med. Sch., 1960; PhD, Australian Nat. U., 1963. Postdoctoral research fellow Nat. Inst. Neurol. Diseases and Blindness, Australian Nat. U., 1960-62, Istituto di Fisiologia, U. Pisa, Italy, 1962-63; from asst. prof. to prof. anatomy, chmn. dept. U. Tex. Southwestern Med. Sch., Dallas, 1963-70; chief lab. comparative neurobiology Marine Biomed. Inst., prof. anatomy and physiology U. Tex. Med. Br., Galveston, 1970—, dir. Marine Biomed. Inst., 1978—2004, chmn. dept. anatomy and neurosci., 1986—2004, Ashbel Smith prof., 1986-95, Cecil and Ida Green prof., 1995—. Mem. neurology B study sect. NIH, 1968-72, chmn., 1970-72, mem. neurol. disorders Program Project rev. com., 1972-76, Nat. Adv. Neurol. and Communicative Disorders and Stroke Coun., 1987-90; tng. grant com. Nat. Inst. of Neurol. Disorders and Stroke, 1994-98. Mem. editl. bd. Neurosci., Exptl. Neurology, 1970-90, Archives Italienne Biologie, Neurosci. Letters, 1976-92; chief editor Jour. Neurophysiology, 1978-83, Pain, 1986-89; assoc. editor Jour. Neurosci., 1986-89, editor-in-chief, 1993-94; sect. editor Exptl. Brain Rsch., 1990-92, 1995-2004. Mem. AAAS, Am. Assn. Anatomists (exec. com. 1980-86), Am. Pain Soc. (pres. 1982-83), Internat. Assn. Study Pain (coun. 1984-90), Am. Physiol. Soc., Soc. Exptl. Biol. Medicine, Soc. Neurosci. (pres. 1984-85), Internat. Brain Rsch. Orgn., Cajal Club, Sigma Xi, Alpha Omega Alpha. Home: 2925 Beluche Dr Galveston TX 77551-1511 Office: U Tex Med Br 301 University Blvd Galveston TX 77555-1069 Office Phone: 409-772-2103. Business E-Mail: wdwillis@utmb.edu.

WILLIS, WILLIAM ERVIN, lawyer; b. Huntington, W.Va., Oct. 11, 1926; s. Asa Hannon and Mae (Davis) W.; m. Joyce Litteral, Sept. 1, 1949; children: Kathryn Cunningham, Anne Dresser, William. Student, Ind. U., 1944, NYU, 1945; AB, Marshall U., 1948; JD, Harvard, 1951; LHD (hon.), Marshall U., 1997. Bar: N.Y. 1952. Pvt. practice, NYC, 1951—; ptnr. Sullivan & Cromwell, 1960-94, sr. counsel, 1994—. Lectr. Practising Law Inst., 1963—; trustee Fed. Bar Council, 1968-72; mem. 2d Circuit Commn. on Reduction Burdens and Costs Civil Litigation, 1977-82. Co-author Doing Business in America; contbr. Edn. Civil Practice Law Rev. Forms and Guidance for Lawyers, also articles to legal jours. Mem. panel arbitrators Pub. Resources; trustee Tenafly (N.J.) Nature Ctr., 1994—2001, pres., 1997—2001; bd. dirs. Soc Yeager Scholars, Marshall U., Huntington, 1995—2004, v.p., 2001—04, pres., 2004—. With AUS, 1944—46. Fellow Am. Coll. Trial Lawyers, Am. Bar Found.; mem. ABA (standing com. on fed. judiciary 1987-95, chair 1992-93, 94-95), N.Y. Bar Assn. (chmn. antitrust sect. 1976-77, exec. com. 1976-83), Assn. Bar City of N.Y. (chmn. profl. discipline com. 1983-86, chmn. ethics 2000 com. 1999—2003, judicial conduct 2000—), Fed. Bar Coun. (trustee 1969-72), Am. Judicature Soc., Am. Arbitration Assn. (panel arbitrators), N.Y. Law Inst., N.Y. County Lawyers, Ins. Jud. Adminstrn., India House. Home: 190 Tekening Dr Tenafly NJ 07670-1219 Also: Otterhole Rd West Milford NJ 07480 Office: Sullivan & Cromwell 125 Broad St 28th Fl New York NY 10004-2498 Business E-Mail: wewillis@nysbar.com.

WILLISCROFT, ROBERT G., retired military officer, writer; s. Paul and Gladys Williscroft; m. D. Christine Leidl, 1964 (div. 1991); m. Viviana Amzel, 1994 (div. 2001); 1 child, Jason. BSc in Oceanography and Meteorology, U. Wash., Seattle, 1969; MSc in Engring., PhD in Engring., Calif. Coast U., Santa Ana, 1983. Qualified in submarines - enlisted USN, 1965, qualified in submarines - commd. USN, 1970, cert. saturation diving officer USN, 1973, Scuba diving instr. Nat. Assn. Underwater Instrs., 1979. Enlisted USN, 1963, advanced through grades to, ret., 1986; sonar technician USN — USS John Marshall (SSBN-611B), Groton, Conn., 1963—66; a. weapons officer, comm officer USN — USS Von Steuben (SSBN-632B), Charleston, SC, 1970—72; navigator, ops. officer USN — USS Ortolan (ASR-22), Phila., 1973—74; ops. officer, 1st lt. USN — USS Pigeon (ASR-21), San Diego, 1974—76; officer in charge, test ops. group USN — Submarine Devel. Group One, San Diego, 1976—77; officer in charge, West Coast NOAA diving program NOAA Commd. Corps, Seattle, 1978—80, officer in charge, East and Gulf Coast NOAA diving program Norfolk, Va., 1980—81, officer in charge, West Coast and Pacific NOAA diving program Seattle, 1983—86; officer in charge, environ. rsch. labs geophys. monitoring program NOAA/NSF, Amundson-Scott South Pole Station, 1981—82; firemarshall NSF, Amundson-Scott South Pole Station, Antarctica, 1981—82; CEO Romar Books, Seattle, 1986—91, Manuscripts Internat., Dayton, Wash., 1986—91; chief staff officer Hyperbaric Technologies, National City, Calif., 1991—93; series 7 stockbroker Morgan Stanley, LA, 1997—98. Author: Basic Pit Diver, 1983 (YMCA Dive Book award, 1983), Advanced PIT Diver, 1984, You Can Dive, 1984, The Chicken Little Agenda - Debunking Experts' Lies, 2006; contbr.; sr. editor: online periodical DefenseWatch; editor: (periodical) San Diego Mensan, L.A. Mentary, Adventurers' Club of Los Angeles News; contbr. various online periodicals. V.p. C. of C., Dayton, 1987—88; state committeeman Rep. Party, Dayton, 1988—90. Decorated Good Conduct medal USN, Nat. Svc. Def. medal, Fleet Ballistic Missile Submarine Patrol Pin (8), Unit Citation (2) NOAA, Antarctic Svc. medal with Winterover Pin; named Diver of Yr., Wash. State Scuba Diving Coun., 1987—88; recipient Spl. Achievement award, US Dept. Commerce, 1982; Navy Enlisted Sci. Edn. Program scholar, USN, 1966—69. Mem.: Kiwanis Internat. (1st vp 1988—89), Adventurers' Club LA (bd.mem., editor 2005—07), Mensa (life; mag. editor 1992—2002), Free and Accepted Order of Masons (32° Scottish Rite Mason 1988). Independent. Achievements include development of Scuba equipment for diving in highly contaminated or radioactive water; Scuba equipment for under-ice diving in the Arctic; atmospheric research at the Geographic South Pole for 13 months; biological baseline research in Arctic for three years; research in feasibility of commercial mining of manganese nodules for a year in Pacific equatorial waters; participated in saturation diving espionage activities during Cold War. Avocations: diving, exploring, writing, travel, space travel. Home: PO Box 1087 Studio City CA 91614 Home Phone: 818-613-9445. Personal E-mail: rgw@argee.net.

WILLISCROFT-BARCUS, BEVERLY RUTH, retired lawyer; b. Conrad, Mont., Feb. 24, 1945; d. Paul A. and Gladys L. (Buck) W.; m. Kent J. Barcus, Oct. 1984. BA in Music, So. Calif. Coll., 1967; JD, John F. Kennedy U., 1977. Bar: Calif. 1977. Elem. tchr., Sunnyvale, Calif., 1968-72; legal sec., legal asst. various law firms, 1972-77; assoc. Neil D. Reid, Inc., San Francisco, 1977-79; sole practice Concord, Calif., 1979—2004. Exam. grader Calif. Bar, 1979-2001; real estate broker, 1980-88; tchr. real estate King Coll., Concord, 1979-80; judge pro-tem Mcpl. Ct., 1981-93; mem. Stage Right Drama Group, Concord, Calif., 1999—; lectr. in adoption law. Co-author: Adoption Law in California, Adoption Practice, Procedure and Pitfalls in California; lectr. in field. Bd. dirs. Contra Costa Musical Theatre, Inc., 1978-82, v.p. adminstrn., 1980-81, v.p. prodn., 1981-82; mem. community devel. adv. com. City of Concord, 1981-83, vice chmn., 1982-83, mem. status of women com., 1980-81, mem. redevel. adv. com., 1984-86, planning commnr. 1986-92, chmn., 1990; mem. exec. bd. Mt. Diablo coun. Boy Scouts Am., 1981-85; bd. dirs. Pregnancy Ctrs. Contra Costa County, 1991-2001, chmn., 1993-2000 Mem. Concord C. of C. (bd. dirs., chmn. govt. affairs com. 1981-83, v.p. 1985-87, pres. 1988-89, Bus. Person of Yr. 1986), Calif. State Bar (chmn. adoptions subcom. north, 1994), Contra Costa County Bar Assn., Christian Legal Soc., Todos Santos Bus. and Profl. Women (co-founder, pres. 1983-84, pub. rels. chmn. 1982-83, Woman of Achievement 1980, 81), Soroptimists (fin. sec. 1980-81). Office: PO Box 981 Pittsburg CA 94565-0098

WILLISON, BRUCE GRAY, dean; b. Riverside, Calif., Oct. 16, 1948; s. Walter G. and Dorothy (Phillips) W.; m. Gretchen A. Illig; children: Patrick, Bruce G., Kristen, Jeffery, Geoffrey, Lea. BA in econs., UCLA, 1970; MBA, U. So. Calif., 1973. With Bank of Am., LA, 1973-79; joined First Interstate Bancorp, LA, 1979, dir. mktg., 1981, sr. v.p., mem. mng. com., 1981—82; sr. v.p. trust divsn. First Interstate Bank of Calif., LA, 1982—83, exec. v.p. world banking group, 1983-85; pres., CEO First Interstate Bank Ltd., LA, 1985-86; chmn., CEO First Interstate Bank Oreg., Portland, 1986-91; chmn., pres., CEO First Interstate Bank of Calif., LA, 1991—96; vice chmn. First Interstate Bancorp, LA, 1995—96; pres., COO H.F. Ahmanson and Co., Irwandale, Calif., 1996—99; dean UCLA Anderson Sch. Mgmt., 1999—2006, John E. Anderson chair in mgmt. Bd. dirs. IndyMac Bancorp., Inc., Sun America, Inc., Health Net Inc., 2000—, Homestore, Inc., 2002—. Bd. dirs. United Way of LA, Operation Hope Inc. Served to lt. USN, 1970—72. *

WILLKE, THEODORE LAWRENCE, research facility director; b. Indpls., Dec. 27, 1944; s. Myron Gustav and Freda (Payne) W.; m. Sue Ellen Koenig, Aug. 1, 1976; children: Theodore II, Chad, Bradford. BS in Astronautical Engring. & Engring. Sci., U.S. Air Force Acad., 1967; MS in Nuclear Engring., MIT, 1968; MBA, U. Dayton, 1971; PhD in Indsl. and Sys. Engring., Ohio State U., 1974. Registered profl. engr., Ohio, Wash. Sys. engr. Battelle, Columbus, Ohio, 1974-77; sect. mgr. Pacific N.W. Labs., Richland, Wash., 1977-82; dir. tech. assessment Gas Rsch. Inst., Chgo., 1982-84, divsn. dir. adminstrn., 1984-86, v.p., 1987-97; dir., CEO Carnegie Mellon Rsch. Inst., Pitts., 1997—2001; pres. TLW Solutions Inc., Pitts., 2002—. Mem. PRC Internat., Arlington, Va., 1994-97; chmn. Internat. Gas Union Com., Chgo., 1994-97; adj. prof. mech. engring. U. Wash., 1979; vis. disting. svc. prof. Carnegie Mellon U., 2001-02. Contbr. articles to profl. jours. including Pub. Utilities Fortnightly, Internat. Jour. Sys. Sci. Mem. tech. adv. com. pipeline safety U.S. Dept. Transp., 1996—; mem. Leadership Pitts. XVI, 1999-2000. Capt. USAF, 1967-71. Recipient award NSPE, 1975. Mem. ASME (mem. bd. on rsch. and tech. devel. 1988-90), AAAS. Achievements include patent in field. Office: TLW Solutions Inc One Oxford Ctr 37th Fl Pittsburgh PA 15219

WILLKE, THOMAS ALOYS, academic administrator, statistician, educator; b. Rome City, Ind., Apr. 22, 1932; s. Gerard Thomas and Marie Margaret (Wuennemann) W.; m. Geraldine Ann Page, Dec. 28, 1954; children: Richard, Susan, Donald, Jeanne, Mary, Kathleen. AB, Xavier U., 1954; MS, Ohio State U., 1956, PhD, 1960. Sr. engr. N.Am. Aviation, Columbus, Ohio, 1959-60; instr. math. Ohio State U., Columbus, 1960-61, assoc. prof., 1966-70, assoc. prof. statistics, 1970-72, prof., 1972-73, dir. stats. lab., 1971-73, vice provost Arts and Scis., 1973-86, acting dean Univ. Coll., 1983-86, dean undergrad. studies Arts and Scis., 1986-87; prof. math. scis. Otterbein coll., Westerville, Ohio, 1987-97, chmn. dept. math. scis., 1988-96; rsch. mathematician U.S. Nat. Bur. Standards, Washington, 1961-66; asst. prof. math. U. Md., College Park, 1963-66; prof. statistics, undergrad. dean Ohio State U., 1987—; prof. math. scis. emeritus Otterbein Coll., 1997—. Contbr. articles on statis. non parametric methods and robustness to profl. jours. Mem. Am. Statis. Assn., Math. Assn. Am. Roman Catholic. Home: 4375 Mumford Dr Columbus OH 43220-4438

WILLKIE, WENDELL LEWIS, II, lawyer; b. Indpls., Oct. 29, 1951; s. Philip Herman Willkie and Rosalie (Heffelfinger) Hall; m. Carlotta Fendig; children: Alexandra Elizabeth, Diana Fendig, Caroline Heffelfinger. AB, Harvard U., 1973; BA, Oxford U., Eng., 1975, MA, 1983; JD, U. Chgo., 1978. Bar: NY 1979. Assoc. Simpson, Thacher & Bartlett, NYC, 1978-82; gen. counsel NEH, Washington, 1982-84; assoc. counsel to Pres. The White House, Washington, 1984-85; chief of staff, counselor to Sec. US Dept. Edn., Washington, 1985, gen. counsel, 1985-88; counsel Office of the Pres.-elect, Washington, 1988-89; gen. counsel Dept. Commerce, Washington, 1989-93; v.p. Westvaco Corp., NYC, 1995-96, sr. v.p., gen. counsel, 1996—2002; sr. v.p., gen. counsel, sec. MeadWestvaco Corp. (formerly Westvaco Corp.), 2002—. Vis. fellow Am. Enterprise Inst., Washington, 1993-94. Co-author, editor: (with J.R. Lilley) Beyond MFN: Trade with China and American Interests, 1994. Harvard U. scholar, 1969-73, Rhodes scholar, 1973-75. Republican. Episcopalian. Office: Mead Westvaco 5 High Ridge Pk Stamford CT 06905 Business E-Mail: wlw2@meadwestvaco.com.

WILLNER, ALAN ELI, electrical engineer, educator; b. Bklyn, Nov. 16, 1962; s. Gerald and Sondra (Bernstein) W.; m. Michelle Frida Green, June 25, 1991. BA, Yeshiva U., 1982; MS, Columbia U., 1984, PhD, 1988. Summer tech. staff David Sarnoff Rsch. Ctr., Princeton, NJ, 1983, 84; grad. rsch. asst. dept. elec. engring. Columbia U., NYC, 1984-88; postdoctoral mem. tech. staff AT&T Bell Labs., Holmdel, NJ, 1988-90; mem. tech. staff Bell Comm. Rsch., Red Bank, NJ, 1990-91; prof. U. So. Calif., LA, 1992—, assoc. dir. Ctr. Photonic Tech., 1994—. Head del. Harvard Model UN Yeshiva U., 1982; instr. Columbia U., 1987; rev. panel mem. NSF, Washington, 1992, Washington, 93, Washington, 94, invited optical comm. workshop, 94; chair panel on optical info. and comm., 94; co-chair Conf. on Lasers and Electro-Optics; steering com. and tech. com. mem. Conf. Optical Fiber Comm. Author 1 book; contbr. articles to profl. jours.; editor-in-chief Jour. Lighwave Tech., IEEE Jour. Selected Topics in Quantum Electronics; assoc. editor Jour. Selected Areas in Comm. Mem. faculty adv. bd. U. So. Calif. Hillel Orgn., 1992. Recipient Disting. Lectr. award, IEEE Lasers and Electro-Optics Soc., Armstrong Found. prize, Columbia U., 1984, Best Engring. Tchr. award, USC/TRW, young investigator award, NSF, 1992, Eddy Paper Award, 2001, USL Assoc. Award for Univ. Wide Excellence in Tchg.; fellow, Semiconductor Rsch. Corp., 1986, Sci. and Engring., David and Lucile Packard Found., 1993, presdl. faculty, NSF, 1994, sr. scholar, Fulbright Found., 1997; grantee NSF, Advanced Rsch. Projects Agy., Packard Found., Powell Found., Ballistic Missile Def. Orgn. Fellow: IEEE, Optical Soc. Am. (symposium organizer ann. mtg. 1992, panel organizer ann. mtg. 1993, symposium organizer ann. mtg. 1995, panel organizer ann. mtg. 1995, program com. for conf. on optical fiber commn. 1996, 1997, program co-chair ann. mtg. 2001, vice chair optical comm. group, tech. council chair-photonics divsn., co-chair sci. and engring. coun., bd. dirs., program co-chair of OSA Annual Mtg., tech. coun. chair photonics divsn.); mem.: IEEE (sr.; editor-in-chief IEEE/OSA Jour. Lightwave Tech.), Soc. Photo-Instrumentation Engring. (program chair telecomm. engring. photonics west 1995, chmn. conf. on emerging techs. for all-optical networks photonics west 1995, program com. for Conf. on Optical Fiber Comm. 1996, conf. program com. components for WDM), IEEE Lasers and Electro-Optics Soc. (chmn. optical comm. subcom. ann. mtg. 1994, bd. govs. 1998—2001, v.p. tech. affairs, mem. optical comm. tech. com., bd. govs., mem. optical networks tech. com., various awards coms., chmn. optical comm. tech. com., awards com. mem. Quantum Electronics, IEEE Fellow, pres.-elect, Disting. Lectr. award), Sigma Xi. Achievements include patents for localized photochemical etching of multilayered semiconductor body, optical star coupler utilizing fiber amplifier tech., and one-to-many simultaneous optical WDM 2-dim. plane interconnections. Home: 9326 Sawyer St Los Angeles CA 90035-4102 Office: U So Calif Dept Elec Engring Eeb 538 Los Angeles CA 90089-0001 Business E-Mail: willner@usc.edu.

WILLNER, ANN RUTH, political scientist, educator; b. NYC, Sept. 2, 1924; d. Norbert and Bella (Richman) W. BA cum laude, Hunter Coll., 1945; MA, Yale U., 1946; PhD, U. Chgo., 1961. Lectr. U. Chgo., 1946-47, rsch. assoc. Ctr. for Econ. Devel. and Cultural Change, 1954-56, 61-62;

advisor on orgn. and tng. Indonesian Ministry for Fgn. Affairs, Jakarta, 1952-53; expert for small scale indsl. planning Indonesian Nat. Planning Bur., Jakarta, 1953-54; fgn. affairs analyst Congl. Reference Svc., Libr. of Congress, 1960; asst. prof. polit. sci. Harpur Coll., Binghamton, NY, 1962-63; postdoctoral fellow polit. sci. and Southeast Asian studies Yale U., New Haven, 1963-64; rsch. assoc. Ctr. Internat. Studies, Princeton U., 1964-69; assoc. prof. polit. sci. U. Kans., Lawrence, 1969-70, prof., 1970-98. Vis. prof. polit. sci. CUNY, 1975; cons. govt. agys. and pvt. industry Polit. sci. editor: Ency. of the Social Scis., 1961; mem. editl. bd. Econ. Devel. and Cultural Change, 1954-57, Jour. Comparative Adminstrn., 1969-74, Comparative Politics, 1977—; author: The Neotraditional Accomodation to Political Independence, 1966, Charismatic Political Leadership: A Theory, 1968, The Spellbinders, 1984, 2004; also monographs, jour. articles, book chpts., newspaper columns. Grantee Rockefeller Found., 1965, Social Sci. Rsch. and Am. Coun. Learned Socs., 1966. Mem. Am. Polit. Sci. Assn. (gov. coun. 1979-81), Nat. Press Club. Home: 560 N St SW # N405 Washington DC 20024-4605 Office Phone: 202-484-2092. Personal E-mail: arwill@earthlink.net.

WILLNER, BARRY A., lawyer; BA cum laude, Lafayette Coll., 1969; JD, Georgetown U., 1972. Bar: NY 1974, US Dist. Ct., So and Ea. Dists. NY, US Ct. Appeals, 2nd Cir. Ptnr. Kaye Scholer LLP, NYC, 1980—, mng. ptnr., mem. exec. com. Co-author: The Shadow Government, 1972. Mem.: ABA, Assn. Bar of City NY. Office: Kaye Scholer LLP 425 Park Ave New York NY 10022 Office Phone: 212-836-8421. E-mail: bwillner@kayescholer.com.

WILLNER, DOROTHY, anthropologist, educator; b. NYC, Aug. 26, 1927; d. Norbert and Bella (Richman) W. Ph.B., U. Chgo., 1947, MA, 1953, PhD, 1961; postgrad., Ecole Pratique des Hautes Etudes, U. Paris, France, 1950—51. Anthropologist Jewish Agy., Israel, 1955-58; tech. asst., adminstrn. expert in community devel. UN, Mexico, 1958; asst. prof. dept. sociology and anthropology U. Iowa, Iowa City, 1959-60; research assoc. U. Chgo., 1961-62; asst. prof. dept. sociology and anthropology U. N.C., Chapel Hill, 1962-63, Hunter Coll., NYC, 1964-65; assoc. prof. dept. anthropology U. Kans., Lawrence, 1967-70, prof., 1970-90; professorial lectr. Johns Hopkins U. Sch. Advanced Internat. Studies, 1992. Cons. Washington Action for Youth, United Planning Orgn., 1964; rsch. in field. Author: Community Leadership, 1960, Nation-Building and Community in Israel, 1969. Contbr. numerous articles to profl. publs. Fellow Am. Anthrop. Assn., Soc. Applied Anthropology, Royal Anthrop. Inst.; mem. Cen. States Anthrop. Soc. (past pres.), Assn. Polit. and Legal Anthropology (past pres.). Home: N 407 560 N St SW Washington DC 20024-4605

WILLNER, JUDITH P., clinical geneticist, pediatrician, educator; b. Bay Shore, NY, July 27, 1945; d. Hyman and Edith (Sclank) Pleasure; m. Joseph Harrison Willner, June 22, 1969; children: Daniel, Rachel, Jonathan. AB, Harvard U., 1967; MD, NYU, 1971. Cert. Am. Bd. Pediatrics, Am. Bd. Med. Genetics. Asst. prof. ob-gyn. and pediatrics N.Y. Hosp./Cornell U. Med. Ctr., NYC, 1982-89; asst. prof. pediatrics, clin. geneticist Mt. Sinai Sch. Medicine, NYC, 1977-80, asst. prof. pediatrics, 1989-93, assoc. prof. human genetics and pediatrics, 1993—. Pres. N.Y. State Genetics Task Force, N.Y.C., 1996—. Mem. schs. com. Harvard U., Radcliffe Coll., 1974—; co-chair 30th reunion Radcliffe Coll., Cambridge, Mass., 1996—. Mem. Am. Soc. Human Genetics. Office: Dept Human Genetics Mt Sinai Hosp 1 Gustave L Levy Pl New York NY 10029-6500

WILLNER, KENNETH M., lawyer; b. Topeka, Feb. 2, 1962; BA with distinction, U.Va., 1984, JD, 1987. Bar: Va. 1987, DC 1988, cert.: U.S. Supreme Ct., U.S. Ct. Appeals, third, fourth, eighth, tenth & D.C. cir., U.S. Dist. Ct., Ea. Dist. Va., U.S. Dist. Ct., D.C., U.S. Dist. Ct., We. Dist. Pa. Profl. pers. ptnr. Paul, Hastings, Janofsky & Walker LLP, Washington. Mem.: D.C. Bar Assn. (employment law sect.), Va. Bar Assn. (employment law sect.), ABA (employment law sect.). Business E-Mail: kenwillner@paulhastings.com.

WILLOCK, MARCELLE MONICA, retired medical educator; b. Georgetown, Guyana, Mar. 30, 1938; came to U.S. 1954; d. George and Renee W. BA, Coll. New Rochelle, 1958; MD, Howard U., 1962; MA, Columbia U., 1982; MBA, Boston U., 1989. Diplomate Am. Bd. Anesthesiology. Asst. clin. prof. med. ctr. NYU, 1968-72, assoc. clin. prof. med. ctr., 1972-74; asst. prof. clin. anesthesiology Columbia U., NYC, 1978-82; prof. Boston U., 1982, chmn. dept. anesthesiology, 1982—98, asst. provost cmty. affairs, 1998—2002; dean Coll. Medicine Charles R. Drew U., LA, 2002—05; ret., 2005. Sec. The Med. Found., Boston, 1991-94. Contbr. articles to profl. jours. Pres. Louis and Marthe Deveaux Found., Panama, 1965—; trustee Coll. New Rochelle, NY, 1976-82, 2006—. Mem. Am. Soc. Anesthesiologists (del. 1986—, alt. dir. 1990-94, bd. dirs. 1994—, asst. sec. 1999-2001), Mass. Soc. Anesthesiologists (pres. 1988-89), Soc. Acad. Anesthesia Chairs (sec.-treas. 1989-91, pres.-elect 1993-94, pres. 1994—), Alpha Omega Alpha. Roman Catholic. Personal E-mail: mwillock@cdrewu.edu.

WILLOCKS, ROBERT MAX, retired librarian; b. Maryville, Tenn., Oct. 1, 1924; s. Willis Lemuel and Hannah (Emert) W.; m. Neysa Nerene Ferguson, May 23, 1947; children— Margaret Sharon, Samuel David, Mark Timothy, Robert Daniel, Kent Max. BA, Maryville Coll., 1949; B.D., Golden Gate Bapt. Theol. Sem., 1951, Th.M., 1962; MA in Library Sci, Peabody Coll., 1962. Ordained to ministry Bapt. Ch., 1950; pastor in Calif., 1950-56; missionary to Korea So. Bapt. Fgn. Mission Bd., Taejon, 1956-65; asso. dir. library Heidelberg Coll., Tiffin, Ohio, 1965-67; dir. library Columbia Coll., SC, 1967-70; asst. dir. libraries Syracuse U., NY, 1970-76; assoc. dir. libraries U. Fla., Gainesville, 1976-83, acting dir. libraries, 1983-84, dep. dir. libraries, 1984-89, ret., 1989; pastor Northwood Bapt. Ch., Gainesville, 1981-92; libr. Bapt. Theol. Sem., Lusaka, Zambia, 1994-97, Ghana Bapt. Sem., Kumasi, 1998—2006. Acting dir. Fla. Ctr. for Libr. Automation, 1984; cons. Choong Chung Nam Province Library Assn., Republic of Korea, 1962—65; dir. Korea Bapt. Press, 1959—61; prof. ch. history Korea Bapt. Sem., 1957—65, acting pres., 1958—59, librarian, 1959—65; vice chmn. Korea Bapt. Mission, 1962—64; del. Fla. Gov.'s Conf. on Libraries, 1978. Editor: Korean translations Thus it is Written, 1963, The Progress of Worldwide Missions, 1965. Chmn. trustees Wallace Meml. Bapt. Hosp., Pusan, Korea, 1963-65; pres. bd. dirs. Phoenix Homeowners Assn., 1980-88. With USNR, 1943-46. Mem. ALA (chmn. telefacsimile com. 1976-78, tech. com. 1980-84, chmn. standards com. 1985-88), Fla. Libr. Assn., Southeastern Library Assn., AAUP, Peabody Coll. Alumni Assn. (pres. S.C. 1968-69) Home: 1326 E Earll Dr Phoenix AZ 85014

WILLOUGHBY, SARAH-MARGARET C., retired chemist, educator, chemical engineer, consultant; b. Bowling Green, KY, Oct. 15, 1917; d. Austin Burrell Claypool and Minerva Dallas Renfrow-Claypool; m. John Richard Evans, II, Aug. 30, 1938 (dec. Dec. 1942); 1 child, Richard Claypool Evans; m. Olief Glenn Willoughby, June 18, 1948 (dec.); children: Sarah, Stephen(dec.). BS, Western Ky. U., 1938; PhD, Purdue U., 1950. Registered profl. engr., Ind., Tex. Chemist Devoe-Reynolds, Inc., Louisville, 1941—42; jr. engr. chem. lab. div. Curtiss-Wright Corp., Louisville, 1942—44; tech. asst. Purdue U., West Lafayette, Ind., 1944—46, fellow, 1946—50; rsch. chemist, coatings divsn. Monsanto Chem. Co., Boston, 1950—52; assoc. prof. of chemistry U. Tex., Arlington, 1954—84, co-dir. Ctr. for Microcrystalline Polymer Rsch. Studies, 1978—82, prof. emeritus chemistry, 1984. Cons. Albert H. Halff Assocs., Dallas, 1980—86. Co-edit., author Engineer-in-Training Manual, 1970. Nominee Dallas-Ft. Worth Trailblazer award, 1996; named to Hall of Disting. Alumni, Western Ky. U., 1994, Am. Men and Women of Sci., Personalities of the South, 1974, Cmty. Leaders and Noteworthy Americans, 1978, Notable Women of Tex., 1984—85, Daughters of Guilds of Colonial Artisans and Tradesmen, 2005; recipient Outstanding Chem. Engr. award, Purdue U., 1996, Cmty. Growth Contbn. award, Arlington Hist. Soc., Tex. Fellow: Am. Inst. Chemists; mem.: Am. Chem. Soc. (emeritus mem.), Peyton Soc. Va. (life), Gold Star Wives Am. (life), NY Acad. Sci. (life), Soc. Women Engrs. (sr.), Nat. Soc. Daughters of Founders and Patriots (v.p. NE Tex. chpt. 1997—, pres. NE Tex. chpt. 2006—08), Plantagenet Soc., Colonial Dames Am., Nat. Soc. DAR (chpt. regent 1967—69, nat. bicentennial com. mem. 1975—76, Nat. Women's Issues essay award 2005), Nat. Soc. Children of Am. Revolution (Tex. sr. state pres. 1968—70), Nat. Soc. Colonial Dames of XVII Century (chpt. regent 1980—82), Magna Charta Dames and Barons (formerly Nat. Soc. Magna Charta Dames) (Tex. state pres. 1986—88, nat. chmn. edn.), Colonial Order of the Crown, Soc. Descendants of Knights of the Most Noble Order of the Garter, Sovereign Colonial Soc. Ams. of Royal Descent, Friends of St. George, Order Ky. Cols., Sigma Xi (pres. 1966—68, emeritus mem.), Alpha Chi Omega (Lambda Epsilon chapt.). Home: 1630 Pecan Park Dr Arlington TX 76012

WILLOUGHBY, STEPHEN SCHUYLER, mathematics professor; b. Madison, Wis., Sept. 27, 1932; s. Alfred and Elizabeth Frances (Cassell) W.; m. Helen Sali Shapiro, Aug. 29, 1954; children: Wendy Valentine (Mrs. Peter Gallen), Todd Alan. AB (scholar), Harvard U., 1953, AM in Teaching, 1955; EdD (Clifford Brewster Upton fellow), Columbia U., 1961. Tchr. Newton (Mass.) Pub. Schs., 1954-57, Greenwich (Conn.) Pub. Schs., 1957-59; instr. U. Wis., Madison, 1960-61, asst. prof. math. edn. and math., 1961-65; prof. math. edn. and math. NYU, 1965-87, dir. math. edn. dept., 1967-83, chmn. math., sci. and stats. edn. dept., 1970-80, 86-87, chmn. U. Faculty Coun., 1981-82; prof. math. U. Ariz., Tucson, 1987—2002; prof. emeritus math. and math. edn. NYU, 1987—; prof. emeritus math. U. Ariz., Tucson, 2002—. Mem. nat. bd. advisor Sq. One TV, 1983-94, U.S. Commn. on Math. Instrn., 1984-95, chmn., 1991-95; math. adv. com. Nat. Tchr. Exam. Successor (Praxis), 1989-94; edn. panel New Am. Schs. Devel. Corp., 1991-97; U.S. Nat. rep. Internat. Commn. on Math. Instrn., 1991-95. Author: Contemporary Teaching of Secondary School Mathematics, 1967, Probability and Statistics, 1968, Teaching Mathematics: What Is Basic, 1981, Mathematics Education for a Changing World, 1990, Real Math, 1981, 85, 87, 91, Math: Explorations and Applications, 1998, College Mathematics Through Applications, 1999, The Other End of the Log: Memoirs of an Education Rebel, 2002, SRA Real Math, K-6, 2007; contbr. articles to profl. jours. and encys., chpts. to yearbooks and anthologies. Recipient Leadership in Math. Edn. Lifetime Achievement medal, 1995. Mem. Nat. Coun. Tchrs. Math. (dir. 1968-71, pres. 1982-84), Coun. Sci. Soc. Pres. (chmn. 1988). Home: 5435 E Gleneagles Dr Tucson AZ 85718-1805 Office: U Ariz Dept Math Tucson AZ 85721-0001 Personal E-mail: sswill@comcast.net.

WILLOUGHBY, WILLIAM FRANKLIN, II, retired physician, researcher; b. Washington, Feb. 4, 1936; s. William Westel and Patricia (De Zychlinska) W.; m. Mary Scott Fishburne, 1963 (div. 1974); children: Westel Woodbury, William Franklin III, Laura Fishburne, Mary Scott; m. Judith Eleanor Barbaras, Oct. 25, 1975; 1 child, Robert Alexander Willoughby. AB, Johns Hopkins U., 1957, MD, 1965, PhD in Microbiology, 1965; grad. with distinction, USAF War Coll., 1985. Diplomate Am. Bd. Pathology. Intern then resident in pathology Johns Hopkins Hosp., 1965-67; asst. prof. depts. pathology and microbiology Case Western Res. U., Cleve.; dir. Virginia Mason Rsch. Ctr., Seattle, 1972-75; assoc. prof. dept. pathology Sch. Medicine, Johns Hopkins U., Balt., 1975-87; prof., chmn. dept. pathology Sch. Medicine, U. S.C., Columbia, 1987-92; dir. labs. Cook County Hosp., Chgo., 1992-98, interim med. dir., 1994-96; ret., 1998. Cons. NIH, Bethesda, Md., 1979-98, mem. pathology A study sect., 1982-86; cons. NRC, Washington, 1981-84; mem. res. component med. coun., Dept. Def., Pentagon, 1991-93; dep. surgeon gen. for res. affairs USAF, Bolling AFB, D.C., 1993-95; asst. surg. gen. USAF, Operation Desert Storm/Desert Shield, 1990-91. Author: The Zycalinski Family: Their Polish Ancestors and American Descendants, 2007; mem. editorial bd. Am. Rev. Respiratory Disease, 1978-84; contbr. articles to profl. jours., reviewer numerous sci. manuscripts. Vestryman Trinity Episcopal Ch., Long Green, Md., 1984-87; bd. dirs. Ctrl. S.C. chpt. ARC, Columbia, 1989-92; bd. fellow Norwich U., 1992-95. Maj. USAFR, 1975-95, advanced through grades to maj. gen., 1992-95. Decorated D.S.M., Legion of Merit; recipient Edwin E. Osgood prize Va. Mason Rsch. Ctr., 1973; Arthritis Found. fellow Scripps Clinic and Rsch. Found., 1967-69; Poncine scholar Poncine Found., 1972-74; NIH rsch. grantee, 1976-91. Fellow Coll. Am. Pathologists; mem. AAAS, Am. Lung Assn. (nat. rsch. grant rev. com. 1978-82, chmn., 1981-82), Am. Soc. Investigative Pathology, Am. Assn. Immunologists, Am. Soc. Cell Biologists, Chgo. Coun. Fgn. Rels., Internat. Acad. Pathology, Assn. Pathology Chmns., Aerospace Med. Assn., Soc. USAF Flight Surgeons (bd. govs. 1993-96), Am. Thoracic Soc., Assn. Mil. Surgeons U.S., Soc. Med. Cons. to Armed Forces, Army Navy Club, Air Force Assn., Univ. Club, Johns Hopkins Club, Silver Wings Club Avocations: music, genealogy, antique automobiles, Chinese art. Home: 1416A S Federal St Chicago IL 60605-3057 Personal E-mail: wwilloughby@sbcglobal.net.

WILLOW, JUDITH ANN LOYE, tax preparer; b. Harrisburg, Pa., Oct. 2, 1939; d. John Steve and Mary Grace (Bergstresser) Loye; m. Robert Glenn Willow, June 14, 1957; 1 child, Robert Allen. Grad. high sch., Harrisburg. Cert. tax preparation, Pa.; enrolled agent IRS, 1997. Legal sec. McNees, Wallace & Nurick, Harrisburg, 1957-58; tax preparer H&R Block, Harrisburg, 1966—. Tax info. source TV interviews, Sta. WHP-TV 21, Harrisburg, 1982—, Sta. WHTM-TV 27, Harrisburg, 1988-89. Dir. Dauphin (Pa.) Recreation Assn., 1970-80; water safety instr. ARC, Harrisburg, 1970-80; v.p. PTA, Dauphin, 1966, sec., 1968. Mem. Nat. Honor Soc. Democrat. Lds. Avocations: reading, swimming, travel. Home: 704 Charles Rd PO Box 171 Dauphin PA 17018-0171 Office: H&R Block Premium Olde Liberty Sq Harrisburg PA 17109 Office Phone: 717-657-0316. E-mail: judytaxldy@aol.com.

WILLS, CHARLES FRANCIS, retired religious organization administrator; b. Avalon, NJ, July 26, 1914; s. Charles H. and Anna Margaret (Diemand) W.; m. Charlotte Emily Robson, Aug. 22, 1936; children: C. Frederic, Emily, Sally and Larry (twins). BS, Wheaton Coll., Ill., 1935; B.D., Eastern Bapt. Theol. Sem., 1938, Th.M., 1941; grad., Air War Coll., 1961. Commd. 1st lt. U.S. Army, 1941; advanced through grades to col. U.S. Air Force, 1963; chaplain AUS, 1941-49, U.S. Air Force, 1949-67; ret., 1967; exec. dir. chaplaincy services Am. Bapt. Chs., Valley Forge, Pa., 1969-75, exec. dir. profl. services, 1975-78; assoc. sec. Bapt. World Alliance, Washington, 1978-80, treas., 1980-81. Mem. Commn. on Doctrine and Interchurch Cooperation, 1980-90. Decorated Legion of Merit, Bronze Star, Purple Heart. Mem. Mil. Chaplains Assn., Mil. Order of Purple Heart. Personal E-mail: willshelton@aol.com.

WILLS, DAVID WOOD, minister, educator; b. Portland, Ind., Jan. 25, 1942; s. Theodore Oscar Mitchell and Elizabeth Lochore (Wood) W.; m. Carolyn Reynolds Montgomery, Aug. 22, 1964; children: John Brookings, Theodore Worcester, Thomas Churchill. BA, Yale U., 1962; BD, Princeton Theol. Sem., 1966; PhD, Harvard U., 1975. Ordained to ministry Presbyn. Ch., 1970. Asst. prof. Sch. of Religion, U. So. Calif., 1970-72; asst. prof. dept. of religion Amherst Coll., Mass., 1972-78, assoc. prof., 1978-83, prof., 1983-90, prof. religion and Black studies, 1990-94, Winthrop H. Smith '16 prof. Am. history and Am. studies, dept. religion and Black studies, 1994—, also dir. Luce Program in Comparative Religious Ethics 1978-88. Author: Christianity in the United States, 2005; editor (with Richard Newman) Black Apostles at Home and Abroad, 1982, (with Albert Raboteau) Afro-American Religion: A Documentary History Project, 1987—. Kent fellow Danforth Found., 1966-70, 75, Ford Found. fellow, 1972, Inst. for Ecumenical and Cultural Rsch. fellow, 1972, Nat. Humanities Ctr. fellow, 1980-81, 94, NEH fellow for Coll. Tchrs., 1988-89, W. E. B. DuBois Inst. for Afro-Am. Rsch. fellow, 1989-91. Mem. Am. Acad. Religion (chair Afro-Am. religious history group 1975-78), Am. Hist. Assn., Am. Soc. Ch. History, Orgn. Am. Historians, Phi Beta Kappa. Home: 47 Stagecoach Rd Amherst MA 01002-3527 Office: Amherst Coll Dept Religion Amherst MA 01002 Office Phone: 413-542-2470. Business E-Mail: dwwills@amherst.edu.

WILLS, GARRY, historian; b. Atlanta, May 22, 1934; s. John and Mayno (Collins) Wills; m. Natalie Cavallo, May 30, 1959; children: John, Garry, Lydia. BA, St. Louis U., 1957; MA, Xavier U., Cin., 1958, Yale U., 1959, PhD, 1961; LittD (hon.), Coll. Holy Cross, 1982, Columbia Coll., 1982, Beloit Coll., 1988, Xavier U., 1993, St. Xavier U., 1993, Union Coll., 1993, Macalester Coll., 1995, Bates Coll., 1995, St. Ambrose, 1997, George Washington U., 1999, Spring Hill Coll., 2000, Siena Heights U., 2001, Gettysburg Coll., 2002, Am. U., 2003, Muhlenberg Coll., 2004. Fellow Ctr. Hellenic Studies, 1961—62; assoc. prof. classics Johns Hopkins U., 1962—67, adj. prof., 1968-80; Henry R. Luce prof. Am. culture and public policy Northwestern U., 1980—88, adj. prof., 1988—2005, prof. history emeritus, 2005—. Author: (book) Chesterton, 1961, Politics and Catholic Freedom, 1964, Roman Culture, 1966, Jack Ruby, 1967, Second Civil War, 1968, Nixon Agonistes, 1970, Bare Ruined Choirs, 1972, Inventing America, 1978, At Button's, 1979, Confessions of a Conservative, 1979, Explaining America, 1980, The Kennedy Imprisonment, 1982, Lead Time, 1983, Cincinnatus, 1984, Reagan's America, 1987, Under God, 1990, Lincoln at Gettysburg, 1992 (Pulitzer Prize for gen. non-fiction, 1993), Certain Trumpets: The Call of Leaders, 1994, Witches and Jesuits: Shakespeare's Macbeth, 1994, John Wayne's America, 1997, St. Augustine, 1999, A Necessary Evil, 1999, Papal Sin, 2000, Venice, Lion City, 2001, St. Augustine's Childhood, 2001, James Madison, 2002, Why Am I a Catholic, 2002, St. Augustine's Memory, 2002, Mr. Jefferson's University, 2002, St. Augustine's Sin, 2003, Negro President, 2003, St. Augustine's Conversion, 2004, The Rosary, 2005, Henry Adams and the Making of America, 2005, St. Augustine's Confessions, 2006, What Jesus Meant, 2006, What Paul Meant, 2006, Head and Heart, 2007. Recipient Merle Curti award, Orgn. Am. Historians, Nat. Book Critics Cir. award (2), Wilbur Cross medal, Yale U., Peabody award, NEH Presdl. medal, 1998, John Hope Franklin award, Chgo. Hist. Soc., First Freedom award, Coun. for the First Freedom, Lincoln Laureate, State of Ill., Lifetime Achievement award, English-Speaking Union. Mem.: AAAL, Am. Philos. Soc., Am. Antiquarian Soc., Am. Acad. Arts and Scis., Mass. Hist. Soc. Roman Catholic. Office: Northwestern U Dept History Evanston IL 60208 Business E-Mail: g-wills@northwestern.edu.

WILLS, J. ROBERT, retired academic administrator, theater educator, writer; b. Akron, Ohio, May 5, 1940; s. J. Robert and Helen Elizabeth (Lapham) W.; m. Barbara T. Salisbury, Aug. 4, 1984 (dec. 1998); m. Jeanne Hokin, June 2002. BA, Coll. of Wooster, 1962; MA, U. Ill., 1963; PhD, Case-Western Res. U., 1971; cert. in arts adminstrn, Harvard U., 1976. Instr. to asst. prof., dir. theatre Wittenberg U., Springfield, Ohio, 1963-72; assoc. prof., dir. grad. studies, chmn. dept. theatre U. Ky., Lexington, 1972-77, prof. theatre, dean Coll. Fine Arts, 1977-81; prof. drama, dean Coll. Fine Arts U. Tex., Austin, 1981-89, Effie Marie Cain Regents chair in Fine Arts, 1986-89; provost, prof. theatre Pacific Luth. U., Tacoma, 1989-94; prof. theatre, dean coll. fine arts Ariz. State U., Tempe, 1994—2006; ret. Cons. colls., univs., arts orgns., govt. agencies Author: The Director in a Changing Theatre, 1976, Directing in the Theatre: A Casebook, 1980, rev. edit., 1994; dir. 95 plays; contbr. articles to profl. jours. Bd. dirs. various art orgns., Ky., Tex., Wash., Ariz. Recipient grants public and pvt. agencies. Mem. Nat. Assn. State Univs. and Land-Grant Colls.(chmn. commn. on arts 1981-83), Coun. Fine Arts Deans (exec. com. 1984-89, sec./treas. 1986-89), Univ. and Coll. Theatre Assn. (pres. 1981-82), Assn. for Communication Adminstrn. (pres. 1986-87), Ky. Theatre Assn. (pres. 1976).

WILLS, JOHN ELLIOT, JR., retired historian, writer; b. Urbana, Ill., Aug. 8, 1936; s. John Elliot and George Anne (Hicks) W.; m. Carolin Connell, July 19, 1958; children: Catherine, Christopher John, Jeffrey David, Joanne, Lucinda. BA in Philosophy, U. Ill., 1956; MA in East Asian Studies, Harvard U., 1960, PhD in History and Far Ea. Langs., 1967. History instr. Stanford (Calif.) U., 1964-65, U. So. Calif., LA, 1965-67, asst. prof., 1967-72, assoc. prof., 1972-84, prof., 1984—2004, prof. emeritus, 2004—, acting chair East Asian Langs. and Cultures, 1987-89; dir. East Asian Studies Ctr. USC-UCLA Joint East Asian Studies Ctr., LA, 1990-94. Rsch. abroad in The Netherlands, Taiwan, China, Japan, Macao, Philippines, Indonesia, India, Italy, Spain, Portugal, Eng. Author: Pepper, Guns, and Parleys: The Dutch East India Company and China, 1662-1681, 1974, Embassies and Illusions: Dutch and Portuguese Envoys to K'ang-hsi, 1666-1687, 1984, Mountain of Fame: Portraits in Chinese History, 1994, 1688: A Global History, 2001; co-editor: (with Jonathan D. Spence) From Ming to Ch'ing: Conquest, Region, and Continuity in Seventeenth-Century China, 1979; editor: Eclipsed Entrepots of the Western Pacific: Taiwan and Central Vietnam, 1500-1800, 2002; contbr. articles to profl. jours. Grantee Nat. Acad. Scis., 1985, Am. Coun. Learned Socs., 1979-80; Younger Humanist fellow NEH, 1972-73. Mem. Assn. for Asian Studies, Am. Hist. Assn., Phi Beta Kappa, Phi Kappa Phi (recognition award 1986, 95). Avocation: travel. Home Phone: 626-449-8048. Business E-Mail: jwills@usc.edu.

WILLS, MICHAEL STEPHEN, nutritionist, quality assurance professional; b. Roslyn, NY, Mar. 10, 1953; s. Thomas Francis and Catherine Ann Wills; m. Svetlana Victorivna Shiryaeva, Jan. 26, 1994 (div. Aug. 2005); m. Barbara Ann Keegan, Jan. 15, 1979 (div. June 20, 1985); stepchildren: Charles Clancy, Kseniya Andreevna Shiryaeva 1 child, Sean Michael. BS with high honors, U. Ariz., 1975. Registered dietitian Am. Dietetics Assn., Ill., 1976. Newspaper carrier LI Newsday, Albertson, NY, 1966—69; dietetic technician Ariz. Med. Ctr., Tucson, 1972—73; dietetic practicum U.S. Army, San Francisco, 1973—73; dietetic technician Tucson Med. Ctr., 1973—75; dietetic internship U. Ariz., Tucson, 1975—76; dir. of food svc. Catskill (N.Y.) Meml. Hosp. and Nursing Home, 1976—77; food svc. dir. New Rochelle (N.Y.) Nursing Home, 1977—79; dir. of food svc. Grace Plz., Inc., Great Neck, NY, 1979—82; corp. dietitian Data Control Info., Inc., Hornell, NY, 1982—84, dir. devel., 1984—86; quality assurance and customer support rep. The CBORD Group, Inc., Ithaca, NY, 1986—87, mgr. support and quality assurance, 1987—88, mgr. quality assurance, 1988—98, dir. quality assurance, 1998—. Cons. ServiceMaster, Downers Grove, Ill., 1986—94, Abbot Labs., Chgo., 1987—88, Brown U., Providence, 1987—92, Hallmark Cards, Kansas City, Kans., 1987—94, 1988 Winter Olympics, Calgary, Alberta, Canada, 1987—88, Disneyland, Paris, 1993—93, The Walt Disney World Co., Orlando, Fla., 1993—, Cornell U., Ithaca, NY, 1995, Kaiser Permanente, LA, 2001—03, NSW Dept. Health, Sydney, 2002—04, Disneyland, Anaheim, Calif., 2003, H.E.B. Markets, San Antonio, 2004—, Calif. Inst. of Tech., Pasadena, Calif., 2004—04, Gordon's Food Svc., 2006—07; presenter in field. Contbr. articles to profl. jours. Alumni bd. dirs. U. Ariz. Coll. Agrl. & Life Scis., 2005—; mem. Unitarian Universalist Assn., Ithaca, 1992—2004. Recipient Photography award, Photographic Soc. Am., 2005; scholar Promising Student, Herricks H.S. PTA, 1971, U. Ariz., 1973—74; NY State Regents scholar, N.Y. State Dept. Edn., 1971, Syntex Dietetic Internship scholar, Syntex Corp., 1975. Mem.: Am. Dietetic Assn. (licentiate), Amercian Soc. for Quality (assoc.; paper reviewer 2002—04), Photographic Soc. Am. (assoc.), Kappa Omicron Nu. Democrat. Roman Catholic. Achievements include development of functional reliability approach for software development; creation of an algorithm for calculating probability of concurrence for multi-user software applications; design of software application for measuring software performance benchmarks; creation of Olvera Valenzuela Memorial Scholarship for University of Arizona. Avocations: photography, astronomy, writing, backpacking. Home: PO 258 20 West Malloryville Rd Freeville NY 13068 Office: The CBORD Group Inc 61 Brown Rd Ithaca NY 14850 Office Phone: 607-257-2410. Personal E-mail: mwills@twcny.rr.com. Business E-Mail: msw@cbord.com.

WILLS, ROBERT HAMILTON, retired publishing executive; b. Colfax, Ill., June 21, 1926; s. Robert Orson and Ressie Mae (Hamilton) W.; m. Sherilyn Lou Niersthelmer, Jan. 16, 1949; children: Robert L., Michael H., Kendall J. BS, MS, Northwestern U., 1950. Reporter Duluth (Minn.) Herald & News-Tribune, 1950-51; reporter Milw. Jour., 1951-59, asst. city editor, 1959-62; city editor Milw. Sentinel, 1962-75, editor, 1975-91; exec. v.p. Jour./Sentinel, Inc., Milw., 1991-92, pres., 1992-93; vice-chmn., 1993; also bd. dirs. Jour./Sentinel, Inc., Milw.; pub. Milw. Jour. Sr. v.p., bd. dirs. Jour. Communications; pres. Wis. Freedom of Info. Council, 1979-86, charter mem., 1979; Pulitzer Prize juror, 1982, 83, 90. Mem. media-law rels. com. State Bar Wis., 1969-99; vice chmn. privacy coun. Wis. Pub. Svc. Commn., 1996-97; mem. Wis. Privacy Coun., 1994-95. Recipient Leadership award Women's Ct. and Civic Conf. Greater Milw., 1987; inducted into Journalism Hall of Achievement Medill Sch. Northwestern U., 1997, Wis. Newspaper Assn. Found. Hall of Fame, 2001. Mem. Wis. Newspaper Assn. (pres. 1985-86, Disting. Svc. award 1992), Wis. AP (pres. 1975-76, Dion Henderson award Svc. 1993), Am. Soc. Newspaper Editors, Internat. Press Inst., Milw. Press Club (Media Hall Fame 1993), Soc. Profl. Journalists (prs. Milw. chpt. 1979-80, nat. pres. 1986-87), Sigma Delta Chi Found. (bd. dirs. 1993-96, Wis. Newsman of Yr. 1973, Freedom of Info. award Milw. chpt. 1988). Home: 2064 Tiger Links Dr Henderson NV 89012-6111 E-mail: wills2064@juno.com.

WILLS, WILLIAM RIDLEY, II, retired insurance company executive, historian; b. Nashville, June 19, 1934; s. Jesse Ely and Ellen (Buckner) W.; m. Irene Weaver Jackson, July 21, 1962; children: William Ridley III, Morgan Jackson, Thomas Weaver. BA, Vanderbilt U., 1956. Agt., staff mgr. Nat. Life & Accident Ins. Co., Nashville, 1958-62, supr., 1962-64, asst. sec., 1964-67, asst. v.p., 1967-70, 2d v.p., 1970-75, v.p., 1975-81, sr. v.p., 1981-83, Am. General Services Co., 1982-83; dir. Nat. Life & Accident Ins. Co., Nashville, 1976-83; pres. Tenn. Hist. Soc., 1985-87; bd. dirs. Nat. Trust for Hist. Preservation, 1988-91. Author: History of Belle Meade: Mansion, Plantation and Stud, 1991, Old Enough to Die, 1996, Touring Tennessee: A Post Card Panorama, 1989-1955, 1996, Tennessee Governors at Home, 1999, Belle Meade Country Club: The First One Hundred Years, 2001, Gentleman, Scholar, Athlete: The History of Montgomery Bell Academy, 2005, Yours to County On-A Nashville Banker Extraordinaire, Sam M. Fleming, Jr., 2007. Nat. chmn. Living Endowment Drive Vanderbilt U., 1974; pres. Cumberland Mus. and Sci. Ctr., Nashville, 1977; gen. chmn. campaign United Way, Nashville and Mid. Tenn., 1978; pres. YMCA of Met. Nashville, 1984; trustee Ladies Hermitage Assn., 1981—90; mem. Tenn. Hist. Commn.; chmn. YMCA Found. Mid. Tenn., 1998—99; chmn. bd. Montgomery Bell Acad., 1988—97, gen. chmn. $43 million capital campaign, 1999—2000; mem. adv. bd. Pub. Libr. of Nashville and Davidson County, 2002—; trustee Tenn. Hist. Soc., 2006—; pres. Monteagle Sundy Sch. Assembly, 2002—04; bd. dirs. Vanderbilt U., 1988—. Lt. USN, 1956—58. Recipient awards YMCA, 1977, 1983, United Way De Tocqueville award, 1989, Tenn. History Book award Tenn. Libr. Assn. and Tenn. Hist. Commn., 1991, Disting. Alumnus award Montgomery Bell Acad., 1996, H.G. Hill award YMCA of Mid. Tenn., 2003. Fellow Life Office Mgmt. Assn.; mem. Assn. Preservation Tenn. Antiquities (pres. Nashville chpt. 1987-89), Belle Meade Country Club, Coffee House Club, Round Table Literary Club. Presbyterian. Personal E-mail: ridleywills@comcast.net.

WILLSE, JAMES PATRICK, newspaper editor; b. NYC, Mar. 17, 1944; s. Sherman Stokes and Katherine (Mackey) W.; m. Sharon Margaret Stack, Sept. 15, 1973; 1 child, Elizabeth Ruth. BA, Hamilton Coll., 1967; MS, Columbia U., 1968. Nat. editor AP, NYC, 1969-74, news editor San Francisco, 1975-78; city editor San Francisco Examiner, 1978-82, mng. editor, 1982-84, NY Daily News, 1984-89, editor, 1989—93, pub., 1992—93; dir. news media Advance Publications, Inc., 1993—94; editor Star Ledger, Newark, 1995—. Named Beveridge Editor of Yr. Nat. Press Found., 2000; fellow Stanford U., 1975. Mem. Am. Soc. Newspaper Editors, AP Mng. Editors. Office: Star Ledger 1 Star Ledger Plz Newark NJ 07102-1291 Office Phone: 973-392-4127. E-mail: jwillse@starledger.com. *

WILLSIE, SANDRA KAY, internist, educator; BS in Med. Tech., Pittsburg State U., Kans., 1975; DO, Kansas City U. Medicine and Biosciences, Mo., 1983. Diplomate in internal medicine, pulmonary diseases and critical care medicine Am. Bd. Internal Medicine, Am. Bd. Osteo. Internists, 2000. Rotating intern Univ. Hosp., Kansas City, Mo., 1983-84; resident in internal medicine U. Mo.-Kansas City Affiliated Hosps., 1984-87; fellow in pulmonary diseases and critical care medicine Truman Med. Ctr.-West, Kansas City, Mo., 1987-89; instr. medicine U. Mo.-Kansas City Sch. Medicine, 1984-89; med. dir. pulmonary clinic Truman Med. Ctr., 1991-2000; asst. prof. medicine U. Mo. Kansas City Sch. Medicine, 1989-94, assoc. prof. medicine, 1994-99, dep. asst. dean, 1994—97, asst. dean, 1997-2000, prof. medicine, 1999-2000, Kansas City U. Medicine and Biosciences, 2000—02, vice dean acad. affairs, adminstrn., med. affairs, 2002—, exec. v.p. acad. affairs, provost, dean, 2002—, exec. v.p. rsch. & med. affairs, dean Coll. Osteo. Medicine, 2007—. Invited bd. question author Am. Bd. Internal Medicine, 1995—, relevance reviewer for pulmonary disease bd. exam, 1996—; internal medicine subspecialty program pre-reviewer Accreditation Coun. for Grad. Med. Edn., 1997—2000; credentials com. Truman Med. Ctr., Inc., 1990—96, med. intensive care unit com., 1992—2000, intermediate care unit com., 1992—2000, exec. com. Truman Health Sys., 1998—2000, profl. standards com., 1998—2000. Contbr. articles to profl. jours. Bd. dirs. Girls to Women, 1995—2000, v.p. bd. dirs., 1996—2000. Fellow: Am. Coll. Physicians (state activities com. 1991—95, chair, state activities com. 1994, scientific presentations judge 1995—96, coun. mem. 1998—2004), Am. Coll. Osteo. Internists (program com. 2002—, rsch. com. 2003—, Rschr. of Yr. 2004); mem.: Met. Med. Soc. (chair women in medicine com. 1995—2000, pres. com. 1995—2000, bd. dirs. 1997—2000, exec. com. 1999—2000, chair women in medicine com. 2002—), Am. Osteo. Assn., Kans. City Pulmonary Roundtable (pres.), Soc. Critical Care Medicine, Am. Lung Assn. Mo. (bd. mem.), Jackson County Osteo. Assn., Mo. Assn. Osteo. Physicians and Surgeons, Am. Thoracic Soc., Am. Coll. Chest Physicians (chair, basic sci. com. 1995—98, scientific program com. 1995—2003, membership com. 1997—2001, gov. for Mo. 1997—2001, chair, scientific presentations and awards com. 1998—2000, vice chair, scientific program com. 1999—2000, chair, scientific program com. 2000—01, regent 2004—, Young Investigator award 1992). Office: Kansas City Univ Medicine and Bioscis 1750 Independence Ave Kansas City MO 64106-1453 Office Phone: 816-283-2308. Business E-Mail: swillsie@kcumb.edu.

WILLSON, C. GRANT, chemical engineering and chemistry professor; b. Vallejo, Calif., Mar. 30, 1939; s. Carlton P. and Margaret Ann (Cosner) Willson; m. Deborah Jeanne Merritt, Dec. 13, 1975; children: William, Andrew. BS in Chemistry, U. Calif., Berkeley, 1962, PhD in Organic Chemistry, 1973; MS in Organic Chemistry, San Diego State U., 1969. With propellent rsch. Aerojet Gen. Corp., Sacramento, 1962-64; tchr., coach Fairfax H.S., LA, 1964-67; prof. Calif. State U., Long Beach, 1973-74, U. Calif., San Diego, 1974-78; mgr. polymer sci. and tech. IBM Almaden Rsch. Ctr., San Jose, Calif., 1978-93; prof. chemistry, chem. engring. U. Tex., Austin, 1993—. Contbr. articles to profl. jours.; patentee in field. Recipient Kosar award, Soc. Imaging Sci. and Tech., 1998, Aristotle award, Semicondr. Rsch. Corp., Photopolymer Sci. award, Japan, 2003. Fellow SPIE; m.Mem. NAE, AAAS, Soc. Photog. and Instrumentation Engrs., Am. Phys. Soc., Am. Chem. Soc. (Arthur K. Doolittle award 1986, ACS Chemistry of Materials 1991, Carothers award 1992, Coop. Rsch. award in Polymer Sci. 1993, Applied Polymer Sci. Award, 2004, Heroes of Chemistry award, Arthur Dehon Little award 2005), NAS (award for chem. in svc. to soc. 1999), Coun. for Chem. Rsch. (Malcom Pruitt award 1997), St. Francis Yacht Club, Sigma Xi. Avocations: sailing, skiing. Office: Univ Texas Dept Chem and Chem Engring Austin TX 78712 Business E-Mail: willson@che.utexas.edu.

WILLSON, CLYDE D., biologist, educator; b. Omaha, May 7, 1935; s. Paul Gallup and Elise Willson; m. Greta Jean Olsen, July 17, 1954; children: Ian, Bjorn, Scott, Gillian. BA in Biochemistry, U. Calif., Berkeley, 1956, PhD in Chemistry, 1960. Postdoctoral fellow Pasteur Inst. NIH, Paris, 1960—62; asst. prof. biology U. Calif., Berkeley, 1962—67, Miller fellow, 1967—69; prof. biology and chemistry Laney Coll., Oakland, Calif., 1969—. Chair biology dept. Laney Coll., 1975—77, 1995—2002, rep. Acad. Senate, 1990—2002. Contbr. articles to profl. jours. Natural scis. docent Oakland Mus., 1969—72. Mem.: AAUP (sec.-treas., U. Calif. at Berkeley 1963—64), No. Calif. Parasitologists, West Coast Bacterial Physiologists. Avocation: keyboard performance. Home: 136 International Blvd Oakland CA 94606 Office: Coll Alameda Chemistry Dept 555 Atlantic Ave Alameda CA 94501

WILLSON, DAVID ALLEN, retired reference librarian, writer; b. Seattle, June 30, 1942; s. Robert Richard and Alice Hansine (Aspen) W.; m. Penelope Poeschl, Dec. 13, 1972 (div. Mar. 1986); children: Mungo Park, Darcy Monroe; m. Michele Geraldine DeBruyne, Mar. 8, 1986; children: Joaquin Sandoval, Alice Maria. BA, U. Wash., 1964, MLS, 1970. Reference libr. Green River C.C., Auburn, Wash., 1970—2000. Author: REMF Diary, 1988, The REMF Returns, 1992, In the Army Now, 1995; co-editor: Vietnam War Literature, 1996, Viet Nam War Jour., 2000—. With US Army, 1966—67. Recipient Disting. Faculty award Puget Power, 1996, Vietnam Vets. Am. Contbn. to Am. Culture award, 1997. Mem.: Popular Culture Assn., Vietnam Vets. Am. Democrat. Lutheran. Avocations: movies, listening to the blues, especially fred mcdowell. Home: 23630 201st Ave SE Maple Valley WA 98038-8633 E-mail: dawillson@earthlink.net.

WILLSON, JOHN MICHAEL, retired mining company executive; b. Sheffield, England, Feb. 21, 1940; s. Jack Desmond and Cicely Rosamond (Long Price) W.; m. Susan Mary Partridge, Aug. 26, 1942; children: Marcus J., Carolyn A. BSc in Mining Engring. with honors, Imperial Coll., London, 1962, MSc in Mining Engring., 1985. With Cominco Ltd., 1966-74, v.p. No. Group Vancouver, B.C., Can., 1981-84; pres. Garaventa (Canada) Ltd., Vancouver, 1974-81; pres., CEO Western Can. Steel Ltd., Vancouver, 1985-88, Pegasus Gold Inc., Spokane, Wash., 1989-92, Placer Dome, Inc., Vancouver, B.C., Can., 1993-2000; ret., 2000. Bd. dirs. Nexen Inc., Finning Internat. Ltd., Garaventa (Can.) Ltd. Pres. N.W.T. Chamber Mines, Yellowknife, Can., 1982-84; chmn. bd. dirs. Western States Pub. Lands Coalition, Pueblo, Colo., 1990-91; bd. dirs. World Gold Coun. Mem. AIME, Can. Inst. Mining and Metallurgy, Inst. Mining and Metallurgy (London), Assn. Profl. Engrs. and Geologists N.W.T., N.W. Mining Assn. (bd. dirs. Corp. Leadership award 1991), World Gold Coun. (chmn. 1999-2001). Avocations: bicycling, tennis, squash, sailing, skiing. Home: 4722 Drummond Dr Vancouver BC Canada V6T 1B4 Fax: 604-228-9664.

WILLUMSTAD, ROBERT B., insurance company executive, retired diversified financial services company executive; b. Bklyn., Aug. 22, 1945; m. Carol Willumstad; 2 children. Grad., Adelphi U., LLD (hon.), 2005. Various ops., retail banking and computer systems positions Chemical Bank, 1967—87; chmn., CEO consumer finance svcs. Travelers Group, chmn., CEO Global Consumer Group, Citigroup Inc., 2000—03; pres. Citigroup, Inc., 2002—05, COO, 2003—05; pres., CEO Citibank N.A., 2003—05; non-exec. chmn. Am. Internat. Group (AIG), 2006—; co-founder Brysam Global Partners, 2007—. Bd. dirs. S.C. Johnson & Son Inc., MasterCard Internat., Am. Internat. Group (AIG), 2006—. Bd. dirs. Habitat for Humanity Internat., 2001—; bd. trustees Am. Scandinavian Found., Adelphia U., 2005—. Recipient Frederick Douglass award, NYC Urban League, 2002. Mem.: Financial Services Roundtable (bd. dirs.). Office: Am Internat Group 70 Pine St New York NY 10270 *

WILLY, THOMAS RALPH, lawyer; b. Phila., Sept. 30, 1943; s. Albert Ralph and Dorothy Rose (Driver) W.; m. Kay Harris, Jan. 12, 1968; children: Elyn Alexandria, Jon Charles. BA in History, U. Mo., Kansas City, 1966, JD with distinction, 1974. Bar: Mo. 1974. Assoc. Deacy & Deacy, Kansas City, 1974-75, Logan, Hentzen, Haitbrink & Moore, Kansas City, 1975; ptnr. Hentzen, Haitbrink & Moore, Kansas City, 1976-78, Hentzen, Moore & Willy, Kansas City, 1978-80, Moore & Willy Profl. Corp., Kansas City, 1980-87, pres., dir., 1987-94; shareholder, dir., v.p. Van Osdol, Magruder, Erickson & Redmond, P.C., Kansas City, 1994—. Cons. Ctr. for Mgmt. Assistance, Kansas City, 1990-2000; presenter living will project, Midwest Bioethics Ctr., 1990-2000. Pres. Kansas City Swiss Soc., 1989-91, bd. dirs. 1993-96, 2004-07; bd. dirs. Greater Kansas City People to People, 1995-98, 2000-03, Friends of Art, Kansas City, Kansas City Consensus, Hist. Kansas City Found. Capt. USAF, 1966-70; sponsor US Army Internat. Officers Info. Program Cmmd and Gen. Staff Coll., Ft. Leavenworth, 1993—. Mem. ABA (sect. intellectual property law, sect. bus. law), Mo. Bar Assn., Lions (bd. dirs. Leawood 1986-88, 90-92, sec. 1988-90, v.p. 1996-97, pres. 2007-). Home: 10314 Lee Blvd Shawnee Mission KS 66206-2629 Office: 2400 Commerce Tower 911 Main St Kansas City MO 64105-2009 Office Phone: 816-421-0644. E-mail: twilly@vomer.com.

WILMER, MARY CHARLES, artist; b. Atlanta, Aug. 25, 1930; d. William Knox and Harriott Creighton (Thomas) Fitzpatrick; m. John Grant Wilmer, Dec. 28, 1950; children: John Grant, Knox Randolph, Charles Inman, Mary Catherine; m. Olin Grigsby Shivers, May 18, 1982. Attended, Wellsley Coll., Mass., 1948—50, Agnes Scott Coll., Decatur, Ga., 1950—51, BA, 1970; BFA, Coll. of Art, 1974. Co-pres. St. Elizabeth's Guild, Cathedral of Saint Philip. Exhibited in one-woman shows at Image South Gallery, 1974, Aronson Gallery, 1977, 79, Heath Gallery, 1982-, Coach House Gallery, 1983, 89; two-person show (with daughter Catherine Wilmer) Swan Coach House Gallery, Atlanta, 2003; group shows include Colony Square, 1975, Coach House Gallery, 1999; portrait painter, 1974—. Bd. dirs. Hillside Cottages, 1963-65, Alliance Theatre Co., 1965-68, Atlanta Child Svcs., 1965-68, Atlanta Coll. Art, 1965-85, Atlanta Puppetry Arts, 1982-87, Atlanta Med. Heritage, 1999-2000; co-chmn. Ga. Commn. Nat. Mus. of Women in the Arts, (pres.) 1985-87; mem. Study Club, 1970-, Book Club, 2001-. Mem. Piedmont Driving Club, Jr. League, Piedmont Garden Club. Episcopalian. Address: 1 Vernon Rd NW Atlanta GA 30305-2964

WILMERDING, JOHN, art historian, educator, curator; b. Boston, Apr. 28, 1938; s. John Currie and Lila Vanderbilt (Webb) W. AB, Harvard U., 1960, AM, 1961, PhD, 1965. Asst. prof. art Dartmouth Coll., 1965-68, assoc. prof., 1968-73, Leon E. Williams prof., 1973-77, chmn. dept. art, 1968-72, chmn. humanities divsn., 1971-72; sr. curator Am. art Nat. Gallery of Art, 1977-83, dep. dir., 1983-88; Sarofim prof. Am. art Princeton U., 1988—, chmn. dept. art and archeology, 1992-99. Vis. lectr. history of art Yale U., 1972; vis. prof. fine arts Harvard U., 1976; vis. prof. art U. Md., 1979; vis. prof. art history U. Del., 1982; hon. curator painting Peabody Mus., Salem, Mass.; vis. curator Met. Mus., 1988—. Author: Fitz Hugh Lane, American Marine Painter, 1964, A History of American Marine Painting, 1968, Pittura Americana dell' Ottocento, 1969, Robert Salmon, Painter of Ship and Shore, 1971, Fitz Hugh Lane, 1971, Winslow Homer, 1972, The Genius of American Painting, 1973, American Art, 1976, American Light, The Luminist Movement, 1980, American Masterpieces from the National Gallery of Art, 1980, An American Perspective, 1981, Important Information Inside, 1982, Andrew Wyeth, The Helga Pictures, 1987, Paintings by Fitz Hugh Lane, 1988; American Views: Essays on American Art, 1991, The Artist's Mount Desert: American Painters on the Maine Coast, 1994, Compass and Clock: Defining Moments in American Culture, 1999, Signs of the Artist: Signatures and Self-Expression in American Paintings, 2003, American Art in the Princeton University Art Museum, Vol. 1, 2004, Richard Estes, 2006. Trustee Nat. Gallery of ARt, Washington, Coll. of the Atlantic, Bar Harbor, Maine, Solomon R. Guggenheim Mus., NYC, N.E. Harbor Libr., Maine, Wyeth Endowment for Am. Art, Wilmington, Del., Nat. Portrait Gallery, Washington. Guggenheim fellow, 1973-74. Fellow Phila. Atheneum (hon.); Mem. Coll. Art Assn., Am. Studies Assn., Am. Philos. Soc. Office: Princeton U Dept Art and Archaeology 105 McCormick Hall Princeton NJ 08544-1018 Home Phone: 609-497-1968; Office Phone: 609-258-3785. E-mail: wilmerdg@princeton.edu.

WILMERS, ROBERT GEORGE, bank executive; b. NYC, Apr. 20, 1934; s. Charles K. and Cecilia (Eitingon) W.; m. Elisabeth Roche de la Rigodiere; children: Robert G. Jr., Christopher C.; stepchildren: Juliette Chevalier, Charlotte deCoupigny, Camille deWouters, Guilaume deWouters. BA, Harvard U., 1956; postgrad., Harvard Bus. Sch., 1958-59. Dep. fin. adminstr. City of N.Y., 1966-70; v.p. Morgan Guaranty Trust Co., NYC and Belgium, 1970-80; CEO M&T Bank Corp., Buffalo, 1983—88, pres., CEO, 1988—2000, chmn., pres., CEO, 2000—05, chmn., 2005—06, chmn., CEO, 2007—. Bd. dirs. Vivian Beaumont Theater Inc., Buffalo Fiscal Stability Authority, The Bus. Coun. N.Y. State, Fin. Svcs. Roundtable. Decorated officer de l'Ordre de la Couronne (Belgium). also: 1 W 64th St New York NY 10023-6734 Office: M&T Bank 1 M&T Plz Buffalo NY 14203 Office Phone: 716-842-5425. Business E-Mail: rwilmers@mtb.com.

WILMORE, DOUGLAS WAYNE, surgeon, educator; b. Newton, Kans., July 22, 1938; s. Waldo Wayne and Hilda Gard (Adrian) W.; m. Judith Kay Shabert; 1 child, Carol Kristann. BA, Washburn U., 1960; MD, Kans. U., 1964; MS (hon.), Harvard U., 1979; PhD (hon.), Washburn U., 1995. Diplomate Am. Bd. Surgery. Intern Hosp. U. Pa., Phila., 1964-65, resident, fellow, 1965-71; chief clin. rsch. and staff surgeon U.S. Army Inst. Surg. Rsch., Ft. Sam Houston, 1971-79; staff surgeon Brigham and Women's Hosp., Boston, 1979—; Frank Sawyer prof. surgery Harvard Med. Sch., Boston, 1989—. Editor Scientific American Surgery, 1988, ACS Surgery, 2001—. Mem. Inst. Medicine, 1999. Lt. Col. U.S. Army, 1971-74. Achievements include development of safe modern techniques for providing parenteral nutrition to critically-ill patients; rehabilitation program for individuals with severe gastrointestinal disease; first to use growth factors and specialized nutrition to rehabilitate patients with the short bowel syndrome; use the amino acid L-glutamine in clinical nutrition.

WILMOT, IRVIN GORSAGE, former hospital administrator, educator, consultant; b. Nanking, China, June 30, 1922; s. Frank Alonzo and Ethel (Ranney) W.; m. Dorothy Agnes Mohlfeld, Feb. 6, 1943; children: Marcia Beth, David Michael. BS, Northwestern U., 1955; MBA, U. Chgo., 1957. With Internat. Register Co., Chgo., 1946-47; buyer U. Chgo., 1947-49; adminstrv. asst., then asst. supt. U. Chgo. Clinics, 1949-61; adminstr. NYU Med. Ctr.-Univ. Hosp., 1961-68, exec. v.p., 1968-81, Blue Cross-Blue Shield Greater N.Y., 1981-83, dir., 1977-81; exec. v.p., COO Montefiore Hosp. and Med. Ctr., NYC, 1984-85; healthcare cons., 1985—. Instr. then asst. prof. U. Chgo., 1957-61; assoc. prof. NYU, 1961-68; prof., 1968—; assoc. dir. U. Chgo. Grad. Program Hosp. Adminstrn., 1959-61; mem. hosp. rev. and planning coun. State of N.Y., 1979-87. Bd. dirs. N.Y. Blood Ctr., 1978-81. With USN, 1940-46. Fellow Am. Coll. Hosp. Adminstrs. (life, chmn. ctrl. com. insts. 1959-65, regent N.Y. State and P.R. 1974—); mem. Assn. U. Programs Hosp. Adminstrs. (exec. sec. 1959-61), Am. Hosp. Assn. (mem. coun. rsch. and planning 1965-68, coun. on mgmt. 1979-80, coun. on fin. 1981-84, trustee 1979-81), Assn. Am. Med. Colls. (chmn. coun. tchg. hosps. 1970-71), Greater N.Y. Hosp. Assn. (bd. govs., pres. 1973-74), Hosp. Assn. N.Y. State (trustee, chmn. 1976-77). Home: 34 Helen Ave Rye NY 10580-2447

WILMOTH, MARSHA H., elementary school educator; d. J.C. and T. Bearnease Bolden; m. Charles DeWayne Wilmoth, Mar. 18, 1972 (dec.); children: Michele H., Sharon L., Leslie D. AA, Coffeyville Cmty. Jr. Coll., Kans., 1972; BS in Edn., Pittsburg State U., 1974; cert. reading specialist, Emporia State U., 1986. Mid. sch. English tchr. Wann (Okla.) Sch., 1974—75; Title 1 reading and math. tchr. K-9th grade, Indian edn. tutoring coord. and tchr. Lincoln Meml. Grade Sch., Caney, 1978—; Title 1 reading tchr. Caney (Kans.) HS, 1981—82; elem. tchr. Caney, 1982—2006; sutstitute tchr. Duncanville (Tex.) Schs., 1976—77. Sponsor youth activities Assemblies of God and Bapt. chs. Named High Qualified Tchr., Kans. State Dept. Edn.; recipient recognition, Unified Sch. Dist. 436, Parent award. Mem.: NEA, Internat. Reading Assn., No. Cherokee Nation, Caney Valley Tchr. Assn., Kans. Edn. Assn., Ducks Unltd., Order Ea. Star, Alpha Upsilon Alpha, Kappa Delta Pi. Avocations: cooking, photography. Office: Caney Valley Unified Schs 201 E 1st Ave Caney KS 67333-1903 E-mail: mwilmoth@caney.com.

WILMOUTH, ROBERT K., commodities trader; b. Worcester, Mass., Nov. 9, 1928; s. Alfred F. and Aileen E. (Kearney) W.; m. Ellen M. Boyle, Sept. 10, 1955; children: Robert J., John J., James P., Thomas G., Anne Marie. BA, Holy Cross Coll., 1949; MA, U. Notre Dame, 1950, LLD, 1984. Exec. v.p., dir. 1st Nat. Bank Chgo., 1972-75; pres., chief adminstrv. officer Crocker Nat. Bank, San Francisco, 1975-77; pres., chief exec. officer Chgo. Bd. Trade, 1977-82; chmn. LaSalle Nat. Bank, 1982-99. Pres., chief exec. officer Nat. Futures Assn., 1982-2002, Spl. Policy Adv. Nat. Futures Assn., 2003-. Life trustee U. Notre Dame; mem. adv. coun. Kellogg Grad. Sch. Mgmt., Northwestern U. Mem. Chgo. Club, Barrington Hill Country Club. Office: Nat Futures Assn 200 W Madison St Ste 1600 Chicago IL 60606-3415

WILMUT, IAN, biologist; b. Hampton Lucey, Eng., July 7, 1944; s. Jack and Eileen Mary (Dalgleish) W.; m. Vivienne Mary Craven, Sept. 9, 1967; children: Helen, Naomi, Dean. BSc in Agrl. Sci., Nottingham U., Eng., 1967, DS, 1998; PhD in Animal Genetic Engring., Cambridge U., Eng., 1971. Sr. scientist ABRO (Animal Rsch. Breeding Station, which is now known as the Roslin Inst.), Edinburgh, Scotland, 1973-93; prin. investigator Roslin Inst., Midlothian, Scotland, 1993—, also mem. sr. mgmt., joint head, dept. gene expression and develop. Scientific advisor Geron Bio-Med, a wholly owned subsidiary of the Geron Corp., Menlo Park, Calif.; lectr. in field. Editor Jour. Reproduction Fertility, 1993—; co-author (with Colin Tudge and Keith Campbell) The Second Creation: Dolly and the Age of Biological Control, 2000, (with Roger Highfield) After Dolly: The Uses and Misuses of Cloning, 2006; contbr. articles to profl. jours. Hon. fellow U. Edinburgh, 1993; recipient Lord Lloyd of Kilgerran prize, Sir John Hammond Meml prize, Soc. Study of Fertility, Rsch. medal, Royal Agrl. Soc. England, Sir William Young award, Royal Highland & Agrl. Soc. Scotland. Mem. Internat. Embryo Transfer Soc. (pres. 1994), NAS (fgn. assoc.), Order of the British Empire; fellow Royal Soc. Edinburgh, Acad. Med. Scis. Achievements include creating the first calf ever produced from a frozen embryo, named Frosty in 1973; with Keith Campbell, the birth of Megan and Morag, two Welsh mountain sheep cloned from differentiated embryo cells in 1995; with Keith Campbell, the production of a mammal cloned from adult cells, the lamb named Dolly in 1996; with Keith Campbell, creating Polly, a sheep cloned from fetal skin cells that had been genetically altered to contain a human gene in 1997; granted a license to clone human embryos for medical research in 2005. Avocations: hill walking, photography, curling, gardening. E-mail: ian.wilmut@bbsrc.ac.uk.

WILNER, ALAN M., retired judge; b. Balt., Jan. 26, 1937; AB, Johns Hopkins U., 1958, MLA, 1966; JD, U. Md., 1962. Assoc. Sherbow, Shea & Doyle, Balt., 1962-65; asst. atty. gen. State of Md., 1965-68; assoc. Venable, Baetjer & Howard, Balt., 1968-71; asst., then chief legis. officer, govs. staff, 1971-77; assoc. judge Ct. of Spl. Appeals, 1977-90, chief judge, 1990-96; judge Md. Ct. of Appeals, 1996—2007. Adj. faculty U. Md. Sch. of Law, U. Balt. Sch. of Law; with Judicial Inst. Md., 1997—, chmn. bd. dirs., 1999—; mem. Md. Alternative Dispute Resolution Commn., 1998—. Mem. ABA, Md. Bar Found., Md. State Bar Assn., Balt. County Bar Assn. *

WILNER, MARION LEONARD, art educator; b. NYC, Sept. 27, 1929; d. Jack Frank and Madeline (Leff) Leonard; m. Myron Wilner, May 28, 1950; children: Andrew, Matthew, David. BS, NYU, 1950, MA, 1952. Prof. of art, coord. art transfer program Bristol CC, Fall River, Mass., 1966-89, prof. emerita, 1993. Advisor dean's adv. coun. coll. visual and performing arts U. Mass., Dartmouth, 1993; lectr. Sacred Hearts Convent, 1992, RI Jewish Hist. Soc., 1992, Brandeis U. Nat. Women's Com., 1991, 90, Universidade Nova, Lisbon, 1988, Universidade Dos Acores, 1987; vis. scholar U. Mass., Dartmouth, 1992; mem. Higher Edn. Nominating Coun., 1990; judge Ea. Edison Poster and Essay Contest, 1989, RI Regional Scholastic Art Awards, 1987, Ann. Regional Art Exhbn. Fall River Festival, 1985; writer art Fall River Herald News, 1994-, judge Portsmouth Arts Guild, 2007. Prin. works exhibited in numerous one-woman and group shows including DeBlois Gallery, Newport, RI, 1992, 94, Bert Gallery, Providence, 1991, Dodge House Gallery, Providence, 1990, Fall River Hist. Soc., 1988, Newport Art Mus., 1987, Escola Superior de Belas Artes, Lisbon, 1986, Eastbourne Gallery, Newport, 1977, Facets Gallery, Fall River, 1993, New England Ctr. Gallery, U. NH, 1992, Fed. Res. Bank Boston, 1992, Deblois Gallery, Newport, RI, 2003, Perkins Gallery, Mass., 2004, Retrosptctive at Bristol CC, Fall River, Mass., 2005, Bristol Art Mus., RI, 2006; prin. works represented in numerous collections including Duro Industries, Inc., Bristol CC, Providence Art Club Mems. Show, Cianfarani award, 1998, RI Econ. Devel. Corp., 1999, Juried RI State Com., Nat. Mus. Women in Arts, 2000, Providence Art Club, Printmaking award, 2001, Deblois Gallery, Newport, RI, 2001, Newport Art Mus., 2002, KRAUSE Gallery, 2003. Trustee Swain Sch. Design, New Bedford, Mass., 1977-91, Fall River Pub. Libr., 1978-91; active Fall River Cultural Commn., 1988—, Fall River Arts Lottery Coun., 1989—; mem. adv. bd. SMU Ctr. for Jewish Culture, 1983; visual arts dir. Festival '82; graphic designer for various community orgns. Gulbenkian grantee Lisbon, Portugal, 1986, 88; recipient Outstanding Cmty. Svc. award Fall River Area C. of C. and Industry, 1996, Ruth Findley award Providence Art Club, 2002. Mem.: Deblois Gallery, 19 on Paper. Home: 786 Madison St Fall River MA 02720-5718 Personal E-mail: mandmwilner@yahoo.com.

WILNER, THOMAS BERNARD, lawyer; b. Toronto, July 7, 1944; came to U.S., 1944; s. Morton H. and Zelda (Dunkelman) W.; m. Jane Ten Broeck; children: Amanda, Adam, David. BA, Yale U., 1966; LLB, U. Pa., 1969. Clk. to Chief Judge William Hastie U.S. Ct. Appeals, Phila., 1969-70; assoc. Debevoise Plimpton, NYC, 1970-72; counsel Amtrak, Washington, 1972-73; ptnr. Arnold & Porter, Washington, 1973-89, Shearman & Sterling, Washington and Tokyo, 1989—.

WILPON, FRED, professional sports team executive; b. Bklyn., Nov. 22, 1936; s. Nathan and Frances (Altman) W.; m. Judith Anne Kessler, Sept. 27, 1958; children: Jeffrey Scott, Robin Lynn, Bruce Nathan. BA, U. Mich., 1958. Vice pres. Hanover Equities Corp., NYC, 1959-69, Peter Sharp & Co., NYC, 1969-71; chmn. bd. Sterling Equities, Inc., Manhasset, NY, 1971—; pres. N.Y. Mets Profl. Baseball Team, 1980—, now also chief exec. officer, 1980—; owner Brooklyn Cyclones, 2000—. Mem. Vol. Urban Cons. Group, Mayor N.Y.C. Housing Task Force; trustee Jewish Inst. Geriatric Care, New Hyde Park, N.Y., 1976—, Green Vale Sch., Glen Head, N.Y., 1977—. Served with USAF, 1959. Mem. Young Pres. Orgn. Clubs: KP. Achievements include unveiling of new NY Mets Stadium plans, 2006.

WILSON, ANGELA LYNN, theater producer, playwright; b. Memphis, Jan. 21, 1955; 1 child, Jennifer. BA in History, U. Tex., Dallas, 1979; MLA, So. Meth. U., Dallas, 1996. Prodr. Theatre Quorum, Dallas, 1998—. Author: (plays) Heart, 1995, (films), 2006, (plays) Perchance, 2002, Dim All the Lights, 2006. Office: Theatre Quorum PO Box 180552 Dallas TX 75218

WILSON, ARMIN, retired chemist; b. Sapulpa, Okla., Dec. 13, 1916; s. Joseph Bartholomew and Amelia (Heller) W.; m. Evelyn Hodes, June 8, 1943; children: Jonathan, Robert. BA, Rice U., 1939, MA, 1941; AM, PhD, Harvard U., 1945. Sr. chemist Merck Labs., Rahway, N.J., 1945-53; dept. head Bristol Myers, Hillside, N.J., 1953-68; prof. Rutgers U., New Brunswick, N.J., 1968-78. Contbr. articles to profl. jours. Fellow N.Y. Acad. Scis.; mem. Phi Beta Kappa, Sigma Xi. Avocation: poetry. Home: 112 Crosslands Dr Kennett Square PA 19348-2014

WILSON, ARTHUR THEODORE, education consultant; b. Newark, July 2, 1945; s. Elmer and Dorothy May (Outlaw-Sloan) W. BA in Humanities, New Sch., 1971, MA in Social Studies Edn., 1974; MA in Philosophy, U. London at Bedford Coll.; PhD in Program History, NYU, 1980. Cert. tchr., N.Y., N.J. Rschr. African Studies, NYC, 1972; tchr. Teaneck Alternative H.S., NJ, 1979—80, Hunter Coll., NYC, 1980—81; cons. gifted and talented program curriculum Bd. Coop. Ednl. Svcs. SUNY, Farmingdale, 1983—; artistic dir. VSA Theatre Co., New Brunswick, NJ, 2004—. Apptd. arts & edn. acad. artist N.J. Performing Arts Ctr., Newark, 1996—; advisor, tutor Master's Degree Program in Acting, New Actors Workshop, Antioch U., N.Y., 1995—; workshop leader Young Playwright's Festival, N.Y.C., 1981—; adj. prof. drama Drew U., Madison, N.J.; co-founder, workshop leader N.J. Young Playwrights Festival, 1983; project dir., playwright Am. Folk Theater Young Co.'s exch. program, London, 1984-85; theater workshop cons. Milneck Sch. for Deaf, L.I., 1984; lit. workshop cons. Orion Gifted and Talented Program, Lindenhurst, N.Y., 1984—; artistic dir. exch. program Manhattan Empire and Tukak Theater, Denmark; dir. playwriting in sch. project N.Y. Shakespeare Festival, 1986—; instr. N.Y. Lit. Assn., N.Y.C., 1984—; poetry reading and workshop with Poet Laureate Gwendolyn Brooks, Union Coll., 1985, guest poet for Mother Hale of Hale House, 1987; dir. playwriting in edn. dept. schs. N.Y. Shakespeare Festival, dir./prodr. Live! (radio edn. program), bd. dirs., cons. arts edn. New Dance Group Ctr., N.Y., 1987—. Editor, writer, pub. Dance Giant Steps, Inc., Bklyn., 1981—; author: (play) The Extended Family, 1987, Peace By Peace, 2004; play and workshop: Words for the Journey; dir. Daddy Say, 1987, Children of Dahomey and Spirit Ensemble, 1986, Bound For Broadway, Broadway N.Y., 2004; dance editor; Feet Mag., 1969-72, Black Creations Mag., 1970-72; editor, pub.: Attitude: The Dancers' Monthly, 1982—; contbr. poetry to Open Mag., Other Countries, New Rain, A Taste of Salt; prodr.: (plays) Life Sea Treasures, 1989-90, Guns Like Candy, 1991, Red High Heels Snap Back, 1995; commns. include: A Tribute for All the Beautiful Black Men, N.Y.C., High Rise Snaps, Washington, D.C., Street Songs, N.Y., Trouble the Water, N.Y., Homeless Monologues, Baca, Bklyn., Hallelujah Roots, N.Y., and others. Workshop leader N.J. Teen Program, 1983-84; advisor, workshop leader, founder N.J. Young Playwrights Festival, 1964-68; rsch. asst. Weeksville Project, Bjlyn., 1969-70; theater dir. local orgns. Recipient numerous scholars, 1970-79; grantee Bklyn. Art and Cultural Assn., 1983, N.Y. Dept. Cultural Affairs, 1983-84, N.Y. State Coun. on Arts, 1982-84, BECA Capezio Found., Heart grant Union County Bd. Freeholders, 1998-2004, N.J. Writers Project, N.J. State Coun. on the Arts, 1999-2005; N.J. State Coun. Arts fellow, 1985-86, Merit award for Poetry, Internat. Soc. Poets Conv., Phila., 2004. Mem. Black Writers Union, Dramatist Guild, Inc., ASSITEJ, Internat. Assn. Children's Theater Professionals, Am. Acad. Poets. Home: 919 Oak St Roselle NJ 07203-2001 Office Phone: 908-887-0782. Personal E-mail: adaddyblack@aol.com.

WILSON, BERTINA IOLIA, retired music educator; b. Southampton, Va., Aug. 17, 1938; d. Purcell Lee and Clarine Branch; m. Aug. 25, 1963 (div. May 1977); children: Brian Keith, Linda Elizabeth. BA, Newark State Coll., 1960; MA, Kean Coll., 1981. Cert. elem. edn. tchr., N.J. Tchr. Newark Bd. Edn., 1960-77, project coord., 1977—95; ch. organist, choir dir. Zion Hill Bapt. Ch., Newark, 1974—; vice prin. Newark Pub. Schs., 1995—97; ret., 1997. Mem. Newark Tchrs. Union, Project Coords. Assn. (exec. bd. Newark chpt. 1981—), Order of Eastern Star (Outstanding Ch. Musician 1986), Phi Delta Kappa (pub. rels. dir. 1987-89). Democrat. Avocations: singing, playing the organ. Home: 345 Mclean Pl Hillside NJ 07205-1748

WILSON, BONNIE JEAN, lawyer, educator, investor; b. Alameda County, Calif. d. August and Violet Adeline (Lockard) Ritzenthaler; m. Allan Nicholas Wilson (dec.); children: Albert Clyde, Bruce Allan. BA, U. Calif., Berkeley, cert. in elem. tchg.; JD, Thomas Jefferson SOL, 1981. Bar: Calif.; cert. tchr., Calif. Elem. sch. tchr. Contra Costa and San Diego Counties; intern San Diego County Dist. Atty. Office, 1981; pvt. practice La Jolla, Calif., 1982—. Mem. La Jolla Presbyn. Ch., San Diego Symphony Assn., Friends of the La Jolla Libr.; adv. dir. San Diego Opera Assn.; edn. activist, 1972-76. Mem. Calif. State Bar Assn., San Diego County Bar Assn., La Jolla Newcomer's Club (bd. dirs. 1968-69), U. Calif. Berkeley Alumni Club (bd. dirs. San Diego chpt. 1961-62), Am. Assn. Ind. Investors (bd. dirs. 1991-97), Pi Lambda Theta, La Jolla Beach and Tennis Club. Presbyterian. Home: 2235 Bahia Dr La Jolla CA 92037-7007

WILSON, BRENDA MARIE, secondary school educator; b. New Orleans, Feb. 4, 1951; d. Chester Simmons, Jr. and Lillie Mae Simmons; m. Eli Wilson, Jr., June 19, 1971; children: Eli III, LaVar Antoine. AS, So. U., 1972; BSc, Rochester Inst. Tech., NY, 1984; MSc, LI U., 1990. Adj. prof. L.I. (N.Y.) U., 1987—89, asst. dean, 1989—93; tchr. Bd. Edn., Bklyn., 1997—98; with accts. payable Chempiah Ministries, Queens, NY, 1998—2000; tchr. Orange County Pub. Schs., Orlando, Fla., 2001—. Mem. sch. adv. com. Orange County Pub. Schs., 2002—. V.p. Eli Wilson Ministries, Orlando, 2002—03. Named Tchr. of Yr., Orange County Pub. Schs., 2004. Mem.: Phi Gamma Nu, Alpha Kappa Alpha. Baptist. Office: Cerokee School 550 S Eola Dr Orlando FL 32801-3999 Home: 6503 Hawdsmoor Dr Orlando FL 32818

WILSON, BRENT LAWRENCE, lawyer, mediator; b. New Orleans, Jan. 9, 1952; s. Commodore Waddell and Mildred Louise (Quave) W.; m. Trojanell Theresa Bordenave, June 22, 1974. BA, Morehouse Coll., 1973; postgrad., U. Ga., 1973-74; JD, SUNY, Buffalo, 1976. Bar: La. 1976, Ga. 1979, U.S. Dist. Ct. (no. dist.) Ga. 1979, U.S. Ct. Appeals (5th and 11th cirs.) 1979, U.S. Ct. Appeals (3d cir.) 1982, U.S. Ct. Appeals (6th cir.) 1986. Field atty. NLRB, Atlanta, 1976-80; assoc. Elarbee, Thompson & Trapnell, Atlanta, 1980-87; ptnr. Elarbee, Thompson, Sapp & Wilson, Atlanta, 1987—. Lectr. Atlanta U., 1984; adj. prof. law Emory U., Atlanta, 1984-85; mem. Study Commn. on Employment Laws, 1997-98. Contbr. articles to profl. jours. Mem. Fulton County Bd. Ethics 1991, Homelessness Task Force United Way of Metropolitan Atlanta, 2005; exec. bd. dirs. Boys and Girls Clubs of Metro Atlanta, 1999—, exec. com., 2005; bd. dirs. St. Judes Recovery Ctr., Inc., 1989—, bd. chair, 2005; active Christ our Hope Cath. Ch. Named one of Top 100 Ga. Super Lawyers, 2004, 2005, 2006; named to Am.'s Top Black Lawyers, Black Enterprise Mag., 2003; recipient, Ga. Legal Elite, 2003, 2006, Best Lawyers for Bus., Chambers USA, 2005, 2006. Mem.: Labors and Employment Rels. Assn., ABA (mem. labor and employment law mgmt. com.), NAACP (life), Coll. Labor and Employment Lawyers, Atlanta Soc. African Am. Human Resources, Soc. Human Resource Mgmt. (legis. com. co-chmn. 1987—88, 1990—91), Nat. Employment Law Coun., Nat. Assn. Securities Dealers (arbitrator), State Bar Ga. (co-chair Ga. Diversity Prog. 1998—99), Nat. Bar Assn. (mem. comml., labor and arbitration sect.), Gate City Bar Assn., Atlanta Bar Assn. (sec., treas. labor and employment law sect. 1985, vice chmn. labor and employment law sect. 1986, chmn. labor and employment law sect. 1987), 100 Blackmen of Atlanta, Atlanta Morehouse, Lawyers Club Atlanta, 191 Club, Atlanta Bus. League, Am. Inns. Ct., Phi Alpha Delta, Omega Psi Phi. Avocations: spectator sports, racquetball, reading, travel. Office: Elarbee Thompson Sapp & Wilson LLP 800 Internat Tower 229 Peachtree St NE Atlanta GA 30303-1614 Home Phone: 770-593-2331; Office Phone: 404-659-6700. Business E-Mail: bwilson@elarbeethompson.com.

WILSON, BRIAN ANDREW, computing performance consultant, educator, writer, editor; b. Denver, July 10, 1967; s. Leonard Tom Jr. and Mary Ann (Slutz) W.; m. Amy Michelle Duncan, Apr. 28, 2001. BA in Music, Cleve. Inst. Music, 1990; BA, Case Western Reserve U., 1990; M in Info. Tech., Am. Intercontinental U., 2002. Cert. Mercury Cert. Product Cons., Mercury cert. instr. Software support, SQA engr. Borland Internat., Inc., Scotts Valley, Calif., 1990-92, software cons., 1992—94; pres., founder OnRamp Internet Svcs., Inc., Atlanta, 1995—96; founder Internet Gadsden, 1995—96, Internet Tuscaloosa, 1995—96; founder, sr. ptnr. Tech-South Consulting, Suwanee, Ga., 1996—. Vis. faculty Ga. Inst. Tech., Atlanta, 2005—. Author: Quattro Pro for Windows: Everything you Need, 1992; tech. editor: Using Quattro Pro 3, 1991, Using Quattro 4, 1992, Using Quattro Pro for Windows, 1992, Paradox for Windows: Programming, 1993, dBase IV 2.5: Quick Reference, 1993. Mem. Ga. Inst. Tech. Coll. Computing Ind. Ptnrs. Assn., Assn. Computing Machinery, Software Contractor's Guild, Berkeley Hills Country Club. Avocations: golf, sailing, tennis, sky-diving. Office: 471 Henderson Lake Dr Canton GA 30115

WILSON, BRUCE BRIGHTON, lawyer, retired transportation executive; b. Boston, Feb. 6, 1936; s. Robert Lee and Jane (Schlotterer) Wilson; m. Elizabeth Ann MacFarland, Dec. 31, 1958; children: Mabeth, Mary, Bruce Robert, Caroline Daly. AB, Princeton U., 1958; LLB, U. Pa., 1961. Bar: Pa. 1962. Assoc. Montgomery, McCracken, Walker & Rhoads, Phila., 1962-69; atty. US Dept. Justice, Washington, 1969-79, dep. asst. atty. gen. antitrust div., 1971-76; spl. counsel Consol. Rail Corp., Phila., 1979-81, gen. counsel litigation and antitrust, 1981-82, v.p., gen. counsel, 1982-84, v.p. law, 1984-87, sr. v.p. law, 1987-97, sr. v.p. merger, 1997. Bd. dirs. Carload Express, Inc., Phila. Indsl. Devel. Corp., Wayne Sr. Ctr., The Phila. Singers; mem. mgmt. com. Concord Resources Group, 1989-91. Chmn. Radnor Twp. Cable Commn. Coun., 1993—2000, mem., 2002—, Radnor Twp. Ethics Commn., 2000—01; vestry St. Mary Episcopal Ch., Wayne, Pa., 2006—. Fellow Salzburg Seminar in Am. Studies (Austria), 1965; fellow Felz Inst. State and Local Govt., 1967. Mem. ABA, Phila. Bar Assn., Corinthian Yacht Club, Merion Cricket Club, Beach Club Cape May. Republican. Episcopalian. Home: 224 Chamounix Rd Wayne PA 19087-3606 Personal E-mail: brucewilson224@comcast.net.

WILSON, BRUCE KEITH, men's health nurse; b. Alton, Ill., Aug. 18, 1946; s. Lewis Philip and Ruth Caroline Wilson; children: Sarah Ann, Andrew James. BSN, U. Tex., San Antonio, 1975, MSN, 1977; PhD, North Tex. State U., Denton, 1987. Coord. Pan Am. U., Edinburg, Tex., 1982-83; house supr. HCA Rio Grande Regional Hosp., McAllen, Tex., 1986-87; program dir. Tex. Southmost Coll., Brownsville, 1983-86; prof. U. Tex.-Pan Am., Edinburg, 1986—. Author: Logical Nursing Math., 1987; contbr. chpts. to books, numerous articles to profl. jours. With U.S. Army, 1966-68. Mem. Am. Assembly for Men in Nursing (bd. dirs. 1997-2001), Tex. League for Nursing (bd. dirs. 1993-97). Avocations: photography, computer. Home: 1702 Ivy Ln Edinburg TX 78539-5367 Office: U Tex-Pan Am Dept Nursing Edinburg TX 78539 Personal E-mail: wilson@hiline.net.

WILSON, C. DANIEL, JR., library director; b. Middletown, Conn., Nov. 8, 1941; s. Clyde D. and Dorothy M. (Neal) W.; m. M. April Jackson, Apr. 1986; children: Christine, Cindy, Clyde, Ben. BA, Elmhurst Coll., 1967; MA, Dominican U., 1968; MPA, U. New Orleans, 1995. Trainee Chgo. Pub. Libr., 1967-68; instr. U. Ill., 1968-70; asst. dir. Perrot Meml. Libr., Greenwich, Conn., 1970-76; dir. Wilton Pub. Libr., Wilton, Conn., 1976-79; assoc. dir. Birmingham Pub. Libr., Birmingham, Ala., 1979-83; dir. Davenport (Iowa) Pub. Libr., 1983-85, New Orleans Pub. Libr., 1985-97, St. Louis County Libr., 1997—. With USMC, 1962-65. Mem. ALA, Internat. Assn. Met. Librs. (pres. 1998-2002), Mo. Libr. Assn., Am. Soc. Pub. Adminstrs., Rotary, Pi Gamma Mu. Episcopalian. Home: 511 W 4th St Hermann MO 65041 E-mail: dwilson@slcl.lib.mo.us.

WILSON, CARL, information technology executive; V.p. info. mgmt. Pillsbury Co. Inc.; sr. v.p., mgmt. info. svc., food and internat. retailing secorts Grand Met. Plc.; v.p. & CIO, info. resources Ga. Pacific Corp.; exec. v.p., dir. & chief info. officer Marriott Internat. Inc., Washington, 1997—. Bd. dir. Global Exchange Services, enamics, Inc., Software Architects, Inc.; bd. dir. (independent mem.) Rivermine, 2005—; mem. AT&T Client Adv. Coun., Microsoft Global Exec. Roundtable. Office: EVP & CIO Marriott Internat One Marriott Dr Washington DC 20058 also: EVP & CIO Marriott Internat 10400 Fernwood Rd Bethesda MD 20817

WILSON, CARL WELDON, JR., construction company executive, civil engineer; b. Norfolk, Va., Sept. 4, 1933; s. Carl Weldon and Janie Marie (Ludford) W.; m. Jean Roberts, Feb. 13, 1960; children: Lisa Ann, Carl Weldon III. BCE, Tex. A&M U., 1954. Registered profl. engr., Tex. Engr. Magnolia Petroleum Co., Morgan City, La., 1954-55, Brown & Root, Houston, 1957-60; project mgr. Claude Everett Constrn. Co., Houston, 1960-62; pres. Falcon Constrn. Co., Houston, 1962-63; pres., owner Wilson Engring. and Constrn. Co., Houston, 1963-68; v.p. Divcon, Inc., Houston, 1968-71, Wilson Industries, Inc., Houston, 1971-81; pres., prin. owner BS&B Engring. Co., Inc., Houston, 1981-86; chmn., majority shareholder Task Internat., Inc., Houston, 1986—. Served to 1st lt. U.S. Army, 1955-57. Republican. Episcopalian. Avocations: tennis, running, painting. Home: 750 Bison Dr Houston TX 77079-4401 Office: Task Internat Inc PO Box 940121 Houston TX 77094-7121 Office Phone: 281-597-8650. Personal E-mail: taskintcww@aol.com. Business E-Mail: cwilson@silverfox.org.

WILSON, CAROLYN ROSS, retired school system administrator; b. Lake Charles, La., June 25, 1941; d. Charles Wesley and Lucille Gertrude (Payne) Ross; m. James David Wilson, Apr. 10, 1971; 1 child, Charlise. BS in Music Edn. cum laude, Xavier U., 1962; MMus in Music Edn., Cath. U., Washington, 1968; postgrad., U. D.C., 1985-86, George Washington U., 1987-88, Harvard U., 1989. Tchr. Xavier U. Jr. Sch. Music, New Orleans, 1960-61, Orleans Parish Schs., New Orleans, 1962-63, D.C. Pub. Schs., Washington, 1964-87, curriculum writer, summer 1984, 85, adminstrv. intern Ea. High Sch., 1987-88, asst. prin. Cardozo High Sch., 1988-89, asst. prin. Duke Ellington Sch. of Arts, 1989-93; prin. Duke Ellington Sch. Arts, Washington, 1993-97—; proposal reader U.S. Dept. Edn., 1998, 98, 99. Curriculum writer music dept. D.C. Pub. Schs., Washington, 1984-85, dir. All City High Sch. Chorus, 1973. Composer: A Dedication to Federal City Alumnae Chapter of Delta, Sigma Theta Sorority, Inc., 1973. Lector Immaculate Conception Ch., Washington, 1986—; named D.C. Tchr. of Yr., 1987. Recipient Cert. of Merit-Outstanding Tchr. and Prin. award D.C. Govt., 1994; U.S. Dept. Edn. Effective Schs. grantee, Washington, 1992. Mem. ASCD, Instn. for Devel. Ednl. Activities (6th yr. fellow, session chair 1988, seminar leader 1991, 92, 93, 94), Delta Sigma Theta (Federal City Alumnae chpt.). Roman Catholic. Avocations: reading, travel, bowling, musical arranging, playing the piano.

WILSON, CARRIE LEE STROUD, principal; b. Bellevue, La., Dec. 14, 1948; d. Jeffrie Edward Stroud and Mary Elizabeth Jones-Stroud; m. Victor George Wilson, Apr. 19, 1972; children: Geoffrey Victor, Kimberly Georgina Elizabeth, James Anderson Stuart. B.A, U. Redlands, 1971; MA in Edn., U. Calif.-Berkeley, 2003. Preliminary Adminstrv. Intern Servicing Credential Calif. Tchg. Credentialing Com., 2002, Preliminary Adminstrv. Servicing Credential Calif. Tchr. Credentialing, 2004, Emergency Tchg. Credential Calif. Tchg. Credentialing, 2001. Counselor Upward Bound/U. Redlands, Vallejo, Calif., 1967; asst. to teen post dir. Redlands City Recreation Dept., Redlands, Calif., 1968; recreation leader Redlands Recreation Dept., Calif., 1969—70, art instr., 1971; docent U. Calif., Berkeley, 1971—72; tchr./ drawing and composition-photography Vallejo City Unified Sch. Dist., 1998—99, asst. prin., 2002—03, vice prin., 2004—; tchr. Berkeley Unified Sch. Dist., Berkeley, Calif., 1973—74; real estate agt. Calif. Sch. Real Estate, Oakland, 1979—80; substitute tchr. Vallejo City Unified Sch. Dist., 1980—84, tchr., 1884—2000; art instr./exploratory art for young people Calif. Coll. Arts and Crafts, Oakland, 1985—86; tchr./summer sch. Vallejo City Unified Sch. Dist., 1999—2000, tchr./secondary/jr. high-middle sch., 1983—98, tchr./art-photography, 1998—99; academic dir. Jesse Bethel HS, Vallejo, 1999—2001, asst. prin., 2002—03, vice prin., 2003—. Chairperson/facilitator Springstowne Jr. HS, Vallejo, 1985—98, dept. head, 1991—98; state conf. presenter Calif. League of Mid. Schs., San Francisco, 1991—92; mentor-master-coach tchr. Springstowne Jr. HS, Vallejo, 1992—98; tchr. leader Jesse Bethel HS, Vallejo, 1998—2001, chairperson digital grant application to the state, 1999—2001, state standardized test coord., 2000—, chairperson com. for accreditation, 2001—02, state sch. intervention program for student achievement, 2001—03. Author: (poetry) What Time Is Fishin Time (pub. Famous Poets Soc., 1995), (essay) The Importance of Nature (pub. Nat. Essay Press, 1967); exhibitions include oil & acrylic painting thesis Journey of Self Expression, ceramics, Vase (Nat. Mus. of Arts- Wash., D.C., 1968), portraits on canvas/oil paintings (Patton State Hospital-Rehabilitation Ctr. For Young Women, 1969), Personal Expressions of African American Suburb Experience (Participant in Exhibit, 1968); contbr. (Cert./Black History Month, 1969); Compilation of Perspectives of an African American Woman (Cert. of Participation/Watts Summer Festival of Arts, L.A., 1965). Mem. ednl. reform programs for student achievement Vallejo City Unified Sch. Dist., 1995—2005; min. Jehovah's Witnesses, Vallejo, 1973—2005; mem. Vallejo Artist Guild, 1990—96; contbr. Continental Omega Boys and Girls Club, Vallejo, 2001—05; advisor Willie B. Atkins Tanner Project, Vallejo, 1998—2005. Nominee Tchr. of Yr., Calif. League Mid. Sch.; recipient, Elks B.P.O.E.; grantee Ednl. Opportunity Grant, Fed. Govt., 1967—71; Behring Scholar, U. Calif. Berkeley, Prin. Leadership Inst., 2001—03. Mem.: Vallejo Schs. Mgrs. Assn., ASCD, Assn. Calif. Sch. Adminstrs. Jehovah'S Witness. Achievements include recipient Phillip Harris Memorial Scholarship; missionary Ministry for Jehovah's Witnesses. Avocations: writing, art. Home: 119 Toni Ct Vallejo CA 94591-4272 Office: Jesse Bethel HS 1800 Ascot Pkwy Vallejo CA 94591-4272 Home Phone: 707-642-9129; Office Phone: 707-556-5700.

WILSON, CECIL BRUCE, internist; b. Columbus, Ga., 1935; m. Betty Jane Wilson; 3 children. BA in History, Emory U., MD. Bd. cert. in internal medicine. Intern US Naval Hosp., Portsmouth, Va., 1961—62, resident in internal medicine San Diego, 1966—69; pvt. practice in internal medicine Fla. Past pres. med. staffs Winter Park Meml. Hosp., Fla. Hosp. Med. Ctr., Orlando; past pres. Fla. Statewide Health Coun.; chair Local Health Coun. of East Cent. Fla. Flight surgeon USN, comdr. USN. Master: Am. Coll.

Physicians (past chair bd. regents); mem.: AMA (mem. ho. del. 1992—, mem. bd. trustees 2002—, chmn.), Orange County Med. Soc. (past pres.), Fla. Med. Assn. (FMA) (pres., chair bd. gov. and exec. com.). Office: 1341 Orange Ave Winter Park FL 32789-4911 Office Phone: 407-647-2122. Office Fax: 407-647-6701. *

WILSON, CHANDRA DANETTE, actress; b. Houston, Aug. 27, 1969; children: Joy, Serena, Michael. BFA in Drama, NYU, 1991. Actor: (plays) The Good Times Are Killing Me (Outstanding Debut Performance, Theatre World award), Paper Moon: The Musical, The Family of Mann, Believing, Caroline, or Change (named one of Eight to Watch, Onstage and Behind the Scenes, NY Times, 2004); (Broadway plays) On the Town; (films) Philadelphia, 1993, Lone Star, 1996, Strangers with Candy, 2005; (TV series) Bob Patterson, 2001, Grey's Anatomy, 2005— (Outstanding Performance by a Female Actor in a Drama Series, SAG, 2007, 2007, Supporting Actress in a Drama Series, NAACP Image Awards, 2007). Mailing: Grey's Anatomy Los Feliz Tower 4th Fl 4151 Prospect Ave Los Angeles CA 90027 *

WILSON, CHARLES A., JR., congressman, funeral director; b. Belmont, Ohio, Jan. 18, 1943; 4 children. BS, Ohio U., 1966; degree, Cin. Coll. Mortuary Sci. Mem. Ohio State Ho. Reps., Columbus, 1997—2004, Ohio State Senate, Columbus, Ohio, 2005—07, US Congress from 6th Ohio dist., 2007—, mem. sci. & tech. com., fin. svcs. com. Mem. banking, pensions and securities com. Ohio State Ho. Reps., mem. fin. and appropriations com., mem. agr. and devel. subcom., mem. rules and reference com.; vice chmn. Belmont (Ohio) Nat. Bank; bd. dirs. East Ohio Regional Hosp. Mem.: Ohio Funeral Dirs. Assn., Blue Dog Coalition, Bridgeport (Ohio) C. of C., St. Clairsville (Ohio) C. of C., Belmont (Ohio) Hills Country Club. Democrat. Roman Catholic. Office: US House Reps 226 Cannon House Office Bldg Washington DC 20515 also: 4137 Boardman Canfield Rd Canfield OH 44406-8087 Office Phone: 330-533-7250. Office Fax: 330-533-7136. *

WILSON, CHARLES BANKS, artist; b. Springdale, Ark., Aug. 6, 1918; s. Charles Bertram and Bertha Juanita (Banks) W.; children: Geoffrey Banks, Carrie Vee. Student, Art Inst. Chgo., 1936—41. Mag. and book illustrator, 1943-60; head art dept. N.E. Okla. A. & M. Coll., Miami, Okla., 1947-61; painter, printmaker. Executed murals, Okla. State Capitol, 1975; represented in permanent collections Met. Mus., NYC, Libr. of Congress, Washington, US Capitol Bldg., DC Corcoran Gallery, Smithsonian Inst., Will Rogers Meml. Mus., Philbrook Art Ctr., Tulsa, Nat. Cowbow Hall of Fame, Oklahoma City, Okla. State Capitol; retrospective exhbn. Gilcreae, 2007; illustrator numerous books; appeared on AETN-TV, Okla., 2006-07, AENBETN-TV, Ark., 2006; subject of profile Am. Artist (PBS), 2007. Bd. dirs. Thomas Gilcrease Mus. History and Art, Tulsa, 1957-61; chmn. Pub. Libr. Bd., Miami, Okla., 1954-59. Named to Okla. Hall of Fame, Okla. Historians Hall of Fame, 2001, named an Okla. Treasure, State of Okla. Arts Commn., 2001; named Charles Banks Wilson Bldg. in his honor Northeast Okla. A&M Coll.; recipient Western Heritage award Cowboy Hall of Fame, Disting. Svc. citation U. Okla., Lifetime Achievement award Ark. Art Coun., 2006; subject of books The Lithographs of Charles Banks Wilson, 1989, Search for the North American Purebloods, 2000, An Oklahoma Portrait, 1989. Mem. Internat. Inst. Arts and Letters (Geneva). Home and Office: 1611 E Mission Blvd Fayetteville AR 72703-3043 Office Phone: 479-442-9891. Personal E-mail: nag-pra-106-@earthlink.net. Business E-Mail: cvwilson@mail.uark.edu.

WILSON, CHARLES NESBITT, lobbyist, former congressman; b. Trinity, Tex., June 1, 1933; s. Charles Edwin and Wilmuth (Nesbitt) Wilson; m. Jerry Wilson (div.); m. Barbara Livshin Alberstadt Zavacky, Feb. 2, 1999. Student, Sam Houston State U., Huntsville, Tex., 1951-52; BS, U.S. Naval Acad., 1956. Commd. ensign U.S. Navy, 1956, advanced through grades to lt.; ret., 1960; mem. Tex. Ho. of Reps., 1960-66, Tex. State Senate, 1966-72, US Congress from 2nd Tex. dist., 1973—97; ranking minority mem. appropriations subcom. on fgn. ops., export financing & related programs; ptnr. Hooper, Owen, Gould & Winburn, 1996—. Mgr. lumber yard, 1962-72 Democrat. Methodist. Office: Hooper Owen Gould & Winburn Ste 730 801 Pennsylvania Ave NW Washington DC 20004-2687

WILSON, CHARLES REGINALD, federal judge; b. Pensacola, Fla., 1954; BS, U. Notre Dame, 1976, JD, 1979. Bar: Fla. 1979. Law clk. to Hon. Joseph W. Hatchett US Ct. Appeals (11th cir.), 1979—80; asst. county atty. Hillsborough county, Fla., 1980—81; county judge 13th Jud. Cir. of Fla., 1986—90; pvt. practice Fla., 1981—86; US magistrate judge US Dist. Ct. (mid. dist.) Fla., 1990—94, US atty., 1994—99; judge US Ct. Appeals (11th cir.), Tampa, Fla., 1999—. Mem.: Ferguson-White Inn of Am. Inn of Ct., Fed. Bar Assn., Am. Law Inst. Office: 11th Cir Ct Appeals 801 N Florida Ave Ste 14B Tampa FL 33602-3849 *

WILSON, CHARLES STEPHEN, cardiologist, educator; b. Geneva, Nebr., June 14, 1938; s. Robert Butler and Naoma Luella (Norgren) Wilson; m. Linda Stern Walt, Aug. 21, 1960; children: Michael Scott, Amy Lynn, Cynthia Lee. BA cum laude, U. Nebr., 1960; MD, Northwestern U., 1964. Diplomate Am. Bd. Internal Medicine subsplty. bd. cardiovascular disease, Nat. Bd. Med. Examiners. Intern Fitzsimons Gen. Hosp., Denver, 1964-65; fellow in internal medicine and cardiology Mayo Grad. Sch. Medicine, Rochester, Minn., 1968-72; practice medicine specializing in cardiology Lincoln, Nebr., 1972—; attending staff Bryan Meml. Hosp., 1972—, chmn. cardiology, 1976-79; clin. prof. medicine and cardiology U. Nebr. Med. Ctr., Omaha; med. dir. Bryan LGH Med. Ctr. Ultrafast CT Scanner, Lincoln, 2001—, Sch. Allied Health, Bryan LGH Coll. of Health Scis., 2002—. Mem. Mayor's Coun. on Emergency Med. Svcs., Lincoln, 1974-78; founder, chmn. Nebr. State Hypertension Screening Program; med. dir. Lincoln Mobile Heart Team, 1977-80, Lincoln Cardiac Rehab. Program, 1978-79; co-founder, pres. Nebr. Heart Inst., 1987; co-founder Lincoln Cardiac Transplant Program, 1987. Contbr. articles to profl. jours.; editorl. cons. Chest, 1975-76; assoc. editor Nebr. Med. Jour., 1981-88. Trustee U. Nebr. Found., 1983—, chmn. Nebr. Coordinating Commn. for Postsecondary Edn., 1984-88; mem. bd. regents U. Nebr., 1991—, chmn. 1994, 2001, 07. Served as maj. M.C., USAR, 1963-68. Gen. Motors Nat. scholar, 1956-60, Nat. Found. med. scholar, 1960-64, Mead Johnson scholar ACP, 1968-71. Fellow ACP, Am. Coll. Cardiology (bd. govs. 1990-93, pres. Nebr. affiliate 1992-93), Am. Coll. Chest Physicans, Am. Heart Assn. (dir. Nebr. affilate 1973-80, pres. 1976-77); mem. Mayo Cardiovascular Soc., Nebr. Cardiovascular Soc. (pres. 1989-90), Nebr. Coun. on Pub. Higher Edn. (steering com. 1991—), Lincoln Heart Assn. (dir. 1972-75, pres. 1974-75), AMA, Nebr. Med. Assn. Lancaster County Med. Soc., Am. Soc. Internal Medicine, Lincoln Found., U. Nebr. Chancellor's Club, Lincoln U. Club (dir. 1981-84), U. Nebr. Pres. Club, Phi Beta Kappa, Sigma Xi, Alpha Omega Alpha, Phi Delta Theta (pres. Nebr. Alpha chpt. 1959-60). Home: 7430 N Hampton Rd Lincoln NE 68506-1624 Office: Bryan LGH Ultrafast CT Scanner 1500 S 48th St Lincoln NE 68506

WILSON, CHERYL YVONNE, elementary and secondary school educator; b. Dayton, Ohio, Sept. 25, 1958; d. Samuel Wesley Wilson Sr. and Hazel Oneida Wilson; m. Henry Heard Cofield Jr., July 27, 1985. Student, Ohio State U., Columbus, 1976—81; AA, Miami U., Oxford, Ohio, 1987. Legal sec. Raymond W. O'Neal, Sr. Atty. at Law, Middletown, Ohio, 1982—83; reorder buyer Dason's Hardware Ctr., 1984—85; Writer's Digest Novel Writing Workshop Middletown City Sch. Dist., 1986—87; deputy clk. Butler County Clk. Cts., Hamilton, 1990—91; mail room clk. Butler County Printing Co., 1992—95; mail courier, security officer Johnson Controls Svcs., Inc., 1998—2000; mail room clk. Dayton Daily News Cox Ohio Publ., 2003—04. Pres., CEO Ohio Writer's Pub. Co., Middletown, 1987—, 1991—; dept. sec. House Reparations 40, 2005—; pres., CEO Carnegie Old Libr., Consortium of Liberal Art and Sci. Found., 2007. Columnist: Dept. Health Regulation Forty Indsl. Inst., 2004—; author: numerous poems, —. Mem. 2006-1966 U.S. Bicentennial Commn., 2003—, curator, exec. dir., 2003; mfr., rep. ILHWA Korean Ginseng Tea Health Food Store Website Products, 2007. Nominee 87th Spingarn medal award, NAACP, 1998, 2001, Coretta Scott King book award, 2002, Oprah Winfrey Angel Network Use Your Life award, 2003. Mem.: NAACP (life Bronze Plaque award 2002), Nat. African Am. Genealogy Rsch. Pub. Assn., Internat. African Am. Genealogy Rsch. Pub. Assn. (curator 2003—, exec. dir. 2003—), Middletown Hist. Soc. (life). Republican. Mem. Lds Ch. Avocations: writing, reading, photography. Personal E-mail: ohioafriamerhistmo@sbcglobal.net.

WILSON, CHRISTOPHER J., lawyer; b. Pensacola, Fla., May 25, 1965; BA cum laude, Thomas More Coll., 1988; JD cum laude, U. Notre Dame, 1991. Bar: Ohio 1991. Ptnr. Frost Brown Todd LLP; assoc. gen. counsel, asst. corp. sec. Cincinnati Bell, Inc. (formerly Broadwing, Inc.), Cincinnati, Ohio, 1999—2003, v.p., gen. counsel, 2003—. Mem. adv. coun. Nat. Assn. Minority and Women Owned Law Firms; mem. steering com. Gr. Cincinnati Minority Counsel Program. Mem.: Ohio State Bar Assn., Cincinnati Bar Assn. Office: Cincinnati Bell Inc 221 E Fourth St Cincinnati OH 45202 Business E-Mail: christopher.wilson@cinbell.com.

WILSON, CLARK R., geophysicist, educator; BA with high honors in Physics, U. Calif. San Diego Revelle Coll., 1970; MS in Earth Sci., U. Calif. San Diego Scripps Instn. Oceanography, 1973, PhD in Earth Sci., 1975. Asst. prof. to assoc. prof. U. Tex., Austin, 1976—89, prof., 1989—, Wallace Pratt prof. geophysics, 1992—. Chmn. dept. geol. scis. U. Tex., Austin, 1990—94, 2004—; geodynamics and geopotential fields prog. specialist NASA, Washington, 1996—99; head Geophys. Fluids Ctr. Hydrology, 1999—2004; mem. directing bd. Internat. Earth Rotation Svc., 2000—. Contbr. articles to sci. jours.; assoc. editor geodesy: Jour. Geophys. Rsch., 1993—99. Office: Geol Scis Dept U Tex 1 Univ Sta C1100 Austin TX 78712-0254 E-mail: crwilson@mail.utexas.edu.

WILSON, CLAUDE RAYMOND, JR., lawyer; b. Dallas, Feb. 22, 1933; s. Claude Raymond and Lottie (Watts) W.; m. Emilynn Wilson; children: Deidra Wilson Graves, Melissa Woodard Utley, Michele Woodard Dunn. BBA, So. Meth. U., Dallas, 1954, JD, 1956. Bar: Tex. 1956; CPA, Calif., Tex. Assoc. firm Cervin & Melton, Dallas, 1956-58; atty. Tex. & Pacific R.R. Co., Dallas, 1958-60; atty. office regional counsel IRS, San Francisco, 1960-63, sr. trial atty. office chief counsel Washington, 1963-65; ptnr. Wilson & White, Dallas, 1965-98, Vial, Hamilton, Koch & Knox LLP, Dallas, 1998—2007, Looper Reed & McGraw, Dallas, 2007—. Chmn., Dallas dist. dir. IRS Adv. Commn., 1990-91. Chmn. Dallas Hist. Soc., 2000-01; mem. fin. com. Dallas Arboretum and Bot. Gardens, 2003—, City of University Park, 2004—; bd. govs., mem. fin. com., mem. ethics com. Dallas Symphony Orch., 2004—. Mem.: AICPA (coun. 1989—93, tax exec. com. 1998—2001), ABA, Tex. Soc. CPAs (pres. 1989—90, pres. Dallas chpt. 1983—84), Dallas Bar Assn. (pres. sect. taxation 1969—70), State Bar Tex., Greater Dallas C. of C. (chmn. appropriations and tax com. 1990—91), Dallas Petroleum Club, Masons, Delta Theta Phi., Delta Sigma Phi. Republican. Episcopalian. Office: Looper Reed & McGraw 4100 Thanksgiving Tower 1601 Elm St Dallas TX 75201 Office Phone: 214-237-6335. Business E-Mail: cwilson@lrmlaw.com.

WILSON, CLEO FRANCINE, foundation administrator; b. Chgo., May 7, 1943; d. Cleo Antonio Chancey and Frances (Page) Watson; divorced; children: SuLyn Silbar. BA in English with distinction, U. Ill., 1976. Supr. Playboy Enterprises, Inc., Chgo., 1980-82; grants mgr. Playboy Found., Chgo., 1982-84, exec. dir., 1984—, v.p. pub. affairs, 2001—. Pres. Intuit: The Ctr. for Intuitive and Outsider Art, 1996—, 2000—. Pres. AIDS Found. Chgo., 1990-93; v.p. Donors Forum Chgo., 1986-88; sec. Chgo. Women in Philanthropy, 1986-87; advisor Chgo. Dept. Cultural Affairs, 1988-90. Recipient Kizzy Image award Black Woman Hall of Fame, 1984;, Friend for Life award Howard Brown Health Ctr, 1991, Handy L. Lindsey award for inclusiveness in philanthropy, 2004; honored by AIDS Found, Chgo, 1999; named one of Chgo's. Up and Coming by Dollars & Sense mag., 1985, Phenomenal Woman award An Expo for Today's Black Woman, 1997. Home: 6571 N Glenwood Ave Chicago IL 60626-5121 Office: Playboy Enterprises Inc 680 N Lake Shore Dr Fl 15 Chicago IL 60611-4455

WILSON, COLIN HENRY, writer; b. Leicester, Eng., June 26, 1931; s. Arthur and Anetta Wilson; m. Joy Stewart; children: Sally, Damon, Rowan; 1 child from previous marriage, Roderick. Writer-in-residence Hollins (Va.) Coll., 1966—67; vis. prof. U. Wash., Seattle, 1967, Rutgers U., New Brunswick, NJ, 1974. Author: The Outsider, 1956, The Glass Cage, 1967, The Angry Years, 2007, Man Hunters, 2007, (novels) The Occult, 1971, The Black Room, 1971, The Space Vampires, 1975, Mysteries, 1978, others, (books) Access to Inner World, 1982, A Criminal History of Mankind, 1983, The Essential Colin Wilson, 1984, The Personality Surgeon, 1986, Spider World, 1987, The Misfits, 1988, Beyond the Occult, 1988, Written in Blood, 1989; author: (with Donald Seaman) Modern Encyclopedia of Murder, 1983, The Serial Killers, 1989; author: (with Damon Wilson) Encyclopedia of Unsolved Mysteries, 1987, Crimes of Passion, 2006; author: others, (plays) Mozart's Journey to Prague, 1991, Spider World: The Magician, 1992, The Strange Life of P. D. Ouspensky, 1993, From Atlantis to The Sphinx, 1996, Atlas of Holy Places and Sacred Sites, 1996, Alien Dawn, 1998, The Books in My Life, 1998, The Devil's Party, 2000, Spider World: The Magician, 2002, Spider World: Shadowland, 2003; author: (with Damon Wilson) Unsolved Mysteries Past and Present, 1993; author: (with Rand Fle'math) Atlantis Blueprint, 2000; author: (autobiography) Dreaming to Some Purpose, 2004, Atlantis and the Kingdom of the Neanderthals, 2006. Mem.: Savage. Business E-Mail: colin@chwilson.demon.co.uk.

WILSON, D. EDWARD, JR., lawyer; b. New Orleans, Dec. 23, 1951; s. Donald Edward and Nellie (Courtney) W.; m. Lynn Whittlesey, Sept. 10, 1981; children: Robert Donald, Thomas Courtney, John Whittlesey. BA, U. Va., 1973; JD, Georgetown U., 1976. Law clk. to Judge R.L. Kunzig U.S. Ct. Appeals (fed. cir.), Washington, 1976-77; assoc. Morgan, Lewis & Bockius, Washington, 1977-81; assoc. counsel to the pres. The White House, Washington, 1981-84, gen. counsel Office of Adminstrn., 1984-85; prin. dep. asst. sec. for mgmt. Dept. of the Treasury, Washington, 1985-86, acting gen. counsel, 1986-88; pvt. practice, 1988—; ptnr., Banking & Fin. Svc., Internat. Bus. practices Venable LLP, Washington, 2003—. Lectr. in field. Chmn Goodwin House, Inc., 1996-2001, Goodwin House Found., 2005-06; mem. vestry St. Peter's Episcopal Ch., Arlington, Va., 1988-91. Recipient Disting. Svc. award Sec. Dept. Treasury, 1988, Gen. Counsel's award, 1988, Chief Counsel's award IRS, 1988. Mem. ABA, D.C. Bar, La. State Bar Assn., Washington Inst. for Affairs, So. Yacht Club (New Orleans), Met. Club (Washington). Republican. Episcopalian. Office: Venable LLP 575 7th St NW Washington DC 20004 Office Phone: 202-344-4000. Business E-Mail: dewilson@venable.com.

WILSON, DANIEL RICHARD, anthropologist, physician; b. Fort Dodge, Iowa, Feb. 22, 1956; m. Sandra Lea Davis; 1 child, Victoria Elizabeth. BA Anthropology, Yale U., 1979; MD, U. Iowa, 1983; PhD Anthropology, Cambridge U., 1995; diploma mental health mgmt., Case Western Res. U., 1996. Cert. FABPN, 1989. Resident in psychiatry Harvard Med. Sch., 1987; neuropsychiatrist McLean Hosp. - Harvard Med. Sch., Belmont, Mass., 1987—92; assoc. prof. psychiatry U. Cin., 1993—98; med. dir. ODMH - Lewis Ctr., 1993—2000, ODMH - Statewide ISS, 1998—2000; prof. psychiatry U. Cin., 1998—2000; prof., chmn. psychiatry, prof. anthropology Creighton U., Omaha, 2000—. Named Nat. Tng. Program of Yr., Nat. Alliance for Mentally Ill, 1995; recipient Huston award, U. Iowa Coll. Medicine, 1983, Nat. Exemplar Training Program award, Am. Psychiat. Assn., 1994; vis. fellow, Clare Hall, Cambridge U., 1992—93, Slyster scholar, AMA, 1982—83, Burroughs-Wellcome fellow, Am. Psychiat. Assn., 1985—87, Overseas fellow, Royal Anthropol. Inst., 1997—, Rotary fellow, Cambridge U., England, 1992—93. Fellow: Am. Bd. Forensic Medicine (life); mem.: World Psychiat. Assn. (chair Psychotherapy 2004—), Internat. Soc. Police Surgeons (life), Alpha Omega Alpha (life). Office: Creighton U Sch Med 3528 Dodge St Omaha NE 68131 Office Phone: 402-345-8828.

WILSON, DAVID GORDON, mechanical engineering educator; b. Sutton Coldfield, Warwick, Eng., Feb. 11, 1928; s. William and Florence Ida (Boulton) W.; m. Anne Ware Sears, July 18, 1963 (div. May 1988); children: John M.B., Erica Sears; m. Ellen Cecilia Warner, Dec. 30, 1988; 1 child, Susan Speck. Postgrad., MIT, Harvard U., 1955-57; BS with honors, U. Birmingham, UK, 1948; PhD, U. Nottingham, UK, 1953. Brush fellow, rsch. asst. Nottingham U., 1950-53; ship's 7th engr. officer Donaldson Line, Glasgow, UK, 1953; engr. Brush Elec. Engring. Co., Ltd., UK, 1953-55; sr. gas-turbine designer Ruston & Hornsby, Lincoln, UK, 1957-58; sr. lectr., mech. engring. U. Ibadan, Zaria, Nigeria, 1958-60; v.p., tech. dir. No. Rsch. and Engring. Corp., Cambridge, Mass., also U.K., 1960-66; assoc. prof. mech. engring. MIT, Cambridge, 1966-71, prof., 1971-94; prof. emeritus, 1994—; co-founder, chief sci. officer Wilson TurboPower, Inc., Woburn, Mass., 2001—. Vis. engr., Boeing Airplane Co., 1956-57; vis. fellow MIT and Harvard U., 1955-56; cons., lectr. in field. Author: The Design of Gas-Turbine Engines, 1991, The Design of High-Efficiency Turbomachinery and Gas Turbines, 1984, (with T.P. Korakianitis), 2d edit., 1998; co-author: (with Frank Rowland Whitt) Bicycling Science, 1974, 2d edit., 1982, 3d edit., 2004, (with Richard Wilson et al) The Health Effects of Fossil-Fuel Burning, 1981, (with Douglas Stephen Beck) Gas-Turbine Regenerators, 1996; co-editor: (with Allan V. Abbott) Human-Powered Vehicles, 1995; editor: Solid-Waste-Management Handbook, 1977, The Treatment and Management of Urban Solid Waste, 1972; editor Human Power, 1984-2002. Recipient T. Bernard Hall prize Inst. Mech. Engrs., 1954, Lord Weir 1st prize Inst. Mech. Engrs., 1955, Indsl. Rsch. IR-100 award, 1974, Reclamation Industries Internat. prize, 1974; Power-Jets-Sch. scholar, 1954; Commonwealth Fund fellow MIT and Harvard U., 1955-57. Avocations: human power, biking, hiking, tennis, music. Office: MIT/Mech Engring Rm 3-137e Cambridge MA 02139 Home Phone: 781-729-2203; Office Phone: 781-368-1000 ext 203. Personal E-mail: dgwilson@mit.edu. Business E-Mail: dave.wilson@wilsonturbopower.com.

WILSON, DAVID JAMES, chemistry researcher, educator; b. Ames, Iowa, June 25, 1930; s. James Calmar and Alice Winona (Olmsted) W.; m. Martha Carolyn Mayers, Sept. 6, 1952; children: John Wesley, Charles Steven, William David, Andrew Lyman, Joyce Ballin. BS in Chemistry, Stanford U., 1952; postgrad., 1952-53, 55-57; PhD, Calif. Inst. Tech., 1958. Mem. faculty U. Rochester, NY, 1957-69, assoc. prof. NY, 1963-67, prof. phys. chemistry NY, 1967-69; prof. Vanderbilt U., Nashville, 1969-95, prof. chemistry and environ. engring., 1977-95, prof. emeritus, 1995—, Alexander Heard disting. service prof., 1983-84; sr. rsch. assoc. Eckenfelder/Brown and Caldwell, Nashville, 1988-95, sr. rsch. fellow, 1995—. Vis. sr. lectr. chemistry U. Ife, Nigeria, 1964-65; vis. prof. U. Málaga, Spain, 1993-94; mem. Rochester Com. for Sci. Info., 1960-69, v.p., 1966-69; chmn. Nashville Com. for Sci. Info., 1971-74. Author: (book) Foam Flotation: Theory and Applications, Hazardous Waste Site Soil Remediation, Modeling of In Situ Techniques for Treatment of Contaminated Soils. Pres. Tenn. Environ. Coun., 1985-87. Sp-3 US Army, 1953—55, Army Chem. Ctr., Md. Recipient award Monroe County Conservation Coun., 1967, Tenn. Conservation League, 1971; Alfred P. Sloan Found. fellow, 1964-66. Mem. AAAS, Am. Chem. Soc., Tenn. Acad. Sci., Sigma Xi, Phi Beta Kappa. Avocations: ornithology, music, travel, hiking. Home: 11544 Quirk Rd Belleville MI 48111 Office Phone: 734-699-7623. Personal E-mail: djw1ls0n@sbcglobal.net.

WILSON, DENA SUZETTE, elementary school educator; b. Lubbock, Tex., Aug. 22, 1964; d. James Leroy and Rena Glyndell Louthan; m. Robert Hugh Wilson Jr., Dec. 16, 1989. BA in Family and Consumer Sci., U. Houston, 1986; M in Elem. Edn., Berry Coll., Mt. Berry, Ga., 2000. Cert. vocat. home econs. tchr. Tex., 1987, kindergarten tchr. Tex., 1988, self-contained elem. tchr. Tex., 2002, tchr. pre-kindergarten-8th grade Ga., Tex., tchr. 6-12 grade Ga., Tex. Tchr. pre-kindergarten Spring Ind. Sch. Dist., Tex., 1986—90; store mgr. Suzette's Cards & Gifts, 1990—97; tchr. grades 1 and 2 Bartow County Schs., Cartersville, Ga., 1997—2002; tchr. grade 3 Llano Ind. Sch. Dist., Tex., 2002—, Renaissance reading leadership team mem., 2006—. Team leader site based leadership team Llano Elem. Sch., Tex., 2004—; site based leadership team Llano Ind. Sch. Dist., Tex., 2006—. Sec. Child Welfare Bd., Llano, Tex., 2004—, Llano Corp. Children in Crisis, 2005—; dir. Awana 1st Bapt., 2003—, dir. vacation bible sch., 2006—. Mem.: Assn. Tex. Profl. Educators, Internat. Reading Assn., Delta Kappa Gamma. Avocations: reading, antiques, cooking. Home: 407 W Sandstone Llano TX 78643 Office: Llano Elem Sch 1600 Oatman St Llano TX 78643 Mailing: PO Box 56 Llano TX 78643 Personal E-mail: robdena@yahoo.com.

WILSON, DENISE See EARLY, TERI

WILSON, DON MATTHEW, III, corporate banking executive; b. Ravenna, Ohio, Jan. 24, 1948; s. Don Matthew and Helen Jane (Strimple) W.; m. Lynn Suzanne Byron, Oct. 13, 1984. AB cum laude, Harvard U., Cambridge, Mass., 1970; MBA, Dartmouth Coll., Hanover, NH, 1973. Mng. dir. Chem. Bank, NYC, 1973—. Republican. Congregationalist Clubs: Harvard (N.Y.C.); Rockaway Hunting (L.I.)

WILSON, DONALD EDWARD, internist, educator, dean; b. Worcester, Mass., Aug. 28, 1936; s. Rivers Rivo and Licine (Bradshaw) Wilson; m. Patricia C. Littell, Aug. 27, 1977; children: Jeffrey D.E., Sean D., Monique, Sheila L. AB, Harvard U., 1958; MD, Tufts U., 1962. Diplomate Am. Bd. Internal Medicine. Intern St. Elizabeth Hosp., Boston, 1962—63; resident in medicine, research fellow in gastroenterology VA Hosp. and Lemuel Shattuck Hosp., Boston, 1963—66; assoc. chief gastroenterology Bklyn. Hosp., 1968—71; instr. medicine SUNY Downstate Med. Center, Bklyn., 1968—71; asst. prof. medicine U. Ill., Chgo., 1971—73, asso. prof., 1973—75, prof., 1975—80, acting head dept. medicine, 1976—77; dir. divsn. gastroenterology U. Ill. Hosp., Chgo., 1971—78, chief of gastroenterology, 1973—80, physician-in-chief, 1976—77; prof., chmn. dept. medicine SUNY Downstate Med. Center, Bklyn., 1980—91; physician-in-chief State U. and Kings County Hosp., 1980—91; dean U. Md. Sch. Medicine, Balt., 1991—, v.p. of med. affairs, 1999—. Vis. prof. medicine U. London, Kings Coll. Med. Sch., 1977—78; mem. gastrointestingal drugs adv. bd. FDA, 1985—87, chmn., 1986—87; mem. Part II test com. Nat. Bd. Med. Examiners, 1985—88; mem. nat. digestive adv. bd. NIH, 1985—87, chmn., 1986—87, mem. gen. clin. rsch. ctrs. com., 1987—; mem. nat. adv. com. Agy. for Health Care Policy and Rsch., Dept. HHS, 1991—94, chmn., 1992—94; mem. residency rev. com. for internal medicine Acque, 1993—; mem. nat. com. fgn. med. edn. and accreditation U.S. Dept. Edn., 1994—; mem. nat. adv. rsch. resources com. NIH, 1997—2000; bd. dirs. Provident Bank Corp., 2002—. Contbr. articles to med. jours.; mem. editl. bd. Tufts Med. Alumni Bulletin, 1993—2002. Bd. vis. Harvard Sch. Pub. Health, 1992—94; bd. overseers Tufts U. Med. Sch., 2002—; bd. dirs. Balt. Symphony Orch., 1997—2004, Kernan Hosp., Balt., 1991—98, bd. dirs., Endowment Fund, 1996—; bd. dirs. Alliance to End Childhood Poisoning, 1992—95, The Baer Sch., Balt., 1992—, Mercy

Med. Ctr., Balt., 1991—, U. Md. Med. Sys., 1991—. Capt. M.C. USAF, 1966—68. Recipient Rsch. award, HEW, 1971, 1974, John A. Hartford Found., Inc., 1972—79, Distilled Spirits Coun. U.S., 1972—74, VA, 1974. Master: ACP; mem.: AAAS, NAS, Inst. of Medicine, Assn. Profs. Medicine (sec.-treas. 1990—91), Am. Clin. and Climatol. Assn., Nat. Med. Assn., Assn. for Acad. Minority Physicians (sec./treas. 1986—), Assn. Am. Physicians, Chgo. Soc. Gastrointestinal Endoscopy (pres. 1979—80), N.Y. Soc. Gastroenterology, N.Y. Acad. Medicine, N.Y. Acad. Scis., Soc. Exptl. Biology and Medicine, Midwest Gut Club, Digestive Disease Found., Chgo. Soc. Gastroenterology (pres. 1978—79), Ctrl. Rsch. Club, Ctrl. Soc. Clin. Rsch., Accreditation Coun. Grad. Med. Edn. (rev. com. internal medicine), Am. Assn. Study Liver Disease, Am. Fedn. Clin. Rsch., Am. Gastroent. Assn., Md. Med Comprehensive Ins. Trust (mem. 1998—, chmn. 1998—2000, 2002—04), The Ctr. Club (Balt.), Med. Club Bklyn., 14 West Hamilton St. Club (Balt.), Harvard Club (Chgo., N.Y.C.), Sigma Pi Phi (grand boule). Office: U Md Sch Medicine 655 W Baltimore St Rm 14029 BRB Baltimore MD 21201-1509 Office Phone: 410-706-7410. Office Fax: 410-706-0235.

WILSON, DONALD EUGENE, management consultant; b. Ventura, Calif., Apr. 12, 1969; s. Randall George and Deborah Ellen (Smith) Wilson; m. Susan Kathleen Johnson, Aug. 29, 1998; children: G. Stephenson Hughes, Georgia Elizabeth Elene, Liam Patrick Ross, Charlotte Reagan. BA in Govt., Calif. State U., Sacramento, 1999, MA in Govt., 2005. Cons. Calif. State Legis. Assembly, Sacramento, 1994—97, Calif. State Legis. Senate, Sacramento, 2001—. Sch. bd. mem. Ctr. Joint United Sch. Dist., Antelope, Calif., 2005—; bd. dirs. Ctr. Endowment Ednl. Excellence, Antelope, 2006—; chmn. Antelope Planning Adv. Coun., 2002—06; mem. state ctrl. com. Calif. Reps., 1993—2004, Calif., 2007—; mem. county ctrl. com. Sacramento Reps., 1996—2000; mem. state exec. bd. Young Rep. Fedn., Calif., 1996—2000. Petty officer USN, 1987—89. Mem.: Pi Sigma Alpha, Phi Kappa Phi. Presbyterian. Avocations: reading, football, gardening, electronics. Office: Senate Vets Affairs Com 1020 N St # 251 Sacramento CA 95814

WILSON, DONALD GREY, engineering management consultant; b. Bridgeport, Conn., Sept. 20, 1917; s. William Gray and Jeannetta McAvoy (Kerr) W.; m. Elizabeth Jean Lanning, Apr. 24, 1943 (div. Mar. 1971, dec. Mar. 2002); children: Kirk Lanning, Craig Gardner, William Grey. BSEE, Rensselaer Poly. Inst., 1938; SM, Harvard U., 1939, MES, 1947, PhD, 1948. Mgr. automatic fire alarm divsn. Sealand Corp., Bridgeport, Conn., 1939-40; instr. elec. engring. Rensselaer Poly. Inst., 1940-42; staff mem. Radiation Lab. MIT, 1942-45; prof. elec. engring. U. Kan., Lawrence, 1947-55, chmn. dept., 1948-55; dir. Phila. Brass & Bronze, 1962-64, Mallory-Xerox Corp., 1964-65. Cons. U.S. Naval Ordance Test Sta., China Lake, Calif., 1953-54; assoc. dir. rsch. dept. Stromberg-Carlson Co., San Diego, 1955-59, gen. mgr., 1959, asst. v.p., 1959-60; v.p. rsch. P.R. Mallory & Co., Indpls., 1960, v.p. rsch. and engring., 1961-71, v.p. rsch., engring. and environ. affairs, 1971-75; alt. dir. Mallory Metal. Products, Eng., 1967; pres. Contemporary Custom Cabinets, San Diego, 1975-76; v.p. Continental Resources and Minerals Corp., Dayton, Ohio, 1978-79; sr. v.p. Tanzi Mergers/Acquisitions, San Diego, 1983-86; mgmt. cons., 1976—; sr. lectr. U. Rochester, 1956-57; lectr. dept. elec. engring. San Diego State U., 1981-92, asst. dean coll. engring., 1987, prof. emeritus, 1992—; mng. dir., exec. bd. Nat. Bur. Cert. Cons., 1988-94, sr. adv. counsel, 1994-2001; sr. advisor Nat. Bur. Energy Solutions, 2007—. Contbr. articles to profl. jours. Bd. dirs. Speech and Hearing Clinic, Indpls., 1960-66, Washington Twp. Sch. Dist., 1964-68, pres., 1966-67. Recipient Outstanding Acad. Advisor award San Diego State U., 1992. Fellow AAAS; mem. IEEE (sr. life, exec. com. San Diego sect. 1986-2003, 2004—, chmn. S.W. area region 6 1999-2000, sec. region 6 2001-02, ethics and mem. conduct com. 2002-03, R&D policy com. 2000—, Third Millennium medal, Region 6 Outstanding Br. Counselor award 1992), Affiliation Profl. Cons. Orgns. (chmn. bd. govs. 1991-93 San Diego Engring. Coun. Outstanding Svc. award 2000), Intertel, Sigma Xi, Sigma Phi Epsilon, Tau Beta Pi, Eta Kappa Nu. Home: 1950 Silverleaf Cir #310 Carlsbad CA 92009 Personal E-mail: don.wilson@ieee.org.

WILSON, DONALD HURST, III, biopharmaceutical industry executive; b. Balt., Mar. 1, 1946; s. Donald H. and Winifred W.; m. Catharine A. MacKinnon, June 21, 1968 (div. 1972); m. Beverly Lee Wright, Oct. 3, 1975 (div. 1998); m. Constance Fisher Neely, Sept. 23, 2000; children: Beverly Callaway, Sarah Elizabeth. AB, Yale U., 1968; MBA, JD, Harvard U., 1976. Bar: Mass. 1977, N.C. 2003; cert. Superior Ct. mediator NC Dispute Resolution Commn., 2004. Cons. Boston Cons. Group, 1976-78; dir. mktg. I/C divsn. Black & Decker, Hampstead, Md., 1978-83; pres. MWI Tng. Svcs., Inc., Hunt Valley, 1983—96; v.p. Innoversity Edn. Ctrs., Global Knowledge Network, Inc., Md., 1996—97; pres. and COO Endacea, Inc. (formerly Link Tech., Inc.), Raleigh, 1997—98, pres. and CEO, 1998—2000, v.p. and COO, 2001—02, v.p., gen. counsel, 2003, pres., CEO and gen. counsel, 2004—. Bd. dirs. Endacea, Inc. (formerly Link Tech., Inc.), Raleigh, 1997—. Mem. vestry St. John's Episcopal Ch., 1993-96, lay eucharistic min., 1995-97; dir. The Bishop Claggett Ctr., 1995-97. Mem.: Info. Tech. Tng. Assn. (founder and dir. 1992—95), Assn. Microcomputer Distbrs. (founder and dir. 1988—90), Archaeol. Soc. Md. (trustee 1994—98). Republican. Avocations: archaeology, golf. Home: 1112 Baslow Brook Ct Raleigh NC 27614-8866

WILSON, DONALD WALLIN, academic administrator, communications educator; b. Poona, India, Jan. 9, 1938; s. Nathaniel Carter and Hannah Myrtle Wilson; children: Carrie, Jennifer, Gregory, Andrew. BA, So. Missionary Coll., 1959; MA, Andrews U., 1961; PhD, Mich. State U., 1966. Dean applied arts and tech. Ont. (Can.) Colls., North Bay, 1968-73; acad. dean Olivet Coll., 1973-76; pres. Castleton State Coll., 1976-79, Southampton Coll., 1979-83, prof. communications and history, 1973-83; pres., prof. Pittsburg State U. (Kans.), 1983-95; pres. Kilang Nusantara Pacific, 1995—; exec. v.p. Shepherd of the Hills Entertainment Group, Branson, Mo., 1997—. Author: The Untapped Source of Power in the Church, 1961, Long Range Planning, 1979, The Long Road From Turmoil to Self Sufficiency, 1989, The Next Twenty-Five Years: Indonesias Journey Into The Future, 1992, The Indispensable Man: Sudomo, 1992. Mem. Kans. Adv. Coun. of C.C.'s; bd. dirs. Internat. U. Thailand; pres. Internat. Univ. Found. Named Alumnus of Achievement Andrews U., 1981; recipient Outstanding Alumni award Mich. State U., 1984. Mem. Speech Communication Assn., Assn. Asian Studies, Internat. Univ. Found. (pres.), Rotary. Methodist. Office: Kilang Nusantara Pacific Office of Pres Frontenac KS 66763 Address: 503 Ohio St Pittsburg KS 66762-6429 E-mail: wdonaldwilson@aol.com.

WILSON, DORIS H., volunteer; b. Akron, Ohio, Jan. 26, 1921; d. Charles Peter and Emma Clara (Howald) Huff; m. Angus Francis Wilson, June 14, 1952; children: Ann Wilson Lambertus, Lea Wilson MacInnis. BS, U. Akron, 1945; postgrad., Framingham State Coll., 1965, Salem State Coll., 1968. Adminstrv. asst. divsn. comml. engr. Ohio Bell Tel. Co., Akron, 1941-52; adminstr. Framingham Ctr. Kindergarten and Nursery Sch., 1965-68. Author: (book) A History of Great Neck, Ipswich, 1984, 1996. Vol. nurse's aide ARC, Akron, 1940; active Gov.'s Coun. Civilian Def., Boston, 1960—66; co-founder, charter mem. Hospice at Home, Wayland, Weston, Natick, Sudbury, Mass., 1978; chmn. W. Suburban Area Boston Symphony Orch., 1978—81; docent Gt. Ho. at Castle Hill, Ipswich, Mass., 1984—2005, Whipple Ho., Ipswich, 1985—2002; treas. Nuc. Freeze Coun., Ipswich, 1986—87; charter mem., bd. dirs. Aplastic Anemia Found. Am. New Eng. region, Brookline, Mass., 1987—92; vol. office asst. Habitat for Humanity, St. Petersburg, Fla., 1988; mem. Ipswich Women's Club, 1981—2006. Recipient Election Poll Officer citation, Gov. of Mass., 1980, 1st pl. Ann. Short Story Contest, Gen. Fedn. Women's Club, 2002. Mem.: AAUW (Mass. state parliamentarian 1966—76, charter, pres. Framingham-Wellesley br., North Shore br., grantee 1974), Ipswich Citizens Advocating Renewable Energy, Friends Glen Magna (Danvers, Mass. dir. 1991—93), Ipswich Hist. Soc., Boston Symphony Assn. Vols., Peace Action, Ipswich Bay Yacht Club (dir. 1981—82), Wayland Women's Club (hon.; pres.). Democrat. Roman Catholic. Home: 8 Bowdoin Rd Ipswich MA 01938-2807

WILSON, DOUGLAS FREDERICK, professional sports team executive, retired professional hockey player; b. Ottawa, Ont., Can., July 5, 1957; s. Douglas and Verna Wilson; m. Katherine Ann Kivisto, July 11, 1981; children: Lacey Anne. Defenseman Chgo. Blackhawks, 1977—91, San Jose Sharks, 1991—93, dir. pro devel., 1997—2003, gen. mgr., 2003—; coord. player rels. and bus. devel. NHL Players Assn., 1993—97. Account exec. Coca-Cola, Chgo. Recipient James Norris Meml. Trophy for best NHL defenseman, 1981-82. Avocations: golf, travel. Office: San Jose Sharks 525 W Santa Clara St San Jose CA 95113 *

WILSON, DOUGLAS LEONARD, minister, educator; b. Lumberton, NC, June 8, 1964; s. James Martin and Ruby Wilson; m. Julia Kaye Roberts, May 19, 1983; children: Martin, Samuel. BS in Math. magna cum laude, N.C. State U., 1986; MRE, Foundations Bible Coll., Dunn, NC, 1990; DRE, Founds. Bible Coll., 1993. Ordained to ministry 1992. Tchr. Raleigh Christian Acad., NC, 1986-90; bookkeeper First Free Will Bapt. Ch., Raleigh, 1987-90; acct. Oscar N. Harris and Assocs., P.A., Dunn, 1990-93; dean Christian Edn. Founds. Bible Coll., Dunn, 1993—. Tchr. Founds. Christian Acad., Dunn, 1993—, prin., 1999—. Vol. Prisoners Hope Ministry, Lillington, NC, 1996—. Recipient Faculty Forum award, Founds. Bible Coll., 1995. Office: PO Box 1166 Dunn NC 28335-1166

WILSON, E. B., manufacturing executive, consultant, writer; b. Albany, NY, May 13, 1931; s. Harold Edgar and Marie Elizabeth (Brush) W.; m. Mary Beth Weilbacher, Aug. 2, 1956. BA, St. Lawrence U., 1953, PhD (hon.), 2002; MBA, Harvard U., 1955. Mkt. dir. Richardson-Vicks, Inc., NYC, Paris, Manila, 1957-64; CEO Japan Kimberly-Clark Corp., Neenah, Wis., 1964-68, France, 1968-71; pres., CEO French ops. Kimberly-Clark, Corp., Neenah, Wis., 1968—73; v.p. internat. div., gen. mgr. Pillsbury Co., Mpls., 1971-76; exec. v.p. Shaklee Corp., San Francisco, 1976-79; pres., CEO Almay Cosmetics, Inc., NYC, 1979-84, Hathaway Group of Warnaco, NYC, 1984—89; chmn. Global Brands, Inc., NYC, 1989—; found., pres. EBI, Inc., Chatham, Mass., 1995—. Chmn., chief exec. officer Sero Co., Branford, Conn., Martin Jonap, Ltd., Hauppauge, NY; bd. dirs. William Schneider, Inc., Miami, HMI, Inc., Norwood, Mass. Author: The Committee on Trustees, 2001; contbr. to columns Trusteeship jour. Trustee Chatham Hist. Soc., 2006-, St. Lawrence U., Canton, NY, 1986-2001, chmn. bd. trustees, 1995-2001, Boston Conservatory, 2000-, San Francisco Ballet, 1978, New Horizons Project, Cambridge, Mass., 2001-; devel. dir. Cen. Park Conservancy, NYC, 1983-89; mem. Pub. Edn. Nominating Coun., Commonwealth of Mass., 2007—. With USAR, 1955-57. Mem. Eastward Ho Club (v.p., gov., 1985-91), Harvard Club NY, Harvard Club Boston, Eagle Scout. Republican. Avocations: cooking, running, golf, reading, international travel. Home and Office: 1114 Orleans Rd North Chatham MA 02650 Personal E-mail: ebi@cape.com.

WILSON, ED, broadcast executive; BS in Fin., U. Ark., 1980. Sales trainee Viacom, NYC, 1980, mgr. Chgo.; sales mgr. KATV, Little Rock; mgr. southern region Paramount, Dallas, 1984, mgr. eastern region NYC; sr. v.p. Sony Pictures TV, LA, 1990; founder MaXaM Entertainment, 1994; pres. CBS Enterprises, NBC Enterprises, 2000—04, Fox TV Network, 2004—. Bd. mem. Univ. Tex. Comm. Bd. mem. Spine in Sports Found., Nat. Assn. TV Programming Executives Ednl. Found.; active mem. ReREAD. Mem.: Hollywood Radio and TV Soc. (bd. mem.), Nat. Assn. TV Programming Executives (bd. dirs., exec. com.). Office: Fox Broadcasting Co 10201 W Pico Blvd Los Angeles CA 90035 *

WILSON, EDWARD CONVERSE, JR., oil and natural gas production company executive; b. Cambridge, Mass., Jan. 1, 1928; s. Edward Converse and Jean (McLean) W.; m. Patricia Ann Cairns, Sept. 10, 1953; children— Amy Cairns, Sarah Converse. AB, Harvard U., 1949. Brokerage trainee Estabrook & Co., Boston, 1951; Midwest Stock Exch. clk. Paul H. Davis & Co., Chgo., 1951-52; mem. Chgo. Bd. Trade, 1952-78, dir., 1966-67, chmn., 1970-71; ptnr. Nolan & Wilson Co. (specialists on Midwest Stock Exchange), 1965-72; sr. ptnr. Wilson Prodn. Co., Ft. Smith, Ark., 1972-74. Mem. devel. com. Chgo. chpt. Nat. Multiple Sclerosis Soc., 1970; mem. vis. com. on univ. resources Harvard, 1971-74, 76-81; Bd. dirs. Franklin Blvd. Community Hosp., 1970-74. Served with USAF, 1946-47. Mem. Racquet Club (Chgo.). Home: 11114 Wickwood Dr Houston TX 77024-7523

WILSON, EDWARD NATHAN, mathematician, educator; b. Warsaw, NY, Dec. 2, 1941; s. Hugh Monroe and Margaret Jane (Northrup) W.; m. Mary Katherine Schooling, Aug. 19, 1976; children: Nathan Edward, Emily Katherine. BA, Cornell U., 1963; MS, Stanford U., 1965; PhD, Washington U., St. Louis, 1971. Instr. Ft. Valley (Ga.) State Coll., 1965-67, Washington U., St. Louis, 1968-69, U. Calif., Irvine, 1970-71, Brandeis U., Waltham, Mass., 1971-73; asst. prof. Washington U., St. Louis, 1973-77, assoc. prof., 1977-87, dean grad. sch., 1983-93, dean univ. coll., 1986-88, prof., 1987—, chair dept. math., 1995-99. Mem. Grad. Record Exams. Bd., Princeton, N.J., 1986-90; sec.-treas. Assn. Grad. Schs. Contbr. articles to profl. jours. Mem. Brentwood Sch. Bd., Mo., 1984. Woodrow Wilson fellow, 1963; NSF fellow, 1963-65; NDEA fellow, 1967-70. Mem. Am. Math. Soc., Math. Assn. of Am. Democrat. Office: Washington U Campus Box 1146 1 Brookings Dr Saint Louis MO 63130-4899 Office Phone: 314-935-6729. Business E-Mail: enwilson@math.wustl.edu.

WILSON, EDWARD OSBORNE, biologist, educator, writer; b. Birmingham, Ala., June 10, 1929; s. Edward Osborne and Inez (Freeman) W.; m. Irene Kelley, Oct. 30, 1955; 1 child, Catherine Irene. BS, U. Ala., 1949, MS, 1950, LHD (hon.), 1980; PhD, Harvard U., 1955; DPhil, Uppsala U., Sweden; DSc (hon.), Duke U., 1978, Grinnell Coll., 1978, U. West Fla., 1979, Lawrence U., 1979, Fitchburg State Coll., 1989, Macalester Coll., 1990, U. Mass., 1990, Oxford U., 1993, Ripon Coll., 1994, U. Conn., 1995, Ohio U., 1996, Bates Coll., 1996, Coll. Wooster, 1997, U. Guelph, 1997, U. Portland, 1997, Kenyon Coll., 2002, U. of the South, 2002, Harvard U., 2004, Clark U., 2005; LHD (hon.), Hofstra U., 1986, Muhlenburg Coll., 1998, Yale U., 1998, Pa. State U., Bradford Coll., 1997, Conn. Coll., 2000, U. South Ala., 2003, Albion Coll., 2005, U. Puget Sound, 2006, Rockefeller U., 2007, Williams Coll., 2007; LLD, Simon Fraser U.; DHC, U. Madrid Complutense, 1995, U. Montreal, 2004; DrRerNat, U. Würzburg, 2000. Jr. fellow Soc. Fellows, Harvard U., 1953—56, faculty, 1956—, Baird prof. sci., 1976—94, Pellegrino U. prof., 1994—97, rsch. prof., 1997—2002, curator entomology, 1971—97, hon. curator entomology, 1997—. Selection com. Guggenheim Found., 1982—89; bd. dirs. World Wildlife Fund, 1983—94, Orgn. Tropical Studies, 1984—91, N.Y. Bot. Garden, 1991—95, Am. Mus. Natural History, 1992—2002, Am. Acad. Liberal Edn., 1993—2004, Nature Conservancy, 1994—2002, Conservation Internat., 1997—. Author: The Insect Societies, 1971, Sociobiology: The New Synthesis, 1975, On Human Nature, 1978 (Pulitzer prize for non-fiction, 1979), Promethean Fire, 1983, Biophilia, 1984, Success and Dominance in Ecosystems, 1990, The Diversity of Life, 1992 (Nat. Wildlife Assn. award, Deutsche Umweltstiftung Book award, Sir Peter Kent Conservation prize), Naturalist, 1994 (L.A. Times Book prize sci., 1995), In Search of Nature, 1996, Consilience: The Unity of Knowledge, 1998 (Forkosch award Internat. Acad. Humanism, 2000), Biological Diversity: The Oldest Human Heritage, 1999, The Future of Life, 2002 (Natural World Book prize, U.K., 2002), Pheidole in the New World: A Dominant, Hyperdiverse Ant Genus, 2003 (Julia Ward Howe prize, 2003), From So Simple A Beginning, 2005, Nature Revealed, 2006, The Creation: An Appeal to Save Life on Earth, 2006; author: (with R.H. MacArthur) The Theory of Island Biogeography, 1967; author: (with C.J. Lumsden) Genes, Mind and Culture, 1981; author: (with Bert Holldobler) The Ants, 1990 (Pulitzer prize for non-fiction, 1991), Journey to the Ants, 1994 (Phi Beta Kappa prize sci., 1995), The Creation, 2006 (Green Book award, Stevens Inst. Tech. Ctr. Sci. Writings, 2007); others. Recipient Cleve.-AAAS Rsch. prize, 1967, Mercer award, Ecol. Soc. Am., 1971, Nat. Medal Sci., 1976, Disting. Svc. award, Am. Inst. Biol. Scis., 1976, Archie Carr medal, U. Fla., 1978, Leidy medal, Acad. Natural Sci., Phila., 1979, Tyler Ecology prize, 1984, Silver medal, Nat. Zool. Park, 1987, German Ecol. Inst. prize, 1987, Weaver award scholarly letters, Ingersoll Found., 1989, Crafoord prize, Royal Swedish Acad. Scis., 1990, Prix di'Inst. de la Vie, Paris, 1990, Revelle medal, 1990, Gold medal, Worldwide Fund for Nature, 1990, Achievement award, Nat. Wildlife Fedn., 1992, Shaw medal, Mo. Bot. Garden, 1993, Internat. prize biology, Govt. of Japan, 1993, Eminent Ecologist award, 1994, Ecol. Soc. Am. Audubon medal, Audubon Soc., 1995, Pub. Understanding Sci. award, AAAS, 1995, John Hay award, Orion Soc., 1995, Schubert prize, Germany, 1996, Washburn medal, Mus. Sci., 1996, Hutchinson medal, Garden Club Am., 1997, Stone award, New Eng. Aquarium, 1999, Nonino prize, Letters and Sci., Italy, 2000, King Faisal Internat. prize for sci., 2000, Kistler prize, Found. for the Future, 2000, Phillips Meml. medal, World Conservation Union, 2000, Lewis Thomas prize, Rockefeller U., 2001, Nierenberg prize, Scripps Oceanographic Inst., 2001, Thoreau medal, Thoreau Soc., 2001, Lifetime Achievement award, Time, 2001, Global Environment Citizens award, Harvard U., 2001, Busk medal, Royal Geog. Soc., 2002, Presdl. medal, Republic of Italy, 2002, Silver Cross of Christopher Columbus, Dominican Republic, 2003, Lowell Thomas award, Explorers Club, 2004, Frances Hutchinson medal, Chgo. Bot. Garden, 2004, Gov.'s award, Island Alliance, Mass., 2004, Rachel Carson award, Internat. Soc. Ecotoxicology and Chemistry, 2004, Rungius medal, Am. Mus. Wildlife Art, 2005, Prince William of Orange medal, Leiden U., 2006, TED prize, Sampling Found., 2006, George B. Stibbitz Comms. Pioneer award, Am. Computer Mus., 2006, TED Biotech. Prize, 2007, Catalonia prize, Spain, 2007; Guggenheim Found. fellow, 1978. Fellow: Deutsche Akad. Naturforsch, Am. Philos. Soc. (Franklin medal 1998), Am. Acad. Arts and Scis.; mem.: NAS, Royal Soc. Sci. Uppsala (Sweden), Russian Acad. Sci., Royal Entomol. Soc. (hon. life), Finnish Acad. Sci. and Letters, Royal Soc. London, Netherlands Entomol. Soc. (hon. life), Royal Soc. Edinburgh (life), Assn. Tropical Biology (hon. life), Acad. Humanism (hon. life), Am. Humanist Assn. (Disting. Svc. award 1982, hon. life, Humanist of Yr.), Zool. Soc. London (hon. life), Entomol. Soc. Am. (Founders Meml. award 1972, L.O. Howard award 1985, hon. life), Brit. Ecol. Soc. (hon. life), Am. Genetics Assn. (hon. life), Explorers Club (life, hon. life). Home: Apt A-208 1010 Waltham St Lexington MA 02421 Office: Harvard U Mus Comparative Zoology Cambridge MA 02138 Office Phone: 617-495-2315. Business E-Mail: ewilson@oeb.harvard.edu.

WILSON, EDWIN, writer, playwright, educator, theater director; b. Nashville, Tenn., Nov. 10, 1927; s. E. Edwin and Catherine (Jones) Wilson; m. Catherine Stuart, July 8, 1967. BA cum laude, Vanderbilt U., 1950; grad. in English, U. Edinburgh, Scotland, 1951; MFA, Yale U., 1957, DFA, 1958. Prof. Yale U. Drama Sch., New Haven, 1957—58, 1961—62, Hofstra U., 1958—60, Vanderbilt U., Nashville, 1959; prof. Grad. Ctr. Hunter Coll. CUNY, NYC, 1966—91; theater critic Wall St. Jour., NYC, 1972—94, sr. cultural writer, 1994—96; moderator TV interviews CUNY-TV, PBS, NYC, 1989—93; chair dept. theater and film CUNY Hunter Coll., 1980—83; v.p. faculty Hunter Coll., NYC, 1973—75; exec. dir. Martin E. Segal Theater Ctr. Hunter Coll., 1987—2003. Mem. N.Y. Drama Critics Cir., 1972—94, pres., 1982—84; mem. Pulitzer Prize Drama Jury, 1977—78, 1979—80, 2000—03; mem. nominating com. Tony awards, NYC, 1975—77, NYC, 1988—99; rep USIA to Romania and German Dem. Republic, 1984. Author: The Theater Experience, 1976, 9th edit., 2004; co-author (with Alvin Goldfarb): Art, 2005, Living Theater 4th edit., 2004; editor (and introduction author): Shaw on Shakespeare, 1961; dir.: (plays, for profl companies as well as student performers.); prodr.(numerous off-Broadway plays and one Broadway Play): Agatha Sue I Love You; playwright: plays Waterfall, The Bettinger Prize, Musical Great Expectations. Pres. Theater Devel. Fund, 1982—84; mem. playwright's com. Rockefeller Found., 1983—86; bd. dir. Theater Devel. Fund, 1981—2003, 1981—, John Golden Fund, 1980—. Grantee grant to report on contemporary Japanese theatre, Milwaukee Rep and Japanese-Am. Friendship Commn., 1978—79. Mem.: Am. Theater Critics Assn., Century Assn., Coffee House Club, Phi Beta Kappa. Home: 55 Central Park W New York NY 10023-5003

WILSON, ELDON RAY, minister; b. Tieton, Wash., Apr. 16, 1931; s. Frank Madison and Beatrice Jane (Snider) W.; m. LouCelle Charlotte Seward, Aug. 3, 1957; children: Randall Wayne, Gary Ray. BTh, Internat. Bible Coll., San Antonio, 1967; PhD, Sussex Coll., Hayward's Heath, Eng., 1972. Ordained to ministry Emmanuel Ch., 1956. Founder, pastor Emmanuel Tabernacle, Port Arthur, Tex., 1958-63; evangelist U.S., Can., 1963-65; founder, pastor Gospel Tabernacle, Ilion, NY, 1965-70; pastor Full Gospel Ch., Halifax, N.S., Canada, 1970-72; missionary Europe, Africa, 1972-77; founder, pastor New Covenant Ch., Columbus, Ohio, 1977-84; missionary New Covenant Ministries, Columbus, 1984-97; acad. dean City Bible Coll., Utica, NY, 1998-2001. Bd. dirs. Good News Mission, Bogota, Colombia, 1985—; trustee Mission Teams Internat., Elkton, Md., 1989—. Author: The New Creation, 1975. Bd. dirs. Kuyahoora Valley Libr., Newport, N.Y., 1985—; overseer Shekinah Ministries, Amsterdam, The Netherlands, Bread of Life Ministries, Bastogne, Belgium. With USN, 1951-55. Republican. Home: 7417 West St Newport NY 13416 Office: PO Box 317 Newport NY 13416

WILSON, ERIC F.G., information technology executive; BSc with honors, Guelph U. Sr. v.p., chief info. officer Philip Svcs. Corp., Houston, 1997—2000; sr. v.p. operations, chief tech. officer Fusionstorm, San Francisco, 2000—03; sr. v.p., chief info. officer Raley's, West Sacramento, Calif., 2003—. Office: Raleys 500 W Capitol Ave West Sacramento CA 95605

WILSON, FLOYD C., oil industry executive; children: Christopher, Andrew. Founder, chmn., pres., CEO Hugoton Energy Corp., 1987—98; chmn., CEO 3TEC Energy Corp., 1999—2003; founder, pres., CEO Petrohawk Energy Corp., Houston, 2003—, chmn., 2004—; ptnr. Wilson Group Companies. Office: Petrohawk Energy Corp 1100 Louisiana Ste 4400 Houston TX 77002

WILSON, FRANCES C., career military officer; BS, Mich. State U.; MEd, Pepperdine U.; MA in Psychology, U. No. Colo.; MS in Bus. Mgmt., Salve Regina Coll.; PhD in Edn., U. So. Calif. Commd. 2d lt. USMC, 1972, advanced through grades to lt. gen., 2006; air traffic control officer Marine Corps Air Sta., Yuma, Ariz., Kaneohe, Hawaii, 1975; tchr. instrnl. mgmt. Marine Corps Devel. & Edn. Ctr., Quantico, Va.; staff sec. 3d Marine Divsn., Okinawa, Japan, 1980-81; asst. prof., co. officer brigade of midshipmen U.S. Naval Acad., Annapolis, Md.; mgmt. analyst HQ USMC, Washington; spl. asst. for gen. and flag officer matters Joint Staff, Pentagon, exec. asst. to vice dir., 1987; comdr. 4th Recruit Tng. Battalion, Parris Island, S.C., 1988-90, Camp H.M. Smith, Svc. Battalion Marine Corps Pacific; sec. Joint Staff, until 1997; commanding gen. Marine Corps Base, Quantico, 1997-99, Third Force Svc. Support Group, Okinawa, Japan, 1999—2001; dir. pers. mgmt. divsn. M&RA Hdqrs. USMC, 2001—03; comdt. Indsl. Coll. Armed Forces, Nat. Def. U., Ft. McNair, DC, 2003—06; pres. Nat. Def. U., Washington, 2006—. Decorated Def.

Superior Svc. medal, Def. Meritorious Svc. medal, Meritorious Svc. medal, Navy Commendation medal, Navy Achievement medal; recipient Leadership award, USMC Women Officer Basic Sch. Office: Nat Def U Ft Lesley J McNair 300 Fifth Ave Marshall Hall Washington DC 20319 *

WILSON, FRANCES HELEN, retired occupational therapist; b. Pitts., Oct. 17, 1929; d. J. Vernon and Margaret Hassler (Prugh) Wilson. BA, Conn. Coll., 1951; advanced standing cert., Columbia Sch. Occupl. Therapy, 1953. Therapist Washington (Pa.) County Soc. Crippled Children and Adults, 1953-54; staff therapist Oakland VA Hosp., U. Pitts., 1955-66; supr. Occupl. Therapy Clinic, Aspinwall VA Hosp., Pitts., 1966-74, 81-85, Occupl. Therapy Clinic, Oakland VA Hosp., Pitts., 1974—85, ret., 1985. Active Jr. League Pitts., Inc.; vol. Pitts. (Pa.) Children's Mus. Mem. Western Pa. (treas. 1967-69), Am. Occupl. Therapy Assns., Presbyn. Univ. Hosp. Pitts. Vol. Assn., Pitts. (Pa.) Symphony Assn., Acad. Lifelong Learning, Conn. Coll. Club (treas. 1971-94), Twentieth Century Club (Pitts.). Republican. Presbyterian. Home: Washington Plz 1116 1420 Centre Ave Pittsburgh PA 15219

WILSON, FRANKLIN D., sociology educator; b. Birmingham, Ala., Sept. 3, 1942; s. Ernest and Ollie Lee (Carter) W.; m. Marion F. Brown; children: Rachel, Chareese BA, Miles Coll., 1964; postgrad., Atlanta U., 1964-65; MA, Wash. State U., 1971, PhD, 1973. Instr. Grambling U., La., 1965-66; William H. Sewell-Bascom prof. sociology U. Wis.-Madison, 1973—, chmn. dept. Afro-Am. studies, 1984-87, chmn. dept. sociology, 1988-91, dir. Ctr. for Demography and Ecology, 1994-99. Author: Residential Consumption, Economic Opportunities and Race, 1979; deputy editor Demography, 1995-98; co-editor Am. Sociol. Rev. Bd. of Census adv. com. Profl. Assns., 1993-99. Served with U.S. Army, 1966-69; Vietnam Decorated Purple Heart, Silver Star, Vietnam medal of Valor; Census fellow Am. Statis. Assn., NSF, 1991-92, Population Coun. fellow, 1971-72. Mem. Population Assn. Am., Sociol. Rsch. Assn., Assn. Black Sociologists, Am. Sociol. Assn. (sec. 2004—). Unitarian Universalist. Avocations: swimming, reading. Office: U Wis Ctr for Demography and Ecology Social Sci Bldg Madison WI 53713 Home Phone: 608-271-8486. Business E-Mail: wilson@ssc.wisc.edu.

WILSON, FRED M., II, ophthalmologist, educator; b. Indpls., Dec. 10, 1940; s. Fred Madison and Elizabeth (Fredrick) W.; m. Karen Joy Lyman, Sept. 10, 1959 (div. June 1962); 1 child, Teresa Wilson Kulick; m. Claytonia Leigh Pemberton, Aug. 28, 1964; children: Yvonne Wilson Hacker, Jennifer Wilson DeLong, Benjamin James. AB in Med. Scis., Ind. U., 1962, MD, 1965. Diplomate Am. Bd. Ophthalmology. Intern Sacred Heart Hosp., Spokane, Wash., 1965-66; resident in ophthalmology Ind. U., Indpls., 1968-71, fellow in ophthalmology, 1971-72, F.I. Proctor Found., San Francisco, 1972-73; from asst. prof. to assoc. prof. ophthalmology Ind. U., Indpls., 1972-76, prof. ophthalmology, 1981—2005, prof. emeritus, 2005—. Med. dir. Ind. Lions Eye Bank, Inc., Indpls., 1973-99; cons. surgeon Ind. U., Indpls., 1973-2005. Contbr. articles to profl. jours., chapters to books. Lt. comdr. USNR, 1966-68, PTO. Mem. Am. Acad. Ophthalmology (assoc. sec. 1988-93, Sr. Teaching award 1989), Assn. Proctor Fellows, Soc. Heed Fellows, Am. Ophthalmol. Soc., Am. Bd. Ophthalmology (bd. dirs. 1993-2000), Ill. Soc. Ophthalmology (hon.), Mont. Acad. Ophthalmology (hon.), Pacific-Coast Ophthalmol. Soc. (hon.). Republican. Avocations: photography, guitar, history, language, natural history. Home: 12262 Crestwood Dr Carmel IN 46033-4323 Office: Ind U Sch Medicine Dept Ophthalmolgy 702 Rotary Cir Indianapolis IN 46202-5133

WILSON, FREDERIC SANDFORD, pharmaceutical company executive; b. Schenectady, NY, Mar. 28, 1944; s. Robert Omer and Isabel May (Sandford) W.; children: Amy Kathleen, Adrienne Ann; m. Judith Ann Goettsche, Feb. 7, 1973; children: Marla Ann, Brian Bennett, Jessica Lea, Jennifer Lynn. BS, Syracuse U., 1968. Acct. exec. Mastropaul Design Inc., Syracuse, N.Y., 1969-70; copy editor Norwich Eaton Pharms., Norwich, N.Y., 1970-72, sales rep. Gary, Ind., 1972-73, asst. product mgr. Norwich, 1974-75, mktg. svcs. mgr., 1975-76, product mgr., 1977-81, bus. devel. mgr., 1981-83, sr. product mgr., 1983-85, mgr. med. foods, 1986-89; assoc. mktg. mgr. P&G Pharms., Norwich, 1989-92; dir. profl. rels. P & G Pharms., Cin., 1993-96; mgr. mktg. svcs. P&G, Cin., 1997-98; category mgr. CME P&G Pharms., Cin., 1998—. Cons. Sandoz Nutrition Corp., Mpls., 1992., bd. dir. Nat. Bd. of Osteopathic Med. Examiners. Inventor Jejunostomy Kit, 1981, Vivonex T.E.N. med. food, 1983, Tolerex med. food, 1987. Bd. dirs. minority access program Syracuse U., 1989-91; nat. task force on continuing med. edn. Provider/Industry Collaboration, chmn. pharm. alliance, 1996-98 Mem.: AMA (affiliate). Office: Procter & Gamble Box 2075 8700 Mason-Montgomery Rd Mason OH 45040-9462 Home Phone: 513-477-2609; Office Phone: 513-622-5456. Business E-Mail: wilson.fs@pg.com.

WILSON, FREDERICK ALLEN, gastroenterologist, health facility administrator, educator; b. Winchester, Mass., Aug. 22, 1937; s. Warren Archibald and Alice Jane (Springall) W.; m. Lynne Stewart Cantley, Feb. 24, 1962; children: Douglas, Victoria. AB, Colgate U., Hamilton, NY, 1959; MD, Albany Med. Coll., NYC, 1963. Intern Hartford Hosp., Conn., 1963-64, resident in medicine, 1964-66; fellow in gastroenterology Albany Med. Coll., 1966-67; USPHS postdoctoral fellow in gastroenterology U. Tex. Southwestern Med. Sch., Dallas, 1969-72; asst. prof. medicine Vanderbilt U. Sch. Medicine, Nashville, 1972-76, assoc. prof., 1976-82, mem. adv. com. clin. rsch. ctr., 1978-81; prof. medicine, chief div. gastroenterology Milton S. Hershey Med. Ctr., Pa. State U., Hershey, 1982-90; prof. medicine, dir. divsn. gastroenterology Med. U. S.C., Charleston, 1990-94, dir. fellowship tng. program in gastroenterology and hepatology, 1990—2003, now prof. medicine divsn. gastroenterology and hepatology, dept. medicine. Mem. ACP Med. Knowledge Self-Assessment Program VI, 1980-81; mem. gastroenterology and clin. nutrition rev. group Nat. Inst. Arthritis, Diabetes, Digestive and Kidney Disease, NIH, Bethesda, Md., 1985-89; pre-reviewer Am. Coun. Grad. Med. Edn., 1994-95. Contbr. numerous articles, abstracts, chpts. to profl. publs.; reviewer for sci. jours. Served to maj. M.C., U.S. Army, 1967-69. Recipient Clin. Investigator award VA Med. Ctr., Nashville, 1972-75; recipient Investigator award Howard Hughes Med. Inst., Vanderbilt U., 1975-78; NIH Fogarty Internat. Ctr. sr. internat. fellow Max Planck Inst. for Biophysics, Frankfurt, Germany, 1979-80. Mem. Am. Fedn. Clin. Rsch., Ctrl. Soc. Clin. Rsch., Am. Gastroenterology Assn., Am. Assn. Study Liver Diseases, Am. Soc. Clin. Investigation, N.Y. Acad. Scis., SC Med. Assn., Ea. Gut Club, Pa. Soc. Gastroenterology. Office: Med U SC Div Gastroenterology 96 Jonathan Lucas St #210 Charleston SC 29425-0001 Business E-Mail: wilsonfa@musc.edu.

WILSON, GARY DEAN, lawyer; b. Wichita, Kans., June 7, 1943; s. Glenn E. and Roe Zella (Mills) W.; m. Diane Kay Williams, Dec. 29, 1965; children: Mark R., Matthew C., Christopher G. BA, Stanford U., 1965, LLB, 1968. Bar: D.C. 1970, U.S. Dist. Ct. D.C. 1970, U.S. Ct. Appeals (D.C. cir.) 1972, U.S. Ct. Appeals (7th cir.) 1979, U.S. Ct. Appeals (2d cir.) 1983. Law clk. U.S. Ct. Appeals, 2d cir., NYC, 1968-69, U.S. Supreme Ct., Washington, 1969-70; assoc. Wilmer, Cutler & Pickering, Washington, 1970-75, ptnr., 1976—. Acting prof. law Stanford (Calif.) Law Sch., 1981-82. Bd. visitors Stanford Law Sch., 1990-92, 2000—. Democrat. Home: 4636 30th St NW Washington DC 20008-2127 E-mail: gwilson@wilmer.com, dwilson1@erols.com.

WILSON, GARY THOMAS, engineering executive; b. Pitts., Sept. 26, 1961; s. Charles Zachary and Doris Jean (Alexander) Wilson; m. Georgiann E. Wilson, Dec. 31, 1994. AB, Dartmouth Coll., 1983, BEEE, 1984; MSEE, Calif. State U., Long Beach, 1992; postgrad., UCLA, 1992-99. Elec. engr. AiResearch, Man., Garrett, Torrance, Calif., 1983; sr. mem. tech. staff TRW Space & Electronics Group, Redondo Beach, Calif., 1984-93; v.p. of R&D CZAND Assocs., LA, 1993—; rsch. asst. UCLA Flight System Rsch. Ctr., Westwood, Calif., 1994-96; sr. scientist payload sys. Hughes Space & Comms., 1996-2000; sr. project mgr. Boeing Satellite Systems, 2000—01; dir. advanced systems Mission Rsch. Corp., 2001—04; v.p. space and sensors sector ATK Mission Rsch., 2004—06; pres. Zuma Engring. & Rsch., 2006—. Cons. CZAND Assocs., L.A., 1985-93; instr. electronics UCLA Smarts Program. Tutor math. and sci. Recipient Meritorious Svc. award United Negro Coll. Fund, 1989; TRW master's fellow, doctoral incentive fellow Calif. State U., 1993. Mem. IEEE, Nat. Soc. Black Engrs., Dartmouth Soc. Engrs. Avocations: tennis, golf, chess, basketball, bicycling. Office: Zuma Engring and Rsch Ste 343 1800 S Robertson Blvd Los Angeles CA 90035-4365 Office Phone: 310-738-4653. Business E-Mail: gwilson@zumaengineering.com.

WILSON, GEORGE MACKLIN, history educator, cultural studies center administrator; b. Columbus, Ohio, Apr. 27, 1937; m. Joyce DeCoster Klain, June 11, 1960; children: George David, Elizabeth Adeline. AB in Politics and Russian Studies, Princeton U., 1958; AM in East Asian Regional Studies, Harvard U., 1960, PhD in History and Far Ea. Langs., 1965. From instr. to asst. prof. history U. Ill., Urbana-Champaign, 1964-67; assoc. prof. history Ind. U., Bloomington, 1967-76, assoc. prof. East Asian langs. and cultures, 1975-76, prof., 1976—, dir. East Asian studies program, 1970-71, 72-73, assoc. dean rsch. and advanced studies, assoc. dean internat. programs, 1972-75, dean internat. programs office of pres., 1975-78, dir. grad. studies dept. history, 1980-83, acting chair dept. history, 1983-84, summer 1981, summer 1982, dir. East Asian studies ctr., 1987—, dir. Title VI nat. resource ctr. East Asian studies, 1991-2000. Vis. lectr. Japanese history U. Mich., Ann Arbor, 1963-64, summer 1964; vist. asst. prof. history summer sch. arts and scis. Harvard U., 1966, assoc. prof. history summer sch., 1975, rsch. assoc. East Asian rsch. ctr., 1966, 75, 78-79; rsch. assoc. faculty letters Kyoto U., 1971-72, vis. prof. faculty edn., 1985; mem., chair various coms. Ind. U., mem. bd. advisors East Asian summer lang. inst., 1985—, chair Japan forum, 1990—; cons. internat. divsn. Ford Found., 1974-77, cons. history Midwest univs. consortium internat. activities, 1979-80; mem. rev. panel divsn. pub. programs NEH, 1978-80; mem. adv. screening com. Japan Coun. Internat. Exch. Scholars, 1978-81, chair, 1980-81; mem. adv. panel Annenberg Sch. Comm. and Corp. Pub. Broadcasting, 1982-84; cons. East Asian history Am. Hist. Rev., 1985-91; mem. Gov. Robert Orr's Higher Edn. Del. to Ind.'s Sister State, Zhejiang Province, China, 1988; chair I.U. Japan Forum, 1988-94; bd. dirs. Ind. Consortium Internat. Programs, 1972-78; Ind. U. mem. bd. dirs. Interuniversity Ctr. Japanese Lang. Studies in Yokohama, 1988—; presenter in field. Author: Radical Nationalist in Japan: Kita Ikki, 1883-1937, 1969, Japanese edit., 1971, Patriots and Redeemers in Japan: Motives in the Meiji Restoration, 1992; editor, contbg. author: Crisis Politics in Prewar Japan: Institutional and Ideological Problems of the 1930s, 1970; Editl. advisor for Japanese and Korean history Encyclopaedia Britannica, 1969-99; book manuscript reader U. Hawaii Press, Ind. U. Press, Princeton U. Press; article manuscript evaluator Am. Hist. Rev., Comparative Studies Soc. and History, Jour. Asian History, Jour. Asian Studies; contbr. articles and book revs. to profl. jours. Grantee U. Ill., 1965, Harvard U., 1966, 75, Ind. U., 1967, 68, 72, Am. Philos. Soc., 1968, Am. Coun. Learned Socs., 1971; Grad. Sch. Arts and Scis. fellow Harvard U., 1959-60, Fgn. Area Tng. fellow Ford Found., 1960-63, Fulbright-Hays Sr. fellow, 1971-72, Profl. fellow Japan Found., 1985. Mem. Am. Hist. Assn. (convener 1984 and 1988 ann. meetings, chair conf. Asian history 1989—), Midwest Conf. Asian Affairs (mem. nominating com. 1990-91), Midwest Univs. Consortium Internat. Activities, Inc. (liaison officer for Ind. U. 1973-78, bd. dirs. 1974-78, sec. corp. 1974-78), Assn. Asian Studies (mem. program com., Japan rep. 1985 ann. meeting), Japan-Am. Soc. Ind., Inc. (founding, mem. steering com. 1987-88, bd. dirs. 1988—), Hudson Inst. (pub.). Office: Indiana University East Asian Studies Ctr Memorial Hall W Rm 207 Bloomington IN 47405

WILSON, GEORGE MALCOLMSON, application developer; b. Mar. 21, 1946; BSEE, U. Ill., Urbana, 1968. Software engr. Cummins-Allison Corp., Mt. Prospect, Ill., 1977—81, 1998—2006; software engr., supr. Recognition Bus. Sys., Elk Grove Village., Ill., 1981—87; software engr. Sun Electric and Suntronic Tech. Group, Crystal Lake, Ill., 1987—98. Recipient award, Math. Assn. Am., 1964. Mem.: Mensa. Mailing: PO Box 1073 Park Ridge IL 60068-7073

WILSON, GERALD EVERETTE, funeral services company executive; b. Houston, Nov. 2, 1953; s. Clifford Dennis and Naomi Betty (Falls) W.; m. Marsherria Ervin, Aug. 14, 1974; children, Gerrad Everette, Garrett, Everette. BA in Econs., MA in Econs., Stanford U., 1976; MS in Acctg., U. Houston, 1978. CPA, Tex. Mem. staff Arthur Young & Co., Houston, 1976-80, mgr., 1980-84, prin., 1984-86; founder, pres., chmn. Wilson Fin. Group, Inc., Houston, 1986—. Bd. dirs. Thompson Funeral Home Inc., Sacramento, So. Funeral Home Inc., Memphis, Whitehaven Chapel Inc., Memphis, Mainland Funeral Home, LaMarque, Tex., Morris-Bates Funeral Home, Ft. Worth, Paradise Funeral Home, Houston, Carl Barnes Funeral Home, Inc., Greater Houston Partnership, 1997-2005, 2007—, govs. bus. coun., exec. com., 1998—, bd. regents Tex. So. U., 1998-2007. Bd. dirs. Stanford U. Athletic Bd., Palo Alto, Calif., 1985—, Leadership Houston, 1985-87, Houston Proud, 1988; chmn. sec. Steering Com. Harris County Parks, Tex., 1986—; mem. adv. bd. Houston Ind. Sch. Dist., 1986—. Named Outstanding Young Houstonian Houston Jaycees, 1985, Outstanding Young Texan Tex. Jaycees, 1985, Outstanding Black Houstonian Riverside Hosp., 1986. Mem. Am. Inst. CPA's, Tex. Soc. CPA's, Inst. Fin. Planning, Houston C. of C., Katy C. of C. Democrat. Baptist. Avocations: golf, jogging. Office: Wilson Fin Group Inc 15415 Katy Fwy Ste 500 Houston TX 77094-1816

WILSON, GLENN, economist, educator; b. East St. Louis, Ill., Feb. 4, 1929; s. Herschel and Regina (Hayes) W.; m. Helen Janice O'Dell, Jan. 28, 1951; children— David, Thomas, Ann. BA, U. Okla., 1951; MA, 1952. Adminstr., Welfare and Retirement Fund United Mine Workers, Pitts., Knoxville, Tenn., 1952-58; dir. med. care research Nationwide Ins. Co., Columbus, 1958-62; exec. dir. Community Health Found., Cleve., 1962-68; exec. v.p. Kaiser Community Health Found., Cleve., 1968-69; assoc. dean U. N.C. Med. Sch., Chapel Hill, 1970-88, prof. dept. social medicine, 1977—, chmn. dept., 1977-89. Cons. Sault Ste. Marie and Dist. Group Health Assn.; health adv. Mayor Stokes, Cleve., 1967-69 Contbr. articles to profl. jours. Office: U NC Med Sc Dept Social Medicine Chapel Hill NC 27514 Home: 349 Cedar Club Cir Chapel Hill NC 27517 E-mail: glenn_wilson@unc.edu.

WILSON, GRETCHEN, vocalist; b. Granite City, Ill., June 26, 1973; 1 child, Grace. Signed by Epic Records, 2003—. Singer: (singles) Redneck Woman, 2004 (Breakthrough Video of Yr., Country Music Television Music award, 2005), When I Think About Cheatin, 2004 (Female Video of Yr., Country Music Television Music award, 2005), (five singles) 5-Mo-Fo-Ya, 2005, (albums) Here for the Party, 2004, All Jacked Up, 2005; TV appearances include: In The Moment, 2004; co-author (with Allen Rucker): Redneck Women: Stories from My Life, 2006. Named Female Vocalist of Yr., Country Music Assn., 2005; recipient Horizon award, 2004, Favorite New Artist, Am. Music Awards, 2004, Favorite Female Country Artist, 2005, Female Country Artist of Yr., Billboard Music Awards, 2004, New Country Artist of Yr., 2004, Top New Artist, Acad. Country Music Awards, 2005, Top Female Vocalist, 2005. Achievements include first new artist to debut at #1 on Billboard's Country LP chart.

WILSON, GROVER GRAY, lawyer; b. Louisville, Apr. 1, 1951; BA, Davidson Coll., 1973; JD, Duke Univ., 1976. Bar: NC 1976. Fellow: Am. Coll. Trial Lawyers; mem.: Am. Bd. Trial Advocates, NC Assn. of Def. Attorneys, Forsyth County Bar Assn., NC Bar Assn. (pres. 2004), Phi Beta Kappa. Office: Wilson & Iseman LLP Ste 400 110 Oakwood Dr Winston Salem NC 27103

WILSON, HAROLD BATTING, treasurer; b. NYC, June 24, 1910; s. William Johnson and May LaForest Wilson; m. Edna Anita Helmling, Jan. 9, 1937 (dec. Apr. 1996). Cert. in acct. and bus. law, Fordham U., 1930—32. Registered pub. acct., N.Y., 1961; cert. data processor Data Processing Mgmt. Assn., 1963, computer technology Inst. Advanced Technology, 1967. Office boy Arthur Andersen & Co., NYC, 1929—32, acct./auditor, 1933—38; acct. Office of Comptr., NYC, 1938—40; prin. systems analyst Divsn. of Employment, NY State, Albany, 1941—70; investment adv. Registered with S.E.C., Naples, Fla., 1975—90; treas. Theatre '90 Inc., Syracuse, NY, 1990—. Corp. dir. Theatre '90 Inc., Syracuse, 1990—. Author: (book) How to Beat Wall St., 1991. Sgt. USAF, 1943—45, US. Recipient NY State cert. of merit, Gov. Nelson A. Rockefeller, 1971. Mem.: SAR Nat. Soc. Avocations: writing, sports. Home: 7235 Canton St Rd Baldwinsville NY 13027

WILSON, HAROLD STACY, history professor, writer; b. Neva, Tenn., June 22, 1935; s. Joseph Hooker Wilson and Bertie Hazel Reece; m. Henrietta Sheppard Fair, June 21, 1968; children: Katherine McCoII, Kyle Stacy. BA, King Coll., 1957; MA, Johns Hopkins U., 1959; PhD, Emory U., 1966. Asst. prof. Wesleyan Coll., Macon, Ga., 1962—66, Old Dominion U., Norfolk, Va., 1966—68, assoc. prof., 1968—2003, prof. history, 2003—, chair, history dept., 1991—98, mem. faculty senate, 1999—, vice-chair faculty senate, 2001—03. Fulbright prof. Fu Ren U., Taipei, Taiwan, 1971—72, Tamkang U., Taipei, 1971—72, Nat. U. Singapore, 1978—80; exch. prof. Kitakyushu U., Japan, 1995. Author: (history book) McClure's Magazine and the Muckrakers, 1970, Confederate Industry: Manufacturers and Quartermasters in the Civil War, 2002; editor: Textile History Rev., 1963—66; assoc. editor: Wesleyan Quar. Rev., 1964—66, editl. asst.: The Great American and The Blue and the Gray; contbr. scholarly articles and book revs. in field. Supporter Union Mission, Norfolk, Va., 1966—, Salvation Army, Norfolk, 1966—, Young Life, Norfolk, 1966—, Stas. WHRO-TV, WHRV-TV, Norfolk, 1966—, Norfolk Pub. Libr., 1966—; founder, Patrick scholarship King Coll., Bristol, Tenn., 1996—; short-term missioner South Am. Missionary Soc., Honduras, 2002—; founding mem. Christ the Redeemer Anglican Ch., Norfolk, 2005—. Nominee Peter Seaborg award, 2002; grantee Tech. and Tchg. grant, U. 21st Century, 1992; Rsch. grant, Nat. Found. Arts and Humanities, 1968, Faculty Field Rsch. grant, US Mil. Acad., 1987. Mem.: So. Hist. Assn. (chair arrangements com. 1987—88), Friends of Old Dominion U. Perry Libr. (life). Independent-Republican. Baptist. Avocations: hiking, swimming, travel. Home: 626 W Princess Anne Rd Norfolk VA 23517-1806 Office: Old Dominion Univ Hampton Blvd Norfolk VA 23529 Home Phone: 757-625-1063; Office Phone: 757-683-3949. Personal E-mail: hwilson@odu.org. Business E-Mail: hwilson@odu.edu.

WILSON, HEATHER ANN, congresswoman; b. Keene, NH, Dec. 30, 1960; d. George Douglas Wilson and Martha Lou Wilson-Kernozicky; m. Jay Hone; 3 children. BS in Internat. Politics, USAF Acad., Colo., 1982; MPhil in Internat. Rels., U. Oxford, Eng., 1984, PhD in Internat. Rels., 1985. US mission NATO, Brussels, 1987—89; dir. def. policy and arms control NSC, Washington, 1989—91; pres. Keystone Internat., Inc., Albuquerque, 1991—95; cabinet sec. N.Mex. Dept. Children, Youth and Families, Santa Fe, 1992—98; mem. US Congress from 1st N.Mex. dist., 1998—, mem. energy and commerce com., mem. permanent select com. on intelligence, ranking mem. tech. and tactical intelligence subcommittee. Adj. prof. U. N.Mex.; mem. Def. Adv. Com. on Women in the Svcs. Contbr. articles to profl. jours. Capt. USAF, 1982—89. Named Rhodes scholar, 1982; recipient Hero of the Taxpayer award, Ams. for Tax Reform, 1999, 2002, Spirit of Free Enterprise award, US C. of C., 2000, Guardian of Small Bus. award, Nat. Fedn. Ind. Bus., 2000, Golden Bulldog award, Watchdog of Treasury, 2000, Disting. Cmty. Health Superhero award, Nat. Assn. Cmty. Health Ctrs., Inc., 2005, Javits-Wagner-O'Day Champion award, 2005. Mem.: Kiwanis. Republican. Methodist. Avocations: hiking, skiing. Office: 20 First Plz NW Ste 603 Albuquerque NM 87102 Office Phone: 202-225-6316, 505-346-6781. Office Fax: 505-346-6723. *

WILSON, HUGH STEVEN, lawyer; b. Paducah, Ky., Nov. 27, 1947; s. Hugh Gipson and Rebekah (Dunn) W.; m. Clare Maloney, Apr. 28, 1973; children: Zachary Hunter, Samuel Gipson. BS, Ind. U., 1968; JD, U. Chgo., 1971; LLM, Harvard U., 1972. Bar: Calif. 1972, U.S. Dist. Ct. (ctrl. dist.) Calif. 1972, U.S. Dist. Ct. (so. dist.) Calif. 1973, U.S. Ct. Appeals (9th cir.) 1975, U.S. Dist. Ct. (no. dist.) Calif. 1977, U.S. Supreme Ct. 1978, U.S. Dist. Ct. (ea. dist.) 1980. Assoc. Latham & Watkins, LA, 1972-78, ptnr. San Diego, 1978—2004; mng. ptnr. Tennenbaum Capital Ptnrs., LLC, Santa Monica, Calif., 2005—. Recipient Jerome N. Frank prize U. Chgo. Law Sch., 1971. Mem. Calif. Club, Coronado Yacht Club, Order of Coif. Republican. Avocations: literature, zoology. Office: Tennenbaum Capital Ptnrs 2951 28th St Ste 1000 Santa Monica CA 90405 Office Phone: 310-566-1007. E-mail: steve.wilson@tennenbaumcapital.com.

WILSON, I. DODD, dean; b. St. Peter, Minn., July 10, 1936; m. Ginger Wilson; 2 children. AB summa cum laude, Dartmouth Coll., 1958; MD, Harvard U., 1961. Diplomate Am. Bd. Internal Medicine. Intern dept. medicine U. Minn. Hosps., Mpls., 1961—62; med. fellow Dept. of Medicine, 1962-63, 65-66; instr. dept. of medicine U. Minn. Med. Sch., Mpls., 1967—68, asst. prof., 1968—71, assoc. prof., 1971—76, dir. sect. of gastroenterology, 1972—83, vice chmn. dept. of medicine, 1983—86, prof. medicine, 1976—86; dean, prof. medicine U. Ark. Coll. of Medicine, Little Rock, 1986—; exec. vice chancellor U. Ark. Med. Scis., 1994—2000, chancellor, 2000—. Mem. Univ. Hosp. Consortium Rsch. Task Force, 1994; adv. bd. UALR Donaghey Project, 1994—; mem. State Crime Lab. Bd., 1992—, chmn. 1991-92; bd. dirs. First Comml. Nat. Bank, Ark. Children's Hosp. Rsch. Inst., Inc.; mem. Ark. Rice Depot Bd., 1988-94; mem. State Med. Examiner's Commn., 1986-90; med. bd. Univ. Hosp., 1986—; mem. chancellor's cabinet U. Ark. for Med. Scis., 1986-2000; chmn. U. Minn. Clin. Assocs., ad hoc com. for fin matters, 1986; vice chmn. U. Minn. Clin. Assocs., 1986, clin. assoc. exec. com., 1985; mem. univ. com. Univ. Press, 1985-86; clin. assoc. planning and mktg. com. U. Minn., 1985; mem. Hosp. Quality Assurance Steering com., 1984-96, chmn. hosp. utilization mgmt. com., 1985; mem. Univ. Bookstore com., 1985; mem. Univ. Senate, 1985-86; chmn. dept. medicine search com. for Dir. of Gen. Internal Medicine, 1985; chmn. med. sch. search com. head of dept. dermatology U. Minn., 1984, chmn. dept. medicine search com. for dir. pulmonary sect. 1984, mem. hosp. bd. govs. com. on planning and devel., 1983-86, med.-surg. hosp. facilities com., 1982-83, mem. steering com. of self-study task force U. of Minn. Med. Sch., 1982-83, many more coms. Contbr. numerous articles to profl. jours. Lt. USNR, 1963—65. Fellow ACP; mem. AMA, Am. Fedn. for Clin. Rsch., Am. Gastroenterol. Assn., Ctrl. Soc. for Clin. Rsch., Am. Assn. for the Study of Liver Disease, Ark. Med. Soc. (editl. bd. 1988-93, ex-officio mem., coun. 1987—), Pulaski County Med. Soc., Assn. of Am. Med. Colls. (coun. of deans, chair 1995-96, mgmt. edn. program planning com. 1993—, adv. panel on strategic positioning for health care reform 1992-95, exec. coun. 1992-97, adminstrv. bd. 1992-97, DEANS-VA coordinating com. 1990-94, ad hoc com. on nursing svcs. and the tchg. hosp. 1989, adv. com. on medicare regulations for payment of physicians in tchg. hosps. 1989), So. Med. Phi Beta Kappa, Alpha Omega Alpha. Office: Univ Ark for Med Scis Mail Slot #541 4301 W Markham St Little Rock AR 72205-7101

WILSON, IAN EDWIN, cultural organization administrator, archivist; b. Montreal, Que., Can., Apr. 2, 1943; s. Andrew and Marion (Mundy) W.; m. Ruth Dyck, Mar. 24, 1979. BA, Queen's U., Kingston, Ont., 1968, MA History, 1974; DLitt York U. (hon.), 2001. Archivist Queen's U., Kingston, Ont., Canada, 1966-76; provincial archivist Sask. (Can.) Archives, 1976-86; archivist of Ont. Ont. Govt., Toronto, 1986-99; dir. gen. info. resource mgmt. divsn. Ministry Culture, Tourism and Recreation, Toronto, 1990-93; nat. archivist Canada, 1999—2004; v.p. Internat. Coun. on Archives, 2000—04; librarian and archivist of Can., 2004—. Sec. Kingston Hist. Soc., 1967-72, v.p., 1972-76; chair cons. group Social Sci. and Humanities Rsch. Coun. Can., Ottawa, 1979-80; adj. prof. Faculty Info. Studies U. Toronto, 1993-2002; spkr. in field. Author: (with J. Douglas Stewart) Heritage Kingston, 1973; editor: Kingston City Hall, 1975; producer: (with J. William Brennan) Regina Before Yesterday, 1978; contbr. articles to profl. jours. Chmn. congregation Mennonite Ch., Regina, 1981-84; mem. Sask. award merit selection com., 1985-86; chair Sask. Heritage adv. bd., 1978-83; Ont. dir. Forum for Young Canadians, 1995-99. Recipient Queen Elizabeth II silver and gold jubilee medal, 1977, 2002, W.G. Leland cert. commendation Soc. Am. Archivists, 1981, W. Kaye Lamb prize Assn. Can. Archivists, 1983; Woodrow Wilson hon. fellow, 1967; apptd. mem. Order of Can., 2002; apptd. comdr. l'ordre des arts et des lettres, France, 2003. Fellow Soc. Am. Archivists; mem. Ont. Hist. Soc. (exec. coun. 1970-73, v.p. 1973-75, pres. 1975-76), Can. Hist. Assn. (past chmn., vice chmn., pres. archives sect. 1972-74), Champlain Soc. (bd. dirs., v.p. 1989-95, pres. 1995-2003). Home: 10 Bayport Priv Ottawa ON Canada K1V 0Z3 Office: Libr and Archives Canada 550 Boul de La Cite Gatineau PQ Canada K1A 0N4 Office Phone: 819-934-5800. E-mail: ian.wilson@lac-bac.gc.ca.

WILSON, IAN HOLROYDE, management consultant, futurist; b. Harrow, Eng., June 16, 1923; came to U.S., 1954; s. William Brash and Dorothy (Holroyde) W.; m. Page Tuttle Hedden, Mar. 17, 1951 (div. Dec. 1983); children: Rebecca, Dorothy, Ellen, Holly, Alexandra; m. Adrianne Marcus, July 12, 1992. MA, Oxford U., 1948. Orgn. cons. Imperial Chem. Industries, London, 1948-54; various staff exec. positions in strategic planning, mgmt. devel. Gen. Electric Co., Fairfield, Conn., 1954—80; sr. cons. to maj. U.S. and internat. cos. SRI Internat., Menlo Park, Calif., 1980-93; prin. Wolf Enterprises, San Rafael, Calif., 1993—. Exec. in residence Va. Commonwealth U., Richmond, 1976; fellow Va. Ctr. for Creative Arts, 1994, 98, 2000. Author: Planning for Major Change, 1976, The Power of Strategic Vision, 1991, Rewriting the Corporate Social Charter, 1992, Managing Strategically in the 1990s, 1993, Executive Leadership, 1995, The New Rules of Corporate Conduct, 2000, The Subtle Art of Strategy, 2003; co-author: The Scenario Planning Handbook, 2006; contbg. editor: Learning from the Future, 1998; mem. editl. bd. Planning Rev., 1973—81; Am. editor: Long Range Planning Jour., 1981—89; sr. editor, mem. editl. bd. Strategy and Leadership, 1993—2004. Mem. adv. bd. Technol. Forecasting and Social Change, 1989—99; chmn. Citizen's Long Range Ednl. Goals Com., Westport, Conn., 1967—70; mem. strategic process com. United Way of Am., Alexandria, Va., 1985—94. Capt. Brit. Army, 1943—45, ETO. Mem. AAAS, Assn. for Strategic Planning, World Future Soc. Unitarian Universalist. Avocations: travel, writing, photography. Home and Office: 79 Twin Oaks Ave San Rafael CA 94901-1915 Home Phone: 415-454-6062; Office Phone: 415-454-6062. Personal E-mail: jason415xx@aol.com.

WILSON, JACK, aeronautical engineer; b. Sheffield, Yorkshire, Jan. 5, 1933; arrived in US, 1956, naturalized, 1980; s. George and Nellie (Place) W.; m. Marjorie Reynolds, June 3, 1961 (div. Jan. 1991); children: Tanya Ruth, Cara; m. Carol Blixen, Jan. 3, 1997. BS in Aero. Engring., with 2d class hon., Imperial Coll., London, 1954; MS in Aero. Engring., Cornell U., Ithaca, NY, 1958, PhD in Aero. Engring., 1962. Cert. power pilot FAA. Sr. scientific officer Royal Aircraft Establishment, Farnborough, England, 1962-63; prin. rsch. sci. Avco-Everett Rsch. Lab., Everett, Mass., 1963-72; vis. prof. Inst. Mecanique des Fluides, Marseille, France, 1972-73; sr. scientist U. Rochester, NY, 1973-80; sr. rsch. assoc. Sohio/BP Am., Cleve., 1980-90; sr. engring. specialist Sverdrup Tech. Inc., Cleve., 1990-93, NYMA, Brook Park, 1994-98, DYNACS Engring. Co., Inc., Brook Park, 1998-2001, QSS Group Inc., Fairview Park, Ohio, 2001—06, ASRC Aerospace Corp., Fairview Park, Ohio, 2006—. Author: (chpt.) "Gas Lasers" of Applied Optics in Engineering VI, 1980, "Laser Sources" of Techniques in Chemistry XVII, 1982; contbr. articles to profl. jours. Glider pilot, instr. Thunderbirgs Gliding Club, Wasworth, Ohio. With U. London Air Squadron, 1952—54, pilot Royal Air Force Vol. Reserve, 1950—54. Co-recipient Manly award, Soc. Automotive Engrs., 1995; recipient Soaring Gold Badge award, Fedn. Aero. Internat., Paris, 1998. Fellow AIAA (assoc.; tech. com. 1991-92). Achievements include first to demonstrate gas-dynamic laser, measurement of air ionization rate at high speeds, wave rotor performance, and unsteady ejector thrust augmentation; patents in application of high speed flow to gas laser media, devel. of antimony dopant sources. Home: 13610 Shaker Blvd Apt 202 Cleveland OH 44120-1564 Office: ASRC Aerospace Corp 21000 Brookpark Rd Cleveland OH 44135-3127 Office Phone: 216-977-1204. Business E-Mail: jack.wilson-1@nasa.gov.

WILSON, JACK FREDRICK, retired federal government official; b. Salt Lake City, Apr. 2, 1920; s. John Lorimer and Mayme J. (James) W.; m. Gwendolyn Gwynn, Nov. 20, 1947; children— Wendy, Elaine, Barbara Ann, Laurel, John F. Jr., James C. BS, Brigham Young U., 1942; postgrad., Mont. State U., 1962, Pa. State U., 1965. Range conservationist Bur. Land Mgmt., Rawlins, Wyo., 1949-57, dist. mgr. Burley, Idaho, 1957-67, dist. and land office mgr. Riverside, Calif., 1967-72; dir. Boise Interagy. Fire Ctr., Idaho, 1972-81; dir. Office Aircraft Services U.S. Dept. Interior, Boise, 1981-87; dir. Boise Interagy. Fire Ctr., 1987-92; ret., 1992. Contbr. articles to profl. jours. Dir. county disaster com. ARC, 1982-88. Maj. USAF, 1942-47 Recipient Meritorious award U.S. Dept. Interior, 1976, Disting. Service award, 1981, EEO Performance award, 1985; Outstanding Contbn. to Fire Mgmt. award U.S. Dept. Agr. Forest Service, 1976, Pub. Lands Found. Life Time Svc. Award 2002. Mem. Soc. Am. Foresters (chmn. fire com. 1980-82), Am. Soc. Range Mgmt. (sec. pres. 1967), So. Calif. Assn. Foresters and Fire Wardens, Lions (sec. 1954-57). Mem. Ch. of Jesus Christ of Latter-day Saints. Avocations: long range weather forecasting, genealogy, reading, golf. Home: 1820 Sunrise Rim Rd Boise ID 83705-5138 Personal E-mail: jfwilson4@cableone.net.

WILSON, JAMES CHARLES, JR., lawyer; b. Birmingham, Ala., Sept. 13, 1947; s. James C. and Angelina (Serio) W.; m. Ann Bullock, Mar. 1, 1975; children: Brent Trammell, Lucy Bullock. BA, Tulane U., New Orleans, 1969, JD, 1972; MBA, Samford U., Birmingham, Ala., 1995. Ptnr. Bradley, Arant, Rose & White, Birmingham, 1972-90, Lange, Simpson, Robinson & Somerville, Birmingham, 1990-93, Sirote & Permutt, P.C., Birmingham, 1993-96; v.p. and gen. counsel Shop-A-Snak Food Mart, Inc., Birmingham, 1996; pres. Lucent Holdings, Inc., Golden, Miss., 1997-98; ptnr. Baker, Johnston & Wilson LLP, Birmingham, Ala., 1999—2002; shareholder Baker Donelson, Bearman, Caldwell & Berkowitz, PC, Birmingham, 2003—. Adj. prof. internat. bus. transactions and internat. law U. Ala., Tuscaloosa, 1983-85, 89-96; internat. bus. transactions Cumberland Sch. Law, 1990-95, adj. prof. corp. fin., 2001—, adj. prof. securities regulation, 2003—. Author: Alabama Business Corporation Law, 1980; co-author: Corporate Law for the Healthcare Provider: Organization, Operation, Merger and Bankruptcy, 1993, Alabama Business Corporation Law Guide, 1995, International Trade Settlements and Negotiations, 2006. Adv. bd. Jr. League of Birmingham, 1984; bd. dirs. Ala. chpt. Am. Liver Found., 1993-97, sec., 1994-95; trustee The Altamont Sch., 1995-2001, v.p., 1996-98, pres., 1998-2000. With U.S. Army, 1972-76. Mem.: ABA (sect. internat. law, tax and corp., banking and bus. law), Birmingham Bar Assn. (chmn. pub. rels. com. 1990, chmn. spl. projects com. 2002, chmn. membership benefits com. 2003), Ala. Law Inst., Ala. Bar Assn., Am. Law Inst., Birmingham Golf Assn. (pres., v.p., treas. 1982—84), Rotary (pres. Birmingham-Sunrise club 1986—87, bd. dirs. 2006—). Office: 1600 Wachovia Tower 420 North 20th St Birmingham AL 35203 Office Phone: 205-244-3829. Business E-Mail: jwilson@bakerdonelson.com.

WILSON, JAMES HARGROVE, JR., lawyer; b. Oliver, Ga., Nov. 26, 1920; s. James Hargrove and Louise (Sealy) W.; m. Frances Audra Schaffer, Dec. 24, 1942 (dec. Nov. 1990); children: Susan Frances, James Hargrove. AB with honors, Emory U., 1940; LL.B. summa cum laude, Harvard U., 1947. Bar: Ga. 1947, D.C. 1951. Assoc. firm Sutherland, Tuttle & Brennan (now Sutherland, Asbill & Brennan LLP), Atlanta and Washington, 1947-53, ptnr., 1953—. Lectr. Emory U., 1959, chmn. bd. visitors, 1967-68; trustee The Northwestern Mut. Life Ins. Co., Milw., 1972-91; mem. advisory group Commr. of Internal Revenue, 1963-64 Pres.: Harvard Law Review, 1946-47. Chmn. bd. trustees Met. Atlanta Crime Commn., 1970-71; mem. Harvard U. Overseers Com. to Visit Law Sch., 1959-65; trustee Emory U., 1983-90, trustee emeritus, 1990—. Served to lt. comdr. USNR, 1942-46. Fellow Am. Bar Found., Am. Coll. Tax Counsel; mem. ABA, State Bar Ga., D.C. Bar, Atlanta Bar Assn., Am. Law Inst. (coun. 1974—), Lawyers Club Atlanta (pres. 1960-61), Am. Judicature Soc., Harvard Law Sch. Assn. (coun. 1981-85), Emory U. Alumni Assn. (pres. 1966-67), Capital City Club, Piedmont Driving Club, Peachtree Club, Phi Beta Kappa, Omicron Delta Kappa, Kappa Alpha. Methodist. Home: 3171 Marne Dr NW Atlanta GA 30305-1931 Office: Sutherland Asbill & Brennan LLP 999 Peachtree St NE Ste 2300 Atlanta GA 30309-3996

WILSON, JAMES LAURENCE, real estate development executive, financial services consultant, educator; b. Jamaica, N.Y., Mar. 20, 1945; s. William Henry and Beulah (Baylis) W.; m. Marilyn Murray, June 13, 1981; children: Leigh William, Robin Steele, Brennen Julian. BS, Union Coll., 1968. Dir. World Assocs., Inc., Ft. Lauderdale, Fla., 1970-77; divsn. head Royal Trust Bank, Miami, Fla., 1976-81; sr. lending officer S.E. Bank, Tampa, 1982-85; pres. Bayshore Investments, Investors and Cons. shopping ctr. devel. co., Tampa, 1984—; exec. v.p., sr. lending officer Boca Bank, Boca Raton, Fla., 1990-92; vice chmn., CEO, organizing dir. So. Security Bank, 1993-2001, sr. v.p., sr. real estate lending officer Fla. Capital Bank, NA, 2002—; adj. faculty Fla. Atlantic Univ. Contbr. articles to profl. jours. Mem. Mortgage Bankers Assn., Am. Bankers Assn., Econ. Soc. South Fla., Am. Inst. Banking, Internat. Coun. Shopping Ctrs. Republican. Home: 21346 Saint Andrews Blvd # 260 Boca Raton FL 33433-2432 Office: Fla Atlantic Univ Boca Raton Campus PO Box 520 Boca Raton FL 33429 Office Phone: 561-416-1100.

WILSON, JAMES LAWRENCE, retired chemical company executive; b. Rosedale, Miss., Mar. 2, 1936; s. James Lawrence and Mary Margaret (Klingman) W.; m. Barbara Louise Burroughs, Aug. 30, 1958; children: Lawrence Burroughs, Alexander Elliott. B.Mech. Engring., Vanderbilt U., 1958; MBA, Harvard, 1963. Vice pres. Nyala Properties, Inc., Phila., 1963-65; staff assoc. Rohm & Haas Co., Phila., 1965-67, exec. asst. to pres., 1971-72, treas., 1972-74, regional dir. Europe, 1974-77, group v.p., 1977-86, vice-chmn., 1986-88, chmn., CEO, 1988-99; ret., 1999. Treas. Warren-Teed Pharms., Inc., Columbus, Ohio, 1967-68, v.p., 1969; pres. Consol. Biomed. Labs., Inc., Dublin, Ohio, 1970-71; bd. dirs. Vanguard Group Investment Cos., Cummins Inc., AmeriSourceBergen Corp. Trustee Vanderbilt U., 1987—, Culver Ednl. Found., 1988—; chmn. Phila. High Sch. Acads., 1989-99. Mem. Chem. Mfrs. Assn. (bd. dirs. 1988-99, chmn. 1996). Office: 175 Strafford Ave Ste 1 Wayne PA 19087-3331

WILSON, JAMES LEE, retired geology educator, consultant; b. Waxahachie, Tex., Dec. 1, 1920; s. James Burney and Hallie Christine (Hawkins) W.; m. Della I. Moore, May 8, 1944; children: James Lee Jr., Burney Grant, Dale Ross (dec.). Student, Rice U., 1938-40; BA, U. Tex., 1942, MA, 1944; PhD, Yale U., 1949. Geologist Carter Oil Co., Tulsa, 1943-44; asst. and assoc. prof. U. Tex., Austin, 1949-52; rsch. geologist Shell Devel. Co., Houston, 1952-66; prof. Rice U., Houston, 1966-79, U. Mich., Ann Arbor, 1979-86; geol. cons. New Braunfels, Tex., 1986—. Cons. Erico Corp., London, 1985-88, Masera Corp., Tulsa, 1988—, Coyote Geol. Svcs., Boulder, Col., 1990—; adj. prof. Rice U., 1986—. Author: Carbonate Facies in Geologic History, 1975; contbr. articles to tech. jours. With C.E., U.S. Army, 1944-46, Italy. Grantee NSF. Fellow: Geol. Soc. Am. (Sloss award); mem.: Con. Soc. Petroleum Geologists, South Tex. Geol. Soc., West Tex. Geol. Soc., Am. Assn. Petroleum Geologists (hon. Disting. Educator award), Paleontological Soc., Soc. Econ. Paleontology and Minerology (pres. 1972—73, field trip guide books 1989, Sidney Powers Meml. award 2002, Twenhofel award, Hedberg award), Internat. Sedimentological Soc. Avocations: piano, languages. Home and Office: 1316 Patio Dr New Braunfels TX 78130-8505 Office Phone: 830-625-6612. Personal E-mail: dwilson6612@sbcglobal.net.

WILSON, JAMES MILLER, IV, cardiovascular surgeon, educator; b. Atlanta, Mar. 11, 1946; s. James Miller Wilson III and Sara Sharp; m. Lisa VanLandingham; children: James Miller V, Robert Paul, Michael Simpson, Sara Ann. Student, Emory U.; MD, Duke U., 1971. Diplomate Am. Bd. Surgery, Am. Bd. Thoracic Surgery. Intern N.Y. Hosp., 1971-72; resident N.Y. Hosp.-Cornell Med. Ctr., 1972-73, U. Calif., San Francisco, 1975-80; attending staff Christ Hosp., Cin., 1980—, Bethesda Hosp., Cin., 1980—, Jewish Hosp., Cin., 1980—, Univ. Hosp., Cin., 1982—, Deaconess Hosp. Cin., 1982—, VA Med Ctr., Cin., 1983—, Children's Hosp., Cin., 1984—, Good Samaritan Hosp., Cin., 1994—; assoc. prof. clin. surgery U. Cin. Coll. Med., 1985—; chmn. dept. cardiovasc. surgery Deaconess Hosp., 1985—2001; dir. cardiac surgery Mercy Hosp., 2001—. Mem. open heart surgery adv. com., Ohio, 1995—; tech. adv. panel on cardiac surgery Nat. Quality Forum, chmn. Contbr. articles to profl. jours. Lt. Comdr. submarine svc. USN, 1973-75. Fellow ACS, Am. Coll. Cardiology, Am. Heart Assn. (cardiovasc. coun.), Am. Coll. Chest Physicians; mem. AMA, U.S. Naval Submarine League, UDT/SEAL Assn., U.S. Submarine Vets., Inc., Am. Assn. Thoracic Surgery, Thoracic Surgery Found., Assn. Acad. Surgery, Soc. Thoracic Surgeons, Ohio State Med. Assn., Cin. Acad. Medicine, Howard C. Nafziger Soc. Avocations: music, diving, hiking, skiing, horses. Office: Heart Hosp #33S 3050 Mack Rd Fairfield OH 45014 Home Phone: 513-271-9060; Office Phone: 513-603-8600. E-mail: jmwilson@alumni.duke.edu.

WILSON, JAMES RAY, small business owner; b. Mar. 7, 1930; s. Ray Crawford and Ruth Lee (Walthers) W.; m. Carolyn Dempsey, Feb. 1, 1952; children: Robin E., Victoria, Mark, Jamie. BA (U.S. Navy Coll. Tng. Program scholar), Miami U., Oxford, Ohio, 1951; postgrad., Miami U., 1967—68; MA, Ohio State U., 1956; PhD, U. Minn., 1984. Grad. asst. Ohio State U., 1955—56; grain mcht. Cargill Inc., Balt., 1956—58; pres. Granexport Corp., Manilla, Philippines, 1959—66; mng. dir. Tradax Graanhandel B.V., Amsterdam, 1966—67; instr. dept. geography Miami U., 1967—68; pres. Cargill Agricola S.A., Sao Paulo, Brazil, 1968—78; dir. indsl. div. Tradax Geneve S.A., Geneva, 1978—80; corp. v.p. Cargill Inc., Mpls., 1980—83; pres. Cargill S.E. Asia, Ltd., Singapore, 1984—88; internat. bus. prof. Miami U. of Ohio, Oxford, Ohio, 1988—92, prof. mgmt., 1994—98; chmn. Cargill Tech. Svcs., Ltd., Thame, England, 1992—94; proprietor Books in Shandon, Shandon, Ohio, 1998—. Served with USN, 1952-55. Fellow Royal Geog. Soc. Congregationalist. Home: 6533 Buckley Rd Oxford OH 45056-9727 Office: Books in Shandon 4795 Cincinnati-Brookville PO Box 8 Shandon OH 45063 Office Phone: 513-738-2962.

WILSON, JAMES REID, JR., publishing executive; b. Phila., Aug. 5, 1934; s. James Reid Wilson and Florence Dunn; m. Eve-Ann Jones; children: Suzanne Winters, Diantha Curtis. BS in Econs., U. Pa., 1956. Assoc. dir. western hemisphere promotion The NY Times, NYC, 1966-69, mgr. indsl. advt., 1969-74; mgr. corp. advt. US News & World Report, NYC, 1974-79, advt. mgr., 1979-85, mktg. mgr., 1985-86; sr. v.p. Newspaper Advt. Bur., NYC, 1986-93; dir. Izvestia/Hearst, WeMbl, NYC and Moscow, 1993-94; pres. Media Ptnr., NYC, 1995-97; ad sales dir. Forbes SIP, NYC, 1997-2000, v.p., 2000—03; mng. dir. Hollywood Stars, 2004—05. Pres. Pa. Assn. Retarded Citizens, 1969-71; sr. v.p. Assn. Retarded Citizens US, Arlington, Tex., 1975-77, pres. 1977-79; bd. mem. Walker Ctr., One-to-One. Mem. St. Nicholas Soc., Union League, Scarsdale Golf Club, Penn Club, NY Sons of the Revolution. Republican. Presbyterian. E-mail: 329wilson@comcast.net.

WILSON, JAMES RICKER, physicist, consultant; b. Berkeley, Calif., Oct. 21, 1922; s. Leslie Ramsey and Ethel Frances (Banker) W.; m. Demetra George Corombos, Feb. 25, 1949; children: Leslie, Marika, George, Tasia, Peter. BS in Chemistry, U. Calif., Berkeley, 1943, PhD in Physics, 1952. With Los Alamos Nat. Lab., N.Mex., 1944—46; physicist Sandia Corp., Alburquerque, 1952-53, Lawrence Livermore Nat. Lab., Calif., 1953-88, lab. assoc., 1991—. Cons. Lawrence Livermore Nat. Lab., 1988-90. Author: Numerical Modeling in Physics, 1991 With U.S. Army, 1944-46. Fellow Am. Phys. Soc. (Hans A. Bethe award 2007), Murdock Found.; mem. Am. Astron. Soc., Internat. Astronomy Union. Democrat. Achievements include establishment of neutrino heating mechanism for supernova and the initiation of thermonucular supernova explosions by black hole steller encounters. Home: 2993 Chateau Way Livermore CA 94550-6845 Office: Lawrence Livermore Nat Lab PO Box L-35 Livermore CA 94551-0808 Home Phone: 925-440-2977; Office Phone: 415-422-1659. E-mail: wilson33@llwl.gov. *

WILSON, JAMES ROSS, communications educator, broadcast executive; b. Petaluma, Calif., Nov. 25, 1939; s. Stanley Thomas and Billie (Ross) W.; m. Elizabeth Ann Buckleman, Dec. 29, 1964 (div. 1982); children: Greg, Tom. BA, Fresno State Coll., 1961; MA, Calif State U., Fresno, 1976. Radio and TV instr. Dept. Def. Info. Sch., Ft. Slocum, N.Y., 1962-65; news dir. Sta. KVON, Napa, Calif., 1965, Sta. KTIM, San Rafael, Calif., 1966; news reporter Sta. KMJ, Fresno, 1966-67, news dir., 1967-71; program dir. Sta. KMJ/KNAX-FM, Fresno, 1971-78, v.p., gen. mgr., 1978-82; news assignment editor Sta. KFSN-TV, Fresno, 1982-83; prof. mass comm., gen. mgr., faculty advisor KFSR-FM Calif. State U., Fresno, 1983—; jazz disk jockey Sta. KVPR, Valley Pub. Radio, Fresno, 1984-90; weekend news anchor KMPH-FM News Radio, 1994-96. Co-author: Mass Media/Mass Culture, 4th edit., 1997, 5th edit., 2000. Recipient Best Newscast award Calif. AP-TV-Radio Assn., 1971, Best News Documentary award Calif. AP-TV-Radio Assn., 1973-74, Broadcast Excellence award Billboard mag., 1976; Calif. State U. grantee, 1987. Mem. Broadcast Edn. Assn., Cen. Calif. Broadcasters Assn. (treas., bd. dirs. 1980-83), Assn. for Edn. in Journalism and Mass Communication, Soc. Profl. Journalists, Alpha Epsilon Rho, Phi Kappa Phi. Home: 4747 E Holland Ave Fresno CA 93726-2914 Office: Calif State U Dept Mass Comm Journalism Fresno CA 93740-0001 E-mail: james_wilson@csufresno.edu.

WILSON, JANE, artist; b. Seymour, Iowa, Apr. 29, 1924; d. Wayne and Cleone (Marquis) Wilson; m. John Gruen, Mar. 28, 1948; 1 child, Julia Gruen. BA, U. Iowa, 1945, MA, 1947. Mem. fine arts faculty Parsons Sch. Design, 1973-83, 89-90. Vis. artist U. Iowa, 1974; adj. assoc. prof. painting and drawing Columbia U., 1975—85, assoc. prof., 1985—86, prof., 1986—88, acting chair, 1986—88; Andrew Mellon vis. prof. painting Cooper Union, 1977—78. One-woman shows include Hansa Gallery, N.Y.C., 1953, 1955, 1957, Stuttman Gallery, 1958, 1959, Tibor de Nagy Gallery, 1960—66, Graham Gallery, 1968, 1969, 1971, 1973, 1975, Fischbach Gallery, 1978, 1981, 1984, 1988, 1990, 1991, 1993, 1995, 1997, Munson-Williams-Proctor Inst., Utica, N.Y., 1980, Cornell U., Ithaca, N.Y., 1982, Compass Rose Gallery, Chgo., 1988, Am. U., Washington, 1989, U. Richmond, Va., 1990, Earl McGratgh Gallery, LA, 1990—91, 1993, Dartmouth Coll., Hanover, N.H., 1991, Arnot Mus., Elmira, N.Y., 1993—94, Parrish Mus., Southampton, N.Y., 1996, Glenn Horowitz Gallery, East Hampton, N.Y., 1996, D. C. Moore Gallery, N.Y.C., 1999, 2001, 2003, 2004, Heckscher Mus., Huntington, N.Y., 2001, McKinney Ave. Contemporary, Dallas, 2003, Represented in permanent collections Met. Mus., Mus. Modern Art, Whitney Mus., Wadsworth Athenaeum, Heron Art Mus., NYU Rockefeller Inst., Vassar Coll., Pa. Acad. Fine Arts, Hirsch Horn Mus., Washington, Nelson-Atkins Mus., Kansas City, Mo., San Francisco Mus. Modern Art, Heckscher Mus., L.I. Mus., Stony Brook, others. Recipient Eloise Spaeth award, Guild Hall, East Hampton, N.Y., 1968, Lifetime Achievement award, 2001, Purchase prize, Childe Hassam Fund, 1971, 1973, 1981, Ranger Fund Purchase prize, 1977; Ingram-Merrill grantee, 1963, Louis Comfort Tiffany grantee, 1967. Mem.: Nat. Acad. Design (academician 1974—, pres. 1992—94), Am. Acad. Arts and Letters (award in Art 1985), Phi Beta Kappa. E-mail: jwi1010@aol.com.

WILSON, JASON, chef; m. Nicole Wilson, 2001. Degree in Culinary Arts, Calif. Culinary Acad., 1995. Cook Aqua, San Francisco, Flying Saucer, San Francisco, Stars, Singapore, 1996, exec. chef Seattle, 1998; founder The Morning Grind coffee cart, South Lake Union, Wash.; caterer Duck Pond Winery, 2001—04; co-owner, exec. chef Crush, Seattle, 2005—. Recipient Best New Chef award, Food and Wine Mag., 2006. Office: Crush Restaurant 2319 E Madison St Seattle WA 98112 Office Phone: 206-302-7874.

WILSON, JEAN DONALD, endocrinologist, educator; b. Wellington, Tex., Aug. 26, 1932; s. J. D. and Maggie E. (Hill) Wilson. BA in Chemistry, U. Tex., 1951, MD, 1955. Diplomate Am. Bd. Internal Medicine. Intern, then resident in internal medicine Parkland Meml. Hosp., Dallas, 1955—58; clin. assoc. Nat. Heart Inst., Bethesda, Md., 1958—60; instr. internal medicine U. Tex. Southwestern Med. Sch., Dallas, 1960—61, prof., 1968—. Editor: Jour. Clin. Investigation, 1972—77. Sr. asst. surgeon USPHS, 1958—60. Recipient Fuller prize, Am. Urol. Assn., 1983, Lita Annenberg Hazen award, 1986, Dale medal, Soc. for Endocrinology, 1991, Pincus medal, Worchester Found., 1992. Fellow: Royal Coll. Physicians; mem.: NAS, Endocrine Soc. (Oppenheimer award 1972, Koch award 1993), Am. Soc. Biochemistry and Molecular Biology, Soc. Exptl. Biology and Medicine, Am. Philos. Soc., Assn. Am. Physicians (Kober medal 1999), Am. Soc. Clin. Investigation, Inst. Medicine, Am. Acad. Arts and Scis. (Amory prize 1977). Office: U Tex Southwestern Med Ctr Dept Internal Medicine 5323 Harry Hines Blvd Dallas TX 75390-8857 Home Phone: 214-351-1837; Office Phone: 214-648-3685. Fax: 214-648-8917. E-mail: jwils1@mednet.swmed.edu.

WILSON, JEAN LOUISE, retired state legislator; b. Phila., June 13, 1928; d. Horace and Catherine (Lennox) Terry; m. Benjamin H. Wilson (dec.); children: Sheryl J. Gordon, Denise T. Munn. BS in Edn., Pa. State U., 1949. Tchr. Columbia Inst., Phila., 1949-50, Wilkes Coll., Wilkes Barre, Pa., 1950-51; office mgr., exec. sec. Camden Fibre Mills, Warminster, Pa., 1969-82; mem. Pa. Ho. of Reps., 1988-92. Legis. chmn. Doylestown V.I.A.; active Benj. H. Wilson Sr. Ctr., Ctr. for Learning in Retirement, Del. Valley Coll.; former mem. bd. Bucks County Opportunity Coun.; treas. Bucks County chpt. Fox Chase Cancer Ctr., 1997—2006. Avocations: duplicate bridge, golf. Home: 12 Far View Rd Chalfont PA 18914-2511

WILSON, JOE (ADDISON GRAVES), congressman, former senator, lawyer; b. Charleston, SC, July 31, 1947; s. Hugh deVeaux And Wray Smart (Graves) Wilson; m. Roxanne Dusenbury McCrory, Dec. 30, 1977; children: Michael Alan, Addison Graves, Julian Dusenbury, Hunter Taylor. BA, Washington and Lee U., Lexington, Va., 1969; JD, U. SC, Columbia, 1972. Bar: SC 1972. Staff mem. US Senator Strom Thurmond, Washington,

1967, US Rep. Floyd Spence, Columbia, SC, 1970-72; ptnr. Kirkland, Wilson, Moore, Taylor & Thomas, West Columbia, 1972—2001; mem. US Congress from 2nd SC dist., 2002—, mem. armed svcs. com., mem. edn. and labor com., mem. fgn. affairs com., asst. majority whip, ranking mem. subcommittee on workforce protections. Dep. gen. counsel US Energy Sec. Jim Edwards, Washington, 1981-82; bd. dirs. Bank Am., Lexington, SC; mem. SC State Senate, Columbia, 1984-2001; presdl. appointee Intergovernmental Adv. Coun. Edn., 1990-91; mem. Internat. Observation Del. for 1990 Bulgarian parliamentary election Vice chmn. SC Rep. Party, 1972-74; campaign mgr. Staff of US Rep. Floyd Spence, Columbia, 1974, 78, 80, 82, 98; dist. campaign mgr. Staff of Gov. Carroll Campbell, 1986 Served in USAR, 1972—75, positions to col. SC Army N.G., 1975—2003. Mem. Rotary, Masons, Shriners. Republican. Presbyterian. Office: US House Reps 212 Cannon House Office Bldg Washington DC 20515 Office Phone: 202-225-2452. Office Fax: 202-225-2455. E-mail: joe.wilson@mail.house.gov. *

WILSON, JOHN HUMAN, III, curator, art historian; b. Fort Worth, Feb. 18, 1956; s. John Human Wilson II and Mary Ryan Wilson; m. Annasue McCleave, Sept. 4, 1982; children: John Human IV, Anna Sophia, Veronica Teresa. BA, So. Meth. U., Dallas, 1978; MA in History of Art, U. London, 1989, PhD in History of Art, 1992. Curator European and Am. art Spencer Mus. Art, U. Kans., Lawrence, 1988—90; curator painting and sculpture Cin. Art Mus., 1990—99; dir. curatorial affairs, curator European art Joslyn Art Mus., Omaha, 2005—. Cons., ind. scholar, Cin., 1999—2005. Author: (collection catalogue) American Paintings from Procter & Gamble: The Historic Cincinnati Collection; art cons. (film) Artworks. Mem.: Historians Brit. Art, Walpole Soc., Assn. Art Mus. Curators (mus. collections and exhibitions com. 2006), Coll. Art Assn., Turner Soc. (life), Athenaeum, Lit. Club Cin. (assoc.). Office: Joslyn Art Mus 2200 Dodge St Omaha NE 45202 Office Fax: 402-342-2376.

WILSON, JOHN I., educational association administrator; b. Burlington, NC, Oct. 25, 1947; BS in Edn., Western Carolina U., 1970; MEd, U. NC, 1971. Spl. edn. tchr. Wake County Sch. Sys., 1972—92; mgr. govt. rels. NC Assn. Educators, 1992—95, exec. dir., 1995—2000, NEA, Washington, 2000—. Pres. Student NC Assn. Educators, 1969—70, Raleigh Assn. Classroom Tchrs., NC, NC Classroom Tchrs. Assn., Wake County Assn. Classroom Tchrs., NC Assn. Educators, 1981; mem. NEA Exec. Com., 1983—89. Co-founder Covenant for NC children; lobbyist NC Educators Assn. Avocation: reading. Office: NEA 1201 16th St NW Washington DC 20036-3290 Office Phone: 202-833-4000. Office Fax: 202-822-7974. *

WILSON, JOHN PASLEY, retired law educator; b. Newark, Apr. 7, 1933; s. Richard Henry and Susan Agnes (Pasley) Wilson; m. Elizabeth Ann Reed, Sept. 10, 1955 (div.); children: David Cables, John Pasley, Cicely Reed. AB, Princeton U., 1955; LLB, Harvard U., 1962. Bar: US Dist. Ct. NJ 1962, Mass. 1963, US Dist. Ct. Mass. 1963. Budget examiner Exec. Office of Pres., Bur. of Budget, Washington, 1955-56; assoc. Riker, Danzig, Scherer & Brown, Newark, 1962-63; asst. dean Harvard U. Law Sch., Cambridge, Mass., 1963-67; assoc. dean Boston U. Law Sch., 1968-82; dean Golden Gate U. Sch. Law, San Francisco, 1982-88, prof., 1988—2003, prof. emeritus, 2003—, dean emeritus, 2003—. Vis. prof. dept. health policy and mgmt. Harvard U., 1988; cons. Nat. Commn. Protection Human Subjects Biomedical and Behavioral Rsch.; mem. Mass. Gov.'s Commn. Civil and Legal Rights Developmentally disabled; former chmn. adv. com. Ctr. Cmty. Legal Edn., San Francisco. Author: (book) The Rights of Adolescents in the Mental Health System; contbr. chapters to books, articles to profl. jours. Bd. dirs. Greater Boston Legal Svcs., Chewonki Found.; mem. Health Facilities Appeals Bd., Mass.; assoc. mem. Dem. Town Com., Concord; chmn. Bd. Assessors, Concord; bd. overseers Boston Hosp. Women, past chmn. med. affairs com.; past mem. instl. rev. bd. Calif. Pacific Hosp., San Francisco. Served to lt. (j.g.) USNR, 1956—59. NIMH grantee, 1973. Mem.: Nat. Assn. Securities Dealers (arbitrator). Democrat. Personal E-mail: jwlsn7@comcast.net.

WILSON, JONATHAN C., lawyer; b. Bristol, Tenn., Dec. 6, 1958; BA pers. mgmt., U. Wyo., 1980, JD with honors, 1983. Bar: Tex. 1983, admitted to practice: US Dist. Ct. (So. Dist.) Tex., US Dist. Ct. (Ea. Dist.) Tex., US Dist. Ct. (We. Dist.) Tex., US Dist. Ct. (No. Dist.) Tex., US Ct. Appeals (5th Cir.), US Ct. Appeals (6th Cir.), US Supreme Ct., cert.: State Bar Tex., Bd. Legal Specialization (specialist), Tex. Supreme Ct. Ptnr. Haynes and Boone LLP, Dallas, chmn., Labor and Employment Law Practice Group. Spkr. in field. Staff editor Wyo. Land & Water Law Rev., 1981—82. Named one of Best in Am. in labor and employment law, Corp. Counsel Mag., 2004. Mem.: Dallas Bar Assn., Tex. State Bar, ABA, Order of Coif. Office: Haynes and Boone LLP 901 Main St Ste 3100 Dallas TX 75202-3789 Office Phone: 214-651-5646. Office Fax: 214-200-0381. Business E-Mail: jonathan.wilson@haynesboone.com.

WILSON, JONATHAN MICHAEL, literature educator, writer; b. London, Feb. 26, 1950; arrived in U.S., 1976; s. Lewis and Doris Wilson; m. Sharon Ann Kaitz, Aug. 30, 1980; children: Adam, Gabriel. BA with honors, U. Essex, Colchester, Eng., 1973; postgrad., Oxford U., Eng., 1974—77; PhD, Hebrew U., Jerusalem, 1980. Asst. prof. English Tufts U., Medford, Mass., 1984—91, assoc. prof. English, 1991—98, chair Dept. English, 1998—2005, prof. English, 1998—, Fletcher Prof. Rhetoric and Debate, 2001—. Vis. scholar Columbia U., NYC, 1976. Author: On Bellow's Planet, 1985, Herzog: The Limits of Ideas, 1990, Schoom, 1994, The Hiding Room, 1995, A Palestine Affair, 2003, An Ambulance Is On The Way, 2005. Simon Guggenheim fellow in fiction, 1994—95. Jewish. Avocation: soccer. Home: 44 Carver Rd Newton MA 02461 Office: Tufts U Dept English Medford MA 02115 E-mail: jonathan.wilson@tufts.edu.

WILSON, JOSEPH CHARLES, IV, former ambassador; b. Bridgeport, Conn., Nov. 6, 1949; s. Joseph Charles III and Phyllis (Finnell) W.; m. Susan Dale Otchis, Apr. 27, 1973 (div. 1986); m. Valerie Elise Plame, Apr. 3, 1998; children: Sabrina Cecile, Joseph Charles, Trevor Rolph, Samantha Finnell Diana. BA in History, U. Calif., Santa Barbara, 1972. Fgn. svc. officer Dept. of State, Washington, 1976-98; congl. fellow Am. Polit. Sci. Assn., Washington, 1985-86; dep. chief of mission Am. Embassy, Bujumbura, Burundi, 1982-85, Brazzaville, Congo, 1986-88, Baghdad, Iraq, 1988-91; amb. Gabon, Sao Tome and Principe, 1992-95; polit. adv. to Commdr. in Chief U.S. Armed Forces Europe, 1995-97; spl. asst. to pres., sr. dir. for African affairs Nat. Security Coun., Washington, 1997-98; pres. JC Wilson Internat. Ventures, Washington, 1998—. Adj. scholar Mid. East Inst., 2002—04. Author: The Politics of Truth: Inside the Lies That Led to a War and Betrayed My Wife's CIA Identity--A Diplomat's Memoirs, 2004 (N.Y. Times Bestseller). Decorated comdr. Order of Equatorial Star (Gabon); recipient Disting. Alumni award U. Calif. Santa Barbara, 1991, 1995, Disting. Def. Dept. Civilian award, 1997; recipient Ron Ridenhour prize, 2003, Am. Patriot award Ams. for Informed Democracy, 2003. Mem. Am. Fgn. Svc. Assn. (William R. Rivkin award 1987), U. Calif. Santa Barbara Alumni Assn., San Onofre Surfing Club. Avocations: golf, bicycling, exercise, skiing. Home Phone: 202-256-0536.

WILSON, JOSEPH MORRIS, III, lawyer; b. Milw., July 26, 1945; s. Joseph Morris Jr. and Phyllis Elizabeth (Cresson) W.; children: Elizabeth J., Eric M.; m. Dixie Lee Brock, Mar. 23, 1984. BA, Calif. State U., Chico, 1967; MA, U. Washington, 1968; JD summa cum laude, Ohio State U., 1976. Bar: Alaska 1976, U.S. Dist. Ct. Alaska 1976, U.S. Ct. Appeals (9th cir.) 1986. Recruiter and vol. U.S. Peace Corps, Republic of Benin, 1969-73; legal intern U.S. Ho. of Reps., Washington, 1975; ptnr. Guess & Rudd P.C., Anchorage, 1976-88, chmn. comml. dept., 1981-82, ptnr. compensation com., 1982-84; mgr. Alaska taxes, sr. tax atty. BP Exploration Inc., Alaska, 1990-99. Bus. law instr. U. Alaska, Anchorage, 1977-78. Mem. Alaska Bar Assn., World Affairs Coun. Democrat. Avocations: music, sports, travel. Home and Office: 2556 Palmera Cir Las Vegas NV 89121-4016 Home Phone: 702-369-7105; Office Phone: 702-369-7105. E-mail: jsphwlsn@aol.com.

WILSON, JULIA ANN YOTHER, lawyer; b. Dallas, Sept. 6, 1958; d. Julian White and Mary Ann (Estes) Yother. BA, East Ctrl. U., Ada, Okla., 1980; JD, U. Okla., 1983. Bar: Okla. 1990, Calif. 1993, D.C. 1995; U.S. Ct. Appeals (9th cir.) Calif. 1993, U.S. Supreme Ct. 1993, U.S. Dist. Ct. (ctrl. dist.) Calif. 1993, U.S. Dist. Ct. (we. dist.) Okla., 1997. Assoc. Law Office of George Rodda Jr., Newport Beach, Calif., 1984-96; sole practice law Oklahoma City, 1996-97; assoc. Coldiron, Wilson & Assocs., Oklahoma City, 1997—2004; pvt. practice Oklahoma City, 2004—. Served to 1st lt. USAR, 1980-86. Mem. ABA, D.C. Bar Assn., Calif. Bar Assn., Oklahoma County Bar Assn., Okla. Bar Assn. (litigation sect.), Orange County Bar Assn. Office: 3233 E Memorial Rd Ste 107B Edmond OK 73013 Home Phone: 405-204-1077; Office Phone: 405-478-8889. Business E-Mail: julia.wilson@lawoklahoma.com.

WILSON, KAREN LEE, museum staff member, researcher; b. Somerville, NJ, Apr. 2, 1949; d. Jon Milton and Laura Virginia (Van Dyke) W.; m. Paul Ernest Walker, 1980; 1 child, Jeremy Nathaniel. AB, Harvard U., 1971; MA, NYU, 1973, PhD, 1985. Rsch. assoc., dir. excavation at Mendes, Egypt Inst. Fine Arts, NYU, 1979-81; coord. exhbn. The Jewish Mus., NYC, 1981-82, adminstrv. cataloguer, 1982-83, coord. curatorial affairs, 1984-86; curator Oriental Inst. Mus. U. Chgo., 1988-96, mus. dir., 1996—2003, rsch. assoc., 1988—; coord. Kish Project Field Mus. Natural History, Chgo., 2004—. Rsch. asso. Oriental Inst. U. Chgo. Author, editor: Mendes, 1982; contbr. articles to profl. jours. Mem.: Coll. Art Assn., Am. Oriental Soc. Office Phone: 312-665-7184. Business E-Mail: k-wilson@uchicago.edu.

WILSON, KAREN LYNN, esthetician; b. Hartford, Conn., Mar. 6, 1956; d. Derwood Alexander and Rita Harriet Briggs; m. Leo Franklin Wilson, Sept. 5, 2003; children: Jeffrey Thomas Haynes, Jason Brian Haynes. BS in Fin. (hon.), Williams Coll., Houston, 1999. Lic. Esthetician Conn. Cosmetology, 2004. Sales and mktg. dir. Bollitierri Tennis Acad., Bradenton, Fla., 1990—95; registrar Nortel Comm., Wethersfield, Conn., 1995—98; sr. fin. assoc. NextiraOne, Wethersfield, Conn., 1998—2002; mktg. staff Total Comm., East Hartford, Conn., 2001—04; esthetician Timeless Reflection @ Cutters' Edge, Rocky Hill, Conn., 2004—. Apptd. to employee counsel Williams Comm., Wethersfield, Conn., 1998—2000, AR task team, 2000—01. Team leader United Way, Wethersfield, Conn., 1998—2000; chairperson Diabetes Found., Wethersfield, 1998—2001; team leader disaster recovery Rebuilding After 911 Tragedy. Recipient Dedication to Customers during 911 Tragedy, NextiraOne, 2001, Tiffany award, Manpower Staffing Svcs., 1996, Cir. of Excellence award, Williams Comm., 2000, Superior Performance; Gold Level, 1996—97, Achieving Customer Excellence award, 2000. Mem.: Continuing Profl. Edn. (assoc.), ABMP (assoc.), Jr. Women's Club (assoc.). Home: 222 Chestnut Hill Rd East Hampton CT 06424 Office: Timeless Reflection @ Cutters' Edge 2162 Silas Deane Hwy Rocky Hill CT 06067 Home Phone: 860-365-0885; Office Phone: 860-563-0243. Personal E-mail: k_lunited@yahoo.com. E-mail: timeless@yahoo.com, skincarebykaren@sbcglobal.net.

WILSON, KAREN WILKERSON, paralegal; b. Reidsville, NC, June 28, 1957; d. William Henry and Jean Gloria (Tiller) W.; married. Student, N.C. State U., 1975-77, Western Carolina U., Cullowhee, NC, 1978-80; diploma, Profl. Ctr. Paralegal Studies, Columbia, SC, 1988. Paralegal Ken H. Lester, Esquire, Columbia, 1989—, Lester & Jones, Columbia. Spkr. Alumni Profl. Ctr. Paralegal Studies, Columbia, 1988-95. Mem. ATLA, S.C. Trial Lawyers Assn. (paralegal rep. 1993-96). Democrat. Presbyterian. Office Phone: 803-252-4700. Business E-Mail: kwilson@lesterandjones.com.

WILSON, KATHY KAY, former foundation administrator, consultant; b. Monticello, Ind., Jan. 25, 1961; d. Kenneth L. and Janet I. Kruger; m. Douglas M. Wilson, July 20, 1991. AS, Ball State U., 1981; BS, Ind. Wesleyan U., 1989. Legal sec. Nesbitt Law Firm, Rensselaer, Ind., 1981-84; asst. to dir. Office of Patents and Copyrights Purdue Rsch. Found., West Lafayette, Ind., 1984-86; legal sec. Barnes & Thornburg, Indpls., 1986-87; rsch. and info. specialist Ind. U. Found., Indpls., 1987-91, dir. rsch. mgmt. and info. svcs. Bloomington, 1991-98, dir. Office of Devel. Svcs., 1998-2001; prin. Wilson Cons., 2003—. Cons. Prospect Rsch., 1991—; mem. faculty Fund Raising Sch., 1988-90. Mem. adv. coun. Bloomington Hosp., 1992-2001. Mem. Am. Prospect Rsch. Assn. (v.p. bd. dirs. 1991, pres. 1992, Ind. chpt. pres. 1988-90), Phi Gamma Nu, Delta Delta Delta. Business E-Mail: wilsondk@home.ffni.com.

WILSON, KEITH DUDLEY, media and music educator, consultant, dean; b. Windermere, July 13, 1936; s. Charles Alexander and Fanny (Shaw) Wilson; 1 child, Nicholas. BA with honors, Kings Coll., Cambridge, 1957, MA, 1960; LittD (hon.), U. Salford, Manchester, Eng., 2000. Lectr. Brit. Coun./Zagreb Univ., Croatia, 1957-58; assoc. prof., dir. TV Brit. Coun. Tehran U., Iran, 1958-64; reader Brit. Coun. Osmania U., Hyderabad, India, 1964-66; head of liberal edn. Salford (Eng.) Coll. Tech., 1967-72, head of humanities, 1972-85; head of performing arts and media U. Coll. Salford, 1985-90; dir. Ctr. Media Performance and Comm. U. Salford, 1990-96, founding chief exec. Internat. Media Ctr., 1993-99, dean faculty of media, music and performance, 1996-99. Tutor, counsellor Open U., 1972—90; dir. TVUK, Adelphi Prodns., Salford, 1988—99, Channel M, 1997—2000; chair PRS John Lennon awards, 1990—93; co-chair NYNEX Cable TV, Manchester, 1993—95; vis. acad. Brit. Coun., Republic of Korea, 1992; founder over 30 higher edn. courses in music, media, drama, rec., entertainment orgns., media and sci., new media; European edn. advisor, cons. media, music and rec. industries, 2000—, Edinburgh Internat. Festival, 1986—97. Musician: (concert tours) Brazil, Belgium, The Netherlands, Iceland, Norway, Denmark, Greece, Ecuador, Russia, Hungary; contbr. articles to profl. jours. and nat. papers. Mem. City of Salford LS Lowry Centenary, 1988, The Lowry, Nat. Landmark Millennium Project for Arts, Digital World Ctr.; founder Salford U. Brass Band, Wind Band, Big Band, Soundworks, Jazz Ensembles, Groove Machine, Aspects Theatre; mem. City Pride Initiative, Manchester, 1993—97, Fellowship Gt. Britain Sasakawa Found., Japan, 1991; mem. centenary com. U. Salford, 1994—96. Fellow: Royal Soc. Arts (chmn. N.W. 2006); mem.: Prodrs. Assn. Cinema and TV, Brit. Acad. Film and TV, Brit. Film Inst., Royal TV Soc. Avocations: wine, walking. Home and Office: 60 Central Rd Didsbury Manchester M204ZA England

WILSON, KENNETH GEDDES, physics research administrator; b. Waltham, Mass., June 8, 1936; s. E. Bright and Emily Fisher (Buckingham) Wilson; m. Alison Brown, 1982. AB, Harvard U., 1956, DSc (hon.), 1981; PhD, Calif. Tech. Inst., 1961; PhD (hon.), U. Chgo., 1976. From asst. prof. to prof. physics Cornell U., Ithaca, NY, 1963—88, James A. Weeks prof. in phys. sci., 1974—87; Hazel C. Youngberg Trustees Disting prof. The Ohio State U., Columbus, 1988—. Co-author: Redesigning Education, 1974. Recipient Nobel prize in physics, 1982, Dannie Heinemann prize, 1973, Boltzmann medal, 1975, Wolf prize in physics, Wolf Found., Israel, 1980, A.C. Eringen medal, 1984, Franklin medal, 1982, Aneesur Rahman prize, 1993. Mem.: NAS, Am. Acad. Arts and Scis., Am. Phys. Soc., Am. Philos. Soc.

WILSON, KENNETH JAY, writer; b. Oklahoma City, Aug. 25, 1944; s. Kenneth J. and Betty Wallace (Bleakmore) W. BA magna cum laude, Yale U., 1966, M.Phil., 1969; postgrad. Queen's Coll., Oxford U., Eng., 1969-70; PhD, Yale U., 1973. From instr. to assoc. prof. English U. Rochester, NY; assoc. Clare Hall, Cambridge U., England; vis. assoc. prof. English Coll. William and Mary, Williamsburg, Va.; dir. of rights and permissions Princeton U. Press. Cons. USIA, 1985 Editor: Letters of Sir Thomas Elyot, 1976, English Works of Thomas More, 1978; author: Incomplete Fictions, 1985, Pope John Paul II, 1992; contbr. essays, book revs. and short fiction to mags. and profl. jours. Woodrow Wilson fellow, 1966, 83; sr. fellow Folger Shakespeare Library, Washington, 1976; Am. Philos. Soc. grantee, 1976; Am. Council Learned Soc. fellow, 1977 Mem. Mory's Club, Elizabethan Club (New Haven), Yale Club (NYC), Palm-Aire Country Club, Phi Beta Kappa. Democrat. Roman Catholic. Home: 5570 Country Club Way Sarasota FL 34243-3759 E-mail: nuboy@comcast.net.

WILSON, KRISTEN ELLEN, psychologist; b. Landsthul, Germany, July 14, 1975; d. Theodore Clark and Nicola Day Wilson. BS, U. South, Sewanee, Tenn., 1993—97; MA, Boston U., 1998—99; PhD, NC State U., Raleigh, 1999—2005. Lic. specialist in sch. psychology Tex. State Bd. Examiners Psychologists, 2005, cert. sch. psychologist Nat. Assn. Sch. Psychology, 2006. Predoctoral intern Coppell Ind. Sch. Dist., Tex., 2004—05; lic. specialist in sch. psychology-trainee Carrollton Farmers Br. Ind. Sch. Dist., Tex., 2005—06, lic. specialist in sch. psychology, 2006—. Contbr. articles to profl. jours. Vol. soccer coach YMCA, Dallas, 2005—. Mem.: Nat. Assn. Sch. Psychology (licentiate). Avocations: soccer, softball, running. Office: Carrollton Farmers Branch ISD 2115 E Frankford Rd Carrollton TX 75007 Home Phone: 214-459-5034.

WILSON, L. C., superintendent; b. Mar. 7, 1949; A, Rockford Bus. Coll., Ill. Prodn. supr. Rockford Powetrain, 1974—2006; plant supt. GKN, Rockford, 2006—. With USN, 1968—70. Home: 2615 Arthur Ave Rockford IL 61101

WILSON, L. MICHELLE (MICHELLE WILSON), lawyer, information technology executive; b. Boise, Idaho, Jan. 20, 1963; d. Tom Martin and George Ann Wilson; m., 1 son. BA, Univ. Wash., Seattle, 1985; JD with honors, Univ. Chgo., 1988. Assoc. Perkins Coie, Seattle, 1988—94, ptnr., 1994—99; assoc. gen. counsel Amazon.com Inc., Seattle, 1999—99, v.p., gen. counsel, sec., 1999—2001; sr. v.p. HR, gen. counsel, sec. Amazon.com, Seattle, 2001—03, sr. v.p., gen. counsel, sec., 2003—. Recipient Dow Jones award Wall St. Jour., 1985. Mem. ABA, Washington State Bar Assn., Order of Coif, Phi Beta Kappa, Beta Gamma Sigma. Office: Amazon.com Inc 1200 12th Ave S Ste 1200 Seattle WA 98144-2734 Office Phone: 206-266-1000. Office Fax: 206-266-1821. *

WILSON, LANFORD, playwright; b. Lebanon, Mo., Apr. 13, 1937; s. Ralph E(ugene) and Violetta (Tate) W. Student, San Diego State Coll., 1955-56; PhD in Humanities (hon.), U. Mo., 1985, Grinnell Coll., Iowa, 1994; PhD in Lit. (hon.), LI U., 1995. Playwright, 1962—; resident playwright, dir., co-founder Cir. Repertory Co., NYC, 1969-95. Instr. playwriting U. Houston, 2003—. Author: (plays) So Long at the Fair, 1963, Home Free!, 1964, No Trespassing, 1964, The Sandcastle, 1964, The Madness of Lady Bright, 1964, Ludlow Fair, 1965, Balm in Gilead, 1965, This is the Rill Speaking, 1965, Days Ahead, 1965, Sex is Between Two People, 1965, The Gingham Dog, 1966, The Rimers of Eldritch, 1966, Wandering, 1966, Lemon Sky, 1969, Serenading Louie, 1970, The Great Nebula in Orion, 1970, The Hot L Baltimore, 1972, The Family Continues, 1972, The Mound Builders, 1975, Fifth of July, 1978, Brontasaurus, 1978, Talley's Folly, 1979, A Tale Told, 1981, Angels Fall, 1983, A Betrothal, 1984, Talley & Son, 1985, Burn This, 1987, A Poster of the Cosmos, 1987, The Moonshot Tape, 1990, Redwood Curtain, 1991, Trinity, 1993, I'm Not the Ocean, 1995, Sympathetic Magic, 1996, A Sense of Place (or Virgil is Still the Frogboy), 1997, Your Everyday Ghost Story, 1997, Book of Days, 1998, Rain Dance, 2003; translator Three Sisters, 1984, Ghosts, 2002; author: (books) Balm in Gilead and Other Plays, 1966, The Rimers of Eldritch and Other Plays, 1968, The Gingham Dog, 1969, Lemon Sky, 1970, The Hot L Baltimore, 1973, The Mound Builders, 1976, Fifth of July, 1979, Talley's Folly, 1980, Angels Fall, 1983, Serenading Louie, 1985, Talley & Son, 1986, Burn This, 1988, Redwood Curtain, 1992, 21 Short Plays, 1994, By the Sea, 1996, Collected Plays, Vol. I, 1997, Vol. II, 1999, Vol. III, 1999, Vol. IV, 2006, A Sense of Place, 1999, Sympathetic Magic, 1999, Book of Days, 2001, Rain Dance, 2005. ABC Yale fellow, 1969; Rockefeller grantee, 1967, 73, Guggenheim grantee, 1970, NEA grantee, 1990; recipient Vernon Rice award, 1966-67, Inst. Arts and Letters award, 1970, Obie award, 1972, 75, 84, 97, Outer Critics Circle award, 1973, Drama Critics Circle award, 1973, 80, Pulitzer prize, 1980, Brandeis award, 1981, John Steinbeck award, 1990, Edward Albee Last Frontier award, 1994, Am. Acad. of Achievement award, 1995, Am. Assn. Theatre Critics Best Play award, 1998, Guild Hall Lifetime Achievement award, 2000, William Inge Lifetime Achievement award, 2002; inducted into Theater Hall of Fame, 1996, Mo. Writers Hall of Fame, 1998; recipient Lucille Lortel's Edith Oliver award for Sustained Excellence, 2001. Mem. Am. Acad. Arts and Letters, Dramatists Guild Am. Council.

WILSON, LEONARD GILCHRIST, medical educator; b. Orillia, Ont., Can., June 11, 1928; s. George Edward and Mary Agnes (MacPhee) W.; m. Adelia Katherine Hans, June 7, 1969; 1 child, George Edward Hans. BA, U. Toronto, Can., 1949; M.Sc., U. London, 1955; PhD, U. Wis., Madison, 1958. Lectr. Mount Allison U., Sackville, N.B., Canada, 1950-53; vis. instr. U. Calif., Berkeley, 1958-59; asst. prof. Cornell U., Ithaca, NY, 1959-60, Yale U., New Haven, 1960-65, assoc. prof., 1965-67; prof., head dept. history of medicine U. Minn., Mpls., 1967-98, prof. emeritus, 1998—. Author: Charles Lyell: The Years to 1841: The Revolution in Geology, 1972, Medical Revolution in Minnesota, 1989, Lyell in America: The Trans Atlantic Years, 1841-1853, 1998; editor: Benjamin Silliman and His Circle, 1979, Sir Charles Lyell's Scientific Journals on the Species Question, 1971; editor Jour. History Medicine and Allied Scis., 1973-82; co-editor: Readings in History of Physiology, 1966; mem. bd. mgrs. Jour. Hist. Medicine, 1962—. Fellow AAAS; mem. Am. Assn. History of Medicine, Am. Hist. Assn., History of Sci. Soc., Minn. Acad. Medicine (pres. 1984-85, sec.-treas. 1989-98), Brit. Soc. for the History of Sci., Soc. for the History of natural History. Home: 797 Goodrich Ave Saint Paul MN 55105-3344 Business E-Mail: wilso004@umn.edu.

WILSON, LEVON EDWARD, lawyer, educator; b. Charlotte, NC, Apr. 2, 1954; s. James A. and Thomasina Wilson. BSBA, Western Carolina U., 1976; JD, N.C. Ctrl. U., 1979; Ed D, 2001. Bar: NC 1981, US Dist. Ct. (mid. dist.) NC 1981, US Tax Ct. 1981, US Ct. Appeals (4th cir.) 1982, US Supreme Ct. 1984, Ga. 2007; lic. real estate broker, NC; cert. mediator NC Alternative Dispute Resolution Commn., arbitrator BBB. Pvt. practice, Greensboro, NC, 1981-85; asst. county atty. Guilford County, Greensboro, 1985-88; asst. prof. N.C. Agrl. & Tech. State U., Greensboro, 1988-91, Western Carolina U., Cullowhee, NC, 1991-96, prof., 1996—, prof., head dept. bus. adminstrn., law and mktg., 1996—2002; pres. Integrated Mgmt. Resources, Inc., 2000—; prof. Sch. Acctg., Ga. So. U., Statesboro, 2005—. Pres. Trade Brokers Cons.; legal counsel, bd. dirs. Rhodes Assocs., Inc., Greensboro, 1982—; legal counsel Guilford County Sheriff's Dept., Greensboro, 1985-88; bd. dirs. Webster Enterprises, Inc. Contbr. articles to profl. jours. Bd. dirs. Post Advocacy Detention Program; active mem. Prison Litigation Study Task Force, Adminstrn. Justice Study Com. Recipient Svc. award Blacks in Mgmt., 1980, Excellence in Tchg. award Jay I. Kneedler Found. of Western Carolina U., 1994-95, 2003-2004; Student in Free Enterprise fellow, Bd of Govs. award for Excellence in Tchg. U. NC Sys, 2004-05. Mem. ABA, N.C. Bar Assn., Acad. Legal Studies in Bus., Southeastern Acad. Legal Studies in Bus. (former editor-in-chief Jour. of Legal Studies in Bus., mng. editor), N.C. Assn. Police Attys., N.C. Real Estate Educators Assn., So. Acad. Legal Studies in

Bus., Phi Delta Phi, Beta Gamma Sigma. Democrat. Methodist. Office: Ga So U Sch Accountancy PO Box 8141 Statesboro GA 30460-8141 Home: PO Box 1414 Statesboro GA 30459-1414 Personal E-mail: levonwilson@msn.com. Business E-Mail: lwilson@georgiasouthern.edu.

WILSON, LEWIS LANSING, insurance executive; b. Cobleskill, NY, Jan. 26, 1932; s. Clarence A. and Ordella (Walker) W.; m. Barbara Jane Kathan, June 7, 1952; children: Susan W. Coleman, Joan, Peter L. (dec.) Grad. high sch., Cobleskill. Cert. profl. ins. agt., ins. cons. Mgr. claims Sterling Ins. Co., Cobleskill, 1950—57; ins. agt. State Farm Ins. Co., Cobleskill, 1957—59; pres. Lewis L. Wilson, Inc., Cobleskill, 1959—91, Fire Mark Ins. Agy., Inc., Cobleskill, 1991—. Pres. Redington Amb. Resort, North Redington, Fla., Point Pleasant Resort, St. Thomas, V.I., bd. dirs.; owner Wilson Travel Agy., 1978—, Wilson Tel. Exch., Cobleskill, 1978-86, Wilson Security, Inc., Cobleskill, 1981-86; rep. NY Mapp Program, 1985-88 Chmn. Cobleskill SUNY Found. Fund Drive; commr. Schoharie County Bd. Elections, 1983—; pres. Cobleskill Ctrl. Sch. Bd., Cmty. Hosp. Schoharie County, Cobleskill; dir. Schoharie Colonial Heritage; past chmn. Nat. PIA PAC, chmn. nat. gov. affairs, 1st v.p.; pres. Cobbleskill Cemetery Assn., 1999—; chmn. Two Million One Hundred Thousand Rescue Fund; mem. Hospice Bd. Deniston; Town chmn. Cobleskill Rep. Party, 1978-83; chmn. Schoharie County Rep. Com., NY, 1983—. Recipient Gold medal, Ronald Reagan, 2004. Mem. Profl. Ins. Agts. (pres. 1989, bd. dirs., v.p. 1987, 1st v.p. 1988, pres. 1989-90, nat. v.p., Ins. Agt. of Yr. 1986), N.Y. Ind. Ins. Agts. (regional v.p.), N.Y. Life Underwriters, Rotary (pres. Cobleskill chpt., gov. dist. 719 1982, Paul Harris fellow 1985-86), Elks (exalted ruler, hon. founder nat. found. 1980), Nat. Assn. Profl. Ins. Agts. (v.p. 2000—, Person of Yr. 1997) Republican. Methodist. Home: 168 Grandview Dr Cobleskill NY 12043 Office: PO Box 39 Cobleskill NY 12043-0039 Office Phone: 518-234-2534. Business E-Mail: lewis@lewiswilsonins.com.

WILSON, LINDA, librarian; b. Rochester, Minn., Nov. 17, 1945; d. Eunice Gloria Irene Wilson. BA, U. Minn., Morris, 1967; MA, U. Minn., 1968. Libr. rsch. svcs. U. Calif., Riverside, 1968-69, head dept. phys. scis. catalog, 1969-71; city libr. Belle Glade (Fla). Mcpl. Libr., 1972-74; instr. part-time Palm Beach Jr. Coll., Belle Glade, 1973; head adult-young adult ext. Kern County Libr. Sys., Bakersfield, Calif., 1974-80; dir. dist. libr. Lake Agassiz Regional Libr. System, Crookston, Minn., 1980-85; supervising libr. San Diego County Libr., 1985-87; county libr. Merced (Calif.) County Libr., 1987-93; learning network mgr. Merced Coll., 1994-95; city libr. Monterey Park (Calif.) Bruggemeyer Libr., 1995—. V.p. legis. Calif. Fedn. Bus., Profl. Women's Clubs, 2007-; mem. Leadership Merced, 1987-88, East Site Based Coordinating Coun., Merced, 1990-92, Merced Gen. Plan Citizens Adv. Com., 1992-95, Sister City Com., Merced, 1992-95. Recipient Libr. award Eagles Aux., 1984, Woman of Achievement award Commn. on the Status of Women, 1990, Libr. award Calif. Libr. Trustees and Commrs., 1990, Woman of Yr. award Merced Bus. and Profl. Women, 1990, People Who Make a Difference award Monterey Pk. United Dems., 2003, Woman of Yr. award 29th Congl. Dist., 2004. Mem. ALA (sec. pub. libr. sys. sect. 1988-89), Met. Coop. Library Sys. (pres. 1999-2000), Calif. Libr. Assn. (sec. govt. rels. com. 1991-92, continuing edn. com. 1993-96, pub. rels. 1997-2000, nominations com. 2000-01), Minn. Libr. Assn. (pres. pub. libr. divsn. 1985), Merced County Mgmt. Coun. (pres. 1989), Merced Bus. and Profl. Women (Woman of Yr. 1987, pres. 1988-89, 1st v.p. Sierra Mar dist., 2006-), East L.A.-Montebello Bus. and Profl. Women (v.p. 1998-2002, pres. 2002-05, 2007-), Rotary (pres. Monterey Park chpt. 1999-2000). Democrat. Lutheran. Avocations: travel, walking, reading, swimming, stamp collecting/philately. Home: 1000 E Newmark Ave Apt 22 Monterey Park CA 91755-3129 Office Phone: 626-307-1418. Business E-Mail: lwilson@montereypark.ca.gov. E-mail: lindalwilson@juno.com.

WILSON, LINDA SMITH, retired academic administrator; b. Washington, Nov. 10, 1936; d. Fred M. and Virginia D. Smith; m. Malcolm C. Whatley, June 29, 1957 (div. 1969); 1 child, Helen K. Whatley; m. Paul A. Wilson, Jan. 22, 1970; 1 stepchild, Beth A. BA, Tulane U., 1957, HLD (hon.), 1993; PhD, U. Wis., 1962; DLitt (hon.), U. Md., 1993. Rsch. assoc. U. Md., College Park, 1962—64, rsch. asst. prof., 1964—67; vis. asst. prof. U. Mo., St. Louis, 1967—68; asst. to vice chancellor for rsch., asst. vice chancellor for rsch., assoc. vice chancellor for rsch. Washington U., St. Louis, 1968—75; assoc. vice chancellor for rsch. U. Ill., Urbana, 1975—85; assoc. dean U. Ill. Grad. Coll., Urbana, 1978—85; v.p. for rsch. U. Mich., Ann Arbor, 1985—89; pres. Radcliffe Coll., Cambridge, Mass., 1989—99, pres. emeritus, 1999; sr. lectr. Harvard Grad. Sch. Edn., 1989—2003; bd. dirs. Myriad Genetics, Tulane U., Tulane Murphy Found. Rsch. resources adv. coun. NIH, Bethesda, Md., 1978—82; mem. Nat. Commn. on Rsch., Washington, 1978—80; dir.'s adv. coun. NSF, Washington, 1980—89; com. on govt.-univ. relationships NAS, 1981—83, govt.-univ.-industry rsch. roundtable, 1984—89, coord. coun. for edn., 1991—93; energy rsch. adv. bd. Dept. of Energy, 1987—90; chmn. adv. com. office sci. and engrng. pers. NRC, 1990—96; adv. com. edn. and human resources NSF, Washington, 1990—95; sci., tech. and states task force Carnegie Commn. on Sci., Tech. and Govt., 1991—92; overser Mus. Sci., Boston, 1992—2001; trustee Mass. Gen. Hosp., 1992—99, hon. trustee, 1999—2002; trustee Com. on Econ. Devel., 1995—; bd. dirs. Inacom, Inc., 1997—2003, Citizens Fin. Group, Inc., 1997—2000, Value Line, Inc., 1998—2000; bd. vis. Coll. Letters and Sci. U. Wis., 1999—2005; dean's adv. coun. Newcomb Coll., 1999—2006. Contbr. articles to profl. jours. and book chpts. Adv. bd. Nat. Coalition for Sci. and Tech., Washington, 1983—87; bd. govs. YMCA, Champaign, Ill., 1980—83. Named One of 100 Emerging Leaders, Am. Coun. Edn. and Change Mag., 1978, Outstanding Alumna, Class of 1957, Tulane U., 2007; recipient Centennial award, Newcomb Coll., 1986, Disting. Alumni award, U. Wis., 1997, Radcliffe medal, 1999. Fellow: AAAS (bd. dirs. 1984—88); mem.: Am. Coun. Edn. (commn. on women in higher edn. 1991—93, chair 1993), Inst. Medicine (coun. mem. 1986—89, com. on setting NIH priorities, com. on govt.-industry collaboration in biomed. edn. and rsch.), Assn. for Biomed. Rsch. (bd. dirs. 1983—86), Nat. Coun. Univ. Rsch. Adminstrs., Soc. Rsch. Adminstrs. (Disting. Contbn. to Rsch. Adminstrn. award 1984), Am. Chem. Soc. (bd. coun. com. on chemistry and pub. affairs 1978—80), Phi Kappa Phi, Phi Delta Kappa, Alpha Lambda Delta, Sigma Xi, Phi Beta Kappa. Home: 47 Keene Neck Rd Bremen ME 04551

WILSON, LIZABETH ANNE (BETSY), dean, library director; b. Waterloo, Iowa, May 21, 1954; d. Martin Lucien and Joanne Hausser Wilson; m. Dean August Pollack, Sept. 1, 1983. BA, Northwestern U., 1972—77; MLS, U. of Ill., 1977—78. Asst. architecture and art libr. U. Ill., 1979—80, asst. undergrad. libr., 1980—86, asst. dir. librs. undergrad. and instrnl. svcs., 1986—92; assoc. dir. librs. for rsch. and instrnl. svcs. U. Wash., Seattle, 1992—2000, dean U. librs., 2001—. Chair of bd. of trustees OCLC, Inc., Dublin, 2003—; exec. dir. Leopoldo Cicognara Program+, Urbana-Champaign, Ill., 1987—2004; co-founder UWired collaboration at the University of Washington. Author (co-author): (journal article) The Bottom Line; contbr. chapters to books, articles. Recipient Margaret E. Monroe Libr. Adult Services award, RUSA/Am. Libr. Assn., 1995, Miriam Dudley Instrn. Libr. award, Assn. of Coll. and Rsch. Libraries, 1995, EDUCAUSE Award for Systemic Progress in Tchg. and Learning, EDUCAUSE, 2000. Mem.: Greater Western Libr. Alliance (pres. 2004), Digital Libr. Fedn. (mem. exec. com. 2004—), OCLC Membs. Coun. (pres. 1999—2000), Assn. Rsch. Librs. (bd. dirs. 2003—), Instrn. Sect. of ACRL (chair 1990—91), Assn. Coll. and Rsch. Librs. (pres. 2000—01, Excellence in Academic Libr. award 2004, Academic/Rsch. Libr. of Yr. 2007). Office: Dean of Libraries University Washington Box 352900 Seattle WA 98195-2900 Office Phone: 206-543-1763. Office Fax: 206-685-8727. Business E-Mail: betsyw@u.washington.edu. *

WILSON, LLOYD LEE, registrar, educator; b. Elkton, Md., Sept. 14, 1947; s. Clifton Laws and Betty Raye (Bare) W.; m. Susan Sieg Wilson, 1992; children: Asa, Ryan, Morgan, Daniel. BS in Mgmt., MIT, 1969, MS in Mgmt., 1977. Bus. mgr. med. clinics Mass. Gen. Hosp., Boston, 1970-73; ptnr. Willow Co., mgmt. cons., Cambridge, Mass., 1974-77; dir. community relations Wilson Neuropsychiat. Hosp., Charlottesville, Va., 1977-78; exec. dir. Jefferson Area United Transp. Inc., Charlottesville, Va., 1978-80, Va. Mountain Housing Inc., Blacksburg, 1980-82; gen. sec. Friends Gen. Conf. Religious Soc. Friends, Phila., 1982-85; dir. rsch. and devel. Va. Mountain Housing, Inc., Christiansburg, 1985-88, dir. multifamily housing, 1989-91, regional dir., 1991-92; pres. Friendly Mgmt. Svcs. Corp., Norfolk, Va., 1992-95, Not-for-Profit Mgmt., Inc., Norfolk, Va., 1995—2004; registrar Chowan U., Murfreesboro, NC, 2002—, asst. prof. religion, 2006—. Dir. instnl. rsch. Chowan Coll., Murfreesboro, N.C., 2000—; Asst. prof. of acctg., 2001—; pres., dir. Va. Housing Coalition, Inc., 1981-82; treas., bd. dirs., Cedar Grove Consulting, LLC, 2004—, Fiddle Hill Farm, Inc., Barboursville, Va., 1982-89; bd. mgrs. Bible Assn. Friends in Am., Phila., 1983-85; mem. com. rec. ministers Balt. Yearly Meeting Friends, Sandy Spring, Md., 1984-86; asst. sec.-treas. Friends Meeting House Fund, Inc., Phila., 1984-85; asst. presiding clk. Comm. Commn. of Friends United Meeting, Richmond, Ind., 1987-88; recorded min. of gospel, Soc. of Friends, 1989— (presiding clk. Va. Beach monthly meeting 1990-92); dir. coordinating cabinet Va. Coun. Chs., 1988; presiding clk. N.C. Yearly Meeting of Friends, 1991-92. Author: Essays on the Quaker Vision of Gospel Order, 1993, Wrestling with one Faith Tradition, 2005; contbr. articles to profl. jours. Treas., bd. dirs. Norfolk (Va.) Quaker House, Inc., 1995-2000; bd. dirs. New Dominion Housing, Inc., Norfolk, 1992-94; vice chmn. Montgomery County Cmty. Svc. Commn., Christianburg, Va., 1980-82; mem. ednl. coun. MIT, 19777-89; bd. dirs. Am. Friends Svc. Com., Inc., Phila., 1980-83; bd. dirs. Interfaith Housing Corp. Cambridge, Inc., 1975-77, treas., 1976-77, also numerous others. Home: PO Box 647 Woodland NC 27897-0647 Office Phone: 252-398-6246. Business E-Mail: llwilson@alum.mit.edu.

WILSON, LOIS FAIR, school system administrator, educator; b. Redlands, Calif., Mar. 17, 1924; d. James Albert and Emma (Lederer) Fair; m. Herbert Blair Wilson (dec. Nov. 1989). BA, U. Redlands, 1945; MEd, U. So. Calif., LA, 1954; EdD, U. Ariz., 1972. Elem. tchr. Long Beach (Calif.) City Schs., San Bernardino County, 1945-51; curriculum cons. Office of San Bernardino (Calif.) County Schs., 1951-61; asst. prof., coord. elem. edn. U. Redlands, Calif., 1961-64, supr. student tchrs. Calif., 1985—; program asst. to coord. for kindergartens Tucson Unified Sch. Dist., 1965-72, curriculum coord. to elem. prin., 1965—83; supr. student tchrs. Calif. State U., San Bernardino, 1985-88; travel escort Hillsen's Tours and Travels, Redlands, 1984-92, Laura's Travel Svc., Redlands, 1992—95; escort San Diego Opera Summer Music Festival, 1993, 94. Tchr. hard of hearing and deaf program fostering learning Easter Seal Pre-Sch., Tucson, 1964—65; summer faculty World Campus Afloat, Chapman Coll., 1974—75, No. Ariz. U., 1978, 80; mem. steering com. Ariz. Young Readers' Conf., U. Ariz., 1975—84; mem. kindergarten curriculum guide com. State of Ariz.; tchr. Summer Demonstration Sch., 1954—56, Stanford U., 1956—58, team staff curriculum workshop, 1959; mem. 1st Ariz. State Kindergarten Curriculum Guide Com.; cons. in field. Contbr. articles to profl. jours. Mem. pre-sch. com. Tucson, 1967-68; bd. dirs. Town and Gown U. Redlands, 1985-92, pres., 1991-92, membership, sec., historian, reunion com., 1984—, class rep.1984—, chair San Bernardino County Agrl. Stabilization and Conservation Svc. Com., 1986-1990; mem. Assocs. of the Redlands Bowl, Assistance League of Redlands, 1988—, heritage aux. 4th grade program, 3d grade drug awareness program, Kimberly Jrs. Reunion Com., 1991; bd. dirs. Redlands Hist. Mus., 2d v.p, 1999—; vol. trainer Head Start. Recipient Cert. of Appreciation Dept. Edn. State of Ariz., 1984, Disting. Svc. award 1993, Hon. Centennial Yr. award 2007. Mem.: ASCD, PEO (chpt. II treas. 1994—95), AAUW (pres. Calif. So. sect. and Ariz. 1960, pres. Ariz. chpt. 1980), Calif. Ret. Tchrs. Assn. (v.p. Redlands-Yucaipa divsn. 1990—92), Ret. Edn. Mgrs. of Calif. (region 12), Calif. Women for Agr., Redlands Art Assn. (endowment com.), U. Redlands Ret. Faculty Assn., Redlands Hist. Glass Mus., Redlands Symphony Assn. and Guild (bd. dirs., 2d v.p. 1988—90, 2003—05, chmn. youth music com. 1988—91, adv. com. 1994—99), Inland Orange Conservancy, Redlands Conservancy, Friends A.K. Smiley Libr., Lincoln Shrine Assn., Redlands Sister City Assn., Redlands Area Hist. Soc., Kimberly-Shirk Assn., Prospect Pk. Assn., Pace Setters (chmn. com. 1992—, scholarship for student in tchr. edn. named in her honor), April Morning Club (membership com. 1988—89, publicity 1989—90, yearbook 1991—92, pres. 1994—95), Redlands Contemporary Club, Alpha Delta Kappa Fidelis Iota (sec. 2001—04, publicity chair, historian 2001—04). Republican. Presbyterian. Avocations: travel, reading, classical music, writing, theater. Home: 1131 Kimberly Pl Redlands CA 92373-6786

WILSON, LOIS M., minister; b. Winnipeg, Man., Can., Apr. 8, 1927; d. Edwin Gardiner Dunn and Ada Minnie (Davis) Freeman; m. Roy F. Wilson, June 9, 1950; children: Ruth, Jean, Neil, Bruce BA, United Coll., Winnipeg, 1947, BDiv, 1969; Diploma in TV prodn., Ryerson Tech. Inst., 1974; DDiv (hon.), Victoria U., Toronto, 1978, United Theol. Coll., Montreal, 1978, Wycliff Coll., 1983, Queens U., Kingston, 1984, U. Winnipeg, 1986, Mt. Allison U., 1988; LLD (hon.), Trent U., Peterborough, 1984, Dalhousie U., 1989, Ripon Coll., Wis., 1992, U. Toronto, 2005, U. Manitoba, 2006; DCL, Acadia U., 1984; DHuml (hon.), Mt. St. Vincent, Halifax, 1984. Ordained to ministry United Church of Can., 1965. Minister, Thunder Bay, 1965-69, Hamilton, 1969-78, Kingston, 1978-80; moderator United Church of Can., Kingston, 1980-82, McGeachy sr. scholar, 1989-91; pres. Can. Council of Chs., Toronto, Ont., 1976-79; co-dir. Ecumenical Forum Can., Toronto, Ont., 1983-89; pres. World Council of Chs., Geneva, 1983-91; chancellor Lakehead U., Thurder Bay, Ont., 1990-2000; chmn. contemporary theology Lafayette-Orinda (Calif.) Presbyn. Ch., 1995; ind. senator Senate of Can., 1998—2002; apptd. ecumenist in residence Toronto Sch. Theology, 2006—. Mem. adv. coun. internt. devel. studies U. Toronto, 1987-93, Fair Oto Can., Across Boundries Multifaith Inst., Mining Watch Can.; spokesperson Project Ploughshares, 1st and 2d UN Conf. on Disarmament, N.Y.C., 1978-82; officer Human Rights Commn., Ont., 1973; mem. bd. regents Victoria U., 1990—; chief Can. Fact finding Mission to Sri Lanka, 1992; team mem. Ctrl. Am. Monitoring Group to El Salvador and Guatemala, 1993; spl. envoy of Can. to The Sudan, 1999-02; lectr. in field. Author: Like a Mighty River, 1980, Turning the World Upside Down, 1989, Miriam, Mary and Me, 1992, Telling Her Story, 1992, Stories Seldom Told, 1997, Nuclear Waste, 2000; mem. adv. bd.: Can. Woman Studies Jour., York U., 1993—2004; contbr. articles to profl. publs.; author: Transforming the Faith of Our Fathers. Apptd. Can. Senator, 1998; pres. Social Planning Coun., Thunder Bay, 1967—68, Can. Com. for Scientists and Scholars, Toronto, 1982; mem. Refugee Status Adv. Com., 1985—89; chmn. Urban Rural Mission, Can., 1990—96; mem. environ. assessment panel Can. Nuclear Fuel Waste Mgmt. and Disposal Concept, 1989—96; bd. dirs. Elizabeth Fry Soc., Hamilton, 1976—79, Amnesty Internat., 1978—90, Can. Inst. for Internat. Peace and Security, 1984—88, Energy Probe, 1981—86, Internat. Ctr. Human Rights and Dem. Devel., 1997—98, Can. Univ. Svc. Overseas, 1983—85; trustee Nelson Mandela Fund, 1990—92. Decorated Order of Can., Order of Ont., Companion of Order of Can.; sr. fellow Massey Coll. U. Toronto, 2005—; recipient Queens Jubilee medal, Commemorative medal for 125th Anniversary of Confederation of Can., 1992, World Federalist Peace award, 1985, Pearson Peace medal UN Assn. of Can., 1985; named hon. pres. Student Christian Movement of Can., Toronto, 1976. Mem. DPR Korea Assoc., Canada (chmn. 2002-), Women, Peace and Security (co-chair 2001-), CAW (pub. rev. bd. 1986—), Can. Assn. Adult Edn. (bd. dirs. 1986-90), Friends Can. Broadcasting (bd. dirs. 1986-94, v.p.), Civil Liberties Assn. (v.p. 1986—), UNIFEM (nat. v.p. 1993-95, mem. CCIC team to monitor El Salvador election 1994), World Federalists (pres. Can. chpt. 1996-2000, v.p. World Federalist Movement intern, 1998-, acting pres., 2004-), Parliament of World's Religions (del. 1993), Christian-Jewish Dialogue Jerusalem (keynote speaker 1994). Mem. United Ch. Of Can. E-mail: royandlois.wilson@sympatico.ca.

WILSON, LUKE, actor; b. Dallas, Sept. 21, 1971; Actor: (films) Bottle Rocket, 1996, Telling Lies in America, 1997, Best Men, 1997, Scream 2, 1997, Bongwater, 1998, Dog Park, 1998, Home Fries, 1998, Rushmore, 1998, Kill the Man, 1999, Blue Streak, 1999, My Dog Skip, 2000, Committed, 2000, Preston Tylk, 2000, Charlie's Angels, 2000, Legally Blonde, 2001, Soul Survivors, 2001, The Royal Tenenbaums, 2001, The Third Wheel, 2002, Masked & Anonymous, 2003, Old School, 2003, Alex and Emma, 2003, Legally Blonde 2: Red, White & Blonde, 2003, Charlie's Angels: Full Throttle, 2003, Around the World in 80 Days, 2004, Anchorman: The Legend of Ron Burgundy, 2004, Mini's First Time, 2006, Hoot, 2006, My Super Ex-Girlfriend, 2006, Idiocracy, 2006, You Kill Me, 2007, Blades of Glory, 2007, Vacancy, 2007; (TV series) The X Files, 1993, That '70s Show, 1998; actor, dir.: (films) The Family Stone, 2005; The Wendell Baker Story, 2005. Office: c/o Creative Artists Agy 9830 Wilshire Blvd Beverly Hills CA 90212 *

WILSON, LYNTON RONALD, retired telecommunications industry executive; b. Port Colborne, Ont., Can., Apr. 3, 1940; s. Ronald Alfred and Blanche Evelyn (Matthews) W.; m. Brenda Jean (Black), Dec. 23, 1968; children: Edward Ronald, Margot Jean, Jennifer Lyn. BA, McMaster U., 1962, LLD, 1995; MA, Cornell U., 1967; D (hon.), U. Montreal, 1995; D in Civil Law, Bishop's U., Lennoxville, Que., Can., 1997; LLD, U. Cape Breton, 1998, Mount Allison U., 2000, Brock U., 2003. Dep. minister Ministry Industry and Tourism, Ont., Canada, 1978-81; pres., CEO Redpath Industries, Ltd., Toronto, Canada, 1981-88; mng. dir. N.Am. Tate and Lyle, PLC, 1986-89; chmn. bd. Redpath Industries, Ltd., Toronto, Canada, 1988-89; vice chmn. Bank of N.S., Toronto, Canada, 1989-90; pres., COO BCE, Inc., Montreal, Canada, 1990-92, pres., CEO, 1992-93, chmn., pres., CEO, 1993-96, chmn., CEO, 1996-98, chmn. bd. dir., 1998-2000. Chmn. bd. dir. CAE, Inc.; chmn. emeritus Nortel Networks Corp.; chmn. Daimler Chrysler Can. Adv. Coun.; mem. supervisory bd. Daimler Chrysler AG; chmn. bd. dirs. Allergen NCE; mem. Prime Minister's adv. com. on public svc. Founding co-chmn. HISTORICA Found., Canada. Decorated officer Order of Can. Mem. The Mount Royal Club of Montreal, York Club, Toronto Golf Club, Rideau Club, Mount Bruno Country Club. Home: 2038 Lakeshore Rd E L6J 1M3 Oakville ON Canada Office: 483 Bay Ste 7th Fl N Tower M5G 2C9 Toronto ON Canada Office Phone: 416-364-4612.

WILSON, M. ROY, academic administrator, medical educator; b. Yokohama, Japan, Nov. 28, 1953; BS, Allegheny Coll., 1976; MD, Harvard Med. Sch., 1980; MS in Epidemiology, UCLA, 1990. Diplomate Nat. Bd. Medicine, Am. Bd. Ophthalmology. Intern Harlem Hosp. Ctr., NYC, 1980-81; resident in ophthalmology Mass. Eye & Ear Infirmary/Harvard Med. Sch., Boston, 1981-84, glaucoma, 1984-85; clin. fellow in ophthalmology Harvard Med. Sch., 1980-85, clin. asst. ophthalmology, 1985-86; clin. instr. dept. surgery, Divsn. Ophthalmology Howard U. Sch. Medicine, Washington, 1985-86; asst. prof. ophthalmology UCLA, 1986-91; asst. prof., chief Divsn. Ophthalmology Charles R. Drew U. of Medicine and Sci., LA, 1986-90, assoc. prof., chief Divsn. Ophthalmology, 1991-94, acad. dean, 1993-95, dean, 1995-98, prof., 1994-98, UCLA, 1994-98; dean sch. medicine Creihton U., Omaha, 1998—, interim v.p., 1999-2000, vice pres. health scis., 2001—; pres. Tex. Tech. U. Health Sci. Ctr., Lubbock, 2003—06; chancellor U. Colo at Denver Health Scis. Ctr., 2006—. Asst. in ophthalmology Mass. Eye and Ear Infirmary, 1985-86; cons. ophthalmologist, Victoria Hosp., Castries, St. Lucia, 1985-86; hosp. appointment, UCLA; chief physician Martin Luther King, Jr. Hosp., L.A., 1986—; project dir. Internat. Eye Found., Ministry of Health, 1985-86; biology lab instr., Allegheny coll., 1975; instr. in biochemistry Harvard U. Summer Sch., 1977-78; instr. Harvard Med. Sch., 1980-85, others; cons. and presenter in field; participant coms. in field. Mem. AMA, APHA, Assn. Rsch. in Vision and Ophthalmology, Chandler-Grant Glaucoma Soc., Nat. Med. Assn., Am. Acad. Ophthalmology, Inst. Medicine (elected 2003), Soc. Eye Surgeons Internat. Eye Found., Mass. Eye and Ear Infirmary Alumni Assn., So. Calif. Glaucoma Soc., West Coast Glaucoma Study Club, Assn. Univ. Profs. in Ophthalmology, L.A. Eye Soc., Calif. Med. Assn., Am. Glaucoma Soc., Soc. Epidemiol. Rsch. Office: U Colo at Denver Health Scis Ctr 35 SYS Boulder CO 80309-0035 *

WILSON, MAGGIE ISABELLE LOVELL, secondary school educator; b. Branchville, Ala., Jan. 26; d. Winston Porter and Ruth Kate (Buckner) Lovell. AB, Samford U., Birmingham, Ala., 1971; MA, EdS, U. Ala., 1978; MFA, Loyola U., 1979; PhD, Sussex U., Eng., 1981. Cert. elem./secondary tchr. Tchr. English Birmingham Pub. Schs., 1972-92; tchr. English secondary edn. Terrell County Schs., Dawson, Ga., 1992-93. Author, illustrator: Carousel of Creative Communication, 1976, Leeds, Her Story, 1979; author: Creative Expressions, 1980, Into Our Third Century, 1984, From Brush Arbor Days to the Twentieth Century, 1992. Historian Leeds (Ala.) First United Meth. Ch., 1990-99; docent Birmingham Mus. Art, 1970-80; pres. Sylacauga dist. United Meth. Women, 1981-84. Recipient numerous awards Ala. Watercolor Soc., Birmingham, 1970—, Pres. award Kappa Pi, Samford U., Birmingham, 1971, Art of Distinction Salon Des Nations, Paris, 1984. Mem. AAUW, Internat. Biog. Assn., Ala. Coun. Tchrs. English (bd. mem. 1976—), Leeds Art Coun., Leeds Hist. Soc., Birmingham Art Assn., Internat. Soc. Artists, Leeds Bus. and Profl. Women (pres. 1971-76, 86, 88—, Woman of Yr. 1996-97), Leeds United Meth. Women (pres. 1972-76, 84—, pres. Sylacauga dist. 1981-84), La. Watercolor Soc. (awards 1986-99), So. Watercolor Soc., Kappa Delta Epsilon, Phi Gamma Mu. Home: 1110 Montevallo Rd SW Leeds AL 35094-1926

WILSON, MALCOLM CAMPBELL, investment trust management executive; b. Phila., Dec. 9, 1942; s. James Murray and Janet (Haines) Wilson; m. Barbara Ann Bahmermann, June 10, 1989; children from previous marriage: Jennifer Marie, David Campbell, Andrew Russel. BS in Bus. Adminstrn., Drexel U., 1966, MBA in Fin., 1968. Chartered fin. analyst. Rsch. analyst Provident Nat. Bank, Phila., 1971—77, co-mgr. rsch. dept., 1977—78, dir. equity rsch., 1978—84, dir. econ. and investment rsch., 1984—88, chief investment officer PNC Fin. div., 1986—88, sr. v.p., mgr. personal svcs. group, 1989—92; exec. v.p., mgr. investment mgmt. and trust Phila. market PNC Bank, N.A., 1993—95; sr. v.p., mgr. Personal Svcs. Group, Mercantile-Safe Deposit and Trust Co., Balt., 1996—98, exec. v.p., mgr. investment mgmt. and trust, 1998—2003; mng. dir., ptnr. Davidson Capital Mgmt., Devon, Pa., 2003—. With USN, 1968—71. Fellow: Fin. Analysts Fedn.; mem.: N.Y. Soc. Security Analysts, Mayflower Soc., Pa. Soc. SAR. Republican. Episcopalian. Avocations: hunting, fishing, golf. Home: 103 Cawley Ct Chester Springs PA 19425 Office: Davidson Capital Mgmt 20 N Waterloo Rd Devon PA 19333 Office Phone: 610-254-2045. Business E-Mail: swilson@davidsoncapmgt.com.

WILSON, MARC FRASER, art museum director; b. Akron, Ohio, Sept. 12, 1941; s. Fraser Eugene and Pauline Christine (Hoff) W.; m. Elizabeth Marie Fulder, Aug. 2, 1975. BA, Yale U., 1963, MA, 1967. Departmental asst. Cleve. Mus. Art, 1964; translator, project cons. Nat. Palace Mus., Taipei, Taiwan, 1968-71; assoc. curator of Chinese art Nelson Gallery-Atkins Mus., Kansas City, Mo., 1971-73, curator of Oriental art, 1973—, interim dir., 1982; curator Oriental art Nelson-Atkins Mus. Art, Kansas City, 1982-99, dir., CEO, 1999—. Mem., rapporteur Indo-US Subcom. on Edn. and Culture, Washington, 1976-79; mem. adv. com. Asia Soc. Galleries, N.Y.C., 1984—, China Inst. in Am., 1985—. Mem. adv. com. Muni-Art Commn. on Urban Sculpture, Kansas City, 1984-87; com. mem.

Kansas City-Xi'an, China, Sister City program, 1986—; mem. humanities coun. Johnson County Cmty. Coll., 1976-79; commr. Japan-U.S. Friendship Commn., Washington, 1986-88; panelist Japan-U.S. Cultural and Edn. Cooperation, Washington, 1986-88; mem. mayor's task force on race relations, 1996—; mem. indemnity adv. panel, 1995—; v.p. Brush Creek Ptnrs. 1995—. Recipient The William Yates Medallion Civic Svc. award William Jewell Coll., 1995, Disting. Svc. award Baker U., 1997. Mem. Assn. Art Mus. Dirs. (treas., trustee 1988-90, chmn. works of art com. 1986-90), Mo. China Coun., Fed. Coun. Arts and Humanities (chmn. arts and artifacts indemnity adv. panel 1986-89, 1995-98). Office: Nelson-Atkins Mus Art 4525 Oak St Kansas City MO 64111-1818 E-mail: mwilson@nelson-atkins.org.

WILSON, MARGARET BUSH, lawyer; b. St. Louis, Jan. 30, 1919; married; 1 child, Robert Edmund. BA cum laude, Talladega Coll., 1940; LL.B., Lincoln U., 1943. Ptnr. Wilson & Wilson, St. Louis, 1947-65; now with firm Wilson & Assocs. Asst. dir. St. Louis Lawyers for Housing, 1969-72; asst. atty. gen. Mo., 1961-62; atty. Rural Electrification Adminstrn., Dept. Agr., St. Louis, 1943-45; instr. civil procedure St. Louis U. Sch. Law, 1971; chmn. St. Louis Land Reutilization Authority, 1975-76; mem. Mo. Coun. Criminal Justice, 1972—; chmn. Intergroup Corp., 1985-87; bd. dirs. Mut. of N.Y. Mem. gen. adv. com. ACDA, 1978-81; trustee emeritus Washington U., St. Louis; chmn. bd. trustees Talladega Coll., Ala., 1988-92; nat. bd. dirs. ARC, 1975-81, United Way, 1978-84, Police Found., 1976-93; treas. NAACP Nat. Housing Corp., 1971-84, chmn. nat. bd., 1975-84; dep. dir./acting dir. St. Louis Model City Agy., 1968-69; adminstr. Mo. Commn. Svc. and Continuing Edn., 1967-68. Recipient Bishop's award Episcopal Diocese Mo., 1962; Juliette Derricotte fellow, 1939-40, Disting. Lawyer award Bar Assn. Metro St. Louis, 1997; Margaret Bush Wilson Endowed Professorship in Arts and Scis. established at Washington U., St. Louis, 2004. Mem. ABA (chmn. youth edn. for citizenship 1991-94, chmn. Nat. Law Day 1998-2000), Nat. Bar Assn., Mo. Bar Assn., Mound City Bar Assn., St. Louis Bar Assn., Alpha Kappa Alpha. Office: Wilson & Assocs 4054 Lindell Blvd Saint Louis MO 63108-3202 Home Phone: 314-531-9276; Office Phone: 314-534-4400. Office Fax: 314-534-4403.

WILSON, MARGARET MARY GEORGIANA, geriatrician, researcher, physician; d. Victoria Arit and Andrew Iyere Wilson. MBBS, U. Ibadan, Nigeria, 1977, MB, 1983. Diplomate Am. Bd. of Internal Medicine, 2000. Sr. registrar U. of Ibadan, Oyo, Nigeria, 1988—90; dir. clin. svcs. St. Louis U., 2004—; clin. rsch. fellow Hammersmith Hosp., London, 1990—91, St. Louis U., 1994—97; assoc. prof. St Louis U., 2000—; med. dir. Tower Village NH, 2000—, Integrated Health Svcs., Big Bend Woods, Mo., 2003—04, Nat. Healthcare, Town and Country, Mo., 2004—. Mem. Nat. Coun. Nutrition, 2001—; mem. editl. bd. Jour. Gerontology: Med. Scis., St. Louis, 2000—; guest editor Clinics in Geriatric Medicine, Phila. Mem. MCC, St Louis, Mo., 2002—04. Recipient Chevening Medicine award, Brit. Fgn. and Commonwealth Office, 1990, Vincent Uzodike; Internal Medicine, Nat. Postgraduate Coll. of Physicians, Nigeria, 1991, Sunderland DGH Excellence in Clin. Presentation, Sunderland DGH, Eng., 1993, Sir William Osler Tchg. award, St. Louis U., 2003, Kathy Humphrey award, 2004; fellow, Nat. Nigerian Med. Postgrad. Coll. Fellow: Nat. Postgrad. Coll. Physicians Nigeria, Acad. Minority Physicians (assoc.); mem.: Royal Coll. Physicians U.K., Am. Geriatric Soc., Brit. Coun. Study Fellows, Am. Med. Dirs. Assn. Christianity. Achievements include development of Geriatric Appetite Evaluation Instrument. Avocation: non-fiction works. Office: Geriatric Div St Louis U 1402 S Grand Blvd Rm M238 Saint Louis MO 63104 Home Phone: 314-918-1622; Office Phone: 314-977-8462, 618-798-3477. Personal E-mail: mmgwilsonmd@yahoo.com. Business E-Mail: wilsonmg@slu.edu.

WILSON, MARGARET SCARBROUGH, retail executive; b. Aug. 7, 1930; Student, Smith Coll., 1948-50; BA, U. Tex., 1952. Mem. staff Bayway Refinery Exxon Corp., NJ, 1960-61; mem. staff psychiat. ward VA Hosp., Houston, 1962; from mem. staff to chmn. Scarbroughs, Austin, Tex., 1952—74, chmn. bd., CEO, 1974—. Mem., bd. dirs. audit and contbns. coms. R.J. Reynolds Industries, 1978-85; hon. bd. dirs. Internat. Longevity Ctr., N.Y.C.; bd. dirs. Scarbrough Devel. Corp., Nat. Retail Fedn., 1991-2002, Am. Productivity & Quality Ctr., 1991-2002; chmn. San Antonio br. Fed. Res. Bank Dallas, 1975-76; trustee Nat. Policy Assn., 1997-98; pres., treas. Scarbrough Ventures LLC, 2001-, MSW-NSG Mgmt. LLC, 2000-, MSW-NSG Enterprises Ltd., 2000-, MSW-NSG Real Estate Ventures Ltd., 2001-. Trustee Com. Econ. Devel., 1973—, Cooper Inst. for Aerobics Rsch., Dallas, 1980-93, St. Stephen's Sch., Austin, 1979-83; mem. Nat. Com. U.S.-China Rels., 1976—, dir. 1980-94; mem. U.S. Coun. Internat. Bus., 1977—, mem. exec. com., 1978—, trustee, 1978—; bd. vistors Babcock Grad. Sch. Mgmt.-Wake Forest U., Winston-Salem, N.C., 1983-86; mem. bus. adv. coun. S.W. Tex. State U., 1983-86; mem. deptl. vis. com. dept. home econs. U. Tex.-Austin, 1983-84, pres.'s assocs., 1992—; mem. univ. coun. Rockefeller U., N.Y.C., 1982-86; mem. chancellor's coun. U. Tex. Sys., 1994—; mem. Tex. Rsch. League, 1977—, dir. audit com. 1986—, Friends of L.B.J. Libr., 1980—; assoc. mem. George Bush Presdl. Libr., 1995—; bd. dirs. World Bus. Coun., 1980-89; mem. adv. coun. Coll. Bus. Adminstrn., U. Tex.-Austin, 1964-68, Dean's Assocs. Coll. Fine Arts, 1985-87, Friends of Free Enterprise com. Coll. Engring., 1985-87; mem. India-U.S. Bus. Coun., 1976-82, dir., 1978-82; mem. Pres.'s Commn. on Pers. Interchange, 1972-73, UN Day Com., 1971-74; mem. Mayor's Bus. Roundtable, Austin, 1985-87; mem. Houston Com. Fgn. Rels., 1994—, Dallas Com. Fgn. Rels., 1997—, SRI Internat. Assocs. Program, 1998-99; mem. Conf. Bd. Mem. Alliance Francaise, Asia Soc. (adv. bd. Houston chpt., 1991-94, mem. N.Y. chpt.), Houston World Affairs Coun., Austin World Affairs Coun., English Speaking Union, Tex. Assn. Taxpayers, Retail Industry Trade Action Coalition (trustee 1984), Nat. Planning Assn. (trustee 1985-97), Am. Enterprise Inst. Am. Mgmt. Assn. (dir. 1969-72), Internat. C. of C., British Am. Bus. Inc., U.S. C. of C. (bd. dirs. 1980-82), Tex. Asian C. of C. (mem. adv. coun. 1997—), Tex. State Soc. Wash., World Econ. Devel. Congress (mem. adv. bd. 1993), Internat. Indsl. Conf. (mem. adv. coun. 1996-97), Coun. Fgn. Rels., World Econ. Forum, Bus. Coun. Internat. Understanding, Ctr. Strategic and Internat. Studies (Washington Round Table 1998—), Am. Enterprise Inst., Pacific Coun. on Internat. Policy, World Pres.'s Orgn. (internat. chpt., met. chpt., Dallas chpt., Houston chpt., Cen. Tex. chpt.), Pres.'s Cir. Nat. Acad. Scis., Inst. of Medicine and Inst. Engrs., Houston Forum, Brookings Instn., Bretton Woods Com., Brit.-N.A. Com., Tarry House, The University Club N.Y., Met. Club (Washington), Headliners Club, Tex. Breakfast Club of Washington, Kappa Kappa Gamma, numerous other local and nat. orgns. Office: 517 W 39th St Austin TX 78751-4904 E-mail: Margaret.Wilson@Scarbroughs.com.

WILSON, MARGARET SULLIVAN, retired executive dean, consultant; b. Norwich, Conn., Mar. 21, 1924; d. John Joseph and Margaret Ellen (Connelly) Sullivan; BS, Eastern Conn. State U., 1944; MA, U. Conn., 1949; m. William Robert Wilson, July 20, 1950 (dec.); children: Margaret Ellen, William Robert. Reading cons. Greenwich (Conn.) Pub. Schs., 1948-50; asst. prof. early childhood, chmn. dept. early childhood Eastern Conn. State U., Willimantic, 1967-77, exec. asst. to pres., 1977-78, v.p. adminstrv. affairs, 1978-80, exec. dean, 1980-89, emeritus dean, 1989—; commr. Nat. Commn. Prevention Infant Mortality, 1986-93, chair Norwich Econ. Devel. Commn., 1988-91, Southeastern Connecticut regional Planning Comm., 1999-2001(mem. 1993—); dir. Rose City Community Land Trust Housing, Com. on City Plan, 1992—; del. White House Conf. on Children, 1970, 80, White House Conf. on Travel and Tourism, 1995; corporator Chelsea Groton Savs. Bank, Norwich, Conn. Mem. Conn. Mental Health Bd., 1979-83; mem. adv. bd. Norwich Hosp.; chmn. rev. com. Conn. Health Coordinating Council; mem. Eastern Regional Mental Health Bd., 1976-83, chmn., 1979-81; mem. Norwich Bd. Edn., 1954-69, 80-83, adv. coun. head start and day care programs, 1986-91; mem. Conn. Dem. Cen. Com., 1966-82, Dem. Town Com., 1964-82, 86-90; chmn. Blue Ribbon Commn. To Establish Goals for U. Conn. Health Ctr., 1975-76; sr. warden Ch. of Resurrection, Norwich., 1988-91, Dio Com on Ministry Higher Edn. Named Citizen of Yr., C. of C., 1970; recipient Disting. Alumni award Eastern Conn. State U., 1972, Mental Health Bell award Conn. Mental Health Assn., 1972, Valiant Women award Council Ch. Women, 1976, Woman of Yr. award Bus. and Profl. Women, 1978, Jefferson award Inst. Pub. Service, 1982, pres. Norwich Mus. Trust, Inc., 1992—; mem., vice chair Southeastern Conn. Regional Planning Commn., 1993—; dir. Family Svc. Southeastern Conn., 1995—, Southeastern Conn. Enterprise Region, Norwich Comm. and Tech. Learning Ctr.; past-pres. Eastern Conn. Cmty. Found.; del. White House Conf. on Aging, 1995. Mem. Norwich Area C. of C. (dir. 1979-81), Greater Willimantic C. of C. (edn. com. 1980-88), United Ch. Women Conn. (bd. dirs.). Democrat. Office: 83 Windham St Willimantic CT 06226-2211 Home: 5 Mills Ln Collinsville CT 06022

WILSON, MARIE C., foundation administrator; b. Ga. 5 children. D in Cmty. Svc. (hon.), Drake U. Dir. women's programs Drake U.; mem. DesMoines City Coun.; pres. Ms. Found. for Women, NYC, 1984—. Co-creator Take Our Daus. To Work Day, 1993—; U.S. govt. del. UN Fourth World Conf. on Women, Beijing, 1995; co-founder, pres. The White House Project, 1998—. Co-author: Mother Daughter Revolution, 1993; author: Closing the Leadership Gap: Why Women Can and Must Help Run the World, 2004. Recipient Robert W. Scrivner award for creative grantmaking, Leadership for Equity and Diversity award, Women & Philanthropy. Office: Ms Found for Women 120 Wall St 33rd Fl New York NY 10005

WILSON, MARK, corporate financial executive; BS in Agrl. Econs.; MBA in Fin. and Acctg., Cornell U. V.p. Thomas Learning MacAndrews & Forbes; CFO Towers Perrin, Stamford, Conn., 2001—. Office: Towers Perrin 1 Stanford Plz Stamford CT 06901

WILSON, MARK LOWELL, philosopher, educator; Student, Reed Coll., 1965—67; BA, Univ. Wash., 1969; PhD, Harvard Univ., 1976. Asst. prof. Univ. Calif., San Diego, 1976—82, assoc. prof., 1982—84, Univ. Ill., Chgo., 1984—91; prof. Ohio State Univ., 1991—98, Univ. Pitts., 1998—. Fellow: Am. Acad. Arts & Scis. Office: Dept Philosophy Univ Pitts 1001 Cathedral of Learning Pittsburgh PA 15260 Office Phone: 412-624-5787. Business E-Mail: mlwilson@pitt.edu. *

WILSON, MARTHA C., physician; b. June 4, 1957; MD, U. Louisville, Ky., 1986. Cert. in facial surgery, opthalmology. Residency, 1990—91; fellowship; pvt. practice San Antonio, 1991—. Office: Eyelid Inst 14615 San Pedro Ave Ste 120 San Antonio TX 78232-4364

WILSON, MARTIN D., pharmaceutical executive; Pres., COO D & K Healthcare Resources, Inc., St. Louis.

WILSON, MARY ALICE, musician, educator; b. Nov. 2, 1939; MusB, Northwestern U., Evanston, Ill., 1961. Orch. band dir., pvt. tchr. Luth. Schs., Deerfield Pub. Schs., 1961-64; pvt. tchr. violin and piano Cleve., 1964-77; dir. Suzuki Program, violin tchr. W.Va. U., 1977—, chmn. music divsn., 2005; founder, leader Seneca String Quartet, Morgantown, W.Va., 1986—. Accompanist. Ch. vol. tchg. and music, Cleve., Chgo., Morgantown, 1960—. Recipient Outstanding Tchr. award, W.Va. U. Music Dept., 2005. Mem.: Am. String Tchrs. Assn. (co-developer, chmn. 5th yr. state solo competition, state sect. 2003—05), W.Va. Music Tchrs. Assn. (dist. chmn. of strings 1977—, state officer pub. 1989—, State Outstanding Tchr. Yr. 1996), Music Tchrs. Nat. Assn. (state office of composition contest 1989—). Home: 237 Poplar Dr Morgantown WV 26505-2519 Personal E-mail: bigmacwil@hotmail.com. Business E-Mail: cbwilson@mail.wvu.edu.

WILSON, MARY ELIZABETH, epidemiologist, physician, educator; b. Indpls., Nov. 19, 1942; d. Ralph Richard and Catheryn Rebecca (Kurtz) Lausch; m. Harvey Vernon Fineberg, May 16, 1975. AB, Ind. U., 1963; MD, U. Wis., 1971. Diplomate Am. Bd. Internal Medicine, Am. Bd. Infectious Diseases. Tchr. of French and English Marquette Sch., Madison, Wis., 1963-66; intern in medicine Beth Israel Hosp., Boston, 1971-72, resident in medicine, 1972-73, fellow in infectious diseases, 1973-75; physician Albert Schweitzer Hosp., Deschapelles, Haiti, 1974-75, Harvard Health Svcs., Cambridge, Mass., 1974-75; asst. physician Cambridge Hosp., 1975-78; hosp. epidemiologist Mt. Auburn Hosp., Cambridge, 1975-79, chief of infectious diseases, 1978—2002, dir. Travel Resource Ctr., 1996—2002, mem. consulting staff, 2003—05. Mem. adv. com. immunization practices CDC, Atlanta, 1988—92; mem. acad. adv. com. Nat. Inst. Pub. Health, Mexico, 1989—91; cons. Ford Found., 1988; site dir. GeoSentinel Network, 1999—2002, spl. cons., 2002—; instr. medicine Harvard Med. Sch., Boston, 1975—93, asst. clin. prof., 1994—99, assoc. prof. medicine, 1999—2004, assoc. clin. prof., 2004—; assoc. Ctr. Health and Global Environment, 1996—2000; asst. prof. depts. epidemiology and population and internat. health Harvard Sch. Pub. Health, 1994—99, assoc. prof. population and internat. health, 1999—; lectr. Sultan Qaboos U., Oman, 1991; chair Woods Hole Workshop, Emerging Infectious Diseases, 1993. Author: A World Guide to Infections: Diseases, Distribution, Diagnosis, 1991; editor (with Richard Levins and Andrew Spielman): Disease in Evolution: Global Changes and Emergence of Infectious Diseases, 1994; mem. editl. bd. Current Issues Pub. Health, 1999—2003, Emerging Infectious Diseases, Global Change and Human Health, 1999—2003; sect. editor travel medicine and tropical diseases: Infectious Diseases Clin. Practices; mem. editl. bd. Infectious Diseases Clin. Practices, 2006—; assoc. editor: Jour. Watch Infectious Diseases, 1997—; mem. editl. adv. bd. Clin. Infectious Diseases, 1999—2004, spl. sect. editor Emerging Infections, Clinical Infectious Diseases, 2006—. Mem. Cambridge Task Force AIDS, 1987—90; bd. dirs. Horizon Comm., West Cornwall, Conn., 1990—97; mem. Nat. Commn. on Indsl. Farm Animal Prodn., 2006—; bd. mem. FXB USA, 2007—. Recipient Lewis E. and Edith Phillips award, U. Wis. Med. Sch., 1969, Cora M. and Edward Van Liere award, 1971, Mosby Scholarship Book award, 1971, Leo Blacklow Tchg. award, 1999; fellow, Ctr. Advanced Study Behavioral Scis., Stanford, Calif., 2002; scholar-in-residence, Bellagio (Italy) Study Ctr., Rockefeller Found., 1996. Fellow: ACP, Royal Soc. Tropical Medicine and Hygiene, Infectious Diseases Soc. Am.; mem.: Am. Soc. Tropical Medicine Hygiene (councilor 2006—), Soc. for Epidemiol. Rsch., Internat. Union Against Tuberculosis and Lung Disease, Soc. for Vector Ecology, Wilderness Med. Soc., Internat. Soc. Travel Medicine, Peabody Soc., Mass. Infectious Diseases Soc., N.Y. Acad. Scis., Am. Soc. Microbiology, Aesculapian Club, Alpha Omega Alpha, Phi Sigma Iota, Sigma Sigma. Avocations: flute, hiking, reading, travel. Business E-Mail: mary_wilson@harvard.edu.

WILSON, MELVIN EDMOND, retired civil engineer; b. Bremerton, Wash., Aug. 3, 1935; s. Edmond Curt and Madeline Rose (Deal) W.; m. Deanna May Stevens, Nov. 22, 1957 (div. Mar. 1971); children: Kathleen, Debra Frank Baldwin. BSCE, U. Wash., 1957, MSCE, 1958. Registered profl. engr., Wash. Asst. civil engr. City of Seattle, 1958-60, assoc. civil engr., 1960-64, sr. civil engr., 1964-66, supervising civil engr., 1966-75, sr. civil engr., 1975-77, mgr. X, 1977-88; owner Wilson Cons. Svcs., Seattle, 1988-89; transp. sys. dir. City of Renton, Wash., 1989-96, ret., 1996. Owner Mel Wilson Photographer, Seattle, 1975-84. Contbr. reports to profl. jours. Rep. Renton transp. work group King County (Wash.) Growth Mgmt. Policy Com.; rep. Renton tech. adv. com. South County Area Transp. Bd., King County, 1992-96, developer svc. policy (adopted by Puget Sound Govtl. Conf.) to encourage travel by transit. successfuly led effort to make Renton first suburban city to receive direct transit svc. under Met. King County Plan, 1994; vol. personal trainer, 1988—; vol. trainer for medical patients, 1988—. Mem. ASCE, Am. Pub. Works Assn., Inst. Transp. Engrs., Tau Beta Pi, Sigma Xi. Avocations: physical fitness, art, psychology.

WILSON, MICHAEL E., lawyer; b. Rantoul, Ill., Oct. 28, 1951; BA cum laude, Washington U., 1973, JD, 1977. Bar: Mo. 1977. Principal Greensfelder, Hemker & Gale, P.C., St. Louis. Instr. legal writing Washington U. Sch. Law, 1979-82; mem. nat. panel constrn. industry arbitrators and co-chmn. St. Louis Constrn. Adv. Com., 1987-97. Mem. ABA, The Mo. Bar (contbr. jour.), Bar Assn. Metro. St. Louis (contbr. jour.), Order Coif. Office: Greensfelder Hemker & Gale PC 2000 Equitable Bldg 10 S Broadway Saint Louis MO 63102-1712

WILSON, MICHAEL HOLCOMBE, ambassador, investment banker, former Canadian government official; b. Toronto, Ont., Can., Nov. 4, 1937; s. Harry Holcombe and Constance L. (Davies) Wilson; m. Margaret Catherine Smellie, Oct. 17, 1964; children: Cameron (dec.), Geoffrey, Lara. Student, Upper Can. Coll.; B in Comm., U. Toronto, 1959. With Harris & Partners Ltd., Toronto, 1961-63, 65-73, v.p., 1972; exec. v.p. following merger with Dominion Securities Ltd., 1973-79; mem. Can. Ho. Commons, Ottawa, 1979-93; min. of state for internat. trade Govt. Can., Ottawa, 1979-80, min. of fin., 1984-91, min. of industry, sci. & tech., min. internat. trade, 1991-93; bus. adv. Michael Wilson Internat., Toronto, 1993—2000; vice chmn. RBC Dominion Securities Inc., 1995-2000; chmn. UBS Global Asset Mgmt. Co. (formerly Brinson Can. Co.), Canada, 2000—04, UBS Can., 2004—06; Can. amb. to US Washington, 2006—. Mem. bd. Ctr. Addiction and Mental Health Found., 2000; chmn. Mental Health Implementation Task Force; bd. mem. Cmty. Found. for Greater Toronto; bd. dirs. BP PLC, Manulife Fin.; chmn. Neuroscience Can. Partnership, Can. Coun. Pub.-Pvt. Partnerships, Can. Coalition for Good Governance; chancellor Trinity Coll. Mem. Toronto Club, Toronto Golf, Badminton and Racquet Club, Osler Bluff Ski Club, Mad River Golf Club, Kappa Alpha. Progressive Conservative. Anglican. Office: Embassy of Canada 501 Pennsylvania Ave NW Washington DC 20001

WILSON, MICHAEL MOUREAU, lawyer, physician; b. Cheverly, Md., Dec. 30, 1952; s. Kenneth Moureau and Helen (Rice) Smith. BS, MIT, 1974; JD, Georgetown U., 1977, MD, 1986. Bar: D.C. 1977, N.Y. 1980, U.S. Dist. Ct. D.C. 1980, U.S. Dist. Ct. Md. 1992, U.S. Ct. Appeals (D.C. cir.) 1980, U.S. Supreme Ct. 1981. Law clk. Hon. John B. Hannum U.S. Dist. Ct., Phila., 1977—78; assoc. Cravath Swaine & Moore, NYC, 1978—79; asst. to gen. counsel NSF, Washington, 1979—82; resident in psychiatry St. Elizabeth Hosp., 1986—89; pvt. practice med. malpractice litigation, 1989—. Notes editor Am. Criminal Law Rev., 1976-77. Mem. ABA, Assn. Trial Lawyers Am., D.C. Trial Lawyers Assn., Phi Beta Kappa. Office: 1120 19th St NW Ste LL-11 Washington DC 20036 Office Phone: 202-223-4488. E-mail: wilson@wilsonlaw.com.

WILSON, MICHELLE See WILSON, L.

WILSON, MIKE, journalist; Police bur. corr. New York Times. Office: The New York Times Police Bur One Police Plz Rm 202C New York NY 10038 Office Phone: 212-349-0193. Office Fax: 212-556-1337. Business E-Mail: wilsonm@nytimes.com.

WILSON, MIRIAM GEISENDORFER, retired physician, educator; b. Yakima, Wash., Dec. 3, 1922; d. Emil and Frances Geisendorfer; m. Howard G. Wilson, June 21, 1947; children— Claire, Paula, Geoffrey, Nicola, Marla. BS, U. Wash., Seattle, 1944, MS, 1945; MD, U. Calif., San Francisco, 1950. Mem. faculty U. So. Calif. Sch. Medicine, LA, 1965—, prof. pediatrics, 1969—2004, emeritus prof. pediatrics, 2004—. Office: U So Calif Med Ctr 1129 N State St Rm 1g24 Los Angeles CA 90033-1044

WILSON, MIRIAM JANET WILLIAMS, publishing executive; b. London, Ont., Can., July 13, 1939; d. Ralph George and Lillian Conn Williams; m. Carson Winnette, Nov. 20, 1960 (div. 1971); children: Barrie Carson Winnette, Rebecca Lynn Winnette; m. Charles Lindsay Wilson, Dec. 14, 1973; 1 child, Charles William Wilson; stepchildren: Kenneth M., Carol Ann, Catherine S., Nancy L., Patrick L. Diploma in nursing, Glendale (Calif.) Sanitarium & Hosp., 1960. RN, Calif., Va., Ohio, Md., W.Va. Head nurse emergency and med. fls. Glendale Sanitarium and Hosp., 1960-65; psychometrist Harding Hosp., Worthington, Ohio, 1969-73; biofeedback specialist in assn. Dr. Randolph P. Johnston, Winchester, Va., 1980-84; dir. Stress Ctr. for Children and Adults, Shepherdstown, W.Va., 1985-87; pres. Rocky River Pubs. LLC, Shepherdstown, 1987—. Lectr. ednl., profl. and civic groups, 1984—. Author: Help For Children, 7 edits., 1987-2004, Stress Stoppers, 2 edits., 1987-89; contbr. articles to profl. publs. Mem. NAFE, Internat. Platform Assn., Am. Booksellers Assn., N.Y. Acad. Scis., Sherpherdstown Women's Club. Avocations: gardening, music, reading. Office: Rocky River Pubs LLC PO Box 1679 Shepherdstown WV 25443-1679 Office Phone: 304-876-1868. E-mail: rockyriverpublishers@citlink.net.

WILSON, MORGAN, chef; Grad., Calif. Culinary Acad., San Francisco; attended, Le Cordon Bleu, Paris. Asst. pastry chef Essex Supper Club; pastry chef EOS Restaurant and Wine Bar, San Francisco, One Market, San Francisco, Cannelle, Brazil, Payard Patisserie and Bistro, Brazil, Supra, Brazil, Aubergine, Newport Beach, Calif.; pastry instr. Calif. Sch. Culinary Arts; exec. pastry chef Bijoux, Dallas. Named one of Dallas' Rising Stars, StarChefs.com, 2007. Office: Bijoux 5450 W Lovers Dallas TX 75209 Office Phone: 214-350-6100. *

WILSON, MYRON ROBERT, JR., retired psychiatrist; b. Helena, Mont., Sept. 21, 1932; s. Myron Robert, Sr. and Constance Ernestine (Bultman) Wilson. *Member of Sons of the American Revolution. Direct descendant of William Wilson, who emigrated to New York from England in 1740. Third generation Montanan, whose family owned and operated hardware jobbing and retail operation in Helena from 1866-1966. Maternal grandfather, D.G.F. Bultman, emigrated from Germany to Sumter, South Carolina in 1890, where he owned and operated dry goods and grocery stores, cotton farms. Sister, Josephine Wilson Boyington married World War II marine flying ace, "Pappy" Boyington.* BA, Stanford U., 1954, MD, 1957. Diplomate Am. Bd. Psychiatry and Neurology. Dir. adolescent psychiatry Mayo Clinic, Rochester, Minn., 1965—71; pres., psychiatrist in chief Wilson Ctr., Faribault, Minn., 1971—86, chmn., 1986—90; ret., 1990. Assoc. clin. prof. UCLA, 1985—99. *Among the first American psychiatrists to limit practice to the new sub-specialty of adolescent psychiatry; developed and directed the adolescent psychiatry program at the Mayo Clinic, including an 18 bed in-patient unit for the long term treatment of (mostly psychotic) adolescents from 1965-71. Acquired the St. James School campus in Faribault, MN where he established the C.B. Wilson Center for adolescents in 1971, as the first facility of its kind in the country. It combined a national referral hospital for teens whose prior treatments had been unsuccessful with an accredited private secondary school for patients and a two- year, master's degree training institute for adolescent psychotherapists.* Contbr. articles to profl. jours. Chmn., CEO C. B. Wilson Found., LA, 1972—2006; bd. dirs. Pasadena (Calif.) Symphony Orch. Assn., 1987; vestryman, treas. St. Thomas' Parish, LA, 1993—96. Lt. comdr. USN, 1958—60. Fellow, Mayo Grad. Sch. Medicine, Rochester, 1960—65. Fellow: Internat. Soc. Adolescent Psychiatry (founder, treas. 1985—88, sec. 1985—88, treas.

1988—92), Am. Soc. Adolescent Psychiatry, Am. Psychiat. Assn.; mem.: Order St. John of Jerusalem, Sigma Xi (Mayo Found. chpt.). Episcopalian. Home Phone: 760-325-4956. Personal E-mail: mrobertwilson@aol.com.

WILSON, NANCY, singer; d. Olden and Lillian (Ryan) W.; m. Kenneth C. Dennis (div. 1969); 1 child, Kenneth C.; m. Wiley Burton, 1974; children: Samantha, Sheryl. Began career as singer with local groups, then joined Rusty Bryant band, 1956; toured Midwest and Can., 1956—58; ind. singer, 1959—; rec. artist Capitol Records, EMI Records, Japan, Nippon Columbia, Japan, Interface, Japan, Columbia Records, USA, Epic/Sony Japan. Singer: I'll Be a Song, How Glad I Am, 1964 (Grammy award for Best R&B Recording, 1965), Keep You Satisfied, 1985 Forbidden Lover, 1987, Nancy Now!, 1989, Lady With A Song, 1990, With My Lover Beside Me, 1991, Love, Nancy, 1994, If I Had My Way, 1997, A Nancy Wilson Christmas, 2001, R.S.V.P., 2004 (Grammy award for Best Jazz Vocal Album, 2005), Turned to Blue, 2006 (Grammy award for Best Jazz Vocal Album, 2007); hostess (TV series) Nancy Wilson Show, Sta. KNBC, LA, 1974-75, Red Hot & Cool (syndicated), 1990—; actor: (films) The Big Score, 1983, The Meteor Man, 1993. Recipient Grammy award for Best R&B Recording, 1965, Grammy award for Best Jazz Vocal Album, 2005, 2007, Best Female Vocalist award Playboy and Down Beat Jazz Polls, Image award NAACP, 1986, award Nat. Med. Assn., Equitable (17th Black Achievement) award, Urban Network Lifetime Achievement award, 1990, Whitney Young awd., Los Angeles Urban League, Essence awd., Essence Magazine, 1992, Jazz Masters award, NEA, 2004; Star on Hollywood Walk of Fame, 1990; inducted into Big Band & Jazz Hall of Fame, 1999. Office: c/o John Levy Enterprises Inc 1828 Coolidge Ave Altadena CA 91001 *

WILSON, NORMAN GLENN, church administrator, writer; b. Rensselaer, NY, Nov. 3, 1936; s. Lawrence Wilbur and Wilhelmena Augusta (Knapp) W.; m. Nancy Ann Deyo, Nov. 17, 1956; children: Beth, Lawrence, Jonathan. BRE in Religious Edn., United Wesleyan Coll., 1958, DD (hon.), 1986; MA in Biblical Studies, Winona Lake Sch. Theology, 1968. Pastor The Wesleyan Ch., 1958-76, Gloversville, NY, 1963-66, North Lakeport, Mich., 1966-70, Owosso, Mich., 1970-76, dir. comm. Indpls., 1992—. Program prodr., speaker The Wesleyan Hour, Indpls., 1975—; mem. gen. adminstrn. coun. The Wesleyan Ch., Indpls., 1992—; disting. lectr. Staley Found., 1986. Author: How to Have a Happy Home, 1976, Christianity in Shoe Leather, 1978, The Constitution of the Kingdom, 1989, People Just Like Us, 1994, Follow the Leader, A Daily Spiritual Journey, 1996; editor, contbr.: Journey Into Holiness, 2000; The Call to Contentment, 2002; editor The Wesleyan Advocate, 1992-2004, Wesleyan Life, 2004-. Mem. Nat. Religious Broadcasters (bd. dirs. 1984-2005, Merit award 1984). Mem. Wesleyan Ch. Avocations: painting, antique cars. Home: 304 Scarborough Way Noblesville IN 46060-3881 Business E-Mail: wilsonn@wesleyan.org.

WILSON, OWEN, actor; b. Dallas, Nov. 18, 1968; s. Robert and Laura Wilson. BA in English, U. Tex., Austin, 1991. Actor: (TV films) Heat Vision and Jack, 1999; (TV series) King of the Hill, 1997; assoc. prodr. (films) As Good as It Gets, 1997, The Royal Tenenbaums, 2001; writer, actor: films Bottle Rocket, 1996; prodr., actor (films) You, Me and Dupree, 2006; actor: (films) The Cable Guy, 1996, Anaconda, 1997, Armageddon, 1998, Permanent Midnight, 1998; exec. prodr., actor: (films) Rushmore, 1998, The Minus Man, 1999, Breakfast of Champions, 1999, The Haunting, 1999, Shanghai Noon, 2000, Meet the Parents, 2000, Zoolander, 2001, Behind Enemy Lines, 2001, I Spy, 2002, Shanghai Knights, 2003, The Big Bounce, 2004, Starsky & Hutch, 2004, The Life Aquatic with Steve Zissou, 2004, Meet the Fockers, 2004, The Wendell Baker Story, 2005, Wedding Crashers, 2005, (voice) Cars, 2006. Recipient Favorite On-Screen Match-Up (with Vince Vaughn), People's Choice Award, 2006, Best On-Screen Team (with Vince Vaughn), MTV Movie awards, 2006. Office: United Talent Agy 9560 Wilshire Blvd Ste 500 Beverly Hills CA 90212

WILSON, OWEN MEREDITH, JR., lawyer, mediator, arbitrator; b. Oakland, Calif., Dec. 22, 1939; s. O. Meredith and Marian Wilson; m. Sandra A. Wilson (div.); children: Ann, Melissa, Jennifer; m. Teddi Anne Wilson; children: Amanda, Lisa. Student, U. Utah, 1957-59; AB, Harvard U., 1961; LLB, U. Minn., 1965. Bar: Oreg. 1965, Wash. 1985. Ptnr. Lane Powell PC, Portland, Oreg., 1969—2005; prin. Wilson Dispute Resolution, Portland, 2005—. Mem. mediation panel U.S. Dist. Ct., 1986—. Mem. bd. visitors Law Sch. U. Minn., 1990-96. Mem. ABA, Oreg. State Bar Assn., Multnomah Bar Assn. Office: 1211 SW 5th Ave Ste 2950 Portland OR 97204-3158 Home Phone: 503-292-6981; Office Phone: 503-972-5090. Business E-Mail: met@wilsonadr.com.

WILSON, PATRICIA POTTER, library and information science educator; b. Jennings, La., May 3, 1946; d. Ralph Harold and Wilda Ruth (Smith) Potter; m. Wendell Merlin Wilson, Aug. 24, 1968. BS, La. State U., 1967; MS, U. Houston-Clear Lake, 1979; EdD, U. Houston, 1985. Cert. tchr., learning resources specialist (libr.), Tex. Tchr. England AFB Elem. Sch., La., 1967-68, Edward White Elem. Sch./Clear Creek Ind. Schs., Seabrook, Tex., 1972-77; libr. C.D. Landolt Elem. Sch., Friendswood, Tex., 1979-81; instr./lectr. children's lit. U. Houston, 1983-86; with U. Houston/Clear Lake, 1984-87, asst. prof. libr. sci. and reading, 1988-94, assoc. prof. learning resources and reading edn., 1994—2001, assoc. prof. emerita, 2001—. Cons. Hermann Hosp., Baywood Hosp., 1986-87, Bedford Meadows Hosp., 1989-90, Wetcher Clinic, 1989; co-owner, v.p. Potter Farms, Inc., 1994—; Longhorn Devel. Bd., NASA & CCISD, 2005-; pres. cabinet U. Houston Ctrl., Clear Lake, U. Tex. Med. Br. Author: Happenings: Developing Successful Programs for School Libraries, 1987, The Professional Collection for Elementary Educators, 1996, Premiere Events: Library Programs That Inspire Elementary Patrons, 2001, Leadership for Today's School Library, 2001, Igniting the Spark: Library Programs that Inspire High School Patrons, 2001, Center Stage: Library Programs That Inspire Middle School Patrons, 2002; editor: A Review Sampler, 1985—86, 1989—90; contbg. editor: Tex. Libr. Jour., 1988—94; contbr. articles to profl. jours. Trustee Freeman Meml. Libr., Houston, 1982—87, v.p., 1985—86, pres., 1986—87; trustee Evelyn Meador Libr., 1993—94, adv. bd., 1994—; bd. dirs. Houston Symphony League-Bay Area, 1996—2005, chair ann. fund campaign, 2005; founder Friends of Neumann Libr., 1998—2001; chmn. hospitality com. Lunar Rendevous Festival, 1998—2001; gen. chmn. Lunar Rendezvous Festival, 2002, mem. adv. bd., 2002—; mem. Assistance League of the Bay Area, 1997—; vol. Houston: A Visit from St. Nicholas Com., 2004—, co-chmn. kick-off event, 2005; mem. adv. bd. Bay Area Soc. Prevention Cruelty Animals, 1994—98, Bay Area Turning Point, 1998—; bd. dirs. Sta. KUHT-TV, 1984—87, Friends of Neumann Libr., 1998—99, Bay Area Houston Ballet and Theatre, 2001—04, vice chair bd. dirs., 2003—04, chmn. kickoff event, 2003; dir. Learning Resources Book Rev. Ctr., 1989—90; bd. dirs. Armand Bayou Nature Ctr., Houston, 1989—94; mem. Bay Area Houston Econ. Partnership, 2002—, mem. banquet com., 2002—. Named Outstanding Vol. of Yr., Houston's Nat. Philanthropy Day, 1999; named one of 10 Men and Women of Heart, Bay Area Turning Point, 2001; recipient Rsch. award, Tex. State Reading Assn., 1993, Pres. award, Tex. Coun. Tchrs. English, Disting. Tchg. award, Enron Corp., 1996, Disting. Alumni award, U. Houston-Clear Lake, 1998, Disting. Alumna award, U. Houston, Coll. Edn., 2002, Disting. Alumni award, U. Houston Ctrl., 2005, Bravo award, Bay Area Houston Ballet & Theater, 2006; grantee, Tex. Libr. Assn., 1993. Mem. ALA, NASA, Clear Creek Ind. Sch. Dist. (Longhorn devel. bd. 2005—), Am. Assn. Sch. Librs., Internat. Reading Assn., Nat. Coun. Tchrs. English (Books for You rev. com. 1985-88, 97-98, Your Reading rev. com. 1993-96), Tex. Coun. Tchrs. English, Antarctican Soc., Bay Area Houston Econ. Partnership (banquet com. 2002-), Clear Lake Panhellenic Assn., Lakewood Yacht Club, Travelers' Century Club, Bay Oaks Country Club, Phi Kappa Phi (sec. 1997-98, pres. 1998-99).

WILSON, PAUL HOLLIDAY, JR., lawyer; b. Schenectady, NY, Sept. 4, 1942; s. Paul H. and Sarah Elizabeth (MacLean) W.; m. Elaine Hawley Griffin, May 30, 1964; children: Hollace, Paul, Kirsten, Katherine. AB, Brown U., 1964; LLB, MBA, Columbia U., 1967. Bar: N.Y. 1967, U.S. Dist. Ct. (so. dist.) 1968. Law clk. U.S. Dist. Ct. (so. dist.) N.Y., NYC, 1967-68; assoc. Debevoise & Plimpton LLP, NYC, 1968-75, ptnr., 1976—, fin. ptnr., 1980-88, 91-93, 2001—, dep. presiding ptnr., 1993-98. Vice-chmn., trustee St. Michael's Montessori Sch., N.Y.C., 1977-79, chmn. bd. trustees, 1979-81. Mem. ABA, Assn. Bar City N.Y. (mem. commn. on securities regulations 1985-88). Clubs: Vineyard Haven Yacht (Mass.) (vice-commodore 1985, commodore 1986-87). Avocations: sailing, reading, music. Office: Debevoise & Plimpton LLP 919 Third Ave 46th Fl New York NY 10022-6225 Home Phone: 212-534-8344; Office Phone: 212-909-6000. Business E-Mail: phwilson@debevoise.com.

WILSON, PAUL LOWELL, mortgage company executive, lawyer; b. May 12, 1951; s. James Joseph and Edna Vivian (Halterman) W.; children: Meredith Elaine, Taylor Halterman; m. Abigail Mayer. AB, W.Va. U., 1973; JD, Coll. of William of Mary, 1976. Bar: W.Va., 1976, U.S. Dist. Ct. (so. dist.) W.Va. 1976, U.S. Dist. Ct. (ea. dist.) Va. 1991. Assoc. Brown & Peyton, Charleston, W.Va., 1976-78; title atty. Lawyers Title Ins. Corp., Williamsburg, Va., 1978-80; assoc. S.J. Baker, Williamsburg, 1981-83; counsel edn. com. W.Va. Legislature, Charleston, 1977-78; gen. counsel A J & L Corp., Williamsburg, 1983-85, v.p., gen. counsel, 1985-91; prin. First Capital Comml. Funding, Inc., 1997—. Bd. dirs. 503 Cert. Devel. Co., Richmond, Sta. WHRO-TV. Mem. York County Sch. Bd., 1986-94, chmn., 1992-94; pres. Nat. Housing Corp., 1986-93, The Preservation Group, Inc., 1991-97. Mem. W.Va. State Bar, Sigma Phi Epsilon. Presbyterian. Office: 5200 Park Rd Ste 207 Charlotte NC 28209 Office Phone: 704-672-9139.

WILSON, PAUL W., economics professor; b. Memphis; BA, Rice U., Houston, 1980; AM, PhD, Brown U., Providence, 1985. Prof. U. Tex., Austin, 1990—2006, Clemson U., SC, 2006—. Office: Clemson U Dept Econs Clemson SC 29634 Office Phone: 864-656-2032. Office Fax: 864-656-4192. Business E-Mail: pww@clemson.edu.

WILSON, PEGGY MAYFIELD, retired chemist; d. Isaac Newton and Ella Lockwood Mayfield; m. Irving Ray Dunlap Jr. (dec.); m. William W. Wilson III, July 25, 1975 (dec.). BS in Chemistry, U. Tex., Austin, 1948, PhD in Chemistry, 1952. Spl. instr. U. Tex., Austin, 1952—53; from rsch. technologist to sr. rsch. technologist Mobil Rsch. Devel. Corp., Dallas, 1953—84, group mgr. dept. rsch., 1984—89; pres. Greater Duncanville Indsl. Corp., Tex., 1991—2000, Stone Gap Indsl. Corp., Duncanville, 1991—2000; ret., 2000. Regent East Tex. State U., Commerce, 1981—87. Founder, econ. devel. City of Cedar Hill, Tex., 1991—96; adv. bd. Cedar Valley C.C.; chmn. bd. dirs. Cedar Hill Econ. Devel. Corp., 1994—96; chmn. Cedar Hill Comprehensive Plan Bd., 1997—99; coun. mem. City of Cedar Hill, 1996—98; active State Rep. Exec. Com., Tex., 1971—80; bd. dirs., treas. Internat. Mus. Cultures. Named Outstanding Rep. Woman, Tex. Fedn. Rep. Women, 1973; recipient Jean Harris award, Rotary, 1998, Golden Cedar Lifetime award, Cedar Hill C. of C., 2001. Mem.: Am. Chem. Soc., Cedar Hill Assn. for Cultural Arts, Cedar Summit Book Club. Republican. Methodist. Achievements include patents in field. Avocation: gardening.

WILSON, PETER SCOTT, lawyer; b. Edinburgh, July 15, 1955; B in Commerce, McGill U., 1976; JD, Harvard U., 1979. Bar: N.Y. 1980. Assoc. Cravath Swaine and Moore LLP, NYC, 1979-87, ptnr., corp., 1987—. Mem. ABA, N.Y. State Bar Assn., Assn. Bar City of N.Y., Internat. Bar Assn. Democrat. Presbyterian. Office: Cravath Swaine & Moore LLP Worldwide Plaza 825 8th Ave New York NY 10019-7475 Office Phone: 212-474-1767. Office Fax: 212-474-3700. Business E-Mail: pwilson@cravath.com.

WILSON, PHIL (SAMUEL PHILIP WILSON), state official; b. 1967; m. Kristen Kincaid. BA in Polit. Sci. & History, Hardin-Simmons U., 1990; MBA in Adminstrn., So. Methodist U. Aide to Senator Phil Gramm US Senate; dir. comm. to R.R. commr. State of Tex., dir. comm. to Gov. Austin, 2002—03, dep. chief of staff to Gov., 2003—07, sec. state, 2007—. Recipient Outstanding Young Alumni award, Hardin-Simmons U., Tomorrow's Leaders Today award, George Skiles Anderson award as Outstanding Male Grad. Office: Office Sec State PO Box 12697 Austin TX 78711 *

WILSON, R. DALE, marketing educator; b. Ironton, Ohio, July 16, 1949; s. Robert J. and Treva L. (Shively) Wilson; m. Emily J. Ray, June 19, 1971; 1 child, Travis Ray. BBA cum laude, Ohio U., 1971; MBA, U. Toledo, 1972; PhD, U. Iowa, Iowa City, 1977. Asst. prof. mktg. Pa. State U., University Park, 1976-80; v.p., dir. mktg. scis. Batten, Barton, Durstine & Osborn, Inc., NYC, 1980-83; vis. prof. Cornell U., Ithaca, NY, 1983-84; assoc. prof. Mich. State U., East Lansing, 1984-87, prof., 1987—. Cons. in field. Contbr. articles to profl. jours. Youth baseball and basketball coach, East Lansing, 1989—98. Grantee, Pa. State U., Mich. State U., IBM Corp. Mem.: Am. Soc. Competitiveness, Inst. Ops. Rsch. and Mgmt. Scis. (assoc. editor interfaces, cert. recognition 1983), Am. Mktg. Assn., Am. Acad. Advt., Beta Gamma Sigma. Office: Mich State U Eli Broad Grad Sch Mgmt Dept Mktg N322 N Business Complex East Lansing MI 48824-1122 Office Phone: 517-432-6403. Business E-Mail: wilsonrr@msu.edu.

WILSON, RAINN D. (RAINN DIETRICH WILSON), actor; b. Seattle, Washington, Jan. 20, 1966; m. Holiday Reinhorn, 1995; 1 child, Walter Mckenzie. Attended, Tufts U., U. Washington; studied acting, NYU grad. acting program; MFA in Acting, NYU, Tisch Sch. Arts, 1989. Writer, dir. The New Bozena, 2005; actor: (films) Galaxy Quest, 1999, Almost Famous, 2000, America's Sweethearts, 2001, Wheelmen, 2002, Full Frontal, 2002, Self Storage, 2002, House of 1000 Corpses, 2003, The Life Coach, 2005, Sahara, 2005, Blue in Green, 2005, Dominion, 2006, My Super Ex-Girlfriend, 2006, The Last Mimzy, 2007; (TV films) The Expendables, 1999, Slice o' Life, 2003; (TV series) Six Feet Under, 2003—05, The Office, 2005—; performer: (Broadway plays) London Assurance, The Tempest, —, (off-broadway) The New Bonzena, Plunge, Venus, Titus Andronicus, Twelfth Night; guest appearances One Life to Live, 1997, When Billie Beat Bobby, 2001, Dark Angel, 2001, CSI: Crime Scene Investigation, 2001, Law & Order: Special Victims Unit, 2002, MDs, 2002, Monk, 2003, Numb3rs, 2005, Entourage, 2005. Avocations: tennis, chess, music.

WILSON, RALPH COOKERLY, JR., professional football team executive; b. Columbus, Ohio, Oct. 17, 1918; s. Ralph Cookerly and Edith (Cole) W.; children: Christy Cole, Linda Brown, Edith Denise. AB, U. Va., 1940; postgrad., U. Mich., 1940-41. Pres. Ralph C. Wilson Jr. Enterprises (privately owned family bus.); engaged in profl. football, roadbuilding Detroit, 1946—; pres., owner Buffalo Bills Profl. Football Club, 1959—. With USNR, 1941-46. Decorated Commendation medal. Mem. Ocean Club of Fla., Country Club of Detroit, Grosse Pointe (Mich.) Club, Buffalo Country Club, Shriners. Presbyterian.

WILSON, RALPH SLOAN, retinal surgeon; b. El Dorado, Ark., Nov. 12, 1937; s. George Evander and Lauree Eta (Doss) W.; AB, Davidson Coll., 1959; BS, U. Ark., 1963, MD (Research fellow), 1963; m. Sarah Mignon Ross, Dec. 27, 1958; m. Ann Jameson, 1987; children: Ralph Sloan, William Gregory, Steven Robert, John Matsek (stepson). Intern, U. Ark. Hosps., Little Rock, 1963-64; postgrad. ophthalmology Harvard Med. Sch., Boston, 1964-65; resident ophthalmology U. Ark. Hosps., 1965, U. Tex. Med. Br., Galveston, 1965-67; Heed fellow retinal pathology and surgery Mass. Eye and Ear Infirmary, Harvard Med. Sch., Boston, 1969: asst. prof. and dir. retina services dept. ophthalmology U. Ark. Med. Center, Little Rock, 1970-75, assoc. prof., 1975-81, prof., 1981—95, prof. emeritus, 1995-, acting chmn. ophthalmology dept., 1974-75; practice medicine specializing in retinal surgery Retinal Group, LTD., Little Rock, 1975-99; mem. Ark. State Bd. Dispensing Opticians; dir. Retina Service, US VA Hosp., Little Rock; chief staff, exec. com. Doctors Hosp.; dir. Ritchie Grocer Co., S.W. Trading Corp. Chmn. admissions com. U. Ark. Coll. Medicine; trustee Lyon Coll. (formerly Ark. Coll.), 1982-; pres., bd. dirs. Retinal Research Fund; bd. dirs. Ark. Eye & Kidney Bank, Ark. Soc. for Prevention of Blindness, 1971-73. Served to lt. comdr. USNR, 1967-69. Diplomate Am. Bd. Ophthalmology (examiner 1973-83); Hoffmann La Roche grantee, 1966-67; recipient AMA Physicians Recognition awards, 1969-99. Mem. Am. Acad. Ophthalmology (speakers bur., hon. award, sr. hon. award Pub. Info. Com.), Am. Acad. Retinal Surgeons (formerly Vitreous Soc., charter mem.), Assn. Rsch. and Vision in Ophthalmology, AMA, Ark., Pulaski County med. socs., Am., Ark. Assns. Ophthalmology, Am. Ophthal. Soc. (athletic chmn.), AAUP, Research to Prevent Blindness, So. Med. Assn., Pan Am. Soc. Ophthalmology, Société Française d'Ophthalmologie, Sociedad Boliviana de Oftalmologia, New Orleans Acad. Ophthalmology, Soc. Eye Surgeons, Internat. Eye Found., U. Tex. Med. Br. Ophthalmology Alumni Assn. (pres. 1970-72), Univ. Med. Group, Soc. Heed Fellows, Little Rock Acad. Surgery, Retina Soc., Ark. Acad. Ophthalmology (pres. 1975-76), Ark. Found. for Med. Care, Assn. VA Ophthalmologists, Ark. Ophthalmology sect. of Ark. Med. Soc. (pres. 1977-78), Assn. Mil. Surgeons, Alpha Omega Alpha, Alpha Tau Omega, Sigma Xi. Contbr. articles to profl. jours., Research in ocular melanomas, ocular fireworks injuries, mechanism of human accomodation and multiple ocular surgical techniques; holder patents in field. Home: 140 Washington Rd Rye NH 03870 E-mail: cottagers@aol.com.

WILSON, RHYS THADDEUS, lawyer; b. Albany, Ga., May 9, 1955; s. Joseph Farr Jr. and Betty Ann W.; m. Carolyn Reid Saffold, June 2, 1984. AB, Duke U., 1976; JD, U. Ga., 1979; LLM, Emory U., 1985. Bar: Ga. 1979. Pvt. practice law, Atlanta, 1979-89; sr. v.p., gen. counsel Monarch Capital Group, Inc., Atlanta, 1989-92, Jackson & Coker, Inc., Atlanta, 1992-93; pres. Jackson & Coker Locum Tenens, Inc., Atlanta, 1993-95; ptnr. Robins, Kaplan, Miller & Ciresi, Atlanta, 1995—2005, Nelson Mullins Riley & Scarborough LLP, 2006—. Spkr. CLE seminars. Contbr. articles to profl. jours. Bd. dirs. Atlanta Opera Co. Named Ga. Super Lawyer, Mergers & Acquisitions, 2004—. Mem. ABA, Ga. Bar Assn. (chmn. internat. law sect. 1987-88, exec. com. corp. and banking law sect. 1987-89, editl. bd. Ga. State Bar Jour. 1986-89), Atlanta Bar Assn. (editor newsletter 1984-86, Outstanding Svc. award 1986), Assn. for Corp. Growth, Atlanta Tech. Angels (bd. dirs.), Visage Internat., Capital City Club. Episcopalian. Office Phone: 404-817-6000.

WILSON, RICHARD A., oil and gas industry support services executive; b. 1938; BS in Petroleum Engring., U. Wyo. Pres. Energy Svc. Co. Inc., Dallas, 1988-89, sr. v.p.- ops., 1989—. Formerly with ESSO Exploration; past v.p. Global Marine Drilling Co.; various positions, then exec. v.p. Schlumberger Tech. Corp. Office: ENSCO 500 N Akard St Ste 4300 Dallas TX 75201-3331

WILSON, RICHARD CHRISTIAN, engineering firm executive; b. Bethlehem, Pa., July 17, 1921; s. Christian and Laura Barrows (Langham) W.; m. Jean M. Avis, July 16, 1949; children— Richard A., Christy. BS, Carnegie-Mellon U., 1943; MS, Lehigh U., 1947; PhD, U. Mich., 1961. Mfg. engr. Westinghouse Electric Corp., East Pittsburgh, 1943; instr. mech. engring. Carnegie-Mellon U., Pitts., 1943-44; vacuum test engr. Kellex Corp., NYC, 1944; area supr. Carbide & Carbon Chem. Co., Oak Ridge, 1945-46; apparatus engr. Westinghouse Electric Corp., Jackson, Mich., 1947-55; instr. indsl. and operation engring. U. Mich., 1955-61, asst. prof., 1961-63, assoc. prof., 1963-66, prof., 1966-85, chmn. dept., 1973-77, assoc. dean Coll. Engring., 1968-72; pres. Techware, Inc., 1985-86, ret., 1986. Dir. Cascade Data Corp., 1969-72 Contbr. articles to profl. jours. Bd. dirs. Ecumenical Assn. Internat. Understanding, 1970-87, pres., 1975-76, 86-87; dir. Washtenaw Trombones and Jazzbones, 1995—. Mem. IEEE, Inst. Mgmt. Sci., Am. Inst. Indsl. Engrs., Ops. Research Soc. Am., Sigma Xi, Beta Theta Pi, Phi Kappa Phi. Clubs: Rotary. Home: 805 Mount Pleasant Ave Ann Arbor MI 48103-4776 Office: U Mich Dept Indsl Engring Ann Arbor MI 48109

WILSON, RICHARD EDWARD, composer, music educator, pianist; b. Cleve., May 15, 1941; s. James F. and Edith Ann (Zingler) Wilson; m. Adene Stevenson Green, May 15, 1971; children: Katherine Blanca, James Graham. AB magna cum laude, Harvard U., 1963; MA, Rutgers U., 1966. Asst. prof. music Vassar Coll., Poughkeepsie, NY, 1966-70, assoc. prof. music, 1970-76, prof. music, 1976—, chmn. dept. music, 1979-82, 85-88, 95-98, Mary Conover Mellon Chair, 1988—. Composer-in-residence Am. Symphony Orch., 1992—. Composer: Music for Violin and Violoncello, 1969; composer: (four string quartets); composer: Eclogue for Piano Solo, 1974 (Burge prize, 1979), Figuration, 1980, Two Symphonies, 1984, 1987, Agitations, 1994, Pamietam, 1995, Five Love Songs, 1995, Transfigured Goat, 1996, A Child's London, 1997, Triple concerto for horn, bass clarinet, marimba and orch., 1998 (Koussevitzky commn.), Intimations for Piano and Orch., 2000, Revelry for Full Orchestra, 2002, Peregrinations for Viola and Orchestra, 2002, others; composer: (opera) Aethelred the Unready, 1994. Recipient Walter Hinrichsen award, Am. Acad. Inst. Arts and Letters, 1986, Cleve. Arts prize, 1988, Exec.'s award Dutchess County, 1989, Stoeger prize, Chamber Music Soc. Lincoln Ctr., 1994, Acad. award in music, Am. Acad. Arts and Letters, 2004;, Guggenheim fellow, 1992. Mem.: ASCAP, Am. Music Ctr., Century Assn., Harvard Club, Phi Beta Kappa. Home: 27 Vassar Lake Dr Poughkeepsie NY 12603-3120 Office: Vassar Coll Dept Music PO Box 18 Poughkeepsie NY 12604-0001

WILSON, RICHARD F., academic administrator; b. Point Pleasant, W.Va. m. Pat Wilson; children: Adam, Rachel. B in Math., Alderson-Broaddus Coll., 1968; MA in Higher Edn., U. Mich., 1970, PhD in Higher Edn., 1978. Math. tchr. Spencerville (Ohio) H.S., 1968—69; dir. admissions Alderson Broaddus Coll., Philippi, W.Va., 1970—74; project asst. to Dr. William Haberl, spl. asst. to the exec. officers U. Mich., Ann Arbor, 1974—75, grad. student rsch. asst. Office Acad. Planning and Analysis, 1975—76, rsch. assoc. Office Acad. Planning Analysis, 1976—78; asst. dir. Office Planning and Evaluation U. Ill., Urbana-Champaign, 1978—80, adj. asst. prof. higher edn., 1981—84, asst. vice chancellor for acad. affairs, 1981—86, assoc. chancellor, 1986—94, interim dir. corp. and found. rels., 1991, adj. prof. higher edn., 1994—2004, assoc. chancellor for devel., 1994—2004; dep. dir. U. Ill. Found., 1994—96, v.p., 1996—2004; pres. Ill. Wesleyan U., 2004—. Mem. Applie Higher Edn. Adv. Group, 1992—. Office: Ill Wesleyan Univ Pres Office Holmes Hall 204 PO Box 2900 Bloomington IL 61702

WILSON, RICHARD HARRY, JR., congressional chief of staff; b. Schnectady, NY, Aug. 19, 1957; s. Richard Harry and Phyllis JoAn Wilson; m. Leslie Jean Frazier, Dec. 5, 1987; children: Robert Dale Gordon, Stefanie Marie Gordon. BS summa cum laude, Martin U., Indpls., 2004; postgrad., Trinity Theol. Sem., Newburgh, Ind., 2007—. Dep. chief of staff Congressman Dan Burton, Indpls., 1993—. Mem. com. Dan Burton for Congress, 1992. Sgt. US Army, 1986—91. Named a Disting. Grad., Class of 1975, William Fremd HS, 2005; named Ky. Col., Gov. of Ky., 1995, Sagamore of the Wabash, Gov. of Ind., 2001; recipient Pres.'s award, Martin U., 2005. Mem.: VFW (life), DAV (life), Am. Polit. Sci. Assn., Acad. Polit. Sci., Am. Legion, Phi Kappa Tau. Republican. Lutheran. Office: Congressman Dan Burton 8900 Keystone Crossing Suite 1050

Indianapolis IN 46240 Home Phone: 317-514-1932; Office Phone: 317-848-0201. Office Fax: 317-846-7306. Personal E-mail: wilson_richard@comcast.net. Business E-Mail: rick.wilson@mail.house.gov.

WILSON, RICHARD LEE, political science professor; b. Worthington, Minn., Dec. 20, 1944; s. G. Roy and Dorothy Eileen (Johnson) W.; m. Carolyn Ann Dirks, Aug. 24, 1968 (div.); 1 child, Kevin Richard. BA, U. Chgo., 1966, postgrad., 1966-67; PhD, Johns Hopkins U., 1971; postgrad., Columbia U., 1988, Stanford U., 1992. Congl. aide 4th Congl. Dist. Md., 1971; asst. prof. polit. sci. U. Tenn., Chattanooga, 1971-76, assoc. prof., 1976-87, prof., 1988—. Registrar-at-large Hamilton County Election Commn., 1977-84; lectr. Robert A. Taft Inst. Govt., U. Tenn., Nashville, 1978, 79, 81; supr. state legis. and met. internship program U. Chattanooga, 1972-86; vis. prof. Govt. Fgn. Affairs Coll., Beijing, 1986-87; Fulbright prof. govt. Beijing U., 1988-89, Samford U., Birmingham, Ala., 1991-93. Author: Tennessee Politics, 1976, American Government, 1993, 2d edit., 1995, American Political Leaders, 2002 (Choice award 2003); editor: Encyclopedia of American Government, 2001; co-editor: Ready Reference: Censorship, 1997 (named Outstanding Ref. Source 1998 ALA), Encyclopedia of the Supreme Court, 2000 (named OUtstanding Ref. Scouce 2002 ALA); contbr. chpts. to books. Chmn. Hamilton County Health Planning Adv. Council, 1975-79; bd. dirs. Ga.-Tenn. Regional Health Commn., 1978-82; active Tenn. State Health Coordinating Council, 1977-81; exec. com. State Health Coordinating Council, 1979-81. Named Outstanding Educator of Yr., Signal Mountain (Tenn.) Jaycees, 1973, Outstanding Prof. of Yr., SGA, 1985-86, Oustanding Reference Source ALA, 2002; recipient Polit. Edn. award NAACP, 1980, Excellent Prof. award Fgn. Affairs Coll., Beijing, 1987, UTC Exceptional Merit award, 1990, 94; NEH grantee, 1988, 92. Mem. So. Polit. Sci. Assn., Midwest Polit. Sci. Assn., Am. Polit. Sci. Assn. (nat. rsch. grant 1995), Nat. Soc. Internships and Exptl. Edn., SAR, China People's Friendship Assn., Aircraft Owners and Pilots Assn. Methodist. Office: Univ of Tenn Dept Political Sci Fletcher Hall 414 Chattanooga TN 37403 Office Phone: 423-425-4226. Business E-Mail: richard-wilson@utc.edu.

WILSON, RICHARD RANDOLPH, lawyer; b. Pasadena, Calif., Apr. 14, 1950; s. Robert James and Phyllis Jean (Blackman) W.; m. Catherine Goodhugh Stevens, Oct. 11, 1980; children: Thomas Randolph, Charles Stevens. BA cum laude, Yale U., 1971; JD, U. Wash., 1976. Bar: Wash. 1976, U.S. Dist. Ct. (we. dist.) Wash. 1976, U.S. Ct. Appeals (9th cir.) 1977. Assoc. Hillis, Phillips, Cairncross, Clark & Martin, Seattle, 1976-81, ptnr., 1981-84, Hillis, Cairncross, Clark & Martin, Seattle, 1984-87, Hillis Clark Martin & Peterson, Seattle, 1987—, mem. mgmt. com., 1991—2007, chmn. land use group, 2007—. Pres. Plymouth Housing Group, Seattle, 1998—2000, trustee, 1994—2001, bd. dirs., 2001—, Quality Child Care Svcs., Inc., Seattle; lectr. various bar assns., 1980—. Contbr. articles to profl. jours. Chmn. class agts. Yale U. Alumni Fund, New Haven, 1985—87, class agt., 1971—2001, mem. class coun., 1991—96, mem. Western Wash. exec. com. Yale capital campaign, 1992—97, vice chmn. leadership gifts com. Yale 25th reunion, 1995—96, 30th reunion, 2000—01; mem., vice chmn. Medina (Wash.) Planning Commn., 1990—92; trustee, performer Gilbert & Sullivan Soc., 1984—91; chmn. capital campaign Plymouth Congl. Ch., 1995, moderator, pres. ch. coun. Seattle, 1998—2000, pres. ch. corp., 2004—05. Mem. ABA, Wash. State Bar Assn. (dir. environ. and land use law sect. 1985-88), Seattle-King County Bar Assn., Kingsley Trust Assn. (trustee 2003-06, pres. 1996-98), Yale Assn. We. Wash. Congregationalist. Avocations: acting, singing, rare book collecting. Home: 2305 86th Ave NE Bellevue WA 98004-2416 Office: Hillis Clark Martin & Peterson 1221 2nd Ave Ste 500 Seattle WA 98101-2925 Office Phone: 206-623-1745. Business E-Mail: rrw@hcmp.com. *Notable cases include: Barrie vs. Kitsap County, 1980; Sore vs. Snohomish County, 1983; Conv. Ctr. Coalition vs. City of Seattle, 1986, Orion Corp. vs. State, 1987, Cougar Mountain Assocs. vs. King County, 1988; King County vs. Central Puget Sound Growth Management Hearings Board, 1998, 1999; Quadrant Corp. v. Central Puget Sound Growth Mgt. Hearings Bd., 2005.*

WILSON, RITA, actress; b. LA, Oct. 26, 1958; m. Tom Hanks; 2 children. Actor: (films) The Day It Came to Earth, 1979, Cheech & Chong's Next Movie, 1980, Volunteers, 1985, The Bonfire of the Vanities, 1990, Sleepless in Seattle, 1993, Mixed Nuts, 1994, Now and Then, 1995, That Thing You Do!, 1996, Jingle All the Way, 1996, No Dogs Allowed, 1996, Psycho, 1998, Runaway Bride, 1999, The Story of Us, 1999, Perfume, 2001, Auto Focus, 2002; (TV films) Barbarians at the Gate, 1993, If These Walls Could Talk, 1996, From the Earth to the Moon, 1998, Invisible Child, 1999; (plays) Distracted, 2007; prodr.: (films) My Big Fat Greek Wedding, 2002, Connie and Carla, 2004; (TV series) My Big Fat Greek Life, 2003. *

WILSON, ROBERT ALLEN, religion educator; b. Geff, Ill., Oct. 7, 1936; s. Perry Arthur and Eva Mae (Dye) W.; m. Patsy Ann Jarrett, June 1, 1957; children: Elizabeth Ann, Angela Dawn, Christine Joy. AB, Lincoln Christian Coll., 1958, Hanover Coll., 1961; MRE, So. Bapt. Sem., 1965, EdD, 1972. Ordained to ministry Ch. of Christ, 1958. Min. Fowler Christian Ch., Ind., 1955—59, Zoah Christian Ch., Scottsburg, Ind., 1959—64; min. edn. and youth Shively Christian Ch., Louisville, 1964—69; prof. Christian edn. and family life Lincoln Christian Seminary, Ill., 1969—2004. Pres. Christian Marriage and Family Enrichment Services, Lincoln, 1980—. Contbr. articles to profl. jours. Mem. Nat. Assn. Profs. Christian Edn. (editor newsletter 1975-79, pres. 1979-80), Religious Edn. Assn., Rotary (bd. dirs. Lincoln chpt. 1988—, pres. 1993-94, asst. gov. dist. 6490 asst. gov. 2007—). Home: 330 Campus View Dr Lincoln IL 62656-2106 Office: Christian Marriage & Family Enrichment Svcs 330 Campus View Dr Lincoln IL 62656 Office Phone: 217-732-1629. Personal E-mail: wilsondrbob99@aol.com.

WILSON, ROBERT E., lawyer; b. Wichita Falls, Tex., Oct. 3, 1943; BBA, So. Meth. U., 1966, JD, 1969. Bar: Tex. 1969. Ptnr., Real Estate, Fin., Corp. Haynes and Boone LLP, Dallas, mng. ptnr. of firm, bd. dir. Contbr. articles to profl. jour.; editor-in-chief Law Jour., 1969. Named a Super Lawyer, D Magazine, Tex. Monthly. Mem.: The Real Estate Coun. (cmty. leadership com.), Am. Coll. Mortgage Attys., US-Japan Bus. Coun., Am. Coll. Real Estate Lawyers (bd. govs.), State Bar Tex. (real property, probate and trust law sect. 1984—), ABA (chmn. mortgages and other debt financing com., real property, probate and trust law sect.), Tex. Bar Assn., Dallas Bar Assn. (chmn. real property law sect. 1982). Office: Haynes & Boone LLP 901 Main St Ste 3100 Dallas TX 75202-3789 Office Phone: 214-651-5601. Office Fax: 214-200-0550. Business E-Mail: robert.wilson@haynesboone.com.

WILSON, ROBERT E., academic administrator; Attended, Culinary Inst. Am. Exec. chef Freedom Plaza, Union Hills Country Club, Club Corp. Am., Del. E. Webb Devel.; chef instr. Scottsdale Culinary Inst., Ariz., 1994—2001, dir. info. technologies Ariz., 1994—2001; pres., co-founder Ariz. Culinary Inst., Scottsdale, 2001—. Office: Arizona Culinary Institute 10585 N 114th St Ste 401 Scottsdale AZ 85259 Office Phone: 866-294-2433. *

WILSON, ROBERT FOSTER, lawyer; b. Windsor, Colo., Apr. 6, 1926; s. Foster W. and Anne Lucille (Svedman) W.; m. Mary Elizabeth Clark, Mar. 4, 1951 (div. Feb. 1972); children: Robert F., Katharine A.; m. Sally Anne Nemec, June 8, 1982. BA in Econs., U. Iowa, 1950, JD, 1951. Bar: Iowa 1951, U.S. Dist. Ct. (no. and so. dists.) Iowa 1956, U.S. Ct. Appeals (8th cir.) 1967. Atty. FTC, Chgo., 1951-55; pvt. practice, Cedar Rapids, Iowa, 1955—. Pres. Lawyer Forms, Inc.; dir. Lawyers Forms, Inc.; mem. Iowa Reapportionment Com., 1968; del. to U.S. and Japan Bilateral Session on Legal and Econ. Rels. Conf., Tokyo, 1988, Moscow Conf. on Law and Bilateral Rels., Moscow, 1990; U.S. del. to Moscow Conf. on Legal and Econ. Rels., 1990. Mem. Iowa Ho. of Reps., 1959-60; pres. Linn County Day Care, Cedar Rapids, 1968-70. Sgt. U.S. Army, 1944-46. Mem. ATLA, Am. Arbitration Assn. (panel arbitrators), Iowa Bar Assn., Iowa Trial Lawyers Assn., Linn County Bar Assn., Am. Legion (judge adv. 1970-75, 87-93), Cedar View Country Club, Elks, Eagles, Delta Theta Phi. Democrat. Home: 2179 Blake Blvd SE Cedar Rapids IA 52403-1128 Office: 810 Dows Bldg Cedar Rapids IA 52403-7010 Office Phone: 319-364-1538. Personal E-mail: rwilsonlaw@aol.com.

WILSON, ROBERT GORDON, investment banker; b. Mt. Vernon, NY, Dec. 16, 1933; s. Gerald and Ella Baxter (Close) W.; m. Valerie Ann Wilson, Apr. 25, 1966 (div. 1986); children: Jennifer Lynn, Kimberly Ann; m. Anne Marie Henriquez, Sept. 27, 1986; 1 child, Anthony H. Crotti. BA, Haverford Coll., 1955; MBA, Columbia U., 1957. Gen. ptnr. Goldman Sachs & Co., NYC, 1967-80, ltd. ptnr., 1981-89; pres. Goldman Sachs Internat., London, 1977-80; chmn., pres. Ecologic Waste Svcs., Inc., Miami, Fla., 1990-94; vice chmn. Carter Kaplan & Co., Richmond, Va., 1993-94; dir., founder LendingTree, Inc., Charlotte, NC, 1997—99. Former chmn. bd. trustees YMCA Greater N.Y., N.Y.C., 1975. Republican. Avocations: golf, wines, travel. Home and Office: Ziani Internat Capital Inc 151 Crandon Blvd Apt 1127 Key Biscayne FL 33149-1596 E-mail: rgw.55@hotmail.com.

WILSON, ROBERT M., diversified financial services company executive; b. St. Louis, Aug. 10, 1952; s. William H. and Mary E. (Sacksteder) W.; m. Joli S. Schneeberger, Oct. 7, 1978; 1 child, William Wilcox. BS, Miami U., Oxford, Ohio, 1974; JD, Cleve. State U., 1977. Bar: Ohio; CPA, Ohio. Ptnr. Touche Ross & Co., Dayton, Ohio, 1972-88, Roberds, Inc., Dayton, 1988-2000, pres., 1998—2000; exec. v.p. Wealthport, Inc., 2000—01; COO CCA Global Ptnrs. Inc., 2001—. Chmn. Dayton Ballet Assn., 1979-91; trustee Carillon Park, 1988-94, City-Wide Devel. Corp., 1991-2000, Cath. Social Svcs., 1995-2000; assoc. bd. Dayton Art Inst., 1989-95. Mem. ABA (com. chmn. 1990-92), Ohio Soc. CPAs (pres. 1985-86). Republican. Roman Catholic.

WILSON, ROBERT WARNE, philanthropist; b. Detroit, Nov. 3, 1926; s. Clarence Warne Wilson and Margaret Ballantyne; m. Marillyn Buelow, Apr. 1957 (div. 1977). BA in Econs. magna cum laude, Amherst Coll., Mass., 1946; MA in Econs., U. Mich., 1947; postgrad., Mich. Law Sch., 1948-49. Trainee First Boston Corp., NYC, 1949-50, 52-53; securities analyst Nat. Bank of Detroit, 1953-58; securities analyst to v.p. Gen. Am. Inv., NYC, 1958-62; securities analyst A.G. Becker & Co., NYC, 1962-68; investor, 1968—86; philanthropist, 1987—. Bd. dirs. Bklyn. Mus., 1974-88, Bklyn. Botanic Garden, 1974-88, NYC Opera, 1977-98, chmn. 1981-93; adv. bd. Met. Opera, 1979-81; trustee Environtl. Def., 1986—, Lyric Opera of Chgo. Nat. Bd., 1995-01, Manhattan Inst., 1986-02, Whitney Mus. of Am. Art, 1978— v.p., World Monuments Fund, 1990— vice chmn., Deafness Rsch. Found., 1998-01. US Army, 1951—52. Mem.: Phi Beta Kappa. Republican. Avocations: opera, museums, theater, movies, sightseeing. Office: 520 83rd St Brooklyn NY 11209-4520 Office Phone: 718-748-6113.

WILSON, ROBERT WOODROW, radio astronomer; b. Houston, Jan. 10, 1936; s. Ralph Woodrow and Fannie May (Willis) W.; m. Elizabeth Rhoads Sawin, Sept. 4, 1958; children: Philip Garrett, Suzanne Katherine, Randal Woodrow. BA with honors in Physics, Rice U., 1957; PhD, Calif. Inst. Tech., 1962. Research fellow Calif. Inst. Tech., Pasadena, 1962-63; mem. tech. staff AT&T Bell Labs., Holmdel, NJ, 1963-76, head wireless tech. rsch. dept., 1976-94; sr. sci. Harvard-Smithsonian Ctr. for Astrophysics, Cambridge, Mass., 1994—. Adj. prof. SUNY, 1978—. Discoverer 3 deg. k microwave background radiation, 1965, CO and other molecules in interstellar space using their millimeter wavelength radiation;. Named Fairchild Disting. scholar, Caltech., 1987; recipient Henry Draper medal, Royal Astron. Soc., London, 1977, Nobel prize in physics, 1978, Herschel Medal, 1977; fellow NSF fellow, 1958—61, Cole fellow, 1957—58. Mem.: AAAS, NAS (Herschel medal 1977), Internat. Sci. Radio Union, Am. Phys. Soc., Internat. Astron. Union, Am. Astron. Soc., Sigma Xi, Phi Beta Kappa. E-mail: rwilson@cfa.com.

WILSON, ROBERTA BUSH, retired psychotherapist, accountant; b. Watertown, NY, Dec. 23, 1937; d. Robert King and Barbara P. (Wiggins) Banks; m. Marvin D. Bush, Feb. 28, 1959 (div. 1977); m. Asa A. Wilson, July 29, 2004. BA, Glenville State Coll., 1977; MS, W.Va. U., Morgantown, 1985. Lic. profl. therapist W.Va. Acct. GE Plastics, Parkensburg, W.Va., 1959—77; lit. vol. Parkensburg, 1977—89; outpatient site head Abraxas, Parkensburg, 1989—95; psychotherapist Westbrook Health Svc., Parkensburg, 1996—97; ret., 1997. Pres., bd. dirs. Lit. Vol. Program of Wood County, Parkersburg. Mem.: Profl. Women's Assn. (pres., bd. dirs., Hall of Fame 1995). Episcoplian. Avocations: gardening, travel, photography. Home: 111 Canterbury Dr Parkersburg WV 26104-8057

WILSON, ROBERTA LOUISE, writer, editor, journalist, activist; b. Hollywood, Calif., June 2, 1954; d. Robert Louis and Noreen Irvine Wilson; life ptnr. Jeff Lynn Moore; stepchildren: Tyron, Dashal, Adrianne 1 child, Dova Lindsay Moore. BA in Psychology, Chapman U., 1976. Editor Career Publs., Orange, Calif., 1976—81; freelance journalist Agoura Valley News, Westlake Mag., Agoura Hills, Calif., 1977—79; tech. writer Ashton-Tate, Torrance, Calif., 1983—87; tech. writer/project lead Microsoft Corp., Redmond, Wash., 1988—2000; freelance tech. writer Aldus Corp., Seattle, 1989—91. Officer Washtech/CWA Local 37083, Seattle, 2002—. Performance art for anti-nuclear UNARM, Business as Usual; contbr. articles to mags., websites. Media/People Power coord. Gt. Peace Mar. for Global Nuc. Disarmament, LA, 1986—86; state coordinating com. Green Party of Wash. State, Seattle, 2001—02; co-organizer/writer bill of rights resolution Bill of Rights Def. Com., Bainbridge Island, Wash., 2003. Mem.: Green Party of Kitsap County (v.p. 2000—05), Winslow Cohousing Group (bd. trustees 1991—93). Mem. Religious Soc. Of Friends. Achievements include walked across the country with the Great Peace March for Global Nuclear Disarmament; co-founding member of first owner-developed cohousing community in the United States. Home Phone: 206-780-2027.

WILSON, ROBIN, interior designer; BA, U. Tex., Austen; MS in Real Estate Fin., NYU. Formerly with Mercer Mgmt. Consulting, Heidrick & Struggles; chmn., CEO Robin Wilson Home, 2000—; national spokesperson Hearst Mag. Home/Shelter Div., 2006—. Commentator O at Home, MarketWatch, Wall Street Journ., CNN, ABC, NBC, NY Daily News, Entrepreneur Mag. Bd. mem. Boston Symphony Orch. Overseers, 1993—2003, YWCA, Austin, Boston & NYC, 1988—98, DoSomething, 2003—05, Public Allies, 2006—. Named one of 50 Most Powerful Women in NY, NY Post, 2007. Mem.: Internat. Interior Design Assn. Office: Robin Wilson Home 230 Park Ave Ste 1000 New York NY 10069 *

WILSON, ROBIN SCOTT, retired academic administrator, writer; b. Columbus, Ohio, Sept. 19, 1928; s. John Harold and Helen Louise (Walker) W.; m. Patricia Ann Van Kirk, Jan. 20, 1951; children: Kelpie, Leslie, Kari, Andrew. BA, Ohio State U., 1950; MA, U. Ill., 1951, PhD, 1959. Fgn. intelligence officer CIA, Washington, 1959-67; prof. English Clarion State Coll., Pa., 1967-70; assoc. dir. Com. Instnl. Cooperation, Evanston, Ill., 1970-77; assoc. provost instrn. Ohio State U., Columbus, 1977-80; univ. pres. Calif. State U., Chico, 1980-93, pres. emeritus, 1993—. Author: Those Who Can, 1973, Death By Degrees, 1995, Paragons, 1996; short stories, criticism, articles on edn. Lt. USN, 1953-57. Mem. AAAS, Phi Kappa Phi E-mail: robinwilson@comcast.net.

WILSON, ROBLEY CONANT, JR., language educator, editor, writer; b. Brunswick, Maine, June 15, 1930; s. Robley Conant and Dorothy May (Stimpson) W.; m. Charlotte A. Lehon, Aug. 20, 1955 (div. 1991); children: Stephen, Philip; m. Susan Hubbard, June 17, 1995. BA, Bowdoin Coll., 1957, D.Litt (hon.), 1987; M.F.A., U. Iowa, 1968. Reporter Raymondville Chronicle, Tex., 1950-1951; asst. publicity dir. N.Y. State Fair Syracuse, 1956; instr. Valparaiso U., Ind., 1958-63; asst. prof. English U. No. Iowa, Cedar Falls, 1963-69, assoc. prof., 1969-75, prof., 1975-2000, prof. emeritus, 2000—, editor N.Am. Rev. Cedar Falls, 1969-2000. Author: The Pleasures of Manhood, 1977, Living Alone, 1978, Dancing for Men, 1983 (Drue Heinz Lit. prize, 1982), Kingdoms of the Ordinary (Agnes Lynch Starrett award, 1986), Terrible Kisses, 1989, A Pleasure Tree, 1990 (Soc. Midland Authors Poetry award, 1990), The Victim's Daughter, 1991, A Walk Through the Human Heart, 1996, Everything Paid For, 1999, The Book of Lost Fathers, 2001, Splendid Omens, 2004, The World Still Melting, 2005; co-editor: 100% Pure Florida Fiction, 2000. Bd. dirs. Associated Writing Programs, Norfolk, Va., 1983-86; pres. Iowa Woman Endeavors, Inc., 1986-90. With USAF, 1951-55. Guggenheim fellow, 1983-84, Nicholl Screenwriting fellow, 1996. Mem.: PEN, Authors' Guild. Home: PO Box 4009 Winter Park FL 32793-4009

WILSON, ROGER GOODWIN, lawyer; b. Evanston, Ill., Sept. 3, 1950; s. G. Turner Jr. and Lois (Shay) W.; m. Giovinella Gonthier, Mar. 7, 1975. AB, Dartmouth Coll., 1972; JD, Harvard U., 1975. Bar: Ill. 1975, US Dist. Ct. (no. dist.) Ill. 1976, US Ct. Appeals (7th cir.) 1977, US Dist. Ct. (no. dist.) Ind. 1985, US Supreme Ct. 2006. Assoc. Kirkland & Ellis, Chgo., 1975-81, ptnr., 1981-86; sr. v.p., gen. counsel, corp. sec. Blue Cross/Blue Shield, 1986—. Speaker Nat. Healthcare Inst., U. Mich., 1987-93, Am. Law Inst.-ABA Conf. on Mng. and Resolving Domestic and Internat. Bus. Disputes, N.Y.C., 1988, Washington, 1990; cert. health cons. program Purdue U., 1993-94, Inst. for Bus. Strategy Devel., Northwestern U., 1993-94, The Health Care Antitrust Forum, Chgo., 1995, Am. Health Lawyers Assn Managed Care Law Inst., 1995, Am. Health Lawyers Assn. Conf. on Tax Issues in Healthcare Orgns., 1996. Contbg. editor: Health Care Fraud and Abuse Newsletter, 1998—2002. Advisor Constl. Rights Found., Chgo., 1982-87; mem. So. Poverty Law Ctr., Montgomery, Ala., 1981—. Mem. ABA, Am. Health Lawyers Assn. (spkr. 1984, 96), Legal Assistance Found. of Chgo. (bd. dirs., pres.), Chgo. Coun. Lawyers (bd. govs. 1988-92), Coun. Chief Legal Officers (conf. bd. 1995—), Coun. Corp. Governance (conf. bd. 1998-00), Dartmouth Lawyers Assn., Chgo. Sinfonietta (bd. dirs. 1987-05), Univ. Club, Mid-Am. Club, Phi Beta Kappa. Home: 330 N Jefferson Ct Unit2004 Chicago IL 60661 Office: Blue Cross/Blue Shield 225 N Michigan Ave Ste 200 Chicago IL 60601-7601 Office Phone: 312-297-6439. Business E-Mail: roger.wilson@bcbsa.com.

WILSON, RONALD A., judge; b. 1968; Special staff asst. Pima County Atty. Barbara La Wall; presiding judge South Tucson City Ct., 2002—. Mem. Pima County Juvenile Ct., Pima County Teen Ct. Mentor In Her Shoes. Named 40 Under 40 Tucson Bus. Edge Man of Yr., 2006; recipient Rosa Parks award, NAACP. Personal E-mail: ronaldawilson@hotmail.com.

WILSON, RONALD LAWRENCE, professional hockey coach; b. Windsor, Ont., Can., May 28, 1955; BA in Econs., Providence Coll. Profl. hockey player Toronto Maple Leafs, 1975-85, Minn. North Stars, 1986-88; asst. coach Milw., Vancouver Canucks, 1989-90, Vancouver Canucks, 1990-93; interim coach Milw. Admirals, 1990; head coach Anaheim (Calif.) Mighty Ducks, 1993-97, Team USA, 1996, Washington Capitals, Landover, Md., 1997—2002, San Jose Sharks, 2002—. Coach Team U.S.A., World Cup of Hockey, 1996, 2004, U.S. Olympic Hockey Team, Nagano, Japan, 1998. Named to NCAA All-Am. East 1st team, 1974-76; Team USA World Cup Champaions, 1996. Office: San Jose Sharks 525 W Santa Clara St San Jose CA 95113

WILSON, ROSS, ambassador; b. Mpls., 1955; m. Margo Squire; 2 children. BA, U. Minn., 1977; MA, Columbia U., 1979; grad., Nat. War Coll., 1995. Intern Office of Soviet Union Affairs US Dept. State, Washington, 1978-80, econ. officer Office of Soviet Union Affairs, 1980-82, 87-90, polit. officer Office of Egyptian Affairs, 1982-84, econ.-comml. officer Prague, 1985-87, spl. asst. to under sec. for econ. & agrl. affairs Washington, 1990-92, dep. exec. sec., 1992-94, US Consul Gen. Melbourne, Australia, 1995-97, prin. dep. to amb.-at-Large, spl. adv. to sec. for new Ind. States of the former Soviet Union Washington, 1997—2000, US amb. to Azerbaijan Baku, 2000—03; US sr. negotiator for the Free Trade Area of the Ams. Office US Trade Rep., Washington, 2003—05; exec. asst. & chief of staff for dep. sec. US Dept. State, Washington, 2005, US amb. to Turkey Ankara, 2005—. Recipient Presdl. Meritorious Svc. award, 2005, Azerbaijan Order of Honor. Office: DOS Amb 7000 Ankara Pl Washington DC 20521 *

WILSON, ROWAN D., lawyer; b. Pomona, Calif., Sept. 3, 1960; AB cum laude, Harvard Coll., 1981; JD cum laude, Harvard Univ., 1984. Bar: Calif. 1985, NY 1987. Law clk., Hon. James R. Browning US Ct. of Appeals, 9th Cir.; assoc. Cravath Swaine & Moore LLP, NYC, 1986—92, ptnr., litig., 1992—. Mem.: Assn. Bar City NY, Fed. Bar Coun., Neighborhood Defender Svc. of Harlem, Lawyers' Com. for Civil Rights (chmn.). Office: Cravath Swaine & Moore LLP Worldwide Plz 825 Eighth Ave New York NY 10019-7475 Office Phone: 212-474-1348. Office Fax: 212-474-3700. Business E-Mail: rwilson@cravath.com.

WILSON, RUSSELL EDWARD, music educator; b. Atlanta, Ga., Jan. 25, 1963; s. Thomas Edward and Vivian Heaton Wilson. M of Music Edn., VanderCook Coll. Music, 1994; MusB, Ga. State U., 1985. Cert. elem., secondary tchr. Ga. Band dir. Hapeville HS, 1987, North Clayton Mid. Sch., College Park, 1987—92, Riverdale Mid. Sch., 1992—98, Mundy's Mill Mid. Sch., Jonesboro, Ga., 1998—2006, Lee Mid. Sch., 2006—, Coweta County, 2006—. Lead tchr. Clayton County Pub. Schools, Jonesboro, Ga., 2001—06; pvt. studio instrn. Oboe Studio, McDonough, Ga., 1981—. Musician (prin. oboist): Tara Winds Concert Band, 1988—. Asst. orch. dir. First Bapt. Ch., Jonesboro, 2004—; comm. dir. Tara Winds Concert Band, Atlanta, 2005—06. Recipient Legion of Honor, John Philip Sousa Found., 2005. Mem.: Ga. Music Educators Assn. (dist. treas. 1990—92), Music Educators Nat. Conf., Internat. Double Reed Soc., Nat. Band Assn. Home: 366 Whitney Ln Mcdonough GA 30253 Home Phone: 678-231-2725. Personal E-mail: oboeman@aol.com. Business E-Mail: russell.wilson@cowetaschools.org.

WILSON, SAMUEL MAYHEW, surgeon; b. Phila., June 26, 1950; m. Dorothy Hay Barrus, June 9, 1990; children: Elisabeth, Mary. BA, Swarthmore Coll., Pa., 1972; MS, Drexel U., Phila., 1975; MD, Temple U., Phila., 1979. Diplomate Am. Bd. Surgery. Resident in surgery Temple U. Hosp., Phila., 1979-84; fellow in vascular surgery Presbyn.-U. Pa. Med. Ctr., 1984-86; attending surgeon Evang. Cmty. Hosp., Lewisburg, 1986-88, Albert Einstein Med. Ctr., Phila., 1988-95. Attending surgeon Elkins Park Hosp., Pa., 1988-95, Frankford Hosp., Phila., 1988-95, JFK Meml. Hosp., Phila., 1988-95; staff surgeon Bayhealth Med. Ctr.-Kent Gen. Hosp., Dover, 1996—, chair dept. surgery, 2006-, med. exec. com., 2005-07, sec./treas., 2005-06; asst. clin. instr. surgery U. Pa. Med. Sch., Phila., 1984-85, assoc. clin. instr., 1985-86; clin. instr. surgery Temple U. Sch. Medicine, Phila., 1988-95; sec.-treas. med. exec. com. Kent Gen. HOsp., 2005-06. Contbr. articles to profl. jours. Active Christ Episcopal Ch.,

Dover, 1996—, vestry, 2005—. Corp. USMCR, 1972-78. Fellow ACS, Southeastern Surg. Congress; mem. AMA (Physician Recognition award), Med. Soc. Del., Kent County Med. Soc., Delaware Valley Vascular Soc., Ea. Vascular Soc. Avocations: sailing, skiing, hiking, photography, reading. Office: 540 S Governors Ave Ste 100A Dover DE 19904-3523 Office Phone: 302-674-0600.

WILSON, SAMUEL V., academic administrator; BA, Hampden-Sydney Coll., LLD, 1979; LHD, Longwood Coll., 1999. Pres. Hampden-Sydney Coll., Va., 1992—2000, pres. emeritus, 2000—, James C. Wheat Vis. Prof. in Leadership, 2000—. Office: Hampden-Sydney Coll Hampden Sydney VA 23943-0128 E-mail: swilson@hsc.edu.

WILSON, SARADA AMELIA PRINCESS, elementary school educator; b. Charleston, SC, Sept. 7, 1980; d. Theodore T. Wilson Jr. and Claudia Wilson. BS in Polit. Sci., Coll. Charleston, SC, 2003; M in Tchg., Pace U., NYC, 2005; M in Adminstrn. and Supervision, Touro Coll., Bklyn., 2007. Coord. social studies test Luisa Dessus Cruz Mid. Sch. 302, Bronx, acad. intervention specialist, dean discipline, tchr. spl. edn.; lead tchr. Edn. Sta., NYC. Democrat. Methodist. Home: 1476 Bryant Ave #B Bronx NY 10460 Office: Luisa Dessus Druz Mid Sch 302 681 Kelly St Bronx NY 10455

WILSON, SCOTT THOMAS, psychologist, researcher; b. Bayonne, NJ, July 29, 1969; s. John Thomas and Patricia Jean Wilson; m. Denise Figlar, May 16, 1999; children: Liam Patrick, Ella Kinsey. BA in Psychology, Rutgers U., 1992; PhD in Clin. Psychology, Columbia U., 2003. Lic. clin. psychologist NY. Predoctoral fellow Columbia U., NYC, 1999—2000, postdoctoral rsch. fellow in psychiatry, 2005—; rsch. scientist NY State Psychiat. Inst., NYC, 2002—05; pvt. practice NYC, 2005—. Cons. Amador and Assocs., LLC, NYC, 2004—. Contbr. Suicide in Schizophrenia. Fellow Nat. Rsch. Svc. award, NIMH, 1999. Mem.: APA. Achievements include research in patients with severe mental illnesses, including schizophrenia and borderline personality disorder. Home Phone: 718-222-4622; Office Phone: 212-543-6236. Business E-Mail: stw16@columbia.edu.

WILSON, STANLEY CHARLES, artist, educator, curator, art gallery director, consultant; b. LA, Feb. 2, 1947; s. Ernest Charles and Eleanor (Reid) W.; m. Jacquelyn Bellard, June 3, 1978; 1 child, Jendayi Asabi. BFA, Otis Art Inst., 1969, MFA, 1971. Asst. prof. Southwestern Coll., Chula Vista, Calif., 1972-73; prof. art Calif. Poly U., Pomona, 1973—; univ. gallery dir. Calif. Poly. U., Pomona, 1988—96; instr. Otis Parsons Watts Towers, LA, 1981-88; prof. emeritus Calif. State Poly. U., Pomona, 2002—. Bd. artists Brockman Gallery Prodns., LA, 1980-85; bd. dirs. Watt Towers Art Ctr., LA; vis. artist dept. art U. Nev., Las Vegas, 1990; vis. prof. sculpture Otis Art Inst., LA, 1991-92; bd. advisors The Armory Gallery, Pasadena, Calif.; apptd. Nat. Edn. Com., Princeton, NJ, 1996; chair Pasadena (Calif.) Arts Commn., 1997; co-chair sculpture panel Coll. Art Assn., LA, 1999; Disting. artist lecture Calif. State U., Northridge, 2001; grad. reviewer Memphis Coll. of Art and Design, Memphis, 2001; co-curator exhbn. Armony Ctr. for Arts, Pasadena, 2002; slide lectr., disting. artist series Calif. State U., Northridge, 2002; vis. artist, grad. reviewer Memphis Coll. Art and Design, 2001; art adv. com. Pasadena Ctr., 2006. One-man shows include Sol Del Rio Gallery, San Antonio, 1980, Brockman Gallery, 1982, Daniel Maher Gallery, 1983, Southwest Coll., 1984; 2 person exhbn. Calif. State U., Bakersfield, 2002; exhibited in group shows at Oranges/Sardines Gallery, 1984, Sparc Gallery, 1985, Mus. African Am. Art, 1985, L.A. Art Gallery, 1986, Muni Art Gallery Calif. State U. Dominguez Hills, Altars, Icons & Sacred Places, San Antonio Art Inst., 1992, Gallery 1078, Chico, Calif., Calif. State U., 2002, Calif. Poly. U., 2003, African AIDS Armory Ctr. for the Arts, Calif., 2004, Calif. African Am. Mus., 2005, Calif. AfroAm. Mus., L.A., 2005, U. Art Gallery Calif. Poly U., 2007; retrospective at Kellogg U. Art Gallery, Calif. State U., Pomona, 2007; represented in permanent collections Calif. Mus. Afro-Am. History and Culture, Prairie View Coll., 1977, Tex. A&M U., 1977, Atlanta Life Ins. Co., 1984, Golden State Life Ins., 1985, Broadway Fed. Savs. & Loan Corp., L.A., 1986, LACTC Metro Rail Commn.; artist in residence Studio Mus. Harlem, N.Y., Spokane (Wash.) Coll., (vis.) Graduate Review Memphis Coll of Art and Design, 2001, Pasadena Art Alliance, 2005; contbr. articles to profl. jours. Chmn. Pasadena Arts Commn. NEA fellow, 1986; Visual Arts fellow Pasadena Art Commn., 1991; advanced placement, Studio Art Devel. Com.; Brody visual art fellow, L.A., 1998; recipient Gold Crown award in visual arts Pasadena Arts Coun., 1998. Progressive. Avocations: music, gardening, architecture, sports. Office: Calif Poly U Dept Art 3801 W Temple Ave Pomona CA 91768-2557 Home Phone: 323-256-2997; Office Phone: 909-869-3519. Business E-Mail: scwilson@csupomona.edu.

WILSON, STEPHANIE D., astronaut; b. Boston, 1966; m. Julius B.J. McCurdy. BS in Engring., Harvard U., Divsn. Engring. and Applied Sciences, 1988; MS in Aerospace Engring., U. Tex., 1992. Loads and dynamic engr. astronautics group Martin Marietta, Denver, 1988—90; mem. attitude and articulation control subsystem for Galileo spacecraft Jet Propulsion Lab., Pasadena, Calif., 1992—96; astronaut NASA, Johnson Space Ctr., Houston, 1996—. Lead CAPCOM (capsule communicator) Columbia Mission, 2003; mission specialist, load master, operating robotic arm STS-121, Return-to-Flight test mission and assembly flight to Internat. Space Station, 2006. Mem.: AIAA. Achievements include research in control and modeling of large, flexible space structures; second African-American women in space. Avocations: skiing, music, astronomy, stamp collecting/philately, travel. Office: Astronaut Office/CB NASA Johnson Space Ctr Houston TX 77058

WILSON, STEPHEN RAY, fertilizer manufacturing company executive; b. DuBois, Pa., Oct. 20, 1948; s. Richard C. and Marilyn J. (Stewart) W.; m. Susan K. Condon, Sept. 5, 1970; children: Jeffrey M., Elizabeth A. BA in Sociology, Northwestern U., 1970, MBA in Fin. and Acctg., 1974. CPA, Ill. Various positions Inland Steel Industries, Chgo., 1974-91, asst. treas., 1985-88; contr., treas. James T. Ryerson & Son, Chgo., 1988-89; v.p. info. mgmt. and fin. Joseph T. Ryerson & Son, Chgo., 1989-90; gen. mgr. corp. planning Inland Steel Industries, Inc., Chgo., 1990-91; sr. v.p., CFO, CF Industries, Inc., Deerfield, Ill., 1991—2003, pres., CEO, 2003—, chmn., 2005—. Bd. dirs. Northwestern Club Chgo., 1982-84; bd. trustees Chgo. Found. for Edn., 1993—. With U.S. Army, 1970-72. Mem. AICPA, Fin. Execs. Inst., Econ. Club Chgo. Avocations: running, golf, travel. Office: CF Industries Inc Ste 400 4 Parkway N Deerfield IL 60015-2590 *

WILSON, STEPHEN RIP, public policy consultant; b. Twin Falls, Idaho, Apr. 26, 1948; s. Jerome P. and Epsy Jane (Griggs) W.; m. Judith Ann Newcomb, June 2, 1972 (dec. Nov. 16, 1977); children: Paul, Sloan; m. Judith E. Allen, Apr. 11, 1992. BA, Columbia U., 1970. Editor Sta. KABC TV, LA, 1970-72; owner, mgr. Oro Verde Farms, Hagerman, Idaho, 1972-77; new dir. Sta. KAET TV, Phoenix, 1978-83; adminstrv. aide U.S. Senator Dennis DeConcini, Phoenix, 1983-89; chief exec. officer Flatt & Assocs., Mesa, Ariz., 1989-90; exec. asst. to Gov. Rose Mofford State of Ariz., Phoenix, 1990-91; pres. SRW Cos., Phoenix, Ariz., 1991—. Commr. Gov.'s Coun. Phys. Fitness, Phoenix, 1988-90; bd. dirs. Crime Victim Found., Phoenix, 1984; mem. Jefferson Forum. Mem. Nucleus Club, Com. on Fgn. Rels. Democrat. Avocations: scuba diving, skiing, tennis, fly fishing, golf, writing. Home: 2017 E Marshall Ave Phoenix AZ 85016-3110 E-mail: Ripp@crwcon.com, dryheataz@hotmail.com.

WILSON, STEVE, museum director; BFA, U. So. Calif.; MFA in acting, Nat. Theatre Conservatory, Denver. Tchr., performing arts chmn. St. Mary's Acad., Colo.; faculty mem. Wolf Theatre Acad. and Stage Eleven; artist-in-residence Cherry Creek and Denver Pub. Sch. Dists., Denver Sch. Arts; exec. artistic dir., acting dir. Mizel Ctr. for Arts and Culture; dir. Wolf Theatre Acad. Office: Mizel Ctr Arts and Culture 350 S Dahlia St Denver CO 80246 Office Phone: 303-316-6363.

WILSON, SYLVIA ALYCE, musician, educator; b. Mpls., June 19, 1950; d. Robert Leighton and Doris Mae (Seim) Butts; m. Dennis Charles Wilson, Sept. 12, 1970; children: Ryan Bradley, Virginia Anne Herzog. BS in Music Edn. with high distinction, U. Minn., Mpls., 1972, MA in Music Edn., 1987. Orch. tchr. Anoka-Hennepin Sch. Dist. No. 11, Coon Rapids, Minn., 1972—77, music tchr., 1986—89, 1992—; substitute music tchr. St. Louis Park (Minn.) Sch. Dist. No. 283, 1978—85; orch. tchr. Wayzata (Minn.) Sch. Dist. #284, 1985—86; orch./choir tchr. Roseville (Minn.) Area Pub. Schs. #623, 1989—90. Musician Lake String Quartet, Mpls., 1982—85; piano tuner, pvt. music tchr., 1982—86; preschool music tchr. West Bank Sch. Music, Mpls., 1983—85; judge Minn. State HS League, St. Paul, 2003—; presenter in field. Contbr. articles to profl. jours. Violinist, violist Cantati Evangelica, Mpls., 1995—2001, Mpls. Civic Orch., 1970—; mentor Minn. Music Edn. Assn., 2006—; VBS tchr. First Bapt. Ch. Mpls., 1990—94, choir dir., bell choir dir., 1992—2000. Named Outstanding Sr., Am. Legion, 1968; recipient Meritorious Orch. Program award, Minn. String Tchrs. Assn., 1987, 2002; grantee, Anoka-Hennepin Ednl. Found., 1999—2001; scholar, U. Minn., 1968. Mem.: NEA, Minn. Educators of the Gifted and Talented, Anoka-Hennepin Edn. Minn. (bldg. rep. 2000—05), Am. String Tchrs. Assn., Music Educators Nat. Conf., Pi Kappa Lambda, Sigma Alpha Iota (pres., v.p., treas., corr. sec. 1970—, co-chair benefit music scholarships, Music scholar 1970, Sword of Honor 1971, Svc. to Chpt. award 2005, Rose of Honor 2006). Home: 2700 Joppa Ave S Saint Louis Park MN 55416 Office: Northdale Mid Sch 11301 Dogwood St Coon Rapids MN 55448 Personal E-mail: swilsonusf@yahoo.com.

WILSON, TAYLOR, lawyer; b. Dallas, Aug. 9, 1963; BA cum laude, Amherst Coll., 1985; JD, So. Meth. U., 1990. Bar: Tex. 1990. Ptnr., corp./securities, venture capital, mergers & acquisitions Haynes and Boone LLP, Dallas, Practice Group Leader, Bus. Trans. Sect., hiring ptnr., co-chmn., Investment Fund Practice Group. Assoc. sr. editor The Internat. Lawyer, 1989—90. Mem.: Dallas Bar Assn., State Bar Tex. (Bus. Law Sect., info./edn. com. 1996—), ABA (Bus. Law Sect., venture capital & pvt. equity com. 2001—). Office: Haynes and Boone LLP 901 Main St Ste 3100 Dallas TX 75202 Office Phone: 214-651-5615. Office Fax: 214-200-0617. Business E-Mail: taylor.wilson@haynesboone.com.

WILSON, TERILYN BARRETT, elementary school educator; b. Logan, W. Va., Aug. 17, 1950; d. Freeman J. and Marie P. Barrett; m. Kenneth Ray Wilson, Nov. 25, 1977; children: Melanie Brooke, Stephanie Marie. BA, Marshall U., 1972, M, 1973. Spl. edn. tchr. Putnam County Sch., Winfield, W.Va., 1972—73, Kanawha County Sch., Charleston, W.Va., 1973—74, Meade County Sch., Brandenburg, Ky., 1974—77, Logan County Sch., Logan, 1978, 1980—85, 2d grade tchr., 1985—90, spl. edn. tchr., 1998—2002, 5th grade tchr., 2003—. Chair, spl. edn. dept. Chapmanville Mid. Sch., Chapmanville, W.Va., 1990—2002, sec., faculty senate, 1994—98. Chief mem. Logan State Pk. Found.; deacon, ch. bd. First Christian Ch., Logan, W.Va., 2003—05. Recipient Tchr. Yr., Logan County, 2007, Walmart, 2007. Mem.: Internat. Reading Assn., Delta Kappa Gamma (v.p. 1992—96). Democrat. Avocations: reading, quilting, travel. Office: Chapmanville Mid Sch 300 Vance St Chapmanville WV 25508 Office Phone: 304-855-8378. Personal E-mail: tbkwilson@verizon.net. Business E-Mail: twilson@access.k12.wv.us.

WILSON, TERRENCE RAYMOND, manufacturing executive; b. St. Louis, July 1, 1943; s. Raymond Lemuel and Eula Ellen (Sutton) W.; m. Judy Marie Coleman, May 23, 1964; children: John Scott, Dustin Marint. Student, Drury Coll., 1961-62, St. Louis Jr. Coll., 1962-64, Mo. U., 1965-67. Program control planning adminstr. McDonnell Aircraft, St. Louis, 1962-65, 67; mgmt. control mgr. Vitro Labs., Silver Spring, Md., 1966; mgr. customer svc. Teledyne Wis. Motor, Milw., 1968-69, dir. ops., 1970-71, dir. mktg., 1972-73; gen. mgr. Teledyne Still-Man, Cookeville, Tenn., 1973-74, pres. multiplant div., 1975-78; group exec. Teledyne, Inc., 1979-84; pres. Teledyne Indsl. Engines, 1984-87; pres., chief exec. officer Morgan Corp., Morgantown, Pa., 1987-92; pres. Magnatech Internat. L.P., Sinking Spring, Pa., 1992-2000; retired, 2000; mng. dir. Spirka Maschinenbau GmbH, Alfeld, Germany, 1996-97. Pres. LINC Preferred Group, Inc., Cookeville, Tenn.; CEO New South Maple Ptnrs., LLC. Bd. dirs. Tenn. Tech. U. Coll. Bus. Found. Mem. Beta Gamma Sigma. Roman Catholic. Office: LINC Preferred Group Inc Cookeville TN 38501 Office Phone: 931-525-6287. Business E-Mail: terrywilson@lincpreferredgroup.com.

WILSON, THEODORE HENRY, retired electronics executive, aerospace engineer; b. Eufaula, Okla., Apr. 23, 1940; s. Theodore V. and Maggie E. (Buie) W.; m. Barbara Ann Tassara, May 16, 1958 (div. 1982); children: Debbie Marie, Nita Leigh, Wilson Axten, Pamela Ann, Brenda Louise, Theodore Henry II, Thomas John, Margaret Mariana; m. Colleen Fagan, Jan. 1, 1983 (div. 1987); m. Karen L. Lerohl, Sept. 26, 1987 (div. 1997); m. Sandra Rivadeneira, Mar. 27, 1997. BSME, U. Calif., Berkeley, 1962; MSME, U. So. Calif., 1964, MBA, 1970, MSBA, 1971. Sr. rsch. engr. N.Am. Aviation Co. div. Rockwell Internat., Downey, Calif., 1962-65; propulsion analyst, supr. div. applied tech. TRW, Redondo Beach, Calif., 1965-67, mem. devel. staff systems group, 1967-71, sr. fin. analyst worldwide automotive dept. Cleve., 1971-72, contr. systems and energy group Redondo Beach, 1972-79, dir. fin. control equipment group Cleve., 1979-82, v.p. fin. control indsl. and energy group, 1982-85, mem. space and def. group Redondo Beach, 1985-93, ret., 1993. Lectr., mem. com. acctg. curriculum UCLA Extension, 1974-79. Mem. Fin. Execs. Inst. (com. govt. bus.), Machinery and Allied Products Inst. (govt. contracts coun.), Nat. Contract Mgmt. Assn. (bd. advisors), Aerospace Industries Assn. (procurement and fin. coun.), UCLA Chancellors Assocs., Tau Beta Pi, Beta Gamma Sigma, Pi Tau Sigma. Republican. Avocations: golf, bridge. Home: 3617 Via La Selva Palos Verdes Peninsula CA 90274-1115

WILSON, THOMAS ALLEN, pediatrician, endocrinologist; s. Gordon Allen Wilson; m. Patricia Westgate; m. Karen Louise Close (div.); children: Tyler Brook, Trevor Close, Jenna Marie, Juliana Rose. MD, U. Pa., Phila., 1973. Diplomate in pediat. Am. Bd. Pediat., 1980, in pediat. endocrinology Am. Bd. Pediat., 1982. Prof. pediat. SUNY, Stony Brook, 1982—, dir. dept. pediatric endocrinology, 1982—. Mem.: Lawson Wilkens Pediatric Endocrine Soc. Office: Divsn Pediatric Endocrinology Dept Pediats SUNY Stony Brook NY 11794-8111 Home Phone: 631-689-9703; Office Phone: 631-444-3429. Office Fax: 631-444-6045.

WILSON, THOMAS DOUGLAS, JR., lawyer; b. Winston-Salem, NC, Aug. 26, 1946; s. Thomas Douglas Wilson and Beatrice Burcham Chapman; m. Betsey Page Bent, Aug. 22, 1984; 1 child, Elizabeth. BA in Econs., U. N.C., Chapel Hill, 1968, JD, 1973. Bar: N.C. 1973, Ga. 1974; cert. arbitrator, mediator Ga., arbitrator N.C. Trial atty. FTC, Atlanta, 1973-78; pvt. practice Atlanta, 1978-81; atty. Ga. Legal Svcs. Corp., Gainesville, 1981-84; mng. ptnr. Wilson, Cobb, Lichstenstein & Lao, Atlanta, 1984-93; pres. Ga. Emission Testing Co., Inc., Atlanta, 1993-95; assoc. McGuire, Wood & Bissette PA, Asheville, NC, 1995-98, mng. ptnr., 1999—2002. Vol. atty. Pisgah Legal Svcs., Asheville, 1996—, v.p., bd. dirs. Author: (manual) Social Security Disability Claims, 1984; co-author: (manual) North Carolina Construction Law: Rights and Remedies, 1998. Chmn. bd. dirs. RiverLink, Asheville, 1997-99; vice chmn. bd. dirs. Regional Waterh Authority Task Force, Asheville, 1996-99; mem. Asheville Econ. Devel. Task Force, 1999-2000; mem. Asheville Econ. Devel. Commn., 1997-99; youth basketball coach YMCA, Asheville Recreation League, 1997-2001; pres., bd. dirs. Asheville HS Booster Club. Mem. ABA, ATLA, Ga. Bar Assn., N.C. Bar Assn. (bd. dirs., constrn. law coun 2000—), N.C. Acad. Trial Lawyers., Asheville N.C. C. of C. (com. Asheville-Bumcombe Water Agreement). Home: 172 Marlborough Rd Asheville NC 28804 Office: 48 Patton Ave Asheville NC 28801-3321 Fax: 828-252-2437. E-mail: tdwilson@mwbavl.com.

WILSON, THOMAS JOSEPH, insurance company executive; m. Jill Garling; 3 children. BSBA, U. Mich., 1979; M of Mgmt., Northwestern U., 1980. Various fin. positions Amoco Corp., Chgo., 1980-86; mng. dir. mergers and acquisitions Dean Witter Reynolds, Chgo., 1986-93; v.p. strategy and analysis Sears, Roebuck and Co., Chgo., 1993-95; sr. v.p., CFO The Allstate Corp., Northbrook, Ill., 1995-98; chmn., pres. Allstate Fin., 1999—2002; pres. Allstate Protection, 2003—05; pres., COO The Allstate Corp., Northbrook, Ill., 2005—06, pres., CEO, 2007—. Bd. dirs. Rush-Presbyn.-St. Luke's Med. Ctr. and Francis W. Parker Sch. Office: The Allstate Corp 2775 Sanders Rd Northbrook IL 60062-6110

WILSON, THOMAS LEON, physicist, researcher; b. Alpine, Tex., May 21, 1942; s. Homer Marvin and Ogarita Maude (Bailey) W.; m. Joyce Ann Krevosky, May 7, 1978; children: Kenneth Edward Byron, Bailey Elizabeth Victoria. BA, Rice U., 1964, BS, 1965, MA, 1974, PhD, 1976. With NASA, Houston, 1965—, astronaut instr., 1965-74, high-energy theoretical physicist, 1969—. Author 3 books; contbr. articles to profl. jours. Recipient Hugo Gernsback award, IEEE, 1964; fellow, NASA, 1969—76. Mem.: AAAS, Am. Nuc. Soc., Am. Assn. Physicists in Medicine, NY Acad. Scis., Am. Phys. Soc. Achievements include research on grand unified field theory, relativistic quantum field theory, quantum chromodynamics, quantum probability theory, supergravity, quantum cosmology, astrophysics, deep inelastic scattering, neutrino astronomy, neutrino tomography; discoverer classical uncertainity principle; subspeciality: relativity and gravitation; patentee in field; contributor to design of NASA's proposed lunar base; originator olive branch as symbol of man's 1st landing on moon (on Susan B. Anthony and Eisenhower dollars); and manual Saturn takeover for Apollo moon program. Home: 206 Woodcombe Dr Houston TX 77062-2538 Office: NASA Johnson Space Ctr Houston TX 77058 Home Phone: 281-480-2194; Office Phone: 281-483-2147. Business E-Mail: twilson@ems.jsc.nasa.gov. E-mail: ThomasWilson@KickapooNovel.com.

WILSON, THOMAS MATTHEW, III, lawyer; b. Ware, Mass., Feb. 22, 1936; s. Thomas Matthew Jr. and Ann Veronica (Shea) W.; m. Deborah Ord Lockhart, Feb. 10, 1962; children: Deborah Veronica, Leslie Lockhart, Thomas Matthew IV. BA, Brown U., 1958; JD, U. Md., 1971. Bar: Md. 1972, U.S. Ct. Appeals (4th cir.) 1976, U.S. Supreme Ct. 1977. Sales mgr. Mid-Ea. Box Mfg. Co., Balt., 1966-74; asst. atty. gen., chief antitrust divsn. State of Md., Balt., 1974-79; ptnr. Tydings & Rosenberg, LLP, Balt., 1979—. Author: Defending an Antitrust Action Brought by a State Attorney General, 1987, The Spectre of Double Recovery in Antitrust Federalism, 1989; co-author: Reciprocity and the Private Plaintiff, 1972; mem. editl. adv. bd.: Bur. of Nat. Affairs Antitrust and Trade Regulation Report, 1979—. Mem. ABA (sect. on antitrust law 1974—, chmn. state antitrust enforcement com. 1986-89, antitrust sect. coun. 1990-93, coord. com. on legal edn. 1993-94), Md. Bar Assn. (antitrust subcom. 1975-78), Internat. Bar Assn. (sect. on bus. law, antitrust law and monopolies com. 1983—), Churchwarden's Chess Club, Annapolis Yacht Club. Republican. Achievements include patents for nail cartons. Home: Baobab Farm Hampstead MD 21074 Office: Tydings & Rosenberg LLP 100 E Pratt St Baltimore MD 21202-1009 Home Phone: 410-239-7950; Office Phone: 410-752-9708. Business E-Mail: twilson@tydingslaw.com.

WILSON, THOMAS S., professional sports team executive; m. Linda Wilson; 3 children. BBA, Wayne State U. Dir. mktg. NBA LA Lakers and NHL LA Kings, 1974—76; sales dir. NBA Detroit Pistons, 1977, exec. dir., 1979, pres., CEO, 1993—; CEO Palace Sports & Entertainment, Inc., pres., 1992—; CEO, gov. NHL Tampa Bay Lightning, 1999—, St. Pete Times Forum, Fla., 1999—. Bd. trustees William Beaumont Hosp. Named Exec. of Yr., Oakland Execs. Assn., 1994; recipient Disting. Citizen award, Boy Scouts Am., 1988, Ernst & Young Master Entrepreneur award for State of Mich., 2002, Gerald R. Sportsperson of Yr. award, Mich. Sports Hall of Fame, 2003. Office: Detroit Pistons 5 Championship Dr Auburn Hills MI 48326-1753 *

WILSON, THOMAS STRONG, JR., (TAM), judge; b. Portland, Oreg., Aug. 13, 1944; s. Thomas Strong and Ruth (Isherwood) W. BA, Dickinson Coll., 1967; JD, U. Miami, 1971. Bar: Fla. 1971, D.C. 1972, U.S. Dist. Ct. (so. dist.) Fla., U.S. Ct. Appeals (5th cir.). Rsch. aide to Justice James Adkins Fla. Supreme Ct., Tallahassee, 1971-72; assoc. Preddy, Haddad, Kutner & Hardy, 1973, John R. Farrell, PA., 1973; asst. pub. defender Pub. Defender's Office, Dade County, Fla., 1974-77; sole practice Dade County, 1978-84; asst. state's atty. State's Atty.'s Office, Dade County, 1984-87, gen. master Family Divsn., 1987-90; judge Circuit Ct., Dade County, 1990. Served to ensign USNR, 1968-69. Named Judge of Yr., Am. Bd. Trial Advocates, Miami chpt., 1999, Dade County Trial Lawyers, 2003; recipient Steven Levine award, Dade County Bar Assn., 2003. Mem. Iron Arrow, Skull and Key. Roman Catholic. Office: 73 W Flagler St Ste 624 Miami FL 33130 Office Phone: 305-349-7161.

WILSON, THOMAS W., pharmacist; b. Aug. 23, 1947; BS in Pharmacy, U. Tex., Austin, PharmD. Registered pharmacist Tex., Colo., cert. psychiat. pharmacist. Pharmacist Dept. Vet. Affairs, Waco, Tex. Mem.: Coll. Psychiat. Neurol. Pharmacists. Address: 145 Bowie Ln Hewitt TX 76643

WILSON, TROY LYNN, technologist; b. Sweetwater, Tex., Dec. 5, 1952; s. Billy Merle and Dorothy Virginia Wilson; m. Connie Lee Wilson, May 25, 1974; children: Corry Lynn, Brad Lee. Grad., Amarillo Coll., Tex. Cert. surg. technologist 1984. Surg. technician N.W. Tex. Hosp., Amarillo. Clin. educator Amarillo Coll. E5 US Army, 1972—78. Mem.: Tex. State Assembly Surg. Technologist. Avocation: golf.

WILSON, TYLER J., medical association administrator; BA, Georgetown U., 1981; JD, Cath. U., 1986. Atty. legis. and regulatory affairs domestic policy divsn. U.S. C. of C.; v.p. govt. affairs Automotive Aftermarket Industry Assn.; exec. dir., sec. Am. Orthotic and Prosthetic Assn., 2000—06; pres., CEO Am. Assn. for Homecare, 2006—. Office: Am Assn for Homecare 625 Slaters Ln Ste 200 Alexandria VA 22314-1171 Office Phone: 703-836-6263. Office Fax: 703-836-6730.

WILSON, VAN RAY, secondary school educator; b. El Dorado, Ark., Mar. 19, 1947; s. Brooks Robert and Marjorie Audrey Wilson; m. Bonnie Young (div.); 1 child, William Brooks; m. Alice Ann McAteer, Sept. 28, 1979; 1 child, Clorinda Ann. BA in Edn., Kensington U., Glendale, Calif., 1992. Cert. tchr. automotive mechanics NY State Edn. Dept. Enlisted US Army, 1965, advanced through grades to sgE8, 1983, ret., 1986; automotive technician Staten Island, NY, 1987—90; HS tchr. NYC Dept. Edn., 1990—. Mem.: Am. Legion, Combat Infantrymen's Assn. (life), Golden Key. Avocations: auto restoration, sailing. Office: Ralph McKee Career-Tech HS 290 St Marks Pl Staten Island NY 10301 Office Phone: 718-420-2600 ext 528.

WILSON, VIRGIL JAMES, III, lawyer, judge; b. San Jose, Calif., July 25, 1953; s. Virgil James Wilson Jr. and Phyllis Emily (Mothorn) Brasser; children: Gabriel James Hekili, Alexander Robert Kaimoku, Hayley Noelani, Maia E. Kailani. BA with honors, U. Calif., Santa Cruz, 1975; JD cum laude, U. Santa Clara, 1981. Bar: US Dist. Ct. (no. dist.) Calif. 1981, US Dist. Ct. Hawaii 1982, US Ct. Appeals (9th cir.) 1987, US Supreme Ct. 1987, Oreg. 1990, US Dist. Ct. Oreg. 1998, US Ct. Fed. Claims 1999. Atty.

James Krueger P.C., Wailuku, Maui, 1981-83; resident counsel Sterns & Ingram, Honolulu, 1983-89; pvt. practice Kailua, Hawaii, 1989—; assoc. Thorp, Purdy, Jewett, Urness & Wilkinson, P.C., Springfield, Oreg., 1998-99; of counsel Law Offices of Ian L. Mattoch, 1993-96, Gaydos, Churnside & Balthrop PC, Eugene, Oreg., 2001—05; pvt. practice, 2005—; mcpl. judge City Coburg, Oreg., 2007—. Owner Wilson Investigations, Santa Cruz, 1978-81, Honolulu, 1981—96, Eugene, 1996—. Mem. Hawaii Bar Assn., Calif. State Bar Assn., Oreg. Bar Assn. Avocation: magic. Office Phone: 541-556-2096. Fax: 541-607-6565. E-mail: VJWILSONiii@msn.com.

WILSON, WALTER CLINTON, retired oil and gas industry executive; b. Brownwood, Tex., Sept. 21, 1942; s. Henry Eliga and Lottie Mae (Palmore) Wilson; m. Debra M. Thompson, Aug. 26, 1965; children: Walter Scott, Aimée Renee. BS cum laude, Howard Payne U., 1965. CPA Tex. Fin. mgmt. Exxon Co. USA, Kingsville, Corpus Christi, Houston, Tex., 1965-81; asst. contr. Superior Oil Co., Houston, 1982-85, fin. cons., 1985-87; contr. EOG Resources, Inc. (formerly Enron Oil and Gas Co.), Houston, 1987-88, sr. v.p., CFO, 1988-2000; ret., 2000. Mem. adv. bd. H. S. Grace & Co., Houston, 2001—. Trustee Fin. Exec. Rsch. Found., 1998—2001; chmn. pers. com. 1st Bapt. Ch., Houston, 1985—87, chmn. deacons, 1994—96; trustee Howard Payne U., Brownwood, 1999—, chmn., 2002—04; bd. dirs. Lyric Performing Arts Co., Brownwood, 2004—, chmn., 2004—. Lt. USNR, 1966—69, Vietnam. Mem.: Tex. Soc. CPAs (Houston chpt.), Fin. Execs. Internat. (Houston chpt.), Kingwood Country Club, Club Corp. Am.-Houston Soc. Republican. Personal E-mail: wwilson2@earthlink.net.

WILSON, WANDA LEE DAVIS, retired casting director; b. Pitts., May 15, 1950; d. James A. Davis, Jr. and Dorothy (Love) Davis Anselmi; m. Kirby L. Wilson Sr., Apr. 23, 1976 (div. July 1984); children: Le Chon Kirb, Lia Shawnyea. Student, Connelly Tech. Sch., Pitts., 1968-71, Allegheny Community Coll., 1968-71, U. Pitts., 1984-86. Stand-in co-host The Together Show Sta. KDKA-TV, CBS, Pitts., 1971; adminstrv. sec. GE, Pitts., 1971-78; sec., notary public Sta. WPCB-TV, Wall, Pa., 1979-80; producer, host The Wanda Wilson Show Am. Cablevision Co., Monroeville, Pa., 1981-84, Warner Cable Co. and Pitts. Telecommunications, Inc., 1984-87; mktg. mgr. The Informer newspaper Homewood Brushton Revitalization and Devel., Pitts., 1984-87; pres. local, nat. internat. pub. rels. W-W Prodns./Wanda Wilson Enterprises, Pitts., 1984; sr. clk./chemical monitor Gencorp Aerojet Tech. Systems, Rancho Cordova, Calif., 1987-90; publicist, cons. Easy Internat., Pitts., 1990; studio camera operator Sta. WPXI-TV, Pitts., 1990-92; casting dir. for commls., film, print media-theatre Wanda Wilson Enterprises, Pitts., 1992; ret., 2006. Scout Modelsearch Am.; occasional writer, copywriter, announcer local radio shows, Pitts., 1972-85; radio show co-host, announcer Internat. People's Radio and TV, Sacramento, 1987; promoter concerts, screenplays, sound tracke Wan Mar Prodns., 1991—. Author (poetry) Love Traces on My Mind, 1972, (songs lyrics) The First Time I Saw You, 1982; performer poetry recitals, Pitts., 1973, (TV movies) $10,000,000 Getaway, 1990, Bump in the Night, 1990, Dead and Alive, 1991, (feature film) Lorenzo's Oil, 1991, Roommates, 1993; producer, hostess WanMar Info. and Talent Showcase Cable TV, Pitts., 1991—; line prodr., casting dir. With Abandon, 1999; casting dir. The Family Tree, 1999, The Matador, 2000, Recollection Rags, 2000. Mem.: Nat. Women's History Mus. Democrat. Avocations: swimming, photography, art, interior decorating. Personal E-mail: wwa02@hotmail.com.

WILSON, WARREN SAMUEL, clergyman; b. New Orleans, May 15, 1927; s. Charlie Price and Warnie (Hart) W.; m. Lillie Pearl Harvey, Apr. 10, 1947; 1 child, Barbara LaJoyce. BA, So. U., Baton Rouge, 1950; DDiv, Moody Coll., Chgo., 1952; DDiv (hon.), Trinity Hall Coll. and Sem., Springfield, Ill., 1975. Ordained to ministry Ch. of God in Christ, 1952, crowned bishop, apptd. state bishop, Calif., 1970, chmn. internat. fin. and budget com. Min. St. Bernard St. Church of God in Christ, New Orleans, 1952—60, Fresno (Calif.) Temple Ch. of God in Christ, 1963—; jurisdictional biship Central Valley Ch. of God in Christ, 1970—; internat. fin. chmn. bd. of biships Ch. of God in Christ, 1974—. Served with USN, 1942-46, PTO. Mem. NAACP (life). Avocations: fishing, boating.

WILSON, WAYNE MAURICE, real estate broker, auctioneer; b. Angola, Ind., Aug. 30, 1948; s. Maurice Edward and Amy Rosinnea (Favourite) W.; m. Virginia Carol Brown, Jan. 21, 1967; children: Brent Jonathan, Julie Renee. Diploma, Superior Sch. Auctioneering, Decatur, Ind., 1966. Lic. auctioneer. Apprentice auctioneer Gorrel Bros. Auctioneers, Hicksville, Ohio, 1966-69; sales mgr. Napco Plastic, Napoleon, Ohio, 1969-73; mfr. rep. Ind. Plastics, 1973-86; sales mgr. Mohre Real Estate & Auction Svc., Edon, Ohio, 1973-78, co-owner Edon, Bryan, Ohio, 1978-91, Mohre-Wilson & Co. Auctions and Realty Unltd., Bryan, 1991—. Pres. Edgerton (Ohio) Devel. Corp., 1982—; adv. bd. Mid-Am. Nat. Bank, Edgerton, Ohio, 1980—. Chmn. adv. bd. Concerned Citizens Edgerton Schs. Mem. Nat. Auctioneers Assn., Cert. Auctioneers Inst. Ohio Auctioneers Assn., Ohio Bd. Realtors, N.W. Ohio Bd. Realtors (bd. dirs. 1987—), Moose. Home: 04522 Rd 5 Edgerton OH 43517-9802 also: Mohre-Wilson & Co 116 E William St Maumee OH 43537-3350 Office: Mohre Wilson Co 6055 County Road 7h Edon OH 43518-9402

WILSON, WENDY MARIE, elementary school educator, consultant; b. Chgo., June 21, 1967; d. Richard John and Carol Lee (Orangias) Ziert; m. Chris Allan Wilson, June 17, 1989; children: Bailey Elizabeth, Grace Amelia Townley. BS in Edn., Loyola U., Chgo., 1991; MAT, Webster U., St. Louis, 1995. Cert. tchr. pre-K - 9 Ill., tchr. pre-K - 6 NY, tchr. gifted edn. ext. grades 5-9. Dir. Champlain Mill Presch., Winooski, Vt., 1990—91; tchr. Montessori K -2 and gifted grade 4 Savannah Chatham City Pub. Schs., Ga., 1991—94; coord. gifted students K - 8 Grant Mid. and Illini Elem. Schs., Fairview Heights, Ill., 1994—95; tchr. 3d grade Lexington Sch., Ky., 1999—2000; tchr. 4th grade Chesapeake Acad., Arnold, Md., 2000—01; tchr. gifted edn. and kindergarten Arlington Pub. Schs., Va., 2001—03; tchr. 1st grade Phelps and Clifton Springs Cen. Sch. Dist., NY, 2003—04; tchr. gifted edn. K-12 and social studies 8-12 Bloomfield Cen. Sch. Dist., NY, 2004—06; tchr. gifted and talented program grades 3-5 Canandaigua Elem/ Sch., NY, 2006—. Intern mus. edn. St. Louis Sci. Ctr., 1995; edn. cons. PBS Tchr. Source, Alexandria, Va., 2001—, mem. adv. bd., 2006—; Arlington County rep. No. Va. Coun. for Gifted/Talented Edn., Arlington, 2001—02. Mem. stained glass restoration com. Dundee Presbyn. Ch., NY, 2005—06. Recipient Canandaigua Nat. Bank Tchr. Recognition award, 2006. Fellow: Wayne-Finger Lakes Leadership Inst. (scholarship 2005—); mem.: ASCD, PEO. Democrat. Avocations: cooking, historic preservation, travel, opera, reading.

WILSON, WENDY SCOTT, history educator; b. Litchfield, Ill., Jan. 21, 1946; d. John Denniston and Shirley Mansfield Wilson; m. Kenneth John Hilty, June 24, 2006; 1 child, Michaela Jane Thompson. BA, Wells Coll., Aurora, NY, 1968; M of Letters, U. Aberdeen, Scotland, 1970. Tchr. Lexington H.S., Mass., 1971—. Sr. lectr. Northeastern U., Boston, 1972—2006; presenter in field. Author: (textbook) American History on the Screen, 2d edit., 2002, World History on the Screen, 2d edit., 2003, Differentiated Instruction for Social Studies, 2006. Sr. warden Grace Episcopal Ch., Newton, Mass., 1998—2000. Recipient Julia Taylor Martin prize in History, Wells Coll., 1968. Mem.: Phi Alpha Theta (life). Episcopalian. Avocations: travel, writing, gardening, auto restoration. Office: Lexington Pub Sch 251 Waltham St Lexington MA 02421 Home Phone: 330-656-3928; Office Phone: 617-921-1902. Personal E-mail: wwhilty@yahoo.com.

WILSON, WILLIAM CAMPBELL MCFARLAND, gastroenterologist; b. Pitts., Pa., June 8, 1953; s. George Lincoln and Nancy Adair (Lytle) W.; m. Marlis Howland, June 25, 1977; children: Sarah, Stephen, Corrie. BS in Biology, Va. Tech, 1975; MD, Hahnemann U., 1979. Intern, residency R.I. Hosp., Providence, 1978-82; staff internist USAF Med. Ctr., Wright-Patterson AFB, Ohio, 1982-86; fellowship Hahnemann U., Phila., 1986-88; with Digestive Care, Dayton, Ohio, 1988—. Chmn. planning com. Dayton Gastroenterology Symposium, 1990—; com. patient edn. Miami Valley Hosp., Dayton, 1990—94, quality assurance com., 1992—, vice chmn. dept. medicine, 1994—96, chmn. dept. medicine, 1996—98, chief of staff-elect, 2002—04, bd. dirs., 2002—, chief of staff, 2004—06. Bd. dirs. Fairhaven Ch., Dayton, 1990—94, 2001—, Dayton Christian Schs., Inc., 1995—. physician, 1993—2003; bd. dirs. In His Name Ministries, 2000—02. Physician USAF, 1979—86. Fellow ACP; Mem. AMA, Am. Gastroenterological Assn., Am. Coll. Gastroenterology, Am. Soc. Gastrointestinal Endoscopy, Montgomery County Med. Assn., Alpha Omega Alpha. Avocations: tennis, woodworking, bicycling, photography, computers. Office: 75 Sylvania Dr Dayton OH 45440-3237 Office Phone: 937-320-5050. E-mail: wcmw@aol.com.

WILSON, WILLIAM HARWELL, psychiatrist, educator; b. Memphis, Feb. 6, 1951; s. Joseph Harwell Wilson and Helen Wilson (Cobb) Carruthers; m. Paula Rea, Oct. 18, 1986; children: Rea Xan, Sanford Shepherd. BA, Brown U., 1973; MD, U. Pa., 1981. Diplomate Am. Bd. Psychiatry and Neurology, Nat. Bd. Med. Examiners. Resident in psychiatry U. Wis., Madison, 1981-85; asst. prof. psychiatry U. Pitts. Sch. Medicine, 1985-86, Med. Coll. Pa., Phila., 1986-89, Oreg. Health Scis. U., Portland, 1989—93, asst. dir. pub. psychiatry tng. program, 1989—94, assoc. prof. psychiatry, 1993—2003, prof. psychiatry, 2003—. Dir. prof. edn. unit Dammasch State Hosp., Wilsonville, Oreg., 1989-94; attending psychiatrist Oreg. Health Scis. U. Hosp., 1994—; dir. Inpatient Psychiatric Svc., 2002-. Contbr. numerous articles on treatment of schizophrenia to sci. jours. Grantee NIMH, 1989-93; Recipient of Mental Health award of Excellence, State Oreg. Disting. fellow Am. Psychiat. Assn.; mem. Soc. for Biol. Psychiatry, Psychiatry, World Fedn. Mental Health, Nat. Alliance for Mentally Ill (Exemplary Psychiatrist award 1992, 98), Am. Soc. Clin. Psychopharmacology. Office: Oreg Health Scis U Mail Code UHN-80 3181 SW Sam Jackson Park Rd Portland OR 97239-3011 Office Phone: 503-494-7353. Business E-Mail: wilsonw@ohsu.edu.

WILSON, WILLIAM J., language educator; b. Oxford, Ind., Sept. 18, 1932; s. William Woodward Wilson and Esta Ella (Burton) Dilley; m. Edith Lucille McElhaney, June 1, 1955 (dec. Mar. 1969); children: Susan Wilson Siener, Maura A., Kyle A. BS summa cum laude, Ill. State U., 1959; MA, Peabody-Vanderbilt U., Nashville, 1968; EdD, Nova U., Ft. Lauderdale, Fla., 1983. Tchr. Manteno (Ill.) High Sch., 1959-60; teaching asst. U. Ill., Urbana, 1960-61; tchr. Wheaton (Ill.) Central High Sch., 1961-67; editor Laidlaw Pubs., Chgo., 1968-69; asst. prof. Ball State U., Muncie, Ind., 1969-70; assoc. prof. English Palm Beach C.C., Lake Worth, Fla., 1970—. Test reader Ednl. Testing Svc., Princeton, N.J., 1965-96; pres. Am. Lang. Rsch. Found., Lake Worth, 1976—. Editor: New Approaches to Language and Composition, 1969; author children's mus. Winter Comes to Florida, 1974, children's mus. play A Cruise on the S.S. Eternal, 1975, Arnold's Answering Apparatus, 1976. Bd. dirs. Village Green Condominiums, Palm Springs, 1985-86. With USN, 1951-55. No. Ill. U. fellow in linguistics, DeKalb, 1965—66, humanities fellow, Peabody-Vanderbilt U., Nashville, 1967. Mem. VFW, NEA, Am. Legion, Nat. Assn. Tchrs. English., Faculty Assn. Palm Beach C.C. (pres. emeritus 1999—), Kappa Delta Pi, Sigma Tau Delta. Democrat. Episcopalian. Avocations: kairos prison ministry, sports, square dancing, travel, collecting timepieces. Home: 2100 Springdale Blvd Apt 216Y Palm Springs FL 33461-6366 Office: Palm Beach C C 4200 Congress Ave Lake Worth FL 33461-6366 Office Phone: 561-967-7222. Personal E-mail: barktree@bellsouth.net. Business E-Mail: wilsonw@pbcc.edu.

WILSON, WILLIAM JAMES, healthcare executive; b. Racine, Wis., Oct. 9, 1948; s. William Henry and Eileen (Tate) W.; m. Deborah Ann Leon, Nov. 14, 1987; children: Jacob Leon, James Tate. Degree in adminstrn. of justice summa cum laude, Am. U., 1972. Asst. dir. promotions Jerry Lewis Telthon, Richmond, Va., 1975; dir. mktg. Mile High Publs., NYC, 1975-76; dir. bur. Travel Comm., Honolulu, 1976-78; founder Hawaii 800, 1979—; v.p. mktg. Video Vacations, NYC, 1982-84; founder Infovision, LA, 1984-87, Conv. TV; chmn. bd. Visitor Cable Network, Honolulu, 1978—; pres. Comcor, Honolulu, 1976—; pres. bus. devel. 3HO Superhealth Hollistic Treatment Ctr., Tucson, 1990-93; pres. Educational Discovery, 1993-94; CEO Advanced Learning Inst., 1994—; mng. dir. Vet. Inst. Integrated Medicine, 1996—98; founder, CEO Inst. Labs., 2001—. Founder Japan Am. News Network. Avocations: skiing, rugby. Home: 1109 Quince Ave Boulder CO 80304-0785 Office: PO Box 88377 Honolulu HI 96830-8377 Office Phone: 720-841-5897. Personal E-mail: jwiearnnow@aol.com.

WILSON, WILLIAM JULIUS, sociology educator; b. Derry Twp., Pa., Dec. 20, 1935; s. Esco and Pauline (Bracy) W.; m. Mildred Marie Hood, Aug. 31, 1957; children: Colleen, Lisa; m. Beverly Ann Huebner, Aug. 30, 1970; children: Carter, Paula. BA, Wilberforce U., 1958; MA, Bowling Green State U., 1961; PhD, Wash. State U., 1966; LHD (hon.), U. Mass., 1982, L.I. U., 1982, Columbia Coll., Santa Clara U., Loyola Coll., 1988, De Paul U., 1989; LLD (hon.), Marquette U., Mt. Holyoke Coll., 1989; LHD (hon.), New Sch. for Social Rsch., 1991, Bard Coll., 1992, John Jay Sch. Criminal Justice, 1992, U. Pa., 1993, So. Ill. U., 1993, Northwestern U., 1993, Bowling Green State U., 1994, SUNY, Binghamton, 1994, Princeton U., 1995, Columbia U., Rutgers U., Haverford Coll., 1996, Johns Hopkins U., Morehouse Coll., Niagara U., 1997, Dartmouth Coll., 1997, U. Amsterdam, 1998, Clarion U., 1999, Colgate U., 1999, Clark U., 1999, Bates Coll., 1999; D (hon.), Northeastern U., 1999, Macalester Coll. Ohio State U., 2001; DHL (hon.), Occidental Coll., 2001, Rensselaer Poly. Inst., 2001, Lawrence U., 2001, U Miami, 2002, others. Asst. prof. U. Mass., Amherst, 1965-69, assoc. prof., 1969-71; vis. asso. prof. U. Chgo., 1971-72, assoc. prof. dept. sociology, 1972-75, prof., 1975—, chmn. dept. sociology, 1978—, Lucy Flower prof. urban sociology, 1980-84, Lucy Flower disting. service prof., 1984—; Lucy Flower Univ. prof., 1990-96; Malcolm Wiener Prof. of social policy Harvard U., 1996-98, Lewis P. and Linda L. Geyser Univ. Prof., 1998—. Mem. bd. univ. publs. U. Chgo. Press, 1975-79; bd. dirs. Ctr. for Nat. Policy, 1987-92, Ctr. Budget and Policy Priorities, 1987—, Ctr. for Advanced Study of Behavioral Scis., 1988-2002, Twentieth Century Fund (now called Century Found., 1992—, Jerome Levy Inst., 1992-2002, Manpower Demonstration Rsch. Corp., 1993—; bd. dirs. Pub./Pvt. Ventures, Phila., 1994-2002, 02-. Author: Power, Racism and Privilege, 1973, Through Different Eyes, 1973, The Declining Significance of Race, 1978, The Truly Disadvantaged, 1987, The Ghetto Underclass, 1993, Sociology and the Public Agenda, 1993, When Work Disappears, 1996 (award Sidney Hillman Found. 1997), The Bridge Over the Racial Divide, 1999. Bd. dirs. Social Sci. Rsch. Coun., 1979-84, Chgo. Urban League, 1983-97, Spencer Found., 1987-97, George M. Pullman Found., 1986-93, Russell Sage Found., 1989-98, Nat. Humanities Ctr., 1990-95, PolicyLink, 2000-; mem. Com. on Sci., Engring. and Pub. Policy, NAS, 1995-2001; nat. bd. dirs. A. Philip Randolph Inst., 1981-, Inst. Rsch. on Poverty, 1983-87; trustee Spelman Coll., 1989-98, Bard Coll., 2001-;bd. govs. Levy Econs. Inst., 2001-; mem. Pres. Commn. on White House Fellowships, 1994-2001; mem. Pres. Com. Nat. Medal Sci., 1994-98; trustee Wilberforce U.; bd. advisors Frederick D. Patterson Rsch. Inst., 1995-, United Negro Coll. Fund, 1996—; mem. scholars' coun. Libr. of Congress, 2002-, coun. academic advisors Congl. Black Caucus Found., 2003-. With U.S. Army, 1958-60. Recipient Disting. Tchr. of Year award U. Mass., Amherst, 1970, Regents Disting. Alumnus award Wash. State U., 1988, Burton Gordon Feldman award Brandeis U., 1991, Frank E. Seidman Disting. award in polit. econ., 1994, Martin Luther King Jr. Nat. award, 1998, Nat. Medal of Sci. 1998, A. Philip Randolph/Bayard Rustin Humanitarian award, 2003; MacArthur Prize fellow, 1987. Fellow AAAS, Am. Acad. Polit. and Social Sci., Am. Acad. Arts and Scis. (Talcott Parsons Social Scis. prize, 2003); mem. NAS, Nat. Acad. Edn., Am. Philos. Soc., Inst. of Medicine, Brit. Acad., Am. Sociol. Assn. (pres. 1989-90, com. for pub. understanding of sociology award 1998, Sydney M. Spivack award 1977, DuBois, Johnson, Frazier award 1990, Lester F. Ward Disting. Contbns. to Applied Sociology award 1998), Soc. for Study Social Problems (C. Wright Mills award 1988), Sociol. Rsch. Assn. (pres. 1987-88), Consortium of Social Sci. Assn. (pres. 1993-94), Internat. Sociol. Assn., Chgo. Urban League (Beautiful People award 1979). Democrat. Home: 75 Cambridge Pkwy Unit E406 Cambridge MA 02142-1229 Office: John F Kennedy Sch Govt Harvard Univ 79 John F Kennedy St Cambridge MA 02138-5801

WILSON, WILLIAM PRESTON, psychiatrist, educator; b. Fayetteville, NC, Nov. 6, 1922; s. Preston Puckett and Rosa Mae (VanHook) W.; m. Dorothy Elizabeth Taylor, Aug. 21, 1950; children: William Preston, Benjamin V., Karen E., Tammy E., Robert E. BS, Duke U., 1943, MD, 1947. Diplomate Am. Bd. Psychiatry and Neurology (examiner). Intern Gorgas Hosp., Ancon, Panama; from resident psychiatry to prof. emeritus Duke U. Med. Ctr., Durham, NC, emeritus prof. psychiatry, 1985—; assoc. prof. psychiatry, dir. psychiat. rsch. U. Tex. Med. Br., Galveston, 1958-60; dir. Inst. Christian Growth, Burlington, NC, 1985—; dist. prof. of counseling Carolina Evang. Divinity Sch., High Point, NC, 1996—. Chief neurophysiol. labs. VA Hosp., Durham, N.C., 1961-76; sec. Am. Bd. Qualification in Electroencephalography, 1971-77; mem. N.C. Gov.'s Task force on Diagnosis and Treatment; mem. med. adv. com. N.C. Found. Mental Health Rsch.; bd. dirs. nat. divsn. Contact Teleminstry USA, also mem. internat. commn. healing; cons. numerous area hosps.; Finch lectr. Fuller Theol. Sem., Pasadena, Calif., 1974; vis. prof. psychiatry Marshall U. Sch. Medicine, Huntington, W.Va., 1985-89. Co-author: The Grace to Grow; editor: Applications of Electroencephalography in Psychiatry; co-editor: EEG and Evoked Potentials in Psychiatry and Behavioral Neurology; contbr. articles to med. jours. Mem. ofcl. bd. Asbury United Meth. Ch., Durham; mem. program and curriculum com. United Meth. Ch., 1973-81; trustee Meth. Retirement Home, Durham; pres. United Meth. Renewal Svcs., Inc., 1978-82. Served with AUS, 1943-46. Recipient Ephraim McDowell award Christian Med. Found., 1982, Pioneer in Christian Psychiatry award Congress on Christian Counseling, 1988; named Educator of Yr., Christian Med. and Dental Soc., 1996; EEG Montreal Neurol. Inst. fellow, 1954-55, postdoctoral fellow NIMH. Mem. Am. Psychiat. Assn., So. Psychiat. Assn. (pres. 1977-78), AMA, So. Med. Assn. (chmn. sect. neurology and psychiatry 1970), Med. Soc. N.C., Durham-Orange County Med. Soc. (chmn. student recruitment com. 1965), Soc. Biol. Psychiatry, Am. EEG Soc. (councillor), So. EEG Soc. (pres. 1964), Assn. Rsch. Nervous and Mental Diseases, Am. Epilepsy Soc., AAAS, Am. Acad. Neurology, Sigma Xi, Alpha Omega Alpha, U.S. Power Squadron Club (comdr. Durham 1971). Republican. Home: 1209 Virginia Ave Durham NC 27705-3263 Office: PO Box 2347 Burlington NC 27216-2347 Office Phone: 336-229-6049. Personal E-mail: williamwilson@verizon.net.

WILSON, WILLIAM R., JR., federal judge; b. 1939; Student, U. Ark., 1957-58; BA, Hendrix Coll., 1962; LLB, Vanderbilt U., 1965. Atty. Autrey & Goodson, Texarkana, Ark., 1965-66, Wright, Lindsey & Jennings, Little Rock, 1969-72, Wilson & Hodge, Little Rock, 1972-74; prin. William R. Wilson Jr., P.A., Little Rock, 1974-80, Wilson & Engstrom, Little Rock, 1980-83, Wilson, Engstrom & Vowell, Little Rock, 1984, Wilson, Engstrom, Corum & Dudley, Little Rock, 1984-93; judge U.S. Dist. Ct. (ea. dist.) Ark., Little Rock, 1993—. Chair Ark. Supreme Ct. Com. on Model Criminal Jury Instrns., 1978—; active Ark. Supreme Ct. Com. on Civil Practice, 1982—. Lt. USN, 1966-69. Named Disting. Alumnus, Hendrix Coll., 1993, Outstanding Lawyer, Pulaski County Bar Assn., 1993. Mem. ABA, ATLA, Am. Bd. Trial Advocates (Nat. Civil Justice award 1992), Am. Coll. Trial Lawyers, Internat. Acad. Trial Lawyers, Internat. Soc. Barristers, Ark. Bar Assn. (Outstanding Lawyer 1991), S.W. Ark. Bar Assn., Ark. Trial Lawyers Assn. (pres. 1982, Outstanding Trial Lawyer 1988-89), Pulaski County Bar Assn. (Outstanding Lawyer 1993). Office: US Dist Ct Ea Dist 600 W Capitol Ave Ste 423 Little Rock AR 72201-3320

WILSON, WILLIAM ROBERTS, JR., (BOB WILSON), lawyer, apparel executive; b. Rosedale, Miss., July 6, 1941; s. William Roberts Wilson Sr. and Mary Elizabeth (Boatner) W.; m. Elizabeth Ann Smith; children: William Roberts Wilson III, Elizabeth Ann, Augusta Elliott. Student, Vanderbilt U., Tenn., 1964; JD, U. Miss., 1969. Pvt. practice, Jackson, Miss.; chmn. bd., owner Dunn's Mid.-South Sporting Goods Co. Chmn. founder The Charitable Food Bank, Miss. Sportsman Against Hunger; active mem. Rep. Nat. Com. Team 100, Newcomen Soc. of U.S., Am. Intertrade Group, Presdl. Round Table, Rep. Senatorial Inner Circle. Mem. NRA (life mem.), Ala. State Bar Assn., Miss. Bar Assn., Miss. Trial Lawyers Assn. (life mem.), Assn. Trial Lawyers of Am. (sustaining mem.), Roscoe Pound Found. (fellow), Miss. State Bar Assn. (former commr.), Nat. Col. Advocacy, United Conservation Alliance (founding bd. mem.), Congressional Sportsmen Found. (bd. dirs.), Quail Unlimited (life mem., life sponsor), Miss. Wildlife Fedn. (life mem.), Ducks Unlimited (sponsoring mem.), Waterfowl, U.S.A., Delta Wildlife Found. (sponsoring founder), British Field Sport Soc. (life mem.), Catfish Point Hunting Club (gen. ptnr.), Athelstan Club, Country Club of Jackson Miss., Delta Kappa Epsilon (bd. dirs. R.O.A.R.), Delta Theta Phi. Office: PO Box 321444 Flowood MS 39232-1444

WILSON-WEBB, NANCY LOU, educational association administrator; b. Maypearl, Tex, Jan. 20, 1932; d. Madison Grady Wise and Mary Nancy Pearson-Bedford (Haney) Wilson; m. John Crawford Webb, July 29, 1972. BS magna cum laude, Abilene Christian U., Tex., 1953; EdM (hon.), Tex. Christian U., 1985. Cert. tchr., mid-mgmt., sch. adminstr., Tex. Tchr. elem. grades Ft. Worth Ind. Sch. Dist., 1953-67, adult edn. tchr., 1967-73; dir. adult edn. consortium for 38 sch. dists. Tex. Edn. Agy., 1973-2000. Pres. Nat. Commn. on Adult Basic Edn., "Most Outstanding adult ed. Admin. in US" by AAAC; 1994-95; pres. Tex. Adult Edn. Adminstrn., 1994; apptd. mem. Tex. State Literacy Coun., 1987-94, Tex. State Sch. Bd. Commn., 1994-99; exec. bd. Tex. Coun. Co-op Dir., 1989-2001, Bd. Nat. Assn. of AAACE, 1988; pres., 1994—; apptd. to Gov. Ann Richard's Task Force for Edn.; ranch owner, mgr., 1998-2003. Cons. to textbooks, 1994-98; editor textbooks, 1999. Pres. Jr. Womans Club, Ft. Worth, 1969, Fine Arts Guild, Tex. Christian U., Ft. Worth, 1970-72, Ft. Worth Womens Civic Club Coun., 1970, pres. Aquarius Women's Club; active Exec. Libr. Bd., Ft. Worth, 1990-2003, Jewel Charity Ball, 1988-2003; bd. dirs. Literacy Plus in North Tex., 1988-99, pres., 2001—; bd. dirs. Greater Ft. Worth Literacy Coun., 1976-88, 2002—, pres., 2001-03; commr. Ed-16 Task Forces Tex. Edn. Agy., 1985-94; literacy bd. dir. Friends of Libr., 1967-2002, Opera Guild Bd. Ft. Worth, 1965-85, Ft. Worth Ballet Guild, Johnson County (Tex.) Corr. Bd., 1990-2000; bd. dirs. Salvation Army, Ft. Worth, 1996-2003, Ft. Worth Libr.; active Tarrant County Bd. on Aging, 1997-98, Commn. Status of Women, Ft. Worth, 1973-99, Southside Ch. of Christ. Recipient Bevy award Jr. Womans Club, 1968, Proclamation Commr. Ct. Outstanding 43 Yr. Literacy Svc. to Tarrant County Com. Ctr., 1994, Tarrant County Woman of Yr. award, Fort Worth Star Telegram, 1995, Outstanding Leadership award Ft. Worth ISD Sch. Bd., 1985, 95, Mayor's Proclamation of Nancy Webb Week, 1996; named one of Most Outstanding Educators in U.S. Nat. Assn. Adult Edn., 1983, Most Outstanding Woman Edn., City of Ft. Worth, 1991, others; nominated to Tex. Hall of Fame for Women, 1991; named to Ft. Worth Hall of Fame, 1992; scholar Germany,

1983. Mem. NEA, DAR (Mary Isham Keith chpt. 1985-2002, Nat. Literacy award 1992, Leadership Literacy award 1985-87, 89, 94, Nat. Educators award 2003), AAUW, Am. Assn. Adult and Continuing Edn. (v.p. 1987-89, chair 1993 internat. conv. 1992, Nat. Adminstr. of Yr. in Adult Edn. 1998, Most Outstanding Adminstr. Adult Edn. in US 1999), Tex. Assn. Adult and Cont. Edn. (pres. 1985-86, Most Outstanding Adult Adminstr. in Tex. 1984), Tex. Coun. Adult Edn. Dirs. (pres. nat. com. on edn., Nat. Dept. Labor award 1992), Coun. World Affairs (bd. dir. 1980-2002), Am. Bus. Women's Assn., Ft. Worth C. of C., Lecture Found., Internat. Reading Assn. (Literacy Challenge award 1991), Ft. Worth Adminstrv. Assn., Southwest Cattle Raisers Assn., Ligon Assn., Zonta, Tanglewood Garden Club, Ft. Worth Garden Club (exec. bd. dirs. 2000-03), Woman's Club, Ft. Worth Petroleum Club, Carousel Dance Club, Met. Dinner Dance Club, Ridglea Country Club, Girls Svc. League, Aquarius (pres. 2001-02), Crescent Club (Dallas), Alpha Delta Kappa (Nat. Literacy award 1992), Greater Ft. Worth Literacy Coun. (pres. 2000-03), Phi Delta Kappa, Mary Isham Keith DAR (Nat. award 1993, Nat. Found. award 2003). Democrat. Mem. Lds Ch. Home: 3716 Fox Hollow St Fort Worth TX 76109-2616

WILSON-WHITAKER, PORTIA ELAINE, school system administrator; b. Durham, NC, June 21, 1946; d. William Jackson Wilson and Beulah Mae Frazier; m. Milton Bernard Whitaker, June 17, 1978; children: Milton Jabar Whitaker, Maurice Brown. BA, NC Ctrl. U., Durham, 1969; student, U. No. Iowa, 1973; student in English, NC Ctrl. U., 1984—87; MA, NC Ctrl. U., Durham, 1984; student, Carleton Coll., Minn., 1992; cert., NC State U., Raleigh, 1997. Cert. Covey leadership trainer Stephen Covey Orgn., 1997, facilitative leadership trainer Interaction Associates, 1998, early childhood administrn. NC Divsn. Child Devel., 1997, mentor NC Dept. Pub. Instrn., 1989. Sec. Frazier Realty Co., Durham, NC, 1963—69; tchr. French Upton County Schs., Thomaston, Ga., 1969—70; tchr. French and English Harnett County Schs., Olivia, NC, 1971—74; long distance operator Gen. Tel. Co., Durham, NC, 1971—72; tchr. French Durham Pub. Schs., 1974—94, coord. fgn. langs., ESL, student exchanges, 1994—2001; site coord. 21st century cmty. learning ctr. Duke U., Durham, 2004—06; coord. fgn. langs. Orange County Schs., Hillsborough, NC, 2005—. Dir. Little Learners Inst., Durham, NC; adj. instr. NC Ctrl. U., Durham, NC, 1984—. Author: This Joy; editor: St. Mark AME Zion Ch. Gazette, 2003—04. Missionary St. Mark A.M.E. Zion Ch., Durham, 1973—2006, chmn. new friends com., 2003—04; bd. dirs. ESL cert. com. NC, 1998—2000; bd. dirs. success by six program United Way, 1997—2001; bd. dirs. academic consortium U. NC, 1999—2001; bd. dirs. cmty. partnership Duke U., 1999—2001. Recipient Outstanding French Tchr. award, WRAL TV-5 and Am. Airlines, 1989, Salem Coll., 1990, Human Rels. Outstanding Educator award, Durham Govt., 2000; scholar, Rotary Internat., 1990. Mem.: TESOL, ASCD, NC So. Assn. Colls. and Schs. (facilitator 1998), Am. Coun. Tchg. Fgn. Langs., Am. Assn. Tchrs. French (scholar 1991), Fgn. Lang. Assn. NC, NC Assn. Educators (rep. 1974—76), U. NC Alliance (chairperson 1983—94), LA Miller Club (sec. 1974—2006). Democrat. African Methodist Episcopal Zion. Achievements include design of ESL registration center. Avocations: travel, cooking, writing. Home: 17 Warbler Ln Durham NC 27712 Office: Little Learners Inst 711 Berwyn Ave Durham NC 27704 Home Phone: 919-477-4249; Office Phone: 919-220-7093. Office Fax: 919-477-4249. Business E-Mail: jamilpo@aaahawk.com.

WILSTED, THOMAS P., archivist, director; b. Detroit, Apr. 16, 1943; s. Barbara J. and Donald E. Wilsted; m. Mary R. Brubaker, Mar. 19, 1966; 1 child, Jeffrey T. BA in History, Kalamazoo Coll., Mich., 1966; MA in Am. History, U. Wis., Madison, 1968. Cert. archivist Acad. Cert. Archivists, 1989. Field archivist Ill. State Hist. Libr., Springfield, 1968—73; manuscripts libr. Alexander Turnbull Libr., Wellington, New Zealand, 1973—78; dir. Salvation Army Archives & Rsch. Ctr., NYC, 1978—90; assoc. dir. Am. Heritage Ctr., U. Wyo., Laramie, 1990—96; dir. Thomas J. Dodd Rsch. Ctr., U. Conn., Storrs, 1996—. Author: (books) Managing Archives and Manuscripts Repositories, 1992 (Waldo Leland Gifford prize, 1992), A New Zealand Seminar, Proceedings of an Archives Seminar Held in Wellington, 21-16, 1975, 1978, Archives Conference Proceedings, 1977 Conference of the Australian Society of Archivists, 1978, Seminar for Local Historians, 1978, Reference Services in Archives, 1986, Planning New and Remodelled Archival Facilities, 2007. Pres. Rotary Club, Coventry, Conn., 1999—2000; gubernatorial appointee Conn. Hist. Records Adv. Bd., Hartford, 2000—. Recipient Arline Custer award, Mid-Atlantic Regional Archives Conf., 1992, Henryetta Berry Meml. award, Wyo. State Hist. Soc., 1994; grantee Paul Harris fellow, Rotary Internat., 1998. Mem.: Acad. Cert. Archivists, New Eng. Archivists, Soc. Rocky Mountain Archivists (pres. 1995—96), Soc. Am. Archivists (Sister M. Claude Ln. award 1990, Philip M. Hamer & Elizabeth Hamer Kegan award 1994), Archives & Records Assn. New Zealand (life; pres. 1976—78). Home: 60 Mountain Ridge Rd Coventry CT 06238 Office: Univ Conn 405 Babbidge Rd Unit 1205 Storrs Mansfield CT 06269-1205 Home Phone: 860-742-7173. Business E-Mail: tom.wilsted@uconn.edu.

WILT, JEFFREY LYNN, pulmonary and critical care physician, educator; b. Fairmont, W.Va., Nov. 15, 1963; s. Paul Lynn and Linda (Amos) W. BA, U. Mich., 1986, MD, 1988. Diplomate Am. Bd. Internal Medicine, Am. Bd. Pulmonary Diseases, Am. Bd. Critical Care Medicine, Am. Bd. Med. Examiners, Am. Bd. Nutrition Support; cert. ACLS instr. Fellow sect. pulmonary and critical care medicine W.Va. U., Morgantown, 1992-95; resident in internal medicine Blodgett-St. Mary's Hosp., Grand Rapids, Mich., 1988-91, chief med. resident in internal medicine, 1990-91; asst. dir. internal medicine residency St. Mary's Hosp., Grand Rapids, 1991-92; pvt. practice, Grand Rapids, 1995—. Asst. dir. med. ICU, Blodgett Meml. Med. Ctr., co-dir. transitional residency, 1997-98, COO internal medicine residency, 1998, program dir., 1998-99; assoc. program dir. internal medicine residency Mich. State U., Grand Rapids, 1999—, asst. prof. medicine, 1999-2003, assoc. prof., 2003—. Fellow ACP (Nat. Clin. Vignette winner 1991), Am. Coll. Chest Physicians (Young Investigators award 1993); mem. AMA, Am. Thoracic Soc., Soc. Crit. Care Medicine. Republican. Avocations: bicycling, Tae Kwon Do, magic, reading, chess. Home: 4995 Sequoia Dr SE Grand Rapids MI 49512-9622 Office: 1900 Wealthy St SE Ste 150 Grand Rapids MI 49506-2969

WILTON, ELISABETH STARR, management consultant; b. Cin., Apr. 1, 1936; d. Frank Starr Wilton Jr. and Bess Virginia (Clausen) Wilton; divorced; 1 child, Bart Wilton Jenkins. BA, Lawrence U., 1958; MEd, U. Md., 1970, PhD, 1978. Cert. clin. hypnotherapist Nat. Bd. Cert. Clin. Hypnotherapists, 2005. With U.S. Govt., Washington, 1959—98, ret., 1998; pres. Wilton Assoc., Inc., McLean, Va., 1999—. Author: Taking Charge: Conversations on Building Life Skills, 2006, (poem) Gifts of the Soul, 1999. Fulbright scholar, Germany, 1958—59. Mem.: Personality Assessment Sys. Found. (sec. 2004—). Home: 7008 Alicent Ct Mc Lean VA 22101 Office: Wilton Assoc Inc 7008 Alicent Ct Mc Lean VA 22101

WILTROUT, ROBERT H., federal agency administrator; b. Kutztown, Pa., Sept. 13, 1950; BA, Kutztown U., 1972; MS in microbiology, Pa. State U., U. Park, 1975; PhD in immunology, Wayne State U., Detroit, 1979; studied, Queens U., Kingston, Ontario, Can., 1981. Postdoctoral studies Lab. Immunodiagnosis NIH; staff fellow Biol. Response Modifiers Program Nat. Cancer Inst. - Frederick Cancer Rsch. and Devel. Ctr.; head exptl. therapeutics sect. of Lab. Expt. Immunology Nat. Cancer Inst, 1986—, dir. Ctr. for Cancer Rsch., 2005—; assoc. dir. Nat. Cancer Inst. at Frederick, 2002—. Fellow USPHS, 1979. Mem.: Soc. Biol. Therapy, Soc. Leukocyte Biology, Am. Assn. Cancer Rsch., Am. Assn. Immunology. Office: Nat Cancer Inst at Frederick Bldg 560 Rm 31-18 1050 Boyles St Frederick MD 21702-1201 E-mail: wiltrour@mail.nih.gov.

WILTSE, JAMES CLARK, civil engineer; b. Dearborn, Mich., Apr. 14, 1927; s. Cecil C. and Mary G. (Brashear) W.; m. Marlyn R. Glatus, Feb. 14, 1953; children: Richard, Mary, Michael. BSCE, U. Mich., 1953. Registered profl. engr., Mass. Civil engr. U.S. Army C.E., Detroit, 1954-67; project engr. USAF Civil Engring., London, 1968-72; civil engr. USN Facilities Engring. Command, Norfolk, Va., 1973-75; chief engr. USN Resident Office, Keflavik, Iceland, 1976-81; staff civil engr. USAF Electronic Systems Div., Kaiserslautern, Germany, 1982-91; spl. asst. ROICC Norfolk, Lantnavfac Eng Com, Norfolk, Va., 1992-93; quality assurance engr. HQ Lantnavfac, 1993-94; ret., 1994. Sgt. U.S. Army, 1946-47, Japan. Fellow ASCE (life); mem. Soc. Am. Mil. Engrs. Home: 8555 Lawson Ave Norfolk VA 23503-5220 Personal E-mail: JCWILTSE@aol.com.

WILTSE, JAMES CORNELIUS, retired electrical engineer; b. Tannersville, NY, Mar. 16, 1926; s. James Cornelius and Leah Ida Wiltse; m. Helen Citron Wiltse, June 20, 1986; m. Margaret Lucille John, Jan. 27, 1950 (div. May 15, 1986); 1 stepchild, David Citron; children: Linda Margaret, Paul James. BSEE, Rensselaer Poly. Inst., Troy, NY, 1946, MSEE, 1951; PhD, Johns Hopkins U., Balt., Md., 1959. Mgr. microwaves and antennas, 1959—63; dir. adv. tech. Electronic Comm., Inc., 1963—64; prin. rsch. scientist, lab chief Martin Marietta Corp., Orlando, Fla., 1964—68, mgr. dept. electromagnetics, 1968—72, dir. rsch. and tech., 1973—77, dir. Electronics Engring. Divsn., 1976; prin. rsch. engr. Ga. Inst. Tech., Atlanta, 1978—. Expert Dept. Electronics, New Delhi, 1993; assoc. dir. Ga. Tech Rsch. Inst., Atlanta, 1979—91. Contbr. articles to profl. jours.; editor, co-author: Millimeter Systems, 1981, Millimeter and Microwave Engineering for Communications and Radar, 1994. Lt. comdr. USNR, 1943—71. Named Author of Yr., Martin Marietta Corp, 1967, Engr. of Yr., Martin Marietta Corp., 1970, Govt. Engr. of Yr., Engrs. Greater Atlanta, 1984. Fellow: IEEE (Microwave Career award 2000), Soc. Photo-Optical Instrumentation Engrs. Independent. Achievements include research in fresnel zone plate antennas; millimeter wave engineering; electromagnetic engineering; development of terahertz technology. Home: 11138 Big Canoe; 9111 Shetland Trace Jasper GA 30143 Home Phone: 706-268-2133. Personal E-mail: james.wiltse@tds.net.

WILTZ, JAMES W., medical products executive; Sales & mgmt. positions Patterson Cos., St. Paul, 1969—80, v.p. midwest div., 1980—86, v.p. sales & dist., 1986—96, pres. dental supply unit, 1996—2003, pres., COO, 2003—05, pres., CEO, 2005—. Office: Patterson Cos 1031 Mendota Heights Rd Saint Paul MN 55120 *

WIMER, ROSS, architect; BA with distinction, Yale U., 1984; M in Architecture with commendation, Harvard U., 1988. Design ptnr. Skidmore, Owings & Merrill LLP, Chgo., 1995—. Vice chmn. Skidmore, Owings & Merrill Found.; adj. prof. Ill. Inst. Tech. Prin. works include Leamouth Peninsula, London, Infinity Tower, Dubai, Shanghai Ctr., Changi Airport Terminal 3, White Magnolia Plz., China, Tyrol Tower, Austria, Qipco West Bay Office Tower, Doha, Qatar, Qatar Sci. Ctr., Doha. Mem.: AIA. Office: Skidmore Owings & Merrill 224 S Michigan Ave Ste 1000 Chicago IL 60604 Office Phone: 312-554-9090. Office Fax: 312-360-4545. *

WIMMER, KATHRYN, retired elementary school educator; b. St. Louis, May 8, 1929; d. Arthur Jordan and Louise Clara Sykes; m. Harry William Wimmer, Aug. 4, 1951; children: Robert William, Richard Jordan. BS in Edn., U. Mo., 1951; postgrad., U. South Fla., 1971—72; PhD in Edn. (hon.), Yorker Internat. U., Milano, Italy, 2007. Cert. tchr. Mo., Fla. Tchr. Affton (Mo.) Sch., 1951—52, Heege Sch., Affton, 1965—67, Gulf Gate Sch., Sarasota, Fla., 1967—72; piano tchr. Crestwood, Mo., 1963—65. Artist, musician, tchr. music and art; tutor IQ, employment and aptitude testing. Oil paintings, watercolor paintings. V.p. Southgate Cmty., Sarasota, 1989—90; pres. bd. dirs. Assoc. Women's Club, Sarasota, 1990—91, bd. dirs., 1986—93; vol. Gulf Gate Libr., Sarasota, 1993—2007. Recipient tennis trophy, Bath and Racquet Tennis Club, Sarasota, 1979, swimming trophy, Southgate Cmty. Assn., 1987, 1988, Wall of Honor cert., Roosevelt H.S., St. Louis, 2003. Mem.: Roosevelt H.S. Alumni Assn., U. Mo. Alumni Assn., Mysterium High IQ Soc., Delta Gamma (scholarship chmn., treas., rush chmn., social chmn.). Democrat. Presbyterian. Achievements include thirteen of the tutored students who were tested successfully were sent to Pine View School for the gifted. Avocations: embroidery, literature, travel, history, genealogy, embroidery. Personal E-mail: HarryKay@peoplepc.com.

WIMMER, KURT A., lawyer; b. Mar. 21, 1959; BJ, U. Mo., 1982; MA, Syracuse U., 1985, JD magna cum laude, 1985. Bar: Kans. 1987, Tex. 1988, DC 1993. Ptnr., Internet/Info. Tech. Practice Group Covington & Burling, Washington, mng. ptnr. London office, 2000—03, ptnr., 1995—2006; sr. v.p., gen. counsel Gannett Co., McLean, Va., 2006—. Co-editor Communications Lawyer, ABA. Recipient Joseph A. Sprague Award, Nat. Press Photographers Assn., 2002. Mem.: Media Law Resources Ctr.-Defense Counsel Sect. (exec. com.), Media Inst. (chmn. Frist Amendment Com.). Office: Gannett Co 7950 Jones Branch Dr Mc Lean VA 22107-0910 Office Phone: 202-662-5278. Office Fax: 202-662-6291. Business E-Mail: kwimmer@cov.com.

WIMMER, MARKUS ANTON, biomedical engineer, educator; PhD, Tech. U. Hamburg, Germany, 1999. Rschr. Arbeitsgemeinsdraft Osteosynthesefragen Rsch. Inst., Davos, Switzerland, 1997—2001; asst. prof., sect. dir. Rush Med. Ctr., Chgo, 2001—. Office: Rush Med Ctr 1653 W Congress Pkwy Ste 1417 Chicago IL 60612 Office Phone: 312-942-2789. Business E-Mail: markus_a_wimmer@rush.edu.

WIMPFFEN, OTTO RUDOLPH, mathematics professor; b. Budapest, Hungary, June 21, 1938; arrived in U.S., 1952; s. John and Susan Wimpffen; m. Verlea Miller (div.); children: Steven, Suzanna Blanchard; m. Laurel Hetherington, Nov. 27, 1993. BS Mech. and Aerospace Engring., Ill. Inst. Tech., 1966; MBA, Loyola U., Chgo., 1972; postgrad., Chgo. State U., 1980—84. Mgr. engring. & prodn. Rep. Packaging, Chgo., 1963—68; engring. staff C. E. Niehoff & Co., Chgo., 1968—75; prof. math. Wilbur Wright Coll., Chgo., 1975—2006; ret., 2006. Bd. dirs. Am.-Spanish Inst., Chgo., 1976—80. 1st lt. N.G. US Army, 1962—63. Recipient Excellence in Tchg. award, Wilbur Wright Coll., 2004—05; Inherited European Title Count Otto Rudolph Wimpffen. Mem.: Math. Assn. Am., Chgo. Yacht Club (race com. 1993—), Little Current Yacht Club. Avocations: sailing, skiing, auto racing, travel.

WIMPFHEIMER, MICHAEL CLARK, lawyer; b. NYC, July 9, 1944; s. Henry and Ruth (Rapp) Wimpfheimer; m. Susanne Rabner, June 11, 1968; children: Jan Steven, Barry Scott, Luba Rachel. BA, Columbia U., 1964; JD, Harvard U., 1967. Bar: N.Y. 1967, U.S. Dist. Ct. (ea. and so. dists.) N.Y. 1974, U.S. Ct. Appeals (2d cir.) 1974, U.S. Ct. Mil. Appeals 1979, U.S. Claims Ct. 1992. Ptnr. Wimpfheimer & Wimpfheimer, NYC, 1970—. V.p. Union Orthodox Jewish Congregations Am., NYC, 1978—2002, sr. v.p., 2002. Comdr. JAGC USN, 1968—70, ret. Mem.: ABA, Bronx County Bar Assn., NY State Bar Assn. Jewish. Home: 2756 Arlington Ave Riverdale Bronx NY 10463-4807 Office: Wimpfheimer & Wimpfheimer 330 W 58th St Ste 209 New York NY 10019-1818 Office Phone: 212-247-8448.

WIMPRESS, GORDON DUNCAN, JR., management consultant, foundation administrator; b. Riverside, Calif., Apr. 10, 1922; s. Gordon Duncan and Maude A. (Waldo) Wimpress; m. Jean Margaret Skerry, Nov. 30, 1946; children: Wendy Jo, Victoria Jean, Gordon Duncan III. BA, U. Oreg., 1946, MA, 1951; PhD, U. Denver, 1958; LLD (hon.), Monmouth Coll., Ill., 1970; LHD (hon.), Tusculum Coll., Greenville, Tenn., 1971. Lic. comml. pilot. Dir. pub. rels., instr. journalism Whittier Coll., Calif., 1946-51; asst. to pres. Colo. Sch. Mines, Golden, 1951-59; pres. Monticello Coll., Alton, Ill., 1959-64, Monmouth Coll., Ill., 1964-70, Trinity U., San Antonio, 1970-77; vice chmn. S.W. Found. Biomed. Rsch., San Antonio, 1977-82, pres., 1982-92, also bd. govs.; pres. Duncan Wimpress & Assocs., Inc., San Antonio, 1992—. Chmn. scholarship commn. Valero Energy Corp.; bd. dirs. SW Rsch. Inst. Author: American Journalism Comes of Age, 1950. Mem. adv. bd. Alamo Area chpt. Am. Diabetes Assn.; ruling elder United Presbyn. Ch., U.S.A.; bd. dirs. ARC, Am. Heart Assn.; trustee San Antonio Med. Found. 1st lt. US Army, 1942—45, ETO. Decorated Bronze Star. Mem.: Pilots Internat. Assn., Nat. Pilots Assn., Am. Assn. Higher Edn., Am. Acad. Polit. and Social Sci., Newcomen Soc. N.Am., Assn. Former Intelligence Officers, Greater San Antonio C. of C., Mensa, North San Antonio C. of C., Confederate Air Force, Aircraft Owners and Pilots Assn., San Antonio Golf Assn., Ptz. Club, San Antonio Country Club, Argyle Club, Rotary (dist. gov. San Antonio club 1983—84), Quiet Birdmen, Sigma Upsilon, Sigma Phi Epsilon (trustee found.), Sigma Delta Pi, Sigma Delta Chi, Pi Gamma Mu. Presbyterian. Avocations: golf, skiing, flying. Home Phone: 210-492-2956; Office Phone: 210-492-8173. Personal E-mail: duncan.w@sbcglobal.net.

WINAWER, SIDNEY J., physician, educator; b. NYC; s. Nathan and Sally Winawer; children: Daniel, Jonathan, Joanna. BA, NYU, 1952; MD, SUNY, 1956; DSc (hon.), SUNY Downstate Med. Ctr., 2005. Asst. in medicine Harvard Med. Sch., Boston, 1962—66; asst. physician Harvard Med. Svc. Boston City Hosp., 1964—66; with Meml. Sloan-Kettering Cancer Ctr., NYC, 1968—, chief gastroent. and nutrition svc., 1978—98, mem. with tenure of title, 1988—, Paul Sherlock chair, 1991—; prof. medicine Cornell U. Coll. Medicine, NYC, 1980—, dir. integrative oncology program, 1997—98. Head Ctr Prevention Cancer WHO, Geneva, 1985—2000; liaison rep Nat Cancer Adv Bd, Washington, 1984—89; mem adv comt cancer prevention Am Cancer Soc, 1988—90; mem sci adv bd ICRF; consult varios rev comts Nat Cancer Inst, Washington. Editor: (book) Prevention Colorectal Cancer, 1980, Basic and Clinical Perspectives of Colorectal Polyps and Cancer, 1988, Lar Bowel Cancers: Policy, Prevention, Research and Treatment, 1991, Management of Gastrointestinal Disease, 1992, Gastrointestinal Cancer, 1992, Cancer of the Colon, Rectum and Anus, 1994, Cancer Free, 1995, Healing Lessons, 1998; contbr. chapters to books, articles to profl jours. Capt USAF, 1959—61. Recipient Clin. Achievement award, Meml. Sloan Kettering Cancer Ctr., 1997, Alumni award, 1998, SUNY Downstate Med. Ctr., 2000, Disting. Gastroenterology award, SUNY, 2003, Constantine Medal, Italian Govt., 2002, Internat. Laurel award, Cancer Rsch. and Prevention Found., 2004, others; grantee Nat. Cancer Inst., 1974, 1977, 1980, 1985, 1988, 1990, 1993, 1999, 2003. Master: Am. Coll. Gastroenterology (pres. 1979—80, Baker Presdl. lectr. 1992, Disting. Sci. Achievement award 1982, Clin. Achievement award 1997); fellow: ACP; mem.: Internat. Digestive Cancer Alliance (co-chair), NY Soc Gastrointestinal Endoscopy (founder, pres. 1978—79, ann. lectr. 1985, Florence Lefcourt disting. svc. award 2006, Florence Lefcourt State of the Art award 2006), Am. Assn. Cancer Rsch., Am. Soc. Clin. Oncology (Am. Cancer Soc. award 2001), Am. Gastroenterol. Assn. (nat. chmn. cancer sect. 1989—91, U.S. multisoc. colorectal cancer task force, Joseph B. Kirsner award 1999), Am. Soc. Gastrointestinal Endoscopy (bd. dirs. 1974—78, disting. lectr. 1985, co-chair guidelines com. 1997—, Schindler award 1994). Jewish. Avocations: opera, cross country skiing, dance, swimming, bicycling. Office: Meml Sloan-Kettering Cancer Ctr 1275 York Ave New York NY 10021-6094 Home Phone: 212-831-1267; Office Phone: 212-639-7678. Business E-Mail: winawers@mskcc.org.

WINBLAD, ANN, investment company executive; BA in Math. and Bus. Adminstrn., U. St. Thomas, St. Paul, Minn., MA in Internat. Econs. and Edn.; LLD (hon.), U. St. Thomas. Systems programmer Fed. Reserve Bank; co-founder Open Systems, Inc., 1976-83; strategic planning cons., IBM, Microsoft, Price Waterhouse, and many start-ups; co-founding ptnr. Hummer Winblad Venture Ptnrs., San Francisco, 1989—. Bd. dirs. Dean & Deluca, Intacct, Market Wire, The Knot, Voltage Security, Arbor Software, Berkeley Systems, Net Perceptions; advisor The Software Forum, San Jose Ctr. for Software Develop., Stanford/MIT Venture Forum. Co-author: Object-Oriented Software, 1990; contbr. articles to profl. publs. Trustee U. St. Thomas, St. Paul, Mich. Office: Hummer Winblad Venture Partners 1 Lombard St Ste 300 San Francisco CA 94111-1130

WINBUSH, OLGA JOYCE, education educator, consultant; d. Harbart Theodore and Claudia Madeleine Tatum; m. Albert Steve Winbush, Oct. 19, 1976; children: LaKetta Denise, Albert Steve, Ari Solomon, Meko Meyatta. BA in Sociology, UCLA, 1976, PhD in Edn., 1999; MA in Human Devel., Pacific Oaks Coll., 1980. Multiple subject clear tchg. credential Commn. on Tchg. Credentialing, Calif., 1992. Tchg. asst. Westland Sch., LA, 1982—83; tchr. Children's Cmty. Sch., Van Nuys, Calif., 1983—93; adj. faculty Antelope Valley Coll., Lancaster, Calif., 1993—98; core faculty, prof. Pacific Oaks Coll., Pasadena, Calif., 1998—. Adj. faculty Chapman U., Lancaster, 1994—98; curriculum cons. Children's Cmty. Sch., Van Nuys, 1996—2003; literacy curriculum cons. First 5/Pacific Oaks Coll., Pasadena, 2003—; literacy cons. Bridging Resources in Tech. and Edn. Afterschool Program, Pasadena, 2003—, CORAL, Pasadena, 2004—05; presenter in field. Editor: (jour.) Pathways, 1992—96; contbr. articles to profl. jours. Mem. Found. for Excellence, Van Nuys, 1985—. Recipient Unsung Hero award, Bridging Resources in Tech. and Edn. Afterschool Prgram, 2004; grantee, First 5 Early Literacy Tng., 2003. Mem.: ND Study Group on Evaluation, Rschrs. of Color, Nat. Black Child Devel. Inst., Jack and Jill Am. (assoc.). Democrat. Avocations: travel, reading, photography. Office: Pacific Oaks College 5 Westmoreland Pl Pasadena CA 91103-3592 Home Phone: 661-946-3915. Business E-Mail: owinbush@pacificoaks.edu.

WINCHELL, MICHAEL GEORGE, lawyer; b. Ardmore, Okla., Oct. 30, 1949; s. George Stockwell and Willis Marion (Woolery) W.; m. Donna Jean Winchell; children: Merriddith Elaine, Candace Michelle, Rachel Elizabeth, Marian Gayle. BBA, Ctrl. State U., Wilberforce, Ohio, 1974; JD, U. Okla., Norman, 1976. Bar: Okla. 1977. Assoc. Sokolsky & Becker, Oklahoma City, 1977; asst. regional counsel GSA, Ft. Worth, 1977-87; adminstrv. judge EEOC Commn., Dallas, 1987-88; counsel S.E. bases USMC, 1988-89; chief counsel John F. Kennedy Space Ctr., 1993-97, Johnson Space Ctr., 1997—2004; ret. Lectr. law U. Okla., 2004—07, asst. prof. dir. legal writing, 2007—. Pres. GSA employee's assn., 1982-84; chief KSC Inter-Tribal Coun., 1993-97. Named Meritorious Exec. of the Federal Sr. Exec. Svc., Pres. Clinton, 2000; recipient Meritorious Civilan Svc. medal, USN, 1993, Exceptional Svc. medal, NASA, 2001. Mem. Fed. Bus. Assn. (pres. 1984-85), FBA (pres. Ft. Worth chpt. 1981-82, bd. dirs. younger lawyers' div. 1981-85, 2d v.p. 5th cir. 1982-83, v.p. 1983-84, sec. cir. officers 1983-84, dep. chmn. cir. officers 1984-85, chmn. rules com. 1985-86), Southeastern Cherokee Confederacy (chief Eagle Clan 1992-93). Office: 700 North 60th Noble OK 73068 Office Phone: 405-325-5919.

WINCHESTER, JAMES R., state supreme court justice; b. Clinton, Okla. m. Susan Winchester; 1 child, Davis. BA, U. Okla.; JD, Okla. City U. Pvt. practice, Weatherford, Okla., Hinton, Okla.; assoc. dist. judge Caddo County, Okla., 1983; dist. judge 6th Jud. Dist. Okla., 1983—97; U.S. adminstrv. law judge, 1997—2000; justice Okla. Supreme Ct., 2000—, vice chief justice, chief justice, 2007—. Mem. exec. bd. Okla. Jud. Conference, pres., 1992-96. Recipient Outstanding State Trial Ct. Judge, Okla. Trial Lawyers Assn., 1986. Office: Oklahoma Supreme Ct Admin Office 1915 N Stiles Ste 305 Oklahoma City OK 73104-2861

WINCHESTER, JESSE GREGORY, finance company executive; b. Charlotte, NC, Mar. 2, 1957; s. Dewey Reece and Ruby Lee (Aldridge) W.; m. Jan Partain, May 14, 1983; children: Dustin, Mary-Elsye, Caleb, Sarah-Anne, Asa, Rebecca-Joy BSBA, U. N.C., 1979; founds. diploma, Am. Inst. Banking, 1979; advanced mgmt. program, Fuqua Sch. Bus., Duke U. Asst. v.p. 1st Nat. Bank Atlanta, 1979—83; exec. v.p. Lomas Mgmt. Inc., Dallas, 1983—96; mng. dir., owner TriMont Real Estate Advisors, Atlanta, 1996—; pres., owner Wineight, LLC. Campaign vol. United Way, Atlanta, 1982—83; participant Opportunity Dallas, 1985, Habitat for Humanity, Dallas and Atlanta, People Helping People, Dallas; leader Awana; cub scout leader Boy Scouts Am., chmn. com., 2007; scoutmaster Nat. Eagle Scout Assn., chmn. scout com.; coach Hopewell Youth Assn., 2003—04, Upward Basketball, 2005—07; mem. Coppell Rep. Club, 1986; deacon Little River Ch., 2002—04; active First Bapt. Ch. of Alpharetta, Ga. Named Hon. Citizen Charlotte, N.C Mem.: Mortgage Bankers Assn., Nat. Assn. Real Estate Investment Mgrs., Comml. Mortgage Securities Assn., Internat. Coun. Shopping Ctrs., Order Arrow, BBL Forum, Appalachia Trail Soc., Forsyth Christian Home Educators (adv. bd. dirs. 1999—2006), Nature Conservancy, Buckhead Club, Haig Pt. Club, U. NC Alumni Assn., Am. Hiking Club, Ga. Tech. Club, Alpha Phi Omega, Beta Gamma Sigma. Avocations: skiing, backpacking, white-water rafting, golf, hiking. Home: Meadowbrook Farm 16035 Westbrook Rd Alpharetta GA 30004-2887 Office: TriMont Real Estate Advisors 3424 Peachtree Rd NE Atlanta GA 30326

WINCHESTER, RICHARD LEE, JR., lawyer; b. Memphis, May 21, 1924; s. Cassius Lee and Harriet Haywood (Bond) Winchester; m. Bette Anne Thompson, July 15, 1944; children: Robin Ann, Richard Lee Jr., John Thompson. LLB, U. Tenn., 1949, JD, 1965. Bar: Tenn. 1949. Sr. ptnr. Winchester Law Firm, Memphis, 1972—; atty. Shelby County, 1961—64; city atty. City of Arlington, Tenn., 1966—. Gen. counsel, bd. chmn. Cmty. Bancshares, Inc.; sec. Beachfront Condos, Inc., N. Fla. Chmn. Germantown Planning Commn., 1958—61; pres., bd. dirs. Mid-South Fair Assn.; bd. dirs. ARC; mem. Gov.'s Commn. on Human Relations, 1962—68; vice chmn., treas. Memphis and Shelby County Dem. Exec. Com., 1958—72; state exec. com., pres. Tenn. Young Dems., 1960—61; del. state and nat. Dem. convs., 1964—68; nat. elector from Tenn., 1960—72; pres. Episc. Planning Commn.; trustee U. Tenn., 1975—84, Episc. Girls Home, Bowld Hosp. Capt. inf. US Army, 1942—46, PTO. Fellow: Tenn. Bar Found. (past pres. jr. sect.); mem.: Omicron Delta Kappa, Phi Kappa Phi, Nat. Assn. Legal Aid and Pub. Defenders, Am. Judicature Soc., Shelby County Bar Assn. (past pres. jr. sect.), Memphis Bar Assn. (past pres.), Tenn. Bar Assn., ABA (past del.), U. Tenn. Alumni Assn. (past bd. govs., 9th dist. rep.), Am. Legion (past post comdr., past state vice comdr.), Kiwanis, Tennessee, 40 and 8, Jesters, VFW (past post vice comdr.), Masons, Shriners, Phi Eta Sigma, Sigma Alpha Epsilon. Episcopalian. Office: Winchester Law Firm 6060 Poplar Ave Ste 38119 Memphis TN 38119 Office Phone: 901-685-9222.

WINCKLER, ALICIA JEAN, human resources director; b. Yankton, SD, Aug. 16, 1972; d. Myron Mark and Barbara Jean Winckler; 1 child, Lucas Hansen. BS in Psychology and Alcohol and Drug Abuse Studies, U. SD, 1994; MA in Indsl. Orgnl. Psychology, U. Colo., Denver, 1997. Project mgr. HR Avantis, Denver, 1996—98; compensation analyst Watson Wyatt Worldwide, Denver, 1997; assessment sys. cons. Sears, Roebuck & Co., Chgo., 1998—2000, mgr. testing and selection, 2000—01, mgr. orgnl. effectiveness, 2001—03, mgr. human resources, 2003—05; south ctrl. region human resource dir. Sears Holdings Corp., Chgo., 2005—06, western region human resources dir., 2006—07, human resources dir. market transformation team, 2007; group dir. orgn. effectiveness Coca Cola Enterprises, 2007—. Adj. faculty mem. Chgo. Sch. Profl. Psychology, 2004. Mem.: APA (assoc.), Kappa Alpha Theta, Omicron Delta Kappa. Democrat. Roman Catholic. Avocations: music, travel. Home: 2020 W Pierce Ave Apt 4 Chicago IL 60622 Office: Coca Cola Enterprises 2500 Windy Trail Pky Office 80062 Atlanta GA 31139 Office Phone: 770-989-3038. Personal E-mail: aliciawinckler@msn.com.

WINCOR, MICHAEL Z., psychopharmacology educator, clinician, researcher, director; b. Chgo., Feb. 9, 1946; s. Emanuel and Rose (Kershner) W.; m. Emily E.M. Smythe; children: Meghan Heather, Katherine Rose. SB in Zoology, U. Chgo., 1966; PharmD, U. So. Calif., 1978. Rsch. project specialist U. Chgo. Sleep Lab., 1968-75; psychiat. pharmacist Brotman Med. Ctr., Culver City, Calif., 1979-83; asst. prof. U. So. Calif., LA, 1983-97, assoc. prof., 1997—, interim chair dept. pharmacy, 2001—02, assoc. dean external programs, 2003—06, dir. continuing pharmacy edn. and internat. programs, 2006—. Cons. Fed. Bur. Prisons Drug Abuse Program, Terminal Island, Calif., 1978—81, Nat. Inst. Drug Abuse, Bethesda, Md., 1981, The Upjohn Co., Kalamazoo, 1982—87, 1991—92, Area XXIV Profl. Stds. Rev. Orgn., LA, 1983, Brotman Med. Ctr., Culver City, Calif., 1983—88, SmithKline Beecham Pharms., Phila., 1990—93, Tokyo Coll. of Pharmacy, 1991, G.D. Searle & Co., Chgo., 1992—97, 1999—2001, Pfizer, NY, 1998—2004, Wyeth-Ayerst, Phila., 1999—2001, Novartis, East Hanover, NJ, 2002—04, AstraZeneca, Wilmington, Del., 2003—04, Nat. Assn. Bd. Pharmacy Continuing Profl. Devel. Com., 2003—04, Sanofi-Aventis, 2004—, Takeda Pharms. N.Am., Inc., 2005—. Contbr. more than 75 articles to profl. jours., chpts. to books, papers presented at nat. and internat. meetings and reviewer. Mem. adv. coun. Franklin Avenue Sch., 1986-89; bd. dirs. K.I. Children's Ctr., 1988-89; trustee Sequoyah Sch., 1992-93; mem. tech. com. Ivanhoe Sch., 1993-96; U. So. Calif. Amb., 2000—. Faculty scholar U. So. Calif. Sch. Pharmacy, 1978; recipient Cert. Appreciation Mayor of LA, 1981, Bristol Labs award, 1978, DuPont Pharma Innovative Pharmacy Practice award, 1995, Pharmacy Coun. Mental Health award, 1996, Outstanding Chpt. Advisor award Am. Pharm. Assn.-Acad. Students of Pharmacy, 2003. Mem. Am. Coll. Clin. Pharmacy (chmn. constn. and bylaws com. 1983-84, mem. credentials com. 1991-93, 95-97, ednl. affairs com. 1994, constn. and bylaws com. 1999-00), Am. Assn. Colls. Pharmacy (focus group on liberalization profl. curriculum 1990-92, mem. pharmacy practice planning commn. 1996-97, chmn. pharmacy practice awards com. 1998-00, mem. bylaws and policy devel. com. 2001-03, mem. computer tech. in edn. task force 2001-02, chmn. coun. of faculties strategic planning and resolutions com. 2001-03, mem. continuing pharmacy edn. ACPE liaison com., 2004-06), Am. Soc. Health-Sys. Pharmacists (chmn. edn. and tng. adv. working group 1985-88, chmn. com. on academia 1996-97), Am. Pharm. Assn. (del. ann. meeting ho. of dels. 1989, 1998), Sleep Rsch. Soc., Nat. Sleep Found., Am. Acad. Sleep Medicine, Calif. Pharmacists Assn. (trustee 1997-01, chmn. editl. rev. com. 1998-03), Hollywood-Wilshire Pharmacists Assn. (pres. 2006—), U. So. Calif. Sch. Pharmacy Alumni Assn. (bd. dirs. 1979—, pres. 1998—), Coll. Psychiat. Neurol. Pharmacists (chmn. recertification com. 2003-06, chmn. program com. 2006-07, Judith J. Saklad Meml. Lecture award 2007), Rho Chi (Alumni award 2007), Phi Lambda Sigma. Avocation: photography. Office: 1985 Zonal Ave Los Angeles CA 90089-9121

WINDELS, PAUL, JR., lawyer; b. Bklyn., Nov. 13, 1921; s. Paul and Louise E. (Gross) W.; m. Patricia Ripley, Sept. 10, 1955 (dec. 1995); children: Paul III, Mary H., James H.R., Patrick D. AB, Princeton U., NJ, 1943; LLB, Harvard U., Cambridge, Mass., 1948. Bar: NY 1949. Spl. asst. counsel NY State Crime Commn., 1951; asst. U.S. atty. Ea. Dist. NY, 1953—56; NY regional adminstr. SEC, 1956—61, also spl. asst, U.S. atty. for prosecution securities frauds, 1956-58; lectr. law Am. Inst. Banking, 1950-57; mem. Windels, Marx, Lane & Mittendorf and predecessor firms, 1961—98, of counsel, 1998—. Author: Our Securities Markets-Some SEC Problems and Techniques, 1962. Trustee Bklyn. Law Sch.; trustee Lexington Sch. for the Deaf, Gerta Charitable Trust; past pres. Fed. Bar Coun. Capt. F.A., AUS, 1943-46, ETO; maj. USAR, ret. Recipient Flemming award for fed. svc.; decorated chevalier Order French Acad. Palms; officer Nat. Order Merit France. Fellow Am. Bar Found.; mem. ABA, NY State Bar Assn., Assn. of Bar of City of NY Republican. Presbyterian. Office: Windels Marx Lane & Mittendorf 156 W 56th St Fl 23 New York NY 10019-3867 Office Phone: 212-237-1210.

WINDER, ALVIN ELIOT, public health educator, clinical psychologist; b. NYC, Feb. 17, 1923; s. Martin Winder and Frances (Erdrick) Isaacson; m. Barbara Ina Dietz, July 19, 1949; children: Mark, Joshua, Sarah, Susan; m. Doris M. Raphael, Aug. 18, 2001. BA, CUNY, 1947; MS, U. Ill., 1948; PhD, U. Chgo., 1952; MPH, U. Calif., Berkeley, 1980. Lic. clin. psychologist, Mass. Chief psychologist VA Hosp., Downey, Ill., 1953-56; rsch. asst., asst. prof. Clark U., Worcester, Mass., 1956-58; chief psychologist VA Clinic, Springfield, Mass., 1958-61; assoc. prof. psychology Springfield Coll., 1961-63; chmn. psychology dept. Westfield (Mass.) State Coll., 1963-65; assoc. prof. counseling edn. Sch. Edn., U. Mass., Amherst, 1965-69, prof., dir. grad. program div. nursing, 1969-78, prof. Sch. Pub. Health, 1978-93; dir. planning, cons. Springfield (Mass.) Pub. Health Dept., 1993-95. Adj. prof. Sch. Pub. Health, Boston U., 1995—; assoc. to exec. sec. Asian Pacific Assn. for Control of Tobacco, 1988—; cons. Mass. Dept. Pub. Health, 1998—. Author: Introduction to Health Education, 1984, Solid Waste Education Recycling Directory, 1989; editor: Adolescence Contemporary Studies, 1974; guest editor Jour. Applied Behavior, 1970; co-editor: Internat. Quar. of Cmty. Health Edn., 1992-96. Sr. selectman Town of Leverett, Mass., 1988-90; Lilly Found. mentor U. Mass., 1989. Grantee U.S. Childrens Bur., 1966, 67, Dexter Found., 1969, NIMH, 1974, Mass. Cancer Soc., 1997, Nat. Cancer Inst., 1986-91. Mem. APHA, APA, Mass. Assn. Older Ams. (v.p. 2002). Avocation: tennis. Home and Office: 70 Seminary Ave Newton MA 02466 Office Phone: 617-969-1482. Personal E-mail: march1931@aol.com.

WINDER, BAYLY PHILIP, bank executive; b. Princeton, NJ, May 19, 1951; s. Richard Bayly and Viola (Hitti) W.; m. Diane Baird Hallock, Oct. 31, 1987; children: Julia Alexandra Rayhill, Bayly Philip Christopher. BA, Haverford Coll., 1973; MS in Fgn. Svc., Georgetown U., 1977. Economist Fed. Reserve Bank of N.Y., NYC, 1974-78; adminstrv. officer Brown Bros. Harriman & Co., NYC, 1978-81; mng. dir. East West Group Ltd., Riyadh, Saudi Arabia, 1981-85; v.p. Nat. Comml. Bank, NYC, 1985-87; dir. Bankers Trust Investment Mgmt., London, 1987—93; head global mktg., sales Credit Suisse Asset Mgmt., 1993—95; dir. head of Middle East Schroders Investment Mgmt., 1995—2002; founder, CEO Polygon Investment Mgmt., 2002—. Contbr. Political Risk in Saudi Arabia, 1979, Arabia After the Oil Boom, 1986; contbr. articles to profl. jours; num TV Appearances. Bd. trustees Am. U. Beirut, Haverford Coll. Internat. Adv. Coun., Renaissance Inst., Le Cercle, Soc. Illustrators. Mem. Union League Club. Avocations: sailing, tennis, skiing. Office: Polygon Investment Mgmt 68 Westerly Rd Princeton NJ 08540 Office Phone: 609-921-2445. Business E-Mail: bpw@polygonim.com.

WINDER, CLARENCE LELAND, psychologist, educator; b. Osborne County, Kans., June 16, 1921; s. Clarence McKinley and Edna (Ikenberry) W.; m. Elizabeth Jane Jacobs, Aug. 14, 1943; children: David William, Christina Louise. Student, Santa Barbara State Coll., 1941; AB with honors, U. Calif. at Los Angeles, 1943; MA, Stanford U., 1946, PhD, 1949. From instr. to assoc. prof. Stanford U., 1949-61; dir. Psychol. Clinic, 1953-61; prof., dir. Psychol. Clinic, Mich. State U., 1961-62, prof. psychology, 1961-91, prof. emeritus, 1991—, chmn. dept., 1963-67; dean Coll. Social Sci. Mich. State U., 1967-74, assoc. provost, 1974-77, provost, 1977-86, provost emeritus, 1991—; prof., dir. Psychol. Svcs. Ctr., U. So. Calif., 1962-63. 1st lt. USAAF, 1943-45. Decorated Air medal with 7 clusters, D.F.C. Fellow APA, AAAS; mem. Sigma Xi. Achievements include research in psychol. aspects schizophrenia, parent-child rels., personality devel., and higher edn. adminstrn. Home: 1776 Hitching Post Rd East Lansing MI 48823-2144

WINDER, RICHARD EARNEST, legal foundation administrator, writer, consultant; b. Vernal, Utah, Sept. 23, 1950; s. William Wallace and Winnifred (Jenkins) W.; m. Janice Fay Walker, Apr. 19, 1975; children: Scott Christian, Eric John, Brian Geoffrey, Laura Jeanne, Amy Elizabeth. BA magna cum laude, Brigham Young U., 1974, JD cum laude, 1978; MBA with honors, U. Mich., Flint, 1988. Lic. life ins. agt. Mich.; bar: Utah 1978, U.S. Dist. Ct. Utah 1978, Mich. 1979, U.S. Dist. Ct. (ea. and we. dists.) Mich. 1979; lic. securities rep. series 6 and 63 NASD, Mich., first mortgage lic. Mich. Tchg. asst., grad. instr. Brigham Young U., Provo, Utah, 1976—78; law clk. Willingham & Coté, East Lansing, Mich., 1978—79, atty., 1979—87; exec. v.p. Mgmt. Leasing, Inc., Battle Creek, Mich., 1987—88, Mgmt. Options, Inc., Lansing, Mich., 1988—91; fin. mgr. Mich. State Bar Found., Lansing, 1991—94, dep. dir., fin. mgr., 1994—; co-founder, prin. Resilience, Inc., 2003—04. Panelist 9th Nat. Legis. Conf. Small Bus., San Antonio, 1987; adj. prof. Davenport Coll. Bus., Lansing, 1990-92, mgmt. adv. com., 1993-96; mem. founding steering com. Capital Quality Initiative, Lansing, 1992-96; liaison State Bar Mich. Long Range Planning Process, 1996-97; co-founder, rsch. prin. Quality Dynamics Rsch. Inst., Haslett, Mich., 1994-97; pres., rsch. prin. Leadership Dynamics Rsch. Inst., Haslett, 1998—; sr. rep. Primerica Fin. Svcs., 2001—; vol. instr. LDS Inst., East Lansing, Mich., 2004—; mem. Legal Svcs. Corp. Tech. Adv. Group, 2007. Author: (with others) Value Sharing: Value Building, 1990, Corporate Orienteering, 1995; contbr., bd. editors: Summary of Utah Real Property Law, 1978. Vol. leader Boy Scouts Am., Chief Okemos Coun., Lansing, 1978—. Fellow Mich. State Bar Found. (life); sr. mem. Am. Soc. Quality (chmn. Lansing-Jackson sect. 1994-95, spkr. and writer); mem. ABA, Mich. Bar Assn., Utah Bar Assn., Lansing Regional C. of C. (small bus. coun., MBA task force Bus. and Edn. com. 1988-92, recipient Chmn.'s award 1992), Beta Gamma Sigma. Republican. Mem. Lds Ch. Avocations: writing, speaking, computer technology, research, teaching. Office: Mich State Bar Found 306 Townsend St Lansing MI 48933-2012 Office Phone: 517-346-6402. Personal E-mail: rwinder@ldri.com. Business E-Mail: rwinder@msbf.org.

WINDER, ROBERT OWEN, mathematician, computer engineer, geophysicist; b. Boston, Oct. 9, 1934; s. Claude V. and Harriet O. W.; m. Kathleen C. Winder; children by previous marriage: Katherine, Amy. AB, U. Chgo., 1954; BS, U. Mich., 1956; MS, Princeton U., 1958, PhD, 1962; MS, Ariz. State U., 2000. With RCA, 1957-78, group head Princeton and Somerville, NJ, 1969-75, dir. microprocessors, 1975-77, dir. systems, 1977-78; mgr. workstation devel. Exxon Enterprises, Inc., Princeton, 1978-85; v.p. Syntex Computer Systems Inc., Bordentown, NJ, 1985-88; mgr. product engring., Princeton Operation, Intel Corp., 1988-93; mgr. engring. ops. video products div., Intel, Chandler, Ariz., 1993-95. Vis. scholar dept. geol. scis. Ariz. State U., Tempe, 2001—06. Contbr. articles to profl. jours.; patentee in field. NSF fellow, 1956-57; Recipient David Sarnoff award RCA, 1975. Fellow IEEE.

WINDHAGER, ERICH ERNST, physiologist, educator; b. Vienna, Nov. 4, 1928; came to U.S., 1954; s. Maximilian and Bertha (Feitzinger) W.; m. Helga A. Rapant, June 18, 1956; children: Evelyn Ann, Karen Alice. MD, U. Vienna, 1954. Rsch. fellow in biophysics Harvard Med. Sch., Boston, 1956—58; instr. in physiology Cornell U. Med. Coll., NYC, 1958—61; vis. scientist U. Copenhagen, 1961—63; asst. to prof. physiology Cornell U. Med. Coll., NYC, 1963—, Maxwell M. Upson prof. physiology and biophysics, 1978—2002, chmn. dept. physiology, 1973—2002, acting chmn. dept. cell biology, 1998—2002. Recipient Homer W. Smith award N.Y. Heart Assn., 1978, Berliner-Abbott award Am. Physiol. Soc., 1999. Office: Weill Med Coll Cornell U Dept Physiology 1300 York Ave New York NY 10021-4805 Home Phone: 201-567-8688; Office Phone: 212-746-6386. E-mail: ewindhag@med.cornell.edu.

WINDHAM, DONALD ERIC, bioinformatics analyst; b. Florence, SC, June 27, 1974; s. Donald Eugene Windham and Deborah Ann Robinson. BS in Zoology, NC State U., Raleigh, 1998, BS in Microbiology and Biology, 2002. Publs. staff NC State U. Computing Svcs., Raleigh, 1996—99; delivery lead IBM, Research Triangle Park, NC, 1999—2000, IT architecture specialist, 2000—02; bioinformatics specialist, sys. adminstr. NC State U. Fungal Genomics Lab., Raleigh, 2003—05; bioinformatics analyst NC State U. Ctr. Biology Nematode Parasitism, 2005—. Recipient One Team award, IBM, 2001. Mem.: Bioinformatics Orgn., Inc., Am. Soc. Microbiology. Office: NC State U Campus Box 7253 Raleigh NC 27603 Home Phone: 919-832-2125.

WINDHAM, JOHN FRANKLIN, lawyer, educator; b. Fayette, Ala., Jan. 21, 1948; s. Grover B. Windham Jr. and Nancy Katherine (McAdams) Haynie; 1 child, John Franklin Jr.; m. Denise Roche McNair, Apr. 6, 1999; 1 stepchild, Brittany Danielle McNair. BA, U. West Fla., 1970; JD, U. N.C., 1975. Bar: Fla. 1975, U.S. Dist. Ct. (no. dist.) Fla. 1976, U.S. Ct. Appeals (11th cir.) 1983, U.S. Supreme Ct. 1984. Acctg. supr. Monsanto Co., Research Triangle Park, N.C., 1970-72; law clk. to U.S. Atty Pensacola, Fla., 1974; assoc. Beggs & Lane, Pensacola, 1975-79, ptnr., 1979—. Adj. asst. prof. bus. law Troy State U., Pensacola, 1983-90. Mem. bd. dirs. Am. Cancer Soc., 1980-06, exec. com. Fla. divsn., 1982-93, 95-2000, chmn. legacies and planned giving, 1984-88, chmn. income devel., 1980-91, chmn. ad hoc adv. com., 1991—, mem. risk adv. subcom., 1991-97, chmn. 1996-97, legal advisor, 1992—, vol. and staff devel. com., 1994-95, planning com., 1994-98, spokesperson tobacco media, 1995-96, mem. cause mktg. work group, 1995-96, mem. scholarship com., 1995-98, chmn. dist. VII steering com., 1995-96, v.p, 1996-97, mem. Winn Dixie adv. com., 1996-99, field ops. com. 1995-98, chmn. field ops. com., 1996-98, mem. task force volunteerism, 1996-97, call ctr. work group, 1996-98, mktg. and comms. com., 1997-2000, divsn. chartering com., 1997-98, chmn.-elect bd. 1997-98, chmn. bd. 1998-99, personnel subcom., 1998-99, patient svc. ctr. work group, 1998-99, audit com., 1999-00, nominating com., 1999-2006, evaluation adv. com., 2001-03, 05—, bylaws com. chmn., 1990-96, triple 5 ad hoc com., 1995-95, cancer control com., 1994-96, stewardship com., 1996-02; mem. Nat. Assembly, 2002-2006, mem. budget and fin. com., nom. ad hoc com., bd. governance task force, 1990—, chmn. bylaws com., 2002—, stewardship com., 2006—; chmn. bd. Escambia Christian Sch., Pensacola, 1976-86; deacon Ch. of Christ, 1985-95, 99-02; adminstrv. team First City Ch., 2002-04, mem. adv. bd.; elder First City Ch., 2004—; mem. adv. bd. Interim Healthcare, 1993-96, Panhandle Rehab. Injury Mgmt. and Evaluation, 1993-96; mem. found. bd. East Hill Christian Sch., 1995-97; bd. govs. Pensacola chpt. Order Granaderos e Dames de Galvez, 1990-98, pres. 1995-98; mem. U. West Fla. Found., 1983-85. Mem. Fla. Bar (workers compensation rules com. 1995-01, drafting subcom. 2000-01), Fla. Def. Lawyers Assn., Fla. Workers Compensation Inst., Southeastern Admiralty Law Inst. (bd. dirs. 1986-89), Northwest Fla. Blood Ctr. Found. (treas. 2002-), N.W. Fla. Blood Ctr. (bd. dirs. 2006—), U. West Fla. Nat. Alumni Assn. (bd. dirs.), Kiwanis (pres. Pensacola 1978-79, 88-89). Republican. Avocation: church activities. Office: Beggs & Lane PO Box 12950 Pensacola FL 32591-2950

WINDHAM, REVISH, poet; b. Panola, Ala., May 31, 1940; s. Ike, Sr. and Lillie (Queen) Windham; m. Janice L. Bowman, Sept. 22, 1985; 1 child, Veronice Wiggins-Windham. BA, Morris Brown Coll., 1962; MPA, NYU, 1989. Cert. mediator N.Y. Case worker N.Y.C. Dept. Social Svcs., 1968—70; youth counselor, group and family counselor, job developer N.Y. State Divsn. Youth, NYC, 1970—90; investigator, unit supr. N.Y. State Divsn. Human Rights, NYC, 1990—99; writer, poet NY, 1999—. Author: Shades of Black, 1970, Shade of Anger, 1972, I Wouldn't Take Nothing for My Journey, 2001, Blues Ain't Nothing but a Tonic, 2005; co-founder Black Forum; poetry editor: Black Forum, editor-in-chief:. Bd. dirs. S.E. Bronx (N.Y.) Neighborhood Ctr., Inc., 2000—, Philipsburg Manor (N.Y.) African Am. Adv. Bd., 2001—. With USN, 1964—68. Mem.: Morris Brown Coll. Alumni Assn., 369th Vets. Assn. (life), Shriners, Pentecost Consistory, Masons, Am. Legion (life), Corinthian, Phi Beta Sigma (life). Democrat. Baptist. Avocations: fishing, travel, reading, gardening. Home: 24 Hickory Rd Briarcliff Manor NY 10510

WINDHAUSER, JOHN WILLIAM, retired journalism educator, consultant; b. Rochester, NY, Jan. 30, 1943; s. Milton Edward and Mary Ellen (McDonald) W.; m. Marlene Marie Most. BS, Tri-State U., 1966; MA, Ball State U., 1967; PhD, Ohio U., 1975. Editor, reporter, advt. and pub. rels. positions, 1964—77; asst. prof. journalism Colo. State U., Ft. Collins, 1971—77, Bradley U., Peoria, Ill., 1977—78; assoc. prof., dir. rsch. ctr. U. Miss., Oxford, 1979—82; prof. La State U., Baton Rouge, 1982—2005, U. Memphis, 2005—; cons. Jomar Assocs. Cons. in field; rsch. judge Soc. Profl. Journalists; editl. bd. Journalism Quarterly, Newspaper Rsch. Jour. Author: The Editorial Process, 1978, 2d edit., 1985; co-editor, co-author: The Media in the 1984 and 1988 Presidential Campaigns, 1991; contbr. numerous articles to profl. jours.; editor Profl. Jour., Coll. Press Rev., 1972-81. Recipient Life Membership award Nat. Coun. Coll. Publs. Advisers, 1981, Presdl. award, 1973-81. Mem. Assn. Edn. in Journalism

WINDHORST, JOHN WILLIAM, JR., lawyer; b. Mpls., July 6, 1940; s. John William and Ardus Ruth (Bottge) W.; divorced; 1 child, Diana Elizabeth. AB, Harvard U., 1962; LLB, U. Minn., 1965. Bar: Minn. 1965, U.S. Tax Ct., U.S. Ct. Appeals (8th cir.) 1965, U.S. Dist. Ct. Minn. 1967, U.S. Supreme Ct. 1975. Law clk. to Hon. H.A. Blackmun U.S. Cir. Ct., Rochester, Minn., 1965-66; assoc. Dorsey & Whitney, Mpls., 1966-70; with office of Revisor of Statutes State of Minn., 1967, 69; ptnr. Dorsey & Whitney, 1971-96, of counsel, 1997—. Bd. dirs. St. Paul Chamber Orch., 1980-86, Harry A. Blackmun Scholarship Found., 1996—, Minn. Taxpayers Assn., 1999—. Mem. ABA (com. on state and local taxes), Minn. Bar Assn., Hennepin County Bar Assn., Harvard Club of Minn. (pres. 1977-78). Home: 1235 Yale Pl Apt 1102 Minneapolis MN 55403-1946 Office: 50 S 6th St Ste 1500 Minneapolis MN 55402 Office Phone: 612-340-2645. Business E-Mail: windhorst.john@dorsey.com.

WINDMAN, ARNOLD LEWIS, retired mechanical engineer; b. NYC, Oct. 17, 1926; s. Raphael and Anna (Wexler) W.; m. Patricia Foley, Dec. 13, 1967; children— Richard, Marjorie, Kevin, Colleen, Sean, JoAnn, Brian, William. B.M.E., Coll. City N.Y., 1947. Bar: registered profl. engr., N.Y., 13 other states. Project engr. F.E. Sutton, NYC, 1947-50; with Syska & Hennessy, Inc., NYC, 1950-90, pres., 1976-86, vice chmn., 1986-90, also bd. dirs. Pres. Am. Cons. Engrs. Coun., 1985-86; chmn. N.Y. State Bd. Engring. and Land Surveying, 1982-84; bd. dirs., v.p. Sea Pines Plantation, 1997-2000. Bd. dirs. Phelps Meml. Hosp., Tarrytown, N.Y., 1974-82; chmn. planning commn. Hilton Head Island, 2000. Mem. Am. Soc. Heating, Refrigerating and Air Conditioning Engrs., chpt. pres. (1965), N.Y. Assn. Cons. Engrs. (pres. 1981-82, dir. 1977), ASME, Tau Beta Pi, Pi Tau Sigma. Democrat. Jewish. Home: 1919 S Beach Club Vl Hilton Head Island SC 29928-4068 *Professional integrity, enthusiasm, and a continuing effort to train younger people for advancement are three key ingredients of a successful career.*

WINDOM, HERBERT LYNN, oceanographer, environmental scientist; b. Macon, Ga., Apr. 23, 1941; m. Patricia Woodruff, 1963; children: Kevin, Elizabeth. BS, Fla. State U., 1963; MS, U. Calif., San Diego, 1965, PhD in Earth Sci., 1968. Prof. oceanography Skidaway Inst. Oceanography, Savannah, Ga., 1968—94, acting dir., 1994-2001, prof. emeritus, 2001—. Mem. Am. Soc. Limnol. and Oceanography, Am. Geophys. Union, Oceanography Soc. Office: Skidaway Inst of Oceanography 10 Ocean Science Cir Savannah GA 31411-1011 E-mail: herb@skio.peachnet.edu.

WINDSOR, ADRIAN SHARON, real estate broker, literature and language professor; b. Adrian, Mich., Oct. 19, 1938; d. LeRoy E. and Delores L. Wood; life ptnr. Ronald V. Knapp; children: Charles L. Proudfit, Kerren L. Bergman. BA, MA, U. Mich., Ann Arbor, PhD, 1967. Cert. internat. property specialist. Assoc. prof. English Colo. Women's Coll., Denver, 1968—77; dir. Sewall & Farrand acad. programs, assoc. prof. English U. Colo., Boulder, 1978—82; stock broker Dain Bosworth, 1982—85; real estate broker Adrian Windsor Broker, Irvine, Calif., 1988—; pres. Sovereign Holdings Internat. Corp. Dir. pub. rels. KGNU Pub. Radio, 1982—83; adj. prof. English Coastline CC, 1991—2006. Author: (book) Seven Tools to Transform Genius Into Practical Power. Bd. mem. Colo. Music Festival, 1978—84, v.p. devel., 1978—84; bd. dirs. LA Fund Raising Reconstruction of Biblioteque Alexendrina. Recipient Outstanding Adj. Faculty award, 1996. Mem.: Fedn. Internation Real Estate Brokers, Calif. Assn. Realtors, Nat. Assn. Realtors, Inside Edge Found. Edn. (bd. dirs. 2002—03, program dir. 2003—). Democrat. Avocations: spiritual counseling, motivation, educational leadership, philanthropic project development. Office: 14252 Culver Dr #205A Irvine CA 92604 Office Phone: 949-310-5538. Personal E-mail: arealwin@aol.com. E-mail: adrianwindsor@sbcglobal.net.

WINDSOR, HARRIET SMITH, state official; b. June 30, 1940; children: James A. Smith Jr., Julia A. Smith-O'Hanlon. BA, Juniata Coll., 1962; PhD, MA, U. Del. Cert. lay spkr. Peninsula Conf. Former English tchr. Seaford Sr. HS; dean instrn., dept. English Chmn. Del. Tech. and Cmty. Coll. Owens Campus; mem., dir. State Personnel Gov. Thomas R. Carper's Cabinet, 1993—2001; sec. state State of Del., Dover, 2001—. Writer, spkr. numerous local, state and nat. bds. Serves Dist. Com. Ordained Ministry; mem., choir dir., organist, ch. sch. tchr., supt., adminstrv. bd. chmn., chmn. Pastor Parish Rels. Com. Millsboro Grace United Meth. Ch., lay leader, 2002—. Named Del. Mother of Yr., 1999, Woman of Yr., Sussex Ctrl. Jr. HS students; named to Del.'s Hall of Fame, 1997; recipient Millsboro's Woman of Year, 1989, Order of the First State, Governor Thomas R. Carper, Del., 2000. Democrat. Methodist. Office: Office Sec of State Townsend Bldg 401 Federal St Ste 3 Dover DE 19901 Office Phone: 302-739-4111. Office Fax: 302-739-3811. E-mail: hnsmith@state.de.us. *

WINDSOR, PATRICIA (KATONAH SUMMERTREE, PERRIN WINTERS, ANNA SEELING), author, educator, lecturer; b. NYC, Sept. 21, 1938; d. Bernhard Edward and Antoinette (Gaus) Seelinger; m. Laurence Charles Windsor, Jr., Apr. 3, 1959 (div. 1978); children: Patience Wells, Laurence Edward; m. Stephen E. Altman, Sept. 21, 1986 (div. 1989). Student, Bennington Coll., 1956—58, Westchester C.C.; AA, NYU. V.p. Windsor-Morehead Assoc., NYC, 1960—63; info. mgr. Family Planning Assn., London, 1974—76; faculty mem. Inst. Children's Lit., Redding Ridge, Conn., 1976—94, 1999—; editor-in-chief AT&T, Washington, 1978—80; instr. U. Md. Writers Inst., Open Univ., Washington, 1980—82; creative developer, faculty mem. Long Ridge Writer's Group, Danbury, Conn., 1988—2000, instr., 2006—; dir. Summertree Studios, Savannah, Ga., 1992—. Dir. Wordspring Lit. Cons., 1989—, Wordworks Writing Cons., 1999—, Born Author Lit. Cons., 2003-; dir. Devel. Writing Workshops, Katonah, NY, 1976-78; judge Internat. Assn. Bus. Communicators, Washington, 1979, 89; lectr. LI U., Jersey City State Coll., Skidmore Coll., others, 1987—; instr. Coastal Ga. Ctr. for Continuing Edn., 1996—, Armstrong Atlantic U. Continuing Edn., 1997-2000, Anne Arundel (Md.) C.C., 2000—, workshop coord., 2000—; dir., founder Born Author-.com, 2002—; dir. Windsomethings Art & Crafts, 2004—; owner, designer Tiger Woman Crafts for Meditation, 2005-. Author: The Summer Before, 1973 (ALA Best Book award 1973, transl. 1980 Austrian State prize 1980, also Brit., Norwegian, German edits.), Something's Waiting for You, Baker D, 1974 (starred selection Libr. Jour., Brit., Japanese edits.), Home Is Where Your Feet Are Standing, 1975, Diving for Roses, 1976 (NY Times Outstanding Book for Young Adults award, starred selection Libr. Jour.), Mad Martin, 1976, Killing Time, 1980, Demon Tree, 1983 (pen name Colin Daniel), The Sandman's Eyes, 1985 (Edgar Allan Poe Best Juvenile Mystery award Mystery Writers Am.), How a Weirdo and a Ghost Can Change Your Life, 1986, The Hero, 1988 (highest rating Voice of Youth Advocate), Just Like the Movies, 1990, The Christmas Killer, 1991 (Edgar nominee, Brit., Danish, French edits.), Two Weirdos and a Ghost, 1991, A Weird and Moogly Christmas, 1991, The Blooding, 1996 (YALSA pick for reluctant readers), The House of Death, 1996, Nightwood (nominated Best Book 2006), 2006; columnist The Blood Rev., 1990-92, Savannah Parent, 1990-92; columnist Coastal Senior, 1997-99; also short stories in anthologies and mags.; actress: The Haunting of Hill House, City Lights Theatre Co., 1991; contr. articles Once Upon a Time Mag., 2003, 04, 05. Mem. City Lights Theatre Co., Savannah, Ga., 1991. Mem. Horror Writers Am., Internat. Women's Writing Guild, Children's Book Guild, Authors Guild, Poetry Soc. Ga., Savannah Storytellers. Avocations: skiing, painting, modern dance. Office: Born Author Dot Com PO Box 799 Severna Park MD 21146 Business E-Mail: info@bornauthor.com.

WINDSOR, WILLIAM EARL, consulting engineer, sales representative; b. Evansville, Ind., Jan. 24, 1927; s. Charles H. and Lora E. (Archey) W.; divorced; children: Kim, William, Robert. Student, Purdue U., 1946-50. Field engr. Philco Corp., Phila., 1950-53, Europe, Africa, Arabia; studio ops. engr. Sta. WFBM, Indpls., 1953-55; field engr. RCA Svc. Co., Cherry Hill, NJ, 1955-56; audio facilities engr. ABC, NYC, 1956-62; rsch. engr. Fine Recording, Inc., NYC, 1962-66; chief engr. A & R Recording, Inc., NYC, 1966-68; chief engr., corp. sec. DB Audio Corp., NYC, 1968-70; pres. Studio Cons., Inc., NYC, 1970-72; sr. v.p., v.p., gen. mgr. Quad Eight Electronics-Quad Eight/Westrex, San Fernando, Calif., 1972-85; sr. mktg. exec. Mitsubishi Pro Audio Group, San Fernando, Calif., 1985-89. Pres., CEO Quad Eight Electronics, Inc., Valencia, Calif., 1989-90; ind. cons., Valencia, 1991—. Inventor monitor mixer for multitrack audio consoles, 1967, update function for audio console automation, 1973; designer of new architecture for film scoring and film re-recording sound mixing consoles, 1974 (Acad. award 1974). Served with USNR, 1945-50. Fellow: Audio Engrng. Soc. (chmn. NY sect. 1970). Avocations: photography, foreign travel, art collecting. Home and Office: 23112 Yvette Ln Valencia CA 91355-3060 Home Phone: 661-255-3265; Office Phone: 661-255-3265. Business E-Mail: wew@aceweb.com.

WINE, L. MARK, lawyer; b. Norfolk, Va., Apr. 16, 1945; s. Melvin Leon and Mildred Sylvia (Weiss) W.; m. Blanche Weintraub, June 8, 1969; children: Kim, Lara, Dana. BA with high honors, U. Va., 1967; JD, U. Chgo., 1970. Bar: D.C. 1970, U.S. Supreme Ct. 1977. Assoc. Kirkland & Ellis LLP, Washington, 1970-72, ptnr., 1978—; trial atty. land and natural resources divsn. Dept. of Justice, Washington, 1972-78. Mem. ABA. Office: Kirkland & Ellis LLP 655 15th St NW Ste 1200 Washington DC 20005-5793 Office Phone: 202-879-5024. Business E-Mail: mwine@kirkland.com.

WINE, MARK PHILIP, lawyer; b. Iowa City, Jan. 6, 1949; s. Donald Arthur and Mary Lepha Schneider; m. Carol Jean Sullivan; children: Nicholas Cox, Meredith Kathryn, Callie Ann, Cassidy Mae. AB, Princeton U., 1971; JD, U. Iowa, 1974. Bar: Iowa 1974, Minn. 1976, Calif. 1997, U.S. Dist. Ct. Minn. 1976, U.S. Ct. Appeals (8th cir.) 1976, U.S. Supreme Ct. 1984, U.S. Ct. Appeals (4th cir.) 1985, U.S. Ct. Appeals (7th and Fed. cirs.) 1992, U.S. Ct. Appeals (9th cir.) 1997, U.S. Dist. Ct. (so., no. and ctrl. dists.) Calif. 1997. Law clk. to judge U.S. Ct. Appeals (8th cir.), St. Louis, 1974-76; ptnr. Oppenheimer Wolff & Donnelly, 1976—2002, McDermott, Will & Emery, LA, 2002—. Mem. ABA, Internat. Assn. Def. Counsel, Calif. Bar Assn., L.A. Bar Assn., L.A. Intellectual Property Law Assn., Princeton Club So. Calif. Democrat. Avocations: cooking, reading, golf. Home: 6220 E Fox Glen Dr Anaheim CA 92807 Office: McDermott Will & Emery 2049 Century Park E Fl 34 Los Angeles CA 90067-3208 Office Phone: 310-551-9322. Personal E-mail: mpwineca@sbcglobal.net. Business E-Mail: mwine@mwe.com.

WINE-BANKS, JILL SUSAN, lawyer; b. Chgo., May 5, 1943; d. Bert S. and Sylvia Dawn (Simon) Wine; m. Ian David Volner, Aug. 21, 1965; m. Michael A. Banks, Jan. 12, 1980. BS, U. Ill., Champaign, Urbana, 1964; JD, Columbia U., 1968; LLD (hon.), Hood Coll., 1975. Bar: N.Y. 1969, U.S. Ct. Appeals (2d, 4th, 5th, 6th, 7th and 9th cirs.), U.S. Supreme Ct. 1974, D.C. 1976, Ill. 1980. Asst. press. and pub. rels. dir. Assembly of Captive European Nations, NYC, 1965-66; trial atty. criminal divsn. organized crime & racketeering U.S. Dept. Justice, 1969-73; asst. spl. prosecutor Watergate Spl. Prosecutor's Office, 1973-75; lectr. law sem. in trial practice Columbia U. Sch. Law, NYC, 1975-77; assoc. Fried, Frank, Harris, Shriver & Kampelman, Washington, 1975-77; gen. counsel Dept. Army, Pentagon, Washington, 1977-79; ptnr. Jenner & Block, Chgo., 1980-84; solicitor gen. State of Ill. Office of Atty. Gen., 1984-86, dep. atty. gen., 1986-87; exec. v.p., chief oper., officer ABA, Chgo., 1987-90; atty. pvt. practice, 1990-92; v.p., dir. transaction and govt. rels. Motorola Internat. Network Ventures, 1992-97; dir. strategic alliances Motorola Cellular Infrastructure Group, 1997—99; v.p. alliance mgmt. Maytag Corp., 1999-2001; CEO Winning Workplaces, Evanston, Ill., 2001—03; chief officer Chgo. Pub. Schs. Edn. to Careers, 2003—. Mem. EEC disting. vis. program European Parliament, 1987; chmn. bd. dirs. St. Petersburg Telecom., Russia, 1994-97, Omni Capital Ptnrs., Inc., 1994-97. Trustee Roosevelt U., 2004—; mem. adv. bd. Project Lead the Way, UIC Econ. Edn. Recipient Spl. Achievement award U.S. Dept. Justice, 1972, Meritorious award, 1973, Cert. Outstanding Svc., 1975; decorated Disting. Civilian Svc. Dept. Army, 1979; named Disting. Vis. to European Econ. Cmty. Mem.: The Chgo. Network, Internat. Women's Forum, Exec. Club (bd. dirs. 1999—2001), Econ. Club. Office: Chgo Pub Schs Edn to Careers 125 S Clark St 12th Fl Chicago IL 60603 Home Phone: 312-861-1433; Office Phone: 773-553-2460. Business E-Mail: jwine-banks@cps.k12.il.us.

WINEGAR, ALBERT LEE, computer company executive; b. Beloit, Wis., Apr. 23, 1931; s. Albert Richard and Theo Rayneta (Hubbell) W.; m. Phyllis M. Everill, June 21, 1953; children: Bradford, Steven, Kristine, Kathleen. BBA, U. Wis., 1954. With IBM Corp., 1956-79, div. dir. mgmt. services, 1977-79; v.p. corp. planning, then group v.p. field ops. Olivetti Corp., Tarrytown, NY, 1979-80, pres., 1980-81; v.p. field ops. NBI Inc., Boulder, Colo., 1981-84; pres., chief exec. officer Sensory, Inc., Santa Clara, Calif., 1984-85, VICOM Systems, Inc., Fremont, Calif., 1985-91, ret., 1991. Bd. dirs. JRL Sys., Inc., Advanced Sys. Integration Group, Acad. Software Inc., Adams Globalization, Inc.; pres. Barton Creek Water Supply Corp. V.p. bd. trustees Valley Hosp., Ridgewood, N.J., 1978-81; pres. NJ Bus. Arts Found., 1977-78, Estates of Barton Creek Homeowners Assn., 1992-94; elder Westlake Hills Presbyn. Ch., stewardship chmn., 2002, fin. chmn., 2003 Capt. AUS, 1954-56. Sloan Exec. fellow, Stanford U., 1970. Mem. Computer and Bus. Equipment Mfrs. Assn. (dir. 1980-81), Barton Creek Country Club, Beta Theta Pi. Republican. Home: 10015 Haynes Bridge Road 6 Alpharetta GA 30022-1909 Home Phone: 678-393-1511.

WINEGAR, BRADFORD CHARLES, otolaryngologist, surgeon, researcher; b. Killeen, Tex., Apr. 27, 1955; s. Albert Lee and Phyllis Marie Winegar; m. Stacy J. Jones, Oct. 28, 1979; children: Bradford Reed, Ross Alan, Chad Evan. MD, Southwestern Med. Sch., Dallas, 1980. Attending physician, ptnr. Austin Ear, Nose & Throat Clinic, Tex., 1985—. Cons. Roxane Labs., Inc., Columbus, Ohio, 2006—; investigator Cedra Clin. Rsch., LLC, Austin, 2006—; mem. adv. bd. Aeriflux, Inc., Austin, 2005—. Morgan Goode fellow, Southwestern Med. Sch., 1977. Fellow: Am. Acad. Otolaryngology, Head and Neck Surgery, Inc.; mem.: AMA (life), Tex. Assn. Otolaryngology, Head and Neck Surgery, Travis County Med. Assn., Tex. Med. Assn., Austin Coun. Fgn. Affairs, Rotary Club. Office: Austin Ear Nose & Throat Clinic 3705 Medical Pky Ste 320 Austin TX 78705-1023 Office Phone: 512-454-0392.

WINEKE, WILLIAM ROBERT, reporter, minister; b. Madison, Wis., Apr. 4, 1942; s. Edward Ervin and Jennie Mae (Lanigan) W.; m. Susan L. Detering, Dec. 9, 1964 (div. June 1975); children: Gregory, Andrew; m. Jacqueline Cone, Mar. 18, 1990. BS, U. Wis., 1965; BDiv, chgo. Theol. Sem., 1969. Reporter Wis. State Jour., Madison, 1963-65; writer United Ch. of Christ, NYC, 1966-68; pub. rels. dir. Chgo. (Ill.) Theol. Sem., Chgo., 1968-69; reporter Wis. State Jour., Madison, 1969—; chaplain Wis. Rescue Mission, Madison, 1977—. Mem. bd. rev. Wis. Health Policy Network, Madison, 1994-2003. Fellow Religions Pub. Rels. Soc., 1974; recipient Disting. Svc. award State Med. Soc. Wis., 1992, Disting. Svc. award LWV, Madison, 1994. Democrat. Home: 1024 Ridgewood Dr Stoughton WI 53589-4125 Office: Wis State Jour 1901 Fish Hatchery Rd Madison WI 53713-1248

WINER, EDWARD L., lawyer; b. Mpls., Nov. 7, 1943; BA, U. Minn., 1965, JD cum laude, 1968. Bar: Minn. 1968, Minn. (US Dist. Ct.) 1969, (US Tax Ct.) 1976, diplomate: Am. Coll. Family Trial Lawyers, cert.: (Family Law Arbitrator). Positions up to shareholder Moss & Barnett, PA, Mpls., 1968—. Law sch. mentor. Co-author: Valuation Strategies in Divorce, 2nd edit., 1992; co-editor: Premarital and Marital Agreements, 1993; contbr. articles to profl. jours. Named one of Top 100 US Attys., Worth Mag., 2006, Top 10 Divorce Lawyers in US, Best Lawyers in Am., Minn. Top 25 Litigators, Minn. Lawyer, Top 100 Super Lawyers, Minn. Law and Politics, Top 40 Vote Getters, Top Appellate Lawyers, Best Lawyers in US, Town and Country Mag.; named to Leading Am. Attys. Fellow: Am. Acad. Matrimonial Lawyers (past pres. Minn. Chpt.); mem.: ABA (family law sect.), Cardozo Soc. (steering com., CLE com.), Hennepin County Bar Assn. (family law sect.), Minn. State Bar Assn. (family law sect.), Phi Alpha Theta, Phi Beta Kappa. Jewish. Avocations: physical fitness, travel. Office: Moss & Barnett PA 4800 Wells Fargo Ctr 90 S 7th St Minneapolis MN 55402-4129 Office Phone: 612-877-5295. E-mail: winere@moss-barnett.com.

WINER, WARD OTIS, mechanical engineer, educator; b. Grand Rapids, Mich., June 27, 1936; s. Mervin Augustus and Ina Katherine (Wood) W.; m. Mary Jo Wielinga, June 15, 1957; children: Mathew Owen, James Edward, Paul Andrew, Mary Margaret. Asso., Grand Rapids Jr. Coll., Mich., 1956; BS, U. Mich., Ann Arbor, 1958; MS, U. Mich., 1959, PhD, 1962; PhD (Cavendish Lab. fellow), Cambridge U., Eng., 1964. Asst. prof. dept. mech. engring. U. Mich., Ann Arbor, 1963-66, assoc. prof., 1966-69; assoc. prof. mech. engring. Ga. Inst. Tech., 1969-71, prof., 1971-84, Regents' prof., 1984—, mem. exec. bd., 1983-88, chmn., 1984-86, dir. and chmn. Sch. Mech. Engring., 1988—, Eugene C. Gwaltney Jr. chair George W. Woodruff Sch. Mech. Engring., 2001—. Chmn. Gordon Research Conf. on Friction, Lubrication and Wear, 1980; mem. NRC, 1980-88; chmn. Com. on Recommendations for U.S. Army Basic Sci. Research, 1985-87; mem. div. mech., structural, materials engring. adv. bd. NSF Engring. Directorate, 1984-89; bd. dirs. Taiho Tribology Rsch. Found. Co-editor: Wear Control Handbook, 1980; tech. editor: Jour. Lubrication Tech., 1980-84, Jour. of Tribology, 1984-87; contbr. articles to profl. jours. Democratic precinct chmn., 1967-68; Mem. exec. bd. Horace H. Rackham Sch. Grad. Studies, U. Mich., 1968. Recipient Disting. Faculty Svc. award Coll. Engring. U. Mich., 1967, Alumni Merit award, 1998, Cert. Recognition, NASA, 1977, Clarence E. Earle Meml. award Nat. Grease Lubricating Inst., 1979, Disting. Prof. award Ga. Inst. Tech., 1987; named Hon. Alumni, Ga. Tech., 2003. Fellow AAAS, ASME (hon.; bd. comms. 1987-91, v.p. rsch. 1989-93, found. trustee 2006—, Melville medal 1975, Centennial medallion 1980, Mayor D. Hersey award 1986, Charles Russ Richards Meml. award 1988), Soc. Tribologists and Lubrication Engrs. (bd. dirs. 1983-86, Internat. award 1997), Brit. Tribology Trust (gold medal 1987), Am. Soc. Engring. Educators (Benjamin Garver Lamme award 1995, Donald Marlowe award 1996); mem. NAE, Metro Atlanta Engring. Soc. (Engr. of Yr. 1989), Am. Acad. Mechanics, Soc. Rheology, Soc. Engring. Sci. (dir. 1980-84), AAUP (pres. Ga. Tech. chpt. 1972-74, v.p. state conf. 1973-75), Sigma Xi (chpt. pres. 1982-83, Sustained Rsch. in Engring. award 1975), Tau Beta Pi, Pi Tau Sigma, Phi Kappa Phi. Home: 1025 Mountain Creek Trl NW Atlanta GA 30328-3535 Office Phone: 404-894-3200. E-mail: ward.winer@me.gatech.edu.

WINERIP, MICHAEL, reporter; married; 4 children. B, Harvard Coll. Suburban reporter NY Times, columnist, investigative reporter, nat. polit. writer, edn. writer, dep. metro editor, staff writer Sunday Mag., nat. edn. columnist. Author: 9 Highland Road: Sane Living for the Mentally Ill, 1995, (children's novel) Adam Canfield of the Slash, 2005. Office: NY Times 229 West 43rd St New York NY 10036 Office Phone: 212-556-4122. Office Fax: 212-556-3758. E-mail: winerip@nytimes.com.

WINESKI, LAWRENCE E., medical educator, biomedical researcher; b. Fort Dix, NJ, June 29, 1949; s. Max E. and Irene R. Wineski; m. Lynn E. Comerford, Aug. 16, 1980; children: Matthew C., Benjamin C. BA, Calif. State U., Fullerton, 1972; MA, San Francisco State U., 1978; PhD, U. of Ill., Chgo., 1981. Sci. officer State U. of Groningen, Netherlands, 1980—81; postdoctoral scholar U. Mich., Ann Arbor, 1981—82; rsch. assoc. U. Ill., Chgo., 1982—83; asst. prof., assoc. prof. Morehouse Sch. Medicine, Atlanta, 1983—. Vis. prof. Emory U. Sch. Medicine, Atlanta, 1999—2000; mem. anatomy adv. bd. Lippincott Williams & Wilkins Publishers, Balt., 2005—; reviewer in field. Author: (educational CD-ROMs) TIPS/Temporal Infratemporal and Pteygopalatine Study Guide, 2002, Introduction to the Face and Scalp, 2005, Introduction to Dissection, 2006; contbr. scientific papers to profl. jours., chapters to books. Grantee Rsch. Grants, NIH, 1986—98, NASA, 1995—2005. Mem.: Am. Soc. Mammalogists, Anatomical Bd. Ga., Am. Assn. Advancement Sci., Am. Assn. Clinical Anatomists, Am. Assn. Anatomists, Soc. for Neuroscience; Soc. for Integrative and Comparative Biology. Avocations: soccer, travel. Office: Morehouse Sch of Medicine 720 Westview Dr SW Atlanta GA 30310-1495 Office Phone: 404-752-1563. Business E-Mail; lwineski@msm.edu.

WINESTOCK, JAMES F., delivery service executive; Grad., Massey Coll. Joined UPS, Atlanta, 1969, coord. corp. schools, dist. mgr. NE Tex., 1992—96, dist. mgr. Mo., 1996—98, region mgr. midwest, 1998—2000, region mgr. no. ctrl., 2000—04, sr. v.p. ops. mem. mgmt. com., 2004—. Trustee March Found., Nat. Urban League. Office: UPS 55 Glendake Pky Atlanta GA 30328 *

WINFIELD, DAVE (DAVID MARK WINFIELD), professional sports team executive, retired professional baseball player; b. St. Paul, Oct. 3, 1951; m. Tonya Winfield; children: Arielle Arline, David Mark II. Student, U. Minn.; LLD (hon.), Syracuse U., 1987. Outfielder San Diego Padres, 1973-80, NY Yankees, 1980-90, Calif. Angels, 1990-91, Toronto Blue Jays, 1991-92, Minn. Twins, 1992-94, Cleve. Indians, 1995; commentator Fox Broadcasting Co., Beverly Hills, Calif., 1996—2002; v.p., sr. adv. San Diego Padres, 2002—. Co-author (with Tom Parker) Winfield: A Player's Life, 1988. Recipient Golden Glove award, 1979-80, 82-85, 87, Silver Slugger award, 1981-85, 92, Babe Ruth award, 1992, Branch Rickey award, 1992, Roberto Clemente award, 1994; named to the Nat. League All-Star Team, 1977-80, Am. League All-Star Team, 1981-88, Sporting News All-Star Team, 1979, 82-84, 92, Major League Baseball Hall of Fame, 2001, Coll. Baseball Hall of Fame, 2006; named Sporting News Am. League Comeback Player of Yr., 1990. He is one of only two men ever drafted in three different pro sports, basketball, football, and baseball; a member of two World Series teams with the Toronto Blue Jays, 1992-93; retired with 3,110 career hits & 465 home runs. Office: San Diego Padres 9449 Friars Rd San Diego CA 92108 *

WINFIELD, JOHN BUCKNER, rheumatologist, educator; b. Kentfield, Calif., Mar. 19, 1942; s. R. Buckner and Margaret G. (Katterfelt) Winfield; m. Patricia Nichols (div. 1968); 1 child, Ann Gibson; m. Teresa Lee McGrath, 1969 (div. 2000); children: John Buckner III, Virginia Lee; m. Leigh Fleming Callahan, 2001. BA, Williams Coll., 1964; MD, Cornell U., 1968. Diplomate Am. Bd. Internal Medicine. Intern in medicine N.Y. Hosp., NYC, 1968-69; staff assoc. LI/Nat. Inst. Allergy and Infectious Diseases NIH, Bethesda, Md., 1969-71; resident in medicine, fellow in rheumatology U. Va. Sch. Medicine, Charlottesville, 1971-73; fellow in immunology Rockefeller U., NYC, 1973-75; asst. prof. medicine U. Va. Sch. Medicine, Charlottesville, 1975-76, assoc. prof. medicine, 1976-78, U. N.C., Chapel Hill, 1978-81, prof. medicine, 1981—2006, chief div. rheumatology and immunology, 1978-99; dir. Thurston Arthritis Rsch. Ctr., U. N.C. Sch. Medicine, Chapel Hill, 1982—2001; dir Daughtridge Arthritis Ctr., Lenoir, NC, 2002—; Smith prof. medicine U. NC Sch. Med., Chapel Hill, 1987—2006, emeritus, 2006—, adj. prof. exercise sports physiology, 2003—; owner Winfield Medical, L.L.C., 2004—. Adv. coun. Nat. Inst. Arthritis and Musculoskeletal and Skin Diseases, NIH, 1988-92; chmn. edn. com. Am. Rheumatism Assn., Atlanta, 1980-84; immunol. scis. study sect. NIH, 1979-83, Arthritis Musculoskeletal and Skin study sect., 1992-96; vice-chair fellowship com. Arthritis Found., 1982; med. coun. Lupus Found. Am., 1987-96. Author more than 130 med. and sci. articles in peer reviewed rheumatology and immunology jours.; mem. editl. bd. Arthritis and Rheumatism, Bull. Rheumatic Diseases, Rheumatology Internat., Clin. Exptl. Rheumatology, Am. Jour. Medicine, Clin. Immunology, Current Rev. Rheumatology. Sr. asst. surgeon with USPHS, NIH, Bethesda, Md., 1968-71. Recipient Borden prize Cornell U. Med. Coll., 1964, numerous rsch. grants NIH and Arthritis Found., 1975—, Sr. Investigator award Arthritis Found., 1976-79, Kenan award U. N.C., 1985, NIH merit award, 1992. Fellow ACP; mem. Am. Assn. Immunologists, Am. Coll. Rheumatology, Am. Fedn. Clin. Rsch., Am. Soc. Clin. Investigation, Assn. Am. Physicians, Am. Clin. Climatol. Assn., Nat. Soc. Clin. Rheumatologists (treas. 1997-02), Henry Kunkel Soc. (councilor 2000-02), Chapel Hill Country Club. Republican. Episcopalian. Avocations: golf, on and off-road motorcycling, scuba diving instructor, skiing. Home: 102 Greenwood Ln Chapel Hill NC 27514-5957 Office Phone: 828-757-6414. Business E-Mail: john_winfield@med.unc.edu.

WINFIELD, RICHARD DIEN, humanities educator; b. NYC, Apr. 7, 1950; s. Sidney Lincoln and Lillian Winfield; m. Sujata Gupta, Apr. 28, 1983; children: Kalindi, Manas Samuel, Rasik Sidd. BA in Philosophy, Yale Coll., New Haven, Conn., 1972; MA in Philosophy, U. Heidelberg, Germany, 1973; PhD in Philosophy, Yale U., New Haven, Conn., 1977. Asst. prof. U. Ga., Athens, 1982—87, assoc. prof., 1987—93, prof., 1993—2001, disting. rsch. prof., 2001—. Author: (books) Reason and Justice, 1988, The Just Economy, 1988, Overcoming Foundations: Studies in Systematic Philosophy, 1989, Freedom and Modernity, 1991, Law in Civil Society, 1995, Systematic Aesthetics, 1995, Stylistics: Rethinking the Artforms After Hegel, 1996, The Just Family, 1998, Autonomy and Normativity: Investigations of Truth, Right, and Beauty, 2001, The Just State: Rethinking Self-Government, 2005, From Concept to Objectivity: Thinking Through Hegel's Subjective Logic, 2006. Mem.: Soc. Systematic Philosophy (pres. 1986—), Hegel Soc. Am. (pres. 2002—04). Office: Univ Ga Dept Philosophy 103 Peabody Hall Athens GA 30602-1627 Home Phone: 706-546-9225. Business E-Mail: winfield@uga.edu.

WINFIELD, RICHARD NEILL, lawyer; b. Chgo., Jan. 20, 1933; s. Richard Paul and Mary B. (Monaghan) Winfield; m. Deobrah Mary Trainer, June 13, 1959; children: Richard Neill Jr., Pamela, Nicole. AB, Villanova U., 1955; LLB, Georgetown U., 1961. Bar: Va. 1961, N.Y. 1962,

U.S. Dist. Ct. (so. dist.) N.Y. 1963. Assoc. Donovan, Leisure, Newton & Irvine, NYC, 1961-65; asst. counsel to Gov. Nelson A. Rockefeller Gov.'s Office, Albany, NY, 1965-67; assoc. Royall, Koegel, Rogers & Wells, NYC, 1967-69; ptnr. Clifford Chance US LLP (formerly known as Rogers & Wells), NYC, 1969—2002. Chmn. bd. consultors Sch. Law Villanova U., Pa., 1980—2004; faculty comm. law confs. Practising Law Inst., NYC, 1977—2001, chmn. libel litig. confs., 1979—2000; prof. Columbia Law Sch., Fordham Law Sch., 2002—. Editor: Libel Litigation, PLI, 1979, 1981, 1984, 1986, 1988, 1990, 1992, 1994, 1996, 1998, 2000; contbr. articles to profl. jours. Chmn. bd. trustees Convent Sacred Heart Sch., NYC, 1987—90; co-chmn. bd. dirs. Fund for Peace, 2000—; mem. bd. visitors Sch. Langs. and Linguistics, Georgetown U., Washington, 1987—93. Lt. USN, 1955—59. Recipient Alumni medallion, Coll. Liberal Arts & Scis. Villanova U., 1984, Loyalty award, Villanova U., 1986, First Amendment award, Deadline Club, 2002. Mem.: ABA (chmn. media law reform working group 1996—, Ctrl. Europe and Eurasian Law Initiative), Internat. Sr. Lawyers Project (co-founder, bd. dirs., treas.), Assn. Bar City of N.Y., N.Y. State Bar Assn., Century Assn. Republican. Roman Catholic. Avocations: travel, history. Home: 40 5th Ave New York NY 10011-8843 Office: Clifford Chance US LLP 31 West 52nd St New York NY 10019 Office Phone: 212-878-8233.

WINFIELD, RODNEY M., artist, retired art educator; b. Manhattan, NY, Feb. 6, 1925; s. Benjamil Lional and Helen Oscar Winfield; m. Margaret Elizabeth MacKenzie Winfield, Sept. 7, 1946; children: Christopher, David, Robin, Nancy. Attended, U. Miami, Coral Gables, Fla., 1942—43, Wash. U., St. Louis, 1970—71. Stained glass designer Emil Frei Co., St. Louis, 1952—57, Emil Frei Assocs., 1957—; art prof. Maryville U., St. Louis, 1964—90; ptnr., v.p., designer Illi Inc., St. Louis, 1967—71. Pres. St. Louis Artists' Guild, 1961—63. Three-dimensional window, US, 1953—53, temple altar wall, 1959—60, chapel, Good Samaritan Hosp., Mt. Vernon, Ill., 1968, space window, Nat. Cathedral, DC, 1970—72, windows, St. Louis U. Chapel, 1983—84, Sheldon Music Hall, St. Louis, 2005, plaque, United Nations Brotherhood Man, Grace Cathedral, 2006. Recipient Tchg. Excellence & Campus Leadership award, Sears Roebuck Found., 1990, Tchr. award, Outstanding Educators Am., 1974—75. Avocations: gardening, poetry, piano. Office: Winfield Gallery PO Box 7393 Carmel CA 93921

WINFREY, CAREY WELLS, journalist, editor; b. NYC, Aug. 1, 1941; s. William Colin and Mary (Robinson) W.; m. Jane Elizabeth Keeney, Feb. 13, 1982; children: Graham William, Wells Millar. AB, Columbia U., 1963, MS in Journalism, 1967. Assoc. editor Time Inc., NYC, 1968-71; exec. producer Ednl. Broadcast Corp., NYC, 1971-77; reporter, fgn. corr. for Africa N.Y. Times, NYC, 1977-80; mng. editor CBS Mags., NYC, 1981-90, editor Cuisine mag., 1983-84, v.p., editorial dir., 1985-87; founding editor-in-chief Memories mag. Diamandis Comm., Inc. (formerly mag. divsn. CBS), NYC, 1987-90; editor-in-chief Am. Health mag. Reader's Digest Publs., NYC, 1990-96; dir. Delacorte Ctr. for Mag. Journalism, Columbia U., NYC, 1996-98; asst. mng. editor People Mag., 1996—2001; editor-in-chief Smithsonian Mag., 2001—. Author: Starts and Finishes, 1975; exec. producer: (TV) Behind the Lines, 1971-75 (Emmy award 1973-74, NYU Don Hollenback award 1974), Assignment America, 1975, WNET Reports, 1976-77; columnist: "Eye on Books" for Book of the Month Club News, 1980, Parenting mag., 1986-89; prodr. CBS Cable; contbr. articles to Mags. Lt. USMC, 1963-66. Pulitzer Travelling fellow, 1967; recipient Meyer Berger award for Disting. Reporting Columbia U., 1978. Home: 3808 Reno Rd NW Washington DC 20008 Office: Smithsonian Mag MRC 513 PO Box 37012 Washington DC 20013-7012 Business E-Mail: cwinfrey@si.edu. *

WINFREY, JOHN CRAWFORD, economist, educator; b. Somerville, Tenn., July 2, 1935; s. Arthur Peter and Frances (Crawford) W.; m. Barbara Ann Strickland, July 20, 1957; 1 child, Mae Millicent. AB, Davidson Coll., 1957; PhD, Duke U., 1965. Asst. dir. data processing Hanes Hosiery, Winston Salem, NC, 1959-62; rsch. asst. in econs. Duke U., Durham, NC, 1963-64; asst. prof. econs. Washington and Lee U., Lexington, Va., 1965-68, assoc. prof., 1969-73, prof., 1974—. Vis. prof. Vanderbilt U., Nashville, 1966, Tufts U., Boston, 1975, UCLA, 1978, U. Ill., 1982, U. Va., 1986, Duke U., 1989, 95, U. Calif., Berkeley, 1993, U. Utrecht, Netherlands, 1995. Co-author: The Motion Commotion, 1972; author: Public Finance, Public Choice and the Public Sector, 1973, Social Issues, The Ethics and Economics of Taxes and Public Programs, 1997. Bd. dirs. Lexington Tennis Clinic, 1968-72, Rockbridge Area Conservation Coun., 1982-84, Rockbridge Area Social Svc., 2002—, Lexington Family Mentoring Program; mem. Rockbridge Area Behavioral Health Adv. Bd., 2001—; pres. Rockbridge Arts Guild, 1986-88, 2001-02. Recipient Cmty. Svc. award Lexington Jaycees, 1971; NEH fellow, 1975, 78, 82, 86, 89, 93; vis. fellow U. Coll. Oxford U., Eng., 1979, 95. Fellow Soc. for Values in Higher Edn.; mem. Am. Econ. Assn., So. Econ. Assn., History of Econs. Soc., Eastern Econ. Assn., High Wheelers Club (Lexington), Sunrise Rotary Club. Democrat. Presbyterian. Home: 160 Kendal Dr #1035 Lexington VA 24450 Office: Washington and Lee U Dept Econs Lexington VA 24450 Business E-Mail: winfreyj@wlu.edu.

WINFREY, MARCELLENE SEDETTA, music educator, church musician; b. Chgo., Dec. 4, 1949; d. Arthur Semon and Nellye Mae Winfrey; m. Darryl Jones, Nov. 27, 1988 (div. Sept. 0, 1994); 1 child, Troy Lamar. B in Music Edn., Roosevelt U., 1980; MS in Elem. Edn., Xavier U., 1994. Cert. Orff-Schulwerk tchr. U. Cin., Coll. Conservatory Music, OH, 2004. Distbn. clk. USPS, Chgo., 1969—74; instr. Chgo. City Wide Coll., 1980—82; educator Chgo. Pub. Schs., 1982—87; adminstr. So. Bapt. Day Care, Cin., 1988—88; min. music Union Bapt. Ch., 1988—93; music specialist Cin. Pub. Schs., 1988—; ch. organist Quinn Chapel AME, 1994—97; ch. musician Allen Temple AME, 1997—. Mem. Local Sch. Dist. Mgmt. Com., Cin., 2004—. Mem., mentor Excel Club, Cin., 2004—05. Mem.: ASCD (assoc.), Ohio Music Educators Assn. (assoc.), Phi Delta Kappa (life). Avocations: travel, genealogy, gardening, walking, dance. Office: Western Hills HS 2144 Ferguson Rd Cincinnati OH 45238-3799 Home Phone: 513-948-0332. Office Fax: 513-363-8751. E-mail: winfrem@cpsboe.k12.oh.us.

WINFREY, OPRAH, television talk show host, actress, television producer; b. Kosciusko, Miss., Jan. 29, 1954; d. Vernon Winfrey and Vernita Lee. BA in Speech Comm. and Performing Arts, Tenn. State U., 1987. News reporter Sta. WVOL Radio, Nashville, 1971-72; reporter, news anchorperson Sta. WTVF-TV, Nashville, 1973-76; news anchorperson Sta. WJZ-TV, Balt., 1976—78, host morning talk show People Are Talking, 1978—83; host talk show A.M. Chgo. Sta. WLS-TV, 1984; host The Oprah Winfrey Show, Chgo., 1985—, Oprah After the Show, Chgo., 2002—; nationally syndicated, 1986—; host series of celebrity interview spls. Oprah: Behind the Scenes; owner, prodr., chmn., CEO Harpo Prodns., 1986—. Ptnr., co-founder Oxygen Media, an Internet and cable TV co., 1998—; founder, editl. dir. O, The Oprah Magazine in conjunction with Hearst Mags., 2000; launched (mag.)first internat. edit., O, The Oprah Magazine in South Africa, 2002-, Oprah, After the Show, 2002-, O at Home, 2004-, Oprah & Friends, XM Satelite Radio Holdings, Inc., 2006-; online leader, Oprah.com, launched Live Your Best Life, 2003-; started Oprah Book Club. Actor (films) The Color Purple, 1985 (nominated Acad. award and Golden Globe award), Native Son, 1986, There Are No Children Here, 1993, Beloved, 1998 (prodr.), Charlotte's Web (voice), 2006, About Us: The Dignity of Children, 1997 (TV), Before Women Had Wings, 1997; prodr. (TV series) Dr. Phil, 2002—; Listen Up: The Lives of Quincy Jones, 1990; prodr., actress (TV mini-series) The Women of Brewster Place, 1989, Brewster Place, 1990; co-prodr. The Color Purple (Broadway), 2005; exec. prodr. (ABC Movie of the Week) Overexposed, 1992; host, supervising prodr. celebrity interview series Oprah: Behind the Scenes, 1992, ABC Aftersch. Spls., 1991-93; host, exec. prodr. Michael Jackson Talks...to Oprah-90 Prime-Time Minutes with the King of Pop, 1993; exec. prodr. (TV movies) Nine, 1992, Oprah Winfrey Presents: Their Eyes Were Watching God, 2005; host Oprah Winfrey's Legends Ball (also exec. prodr.), 2006, Building a Dream: The Oprah Winfrey Leadership Acad. (also exec. prodr.), 2007, The Oprah Winfrey Oscar Special, 2007; exec. prodr. (TV miniseries) Oprah Winfrey Presents: The Wedding, 1998, David and Lisa, 1998, Tuesdays with Morrie, 1999, Amy and Isabelle, 2001, Their Eyes Were Watching God, 2005; voice (video) Our Friend, Martin, 1999; guest appearances The Fresh Prince of Bel-Air, 1992, Ellen, 1997, Home Improvement, 1999, The Hughleys, 1999, Mad TV, 2002 and several others. Established Oprah Winfrey Found., 1987—, Oprah's Angel Network, 1997—, ChristmasKindness South Africa, 2002—, Oprah Winfrey Scholars Program, Oprah Winfrey Leadership Academy for Girls, Henley-on-Klip, South Africa, 2006, Seven Fountains Primary Sch, South Africa, 2007. Recipient Woman of Achievement award NOW, 1986, Emmy award for Best Daytime Talk Show Host, 1987, 91, 92, 94, 95, 97, Hon. Nat. Book Award for influential contbn. to reading and books, 1999, Nat. Book Found's 50th Anniversary gold medal, 1999, America's Hope award, 1990, Industry Achievement award Broadcast Promotion Mktg. Execs./Broadcast Design Assn., 1991, Image awards NAACP, 1989, 91, 92, 94, Entertainer of Yr. award NAACP, 1989, CEBA awards, 1989, 90, 91, George Foster Peabody's 1995 Individual Achievement award, 1996, Gold Medal award IRTS, 1996, Lifetime Achievement award NATAS, 1998, People's Choice award, 1997, 98, Horatio Alger award, 1993, Bob Hope Humanitarian award, 54th Ann. Primetime Emmy Awards, 2002, Marian Anderson Award, Phila., 2003, AAP Honors award, Assn. Am. Publishers, 2003, Disting. Svc. award, Nat. Assn. Broadcasters, 2004, Global Humanitarian Action award, UN Assn. USA, 2004, Nat. Freedom award, Nat. Civil Rights Mus., 2005, Nat. Mag. award, Am. Soc. Mag. Editors, 2007, Humanitarian award, Elie Wiesel Found., 2007; ranked #1 Most Powerful In Industry, Entertainment Weekly, 1998, 200 Greatest Pop Culture Icons, VH1, 2003; named Broadcaster of Yr. Internat. Radio and TV Soc., 1988, TV Performer of Yr., TV Guide, 1997, Most Important Person in Books and Media, Newsweek, 1997; named one of 50 Most Beautiful in the World, People, 1997, America's 25 Most Influential People of the 20th Century, Time, 1998, 100 Most Powerful Women in Entertainment, Hollywood Reporter, 2004, 2006, 100 Most Influential People, Time Mag., 2004, 2005, 2007, Most Powerful Women, Forbes mag., 2005-2006, 50 Women to Watch, Wall St. Journal, 2005, 100 Most Influential People, Time Mag., 2006, 100 Most Influential Black Ams., Ebony mag., 2006, 50 Most Powerful Women in Bus., Fortune mag., 2006, 50 Who Matter Now, CNNMoney.com Bus. 2.0, 2006, 100 Most Powerful Celebrities, Forbes-.com, 2007; named to List American Billionaires, Fortune, 2003, 400 Richest Americans, 1999-, World's Richest People, 2003-; inducted to Television Hall of Fame, 1994, Broadcasting and Cable Hall of Fame, 2002, NAACP Hall of Fame, 2005; elected to Nat. Women's Hall of Fame, Seneca Falls, NY. Initiated a campaign to establish a national database of convicted child abusers, and testified before U.S. Senate Judiciary Committee on behalf of National Child Protection Act in 1991, as a result, President Clinton signed the "Oprah Bill" into Law on December 20, 1993, establishing the national database used by law enforcement agencies around the world; third woman in American entertainment industry to own her own studio; first African-American woman to reach billionaire status; after receiving Lifetime Acheivement Award in 1998, permanently withdrew name from Daytime Emmy Award consideration; Oprah and Oprah Winfrey Show received a total of 39 Daytime Emmy awards: seven for Outstanding Host; nine for Outstanding Talk Show; twenty-one in the Creative Arts categories; and one for supervising producer of the ABC School Special, Shades of Single Protein; celebrated the 20th year anniversary of the Oprah Winfrey Show in November, 2005. Office: Oprah Winfrey Show Harpo Studios 1058 W Washington Blvd Chicago IL 60607 Address: Harpo Prodn PO Box 909715 Chicago IL 60607 Office Phone: 312-633-0808. *

WING, ADRIEN KATHERINE, law educator; b. Aug. 7, 1956; d. John Ellison and Katherine (Pruitt) Wing; children: Che-Cabral, Nolan Felipe. AB magna cum laude, Princeton U., 1978; MA, UCLA, 1979; JD, Stanford, 1982. Bar: N.Y. 1983, U.S. Dist. Ct. (so. and ea. dists.) N.Y. 1983, U.S. Ct. Appeals (5th and 9th cirs.). Assoc. Curtis, Mallet-Prevost, Colt & Mosle, NYC, 1982-86, Rabinowitz, Boudin, Standard, Krinsky & Lieberman, 1986-87; assoc. prof. law U. Iowa, Iowa City, 1987-93, prof., 1993—, disting. prof. law, 2001—, assoc. dean faculty R&D, 2006—. Mem. alumni council Princeton U., 1983-85, 96-2000, mem. exec. com., 2002—, trustee Class of '78 Alumni Found., 1984-87, 93—, v.p. Princeton Class of 1978 Alumni, 1993-98, trustee Princeton U. 1995; mem. bd. visitors Stanford Law Sch., 1993-96; vis. prof. U. Mich., 2002. Mem. bd. editors Am. J. Comp. Law, 1993—. Mem. Iowa Commn. on African Ams. in Prisons, 1999—. Recipient Disting. Alum award, Newark Acad., 2004, Gertrude Rush award, 2006. Mem.: ABA (exec. com. young lawyers sect. 1985—87, law sch. site inspector 2002—), U.S. Assn. Constl. Law (bd. dir.), Am. Assn. of Law Schs. (minority sect. bd. 1996—, chair 2002), Am. Friends Svc. Com. (bd. dirs. Mid. East 1998—2004), Am. Soc. Internat. Law (exec. coun. 1986—89, exec. com. 1988—99, nominating com. 1991, 1993, group chair S. Africa 1993—95, membership com. 1994—95, exec. coun. 1996—99, v.p. 2007—), Internat. Assn. Dem. Lawyers (UN rep. 1984—87), Nat. Conf. Black Lawyers (chmn. internat. affairs sect. 1982—95, UN rep.), Internat. Third World Legal Studies Assn. (bd. dirs. 1996—, nominating trustee Princeton com. 1997—2000), Coun. on Fgn. Rels., Iowa Peace Inst. (bd. dirs. 1993—95), Iowa City Fgn. Rels. Coun. (bd. dirs. 1989—94), Transafrica Scholars Forum Coun. (bd. dirs. 1993—95), Black Alumni of Princeton U. (bd. dirs. 1982—87). Democrat. Avocations: photography, writing, poetry. Office: U Iowa Sch Law Boyd Law Bldg Iowa City IA 52242 Home Phone: 319-354-2849; Office Phone: 319-335-9129. E-mail: adrien-wing@uiowa.edu.

WING, ELIZABETH SCHWARZ, museum curator, educator; b. Cambridge, Mass., Mar. 5, 1932; d. Henry F. and Maria Lisa Schwarz; m. James E. Wing, Apr. 18, 1957; children: Mary Elizabeth Wing-Berman, Stephen R. BA, Mt. Holyoke Coll., 1955; MS, U. Fla., 1957, PhD, 1962. Interim asst. curator Fla. Mus. Natural History, U. Fla., Gainesville, 1961-69, asst. curator, 1969-73, assoc. curator, 1973-78, curator, 1978—2001, curator emeritus, 2001—; prof. anthropology dept. U. Fla., 1979—2001, prof. zoology dept., 1988—2001. US rep. Internat. Congress Archaeozoology, 1981—2001. Author: (with A.B. Brown) Paleonutrition, 1979, (with E.J. Reitz) Zooarcheology, 1999, (with Lee A. Newsom) On Land and Sea, 2004; editor (with J.C. Wheeler) Economic Prehistory of the Central Andes, 1988; contbr. articles to profl. jours. Recipient Fryxell award Soc. Am. Archaeology, 1996; NSF grantee, 1961-64, 68-73, 79-80, 84-85, 89-91, 92-95. Mem. NAS, Soc. Ethnobiology (pres. 1989-91, trustee 1991-). Office: U Fla Dickinson Hall/Fla Mus Natural History PO Box 117800 Gainesville FL 32611-7800

WING, JAMES DAVID, lawyer; b. Milw., May 4, 1943; s. William H. and Elaine E. (Koehler) W.; children: Benjamin, Tracy, Nathaniel, John. BA, Beloit Coll., Wis., 1965; MA, U. Chgo., 1966, JD, 1969. Bar: Wis. 1969, Fla. 1975, U.S. Ct. Appeals (7th cir.) 1973, U.S. Dist. Ct. (mid. dist.) Fla. 1975, U.S. Ct. Appeals (5th cir.) 1978, U.S. Dist. Ct. (so. dist.) Fla. 1981, U.S. Ct. Appeals (11th cir.) 1981, U.S. Supreme Ct. 1979. Assoc. Whyte, Hirschboeck, Minahan, Harding & Harland, Milw., 1969-75, Carlton, Fields, Ward, Emmanuel, Smith & Cutler, Tampa, Fla., 1975-85, Myers, Kenin, Levinson, Frank & Richards/Shea & Gould, Miami, Fla., 1985-88, Fine, Jacobson, Schwartz, Nash, Block & England, Miami, 1988-94, Holland & Knight, Miami, 1994—. Fellow Ctr. for Internat. Legal Studies, Salzburg, Austria. Mem. Phi Beta Kappa, Phi Eta Sigma, Omicron Delta Kappa. Avocations: germanistics, tennis. Office: Holland & Knight LLP 701 Brickell Ave Ste 3000 Miami FL 33131 Office Phone: 305-374-8500, 305-789-7768. Fax: 305 789 7799. E-mail: james.wing@hklaw.com.

WING, JOHN RUSSELL, lawyer; b. Mt. Vernon, NY, Jan. 20, 1937; s. John R. and Elinore (Smith) W.; m. Mary Zeller, Aug. 24, 1963 (div. June 1975); children: Ethan Lincoln, Catherine Dorothy; m. Audrey Strauss, Aug. 12, 1979; children: Carlin Elinore, Matthew Lawrence. BA, Yale U., 1960; JD, U. Chgo., 1963. Bar: N.Y. 1964. Assoc. Sherman & Sterling, NYC, 1963-66; asst. U.S. atty. So. Dist. N.Y., NYC, 1966-78; chief fraud unit U.S. Dist. Atty. So. Dist. N.Y., 1971-78; ptnr. Weil, Gotshal & Manges, NYC, 1978—. Contbr. articles to profl. jours. Fellow Am. Coll. Trial Lawyers; mem. ABA (white collar crime com. criminal justice sect. 1978—, environ. task force com. 1983-85), Assn. Bar of City of N.Y. (criminal advocacy com. 1985-88), Fed. Bar Coun. (2d cir. cts. com. 1982-84), N.Y. Coun. Def. Lawyers (bd. dirs. 1986-90). Republican. Episcopalian. Avocation: sailing. Home: 52 Livingston St Brooklyn NY 11201-4813 Office: Weil Gotshal & Manges 767 5th Ave Fl Concl New York NY 10153-0119 Office Phone: 212-310-8364. Business E-Mail: john.wing@weil.com.

WING, THOMAS M., military officer, systems engineer; b. LA, Dec. 8, 1962; s. Wilbur Bill L. and Donna M. Wing; m. Elisa R. Martinez, Aug. 4, 1988; 1 child, Emily Rose. BS in Aerospace Engring., US Naval Acad., Annapolis, Md., 1984; diploma, US Naval War Coll., Newport, RI, 2004. Cert. master vessels to 1600 GT USCG, 1999, 2nd mate, unlimited tonnage, all oceans USCG, 1999, able seaman, unlimited tonnage, all oceans USCG, 1999. Commd. ensign USN, 1980, advanced through grades to comdr., 1999, divsn. officer USS Benjamin Stoddert Pearl Harbor, Hawaii, 1985—87, navigator USS Lynde Mccormick San Diego, 1987—90, instr., curriculum developer fleet combat tng. ctr., 1990—92, combat sys. officer USS Robert G. Bradley Charleston, SC, 1993—95, variouis positions San Diego, 1995—2003, officer command control computers comms. Everett, Wash., 2003—04, liaison officer joint theater air and ballistic missile def. Prince Sultan Air Base, Saudi Arabia, 2003—03, comdr. ctrl. commd. Manama, Bahrain, 2004—, br. head Spawar sys. ctr. San Diego, 2006—. Mem. vestry St. Timothy's Episc. Ch., San Diego, 2002—03. Decorated Combat Action ribbon USN, Civilian Meritorious Svc. award, Joint Svc. Commendation medal. Mem.: US Naval Acad. Alumni Assn. (life), US Naval Inst. (life), Wing Family Am. (assoc.). Episcopalian. Avocations: sailing, skiing, reading, writing. Office: Space and Naval Warfare Syst Ctr 53560 Hull St San Diego CA 92152-5001 Home Phone: 858-271-4890; Office Phone: 619-553-8995. Office Fax: 619-553-6307. Personal E-mail: tmwing@san.rr.com. Business E-Mail: tom.wing@navy.mil.

WINGARD, JOHN REID, medical educator; b. Charleston, SC, Jan. 30, 1947; m. Frances Diane Phillips, 1974; children: Ellen, Emily, Sally, Benjamin. BA in English, Yale U., 1969; MD, The Johns Hopkins U., 1973. Diplomate Am. Bd. Internal Medicine, subspecialty of Med. Oncology. Intern City of Memphis Hosp./U. Tenn. Ctr. for Health Scis., 1973-74, resident, 1974-76; chief resident V.A. Hosp., Memphis, 1976-77; instr. in medicine U. Tenn. Ctr. for Health Scis., Memphis, 1976-77; fellow in oncology and internal medicine The Johns Hopkins U. Sch. Medicine, Balt., 1977-79, various to asst. prof. oncology, 1977-87, assoc. prof. oncology, 1987-91, assoc. prof. medicine, 1990-91; prof. medicine Emory U. Sch. Medicine, Atlanta, 1991-96, prof. Winship Cancer Ctr., 1992-96; dir. bone marrow transplant program, prof. medicine U. Fla., Gainesville, 1996—; dep. dir. U. Fla. Shands Cancer Ctr., 2004—. Dir. bone marrow transplant program Emory U. Sch. Medicine, 1991-96; dir. Bone Marrow Transplant Outpatient Clinic, Johns Hopkins Oncology Ctr., 1984-91; cons. Office of Disability Programs, Social Security Adminstrn., Balt., 1981-91; study group Nat. Inst. Allergy and Infectious Diseases, 1988—; adv. com. Internat. Bone Marrow Transplant Registry, 1989-91, 95—, sec.-treas., 1998—; chair, steering com. Blood and Marrow Transplant Clin. Trials Network, 2001—; bd. dirs. Found. Cellular Therapies, Nat. Marrow Donor Program. Contbr. articles to profl. jours.; contbr. chpts. to books; assoc. editor: Biology of Blood and Marrow Transplantation. Mem. Am. Soc. Microbiology, Am. Soc. Clin. Oncology, Am. Soc. Hematology, Internat. Soc. Exptl. Hematology, Am. Soc. Blood and Marrow Transplantation (pres. 2002-2003). Office: U Fla Coll Medicine PO Box 100277 Gainesville FL 32610-0277 Office Phone: 352-273-8010. Business E-Mail: wingajr@medicine.ufl.edu.

WINGATE, C. KEITH, law educator; b. Darlington, SC, May 12, 1953; s. Clarence L. and Lilly W.; m. Gloria Farley; stepchildren: Brenda, Marvin, Terry and Oliver Champion. BA in Polit. Sci., U. Ill., 1974, JD cum laude, 1978. Bar: Calif., 1978. Assoc. litigation dept. Morrison & Foerster, San Francisco, 1978-80; from asst. to assoc. prof. law U. Calif.-Hastings, San Francisco, 1980-86, prof., 1986—. Dir. Coun. Legal Edn. Opportunity Region I Inst., 1989; vis. prof. law Stanford Law Sch., fall 1990, 94, spring 1998; chair Minority Law Tchrs.' Conf. Com., 1990; mem. acad. assistance work group, 1991; trustee Law Sch. Admission Coun., 1997-2001. Author: (with David I. Levine and William R. Slomanson) Cases and Materials on California Civil Procedure, 1991, (with William R. Slomanson) California Civil Procedure in a Nutshell, 1992, (with Donald L. Doernberg) Federal Courts, Federalism and Separation of Powers, 1994, 2nd edit., 2000. Bd. dirs. Cmty. Housing Devel. Corp., North Richmond, 1990-99. Recipient 10 Outstanding Persons award U. Ill. Black Alumni Assn., 1980; Harno fellow U. Ill., Coll. of Law, 1976. Mem. Assn. Am. Law Schs. (chair sect. minority groups 1990, exec. com. mem. sect. civil proceedure 1991), Charles Houston Bar Assn., Phi Sigma Alpha. Office: U Calif Hastings Coll Law 200 Mcallister St San Francisco CA 94102-4707

WINGATE, CONSTANCE BLANDY, retired librarian; b. Woodbury, NJ, Mar. 7, 1935; d. John Chase and Josephine Spond (Black) Blandy; m. Len B. Cooke Jr., 1978 (div. 1987); m. John B. Wingate, Mar. 12, 1999. BA, U. Pa., 1956; MA, U. Denver, 1957. Adult cons. Onondaga Library System, Syracuse, 1965-66; asst. dir. Mt. Vernon (N.Y.) Public Library, 1966-75; dep. dir. Queens Borough Public Library, Jamaica, NY, 1975-79, dir., 1980-94; ret., 1994. Founder pres. Literacy Vols. Mt. Vernon, 1972-74. Trustee METRO, 1980-91, v.p., 1985-88, pres., 1988-91; mem. N.Y. State Libr. Svcs. and Constrn. Act Adv. Coun., 1982-88, chmn., 1986-87; bd. dirs. Queens Coun. on the Arts, 1988-94, v.p., 1989-93; bd. dirs. Queens Mus. of Art, 1988-98, v.p., 1994-96, pres. 1996-98; bd. dirs. Queens Libr. Found., 1996-2003. Mem.: ALA, Circumnavigators Club (internat. sec. 2002—06, internat. bd. govs. 2006—). Republican. Episcopalian. Home: 166-25 Powells Cove Blvd Beechhurst NY 11357

WINGATE, ROBERT LEE, JR., internist; b. Columbia, SC, May 28, 1936; s. Robert Lee and Helen (Owen) W.; m. Ritanne Cooper, Apr. 19, 1962 (div. 1965); 1 child, Elizabeth Anne Butterfield-Wingate; m. Jeannette DeLatte, Mar. 27, 1968 (div. 1980); children: Laura Owen Wingate, Charlotte Cramer; m. Ann Phyfer, Apr. 1, 1999; 1 child, Jeff Stamm. BS, U. S.C., 1957; MD, Med. Coll. S.C., 1961. Intern Cin. Gen. Hosp., 1961-62, jr. resident internal medicine, 1964-65; asst. resident in internal medicine Med. Coll. of Va., Richmond, 1965-66; resident in internal medicine Charity Hosp. of La., New Orleans, 1966-67, resident in neurology, 1967-68; pvt. practice Columbia, 1968-78; PruCare physician Memphis, 1983-85; med. dir. M. Lowenstein and Celanese Corps., Rock Hill, SC, 1978-80; med. dir. nursing home care unit Dorn VA Hosp., Columbia, 1980-82; med. cons. disability determination div. Vocat. Rehab. S.C., Columbia, 1982-83; cons. Student Health Ctr. U. S.C., Columbia, 1985-86; cons. Urgent Care Ctrs. S.C., 1986-87; pvt. practice Pelion, SC,

1987-92; staff internist, chief of staff, cons. internal medicine Western Mental Health Inst., Western Institute, Tenn., 1992-2000; with Memphis Mental Health Inst., 2000—03. Med. dir. Forest Hills Nursing Ctr., Columbia, 1968-78; med. cons. S.C. Commn. for Blind, Columbia, 1970-78, Mid-Carolina Coun. on Alcoholism, Columbia, 1970-74; instr. internal medicine U. S.C. Sch. Medicine, 1980-82; cons. internal medicine and urgent care Pelion Cmty. Care Ctr., 1989-92; instr. Sch. Nursing, Med. Coll. S.C., Winthrop divsn., 1978-80; lectr. in field; mem. adv. bd. Vector Med. Techs. and Nutrition Superstores; cardiology cons. Western Mental Health Inst., 2000-2003; pvt. practice gen. internal medicine, 2003. Contbr. articles to newspapers; reviewer Annal of Internal Medicine. Ofcl. physician Peanut Party S.C., 1990-92. Lt. comdr. M.C., USNR, 1958-66. Grantee Burroughs-Wellcome Co., 1958, Med. Coll. S.C., 1960, Congress of U.S. 1987. Fellow ACP; mem. AMA (life mem., Physician's Recognition award 1969, 74, 79, 85, 86, 94-96, 96-99, 99-2002), Am. Soc. Internal Medicine, Am. Occupational Med. Assn., So. Med. Assn., West Tenn. Consolidated Med. Assembly, Soc. of 1824, State of Tenn. Med. Assn-.Consol. Med. Assembly of West Tenn. Avocations: chess, hunting, fishing, gardening, billiards.

WINGATE, THOMAS RUSSELL, writer; b. Corning, NY, Feb. 27, 1947; s. Paul Michael and Shirley Janet Smith; m. Martha Anne Guice, May 25, 1985; m. Naomi Loftus Wingate (div.); children: James, Rebecca. BA in History, U. Calif., LA, 1968; MA in History, U. Calif., Santa Barbara, 1970; MBA, U. Phoenix, 1989. Critic Writer's Digest Criticism Svc., Cin., 1992—98; sr. ptnr. Pink Tree Press, Salt Lake City, 1993—2002, Wingate & Wingate Writers, Salt Lake City, 1989—; CFO Project Gutenberg Literary Archive Found., Inc., Salt Lake City, 2001—. Mem.: NRA (life), Am. Mensa (life). Republican. Mem. Lds Ch. Avocations: reading, astronomy, history, poetry, movies. Office: Wingate & Wingate Writers PO Box 16536 Salt Lake City UT 84116 Office Phone: 801-596-1887. Personal E-mail: utahpindar@aol.com.

WINGBLADE, LOREN CHARLES, education educator; b. Chgo., Dec. 23, 1941; s. Loren Milton and Wanda S. Wingblade; m. Susan Leah Bozarth, Apr. 4, 1970. BS in Zoology, U. Wis., Madison, 1966; MA in Psychology, No. Ill. U., DeKalb, 1970; PhD in Psychology, Ind. U., Bloomington, 1977, MA in Sociology, 1988. Cert. bioethics Med. Coll. Wis.-Milw. Asst. prof. Westminster Coll., Fulton, Mo., 1977—83; vis. prof. Ind. U., 1983—89; prof. Jackson C.C., Mich., 1989—. Tchr. Ind. U., Purdue U.; adj. instr. Siena Heights U. Mem. bioethics com. W.A. Foote Hosp., Jackson, 2001—. Mem.: North Ctrl. Sociol. Assn., Midwest Sociol. Assn., Carnegie Coun. on Ethics and Internat. Affairs, NEA, Am. Assn. for the Advancement of Sci., Am. Soc. Bioethics and Humanities, Am. Sociol. Asn., APA. Democrat. Lutheran. Achievements include development of IBM-PC exercises for introductory psychology lab, assessment tool for introductory sociology course. Office: Jackson CC 2111 Emmons Rd Jackson MI 49201 Business E-Mail: loren_c_wingblade@jccmi.edu.

WINGER, ROGER ELSON, retired church administrator; b. Fisherville, Ont., Can., Dec. 25, 1933; s. Elson Clare and Bertha Caroline (Schweyer) W.; m. Della Bertha Lebien, June 7, 1958; children: Jeffrey, Karen Mohr, David, Thomas, Susan. AA, Concordia Jr. Coll., Ft. Wayne, Ind., 1953; BA, Concordia Sem., St. Louis, 1955, theol. diploma, 1958; DD (hon.), Concordia Luth. Sem., Edmonton, Alta., Can., 1991. Ordained to ministry, Luth. Ch., 1958. Pastor Holy Trinity Luth. Ch., London, 1958-64, Good Shepherd Luth. Ch., Coventry, Eng., 1964-69, Luth. Mission, Liverpool, Eng., 1969-72, Faith Luth. Ch., Dunnville, Ont., 1972-78, St. Matthew Luth. Ch., Smithville, Ont., 1972-78, St. Paul's Luth. Ch., Kitchener, Ont., 1978-91; pres. ea. dist. Luth. Ch.-Can., Kitchener, 1991-2000; ret., 2000. V.p. Ont. dist. Luth. Ch.-Can., 1982-88; sec. Luth. Ch.-Can., Winnipeg, Man., 1988-91; mem. bd. regents Concordia Luth. Sem., Edmonton, Alta., 1984-88, Concordia Luth. Sem., St. Catharines Ont., 1991-2000; bd. govs. Lutherwood; bd. dirs. Luth. Bible Translators Can. Lutheran. Avocations: photography, golf, woodworking. Home: 76 Deerwood Crescent Kitchener ON Canada N2N 1R3 E-mail: rogerdella@rogers.com.

WINGERT, HANNELORE CHRISTIANE, realtor, chemicals executive; b. Karlsbad, Czechoslavakia; came to US, 1962, naturalized, 1967; d. Andreas and Gisela Maria (Ciharz) Zwickel; m. Rudolf Wingert, Feb. 9, 1963; children: Angela Helene, Christopher Rudolf. I.BA, Stadt. Berufsschule, Germany, 1961; postgrad. in mgmt., Bergen C.C., 1983. Lic. real estate, NJ, Calif. Clk. various cos., NJ, 1963, bilingual sec. NJ, 1963-78; exec. sec., adminstrv. asst. Lurgi Corp., Hasbrouck Heights, NJ, 1978-81; sr. exec. sec. Degussa Corp., Teterboro, NJ, 1981-83, asst. product mgr. silica, 1983-85, asst. product mgr. H202, 1985-87, sales promotion coord., 1987; sales assoc. Schlott Realtors, Kinnelon, NJ, 1987-90, Coldwell Banker, 1990—2001, Hanson/McMillin Realty, Escondido, Calif., 2002—07, Windermere Exclusive Properties, Escondido, 2007—. Author real estate newsletter, 1992—, cmty. newsletter, 1977-79. Mem. Garden State Multiple Listing Svc.; chmn. master planning com. High Crest Lake, West Milford, NJ, 1974-75; advisor Jr. Woman's Club Kinnelon-Butler, NJ, 1973-74; techr. computer classes Bd. Realtors, Passaic County, 1989-92; vol. usher Ctr. of Arts, Escondido, 2006-. Mem. Nat. Assn. Realtors, Calif. Assn. Realtors, No. San Diego County Assn. Realtors, Sandicor Multiple Listing Svcs., Fed. Woman's Clubs (past pres.), High Crest Lake Woman's Club (West Milford, NJ, pres. 1972-73). Republican. Roman Catholic. Home: 743 Atwood Pl San Marcos CA 92069 Office Phone: 760-233-5320. Personal E-mail: hcwingert@cox.net.

WINGERT, MICHAEL J., computer company executive; BSEE, Univ. Minn. With Maxtor Corp., Milpitas, Calif., 1994—96, v.p. engring., 1996—99, v.p. desktop engring., 1999—2001, sr. v.p. engring., 2001—04; pres., COO, CEO Cornice Inc., Longmont, Colo., 2004; pres., COO Maxtor Corp., Milpitas, Calif., 2004—06; exec. v.p. Maxtor integration Seagate Tech., Scotts Valley, Calif., 2006. Office: Seagate Technology 920 Disc Dr Scotts Valley CA 95066

WINGET, LARRY J., SR., automotive industry executive; Chmn., CEO, pres. Venture Global Engring. Indus., Fraser, Mich. Office: Venture PO Box 278 Fraser MI 48026-0278

WINGET, WALTER WINFIELD, retired lawyer; b. Peoria, Ill., Sept. 12, 1936; s. Walter W. Winget and Arabella (Robinson) Richardson; m. Alice B. Winget, Sept. 23, 1993; children: Marie, Marshall. AB cum laude, Princeton U., 1958; JD, U. Mich., 1961. Bar: RI 1962, Ill. 1962, US Supreme Ct. 1971. Assoc. Edwards & Angell, Providence, 1961-64; ptnr. Winget & Winget, 1964—69, Winget & Kane, Peoria, 1977-2000, of counsel, 2000—07; sole practice Peoria, 1969—77; ret., 2007. Asst. pub. defender Peoria, 1969-70; bd. dirs. various corps. Atty., bd. dirs. Better Bus. Bur. Cen. Ill., Inc. 1973-92, chmn., 1979-81. Served to sgt. U.S. Army, 1961-62. Mem. Ill. Bar Assn., Peoria County Bar Assn. (pres. 1991-92), Peoria Country Club, Princeton Club Chgo. (mem. schs. com. 1980-2006), Safari Club, Oakland Hall Club. Republican. Episcopalian. Avocations: competitive target shooting, big game and duck hunting, farm management. Home: 6712 N Post Oak Rd Peoria IL 61615-2347 Office: Ste 1711 411 Hamilton Blvd Peoria IL 61602-1104 Office Phone: 309-674-2310.

WINICK, BERNYCE ALPERT, artist, photographer; b. NYC; Student, Bklyn. Mus. Art Sch., 1938—41; BA in Fine Arts and Music, NYU; pvt. studies with, Mario Cooper, NYC, 1969—86; student, Traphagen Sch. Fashion, 1958—61, Art Students League N.Y., 1961—64, Nat. Acad. Design Sch. Fine Arts, 1968—72. Artist, Woodmere, L.I., N.Y., 1969—. Designer, fashion artist, fashion con. in field. One-woman shows include Hewlett-Woodmere Pub. Libr., LI, 1969, Galerie Internat., NY, 1977, Thomas Moran (First prize Nat. Acad. Sch., 1972, Salmagundi Club 1981, 82, 87, 90, Nat. Arts Club, 1985, 2002, Nat. Acad. Sch., 1972 (First Prize Meml. award 2002), Gallery Internat. 57, NY, 1989, Discovery Art Gallery, Sea Cliff, LI, 1989, 96, 98, Glen Cove, NY, 1993-94, Chelsea Ctr., East Norwich, NY, 1993, 96, 98, 2000, 02, Z Gallery, SoHo, NY, 1994, County Exec. Bldg., 1997, Fine Arts Mus. LI, 1997, Town Hall, Hempstead, NY, 2000, Wisser Meml. Libr., 2003, NY Inst. Tech., 2004, Wiser Meml. Libr., NY Inst. Tech., Old Westbury, 2007; exhibited in group shows at Discovery Art Gallery, Glen Cove, NY, 1988, 91-93, 1996, 2000, 02, Nat. Acad. Sch. Fine Arts, NY, 1972, Long Beach Mus., LI, 1979, 81-85, 89 (2d prize 1989), Chen Chung Gallery of St. John's U., NY, 1980, Salmagundi Club, NY, 1980-81, 2002 (Thomas Moran Meml. award, 1st prize), Am. Watercolor Soc., NY, 1982, 85, 88, 92, Fine Arts Mus. LI, 1983, 88-89, 91-92, 96 (2d prize), 97, Nat. Arts Club, NY, 1985-86, 88-89, 2002, Nassau County Mus., LI, 1985-86, 88, Nat. Assn. Women Artists, NY, 1986, 88, 91-93, C.W. Post Coll., LI, LI Arts Coun. Freeport, 1995-96, 1999 (First prize in black and white photography), 2006 (Fabian Adler Meml. award), Chelsea Cultural Ctr., NY, 1995, 2001, (Suburban Art League award), Rockville Ctr. Guild for the Arts, NY, 1995, 97 (Best in Show for photography), Chelsea Ctr. (Peacock Showcase award, First prize 2000, Merit award 2001), East Norwich, NY, Discovery Art Gallery, Sea Cliff, NY, 1998, Canton Art Inst. Ohio, Galerie Internat., Gallery Internat. 57, Z Gallery, Salle Augustin-Chenier, Quebec, Can., Town Hall, Town of Hempstead, NY, 2000, NY Inst. Tech., Wisser Meml. Libr., 2001, Nat. Arts Club (First photography prize 2002), Heckscher Mus., Huntington, NY, 2003, Mills Pond House, St. James, NY, 2002, 05 (1st prize watercolor), Nat. Arts Club, NY, 2001 (1st prize), NY Inst. Tech. Wissen Meml. Libr., Old Westbury, 2004, others; work included in US Dept. State Art in Embassies program, pvt. and corp. collections including Carnegie Hall; photographs in publs. including South Shore Record, 1995, Encyclopedia of Watercolour Landscape Techniques, 1996, Popular Photography, 1996-97, 99-00, 04, Photography on America Online, 1997, 99-2000, New York: Sterling Pub. Co., Inc., 1998, Watercolor Planning and Painting, 1998, Abstracts in Watercolor, 1996, NY Times, 1999, 2001, NY Inst. Tech., 2003, Wisser Meml. Libr., Old Westbury, NY, 2004, Mills Pond House (1st prize watercolor 2005), St. James, NY, 2005; photography in (books) Capturing the Seen and Unseen in Photographs, 2001, Thirty Nine Musical Photographs, 2003, Town and Country Mag.; photographs exhibited in Mill Pond House, Salmagundi Club, NYU, Nat. Assn. Women Artists, Artists Unlimited, Tampa, Fla.; author poetry; contbr. articles to profl. jours. Recipient award, Salmagundi Club, 2004, 2005, other awards, Fabian Adler Meml. award, L.I. Arts Coun., 2006. Fellow Royal Soc. Encouragement Arts Manufactures and Commerce; mem. Am. Watercolor Soc., Nat. Assn. Women Artists, Tri County Artists, Long Beach Art League, Art League of LI, Harvard Club, Arts Group, Poetry Group. Avocations: fashion design, piano, poetry. Home and Office: 923 Beth Ln Woodmere NY 11598-1507 Office Phone: 516-374-6415.

WINICK, MARTIN, pediatric surgeon; b. NYC, Feb. 20, 1935; s. David Winick and Sadie Zubress Winicj; m. Marianne Winick; children: Stephen, Suzanne, Vanessa, Jonathon. BS magna cum laude, CCNY, 1956; MD, SUNY, Bklyn., 1960. Rotating intern Jewish Hosp. Bklyn., 1960—61, gen. surgery resident, 1961—65; pediat. surgery resident St. Christopher's Hosp. for Children., Phila.; pediatric surgeon pvt. practice, Suffolk, NY, 1968. Lt. comdr. USPHS, 1966—68. Fellow: Am. Coll. Surgeons; mem.: Am. Pediatric Surg. Assn. Republican. Jewish. Home: 5 Pine Point Huntington NY 11743 Office: 158 E Main St Huntington NY 11743-2988 Office Phone: 631-427-1300.

WINICK, MYRON, nutrition professor, physician; b. NYC, May 4, 1929; s. Charles B. and Ruth E. (Gesser) W.; m. Elaine L. Lasky, Sept. 19, 1964; children: Jonathan, Stephen. AB, Columbia U., 1951; MS, U. Ill., 1952; MD, SUNY, 1956. Intern U. Pa., Phila., 1956-57; asst. resident pediatrics Cornell U. Med. Coll., NYC, 1957-59, chief resident, 1959-60; attending pediatrician Stanford U. Hosp., 1963-64; asst. prof. pediatrics Cornell U. Med. Coll., NYC, 1964-68, assoc. prof. pediatrics and nutrition, 1968-70, prof., 1970-71; dir. Inst. Human Nutrition Columbia U. Inst. Human Nutrition, 1972-87, prof. pediatrics, 1972-89, R.R. Williams prof. nutrition, 1973-89, R.R. Williams prof. emeritus, 1990—; pres. U. Health Scis./Chgo. Med. Sch., North Chgo., Ill., 1990-93; dir. Ctr. for Nutrition, Genetics and Human Devel., 1975-87. Vis. prof. pediatrics U. Chile, Santiago, 1967; asst. attending pediatrician NY Hosp., NYC, 1964-68, assoc. attending pediatrician, 1968-70, attending pediatrician, 1970-71; attending pediatrician Presbyn. Hosp., NYC, 1972-89; cons. Pan Am. Health Orgn., 1966—; med. dir. Weight Watchers Internat., 1997—; sr. scientist Am. Health Found., 1999—. Author: Malnutrition and Brain Development, 1976; textbook Nutrition in Health and Disease, 1980; Growing Up Healthy; A Parent's Guide to Good Nutrition, 1982; For Mothers and Daughters: A Guide to Good Nutrition for Women, 1983; Your Personalized Health Profile: Choosing the Diet That's Right for You, 1985; Nutrition, Pregnancy and Early Infancy, 1989; The Fiber Prescription, 1992; editor: textbook Current Concepts in Nutrition, 1972—, Nutrition: Pre- and Postnatal Development, Vol. I, Human Nutrition: A Comprehensive Treatise, 1979, Columbia Ency. of Nutrition, 1988, (with Joan Lunden) Growing Up Healthy, 2004, Final Stamp: The Jewish Doctors in the Warsaw Ghetto, 2007; contbg. editor Nutrition Revs., 1969-76; mem. editl. bd. Jour. Nutrition, 1972-76, 82-86, The Year in Metabolism (now Contemporary Metabolism), 1975—; assoc. editor Growth, 1984—; nutrition editor Cancer Prevention, 1994—. Trustee Found. for Internat. Child Health; mem. nutrition interdisciplinary cluster Pres.' Biomed. Research Panel, 1975; mem. panel on infants and children Pres.' Commn. on Mental Health, 1977; cons. Office of Tech. Assessment, U.S. Congress, 1976-78; mem. Food and Nutrition Bd. NRC, 1982-88. With USNR, 1960-62. Bank of Am.-Gianini Found. fellow Stanford, 1962; NIH Spl. fellow, 1963; recipient NIH Career Devel. award, 1968-71; E. Mead Johnson award pediatric research, 1970; Osborne and Mendel award Am. Inst. Nutrition, 1976; Agnes Higgins award March of Dimes Found., 1983 Fellow Royal Soc. Health, Am. Soc. Nutritional Scis., Am. Acad. Pediatrics; mem. AAAS, Am. Soc. Cell Biology, Soc. Developmental Biology, Harvey Soc., Soc. Pediatric Rsch., Royal Soc. Medicine, Brit. Nutrition Soc., Am. Soc. Clin. Nutrition, NY Acad. Scis., NY Acad. Medicine, (cons.), Soc. for Exptl. Biology and Medicine, Soc. for Neurosci., Internat. Soc. for Devel. Neurosci., Cosmos Club. Home: 165 West End Ave Apt 10K New York NY 10023 Business E-Mail: mw29@columbia.edu.

WINK, ANDRE, history professor; s. Andries Wink and Catharina Jacoba Mathijsse. PhD, U. Leiden, Netherlands, 1984. C&C Huygens fellow NWO, The Hague, Netherlands, 1984—89; prof. history U. Wis., Madison, 1989—. Author: Al-Hind:The Making of the Indo-Islamic World, 3 vols. Office: Univ Wis 455 N Park St Madison WI 53706 Home Phone: 312-397-9798; Office Phone: 608-263-5092. Business E-Mail: awink@wisc.edu.

WINKEL, RAYMOND NORMAN, aerospace scientist, consultant, retired military officer; b. Flint, Mich., Dec. 8, 1928; s. Norman Martin and Evelyn Matilda (Hylen) W.; m. Ellen Stefula, Dec. 29, 1955 (dec. Feb. 2006); children: Raymond Norman, Ann, Maryellen. *Moved to Muskegon, Michigan at age 1. Raised in Muskegon and graduated from Muskegon High School in 1946.* BS, U.S. Naval Postgrad. Sch., Monterey, Calif., 1964; MS, Villanova U., Pa., 1967; grad. advanced mgmt. program, Harvard U., 1973. Enlisted in USN, 1948, commd. ensign, designated naval aviator, 1951, advanced through grades to rear adm., 1979; service in Far East; comdg. officer Naval Electronics Systems Test and Evaluation Facility St. Inigoes, Md., 1969-71; dir. avionics U.S. Navy, 1973-76; project mgr. Navy/Marine Corps heavy lift helicopter, 1976-78; gen. mgr. Navy/industry team to develop new ship/aircraft weapon system for anti-submarine warfare LAMPS Mark III, 1978-81; ret. USN, 1981; v.p. Washington ops. Telephonics Corp., Huntington, NY, 1981-82; v.p. programs and contracts Astronautics Corp. Am., Milw., 1982-94; aerospace industry cons. Heathsville, Va., 1994-95. Decorated Legion of Merit, Air medal, Navy Achievement medal. Mem. Exptl. Aircraft Assn., U.S. Naval Inst., Assn. Naval Aviation, Mil. Officers Assn. Am., Kiwanis, Indian Creek Yacht and Country Club, U.S. Power Squadron. Republican. Roman Catholic. Home: 1860 Island Point Rd Heathsville VA 22473-3729 E-mail: rwinkel@crosslink.net.

WINKELRIED, JON A., investment banker; b. Millburn, NJ, 1959; m. Abby Ellen Lipsey, Feb. 23, 1986. AB, U. of Chicago, 1981, MBA, 1982. Joined Goldman, Sachs & Co., Chgo., 1982, ptnr., 1990, head leveraged fin., 1995, mem. mgmt. com., 1999—, global co-head fixed income, currency and commodities London, 2000; co-head investment banking divsn. The Goldman Sachs Group, Inc., 2005—06, pres., co-COO NYC, 2006—. Office: The Goldman Sachs Group Inc 85 Broad St New York NY 10004

WINKELSTEIN, WARREN, JR., physician, educator; b. Syracuse, NY, July 1, 1922; s. Warren and Evelyn (Neiman) W.; children: Rebecca Winkelstein Yamin, Joshua, Shoshana; m. Veva Kerrigan, Feb. 14, 1976. BA, U. N.C., 1942; MD cum laude, Syracuse U., 1947; MPH, Columbia U., 1950. Diplomate Am. Bd. Preventive Medicine. Intern Charity Hosp., New Orleans, 1947-48; with ICA (Vietnam), 1951-53; from dir. div. communicable disease control to 1st dep. comdr. local, environ. health svcs. Erie County Health Dept., 1953-62; from assoc. prof. to prof. SUNY, Buffalo, 1962-68; prof. epidemiology, dean pub. health U. Calif., Berkeley, 1972-96, prof. emeritus, 1996. Dir. Internat. Environ. Epidemiology Inst., 1997. Author: Basic Readings in Epidemiology, 1972; contbr. articles profl. jours. With AUS, 1944-46. Mem. APHA, AAAS, Internat. Am. Epidemiol. Socs., Am. Heart Assn. Address: Dept Epidemiol Univ Calif Sch Pub Health Berkeley CA 94720-7360

WINKENWERDER, WILLIAM, JR., former federal agency administrator; b. Ashville, NC, Apr. 27, 1954; BS, Davidson Coll., 1976; MD, U. N.C., 1981; MBA, U. Pa., 1986; postgrad., Stanford U., 1991. Resident internal medicine N.C. Meml. Hosp. U. N.C., 1981-84; instr. dept. medicine Sch. Medicine U. Pa., 1984-87; spl. asst. to adminstr. Health Care Financing Adminstrn. US Dept. Health & Human Services, 1987-88; dir. quality assurance and utilization mgmt. Southeast Permanente Med. Group, Kaiser Permanente, Atlanta, 1988-90, assoc. med. dir., 1990-92; v.p. CMO so. ops. Prudential Health Care, Atlanta, 1992-95; v.p. primary care svcs. Emory Health Care, Atlanta, 1996-98; assoc. v.p. health affairs Robert Woodruff Health Scis. Ctr. Emory U., 1996-98; exec. v.p. health care svcs., vice chmn. Blue Cross Blue Shield Mass., Boston, 1998—; asst. sec. for health affairs US Dept. Def., Washington, 2001—07. Mem. exec. com. Emory Healthcare, Emory Clinic, 1996-98; chmn. CMO com. Prudential Healthcare, 1992-95; bd. dirs. Care Sci. Corp., Wharton Sch. Bus. Health Care Alumni, Fed. Employees Program-Blue Cross Blue Shield Assn., The Reed and Barton Co.; founder HCFA Effectiveness Initiative, U.S. Dept. Health and Human Svcs., participant Task Forces on Health and Human Svcs. AIDS and Minority Health, 1987-88, U.S. Pub. Health Risk Assessment and Quality Assurance, Sec.'s Minority Health, Sec.'s Catastophic Illness; rep. Prudential on Med. Dirs. Com. on Group Health Assn. Am.; spkr. in field. Contbr. articles to profl. jours. Kaiser Family Found. fellow, 1984-86, 87-88, Kellogg Pub. Health Policy fellow U. Pa., 1986, Wharton Washington fellow U. Pa., 1986. Mem.: AMA, Am. Soc. Internal Medicine, Health Care Forum's Physician Leader Network, Am. Assn. Health Plans (bd. dirs.), Am. Coll. Physician Execs., Am. Coll. Physicians, Davidson Coll. Alumni Assn. *

WINKLEBLACK, ARTHUR B., food products executive; BA in Bus. and Econs., UCLA; MBA, U. Pa. Exec. v.p., CFO C. Dean Metropoulos & Co., 1998—99; acting COO Perform.com, 1999—2001; CEO Freeride-.com at Indigo Capital, 1999—2001; exec. v.p., CFO H.J. Heinz Co., Pitts., 2002—. Office: HJ Heinz Co 600 Grant St Pittsburgh PA 15219 *

WINKLEBLECH, EILEEN, computer technology educator, career planning administrator; b. Newark, Dec. 17, 1966; d. William John Glagola and Rose Sharon Reed; m. Vincent Anthony Winkleblech, July 12, 1992; children: Zachary Charles, Erik William, Cameron Allan. B in Edn., Caldwell Coll., NJ, 1988. Cert. Tchr. of Elem. Edn. N.J. State Dept. of Edn., 1988. Self- contained multidisciplinary instr. grade 8 Wash. Sch., Harrison, NJ, 1988—89, life skills, health, career edn., computer tech. edn. instr., 1999—2002; adult a.c.e. tech. grant program instr., 2000—01; basic skills math. instr. grades 6-8, 2003—05; after-school improvement program instr. grade 8, 2005; strategies in math. instr. grades 6—8, 2005; computer tech., career edn. instr. grades 6-8 Wash. Sch., Harrison, NJ, 2006—. Student/staff support team mem. Wash. Sch., Harrison, NJ, 1999—; a.c.e. tech. grant summer camp coord. Harrison (N.J.) Bd. of Edn., 2001; tech. com. chairperson Wash. Sch., Harrison, NJ, 2004—; after sch. improvement program coord. Wash. Sch./ Lincoln Sch., Harrison, NJ, 2004—05; math. team leader Wash. Sch., Harrison, NJ, 2006—. Office: Washington Sch 223 Hamilton St Harrison NJ 07029 Home Phone: 973-497-2125; Office Phone: 973-482-2285. Business E-Mail: ewinkleblech@harrison.k12.nj.us.

WINKLER, AGNIESZKA M., marketing executive; b. Rome, Feb. 22, 1946; came to U.S., 1953; naturalized, 1959; d. Wojciech A. and Halina Z. (Owsiany) W.; children from previous marriage: children: Renata G. Ritcheson, Dana C Sworakowski; m. Arthur K. Lund. BA, Coll. Holy Name, 1967; MA, San Jose State U., 1971; MBA, U. Santa Clara, 1981. Tchg. asst. San Jose State U., 1968-70; cons. to Ea. European bus. Palo Alto, Calif., 1970-72; pres./founder Commart Communications, Palo Alto, 1973-84; pres./founder, chmn. bd. Winkler Advt., Santa Clara, Calif., 1984—; chmn. bd. SuperCuts, Inc.; chmn., founder TeamToolz, 2000—04, The Winkler Group, 2004—. Bd. dirs. Reno Air, Lifeguard, Lifeguard Life Ins., IP Locks, C200, Inter-tel, Western Folklife Ctr., The Cheesecake Factory Inc., 2007-; exec. com. C200. Author: Warp Speed Branding, 1999. Trustee Santa Clara U., 1991—; trustee O'Connor Found., 1987-93, mem. exec. com., 1988—, mem. Capital Campaign steering com., 1989; mem. nat. adv. bd. Comprehensive Health Enhancement Support System, 1991—; mem. mgmt. west com. A.A.A.A. Agy., 1991—, vice chair no. Calif. coun., 1996—; project dir. Poland Free Enterprise Plan, 1989-92; mem. adv. bd. Normandy France Bus. Devel., 1989-92; mem. bd. regents Holy Names Coll., 1987—; bd. dirs. San Jose Mus. Art, 1987; mem. San Jose Symphony, Gold Baton, 1986; mem. nat. adv. com. Chess, 1991—; dir. Bay Area Coun., 1994—. Recipient CLIO award in Advt., Addy award, others; named to 100 Best Women in Advt., Ad Age, 1988, Best Woman in Advt., AdWeek and McCall's Mag., 1993, one of 100 Best and Brightest Women in Mktg. & Advt., Nat. Assn. Women Bus. Owners, 1996. Mem. Family Svc. Assn. (trustee 1980-82), Am. Assn. Advt. Agys. (agy. mgmt. west com. 1991), Bus. Profl. Advt. Assn., Polish Am. Congress, San Jose Advt. Club, San Francisco Ad Club, Beta Gamma Sigma (hon.), Pi Gamma Mu, Pi Delta Phi (Lester-Tinneman award 1966, Bill Raskob Found. grantee 1965).

WINKLER, ALLEN WARREN, lawyer, educator; b. Chgo., Dec. 11, 1954; s. Maurice A. and Florence (Klein) W.; m. Bett C. Gibson, Nov. 1, 1986. BS, No. Ill. U., 1977; JD, Tulane U., 1981. Bar: La. 1980, Ill. 1982, U.S. Dist. Ct. (ea. dist.) La. 1982, U.S. Dist. Ct. (mid. dist.) La. 1987. Atty. Tulane Law Clinic, New Orleans, 1980—81, La. Legal Clinic, New Orleans, 1982-84; pvt. practice law New Orleans, 1984-85; staff atty. Oak Tree Savs. Bank, S.S.B., New Orleans, 1985-87, sr. atty., asst. v.p.,

1987-90; atty. FDIC/Resolution Trust Corp., Baton Rouge, 1991-92, sr. atty. Atlanta, 1992-95; sr. corp. counsel Fleet Fin., Inc., Atlanta, 1996-97; pres. Legal Ease Inc., Atlanta, 1996—; corp. counsel Prudential Bank, Atlanta, 1997; gen. counsel, v.p. NCS Mortgage Svcs., Norcross, Ga., 1998-2000, gen. counsel, 1999-2000; exec. v.p., COO Companion Servicing Co., LLC, 1999-2000; corp. counsel Provident Bank, Atlanta, 2000-2001; first v.p. sr. counsel SunTrust Banks, Inc., Atlanta, 2001—. Mem. faculty Franklin Coll. Ct. Reporting, Metairie, La., 1981-88; cons., guest lectr. paralegal studies Tulane U., New Orleans, 1982-90; guest lectr. U. New Orleans, 1988-90. Vol. Hawkins for Judge campaign, New Orleans. Mem. La. Bar Assn., Ill. Bar Assn. Home: 4754 Forest Glen Court Marietta GA 30066 Office: SunTrust Bank 3600 SunTrust Plz 303 Peachtree St NE Atlanta GA 30308 Home Phone: 770-928-1820; Office Phone: 404-658-4363. Business E-Mail: allen.winkler@suntrust.com.

WINKLER, CHARLES HOWARD, investment company executive; b. NYC, Aug. 4, 1954; s. Joseph Conrad and Geraldine Miriam (Borok) W.; m. Joni S. Taylor, Aug. 28, 1993. BBA with highest distinction, Emory U., 1976; JD, Northwestern U., 1979. Bar: Ill. 1979, U.S. Dist. Ct (no. dist.) Ill. 1979. Assoc. Levenfeld & Kanter, Chgo., 1979-80, Kanter & Eisenberg, Chgo., 1980-84, ptnr., 1985-86, Neal Gerber & Eisenberg, Chgo., 1986-96; sr. mng. dir., COO Citadel Investment Group, LLC, Chgo., 1996—2001; sr. mng. dir. Citadel Trading Group, Chgo., 1996—2000, Aragon Investments Ltd., Chgo., 1996—2000. Bd. dirs. Kensington Global Strategies Fund, Ltd., Antaeus Internat. Investments, Ltd., Jackson Investment Fund Ltd., Citadel Investment Group (Europe) Ltd., chief oper. officer, and sr. mng. dir. Amaranth Group Inc., 2001—.; hedge fund mgr. Author: (with others) Basic Tax Shelters, 1982, Limited Liability Companies: The Entity of Choice, 1995; mng. editor Northwestern Jour. Internat. Law and Bus., 1979. Mem. ABA (mem. sect. on taxation), Beta Gamma Sigma. Office: Amaranth Group Inc One American Ln Greenwich CT 06831 Office Phone: 203-422-3320. Business E-Mail: cwinkler@amaranthllc.com.

WINKLER, DANA JOHN, lawyer; b. Wichita, Kans., Jan. 2, 1944; s. Donald Emil and Hazel Claire (Schmitter) W.; m. Mary Ann Seiwert, Oct. 14, 1967; 1 child, Jonathan. BA, Wichita State U., 1967; JD, Washburn Law Sch., 1971. Staff writer Wichita Eagle & Beacon, 1961-67; ptnr. Davis, Bruce, Davis & Winkler, Wichita, 1972-77; asst. city atty. City of Wichita, 1977-99; dir. Wichita Mcpl. Fed. Credit Union, 1980—, pres., 1982, 99-2000, sec.-treas., 1994-98, v.p., 1998-99. Dir. Deaf and Hard of Hearing Counseling Svc., 1979-80. Vol. Sedgwick County United Way, Wichita, 1973-74; vice-chmn. Wichita Pub. Schs. Spl. Edn. Adv. Coun., 1987-89. 1st lt. U.S. Army, 1967-69. Mem. Kans. Bar Assn., Wichita Bar Assn. Republican. Roman Catholic. Home and Office: 1621 Harlan St Wichita KS 67212-1842 Personal E-mail: djwinkler@cox.net.

WINKLER, GAIL CASKEY, historian, writer; b. Chgo., Aug. 5, 1942; d. Robert E. and Ethel (Barquist) Caskey; m. Robert H. Winkler, Jan. 22, 1964 (div. 1976); m. Roger W. Moss, July 19, 1981. BA, Beloit Coll., Wis., 1964; MA, U. Wis., 1971, MS, 1977, PhD, 1988. Instr. U. Wis., Madison, 1976-81; sr. ptnr. LCA Assocs., Phila., 1982—; adj. faculty U. Pa., Phila., 1986—; asst. prof. U. Del., 1991-93. Author: Victorian Interior Decoration, 1986, Victorian Exterior Decoration, 1987, Floor Coverings for Historic Buildings, 1988, The Well-Appointed Bath, 1989, An Analysis of Drapery, 1993; (museum installations include), William Conner House, Conner Prairie, Fishers, Ind., Lanier Mansion, Madison, Ind., Tudor Hall in Pamplin Park, Petersburg, Va., Fairlawn Mansion, Superior, Wis., Adams House Mus., Deadwood, S.D., Villa Louis, Prairie du Chien, Wis., Hixon House, LaCrosse, Wis., Campbell House Mus., St. Louis, Dr. Richard Eells House, Quincy, Ill., (projects include) studies of the historic finishes and furnishings of the U.S. Senate and House, Chambers, Va. State Capitol, Richmond, City Hall, Phila., Capitol of the Commonwealth Pa., Rutherford B. Hayes house, Fremont, Ohio, Buchanan house, U.S. Naval Acad., Anderson Cottage (summer White House Abraham Lincoln), Washington, D.C., Wright Bros.' Printing Shop, Dayton, Ohio. Fellow Am. Soc. Interior Designers (bd. dirs. Pa. East chap. 1983-88, 2001—, Athena award 1989, Medallist award 1995), Found. Interior Design Edn. and Rsch. (rsch. com. 1986-96). Office: 604 S Washington Sq Philadelphia PA 19106-4118 Office Phone: 215-925-8367.

WINKLER, HENRY FRANKLIN, actor, film producer, director; b. NYC, Oct. 30, 1945; s. Harry Irving and Ilse Anna Maria (Hadra) W.; m. Stacey Weitzman, May 5, 1978; children: Zoe Emily, Max Daniel, (stepchildren) Jed Weitzman. BA, Emerson Coll., 1967, PhD, 1978; MA, Yale Sch. Drama, 1970. With Yale Repertory Theatre, 1970-71. Founder New Haven Free Theatre, 1968, Off The Wall N.Y., improvisation co., 1972; tchr. drama UCLA Adult Extension; founding mem. Children's Action Network. Off-Broadway shows, 1972-73, Cin. Playhouse, 1973; Broadway shows, The Dinner Party; London Theatre, Peter Pan, 2006; films include The Lords of Flatbush, 1972, Crazy Joe, 1974, Heroes, 1977, The One and Only, 1977, Night Shift, 1983, Wes Craven's Scream, 1996, Ground Control, 1998, The Water Boy, 1998, Ugly Naked People, 1999, Elevator Seeking, 1999, Dill Scallion, 1999, P.U.N.K.S., 1999, Down to You, 2000, I Shaved My Legs for This, 2001, Holes, 2003, Fronterz, 2004, Unbeatable Harold, 2005, Berkeley, 2005, The Kid and I, 2005, The King of Central Park, 2006, Click, 2006; starred in TV series Happy Days, 1973-84, Fonz and the Happy Days Gang (voice), 1980, The Mork & Mindy/Laverne & Shirley with the Fonz Show (voice), 1982, Monty, 1994 (also exec. prodr.), Mr. Sunshine, (voice) Clifford's Puppy Days, 2003 (Performer for an animated program, Daytime Emmy award, Acad. TV Arts & Scis., 2005), Out of Practice, 2005-; appeared in TV films Katherine, 1975, America Salutes Richard Rodgers: The Sound of His Music, 1976, An American Christmas Carol, 1979 (ABC), Absolute Strangers, 1991 (CBS), The Only Way Out, 1994 (ABC), Truman Capote's One Christmas, 1994 (NBC), A Child is Missing, 1995 (CBS) (also exec. prodr.), Dad's Week Off, 1996 (Showtime), National Lampoon's Dad's Week Off, 1997, Detention: The Siege at Johnson High, 1997, Beverly Hills S.U.V., 2006; exec. producer (TV) Who Are the Debolts? Where Did They Get Nineteen Kids?, 1977, Starflight:The Plane That Couldn't Land, 1983, Ryan's Four, 1983, When Your Lover Leaves, 1983, Scandal Sheet, 1984, MacGyver, 1985-94 (several episodes), Mr. Sunshine, 1986, A Family Again, 1988, Starting Now, 1989, Sightings, 1992, Dead Man's Gun, 1997, 1999, So Weird, 1999, Sightings: Heartland Ghosts, 2002, WinTuition, 2002, Hollywood Squares, 2002-04, Young MacGyver, 2003, Unexplained Mysteries, 2003, Dallas Reunion: Return to Southfork, 2004, Happy Days: 30th Anniversary Reunion, 2005, Knots Landing Reunion: Together Again, 2005; prodr. (films) The Sure Thing, 1985; prodr., host home video Strong Kids, Safe Kids, 1985, PBS animated spl. Happy Ever After, 1985, Two Daddies to Love Me, 1988; prodr. (films) Young Sherlock Holmes, 1985; prodr. (TV films) Losing a Sister, 1988; pres. Fair Dinkum Prodns., Hollywood, Calif., 1979—, Winkler-Daniels Prodns., Hollywood, 1987-91; prodr. (TV) Run, Don't Walk for own co. JZM Prodns., 1981; dir. (TV) Joanie Loves Chachi, 1982; dir. (TV films) All the Kids Do It, 1984, A Smokey Mountain Christmas, 1986, Memories of Me, 1988, Cop and a Half, 1993, Dave's World, 1993, Too Something, 1995, Clueless, 1996, Sabrina, the Teenage Witch, 1996; TV guest appearances include Mary Tyler Moore, 1973, The Bob Newhart Show, 1974, Laverne & Shirley, 1976, 1979, Saturday Night Live, 1977, Mork & Mindy, 1978, Joanie Loves Chachi, 1982, Macgyver, 1990, (voice) Street Sharks, 1995, (voice) South Park, 1998, The Practice, 1999, 2000, (voice) The Simpsons, 1999, The Drew Carey Show, 2001, Law & Order: Special Victims Unit, 2002, Hollywood Squares, 2003, Arrested Development, 2003-05 (several episodes), Third Watch, 2004, Crossing Jordon, 2005; co-author (with Lin Oliver) (children's book series): Hank Zipzer:The World's Greatest Underachiever. Recipient Golden Globe award 1976, 77, 78, Golden Plate award Am. Acad. Achievement 1980, Daytime Emmy nomination best dir. All The Kids Do It, produced for JZM Prodns., 1985, Sorrisi e Canzoni Telegatto award (Italian TV award) 1980, Humanitarian award Women in Film, 1988, UN Peace prize, Chevalier de l'Ordre des Arts et des Lettres; named hon. youth chmn. Epilepsy Found., chmn. Toys for Tots, 1977, Best Actor in Comedy Series, Photoplay mag. 1976-77, King of Baccus, Mardi Gras, New Orleans 1977, Emmy nominee 1975, 76, 77, nat. spokesperson United Friends of the Children, 1982—. Mem. AFTRA, Screen Actors Guild, Actors Equity. Address: Evan Tripoli Internat Creative Mgmt 8942 Wilshire Blvd Beverly Hills CA 90211 *

WINKLER, HENRY RALPH, retired academic administrator, historian; b. Waterbury, Conn., Oct. 27, 1916; s. Jacob and Ethel (Rieger) W.; m. Clare Sapadin, Aug. 18, 1940; children— Allan Michael, Karen Jean; m. Beatrice Ross, Jan. 28, 1973. AB, U. Cin., 1938, MA, 1940; PhD, U. Chgo., 1947; degree (hon.), Lehigh U., 1974, Rutgers U., 1977, No. Ky. U., 1978, St. Thomas Inst., 1979, Hebrew Union Coll., 1980, Xavier U., 1981, U. Akron, 1984, U. Cin., 1987, Thomas More Coll., 1989. Instr. U. Cin., 1939-40; asst. prof. Roosevelt Coll., 1946-47; mem. faculty Rutgers U., 1947-77, prof. history, 1958-77, chmn. dept., 1960-64; dean Faculty Liberal Arts, 1967, vice provost, 1968-70, acting provost, 1970, v.p. for acad. affairs, 1970-72, sr. v.p. for acad. affairs, 1972-76, exec. v.p., 1976-77, U. Cin., 1977, pres., 1977-84, pres. emeritus, 1984—, Univ. prof. history, 1977-86, prof. emeritus, 1986—. Mng. editor Am. Hist. Rev., 1964-68; vis. prof. Bryn Mawr Coll., 1959-60, Harvard, summer 1964, Columbia, summer 1967; faculty John Hay Fellows Inst. Humanities, 1960-65; bd. overseers Hebrew Union Coll., 1984—. Author: The League of Nations Movement in Great Britain, 1914-19, 1952, Great Britain in the Twentieth Century, 1960, 2d edit., 1966; editor: (with K.M. Setton) Great Problems in European Civilization, 1954, 2d edit., 1966, Twentieth-Century Britain, 1977, Paths Not Taken: British Labour and International Policy in the Nineteen Twenties, 1994, British Labour Seeks a Foreign Policy, 2004; mem. editorial bd. Historian, 1958-64, Liberal Edn., 1986—; mem. adv. bd. Partisan Rev., 1972-79; contbr. articles to jours., revs. Nat. chmn. European history advanced placement com. Coll. Entrance Exam. Bd., 1960-64; mem. Nat. Commn. on Humanities in Schs., 1967-68, Am. specialist Eastern Asia, 1968; exec. com. Conf. on Brit. Studies, 1968-75; chmn. bd. Nat. Humanities Faculty, 1970-73; chmn. adv. com. on history Coll. Entrance Exam. Bd., 1977-80; mem. council on acad. affairs, mem. bd. trustees, chmn., 1982-84; pres. Highland Park (N.J.). Bd. Edn., 1962-63; mem. exec. com. Nat. Assn. State Univs. and Land-Grant Colls., 1978-81, mem. Cin. Lit. Club, 1978—, pres., 1993—; bd. dirs. Am. Council on Edn., 1979-81; trustee Seasengood Good Govt. Found., 1979—, pres., 1991-93; trustee Thomas More Coll., 1986-93; mem. Ohio Indsl. Tech. and Enterprise Bd., 1983-89; bd. dirs. Nat. Civic League, 1986—, Planning Accreditation Bd., 1988—; mem. adv coun. U. Va.'s Coll at Wise, Ohio Humanities Coun., 1994— With USNR, 1943-46. Recipient Lifetime Achievement award N.Am. Conf. on Brit. Studies, 1995, Bishop William Hughes award for disting. svc. to Cath. higher edn. Thomas More Coll., 1997, Leadership Medallion, Xavier U., 2003, Excellence award U. Cin., 2006. Mem. Am. Hist. Assn., Phi Beta Kappa, Tau Kappa Alpha, Phi Alpha Theta. Clubs: Comml., Bankers, Cin., Lit. Office: U Cin 571 Langsam Library Cincinnati OH 45221-0001 Business E-Mail: Henry.Winkler@uc.edu.

WINKLER, IRWIN, motion picture producer; b. NYC, May 28, 1931; s. Sol and Anna Winkler; m. Margo Winkler; 1 child. BA, NYU, 1955. Mailroom messenger William Morris Agy., NYC, 1955-62; motion picture producer, owner Winkler Films, Culver City, Calif., 1982—. Pres., Chartoff-Winkler Prodns., 1966—. Prodr.: Rocky, 1976 (10 Acad. award nominations, winner 3 including Best Picture, Los Angeles Film Critics award for best picture), They Shoot Horses Don't They, 1969 (9 Acad. award nominations), Nickelodeon, 1976, The Gambler, 1974, Up the Sandbox, 1972, The New Centurions, 1972, Point Blank, 1967, Double Trouble, 1967, Leo the Last, 1970 (Best Dir. award Cannes Film Festival, Belgrade Film Festival), The Strawberry Statement, 1970 (Jury prize Cannes Film Festival), The Split, 1968, Breakout, 1975, Believe in Me, 1971, The Gang That Couldn't Shoot Straight, 1971, The Mechanic, 1972, Busting, 1974, S.P.Y.S, 1974, Peeper, 1975, New York, New York, 1977, Valentino, 1977, Uncle Joe Shannon, 1978, Rocky II, 1979, Raging Bull, 1980 (8 Acad. award nominations, winner 2, Los Angeles Film Critics award for best picture), Rocky III, 1981, True Confessions, 1981, Author, Author, 1982, The Right Stuff, 1983 (8 Acad. award nominations), Rocky IV, 1984, Revolution, 1985, 'Round Midnight, 1986 (2 Acad. award nomiations, Acad. award Best Original Score), Betrayed, 1988 (Chgo. Film Festival Lifetime Irwin Achievement award 1987), Goodfellas, 1990 (6 Acad. award nominations) The Net, 1995, The Juror, 1996, The Shipping News, 2001, Enough, 2002; exec. prodr.: Comes a Horseman, 1978, Rocky Balboa, 2006; dir, writer: Guilty by Suspicion, 1991 (U.S. selection Cannes Film Festival, winner 1, Brit. Acad. award Best Picture, N.Y. Film Critics Best Picture, L.A. Film Critics Best Picture), Rocky V, 1990, Music Box, 1990 (Golden Bear award for best film Berlin Film Festival); prodr., dir.: Night and the City, 1992 (N.Y. Film Festival, London Film Festival), The Net, 1995, The Juror, 1997, At First Sight, 1998, Life as a House, 2001, De-Lovely, 2004; retrospectives Brit. Film Inst., 1989, Chgo. Film Festival, 1989, Mus. Modern Art, N.Y.C., 1990, L.A. County Mus. Art, 1992. Served with U.S. Army, 1951-53. Named Commander d'Artes et de Lettres, French Govt. Minister of Culture, 1985; recipient Career Achievement in Producing Award Nat. Bd. Review, 2006. Mem. Am. Film Inst. (bd. govs.), Prodrs. Guild Am. (bd. dirs.). Office: Winkler Films 211 S Beverly Dr Ste 200 Beverly Hills CA 90212-3882

WINKLER, JEFFREY D., chemist; b. 1956; AB, Harvard Coll., 1977; MA, MPhil, PhD, Columbia U., 1981-83. Prof. chemistry U. Pa. Recipient NIH-NCI Rsch. Career Devel. award, 1988-93, Am. Cyanamid Young Faculty award, 1988-93, Arthur C. Cope scholar award Am. Chem. Soc., 2000; Alfred P. Sloan rsch. fellow, 1987-89. Achievements include research on total synthesis of naturally occurring compounds with important biological activity; development of new reactions and strategies in organic synthesis; design and synthesis of small molecules that mimic the functions of biological catalysts; preparation of macromolecular structures with well-defined structures and functions such as conducting or non-linear optical properties. Office: U Pa Dept Chemistry 231 S 34th St Philadelphia PA 19104-6323 Office Phone: 215-898-0052. E-mail: winkler@sas.upenn.edu.

WINKLER, JOHN FREDERICK, lawyer, educator; b. Gallipolis, Ohio, May 26, 1946; s. Carl Frederick and Anna (Reed) W.; m. Wendy Stephenson, May 2, 1970; children: Jonathan Reed, Asa Benjamin, Mary Susannah. BA, Yale U., New Haven, 1968; MA, McGill U., Montreal, 1972; AM, Harvard U., Cambridge, Mass., 1973; JD, Ohio State U., 1982. Bar: Ohio 1983, U.S. Supreme Ct. 1992. Assoc. Baker & Hostetler, Columbus, Ohio, 1983-90, ptnr., 1991-97, Christensen, Shoemaker & Winkler, Columbus, 1997—2002; counsel Ohio Supreme Ct. Rules Com., 1998—, Shoemaker, Winkler, Howarth & Taylor LLC, Columbus, 2003, Winkler & Winkler LLC, Columbus, Ohio, 2004—. Adj. prof. law Capital U., Columbus, 1987-98; teaching fellow Harvard U., Cambridge, Mass., 1974-77; lectr. in field. Author: (with M.L. Benedict) The History of Ohio Law, 2004; contbr. articles to profl. jours. Mem. ABA, Am. Inns. of Ct., Ohio Bar Assn., Columbus Bar Assn. (mem. editl. bd. 1995—1996). Home: 253 N Remington Rd Bexley OH 43209-1444 Office: Winkler & Winkler LLC 3220 Riverside Dr Ste B 1 Columbus OH 43221 Office Phone: 614-668-8221. E-mail: jwinkler@aya.yale.edu.

WINKLER, JOSEPH CONRAD, former recreational products manufacturing executive; b. Newark, May 20, 1916; s. Charles and Mollie (Abrams) W.; m. Geraldine M. Borok, Sept. 20, 1953; children: Charles H., David J. BS, NYU, 1941. Gen. mgr. Indsl. Washing Machine Corp., New Brunswick, NJ, 1941-48; controller Mojud Corp., NYC, 1948-52; controller, asst. treas. Barbizon Corp., NYC, 1952-57; controller Ideal Toy Corp., NYC, 1957-58, McGregor-Doniger, Inc., NYC, 1958-59; dir. fin. and adminstrn. Ideal Toy Corp., NYC, 1960-62, v.p. fin., 1962-68, sr. v.p. fin., 1968-78, exec. v.p., COO, dir., 1978-81, pres., dir., 1981-83; exec. in residence, bus. adv. coun. Sch. Bus. Adminstrn., Montclair (N.J.) State U., 1983-90. Dir. Ideal of Australia Ltd., Melbourne, 1963-82, Ideal of Canada Ltd., Toronto, 1963-82, Ideal of Japan Ltd., Tokyo and Kiowa, 1963-80, Ideal Toy Co. Ltd., High Wycombe and Wokingham, Eng., 1966-82, Arxon Spiel & Freizeit GmbH, Rotgau, Germany, 1968-82, Perfekta Ltd. and Hollis Industries Ltd., Hong Kong, 1970-74, Ideal Loisirs S.A., Paris, 1972-82. Mem. editl. bd. Issues in Internat. Bus., 1985-92. Committeeman, troop treas. Boy Scouts Am., Tenafly, N.J., 1965-71; bd. dirs. N.Y. League Hard of Hearing, 1982-88; active Nat. Roster Sci. and Splized. Pers., War Manpower Commn., 1941-46. Served with Office Statis. Control USAAF, 1945. Mem. Fin. Execs. Inst. Office Phone: 561-588-0952. E-mail: chada@worldnet.att.net.

WINKLER, LEE B., business consultant; b. Buffalo; s. Jack W. and Caroline (Marienthal) W.; 1 child, James; m. Maria Mal Verde. BS cum laude, NYU, 1945, MS cum laude, 1947. Pres. LBW, Inc. (formerly Winkler Assocs. Ltd.), NYC, Beverly Hills, Calif., 1948—, Winkler Assocs. Ltd., Beverly Hills, Calif., and N.Y.C., 1958—; exec. dir. Global Bus. Mgmt. Inc., Beverly Hills, 1967—. V.p. Bayly Martin & Fay Inc., N.Y.C., 1965-68, John C. Paige & Co., N.Y.C., 1968-71; cons. Albert G. Ruben Co., Beverly Hills, 1971— Served with AUS, 1943-45. Decorated chevalier comdr. Order Holy Cross Jerusalem, also spl. exec. asst., charge d'affaires, 1970; chevalier comdr. Sovereign Order Cyprus, 1970 Mem. Nat. Acad. TV Arts and Scis., Nat. Acad. Recording Arts and Scis., Beverly Hills C. of C., Phi Beta Kappa, Beta Gamma Sigma, Mu Gamma Tau, Psi Chi Omega. *In the final analysis, the bottom line, if you will— the only thing that truly matters in life are those friends and family that hold you dear to them. Success, and its attendant monies, rise and fall like the tides, and even vanish at times, but earned love is as constant as the earth's rotation is independent of the tides.*

WINKLER, MATTHEW ADAM, editor-in-chief, reporter; b. June 1, 1955; m. Lisa Winkler; 3 children. AB in History, Kenyon Coll., 1977, LLD. Reporter Mount Vernon News, Ohio, 1976—77; pub. rels. specialist Gehrung Assocs., Keene, NH, 1977—78; reporter, asst. editor Bond Buyer, 1978—80; with Dow Jones Capital Markets Reports, 1980; reporter Wall Street Jour., 1980—90; European Fin. corr. Wall Street Jour. Europe, Jour. London, 1982—87; with Bloomberg L.P.; editor-in-chief Bloomberg Bus. News (Now Bloomberg News), NYC, 1990—. Chmn. bd. trustees Kenyon Rev. Co-author: Bloomberg by Bloomberg, 1997. Trustee N.J. Symphony Orch., Overseas Press Club, 1998, Knight-Bagehot Fellowship Columbia U. Office: Bloomberg News 499 Park Ave New York NY 10022-1240 *

WINKLER, MICHAEL, computer company executive; BS in Elec. Engring., Lehigh U.; MBA, Harvard Bus. Sch. Various mgmt. positions Xerox Corp.; v.p., gen. mgr. comp. systems Toshiba Am. Info. Systems, Inc., 1992—95; sr. v.p., group gen. mgr. Compaq Computer Corp. (later acquired by Hewlett-Packard Co.), Houston, 1996—2000, exec. v.p. global bus. units, 2000—01; exec. v.p. global ops. Hewlett-Packard Co., 2001—02, exec. v.p., chief mktg. officer, 2002—. Office: Hewlett-Packard Co 3000 Hanover St Palo Alto CA 94304-1185 Office Phone: 650-857-1501.

WINKLER, PAUL FRANK, JR., astrophysicist, educator; b. Nashville, Nov. 10, 1942; s. Paul Frank and Estelle (Pye) W.; m. Geraldine Huck, Aug. 20, 1966 (div. 1979); children: Katharine Winkler Corcoran, Johanna Winkler Durrett; m. Janet Pippitt Beers, June 25, 1983; stepchildren: Sarah Creighton Beers, Nathan Pippitt Beers. BS, Calif. Inst. Tech., 1964; A.M., Harvard U., 1965, PhD, 1970. From instr. to prof. physics Middlebury Coll., Vt., 1969—84, William R. Kenan Jr. prof. physics, 1984-87, chmn. nat. scis. div., 1988-93, asst. to pres. for sci. planning, 1993-96, Gamaliel Painter Bicentennial prof. physics, 1997—. Vis. scientist MIT, Cambridge, 1973-74, 78-80; sr. vis. fellow Inst. Astronomy, U. Cambridge, 1985-86; vis. resident astronomer Cerro Tololo InterAm. Observatory, La Serena, Chile, 1990-91, 96-97; vis. fellow Joint Inst. for Laboratory Astrophysics, U. Colo., Boulder, 1991. Contbr. articles to profl. jours. NSF fellow, 1965-69, Alfred P. Sloan Found. fellow, 1976-80 Mem. Vt. Acad. Sci. and Engring., Am. Phys. Soc., Am. Astron. Soc., Internat. Astron. Union, Coun. on Undergrad. Rsch., Sigma Xi. Office: Middlebury Coll Dept Physics Middlebury VT 05753 Business E-Mail: winkler@middlebury.edu.

WINKLER, SHELDON, dentist, educator; b. NYC, Jan. 25, 1932; s. Ben and Lillian (Barsh) W.; m. Sandra M. Cohen, Aug. 13, 1961; children: Mitchell, Lori. BA, Washington Sq. Coll., 1953; DDS, NYU, 1956. Asst. prof. denture prosthesis NYU Coll. Dentistry, NYC, 1958-61, 66-68, rsch. asst. prof., 1962-63; dir. materials rsch. Consol. Metal Products Industries Inc., Albany, NY, 1963-65, cons. materials rsch., 1966-68; asst. prof. removable prosthodontics sch. dentistry SUNY, Buffalo, 1968-70, assoc. prof., 1970-79; prof., chmn. dept. prosthodontics Temple U. Sch. Dentistry, Phila., 1979-86, 94-96, asst. dean for advanced studies, continuing edn./rsch., 1987-89, acting asst. dean, 1993-95, prof. restorative dentistry, 1996—2006; prof. dentistry Ariz. Sch. Dentistry and Oral Health, Mesa, 2006—07, Midwestern U. Coll. Dental Medicine, Glendale, Ariz., 2007—. Asst. dir. dental dept. NYU Med. Ctr. Goldwater Meml. Hosp., NYC, 1966—68, vis. dentist dental dept., 1966—68; attending in prosthodontics E.J. Meyer Meml. Hosp., Buffalo, 1975—79; postgrad instr. First Dist. Dental Soc. NY, NYC, 1963—; cons. Coe Labs., Chgo., 1967—87, Harkness Ctr., Buffalo, Rosa Coplon Home & Infirmary, Buffalo, 1970—79, Erie C.C., Buffalo, 1979—, Lever Bros. Co., NYC, 1981—, VA Hosp., Phila., 1989—, Ivoclar N. Am., Amherst, NY, 2000—; lectr. dept. dental hygiene NYC C.C., 1967—68; hon. prof. Pierre Fauchard Sch. Dentistry, Asuncion, Paraguay, 1999—. Author: (with A. Davidoff and M.H.M. Lee) Dentistry for the Special Patient: The Aged, Chronically Ill and Handicapped, 1972, Essentials of Complete Denture Prosthodontics, 1979, 2d edit., 1988; editor: Resins in Dentistry, 1975, Complete Dentures, 1977, Removable Prosthodontics, 1984, (with B.R. Lang, F.R. Lauciello and G.P. McGivney) Contemporary Complete Denture Occlusion, 2001; editor Jour. Implant Dentistry, 1990-97; sr. editor Jour. Oral Implantology, 2000—; contbr. articles to profl. lit.; co-designer McGowan-Winkler complete denture trays. Served as capt. AUS, 1956-58, 61-62. Recipient Outstanding Layman award Vocat. Tech. Alumni and Student Assn., SUNY, Buffalo, 1974, Internat. Edn. award Internat. Congress Oral Implantologists, 1992, journalism award Internat. Coll. Dentists, 1993, Academic Devotion award Chulalongkorn U., Bangkok, 1995. Fellow Am. Coll. Dentists, Greater N.Y. Acad. Prosthodontics; mem. ADA, Internat. Assn. Dental Rsch., Am. Assn. Dental Schs., Am. Acad. Implant Prosthodontics (Outstanding Personality Implant Prosthodontics award, 2002), Sci. Rsch. Soc. Am., Acad. Plastics Rsch., Am. Prosthodontic Soc., Am. Soc. Geriatric Dentistry, Internat. Congress of Oral Implantologists, Sigma Xi, Sigma Epsilon Delta, Omicron Kappa Upsilon. Home: 8672 E Eagle Claw Dr Scottsdale AZ 85262-1058 Office Phone: 480-588-8062. E-mail: swinkdent@cox.net.

WINLAND, THOMAS W., lawyer; b. Lancaster, Ohio, Mar. 18, 1949; BS, Ohio State U., 1971; JD, Duke U., 1974. Bar: Ohio 1974, D.C. 1982. U.S. Patent and Trademark Office, U.S. Ct. Customs and Patent Appeals 1980, U.S. Claims Ct. 1982, U.S. Ct. Appeals (fed. cir.) 1982. Ptnr. Finnegan, Henderson, Farabow, Garrett & Dunner, Washington. Named one of best lawyers in intellectual property law, Best Lawyers in Am., 2005—06. Mem. ABA (patent, trademark and copyright law sects., pub.

contract law), Am. Intellectual Property Law Assn., D.C. Bar, Bar Assn. of D.C., Ohio State Bar Assn. Office: Finnegan Henderson Farabow Garrett & Dunner LLP 901 New York Ave NW Washington DC 20001-3315 Office Phone: 202-408-4000. Office Fax: 202-408-4400. Business E-Mail: tom.winland@finnegan.com.

WINMILL, B. LYNN, federal judge; m. Judy Jones; 4 children. BA, Idaho State U., 1974; JD, Harvard U., 1977. Atty. Holland and Hart, Denver, 1977-79, Hawley, Troxell, Ennis and Hawley, Pocatello, Idaho, 1984-87; judge Idaho Sixth Jud. Dist. Ct., Pocatello, 1987-95, US Dist. Ct. Idaho, Boise, 1995—, chief judge, 1999—. Adj. prof. law Idaho State Univ., 1991—95. Mem.: Colo. Bar Assn., 6th Dist. Bar Assn., Idaho State Bar Assn. Office: US Dist Ct Idaho US Courthouse 550 W Fort St 6th Fl Boise ID 83724-0001 Office Phone: 208-334-9145. Fax: 208-334-9209.

WINN, ALBERT CURRY, clergyman; b. Ocala, Fla., Aug. 16, 1921; s. James Anderson and Elizabeth (Curry) W.; m. Grace Neely Walker, Aug. 29, 1944; children: Grace Walker (Mrs. Stewart E. Ellis), James Anderson, Albert Bruce Curry, Randolph Axson. AB, Davidson Coll., 1942, LLD, 1968; BD, Union Theol. Sem., Va., 1945, ThD, 1956; ThM, Princeton Theol. Sem., 1949; LLD, Stillman Coll., 1975. Ordained min. Presbyn. Ch., 1945. Asst. prof. Davidson Coll., 1946-47; pastor Potomac Rural Parish, Va., 1948-53; prof. Bible Stillman Coll., 1953-60; prof. theology Louisville Presbyn. Theol. Sem., 1960-73, pres., 1966-73; pastor 2d Presbyn. Ch., Richmond, Va., 1974-81, N. Decatur Presbyn. Ch., Decatur, Ga., 1981-86. Moderator Presbyn. Synod Ala., 1958, Presbyn. Synod Ky., 1969, Gen. Assembly, Presbyn. Ch. in U.S., 1979; vis. prof. Union Theol. Sem. in Va., 1987, Columbia Theol. Sem., 1987, Louisville Presbyn. Theol. Sem., 1988; interim pastor Cen. Presbyn. Ch., Atlanta, 1989-90, St. Andrews Presbyn. Ch., Tucker, Ga., 1993-94; parish assoc. Trinity Prebyn. Ch., Winston-Salem, NC, 1999—. Author: Layman's Bible Commentary on Acts, 1960, The Worry and Wonder of Being Human, 1966, Where Do I Go From Here, 1972, Proclamation Two: Epiphany, 1980, A Sense of Mission, 1981, Christ the Peacemaker, 1982, Plain Talk about the Apostles' Creed, 1985, The Christian Primer, 1990, Ain't Gonna Study War No More, 1993. Chmn. trustees Stillman Coll., 1965-70. Served as chaplain USNR, 1945-46. Mem. Phi Beta Kappa, Beta Theta Pi, Omicron Delta Kappa. Office: 212 Oakwood Ct Winston Salem NC 27103-1952 E-mail: al.winn@juno.com.

WINN, CAROLYN PAUTKE, librarian, consultant; b. Detroit, June 5, 1927; d. Benno Edgar and Caroline Amelia (Milatz) Pautke; divorced; children: Eric, Gregory, Mathew. BS in Zoology, U. Mich., 1949, MA in Zoology, 1950; MLS, U. R.I., 1970. Cataloguer Mus. Zoology U. Mich., Ann Arbor, 1950-54; rsch. asst. U. Md., College Park, 1963-65, U. R.I., Kingston, 1965-67, cataloger, 1968-69, ast. ref. libr., 1969-70, instr. sci. ref. libr., 1970-73, asst. prof., sci. ref. libr., 1973-75; rsch. libr. Woods Hole (Mass.) Oceanographic Instn., 1975-95. Cons. Marine Biol. Lab./Woods Hole Oceanog. Instn. Libr., 1994—. Contbr. articles to profl. jours. Observer, vol. White House Conf. Librs. and Info. Svcs., Washington, 1979; adv. com. N.E. Academic Sci. Info. Ctr., New Eng. Bd. Higher Edn., 1978. Grantee U. R.I., 1974-75, Woods Hole Oceanographic Instn., 1976-77, 80-81, 86-87, Bur. Land Mgmtm., 1982-84. Mem. ALA, Am. Geophys. Union. (subcom. electronic pub. 1983-87), Internat. Assn. Marine Sci. Librs. and Info. Ctrs. (editor jour. 1989-90, pres. 1982-83), New Eng. On-Line Users Group (database com. 1979-86), New Eng. Libr. Assn., R.I. Libr. Assn., R.I. Health Scis. Librs. Consortium, Nat. Micrographics Assn., Soc. Scholarly Pub., New Eng. Microcomputer Users Group, Boston Libr. Consortium (collection mgmt. com. 1992-94), Cape Librs. Automated Materials Sharing, Inc. (pres. 1989-90, mem. coms.) E-mail: cpwinn90@hotmail.com.

WINN, H. RICHARD, surgeon; b. Chester, Pa., 1942; BA, Princeton U., 1964; MD, U. Pa., 1968. Diplomate Am Bd. Neurol. Surgeons. Intern U. Hosp., Cleve., 1968-69, resident surgery, 1969-70; resident neurolog. surgery U. Hosp. Va., Charlottesville, 1970-74; neurol. surgeon U. Wash. Hosp., Seattle, 1983—2002; prof., chmn. neurol. surgery U. Wash., Seattle, 1983—2002; prof. neurosurgery and neurosci. Mt. Sinai Med. Sch., NYC, 2003—. Bd. dirs. Am. Bd. Neurol. Surgery, 1995-2001, vice chmn., 2000-01. Founding editor Neurosurgical Clinics of North America; mem. editl. bd. Jour. Neurosurgery, 1995-2001, chair, 2001-2002; mem. editl. bd. Am. Physiology, 1995-2000, Am. Jour. Surgery. Recipient Disting. Alumnus, Haverford Sch., 2000. Fellow AAAS, Soc. Brit. Neurol. Surgeons (hon.); mem. AMA, Am. Assn. Neurol. Surgeons, Soc. Neurol. Surgeons (Grass prize 1999, Disting. Svc. award 2005), Congress Neurol. Surgeons. Office: Dept Neurosurgery Mount Sinai Sch Medicine One Gustave L Levy PO Box 1136 New York NY 10029 Office Phone: 212-241-9128. Business E-Mail: richard.winn@mountsinai.org.

WINN, JAMES JULIUS, JR., lawyer; b. Colon, Panama, Nov. 7, 1941; came to U.S., 1941; s. James Julius and Molly (Brown) W.; m. Elizabeth Kokernot Lacy, Aug. 15, 1970; children: Mary Ann W. Burns, E. Lacy W. Sakellaris, James Julius VI. AB, Princeton U., 1964; JD cum laude, Washington and Lee U., 1970. Bar: Md. 1970, U.S. Dist. Ct. Md. 1971, U.S. Dist. Ct. D.C. 1982. Assoc. Piper & Marbury, Balt., 1970-78; ptnr. Piper Rudnick LLP, Balt., 1978—2004; mem. Winn Group LLC, 2001—; gen. counsel Kokernot 06 Ranch, Inc., 2006—. Bd. dirs. The Columbia Bank. Assoc. editor, contbr. author Washington & Lee U. Law Rev., 1968-70. Counselor St. John's Ch., Western Run Parish, Glyndon, Md., 1974—; mem. com. on canons and other bus. Episc. Diocese Md., 1986—; dir. Ctr. for Ethics and Corp. Policy, 1988-95, chmn., 1991-95; dir. Ctr. Stage, 1986-2004; dir. Oldfields Sch., 1991-96; v.p., dir. Ruxton Country Sch., 1988-91; dir. The Jemicy Sch., 1999—, chmn. 2005—. Mem. Md. State Bar Assn. (com. on corp. law of sect. of bus. law). Office: DLA Piper US LLP 6225 Smith Ave Baltimore MD 21209-3600

WINN, JOAN, adult education educator; BS, Ill. State U., Chgo.; MBA, Boise State U., Idaho; MS, U. Wis., Madison; PhD, U. Ga., Athens. Prof. U. Denver, 1988—. Pres. Western Casewriters Assn., 1996—2007, US-ASBE, 2001—02. Mem. editl. bd.: Case Rsch. Jour. Scholar, Fulbright Found., 2004—05. Achievements include research in entrepreneurship. Office: University of Denver Daniels College Business Denver CO 80208 Office Phone: 303-871-2192. Business E-Mail: jwinn@du.edu.

WINN, JOHN ARTHUR, JR., mathematics educator; b. Norfolk, Va., Apr. 8, 1945; s. John Arthur Sr. and Doris Marie (Beudert) W.; m. Elizabeth Ann Westcott, Dec. 17, 1988. BA with honors, SUNY, Oneonta, 1966; MS, C.W. Post Coll., 1969; PhD, Adelphi U., 1980. Cert. math. tchr., N.Y. Computer programmer Grumman Corp., Bethpage, N.Y., 1969-72, Electronic Assocs., Inc., Hampton Roads, Va., 1973-74; distinguished prof. math. SUNY, Farmingdale, 1974—, chair math., 1992—. Coord. Discrete Math. Conf., Farmingdale, 1986; dir. Farmingdale Faculty Conf., 1987—. Author: Asymptotic Bounds for Classical Ramsey Numbers, 1988; contbr. articles to profl. jours. Mem. Math. Assn. Am. (del. 1987—, coord. regional conf. 1989, bd. govs. 2005—, Distinguished Tchg. award Metro NY, 2006), Am. Math. Soc. Avocation: trombone. Office: SUNY Melville Rd Farmingdale NY 11735-2221

WINN, JOHN L., school system administrator; b. Brunswick, Ga., Oct. 23, 1948; BA, Fla. State U., 1970; MA in Philosophy, U. Fla., 1973. Dir. prevention ctr. Fla. Dept. of Edn., Tallahassee, 1987—89, edn. policy dir. to commr. of edn., 1989—91, dir. Office of Policy Rsch. and Accountability, 1991—96, coord. policy rsch., 1996—99, edn. policy coord. to gov., 1999—2001, asst. sec. of edn., 2001—02, dep. commr. for Accountability, Rsch., and Measurement, 2002—03, chief of staff to commr. of edn., 2003—04, commr. of edn., 2004—. Office: Fla Dept of Edn / Off of Commr Turlington Bldg, Ste 1514 325 W Gaines St Tallahassee FL 32399 Office Phone: 850-245-0505. *

WINN, JOSEPH LAMPHER, retired electronics executive; b. Cambridge, Mass., Aug. 12, 1951; s. Joseph L. and Alicia M. (Muir) W.; m. Gail A. Cadogan, June 19, 1976; children: Kelly, Caroline, Joseph. BS in Fin., Boston Coll., 1973; MBA, Babson Coll., 1974. Fin. mgr. program Sanders Assocs. Inc., Nashua, N.H., 1974-78; fin. mgr. Digital Equipment Corp., Maynard, Mass., 1978-83; sr. v.p., controller Am. Cablesystems Corp., Beverly, Mass., 1983-88; exec. v.p., chief fin. officer Atlantic Radio Corp., Manchester, Mass., 1988—93; CFO & dir. Am. Radiosystems Corp., 1993—98; CFO Am. Tower Corp., Boston, 1998—2001, vice chmn., 2002—03. Bd. dirs. OnePIN, Westborough, Mass. Bd. trustees The Carroll Sch., 2002—03; trutee Babson Coll., 2001—. Roman Catholic. E-mail: joe.winn@americantower.com.

WINN, MORRIS X., former federal agency administrator; Grad., Prairie View A&M U. Divsn. dir. support svcs. Tex. Atty. Gen.'s Office, 1984—92, dir. employee rels., 1992—94; deputy commr. human resources Tex. Dept. Ins., 1994—99; divsn. mgr. human resources Tex. Comptroller Pub. Accts., 1999—2002; asst. adminstr. adminstrn. and resources mgmt. EPA, Washington, 2002—04.

WINN, STEVEN JAY, critic; b. Phila., Apr. 25, 1951; s. Willis Jay and Lois (Gengelbach) W.; m. Katharine Weber, Sept. 15, 1979 (div. Dec. 1985); m. Sally Ann Noble, July 22, 1989; 1 child, Phoebe Ann. BA, U. Pa., 1973; MA, U. Wash., 1975. Staff writer, editor Seattle Weekly, 1975-79; theater critic San Francisco Chronicle, 1980—2002, arts and culture critic, 2002—. Co-author: Ted Bundy: The Killer Next Door, 1980, Great Performances: A Celebration, 1997; contbr. articles to various publs. Wallace Stegner fellow Stanford U., 1979-80; recipient first prize Excellence in Writing award Am. Assn. of Sunday and Feature Editors, 2002, 2003. Office: San Francisco Chronicle 901 Mission St San Francisco CA 94103-2905 Office Phone: 415-777-8869. E-mail: swinn@sfchronide.com.

WINNER, GEORGE HENRY, lawyer; b. Elmira, NY, July 31, 1949; s. George H. and Beverly S. (Sweet) W.; m. Lynn Hardman, Dec. 4, 1976; children: Catherine H., Elizabeth H., Meredith F. BA, St. Lawrence U., 1971. Bar: N.Y. 1977, U.S. Dist. Ct. (no. and we. dists.) N.Y. 1977. Adminstrv. asst. N.Y. State Senate, Albany, NY, 1972-76, counsel, 1977-78, minority leader pro-tem, 1990—; N.Y. state assemblyman 127th Dist., Albany, NY, 1979—2004; ptnr., assoc. Winner, Sullivan & Delaney, Elmira, NY, 1977-84; ptnr. Winner & Denton, Elmira, NY, 1984-94, Denton, Keyser, LaBreque & Moore, Elmira, 1995—2002, Keyser Maloney & Winner LLP, 2002—; sen. 53d Dist., Albany, 2005—. Dir. Peak Resorts, Inc., Virgil, N.Y., 1994—. Chemung County GOP exec. com., Elmira, 1980—. Mem. N.Y. State Bar Assn., Chemung County Bar Assn. Republican. Avocations: skiing, golf, scuba diving. Home: 15 Abbey Rd Elmira NY 14905 Office: Keyser Maloney & Winner 150 Lake St Elmira NY 14901-3401 Office Phone: 607-734-0990.

WINNER, KARIN E., editor-in-chief; b. White Plains, NY, Dec. 27, 1945; BA in Journalism, U. So. Calif. West coast editor Women's Wear Daily; co-founder W mag.; features editor San Diego Union (merged with Evening Tribune to become San Diego Union-Tribune, 1991), 1976; exec. editor San Diego Union-Tribune, 1991—95, editor, 1995—. Mem.: Am. Soc. Newspaper Editors, Calif. Soc. Newspaper Editors. Office: San Diego Union-Tribune 350 Camino De La Reina San Diego CA 92108 Mailing: San Diego Union-Tribune PO Box 120191 San Diego CA 92112-0191 Office Phone: 619-293-1201, 619-293-1354. E-mail: Karin.winner@uniontrib.com. *

WINNER, MICHAEL ROBERT, film director, film producer, writer; b. London, Oct. 30, 1935; s. George Joseph and Helen (Zloty) W. Degree in law and econs. with honors, Cambridge U., Eng., 1956. Writer Fleet St. (newspapers), London, 1956-58. Columnist London Sunday Times, 1990, London News of the World, 1995. Engaged in film prodn., 1956; dir. films Play it Cool, 1962, West 11, 1963, The Mechanic, 1972, Death Wish II, 1981; dir., writer The Cool Mikado, 1962, You Must be Joking, 1965, The Wicked Lady, 1982; producer, dir. The System, 1963, I'll Never Forget What's 'isname, 1967, The Games, 1969, Lawman, 1970, The Nightcomers, 1971, Chato's Land, 1971, Scorpio, 1972, The Stone Killer, 1973, Death Wish, 1974, Won Ton Ton The Dog Who Saved Hollywood, 1975, Firepower, 1978, Scream for Help, 1983, Death Wish III, 1985; producer, writer, dir. films The Jokers, 1966, Hannibal Brooks, 1968, The Sentinel, 1976, The Big Sleep, 1977, Appointment With Death, 1987, A Chorus of Disapproval, 1988, Bullseye!, 1989, Dirty Weekend, 1992, Parting Shots, 1997; producer plays Nights at the Comedy, Comedy Theatre, London, 1960, The Silence of St. Just, Gardner Centre, Brighton, 1971, The Tempest, Wyndhams Theatre, London, 1974, A Day in Hollywood, A Night in the Ukraine, Mayfair Theatre, London, 1978, (TV series London Weekend TV) Michael Winner's True Crimes, 1990, 91, 92, 93, 94; author: Winner's Dinners, 1999, rev. edit., 2000, Winner Guide to Whining and Dining, 2002, (autobiography) Winner Takes All, 2004, paperback edit., 2005, The Fat Pig Diet, 2007; actor: (BBC film) For the Greater Good, 1990, Decadence, 1993, The Flump, 2000; actor and/or dir. commls. including Esure Ins., Kenco, Doritos, Books for Schs. Founder, chmn. Police Meml. Trust, 1984. Mem. Dirs. Guild Gt. Britain (coun.) Office: Scimitar Films Ltd 219 Kensington High St London W8 6BD England Home Phone: 0207 603 5510; Office Phone: 0207 603 4820. E-mail: winner@ftech.co.uk.

WINNICK, STEVEN YALE, lawyer; b. New Haven, Nov. 18, 1944; s. Morris Jerry and Ruth (Greenberg) Winnick; m. Martha Jo Jacobs, June 2, 1985; children: Seth, Rebecca, Matthew. BA cum laude, Yale U., New Haven, 1966; JD cum laude, U. Mich., Ann Arbor, 1969. Bar: Mich. 1969, DC 2005. Spl. asst. US Dept. Edn., Washington, 1972—80, asst. gen. counsel, 1980—86, designated agy. ethics ofcl., 1985—2005, dep. gen. counsel, 1989—2005; sr. counsel Holland & Knight, Washington, 2005—. Treas. Citizens for Integrated Schs., Montgomery County, Md., 1975—76. Named Best Boss in Am. for Working Moms, Redbook Mag., 1996; recipient Justice Tom C. Clark Outstanding Lawyer award, Fed. Bar Assn., 1995, Exec. Branchwide Disting. Svc. award, US Office Govt. Ethics First, 1997, Presdl. Meritorious Exec. award, Pres. of US, 1990, Presdl. Disting. Exec. award, 1997, 2003. Avocations: running, tennis, reading. Home: 8903 Clifford Ave Chevy Chase MD 20815 Office: Holland & Knight LLP 2099 Pennsylvania Ave NW Washington DC 20006

WINNING, J. PATRICK, lawyer; b. Murphysboro, Ill., Oct. 29, 1952; s. William T. Jr. and Lillian (Albers) Winning; m. Jessica Anne Yoder, June 17, 1978 (div. July 1999); children: Erika Anne, Brian Patrick, Derek Matthew; m. Lisa A. Baue, June 3, 2006. AB with distinction, Mo. Bapt. Coll., 1974; JD, St. Louis U., 1979. Bar: Mo. 1979, U.S. Dist. Ct. (ea. dist.) Mo. 1979, U.S. Ct. Appeals (8th cir.) 1979, U.S. Dist. Ct. (so. dist.) Tex. 1985, U.S. Ct. Appeals (5th cir.) 1987, U.S. Dist. Ct. (we. dist.) Tex. 1988, Tex. 1989. Assoc. Chused, Strauss, Chorlins, Goldfarb, Bini & Kohn, St. Louis, 1979-81, Vogler Law Firm, St. Louis, 2000—01; assoc. counsel Mfrs. Hanover Fin. Svcs., Phila., 1981-83; corp. counsel Cessna Fin. Corp., Wichita, Kans., 1983-85; atty. Southwestern Bell Publs., Inc., St. Louis, 1985-90; pres. Butler Hill Investments, Inc., St. Louis, 1990-91; pvt. practice, 1990—2000, 2001—04; v.p., gen. counsel Winning Equipment Co., Herculaneum, Mo., 2000-01; with Elco Chevrolet, Ballwin, Mo., 2002—03; gen. counsel Right Choice Mortgage, 2004—05; pres., CEO Omega Title Co., 2005—. Prin. Success Mgmt. Group, 1991—96, DPPC Mgmt. Group, St. Louis, 1996—97; sec., bd. dirs. Winning Equipment Co.; asst. prof. bus. adminstrn. Mo. Bapt. Coll., 1986—2001, Mo. Bapt. U., 2003—05. Treas. Concerned Citizens Chesterfield, 1989-91; deacon, mem. fin. com. 1st Bapt. Ch., Ellisville, Mo., 1992-93, vice chmn. fin. com., 1993-94, chmn. fin. com., 1994-95, vice chmn. deacons, 1993-95, chmn. deacons, 1997-98, dir. Sunday sch., 1993-94, trustee, chmn. athletic com., 1992-97, 98-2000; chmn. by-laws com. Mo. Bapt. Coll., 1992-96, sec. presdl. search com., 1994, mem., exec. com. bd. trustees, 1994-97, 98-2000; mgr. St. Louis Flames Youth Baseball, 1992-95, St. Louis Thunder Youth Baseball, 1995-97; coach St. Clare Bulls Basketball Team, 1994-97, St. Louis Wolfpack Youth Baseball, 1997-98; asst. scoutmaster troop 313, merit badge counselor Boy Scouts Am., 1997-2002, camporee staff New Horizons dist., 1998-2000, 2005—, adult leader tng. staff, 1998—, camping com., 1998-2000, 2005-, dist. roundtable staff, 1999-2003, chmn. membership com. New Horizons dist., 1999-2002, merit badge counselor, 1997-2002, fall camporee campmaster advisor, 2006; mem. evangelism com. Immanuel Luth. Ch., St. Charles, Mo., 2006—. Named one of Outstanding Young Men of Am., 1987, Outstanding Alumnus, Mo. Bapt. Coll., 1987-88; named to Athletic Hall of Fame, Mo. Bapt. Coll., 1989; recipient Wood Badge Adult Leadership Tng. award Boy Scouts Am., 1998. Mem. Nat. Lawyers Assn., Nat. Eagle Scouts Assn., Met. St. Louis Bar Assn., Christian Legal Soc., Acad. Family Mediators, Assn. Family and Conciliation Cts., Mo. Bapt. Coll. Alumni Assn. (pres. 1980-81, 88-90, 2006-), St. Charles C. of C., St. Peter's C. of C., St. Louis Assn., Christian Attys., Mo. Assn. Mortgage Brokers, Nat. Assn. Mortgage Brokers, Am. Land Title Assn., Mo. Land Title Assn., West County C. of C., Chesterfield C. of C. Republican. Southern Baptist. Avocations: coaching baseball and basketball, reading, camping. Office: 1000 Fairgrounds Dr Ste 102 Saint Charles MO 63301 Office Phone: 636-757-0400. Business E-Mail: pwinning@omegatitle.net.

WINNOWSKI, THADDEUS RICHARD (TED WINNOWSKI), investment banker, consultant; b. Albany, NY, Feb. 20, 1942; s. Thaddeus Walter and Harriet Frances (Witko) W.; m. Sheila Margaret Neary, June 15, 1968; children: Dona, Paul. BS in Econs., Siena Coll., 1963; postgrad., Rensselaer Poly. Inst., 1968-72. Adminstrv. v.p. Key Bank N.A., Albany, N.Y., 1978-80; pres. Key Bank L.I., Sayville, N.Y., 1980-85; pres., CEO Key Bank Oreg., Woodburn, 1985-86, chmn., CEO Portland, 1986-95, chmn., 1995-97; exec. v.p., group exec. N.W. region Key Corp., Seattle, 1995-97, chmn., CEO, 1996-97; pres., CEO Centennial Bank, Eugene, Oreg., 1998—2002. Mem. adv. bd. Blue Cross/Blue Shield Oreg.; chmn. bd. regents U. Portland. 1st lt. U.S. Army, 1964-66. Mem. Portland Met. C. of C. (hon. bd. dirs., former chmn.). Roman Catholic. Office Phone: 503-819-8198. Personal E-mail: tedwinnowski@centennialbank.com, twinnowski@earthlink.net.

WINOGRAD, AUDREY LESSER, retired advertising executive; b. NYC, Oct. 6, 1933; d. Jack J. and Theresa Lorraine (Elkind) Lesser; m. Melvin H. Winograd, Apr. 29, 1956; 1 child, Hope Elise. BA, U. Conn., 1953. Asst. advt. mgr. T. Baumritter Co., Inc., NYC, 1953-54; asst. dir. pub. rels. and creative merchandising Kirby, Block & Co., Inc., NYC, 1954-56; divsn. mdse. mgr., dir. advt. and sales promotion Winograd's Dept. Store, Inc., Point Pleasant, NJ, 1956-73, v.p., 1960-73, exec. v.p., 1973-86; pres., CEO AMW Assocs., Atlanta, 1976—2002, ret., 2002—. Editor bus. newsletters. Bd. dirs. Temple Beth Am, Lakewood, N.J., 1970-72, Temple Emanuel, Atlanta, 1999-2001; active Alley Cat Allies, Fund for Animals. Mem. NAFE, LWV, Jersey Pub. Rels. and Advt. Assn. (pres. 1982-83, bd. dirs.), Retail Advt. and Mktg. Assn. Internat., Monmouth Ocean Devel. Coun., Monmouth County Bus. Assn. (bd. dirs. 1985-97, pres. 1988-90, Woman of Yr. 1992-93, Person of Yr. 1995), N.J. Assn. Women Bus. Owners, Am. Soc. Advt. and Promotion, Ocean C. of C. (bd. dirs. 1994-97, award 1993, 94), Retail Advt. Conf. (Career Achievements and Contbns. to Soc. award 1993), Soc. Prevention Cruelty to Animals, Animal Protection Inst. Am., Human Soc., Internat. Fund Animal Welfare, World Wildlife Fund, Friends of Animals, Defenders of Wildlife, Nat. Humane Edn. Soc., In Defense of Animals, Atlanta Humane Soc., Sierra Club, Peta, Natural Resources Def. Coun., Delta Rescue, Last Chance for Animals, Best Friends, Humane Soc. of U.S., United Animal Nat., Wilderness Soc., Lifesavers Wild Horse Rescue, Environ. Defense, Audobon, Greenpeace. Avocations: collecting animal collectibles, gourmet cooking, environmental protection, exercise. Office: AMW Assocs 5304 Vernon Lake Dr Atlanta GA 30338-3527 Personal E-mail: audwin@comcast.net.

WINOGRAD, NICHOLAS, chemist; b. New London, Conn., Dec. 27, 1945; s. Arthur Selig Winograd and Winifred (Schaefer) Winograd Mayes; m. Barbara J. Garrison. BS, Rensselaer Poly. Inst., 1967; PhD, Case We. Res. U., 1970. Asst. prof. chemistry Purdue U., West Lafayette, Ind., 1970-75, assoc. prof. chemistry, 1975-79; prof. chemistry Pa. State U., University Park, 1979-85, Evan Pugh prof. chemistry, 1985—. Cons. Lawrence Livermore Lab., 1997-2003; mem. chemistry adv. bd. NSF, Washington, 1987-90, analytical chemistry adv. bd., 1986-89. Contbr. articles to profl. jours. A.P. Sloan Found. fellow, 1974; Guggenheim Found. fellow, 1977; recipient Founder's prize Tex. Instruments Found., 1984, Faculty Scholar's Pa. State U., 1985, Bennedetti Pichler award Am. Microchem. Soc., 1991, Outstanding Alumnus award Case We. Res. U., 1991. Fellow AAAS (Sect. award); mem. Am. Chem. Soc. Avocation: running. Home: 138 Chemistry Ln Spring Mills PA 16875-9703 Office: Pa State U Dept of Chemistry 209 Chemistry Bldg University Park PA 16802-6300 Home Phone: 814-422-8069; Office Phone: 814-863-0001. Business E-Mail: nxw@psu.edu.

WINOGRAD, SHMUEL, mathematician; b. Tel Aviv, Jan. 4, 1936; came to U.S., 1956, naturalized, 1965; s. Pinchas Mordechai and Rachel Winograd; m. Elaine Ruth Tates, Jan 5, 1958; children: Daniel H., Sharon A. BSEE, MSEE, MIT; PhD in Math., NYU, 1968. Mem. research staff IBM, Yorktown Heights, NY, 1961-70, dir. math. sci. dept., 1970-74, 81-94; IBM fellow, 1972—. Permanent vis. prof. Technion, Israel. Author: (with J.D. Cowan) Reliable Computations in the Presence of Noise; research on complexity of computations and algorithms for signal processing. Fellow IEEE (W. Wallace McDowell award 1974), Assn. Computing Machinery, N.Y. Acad. Scis.; mem. NAS, Am. Math. Soc., Math. Assn. Am., Am. Philos. Soc., Soc. Indsl. and Applied Math., Am. Acad. Arts & Scis. Home: 235 Glendale Rd Scarsdale NY 10583-1533 Office: IBM Research PO Box 218 Yorktown Heights NY 10598-0218 Business E-Mail: swino@us.ibm.com.

WINOKUR, MARISSA JARET, actress; b. NYC, Feb. 2, 1973; Studied at, Am. Musical and Dramatic Acad. Actor: (plays, Broadway) Grease, 1995, Hairspray, 2002 (Tony award for best actress, 2003), 2005; (plays) Guys and Dolls, Peter Pan, Little Shop of Horrors, Romeo and Juliet, Nunsense II, Grandma Sylvia's Funeral, Hair, Happy Days; (films) Demo Real, 1998, Why Love Doesn't Work, 1999, Never Been Kissed, 1999, American Beauty, 1999, Sleep Easy, Hutch Rimes, 2000, Scary Movie, 2000, Amy's Orgasm, 2001, On Edge, 2001, Now You Know, 2002; (TV films) Beautiful Girl, 2003; co-exec. prodr. (TV films) Beautiful Girl, 2003; actor(guest appearances): (TV series) The Steve Harvey Show, 1998, Felicity, 1999, Dharma & Greg, 1999, 2000, Moesha, 2000, Curb Your Enthusiasm, 2000, Just Shoot Me, 2000, The Ellen Show, 2001, Boston Public, 2001. Office Phone: 310-288-5888. Office Fax: 310-288-5868.

WINROTH, ANDERS, historian, educator; children: Hjalmar, Elsa. BA, Stockholm U., 1990; PhD, Columbia U., 1996. Rsch. fellow U. Newcastle upon Tyne, 1996—98; asst. prof. dept. history Yale U., 1998—2003, assoc. prof., 2003—04, prof., 2004—. Author: The Making of Gratian's Decretum, 2000; co-editor: Charters, Cartularies and Archives: The preservation and transmission of Documents in the Medieval West, 2002. Morse fellow, Yale U., 2001—02, MacArthur Found. fellow, 2003. Office: Yale Univ Dept of History PO Box 208324 New Haven CT 06520 Home Phone: 203-781-8429; Office Phone: 203-432-7657.

WINSBERG, HARRIS BRYAN, lawyer; s. Larry and Brenda Winsberg; m. Jennifer Manning, Sept. 28, 2002; 1 child, Andrew Thomas. BA, U. Fla., Gainesville, 1994, JD, 1997. Bar: Fla. 1998, Ga. 2000. Law clk. to Hon. Karen Jennermann, Orlando, Fla., 1997—98; assoc. Kay Gronek & Latham, Orlando, 1998—2000, Troutman Sanders, Atlanta, 2000—05, ptnr., 2005—. Mem.: Ga. Bar (treas. bankruptcy sect. 2006). Office: Troutman Sanders LLP 600 Peachtree St Atlanta GA 30308

WINSHIP, FREDERICK MOERY, journalist; b. Franklin, Ohio, Sept. 24, 1924; s. Wilbur William and Edna B. (Moery) W.; m. Joanne Tree Thompson, Aug. 29, 1967. AB, DePauw U., 1945; MS, Columbia, 1946. Corr. UPI, 1946—; assigned UN, 1947-49; editorial staff N.Y.C., 1950-60, cultural affairs editor, 1960-72, sr. editor, 1972-75, asst. mng. editor, 1975-80; sr. editor arts/theater NYC, 1980-98; Broadway critic, 1985-98; arts critic at large, 2000—. Contbr. articles mags. Pres. Letters Abroad, Inc., 1962-83; chmn. Easter Seal Soc., N.Y.C., 1964-73, Oratorio Soc. N.Y., 1965-75, N.Y. Conf. Patriotic Socs., 1967-72; Bd. dirs. Odell House-Rochambeau Hdgrs., 1965-75, N.Y. State Easter Seal Soc., 1969-72, Mus. of City of N.Y., 1974—, Am. Philharm. Orch., 1981-82, Friends of the Am. Theater Wing, 1990—. Recipient Am. Legion Journalism award, 1955; Whitelaw Reid Journalism fellow India, 1958; Creative Club Journalism award, 1962 Mem. S.A.R. (sec. N.Y. chpt. 1963-68), St. Nicholas, Founders and Patriots, Mayflower Descs., Soc. Colonial Wars (bd. dirs.), S.R., Soc. Cincinnati, Sigma Delta Chi. Republican. Episcopalian. Home: 419 E 57th St New York NY 10022-3060

WINSLET, KATE, actress; b. Reading, Berkshire, Eng., Oct. 5, 1975; d. Roger and Sally Bridges Winslet; m. James Threapleton, Nov. 22, 1998 (div. Dec. 13, 2001); 1 child, Mia; m. Sam Mendes, May 24, 2003; 1 child, Joe Alfie. Appeared in plays including Peter Pan, What the Butler Saw (Manchester Evening News award for Best Supporting Actress), A Game of Soldiers, (musical) Adrian Mole; actress (films) Heavenly Creatures, 1994 (Best Fgn. Actress award New Zealand Film and TV Awards, Best Brit. Actress London Film Critics Cir. Awards, Best Brit. Empire Mag. Awards), Sense and Sensibility, 1995 (SAG award, Brit. Acad. Film and TV award for Best Supporting Actress, Golden Globe nominee, Acad. Award nominee for Best Supporting Actress), A Kid in King Arthur's Court, 1995, Jude, 1996, Hamlet, 1996, Titanic, 1997 (BAFTA award, Best Brit. Actress Empire Mag., Golden Globe nominee, Best European Actress European Film Acad., Acad. Award nominee for Best Actress), Hideous Kinky, 1998, Holy Smoke, 1999, (voice only) Faeries, 1999, Quills, 2000 (Best Actress Evening Std. Brit. Film award, nominee Best Supporting Actress SAG award 2000), Enigma, 2001 (Best Brit. Actress Empire Awards), (voice only) Christmas Carol: The Movie, 2001, Iris: A Memoir of Iris Murdoch, 2001(Acad. Award nominee for Best Supporting Actress, Golden Globe nominee, BAFTA nominee), War Game, 2001 The Life of David Gale, 2003, Plunge: The Movie, 2003, Eternal Sunshine of the Spotless Mind, 2004 (Best Brit. Actress London Film Critics Cir. Awards, Best Brit. Actress Empire Mag. Awards, Acad. Award nominee, Golden Globe nominee, SAG nominee, BAFTA nominee), Finding Neverland, 2004 (BAFTA nominee), Romance & Cigarettes, 2005, All The King's Men, 2006, Little Children, 2006, (voice only) Flushed Away, 2006, The Holiday, 2006; (TV movies) Anglo Saxon Attitudes, 1992, (voice only) Pride, 2004; (TV series) Dark Season, 1991, Get Back, 1992; (TV appearances) Casualty, 1993; co-creator: Listen to the Storyteller, 2000 (Grammy award for Best Spoken Word Album for Children) Recipient Gotham award, Independent Feature Projects, 2006, Desert Palm Achievement for Acting, Palm Springs Internat. Film Soc., Palm Springs Internat. Film Festival, 2007. *

WINSLETT, STONER, artistic director; b. Jacksonville, Fla., Aug. 17, 1958; m. Donald Paulding Irwin; children: Louise Gray Irwin, Elizabeth Irwin, Alexander Pankoff, Caroline Irwin. Student, Am. Ballet Theatre Sch., N.C. Sch. of the Arts; BFA summa cum laude, Smith Coll., 1980. Artistic dir. Richmond Ballet, 1980—. Pres. John Butler Found. Mem.: Phi Beta Kappa. Office: Richmond Ballet 407 E Canal St Richmond VA 23219-3811 *

WINSLOW, CATHERINE P., plastic surgeon; d. Lawrence Anthony Shideler and Sharon Ann Muller; m. Timothy J. Winslow, Sept. 12, 1992; children: Joshua, Jordan. BS, Purdue U., West Lafayette, Ind., 1990; MD, Ind. U., Indpls., 1994. Chief facial plastic surgery Walter Reed Army Med. Ctr., Washington, 2000—04; owner Winslow Facial Plastic Surgery, Carmel, Ind., 2004—. Asst. clin. prof. Ind. U. Sch. Medicine, Indpls., 2004—; examiner Am. Bd. Facial Plastic Surgery, Washington, 2004—06, Am. Bd. Otolaryngology, Chgo., 2006. Host Evening of Elegance Benefit Komen Found., Carmel, 2004—06. Maj. US Army, 2000—04. Recipient Jack Anderson award, Am. Bd. Facial Plastic Surgery, 2003, Torch Bearer award, State of Ind., 2005. Fellow: ACS, Am. Acad. Otolaryngology (com. mem. 2000—), Am. Acad. Facial Plastic Surgery (com. mem. 2000—). Achievements include selected to be the first otolaryngologist consultant to The White House. Office: Winslow Facial Plastic Surgery 755 W Carmel Dr Ste 116 Carmel IN 46032

WINSLOW, DAVID ALLEN, chaplain, retired military officer; b. Dexter, Iowa, July 12, 1944; s. Franklin E. and Inez Maude (McPherson) W.; children: Frances, David. BA, So. Nazarene U., 1968; MDiv, Drew U., 1971, STM, 1974; cert. of achievement, Emergency Mgmt. Inst., FEMA, 1997. Ordained to ministry United Meth. Ch. Detroit Annual Conf., 1969; cert. FEMA instr. Clergyman, 1969—; assoc. min. All Sts. Episcopal. Ch., Millington, NJ, 1969-70; asst. min. Marble Collegiate Ch., NYC, 1970-71; min. No. NJ Conf. United Meth. Ch., 1971-75; joined chaplain corps USN, 1974, advanced through grades to lt. comdr., 1980, ret., 1995; chaplain Oak Knoll Naval Med. Ctr., Oakland, Calif., 1993-95; command chaplain USNS Mercy T-AH19, Oakland, 1993—95; disaster cons. Ch. World Svc., Cupertino, Calif., 1997—2001. Chaplain med. assistance team CA-6/nat. disaster med. sys. Contra/Costa County, Calif., 1997—2005; founding mem. Dept. Homeland Security, 2003; salesperson Dept. real estate State of Calif., 2000—. Author: The Utmost for the Highest, 1993, Epiphany: God Still Speaks, 1994, Be Thou My Vision, 1994, Evening Prayers At Sea, 1995, Wiseman Still Adore Him, 1995, God's Power At Work, 1996; (with Walsh) A Year of Promise: Meditations, 1995, editor: The Road to Bethlehem: Advent, 1993, Preparation for Resurrecton: Lent, 1994, God's Promise: Advent, 1994, The Way of the Cross: Lent, 1995; contbr. articles to profl. jours. Bd. dirs. disaster svcs. and family svcs. ARC, Santa Ana, Calif., 1988-91, Child Abuse Prevention Ctr., Orange, Calif., 1990-91; bd. dirs. Santa Clara County Coun. Chs., 1993-94, del., 1995-98; bd. dirs. Salvation Army Adult Rehab. Ctr. Adv. Coun., San Jose, Calif., 1995-2002; bd. dirs. emergency svcs. Santa Clara Valley chpt. ARC, San Jose, 1995-98; bd. dirs. disaster svcs. Interfaith Svc., Inc., San Jose Internat. Airport. Recipient Navy Achievement medal, Navy Commendation medal with Gold Star in lieu of 2nd award, Navy Expeditionary medal, Humanitarian Svc. medal, Battle "E" award, Nat. Def. Svc. medal, sea svc. deployment ribbon with silver star. Fellow Am. Acad. Experts in Traumatic Stress (cert. expert), USN League (hon.), Disabled Am. Vets. (life), Internat. Assn. Civil Aviation Chaplains, Sunrise Exch. Club (chaplain 1989-91), Dick Richards Breakfast Club (chaplain 1988-91), Kiwanis, Masons (life), Shriners. Avocations: golf, skiing, sailing. Office Phone: 408-858-5983.

WINSLOW, HELEN LITTELL, lawyer; b. Wilmington, Del., May 11, 1952; d. Julian Dallas and Jean (Littell) W.; m. Jonathan David Jaffe, Nov. 8, 1980; children: Kenan Winslow Jaffe, Nathaniel Harrington Jaffe, Saul Handler Jaffe. AB, Bryn Mawr Coll., 1974; JD, U. N.C., 1977. Bar: Del. 1977, U.S. Dist. Ct. Del. 1977, U.S. Ct. Appeals (3d cir.) 1980, U.S. Supreme Ct.1980. Law clk. to presiding judge U.S. Dist. Ct. Del., Wilmington, 1977-79; assoc. Richards, Layton & Finger, Wilmington, 1979—2001; asst. gen. counsel H.D. Lee Co., Inc., 2001—. Mem. ABA, Fed. Bar Assn. (v.p. Del. chpt. 1985-86, pres. Del. chpt. 1987—89), Del. Bar Assn. (pres. 2005-06), Am. Judicature Soc. Democrat. Jewish. Avocation: singing. Office: HD Lee Co 3411 Silverside Rd Concord Pike Wilmington DE 19810

WINSLOW, JOHN FRANKLIN, lawyer; b. Houston, Nov. 15, 1933; s. Franklin Jarnigan and Jane (Shipley) W. BA, U. Tex., 1957, LLB, 1960. Bar: Tex. 1959, DC 1961. Atty., Hispanic law div. Libr. of Congress, Washington, 1965-68; counsel, com. on the judiciary House of Reps., 1968-71; atty., editor Matthew Bender & Co., Washington, 1973-79; atty. FERC, Washington, 1979-84; pvt. practice Washington, 1984—. Rschr. Hispanic Law Rsch., Washington, 1979—. Author: Conglomerates Unlimited: The Failure of Regulation, 1974; editor: Fed. Power Service, 1974-79; contbr. articles to Washington Monthly, Nation, 1975—. Mem. Tex. Bar Assn., D.C. Bar Assn. Office Phone: 202-338-4747. Personal E-mail: jfwinslow@aol.com.

WINSLOW, NORMAN ELDON, small business owner; b. Oakland, Calif., Apr. 4, 1938; s. Merton Conrad and Roberta Eilene (Drennen) W.; m. Betty June Cady, Jan. 14, 1962 (div. Aug. 1971); 1 child, Todd Kenelm; m. Ilene Ruth Jackson, Feb. 3, 1979. BS, Fresno State U., Calif., 1959. Asst. mgr. Proctors Jewelers, Fresno, 1959-62; from agt. to dist. mgr. Allstate Ins. Co., Fresno, 1962-69; ins. agt. Fidelity Union Life Ins., Dallas, 1969-71; dist. and zone mgr. 7-Eleven, Inc., Dallas, 1971-78; owner Ser-Vis-Etc. LLC, Fresno, Calif., 1978—. Expert witness, cons. Am. Arbitration/Calif. Superior Cts. Pub./editor FranchiserviceNews; author: Hands in Your Pockets, 1992; contbr. numerous articles to profl. jours. With USAFNG, 1961-67. Mem. Nat. Coalition of Assn. of 7-11 Franchises (affiliate, mem. adv. bd. 1984-90). Republican. Methodist. Avocations: gardening, photography, travel, model railroading. Home: 1293 N Fancher Ave Fresno CA 93727 Office: Ser-Vis-Etc LLC PO Box 8444 Fresno CA 93747-8444 Personal E-mail: servisetc@aol.com.

WINSLOW, ROBERT A., real estate company executive; With IDC Real Estate (now JonesLangLaSalle), Tex., 1971; mktg. exec. IBM Corp.; co-founder, chmn., CEO US Equities Realty, Chgo., 1978—. Former co-chmn. Chgo. Devel. Coun.; mem. Mayor's Fellows Program, Fin. Rsch. and Adv. Com.; bd. mem. Metra, MB Fin. Inc. Founding chmn. Sculpture Chgo.; former bd. mem. Mus. Contemporary Art; mem. bd. overseers Rush Med. Coll.; trustee Rush-Presbyn.-St. Luke's Med. Ctr., North Ctrl. Coll., Ill. Masonic Med. Ctr., Columbia Coll., Chgo.; active Boy Scouts Am./Chgo. Area Coun., Bright New City, 1989—97; dir. Arts Club Chgo., The Marwen Found.; bd. mem. The Graham Found., Chgo. Pub. Libr. Found. Mem.: Chicagoland C. of C. (v.p. bd. dirs. 1982—91, bd. mem. 1990—, pres. adv. bd. 1991). Office: US Equities Realty Ste 400 20 N Michigan Ave Chicago IL 60602

WINSLOW, WALTER WILLIAM, psychiatrist, educator; b. Lacombe, Alta., Can., Nov. 23, 1925; came to U.S., 1959, naturalized, 1964; s. Floyd Raymond and Lily Evangeline (Palmer) W.; m. Barbara Ann Spiker; children: Colleen Denise, Dwight Walter, Barbara Jean, Wendi Jae. BS, La Sierra Coll., 1949; MD, Loma Linda U., 1952. Diplomate: Am. Bd. Psychiatry and Neurology. Intern Vancouver Gen. Hosp., 1952; psychiat. resident Provincial Mental Hosp., Essondale, B.C., 1957-59, Harding Hosp., Worthington, Ohio, 1959-60; instr. dept. psychiatry and indsl. medicine U. Cin., 1960-66, dept. preventive medicine, 1964-66; asst. prof. psychiatry U. N.Mex., Albuquerque, 1966-68, assoc. prof. psychiatry, 1969-74, prof., chmn. dept. psychiatry, 1974-91, dir. mental health programs, 1976-91; med. dir. Charter Hosp. of Albuquerque, 1991-95, Charter-Heights BHS, Albuquerque, 1995—99; ret. Assoc. prof. psychiatry Georgetown U., Washington, 1968-69; dir. bernalillo County Mental Health/Mental Retardation Ctr., 1970-78, 81-91. Author: The History of Psychiatry in New Mexico, 1889-1989, 2005; contbr. articles to profl. jours. Recipient N.Mex. Gov.'s Commendation for 10 yrs. service in mental health, 1979 Fellow Am. Psychiat. Assn. (life, area VII rep. 1981-85, Assembly Speaker's award 1984), Am. Coll. of Psychiatrists (life), Am. Assn. Community Psychiatrists (hon.); mem. AMA, Am. Assn. Psychiatry and the Law, N.Mex. Psychiat. Assn. (pres. 1974-75) Republican.

WINSON, ELLEN-MARIE (MACONE), school system administrator, reading specialist; b. Woburn, Mass., Sept. 6, 1941; d. Fred Charles and Edna McKay Macone; m. Robert Arthur Winson, Aug. 7, 1971 (dec. Dec. 2005); children: Maura Jane Mann, Suzanne Marie DiPalma, Peter Robert. BS, U. of Mass., 1958—62; MEd, Northeastern U., 1963—66. Teacher Elementary K-8 Mass. Dept of Edn., 1962, Reading Specialist K-12 Mass. Dept of Edn., 1965, Supervisor of Reading K-12 Mass. Dept. of Edn., 1968. Elem. tchr. Woburn Pub. Schools, Woburn, Mass., 1962—66, reading specialist k-12, 1966—76, Title 1 tchr., 1987—2000, Title 1 dir., 2000—: Remedial reading coord. Woburn Pub. Schools, Mass., 1968—77. V.p. Friends of the Libr., Woburn, Mass., 2001; bd. dirs. Title 1 Dissemination Project, Melrose, Mass., 1990—2005. Recipient State Leadership award, Nat. Assn. of Fed. Edn. Program Administrators, 2005. Mem.: Coun. of Administrators of Compensatory Edn. (rec. sec. 2003—05), Internat. Reading Assn. Avocations: travel, reading. Home: 23 Clinton St Woburn MA 01801 Office: Woburn Public Schools 55 Locust St Woburn MA 01801 Home Phone: 781-933-1210; Office Phone: 781-937-8233 x 230. Office Fax: 781-937-0715. Personal E-mail: ewinson@aol.com. E-mail: emwinson@woburnpublicschools.com.

WINSOR, WILLIAM JOHN, III, engineer, consultant; b. Ft. Worth, Apr. 26, 1952; s. William John Winsor and Marguerite Powell; m. Rebecca Anne Taylor. BS, U. Tenn., Martin, 1976, U. New Orleans, 1987. US customs inspector US Customs, New Orleans, 1981—82; sr. facility staff engr. Lockheed Martin, New Orleans, 1986—; sr. staff engr. Winsor and Assocs., New Orleans, 2005—. Dir. Winsor and Assocs., Slidell, La. E-4 US Army N.G., 1971—77. Mem.: ASHRAE, Instruemntation Soc. Am. Avocation: automobile restoration. Office: Winsor and Assocs 35621 Garden Dr Slidell LA 70460

WINSTANLY, DEREK MILES, medical practitioner, company executive; b. Pretoria, South Africa, June 25, 1946; s. Miles Winstanly and Gwen Cathrine Christie Gibbings; m. Heather Bucke (div. 1978); 1 child, Janet Hilary Winstanly; m. Louise Marie Teichler, Jan. 31, 1997. MB ChB, U. Pretoria, 1972. Cert. med. practitioner, aviation and space medicine. Gen. practitioner, Pretoria, 1976-80; med. adviser clin. devel., regulatory, and med. affairs Glaxo Pty Ltd., S. Africa, 1984-87, dir. mktg. and sales, 1987-89, dir. strategy and new bus. devel., 1989-90, chief exec., 1990-93, chmn., chief exec., 1993-94, dir. migraine and new therapy areas U.K., 1994-95; dir. emerging diseases Glaxo Wellcome Plc, U.K., 1995-97; pres. Nippon Wellcome KK, Japan, 1997-99; pres. and chmn. Quintiles Transnational, Japan, 1999—2005; exec. v.p. Quintiles Transnational Rsch., Triangle Pk., NC, 2005—. 1st gov. Med. U. South Africa, 1992—93, now trustee; prin. med. officer Inst. Aviation Medicine. With S. African Def. Force, 1980-84. Mem. S. African Aerospace Med. Soc. (past pres.). Avocations: tennis, golf, reading. Home: 104 N Boundary St Chapel Hill NC 27514 Office Phone: 919-998-2000.

WINSTEAD, DWIGHT, medical products executive; BS in Med. Tech., Delta State U. Health care salesman Worthington Diagnostics, Johnson & Johnson; dir. materials mgmt., adminstrv. dir. clin. labs. Alton Ochsner Found. Hosp., New Orleans; exec. v.p. VHA, Inc.; pres. Owen Healthcare, 1997—2001; grp. pres. Clin. Svcs. and Consulting Cardinal Health, 2001, group pres. Automation and Info. Svcs., COO Clin. Technologies and Svcs., grp. pres. Clin. Technologies and Svcs., 2006—. Bd. dirs. Sonus Pharms., 1995—. Office: Cardinal Health 7000 Cardinal Pl Dublin OH 43017

WINSTEAD, GEORGE ALVIS, law librarian, director; b. Owensboro, Ky., Jan. 14, 1916; s. Robert Lee and Mary Oma (Dempsey) Winstead; m. Elisabeth Donelson Weaver, July 18, 1942. BS, We. Ky. U., 1938; MA, George Peabody Coll., 1940, MLS, 1957, MEd, 1958. Head chemistry and biology dept. Belmont Coll., Nashville, 1952-56; head chemistry dept. George Peabody Coll., Vanderbilt U., Nashville, 1956-58; assoc. law librarian Vanderbilt U., Nashville, 1958-76; dir. Tenn. State Supreme Ct. Law Libraries, Nashville, 1976—. Law cons. Tenn. Youth Legis., Nashville, 1976—; cons. civic clubs, local colls., 1976—, Tenn. State Govt. Depts. Archives, Nashville, 1976—. Author: Tenn. State Law Library Progress Reports, 1975, Supreme Court Library Personnel Guide, 1981, Designing Future Law Libraries' Growth and Expansion, 1982, Problem Identification and Solutions in Law Libraries, Tenn. Supreme Courts, 1985; mem. editl. bd. A Dictionary of Chemical Equations, 1952—. Mem. Col. Tenn. Gov.'s staff, Nashville, 1978. With USAAF, 1943-46. Named to Gov.'s Staff of Ky. Cols., Lexington, 1988. Fellow Am. Inst. Chemists, SAR. Baptist. Avocations: camping, hiking, travel, crafts, antique cars. Office: Tenn Supreme Ct Libr Nashville TN 37219

WINSTEAD, MELODY, science educator; d. Teryl Washington. BA, Coll. New Rochelle, NYC, 1980; MA, CCNY, NYC, 1993. Cert. secondary sci. edn. tchr. NY State, 1987. Staff developer sci. NYC Dept. Edn. Dist. 5, NYC, 1979—2004, tchr., 1997—99, NYC Dept. Edn., NYC, 1987—. Sci. inquiry specialist, New Rochelle, NY. Home: 23 Lathers Park New Rochelle NY 10801-3910 Personal E-mail: melodywinstead@yahoo.com.

WINSTEAD, NASH NICKS, academic administrator, plant pathologist; b. Durham County, NC, June 12, 1925; s. Nash L. and Lizzy (Featherston) W.; m. Geraldine Larkin Kelly, Sept. 17, 1949; 1 dau., Karen Jewell. BS, N.C. State U., 1948, MS, 1951; PhD, U. Wis., 1953. Asst. prof. plant pathology, Raleigh, 1953-58; assoc. prof. N.C. State U., Raleigh, 1958-61, prof., 1961-90, prof. emeritus, 1991—, dir. inst. biol. scis., 1965-67, asst. dir. agrl. exptl. sta., 1965-67, asst. provost, 1967-73, assoc. provost, 1973-74, provost and vice chancellor, 1974-90, acting chancellor, 1981-82. Phillip Found. intern acad. adminstrn. Ind. U., 1965-66; bd. trustees N.C. Sch. Sci. and Math., 1985-90. Author: Home grown and Homemade, 1997, Mama's Book, 1998, The Provost's Office N.C. State U., An Informal History, 1955-93, 1999, The Civil War Campaigns Involving Corporal James Fletcher Winstead, 1999, Featherston Memories, 2002, Start Where You Are and Use What You've Got, 2005; contbr. articles profl. jours. Mem. N.C. Council on Higher Edn. for Adults, 1967-75; inst. rep. So. Assn. for Colls. and Schs., 1967-74; mem. Cooperating Raleigh Colls., 1968-90, pres., 1971-73, 83-85; chmn. interaction between protoplasm and toxicants com. So. Regional Edn. Bd., 1964-65; Bd. dirs. N.C. State U. YMCA, 1963-65; trustee Meth. Home for Children, 1980-88, pres., 1983-84, N.C. Wesleyan Coll., 1987-97. Served with USAAF, 1943-46. Recipient Sigma Xi research award, 1960 Fellow AAAS; Mem. Am. Phytopath. Soc. (chmn. disease, pathogen physiology com.), Am. Inst. Biol. Scis., N.C. Assn. Colls. and Univs. (exec. com. 1974-80, pres. 1978-79), Nat. Assn. State Univs. and Land Grant Colls. (edn. telecommunications com. 1980-85, equal opportunity com. 1985-88). Acad. Deans for So. States, N.C. Assn. of Acad. Officers (exec. com. 1986-89, v.p., pres. 1987-88), Sigma Xi, Phi Kappa Phi, Omicron Delta Kappa. Clubs: Torch Internat. (sec.). Home: 1109 Glendale Dr Raleigh NC 27612-4709

WINSTEAD, NATHANIEL SCOTT, gastroenterologist; b. Cin., Jan. 10, 1973; s. Daniel Keith and Jennifer Lee Winstead; m. Amanda Lee Mantle, June 21, 1997. MD, Tulane U., New Orleans, 1996—2000. Diplomate Am. Bd. Internal Medicine, 2003. Chief resident internal medicine Tulane U. Sch. Medicine, 2003—04; fellow sect. gastroenterology & hepatology U. Ala., Birmingham, 2004—. Mem.: AMA, Am. Soc. Gastrointestinal Endoscopy, Am. Gastroent. Assn. Avocations: running, golf, running. Office: Univ Ala MT401E2 1530 3d Ave S Birmingham AL 35294-4410 Home Phone: 205-996-2877. Home Fax: 205-934-4888.

WINSTEIN, BRUCE DARRELL, physics professor; BS, UCLA; PhD, Calif. Inst. Tech., 1970. Samuel K. Allison disting. svc. prof. physics Univ. Chgo. Recipient W.K.H. Panofsky Prize in Experimental Particle Physics, Am. Phys. Soc., 2007. Fellow: Am. Acad. Arts & Scis.; mem.: NAS. Office: Physics Dept Univ Chgo 5640 S Ellis Ave Chicago IL 60637 Office Phone: 773-702-7594. Office Fax: 773-702-6645. Business E-Mail: bruce@hep.uchicago.edu. *

WINSTEN, SAUL NATHAN, lawyer; b. Providence, Feb. 23, 1953; s. Harold H. and Anita E. Winsten; m. Patricia J. Miller, Aug. 7, 1977; children: David A., J. Benjamin, Jennifer M. BA, Beloit Coll., Wis., 1976; JD, Drake U., Des Moines, 1980. Shareholder DeWitt Ross & Stevens, Brookfield, Wis.; chmn. corp. counsel com. Wis. Mfrs. Commn., 2004—. Contbr. articles to profl. jours. Active Wis. Gov.'s Adv. Coun. on Internat. Trade, 1996-2003, co-chmn., 1999-2002; active Wis. Gov.'s Internat. Edn. Task Force, 1997-98; chmn. Wis. Mfrs. and Commerce Corp. Counsel Com., 2004-; adv. com. Great Lakes Area IRS Adv. Com. Tax Exempt Orgn./Govt. Entities Coun., 2005—. Mem. ABA (chmn. com. young lawyers divsn. 1989-90, governing coun., antitrust, bus. and internat. law sects.), Wis. Bar Assn. (chair tax exempt orgn. com. of bus law sect. 2005-06), Internat. Bar Assn., Japan-Am. Soc. Wis. (pres. 1993-94, co-founder 1990, sec. 1990-92), Nat. Assn. Japan-Am. Socs. (bd. dirs. 1991-97, exec. com. 1993-97), Order of Barristers, Hessen-Wisconsin, Inc. (bd. dirs.), Internat. Bar Assn. Office: DeWitt Ross & Stevens 13935 Bishops Dr Brookfield WI 53005-6605 Office Phone: 262-754-2852. Business E-Mail: snw@dewittross.com.

WINSTON, ARTHUR WILLIAM, physicist; b. Toronto, Can., Feb. 11, 1930; arrived in U.S., 1951, naturalized, 1959; s. Maurice and Alma (Freedman) Winston; m. Lily Baum, Sept. 4, 1949; children: Leslie, Pamela, David, Matthew. BSc, U. Toronto, 1951; PhD, MIT, 1954. Physicist NRC, Toronto, Canada, 1949—51; rsch. asst. MIT, Cambridge, Mass., 1951—54; sr. engr. Schlumberger Corp., Houston, 1954—57; physicist Nat. Rsch. Corp., Cambridge, 1957—59; chief scientist Allied Rsch. Assocs., Boston, 1959—61; pres. Space Scis., Inc., Waltham, Mass., 1961—65, Ikor Inc., Burlington, Mass., 1965—75; v.p. Omni-Wave Electronics Corp., Gloucester, Mass., 1976—78; pres. Wincom Corp., Lawrence, Mass., 1979—86; coord. and prof. advanced tech. and engrng. The Gordon Inst., Lawrence, 1986—, dir. Dir. Granite State Controls, Inc.; adj. prof. Northeastern U., 1978—; mem. US Dept. Commerce European Pollution Control Trade Mission, 1971; chmn. Electro Conf., 1960, MIT Boston Seminar Series, 1988—; judge Mass. State Sci. Fair, 1957—; chmn. internat. intercultural progs. com. Lexington chpt. Am. Field Svc., 1977—. Contbr. articles to profl. jours. Co-recipient Bernard M. Gordon prize, NAE, 2007; recipient Cert. Appreciation, U.S. Dept. Commerce, 1971, Inventor's award, 1986; scholar Wallberg Meml. scholar, 1949, Assn. Profl. Engrs., 1949, others. Mem.: AIME, AIAA, IEEE (pres. 2004, Millennium medal 2000), Air Pollution Control Assn., Am. Geophys. Union, Am. Phys. Soc., Appalachian Mountain Club, Sigma Xi. Home: 7 Wainwright Rd Unit 15 Winchester MA 01890-2388 *

WINSTON, DAVID CHARLES, pathologist; b. St. Louis, Sept. 25, 1963; s. Donald Francis and Maxine Marie (Kertz) W.; m. Cynthia Lucille McDougal, June 17, 1989; 1 child, Zachary Lewis. BS, St. Louis U., 1985; PhD, Med. U. S.C., 1991, MD, 1993. Resident in pathology U. Va. Health Scis. Ctr., Charlottesville, 1993-97; fellow in forensic pathology Office of Med. Investigator U. N.Mex. Sch. Medicine, Albuquerque, 1997-98. Contbr. articles to profl. jours. Mem. AMA, Royal Microscopic Soc., Coll. Am. Pathologists, Am. Soc. Clin. Pathologists, Va. Soc. Pathologists, Va. Med. Soc., U.S. and Can. Acad. Pathology. Office: U Va Health Scis Ctr Dept Pathology PO Box 214 Charlottesville VA 22902-0214

WINSTON, FLAURA K., engineering researcher; Ph. D., Univ. of Penn. School of Medicine. Asst. physician Children's Hosp. of Phila., 1994—; founder, dir. TraumaLink. Recipient Melville medal ASME, 1995. Fellow: Bloomberg School of Public Health, John's Hopkins Univ. Office: The Children's Hosp of Phila 3535 TraumaLink 10th Fl 34th St and Civic Ctr Blvd Philadelphia PA 19104

WINSTON, GEORGE, solo pianist, guitarist, harmonica player; b. Hart, Mich., 1949; Ind. musician, 1967—; founder Dancing Cat Productions, Santa Cruz, Calif., 1983—. Ten solo piano albums including Ballads and Blues, 1972, Autumn, 1980, Winter Into Spring, 1982, December, 1982, Summer, 1991, Forest, 1994, Linus & Lucy: The Music of Vince Guaraldi, 1996, Plains, 1999, Night Divides the Day--The Music of the Doors, 2002, Montana, A Love Story, 2004; audiobook soundtracks: (with Meryl Streep) The Velveteen Rabbit, 1984, This is America Charlie Brown--Birth of the Constitution, 1988, (with Liv Ullmann) Sadako and the Thousand Paper Cranes Benefit CD, 1995, Remembrance-9/11 Memorial Benefit CD, 2001; prodr., co-prodr. 36 albums of the masters of traditional Hawaiian slack key (finger style) guitar. Office: c/o Dancing Cat Prodns PO Box 639 Santa Cruz CA 95061-0639 Office Phone: 831-429-5085. E-mail: ml@dancingcat.com.

WINSTON, HAROLD RONALD, lawyer; b. Atlantic, Iowa, Feb. 7, 1932; s. Louis D. and Leta B. (Carter) W.; m. Carol J. Sundeen, June 11, 1955; children: Leslie Winston Yannetti, Lisa Winston Shaw, Laura Winston Moritz. BA, U. Iowa, 1954, JD, 1958. Bar: Iowa 1958, U.S. Dist. Ct. (no. and so. dists.) Iowa 1962, U.S. Tax Ct. 1962, U.S. Ct. Appeals (8th cir.) 1970, U.S. Supreme Ct. 1969. Trust officer United Home Bank & Trust Co., Mason City, Iowa, 1958-59; mem. Breese & Cornwell, Mason City, 1960-62, Breese, Cornwell, Winston & Reuber, Mason City, 1963-73, Winston, Schroeder & Reuber, Mason City, 1974-79, Winston, Reuber, Swanson & Byrne, P.C., Mason City, 1980-92, Winston, Reuber & Byrne, Mason City, 1992-96, Winston & Byrne, P.C., Mason City, 1996—. Police judge, Mason City, 1961-73. Contbr. articles to profl. jours. Past pres. Family YMCA, Mason City, Cerro Gordo County Estate Planning Coun.; active local charitable orgns. Capt. USAF, 1955-57. Fellow Am. Coll. Trust and Estate Counsel, Am. Bar Found. (life), Iowa Bar Found. (life); mem. ABA, ATLA, Iowa Bar Assn. (gov., lectr. ann. meeting 1977-79), 2d Jud. Dist. Bar Assn. (lectr. meeting 1981-82), Cerro Gordo County Bar Assn. (past pres.), Am. Judicature Soc., Mason City Country Club, Kiwanis, Masons. Republican. Presbyterian. Office: Winston & Byrne 119 2d St NW Mason City IA 50401-3105 Office Phone: 641-423-1913. Business E-Mail: hwinston@mchsi.com.

WINSTON, JUDITH ANN, lawyer; b. Atlantic City, Nov. 23, 1943; d. Edward Carlton and Margaret Ann (Goodman) Marianno; m. Michael Russell Winston, Aug. 10, 1963; children: Lisa Marie, Cynthia Eileen. BA magna cum laude, Howard U., Washington, 1966; JD, Georgetown U., 1977. Bar: DC 1977, US Supreme Ct. Dir. EEO project Coun. Great City Schs., Washington, 1971-74; legal asst. Lawyers Com. for Civil Rights Under Law, Washington, 1975-77; spl. asst. to dir. Office for Civil Rights, HEW, Washington, 1977-79; exec. asst., legal counsel to chair U.S. EEO Commn., Washington, 1979-80; asst. gen. counsel U.S. Dept. Edn., 1980-86; dep. dir. Lawyers Com. for Civil Rights Under Law, 1986-88; dep. dir. pub. policy Women's Legal Def. Fund, Washington, 1988-90, chair employment discrimination com., 1979-88, ednl. cons., 1974-77; asst. prof. law Washington Coll. Law of Am. U., 1990-93, assoc. prof. law, 1993-95; gen. counsel U.S. Dept. Edn., Washington, 1993-2001; exec. dir. Pres.'s Initiative on Race, 1997-98; undersec. U.S. Dept. Edn., 2000-01; rsch. prof law Washington Coll. Law Am. U., Washington, 2001—02; ptnr. Winston Withers & Assocs., LLC, Washington, 2002—. Author: (book) Desegregating Schools in the Great Cities: Philadelphia, 1970, Chronicle of a Decade 1961-70, 1970, Desegregating Urban Schools: Educational Equality/Quality, 1970; contbr. articles to profl jours. Pres. bd. dirs. Higher Achievement Program; bd. dirs. Ptnrs. for Dem. Change, Nat. Pub. Radio, So. Edn. Found., Nat. Law Ctr. on Poverty and Homelessness, Hist. Soc. DC Cir. Ct. Appeals, 2004—. Named Woman Lawyer of the Yr, Women's Bar Asn, 1997; recipient Margaret Brent, Am Bar Asn Comn Women in the Profession, 1998, Thurgood Marshall award, DC Bar, 1999. Fellow: ABA Found.; mem.: ACLU, Lawyers Com. Civil Rights Under Law, Nat. Bar Assn., Washington Bar Assn., Washington Coun. Lawyers, DC Bar Asn, Fed. Bar Assn., Links Inc., Phi Beta Kappa, Delta Theta Phi, Alpha Kappa Alpha. Democrat. Episcopalian. Home: 1371 Kalmia Rd NW Washington DC 20012-1444 Office: Winston Withers & Assocs 1730 M St NW # 413 Washington DC 20036 Home Phone: 202-829-4085; Office Phone: 202-887-8202. Business E-Mail: jwinston@winwithassocs.com.

WINSTON, LELAND A., orthopedic surgeon, educator; b. Wharton, Tex., Sept. 12, 1946; BA, Rice U., Houston, Tex., 1969; MD, U. Tex., Galveston, 1973. Cert. Am. Bd. Orthop. Surgeons, lic. Tex. Intern, orthop. U. Tex., Houston, 1973—74, resident, orthop. surgery, 1974—78; clin. assoc. prof. dept. orthop. surgery U. Tex. Health Sci. Ctr. at Houston Med. Sch.; clin. instr., dept. orthop. surgery Baylor Coll. Medicine. Co-team physician Rice U., Dept. Athletics. Contbr. articles to profl. jours. Named one of Golf Digest 2006 Top Golf Doctors in Am. Fellow: Am. Acad. Orthop. Surgeons; mem.: AMA, Am. Orthop. Soc. for Sports Medicine, Houston Orthop. Soc., Tex. Med. Assn., Harris County Med. Soc. (mem. com. ethics). Office: 6500 Fannin Ste 1006 Houston TX 77030 *

WINSTON, MICHAEL RUSSELL, foundation executive, historian; b. NYC, May 26, 1941; s. Charles Russell and Jocelyn Anita Prem Das Winston; m. Judith Ann Marianno, Aug. 10, 1963; children: Lisa Marie, Cynthia Eileen. BA magna cum laude, Howard U., 1962; MA, U. Calif.-Berkeley, 1964, PhD, 1974. Instr. dept. history Howard U., Washington, 1964-66, asst. dean Coll. Liberal Arts, 1968-69, asst. prof. dept. history, 1970-73, v.p. acad. affairs, 1983-90, prof. emeritus, 1990—; assoc. dir. Inst. Svc. to Edn., Washington, 1966; fellow Haus. Hof-und Staatsarchiv, Vienna, 1969; dir. Moorland Spingarn Rsch. Ctr., 1973-83; v.p., bd. dirs. Alfred Harcourt Found., Silver Spring, Md., 1992-93, pres., treas., 1993—. Cons. Smithsonian Instn., 1979—, nat. Inst. Edn., 1978-85, NSF, 1985—. Author: (with R.W. Logan) The Negro in the United States, 1970, The Howard Univ.Dept. of History, 1913-73, 1973; editor: (with R.W. Logan) Dictionary of Am. Negro Biography, 1982, (with G.R. McNeil) Hist. Judgements Reconsidered, 1988; mem. editl. bd. Washington History, 1993-97. Mem. exec. bd. Nat. Capital Area coun. Boy Scouts Am., 1988—90; trustee spl. contbn. fund NAACP, 1980—82; trustee D.C. Pub. Defender Svc., 1985—88; bd. trustees Woodrow Wilson Nat. Fellowship Found., 1997—2006; bd. mgrs. Hist. Soc. Washington; bd. dirs. Harcourt Brace Jovanovich, 1980—91, D.C. Pub. Libr. Found., 1994—2002, pres., 1995—99, Nat. Coun. for History Standards; mem. bd. overseers' com. to visit dept. history Harvard U., 1996—; mem. nat. adv. com. and coun. of scholars Libr. of Congress; nat. adv. bd. Protect Historic Am.; mem. Commn. on Coll. and Univ. Nonprofit. Studies ABA; mem. Nat. Ctr. for History in the Schs. UCLA/NEH. Moten fellow U. Edinburgh, 1962, Wilson fellow U. Calif., 1962, Ford fellow, 1969-70, Woodrow Wilson Internat. Ctr. Scholars fellow, 1979-80; sr. scholar, 2001—. Mem.: Nat. Coun. for History Standards, Coun. on Foreign Relations, Atlantic Coun. of U.S., Hist. Soc. Washington, Am. Antiquarian Soc., Orgn. Am. Historians, Am. Hist. Assn., Grolier Club, Century Assn., Cosmos Club (Washington), Phi Beta Kappa (Ralph Waldo Emerson prize com. 2000). Democrat. Episcopalian. Home: 1371 Kalmia Rd NW Washington DC 20012-1444 Office: Alfred Harcourt Found 8401 Colesville Rd Silver Spring MD 20910-3352 Home Phone: 202-829-4085; Office Phone: 301-589-1551. E-mail: mwinston@erols.com, michaelrwinston@aol.com.

WINT, DENNIS MICHAEL, museum director; b. Macon, Ga., Mar. 17, 1943; s. Paul Kenneth and Mary (McClure) W. BS, U. Mich., 1965; tchr.'s cert., Lake Erie Coll., 1970; PhD, Case Western Res. U., 1977. Dir. environ. edn. Wiloughby Eastlake City Schs., 1968-70; dir. Ctr. Devel. Environment Curiculum, 1970-75; cons. Ohio Dept. Edn., 1975-77; dir. mus. and edn. Acad. Natural Scis., Phila., 1977-79, v.p., dir. natural history mus., 1979-82; dir. Cranbrook Inst. Sci., Bloomfield Hills, Mich., 1982-86; pres. St. Louis Sci. Ctr., 1986-95; pres., CEO The Franklin Inst., Phila., 1995—. Adj. asst. prof. Temple U.; past chmn. edn. and human resources adv. com. NSF, 1991-92; past pres. St. Louis Area Mus. Collaborative, 1991-92, mem. exec. com. Bd. govts. Greater Phila. 1st Partnership for Reform, 1995—98, mem. leadership com., 1995—98. Mem. Am. Assn. Mus. (bd. dirs. 2003-), Assn. Sci.-Tech. Ctrs. (mem. nominating com., v.p. 1993-95, pres. 1995-97, chmn. internat. com. 2000-05, strategic planning com. 2002-05), Greater Phila. Cultural Alliance (bd. dirs. 1996-05, chmn. strategic planning com. 2000-05), Benjamin Franklin Fed. Tchg. Commn. (co-chair). Home: 222 N 20th St Philadelphia PA 19103

WINTER, CHESTER CALDWELL, surgeon, educator, historian, writer; b. Cazenovia, NY, June 2, 1922; s. Chester Caldwell and Cora Evelyn (Martin) W.; m. Mary Antonia Merullo, Oct. 22, 1983; children by previous marriage: Paul, Ann, Jane. BA, U. Iowa, 1943, MD, 1946. Diplomate: Am. Bd. Urology. Intern Meth. Hosp., Indpls., 1946-47; med. resident St. Luke's Hosp., Cedar Rapids, Iowa, 1947; physician Calif., 1950-51; resident gen. surgery VA Hosp., Los Angeles, 1952-53; resident urology VA Hosp.-UCLA Med. Ctr., 1953-57; clin. asst. surgery UCLA, 1954-57, instr. surgery and urology, 1957-58, asst. prof. surgery and urology, 1958-59, asst. prof. Step II, 1959-60; prof. surgery and urology Ohio State U., 1960-88, prof. emeritus surgery and urology, 1988—, Louis Levy prof. urology, 1980-88. Dir. urology Ohio State U. Hosp., Columbus, 1960-78; cons. urology VA, Air Force hosps., Dayton, 1960-80. Author: Radioisotope Renography, 1963, Correctable Renal Hypertension, 1964, Nursing Care of Patients with Urologic Diseases, 4th edit, 1977, Practical Urology, 1969, Vesicoureteral Reflux, 1969, A Concise History of the U.S. and the State of Ohio, 2002, A Bicentennial History of the State of Ohio, 2003, Ohio Cities: Historical Descriptions, 2004, Concise Biographies of Notable Ohioans, 2005; editl. cons. Exerpta Medica: Nuclear Medicine, Jour. AMA; mem. editl. bd. Andrology, Jour. Urology; contbr. articles to profl. jours. Served to capt. M.C. U.S. Army, 1943-46, 48-49. Fellow Am. Acad. Pediatricians, Am. Coll. Surgeons; mem. Am. Assn. Genitourinary Surgeons, Am. Urol. Assn., Soc. Univ. Surgeons, Soc. Pediatric Urology, Soc. Univ. Urologists, Internat. Soc. Urology, Urol. Investigators Forum, Ohio State Med. Assn., Columbus Surg. Soc., Central Ohio Urology Soc., Columbus Acad. Medicine, Ohio State U. Med. Soc. Home: 6425 Evening St Worthington OH 43085-3054 E-mail: cwinter3@ameritech.net.

WINTER, DAVID FERDINAND, electrical engineering educator, consultant; b. St. Louis, Nov. 9, 1920; s. Ferdinand Conrad and Annie (Schaffer) W.; m. Bettie Jeanne Turner; children: Suzanne, Sharie Winter Chappeau. BSEE, Washington U., St. Louis, 1942; MSEE, MIT, 1948. Registered profl. engr., Mo. Staff mem. radiation lab. MIT, Cambridge, 1942-45, rsch. assoc. electronics lab., 1945-48; prof. elec. engring. Washington U., St. Louis, 1948-55, affiliate prof. elec. engring., 1955-67; v.p. engring. and rsch. Moloney Elec. Co., St. Louis, 1955-74; v.p. rsch. and engring. Blackburn div. IT&T, St. Louis, 1974-82, dir. advanced tech. devel., 1982-86; pvt. practice cons. St. Louis, 1986—. Ct. recognized tech. expert on sources, mitigation, and effects of stray voltage on dairy cattle cons. Wis. Pub. Svc. Commn.; cons. Naval Ordanance Lab. of Ind., Indpls., 1950-53, other industries, St. Louis, 1979—. Contbr. articles to profl. jours.; holder 28 patents. Elder, pastor Maplewood Bible Chapel, St. Louis. Recipient Alumni Achievement award, Wash. U., Sch. Engring. & Applied Sci., St. Louis. Mo., 2003, Washington U., 2003. Fellow IEEE (life), Inst. Radio Engrs.; mem. NSPE, Am. Soc. Agrl. Engrs., Mo. Soc. Profl. Engrs., Sigma Xi, Tau Beta Pi, Eta Kappa Nu. Avocations: cabinet maker, photography, music instruments. Home and Office: 735 Harvard Ave University City MO 63130-3135 Office Phone: 314-727-4532. E-mail: dfwinter@hotmail.com.

WINTER, DAVID LOUIS, retired systems engineer, human factors scientist; b. Pitts., July 30, 1930; s. Louis A. and Gladys M. (Quinn) W.; m. Nancy L. Tear, July 1, 1952; children: Leeson, Blaise, Gregory, Lauren. BA, U. Pitts., 1952; MA, Columbia U., 1960; cert. computer sci., Northeastern U., 1971. Assoc. rsch. scientist Am. Insts. Rsch., Washington, 1961-66, sr. rsch. scientist Bedford, Mass., 1966-71, prin. rsch. scientist, 1976-94, retired, 1995; sr. systems analyst RCA Corp.-Sarnoff Labs., Princeton, NJ, 1971-73; mgr. systems engring. Codon Corp., Bedford, 1973-76. Computer systems cons. Mass. Dept. Mental Health, 1971-73. Pres. Mayo Peninsula Civic Assn., Edgewater, Md., 1964-65; v.p. Bedford Human Rels. Coun., 1992-94. Capt. USAF, 1952-64. Mem. Am. Acad. Polit. Sci., Human Factors Soc., Soc. Ednl. Tech. Democrat. Roman Catholic. Achievements include design and human factors test for 8 USAF electronic, intelligence and backscatter radar systems; design of 4 computer-assisted training systems for USAF E3 AWACS radar, computer displays, communications and navigation subsystems; cons. engr. for design and test of E6 Joint Stars battlefield surveillance system. Office: MicroVentures Ltd 27 Gould Rd Bedford MA 01730-1250

WINTER, DONALD C., civilian military employee, former science administrator; b. 1948; BS in Physics with high distinction, U. Rochester, 1969; MS, U. Mich., 1970, PhD, 1972; grad., U. SC Mgmt. Policy Inst., 1979; grad. exec. program, UCLA, 1987; grad. program for sr. execs. in nat. and internat. security, Harvard U., 1991. Dir. rsch. & devel. in laser physics & applications TRW Sys., 1972—80, sr. sys. engring. & program mgr., 1982—90, v.p., gen. mgr. Def. Sys., Divsn. Space & Electronics, 1990—97, v.p., dep. gen. mgr. for group devel. space & electronics, 1998—99, pres., CEO, 2000—02; corp. v.p., pres. mission sys. Northrop Grumman Corp., LA, 2002—05; program mgr. for space acquisition, tracking and pointing programs Def. Advanced Rsch. Projects Agy. US Dept. Def., 1980—82, sec. Dept. of Navy, 2006—. Bd. dirs. Wolf Trap Found., Electronic Industries Alliance, USO Met. Washington. Mem.: Nat. Acad. Engring. Office: US Dept Def Sec of Navy The Pentagon Rm 4E686 Washington DC 20350 *

WINTER, DOUGLAS E., lawyer, writer; b. St. Louis, Oct. 30, 1950; s. William E. and Dorothy E. (Schuster) W.; m. Lynne G. Turner, July 9, 1977; step-children: Carl, John, Stephen. BS, U. Ill., 1971, MS, 1972; JD, Harvard U., 1975; postgrad., Judge Advocate Gen.'s Sch., 1977. Bar: Mo. 1975, Ill. 1976, DC 1976. Clk. to Hon. William H. Webster U.S. Ct. Appeals (8th cir.), St. Louis, 1975-76; assoc. Covington & Burling, Washington, 1976-84; ptnr. Bryan Cave LLP, Washington, 1985—. Vis. prof. U. Iowa, Iowa City, 1980-81. Author: Stephen King, 1982, Shadowings: The Reader's Guide to Horror Fiction, 1983, Stephen King: The Art of Darkness, 1984, Faces of Fear, 1985, Black Wine, 1986, Splatter: A Cautionary Tale, 1987, Prime Evil, 1988, Darkness Absolute, 1991, Black Sun, 1994, Millennium, 1997, Revelations, 1997, Run, 2000, Clive Barker: The Dark Fantastic, 2001, Introduction to Legal Writing, 2004, A Little Brass Book of Full Metal Fiction, 2006, American Zombie, 2007; contbr. articles to popular mags. and nat. newspapers. Capt. US Army, 1973-77. Recipient world fantasy award World Fantasy Conv., 1986, award Internat. Horror Guild, 1995, 96, 98. Mem. Nat. Book Critics Circle, Horror Writers Assn. (chmn. grievance com. 1989—, trustee 1997—). Office: Bryan Cave LLP 700 13th St NW Fl 6 Washington DC 20005-3960 Office Phone: 202-508-6000. Business E-Mail: dewinter@bryancave.com.

WINTER, FREDERICK ELLIOT, fine arts educator; b. Barbados, WI, June 19, 1922; s. Edward Elliot and Constance Mabel (Gill) W.; m. Joan Elizabeth Hay, June 9, 1951; children: Elizabeth, Penelope, Mary, Michael. BA, McGill U., 1945; PhD, U. Toronto, 1957. Instr. U. Toronto, 1947-49, 50-51, lectr., 1951-57, asst. prof., 1957-61, asso. prof., 1961-68, prof., 1968-90, prof. emeritus, 1990—, chmn. dept. fine art, 1971-77, grad. coord. history of art, 1978-81, spl. lectr. history of art, 1990-98; chmn. U. Toronto Assn. Teaching Staff, 1968-69. Mem. mng. com. Am. Sch. Classical Studies, Athens, Greece, 1968-90, chair pers. com., 1975-77; mem. programme com. Can. Archaeol. Inst. at Athens, 1990-94; bd. dirs. Can. Acad. Inst., Athens. Author: (with G.S. Vickers, P.H. Brieger) Art and Man, Vol. I, 1963, Greek Fortifications, 1971, Studies in Hellenistic Architecture, 2006; contbr. articles Jour. Classical Assn. Can., Am. Jour. of Archaeology, Echos du Monde Classique/Classical Views. Recipient Gold medal in classics McGill U., 1945; Flavelle fellow U. Toronto, 1947-48; White fellow Am. Sch., Athens, 1949-50; spl. research fellow, 1977-78, 87-88; sr. assoc. fellow, 1982, 83-84, 86, 91; Am. Philos. Soc. grantee, 1957; grantee Soc. Sci. Humanities Rsch. Coun. Can., 1962, 68, 71, 75, 77-78, 82, 83-84, 86, 87-88, 91; grantee U. Toronto Humanities and Social Scis. Rsch. Com., 1993. Mem. Classical Assn. Can., Archeol. Inst. Am. (editorial adv. bd. Am. Jour. Archaeology 1981-85) Home: 164 Highgate Ave Willowdale ON Canada M2N 5G8

WINTER, HARVEY JOHN, retired government official; b. New Albion, NY, Apr. 6, 1915; s. George J. and Irene (Harvey) W.; m. Virginia M. Shaw, Sept. 2, 1939; 1 child, Jeffrey S. BA magna cum laude, U. Buffalo, 1938, MA, 1939; teaching fellow, George Washington U., 1939-40. Historian U.S. Nat. Park Service, 1940-42; archivist U.S. Nat. Archives, 1942-43; with U.S. Office Alien Property Custodian, 1943-51, chief reports and stats. sect., 1948- 51; with State Dept., 1951—, chief internat. bus. practices div., 1959- 61, asst. chief, 1961-70, chief bus. practices div., 1970-71, dir. office bus. protection, 1971-73, dir. office bus. practices, 1973-90; dir. office intellectual property and competition, 1991-92; U.S. del. European Productivity Agy. cartel meetings, Paris, 1958-60; mem. U.S. del. diplomatic confs. Internat. Design Agreement, The Hague, 1960, 17th session GATT, Geneva, 1960; U.S. alt. rep. 5th session Intergovtl. Copyright Com., London, 1960, 6th session, Madrid, 1961, 7th session, New Delhi, 1963; U.S. alt. rep. Interunion Coordinating Com., Geneva, 1963-69; U.S. observer African Seminar on Indsl. Property, Brazzaville, Congo, 1963; U.S. alt. observer Latin Am. Indsl. Property Seminar, Bogota, Colombia, 1964, Asian Indsl. Property Seminar, Colombo, Ceylon, 1966, Com. of Experts on Inventors' Certificates, Geneva, 1965, Com. of Experts on Adminstrv. Agreement, Geneva, 1965, Intellectual Property Diplomatic Conf., Stockholm, 1967, Diplomatic Conf. on Agreement for Classification of Indsl. Designs, Locarno, Switzerland, 1968, Diplomatic Conf. on Patent Cooperation Treaty, Washington, 1970, Diplomatic Conf. on Agreement for Internat. Patent Classification, Strasbourg, France, 1971, Diplomatic Conf. on Universal Copyright Conv., Paris, 1971; U.S. alt. rep. Diplomatic Conf. on Phonogram Conv., Geneva, 1971, Diplomatic Conf. on Indsl. Property, Vienna, 1973; U.S. rep. Com. Experts on Type Face Agreement, Geneva, 1972, Com. Experts on Communications Satellites Problems, Nairobi, Kenya, 1973; U.S. del. Diplomatic Conf. on Communications Satellites Conv., Brussels, 1974, Diplomatic Conf. on Treaty for Deposit Microorganisms, Budapest, Hungary, 1977, Diplomatic Conf. on Plant Protection Conv., Geneva, 1978, World Intellectual Property Orgn. Governing Bodies, Geneva, 1979-82, alt. del., 1983-91; alt. U.S. del. Diplomatic Conf. on Revision of Paris Conv., Geneva, 1980, 82, 83, 84 Nairobi, 1981; ret., 1992. U.S. del. UNESCO Experts on Rental of Videograms, Paris, 1984, Com. Govtl. Experts on Audiovisual Works and Phonograms, Paris, 1986, Com. Govtl. Experts on Internat. Register of Audiovisual Works, Geneva, 1988, Diplomatic Conf. on Treaty for Internat. Registration of Audiovisual Works, Geneva, 1989, Com. Experts on Disputes Steelement Treaty on Intellectual Property, 1990; chmn. Internat. Patent Classification Assembly, 1992. Recipient Superior Honor award Dept. State, 1971, 75, 89, 92, 50-Yr. Svc. award, 1990, Jefferson medal, N.J. Patent Law Assn., 1982; honoree Copyright Soc. U.S.A., 1989. Mem. Phi Beta Kappa. Episcopalian (vestry).

WINTER, HORST HENNING, chemical engineer, educator; b. Stuttgart, Sept. 9, 1941; s. Simon Wilhelm and Hanna (Schwenn) W.; m. Karin Eckert, Aug. 29, 1969; children: Dirk Christopher, Lisa Susanne, Caroline Elke, Peter Benjamin. D of Engring., U. Stuttgart, 1973. Privatdozent U. Stuttgart, 1976-79; prof. U. Mass., Amherst, 1979—; owner IRIS Devel. LLC. Editor Rheologica Acta, 1989-2005; mem. edit. bd. Jour. Rheology, 1989—, Jour. Non-Newtonian Fluid Mechanics, 1989—; contbr. articles to sci. and profl. jours., 1977—. Recipient Bingham medal, 1996, NSF Creativity award, 1997, Alexander von Humboldt prize, 1999. Mem. Am. Soc. Rheology (exec. com. 1990-91), Am. Inst. Chem. Engrs., N.Y. Acad. Sci. Achievements include development of novel rheological techniques; discovery of self-similar relaxation of polymers at the gel point; universal time spectrum of linear flexible polymers of uniform length; invention of CSX process for making ultra-clean porous polymers; co-architect of the cyberinfrastructure platform for rheology. Office: U Mass Dept Chem Engring Amherst MA 01003 E-mail: winter@ecs.umass.edu.

WINTER, JEFFREY B., elementary school educator; BA, St. Ambrose U., Davenport, Iowa, 1970; MA, Western Ill. U., Malcomb, 1989. Cert. tchr. Iowa, 2007. Tchr. Bettendorf Cmty. Schs., Iowa, 1974—. Avocations: reading, movies, walking, gardening. Home Phone: 309-786-2119; Office Phone: 563-359-3686.

WINTER, JIMMY, entrepreneur, systems administrator; b. 1982; Web site designer Fastmusic Label, NYC, 1999; founder Music Arsenal, Omaha, 2003—. Named one of Best Entrepreneurs Under 25, BusinessWeek, 2006. Office: Music Arsenal Ste 280 12105 W Center Rd Omaha NE 68137 Office Phone: 800-231-9273. E-mail: info@musicarsenal.com.

WINTER, JUDY ELAINE, freelance/self-employed journalist, speaker; d. Lester App and Marie Pitcowicz; m. Richard Kent Winter, Aug. 7, 1976; children: Jenna Marie, Eric Richard(dec.). BA in Comm., Mich. State U., 1980. From advt. mgr. to corp. devel. assoc. WKAR-TV, East Lansing, Mich., 1985—88, corp. devel. assoc., 1988—92; freelance columnist DeWitt, Mich., 1996—. Cmty. adv. panel Lansing State Jour. Author: Breakthrough Parenting for Children with Special Needs: Raising the Bar of Expectations, 2006; contbr. articles to profl. jours. and periodicals, chapters to books. Co-chmn. Eric RicStar Winter Music Therapy Summer Camp, Mich. State U., 2003—. Named to Wall of Tolerance, Montgomery, Ala., 2003; recipient Cmty. Achievement award, Mich. Week, 2000, Disting. Achievement award, The Assn. Ednl. Pubs., 2000, 2002, Exceptional Parent award, Mich. Federated Chpts. Coun. Exceptional Children, 2002, Chief Everything Officer award, AOL and Dove, 2006, Outstanding Alumni award, Mich. State U. Coll. Com. Arts and Sci., 2007. Avocations: travel, gardening, walking, photography, community outreach. E-mail: jappwinter@aol.com.

WINTER, LEIGH ELLEN, artist, educator; b. St. Louis, Mar. 31, 1969; d. Richard Lawrence and Vicki Hunt Winter, Kathryn Ann Winter (Stepmother); m. Gabriel Paul Katz, Sept. 29, 2001. BFA in Metalsmithing, U. Kans., Lawrence, 1992; MFA in Sculpture, Pratt Inst., NYC, 1997. Asst.

to art critic Robert C. Morgan, NYC, 1996—98; artist's asst. Artist-Angiola Churchill, NYC, 1997; curatorial asst./registrar Ian Woodner Family Collection, NYC, 1998—99; asst. to the chair, art & design edn. Pratt Inst., Bklyn., instr., 2000—04, Sch. Visual Arts, NYC, internship coord., 2004—06, asst. dir. office career devel., 2006—. Artist's lecture Villa Duchesne, St. Louis, 1996; mem. grad. admissions com., art and design edn. Pratt Inst., Bklyn., 2000—04, mem. internship coun., 2001—04, mem. faculty search com., art and design edn., 2001—02, mem. peer rev. com., art and design edn., 2001—02, mem. sen. academic initiatives com., 2002—04. Exhibitions include Convergence, Pratt Inst., Bklyn., U. Kans., Lawrence, Kans., Wash. U., St. Louis, Olivette Cmty. Ctr. (Second Pl., 1984, Hon. Mention, 1984), St. Louis Artists Guild, Williamsburg Art and Hist. Soc., Bklyn., Caitlyn Gallery, St. Louis, The Bronx Mus. for the Arts, Bronx, NY, Monk Gallery, Williamsburg, Bklyn., NY, Mercer SS Gallery, NYC, 2004, prin. works include Point Lookout, East Windham, NY. Recipient Drawing and Painting, Villa Duchesne, Sculpture, Visual Arts; Artist's Residency, Vt. Studio Ctr., 2003, Artists in the Marketplace Program, Bronx Mus. of the Arts, 1997. Mem.: Nat. Assn. Colleges and Employers, Coll. Art Assn., Soc. Ethical Culture. Personal E-mail: leighwinter@optonline.net.

WINTER, MILDRED M., educational administrator; BA summa cum laude, Harris Tchrs. Coll.; MEd, U. Mo.; postgrad., Harvard U., U. Cin. Exec. dir. Parents As Tchrs. Nat. Ctr. Inc., St. Louis. Tchr., cons., Mo., 1962-68; developer, dir. Ferguson-Florissant Parent-Child Early Edn. Program, Mo., 1969-72; first dir. early childhood edn. Mo. Dept. Elem. and Secondary Edn., 1972-84; sr. lectr. dept. elem. and early childhood edn. U. Mo., St. Louis; cons. in field. Contbr. articles to profl. jours. Named Outstanding Leader in Field of Edn., Mo. House of Reps., 1982, Outstanding Educator and Adv. for Young Children, Mo. Gov. Christopher S. Bond, 1984, Pioneer in Edn., State Bd. Edn., Mo. Dept. Edn., 1991, St. Louis Woman of Achievement in Edn., 1992; cited for Pioneering Leadership in Edn. Resolution, Mo. Senate, 1995; recipient Outstanding Svc. award Assn. Edn. of Young Children, 1984, Vol. Accreditation Leadership award, 1993, Spl. award Nat. Soc. Behavioral Pediat., 1992, Charles A. Dana Pioneering Achievements Health and Edn. Inst. Medicine award NAS, 1995. Office: Parents as Teachers Patnc 2228 Ball Dr Saint Louis MO 63146-8602

WINTER, MIRIAM THERESE (GLORIA FRANCES WINTER), nun, religious studies educator; b. Passaic, NJ, June 14, 1938; d. Mathias William and Irene Theresa (Marton) W. BMus, Cath. U. Am., Washington, DC, 1964; M in Religious Edn., McMaster Divinity Coll., Hamilton, Ont., Can., 1976; PhD in Liturgical Studies, Princeton Theol. Sem., NJ, 1983; LHD (hon.), Albertus Magnus Coll., New Haven, Conn., 1991, St. Joseph Coll., West Hartford, Conn., 1993, Mount St. Vincent U., Halifax, Nova Scotia, 2004. Joined Med. Mission Sisters, Roman Cath. Ch., 1955. Dir. liturgy and liturgical music Med. Mission Sisters, Phila., 1960-76, pub. rels. dir., coord., 1963-72; assoc. prof. liturgy, worship and spirituality Hartford (Conn.) Sem., 1980-85, prof., 1985—, prof. liturgy, worship, spirituality, and feminist studies, 1994—; founder, dir. Women's Leadership Inst., 1996—. Mem. faculty St. Therese's Inst., Phila., 1964-68, acad. dir., 1968-72, Immaculate Conception Sem. Summer Program, Mo., 1969, Cath. U. Summer Grad. Program, Washington, 1970, Hope Ecumenical Inst., Jerusalem, summer 1974, 75, 76, McMaster Divinity Coll. Grad. Program, 1976, Continuing Edn. Program, 1976, NY Archdiocesan Sch. Liturgical Music, summer 1980, 82, Vancouver Sch. Theology, summer 1982, USN Chaplains through Auburn Theol. Sem., 1990; mem. adj. faculty Union Inst., Cin., 1992-94, Sophia Ctr. Holy Names U., Oakland, Calif., 2002-; vis. faculty Islamic Religious Coun. of Singapore, 2007; with emergency relief work Internat. Rescue Com., Cambodia, 1979-80, Malteser-Hilfsdienst Auslandsdienst, Germany, 1984, Med. Mission Sisters, Ethiopia, 1985; lectr., instr., performer, worship leader, song leader for various groups by invitation, nat. and internat., 1967—. Author: Preparing the Way of the Lord, 1978, God-With-Us: Resources for Prayer and Praise, 1979, An Anthology of Scripture Songs, 1982, Why Sing? Toward a Theology of Catholic Church Music, 1984, WomanPrayer, Woman Song: Resources for Ritual, 1987, WomanWord: A Feminist Lectionary and Psalter, 1990, WomanWisdom: A Feminist Lectionary and Psalter, Women of the Hebrew Scriptures, Part I, 1992 (1st pl. award for books on liturgy Cath. Press Assn., 1992), WomanWitness: A Feminist Lectionary and Psalter, Women of the Hebrew Scriptures, Part II, 1992 (1st pl. award for books on liturgy Cath. Press Assn., 1993), The Gospel According to Mary: A New Testament for Women, 1993; co-author: Defecting in Place: Women Claiming Responsibility for Their Own Spiritual Lives, 1994 (2d pl. award for books on gender studies Cath. Press Assn., 1995), The Chronicles of Noah and Her Sisters: Genesis and Exodus According to Women, 1995 (2d pl. award for books on gender studies Cath. Press Assn., 1996), Songlines: Hymns, Songs, Rounds and Refrains, 1996, The Singer and the Song: An Autobiography of the Spirit, 1999, Out of the Depths, The Story of Ludmila Javorova, Ordained Roman Catholic Priest, 2001 (1st pl. award for books on popular presentation of the Cath. faith Cath. Press Assn., 2002), Eucharist with a small "e", 2005 (3d pl. award for books on liturgy, 2006); author: numerous songs including albums Keepsake, Hymns Re-Imagined, SpiritSong, EarthSong, WomanSong, Remember Me, Sandstone, Songs of Promise, RSVP: Let Us Pray, Gold, Incense and Myrrh, In Love, Seasons (Christian Oscar award Nat. Evang. Film Found., 1971), Knock, Knock, Praise the Lord in Many Voices (live rec. of Mass of a Pilgrim People premiered at Carnegie Hall), 1967, I Know the Secret, Joy is Like the Rain (Gold album in USA and Australia); contbr. articles to profl. jours. Bd. dirs. Capitol Region Conf. Chs., 1984-91, v.p., 1986-88. pres. bd. dirs., 1988-90, past pres., 1990-91, Archdiocesan Office Urban Affairs, 1986-95; mem. Christian Conf. ann. event WINFEST, 1986, 87; mem. small christian communities design team Archdiocese of Hartford, 1987-91; mem. major events design team RENEW, 1986; subcommn. chair Archdiocesan Office of Synod, 1991; mem. New Eng. team Ministry of Money, 1984-90, 93; mem. The New Century Hymnal editl. com. United Ch. of Christ, 1993-95; active Pediats. AIDS Unit Yale-New Haven Hosp., Covenant to Care, Voices of Joy Gospel Choir women imprisioned at Niantic. Grantee Lilly Endowment, 1989-90, 91-93; recipient Ho. of Reps. citation Commonwealth of Pa., 1968, Women in Leadership Edn. award YWCA Conn., 1989, Convenant to Care award for ministry to children, 1993; named to McMaster U. Alumni Gallery, 1982, Celebration of 120 Women in Leadership, 1987, Bayley-Ellard H.S. Hall of Fame, 1993, Conn. Women's Hall of Fame, 2002. Mem. ASCAP (Popular Awards list 1968—), AAUW (Excellence in Equity award Conn. chpt. 1995), Nat. Assn. Pastoral Musicians, N.Am. Acad. of Liturgy, Societas Liturgica. Avocations: photography, calligraphy. Office: Hartford Sem 77 Sherman St Hartford CT 06105-2260 Home Phone: 860-233-0875; Office Phone: 860-509-9558.

WINTER, PETER MICHAEL, anesthesiologist, educator; b. Sverdlovsk, Russia, Aug. 5, 1934; arrived in U.S., 1938, naturalized, 1944; s. George and Anne Winter; m. Michelle Yakopec, Dec. 28, 1991; children: Karin Anne, Christopher George, Lia Lynn, Tori Anne. BA, Cornell U., 1958; MD, U. Rochester, 1962. Diplomate Am. Bd. Anesthesiology. Intern U. Utah, Salt Lake City, 1962-63; resident in anesthesiology, pharmacology and respiratory physiology Mass. Gen. Hosp., Boston, 1963-65; USPHS fellow Harvard U. Med. Sch., Mass., 1964-66; Buswell fellow dept. physiology, asst. prof. SUNY, Buffalo, 1966-69; assoc. prof. dept. anesthesiology Sch. Medicine, U. Wash., Seattle, 1969-74, prof., 1974-79; prof., chmn. dept. anesthesiology and critical care medicine U. Pitts. Sch. Medicine, 1979-96, Peter and Eva Safar prof. anesthesiology/critical care med., 1987—96, prof. emeritus, dir. faculty devel., 1996—. Anesthesiologist in chief Univ. Health Ctr. Hosps., Pitts., 1979—96. Editl. cons.: Anesthesiology CCMJ; contbr. chapters to books, papers and abstracts to publs. With US Army, 1953—56. Recipient Career Devel. award, NIH, 1971. Mem.: AMA, Assn. univ. Anesthetists, Internat. Anesthesia Rsch. Soc., Undersea Med. Soc., Soc. Critical Care Medicine, N.Y. Acad. Scis., Royal Soc. Medicine, Am. Soc. Anesthesiologists, Am. Coll. Chest Physicians, Morton Soc., Am. Alpine Club. Office: 3471 5th Ave Ste 910 Pittsburgh PA 15213-3221

WINTER, RALPH D., Christian world missionary, professor; b. 1925; BS in civil engr., Caltech; MA in teaching Eng. as a second language, Columbia U.; BD, Princeton Theological Seminary; stud., Fuller Theological Seminary, Pasadena, CA; PhD. in Structural Linguistics, Cornell U. Student pastor Lamington Presbyterian Church, 1953—56; rural devel. specialist Presbyterian Church, Guatemala, 1956—66; founder, dir. Industrias Técnicas (indsl. tng. for Guatemalan Indian pastors), 1958—66, Union Abraham Lincoln (adult edn. extension program), Guatemala, 1961—66; professor of anthropology Landivar U., Guatemala, 1961—66; exec. dir. Asociacion latinoamericana de escuelas teológicas, reg. norte, 1965—66; prof. historical devel. of the christian movement Fuller Seminary, 1966—76; co-founder, sec.-treasurer American Soc. of Missiology, 1972—75; founder, gen. dir. Frontier Mission Fellowship, 1976—; gen. dir. U.S. Ctr. for World Mission, 1976—90; pres. William Carey Internat. U., 1977—80; editor Mission Frontiers Bulletin, 1977—; pres. American Society of Missiology, 1979—80, William Carey Internat. U., 1990—97; dir. Inst. of Internat. Studies, U.S. Ctr. for World Mission, 1990—97; v.p. Southwest, Evangelical Missiological Soc., 1992—99; chancellor William Carey Internat. U., 1997—99; distinguished missiologist in residence Fuller Theological Seminary, 1998—; pres. William Carey Internat. U., 2000—04, chancellor, 2005—. Founder Inst. for the Study of the Origins of Disease, 1999, William Carey Library, 1969; co-founder Assoc. of Church Mission Committees, 1975; founder Presbyterian Frontier Fellowship, 1975, Internat. Soc. for Frontier Missiology, 1985, Presbyterian Ctr. for Mission Studies, 1973. Named one of The 25 Most Influential Evangelicals in America, Time Magazine, 2005. Office: William Carey International University 1539 East Howard St Pasadena CA 91104 Personal E-mail: winter@ralphwinter.org. *

WINTER, RALPH KARL, JR., federal judge; b. Waterbury, Conn., July 30, 1935; married. BA, Yale U., 1957, JD, 1960; JD (hon.), Bklyn. Law Sch., NY Law Sch. Bar: Conn. 1973. Rsch. assoc., lectr. Yale U., 1962—64, from asst. prof. assoc. prof. law, 1967—78, William K. Townsend prof. law, 1978—82, adj. prof. law, 1982—; spl. cons. subcom. on separation of powers U.S. Senate Com. on Judiciary, 1968—72; sr. fellow Brookings Inst., 1968—70; adj. scholar Am. Enterprise Inst., 1972—82; judge US Ct. Appeals (2d cir.), New Haven, 1982—97, chief judge, 1997—2000, sr. judge, 2000—; judge Fgn. Intelligence Surveillance Ct., 2003—. Vis. prof. law U. Chgo., 1966; adv. com. civil rules Jud. Conf. US, 1987—92, chmn. adv. com. rules evidence, 1993—96, exec. com., 1998—2000, chmn. exec. com., 1999—2000. Contbr. articles to profl. jours. Recipient Conn. Law Rev. award, Learned Hand award, Fed. Bar Coun. Office: US Ct Appeals 2nd Cir US Courthouse 141 Church St New Haven CT 06510-2030 *

WINTER, RICHARD LAWRENCE, diversified financial services company executive; b. St. Louis, Dec. 17, 1945; s. Melvin Lawrence and Kathleen Jane (O'Leary) Winter; m. Kathryn Ann Geppert, Dec. 4, 1993; children from previous marriage: Leigh Ellen, Jessica Marie, George Bradford. BS in Math., St. Louis U., 1967, MS in Math. (fellow), 1969; MBA, U. Mo., St. Louis, 1976. Rsch. analyst Mo. Pacific R.R., St. Louis, 1971-73; dir. fin. rels. Linclay Corp., St. Louis, 1973-74; asst. v.p. 1st Nat. Bank in St. Louis (now Centerre Bank, NA) subs. Boatmen's Nat. Bank, 1974-79; v.p. fin. UDE Corp., St. Louis, 1979-81; pres. Health Care Investments, Ltd., St. Louis, 1981—, Larus Corp., St. Louis, 1981—, Garden View Care Ctr., Inc., O'Fallon, Mo., 1987—, Garden View Care Ctr. of Chesterfield, Inc., 1990—, Garden View Care Ctr. of St. Louis, Inc., Valley Park, Mo., 1998—. Exec. bd. Duchesne Bank, St. Peters, Mo., 1989—97; lectr. math. U. Mo., St. Louis, 1972—74, St. Louis U., 1982—90. Chmn. Mo. State Coun. Arts, 2005—06; cmty. adv. bd. Coll. Fine Arts and Comm. U. Mo., St. Louis, 2003—; bd. dirs. Dance St. Louis, 1998—2004, 2006—, Mid-Am. Arts Alliance, 2005—06, Jazz St. Louis, 2006—; mem. fundraising staff St. Louis Symphony; exec. adv. bd. St. Louis U. Coll. Arts and Scis., 2000—; mem. fundraising staff Jr. Achievement; fundraising staff United Way St. Louis, Arts and Edn. Fund, St. Louis, 1974—79. With US Army, 1969—71. Mem.: Nat. Health Lawyers Assn., Mo. Athletic Club (St. Louis), Pi Mu Epsilon. Roman Catholic. Office: Ste 170 12444 Powerscourt Dr Saint Louis MO 63131-3659 Home: Ten Aragon Ave # 1208 Coral Gables FL 33134 Office Phone: 314-965-1991. Business E-Mail: richard-l-winter@gvcc.com.

WINTER, ROBIN OKNER, health facility administrator; b. Newark, Mar. 10, 1953; BA, Haverford Coll., Haverford, Pa., 1974; MD, Albert Einstein Coll. Medicine, 1978; M in Med. Mgmt., Carnegie Mellon U., 1999. Diplomate Am. Bd. Family Medicine (cert. in geriatric medicine). Dir. family medicine residency program JFK Med. Ctr., Edison, NJ, 1989—. Mem.: Assn. Family Medicine Residency Dirs. (pres. 2003—04). Office: JFK Med Ctr 65 James St Edison NJ 08818 Office Phone: 732-321-7493. Office Fax: 732-906-4986.

WINTER, ROGER PAUL, former federal agency administrator; b. Hartford, Conn., July 13, 1942; s. Raymond Gustav and Marion Nellie (Stafford) W.; m. Delorise Allen, Aug. 22, 1966; children: Jonathan, Raymond Todd, Nicole. BA in Psychology, Wheaton Coll., 1964; LLD (hon.), Holy Family Coll., 1993. Asst. sec. Md. Dept. Human Resources, Balt., 1970-79, Md. Dept. Budget and Fiscal Planning, Annapolis, 1979-80; dir. Office of Refugee Resettlement, HHS, Washington, 1980-81, U.S. Com. for Refugees, Washington, 1981-2001; exec. dir. Immigration and Refugee Svcs. Am., Washington, 1994-2001; dir. Office U.S. Fgn. Disaster Assistance, Washington, 2001—02; asst. adminstr. Bur. Democracy Conflict & Humanitarian Response USAID, Washington, 2002—05; spl. rep. to Sudan US Dept. of State, 2005—06. Cons. on refugee affairs Women's Refugee Project, Washington, 1981-84; adv. bd. Refugee Policy Group, 1981-86; mem. bd. Refugee Voices, 1988-96; mem. exec. com. Coun. Washington Reps. on UN, 1989-91. Recipient Disting. Service Cambodian Assn. Am., 1982, Disting. Service award Indochina Resource Action Ctr., 1988. Mem. Nat. Ry. Hist. Soc.-Balt., Sudan Relief and Rehab. Assn. (bd. dirs., sec. 1991-93). Lodges: Eagles. Personal E-mail: rwinter4700@yahoo.com.

WINTER, RUTH GROSMAN (MRS. ARTHUR WINTER), journalist; b. Newark, May 29, 1930; d. Robert Delmas and Rose (Rich) Grosman; m. Arthur Winter, June 16, 1955; children: Robin, Craig, Grant. BA, Upsala Coll., 1951; MS, Pace U., 1989. With Houston Press, 1955-56; gen. assignment Newark Star Ledger, 1951-55, sci. editor, 1956-69; columnist L.A. Times Syndicate, 1973-78, Register and Tribune, syndicate, 1981-85, isyndicate.com, 1999-2001; co-owner Feed Your Family Right, 2007—. Columnist myskinMD.com, 2000-01; contbr. to consumer mags.; instr. St. Peters Coll., Jersey City.; vis. lectr. mag. writing Rutgers U. Author: Poisons in Your Food, rev. edits., 1971, 91, 99, 2004, How to Reduce Your Medical Bills, 1970, A Consumer's Dictionary of Food Additives, 1972, 3d rev. edit., 1994, 99, 2004, Vitamin E, The Miracle Worker, 1972, So You Have Sinus Trouble, 1973, Ageless Aging, 1973, So You Have a Pain in the Neck, 1974, rev. edit., 2000, A Consumer's Dictionary of Cosmetic Ingredients, 1974, 4th rev. edit., 1994, 6th rev. edit., 2005, Don't Panic, 1975, The Fragile Bond: Marriage in the 70's, 1976, Triumph Over Tension, 1976 (N.J. Press Women's Book award), Scent Talks Among Animals, 1977, Cancer Causing Agents: A Preventive Guide, 1979, The Great Self-Improvement Sourcebook, 1980, The Scientific Case Against Smoking, 1980, People's Guide to Allergies and Allergens, 1984, A Consumer's Guide to Medicines in Food, 1995, So What Can I Eat?, 2006; co-author: The Lean Line One Month Lighter Program, 1985, Thin Kids Program, 1985, Build Your Brain Power, 1986, Eat Right: Be Bright, 1988, A Consumer's Dictionary of Medicines: Prescription, Over-the-Counter and Herbal, 1994, 97, Super Soy,: The Miracle Bean, 1996, rev. edit., 2000, Pain in the Neck, 1997, rev. edit., 2000, Anti Aging Hormones, 1997, Brain Workout, 1997, 2003, Vitamin E: Your Protection Against Exercise Fatigue, Weakened Immunity, Heart Disease, Cancer, Aging, Diabetic Damage, Environmental Toxins, 1998, Smart Food, 1999, rev. edit., 2007, The Female Athlete's Body Book: Preventing and Treating Sports Injuries in Women and Girls, 2003, What Can I Eat? 2006, Feed Your Family Right, 2006. Recipient award of merit ADA, 1966, Cecil award Arthritis Found., 1967, Am. Soc. Anesthesiologists award, 1969, Arthritis Found. award, 1978; named Alumnus of Year Upsala Coll., 1971, Woman of Year N.J. Daily Newspaper Women, 1971, Woman of Achievement Millburn Short Hills Profl. and Bus. Women's Assn., 1991, Golden Triangle award Am. Dermatol. Assn., 1998. Mem. Soc. Mag. Writers, Authors League, Nat. Assn. Sci. Writers (Svc. award 2006, 07), Am. Med. Writers Assn. (Eric Martin Meml. award), N.J. Daily Newspaper Women (awards news series 1958, 70, named Woman of Achievement 1971, 83), Am. Soc. Journalists and Authors (pres. 1977-78, spl. service award 1983, Lifetime Achievement award 2004), N.J. Press Women (pres. 1982-84) Home and Office: 44 Holly Dr Short Hills NJ 07078-1318 Personal E-mail: writer@brainbody.com.

WINTER, TERENCE, writer; BA, NYU; JD, St. John's U. Sch. Law. Practiced law (2 years), NYC. Co-prodr., writer (TV series) Sister, Sister, 1994, Flipper, 1995, DiResta, 1998, The PJs, 1999, exec. prodr., writer Brooklyn Rules, 2006, The Sopranos, 2000— (co-recipient, Writers Guild award and Edgar Award for the episode, Pine Barrens, 2001, Emmy award for Best Writing in a Drama Series for the episode, Long Term Parking, 2004, Emmy award for Outstanding Writing for a Drama Series the episode, Members Only, 2006), guest appearances (TV series), 2000, 2004; writer: TV series Diagnosis Murder, 1993; writer (TV series) The Cosby Mysteries, 1994, Charlie Grace, 1995, Xena: Warrior Princess (3 episodes: 1995, 1996, 1998), (TV episode) The Great Defender, 1995, Get Rich or Die Tryin', 2005, (video game) 50 Cent: Bulletproof. Mem.: Conn. Bar, NY Bar.

WINTER, THOMAS SWANSON, publishing executive; b. Teaneck, NJ, Dec. 28, 1937; s. Frank J. and Beulah (Swanson) W.; m. Dawne Cina, Mar. 28, 1978; children: Victoria Ruth, Abigail Swanson. AB, Harvard U., 1959, MBA, 1961. Asst. editor Human Events newspaper Human Events, Inc., Washington, 1961-64, editor, 1964—, co-owner, pres., 1966-99, pres., editor-in-chief, 1999—; pres. Fund for Objective News Reporting. Treas. Conservative Victory Fund, Washington, 1975—; 1st vice-chmn. Am. Conservative Union, 1972—. Mem.: Nat. Press, Capitol Hill. Lutheran. Home: 16 4th St SE Washington DC 20003-3804 Office: Human Events 1 Massachusetts Ave NW Washington DC 20001-1401 Office Phone: 202-216-0600. Business E-Mail: twinter@eaglepub.com.

WINTER, TRAVIS FORD, social worker; b. Poughkipsee, NY, Dec. 24, 1970; s. Hurf Tuttle (Stepfather) and Melissa Michael Sheldon; m. Kimberly Lynn Tuttle, Apr. 13, 2002; children: Keely Marie, Morgan Eimile. A, Tompkins Cortland CC, Dryden, NY, 1991; BA in Psychology, Ithaca Coll., NY, 1995; MS in Social Work, U. Pa., Phila., 1997. Lic. clinical social worker NY, 2001; cert. adminstrv. mgmt. U. Buffalo, 2006. Clin. cons. Urban Health Svcs., Phila., 1997—98; day treatment counselor Franziska Racker Ctrs., Ithaca, 1998—. Contbr. articles to profl. jours. Disaster mental health vol. Am. Red Cross, NY, 2000, disaster action team mem., Tompkins county chpt. Ithaca, 1999; ESL vol. Literacy Vols. Tompkins County, Ithaca, 2000—02; mental health vol. Tompkins County Critical Incident Stress Mgmt. Team, Ithaca, 2001; postvention vol. Suicide Prevention & Crisis Svc., Ithaca, 2002; bd. mem., Tompkins County Chpt. ARC, Ithaca, 2003—06. Recipient Graceful Giving award, Graceful Giving Com., 2002. D-Liberal. Home: 4382 Iradell Rd Ithaca NY 14850 Office: Franziska Racker Ctrs 555 Warren Rd Ithaca NY 14850 Personal E-mail: traviswinter@msnc.om. Business E-Mail: traviswcss@rackercenters.org.

WINTER, WILLIAM EARL, retired beverage company executive; b. Granite City, Ill., Sept. 21, 1920; s. William M. and Ada M. (Compton) W.; m. Dorothy E. Schuster, Feb. 20, 1944 (dec. 1976); children: William C., Douglas E.; m. Mildred E. Stiebel, Mar. 18, 1977. AB, U. Ill., 1942. With Seven-Up Co., St. Louis, 1946-81, v.p., dir. mktg., 1969-71, exec. v.p., 1971-74, pres., chief operating officer, 1974-76, pres., chief exec. officer, 1976-79, chmn. bd., 1979-81, also former dir., cons.; chmn. emeritus, 1996—; cons. Cadbury Beverages/Seven-Up, chmn. emeritus, 1996. Bd. dirs. YMCA Greater St. Louis, U. Ill. Found.; mem. exec. bd. St. Louis Area coun. Boy Scouts Am. Capt. U.S. Army, 1942-46. Named to Promotion Mktg. Hall of Fame, 1979, Beverage World Hall of Fame, 1986 Mem. Am. Mktg. Assn., Sales and Mktg. Execs. St. Louis, Promotion Mktg. Assn. Am. (chmn. bd. 1971-72), Phi Beta Kappa, Phi Eta Sigma, Omicron Delta Gamma. Home: 14112 Baywood Villages Dr Chesterfield MO 63017-3421 Home Phone: 314-878-9870.

WINTER, WILLIAM FORREST, retired governor, lawyer; b. Grenada, Miss., Feb. 21, 1923; s. William Aylmer and Inez (Parker) W.; m. Elise Varner, Oct. 10, 1950; children: Anne, Elise, Eleanor. BA, U. Miss., 1943, LLB, 1949; LLD, William Carey Coll., 1980, Millsaps Coll., 1983, Troy State U., 1988, Davidson Coll., 1996, Miss. U. for Women, 2000, U. N.C., 2004, Tougaloo Coll., 2004. Bar: Miss. 1949. Practice in Grenada, 1949-58; practice in Jackson, Miss., 1968—; ptnr. Watkins, Pyle, Ludlam, Winter and Stennis, 1968-80; sr. ptnr. Watkins Ludlam Winter & Stennis, 1985—; mem. Miss. Ho. of Reps., 1948-56; state tax collector, 1956-64; state treas., 1964-68; lt. gov. Miss., 1972-76; gov., 1980-84. Eudora Welty prof. So. studies Millsaps Coll., 1989; Jamie Whitten prof. law U. Miss., 1989; prof. pub. policy Miss. Valley State U., 2001—05; chmn. So. Growth Policies Bd., 1981, So. Regional Edn. Bd., 1982, MDC, Inc.; mem. Pres.'s Adv. Bd. on Race, 1997—99; chmn. Adv. Commn. on Intergovtl. Rels., 1993—97. Pres. bd. trustees Miss. Dept. Archives and History; chmn. Kettering Found., 1990-93, Appalachian Regional Commn., 1983, Commn. on Future of South, 1986, Nat. Civic League, 1987-88, Nat. Commn. on State and Local Pub. Svc., Stennis Ctr. for Pub. Svc., Found. for the Mid South. With AUS, 1943-46, 51. Harvard U. Inst. Politics fellow, 1985. Mem. Am., Miss., Hinds County bar assns., U. Miss. Alumni Assn. (pres. 1979), Phi Delta Phi, Omicron Delta Kappa, Phi Delta Theta. Clubs: Univ. (Jackson). Democrat. Presbyterian. Office: 633 N State St Jackson MS 39202-3306 Home Phone: 601-366-1741; Office Phone: 601-949-4800.

WINTER, WILLIAM THOMAS, chemistry educator; b. NYC, Nov. 14, 1944; s. Garrett Henry and Dorothea (Babcock) W.; m. JEanna Swanson, June 27, 2002. BS in Polymer Chemistry, SUNY, Syracuse, 1966, PhD in Phys. Chemistry, 1974. Sr. subject tchr. Sultan Ismail Coll., Kota Bharu, Malaysia, 1967-68; rsch. asst. SUNY Coll. Environ. Sci. and Forestry, Syracuse, 1969-73, prof. chemistry, 1988—; vis. asst. prof. Purdue U., West Lafayette, Ind., 1973-77; assoc. prof. Poly. U., Bklyn., 1977-88; dir. Cellulose Rsch. Inst., 1997—. Cons. Johnson and Johnson, New Brunswick, N.J., 1978-88, Stanford, Conn., 1985, 93, Xerox Corp., Mississauga, Ont., Can., 1985-86. Contbr. articles to profl. jours., chpts. to books; editorial bd., Cellulose, 1993—. Recipient rsch. award Am. Chem. Soc., 1977-89, NIH, 1978-81, NSF, 1984, 88, USDA, 1990, US Dept. Edn., 2001—, NASA, 2006. Mem. AAAS, Am. Chem. Soc. (treas. cellulose div.

1990-92, program com., fin. com., polymer, biotech. and computer div., awards chair 2006—). Office: SUNY Coll Environ Sci 108 Jahn Lab 1 Forestry Dr Syracuse NY 13210-2712

WINTER, WINTON ALLEN, JR., lawyer, state senator; b. Ft. Knox, Ky., Apr. 19, 1953; s. Winton A. and Nancy (Morsbach) W.; m. Mary Boyd, July 28, 1978; children: Katie, Molly, Elizabeth. BA, U. Kans., 1975, JD, 1978. Bar: Kans. 1978. Ptnr. law firm Stevens & Brand, LLP, Lawrence, Kans., 1978—; v.p., gen. counsel Peoples, Inc., 2000-02; pres., CEO Peoples Bank, 2002—; pres. Corp. for Change; mem. Kans. Senate, 1982-92. Bd. dirs. Lawrence United Fund, Boys Club of Lawrence. Mem. ABA, Kans. Bar Assn., Douglas County Bar Assn. Kans. U. Law Soc., Rotary. Republican. Roman Catholic. Note and comment editor Kans. Law Rev., 1977-78. Office: PO Box 1795 4831 W 6th St Lawrence KS 66049 Home Phone: 785-843-4479; Office Phone: 785-842-4004. Personal E-mail: wwinter@epeoples.com. Business E-Mail: wwinter@bankingunusual1.com.

WINTERER, PHILIP STEELE, lawyer; b. San Francisco, July 8, 1931; s. Steele Leland and Esther (Hardy) W.; m. Patricia Dowling, June 15, 1955; children: Edward J., Amey W. Marrella. BA, Amherst Coll., 1953; LLB with honors, Harvard U., 1956. Bar: N.Y. 1957, Republic of Korea 1958. Assoc., ptnr., head tax dept., dep. presiding ptnr. Debevoise & Plimpton, NYC, 1956—93, of counsel, 1994—96; ret., 1996. Treas. Harvard Law Rev. Contbr. articles to profl. jours. Past pres. Am. Italy Soc.; life trustee Amherst Coll.; chmn. emeritus Sch. of Am. Ballet; chmn. exec. com. Phipps Houses; trustee emeritus N.Y. State Bd. Nature Conservancy; past chmn. Austen Riggs Ctr.; past vice chmn. Adelphi U.; bd. govs. Emily Dickinson Mus., Folger Shakespeare Libr.; mem. adv. coun., past v.p. Adirondack Trail Improvement Soc. Recipient Amherst Coll. medal for Eminent Svc., 1980, Pres. medal Adelphi U., 2004. Mem.: Am. Coll. Tax Counsel, Tax Forum, Citizens Housing and Planning Coun. N.Y., Am. Law Inst., Coun. Fgn. Rels., Century Assn., Ausable Club (past pres.), Phi Beta Kappa (dir. fellows). Home: 57 Gulf Brook Way Keene NY 12942 also: 1165 5th Ave New York NY 10029-6931 Office: Debevoise & Plimpton 919 3rd Ave New York NY 10022 Personal E-mail: winterhill95@aol.com.

WINTERER-SCHULZ, BARBARA JEAN, graphics designer, writer; b. Manchester, NH, Apr. 1, 1938; d. John Edward and Elizabeth Virginia Grace; m. Allen George Winterer, Mar. 30, 1959 (div. 1977); children: Audrey Lyn Winterer-Chavez, Amy Jo Winterer DeNoble. AA, Mesa CC, Ariz., 1980; BS summa cum laude, U. Md., Heidelberg, Germany, 1996; postgrad. Sheriff's Tng. Acad., Montezuma County, Colo.; grad., U. Colo., 2004. Art designer Morningstar Art Design Studio, Dolores, Colo., 1988—. Interpreter Colo. State Pk.; U.S. rail ranger Durango-Silverton R.R.; master gardener Colo. State U.; bd. dirs. S.W. Cmty. Resources; health care provider Archuleta County Sch. Dist., Pagosa Springs, Colo.; farm medic.; guest lectr. Northern Ariz. Univ., Mesa Verda Nat. Pk., UNESCO World Heritage Ctr. Contbr. articles to newspapers and jours. Asst. dir. Ariz. Myasthenia Gravis Found., 1977—80; ofcl. U.S. reporter World Eskimo Indian Olympics, Fairbanks, Alaska, 1994; mem. disaster response team ARC, Pagosa Springs, mem. Durango chpt.; bd. dirs., chmn. pub. rels. com. Habitat for Humanity, Pagosa Springs; interpreter Chimney Rock Hist. Archeol. Site; interpretive docent, vol. Bur. Land Mgmt., Anasazi Heritage Ctr. Mus., 2004—; mem. Friends of Libr., Dolores, Colo. Recipient Humanitarian award, Phila. Inst. Human Potential, 1972, Chancellor of Germany award for Acad. Achievement, 1986, citation of Meritorious Achievement award in the Arts and Humanitarianism, Internat. Biog. Ctr., 1997; scholar, Chancellor of Germany. Mem.: AAUW, Colo. Archeology Soc., Hihitsanom Archeol. Soc., Pub. Lands Interpretive Assn., Libr. of Congress (assoc.), Internat. Rotary Club, Nat. Fedn. Garden Clubs, Cortez Garden Club (pres.), Colo. Fedn. Garden Clubs, Phi Theta Kappa, Alpha Sigma Lambda. Avocations: gardening, gourmet cooking. Office: Morningstar Art Design Studio PO Box 388 Dolores CO 81323-0388

WINTERMAN, CRAIG L., lawyer; b. Denver, Oct. 29, 1950; BS, U. Oreg., 1973; JD, Southwestern U., 1976. Bar: Calif. 1977, U.S. Dist. Ct. (cen. dist.) Calif. 1977, U.S. Dist. Ct. (so. and no. dists.) Calif. 1980, U.S. Ct. Appeals (9th cir.) 1980, U.S. Supreme Ct. 1980. Ptnr. Herzfeld & Rubin, LA, 1986—. Mem. State Bar Calif., Assn. So. Calif. Def. Counsel, Assn. Advancement Auto. Medicine, U. Oreg. Alumni Assn. (pres. so. Calif. chpt. 1999-2001). Office: Herzfeld & Rubin 1925 Century Park E Ste 600 Los Angeles CA 90067-2783 E-mail: cwinterman@hrla.net.

WINTER-NEIGHBORS, GWEN CAROLE, special education and art educator, consultant; b. Greenville, SC, July 14, 1938; d. James Edward (dec. 2002) and Evelyn (Lee) Walters (dec. 1998); m. David M. Winter Jr., Aug., 1963 (dec. Feb. 1980); children: Robin Carole Winter, Charles G. McCuen, Dustin Winter TeBrugge; m. Thomas Frederick Neighbors, Mar. 24, 1989. BA in Edn. and Art, Furman U., Greenville, SC, 1960, MA in Psychology, 1967; cert. in guidance/pers., Clemson U., SC, 1981; EdD in Youth and Mid. Childhood Edn., Nova Southeastern U., Ft. Lauderdale, Fla., 1988; postgrad., U. SC, Spartanburg, 1981-89; cert. clear specialist instrn. with honors, Calif. State U., Northridge, 1991; art edn. cert., Calif. State U., LA, 1991; JD, Glendale U., Calif., 1999. Cert. tchr. art, elem. edn., psychology, secondary guidance, SC. Tchr. 7th grade Greenville Jr. H.S., 1960—63; art tchr. Wade Hampton H.S., Greenville, 1963—67; prin. adult edn. Woodmont H.S., Piedmont, SC, 1983—85, Mauldin H.S., Greenville and Mauldin, SC, 1981; tchr. ednl. psychology edn. dept. Allen U., Columbia, SC, 1969; activity therapist edn. dept. SC Dept. of Corrections, Columbia, 1973—76; art specialist gifted edn. Westcliffe Elem. Sch., Greenville, 1976—89; tchr. self-contained spl. day class Elysian Heights Elem. Sch., Echo Park and L.A., Calif., 1989—91; art tchr. med. drawing Sch. Dist. Greenville County Blue Ridge Mid. Sch., Greer, 1991—95; tchr./asst. head edn. dept. N. Creenville Coll., 2001—02. Participant nat. conf. US Dept. Edn./So. Bell, Columbia, 1989; com. mem. nat. exec. com. Nova Southeastern U., 1988—89; asst. chmn., tchr. edn. dept. North Greenville Coll., 2001, adm., staff, 01, U. SC, Spartanburg, adj., student tchr., supr., 2002; adv. bd. SC Gov. Sch. for Arts and Humanities; parent/tchr. adv. bd. Spl. Edn.; adj. prof U. SC Univ. Ctr., Greenville, 2002—03; ind. rep. Primerica Fin. Svs., 2003—06; ind. agt. Will Robinson/Horace Mann Ins. Co. Mozart Book, 1988; author: Let's Sing a Song About America, 1988 (1st pl. Nat. Music award, 1990), numerous poems. Life mem. Rep. Presdl. Task Force, 1970—; mem. voter registration com. Lexington County Rep. Party, 1970—80; grand jury participant 13th Jud. Ct. Sys., Greenville, 1986—88, guardian ad litem, 1988—2005; mem. arts educators adv. task force SC Gov. Sch. Arts and Humanities, 2002—04; mem. spl. edn. parent adv. bd. representing Sue Cleveland Elem. Sch. Greenville Co. Sch. Dist., Spl. Edn. Topics and Trends, 2001—07; poll mgr. Greenville Co. Tchr. Incentive grantee Sch. Dist. Greenville County, 1986-88, Project Earth grantee Bell South, 1988-89, 94-95, Edn. Improvement Act/Nat. Dissimination Network grantee SC State Dept. Edn., 1987-88, Targett 2,000 Arts in Curricular grantee SC Dept. Edn., 1994-95, Alliance grantee Bus. Cmty. Greenville, 1992-95, Greer Art Rsch. grantee, 1993-94, SC Govs. Sch. Study grantee, 1994, Edn. Improvement Act Competitive Tchr. grantee SC Dept. Edn., 1994-95, Alliance Grand grant, 1995-96; recipient Am. Jurisprudence Bancroft-Whitney award Glendale U. Sch. Law, 1997, 98, Excellence Recognition in Real Property award Glendale Law Faculty, 1997, Excellence in Art of Appellate Advocacy, Glendale U. Sch. Law, 1998, Am. Jurisprudence Bancroft-Whitney award Constl. Law I, 1998. Mem.: AAUW, ABA, Palmetto State Tchr. Assn., SC Art Edn. Assn., SC Arts Alliance, Nat. Mus. Women in Arts, Nat. Art Edn. Assn., Furman U. Singer Alumni, Phi Delta Kappa. Baptist Avocations: computers, art, writing, music. Personal E-mail: gwen.neighbors@gmail.com.

WINTEROWD, WALTER ROSS, language educator; b. Salt Lake City, Jan. 24, 1930; s. Harold Ross and Henrietta Ethel (Fike) W.; m. Norma Graham, Aug. 2, 1952; children: Geoffrey Ross, Anthony Gordon. BS, Utah State U., 1952; PhD, U. Utah, 1962. Asst. prof. U. Mont., Missoula, 1962-66; assoc. prof. U. So. Calif., Los Angeles, 1966-71, prof. English, 1971-79, McElderry prof. English, 1979-97, prof. emeritus, 1997—. Author: Rhetoric: A Synthesis, 1967, Contemporary Rhetoric, 1975, The Contemporary Writer, 1975, Composition/Rhetoric: A Synthesis, 1986, The Culture and Politics of Literacy, 1989, The Rhetoric of the "Other" Literature, 1990, (with Geoffrey Winterowd) The Critical Reader, Thinker, and Writer, 1992, The English Department: A Personal and Institutional History, 1998, Searching for Faith, 2005, (with Judith Rodby) the Uses of Grammar, 2005. Served with U.S. Army, 1953-55. Mem. Nat. Council Tchrs. English, AAUP Democrat. Home: 17551 San Roque Ln Huntington Beach CA 92647-6641 Personal E-mail: wrossw@msn.com.

WINTERS, BARBARA JO, musician; b. Salt Lake City; d. Louis McClain and Gwendolyn (Bradley) W. AB cum laude, UCLA, 1960, postgrad., 1961, Yale, 1960. Mem. oboe sect. L.A. Philharm., 1961-94, prin. oboist, 1972-94; ret. Clinician oboe, English horn, Oboe d'amore. Recs. movie, TV sound tracks. Avocations: painting, piano. Home: 3529 Coldwater Canyon Ave Studio City CA 91604-4060 Office: 151 S Grand Ave Los Angeles CA 90012-3013

WINTERS, BRIAN JOSEPH, professional basketball coach; b. Rockaway, NY, Mar. 1, 1952; m. Julie Winters; children: Cara, Keelin, Meghan, Brendan, Kevin, Ryan. Grad., U. SC, 1974. Profl. basketball player NBA LA Lakers, 1974—75, NBA Milw. Bucks, 1975—83; asst. coach Princeton U., 1984—86, NBA Cleve. Cavaliers, 1986—93, NBA Atlanta Hawks, 1993—95, NBA Denver Nuggets, 1997—98, NBA Golden State Warriors, 1999—2001, head coach, 2001—02, NBA Vancouver Grizzlies, 1995—97, WNBA Ind. Fever, 2003—. Named to NBA All-Rookie Team, 1974, NBA All-Star Team, 1976, 1978. Office: Ind Fever Conseco Fieldhouse One Conseco Ct 125 S Pennsylvania St Indianapolis IN 46204 *

WINTERS, DAVID DOUGLAS, lawyer; s. Frederick Douglas and Wanda Mae Hudson Winters; m. Debbie Elaine Tipton, Apr. 23, 1977; children: Charity, Patience, Ian. BS, US Naval Acad., Annapolis, Md., 1976; MS, U. So. Miss., Gulfort, 1987; LLD, Oxford Brookes, Eng., 1996; JD, So. Ill. U., Carbondale, 2002. Bar: US Patent Office 2001, Tenn. 2002, US Supreme Ct. 2003. With US Navy, 1971—94; internat. cons. group mng. dir. London, 1994—96; internat. bus. cons., negotiator Nagasaki, Japan, 1996—99; patent atty. Clarksville and Nashville, Tenn., 2002—. Standing city judge pro tem, Clarksville, 2004—. Author: The Boat Officer's Handbook, 1981, 1991. Founder Charles M. Hudson grant for excellence in patent law So. Ill. U., Sch. Law, 2005. Mem.: Tenn. Bar Assn. (del. 2007), Nashville Bar Assn., US Naval Inst., Brit. Spl. Forces Club, Mensa, Phi Delta Phi. Avocations: flying, yachting, scuba diving. Office: Winters Patent Law 227-C Wilma Rudolph Blvd Ste 237 Clarksville TN 37040

WINTERS, HAROLD FRANKLIN, physicist; b. Renton, Wash., May 19, 1932; s. Walter Wade and Ruth Elizabeth (Meyer) W.; m. Marjorie Ann Neiswender, June 9, 1956; children: Kathie Moe, David Winters, John Winters, Janice Assadi, Judy Ahlquist. Attended, Biola Coll., 1950-51; BS, Whitworth Coll., 1958; PhD, Washington State U., 1963. Rsch. staff mem. IBM Almaden Rsch. Ctr., San Jose, Calif., 1963-93, emeritus, 1993—. Vis. prof. Odense U., Denmark, 1979-80; past N.Am. rep. Subcom. on Plasma Chemistry, Internat. Union Pure and Applied Chemistry; past trustee Am. Vacuum Soc.; past lectr. numerous major nat. and internat. confs. throughout the world. Past mem. editl. bd. Plasma Materials Interactions, Jour. Nuc. Instruments and Methods; contbr. numerous articles to sci. jours. Corp. U.S. Army, 1952-54. Recipient (with John Coburn) Thinkers award Tegal Corp., 1983, Disting. Alumni Achievement award Wash. State U., 1992. Fellow Am. Vacuum Soc. (John A. Thornton Meml. award and lectr. 1993, plasma sci. divsn. named grad. student award in honor of John Coburn and Harold Winters 1994); mem. AAAS, Am. Sci. Affiliation. Baptist. Achievements include patents for plasma processing, ion sources and ion pumps; scientific contributions in the fields of plasma science, surface science, thin films, ion bombardment of solids, dissociation of gases by electron impact. Home: 632 Lanfair Dr San Jose CA 95136-1947 Personal E-mail: htxc88a@yahoo.com. *My conversion to evangelical Christianity in high school led to a change in my attitude, lifesyle, behavior, and study habits. I changed from a poor student with a bad attitude to an excellent student with a great love for science. These changes led to a successful and enjoyable scientific career. I find no contradiction or conflict between science and my Christian faith; on the contrary science has increased my respect for God.*

WINTERS, JILL MARY, nursing educator, director; b. Milw., June 30, 1955; d. John Paul Gabor and Ann Lorraine (Ladish) Gordy; m. Jack Mark Winters; children: David, Michael. BSN, U. Wis., Milw., 1978; MS in Nursing, Marquette U., 1991; PhD, U. Wis., 1996. Cert. CCRN. Nurse various hosps., Milw., 1978—85, Peck Foods Corp., Milw., 1985-88; asst. prof. U. Wis.-Milw., 1996—2001; assoc. prof., dir. rsch. Marquette U., Milw., 2001—. Contbr. numerous book chpts. and articles to profl. jours. Grantee, Nat. Inst. Nursing Rsch., Wis. Women's Health Found., Nat. Inst. Disability and Rehab. Rsch., Nat. Inst. Child Health and Human Devel., Children's Hosp. Wis. Mem. AACCN (grantee 1997), ANA, Midwest Nursing Rsch. Soc., Am. Nurses Found., Sigma Theta Tau (v.p. local chpt. 1997-99). Roman Catholic. Achievements include research in use of music to improve cardiac function and reduce anxiety after myocardial infarction, heart rate variability in infants with serious congenital heart defects and prematurity; heart rate variability with myocardial infarction and heart failure, accessibility of medical equipment for persons with disabilities, exercise and heart failure, and telehealth applications. Avocations: golf, running, cross country skiing. Home: 10320 N Provence Ct Mequon WI 53092-5228 Office: Marquette U Coll Nursing PO Box 1881 Milwaukee WI 53201-1881 Home Phone: 262-242-3922; Office Phone: 414-288-3848. Business E-Mail: jill.winters@marquette.edu.

WINTERS, JONATHAN, actor; b. Dayton, Ohio, Nov. 11, 1925; s. Jonathan H. and Alice Kilgore (Rodgers) W.; m. Eileen Ann Schauder, Sept. 11, 1948; children: Jonathan IV, Lucinda Kelley. Student, Kenyon Coll., 1946; B.F.A., Dayton Art Inst., 1950. With radio sta. WING, Dayton, 1949; disc jockey sta. WBNS-TV, Columbus, Ohio, 1950-53. Appeared on: Garry Moore Show, 1954-63, Steve Allen Show, 1954-61, Omnibus, 1954, NBC Comedy Hour, 1956, Jonathan Winters Show, 1956-57, Jack Paar Show, 1963-64, Andy Williams Show, 1966-67, Dean Martin Show, 1966-67, Jonathan Winters Show, CBS-TV, 1968-69, Wacky World of Jonathan Winters, 1972-73; numerous appearances NBC Monitor show, 1963—, Hollywood Squares, 1975—; TV series include Mork & Mindy, 1982-83, Davis Rules, (Emmy award for best supporting actor) 1991-92, 5 spls. Showtime Cable TV; night club appearances, 1953-60; motion picture appearances: It's a Mad, Mad, Mad World, 1963, The Loved One, 1964, The Russians Are Coming, The Russians Are Coming, 1966, Penelope, 1967, The Midnight Oil, 1967, 8 On the Lam, 1967, Oh Dad, Poor Dad, 1968, Viva Max, 1969, The Fish That Saved Pittsburgh, 1979, The Longshot, 1986, Say Yes, 1986, Moon Over Parador, 1988, The Flintstones, 1994, The Shadow, 1994, The Adventures of Rocky and Bullwinkle, 2000, Edward Fudwupper Fibbed Big, 2000, Swing, 2003; rec. artist, Columbia Records.; author: Mouse Breath, Conformity and Other Social Ills, 1965, Winter's Tales, 1987, Hang-Ups, 1990; voice: Arabian Knights, 1995, Santa vs. the Snoman, 1997, also numerous cartoon characters. Served with USMCR, 1943-46, PTO. Named to Comedy Hall of Fame U.S., 1993, Comedy Hall of Fame Can., 1994; recipient Grammy for Comedy Album of Yr., 1996, Mark Twain Prize for Am. Humor, Kennedy Center, 2000.

WINTERS, MARTHA P., history and language educator; d. Charles LeRoy and Jacqueline Cleve Winters. BA in Letters, U. Okla., Norman, 1975, MA in Latin, 1978. Tchr. Latin, world history Ardmore H.S., Okla., 1978—85, Ctrl. Mid-H.S., Norman, Okla., 1985—97; tchr. world history Norman North H.S., Okla., 1997—2005, tchr. Latin, world history, 2005—. Pres. Okla. Fgn. Lang. Tchrs. Assn., 1980—81; com. People to People-Social Studies, South Africa, 2004. Mem.: Nat. Coun. for Social Studies, Am. Classical League. Republican. Office: Norman North HS 1809 Stubbeman Ave Norman OK 73069 Business E-Mail: mwinters@norman.k12.ok.us.

WINTERS, RICHARD ALLEN, mineral economist; b. Butte, Mont., Feb. 19, 1963; s. Allen S. and Doris Ellen Winters. BS in Fin. and Econs., U. Mont., 1986; MS in Mineral Econs., Colo. Sch. Mines, 1990, postgrad., 1991-93. Office engr. Morrison Knudsen Engrs., Richland, Wash., 1986-88, project acct., 1987-88; ops. analyst Echo Bay Mines, Denver, 1989; instr. Colo. Sch. Mines, Golden, Colo., 1991-92; cons. Coors Brewing Co., Golden, 1991-92; sr. rsch. engr. Phelps Dodge Mining Co., Morenci, Ariz., 1992-94; gold analyst Robertson, Stephens and Co., San Francisco, 1994-95; v.p. corp. devel. Golden Star Resources Ltd., Denver, 1995-99; v.p. RMB Resources, 2000—04, pres., 2005—. Pres. Mineral Econ. Grad. Student Assn., 1989-90. Mem. Soc. Mining, Metallurgy and Exploration, Assn. Environ. Resource Economists, Mineral, Econs. and Mgmt. Soc. Avocations: outdoors, jewelry craft. Office: 143 Union Blvd Ste 900 Lakewood CO 80228

WINTERS, ROBERT CUSHING, insurance company executive; b. Hartford, Conn., Dec. 8, 1931; s. George Warren and Hazel Keith (Cushing) W.; m. Patricia Ann Martini, Feb. 10, 1962; children: Sally, Beth. BA, Yale U., 1953; MBA, Boston U., 1963; LHD, Montclair State Coll., 1991, St. Peter's Coll., 1993. With Prudential Ins. Co. Am., 1953—, v.p. actuary, 1969-75, sr. v.p. Cen. Atlantic home office, 1975-78, exec. v.p., Newark, 1978-84, vice chmn., 1984-86, chmn., CEO, 1987-94, chmn. emeritus Newark, 1995—. Trustee, Episcopal Divinity Sch., Boston Symphony Orch. With U.S. Army, 1954-56. Fellow Soc. Actuaries; mem. Am. Acad. Actuaries (past pres.), Am. Coun. Life Ins. (chmn. bd. dirs. 1990-91), Sigma Xi. Office: Prudential Ins Co Am 751 Broad St 10th Fl Newark NJ 07102-3714 E-mail: robert.c.winters@prudential.com.

WINTERS, SAM, lawyer; b. Tex. BA, U. Tex., 1944, JD, 1948. Bar: Tex. 1948. Shareholder Clark, Thomas & Winters, Austin, Tex.; bd. govs. U.S. Postal Svc., Washington, 1991—2000, vice chair, 1996-97, chmn. bd. govs., 1994-95, 98. Chmn. Tex. Rsch. League, 1990, 91; past mem. Nat. Hwy. Safety Adv. Com.; mem. devel. bd. U. Tex., Austin. With USN, World War II. Mem. ABA (past chair sect. pub. utilities, comm. and transp.), Am. Law Inst. (life), State Bar Tex. Office: Clark, Thomas & Winters PO Box 1148 Austin TX 78767

WINTERS, STANLEY B., history professor, consultant, writer; b. NYC, June 5, 1924; m. Helen Plavner, Sept. 12, 1948 (div. Dec. 1969); children: Jenifer O'Neill, Neal Winters; m. Zdenka Müllerová, Jan. 9, 1970. AB, NYU, 1948; AM, Columbia U., 1950; PhD, Rutgers U., 1966. Cert. secondary social studies educator, N.J. Artist, draftsman Art Glass Co., NYC, 1942-43; instr. history NYU, 1949-50; dir., co-propr. Clinton Hill Day Sch., Newark, 1950-56; tchr. social studies Livingston (N.J.) H.S., 1956-57; disting. prof. history Newark Coll. Engring./N.J. Inst. Tech., 1957-91; disting. prof. emeritus history N.J. Inst. Tech., Newark, 1991—. Adj. prof. history Rutgers U., Newark, 1980-91, rsch. assoc. Urban Studies Ctr., New Brunswick, 1961-62; cons., columnist Office of Info., Newark, 1972-80. Author: Karel Kramář's Early Political Career, 1966, From Riot to Recovery: Newark After Ten Years, 1979, T.G. Masaryk, 1850-1937: Thinker and Politician, 1990; co-author, editor: Intellectual and Social Developments in the Habsburg Empire, 1975, Great Britain, the USA and the Bohemian Lands 1848-1938 1991; editor: Dynasty, Politics and Culture, 1991, East Ctrl. Europe jour., 1975-91; mem. editl. bd. Bohemia-Zeitschrift, Munich, 1985-2003; columnist (pseudonymous weekly) NJ Afro-Am. newspaper, 1958-64; contbr. over 200 articles to profl. jours. and publs. Pres., co-founder Clinton Hill Neighborhood Coun., Newark, 1955-61; chmn. edn. com. br. NAACP, Newark, 1960-64; candidate city coun., Newark, 1962; candidate Essex County Freeholder, 1965; trustee Preservation and Landmarks Com., Newark, 1980-93; pres. Czechoslovak History Conf., Chapel Hill, N.C., 1988-90. Staff sgt. U.S. Army, 1943-46, ETO. Recipient Szendzimir award, Polish Inst. Arts and Scis., N.Y.C., 1971, N.J. Inst. Tech. Pub. Svc. award, 1982, Josef Hlávka Meml. medal, Czechoslovak Acad. Scis., Prague, 1991, Disting. Svc. award, Czechoslovak History Conf., 1995, František Palacky Hon. medal, Acad. Scis. Czech Republic, 2003; grantee, NEH, 1967, N.J. Com. Humanities, 1976—77, 1985. Mem. Am. Hist. Assn. (life, nominated first Czech historian as hon. fgn. mem.), Organization Am. Historians, Am. Assn. Advancement Slavic Studies, Collegium Carolinum, Josef Pekař Hist. Soc. (hon.), Hist. Assn. of Czech Republic (hon.), Phi Beta Kappa. Avocations: chess, travel, walking, correspondence, pre-contemporary music. Home: 463 MacArthur Dr Port Charlotte FL 33954-3432

WINTERS, WILLIAM THOMAS, bank executive; b. NYC, Sept. 27, 1961; s. William Thomas and Ann Wilson (Vickey) W.; m. Adriane Besonc, Sept. 19, 1984. BA, Colgate U., 1983; MBA, Wharton Bus. Sch., 1988. V.p., head global commodity swop group J P Morgan, NYC, 1988-91. Office: J P Morgan 60 Wall St New York NY 10005-2888

WINTERSHEIMER, DONALD CARL, retired state supreme court justice; b. Covington, Ky., Apr. 21, 1931; s. Carl E. and Marie A. (Kohl) W.; m. Alice T. Rabe, June 24, 1961; children: Mark D., Lisa Ann, Craig P., Amy T., Blaise Q. BA, Thomas More Coll., 1953; MA, Xavier U., 1956; JD, U. Cin., 1959; LHD (hon.), No. Ky. U., 1999. Pvt. practice, Covington, 1960-76; city solicitor City of Covington, 1962-76; judge Ky. Ct. Appeals, Frankfort, 1976-83; justice Ky. Supreme Ct., Frankfort, 1983—2007. Chmn. Ky. Supreme Ct. Criminal Rules Com., 1988-94, Continuing Jud. Edn. Com., 1983—2007, Rules Com., 1994—2007; del. Foster Parent Rev. Bd., 1985-2002; mem. adv. bd. Sta. WNKU-FM, 1984-94, Am. Soc. Writers on Legal Subjects. Published articles in Law Jour. of Nat. Legal Ctr. for Medically Disabled, Issues in Law & Medicine, Albany Law Review, Quinnipiac Law Review, Temple Law Review, No. Ky. U. Chase Law Rev., NYU Annual Survey of Am. Law. Trustee Sta. WNKU-FM. Recipient Cmty. Svc. award Thomas More Coll., 1968, Disting. Alumnus award, 1982, Monsignor Murphy award, 2007, Disting. Alumni award Coll. Law/U.Cin., 1998, Lincoln award No. Ky. U., 2007; named Disting. Jurist Chase Coll. Law, 1983, Outstanding Jurist Phi Alpha Delta Law Frat., 1990. Mem. ABA, Am. Judicature Soc., Ky. Bar Assn., Ohio Bar Assn., Cin. Bar Assn., Inst. Jud. Adminstrn., Am. Inns of Ct. (founder Chase chpt.). Democrat. Roman Catholic. Home Phone: 859-581-8781; Office Phone: 859-292-6300.

WINTERSTEIN, JAMES FREDRICK, academic administrator; b. Copperas Cove, Tex., Apr. 8, 1943; s. Arno Fredrick Herman and Ada Amanda Johanna (Wagnr) W.; m. Diane Marie Bochmann, July 13, 1963; children: Russell, Lisa, Steven, Amy. Student, U. N.M., 1962; D of Chiropractic cum laude, Nat. Coll. Chiropractic, 1968; cert., Harvard Inst. for Ednl. Mgmt., 1988. Diplomate Am. Chiropractic Bd. Radiology; lic. chiropractic, Ill., Fla., S.D., Md. Night supr. x-ray dept. DuPage Meml. Hosp., Elmhurst, Ill.,

1964-66; x-ray technologist Lombard (Ill.) Chiropractic Clinic, 1966-68, asst. dir., 1968-71; chmn. dept. diagnostic imaging Nat. Coll. Chiropractic, Lombard, Ill., 1971-73, chief of staff, 1985-86; pres. Nat. U. Health Scis., Lombard, Ill., 1986—; pvt. practice West Chicago, Ill., 1968-73, Fla., 1973-85. Faculty Nat. Lincoln Coll. Post-Profl., Grad. and Continuing Edn., 1967—; chmn. x-ray test com. Nat. Bd. Chiropractic Examiners, 1971-73; govs. adv. panel on coal worker's pneumoconiosis and chiropractic State of Pa., 1979; v.p. Am. Chiropractic Coll. Radiology, 1981-83; mem. adv. coun. on radiation protection Dept. Health and Rehabilitative Svcs. State of Fla., 1984-85; cons. to bd. examiners State of S.C., 1983-84, State of Fla., 1980-85; cons. to peer review bd. State of Fla., 1980-84; trustee Chiropractic Centennial Found., 1989-90; mem. adv. com. Aids Alternative Health Ptnrs., 1996-2000, Consortial Ctr. for Chiropractic Rsch., 1998—; bd. dirs. Fedn. Ill. Ind. Colls. and Univs., 1995—; bd. dirs. Alternative Medicine, Inc., 1999—; spkr. in field. Pub. Outreach (Nat. Univ. Health Scis. monthly); author numerous monographs on chiropractic edn. and practice; co-inventor composite shielding and mounting means for x-ray machines; contbr. articles to profl. jours. Chmn., bd. dirs. Trinity Luth. Ch., West Chgo., 1970-72, Luth. High Sch., Pinellas County, Fla., 1979-82, St. John Luth. Ch., Lombard, 1988; chmn. bd. edn. First Luth. Sch., 1975-79; chmn. First Luth. Congregation, Clearwater, Fla., 1979-82; chmn. bldg. planning com. Grace Luth. Ch. and Sch., St. Petersburg, Fla., 1984-85; bldg. planning com. ch. expansion, new elem. sch., First Luth. Sch., 1975-79; stewardship adv. coun. Fla./Ga. dist. Luth. Ch. Mo. Synod, 1983-85; trustee West Suburban Regional Acad. Consortium, 1993-99. With U.S. Army, 1961-64. Recipient Cert. Meritorious Svc. Am. Chiropractic Registry of Radiologic Technologists, Cert. Recognition for Inspiration, Guidance, and Support Delta Tau Alpha, 1989, Cert. Appreciation Chiropractic Assn. South Africa, 1988, 1st pl. Fund Raiser Ride for Kids award Pediat. Brain Tumor Found. U.S., 1997, Cert. Appreciation Ill. Chiropractic Soc., 1997, Hope and Support award Alternative Health Ptnrs., 1998, Chiropractor of Yr., Ill. Chiropractic Soc., 2000, Person of the Yr., Alternative Medicine, Inc., 2001, NUHS Bd. Trustees Disting. Svc. award, 2002, President's citation award Maryland Chiropractic Assn., 2003. Mem. APHA, Am. Chiropractic Assn., Am. Chiropractic Coll. Radiology (pres. 1983-85, exec. com. 1985-86), Am. Chiropractic Coun. on Diagnostic Imaging, Am. Chiropractic Coun. on Diagnosis and Internal Disorders, Am. Chiropractic Coun. on Nutrition, Nat. Univ. Alumni Assn., Am. Acad. Chiropractic Physicians (sec.), Assn. Chiropractic Colls. (sec.-treas. 1986-91), Coun. Chiropractic Edn. (sec.-treas. 1988-90, v.p. 1990-92, pres. 1992-94, immediate past pres. 1994-96), Fla. Chiropractic Assn. (chmn. radiol. health com. 1977-85, Disting. Svc. award 1999). Republican. Lutheran. Avocations: reading, automobile rehabilitation, harley-davidson motorcycles, fishing.

WINTER-SWITZ, CHERYL DONNA, travel company executive; b. Jacksonville, Fla., Dec. 6, 1947; d. Jacqueline Marie (Carroll) Winter; m. Frank C. Snedaker, June 24, 1974 (div. May 1976); m. Robert William Switz, July 1, 1981. AA, City Coll. of San Francisco, 1986; BS, Golden Gate U., 1990, MBA, 1992. Bookkeeper, agt. McQuade Tours, Ft. Lauderdale, Fla., 1967-69; mgr. Boca Raton (Fla.) Travel, 1969-76; owner, mgr. Ocean Travel, Boca Raton, 1976-79; ind. contractor Far Horizons Travel, Boca Raton, 1979-80; mgr. Tara/BPF Travel, San Francisco, 1981-84; mgr. travel. dept. Ernst & Whinney/Lifeco Travel, San Francisco, 1984-86; travel cons. Golden Gate U., San Francisco, 1986-99, Siemer & Hand Travel, San Francisco, 1989-99, Ravenel Travel, Charleston, SC, 1999-2000, Carlson Carolina Travel, Mt. Pleasant, SC, 2000—02, Sato/Navigant Travel, 2003—04; mgr. travel dept. WareOnEarth Comm., Inc., Charleston, 2004—. Instr. Golden Gate U., 1986-99, U. San Francisco. Mem. Amateur Trapshooting Assn., Hotel and Restaurant Mgmt. Club. Republican. Episcopalian. Avocations: trap shooting, gardening, cooking, travel, reading. Home: 1189 W Park View Pl Mount Pleasant SC 29466-7910 Office: WareOnEarth Comm Inc 2457 Aviation Ave Ste 200 N Charleston SC 29406

WINTERTON, JOSEPH HENRY, computer software executive; b. Oneida, NY, July 22, 1948; s. Stewart Grant and Margaret (Durant) W.; m. Susan Marie Briggs, May 29, 1971; children: Tamara Leigh, Danielle Marie, Derek James. AAS, Canton Coll., NY, 1968; BA, SUNY, Potsdam, 1970. Adv. programmer IBM Corp., Poughkeepsie, N.Y., 1970-81; mgr. R & D Candle Corp., LA, 1981-83, dir. R&D White Plains, NY, 1983-96, sr. dir. R&D, 1996—2003; v.p., sr. mgr. Bank One, Columbus, Ohio, 2003—04; mgr. IBM Corp., Somers, NY, 2004—. Coach Yorktown (N.Y.) Athletic Club, 1988—2001; treas. Hudson Valley Christian Acad., Mahopac, NY, 1986—87, Yorktown Theatre Workshop, Yorktown Heights, NY, 1989—92; trustee Calvary Bapt. Ch., Ossining, NY, 1986, midnight run vol., 1993—; bd. dirs. Yorktown Theatre Co. With US Army, 1970—76, N.G. Republican. Mem. Christian Ch. Avocations: photography, teaching Sunday sch., coaching youth sports, golf. Home: 1521 Hanover St Yorktown Heights NY 10598-4709 E-mail: jowinterton@aol.com.

WINTHROP, JOHN, wines and spirits company executive; b. Salt Lake City, Apr. 20, 1947; children: Grant Gordon, Clayton Hanford. AB cum laude, Yale U., 1969; JD magna cum laude, U. Tex., 1972. Bar: Calif. 1972. Law clk. 9th cir. U.S. Ct. Appeals, LA, 1972-73; conseil juridique Coudert Freres, Paris, 1973-75; v.p. gen. counsel MacDonald Group, Ltd., LA, 1976-82; pres., CEO MacDonald Mgmt. Corp. and MacDonald Group Ltd., LA, 1982-86; pres., chief exec. officer MacDonald Corp. (gen. contractors), LA, 1982-86; chmn., CEO Comstock Mgmt. Co., LA, 1986—; pres., CEO Winthrop Investment Properties, Los Angeles, 1986—; CEO Veritas Imports, LA, 1995—. Bd. dirs. Plus Prods., Tiger's Milk Prods., Irvine, Calif., 1977-80. Contbr. articles to profl. jours. Bd. dirs., sec. L.A. Sheriff's Dept. Found.; bd. dirs. L.A. Opera. Mem. Nat. Eagle Scout Assn. (life), French-Am. C. of C. (bd. dirs. 1982-87), Urban Land Inst., Yale Club N.Y., Calif. Club, The Beach Club, Jonathan Club, Order of the Coif, Beta Theta Pi. Office: Veritas Imports Penthouse 9460 Wilshire Blvd Beverly Hills CA 90212-2720 E-mail: jwinthrop@veritaswine.com.

WINTHROP, KENNETH RAY, insurance executive; b. NYC, Dec. 29, 1950; s. Ralph and Lore (Bruck) W.; m. Sharon Swinnich, 1976 (div. 1978); m. Diane Louise Denney, June 27, 1981; children: Alyssa Louise, Matthew Lawrence, Andrew Lee. BA in English, SUNY, Buffalo, 1972. CLU. Agt. Northwestern Mut. Life Ins., Woodland Hills, Calif., 1975-78, Nat. Life of Vermont, LA, 1978-93; mgr. Mass Mut., LA, 1993-97, agt., 1997—. Referee Am. Youth Soccer Orgn., L.A., 1996—. Mem. Million Dollar Round Table (life). Avocations: racquetball, skiing, fishing, gardening. Home: 1404 5th St Manhattan Beach CA 90266-6338 Office: 2200 Pacific Coast Hwy 318 Hermosa Beach CA 90254 Office Phone: 310-406-1800. Business E-Mail: kwinthrop@finsvcs.com.

WINTHROP, LAWRENCE FREDRICK, judge; b. Apr. 18, 1952; s. Murray and Vauneta (Cardwell) W. BA with honors, Whittier Coll., 1974; JD magna cum laude, Calif. Western Sch., 1977. Bar: Ariz. 1977, Calif. 1977, U.S. Dist. Ct. Ariz. 1977, U.S. Dist. Ct. (so. dist.) Calif. 1981, U.S. Ct. Appeals (9th cir.) 1981, U.S. Dist. Ct. (cen. dist.) Calif. 1983, U.S. Supreme Ct. 1983. Assoc. Snell and Wilmer, Phoenix, 1977—83, ptnr., 1984—93, Doyle, Winthrop, P.C., Phoenix, 1993—2002; judge divsn. one Ariz. Ct. Appeals, Phoenix, 2002—. Judge pro tem Maricopa County Superior Ct., 1987-97; lectr. Ariz. personal injury law and practice and state and local tax law Tax Exec. Inst., Nat. Bus. Inst., Profl. Edn. Systems, Inc., Ariz. Trial Lawyers Assn., Maricopa County Bar. Editor-in-chief: Calif. Western Law Rev., 1976-77. Fellow, Ariz. Found. Legal Svcs. and Edn.(bd. dir. 2005-, v.p. 2007-); Charter benefactor, Maricopa County Bar Found.; mem. Ariz. Supreme Ct. Com. on Examinations, 1995-2002; bd. dir. Ariz. Tax Rsch. Assn., 1989-99; bd. dir. Ariz. Assn. Defense Counsel, past. pres. 1988-89; chmn. Valley of Sun Sch. & Habilitation Ctr., 1994-96, bd. dir. 1989-97; mem. Vol. Lawyers' Program, 1980-2002. Mem. Calif. Bar Assn., Ariz. Bar Assn., Am. Bd. Trial Advs., Aspen Valley Golf Club, Lorna Lockwood Inn Ct. (co-pres. 2005-06), Forest Highlands Club Republican. Methodist. Avocations: music, golf. Home: 83 W Cypress St Phoenix AZ 85003 Office: 1501 W Washington St Phoenix AZ 85007 Office Phone: 602-542-1430. Business E-Mail: lwinthrop@appeals.az.gov.

WINTLE, SUZANNE, elementary school educator; BA in Elem. Edn., Univ. Omaha, Nebr. Tchr., Nebr., 1970—71, Westchester, Ill., 1971—76, Florence Sawyer Sch., Bolton, Mass., 1976—. Facilitator Sawyer Sch. Study Group. Named Mass. Tchr. of Yr., 2006. Office: Florence Sawyer Sch 100 Mechanic St Bolton MA 01740 Office Phone: 718-338-3635. Business E-Mail: swintle@nrsd.net. *

WINTNER, MARK S., lawyer; b. Bronx, NY, 1947; BA cum laude, Queens Coll., 1968; JD, U. Chgo., 1972, LLM in Taxation, 1977. Bar: N.Y. 1973. Ptnr., employee benefits law, exec. compensation Stroock & Stroock & Lavan LLP, NYC. Mem. ABA, N.Y. State Bar Assn., Order Coif. Office: Stroock & Stroock & Lavan LLP 180 Maiden Ln New York NY 10038-4982 Office Phone: 212-806-6020. Office Fax: 212-806-6006. Business E-Mail: mwintner@stroock.com.

WINTON, CALHOUN, literature educator; b. Ft. Benning, Ga., Jan. 21, 1927; s. George Peterson and Dorothy (Calhoun) W.; m. Elizabeth Jefferys Myers, June 30, 1948; children: Jefferys Hobart, William Calhoun. Student, Ga. Inst. Tech., 1944-46; BA, U. of the South, 1948; MA, Vanderbilt U., 1950, Princeton U., 1954, PhD, 1955. Instr. Dartmouth Coll., Hanover, NH, 1954-57; asst. prof. U. Va., Charlottesville, 1957-60; asst. prof. then assoc. prof., asst. dean Grad. Sch. U. Del., 1960-67; prof. dept. English U. S.C., Columbia, 1967-75, chmn. dept., 1970-73; prof. U. Md., College Park, 1975-97, dir. Rsch. Ctr. for Humanities, 1988-90, prof. emeritus, 1997—. Del. Joint Nat. Com. on Langs., Washington, 1986-90, 95-99. Author: (biography) Captain Steele, 1964, Sir Richard Steele, 1970; editor: Plays of Aaron Hill, 1981, John Gay and the London Theatre, 1993; author (with others) Colonial Book in the Atlantic World, 2000; contbr. entries Oxford Dictionary of National Biography, 2004, Agent of Change, 2007. Pres. faculty guild U. Md., 1986-89; bd. dirs. Md. Fedn. Tchrs., Balt., 1986-89. Capt. USN, 1944-47, 50-52. Am. Philos. Soc. grantee, 1960; Guggenheim Found. fellow, 1965-66, Folger Shakespeare Libr. fellow, Washington, 1970, John Carter Brown Libr. fellow, Providence, 1995, 2003 Fulbright Commn. lectureship, Ankara, Turkey, 1979-80. Mem. MLA (exec. com. South Atlantic chpt. 1977-80), Am. Soc. 18th-Century Studies (founder 1970—), East Cen. Soc. 18th Century Studies (pres. 1987), Assn. Princeton Grad. Alumni (exec. bd. 1986-90), Cosmos Club Washington, Princeton Club (N.Y. and Washington), Am. Antiquarian Soc., Literary Soc. Washington. Democrat. Episcopalian. Avocations: swimming, book collecting. Office: The Univ of the South PO Box 3128 Sewanee TN 37375-3128 Business E-Mail: cwinton@mail.umd.edu.

WINTON, LINDA, international trainer, consultant; b. Phila. BA in Secondary Edn. and Spanish, La Salle Coll., Phila., 1971—75; MA in Spanish Lang. and Lit., NYU, Madrid, 1978—79; MS in Adult Edn. and Human Resource Tng. and Devel., U. So. Maine, Gorham, 1990—91. Cert. Tchr. Spanish Pa. Dept. Edn., 1975, NJ Dept. Edn., 1975, Tchr. French NJ Dept. Edn., 1977, Exhbn. Mgr. Internat. Assn. Exhbn. Mgmt., 2003. Spanish and French tchr. Willingboro HS, NJ, 1975—77; ESL instr. Camden Learning Ctr., NJ, 1975—77, Shell Oil Co., Madrid, 1977—79, Inst. Internat. Madrid, 1977—79, Aldeasa, Madrid, 1977—79; export sales Wheatland Tube Co., EMSI, Pa., 1979—81; Spanish and French tchr. Haddonfield HS, 1981—82; Spanish instr. U. Ky., 1982—84; dir. Gorham Adult and Cmty. Edn., Maine, 1989—93, prin. Tng. Assocs. Maine, 1990—91; sales rep., account exec. Diversified Expn., Maine, 1994—97; pres., CEO New Markets Internat. LLC, Falmouth, Maine, 1997—. Programmer Tampa Bay Coun. Internat. Visitors, Fla., 1986—87; sr. programmer Maine Coun. Internat. Visitors, 2000—. Recipient Ofines award for study linguistics, 1978; fellow, Nat. Endowment Humanities, 1984. Mem.: Meeting Profls. Internat. (internat. devel. com. 2000—01, global issues adv. group 2001—02, New Eng. chpt. fin. com. 2001—02, New Eng. chpt. internat. membership com. 2002—03, New Eng. chpt. membership com. 2002—04, New Eng. chpt. liaison to multicultural initiative 2003—05, New Eng. chpt. bd. dirs. 2004—05), Internat. Assn. Exhbn. Mgmt. (dept. commerce liaison com. 2001—03, CEM commn. 2003—06). Office: New Markets Internat LLC 12 Arbor Rd Falmouth ME 04105 Office Phone: 207-781-2019. Business E-Mail: nmi@maine.rr.com.

WINTOUR, ANNA, editor-in-chief; b. London, Nov. 3, 1949; arrived in U.S., 1976; d. Charles and Elinor Wintour; m. David Shaffer, Sept. 1984 (div. 2001); children: Charles, Kate; m. J. Shelby Bryan. Student, Queens Coll., 1963—67. Deputy fashion editor Harper's and Queen Mag., London, 1970—76; fashion editor Harper's Bazaar, NY, 1976—77; fashion and beauty editor Viva Mag., NY, 1977—78; contbg. editor fashion and style Savvy Mag., NY, 1980—81; sr. editor NY Mag., 1981—83; creative dir. US Vogue, NY, 1983—86; editor-in-chief British Vogue, London, 1986—87, House and Garden, NY, 1987—88, Vogue, NY, 1988—. Trustee Metropolitan Museum of Art, NYC. Named one of 10 Most Fascinating People of 2006, Barbara Walters. Office: Vogue 4 Times Sq New York NY 10036 *

WINTROB, JAY S., insurance company executive; Grad. summa cum laude, U. Calif., Berkeley, 1979; JD, U. Calif., 1982. With O'Melveny & Myers, LA; asst. to chmn. AIG Sun Am., 1987, corp. v.p., 1987—89, sr. v.p., 1989—91, exec. v.p., 1991—95, vice chmn., 1995—98, CEO, 1998—2000, pres., 2000—, CEO, 2001—; exec. v.p. Am. Internat. Group, 2002—. Bd. dirs. AIG Sun Am., AIG; bd. trustees J. Paul Getty Trust, 2004—. Recipient Ecumenical Coun. Leadership award, Archdiocese LA, 2001, Luis Lainer Founder's award, Bet Tzedel Legal Services, 2002. Mem.: Order of Coif. Office: Am Internat Group 70 Pine St New York NY 10270

WINTRODE, RALPH CHARLES, lawyer; b. Hollywood, Calif., Dec. 21, 1942; s. Ralph Osborne and Maureen (Kavanagh) W.; m. Leslie Ann O'Rourke, July 2, 1966 (div. Feb. 1994); children: R. Christopher, Patrick L., Ryan B.; m. Denise A. Beetham, Aug. 24, 1999. BS in Acctg., U. So. Calif., 1966, JD, 1967. Bar: Calif. 1967, N.Y. 1984, Japan 1989. From assoc. to ptnr. to of counsel Gibson, Dunn & Crutcher, Tokyo, L.A., Newport Beach and Irvine, Calif., 1967—. Sec. Music Ctr. Los Angeles County, 1986-88; bd. dirs. Coro Found., L.A. County, 1986-87. Mem. Newport Harbor Club, Am. Club Tokyo. Avocations: sailboat racing, auto racing, flying. Office: Gibson Dunn & Crutcher 4 Park Plz Ste 1400 Irvine CA 92614-8557 also: 333 S Grand Ave Ste 4400 Los Angeles CA 90071-1548 E-mail: wintrode@cox.net.

WINTROL, JOHN PATRICK, lawyer; b. Wichita, Kans., Feb. 13, 1941; s. Clarence Joseph and Margaret (Gill) W.; m. Janet Lee Mitchell; children: John Howard, Joanna Lee. BA cum laude, Rockhurst Coll., 1963; JD, Georgetown U., 1969. Bar: DC 1969, U.S. Ct. Appeals (4th, 5th, 11th and DC cirs.) 1981, U.S. Dist. Ct. Md. 1984. Law clk. to Hon. Howard Corcoran U.S. Dist. Ct., Washington, 1969-71; assoc. Howrey & Simon, Washington, 1971-77; mng. ptnr. Perito, Duerk & Pinco, Washington, 1978-85; ptnr. Finley Kumble, Washington, 1985-87, Laxalt, Washington, Perito & Dubuc, Washington, 1988-91, McDermott, Will & Emery, Washington, 1991—2002, John P. Wintrol L.L.C., Washington, 2003—. Mem. jud. conf. U.S. Ct. Appeals (D.C. cir.); adj. prof. George Washington Sch. Law, 2007—. Vol. Peace Corps, Turkey, 1963-65; pres. bd. trustees Holton Arms Sch. Mem.: ABA. Roman Catholic. Office: 2000 M St NW Ste 700 Washington DC 20036 Home Phone: 301-229-6208; Office Phone: 202-261-1056. Business E-Mail: jwintrol@jpwlaw.net.

WINTROUB, BRUCE URICH, dermatologist, educator, researcher; b. Milw., Nov. 8, 1943; s. Ernest Bernard and Janet (Zien) W.; m. Marya Kraus, Jan. 20, 1973; children: Annie, Ben, Molly. BA, Amherst Coll., 1965; MD, Washington U., St. Louis, 1969. Diplomate Am. Bd. Internal Medicine, Am. Bd. Dermatology. Intern in medicine Peter Bent Brigham Hosp., Boston, 1969-70, jr. asst. resident in medicine, 1970-71, jr. assoc. in medicine, 1976-80, asst. then attending physician, 1976-81; resident in dermatology Harvard Med. Sch., Boston, 1974-76, instr., 1976-78, asst. prof., 1978-82; assoc. prof. dermatology Sch. Medicine, U. Calif., San Francisco, 1982-85, attending physician med. ctr., 1982—, prof., mem. exec. com. dept. dermatology, 1985-95, 2000—, mem. dean's adv. com., governing bd. continuing med. edn., other coms., 1986-95; chmn. exec. com. dept. dermatology U. Calif., San Francisco, 1985-95, 2000—, exec. vice dean Sch. Medicine, 1995-97, assoc. dean sch. medicine, 1990—95, 2000—04, vice-dean sch. med., 2004—; chief med. officer U. Calif.-San Francisco Stanford Health Care, San Francisco, 1997-99; assoc. dean Sch. Medicine Stanford (Calif.) U., 1997—99; dir. Dermatology Assocs., San Francisco, 1982-85; prof. & chair, dept. dermatology U. Calif.-San Francisco, 1986—95, 1999. Cons. in dermatology Mass. Gen. Hosp., Boston, 1976-82, Beth Israel Hosp. and Children's Hosp. Med. Ctr., Boston, 1978-82, Parker Hill Med. Ctr., Boston, 1980-82; attending physician Robert B. Brigham Hosp. div. Brigham and Women's Hosp., Boston, 1980-81, assoc., 1980-82; chief dermatology svc. Brockton (Mass.) VA Med. Ctr., 1980-82; asst. chief dermatology VA Med. Ctr., San Francisco, 1982-85, mem. space com., 1984-85, dean's adv. com., 1985—, chmn. budget com., 1987—; clin. investigator Nat. Inst. Allergy, Metabolism and Digestive Disease, NIH, 1978; assoc. dean Sch. Medicine Stanford U., 1997—. Author: (with others) Biochemistry of the Acute Allergic Reactions, Fifth International Symposium, 1988; contbr. numerous articles, abstracts to profl. jours. Grantee Clin. fellow and grantee, NIH, 1967—69. Fellow Am. Acad. Dermatology (com. evaluations 1985—, coun. govt. liaison 1987—, congress on tech. plannning commn. 1988—, assoc. editor Dialogues in Dermatology jour. 1982-85, Stellwagon prize 1976); mem. Soc. Investigative Dermatology (chmn. pub. rels. com. 1987-88), Assn. Profs. Dermatology (chmn. program com. 1987—, bd. dirs.), Pacific Dermatol. Assn. (chmn. program com. 1987—), San Francisco Dermatol. Soc., Am. Fedn. Clin. Rsch. (chmn. dermatology program 1988-89), Am. Assn. Immunology, Dystrophic Epidermolysis Bullosa Rsch. Am. (bd. dirs. 1981), Internat. Soc. Dermatology, Internat. Soc. Cutaneous Pharmacology (founding mem.), Am. Soc. Clin. Investigation, Skin Pharmacology Soc., Calif. Med. Soc., San Francisco Med. Soc., Clin. Immunology Soc., Dermatology Found., (bd. dirs., exec. com.), AAAS, Am. Assn. Physicians, Calif. Acad. Medicine, Am. Dermatol. Assn., Sigma Xi, Alpha Omega Alpha. Avocation: golf. Office: Dept Dermatology U Calif San Francisco 1701 Divisadero St Rm 342 San Francisco CA 94143-0316 Office Phone: 415-353-7597. Business E-Mail: wintroub@medsch.ucsf.edu.

WINWOOD, STEPHEN LAWRENCE, musician, composer; b. Birmingham, Eng., May 12, 1948; s. Lawrence Samuel and Lillian Mary (Saunders) W.; m. Eugenia Crafton, Jan. 17, 1987; children: Mary Clare, Elizabeth Dawn, Stephen Calhoun, Lillian Eugenia. Rec. artist Spencer Davis Group, 1964-67, Blind Faith, 1970, Traffic, 1967-74; solo artist N.Y.C. and in England, 1974—. Dir. F.S. Ltd. Albums include: Arc of a Diver, 1980, Talking Back to the Night, 1982, Back in the High Life, 1986, Roll With It, 1988 (Grammy 1989), Chronicles, Refugees of the Heart, 1991, Traffic: Far From Home, 1994, Junction 7, 1997, About Time, 2003. Recipient 14 Gold Record awards, 4 Platinum Record awards, 2 Grammy awards, Lifetime Achievement award Ivor Novello's, 2002; inductee (with band Traffic) Rock 'N Roll Hall of Fame, 2004. Address: 41 Rodney Rd Cheltenham Gloucestershire GL50 1HX England

WINZENREID, JAMES ERNEST, lawyer, entrepreneur; b. Wheeling, W.Va., June 9, 1951; s. Ernest Christian and Dorothy Emma (Wolf) Winzenreid; m. Rebecca Lee Rice, Aug. 11, 1979; children: Diana Lee, Lauren Rice. AB, W. Liberty State Coll., W.Va., 1973; MBA, W.Va. U., Morgantown, 1979; JD, Duquesne U., Pitts., 1987; LLM, Wayne State U., Detroit, 1989. Bar: Pa. 1987, U.S. Dist. Ct. (we. dist.) Pa. 1987. Staff asst. Wheeling Pitts. Steel Corp., Wheeling, 1974—78, supr. indsl. rels., 1978; mgr. profl. planning and devel. Copperweld Corp., Pitts., 1978—79, mgr. human resources Glassport, Pa., 1979—81, plant mgr., 1981—83, group mgr. human resources Pitts., 1984—85, market program mgr., 1986—87; with lab. and employment dept. Eckert, Seamans, Cherin & Mellott, Pitts., 1986—87; corp. staff rep. Tecumseh Products Co., Mich., 1987—89; v.p. human resources devel. Lafarge Corp., Va., 1989—94; v.p. human resources western region Lafarge Constrn. Materials, Calgary, Alta., Canada, 1994—96, Lafarge Can. Inc., Calgary, 1996—99; mgr. union rels. GE, Bloomington, Ind., 2000—02; dir. labor rels. and compliance Metaldyne Corp., Plymouth, Mich., 2002—04; dir. employee rels. Lear Corp, Southfield, 2004—06; pvt. practice arbitration Washington, Pa., 2006—; labor relations dir. Aramark Corp., Phila., 2007—. Mng. editor: Juris mag., 1986. Bd. dirs. Wheeling Symphony Soc., 1977—86, Wheeling Jaycees, 1976—78; mem. adv. bd. Jr. Achievement Southwestern Pa., 1981—83. Named Outstanding Young Men, Am. U.S. Jaycees, 1979. Mem.: ABA, Indsl. Rels. Rsch. Assn., Human Resource Planning Soc., Am. Soc. Human Resources Mgmt., Allegheny Bar Assn., Pa. Bar Assn., Phi Alpha Delta. Republican. Lutheran. Avocations: golf, reading. Home: 924 Mill Pond Ct Northville MI 48167 Office: 39255 Country Club Dr Ste B-1 Farmington Hills MI 48331 Office Phone: 248-848-2070. Personal E-mail: jimwinzenreid@aol.com.

WINZER, P.J., lawyer; b. Shreveport, La., June 7, 1947; d. C.W. Winzer and Pearlene Hall Winzer Tobin. BA in Polit. Sci., So. U., Baton Rouge, 1968; JD, UCLA, 1971. Bar: Bar: Calif. 1972, U.S. Supreme Ct. 1986. Staff atty. Office of Gen. Counsel, U.S. HEW, Washington, 1971-80; asst. spl. counsel U.S. Office of Spl. Counsel Merit Systems Protection Bd., Dallas, 1980-82; regional dir. U.S. Merit Systems Protection Bd., Alexandria, Va., 1982—. Mem. Calif. Bar Assn., Fed. Cir. Bar Assn., Delta Sigma Theta. Office: US Merit System Protection 1800 Diagnol Rd Ste 205 Alexandria VA 22314-2840

WIORKOWSKI, JOHN JAMES, mathematics professor; b. Chgo., Sept. 30, 1943; BS, U. Chgo., 1965, MS, 1966, PhD, 1972. Rsch. assoc. U. Chgo., 1972; asst. prof. Pa. State U., University Park, 1973-74; assoc. prof. U. Tex. at Dallas, Richardson, 1975, assoc. prof. and program head Math. Scis. Program, 1979-81, prof., 1981—, asst. to v.p. acad. affairs, 1980-85, asst. v.p. acad. affairs, 1985-94, assoc. provost, 1994-2001, vice-provost, 2001—, head math. scis. program, 1996-98. Cons. to Fed. Energy Adminstrn., 1975, Tex. Instruments, 1977, Frito-Lay Inc., 1977-78, Republic Nat. Bank, 1979; mem. panel studying 55 mile per hour speed limit Nat. Acad. Sci. Contbr. articles to profl. jours. Served to capt. U.S. Army, 1968-71. Decorated Army Commendation medal, NSF grantee, 1975—; Am. Coun. Edn. fellow, 1981-82. Mem. Am. Statis. Assn. (chpt. pres. 1974, v.p. 1977, chpt. pres. 1978), AAAS, Inst. Math. Stats., Biometric Soc., Sigma Xi. Unitarian Universalist. Home: 9922 Lincolnshire Ct Rockwall TX 75087-4509 Office: U Tex at Dallas PO Box 830688 Richardson TX 75083-0688 Office Phone: 972-883-2274. Personal E-mail: wiorkow@msn.com. Business E-Mail: wiorkow@utdallas.edu.

WIOT, JEROME FRANCIS, radiologist; b. Cin., Aug. 24, 1927; s. Daniel and Elvera (Weisgerber) W.; m. Andrea Kockritz, July 29, 1972; children— J. Geoffrey, Jason. MD, U. Cin., 1953. Diplomate: Am. Bd.

Radiology (trustee, pres.). Intern Cin. Gen. Hosp., 1953-54, resident, 1954-55, 58-59; gen. practice medicine Wyoming, Ohio, 1955-57; mem. faculty U. Cin., 1959-67, 68—, prof., chmn. radiology, 1973-93, acting sr. v.p., provost for med. affairs, 1985-86, prof. emeritus, 1998—; practice medicine specializing in radiology Tampa, Fla., 1967-68. Contbr. articles to med. jours. Bd. dirs. Ruth Lyons Fund, U. Cin. Found., 1997—2003, U. Cin. Hosp., 2005—. Served with USN, 1945-46. Fellow Am. Coll. Radiology (pres. 1983-84, chmn. commn. on diagnostic radiology); mem. Radiol. Soc. N.Am., Am. Roentgen Ray Soc. (pres. 1986-87), Am. Bd. Radiology (pres. 1982-84), Ohio Med. Assn., Cin. Acad. Medicine, Radiol. Soc. Greater Cin., Ohio Radiol. Soc. Office: U Cin Med Ctr Dept Radiology 234 Goodman St Cincinnati OH 45267-1000 Office Phone: 513-475-8755. E-mail: jfwiot@hotmail.com.

WIPFLER, WILLIAM JOHN, health facility administrator; s. William Louis and Pauline P. Wipfler; m. Valerie S. Libby, Aug. 10; children: Ashley, Michaela, Vanessa, Isaac. BA, Antioch Coll., Yellow Springs, Ohio, 1980; JD, MBA, Boston Coll., Newton, 1987. Atty. Pierce Atwood, Portland, Maine, 1987—88; asst. atty. gen. Maine Atty. Gen., Augusta, 1989—92; gen. counsel Maine Healthcare Fin. Corp., Augusta, 1992—94, exec. dir., 1994—96; CEO Eyecare Med. Group, Portland, 1996—2006, Orthop. Assocs., 2006—. Founder, bd. mem. Maine ASU Coalition, Portland, 2003—. Bd. mem. State of Maine Social Worker Bd., Augusta, 2000—04; bd. chair Inst. for Civic Leadership, Portland, 2002—; bd. Boys to Men, Portland, 2002—05. Office: Orthopaedic Assocs 33 Sewall St Portland ME 04102

WIPKE, W. TODD, chemistry professor; b. Dec. 16, 1940; BS, U. Mo., Columbia, 1962; PhD, U. Calif., Berkeley, 1965. Rsch. chemist Esso Rsch. and Engring. Co., Baton Rouge, 1962; postdoctoral rsch. fellow Harvard U., 1967-69; asst. prof. Princeton U., 1969-75; assoc. prof. chemistry U. Calif., Santa Cruz, 1975-81, prof. chemistry, 1981—. Founder, sr. v.p. Molecular Design Ltd., San Leandro, Calif., 1978-91; founder, chmn. bd. GluMetrics Inc., 2002-04, dir. 2005-; founder, dir. Leptogen, Inc., 2006—; cons. Ciba-Geigy, Basle, Switzerland, 1978-82, BASF, Ludwigshafen, Fed. Republic Germany, 1974-78, Squibb, Princeton, N.J., 1976-81; adv. EPA, 1984—; mem. sci. adv. bd. Pharmix, Scitegic, Tosk; co-founder Leptogen, 2006. Editor: Computer Representation and Manipulation of Chemical Information, 1973, Computer-Assisted Organic Synthesis, 1977; editor-in-chief: (jour.) Tetrahedron Computer Methodology, 1987-92; editor: Tetrahedron and Tetrahedron Letters, 1987-92; contbr. articles to profl. jours. Capt. US Army, 1966—67. Recipient Eastman Kodak Rsch. award, 1964, Texaco Outstanding Rsch. award, 1962, Alexander von Humboldt Sr. Scientist award, 1987; Merck Career Devel. grantee, 1970; NIH fellow, 1964-65. Mem. Am. Chem. Soc. (assoc., Computers in Chemistry award 1987, St. Charles Found. Alumni award 1996), Assn. Computing Machinery, Chem. Soc., Am. Assn. Artificial Intelligence (charter), Chem. Structure Assn. (charter), Internat. Soc. Study Xenobiotics. Office: U Calif Dept Chemistry Santa Cruz CA 95064

WIRASINHA, HEMAMALI ANUSHKA, computer scientist, researcher; b. Colombo, Sri Lanka, Mar. 1, 1972; d. Armyne Edwin and Hemamali Cornelia Wirasinha. Diploma in econ., London U., 1991; BS in Econ. with honors, U. London, 1994; postgrad., Harvard U., 1996; PhD in Computers and Info. Sci. (hon.), Cosmopolitan U., Miami, Fla., 2004. Jr. mgmt. exec. Ceylon Shipping Lines Ltd., Colombo, Sri Lanka, 1994—95; assisting lectr. in micro computers and info. tech. Harvard U., Cambridge, Mass., 1996—98. Dir. Ceylon Shipping Lines Ltd., Colombo, Sri Lanka, 1998—; author Prentice Hall India, Delhi, India, 2002—, Publish Am., Frederick, Md.; advanced level GCE AS/A2 examiner and moderator in computing U. London Edexcel; Sigma Xi ambassador Packard Internat. Sci. Networking Initiative, Sri Lanka, India, Maldives. Author: (book) Spread the Word Around: MS Word, 2001, Cyber Ethics, 2001, Study Buddy, 2001, Digital Art, 2001, Computer Tutor, 2001, Java Essence, 2002, PC Private Eye, 2002, Doctor PC, 2002, I Want to Teach the World to Click!: Computing for the Visually Impaired, 2002, Office Essentials: MS Office XP, 2002, Visually Learn PC (India Times Bestseller 2003), 2002, On Your Marks Net Set Go! Surviving in an E-World (India Times Bestseller 2003), 2002, Flash in a Flash: Web Development, 2002, Computing for the Asian Woman and the Curious Man, 2003, Microchip Militant, 2004. Establishing chpt. Young Politicians of Am., Cambridge, Mass.; contributory America's first responders alliance, Cambridge, Mass., 2004. Recipient Excellence award, Internat. Modeling and Talent Assn., 1997. Mem.: IEEE, AAAS, Brit. Computer Soc., Women in Tech. Internat., Assn. for Women in Computing, Am. Assn. for Artificial Intelligence, Harvard Faculty Club, Sigma Xi, Outstanding Student Honor Soc. Achievements include research in computer security; viability and usability of microchip implantations and advanced tech. to aid the visually impaired. Avocations: writing, travel, fashion, sports, swimming. Home: Apt 401 950 Massachusetts Ave Cambridge MA 02139 Address: 6 Charles Way Colombo 3 Sri Lanka Home Phone: 617-864-1094; Office Phone: 617-864-0041. Fax: 011 941 5725065; Home Fax: 617-864-1094. Personal E-mail: anushkawirasinha@post.harvard.edu. E-mail: anushka1@sigmaxi.org.

WIRE, WILLIAM SHIDAKER, II, retired apparel and footwear manufacturing company executive; b. Cin., Jan. 5, 1932; s. William Shidaker and Gladys (Buckmaster) W.; m. Alice Dumas Jones, Aug. 31, 1957 (dec.); children: Alice Wire Freeman (dec.), Deborah Wire Suber; m. Cheryl C Yates, Sept. 25, 2004. Student, U. of South, 1950; AB, U. Ala., 1954, JD, 1956; LLM, NYU, 1957. Bar: Ala. 1956. Atty. Hamilton, Denniston, Butler & Riddick, Mobile, 1959-60; with Talladega Ins. Agy., Ala., 1961-62, Genesco, Inc., Nashville, 1962-94, former chmn. and CEO. Bd. dirs. Genesco Inc., Dollar Gen. Corp., Am. Endoscopy Svcs., Inc., Nashville Bank & Trust Co. Mem.: Burnt Pine Golf Club (Destin, Fla.), Golf Club Tenn., Univ. Club (NY), Belle Meade Country Club (Nashville), Kappa Alpha. Presbyterian. Home: 706 Overton Park Nashville TN 37215-2452

WIRKEN, CHARLES WILLIAM, lawyer; b. Moline, Ill., Aug. 29, 1951; s. Walter William and Elizabeth Claire Wirken; children: Nicole, Michelle. BS, U. Ariz., 1972, JD, 1975. Bar: Ariz. 1975, U.S. Dist. Ct. Ariz. 1976, U.S. Ct. Appeals (9th cir.) 1980, U.S. Ct. Appeals (Fed. cir.) 1985, U.S. Ct. Appeals (10th cir.) 2004, U.S. Supreme Ct. 1980. Assoc. Killian, Legg & Nicholas, Mesa, Ariz., 1975-79; ptnr. Killian, Nicholas, Fischer, Wirken, Cook & Pew, Mesa, 1980-97, Gust Rosenfeld P.L.C., 1997—. Pres. Vol. Lawyers Project, Phoenix, 1981-83; judge pro tem Ariz. Ct. Appeals, 1985-99, Maricopa County Superior Ct., 1986—; mem. civil study com. Maricopa County Superior Ct., 1984—; bd. dirs. Cmty. Legal Svcs., Phoenix, 1979-82. Exec. v.p. East Valley Partnership, Mesa, 1984; pres. Tri-City Cath. Social Svc., Mesa, 1983, 84; bd. dirs. East Valley Cultural Alliance, Mesa, 1984. Mem. State Bar Ariz. (bd. govs. 1995-06, pres. 2004-05, chair trial practice sect. 2001-02, chair civil practice and procedure com. 2006-07), Maricopa County Bar Assn. (bd. dirs. 1983-91, pres. 1989-90), East Valley Bar Assn. (pres. 1979-80), Mesa C. of C. (dir. 1980-83, v.p. 1982-83), Rotary (bd. dirs. 1980-89, pres. 1987-88). Democrat. Roman Catholic. Home: 1708 E Knoll St Mesa AZ 85203-2171 Office: Gust Rosenfeld PLC 201 E Washington Ste 800 Phoenix AZ 85004-2327 Home Phone: 480-644-9657; Office Phone: 602-257-7959. Business E-Mail: cwirken@gustlaw.com.

WIRKEN, JAMES CHARLES, lawyer; b. Lansing, Mich., July 3, 1944; s. Frank and Mary (Brosnahan) W.; m. Mary Morse, June 12, 1971; children: Christopher, Erika, Kurt, Gretchen, Jeffrey, Matthew. BA in English, Rockhurst Coll., 1967; JD, St. Louis U., 1970. Bar: Mo. 1970, U.S. Dist. Ct. (we. dist.) Mo. 1970. Asst. prosecuter Jackson County, Kansas City, Mo., 1970-72; assoc. Morris, Larson, King, Stamper & Bold, Kansas City, 1972-75; dir. Spradley, Wirken, Reismeyer & King, Kansas City, 1976-88, Wirken & King, Kansas City, 1988-93; CEO The Wirken Law Group, Kansas City, 1993—. Adj. prof. U. Mo., Kansas City, 1984—89, 2001—; columnist Wirken Tips: Law Office Mktg., Mgmt. and Econ. The Daily Record, 2006, Wirkens Quips Quotes, Wit and Wisdom The Daily Record, 2003—06. Author: (books) Managing a Practice and Avoiding Malpractice, 1983; co-author: Missouri Civil Procedure Form Book, 1984; mem. editl. bd.: jours. Missouri Law Weekly, 1989—, Lender Liability News, 1990—, Emerging Trends and Theories of Lender Liability, 1991, host: Wirken on the Law KMBZ-FM, 1998—2007, Kans. City Morning News Sunday Edit. KMBZ-FM, 2007. Named Best the Bar, Kans. City Bus. Jour., 2005—07, Mo. Super Lawyer, 2006, 2007. Mem. ABA (exec. coun.), Nat. Conf. Bar Pres. (coun. 1992-96), Nat. Caucus of Met. Bar Leaders (exec. coun., pres. 1988-94), Am. Trial Lawyers Assn., L.P. Gas Group (founder, chair 1986-90, founder, chair lender liability group 1987-96), Mo. Bar Assn. (bd. govs. 1977-78, 2004—, chmn. econs. and methods practice com. 1982-84, quality and methods of practice com. 1989-91, vice chmn. young lawyers sect. 1976-78), Mo. Assn. Trial Attys. (bd. govs. 1983-85), Kansas City Met. Bar Assn. (pres. young lawyers sect. 1975, chair legal assistance com. 1977-78, chair tort law com. 1982, pres. 1990). Home: 47 W 53rd Kansas City MO 64112 Office: The Wirken Law Group PC 4740 Grand Blvd Ste 200 Kansas City MO 64112 Office Phone: 816-471-0330. Business E-Mail: jwirken@wirkenlaw.com.

WIRSCHING, CHARLES PHILIPP, JR., retired brokerage house executive, securities trader; b. Chgo., Oct. 26, 1935; s. Charles Philipp and Mamie Ethel (York) W.; m. Beverly Ann Bryan, May 28, 1966. BA, U. N.C., 1957. Sales rep. Adams-Millis Corp., Chgo., 1963-67; ptnr. Schwartz-Wirsching, Chgo., 1968-70; sec., dir. Edwin H. Mann, Inc., Chgo., 1971-74; stockbroker Paine Webber, Inc., Chgo., 1975-85, account v.p., 1986-95; ret., 1995. Cons. Paine Webber, Inc. Chgo., 1996-99. Adv. coun. John Nuveen & Co., Inc., 1993-95; trustee Wirsching Charitable Trust, 1987—. Mem.: Organ Hist. Soc., Salem (Ohio) Hist. Soc. Republican. Episcopalian. Avocation: foreign travel. Home and Office: 434 Clinton Pl River Forest IL 60305-2249

WIRSZUP, IZAAK, mathematician, educator; b. Wilno, Poland, Jan. 5, 1915; came to US, 1949, naturalized, 1955; s. Samuel and Pera (Golomb) W.; m. Pola Ofman, July 19, 1940 (dec. 1943); 1 son, Vladimir (dec. 1943); m. Pera Poswianska, Apr. 23, 1949; 1 dau., Marina (Mrs. Arnold M. Tatar). *Izaak Wirszup and his wife Pera (Poswianska Deull) are both survivors of the Nazi Holocaust. Izaak's entire family, including: his first wife Pola (Ofman), their 2 year old son Vladimir, both of Izaak's parents Samuel and Pera (Golomb) Wirszup, Izaak's brother Naum and sister Golda, and their families, were all killed by the Nazis. From September 1941, Izaak Wirszup was imprisoned first in the Ghetto Wilno, then in several Nazi concentration camps in Estonia and Germany. He was liberated by the American Army on April 30, 1945 from camp Allach-Dachau (near Munich, Germany).* Magister of Philosophy in Math, U. Wilno, 1939; PhD in Math, U. Chgo., 1955. Lectr. math. Tech. Inst. Wilno, 1939-41; dir. Bur. d'Études et de Statistiques Spéciales, Société Centrale d'Achat-Société Anonyme des Monoprix, Paris, 1946-49; mem. faculty U. Chgo., 1949—, prof. math., 1965-85, prof. math. emeritus, 1985—, prin. investigator U. Chgo. Sch. Math. Project (sponsored by Amoco Found., also dir. resource devel. component), 1983—, dir. Internat. Math. Edn. Resource Ctr., 1988—. Dir. NSF Survey Applied Soviet Rsch. in Math. Edn., 1985-91; cons. Ford Found., Colombia, Peru, 1965-66, Sch. Math Study Group, 1960, 61, 66-68; participant, writer tchr. tng. material African Math. Program, Entebbe, Uganda, summer 1964, Mombasa, Kenya, summers 1965-66; assoc. dir. Survey Recent Ea. European Math. Lit., 1956-68, dir., 1968-84; dir. NSF program application computers to mgmt., 1976-83; cons. NSF-AID Sci. Edn. Program, India, 1969; mem. US Commn. on Math. Instn., 1969-73; co-prin. investigator U. Chgo.-Polk Bros. Found. Program for the Devel. of Math. Tchrs. in Chgo. Pub. Schs., 1999—. *A December 1979 comparative studies report by Izaak Wirszup to the National Science Foundation, which revealed a crisis in mathematics and science education in the U.S., came to the attention of President Jimmy Carter. The President ordered a review of U.S. science and engineering education policies. Wirszup was subsequently invited to testify six times before the U.S. Senate. With an 8.4 million dollar grant from the Amoco Foundation, Wirszup founded the University of Chicago School Mathematics Project in 1983. More than three million students and teachers are now using UCSMP texts.* Contbr. articles to profl. jours.; Editor Math. books, transls., adaptions from Russian.; Adviser math.: Ency. Brit., 1971—. Recipient Lewellyn John and Harriet Manchester Quantrell award U. Chgo., 1958, Univ. Alumni Svc. medal, U. Chgo., 1994; resident master Woodward Ct., U. Chgo., 1971-85; endowed Wirszup Lecture Series, U. Chgo., 1986. Mem. NY Acad. Scis., Am. Math. Soc., Math. Assn. Am., AAAS, Nat. Council Tchrs. Math. (chmn. com. internat. math. edn. 1967-69, Lifetime Achievement medal for Leadership, Tchg., and Svc. in Math. Edn. 1996) Home: 5750 S Kenwood Ave Chicago IL 60637-1744 Office: U Chgo Dept Math 5734 S University Ave Chicago IL 60637-1514 Office Phone: 773-667-1967.

WIRT, FREDERICK MARSHALL, retired political scientist, educator; b. Radford, Va., July 27, 1924; s. Harry Johnson, Sr. and Goldie (Turpin) W.; m. Elizabeth Cook, Sept. 6, 1947; children: Leslie Lee, Sandra Sue, Wendy Ann. BA, DePauw U., 1948; MA, Ohio State U., 1949, PhD, 1956. Instr. to prof. polit. sci. Denison U., Granville, Ohio, 1952-66; vis. prof., lectr. U. Calif., Berkeley, 1966-68, 69-72; dir. policy scis. grad. program U. Md. Balt. County, 1972-75; prof. polit. sci. U. Ill., Urbana, 1975-2000; ret., 2000. Dir. Inst. for Desegregation Problems, U. Calif.-Berkeley, 1970-72; cons. Motion Picture Assn. Am., Rand Corp., Nat. Inst. Edn., SUNY Sch. Edn. Albany; vis. prof. U. Rochester, Nova U., U. Melbourne; acad. visitor London Sch. Econs. Author: Politics of Southern Equality, 1970 (honorable mention for best book 1972), Power in the City, 1974; (with others) School Desegregation in the North, 1967, The Polity of the School, 1975, Political Science and School Politics, 1977, Education, Recession, and the World Village, 1986, (with others) Culture and Education Policy in the American States, 1992, Ain't What We Was: Civil Rights in the New South, 1997 (Best Book on So. Politics award So. Polit. Sci. Assn., 1998), The Political Dynamics of American Education, 3d edit., 2005. Mem. Granville City Charter Commn., 1964. Grantee Am. Philos. Soc., Denison Rsch. Assn., U. Ill. Rsch. Bd., NEH, Ford Found., Ctr. Advanced Studies; fellow U. Ill., Dept. Edn., Spencer Found.; recipient Lifetime Achievement award Am. Ednl. Rsch. Assn., 1995, Am. Polit. Sci. Assn., 1994. Mem. Am. Polit. Sci. Assn. (nat. council), Midwestern Polit. Sci. Assn., Am. Ednl. Rsch. Assn., Policy Studies Orgn. Office: U Ill Dept of Polit Sci Urbana IL 61801 Home: 2340 W Seltice Way Apt 129 Coeur D' Alene ID 83814 E-mail: fmwirt@verizon.net.

WIRT, MICHAEL JAMES, library director; b. Sault Sainte Marie, Mich., Mar. 21, 1947; s. Arthur James and Blanche Marian (Carruth) W.; m. Barbara Ann Hallesy, Aug. 12, 1972; 1 child, Brendan. BA, Mich. State U., 1969; MLS, U. Mich., 1971; postgrad., U. Wash., 1990. Cert. libr., Wash. Acting libr. U. Mich. Ctr. for Rsch. on Econ. Devel., Ann Arbor, 1971-72; instnl. svcs. libr. Spokane County (Wash.) Libr. Dist., 1972-76, asst. dir., 1976-79, acting dir., 1979, dir., 1980—. Mem. adv. com. Partnership for Rural Improvement, Spokane, 1982-85, Wash. State Libr. Planning and Devel. Com., 1984-85, Ea. Wash. U. Young Writers Project Adv. Bd., 1988-89; mem. issues selection com. Citizens League of Greater Spokane, 1991-93, City of Spokane Indian Trail Specific Plan Task force, 1992-95; mem. comm. com. United Way Spokane County, 1994, campaign chair local govt. divsn., 1996. Mem. Wash. Libr. Assn. (2d v.p. 1984-86, dir. 1989-91, pub. rels. com. 1993-2001, chair legis. planning com. 2003—, conf. coord. 2003-05, Merit award 1984, Pres. award 1998), Wash. Libr. Network (rep. Computer Svc. Coun. 1983-86, v.p., treas. State Users Group 1986-87), Am. Libr. Assn. (Pub. Libr. Affiliates Network 1990-93, PLA Bus. Coun. 1990-94, chmn. 1991-94), Spokane Valley C. of C. (local govt. affairs com. 1987-2000, co-chair 1996-98, pub. policy com. 2000-2005, mem. local governance com. 2003-2005, governence com. 2005—), Spokane Regional C. of C. (local govt. com. 1990-94, human svcs. com. 1990-92, chmn. 1991-92, govt. reorgn. task force 1995), Spokane Civic Theatre (bd. dirs. 1996-2001, v.p. 1997-98, 2000, sec. 1998-2000), Inland N.W. Legis. Coalition, Momentum (local govt. strategy com. 1992-94), New Century (govt. collaboration com. 1997-98), Inland N.W. Coun. Librs. (bd. dirs. 1979—, chmn. 1997-98). Office: Spokane County Libr Dist 4322 N Argonne Rd Spokane WA 99212-1853 Office Phone: 509-924-4122. Business E-Mail: mwirt@scld.org.

WIRTH, DYANN FERGUS, public health educator, microbiologist; b. Racine, Wis., Jan. 31, 1951; d. Russell and Phyllis Rose (Muratone) Fergus; m. Peter Wirth, Aug. 25, 1973. BA with highest honors, U. Wis., 1972; PhD, MIT, 1978; AM (hon.), Harvard U., 1990. Instr. Marine Biol. Lab., Woods Hole, Mass., 1980-84; asst. prof. Harvard Sch. Pub. Health, Boston, 1981-86, assoc. prof., 1986-90, prof., 1990—, dir. Harvard Malaria Initiative, 1997—; editor-in-chief Acad. Press Exptl. Parasitology, Boston, 1987—. NIH study sect. mem. tropical medicine and parasitology NIH, Bethesda, 1987-91; chmn. steering com. on chemotherapy of Malaria WHO, Geneva, 1986-91, 91—, chair steering com. on drug devel., mem. rsch. capacity strengthening, mem. strategic rsch. com., 1997—; mem. sci. adv. bd. Edna McConnell Clark Found.; chair sci. adv. com. Burroughs Wellcome Fund Career Awards, 1994—. Contbr. numerous articles to profl. jours. Fellowship Fulbright Found., 1972-73, Predoctoral fellowship NIH, 1973-78, Helen Hay Whitney fellowship, 1978-81; recipient Burroughs-Wellcome award in Molecular Parasitology, 1982, 85-90. Mem. AAAS, Am. Soc. Microbiology, Am. Soc. Tropical Medicine and Hygiene (pres. 1999, Bailey K. Ashford award 1995), Am. Soc. Virology, Inst. Medicine, Phi Beta Kappa. Office: Harvard Sch Pub Health Dept Immunology & Infectious Diseases 665 Huntington Ave Boston MA 02115 E-mail: dfwirth@hsph.harvard.edu.

WIRTH, ERIN MASSON, lawyer; d. Robert and Grace Masson; m. Kevin Edward Wirth, 1998. BA, Smith Coll., Northampton, Mass., 1986—90; JD, Coll. William & Mary, Williamsburg, Va., 1992—95. Bar: Md., Fla., Hawaii, Mich. Atty. Semmes, Bowen & Semmes, 1995—97; asst. state atty., 1997—2000; edn. coord. Kapiolani Med. Ctr., 2000—01; atty. Lyons, Brandt, Cook & Hiramatsu, 2001—02; atty. advisor FTC, DC, 2003—06; mng. atty. Legal Aid of Northeastern Minn., Duluth, Minn., 2007—. Contbr. articles to profl. jours. Mem.: ABA. Office: Legal Aid NE Minn 302 Ordean Bldg 424 W Superior St Duluth MN 55802 Home Phone: 218-728-1458; Office Phone: 218-726-4707. E-mail: briefcounsel@msn.com.

WIRTH, FREMONT PHILIP, JR., neurosurgeon, educator; b. Nashville, July 23, 1940; s. Fremont P. and Willa (Dean) W.; children: Fremont Philip III, Andrew Simpson, Carolyn Howe. BA with honors in History, Williams Coll., 1962; MD, Vanderbilt U., 1966. Diplomate Am. Bd. Neurol. Surgery (guest examiner 1989, bd. dirs. 1992-98, vice chmn. 1997-98), Nat. Bd. Med. Examiners; cert. advanced trauma life support ACS. Surg. intern Johns Hopkins Hosp., Balt., 1966-67, resident and fellow in surgery, 1967-68; asst. resident in neurosurgery Barnes Hosp., Washington U., St. Louis, 1970-72, fellow in neurosurgery, 1972-74; pvt. practice, Savannah, Ga., 1974—. Asst. clin. prof. neurosurgery Med. Coll. Ga., Augusta, 1991—, vis. prof., 1978, 79, 86, 87; mem. staff, neurosurg. ICU, St. Joseph's Hosp., 1974—, dir. neurosurg. ICU, 1978—; mem. staff Meml. Med. Ctr., 1974-75, dir. rehab., 1983; mem. staff Candler Gen. Hosp., 1974—; med. dir. Head and Spinal Cord Injury Prevention Project for Ga., 1984-96; presenter in field, 1970—; vis. prof. U. Md., Balt., 1981, Tufts New Eng. Med. Ctr., Boston, 1982. Series editor (with R.A. Ratcheson) Concepts in Neurosurgery, 1986-93; editor: (with Ratcheson) Neurosurgical Critical Care, Concepts in Neurological Surgery, Vol. 1, 1987, Ruptured Cerebral Aneurysms, Concepts in Neurological Surgery, Vol. 6, 1994; contbr. articles and book revs. to med. jours., chpts. to books. Elder Skidaway Island Presbyn. Ch., 1981-83; mem. pack 57 com. Cub Scouts Am., Savannah, 1979-84; mem. troop 57 com. Boy Scouts Am., Savannah, 1980-85, mem. fin. com. Coastal Empire coun., 1987-90, mem. adv. bd., 1990-96; chmn. physicians' solicitation United Way Coastal Empire, 1987; bd. dirs. Think First Found., 1990-95. With USPHS, 1968-70. Fellow ACS (bd. govs. 1984-90, sr. mem. trauma com. 1991-93); mem. AMA (physician's recognition award 1973-76, 77-79, 80-82, 83-85, 88-91, 91-94, 95-98, 98—), Congress Neurol. Surgeons (profl. conduct com. 1989-93, v.p. 1985-86, Disting. Svc. award 1989), Am. Acad. Neurol. Surgeons, Neurosurg. Soc. Am., Am. Assn. Neurologic Surgeons (nominating com. 1994-96, bd. dirs. 1998-2001, v.p. 2002-03, pres. 2005-06), Brain Surgery Soc., Ga. Med. Soc. (pres. 1995, bd. trustees 1996-2001, chmn. 2000-01), Med. Assn. Ga. (editl. bd. 1987-93), Ga. Neurosurg. Soc. (exec. com. 1981-88, pres. 1988-89), So. Neurosurg. Soc. (exec. com. 1982-91, pres. 1988-89, Semmes lectr. 1997), N.Am. Skull Base Soc., Am. Heart Assn. (fellow stroke coun.). Avocations: golf, fly fishing, hunting. Office: Neurol Inst Savannah 4 E Jackson Blvd Savannah GA 31405-5810

WIRTH, KELLEY K., state representative; b. Panorama City, Calif., Aug. 2, 1965; children: Kennedy, Meghan. BS, Oreg. State U., 1989; MS, U. So. Calif., 1992. State rep., dist. 16 Oreg. House Rep., Salem, 2001—; sys. analyst, planning commr. City of Corvallis, Oreg., 1996—; sys. analyst Asst. to 3d Infantry Divsn. Chief of Staff, 1993—99. Adj. computer tech. faculty City Colls. Chgo.-Europe, 1992; bd. mem. Land Devel. Hearings Bd. City of Corvallis, 1998—, mem. Neighborhood Tech. Rev. Group, 1997—. Mem.: Corvallis LWV. Democrat. Episcopalian.

WIRTH, MICHAEL K. (MIKE WIRTH), oil company executive; b. Oct. 1960; m. Julie Wirth; 4 children. BS, U. Colo. With Chevron Corp., 1982—, design engr., 1982, sr. retail mgr. mktg. Western Ops., 1998—99, gen. mgr. retail mktg., 1999—2000; pres. mktg. Caltex Corp., Singapore, 2000—01; pres. mktg. Asia/Middle East/Africa ChevronTexaco Corp, 2001—04, pres. Global Supply and Trading, 2004—06, exec. v.p. Global Downstream, 2006—. Office: Chevron Hdqs 6001 Bollinger Canyon Rd San Ramon CA 94583

WIRTH, PETER, lawyer; b. Halgehausen, Germany, July 17, 1950; U.S., 1956; BA, U. Wis., 1972; JD, Harvard U., 1975. Bar: Mass. 1975. Assoc. Palmer & Dodge, Boston, 1975-81, ptnr., 1982-96, of counsel, 1996—; exec. v.p. legal and corp. devel., chief legal officer, sec. Genzyme Corp., Cambridge, 1996—. Lectr. grad. tax program Boston U., 1982-85. Mem. ABA, Mass. Bar Assn., Phi Beta Kappa. Office: Genzyme Corporation 500 Kendall St Cambridge MA 02142 Office Phone: 617-768-6882, 617-252-7600.

WIRTH, SANDRA LEE, real estate company owner; b. Buffalo, June 8, 1945; d. Dominic A. and Santina (Lopez) Liberatore; 1 child, H. William III. Prin. Metro Sandra Lee Wirth Robshaw Gallery of Homes, Tonawanda, N.Y.; regional mgr. Paul Robshaw Galler of Homes, Tonawanda, N.Y., mgr. line Cheektowaga, N.Y.; broker assoc. B.W. Morris and Son Realtors, Buffalo; owner Metro Sandra Lee Wirth, Real Estate; mem. N.Y. Assembly, Dist. 148, Albany, 1994—. Chmn., past pres. West Seneca Druga Abuse Prevention Coun.; sponsor Call Home Free Program, Nat. Crime Prevention Coun.'s Nat. Night Out. Named Realtor of the Yr., Elma Bus. Person of the Yr. Mem. Nat. Assn. Realtors (cert.), N.Y. Assn. Realtors (state dir.), Greater Buffalo Bd. Realtors (1st v.p. 1988, treas. 1989, pres. elect 1990), Greater Buffalo Assn. Realtors (pres.), Buffalo and West Seneca C. of C. Office: NYS Assembly 148th District 5763 Seneca St Elma NY 14059-9615

WIRTH, TAMARA L., music educator; b. Stuebenville, Ohio, July 18, 1968; d. William Harry and Elva Elizabeth Jones; m. Douglas Harry Wirth; children: Matthew Robert, Bradley Douglas. BS in Music Edn., Ind. U., Pa., 1990; MA in Edn., Marygrove Coll., 2005. Organist, choir dir. Paris (Pa.) Presbyn. Ch., 1985—92; organist Trinity United Meth. Ch., Spencerville, 1993—97; substitute tchr. various sch., Allen and Auglaize counties, Ohio, 1993—98; music tchr. St. Joseph Cath., Wapakoneta, Ohio, 1998—. Sec. St. Joseph PTO, Wapakoneta, 1999—2003, Spencerville PTO, 1998—2002. Democrat. Avocations: crafts, sewing, aerobics. Home: 8656 Deep Cut Rd Spencerville OH 45887 Office: St Joseph Cath Sch 1101 Lincoln Hwy Wapakoneta OH 45895

WIRTH, TIMOTHY ENDICOTT, foundation administrator, retired senator; b. Santa Fe, Sept. 22, 1939; s. Cecil and Virginia Maude (Davis) W.; m. Wren Winslow, Nov. 26, 1965; children: Christopher, Kelsey. BA, Harvard U., 1961, MEd, 1964; PhD, Stanford U., 1973; degree (hon.), U. Colo., Denver U., Colo. Coll., Washington Coll., Clark U. White House fellow, spl. asst. to sec. HEW, Washington, 1967; asst. to chmn. Nat. Urban Coalition, Washington, 1968; dep. asst. sec. for edn. HEW, Washington, 1969; v.p. Great Western United Corp., Denver, 1970; mgr. Rocky Mountain office Arthur D. Little, Inc. (cons. firm), Denver, 1971-73; mem. 94th-99th Congresses from 2d Colo. Dist., 1975-87, mem. energy and commerce com., sci. and tech. com., budget com., chmn. subcom. telecommunications, fin. and consumer protection; U.S. senator from Colo., 1987-93; counselor U.S. Dept. State, Washington, 1993-94, Under Sec. of State for global affairs, 1994-97; pres. UN Found. and Better World Fund, Washington, 1997—. Mem. bd. overseers Harvard U.; chair vis. com. Harvard Grad. Sch. Edn. Recipient Disting. Service award HEW, 1969; Ford Found. fellow, 1964-66 Fellow: Am. Acad. Arts & Sci. Mem. White House Fellows Assn. (pres. 1968-69), Denver Council Fgn. Relations (exec. com. 1974-75), Alliance to Save Energy (chmn. 1987-93). Office: UN Found 1800 Massachusetts Ave NW Ste 400 Washington DC 20036

WIRTHLIN, RICHARD BITNER, researcher; b. Salt Lake City, Mar. 15, 1931; s. Joseph L. and Madeline (Bitner) W.; m. Jeralie Chandler, Nov. 23, 1956; children: Richard L., Mary Ann, J. Mark, Carolyn, Michael, Jill, Susan, John BS, U. Utah, 1956, MA, 1957; PhD, U. Calif.-Berkeley, 1964. Lectr. U. Calif. Med. Ctr., San Francisco, 1960-61; chmn. dept. econs. Brigham Young U., Provo, Utah, 1964-69; ptnr. Merrill-Wirthlin Assocs., Provo, 1964-69; pres., chmn. bd. dirs. Decision/Making/Info., McLean, Va., 1969-84; chmn. bd. dirs., CEO The Wirthlin Group, Salt Lake City, 1987—. Co-author (with Wynton C. Hall): (book) The Greatest Communicator: What Ronald Reagan Taught Me about Politics, Leadership, and Life, 2004. Dir. planning and strategy Reagan/Bush Campaign, 1980, campaign dir. research, planning and policy, 1980-81; dir. planning and evaluation Pres.-Elect Transition Com., 1980-81; cons. to Prime Minister Margaret Thatcher and Brit. Conservative Party, 1989—; bd. dirs. Harris Interactive, 2004—. Recipient Disting. Alumni award U. Utah, 1986, Disting. Alumni Service award Brigham Young U., 1987; named Advt. Man of Yr., Advt. Age, 1981, Pollster of Yr. Polit. Cons., 1981. Mem. Acad. Polit. Sci., Am. Econ. Assn., Am. Mktg. Assn., Am. Assn. Pub. Opinion/Research, Council Survey Research Orgns., Sigma Chi, Omicron Delta Epsilon Republican. Office: 2625 Old Orchard Cir Salt Lake City UT 84121

WIRTSCHAFTER, DAVID, talent agency executive; Agent William Morris Motion Picture Divsn., Beverly Hills, Calif.; pres. William Morris Agency, Beverly Hills, Calif., 2005—. Office: William Morris Agy Inc 151 S El Camino Dr Beverly Hills CA 90212-2775

WIRTZ, WILLIAM WADSWORTH, real estate company executive, professional sports team executive; b. Chgo., Oct. 5, 1929; s. Arthur Michael and Virginia (Wadsworth) Wirtz; m. Joan Roney, Dec. 15, 1950 (dec. May 1983); children: William R., Gail W., Karen K., Peter R., Alison M.; m. Alice Pirie Hargrave, Dec. 1, 1987. AB, Brown U., 1950. Pres. Chgo. Blackhawk Hockey Team, Inc., 1966—, Chgo. Stadium Corp., 1966—, Consol. Enterprises, Inc., Chgo., 1966—, Forman Realty Corp., Chgo., 1965—, 333 Bldg. Corp., Chgo., 1966—, Wirtz Corp., Chgo., 1964—. Chmn. bd. govs. Nat. Hockey League. Named to NHL Hall of Fame, 1976; recipient Lester Patrick trophy, 1978. Mem.: Sunset Ridge Country Club (Northbrook, Ill.), Fin and Feather Club (Elgin, Ill.), Mid-America Club (Chgo.), Racquet Club (Chgo.), Saddle and Cycle Club (Chgo.). Office: Wirtz 680 N Lake Shore Dr Fl 19 Chicago IL 60611-3495 also: United Ctr 1901 W Madison St Chicago IL 60612-2459 also: Nat Hockey Leage 1155 Metcalfe St Ste 960 Montreal PQ Canada H3B 2W2

WIRUM, ANDREA A., lawyer; b. Okla. City, Feb. 24, 1956; BA, Mich. State Univ., 1977; JD, Univ. Calif., Hastings, 1980. CPA 1977; bar: Calif. 1980. Ptnr. Corp. & Securities practice, mem. mng. bd. Pillsbury Winthrop Shaw Pittman, San Francisco. Office: Pillsbury Winthrop Shaw Pittman 50 Fremont St San Francisco CA 94105 Office Phone: 415-983-1735. Office Fax: 415-983-1200. Business E-Mail: andrea.wirum@pillsburylaw.com.

WISBAUM, WAYNE DAVID, lawyer; b. Niagara Falls, NY, May 29, 1935; s. Franklin C. and Elizabeth (Boff) W.; m. Janet Katz, July 3, 1960; children: Karen, Wendy, Deborah. BA, Cornell U., 1956; LL.B., Harvard U., 1959. Bar: N.Y. 1960. Assoc. Kavinoky & Cook, Buffalo, 1960-66, sr. ptnr., 1966—. Pres., chmn. bd. dirs. Kleinhans Music Hall Mgmt. Inc., 1990-2000, life emeritus, 2003-. Pres. Buffalo Coun. on World Affairs, 1968-70; mem. Young Leadership Cabinet Nat. United Jewish Appeal, 1967-73; mem. com. on leadership devel. Nat. Coun. Jewish Fedn. and Welfare Funds, 1967—; mem. Mayor's Com. on Youth Opportunity; bd. dirs. Anti-Defamation League; mem. Coun. Internat. Studies, SUNY, Buffalo; chmn. Buffalo chpt. Am. Jewish Com.; pres., chmn. bd. dirs. Buffalo Found. Jewish Philanthropies, 2001—; bd. govs. United Jewish Fedn., Buffalo; chmn. bd. dirs. Buffalo Philharm. Orch. Soc.; bd. dirs., mem. exec. com. Burchfield Art Ctr.; bd. dirs., pres. Jewish Family Svc. of Erie County; vice chmn., bd. dirs. Artpark, Irish Classical Theatre; trustee Buffalo and Erie County Park Libr., Daemen Coll., 2004—; dir. emeritus Zool. Soc. Buffalo and Erie County, 2005—. Served to capt. U.S. Army, 1964. Recipient United Jewish Fedn. Buffalo Leadership award, 1967, Cmty. Rels. award Am. Jewish Com., 1985, Abram Pugash award Jewish Family Service, 1985, Cmty. Leadership award Israel Bonds, 2001, honoree Citation banquet Nat. Conf. for Cmty. and Justice, 2004, Citizen of Yr. award Buffalo News, 2003; named Harvard Alumnus of Yr., 1990. Mem. ABA, N.Y. State Bar Assn. (chmn. com. lawyers title guaranty funds, Root/Stimson award 2003), Erie County Bar Assn., Am. Law Inst., Harvard Law Sch. Assn. Western N.Y. (sec.), Zool. Soc. Buffalo (dir., mem. exec. com.), Harvard Club (pres. Buffalo chpt., mem. N.Y.C. chpt.), Buffalo Club, Cornell Club (N.Y.C. chpt.), Zeta Beta Tau. Home: 180 Greenaway Rd Buffalo NY 14226-4166 Office: Kavinoky & Cook 120 Delaware Ave Rm 600 Buffalo NY 14202-2793 Office Phone: 716-845-6000. Business E-Mail: wwisbaum@kavinokybook.com.

WISDOM, PEGGY JEAN, neurologist; b. OKeene, Okla., Nov. 4, 1947; d. Clarence W. and Grace V. Wisdom. BS in Biology/Chemistry, Northwestern State Coll., Evanston, Ill., 1968; MD, U. Okla., Norman, 1972. Diplomate Am. Bd. Psychiatry and Neurology. Resident in neurology U. Fla., 1972-76; asst. prof. neurology U. Okla., Oklahoma City, 1976-90, assoc. prof. neurology, 1990—2002, prof. neurology, 2002—, vice chair dept. neurology, 1981—; med. dir. neurologic rehab. O'Donoghue Rehab. Inst., Oklahoma City, 1981-89, chief of staff, 1986-90; chief neurology VA Med. Ctr., Oklahoma City, 1994-97, chief neurology/rehab., 1997—. Cons. Commn. on Accreditation of Rehab. Facilities, Tuscon, 1990-2006, Okla. Dept. Rehab. Svcs., Oklahoma City, 1993-96. Sci. adv. bd. Omniplex Mus., Oklahoma City, 1994. Mem. Am. Acad. Neurology, Am. Acad. Neurology (chmn. women issues in neurology sect. 1999-2001), Assn. of VA Neurologists, Am. Epilepsy Soc. Republican. Presbyterian. Office: U Okla Health Scis Ctr # 215 711 Stanton L Young Blvd Oklahoma City OK 73104-5021 Home Phone: 405-340-7602; Office Phone: 405-271-4113. Business E-Mail: peggy-wisdom@ouhsc.edu.

WISE, AARON NOAH, lawyer; b. Hartford, Conn., Feb. 14, 1940; s. Joseph J. and Ethel (Sklar) W.; m. Genevieve Ehrlich, Dec. 17. 1966; children: Haywood Martin, Paul Russell, Renee Alicia AB, Boston U., 1962; JD, Boston Coll., 1965; LLM in Comparative/Internat. Law, NYU, 1971; certificat de Doctorat, d' Université en Droit U. Paris, 1970. Bar: NY 1965, US Dist. Ct. (so. dist.) NY 1965. Internat. atty. Schering-Plough, Kenilworth, NJ, 1969-74; ptnr. Conboy Hewitt O'Brien & Boardman, NYC, 1974-80, Wise Lerman & Katz PC (formerly Rosenbaum Wise Lerman & Katz), NYC, 1981-95, Klepner & Cayea, NYC, 1995-98, Brand, Cayea & Brand, LLC, 1998-2000, Siller Wilk LLP, NYC, 2000—02, Gallet Dreyer & Berkey, LLP, NYC, 2002—. Author: International Sports Law and Business (Kluwer Law Internat., 1997, 3 vols.), Foreign Businessman's Guide to U.S. Law-Practice-Taxation, 2004; contbr. articles to pubs. in U.S. and Europe. Mem.: ABA, NY State Bar Assn. Avocation: multi-lingual including French, German, Spanish, Portuguese, Italian, Russian and Japanese. Home: 38 Cummings Cir West Orange NJ 07052-2264 Office: Gallet Dreyer & Berkey LLP 845 Third Ave New York NY 10022-6601 Office Phone: 212-935-3131. Business E-Mail: anw@gdblaw.com.

WISE, ALLEN F., health care company executive; b. Wichita, Kans., Aug. 20, 1942; BS, Wichita State U. Exec. v.p. of operations Health Care Systems Inc., 1985—90; pres., CEO Keystone Health Plan, 1991-94; COO Independence Blue Cross, Phila., 1991—94; exec. v.p. Metra Health Co., 1994—95; pres., CEO Wise Health System, 1994; exec. v.p. United HealthCare Corp., 1995—96; pres., CEO Coventry Health Care, Inc., Bethesda, Md., 1996—2004, non-exec. chmn., 2004—. Bd. dir., chmn. HealthMarkets Inc.; bd. dir. Magellan Health Services Inc., NCP Group Inc. Office: 6705 Rockledge Dr Ste 900 Bethesda MD 20817-1814 *

WISE, BOB (ROBERT ELLSWORTH WISE JR.), former governor, former congressman; b. Washington, Jan. 6, 1948; m. Sandy Casber; children: Robert, Alexandra. BA, Duke U., 1970; JD, Tulane U., 1975. Bar: W.Va. 1985. Sole practice, Charleston, W.Va., 1975—80; atty., legis. coun. for judiciary com. W.Va. Ho. of Dels., 1977—78; mem. W.Va. Senate, 1980—82, 97th-106th Congresses from 2nd W.Va. dist., Washington, 1983—2001; whip at large, 1986—2001; mem. govt. reform and oversight com., transp. and infrastructure com.; gov. State of W.Va., 2001—05. Pres. Alliance for Excellent Edn., Washington, 2005. Dir. West Virginians for Fair and Equitable Assessment of Taxes, Inc. Mem.: ABA, W.Va. State Bar Assn. Democrat. Avocations: physical fitness, bluegrass music. Mailing: Alliance for Excellent Edn 1201 Connecticut Ave NW Ste 901 Washington DC 20036

WISE, BRET W., chemical company executive; m. June Wise; 3 children. BS, Ind. U. CPA. Ptnr. KPMG; v.p., CFO WCI Steel, Inc., Warren, Ohio; sr. v.p., CFO Ferro Corp., Cleve., 1999—2002; CFO, sr. v.p. DENTSPLY Internat. Inc., York, Pa., 2002—05, exec. v.p., 2005—06, pres., COO, 2006, chmn., CEO, 2006—. Bd. dir. Dental Trade Alliance. Mem. AICPA, Fin. Execs. Inst. Office: DENTSPLY Internat Inc Susquehanna Commerce Ctr 221 W Philadelphia St York PA 17405 *

WISE, CHARLA KAMM, aeronautics company executive; m. Michael Wise; 3 children. B in Aero. and Aerospace Engring., U. Mich., Ann Arbor, 1975. Assoc. engr. Gen. Dynamics, Ft. Worth, prog. dir. F-16 USAF progs., 1987; v.p., prog. dir. F-22 prog. Lockheed Martin Corp., Ft. Worth, v.p., dep. co. ops., v.p. engring. home dept., 1998—2003; v.p. bus. ops. Lockheed Martin Aeronautics Co., Ft. Worth. Pres. Lockheed Martin Aeronautics Employees' Reaching Out Club, Ft. Worth; pres. bd. dirs. Goodwill Industries Ft. Worth. Recipient Upward Mobility award, Soc. Women Engrs., 1996, Henry Laurence Gantt medal, ASME, 2006. Mem.: Women in Aerospace, Soc. Aerospace Engrs., Rotary Internat. Office: Lockheed Martin Aeronautics Lockheed Blvd Fort Worth TX 76108 *

WISE, CHARLES DAVIDSON, science educator; b. Huntington, W. Va., June 13, 1926; s. Fred Eugene Wise and Maggie M. Harshbarger; m. Juanita Irene Meadows, Mar. 22, 1947; 1 child, Sandra. AB, MS, W. Va. U., 1950; PhD, U. N.Mex., 1962. Cert. tchr. N.Mex., W. Va., Tex. Tchr. St. Albans (W. Va.) High Sch., 1951-53; lab. assst. Marshall U., 1950-51; grad. fellow U. N.Mex., Albuquerque, 1953-55, grad. asst., 1960-61; rsch. scientist U. Tex., Port Aransas, Tex., 1958-60; prof. Ball State U., Muncie, Ind., 1961-91; rep. Ind. State Legislature, Indpls., 1967-69; senator Ind. State Senate, Indpls., 1969-73. Contbr. articles to profl. jours., 1958—. Bd. dirs. Mental Health Svc. East Cen. Ind., 1974-77; pres. Muncie Bicentennial Festival Com., 1975-77. With U.S. Army, 1944-46. Recipient fellowship U. Ind., 1957, U. Tex., 1957-58, Marshall U. Alumni Community Achievement award, 1993; named Alumnus of Yr., East Bank High Sch., W.Va., 1977. Fellow Ind. Acad. Sci.; mem. Nat. Assn. State Legislators (life mem.), Nat. Audubon Soc., Ind. Audubon Soc. (past pres., conservation award 1977), E. Cen. Ind. Audubon Soc. (pres. 1988-90, conservation award 1984), Sigma Xi Rsch. Soc. (pres. Ball State U. chpt., bd. dir. Hoosier Environ. coun. 1990-93). Republican. Presbyterian. Avocations: birdwatching, travel, languages, genealogy, history. Home: 1032 Brickyard Ave Milton WV 25541 Office: Ball State Univ Muncie IN 47306-0001 Office Phone: 765-285-8820.

WISE, CHARLES WILLIAM, III, financial advisor; b. York, Pa., Oct. 7, 1951; s. Charles W. and Charlotte Louise; m. Holly Sue Smith, Dec. 7, 1974; 1 child, Heather Britta. BSBA, Ind. U. Pa., 1973. CPA Pa., cert. PFS; registered investment advisor rep. NASD. Staff, sr., in charge acct. Miller & Co. CPAs, York, Pa., 1973-77; supr. fin./operational audit Pa. Blue Shield, Camp Hill, Pa., 1977-79, various mgmt. positions audit, info. sys. audit, account svcs. and support, special investigations., 1979-85, dir. corp. audit, 1986-94; dir. audit/reimbursement Xact Medicare Svcs., Camp Hill, 1995—97; dir. audit and performance analysis HGSA, Camp Hill, 1998—99, dir. spl. projects, 1999—2000; chief security officer Highmark, Inc., Camp Hill, 2001—03; fin. advisor Citigroup/SmithBarney, 2004—. Life mem. Laurel Fire Co.; officer, bd. dirs. Strand Capitol Performing Arts Ctr.; mem. Art Forever Adv. Bd. Mem.: AICPA, York 100, Friends of Drum Corps Internat. Home: 60 Polaris Dr Mount Wolf PA 17347-9711 Office: SmithBarney 204 N George St 3d Fl York PA 17401 Home Phone: 717-266-0127; Office Phone: 717-854-5553, 800-343-5235.

WISE, DAMON, chef; B in Psych. and Liberal Arts, West Va. U., 1993; grad., Balt. Internat. Culinary Coll., 1996. Cook Le Bec Fin, Phila., The Greenbrier, Sulpher Springs, W.Va., Lespinasse, Cello; stagiaire Taillevent, Paris, Apicius, Paris; line cook Gramercy Tavern, NYC; chef de cuisine Craft, NYC; exec. chef Craft Restaurants, 2007—. Named one of NYC's Rising Stars, StarChefs.com, 2007. Office: Craft Restaurants 43 E 19th St New York NY 10003 *

WISE, GARY LAMAR, electrical engineering and mathematics educator, investment researcher; b. Texas City, Tex., July 29, 1945; s. Calder Lamar and Ruby Lavon (Strom) W.; m. Mary Estella Warren, Dec. 28, 1974; 1 child, Tanna Estella. BA summa cum laude, Rice U., 1971; MSE, Princeton U., 1973, MA 1973, PhD, 1974. Postdoctoral rsch. assoc. Princeton U., N.J., 1974; asst. prof. Tex. Tech U., Lubbock, 1975-76; asst. prof. U. Tex., Austin, 1976-80, assoc. prof., 1980-84, prof. elec. and computer engring. and math., 1984—; rsch. assoc. in stats. U. Calif. Berkeley, 1989; tech. reviewer Rsch. Office U.S. Army, Durham, N.C., 1976, office sci. rsch. USAF, Washington, 1980-83, Harper and Row Pubs., N.Y.C., 1982-83, NSF, 1984, 87, 89, 90, Springer-Verlog Pubs., N.Y.C., 1987-88, John Wiley and Sons Pubs., N.Y.C., 1988, PWS-Kent Pubs., Boston, 1990; cons. Baylor Coll. Medicine, Houston, 1972; mem. control group League City Nat. Bank, 1978-82; speaker at numerous tech. confs. Contbr. chpts., numerous articles to profl. publs. Recipient award for outstanding contbns. to Coll. Engring., U. Tex. Engring. Found., 1979, 81; USAF Sci. rsch. grantee, 1976-90, Office of Naval Rsch. grantee, 1990—; rsch. contracts E-Systems, Inc., 1983-85; Carroll D. Simmons Centennial teaching fellow U. Tex., Austin, 1982-84. Mem. IEEE, Soc. Indsl. and Applied Math., Am. Math. Soc., Inst. Math. Stats., Math. Assn. Am., Eta Kappa Nu, Phi Beta Kappa, Tau Beta Pi. Methodist. Home: 40 N I H 35 Apt 5c2 Austin TX 78701-4351

WISE, GEORGE EDWARD, lawyer; b. Chgo., Feb. 26, 1924; s. George E. and Helen L. (Gray) W.; m. Patricia E. Finn, Aug. 3, 1945; children: Erich, Peter, Abbe, Raoul, John. JD, U. Chgo. Bar: Calif. 1949, U.S. Dist. Ct. (no. dist.) Calif. 1948, U.S. Ct. Appeals (9th cir.) 1948, U.S. Dist. Ct. (cen. dist.) 1950, U.S. Supreme CT. 1955. Law clk. Calif. Supreme Ct., 1948-49; sr. ptnr. Wise, Wiezorek, Timmons & Wise, Long Beach, 1949—; of counsel Wise Pearce Yocis & Smith, Long Beach. With USNR, 1943-45. Fellow Am. Coll. Trial Lawyers; mem. ABA, Los Angeles County Bar Assn., Long Beach Bar Assn. (pres. 1970, Atty. of Yr. 1990), Calif. State Bar. Home: 5401 E El Cedral St Long Beach CA 90815-4112 Office: Wise Pearce Yocis & Smith 249 E Ocean Blvd Ste 440 Long Beach CA 90802-4806 Personal E-mail: georgewise@yahoo.com.

WISE, JACK RONALD, music educator; b. Watseka, Ill., June 17, 1951; s. John Carroll and Rachel Mary Wise; m. Barbara Jean Given; children: Colin Jeffery, Erin Elizabeth, Sean Robert. BS in Music Edn., U. Ill., 1974; MusM, No. Ill. U., 1992. Cert. tchr. Ill., 1974. Tchr. music Decatur (Ill.) Pub. Schs., 1974—75, Orland Pk. (Ill.) Elem. Sch. Dist., 1975—76; from dir. band. elem. sch. to tchr. music Carptentersville (Ill.) Unified Sch. Dist., 1976—2001, tchr. music, 2001—. Cons. Crystal Lake (Ill.) Elem. Sch. Dist., 1992. Organizer, leader Appalachian Svc. Project Trips, Hampshire, Ill., 1996—2004. Mem.: NEA, Ill. Music Educator's Assn., Ill. Edn. Assn., Local Edn. Assn. Dundee (bldg. rep. 2002—06), Music Educator's Nat. Conf., Pi Kappa Phi. Methodist. Avocations: reading, musical performance, sports, mechanical work on instruments, woodworking. Office: Algonquin Middle School C U S D 300 520 Longwood Place Algonquin IL 60102 Office Phone: 847-658-2545. Business E-Mail: jack.wise@d300.org.

WISE, JOAN S., lawyer; b. Trenton, NJ, Aug. 11, 1941; BS in Edn., George Washington U., 1976; MA in Remedial Reading, U. Calif., 1979; JD, Georgetown U. Bar: Md. 1984, DC 1987, US Supreme Ct. 1988. Asst. atty. gen. consumer protection State of Md., staff atty. to atty. gen.; atty. to assoc. gen. counsel Am. Assn. Retired People (AARP), 1987—99, gen. counsel, 1999—. Mem.: Md. State Bar Assn., Inc., DC Bar Assn. Office: AARP 601 E St NW Washington DC 20049 *

WISE, JOHN AUGUSTUS, lawyer, director; b. Detroit, Mar. 30, 1938; s. John Augustus and Mary Blanche (Parent) W.; m. Helga M. Bessin, Nov. 27, 1965; children: Monique Elizabeth, John Eric. Student, U. Vienna, 1957—58; AB honors cum laude, Coll. Holy Cross, 1959; JD, U. Mich., 1962; postgrad., U. Munich Law Faculty, 1962—63. Bar: Mich. 1963, D.C. 1966. Assoc. Dykema, Gossett, Detroit, 1962-64; asst. to pres. Internat. Econ. Policy Assn., Washington, 1964-66; assoc. Parsons, Tennent, Hammond, Hardig & Ziegelman, Detroit, 1967-70; pres. Wise & Marsac P.C., Detroit, 1970-2001; sr. ptnr. Williams, Mullen, Clark & Dobbins, PLLC, Detroit, 2001—04; of counsel, ptnr. Howard & Howard, P.C., Detroit, 2004—. Dir. Peltzer & Ehlers Am. Corp., 1975-80, Colombian Am. Friends Inc., 1974-89. Bd. dirs. Hyde Park Coop., 1974-77; trustee Friends Sch., Detroit, 1977-81, Brighton Health Svcs. Corp., 1991-94, Providence Hosp., 2001—; chmn. bd. dirs. Brighton Hosp., 1995—; mem. Detroit Com. on Fgn. Rels. Ford Found. grantee U. Munich, 1962-63. Mem. ABA, Mich. Bar Assn., Detroit Bar Assn., Internat. Bar Assn., Detroit Athletic Club, Detroit Econ. Club. Roman Catholic. Home: 1221 Yorkshire Rd Grosse Pointe Park MI 48230-1105 Office: Pinehurst Ctr Ste 101 39400 Woodward Ave Bloomfield Hills MI 48304-5151 Office Phone: 248-723-0435. E-mail: jwise@howardandhoward.com.

WISE, JOHN MACGREGOR, speech educator; b. Napa, Calif., May 13, 1966; BA in Comm. and English, Trinity U., San Antonio, 1988; MA in Speech Comm., U. Ill., Urbana, 1990, PhD in Speech Comm., 1995. Asst. prof. Clemson U., SC, 1995—99, Ariz. State U., Phoenix, 1999—2003, assoc. prof., 2003—, chair, 2003—06. Author: Exploring Technology and Social Space, 1997, Culture and Technology:, 2005, Mediamaking, 2d edit., 2005. Mem.: Nat. Comm. assn., Internat. Comm. Assn. Office: Ariz State U 4701 West Thunderbird Rd Glendale AZ 85306

WISE, KIMBERLY ANNE (SCHILLACI), musician, educator; b. Painesville, Ohio, Apr. 15, 1975; d. Cynthia E and Kinton Connelly (Stepfather), Joseph S and Brenda Schillaci (Stepmother); m. Jeff Wise, June 16, 2000. MusB in Edn., Baldwin-Wallace Coll., 1998; MusM in Edn., VanderCook Coll. Music, 2004. Cert. tchr. N.C., 2002. Asst. dir. bands Parkwood Mid. and High Schs., Monroe, NC, 1998—2002; dir. bands and music East Lincoln Mid. Sch., Iron Station, 2002—; asst. dir. marching band East Lincoln H.S., Denver, 2002—. Brass performer Theatre Charlotte, 1999—99; asst. prin. horn Winthrop U. Olde English Wind Ensemble, Rock Hill, 2001—; prin. horn U. N.C. Charlotte Cmty. Band, 2003—. Musician: (performance) Winthrop Olde English Wind Ensemble (Selected to perform at the Am. Bandmasters Assn. Ann. Conv., 2005). V.p., sec. treas. VanderCook Coll. Music, 2004. Recipient John Philip Sousa Outstanding Band Mem. award, Riverside H.S. Band, 1993; scholar, U.S. Achievement Acad., 1997. Mem.: South Ctrl. Dist. Bandmasters Assn., Nat. Band Assn., Music Educator's Nat. Conf., Omicron Delta Kappa, Mu Phi Epsilon. Avocations: french horn, travel. Home: 12251 Fullerton Ct Charlotte NC 28214 Office: East Lincoln Mid Sch 4137 Highway 73 Iron Station NC 28080 Home Phone: 704-697-8776; Office Phone: 704-732-0761. Office Fax: 704-732-4456. Personal E-mail: kimberly@oldmedia.com. E-mail: kwise3@lincoln.k12.nc.us.

WISE, LORRAINE E., educational consultant; d. Alonza Jerome and Elsie Virginia Beulah; 1 child, Hillary Lauren Beulah. BA, Fed. City Coll., 1974; MSW, Howard U., 1977. From program asst. to sr. policy specialist US Dept. Edn., 1974—94, sr. policy specialist student achievement and sch. accountability programs, 1994—. Nat. parental involvement expert US Dept. Edn., Office Elem. and Secondary Edn., Student Achievement ans Sch. Accountability, Washington, 1994—. Contbg. author Reaching All Families: Creating Family-Friendly Schools, Family Involvement in Children's Education:Successful Local Approaches, discussant (various profl. symposiums), expert (various parental involvement programs); contbr. chapters to books. Recipient Plaque for Continued Support, Nat. Coalition Title I Chpt. 1 Parents Bd. Dirs., 2001, VIP award, Nat. Coalition Title I Parents, 2003, Plaque, NJ Assn. Parent Coord., Commitment and Dedication to Parents, 2003, Nat. Coalition of ESEA Title I Parents, 2005. Mem.: Am. Ednl. Rsch. Assn. Office: US Dept Edn 400 Md Ave SW Washington DC 20202 Office Phone: 202-260-1406. Business E-Mail: lorraine.wise@ed.gov.

WISE, MARK B., physics professor; b. Montreal, Canada, Nov. 9, 1953; BSc, U. Toronto, 1976, MSc, 1977; PhD, Stanford U., Calif., 1980. Asst. prof. theoretical physics Calif. Inst. Tech., 1982—84, assoc. prof.,

1984—85, prof., 1985—92, John A. McCone prof. high energy physics, 1992—. Recipient Loeb lectr., Harvard U., 1998, Sakurai prize, Am. Phys. Soc., 2001; Alfred P. Sloan fellowship, Alfred P. Sloan Found., 1984—86. Fellow: Am. Acad. Arts and Scis.; mem.: NAS, Harvard Soc. Fellows (jr. fellow 1980—83). Office: Calif Inst Tech Particle Theory Group Mail Code 452-48 1200 E California Blvd Pasadena CA 91125 Office Phone: 626-395-6687. Office Fax: 626-568-8473. E-mail: wise@theory.caltech.edu. *

WISE, PATRICIA, opera singer, educator; b. Wichita, Kans. d. Melvin R. and Genevieve F. (Dotson) W.; 1 child, Jennifer. B. Music Edn., U. Kans., Lawrence, 1966. Prof. voice Ind. U. Sch. Music, Bloomington, 1995—; tchr. master classes San Francisco, Vienna Conservatory, Salzburg (Austria) Mozarteum; voice tchr. Domingo Young Artist program Washington Opera. Debut as Susanna in Marriage of Figaro, Kansas City, 1966; prin. roles include Lucia, Gilda, Micaela, Juliette, Zerbinetta, Pamina, Musetta, Lulu, Violetta, Nedda, others; appeared with leading Am. opera cos. including, Chgo., Santa Fe, N.Y.C., San Francisco, Houston, San Diego, Miami, Balt., Phila., Pitts.; European appearances, 1971-76, London Royal Opera, Glyndebourne Festival, Vienna Volksoper, Geneva Opera; guest artist with Vienna, Hamburg, Munich, Cologne, Frankfurt, and Berlin State Operas; guest appearances in Madrid, Barcelona, Rome, La Scala Milan, Nice, Paris Chatelet, Zurich, Dresden, Salzburg Festival, Theatro Colon, Buenos Aires; appeared with orchs. including, Chgo. Symphony Orch., Los Angeles Symphony Orch., N.Y. Handel Soc., Israel Philharm. Orch., Vienna Philharm. Orch., N.Y. Philharm., Cleve. Orch., Berlin Symphonic Orch., BBC Orch., Nat. Orch. France; Angel Recordings; internat. TV, film appearances. Recipient Morton Baum award N.Y.C. Ctr., 1971, Dealey Meml. award Dallas Symphony, 1966, Naftzger young Artist award Wichita Symphony, 1966, Midland Young Artist award Midland (Tex.) Symphony Orch., 1966; M.B. Rockefeller Fund grantee, 1967-70; Sullivan Found. grantee, 1967-68; named Kammersänger Vienna Staatsoper, 1989. E-mail: patwise@indiana.edu.

WISE, ROBERT F., JR., lawyer; b. Bronxville, NY, Oct. 1, 1947; m. Alison Bell; children: Katherine B., Robert A. BA with high distinction, U. Va., 1969; JD, Yale U., 1972. Bar: NY 1973, US Dist. Ct. (so. and ea. dists.) NY 1973, US Ct. Appeals (2d cir.) 1973, US Supreme Ct. 1980. Assoc. Davis Polk & Wardwell, NYC, 1972—79, ptnr., 1979—. Taught U. New Haven. Contbr. articles to profl. jours. Pres. Purchase (NY) Environ. Protective Assn., 1988-92, 1st lt. USAFR, 1969-73. Mem. ABA (chaired fin. markets subcom. ins. com. antitrust sect.), Fed. Bar Coun., NY Bar Assn. (chmn. fed. procedure com. 1991-), NYC Bar Assn. (com. on State Cts. superior jurisdiction and juvenile justice com.), Westchester Country Club (bd. govs. 1993-), co-chair Joint com. on Local Rules So. and ea. Dist. NY, fellow Am. coll. Trial Lawyers. Office: Davis Polk & Wardwell 450 Lexington Ave Fl 31 New York NY 10017-3982 Office Phone: 212-450-4512. Office Fax: 212-450-3512. E-mail: robert.wise@dpw.com.

WISE, ROBERT POWELL, lawyer; b. Jackson, Miss., Nov. 13, 1951; s. Sherwood Willing and Elizabeth (Powell) W. AB, Colgate U., 1973; MA, U. Va., 1975; JD, Washington & Lee U., 1979. Bar: Miss. 1979, U.S. Dist. Ct. Miss. 1979, U.S. Ct. Appeals (5th cir.) 1988. Ptnr. Wise, Carter, Child & Caraway, Jackson, 1979—. Lic. lay reader, chalice bearer St. Andrews Episc. Cathedral, Jackson, 1984—; pres. Caledonian Soc. Miss., Jackson, 1987, bd. dirs., 1985-90; bd. dirs. Belhaven Improvement Assn., 1991—, pres., 1994-97, v.p., 1999—, English Speaking Union of Miss., Jackson, 1985-92, Nat. Kidney Found. Miss., 1987—, v.p., 1988-92, pres. 1993-94; pres. Belhaven Security Assn., 1992-93. Mem. ABA (forums on constrn. and comm. law), Fed. Comm. Bar Assn., Miss. Bar Assn. Office: 600 Heritage Bldg PO Box 651 Jackson MS 39205-0651 Home: 656 Highleadon Pl Madison MS 39110-7655 Office Phone: 601-968-5561, 601-968-5500. Business E-Mail: rpw@wisecarter.com.

WISE, THERESA, air transportation executive; BA in Math. and Chemistry, St. Olaf Coll., Northfield, Minn.; MS in Ops. Rsch. and Applied Math., PhD in Ops. Rsch. and Applied Math., Cornell U., Ithaca, NY. With NW Airlines Corp., Minn., 1993—, mng. dir. info. svcs., v.p. Info. Svcs. Group, 2001—07, sr. v.p., chief info. officer, 2007—. Office: NW Airlines Corp 2700 Lone Oak Pky Eagan MN 55121 Office Phone: 612-726-2111. *

WISE, WILLIAM EDWARD, JR., colon and rectal surgeon, oncologist; b. St. Louis, Mo., July 5, 1954; MD, Boston U. Sch. Medicine, 1983. Cert. Colon & Rectal Surgery, Surgery. Intern, surgery Ohio State U., Columbus, Ohio, 1983—84, resident, colon & rectal surgery, 1984—89, clin. asst. prof.; fellow Grant Med. Ctr., Columbus, Ohio, 1989—90, hosp. appointment, 1990—, Riverside Methodist Hosp., Columbus, Ohio, 1990—; with practice Colon & Rectal Surgery Assocs., Columbus, Ohio. Office: Colon & Rectal Surgical Assocs 3545 Olentangy River Rd #500 Columbus OH 43214 Office Phone: 614-263-2138. Office Fax: 614-263-8893. *

WISE, WILLIAM JERRARD, lawyer; b. Chgo., May 27, 1934; s. Gerald Paul and Harriet Muriel (Rosenblum) Wise; m. Peggy Spero, Sept. 3, 1959; children: Deborah, Stephen, Betsy, Lynne. BBA, U. Mich., 1955, MBA, 1958, JD with distinction, 1958. Bar: Ill. 1959. Spl. atty. Office Regional Counsel, IRS, Milw., 1959-63; with McDermott, Will & Emery, Chgo., 1963-70, Coles & Wise, Ltd., Chgo., 1971—80, Wise & Stracks, Ltd., Chgo., 1980—2000, Querrey & Harrow, Chgo., 2000—. Lectr., contbr. Ill. Inst. Continuing Legal Edn.; arbitrator Cir. Ct. Cook County Ill., 1990—. Bd. dirs. Blind Svc. Assn., Chgo., 1964—74; active Village of Winnetka, Ill., 1974—75; dir., treas. Suzuki Orff Sch. Young Musicians, Chgo., 1981—91. With US Army, 1958—59. Mem.: Chgo. Bar Assn. Home: 1401 Tower Rd Winnetka IL 60093-1628 Office: Querrey & Harrow 175 W Jackson Blvd Ste 1600 Chicago IL 60604-2827 Home Phone: 847-446-2079; Office Phone: 312-540-7104. Personal E-mail: dididoe@yahoo.com. *I believe that one succeeds best in our society if one gives as little thought as possible to one's personal well being.*

WISEHART, MARY RUTH, retired religious organization administrator; b. Myrtle, Mo., Nov. 2, 1932; d. William Henry and Ora (Harbison) W. BA, Free Will Bapt. Bible Coll., 1955, George Peabody Coll. Tchrs., 1959, MA, 1960, PhD, 1976. Tchr. Free Will Bapt. Bible Coll., Nashville, 1956-60, chmn. English dept., 1961-85; exec. sec.-treas. Free Will Bapt. Women Nat. Active for Christ, 1985-98. Author: Sparks Into Flame, 1985, Beyond the Gate, 1998; contbr. poetry to jours. Mem. Scribbler's Club. Free Will Baptist. Avocations: photography, music, drama. Personal E-mail: wisemrw@aol.com.

WISEHEART, MALCOLM BOYD, JR., lawyer; b. Miami, Fla., Sept. 18, 1942; s. Malcolm B. and Dorothy E. (Allen) Wiseheart; m. Michele I. Romanens, Dec. 11, 1976. BA, Yale U., 1965; MA in English Jurisprudence, Cambridge U., 1973; JD with honors, U. Fla., 1970. Bar: Fla. 1970, Eng. 1970, Wales 1970, Jamaica 1970, Trinidad and Tobago 1971, DC 1980. Assoc. Helliwell, Melrose & DeWolf, Miami, 1970-72; pvt. practice Miami, 1973—86, 1987—; sr. ptnr. Wiseheart & Joyce, P.A., Miami, 1986—87. Sec., gen. counsel Wiseheart Found., pres., 1985—2007; spl. master Dade County Property Appraisal Adjustment Bd., 1977—90; pres. Fla. Law Inst., 1980—2007; bd. dirs. Sta. WLRN Pub. Radio, 1982; dir. Yale Alumni Schs. Com. S. Fla., 2001—06; bd. dirs. Coun. Internat. Visitors. Bd. trustees Ransom Everglades Sch., 1995—97; bd. trustees, mem. exec. com. Players State Theater, 1982—84. Named Most Outstanding, U. Fla. Law Rev. Alumnus, 1981. Mem.: Gray's Inn of Ct., London (barrister), Order of Coif, Dade County Bar Assn. (dir. 1971—74, treas. 1974—75, sec. 1975—77, dir. 1986—89), Fla. Bar (chmn. grievance com. 1978—81), United Oxford and Cambridge Univs. Club (London), Yale Club (Miami pres. 1976—77). Office: Wiseheart Bldg 2840 SW 3rd Ave Miami FL 33129-2317 Home Phone: 305-667-8976; Office Phone: 305-285-1222. E-mail: mbwjr@bellsouth.net.

WISEMAN, ALAN M(ITCHELL), lawyer; b. Long Branch, NJ, July 6, 1944; s. Lincoln B. and Gertrude (Gorcey) W.; m. Paula Wiseman, July 8, 1965; children: Steven, David, Julie. BA, Johns Hopkins U., 1965; JD, Georgetown U., 1968. Bar: Md. 1968, Ill. 1970, DC 1973. Law clk. Hon. William J. McWilliams, Md. Ct. Appeals, 1968-69; assoc. Schiff, Hardin & Waite, Chgo., 1970-74; ptnr. Howrey Simon Arnold White, LLP, Washington, 1976—, co-chair antitrust practice group, chmn. pro bono and charitable activities com. Editor Georgetown Law Jour., 1967-68. Mem. US C. of C. (coun. antitrust policy 1983-2001). Office: 1299 Pennsylvania Ave NW Washington DC 20004-2400 Office Phone: 202-383-6638, 202-783-0800. Business E-Mail: wisemana@howrey.com.

WISEMAN, CARTER STERLING, writer, educator; b. NYC, Oct. 8, 1945; s. Mark Huntington Wiseman and Eleanor (Carter) Wood; m. Eileen Condon, Oct. 19, 1985; children: Emma, Owen, Damian. BA, Yale U., 1968; MA, Columbia U., 1972. Newsman AP, NYC, 1972-74; assoc. editor Newsweek Mag., NYC, 1974-77; sr. editor Horizon Mag., NYC, 1977-79; mng. editor Portfolio Mag., NYC, 1979-80; archtl. critic N.Y. Mag., NYC, 1980-96; editor Yale Alumni Mag., New Haven, 1986—2002; lectr. Yale Sch. Architecture, New Haven, 2002—. Bd. dirs. MacDowell Colony, Peterborough, NH, pres., 1999—; tchr. The Reading Co., Westport, Conn., 2003—07, Ednl. Solutions Group, Westport, Conn., 2007—. Author: Twentieth Century American Architecture, 2000, I.M. Pei, 2001, Louis I. Kahn, 2007; contbg. editor: ARTnews, 1996—; editor: A Place for the Arts, 2006. Chair Loeb Fellowship Assn. Harvard U., 1986—95. With US Army, 1968—71. Recipient Spl. Citation award, Am. Inst. Arch., 1984, Inst. Honor award, Am. Inst. Archs., 1987, Interpretative Writing award, Soc. Silurians, 1985, Roger Starr award, Citizens Housing and Planning Coun., 1987, 1990; Loeb fellow, Harvard U., 1985. Mem.: Century Assn., Yale Club N.Y. Office: 16 W Branch Rd Weston CT 06883-2917 Personal E-mail: writertime@aol.com.

WISEMAN, CRAIG, song writer, publisher; b. Hattiesburg, Miss. With Almo Irving Music Publishing, 1990—2000, BMG Music Publishing, 2000—04; owner Big Loud Shirt Industries, 2004—. Mem. adv. bd. ASCAP. Composer over 11 number one country singles including, (Kenny Chesney) Young, She's Got It All, The Good Stuff (Country Song of Yr. Billboard Mag., 2002, ASCAP Song of Yr., 2004), (Tim McGraw) Everywhere, The Cowboy in Me, Live Like You Were Dying (Country Music Assn. Song of Yr. & Single of Yr., 2004, Acad. Country Music Song of Yr. & Single of Yr., 2005, Grammy award for Best Country Song, 2005), (Phil Vasser) Just Another Day in Paradise, (Lonestar) Tell Her, (Brooks & Dunn) Believe (Country Music Assn. Song of Yr., 2006). Named Writer of Yr., Music Row Mag., 1997, Nashville Songwriters Assn., 1997; recipient Songwriter of Yr. award, ASCAP, 2004. Mem.: Nashville Songwriter's Assn. Internat. (mem. exec. bd.), Country Music Assn. Office: Big Loud Shirt Industries LLC 1105 17th Ave S Nashville TN 37212

WISEMAN, DENNIS R., science educator; b. Jeffersonville, Ind., Apr. 21, 1952; s. Helen P. Wiseman. BS in Elem. Edn., Ind. U., New Albany, 1970—80; MEd, U. Louisville, Ky., 1984—87. Tchr. Jefferson County Pub. Schs., Louisville, 1984—2006, sci. consulting tchr., 2006—. Mem.: NEA. Home: 4525 Estate Dr Louisville KY 40216 Office: 4309 Bishop Ln Louisville KY 40218 Home Phone: 502-380-9060.

WISEMAN, DONALD F., lawyer; b. Cairo, Ill., 1946; BA, Univ. Va., 1968; JD, Memphis State Univ., 1976. Bar: Tenn. 1976. Atty. Fed. Express Corp., 1976—79, private practice, 1979—91; v.p., gen. counsel, sec. The Restaurant Co., 1991—2003, Swift & Co., Colo., 2003—06, sr. v.p., gen. counsel, sec., 2006—. Served as helicopter pilot US Army, Vietnam. Office: Swift & Co 1770 Promontory Circle Greeley CO 80634

WISEMAN, DOUGLAS CARL, education educator, department chairman, dean; b. Nashua, NH, Feb. 28, 1935; s. Howard W. and Ruth D. (Aiken) W.; m. Donna Wiseman; children: Mark, Cynthia, Lori, Alan, Kathleen, Steve. BEd, Plymouth State Coll., NH, 1961; MS, Ind. U., 1962, PED, 1970. Cert. tchr. health, math., phys. edn., sci. Tchr., track coach Nashua (N.H.) Pub. Schs., 1960-61, tchr., baseball coach, 1962-63; tchg. asst. Ind. U., Bloomington, 1961-62; tchr. high sch., wrestling coach Portage (Mich.) High Sch., 1963-64; instr., asst. prof., soccer, wrestling and tennis coach Plymouth (N.H.) State Coll., 1964-69; asst. prof. Northeastern U., Boston, 1969-71; dir. athletics, chmn. phys. edn. dept. Plymouth State Coll., 1971-80, assoc. dean, dir. undergrad. studies, 1993-96, prof., accreditation coord., 1996-98, ret., 1998, prof. emeritus, 1998—; prof., chair dept. edn. Univ. Sys. of N.H., 1980—. Aquatics cons. Am./Nat. Red Cross, Laconia, N.H., 1971-98, State Dept. Edn., Concord, 1980-98. Author, contbg. editor: Adapted Physical Education, 1982, Practical Research, 1989, Quantitative Research, 1992, Physical Education for Exceptional Students, 1994, Introduction to Educational Research, 1995, Educational Research, 1996, Research Strategies for Education, 1999; contbr. more than 50 articles to profl. jours. Cert. police officer Ashland, N.H., 1992-98; chair sch. bd. Plymouth Regional Sch. Dist., 1989-91; divsn. staff officer-pub. edn., flotilla career counseling officer USCG Aux., 2001-2002; deacon Superstition Foothills Baptist Ch., 2007-. with US Army, 1953-56, US Paratroopers, 1954—56; hon. discharge 1956. AAHPERD Ea. Dist. scholar, 1990-91. Republican. Avocations: reading, hiking, boating, Tae Kwon Do. Personal E-mail: seaquest05@msn.com.

WISEMAN, ERIC C., apparel executive; BS, MBA, Wake Forest Univ. Exec. v.p. JanSport VF Corp., Greensboro, NC, 1995—98, pres. Bestform Intimates, 1998—2000, v.p. & chmn. global intimate apparel, 2000—03, v.p. & chmn. sportswear coalition, 2003—04, v.p. & chmn. outdoor & sportswear coalitions, 2004—05, exec. v.p. global brands, 2005—06, pres., COO, 2006—. Office: VF Corp 105 Corporate Ctr Blvd Greensboro NC 27408 Mailing: VF Corp PO Box 21488 Greensboro NC 27420-1488 *

WISEMAN, FLOYD LANDIS, chemist; b. Oakland, Calif., Mar. 21, 1956; s. James Edward and Nora Gail Wiseman; m. Jacqueline Sue Snider, Jan. 13, 1978; children: James Matthew, John Mark, Fallon Rene. BS in Chemistry, U. Tenn., Martin, 1978; PhD in Chemistry, La. State U., Baton Rouge, 1982. Postdoctoral assoc. La. State U., 1982—84; commd. 2d lt. USAF, 1984, advanced through grades to maj., 1996; prof. USAF Acad., Colorado Springs, Colo., 1988—92, US Mil. Acad., West Point, NY, 1999—2004; ret. USAF, 2004; sr. scientist ENSCO, Inc., Melbourne, Fla., 2004—. Contbr. articles to profl. jours. Missions coord. River of Life Ch., Merritt Island, Fla. Decorated Commendation medal USAF, Meritorious Svc. medal. Republican. Mem. Assemblies Of God. Avocations: music, writing. Home: 1740 Curlew Ct Viera FL 32955 Office: ENSCO, Inc 4849 N Wickham Rd Melbourne FL 32940

WISEMAN, FRANK L., JR., chemistry professor; Prof., chair chemistry dept. Georgetown Coll., Ky. Recipient US Prof. of Yr. award, Carnegie Found. for Advancement of Tchg. and Coun. for Advancement and Support of Edn., 2006. Avocations: painting, hunting. Office: Chemistry Dept Georgetown Coll 400 E College St Georgetown KY 40324 Office Phone: 502-863-8103. E-mail: Frank_Wiseman@georgetowncollege.edu. *

WISEMAN, JANE, broadcast executive; b. Aug. 24, 1971; m. Joe Wiseman. Asst. to head writer of Gen. Hosp. ABC; asst. on Ink CBS; exec. comedy dept. Fox Broadcasting Co., 2000; v.p. comedy devel. NBC Entertainment, Burbank, Calif. Achievements include working on the TV shows Andy Richter Controls the Universe, The Bernie Mac Show, Undeclared, Arrested Development, The Simple Life, Twenty Good Years, 30 Rock and the upcoming The Singles Table. Office: NBC Entertainment 3000 W Alameda Ave Burbank CA 91523 *

WISEMAN, LAURENCE DONALD, foundation executive; b. Washington, Feb. 24, 1947; s. Leon Robert and Marion (Wiseman; m. Robin Lynn Jeweler, May 29, 1978; children: Justin J., David B. AB with highest distinction, Dartmouth Coll., 1969; M in Pub. Affairs, Princeton U., 1971. Exec. producer Sta. WQED-TV (pub. broadcasting), Pitts., 1971-75; prin. Moses, Epstein and Wiseman, Washington, 1975-78; v.p. Yankelovich, Skelly and White, NYC, 1978-81, Am. Forest Council, Washington, 1981-84, pres., 1984—. Pres. Am. Forest Coun., 1984-92, Am. Forest Found., 1993—; external adv. bd. mem., Global Inst. Sustainable Forestry, Yale U., 2005-. Author: Coalition Building, 1977. Bd. dirs. Cystic Fibrosis Found., N.Y.C., 1979-80, Urban Philharm., Washington, 1980-83, Sasha Bruce House, Washington, 1980-82; adv. com. Soc. for Profl. Journalists, Washington, 1984; trustee Nat. Ctr. for Housing and the Environment, 2001—; hon. trustee Nat. Arbor Day Found., Nebraska City, Nebr., 1984—; chair Nat. Coun. on Pvt. Forests, 1997-98, Inst. for Journalism and Natural Resources, 1998—. Mem. Am. Forestry Assn., Soc. Am. Foresters, Pub. Rels. Soc. Am. Home: 10621 Democracy Ln Potomac MD 20854-4016 Office: Am Forest Found 1111 19th St NW Washington DC 20036-3603 Business E-Mail: lwiseman@forestfoundation.org. E-mail: lwiseman@affoundation.org.

WISEMAN, MICHAEL MARTIN, lawyer; b. NYC, Oct. 25, 1953; s. Robert Lawrence and Katherine Loise (Martin) W.; m. Helen Ann Garten, May 18, 1984. BA, Harvard U., 1975, JD, 1978. Bar: NY 1979, Mass. 1978, US Dist. Ct. (so. and ea. dists.) NY 1979, US Supreme Ct. 1988. Assoc. Sullivan & Cromwell, NYC, 1978-85, ptnr., 1985—, and mng. ptnr. fin. institutions practice area. Mem. NY State Bar Banking Law Com.; former mem. Russian-Am. Bankers Forum. Contbr. articles to profl. jours. Fellow Am. Bar Found.; mem. ABA (vice chair banking, currency and treasury com. of adminstrv. law sect. 1991-94), Assn. Bar City NY (chair com. on banking law 1985-91, chair 1988-91), Am. Law Inst. Office: Sullivan & Cromwell 125 Broad St Fl 28 New York NY 10004-2489 Office Phone: 212-558-3846. Office Fax: 212-558-3588. Business E-Mail: wisemanm@sullcrom.com.

WISEMAN, THOMAS ANDERTON, JR., federal judge; b. Tullahoma, Tenn., Nov. 3, 1930; s. Thomas Anderton and Vera Seleta (Poe) W.; m. Emily Barbara Matlack, Mar. 30, 1957; children: Thomas Anderton III, Mary Alice, Sarah Emily. BA, Vanderbilt U., 1952, LL.B., 1954; LLM, U. Va., 1990. Bar: Tenn. Pvt. practice, Tullahoma, 1956-63; ptnr. Haynes, Wiseman & Hull, Tullahoma and Winchester, Tenn., 1963-71; treas. Tenn., 1971-74; ptnr. Chambers & Wiseman, 1974-78; judge U.S. Dist. Ct. (mid. dist.) Tenn., Nashville, 1978—, chief judge, 1984-91, sr. judge, 1995—; 6th cir. rep. Jud. Conf. of the U.S., 1996—2001, chair dist. judges conf., 1998-99. Mem. Tenn. Ho. of Reps., 1964-68; adj. prof. law Vanderbilt U. Sch. Law; cons. to judiciary of Brcko, Bosnia, 2002; mem. pattern jury instrn. com. 6th cir., 1988—. Asso. editor: Vanderbilt Law Rev, 1953-54. Democratic candidate for gov., Tenn., 1974; Chmn. Tenn. Heart Fund, 1973, Middle Tenn. Heart Fund, 1972. Served with U.S. Army, 1954-56. Fellow Tenn. Bar Found.; mem. Fed. Judges Assn. (bd. dirs. 1982-87, v.p. 1982-91, 87-91), Masons (33 deg.), Shriners, Amateur Chefs Soc. Presbyterian. Office: US Dist Ct 777 US Courthouse 801 Broadway Nashville TN 37203-3816 Office Phone: 615-736-7013.

WISEMAN, THOMAS G., lawyer; b. Bklyn., Sept. 8, 1947; BS, L.I. Univ., 1969; MS, Pa. State Univ., 1971; JD, Univ. Balt., 1982. Bar: Va. 1984, DC 1998, US Patent & Trademark Office. Primary patent examiner U.S. Patent & Trademark Office, 1972—83, supervising patent examiner, 1983—90, examiner in chief, 1990—91; acting patent branch chief Office Tech. Transfer, NIH, 1991—93; ptnr., Patent Prosecution, Intellectual Property Litigation practices Venable LLP, Washington. Lectr. L.I. Univ., 1972. Mem.: ABA, Am. Intellectual Property Assn., Va. State Bar Assn., DC Bar Assn., Am. Chemical Soc., Am. Assn. for Advancement of Sci. Office: Venable LLP 575 7th St NW Washington DC 20004 Office Phone: 202-344-4614. Office Fax: 202-344-8300. Business E-Mail: tgwiseman@venable.com.

WISH, JAY BARRY, nephrologist, specialist; b. Hartford, Mar. 30, 1950; s. Martin and Evelyn Lillian (Lassman) W.; m. Linda Kristina Hansen, June 29, 1971; (div. 1980); children: Allen Jeremy, Robin Lindsey; m. Diane Elizabeth Perkins, June 5, 1983 (div. 2006); children: Jeffrey Bryan, David Phillip. BA, Wesleyan U., 1970; MD, Tufts U., 1974. Diplomate Am. Bd. Internal Medicine, Am. Bd. Nephrology. Resident in medicine New England Med. Ctr., Boston, 1974-79; instr. in medicine Tufts U., Boston, 1978-79; lectr. in health sci. Northeastern U., Boston, 1978-79; asst. prof. of medicine Case Western Res. U., Cleve., 1979-85, assoc. prof. of medicine, 1985-96, prof. medicine, 1996—; dir. hemodialysis U. Hosps. of Cleve., 1980—, dir. continuing edn., 1987-95. Chmn. Med. Adv. Bd. Kidney Found. of Ohio, Cleve., 1985-88. Author: Renal Disease and Hypertension, 1982, Disorders of Potassium, 1984, Metabolic Diseases, 1986, Rheumatic Diseases of the Kidney, 1993, Acid-Base and Electrolyte Disorders in the Critically Ill Patient, 1993, Assuring Quality of Care in Dialysis Patients, 1994, Algorithms and Care Paths for Quality Improvement, 2000, Adequacy of Hemodialysis, 2002, Quality, Safety and Accountability in Dialysis, 2004; contbr. articles to med. jours. Chmn. med. rev. bd. End-Stage Renal Disease Network #22, Pitts., 1982-87, End-State Renal Disease Network #9, Indpls., 1992-2000, pres., 2001-06; mem. exec. com. Forum of End-Stage Renal Disease Networks, 1992-2006, v.p., 1996-98, pres., 1998-2001; bd. dirs. Renal Phys. Assn., 1993-99, sec. 1996-97, treas., 1997-98; mem. Nat. Kidney Found. Fellow Am. Coll. of Physicians; mem. Cleve. Restoration Soc., Am. Soc. of Nephrology, Internat. Soc. of Nephrology, Alpha Omega Alpha. Democrat. Jewish. Avocation: performing arts. Office: U Hosps Cleve 11100 Euclid Ave Cleveland OH 44106-1736 Home Phone: 216-849-3950; Office Phone: 216-844-3163. Personal E-mail: jaywish@earthlink.net.

WISH, LESLIEBETH BERGER, psychotherapist, writer, management consultant; d. Irving L. and Miriam Solomon Berger; m. Peter A. Wish, Nov. 16, 1984; 1 stepchild, Carly Sidra. AB in History & English, Carnegie Mellon U., 1970; MA in English, Ohio U., 1971; MA in Social Svc. Mgmt., Byrn Mawr Coll., 1976; EdD in Human Devel., U. Mass., 1996. Lic. clin. social worker Md., 1980, Mass., 1982, Fla., 2003, diplomate clin. social work Bd. Examiners, 1988; cert. aquatics fitness instr. 2005. Post doctoral tng. in marriage & family therapy sys. Georgetown U. Med. Sch., DC, 1979—82; dir. social work & families The Linwood Sch., Ellicott City, Md., 1980—81; dir. human resource devel. & clin. svcs. The New England Inst. Family Rels., Framingham, Mass., 1982—94; faculty coord., admissions acad. advisor Grad. Ctr. Bus. & Counseling Webster U., Sarasota, 2001—04; v.p. Gulfcoast Healthstyle, Sarasota, Fla., 1994—. Girls' career workshop developer Girls, Inc., Sarasota, Fla., 2006—; lectr., cons. in field. Author: Incest, Women & Work, 1998; author, contbg. editor: Trafalgar Publs., 2001—06; contbr. articles to popular mags.; author numerous poems. Chair Sarasota Women's Advisory Commn., 1994—2001; pres. coun. Easter Seals, 2002—; co-coord. counseling network, spl. ops. Warrior Found., 2006—; co-coord. counselor network Spl. Ops. Warrior Found.; co-coord. Child Abuse Task Force, Sarasota, 2006—07; active Girls, Inc., Sarasota, 2006—, program and workshop devel., 2006—, The Women's Resource Ctr., Sarasota, 2007—. Recipient Md.'s Best Small Press award, Md. Arts Commn., 1981. Mem.: Am. Biog. Inst. (Woman Yr. 2006), Women's Leadership & Acad. Honor Society (mortar bd. 1970), Phi

Kappa Phi. Achievements include first to expand sex education and awareness of sexual issues at work and home for The New England Institute of Family Relations; research in the connection between childhood sexual abuse and its impact on work and career in women; on career-family history inventory. Avocations: travel, opera, writing, painting.

WISHARD, DELLA MAE, former newspaper editor; b. Bison, SD, Oct. 21, 1934; d. Ervin E. and Alma J. (Albertson) Preszler; m. Glenn L. Wishard, Oct. 18, 1953; children: Glenda Lee, Pamela A., Glen Evin. Grad. HS, Bison. Mem. SD Ho. of Reps., Pierre, 1984-96; pub., editor Bison Courier, SD, 1996-2000; owner Wishards Rentals, Rapid City, SD, 2004—. Colunist: County Farm Bur., 1970—96. State comitteewoman Rep. Ctrl. Com., Perkins County, SD, 1980—84, SD, 1998—2001; Rep. precinct comitteewoman Pennington County, 2006—; chmn. Perkins County Rep., 2000—03. Mem.: SD Farm Bur. (state officer 1982), Am. Legis. Exch. Coun. (state coord. 1985—91, state chmn. 1991—96), Fed. Rep. Women (chmn. Perkins County chpt. 1978—84). Lutheran. Avocations: writing, gardening. Home and Office: 3900 S Valley Dr Rapid City SD 57703 Personal E-mail: wishd@wes.comm.com.

WISHARD, GORDON DAVIS, lawyer; b. Indpls., Jan. 7, 1945; s. William Niles Jr. and Caroline (Davis) W.; m. Anne Emison; children: Claire Wishard Hoppenworth, Gordon Davis Jr. BA, Williams Coll., 1966; JD, Ind. U., 1969. Bar: Ind. 1969, US Dist. Ct. (so. dist.) Ind. 1969, US Ct. Appeals (7th cir.) 1976, US Supreme Ct. 1980, US Tax Ct. 1983. Ptnr. Ice Miller, Indpls. Mem. Am. Coll. Trust and Estate Coun. (Ind. chmn. 1990-95). Avocations: hunting, fishing. Office: Ice Miller 1 American Sq Indianapolis IN 46282-0020 Office Phone: 317-236-2331.

WISHART, RONALD SINCLAIR, retired chemical company executive; b. Bklyn., Mar. 1, 1925; s. Ronald Sinclair and Elizabeth Lathrop (Phillips) W.; m. Betty B. Burnup, Sept. 14, 1951 (dec. Dec. 1973); children: Michael Sinclair, James Ronald; m. Eleanor Dorothy Parrish Dooley, Jan. 11, 1975; stepchildren: Donna Dooley Willix, Arthur D. Dooley. BChemE, Rensselaer Poly. Inst., Troy, NY, 1948. Engr., chemist Linde air divsn. Union Carbide Corp., Tonawanda, NY, 1948-51; sales rep. Chgo., Cleve., 1951-56; region mgr. Chgo., 1956-57; product mgr., mktg. mgr. Silicones divsn. NYC, 1957-64; gen. mgr., pres., 1964-66; pres. devel. and coating materials divsns., 1966-71; corp. dir. energy and transp. policy, 1972-82; v.p. fed. govt. rels., 1983-85; v.p. pub. affairs Danbury, Conn., 1985-90; chief of staff to chmn. of corp. Union Carbide, NYC, 1984-85. Mem. adv. coun. Gas Rsch. Inst., Energy Modeling Ctr., Stanford U., 1979-83, Environ. and Energy Policy Ctr., John F. Kennedy Sch. Pub. Policy, Harvard U., 1980-87; energy com. Aspen Inst., 1976-88; chmn., exec. dir. Electricity Consumers Resource Coun., Washington, 1976-79. Author: The Marketing Factor, 1966; contbr. chpts. to books and articles to profl. jours.; patentee silicone formulas. Vol. Am. Field Svc., Burma, 1944-45; pres., trustee, elder White Plains Presbyn. Ch., NY, 1987-90; elder Palm City Presbyn. Ch., 1996-2002; treas., bd. dirs. St. Christopher's Jenni Clarkson Home, 1968-91; mem. exec. bd. Westchester Putnam coun. Boy Scouts Am., White Plains, 1985-91; v.p. Carbide Retiree Corps.; v.p. Hospice Martin and St. Lucie, Inc., 1994-99, pres. 2000-02; pres. Lancewood Assn., 1997. Mem. NAM (mem. energy com.), Am. Mgmt. Assn. (v.p. 1966-69), Chem. Mfrs. Assn. (chmn. energy com. 1974-78), Nat. Petroleum Refiners Assn. (v.p. 1972-76, chmn. issues com. 1985-89), Internat. Fedn. Ind. Energy Users (chmn. 1978), Am. Chem. Soc., Soc. Chem. Industry, US C. of C. (mem. energy com.), Met. Club Washington, Harbor Ridge Yacht and Country Club. Republican. Presbyterian. Avocations: golf, reading, bridge. Home: 1329 Lancewood Ter Palm City FL 34990

WISHEK, MICHAEL BRADLEY, lawyer; b. Pasadena, Calif., June 25, 1959; s. Homer Cedric and Donna Jean (Arnold) W.; m. Shari Patrice Rubin, June 7, 1981 (div. Feb. 1986); m. Dorothea Jean Palo, Feb. 12, 1988; children: Kirstin Alyce, Lauren Ashley. BS in Polit. Sci and Philosophy, Claremont Men's Coll., 1981; JD, U. Calif., Davis, 1985. Bar: Calif. 1986, U.S. Dist. Ct. (ea. dist.) Calif. 1986. Assoc. Michael S. Sands, Inc., Sacramento, 1986-91; ptnr. Rothschild & Wishek, Sacramento, 1991—96, Rothschild, Wishek & Sands, 1996—2005, Rothschild, Wishek & Sands LLP, 2006—. Mem. Milton L. Schwartz Am. Inn of Ct., 2000—; adj. instr. trial practice U. Calif., Sch. Law, Davis. Mem. ABA, Calif. Bar Assn., Sacramento County Bar Assn. (co-chmn. criminal law sect. 1988-90), Calif. Attys. for Criminal Justice. Office: 901 F St Ste 200 Sacramento CA 95814-0733 Office Phone: 916-444-9845. Business E-Mail: bwishek@rwslaw.com.

WISHNER, MAYNARD IRA, retired finance company executive, lawyer; b. Chgo., Sept. 17, 1923; s. Hyman L. and Frances (Fisher) W.; m. Elaine Loewenberg, July 4, 1954; children: Ellen Kenemore, Jane Wishner, Miriam Segel. BA, U. Chgo., 1944, JD, 1947; LHD (hon.), Spertus Inst., 1998, Hebrew Union Coll., 2001, Spertus Coll. Judaica, 2001. Bar: Ill. 1947. Exec. dir. Chgo. Commn. on Human Relations, 1947-52; chief ordinance enforcement div. Law Dept., City of Chgo., 1952-55; mem. law firm Cole, Wishner, Epstein & Manilow, Chgo., 1955-63; with Walter E. Heller & Co., Chgo., 1963-86, pres., 1974-86; of counsel Rosenthal and Schanfield, Chgo., 1986-95, ret., 1995—. Dir. Walter E. Heller Internat. Corp., Am. Nat. Bank & Trust Co., and br. cos., Chgo. Pres. Jewish Fedn. Met. Chgo., 1987-89; chair Nat. Jewish Community Rels., 1992-94, pres. Coun. Jewish Fedn., 1993-96; chmn. bd. govs. Am. Jewish Com., 1977-80, nat. pres. 1980-83, hon. pres., recipient Human Rights medallion, 1975; bd. dirs. Nat. Found. for Jewish Culture; chmn. Ill. Humanities Coun.; commr. Nat. Hillel Found.; mem. vis. com. U. Chgo. Sch. Social Svc. Adminstrn. and Divsn. of the Humanities; chair Ill. Humanities Coun., 1991-93; bd. govs. Jewish Agy. for Israel. Recipient Rosenwald award Jewish Fedn. Met. Chgo., Officers Merit medal Republic of Poland, United Hellenic Leadership Coun. Frisis award, Civic Achievement award U. Chgo. Home: 1410 Sheridan Rd Wilmette IL 60091-1895 Home Phone: 847-256-5015. E-mail: maynwish@aol.com.

WISHNICK, MARCIA MARGOLIS, pediatrician, geneticist, educator; b. NYC, Oct. 10, 1938; d. Hyman and Tillie (Stoller) Margolis; m. Stanley Wishnick, June 12, 1960; 1 child, Elizabeth Anne. BA, Barnard Coll., 1960; PhD, NYU, 1970, MD, 1974. Diplomate Am. Bd. Pediatrics, Nat. Bd. Med. Examiners. Rsch. technician Lederle Labs./Am. Cyanamid, Pearl River, NY, 1960-66; postdoctoral fellow N.Y. Pub. Health Lab., NYC, 1970-71; resident in pediatrics NYU-Bellevue Med. Ctr., NYC, 1974-77, asst. prof. pediatrics, 1977-82; clin. assoc. prof. pediatrics Bellevue Med. Ctr. NYU Med. Ctr., NYC, 1982-87; clin. prof. pediatrics NYU-Bellevue Med. Ctr., NYC, 1987—2003; pvt. practice, NYC, 1977—2003. Contbr. articles to profl. jours. Fellow Am. Acad. Pediatrics; mem. AMA, N.Y. Pediatric Soc., N.Y. Med. Soc. Home Phone: 808-882-7959; Office Phone: 808-937-0312. Business E-Mail: docwishnick@earthlink.net.

WISKOCIL, ANGIOLINA, telecommunications industry executive; b. Ecuador; B, Univ. Calif. Acctg. clerk Pacific Bell, 1973, v.p., network engrng. West; now sr. v.p.-network svcs. AT&T Inc. (formerly SBC Comm., Inc.), San Antonio. Served on Calif. United Task Force to bridge digital divide; rep. to Leadership Am. Named one of 80 Elite Hispanic Women, Hispanic Bus. Mag., 2005, 50 Most Important Hispanics in Tech., Bus., Hispanic Engineer and Info. Tech. mag., 2005. Office: AT&T Inc 175 E Houston San Antonio TX 78205 Office Phone: 210-821-4105. Office Fax: 210-351-2071.

WISLER, DAVID CHARLES, aerospace engineer; b. Pottstown, Pa., Apr. 21, 1941; s. Lloyd William and Ruth Georgiana (Enos) W.; m. Judith Ann Caleen, Aug. 22, 1964 (dec. Mar. 1979); children: Scott David, Cheryl Lynn; m. Beth Ellen Howard, Jan. 5, 1980; 1 child, Daniel James; step children: Chad Wihtford, Christen Whitford. BS in Aero Engrng., Pa. State U., 1963; MS in Aero. Engrng., Cornell U., 1965; PhD in Aero. Engrng., U. Colo., 1970. Rsch. engr. GE R & D Ctr., Schenectady, 1965-67; mgr. aero tech. labs. GE Aircraft Engines, Evendale, Ohio, 1985—. Mgr. univ. programs and aero tech. labs.; adj. prof. Ohio State U., U. Cin., Tsinghua U., Beijing. Editor: Jour. Turbomachinery, 2003; contbr. articles to profl. jours., chpts. to books; patentee in sloped trenches in compressors. Fellow ASME (chmn. turbomachinery com. 1993-, bd. dirs. Internat. Gas Turbine Inst. 1997-, v.p. 2003—, Melville medal for best tech. paper 1989, 98, 2003, Gas Turbine award, 1990, 92); mem. AIAA (assoc.), NAE. Achievements include patents in field. Avocation: photography. Home: 40 Trappist Walk Fairfield OH 45014-4465 Office: GE Aviation 1 Neumann Way # G407 Cincinnati OH 45215-1915 Home Phone: 513-829-2286; Office Phone: 513-243-2905. Business E-Mail: dave.wisler@ae.ge.com.

WISMER, PATRICIA ANN, retired secondary school educator; b. York, Pa., Mar. 23, 1936; d. John Bernhardt and Frances Elizabeth Loreen Marie (Fry) Feiser; m. Lawrence Howard Wismer, Aug. 4, 1961. BA in English, Mt. Holyoke Coll., 1958; MA in Speech/Drama, U. Wis., 1960; postgrad., U. Oreg., 1962, Calif. State U., Chico, 1963-64, U. So. Calif., 1973-74. Tchr., co-dir. drama program William Penn Sr. High Sch., York, 1960-61; instr. English, dir. drama York Jr. Coll., 1961-62; assoc. church editor San Francisco Examiner, 1962-63; reporter, publicist News Bur. Calif. State U., Chico, 1963-64; chmn. English Dept. Chico Sr. H.S., 1966-96; mentor tchr. Chico Sr. High Sch., Chico Unified Sch. Dist., 1983-93. Judge writing awards Nat. Coun. Tchr. English, 1970—; cons. No. Calif. Writing Project, 1977—; curriculum cons., freelance writer and photographer, 1996—. Author: My Life with Vanessa: A Journal of the Plagued Years, 1998, 40 Year Photo Retrospective, 2002; newsletter editor Chico Cat Coalition, 1999-2004; (poetry/ photo book project) Ambient Light and Shadow, 2005. Mem. Educators for Social Responsibility, Planetary Soc., Upper Calif. Coun. Tchrs. English (bd. dirs. 1966-85, pres. 1970-71), Calif. Assn. Tchrs. English, Nat. Coun. Tchrs. English, NEA, Calif. Tchrs. Assn., Chico Unified Tchrs. Assn. Democrat. Lutheran. Avocations: photography, play production, video production. Home: 623 Arcadian Ave Chico CA 95926-4504 Office: PO Box 1235 Cannon Beach OR 97110-1235 Personal E-mail: pwismer@aol.com.

WISNER, FRANK GEORGE, insurance company executive, former ambassador; b. NYC, July 2, 1938; s. Frank Gardiner W. and Mary Knowles (Fritchey) W.; m. Genevieve de Virel, July, 1969 (dec. 1974); 1 dau., Sabrina; m. Christine de Ganay, June, 1976; 1 son, David; stepchildren: Caroline Sarkozy, Olivier Sarkozy. BA, Princeton U., 1961. With Fgn. Svc. Dept. U.S. Dept. State, Algiers, Morocco, 1962-64; from dep. amabassador's staff aide to sr. advisor Vietnamese province Tuyen Duc Agy. Internat. Devel., Vietnam, 1964-68; officer-in-charge Tunisian affairs U.S. Dept. State, Washington, 1968-71; chief econ.-comml. sect. Am. Embassy, Tunis, Tunisia, 1971-73, chief polit. sect. Dacca, Bangladesh, 1973-74; dir. plans and mgmt. Bur. Pub. Affairs, Washington, 1974-75; spl. asst. to dir., then dep. dir. Pres.' Interagy. Task Force Refugee Resettlement, Washington, 1975; spl. asst. to undersec. polit. affairs, 1975-76; dir. office So. African affairs U.S. Dept. State, Washington, 1976-77, dep. exec. sec., 1977-79; U.S. amb. to Zambia Lusaka, 1977-82; dep. asst. sec. African affairs U.S. Dept. State, Washington, 1982-86; U.S. amb. to Egypt Cairo, 1986-91; U.S. amb. to Philippines Manila, 1991-92; under sec. of state for internat. security affairs Washington, 1992-93; under sec. of def. for policy Dept. Def., Washington, 1993-94; U.S. amb. to India U.S. Dept. State, 1994-97; vice chmn. external affairs Am. Internat. Group Inc., NYC, 1997—. Bd. dirs. EOG Resources; trustee Am. U. of Beirut, Am. U. Cairo; mem. bd. bus. Coun. Internat. Understanding; bd. U.S.-India Bus. Coun.; bd. refugees Internat., United Svcs. Orgn. Decorated Legion of Honor (Romania); recipient meritorious honor award Dept. State, 1973, superior honor award, 1992, disting. svc. award, 1997; recipient Mil. Medal of Honor Govt. Vietnam, 1968, Social Welfare medal of honor, 1968. Mem. Coun. on Fgn. Relations, Metropolitan Club (Washington), Ivy Club (Princeton, N.J.), Knickerbocker Club (N.Y.), Brook Club (N.Y.). Episcopalian. Office: Am Internat Group Inc 18th Fl 70 Pine St New York NY 10270-0002 *

WISNER, PAMELA L., social worker; b. Stevensville, Newfoundland, Can., Dec. 4, 1958; d. John R. Wisner, Leslie S. Wisner. BA in Psychology and Sociology, U. Mobile, 1980; M in Counseling, La. Bapt. U., 1998. LCSW Ala. Bd. Social Work Examiners, 1995, cert. Cognitive Behavioral Therapist 1999, Forensic Counselor 1999, Addictions specialist, Domestic Violence Counselor endorsement 1999. Dir. cmty. svc. RAPHA, Mobile, Ala., 1995—96; coord., counselor Charter of Mobile, 1996—2000; therapist, family cons. Gulf Coast Therapeutic Program, Inc., Mobile, 2000—. Mem.: Nat. Bd. Cognitive Behavioral Therapists, Am. Psychotherapy Assn. (diplomate 1999). Avocation: Avocations: travel, reading, cats, crafts, cooking. Office: Therapeutic Programs 601 Bel Air Blvd Ste 200 Mobile AL 36606-3524 Home: 6213 Burnt Wood Dr S Mobile AL 36695

WISNESKI, KURT, art educator; b. Northampton, Mass., Apr. 14, 1948; s. Henry Wisneski and Jacqueline Lavoie; m. Wendy J. Goldsmith, Sept. 4, 1979; children: Daniel Goldsmith, Jordan Goldsmith. BFA, U. Mass., Amherst, 1972; MFA, Syracuse U., NY, 1974. Lab. asst. printmaking U. Mich., Ann Arbor, 1974—75, printmaking lab. demonstrator, 1975—76; printmaking staff asst. U. Mass., Amherst, 1976—80, vis. lectr. Dartmouth, 1980—86, asst. prof., 1986—91, assoc. prof., 1991—96, prof., 1996—. Author: Monotype/Monoprint: History and Techniques, 1995; one-man shows include U. Mass. Med. Ctr. Gallery, Worcester, 1992, Benson Hall, RI Sch. Design, Providence, 1997, Ark. State U., 1999, Brown U. Art Gallery, Providence, 2000, exhibited in group shows at Attleboro Mus., Mass., 1989, exhibitions include Met. Mus., Miami, Fla., 1982, Fall River Arts Festival Regional Exhbn., Mass., 1985 (2d prize), 1990 (2d prize), Taller Galeria, Barcelona, 1985, 1987, 1988, U. NH, Durham, 1987, Fine Arts Acad., Warsaw, Poland, 1988, Miriam Perlman Gallery, Chgo., 1988, Provincetown Art Mus., Mass., 1988, Fed. Res. Bank of Boston, 1989, 1992, 1998, U. ND Print and Drawing Annual, Grand Forks, 1990, Mass. Med. Ctr. Gallery, 1990 (Purchase prize), Neworld Bank Corp. Art Gallery, Boston, 1992, Arnold Art Store and Gallery, Newport, RI, 1992, Ind. U., South Bend, 1994, The Brush Gallery, Lowell, Mass., 1995, DePauw U., Greencastle, Ind., 1995, U. Wis. Parkside, Kenosha, 1995, Ctrl. Conn. State U., New Haven, 1996, U. Minn., Mpls., 1996, Blackbridge Hall Gallery, Ga. Coll. and State U., 1999, Newport Art Mus., RI, 1999, Duxbury Art Complex, 1999, Art Adv., Boston, 2000, NH Inst. Art Print Exhbn., 2001, Bridgewater State U., Mass., 2001, Target Gallery, Torpedo Factory, Alexandria, Va., 2002 (hon. mention), U. Mass. Dartmouth Art Gallery, 2003, The Art Complex Mus., Duxbury, Mass., 2004 (1st prize in printmaking), Providence Art Club (Florence Breevoort Kane prize, 1990, Bradford Swain prize, 1995, Providence Art Club award, 2001), Represented in permanent collections Midwest Mus. Am. Art, Elkhart, Ind., Provincetown Art Assn. and Mus., Univ. Art Gallery, U. NH, Fed. Res. Bank of Boston, Appalachian State U., Boone, NC, Fidelity Corp., Boston, Berkshire Mus., Pittsfield, Mass., Smithsonian Inst., RI Sch. Design, U. Wis., Madison. Mem.: So. Graphics Coun. Home: 224 Gaffney Rd South Dartmouth MA 02748 Office: U Mass Dartmouth 285 Old Westport Rd Dartmouth MA 02747

WISNICKI, JEFFREY LEONARD, plastic surgeon; b. NYC, May 15, 1957; s. Joseph and Lorraine (Justman) Wisnicki; m. Rebecca Lynn O'Shields, Feb. 2, 1997; children: Justin Robert, Brandon Lawrence. BS summa cum laude, Rensselaer Poly. Inst., 1976; MD cum laude with honors, Union U., 1980. Diplomate Am. Bd. Plastic Surgery. Intern in surgery Stanford (Calif.) U. Med. Ctr., 1980-81, resident in gen., plastic and reconstructive surgery, 1981-84, chief resident in plastic and reconstructive surgery, 1985-86; fellow in plastic and reconstructive surgery Dartmouth-Hitchcock Med. Ctr., Hanover, NH, 1984; active staff Good Samaritan Hosp., West Palm Beach, Fla., 1986—, Wellington Regional Hosp., West Palm Beach, 1986—; chief divsn. plastic surgery John F. Kennedy Meml. Hosp., West Palm Beach, 1990-93; chmn. dept. surgery Palms West Hosp., West Palm Beach, 1991-93, chief med. staff, 1994-97, chmn. bd. trustees, 1997—2002, trustee, 2002—03; chief divsn. plastic surgery Good Samaritan and St. Mary's Hosp., West Palm Beach, 1997—2001, Good Samaritan Hosp., 2004—. Clin. instr. surgery U. Calif., San Francisco, 1985; bd. dirs. Interplast, 1985-86, clin. faculty, 1986—90; presenter in field. Contbr. chpts. to books and articles to profl. jours. Named Best Plastic Surgeon, Palm Beach Mag., 1998. Fellow ACS; mem. Am. Soc. Plastic & Reconstructive Surgeons, Alpha Omega Alpha. Office: Ste 133 13005 Southern Blvd Loxahatchee FL 33470 Home Phone: 561-790-0444; Office Phone: 561-798-1400.

WISNIEWSKI, P. MICHELLE, retired obstetrician, gynecologist; b. Oneida, NY, June 26, 1945; d. Henry Francis Wisniewski and Kathryn Starr Holloway; m. Anna Cebula Costello, Sept. 20, 1998; m. Louise Marie Benyovszky, Sept. 22, 1984 (div.); children: Ladislaus Michael, Alexander Paul. BS, Georgetown U., 1967; MD, Universidad Autonoma de Guadalajara, Mexico, 1975. Bd. Cert. Am. Bd. of Ob/Gyn, 1983, lic. Physican and Surgeon NJ, Pa., 1977, Residency in Ob/Gyn Hahnemann U., 1980. Chairperson, dept of ob/gyn Health Care Plan of NJ., Cherry Hill, NJ, 1980—82; attending physician ob/gyn NE Hosp., Phila., 1882—1987, Nazareth Hosp., Phila., 1984—90, Pa. Hosp., Phila., 1987—91; chairperson, dept. of ob/gyn Mercy Hosp., Wilkes-Barre, Pa., 1991—92. Author: (medical research) Journal of Reproductive Medicine (Fellowship, Internat. Soc. for the Study of Vulvovaginal Disease, 1987), (photographic exhibit) The Natural and Scenic Beauty of the Florida Keys, 2003. Chairperson Fla. Keys Coun. for People with Disabilities, Key West, Fla., 2000—06; sr. dir. Disability and Disaster: Surviving the Fla. Keys; lobbyist Key West City Coun., Monroe County Commn., Key West, Fla., 2001—06; active plaintiff Assn. for Disabled Am., Miami, Fla., 2001—06, pres., 2006—. 1st lt. US Army, 1967—70, Rep. Vietnam. Decorated Air Medal for Valor USARV, Mil. Medal of Honor & Gallantry Cross Rep. Vietnam; recipient Hon. Conch Cert., Monroe Fla. County Mayor, 2002. Fellow: Am. Coll. Ob-Gyn. (life). Achievements include first to led the struggle to make the Florida Keys accessible for people with disabilities; aided passage of transgender civil rights legislation. Office: FKCFPWD Chairperson 1100 Simonton St Ste 2 257 Key West FL 33040 Home Phone: 305-745-8722. Personal E-mail: kwimages@bellsouth.net.

WISNIEWSKI, STEPHEN ADAM, professional football player; b. Rutland, Vt., Apr. 7, 1967; Student, Pa. State U. Offensive guard L.A. Raiders/Oakland Raiders, 1989—. Named All-Pro Team Guard by Sporting News, 1990-93, Coll. All-Am. Team, 1987, 88. Played in Pro Bowl, 1990-91, 93. Home: 36 El Alamo Ct Danville CA 94526-1455

WISNIEWSKI, THOMAS JOSEPH, music educator; b. Chgo., Sept. 17, 1926; s. George Wisniewski and Rose (Jelewski) W.; children: Dieter, Lisa Ann, Ericka (dec.). MusB, Am. Conservatory of Music, Chgo., 1948; MusM, No. Ill. U., DeKalb, 1964. Instr. string instrument Sch. Dist. 89, Maywood, Ill., 1950-55; orch. dir. Sch. Dist. 44, Lombard, Ill., 1955-67; dir. orchs. Glenbard East High Sch., Lombard, 1959-67; acting head extension in music, divsn. u. extension U. Ill., Urbana, 1965—69, prof. music, 1967, emeritus prof., acting chair, 1994, chair music edn. div., 1988-92. Clinician and guest condr. internationally; music cons. Webster Internat. Illustrated Dictionary, 1993; ednl. cons. Wm. Lewis and Son, Chgo., 1965-70, Hal Leonard Pubs., Milw., 1975-84., Glaesel divsn. Selmer Corp., Elkhart, Ind., 1975-90. Prodr. films Playing the String Bass, 1967, Playing the Cello, 1968; developer (with Rodney Mueller) computer software program Visualized Vibrato, 1995, version 2.0, 1998; author: Learning Unlimited String Program, Vol. 1, 1975, (with John Higgins) Vol. 2, 1976; editor Orch. Publs., 1990; music editor Webster International Illustrated Dictionary, 1994. Mem. Am. String Tchrs. Assn. Assn. (Disting. Svc. award Ill. unit 1991, Disting. Svc. award Tenn. unit 1993), Ill. Music Educators Assn. (Pres.'s award 1996), Music Educators Nat. Conf., Ill. String Tchrs. Assn. (editor 1967, 87, pres. 1970), Nat. Jazz Educators Assn. (nat. orch. chmn. 1976), Pi Kappa Lambda, Phi Mu Alpha. Personal E-mail: thomaswisniewski@mac.com.

WISS, MARCIA A., lawyer; b. Columbus, Ohio, May 15, 1947; d. John William and Margaret Ann (Cook) W.; m. Donald G. MacDonald (dec.); children: Christopher C. Wiss MacDonald, Joan Merle MacDonald. BS in Fgn. Svc., Georgetown U., 1969, JD, 1972. Bar: D.C. 1972. Econ. analyst World Bank, Washington, 1969; atty. U.S. Dept. Justice, 1972-73; atty. office gen. counsel Overseas Pvt. Investment Corp., 1973-78; gen counsel-designate Inst. for Sci. and Tech. Cooperation, 1979; ptnr. Kaplan Russin & Vecchi, 1987-92, Whitman & Ransom, 1992-93, Whitman, Breed, Abbott & Morgan, Washington, 1993-96; counsel Wilmer, Cutler & Pickering, 1996-2000; ptnr. Hogan & Hartson, 2000—. Gen. counsel Washington chpt., Soc. Internat. Devel., 1980-2001; gen. counsel, Assn. for Women in Devel., 1982—; bd. advisers, Procedural Aspects of Internat. Law Inst., 1985—; gen. counsel internat. policy coun. agr., adj. prof. of law Georgetown U. Law Ctr., 1984—, Johns Hopkins Sch. of Advanced Internat. Studies, 2001—. Editor Georgetown Law Ctr. Jour. Law and Policy in Internat. Bus., 1971-72. Chair Holy Trinity Parish Coun., Washington, 1976. Mem. Am. Fedn. Govt. Employees (chmn. 1975-76), D.C. Bar (steering com. divsn. 12, 1985-88, co-chmn. fin. and banking com. 1985), Am. Soc. Internat. Law (v.p. 1991-94, exec. coun. 1987-90), Washington Fgn. Law Soc. (pres. 1983-84). Roman Catholic. Office: Hogan & Hartson 555 13th St NW Washington DC 20004 Office Phone: 202-637-5429.

WISSEL-LITTMANN, JEFFREY G., health facility executive; b. May 1968; Pres., trustee TIRR Rehab. Ctr., Houston, 2003—. Mem.: Am. Phys. Therapy Assn. Office Phone: 713-521-0020. *

WISWALL, DOROTHY ROLLER, language educator; b. Alpirsbach, Germany, Aug. 6, 1947; d. Albert and Else Roller; m. Thomas S. Wiswall, June 5, 1976; children: James, Karen. AB, Cornell Univ., 1971; AM, Univ. Mich., 1972, PhD, 1979. Instr. Sch. for Internat. Tng., Brattleboro, Vt., 1971; tchg. fellow Univ. Mich., Ann Arbor, 1971—75; adj. prof. Niagara Univ., 1981—91, Canisius Coll., Buffalo, 1991—2003, Buffalo State Coll., Buffalo, 2001—. Workshop presenter BOCES, Buffalo, 1998—99; vice pres. Am. Assn. of Teachers of German, Buffalo, 1998—2002; docent Buffalo Mus. Sci., 2004—; tutor Lit. Vols. Buffalo, 2004—. Author: A Comparison of Selected Poetic and Scientific Works of Albrecht von Haller, 1981, poetry. Treas. Grand Island Cmty. Chorus, 2006—; mem. coun. St. Timothy Luth. Ch., Grand Island, NY, 1999—2005, deacon, 2004—; pres. bd. dirs. STLCC Child Care Ctr., Grand Island, NY, 1995—99. Recipient 2d prize, Faculty divsn. Martin Luther King Poetry Contest at Canisius Coll., 2003; Travel grantee, U., Bern, Switzerland, 1977. Mem.: Am. Assn. Tchrs. German (v.p. 1998—2002), Zonta Internat. Club Buffalo (bd. dirs. 2004—06, sec. 2006—), Phi Sigma Iota. Lutheran. Avocations: swimming, playing violin, sewing, history of science, writing poetry. E-mail: wiswall@localnet.com.

WISWALL, FRANK LAWRENCE, JR., lawyer, educator; b. Albany, NY, Sept. 21, 1939; s. Frank Lawrence and Clara Elizabeth (Chapman) W.; m. Elizabeth Curtiss Nelson, Aug. 9, 1975; children by previous marriage:

Anne W. Kowalski, Frank Lawrence III. BA, Colby Coll., 1962; JD, Cornell U., 1965; PhD in Law, Cambridge U., 1967. Bar: Maine 1965, NY 1968, Va. 1974, US Supreme Ct. 1968; lic. master near coastal steam and motor vessels, 1960—. Assoc. Burlingham, Underwood, NYC, 1967-73; maritime legal adviser Rep. of Liberia, 1968-88; prof. (ad honorem) Internat. Maritime Law Inst., 1999; vice-capt. coxswain ano divsn. US Coast Guard Aux., 2006—; writer, cons. in field internat. maritime law, 1988—. Legal com. Internat. Maritime Orgn., London, 1972-74, vice-chmn. 1974-79, chmn., 1980-84; tutorial supr. internat. law Clare Coll., Cambridge, Eng., 1966-67; vis. lectr. Cornell Law Sch., 1969-76, 82; lectr. U. Va. Law Sch. and Ctr. Oceans Law and Policy, 1978-82; prof. law Cornell U., 1984; Johnsen prof. maritime law Tulane U., 1985; vis. prof. law World Maritime U., Malmo, Sweden, 1986-2003; prof.,fellow Internat. Maritime Law Inst., Malta, 1991—, governing bd., 1992—; del. Internat. Conf. Marine Pollution, London, 1973; del., chmn. drafting com. Internat. Conf. Carriage of Passengers and Luggage by Sea, Athens, 1974; del. Internat. Conf. Safety of Life at Sea, London, 1974, UN Conf. Carriage of Goods by Sea, Hamburg, 1978, XIII Diplomatic Conf. Maritime Law, Brussels, 1979, UN Conf. Law of Sea, Caracas, Venezuela, 1974, NY, 1980; del., chmn. com. final clauses Internat. Conf. Limitation of Liability for Maritime Claims, London, 1976; chmn. com. of whole Internat. Conf. Carriage Hazardous Substances by Sea, 1984; del. internat. conf. Maritime Terrorism, Rome, 1988; counsel various marine casualty bds. investigation, 1970-90, harbormaster, Port of Castine, 1960-62; chmn. joint internat. working group acts piracy and maritime violence, 1998-2001, joint internat. working group criminal offenses on high seas, various orgns., 2004-07. Author: The Development of Admiralty Jurisdiction and Practice Since 1800, 1970; editor-in-chief Benedict on Admiralty, Vols. 6, 6A-6F (Internat. Maritime Law), 1992—, Com. Maritime Internat. Handbook of Maritime Convs., 1997, 2001, 04; mem. editl. bd. Jour. Maritime Law and Commerce, 1993—, Benedict's Maritime Law Bull., 2002—, World Maritime U. Jour. Maritime Affairs; contbr. articles to profl. jours. Ofcl. prin. Diocese Mid-Atlantic States, 1988—, Diocese UK, 1997—, Anglican Cath. Ch.; chancellor Missionary Diocese NE, 1993—, Diocese Australia, 1998—; spkr. assembly laity Anglican Cath. Ch., 1995—2007; chmn. Am. Maritime Law Found., 2002—. Recipient Yorke prize U. Cambridge, 1968-69. Fellow Royal Hist. Soc.; mem. Nat. Lawyers Assn., Comité Maritime Internat. (titulary mem., exec. councillor 1989-96, v.p. 1997-2005, v.p. honoris causa 2005-), Maritime Law Assn. US (chmn. com. intergovtl. orgns. 1983-87, chmn. com. CMI 1987-95), Ecclesiastical Law Soc., Selden Soc., Am. Soc. Legal History, US Navy League (pres. Penobscot coun. 1997), Oxford and Cambridge Club (London), Century Assn., Alpha Delta Phi, Phi Delta Phi. Office: PO Box 201 Castine ME 04421-0201

WIT, DAVID EDMUND, software company executive; b. NYC, Feb. 25, 1962; s. Harold Maurice W. and Joan Leta (Rosenthal) Sovern; m. Kathleen Mary Bentley, Sept. 9, 1989. BA summa cum laude, Hamilton Coll., 1985. Rsch. assoc. E.M. Warburg Pincus and Co., NYC, 1985-86; CEO Logicat Inc., NYC, 1986—2002; co-CEO Micron Sys. Inc., Washington Crossing, Pa., 2003—; CEO Oakdale Capital, LLC, Larchmont, NY, 2003—. Mem. Phi Beta Kappa. Avocation: exercise. Home: 3 Stratford Rd Larchmont NY 10538-1341 Office Phone: 914-834-1343.

WIT, HAROLD MAURICE, retired investment banker, lawyer; b. Boston, Sept. 6, 1928; s. Maurice and Martha (Bassist) W.; children from previous marriage: David Edmund, Hannah Edna (dec.); 1 stepchild, Simon; m. Susan King, Sept. 16, 1999. AB magna cum laude, Harvard, 1949; JD (editor law jour.), Yale, 1954. Bar: N.Y. 1954. Assoc. Cravath, Swaine & Moore, NYC, 1954-58; asst. sec. One William St. Fund, Inc., NYC, 1958-59, v.p., sec., 1959-60; assoc. Allen & Co., 1960-70; assoc Allen & Co., Inc., 1965—, v.p., 1965-70, exec. v.p., 1970-98, mng. dir., mem. exec. com.; ret. Mgr. Allen Investments II LLC. Former trustee South Folk-Shelter Island chpt. Nature Conservancy, 1993-2000; co-founder Group for South Fork; pres. South Fork Watchdogs, Inc.; mem. Panel on Future of Govt. in N.Y., 1979-80; mem. vis. com. Harvard U. Div. Sch., 1990-97. With Mass. N.G., 1947-50; lt. (j.g.) USNR, 1951-53, Korea. Mem. VFW, Am. Legion, Korean War Vets. Assn., University Club (N.Y.C.), Harvard Club (N.Y.C.), Phi Beta Kappa, Phi Delta Phi. Home: 150 E 69th St New York NY 10021-5704 also: 57 Cross Hwy East Hampton NY 11937-0348 Office: Allen & Co Inc 711 5th Ave New York NY 10022-3111 Office Phone: 212-832-8000.

WITCHER, MICHAEL H., homeland and national security expert; b. Birmingham, Ala., Apr. 27, 1970; s. Pam Grass and James S. Witcher. BS in Bus. Adminstrn., Birmingham-Southern Coll., Ala., 1993. Bus. account exec. GTE Wireless, Birmingham, Ala., 1998—99; dir. sales, mktg. and pub. rels. Vazda Studios, Birmingham, 1999—2001; west coast IT/control systems sales mgr. Prophet Systems Innovations, Denver, 2001—02; dir. of govt. and internat. bus. devel. affairs BSI2000, Washington, DC, 2002—04; homeland and nat. security cons. Omega Force, Birmingham, 2004—; dir. homeland security Praetorian Systems, Birmingham, 2006—. Capt. Mountain Brook Police Dept., Explorers, Mountain Brook, Ala., 1985—88; co-chairman Pub. Rels. Com., Operation New Birmingham, Ala., 1995—97; fundraiser Ala. Symphonic Assn., Birmingham, 1995—97; govtl. affairs com. Chamber of Commerce, Birmingham, 1997—, law enforcement com., 1997—; fin. com. mem. Colo. State Rep. Party, Denver, 2002—05; program mem. Infraguard, Birmingham, 2006—; citizen's acad. class mem. FBI, Birmingham, 2006—, bd. dirs., P.U.S.H. Program, 2006—. Author: (poetry) Over 300 poems, 6 published poems (Top 50 Poetic Works award, 2006); dir.: (wrote, directed, and edited video) Rebuilding a City Center;, author multiple marketing pieces and op-eds. Campaign mgr. multiple polit. campaigns, Birmingham, 1996—2000; founder, chmn. Omega Polit. Action Com., Birmingham, 1996—2004; bd. mem., treas. Birmingham Advt. Fedn., Birmingham, 1999—2001; bd. mem. Ala. Zool. Soc., Birmingham Zoo, Ala., 1999—2005, Rocky Mountain Butterfly Consortium, Denver, 2002—03. Mem.: Birmingham Mus. of Art (assoc.), Alpha Tau Omega (life). Achievements include listing in Top 40 Under 40, Birmingham Business Journal. Avocations: horseback riding, soccer, Karate, sailing, travel. Personal E-mail: michael@michaelwitcher.com.

WITCHER, ROBERT CAMPBELL, SR., bishop; b. New Orleans, Oct. 5, 1926; s. Charles Swanson and Lily Sebastian (Campbell) W.; m. Elisabeth Alice Cole, June 4, 1957; 2 children. BA, Tulane U., 1949; MDiv, Seabury-Western Theol. Sem., 1952, DD, 1974; MA, La. State U., 1960, PhD, 1968; DCL (hon.), Nashotah House, 1989. Ordained priest Episcopal Ch., 1953; consecrated bishop, 1975. Priest-in-charge St. Andrew Ch., Clinton, La., Zachary, La., 1953-56, St. Augustine Ch., Baton Rouge, 1953-54, rector, 1954-61; canon pastor Christ Ch. Cathedral, New Orleans, 1961-62; rector St. James Ch., Baton Rouge, 1962-75; coadjutor bishop LI, 1975-77; bishop, 1977-91; prof. ch. history Mercer Sch. Theology, 1975-91; interim bishop of Armed Forces, 1989-90; bishop in residence Baton Rouge, New Orleans, 1991-92. Pres. Mercer Scholarship Fund; trustee Ch. Pension Fund, 1991-92; pres. bd. trustees estate belonging to Diocese of L.I., 1975-91; pres. Anglican Soc. N.Am., 1980-83; chmn. pastoral com. House of Bishops, 1980-90, Com. to Revise Title III, 1980-90; chmn. Com. on Developing Guidelines for Theol. Edn.; cons. Episc. Health Fund L.I.; historiographer Diocese of La. Author: The Episcopal Church in Louisiana, 1801-1861. Trustee U. of South, 1963-69, Seabury-Western Theol. Sem., 1963-82, Gen. Theol. Sem., 1979-88, Ch. Pension Fund, 1985-91, Bch. Reins. Corp., Killough Charitable Trust, Gen. Health Med. Ctr., Gen. Health Found.; pres. Episc. Health Svcs.; bd. dirs. Nat. Coun. Alcoholism, L.I. Coun. Alcoholism, Alcohol and Drug Abuse Coun., Baton Rouge, St. Mary's Hosp. for Children, Baton Rouge Green, La. Urban Forestry Coun., United Way, Gen. Health Sys., GHS Found.; bd. dirs., trustee St. James Place; active NCCJ (Baton Rouge chpt.). Capt. USNR, ret. Recipient Nat. Gold medal, SAR, Sesquicentennial medal, Tulane U., Gold Good Citizenship medal, NSSAR. Mem. N.Y. State Coun. Chs., L.I. Coun. Chs. (com. social justice), Am. Legion, Mil. Order of World Wars, Naval Res. Assn., Res. Officers Assn., Mil. and Hospitaller Order of St. Lazarus, Soc. Colonial Wars, Phi Kappa Phi, Phi Alpha Theta, Eta Sigma Phi. Episcopalian. Address: 1934 Steele Blvd Baton Rouge LA 70808-1673 Personal E-mail: cusnr@aol.com.

WITCOFF, SHELDON WILLIAM, lawyer; b. Washington, July 10, 1925; s. Joseph and Zina (Ceppos) W.; m. Margot Gail Hoffner, Sept. 6, 1953; children: Lauren Jill, David Lawrence, Lisa Ann, Julie Beth. BS in Elec. Engring, U. Md., 1949; JD, George Washington U., 1953. Bar: D.C. 1953, N.Y. 1955, Ill. 1956. Patent examiner Patent Office, Dept. Commerce, 1949-53; patent lawyer Bell Telephone Labs., Murray Hill, NJ, 1953-55; ptnr. Bair, Freeman & Molinare, Chgo., 1955-69, Allegretti, Newitt, Witcoff & McAndrews, Chgo., 1970-88, Allegretti & Witcoff, LTD, Chgo., 1988-95, Banner & Witcoff Ltd., Chgo., 1995—. V.p., dir. Art Splty. Co., Chgo., 1967-84; v.p. Caspian Fur Trading Co., N.Y.C.; co-founder Child Abuse Unit for Studies, Edn. and Svcs., Chgo. Fire and police commr., Skokie, Ill., 1960-63. Served with USNR, 1943-46. Mem. Am. Bar Assn., Intellectual Property Assn. of Chgo., Order of Coif, Tau Epsilon Phi, Phi Delta Phi., B'nai B'rith. Office: 10 S Wacker Dr Chicago IL 60606-7407 Office Phone: 312-463-5000. Personal E-mail: witcoff@hotmail.com. Business E-Mail: switcoff@bannerwitcoff.com.

WITCOVER, JULES JOSEPH, columnist, writer; b. Union City, NJ, July 16, 1927; s. Samuel and Sarah (Carpenter) W.; m. Marian Laverty, June 14, 1952 (div. Oct. 1990); children: Paul, Amy, Julie, Peter; m. Marion Elizabeth Rodgers, June 21, 1997. AB, Columbia Coll., 1949; MS, Columbia Grad Sch. Journalism, 1951. Reporter Hackensack (NJ) Star-Telegram, 1949-50, Providence Jour., 1951-52, Newark Star-Ledger, 1953, Washington Bur. Newhouse Newspapers, 1954-69, LA Times, Washington, 1970-72, Washington Post, 1973-76; columnist Washington Star, 1977—81, Balt. Sun, Washington, 1981—2005, Tribune Media Svcs., 1977—. Author: 85 Days: The Last Campaign of Robert Kennedy, 1969, The Resurrection of Richard Nixon, 1970, White Knight: The Rise of Spiro Agnew, 1972, (with Richard M. Cohen) A Heartbeat Away: The Investigation and Resignation of Vice President Spiro T. Agnew, 1974, Marathon: The Pursuit of the Presidency, 1972-76, 1977, (novel) The Main Chance, 1978, (with Jack W. Germond) Blue Smoke and Mirrors: How Reagan Won and Why Carter Lost the Election of 1980, 1981, (with Germond) Wake Us When It's Over: Presidential Politics of 1984, 1985, (with Germond) Whose Broad Stripes and Bright Stars?: The Trivial Pursuit of the Presidency 1988, 1989, Sabotage at Black Tom: Imperial Germany's Secret War in America, 1914-1917, 1989, Crapshoot: Rolling the Dice on the Vice Presidency, 1992, (with Germond) Mad as Hell: Revolt at the Ballot Box 1992, 1993, The Year the Dream Died: Revisiting 1968 in America, 1997, No Way to Pick a President: How Money and Hired Guns Have Debased American Elections, 1999, Party of the People: A History of the Democrats, 2003, The Making of an Ink Staired Wretch: Half a Century Pounding the Political Beat, 2005, Very Strange Bedfellows: The Short and Unhappy Marriage of Richard Nixon and Spiro Agnew, 2007. With USN, 1945-46. Recipient Washington Corr. award Sigma Delta Chi, 1963, Alumni award Columbia Grad. Sch. Journalism, 1972; Reid Found. fellow, Europe, 1958. Roman Catholic.

WITEK, JAMES EUGENE, retired public relations executive; b. LaPorte, Ind., Sept. 14, 1932; s. Stanley and Victoria (Peret) W.; m. Mary Carolyn Hood, June 18, 1955; children: James Jay, Janet Marie, Jeffrey Patrick, Jean Theresa. AB, Ind. U., 1954; MA, U. Mo., 1970. Joined U.S. Army, 1954, commd. 2d lt., 1954, advanced through grades to lt. col., 1968; editor, pub. Infantry Mag., Fort Benning, Ga., 1968-70; advisor to Vietnamese Mil. Region IV Ranger Comdr., 1970-71; plans officer CINCPAC, Hawaii, 1971-75; exec. editor Soldiers, Washington, 1975-77, editor in chief, 1977-79; dir. public affairs Nat. Com. for Employer Support Guard and Res., Arlington, Va., 1979-82, ret., 1982; dep. dir. pub. relations Am. Legion, Washington, 1982-86; mgr. pub. rels. Dowty Aerospace, Sterling, Va., 1986-99; ret. Decorated Legion of Merit, Bronze Star, Air Medal, Purple Heart, Vietnamese Cross of Gallantry with Silver Star. Mem. Am. Legion, Ret. Officers Assn., Disabled Am. Vets., Phi Beta Kappa, Tau Kappa Alpha, Pi Kappa Phi. Roman Catholic. Home: 3240 Atlanta St Fairfax VA 22030-2128

WITEK, JOHN W., history professor; b. Chgo., Sept. 13, 1933; s. John Andrew and Antoinette T. Witek. BA, Loyola U., 1957, MA, 1964; Ph. L., West Baden Coll., 1959; S.T.L., Bellarmine Sch. Theology, 1966; PhD, Georgetown U., 1973. Asst. prof. East Asian history Xavier U., Cin., 1973—75, Georgetown U., Wash., 1975—81, assoc. prof. East Asian history, 1981—2003, prof. East Asian history, 2003—. Chmn. scholars' coun. Ricci Inst., U. San Francisco, 1999—. Author: Controversial Ideas in China and in Europe, 1982; editor: Ferdinand Verbiest, 1623-1688, 1994, Dicionario Portugues-Chines, 2001, Monumenta Sinica, vol. 1, 2002. Mem. bd. dirs. Asian divsn. Libr. Congress Friends Soc., 2004—. Mem.: Am. Hist. Assn., Am. Cath. Hist. Assn. (2nd v.p. 1999—2001), Assn. Asian Studies (pres., Mid-Atlantic region 1989—90), Phi Beta Kappa. Roman Catholic. Home: Jesuit residence Georgetown U Washington DC 20057 Office: Dept History Georgetown U Washington DC 20057 Office Phone: 202-687-6061. Fax: 202-687-7245.

WITHEE, DIANA KEERAN, art historian, art dealer, educator; d. Royal Victor and Johanna Polterock Keeran; m. Gregory Wallace Withee, June 8, 1968 (div. 2007); children: Christopher Edward, Jefftrey Wallace, Brett Andrew. BA in Art History cum laude, Pomona Coll., Claremont, CA, 1969; MA in Art History, Tulane U., 1976; ABD in Art History, U. Md., College Park, 1994. Rsch. & prodn. asst., art documentaries Nat. Mus. of Am. Art, Washington, 1980—83; art history instr. Montgomery Coll., Rockville, Md., 1984—85; art history instr. & cons. Montgomery County Pub. Schs., Rockville, Md., 1986—87; curatorial asst., manuscripts and rare books Walters Art Gallery, Baltimore, Md., 1988—90; mus. educator Nat. Gallery of Art, Washington, 1990—93; guide supr., mus. educator Hillwood Mus., Washington, 1993—98; art dealer Sumner and Dene Gallery, San Diego, 1999—2002, Whitt-Krauss Objects of Fine Art, San Diego, 1999; art instr. Ctrl. Tex. Coll., San Diego, 2001—04; art dealer Susan St. Fine Art Gallery, Solana Beach, Calif., 2002—; co-owner Keeran Properties, Helendale, Calif., 2004—. Cons. Time-Life Books, Alexandria, Va., 1992; bd. dirs. San Diego State U. Arts Coun.; panelist, art critic San Diego Inst. The Living Artist, 2002—05. Prodn. asst. (videotape) Anni Albers, William H. Johnson, Reuben Nakian, Jacob Kainen:Five Decades as an Artist, asst. prodr. Americans in Brittany and Normandy, curator (art exhibition) More than a Miniature: Works of Art in Medieval Manuscripts, (exhibition) The Power of the Press: Revolution & Communications 1450-1600; author: (mag. articles) The Walters Art Gallery Bulletin, (contributing author) Culture et Revolution: The French Revolution and Its Aftermath, (instructor's manual) The Inquiring Eye: The European Renaissance, (book) Teacher Programs in Art Museums: A Directory; contributing author (magazine) The Post, presenter (symposium paper) Intimate Portrayals of Napoleon's Family, (scholarly conference paper) Anatomical Observations of Women's Life Stages in the Frescoes of Thera, (scholarly conference presentation) An Altar in the Miniature Fresco at Thera and Its Implications, lecturer (scholarly lecture) Timeless Cycles: Youth, Beauty and Ag in the Bronze Age Frescoes of Thera, scholarly presenter (scholarly conference presentation) The Boxing Boys and Fishermen Frescoes at Thera: An Analysis of their Physical Ages and Its Implications, Physical Growth and Aging Characteristics Depicted in the Theran Frescoes at Thera, conference presenter (conference presentations) Developing Good Relationships Between Guides and Security, lecturer (museum lecture series) C.W.Post and the Breakfast Cereal Revolution, The Gilded Age: The Newport Mansions; editor: (newsletter) COVA Newsletter. Recipient Letter of Commendation, Nat. Gallery of Art, 1991, Cash Bonus award, 1992; scholar Grad. assistantship, U. Md., 1986-1988; Mus. fellowship, U. of Md., 1988-89, Travel fellowship, Wash. Chpt., Am. Inst. of Archaeology, 1991. Mem.: Phi Kappa Phi. Achievements include development of new methodology of deciphering Aegean Bronze Age art; ran numerous national programs in museum education for National Gallery of Art; re-organization of entire Hillwood guide program; volunteered to teach Navy & Marine personnel aboard the aircraft carrier John C. Stennis on its deployment to participate in war in Afghanistan two months after 9/11. Home: 850 State St #128 San Diego CA 92101 Personal E-mail: dkkeeran@cox.net.

WITHERELL, DENNIS PATRICK, lawyer; b. Dec. 15, 1951; s. Thomas William and Kathryn Marie (Savage) Witherell; m. Suzanne Witherell; children: Natalie, Jay stepchildren: Jodi Brouilette, Shelby Watson, Shane Allen. AB with highest honors, U. Mich., Ann Arbor, 1973; JD summa cum laude, Ohio State U., Columbus, 1977. Bar: Ohio, US Dist. Ct. (no. dist.) Ohio, US Ct. Appeals (6th cir.). Law clk. U.S. Ct. Appeals (6th cir.), Cin., 1977—78; assoc. Shumaker, Loop & Kendrick LLP, Toledo, 1978—83, ptnr., 1983—. Exec. bd. NW Ohio chpt. March of Dimes Birth Defects Found., Toledo, 1978—91; chmn. March of Dimes Birth Defects Found., N.W. Ohio chpt., 1982—84; trustee Kidney Found. of Northwest Ohio, 1988—94, pres., 1992—93; trustee Life Connection of Ohio, 1991—2004, 2006—, Vis. Nurse-Extra Care, 1994—99. Mem.: ABA, Nat. Multiple Sclerosis Soc. (bd. trustees Northwest Ohio chpt. 1999—, chmn. 2004—06), Soc. of Ohio Hosp. Attys., Toledo Bar Assn, Ohio State Bar Assn. (chmn. health care law com. 1988—92), Am. Health Lawyers Assn. Roman Catholic. Home: 3218 Stonegate Dr Maumee OH 43537-9476 Office Phone: 419-321-1221.

WITHERELL, MICHAEL S., physicist, educator; b. Toledo, Sept. 22, 1949; s. Thomas W. and Marie (Savage) W.; m. Elizabeth Hall. BS in Physics, U. Mich., 1968; MS, U. Wis., 1970; PhD in Physics, U. Wis., Madison, 1973. Instr. Princeton (N.J.) U., 1973-75, asst. prof., 1975-81, U. Calif., Santa Barbara, 1981-83, assoc. prof., 1983-86, prof., 1986-99, prof. physics, 2005—, vice chancellor for rsch., 2005—; dir. Fermi Nat. Accelerator Lab. (Fermilab), Batavia, Ill., 1999—2005. Guggenheim fellow John S. Guggenheim Found., 1989-90; recipient Gold award US Sec. Energy, 2004 Fellow AAAS, Am. Physical Soc. (W.K.H. Panofsky prize 1990); mem. NAS Achievements include research in application of technologies to study particle physics: silicon vertex detectors and high-speed data acquisition sys. Office: U Calif Santa Barbara Office of Rsch 3227 Cheadle Hall Santa Barbara CA 93106-2050 Office Phone: 805-893-8270. Business E-Mail: witherell@research.ucsb.edu.

WITHERS, CARL RAYMOND, lawyer; b. Reading, Pa., Jan. 26, 1924; s. Stuart Snable Withers and Edith Garman; m. Jenny Constance Cory, Sept. 2, 1950; children: Wren, Jill, Bradford. AB, Wittenberg U., 1950; JD, U. Mich., 1953. Bar: Ohio 1954. Pvt. practice, Cleve., 1954—. Former pres. mus. Shaker Hist. Soc., Shaker Heights, Ohio, 1970—; former trustee, treas. N.E. Inter Mus. Coun., Cleve., 1980—; exec. com. Cuyahoga County Rep. Party, Cleve., 1984-94; former deacon and trustee Fairmount Presbyn. Ch.; former trustee Cleve. Soldiers' and Sailors' Monument. Mem. Ohio State Bar Assn. (former coun. of dels. 1955), Cleve. Bar Assn., Am. Legion (Army-Navy Shaker post 54, former comdr., adjutant), Gt. Lakes Curling Assn. (treas., pres. 1985-96), Cleve. Grays, Estate Planning Coun. Cleve., Cleve. Rotary (former trustee), Cleve. City Club, Beta Theta Pi (former pres.), Delta Theta Phi. Republican. Presbyterian. Avocation: genealogy. Home: 103 Laurel Lake Dr Hudson OH 44236-2153 Home Phone: 330-528-6132; Office Phone: 216-650-1199.

WITHERS, HUBERT RODNEY, radiotherapist, radiobiologist, educator; b. Queensland, Australia, Sept. 21, 1932; arrived in U.S., 1966; s. Hubert and Gertrude Ethel (Tremayne) W.; m. Janet Macfie, Oct. 9, 1959; 1 child, Genevieve. MB BS, U. Queensland, Brisbane, Australia, 1956; PhD, U. London, 1965, DSc, 1982. Bd. cert. Ednl. Coun. Fgn. Med. Grads. Intern Royal Brisbane and Associated Hosps., 1957; resident in radiotherapy and pathology Queensland Radium Inst. and Royal Brisbane Hosp., 1958-63; U. Queensland Gaggin fellow Gray Lab., Mt. Vernon Hosp., Northwood, Middlesex, England, 1963—65, Royal Brisbane Hosp., 1966; radiotherapist Prince of Wales Hosp., Randwick, Sydney, Australia, 1966; vis. rsch. scientist lab. physiology Nat. Cancer Inst., Bethesda, Md., 1966-68; assoc. prof. radiotherapy sect. exptl. radiotherapy U. Tex. Sys. Cancer Ctr. M.D. Anderson Hosp. & Tumor Inst., Houston, 1968-71, prof. radiotherapy, chief sect. sect. exptl. radiotherapy, 1971-80; prof. dir. exptl. radiation oncology dept. radiation oncology UCLA, 1980-89, 1991—94, prof. vice chair, dir. exptl. radiation oncology dept. radiation oncology, 1991—94, Am. Cancer Soc. Clin. Rsch. prof. dept. radiation oncology, 1992—94, interim dir. Jonsson Comprehensive Cancer Ctr., 1994—95, chmn. radiation oncology, 1994—2005. Assoc. grad. faculty U. Tex., Grad. Sch. Biomed. Scis, Houston, 1969-73, mem. grad. faculty, 1973-80; prof. dept. radiotherapy Med. Sch., U. Tex. Health Sci. Ctr., Houston, U. Tex. Med. Sch., Houston, 1975-80; prof., dir. Inst. Oncology, The Prince of Wales Hosp., U. NSW, Sydney, Australia, 1989-91; mem. com. mortality mil. pers. present-at-atmosphere tests of nuc. weapons Inst. Medicine, 1993-94; mem. radiation effects rsch. bd. NRC, 1993-99; mem. com. neutron dose reporting Internat. Commn. Radiation Units and Measurements, 1982-93, mem. report com. clin. dosimetry for neutrons, 1993-98; mem. task force non-stochastic effects radiation Internat. Com. Radiation Protection, 1980-84, mem. com. 1, 1992-00; mem. radiobiology com. Radiation Therapy Oncology Group, 1979-89, mem. dose-time com., 1980-89, mem. gastroenterology com., 1982-89; fellow Royal Australian Coll. Radiologists Edn. Bd., 1989-91; trustee Am. Bd. Radiology, 1995-04; mem. cancer rsch. coord. com. U. Calif., 1991-97, mem. standing curriculum com. UCLA biomed. physics grad. program, 1993-2007; cons. exptl. radiotherapy U. Tex. Sys. Cancer Ctr., 1980—. Mem. Am. editl. bd.: Internat. Jour. Radiat. Oncol. Biol. Phys., 1982-89, 1991-2007, internat. editl. bd., 1989-91; cons. editor: The European Jour. Cancer, 1990-95; editl. bd. dirs.: Endocurietherapy/Hyperthermia Oncology, 1991—2001, Radiation Oncology Investigations, 1992-2002; assoc. editor: Cancer Rsch., 1993-94, editl. bd. 1995-97. Mem. Kettering selection com. Gen. Motors Cancer Rsch. Found., 1988-89, chmn., 2002-03, awards assembly, 1990-94, 2002-04, adv. coun., 1994—. Decorated officer Order of Australia, 1998; Named Gilbert H. Fletcher lectr. U. Tex. Sys. Cancer Ctr., 1989, Clifford Ash lectr. Ont. Cancer Inst., Princess Margaret Hosp., 1987, Erskine lectr. Radiol. Soc. N.Am., 1988, Ruvelson lectr. U. Minn., 1988, Milford Schultz lectr. Mass. Gen. Hosp., 1989, Del Regato Found. lectr. Hahnemann U., 1990, Bruce Cain Meml. lectr. New Zealand Soc. Oncology, 1990; recipient Medicine prize Polish Acad. Sci., 1989, Second HS Kaplan Disting. Scientist award Internat. Assn. Radiation Rsch., 1991, Gray medal Internat. Commn. Radiation Units, 1995, U.S. Dept. Energy Fermi award 1997, Radiation Rsch. Soc. Failla award, 1988, Gold medal Royal Australian and N.Z. Coll. Radiologists, 1997, Charles F. Kettering prize GM Cancer Rsch. Found., 1998; Emmanuel van der Schueren medal, 2004, Gold medal Gilbert H. Fletcher Soc., 2005, Gold medal Radiol. Soc. N.Am., 2005. Fellow Am. Coll. Radiology, ACS Oncology Group (ethics com. oncology 2002—), Royal Australasian Coll. Radiologists (bd. cert., Gold medal 1997), Am. Bd. Radiology (bd. cert. therapeutic radiology 1977, Am. Coll. Radiology adv. com. patterns of care study 1988-93, radiation oncology adv. group 1993-98, others, Gold medal 2004), Am. Radium Soc. (credential com. 1986-89, 93-94, treas. 1993-94, pres. 1996-97, others, Janeway medal 1994), Am. Soc. Therapeutic Radiology and Oncology (Gold Medal awards com. 1982, 93, 00, publs. com.

1993-97, vice-chair publs. com., 1996-97, keynote address 1990, Gold medal 1991), Nat. Cancer Inst. (ad-hoc rev. coms. 1970—, radiation sudy sect. 1971-75, cons. U.S.-Japan Coop. Study high LET Radiotherapy 1975-77, cancer rsch. emphasis grant rev. com. 1976, clin. cancer ctr. rev. com. 1976-79, toxicology working group 1977-78, reviewer outstanding investigator grants 1984-93, bd. sci. counselors, 1986-88), Nat. Cancer Inst. Can. (adv. com. rsch. 1992-95), Pacific N.W. Radiol. Soc. (hon.), Tex. Radiol. Soc. (hon.), So. Calif. Radiation Oncology Soc. (sec., treas., 1992-94, pres. 1997-98), European Soc. Therapeutic Radiology and Oncology (hon.; Regaud lectr. 2000), Polish Oncology Soc. (hon., Gold medal 2002), Austrian Radiation Oncology Soc. (hon.), Phila. Roentgen Ray Soc. (hon.), Radiation Rsch. Soc. (pres. 1982-83, honors and awards com. 1984-88, ad hoc com. funds utilization 1987-89, adv. com. Radiation Rsch. Jour. 1988-96). Office: David Geffen Sch Medicine UCLA 10833 Le Conte Ave Los Angeles CA 90095-1714 Business E-Mail: hwithers@mednet.ucla.edu.

WITHERS, W. RUSSELL, JR., broadcast executive; b. Cape Girardeau, Mo., Dec. 10, 1936; s. Waldo Russell Sr. and Dorothy Ruth (Harrelson) W.; 1 child, Dana Ruth. BA, S.E. Mo. State U., 1958. Disc jockey Sta. KGMO Radio, Cape Girardeau, 1955-58; account exec. Sta. WGGH Radio, Marion, Ill., 1961-62; v.p. LIN Broadcasting Corp., Nashville, 1962-69; exec. v.p., dir. Laser Link Corp., Woodbury, NY, 1970-72; owner Withers Broadcasting of Hawaii, 1975-79, Withers Broadcasting of Minn., 1974-79, Withers Broadcasting Cos., Iowa, 1981—, Mood Music Ill., Mt. Vernon, 1973—, Mood Music, Inc., Cape Girardeau, 1972—, Royal Hawaiian Radio Co., Inc., others. Owner various radio and TV stas. including KREX-TV, Grand Junction, Colo., KREY-TV, Montrose, Colo., KREG-TV, Glenwood Springs, Colo., Page Ins. and Real Estate, Mt. Vernon, Ill.; chmn. bd., CEO Withers Beverage Corp., Mobile, Ala., 1973—79; chmn. adv. bd. Mut. Network; bd. dirs. Theatrevision, Inc., Turneffe Island Lodge, Ltd., Belize, Sta. WDTV, Clarksburg, W.Va., WMIX-AM-TV, Mt. Vernon, KGMO-KAPE, Cape Girardeau, KOKX AM-FM, Keokuk, Iowa, KTRC, Santa Fe, KRHW and KBXB, Sikeston, Mo., WKIB Anna, Cape Girardeau, WMOK, WREZ and WZZL, Paducah, Ky., WSDR-WSSQ, WZZL, Sterling Rock Falls, Ill., WILY, WRXX (FM), Centralia, Ill., WEBQ and WEBQ-FM, Harrisburg, Ill.; pres. Ill. Pub. Airports Assn.; co-chmn. TARPAC. Bd. dir., chmn. bd. Mt. Vernon Tourism and Conv. Bur.; chmn. Mt. Vernon Airport Authority; bd. regents Lincoln Acad.; past pres. IPAA; past chmn. Conv. & Visitors, Airport Authority; bd. dir. No. Colo. C.C., Libr. Am. Broadcasters, Radio Bd., AP. With U.S. Army, 1957-58. Mem. Mt. Vernon C. of C. (bd. dir.), Nat. Assn. Broadcasters (bd. dir., exec. com.), Ill. Broadcasters Assn., Stadium Club, Mo. Athletic Club, Elks, Moose, AmVets, Masons, Shriners, Sigma Chi. Christian Scientist. Home: 16074 Hawthorne Rd Mount Vernon IL 62864-2852 Office: PO Box 1508 Mount Vernon IL 62864-0030 Home Phone: 618-244-4300; Office Phone: 618-242-3500. Personal E-mail: wrwithers@mvn.net.

WITHERS, W. WAYNE, lawyer; b. Enid, Okla., Nov. 4, 1940; s. Walter O. and Ruby (Mackey) W.; m. Patricia Ann Peppers, Dec. 12, 1974; children: Jennifer Lynn, Whitney Lee. BA, U. Okla., 1962; JD, Northwestern U., 1965. Bar: Okla. 1965, Mo. 1970, US Ct. Appeals (8th cir.), 1972, US Supreme Ct. 1972, US Ct. Appeals (fed. cir.) 1984, US Ct. Appeals (DC cir.) 1985, US Ct. Claims, 1984. Staff atty. FTC, Washington, 1965-68; co. atty. Monsanto Co., St. Louis, 1968-78, asst. gen. counsel, 1978—82; v.p., gen. counsel Monsanto Agrl. Co., St. Louis, 1978—89; exec. v.p., sec., gen. counsel Emerson Electric Co., St. Louis, 1989—. V.p. Internat. Food Biotechnology Coun., Washington, 1989-90; bd. dirs. Internat. Life Scis. Inst., Washington, 1988-89. Contbr. articles to profl. jours. Chmn. bd. Mo. Hist. Soc., 2002—04; trustee MHS, 1995—; bd. dirs. World Agrl. Forum, 1999—. Mem. ABA (sect. bus. law, com. gen. counsel, antitrust, litig.), Am. Law Inst., Bar Assn. Met. St. Louis, Am. Corp. Counsel Assn., Am. Soc. Corp. Secs., Supreme Ct. Hist. Soc., Warren E. Burger Soc., Nat. Ctr. State Cts., Washington Legal Found., Indsl. Biotechnology Assn. (chmn. law com. 1985-88), Environ. Law Inst. (assoc.), Nat. Agrl. Chem. Assn. (chmn. law com. 1983-85), The Conf. Bd. Coun. for Gen. Counsel (vice chmn. 1992-98), MAPI Law Coun. Office: Emerson Electric Co 8000 W Florissant Ave Saint Louis MO 63136-8506 *

WITHERSPOON, CAROLYN BRACK, lawyer; b. Little Rock, Mar. 29, 1950; d. Gordon Paisley and Mildred Louise (Lemon) Brack; m. Joseph Roger Armbrust, July 25, 1970 (div. 1976); 1 child, Catherine Paisley Armbrust; m. John Leslie Witherspoon, June 15, 1979. Student, So. Meth. U., 1970; BA, U. Ark., 1974, JD with honors, 1978. Bar: Ark. 1978, U.S. Dist. Ct. (ea. and we. dists.) Ark. 1978, U.S. Ct. Appeals (8th cir.) 1979, U.S. Supreme Ct. 1981. Asst. atty. City of Little Rock, 1978, chief dep. atty., acting city atty., 1984—85; assoc. House, Wallace & Jewell, Little Rock, 1985—87, ptnr., 1987—90; dir. McGlinchey Stafford Lang, Little Rock, 1990—97, Cross, Gunter, Witherspoon & Galchus, Little Rock, 1997—. Mem. com. Fed. Ct. Practice, 1988—91; mem. civil practice com. Ark. Supreme Ct., 1989—97, mem. continuing legal edn. bd., 1998—2001; chair adv. com. Civil Justice Reform Act, 1993—95; chair State Bd. Bar Examiners, 2001—05. Contbr. articles to profl. jours. Commr. Ark. Real Estate Commn., 1978—81; past chmn. Little Rock Housing Authority Bd. Commn.; past pres., bd. dirs. Advs. for Battered Women; past pres. Women's Found. Ark., Ark. Women's History Inst. Recipient Labor Law award, Am. Jurisprudence, 1977. Fellow: Coll. Labor and Employment Lawyers, Am. Bar Found. (Ark. Fellows chair); mem.: ABA (ho. dels. 1997—, trial and ins. practice sect., equal employment opportunity com.), Am. Employment Law Coun., William R. Overton Inn of Ct. (pres. 1992—93), Nat. Inst. Mcpl. Law Officers (state chmn. 1985—87, v.p. 1987—89), Pulaski County Bar Assn. (pres. 1989—90), Ark. Assn. Women Lawyers (pres. 1982—83), Ark. Bar Assn. (pres. 1995—96, Golden Gavel award 1989, Ark. Inst. Cont. Legal Edn. award 1991, Golden Gavel award 1993, Charles L. Carpenter award 2005), Transp. Lawyers Assn. (mem. exec. com. 1997—99), Nat. Conf. Bar Pres. (mem. exec. coun. 1996—99), Am. Jur Soc., Am. Law Inst. Avocations: hunting, fishing, reading, travel. Office: Cross Gunter Witherspoon and Galchus 500 President Clinton Ave Ste 200 Little Rock AR 72201-1747 Office Phone: 501-371-9999. Business E-Mail: cspoon@cgwg.com.

WITHERSPOON, MARIA BERNARDA PENA, principal; b. San Cristobal, Dominican Republic, Dec. 20, 1955; came to U.S., 1969; d. Benjamin de Jesus and Belen Pena; m. James Howard Witherspoon, Aug. 6, 1977 (div. Feb. 1991). AA in Social Svcs., Pima CC, Ariz., 1980; BS in Child Devel. and Family, U. Ariz., 1981, MEd in Bilingual Edn., 1986, ednl. adminstrn. cert., 1989. Cert. basic elem. tchr. with bilingual endorsement Ariz., prin. Ariz., bilingual elem. edn. NY, sch. adminstr., supr. NY. Family counselor El Rio Neighborhood Ctr., Tucson, 1979; pre-sch. tchr. Project Head Start, Tucson, 1980; data collector U. Ariz., Tucson, 1982; bilingual educator Tucson Unified Sch. Dist., 1984-88; bilingual curriculum specialist Stafford Engring. and Tech. Magnet Sch., Tucson, 1988—; asst. prin. Leonardo da Vinci Intermediate Sch., 1999—2002; prin. Roberto Clemente Pub. Sch., 2002—. Mem. Spanish Lang. Arts Adoption com. Tucson Unified Sch. Dist. Mem. Task Force on Native Am. Studies, Tucson, 1986. Mem. AAUW, NEA, Tucson Edn. Assn. (alt. state del., assembly rep.), Nat. Assn. Bilingual Edn., Assn. for Supervision and Curriculum Devel., Am. Home Econs. Assn., Nat. Assn. Female Execs, N.Y.C. Elem. Sch. Prin.'s Assn., Assn. Family and Consumer Svc. Republican. Roman Catholic. Home: 9550 113th St South Richmond Hill NY 11419-1111 Office: Roberto Clemente Primary Sch PS19K 325 S 3d St Brooklyn NY 11211 Office Phone: 718-387-8554. Personal E-mail: mariawith@aol.com.

WITHERSPOON, REESE (LAURA JEAN REESE WITHERSPOON), actress; b. New Orleans, Mar. 22, 1976; d. John and Betty Witherspoon; m. Ryan Phillippe, June 5, 1999 (separated); children: Ava Elizabeth, Deacon. Co-owner prodn. co. Type A Films; global amb. Avon cosmetics, 2007—. Actor: (films) The Man in the Moon, 1991, A Far Off Place, 1993, Jack the Bear, 1993, S.F.W., 1994, Freeway, 1996, Fear, 1996, Twilight, 1998, Overnight Delivery, 1998, Pleasantville, 1998, Cruel Intentions, 1999, Election, 1999, Best Laid Plans, 1999, American Psycho, 2000, Little Nicky, 2000, (voice only) The Trumpet of the Swan, 2001, Legally Blonde, 2001, The Importance of Being Earnest, 2002, Sweet Home Alabama, 2002, Vanity Fair, 2004, Just Like Heaven, 2005, Walk the Line, 2005 (Best Actress, NY Film Critics Circle, 2005, Boston Soc. Film Critic award, 2005, Broadcast Film Assn., 2006, Nat. Soc. Film Critics award, 2006, Best Performance by an Actress in a Motion Picture-Musical or Comedy, Hollywood Fgn. Press Assn. (Golden Globe award), 2006, Outstanding Performance by a Female Actor in a Leading Role, Screen Actors Guild award, 2006, Actress in a Leading Role, British Acad. Film and TV Arts, 2006, Performance by an Actress in a Leading Role, Acad. Motion Picture Arts & Sciences, 2006, Choice Movie Actress: Drama/Action Adventure, Teen Choice awards, 2006); actor, exec. prodr.: (films) Legally Blonde 2: Red, White & Blonde, 2003; actor, prodr.:(films) Penelope, 2006; actor: (TV films) Wildflower, 1991, Desperate Choices: To Save My Child, 1992; (mini-series) Return to Lonsome Dove, 1993 (TV appearances) Friends, 2000, (voice only) King of the Hill, 2000, The Simpsons, 2002 Named 25 Most Intriguing People, People, 2001, 50 Most Beautiful People, 2002, Favorite Female Film Star, 2004; named one of 100 Most Influential People, Time Mag., 2006, 50 Most Powerful People in Hollywood, Premiere mag., 2006; recipient Catalan Internat. Film Festival Award Best Actress, 1997, Movieline Young Hollywood Award for Breakthrough Performance (Female), 1999, Online Film Critics Soc. Award for Best Actress, 1999, National Soc. of Film Critics Award for Best Actress, 1999, Favorite Leading Lady, People's Choice Award, 2006. Office: Creative Artists Agy 2000 Ave of the Stars Los Angeles CA 90067

WITHERSPOON, WALTER PENNINGTON, JR., orthodontist; b. Sept. 3, 1938; s. Walter P. and Florence Evelyn (Jones) W.; m. Joyce Ann Smith, Sept. 6, 1970; 1 child, Annie Melissa. BS, U. S.C., 1960; DDS, U. N.C., 1964, MSO, 1969. Pvt. practice, Columbia, 1969—. Med. staff Bapt. Med. Ctr., Columbia, 1970—, Lexington County Hosp., West Columbia, 1974—. Host Nite Line Broadcasting Co. Adv. bd. 1st Palmetto Bank and Trust, West Columbia, 1982; mem. adv. bd. 1st Citizens Bank; candidate S.C. Ho. of Reps., 1994; del. S.C. Rep. Com., 1989—; mem. platform com. S.C. Rep. Party Conv., poll com., 1992; del. Rep. Nat. Conv., Houston, 1992, rules com., task force on edn.; Rep. nat. committeeman, 1996—, rules com., rep. nat. com., 1996; pres. Rep. Electoral Coll., 1996, 2000; bd. dirs. Southeastern Coll. Assemblies of God, Lakeland, Fla., 1984, Brookland Plantation Home for Boys, Orangeburg, S.C.; pres. Friends of Irmo Libr.; chmn. Lexington County Rep. Party; commr. Richland/Lexington Counties Commn. for Tech. Edn., S.C. Commn. on Alcohol and Drug Abuse; bd. dirs. Centerplace for Homeless; mem. Presdl. Visit-Ticket Com.; amb. Irmo C. of C.; vol. lockup telethon Muscular Dystrophy Assn. Lt. USN, 1964-66. Recipient Century Mem. award Boy Scouts Am., 1984. Mem. ADA, Greater Columbia Dental Assn. (pres. 1975-76), U. NC Dental Alumni Assn. (bd. dirs.), SC Dental Assn. (ho. of dels. 1971-73, 91-96, legis. com. 1993), SC Orthodontic Assn. (ctrl. dist. dir., state rep.), Am. Assn. Orthodontists, (polit. action com.), Sertoma (pres. 1975-76), Am. Legion (mem. baseball com.), So. Assn. Orthodontists (SC rep. Am. Assn. Orthodontists polit. action com.), Cen. Dist. Dental Soc. Home: 250 Lancer Dr Columbia SC 29212-1216 Office: 205 Med Cir W West Columbia SC 29169-3653

WITHERSPOON, WILLIAM, investment economist; b. St. Louis, Nov. 21, 1909; s. William Conner and Mary Louise (Houston) W.; m. Margaret Telford Johanson, June 25, 1938; children: James Tomlin, Jane Telford, Elizabeth Witherspoon McElroy. Student, Washington U. Evening Sch., 1928-47. Chartered fin. analyst; registered investment advisor. Rsch. dept. A. G. Edwards & Sons, 1928-31; pres. Witherspoon Investment Co., 1931-34; head rsch. dept. Newhard Cook & Co. Ltd., 1934-43, 45-53, economist, investment analyst, 1965—68; chief price analysis St. Louis Ordnance Dist., 1943-45; owner Witherspoon Investment Counsel, 1953-64; v.p. rsch. Stifel, Nicolaus & Co., 1968-81; registered investment advisor St. Louis, 1981—. Lectr. on investments Washington U., 1948-67. Contbr. articles to profl. jours. Mem. Clayton Bd. Edn., 1955-68, treas., 1956-68, pres., 1966-67; mem. Clayton Park and Recreation Commn., 1959-60; trustee Ednl. TV, KETC, 1963-64; mem. investment com. Gen. Assembly Mission Bd. Presbyn. Ch. (USA), Atlanta, 1976-79, mem. permanent com. ordination exams, 1979-85; cons. to investment com. Ctr. Theol. Inquiry, Princeton, N.J., 1995-97. Served as civilian Ordnance Dept., AUS, 1943-45. Mem. St. Louis soc. Fin. Analysts (pres. 1949-50), Mo. Athletic Club (St. Louis). Home: 6401 Ellenwood Ave Saint Louis MO 63105-2228 Personal E-mail: wwspoon@swbell.net. *Many of the current social and ethical problems of today might be partially resolved if theology would be influenced by the 4th dimension of spacetime plus the 5th dimension of the mind, the 6th dimension of the spirit and the 7th dimension of God the Father.*

WITHROW, GREGORY B., director, accountant; s. Roy Preston and Mary Leola Withrow; m. Jeanette Marie Cleveland, Mar. 18, 1989; 1 child, Julie Marie. MusB in Piano Performance magna cum laude, No. Ky. U., 1980, BS in Acctg., 1987; MBA, U. Ky., 1983; cert. in computer programming, Longview C.C., Lee's Summit, Mo., 1997; cert. in mgmt., SUNY, Plattsburgh, 2004, cert. in strategic leadership, 2005. Internal auditor Fifth Third Bank, Cin., 1987—90; acct. Nazarene Theol. Sem., Kansas City, Mo., 1990—95; contr. Cleve. Chiropractic Coll., Kansas City, Mo., 1995—97; fiscal mgr. United Services Cmty. Action Agy., Kansas City, Mo., 1997—98; dir. corp. services Ctr. for Mgmt. Assistance, Kansas City, Mo., 1998—2002; dir. student accounts SUNY Plattsburgh, 2003—. Dir. acad. rels. and ednl. projects Inst. Mgmt. Accts.-Kansas City Chpt., 1993—94, dir. program roster, 1994—95, treas., 1995—96; mem. steering com. NonprofitBooks (sponsored by B2P Commerce Corp.), Chgo., 2001—02; membership com. Cmty. Assn. Nonprofit Bus. Execs., Kansas City, 2002—02. Pianist Ch. of the Nazarene, Plattsburgh, NY, 2003—. Presdl. scholar, No. Ky. U., 1976—80. Avocations: piano, hiking. Office: SUNY Plattsburgh 101 Broad St Plattsburgh NY 12901

WITHROW, JAMES A., music educator; b. Harrisburg, Pa., Nov. 24, 1964; s. James L. and Joyce M. (Yeckley) Withrow. BS in Edn., Clarion U. of Pa., Pa., 1987. Instructional II Pa., 1993. Music educator South Ea. Sch. Dist., Fawn Grove, Pa., 1988—; vol. Leo Enterprises/Red Lion Fire Co., Red Lion, Pa., 2005—. Yearbook adv. Delta-Peach Bottom Elem. Sch., Delta, Pa., 2001—. Vol. Leo Enterprises/Red Lion Fire Dept., Red Lion, Pa., 2005. Mem.: Pa. Music Educators Assn. (assoc.), Nat. Assn. for Music Edn. (assoc.). Office: Delta-Peach Bottom Elem Sch 1081 Atom Rd Delta PA 17314 Office Phone: 717-456-5313.

WITHROW, LUCILLE MONNOT, nursing home administrator; b. Alliance, Ohio, July 28, 1923; d. Charles Edward Monnot and Freda Aldine (Guy) Monnot Cameron; m. Alvin Robert Withrow, June 6, 1945 (dec. 1984); children: Cindi Withrow Johnson, Nancy Withrow Townley, Sharon Withrow Hodgkins (dec.), Wendel Alvin. AA in Health Adminstrn., Eastfield Coll., Mesquite, Tex., 1976. Lic. nursing home adminstr., Tex.; cert. nursing home ombudsman. Held various clerical positions, Dallas, 1950-72; office mgr., asst. adminstr. Christian Care Ctr. Nursing Home, Mesquite, Tex., 1972-76; head adminstr. Christian Care Ctr. Nursing Home and Retirement Complex, Mesquite, 1976-91; nursing home ombudsman Tex. Dept. Aging and Tex. Dept. Health, Dallas, 1991-93; legal asst. Law Offices of Wendel A. Withrow, Carrollton, Tex., 1993—. Com. on geriatric curriculum devel. Eastfield Coll., Mesquite, 1979, 87; ombudsman adv. com. Sr. Citizens Greater Dallas; cons. in field. Vol. Dallas Arboretum and Bot. Soc.; mem. Ombudsman adv. com. Sr. Citizens of Greater Dallas; charter mem. Stage Show Prodns. Recipient Volunteerism award, Tex. Atty. Gen., 1987, Tex. Gov., 1992. Mem. Tex. Assn. Homes for Aging, Am. Assn. Homes for Aging, Health Svcs. Speakers Bur., White Rock Kiwanis. Mem. Ch. Of Christ. Avocations: reading, travel, theater. Home: 11344 Lippitt Ave Dallas TX 75218-1922 Office: Law Office of W A Withrow 1120 Metrocrest Dr Ste 200 Carrollton TX 75006-5872

WITHROW, MARY ELLEN, federal agency administrator; b. Marion, Ohio, Oct. 2, 1930; d. Clyde Welsh and Mildred (Stump) Hinamon; m. Norman David Withrow, Sept. 4, 1948; children: Linda Rizzo, Leslie Legge, Norma, Rebecca Gooding. Mem. Elgin Local Bd. Edn., Marion, Ohio, 1969-73, pres., 1972; safety programs dir. ARC, Marion, 1968-72; dep. registrar State of Ohio, Marion, 1972-75; dep. county auditor Marion County, Ohio, 1975-77, county treas. Ohio, 1977-83; treas. State of Ohio, Columbus, 1983-94; treas. of the U.S. Dept. Treasury, Washington, 1994—2001. Chmn. Ohio Bd. Deposits, 1983—. Mem. exec. com. Ohio Dem. Com., mem. exec. com. women's caucus; mem. Dem. Nat. Com.; mem. Met. Women's Ctr.; pres. Marion County Dem. Club, 1976; participant Harvard U. Strategic Leadership Conf., 1990; mem. Dem. Leadership Coun.; mem. Internat. Currency News Bd., 2002—, Robert Wood Johnson Fellowhisp Bd, 1997—. Recipient Donald L. Scantlebury Meml. award, 1991, Women of Achievement award YWCA of Met. Columbus, 1993, Outstanding Govt. Svc. award Am. Numis. Assn., 1995; inducted Ohio Women's Hall of Fame, 1986; named Outstanding Elected Dem. Woman Holding Pub. Office, Nat. Fedn. Dem. Women, 1987, Advocate of Yr., SBA, 1988, Most Valuable State Pub. Ofcl., City and State newspaper, 1990; Women Execs. in State Govt. fellow Harvard U., 1987. Mem. LWV (dem. leadership coun.), State Assn. County Treas. (legis. com. 1979-83, treas. 1982), Nat. Assn. State Treas. (pres. 1992, Jesse Unruh award 1993, chair long range planning com., mem. exec. com.), Nat. Assn. State Auditors Comtps. and Treas. (pres. 1990, strategic planning com., intergov. rels. com., chair state and mcpl. bonds com.), Treasury Hist. Assn., I Safe Bd, Coun. State Govts. (exec. com., internat. affairs com., orgnl. planning and coord. com., strategic planning task force), Women Execs. in State Govt. (chair fund devel. com.), Altrusa Bus. and Profl. Women's Club (hon.), Delta Kappa Gamma (hon.), Delta Sigma Pi (hon.). Clubs: Bus. and Profl. Women's.

WITHROW, WILLIAM N., JR., lawyer; b. Toccoa, Ga., June 26, 1954; BA magna cum laude, U. Ga., 1975, JD magna cum laude, 1978. Bar: Ga. 1978. Law clk. to Hon. James C. Hill US Ct. Appeals, 5th Cir., 1978-79; ptnr., complex litig. Troutman Sanders LLP, Atlanta, 1986—, and sect. chief, litig. dept. Mem. ABA, State Bar Ga., Atlanta Bar Assn. Office: Troutman Sanders 5200 Bank of Am Plz 600 Peachtree St NE Ste 5200 Atlanta GA 30308-2216 Office Phone: 404-885-3244. Office Fax: 404-962-6726. E-mail: william.withrow@troutmansanders.com.

WITKE, DAVID RODNEY, retired newspaper editor, consultant; b. Council Bluffs, Iowa, Mar. 24, 1937; s. Arnold and Rosamond Louise (Storer) W.; m. Priscilla Bill Smith, Oct. 8, 1960; 1 son, Carl. BS in Journalism, Northwestern U., 1959. Reporter, editor The Courier, Champaign-Urbana, Ill., 1962-66; copy editor The Register, Des Moines, 1966-70, city editor, 1970-73, asst. mng. editor adminstrn., 1973-74, asst. mng. editor electronics, 1974-75, mng. editor, 1975-83, dir. ops., 1983-85, dep. editor, omsbudsman, 1985-87, exec. sports editor, 1987-98, sr. editor, 1998—2002, ret., 2002; freelance cons., 2002—. Rep. Iowa Freedom of Info. Coun., Des Moines, 1973—, pres., 1986-88; vis. lectr. Drake U., 1986—, Iowa State U., 1990—; adj. faculty Simpson Coll., 2003—, adv. bd., 2007—; juror Pulitzer Prize, 1989-91; tng. cons. The Register, Des Moines, 2003—; lectr. in field Bd. dirs. Des Moines Pastoral Counseling Ctr., 2005—. Served to lt. (j.g.) USN, 1959-62, PTO. Mem. Assoc. Press Mng. Editors Assn., Mid-Am. Newspaper Assn., AP Sports Editors Assn., Iowa Newspaper Found., The Prairie Club, Sigma Delta Chi. Unitarian Universalist. Home and Office: 2521 48th Pl Des Moines IA 50310-2506 Office Phone: 515-274-0578.

WITKIN, ERIC DOUGLAS, lawyer; b. Trenton, NJ, May 14, 1948; s. Nathan and Norma Shirley (Stein) W.; m. Regina Ann Bilotta, June 8, 1980; children: Daniel Robert, Sarah Ann. AB magna cum laude, Columbia U., 1969; JD, Harvard U., 1972. Bar: N.Y. 1973, D.C. 1989, U.S. Dist. Ct. (so. and ea. dists.) N.Y. 1974, U.S. Dist. Ct. (we. dist.) N.Y. 2001, U.S. Ct. Appeals (2d and D.C. cirs.) 1974, U.S. Supreme Ct. 1977, U.S. Dist. Ct. D.C. 1989. Assoc. Poletti, Freidin, Prashker & Gartner, NYC, 1972-80, ptnr., 1980-85; sr. atty. labor Kaye, Scholer, Fierman, Hays & Handler, NYC, 1985-88; of counsel Akin, Gump, Strauss, Hauer & Feld, Washington, 1988-90; counsel Benetar, Bernstein, Schair & Stein, NYC, 1990-99; ptnr. Roberts & Finger, LLP, NYC, 1999-2001, Greble & Finger, LLP, NYC, 2001; counsel Brown, Raysman, Millstein, Felder, & Steiner LLP, NYC, 2001—06, Thelen Reid Brown Raysman and Steiner, LLP, NYC, 2006—. Treas., founder Property Owners Against Unfair Taxation, NYC, 1983-90, Park Ridge Neighborhood Assn., Harrison, NY, 2000-; trustee Congregation Emanu-El of Westchester, 1996—, pres., 2002-04. Lawrence Chamberlain scholar Columbia U., NYC, 1968; recipient Alumni medal Alumni Fedn. Columbia U., 1982 Mem. ABA (labor and employment law sect.), N.Y. State Bar Assn. (labor and employment law sect., com. on equal employment opportunity law), Assn. of Bar of City of NY (spl. com. on sex and law 1975-82, com. on labor and employment law 1982-85, 92-94), Westchester County Bar Assn., Columbia Coll. Alumni Assn. (pres. 1988-90, bd. dirs. 1974—, Robert Lincoln Carey prize, Alumni prize 1969, Lions award 1990), Alumni Fedn. Columbia U. (alumni trustee nominating com. 1990-97, pres. 1997-99), Am. Soc. Pers. Adminstrn. (contbr. monthly newsletter 1986-88), Soc. Human Resource Mgmt., Soc. Columbia Grads. (bd. dirs. 1994-97), Human Resources Assn. NY, Phi Beta Kappa. Clubs: Harvard (NYC), Am. Yacht (Rye, NY) Avocations: piano, sailing. Home: 103 Wendover Rd Rye NY 10580-1939 Office: Thelen Reid Brown Raysman and Steiner LLP 900 3rd Ave Fl 21 New York NY 10022 Office Phone: 212-895-2313. Personal E-mail: ericwitkin@aol.com. Business E-Mail: ewitkin@thelen.com.

WITKIN, EVELYN MAISEL, retired geneticist; b. NYC, Mar. 9, 1921; d. Joseph and Mary (Levin) Maisel; m. Herman A. Witkin, July 9, 1943 (dec. July 1979); children— Joseph, Andrew. AB, NYU, 1941; MA, Columbia U., 1943, PhD, 1947; DSc honoris causa, N.Y. Med. Coll., 1978, Rutgers U., 1995. Mem. staff genetics dept. Carnegie Inst., Washington, 1950-55; mem. faculty State U. N.Y. Downstate Med. Center, Bklyn., 1955-71, prof. medicine, 1968-71; prof. biol. scis. Douglass Coll., Rutgers U., 1971-79, Barbara McClintock prof. genetics, 1979-83, Waksman Inst. Microbiology, 1983-91; Barbara McClintock prof. emerita Waksman Inst. Microbiology, Rutgers U., 1991—. Author articles; mem. editorial bds. profl. jours. Postdoctoral fellow Am. Cancer Soc., 1947-49; fellow Carnegie Instn., 1957; Selman A. Waksman lectr., 1960; Phi Beta Kappa vis. scholar, 1980-81; grantee NIH, 1956-89; recipient Prix Charles Leopold Mayer French Acad. Scis., 1977, Lindback award, 1979, Nat. Medal of Science award, 2002. Fellow AAAS, Am. Acad. Microbiology; mem. NAS, Am. Acad. Arts and Scis., Environ. Mutagen Soc., Am. Genetics Soc. (Thomas Hunt Morgan medal, 2000), Am. Soc. Microbiology. Home: 1 Firestone Ct Princeton NJ 08540-5220 E-mail: ewitkin@aol.com.

WITKIN, JOEL-PETER, photographer, poet; b. Bklyn., Sept. 13, 1939; s. Max and Mary (Pellegrino) W.; 1 child, Kersen Ahanu; m. Barbara Anne Gilbert, 2005. B.F.A., Cooper Union, 1974; M.F.A., U. N.Mex., 1986; student (fellow), Columbia U., 1973-74. Artist in residence Zerybthia

Rome, Italy, summer 1996; represented by Galerie Baudoin Lebon, Paris, Catherine Edelman Gallery, Chgo., Silverstein Photography, NYC; artist in residence Berlin, fall 1998, Paris, winter 1998. Lectr. Am. Acad. Rome, 1996, Camera Work, Berlin, El Escorial, Spain, 1998, Yale U., 2001, Internat. Ctr. Photography, 1999, Moscow Ho. Photography, 2001, Ecole Beaux Arts Superior, Paris, 2005. Exhibited in Projects Studio One, NYC, 1980, Galerie Texbraun, Paris, 1982, Baudoin Lebon, Paris, 1982, 86, 90, 94, 97, 2000, 02, 04, Kansas Ctiy Art Inst., 1983, Stedelijk Mus., Amsterdam, 1983, Fraenkel Gallery, 1983-84, 87, 91, 93, 95, 97, Pace WildenStein MacGill Gallery, NYC, 1983, 84, 87, 89, 91, 93, 95, 97, San Francisco Mus. Modern Art, 1985, Bklyn. Mus., 1986, Galerie Baudoin Lebon, Paris, 1987, 89, 91, 95, 97, 2000, 02, 04, 07, Centro de Arte Reina Sofia Mus., Madrid, 1988, Palais de Tokyo, Paris, 1989, Fahey/Klein Gallery, LA, 1987, 89, 91, 97, 98, 2005, Mus. Modern Art, Haifa, Israel, 1991, Photo Picture Space Gallery, Osaka, Japan, 1993, 95, 2001, Guggenheim Mus., NYC, 1995, Interkamera, Prague, 1995, Il Castello de Rivoli Mus., Turin, 1995, Encontros de Fotografia, Colombia, Portugal, 1996, 98, Rencontres de la Photographie, Arles, France, 1996, Taipei Photo Gallery, Taiwan, 1994, 96, 98, Mus. of Fine Arts, Santa Fe, 1998, Wildenstein Gallery, Tokyo, 1998, Pace Wildenstein, LA, 1998, Sternburg Mus., Prauge, 1999, Mesiac Fotographie, Slovakia, 1999, Hotel De Sully, Paris, 2000, Catherine Edelman Gallery, Chgo., 2000, 05, Ricco/Maresca Gallery, NYC, 1997, 99, Athens Sch. Fine Art, 2000, Ctr. Contemporary Art, Honolulu, 2000, Hasted/Hunt Gallery, NYC, 2001, 04, Etherton Gallery, Tucson, 2001, 05, Linda Durham Gallery, Santa Fe, 2005, Stadt Mus., Jena, 2002, Picture Photo Space, Osaka, 2002, Infinito Gallery, Turin, 2002, Galeria Juana de Aizpuru, Madrid, 2003, Photoes Pana, Madrid, 2003, Le Garage Galerie, Toulouse, 2003, ARCO, Madrid, 2004, Gary Tatintsian Gallery, Moscow, 2005, Moscow House Photography, 2005, Witkin Vintage, Hasted/Hunt, NYC, 2006, Café Françoise, Brussels, Paris-Photo, 2006, Chgo. Art Fair, 2007, Cite Internat. des Arts, Paris, 2006, Medici Palace, Seravezza, Italy, 2007, Galleria Ca Di Fra, Milano, 2007, Maison de la Culture de Namur, Belgium, 2007, Luz Bienal de las Artes, Zaragoza, 2007, Mus. Photography, Bogata, Columbia, 2007; group shows: Mus. Modern Art, NYC, 1959, San Francisco Mus. Moder Art, 1981, Whitney Biennial, 1985, Palais de Tokyo, Paris, 1986, La Photographie Contemporaine en France, 1996, Foto Masson, Goteberg, Sweden, 1997, Hanlin Museum, So. Korea, 1997, Bogardenkapel, Bruges, 1998, Hayward Gallery, London, 1997, Strasborg Mus. d'Art Moderne et Contemporaine, 1998, The Ansel Adams Ctr., San Francisco, 1999, Camera Work, San Francisco, 1999, The Louvre, Paris, 2000, Museé Bourdelle, Paris, 2000, John Gibson Gallery, NYC, 2000, The High Mus. Art, Ga., 2000, Fotografie Forum, Frankfort, 2001, Nat. Gallery of Can., 2002, Hotel de Sully, Paris, 2002, The Israel Mus., Jerusalem, 2002, The Whitney Mus., NYC, 2002, H. Lunn Collection, Lille, 2003, Photology, Milan, 2003, Akira Ikeda Gallery, Berlin, 2003, Aperture: Photography Past/Forward, NYC, 2003, Nat. Gallery Can., Ottawa, 2004, Yancey Richardson Gallery, NYC, 2004, Guggenheim, Bilbao, 2005, Bruce Silverstein, NYC, 2005, Ctr. D'Art Del'Yonne, 2005, Wessel and O'Connor Fine Art, NYC, 2005, Mus. Contemporary Photography, Chgo., 2005, Cité Internat.: "The Book", Paris, 2006, Houston Ctr. for Photography, Silver Retrospective, 2006, "Eye of the Beholder", Richard Avedon collection, 2006, "The Invisible Landscape", Nat. Gallery Can., 2007, Miami Mus., Charles Cowles collection, 2007, Photo London, Silverstein-Photography, 2007, Terry Etherton Gallery, Tucson, Ariz., 2007, others; represented in permanent collections, Mus. Modern Art, NYC, San Francisco Mus. Modern Art, 1980, Nat. Gallery Art, Washington, Victoria and Albert Mus., London, George Eastman House, NY, Getty Collection, Moder Museet, Stockholm, Sweden, Whitney Mus., NYC, Guggenheim Mus., NYC, Met. Mus., NYC, Tokyo Met. Mus. Photography, Nat. Gallery Can., Metropolitan Mus. Art, NYC, Phila. Mus. Art; subject of monographs: Joel-Peter Witkin, 1985, 88-89, 91, 93, 95-96, 98-2003, 06—; editor: Masterpieces of Medical Photography, 1987, Harms Way, 1994; visual editor: Songs of Experience, 2002, Songs of Innocence, 2003, Songs of Experience and Songs of Innocence, 2004, Bourgeoisie-in-de-Nile, 2006, The History of Hats in Art, NY Times, 2006, Maestro Witkin, Delpire Editeuyr, 2007; artist in residence: Paris, 1994, 98, 2000, Rome, 1996, Berlin, 1998, Buenos Aires, 2003, Moscow, 2005. Served with U.S. Army, 1961-64. Decorated Commandeur des Arts et de Lettres (France); recipient The Augustus Saint Gaudens medal The Cooper Union, 1996, Disting. Alumni award The Cooper Union, 1986, Internat. Ctr. Photography award, 1988, award for N.Y. Times "The Plague Yr.," Soc. Publ. Designers, 2000; Ford Found. grantee, 1977, 78, Nat. Endowment in Photography grantee, 1980, 81, 86, 92. Address: 1707 Five Points Rd SW Albuquerque NM 87105-3017 Office Phone: 505-843-6682. Personal E-mail: jwitkin1@comcast.net. *My need is to understand existence. That need becomes art when it reaches into the extreme limit of the possible with grace and truth.*

WITKOP, BERNHARD, chemist; b. Freiburg, Baden, Germany, May 9, 1917; came to U.S., 1947, naturalized, 1953; s. Philipp W. and Hedwig M. (Hirschhorn) W.; m. Marlene Prinz, Aug. 8, 1945; children: Cornelia Johanna, Phyllis, Thomas. Diploma, U. Munich, 1938, PhD, 1940, Golden Dr. Diploma, 1990; ScD, Privat-Dozent, 1947. Matthew T. Mellon research fellow Harvard U., 1947-48, mem. faculty, 1948-50; spl. USPHS fellow Nat. Heart Inst., NIH, 1950-52; vis. scientist Nat. Inst. Arthritis and Metabolic Diseases, 1953, chemist, 1954-55, chief sect. metabolites, 1956-87, chief lab. chemistry, 1957-87, scholar, 1987-92, hon. scholar emeritus, 1993; vis. prof. U. Kyoto, Japan, 1961, U. Freiburg, Fed. Repubic Germany, 1962; adj. prof. U. Md. Med. Sch., Balt.; Nobel symposium lectr. Stockholm-Karlskoga, 1981. Mem. bd. Internat. Sci. Exchange, 1974; exec. com. NRC, 1975; mem. Com. Internat. Exchange, 1977, Paul Ehrlich Award Com., Frankfurt, 1980-97; bd. dirs. Leo Baeck Inst., NY. Editor: Fedn. European Biochem. Soc. Letters, 1979-90. Recipient Superior Svc. award USPHS, 1967; Paul Karrer Gold medal U. Zurich, 1971; Kun-ni-to (medal of sci. and culture 2d class) Emperor of Japan, 1975; Alexander von Humboldt award for sr. U.S. scientists, 1978 Mem. NAS, Am. Chem. Soc. (Hillebrand award 1958, Golden Membership 1997), Am. Acad. Arts and Sci., Am. Philos. Soc., Acad. Leopoldina (fgn.), Pharm. Soc. Japan (hon.), Chem. Soc. Japan (hon.), Japanese Biochem. Soc. (hon.), Acad. Scientarium et Artium Europaea, Rheinisch-Westfälische Akademie der Wissenschaften. Office: NIH-Dept Health Edn & Welfare 2A 04 Bldg 8 Bethesda MD 20892-0001 *A career between two worlds and two wars, spanning 50 years of research aims changing from structural to dynamic aspects, may be considered epigonal in the sense that my teacher H. Wieland (Nobel Prize 1928) always considered biochemistry as a neglected area of organic chemistry. In a small way I tried to follow his example and interests, such as oxidation mechanisms, natural products and highly active toxins.*

WITKOSKY, DAVID V., language educator; s. Vernon and Jeanne Witkosky. BA, U. Ill., Chgo., 1980, MA, 1982; PhD, U. Ill., Urbana-Champaign, 1988. Asst. prof. Auburn U., Montgomery, 1989—97, assoc. prof., 1997—2007, prof., 2007—, dir. honors program, 1997—2003, dir. master liberal arts program, 2003—. Vis. asst. prof. Ill. Wesleyan U., Bloomington, 1988—89; reviewer in field. Author: (book reviews) Unterrichtspraxis: Teaching German, (biographical dictionary entries) Key Thinkers in Linguistics and the Philosophy of Language; contbr. articles to profl. jours., monographs; mem. editl. bd.: Am. Ednl. History Jour., 2001—. Grantee, Auburn U., 1993—96. Mem.: MLA, Nat. Social Sci. Assn., Midwest History Edn. Soc., So. Coun. Lang. Tchg., Am. Coun. Tchg. Fgn. Languages, Am. Assn. Tchrs. German, Ala. Assn. Fgn. Lang. Tchrs., German-Am. Soc., Omicron Delta Kappa, Phi Kappa Phi, Phi Beta Kappa. Avocations: reading, hiking, stamp collecting/philately, travel. Office: Auburn University Montgomery PO Box 244023 Montgomery AL 36124-4023 E-mail: dwitkosk@mail.aum.edu.

WITMER, GEORGE ROBERT, JR., lawyer; b. Rochester, NY, Mar. 23, 1937; s. George Robert and Marian Pauline (Costello) W.; m. Nancy Rosetta Wenner, Dec. 28, 1968; children: Wendy Lynn, Heidi Dawn, George Robert, III, Frank David. AB, U. Rochester, 1959; LL.B., Harvard U., 1962. Bar: N.Y. 1962, U.S. Dist. Ct. (we. dist.) N.Y. 1963, U.S. Supreme Ct. 1967, U.S. Dist. Ct. (no. dist.) N.Y. 1977, U.S. Ct. Appeals (2d cir.) 1998. Assoc. Nixon, Hargrave, Devans & Doyle, Rochester, 1962-70, ptnr., 1970-99, Nixon Peabody, Rochester, 1999—2005, sr. counsel, 2005—. Instr. in bus. law U. Rochester, 1965-66; mem. com. to advise and cons. Jud. Conf. State N.Y. on Civil Practice Law and Rules, 1970-77; mem. N.Y. State Jud. Inst. on Professionalism in the Law, 1999—; mem. Adv. Group to N.Y. State and Fed. Jud. Coun., 1999—. Mem. N.Y. State Rep. Com., 1976—93; trustee Eastman Dental Ctr. Rochester, 1977—97, pres. bd. trustees, 1989—90; trustee U. Rochester, 1979—, chmn., 2003—. Fellow: ABA, N.Y. Bar Found. (dir. 1991—96); mem.: N.Y. State Bar Assn. (ho. dels. 1978—, exec. com. environ. law sect. 1981—96, pres. 1994—95, Disting. Svc. award environ. law sect.), Monroe County (N.Y.) Bar Assn., Am. Law Inst. (life), ABA, Rotary (dir. Rochester club 1977—79, pres. 2001—02), Masons (master local lodge 1971), Phi Beta Kappa. Republican. Lutheran. Home: 892 Lake Rd Webster NY 14580-9008 Office: Nixon Peabody LLP PO Box 31051 Clinton Sq Rochester NY 14604-1729 Business E-Mail: grwitmer@nixonpeabody.com.

WITMEYER, JOHN JACOB, III, lawyer; b. New Orleans, Dec. 18, 1946; s. John J. and Thais Audrey (Dolese) W. BS, Tulane U., 1968; JD with distinction, Duke U., 1971. Bar: NY. Assoc. Mudge Rose Guthrie & Alexander, NYC, 1971-76; ptnr. Ford Marrin Esposito & Witmeyer (now Ford, Marrin, Esposito, Witmeyer & Gleser LLP), NYC, 1976—. Bd. trustees Gregorian U. Found., 1999—; adv. coun. Paul Tulane Coll., Tulane U., 1998—2006, Sch. Arts & Scis. Tulane U., 2006—; bd. dirs. Tulane Assocs., Tulane U., 2001—. Col. US Army. Mem.: Order of the Holy Sepulchre (knight commander). Office: Ford Marrin Esposito Witmeyer & Gleser LLP Wall St Plz New York NY 10005-1875 Business E-Mail: jjwitmeyer@fmew.com.

WITORSCH, PHILIP, internist, educator; b. NYC, July 11, 1937; s. Benjamin and Sarah (Etkin) Witorsch; m. Joan Linda Pellman, June 7, 1959; children: Beth Joy, Jeffrey Lee. BA, NYU, 1958, MD, 1962. Diplomate Am. Bd. Internal Medicine, Am. Bd. Pulmonary Disease. Intern, resident internal medicine Yale U., New Haven Hosp., 1962—64; clin. assoc., clin. investigator Nat. Inst. Allergy and Infectious Diseases NIH, Bethesda, Md., 1964—67; resident, chief resident in internal medicine, fellow pulmonary diseases VA. Hosp., Washington, 1967—69; chmn. pulmonary and critical care medicine, dir. med. intensive care unit, med. dir. respiratory therapy Washington Hosp. Ctr., 1969—82, sr. attending in medicine, 1969—2005; prof. medicine and physiology, dir. sect. environ. medicine and toxicology, divsn. pulmonary diseases and allergy, med. dir. for respiratory care George Washington U., 1983—95; prof. medicine and pharmacology Georgetown U. Med. Ctr. and Hosp., 1995—, dir. environ. occupl. toxicology assessment program, 1995—; attending physician medicine Georgetown U. Hosp., 1995—; dir. clin. cons. svc. clin. pharmacology divsn. Georgetown U. Med. Ctr. and Georgetown U. Hosp., 1995—; med. dir. occupl. health program Georgetown U. Med. Ctr., 2005—. Cons. pulmonary disease VA Hosp. NIH, Dept. State, Andrews AFB, Dept. Justice, Dept. Labor. Contbr. articles to profl. jours. With USPHS, 1964—67. Fellow: ACP, Royal Soc. Medicine, Am. Geriatric Soc., Am. Coll. Chest Physicians (gov. Washington chpt. 1995—97); mem.: AMA (Physicians Recognition award 1972, 1975, 1978, 1981, 1984, 1987, 1990, 1993, 1996, 1999), Montgomery County Med. Soc., Am. Coll. Occupl. and Environ. Medicine, Am. Coll. Toxicology, Am. Soc. Internal Medicine, Am. Heart Assn., Am. Assn. Respiratory Therapy, Am. Fedn. Clin. Rsch., Med. Chirurgical Faculty Md., Med. Soc. DC, DC Thoracic Soc., Am. Thoracic Soc., Soc. Critical Care Medicine, Phi Beta Kappa, Alpha Omega Alpha. Office: Dept Pharmacology Georgetown Univ Med Ctr MED-DENT SE 402 Box 571443 3900 Reservoir Rd NW Washington DC 20057-1443 Home Phone: 301-983-0758; Office Phone: 202-687-0398. Business E-Mail: Witorscp@georgetown.edu.

WITORT, JANET LEE, lawyer; b. Cedar Rapids, Iowa, Mar. 10, 1950; d. Charles Francis Svoboda and Phyllis Harriet (Wilber) Miller; m. Stephen Francis Witort, Oct. 27, 1979. Student, U. Colo., 1968-69, U. Iowa, 1971; BA, U. No. Colo., 1972; JD, Loyola U., 1979. Bar: Ill. 1979, U.S. Dist. Ct. (no. dist.) Ill. 1979, U.S. Dist. Ct. (no. dist.) Ill. 1979, U.S. Supreme Ct. 1987. Paralegal Fed. Nat. Mortgage Assn., Chgo., 1973-75, Sidley & Austin, Chgo., 1975-76; assoc. Frankel, McKay & Orlikoff, Chgo., 1979-81; atty. Mut. Trust Life Ins. Co., Oak Brook, Ill., 1981-86; assoc. counsel, asst. sec. N.Am. Co. for Life and Health Ins., Chgo., 1986-88; sr. atty. AMA, Chgo., 1988-89; gen. coun., sec. AMA Ins., Chgo., 1989-91, v.p. gen. counsel, sec., 1991-93; asst. gen. counsel Prudential Ins. and Fin. Svcs., Chgo., 1994—98; sr. counsel Allianz Life Ins. Co. of N.Am., 1998—99, v.p., dep. gen. counsel, 1999—. Author: (with others) The Legal Assistant-A Self Statement, 1974, (with others) Requirements and Limitations Imposed by Corporate Law, 1989, updated, 1992. Vol. Rep. Campaign, Chgo., 1974-76, 90-93, Children's Hosp. Guild, North Oaks, Minn., 1993—, v.p. 1994-95, pres. 1996; vol. Sci. Mus. Minn., St. Paul, 1994-2001; trustee Hindsdale Ill. Pub. Libr., 1987-93, v.p., 1991-93; bd. dirs. Suburban Libr. Sys., Burr Ridge, Ill., 1988-91, sec. 1990-91; bd. dirs. Children's Hosp. Assn., St. Paul, 1995-96; active Jr. League, St. Paul, 1997-02, bd. dirs., 2000-01, sustainer, 1993, sustainer, Washington, 1993-; mem. North Oaks Planning Commn., Minn., 2000—; del. Mo. State Rep. Conv., 2000; docent Freer and Sackler Galleries Art Smithsonian, 2006—; docent Freer Gallery Art, 2006—. Mem. ABA, Am. Soc. Med. Assn. Coun., Ill. Bar Assn., Chgo. Assn. Paralegal Assts. (sec. 1973-74), Chgo. Bar Assn. (chair life & health ins. subcom. 1992-93), Womans Bar Assn. of Ill. (mem. ins. com. 1987-93), Ill. Paralegal Assn. (v.p. 1975-76), Nat. Fed. Paralegal Assns. (midwest reg. dir. 1975-76), Am. Corp. Counsel Assn. (membership com. 1988-90), Phi Alpha Delta, Student Bar Assn. (class rep. 1976-77). Republican. Avocations: golf, travel, skiing. Office: 1047 N Stuart St Arlington VA 22201

WITT, ALICIA, actress; b. Worcester, Mass., Aug. 21, 1975; d. Robert and Diane W. Home edn. Actress Internat. Creative Mgmt., Beverly Hills, Calif. TV appearances: Cybill, 1995-98, The Disappearance of Vonnie, 1994, Blackout, 1993, Twin Peaks, 1991, Hotel Room, Ally McBeal, 2000, Ring of the Nibelungs, 2004; film appearances: Dune, 1984, Liebestraum, 1991, Bodies, Rest and Motion, 1993, Fun, 1994 (Spl. Jury Recognition award Sundance Film Festival 1994), Four Rooms, 1995, Mr. Holland's Opus, 1995, Citizen Ruth, 1996, The Reef, 1997, Bongwater, 1998, Urban Legend, 1998, (voice) Gen 13, 1998, Cecil B. DeMented, 2000, Playing with Mona Lisa, 2000 (Best Actress award U.S. Comedy Arts Festival 2000), Vanilla Sky, 2001, Ten Tiny Love Stories, 2001, American Girl, 2002, Two Weeks Notice, 2002, The Upside of Anger, 2005; prodr. On the Wise, 2005; actor, prodr. Girls' Lunch, 2004; TV guest appearances Twin Peaks, 1990, Hotel Room, 1993, The Sopranos, 2000, Ally McBeal, 2000, The Twilight Zone, 2003, (mus. theater) The Gift, 2000; stage appearances Dissonance, 2007. Recipient Spl. Jury Recognition for acting, Sundance Film Festival, 1994, Ind. Spirit Award nomination, 1995. Avocations: listening to big-band recordings, chess, backgammon, bowling. *

WITT, CATHERINE LEWIS, neonatal nurse practitioner, writer; b. Burlington, Iowa, Nov. 21, 1957; d. Rodney Darrell and Neola Ann (Wharton) Lewis; m. John Robert Witt, Mar. 31, 1984; children: Jeffrey Lewis, Jennifer Diane. BSN, U. No. Colo., Greeley, 1980; MSN, U. Colo., 1987. Cert. neonatal nurse practitioner. Staff nurse St. Joseph's Hosp., Denver, 1980-85; neonatal nurse practitioner Denver Children's Hosp., 1986-88; coord. neonatal nurse practitioner and neonatal transport Presbyn.-St. Luke's Med. Ctr., Denver, 1988—2002; neotal nurse practitioner NNP Svcs. of Colo., 2003—. Mem clin faculty neonatal nurse practitioner program Regis U. Editor-in-chief: Advances in Neonatal Care; contbr. chapters to books, articles to profl. jours. Troop leader Girl Scouts US; children's Bible tchr., altar guild Episcopal Ch. Mem. Nat. Assn. Neonatal Nurses (co-chair program com. 1992-94, bd. dir., dir.-at-large 1997-99, sec. 1999-2000, pres. 2003-04, past pres. 2005—), Nat. Cert. Corp. (test. com. 1994-96, nominations com. 2004-05). Democrat. Episcopalian. Avocations: altar guild, reading, sewing, dance. Home: 17586 E Dickenson Pl Aurora CO 80013-4180 Office: Presbyn-St Luke's Med Ctr 1719 E 19th Ave Denver CO 80218-1235 Office Phone: 303-839-7735. Personal E-mail: 70044.2401@compuserve.com. Business E-Mail: catherine.witt@healthonecares.com.

WITT, DAVID L., curator, writer; b. Kansas City, Mo., Nov. 3, 1951; s. Lloyd Vernon and Dean Witt. BS in Polit. Sci., Kans. State U., 1974; M Liberal Studies, U. Okla., 2000. Naturalist Naish Nature Ctr., Edwardsville, Kans., summers 1967-70; asst. curator Seton Mus., Cimarron, N.Mex., summers 1972-74; curatorial asst. Riley County Hist. Mus., Manhattan, Kans., 1973-74; mus. asst. Millicent Rogers Mus., Taos, N.Mex., 1976-77; curator The Gaspard House Mus., Taos, N.Mex., 1978-79, The Harwood Found., Taos, N.Mex., 1979—2005, Acad. for Love of Learning, Santa Fe, 2005—. Author: The Taos Artists, 1984, Taos Moderns: Art of the New, 1992 (Southwest Book award Border Regional Libr. Assn. 1993), Modernists in Taos from Martin to Dasburg, 2002 (S.W. Book award Border Regional Libr. Assn. 2003, Ralph Emerson Twitchell award N.Mex. Hist. Soc. 2003); co-author: Spirit Ascendant: The Art and Life of Patrociño Barela, 1996 (S.W. Book award Border Regional Libr. Assn. 1997); contbr. Taos Artists and Their Patrons, 1898-1950; contbr. articles to profl. jour. Organizer first N.Mex. Art History Conf., 1986; founder S.W. Art Hist. Coun., 1990. Mem. PEN, Am. Assn. Mus., N.Mex. Assn. Mus. (pres. 1986-88). Home: PO Box 317 Taos NM 87571-0317 Personal E-mail: davidlwitt@cybermesa.com.

WITT, HUGH ERNEST, manufacturing executive, consultant; b. Winchester, Ky., Nov. 18, 1921; s. Hugh E. and Louella (Milliken) W.; m. Janie Bryan (dec. Oct. 1990); m. Evelyn Chapman, Apr. 22, 1993. Student, Transylvania U., 1941-43; BS, U. Ky., 1945; MS, MIT, 1957. Asst. to dep. asst. sec. Dept. of Air Force, Washington, 1954-61, dep. asst. sec., 1961-70, Dept. of Navy, Washington, 1970-73; prin. dep. asst. Sec. of Def., Washington, 1973-74; fed. procurement policy adminstr. Office Mgmt. and Budget, Washington, 1974-77; dir., govt. liaison United Techs. Corp., Washington, 1977-81, v.p., govt. liaison, 1981-87, cons. to United Techs. Corp., 1987—. Pres. Old Town Civic Assn., Alexandria, Va., 1961-63; bd. dirs. Alexandria Hist. Found.; mem. Alexandria Bd. Archtl. Rev., 1964-77; trustee Alexandria Hosp. Found., 1992-94. Alfred P. Sloan fellow MIT, Cambridge, Mass., 1956-57. Fellow Nat. Contract Mgmt. Assn.; mem. Aerospace Industries Assn., Nat. Security Indsl. Assn., MIT Alumni Assn., Soc. Sloan Fellows, Kappa Alpha.

WITT, JAMES LEE, management consultant, former federal agency administrator; b. Dardanelle, Ark., 1944; m. Lea; children: Jimmy, Michael. Founder Witt Constrn. Co.; county judge Yell County, Ark.; state dir. Office Emergency Svcs., Ark.; dir. Fed. Emergency Mgmt. Agy. (FEMA), Washington, 1993—2001; chmn., CEO James Lee Witt Assoc., LLC, Washington, 2002—; CEO Internat. Code Coun., 2003—; nat. co-chmn. ProtectingAmerica.org, Washington, 2006—. Chmn. bd. Child Devel., Inc., charter; Gov.'s rep. state disasters, Presdl. disasters; bd. govs. ARC. Recognized for reinvention efforts Nat. Assn. Counties. Office: James Lee Witt Associates LLC 701 13th St NW Ste 800 Washington DC 20005-3967

WITT, JIM, executive editor; Grad., Tex. State U., San Marcos, 1974. Asst. mng. editor, news Star-Telegram Arlington, 1986—92, editor, 1992—95; pub. Star Telegram Northeast Tarrant County Ed., 1995—95; sr. v.p. & exec. editor Ft. Worth Star-Telegram, 1996—. Named to University Star Hall of Fame, Tex. State U.-San Marcos, 2007. Mem.: Tex. AP Mng. Editors, Am. Soc. Newspaper Editors. Office: Ft Worth Star-Telegram 400 W 7th St Fort Worth TX 76102-4701 Office Phone: 817-390-7704. E-mail: jwitt@star-telegram.com. *

WITT, ROBERT E., academic administrator; b. Sept. 16, 1940; m. Anne Witt; children: Peter, Karen. BA in Econs., Bates Coll., 1962; MBA, Dartmouth Coll., 1964; PhD in Bus. Adminstrn., Pa. State U., 1968. Rsch. asst. Amos Tuck Sch., Dartmouth Coll., Hanover, N.H., 1964-65; instr. mktg. Pa. State U., 1967-68; asst. prof. Coll. and Grad. Sch. Bus., U. Tex., Austin, 1968-71, assoc. prof., 1971-75, chmn. dept. mktg., 1973-83, prof., 1975-83, Zale Corp. centennial prof. bus., 1983-85, Betty and Glenn Mortimer centennial prof. bus., 1985-95, centennial chairperson bus. edn. leadership, 1986-95, acting dean, then dean, 1985—95; interim pres. U. Tex., Arlington, 1995-96, pres., 1996—2003, U. Ala., 2003—. Mem. budget coun. dept. mktg. adminstrn. U. Tex., Austin, 1969-85, mem. faculty exec. devel. program 1969—, mem. dean's coun., 1986—; mem. athletes adv. com. NCAA, 1986—; mem. acad. adv. bd. World Mgmt. Coun., 1988; mem. future directions coun. U. Tex. Ex-Students Assn., 1978-88, mem. exec. coun., 1981-83, 87-89; mem. adv. bd. dirs. Post Oak Bank, 1993—, Frost Nat. Bank, 1993—; mem. Acctg. Edn. Change Commn., 1992—; bd. dirs. Life Ptnrs. Group. Assoc. editor Social Sci. Quar., 1970-72; mem. editl. rev. bd. Jour. Mktg., 1971-73, 82-85; contbr. articles to profl. jours. Bd. dirs. Austin Symphony, 1991—, Univ. Coop. Soc., 1978-82. Recipient Top Hand award U. Tex. Ex-Students Assn., 1988. Mem. Am. Mktg. Assn. (fellow doctoral consortium 1967, program chmn. doctoral consortium 1972, reviewer, presenter), Assn. for Consumer Rsch. (treas. 1976, mem. exec. com. 1975-76, reviewer, conf. session chmn.), Am. Assembly Collegiate Schs. of Bus. (bd. dirs. 1991—, mem. visitation com. 1991, mem. govtl. rels. com. 1986-89, chmn. govtl. rels. com. 1987-89), So. Mktg. Assn. (conf. trach chmn., presenter), Beta Gamma Sigma (v.p. U. Tex. chpt. 1973-74, pres. chpt. 1974-75), Phi Kappa Phi. Office: Office of Pres PO Box 870100 203 Rose Administration Tuscaloosa AL 35487-0100 Office Phone: 205-348-5100. Office Fax: 205-348-8377. E-mail: witt@pres.ua.edu. *

WITT, RUTH HUTT, management consultant; b. Columbus, Aug. 8, 1957; d. Thomas Micijah and Mary Barnes; children: Jeffrey Tyler Sheppar, William Fisher III. B of Elec. Engring. Tech., Ohio Inst. Tech., Columbus, 1979. Metallurgical tech. Reynolds Metal, Richmond, Va.; bus. analyst Va. Power, Lavisa; mng. prin. Oracle, Reston. Home: 15255 Brazil Cir Dale City VA 22193 Office: Oracle 1910 Oracle Way Reston VA 20190

WITT, TOM, economics researcher, educator; b. Borger, Tex., Apr. 22, 1944; s. Eugene Thomason and Helen C. (Hathaway) W.; m. Grethe A. Myles, Mar. 4, 1976. BA, Okla. State U., Stillwater, 1966; MA, Washington U., St. Louis, 1968, PhD, 1974. Asst. prof. dept. econs. W.Va. U., Morgantown, 1970-75, assoc. prof. dept. econs., 1975-80, acting asst. dean Grad. Sch., 1977-78, exec. dir. Bur. Bus. Rsch., 1985—, dir. Ctr. Econs. Rsch., 1985—, acting assoc. dean Coll. Bus. and Econs., 1985-86, assoc. dean rsch. and outreach Coll. Bus. and Econs., 1994—2006. Cons. Nat. Regulatory Rsch. Inst., Columbia, Ohio, 1980-81, Am. Electric Power, 1995—, Allegheny Power, 1997—, exec. legis. br. Govt. W.Va., 1985—; cons., expert witness W.Va. Human Rights Commn., Charleston, 1984; expert witness W.Va. Atty. Gen., 1987-88, Ashland Oil, 1992-93. Author: Power from the Appalachians, 1989, also monographs; co-editor: West Virginia in the Nineties: Policies for Econ. Progress; econs. columnist The State Jour., Charleston; contbr. articles to profl. jours. Pres. Cheat Canyon Park Homeowners, Morgantown, 1979-87, Monongalia Arts Ctr., 1980-81; bd. dirs., treas. Friends of W.Va. Pub. Radio, Charleston, 1985-93, chmn.,

1989-91; sec.-treas. Cheat Neck Pub. Svc. Dist., 1989-95; mem. Monongalia County Econ. Devel. Authority, 1994—. Mem. Am. Econ. Assn., Regional Sci. Assn., Assn. for Univ. Bus. and Econ. Rsch. (pres. 2000-2001). Home: 3202 Deerfield Ct Morgantown WV 26508-8612 Office: Bureau of Bus & Econ Rsch WV U PO Box 6025 Morgantown WV 26506-6025 Business E-Mail: twitt@wvu.edu.

WITT, WALTER FRANCIS, JR., lawyer; b. Richmond, Va., Feb. 18, 1933; s. Walter Francis and Evelyn Virginia (Riggleman) W.; m. Rosemary Winter, Sept. 5, 1964; children: Leslie Anne Millman, Walter Francis III. BS, U. Richmond, 1954, JD, 1966. Bar: Va. 1966, DC 1974. Assoc. Hunton and Williams, Richmond, 1966-74, ptnr., 1974—. Contbr. articles to profl. jours. 1st lt. US Army, 1955-57. Mem. ABA (chmn. real property com. sect. gen. practice 1995-2000, Va. Bar Assn., Richmond Bar Assn., DC Bar Assn., Phi Beta Kappa, Phi Delta Phi. Home: 8901 Tresco Rd Richmond VA 23229-7725 Office Phone: 804-788-8391.

WITTBRODT, EDWIN STANLEY, financial planner, consultant, retired military officer; b. Flint, Mich., Aug. 13, 1918; s. Stanley Frank and Marie (Ross) W.; m. Joan Helen Miller, Apr. 22, 1950; children: Stephanie Rita, Candace Lee, Edwin Stanley. Student, Gen. Motors Inst. Tech., 1936-38, Grad. Sch. Dept. Agr., 1950-51, Indsl. Coll. Defense U., 1961-62, George Washington U., 1962, U. So. Calif., 1963-64, Defense Computer Inst., 1967, U. NH, 1976. Joined U.S. Army, 1941, commd. 2d lt., 1942; advanced through grades to brig. gen. USAF, 1968; various assignments, 1941-49; budget officer Hdqrs. USAF, 1949-53, 56-61; dir. budget and acctg. Hdqrs. N.E. Air Command, Nfld., 1953-56; comptroller space systems div. Los Angeles, 1962-64; comptroller aero., systems div. Wright-Patterson AFB, 1964-66; asst. comptroller USAF, 1966-67; dir. acctg. and fin. Hdqrs. USAF, 1967-68; asst. comptroller air force for acctg. and fin., comdr. Air Force Acctg. and Fin. Ctr., Denver, 1968-71; v.p. systems Cen. Bank Denver, 1971-81, v.p. info. resources mgmt., 1981-84. Bd. dirs. Computer Congenerics Corp. Colo., Hasa Corp. Co-chmn. Combined Fed. Campaign, Denver, 1968-87; Hon. dir. USO, Denver, 1968-71, mem. council, 1971-87. Decorated D.S.M., Legion of Merit, Soldier's medal, Commendation medal with oak leaf cluster; recipient Gen. Jimmy Doolittle Disting. Fellow award, Flint No. Alumni Assn. Disting. Fellow award, 1990, Treas. Dept. Pioneer in Elec. Commerce award, 1995. Mem. Am. Soc. Mil. Comptrollers (past pres. Washington chpt., nat. v.p. 1968-70, pres. Denver chpt. 1971-72), Assn. Govt. Accountants, Assn. Mil. Banks (dir. 1974-84), Am. Inst. Banking, Denver C. of C. (chmn. mil. affairs com. 1979-82), Aurora C. of C. (def. coun. 1987—), Air Force Assn. (v.p. N. Colo. 1971-72, pres. Silver and Gold chpt. 1972-73, state treas. 1976-83, pres. Mile High chpt. 1987-88) Clubs: Columbine Country. Home: 3091 Mill Vista Rd #1301 Highlands Ranch CO 80129 *I have adopted two attitudes that I believe assisted me in all of my undertakings: (1)— that of being what I call a "responsible non-conformist" and (2)— "no problems— just opportunities".*

WITTBRODT, ELIZABETH S., occupational therapist, educator; BS in Occupl. Therpay, Western Mich. U., Kalamazoo, 1982; M Health Sci., Govs.State U., Chgo., 1990; EdD, Loyola U., Chgo., 1997. Cert. Nat. Bd. of Occupl. Therapy Bethesda, 1982. Staff occupl. therapist Jewish Hosp. of Cin., Cincinnati, Ohio, 1982—85; staff occupl. therapist neuro-trauma Loyola U. Med. Ctr., Maywood, Ill., 1985—86; clin. coord. Hinsdale Hosp., Hinsdale, Ill., 1986—87; assoc. prof. occupl. therapy Chgo. State U., Chgo., 1987—; registry staff Hinsdale Hosp., Hinsdale, Ill., 1990—. Roster accreditation evaluators for occupl. therapy edn., Bethesda, Md., 2003—. Contbr. articles to profl. jours. Bd. mem. Riverside Twp. Mental Health Bd., Riverside Township, Ill., 2003—06; adv. bd. mem. Health Care Adv. Bd., Congressional Dist., Ill., 1999—2000; v.p. Youth Scholarship Com., North Riverside, Ill., 2000—. Recipient Faculty Excellence, Chgo. State U., 1993, 1994, 1996, 1997, 2001, Occupl. Therapist of the Yr., Ill. Occupl. Therapy Assn., 1995. Mem.: Ill. Occupl. Therapy Assn. (dir. membership 1997—2006, pres. 2006—07, Ill. Occupl. Therapist of the Yr. 1995), Am. Occupl. Therapy Assn., Phi Delta Kappa. Office: Chgo State Univ 9501 King Dr Chicago IL 60628 Home Phone: 708-442-0390. Office Fax: 773-995-2839; Home Fax: 708-442-6585. Personal E-mail: elizawitt1@aol.com. Business E-Mail: ewittbro@csu.edu.

WITTCOFF, HAROLD AARON, chemist; b. Marion, Ind., July 3, 1918; s. Morris and Bessie (Pruss) W.; m. Dorothy Brochin, 1946; 2 sons AB magna cum laude, DePauw U., Greencastle, Ind., 1940; PhD, Northwestern U., Evanston, Ill., 1943; grad., Advanced Mgmt. Program, Harvard U., Cambridge, Mass., 1964. From mem. staff to v.p., dir. chem. R&D Gen. Mills, Inc., Mpls., 1943—79; v.p., dir. corp. rsch. Gen. Mills Chemicals, Inc., 1969—79; dir. R & D Koor Chems., Beer Sheva, Israel, 1979-82; dir. process evaluation and rsch. planning Chem Systems, Tarrytown, N.Y., 1982-85; sci. adviser NEXANT/Chem Systems, White Plains, NY, 1985—; adj. prof. chemistry U. Minn., 1973-82. Vis. prof. Chulalongkorn U., Thailand, 1995-2005; adj. prof. chemistry Weizmann Inst., Israel, 1979-2005. Author: The Phosphatides, 1951, Industrial Organic Chemistry: A Perspective 2 vols. 1980; Pharmaceutical Chemicals in Perspective, 1989, Industrial Organic Chemicals, 1996, 2nd edit., 2004, Organic Chemistry Principles and Industrial Practice, 2003; patentee in field. Recipient Minn. award Am. Chem. Soc., 1976 Mem. Phi Beta Kappa, Sigma Xi, Phi Eta Sigma. Home: Box 307 Scarborough NY 10510 Office: Nexant Inc 4450 S White Plains NY 10601 Office Phone: 914-609-0330. Personal E-mail: hawittcoff@yahoo.com. Business E-Mail: hwittcoff@nexant.com.

WITTE, ARNOLD STEWART, neurologist; b. NYC, Dec. 14, 1952; s. Henry Dennis Witte and Shirley Block; m. Debra J. DeLuca, Apr. 29, 1984; children: Samantha, Russell, Daniel, Larissa. BS, SUNY, Stony Brook, 1973; MD, Tufts U., 1977. Diplomate Am. Bd. Internal Medicine, Am. Bd. Neurology & Psychiatry, Am. Bd. Electrodiagnostic Medicine, lic. NJ, Pa. Intern U. Hosps. Cleve., Cleve., 1977—78, resident, 1978—79; resident in neurology Hosp. of U. Pa., Phila., 1980—81, fellow, 1982—83; asst. prof. neurology Thomas Jefferson U. Hosp., 1983—86; mem. staff Capital Health Sys. at Mercer, 1986—, chief dept. neurology, 1989—96, 1999, vice chief dept. neurology, 2000—. Cons. Trenton Psychiat. Hosp., 1987—, Forensic Psychiat. Hosp., 1987—; courtesy staff St. Francis Med. Ctr., 1993—; active staff Robert Wood U. Hosp., Hamilton. Contbr. articles to profl. jours. Mem.: AMA, Mercer County Med. Soc., Am. Acad. Neurology, Alpha Omega Alpha. Office: 2 Princess Rd Lawrenceville NJ 08648 Office Phone: 609-895-9000.

WITTE, DALE ANDREW, choral director, educator; b. Marshfield, Wis., Nov. 20, 1967; s. David Albert and Dorothy Lee Witte; m. Renee Sue Heckendorf, June 22, 1991; children: Jonathan David, Hannah Beth. BS, Dr. Martin Luther Coll., New Ulm, Minn., 1989; M in Ch. Music, Concordia U., River Forest, Ill., 1997. Tchr., choir dir. St. Paul Luth. Ch., Tomah, Wis., 1989—93; choral dir., music tchr. Winnebago Luth. Acad., Fond du Lac, Wis., 1993—2006. Music Tech. Lab grantee, Internat. Paper, 2006. Mem.: Music Educators Nat. Conf. (assoc.), Am. Choral Dirs. Assn. (assoc.). Home: 51 E Arndt St Fond Du Lac WI 54935 Office: Winnebago Luth Acad 475 E Merrill Ave Fond Du Lac WI 54935 Home Phone: 920-923-3059; Office Phone: 920-921-4930.

WITTE, OWEN NEIL, microbiologist, molecular biologist, educator; b. Bklyn., May 17, 1949; BS, Cornell U., 1971; MD, Stanford U., 1976. Predoctoral fellow Stanford U. Med. Sch., Palo Alto, Calif., 1971-76, MIT Ctr. Cancer Rsch., Cambridge, Mass., 1976-80; asst. prof., Dept. Microbiology, Molecular Genetics UCLA, 1980-82, assoc. prof., Dept. Microbiology, Molecular Genetics, 1982-86, prof., Dept. Microbiology, Molecular Genetics, 1986—, pres.'s chair in devel. immunology, Dept. Microbiology, Molecular Genetics, 1989—, founding dir., Inst. for Stem Cell Biology and Medicine, 2005—; investigator UCLA Howard Hughes Med. Inst., 1986—; prof., microbiology, immunology & molecular genetics UCLA David Geffen Sch. Medicine, 1996—, prof. molecular and med. pharmacology. Adv. bd. mem. Pew Scholars in Biomedical Sci., Damon Runyon Scholars Bd., Lasker Prize Award Jury. Contbr. articles to profl. jours. Am. Cancer Soc. faculty scholar, 1982-87; recipient Faculty award UCLA, 1990, award in basic cancer rsch. Milken Family Med. Found., 1990, Richard and Hinda Rosenthal Found. award Am. Assn. Cancer Rsch., 1991, William Dameshek prize Am. Soc. Hematology, 1993; Outstanding Investigator grantee Nat. Cancer Inst., 50th Anniversary Commemorative award, Leukemia Soc. of Amer., 1999, Warren Alpert Found. prize, 2000, de Villiers Internat. Achievement award, Leukemia and Lymphoma Soc., 2003 Fellow Am. Acad. Arts and Scis., 1996, Am. Acad. Microbiology, 1997; mem. NAS, Inst. Medicine. Office Phone: 310-206-0386. E-mail: owenw@microbio.ucla.edu. *

WITTE, ROBERT JAY, lawyer; b. Oklahoma City, May 16, 1968; s. Richard Owen and Janice (Hester) W.; m. Deborah Lynn Hammond, June 15, 1991; children, Brandon Ryan, Courtney Nicole. BA with highest honors, U. Okla, 1990; JD cum laude, So. Meth. U., Dallas, 1993. Bar: Tex. 1993, US Dist. Ct. 1994, US Ct. Appeals (5th cir.) 1994, US Supreme Ct., 1999, US Ct. Appeals (10th cir.) 2002. Atty. Winstead, P.C., Dallas, 1993—. Bd. dirs. Tex. Young Lawyers Assn., 2000—05. Bd. dirs. Dallas Summer Musicals, 2005-, DSM Gala co-chair, 2008; bd. dirs. Dallas Arts Dist. Alliance, 2005-, Am. Heart Assn., 1997-2001; bd. dirs., pres. U. Okla. Club of Dallas, 2002—; bd. dirs., chair. Make-A-Wish Found. of North Tex., 1996—; founding chair Muscular Dystrophy Assn. Dallas Legal Leaders: Hot Hundred Who Care. Named a Tex. Super Lawyer, Tex. Monthly, 2003—06; named one of Best Dallas Lawyers Under 40, D Mag., 2002, 2004, 2006, Best Lawyers in Dallas, 2005, 2007, Top 40 Bus. Leaders Under 40, Dallas Bus. Jour., 2002, 2005, 2006; recipient Dallas Heart Ball Debra Sue Payne award, Nat. Philanthropy Day award, 2001. Mem. Dallas Bar Assn., Dallas Assn. Young Lawyers (Com. chair leadership devel. 1997—, bd. dirs. 1999-2005, trustee), ABA, Tex. Bar Found., Dallas Bar Found., Leadership Dallas Alumni Assn. Republican. Methodist. Avocations: golf, softball, following college and professional sports, politics. Office: Winstead PC 5400 Renaissance Tower 1201 Elm St Dallas TX 75270-2199 Office Phone: 214-745-5861. Office Fax: 214-745-5390. Business E-Mail: rwitte@winstead.com.

WITTELS, BARNABY CAESAR, lawyer, writer; b. Phila., Mar. 28, 1948; s. David G. and Beatrice Tanya (Graitcer) Wittels; m. Heidi Jo Linsk, Sept. 8, 1974 (div. Aug. 1997); children: Kate Sophie, William David; m. Mary M. Labaree, Sept. 20, 1998. BA cum laude, Temple U., 1970; MA in Pol. Sci., Boston U., 1972, JD, 1975. Bar: Pa. 1975, U.S. Dist. Ct. (ea. dist.) Pa. 1985, U.S. Dist. Ct. Appeals (2d, 3d and 4th cirs.) 1986. Asst. defender Defender Assn. Phila., 1975-80; law clk. to Hon. Stanley Kubacki Ct. Common Pleas Phila. County, 1980-84; ptnr. Wittels, Newman & Bomstein, Phila., 1980-82; assoc. LaCheen & Alva, Phila., 1982-86; ptnr. LaCheen & Assoc., Phila., 1986—2003, LaCheen, Dixon, Wittels & Greenburg, Phila., 2003—. Advisor Temple U. Parliamentary Debate Team, 2004—; mem. lawyers assistance com. Pa. Supreme Ct. Contbr. columns in newspapers. Chair N.W. Victim Svcs., Phila., 1981—84, mem. counsel, 1984—90, bd. dirs., 1983—90, chair, 1997—2003, founding mem., mem. bd. dirs. counsel, 2003—; baseball coach Chestnut Hill Fathers Club, 1985—98, commr., 1991—93, 1992—98; vol. Lawyers Concerned for Lawyers, 2003—; committeeman 21st divsn. Dems., Phila., 1985—90; active various polit. and jud. campaigns, 1980—; mem. exec. com. N.W. Interfaith Movement, 1985—86. Mem.: ABA, NACDL, Phila. Bar Found. (Apothaker award 1983), Pa. Bar Assn., Phila. Bar Assn. (mem. fee dispute com. 1996—, mem. com. to elect good judges 1987—88, mem. lawyers assistance com. 2003—), Pa. Assn. Criminal Def. Lawyers. Jewish. Avocations: writing, baseball, football, reading, woodworking. Office: LaCheen Dixon Wittels & Greenberg 1429 Walnut St 13th Fl Philadelphia PA 19102 Office Phone: 215-735-5900. Office Fax: 215-735-4649. Personal E-mail: barnabyw@aol.com.

WITTEMYER, JOHN, lawyer; b. Boulder, Colo., Dec. 19, 1939; s. Leonard and Beatrice Augusta (Dickhut) W.; m. Nancy Jean Vincent, June 6, 1964; children— Jon Vincent, Christopher Glen, Luke Leonard. B.S.C.E., U. Colo., 1962, B.S. in Bus., 1962, LL.B., 1965. Bar: Colo. 1965, Alaska 1965. Law clk. U.S. Supreme Ct. Alaska, 1965; dist. atty. 1st Jud. Dist. Alaska, Juneau, 1966-67; sole practice, Boulder, 1967-73; ptnr. Moses, Wittemyer, Harrison & Woodruff, P.C., Boulder, 1973—; gen. counsel Platte River Power Authority, 1975—2002; chmn. bd., chief exec. officer Crowley land and Devel. Co., subs. Aetna Casualty and Surety Co., Ordway, Colo., 1970-75. Mem. ABA, Colo. Bar Assn., Boulder Bar Assn., Colo. Cattlemen's Assn. Republican. Methodist. Club: Country. Home: Sunshine Canyon PO Box 4575 Boulder CO 80306-4575 Office: PO Box PO Box 1440 Boulder CO 80306-1440

WITTEN, DAVID MELVIN, retired radiology educator; b. Trenton, Mo., Aug. 16, 1926; s. Buford Isom and Mary Louise (Melvin) W.; m. Netta Lee Watkins, Dec. 23, 1950; children— David Melvin, II, Michael Lee. Student, Trenton Jr. Coll., 1943-44, 46-47; AB, Washington U., St. Louis, 1950, MD, 1954; MS in Radiology, U. Minn., 1960. Diplomate: Am. Bd. Radiology. Intern Virginia Mason Hosp., Seattle, 1954-55; practice medicine specializing in family medicine Trenton, Mo., 1955-57; fellow in radiology Mayo Clinic/Mayo Found., Rochester, Minn., 1957-60; cons. in diagnostic roentgenology Mayo Clinic, 1960-70; instr. Mayo Grad. Sch. Medicine, Rochester, 1960-66, asst. prof. radiology, 1966-70; pvt. practice medicine specializing in radiology Aberdeen, Wash., 1970-71; clin. assoc. prof. U. Wash., 1970-71; prof. diagnostic radiology, chmn. dept. diagnostic radiology U. Ala., Birmingham, 1971-82; diagnostic radiologist in chief Univ. Hosp., Birmingham, 1971-82; prof., chmn. dept. radiology U. Mo., Columbia, 1982-87, prof. emeritus, 1987—, interim chmn. dept. radiology, 1998-99. Pres. U. Ala. Health Services Found., 1973-75 Author: Atlas of Tumor Radiology-The Breast, 1969, Clinical Urography, 1970, 77; contbr. articles on radiology of breast cancer, urologic and gastrointestinal disease to profl. jours.; mem. editorial bd. Am. Jour. Roentgenology, 1976-87, Applied Radiology, 1978-87, Urologic Radiology, 1979-87, Radiographics, 1983-87. Served with USNR, 1944-46. Fellow Am. Coll. Radiology; mem. AAAS, AMA, Radiol. Soc. N.Am., Am. Roentgen Ray Soc., Soc. Uroradiology (pres. 1981-82, Gold medal 2003), Soc. Uroradiology (gold medal 2003), Assn. Univ. Radiologists, Mo. Radiol. Soc. (pres. 1988-89), Mo. State Med. Assn., Can. Assn. Radiologists (hon.), Audubon Soc. (editor The Bluebird chpt. 1990-98). Home: 601 W Covered Bridge Rd Columbia MO 65203-9562 Office: Univ Mo Health Scis Ctr 1 Hospital Dr Columbia MO 65201-5276 Office Phone: 573-282-1026. Personal E-mail: dmw8@tranquility.net.

WITTEN, EDWARD, mathematical physicist; b. Balt., Aug. 26, 1951; s. Louis Witten; m. Chiara Nappi; 3 children. BA in history, Brandeis U., 1971; MA, Princeton U., 1974, PhD, 1976; PhD (hon.), Brandeis U., 1988, Hebrew U. of Jerusalem, 1993, Columbia U., 1996, U. Southern Calif., 2004. Postdoctoral fellow Harvard U., 1976—77, jr. fellow, 1977—80; prof. physics Princeton U., NJ, 1980—87; prof. Sch. Natural Scis, Inst. for Advanced Study, Princeton, NJ, 1987—; Charles Simonyi prof. Princeton U., NJ, 1997—. Vis. prof. Calif. Inst. Tech., 1999—2001. Contbr. articles to mags. and profl. jours.; co-author (with M.B. Green and J.H. Schwarz): Supersting Theory, Vol. 1 and 2, Cambridge Univ. Press. Bd. dirs. Americans for Peace Now, 1992—. MacArthur Fellow, 1982; recipient Einstein medal Einstein Soc. Berne, Switzerland, 1985, Phys. and Math. Sci. award N.Y. Acad. Sci., 1985, Dirac medal Internat. Ctr. Theoretical Physics, 1985, Alan Waterman award NSF 1986, Fields Medal, Internat. Union of Mathematicians, 1990, Madison medal, Princeton Univ., 1992, NJ Pride award, 1996, Award of the Golden Plate, Am. Acad. of Achievement, 1997, Klein medal, Stockholm U., 1998, Dannie Heineman prize, Am. Inst. of Physics, 1998, Nemmers prize in Math., Northwestern U., 2000, Clay Rsch. award, Clay Math. Inst., 2001, Shalom award, Americans for Peace Now, 2002, Nat. Medal of Science, 2002. Fellow: Am. Philosophical Soc., Am. Phys. Soc., Am. Acad. Arts & Scis., NAS; mem.: Acad. of Sciences of Paris (assoc.). Office: Inst for Advanced Study Sch Natural Scis Einstein Dr Princeton NJ 08540-4920

WITTEN, LOUIS, physics professor; b. Balt., Apr. 13, 1921; s. Abraham and Bessie (Perman) W.; m. Lorraine Wollach, Mar. 27, 1949 (dec. 1987); children: Edward, Celia, Matthew, Jesse; m. Francis L. White, Jan. 2, 1992. BE, Johns Hopkins U., Balt., 1941, PhD, 1951; BS, NYU, 1944. Research assoc. Princeton U., NJ, 1951-53; research assoc. U. Md., College Park, 1953-54; staff scientist Lincoln Lab., MIT, 1954-55; assoc. dir. Martin Marietta Research Lab., Balt., 1955-68; prof. physics U. Cin., 1968-91, prof. emeritus, 1991—. Trustee Gravity Research Found. Editor: Gravitation: An Introduction to Current Research, 1962, Relativity: Procs. of Relative Conf. in Midwest of 1969, Symposium on Asymptotic Structure of Space-Time, 1976; patentee in field; contbr. numerous articles to sci. jours. First lt. Air Corps US Army, 1942—46. Fulbright lectr. Weitzmann Inst. Scis., Rehovot, Israel, 1963-64 Fellow Am. Phys. Soc.; mem. Am. Math. Soc., Internat. Astron. Union, AAAS. Office: Univ Cincinnati Dept Physics Cincinnati OH 45221-0011 Office Phone: 513-556-0532. Business E-Mail: witten@physics.uc.edu.

WITTEN, ROGER MICHAEL, lawyer; b. Atlantic City, Nov. 13, 1946; s. H. Davis and Miriam P. (Popkin) Witten; m. Jill S. Judd, June 5, 1971; children: Wendy D., Katherine J. BA magna cum laude, Dartmouth Coll., 1968; JD cum laude, Harvard Univ., 1972. Bar: Mass. 1973, NY, US Supreme Ct. 1976. Law clk. Judge Harrison L. Winter, US Ct. Appeals (4th cir.), 1972—73; asst. spl. prosecutor Watergate Spl. Prosecution Force, Washington, 1973—74; ptnr. Wilmer Cutler Pickering, Washington, 1975—2004; ptnr., co-chmn. Internat. Litigation group, mem. mgmt. com. Wilmer Cutler Pickering Hale & Dorr, NYC, 2004—. Counsel Common Cause, 1982—; chmn. 20th Century Fund Working Group on Campaign Fin. Reform, 1998. Contbr. articles to profl. jours. Mem.: ABA (chmn. Election Law com. 1988—90), DC Bar Assn., Phi Beta Kappa. Office: Wilmer Cutler Pickering Hale & Dorr 399 Park Ave New York NY 10022 Office Phone: 212-230-8850. Office Fax: 212-230-8888. Business E-Mail: roger.witten@wilmerhale.com.

WITTENBERG, HENRY TAYLOR, JR., physician, surgeon; b. Kansas City, July 5, 1933; s. Henry Taylor and Ruby Lena (Pratt) Wittenberg; m. Helen Marie Marlar, Sept. 7, 1963; children: Heather Melanee, Henry Taylor III. BS in Pharmacy, U. Kans., Lawrence, 1956; DO, Kansas City U. Medicine and Bioscis., 1960. Lic. Mo., 1960, Okla., 1962, cert. Am. med. dir. 1998. Intern Lakeside Hosp., Kansas City, 1960—61; preceptor Claremore Health Ctr., Okla., 1962—64; physician pvt. practice, Independence, Mo., 1961—62, Blue Star Clinic, Claremore, 1962—, Claremore Regional Hosp., 1962—; interim home health med. dir., 2004—. Chief staff Claremore Regional Hosp., 1962—; founder, bd. mem. First Bank of Okla., 1977, v.p. bd., 1977—87; founding mem. Okla. chpt. Am. Med. Dirs., 1991, v.p. bd., 1991—95; med. dir. Wood Manor Nursing Home, 1987—, Claremore Nursing Home, 1989—, Trinity Hospice, 2000—, Colonial Care Nursing Home, 2002—; mem. gov.'s com. Emergency Med. Svc., 1995—2000; mem. adv. bd. Unicare Welfare HMO, 2002—04. Editor-in-chief: U. Kans. Jayhawker U. Kans. Yearbook, 1956. Founding mem., pres. Claremore Jaycees; chmn. Rogers County March of Dimes, 1965—67; Jaycee founder group, original cast mem. Claremore Gridiron, 1966—; lay reader St. Paul's Episcopal Ch., jr. warden, 1998, sr. warden, 1999. Named Physician of Yr., Claremore, Okla., 1996, Rep. of Yr., Nat. Rep. Congressional Com. and Bus. Adv. Coun., 2001; named one of Am.'s Top Family Doctors, Consumer Rsch. Coun. Am., 2004, 2007; recipient Omicron Delta Kappa Scholastic award, Kans. U., Otto Schnellbacjer award Outstanding Contbr. Campus L:ife, Nat. Leadership award, Nat. Rep. Congressional Com., cert. for contbns. to ambulatory care and pub. health, CDC. Mem.: Rogers County Med. Soc. (v.p. 1986, program dir. 1986—97), Okla. Osteo. Assn. (life), U. Kans. Gold Medal Club, Shrine (Potentate's Honor award 2003), Scottish Rite, Masons, Rho Sigma Chi, Sigma Sigma Phi, Psi Sigma Alpha, Kappa Psi (pres.), Delta Chi. Episcopalian. Achievements include delivery over 3000 babies. Office: Blue Star Clinic 206 E Blue Star Dr Claremore OK 74017 Home Phone: 918-341-4278; Office Phone: 918-341-4040.

WITTENBORG, KARIN, university librarian; m. Michael B. Sullivan. BA, Brown U., 1969; MLS, SUNY Buffalo, 1976. Various positions SUNY Buffalo, 1976—79; libr. mgmt. intern MIT, 1981—82; chief gen. reference dept. and curator social sci. collections Stanford U., 1979—85; assoc. univ. libr. collections UCLA, 1985—93; univ. libr. U. Va., 1993—. Adv. coun. Academic Computing and Libr. Stanford U.; mem. com. info. resources Brown U.; exec. com. Digital Libr. Fedn. Recipient Zintl Leadership award, U. Va., 2005. Avocations: cooking, running, gardening. Office: Univ Virginia Library PO Box 400113 Charlottesville VA 22904 Office Phone: 434-924-7849. Fax: 434-924-1431. E-mail: kw7g@virginia.edu. *

WITTENBRAKER, RICK L., lawyer, waste management executive; b. New Castle, Ind., Mar. 25, 1948; BBA cum laude, Tex. Christian U., Ft. Worth, 1970; JD, U. Tex., Austin, 1973. Bar: Tex. 1973. Ptnr. Bracewell & Patterson, LLP, Houston, 1983—2003; sr. v.p., gen. counsel, chief compliance officer Waste Mgmt. Inc., Houston, 2003—. Mem. exec. com. bd. dirs. Spring Branch Edn. Found., Houston; bd. trustees Tex. Christian U.; bd. dirs. Assn. Cmty. Broadcasting (Houston Pub. Broadcasting). Mem.: Beta Gamma Sigma. Office: Waste Mgmt Inc 1001 Fannin St Ste 4000 Houston TX 77002 Office Phone: 713-512-6361. E-mail: rwittenbraker@wm.com. *

WITTENBURG, MICHAEL SHANE, concert pianist, music educator; b. Saarbrücken, Germany, Nov. 26, 1973; s. John Steven and Margaret Wittenburg; 1 child, Karl Frederick. MusB in Performance-Piano, Eastman Sch. Music, 1996, MusM in Performance and Lit.-Piano, 1998; MusM in Performance-Orchestral Conducting, U. Tenn., Chattanooga, 2001. Instr. music Lee U., Cleveland, Tenn., 2001—04, asst. prof. music, 2004—; organist Christ United Meth. Ch., Chattanooga, 1999—; sect. violin Chattanooga Symphony and Opera, 1999—. Named Oustanding Grad. Student in Music: Performance, U. Tenn., Chattanooga, 2000; recipient Performer's cert. in Piano, Eastman Sch. Music, 1996; fellow Opera Coaching, 1996—98. Mem.: Am. Fedn. Musicians (mem. local 80), Pi Kappa Lambda (Faculty Inductee 2005). Conservative. Avocations: tennis, travel. Home: 621 Memorial Dr #1501 Chattanooga TN 37415 Office: Lee Univ Cleveland TN Home Phone: 423-875-6579. Personal E-mail: deliusfan@aol.com. E-mail: mwittenburg@leeuniversity.edu.

WITTES, ROBERT E., physician, science foundation director; b. NYC, Mar. 20, 1943; married; 3 children. AB magna cum laude, Harvard U., 1964, MD cum laude, 1968. Intern in medicine Beth Israel Hosp., Boston, 1968-69, resident, 1969-70; rsch. assoc. lab. biochemistry Nat. Cancer Inst., NIH, Bethesda, Md., 1970-72; fellow in med. oncology Meml. Hosp., 1972-73, clin. asst. physician med. oncology svc., 1973-74, 74-75; physician to outpatients N.Y. Hosp., NYC, 1974-76; asst., then assoc. attending physician solid tumor svc. Meml. Hosp., 1975-83, asst. chief, 1979-83; assoc. dir. cancer therapy evaluation program Nat. Cancer Inst., NIH, Bethesda, 1983-88, chief medicine br. clin. oncology program, 1990-95, dir. divsn. cancer treatment, diagnosis and ctrs., 1995—2002, dep. dir. extramural sci., 1997—2002; Physician in Chief Memorial Sloan-Kettering Cancer Center, 2002—. Asst. in medicine, Harvard U. Sch. Medicine,

1969-70; instr. medicine Georgetown U. Sch. Medicine, Washington, 1970-72; fellow in medicine, Cornell U. Med. Coll., 1972-74, instr. 1974-75, asst. prof., 1975-79, assoc. prof., 1980-83; rsch. assoc. Sloan-Kettering Inst., 1975-83; vis. physician Walter Reed Army Med. Ctr., Washington, 1987-88. Mem. editorial bd. Jour. clin. Oncology, 1983-86, Internat. Jour. Radiation Oncology, Biology and physis, 1987—, Am. Jour. clin. Oncology, 1985—, Cancer Investigation, 1983—, Current Opinion in Oncology, 1988—; editor-in-chief Cancer Treatment Reports, 1983-87, Primry Care and Cancer, 1982—, NCI Monographs, 1986-88, Jour. Nat. Cancer Inst., 1988, Oncology, 1987—. With USPHS. Fellow ACP; mem. AAAS, Am. Assn. Cancer Rsch., Am. Fedn. for Clin. Rsch., Am. Soc. Clin. Oncology, Internat. Assn. for Study of Lung Cancer, Soc. Head and Neck Surgeons (cons.). Office: Meml Sloan-Kettering Cancer Ctr 1275 York Ave New York NY 10021-0001

WITTICH, JOHN JACOB, retired academic administrator, finance company executive; b. Huntley, Ill., Nov. 13, 1921; s. John and Eva (Karl) W.; m. Leah Elliott, Apr. 2, 1944; children: Karen Ann Zvonar, Jane Ellen Tock, John Elliott. BA, DePauw U., 1943, LLD (hon.), 1971; MA, U. N.Mex., 1949; PhD, Stanford U., 1952; LHD (hon.), Ill. Coll., 1979; DPS (hon.), MacMurray Coll., 1980. Tchr. Albuquerque H.S., 1948-49; tchg. asst. Stanford, 1949-51; asst. prof. psychology Coll. of Pacific, Stockton, Calif., 1951-52; dean of admissions and fin. aid, assoc. prof. DePauw U., Greencastle, Ind., 1952-61; exec. dir. Coll. Center of Finger Lakes, Corning, NY, 1961-63, Coll. Student Personnel Inst., Claremont, Calif., 1963-68; adj. prof., dir. grad. studies in student pers. Claremont Grad. Sch., 1963-68; pres. MacMurray Coll., Jacksonville, Ill., 1968-80; dir. Fla. Assn. Colls. and Univs., 1980-84; dir. higher edn. program Stetson U., 1981-88; v.p. Capital Formation Counselors, Inc., Belleair Bluffs, Fla., 1983—2005. Contbr. articles to profl. jours. Exec. com. Divsn. Higher Edn., Ctrl. Ill. Conf. of United Meth. Ch., 1968-80; exec. com. Fedn. Independent Ill. Colls. and Univs. and Assoc. Colls. Ill.; non-pub. adv. com. Ill. Bd. Higher Edn., 1972-78; mem. Nat. Merit Scholarship Selection Com., 1956, 61; cons. Calif. Gov.'s Conf. on Edn., 1965, on Youth, 1966; trustee Fla. Endowment for Humanities, 1982-85; presdl. counsellor Stetson U., 1987—; bd. dirs. DeLand House Next Door, 1990-94; citizens adv. com. West Volusia Hosp. Authority, 1992-2002, vice-chmn., 2001-02; rsch. project evaluator for human subjects regional office U.S. FDA, 2003-06. With USMC, 1943-46, PTO. Recipient DePauw Achievement award, 1969, Alumni citation DePauw U., 1994; Rockefeller fellow Aspen Inst. for Humanistic Studies, 1979. Mem. APA, Am. Coll. Pers. Assn. (commn. chmn.), Nat. Assn. Coll. Admissions Counselors (exec. bd. 1955-58), Cen. States Coll. Assn. (exec. com. 1969-77, sec.-treas. 1970-77), 4th Marine Divsn. Assn. WW II, Sigma Chi. Office Phone: 217-352-4617. Personal E-mail: john.wittich@gmail.com.

WITTIG, RAYMOND SHAFFER, lawyer, intellectual property technology manager; b. Allentown, Pa., Dec. 13, 1944; s. Raymond Battie and Alice (Shaffer) Wittig; m. Beth Glover, June 21, 1975; children: Meaghan G., Allison G. BA, Pa. State U., 1966, MEd, 1968; JD, Dickinson Sch. Law, 1974. Bar: U.S. Ct. Appeals (DC cir.) 1978. Rsch. psychologist Intext Corp., Scranton, Pa., 1968; minority counsel Small Bus. Com., U.S. Ho. of Reps., Washington, 1975-84; pvt. practice Washington, 1984-92; tech. mgmt. group leader Geo-Ctrs., Inc., Newton, Mass., 1992—2005; prin. Sci. Apps. Internat. Corp. Tech. Mgmt. Advisors, 2005—. Capt. US Army, 1969—71. Mem.: ABA, AAAS, Assn. Univ. Tech. Mgrs., Am. Intellectual Property Law Assn., Fed. Lab. Consortium, Nat. Order Barristers, Licensing Execs. Soc. Office Phone: 202-841-0655.

WITTLINGER, TIMOTHY DAVID, lawyer; b. Dayton, Ohio, Oct. 12, 1940; s. Charles Frederick and Dorothy Elizabeth (Golden) W.; m. Diane Cleo Dominy, May 20, 1967; children: Kristine Elizabeth, David Matthew. BS in Math., Purdue U., 1962; JD with distinction, U. Mich., 1965. Bar: Mich. 1966, U.S. Dist. Ct. (ea. dist.) Mich. 1966, U.S. Ct. Appeals (6th cir.) 1968, U.S. Supreme Ct. 1971. Assoc. Clark Hill (formerly Hill Lewis), Detroit, 1965-72, ptnr., 1973—, head litigation dept., 1976-91, gen. counsel, 1997—, chief legal officer, 1997—. Profl. assistance com. U.S. Dist. Ct. (ea. dist.) Mich., 1981-82; mem. Mich. Supreme Ct. Com. to Evaluate Mediation Ct. Rule, 1997-98; author, lectr. Ctr. for Internat. Legal Studies, 1999—; mem. coll. fellows Ctr. Internat. Legal Studies, Salzburg, Austria; vis. prof. Southern Fed. U. Rstov-un-dun, Russia. Mem. ho. of deps. Episc. Ch., NYC, 1979-2003; vice chmn. Robert Whitaker Sch. Theology, 1983-87; sec. bd. trustees Episc. Ch., Diocese of Mich., Detroit, 1983—, sec. conv. Episc. Diocese of Mich., 1990—, ch. atty., 1997—, sec. Episc. nat. econ. justice implementation com., 1988-95, Episc. nat. exec. coun., 1991-97, nat. audit com., 2000-03; mem. Nat. Standing Commn. on Ministry Devel., 2000-06; ministry com. Nat. Episc. Jubilee, Nat. Episc. Coalition for Social Witness and Justice, Fifth Province Episc. Ecclesiastical Ct. Appeal, 1997-2000; treas. Episcopal Ch. Province V, 2006-; bd. dirs. Episc. Student Found., U. Mich., 1990-93, 2000-2002; chair Grubb Inst. Behavioral Studies Ltd., Washington, 1986—, London, 1986—; bd. dirs., treas., Birmingham Village Playhouse, 2000—; bd. trustees, Michigan Interfaith Trust Fund, 2007-. Mem. ABA, Engring. Soc. Detroit, Assn. Profl. Responsibility Lawyers. Home: 736 N Glenhurst Dr Birmingham MI 48009-1143 Office: Clark Hill 500 Woodward Ave Ste 3500 Detroit MI 48226-3435

WITTMAN, RANDY SCOTT, professional basketball coach; b. Indpls., Oct. 28, 1959; m. Kathy Wittman; children: Ryan, Lauren. BS, Ind. U., 1983. Draft pick Washington Bullets, 1983; player Atlanta Hawks, 1983—88, Sacramento Kings, 1988—89, Ind. Pacers, 1989—92, asst. coach, 1992—93, Dallas Mavericks, 1993—94, Minn. Timberwolves, 1994—99, 2001—05, 2006—07, head coach, 2007—; asst. coach Orlando Magic, 2005—06; head coach Cleve. Cavaliers, 1999—2001. Named to Ind. U. Hall of Fame, 1995. Office: Minn Timberwolves Target Center 600 First Ave N Minneapolis MN 55403-1416 *

WITTMAN, VANESSA AMES, communications executive; b. New London, Conn., Apr. 16, 1967; m. Drew M. Wittman; children: Parker, Mason. BS, U. N.C., 1989; MBA, U. Va., 1993. Assoc. Anderson Consulting, 1989—91; investment banker Morgan Stanley, 1993—96; ptnr. Sterling Payot, 1996—97; CFO Metricom, Inc., 1997—99; sr. dir. corp. devel. Microsoft Corp., 1999—2000; v.p., corp. devel. 360networks, 2000—02, CFO broadband network svcs., 2002—03; exec. v.p., CFO Adelphia Comm. Corp., 2003—. Bd. dirs. InfoSpace, Inc., Bellevue, Wash. Avocations: tennis, skiing. Office: Adelphia Comm Corp 5619 DTC Pkwy Greenwood Village CO 80111 Office Phone: 303-268-6300. Office Fax: 303-268-6495. *

WITTMANN, MARSHALL, political organization worker; b. Waco, Tex., 1953; m. Karen L. Wittmann; 2 children. Student, NYU; BA in Elem. Edn., Univ. Mich., 1975. Campaign worker Ralph Yarborough, Lyndon B. Johnson, Eugene McCarthy; with United Farm Workers, 1975—76; lobbyist Nat. Treasury Employees Union, Washington, 1980—84, 1984—86; press sec. Linda Chavez for Senate campaign, Md., 1986, Connie Morella for Congress campaign, Md., 1986; dep. asst. sec. US Dept. Health & Human Services, Washington, 1989—92; spokesman Christian Coalition, 1992—95; with Heritage Found., 1995—2000, Hudson Inst., 2000—02; press sec. to Senator John McCain US Senate, Washington, 2002—04, comm. dir. & spokesman to Senator Joseph Lieberman, 2006—; sr. fellow Dem. Leadership Coun., Washington, 2004—06. Founder Jews for George, 1988. Independent. Jewish. Widely known as a political pundit. *

WITTMER, ELYSE MARIE, academic administrator; b. Abington, Pa., Dec. 19, 1980; d. Wayne John and Janet Elise Wittmer. BA, York Coll. Pa., 2003. Devel. asst. Susquehanna Assn. Blind and Vision Impaired, Lancaster, Pa., 2003—05; devel. assoc. York Coll. Pa., 2005—07, dir. prospect mgmt. and rsch., 2007—. Chmn. pub. rels. and mktg. com. Olivia's Ho., York, 2003—06. Mem.: Assn. Fundraising Profls. (chmn. pub. rels. com. 2005—07), Jr. League NY, York Young Profls. (assoc.), Pub. Rels. Soc. Am. (life), Phi Sigma Pi (life). Office: York Coll Pa Country Club Rd York PA 17405 Home Phone: 215-815-7682; Office Phone: 717-815-6861. Business E-Mail: ewittmer@ycp.edu.

WITTMER, JAMES FREDERICK, preventive medicine physician, educator; b. Carlinville, Ill., Dec. 30, 1932; s. Franklin Benjamin and Eva Caroline (Zihlman) W.; m. Juanita Lou Wilkey, June 29, 1962; children: Ellen, Carol, Nancy. MD, Washington U., St. Louis, 1957; MPH, Harvard U., 1961. Diplomate Am. Bd. Preventive Medicine. Intern U. Va. Hosp., Charlottesville, 1857-58; commd. capt. USAF, 1958, advanced through grades to col., 1971; ret., 1979; dean allied health U. Tex. Health Sci. Ctr., San Antonio, 1979-80; asst. med. dir. Conoco Oil Co., Ponca City, Okla., 1980-81; assoc. med. dir. Mobil Oil Corp., NYC, 1981-83; dir. health, environ. and safety ITT, NYC, 1983-95, corp. v.p., 1990-95. Clin. prof. medicine Cornell U. Med. Coll., NYC, 1984—; lectr. environ. medicine NYU, NYC, 1984—; adj. prof. U. Tex. Sch. Pub. Health, Houston, 1987—, prof. occupl. health, 1996—97; nat. coord. com. on clin. preventive svcs. USPHS, 1994—97; cons. office hearings and appeals U.S. Social Security Adminstrn., 1997—2003; cons. Met. Health Dist., San Antonio, 2002—. Mem. Pres.'s Com. on Employment People with Disabilities, Washington, 1986-2000, chmn. med. and ins. com., 1986-90. Fellow ACP, Am. Coll. Occupational and Environ. Medicine (bd. dirs. 1990-97, sec. 1992-94), Am. Coll. Preventive Medicine, Aerospace Med. Assn., N.Y. Acad. Medicine; mem. AMA. Home and Office: 159 Sabine Rd Boerne TX 78006-6217 Home Phone: 830-537-4782; Office Phone: 830-537-4782. Business E-Mail: wittmer@gvtc.com.

WITTNER, LAWRENCE STEPHEN, history professor; b. NYC, May 5, 1941; s. Jacob and Rose (Barnett) W.; m. Patricia Ellen Sheinblatt (div. May 1981); 1 child, Julia; m. Dorothy Tristman, Aug. 31, 1999. AB, Columbia U., 1962, PhD, 1967; MA, U. Wis., 1963. Asst. prof. history Hampton Inst., Va., 1967—68, Vassar Coll., Poughkeepsie, NY, 1968—73; Fulbright sr. lectr. Fulbright-Hays Ednl. Exch. Program, Tokyo and Kyoto, Japan, 1973-74; lectr. history SUNY, Albany, 1974—76, asst. prof., 1976—77, assoc. prof., 1977—83, prof., 1983—. Pres. Conf. on Peace Rsch. in History (now Peace History Soc.), 1977-79; mem. exec. com. Albany chpt. United Univ. Professions, 1980—. Author: Rebels Against War: The American Peace Movement, 1941-60, 1969, rev. edit. Rebels Against War: The American Peace Movement, 1933-1983, 1984, Cold War America: From Hiroshima to Watergate, 1974, rev. edit., 1978, American Intervention in Greece, 1943-1949, 1982, One World or None: A History of the World Nuclear Disarmament Movement through 1953, vol. 1 of The Struggle Against the Bomb, 1993, Vol. 2, Resisting the Bomb: A History of the World Nuclear Disarmament Movement, 1954-70, 1997, Vol. 3, Toward Nuclear Abolition: A History of the World Nuclear Disarmament Movement, 1971 to the Present, 2003; co-exec. editor Peace and Change: Jour. Peace Rsch., 1984—87. Co-chmn. Capital Dist. Labor-Religion Coalition, Albany, 1982-84; treas. Solidarity Com. Capital Dist., Albany, 1986—. Recipient Charles DeBenedetti prize Conf. on Peace Rsch. in History, 1989, excellence award N.Y. State and United Univ. Professions, 1990; fellow NEH, 1980-81, Am. Coun. Learned Socs. and Ford Found., 1987-88, U.S. Inst. Peace, 2002; rsch. grantee Nonprofit Sector Rsch. Fund, Aspen Inst., Washington, 1998-99, John D. and Catherine T. MacArthur Found., 2002. Mem. Internat. Peace Rsch. Assn. (chmn. Peace History Commn. 1998-2001), Peace History Soc. (N.Am. bd. 1990-94, 97-2000, 2004-), Peace Action (bd. dirs., 2005—). Democrat. Avocation: music. Office: SUNY History Dept 1400 Washington Ave Albany NY 12222-0100 Office Phone: 518-442-4789. Fax: 518-442-3477. E-mail: wittner@albany.edu.

WITTROCK, MERLIN CARL, educational psychologist; b. Twin Falls, Idaho, 1931; s. Herman C. and Mary Ellen W.; m. Nancy McNulty, Apr. 3; children: Steven, Catherine, Rebecca. BS in Edn. and Biology, U. Mo., 1953, MEd in Ednl. Psychology, 1956; PhD in Ednl. Psychology, U. Ill., 1960. Prof. grad. sch. edn. UCLA, 1960—, disting. univ. tchr., founder Ctr. Study Evaluation, chmn. faculty, chmn. divsn. ednl. psychology, supr. UNEX Intern Tchr. Preparation Program, 1996—2006. Dir. math. and humanities program, co-founder Urban Tchr. Edn. Program; fellow Ctr. for Advanced Study in Behavioral Scis., 1967—68; vis. prof. U. Wis., U. Ill., Ind. U., Monash U., Australia; co-prin. investigator Calif. Reading Tchr's Insts.; chmn. com. on evaluation and assessment L.A. Unified Sch. Dist.; nat. adv. panel for math. scis. NRC of NAS; chmn. nat. bd. Nat. Ctr. for Rsch. in Math. Scis. Edn., U. Wis., Madison; chmn. charges com. UCLA; adv. bd. Kauffman Found.; dir. evaluation Calif. Reading Tchrs. Profl. Devel. Program; steering com. tchr. cert. program L.A. Unified Sch. Dist. Author, editor: The Evaluation of Instruction, 1970, Changing Education, 1973, Learning and Instruction, 1977, The Human Brain, 1977, Danish transl., 1980, Spanish transl., 1982, The Brain and Psychology, 1980, Instructional Psychology: Education and Cognitive Processes of the Brain, Neuropsychological and Cognitive Processes of Reading, 1981, Handbook of Research on Teaching, 3d edit., 1986, The Future of Educational Psychology, 1989, Research in Learning and Teaching, 1990, Testing and Cognition, 1991, Generative Science Teaching, 1994, Problem-Solving Transfer, 1996, Taxonomy for Learning, Teaching and Assessing, 2001. Mentor Edn. Leadership Program; bd. dirs. WestEd R & D Ctr., 1989—2001. Capt. USAF, 1953—55. Recipient Disting. Tchr. of Univ., UCLA; grantee, Ford Found. Fellow: APA (pres. divsn. ednl. psychology 1984—85, assn. coun. 1988—91, award for Outstanding Svc. to Ednl. Psychology 1991, 1993, Disting. Svc. award for svc. to sci. adv. coun., Thorndike award for outstanding psychol. rsch. 1987), AAAS, Am. Ednl. Rsch. Assn. (chmn. ann. conv., chmn. publs. 1980—83, assn. coun. 1986—89, bd. dirs. 1987—89, chmn. com. on ednl. TV, Outstanding Contbns. award 1986, Outstanding Svc. award 1989), Am. Psychol. Soc. (charter fellow); mem.: Phi Delta Kappa. Office: UCLA 3021 Moore Hl Los Angeles CA 90095-1521 Office Phone: 310-825-8329. Business E-Mail: wittrock@ucla.edu.

WITTRY, DAVID BERYLE, physicist, researcher; b. Mason City, Iowa, Feb. 7, 1929; s. Herman Joseph and Edna Pearl (Filbey) W.; m. Mildred Elizabeth DuBois, July 1, 1955; children: James David, Robert Andrew, Kristopher Lee, Diane Marie, Linda Beryle. BS, U. Wis., 1951; MS, Calif. Inst. Tech., 1953, PhD, 1957. Research fellow Calif. Inst. Tech., Pasadena, 1957-59; asst. prof. U. So. Calif., Los Angeles, 1959-61, assoc. prof. dept. elec. engring., 1961-69, prof. dept. materials sci. and elec. engring., 1969-98, disting. prof. emeritus, 1998—. Cons. Hughes Semiconductors, 1958-59, Applied Research Labs., Inc., 1958-83, Exptl. Sta., E.I. du Pont de Nemours & Co., 1962-71, Gen. Telephone and Electronics Research Labs., 1966-72, Autonetics div. N. Am. Aviation, 1961-63, Electronics Research div. Rockwell Internat., 1976-81, Atlantic Richfield Co. Corp. Tech. Lab., 1981-87, Jet Propulsion Lab., 1985-88, Hitachi Instruments, 1989-90; vis. scientist Japan Soc. Promotion of Sci., U. Osaka Prefecture, 1974. Editor 3 proceedings of cons. Contbr. articles to profl. jours. Patentee in field. Recipient first award essays on gravity, Gravity Research Found., 1949, Disting. Scientist award phys. scis. Microscopy Soc. Am., 1995, Disting. Svc. citation U. Wis. Coll. Engring., 1996; Guggenheim fellow, 1967-68; Knapp scholar U. Wis., 1949-51. Mem. IEEE, Electron Microscopy Soc. Am. (dir. phys. scis. 1979-81, pres. 1983), Microbeam Analysis Soc. (sec. organizing com. 1966, exec. council 1970-72, pres. 1988, Presdl. award 1980, Birks award 1987, 89, hon. mem.), Am. Phys. Soc., Sigma Xi. Methodist. Office: U So Calif Dept Materials Sci Los Angeles CA 90089-0001

WITTRY, DIANE MARIE, conductor, musician; d. David Beryl and Mildred Elizabeth Wittry; m. Richard Edward Peckham. MusB, U. So. Calif., 1983, MusM, 1985; studies with Leonid Korchmar, St. Petersburg Conservatory Music. Asst. condr. Pasadena Symphony, 1988—95; music dir., condr. Greater Miami (Fla.) Youth Symphony, 1989—91, Symphony S.E. Tex., Beaumont, 1991—2000, Allentown (Pa.) Symphony, 1996—, Norwalk (Conn.) Symphony, 2001—. Guest condr. LA Philharm., San Diego Symphony, N.J. Symphony, Houston Symphony, Fla. Philharm., others. Author: Beyond the Baton, 2005. Named Top prize winner, Conducting Competition, Italy, 2001; recipient Gold Crown award, City of Pasadena, 1991, Outstanding Merit award, Chamber Music Am., 1992, Helen M. Thompson award, Am. Symphony Orch. League, 1996, Arts Ovation award, City of Allentown, 1999, Women of Excellence award, City of Beaumont, 1999, Women of Distinction award, Lehigh Valley, Pa., 2000, Florino Doro award, City of Vince, Italy, 2003. Mem.: Am. Symphony Orch. League, Condr.'s Guild (bd. dirs.), Phi Kappa Lambda. Methodist.

WITTSTEIN, EDWIN FRANK, theater director, set designer; b. Mt. Vernon, NY, Apr. 7, 1929; s. Nathan Harry and Miriam (Goldman) W. Student, Parsons Sch. Design, 1946-50; BS, NYU, 1950; postgrad., Cooper Union, 1950-52. Stage designer Dramatic Workshop prodn. The Inspector General, 1947; set designer Gertrude Stein's Yes Is for a Very Young Man; set and costume designer Ounga Opera, Phila., 1950, (opera) The Celebrated Jumping Frog of Calaveras County, Venice, Italy, 1953, The Transposed Heads, 1958, The Fantasticks, 1960-2002; designer Broadway prodn. Kean, 1961; set and costume designer The Gondoliers, N.Y.C. Opera, 1963, The Knack (directed by Mike Nichols), 1964, The Marriage of Figaro, N.Y.C. Opera, 1965, The Amen Corner, 1965, Happy Birthday Wanda June, Enter Laughing, 1965, The Room, A Slight Ache, 1965, The Yearling, 1965, Serjeant Musgrave's Dance, 1966 (Obie award 1966), You Know I Can't Hear You When the Water's Running, 1967, set designer Merchant of Venice, Shakespeare Festival Conn., 1967, As You Like It, Richard II, Shakespeare Festival Conn., 1968, The Man in the Glass Booth, 1968, The Basement, The Tea Party, Celebration, 1969, (for Cin. Playhouse) The Miser, Volpone, The Good Woman of Setzuan, Angel Street, He Who Gets Slapped, 1968-70, The Country Wife, Shakespeare Theatre, Conn., 1973, Ulysses in Nightown, 1974 (Tony award nomination 1974, Maharam award 1974), The Torchbearers, 1978, The Aspern Papers, 1978, Love's Labors Lost, 1983, Berkshire Theatre Festival, 1988, Tusitala, 1988, Tete a Tete, 1989, The Hasty Heart, 1990, Trains, 1991, (sets, costumes 30th anniversary tour) The Fantasticks, 1990, Sarah, Plain and Tall, 1991 (Emmy nomination 1991), Colette Collage, 1991, March of the Falsettos, 1991, Falsettoland, 1991, (prodn. designer Hallmark Hall of Fame TV) An American Story, 1992, (prodn. designer Hallmark Hall of Fame TV) Skylark, 1993, (prodn. designer Hallmark Hall of Fame TV) A Place for Annie, 1993, (set designer off-Broadway) I Do! I Do!, 1996, The Fantasticks, 2006; designer TV shows Armstrong Circle Theatre, The Tonight Show with Steve Allen, NBC operas Cosi Fan Tutte, La Traviata, La Boheme, Boris Godounov, Cavalleria Rusticana, Blithe Spirit, The Diary of Anne Frank, Camino Real, The Royal Family, The Prince of Homburg; prodn. designer TV series The Adams Chronicles (Emmy nomination 1975); designer TV films A Memory of Two Mondays, 1971, For Ladies Only, 1982, Legs, 1982, Samson and Delilah, 1983, Heartsounds, 1984; designer TV spl. Echoes in the Darkness, 1987; designer films Bananas, 1971, Play It Again Sam, 1971, The Seven-Ups, 1972; art dir. films Smile, 1975, Fame, 1979; prodn. designer film Endless Love, 1981; set and costume designer (ballet) Coppelia, 1992; one-man show (painting) Hammond Museum, N. Salem, N.Y., 1999; drawer, writer Positano Sketch Book, 2000; designer sets and costumes for new revival of The Fantasticks, Broadway, 2006. Home: 339 E 87th St New York NY 10128-4801

WITTY, CHRISTINE (CHRIS WITTY), speed skater; b. West Allis, Wis., June 23, 1975; Student, Carroll Coll. Speed skater, 1985—. Mem. U.S. nat. team, 1988—. Recipient 1000 meter Silver medal Olympic Games, Nagano, Japan, 1998, 1500 meter Bronze medal, 1998; finished 2nd U.S. Olympic Team Trials, 2000. Achievements include U.S. flag bearer, Torino Olympic Winter Games, 2006. Avocations: cycling, movies, mountain biking. Home: PO Box 9694 Salt Lake City UT 84109-9694

WITZEL, BRADLEY STEVEN, special education educator; s. Ronald and Elizabeth Witzel; m. Isabelle Laramee; children: Laura, Caroline. PhD, U. Fla., Gainesville, 2001. Lic. spl. edn. Va., 1994. Asst. prof. Winthrop U., Rock Hill, SC, 2002—. Contbr. articles to profl. jours. Pres. SC divsn. Learning Disabilities, Rock Hill, 2005—06. Fellow, U. Fla., 2000—01. Mem.: Internat. Dyslexia Assn. (assoc.). Achievements include patents for algebra model for instruction. Office: Winthrop Univ 701 Oakland Ave Rock Hill SC 29733 Office Phone: 803-323-2211.

WIVEL, NELSON AUBURN, physician, medical researcher, educator, biotechnology consultant; b. Denver, Sept. 4, 1935; s. Claude Burns and Aubrey (Angus) W.; m. Carol Henderson, June 16, 1963 (dec. 1999); children: Mark Auburn, Ashley Elizabeth. BS, Ea. N.Mex. U., 1957; MD, Stanford U., 1961. Diplomate Am. Bd. Pathology. Intern Cornell U., NYC, 1961-62, asst. resident in medicine, 1962-63; asst. resident in pathology Stanford U., Calif., 1963-65; rsch. trainee in pathology Washington U., St. Louis, 1965-66; head ultrastructural studies sect. Nat. Cancer Inst., Bethesda, Md., 1966-70, head ultrastructural biology sect., 1970-86; med. officer for AIDS rsch. Gen. Clin. Rsch. Ctrs., NIH, Bethesda, 1986-89, dir. Office of Recombinant DNA Activities, 1989-96; dep. dir. Inst. Human Gene Therapy Sch. Medicine U. Pa., Phila., 1996—2007. Adj. prof. molecular and cellular engring., program chair ethics and pub. policy rsch. program U. Pa. Med. Ctr., Phila., 1996-2007; exec. dir. recombinant DNA adv. com. NIH; biotech. cons., 2007—. Assoc. editor Jour. Nat. Cancer Inst., 1968-70, Human Gene Therapy, 1993—, Jour. Biolaw and Bus., 1996—, Transplant Video Jour., 2002-04, Pre Clinica, 2003-05; contbr. more than 100 articles to profl. jours. including Sci., Nature, Jour. of Virology, Virology. Recipient Commendation medal USPHS, 1990. Mem. Am. Soc. Cell Biology, Am. Soc. Virology, Am. Soc. Gene Therapy. Achievements include research on murine retroviruses that can function as moveable genetic elements (transposons). Office Phone: 215-836-1519.

WIXEN, JOAN SAUNDERS, journalist; b. Boston, Dec. 26, 1931; d. Harry Hyman and Sadye (Ginsburg) Saunders; m. Burton N. Wixen, Aug. 9, 1953; children: Randall, Warren, Bradford. BA, U. So. Calif., LA, 1952; MS, UCLA, 1953. West coast corr. Sunday Mag., Detroit News, 1972—78; journalist LA Times, Christian Sci. Monitor, Chgo. Sun Times, Miami Herald, Fla., San Francisco Chronicle, Washington Star, Buffalo Evening News, LA Daily News, Parade. Contbr. articles to mags. including Family Cir., New Woman, Pageant, Modern Maturity, Eve, to syndicates including United Features, LA Times-Washington Post, N.Am. Newspaper Alliance, Universal Press Syndicate, others. E-mail: saunderswixen@earthlink.net.

WIXOM, WILLIAM DAVID, art historian, museum administrator, educator; b. Phila., July 17, 1929; s. Clinton Wood and Beatrice Rachel (Hunt) W.; m. Nancy Coe, Aug. 8, 1959; 3 children. BA, Haverford Coll., Pa., 1951; MA, Inst. Fine Arts NYU, 1963. Asst. curator to curator medieval and renaissance decorative arts Cleve. Mus. Art, 1958-78, chief curator early western art, 1979; chmn. dept. medieval art and The Cloisters Met. Mus. Art, NYC, 1979-98, curator emeritus. Lectr. Barnes Found., Merion, Pa., 1951—52, curatorial cons. for medieval art, mem. curatorial adv. com., 2002—05; adj. assoc. prof. history of art Case Western Res. U., Cleve., 1967—78, adj. prof., 1978, NYU, 1981—82; mem. adv. coun. Snite Mus. Art Notre Dame U., 1974—95. Author: Treasures from Medieval France, 1967, Renaissance Bronzes from Ohio Collections, 1975, Picturing the

Apocalypse: Illustrated Leaves from a Medieval Spanish Manuscript, 2002, A Glimpse at the Fountains of the Middle Ages, 2003, Medieval Sculptures at the Metropolitan, 800 to 1400, 2005, Late Medieval Sculpture at the Metropolitan, 1400 to 1530, 2007; contbg. author The Royal Abbey of Saint Denis in the Time of Abbot suger, 1981, The Treasury of San Marco, 1985, Gothic and Renaissance Art in Nuremberg, 1986, Festschrift Gerhard Bott, 1987, Hommage a Hubert Landais, 1987, The Cloisters, Studies in Honor of the Fiftieth Anniversary, 1992, Festschrift Gerhard Schmidt, 1994, Enamels of Limoges 1100-1350, 1996, Studies in Honor of Kurt Weitzmann, 1995, The Dictionary of Art, 1996, The Glory of Byzantium, Art and Culture of the Middle Byzantine Era, AD-843-1261, 1997, Sculptures hors contexte, Louvre conférences et colloques, 1997, Mirror of the Medieval World, 1999, Romanesque Sculpture in American Collections, 1999, Tilman Riemenschneider, Master Sculptor of the Late Middle Ages, 1999; contbr. articles to profl. jours. Bd. dirs. Internat. Ctr. Medieval Art, N.Y.C., 1971-82, pres., 1971-74. Belgium-Am. Ednl. Found. fellow, 1962; Nat. Endowment Arts grantee, 1973; fellow Pierpont Morgan Libr., 1979-2001; J. Paul Getty Mus. Guest Scholar, 1996. Fellow Soc. of Antiquaries of London; mem. Coll. Art Assn. (dir. 1979-83), Medieval Acad. Am., Internat. Ctr. Medieval Art. Mem. Soc. Of Friends. Office: Dept Medieval Art Met Mus Art New York NY 10028

WIXON, HENRY N., lawyer; b. 1954; BS, U. Md., 1976, MS, 1980; JD, George Washington U., 1986. Bar: Md. 1986, DC 1989, US Patent & Trademark Office, US Supreme Ct. 1990. Ptnr., vice chmn. Intellectual Property dept. Wilmer Cutler Pickering Hale & Dorr, Washington. Mem.: Fed. Bar Assn. (past chmn. Comm. & IP Law sect., Patent, Trademark & Copyright com.), Am. Intellectual Property Law Assn. (charter mem. Biotechnology Practice com.), ABA, Md. Bar Assn. (mem. Com. on Representing Emerging Companies), DC Bar Assn., Biotechnology Ind. Assn. (mem. Intellectual Property Com.), Internat. Fedn. Advancement of Genetic Engring. & Biotechnology, No. Va. Biotechnology Council, Va. Biotechnology Assn. Office: Wilmer Cutler Pickering Hale & Dorr Willard Office Bldg 1455 Pennsylvania Ave NW Washington DC 20004 Office Fax: 202-942-8459, 202-942-8484. Business E-Mail: henry.wixon@wilmerhale.com.

WIXTROM, DONALD JOSEPH, translator; b. Republic, Mich., Oct. 14, 1928; s. Joseph Albert and Edith (Johnson) W.; m. Marilyn Jean Sjoquist, Oct. 14, 1961; children: Joe Alan, Lorna Jean, Aaron Matthew. Free lance translator, Republic, 1966—. Mem. Am. Translators Assn. Baptist. Home and Office: 6035 Dogwood Rd Republic MI 49879-9214

WIZARD, BRIAN, publisher, author; b. Newburyport, Mass., June 24, 1949; s. Russell and Ruth (Hidden) Willard. BA, Sonoma State U., Calif., 1976; D of Metaphysics, Universal Life Ch., 1997. Ordained to ministry Universal Life Ch., 1997. Pvt. practice as jeweler, sculptor and craftsman, Calif., 1974-79; Wallowa, Oreg., 1991—; prin. The Starquill Pub., Port Douglas, Queensland, Australia, 1981-86; owner Starquill Internat., Wallowa, Oreg. Author: (trilogy) The Will He Make it Saga (contender 1998 Pulitzer prize), Permission to Kill, 1985, Permission to Live, 1992 (Nobel Prize for lit. nominee 2000), Back in the World, 1995; (novels) Shindara, 1990, Heaven on Earth, 1998, Coming of Age, 1990, Pollution IV, 1993, 2d edit. 2006; Nigerian 419 Scam "Game Over!", 2000, Brazilian, Portuguese transl., 2005; (short stories) Tropical Pair, 1986, Metempsychosis, 1988 (In Search of) The Silver Lining, 1994, The Moon Whistling By on a Cloud, 1994, (The Princess of the) Wildflowers, 1995, Mushroom Magic, 1996, Vietnam 1999! Make Friends Not War, (novella) Beware of the Reload, 2003, Beware of Classified Ad Fraud, 2004, Psychology of Financial Terrorism, 2004, Beware of the 419 Employment Scam, 2005, Beware of the 419 Chat Scam, 2005, Space Egg, 2005, Don't Be Scammed-Be Informed, 2006; contbr. to Smithsonian Inst.'s The Vietnam War Generation, (audio version) Game Over!, 2002; contbr. to SpaceArc; prodr. (video documentary) Thunderhawks, 1987 (winner best documentary NY Ind. Film Festival 2005), Swift Action Newsteam, Tope Creek Lookout, 1995, Make Friends Not War: Return to Vietnam, 1999 (Aorence Vietnam Short Story winner); songwriter, prodr. (cassette) Brian Wizard Sings for His Supper, 1989 (cert. of achievement Billboard 1993); songwriter, singer, prodr. (I Don't Want) Permission to Kill, 1989, Busker's Theme Song, Living in North Queensland, Circus Act, Hitch Hiking Man, Self-Portrait, The Love We Share Will Never End, 1994, Never Met a Girl Like You, Folk-Rock Opera: A Cover Story: After That Ugly Saloon Incident; contbr. to America's Finest Songwriter and Lyricists CD, 1997, (novels, video and music) Brian Wizard's 20th Century Anthology, 1998 (nominee Nobel Prize in Lit. 2000), (video) Vietnam '99, (audio book) Nigerian 419 Scam Game Over, 2003, (opera) The Rocky Raccoon Folk Rock, 2004, (Honorable Mention 2006), Roadkill Stew, 2004 (Honorable Mention 2006); contbr. to TV documentaries History of the Machine Gun, 2000, Vietnam, The Personal Experience, 2001; contbr. (video documentary) Vietnam: Then and Again, 2005. Renovator hist. landmark The Tope Creek Lookout (Skyship); mem. Nat. Hist. Lookout Register; sponsor Adopt A Hwy., 1995; min. Universal Life Ch.; amb. at large Africa Anti Fraud Alliance. With U.S. Army, 1967-70. Decorated Air medals (26), Aviator Flight Wings; recipient Cert. of Appreciation, Pres. Richard M. Nixon, Combat Flight Helmet, Platoon Scarf Smithsonian Instn. Nat. Air and Space Mus., Gold Book award, Mil. Writers Assn., Silver Book award, Am. Authors Assn., Best Documentary, NY Internat. Ind. Film Festival, Las Vegas, 2005. Mem. 145th Combat Aviation Bn. Assn., Vietnam Combat Vets. Assn., Vietnam Vets. Am., Vietnam Vets. Australia Assn., NRA (cert. handgun instr., 2002). Office: PO Box 42 Wallowa OR 97885-0042

WIZDA, CHRISTINE ANNE, history professor; b. Flemington, NJ, Sept. 21, 1977; d. Thomas Steven and Elaine Ann Wizda. BA, Rider U., 1999; MA, U. Houston, 2003, M in Applied Med. Anthropology, 2004, PhD, 2004—. Tutor Rider U., Lawrenceville, NJ, 1996—99; tchg. asst. U. Houston, 1999—2006. Named to The Chancellor's List, 2006; recipient, 2003; grantee scholarship, U. Coll., Cork, Ireland, 1998; Murry Miller scholar, U. Houston, 2002, conf. grantee, 2003, scholar for field work in Belize, Office Internat. Studies, 2003. Mem.: Soc. Mil. History, Orgn. Am. Historians, Am. Hist. Assn., Phi Beta Delta, Phi Alpha Theta, Pi Gamma Mu.

WLADAWSKY-BERGER, IRVING, communications executive; b. Cuba; MS in Physics, PhD in Physics, U. Chgo. Various managerial and professional positions, Thomas J. Watson Rsch. Ctr. IBM, Armonk, NY, 1970—84, v.p. computer sciences Thomas J. Watson Rsch. Ctr., 1984—85, various exec. positions large-systems develop. org., 1985—91, gen. mgr. POWER Parallel Systems Armonk, NY, 1991—95, gen. mgr. internet divsn. Somers, NY, 1995—99, v.p. tech. and strategy, 2000—. Mem. commn. on physical sciences, mathematics, and resources Nat. Rsch. Coun., 1984—87, founding mem. computer sciences and telecommunications bd.; mem. U. Chgo. bd. governors Argonne Nat. Laboratories; mem. technol. advisory coun. BP Internat.; co-chair President's Information Technol. Advisory Com., 1999—. Named one of 50 Most Important Hispanics in Tech., Bus., Hispanic Engineer and Info. Tech. mag., 2005; recipient Hispanic Engineer of the Year, 2001; fellow, Am. Academy of Arts and Sciences. Office: IBM Rte 100 Somers NY 10589

WLASCHIN, KEN, cultural organization administrator, writer; b. Bradish, Nebr., July 12, 1934; s. Bernard A. and Lucy M. (Stevens) W.; m. Maureen N. Kennedy Martin, Mar. 22, 1961; 1 child, Scott Martin. BA, Dartmouth Coll., 1956; MA, U. Coll., Dublin, Ireland, 1957; postgrad., U. Poitiers, France, 1960. Program dir. Nat. Film Theater, London, 1969-83, London Film Festival, 1970-83; artistic dir. LA Film Expn., 1984-86; dir. exhbn. Am. Film Inst., LA, 1986-97, dir. creative affairs and preservation, 1998—. Theater critic Rome Daily Am. & Daily Sketch, Rome and London, 1962-67; art critic Art Voices Mag., Rome, 1962-68; film critic Films and Filming Mag., London, 1973-82; story editor London Weekend TV, 1968. Author: (TV play) Ticket to Trieste, 1961, (novel), The Italian Job, 1964, Rome A City, 1964, Guide to Cinema, 1970, Encyclopedia of Movie Stars, 1979, Faber Book of Movie Verse, 1994, Opera on Screen, 1997, Gian Carlo Menotti on Screen, 1999, Encyclopedia of Opera on screen, 2004, Encyclopedia of American Opera, 2005. With US Army, 1958-61, ETO. Mem. Brit. Film Inst., Brit. Film Acad. Avocation: opera. Home: 1050 E Ramon Rd #35 Palm Springs CA 92264 Office: Am Film Inst 2021 N Western Ave Los Angeles CA 90027-1625 Office Phone: 323-856-7708. Business E-Mail: kwlaschin@afi.com.

WLEUGEL, JOHN PETER, manufacturing executive; b. Hoyanger, Sogn, Norway, July 1, 1929; s. Johan and Helga (Faye) W.; m. Leonor Abaroa, Dec. 1959; children— Jan Andrew, Cecilia Maria. BA, U. Copenhagen, 1953; MBA, U. Toronto, 1957. With Belgium Machine Tool Assn., 1953-54, Massey-Ferguson Ltd., Toronto, 1954-71, treas., 1968-71; sr. v.p. Bata Ltd., Toronto; dir., officer several subsidiaries (Bata Shoe Orgn.), Don Mills, Ont., Canada, 1972-89; prof., exec.-in-residence, internat. adv. bd. Schulich Sch. Bus., York U., North York, Canada, 1990—. Mem.: Financial Execs. Inst. Home: 5 Campbell Crescent Toronto ON Canada M2P 1P1 Office: Schulich Sch Bus York U 4700 Keele St Toronto ON Canada M3J 1P3

WOBROCK, JESSE LUCAS, biomechanical engineer; b. St. Charles, Mo., Apr. 30, 1976; s. David Edward and Deborah Louise Wobrock; m. Julie Diane Burton, June 27, 1979; 1 child, Luke David. PhD in Biomedical Engring., UCLA, 2005. Pres., sr. engr. Accident Reconstruction & Biomechanics, Arroyo Grande, Calif., 2005—; accident reconstruction, biomechanics expert, 2000—06. Mem.: Am. Mensa (assoc.). Conservative. Lutheran. Achievements include research in motorcycle helmet and vehicle design. Avocations: baseball, golf, travel. Home and Office: 604 Village Ct Arroyo Grande CA 93420 Office Phone: 805-474-8196. Office Fax: 805-474-8496. Personal E-mail: jwobrock@hotmail.com.

WOBUS, REINHARD ARTHUR, geologist, educator; b. Norfolk, Va., Jan. 11, 1941; s. Reinhard Schaffer and Oral (Phares) W.; m. Sheridan Whitcher, Mar. 18, 1967; children: Erik Reinhard, Cameron Wright. BA, Washington U., St. Louis, 1962; MA, Harvard U., 1963; PhD, Stanford U., 1966. Asst. prof. geology Williams Coll., Williamstown, Mass., 1966-72, assoc. prof., 1972-78, prof., 1978-85, Edna McConnell Clark prof. geology, 1985—, dept. chmn., 1988-96. Geologist U.S. Geol. Survey, Denver, 1967-86; vis. prof. Colo. Coll., Colorado Springs, 1976, 82-83, Colo. State U., Ft. Collins, summers 1977-84; bd. dirs. Colo. Outdoor Edn. Ct., Florissant, Williamstown Rural Lands Found.; co-founder Keck Twelve-Coll. Geol. Consortium, mem. governing bd., 1986—, exec. com., 2005—. Contbr. maps and articles on Precambrian geology of So. Rocky Mountains to profl. jours. Danforth fellow, 1962, Woodrow Wilson fellow, 1962, NSF fellow, 1962-66. Fellow Geol. Soc. Am.; mem. Am. Geophys. Union, Nat. Assn. Geosci. Tchrs., Coun. on Undergrad. Rsch., Colo. Sci. Soc., Mineral Soc. Am., Phi Beta Kappa, Sigma Xi. Current work includes petrology and geochronology of Precambrian igneous and metamorphic rocks and mid-Tertiary volcanic rocks, so. Rocky Mountains, Silurian volcanic rocks, coastal Maine. Home: 20 Grandview Dr Williamstown MA 01267-2528 Office: Williams Coll Dept Geoscis Williamstown MA 01267 Office Phone: 413-597-2470. Business E-Mail: rwobus@williams.edu.

WODICZKO, KRZYSZTOF, artist, architect, educator; b. Warsaw, 1943; arrived in Can., 1977, arrived in US, 1991; MFA, Acad. Fine Arts, Warsaw, Poland, 1968. Designer Polish Optical Works; asst. prof. intermedia and photography Nova Scotia Coll. Art and Design, 1980—81; asst. prof. photography U. Hartford, 1988—89, Calif. Inst. Tech., 1991; prof. sculpture Ecole Nationale Superieure des Beaux Arts, France, 1991—95; joined faculty MIT, Cambridge, 1991, prof. visual arts, 1997—, dir. Ctr. Advanced Visual Studies (CAVS), 1994—96, 2003—, dir. Interrogative Design Group, 1994—. Adj. prof. Warsaw Poly. Inst., 1970—75; vis. prof. design and mixed media Nova Scotia Coll. Art and Design, 1977—79; adj. prof. indsl. design Ont. Coll. Art, 1979; vis. prof. photography and studio art Calif. Inst. Arts, 1988; guest prof. sculpture Cooper Union Sch. Art, 1987, 89. One-man shows include Foksal Gallery, Warsaw, 1973, 1974, 1975, 1976, 1977, Hal Broom Gallery, NYC, 1977, 1978, 1980, 1984, 49th Paralle, 1986, Clocktower, 1988, Hirschhorn Mus., Washington, 1988, Galerie Gabrielle Maubrie, Paris, 1989, 1992, 1996, Exit Art, NYC, 1989—90, Josh Baer Gallery, 1991, Galerie Lelong, 1996, Hiroshima City Contemporary Art Mus., 1999, Zacheta Nat. Gallery Contemporary Art, Warsaw, Poland, (in preparation), 2006, others, exhibited in group shows at Edinburgh Festival, 1988, Wiener Festwochen, 1988, Whitney Mus., 1989, Ctr. Georges Pompidou, Paris, 1989, 1996—97, The Israel Mus., Jerusalem, 1990, Mus. Modern Art, San Francisco, 1991, Mus. d'Art Contemporain, Montreal, 1992, Mus. Fine Arts, Boston, 1993—94, Kunstmus., Bonn, Germany, 1994, Setagaya Mus. Art, Tokyo, 1995, Sonje Mus. Contemporary Art, Seoul, 1996, Louisiana Mus., Denmark, 1996, Nat. Mus. Modern Art, Kyoto, Japan, 1996, Uchwtz (The Handle), Museum Sztuki, Lodz, Poland, 1999, Venice Architectural Biennale, 2000, Whitney Bienniale, Whitney Mus. Art, NYC, 2000, The Generali Found., Vienna, 2002, Internat. Ctr. Photography, NYC, 2003, Mass. Mus. Contemporary Art, 2004, Basque Mus. Contemporary Art, Spain, 2004, others, projections, The Bunker Hill Monument, Boston, 1998, The A-bomb Dome, Hiroshima, 1999, El Centro Cultural, Tijuana, Mex., 2001, The Central Library, St. Louis, 2004, Barcelona, 2005, others, instrumentations, Dis-Armor, 1999—, Aegis, 2000—, others; Commd. (with Julian Bonder) to design a Meml. to the Abolition of Slavery, City of Nantes, France, 2004—; author: Critical Vehicles: Writings, Projects, Interviews, 1999. Recipient Hiroshima Art Prize, 1998, Kepes Art Prize, Coun. for Arts, MIT, 2004, Artist Award for Disting. Body of Work, Coll. Art Assn., 2004. Office: MIT Ctr Advanced Visual Studies 265 Massachusetts Ave N51-315H Cambridge MA 02139

WODLINGER, MARK LOUIS, broadcast executive; b. Jacksonville, Fla., July 13, 1922; s. Mark H. and Beatrice Mae (Boney) W.; m. Marilyn Stone-Birk; children: Kevin, Michael, Stephen, Mark. BS, U. Fla., 1943. Salesman Sta. WQUA, Moline, Ill., 1948; mgr. Sta. WOC-AM-FM-TV, Davenport, Iowa, 1949-58; v.p. Sta. WMBD-TV, Peoria, Ill., 1959-61; v.p., gen. mgr. Sta. WZZM-TV, Grand Rapids, Mich., 1962-63, Sta. KMBC-TV, Kansas City, Mo., 1963-69; pres. Intermedia, Kansas City, 1969-73; builder, owner comml. radio stas. Swaziland, Africa; operator Radio Malawi, Blantyre, and Marknews TV and Radio News Bur., Nairobe, Kenya, 1971-74; owner, pres. Sta. KBEQ, Kansas City, 1973-77; owner Sta. WCJX-FM, Miami, 1985-86, Sta. WIXI-FM, Naples and Ft. Myers, Fla., 1986-95, Sta. KKLO-AM, Leavenworth, Kans., 1982-92, Sta. KCWV, Kansas City, Mo., 1982-90, TV-5, Hit Video USA, Satellite Music Network, Houston, 1985-88, SMR-2-way radio/telephone, Naples, Fla., 1993—, San Francisco, 1993—; owner, mng. dir. Radio Hirszolgalat; owner Roxy Radio, Budapest, Hungary, 2007—, Roxy Advt. Network, 2007—. Chmn. bd. dirs. Wodlinger Broadcasting Co., Naples, 1978—; ptnr. Wireless Cable, Naples, 1990—; owner, ptnr. KABELTEL KFT (Hungary), Budapest, Sopron, Nagykanizsa, Szombathely, 1991-96; comml. FM Radio Ikva, Sopron, 1993—, comml. FM Radio Kecskemet, Hungary, 1995—, FM Radio Zalaegerszeg, 1995—, comml. FM Reflex Radio 99.2 MHz, Szekesfehervar, Hungary, 1996—, FM Love Radio 97.8, Tallinn, Paide, Rakvere, Tartu, Sindi, Viliandi and marjamaa, Estonia, 1993—; ptnr., chmn. bd. dirs. wireless cable TV Ukrainian-Am. Broadcasting, Kiev, Ukraine, 1990—, comml. TV Channel 7, 1990—, comml. FM Radio 69.89, Kiev, 1992—; owner, ptnr. comml. FM Radiocentras, Vilnius, Lithuania, 1992-96; owner, ptnr. comml. FM Radiola 99.70 MHz, 1996—; ptnr. joint mktg. AT&T Paradyne, Largo, Fla., 1992-94, Bellcore, Morristown, N.J., 1995—; owner, ptnr., chmn. bd. dirs. real estate devel., Croatia, 1991—; owner outdoor advt. billboards, Tallinn, Estonia, 1993-95; owner, ptnr. real estate devel., Hungary, 1991—. Bd. dirs. Kansas City Philharm., Kansas City Civic Coun., Naples YMCA; mem. Conservancy, Naples Civic Assn. Served to lt. USN, 1941-45. Mem. Nat. Assn. Broadcasters, Mo. Assn. Broadcasters, Broadcast Pioneers. Clubs: Kansas City, Univ., Vanguard, Carriage, Port Royal, Naples Yacht, Houston Yacht, White Lake Yacht (Whitehall, Mich.), Haile Plantation Country Club. Lodges: Rotary. Republican. Episcopalian. Home Phone: 352-372-2666; Office Phone: 352-870-8784. E-mail: wodlinger@radionews.hu.

WODNICKI, ADAM JULIUSZ, pianist, educator; arrived in US, 1986, naturalized; s. Bronislaw Wodnicki and Malwina Wodnicka; m. Marta Janina Hoffman-Wodnicka, Nov. 15, 1973; children: Maya Andrea Wodnicka, Natalia Eva Wodnicka. MusM, Acad. of Music, Cracow, Poland, 1974. Faculty mem. Acad. of Music, Cracow, Poland, 1973—77; asst. prof. U. of Tex. at Austin, 1979—80; prof. of piano U. of North Tex. Coll. of Music, 1980—. Artistic co-dir. Internat. Piano Masterclasses, Varna, Bulgaria, 2000—; mem. bd. of artistic advisors Internat. Piano Festival and Course, Aveiro, Portugal, 2001—04. Performance editor (music score) I.J.Paderewski: Complete Works; performer: (albums) CDCM Computer Music Series, vol.1, Computer Music Compositions, K. Szymanowski: 12 Studies op.33, R. Muczynski: Piano Trios, I.J.Paderewski: Piano works, vol.1, I.J.Paderewski: Piano works, vol.2, D.Dzubay, R.Muczynski, D, Shostakovich:Sonatas for Cello and Piano, CDCM Computer Music Series, vol.27, J.Schwantner:and the Mountains Rising Nowhere, CDCM Computer Music Series, vol.14, Computer Music Currents 8; performer: (with Joseph Banowetz and Vladimir Ashkenazy) Sergey Taneyev: The Composer's Birthday, for narrator and piano four hands. Recipient 3 prizes, VIII Festival of Polish Pianists, 1974, nat. competition prize, Chopin Soc., Warsaw, Poland, 1969—71, Worldwide Steinway Artists Roster, Steinway&Sons, NY, 1997—; Touring Artists Roster, Tex. Commn. on the Arts, 1996—. Mem.: Music Teachers Nat. Assn., Am. Liszt Soc. Office: Univ of North Tex Coll of Mus PO Box 311367 Denton TX 76203-1367 Home Phone: 940-566-1393; Office Phone: 940-565-3715. Personal E-mail: mnawod@juno.com.

WOELFEL, JAMES WARREN, philosophy and humanities educator; b. Galveston, Tex., Aug. 16, 1937; s. Warren Charles and Mary Frances (Washinka) W.; m. Sarah Chappell Trulove, Nov. 24, 1982; children by previous marriages: Skye Caitlin, Allegra Eve, Sarah Judith; stepchildren: Ann Marie and Paul Trulove. BA, U. Okla., 1959; MDiv, Episcopal Div. Sch., Cambridge, Mass., 1962; MA, Yale U., 1964; PhD, U. St. Andrews, Scotland, 1967. Asst. prof. philosophy and religion U. Kans., Lawrence, 1966-70, asst. prof. philosophy, 1970-71, assoc. prof. philosophy and religion, 1971-75, prof. philosophy and religious studies, 1975-88, prof. philosophy, 1988—, acting chmn. dept. religious studies, 1983-84, dir. Humanities and Western civilization program, 1985—. Manuscript reader for various presses, jours. Author: Bonhoeffer's Theology, 1970, Borderland Christianity, 1973, Camus: A Theological Perspective (republished as Albert Camus on the Sacred and the Secular, 1987), 1975, Augustinian Humanism, 1979, The Agnostic Spirit as a Common Motif in Liberal Theology and Liberal Scepticism, 1990, Portraits in Victorian Religious Thought, 1997, The Existentialist Legacy and Other Essays on Philosophy and Religion, 2006; co-editor (with Sarah Chappell Trulove): Patterns in Western Civilization, 1991, 4th edit., 2006; contbr. essays, revs. to profl. jours.; contbr. articles to profl. jours. Danforth grad. fellow Episcopal Div. Sch., Cambridge, Mass., 1959-62, U. St. Andrews, 1962-63, 65-66, Yale U., New Haven, 1963-65; Fulbright scholar U. St. Andrews, 1962-63, Pub. Scholar award Kans. Humanities Coun., 1997; grantee NEH, Exxon Found., Mellon Found., Menninger Found., Inst. for Ecumenical and Cultural Rsch. Mem. Am. Philos. Assn., Assn. for Core Texts and Courses, Phi Beta Kappa. Democrat. Avocations: piano, walking. Home: 808 Alabama St Lawrence KS 66044-3942 Office: U Kans Humanities & Western Civilization Program Bailey Hall 1440 Jayhawk Blvd Rm 308 Lawrence KS 66045-7574 Office Phone: 785-864-3011. E-mail: woelfel@ku.edu.

WOERNER, ROBERT EUGENE, retired editor, writer; b. Cadillac, Mich., Sept. 23, 1947; s. William Reginald and Ellen Hazel (Van Zoeren) W. BA in English with high honor, Grand Valley State U., 1969. Logistics coord. Colo. Outward Bound, 1979-80; writer, editor Bur. of Land Mgmt., U.S. Dept. Interior, Grand Junction, Colo., 1977-78, Elko, Nev., 1980-82, Craig, Colo., 1982-84, Denver, 1984—2006; ret. Free-lance writer, Buena Vista, Colo., 1976-77; mem. computer tech. adv. bd. Warren Tech, Golden, Colo., 1994-97. Newsletter editor Urban Peak, Denver, 1989-95; author book rev.; contbr. articles to profl. jours. including Jour. of Forestry, Govt. Exec. Vol. Craig Hosp., Englewood, Colo., 1994; vol. cmty. friend U. Denver's Office Internationalization Global Amb. Program., 2005—. Capt. USAF, 1970—76. Honors scholar Grand Valley State U., 1966-69; recipient 4 STAR awards Bur. of Land Mgmt., 1999-2002, cert. Excellence in Accountability Reporting Assn. Govt. Accts. U.S. Dept of Interior, 2001. Mem.: So. Utah Wilderness Alliance, Sister Cities Internat., Japan Am. Soc. Colo. Avocations: hiking, astronomy, travel, reading, music.

WOERTZ, PATRICIA ANN, agricultural company executive, retired oil company executive; b. Pitts., Mar. 17, 1953; married; 3 children. BS in Acctg., Pa. State U., 1974; grad. Internat. Exec. Devel. Program, Columbia U., 1994. Acct. Ernst & Young, Pitts., 1974—77; with Gulf Oil Corp., Pitts., 1977-81, Houston, 1981-85; with debt. reduction process, merger of Gulf and Chevron, 1985-87; fin. mgr. Chevron Info. Tech. Co., 1989-91, strategic planning mgr., 1991-93; pres. Chevron Can. Ltd., Vancouver, B.C., 1993-96, Chevron Internat. Oil Co., 1996-98; v.p. logistics and trading Chevron Products Co., Chevron Corp., 1996-98, v.p., 1998—2001; pres. Chevron Products Co., 1998—2001; exec. v.p. Global Downstream ChevronTexaco Corp, San Francisco, 2001—06; pres., CEO Archer Daniels Midland Co., Decatur, Ill., 2006—07, chmn., pres., CEO, 2007—. Bd. dirs. Archer Daniels Midland Co., 2006—. Bd. trustees U. San Diego; bd. visitors Pa. State U. Named a Disting. Alumna, Pa. State U., 2005; named one of Most Powerful Women in Bus., Fortune mag., 2005, 50 Most Powerful Women in Bus., 2006, 100 Most Powerful Women, Forbes mag., 2006, 50 Who Matter Now, CNNMoney.com Bus. 2.0, 2006, 50 Women to Watch, Wall St. Jour., 2006; recipient Alumni Fellow award, 2002. Mem.: Calif. C. of C. (bd. mem. 1999—), Am. Petroleum Inst. (bd. dirs.). Office: Archer Daniels Midland Co 4666 Faries Pkwy Decatur IL 62526 *

WOESE, CARL R., biophysicist, microbiology educator; b. Syracuse, NY, July 15, 1928; AB in Math. and Physics, Amherst Coll., 1950, DSc (hon.), 1985; PhD in Biophysics, Yale U., 1953; postgrad., U. Rochester, 1953-55; DSc (hon.), Syracuse U., 1994. Rsch. assoc. biophysics Yale U., New Haven, 1955-60; Biophysicist GE Rsch. Lab., 1960-63; prof. microbiology U. Ill., Urbana, 1964—. Stanley O. Ikenberry Endowed chair U. Ill., 1996. Contbr. articles to profl. jours. Recipient Bergey award Bergey's Manual Trust, 1983, John D. and Catherine T. MacArthur award, 1984, Leeuwenhoek medal 1990, 1992, 23d Brown-Hazen Lctrs. award, 1992, Roger W. Stanier Meml. Lctr. award U. Calif., Berkeley, 1993, Nat. Medal Sci., 2000, Crafoord prize, 2003; Univ. Sr. scholar U. Ill., 1986. Fellow Explorer's Club, Indian NAS, Am. Acad. Arts and Scis., Am. Acad. Microbiology; mem. Deutsche Gesellschaft fur Hygiene und Mikrobiologie (corr.), Deutsche Akademie Der Naturforscher Leopoldina, Bayerische Akademie der Wissenschaften (corr.), Max-Planck Soc., NAS (Selman A. Waksman award 1997), Ctr. Advanced Study U. Ill. Office: U Ill Chem & Life Scis Lab 131 Burrill Hall 601 S Goodwin Ave Urbana IL 61801-3709

WOESTENDIEK, JOHN, JR., (WILLIAM JOHN WOESTENDIEK), newspaper reporter; b. Winston-Salem, NC, Sept. 5, 1953; s. William John Sr. and Josephine (Pugh) W.; 1 child, Joseph Yoon Tae. BJ, U. N.C., 1975. Reporter Ariz. Daily Star, Tucson, 1975-78; reporter, asst. city editor, city editor Lexington (Ky.) Herald-Leader, 1978-81; reporter Phila. Inquirer, 1981-90, nat. corr. West Coast bur. Newport Beach, Calif., 1990-93, reporter, 1994-96, columnist, 1996-2000; enterprise editor Charlotte (N.C.) Observer, 2000-01; reporter Baltimore Sun, 2001—. Recipient Paul Tobenkin Meml. award Columbia U., 1984, Nat. Headliners award Press Club Atlantic City, 1987, Pulitzer Prize for Investigative Reporting Columbia U., 1987, Ernie Pyle award, 1994, Best Feature Story award Ky. Press. Assn., 1978, Best Investigative Story award Ky. Press Assn., 1979, Nat. Arc of Excellence Nat. Assn. Retarded Citizens, 1984, Best News Reporting First Place award AP Mng. Editors Pa., 1985, Sigma Delta Chi award for Feature Writing, 1994, Best Feature Story award Chesapeake Associated Press, 2004; John S. Knight fellow Stanford U., 1988-89; named to N.C. Journalism Hall of Fame, 2003.

WOETZEL, KURT D., banking executive; With Adolph Coors Co., 1978—84; joined The Bank of NY Co., Inc., 1985, now exec. v.p., chief info. officer. Named Leader in Fin., CNBC Tech. Leadership Awards, 2005; named one of Premier 100 IT Leaders, Computerworld, 2005. Office: The Bank of NY Co Inc One Wall St New York NY 10286 Office Phone: 212-495-1784. Office Fax: 212-809-9528. E-mail: kwoetzel@bankofny.com.

WOFFORD, CHLOE ANTHONY See MORRISON, TONI

WOFFORD, HARRIS, senator, lawyer; b. NYC, Apr. 9, 1926; s. Harris Llewellyn and Estelle (Gardner) W.; m. Emmy Lou Clare Lindgren, Aug. 14, 1948 (dec. Jan. 1996); children: Susanne, Daniel, David. BA, U. Chgo., 1948; study fellow, India, 1949, Israel, 1950; LLB, Yale U., 1954, Howard U., 1954. Bar: D.C. 1954, U.S. Supreme Ct. 1958, Pa. 1978. Asst. to Chester Bowles, 1953-54; law assoc. Covington & Burling, Washington, 1954-58; legal asst. to Rev. Theodore Hesburgh, Commn. on Civil Rights, 1958-59; assoc. prof. Notre Dame Law Sch., 1959-60, on leave, 1961-66; asst. to Senator Kennedy, 1960; spl. asst. to Pres. Kennedy, 1961-62; spl. rep. for Africa, dir. Ethiopian program U.S. Peace Corps, 1962-64; assoc. dir. Peace Corps, Washington, 1964-66; pres. Coll. at Old Westbury, SUNY, 1966-70, Bryn Mawr (Pa.) Coll., 1970-78; counsel firm Schnader, Harrison, Segal and Lewis, Phila., 1979-86; chmn. Pa. Dem. State Com., 1986; sec. labor and industry Commonwealth of Pa., 1987-91; U.S. senator from Pa., 1991-95; CEO Corp. Nat. Svc., Washington, 1995—2001; co-chair America's Promise: The Alliance for Youth, Alexandria, Va., 2001—04. Vis. lectr. Howard Law Sch., 1956; prof. of practice U. Md., 2003—. Author: It's Up to Us, 1946, (with Clare Wofford) India Afire, 1951, Of Kennedys and Kings, 1980; editor: Embers of the World, 1970; co-editor: Report of the U.S. Commission on Civil Rights, 1959. Mem. Coun. Fgn. Rels., 1968—; co-chmn. Com. for Study of Nat. Svc., 1977-80; mem. U.S. Adv. Com. on Nat. Growth Policy Processes, 1975-76; trustee The Am. Coll., Bryn Mawr, 1975-83; mem. coun. U.S.-South Africa Leader Exch. Program, 1971-87; bd. dirs. Internat. League for Human Rights, 1979-87, pres., 1980-81; bd. dirs. After-Sch. All-Stars, Campus Compact, Points of Light Found., Youth Svc. Am.; trustee Martin Luther King Ctr. for Nonviolent Social Change, 1983-87; governing coun. Wilderness Soc., 1983-87. With USAF, 1944-45. Mem.: ABA. Democrat. Roman Catholic. Home: 955 26th St NW Apt 501 Washington DC 20037-2040 E-mail: hlwofford@aol.com.

WOGAMAN, GEORGE ELSWORTH, insurance company executive, financial consultant; b. Mikado, Mich., May 29, 1937; s. Edgar R. and Leah Katherine (McGuire) W.; m. Sandra Lee Jensen, Apr. 10, 1965; children: Jennifer, Christopher. Grad. various ins. courses. CLU, registered rep.; cert. ChFc. With Blair Transit Co., Dun & Bradstreet, Chrysler Engring. Co., 1955-61; exec. chef Westward Ho!, 1961-68; owner, mgr. George Wogaman Ins. Agy., Grand Forks, N.D., 1969—. Mem. pres. coun. Farmers Ins. Group, 1988—98, 1999—2004; alderman East Grand Forks (Minn.) City Coun., 1979—2000, v.p., 1982—2006. Corp. mem. Altru Health Sys., Grand Forks, 1982—; mem. Nat. Rep. Congl. Com., Rep. Presdl. Task Force; mem. Red River Valley Estate Planning Coun.; mem. Wesley United Meth. Ch., Grand Forks; pres. bd. dirs. Econ. Devel. and Housing Authority, East Grand Forks, Minn., 2007. Recipient Pub. Svc. award East Grand Forks City Coun., 1979. Mem. Am. Soc. CLU's, North Valley Life Underwriters Assn. (Life Underwriter of Yr. 1988), Famers Financial Solutions. Home: 1818 19 h St NW East Grand Forks MN 56721-1013 Office: 2612 Gateway Dr Grand Forks ND 58203-1406 Home Phone: 218-773-9465; Office Phone: 701-772-7108. Business E-Mail: gwogaman@farmersagent.com.

WOGER, JOHN ALLEN, band director, department chairman; b. Nov. 23, 1960; BFA, U. Wis., Milwaukee, 1985. Cert. gen. music tchr. 6-12 Wis., k-12 tchr. Wis. Band dir. Deerfield HS, Wis., 1985—90, Menomonee Falls North Jr. High, Menomonee Falls, Wis., 1990—. Named Tchr. of Yr., North PTSA, 1996, 2005; fellowship, Herb Kohl Ednl. Found., 1999. Mem.: Wis. Sch. Music Assn. Home: N76 W15942 Hunters Ridge Cir Menomonee Falls WI 53051

WOHL, FRANK HAROLD, lawyer; b. Richmond, Va., June 5, 1942; AB, Dartmouth Coll., 1963; JD, U. Chgo. Law, 1966. Bar: NY 1967. Asst. U.S. atty. So. Dist. NY, NYC, 1971—79; ptnr. Rosenman & Colin, NYC, 1979—84, Lankler Siffert & Wohl, LLP, NYC, 1984—. Chair NYC Civilian Complaint Rev. Bd., 1999—2002. Fed. RICO adminstr. Fulton Fish Market, NYC, 1988—92; dir. Broodwood Child Care, Bklyn., 1992—99. Lt. comdr. JAGC USNR, 1967—71. Fellow: Am. Coll. Trial Lawyers (Access to Justice award 2000); mem.: Fed. Bar Coun. (trustee 2004—), NY Coun. Def. Lawyers (bd. mem. 1998—2002), Fed. Bar Found. (dir. 1996—2002), Bar Assn. City of NY. Office: Lankler Siffert & Wohl LLP 500 Fifth Ave New York NY 10110-3398 Home Phone: 718-834-9583; Office Phone: 212-921-8399.

WOHLBERG, BRENDT, electrical engineer, researcher; b. Pietermaritzburg, South Africa, Jan. 22, 1969; s. Rolf and Lorna Wohlberg; m. Alison Sawyer; children: Olivia, Alexander. MSc in Applied Sci., U. Cape Town, South Africa, 1993, PhD, 1996. Postdoctoral rschr. elec. engring. dept. U. Cape Town, 1997—98; postdoctoral rschr. Ctr. Nonlinear Studies Los Alamos Nat. Lab., 1999—2002, tech. staff mem. T-7 Math. Modeling and Analysis, 2002—. Contbr. articles to profl. jours. Office: Los Alamos Nat Lab T7 MS B284 Los Alamos NM 87545 Office Phone: 505-667-6886.

WOHLEBER, LYNNE FARR, archivist, librarian; b. Pitts., Mar. 16, 1939; d. Donald Elmer and Helen Rose (Lula) F.; m. David Louis Wohleber, Oct. 14, 1972 (div. Sept. 1989); 1 child, Jeffrey David. AB, Allegheny Coll., 1961; MLS, U. Pitts., 1991. Sec. comm. Aluminum Co. Am., Pitts., 1968—73; shop mgr. The Thread Shed, Pitts., 1986—90; libr. Coun. Am. Embroiderer's Libr., Carnegie, Pa., 1985—93; archivist Episcopal Diocese Pitts., 1989—. Cons. Calvary Episcopal Ch. Archives, Pitts., 1992—93, Bapt. Home Libr., Mt. Lebanon, Pa., 1994, First United Meth. Ch. Archives, Pitts., 1995, Episcopal Diocese of Albany, 2000; archival cons. Christ Ch., New Brighton, 2001, Old St. Luke's, Scott Twp., 2002, Grace Ch., Pitts., 2005; bldg. archives workshop instr., 1995, 2000—; 250th anniversary comm. com. Episcopal Diocese of Pitts., 2007—; presenter in field. Libr. com., bd. deacons, rec. sec. Bower Hill Cmty. Ch., 1996-99, nominating com. 1998-99, elder, 2003-06; contemporary svc. task force, 2002-04; coord. presch. program Am. Lung Assn., Pitts., 1977-87; capt., ward chair Am. Cancer Soc., Pitts., 1978-84; newsletter editor Mendelssohn Choir of Pitts., 1973-87; den leader Boy Scouts Am., Mt. Lebanon, Pa., 1983-84. Mem. Soc. Am. Archivists (planning com. 1999 Pitts. conf.), Mid-Atlantic Regional Archives Conf. (co-chair spl. events 1992, publs. com. 1996-2001, panelist 1999 spring conf., conf. local arrangements publicity com. 2003—04), Nat. Episcopal Historians and Archivists (Pitts. coord. for 1997 Episcopal Tri-History Conf., bd. dirs. 1996-2004, treas. 1999-2004, membership sec. 2005—), Hist. Soc. Episcopal Ch., Curators, Archivists and Record Profls. We. Pa. (co-chair Archives Week 1999 com.), Women's Episcopal History Project, Episcopal Archivists Network, Beta Phi Mu. Republican. Presbyterian and Episcopalian. Home: 110 Skylark Cir Pittsburgh PA 15234-1018 Office: Episcopal Diocese of Pitts 900 Oliver Bldg 535 Smithfield St Pittsburgh PA 15222-2403 Office Phone: 412-325-0087 ext. 138. Business E-Mail: wohleber@pgh.anglican.org.

WOHLER, WAYNE L., information scientist; b. Topeka, Nov. 9, 1955; s. Walter Bernard Wohler and Eileen Geneva Huff; m. Lorilynn King (div.); children: Brian, Walter, Diana. BSEE summa cum laude, U. Idaho, Moscow, 1977. Engr. IBM, Boulder, Colo., 1977—84, mgr., 1984—88, info. tech. arch., 1988—. Mem. info. tech. arch. cert. bd. IBM, Longmont, Colo., 1998—. Patentee in field. Mem. Airport Bd., Longmont, 1995. Mem.: U. Idaho Alumni Assn. (bd. dirs.), Lions. Avocations: flying, programming, reading, genealogy. Home: PO Box 1762 Longmont CO 80502

WOHLERS, TERESA DAHMUS, lawyer; BA in Internat. Studies and French magna cum laude, Tex. A&M U., Coll. Sta., 1997; student, Université Stendhal, Grenoble, France, 1997; M in Pub. Affairs, U. Tex., 2003, JD, 2003. Bar: Tex. 2003. Atty. Eggleston & Briscoe, Houston, 2003—04, Popp & Ikard, L.L.P., Austin, Tex., 2004—05, Ikard, Wynne & Ratliff, L.L.P., Austin, Tex. Contbr. articles to profl. jours. Named a Rising Star, Tex. Super Lawyers mag., 2006. Mem.: Austin Young Lawyers Assn., Austin Bar Assn. Office: Office Atty Gen Adminstrv Law Divsn PO Box 12548 Austin TX 78711-2548 Business E-Mail: teresa.wohlers@oag.state.tx.us.

WOHLFORTH, ERIC EVANS, lawyer; b. NYC, Apr. 17, 1932; s. Robert Martin and Mildred Campbell (Evans) W.; m. Caroline Penniman, Aug. 3, 1957; children: Eric Evans, Charles Penniman. AB, Princeton U., 1954; LLB, U. Va., 1957. Bar: N.Y. 1958, Alaska, 1967. Assoc. Hawkins, Delafield & Wood, NYC, 1957-66; ptnr. McGrath & Wohlforth, Anchorage, 1966-70; commr. revenue State of Alaska, Anchorage, 1970-72; ptnr. McGrath, Wohlforth & Flint, Anchorage, 1972-74, Wohlforth & Flint, Anchorage, 1974-87, Wohlforth, Argetsinger, Johnson & Brecht, Anchorage, 1988-98, Wohlforth, Vassar, Johnson & Brecht, Anchorage, 1999—2005, Wohlforth, Johnson, Brecht, Cartledge & Brooking, Anchorage, 2005—. Mem. Alaska Investment Adv. Com., 1973-80. Vice-chair Alaska Permanent Fund Corp., 1995—97, trustee, 1995—2006, vice-chair, 2001—02, chmn., 1997—99, 2002—03; mem. investment com. U. Alaska Found., 2002—, chair, 2004—; chancellor Episcopal Diocese of Alaska, 1972—; trustee Alaska Pacific U., 2003—; bd. dirs. Commonwealth North, 2004—, Alaska Growth Capital, 2007—; trustee U. Alaska Found., 2007—. Mem. Alaska Bar Assn., Assn. of Bar of City of N.Y. Home: 7831 Ingram St Anchorage AK 99502-3965 Office: 900 W 5th Ave Ste 600 Anchorage AK 99501-2044 E-mail: ewohlforth@akatty.com.

WOHLGENANT, RICHARD GLEN, lawyer, director; b. Porterville, Calif., Dec. 2, 1930; s. Carl Ferdinand and Sara Alice (Moore) W.; m. Teresa Joan Bristow, Dec. 27, 1959; children: Mark Thomas, Tracy Patrice, Timothy James. BA, U. Mont., Missoula, 1952; LL.B., Harvard U., Cambridge, Mass., 1957. Bar: Colo. 1957, U.S. Dist. Ct. Colo. 1957. Assoc. Holme Roberts & Owen LLP, Denver, 1957-62; ptnr./mem. Holme Roberts & Owen, Denver, 1962-99, of counsel, 2000—. Bd. dirs. Adopt-A-Sch., Denver, 1976-80, St. Joseph Found., Denver, 1990-93, Denver Com. Coun. Fgn. Rels., 1988-98, Japanese-Am. Soc. Colo., 1993-98, Rocky Mountain chpt. U.S. Mex. C. of C., 1993-00; bi-nat. bd. U.S./Mex. C. of C., 2000—01; mem. Chamber of the Americas, 2001—03; adv. bd. Human Med. Genetics Prgm., U. Colo. H.S.C., 2000—03; trustee Helen K.and Arthur E. Johnson Found., 2003—. Mem. ABA, Colo. Bar Assn., Denver Bar Assn., Am. Coll. Real Estate Lawyers, Univ. Club, Law Club, City Club, Cactus Club, Denver Press Club, Mile High Club. Republican. Roman Catholic. Home: 300 Ivy St Denver CO 80220-5855 Office: Holme Roberts & Owen LLP 1700 Lincoln St Denver CO 80203-4500

WOHLTMANN, HULDA JUSTINE, pediatrician, endocrinologist; b. Charleston, SC, Apr. 10, 1923; d. John Diedrich and Emma Lucia (Mohrmann) W. BS, Coll. Charleston, 1944; MD, Med. U. S.C., 1949. Diplomate Am. Bd. Pediatrics. Intern Louisville Gen. Hosp., 1949-50; resident in pediatrics St. Louis Children's Hosp., 1950-53, 1953-65, instr., 1953-58, asst. prof., 1958-65, postdoctoral fellow biochemistry, 1961-63; assoc. prof. pediatrics, head pediatric endocrinology Med. U. S.C., Charleston, 1965-70, prof., 1970-90, prof. emeritus, 1990—. Bd. dirs. Franke Home, Charleston, 1975-97, treas., 1989-91; mem. adv. bd. for ethics ctr. Newberry (S.C.) Coll., 1989—; trustee Luth. Theol. So. Sem., 1991-97. Contbr. articles to sci. jours. Mem. Am. Pediatric Soc., Ambulatory Pediatric Assn., Endocrine Soc., Am. Diabetes Assn., Am. Acad. Pediatrics, Midwest Soc. Pediatric Rsch., So. Soc. Pediatric Rsch., S.C. Diabetes Assn. (bd. dirs. 1970-86, pres. 1970-73, 84-85, v.p. 1982-83, Profl. Svc. award 1977), Lawson Wilkins Endocrine Soc., Sugar Club; fell. Am. Acad. Pediatrics. Lutheran. Home: 3 46th Ave Isle Of Palms SC 29451-2607

WOHRLE, MARTA, publishing executive; b. Manchester, Eng. Ptnr., co-founder Informed Sources, 1993—2002; dir. Mercer Mgmt. Cons., 2002—06; sr. v.p., dir. digital media Hachette Filipacchi Media U.S., NYC, 2006—. Named a Woman to Watch, Advt. Age, 2007. Office: Hachette Filipacchi Media US 1633 Broadway Fl 45 New York NY 10019 Office Phone: 212-767-6000. *

WOJCICKI, ANDREW ADALBERT, chemist, educator; b. Warsaw, May 5, 1935; s. Franciszek Wojcicki and Janina (Kozlowa) Hoskins; m. Marba L. Hart, Dec. 21, 1968; children: Katherine, Christina. BS, Brown U., 1956; PhD, Northwestern U., 1960; postdoctoral fellow, U. Nottingham, Eng., 1960-61. Asst. prof. chemistry Ohio State U., Columbus, 1961-66, assoc. prof., 1966-69, prof., 1969-2000, prof. emeritus, 2001—, acting chmn., 1981-82, assoc. chmn., 1982-83, 84-86. Vis. prof. Academia Sinica, Taipei, Taiwan, 2002-03, Case Western Res. U., 1967, U. Bologna, Italy, 1988, Nat. Sci. Council Chemistry Rsch. Promotion Ctr., Taiwan, 1994, U. Sydney, Australia, 1998; vis. researcher U. Coll. London, 1969; sr. U.S. scientist Alexander von Humboldt Found., Mulheim/Ruhr, Germany, 1975-76; vis. scholar U. Calif.-Berkeley, 1984; assoc. dean Coll. of Math. and Phys. Scis., Ohio State U., 1996-98. Contbr. articles to profl. jours. Guggenheim fellow U. Cambridge (Eng.), 1976; recipient Disting. Teaching award Ohio State U., 1968, Humboldt Sr. award Humboldt Found., 1975-76, Casimir Funk Natural Sci. award, Polish Inst. of Arts and Scis. in Am., 2001. Mem.: Am. Chem. Soc. (Columbus sect. award 1992), Phi Lambda Upsilon, Sigma Xi. Home: 825 Greenridge Rd Columbus OH 43235-3411 Office: Ohio State U 100 W 18th Ave Columbus OH 43210-1185 Office Phone: 614-292-4750.

WOJCICKI, STANLEY GEORGE, physicist, researcher; b. Warsaw, Mar. 30, 1937; came to U.S., 1950; s. Franciszek and Janina (Kozlow) W.; m. Esther Denise Hochman, Nov. 17, 1961; children: Susan Diane, Janet Maia, Anne Elizabeth. AB, Harvard U., 1957; PhD, U. Calif., Berkeley, 1962. Physicist Lawrence Radiation Lab., Berkeley, 1961-66; asst. prof. physics Stanford U., 1966-68, assoc. prof., 1968-74, prof., 1974—, chmn. dept., 1982-85, dep. dir. Superconducting Supercollider Central Design Group, 1984-89, chmn. physics dept., 2004—; chmn. Stanford Linear Accelerator Center Exptl. Program Adv. Com., 1979-81. Chmn. High Energy Physics Adv. Panel, 1990-96; spokesperson FermiLab Main Injector Neutrine Oscillation Search expt. Assoc. editor Phys. Rev. Letters for Exptl. High Energy Physics, 1978-80. Recipient Alexander von Humboldt Sr. Am. Scientist award, 1981; NSF fellow, 1964-65; Sloan Found. fellow, 1968-72; Guggenheim fellow, 1973-74 Fellow Am. Phys. Soc. Office: Stanford U Dept Physics Stanford CA 94305-4060 Home Phone: 650-493-0919; Office Phone: 650-926-2806. Business E-Mail: sgweg@slac.stanford.edu.

WOJCIK, BARBARA ELZBIETA, statistician, researcher; arrived in US, 1987; d. Stanislaw and Stanislawa Marciniak; m. Zbigniew M. Wojcik, 1974; children: Martin R., Paulina M. BSEE, MSEE, Tech. U. Warsaw, 1973; PhD, Polish Acad. Scis., 1979. From asst. to asst. prof. Sys. Rsch. Inst., Polish Acad. Scis., Warsaw, 1975—89; instr. Wichita State U., Kans., 1988; engr., data analyst Beech Aircraft, Fort Sam Houston, 1988—90; vis. asst. prof. U. Tex., San Antonio, 1990—91; supervisory statistician Ctr. for Healthcare Edn. and Studies, Fort Sam Houston, Tex., 1993—2001; dep. dir. Ctr. for AMEDD Strategic Studies, Fort Sam Houston, 2001—. Adj. prof. Webster U., Fort Sam Houston, Tex., 1992—94; asst. prof. US Army, Baylor U., 1993—2001. Contbr. numerous papers and articles to profl. jours. and pubs. Named one of the Top 25 Cancer Rschrs. in the U.S., Am. Cancer Soc., 1998; recipient Rschr. of Yr. award, US Army, Baylor U., 1996, 1999. Mem.: APHA. Achievements include research in healthcare, epidemiology, statistics, rough sets. Office: Ctr for AMEDD Strategic Studies 1608 Stanley Rd Bldg 2268 Fort Sam Houston TX 78234 Office Phone: 210-221-9633. Business E-Mail: barbara.wojcik@amedd.army.mil.

WOJCIK, CASS, decorative supply company executive, retired municipal official; b. Rochester, NY, Dec. 1920; s. Emit M. and Casimira C. (Krawiecz) Wojcik; m. Lillian Leocadia Lendzion, Sept. 25, 1948 (dec. Jan. 2007); 1 child, Robert Cass. Student, Lawrence Inst. Tech., 1941—43, Yale U., 1943—44, US Sch. for European Pers., Czech Republic, 1945. Owner Nat. Florists Supply Co., Detroit, 1948—88, Nat. Decorative, Detroit, 1950—89; co-owner Creaton Ctr., Detroit, 1955—60, Wojcik Family Collection Collectqables Mktg., 1995—. Cons.-contr. hort-bot. design auto show displqays, TV prodrs., designers and decorators. Nen, Regional Planning and Evaluation Coun., 1969—75; city-wide mem. Detroit Bd. Edn., 1970—75; commr. Detroit Pub. Schs. Employees Retirement Commn., 1975; mem. Area Occupl. Ednl. Commn., Ednl. Task Force; chmn., grand marshal Ann. Gen. Pulaski Day Parade, Detroit, 1970—71; mem. Friends of Belle iSLE; mem. pastoral coun. Archdiocese of Detroit, ', 1983—86, 1988—92; v.p. rsch. Bama Coll., Ft. Lauderdale, Fla., 1989—94; vice chmn. '13th Congl. Dist. Rep. Party Mich., 1987—91; elected Electoral Coll., 1988. Withy US Army, 1944—46. Decorated Bronze Star; recipient citation, Polish-Am. Congress, 1971, 3d prize Art in Park, City of Oakland Park, Fla. Mem.: Mich. Heritage Coun., Internat. Platform Assn., Nat. Coun. Tchr. Retirement, Mcpl. Fin. Officers Assn. US, Nat. Coun. Great Cities Schs., Big Cities Sch. Bd. Com., Nat. Sch. Bd. Assn., Mich. Sch. Bd. Assn., SE Mich. Coun. Govts., Nat. Geog. Soc., Polish Century Club. Home: 1729 SW 14th Ct Fort Lauderdale FL 33312-4109 Office Phone: 561-750-9033.

WOJCIK, JASON PAUL, history professor; s. Walter and Sandra Wojcik; m. Valerie Beth Wiley, Aug. 1, 1998; children: Baylee Nicole, Braydon Alexander. BA, U. Pitts., Johnstown, Pa., 1996; MAT, U. Pitts., 1997; MA, Duquesne U., Pitts., Pa., 2000. Cert. tchr. social studies Pa., 1997. Assoc. prof. history and cultural studies Pa. Highlands C.C., Johnstown, 2000—, coord. student life, 2005—06. Office: Penn Highlands C 881 Hills Plz Dr Ste 450 Ebensburg PA 15931 Office Phone: 814-262-6413.

WOJCIK, JOHN CASIMIR, music educator, director; b. South Haven, Mich., Aug. 19, 1952; s. Casimir Joseph and Mary Josephine Wojcik; m. Kimberly Kristine Allison, Mar. 25, 2000; 1 child, Jacob Casimir. MusB in Edn., Mich. State U., East Lansing, 1978; MusM in Trumpet Performance, U. Okla., Norman, 1981; MusD in Instrumental Conducting, U. Kans., Lawrence, 1989. Asst. dir. bands Enid H.S., Okla., 1980—84; dir. bands Phillips U., Enid, 1984—87, Graceland U., Lamoni, Iowa, 1989—2001; dir. bands, instr. trumpet Tex. A&M U., Corpus Christi, Tex., 2001—05; dir. bands Delta State U., Cleve., Miss., 2005—. Contbr. articles to profl. jours. Mem.: World Assn. Symphonic Bands and Ensembles, Miss.Bandmasters Assn., Nat. Band Assn., Music Educators Nat. Conf., Coll. Band Dirs. Nat. Assn., Tau Beta Sigma, Kappa Kappa Psi, Pi Kappa Lambda, Phi Kappa Phi, Phi Mu Alpha Sinfonia (rec. sec. 1976—77, pres. 1977—78). Democrat. Roman Catholic. Avocations: golf, jogging, history. Office: Delta State U PO Box 3256 Cleveland MS 38733 Home: 1202 Farmer St Cleveland MS 38732 Office Phone: 662-846-4629. Office Fax: 662-846-4605. Personal E-mail: jkwojcik@bellsouth.net. Business E-Mail: jwojcik@deltastate.edu.

WOJCIK, MARTIN HENRY, not-for-profit executive; b. Chgo., May 10, 1948; s. Henry Martin and Mary Lorraine (Naughton) W. BS, Ill. Inst. Tech., 1970; M. in Humanities, Bonn U., W. Ger., 1975. Price adminstr. R.R. Donnelley & Sons., Chgo., 1970-72; dir. devel. Citizens for a Better Environment, Milw., 1976-79, pres. Chgo., 1979-85; dir. found. rels. Northwestern U., Evanston, Ill., 1987-89; dir. corp. and found. rels. Mayo Found., Rochester, Minn., 1989—2002; sr. v.p., COO, Scripps Health Found., La Jolla, Calif., 2002—04; dir. devel. The Biodesign Inst., Ariz. State U., Tempe, 2005—. Bd. dir. Citizens for Better Environment, Chgo., chmn. bd. dir., 1990—91, 1999—2001; mem. policy adv. com. Ill. EPA, Springfield, Ill., 1980—82. Bd. dir. Rochester Civic Theatre, 1991-97, pres. bd. dir. 1994-95; bd. dir. Wasie Found., 2003—; mem. adv. panel Minn. State Arts Bd., 1995, 97, 99, 2001; adv. coun. KSDS Pub. Radio, San Diego, 2003-; panelist, Ariz. Commn. on the Arts, 2007. Mem. Ill. Inst. Tech. Alumni Assn. Roman Catholic. Home: 8507 N 84th Pl Scottsdale AZ 85258-2401

WOLANDE, CHARLES SANFORD, former computer company executive; b. Chgo., July 25, 1954; s. Sam C. and Marie Helene (Riccio) W.; children: Eric, Jill, Patrick, Ryan, Haley. B, St. Mary's Coll., Winona, Minn., 1976. Lab. tech. Jefferson Electric, Bellwood, Ill., 1976-73; pres. Comark, Inc., Glendale Heights, Ill., 1978—2002, also CFO Bloomingdale, Ill., 1978—2002. Named High Tech. Entrepreneur of the yr., Peat, Marwick, Mitchell, Chgo., 1987; named to CRN Industry Hall of Fame, 2003. Mem. C. of C. Glendale Heights. Republican. Roman Catholic. Avocations: golf, skiing. Office: 444 Scott Dr Bloomingdale IL 60108-3111

WOLANIN, BARBARA ANN BOESE, curator, art historian; b. Dayton, Ohio, Dec. 12, 1943; d. William Carl and Elisabeth Cassell Boese; m. Thomas R. Wolanin, 1966 (div. 1980); children: Peter, Andrew; m. Phillip F. Brown, 2001. AB, Oberlin Coll., 1966, AM, 1969; MAT, Harvard U., 1967; PhD, U. Wis., 1981. Art tchr. Newton (Mass.) Pub. Schs., 1969-71; asst. prof. art history Trinity Coll., Washington, 1978-83, James Madison U., Harrisonburg, Va., 1983-85; curator U.S. Capitol, Arch. of the Capitol, Washington, 1985—. Author: (exhbn. catalog) Arthur B. Carles, 1983, 2000, Constantino Brumidi, 1998; contbr. articles to profl. jours. Recipient Faculty Devel. award, James Madison U., 1985; Woodrow Wilson fellow, 1967, Kress fellow, U. Wis., 1974, Smithsonian fellow, 1976. Mem.: Am. Inst. Conservation, Coll. Art Assn., ArtTable (bd. dirs. DC chpt. 2003—05), Women's Caucus Art (pres. DC chpt. 1998—2001, nat. bd. dirs. 2002—), Phi Beta Kappa (pres. Trinity Coll. 1982—83). Home: 7807 Hamilton Spring Rd Bethesda MD 20817 Office: US Capitol Office Architect Washington DC 20515-0001

WOLANIN, THOMAS RICHARD, federal agency administrator, educator; b. Detroit, Dec. 1, 1942; s. Chester Richard and Helen Theresa (Luszki) W.; m. Donna M. Christian; children: Peter, Andrew. BA magna cum laude, Oberlin Coll., 1965; MA, Harvard U., 1970, PhD, 1972. Staff dir. subcom. on labor-mgmt. rels. House Edn. and Labor Com., 1975-77, dep. staff dir. subcom. on select edn., 1977-78; exec. asst. to pres. NYU, 1981-82; analyst Senate Budget Com., 1982-83; staff dir. subcom. on investigations House P.O. and Civil Svc. Com., 1983-85, 87-91; staff dir. subcom. on postsecondary edn. House Edn. and Labor Com., 1978-81, 85-87;, 91-93; dep. ast. sec. legis. and congl. affairs U.S. Dept. Edn., Washington, 1993-96; sr. assoc. The Inst. for Higher Edn. Policy, Washington, 1996—. Instr. govt. Oberlin Coll., 1967-69; asst. prof. polit. sci. U. Wis., Madison, 1971-78; rsch. prof. edn. policy and polit. sci. George Washington U., Washington, 1997-00. Author: Presidential Advisory Commissions: Truman to Nixon, 1975; co-author: Congress and the Colleges: Higher Education in National Politics, 1976; contbr. articles to profl. jours. Bd. dirs. Am. Youth Policy Forum. Woodrow Wilson fellow, 1965-66, fellow Harvard U., 1965-67, 69-71, Congl. fellow, 1971-72, Spencer fellow Nat. Acad. Edn., 1975-81, Fulbright Found., 2005; grantee Ford Found., 1972-73, 73-74, USIA, 1990; scholar The Brookings Instn., 1970 Mem. Polish Am. Arts Assn. Washington, Congl. Fellowship Alumni Assn., Phi Beta Kappa. Democrat. Avocations: military history, polish history, literature. Office: Inst Higher Edn Policy 1320 19th St NW Ste 400 Washington DC 20036-1635 Office Phone: 202-861-8223 214. E-mail: tom@ihep.com.

WOLAVER, STEPHEN ARTHUR, judge; b. Springfield, Ill., Sept. 4, 1950; s. Lynn Ellsworth and Arah Dean Phyllis W.; m. Gayla Sue Howard, Feb. 28, 1987; children: Lindy Allison, Scott. BS, Miami U., Oxford, Ohio, 1972; JD, Valparaiso U., 1975. Bar: Ohio 1975, U.S. Dist. Ct. (so. dist.) Ohio 1976, U.S. Ct. Appeals (6th cir.) 1997, U.S. Tax Ct. 1990, U.S. Supreme Ct. 1979. Ptnr. Gill, Wolaver & Welch, Fairborn, Ohio, 1975-81; asst. pros. atty. Greene County (Ohio), Xenia, 1976—, chief trial counsel, 1989—2003, elected Common Pleas judge, 2003—; ptnr. Wolaver, Sheets & Lewis, Fairborn, 1981—2001, Wolaver, Mayer & Cusack, 2002. Instr. Fairborn Bd. Edn., 1978—; adj. prof. Clark Tech. Coll., 1979-85; instr. Greene County Law Enforcement Police Acad., 1988—, Greene County Career Ctr. Police Acad., 2004; faculty Nat. Advocacy Ctr. U. So. Carolina, 2001; lectr., 1982—, law enforcement adv. com., 1983-86; advisor Fairborn (Ohio) H.S. Mock Trial Team, 1987-96. Greene County campaign chmn. Gov. Rhodes re-election com., 1978, 86, Voinovich for U.S. Senate; active Greene County Rep. Ctrl. Com., 1978-2002; youth counselor Bethlehem Luth. Ch., Fairborn, 1980-96, head usher com. pres. Rona Village Homeowners Assn., 1981; pres. Greene County Rep. Club, 1999-2000. Named one of Outstanding Young Men Am., Jaycees, 1981, Greene County Legal Secs. Boss of Yr. award, 1985; named to Fairborn H.S. Hall of Honor, 2003; recipient Outstanding Asst. Prosecutor of Yr. award Ohio Pros. Attys. Assn., 1998, Outstanding Trial award Nat. Assn. Govt. Attys. in Capital Litigation, 2002, Meritorious Achievement award Ohio Pros. Attys. Assn., 2002. Mem. Greene County Bar Assn. (sec.-treas. 1997, v.p. 1998, pres. 2000), Ohio Bar Assn., Assn. Trial Lawyers Am., Nat. Dist. Attys. Assn., Sertoma (pres. 1982-83), Ohio Jud. Conf. (com. mem. 2003-), Delta Tau Delta. Office: Courthouse 45 N Detroit Ave Xenia OH 45385 Office Phone: 937-562-5218. Business E-Mail: swolaver@co.greene.oh.us.

WOLCOTT, HUGH DIXON, obstetrics and gynecology educator; b. NYC, Jan. 12, 1946; s. Charles Edmund and Joan Degrau (Loveland) W.; m. Jane Jarrell Smith; children: Allison, James. BS, U.S. Naval Acad., 1967; MSE, Princeton U., 1969; MD, Northwestern U., 1979. Diplomate Am. Bd. Ob-Gyn, Am. Bd. Med. Examiners. Commd. ensign USN, 1967, advanced through grades to capt., 1990; aviator, Fighter Squadron 14 Naval Air Station, Oceana, Va., 1971-74; test pilot Naval Air Test Ctr., Patuxent River, Md., 1974-76; staff physician Naval Hosp., Portsmouth, Va., 1984, Jacksonville, Fla., 1984-86, dir. colposcopy and laser clins. Portsmouth, Va., 1986-89, dir. ob-gyn. residency program, 1989-91, acting chmn. dept. ob-gyn., 1990-91; ret., 1991; asst. prof. Med. Coll. Hampton Roads, Norfolk, Va., 1991—. Chmn. dept. ob-gyn. Sentara Hosps, Norfolk, 1996—2001; ob-gyn. splty. advisor Sentara Health Mgmt. Corp., 2000—; chmn. bd. mgr.s Mid-Atlantic Women's Care, LLC, 2005—. Contbr. articles profl. jours. Mem. steering com. Sentara ObRight Patient Safety Initiative, 2005—. Awarded 1st prize scientific paper by resident physician Am. Coll. Obstetricans and Gynecologists; recipient Guggenheim fellowship Princeton U., 1967-68; Trident scholar U.S. Naval Acad., 1966-67. Fellow Am. Coll. Ob.-Gyns. (chmn. Navy sect. armed forces dist. 1989-91), Assn. Profs. Ob.-Gyns. (assoc.); mem. Am. Assn. Gynecol. Laparoscopists. Episcopalian. Home: 835 Botetourt Gdns Norfolk VA 23507-1814 Office: Woman Care Ctrs 100 Kingsley Ln Ste 400 Norfolk VA 23505 Home Phone: 757-627-1290; Office Phone: 757-451-0929. Personal E-mail: hdwolcott@aol.com.

WOLCOTT, JOHN WINTHROP, III, retired manufacturing executive; b. Balt., Dec. 3, 1924; s. John Winthrop, Jr. and Dorothy C. (Fraser) W.; m. Elizabeth Thelin Hooper, Apr. 24, 1948 (div. 1985); children: John Winthrop IV (dec.), Elizabeth T., Katherine C.; m. Karen E. Jones, Oct. 1, 1985; 1 child, Oliver Lund. B.Indsl. Engring., Gen. Motors Inst., 1951. Registered profl. engr., Ohio. With Gen. Motors Corp., 1946-53, Weatherhead Co., Cleve., 1957-60; v.p. H.K. Porter Co., Inc., Pitts., 1960-64; pres., dir., CEO Ametek, Inc., NYC, 1964-66; v.p. Am. Machine & Foundry Co., 1966-77, group exec. process equipment group, 1967-70; exec. v.p. ops., dir. AMF, Inc., 1970-77; pres., chief exec. officer, dir. Transway Internat. Corp., NYC, 1978-86, chmn. bd., 1982-86. Served with USCGR, 1943-46. Mem. Soc. Colonial Wars, Md. Club (Balt.) Episcopalian. Home: 210 Carrsbrook Dr Charlottesville VA 22901-1004

WOLD, JOHN SCHILLER, geologist, former congressman; b. East Orange, NJ, Aug. 31, 1916; s. Peter Irving and Mary (Helff) W.; m. Jane Adele Pearson, Sept. 28, 1946; children: Peter Irving, Priscilla Adele, John Pearson. AB, St. Andrews U., Scotland and Union Coll., Schenectady, 1938; MS, Cornell U., 1939; LLD (hon.), U. Wyo., 1991. Dir. Fedn. Rocky Mountain States, 1966-68; v.p. Rocky Mountain Oil and Gas Assn., 1967, 68; mem. Wyo. Ho. of Reps., 1957-59; Wyo. Republican candidate for U.S. Senate, 1964, 70; mem. 91st Congress at large from Wyo.; chmn., CEO Wold Trona Co., Inc.; pres., chmn. Wold Talc Co.; ret. Wold Nuclear Co., Wold Mineral Exploration Co., Casper, Wyo.; founding pres. Wyo. Heritage Soc.; founder Central Wyo. Ski Corp. Chmn. Wyo. Natural Gas Pipeline Authority, 1987-91; chmn. bd. Nuclear Exploration and Devel. Corp., Mineral Engring. Co., chmn., CEO Gastech, 2005—. Chmn. Wyo. Rep. Com., 1960-64, Western State Rep. Chmns. Assn., 1963-64; mem. exec. com. Rep. Nat. Com., 1962-64; chmn. Wyo. Rep. State Fin. Com.; Active Little League Baseball, Boy Scouts Am., United Fund, YMCA, Boys Clubs Am.; former pres. bd. trustees Casper Coll.; trustee Union Coll. Served to lt. USNR, World War II. Named Wyo. Man of Yr. AP-UPI, 1968; Wyo. Mineral Man of Yr., 1979, Wyo. Heritage award, 1992, Wyo. Oil/Gas and Mineral Man of 20th Century, Am. Heritage Ctr. of U. Wyo., 1999; named Benefactor of Yr., Nat. Coun. for Resource Devel., 1993. Mem. Wyo. Geol. Assn. (hon. life, pres. 1956), Am. Assn. Petroleum Geologists, Ind. Petroleum Assn. Am., AAAS, Wyo. Mining Assn., Sigma Xi, Alpha Delta Phi. Episcopalian (past vestryman, warden). Home: 1231 W 30th St Casper WY 82601-5372 Office: Mineral Resource Ctr 139 W 2nd St Casper WY 82601-2473 Office Phone: 307-265-7252. Business E-Mail: gastech@woldoil.com.

WOLDEN, SUZANNE LEESA, pediatric radiation oncologist; b. West Covina, Calif., June 30, 1969; MD, U. Calif. San Francisco Sch. Medicine, 1994. Cert. Radiation Oncology. Intern Cornell Med. Ctr., NY, 1994—95; resident Stanford U. Med. Ctr., Calif., 1995—98; asst. attending Meml. Sloan-Kettering Cancer Ctr., NY, 1998—. Contbr. articles to profl. jours. Named one of Medical Marvel, NY Mag., 2006. Office: Meml Sloan-Kettering Cancer Ctr 1275 York Ave New York NY 10021 Office Phone: 212-639-5148. *

WOLDMAN, SHERMAN, pediatrician; b. Buffalo, Apr. 1, 1932; s. Joseph Harry and Sadie (Weinstein) W. m. Fern Marlene Weinstein, Dec. 28, 1952; children: Deborah Janine Case, Scott Alan, Sabina Heide Muller. BS in Pharmacy magna cum laude, U. Buffalo, 1953, MD with high honors, 1957. Diplomate Am. Bd. Pediat. Intern Millard Fillmore Hosp., Buffalo, 1957-58; resident in pediat. Womens & Children's Hosp., Buffalo, 1958—60, active staff, 1961—2004, emeritus, 2005; pvt. practice Buffalo, 1961-66, Cheektowaga, NY, 1962—2004; med. insp. Lover Twp. Elem. Schs., Cape May, NJ, 2005—; mem. active staff Millard Fillmore Hosp., Buffalo, 1961—2004, chmn. dept. pediat., 1985-91, emeritus, 2005; pediatrician pvt. practice, 2005, Clermont, 2006—. Clin. asst. pediat. SUNY Sch. Medicine, Buffalo, 1962, clin. assoc. 1970, clin. asst. prof., 1973, clin. assoc. prof., 2001, preceptor Sch. Nursing, 1976-82; attending pediatrician Booth Meml. Hosp., Buffalo, 1969-72; sch. physician Williamsville Ctrl. Schs., NY, 1962-94, chmn. of physicians, 1970-94; courtesy staff St. Joseph Intercmty. Hosp., Cheektowaga, 1963-80, Kenmore Mercy Hosp., NY, 1963-70, 1974-82, Sisters of Charity Hosp., Buffalo, 1991-2003, Erie County Med. Ctr., Buffalo, 1979-83, Buffalo Gen. Hosp., 1987-95; provisional staff Mercy Hosp., Buffalo, 1982-83, courtesy staff, 2000-03. Vol. Leukemia and Lymphoma Soc., 1975—, bd. trustees Western NY and Finger Lakes chpt. 1975-2005, pres. 1977-79, v.p. 1979-81, profl. edn. com. 1975-2005, nat. bd. trustees 1978-87, vice chmn. patient aid com., 1980-87; task force on sch. health Erie County Health Dept., NY; trustee Temple Beth David Ner-Israel, Buffalo, 1964-65; vol. staff pediatrician Clinic Cape May County House, NJ, 2006—. Co-recipient recognition cert. Cheektowaga NY C. of C., 1982; Myron L. Woldman Vol. of Yr. award Western NY chpt. Leukemia Soc. Am., 1987, nat. chmn.'s citation 1999; Disting. Physician award Millard Fillmore Health Sys., 1995. Mem.: Maimonides Med. Soc. (pres. Buffalo chpt. 1982—83), Med. Soc. County of Erie, N.Y. (chmn. pub. health com. 1978—79), Buffalo Pediat. Soc. (pres. 1969—70), Med. Soc. State of N.Y., Am. Acad. Pediat. (PREP fellow 1979—85, 1992—94, 1994—96, 1997—99, 2000—02), Gibson Anat. Soc. (hon.), Phi Lambda Kappa (alumni pres. 1965, v.p. alumni 1980—81), Rho Chi, Alpha Omega Alpha. Avocations: gardening, computers. Personal E-mail: swoldman@comcast.net.

WOLD-OLSEN, PER, pharmaceutical executive; b. Nov. 6, 1947; MBA in Econs. Adminstrn., Norwegian Sch. Mgmt., 1972; MBA in Mgmt. and Mktg., U. Wis., 1973. Mgmt. trainee Sarpsborg Paper Co., 1968—69; product mgr. trainee MSD Norway Merck & Co., Inc., 1973, European area intern, Rahway, 1974, spl. project mgr. MSD Norway, 1974, fin. and adminstrn. mgr. MSD Norway, 1975, mng. dir. MSD Norway, 1976, regional dir. Scandinavia, 1986, v.p. MSD Europe and regional dir. Scandinavia, 1990, sr. v.p. mktg. human health divsn., 1991—94; pres. Merck Human Health Merck & Co. Inc., Whitehouse Station, NJ, 1994—97, pres. Human Health Europe, Middle East & Africa, 1997—2005, pres. intercontinental health, 2005—.

WOLDT, HAROLD FREDERICK, JR., newspaper publishing executive; b. Atlanta, July 4, 1947; s. Harold Frederick and Dorothy Rose (Lansdowne) W.; m. Lisa Diane Neves; children: Lauren Rae, Katherine Neves, Caroline Neves. BS in Journalism, So. Ill. U., 1969. Classified advt. rep. Chgo. Tribune, 1969-70, classified automobile staff mgr., 1970-72; nat. advt. sales rep. Chgo. Tribune newspapers, NYC, 1972-74, city circulation mgr., 1974-77; nat. circulation mgr. Chgo. Tribune, 1977-80, circulation mgr., 1980-84; v.p., circulation News & Sun Sentinel Co., Ft. Lauderdale, Fla., 1985; circulation dir. Newsday, Inc., Melville, NY, 1986-88, v.p. circulation LI, NY, 1988-94; sr. v.p. circulation Newsday, pres. Distbn. Systems. Am. subs. of Newsday, Inc., 1994-98; v.p. sales circulation mktg. The N.Y. Times, NYC, 1998—2000; dir. circulation Omaha World-Herald; v.p. circulation San Jose Mercury News, Calif., 2001—04, 2006—; sr. v.p. circulation LA Newspaper Group, 2007—, dir. circulation LA Daily News, 2007—. Speaker, participant Am. Press Inst.; bd. dirs. Abilities Health and Rehab. Svcs. (Nat. Ctr. for Disability Svcs.), Albertson, LI, N.Y., 1992-94. Bd. dirs. Robert R. McCormick Boys Club, Chgo., 1980-81; chmn. United Way campaign, Chgo. Tribune, 1980, Omaha World-Herald United Way Campaign, 1999-2000, bd. dir. San Jose Children's Discovery Mus. Calif., Ronald McDonald House Charities of the Bay Area, San Francisco, 2002—. Mem. Am. Pubs. Newspaper Assn. (circulation and readership com. 1988-93), Internat. Circulation Mgrs. Assn. (pres. 1991-92), Alpha Delta Sigma, Tau Kappa Epsilon. Office Phone: 818-713-3101. Personal E-mail: hfwoldt@aol.com. Business E-Mail: harry.woldt@langnews.com.

WOLETZ, ROBERT G., editor; b. 1953; Cable tv advt. editor Paul Kagan & Assocs.; founder RGW Media, 1984; pub. rels. mgr. ABC Video Enterprises, 1985—86; with NY Times, 1986—, Vows columnist, Sunday Styles sect., Society News editor. Office: NY Times 229 W 43rd St New York NY 10036 Office Phone: 212-556-4588. Office Fax: 212-556-5999, 212-556-7689.

WOLF, AIZIK LOFT, neurosurgeon; b. Bogota, Colombia, Jan. 17, 1956; came to U.S., 1963; s. Jose Wolf and Judy Grimberg Loft. AB, U. Chgo., 1977; MD, Yale U., 1981. Diplomate Am. Bd. Neurol. Surgery. Asst. prof. neurosurgery, chief epilepsy surgery U. Md. Hosp., Balt., 1987-93, asst. prof. neurology, chief Gamma knife skull base surgery, 1990-93; dir. Miami Neurosci. Ctr. Doctors Hosp., Coral Gables, Fla., 1993—. Office: Doctors Hosp 5000 University Dr Coral Gables FL 33146-2094 Office Phone: 786-308-3700. E-mail: drwolf@miamineurosciencecenter.com.

WOLF, ALAN STEVEN, lawyer; b. Jersey City, Jan. 5, 1955; s. Lester Joel and Beatrice (Spiegel) W.; m. Donna Snow Wolf, Aug. 31, 1980; children: Lauren, Bradley. BA, Dartmouth Coll., 1977; JD, Southwestern U., LA, 1980. Bar: Calif. 1980, U.S. Dist. Ct. (no., so., ea. and cen. dists.) Calif. 1980. With Alvarado, Rus & McClellen, Orange, Calif., 1981-84; ptnr. Cameron Dreyfuss & Wolf, Orange, 1984-89; pres. Gordon & Wolf, Newport Beach, Calif., 1989-91, Wolf & Pfeifer, Newport Beach, Calif., 1991-97, Wolf & Richards, Newport Beach, 1997—. Pres., founding dir. Laguna Beach (Calif.) Pop Warner Football, 1995-99, sec., 1996; chief Indian Princess Tribe, Laguna Beach, 1993; charter bd. dirs. Irvine Swim League, 1985. Mem. U.S. Foreclosure Network (bd. dirs. 1990-95, Com. Mem. of Yr. 1994), Calif. Mortgage Bankers Assn. (chmn. legal issues com. 1994-95), Dartmouth Club (pres. Orange County club 1991); fellow Am. Coll. Mortgage Attys. Avocations: computers, internet.

WOLF, ALFRED A., physicist, educator; b. Phila., July 21, 1925; s. Jacob Wolf, Anna Marcus W.; m. Enid G. Wolf, Nov. 24, 1957 (div. Dec. 1981); children: Marcus M., Laurence J. BSEE, Drexel U., Phila., 1948; MSEE, U. Pa., Phila., 1954, PhD, 1958; ScD, U. Juarez, Mexico, 1977, MD, 1978. Engr.-in-charge Naval Air Devel., Johnsville, Pa., 1949—56; chief scientist Gen. Dynamics, Rochester, NY, 1957—60; dir. rsch. Litton Industries, Silver Spring, Md., 1960—63; disting. prof. elec. engring. Drexel U., Phila., 1963—65; tech. dir. RCA, Burlington, Mass., 1965—67; assoc. tech. dir. Naval Ship R&D Ctr., Annapolis, Md., 1967—78; pres. Prime Rsch. Found., Annapolis, 1978—. Asst. prof. elec. engring. U. Pa., Phila., 1949—59; Pa. scholar, 1952—54; sr. sci. advisor USN, 1971—76; adj. assoc. prof. U. Rochester, 1960—62; adj. prof. U. Md., Annapolis, 1967—69, George Washington U., Washington, 1969—99. Author (prize winning): Biophysics of Wound Healing, 1989; contbr. 105 articles to profl. jours. (14 awards). Cpl. US Army, 1943—46. Nominee Nobel Prize in Physics, 1972; named Notable Am. of Bicentennial Era, Am. Biog. Inst., 1976; recipient Citation of Honor, Drexel U., 1961, Honor citations (8), USN, 1972—83; grantee, NSF, 1956—59; Pa. scholar, 1952—54. Mem.: IEEE (life), Engring. in Medicine and Biology Soc. (chmn. Balt. sect. 1990—95), Sigma Xi. Democrat. Jewish. Achievements include discovery of first high temperature superconductor; 24 patents for electronics devices and systems. Avocation: writing. Home and Office: Prime Rsch Found 562 Ferry Point Rd Annapolis MD 21403-1308

WOLF, ALICE KOERNER, state legislator, former mayor; b. Vienna, Dec. 24, 1933; d. Frederick Koerner and Renee (Engel) K.; m. Robert A. Wolf, 1955; children: Eric Jeffrey, Adam Nathaniel. BS, Simmons Coll., 1955; MPA, Harvard U., 1978; EdD (hon.), Wheelock Coll., 2001. Residence staff MIT, Lincoln Lab, 1955-62, Computer Corp Am., 1967-71, pers. dir., 1971-76; mem. Cambridge Sch. Com., 1974-81, vicechairwoman, 1976—77, 1980—81; mem. Cambridge City Coun., 1984—93; vice mayor Cambridge, Mass., 1990—91; mem. 25th Middlesex, Mass. House of Reps., Boston, 1997—. Del. Dem. Nat. Conv., 1980, 84, 88, 92, State Conv. Mem. NOW, Mass. Women's Polit. Caucas Cambridge Mental Health Assn., Am. for Dem. Action, Nat. Orgn. Women Am. Civil Liberties Union, Nat. Democrat. Office: Mass Ho of Reps State House Rm 134 Boston MA 02133 Home: 48 Huron Ave Cambridge MA 02138-6706 Office Phone: 617-722-2400. Personal E-mail: alice@alicewolf.org. Business E-Mail: rep.alicewolf@hou.state.ma.us.

WOLF, BARRY, geneticist, pediatric educator; b. Chgo., June 19, 1947; s. Bert D. and Toby E. (Urkoff) W.; children: Michael Loren, Bryan Phillip. BS, U. Ill., 1969; MD, U. Ill. Coll. Medicine, 1974; PhD, U. Ill., 1974. Diplomate Am. Bd. Pediatrics, Med. and Biochem. Genetics. Intern, resident in pediatrics Childrens Meml. Hosp., Northwestern U., Chgo., 1974-76; fellow Yale U. Sch. Medicine, New Haven, 1976-78; prof. human genetics Med. Coll. Va., Richmond, 1978-2001, vice chair for rsch. dept. pediatrics, 1996-2000; dir. rsch. Conn. Children's Med. Ctr., 2001—05; assoc. chmn., dir. rsch. Dept. Pediats. Sch. Medicine U. Conn., 2001—01; chmn. Dept. Med. Genetics Henry Ford Hosp., Detroit, 2005—. Author over 175 jour. articles and book chpts. dealing with inherited disorders of metabolism and biochem. genetics, specifically disorders of biotin metabolism. Recipient E. Mead Johnson award for pediatric rsch. Am. Acad. Pediatrics, 1988, Borden award in nutrition Am. Inst. Nutrition, 1987, Outstanding Scientist of Va. award Va. Sci. Mus., 1986, Ounce of Prevention award Action for Prevention of Va., 1985. Mem. Am. Soc. Clin. Investigation, Am. Pediat. Soc., Soc. Pediatric Rsch., Soc. Inherited Metabolic Diseases, Soc. Study Inborn Errors of Metabolism, Am. Soc. Human Genetics. Avocation: japanese cloisonne. Office: Henry Ford Hosp Dept Med Genetics 2799 W Grand Blvd CFP-4 Detroit MI 48202 Home Phone: 248-433-9003; Office Phone: 313-916-3116. Business E-Mail: bwolf1@hfhs.org.

WOLF, BARRY M., lawyer; b. NYC, Nov. 14, 1959; BS summa cum laude, SUNY, Albany, 1981; JD cum laude, U. Mich., 1984; LLM, NYU, 1989. Bar: N.Y. 1985. Ptnr. Weil, Gotshal & Manges LLP, NYC, co-head global corp. dept., 2000—. Mem.: ABA, Private Investment Fund Forum, N.Y. State Bar Assn. Office: Weil, Gotshal & Manges LLP 767 Fifth Ave New York NY 10153 Office Phone: 212-310-8209. E-mail: barry.wolf@weil.com.

WOLF, BRANDON B., lawyer; BS, Nova Southeastern U., 1995; JD, South Tex. Coll. Law, 1999. Bar: Tex. 2000. Mng. atty. gen. counsel grp., Tex. Foreclosure Divsn. Barrett, Burke, Wilson, Castle, Daffin & Frappier, L.L.P., Addison, Tex. Named a Rising Star, Tex. Super Lawyers mag., 2006. Mem.: ABA, Dallas Bar Assn. Office: Barrett Burke Wilson Castle Daffin & Frappier LLP 15000 Surveyor Blvd Ste 100 Addison TX 75001 Office Phone: 972-386-5040. E-mail: brandonw@bbwcdf.com. *

WOLF, BRUCE, lawyer; b. Phila., Dec. 16, 1955; s. Charles and Mary (Saionz) W. BA, Temple U., 1977; JD, Drake U., 1981. Bar: Pa. 1981, U.S. Dist. Ct. (ea dist.) Pa. 1981, U.S. Ct. Appeals (3d cir.) 1981. Assoc. LaCheen & Alva, Phila., 1981-88; pvt. practice Phila., 1989—. Mem. Fed. Criminal Justice Act Panel, Phila., 1998—. Committeeman Phila. Dem. Party 63rd ward, 1994-2000. Mem. Phila. Bar Assn., Pa. Assn. Criminal Def. Lawyers. Democrat. Jewish. Office: 612 S 6th St 1st Fl Philadelphia PA 19147-2108 Home Phone: 215-512-4274; Office Phone: 215-627-2782. Fax: (215) 922-2194. E-mail: bwolf.esq@erols.com.

WOLF, CHARLES, JR., economist, educator; b. NYC, Aug. 1, 1924; s. Charles and Rosalie W.; m. Theresa van de Wint, Mar. 1, 1947; children: Charles Theodore, Timothy van de Wint. BS, Harvard U., Cambridge, Mass., 1943, M.P.A., 1948, PhD in Econs., 1949. Economist, fgn. service officer U.S. Dept. State, 1945-47, 49-53; mem. faculty Cornell U., 1953-54, U. Calif., Berkeley, 1954-55; sr. economist The Rand Corp., Santa Monica, Calif., 1955-67, head econs. dept., 1967-81; dean The Rand Grad. Sch., 1970-97, prof. pub. policy, 1997—, sr. econ. advisor, 1981—, corp. fellow in internat. econs., 1996—; sr. fellow Hoover Inst., 1988—. Bd. dirs. Capital Income Builder Fund, Capital World Growth Fund; lectr. econs. UCLA, 1960-72; mem. adv. bd. ctr. internat. bus. and econ. rsch., UCLA Anderson Grad. Sch. Bus., 1996—. Author: The Costs and Benefits of the Soviet Empire, 1986, Markets or Governments: Choosing Between Imperfect Alternatives, 1989, 2d edit., 1993, Linking Economic Policy and Foreign Policy, 1991, Long-Term Economic and Military Trends: The United States and Asia, 1994-2015, 1995, The Economic Pivot in a Political Context, 1997; co-author: Economic Openness: Many Facets, Many Metrics, 1999, Asian Economic Trends and Their Security Implications, 2000, European Military Prospects, Economic Constraints and the Rapid Reaction Force, 2001, Straddling Economics and Politics: Cross-Cutting Issues, in Asia, the United States and the Global Economy, 2002, Fault Lines in China's Economic Terrain, 2003, North Korean Paradoxes, 2005, The Russian Economy: Progress and Retreat on the Transitional Road, 2006; contbr. articles to profl. jours. Mem. Assn. for Public Policy Analysis and Mgmt. (pres. 1980-81), Am. Econs. Assn., Econometric Soc., Coun. on Fgn. Rels., Pacific Coun. Internat. Policy, Internat. Inst. Strategic Studies London. Clubs: Cosmos (Washington); Riviera Tennis (Los Angeles); Harvard (N.Y.). Office: The Rand Corp 1776 Main St Santa Monica CA 90407-2138 Office Phone: 310-451-6926. Business E-Mail: wolf@rand.org.

WOLF, CHARLES BENNO, lawyer; b. Chgo., Apr. 16, 1950; s. Ludwig and Hilde (Mandelbaum) W.; m. Sarah Lloyd, Sept. 1, 1973; children: Walter Ludwig, Peter Barton. AB, Brown U., 1972; JD, U. Chgo., 1975. Bar: Ill. 1975, U.S. Dist. Ct. (no. dist.) Ill. 1975, U.S. Ct. Appeals (3rd, 4th, 5th, 6th, 7th, 8th, 9th, 10th, and 11th cirs.) 1985, U.S. Supreme Ct. 1985. Ptnr. Vedder, Price, Kaufman & Kammholz, Chgo., 1975—, exec. com., 1999—. Co-author: ERISA Claims and Litigation, 10th edit., 1995; sr. editor: Employee Benefit Law, 2007-; contbr. articles to profl. jours. Fellow Am. Coll. Employee Benefits Counsel; mem. ABA (co-chair labor sect. subcom. on collective bargaining and employee benefits, past co-chair subcom. on multi-employer plans), Internat. Found. Employee Benefit Plans. Office: Vedder Price Kaufman & Kammholz 222 N La Salle St Ste 2600 Chicago IL 60601-1100 Office Phone: 312-609-7888. Business E-Mail: cwolf@vedderprice.com.

WOLF, CRAIG (M. CRAIG WOLF), trade association administrator; married; 2 children. Asst. state atty. County of Alleghany, Md., 1990—95; trial atty. U.S. Dept. Justice, 1995—98; counsel com. on judiciary U.S. Senate, 1998—2000; gen. counsel Wine & Spirits Wholesalers of Am., Inc., 2000—06, interim pres. to pres., 2006—, CEO, 2006—. Capt. JAG Corp. USAR. Office: Wine & Spirits Wholesalers of Am Inc 805 15th St NW Ste 430 Washington DC 20005 *

WOLF, CYD BETH, lawyer, entrepreneur; b. NYC, Oct. 6, 1957; d. Aaron Joseph and Sally (Marcus) Wolf; m. Germano Fabio Fabiani, Nov. 18, 1990; children: Alessandra Julia Fabiani, Francesca Isabella Fabiani. BA in Urban Studies with honors, U. Pa., 1977; JD, U. Balt., 1983. Bar: Md 1983, US Dist Ct Md 1983, US Ct Appeals (6th and 11th cir) 1986, US Ct Appeals (4th and 5th cir) 1989. Assoc. Weinberger, Weinstock, Sagner, Stevan & Harris, Balt., 1983-86, Semmes, Bowen & Semmes, Balt., 1986-90, Piper & Marbury, Balt., 1990-95; pvt. practice Balt., 1995—2002; asst. atty. gen. Md. State Dept. Bus. and Econ. Devel., Balt., 2002—07; pvt. practice Balt., 2007—. Contbr. articles to profl. jours. Mem. leadership com., fundraiser, mentor U. Balt. Edn. Found. Mem.: ABA, Bar Assn. Balt. City (banking, bankruptcy and bus. law sect.), Bankruptcy Bar Assn. (rules com. dist. Md. 1997), Md. State Bar Assn. (banking and bus. sect.). Avocations: tennis, painting, drawing, fiction and non-fiction reading and writing. Home: 5 Hillchase Ct Baltimore MD 21208-6306 Office: 300 S High St Baltimore MD 21202 Home Phone: 410-484-3213.

WOLF, DALE B., health care company executive; BA, Univ. Colorado; MBA, Univ. Denver. V.p. specialty ops. The Travelers, 1988—94; sr. v.p. bus. devel. MetraHealth Cos., Inc., 1995; exec. v.p. SpectraScan Health Svcs., Inc., 1995—96; sr. v.p. Coventry Health Care, Bethesda, Md., 1996—98, CFO, 1996—2004, treas., 1996—2004, exec. v.p., 1998—2004, CEO, 2004—. Bd. dir. HealthExtras Inc. Mem.: Soc. of Actuaries. Office: Coventry Health Care 6705 Rockledge Dr Bethesda MD 20817 *

WOLF, DALE EDWARD, state official; b. Kearney, Nebr., Sept. 6, 1924; m. Clarice Wolf; 4 children. BSc, U. Nebr., 1945; PhD in Agronomy and Weed Control, Rutgers U., 1949. With Dept. Agr., 1946; assoc. prof. agronomy Rutgers U., 1949; with E.I. duPont de Nemours & Co., Inc., from 1950, dir. agrichem. mktg., then gen. mgr. biochem. dept., 1972-79; v.p. biochems., also chmn. bd. subs. Endo Labs., Inc., Wilmington, Del., from 1979; group v.p. Agrl. Products, Wilmington, Del., from 1983; dir. Del. Devel. Office, Dover, 1987-89; lt. gov. of Del. Dover, 1989-93; gov. State of Del., Dover, 1992—93. Vice chmn. WSFS Bank, 1998-2005; trustee Christiana Care Health Svcs., 2002—. Co-author: Principles of Weed Control, 1951. Bd. dirs. Del. chpt. ARC, 1975; gen. campaign chmn. United Way Del., 1978, also bd. dirs.; gen. campaign chmn. Girls Club Del., 1987; chmn. Del. Found. for Literacy, 1993-98; mem. adv. bd. U. Del. Hotel, Restaurant Mgmt. Sch., 1993—; chmn. Stand Up for What is Right and Just, 2003-07, vice chmn., 2007—. 1st lt. AUS, 1943-46. Decorated Bronze Star, Purple Heart; recipient Josiah Marvel award, Del. State C. of C., 2005, Liberty Bell award, Del. Bar Assn., 2007. Mem. Nat. Agrl. Chem. Assn. (chmn. 1981-83), Pharm. Mfrs. Assn. (dir.), Masons, Farmhouse Fraternity, Sigma Xi, Alpha Zeta. Republican.

WOLF, DICK (RICHARD A. WOLF), television producer; b. NYC, Dec. 20, 1946; m. Susan Scranton, 1970 (div. 1981); m. Christine Marburg, 1983; 3 children. Student, U. Pa. Exec. producer, pres. Wolf Films, Inc. Copywriter, producer over a dozen campaigns and 100 TV commls., 1969-76; producer, writer (screenplay) Skateboard, 1978, School Ties, 1992; writer, script cons. (TV series) Hill Street Blues, 1985 (Emmy award, Writer's Guild nominations for episode What are Friends For); writer, producer (film) No Man's Land, 1987; writer, producer and actor (film) Masquerade, 1988; writer, exec. producer 4 installments (series TV movies) Gideon Oliver, 1989; writer, creator, exec. producer (series TV movies) Christine Cromwell, 1989-90, (TV series) Nasty Boys, 1990, H.E.L.P., Law & Order, 1990, (Producers Guild Am. shared award Episodic TV 1996, Emmy award Outstanding Drama Series, 1996/97), Mann & Machine, 1992, The Human Factor, 1992, Crime and Punishment, 1993, South Beach, 1993, New York Undercover, 1994, Swift Justice, 1996, Arrest and Trial, 2000, Dragnet, 2003-04; creator, exec. producer (TV series) Feds, 1997, Players; exec. producer (TV series) Law & Order: Special Victims Unit, 1999—, D.C., 2000, Deadline, 2000-01, Law & Order Crime & Punishment, 2002—; exec. prodr., writer Law & Order Criminal Intent, 2001—; prodr. (TV documentary) Twin Towers, 2003. Office: Wolf Films Inc c/o Universal TV 100 Universal City Plz Universal City CA 91608-1002

WOLF, EDWARD LINCOLN, physicist, educator; b. Cocoa, Fla., Nov. 22, 1936; s. Norman Lincoln and Harriet (Burgess) W.; m. Carol Joyce Euwema, June 15, 1958; children: Douglas Wakefield, David Lincoln. BA, Swarthmore Coll., 1958; PhD, Cornell U., 1964. Postdoctoral fellow U. Ill. Dept. Physics, Urbana, 1964-66; research assoc. Eastman Kodak Co., Rochester, NY, 1967-75; prof. physics Iowa State U., Ames, 1975-85; head dept. physics, prof. Polytechnic U., Bklyn., 1986—95, prof. physics, 1986—. Sr. vis. fellow Cavendish Lab. U. Cambridge, U.K., 1973-74; vis. prof. U. Pa., Phila., 1982; program dir. condensed matter physics NSF, 1996-98. Author: Principles of Electron Tunneling Spectroscopy, 1985; editor: Materials and Mechanisms of Superconductivity, 1985, Nanophysics and Nanotechnology, 2004, 2d edit., 2006. Fellow Am. Phys. Soc.; mem. AAAS, Materials Rsch. Soc., Phi Beta Kappa, Sigma Xi. Presbyterian. Avocations: jogging, bicycling, music. Office: Polytechnic U Dept Physics Six Metrotech Ctr Brooklyn NY 11201-3850 Office Phone: 718-260-3629. E-mail: ewolf@poly.edu.

WOLF, FRANK RUDOLPH, congressman, lawyer; b. Phila., Jan. 30, 1939; m. Carolyn Stover; children: Frank, Virginia, Anne, Brenda, Rebecca. Student, U. Miss., Oxford, 1957—58; BA, Pa. State U., 1961; LLB, Georgetown U. Sch. Law, 1965. Bar: Va., Washington, DC. Lawyer pvt. practice; legis. asst. Staff of US Rep. Edward G. Biester, Jr. of Pa., 1968-71; asst. Staff of US Sec. Interior Rogers C.B. Morton, 1971-74; dep. asst. sec. Congl. and Legis. Affairs US Dept. Interior, 1974-75; mem. US Congress from 10th Va. dist., 1981—. Mem. appropriations com., US Congress, mem. sci., the depts. of state, justice, and commerce, and related agencies subcommittee, 2001-. Served in US Army, 1962—63, served in USAR, 1963—67. Republican. Presbyterian. Office: US Ho Reps 241 Cannon Ho Office Bldg Washington DC 20515-4610 Office Phone: 202-225-5136. *

WOLF, G. VAN VELSOR, JR., lawyer; b. Balt., Feb. 19, 1944; s. G. Van Velsor (dec.) and Alice Roberts (Kimberly) W. (dec.); m. Ann Holmes Kavanagh, May 19, 1984; children: George Van Velsor III, Timothy Kavanagh (dec.), Christopher Kavanagh, Elisabeth Huxley. BA, Yale U., 1966; JD, Vanderbilt U., 1973. Bar: N.Y. 1974, U.S. Dist. Ct. (so. dist.) N.Y. 1974, U.S. Ct. Appeals (2d cir.) 1974, Ariz. 1982, U.S. Dist. Ct. Ariz. 1982, U.S. Ct. Appeals (9th cir.) 1982. Agrl. advisor U.S. Peace Corps., 1966-70; assoc. Milbank, Tweed, Hadley & McCloy, NYC, 1973-75; vis. lectr. law Airlangga U., Surabaya, Indonesia, 1975-76; editor-in-chief Environ. Law Reporter, Washington, 1976-81; assoc. Lewis & Roca, Phoenix, 1981-84, ptnr., 1984-91, Snell & Wilmer, Phoenix, 1991—. Vis. lectr. law U. Ariz., 1990, Vanderbilt U., 1991, U. Md., 1994, Ariz. State U., 1995; cons. Nat. Trust Hist. Preservation, Washington, 1981. Editor: Toxic Substances Control, 1980; editor in chief Environ. Law Reporter 1976-81; contbr. articles to profl. jours. Bd. dirs. Ariz. divsn. Am. Cancer Soc., 1985—96, sec. Ariz. divsn., 1990—92, vice-chmn. Ariz. divsn., 1992—94, chmn. Ariz. divsn., 1994—96, bd. dirs. S.W. divsn., 1996—2003, chmn., 1996—98, nat. bd. dirs., 1999—, bd. dirs. Gt. West divsn., 2003—, bd. dirs., Cancer Action Network, 2002—05, pres. Cancer Action Network, 2003—04, nat. treas., 2004—06, nat. vice chair, 2006—; bd. dirs. Herberger Theatre Ctr., 1998—2006, sec., 2001—03, vice chmn., 2003—04; bd. dirs. Phoenix Little Theatre, 1983—89, chmn., 1985—87. Recipient St. George medal Am. Cancer Soc., 1998 Mem. ABA (vice-chmn. SONREEL commn. state and regional environ. coop. 1995-98, co-chmn. 1998-2000, vice-chmn. environ. audits task force 1998-99, vice-chmn. SONREEL ann. meeting planning com. 1998-99), Assn. of Bar of City of N.Y., Ariz. State Bar Assn. (coun. environ. & nat. res. law sect. 1988-93, chmn. 1991-92, CLE com. 1992-98, chmn. 1997-98), Maricopa County Bar Assn., Ariz. Acad., Union Club N.Y.C., Univ. Club Phoenix, Phoenix Country Club. Office: Snell & Wilmer 1 Arizona Ctr Phoenix AZ 85004-2202 Office Phone: 602-382-6201. Business E-Mail: vwolf@swlaw.com.

WOLF, GERALYN, bishop; b. Apr. 30, 1947; BS, West Chester U., Pa., 1968; MA in Edn., Trenton State Coll., NJ, 1971; MDiv, Episcopal Div. Sch., Cambridge, Mass., 1977. Tchr. George Sch., Newtown, Pa., 1970—74; ordained deacon, 1977, priest, 1978; served several Phila. area congregations, 1977—81; vicar St. Mary's Episcopal Ch., Phila., 1981—87; dean Christ Ch. Cathedral, Louisville, 1987—95; consecrated bishop, 1996; bishop Episcopal Diocese of RI, 1996—. Retreat leader and spkr. for the homeless. Author: Down and Out in Providence, various hymn texts. Episcopalian. Achievements include serving as the first female Dean of a Cathedral; mem. US Field Hockey Touring Team, Argentina, 1973. Office: Episcopal Diocese of RI Diocesan House & Resource Ctr 275 N Main St Providence RI 02903-1298 Office Phone: 401-274-4500. Office Fax: 401-331-9430. Business E-Mail: beeplepeople@cox.net.

WOLF, HAROLD HERBERT, pharmacy educator; b. Quincy, Mass., Dec. 19, 1934; s. John I. and Bertha F. (Sussman) W.; m. Joan Z. Silverman, Aug. 11, 1957; children: Gary Jerome, David Neal. BS, Mass. Coll. Pharmacy, 1956; PhD, U. Utah, 1961; LLD (hon.), U. Md., 1994. Asst. prof. pharmacology Coll. Pharmacy Ohio State U., 1961-64, assoc. prof., 1964-69, prof., 1969-76, Kimberly prof., 1975-76, chmn. divsn. pharmacology, 1973-76; dean Coll. of Pharmacy, U. Utah, Salt Lake City, 1976-89, prof. pharmacology, 1976—2005, dir. Anticonvulsant Drug Devel. Program, 1989—2002, prof. emeritus, 2005—. Vis. prof. U. Sains Malaysia, 1973-74; mem. Nat. Joint Commn. on Prescription Drug Use, 1976-80; mem. NIH rev. com. Biomed. Rsch. Devel. Grant Program, 1978-79; external examiner U. Malaya, 1978, 92, 96, U. Sains Malaysia, 1980. Contbr. articles in field of ctrl. nervous sys. pharmacology and field of pharm. edn. Recipient Alumni Achievement award Mass. Coll. Pharmacy, 1978, Disting. Faculty award U. Utah, 1989, Rosenblatt prize, 1989, Disting. Alumnus award Coll. Pharmacy, U. Utah, 1991, Weaver prize, 2000. Fellow AAAS, Acad. Pharm. Scis.; mem. Am. Soc. Pharmacology and Exptl. Therapeutics, Am. Pharm. Assn. (task force on edn. 1982-84), Am. Assn. Colls. of Pharmacy (pres. 1977, Disting. Pharmacy Educator award 1988, scholar in residence 1989, chmn. commn. on implementing change in pharmacy edn. 1989-92, 95-96), Am. Soc. Hosp. Pharmacists (commn. on goals 1982-84), Am. Coun. on Pharm. Edn. (bd. dirs. 1985-88), Soc. Neurosci. Jewish. Home: 4467 Adonis Dr Salt Lake City UT 84124-3922 Office: Univ Utah Coll Pharmacy Salt Lake City UT 84112

WOLF, HEATHER, library director; Grad. in Bus. Adminstrn., U. Pacific, Stockton, Calif.; MLS, U. Ariz. Br. mgr., regional br. coord. Maricopa County Libr. Dist., Ariz.; br. mgr., supervisory reference libr. and supervisory libr. collection support svcs. City of Mesa Libr., Ariz., acting dir., 2006, dir., 2006—. Office: City of Mesa Libr 64 E First St Mesa AZ 85201 Office Phone: 480-644-2712. E-mail: heather.wolf@cityofmesa.org.

WOLF, IRNA LYNN, psychologist; b. Dunottar, South Africa, Aug. 30, 1949; came to U.S., 1977; d. John and Tolsa W.; m. Raymond Frank Shamos, Feb. 22, 1976; children: Lorin Iver, Richard Lance, Ilan Hiram, Troy Joseph. MFA cum laude, U. Witwatersrand, 1976; MA, U. Rochester, 1983; PhD, Ariz. State U., 1991, postgrad., 1997. Lic. psychologist, Ariz., diplomate Am. Bd. Psychology; cert. sch. psychologist. Rsch., tchg. asst. Ariz. State U., Tempe, 1984-89; ind. rsch., 1989-97; pvt. practice Phoenix, 1997—. Lectr. in field; cons. Human Info. Processing, 1997—. Contbr. articles to profl. jours. Recipient Certificate of Appreciation Paradise Valley Police Dept., 1992. Mem. APA, Am. Psychol. Soc., Nat. Assn. Sch. Psychologists, We. Psychol. Assn., Ariz. Psychol. Assn., Phi Kappa Phi. Republican. Avocations: painting, drawing, hiking, swimming. Home: 4516 E Onyx Ave Phoenix AZ 85028-4200

WOLF, JACQUELINE L., gastroenterologist; b. Indpls. BA, Radcliffe Coll., Boston, 1971; MD, Tufts U. Sch. Medicine, Boston, 1975. Intern U. Chgo. Hosp. Clinics, 1975—76, resident, 1976—77; third yr. resident Peter Bent Brigham Hosp., 1977—78, rsch. fellow, 1978—80; clinical fellow Harvard Med. Sch., 1977—78, rsch. fellow, 1978—80, instr. medicine, 1980—83, asst. prof. medicine, 1983—97, assoc. prof. medicine, 1998—, assoc. prof. clin. medicine, 1997—98; attending physician West Roxbury Vet. Adminstrn. Hosp., Mass., 1979—2002, 1980—85; jr. assoc. medicine Brigham and Women's Hosp., Boston, 1980—82, attending physician, 1980—2001, assoc. physician, 1982—96, attending physician, 1985—2001, screening sigmoidoscopy clinic coord., 1988—95, co-dir., Inflammatory Bowel Disease Ctr., 1991—96, attending physician, 1991—2001, co-dir., Colon Cancer Screening Clinic, 1995—98, physician, 1996—2002; cons. physician Dana Farber Cancer Inst., 2000—02; physician Faulkner Hosp., 2000—; staff physician Beth Israel Deaconess Med. Ctr., Boston, 2002—, attending physician, 2002—. Sec. bd. dirs. Soc. Advancement Women's Health Rsch., Washington, 2005—; co-chair Harvard Med. Sch., Ctr. Excellence Women's Health, Boston, 2004—; mem., exec. com. Harvard Med. Sch. Ctr. for Excellence Women's Health Rsch., Fund for Women's Health Rsch., Boston, 2005—; cons. in field. Recipient Jerry S. Trier Excellence Tchg. award, Brigham and Women's Hosp., 2000; scholar, Sandox, 1987. Mem.: Am. Gastroent. Assn. (co-chair person 1993—95, task force on tng. women's health issues digestive disease, rep., chair 1992), Alpha Omega Alpha. Office Phone: 617-667-4241.

WOLF, JEFFREY STEPHEN, physician; b. Hartford, Conn., July 30, 1946; s. Abraham and Norma Wolf; m. Nina Loving Lockridge; children: Sarah Loving, Lawren Hiley. BS, McGill U., 1968; MD, Med. Coll. Va., 1972, MS, 1973. Diplomate Am. Bd. Colon and Rectal Surgery. Intern in surgery Mt. Sinai Hosp., NYC, 1972-73, resident, 1973-75, N.Y. Med. Coll.-Met. Hosp., NYC, 1975-77; chief resident in surgery Met. Hosp., NYC, 1977-78; fellow colon-rectal surgery Grtr. Balt. Med. Ctr., 1978-79; colon-rectal surgeon Portsmouth, Va., 1979—. Fellow ACS, Am. Soc. Colon and Rectal Surgery; mem. AMA, Portsmouth Acad. Medicine, Med. Soc. Va., Am. Soc. Colon and Rectal Surgeons, So. Med. Assn., Chesapeake Colon-Rectal Soc., S.E. Va. Soc. Colon-Rectal Surgeons. Office: 3235 Academy Ave Ste 200 Portsmouth VA 23703-3200 Office Phone: 757-484-9653.

WOLF, JEROME L., lawyer; BA, George Washington U., Washington, 1970; JD, Duquesne U. Sch. Law, Pitts., 1973. Bar: NY 1974, Fla. 1984, cert.: Fla. Bd. Legal Specialization and Edn. (wills, trusts and estates). Ptnr. Berger Singerman, Boca Raton, Fla., Duane Morris LLP, Boca Raton. Contbr. articles to profl. publs. Named one of Top 100 Attys., Worth mag., 2005—06, Top South Fla. Lawyers in Tax and Estate Law, South Fla. Legal Guide, 2007. Mem.: South Palm Beach County Bar Assn., ABA, Fla. Bar (mem. real property and probate and trust law sects., chmn. trust law com. 1991—95, chmn., lectr. bi-ann. will and trust drafting seminar, recipient Ann. Svc. award from real property, probate and trust law sect. 1993), NY State Bar Assn. (mem. trusts and estates sect., mem. com. on estate planning, chmn. subcommittee on fin. planning 1983—84, chmn. subcommittee on cmty. property 1979—82, mem. com. on estate planning for the disabled), Palm Beach County Bar Assn. (mem. estate and probate continuing legal edn. com. 1986—, lectr. ann. probate and guardianship law seminar 1987—89, 1993). Office: Duane Morris LLP Ste 324A 2255 Glades Rd Boca Raton FL 33431 Office Phone: 561-988-8710. Office Fax: 561-988-8716. E-mail: jwolf@duanemorris.com.

WOLF, JOHN MICHAEL, adult education seminar consultant; b. Upper Darby, Pa., Aug. 21, 1946; s. Herbert Michael and Elizabeth (Collins) W.; m. Gloria Ann Pettinati, Feb. 1, 1969 (div. 1978); m. Diane Elaine Batterson, Sept. 10, 1983 (div. 1994); children: John Michael Jr., Jessica Diane. BS, Drexel U., 1969; MBA, Temple U., 1972; PhD, Walden U., 1990. Salesman Lit Bros., Upper Darby, 1961-63, Cousins Shoes, Upper Darby, 1963-69; purchasing agt. Philco-Ford Co., Phila., 1969-70; sales rep. Conn. Gen. Life Ins. Co., Phila., 1970-75, Provident Life & Accident Ins. Co., Cherry Hill, NJ, 1975-78; pres. Associated Cons., Haddonfield, NJ, 1978-96; sr. ptnr. Lifelong Learning Ptnrs., Bradenton, Fla., 1996—. Cons. in field. Chmn. U.S. Jaycees, Haddonfield, 1979; co-chmn. March of Dimes, Haddonfield, 1983. Mem. Am. Mgmt. Assn., Soc. for Accelerative Learning & Tchg., Internat. Alliance Learning Creative Edn. Found., Statue of Liberty Found., Tau Kappa Epsilon. Avocations: soccer, music, travel, skiing. Office: Lifelong Learning Ptnrs 4115 Pinar Dr Bradenton FL 34210 Office Phone: 941-758-1800. Personal E-mail: wolfman73@aol.com.

WOLF, JOHN S., ambassador, federal agency administrator; b. Sept. 12, 1948; BA, Dartmouth Coll., 1970; postgrad., Princeton U., 1978-79. Fgn. svc. officer, 1970—; prin. dep. asst. sec. for int. orgn. affairs U.S. Dept. State, 1989—92; amb. to Malaysia Kuala Lumpur, 1992—95; coord. APEC, 1996, amb., 1997; spl. advisor to Pres. and Sec. of State, Caspian Basin Energy Diplomacy, 1999—2000; asst. sec. for non-proliferation U.S. Dept State, 2001—, chief U.S. Coordination Monitoring Mission (Middle East), 2003—. Recipient Pres.'s Meritorious Svc. award, 1992, APCAC award, Asia Pacific Coun. Am. C. of C., 1996. Office: US Dept State Non-Proliferation Bureau 2201 C St NW Washington DC 20520

WOLF, JOSEPH ALBERT, mathematician, educator; b. Chgo., Oct. 18, 1936; s. Albert M. and Goldie (Wikoff) W. BS, U. Chgo., 1956, MS, 1957, PhD, 1959. Mem. Inst. for Advanced Study, Princeton, 1960-62, 65-66; asst. prof. U. Calif., Berkeley, 1962-64, assoc. prof., 1964-66, prof., 1966—94, Miller research prof., 1972-73, 83-84, prof. grad. sch., 1994—; prof. honorario Universidad Nacional de Cordoba, Argentina, 1989. Vis. prof. Rutgers U., 1969-70, Hebrew U., Jerusalem, 1974-76, Tel Aviv U., 1974-76, Harvard U., 1979-80, 86 Author: Spaces of Constant Curvature, 1967, 5th edit., 1984, Unitary Representations on Partially Holomorphic Cohomology Spaces, 1974, Unitary Representations of Maximal Parabolic Subgroups of the Classical Groups, 1976, Classification and Fourier Inversion for Parabolic Subgroups with Square Integrable Nilradical, 1979; (with G. Fels, A.T. Huckleberry) Cycle Spaces of Flag Domains: A Complex Geometric Approach, 2005; Harmonic Analysis on Commutative Spaces, 2007; co-editor, author: Harmonic Analysis and Representations of Semisimple Lie Groups, 1980, The Penrose Transform and Analytic Cohomology in Representation Theory, 1993, Geometry and Representation Theory of Real and P-Adic Grps., 1997, Global Differential Geometry: The Mathematical Legacy of Alfred Gray, 2000; editor Letters in Math. Physics, Jour. of Group Theory in Physics; contbr. articles to profl. jours. Alfred P. Sloan rsch. fellow, 1965-67, NSF fellow, 1959-62; recipient Médaille de l'Université de Liège, 1977, Humboldt prize, 1995. Mem. Am., Swiss Math. Socs. Office: U Calif Dept Math Berkeley CA 94720-3840 Business E-Mail: jawolf@math.berkeley.edu.

WOLF, KARL EVERETT, aerospace transportation executive, communications executive; b. Hartford, Conn., Aug. 19, 1921; s. Carl Fred and Anna (Voss) W.; m. Lola Sue Stoner, Aug. 1, 1948; children: Paula R., Gloria J., Glenn K. BS, U.S. Mil. Acad., 1943; JD, U. Pa., 1953; SJD, George Washington U., 1963. Bar: D.C. 1953, Conn. 1953, U.S. Supreme Ct. 1960, Calif. 1971, Mich. 1975. Commd. 2d lt. U.S. Army, 1943, advanced through grades to lt. col., 1959, ret., 1963; assoc. counsel Philco. Corp., Phila., 1963-73; v.p., gen. counsel Ford Aerospace Corp., Detroit, 1973-88; ret., 1988. Mem. adv. bd. Bur. Nat. Affairs, Fed. Contract Reports, Washington, 1963-73 Author: State Taxation of Government Contractors, 1964. Decorated Silver Star, Bronze Star, Purple Heart, Croix de Guerre (Belgium). Mem. ABA, Calif. Bar Assn. Home: Apt 309 25412 Sea Bluffs Dr Dana Point CA 92629-2198 E-mail: karlwolf@cox.net.

WOLF, LARRY M., lawyer; b. Balt., July 11, 1937; d. William W. and Mildred Livingston Wolf; m. Lois Twersky Wolf, Aug. 23, 1960. BA, John Hopkins U., Balt., 1958; LLB, Yale Law Sch., New Haven, Conn., 1961. Bar: Md. 1961, cert.: US Supreme Ct. Bar 1998. Assoc. atty. Shawe & Rosenthal, Balt., 1961—71; ptnr. Wolf, Pokempner & Hillman, Balt., 1972—86, Whiteford, Taylor & Preston, Balt., 1986—. Pres. Bd. Jewish Edn., Balt., 1982—84, Liberty Randallstown Coalition, Md., 1998—2000, Comprehensive Housing Assistance, Inc., Balt., 2002—04, Beth Israel Congregation, Owings Mills, Md., 1985—88. Jewish. Home: 8920 Griffin Way Pikesville MD 21208 Office: Whiteford Taylor Preston 7 St Paul St Baltimore MD 21202

WOLF, MARCUS ALAN, lawyer; b. Mansfield, Ohio, July 6, 1946; s. Carl Merle and Eunice Virginia (Beekman) W.; children: Stephanie Ariah, Marcus André. BA, Northeast La. U., 1969; JD, Ohio No. U., 1980. Bar: Ohio 1980, U.S. Dist. Ct. (no. dist.) Ohio 1980. Tchr. Clearfork Valley Schs., Butler, Ohio, 1969-70, Shelby City Schools, Shelby, Ohio, 1972-77; prin. Marcus A. Wolf Co. L.P.A. (formerly Thompson & Wolf Co. L.P.A.), Mansfield, 1980—. Mem. dist. 7 Mansfield Power Squadron, 1985—. Mem. ABA, Ohio Bar Assn., Richland County Bar Assn. (chmn. cert. grievance com.), Masons, Elks. Methodist. Avocations: boating, fishing, skiing, hunting. Home: 457 Davis Rd Mansfield OH 44907-1121 Office: 371 Lexington Ave Mansfield OH 44904-1714 Office Phone: 419-524-5257.

WOLF, MARTIN EUGENE, lawyer, educator; b. Balt., Sept. 9, 1958; s. Eugene Bernard and Mary Anna (O'Neil) W.; m. Nancy Ann Reinsfelder, May 9, 1980; children: Matthew Adam, Allison Maria, Emily Elizabeth. BA, Johns Hopkins U., 1980; JD, U. Md., 1991. Bar: Md. 1991, US Dist. Ct. Md. 1992, US Ct. Appeals (4th cir.) 1992, US Ct. Appeals (2nd cir.) 1993, US Ct. Appeals (3rd cir.) 1998, US Ct. Appeals (11th cir.) 2000, US Ct. Fed. Claims 2001, US Ct. Appeals (Fed. cir.) 2003, US Supreme Ct. 2006, US Ct. Appeals (6th cir.) 2007. Mgmt. trainee Giant Foods, Inc., Landover, Md., 1980-82, dept. mgr., 1982-83, ops. analyst, 1983-86, fin. coord., 1986-89; law clk. Piper & Marbury, LLP, Balt., 1989—91, assoc., 1991—96; prin. Law Office of Martin E. Wolf, Abingdon, Md., 1996—99; ptnr. Quinn, Gordon & Wolf Chartered, Towson, Md., 2000—. Pres. bd. dirs. Chesapeake Search & Rescue Dog Assn., Inc., 2000—02. Mem. ABA, Md. State Bar Assn., Harford County Bar Assn., Harford County Bar Found. (Vol. Svc. award 1992, 94), Assn. Am. Justice. Democrat. Roman Catholic. Avocations: lacrosse, hockey. Home: 11 Mitchell Dr Abingdon MD 21009-1628 Office Phone: 410-825-2300. Business E-Mail: mwolf@quinnlaw.com.

WOLF, NAOMI, writer; b. San Francisco, Nov. 12, 1962; d. Leonard and Deborah W.; m. David Shipley, Sept. 1993. BA, Yale U., 1984. Author: The Beauty Myth: How Images of Beauty Are Used Against Women, 1990, Fire With Fire: The New Female Power and How It Will Change the 21st Century, 1993, The Treehouse: Eccentric Wisdom from My Father on How to Live, Love and See, 2005; contbr. to periodicals including New Republic, N.Y. Times, Wall Street Journal. Rhodes scholar, 1986. Office: c/o John Brockman Inc 5 E 59th St New York NY 10022

WOLF, PETER MICHAEL, investment manager, consultant, writer; b. New Orleans, Dec. 6, 1935; s. Morris and Ruth (New) W.; m. Alessandra Cantey, July 3, 1967; children: Phelan Godchaux, Alexis Ambler. BA, Yale U., 1957; MA, Tulane U., 1963; PhD, NYU, 1968. Ptnr. Wolf and Co., New Orleans, 1958-62; assoc. Wilbur Smith & Assocs., NYC, 1968-70; faculty mem. NYU, 1966-67, Pratt Inst., NYC, 1968-70; adj. prof. Cooper Union, NYC, 1971-87; chmn. bd. fellows, mem. faculty Inst. Arch. and Urban Studies, NYC, 1972-82; prin. Peter Wolf Assocs., NYC, 1970—. Participant, advisor Investment Policy com. Fiduciary Counsel Inc., 2000-04; organizer of exhbns. Mus. Modern Art, NYC, 1969; writer exhbns. Whitney Mus. Art, NYC, 1970; contbr. exhbns. Mus. Modern Art, NYC, 1973, Albany Inst Art, 1975; vis. scholar/artist Am. Acad. in Rome, 2001 Author: Hot Towns: The Future of the Fastest Growing Communities in America, 1999; Land in America: Its Value, Use and Control, 1981; On Streets, 1979; The Future of the City: New Directions in Urban Planning, 1974; The Evolving City, Urban Design Proposals by Ulrich Franzen and Paul Rudolph, 1974, Another Chance for Cities, 1970, Eugene Hénard and the Beginning of Urbanism in France 1900-1914, 1969. Trustee Guild Hall, East Hampton, NY, 1981-86, 99—, Van Allen Inst., 1995—, Godchaux Res. Plantation Fund, pres., 1994—; chmn. bd. trustees Van Allen Inst., NY, 1999-2000; adv. bd. Nat. Acad. Design, 1999—; dir. Franklin Realty Co., 2005—; trustee Village Preservation Soc. 2005—; founder, trustee, chmn. Thomas Moran Trust, 2006—. NEA fellow, 1979; Graham Found. fellow, 1967-68, 94-95; Fulbright fellow, 1965-66; Ford Found. grantee, 1971-74; recipient Charles P. Shattuck award Nat. Rsch. Ednl. Trust Fund, 1983. Mem.: Inst. Pvt. Investors, Contemporary Arts Coun. Mus. Modern Art. Avocation: tennis. Home: 325 West End Ave New York NY 10023-8135 Office: 19 W 44th St Ste 812 New York NY 10036 Home Phone: 212-874-2489; Office Phone: 212-302-4240.

WOLF, ROBERT EDWARD, physician, educator; b. Houston, Jan. 20, 1942; s. John Eaton and Ruby Lucile (Bukowski) W.; m. Ann Elizabeth Killebrew, Dec. 23, 1967; 1 child, Robert Edward, Jr. BA, Baylor U., 1964; MA, U. Tex. Med. Br., 1968, MD, 1969, PhD, 1973. Diplomate Am. Bd. Internal Medicine. Intern in internal medicine U. Tex. Med. Br., Galveston, 1969-70, resident in internal medicine, 1970-71; fellowship in rheumatology U. Tex. Health Scis. Ctr., Dallas, 1973-75; rsch. assoc. VAMC, Dallas, 1975-77; asst. prof. of medicine U. Tex. Health Scis. Ctr., Dallas, 1975-77; staff physician, chief rheumatology VA Med. Ctr., Shreveport, La., 1977—; chief rheumatology La. State U. Health Scis. Ctr., 1997—2003, assoc. prof. medicine, 1977-89, prof. medicine, 1989—2003, dir. Arthritis Ctr., 1990—2003, prof. emeritus, 2004—. Mem. faculty promotions com. La. State U. Health Scis. Ctr., 1994—98, rsch. adv. coun., 1992—2003, adminstrv. coun., 1994—2003, utilization rev. com., 1983—95. Contbg. author: Selected Topics in Clinical Chemistry, 1972, Serum Protein Abnormalities, 1975; contbr. articles to profl. jours. Undergrad. edn. com. Arthritis Found., Atlanta, 1979-82, pres., 1983-85, exec. com.; active Lupus Found., Shreveport. Lt. comdr. USPHS, 1971-73. Recipient Grand (Student) award Nat. Rsch. Forum, Galveston, 1968, 3rd (Resident) award, 1970, Multipurpose Arthritis Ctr. award NIH, Bethesda, Md., 1977, Ctr. of Excellence-Arthritis award State of La., Baton Rouge, 1990-2003. Fellow: Am. Coll. Rheumatology. Office: VA Med Ctr 510 E Stoner Ave Shreveport LA 71101

WOLF, STEPHEN M., consumer products company executive, former airline executive; b. Oakland, Calif., Aug. 7, 1941; BA, San Francisco State U., 1965. Various positions Am. Airlines, Los Angeles, 1965-79, v.p. western div., 1979-81; sr. v.p. mktg. Pan Am. World Airlines, NYC, 1981-82; pres., chief operating officer Continental Airlines, Houston, 1982-83; pres. Republic Airlines, Mpls., 1984-85, pres., chief exec. officer, 1985-86; chmn., pres., chief exec. officer Tiger Internat., Los Angeles, 1986-87, UAL Corp. and United Airlines, Chgo., 1987-92, chmn., CEO, 1992-94, former pres., dir.; adviser Air France, 1994-96; chmn., CEO USAIR Inc, Arlington, Va., 1996-98, chmn., 1998—2001, non exec. chmn., 2002—03; mng. ptnr. Alpilles LLC, 2003—; chmn. R.R. Donnelley & Sons Co., 2004—. Bd. dirs. Air Transport Assn., Bus. Roundtable, Washington, Altria Group Inc., conf. bd. N.Y. Internat. Air Transport Assn., Geneva, World Travel and Tourism Coun., London. Bd. dirs. Alzheimer's Disease and Related Disorders Assn., Chgo., Art Inst., Chgo., Chgo. Symphony Orch., Muscular Dystrophy Assn., Rush-Presbyn.-St. Luke's Med. Ctr., Chgo., J.L. Kellogg Sch. Bus. Adv. Coun., Northwestern U. Trustee Northwestern U., mem. bus. adv. com. Transportation Ctr. *

WOLF, TIMOTHY VAN DE WINT, food products executive; b. Apr. 27, 1953; s. Charles and Theresa Wolf; m. Mary Therese Merritt. BA in Econs. cum laude, Harvard U., 1974; MBA, U. Chgo., 1976. Fin. analyst to sr. fin. analyst Tennant Co., Mpls., 1976-79; mgr. mktg. planning and analysis Electrolux div. Consolidated Food Corp., Stamford, Conn., 1979-80; mgr. bus. planning Pepsi USA, Purchase, NY, 1980-81, mgr. bus. devel. and competitive analysis, 1981-82, dir. bus. planning fountain beverage div., 1982-84; sr. dir. bus. planning Taco Bell Corp., Irvine, Calif., 1984-86; v.p., controller Taco Bell & other sr. fin. mgmt. positions Pepsico, Purchase, NY, 1986—95; CFO Adolph Coors Co. & Coors Brewing Co., 1995—2005; global CFO Molson Coors Brewing Co., Denver, 2005—. Bd. dirs. Irvine Med. Ctr. Harvard Coll. scholar, Cambridge, Mass. Mem.: Harvard of So. Calif., U. Calif. Chancellor's (Irvine). Avocations: tennis, skiing, golf, German history, international relations. Office: Molson Coors Brewing Co 1225 17th St Ste 3200 Denver CO 80202 *

WOLF, WERNER PAUL, physicist, researcher; b. Vienna, Apr. 22, 1930; arrived in U.S., 1963, naturalized, 1977; s. Paul and Wilhelmina Wolf; m. Elizabeth Eliot, Sept. 23, 1954; children: Peter Paul, Mary-Anne Githa. BA, Oxford U., Eng., 1951, DPhil, MA, Oxford U., Eng., 1954; MA (hon.), Yale U., 1965. Rsch. fellow Harvard U., 1956-57; Fulbright travelling fellow, 1956-57; Imperial Chem. Industries rsch. fellow Oxford U., 1957-59, univ. demonstrator, lectr., 1959-62; lectr. New Coll., 1957-62; faculty Yale U., 1963—2001, prof. physics and applied sci., 1965-76, dir. grad. studies dept. engring. and applied sci., 1973-76, Becton prof., 1976-84, chmn. dept. engring. and applied sci., 1976-81, chmn. council engring., 1981-84, Raymond J. Wean prof. engring. and applied sci., prof. physics, 1984—2001, prof. emeritus, 2002—, dir. undergrad. studies dept. applied physics, 1987-94, dir. grad. studies coun. engring., 1989, chmn. dept. applied physics, 1990-97, chair commn. on econ. status of faculty, 1990-92, dir. ednl. affairs for engring., 1994-99. Cons. Dupont Exptl. Sta., Wilmington, Del., 1957, Hughes Aircraft, Culver City, Calif., 1957, GE Rsch. Lab., Schenectady, N.Y., 1960, Mullard Rsch. Labs., Salfords, England, 1961, IBM, Yorktown Heights, N.Y., 1962-66, Brookhaven Nat. Lab., 1966-80, GE R & D Ctr., Schenectady, 1966-93, U. Bridgeport, 1995-96, Nat. U. Singapore, 1994-96; vis. prof. Technische Hochschule, Munich, Germany, 1969; Sci. Research Council sr. vis. fellow Oxford U., 1980, 84; vis. fellow Corpus Christi Coll., 1984, 87; mem. program com. Conf. Magnetism and Magnetic Materials, 1963, 65, 86, chmn., 1968, mem. adv. com., 1964-65, 70-76, 85-88, chmn., 1972, steering com., 1970-71, conf. gen. chmn., 1971; mem. organizing, program coms. Internat. Congress on Magnetism, 1967, internat. program com., 1978-79, planning com., 1979-85; vis. physicist Brookhaven Nat. Lab., 1966, 68, vis. sr. physicist, 1970, research collaborator, 1972, 74, 75, 77, 80; mem. vis. com. dept. phys./sci. U. Del., 1980, 84, 86; mem. NATO Advanced Study Inst. Program Com., 1983, 85, internat. adv. bd. Yamada Conf. XXV on Magnetic Phase Transitions, 1990; mem. bd. visitors Fairfield U. Sch. Engring., 1996-2005. Editor: CASE Reports, 1988-90; contbr. articles to profl. jours. Named vis. guest fellow, Royal Soc. London, 1987; recipient sr. U.S. scientist award, Alexander von Humboldt Found, 1983, Sheffield Disting. Tchg. award, Yale U. Faculty Engring., 2000. Fellow IEEE (life), Am. Phys. Soc. (edn. com. 1977-80, program dir. Indsl. Grad. Intern Program 1978-79, chmn. fellowship com., Div. Condensed Matter Physics 1981-83); mem. Conn. Acad. Sci. and Engring., Yale Sci. and Engring. Assn. (Meritorious Svc. award 1985). Home: 37 Apple Tree Ln Woodbridge CT 06525-1258 Office: Yale U Dept Applied Physics PO Box 208284 New Haven CT 06520-8284 Business E-Mail: werner.wolf@yale.edu.

WOLF, WILLIAM B., JR., lawyer; b. Washington, Sept. 11, 1927; s. William B. and Ruth (Pack) W.; m. Edna Russell Jacobs, Aug. 8, 1952 (div. Oct. 1976); children: Susan Marcia, William B. III, Victoria Katharine; m. Audrey Ann Riven, Nov. 29, 1980. AB, Princeton, 1948; postgrad., Oxford U., 1950; LLB, Yale U., 1951. Bar: D.C. 1951, U.S. Supreme Ct. 1954, Md. 1963. Ptnr. Wolf & Wolf, Washington, 1951-64, 82—; sole practice Washington, 1964-72, 75-81; ptnr. Wolf & Rosenblatt, Washington, 1972-75, Wolf, Amram & Hahn, P.C., Washington, 1981-82. Vice chmn. Security Nat. Bank, Washington, 1984-85. Author: Lawyers Are a Dime a Dozen, 1999. Pres. Nat. Capital USO, 1966—67, Jewish Hist. Soc. Greater WAshington, Brotherhood Washington Hebrew Congregation, 1967—68. With USN, 1945, sgt. US Army, 1946—48. Mem.: ABA, Bar Assn. D.C., University (Washington), Nassau (Princeton, N.J.), Edgartown (Mass.) Yacht, Woodmont Country. Republican. Jewish. Home: Watergate East Washington DC 20037 Office: Wolf & Wolf 2510 Virginia Ave NW Washington DC 20037 Home Phone: 202-965-3456; Office Phone: 202-298-6000. E-mail: visible@abanet.org.

WOLF, WILLIAM MARTIN, computer company executive, consultant; b. Watertown, NY, Aug. 29, 1928; s. John and Rose (Emrich) Wolf; m. Eileen Marie Jolly, Aug. 19, 1952 (div. 1972); children: Rose(dec.), Sylvia, William. BS, St. Lawrence U., 1950; MS, U. N.H., 1951; postgrad., U. Pa., 1951—52, MIT, 1952—55. Programmer digital computer lab. MIT, Cambridge, 1952—54, dir., exec. dir. Tech. Capital Network, 1992—94; pres. Wolf R & D Corp., Boston, 1954—69, Wolf Computer Corp., Boston, 1966—76, Planning Sys. Internat., Boston, 1976—81, Micro Computer Software Inc., Cambridge, 1981—88, Tech. Acquisition Corp., Boston, 1989—91, Planning Internat., Inc., Boston, 1989—94, Wolfsort Corp., Boston, 1989—; chmn. Wolf & McManus, Brookline, Mass., 1995—; founder Year 2000 Software Corp., Brookline, Mass., 1996—2000; co-founder, pres., CEO Eureka.Com, Inc., Rockport, Mass., 1999—2000, FocuSystems, Inc., Rockport, Mass., 2000—; founder, pres., CEO Mass. Med. Agy., 2002—. Co-founder, pres. Assn. Ind. Software Cos., Washington, 1965—67, Design Sci. Inst., Phila., 1969—73, Nat. Coun. Profl. Svc. Firms, Washington, 1970—75; seminar leader MIT Sloan Sch., Cambridge, 1970; co-founder, bd. dirs. Harbor Nat. Bank, Boston. Author: (autobiography) No "e", 2005. Trustee Addison Gilbert Hosp., Gloucester, Mass., 1963; co-founder X-10 Orgn., Boston, 1962; v.p. Young Pres. Orgn., Boston, 1970; overseer Mus. Sci., Boston, 1989—97. Named Outstanding Young Man in Boston, Jaycees, 1962; recipient Spkr.'s award, Data Processing Mgmt. Assn., 1966. Mem.: World Bus. Coun., MIT Club (Alumni award 1991), Forty-Niners. Achievements include invention of management system; orbit calculator; patents for sorting method; method for solving Year 2000 problem. Personal E-mail: wmwolf@aol.com.

WOLFBERG, MELVIN DONALD, optometrist, educational association administrator, consultant; b. Altoona, Pa., June 24, 1926; s. Max Alex and Claire (Schiffman) Wolfberg; m. Audrey Iris Koch, Apr. 26, 1952; children: Debra Lynn, Michael Alex, Daniel Ben; m. Linda Diane Machesic, Dec. 4, 1979. OD, Pa. Coll. Optometry, Phila., 1951; D of Ocular Sci. (hon.), New England Coll. Optometry, 1989, Ill. Coll. Optometry, 1990; LHD (hon.), Pa. Coll. Optometry, 1998. Lic. optometrist, Pa. Pvt. practice and ptnr. optometric practice, Selinsgrove, Pa., 1951-79; pres. Pa. Coll. Optometry, Phila., 1979-89, chmn. bd., 1976-79; v.p. profl. rels. Bausch and Lomb, Rochester, NY, 1991-95; pres. In Vision Inst., Boston, 1991-95; ptnr./dir. Sylvan Learning Ctr., Vero Beach, Fla., 1996—. Cons. to sec. HEW, Washington, 1970-77; dir. Better Vision Inst., N.Y.C., 1960-80. Mem. Selinsgrove City Coun., 1961-62; pres. Selinsgrove Community Chest, 1957; chmn. Optometrists Rep. Nat. Com., 1972, 76; chmn. Nat. Inter-Profl. Health Coun., Washington, 1972-77; dir. Univ. City Sci. Ctr., Phila., 1980-87; adv. com. Coun. Higher Edn., Commonwealth Pa., 1980-89. Served with U.S. Army, 1944-46, ETO. Decorated Purple Heart, Bronze Star, Silver Star; named Man of Yr. Central Pa. Optometric Soc., 1964, Alumnus of Yr. Pa. Coll. Optometry, 1970; recipient Carel C. Koch Meml. medal, 1989. Fellow Am. Acad. Optometry (pres. 1985-86, Eminent Svc. award, 2005); mem. Pa. Assn. Colls. and Univs. (exec. com. 1982-89, sec.-treas. 1985-88, vice chmn. 1988-89), Pa. Optometric Assn. (pres. 1959-61, Optometrist of Yr., Ewalt Meritorious Svc. award 2003), Am. Optometric Assn. (pres. 1969-70, Disting. Svc. award 1994, named to Nat. Optometry Hall Fame 2004), Pa. Coll. Optometry Alumni Assn. (pres. 1957), Beta Sigma Kappa. Office Phone: 772-299-0502. Business E-Mail: ilovesylvan@bellsouth.net.

WOLFE, BARBARA L., economics professor, researcher; b. Phila., Feb. 15, 1943; d. Manfred and Edith (Heimann) Kingshoff; m. Stanley R. Wolfe, Mar. 20, 1965 (div. Mar. 1978); m. Robert H. Haveman, July 29, 1983; children: Jennifer Ann Wolfe, Ari Michael Wolfe. BA, Cornell U., Ithaca, NY, 1965; MA, U. Pa., 1971; PhD, U Pa., 1973. Asst. prof. Bryn Mawr (Pa.) Coll., 1973-76; rsch. assoc. Inst. Rsch. on Poverty, Madison, Wis., 1976-77, dir., 1994—2000; from asst. prof. to assoc. prof. U. Wis., Madison, 1977-88, prof., 1988—, dir., LaFollette Sch. Pub. Affairs, 2006—. Adj. prof. Australian Nat. U., 2002-; resident scholar NIAS, Wassenear, Netherlands, 1984-85, 96-97, 2007; vis. scholar Russell Sage Found., N.Y., 1991-92. Co-author: Succeeding Generations, 1994; editor: (book) Role of Budgetary Policy in Demographic Transitions, 1994, contbr. articles to profl. jours. Mem. Commn. on Children with Disabilities, Washington 1994-95, Tech. Adv. Panel Social Security, Washington, 1994-95; vice chair bd. on children, youth and families IOM and NAS, 2005; mem. adv. comm. dir., NIH, 2006-. Recipient Best Article of Yr. award Rev. Income and Wealth, 1992, Fulbright award Coun. Internat. Exch. of Scholars, 1984. Mem.: Am. Soc. for Health Econ., Internat. Health Econ. Assn., Inst. of Medicine, Assn. Pub. Policy Mgmt. (policy coun. 2001—04), Internat. Inst. Pub. Fin. (bd. mgmt. 1994—2000, v.p. 2000—03), Am. Econ. Assn. (bd. CSWERP com. 1989—92, exec. bd. 1996—99). Office: U Wis Inst Rsch on Poverty 1180 Observatory Dr Madison WI 53706-1320 Office Phone: 608-262-3581. Business E-Mail: wolfe@lafollette.wisc.edu, bwolfe@wisc.edu.

WOLFE, CAMERON WITHGOT, JR., lawyer; b. Oakland, Calif., July 7, 1939; s. Cameron W. and Jean (Brown) W.; m. Frances Evelyn Bishopric, Sept. 2, 1964; children: Brent Everett, Julie Frances, Karen Jean. AB, U. Calif., Berkeley, 1961, JD, 1964. Bar: Calif. 1965, U.S. Dist. Ct. (no. dist.) Calif. 1965, U.S. Ct. Appeals (9th cir.) 1965, U.S. Tax Ct. 1966, U.S. Ct. Claims 1977, U.S. Ct. Appeals (3d cir.) 1980, U.S. Supreme Ct. 1986. Assoc., then ptnr. Orrick, Herrington & Sutcliffe, San Francisco, 1964—. Bd. dirs. Crowley Maritime Corp.; mem. steering com. Western Pension Conf. Pres. League To Save Lake Tahoe, 1979, 80; chmn. League To Save Lake Tahoe Charitable Truste, 1966-91, Piedmont Ednl. Fund Campaign, 1982-83; pres. Piedmont Ednl. Found., 1986-90; bd. dirs. Yosemite Fund, 1993—. With U.S. Army, 1957; with USAR, 1957-65. Mem. ABA (taxation com.), Calif. State Bar, San Francisco Bar Assn., San Francisco Tax Club (pres. 1997-98), Pacific Union Club, Claremont Country Club (Oakland, Calif.), Order of Coif, Phi Beta Kapa. Home: 59 Lakeview Ave Piedmont CA 94611-3514 Office: Orrick Herrington Sutcliffe 405 Howard St Fl 11 San Francisco CA 94105-2680

WOLFE, CHARLES MORGAN, electrical engineering educator; b. Morgantown, W.Va., Dec. 21, 1935; s. Slidell Brown and Mae Louise (Maness) W.; children— David Morgan, Diana Michele BSE.E., W.Va. U., Morgantown, 1961, MSE.E., 1962; PhD, U. Ill., 1965. Research assoc. U. Ill., Urbana, 1965; mem. staff MIT Lincoln Lab., Lexington, Mass., 1965-75; prof. elec. engring Washington U., St. Louis, 1975-97, Samuel C. Sachs prof., 1982-90, dir. semicondr. research lab., sr. prof., 1979-90. Cons. MIT Lincoln Lab., 1975-76, Fairchild Semicondr., Palo Alto, Calif., 1975-76, Air Force Avionics Lab., Dayton, Ohio, 1976-79, U. Ill., 1983-85 Author: Physical Properties of Semiconductors, 1989; editor: Gallium Arsenide and Related Compounds, 1979; contbr. articles to profl. jours., chpts. to books Served as sgt. USMC, 1955-58 Fellow: IEEE (field awards com. 1984—87, Jack A. Morton award 1990); mem.: NAE, Electrochem. Soc. (Electronics divsn. award 1978).

WOLFE, DAVID LOUIS, lawyer; b. Kankakee, Ill., July 24, 1951; s. August Christian and Irma Marie (Nordmeyer) W.; m. Gail Lauret Fritz, Aug. 25, 1972; children: Laura Beth, Brian David, Kaitlin Ann. BS, U. Ill., 1973; JD, U. Mich., 1976. Bar: Ill. 1976, U.S. Dist. Ct. (no. dist.) Ill. 1976. Assoc., Gardner, Carton & Douglas, Chgo., 1976-82, ptnr., 1983—, mem. Mgmt. Com., 2002-06, HR law dept; lectr. ABA, Estate Planning Aid Assn. for Lutherans SMART Program, Chgo., 1980-84, Ill. Inst. Continuing Legal Edn., Employee Benefits Sec. Coun., Chgo. Bar Assn., Lake Shore Nat. Bank, Ill. State Bar Assn., Daughters Charity Nat. Health Sys., Lutheran Health Sys., AM. Assn. Homes & Svcs. for Aging, Mich. Assn. Cert. Pub. Accts., Diversified Investment Advisors, Decalogue Soc., Conf Cons. Actuaries, Ind. Pension Conf., Inst Internat. Rsch., Lake Shore Bank Chgo. Contbr. articles to legal publs. Co-founder, mem. steering com. adv. bd. HR Hosp.; bd. dirs. World Law Group. Recipient Recognition award Ill. Inst. Continuing Legal Edn., 1981-84, Named to Best Lawyers Am., 1993-2006; named Leader in Field, Chambers USA, 2006. Mem. ABA (sects. on taxation, corp. banking and bus. law 1981-90, lectr.), NFL Players Assn. (cert. contract advisor 1983-88), NCAA (cert. contract advisor), Ill. State Bar Assn. (employee benefits sect. council, 1986-95, past chmn., recognition award 1983), Phi Kappa Phi, Beta Alpha Psi, Beta Gamma Sigma, Sigma Iota Lambda, Phi Eta Sigma. Office: Drinker Biddle Gardner Carton 191 N Wacker Dr Ste 3700 Chicago IL 60606 Office Phone: 312-569-1313. Personal E-mail: dwolfe@gcd.com. Business E-Mail: david.wolfe@dbr.com.

WOLFE, DEBORAH ANN, lawyer; b. Detroit, May 4, 1955; d. Adam and Mary A. (Smyth) Wolfe; m. Lester D. McDonald, May 23, 1987; children: Molly, Thomas. Student, Ariz. State U., Tempe, 1973-76; BA in Polit. Sci., Bus., Tex. Christian U., Ft. Worth, 1977; postgrad., So. Meth. U., Dallas, 1977-78; JD, U. San Diego, 1980; grad., Gerry Spence's Trial Lawyers Coll., 1999. Bar: Calif. 1981, Ariz. 1982. Pvt. practice, San Diego, 1981—83, 1989-91; ptnr. Kremer & Wolfe, San Diego, 1983-86; assoc. D. Dwight Worden, Solana Beach, Calif., 1986-89; owner Wolfe & McDonald, 1991-96; shareholder Nugent & Newnham, San Diego, 1996—2003, Nugent Weinman Abbene Alcock & Wolfe, San Diego, 2004—06; owner Wolfe Legal Group, San Diego, 2006—. Instr. San Diego Inn of Ct. Evidence, 1988-95. Floutist San Diego City Guard Band, 1981-93, Grossmont Sinfonia, La Mesa, 1982-83, Classical/Chamber Music Quartet, San Diego, 1983-87, Foothills United Meth. Ch. band, 1997—; leader Girl Scouts. Named one of Lawyers of the Yr. Calif. Lawyer Mag., 1996, one of top ten plaintiff legal malpractice lawyers in Calif., 2001. Mem. Am. Assn. Justice, Consumer Attys. Calif., Consumer Attys. San Diego (pres. 1996, Outstanding Trial Lawyer award 1996, 2000, 02, Trial Lawyer of Yr. award 1996, 2005), Lawyers Club (San Diego), San Diego Trial Lawyers Assn. (Outstanding Trial Lawyers award 1987), Am. Inns of Ct. (master), Nat. Bd. Trial Advocates. Office: Wolfe Legal Group 401 W A St Ste 2200 San Diego CA 92101-3536 Office Phone: 619-234-3363. Business E-Mail: dwolfe@wolfelegalgroup.com.

WOLFE, ELLEN DARLENE, school librarian, elementary school educator; b. Mattoon, Ill., Dec. 16, 1952; d. Floyd Dale and Irma Jane (Hensley) Robinson; m. Walter Ray Wolfe, Mar. 12, 1994; children: Gregory David, William Scott, Joseph Dean, Brian Matthew, Joshua Paul. BS, Ind. State U., 1987. Cert. elem. educator, Ill. Reading tchr. Marshall (Ill.) Community Dist. 2, 1987-91; law libr. Robinson (Ill.) Correctional Ctr., 1991-94; libr. Palestine (Ill.) Cmty. Unit Sch. Dist. # 3, 1994—. Libr. City of Marshall, 1986—; dir. summer camp Clark County Handicapped Assn., Marshall, 1988—; law libr. Robinson Correctional Ctr., 1991. Coord. Jr. youth group St. Mary's Cath. Ch. Mem. Correctional Edn. Assn., Home Ext. Club, Kappa Delta Pi, Phi Delta Kappa. Roman Catholic. Home: 18993 E River Rd Palestine IL 62451-2430 Office: Robinson Correctional Ctr PO Box 1000 Robinson IL 62454-0919

WOLFE, ETHYLE RENEE, academic administrator; b. Burlington, Vt., Mar. 14, 1919; d. Max M. and Rose (Saiger) Wolfe; m. Coleman Hamilton Benedict, Dec. 4, 1954. BA, U. Vt., 1940, MA, 1942; postgrad., Bryn Mawr Coll., 1942—43; PhD, NYU, 1950; LHD (hon.), CUNY, 1989; LittD (hon.), Iona Coll., 1989. Tchg. fellow U. Vt., 1940—42; rsch. fellow Latin Bryn Mawr (Pa.) Coll., 1942—43; instr. classics Bklyn. Coll., 1947—49, instr. classical langs., 1949—54, asst. prof., 1954—59, assoc. prof., 1960—68, prof., 1968—, acting chmn. dept. classics and comparative lit., 1962—63, chmn. dept., 1967—72; dean Bklyn. Coll. Sch. Humanities, 1971—78; exec. officer Bklyn. Coll. Humanities Inst., 1980—89; provost and v.p. for acad. affairs Bklyn. Coll., 1982—88, provost emeritus, 1989. Exec. com., chmn. com. on undergrad. affairs, com. on univ.-wide programs CUNY; study group AAAS, 1987—89, pub., 1987—89; dir. Nat. Core Visitors Programs, 1985—89, Fund for Improvement of Postsecondary Edn.-funded Ctr. for Core Studies, 1987—88; co-chair senate report Chancellor's Coll. Prep. Initiative, 1991; exec. com The Liberal Art of Sci.: Agenda for Action. Mem. editl. bd.: Classical World, 1965—71; co-editor: The Am. Classical Rev., 1971—76; contbr. articles to profl. jours. Named Ethyle R. Wolfe Inst. for the Humanities Bklyn. Coll. in her honor, 1989; named to Hall of Honor, U. Vt., 1991, Disting. U. Faculty Sen. Emeritus, CUNY, 1992; recipient Kirby Flower Smith award, 1939, Goethe prize, U. Vt., 1940, Alumni Achievement award, 1985, Nat. Presdl. medal, NEH, Charles Frankel prize, 1990; grantee, 1971, 1982—84, Mellon Found., 1982—85, 1986—89, Exxon, 1986—89, Josiah Macy, 1986—90. Mem.: Am. Soc. Papyrologists, Classical Assn. Atlantic States (exec. com.), Vergilian Soc. Am., Archeol. Inst. Am., Am. Philol. Assn., N.Y. Classical Club (past pres., exec. com.), Phi Beta Kappa (pres. 1988—90, past pres. Rho of N.Y. chpt., Spl. Citation of Honor on Sesquicentennial U. Vt. 1998). Home: 360 W 22nd St New York NY 10011-2600 Office: care Ethyle R Wolfe Inst Humanities Bklyn Coll Bedford Ave # H Brooklyn NY 11222

WOLFE, GARY DONALD, commissioner, retired librarian; b. Altoona, Pa., Mar. 19, 1941; s. Donald George and Norma Rosmond (Cooper) W.; m. Mary Susan Olex, Aug. 5, 1967; children: Mark Douglas, Michelle Marie. BS in Elem. Edn., St. Francis Coll., Loretto, Pa., 1970; MLS, U. Pitts., Pa., 1972. Libr. clk. Altoona Pub. Libr., 1959-61; acting children's libr. Coyle Free Libr., Chambersburg, Pa., 1961-63; asst. prof. librarianship St. Francis Coll., 1963-75; adminstr. Centre County Libr., Bellefonte, Pa., 1975-89; dir. libr. devel. State Libr. Pa., Harrisburg, Pa., 1989-95; dep. sec. edn., commr. for libs. State of Pa., Harrisburg, Pa., 1995—. Editor: Automated Circulation: A Study, 1981. Vol. driver Am. Cancer Soc., Lower Paxton Twp. Sr. Vol. Van Svc. Sgt. USAR, 1963—69. Recipient Disting. Alumni award St. Francis Coll., 1997, Cert. of Commendation, Am. Assn. Sch. Librs., 2003. Mem. Pa. Libr. Assn. (treas. 1983-85, cert. of merit 1986, Disting. Svc. award 1997), Pa. Citizens for Better Librs. (bd. mem. 2003-, Lifetime Achievement award 2003). Republican. Avocation: reading. Home: 2407 Wicklow Dr Harrisburg PA 17112-9620 Personal E-mail: garydwolfe@comcast.net.

WOLFE, GEORGE C., theater director, producer, playwright; b. Frankfurt, Ky., Sept. 23, 1954; s. Costello and Anna Wolfe. BA, Pomona Coll., 1976; MFA, NYU, 1983. With Inner City Cultural Center, Los Angeles, Calif., 1975—78; teacher City Coll. of N.Y. & Richard Allen Ctr. for Cultural Art; resident dir. Public Theatre, NYC, 1990—93; prodr. N.Y. Shakespeare Festival, NYC, 1993—; head prodr. Public Theatre, NYC, 1992—2004. Works include: writer, lyricist (plays) Paradise!, 1985; writer, dir. The Colored Museum, 1986 (Elizabeth Hull-Kate Warriner award, Dramatists Guild, 1986), Jelly's Last Jam, 1992 (Drama Desk award, 1992,

Joe A. Callaway award, Stage Dirs. and Choreographers Found., 1993); writer Queenie Pie, 1987, The Wild Party, 2000; scene contbr. Urban Blight, 1988; curator Festival of New Voices, 1990, 92; adaptor, dir. Spunk, 1990 (Obie award best dir., 1990); dir., prodr. (Broadway shows) Angels in America: Millennium Approaches, 1992, (Tony award best dir., 1993), Angels in America: Perestroika, 1993 (Tony award nominee best dir., 1994), Twilight: Los Angeles, 1994, The Tempest, 1995, On the Town, 1998, Elaine Stritch At Liberty, 2002, Topdog/Underdog, 2002, Caroline, or Change, 2004 (Tony nom. best dir. of a musical, 2004); dir. (NY theater) Mother Courage and Her Children, 2006; prodr., lyrics, Bring in Da Noise, Bring in Da Funk, 1996 (Tony award for best dir., 1996); prodr. Golden Child, 1998, Take Me Out, 2003; dir. (TV movie), Lackawanna Blues, 2005 (Outstanding Directorial Achievement in Movies for TV, Director's Guild Am., 2005); actor: A Delicate Balance, 1996 (Tony award best leading actor, 1996). Grantee Rockefeller Found., Nat. Endowment for Arts, Nat. Inst. Musical Theatre; recipient Hull-Warriner award, 2 Audleco awards, The George Oppenheimer/Newsday award, CBS-FDG New Play award, NYU Disting. Alumni award, HBO/USA Playwrights award, Person of Yr. award Nat. Theatre Conf., Spl. Achievement award Audleco, Spirit of the City award, LAMBDA award, Career Achievement award, New Dramatists, 2005; named A Living Landmark, N.Y. Landmarks Conservancy. Mem. Dramatists Guild (mem. exec. bd.), Dir. Guild of Amer., Writers Guild of Amer., bd. dirs. Young Playwrights Festival, N.Y.C. Office: Joseph Papp Pub Theater 425 Lafayette St New York NY 10003-7087

WOLFE, GEORGE CROPPER, retired private school educator, artist, writer; b. New Orleans, Sept. 6, 1933; s. Howard Edward and Amaryllis (Brannen) Wolfe; m. Catherine Vasterling, June 2, 1955; children: David, Michael, Philip. BFA, La. State U., 1956; MEd, U. New Orleans, 1972, MS in Urban Planning, 1975; postgrad., Tex. Tech U., Junction, 1986-93; MA in Art, Northwestern State U., Natchitoches, La., 2007. Cert. tchr. art, social studies La. Elem. tchr. Live Oak Manor Sch., Waggaman, La., 1962-65; tchr. art Isidore Newman Sch., New Orleans, 1965-96; adj. prof. art Northwestern State U., Natchitoches, La., 1997-99; co-owner design studio Wolf Patrol Prodns. Author: (book) 3D-Wizardry: Design in Papier Mache Plaster and Foam, 1995, (video) Sculpture in Motion, 2000 (Silver Telly award, 2001), 3-D Wizardry (Telly award, 1996), Papier Maché Plaster and Foam; one-man shows include Hanchley Gallery, Northwestern U., 1999, Dragons of the Mind, Northwestern State U., 2006, 50 Yr. Retrospective Art Show, Hauchley Gallery, 2006, exhibited in group shows at New Alexandria (La.) Mus. Art, commn. sculpture, Echo Totem, Alexandria Mus. Art, 1998, Alex the Red, 1998, Hands Supporting Hands, Wesley Found., 1999, commn. life size puppets, Two by Two, Northwestern State U. Summer Theatre, 1999, commn. sculpture, Rhino, Northwestern State U., 2004; contbr. articles to profl. jours. With USCG, 1956—58. Mem.: La. Art Edn. Assn. (pres. 1978—79, coord. conf. 2005), Nat. Art Edn. Assn. (La. Art Educator of the Yr. 1990, Ret. Art Educator of the Yr. 2000—01, Victor Lowenfeld award 2002), Phi Delta Kappa (v.p., Rsch. award 1996), Kappa Delta Pi. Home: 342 Jefferson St Natchitoches LA 71457-4382

WOLFE, GREGORY BAKER, international relations educator; b. LA, Jan. 27, 1922; s. Harry Norton and Laura May (Baker) W.; m. Mary Ann Nelson, June 15, 1946; children: Gregory Nelson, Laura Ann, Melissa Helene. AB, Reed Coll., 1943; MA, Fletcher Sch. Law and Diplomacy, 1947, PhD, 1961; Dr. honoris causa, U. Autonoma de Guadalajara, Mex., 1984; D.H.L., S.E. Coll. Osteo. Medicine, Miami, Fla., 1985; DHL, U. Tecnologica Equinoccial, Quito, Ecuador, 2000, U. Tecnologica de Santiago, Dominican Republic, 2001. With internat. div. Arthur D. Little, Inc., Cambridge, Mass., 1951-57; dir. Greater Boston Econ. Study Com., 1957-61; dir. Latin Am. program Com. Econ. Devel., 1961-64; dir. intelligence and rsch. for Am. republics State Dept., 1964-68; pres. Portland State U., 1968-74; dean Sch. Internat. Svc. Am. U., Washington, 1975-79; pres. Fla. Internat. U., Miami, 1979-86, prof. internat. rels., 1979—83, emeritus pres. and prof., 1983—; vis. scholar Cambridge U., Eng., 1986-87; chmn. Ednl. Facility Authority, Dade County, Fla., 1998—. Fed. negotiator Joint Transp. Com. Washington 1962-66 Contbr. articles to profl. jours. Chmn. bd. trustees Internat. Fine Arts Coll., 1993—2004, U. de Palermo Found., Buenos Aires, 1998—; bd. dirs. Chopin Found. U.S., Inc., 1988-96, Concert Assn. Fla., Inc., 1988—; founding chmn. Brickell Ave. Lit. Soc., 1 988-96. Recipient Fla. Internat. Ctr. award, 1980, Leonard Abess award, 1984, Orden del Merito Civil, King of Spain, 1986, Fulbright lectr., Ecuador, 1989. Personal E-mail: andes79@hotmail.com.

WOLFE, HARRIET MUNRETT, lawyer; b. Mt. Vernon, NY, Aug. 18, 1953; d. Lester John Francis Jr. and Olga Harriet (Miller) Munrett; m. Charles Briant Wolfe, Sept. 10, 1983 (div. Dec. 2004). BA, U. Conn., 1975; postgrad., Oxford U., Eng., 1976; JD, Pepperdine U., 1978. Bar: Conn. 1979. Assoc. legal counsel, asst. sec. Citytrust, Bridgeport, Conn., 1979-90; v.p., sr. counsel, asst. sec. legal dept. Shawmut Bank Conn., N.A., Hartford, 1990-96, pvt. practice, 1996-97; exec. v.p., gen. counsel, sec. Webster Fin. Corp., Waterbury, Conn., 1997—. Govt. rels. com. Electronic Funds Transfer Assn., Washington, 1983—. Mem. ABA, Conn. Bar Assn. (legis. com. banking law sect.), Conn. Bankers Assn. (trust legis.com.), Guilford Flotilla Coast Guard Aux., U.S. Sailing Assn., Phi Alpha Delta Internat. (Frank E. Gray award 1978, Shepherd chpt. Outstanding Student award 1977-78). Home: 621 Northwood Dr Guilford CT 06437-1124 Office: Webster Fin Corp Webster Plaza Waterbury CT 06702 Office Phone: 203-578-2423. Business E-Mail: hwolfe@websterbank.com.

WOLFE, JAMES RONALD, retired lawyer; b. Pitts., Dec. 10, 1932; s. James Thaddeus and Helen Matilda (Corey) W.; m. Anne Lisbeth Dahle Eriksen, May 28, 1960 (dec. 1996); children: Ronald, Christopher, Geoffrey; m. Patricia D. Yoder, Oct. 30, 1999. BA summa cum laude, Duquesne U., 1954, DHL (hon.), 1997; LLB cum laude, NYU, 1959. Bar: N.Y. 1959. Assoc. Simpson Thacher & Bartlett, NYC, 1959-69, ptnr., 1969-95, counsel, 1996-99, ret., 1999—. Co-editor: West's McKinney's Forms, Uniform Commercial Code, 1965. Served to 1st lt. U.S. Army, 1955-57. Mem. Assn. Bar City N.Y. Roman Catholic. Home: 500 SE 5th Ave Apt 601 Boca Raton FL 33432-5510 Office: Simpson Thacher & Bartlett 425 Lexington Ave New York NY 10017-3954

WOLFE, JOHN HALL, medical researcher, educator, consultant; b. Davenport, Iowa, Oct. 16, 1947; s. Donald E. and Peggy V. (Hall) Wolfe; m. Ruth M. Lamdan, July 19, 1986. AB, Ripon Coll., Wis., 1965—69; VMD, U. Pa., Phila., 1978—82, PhD, 1978—86. Fellow Sloan-Kettering Inst. Cancer Rsch., NYC, 1985—87; prof. U. Pa., Phila., 1987—; adj. prof. Wistar Inst., Phila., 1993—; dir. W. F. Goodman Ctr. for Comparative Med. Genetics U. Pa. Sch. Vet. Medicine, Phila., 1998—; stokes investigator Children's Hosp. Phila., 1998—. Cons. NIH, 1990—, Welcome Trust, London; sci. adv. bd. Nat. MPS Soc., 2000—, Internat. Soc. Mannosidosis & Related Diseases, 2002—. Contbr. articles to profl. jours. Capt. US Army, 1969—72, Germany. Decorated Commendation medal US Army; recipient Auxillary to SCAVMA prize, U. Pa. Sch. Vet. Medicine, 1982, SmithKline Beecham Rsch. award, 1991, Spl. Emphhasis Rsch. Career award, NIH, 1992—97; fellow, Med. Scientist Tng. Program of NIH, U. Pa., 1978—84; grantee Exxon Fellow, Sloan-Kettering Inst. Cancer Rsch., 1985—87; Rsch. grants, NIH, 1990—. Mem.: Am. Soc. Human Genetics, Soc. Neuroscience, Am. Soc. Gene Therapy, Am. Soc. Microbiology, Sierra Club (life). Achievements include patents for human neural stem cells. Avocation: sailing. Office: Univ Pa Childrens Hosp Phila 502G ARC 3516 Civic Ctr Blvd Philadelphia PA 19104 Home Phone: 215-242-3995.

WOLFE, JOHN LESLIE, lawyer; b. Cuyahoga Falls, Ohio, Dec. 6, 1926; s. Leslie George and Phyllis (Bond) W.; m. Barbara Lou Carle, Dec. 27, 1950 (div.); children: David, Karla. AB, U. Akron, 1950; JD, U. Mich., 1953. Bar: Ohio 1953, U.S. Dist. Ct. (no. dist.) Ohio 1955, U.S. Ct. Appeals (6th cir.) 1966, U.S. Supreme Ct. 1970. Sole practice, Akron, 1953—56; asst. pros. atty. Summit County, Akron, 1956—57; assoc. Hershey & Browne, Akron, 1957—61, ptnr., 1961—85, Wolfe, Williams & Abdenour, Akron, 1986—90; sole practice Akron, 1991—. Asst. atty. gen. State of Ohio, 1971-74; adj. prof. trial practice U. Akron, 1975-80; counsel Tri County Regional Planning Commn. of Portage, Summit and Medina Counties, 1960-74. Trustee Akron Law Libr., 1961—; past pres. Progress Through Preservation. Served with U.S. Army, 1945-47. Recipient Ohio Legal Ctr. Inst. award of merit, 1966. Mem.: ATLA, ABA, Nat. Employment Lawyers Assn., Ohio Acad. Trial Lawyers, Akron Bar Assn., Ohio State Bar Assn. Office: National City Center 1 Cascade Plz Ste 740 Akron OH 44308-1154 Home: 45 Mayfield Ave Akron OH 44313 Office Phone: 330-535-2441. Personal E-mail: wolfe81@sbcglobal.net.

WOLFE, LAWRENCE J., lawyer; b. 1951; BA, U. Calif. Davis, 1974; JD, U. Wyo, 1980. Asst. atty. gen. Office of Atty. Gen., Wyo., 1980—85, chief nat. resources divsn. Wyo., 1983—85; chair resources dept. Holland & Hart LLP, Cheyenne, Wyo., 2001—06, mng. ptnr., 2007—. Mem.: Cheyenne Rotary Club. Office: Holland & Hart LLP 215 Warren Ave Ste 450 Cheyenne WY 82001-3162 Office Phone: 307-778-4218. Office Fax: 307-778-8175. E-mail: lwolfe@hollandhart.com. *

WOLFE, LESLIE R., think-tank executive; Exec. dir. Ctr. for Women Policy Studies, Washington, D.C., pres. Office: Ctr Women Policy Studies 1211 Connecticut Ave NW Ste 312 Washington DC 20036-2709

WOLFE, LINDA, writer; b. NYC, Nov. 15, 1932; d. Harry M. Friedman and Mina Romanoff Kaufman; m. Max Pollack; 1 child, Jessica Wolfe Bernstein; stepchildren: Deborah Pollack, Jude Pollack. MA, NYU, 1958. Editl. asst. Oxford U. Press, NYC, 1955—60, Partisan Rev., NYC, 1958—60; writer, rschr. Time, Inc., NYC, 1960—71; contbg. editor N.Y. Mag., NYC, 1971—96; consulting editor Woman Mag. (Conde Nast), NYC, 1990—90. Author: (book) The Literary Gourmet, 1962, The Cooking of the Caribbean Islands, 1970, Playing Around: Women and Adultery, 1975, The Cosmo Report: Women and Sex in the Nineteen-Eighties, 1981, Private Practices (a novel), 1981, The Professor and the Prostitute and Other True Tales of Murder and Madness, 1986, Wasted: The Preppie Murder, 1989 (Notable Book of Yr., N.Y. Times, 1989), Double Life: The Shattering Affair Between New York's Chief Judge Sol Wachtler & Socialite Joy Silverman, 1994, Love Me To Death: A Journalist's Memoir of the Hunt for her Friend's Killer, 1998, The Murder of Dr. Chapman: The Legendary Trials of Lucretia Chapman and Her Lover, 2004. Recipient Edgar Allan Poe award nominee, Mystery Writers of Am., 1989. Mem.: PEN (exec. bd. dirs. 1994—95), Nat. Book Critics Circle (v.p. 1997—2002, exec. bd. 2005—). Avocations: 18th century English dance, travel.

WOLFE, MARGARET RIPLEY, historian, educator, consultant; b. Kingsport, Tenn., Feb. 3, 1947; d. Clarence Estill and Gertrude Blessing Ripley; m. David Earley Wolfe, Dec. 17, 1966; 1 child, Stephanie Ripley. BS magna cum laude, East Tenn. State U., 1967, MA, 1969; PhD, U. Ky., 1974. Instr. history East Tenn. State U., 1969-73, asst. prof., 1973-77, assoc. prof., 1977-80, prof., 1980—, prof. history emerita, 2004—, sr. rsch. prof. history, 1999—2004, prof. history emerita, sr. faculty affiliate, 2004—06. Disting. vis. prof. in history Washington and Lee U., 2006. Author: Lucius Polk Brown and Progressive Food and Drug Control, Tennessee and New York City, 1908-1920, 1978, An Industrial History of Hawkins County, Tennessee, 1983, Kingsport, Tennessee: A Planned American City, 1987, Daughters of Canaan: A Saga of Southern Women, 1995; gen. editor: Women in Southern Culture Series, 1995-2004; contbg. author to books, also introductions to books; contbr. articles to profl. jours. Mem. Tenn. Com. for Humanities, 1985-85, exec. coun. mem., 1984-85; mem. Women's Symphony Com., Kingsport, 1990-95; exec. com. Tenn. Commemorative Woman's Suffrage Comm., 1994-95; mem. state rev. bd. Tenn. Hist. Commn., 1995—2005. Haggin fellow U. Ky., 1972-73; recipient Disting. Faculty award East Tenn. State U., 1977, East Tenn. State U. Found. rsch. award, 1979, Alumni cert. merit, 1984. Mem. AAUP, ACLU (exec. com. Tenn. 1991-92), NOW, Tenn. State Employees Assn., Am. Studies Assn. (John Hope Franklin Prize com. 1992), Am. Hist. Assn., Orgn. Am. Historians, So. Assn. Women Historians (pres. 1983-84, exec. com. 1984-86), So. Hist. Assn. (com. on status of women 1987, program com. 1988, interim chair program com. 1988, mem. com. 1993, 94, 95, nominating com. 1994, chair nominating com. 1995, chmn. mem. com. 1997, exec. coun. 1998-2000), Smithsonian Assocs, Tenn. Hist Commn. (state rev. bd. 1995-2005), Tenn. Hist. Soc. (editl. bd. 1995—2004), Coordinating Com. for Women in History, East Tenn. Hist. Soc. (mem. editl. bd. Jour. East Tenn. History 1995-2004), St. George Tucker Soc., Phi Kappa Phi. E-mail: mrwolfe47@earthlink.net.

WOLFE, MARY JOAN, physician; d. Dermot F. and Jean M. Wolfe; m. Thomas R. Roberts, June 9, 1979; children: Douglas Roberts-Wolfe, Rebecca Roberts-Wolfe. AB Chemistry, Cornell U., 1971; MD, Hershey Med. Ctr., Pa., 1976. Diplomate Am. Bd. Internal Medicine, Am. Bd. Emergency Medicine. Intern Rochester Gen. Hosp., NY, 1976—77; resident internal medicine Westchester County Med. Ctr., Valhalla, NY, 1977—79, attending physician emergency dept., 1979—83; practice medicine specializing internal medicine Ossining, NY, 1986—; sr. attending physician Phelps Meml. Hosp. Ctr., NY, 1992—; founding mem., lab. dir. North Star Med. Group, PC, 2006—. Attending physician emergency room No. Westchester Hosp., Mt. Kisco, NY, 1986—89; founding mem., dir. lab. North Star Med. Group, 2006—, chmn. ancillary com., 2006—. Mem. ethics com. Phelps Meml. Hosp., 1994-97, mem. bylaws com., 1989-96, chmn., 1996-2004. Avocations: computers, painting, quilting. Home: 6 Cecilia Ln Pleasantville NY 10570-1502 Office: 14 Church St Ossining NY 10562-4831 Office Phone: 914-941-1334.

WOLFE, MAURICE RAYMOND, retired museum director, educator; b. Paris (Neuilly), France, Oct. 13, 1924; s. Guy Ellsworth and Genevieve (Plion) W.; m. Warwick Ellen Griffin, Nov. 4, 1955; 1 child, Shavaun. BA, U. Calif. in Sociology, Berkeley, 1948; MA in Sociology, U. Calif., Berkeley, 1952; postgrad. study, U. Paris Sorbonne, 1951; Cert. of Completion Sch. of Edn., U. Calif., Berkeley, 1954, postgrad., 1955. Rsch. asst. dept. of edn. U. Calif., Berkeley, 1949; tchr. of English and history Castlemont H.S., Oakland, Calif., 1954; lectr. in anthropology, philosophy, sociology and edn. U. Md. Overseas, 1956-59; lectr., instr. in philosopy and sociology U. Md., Munich, 1960-62; faculty mem. Merritt Coll., Oakland, Calif., 1962-88, chmn. dept. behavioral scis., 1967-87; dir. and founder Merritt Coll. Anthropology Mus., Oakland, 1973-88; rsch. assoc. U. Calif. Lowie Mus. of Anthropology, 1985-89. Lectr. Pers. Mgmt. for Execs., U.S. Govt. Sponsored, Berkeley, Calif. 1966-67, San Francisco State U., 1967-68, Calif. State U., Hayward, Dept. Sociology, 1970-71; adj. instr. Monterey Peninsula Coll., 1990, 91, Hartnell Coll., Salinas, Calif., Chapman U., 1992-95, Golden Gate U., 1995-98; adj. prof. Golden Gate U., 1997—. Editor: (jour.) Socioloqus, 1952. Recipient French Govt fellowship, Sorbonne, Paris, 1956; named to list of Great Teachers of Calif., Calif. Assn. Comty. Colls., Santa Barbara, 1984. Home: 33751 E Carmel Valley Rd Carmel Valley CA 93924-9303 Personal E-mail: warwickwolfe@aol.com.

WOLFE, NATHAN, epidemiologist; MA in Biol. Anthropology, Harvard U., DSc in Immunology & Infectious Disease. Asst. prof. Bloomberg Sch. Pub. Health Johns Hopkins U., Balt. Contbr. articles to profl. jours. Named one of Brilliant 10, Popular Sci. mag., 2006; recipient Internat. Rsch. Scientist Devel. award, NIH Fogarty Internat. Ctr., 1999—2006, Dir.'s Pioneer award, NIH, 2005—; Fulbright fellow, 1997—98. Office: Bloomberg Sch Pub Health Johns Hopkins U 615 N Wolfe St E7132 Baltimore MD 21205 Office Phone: 410-614-2539. Office Fax: 410-502-0530. E-mail: nwolfe@jhsph.edu. *

WOLFE, RICHARD PEEL, lawyer; b. Brookhaven, Miss., May 31, 1937; s. Hubert Heuck and Nell (Peel) W.; m. Ann Perkins Terrell, Aug. 20, 1960; children: Susan W. Huppman, Emily W. Leigh. AB magna cum laude, Princeton U., 1959; JD, Harvard U., 1962; M in Civil Law, Tulane U., 1965. Bar: La. 1963, U.S. Dist. Ct. (ea. dist.) La. 1963, U.S. Ct. Appeals (5th cir.) 1963. Assoc. Monroe & Lemann, Attys., New Orleans, 1963—68, ptnr., 1968—96, sect. head, corp. sect., 1974—96, mgmt. com., 1989—93; ptnr. Jones, Walker, Waechter, Poitevent, Carrère & Denègre, Attys., New Orleans, 1997—2005, of counsel, 2006—. Mem. IRS-Tax Lawyers S.W. Regional Liaison Com., 1976-77; presenter in field. Mem. Bd. Liquidation, City Debt for City of New Orleans, 2004—; bd. deacons St. Charles Ave. Presbyn. Ch., 1967—70, 1972—75, chmn., 1970; bd. dirs. New Orleans Opera Assn., 2005—; mem. planning com. Tulane Corp. Law Inst., Tulane Law Sch., 1988—2000; bd. dirs. Met. Crime Commn. of New Orleans, 1997—2001, Bur. Govtl. Rsch., 1984—90; trustee La. Nature and Sci. Ctr., 1980—84; chmn. Gallier Ho. Mus. Coun., Tulane U., 1986—88, trustee, 1978—86; mem. com. to nominate alumni trustees Princeton U., 1979—81, chmn., 1981; mem. Audubon Pk. Commn., New Orleans, 1971—77; trustee Metairie Pk. Country Day Sch., 1973—77; mem. agy. rels. com. United Way of Greater New Orleans, 1973—75; bd. dirs. La. Mus. Found., 2006—. Mem.: ABA (corp. stockholder relationships com. 1967—77, sect. of taxation 1967—97), La. State Bar Assn. (liaison com. with dist. dir. IRS 1974—80, chmn. sect. on taxation 1975—76, task force on legal practice designation and specialization 1981—83, cert. tax law specialist 1986—96), Soc. of War of 1812, Cap and Gown Club (Princeton U.), Harvard Club (N.Y.C.), New Orleans Country Club, Boston Club, La. Club, New Orleans Lawn Tennis Club, Phi Beta Kappa. Republican. Presbyterian. Home: 7916 Plum St New Orleans LA 70118 Office: Jones Walker 201 St Charles Ave Ste 5100 New Orleans LA 70170 Office Phone: 504-582-8182.

WOLFE, SARAH CATHARINE, curator; b. Washington, Nov. 21, 1976; d. David Richard and Ann Furr Wolfe. B in History and Anthropology, Colo. State U., Fort Collins, 1998; M of Maritime History and Underwater Archaeology, East Carolina U., Greenville, NC, 2001. Conservation technician East Carolina U. Maritime Conservation Lab./Joyner Libr., 1999—2001; archaeological rschr. Md. Archaeological Conservation Lab., Prince Frederick, 2001—02; curator of collections and exhibits Mus. Aviation Flight and Tech. Ctr., Robins AFB, Ga., 2002—. Author: (publication) Anglo-American Naval Edged Weapons in the Age of Fighting Sail: Historiographical and Cultural Analysis of the Axe, Pike and Sword as Weapons and Symbols, 1775 — 1865; exhibitions include Total Force: The Workers Behind Robins Air Force Base. Roy N. Lokken Meml. scholar, East Carolina U., 2000. Mem.: Am. Assn. Museums (project head Mus. Aviation 2005), Soc. Hist. Archaeology, Golden Key Nat. Honor Soc., Phi Alpha Theta (v.p. 1997—98), Phi Theta Kappa. Liberal. Avocations: history, underwater archaeology, animals, travel. Office: Mus Aviation Flight and Tech Ctr 1942 Heritage Blvd Robins Afb GA 31098-2442 Home Phone: 478-335-3294; Office Phone: 478-926-7313.

WOLFE, SCOTT W., orthopedic hand surgeon; b. Rye, NY, Aug. 28, 1958; MD, Cornell U., 1984. Intern Roosevelt Hospital, NYC, 1984—86; orthopedics resident Hospital for Special Surgery, NYC, 1986—89; fellowship in hand surgery Columbia U. Coll. of Physicians & Surgeons, NYC, 1989—90; prof. Yale U. Sch. of Medicine, New Haven, dir. hand & upper extremity div.; prof. orthopedic surgery Cornell-Weill Med. Ctr., NYC; chief hand service Hospital for Special Surgery, NYC, clin. dir. orthopedic surgery & attending orthopedic surgeon, dir. hand surgical fellowship; assoc. dir. clinical rsch. Alberto Vilar Ctr. for Hand and Upper Extremity Surgery; chief hand and upper extremity surgery. Named one of NY Mag. Best Doctors in NY, 2001—05. Office: Hospital for Special Surgery 535 E 70th St New York NY 10021 Office Phone: 212-606-1529. Business E-Mail: wolfes@hss.edu.

WOLFE, SIDNEY MANUEL, physician; b. June 12, 1937; s. Fred and Sophia Esther (Marks) W.; m. Suzanne M. Goldberg; children: Hannah, Leah, Rachel, Sarah. BS, Western Res. U., 1960, MD, 1965. Intern. Cleve. Met. Gen. Hosp., 1965-66, resident internal medicine, 1969-70; staff assoc. NIH, 1966-72; dir. Pub. Citizens Health Research Group, Washington, 1972—. Contbr. articles to med. jours. Served with USPHS, 1966-69. McArthur fellowship, 1990—. Office: Pub Citizen Health Rsch Group 1600 20th St NW Washington DC 20009 *

WOLFE, THAD ALLISON, air force officer; b. Coulee Dam, Wash., Oct. 26, 1942; s. Clyde Allison and Leona (Ruffner) W.; m. Jill Ann Strathern, June 4, 1964; children: Thori, Christian, Molly. BS in Mil. Sci., USAF Acad., 1964; MSEE, U. Wyo., 1969; grad., Squadron Officer Sch., 1972, Air Command and Staff Coll., 1978, Nat. War Coll., 1985; grad. sr. exec. program in nat. and internat. security, Harvard U., 1992. Commd. 2nd lt. USAF, 1964, advanced through grades to lt. gen., 1993; ops. flight comdr. 6950th Security Wing, RAF Sta. Chicksands, Eng., 1965-66; signals intelligence ops. officer 6994th Security Squadron, Pleiku, South Vietnam, 1966-67; devel. engr. Def. Intelligence Agy., Va., 1969-70; instr. pilot, flight comdr., asst. sect. comdr. Vance AFB, Okla., 1970-74; aircrew tng. Castle AFB, Calif., 1974-75; crew comdr., ops. officer 325th Bombardment Squadron, Fairchild AFB, Wash., 1975-77; readiness analyst, chief of pers. and adminstrn., exec. officer to dir., directorate ops. and readiness Hdqs. USAF, Washington, 1978-81; comdr. 9th Bombardment Squadron, Carswell AFB, Tex., 1981; dep. comdr. for standardization and evaluation 1st Combat Evaluation Group, Barksdale AFB, La., 1982; command ctr. sr. contr. Hdqs. Strategic Air Command, Offutt AFB, Nebr., 1982-84; vice comdr., then comdr. 509th Bombardment Wing, Pease AFB, N.H., 1985-88; spl. asst. to comdr. for officer profl. devel. Hdqs. Strategic Air Command, Offutt AFB, Nebr., 1988, dep. dir. nat. strategic target list, joint strategic target planning staff, 1988-90; comdr. Strategic Warfare Ctr., Ellsworth AFB, S.D., 1990-92; asst. dep. dir. for ops. Nat. Security Agy., Ft. George G. Meade, Md., 1992-93; vice comdr. Air Combat Command, Langley AFB, Va., 1993-95. Chmn., CEO Internat. Youth Inst., 1996—; chmn. profl. mil. edn. bd. dirs. Air Combat Command, Langley AFB, Va., 1993-95, chief environ. leadership coun., 1993-95; bd. dirs. Air U., Maxwell AFB, Ala., 1995, Inst. Environ. and Natural Resources, Rsch. and Policy, U. Wyo., Laramie, 1995—, Western Rsch. Inst., Laramie, 1995—. Chmn. membership Boy Scouts Am., Rapid City, S.D., 1991. Decorated D.D.S.M., D.S.S.M., Legion of Merit, Bronze Star, Meritorious Svc. medal with three oak leaf clusters, Air medal, Air Force Commendation medal, Vietnam Svc. medal with svc. star, Republic of Vietnam Campaign medal. Mem. USAF Acad. Assn. of Grads., U. Wyo. Alumni Assn., Air Force Assn., Daedalians. Avocations: reading, sports, antiques, gardening. Office: Internat Youth Inst Inc 128 S Royal St Alexandria VA 22314-3337

WOLFE, TOM (THOMAS KENNERLY WOLFE JR.), writer, journalist; b. Richmond, Va., Mar. 2, 1931; s. Thomas Kennerly and Helen (Hughes) W.; m. Sheila Berger; children: Alexandra, Thomas AB, Washington and Lee U., 1951, DLitt (hon.), 1974; PhD in Am. Studies, Yale U., 1957; DFA (hon.), Mpls. Coll. Art, 1971, Sch. of Visual Arts, 1987; LHD (hon.), Va. Commonwealth U., 1983, Southampton Coll., NY, 1984, Randolph-Macon Coll., 1988, Manhattanville Coll., 1988, Longwood Coll., 1989; DLitt (hon.), St. Andrews Presbyn. Coll., 1990, Johns Hopkins U., 1990, U. Richmond, 1993. Reporter Springfield (Mass.) Union,

1956-59; reporter, Latin Am. corr. Washington Post, 1959-62; city reporter N.Y. Herald Tribune, 1962-66; mag. writer N.Y. World Jour. Tribune, 1966-67; contbg. editor New York mag., 1968-76, Esquire Mag., NYC, from 1977. Writer N.Y. Sunday Mag., 1962-66; contbg. artist Harper's Mag., NYC, 1978-81. One-man show of drawings include Maynard Walker Gallery, NYC, 1965, Tunnel Gallery, NYC, 1974; author: The Kandy-Kolored Tangerine-Flake Streamline Baby, 1965, The Electric Kool-Aid Acid Test, 1968, The Pump House Gang, 1968, Radical Chic and Mau-mauing the Flak Catchers, 1970, The Painted Word, 1975, Mauve Gloves and Madmen, Clutter and Vine, 1976, The Right Stuff, 1979 (Am. Book award 1980), In Our Time, 1980, From Bauhaus to Our House, 1981, The Purple Decades: A Reader, 1982, The Bonfire of the Vanities, 1987, A Man in Full, 1998, Ambush at Fort Bragg (audio), 1997, Hooking Up, 2000, I Am Charlotte Simmons, 2004; editor, contbr. The New Journalism, 1973; contbr. articles to Esquire Mag., others. Recipient Front Page awards for humor and fgn. news reporting Washington Newspaper Guild, 1961, Soc. Mag. Writers award for excellence, 1970, Frank Luther Mott Rsch. award, 1973, Harold D. Vursell Meml. award Am. Acad. and Inst. Arts and Letters, 1980, Columbia Journalism award, 1980, Nat. Sculpture Soc. citation for art history, 1980, John Dos Passos award, 1984, Gari Melchers medal, 1986, Benjamin Pierce Cheney medal Ea. Wash. U., 1986, Washington Irving medal St. Nicholas Soc., 1986, Theodore Roosevelt medal Theodore Roosevelt Assn., 1990, Wilbur Cross medal Yale Grad. Sch. Alumni Assn., 1990, St. Louis Literary award, 1990, Quinnipiac Coll. Pres. award, 1993, Golden Plate award, Acad. Achievement, 2005; named Va. Laureate for Lit., 1977; Chicago Tribune Literary Prize for lifetime achievement, 2003. Office: Farrar Straus & Giroux Inc 19 Union Sq W 11th Fl New York NY 10003-3304 *

WOLFE, VERDA NELL, pension consultant, financial planner; b. Sulphur Springs, Tex., Jan. 31, 1927; d. Marvin Alvin and Winnie Davis (Bass) Hamiter; m. James Braddy Wolfe, May 3, 1947; children: James Gordon, William Gregory, Charles Gary. Student, Baylor U., 1948-52, Tex. Tech U., 1974-76. CLU, CFP; cert. pension cons. Estate analyst Estate Fin. Planning Svc., Lubbock, Tex., 1973-76, Planning Cons., Lubbock, 1977-81; pres. DDRW Fin. Svcs., Lubbock, 1982-85, Pension Concepts and Administration, Lubbock, 1986—. Mem. Soc. Fin. Svcs. Profls. (chpt. pres. 1988-89), Inst. Cert. Fin. Planners, Am. Soc. Pension Actuaries and Cons. Avocations: music, painting, gardening. Home: 2125 57th St Lubbock TX 79412-2625 Office: Pension Concepts & Adminstn 2811A 74th St Lubbock TX 79423-1437 Personal E-mail: v_wolfe@sbcglobal.net. Business E-Mail: vwolfe@door.net.

WOLFEN, WERNER F., lawyer; b. Berlin, May 15, 1930; came to U.S., 1939; s. Martin and Ruth Eva (Hamburger) W.; m. Mary Glasier, July 1, 1956; children: Richard, James, Lawrence (dec.). BS, U. Calif., Berkeley, 1950, JD, 1953. Bar: Calif. 1953. Assoc. Irell & Manella, LA, 1953-57, ptnr., 1957-98, sr. ptnr. emeritus, 1999—; pres. Capri Investment Co. LLC, 1999—. Bd. dirs. Broadcom Corp., Calhoun Vision, Inc., Pre-Cash Corp.; bd. visitors UCLA Sch. Arts and Arch., 1995—. Bd. dirs. UCLA Found., 1992-2003; bd. dirs. L.A. Goal, 1994-, pres., 1994-99. Mem. ABA. Democrat. Jewish. Office: Capri Investment Co LLC 1800 Avenue of the Stars Los Angeles CA 90067-4212 Home Phone: 310-472-0032; Office Phone: 310-203-7521. Business E-Mail: wwolfen@irell.com.

WOLFENDEN, RICHARD VANCE, biochemistry educator; b. Oxford, Eng., May 17, 1935; s. John Hulton and Josephine (Vance) W.; m. Anita Gaunitz, June 25, 1965; children: Peter, John. BA, MA, Exeter Coll., Oxford U., Eng., 1958; PhD, Rockefeller Inst., 1964. Asst. prof. chemistry Princeton U., NJ, 1964-70; assoc. prof. biochemistry U. N.C., Chapel Hill, 1970-73, prof. biochemistry, 1973-83, alumni disting. prof., 1983—. Vis. fellow Exeter Coll., Oxford, 1969, vis. prof. U. Montpellier, France, 1976; mem. molecular biology panel NSF, Washington, 1973-76; mem. bio-organic and natural products study sect. NIH, Washington, 1981-86. Mem. editl. bd. Bioorganic Chemistry, 1983—, Biomed. Chem. Letters, 1993—. Fellow AAAS, Am. Acad. Arts and Scis.; mem. NAS, Am. Chem. Soc. (chair biol. divsn. 2000-02), Am. Soc. Biol. Chemists. Democrat. Home: 104 Jolyn Place Chapel Hill NC 27517 Office: U North Carolina Dept Biochemistry Chapel Hill NC 27514

WOLFENSON, AZI U., electrical, mechanical and industrial engineer, consultant; b. Rumania, Aug. 1, 1933; arrived in Peru, 1937; s. Samuel G. and Polea S. (Ulanowski) Wolfenson; m. Rebeca Sterental, Jan. 10, 1983; 1 child, Michael Ben;children from previous marriage: Ida, Jeannette, Ruth, Moises, Alex. Mech., Elec. Engr., U. Nacional de Ingenieria, Peru, 1955; Indsl. Engr., U. Nacional de Ingenieria, 1967; MSc in Indsl. Engring., U. Mich., 1966; PhD in Engring. Mgmt., Pacific Western U., 1983; PhD in Engring. Energy, Century U., 1985; D in Philosophy of Engring. (hon.), World U. Roundtable, Ariz., 1987. Power engr. Peruvian Trading Co., 1956-57; gen. mgr. AMSA ingenieros S.A., 1957-60; prof. U. Nacional de Ingenieria, Peru, 1956-72, dean mech. and elec. engring., 1964-66, dean indsl. engring., 1967-72; dir. SWSA Automotive Parts, Peru, 1954-77; project mgr. Nat. Fin. Corp., Cofide, 1971-73; Peruvian dir. Corporacion Andina de Fomento, CAF, 1971-73; rep. in Peru CAF, 1973-74; pres. DESPRO cons. firm, 1973-76; exec. pres. Electroperu, 1976-80. Cons. engr., 1964—; dir. Tech. Transference Studies, 1971—72. Author: (book) Work Communications, 1966, Programmed Learning, 1966, Production Planning and Control, 1968, Transfer of Technology, 1971, National Electrical Development, 1977, Energy and Development, 1979, El Gran Desafio, 1981, Hacia una politica economica alternativa, 1982, The Power of Communications: The Media, 1987; contbr. articles to newspapers and jours. Mem. Nat. Coun. Fgn. Investment and Tech. Transfer, 1972—73, Superior Coun. Electricity, 1964—66; metal mech. expert for andean group, 1970—71; promoter, co-founder, gen. mgr. La Republica Newspaper, Peru, 1981; pres. PROA Project promotion AG, Switzerland, 1982—; chmn. Inst. for the Devel. of the Ams., Inc., Fla., 1993—; co-founder El Popular, 1983, El Nacional, 1985, Todo Sport, 1993, El Chino, 1994, La Reforma, 1997, El Men, 1999, La Razon, 2001; pres. bd. dirs., newspapers; v.p. bd. dirs. Island Way Cmty. Assn., 1995—97; mem. exec. bd. dirs. Miami State Israel Bonds, 1997; mem. consultative coun. Instituto Peruano de Deportes, 1999; mem. consultive coun. Min. Econ. and Fin., 1973—74; councilman at the Concejo Provincial De Lima, 1969—75; pres. Peruvian Jewish Cmty., 1966—70, Peruvian Hebrew Sch., 1976—78. Named Exec., Gente Mag., 1979; recipient Recognition award, Israel Govt., 1967, Disting. Contbn. award, City of Lima, 1970, 1971, Disting. award, Trujillo, 1978, Huaral, 1979, City Coun. Huancayo, 1980, Piura, 1980, Disting. Contbn. to Elec. Devel. in Peru, 1979, Disting. Svc. awards, Order Merit, Peru, 1980, Disting. Comision Integracion Electrica Regional medal, CIER, 1984, El Sol Radiante, City Hall of Magdalena, Peru, 1995, Medal of Honor, Electrical Engring. Colegio de Ingenieros del Peru, 2003, Spl. award, Gente mag., 2006. Fellow: Brit. Inst. Mgmt., Inst. Prodn. Engrs.; mem.: J.C.C. Fla., FCL, AIIE (sr.), ASME, MTM Assn., AAAS, World Assn. Newspapers (exec. mem. 2003), Asociacion Periodistas Peru, Circulo Periodistas Peru, Swiss sect. PEN Club INternat., Swiss Soc. Writers, United Writers Assn., Assn. Energy Engrs., Am. Nuc. Soc. (vice chmn. 1988, 1990, chmn. Swiss sect. 1991—93, Significant Contbn. to Advancement of Nuc. Sci. award 1995), Inst. Adminstrv. Mgmt., Asociacion Peruana Avance Ciencia, Assn. Mgmt. Sci. (dir. 1968), Am. Inst. Mgmt. Sci., Am. Soc. Engring. Edn., Asociacion Electrotechnica del Peru, Inst. Peruano Ingenieros Mecanicos (pres. 1965—66, v.p. 1967, dir. 1969, 1970, 1976), Colegio Ingenieros Peru (medal of honor award 2003), Alumni Assn. Mich., Pacific Western and Century U., Hebraica Club, Club dr 2000. Home: 3781 NE 208th Ter Miami FL 33180-3835 Office: 3601 NE 207th St Ste 1205 Aventura FL 33180 Personal E-mail: aziwolfenson@aol.com.

WOLFER, DALE, retired music educator; b. Denver, June 2, 1928; s. George Earl and Hazel Grace Wolfer; m. Annette Baldwin, June 26, 1931; children: Chrisann, Suzanne, Michael Shane, Eric Jon. B in music edn., Colo. A&M, 1951; M in music edn., Denver U., 1958. Music dir. Olathe HS, Colo., 1953—54; choral dir. Grand Junction HS, Colo., 1954—58, Littleton HS, Colo., 1958—72, Lanier HS, U. Tex, Austin, Tex., 1972—88; music dir. Hillcrest Sch., Jos, Nigeria, 1988—90; prof. Lutheran Ch. HS, Bratislava, Slovakia, 1990—91; ret., 1991. Ch. worker Lutheran Hour Ministries, Istebna, Poland, 1998, Tikhovitsy, Russia, 99, Wittenberg, Germany, 2000. Summer music studies Western State Coll., Gunnison, Colo., 1948—50, U. Salzburg, Salzburg, Austria, 1968, Fred Waring Workshop, Paul Christiansen Workshop, 1968; mem. nat. com. Nat. Intercollegiate Band, Denver, 1951; host/docent Cherokee Ranch Castle, Sedalia, 2007; ch. choir dir. various denominations, 1983—90, ch. handbell dir., 1994—2003. 1st lt. US Army, 1951—53, Korea. Decorated Purple Heart US Army, Korea, Air medal. Mem.: Am. Choral Dir. (life). Lutheran. Avocations: travel, fishing, hiking, handbells, stained glass art. Home: 1447 Pineridge Ln Castle Rock CO 80108-0213

WOLFERSTEIG, ELOISE SMITH, retired music educator; b. Bklyn., Oct. 7, 1930; d. George Francis and Louise C. (Becker) Smith; m. Robert Frederick Wolfersteig; 1 child, Patricia Lynn Albritton. MusB, West Minster Choir Coll., Princeton, NJ, 1953; MusM, Jamestown Coll., ND, 1958; MEd, Ga. Coll., 1973. Choir dir. St. Francis Assisi Cath. Ch.; tchr. Jacob Tome Inst., Md., 1953—54, Bainbridge (Md.) Elem. Sch., 1954—55; dir. Officers' Wives Nursery Sch., Bermuda, 1955—56; music tchr. Baldwin City Schs., Milledgesville, Ga., 1965—75; gifted edn. tchr. Bibb City Sch., Macon, Ga., 1975—90; music tchr. Cherokee City Sch., Andrews, NC, 1990—91; gifted edn. tchr. Clay City Schs., Hayesville, NC, 1991—95; tech. cons. Andrews, NC, 1995—99; dir. sch. age choirs Blairsville, Ga., 1998—. Finalist Excellence in Singing, Met. Opera, 1958; recipient District Star Tchr., Macon, Ga., 1985, Tchr. of Yr., Spl. Edn., Macon, Ga., 1988. Mem.: DAR (pres., regent), Delta Kappa Gamma, Phi Delta Kappa, Sigma Alpha Iota. Avocations: poetry, art, writing, drawing. Home: 5316 Pine Crest Rd Young Harris GA 30582 Personal E-mail: rfwolfer@alltel.net.

WOLFERSTEIG, JEAN LOIS, medical association administrator, educator; b. Kingston, NY, July 13, 1950; d. Evelyn Anna Schupp and John Raymond Wolfersteig; life ptnr. William Edward Miller. AS in Liberal Arts, Ulster County CC, 1970; BA in Secondary Edn., State U. Coll., 1972; MS in Pub. Svc. Adminstrn., Russell Sage Coll., Albany, New York, 1983. Unit mgr. Wassaic Devel. Ctr., Wingdale, NY, 1972—75, staff devel. specialist, 1976—79; dir. of staff devel. and tng. Westchester Devel. Disabilities Svcs. Office, Tarrytown, NY, 1979—84, Hudson River Psychiat. Ctr., Poughkeepsie, NY, 1984—92, quality mgmt. dir., 1992—98, dir. for facility admin. svcs., 1998—2002, CEO, 2002—. Bd. mem. Cmty. Adv. Bd. for Marist Coll., Poughkeepsie, 1985—90; adj. faculty Westchester CC, Valhalla, 1981—84; bd. mem. Adv. Bd. for Orange County CC. Forensic Mental Health Program, Middletown, NY, 1985—85. Co-author: (international presentations) Balanced Scorecard and Performance Improvement. Chairperson of selection com. Herman B. Snow Scholarship Fund, Poughkeepsie, 1991—2001. Recipient Salute to Women in Industry, Dutchess County YWCA, 1992, Leadership and Svc. award, Nat. Alliance for Mentally Ill (Mid-Hudson), 2006. Mem.: Nat. Alliance Mentally Ill (Leadership award 2006), Nat. Assn. of State Mental Health Dirs., Phi Kappa Phi. Avocations: writing, sailing, travel, gardening. Office: Hudson River Psychiatric Center 10 Ross Cir Poughkeepsie NY 12601 Home Phone: 845-331-5452; Office Phone: 845-483-3400. Business E-Mail: hrqajlw@omh.state.ny.us.

WOLFF, ALEJANDRO DANIEL, ambassador; b. 1956; d. Gerard and Toni Wolff; m. Alexandra Wolff; children: Philip, Michael. Grad. magna cum laude, UCLA, 1978. Fgn. svc. officer US Dept. State, 1979—, mem. policy planning staff Washington, 1981—82; amb. Am. Embassy, Rabat, 1983—85, Brussels, 1985—88; with Office of Soviet Union Affairs US Dept. State, Washington, 1988—89, with Office Under Sec. Polit. Affairs, 1989—91; amb. Am. Embassy, Santiago, Chile, 1991—94, dep. chief of mission to Cyprus Nicosia, 1994—96; dep. exec. sec. US Dept. State, Washington, 1996—98, exec. asst. to Sec. of State Madeleine Albright and Colin Powell, 1998—2001; dep. chief of mission US Mission to UN, Paris, 2001—05; dep. US rep. to UN US Dept. State, NYC, 2005—, acting permanent US rep. to UN, 2006—07. Office: UN 140 E 45th St 7th Fl New York NY 10017

WOLFF, BRIAN RICHARD, metal products executive; b. LA, Dec. 11, 1955; s. Arthur Richard and Dorothy Virginia (Johnson) Wolff; children from previous marriage: Ashley Rachael, Taryn Nicole. BSBA, Calif. State U., Chico, 1980; postgrad., U. Phoenix, 1990—. Registered counseling practitioner Calif., cert. emergency response team Huntington Beach Fire Dept., 2003; ordained min. Prog. Universal Life Ch., 1996; registered guidance practitioner Calif. Sales rep. Federated Metals Corp./ASARCO, Long Beach, Calif., 1980-82, dist. sales mgr., 1983-84; sales mgr. Copper Alloys Corp., Beverly Hills, Calif., 1982-83; dir. mktg. Federarted-Fry Metals/Cookson, Long Beach, Industry and Paramount, Calif., 1984-87; regional sales mgr. Colonial Metals Co., LA, 1987-91; nat. sales mgr. Calif. Metal X/Metal Briquetting Co., LA, 1991-93; sales engr. Ervin Industries, Inc., Ann Arbor, Mich., 1993-95. Tech. sales mgr. GSP Metals & Chems. Co., 1987—91; cons. sales Calif. Metal Exch., LA, 1987—91, Atlas Pacific, Inc., Bloomington, 1993—2005, mgr. sales, 2005—. Contbr. poetry to various publs. Mem. citizens adv. com. bus. Calif. Legislature., 1983; bd. trustees Newport Beach (Calif.) Alano Club, 2002—, pres., 2003—; bd. dirs. H.O.W. Hall, Huntington Beach, Calif., 2006—. Mem.: NRA, Soc. Die Cast Engrs., Am. Electroplaters Soc., Steel Structures Painting Coun., Calif. Cast Metals Assn., Am. Foundrymen Soc., Non Ferrous Founders Soc., Internat. Sculpture Ctr. Republican. Presbyterian. Avocations: scuba diving, tennis, fishing, trap shooting, hunting. Office Phone: 909-421-1200. E-mail: brian@atlaspacific.net.

WOLFF, CANDIDA (CANDI), federal official; b. Sharon, Conn., June 9, 1964; m. Mark Roger Wolff; 2 children. BA in Math & Polit. Sci., Mount Holyoke Coll., 1986; JD, George Washington U., 1989. Pub. policy lobbyist Akin, Gump, Strauss, Hauer & Feld, LLP, 1989—93; tax counsel to Senator Malcolm Wallop US Senate, 1993—95; legis. counsel US Senate Steering Com., 1995—96, dep. staff dir. Senate Rep. Policy Com., 1997—2000; dep. asst. to v.p. for legis. affairs The White House, 2001—02, asst. to v.p. for legis. affairs., 2002—04, asst. to pres., dir. legis. affairs, 2005—; ptnr. Washington Coun. Ernst & Young, 2004. Office: The White House 2nd Fl, West Wing 1600 Pennsylvania Ave NW Washington DC 20500 Office Phone: 202-456-2230. Office Fax: 202-456-0200.

WOLFF, CATHERINE ELIZABETH, opera company executive; b. Evanston, Ill., June 11, 1957; AB with honors, Vassar Coll., 1979; MA in Performing Arts Mgmt., Am. U., 1982. Cert. exec. program for non-profits arts leaders Stanford Graduate Sch. Bus., Ctr. for Social Innovation/Nat. Arts Strategies, 2007. Adminstrv. asst. Opera Am., 1982-85; artistic adminstr. Pitts. Opera, 1985-94; exec. dir. Del. Symphony Orch., Wilmington, 1994-95; gen. dir. Syracuse (N.Y.) Opera Co., 1996—. Music panelist NYS Coun. Arts, 2000—02, co-chair music panel, 2003, auditor, 2004—. Mem. steering com. Arts and Culture Leadership Alliance Ctrl. NY, 2004—07, founding pres., 2005—06. McGuire fellow Vassar Coll., 1979. Mem. Opera Am.(Career Svc. award 2006), Am. Symphony Orch. League, Phi Beta Kappa. Office: Syracuse Opera Co PO Box 1223 Syracuse NY 13201-1223 Business E-Mail: cwolff@syracuseopera.com.

WOLFF, CHRISTOPH JOHANNES, music historian, educator; b. Solingen, Germany, May 24, 1940; came to U.S., 1970; s. Hans Walter and Annemarie (Halstenbach) W.; m. Barbara Mahrenholz, Aug. 28, 1964; children: Katharina, Dorothea, Stephanie. Student, U. Berlin, 1960-63, U. Freiburg, Germany, 1963-65; Dr. Phil., U. Erlangen, Germany, 1966; MusD, New Eng. Conservatory, 1999; LHD, Valparaiso U., 2002; PhD (hon.), U. Jena, Germany, 2005. Lectr. U. Erlangen, 1966-69; asst. prof. U. Toronto, Ont., Can., 1968-70; assoc. prof. musicology Columbia U., 1970-73, prof., 1973-76; prof. musicology Harvard U., 1976—, William Powell Mason prof., 1985—2002, Adams Univ. prof., 2002—, dept. chmn., 1980-88, 90-91. Vis. prof. Princeton U., 1973, 75; hon. prof. U. Freiburg, Germany, 1990—; acting dir. Harvard U. Libr., 1991—92; dir. Bach Archive, Leipzig, Germany, 2001—; dean Grad. Sch. Arts and Scis., 1992—2000. Author: Der Stile Antico in der Musik J.S. Bachs, 1968, The String Quartets of Haydn, Mozart and Beethoven, 1980, Bach Compendium, 7 vols., 1986—89, Bach: Essays on His Life and Music, 1991, Mozart's Requiem, 1994, The World of Bach Cantatas, 1997, The New Bach Reader, 1998, Johann Sebastian Bach: The Learned Musician, 2000; contbr. articles to profl. jours.; editor: Bach-Jahrbuch, 1974—2004, critical edits. of music by Scheidt, Buxtehude, Bach, Mozart and Hindemith. Recipient Dent medal, Royal Mus. Assn., London, 1978, Humboldt prize, Alexander von Humboldt Found., 1996. Fellow: Am. Philos. Soc., Am. Acad. Arts and Scis.; mem.: Gesellschaft fuer Musikforschung, Saxon Acad. of Scis. (Leipzig), Am. Musicol. Soc., Internat. Musicol. Soc. Home: 182 Washington St Belmont MA 02478-3560 Office: Harvard U Dept Music Cambridge MA 02138-5723

WOLFF, DEBORAH H(OROWITZ), lawyer; b. Phila., Apr. 6, 1940; d. Samuel and Anne (Manstein) Horowitz; m. Morris H. Wolff, May 15, 1966 (div.); children: Michelle Lynn, Lesley Anne; m. Walter Allan Levy, June 7, 1987. BS, U. Pa., 1962, MS, 1966; postgrad., Sophia U., Tokyo, 1968; JD, Villanova U., 1979, LLM, 1988. Tchr. Overbrook H.S., Phila., 1962-68; homebound tchr. Lower Merior Twp., Mongomery County, 1968-71; asst. dean U. Pa., Phila., 1975-76; law clk. Stassen, Kostos and Mason, Phila., 1977-78; assoc. Spencer, Sherr, Moses and Zuckerman, Norristown, Pa., 1980-81; ptnr. Wolff Assocs., Phila., 1981—. Lectr. law and estate planning, Phila., 1980—. Founder Take a Brother Program; bd. dirs. Germantown Jewish Ctr.; h.s. sponsor World Affairs Club, Phila., 1962-68; mem. exec. com., sec. bd. Crime Prevention Assn., Phila., treas., bd. dirs., 1965—; v.p. bd. dirs. U. Pa. Alumnae Bd., Phila., 1965—, pres. bd. dirs., 1993—, v.p. organized classes, bd. crime prevention; chmn. urban conf. Boys Club Am., 1987, treas., 1999; active Hahnmann Brain Tumor Rsch. Bd.; v.p., bd. dirs. Crime Prevention; treas. Assn. of Alumnae ds.; mem. Alumni Class Leadership Counsel bd. U. Pa., 2001—, sec., 2006-. Recipient 3d Ann. Cmty. Svc. award Phila. Mayor's Com. for Women, 1984; named Pa. Heroine of Month, Ladies Home Jour., 1984. Mem.: Lions (pres. Germantown Club 1997—). Avocations: bridge, tennis. Home and Office: 422 W Mermaid Ln Philadelphia PA 19118-4204 Personal E-mail: debbyw@comcast.net.

WOLFF, DERISH MICHAEL, economist; b. Boston, May 14, 1935; s. Nathan and Ruth Mae (Derish) W.; m. Maureen Robinson; children: Jeffrey Scott, Hayley Beth. BA, U. Pa., Phila., 1957; MBA, Harvard U., Cambridge, Mass., 1959. Fin. analyst Sigmund Werner, Inc., Belleville, NJ, 1959-61; devel. economist Louis Berger, Inc., East Orange, NJ, 1961-65, chief economist, 1965-67, v.p., 1968-75, exec. v.p., 1976-82, pres., CEO, 1982—2002, chmn., 2002—. Dir. Berger Group Holdings, CHELBI, Ammann & Whitney, Va. Maintenance Svcs., Klohn-Crippen, Berger, Devine, Yaeger; guest lectr. UN, Fgn. Svc. Inst., Newark Inst. Tech., U. Nev., Ga. Inst. Tech., The New Sch., Harvard U., Rutgers U., U. Denver; vis. lectr. MIT, 2001—; mem. industry adv. panel Dept. of State, 2001-05; mem. Bretton Woods Com., 1987—. Mem. editl. bd. Modern Engring. Tech, 1978-80, Nat. Devel.-Modern Govt., 1972-79, Constrn. Bus. Review, 1991-95. Mem. adv. com. NJ Inst. Tech., 1995-2006; class chmn. U. Pa. Ann. Giving, 1975-82; mem. adv. bd. Huntsman Program Internat. Studies and Bus., U. Pa., 1997—; U.S. presdl. trade del. to Japan, 1986; indsl. sector adv. com. Dept. of Commerce, 1988-92; adv. com. US Trade and Devel. Program, 1989-92; bd. overseers NJ Inst. Tech., 2006. Recipient Pres.'s medal for lifetime achievement, N.J. Inst. Tech., 2003. Mem. Am. Cons. Engrs. Coun. (chair internat. engring. com. 1983-85, vice chair 1986-93), Internat. Engring. and Constrn. Industries Coun. (del. 1986, 87, chmn. 1988-90), Bldg. Futures Coun. (co-chmn. 1994-), Ctr. for Strategic and Internat. Studies (steering group/GATT negotiations 1989), Phi Beta Kappa. Clubs: Harvard, Penn. Jewish. Office: Berger Group Holdings Inc 100 Halsted St East Orange NJ 07018-2699 Home Phone: 908-854-2939; Office Phone: 973-678-1960. Business E-Mail: dwolff@louisberger.com.

WOLFF, EDWARD, physician; b. NYC, Apr. 15, 1941; s. Julius and Molly W.; m. Marilyn Alice Pels; children: Shanna, Loryn, Kimberly. BS, Muhlenberg Coll., 1962; MD, Georgetown U., 1966. Intern U. Ala. Hosp., Brimingham, 1966-67; resident N.Y. Med. Coll., NYC, 1967-71; physician pvt. practice, Great Neck, NY, 1976—. Attending physician North Shore U. Hosp., Manhasset, NY, St. Francis Hosp. Heart Ctr., Roslyn, NY. Fellow Am. Coll. Physicians; mem. AMA, N.Y. State Med. Soc., Nassau County Med. Soc. Office: Ste 404 107 Northern Blvd Great Neck NY 11021 Office Phone: 516-498-1818.

WOLFF, EDWARD ALVIN, electronics engineer; b. Chgo., Oct. 31, 1929; s. Samuel S. and Lillian P. Wolff; m. Anna Lee Tishk, June 19, 1951; children: David Steven, Eliot Marvin, Susan Toby. BSEE, U. Ill., 1951, MS, 1953; PhD, U. Md., 1961. Electronic scientist Naval Research Lab., Washington, 1951-54; project engr. Md. Electronic Mfg. Corp., Litton Industries, College Park, Md., 1956-59, Electromagnetic Research Corp., College Park, Md., 1959-61; engring. mgr. Aero Geo Astro-Keltec Industries/Aiken Industries, Alexandria, Va., 1961-67; v.p. Geotronics, Inc., Falls Church, Va., 1967-71; supervisory electronics engr. NASA Goddard Space Flight Ctr., Greenbelt, Md., 1971—; system mgr. Network TDRS System, 1981-89, MRJ, Inc., Oakton, Va., 1989-98; cons. in field, 1998—. Instr. Tex. A&M U., 1962. Author: Spacecraft Technology, 1962, Antenna Analysis, 1966, 2d edit., 1988, Geoscience Instrumentation, 1974, Urban Alternatives, 1975, Microwave Engineering and Systems Applications, 1988. Mem. Md. Gov.'s Sci. Resources Adv. Bd., 1963—67; pres. U.S. Environment and Resources Coun., 1972—75; treas. World Environment and Resources Coun., 1975—81. With US Army, 1954—56. Fellow: IEEE (life; bd. dirs. 1971—72), Washington Acad. Scis.; mem.: NSPE, AIAA, Phi Eta Sigma, Sigma Tau, Eta Kappa Nu. Home: 16870 Island Cove Dr Apt 130 Jupiter FL 33477-2356 Personal E-mail: ewolff@bigfoot.com. *Everything I have done has been with the help of others. In return, as I have acquired management responsibilities, a primary objective has been to help others achieve their goals.*

WOLFF, EDWARD NATHAN, economist, educator; b. Long Branch, NJ, Apr. 10, 1946; s. Arthur Seymour and Ethel (Kalmenoff) Wolff; m. Jane Zandra Forman, Nov. 27, 1977; children: Spencer, Ashley. BA, Harvard U., 1968; PhD, Yale U., 1974. Rsch. assoc. Nat. Bur. Econ. Rsch., NYC, 1974-77, 2001—; asst. prof. NYU, NYC, 1974-79, assoc. prof., 1979-84, prof., 1984—; mng. editor Rev. Income and Wealth, 1987—2004; sr. scholar Levy Econs. Inst., 1999—. Cons. Aspen Inst., 1993, World Bank, 1994—97, Jerome Levy Econs. Inst., 1995—96, Century Found., 1999—2002, UN, 2000—02, 2005—06, Math. Policy Rsch., 2002—03, Econ. Policy Inst., 2000—06; others; vis. scholar Russell Sage Found., 2003—04. Author: Growth, Accumulation and Unproductive Activity, 1987, Top Heavy: A Study of Increasing Unequality of Wealth in America, 1995, Economics of Poverty, Inequality, and Discrimination, 1997, Retirement Insecurity, 2002, Does Education Really Help? Skill, Work and Inequality, 2006; editor: International Comparisons of Household Wealth

Distribution, 1987, Research in Economic Inequality, Vol. 4, 1993, The Economics of Productivity, 1997, Quality of Life in Advanced Industrialized Nations, 2004, International Perspectives on Household Wealth, 2006; co-author: Productivity and American Leadership: The Long View, 1989, Competitiveness, Convergence, and International Specialization, 1993, Downsizing in America, 2003, Retirement Income: The Crucial Role of Social Security, 2005; co-editor: International Perspectives on Profitability and Accumulation, 1992, Poverty and Prosperity in the USA in the Late Twentieth Century, 1993, Convergence of Productivity, 1994, Assets for the Poor, 2001; contbr. articles to profl. jours. Grantee, NSF, 1984—90, Exxon Found., 1984—88, Fishman-Davidson Ctr. U. Pa., 1987—89, Sloan Found., 1990—98, 2006—, Mellon Found., 1991—95, Russell Sage Found., 1997—2003, Ford Found., 1997—2005, Kauffman Found., 2004—07, Sloan Found., 2006—. Mem.: Eastern Econs. Assn. (pres. 2002—03), Internat. Input-Output Assn. (coun. 1995—2003), Internat. Assn. Rsch. Income and Wealth (coun. mem. 1987—), Am. Econ. Assn. Avocations: tennis, skiing. Office: NYU Dept Econs 269 Mercer St Rm 700 New York NY 10003-6633 Home Phone: 212-924-4386; Office Phone: 212-998-8917. Business E-Mail: ew1@nyu.edu.

WOLFF, EDWIN RAY, retired construction engineer, consultant; b. Continental, Ohio, Mar. 24, 1933; s. Ray Simeon and Datha Ruth (Donaldson) W.; m. Elizabeth I. Sutterlin, Feb. 16, 1963; children: Sandra Jean, Donald Scott. BSME, U. Toledo, 1969. Registered profl. engr., Ohio. Mem. design staff City of Ft. Lauderdale, Fla., 1965-67; mem. design/spl. orders staff Devilbliss Co., Toledo, 1967-69; engineer, mem. R & D staff Toledo Scale, 1969-70; design/constrn. engr. Lucas County Engr., Toledo, 1970-98, ret., 1998. Cons. G.A.F., Inc., Oregon, Ohio, 1980—. Vol. Spl. Olympics, Lucas County, 1989—; trustee, bd. elders Fairgreen Ch., Toledo, 1975—; trustee Beneficial Union Pittsburg, 1986—2007; former bd. dirs. Lucas County ARC; bd. dirs. Cmty. Residential Svcs., Inc. With Combat Engrs. Corps, 1956-58. Mem. Phi Kappa Chi, Pi Kappa Alpha. Democrat. Presbyterian. Home: 4312 Grantley Rd Toledo OH 43613-3738

WOLFF, ELEANOR BLUNK, actress; b. Bklyn., July 10, 1931; d. Sol and Bessie (Schultz) Blunk; m. William Howard Wolff, June 19, 1955; children: Ellen Jill, Rebecca Louise. BA in Edn., Speech and Theatre, Bklyn. Coll., 1972, MS in Spl. Edn., 1975; postgrad., Adelphi U., Garden City, NY, 1980-81. Cert. tchr., N.Y. Fashion model Garment Ctr., NYC, 1949—50; sec. to v.p. out-of-town/export sales Liebmann Breweries Inc., Bklyn., 1950—58; tchr. N.Y.C. Bd. Edn., Bklyn., 1971-76; sec. to dir. environ. programs, pub. affairs officers, speakers bur. project leader Power Authority State of N.Y., NYC, 1976-85; tchr. Hewlett-Woodmere (N.Y.) Sch. Dist., 1986-89; instr. adult edn. County of Nassau, NY, 1986-97. Actress/model, N.Y.C., 1992—; mem. Love Creek Prodns. V.p. program devel. for youth ctr. Wavecrest Gardens Cmty. Assn., Far Rockaway, NY, 1959-63; teen leader Far Rockaway Jewish Ctr. Youth Coun., 1965-68; pres. Parents Assn. P.S. 215Q, Far Rockaway, 1966-67; tutor NYC Bd. Edn. Sch. Vol. Program, Far Rockaway, 1969-71, New Ground Inc., Mineola, NY, 2004—; chair civic affairs Dem. Club, Far Rockaway, 1961-63; committeewoman Dem. Ctrl. Com., Queens County, NY, 1963-64, Nassau County Dem. Party, 1998-; v.p. membership, constn. com. Nassau County Dem. Women's Caucus, 1988, 89; awards com. Bklyn. Coll., 1993-97, chair theatre arts affiliate, 1990-94, 2001-; comm. adv. com. Hewlett-Woodmere Sch. Dist. 14, 1996-97, zone leader, 2007—; press/media steward vol. Goodwill Games, 1998; vol. program presenter Child Abuse Prevention Svcs., Roslyn, NY, 2003-05; vol. income tax assistance IRS, 2004-. Named Mother of Yr. Congregation Shaaray Tefila, Far Rockaway, 1968; recipient Merit award Wavecrest Gardens Cmty. Assn., 1960, Theater Arts Trophy for disting. svc. Bklyn. Coll. Alumni, 1992. Mem.: SAG (awards nominating com. 2000—01, 2006—07), AFTRA, Actors Equity Assn., Alumni Assn. Bklyn. Coll. (life), Cmty. Garden Club of North Woodmere Park (corr. sec. 2001—03, rec. sec. 2006—). Avocations: painting, piano, gardening. Home Phone: 516-295-1649. Personal E-mail: eleanorwolff@cs.com.

WOLFF, ELROY HARRIS, lawyer; b. NYC, May 20, 1935; s. Samuel and Rose Marian (Katz) W.; children: Ethan, Anna Louise. AB, Columbia U., 1957, LL.B., 1963. Bar: N.Y. 1963, D.C. 1969. Assoc. Kaye, Scholer, Fierman, Hays & Handler, NYC, 1963-65; atty.-adviser to commr. FTC, Washington, 1965-67; sr. trial atty. Dept. Transp., 1967-69; assoc. Leibman, Williams, Bennett, Baird & Minow, Washington, 1969-70, ptnr., 1970-72, Sidley & Austin, Washington, 1972-99; sr. counsel Sidley Austin Brown & Wood, Washington, 2000—04. Mem. adv. com. on practice and procedure FTC, 1969-71; chmn. adv. com. on procedural reform CAB, 1975 Served to 1st lt. USAF, 1957-60. Mem. ABA (chmn. spring meeting program 1992-94, coun. 1995-98), Union Internationale des advocats (chmn. competition law com. 1994-98), Army and Navy Club. Office: 1629 K St NW Ste 300 Washington DC 20036 Home Phone: 302-539-7311; Office Phone: 202-257-4035. Business E-Mail: e.wolff@mchsi.com.

WOLFF, FRANK PIERCE, JR., lawyer; b. St. Louis, Feb. 27, 1946; s. Frank P. and Beatrice (Stein) W.; m. Susan Scallet, May 11, 1984; children: Elizabeth McLane, Victoria Hancox. BA, Middlebury Coll., 1968; JD, U. Va., 1971. Bar: Mo. 1971, U.S. Ct. Appeals (5th cir.) 1974, U.S. Ct. Appeals (8th cir.) 1975, U.S. Supreme Ct. 1975. Ptnr. Lewis, Rice & Fingersh, St. Louis, 1971—90; ptnr., sect. leader, bus. and transactional counseling sect., mem. oper. group Bryan Cave LLP, St. Louis, 1997—. Bd. dirs. Misco Shawnee, Inc. Bd. dirs. Leadership St. Louis, 1985-88, Washington U. Child Guidance Clinic, St. Louis, 1976-79, Jewish Family and Children's Svc., St. Louis, 1981-83, John Burroughs Sch., 1995-2000, BJC Health Sys., Inc., 1998-2001, The Butterfly House, 2001—; gen. counsel Mo. Bot. Garden, St. Louis, 1981—, Mo. Hist. Soc., St. Louis, 1997—; trustee St. Louis Children's Hosp., 1995-2001, chairperson mission vision and values com., 1996-2001, mem. exec. com., 1997-99; co-chmn. Parks Task Force, 2004 Inc. Capt. USAR, 1968-76. Mem. ABA, Mo. Bar Assn., Bar Assn. Met. St. Louis (chmn. corp. sect. 1984-85), Noonday Club, Westwood County Club (chmn. fin. com. 1989-91, treas. 1989-91, v.p. 1991-93, pres. 1994-95, exec. com. 1989-95). Home: 17 Clerbrook Ln Saint Louis MO 63124-1202 Office: Bryan Cave LLP One Metropolitan Square 211 N Broadway Ste 3600 Saint Louis MO 63102-2733 Office Phone: 314-259-2330. Business E-Mail: fpwolff@bryancave.com.

WOLFF, GRACE SUSAN, pediatric cardiologist; b. Rome, NY; BS, Le Moyne Coll., 1961; MD, Med. Coll. Wis., 1965. Diplomate Am. Bd. Pediatrics, Pediatric Cardiology. Intern St. Vincents Hosp., NYC, 1965-66; pediat. resident Babies Hosp.-Columbia Presbyn., 1967-69; fellow in pediat. cardiology Childrens Hosp., Boston, 1969-71; chief divsn. pediat. cardiology U. Miami-Jackson Meml. Hosp., 1995—2005; prof. U. Miami, 1984; pediatrician, pediatric cardiologist U. Miami-Jackson Meml. Hosp., 1977—. Mem. Am. Acad. Pediats., Am. Bd. Pediats., NASPE, Am. Acad. Pediat., Am. Coll. Cardiology, Am. Heart Assn. Office: U Miami-Jackson Meml Hosp PO Box 016960-R76 Miami FL 33101 Office Phone: 305-585-6683. Business E-Mail: gwolff@med.miami.edu.

WOLFF, GREGORY STEVEN, insurance company executive; b. Manchester, Conn., Dec. 10, 1951; s. Thomas J. and M. Elizabeth (Grandburg) W.; m. Elizabeth Mae Heppenstall, June 3, 1971; children: Keith J., James T., Kyle M. BA in Edn., U. Conn., 1974. Cert. fin. planner. Insurance salesman Northwestern Mut. Life, Glastonbury, Conn., 1974-76, Wolff-Zackin & Assocs., Inc., Vernon, Conn., 1976—2001; chmn. bd. dirs., mng. mem. Wolff-Zackin Fin. LLC, Vernon, 2001—. Lectr. in field; bd. dirs. Savs. Bank of Manchester Found., bd. dirs., Ea. Conn. Health Network, bd.overseers Internat. Inst. Sport. Contbr. articles to profl. jours.; co-author: Financial Need Analysis I, cassette prog. Co-founder Manchester Soccer Camp, 1981; bd. overseers Internat. Inst. of Sport. Mem. Nat. Assn. Life Underwriters, Conn. Assn. Life Underwriters, Hartford Assn. Life Underwriters (past pres.), Million Dollar Round Table, Ct. of Table. Methodist. Avocations: tennis, golf, coaching youth sports. Home: 126 Tamarac Dr Glastonbury CT 06033-1941 Office: Wolff-Zackin Fin LLC PO Box H Vernon Rockville CT 06066-1620

WOLFF, HERBERT ERIC, banker, former army officer; b. Cologne, Germany, May 24, 1925; s. Hugo and Juanna Anna (Van Dam) W.; m. Alice (Billy) Rafael, Nov. 13, 1946 (dec. July, 1987); children: Karen (dec. Jan., 1992), Herbert E., Allen R. BA, Rutgers U., 1953; BS, U. Md., 1957; MA, George Washington U., 1962; grad., US Army War Coll., 1962, Harvard U., 1979. Commd. 2nd lt. US Army, 1945, advanced through grades to maj. gen.; served in Fed. Republic of Germany, Greece, Iran, Republic of Korea, Australia, New Guinea, The Phillipines, Japan and Socialist Republic of Vietnam; dep. dir. ops. NSA and Chief CSS, Ft. Meade, Md., 1973—75; dep. corps. comdr. V. Corps US Army, Frankfurt, Germany, 1975-77, comdr. gen. US Army Western Command Hawaii, 1977-81; with First Hawaiian Bank, Honolulu, 1981-2000, sr. v.p., corp. sec., to 2000; hon. consul gen. (Dató) US Pacific region Govt. of Malaysia, Honolulu, 1985—. Author: The Man on Horseback, 1962, The Tenth Principle of War Public Support, 1964, The Military Instructor, 1968. Exec. bd. Aloha coun. Boy Scouts Am.; bd. dirs. USO, Girl Scouts of US, Hawaii, Found. Armed Forces Ctr. Security Studies; vice chmn. March of Dimes; v.p. Hawaii Com. Fgn. Rels.; past pres. Pacific Asian Affairs Coun., Hawaii Army Mus. Soc. Decorated Bronze Star with V and 3 oak leaf clusters, Air medal (24) US Army, Purple Heart, Gallantry Cross with 2 palms, Gallantry Cross with palm and silver star Nat. Order 5th class South Vietnam, Order Nat. Security Merit Choen-Su S. Korea, D.S.M. with oak leaf clusters (2), Silver Star with oak leaf cluster US Army, Legion of Merit with 3 oak leaf clusters, D.F.C., Combat Infantry Badge with two stars, master parachutist, Army aviator; named Citizen of Yr. Fed. Exec. Bd., 1987. Mem. 1st Inf. Divsn. Assn., 1st Cav. Divsn. Assn., Plaza Club (pres., bd. dirs.), Waialae Country Club, Rotary, Phi Kappa Phi. Office: First Hawaiian Ctr 999 Bishop St Honolulu HI 96813-0001 Personal E-mail: generalherbwolff@aol.com. *History is a gift we borrow and hope to pass on. Forget the past and be doomed to repeat it. Remember the past and accept the challenge to convince others.*

WOLFF, JESSE DAVID, lawyer; b. Mpls., Aug. 26, 1913; s. Maurice I. and Annalee (Weiskopf) W.; m. Elizabeth Hess, Nov. 22, 1939; children: Nancy Nicholas, Paula, Daniel Jesse. BA summa cum laude, Dartmouth Coll., 1935; JD, Harvard U., 1938. Bar: N.Y. 1938. Practiced in, NYC, 1938—; assoc., then ptnr., to counsel Weil, Gotshal & Manges, 1938-88, 88—, sr. mng. ptnr., 1966-86. Past dir., dep. chmn. Sotheby Parke Bernet Group (Eng.); past mem. adv. bd. Sotheby's Inc. Past hon. trustee Greater N.Y. ARC; past mem. exec. com. Salvation Army, N.Y.C. Served with AUS, 1942-45. Mem. ABA, Judge Adv. Gen. Assn. Office: Weil Gotshal & Manges 767 5th Ave 31st Fl New York NY 10153-0119 Business E-Mail: jesse.wolff@weil.com.

WOLFF, JOSH, professional soccer player; b. Stone Mountain, Ga., Feb. 25, 1977; m. Angela Wolff, Nov. 11, 2000; 2 children. Attended, Univ. S.C. Forward Chgo. Fire, 1998—2003, Kansas City Wizards, 2003—06, TSV 1860 München, Germany, 2006—. 47 caps, 10 goals U.S. Nat. Soccer Team, 1999—; mem. U.S. World Cup team, 2002, 06. Named to Major League Soccer All-Star team, 2002, 2004. Mailing: US Soccer Fedn 1801 S Prairie AVe Chicago IL 60616

WOLFF, L. THOMAS, physician, educator; b. Suffern, NY, 1942; MD, Albany Med. Coll., 1968. Dir. emeritus rural med. edn. program Upstate Med. U., Syracuse, NY; co-founder N.Y. State Area Health Edn. Sys.; disting. teaching prof. emeritus family medicine SUNY Upstate Med. U., NY. Co-investigator IDEATEL. Mem.: ABFP (pres. 1998—2003). Office: SUNY Upstate Med U Div Family Medicine 200 Madison Irving Med Ctr Syracuse NY 13210

WOLFF, LARRY, history professor; s. Robert and Renee Wolff; m. Perri Klass; children: Benjamin Orlando Klass, Josephine Charlotte Paulina, Anatol Elvis Klass. AB, Harvard Coll., Cambridge, Mass., 1979; PhD in History, Stanford U., Calif., 1984. Prof. history Boston Coll., 1986—2006, NYU, 2006—. Author: (history book) Venice and the Slavs: The Discovery of Dalmatia in the Age of Enlightenment (Barbara Jelavich prize, 2002), Inventing Eastern Europe: The Map of Civilization on the Mind of the Enlightenment, Postcards from the End of the World: Child Abuse in Freud's Vienna, The Vatican and Poland in the Age of the Partitions, (novel) The Boys and their Baby. Fellow Guggenheim fellowship, Guggenheim Found., 2002, Am. Coun. of Learned Societies fellowship, Am. Coun. of Learned Societies, 1996, Fulbright fellowship, U.S. Fulbright Commn., 1981. Mem.: Soc. for Austrian and Habsburg History (assoc.; exec. com. mem. 2002—06), Am. Soc. for Eighteenth-Century Studies (assoc.; exec. bd. mem. 2005), Am. Assn. for the Advancement of Slavic Studies (assoc.), Am. Hist. Assn. (assoc.; officer, rsch. divsn. 2002—05), Am. Acad. of Arts and Sciences (life). Achievements include research concerning the "invention" of Eastern Europe, how Europe came to be conceived as being divided into an East and a West, that is, Eastern Europe and Western Europe. Avocations: opera, baseball, music, movies. Office: NYU History Dept 53 Washington Square South New York NY 10012

WOLFF, MANFRED ERNST, chemist, pharmaceutical executive; b. Berlin, Feb. 14, 1930; came to U.S., 1933; s. Adolph Abraham and Kate (Fraenkel) W.; m. Helen S. Scandalis, Aug. 1, 1953 (div. 1971); children: Stephen Andrew, David James, Edward Allen; m. Susan E. Hurbert, Jan. 19, 1973 (div. 1975); m. A. Gloria Johnson, Dec. 25, 1982. BS, U. Calif., Berkeley, 1951, MS, 1953, PhD, 1955. Registered U.S. patent agt. Rsch. fellow U. Va., 1955-57; sr. medicinal chemist Smith, Kline & French Labs., Phila., 1957-60; mem. faculty U. Calif., San Francisco, 1960-82, prof. medicinal chemistry, 1965-82, chmn. dept. pharm. chemistry, 1970-82; dir. discovery rsch. Allergan Labs, Irvine, Calif., 1982-84; v.p. discovery rsch. Allergan Pharms., Irvine, 1984-89; v.p. R & D Immunopharmaceutics Inc., San Diego, 1989-91, sr. v.p. R & D, 1991-95; pres. Intellepharm., Inc., Laguna Beach, Calif., 1997—. Adj. prof. medicinal chemistry U. So. Calif., 1982—; elected mem. U.S. Pharm. Conv. Com. of Revision, 1990—; lectr. Sch. Med. Chemistry Drew U., NJ, 1998-. Editor: Burger's Medicinal Chemistry and Drug Discovery, Vol. 1-5, 5th edit., 1995-97; asst. editor Jour. Medicinal Chemistry, 1968-71; mem. editl. bd. Medicinal Chemistry Rsch., 1991-95, PharmSci., 1999-2004; contbr. articles to profl. jours.; patentee in field. Fellow AAAS, Am Assn. Pharm. Scientists; mem. Am. Chem. Soc. Achievements include discovery of Alphagan and Lumigan medicines for glaucoma, Tazorac medicine for psoriasis, and Thelin medicine for pulmonary arterial hypertension. Office Phone: 949-494-5458. E-mail: drwolff@aol.com.

WOLFF, MICHAEL A., state supreme court judge; Grad., Dartmouth Coll., 1967; JD, U. Minn., 1970. Lawyer Legal Svcs.; mem. faculty St. Louis U. Sch. Law, 1975-98; judge Mo. Supreme Ct., 1998—, chief justice, 2005—. Chief counsel to gov., 1993-94, spl. counsel, 1994-98. Co-author: Federal Jury Practice and Instructions, 4th edit; author monthly column Law Matters: Reflections of Chief Justice Michael A. Wolff, 2005. Chief counsel to Gov. St. Louis, 1993-94, spl. counsel, 1994-98. Office: Supreme Ct Mo PO Box 150 Jefferson City MO 65102-0150 *

WOLFF, OTTO J., federal agency administrator; b. 1942; BS in Fin., Pa. State U. Profl. staff mem. com. on house adminstrn. U.S. Ho. Reps.; dep. asst. sec. for adminstrn. US Dept. Commerce, 1981—93, asst. sec. for adminstrn., CFO Washington, 2001—. Office: US Dept Commerce 1401 Constitution Ave NW Washington DC 20230

WOLFF, PAUL MARTIN, lawyer, sculptor; b. Kansas City, Mo., July 22, 1941; s. Joseph L. and Eleanor B. Wolff; m. Rhea S. Schwartz, Oct. 9, 1976. BA, U. Wis., 1963; LLB, Harvard U., 1966. Bar: D.C. 1968, U.S. Ct. Appeals (D.C. and 2d cir.) 1968, U.S. Supreme Ct. 1975, U.S. Ct. Appeals (10th and fed. cirs.) 1981, U.S. Ct. Appeals (8th cir.) 1982, U.S. Tax Ct. 1982, U.S. Ct. Claims 1984. Law clk. to Judge James R. Durfee U.S. Ct. Claims, Washington, 1966-67; assoc. Williams & Connolly, Washington, 1967-75, ptnr., 1976—. Adj. prof. Catholic U. Law Sch., 1970-73. Co-author: Forensic Sciences; contbr. articles to legal jours.; artist (one-man shows): Trinity U., Washington, 2005, Zenith Gallery, Washington, 2005, 06, 07. Bd. dirs. Washington Coun. for Civil Rights Under Law, 1980-90, Renwick Alliance, Washington, 1987-93, Am. Jewish Com., Washington, 1988-92, Washington Legal Clinic for Homeless, 1988-99, Opportunities for Older Ams. Found., 1988-92, Emeritus Found., 1992-99; bd. dirs. Washington Performing Arts Soc., 1990-2002, hon. dir., 2002—; vice chmn. D.C. Pub. Charter Schs. Resource Ctr., 1999-2003; dir. D.C. Sports Commn., 1994-2000; dir. Com. Pub. Edn., 1994-99; trustee Fed. City Coun., bd. trustees, 1996—; trustee Am. U., 1996-2005; overseer Corcoran Mus. of Art, 1997-2005; mem. adv. bd. Woodrow Wilson Ctr. for Internat. Studies, 1999—; co-chmn. Triad Automotive Group LLC; mem. acquisitions com. Jewish Mus., 2003—. Recipient Learned Hand award, Am. Jewish Com., 2004. Mem. Georgetown Club, Econ. Club Washington (dir.), Phi Beta Kappa. Independent. Avocations: photography, gardening, fly fishing, sculpting. Home: 4770 Reservoir Rd NW Washington DC 20007-1905 also: Oak Ridge Warrenton VA 20186 Office: Williams & Connolly 725 12th St NW Washington DC 20005-5901: 1250 Villager Sun Valley ID 83353 Fax: 202-434-5580. E-mail: pwolff@wc.com, dcpmw@aol.com.

WOLFF, PETER ADALBERT, retired physics professor, researcher; b. Oakland, Calif., Nov. 15, 1923; s. Adalbert and Ruth Margaret W.; m. Catherine C. Carroll, Sept. 11, 1948; children: Catherine Mia, Peter Whitney. AB in Physics, U. Calif., Berkeley, 1945, PhD in Physics, 1951. Rsch. scientist Lawrence Radiation Lab., 1951-52; staff scientist Bell Telephone Lab., Murray Hill, NJ, 1952-63, dept. head, dir. electronic rsch. lab., 1964-70; prof. physics U. Calif., San Diego, 1963-64; prof. physics, head solid state and atomic physics div., assoc. dir. Material Sci. Ctr. MIT, Cambridge, 1970-76, dir. rsch. lab. of electronics, 1976-81, prof. physics Cambridge, 1976-89, prof. emeritus, 1994—, 1994—; dir. Francis Bitter Nat. Magnet Lab., 1981-87. Dir. Draper Lab. Contbr. articles to profl. jours. Served with C.E. U.S. Army, 1945-46. Fellow Nippon Electric Co. Rsch. Inst., Princeton, 1989-94. Mem. Am. Phys. Soc. Home: 321 Greew Way Wayland MA 01778

WOLFF, RICHARD JOSEPH, public relations executive, consultant, historian; b. Hackensack, NJ, Oct. 13, 1952; s. Richard Hamilton and Irene Marie (Ciruzzi) W. AB, Georgetown U., 1974; MA, Columbia U., 1976, PhD, 1979. Asst. dean, prof. St. John's U., Queens, NY, 1980-85; ptnr. pub. rels. Kekst & Co., Inc., NYC, 1985-97; mng. dir. Eastern region and L.Am. Golin/Harris Internat., NYC, 1997—2002, worldwide mng. divsn. G/H Fin., 1997—2002; CEO, The Global Cons. Group, NYC, 2002—. Mem. Columbia U. Seminar Modern Italy, NYC, 1983—; founding mem. St. John's U. Seminar Vatican Studies, Queens, 1994—. Author: Between Pope and Duce, 1990, Dorothy Day, 1994; contbr. articles to profl. jours.; editor Catholics, the State and the European Radical Right, 1987. Chmn., commr. North Hudson Sewerage Authority, Hudson County, NJ, 1988—; mem. adv. com. Senator Robert Menendez, NJ, 1994—. Recipient Howard Marraro prize Am. Cath. Hist. Assn., 1982, Internat. fellow Columbia U., 1977; named to Order of Malta, Knight of Magistral Grace. Mem. Order of Malta, Phi Beta Kappa. Roman Catholic. Avocations: golf, reading, travel, politics. Office: The Global Consulting Group 22 Cortlandt St 14th Fl New York NY 10007

WOLFF, ROBERT PAUL, philosophy educator; b. NYC, Dec. 27, 1933; s. Walter Harold and Charlotte (Ornstein) W.; m. Cynthia Griffin, June 9, 1962 (div. 1986); children: Patrick Gideon, Tobias Barrington; m. Susan Gould, Aug. 25, 1987. AB, Harvard U., 1953, MA in Philosophy, 1954, PhD, 1957. Instr. Harvard U., 1958-61; asst. prof. philosophy U. Chgo., 1961-63; vis. lectr. Wellesley Coll., 1963-64; assoc. prof. philosophy Columbia, 1964-69, prof., 1969-71; prof. philosophy U. Mass., Amherst, 1971-92, prof. Afro-Am. studies, 1992—; grad. program dir. doctoral program in Afro-Am.; devel. cons. U. QwaQwa, South Africa, 1998—. Author: Kant's Theory of Mental Activity, 1963, A Critique of Pure Tolerance, 1965, Political Man and Social Man, 1966, Kant: A Collection of Critical Essays, 1967, Poverty of Liberalism, 1968, The Ideal of the University, 1969, In Defense of Anarchism, 1970, 2d edit., 1998, Ten Great Works of Philosophy, 1970, The Rule of Law, 1971, Styles of Political Action in America, 1971, Philosophy: A Modern Encounter, 1971, The Autonomy of Reason, 1973, 1984 Revisited, 1973, About Philosophy, 1975, 9th edit., 2005, Understanding Rawls, 1977, Understanding Marx, 1985, Moneybags Must Be So Lucky, 1988, Autobiography of an Ex-White Man, 2005. Exec. dir. Harvard-Radcliffe Alumni/ae Against Apartheid, 1988-90; pres., exec. dir. Univ. Scholarships for South African Students, 1990—; co-dir. Inst. Advanced Study in Humanities U. Mass., 1992-98, dir. Doctoral Program in Afro-Am. Studies, 1996—, dir. Undergrad. Mentoring and Achievement Program, 2006—. Home: 107 Buffam Rd Amherst MA 01002-9723 also: 17 rue Maître Albert 75005 Paris France Office Phone: 413-545-2751. Personal E-mail: rwolff12@comcast.net. Business E-Mail: rwolff@afroam.umass.edu.

WOLFF, RONALD KEITH, toxicologist, researcher; b. Brantford, Ont., Can., July 25, 1946; s. Roy Clifford and Agnes Audrey (Stratton) W.; m. Mary Carole Cromien Wolff, Aug. 26, 1972; children: Mark, Sarah, Andrew, Brian. BS, U. Toronto, 1964-68; MS, 1968-69, PhD, 1969-72. Diplomate Am. Bd. Toxicology, 1983. Rsch. assoc. McMaster U., Hamilton, Can., 1973-76; scientist Lovelace Inhalation Toxicology Rsch. Inst., Albuquerque, N.Mex., 1976-88; sr. rsch. scientist Eli Lilly and Co., Greenfield, Ind., 1988—2004; rsch. fellow Nektar Therapeutics, San Carlos, Calif., 2004—. Author: (book chpt.) Comprehensive Treatise on Pulmonary Toxicology, 1992, Comprehensive Toxicology, 1997; contbr. articles to profl. jours. Recipient Frank Blood award Soc. Toxicology, 1989, Thomas T. Mercer joint prize Am. Assn. for Aerosol Rsch. and Internat. Soc. Aerosols in Medicine, 2002. Mem. Am. Assn. for Aerosol Rsch., Internat. Soc. Aerosols in Medicine, Soc. Toxicology, Am. Indsl. Hygiene Assn. Avocations: camping, hiking, hockey. Office: Nektar Therapeutics 150 Industrial Rd San Carlos CA 94070 Office Phone: 650-620-6581. Business E-Mail: rwolff@nektar.com.

WOLFF, RUSSELL, broadcast executive; AB, Dartmouth Coll., 1989; MBA, Amos Tuck Sch. Bus. Admin. With Leo Burnett Co., Chgo., 1989—92; dir. market devel. MTV Networks, 1994—97; v.p., Pacific Rim Bus. Interests ESPN, 1997, v.p., programming star sports div., 1998, sr. v.p., 2000, ESPN Deportes, 2002—04, exec. v.p., 2004—. Chmn. CTV Spl. Television, Inc. Named one of 40 Under 40, Sports Bus. Jour., 2006. Office: ESPN ESPN Plz 935 Middle St Bristol CT 06010 *

WOLFF, SANFORD IRVING, lawyer; b. Chgo., Apr. 13, 1915; s. Herbert Barron and Libby (Levey) W.; m. Ann Barry, Mar. 21, 1970; children: Paul, David, Laura. BA, Knox Coll., 1936; grad., John Marshall Law Sch., U. Chgo., 1940. Bar: Ill. 1940, N.Y. 1973. Pvt. practice, Chgo.

and NYC, 1945—; chief exec. AFTRA, AFL-CIO, NYC, 1968-85; of counsel Becker, London & Kossow, NYC, 1985—; chief exec. and counsel Am. Guild of Musical Artist, AFL-CIO, 1988-93. Trustee Harris Sch., Chgo. Served with AUS, 1940-45. Decorated Combat Inf. badge, Purple Heart, Bronze Star with cluster, Silver Star. Mem. ABA, Chgo. Bar Assn., NY Bar Assn. Home: 19 Prides Crossing New Canaan CT 06840-5502 Office Phone: 203-966-0300.

WOLFF, SHELDON, radiobiology educator; b. Peabody, Mass., Sept. 22, 1928; s. Henry Herman and Goldie (Lipchitz) W.; m. Frances Faye Farbstein, Oct. 23, 1954; children: Victor Charles, Roger Kenneth, Jessica Raye. BS magna cum laude, Tufts U., 1950; MA, Harvard U., 1951, PhD in Biology, 1953. Teaching fellow Harvard U., 1951-52; sr. rsch. staff biology div. Oak Ridge Nat. Lab., 1953-66; prof. cytogenetics, anatomy and radiology U. Calif., San Francisco, 1966-94; prof. emeritus, 1994—; dir. Lab. Radiobiology and Environ. Health U. Calif., San Francisco, 1983-95; vice chmn., chief rsch. Radiation Effects Rsch. Found., Hiroshima, Nagasaki, Japan, 1996—2000. Vis. prof. radiation biology U. Tenn., 1962, lectr., 1953-65; cons. several fed. sci. agys.; mem. health and environ. rsch. adv. com. U.S. Dept. Energy, 1986—, chmn., 1987-95; co-chmn. Joint NIH/Dept. Energy Subcom. on Human Genome, 1989-94. Editor: Chromosoma, 1983-97; assoc. editor: Cancer Research, 1983-97; Editorial bd.: Radiation Research, 1968-72, Photochemistry and Photobiology, 1962-72, Radiation Botany, 1964-86, Mutation Research, 1964-97, Caryologia, 1967-96, Radiation Effects, 1969-81, Genetics, 1972-85; Contbr. articles to sci. jours. Mem. Marin County (Calif.) Civil Grand Jury, 2003—05; Marin County Grand Jury Assn., 2003—; Calif. Grand Jury Assn., 2004—. Recipient E.O. Lawrence meml. award U.S. AEC, 1973, 1st ann. Belle award, 1998. Mem. Genetics Soc. Am., Radiation Rsch. Soc. (counselor for biology 1968-72, Failla lectr. 1992, medal 1992), Am. Soc. Cell Biology, Environmental Mutagen Soc. (coun. 1972-75, pres. 1980-81, award 1982), Internat. Assn. Environ. Mutagen Socs. (treas. 1978-85), Sigma Xi. Democrat. Home: 41 Eugene St Mill Valley CA 94941-1717 Office: U Calif Dept Radiology San Francisco CA 94143-0628 Business E-Mail: shellyw@radmail.ucsf.edu.

WOLFF, SIDNEY CARNE, astronomer, science administrator; b. Sioux City, Iowa, June 6, 1941; d. George Albert and Ethel (Smith) Carne; m. Richard J. Wolff, Aug. 29, 1962 BA, Carleton Coll., 1962, DSc (hon.), 1985; PhD, U. Calif., Berkeley, 1966. Postgrad. research fellow Lick Obs, Santa Cruz, Calif., 1969; asst. astronomer U. Hawaii, Honolulu, 1967-71, assoc. astronomer, 1971-76; astronomer, assoc. dir. Inst. Astronomy, Honolulu, 1976-83, acting dir., 1983-84; dir. Kitt Peak Nat. Obs., Tucson, 1984-87, Nat. Optical Astronomy Observatories, 1987-2001; dir. Gemini Project Gemini 8-Meter Telescopes Project, 1992-94; astronomer, project scientist Large Synoptic Survey Telescope, 2001—04. Pres. SOAR Inc., 1999-2003; project scientist Large Synoptic Survey Telescope, 2002-04. treas. 2005; bd. mem. LSST Corp. Author: The A-Type Stars--Problems and Perspectives, 1983, (with others) Exploration of the Universe, 1987, Realm of the Universe, 1988, Frontiers of Astronomy, 1990, Voyages Through the Universe, 1996, 2nd edit., 2003, Voyages to the Planets, 1999, 2nd edit., 2003, Voyages to the Stars and Galaxies, 1999, 2nd edit., 2003; founding editor: Astronomy Edn. Rev., 2002; contbr. articles to profl. jours. Trustee Carleton Coll., 1989—, chair acad. affairs com., 1995-2005. Rsch. fellow Lick Obs. Santa Cruz, Calif., 1967; recipient Nat. Meritorious Svc. award NSF, 1994. Fellow Royal Astronical Soc.; mem. Astron. Soc. Pacific (pres. 1984-86, bd. dirs. 1979-85), Am. Astron. Soc. (coun. 1983-86, pres.-elect 1991, pres. 1992-94, Edn. prize 2006). Office: Nat Optical Astronomy Obs PO Box 26732 950 N Cherry Ave Tucson AZ 85719-4933 Business E-Mail: swolff@noao.edu.

WOLFF, STUART, online real estate executive; BSEE, Brown U.; MSEE, Princeton U., D in Elec. Engring. Former founder and CEO CareNet Am., others.; former v.p. And Interactive; former v.p. bus. svcs. TCI Interactive (subs. Telecomms. Inc.); chmn., pres. Real Select, Inc. (subs. Homestore.com, Inc.), Thousand Oaks, Calif. Recipient MONBUSHO fellowship, Japanese Min. of Edn., Tokyo Inst. Technology, 1986. Office: Homestore.com Inc 225 W Hillcrest Dr Ste 100 Thousand Oaks CA 91360-7884

WOLFF, TOBIAS (JONATHAN ANSELL WOLFF), writer; b. Birmingham, Ala., June 19, 1945; s. Arthur Saunders and Rosemary (Loftus) Wolff; m. Catherine Dolores Spohn, 1975; children: Michael, Patrick, Mary Elizabeth. BA, Oxford U., 1972, MA, 1975, Stanford Univ., 1978; LHD (hon.), Santa Clara Univ., 1996. Mem. faculty Stanford (Calif.) U., Goddard Coll., Plainfield, Vt., Ariz. State U., Tempe, Syracuse (N.Y.) U., Stanford (Calif.) U., 1997—, dir. creative writing program, 2000—02; reporter Washington Post. Author: In the Garden of the North American Martyrs, 1981 (St. Lawrence award for fiction 1982), The Barracks Thief, 1984 (PEN/Faulkner award for fiction 1985), Back in the World, 1985, This Boy's Life: A Memoir, 1989 (L.A. Times Book prize 1989), In Pharaoh's Army: Memories of the Lost War, 1994 (Esquire-Volvo-Winterstone's award, Eng., 1994), The Night in Question, 1996, Old School, 2003 (PEN/Faulkner Award for Fiction finalist, 2004, Nat. Book Critics Circle finalist, LA Times Book award finalist, 2004, Prix de Medicis finalist, France, 2005); editor: Matters of Life and Death: New American Stories, 1983, The Stories of Anton Chekhov, 1987, Best American Short Stories, 1994, The Vintage Book of Contemporary American Stories, 1994, A Doctor's Visit: The Short Stories of Anton Chekov. Recipient Wallace Stegner fellowship in creative writing, 1975-76, Mary Roberts Rinehart award, 1979, Rea award, 1989, Whiting Writer's award, 1989, Lila-Wallace-Reader's Digest award, 1993, Lyndhurst Found. award, 1994, award merit Am. Acad. Arts and Letters, 2001, Fairfax prize for lit. George Mason U., 2003; Nat. Endowment for the Arts fellowship in creative writing, 1978, 85, Ariz. Coun. on Arts and Humanities fellowship in creative writing, 1980, Guggenheim fellowship, 1982. Office: Stanford U Dept English Stanford CA 94305-2087 Office Phone: 650-723-0504.

WOLFF, VIRGINIA EUWER, writer; b. Portland, Oreg., Aug. 25, 1937; d. Eugene Courtney and Florence Evelyn (Craven) Euwer; m. Art Wolff, July 19, 1959 (div. July 1976); children: Anthony Richard, Juliet Dianne. AB, Smith Coll., 1959; postgrad., Goddard Coll., Warren Wilson Coll., L.I. U., Portland State U., Lewis & Clark Coll. Cert. tchr., Oreg. Tchr. The Miquon Sch., Phila., 1968-72, The Fiedel Sch., Glen Cove, NY, 1972-75, Hood River Valley (Oreg.) H.S., 1976-86, Mt. Hood Acad., Govt. Camp, Oreg., 1986-98. 2d violinist Quartet con brio, Portland, 1989-94, Parnassius Quintet, Portland, 1996—. Author: Probably Still Nick Swansen, 1988, The Mozart Season, 1991, Make Lemonade, 1993, Bat 6, 1998, True Believer (Nat. Book award, Michael L. Printz honor, Pacific N.W. Booksellers Assn. award, Jane Addams Book honor, 2002), 2001, represented US, honor book, Internat. Board on Books for Young People, 2004. Violinist Mid-Columbia Sinfonietta, Hood River, 1976—92, Oreg. Sinfonietta, Portland, 1988—, Parnassius Chamber Ensemble, 2000-. Recipient Young Adult Book award Internat. Reading Assn., 1989, PEN U.S.A. Ctr. West, 1989, Best Young Adult Book of Yr. award Mich. Libr. Assn., 1993, Child Study Children's Book award Bank Street Coll., 1994, Oreg. Book award Oreg. Lit. Arts, 1994, 2001, Jane Addams Children's Book award Jane Addams Peace Assn. and the Women's Internat. League for Peace and Freedom, 1999, Nat. Book award, 2001, Printz Honor Book award, 2002, Jane Addams Honor Plaque, 2002, Evelyn Sibley Lampman award for svc. to the children of Oreg., Oreg. Libr. Assn., 2005; named to Carnegie medal Shortlist, ALA, 2002. Mem. Soc. Children's Book Writers/Illustrators (Golden Kite 1994, 2002), Chamber Music Soc. Oreg. Avocations: chamber music, swimming, hiking, playing violin, gardening. Office: Curtis Brown Ltd care Elizabeth Harding 10 Astor Pl Fl 3 New York NY 10003-6982

WOLFF, WILLIAM F., III, investment banker; b. NYC, Apr. 12, 1945; s. William F., Jr. and Nancy (Wimpfheimer) Wolff; m. Phyllis Fox, June 1, 1969; children: Kenneth, Laura, Jonathan, Gillian. BA, U. Mich., 1967; JD, Columbia U., 1970, MBA, 1971. Bar: N.Y. 1970. V.p. Salomon Bros., Inc., NYC, 1971-78; prin. Morgan Stanley & Co., NYC, 1978-83; mng. dir. Lehman Bros., NYC, 1983-2000, UBS Warburg, NYC, 2000—02, Endurance Capital, NYC, 2002—03; mng. ptnr. Lykos Capital Mgmt., 2003—. Trustee St. David's Sch., NYC, 1985—2004; dir. City Harvest, 1999—2005. Mem.: Ocean Beach Club (Elberon, N.J.) (trustee 1985—89), Univ. Club (N.Y.). Office: 909 3d Ave New York NY 10022 Personal E-mail: rwolff3@yahoo.com.

WOLFF, WILLIAM I., surgeon, educator; b. NYC, Oct. 24, 1916; s. Julius Louis and Matilda (Brick) W.; m. Lillian Myrick, June 30, 1952 (div. 1967); children: Richard, Deborah, David, Alan, Lisa, Mitchell, George, Rebecca, Barbara; m. Rita T. Smith, Feb. 15, 1972. BS, NYU, 1936; MD, U. Md., 1940. Diplomate Am. Bd. Surgery, Am. Bd. Thoracic Surgery. Intern Cornell U. divsn. Bellevue Hosp., 1940-42, resident specializing in chest surgery Columbia U. divsn., 1942-43; resident, chief Bronx Vets. Hosp., 1946-48; chief thoracic surgery Deshon Vets. Hosp., 1949; practice medicine specializing in surgery NYC, 1950—; emeritus dir. surgery Beth Israel Med. Ctr., NYC, 1962-76; prof. surgery Mt. Sinai Sch. Medicine, NYC, 1965—. 1st disting. lectr. soc. Am. Gastrointestinal Surgeons, 1987; vis. prof. or invited guest lectr. over 40 med. schs. univ. ctrs., over 150 tchg. hosps., numerous nat. and internat. cancer confs. in U.S., Eng., South Africa, Kenya, Israel, Mex., Can., USSR, France and P.R. Contbr. over 120 articles to med. jours., chpts. to books. Served to maj. M.C. AUS, 1943-46, ETO. Mem. ACS, Am. Coll. Gastroenterology (bd. govs.), Am. Assn. for Thoracic Surgery, Soc. Thoracic Surgeons (founding), Soc. for Surgery Alimentary Tract, Am. Coll. Chest Physicians, Am. Gastroenterologic Assn., Internat. Soc. Surgery, Internat. Cardiovasc. Surg. Soc., N.Y. Surg. Soc. (pres. 1980-81), N.Y. Acad. Medicine (chmn. sect. on surgery), Assn. Alumni Bellevue Hosp. (pres. 1982), Aspetuck Valley Country Club. Achievements include early contributor to subject of cardiac resuscitation by ccardiac message; originator of scientific procedure of colonoscopy and removal of colonic polyps. Home: 200 E 24th St Apt 1503 New York NY 10010-3919 Home Phone: 203-226-0567; Office Phone: 212-755-4144.

WOLFHARD, HANS GEORG, retired research scientist; b. Basel, Switzerland, Apr. 2, 1912; arrived in U.S., 1956, naturalized, 1961; s. Albert Georg and Helen (Buerck) W.; m. Adelheid Rohde, Jan. 18, 1940 (dec. 1995); children: George, John (dec. 2002), Bernie; m. Clara Ralston, Jan. 4, 1997. Student, U. Berlin, 1934-35; Dr.Rer.Nat., U. Goettingen, 1938. Scientist Aero. Rsch. Sta., Brunswick, Germany, 1939—46; rsch. scientist Imperial Coll., London, Royal Aircraft Establishment, England, 1946—56; sr. prin. scientific officer Bur. Mines, Pitts., 1956—59; head dept. physics reaction motors divsn. Thiokol Chem. Corp., Denville, NJ, 1959—63; mem. sr. rsch. staff Inst. Def. Analyses, Alexandria, Va., 1963—96; ret. Cons. Sverdrup Tech., AEDC-Arnold AFB, Tenn., 1996—2004. Co-author: Flames, 4th edit., 1979, Chinese transl., 1990. Fellow Ballistic Missle Def., Def. Dept.; recipient 1st Gen. Goodpastor award for Excellence in Rsch., 1983. Fellow Am. Optical Soc., Mil. Sensor Symposium (First Jamieson award); mem. AIAA, Combustion Inst. Presbyterian. Home: 711 Bright Ave Fayetteville TN 37334-2255

WOLFINGER, NICHOLAS H., educator; b. Palo Alto, Calif., May 2, 1966; s. Raymond E. and Barbara Kaye Wolfinger; AB, U. Calif., Berkeley, 1990; MA, UCLA, LA, 1992, PhD, 1998. Assoc. prof. U. Utah, Salt Lake City, 2005—. Author: (research monograph) Understanding the Divorce Cycle. Liberal. Office: Univ Utah 225 S 1400 East AEB 228 Salt Lake City UT 84112 Office Phone: 801-581-7491. Office Fax: 801-581-5156. Personal E-mail: nick.wolfinger@fcs.utah.edu.

WOLFINGER, RAYMOND EDWIN, retired political science professor; b. San Francisco, June 29, 1931; s. Raymond Edwin and Hilda (Holm) W.; m. Barbara Kaye, Aug. 7, 1960; 1 son, Nicholas Holm. AB, U. Calif.-Berkeley, 1951; MA, U. Ill., 1955; PhD, Yale U., 1961. Asst. prof. polit. sci. Stanford U., Calif., 1961—66, assoc. prof., 1966-70, prof., 1970-71, U. Calif., Berkeley, 1971—, Heller prof. polit. sci., 1995—2006; ret., 2006. Dir. U. Calif. Data Archive and Tech. Assistance, 1980-92; chmn. bd. overseers Nat. Election Studies, Ann Arbor, Mich., 1982-86 Author: The Politics of Progress, 1974, (with others) Dynamics of American Politics, 1976, 80, (with Steven J. Rosenstone) Who Votes, 1980, (with others) The Myth of the Independent Voter, 1992; mem. editorial bd. Brit. Jour. Polit. Sci., 1980-84, Am. Polit. Sci. Rev., 1985-88. Bd. dirs. S.W. Voter Rsch. Inst., San Antonio, 1988-96, Consortium of Social Sci. Assns., 1987-93, pres. 1988-90. 1st lt. U.S. Army, 1951-53. Fellow Ctr. for Advanced Study in Behavioral Scis., 1960-61; Guggenheim fellow, 1965; Ford Found. faculty research fellow, 1970-71 Fellow Am. Acad. Arts and Scis. (chair Class III membership com. 1998-99); mem. Am. Polit. Sci. Assn. (sec. 1981-82), AAUP (council 1981-84), Western Polit. Sci. Assn. (v.p. 1988-89, pres. 1989-90). Democrat. Office: U Calif Dept Polit Sci Berkeley CA 94720-1950

WOLF-KLEIN, GISELE PATRICIA, geriatrician; b. Geneva, June 11, 1951; came to U.S., 1976; d. Francis and Patricia (Johnston) Wolf; m. Allen Klein. MD, Geneva U., 1975. Diplomate Am. Bd. Internal Medicine. Intern., resident L.I. Jewish Med. Ctr., 1976-78, fellow in geriatric medicine New Hyde Park, NY, 1978-80, chief geriatric medicine, 1991—. Assoc. prof. medicine Albert Einstein Coll. of Medicine, N.Y. Author: Keys to Alzheimers Disease, 1992; contbr. numerous articles to profl. jours. Recipient 1 of Best Drs. in USA award Woodward-White, 1992-93. Fellow ACP, Am. Geriatric Soc.; mem. Gerontol. Soc. Am., Met. Area Geriatric Soc. (bd. dirs. 1991—), Sigma Xi. Avocations: skiing, mountain climbing, sculpture. Office: Parker Jewish Geriatric Inst 27111 76th Ave New Hyde Park NY 11040-1436 E-mail: gwolfklein@parkerinstitute.org.

WOLFMAN, BERNARD, lawyer, educator; b. Phila., July 8, 1924; s. Nathan and Elizabeth (Coff) W.; m. Zelda Bernstein, Dec. 25, 1948 (dec. Oct. 1973); children: Jonathan L., Brian S., Dina A.; m. Toni A. Grotta, June 12, 1977. AB, U. Pa., 1946, JD, 1948; LLD (hon.), Jewish Theol. Sem., 1971, Capital U., 1990. Bar: Pa. 1949, Mass. 1976. Mem. law firm Wolf, Block, Schorr & Solis-Cohen, Phila., 1948-63; prof. law U. Pa. Law Sch., 1963-76, dean, 1970-75, Kenneth W. Gemmill prof. tax law and tax policy, 1973-76, chmn. Faculty Senate, 1969-70; Fessenden prof. law Harvard U., 1976—2007, Fessenden prof. emeritus, 2007—. Vis. prof. Stanford U. Law Sch., 1982, NYU Law Sch., 1987-88; Irvine lectr. Cornell U. Law Sch., 1980; Halle lectr. Case Western Res. U. Law Sch., 1983; Cleve. State U. Sch. Law; Sugarman lectr., 1989; Altheimer lectr. U. Ark. Sch. Law, Little Rock, 1994; Polisher lectr. Dickinson Coll. Law, 1998; mem. editl. bds. law divsn. Aspen Law & Bus. (formerly Little Brown & Co.), Jour. Corp. Taxation; gen. counsel AAUP, 1966-68, mem. coun., 1979-82; prof.-in-residence tax divsn. Dept. Justice, 2003; cons. to ind. counsel Lawrence E. Walsh (Iran-Contra prosecution), 1987-89; adv. group to commr. internal revenue, 1966-67; cons. tax policy U.S. Treasury Dept., 1963-68, 77-80; chmn. Task Force Univ. Governance, U. Pa., 1968-70; steering com. IRS project Adminstrv. Conf. US, 1974-80; vice chmn. bd. advs. NYU-IRS Continuing Profl. Edn. Project, 1981-85; mem. legal activities policy bd. Tax Analysts, 1974—; exec. com. Fed. Tax Inst. New Eng., 1976—; pres. Fed. Tax Inst. New Eng., 2004—. Author: (with Diane M. Ring)Federal Income Taxation of Corporate Enterprise, 1971, 4th edit., 2005; (with J. Holden and D. Schenk) Ethical Problems in Federal Tax Practice, 1981, 3dedit., 1995, (with J. Holden and K. Harris) Standards of Tax Practice, 1991, 6th edit. 2004; sr. author: Dissent Without Opinion: The Behavior of Justice William O. Douglas in Federal Tax Cases, 1975; contbr. articles to profl. jours. Adv. com. Commn. Philanthropy and Pub. Needs, 1973-75; mem. Phila. regional council Pa. Gov.'s Justice Commn., 1973-75; trustee Found. Center, NYC, 1970-76, Fedn. Jewish Agys. Greater Phila., 1968-74; bd. dirs. Phila. Lawyers Com. Civil Rights Under Law, 1970-74, Phila. Defender Assn., 1955-69; mem. Nat. Lawyers Adv. Council of Earl Warren Legal Tng. Program. Served with AUS, 1943-45. Fellow Am. Bar Found., Am. Coll. Tax Counsel (past regent 1st cir.); mem. ABA (past chmn. com. on taxation, coun. sect. individual rights and responsibilities 1978-82, coun. sect. taxation 1982-85), Am. Law Inst., ACLU (nat. dir. 1973-75), Order of Coif (exec. com. 1982-91, v.p. 1986-89, pres. 1989-91), Phi Beta Kappa. Home: 229 Brattle St Cambridge MA 02138-4623 Office: Harvard Law Sch 1545 Mass Ave Cambridge MA 02138 Office Phone: 617-495-4623. E-mail: wolfman@law.harvard.edu.

WOLFMAN, EARL FRANK, JR., surgeon, educator; b. Buffalo, Sept. 14, 1926; s. Earl Frank and Alfreda (Peterson) W.; m. Lois Jeannette Walker, Dec. 28, 1946; children— Nancy Jeannette, David Earl, Carol Anne. BS cum laude, Harvard U., Cambridge, Mass., 1946; MD cum laude, U. Mich., 1950. Diplomate Am. Bd. Surgery. Intern U. Mich., Ann Arbor, 1950-51, asst. resident in surgery, 1951-52, resident in surgery, 1954-55, from jr. clin. instr. surgery to assoc. prof., 1955-66, asst. to dean, 1960-61, asst. dean, 1961-64; practice medicine specializing in surgery, 1957—, Sacramento, 1966—; prof. surgery Sch. Medicine, U. Calif., Davis, 1966—, founding chmn. dept. surgery, 1966-78, founding assoc. dean, 1966-76, mem. staff, chief surg. svcs. Med. Ctr., 1966-78, founding chmn. div. surg. scis., 1966-78. Contbr. articles to profl. jours. Served to lt. M.C. USNR, 1952-54. Fellow ACS; mem. AMA (del. 1987-99), Ctrl. Surg. Soc., Western Surg. Soc., Sacramento Surg. Soc., Pacific Coast Surg. Soc., Frederick A. Coller Surg. Soc., Soc. Surgery Alimentary Tract, Am. Assn. Endocrine Surgeons, Sierra Sacramento Valley Med. Soc., Calif. Med. Assn. (trustee 1991-2000), Am. Soc. Gen. Surgeons. Methodist. Office: U Calif Davis Sch Medicine Dept Surgery 2221 Stockton Blvd Fl 3 Sacramento CA 95817-2214 Business E-Mail: efwolfman@ucdavis.edu.

WOLFMAN, IRA JOEL, editor, writer; b. Oct. 7, 1950; s. Aaron and Beatrice Ruth (Perlo) W.; m. Julia Diamant, June 24, 1979 (dec. 1982); m. Ronda Small, Dec. 20, 1991. BA cum laude, SUNY, Albany, 1971. News editor Washington Park Spirit, Albany, NY, 1971-73; sr. editor Smash mag., NYC, 1975-76, Circus mag., NYC, 1976-79; assoc. editor 3-2-1 Contact mag., NYC, 1979-80; editor Sesame St Parents' Newsletter, NYC, 1980-83; editor-in-chief Enter mag., NYC, 1983-85, Sesame St. mag., Parents Guide, 1990-94; v.p., editor-in-chief Adult Consumer mags. Children's Television Workshop, NYC, 1994-97, v.p., editorial dir. mags. and sch. products, 1997-2000, group v.p., publ. mags. Sesame Workshop, 2000-01; prin. POE Comms., 2001—; sr. v.p. editl. Weekly Reader Pub., 2004—. Newsletter editor Found. for Grandparenting, Mt. Kisco, N.Y., 1984-87; editor Am. Writer, 1988-89; freelance writer and editor, contbr. to Travel & Leisure, Reader's Digest, Archtl. Record, Metropolis, N.Y. Daily News, Ms., Spy, 1985—. Author: Do People Grow on Family Trees? Genealogy for Kids and Other Beginners, 1991, My World and Globe, 1991, Climbing Your Family Tree: Online and Offline Genealogy, 2002, Jewish New York: Notable Neighborhoods and Memorable Moments, 2003. N.Y. State Legis. Corrs. scholar, 1970. Jewish. Personal E-mail: iwolfman@weeklyreader.com.

WOLFORD, KATHRYN FRANCES, foundation administrator; b. Reading, Pa., Dec. 12, 1957; d. Howard Francis Wolford and Katherine Eva (Auker) Carbaugh. BA in History, Gettysburg Coll., 1979; MA in Religious Studies, U. Chgo. Divinity Sch., 1980; MA in Pub. Policy, U. Chgo., 1981; PhD (hon.), Gettysburg Coll., 1995; PhD (hon.), Muhlenberg Coll., 2003. Country program rep. Ch. World Svc., Dominican Republic, 1983-85; regional rep. Nat. Coun. Chs. USA, NYC, 1985-90; program dir. for L.Am., Luth. World Relief, Balt., 1991-93, pres., 1993—2006, McKnight Found., Mpls., 2006—. Former bd. mem. Md. Assn. Nonprofit Organizations, Gettysburg Coll., Foods Resource Bank; former bd. chair InterAction, Action by Churches Together; former bd. mem. Lutheran Cmty. Found.; mem., adv. com. Johns Hopkins U. Inst. for Policy Studies. Named Md. Top 100 Women, Md. Daily Record, 2002, 2004; recipient Young Alumni Achievement award, Gettysburg Coll., Woman of Distinction award. Democrat. Lutheran. Avocation: sailing. Office: McKnight Foundation 710 S 2nd St Ste 400 Minneapolis MN 55401 Office Phone: 612-333-4220. Office Fax: 612-332-3833. *

WOLFORD, LARRY M., surgeon; s. Donald Ralph and Irene Wilma W.; m. Denise Hazel LeBlanc, June 11, 1983; children: Dax Patrick, Dallas Danielle, Demi Denise, Dylan Dion, Dash Larry. BS, U. Pitts., 1965; DMD, Temple U., Phila., 1969; cert. in Oral Surgery, U.Tex. Southwestern Med. Sch., Dallas, 1973; diploma of Hon. Merit (hon.), U. São Paulo, Brazil, 1995. Diplomate Am. Bd. Oral and Maxillofacial Surgery. Asst. dir. dept oral and maxillofacial surgery and ctr. for correction dentofacial deformities John Peter Smith Hosp., Fort Worth, 1973—83, coord. Ft. Worth cleft palate program, 1973—83; prof. oral and maxillofacial surgery Baylor Coll. Dentistry, Dallas, 1983—87, dir. of oral and maxillofacial surgery grad. program, 1984—86, clin. prof. of oral and maxillofacial surgery, 1987—; dir. oral and maxillofacial surgery fellowship program Baylor Coll. Dentistry Tex. A&M U. Sys. and Baylor U. Med. Ctr., Dallas, 1985—. Mem. adv. com. Am. Bd. Oral and Maxillofacial Surgery, 1985—91. Co-author: Dentofacial Deformities: Surgical Orthodontic Correction, Surgical Treatment Objective: A Systematic Approach to the Prediction Tracing; co-editor: Cleft / Craniofacial / Cosmetic Surgery; contbr. 20 chapters to books;, author 155 manuscripts. Recipient 1st William F. Harrigan award, William F. Harrigan Soc., 1982, Diplomat Am. Coll. Dentists award, Am. Coll. Dentistry, 1987, William J. Gies Found. Oral and Maxillofacial award for major contributions, 1990. Mem.: ADA, Am. Soc. TMJ Surgeons, Am. Assn. Oral and Maxillofacial Surgeons (mem. com. ann. sci. sessions 1977—83, chmn. planning com. combined meeting AAO/AAOMS 1980, chmn. com. annual sci. sessions 1980—82, spl. cons. com. annual sci. sessions 1982—83, mem. planning com. combined meeting AAO/AAOMS 1983). Achievements include research leading to FDA approval of the following products: Porous block hydroxyapatite (Interpore 200) for bone grafting in the craniofacial area; TMJ Concepts total joint prostheses for TMJ reconstruction; Mitek mini anchors for disc repositioning in TMJ surgery; development of many surgical procedures and instruments. Avocation: sports cars. Office: 3409 Worth St Ste 400 Dallas TX 75246

WOLFORD, RICHARD G., food products executive; With Dole Foods, 1967—87, pres. packaged foods, 1982—87; CEO HK Acquisition Corp., 1988—96, Del Monte Foods Co., San Francisco, 1997—98, pres., CEO, 1998—2000, chmn., pres., CEO, 2000—. Office: Del Monte Foods Co One Market The Landmark San Francisco CA 94105 *

WOLFOWITZ, PAUL DUNDES, former President of the World Bank, former federal agency administrator; b. NYC, Dec. 22, 1943; s. Jacob and Lillian (Dundes) W.; m. Clare Selgin, Nov. 25, 1968 (div. 2002); children: Sara Elizabeth, David Samuel, Rachel Dahlia. BA in Math. and Chemistry, Cornell U., 1965; MA, U. Chgo., 1967, PhD in Polit. Sci., 1972. Lectr., asst. prof. Yale U., 1970-73; with US Arms Control & Disarmament Agy., 1973-77, spl. asst. to dir., 1974-75, dep. asst. dir., 1976, spl. asst. for Strategic Arms Limitation Talks (SALT), 1976-77; dep. asst. sec. for regional progs., prog. analysis & evaluation US Dept. Def., Washington, 1977-80; vis. assoc. prof. Paul H. Nitze Sch. Advanced Internat. Studies, Johns Hopkins U., 1980-81, dean, prof internat. rels., 1994—2001; dir. policy planning staff US Dept. State, Washington, 1981-82, asst. sec. for East Asian & Pacific affairs, 1982-86, US amb. to Indonesia Jakarta, 1986-89; under sec. for policy US Dept. Def., Washington, 1989—93, dep.

sec., 2001—05; pres. The World Bank Group, Washington, 2005—07; vis. scholar Am. Enterprise Inst., 2007—. Recipient Presdl. Citizens medal. Office: Am Enterprise Inst 1150 Seventeenth St NW Washington DC 20036 *

WOLFRAM, CHARLES WILLIAM, law educator; b. Cleve., Feb. 28, 1937; s. Carl P. and Dona M. (Minitch) W.; m. Nancy Russell Bass, Dec. 18, 1965; children: Catherine Dana, Peter Russell. AB, Notre Dame U., 1959; LLB, U. Tex., 1962. Bar: D.C. 1962, Minn. 1974. Assoc. Covington & Burling, Washington, 1962-64; mem. FAA Contract Appeals Panel, Washington, 1964-65; asst. prof. law U. Minn., 1965-67, assoc. prof., 1967-70, prof., 1970-81; prof. law Cornell U., Ithaca, N.Y., 1982-84, Charles Frank Reavis Sr. prof. law, 1984-99, Charles Frank Reavis Sr. prof. emeritus, 1999—. Assoc. dean acad. affairs Cornell U., Ithaca, 1986-90, interim dean, 1998-99; vis. prof. U. So. Calif. Law Center, 1976-77. Author: (with J. Morris Clark) Professional Responsibilty: Issues for Minnesota Attorneys, 1976, Modern Legal Ethics, 1986; contbr. chpts. to books, articles to profl. jours. Mem. Am. Law Inst. (chief reporter Restatement of Law Governing Lawyers, 1986- 2000), Order of Coif. Democrat. Office: 2887 College Ave #148 Berkeley CA 94705 Office Phone: 510-841-5542. E-mail: chuwolfram@aol.com.

WOLFRAM, DAVID ANTHONY, information technology manager; b. Melbourne, Australia, Sept. 20, 1962; s. Hans Gerhard (dec.) and Bettine Rosalind (Kauffmann) W. BSc with honors, U. Melbourne, 1984, MSc, 1986; PhD, Cambridge U., Eng., 1990, Oxford U., 1991; Exec. MBA, Australian Grad. Sch. Mgmt., 2003. Cert. european engr., chartered IT profl., PMP; chartered engr. Rsch. asst. U. Oxford, 1990; jr. rsch. fellow Christ Ch., Oxford, 1990-94, BT fellow, 1994; lectr. in computer sci. Australian Nat. U., Canberra, 1995-2000, vis. fellow Rsch. Sch. Info. Sci. and Engring., 2000; with Microsoft Corp., USA, Redmond, Wash., 2000—02; project mgr. Expert Info. Svc. (now Infosys Tech. Australia), Melbourne, 2003—07; sr. mgr. Infosys Tech., Australia, 2007—. Mem. program com CATS Computing: The Australasian Theory Symposium, 1999, 2000, 03, 04, program chair, 00, mem. steering com., 2000—. Author: The Clausal Theory of Types, 1993; contbr. articles to profl. jours.; guest editor: Electronic Notes in Theoretical Computer Science, Vol. 31, 2000; guest editor spl. issue Theoretical Computer Science, 2003. Mem. Trinity Coll., Cambridge, England, Christ Ch., Oxford, England. Recipient Commonwealth Postgraduate Rsch. award, Australian Govt., 1984—85; grantee Lockey Fund Travel Grant, U. Oxford, 1993; recipient, Rae & Edith Bennett Travelling Scholarship, U. Melbourne, 1988—90, Rouse Ball Fund Travel Grant, Trinity Coll., Cambridge, 1990. Fellow: Royal Soc. Arts, Brit. Computer Soc., Cambridge Philos. Soc. (life); mem.: IEEE (sr.), Project Mgmt. Inst. (bd. dirs. Melbourne chpt. 2006—), Assn. Computing Machinery, IEEE Computer Soc., London Math. Soc., Internat. Soc. for Philos. Enquiry (diplomate), Melbourne Cricket Club, Am. Australian Assn., Ordre du Tastevin (chevalier). Avocations: photography, tennis, chess. Office: Infosys Tech Australia Pty Ltd Level 3 484 St Kilda Rd Melbourne VIC 3004 Australia

WOLFRAM, STEPHEN, physicist, computer company executive; b. London, Aug. 29, 1959; came to U.S., 1978; Degree, Eton Coll., 1976, Oxford U., 1978; PhD in Theoretical Physics, Calif. Inst. Tech., 1979. With Calif. Inst. Tech., Pasadena, 1979-82, Inst. for Advanced Study, Princeton, NJ, 1983-86; prof. physics, math, computer sci. U. Ill., Champaign, 1986-90; founder, dir. Ctr. for Complex Sys. Rsch., 1996—98; pres., CEO Wolfram Rsch. Inc., Champaign, 1987—. Author: Theory and Applications of Cellular Automata, 1986, Mathematica: A System for Doing Mathematics by Computer, 1998, 2d edit., 1991, Mathematica Reference Guide, 1992, Mathematica: The Student Book, 1994, The Mathematica Book, 3rd edit., 1996, 5th edit., 2003, Cellular Automata and Complexity, 1994, A New Kind of Science, 2002; editor jour. Complex Systems, 1986— Fellow MacArthur Found., 1981; recipient World Leaders of Tomorrow award, World Economic Forum, 1999; named Scientist of Yr., R&D Mag., 2002. Office: Wolfram Rsch Inc 100 Trade Centre Dr Champaign IL 61820-7237 Business E-Mail: s.wolfram@wolfram.com.

WOLFRAM, THOMAS, physicist, educator; b. St. Louis, July 27, 1936; s. Ferdinand I. and Audrey H. (Calvert) W.; m. Eleanor Elaine Burger, May 22, 1965; children: Michael, Gregory, Melanie, Susan, Steven. BA, U. Calif., Riverside, 1959, PhD in Physics, 1963; MA in Physics, UCLA, 1960. Engr. Atomics Internat., Canoga Park, Calif., 1960-63; mem. tech. staff N.Am. Aviation Corp. Sci. Ctr., Thousand Oaks, Calif., 1963-68; group leader in solid state physics Rockwell Internat. Sci. Ctr., Thousand Oaks, 1968-72, dir. div. physics and chemistry, 1972-74; prof. physics, chmn. dept. physics and astronomy U. Mo., Columbia, 1974-83; dir. phys. tech. divsn. AMOCO Corp., 1983-87; v.p., gen. mgr. AMOCO Laser Co., 1987-95; bus. cons., 1995—. Cons. in field. Author: The Venture, The Dragon Tamers, Electronic and Optical Properties of d-Band Perovskites; editor: Inelastic Electron Tunneling Spectroscopy, 1978; contbr. articles to profl. jours. Recipient Disting. Prof. award Argonne Univs. Assn., 1977 Fellow: Am. Phys. Soc. Home and Office: 228 Trafalgar Ln San Clemente CA 92672 Personal E-mail: ewolfram@cox.net. *Crisis is the catalyst for constructive change.*

WOLFRAM, WILLIAM RAY, artist, educator; b. Mason City, Iowa, July 5, 1936; s. Theodore Martin and Rose Wolfram; m. Carmen Louise Sunde, Aug. 9, 1958; children: William Ray, Ward Kenneth. MFA, U. Ariz., Tucson, 1960. Prof. art Concordia U., Seward, Nebr., 1960—. Acrylic and digital painting. Home: 1036 Sunrise Seward NE 68434 Office: Concordia Univ 800 North Columbia Seward NE 68434 Home Phone: 402-643-2535; Office Phone: 402-643-7499. Personal E-mail: wwolfram@alltel.net. Business E-Mail: william.wolfram@cune.edu.

WOLFSCHMIDT, WILLI See FLINT, WILLIS

WOLFSON, AARON HOWARD, radiation oncologist, educator; b. Nashville, May 13, 1955; s. Sorrell Louis and Jacqueline Adele (Falis) W.; m. Adrienne Sue Mates, Dec. 16, 1979; children: Alexis Ellyn, Andrew Lane. BA, U. Fla., 1978, MD, 1982. Diplomate Am. Bd. Radiology. Intern internal medicine Jackson Meml. Hosp., Miami, Fla., 1982—83; staff physician Pub. Health Svc., Miami, 1983—85; pvt. practice Palm Beach Gardens, Fla., 1985—86; resident in radiation oncology Med. Coll. Va., Richmond, 1986—89; from instr. to assoc. prof. radiation oncology U. Miami, Miller Sch. Medicine, 1989—2003, prof., 2003—, vice chair dept. radiation oncology, 2005—. Co-dir. Gynecology Site dis. group Sylvester Cancer Ctr., 2001—. Contbr. articles to profl. jours. Bd. dirs. Children's Home Soc., Ft. Lauderdale, Fla., 1993—, Temple Beth Israel, Sunrise, Fla., 1994—; mem. spkrs. bur. U. Miami, 1993—; vol. spkr. Broward County Schs., 1990—; exec. v.p. Temple Beth Israel, 1996-98, pres., 1998-99. Sylvester Cancer Ctr. grantee, 1992. Mem. Gynecologic Oncology Group, Radiation Therapy Oncology Group, Am. Soc. Therapeutic Radiology and Oncology. Jewish. Achievements include research on malignant tumors of the female genital tract; patent for radiation implant for gynecologic cancer. Office: Univ Miami 1475 NW 12th Ave # D-31 Miami FL 33136-1002 Home Phone: 954-370-8038; Office Phone: 305-243-4210. Business E-Mail: awolfson@med.miami.edu.

WOLFSON, HOWARD, political analyst; b. NYC; m. Terri McCullough; 1 child, Sarah. BA, U. Chgo.; MA in US History, Duke U., 1991. Reporter local politics northern Va. newspaper; chief of staff and press sec. US Rep. Nita M. Lowey, 1993; comm. dir., spokeperson Charles Shumer campaign for US Senate, 1998; comm. dir. Hillary Rodham Clinton campaign for US Senate, 1999—2000, 2005—06; exec. dir. Dem. Congl. Campaign Com., 2001—02; ptnr. The Glover Park Group, NYC. Commentator Meet the Press, This Week With George Stephanopoulis, Larry King Live. Named one of 40 Under 40, Crain's NY, 2005. Office: The Glover Park Goup Ste 702 86 Chambers St New York NY 10007 Office Phone: 646-495-2700. Office Fax: 646-495-2710. *

WOLFSON, IVAN RICHARD, management consultant; b. Phila., Aug. 31, 1945; m. Michele Karen Veiser; 1 child, Mark. BS in Bus., Drexel U., Phila., 1968. Pres. A.R. Wolfson Assoc., Wyncote, Pa., 1963—. Office: AR Wolfson Assoc 409 Salisbury Rd Wyncote PA 19095-2023 Office Phone: 215-884-1500.

WOLFSON, JAY, public health and medical educator, researcher, consultant, lawyer; b. Chgo., July 13, 1952; s. Max Joseph and Ida (Kolender) W.; m. Maxine Loren Coplan, May 4, 1988; children: Alan H., Marc J., Joel L. AB, U. Ill., 1973; MA, NYU, 1974; MPH, Ind. U., 1975; DPH, U. Tex., 1981; JD, Stetson Coll., 1993. Asst. prof. health adminstrn. Sch. Pub. Health U. S.C., Columbia, 1978-80; assoc. prof. health adminstrn. Coll. of Pub. Health U. Okla., Oklahoma City, 1981-84; v.p. Health Cost Mgmt., Inc., Tampa, Fla., 1984—; assoc. prof. healthcare, fin. & poicy Coll. Pub. Health, U. South Fla., Tampa, 1991-95; prof. health law and fin. U. South Fla. Coll. Pub. Health, Tampa, 1995—; prof. medicine U. South Fla., Tampa, 1997—, chmn. dept. pub. health policy and mgmt. Coll. Pub. Health, dir. Fla. Pub. Health Info. Ctr., 1991—; trustee Tampa Gen. Hosp., 1988—99; prof. medicine Fla. State U., 2003, disting. svc. prof. pub. health and medicine, 2005; assoc. v.p. health law, policy and safety USP Health, 2005—. Co-dir. Stetson-U. South Fla. Ctr. for Law and Medicine, 2000—; spl. guardian ad litem for Theresa Marie Schiavo, 2002-04; dir. Fla. Pub. Health Info. Ctr., 1990—; vis. prof. Tokyo U. Coll. Medicine, 1985; sr. fin. cons. Fla. Office Pub. Counsel, Tallahassee, 1986—; cons. Fla. Dept. Ins., Tallahassee, 1987—, Fla. Dept. Health and Rehab. Svcs., Tallahassee, 1987—, Dun & Bradstreet Co., N.Y.C., 1987—; mem. medicare competitive pricing review com., 1998-2004; gen. counsel Am. Bd. Healthcare Risk Mgmt., 1994—. Author: Managing Employee Health Benefits, 1985; contbr. articles to profl. jours. Trustee Hillsborough County Hosp. Authority, Tampa, 1988-1999, Fla. Health Scis. Ctr., Inc., 1998-1999; pres. Kids Health Care Found., Inc., 1997—. Marcus and Teresa Levi scholar NYU, 1974; W.K. Kellogg Found. fellow, 1983; Sr. Fulbright scholar to Japan, 1985, Faculty scholar US Ctr Disease Control and Prevention, 1998-1999. Mem. Am. Pub. Health Assn., Health Care Fin. Mgmt. Assn., Am. Coll. Healthcare Execs. Jewish. Avocation: writing. Office: U South Fla Coll Pub Health 13301 N 30th St Tampa FL 33612-3807 E-mail: jwolfson@hsc.usf.edu.

WOLFSON, JORDAN, artist; b. NYC, 1980; BFA, Rhode Island Sch. Design, Providence, RI, 2003; studied, Konfstack Coll. Arts & Krafts, Stockholm, Sweden, 2003. One-man shows include Radar, Galleri Brandstrom & Stene, STOCKHOLM, 2002, Nostalgia is Fear, Irma Vep Lap, Champagne, France, 2004, Jordan Wolfson, Kunsthalle Zurich, 2004, Neverland, Jordan Wolfson, Yvon Lambert, Paris, 2005, Jiem-no-Pedti, t293 Naples, 2005, Wako Works of Art, Tokyo, 2006, exhibited in group shows at Fort Thuder, Providence, RI, 2000, Nada Art Fair, Miami, 2003, Palm D'Or Social Club, Berlin Art Fair, 2004, Festival of Dreams, Lombard-Freid Gallery, NYC, 2004, None of the Above, Swiss Inst., NYC, 2004, There is No Such Thing As The Real World, Galleri MGM, Oslo, 2005, BUIA Gallery, 2005, Post note, Midway Contemporary Art Mus., Minn., 2005, U-Move, Utopia and Image on the Move, Gallery Contemporary Art, Monfalcone, Italy, 2005, Sold Out, Spazio, More Fools In Town, Turin, 2005, Hudson Valley Ctr. Contemporary Art, 2006, Uncertain States of Am., 2006, Whitney Biennial, Whitney Mus. Art, 2006. Office: c/o Whitney Mus 945 Madison Ave New York NY 10021

WOLFSON, MARK ALAN, investor, educator, dean; b. Chgo., Sept. 25, 1952; s. Jack and Maribelle (Simen) W.; m. Sheila Rae Aronesti, Aug. 3, 1975; children: Laura Rachel, Charles Michael. BS in Acctg. and Fin., U. Ill., 1973, M in Acctg. Sci., 1974; PhD in Acctg., U. Tex., 1977. Asst. prof. acctg. Stanford (Calif.) U., 1977-81, assoc. prof., 1981-85, prof., 1985-87, Joseph McDonald prof., 1987-92, assoc. dean, 1990-93, Dean Witter prof. acctg. and fin., 1992-96, cons. prof., 2001—; mng. ptnr. Oak Hill Capital Mgmt., 1998—; established Oak Hill Strategic Ptnrs., 1996—, Oak Hill Investment Mgmt., 2000—; prin. Oak Hill REIT Ptnrs., 2004—, Oak Hill Spl. Opportunities Fund, 2004—. Ford Found. vis. assoc. prof. U. Chgo., 1981-82; Thomas Henry Carroll vis. prof. Harvard U., Boston, 1988-89; cons. Fin. Acctg. Stds. Bd., Norwalk, Conn., 1985, 89-92; rsch. assoc. Nat. Bur. Econ. Rsch., Cambridge, Mass., 1988—; steering com. Stanford Inst. Econ. Policy Rsch., 1990-2000, exec. com. 2001—; task force Fed. Home Loan Bank Bd., 1989; bd. dirs. eGain Comm., Fin. Engines, Inc., Accretive Healthcare; mem. investment com. William and Flora Hewlett Found., 2004—. Contbr. numerous articles to profl. jours. Recipient Pomerance prize Chgo. Bd. Options Exch., 1981, Disting. Tchg. award Stanford U., 1990, Notable Contbn. to Lit. award AICPA-Am. Acctg. Assn., 1990, 92, Wildman award, 1991; named Disting. Accountancy Alumnus, U. Ill., 1989. Jewish. Office: Oak Hill Capital 2775 Sand Hill Rd Ste 220 Menlo Park CA 94025-7019

WOLFSON, MICHAEL GEORGE, retired lawyer; b. Chgo., Sept. 1, 1938; s. A. Lincoln M. Weingarten and Brina (Nelson) W.; m. Rita Sue Parsont, Sept. 11, 1966; children: Bethany Lynne, Sara Wynne, Deborah Kay. Student, MIT, 1956-58; BA, U. Chgo., 1961, JD, 1964, postdoctoral, 1964-65. Bar: Ill. 1964, N.Y. 1969. Assoc. Cravath, Swaine & Moore, NYC, 1965-71, Brown, Wood, Fuller, Caldwell & Ivey, NYC, 1971-73; ptnr. Sidley Austin LLP, NYC, 1974—2002, sr. counsel, 2003—06, ret., 2006. Mediator, specializing in comml. and internat. disputes. Woodrow Wilson fellow, 1961; Ford Found. fellow in internat. trade and devel., 1965. Fellow Am. Bar Found. (life); mem. ABA. Avocations: reading, photography, fly fishing, bicycling. Home Phone: 212-517-7759; Office Phone: 212-839-5321. Business E-Mail: mwolfson@sidley.com.

WOLGEMUTH, RICHARD LEE, pharmaceutical executive; b. Lebanon, Pa., June 29, 1945; s. Clyde Hess and Mary Grace (Longenecker) W.; m. Cheryl Ann Hamman, May 1968; children: Richard Brent, Erryl Clyde, Christina Jo, Travis Grant. BSc in Biology and Chemistry, Ashland Coll., Ohio, 1968; MS in Gastrointestinal Physiology, Ohio State U., PhD in Gastrointestinal Physiology, 1975. Jr. pharmacologist Warren Teed Pharms., Columbus, Ohio, 1969-75; scientist I Rohm & Haas Co., Phila., 1975-77; sr. rsch. scientist Adria Labs., Columbus, Ohio, 1977-83, mgr. pharms. and med. chems., 1984-85, dir., project coord., 1985-87, dir. regulatory affairs, 1987-92; group dir. to v.p. global regulatory affairs GlaxoSmithKline, 1992—2003; sr. v.p. global regulatory scis. Bristol-Myers Squibb, 2003—. Cons. Nat. Inst. Occupl. Safety and Health, Cin., 1975-77. Author: Drug Design & Delivery, 1990; contbr. articles to Jour. Med. Chemistry, Jour. Organic Chemistry, Biochemical Medicine. Pres. Kimberly Woods Assn., Plain City, Ohio, 1987; co-chmn. Johnathan Alder Tax Levy Com., Plain City, 1982; bd. trustees Plain City Libr., 1985. Mem. Am. Soc. Cancer Chemotherapy, NY Acad. Scis., Soc. Exptl. Biology and Medicine, Regulatory Affairs Profl. Soc. Republican. Mem. Ch. of the Brethren. Achievements include patents for Anthracycline anti-cancer antibiotics, anti-convulsants, diagnostics; methods for treating kidney stones. Office: Bristol Myers Squibb 345 Park Ave New York NY 10154-0037 *

WOLIN, NEAL STEVEN, lawyer; b. Chgo., Dec. 9, 1961; m. Nicole Elkon; 1 child, Ethan. BA summa cum laude in Hist., Yale U., 1983; MS in Devel. Econs., U. Oxford, Eng., 1985; JD, Yale U., 1988. Bar: Ill. 1989, DC 1989, Conn. 2002, US Supreme Ct. 1995. Law clk. US Judge Eugene H. Nickerson, Bklyn., 1988-89; adj. asst. prof. law Bklyn. Law Sch., 1989; assoc. Wilmer, Cutler & Pickering, Washington, 1989-90; spl. asst. to dir. ctrl. intelligence, 1990-93; dep. legal adv. NSC The White House, 1993-94, exec. asst. to the nat. security adv., 1994-95; dep. gen. counsel US Dept. Treasury, 1995-99, gen. counsel, 1999-2001; exec. v.p., gen. counsel Hartford Fin. Svcs. Grp., Inc., 2001—07, pres., COO property-casualty ops., 2007—. Vis. fellow Brookings Instn., Washington, 2001; adj. lectr. in pub. policy JFK Sch. Govt., Harvard U., 2001; bd. dirs. Greater Hartford Legal Assistance Found. Bd. overseers RAND Corp. Inst. Civil Justice; mem. bd. regents U. Hartford; mem. Presdl. Adv. Commn. on Holocaust Assets in US, 1999—2000. Named one of 100 People to Watch, Washingtonian mag., 1999; recipient Alexander Hamilton award, Sec. Treasury, 2001; Charles and Julia Henry Fellow, Henry Trust, Oxford U., 1983—84, Coker Tchg. Fellow, Yale Law Sch., 1987—88. Mem.: Coun. Fgn. Rels., Phi Beta Kappa. Office: Hartford Fin Svcs Grp Inc Hartford Plz Hartford CT 06115 Office Phone: 860-547-3100. Business E-Mail: nwolin@thehartford.com. *

WOLIN, ROBERT EVERETT, lawyer; BA, Lafayette Coll., 1969; JD, NYU, 1973. Bar: N.Y. 1974, Pa. 1979, Tex. 1983, US Dist. Ct. (so. N.Y., ea. Pa., No. Tex. dist.). Law clk. Judge James A. Coolahan, US Dist. Ct. N.J., 1973—75; adminstrv. ptnr. & mem. mgmt. com. Kirkpatrick & Lockhart Nicholson Graham LLP, Dallas. Mem.: ABA, N.Y. State Bar Assn., Tex. Bar Assn., Dallas Bar Assn., Phi Beta Kappa. Office: Kirkpatrick & Lockhart Nicholson Graham LLP Suite 1800 2828 N Harwood St Dallas TX 75201-6966 Office Phone: 214-939-4909. Office Fax: 214-939-4949. Business E-Mail: rwolin@klng.com.

WOLINSKY, EMANUEL, internist, educator; b. NYC, Sept. 23, 1917; s. Jacob and Bertha (Siegel) W.; m. Marjorie Claster, Nov. 15, 1946; children: Douglas, Peter. BA, Cornell U., 1938, MD, 1941. Diplomate Am. Bd. Med. Microbiology. Intern, resident medicine N.Y. Hosp., 1943-45; bacteriologist Trudeau Lab., Saranac Lake, NY, 1947-56; mem. faculty Case Western Res. U. Sch. Medicine, 1956-98, prof. medicine, 1968-88, prof. pathology, 1981-88, prof. emeritus, 1988-98, ret., 1998. Dir. microbiology Cleve. Met. Gen. Hosp., 1959-91, acting dir. dept. pathology, 1980-86, chief div. infectious diseases, 1961-83. Co-editor Textbook of Pulmonary Diseases, 5th edit., 1993; Asso. editor: Am. Rev. Respiratory Diseases, 1973-79; Contbr. articles to profl. jours., textbooks. Mem. Tb panel U.S.-Japan Co-op. Med. Sci. Program, 1969-75. Recipient Crystal Cross award Ohio Thoracic Soc., 1995, Louis Weinstein award Clin. Infectious Diseases, 1995, Maurice Saltzman award Mt. Sinai Healthcare Found., 1999; named to Med. Hall of Fame, Cleve. Mag., 1998. Mem. Am. Soc. Microbiology (Gardner Middlebrook award 1998), Am. Thoracic Soc. (Trudeau medal 1986), Infectious Diseases Soc. Am. (Soc. Citation award, 2004), Phi Beta Kappa, Alpha Omega Alpha. Home: 24761 S Woodland Rd Cleveland OH 44122-3327

WOLINTZ, ARTHUR HARRY, neurologist, ophthalmologist; b. Bklyn., May 30, 1937; s. Louis and Celia (Ragofsky) W.; m. Carol Sue Bergstein, Nov. 28, 1963; children: Robyn Joy, Ellen Sharon. Student, NYU, 1955-58; MD summa cum laude, SUNY, Bklyn., 1962; postgrad., Columbia U., 1967-68. Diplomate Am. Bd. Psychiatry and Neurology, Am. Bd. Ophthalmology; licensee Nat. Bd. Med. Examiners, U. State of N.Y. Intern Maimonides Hosp., Bklyn., 1962-63, jr. resident in medicine, 1963-64; resident Nat. Inst. Neurol. Diseases and Blindness, Bethesda, Md., 1964-66; chief resident Mt. Sinai Hosp., NYC, 1966-67; clin. asst. prof. neurology Downstate Med. Ctr. SUNY, Bklyn., 1968-69, resident in ophthalmology, 1969-71, from asst. prof. to prof., 1971—, prof. clin. ophthalmology and clin. neurology, 1977—, interim chief ophthalmology, 1983, acting regional chmn. dept. ophthalmology, 1984, prof. ophthalmology, 1987—, chmn. dept. ophthalmology, 1987-96; Disting. tchg. prof., chair emeritus dept. ophthalmology SUNY-Health Sci. Ctr. Bklyn., 1995, 96—; asst. neurologist Presbyn. Hosp., NYC, 1967-68; instr. neuropathology Coll. Physicians and Surgeons Columbia U., NYC, 1967-68; instr. neurology Mt. Sinai Sch. Medicine, NYC, 1967-68; assoc. dir. neurology Maimonides Med. Ctr., Bklyn., 1968-69; asst. neurologist Coney Island Hosp., Bklyn., 1968-69. Vis. neurologist Kings County Hosp. Ctr., Bklyn, 1968-69; chief divsn. ophthalmology and neuro-ophthalmology Kingsbrook Jewish Med. Ctr., Bklyn., 1971, sec. med. and dental staff 1976-77, v.p. 1978-79, pres. 1980-81, dir. ophthalmology 1981; attending physician State Univ. Hosp., Bklyn., 1971, Kings County Hosp. Ctr., Bklyn., 1971; cons. Luth. Med. Ctr., Beth Israel Med. Ctr., Brookdale Hosp. Med. Ctr., Bklyn., L.I. Coll. Hosp., Bklyn., Maimonides Med. Ctr., Cath. Med. Ctr. Bklyn. and Queens, Bklyn. VA Hosp. Author: Essentials of Clinical Neuro-Ophthalmology, 1976; contbr. chpts. to sci. textbooks and handbooks, articles to profl. jours. Pres. Flatbush Jewish Ctr., Bklyn. With USPHS 1964-66. Recipient J. Eugene Chalfin Meml. Lectr. award Alumni Assn. State Univ.-Kings County, 1981, Tchr. of Yr. award dept. ophthalmology Interfaith Med. Ctr., 1988, Greats in Ophthalmology in Bklyn. award SUNY Downstate Med. Ctr. Dept. Ophthalmology, 2004, Alumni Svc. award SUNY Downstate Med. Ctr. Coll. Medicine, 2007. Fellow ACP, ACS, Am. Acad. Ophthalmology and Otolaryngology, Am. Acad. Neurology; mem. AMA, AAAS, Med. Soc. County Kings, Med. Soc. State N.Y., Bklyn. Ophthal. Soc., N.Y. Acad. Medicine, Am. Acad. Neurology, Alumni Assn. SUNY (pres.-elect 1989, pres. 1990-91, Richard C. Troutman M.D. Master Tchr. award in ophthalmology 1987, Disting. Alumni Achievement award 1997, Frank L. Babbott M.D. Meml. award 2002, Clarence and Mary Dennis Dedicated Svc. award 2004, Kingbrook Pres.'s award 2004), Oddfellows, Alpha Omega Alpha. Avocations: Torah reader, cantor. Home and Office: 100 Ocean Pky Apt 4H Brooklyn NY 11218-1755 Office Phone: 718-854-7360. Personal E-mail: ahwolintz@aol.com.

WOLITZER, STEVEN BARRY, investment banker; b. Bklyn., Mar. 14, 1953; s. Philip and Regina (Wurm) W.; m. Joyce Sue Lindower, Dec. 7, 1985; children: David Joel, Scott Richard, Rachel. BS, NYU, 1973; MBA, Harvard U., 1977. CPA, N.Y. Mng. dir. Lehman Bros. Inc., NYC, 1977—, head global mergers and acquisitions, 1996—. Home: 1185 Park Ave Apt 6A New York NY 10128-1309 Office: Lehman Bros Inc 745 Seventh Ave New York NY 10019 Office Phone: 212-526-2345. Business E-Mail: swolitze@lehman.com.

WOLK, BRUCE ALAN, law educator; b. Bklyn., Mar. 2, 1946; s. Morton and Gertrude W.; m. Lois Gloria Krepliak, June 22, 1968; children: Adam, Daniel. BS, Antioch Coll., 1968; MS, Stanford U., 1972; JD, Harvard U., 1975. Bar: D.C. 1975. Assoc. Hogan & Hartson, Washington, 1975-78; prof. U. Calif. Sch. Law, Davis, 1978—, acting dean, 1990-91, dean, 1993-98. Danforth Found. fellow, 1970-74, NSF fellow, 1970-72, Fulbright sr. research fellow, 1985-86. Mem. ABA, Am. Law Inst. Office: Univ Cal Davis Sch Law King Hall 400 Mrak Hall Dr Davis CA 95616-5201

WOLKOFF, EUGENE ARNOLD, lawyer; b. NYC, June 9, 1932; s. Oscar and Jean (Zablow) W.; m. Judith Gail Edwards, Oct. 15, 1967; children: Mandy, Elana, Alexa, Justine. AB, Bklyn. Coll., 1953; LLB, St. John's U., 1961. Bar: NY 1962, N.Mex. 1994. Practiced in, NYC and Santa Fe; mem. Callahan & Wolkoff, NYC, 1965—; gen. counsel BGK Group of Cos. Served to lt. col. USAFR, 1953-75. Mem. NY State Bar Assn., N.Mex. Bar Assn., Phi Beta Gamma. Office: 330 Garfield St Santa Fe NM 87501-2640 also: 240 W 35 St Ste 700 New York NY 10001 Office Phone: 505-992-5100, 212-332-9069. E-mail: gene@bgkgroup.com.

WOLKOFF, NEAL L., stock exchange executive; s. Martin and Evelyn Wolkoff; m. Janet Lynn Armuth, May 30, 1983; 3 children. BA, Columbia U., 1977; JD, Boston U., 1980. Bar: New York. Atty. NY Mercantile Exch., Inc., NYC, 1981—93, exec. v.p., 1993—2002, acting pres., 2000—01, exec. v.p., COO, 2002—03; cons. Am. Stock Exchange LLC, acting CEO, 2005, chmn., CEO, 2005—. Office: Am Stock Exch LLC 86 Trinity Place New York NY 10006 Business E-Mail: neal.wolkoff@amex.com. *

WOLKOV, HARVEY BRIAN, oncologist, researcher; b. Cleve., Feb. 8, 1953; s. Sidney and Norma Wolkov; m. Lauren Cronin, Jan. 9, 1993; 1 child, Nicole. BSc, Purdue U., West Lafayette, Ind., 1975, MSc, 1977; MD, Med. Coll. Ohio, Toledo, 1979. Diplomate Am. Bd. Radiology. Intern U. Calif., San Francisco, 1979-80; resident Stanford Med. Ctr., Calif., 1980-83; rsch. asst. Stanford U., 1982; from asst. clin. prof. to assoc. clin. prof. U. Calif., Davis, 1983-97, assoc. clin. prof., 1997—; med. dir. Mercy Hosps., Sacramento, 1987-90, Sutter Cancer Ctr. Dept. Radiation Oncology, Sacramento, 1990—. Mem. adv. bd. Nat. Graves Disease Found., Jacksonville, Fla., 1993—; dir. Sutter Gamma Knife Ctr., 1997—; co-prin. investigator radiation oncology Children's Oncology Group, 2001—. Author (with others): (book) Intraoperative Radiation, 1989, Frontiers in Radiation, 1991, Textbook Radiation Oncology, 2004; contbr. articles to profl. jours. Bd. dirs. Sutter Hosps. Found., Sacramento. Mem.: Calif. Radiol. Soc. (exec. com. 2001—), Sutter Inst. Med. Rsch. (chair rsch. com. 1996—, hosp. chair oncology com. 2003—, neuroscience inst. leadership com. 2003—), Calif. Radiation Oncology Soc. (pres.-elect 1999, pres. 2000—01), Am. Soc. Therapeutic Radiology and Oncology (bd. dirs. 2000—03, vice chair outcome rsch., fin. com., corp. rels., workforce, comm., coronary artery radiation therapy coms., Internat. Travel award 1987, inaugural fellow 2006), Radiation Therapy Oncology Group (com. chair 1986—90, publ. com. 1990—, mem. com. 1990—, lung and brain com. 1990—), No. Calif. Radiation Oncology Soc. (pres. 1999—2001), Coun. Affiliated Radiation Oncology Soc. (pres. 1999—2000), Assn. Residents Radiation Oncology (exec. com. 1997—2000, advisor emeritus 2000—, faculty advisor 1997—2000), Am. Cancer Soc. (reviewer 1990—, fellow 1978, 1983), Am. Coll. Radiology (chmn. stds. accreditation com. 1997—2003, councilor at large 1999, alt. councilor 2000—03, councillor 2003—, mem. expert panels, credentials com., fellow 1997). Avocations: painting, sculpture, travel, cello. Office: Sutter Cancer Ctr 2800 L St Ste 10 Sacramento CA 95816-5616 Personal E-mail: hbwolkov@comcast.net. Business E-Mail: wolkovh@radiological.com.

WOLL, HARRY J., electrical engineer; b. Farmington, Minn., Aug. 25, 1920; s. Henry L. and Clara M. (Fredrickson) W.; m. Mary V. Cowan, Feb. 15, 1947; children: Daniel, Alice. BSE.E., N.D. State U., 1940; postgrad., Ill. Inst. Tech., 1940-41; PhD, U. Pa., 1953. With RCA Corp., 1941-85, chief engr. aerospace systems div. Burlington, Mass., 1963-69, div. v.p. govt. engring. Moorestown, NJ, 1969-75; div. v.p., gen. mgr. RCA Automated Systems, Burlington, 1975-81; staff v.p., chief engr. RCA Electronic Products and Labs., Princeton, NJ, 1981-85. Patentee in field. Chmn. bd. trustees Moore Sch. Elec. Engring., U. Pa. 1976-90; trustee U. Pa., 1989-91. Recipient 50th Anniversary gold medal Moore Sch. Elec. Engring., U. Pa., 1973 Fellow AAAS, IEEE (past chmn. Phila. sect., past chmn. fellow com.), Aerospace Industries Tech. Council (past chmn.); mem. KC, Sigma Phi Delta, Phi Kappa Phi. Roman Catholic. Home Phone: 608-230-3725. E-mail: hjwoll@cs.com.

WOLLACK, EDWARD J., astrophysicist; s. Edward F. and Donna K. Wollack; m. Allison Pihl, Aug. 25, 1990; children: Alex, Andrew. BS in Physics summa cum laude, U. Minn., Mpls., 1987; PhD, Princeton U., NJ, 1994. Upper atmosphere rsch. scientist Bartol Rsch. Inst., U. Del., Newark, 1987—88; millimeter wave sensor design engr. Honeywell Def. Sys. Grp., Minnetonka, Minn., 1988—89; rsch. assoc. Nat. Radio Astronomy Obs., Charlottesville, Va., 1994—98; astrophysicist NASA Goddard Space Flight Ctr., Greenbelt, Md., 1998—. Contbr. articles to profl. jours. Cubmaster, den leader Boy Scouts Am., Fulton, Md., 2002—07. Recipient Antartic Svc. medal, NSF, 1988, Exceptional Achievement medal, NASA, 2002. Mem.: AAAS, IEEE, Am. Inst. Physics, Am. Astron. Soc. Achievements include patents for charge dissipative electrical interconnect; patents pending for wire ribbon stripping fixture; broadband high spurious-suppression microwave bandpass filter; interferometric polarization control; polarization preserving bandpass filter with large stop-band. Office: NASA Goddard Space Flight Ctr Code 665 Bldg 21 Greenbelt MD 20771

WOLLAM, JEAN FARR, retired diplomat; b. Holyoke, Mass., Oct. 5, 1917; d. Howard George and Nettie Hillman Farr; m. Park Fields Wollam, July 7, 1982 (dec.). Sec. pvt. industry, Holyoke, 1935—40; civil servant US Govt., Washington, 1941—46; passport clk. US Consulate, Berlin and Frankfurt, Germany, 1946—49; econ. asst. US Embassy, Bogota, Colombia, 1949—51, US Consulate, Monterrey, Mexico, 1952—54; adminstrv. asst. US Dept. State L.Am. Affairs, Washington, 1954—58; pers. officer US Embassy, Saigon, Vietnam, 1958—59, Phnom Penh, Cambodia, 1959—61, Athens, Greece, 1966—70, Lagos, Nigeria, 1971—73, Rome, 1973—76; placement officer Dept. State, Washington, 1961—66. Mem.: Gen. Soc. Mayflower Descs. Episcopalian. Avocations: bridge, writing. Home: 201 Grand Ave Carlsbad CA 92008 Personal E-mail: jfwollam@roadrunner.com.

WOLLAN, CURTIS NOEL, theater producer, theater director; b. Mpls., Nov. 10, 1951; s. Curtis Berdins and Lorraine Alice (Walser) Wollan; m. Jane Ellen Deter, May 17, 1980; children: Alexis Lorraine, Chet Curtis. BA in Speech and Theatre, Luther Coll., Decorah, Iowa, 1973; MFA in Directing, U. Iowa, 1976. Ptnr., artistic dir. Stage Two Prodns., Mpls., 1977-85; artistic dir. Chimera Theatre Co., St. Paul, 1985-87; ptnr., artistic dir. T.C.C. Prodns., Mpls., 1990-92; pres., prodr., dir. Troupe Am., Inc., Mpls., 1987—. Guest dir. Circa 21 Prodns., Rock Island, Ill., 1983—, Big League Theatricals, NYC, 1988—93, Ryman Auditorium, Nashville, 1999, Lucas Theatre for the Arts, Savannah, 2001, Theatre Under the Stars, Houston, 2001, Dollywood Holiday Show, 2003—, Foothills Repertory Theatre, Worcester, Mass., 2004—05; past sec., bd. dirs. Midwest Citizens for Arts, Mpls., 1985—87; dir., asst. prodr. Sheehan Prodns. Medora Mus., Mpls., 1987—91; prodr., dir. Medora Musical, 1992—. Creator, dir. mus. concept revue: (plays) The Lovely Liebowitz Sisters, 1986—; dir.(nat. tour): Pump Boys and Dinettes, 1987—88, 1995, 2000, Big River, 1988—89, Oil City Symphony, 1989—90, Gifts of the Magi, 1990, Driving Miss Daisy, 1991—92, Steel Magnolias, 1992—93, Steven King's Ghost Stories, 1993, 1994, On Golden Pond, 1994, A Christmas Carol, 1996—2005, The Odd Couple, 1997, Moon Over Buffalo, 1998—99, Hank Williams, Lost Highway, 2000—01, The Sunshine Boys, 2001—05, Same Time, Next Year, 2002; co-author, dir. nat. tour: Mr. Pickwick's Christmas, 1987—92; prodr., dir. nat. tour 1940's Radio Hour, 1988, 1990; prodr.(nat. tour): A Child's Christmas in Wales, 1988—89, Forbidden Broadway, 1990—91, 1994, Babes in Toyland, 1992—96, 2004, Tap Dance Kid, 1995, Mahalia, 1996, Miracle on 34th St., The Musical, 1997—98, Schoolhouse Rock Live!, 1997—2000, Here's Love, 1999; prodr., dir.: Pump Boys and Dinettes, 1999—; Hank and My Honky Tonk Heroes, 1999—2003; Forever Plaid, 1999—; Church Basement Ladies, 2005—; How to Talk Minnesotan, The Musical, 2005—; actor: (films) Bix, 1990, The Childhood Friend, 1993. Recipient Best Prodn. award, Twin Cities Critics Cir., 1981, Best Direction award, 1981, Patriotism award, Am. Legion, 1995. Mem.: Southeastern Theatre Conf. Lutheran. Avocations: movies, restaurants, travel, history, horseback riding. Office: Troupe Am Inc 528 Hennepin Ave Ste 206 Minneapolis MN 55403-1810 Home Phone: 612-789-7841. Personal E-mail: cw@troupeamerica.com.

WOLLAN, EUGENE, lawyer; b. NYC, Nov. 2, 1928; s. Isidor and Mollie (Elterman) W.; m. Jean B. Sack, June 6, 1954 (div. 1974); children— Eric G., Jennifer J.; m. Marjorie Cama, Nov. 25, 1977; stepchildren: Valerie M. Rosenwasser, Jon J. Rosenwasser. BA cum laude, Harvard U., 1948, JD, 1950. Bar: NY, 1950, US Dist. Ct. (so. and ea. dists.) NY 1953. US Ct. Appeals (2d cir.) 1955, US Ct. Mil. Appeals 1951, US Supreme Ct. 1960; cert. arbitrator and umpire. Assoc. Rein Mound & Cotton, NYC, 1953-62, ptnr., 1963-87, Mound, Cotton, Wollan & Greengrass, 1987—. Col. USAR, 1951-81. Mem. Internat. Assn. Ins. Counsel, Def. Rsch. Inst., Internat. Soc. Barristers, Assn. Internationale De Droit Des Assurances, NYC Bar Assn., NY County Lawyers, Judge Advocates Assn., Aida Reins. and Ins. Arbitration Soc., Harvard Club, NYC, Met. Opera Guild, NYC. Home: 430 E 57th St New York NY 10022-3061 Office: Mound Cotton Wollan & Greengrass One Battery Park Plz New York NY 10004 Home Phone: 212-421-3770; Office Phone: 212-804-4222. Business E-Mail: ewollan@moundcotton.com.

WOLLE, CHARLES ROBERT, judge; b. Sioux City, Iowa, Oct. 16, 1935; s. William Carl and Vivian (Down) W.; m. Kerstin Birgitta Wennerstrom, June 26, 1961; children: Karl Johan Knut, Erik Vernon, Thomas Dag, Aaron Charles. AB, Harvard U., 1959; JD, Iowa Law Sch., 1961. Bar: Iowa 1961. Assoc. Shull, Marshall & Marks, Sioux City, 1961-67, ptnr., 1968-80; judge Dist. Ct. Iowa, Sioux City, 1981-83; justice Iowa Supreme Ct., Sioux City and Des Moines, 1983-87; judge U.S. Dist. Ct. (so. dist.) Iowa, Des Moines, 1987-92, chief judge, 1992-99, sr. U.S. dist. judge, 2001—. Faculty Nat. Jud. Coll., Reno, 1983-2004 Editor Iowa Law Rev., 1960-61. V.p. bd. dirs. Sioux City Symphony, 1972-77; bd. dirs. Morningside Coll., Sioux City, 1977-81. Fellow Am. Coll. Trial Lawyers; mem. Sioux City C. of C. (bd. dirs. 1977-78); Iowa State Bar Assn. Avocations: sports, art, music, literature, skiing. Office: Sr US Dist Judge US Dist Ct SD IA 110 E Ct St Des Moines IA 50309 Office Phone: 775-265-3736. Business E-Mail: charles_wolle@iasd.uscourts.gov.

WOLLENBERG, BRUCE FREDERICK, electrical engineering educator, consultant; b. Buffalo, June 14, 1942; s. Henry William and Louise Viola (Swanson) W.; m. Ruth Elsie Kunz, June 5, 1965; children: Anne Louise, Allen Louis, Amy Lynn, Aaron Lee BEE, Rensselaer Poly. Inst., 1964, M Engring., 1966; PhD, U. Pa., 1974. Sr. engr. Leeds & Northrup Co., North Wales, Pa., 1966—74, Power Techs. Inc., Schenectady, 1974—84; prin. cons. Control Data Corp., Plymouth, Minn., 1984—89; prof. elec. engring. U. Minn., Mpls., 1989—, dir. grad. studies, dir. Ctr. for Electric Energy. Adj. prof. Rensselaer Poly. Inst., Troy, N.Y., 1979-84; cons. Empros Systems Internat., Plymouth, 1989—, No. States Power Co., Mpls., 1990—, Energy Control Cons., Fairfax, Va., 1990—; cons. on electric utility engring Author: Power Generation Operation and Control, 1984, 1996; also articles Chmn. bd. dirs. Loudonville (N.Y.) Christian Sch., 1978-83; chmn. Colonie (N.Y.) Zoning Bd., 1979-84; bd. dirs. Minn. Youth Symphony, Mpls., 1985-87 Named Outstanding Tchg. Prof., HKN, 2002—03; recipient Tech. Excellence award, Control Data Corp., 1987. Fellow IEEE (Power Engring. Soc., Third Millenium medal 2000, Oustanding Power Engring. Educator award 2002); mem. Nat. Acad. Engring., U. Minn. Acad. Disting. Prof., Tau Beta Pi, Eta Kappa Nu, Sigma Xi. Republican. Avocation: collecting records and cds. Home: 5100 Prescott Dr Minnetonka MN 55345-4847 Office: Univ of Minn Elec Engring Dept 200 Union St SE Minneapolis MN 55455-0154 Home Phone: 952-933-7456; Office Phone: 612-626-7192. E-mail: wollenbe@umn.edu.

WOLLER, JAMES ALAN, lawyer; b. Adrian, Mich., Dec. 27, 1946; s. Robert Arthur and Florence Emma (Jacob) W.; m. Jill Ann Samis, Aug. 18, 1968 (div. Aug. 1978); 1 child, Emily Erin; m. Elizabeth Julia Frey, May 22, 1982 (div. Apr. 1999); m. Carol Pierini, Oct. 29, 1999. BA, U. Mich., 1969; JD, Columbia U., 1974. Bar: N.J. 1974, U.S. Dist. Ct. N.J. 1974, U.S. Tax Ct. 1976, U.S. Supreme Ct. 1995. Assoc. McCarter & English, Newark, 1974-79; v.p. Pfaltz & Woller, PA, Summit, NJ, 1979-86, pres., 1987—. Editor Columbia U. Human Rights Law Rev., 1973-74; author New Jersey Real Property Statutes Annotated Deskbook, 2007. Mem.: ABA, Summit Bar Assn. (pres. 1987—88), Union County Bar Assn., NJ Bar Assn., Columbia Law Sch. Assn. NJ (trustee 1992—97, v.p. 1997—2001, pres. 2001—03), Raritan Yacht Club (Perth Amboy, NJ) (fin. sec. 1988—89, treas. 1989—92, vice commodore 1993—94, commodore 1994—95), Downtown Club (trustee 1997—99, treas. 1999, v.p. 2000, pres. 2001). Republican. Methodist. Avocation: sailing. Home: 187 High St Perth Amboy NJ 08861 Office: Pfaltz & Woller PA 382 Springfield Ave Ste 217 Summit NJ 07901-2780 Home Phone: 732-324-8460; Office Phone: 908-273-1974. Personal E-mail: jimwoller@aol.com.

WOLLER, KEVIN MARC PETER, psychology professor, researcher; s. Tilman Wilhelm Meinrad and Helen Emma Rosa Woller; m. Kimberly Rachele Moore, Mar. 27, 1999; children: Taylor Danielle Hawkins, Logan Loyd Tilman, McKenzie Gabrielle Sara. BA, U. Wash., 1989; PhD, Kent State U., 1999. Acting asst. prof. La. Tech. U., Ruston, 1996—97; asst. prof. La. State U., Alexandria, 1997—2000; assoc. prof. Rogers State U., Claremore, Okla., 2000—. Mem. human subjects rev. bd. Rogers State U., Claremore, Okla., 2003—. Contbr. articles to profl. jours. Named Advisor of Yr., La. State U., Alexandria, 1998—99. Mem.: APA, Psi Chi (faculty advisor 2003—). Office: Rogers State Univ 1701 W Will Rogers Blvd Claremore OK 74017 Home Phone: 918-343-0086; Office Phone: 918-343-7568. E-mail: kwoller@rsu.edu.

WOLLERSHEIM, JANET PUCCINELLI, psychology professor; b. Anaconda, Mont., July 24, 1936; d. Nello J. and Inez Marie (Ungaretti) Puccinelli; m. David E. Wollersheim, Aug. 1, 1959 (div. June 1972); children: Danette Marie, Tod Neil; m. Daniel J. Smith, July 17, 1976. AB, Gonzaga U., 1958; MA, St. Louis U., 1960; PhD, U. Ill., 1968. Lic. psychologist Mont. Asst. prof. psychology, asst. dir. testing/counseling ctr. U. Mo., 1968-71; prof. psychology U. Mont., Missoula, 1971—, dir. chin. psychology, 1980-87; chair Mont. Bd. Psychologists, 1977-78; cons. Mont. State Prison, 1971-85, Trapper Creek Job Corps, 1973—2003; pvt. practice Missoula, 1971—. Author numerous rsch. articles. Bd. dir. Crisis Ctr., Missoula, 1972-73; mem. profl. adv. bd. Head Start, Missoula, 1972-79. Recipient Disting. scholar award, U. Mont., 1991. Fellow Am. Psychol. Assn. (bd. dirs. div. clin. psychology 1990-92); mem. Rocky Mountain Psychol. Assn. (pres. 1983-84), Nat. Coun. Univ. Dirs. Clin. Psychology (bd. dirs. 1982-88). Home and Office: 105 Greenwood Ln Missoula MT 59803-2401 Home Phone: 406-543-6946; Office Phone: 406-543-6946. Personal E-mail: jpwoller2000@yahoo.com.

WOLLERT, GERALD DALE, retired food products executive, securities trader; b. LaPorte, Ind., Jan. 21, 1935; s. Delmar Everette and Esther Mae W.; m. Carol Jean Burchby, Jan. 26, 1957; children— Karen Lynn, Edwin Del. BS, Purdue U., 1957. With Gen. Foods Corp., 1959-89, dir. consumer affairs White Plains, N.Y., 1973-74, mng. dir. Cottee Foods div. Sydney, Australia, 1974-76, gen. mgr. Mexico div. Mexico City, 1978-79, pres. Asia/Pacific ops. Honolulu; corp. v.p. worldwide coffee and internat. div. Kraft Gen. Foods Corp., Honolulu, 1979—89; ret., 1989; pres. GDW Investment Systems LLC, 2004—. Dir. Gen. Foods cos., Japan, Peoples Republic China, Korea, India, Taiwan, Singapore, Philippines. Webelos leader Boy Scouts Am., Mexico City, 1978-79; co. gen. chmn. United Fund campaign, Battle Creek, Mich., 1964-65, White Plains, N.Y., 1972-73. Served with U.S. Army, 1958. Mem. Asian-U.S. Bus. Coun., Oahu Country Club (Hawaii), Venice Golf and Country Club (Fla.), Legacy Hills (Ind.) Club.

WOLLMAN, ROGER LELAND, federal judge; b. Frankfort, SD, May 29, 1934; s. Edwin and Katherine Wollman; m. Diane Marie Schroeder, June 21, 1959; children: Steven James, John Mark, Thomas Roger. BA, Tabor Coll., Hillsboro, Kans., 1957; JD magna cum laude, U. S.D., 1962; LLM, Harvard U., 1964. Bar: S.D. 1964. Law clerk Hon. George T. Mickleson US Dist. Ct (So. Dist, SC), 1962—63; sole practice Aberdeen, 1964—71; states atty. Brown County, Aberdeen, 1967—71; justice S.D. Supreme Ct., 1971—85, chief justice, 1978—82; judge US Ct. Appeals (8th cir.), 1985—, chief judge, 1999—2002. Mem. Jud. Conference of US, 1999—2002. With US Army, 1957—59. Mem.: Am. Jud. Soc. Office: US Ct Appeals US Courthouse & Fed Bldg 400 S Phillips Ave Rm 315 Sioux Falls SD 57104-6851 *

WOLLMER, RICHARD DIETRICH, statistics and operations research educator; b. LA, July 27, 1938; s. Herman Dietrich and Alice Myrtle (Roberts) W. BA in Math., Pomona Coll., 1960; MA in Applied Math., Columbia U., 1962; MS in Engring. Sci., U. Calif., Berkeley, 1963, PhD Engring. Sci., 1965. Scientist Rand Corp., Santa Monica, Calif., 1965-70; prof. info. systems Calif. State U., Long Beach, 1970—, dept. chair, 2000—03, vis. prof. Northridge, 1981—82. Cons. McDonnell Douglas, Long Beach, Calif., 1978-80, 82, 85-91, Logicon, San Pedro, Calif., 1979-81, Behavioral Tech. Labs., U. So. Calif., 1973-75; vis. assoc. prof. Stanford U., 1976; rsch. scientist Electric Power Rsch. Inst., Palo Alto, Calif., 1977; rsch. engr. Jet Propulsion Lab., Pasadena, Calif., 1971. Contbr. articles to profl. jours. Deacon Bel Air Presbyn. Ch., L.A., 1982-84, treas. 1983; mem. St. Andrews Presbyn. Ch., Newport Beach, Calif., 1999—. Mem.: Internat. Fedn. Ops. Rsch. Mgmt. Sci. (So. Calif.), Internat. Fedn. Ops. Rsch. Mgmt. Sci. (treas. 1999, sec. 2003, v.p. mem. 2006), Ops. Rsch. Soc. Am., So. Calif. Inst. Mgmt. Sci.-Ops. Rsch. Soc. (treas. 1979, vice chmn. 1980, chmn. 1981, vice chmn. 1988, chmn. 1989). Republican. Avocations: classical music, sports, reading, antique cars. Home: 6132 Fernwood Dr Huntington Beach CA 92648-5574 Office: Calif State U 1250 N Bellflower Blvd Long Beach CA 90840-8306 Business E-Mail: rwollmer@csulb.edu.

WOLMAN, ERIC, health care consultant; b. NYC, Sept. 25, 1931; s. Leo and Cecil (Clark) W.; m. Sandra Rosman, July 27, 1963; children: Karin, Alastair. AB in Math., Harvard Coll., 1953; PhD in Applied Math., Harvard U., 1957. Mem. tech. staff AT&T Bell Labs., Murray Hill, Holmdel, NJ, 1957—66, dept. head traffic rsch. and network engring. Holmdel, NJ, 1966—77, dept. head ops. rsch. and computing sys. West Long Branch, NJ, 1977—82, dept. head human performance engring. Piscataway, Summit, NJ, 1983—87; v.p. cmty. programs and rsch. Mich. Cancer Found., Detroit, 1988—91; asst. leader cancer prevention and control program Prentis Comprehensive Cancer Ctr. Met. Detroit, 1990—94; mem. faculty grad. program in cancer biology Wayne State U. Sch. of Medicine, Detroit, 1992—96; vis. rsch. prof. dept. sys. engring and ops. rsch. George Mason U., Fairfax, Va., 1996—. Mem. evaluation panel for fire programs Nat. Bur. of Standards, Gaithersburg, Md., 1966-74, evaluation panel for nat. engring. lab., 1974-80, working group on info. tech. NSF, Arlington, Va., 1980-81. Contbr. articles to profl. jours. Trustee Rumson (N.J.) Country Day Sch., 1973-81, Sea Edn. Assn., Woods Hole, Mass., 1981—. Fellow AAAS, Inst. Ops. Rsch. and The Mgmt. Scis. (coun. 1979-82), INFORMS; mem. Seabright Beach Club, Harvard Club (NYC). Avocation: cruising. Home: 7806 Hidden Meadow Ter Potomac MD 20854-1792 Office Phone: 301-983-0698. Personal E-mail: eric.wolman@erols.com.

WOLMAN, JONATHAN PALEY, journalist; b. Madison, Wis., Aug. 1, 1950; s. Joseph Martin and Anne (Paley) W.; m. Deborah Eve Lamm, Sept. 24, 1978; children: Jacob, Emma, Sophia. BA, U. Wis., 1972. Reporter AP, Detroit, 1973-74, Madison, 1973, news editor Mich. news Mich., 1975, Urban Affairs Team Washington, 1976-77, news editor Wash. (D.C.) news, 1978-80, news editor, 1980-84, asst. bur. chief Washington (D.C.) Divsn., 1984-88, bur. chief Washington, 1989-98, mng. editor New York, 1998-2000, exec. editor, 2000—02, sr. v.p., 2002—04; editl. page editor Denver Post, 2004—. Mem. Am. Soc. Newspaper Editors, 1994—. Office: Denver Post 101 W Colfax Denver CO 80202 Office Phone: 303-954-1780. Business E-Mail: jwolman@denverpost.com.

WOLMAN, M. GORDON, geography educator; b. Balt., Aug. 16, 1924; s. Abel and Anna (Gordon) W.; m. Elaine Mielke, June 20, 1951; children: Elsa Anne, Abel Gordon, Abby Lucille, Fredericka Jeannette. Student, Haverford Coll.; AB in Geology, Johns Hopkins U., 1949; MA in Geology, Harvard U., 1951, PhD in Geology, 1953. Geologist U.S. Geol. Survey, 1951-58, part-time, 1958—; assoc. prof. geography Johns Hopkins U., Balt., 1958-62, B. Howell Griswold, Jr. prof., geography and internat. affairs, 1962—. Prof. Johns Hopkins U., 1962—, chmn. dept. geography and environ. engring., 1958—90, interim provost, 1987, 90, prof. environ. health sci., 1998—; adv. com. geography U.S. Office Naval Rsch., Oak Ridge Nat. Lab.; exec. com. divsn. earth sci. NRC; internat. environ. programs com., environ. studies bd., com. water, com. mineral resources and environ., chmn. nat. commn. water quality policy NAS; chmn. NRC Com. Adv. U.S. Geol. Survey; chmn. NAS Commn. Geoscis., Environment and Resources, NRC Bd. Sustainability, 1995—2000; chmn. study land use and populationNRC Tri-Acad., China, India; environ. adv. com. Savannah River Tech. ctr.; chmn. U.S. Com. for IIASA, 1999—2003; chmn. adv. com. mgmt. and protection of water resources State. of Md., 2004—. Author: Fluvial Processes in Geomorphology, 1964; editl. bd.: Science mag. Pres. bd. trustees Park Sch., Balt.; pres. bd. dirs. Sinai Hosp., Balt., Resources for Future, 1980-87; adv. com. Inst. Nuc. Power Ops., 1982-85; active Balt. City Charter Revision Commn., Cmty. Action Com., Balt. With USNR, 1943-46. Recipient Meritorious Contbn. award Assn. Am. Geographers, 1972, Disting. Career award Geomorphology, 1993, D.L. Linton award Brit. Geomorphological Rsch. Group, 1994, Rachel Carson award Chesapeake Appreciation Inc., Ian Campbell medal Am. Geol. Inst., 1997, Nev. Med. Desert Rsch. Inst., Abel Wolman award Chesapeake sect. AWWA, 2003, Lifetime Achievement award Nat. Coun. for Sci. and the Environment, 2004, Outstanding Contbn. to Water Environment award Water Environment Fedn., 2004, Eisenhower medal Johns Hopkins U., 2005, Benjamin Franklin medal in Earth and Environ. Sci., Franklin Inst., 2006. Fellow Am. Acad. Arts and Scis., AAAS; mem. ASCE, NAS, NAE, Am. Geophys. Union (chmn. subcom. sedimentation, pres. hydrol. sect., Robert Horton medal 2000), Geol. Soc. Am. (v.p. 1983, pres. 1984, Penrose medal 1999), Am. Philos. Soc., Am. Geog. Soc. (councillor 1965-70, Cullum Geog. medal 1989), Washington Geol. Soc., Agrl. Hist. Soc., Md. Acad. Scis. (exec. com. 1970-75), Am. Geophysical Union, Phi Beta Kappa, Sigma Xi. Home: 2104 W Rogers Ave Baltimore MD 21209-4553 Office: Johns Hopkins U Dept Geography/Environ Engr Baltimore MD 21218 Home Phone: 410-664-2816; Office Phone: 410-516-7090. Business E-Mail: wolman@jhu.edu.

WOLMAN, MARTIN, lawyer; b. Albany, NY, Feb. 2, 1937; s. Benjamin S. and Sonya (Kogan) W.; children: Koren M. Wolman-Tardy, Barton T., William B., Brandon S. AB, Brown U., 1958; LLB, U. Calif., Berkeley, 1964. Bar: Calif., 1964, Conn., 1965. Atty. Conn. Bank & Trust Co., Hartford, 1964-67; assoc. Day Pitney (formerly Day, Berry & Howard), Hartford, 1967-72, ptnr., 1972—. Mem. Conn. Law Revision Commn., 1985-2002. Trustee Russell-Sage Coll., Troy, NY, 1990-96, Wadsworth Atheneum, 1994-2002, Lyme Acad. Coll. Fine Arts, 2003—; trustee Kingswood-Oxford Sch., West Hartford, Conn., 1980-93, chmn., 1986-89; bd. dirs. Hartford Hosp., 1991—, chmn., 2003—; bd. dirs. Inst. Living, 1994, Hartford Health Care Corp., 1996—; bd. govs. Hill-Stead Mus., Farmington, Conn., 1990-94. Lt. (j.g.) USN, 1958-61. Fellow Am. Coll. Trust and Estate Counsel (chmn. Conn. chpt. 1981-86); mem. Conn. Bar Assn. (chmn. exec. com. probate sect. 1979-82). Office: Day Pitney 29 S Main St West Hartford CT 06107 Office Phone: 860-275-0221. Business E-Mail: mwolman@daypitney.com.

WOLNITZEK, STEPHEN DALE, lawyer; b. Covington, Ky., Mar. 13, 1949; s. Frederick William Jr. and Mary Ruth (Meiners) W.; m. Katherine Anita Bishop, Dec. 15, 1972; children: Marcus Stephen, Justin Bishop. BA cum laude, U. Notre Dame, Ind., 1970; JD, U. Cin., 1974. Bar: Ky. 1975, US Dist. Ct. (ea. dist.) Ky. 1976, US Supreme Ct. 1978, US Dist. Ct. (we. dist.) Ky. 1981, US Ct. Appeals (6th cir.) 1991. Dep. sheriff Kenton County,

Covington, 1971—74; assoc. Taliaferro & Smith, Covington, 1975—80; ptnr. Taliaferro, Smith, Mann, Wolnitzek & Schachter, Covington, 1980—86; officer Smith, Wolnitzek, Schachter & Rowekamp P.S.C., Covington, 1986—96; pres. Wolnitzek, Rowekamp, Bender & Bonar, P.S.C., Covington, 1996—98, Wolnitzek, Rowekamp & Bonar, P.S.C., Covington, 1998—2002, Wolnitzek & Rowekamp PSC, Covington, 2002—. Bd. dirs. Ky. Legal Svcs. Plan Inc., 1984-96; adj. prof. Samuel Chase Coll. Law, No. Ky. U., 1995-98; mem. Ky. Jud. Retirement and Removal Commn. (now Ky. Jud. Conduct Commn.), 1995—, chair, 1996—. Mem. exec. com. Kenton County Boys-Girls Club, 1981-2003, sec., 1995, v.p., 1996, pres., 1997; mem. exec. com. Ky. Law Enforcement Coun., Frankfort, 1984-93, vice chmn., 1991-93, chair cert. com., 1986-93; mem. City Coun., Ft. Wright, Ky., 1984-85, mem. Bd. Adjustment, 1986-97, vice chair, 1995-97; pres. No. Ky. Cmty. Ctr., Covington, 1985-86; mem. bd. visitors Chase Coll. Law, No. Ky. U., 1995-97, U. Cin. Coll. Law, 2006—; bd. dirs. Kenton Housing Inc., 1985-2006, sec., 1991-93, v.p., 1993-95, pres., 1995-97; trustee No. Ky. Youth Leadership Found., 1992-2003, exec. com. bd. dirs., 1992-2003, pres., 1996-2001; gen. chair diocesean annual appeal Diocese of Covington, 2001; chair fin. com. St. Tynes Roman Cath. Ch., 1998-. Recipient Roy Taylor award No. Ky. Legal Aid Soc., 1985, Disting. Lawyer award No. Ky. Bar Assn., 1998; named Vol. of Yr., Cmty. Chest United Appeal, Cin., 1986. Fellow: No. Ky. Bar Found. (charter life), Ky. Bar Found. (bd. dirs. 1989—94, 1995—2000, 2003—06, charter life), Am. Bar Found.; mem.: So. Conf. Bar Presidents, Nat. Conf. Bar Presidents, Fraternal Order Police (Ky. gen. counsel 1975—), U. Cin. Alumni Assn. (trustee, bd. dirs. 1999—, treas. 2002—03, v.p. 2004—06, pres. 2006—), Def. Rsch. Inst., Ky. Def. Counsel. (bd. dirs. 1982—86), Nat. Coun. Sch. Bd. Attys., Ky. Coun. Sch. Bd. Attys. (bd. dirs. 1981—87), Assn. Def. Trial Attys., Ky. Bar Assn. (bd. govs. 1984—96, chmn. ann. conv. 1986, chmn. ho. of dels. 1986, v.p. 1992—93, pres. 1994—95), Notre Dame Club Cin. Democrat. Roman Catholic. Avocations: sports, reading. Home: 1836 Beacon Hl Covington KY 41011-3684 Office: PO Box 352 502 Greenup St Covington KY 41011-2522 Office Phone: 859-491-4444. Personal E-mail: wolnitfam@fuse.net. Business E-Mail: swolnitzek@wblaw.com.

WOLPE, DAVID, rabbi; b. 1958; Prof., Dept. Theology Jewish Theological Seminary of America, NYC, Univ. Judaism, LA, Hunter Coll.; rabbi Sinai Temple, NYC. Contbr. articles to numerous mag. and jours. incl. Newsweek, U.S. News and World Report, The Los Angeles Times, The New York Times, USA Today; appearances: PBS; CNN; CBS This Morning; A & E Mysteries of the Bible; author: The Healer of Shattered Hearts: A Jewish View of God, In Speech and In Silence: The Jewish Quest for God from Henry Holt, Teaching your Children About God, Why Be Jewish?, Making Loss Matter: Creating Meaning in Difficult Times, Floating Takes Faith: Ancient Wisdom for a Modern World. Named one of The Top 50 Rabbis in America, Newsweek Mag., 2007. Office: Sinai Temple 10400 Wilshire Blvd Los Angeles CA 90024 Fax: 310-474-6801. *

WOLPER, DAVID LLOYD, motion picture and television executive; b. NYC, Jan. 11, 1928; s. Irving S. and Anna (Fass) W.; m. Margaret Dawn Richard, May 11, 1958 (div.); children: Mark, Michael, Leslie; m. Gloria Diane Hill, July 11, 1974. Student, Drake U., 1946, U. So. Calif., 1948. V.p., treas. Flamingo Films, TV sales co., 1948-50, v.p. West Coast Ops., 1954-58; chmn., pres. Wolper Prodns., LA, 1958—. Cons., exec. producer Warner Bros., Inc., 1976—. TV prodns. include Race for Space, Making of the President 1960, 64, Biography series, Story of... series, The Yanks are Coming, Berlin: Kaiser to Khrushchev, December 7: Day of Infamy, The American Woman in the 20th Century, Hollywood and The Stars, March of Time Specials, The Rise and Fall of the Third Reich, The Legend of Marilyn Monroe, Four Days in November, Krebiozen and Cancer, National Geographic, Undersea World of Jacques Cousteau, China: Roots of Madness, The Journey of Robert F. Kennedy, Say Goodbye, George Plimpton, Appointment With Destiny, American Heritage, Smithsonian, They've Killed President Lincoln, Sandburg's Lincoln, Primal Man, The First Woman President, Chico and the Man, Get Christie Love, Welcome Back, Kotter!, Collison Course, Roots, Victory at Entebbe, Roots: The Next Generations, Moviola, The Thorn Birds, North and South Books I, II, III, Napoleon and Josephine, Alex Haley's Queen, Men Of The Dragon, Unwed Father, The Morning After; feature films include The Hellstrom Chronicle, Devil's Brigade, The Bridge at Remagen, If It's Tuesday, This Must Be Belgium, Willy Wonka and The Chocolate Factory, Visions of Eight, This is Elvis, Murder in the First, Surviving Picasso, L.A. Confidential; live spl. events include Opening and Closing Ceremonies 1984 Olympic Games, Liberty Weekend July 3-6, 1986. Trustee L.A. County Mus. Art, Am. Film Inst., L.A. Thoracic and Cardiovascular Found., Boys and Girls Clubs Am., U.S. Golf Assn. Found.; bd. dirs. Amateur Athletic Assn. L.A., L.A. Heart Inst., Acad. TV Arts and Scis. Found., So. Calif. Com. for Olympic Games, U. Soc. Calif. Cinema/TV Dept.; bd. govs. Cedars Sinai Med. Ctr.; com. mem. U.S. Olympic Team Benefit; mem. adv. com. Nat. Ctr. Jewish Film. Named to TV Hall of Fame, 1988; recipient award for documentaries, San Francisco Internat. Film Festival, 1960, 7 Golden Globe awards, 5 George Foster Peabody awards, Disting. Svc. award, US Jr. C. of C., award, Monte Carlo Internat. Film Festival, 1964, Grand Prix for TV Programs, Cannes Film Festival, 1964, medal of Chevalier, French Nat. Legion of Honor, 1990, Disting. Svc. award, Nat. Assn. Broadcasters, 2007, David L. Wolper Student Documentary Achievement award named in his honor, Internat. Documentary Assn., David L. Wolper Ctr. for Study of Documentary named in his honor, U. So. Calif. Mem.: NATAS (50 Emmy awards, 145 Emmy nominations), Caucus for Prodrs., Writers and Dirs., Prodrs. Guild Am. (David L. Wolper Prodr. of Yr. award named in his honor), Acad. Motion Picture Arts and Scis. (Oscar award, 11 Oscar nominations). Office: The David L Wolper Co Inc 617 N Rodeo Dr Beverly Hills CA 90210 Business E-Mail: thewolperletter@msn.com.

WOLPERT, ANN J., library director; BA, Boston U.; MLS, Simmons Coll., Boston. Libr. Boston Redevelopment Authority, 1967—76; with Arthur D. Little Inc., 1976—92, from tech. info. specialist, to mgr. Rsch. Libr., to dir. Cambridge Info. Ctr.; dir. Rsch. and Info. Svc. Harvard Bus. Sch., 1992—93, exec. dir. Libr. and Info. Svc., 1993—95; dir. Mass. Inst. Tech. Librs., 1996—. Mem. Strategic Planning Com. Mass. Bd. Libr. Commr., 1992—; cons. U. N.Mex., Cornell U., Adelphi U., NYC, INCAE campuses, Costa Rica, Nicaragua, League European Rsch. Librs., Amsterdam, Nat. Libr. China, Malaysia U. Sci. and Tech.; spkr. in field; chmn. mgmt. bd. Mass. Inst. Tech. Press; bd. dirs. Tech. Rev., Inc. Mem. edtl. bd. Libr. and Info. Sci. Rsch., The Jour. Libr. Adminstrn., mem. adv. com. Sci. and Engring. Indicators; contbr. libr. papers to various publs.; reviewer Tech. Rev. Advisor Publ. Com. Mass. Med. Soc.; bd. dir. Boston Libr. Consortium; hon. bd. trustees Simmons Coll.; mem. bd. dirs. Boston Libr. Consortium, NIH's Pub. Access Working Group, Steering Coms. Coalition Networked Info., Digital Libr. Fedn.; mem. Nat. Network Women Leaders Higher Edn. Am. Coun. Edn., Dean's Com., Pres.'s Acad. Coun., OpenCourseWare Faculty. Named to Nat. Network for Women Leaders in Higher Edn., Am. Coun. Edn. Mem.: Info. Tech. Strategic Planning and Resources Coordinating Com., Coun. Ednl. Tech., Com. Intellectual Property, Assn. Rsch. Libr. (past pres. 2004—05, v.p. to pres., mem. intellectual property and copyright com.). Office: Building 14S-216 MIT 77 Massachusetts Ave Cambridge MA 02139-4307 Office Phone: 617-253-5297. Office Fax: 617-253-8894. E-mail: awolpert@mit.edu. *

WOLPERT-DEFILIPPES, MARY K., science administrator; BS in Pharmacy cum laude, Creighton U., 1963; MS in Pharmacology, U. Mich., 1966, PhD in Pharmacology, 1969; postdoctoral student, Yale U., 1969—. Rsch. assoc. in pharmacology Yale U., New Haven, 1970-71; staff fellow lab. chem. pharmacology NIH, Bethesda, Md., 1971-75, pharmacologist drug evaluation br., 1976-81, supervisory pharmacologist drug evaluation br., 1981-82, dep. chief drug evaluation br., 1982-85, pharmacologist Office of Assoc. Dir., 1985-88, program dir. Grants and Contracts Ops. Br., 1988-97, chief Grants and Contracts Ops. Br., 1997—. Contbr. articles to profl. jours.; patentee in field. Mem. Gamma Pi Epsilon, Rho Chi. Office: Nat Cancer Inst Divsn Cancer Treatment and Diagnosis Exec Pla N Rm 8150 Bethesda MD 20892 Office Phone: 301-496-8783. Business E-Mail: wolpertm@exchange.nih.gov.

WOLPERT RICHARD, CHAVA, artist; b. Frankfurt, Germany, Feb. 26, 1933; arrived in Palestine, 1934, arrived in U.S., 1958; d. Ludwig Y. and Else (Ahrens) Wolpert; m. Henry A. Richard, 1959 (dec. 1971). Student, Bezalel Acad. Arts and Design, Jerusalem, 1954—56. Artist-in-residence The Jewish Mus., NYC, 1958—88. Painter, designer/creator of contemporary style ceremonial Judaica such as candelabra, Passover sets, Torah ornaments, decorative Judaica in enamel, silver, other metals, glass, porcelain, wood, acrylics, fabrics and oil painting; represented in 11 mus. collections in U.S., Australia, Europe, Israel. Pvt. Israeli Army, 1951—53. Recipient 2 Merit awards Interfaith Forum on Religion, Art and Arch., 1980, 83, Jurors' Choice award Liturgical Art Guild, 1991, Best in Judaica award Liturgical Art Guild, 1997. Mem. Judaic Art Guild, Liturgical Art Guild. Avocations: reflexology, healing with herbs. Office Phone: 718-896-4451.

WOLRAICH, MARK LEE, pediatrician, educator; BA, SUNY, Binghamton, 1966; MD, SUNY, Syracuse, 1970. Diplomate Am. Bd. Pediat. Pediatric intern SUNY, Syracuse, 1970-71; pediatric resident U. Okla. Health Scis. Ctr., Oklahoma City, 1973-74; pediatric fellowship U. Oreg. Health Scis. Ctr., 1974-76; asst. prof. U. Iowa, 1976-81, assoc. prof., 1981-86, prof., 1986-90, Vanderbilt U., 1990-2001, dir. divsn. child devel., dir. child devel. ctr., 1990-99, dir. ctr. for chronic illnesses and disabilities in children, 1990-2000; investigator J.F. Kennedy Ctr. for Rsch. on Edn. and Human Devel., 1990-2001; prof. pediat., dir. Child Study Ctr. Okla. U. Health Scis. Ctr., 2001—. Med. supr. U. Iowa Divsn. of Devel. Disabilities, 1980-90; vis. prof. Great Ormond St. Hosp. for Sick Children, London, 1983, U. Cape Town, Rondebosch Cape, South Africa, 1986, Columbus Children's Hosp., Ohio State U., Dept. Pediat., 1988; mem. Iowa State Foster Care Rev. Bd. Co-editor Advances in Developmental and Behavioral Pediatrics, 1981-92; cons. editor Am. Jour. on Mental Deficiency; editl. adv. bd. A Guide to Parent Counseling; editor The Classification of Child and Adolescent Mental Disorders in Primary Care-Diagnostic and Statistical Manual for Mental Disorders in Primary Care Child and Adolescent Version, 1996; cons. reviewer Developmental Medicine and Child Neurology, Pediatrics, Nutrition and Behavior, Jour. Pediatrics, Jour. of Social and Personal Relationships, Applied Rsch. in Mental Retardation, Jour. of Clin. Psychology, Jour. Developmental and Behavioral Pediatrics, Clin. Pediatrics, others; contbr. numerous articles to profl. publs. Recipient Disting. and Dedicated Svc. award Spina Bifida Assn. Iowa, 1979, Lou Holloway award Health Scis. Edn.; grantee NIMH, 1987-90, 98-2001, Nat. Inst. on Disability and Rehab. Rsch., 1987-89, NIH, 1988-91, Iowa Dept. Human Svcs., 1986-89, U. Iowa, 1979-87, United Cerebral Palsy Rsch. and Endl. Found., Inc., 1978-87, Iowa March of Dimes, 1980, Sugar Assn., Inc., 1983, Internat. Life Scis. Inst., 1988-91, W.T. Grant Found., 1989; MCH Lend grant, 1999—, CDC grant, 2002; named to Children and Adults with Attention-Deficit/Hyperactivity Disorder Hall of Fame, 2003. Fellow Am. Acad. Pediat. (com. 1992-2000, chair com. on psychosocial aspects child and family health 1997-2000, chair child and adolescent health action group 2000-04, chair-elect mgmt. com., 2004-, chmn. mgmt. com. 2006—), Am. Acad. Cerebral Palsy and Devel. Medicine; mem. Soc. for Devel. and Behavioral Pediat. (pres. 1994-95, program dir. 1990-93), Soc. Pediatric Psychology Assn. (assoc., Lee Salk award for disting. svc.), Soc. for Pediatric Rsch. (sr.), Am. Acad. Physician and Patient (charter), Am. Pediatric Soc. Office: Okla U Health Scis Ctr 1100 NE 13th St Oklahoma City OK 73117

WOLSKI, VICTOR J., federal judge, lawyer; m. Lisa Wolski. BA in Hist., U. Pa., 1984, BS in Econs., 1984; JD, U. Va., 1991. Bar: Calif., DC, Oreg., Wash., US Ct. Fed. Claims, US Ct. Appeals, 9th & Fed. cir., US Supreme Ct. Asst. to sec. USDA, 1988; asst. to gen. counsel US Dept. Energy; law clerk US Dist. Ct. (no. dist. Calif.), 1991—92; atty. Pacific Legal Found., 1992—97; tax counsel to Senator Connie Mack US Senate, Washington, 1997—2000; gen. counsel & chief tax adv. Joint Econ. Com., US Congress, 1999—2000; atty. Cooper & Kirk, Washington, 2000—03; judge US Ct. Fed. Claims, Washington, 2003—. Office: US Ct Fed Claims 717 Madison Pl NW Washington DC 20005 Home Phone: 703-920-8740. *

WOLSKY, JACK, retired art educator; b. Rochester, NY, Aug. 5, 1930; s. Benjamin and Mary Wolsky; m. Gladys Mindlin Wolsky, Dec. 20, 1953; children: Bonnie, Sharon, Marsha. AS, Rochester Inst. Tech., 1951; BS, SUNY, Buffalo, 1955, MS, 1957. Prof. art SUNY, Brockport, NY, 1959—85, prof. emeritus, 1985—; ret., 1985. Mem. adv. bd. Jewish Cultural Arts Commn., Rochester, NY, Modern Arts Adv. Evaluation Com., Rochester and Monroe County, NY, Rochester Inst. Tech. Alumni Assn. Exec. Coun.; juror Western Gateway project N.Y. State Dept. Transp.; juror Monroe County-Greater Rochester Internat. Airport Competition, 2001—. Represented in permanent collections Meml. Art Gallery, Rochester, Munson-Williams-Proctor Inst., Utica, N.Y., State Univ. Coll. at Brockport, New Britain (Conn.) Mus. Am. Art, Rochester Inst. Tech. Adviser, vol. Rochester chpt. ARC, 1993—; bd. dirs. Temple B'rith Kodesh, Rochester, Friends of Sch. of Arts, Rochester. Recipient Kosciuszko Found. award, 1963, Juror's award, Rochester Finger Lakes Show, 1962, Harry Hoffman Meml. award, Albright Art Gallery, 1964, Rochester C. of C. Civic award in culture and arts, 1999, Chancellor's award for excellence in tchg., SUNY, 1979, SUNY Faculty Rsch. fellowship, 1968, 1970, 1973, Visual Arts award, Arts and Cultural Coun. Greater Rochester, 2002, Lillian Fairchild award, U. Rochester, Faculty Exch. scholarship, SUNY. Avocations: tennis, gardening. Home: 295 Washington St Spencerport NY 14559 Personal E-mail: gwolsky823@aol.com.

WOLSON, CRAIG ALAN, lawyer; b. Toledo, Feb. 20, 1949; s. Max A. and Elaine B. (Cohn) Wolson; m. Ellen Carol Schulgasser, Oct. 26, 1986; children: Lindsey, Michael, Geoffrey. BA, U. Mich., 1971, JD, 1974. Bar: NY 1975, US Dist. Ct. (so. and ea. dists.) NY 1975, US Ct. Appeals (2d cir.) 1975, US Supreme Ct. 1978. Assoc. Shearman & Sterling, NYC, 1974—81; v.p., asst. gen. counsel Thomson McKinnon Securities Inc., NYC, 1981—85; v.p., sec., gen. counsel J.D. Mattus Co., Inc., Greenwich, Conn., 1985—88; also bd. dirs. J.D. Mattus Co., Inc. and affiliated cos., Greenwich, Conn.; v.p., asst. gen. counsel Chem. Bank, NYC, 1988—95; of counsel Williams & Harris, NYC, 1995-96; ptnr. Williams & Harris LLP, NYC, 1996-97; counsel Brown & Wood L.L.P., NYC, 1997-98, Mayer, Brown & Platt, NYC, 1999-2001; spl. counsel Schulte Roth & Zabel LLP, NYC, 2001—03; ptnr. Duane Morris, LLP, NYC, 2003—06; spl. counsel Cadwalader, Wickersham & Taft LLP, Charlotte, NC, 2006—. Dep. clk. Lucas County Courthouse, Toledo, 1968-69, 71-72. Articles and administrv. editor U. Mich. Law Rev., 1973-74. Named a NY Super Lawyer, Law and Politics, 2006. Mem.: ABA, Assn. of Bar of City of N.Y. (securities regulation com. 1994—97, corp. law com. 1997—2000, project fin. com. 2000—03, corp. law com. 2003—05, chmn. structured fin. com. 2004—), N.Y. State Bar Assn. (NY Super Lawyer 2006), Pi Sigma Alpha, Phi Eta Sigma, Phi Beta Kappa. Avocations: reading, piano, theater. Home: 29 Punch Bowl Dr Westport CT 06880-2130 Office: Cadwalader Wickersham & Taft LLP 227 W Trade St Charlotte NC 28202 Home Phone: 203-222-8687; Office Phone: 704-348-5363. Business E-Mail: craig.wolson@cwt.com.

WOLTER, JOHN AMADEUS, librarian, federal official; b. St. Paul, July 25, 1925; s. Amadeus Frank and Marjorie (Wears) W.; m. Joan Patricia Venard, July 6, 1956; children: Mark, Thomas, Matthew, David. Student, Coll. of St. Thomas, 1950; BA, U. Minn., 1956, MA, 1965, PhD, 1975; postgrad., Georgetown U., 1957. Officer, seaman Isthmian Lines Inc., NYC, 1943-50, 57-60; marine transp. officer Mil. Sea Transp. Ser., Washington, 1956-57; instr., map libr. U. Minn., 1961-64, asst. to dir. univ. librs., 1964-65, research fellow, 1965-66; asst. prof. Wis. State U., River Falls, 1966-68; asst. chief geography and map. div. Libr. of Congress, Washington, 1968-78, chief, 1978-91, acting dir. pub. svc. and collections MGMT I, 1989-90; cons. in geography, 1991-93. Mem. U.S. Bd. Geog. Names, 1969-83, vice chmn., 1980-81, chmn., 1981-83. Editor: Progress of Discovery: Johann Georg Kohl, 1993, Images of the World: The Atlas Through History, 1996, The Napoleonic War in the Dutch East Indies. The Minto Collection: Essay and Bibliography, 1999; rev. editor cartography divsn. Surveying and Mapping, 1971-72; mem. editl. bd. Cartographica, 1971-80, Am. Cartographer, 1974-79, Terrae Incognitae, 1973-75, ACSM Bull., 1974-80, Surveying and Mapping, 1972-80; editl. advisor The Portolan, 1986—; contbg. editor Imago Mundi, 1979-91; contbr. articles to profl. jours. Served with U.S. Army, 1950-56. Libr. of Congress Disting. Svc. award, 1992, Smithsonian Inst. Cert. of award, 1986. Mem. Internat. Geog. Union (U.S. nat. com. 1972-80, 84-88), Internat. Cartographic Assn. (U.S. mem. commn. on history of cartography 1972-76, corr. 1976-92, Assn. Am. Geographers (editorial bd. Annals 1988-92), Spl. Librs. Assn. (sec.-treas. geog.and map div. 1965), Soc. History Discoveries (sec.-treas. 1972-75, coun. 1976-78, v.p. 1983-85, pres. 1985-87), Am. Congress Surveying and Mapping (chmn. publs. com. 1978-80, Presdl. citation 1985), N.Am. Soc. Oceanic History, Soc. for History of Discoveries, Washington Map Soc., Soc. Nautical Rsch., U.S. Naval Hist. Found., Philip Lee Phillips Soc. (bd. dirs. ex officio), DAV, Am. Legion, Am. Mcht. Marine Vets., Theta Delta Chi. Home: 712 Canvasback Court Salisbury MD 21804 Personal E-mail: jawjo@comcast.net.

WOLTERING, MARGARET MAE, retired educational association administrator; b. Trenton, Ohio, July 24, 1913; d. David Lindy and Nellie Stevenson; m. Elmer Charles Woltering, Apr. 9, 1938 (dec. Oct. 1994); 1 child, Eugene Anthony. Student, Mercy Sch. Nursing, Hamilton, Ohio, 1931-34; BS, Miami U., 1962, MEd, 1968, postgrad., 1975. RN Ohio, cert. tchr., curriculum supr., Ohio Pub. Health. Pub. health nurse Ohio State Dept. Health, Butler County, 1936-49; supr. Swedish Hosp., Seattle, 1944-45; various h.s. teaching positions Cin., 1968-78; ednl. cons. Ohio, 1981-94. Cons., Ohio, 1981—96; ednl. cons. specializing in curriculum devel., 1980—91; book reviewer Friends of Libr., 1991—93; lectr. Sr. Citizens Ctr., 1992—98; instr. Bible Study, 2000—05. Author: The National Library of Poetry Anthology, 2000—03, spelling book, numerous poems; contbg. author: Theater of the Mind, 2003. Chmn. Hosp. Svc. for Children, Hamilton, 1981—85; chmn. vol. tutorial program Hamilton H.S., 1989—93, 1994—2000; taught adults Bible Study, 1995—2005. Recipient Order of St. Louis IX medallion, 2003, Champion-Tenet award, 2003. Mem.: AAUW, Toastmasters. Democrat. Roman Catholic. Avocations: reading, theater, art collecting, China porcelain painting.

WOLTERS, CURT CORNELIS FREDERIK, foreign service officer; b. Nymegen, The Netherlands, Mar. 13, 1938; came to U.S., 1957; s. Frederik and Cornelia Johanna (Jansen) W.; m. Sara J. Daughters, June 10, 1962 (div. 1980); children: Gwyneth, Chad; m. Charlotte Cooper, Sept. 22, 1980 (div. 1988); children: Lottena, Cicely; m. Sylvana K. Perry, Apr. 1989; 1 child, Roger. Student, Wash. State U., 1958-61, U. Bonn, Fed. Republic Germany, 1962-63; BA, U. Oreg., 1964, MA, 1966; MBA, U. Washington, 1976; PhD, Pacific Western U., 1989. Asst. sec. Rep. Botswana Govt., Gaborone, 1966-68; program advisor The Ford Found., NYC, 1968-74; sr. rsch. analyst Seattle C. of C., 1974-76; sr. assoc. Inst. Pub. Adminstrn. N.Y., NYC, 1976-78; freelance economist Africa, 1978-79; econ. program officer, diplomat (AID) Dept. State, Washington, 1979—. Cons. Inst. for Puget Sound Needs, Seattle, 1975-76, Pacific Cons., Washington, 1976; chair Am. Cmty. Assoc., U.S. Embassy, Lusaka, Zambia, 1998—. Contbr. numerous articles to profl. jours.; author project evaluations. Mem. civic action com. Congress of Racial Equality, Eugene, Oreg., 1965-66; vol. campaign Dixie Lee Ray Gubernatorial Campaign, Seattle, 1976; treas., chmn. fin. com. Internat. Sch. Islamabad, 1989-92. Carnegie Found. fellow, 1964-65, Africa-Asia pub. svc. fellow Maxwell Sch., 1966-68, fellow German Govt., U. Bonn, 1962-63; recipient Air Def. Command Outstanding Achievement award USAF, 1960, Cmty. Svc. award U.S. Embassy, Islamabad, 1992-93, 93-94, Meml. Order of Tin Hats, Kabaw Valley Shellhole chpt. Lusaka, Zambia, 1997—. Mem. Am. Econ. Assn., Air Force Assn., Wilson Ctr. (assoc. of Smithsonian Instn.), Am. Fgn. Svc. Assn., Holland Am. Club (treas. Greater Seattle area 1975-76), Am. Legion. Office: Dept Of State 210 Lusaka Pl Washington DC 20521-2310 E-mail: cuwolters@usaid.gov, curtwolters@yahoo.com.

WOLTERS, RAYMOND, historian, educator; b. Kansas City, Mo., July 25, 1938; s. Raymond M. and Margaret G. (Reilly) W.; m. Mary McCullough, June 23, 1962; children: Jeffrey, Kevin, Thomas. BA, Stanford U., 1960; MA, U. Calif.-Berkeley, 1962, PhD, 1967. Instr. dept. history U. Del., Newark, 1965-67, asst. prof., 1967-70, assoc. prof., 1970-75, prof., 1975-96, Thomas Muncy Keith prof., 1996—. Mem. editl. adv. bd. Acad. Am. Ency.; author: The New Negro on Campus, 1975, The Burden of Brown, 1984, Right Turn, 1996, Du Bois and His Rivals, 2002. Fellow NEH, 1971-72, Am. Coun. Learned Socs., 1978-79, Earhart Found., 1989-90; recipient Silver Gavel award ABA. Mem. Am. Hist. Assn., Orgn. Am. Historians, So. Hist. Assn. Home: 20 Bridlebrook Ln Newark DE 19711-2061 Office: U Del History Dept Newark DE 19716 Home Phone: 302-731-4181; Office Phone: 302-831-2378. Business E-Mail: wolters@udel.edu.

WOLTERSTORFF, NICHOLAS PAUL, philosophical theology educator; b. Bigelow, Minn., Jan. 21, 1932; s. Matthew and Agnes (Feenstra) W.; m. Claire Kingma, May 29, 1935; children: Amy, Eric, Robert, Klaas, Christopher. BA, Calvin Coll., 1953; MA, Harvard U., 1954, PhD in Philosophy, 1957; LittD (hon.), Northwestern Coll., 1989. Instr. Yale U., New Haven, 1957-59; prof. Calvin Coll., Grand Rapids, Mich., 1959-89; Noah Porter prof. philosophical theology Yale U., New Haven, 1989—2002, prof. emeritus, 2002—. Vis. prof. U. Tex., Austin, 1969, U. Mich., Ann Arbor, 1971, Princeton (N.J.) U., 1985, Notre Dame (Ind.) U., 1987; part-time prof. Free U., Amsterdam, The Netherlands, 1984-89; Wilde lectr. Oxford U., 1993. Author: On Universals, 1970, Reason Within Bounds of Religion, 1976, Works and Worlds of Art, 1980, Art in Action, 1980, Until Justice and Peace Embrace, 1983, Divine Discourse, 1995, John Locke and Ethics of Belief, 1996, Religion in the Public Square, 1997, Thomas Reid and the Story of Epistemology, 2001; co-edit. (with Alvin Plantinga) Faith and Rationality, 1984. Recipient Harbison award Danforth Found., 1980; NEH fellow, 1980. Mem. Am. Philos. Assn. (pres. 1991-92), Soc. Christian Philosophers (past pres.). Democrat. Avocations: gardening, woodworking. Office: Yale U Divinity Sch 409 Prospect St New Haven CT 06511-2167 Office Phone: 203-432-5343. Office Fax: 203-432-5356. E-mail: nicholas.wolterstorff@yale.edu.

WOLTZ, HOWARD OSLER, JR., retired metal products executive; b. Mt. Airy, NC, Apr. 2, 1925; s. Howard Osler and Louise (Elliott) W.; m. Joan Elizabeth Moore, Dec. 29, 1949; children: Louise, Joan Woltz Robins, Howard O. III, Edwin Moore. LLB, U. Va., 1948. Bar: N.C., 1948. Ptnr. law firm, Mt. Airy, 1948-54; pres., founder Dixie Concrete Products, Inc., Mt. Airy, 1953-69; founder Dixie Exposaic, Inc., Mt. Airy, 1963; pres., chmn. bd. Insteel Industries (formerly Exposaic Industries, Inc.), Mt. Airy, 1969-89, chmn., CEO, 1989-91, non-exec. chmn., 2005—; ret., 2005. Mem. N.C. Ho. of Reps., 1951-53; chmn. Mt. Airy-Surry County Airport

Authority, 1987-93; former pres. Greater Mt. Airy United Fund. Mem. Nat. Concrete Masonry Assn. (pres. 1965), N.C. Concrete Masonry Assn. (pres. 1959), Wire Reinforcement Inst. (chmn. 1982), Am. Wire Producers Assn. (bd. dirs. 1987-91), N.C. State Bar Assn., Mt. Airy C. of C. (Citizen of Yr. 1991). Rotary (past pres. Mt. Airy). Republican. Home: 243 Old Green Hill Rd Mount Airy NC 27030-9240 E-mail: howardwoltz@earthlink.net.

WOLTZ, KENNETH ALLEN, retired management consultant; b. Phila., Mar. 2, 1943; s. Herman and Florence (Varell) M.; m. Barbara Hand, June 18, 1966; children: Karyn, Diane, Kenneth. BS, U.S. Mil. Acad., 1966; MBA, Xavier U., 1971. Cert. mgmt. cons. Various mgmt. positions GE, Evansdale, Ohio and Bethesda, Md., 1968-73; mgr. systems Xerox Corp., Rochester, N.Y., 1973-75; dir. info. svcs. McGraw Edison, Des Plaines, Ill., 1975-77; mng. dir., mgmt. cons. KPMG, Chgo., 1977-80; mgmt. cons., CEO, Woltz & Assoc., Inc., Barrington, Ill., 1980—; mgmt. cons. Speaker at various Univs. With U.S. Army, 1966-68. Mem. Soc. Mgmt. Info. Systems, Inst. Mgmt. Cons., West Point Soc. (treas. 1975), Assn. Corp. Growth, Assn. Mgmt. Consulting Firms, Ind. Computer Cons. Assn. Home: 800 Ocean Dr Unit 1105 Juno Beach FL 33408-1724

WOLVEN, ANN REED, literature and language professor, journalist; b. Washington, May 12, 1959; d. William Thomas III and Winifred Vycital Reed; m. Gregory Allen Wolven, Nov. 6, 1982; children: Christopher James, Katherine Erienne. BA in English, Mary Baldwin Coll., Staunton, Va., 1981; MS in Journalism, Northwestern U., Evanston, Ill., 1982; M in Secondary English Edn., Lynchburg Coll., Va., 1989. Gen. assignment reporter The Potomac News, Md., 1978—80; corr. Lerner Newspapers, Washington, 1982; gen. assignment reporter Amherst-Nelson Pub. Coll., Va., 1983—86; journalism educator Lynchburg Coll., Va., 1986—89; English educator Mecklenburg County Pub. Schs., Skipwith, Va., 1992—97; English/Reading/ESL educator Vincennes U., Ind., 1998—2001; English educator Lincoln Trail Coll., Robinson, Ill., 2001—. Freelance journalist, Vincennes, 1992—. Mem. Lincoln HS Athletic Assn., Vincennes, 1993—2006; girl scout leader Shagbark Girl Scout Coun., Vincennes, 1998—2001; leader Jr. Achievement, Vincennes, 1999—2000; pres. Riley Elem. PTO, Vincennes, 2000—01; seedling grants chair Clark Academic Boosters, Vincennes, 2000—05, pres., 2004—05; mem. Lincoln HS Football Parents, Vincennes, 2003—06, Lincoln HS Volleyball Parents, Vincennes, 2004—06, Lincoln HS Girls Basketball Parents, Vincennes, 2005—06. Recipient Gen. Assignment Reporting award, Va. Press Assn., 1984, 1985, First Pl. Yearbook, Am. Scholastic Press Assn., 1995, 1996, 1997; grantee, Eisenhower Profl. Devel. Program, 2000—01. Mem.: IEA, NEA, NCTE, MLA, Tri-State U. Football Assn., Tri-State U. Parents Assn. Achievements include design of online composition and analysis course; online introduction to literature course; online English literature since 1800 course. Avocations: fossil hunting, gardening, reading, computers, travel. Home: 1403 Old Orchard Rd Vincennes IN 47591 Office: Lincoln Trail Coll 11220 State Hwy 1 Robinson IL 62454 Home Phone: 812-886-3815; Office Phone: 618-544-8657. Business E-Mail: wolvena@iecc.edu.

WOLYNES, PETER GUY, chemistry researcher, educator; b. Chgo., Apr. 21, 1953; s. Peter and Evelyn Eleanor (Etter) W.; m. Jane Lee Fox, Nov. 26, 1976 (div. 1980); m. Kathleen Cull Bucher, Dec. 22, 1984; children: Margrethe Cull, Eve Cordelia, Julia Jean. AB with highest distinction, Ind. U., 1971; AM, Harvard U., 1972, PhD in Chem. Physics, 1976; DSc (hon.), Ind. U., 1988. Rsch. assoc. MIT, Cambridge, 1975-76; asst. prof., assoc. prof. Harvard U., Cambridge, 1976-80; vis. scientist Max Planck Inst. für Biophysikalische Chemie, Gottingen, Fed. Republic Germany, 1977; assoc. prof. chemistry U. Ill., Urbana, 1980-83, prof. chemistry, 1983-2000, prof. physics, 1985-2000, prof. physics and biophysics, 1989-2000, mem. Ctr. for Advanced Study, 1989-2000; William H. and Janet LyCan prof. chemistry Ctr. for Advanced Study U. Ill., Urbana, 1993-96, Robert Eiszner prof., 1996-2000; prof. chemistry and biochemistry U. Calif., San Diego, 2000—, Francis H.C. Crick prof., 2001—, prof. physcis, 2003—. Vis. prof. Inst. for Molecular Sci., Okazaki, Japan, 1982, 87; vis. scientist Inst. for Theoretical Physics, Santa Barbara, Calif., 1987, Ecole normale Supérieure, Paris, 1992; Merski lectr. U. Nebr., 1986; Denkewalter lectr. Loyola U., 1986; Hinshelwood lectr. Oxford U., 1997; Harkins lectr. U. Chgo., 1997; FMC lectr. Princeton U., 1998; Matsen lectr. U. Tex., 2002; Rice lectr. U. NC, 2005. Contbr. numerous articles to profl. jours. Sloan fellow, 1981-83, J.S. Guggenheim fellow, 1986-87; Beckman assoc. Ctr. for Advanced Study, Urbana, 1984-85; Fogarty scholar NIH, 1994-98. Fellow AAAS, Am. Phys. Soc. (Biol. Physics prize 2004), Am. Acad. Arts and Scis., The Biophys. Soc.; mem. NAS, Am. Chem. Soc. (Pure Chemistry award 1986, Peter Debye award 2000, Edgar Fahs Smith award Phila. sect. 2005), NY Acad. Scis., Royal Soc. UK (fgn.), Phi Beta Kappa, Sigma Xi, Phi Lambda Upsilon (Fresenius award 1988), Sigma Pi Sigma, Alpha Chi Sigma. Home: 12737 Sandy Crest Ct San Diego CA 92130-2795 Office: U Calif San Diego Dept Chem and Biochemistry 9500 Gilman Dr MC 0371 La Jolla CA 92093-0371 Home Phone: 858-509-2730; Office Phone: 858-822-4825. Business E-Mail: pwolynes@ucsd.edu. *

WOMACK, EDGAR ALLEN, JR., energy executive, nuclear technology consultant; b. Humboldt, Tenn., Oct. 29, 1942; s. Edgar Allen Sr. and Lucy Opal (George) W.; m. Linda Jane Cochran, Dec. 28, 1963; children: Connie Britton, Cynthia Womack. BS, MIT, 1963, MS, 1965, PhD, 1969. With U.S. Atomic Energy Commn., Washington, 1968-73, Babcock and Wilcox Co., 1975-85, v.p. sales and mktg., 1983-85; v.p. R&D, chief tech. officer McDermott Internat., 1985—98; pres., COO BWX Techs., 1998—2002; prin. Cyncon LLC, 2003—. Mem. bd. Naval Submarine League. Patentee in field. Served to lt. USNR, 1968-70. Hon. Woodrow Wilson Found. fellow. Fellow ASME (ind. adv. bd. 1988—, chmn. 1997), AAAS, Indsl. Research Inst. (bd. 1989-96, pres. 1994-95), Sigma Xi. Presbyterian. Avocations: photography, diving, golf. Home: 401 Saint Andrews Cir Lynchburg VA 24503-3750 Personal E-mail: cyncon@adelphia.net.

WOMACK, JAMES ERROL, college president; b. Eugene, Oreg., June 27, 1940; s. John Leon and Dorothy Laverne (Yarbrough) W.; m. Sharron Kay McCullough, June 8, 1963; children: Timothy, Stephen, Joseph, Marilee. BS, N.W. Christian Coll., 1963; M Teaching, Cen. Okla. State U., 1968; postgrad., Pacific Luth. U., 1958-60, U. Oreg., 1960-63, Phillips U., 1966-68, DHum (hon.), 1987. Cert. tchr., Okla., Calif.; cert. fund raising exec.; ordained to ministry Christian Ch. (Disciples of Christ), 1963. Youth min. Lowell (Oreg.) Christian Ch., 1962-63, First Christian Ch., The Dalles, Oreg., 1963-65; youth and edn. min. Putnam City Christian Ch., Oklahoma City, 1965-68; tchr. English and social studies, coach basketball Patterson (Calif.) High Sch., 1968-71; min. youth and edn. Maze Blvd. Christian Ch., Modesto, Calif., 1968-71; dir. devel. Nat. Benevolent Assn. (Colo. Christian Home), Denver, 1976-86; coord. campus activities, coach basketball N.W. Christian Coll., Eugene, 1971-73, dir. planned giving, 1973-76, pres., 1986—. Cons. Luth. Social Svcs. Colo., Denver, 1984-85, Dayton, Ohio, 1986-89, Florence Crittenton Home Svcs., Little Rock, 1985-98; presenter in field. Mem. devel. coun. Woodhaven Learning Ctr.; mem. fin. com. and nurture commn. Cen. Rocky Mountain Region Christian Ch.; chmn. N.W. Oklahoma City Youth Week Activities; trustee N.W. Christian Coll.; active Denver Planned Giving Roundtable; regional bd. dirs. N.W. Regional Ch., Christian Ch. in Kans. Recipient Book Award for Acad. Excellence Christian Bd. of Pub. Mem. Nat. Soc. Fund Raising Execs., Nat. Benevolent Assn. (trustee best of caring fund), Oreg. Ind. Coll. Assn. (mem. exec. com.), Colo. Assn. Fund Raisers (past sec., bd. dirs.), Emerald Empire Fellowship of Christian Athletes (charter mem., sec., bd. dirs.), Ministerial Alliance (chmn. migrant ministries), Rotary (mem. program com. Eugene chpt. 1990), Optimists (bd. dirs. Highland Park chpt.), Civitan, Denver City Club. Avocations: fishing, reading, sports. Home: 1363 Windsor Ct Springfield OR 97477-8107 Office: NW Christian Coll 828 E 11th Ave Eugene OR 97401-3745 E-mail: pres@nwcc.edu.

WOMACK, LEE ANN, country musician; b. Jacksonville, TX, Aug. 19, 1966; married; 2 children. Singer: (albums) Lee Ann Womack, 1997, Some Things I Know, 1998, I Hope You Dance, 2000, The Season for Romance, 2002, Something Worth Leaving Behind, 2002, Greatest Hits, 2004, There's More Where That Came From, 2005 (Album of Yr., Country Music Assn., 2005), (singles) The Fool, 1997, Does My Ring Burn Your Finger, 2000 (USA Today song of yr., 2001), I Hope You Dance, 2000, I May Hate Myself in the Morning, 2005 (Single of Yr., Country Music Assn., 2005); with Willie Nelson (duet) Mendonceno County Line, 2002 (Country Music Assn. Vocal Event of Yr.). Studio: MCA Records Inc 60 Music Sq E Nashville TN 37203 Office: Richard De la Font Agency Inc Ste 505 4845 S Sheridan Rd Tulsa OK 74145 Office Phone: 615-244-8944, 918-665-6200.

WOMACK, ROBERT ROBINSON, artist; m. Catherine Roseberry. BFA in Painting and Printmaking, Va. Commonwealth U., Richmond, 1980. Pvt. practice artist Coloratura, Richmond, 1983—. Founding mem. Folk Art Soc. Am., Richmond, 1987; juror Richmond Craft and Design Show, 1999; spkr. in field. Featured artist: brochure Coloratura: Stories and Scenarios, 1992, Right at Home: American Studio Furniture, 2004, catalog Sleight of Hand, McDonough Mus., 2004; Represented in permanent collections Renwick Gallery Collections, Smithsonian Am. Art Mus., Washington, numerous pvt. collections. Visual Artist fellow, Nat. Endowment for the Arts, 1994, Individual Artist fellow, Va. Commn. for the Arts, 1994, 1999, Residency fellow, Va. Ctr. for the Creative Arts, 2001, 2002, 2004, 2007. Home: 3810 Thimble Ln Richmond VA 23222

WOMACK, THOMAS HOUSTON, manufacturing executive; b. Gallatin, Tenn., June 22, 1940; s. Thomas Houston and Jessie (Eckel) Womack; m. Linda Walker, July 20, 1963 (div. Dec. 1989); children: Britton Ryan, Kelley Elizabeth; m. Pamela Ann Reed, Apr. 20, 1991. BSME, Tenn. Tech. U., Cookeville, 1963. Project engr. U.S. Gypsum Co., Jacksonville, Fla., 1963-65; project mgr. Maxwell House Divsn. Gen. Foods Corp., Jacksonville, 1965-68, mfg. mgr. Hoboken, NJ, 1968-71, divsn. ops. planning mgr., 1971-73; industry sales mgr. J.R. Schneider Co., Tiburon, Calif., 1973-79; pres. and CEO Womack Internat., Inc., Mare Island, 1979—; chmn. and CEO Ceramic Microlight Techs., Inc., 1995—; pres. and CEO Micronic Filtration Tech., LLC, 2005—. Mem.: Am. Soc. Chem. Engrs., Soc. Mfg. Engrs., Am. Filtration Soc., Soc. Tribologists and Lubrication Engrs. Achievements include patents for. Avocations: skiing, vintage exotic sports cars. Office: Womack Internat Inc PO Box 2175 Vallejo CA 94592-0175 Office Phone: 707-562-1000. Office Fax: 707-562-1010. Business E-Mail: womack@womack.com.

WOMBLE, KEN, theater educator, film director, writer, actor; s. Maxine Womble; m. Sandy Womble. BFA in Theatre, Fla. State U., Tallahassee, 1976; MFA in Theatre, So. Meth. U., Dallas, 1978. Dir. of performing arts St. Margaret's Episcopal Sch., San Juan Capistrano, Calif., 1997—2005; theatre instr. Saddleback Coll., Mission Viejo, 2000—05; asst. prof., theatre U. No. Colo., Greeley, 2005—. Author: (play) A Midsummer Night's Dream, An Adaptation, 2003; dir.: (documentary film) Wally Huntoon, A Life By Design, 2005; author: (play) Romeo and Juliet, An Adaptation, 2006; actor: (theatre, film and television) Over 100 appearances. Mem.: AFTRA, SAG, Actors' Equity Assn. Office: Univ No Colo 501 20th St Campus Box 49 Greeley CO 80639 Home Phone: 970-351-1193; Office Phone: 970-351-1193.

WOMBLE, WILLIAM FLETCHER, lawyer; b. Winston-Salem, NC, Oct. 29, 1916; s. Bunyan Snipes and Edith (Willingham) Womble; m. Jane Payne Gilbert, Oct. 11, 1941; children: William Fletcher, Jr., Jane Womble Haver, Russell G., Ann Womble Strader. AB, Duke U., 1937, JD, 1939; LHT (hon.), High Point U., 2000. Bar: NC 1939. Assoc. Womble Carlyle Sandridge & Rice P.L.L.C. and predecessors, Winston-Salem, 1939-47, mem., 1947—. Campaign chmn. Forsyth County Cmty. Chest, 1949; mem. NC Gen. Statutes Commn., 1953—55, NC Bd. Higher Edn., 1955—57, 1960—63, NC Adv. Budget Commn., 1957—58; trustee, past chmn. High Point Coll. (now High Point U.), 1950—; trustee Winston-Salem State U., 1953—55; pres. Children's Home, 1959—75; bd. dirs. Triad United Meth. Home (now Arbor Acres United Meth. Retirement Cmty.), 1976—87, 1989—97, treas., 1975—79, pres., 1979—85; hon. chair United Way, Forsyth County, 1998; mem. People-to-People Citizen Amb. Program, 1981, 1986, NC Ho. of Reps., 1953—58, chmn. com. higher edn., vice chmn. fin. com., 1957; chmn. adminstrv. bd. Centenary United Meth. Ch., 1961—63, chmn. bd. trustees, 1983—85; trustee Sr. Svcs., Inc., 1998—2005, chair ann. fund., 2004—05. Served to maj. USAF, 1941—46. Named Trustee of the Yr., Gen. Bd. Global Mins. of United Meth. Ch., Health and Wlfare Minst. Dept., 1989. Fellow: Am. Bar Found. (life; state chmn. 1984—89, Fifty Yr. award 1995); mem.: ABA (ho. dels. 1978—87, bd. govs. 1982—85, exec. coun. Nat. Conf. Bar Pres. 1985—88, ethics com. 1985—91, resource devel. coun. 1986—92, chmn. jud. code subcom. 1988—91, chair affiliate outreach com. 1994—97, coun. mem. sr. lawyers divsn. 1995—97), Forsyth County Bar Assn. (pres. 1962), Am. Judicature Soc., NC State Bar (trustee Interest on Lawyers Trust Accounts 1983—91, vice chmn. 1989—91, Chief Justice's Professionalism award 2001), NC Bar Assn. (pres. 1966—67, chmn. endowment founders campaign 1986—87, chair sr. lawyers divsn. 1994—95, Judge John J. Parker award 1984), Soc. Cin., Winston-Salem C. of C. (pres. 1960—61), Old Town Club, Rotary (local pres. 1964). Democrat. Home: 1244 Arbor Rd 441 Winston Salem NC 27104-1139 Office: Womble Carlyle Sandridge & Rice One W 4th St Winston Salem NC 27101 Office Phone: 336-721-3603. Office Fax: 336-733-8369. Business E-Mail: wwomble@wcsr.com.

WOMMACK, RON, architect; Prin. Ron Wommack Arch., Dallas. Prin. works include Parkwood Lofts (Honor award, AIA Dallas, 1995, Honor award, Tex. Soc. Archs., 1996), Parkwood Terrace (Citation award, AIA Dallas, 1996), Mitchell Lofts (Preservation Dallas Achievement award, 2000), Powerstation (Honor award, AIA Dallas, 2002, D Mag. Home award, 2002), Miro Townhomes (Merit award, AIA Dallas, 2002), Commerce Street Townhomes, Mario Sinacola & Sons hdqs., 3500 Gillon (D Mag. Home award, 2002), 4222 Buena Vista, Skinceuticals Corp. Offices. Fellow: AIA; mem.: Dallas Architecture Forum (bd. mem., pres.), Tex. Soc. Archs. Office: 918 Dragon St Dallas TX 75207 Office Phone: 214-915-0923. Office Fax: 214-915-0901. E-mail: ron@ronwommack.com. *

WON, YOU-YEON, engineering educator; b. Seoul, Republic of Korea; BS, Seoul Nat. U., 1992; PhD, U. Minn., Mpls., 2000. Postdoctoral assoc. in materials sci. and engring. MIT, Cambridge, Mass., 2000—01; postdoctoral fellow in applied physics Harvard U., Cambridge, 2001—03; asst. prof. chem. engring. Purdue U., West Lafayette, Ind., 2003—. Mem.: AIChE, Materials Rsch. Soc., Am. Chem. Soc., Am. Phys. Soc. Achievements include research in polymer and colloid sciences, nanobiotechnology. Office: Purdue U 480 Stadium Mall Dr West Lafayette IN 47907 Office Phone: 765-497-3959.

WONDER, STEVIE (STEVELAND HARDAWAY JUDKINS, STEVLAND MORRIS), musician; b. Saginaw, Mich., May 13, 1950; m. Syreeta Wright, 1971 (div. 1972); m. Kai Milla Wonder, 2001; children: Kailand, Mandla Kadjaly Carl Stevland Morris; children: Aisha, Keita, Mumtaz. Student pub. schs. in Detroit until age 12; then transferred to, Mich. Sch. for Blind. Recording artist Motown Records, Detroit, 1963—70; founder, pres. music pub. co. Black Bull Music, Inc., 1970—, Wondirection Records, Inc., 1982—. (singles) Fingertips, 1963, Uptight/Purple Raindrops, 1965, Someday At Christmas/The Miracles of Christmas, I'm Wondering/Everytime I See You I Go Wild, 1966, I Was Made To Love Her/Hold Me, 1967, Shoo-Be-Doo-Be-Doo-Da-Day/Why Don't You Lead Me To Love, You Met Your Match/My Girl, 1968, For Once In My Life, I Don't Know Why, My Cherie Amour, Yester-Me, Yester-You, Yesterday, Never Had a Dream Come True, Signed, Sealed, Delivered I'm Yours, Heaven Help Us All, I Wish (Grammy award, 1977), Don't You Worry 'Bout a Thing, You Haven't Done Nothin', Boogie on Reggae Woman (Grammy award, 1975), Isn't She Lovely, Sir Duke, Another Star, As, You Are the Sunshine of My Life (Grammy award, 1974), Superstition (Grammy award, 1974), Higher Ground, Living For the City (Grammy award, 1975), I Just Called to Say I Love You; singer: (albums) Tribute to Uncle Ray, 1962, With a Song In My Heart, 1963, The Jazz Soul of Little Stevie, 1963, The Twelve-Year Old-Genius, 1963, Stevie At The Beach, 1964, Down to Earth, 1966, Uptight, 1966, Someday at Christmas, 1967, I Was Made To Love Her, Someday At Christmas, 1967, Eivets Rednow (Featuring Alfie), 1968, For Once in My Life, 1968, Stevie Wonder's Greatest Hits, 1968, My Cheric Amour, Talk of The Town, 1969, Live at the Talk of the Town, 1970, Signed, Sealed and Delivered, 1970, Live In Person, 1970, Steve Wonder's Greatest Hits Vol. 2, 1971, Where I'm Coming From, 1971, Talking Book, 1972, Music of My Mind, Stevie Wonder Live, Where I'm Coming From, Talking Book, 1972, Portrait, 1976, Innervisions, 1973 (Grammy award, 1974), Fulfillingness' First Finale, 1974 (Grammy award, 1975), Songs In the Key of Life, 1976 (Grammy award, 1977), Looking Back, 1977, Stevie Wonder's Journey Through the Secret Life of Plants, 1979, Hotter than July, 1980, Stevie Wonder's Original Musiquarium, 1982, Woman in Red, 1984, In Square Circle, 1985 (best soul/R&B album of yr., Down Beat mag. Readers' poll, 1986), I Just Called to Say I love You, 1984 (Acad. award, Golden Globe award for single, 1984), Characters, 1987, Jungle Fever, 1991, Inner Peace, Motown Legends, 1995, Natural Wonders, 1995, Conversation Peace, 1996, Song Review, 1996, At the Close of a Century, 1999, The Definitive Collection, 2002, A Time to Love, 2005 (Grammy for Best Male Pop Vocal Performance, 2006), (Soundtrack) Bamboozled; actor: (films) Bikini Beach, Muscle Beach Party, 1964; frequent appearances (TV series) Mike Douglas Show, guest host Saturday Night Live. Named Musician of Year, Down Beat mag. Rock/Blues Poll, 1973—75, 1977—78, Best Selling Male Soul Artist of Year, Nat. Assn. Rec. Merchandisers, 1974; named to Songwriters Hall of Fame, 1982, Rock and Roll Hall of Fame, 1989; recipient Nelson Mandela Courage award, 1991, numerous Grammy awards, numerous awards for best singer/songwriter, Rock Music award, 1977, Am. Music award, 1978, Am. Video award for best rhythm and blues video for Ebony and Ivory, 1982, Century award, Billboard Music Awards, 2004, Grammy Award (with Beyoncé) for Best R&B Performance by Duo, 2006, Grammy Award (with Tony Bennett) for Best Pop Collaboration with Vocals, 2007, Lifetime Achievement award, Nat. Civil Rights Mus., 2006. Office: 4616 W Magnolia Blvd Burbank CA 91505-2731

WONDERS, PAMELA KIM, music educator; b. East Liverpool, Ohio, Aug. 3, 1955; d. Richard Daniel and Lila Lee Wonders. BS in music edn., Trevecca Nazarene U., 1978; MEd, Tenn. State U., 1991. Band dir. Hillsboro H.S., Nashville, 1978—79, DuPont Elem., Nashville, 1979—80; choral dir. Maplewood H.S., Nashville, 1980—86, Hunters Lane H.S., Nashville, 1986—. Regional mgmt. team Sweet Adelweiss Internat., Tulsa, Okla., 2000—03, dir. musical activities, 1986—89; dir. Metro Nashville Chorus, 1988—. Mem.: Mid. Tenn. Vocal Assn., Music Educators Nat. Conf., Nat. Edn. Assn. Home: 590 Thomas Jefferson Circle Madison TN 37115 Office: Hunters Lane HS 1150 Hunters Lane Nashville TN 37207 Personal E-mail: wondersk@aol.com.

WONDERS, WILLIAM CLARE, geography educator; b. Toronto, Apr. 22, 1924; s. George Clarence and Ann Mary (Bell) W.; m. Lillian Paradise Johnson, June 2, 1951; children: Karen Elizabeth, Jennifer Anne, Glen William. BA with honors, Victoria Coll., U. Toronto, 1946; MA, Syracuse U., 1948; PhD, U. Toronto, 1951; Fil. Dr. h.c., Uppsala U., 1981. Teaching asst. dept. geography Syracuse U., 1946-48; lectr. dept. geography U. Toronto, 1948-53; asst. prof. geography dept. polit. economy U. Alta., 1953-55, assoc. prof. geography, 1955-57, prof., head dept. geography, 1957-67, prof. dept. geography, 1967-87, Univ. prof., 1983—, prof. emeritus, 1987—. Vis. prof. geography U. B.C., 1954, U. Okla., 1965-66, St. Mary's U., 1977, U. Victoria, 1989, J.F. Kennedy Inst., Free U. Berlin, 1990; guest prof. Inst. Geography, Uppsala (Sweden) U., 1962-63; rsch. fellow in Geography U. Aberdeen, Scotland, 1970-71, 78; vis. fellow in Can. Studies, U. Edinburgh, Scotland, 1987. Author: Looking at Maps, 1960, The Sawdust Fusiliers, 1991, Norden and Canada-A Geographer's Perspective, 1992, Alaska Highway Explorer, 1994; author: (with T. Drinkwater et al.) Junior Atlas of Alberta, 1979; contbr., editor: Canada's Changing North, 1971, rev. edit., 2003, The North, 1972, The Arctic Circle, 1976, Knowing the North, 1988, Geographica's Pocket World Reference, 2000, Frontiersmen & Settlers, 2002, Geordies, Yankees and Canucks, 2006; contbr. articles to jours. and encys., chapters to books. Active Nat. Adv. Com. on Geog. Rsch., 1965-69; chmn. Boreal Inst. No. Studies (Can. Circumpolar Inst.), 1960-62; mem. Can. Permanent Com. on Geog. Names, 1981-94, Alta. Hist. Sites Bd., 1978-83, vice-chmn., 1982-83; policy bd. Can. Plains Rsch. Centre, U. Regina (Sask.), 1975-86; adv. bd. Royal Tyrrell Mus. Paleontology, 1984-89; bd. dirs. Muttart Found., 1986-93, 95-98, v.p., 1991-93. Decorated Order of Can., Can. Forces Decoration; recipient Queen's Jubilee medal; NSF sr. fgn. scientist fellow, 1965-66; Can. Coun. leave fellow, 1969-70, 77-78; Nuffield Found. fellow, 1970-71. Fellow Arctic Inst. N.Am., Royal Soc. Can., Royal Can. Geog. Soc. (Massey medalist 1998); mem. Can. Assn. Geographers (past pres.), Can. Assn. Scottish Studies (councillor 1974-77), Scottish Soc. No. Studies, Champlain Soc. (councillor 1981-86), Sigma Xi, Gamma Theta Upsilon. E-mail: wwonders@shaw.ca.

WONG, AH-SAN, planetary scientist, musician, writer; d. Chuen Wong and Mei Leung; m. Michael T. Elliott, Oct. 3, 2005; 1 child, Logan Tian-Yang. BS in Physics, Calif. State U., Fresno, 1992; MS in Physics, Calif. Inst. Tech., Pasadena, 1995, PhD in Physics, 2002. Sr. rsch. fellow U. Mich., Ann Arbor, 2002—06; rsch. fellow Calif. Inst. Tech., Calif., 2006—. Mem.: Am. Astron. Soc. (mem. divsn. planetary sci.), Am. Geophys. Union.

WONG, ANDREA J., broadcast executive; b. 1966; BS in Elec. Engring., MIT, 1988; MBA, Stanford U., 1993. Rschr. ABC News PrimeTime Live, 1993—94; exec. asst. pres. ABC TV Network, 1994—95; exec. asst. to pres. ABC, Inc., 1995—97, v.p., exec. asst. pres., 1997—98; v.p. alt. series & specials. ABC Entertainment, 1998—2000, sr. v.p. alt. series & specials., 2000—04, exec. v.p. alt. programming, specials & late night, 2004—07; pres., CEO Lifetime Entertainment Services, 2007—. Named one of 100 Most Powerful Women in Entertainment, Hollywood Reporter, 2006. Office: Lifetime Entertainment Services World Wide Plz 309 W 49th St New York NY 10019 *

WONG, B.D. (BRADLEY DARYL WONG), actor; b. San Francisco, Oct. 24, 1962; s. William D. and Roberta Christine (Leong) W.; 1 child, Jackson Foo. Grad. high sch., San Francisco. Bd. dirs. Alliance of Resident Theatres, N.Y.C.; lectr. Royce Carlton Inc. Speakers, N.Y.C., 1991—. Appeared (Broadway play) M. Butterfly, 1988-90 (Tony award, N.Y. Drama Desk award, N.Y. Outer Critics Circle award, Theatre World award, Clarence Derwent award, 1988), You're a Good Man, Charlie Brown, 1999, Pacific Overtures, 2004, Children and Art, 2005; (regional theatre) Pippin, 2005, Chaucer in Rome, Shanghai Moon, Herringbone, 2007; (films) Family Business, 1990, The Freshman, 1990, Mystery Date, 1991, The Lounge People, 1991, Father of the Bride, 1991, The Lounge People, 1992, Jurassic Park, 1993, Men of War, 1994, The Ref, 1994, Father of the Bride II, 1995, Executive Decision, 1996, Stinkers, 1997, Seven Years in Tibet, 1997, Mulan, 1998, Slappy and the Stinkers, 1998, The Salton Sea, 2002, Stay, 2005; (TV movies) And the Band Played On, 1993, Judith Krantz's Dazzle, 1995, Dazzle, 1995, The Substitute 2: School's Out, 1998, (voice) Reflections on Ice: Michelle Kwan Skates to the Music of Disney's Mulan, 1998, Miss USA, 2004; (TV series) The X Files, 1996, Oz, 1997, Chicago Hope, 1999, Law & Order: Special Victims Unit, 2002—; TV guest appearances include (voice) Kim Possible, 2002. Recipient Arts in Leadership award, Coro Found., San Francisco, 1991, Jimmie award for Arts Advocacy, Assn. Asian- Pacific Am. Artists, L.A., 1991. Mem. SAG, AFTRA, Asian-Pacific Alliance for Creative Equality (co-founder 1990), Asian Am. Legal Def. and Edn. Fund (Justice in Action award, 1991), Actors' Equity Assn. *

WONG, BRIAN JET-FEI, surgeon; b. LA, Sept. 23, 1963; s. Richard Toy and Hazel F. (Lue) W. BS, U. So. Calif., 1985; postgrad., Oxford U., 1985-86; MD, Johns Hopkins U., 1990; PhD, U. Amsterdam, 2001. Resident U. Calif., Irvine, 1990-96, clin. instr., 1997-98, asst. prof., 1998—2001, assoc. prof., 2001—06, prof., 2006—. Rsch. assoc. Beckman Laser Inst., Irvine, 1994—. Mem. ACS, Biomed. Optical Soc., SPIE, Am. Acad. Facial Plastic Surgery. Avocation: surfing. Office: U Calif Dept Otolaryngology 101 City Dr S # B25r81 Orange CA 92868-3201 Office Phone: 714-456-5753.

WONG, CHING-PING, chemist, materials engineer; b. Canton, China, Mar. 29, 1947; came to U.S., 1966; s. Kwok-Keung and Yun-Kwan W. BS in Chemistry, Purdue U., 1969; PhD in Organic/Inorganic Chemistry, Pa. State U., 1975. Postdoctoral scholar Stanford (Calif.) U., 1975-77; mem. rsch. staff AT&T Bell Labs., Princeton, NJ, 1977-82, sr. mem. tech. staff, 1982-87, disting. mem. tech. staff, 1987-92; AT&T Bell Labs. fellow, 1992-96; Regents, Charles Smithgall Inst. endowed chair, disting. prof. Sch. of Materials Sci. and Engring., Ga. Inst. Tech., Atlanta, 1996—; assembly, reliability and thermal mgmt. rsch. dir. NSF Packaging Rsch. Ctr. Program chmn. 39th Electronic Components Conf., 1989; gen. chmn. 41st Electronic Components and Tech. Conf., 1991; bd. govs. IEEE-Components, Hybrids and Mfg. Tech. Soc., 1987-89, tech. v.p., 1990-91, pres., 1992-93. Author, editor: Polymers for Electronic and Photonic Applications, 1993; contbr. articles to profl. jours. Recipient Outstanding Papers and Contbns. award IEEE-Components, Hybrids and Mfg. Tech. Soc., 1990, 91, 94, 96, 1998, 2001, Ga. Tech. Outstanding Faculty award, London, 1999, award of excellence Univ. Press, 2000, Ga. Tech. Disting. Profl award, 2004. Fellow: Nat. Acad. Engring., IEEE (Outstanding Sustained Tech. Contbns. award 1995, Millenium medal 2000, EAB Exceptional Continuation Edn. award 2001, CPMT Outstanding Exceptional Tech.Contbn. award 2002, CPMT Field award 2006). Achievements include over 50 U.S. and numerous internat. patents for integrated device passivation and encepsulation area; pioneer in application of gel polymers for device reliability without hermeticity, nano technology, a new application on electronic device packaging. Office: Ga Inst Tech Sch Materials Sci & Engring 771 Ferst Dr Atlanta GA 30332-0001 Office Phone: 404-894-8391. Business E-Mail: cp.wong@mse.gatech.edu.

WONG, DAVID T., biochemist, researcher; b. Hong Kong, Nov. 6, 1935; arrived in US, 1957; s. Chi-Keung and Pui-King Wong; m. Christina Lee, Dec. 28, 1963; children: Conrad, Melvin, Vincent. Student, Nat. Taiwan U., 1955—56; BS, Seattle Pacific U., 1961; MS, Oreg. State U., 1964; PhD, U. Oreg., 1966. Post doctoral fellow U. Pa., Phila, 1966—67; sr. biochemist Lilly Rsch. Labs., Indpls., 1968-72, rsch. biochemist, 1973-77, sr. rsch. scientist, 1978-89, rsch. advisor, 1990-97, Lilly Disting. Rsch. fellow, 1997-99, cons., 2000—. Adj. prof. biochemistry and molecular biology Ind. U. Sch. Medicine, 1986—96, adj. prof. neurobiology, 1991—. Mem. editl. bd.: Chinese Jour. Physiology, 1996—2000; contbr. articles to sci. jours. Named Alumnus of Growing Vision, Seattle Pacific U., 1991, Alumnus of Yr., 1998, Disting. Alumni Scientist award, Oreg. Health and Sci. U., 2004; recipient Scientist of Yr. Pres.' award, Chinese Neurosci. Soc., 1991, Discoverers award, Pharm. Mfr. Assn., 1993, Lifetime Rsch. award, Mental Health Assn. Ind., 1996, World Difference award, Ind. Health Industry Forum, 1996, Pharm. Discoverer's award Prozac, Nat. Alliance Rsch. Schizophrenia and Depression, 1996, Outstanding Achievement in Neurosci. Rsch. award, Lilly Neuroscience Eli Lilly and Co., 2000, Cornerstone award, Am. Drugstore Mus. Indpls., 2000, Excellence award, Asian Am. Alliance, Inc., 2002, Pioneer Recognition award, Com. 100, 2002, Excellence award, U.S. Pan Asian Am. C. of C., 2002, Hon. Ga. Citizen, mem. Goodwill Amb. Corp., State of Ga., 2003; Alumni fellow, Oreg. State U., 2003. Mem.: Ind. Chinese-Am. Profls. Assn. (pres. 2000), Soc. Chinese Bioscientists Am. (Disting. Scientist award for drug discovery 2004), Soc. Neurosci. (pres. Indpls. chpt. 1987, 1988), Am. Soc. Pharmacology and Exptl. Therapeutics, Am. Coll. Neuropsychopharamcology, Indpls. Assn. Chinese Ams. (pres. 1987). Achievements include patents in field; research in biochemistry and pharmacology of neurotransmission; development of other drugs including Strattera (Atomoxetive) for attention deficit hyperactivity disorder; co-inventor and developer of antidepressant drugs, Prozac (Fluoxetine)and Cymbalta (Duloxetine, a serotonin and norepinephrine uptake inhibitor); co-inventor dapoxetine (serotonin uptake inhibitor); research in potentially useful substances which enhance transmission of norepinephrine, dopamine, serotonin, acetylcholine, and GABA-neurons; natural products led to the discovery of caboxylic ionophores: Narasin and A204, which increase transport of cations across biomembranes. Home: 5812 E Fall Creek Parkway N D Indianapolis IN 46226-1051 Home Fax: 317-254-8288. Personal E-mail: dtwongindy@iquest.net.

WONG, EDWARD VINCENT, investment company executive; b. Houston, Nov. 12, 1927; s. Samuel Bark and Mary Eng-Shee Wong; m. Ernestine Elizabeth Kobl (dec.). BS, Stewart Inst., NJ; BA, Inst. Culinary Arts, New Haven, 1956; MBA, Hartford Grad. Ctr., Conn., 1978; D, Pace U., NYC, 1980. Investment exec. Far East Asian Group, Hong Kong. Mem. US Trade Commn.; sr. fellow Overseas Devel. Coun. Far East. Author: International Monetary. Mentor Holy Name Soc., Hartford, Conn., St. Joseph Catheral, Hartford, Conn. Col. US Army. Named Knight of St. Gregory, Vatican, Pope Pius XII, 1952. Fellow: Les Amis Escoffer Soc., Soc. Culinaire Philanthropique. Democrat. Roman Catholic. Avocations: piano, poetry, chess, art. Office: Far East Asian Group PO Box 189 Lynbrook NY 11563

WONG, ELIZABETH HUNG, organist, choirmaster; m. James Wong, Jan. 5, 2002. MusM, Performer's Cert., Northwestern U., Evanston, Ill., 1995. Asst. organist, choirmaster Christ Ch., Bronxville, NY, 2001—02; organist, choirmaster Ch. of the Epiphany, N.Y.C., 2004—. Mem.: Assn. Anglican Musicians, Am. Guild Organists (sec. 2004). Office: Church of the Epiphany 1393 York Ave at 74th St New York NY 10708 Office Phone: 212-737-2720/24. Business E-Mail: wongehyh@gmail.com.

WONG, JAMES BOK, economist, chemical engineer, technologist, consultant; b. Canton, China, Dec. 9, 1922; came to U.S., 1938, naturalized, 1962; s. Gen Ham and Chen (Yee) W.; m. Wai Ping Lim, Aug. 3, 1946, (dec.); children: John, Jane Doris, Julia Ann; m. Betty K.C. Yeow, May 25, 2002. BS summa cum laude in Agr., U. Md., 1949, BS summa cum laude in Chem. Engring., 1950; MS, U. Ill., 1951, PhD, 1954. Rsch. asst. U. Ill., Champaign-Urbana, 1950-53; chem. engr. Std. Oil of Ind., Whiting, 1953-55; process design engr., rsch. engr. Shell Devel. Co., Emeryville, Calif., 1955-61; sr. planning engr., prin. planning engr. Chem. Plastics Group, Dart Industries, Inc. (formerly Rexall Drug & Chem. Co.), LA, 1961-66, supr. planning and econs., 1966-67, mgr. long range planning and econs., 1967, chief economist, 1967-72, dir. econs. and ops. analysis, 1972-78, dir. internat. techs., 1978-81; pres. James B. Wong Assocs., LA, 1981—. Chmn. bd. dirs. United Pacific Bank, 1988—; tech. cons. various corps. Author: Jade Eagle, 2000; contbr. articles to profl. jours. Bd. dirs., pres. Chinese Am. Citizens Alliance Found.; mem. Asian Am. Edn. Commn., 1971-81. Served with USAAF, 1943-46. Recipient L.A. Outstanding Vol. Svc. award, 1977. Mem. Am. Chem. Soc., Am. Inst. Chem. Engrs., VFW (vice comdr. 1959), Commodores (named to exec. order 1982), Sigma Xi, Tau Beta Pi, Phi Kappa Phi, Pi Mu Epsilon, Phi Lambda Upsilon, Phi Eta Sigma. Home: 2460 Venus Dr Los Angeles CA 90046-1646 Office Phone: 323-876-4083. *Personal philisophy: A man's reputation is his most prized possession.*

WONG, JOE BING, retired architect; b. Clifton, Ariz., Aug. 17, 1921; s. Hing Chong and Mock See Wong; m. Lillian Phyllis Jew, Dec. 19, 1942; children: Jeffrey(dec.), Judy Margaret. Student, U. Calif., Berkeley, 1938—41, Calif. Sch. Fine Arts, 1946—48. Registered arch., Calif., 1952, Ariz., 1954, Nev., 1963, Colo., 1968, Tex., 1990, Nat. Coun. Archtl. Registration, 1964. Ship conversion engr. Gen. Engring.-Drydock, San Francisco, 1941—42; designer, chief draftsman Higgins & Root Archs., San Jose, Calif., 1946—53, Nichols-White Archs., Palo Alto, Calif., 1945—46; arch., owner Wong Assocs., Scottsdale, Ariz., 1954—98; ret., 1998. Pres. Associated Scottsdale Archs., 1968—85. Active Scottsdale Libr. Bd., 1962—68; mem., chmn. Scottsdale Design Rev. Bd., 1968—71, Scottsdale Bldg. Adv. Bd., 1971—83, Scottsdale Adv. Bd. Appeals, 1983—90. With US Army, 1943—46. Fellow: Internat. Inst. Arts and Letters (life); mem.: AIA (emeritus), Nat. Soc. Lit. and the Arts, Scottsdale Charros (life). Avocations: fishing, painting. Home: 7782 Via Sonrisa Scottsdale AZ 85258

WONG, KON MAX, electrical engineer educator; b. Macau, China, June 11, 1945; arrived in Can., 1976; s. Ho Ting and Sin Hung (Yung) Wong; m. Margaret Ellen Rumsey, Aug. 25, 1984; children: An Zhong Alexander, Hui Zhong Richard. BSc in Engring., U. London, 1969; DIC, Imperial Coll., London, 1972; PhD, U. London, 1974, DSc, 1995. Rsch. engr. Plessey Telecom Rsch., Taplow, 1969-76; assoc. prof. Tech. U. Nova Scotia, Halifax, Can., 1976-81; prof. McMaster U., Hamilton, Canada, 1981—, Mitel Prof. signal processing, 1999—, chmn. dept. elec. engring., 1985—86, 1988—94, 2003—; hon. prof. South East U., Nanjing, China, 1995—; vis. prof. Chinese U. Hong Kong, Hong Kong, 1997—. Cons. Defence Rsch. Establishments, Can., 1986—, Mitel Corp., Ottawa, Can., 1993—, Lockheed-Martin, Ottawa, 1993-94, Canadian Marconi, Ottawa, 1995-97, Spotwave wireless, 2000—; assoc. editor IEEE Transaction on Signal Processing, 1997-99. Contbr. articles to textbooks, to profl. jours. Fellow: IEEE, Canadian Acad. Engring., Royal Statistics Soc., Inst. Physics, Inst. Elec. Engrs. Avocations: ping pong/table tennis, swimming, squash, piano playing, painting. Office: Dept Elec & Computer Engring McMaster U Hamilton ON Canada

WONG, KUOK-SHOONG DANIEL, research scientist; BSE in Elec. Engring., Princeton U., 1992; MS in Elec. Engring., Stanford U., 1994, PhD in Elec. Engring., 1998. Rsch. scientist Telcordia Techs., Red Bank, NJ, 1998—2006. Invited external Phd examiner, computer sci. dept. Nat. U. Singapore; prof. Malaysia U. Sci. and Tech., Petaling Jaya, 2003—. Author: Wireless Internet Telecommunications; co-author: Wireless IP and Building the Mobile Internet; contbr. articles to profl. jours. including IEEE Transactions on Vehicular Tech., IEEE Jour. on Selected Areas in Comms., Internat. Jour. on Parallel and Distributed Sys. and Networks, IEEE Comms. Letters, IEEE Personal Comms. Mag., IEEE Comms. Mag. Pianist, leader small group bible studies Monmouth Chinese Christian Ch., NJ, 1999—2003. Fellowship, Stanford U. Sch. of Engring., 1992—93. Mem.: IEEE (sr.; vice-chair, NJ coast sect., comm. chpt. 2000—03, conf. tech. program com., session organizer, chair, tutorial tchr. 2001—, bd. dirs. Comsoc Sister Soc. 2004—), Sigma Xi, Phi Beta Kappa, Tau Beta Pi. Achievements include patents for Multicarrier personal access comms. sys. Address: B-09-3A Ken Condo Jalan SS 2/72 Petaling Jaya Selangor 47400 Malaysia

WONG, LILIANE, architect, educator; BA, Vassar Coll., 1981—81; MA, Harvard U., 1985. Registered arch. Assoc. Perry Dean Rogers & Ptnrs., Boston, 1985—94; prin. Mahon Wong Assocs., Cambridge, Mass., 1994—; assoc. prof. RISD, Providence, 1998—. Furniture line, Kore libr. furnishings line, 1995. Named Bulfinch Arch Competition winner, Hist. Neighborhood Found., 1987. Mem.: AIA, Boston Soc. Archs. (Women in Architecture award 1994, Women in Design aard 2002).

WONG, MARGARET WAI, lawyer; b. Hong Kong, July 27, 1950; d. Mien Lin and Kuan Kuo (Kwan) Hwang; m. Kam M. Chan, Jan. 3, 1983. AA, Ottumwa Heights Coll. (Iowa), 1971; BSc in Chemistry-Biology, Western Ill. U., 1973; JD, SUNY-Buffalo, 1976. Bar: Ohio 1977, N.Y. 1977, D.C. 1980, U.S. Dist. Ct. 1980, U.S. Ct. Appeals (6th cir.) 1983. Instr. bus. law SUNY-Fredonia, 1977; mgmt. trainee Cen. Nat. Bank, Cleve., 1977-78; chief legal and fin. officer Buffalo City Govt., 1979-80; assoc. Berger & Kirchenbaum, Cleve., 1980-81; prin. Margaret W. Wong & Assocs., Cleve., 1981—; co-founder, co-owner Pearl of the Orient Restaurant, Cleve., 1978—; co-founder, cons. Richmond Apothe-Care, Inc. Pharmcy, Cleve., 1982-95, Cleve. Apothe-Care, Inc. Pharmacy, 1986—. Contbr. articles to legal jours. Trustee, Women Space, Cleve., 1982—, Fedn. Community Planning, Cleve., 1983-84, Women City Club, Cleve., 1983—, Orgn. Chinese Ams., Cleve., 1983—, Cleve. Coun. Human Relations, 1983—; sec., trustee Chinese Assn. Greater Cleve., 1980—; bd. dirs. Greater Cleve. Growth Assn., Inter-Mus. Conservation Assn., Notre Dame Coll., Greater Cleve. Roundtable, NCCJ. Named one of Top Ten Outstanding Young Women, Glamour mag., 1983; YWCA Career Woman of Yr., 1984. Mem. ABA (vice chmn. immigration, naturalization and aliens sect. 1993-94), Fed. Bar Assn. (pres.-elect 1993, pres. 1994), N.Y. State Bar Assn., D.C. Bar Assn., Cuyahoga County Bar Assn., Cleve. Bar Assn., Ohio Bar Assn., Cleve. Trial Lawyers Assn., Am. Assn. Immigration Lawyers. Club: Zonta (trustee 1983-84) (Cleve.). Office: Margaret W Wong & Assoc 3150 Chester Ave Cleveland OH 44114 Office Phone: 216-566-9908. Business E-Mail: wong@imwong.com.

WONG, NATHAN DONALD, medicine and epidemiology researcher, educator; b. Downey, Calif., Apr. 18, 1961; s. Donald Wah and Mew Lun (Hee) W.; m. Mia K. Park, July 21, 1996; 1 child, David. BA, Pomona Coll., Claremont, Calif., 1983; MPH, Yale U., New Haven, Conn., 1985, PhD, 1987. Lectr. medicine Yale U., New Haven, 1987; asst. prof. U. Calif., Irvine, 1988—94, assoc. prof., 1994—2002, dir. heart disease prevention program, dept. medicine, 1991—, prof., 2003—; prof. dept. epidemiology UCLA, 2003—. Prin. investigator Antihypertensive Lipid-Lowering to Prevent Heart Attack Trial and other lipid and cardiovasc. prevention trials, 1994—; co-prin. investigator Women's Health Initiative, 1995—; investigator NIH Multiethnic Study of Atherosclerosis (MESA), Coronary Artery Risk Development in Young Adults, Cardiovascular Health Study, and epidemiology of diabetes interventions and complications studies; interviewed for various publs. and programs, including ABC Eyewitness News, L.A. Times, Orange County Register, CBS News, USA Today, N.Y. Times, others; profl. cons. Cedars-Sinai Med. Ctr., 2002—; editor-in-chief textbook Preventive Cardiology, Mcgraw-Hill, 2000, 2d edit, 2005; co-editor (textbook) Metabolic Syndrome and Cardiovascular Disease, 2007. Co-editor: (textbook) Metabolic Syndrome and Carciovascular Disease, 2007; mem. editl. bd.: Preventive Cardiology, Jour. Cardiovascular Drugs, Jour. Cardiometabolic Risk; contbr. chapters to books, over 100 articles to profl. jours. Mem. Calif. Senate Hearing Panel on Youth Phys. Edn. and Fitness, 1991; chair Calif. Cardiovasc. Disease Prevention Coalition, 1998-99; spkr. numerous internat., nat. and local confs., hosps., and med. spkrs. burs. Rsch. grantee, Bristol Myers-Squibb, Pfizer, Merck. Fellow Am. Coll. Cardiology (membership and credentialing com. 2003—, prevention of cardiovasc. disease com. 2003-04, taskforce 4, 34th Bethesda Conf. 2003), Am. Heart Assn. Coun. on Epidemiology and Prevention. Achievements include research in computed tomography, metabolic syndrome, diabetes, lipids, hypertension, preventive cardiology, coronary and aortic calcium. Avocations: running, hiking, skiing, photography. Office: UCI Heart Disease Prevention Program C240 Medsci I Irvine CA 92697-0001 Home Phone: 949-240-2840. Business E-Mail: ndwong@uci.edu.

WONG, OTTO, epidemiologist; b. Canton, China, Nov. 14, 1947; came to U.S., 1967, naturalized, 1976; m. Betty Yeung, Feb. 14, 1970; children: Elaine, Jonathan. BS, U. Ariz., 1970; MS, Carnegie Mellon U., 1972, U. Pitts., 1973, ScD, 1975. Cert. epidemsiologist Am. Coll. Epidemiology, 1982. USPHS fellow U. Pitts., 1972-75; asst. prof. epidemiology Georgetown U. Med. Sch., 1975-78; mgr. epidemiology Equitable Environ. Health Inc., Rockville, Md., 1977-78; dir. epidemiology Tabershaw Occuopational Med. Assocs., Rockville, 1978-80; dir. occupational rsch. Biometric Rsch. Inst., Washington, 1980-81; exec. v.p., chief epidemiologist ENSR Health Scis., Alameda, Calif., 1981—; chief epidemiologist, pres. Applied Health Scis., San Mateo, Calif., 1991—. Adj. prof. epidemiology and biostats. Tulane U. Med. Ctr., New Orleans, dept. cmty. and family medicine Chinese U. Hong Kong, U. No. Tex. Med. Ctr., epidemiology U. North Tex., Ft. Worth, 2007; vis. prof. epidemiology and occupl. health Nat. Def. Med. Ctr., Taipei, Taiwan, Shanghai Med. U.; hon. prof. cmty. medicine U. Hong Kong; cons. WHO, Nat. Cancer Inst., Nat. Inst. Occupl. Safety and Health, Occupl. Safety and Health Adminstrn., Nat. Heart, Lung and Blood Inst., Internat. Agy. for Rsch. on Cancer, U.S. EPA, Ford Motors Co., Gen. Electric, Mobil, Chevron, Union Carbide, Fairfax (Va.) Hosp., Agy. for Toxic Substances and Disease Registry, U. Ariz. scholar, 1967-68 Mem. editl. bd. The Annals of Epidemiology, Occupl. and Environ. Medicine.; contbr. articles to profl. jours. Fellow Am. Coll. Epidemiology, Human Biology Council; mem. Am. Pub. Health Assn., Biometric Soc., Soc. Epidemiologic Rsch., Phi Beta Kappa, Pi Mu Epsilon. Republican. Office: Applied Health Scis PO Box 2078 181 2nd Ave Ste 628 San Mateo CA 94401-3812

WONG, PATRICIA M.Y., library director; BA, Univ. Calif., Berkeley, 1983, MLIS, 1984. Cataloger Oakland Unified Sch. Dist., 1984—85; children's libr. Oakland Pub. Libr., 1984—87, Berkeley Pub. Libr., 1989, supervising libr., 1989—99, prog. dir. Partnerships for Change, 1990—95; libr. prog. mgr. Oakland Pub. Libr., 1999—2001; dep. dir. libr. services Stockton-San Joaquin County Pub. Libr., 2001—, interim dir. libr. services, 2005. Trainer, various programs Calif. State Libr., 2001—04; trainer, cons. Calif. Cultural Crossroads, Calif. State Libr., 2004—; lectr. Sch. Libr. & Info. Sci., San Jose State Univ., 2006—. Contbr. chapters to books, articles to profl. jours. Named one of the Movers & Shakers, Libr. Jour., 2007. Mem.: ALA (councilor-at-large 1996—2007, mem. exec. bd. 2001—05, chair budget & rev. com. 2005—), U.S. Bd. on Books for Young People (bd. dir. 1995—96), Asian/Pacific Am. Libr. Assn. (pres. 1999, Advocacy award 2006), Chinese Am. Libr. Assn. (bd. dir. 1991—93, pres. Calif. chapt. 1993). Office: Stockton-San Joaquin County Pub Libr 605 N El Dorado St Stockton CA 95202 E-mail: pattywong61@comcast.net.

WONG, RAYMOND SHIU-LOONG, radiologist; b. Hong Kong, Jan. 25, 1942; came to U.S., 1958; s. Jason Y. and Nancy L. (Tamm) W.; m. Jo-Lien Hsieh; 1 child, Florence W. BS in Chemistry, UCLA, 1962; MD, U. Chgo., 1966. Diplomate Am. Bd. Radiology with subspecialty in nuclear radiology, Am. Bd. Pediats. Diagnostic radiologist Hollywood Presbyn. Med. Ctr., LA, 1981-94, Huntington Meml. Hosp., Pasadena, Calif., 1994—. Contbr. articles to profl. jours. Mem. Am. Coll. Radiology, Soc. Nuclear Medicine, Calif. Radiol. Soc., L.A. Radiol. Soc., Radiol. Soc. N.Am. Office: Huntington Meml Hosp 100 W California Blvd Pasadena CA 91105-3097

WONG, RICHARD, music educator; b. Berkeley, Calif. s. Sun and Jik Wong. BA in Music, U. Calif., Berkeley, 1992; MA in Music, Calif. State U., Hayward, 1997. Cert. tchr. Calif. Music educator Am. H.S., Fremont, Calif., 1995—2006. Elem. band dir., Fremont, Calif., 1996—. Musician: (concerts) Community Band. Named Staff Mem. of Month, Am. H.S., 2003; recipient Most Promising New Tchr. award, Fremont Unified Sch. Dist., 1995, Founder's Day award, Fremont Unified Sch. Dist. PTA, 2000; grantee, Fremont Edn. Found., 1999. Mem.: NEA, Internat. Soc. Music Edn., Calif. Music Educators Assn., Calif. Teachers Assn., Calif. Band Dirs. Assn., No. Calif. Band Assn., Internat. Assn. Jazz Educators, Nat. Assn. Music Edn., Am. Choral Dirs. Assn. (life). Avocation: reading. Home Phone: 510-744-9632; Office Phone: 510-796-1776.

WONG, STANTON D., lawyer; b. San Francisco, Nov. 4, 1957; AB, Univ. Calif., Berkeley, 1979, MBA, JD, Univ. Calif., Berkeley, 1983. Bar: Calif. 1983. Ptnr., ch-chmn. Securities practice Pillsbury Winthrop Shaw Pittman, San Francisco. Contbr. articles to profl. jours. Office: Pillsbury Winthrop Shaw Pittman 50 Fremont St San Francisco CA 94105 also: 2475 Hanover St Palo Alto CA 94304-1114 Office Phone: 415-983-1790. Office Fax: 415-983-1200. Business E-Mail: stanton.wong@pillsburylaw.com.

WONG, STOVA, law firm executive; Dir. networks and telecom. Paul, Hastings, Janofsky & Walker LLP, chief info. officer. Recipient Premier 100 IT Leadership award, Computerworld, 2005, CIO 100 award, 2005.

WONG, SUN YET, engineer, consultant; b. Honolulu, Dec. 6, 1932; s. Chip Tong and Shiu Inn (Chang) W.; m. Janet Siu Hung Lau; children: Cathleen, Bryan, Jonathan. BS in Civil Engring. with honors, U. Hawaii, 1954; MS in Civil Engring., Yale U., 1955. Engr. N.Am. Aviation, Downey, Calif., 1955-58; mem. tech. staff Ramo Woolridge Space Tech. Labs., Redondo Beach, Calif., 1958-64; exec. v.p., treas., tech. dir. Mechanics Rsch. Inc., El Segundo, Calif., 1964-77; treas. System Devel. Corp., Santa Monica, Calif., 1977-79; chmn. bd., pres., treas. Applied Rsch. Inc., El Segundo, 1979-81; ind. cons. Rolling Hills Estates, Calif., 1981—. Cons. J.H. Wiggins Co., Redondo Beach, 1982—84, Intercon, Cerriots, Calif., 1982—84, Acurex, Mountain View, Calif., 1983, Applied Tech., Mountain View, Calif., 1983—85, Aston., Mountain View, 1983—85, Electromech. Sys. Inc., Anaheim, Calif., 1984, Measurement Analysis Corp., Torrance, Calif., 1984—96, MRJ, Fairfax, Va., 1984, Tompkins and Assocs., Torrance, 1984—2003, TRW, Redondo Beach, 1984, E Sys., Garland, 1986—93, Statis. Scis., Inc., Beverly Hills, Calif., 1986, Kodak Datatape, Pasadena, Calif., 1989, Odectics, Anaheim, 1990, Ampex, Redwood City, Calif., 1991, Swales & Assocs., Beltsville, Md., 1992—93, Hughes Space and Comms. Co., El Segundo, 1992, El Segundo, 94, El Segundo, 1996—2000, Lion Engring., Rancho Palos Verdes, Calif., 1994—2002, NASA Goddard, Greenbelt, Md., 1997, Boeing Space Sys., El Segundo, 2000—, Raytheon, El Segundo, 2000—02, Boeing Space and Intelligence, Seal Beach, 2003—06, TriSept, Washington, 2003—. Recipient Intelligence Cmty. Seal medallion, U.S. Govt., 2001, Nat. Reconnaisance Office Dir.'s award, 2001, Tech. Excellence award, Boeing Co., 2002. Avocation: metal machining. Home and Office: 7 Club View Ln Rolling Hills Estates CA 90274 Office Phone: 310-534-4713. Personal E-mail: sywong@dslextreme.com.

WONG, THOMAS TANG YUM, engineering educator; b. Hong Kong, July 27, 1952; arrived in U.S., 1976; s. Kwai Sun and Yee Yuen (Fung) W.; m. Min-I Lee, June 9, 1984; children: Clara Joyce, Lillian Denise. BSc in Engring., U. Hong Kong, 1975; MS, Northwestern U., Evanston, Ill., 1978, PhD, 1981. Product engr. Motorola Semiconductor, Inc., Hong Kong, 1975-76; teaching asst. Northwestern U., 1976-78, rsch. asst., 1978-80, postdoctoral fellow, 1980-81; asst. prof. Ill. Inst. Tech., Chgo., 1981-86, assoc. prof., 1986-96, prof., 1996—, dir. grad. program dept. elec. engring., 1987-95, chmn. dept. elec. and computer engring., 2001—05; dir. rsch. and devel. Telecomm. Equipment Corp., Chgo., 1994—2001; chief sci. authority Quintech Electronics & Comms., Inc., Indiana, Pa., 1997-99. Cons. to pvt. industry, 1981—; chmn. Chicagoland Microwave Symposium, 1988. Author: Fundamentals of Distributed Amplification, 1993; co-author: Electromagnetic Fields and Waves, 2006; contbr. articles to profl. jours.; book reviewer tech. publs.:. Trustee Sch. Dist. 73.5, Ill., 1995—2001. GE fellow, 1983; rsch. grantee NASA, 1989-91, U.S. Dept. Energy, 1992—. pvt. industry, 1993—. Mem. IEEE (chmn. joint Chgo. chpt. Antenna Propagation and Microwave Theory Techniques Soc. 1987-88, mem. steering com. joint symposium Antennas Propagation Soc./Internat. Union of Radio Sci./Nuclear Electromagnetic Pulse 1992), AAUP, Am. Soc. Engring. Edn., Am. Phys. Soc., Tau Beta Pi, Eta Kappa Nu. Achievements include patents for microwave electronics and communications. Office: Ill Inst Tech Dept Elec/Computer Engring Chicago IL 60616 Business E-Mail: twong@ece.iit.edu.

WONG, TIMOTHY C., language and literature educator; b. Hong Kong, Jan. 24, 1941; came to U.S., 1951; s. Patrick J. and Rose (Poon) W.; m. Elizabeth Ann Steffens, Dec. 18, 1970; children: Sharon Elizabeth, Rachel Margaret, Laura Katherine. BA, St. Mary's Coll., Moraga, Calif., 1963; MA, U. Hawaii, 1968; PhD, Stanford U., 1975. Vol. U.S. Peace Corps, Thailand, 1963-65; asst. prof. Ariz. State U., Tempe, 1974-79, assoc. prof., 1979-85; resident dir. Coun. on Internat. Ednl. Exchange Peking Univ., China, 1984-85; assoc. prof. Ohio State U., Columbus, 1985-95; prof. Ariz. State U., Tempe, 1995—, dir. Ctr. for Asian Studies, 1995—2002, grad. dir. Asian langs. and civilizations program, 2002—. Author: Wu Ching-tzu, 1978, Stories for Saturday: Twentieth-Century Chinese Popular Fiction, 2003. Mem. Chinese Lang. Tchrs. Assn., Assn. Asian Studies, Am. Oriental Soc. (dir.-at-large 1996-2000, v.p. western br. 2000-01, pres. 2001-03). Democrat. Roman Catholic. Office: Ariz State U Dept Langs and Lits Tempe AZ 85287-0202 Home Phone: 480-705-0316. E-mail: timothy.wong@asu.edu.

WONG, WADE HWU, radiologist, educator; b. Honolulu, June 24, 1946; s. Arthur Y. and Margaret An Wong; m. Louise Marie Ward; children: Rob, Lisa. BS, U. So. Calif., LA, 1968; DO, Kirksville Coll. Osteo. Medicine, Mo. Diplomate Am. Bd. Radiology, Am. Bd. Neuroradiology, 1995. Med. dir. Polk Cmty. Hosp., Salem, Oreg., 1980—81; shareholder Evergreen Radiology, Bremerton, Wash., 1981—91; clin. instr. U. Calif., San Diego, 1991—93, asst. prof. radiology, 1993—95, assoc. prof., 1995—2000, prof. radiology, 2000—. Cons. Spinal Specialties, San Antonio, 2000—, X-Stent, Denver, 2006; mem. tng. faculty Kyphon, Sunnyvale, Calif., 2000—. Author: 100 Interventional Procedures, 2001. Comdr. USN, 1972—79. Named Tchr. of Yr. Neuroscis., U. Calif., San Diego; recipient Silver Spoon for Tchr. of Yr., 1993, 1995, 1999, Gabriel Wilson award, WURS, 2006. Fellow: AOCDMR, Am. Osteo. Coll. Radiology, Am. Coll. Radiology; mem.: Western Neuroradiol. Soc. (pres.), Am. Soc. Neuroradiology (sr.), Am. Soc. Spine Radiology (pres.). Avocations: kayaking, hunting, sailing, travel. Office: U Calif 9300 Campus Point Dr La Jolla CA 92037

WONG, WAI HING, marine biologist, researcher; b. Zibo, China; arrived in U.S., 2000; s. Naizhong Wang and Cuiying Chen; m. Ting Sun, Dec. 16, 1998. BS, Ocean U. Qingdao, China, 1993; MS, Ocean U. Qingdao, 1996; PhD, City U. Hong Kong, 2001. Rsch. asst. City U. Hong Kong, 1996—97; postdoctoral rsch. assoc. SUNY, Stony Brook, 2000—02, La. U. Marine Consortium, Chauvin, 2003—05, La. State U. Aquaculture Rsch. Sta., Baton Rouge, 2005—. Mem.: Marine Biol. Assn. Hong Kong, Nat. Shellfisheries Assn., Estuarine Rsch. Fedn. Achievements include discovery of evolutionary traits in digestive investments and feeding morphology of green mussels in different environments; demonstration of top-down control of bivalves on phytoplankton community with fatty acid analysis; elucidation of the selective feeding behavior of green mussels Perna viridis; discovery of the benthoszooplankton loop (BZ loop) in the zebra mussel Dreissena polymorpha. Avocations: basketball, soccer, running. Office: La State U Aquaculture Rsch Sta 2410 Ben Hur Rd Baton Rouge LA 70820 Office Phone: 225-765-2848. Office Fax: 225-765-2877. Business E-Mail: wong@lsu.edu.

WONG, WALLACE, real estate investor; b. Honolulu, July 13, 1941; s. Jack Yung Hung and Theresa (Goo) W.; m. Amy Ju, June 17, 1963; children: Chris, Bradley, Jeffery. Student, UCLA, 1960-63. Chmn., pres. South Bay Coll., Hawthorne, Calif., 1965-86; chmn. Santa Barbara (Calif.) Bus. Coll., 1975—; gen. ptnr. W B Co., Redondo Beach, Calif., 1982—; CEO Pacific Am. Group, Rancho Santa Margarita, 1991-96; chmn., CEO Alpine, Inc., Rancho Santa Margarita, Calif., 1993-96; pres. Bayside Properties, Laguna Beach, Calif., 1993—, San Juan Capistrano, Calif., 1993—. Bd. dirs. Metrobank, L.A. FFF Enterprises; chmn. bd. 1st Ind. Fin. Group., San Juan Capistrano, 1994—. Acting sec. of state State of Calif., Sacramento, 1982; founding mem. Opera Pacific, Orange County, Calif., 1985; mem. Hist. and Cultural Found., Orange County, 1986; v.p. Orange County Chinese Cultural Club, Orange County, 1985. Named for Spirit of Enterprise Resolution, Hist. & Cultural Found., Orange Country, 1987; recipient resolution City of Hawthorne, 1973. Mem. Westren Accred Schs. & Colls. (v.p. 1978-79), Magic Castle (life), Singapore Club. Avocations: travel, skiing. Address: 884 Molokua Dr Kailua HI 96734 Business E-Mail: wwong1025@hawaii.rr.com.

WONG, WING-YEN, hematologist, educator; b. Malaysia; BA, Occidental Coll., LA, 1979; MD, U. So. Calif., 1983. Intern U. So. Calif. Med. Sch., LA, 1979—83, resident, 1983—86, 1987, fellowship, 1987—91; dir., hemostasis and thrombosis Childrens Hosp. L.A., 2001—; assoc. prof. pediat. U. So. Calif., 2001—. Editl. bd. Haemophilia Forum, 2001—; jour. reviewer Jour. Pediatric Hematology-Oncology, Haemophilia, Lancet; adv. task force on pediatric hemostasis Nat. Hemophilia Found., 2002; med. dir. Hemophilia Found. So. Calif., 2002; mem. various rev. and study coms.; adv. com. blood safety and availability Sec. HHS, Washington, 2003—; expert in field. Contbr. articles to profl. jours., chapters to books. Physician Hemophilia Camp, 1997—. Mem.: Internat. Soc. Thrombosis and Haemostasis, World Fedn. Hemophilia, Am. Assn. Blood Banks, Hemophilia Rsch. Soc., Am. Soc. Hematology, Am. Acad. Pediat., Soc. Pediatric Rsch., Women Faculty Health Sci. Assn., We. Soc. Pediatric Rsch., L.A. Pediatric Soc., U. So. Calif. Salerni Collegium Alumni Assn. (bd. dirs. 1997—). Office: Childrens Hosp LA 4650 Sunset Blvd MS 54 Los Angeles CA 90027 Home: One Baxter Way Westlake Village CA 91362 Office Phone: 323-669-4141. Business E-Mail: wwong@chla.usc.edu.

WONG, YANYI LIU, physicist, researcher; arrived in US, 1998, naturalized, 2004; s. Mingpai Wong and Lilun Liu. BSEE, U. Md., Coll. Pk., 2001, MSEE, 2004, PhD in Elec. Engring., 2007. Tchg. asst. microelectronics U. Md., 2001—03; assoc. staff, applied physics lab. Johns Hopkins U., Laurel, Md., 2003—; sr. device engr. Impinj, Inc., Seattle, 2007—. Contbr. articles to profl. jours. Mem.: IEEE (finalist Best Paper award 2005). Buddhist. Office Phone: 240-899-0509. Business E-Mail: yanyi.wong@ieee.org.

WONG, Y(ING) WOOD, real estate investment company executive, real estate development company executive, venture capital investment company executive; b. Hong Kong, Apr. 28, 1950; came to U.S., 1969; s. Loyee K.H. and Margaret M.C.L. Wong; m. Leslie K.P. Chan, Dec. 18, 1977; children: Joshua H., Jonathan H. AA in Biology, Menlo Coll., Atherton, Calif., 1971, BS in Bus. Adminstrn., 1974; BA in Zoology, U. Calif., Berkeley, 1972; MBA, Northwestern U., Evanston, Ill., 1976. Auditor Touche Ross & Co., CPAs, San Francisco, 1976-78; founder, mng. dir. Wong Properties, Palo Alto, Calif., 1976—; founder, venture capital ptnr. Wongfratris Investment Co., Palo Alto, 1986—; founder, ptnr. Corona Main Devel., L.L.C., Palo Alto, 2003—. Instr. Golden Gate U., 1977. Trustee Crystal Springs Uplands Sch., Hillsborough, Calif., 1993-98; advisor The Pei Ying Mid. Sch., Guangzhou, China, The Pui Ying Christian Svcs. Soc., Vancouver, Can.; bd. dirs. Peninsula Symphony, Los Altos, Calif., 2002-03. Named Hon. Citizen of Taishan City, China; established Wood Wong Fgn. Students Exch. Grant, Menlo Coll., 1997—, established Margaret Wong Meml. Music award endowment, Taishan (China) Pei Ying Mid. Sch., 2004—. Mem. Internat. Platform Assn., Commonwealth Club Calif., Beta Alpha Psi. Office: 51 Jordan Pl Palo Alto CA 94303-2903 E-mail: wood.wong@wongfratris.com.

WONG-DIAZ, FRANCISCO RAIMUNDO, lawyer, educator; b. Havana, Cuba, Oct. 29, 1944; came to U.S., 1961; s. Juan and Teresa (Diaz de Villegas) Wong; 1 child, Richard Alan. BA with honors, No. Mich. U., 1965; MA with highest honors, U. Detroit, 1967; PhD, MA, U. Mich., 1974; JD, U. Calif., Berkeley, 1976. Bar: Calif. 1980, U.S. Dist. Ct. (no. dist.) Calif. 1990, Fla. 1987. Prof. City Coll. San Francisco, 1975—, dept. chmn., 1978-85; rsch. atty. Marin Superior Ct., 1980-81; ct. arbitrator Marin Mcpl. Ct., 1985; atty. pvt. practice, Kentfield, Calif., 1980—; academic fellow FDD, 2007—. Adj. asst. prof. San Francisco State U., 1977; assoc. dean Miami-Dade Coll., 1986; dir. Cutcliffe Cons., Inc., Hawthorne, LaFamila Ctr., Inc., San Rafael, Calif., 1980-85, Small Bus. Inst., Kentfield, 1982-86; cons. ICC Internat., San Francisco, 1980-82; polit. commentator Univision KDTV, 1980—; bd. dirs. Pedro Pan Group, Inc.; prostate cancer devel. rsch. com. U. Calif. San Francisco Cancer Ctr. Author: American Politics in a Changing World, 1999, 2d edit., 2004; bd. editors Indsl. Rels. Law Jour., 1975-76; mem. editl. bd. Calif. Lawyer, 1991-93. Lector St. Sebastian's Ch., 1984—, parish coun., 1995; bd. dir. Am. Cancer Soc., 1999—; mem. devel. rsch. program, fellowship com. U. Calif.-San Francisco, 2002—; mem. adv. bd. Redes en Accion, 2002—; mem. Com. on the Present Danger, 2005—; mem. World Assn. Internat. Studies. Vis. scholar U. Calif. Berkeley Sch. Bus., 1983-84, US Dept. State scholar, Washington, 1976; Horace C. Rackham fellow U. Mich., 1970, summer fellow U. Calif. Berkeley, 1995, Nat. Security Law Ctr. U. Va., 1996, Acad. fellow Found. for the Def. Democracies, 2007—; recipient Patient Courage award, ACS, 2004; named Best New Vol. of Yr., Am. Cancer Soc., 2000, One of One Hundred Most Influential Hispanics in the Nation, Hispanic Bus. Mag., 2000. Mem. ABA, Am. Polit. Sci. assn., Latino Ednl. Assn. (co-founder, treas. 1985), Cuban Am. Nat. Coun., World Affairs Coun. (sem. leader San Francisco 1980), World Assn. Internat. Studies, Pacific Coun. Internat. Policy, U. Calif. San Francisco PC Advocates, Commonwealth Club. Roman Catholic. Business E-Mail: fwong@ccsf.edu.

WONG-LIANG, EIRENE MING, psychologist; b. Nassau, Bahamas, Nov. 20, 1961; came to U.S., 1969; d. Menyu and Lim Ming (Chow) Wong; m. Danqing Liang. BA, Trinity U., San Antonio, 1984; PhD, Calif. Sch. Profl. Psychology, 1992, postdoc. MS in Clin.Psychopharmacology, 2002. Crisis counselor United Way Crisis Hotline, San Antonio, 1983; lab. asst. Trinity U., 1983; counselor Bayer County Women's Ctr., San Antonio, 1984, Turning Point Juvenile Diversion Project, Garden Grove, Calif., 1985-86; psychol. trainee Wolters Elem. Sch., Fresno, 1987, San Luis Obispo (Calif.) Youth Day Treatment, 1987-88, Calif. Sch. Profl. Psychology Svc. Ctr., Fresno, 1988-89; staff psychologist 314th Med. Ctr., Little Rock, Ark., 1989-93; pvt. practice, clin. psychologist Houston, 1993—. Psychologist USAFR, 1990-93. Mem. APA, Am. Soc. Clin. Hypnosis, Nat. Register Health Svc. Providers in Psychology, Tex. Psychol. Assn., Houston Psychol. Assn., Houston Assn. Clin. Hypnosis (charter, treas. 1996-97, pres. 1997-98), Internat. Soc. Clin. Hypnosis, Fort Bend Mental Health Assn. (bd. dirs. 1998, 99, chair bd. govs. 1999), Am. Soc. Clin. Hypnosis (rep. bd. govs. 1997, 98, 99). Office: 8323 Southwest Fwy Ste 760 Houston TX 77074-1609 Office Phone: 713-981-8325.

WONG SMITH, HELEN MEI LIN, librarian, archivist, consultant; b. Honolulu, July 29, 1959; d. Wilbert Wah Wai and Barbara Jean Wong; m. Thomas Ernest Ward Smith Jr., July 4, 1987; children: Barbara Kaonohiokala Mei Lin Smith, Thomas Piilani Wah Wai Smith. BA in Hawaiian Studies, U. Hawaii-Manoa, Honolulu, 1986, M Libr. and Info. Sci., 1991. Cert. Acad. Cert. Archivists, 2006. Archivist Hawaii Med. Libr., Honolulu, 1996—2000; asst. libr. Gemini North Obs., Hilo, Hawaii, 1999—2001; libr. Kamehameha Schs., Keaau, Hawaii, 2001—04, hist., cultural specialist Honolulu, 2001—; libr. Hawaiian collection U. Hawaii-Hilo, 2007—. Archiva and hist. cons., Hilo, 1993—. Hawaiian quilt, Na kalo no Kahealani; compiler: bibliography Kona in History: A Guide to Resources. Bd. dirs. Volcano Art Ctr., Hawaii, 2002—03. Recipient Mary Edward Profl. award, Libr. and Info. Sci. Program, 2002; fellow, Jessie Smith Noyes Found., 1986—87; Hawaiian Quilting Design fellow, State Found. Culture and Arts, 1996. Fellow: Assn. Hawaii Archivists (pres. 2007—); mem.: Hawaii Libr. Assn. (pres. 1997—98), Soc. Am. Archivists, Hawaiian Hist. Soc., Beta Phi Mu. Achievements include development of Land Legacy database. Home Phone: 808-935-0925. Business E-Mail: smith@hawaii.edu.

WONGSWAN, JON, economist; b. Gainesville, Fla., Mar. 13, 1975; s. John C.S. and Mallika Tang; m. Pimkae Briksawan, Aug. 9, 2002; 1 child, Pim J. BA, Chulalongkorn U., Bangkok, 1996; PhD, Duke U., Durham, N.C., 1996—2002. Economist Fed. Res. Bd., Washington, 2002—. Emerging markets rschr. Barclays Global Investors, San Francisco, 2007. Contbr. chapters to books, articles to profl. jours. Recipient Gold medal, Chulalongkorn U., 2002; scholar, Sanwa Bank, 1997—2002, Japanese Govt. and IMF, 2002—04. Mem.: Western Fin. Assn. (life). Home: 1142 N Vernon St Arlington VA 22201 Office: Fed Res Bd 20th and C Streets NW Washington DC 20551 Home Phone: 703-469-2148. Personal E-mail: jon_wongswan@yahoo.com. Business E-Mail: jon.wongswan@frb.gov.

WONHAM, WALTER MURRAY, electrical engineer, educator; b. Montreal, Que., Can., Nov. 1, 1934; m. Vera Anne Hale; children: Marjorie Jane, Cynthia Margaret. B of Engring., McGill U., Montreal, 1956; PhD, U. Cambridge, Eng., 1961. Asst. prof. elec. engring. Purdue U., Lafayette, Ind., 1961-62; rsch. scientist Rsch. Inst. for Advanced Studies, Balt., 1962-64; assoc. prof. Brown U., Providence, 1964-69; rsch. assoc. NASA, Cambridge, Mass., 1967-69, cons., 1969; prof. elec. engring. U. Toronto, Ont., Canada, 1970—, J. Roy Cockburn prof., 1991-96, Cockburn chair, 1991, univ. prof., 1996—2000, univ. prof. emeritus, 2000—. Author: Linear Multivariable Control: A Geometric Approach, 1974, 3d edit., 1985 (Russian transl. 1980, Chinese transl. 1984); assoc. editor Soc. for Indsl. and Applied Math., Jour. on Control and Optimization, 1965-79, Sys. Control Letter, 1981-85. Recipient Brouwer medal Netherlands Math Soc., 1990; Athlone fellow, Gt. Britain, 1956-58; spl. scholar Nat. Rsch. Coun. Can., 1958-60; sr. postdoctoral resident rsch. assoc. NAS USA, 1967-69. Fellow IEEE (life, Control Sys. Sci. and Engring. award 1987), Royal Soc. Can.; mem. U.S. NAE (fgn. assoc.). Office: U Toronto Dept Elec Engring 35 St George St Toronto ON Canada M5S 3G4 Personal E-mail: wonham@control.utoronto.ca.

WONNACOTT, PAUL, retired economics professor; b. London, Ont., Can., Mar. 16, 1933; s. Gordon Elliott and Muriel Johnston Wonnacott; m. Donna Elizabeth Cochrane, July 2, 1960; children: David, Ann, Alan, Bruce. BA, U. Western Ont., 1955; MA, Princeton U., 1957, PhD, 1959. Instr., asst. prof. econs. Columbia U., NYC, 1958-62; from assoc. prof. to prof. econs. U. Md., College Park, 1962—91, prof. emeritus, 1992. Rsch. staff Royal Commn. Banking and Fin., Toronto, 1962; sr. staff economist Coun. Econ. Advisers, Washington, 1968-70; assoc. dir. divsn. internat. fin. Fed. Res. Bd., Washington, 1974-75; vis. scholar Office Internat. Monetary Rsch., U.S. Treasury, 1980; econ. adviser to Under Sec. of State, 1990-91; mem. Pres.'s Coun. Econ. Advisers, 1991-93; Alan Holmes prof. econs. Middlebury Coll., 1994-2000, ret., 2000. Author: The Canadian Dollar, 1960, 2d rev. edit., 1965, (with R.J. Wonnacott) Free Trade between the United States and Canada: The Potential Economic Effects, 1967, (with H.G. Johnson and H. Shibata) Harmonization of National Economic Policies under Free Trade, 1968, Macroeconomics, 1974, 3d rev. edit., 1984, (with R.J. Wonnacott) Economics, 1979, 4th rev. edit. 1990, Spanish edit., 1981, 3d rev. edit., 1987, (with Y. and C. Crusius) Portuguese edit., 1982, 2d rev. edit., 1985, (with A. Blomquist) Can. edit., 1983, 4th rev. edit., 1994, Lithuanian edit., 1998, The United States and Canada: The Quest for Free Trade, 1987, The Last Good War: A Novel, 2007; contbr. articles to profl. jours. Fellow Brooking Inst., 1957-58, Ford Found., 1963-64; vis. fellow Inst. Internat. Econs., 1986, 93-94. Home: 10100 Bevern Ln Potomac MD 20854 Personal E-mail: paulwon@refraction.org.

WONNACOTT, RONALD JOHNSTON, retired economics professor; b. London, Ont., Can., Sept. 11, 1930; s. Gordon and and Muriel (Johnston) W.; m. Eloise Howlett, Sept. 11, 1954; children: Douglas, Robert, Cathy Anne. BA, U. We. Ont., 1955; AM, Harvard U., 1957, PhD, 1959. Mem. faculty U. We. Ont., London, 1958—96, prof. econs., 1964—96, chmn. dept., 1969—72, prof. emeritus, 1996—. Vis. assoc. prof. U. Minn., Mpls., 1961-62; cons. Resources for the Future, Econ. Council Can., Can.-Am. Com., C.D. Howe Inst. Author: Canadian-American Dependence: An Interindustry Analysis of Production and Prices, 1961, Canada's Trade Options, 1975, Selected New Developments in International Trade Theory, 1984, The Economics of Overlapping Free Trade Areas and the Mexican Challenge, 1991, (with G.L. Reuber) The Cost of Capital in Canada, 1961, (with Paul Wonnacott) Free Trade Between the U.S. and Canada, 1967, Economics, 1979, 4th edit., 1990, (with Thomas H. Wonnacott) Introductory Statistics, 1969, 5th edit., 1990, Econometrics, 1970, 2d edit., 1979, Regression, 1981 Fellow Royal Soc. Can.; mem. Am. Econ. Assn., Can. Econ. Assn. (pres. 1981), London Hunt Club, Sunningdale Golf Club (Eng.), Hon. Co. Edinburgh Golfers, Craigleith Ski Club. Home: 171 Wychwood Pk London ON Canada N6G 1S1 Personal E-mail: wonnacot@uwo.ca.

WONNER, PAUL JOHN, painter; b. Tucson, Apr. 24, 1920; Student, Calif. Coll. Arts and Crafts; MA, MLS, U. Calif., Berkeley, 1953. Instr. painting UCLA, 1963-64, Otis Art Inst., 1966-68, Coll. Creative Studies, Santa Barbara, Calif., 1968-71, U. Calif., Davis, 1975-76, U. Calif., Long Beach, 1981. Represented in permanent collections Guggenheim Mus., N.Y.C., San Francisco Mus. Art, Nat. Collection Fine Arts, Smithsonian Inst., Oakland Mus., Joseph H. Hirshhorn Found., Boston Mus. Fine Arts, Charles A. Wustum Mus. Fine Art, Mpls. Inst. Art; one-man shows include San Francisco Art Assn. Gallery, Los Angeles, 1956, Whitney Mus. Am. Art, N.Y.C., 1959, Art Inst. of Chgo., 1961, 64, U. Ill., 1961, 63-65, Mus. Modern Art, N.Y.C., 1962, Waddington Galleries, London, 1965, Poindexter Gallery, N.Y.C., 1971, Charles Campbell Gallery, San Francisco, 1974, Calif. State U., Long Beach, 1975, 81, James Corcoran Gallery, Los Angeles, 1979, Los Angeles Munic Art Mus., 1982, John Berggruen, San Francisco, 1985-86, DC Moore Gallery, NYC, 1998, 99. Office: 403 Main St # 709 San Francisco CA 94105-2067 Address: John Berggruen Gallery 228 Grant St San Francisco CA 94108

WOO, ALEX, jewelry designer; BA, Cornell Univ. Owner and designer Alex Woo Jewelry, NYC, 1999—. Named NY's Rising Star, Crain's Bus. 40 Under 40, 2005, Rising Star, JCK Show, Design Ctr., 2006; named to Elite Women, Hispanic Bus. Mag., 2005; recipient Design Award, Women's Jewelry Assn., 1998. Office: Alex Woo Inc 70 Bowery Ste 208 New York NY 10013 Office Phone: 212-226-1352. Office Fax: 212-226-5533.

WOO, BENJAMIN KAI PAN, psychiatrist; MD, U. Calif., La Jolla, Calif., 2000—05. Lic. physician & surgeon Calif., 2006. Resident physician Kern Psychiatry UCLA, Bakersfield, 2005—. Prin. investigator Kern Med. Ctr., Bakersfield, 2005—. Author: General Hospital Psychiatry; contbr. articles to profl. jours. Recipient Howard G. Clark award in biomed. engring. rsch., Duke U., 2000; grantee Ford Internat. Rsch. award in economics & polit. sci., 1998, Geriatric Mental Health fellowship, UCSD Divsn. Geriatric Psychiatry, 2004; UCSD Academic Geriatric Rsch. Ctr. mini-grant, U. Calif., 2005. Fellow: Am. Assn. Geriatric Psychiatry (Stepping Stones fellow 2006); mem.: Am. Psychiat. Assn.

WOO, CAROLYN YAUYAN, dean; b. Hong Kong, Apr. 19, 1954; arrived in US, 1972; m. David E. Bartkus; children: Ryan, Justin. BS in Economics, with honors and highest distinction, Purdue U., 1975, MS in Indsl. Adminstrn., 1976, PhD in Strategic Mgmt., 1979. Asst. prof. mgmt. Purdue U., 1981—85, assoc. to full prof., 1985—93, assoc. exec. v.p. acad. affairs, 1995—97; dir. profl. master's programs Purdue U. Krannert Sch. Mgmt., 1993—95; Martin J. Gillen dean Mendoza Sch. Bus., Notre Dame U., 1997—, Ray and Milann Siegfried chair entrepreneurial studies, 1997—. Bd. dirs. Aon Corp., 1998—, Nisource Industries Inc., 1998—, Circuit City Stores Inc., 2001—. Bd. dirs. Catholic Relief Services, 2004—; bd. regents U. Portland, 2004—. Recipient TIEM Found. Disting. Scholar award, Internat. Coun. Small Bus., 1987, Excellence award for edn., Asian Am. Alliance, 2002, John S. Day alumni academic svc. award, Krannert Sch. Mgmt., Purdue U., 2003. Mem.: Com. of 100, Assn. to Advance Collegiate Schools Bus. Internat. (bd. dirs. 1999—, vice chair 2002—03, chair 2003—04). Office: Notre Dame Univ 204 Mendoza College Business Notre Dame IN 46556-5646 Office Phone: 574-631-7992. Business E-Mail: Carolyn.Y.Woo.5@nd.edu. *

WOO, DEREK, electrical and computer engineer; b. Sarnia, Ont., Can., Oct. 19, 1969; s. Charles and Shirley Woo; m. Yvonne Fennema, Mar. 9, 1996; children: Gabriel, Julian. BScEE, U. Western Ont., London, 1991. Design engr. Ont. Power Generation (Ont. Hydro), Toronto, 1989—93; cons. Siemens AG, Toronto, 1993—94, Accenture (formerly Andersen Consulting), Toronto, NYC, Chgo., 1994—96; pres. Eidetic Sys. Inc., NYC, 1996—; v.p., firmwide tech. Goldman, Sachs & Co., NYC, 2004—. Grantee, Govt. of China, 1987; scholar, Imperial Oil (Esso), 1987—91. Mem.: IEEE, IEEE Stds. Assn. Home Phone: 212-357-1349.

WOO, JOHN See WU, YUSEN

WOO, KENNETH ROGER, urologist; b. LA, July 27, 1969; s. Roger and Julie Woo; m. Christine H. Sohn, May 16, 1998. BS in Molecular Biology magna cum laude, UCLA, 1992; MD with distinction, Mt. Sinai Sch. Medicine, NYC, 1996. Resident urology NYU Med. Ctr., 1996—2002. Contbr. articles to profl. jours. Grantee Yamanouchi USA Rsch., 1999. Mem.: AMA, Endourol. Soc., Am. Assn. Clin. Urologists, Am. Urol. Assn., Golden Key, Phi Beta Kappa. Avocations: tennis, hiking. Home Phone: 410-663-1301; Office Phone: 410-879-4879. Personal E-mail: kennethwoo@comcast.net.

WOO, S. B. (SHIEN-BIAU WOO), retired state official, physicist, educator; b. Shanghai, Aug. 13, 1937; came to US, 1955; s. C.K. and Kuo-Ying (Chang) W.; m. Katy K.N. Wu, July 20, 1963; children: Chih-I, Chih-Lan. BS in Physics and Math. summa cum laude, Georgetown Coll., Ky., 1956; MS in Physics, Washington U., St. Louis, 1962, PhD in Physics, 1964. Prof. physics U. Del., Newark, 1966—2002; lt. gov. State of Del., Dover, 1985-89. Pres. Del. State Senate; chmn. Bd. Pardons; cons. E.I. DuPont Co., Wilmington, Del., 1968, Del. State Coll., Dover, 1980—81; steering com. 80-20 initiative, 1998—2001; pres. 80-20 PAC, 2001—06, 80-20 Ednl. Found., 2005—. Contbr. articles to profl. jours. Chmn. bd., chief exec. officer Chinese Am. Community Ctr., Hockessin, Del., 1982-83; sec. Asian-Am. caucus Democratic Nat. Conv., 1983-84; pres., co-chmn. Gov.'s Internat. Trade Council, 1985-89; chmn. Gov.'s task force on High Tech., 1985-89. Recipient Highest Achievement award Asian Am. High Tech. Conv., 1985; Army Rsch. grantee, 1972-87, NSF grantee, 1978-81; Inst. fellow Kennedy Sch., Harvard U. Mem. Am. Phys. Soc., AAAS,

AAUP (exec. com. nat. council 1974-77), Orgn. Chinese Ams. (bd. dirs. 1977-79, nat. pres. 1990-91), Sigma Xi. Independent. Home: 5 Farm House Rd Newark DE 19711-7458 Office Phone: 866-367-8020. Business E-Mail: sbw@udel.edu.

WOO, SAVIO LAU-YUEN, bioengineering educator; b. Shanghai, June 3, 1942; naturalized; s. Kwok Chong and Fung Sing Woo; m. Patricia Tak-kit Cheong, Sept. 6, 1969; children: Kirstin Wei-Chi, Jonathan I-Huei. BSME, Chico State U., 1965; MS, U. Wash., 1966, PhD, 1971; DSc (hon.), Calif. State U., 1998. Rsch. assoc. U. Wash., Seattle, 1965—70; asst. research prof. U. Calif.-San Diego, La Jolla, 1970—74, assoc. rsch. prof., 1974—75, assoc. prof., 1975—80, prof. surgery and bioengring., 1980—90; vice chmn. for rsch., dir. Musculoskeletal Rsch. Ctr., U. Pitts., 1990—; prof. ortho surgery U. Pitts., 1990—93, prof. mech. engring., 1990—, Albert B. Ferguson Jr. prof. orthopaedic surgery, 1993—2004, prof. civil and environ. engring., 1994—2000, prof. rehab. sci. and tech., 1994—, W.K. Whiteford prof. bioengring., 1998—2007, Carnegie centenary prof., 2002, prof. bioengring., 2007—. Prin. investigator VA Med. Ctr., San Diego, 1972—90, Pitts., 1990—; cons. bioengr. Children's Hosp., San Diego, 1973—80; cons. med. implant cos., 1978—85; vis. prof. biomechanics Kobe (Japan) U., 1981—82; dir., CEO M&D Coutts Inst. for Joint Reconstrn. and Rsch., 1984—90; sci. adv. com. Whitaker Found., 1986—95, Steadman-Hawkins Sports Medicine Found., 1990—, Aircast Found., 1998—2004, OsteoArthritis Scis. Inc., 1992—95; adv. bd. Coll. Engring., Computer Sci. and Tech. Calif. State U., Chico, 1994—; adv. com. coord. grad. program in biomed. engring. U. Edmunton, U. Calgary, 1997—99; bioengring. adv. com. Nat. Health Rsch. Inst., Taiwan, 1996—; biomed. engr. dept. adv. bd. Wayne State U., 1996—; bioengring. dept. adv. bd. Med. Coll. Ohio, 2004—. Assoc. editor Jour. Biomech. Engring., 1979—87, Jour. Biomechanics, 1978—, Jour. Orthopedic Rsch., 1983—2001, Materials Sci. Reports, 1990—97, Jour. Inst. Mech. Engrs., 1990—94, mem. internat. adv. bd. Jour. Knee Surgery, Sports Tramuatology, Arthroscopy, 1993—, mem. editl. bd. Jour. Ortho. Sci., 1995—, Jour. Ortho. Surgery, 1998—2002, Jour. Musculoskeletal Rsch., 1998—, Am. Jour. Sports Medicine, 1995, Am. Acad. Ortho. Surgery, 1995—2000, Healthcare Eng., 1999—, Tech. and Health Care, 2000—05, Jour. Mechanics in Medicine and Biology, 2001—, Frontiers in Bioscience Jour., 2001—, Acta Clinica, 2002—, Jour. Biomed. Engring., 2006—, Jour. Molecular and Cellular Biomechanics, 2005—, Jour. Biomed. Engring., 2006—, Jour. Ortho. Surgery and Rsch., 2006—. Recipient Rsch. Career Devel. award, NIH, 1977—82, Elizabeth Winston Lanier Kappa Delta award, 1983, awards for excellence in basic sci. rsch., Orthopaedic Rsch. Soc. and Am. Acad. Orthopaedic Surgeons, 1983, 1986, 1990, 1993, 2002, Wartenweiler Meml. Lectureship, 1987, Citation award, Am. Coll. Sports Medicine, 1988, O'Donoghue award, Am. Orthopaedic Soc. Sports Medicine, 1990, 1997, H.R. Lissner award, 1991, Giovanni Borelli award, 1993, Muybridge medal, Internat. Soc. Internat. Biomechanics, 1995, GOTS-Beiersdorf AG Res. award, 1996, Olympic Gold Medalist and prize, 1998, Cabaud Meml. award, AOSSM, 1999, Albert Trillat Young Inventors award, ISAKOS, 1999, Chancellor's Disting. Res. award, U. Pitts., 1999. Fellow: ASME (chmn. honors com. bioengring. divsn. 1978—83, mem. exec. com. 1984—89, chmn. bioengring. divsn. 1986—87, sec., chmn. biomechanics com., Robert Henry Thurston award 2005), Biomed. Engring. Soc. (bd. dirs. 1984—86, 2005—07, Disting. Lectr. 2005), Am. Inst. Med. and Biol. Engring. (founding chmn. coll. fellows 1992—94, bd. dirs. 1992—94); mem.: NAS, NAE, Internat. Soc. Arthroscopy, Knee Surgery and Orthop. Sports Medicine (chmn. scientific com. 2007—), World Assn. Chinese Biomed. Engring. (founding pres. 2002—), US Nat. Comm. Biomechanics (exec. com. 1988—2000, chmn. 1994—97), Chinese Speaking Ortho Soc. (chmn. edn. com. 1997—2000, bd. dirs. 1997—2003), Internat. Soc. Fractures Repair (bd. dirs. 1986—94, v.p. 1987—90, pres. 1990—92), Am. Soc. Biomechanics (bd. dirs. 1977—87, pres. 1985—86), Soc. for Tennis Medicine and Sci. (hon.; bd. dir. 1997—2005), We. Orthopaedic Assn. (hon.), Can. Orthopedic Rsch Soc. (hon.), Arthroscopy Assn. N. Am. (hon.), Herodicus Soc. (hon.), Orthopaedic Rsch. Soc. (chmn. program com. 1983—84, bd. dirs. 1983—87, pres. 1985—86), Am. Acad. Orthopedic Surgeons, World Coun. for Biomechanics (chmn. 1998—2002), Internat. Olympic Com. Olympic Acad. of Scis., Acad. Sinica, Inst. Medicine (chmn. sect. I 1996—98). Office: U Pitts 300 Tech Dr 405 Ctr for Bioengring Pittsburgh PA 15219

WOO, SOOK-BIN, dentist, educator; d. Sup-Yik Woo and Kit-Meng Wong; m. Roger S. Warner; children: Christopher I. Warner, Sarah J. Warner. DMD, Harvard u., Boston, 1989. Lic. oral & maxillofacial pathologist Am. Bd. Oral & Maxillofacial Pathology, 1990, oral medicine Am. Bd. Oral Medicine, 2003. Staff pathologist Pathology Svcs. Inc., Cambridge, Mass., 1991—; attending dentist Brigham & Women's Hosp., Boston, 1991—; asst. prof. Harvard Sch. Dental Medicine, Boston, 1997—. Chief clin. affairs Divsn. Oral & Maxillofacial Surgery, Oral Medicine & Gen. Dentistry, Brigham & Women's Hosp., 2004—. Recipient Nat. Rsch. Svc. award, NIH, 1988—91, Career Devel. award, Am. Cancer Soc., 1993—97. Fellow: Am. Acad. Oral Medicine, Am. Acad. Oral and Maxillofacial Pathology (councillor exec. com. 2005—). Office: Brigham & Women's Hosp 1620 Tremont St #3-028 Boston MA 02120

WOO, STANLEY Y., medical educator, director, optometrist; m. Lisa Tran, 2000; 1 child, Kate Judy. BS, U. Toronto, Ontario, 1990; OD, U. Calif., Berkeley, 1994; MS, U. Houston, 2000. Diplomate Low Vision Rehab. Am. Acad. Optometry, 1999, lic. Laser Therapy for Anterior Segment Northeastern State U., 2006. Vis. asst. prof. U. Houston, 1995—2001, dir. residency program in low vision rehab., 1999—, clin. assoc. prof., 2001—; dir. clin. svcs. Lighthouse Houston, 1995—97; assoc. dir. Houston Delta Gamma Found., 1997—98; founding dir. Ctr. for Sight Enhancement, U. Houston, 1998—2000. Pres. Harris County Optometric Soc., Houston, 2001—02; cons. Nat. Bd. Examiners in Optometry. Clin. Sci. Com. for Refractive/Oculomotor/Sensory Integrative Conditions, Charlotte, NC, 2005—; chair, sci. merit rev. adv. bd., rehab. R&D svc., vision panel Dept. Vets. Affairs, Washington, 2006—. Recipient George Wash. Honor medal, Freedoms Found. at Valley Forge, 2006. Fellow: Am. Acad. Optometry (chair, region II fellowship admittance com. 2003); mem.: Tex. Optometric Assn. (bd. dirs. 1999—2006, Young Optometrist Yr. 2006, Humanitarian award 2006), Am. Optometric Assn. Achievements include patents pending for application of visual orientation sensitivity in early macular disease. Avocations: travel, bicycling. Office: U Houston 505 J Davis Armistead Houston TX 77204-2020 Home Phone: 713-426-1526; Office Phone: 713-743-0799. Home Fax: 713-743-0190.

WOO, VERNON YING-TSAI, lawyer, real estate developer; b. Honolulu, Aug. 7, 1942; s. William Shu-Bin and Hilda Woo; children: Christopher Shu-Bin, Lia Gay. BA, U. Hawaii, 1964, MA, 1966; JD, Harvard U., 1969. Pres. Woo Kessner Duca & Maki, Honolulu, 1972-87; pvt. practice law Honolulu, 1987—. Judge per diem Honolulu Dist. Family Ct., 1978-84, 1995-2002. Bd. dirs. Boys and Girls Club of Honolulu,. 1985-95, pres., 1990-92. Mem.: ABA, Honolulu Bd. Realtors, Hawaii Bar Assn. Home: 3936 Waokanaka St Honolulu HI 96817 Office: 700 Richards St Ste 2306 Honolulu HI 96813 Home Phone: 808-595-3344; Office Phone: 808-529-8822. Personal E-mail: vwoo@hawaii.rr.com.

WOOD, ANDRÉE ROBITAILLE, archaeologist, researcher; b. Chgo., Feb. 10, 1929; d. Andrew George and Alice Marie (Fortier) Robitaille; m. Richard Lawrence Wood, Jan. 14, 1956; children: Mary Wood Molo, Matthew William Wood, Melissa Irene Wood, Elizabeth Wood Wesel, John Andrew Wood. BA, No. Ill. Univ., DeKalb, 1977, MA, 1982. Freelance archaeologist, 1981—84; rsch. asst. Prehistoric Project Oriental Inst., Univ. Chgo., Ill., 1984—98. Rsch., discovery, removal, analysis and identification of ancient blood residues on lithic material excavated at ten millenium old site, Çayönü in Ergani, Turkey. Contbr. articles to profl. jours. Avocations: poetry, boating, tennis. Home: 356 Old Sutton Rd Barrington IL 60010-9113 also: 8735 Midnight Pass Rd Apt 604B Sarasota FL 34242-2892

WOOD, BETTY JEAN, conceptual artist, art educator; b. Pitts., Ind., Mar. 2, 1942; d. Ralph Alphas and Mary Cordis Blanton; m. John E. Ayers, Aug. 25, 1963 (div. May 1987); children: Mark Ayers, Kristin Ayers Torres; m. Frederick Harrison Wood, Jr., Nov. 28, 1987 (dec. Jan. 2002); children: Andrew, Christopher. BA with honors, Pa. State U., 1984; MFA, U. Okla., 1992. Artist-in-residence Okla. Arts Coun., 1993—2003; asst. instr. Okla. Arts Inst., Okla. State U., Stillwater, 1998; guest lectr. Southwestern State U., Weatherford, Okla., 2001; instr. Oklahoma City Mus. of Art., 2002—; guest lectr. Goddard Art Ctr., Ardmore, Okla., 2003. Spl. project asst. ConservArt Assoc., Culver City, Calif., 1991—93; asst. preparator Fred Jones, Jr. Mus. of Art, U. Okla., 1992—2005, installation asst., 1992; co-coord. SummerWind Arts Festival, Norman, 1994—96; coord. SummerWind Arts Festival, Children's Events, 1995—; art cons. Dept. Edn., San Juan, 1986; bd. dirs. Children's Art Network, Norman, 1996—2001; coord./curator spl. exhbn. Ctrl. Pa. Festival of the Arts, State College, 1973—87; adj. prof. U. Okla., Norman, Okla., 1997—98, 2004—06; artist in residence, Costa Rica, 2006, Vt. Studio Ctr., Johnson, 2007. Author: (book reviews) Museologist, 1986—87, Community Based Art Education, 1995; one-woman shows include Bricktown Fin. Inst., Okla., numerous others, exhibited in group shows at 50th Anniversary Nat. Art Exhibit, Wind River Valley Artist's Guild, Wyo., Leslie Powell Gallery, Okla., IAO Gallery, Okla., Gallery on the Sq., Ky., Period Gallery, Nebr., Suite 2 Portfolio, Okla., Kirkpatrick Galleries of Omniplex, Okla., Goddard Art Ctr., Ardmore, Okla., East Ctrl. U., Ada, Okla., Purdue U., West Lafayette, Ind., Lamar U., Beaumont, Tex., Mus. Great Plains, Lawton, Okla., Soho Art Dist., NYC, Murray State Coll., Tishomingo, Okla., Mainsite Art Gallery, Norman, Okla., Internat. Print Exhbn., Barcelona, Spain, Taiwan, Ponca City Gallery, Okla., Pass Gallery, Norman, 2007, U. Okla., 2007, Southwestern State U., Okla., 2007, Oklahoma City U. Gallery, 2007, Am. Print Alliance, Peachtree City, Ga., 2007, Internat. Print Exhbn., Spain, Eng. and France, 2007, Internat. Visions Exhbn., Oklahoma City, 2007, others, Represented in permanent collections Okla. Visual Arts Coalition, Oklahoma City, Sch. of Art, U. Okla., Okla., exhibited in group shows at others, over 350 exhbns., Represented in permanent collections Fred Jones, Jr. Mus. of Art, Okla., Okla. Sch. of Arts and Scis., Sch. of Visual Arts, Pa. State U., Okla. City Art Mus., pvt. collections U.S. and abroad. Recipient numerous awards for art. Mem.: Fred Jones Jr. Mus. Art, Oklahoma City Mus. Art, Mus. Women in Art, Nat. Mus. for Women in Art, Five to Nine Artists, Jacobson House Found., U. Okla. Art Alumni Assn. (pres. 1993), Pa. State U. Alumni Assn., Beta Sigma Phi Sorority (pres. 1983—84). Democrat. Avocations: children's/adult's workshops, reading, antiques, art. Home: 3316 Riviera Dr Norman OK 73072-7613 Office Phone: 405-850-2051. Business E-Mail: fredwood@ou.edu.

WOOD, BRENDA JEAN, pastor, evangelist; b. Patrick AFB, Fla., Sept. 24, 1961; d. Terry Robert Hubbard and Cherry Ann Redwine, James William Redwine (Stepfather); m. Ross Landan Wood, Apr. 11, 1981; children: Jared Ross, Dwight Adam Myers, Christopher Wayne Pitts, Leslie Anne. AA, Weatherford Coll., Weatherford, Texas, 1981; BA Psychology, Calif. State U., San Bernardino, Calif., 1995; MS Marriage & Family Therapy, Fuller Theol. Sem., Pasadena, Calif., 1999, MA in Theology, 2002. Ordained min. Bethel Christian Ctr., 2004, lic. min. Assemblies of God, Calif., 1999. Youth pastor Full Gospel Assembly of God, Norco, Calif., 1995—97; intern counselor Turning Point Counseling, Diamond Bar, Calif., 1997—99; christian edn. dir. New Life Christian Fellowship, Riverside, Calif., 1998—98, youth pastor, 1998—98, sr. pastor, 1998—2004; pastor, founder Word of Life Ministries Internat., 2005—; evangelist Word of Life Ministries in Nigeria and India. Spkr. Religious and Civic Functions, 1995—; evangelist New Life Christian Fellowship, Mexico, 2002—, Nigeria, 2003, pastoral counselor, Calif., 1995—; parenting educator Safe Haven Program, Riverside, Calif., 2002—03. Chaplain Calif. Dept. of Forestry, Riverside, Calif., 2001—04; mem. Cops and Clergy, Riverside, Calif., 2002, bd. mem., 2002; mem. Jurupa C. of C., Riverside, Calif., 2003, Pastors Prayer Fellowship, Riverside, Calif., 2001. Scholar Music, Weatherford Coll., 1979. Assemblies Of God. Avocations: spending time with my family, gardening, travel. Home: 1804 Noah Dr Corona CA 92880 E-mail: pastorbrenda@theword.us.

WOOD, CATHERINE T., special education educator; b. Mineola, NY, Jan. 17, 1950; d. Owen Joseph Sheehan and Dorothy Margaret Carnaghan; m. David Patrick Wood, Aug. 7, 1976; 1 child, Khalie Tamara. BS in Psychology, Spanish and Edn., Molloy Coll., Rockville Ctr., NY, 1971; MS in Spl. Edn., Hofstra U., 1975, postgrad. in Speech and Lang., 1975—; postgrad., Nov Southeastern U., 2005—. Cert. tchr. N.Y., in sign lang. Spl. edn. tchr. Malverne Sch. Dist., NY, 1971—80; spl. edn. math specialist Horizion Sch. for Perceptual Devel., Bayside, NY, 1980—84; spl. edn. tchr. Valley Stream Dist. 30, NY, 1984—. Pres. sch. bd. Our Lady of Peace Sch., Lynbrook, NY, 1995—97; mem. regional sch. bd. Region#24, Lynbrook, NY, 1995—97; religous edn. tchr. Our Lady of Peace, Lynbrook, NY, 1994—98. Vol. Full Cir., NYC, 1969—73; tchr. vol. Vocat. Edn. Extension Bd., Hempstead, 1994—98. Recipient Master Tchrs. Award, Molloy Coll., N.Y., 1995. Mem.: ASCD, NY Student Speech Lang. Hearing Assn., Valley Stream Tchrs. Assn., Nassau Reading Coun., Nat. Coun. Tchrs. English, Nassau County Math Tchr. Assn., Kappa Delta Pi. Roman Catholic. Avocations: sewing, knitting, kayaking, music, pottery. Office: Forest Rd Sch 16 Forest Rd Valley Stream NY 11581

WOOD, CHERYL RALEY, minister, musician; b. Okla. City, Jan. 24, 1955; d. Coleman LaVan and Fern Norwood Raley; m. Timothy Michael Wood, June 16, 1984; children: Daniel Raley, Michael James. MusB with honors, Okla. Bapt. U., Shawnee, 1977; MusM, The U. Mich., Ann Arbor, 1979; student in Deacon Studies, Garrett-Evang. Theol. Sem., Evanston, Ill., 2003. Ordained minister United Meth. Ch., 2007. Organist First Bapt. Ch., Bartlesville, Okla., 1981—84; ind. music tchr., freelance organist, 1984—88; organist First United Meth. Ch., Weatherford, Tex., 1988—96; dir. of music/organist Craft Meml. United Meth. Ch., Columbia, Tenn., 1996—2001; organist Bellevue United Meth. Ch., Nashville, 2001—03; min. music First United Meth. Ch., Pulaski, Tenn., 2004—. Adj. instr. music Bartlesville Wesleyan Coll., Okla., 1981—83, Martin Meth. Coll., Pulaski, Tenn., 2000—03. Musician: Cmty. Chorus, Tenn. Ann. Conf. Clergy mem. Tenn. Ann. Conf. United Meth. Ch., 2007—. Mem.: Fellowship United Meths. Music and Worship Arts, Choristers Guild (musician choir Mid. Tenn. chpt.), Am. Guild Organists. Home Phone: 931-540-8484; Office Phone: 931-363-2595.

WOOD, CORINNE GIESEKE, former lieutenant governor; b. Barrington, Ill., May 28, 1954; m. Paul R. Wood; children: Ashley, Brandon, Courtney. BS, U. Ill., 1976; JD, Loyola U., 1979. Bar: Ill. 1979. Pvt. practice; counsel Ill. Savs. and Residential Fin. Bd.; atty. Hopkins & Sutter, Chgo.; gen. counsel Ill. Commr. of Banks and trusts; state rep. 59th dist. 90th Ill. Gen. Assembly, Springfield; rep. State of Ill., 1997—99, former lt. gov. Springfield, 1999—2003. Appointed spec. asst., Ill. Atty. Gen. Former co-capt. Shields Twp. Rep. Precinct; Lake Forest chmn. John E. Porter for Congress, 1994, 96; adv. mem. Coun. of Women Advisors to U.S. Congress; past 1st v.p., bd. dirs. Women's Rep. Club, past pres., bd. mem. 10th Congl. Dist. of Lake Forest/Lake Bluff chpt.; past pres. (fin. chmn.), mem. bd. govs. Lake County Rep. Fedn.; bd. dirs. Allendale Shelter Club, Allendale Assn.; adv. bd. A Safe Place; transition bd. dirs. Anne M. Kiley Ctr. for the Developmentally Disabled; mem. LWV of Lake Forest/Lake Bluff; mem. Lake Forest Open Lands Assn.; former Lake Forest chmn., sustaining mem. Jr. League of Chgo.; former new mems. chair, membership com., Sunday sch. tchr. First Presbyn. Ch. of Lake Forest; den leader Pack 43, Boy Scouts Am.; plan commr. City of Lake Forest, 1993-97, sr. housing commr., 1993-97, ad hoc com. on sr. housing bd. mem. Recipient City of Lake Forest Spl. Recognition of Pub. Svc. award. Mem. ABA, Ill. Bar Assn., Lake County Bar Assn., Chgo. Bar Assn., House Financial Insts. Comm., Comm. on Aging, Edn. Appropriations Comm., Labor and Commerce Comm., appointed mem., Legislative Rsch. Bureau, bd. mem. Republican.

WOOD, CRAIG BRECKINRIDGE, paleobiologist, natural sciences educator; b. Washington, Jan. 27, 1943; s. William Ernest Wood and Christina Mae (DeBrito) Phillips; m. Sung He Lee, May 21, 1982; children: William, Violet, Virginia. AB in Geology, U. N.C., 1966; MS in Geology, U. Wyo., 1967; MA in Geology, Harvard U., 1980, PhD in Geology, 1992. Tchg. fellow geology, anthropology, biology depts. Harvard U., Cambridge, Mass., 1968-70, 73-74; rsch. assoc. geology dept. Princeton (N.J.) U., 1970-71; geologist Herbert & Assocs. Ltd., Virginia Beach, Va., 1972-73; instr. natural sci. Providence Coll., 1974—79, asst. prof. natural sci., spl. lectr. geology, 1979—, assoc. prof. natural sci., 1993—2001, prof., 2001—, dir. natural sci. program, 1993—95, chmn. dept. biology, 2006—. Harvard U. exch. scholar dept. paleontology U. Calif., Berkeley, 1988-89; rsch. assoc. in mammalogy Mus. Comparative Zoology, Harvard U., 1994-2006; hon. guest prof. Jilin U., 2002—; expdn. mem. Rift Valley Rsch. Mission in Ethiopia, Addis Ababa, 1976, Blue Nile region, Ethiopia, 1993, 96, 97, 98; Mesozoic fieldwork in Gyeongsangdo, Korea, 1998-2000, 03; fieldwork in Jilin Province, China, 2000, 2002, 2003. Co-discoverer of "Bodo Man", 1976, first Ethiopian highland Mezozoic vertebrates, 1993, first Ethiopian dinosaurs, 1996, first Triassic vertebrates in Tigray Province, 1997-98, first Ethiopian Mesozoic mammal, 1999, first Mesozoic mammals in Jilin Province, China, 2000; assoc. editor: Jour. Paleontology Soc. Korea, 2001-07. Mem. Soc. Vertebrate Paleontology, R.I. Carolina Club (treas. 1994-97), Sigma Xi, Phi Mu Alpha Sinfonia. Office: Providence Coll Biology Dept Providence RI 02918-0001 Office Phone: 401-865-2250. Business E-Mail: cbwood@providence.edu.

WOOD, CYNTHIA WILDER, elementary school educator; b. West Point, NY, July 4, 1952; d. Robert Morse and Cynthia Rich Wood. AA in Early Childhood Edn., Centenary Coll., 1974; BS in Health Edn., U. Conn., 1984; MAT in Elem. Edn., U. Portland, 1989. Med. assoc. pvt. med. office, Greenwich, Conn., 1974—80; radiol. tech. United Hosp., Port Chester, NY, 1980—84, Providence Milw. Hosp., Clackamas, Oreg., 1985—88, Williamette Falls Hosp., Oregon City, 1988—90; tchr. elem. sch. Portland Pub. Schs., 1990—2003, mentor reading coach, 2003—. Mem. Consortium Ednl. Advancement and Devel., Portland, 1994—2007; presenter in field. Mem. Alameda Tuesday Club, Portland, 1992—2000. Mem.: ASCD, Alpha Delta Kappa. Democrat. Episcopalian. Avocations: reading, needlepoint, gardening. Home: 5022 NE Sumner St Portland OR 97218 Office: Whitman Elem Sch 7326 SE Flavel St Portland OR 97206 Office Phone: 503-916-6370. Business E-Mail: cwood@pps.k12.or.us.

WOOD, D. ANN, language and music educator; b. Albuquerque, Aug. 20, 1949; adopted d. Arol Edmund and Margaret Dudley Beck, d. Ray Ruff and Jeanne Ann Short; m. Patrick David Kennedy, July 26, 1969 (div. Jan. 15, 1991); children: Ryan Patrick Kennedy, Deirdre Ann Kennedy; m. Brian Claude Wood, Feb. 23, 1991; 1 child, Victoria Ann. BA in Speech and Theater, U. Mich., 1970; M Ch. Music, Concordia U. Wis., 2001. Ordained elder Presbyn. Ch. Instr. Wood Music Studio, Escanaba, Mich., 1977—; adj. faculty English and comm. Bay de Noc CC, Escanaba, 1981—; dir. music First Presbyn. Ch., Escanaba, 1989—. Musical dir. Bay de Noc Choral Soc., Escanaba, 1992—. Composer: (handbell composition) Amazing, Wondrous!. Bd. dirs. Bay Area Campus Ministry, Escanaba, 1997—. Named Outstanding Part-time Faculty Mem., Bay de Noc CC, 2005. Mem.: Choristers Guild, Suzuki Assn. Americas, Am. String Tchrs. Assn., Am. Choral Dirs. Assn., Am. Guild English Handbell Ringers (cert.). Presbyterian. Avocations: travel, community theater, music performance. Home: 2543 Lake Shore Dr Escanaba MI 49829 Office: Bay de Noc CC 2001 N Lincoln Rd Escanaba MI 49829 Office Phone: 906-786-5802 1248. Personal E-mail: dawood@charter.net.

WOOD, DAVID M., oil industry executive; B in Geology, Nottingham U., Eng. Mgr. frontier exploration Murphy Oil Corp., 1994—95, gen. mgr. frontier exploration, 1995—97, v.p. frontier exploration & prodn., 1997—99, sr. v.p. frontier exploration & prodn., 1999—2003, pres. Murphy Exploration & Prodn. Co.-Internat., 2003—06, exec. v.p., 2007—. Office: Murphy Oil Corp PO Box 7000 El Dorado AR 71731-7000 Office Phone: 870-862-6411. *

WOOD, DIANE PAMELA, federal judge; b. Plainfield, NJ, July 4, 1950; d. Kenneth Reed and Lucille (Padmore) Wood; children: Kathryn Hutchinson, David Hutchinson, Jane Hutchinson; m. Robert L. Sufit, 2006. BA, U. Tex., 1971, JD, 1975; JD (hon.), Georgetown U., 2003, Ill. Inst. Tech., 2004. Bar: Tex. 1975, DC 1978, Ill. 1993. Law clk. US Ct. Appeals (5th cir.), 1975—76, US Supreme Ct., 1976—77; atty.-adv. US Dept. State, Washington, 1977—78; assoc. Covington & Burling, Washington, 1978—80; asst. prof. law Georgetown U. Law Ctr., Washington, 1980—81, U. Chgo., 1981—88, prof. law, 1988—95, assoc. dean, 1989—92, Harold J. and Marion F. Green prof. internat. legal studies, 1990—95, sr. lectr. law, 1995—; spl. cons. antitrust divsn. internat. guide US Dept. Justice, 1986—87, dep. asst. atty. gen. antitrust divsn., 1993—95; judge US Ct. Appeals (7th cir.), 1995—. Contbr. articles to profl. jours.; bd. editors: Am. Jour. Internat. Law. Bd. dirs. Hyde Park-Kenwood Cmty. Health Ctr., 1983—85. Fellow: Am. Acad. Arts and Scis.; mem.: Am. Law Inst. (elected coun. mem. 2003), Am. Soc. Internat. Law, Phi Alpha Delta. Democrat. Office: US Courthouse 219 S Dearborn St Chicago IL 60604-1803 *

WOOD, DIRK GREGORY, surgeon, physician, forensic consultant; b. Springfield, Ohio, Sept. 19, 1953; s. Carlos Paul and Evelyn Cecelia (Bird) W. BA magna cum laude, Urbana U., Ohio, 1973; postgrad., Ohio State U., 1973-75; MD, UAG Facultad de Medicina, Guadalajara, Mexico, 1980; mini pupilage, Inns of Court School of Law, London, 1990; JD, Capital Law Sch., Columbus, Ohio, 1991. Diplomate Am. Bd. Ob-Gyn, Am. Bd. Forensic Medicine. Intern Bronx Lebanon Hosp., NY, 1981-82; resident William Beaumont Hosp., Royal Oak, Mich., 1982-86; physician, surgeon Her Care, Inc., Springfield, 1986—2001. CEO Just What the Doctor Ordered, Springfield, 1992-2001; dir. of obstetrics Mercy Med. Ctr., Springfield, Ohio, 1999-2000; chief collaborative physician Nurse Midwives Ctr., 1999-2000. Coroner Clark County, Ohio, 1991-97; mem. Clark County Rep. Ctrl. Com., Clark County Dist. 14, 1992-96. Named Ky. col., Ala. col. Fellow Internat. Coll. Surgeons, Am. Coll. Legal Medicine, Am. Coll. Forensic Examiners, Interam. Coll. Physicians and Surgeons; mem. SAR, Am. Soc. Law and Medicine, Phi Delta Epsilon (past chpt. pres.), Phi Alpha Delta. Avocations: scuba diving, bibliophilia, travel. Home: 2900 Cleveland Ave Saint Joseph MI 49085 Personal E-mail: drdirkwood@comcast.net.

WOOD, DONALD CRAIG, retired marketing professional; b. Wilmington, Del., June 24, 1937; s. Thomas Henry and Madelyn (Brehm) W.; m. Elizabeth Haring, Apr. 28, 1962; children: Craig Standish, Allison Jean. BA, U. Del., 1959; MBA, Northwestern U., 1967. Sales engr. NVF Corp., Broadview, Ill., 1960-62, Synthane Corp., Morton Grove, Ill., 1962-68; account exec., mgr. sales Donnelley Mktg. subs. Dun and Bradstreet Corp., Oakbrook, Ill., 1968-76, from dir. to v.p. market devel. to v.p. mktg. Stamford, Conn., 1977-1980; from v.p., gen. mgr. to pres. Donnelley Mktg. Info. Svcs. subs. Dun and Bradstreet Corp., Stamford, 1980-86; sr. v.p.

Donnelley Mktg. Inc. subs. Dun and Bradstreet Corp., Stamford, 1987-90; v.p., gen. mgr. info. svcs. Triad Systems Corp., Livermore, Calif., 1990-96; ret., 1996. Served to 1st lt. U.S. Army, 1959-60. Home: 6312 Providence CC Dr Charlotte NC 28277

WOOD, DONALD EURIAH, retired lawyer; b. Guymon, Okla., May 27, 1935; s. Theodore and Lula Elizabeth (Rider) W.; m. Lynda Sharon Harris, Sept. 30, 1960; children: Donald Craig, Tana Dawn, Kristen Lynn. BA, Panhandle A&M Coll., 1958; LLB, Okla. U., 1964, JD, 1970. Bar: Okla. 1964. Asst. county atty., Texas County, 1964; county atty., 1965-67; dist. atty. Okla. 1st Jud. Dist., Guymon, 1967—2002; ret., 2002. Adv. com. Okla. Commn. Criminal and Traffic Enforcement Systems, 1972; active Gov.'s Commn. Cmty. Affairs and Planning, 1972-75; faculty Panhandle State Coll., 1974-92; mem. Okla. Dist. Atty. Tng. Coun., 1976-2001; active Okla. Bur. Narcotics and Dangerous Drugs Commn., 1992-98. Served with inf. AUS, 1958-60. Named Okla. Prosecutor of Yr., Assn. Okla. Narcotic Enforcers, 1994-95. Mem. Okla. Bar Assn. (legal ethics com. 1971-72), Texas County Bar Assn. (pres. 1966, 1970-71), Nat. Dist. Attys. Assn., Okla. Dist. Attys. Assn. (pres. 1972, exec. com. 1971-2001), Elks Club, Rotarian Club, Phi Alpha Delta. Presbyterian. Home: Woodland Ter 9524 E 71st St Apt 124 Tulsa OK 74133 Personal E-mail: done@ptsi.net.

WOOD, DONALD F., lawyer; b. Bonne Terre, Mo., July 25, 1944; BSBA, Washington U., 1966; JD, Harvard U., 1969. Bar: Tex. 1970. Adminstrv. ptnr. Vinson & Elkins, L.L.P., Austin. Fellow Houston Bar Found. (chmn. 1991); mem. Beta Gamma Sigma, Omicron Delta Kappa. Office: Vinson & Elkins LLP 2801 Via Fortuna Ste 100 Austin TX 78746 Business E-Mail: dwood@velaw.com.

WOOD, DOUGLAS LYNN, medical educator; b. Columbia, Mo., June 24, 1951; s. Cecil Vernon and Wilda Fay (Palmer) W.; m. Julia Ann Sandbothe, May 28, 1977; children: Ethan, Amanda, Paul, Benjamin. BA cum laude with distinction in Biology, Carleton Coll., 1973; MD magna cum laude, U. Mo., 1977. Diplomate Am. Bd. Internal Medicine, Am. Bd. Cardiovasc. Diseases. Asst. prof. medicine Mayo Grad. Sch. Medicine, Rochester, Minn., 1983—91, assoc. prof. medicine, 1991—2003, prof. medicine, 2003—. Cons. cardiovasc. diseases Mayo Clinic, Rochester, 1983—, vice-chair dept. medicine, 1993—, chair divsn. health care policy and rsch., 2007—; pres., CEO, chmn. bd. dirs. Immanuel-St. Joseph's Mayo Health Sys., Mankato, Minn.; chair Sec.'s Adv. Com. on Regulatory Reform, Dept. HHS, 2001-02, mem. practicing physicians adv. com., 2000-04. Contbr. articles to profl. jours. Mem. coun. on performance measurement Joint Commn. on Accreditation of Healthcare Orgns., Oakbrook Terrace, Ill., 1995-2007; mem. CPT editl. panel AMA, Chgo., 1994-97; chair fin. coun. St. Pius X Ch., Rochester, 1993-97; mem. Minn. Citizens Forum on Health Care Costs, 2003-04; mem. Gov.'s Quality Control Coun., 2006—. Fellow ACP, Am. Coll. Cardiology; mem. Am. Coll. Physician Execs., Alpha Omega Alpha, Sigma Xi. Office: Mayo Clinic 200 1st St SW Rochester MN 55905-0002 Home Phone: 507-285-1624; Office Phone: 507-284-3725. Business E-Mail: wood.douglas@mayo.edu.

WOOD, ELIJAH, actor; b. Cedar Rapids, Iowa, Jan. 28, 1981; Appeared in films Back to the Future Part II, 1989, Internal Affairs, 1990, Avalon, 1990, Paradise, 1991, Radio Flyer, 1992, Forever Young, 1992, The Adventures of Huck Finn, 1993, The Good Son, 1993, North, 1994, The War, 1994, Flipper, 1996, The Ice Storm, 1997, Deep Impact, 1998, Black and White, 1999, The Bumblebee Flies Anyway, 2000, Chain of Fools, 2000, The Lord of the Rings: The Fellowship of the Ring, 2001, The Lord of the Rings: The Two Towers, 2002, The Lord of the Rings: The Return of the King, 2003, Spy Kids 3-D: Game Over, 2003, Eternal Sunshine of a Spotless Mind, 2004, Hooligans, 2005, Sin City, 2005, Everything is Illuminated, 2005, Paris, Je t'aime, 2006, (voice) Happy Feet, 2006; TV movies include Child in the Night, 1990, Day-O, 1992, Oliver Twist, 1997; also appeared in music video Paula Abdul's Forever Your Girl. Office: William Morris Agency c/o Nichole David 151 S El Camino Dr Beverly Hills CA 90212-2775 *

WOOD, ELIZABETH ANN, special education educator; b. Pittsfield, Mass., Aug. 2, 1979; d. Dennis Roy Luczynski and Tami Lee Daley; m. Jason Richard Wood, Aug. 31, 2000; 1 child, Haley Elizabeth. BA in Sociology, BA in Early Childhood Edn., Mass. Coll. Liberal Arts, 2001, MEd in Spl. Needs, 2003. Cert. early childhood and moderate disability tcur. Mass. Mgr. Subway, North Adams, Mass., 1996—2002; lead pre-kindergarten tchr. North Berkshire YMCA, North Adams, 2001—03; spl. needs tchr. Hillcrest Edn. Ctrs., Pittsfield, Mass., 2003—. Mem.: Nat. Honor Soc. Roman Catholic. Avocations: sewing, exercise, scrapbooks. Home: 2 Daniels Ct Adams MA 01220 Office: Hillcrest Ednl Ctrs 1450 W Housatanic St Pittsfield MA 01201 Business E-Mail: lwood@hillcrestec.org.

WOOD, EMILY CHURCHILL, special education and social studies educator, consultant; b. Summit, NJ, Apr. 11, 1925; d. Arthur Burdett and Ruth Vail (Pierson) Churchill; m. Philip Warren Wood, June 22, 1946; children: Martha, Arthur, Warren, Benjamin. BA, Smith Coll., 1946; MA in Teaching, Manhattanville Coll., 1971; postgrad., U. Tulsa, 1974-79, Langston U., 1990-92. Cert. tchr. social studies, learning disabilities, elem. edn., econs., Am. history, world history. Tchr. Miss Fines Sch., Princeton, NJ, 1946-47, Hallen Ctr. for Edn., Portchester, NY, 1973-74, Town and Country Sch., Tulsa, Okla., 1974-79, Tulsa Pub. Schs., 1979-97, Heritage Acad., Tulsa, 1998—; adj. instr. Tulsa C.C., Tulsa, 1998—2007. Ednl. cons. Tulsa, 1997—: exchange coord., Tulsa Pub. Sch., 2005—, culture box coord. Tulsa Global Alliance, 2004—; leader colloquia Bill of Rights Arts and Humanities Coun., Tulsa, 1989; mem. literacy task force Tulsa 2000 Edn. Com., 1990-92; chmn. internat. student exch. Eisenhower Internat. Sch., Tulsa, 1992—. Author: (with others) Visual Arts in China, 1988, Applauding Our Constitution, 1989, The Bill of Rights: Who Guarantees What, 1993; contbr. articles to profl. jours. Leader, founder Am. Field Svc., Tulsa, 1982—84; pres., v.p. Booker T. Washington H.S. PTA, Tulsa, 1985; campaign mgr. auditors race Dem. Party, Tulsa, 1988, 1992, 1994, 2006; bd. dirs. Smith Coll. Alumnae, Northampton, Mass., 1956—59, Sister Cities Internat., Tulsa, 1992—2001, nominations chair, 1999—2001; bd. dirs. Tulsa Global Alliance; trustee Okla. Found. for Excellence, 2000—. Named Tulsa Tchr. of Yr. Tulsa Classroom Tchrs. Assn., 1988, Nat. Elem. Tchr. of Yr., Nat. Bar Aux., 1992, Outstanding Elem. Social Studies Tchr., Nat. Cound. or Social Studies, 1999; recipient Elem. Medal of Excellence, Okla. Found. for Excellence, 1990, Valley Forge Tchrs. medal Freedoms Found., 1992, Paragon award Tulsa Commn. on Status of Women, 1996, Pinnacle award Mayor's Commn. on Status of Women, 1998, Liberty Bell award Tulsa Bar Assn., 1998, Global Vision award Tulsa Global Alliance, 2002. Mem. UN Assn. Ea. Okla. (pres. 1998-2000), Nat. Coun. Social Studies (religion program com. 1984—, bd. dirs. 1997—), DAR, Okla. Edn. Assn., Okla. Coun. Social Studies (pres. 1995, tchr. of yr. 1984), Okla. Bar Assn. (law related com. 1988—, tchr. of yr. 1990), Okla. Coun. Econ. Edn. (state and nat. awards 1981, 89, 92), Kent Place Alumnae Assn. (Disting. Alumna award 1992, Alumna Career award 2007). Avocations: reading, swimming, travel, walking. Home: 3622 S Yorktown Pl Tulsa OK 74105-3452 E-mail: emily_wood46@hotmail.com.

WOOD, EVAN RACHEL, actress; b. Raleigh, NC, Sept. 7, 1987; d. Ira David Wood and Sara Lynn Moore. Actor: (films) Digging to China, 1998, Practical Magic, 1998, Detour, 1999, Little Secrets, 2001, S1m0ne, 2002, Thirteen, 2003, The Missing, 2003, Down in the Valley, 2005, Pretty Persuasion, 2005, The Upside of Anger, 2005, Running with Scissors, 2006, (voice) Asterix and the Vikings, 2006, Shark Bait, 2006,: (TV films) In the Best of Families: Marriage, Pride & Madness, 1994, Search for Grace, 1994, A Father for Charlie, 1995, Death in Small Doses, 1995, Get to the Heart: The Barbara Mandrell Story, 1997, Down Will Come Baby, 1999; (TV series) Profiler, 1998—99, Once and Again, 1999—2002, (guest appearances) American Gothic, 1995—98, Touched by an Angel, 2000, The West Wing, 2002, CSI: Crime Scene Investigation, 2003. *

WOOD, FRANCES DIANE, medical secretary, artist; b. Caddo, Okla., Mar. 7, 1950; d. Clovis Lynn and Hilda Dee (Guthrie) Wood; m. Samuel Dante Wolfe, Aug. 20, 1990 (div. Mar. 1992). BA, Southea. Okla. State U., 1972; postgrad., Grayson County Coll., 1987, Rose State Coll., 2002, U. Ctrl. Okla., 2004. Cert. master gardener Okla., 2006. Ins. clk. Sherman Cmty. Hosp., Tex., 1973—74; med. sec. Essin Clinic, Sherman, 1980—83; med. transcriptionist Texoma Med. Ctr., Denison, Tex., 1983—88, Wilson N. Jones Meml. Hosp., Sherman, 1989—95; CEO Designs by Diane, Caddo, 1995—. Conv. del. Blue Cross-Blue Shield Tex., Dallas, 1980—83; v.p. Jett Transcription, Denison, 1988. Exhibitions include paintings in cmty. art shows, Represented in permanent collections Shamrock Bank, Caddo, Indian Terr. Mus., Caddo. Charter mem. Caddo Edn. Found., Okla., 1993-95; sponsor Save the Children, Philippines, 1995. Named Okla. Master Gardener, 2006—. Mem. ASPCA, Friends Internat. Fellowship of Christians and Jews, Physicians Com. for Responsible Medicine, Nat. Trust Hist. Preservation, Okla. Sheriffs Assn. (hon.), Arts Coun. Co-op (life), Nat. Arbor Day Found., Sierra Club, Sacred Heart Auto League, People for Ethical Treatment Animals, Urban League Greater Oklahoma City Democrat. Avocations: pet care and pet psychology, interior decorating, astronomy, holistic and naturopathic medicine, gardening.

WOOD, FRANK, actor; b. Lincoln, Mass. Grad. acting program, NYU; grad. theater program, Wesleyan U. Broadway debut in Side Man (Tony award, 1999); actor: (plays) Three Sisters, Tomorrowland, King of Rats, Dark Ride, Hollywood Arms, 2002, The Rainmaker, 2006, Spring Awakening, 2006; many roles in Gil Kofman plays at Soho Rep, Adobe Theater and Dallas Theater Ctr., has worked with Fifty Second Street Project; actor: (TV appearances) Ed, 2001, The Sopranos, 2001, Third Watch, 2001, Law and Order, 2002; (films) Down to You, 2000, Small Time Crooks, 2000, Pollock, 2000, Thirteen Days, 2000, The Royal Tenenbaums, 2001, In America, 2002, People I Know, 2002, The Undeserved, 2004, King of the Corner, 2004, Keane, 2004, The Favor, 2006. Recipient 1995 Drama-Logue award for best ensemble in Kofman's Entrevista 187, Padua Hills Playwrights Festival. Mem.: East Coast Artists.

WOOD, FRANK MAXWELL, prosecutor, lawyer; b. Forest Park, Ga. m. Suzanne Brunson; children: Frank, Sydney, James. BA, LaGrange Coll., 1981; JD, U. Ga., 1985. Law clk. Floyd County Superior Ct., 1985—87; staff atty. Pros. Attys.' Coun. Ga., 1992—94; asst. dist. atty. Ocmulgee Dist. Atty.'s Office, 1994—97; pvt. practice Macon, Ga.; US atty. (mid. dist.) Ga. US Dept. Justice, 2001—. Mem. Martha Bowman Meml. United Meth. Ch. With USAF, col. Ga. Air Nat. Guard. Office: US Attys Office Gateway Plz 300 Mulberry St 4th Fl Macon GA 31201 Office Phone: 478-752-3511. *

WOOD, GORDON STEWART, historian, educator, writer; b. Concord, Mass., Nov. 27, 1933; s. Herbert G. and Marion (Friberg) W.; m. Louise Goss, Apr. 30, 1956; children: Christopher, Elizabeth, Amy. AB, Tufts U., 1955; AM, Harvard, 1959; PhD, Harvard U., 1964. Fellow Inst. Early Am. History and Culture, Williamsburg, Va., 1964-66; asst. prof. Harvard U., Cambridge, Mass., 1966-67; assoc. prof. U. Mich., Ann Arbor, 1967-69; prof. history Brown U., Providence, 1969—; Pitt. prof. Cambridge U., 1982-83. Bancroft lectr. U.S. Naval Acad., 1986; Anson G. Phelps lectr. NYU, 1986; Charles Edmundson lectr. Baylor U., 1987; Samuel Paley lectr. Hebrew U., Jerusalem, 1987; presdl. lecture series on presidency, 1991; trustee, visiting prof. history & law Northwestern U., 2003; bd. trustees Tufts U. Author: The Creation of the American Republic, 1776-1787, 1969, The Rising Glory of America, 1760-1820, 1971; co-author: The Great Republic, 1977, The Radicalism of the American Revolution, 1992 (Pulitzer Prize for history 1993); co-editor: Imagined Histories: American Historians Interpret the Past, 1998, The American Revolution: A History, 2002, The Americanization of Benjamin Franklin, 2004, Revolutionary Characters: What Made the Founders Different, 2006. Mem. coun. Inst. Early Am. History and Culture, 1980-83; bd. trustees Colonial Williamsburg. With USAF, 1955-58. Recipient Bancroft prize Columbia U., 1970, Disting. Visitor award Australian-Am. Ednl. Found., 1976, Douglass Adair prize, 1984, Emerson prize Phi Beta Kappa, 1992, Kidger award New Eng. Tchrs. Assn., 2001, Boston Authors Club prize, 2005; Sunderland fellow U. Mich. Law Sch., 1990, All Souls Coll. fellow, 1991, Fletcher Jones Found. Disting. fellow The Huntington, 1997-98; Woodrow Wilson Ctr. guest-scholar, 1993-94; named to Rhode Island Heritage Hall of Fame, 2000; Dr. of Letters, La Trobe Univ., Austrailia. Mem. Am. Hist. Assn. (John Dunning prize), Orgn. Am. Historians, Soc. Am. Historians, Nat. Hist. Soc. (chmn. bd. advisors), Soc. Historians of the Early Am. Republic (pres.), Am. Acad. Arts and Scis., Am. Philos. Soc. Office: Brown Univ Dept of History Box N Providence RI 02912-9040

WOOD, HARLINGTON, JR., federal judge; b. Springfield, Ill., Apr. 17, 1920; s. Harlington and Marie (Green) W. AB, U. Ill., 1942, JD, 1948. Bar: Ill. 1948. Practiced in, Springfield, 1948-69; mem. firm Wood & Wood, 1948—58, 1961—69; U.S. atty. So. Dist. Ill., 1958-61; assoc. dep. atty. gen. for U.S. attys. Justice Dept., Washington, 1969-70, assoc. dep. atty. gen., 1970-72, asst. atty. gen. civil div., 1972-73; U.S. dist. judge So. Dist. Ill., Springfield, 1973-76; circuit judge U.S. Ct. Appeals (7th cir.), Springfield, 1976—92, sr. judge, 1992—. Adj. prof. Sch. Law, U. Ill., Champaign, 1993; disting. vis. prof. St. Louis U. Law Sch., 1996-2000. Chmn. Adminstrv. Office Oversight Com., 1988-90; mem. Long Range Planning Com., 1991-96. US Army, 1942—46. Recipient Profl. Lifetime Achievement award, Inns of Ct., 2002. As rep. of US govt., his refusal to authorize use of force at Wounded Knee in 1973 is credited with helping bring a nonviolent end to the conflict. Office: US Ct Appeals PO Box 233 Petersburg IL 62675-0233 *

WOOD, H(OWARD) JOHN, III, astrophysicist, astronomer; b. Balt., July 19, 1938; s. Howard John Jr. and Cara (Loss) W.; m. Austine Barton Read, June 10, 1961 (div. Jan. 1975); children: Cara Loss, Erika Barton; m. Maria Ilona Kovacs, May 22, 1977; 1 child, Andreas M. BA in Astronomy, Swarthmore Coll., 1960; MA, Ind. U., 1962, PhD, 1965. Lectr., asst. prof. then assoc. prof. U. Va., Charlottesville, 1964-70; staff astronomer European So. Obs., Santiago, Chile, 1970-75; Fulbright Rsch. fellow U. Vienna Obs., 1976-78; rsch. assoc. Ind. U., Bloomington, 1978-81; asst. to the dir. Cerro Tololo Inter-Am. Obs., La Serena, Chile, 1982-83; physicist, astronomer NASA/Goddard Space Flight Ctr., Greenbelt, Md., 1984—, mgr. instrument synthesis and analysis lab., 2000—. Optics lead engr. Mars Observer Laser Altimeter, 1989-90, Hubble Space Telescope, 1990—; advisor optics and outreach James Webb Space Telescope, 1996—; advisor, participant Hubble Space Telescope Allen Comm., NASA, Danbury, Conn., 1990; co-chmn. Hubble Space Telescope Ind. Optical Rev. Panel, Columbia, Md., 1990-91; mem. panel The Townes/SAGE Panel-Jet Propulsion Lab., Pasadena, 1991-92 Co-author: (Book) Physics of Ap Stars, 1976; contbr. articles to profl. jours. Grantee NSF (10), 1965-82, Am. Astron. Soc., 1978. Mem. Internat. Astron. Union (Commn. 29 1962—), Optical Soc. Am. (chair optical tech. divsn. 1999-2001, co-chair ann. meeting 2002), Am. Astronomical Soc., Sigma Xi. Achievements include discovery of Balmer-Line variability of Ap stars; discovery of magnetic fields in southern Ap stars; alignment testing and delivery of the DIRBE photometric cryogenic telescope on the COBE spacecraft; alignment and optical prescription for Hubble Space Telescope while in orbit. Office: NASA/Goddard Space Flight Ctr Code # 551 Greenbelt MD 20771-0001 Office Phone: 301-286-8278. Business E-Mail: howard.j.wood@nasa.gov.

WOOD, JACKIE DALE, physiologist, educator, researcher; b. Picher, Okla., Feb. 16, 1937; s. Aubrey T. Wood and Wilma J. (Coleman) Wood Patterson. BS, Kans. State U., 1964, MS, 1966; PhD, U. Ill., 1969. Asst. prof. physiology Williams Coll., Williamstown, Mass., 1969-71; asst. prof. U. Kans. Med. Ctr., Kansas City, 1971-74, assoc. prof., 1974-78, prof., 1978-79; prof., chmn. dept. physiology Sch. Medicine, U. Nev., Reno, 1979-85; chmn. dept. physiology coll. medicine Ohio State U., Columbus, 1985-97, prof. physiology and internal medicine, 1997—. Cons. NIH, Bethesda, Md., 1982-88. Recipient Rsch. Career Devel. award NIH, 1974; named Hon. Citizen City of Atzugi Japan, 1987; Alexander von Humboldt fellow, W.Ger., 1976, grantee NIH, 1971—. Fellow Am. Gastroent. Assn.; mem. AAAS, Am. Physiol. Soc. (assoc. editor 1984-96, rsch. award 1986), Soc. Neuroscience. Office: Ohio State U Dept Physiology and Cell Biology 304 Hamilton Hall 1645 Neil Ave Columbus OH 43210-1218 Home Phone: 614-457-2820; Office Phone: 614-292-5449. Business E-Mail: wood.13@osu.edu.

WOOD, JAMES, magazine editor, literary critic; b. Durham, Eng., 1965; m. Claire Messud; 2 children. Chief lit. critic The Guardian, London, 1990—; sr. editor The New Republic, Washington, 1996—; also editor-at-large Kenyon Rev.; prof., practice lit. criticism Harvard Univ., 2003—. Author: The Broken Estate, 2000, The Book Against God, 2003, The Irresponsible Self, 2004. Recipient British Press Young Journalist of Yr. award, 1990. Fellow: Am. Acad. Arts & Scis. Office: New Republic 1331 H St NW Suite 700 Washington DC 20005 Office Phone: 202-508-4444. *

WOOD, JAMES ANDERSON, cardiac surgeon; b. Newton, Mo., Nov. 5, 1926; s. Frank and Lula Wood; m. Joann Wood, 1950; children: Diane, James, Jeff, Carol. BA, Reed Coll., 1953; MD, U. Oreg., 1957. Diplomate Am. Bd. Thoracic Surgey, Am. Bd. Surgery. Prof. cardiac surgery, 1974—94. Co-founder St. Vincent Hosp. Cardiac Surg. Program, Portland, VA Hosp. Cardiac Surg. Program, Portland; founder Bend OR Cardiac Surg. Program, Portland, Corvallis OR Cardiac Surg. Contbr. articles to profl. jours. With Marine Corps. Recipient Young Rschr. award Am. Heart Assn., Meritorious award AMA, 1965. Mem. AMA, Portland Surg. Soc., U.S. Polo Assn., Robert Wise Surg. Soc., El Dorado Polo Club, William Conklin Surg. Soc., Albert Starr Club, Am. Soc. of Thoracic Surgeons, Portland Acad. of Medicine, Dant Found., Wesley Eager Cardiac Surg. Found. (pres.), Pan Pacific Assn., Pacific Coast Surg., North Pacific Surg., Internat. Cardiovascular. Home: PO Box 5 North Plains OR 97133-0005

WOOD, JAMES EDWARD, JR., religion educator, author; b. Portsmouth, Va., July 29, 1922; s. James E. and Elsie Elizabeth (Bryant) W.; m. Alma Leacy McKenzie, Aug. 12, 1943 (dec. Oct. 2000); 1 son, James Edward III BA, Carson-Newman Coll., 1943; BD, So. Bapt. Theol. Sem., 1947, ThM, 1948; MA, Columbia U., 1949; postgrad., U. Tenn., 1943-44; cert. in Chinese, Yale U., 1949-50; Japanese diploma, Naganuma Sch. Japanese Studies, Tokyo, 1950-51; PhD., So. Bapt. Theol. Sem., 1957; LLD, Seinan Gakuin U., Japan, 1983; LLD (hon.), Capital U., 1996; DHC (hon.), Bucharest U., Romania, 1998. Ordained to ministry So. Bapt. Ch., 1942. Pastor Bapt. chs., Tenn. and Ky., 1942-48; Bapt. missionary to Japan, 1950-55; prof. religion and lit. Seinan Gakuin U., Japan, 1951-55; assoc. prof. history of religions Baylor U., Waco, Tex., 1955-58, prof. hist. religions, dir. J. M. Dawson Inst. Ch. State Studies, 1958—73, 1980—99, 1st dir. honors program, 1959-64, founder chmn. interdeptl. grad. degree program in ch.-state studies, 1962-73, 80-95, founder Baylor Univ. Ch. State Rsch. Ctr., 1968, founder, chmn. faculty-student Far Eastern exch. program, 1970-72, Simon and Ethel Bunn Disting. prof. ch.-state studies, 1980-99, Simon and Ethel Bunn Disting. prof. emeritus, 1999—. Exec. dir. Bapt. Joint Com. on Pub. Affairs, Washington, 1972—80; mem. ctrl. panel Bapt. World Alliance Commn. on Religious Liberty and Human Rights, 1965—75, 1980—2000, Commn. on Freedom, Justice and Peace, 1975—80; chmn. Bapt. Com. on USA Bicentennial, 1973—76; mem. So. Bapt. Inter-Agy. Coun., 1972—80, vice chmn., 1975—76, sec., 1976—77; fellow Internat. Acad. for Freedom of Religion and Belief, 1985—, pres., 1990—2000, hon. pres., 2000—; vis. prof. So. Bapt. Theol. Sem., 1974, N.Am. Bapt. Theol. Sem., Sioux Falls, SD, 1974, Sioux Falls, 79, Okla. Bapt. U., Shawnee, 1977; vis. scholar Christ Coll. Oxford U., 1983; vis. prof. Bulgarian Bapt. Theol. Sem., Sofia, Bulgaria, 1998; vis. prof. Faculty of Canon Law Cath. U., Leuven, Belgium, 1999; vis. prof. others; vis. lectr. Tex. A&M U., 1962, 65, 68, Ashland Theol. Sem., Ohio, 1971; lectr. Union Theol. Sem., NYC, 1974, Va., 89; Vernon Richardson lectr. U. Bapt. Ch., Balt., 1975; lectr. Ea. Bapt. Theol. Sem., Phila., 1975, Duquesne U., 1976, Wake Forest U., 1978, U. Richmond, 1979, First World Congress on Religious Liberty, Amsterdam, 1977, Rice U., 1977, 84, Notre Dame Law Sch., 1980, U. Kans., 1982, 2d World Congress on Religious Liberty, Rome, 1984, U. Faculty of Law, Warsaw, 1984, Loyola U., 1985, U. So. Calif., 1983, U. Oviedo, Spain, 1989, Chinese Inst. Religion, Beijing, 1986, Brigham Young U., 1986, 95, 97, 2005, Naval Coll. Chaplains, Providence, 1988—95, U. Kans. Law Sch., 1990, U. Tirana, Albania, 1992, U. Malta, 1994, Austin Coll., 1989, 95, U. Pitts. Law Sch., 1997, U. Kiev, 1998; chair Internat. Consultation on Religious Rights and Ethnic Identity, Budapest, 1992; co-chair Internat. Conf. Religious Freedom, Moscow, 1993; mem. internat. adv. bd. World Report on Freedom Conscience Human Rights Ctr. U. Sussex, England; co-chair consultation on Freedom of Conscience Human Rights and Belief, Moscow, 1993; chair Internat. Consultation Religious Liberty and Social Peace, Malta, 1994; Carver-Barnes lectr. Southeastern Bapt. Theol. Sem., 1981; Asian Found. lectr. Seinan Gakuin U., Japan, 1983; ecumenical consultation on edn. Nat. Coun. Chs., 1974; spkr. in field. Co-author: Church and State in Scripture, History and Constitutional Law, 1958; author: A History of American Literature: An Anthology, 1952, The Problem of Nationalism, 1969, Nationhood and the Kingdom, 1977, Secular Humanism and the Public Schools, 1986, Reflections on Church and State, 1995; (edited by Derek H. Davis) The Separation of Church and State Defended: Selected Writings of James E. Wood, Jr., 1995, Church-State Relations in the Modern World, 1999, Church and State In Historical Perspective, vol. 1, 2005, Church and State In the Modern World, vol. 2, 2005, and numerous others; editor: Markham Press Fund, Baylor U. Press, 1970-72; editor, contr.: Jewish-Christian Relations in Today's World, 1971, Baptists and the American Experience, 1976, Religion and Politics, 1983, Religion, the State, and Education, 1984, Religion and the State: Essays in Honor of Leo Pfeffer, 1985, Ecumenical Perspectives on Church and State, Protestant, Catholic and Jewish, 1988, Readings on Church and State, 1989, The First Freedom: Religion and the Bill of Rights, 1990, contr. co-editor: The Role of Religion in the Making of Public Policy, 1991, The Role of Government in Monitoring and Regulating Religion in Public Life, 1993, Problems and Conflicts Between Law and Morality in a Free Society, 1994, founding editor Jour. Ch. and State, 1959-73, 80-93, mem. editl. coun., 1973-80, mem. editl. bd., 1993-99; mem. editl. bd. Religion and Public Edn., Religious Freedom Reporter; area editor, contbr. Ency. So. Bapts., 1982, Church and State in Am. History, 1987; contbr. Changing Trends in Education, 1992, Law, Religion and Human Rights in Global Perspective, 1995, Dialogue of Democracy: An American Politics Reader, 1996, United Nations' Contributions to the Prevention and Settlement of Conflicts, 2003, The New Inquisitors, 2004, many others; contbr. over 300 articles to profl. jours. Sponsor Ams. for Pub. Schs., 1963-68; bd. dirs. Waco (Tex.) Planned Parenthood, 1966-72, pres., 1971-72; sponsor Christians Concerned for Israel, 1968—, Tex. Conf. Chs. Consultation on Religion and Public Edn., 1971, Nat. Christian Leadership Conf. for Israel, 1978—; pres. Waco area ACLU, bd. dirs. Tex. unit, 1968-72; pres. Nat. Coun. Religion and Pub. Edn., 1979-83. exec. com., 1975-90, bd. dirs., 1972-90; chmn. exec. com.

Coun. Washington Reps. on UN, 1977-80, mem. council exec. com., 1973-80; exec. com. Nat. Coalition on Pub. Edn. and Religious Liberty, 1973-95; mem. religious liberty com. Nat. Coun. Chs. U.S.A., 1972—, mem. com. internat. concerns on human rights, 1973-80; Am. rep. Chs. Montreux Colloquium on Helsinki Final Act, 1977; v.p. Waco Conf. Christians and Jews, 1983-86, Internat. Acad. for Freedom of Religion and Belief, 1985-90, pres., 1990-2000, hon. pres., 2000—; mem. internat. adv. bd. World Report on Freedom of Conscience, Human Rights Ctr., U. Sussex, Eng.; trustee Internat. Devel. Conf., 1974-80; nat. coun. Am.-Israel Friendship League, 1977—; founder, chmn. Waco Human Rights Week, 1981-86; mem. ch. rels. com., U.S. Holocaust Meml. Coun., 1990-97; adv. com. on religious freedom abroad U.S. State Dept., 1998-2004. Recipient Disting. Alumnus award, Carson-Newman Coll., 1974, Religious Liberty award, Alliance for Preservation of Religious Liberty, 1980, Henrietta Szold award, Tex. region Hadassah, 1981, Human Rights award, Waco Conf. Christians and Jews, 1986, Cir. of Achievement award, Baylor U. Mortar Bd., 1991, Religious Freedom Lifetime award, Ams. United Ctrl. Tex., 1993, W.R. White Meritorious Svc. award, 1996, Human Rights Leadership award, Freedom mag., 1998, Herbert H. Reynolds Exemplary award, 2004, Alma M. and James E. Wood, Jr. endowed scholarship, Baylor U., 2004—, Disting. Svc. in Promoting Religious Freedom award, Brigham Young U. Internat. Ctr. for Religious Studies, 2005. Mem. Am. Soc. Ch. History, Am. Acad. Religion, Am. Soc. Internat. Law, Am. Soc. Sci. Study of Religion, N. Am. Soc. Ecumenists, NCCJ (ad. com. on ch. state and taxation 1979-85), ACLU, Supreme Court Hist. Soc., Soc. for Scholarly Publishing, Va. Hist. Soc., Phi Eta Sigma, Pi Kappa Delta, Alpha Psi Omega. Democrat. Home: 203 Barrington Ln Yorktown VA 23693-5622 Business E-Mail: james_wood@baylor.edu.

WOOD, JAMES JERRY, lawyer; b. Rockford, Ala., Aug. 13, 1940; s. James Ronald and Ada Love Wood; m. Earline Luckie, Aug. 9, 1959; children: James Jerry, William Gregory, Diana Lynn. AB, Samford U., 1964, JD, 1969. Bar: Ala. 1969, U.S. Supreme Ct. 1976. Dir. legal affairs Med. Assn. State of Ala., Montgomery, 1969-70; asst. atty. gen. State of Ala., Montgomery, 1970-72; asst. U.S. atty. Middle Dist. Ala., Montgomery, 1972-76; pvt. practice, 1977-78; pres. Wood & Parnell, P.A., Montgomery, Ala., 1979-89; pvt. practice Montgomery, 1990—. Gen. counsel Ala. Builders Self-Insurers Fund, Home Builders Assn. of Ala.; chmn. character and fitness com. Ala. State Bar, 1981-84, 86-89, chair task force on quality of life, 1990-92, chair task force on mem. svcs., 1994-96. Capt. USAR, 1974-79. Fellow: Ala. Law Found., Am. Bar Found.; mem.: FBA (pres. Montgomery chpt. 1974—75), ABA (ho. of dels. 1990—98), Def. Rsch. Inst., Ala. Coun. Assn. Execs. (pres. 2001), Ala. Bar Assn., Ala. Assn. Workers Compensation Group Self-Insured Funds (chmn.), Am. Soc. Assn. Execs., Am. Nat. Inns of Ct., Rotary (pres. Montgomery Capital chpt. 1986—87, 1996—97). Republican. Baptist. Office: PO Box 241206 Montgomery AL 36124-1206 Home Phone: 334-356-0573; Office Phone: 334-834-3006. E-mail: jjwood@mindspring.com.

WOOD, JAMES MCKEAN, application developer; b. Pitts., Mar. 30, 1963; s. Allen Rice Wood and Elizabeth Cornelia Barlow. BS, Carnegie-Mellon U., Pitts., 1988; MS, U. Pa., Phila., 1988. Software engr. Carnegie Group, Inc., Pitts., 1985—88; mem. tech. staff Siemens Corp. Rsch., Princeton, NJ, 1990—98; disting. mem. tech. staff Siemens Comms., Boca Raton, Fla., 1998—. Mem.: IEEE, Assn. Computing Machinery. Democrat. Episcopalian. Avocations: piano, weightlifting, reading. Home: 333 Sunset Dr Fort Lauderdale FL 33301

WOOD, JAMES MICHAEL, lawyer; b. Oakland, Calif., Mar. 22, 1948; s. Donald James and Helen Winifred (Reimann) Wood; m. Cynthia Ahart Wood; children from previous marriage: Nathan, Sarah, Ruth 1 stepchild, Alexandra. BA, St. Mary's Coll., 1970; JD, U. San Francisco, 1973. Bar: Calif. 1973, U.S. Dist. Ct. (no., ctrl. and so. dists.) Calif. 1973. Rsch. atty. Alameda County Superior Ct., Oakland, 1973-76; ptnr. Reed Smith LLP, Oakland, 1976—. Presenter profl. confs. Contbr. articles to profl. jours. Chair of bd. dirs. Food and Drug Law Inst., Washington, DC. Named Atty. of Yr., Aids Legal Referral Panel, 2006; recipient Disting. Pro Bono Svc. award, Reed Smith Sean Halpin. Mem.: ABA (litig. sect., health litig. com., litig. products liability com.), Food Drug Law Inst. (bd. dirs., adv. com. 1999—), Nat. Health Lawyers Assn., Am. Acad. Hosp. Attys., Def. Rsch. Inst., Alameda County Bar Assn., No. Calif. Assn. Def. Counsel, State Bar Calif. Office: Reed Smith LLP 1999 Harrison St Ste 2200 Oakland CA 94612-3572 Office Phone: 510-466-6758. Business E-Mail: jmwood@reedsmith.com.

WOOD, JAMES NOWELL, foundation administrator, former museum director; b. Boston, Mar. 20, 1941; s. Charles H. and Helen N. (Nowell) W.; m. Emese Forizs, Dec. 30, 1966; children: Lenke Hancock, Rebecca Nowell. Diploma, Universita per Stranieri, Perugia, Italy, 1962; BA, Williams Coll., Williamstown, Mass., 1963; MA (Ford Mus. Tng. fellow), NYU, 1966. Asst. to dir. Met. Mus., NYC, 1967-68, asst. curator dept. 20th century art, 1968-70; curator Albright-Knox Art Gallery, Buffalo, 1970-73, assoc. dir., 1973-75; dir. St. Louis Art Mus., 1975-80; pres., dir. Art Inst. Chgo., 1980—2004; pres., CEO J. Paul Getty Trust, LA, 2007—. Vis. com. visual arts U. Chgo., 1980-94; head com. Nat. Endowment Arts; pres., Pulitzer Found. Arts, 2005- Mem. Intermuseum Conservation Assn. (past pres.), Assn. Art Mus. Dirs. Office: J Paul Getty Trust 1200 Getty Ctr Dr Los Angeles CA 90049 Office Phone: 310-440-7600. Business E-Mail: jwood@getty.edu.

WOOD, JANIS LOUISE, retired assistant principal; b. Wichita Falls, Tex., June 26, 1947; d. J. D. Richmond and Sarah Helena Stevens; m. Tommy Joe Kennedy (div.); children: Pamela Kathleen Leidy, John David; m. Jack Kelsey Wood, Aug. 7, 1970. AA, Eastfield Coll., Dallas, 1973; BA cum laude, U. Tex., Dallas, 1976; MEd, E. Tex. U., Commerce, 1997. Cert. tchr. Tex. Tchr. Plano Ind. Sch., Tex., 1978—82; owner, designer Wood Studios, Plano, 1984—90; tchr. Garland Ind. Sch. Dist., Tex., 1992—97, asst. prin., 1997—98, HS asst. prin., 1998—2001; ret., 2001. Instr. writing Collin County CC, Plano, 1992—94, Richland CC, Richardson, Tex., 1992—94; cons. human resources Millennium Cirs., Dallas, 2004—06. Bd. dirs. Garland Sports Hall of Fame, 2004—06. Recipient Super Tchr. award, Naaman Forest HS, 1992, Life Saving award, Garland Police, 2000. Mem.: Phi Theta Kappa. Republican. Avocations: gardening, reading.

WOOD, JEREMY SCOTT, architect, urban designer; b. Glen Ridge, NJ, Oct. 23, 1941; s. William Gamble and Alice-Marguerite (Scott) W.; m. Robin Benensohn-Rosefsky, June 14, 1970; children: Alexis, Jonas, Augusta. AB, Yale U., New Haven, Conn., 1964, M in Architecture, 1970. Registered architect, Ma. Sr. assoc. TAC/The Architects Collaborative, Inc., Cambridge, Mass., 1970-94; sr. project mgr. Domenech Hicks & Krockmalnic, Inc., Boston, 1995-97; sr. project architect Elkus/Manfredi Architects, Ltd., Boston, 1997—. Instr. Boston Archtl. Ctr., 1970-76; head tutor dept. art history, history of modern architecture Yale U., 1969-70, Emerson Coll. Performance and Prodn. Ctr./Cutler Majestic Theatre Renovation, Boston, 2001-03, Emerson Coll. Paramount Ctr. and Dormitory, Boston, 2004-. Author: (sect. and chpt. in books) Adaptive Reuse: Issues and Case Studies in Building Preservation, 1988, Office Buildings, 1989, Exposed Structure in Building Design, 1993; prin. works include Emerson Coll. Prodn. and Performance Ctr., Boston, 2001—03, Allen House Restoration & Condominiums, South End, Boston, 1998, MBTA/AMTRAK North-South Rail Link Stations (Boston), MBTA Subway Station Modernization State St. and Govt. Ctr. Stations (Boston), Complejo Medico de las Americas, Guatemala City, Guatemala, Health Care Internat. Hosp. and Hotel, Clydebank, Glasgow, Scotland, Copley, Place, Boston, The Westin Hotel at Copley Place, Boston, Liberty Ctr. and Vista Internat. Hotel, Pitts., Wellington Bus. Ctr. Offices, Medford, Mass., Two Portland (Maine) Sq. Office Bldg., One Mifflin Pl., Cambridge, Groton (Mass.) Sch. Dormitories, Coll. Engring. and Applied Sci., Shuwaikh Campus, Kuwait U., Kuwait City, Kuwait, Hosp. U. Pa., Phila.; asst. editor Perspecta 11; corr. Architecture and Urbanism, 1976; contbr. articles to profl. jours. Recipient Award of Excellence, Assn. Sch. Bus. Ofcls., Coun. Ednl. Facilities Planners, AIA, 1976, Concrete Industry Bd. Spl. Recognition award The Westin Hotel, Boston, 1983, Prestressed Concrete Inst. award, 1983, Honor award Associated Gen. Contractors of Mass., 1985, Grand award Urban Land Inst., 1988, hon. mention New Eng. Healthcare Design Awards, 1994, 1997 Move Massachusetts 2000 design award for engring. and arch. of North South Rail Link Project, Boston Preservation Alliance award for renovation of Cutler Majestic Theatre, 2003, Nat. Trust Hist. Preservation Honor award, 2004. Mem. AIA, Boston Soc. Architects (Honor awards), Mass. State Assn. Architects, Am. Planning Assn., Soc. Archtl. Hists. (life, Nat. chpt.), The Archtl. League N.Y. Home: 10 Pigeon Hill Rd Weston MA 02493-1620

WOOD, JOHN ARMSTEAD, planetary scientist, geological sciences educator, artist; b. Roanoke, Va., July 28, 1932; s. John Armstead and Lillian Cary (Hall) W.; m. Elisabeth Mathilde Heuser, June 12, 1958 (div.); children: Crispin S., Georgia K.; m. Julie Marie Nason, Sept. 9, 1989. BS in Geology, Va. Polytech. Inst., 1954; PhD in Geology, Mass. Inst. Tech., 1958; post-doctoral study, U. Cambridge, Eng., 1959-60. Staff scientist Smithsonian Astrophys. Obs., Cambridge, Mass., 1959, 1961—62, 1965—2004, ret., 2004; research asso. Enrico Fermi Inst. U. Chgo., 1962-65; prof. Harvard U., Geol. Scis. Dept., 1976-95; assoc. dir. Harvard-Smithsonian Center for Astrophysics, 1981—86. Vice chmn. Lunar Sample Analysis Planning Team, 1971—72; mem. NRC, Space Studies Bd., 1998—2001; chair Com. on Lunar and Planetary Exploration, 1999—2001. Author: Meteorites and the Origin of Planets, 1968, The Solar System, 1979, 2d edit., 2000. Recipient NASA medal for exceptional sci. achievement, 1973, J.L. Smith medal NAS, 1976, G.K. Gilbert award Geol. Soc. Am., 1992. Fellow AAAS, Am. Geophys. Union (F.L. Whipple award 2004), Meteoritical Soc. (pres. 1971-72, Leonard medal 1980); mem. NAS, Am. Acad. Arts and Scis., Cambridge Art Assn., Cosmos Club. Achievements include having asteroid no. 4736 named in his honor Johnwood. Home: 71 Langdon St Cambridge MA 02138-2501 Personal E-mail: JAWood@alum.mit.edu.

WOOD, JOHN F., prosecutor; m. Julie Myers, 2005. Grad., U. Va.; JD, Harvard Law Sch. Staff mem. to Senator John C. Danforth US Senate, Washington; law clk. to Hon. J. Michael Luttig, US Ct. Appeals (4th Cir.), 1996—97; law clk. to Justice Clarence Thomas US Supreme Ct., 1997—98; assoc. Kirkland & Ellis LLP, 1998—2001; dep. assoc. atty. gen., counsel to assoc. atty. gen. US Dept. Justice, 2001—02; dep. gen. counsel, Office Mgmt. & Budget Exec. Office of the Pres., 2002—03; chief of staff to sec. US Dept. Homeland Security, 2005—07; US atty. (we. dist.) Mo. US Dept. Justice, Kans. City, 2007—. Office: US Attys Office Charles E Whittaker Courthouse 400 E 9th St Rm 5510 Kansas City MO 64106 Office Phone: 816-426-3122. Office Fax: 816-426-4210. *

WOOD, JOHN MARTIN, lawyer; b. Detroit, Mar. 29, 1944; s. John Francis and Margaret Kathleen (Lynch) Wood; m. Judith Anne Messer; children: Timothy Peter, Meagan Anne. BA, Boston Coll., 1966; JD, Cath. U. Am., 1969. Bar: D.C. 1970, Va. 2001, U.S. Dist. Ct. D.C. 1970, U.S. Dist. Ct. Va. 2001, U.S. Ct. Appeals (D.C. cir.) 1973, U.S. Ct. Appeals (3d cir.) 1973, U.S. Ct. Appeals (4th cir.) 1973, U.S. Supreme Ct. 1973. Trial atty, tax divsn. Dept. Justice, Washington, 1969-73; assoc. Reed Smith LLP, Washington, 1973-80, ptnr., 1980—, mng. ptnr., 1989-95, dir. legal pers., 1995-98. Dir. adv. bd. Salvation Army, Va. and Met. Washington, Leadership Washington, 1993—. Mem.: Fed. Bar Assn., Fairfax Bar Assn., The Currituck Club N.C., River Bend Golf and Country Club, Barristers Club Washington, Delta Sigma Pi, Phi Alpha Delta. Home: 9490 Oak Falls Ct Great Falls VA 22066-4143 Office: Reed Smith LLP 3110 Fairview Park Dr Ste 1400 Falls Church VA 22042 Office Phone: 703-641-4248. Business E-Mail: jwood@reedsmith.com.

WOOD, JONATHAN STUART, economist, educator; b. New Orleans, Nov. 14, 1944; s. John Joseph and Linelle Marie (Waguespack) W.; m. Ann M., Apr. 7, 1973; children: Elizabeth, Christopher, Julie, Jonathan. Grad., NASA Summer Inst. in Space and Engring., 1965; BS in Mech. Engring., Tulane U., 1966; MS in Aerospace Engring., Princeton U., 1970; MBA in Econs., NYU, 1975, MPhil in Econs. and Fin., 1978, PhD in Econs. and Fin., 1980. Rschr. on bio-engring study of neck whiplashes Tulane Med. Sch. and Tulane Sch. Engring. (for US Dept Health, Edn. and Welfare), 1963; materials tester and lab. analyst Svc. Foundry, New Orleans, 1964; ops. rsch. & econ. analyst Grumman Aerospace Corp., Bethpage, NY, 1969-74; sr. investment analyst, cons. to common stock dept. Prudential Ins. Co., Newark, 1974-76; instr. fin. & acctg. Sch. Bus. U. Conn., Storrs, 1976-78; Liberty Fund Rsch. fellow Stanford U. Inst. Humane Studies Rsch. Seminar in Econs., Palo Alto, Calif., 1977; asst. prof. econs. & fin. Tulane U., New Orleans, 1978-84; assoc. prof. econs. & fin. Coll. Bus. Adminstrn. Loyola U., New Orleans, 1984—. Prof. econs. and fin. Pace U. Grad. Sch. Bus. Adminstrn., N.Y.C., 1975-76; vis. prof. fin. Grad. Sch. Bus. Adminstrn. NYU, 1980; vis. prof. fin. Grad. Sch. Bus. Tulane U., 1985, 91, lectr., 1990; presenter in field.; cons. economist; expert in bus. valuation; adj. prof. in econ. and fin. Pace U. Grad. Sch. Bus. Adminstrn., N.Y., 1975-76; appeared on WWL-TV discussing current econ. and fin. events focusing on La. econ. matters; rschr., lectr. in field; conducted interviews and seminars in field. Author: Chemical Kinetic Influences, 1968, Chemical Kinetic Influences in Liquid Propellant Rocket Combustion Instability, 1969, 70, Effectiveness Evaluation of Orbital Observatories (with Joseph R. Fragola), 1975, Heterogeneous Expectations and Security Price Distributions, 1978, Entrepreneurship and the Co-Ordination of Expectations in the Stock Market, 1980, 82, Some Refinements in the Austrian Trade-Cycle Theory, 1984, Capital Formation Problems in the United States and the Question of a Capital Shortage, 1984, Methodologies for Valuation of Closely-Held Companies (with Dr. Michael A. Dalton and Robert I. Glover), 1989, Valuation of Closely-Held Companies & Professional Practices by Experts (with Dr. Michael A. Dalton and Dr. Robert I. Glover), 1989, Real Value of Damage Caps for Medical Malpractice in Louisiana (with Michael A. Dalton), 1997; referee Quarterly Rev. Econs. and Bus., 1982, Rev. Austrian Econs., 1989; contbr. chpts., reviews to books. Chmn. fin. com., mem. exec. bd. Short-Fern St. Neighborhood Assn., 1984-85; lectro, Eucharistic min., mem. com. Univ. Parish St. Thomas More Tulane U.; dir. Operation New Start, Inc.; softball coach Carrollton Boosters; elected to u. senate, 1986—; U. Senate Parking Com., 1986-87; faculty acad. affairs budget com., 1986-89, 89-92; Blue Ribbon Task Force for libr.'s acad. future, 1986-87; u. senate designatee to Fin. Com. of bd. trustees, 1991-92, 92-93; advisor to Endowment Com. of Bd. Trustees, 1991-93. Recipient MBA Top Gun award as Outstanding Tchr., Loyola U., 1993. Mem. Am. Econ. Assn., Am. Fin. Assn., We. Econ. Assn., We. Fin. Assn., So. Econ. Assn., So. Fin. Assn., Ea. Fin. Assn., Southwestern Social Scis. Assn., Opers. Rsch. Soc. Am./Inst. Mgmt. Sci., Pontchartrain Astronomy Soc., Student Recruitment Team, Grad. Edn. Task Force, Entrepreneurship Task Force, Curriculum Com., Advising Com. (chmn. 1986-87), MBA Curriculum Task Force. Avocations: astronomy, music. Home and Office: 500 Arlington Dr Metairie LA 70001-5516 Office Phone: 504-866-7200. Personal E-mail: stuartwood13@msn.com.

WOOD, JOSEPH S., academic administrator; b. 1947; m. Diane Wood. AB, Middlebury Coll., 1968; MA, U. Vt., 1974; PhD, Pa. State U., 1978. Ops. asst. Interlake Steamship Co., Cleve., 1968—69; mem. faculty U. Nebr., Omaha, 1977—88; vis. assoc. prof. geography George Mason U., Fairfax, Va., 1987—88, vice provost academic affairs, prof. geography, 1987—2000, assoc. prof. geography, 1988—97, chmn. geography & earth systems sci. dept., 1990—97, course leader integrative studies, New Century Coll., 1995—97, interim provost, 1999; prof. geography U. So. Maine, Portland, Maine, 2000—, provost & v.p. academic affairs, 2000—07, interim pres., 2007—. Vis. prof. S. China Normal U., Guangzhou, China, 1984; project assoc. Assn. Am. Geographers, Washington, 1987—88. Mem. Creative Econ. Steering Com. City of Portland, Maine; mem. bd. dirs. Maine Philanthropy Ctr.; pres. bd. dirs. Ctr. Prevention of Hate Violence, Maine. Combat engr. US Army, 1969—71, Vietnam. Office: Office of the Provost PO Box 9300 Portland ME 04104-9300 Office Phone: 207-780-4485. Office Fax: 207-780-4480. E-mail: jswood@usm.maine.edu. *

WOOD, J(OSHUA) WARREN, III, lawyer; b. Portsmouth, Va., Aug. 31, 1941; s. Joshua Warren and Mary Evelyn (Carter) Wood; m. Marcia Neal Ramsey, Feb. 29, 1964; children: Lauren Elaine Yeh, Joshua Warren IV. AB, Princeton U., 1963; JD, U. Va., 1971. Bar: Va. 1971, NJ 1976, US Supreme Ct. 1977, NY 1982. Comml. banking asst. Bankers Trust Co., NYC, 1967-68; assoc. McGuire, Woods & Battle, Richmond, Va., 1971-75; v.p., gen. counsel, sec. Robert Wood Johnson Found., Princeton, NJ, 1975—2003; pres., gen. counsel Global Ctr. Dispute Resolution Rsch., NYC, 2004—05; of counsel Greenbaum, Rowe, Smith & Davis LLP, Woodbridge, NJ, 2005—07, The Legato Law Firm LLC, Bridgewater, NJ, 2007—. Mem. AAA/ABA/AMA Commn. Alternative Dispute Resolution Health Care; master Marie L. Garbaldi Am. Inn Ct. Alternative Dispute Resolution. Mem. editl. bd. Va. Law Rev., 1969—71. Mem. coun. internat. advisors Internat. Ctr. for Corp. Accountability, NYC; bd. dirs. Biotech. Found. Inc., Phila. Capt. arty. US Army, 1963—67. Decorated Army Commendation medal. Mem.: ABA, Internat. Bar Assn. (mem. arbitration com.), Am. Arbitration Assn. (bd. dirs., mem. panel arbitrators, task force mass torts and alternative dispute resolution), NJ Bar Assn., Va. Bar Assn., NY Bar Assn., Princeton Club, Order of Coif. Office: 757 Route 202/206 N Bridgewater NJ 08807 Home Phone: 609-921-2890; Office Phone: 908-725-9800. Office Fax: 908-725-9890. Business E-Mail: jw.wood3@verizon.net.

WOOD, JULIENNE LOUISE, librarian, historian; d. John Henry Wood and Lilas Naomi Lothen; m. Samuel Claude Shepherd, Jr., Sept. 2, 1978. BA magna cum laude, Gustavus Adolphus Coll., 1970; MA U.S. History, U. Wis., Madison, 1972; MLS, U. Wis., Milw., 1978; PhD U.S. History, U. Wis., Madison, 1994. Libr. copyright acquisitions Libr. Congress, Washington, 1979—80, sr. libr. copyright acquisitions, 1980—83, supr. libr. copyright office, 1983—85; dir. Barksdale Air Force Base Libr., Bossier City, La., 1985—87; lectr. history Centenary Coll., Shreveport, La., 1995—98; libr. govt. info. La. State U., Shreveport, 1999—2000, head rsch. svc. Noel Meml. Libr., 2000—. Subject advisor Hist. of the Americas, Gen. Works Libr. Sci., Bowkers Best Books for Academic Librs., 2002—04. Author: (hist. articles) Dictionary of American History, 2003, (biog. articles) American National Biography, 1999; book reviewer (reference book reviews) American Reference Books, Annual, 2001—, subject adv. Vol. 4 and Vol. 10, The Best Books, Inc., 2003. Co-chmn. program com. La. Hist. Assn., Forty-second ann. meeting, Lafayette, La., 2000; bd. dirs. La. Hist. Assn., 2004—07; mem. bd. dir. Ark.-La.-Tex. Genealogical Assn., Shreveport, 1990; mem., treas., show chair. Red River Quilters, Shreveport, 1992—; grants reviewer Alliance Edn., Shreveport, 2001—. Higher Edn. Act Title II-B fellow, U. Wis.-Milw. Sch. Libr. Sci. Mem.: ALA (nat. com. 2000—), La. Libr. Assn. (state com. 2001—03, 2007—), So. Hist. Assn., Orgn. Am. Historians, Phi Kappa Phi, Beta Phi Mu, Phi Alpha Theta. Office: Noel Memorial Libr LSU Shreveport One Univ Pl Shreveport LA 71115-2399

WOOD, KENNETH ANDERSON, small business owner, display designer; b. Cleve., May 11, 1913; s. George Robert and Leonore (Anderson) Wood; m. Ruth Eleanor Diehm, Sept. 14, 1937 (dec. May 1999). Student, Fenn Coll., Cleve., 1932-34, Cleve. Inst. Art, 1935-45. Artist Patterson Displays, Cleve., 1934-35; art dir. Bailey Meter Co., Wickliffe, Ohio, 1936-71; owner Kenwood Designers and Assocs., Chesterland, Ohio, 1971—; designer of stained glass windows, 1979—. Pres. Artist and Craftsman Assocs., Cleve., 1940—44, Geauga Artists Assn., Geauga County, Ohio, 1950—53. Exhibitions include nat., regional and local, 1939—97, Represented in permanent collections Butler Mus. Am., Youngstown, Ohio, Inlander Collection of Gt. Lakes Regional Paintings, Cleve. Mus. Art, numerous pvt. collections; patents for product design. Mem.: Indsl. Designers Soc. Am. (life). Republican. Seventh Day Adventist. Avocation: travel. Office: Kenwood Design and Assocs 11950 Sperry Rd Chesterland OH 44026-2225 Office Phone: 440-729-7778. E-mail: kennethwood@kennethwood.com.

WOOD, KENNETH ARTHUR, retired editor, writer; b. Hastings, Sussex, Eng., Feb. 25, 1926; came to U.S., 1965; s. Arthur Charles and Ellen Mary (Cox) W.; m. Hilda Muriel Harloe, Sept. 13, 1952. Editor Stamp Collector newspaper Van Dahl Publs., Albany, Oreg., 1968—80, editor emeritus, 1980—. Author (ency.) This Is Philately, 1982, (atlas) Where in the World, 1983, Basic Philately, 1984, Post Dates, 1985, Modern World, 1987; author several hundred articles and columns published in the U.K. and U.S.A., 1960—. Served with Brit. Army WW II. Recipient Disting. Philatelist award Northwest Fedn. Stamp Clubs, 1974, Phoenix award Ariz. State Philatelic Hall of Fame, 1979, Disting. Philatelist award Am. Topical Assn., 1979. Fellow Royal Philatelic Soc. (London); mem. Am. Philatelic Soc. (hon. life, Luff award 1987, Hall of Fame Writers Unit, 1984). Avocations: stamp collecting/philately, aviation history, modern history, gardening. Office: 2430 Tudor Way SE Albany OR 97322-5661

WOOD, KERRY, professional baseball player; b. Irving, Texas, June 17, 1977; Pitcher Chicago Cubs, 1998—. Named Nat. League Rookie of the Yr., 1998; named to Nat. League All-Star Team, 2003. Achievements include led Nat. League in strikeouts (266), 2003; over 3,000 career strikeouts. Office: c/o Chicago Cubs 1060 W Addison Chicago IL 60613

WOOD, KIMBA M., federal judge; b. Port Townsend, Wash., Jan. 2, 1944. BA cum laude, Conn. Coll., 1965; MSc, London Sch. Econs., 1966; JD, Harvard U., 1969. Bar: U.S. Dist. Ct. D.C. 1969, U.S. Ct. Appeals D.C. 1969, N.Y. 1972, U.S. Dist. Ct. (ea. and so. dists.) N.Y. 1974, U.S. Ct. Appeals (2d cir.) 1975, U.S. Supreme Ct. 1980, U.S. Dist. Ct. (we. dist.) N.Y. 1981. Assoc. Steptoe & Johnson, Washington, 1969-70; with Office Spl. Counsel, OEO Legal Svcs., Washington, 1970-71; assoc., then ptnr. LeBoeuf, Lamb, Leiby & MacRae, N.Y.C., 1971-88; judge, U.S. Dist. Ct. (So. Dist.), NY, 1988—. Mem. ABA (chmn. civil practice, procedure com. 1982-85, mem. coun. 1985-88, jud. rep. 1989-91), N.Y. State Bar Assn. (chmn. antitrust sect. 1983-84), Fed. Bar Coun. (trustee from 1978, v.p., 1984-85), Am. Law Inst. Office: US Dist Ct US Courthouse 500 Pearl St Rm 1610 New York NY 10007-1316

WOOD, L. LIN, JR., lawyer; b. Raleigh, NC, Oct. 19, 1952; s. Lucian Lincoln and Josephien (Currin) Wood; m. Deborah Anne Jamison, July 25, 1987; children: Elizabeth, Ashley, Matthew Carlton. BA cum laude, Mercer U., 1974, JD cum laude, 1977. Bar: Ga. 1977, US Dist. Ct. (No. Dist.) Ga. 1977, US Dist. Ct. (Mid. Dist.) Ga. 1977, US Dist. Ct. (Dist. Colo.), US Ct. Appeals (5th Cir.) 1977, US Ct. Appeals (11th Cir.) 1981, US Supreme Ct. Assoc. Jones, Cork, Miller & Benton, Macon, Ga., 1977—80, Freeman & Hawkins, Atlanta, 1980—83; ptnr. Wood & Grant, Atlanta, 1983, Powell Goldstein LLP, Atlanta. Staff mem. Mercer Law Rev., 1975—77. Recipient Am. Jurisprudence award, 1976, 1977, US Law Week award, 1977. Mem.: Atlanta City Club, Ga. Trial Lawyers Assn., Lawyers Club Atlanta, Atlanta Bar Assn., State Bar Ga., Assn. Trial Lawyers Am., ABA (vice-chmn. media law & defamation torts com.). Republican. Methodist. Office: Powell Goldstein LLP One Atlanta Ctr 14th Floor 1201 W Peachtree St

NW Atlanta GA 30309 Office Phone: 404-572-6633. Office Fax: 404-572-6999. E-mail: llwood@pogolaw.com. *

WOOD, LARRY (MARY LAIRD), journalist, writer, public relations executive, educator, environmental consultant; b. Sandpoint, Idaho; d. Edward Hayes and Alice (McNeel) Small; children: Mary, Marcia, Barry. BA summa cum laude, U. Wash., 1939, MA summa cum laude, 1940; postgrad., Stanford U., 1940—43, U. Calif., Berkeley, 1946—47, U. Wis., 1971—72, U. Minn., 1971—72, U. Ga., 1972—73, U. Calif., Santa Cruz, 1974—76, Stanford Hopkins Marine Sta., 1977—80. Cert. secondary and jr. coll. tchr., Wash., Calif. Feature writer and columnist Oakland Tribune and San Francisco Chronicle, Calif., 1939—; archtl. and environ. feature and travel writer and columnist San Jose Mercury News (Knight Ridder), Calif., 1972-90; tchg. fellow Stanford U., 1940-43; dir. pub. rels. 2-counties, 65-park 100,000 acre East Bay Regional Park Dist., No. Calif., 1948-68; pres. Larry Wood Pub. Rels., 1946—; pub. rels. dir. Calif. Children's Home Soc., 1947-58. Prof. pub. rels., mag. writing, journalism, investigative reporting San Diego State U., 1974-75; disting. vis. prof. journalism San Jose State U., 1976; assoc. prof. journalism Calif. State U., Hayward, 1978; prof. sci. and environ. journalism U. Calif. Berkeley Ext. grad. divsn., 1979—; press del. nat. convs. Am. Geophys. Union Internat. Conf., 1986—, AAAS, 1989—, Nat. Park Svc. VIP Press Tour, Yellowstone after the fire, 1989—, Nat. Assn. Sci. Writers, 1989—, George Washington U./Am. Assn. Neurol. Surgeons Sci. Writers Conf., 1990, Am. Inst. Biol. Scis. Conf., 1990, Nat. Conf. Sci. Writers, Am. Heart Assn., 1995, Internat. Cardiologists Symposium for Med./Sci. Writers, 1995, Annenberg Program Electronic Media Symposium, Washington, 1995; EPA del. to USSR and Ea. Europe; expert witness on edn., pub. rels., journalism and copyright; spl. media guest Sigma Xi, 1990—; mem. numerous spl. press corps; selected White House Spl. Media, 1993—; selected mem. Duke U. 14th Ann. Sci. Reporters Conf., 1995; internat. press guest Can. Consulate Gen. Dateline Can., 1995—, French Govt. Tourist Office, 1996—, Ministerio delle Risorse Agricole Alimentarie Forestali and Assocs. Conf., 1995; appeared in TV documentary Larry Wood Covers Visit of Queen Elizabeth II; cons. in field. Contbr. over 5,500 articles to newspapers, nat. mags., nat. and internat. newspapers including L.A. Times-Mirror Syndicate, Knight-Ridder Syndicate, Washington Post, Phila. Inquirer, Chgo. Tribune, Miami Herald, Oakland Tribune, Seattle Times, San Francisco Chronicle, 36 Million Circulation Parade, San Jose Mercury News, LA Time/Monitor Worldwide News Syndicate (4 Nat. Headliner awards), Monterey Peninsula Herald, Calif., Washington Post, Phila. Inquirer, Hawaiian Airlines In Paradise, MonitoRadio, Donnelly Pubs., Sports Illus., Life, Mechanix Illus., Popular Mechanics, Parents (contbg. editor), House Beautiful, Am. Home (awards 1988-89), Travelday, Better Homes and Gardens, Sunset, Archtl. Digest, National Geographic World, Travel & Leisure, Chevron USA/Odyssey (Calif. Pub.'s award 1984), Xerox Edn. Publs., Europe's Linguapress, PSA Mag., Off Duty, Oceans, Sea Frontiers, AAA Westways, AAA Via, Travelin', others; home and garden columnist, editor, 5-part series Pacific Coast Ports, 5-part series Railroads of the West, series Immigration, Youth Gangs, Endangered Species, Calif. Lighthouse Chain, Lighthouses of the World, Pacific Coast Wetlands, Elkhorn Slough Nat. Estuarine Res., Ebey's Landing Nat. Hist. Island Res., Calif. Water Wars, BLM's Adopt a Horse Program, Mt. St. Helen's Eruption, Oreg's Covered Bridges, Loma Prieta Earthquake, Oakland Firestorm, Missing Children, Calif. Prison Reform, Columbia-Alaska's Receding Glacier, Calif. Underwater Parks, others; author: Wonderful U.S.A.: A State-by-State Guide to Its Natural Resources, 1989; co-author: McGraw-Hill English for Social Living, 1944, Fawcett Boating Books, 1956-66, Fodor's San Francisco, Fodor's California, 1982-89, Bell and Howell/Charles Merrill Focus on Life Science, Focus on Physical Science, Focus on Earth Science, 1983, 2d edit, 1987, State of California's Golden State Travel Guide, 1998; contbr. Earth Science 1987; author: (with others) anthology West Winds, 1989; reviewer Charles Merrill texts, 1983-84; book reviewer Profl. Communicator, 1987—; selected writings in permanent collections Oakland Pub. Libr., U. Wash. Main Libr.; contbr., author Journalism Quar.; author script PBS/AAA America series, 1992; contbg. editor: Parents, Fashion Showcase, Spokane Mag.; contbr. chpt. to books. Nat. chmn. travel writing contest Assn. for Edn. in Journalism and Mass Comm. Soc. Am. Travel Writers, 1979-83; judge writing contest for Nat. Assn. Real Estate Editors, 1982—; invited Nat. Park Svc. Nat. Conf. Sci. Writers, 1985, Postmaster Gen.'s 1992 Stamps, 1991, Internat. Geophys. Union Conf., 1982—, The Conf. Bd., 1995—, Corp. Comm. Conf., Calif. Inst. Tech. Media and Sci. Seminar, 1995—, Med. Writers Delegation to Russia and Estonia, 1997, NY Times Opinion Rsch. Co. Corp. Image Conf., 1999, EPA and Dept. Energy Tech. Conf., 1992, Am. Soc. Photogrammetry and Remote Sensing Internat. Conv. Mapping Global Change, 1992-, US Conf. on Oceans, 1998, NY Mus. Modern Art Matisse Retrospective Press Rev. and all media previews, 1992—, celebration 150th anniversary Oreg. Trail, 1993, Nat. Coun. Advancement Sci. Writing, 1977-2003, Sigma Xi Nat. Conf., 1988-2003, Nat. Sci. Writers Confs., 1977-2003, PRSA Travel and Tourism Conf., 1993—, Internat. Conf. Environment, 1994-95, Quality Life Europe, Prague, 1994, Calif. Sesquicentennial, 1996, 14th Ann. Sci. Writers Conf., 1996, Picasso Retrospective, 1996, others; mem. Gov.'s Conf. Tourism NC, 1993-2002, Calif., 1976—, Fla., 1987—, NC Govs. conf. on tourism and film, 2000-, U.C. Irvine Calif. Computer Sci. Symposium, 2000, Sea Grant's conf. on sci. in the news, 2000, NY conf. bd. conf. on environ. journalism, 2000, on economics, 2001; press guest 14 US states and 12 fgn. countries' Depts. Tourism, 1986—; chmn. New Com. for Sci./Journalism Curricula U. Wash., 2006-. Named to Broadway Hall of Fame, U. Wash., 1984; recipient Broadway Disting. Alumnus award, 1995; citations for environ. writing Nat. Park Svc., US Forest Svc., Bur. Land Mgmt., Oakland Mus. Assn., Oakland C. of C., Chevron USA, USN plaque and citation, Best Mag. articles citation Calif. Pubs. Assn., 1984, US Treasury award, 1946; co-recipient award for best Sunday newspaper mag. Nat. Headliners, citation for archtl. features Oakland Mus., 1983; honoree for achievements in journalism Nat. Mortar Bd., 1988, 89; named one of 10 V.I.P. press 1989; one of Calif.'s top 40 Contemporary Authors, 1989; nat. honoree Social Issues Resources Series, 1987; recipient, Gov.'s Calif. Women of Achievement award, 1988-90. Mem.: AAAS, Calif. Acad. Scis., Am. Bd. Forensic Examiners, Pub. Rels. Soc. Am. (charter mem. travel, tourism, environment and edn. divsns.), Nat. Sch. Pub. Rels. Assn., Environ. Cons. N.Am., Am. Assn. Edn. in Journalism and Comm. (exec. bd. nat. mag. divsn. 1978, panel chmn. 1979—80, author Journalism Quart. jour.), Women in Comm. (nat. bd. officer 1975—77, book reviewer Prof. Communicator), Soc. Profl. Journalists (nat. bd. for hist. sites 1980—), Nat. Press Photographers Assn. (Bay area internet project 1989—, hon. life, honoree 1995), Investigative Reporters and Editors (charter), Nat. Assn. Sci. Writers, Bay Area Advt. and Mktg. Assn., Internat. Assn. Bus. Communicators, Am. Assn. Med. Writers, Soc. Am. Travel Writers, Am. Film Inst., Soc. Environ. Journalists (charter), Calif. Acad. Environ. News Writers, Am. Mgmt. Assn., Nat. Soc. Environ. Journalists (charter), Calif. Environ. Leadership Roundtable, Am. Heritage Found. (citation 1986—88), Fine Arts Mus., San Francisco, Calif. State Parks Found., Purple and Gold Soc., Mortar Board Alumnae Assn. (life honoree 1988—89), Stanford Alumni (life), U. Calif., Berkeley Alumni (life; v.p., scholarship chmn. 1975—81), U. Wash. Com. (life; charter mem. ocean scis. alumni, dept. adv. sci. journalism, disting. alumni 1987), Nat. Parks and Conservation Assn., Calif. Environ. Leadership Roundtable (trustee), Nat. Wildlife Fedn., Oceanic Soc., Nature Conservancy, Smithsonian Audubon Soc., Internat. Oceanog. Found., Calif. Writers Club (state bd., Berkeley bd. 1989—, honoree ann. conv. Asilomar, Calif. 1990), Nat. Press Club, San Francisco Press Club, Seattle Advt. and Sales Club (former officer), Seattle Jr. Advt. Club (charter), Phi Beta Kappa (statewide chmn. scholarship awards 1975—81, v.p., bd. dirs. Calif. Alumni Assn.), Pi Lambda Theta (charter 1995—, planning com.), Theta Sigma Phi. Home and Office: Piedmont Pines 6161 Castle Dr Oakland CA 94611-2737 Office Phone: 510-531-0977. *A creed I follow is Ralph Waldo Emerson's statement: "Nothing great was ever achieved without enthusiasm."*.

WOOD, LINCOLN JACKSON, aerospace engineer; b. Lyons, NY, Sept. 30, 1947; s. William Hulbert and Sarah Brock (Strumsky) Wood. BS with distinction, Cornell U., 1968; MS in Aeronautics and Astronautics, Stanford U., 1969, PhD, 1972. Staff engr. Hughes Aircraft Co., El Segundo, Calif., 1974-77; tech. staff Jet Propulsion Lab. Calif. Inst. Tech., Pasadena, 1977-81, tech. group supr. Jet Propulsion Lab., 1981-89, tech. mgr., 1989-91, dep. tech. sect. mgr., 1991-99, dep. leader Ctr. of Excellence for Deep Space Comm./Nav. Sys., 2000—03, tracking and nav. svc. sys. mgr., deep space mission sys. engring. and ops. programs, 2003—04, program mgr., 2004—. Bechtel instr. engring. Calif. Inst. Tech., Pasadena, 1972—74, lectr. in sys. engring., 1975—76, vis. asst. prof., 1976—78, vis. assoc. prof., 1978—84; cons. in field. Contbr. articles to profl. jours. Bd. dirs. Boys Republic, Chino Hills, Calif., 1991, 1997—2007. Fellow: AIAA (assoc.; assoc. editor Jour. Guidance, Control and Dynamics 1983—89, tech. com. astrodynamics 1985—86, chmn. 1986—88); mem.: AAAS, IEEE (sr.), Am. Astron. Soc. (sr.; assoc. editor Jour. Astron. Scis. 1980—83, space flight mechanics com. 1980—97, gen. chmn. AAS/AIAA Space Flight Mechanics Meeting 1993, chmn. space flight mechanics com. 1993—95), Los Solteros (pres. 1991, 1997—2005), Sigma Xi. Office: Jet Propulsion Lab 4800 Oak Grove Dr Mail Stop 301-150 Pasadena CA 91109 Business E-Mail: lincoln.j.wood@jpl.nasa.gov.

WOOD, LINDA MAY, librarian; b. Ft. Dodge, Iowa, Nov. 6, 1942; d. John Albert and Beth Ida (Riggs) Wiley; m. C. James Wood, Sept. 15, 1964 (div. Oct. 1984). BA, Portland State U., 1964; M in Librarianship, U. Wash., 1965. Reference libr. Multnomah County Libr., Portland, Oreg., 1965-67, br. libr., 1967-72, adminstrv. asst. to libr., 1972-73, asst. libr., asst. dir., 1973-77; asst. city libr. L.A. Pub. Libr., 1977-80; libr. dir. Riverside (Calif.) City and County Pub. Libr., 1980-91; county libr. Alameda County Libr., Fremont, Calif., 1991—. Adminstrv. coun. mem. Bay Area Libr. and Info. Svcs., Oakland, Calif., 1991—. Chair combined charities campaign County of Alameda, Oakland, Calif., 1992; bd. dirs. Inland AIDS project, Riverside, 1990-91; vol. United Way of Inland Valleys, Riverside, 1986-87, Bicentennial Competition on the Constitution, 36th Congl. Dist., Colton, Calif., 1988-90. Mem. ALA (CLA chpt. councilor 1992-95), Calif. Libr. Assn. (pres. 1985, exec. com., ALA chpt. councilor 1992-95), Calif. County Librs. Assn. (pres. 1984), League of Calif. Cities (cmty. svcs. policy com. 1985-90), OCLC Users Coun. (Pacific Network del. 1986-89). Democrat. Avocations: dance, opera, reading. Office: Alameda County Libr 2450 Stevenson Blvd Fremont CA 94538-2326 Home Phone: 510-841-3223; Office Phone: 510-745-1536. E-mail: lwood@aclibrary.org.

WOOD, LISA GODBEY, federal judge, former prosecutor; b. Lexington, Ky., Jan. 28, 1963; married; 2 children. BA summa cum laude, U. Ga., 1985, JD summa cum laude, 1990. Bar: Ga. 1990. Law clk. to Hon. Anthony A. Alaimo US Dist. Ct. (so. dist.) Ga., 1990; assoc. Gilbert, Harrell, Summerford & Martin, Brunswick, Ga., 1991—2004, ptnr., 1995—2004; US atty. (so. dist.) Ga. US Dept. Justice, Savannah, Ga., 2004—07; judge US Dist. Ct. (so. dist.) Ga., 2007—. Adv. com. US Dist. Ct.; disciplinary review panel State Bar Ga.; mem. Ga. Bd. Pub. Safety. Mem.: ABA, Def. Rsch. Inst. Office: Fed Justice Ctr 600 James Brown Blvd Augusta GA 30901 *

WOOD, MARCUS ANDREW, lawyer; b. Mobile, Ala., Jan. 18, 1947; s. George Franklin and Helen Eugenia (Fletcher) W.; m. Sandra Lee Pellonari, July 25, 1971; children: Edward Alan, Melinda Janel. BA cum laude, Vanderbilt U., 1969; JD, Yale U., 1974. Bar: Oreg. 1974, U.S. Dist. Ct. Oreg. 1974, U.S. Ct. Appeals (9th cir.) 1982. Assoc., then ptnr. Rives, Bonihadi & Smith, Portland, Oreg., 1974-78; ptnr. Stoel Rives LLP and predecessor firms, Portland, 1974—. Pres., bd. dirs. Indochinese Refugee Ctr., Portland, 1980, Pacific Ballet Theatre, Portland, 1986-87; bd. dirs. Outside In, Portland, 1989-2006. Lt. USNR, 1969—71. Mem.: ABA, Phi Beta Kappa. Home: 9300 NW Finzer Ct Portland OR 97229-8035 Office: Stoel Rives 900 SW 5th Ave Ste 2300 Portland OR 97204-1229 Home Phone: 503-203-1359. Business E-Mail: mwood@stoel.com.

WOOD, MARGARET, performing company executive; Entertainment and spl. events dir. Stratton Mountain Resort, Stratton, Va.; gen. mgr. Broward Ctr. for the Performing Arts, Ft. Lauderdale, Fla.; interim gen. dir. Anchorage Opera; gen. dir. Dance Conneticut, 2000—. Co-founder Performing Artservices Inc., NY; founder Dance Umbrella, 1975.

WOOD, MARIAN STARR, publishing executive; b. NYC, Mar. 30, 1938; d. Edward James and Betty (Starr) Markow; m. Anthony Stuart Wood, Mar. 21, 1963. BA, Barnard Coll., 1959; postgrad., Columbia U., 1959—64. Tchg. asst., lectr. Columbia U., NYC, 1960-64; editor Praeger Pubs., NYC, 1965-71; sr. editor Henry Holt & Co., NYC, 1972-81, exec. editor, 1981-96, assoc. pub. Marian Wood Books, 1996-99; v.p. Marian Wood Books at G.P. Putnam's Sons, NYC, 1999—. Recipient Roger Klein Found. award for career achievement, 2001. Office Phone: 631-477-0618. E-mail: marian.wood@us.penguingroup.com.

WOOD, MARK D., lawyer; b. Chgo., Jan. 8, 1966; BS with high honors, U. Ill., 1987; JD cum laude, U. Mich., 1990. CPA Ill., 1987; bar: Ill. 1990, US Dist. Ct., No. Dist. Ill. Ptnr., co-chair securities practice Katten Muchin Rosenman LLP, Chgo. Mem.: ABA, Am. Bar Assn. Office: Katten Muchin Rosenman LLP 525 W Monroe St Chicago IL 60661 Office Phone: 312-902-5493. Office Fax: 312-577-8858. E-mail: mark.wood@kattenlaw.com.

WOOD, MARY ELIZABETH, retired secondary school educator, church musician; b. Berwyn, Ill., Apr. 15, 1929; d. Ralph Jerome Compton and Dora Mary Langlois; m. Harvey Eugene Wood, Aug. 21, 1954 (dec.); children: Joseph, Ann, Kim, Lynn, Christopher, Curtis, Carol, John, Nicole. BA in English and Edn., Marycrest U., Davenport, Iowa, 1951; MA in English and Edn., Mich. State U., East Lansing, 1958; AA in Music summa cum laude, Lansing C.C., Mich., 1980. Cert. permanent tchr. Mich. Tchr. H.S. Oxford (Iowa) Schs., 1951—52; tchr. jr. and sr. H.S. Gobles (Mich.) Schs., 1952—55; tchr. Cement City H.S., 1957—58, Portland H.S., 1958—60, Dimondale H.S., 1960—62; tchr. H.S. completion adults Holt Pub. Schs., 1965—95. Cantor Immaculate Heart Mary Ch., Lansing, Mich., 1970—84; dir. music Holy Cross Ch., Lansing, 1983—88, St. Peter Cath. Ch., Eaton Rapids, Mich., 1989—91, St. Jude Cath. Ch., DeWitt, Mich., 1992—2002; painter religious iconography; musician Ch. Resurrection, Lansing. Singer: (albums) Jesus Lives by Fr. Lucien Deiss; composer: (children's operettas) The Country Cousin, 1984, The Touch, 1994, (liturgical music) Dedication Mass of St. Peter, 1992. Mem.: Nat. Assn. Pastoral Musicians (co-chmn. Lansing chpt. 1995—). Roman Catholic. Avocations: sewing, reading, singing, music, writing. Home: 5102 Killarney Dr Holt MI 48842 Personal E-mail: tinlizzy29@aim.com.

WOOD, MAURICE, medical educator; b. Pelton, Eng., June 28, 1922; came to U.S., 1971; s. Joseph and Eugenie (Lumley) W.; m. Erica Joan Noble, May 1, 1948; children: Roger Lumley, Ashley Michael, Frances Jane. MB BS, U. Durham, Eng., 1945. Diplomate Am. Bd. Family Practice. Sr. ptnr. med. practice South Shields County, Durham, 1950-71; gen. practice teaching group U. Newcastle, Newcastle-on-Tyne, Eng., 1969-71; gen. clin. asst. dept. psychology-medicine South Shields Gen. Hosp., 1966-71; assoc. prof., dir. rsch. in family practice Med. Coll. Va.-Va. Commonwealth U., Richmond, 1971-73, prof., dir. rsch. in family practice, 1973-87, prof. emeritus, 1987—. Cons. advisor WHO, Geneva, 1979-90, chmn. working party to develop a classification for primary care, 1979-90; founding mem. exec. dir. N.Am. Primary Care Rsch. Group, Richmond, 1983-92, past pres., pres. emeritus, 1993—; chmn. com. on cmty. oriented primary care Insts. of Medicine, 1982-84. Assoc. editor Jour. Family Practice, 1976-83. Recipient award for meritorious svc. Va. Acad. Family Physicians, 1976; Maurice Wood award for career achievement in primary care rsch. founded in his honor, 1995. Fellow Royal Coll. Gen. Practitioners, Am. Acad. Family Physicians, World Orgn. Family Doctors (internat. classification com. 1986—),; mem. Inst. Medicine-Nat. Acad. Sci., Soc. Tchrs. Family Medicine (Curtis Hames Career Research award 1984), Ambulatory Sentinel Practice Network, Internat. Primary Care Network (treas., bd. dirs.), N.Am. Primary Care Rsch. Group (treas., bd. dirs., exec. dir., 1982-92), Rotary. Episcopalian. Personal E-mail: wood150w@verizon.net.

WOOD, MICHAEL M., ambassador; married; 2 children. Co-founder, CEO Hanley Wood, LLC, 1976—2005; mem. bd. advisors Weronis Suhler Stevenson, 2005; founder Redwood Investments, LLC, 2005; U.S. amb. to Sweden, 2006—. Former mem. Harvard Joint Ctr. for Housing Studies, long range planning com. Nat. Assn. Home Builders. Recipient Top Exec. of Yr. award, Media Bus. mag., 2005. Office: US Embassy 5750 Stockholm Pl Washington DC 20521

WOOD, MICHAEL W, lawyer; b. Austin, Tex. B, Rice Univ., Houston, 1967; JD, Univ. Tex., 1970. Bar: Tex. 1971, US Supreme Ct., US Ct. of Appeals (5th cir.), US Tax Ct. Co-founder Wood Campbell Moody & Gibbs, 1971; ptnr. Nathan Wood Sommers & Lippman; sr. v.p. and CEO Azurix Water Resources; co-ptnr. in charge of Houston office Akin Gump Strauss Hauer & Feld LLP, Houston, 2002—. Bd. trustees Houston Grand Opera; former bd. dir. Houston Ballet Found. and Wortham Theater Ctr. Mem.: ABA, Houston Bar Assn. Office: Akin Gump Strauss Hauer & Feld LLP 44th Fl 1111 Louisiana St Houston TX 77002-5200 Office Phone: 713-220-8111. Office Fax: 713-236-0822. Business E-Mail: mwood@akingump.com.

WOOD, MYRA LINDEN FRANK, consultant; b. Richmond, Va., Oct. 26, 1950; d. J. C. and Myra Teresa (Lanzarone) Frank; m. Timothy Franklin Long (div. Jan. 1981); m. Robert Andrew Hudson (div. 1994); m. Frederick W. Wood, Sept. 25, 1999. BA, Erskine Coll., Due West, SC, 1972; student, Inst. Fin. Edn., 1982-88. Chief activities therapist S.C. Dept. Corrections, Columbia, 1973-75, acting prin., 1975-77, coll. coord., 1977-78; owner, operator Carolina Coast Seafood, Aiken and Beaufort, S.C., 1978-80; from teller to savs. counselor Security Fed. Savs. & Loan, Aiken, 1981-83; customer svc. rep. Bankers 1st Savs. & Loans, Augusta, Ga., 1983-84, mgr. br. adminstrn., 1984-85; coord. automated teller machines, banking officer 1st Fed. Savs. Bank, Brunswick, Ga., 1985-88; ptnr., cons. electronic banking/software devel. RAH Systems, Brunswick, 1988-93; ptnr. specific application computer programming, software tng. Details & More, Greenville, S.C., 1989-90, ptnr. event planning, various mfg. positions and mktg./sales, 1989-91; cons. office and computer svcs. Mauldin, S.C., 1992-93. Lectr. S.C. Edn. Tchrs. Assn., Columbia, 1974, S.C. Assn. Social Workers, Columbia, 1975, Bus. and Profl. Women's Club, Columbia, 1978; small bus. owner, distbr. Nuskin product line, 1987—90; ind. mktg. rep. Network 2000/U.S. Spring, 1988—92; computer specialist Top Food Svcs. Carolina, Inc., Duncan, SC, 1989—90; admintrv./sales mgr. Cusom Catering, Duncan, 1990; cons. Contract Office/Computer Svcs., Greenville, 1992—2004; Shaklee ind. distbr., 1998—; dir., v.p., CFO FMW Holdings, Inc., 2000—; assoc. World Leadership Group/Global Equity Lending, 2004—; br. mgr. World Leadership Group/Global Equity Landing, 2005—. Book rev. writer A Class Act, Greenville, 1996—, appeared with Aiken Cmty. Theatre, 1981. Bd. dirs. Quest Soc., Greenville, 1992-95; mem. hospice com. Am. Cancer Soc., Augusta, 1981; lectr. St. John's United Meth. Ch., 1981-82, A Class Act, 1998; registrar, treas. Sugar Creek Soccer Club, Greenville, 1996-97. Mem. A Creative Gathering Writers Group, Writer's Roundtable. Democrat. Avocations: writing, reading, travel, study/research exploring the internet. Home and Office: PO Box 333 Mauldin SC 29662-0333 E-mail: cobfrank@charter.net.

WOOD, NANCY ELIZABETH, psychologist, educator; d. Donald Sterret and Orne Louise (Erwin) W. BS, Ohio U., 1943, MA, 1947; PhD, Northwestern U., 1952. Prof. Case We. Res. U., Cleve., 1952—60; specialist, expert HEW, Washington, 1960—62; chief rschr. USPHS, Washington, 1962—64; prof. U. So. Calif., LA, 1965—. Learning disabilities cons., 1960-70; assoc. dir. Cleve. Hearing and Speech Ctr., 1952-60; dir. licensing program Brit. Nat. Trust, London. Author: Language Disorders, 1964, Language Development, 1970, Verbal Learning, 1975 (monograph) Auditory Disorders, 1978, Levity, 1980, Stoneskipping, 1989, Bird Cage, 1994, Out of Control, 1999. Pres. faculty senate U. So. Calif., 1987—88. Recipient Outstanding Faculty award, Trojan Fourth Estate, 1982, Pres.' Svc. award, U. So. Calif., 1992. Fellow APA (cert.), AAAS, Am. Speech and Hearing Assn. (legis. coun. 1965-68); mem. Internat. Assn. Scientists. Republican. Methodist. Office: U So Calif University Park Los Angeles CA 90089-0001 Personal E-mail: woodn@adelphia.net, woodn@woodvunev.com.

WOOD, PAMELA SHARON, music educator, soprano; b. San Francisco, Mar. 29, 1944; d. Clinton Barford and Pearl (Henderson) Wood; m. Eric Scott Fraley, Dec. 28, 1968 (div. 1981); children: Ayanna Fraley Moore, Amara Fraley; m. Stephen B. Ambush, July 25, 1982 (div. 1996). B in Music Edn. summa cum laude, Howard U., Washington, 1967; MusM in Vocal Performance, U. Mass., 1980. Cert. in Music Divsn. Yale Summer Sch. Mus. Art, 1968, in tchg. and musicianship Kodaly Musical Tng. Inst. Inc., 1976, assoc. cert. Kodaly Ctr. Am., Wellesley, Mass., 2000. Music instr. and choral dir. Baccus and Hamilton Jr. High Schs., Wash., DC, 1967—69; music instr. and choral dir., elem. and jr. high sch. music specialist pub. schs., Stoneham, Mass., 1969—70; chmn. dept. music theory and edn. Elma Lewis Sch. of Fine Arts, Nat. Ctr. of Afro-American Artists, Inc., Boston, 1970—76; music tchr. Boston Pub. Schs. and Kodaly Ctr. of Am., 1981—82; voice tchr. Tufts U., Medford, Mass., 1982—87; music instr. Wheelock Coll., Boston, 1983—87, Roxbury CC, Boston, 1986—87; lectr. music MIT Sch. Humanities, Arts and Social Scis., Cambridge, Mass., 1987—96, sr. lectr. music, 1996—. Condr. Women's Inn at Pine St., Boston, 1995—2001, Sisters St. Joseph Cmty. Chorus, Brighton, Mass., 1996—2004, Pine Manor Coll., Chestnut Hill, Mass., 2004—05, voice tchr., 2002—05; faculty Kodály Music Inst., Boston, 1999—; devel. Solfege course Mass. Inst. Tech., 2000; presenter in field, 1971—. Singer (soprano soloist): Steve Reich & Musicians, 1974—88, NY and Israel Philharm., London, Boston, Chgo., San Francisco Symphonies, 1974—96. Bd. overseers New Eng. Conservatory of Music, Boston, 1996—2004; assoc. bd. mem. Kodaly Ctr. Am., Wellesley, Mass., 1996—; panelist Mass. Coun. Arts Humanities, 1982—83; bd. dirs. Boston Orch. & Chorale, 1991—94, Boston Children's Chorus, 2006—; convener, chair adv. com. New Eng. Conservatory Music, Boston, 1992—95; adjudicator Nat. Assn. Negro Bus. Profl. Women's Clubs, 1995, 1997, 2001, 2002; search com. Boston Children's Chorus, 2003; nat. conf. program team Orgn. Am. Kodaly Educators, 2004—05. Recipient Sponsors and Patrons award, Met. Opera Co., 1972, Nat. Assn. Tchrs. of Singing, 1981, Black Achiever, Greater Boston YMCA, 1994; honoree, Oberlin Black Musicians' Guild, Oberlin Conservatory of Music, 2003. Mem.: Internat. Kodaly Soc., Orgn. Am. Kodaly Educators (nat. conf. team 2004—05), Nat. Assn. Study and Performance of African-Am. Music, Ctr. Black Music Rsch., Boston Area Kodaly Educators, Pi Kappa Lambda. Office: Mass Inst of Tech 77 Massachusetts Ave Cambridge MA 02139 Home Phone: 508-879-1145; Office Phone: 617-253-8778.

WOOD, PATRICK HENRY, III, former federal official; b. Port Arthur, Tex., July 4, 1962; m. Kathleen Ryder; 4 children. BS in Civil Engring., Tex. A&M U.; JD, Harvard Law Sch. Atty. Baker & Botts LLP, Washington; engr. Arco Indonesia; legal counsel to chmn. Tex. Railroad Commn.; advisor to Fed. Energy Regulatory Commr. Jerry Langdon Fed. Energy Regulatory Commn., US Dept. Energy, Washington, staff mem., 1991—93, chmn., 2001—05, Pub. Utility Commn. Tex., 1995—2001. Bd. dirs. SunPower Corp., 2005—; chmn. advisory bd. Airtricity N. Am., Chgo., 2006—. Office: Airtricity Inc 401 N Michigan Ave Ste 3020 Chicago IL 60611

WOOD, QUENTIN EUGENE, oil industry executive; b. Mechanicsburg, Pa., Mar. 5, 1923; s. Lloyd Paul and Greta (Myers) W.; m. Louise Lowe, Apr. 14, 1958. BS, Pa. State U., 1948. Petroleum engr. Quaker State Oil Refining Corp., Parkersburg, W.Va., 1948-52, chief engr. Bradford, Pa., 1952-55, mgr. prodn., 1955-68, v.p. prodn. Oil City, Pa., 1968-70, exec. v.p., 1970-73, pres., chief ops. officer, 1973-75, pres., chief exec. officer, 1975-82, chmn., chief executive officer, 1982-88, chmn. bd., 1988-90, dir., 1990-93. Bd. dirs. Pa. Mfrs. Ins. Co.; chmn. industry tech. adv. com. U.S. Bur. Mines, 1960-70, Penn Grade Tech. Adv. Com., 1955-69, Pa. Oil and Gas Conservation Commn., 1961-71. Trustee Pa. State U., 1976-94, pres., 1979-87. 1st lt. USAAF, 1943-46. Mem. Am. Inst. Metall. Engrs., Pa. Grade Crude Oil Assn. (dir.), Pa. Oil Producers Assn. (past pres., dir. Bradford dist.), Am. Petroleum Inst. (dir.), Nat. Petroleum Refiners Assn. (dir.). Home: 1402 Spinnakers Reach Dr Ponte Vedra Beach FL 32082

WOOD, R. STEWART, JR., retired bishop; b. Detroit, June 25, 1934; s. Raymond and Marjorie Wood; m. Kristin Lie Miller, June 25, 1955; children: Lisa, Raymond, Michael. AB, Dartmouth Coll., 1956; MDiv, Va. Theol. Sem., 1959; MA in Counseling and Sociology, Ball State U., 1973; postgrad., Va. Seminary. Ordained to diaconate and priesthood Episc. Ch., 1959. Assoc. rector St. Paul's, Columbus, Ind., 1959—60; vicar Episc. Ch., Seymour and Bean Blossom, Ind., 1960—63; assoc. rector Grace Ch., Muncie, Ind., 1963—66, rector, 1966—70; exec. dir. Episc. Cmty. Svcs., Indpls., 1970—76; rector All Saint's Episc. Ch., Indpls., 1973—76, Christ Ch., Glendale, Ohio, 1976—84, St. John's Ch., Memphis, 1984—88; elected Bishop Coadjutor Diocese Mich., Detroit, 1988—89, diocesan bishop, 1990—2000; ret., 2000. Dir. summer camps, conf. ctr.; dep. Gen. Conv. 1970, 73, 76, 82; exec. coun. 1972-76, Coalition for Ordination of Women, bd. dirs. Episcopalian. Avocations: camping, golf, tennis, photography. Office: Box 968 255 Robert Frost Ln Quechee VT 05059-0968 Office Phone: 802-295-8912. E-mail: stemwood@aol.com.

WOOD, RICHARD COURTNEY, library director, educator; b. Spartanburg, SC, Aug. 8, 1943; s. Herman Alva and Mildred Eloise (Porter) W.; m. Amy Louise Black, Aug. 16, 1974. BA, U. Tex., 1966; MLS, U. S.C., 1977. Head cataloging Wofford Coll. Libr., Spartanburg, 1969-78; hosp. libr. John Peter Smith Hosp., Ft. Worth, 1978-80; reference libr. Tex. Coll. Osteo. Medicine, Ft. Worth, 1980-82, assoc. dir. libr., 1982-91; exec. dir. librs., assoc. prof. Sch. Medicine, chair HCOM dept. Tex. Tech U. Health Scis. Ctr., Lubbock, 1991—. Cons. Tarrant County Med. Libr. Assn., Fort Worth, 1978-82, 84, Med. Plaza Hosp., Fort Worth, 1979-82, Grand Prairie (Tex.) Community Hosp., 1980-81, Cook-Fort Worth Children's Hosp., 1988-91. Patron Kimball Art Mus. Fort Worth, 1987—; spokesman Neighborhood Assn., Fort Worth, 1989; vis. exec. United Way, Fort Worth, 1990. Recipient Dean's award Sch. Nursing, Tex. Tech U. Health Sci. Ctr., 1998. Mem. Dallas-Tarrant County Consortium (chmn. 1980-81), Metroplex Consortium Health Scis. (chmn. 1980-81), South Cen. Regional Group, Med. Libr. Assn. (chmn. osteo. librs. sect. 1986-87), South Cen. Acad. Med. Librs. (bd. dirs. 1991—, past chair), Nat. Network Librs. Medicine (bd. dirs. South Cen. region 1991-93), Deutsche Gesellschaft für Heereskunde, LIS Users Group (chair exec. bd.), Sigma Tau Delta. Republican. Presbyterian. Avocations: languages, travel, history, gardening, music. Home: 1805 Bangor Ave Lubbock TX 79416-5518 Office: Preston Smith Libr Health Scis 3601 4th St Lubbock TX 79430-0001 Home Phone: 806-791-2724; Office Phone: 806-743-2203. Office Fax: 806-743-2218. Business E-Mail: richard.wood@ttuhsc.edu.

WOOD, RICHARD ROBINSON, real estate company executive; b. Salem, Mass., Nov. 8, 1922; s. Reginald and Irene Margaret (Robinson) Wood; m. Pamela Vander Wiele, Mar. 8, 1951 (div. Apr. 1969); children: Christopher Robinson, Bryant Cornelius, Marcella Wood Mackenzie; m. Jane Philbin, Sept. 19, 1970. AB, Harvard Coll., 1944; postgrad., Mass. Inst. Tech., 1947-48. V.p. Hunneman & Co., Boston, 1959-72; trustee, sec. Mass. Real Estate Investment Trust, Boston, 1967-69; trustee Suffolk Franklin Savings Bank, 1967-74; pres., chmn. Continential Real Estate Equity, Boston, 1972-74; exec. v.p. ITEL Real Estate Corp., San Francisco, 1974-75; v.p. Baird & Warner, Chgo., 1976-80; pres., chmn. Renwood Properties, Inc., Cambridge, Mass., 1981—. Founder Real Estate Securities 2d Syndication Inst., 1972, pres., 1976—78; pres., chmn. ILCO Properties, Chgo., 1981—87; v.p., dir. Common Goal Capitol Group, Balt., 1986—; gen. ptnr. Common Goal Mortgage Fund, Balt., 1986—; mem. Coun. Rural Housing and Devel., 1988—; v.p., bd. dirs. St. Katherines Care Ctrs., 1990—; chmn. Inst. Responsible Housing Preservation, 1994—99, 19 Chauncy St. Trust, 1995—. Mem. Mayor's Citizen Adv. Bd., Boston, 1965—67, Coun. Rural Housing and Devel., 1988—; committeeman, treas. Mass. Rep. State Com., Boston, 1964—72; pres. Boston Rep. City Com., 1965—67. With M.C. US Army, 1943—44. Mem.: Nat. Leased Housing Assn., White Mountain Ski Runners, Badminton and Tennis Club, Harvard Club N.Y., Longwood Cricket Club, Harvard Club Boston. Avocations: tennis, skiing. Home: 19 Chauncy St Cambridge MA 02138-2549 Office: Renwood Properties Inc Ste 44 875 Massachusetts Ave Cambridge MA 02139-3067 Home Phone: 617-354-5182; Office Phone: 617-876-4455. Personal E-mail: renwoodprops@aol.com.

WOOD, ROBERT CHARLES, lawyer, real estate developer; b. Chgo., Apr. 8, 1956; s. Roy Edward and Mildred Lucille (Jones) W.; m. Jennifer Jo Briggs, Oct. 1984; children: Jacqueline Jones, Reagan Keith. BA in History, So. Meth. U., 1979, BBA in Real Estate, 1979, JD, 1982. Bar: Tex. 1983. Appraiser McClellan-Massey, Dallas, 1977—79; rschr., acquisitions officer Amstar Fin. Corp., Dallas, 1979—80; prin. Robert Wood Cons., Dallas, 1981—98; prin. Welch & Wood Attys. and Y2K Cons., Dallas, 1998—2000; pvt. practice Dallas, 1995—; real estate investor and developer, 1998—. Cons. Plan Mktg. Cos., 1983-84; pvt. practice law, Dallas, 1983-84; gen. counsel Diversified Benefits, Inc., Dallas, 1984-86; nat. accts. mgr. Lomas & Nettleton Real Estate Group, Dallas, 1987-88; sr. pension cons., prin. Eppler, Guerin &Turner, 1988-93; chmn. adv. coun. on devel. Medisend, 1991; nat. consulting coord. fin. advisors coun., v.p. Callan Assocs., San Francisco, 1994-95; atty. at law, 1995—; exec. v.p., gen. counsel, Rushmore Investment Advisors, Plano, Tex., 2002-06. Author: Electionomics: How the Money Managers View the Election, 1992, After the Congress Vote: How the Managers See Things Now, 1993, Y2K--The Year 2000 Issue: How Y2K Affects the Markets, 1998; mem. So. Meth. U. Law Rev., 1981-82; contbr. articles to profl. publs. Bd. dirs. Dallas unit Am. Cancer Soc., 1982-87, mem. spl. events com., 1986-87, mem. crusade com., 1987-88, mem. medisend adv. com., 1988-94, chmn. corp. devel. bd., 1989-95. Mem. Tex. Bar Assn., Phila. Bar Assn., Phi Gamma Delta. Avocations: skiing, tennis, bicycling. Office Phone: 214-369-3209. E-mail: rccwood@aol.com.

WOOD, ROBERT E., philosopher, educator; b. Racine, Wis., Oct. 20, 1934; s. Earl J. and Cathryn M. Wood; m. Marjorie M. Simanek; children: Robert L., Gregory T., Mary T. Kubala, David J., Mark C. BA, Marquette U., Milw., 1958, MA, 1961, PhD. From asst. to prof. St. Joseph's Coll., Rensselaer, Ind., 1961—76; assoc. prof. St. Joseph's U., Phila., 1976—79; from asst. to prof. U. Dallas, Irving, 1979—. Vis. assoc. Cath. U. Am., Washington, 1968—69, Duquesne U., Pitts., 1974; vis. prof. Marquette U., 1995; chmn. dept. philosophy St. Joseph's Coll., 1969—77, U. Dallas, 1984—96, dean, 1987—90, acting provost, dean Constantin Coll., 1988, interim provost, dean Constantin Coll., 1990—91, chair acad. senate, 1996. Author: Martin Buber's Onthology, 1969, A Path Into Metaphysics, 1991, Placing Aesthetics, 1999; editor: The Future of Metaphysics, 1970; contbr. articles to profl. jours. Fulbright grantee, Tubingen, Germany, 1989. Mem.: Am. Cath. Philos. Assn. (mem. exec. con. 1989—). Democrat. Roman Catholic. Avocations: sculpting, gardening. Home: 209 E Scotland Dr Irving TX 75062 Office: U Dallas Dept Philosophy 1845 E Northgate Dr Irving TX 75062

WOOD, ROBERT EMERSON, pediatrics educator; b. Jacksonville, Fla., Nov. 15, 1942; s. Waldo E. and Verda V. Wood. BS in Chemistry magna cum laude, Stetson U., 1963; PhD in Physiology, Vanderbilt U., 1968, MD, 1970. Bd. cert. pediatrics; bd. cert. pediatric pulmonology. Intern in pediatrics Duke U. Med. Ctr., Durham, 1970-71, resident in pediatrics, 1971-72; fellow pediatric pulmonology Case Western Res. U., Cleve., 1974-76, asst. prof. pediatrics, 1976-82, assoc. prof. pediatrics, 1982-83; assoc. prof. pediatrics, chief divsn. pediatric pulmonary medicine Dept. Pediatrics, U. N.C., Chapel Hill, 1983-88, prof. pediatrics, chief divsn. pediatric pulmonary medicine, 1988-94, dir. pediat. ICU, 1984-86, dir. Ctr. Pediat. Bronchology, 1994-99; prof. pediats. and otolaryngology Cin. Children's Hosp. Med. Ctr., U. Cin., 1999—; chief, divsn. pulmonary medicine Children's Hosp. Med. Ctr., U. Cin., 2001—05. Mem. editorial bd.: Pediatric Pulmonology, 1992—, Jour. Bronchology, 1993—; contbr. chpts. to books and articles to profl. jours. Lt. comdr. USPHS, 1972-74. Named Grad. fellow Danforth Found., 1963-68, Med. Scientist fellow Life Ins. Med. Rsch. Found., 1965-70, Clin. Rsch. fellow Cystic Fibrosis Found., 1974-76. Mem. Am. Bronchesophagological Assn., Am. Assn. for Bronchology, Soc. for Pediatric Rsch., Am. Thoracic Soc., N.C. Pediatric Soc. Office: Cin Children's Hosp Med Ctr Pediat Pulmonary Medicine 3333 Burnet Ave Cincinnati OH 45229-3039 Office Phone: 513-636-2776. Fax: 513-636-7734. Business E-Mail: rewood@cchmc.org.

WOOD, ROBERT L., chemicals executive; BA in History, U. Mich. Field seller Dow Chem. Co., Cleveland, Ohio, 1978—80, mktg. recruiting and placement dept. Midland, Mich., 1980—82, product sales mgr., 1982—84, mktg. mgr., 1984—87, dir. mktg., 1987—89, v.p. mktg. Indpls., 1989—90, v.p. sales, household products, 1990—93, group v.p. and gen. mgr. household products, 1993—94, v.p. polyolefins and elastomers, 1994—95, bus. v.p. engring. plastics, 1995—97, bus. v.p. polyurethanes, 1997—2000, bus. group pres. thermosets and Dow automotive, 2000—04; joined Crompton Corp., Middlebury, Conn., 2004; chmn., pres., CEO Chemtura Corp. (formed in merger of Crompton and Great Lakes), Middlebury, Conn., 2005—. Mem. Big Brothers Big Sisters of Am. Mem.: Jarden Corp. (bd. dirs.). Office: Chemtura Corp 199 Benson Rd Waterbury CT 06749 *

WOOD, ROBERT WARREN, lawyer; b. Des Moines, July 5, 1955; s. Merle Warren and Cecily Ann (Sherk) W.; m. Beatrice Wood, Aug. 4, 1979; 1 child, Bryce Mercedes. Student, U. Sheffield, Eng., 1975-76; AB, Humboldt State U., 1976; JD, U. Chgo., 1979. Bar: Ariz. 1979, Calif. 1980, Wyo. 2000, NY 1989, D.C. 1993, Mont. 1998, US Tax Ct. 1980, Wyo.; Roll of Solicitors of Eng. and Wales, 1998. Assoc. Jennings, Strouss, Phoenix, 1979-80, McCutchen, Doyle, San Francisco, 1980-82, Broad, Khourie, 1982-85, Steefel, Levitt & Weiss, 1985-87, ptnr., 1987-91, Bancroft & McAlister, 1991-93; prin. Robert W. Wood, P.C., 1993—2005; ptnr. Wood & Porter, 2006—. Instr. in law U. Calif., San Francisco, 1981—82. Author: Taxation of Corporate Liquidations: A Complete Planning Guide, 1987, 2nd edit., 1994, The Executive's Complete Guide to Business Taxes, 1989, Corporate Taxation: Complete Planning and Practice Guide, 1989, S Corporations, 1990, The Ultimate Tax Planning Guide for Growing Companies, 1991, Taxation of Damage Awards and Settlement Payments, 1991, 3d edit., 2005, Office Tax Guide, 1991; co-author: (with others) California Closely Held Corporations: Tax Planning and Practice Guide, 1987, Legal Guide to Independent Contractor Status, 3d edit., 2000; editor: California Small Busines Guide, 4 vols., 1998, Home Office Money & Tax Guide, 1992, Tax Aspects of Settlements and Judgements, 1993, 2d edit., 1998, 3d edit., 2005; editor-in-chief The M & A Tax Report; editor: Limited Liability Companies: Formation, Operation and Conversion, 1994, 2d edit., 2001, Limited Liability Partnerships: Formation, Operation and Taxation, 1996; mem. editl. bd. Real Estate Tax Digest, The Practical Accountant, Jour. Real Estate Taxation. Fellow Am. Coll. Tax Counsel; mem. Calif. Bd. Legal Specialization (cert. specialist taxation), Can. Bar Assn., Bohemian Club, Law Coun. Australia. Republican. Office: Wood & Porter 333 Sacramento St San Francisco CA 94111 Office Phone: 415-834-1800. Business E-Mail: wood@woodporter.com.

WOOD, ROGER F., lawyer; b. Washington, Aug. 26, 1947; BA, Swarthmore Coll., 1969; postgrad., Merton Coll., Oxford, England, 1969-70; JD, Harvard U., 1973. Bar: Pa. 1973. Law clk. to Hon. John P. Fullam U.S. Dist. Ct. (ea. dist.) Pa., 1973-75; with Dillworth, Paxdon, Kalish & Kauffman, Phila.; atty. Dilworth Paxson LLP, Phila. Mem., bd. trustees Anna T. Jeanes Found. and Friends Fiduciary Corp. Mem. Phi Beta Kappa. Office: Dilworth Paxson LLP 1735 Market St Ste 3200 Mellon Bank Ctr Philadelphia PA 19103-7501 Office Phone: 215-575-7068. Office Fax: 215-575-7200. E-mail: woodrf@dilworthlaw.com.

WOOD, RONALD, musician; b. London, June 1, 1947; Owner Woody's on the Beach (nightclub), Miami, 1987—. Guitarist and bassist with Jeff Beck Group, 1966—69, Faces, 1969—75, Rolling Stones, 1975—, New Barbarians, 1979, solo (albums) Gimme Some Neck, 1979, I've Got My Own Album To Do, Now Look, albums (with Rolling Stones) Black and Blue, 1976, Love You Live, 1977, Some Girls, 1979, Emotional Rescue, 1979, Sucking in the Seventies, 1981, Tattoo You, Still Life, 1982, Undercover, 1983, Between the Sheets, 1985, Dirty Work, Rewind, 1986, Steel Wheel, 1988, Flashpoint, 1991, Voodoo Lounge, 1994 (Grammy award Best Rock Album), Bridges to Babylon, No Security, 1997, A Bigger Bang, 2005, (with Faces) Long Player, A Nod's As Good As A Wink..., To a Blind Horse, Ooh-La-La, (with Small Faces) First Step, Ogden's Nut Gone Flake, There Are But Four Small Faces, 1991, All or Nothing, 1992, films Let's Spend the Night Together, 1982, Digital Dreams, 1983. Named Greatest Touring Band of All Time, World Music Awards, 2006; named to Rock and Roll Hall of Fame, 1989. Office: Virgin Records 1540 Broadway New York NY 10036-4039

WOOD, SHELTON EUGENE, education educator, minister, consultant; b. Douglas, Ga., May 20, 1938; s. Shelton and Mae Lillie (Pheil) Wood; m. Edna Louise Wood, Aug. 25, 1961; children: Shelton John, Deirdre Louise. AA, St. John's U., 1958; BA, U. Nebr., 1959; MEd, Coll. William and Mary, Williamsburg, Va., 1971; PhD, Sussex U., 1973; EdD, Southeastern U., Washington, DC, 1975; MBA, Ctrl. Mich. U., Mount Pleasant, 1977; MA, U. Okla., Norman, 1980; D in Ministry, Wesleyan Bible Coll., 1999; Cert. in Internt. Rels., Fgn. Svc. Inst., 1971; Cert. in Mgmt., Indsl. Coll. Armed Forces, 1970. Area mgr. Marshall Fields Corp., Fla., 1957-58; transp. supr. Greyhound Corp., Jacksonville, Fla., 1959-62; officer US Army, 1963, advanced through grades to inf. col., 1996; with Redstone Readiness Group, 1977-80; chief studies and analysis divsn. Korean Inst. for Def. Analysis, 1981-83; faculty St. John River C.C., 1984-90; nat. and internat. bus. and mgmt. cons., 1995—; sr. pastor Fellowship Wesleyan Ch., Spring Hill, Fla., 1998—2005, asst. dist. supt. Fla., 2005—. Faculty Wesleyan Bible U., 1997—; pres. Georgetown Wesleyan U. of the Americas, 2005-. Author: Strategic for Implementing A Family Life Ministry Ctr., 1997; contbr. articles to profl. jours. Active Boy Scouts Am., 1977—90; lay leader United Meth. Ch., Falls Ch., Va., 1977—79, St. James United Meth. Ch., 1986—90; mem. dist. bd. ministerial develop. Fla. Dist. of Wesleyan Ch., 1999, chair evangelism and ch. growth com., 1999—; bd. dirs. Baby Love. Decorated Bronze Star with 2 oak leaf clusters, Air medal with 3 oak leaf clusters, Purple Heart with 2 oak leaf clusters; Sussex Coll. fellow, 1969-70. Mem. NEA, Am. Soc. Trainers and Developers (pres. S.E. chpt. 1974-75), Am. Def. Preparedness Assn., Putnam County C. of C. (pres. 1990-91), Toastmasters Internat. (Disting. Toastmaster 1989), Kiwanis (pres. 1989-90), Phi Kappa Delta, Phi Delta Kappa. Address: 8485 Chatsworth St Spring Hill FL 34608 Personal E-mail: ewood11@tampabay.rr.com.

WOOD, STEPHEN WRAY, minister, educator, legislator, singer, songwriter; b. Winston Salem, NC, Oct. 6, 1948; s. D.W. and Annie Lee (Harris) W.; m. Starr Smith, June 18, 1978; children: Allyson, Joshua. BTh., John Wesley Coll., 1970; BA, Asbury Coll., 1973; MA, U. NC, Greensboro, 1979; DMin, Luther Rice U., Ga., 1980; MDiv, Houston Grad. Sch. Theology, 1990. Asst. dean, asst. prof. John Wesley Coll., High Point, NC, 1975-81; min. Soc. of Friends, 1980—. Adj. prof. Luther Rice U.; assoc. prof. Houston Grad. Sch. Theology; pres. Triad Christian Counseling, Greensboro, 1979. Contbr. articles to hist., ednl. and religious jours., Dictionary of NC Biography, Oxford Internat. Roundtable, 1997—; composer, singer religious music. Trustee John Wesley Coll., High Point, 1981—; bd. dirs. Friends Ctr.-Guilford Coll., Greensboro, 1982-89; vice chmn. Guilford County Rep. Party, NC, 1981-85; mem. NC State Ho. Reps., 1985-86, 89-90, 91-92, 93-94, 95-96, 97-98, 99-2000, 2003-05, spkr. pro tem, 1997—; apptd. mem. Selective Svc. Commn., 2001—; chaplain High Point Jaycees. With US Army, 1970-71; capt. NC State Militia. Mem. BMI (affiliate songwriter 1978—). Avocations: golf, book collecting, reading, cowboy boots. Office: 8098 Reynolda Rd Pfafftown NC 27040 Personal E-mail: repstevewood@juno.com. *I often reflect upon the maternal advice proffered me as a child, "Steve, if at first you don't succeed, try, try again." We may be down but not out. Therefore is no such thing as the good old days because the future is just as bright as the promises of God. We conquer by continuing. Life is not a problem to be solved, it is a gift to be enjoyed.*

WOOD, TERRY DAVID, broadcasting executive; b. Hollywood, Calif., July 1, 1942; s. Gordon Dale and Mabel Catherine (Fierbringer) W.; m. Jane Anne Forte, July 2, 1977; children: Patricia Rae, Terry David Jr., Heather Dyan. Student, U. South Fla., 1960-61. Prodn. mgr., announcer, program mgr. various radio and TV stas., Fla., Ill. and Ohio, 1959-69; ops. mgr. Sta. WONE-AM/FM, Dayton, Ohio, 1969-78; program dir. Sta. WWSW-AM, Pitts., 1978-79, Sta. WSAI-AM, Cin., 1979-80; v.p., gen. mgr. Sta. WRVR-AM/FM, Memphis, 1980-88, Sta. WLTI-FM, Detroit, 1988—. Bd. dirs., exec. v.p. Country Radio Seminar, Inc., Nashville, 1973-81. Bd. dirs. Memphis chpt. Nat. Kidney Found., 1981-82, Memphis March of Dimes, 1986-88, Memphis Youth Villages, 1986-88, Detroit, Big Bros. and Big Sisters, 1989—, Detroit Sci. Ctr., 1989—, Beaumont Found., 1990—. Named one of 100 Most Powerful Women in Entertainment, Hollywood Reporter, 2006. Mem. Tenn. Assn. Broadcaster (bd. dirs., conv. chmn. 1984-85), Memphis Area Broadcasters Assn. (past officer), Nat. Assn. Broadcasters (legis. liaison 1987-88). Republican. Roman Catholic. Avocations: golf, swimming. Office: Sta WLTI-FM 28411 Northwestern Hwy Ste 100 Southfield MI 48034-5544 *

WOOD, TERRY LEE, mathematics educator; BA, Mich. State U., 1964, MA, 1968, PhD, 1976. Cert. tchr., Mich. Elem. tchr. Lansing (Mich.) Pub. Schs., 1964-65, 66-68; tchr., researcher The Lab. Schs., Chgo., 1979-80; vis. asst. prof. Purdue U., West Lafayette, Ind., 1985-88, asst. prof. math. edn., 1988-93, assoc. prof., 1993-98, prof., 1998—. Co-editor: Transforming Children's Mathematics Education, 1990, Recreating Elementary Mathematics Education: Insights and Issues, 1993, Mathematics Teacher Education International Perspectives, 1999, Beyond Classical Pedagogy: Teaching Elementary School Mathematics, 2001; asst. editor Jour. Math. Tchr. Edn.; mem. editl. bd. Ednl. Studies in Math., Jour. Tchr. Edn., Brit. Soc. for Learning Math., Child Devel., Math. Tchr. Edn. and Devel. Robert L. Snodgrass scholar. Mem. AAAS, APA, Am. Ednl. Rsch. Assn., Nat. Coun. Tchrs. Math., Psychology Math. Edn. Internat., Psychology Math. Edn. N.Am., Soc. Rsch. in Child Devel. Office: Purdue U Curriculum & Instrn Beering Hall 100 N University St West Lafayette IN 47907-1622 Office Phone: 765-494-2353. Business E-Mail: twood@purdue.edu.

WOOD, THOMAS E., lawyer; b. LA, Apr. 20, 1939; s. Louis Earl and Youda (Hays) Wood; m. Sally Ann Wood, June 22, 1963; children: Julia W. DeVuono, Melissa W. Brewster. BA, Amherst Coll., 1961; LLB, U. Pa., 1966. Bar: Pa. 1966. Assoc. Drinker Biddle & Reath LLP, Phila., 1966-72, ptnr., 1972—2006, ptnr.-in-charge Berwyn office, 2001—06, of counsel, 2006—; bd. dirs. Vertex, Inc. Chmn. Easttown Zoning Hearing Bd., Easttown Twp., Pa., 1976—; trustee Atlantic Challenge Found. Mem. Phila. Club. Office: Drinker Biddle & Reath LLP 1000 Westlakes Dr Ste 300 Berwyn PA 19312-2409 Home Phone: 610-688-0734; Office Phone: 610-993-2211. Office Fax: 610-993-8585. E-mail: thomas.wood@dbr.com.

WOOD, THOMAS WESLEY, humanities educator, editor; b. Hugo, Okla., Mar. 16, 1920; s. Thomas Wesley Wood Sr. and Alma Elora (Rogers) Daniel; m. L. Deloris Gray, May 31, 1968; m. Doreen Anderson, June, 1950 (div. 1966); children: John William, Thomas Wakefield. BA in History and Journalism, Tulsa U., 1951, MA in History, 1952; MS in Journalism, Northwestern U., 1953; PhD in European History, U. Okla., 1966. Reporter City News Bur. Chgo., 1952-54; prof. Tulsa (Okla.) U., 1954-73, So. Ill. U., Carbondale, 1973-76; vis. prof. Am. U., Cairo, Egypt, 1976-78, U. Ark., Little Rock, 1978-80; prof. Temple U., Phila., 1980-90, emeritus prof., 1990—. Reporter, corr. Tulsa World, 1954-84; editor, pub., founder Lost Generation Jour., Salem, Mo., 1973—. Author: Tulsa U. Editing Hankbook, 1956, 60, Tulsa U. Reporting Handbook, 1958, 60, 69, Outline History of American Journalism, 1961, Influence of the Paris Herald on the Lost Generation Writers, 1966; sub.-editor Egyptian Gazette, 1977-78. Recipient editing and writing award Mo. Press Women, 1985, writing award Pa. Press Club, 1983, writing award Ark. Press Women, 1979, 80, photography award Soc. Profl. Journalists, 1972. Mem. Overseas Press Club Am., Assn. Edn. Journalism and Mass Comm., Hemingway Soc., Soc. Scholar Editors, Coun. Editors Learned Journals, Pi Alpha Mu (nat. pres. 1956-60). Republican. Baptist. Avocations: fly fishing, travel, interviewing expatriate 20's americans. Home: RR 5 Box 134 Salem MO 65560-9008 Office: Lost Generation Jour RR 3 Box 387 Salem MO 65560-9315

WOOD, VIRCHEL EDGAR, orthopedist, surgeon, educator; s. Virchel Edgar and Gladys Brome Wood; m. Esther June Wood, Aug. 15, 1958; children: Tamarin, Laurel, Garry, Darrell, Victoria. BA in Chemistry, Atlantic Union Coll., Lancaster, Mass., 1956; MD, Loma Linda U., Calif., 1960. Diplomate Am. Bd. Orthop. Surgery, 1969. Rotating internship Wash. Sanitarium & Hosp., Takoma Park, Md., 1960—61; resident gen. surgery Harbor Gen. Hosp., Torrance, Calif., 1961—63; resident orthop. surgery U. Mass., Worcester, 1963—66; chief, orthop. svc. US Army Hosp., Fort Leonard Wood, Mo., 1967—69; fellow hand surgery Columbia-Presbyn. Hosp., NYC, 1970, U. Iowa, Iowa City, 1970; orthopaedic hand surgeon Loma Linda U. Med. Ctr., 1971—. Chief hand surgery svc. Loma Linda U., 1971—2000, prof. orthop. surgery, 1986—, dir. microsurgery lab., 1989—92, consulting chief hand surgery svc., 2000—06, vice-chair dept. orthop., 2000—. Contbr. chapters to books, scientific papers. With MC US Army, 1967—69. Named Outstanding Tchr. of Yr., Loma Linda U. Sch. Medicine, 1973, Outstanding Faculty Rschr., Walter E. Macpherson Soc. Loma Linda U., 1994, 1995, Alumnus of Yr., Neufeld Soc. Loma Linda U., 1996, Honored Alumnus, President's Coun. Loma Linda U. Alumni Assn., 1999; recipient U. Disting. Svc. award, Loma Linda U. Sch. of Medicine, 2004, Editor's Choice award, Nat. Libr.

of Poetry, 1998, Centennial Vanguard award, Loma Linda U. Allied Health Sci. Ctrs., 2006. Mem.: AAUP, ACS, AMA, Academic Orthop. Soc., Am. Orthop. Assn., Am. Soc. Surgery of Hand (Most Frequently Cited Author in Congenital Hand Lit. Past 50 Years 1995), Am. Acad. Orthop. Surgeons, Inland Orthop. Soc., Calif. Med. Assn., Internat. Congenital Hand Anomalies Study Group, Internat. Soc. Poets (assoc.), Alpha Omega Alpha. Seventh-Day Adventist. Avocations: travel, museums, gemology, archaeology, poetry. Office: Loma Linda Univ Orthopaedics Ste 218 11406 Loma Linda Dr Loma Linda CA 92354 Office Phone: 909-558-6444. Office Fax: 909-558-6118.

WOOD, VIVIAN POATES, mezzo soprano, educator; b. Washington, Aug. 19, 1923; d. Harold Poates and Mildred Georgette (Patterson) W. Studies with Walter Anderson, Antioch Coll., 1953-55; studies with Denise Restout, Saint-Leu-A-Forêt, France and Lakeville, Conn., 1960—62, studies with Denise Restout, 1964—70; studies with Paul A. Pisk, 1968—71; studies with Paul Ulanowsky, NYC, 1958—68; Elemer Nagy, 1965-68, Vyautas Marijosius, 1967-68; MusB, Hartt Coll. Music, 1968; postgrad. (fellow), Yale U., 1968; MusM (fellow), Washington U., St. Louis, 1971, PhD (fellow), 1973. Debut in recital series Internat. Jeunesse Musicals Arts Festival, 1953; solo fellowship Boston Symphony Orch., Berkshire Music Ctr., Tanglewood, 1964, St. Louis Symphony Orch., 1969, Washington Orch., 1949, Bach Cantata Series Berkshire Chamber Orch., 1964, Yale Symphony Orch., 1968. Appearances in U.S. and European recitals, oratorios, operas, radio and TV, 1953-68; soloist Landowska Ctr., Lakeville, 1969, Internat. Harpsichord Festival, Westminister Choir Coll., Princeton, N.J., 1973; prof. voice, head voice area Sch. of Music, U. So. Miss., Hattiesburg, 1971-2000, ret. 2000, prof. emerita, 2000—; asst. dean Coll. Fine Arts, 1974-76, acting dean, 1976-77; guest prof. Hochschüle für Musik, Munich, 1978-79; prof. Italian Internat. Studies Program, Rome, 1986; Miss. coord. Alliance for Arts Edn., Kennedy Ctr. Performing Arts, 1974—; mem. Miss. Gov.'s Adv. Panel for Gifted and Talented Children, 1974—, 1st Miss. Gov.'s Conf. on the Arts, 1974—. Author: Polenc's Songs: An Analysis of Style, 1971. Recipient Young Am. Artists Concert award N.Y.C., 1955; Wanda Landowska fellow 1961-68. Mem. Miss. Music Tchrs. Assn., Nat. Assn. Tchrs. of Singing, Music Tchrs. Nat. Assn., Am. Musicology Soc., Golden Key, Mu Phi Epsilon, Delta Kappa Gamma, Tau Beta Kappa (hon.), Pi Kappa Lambda. Democrat. Episcopalian.

WOOD, WILLARD MARK, lawyer; b. Traverse City, Mich., Nov. 30, 1942; s. William Mark and Ebba Forsman Wood; m. Sharon McDermott, June 19, 1965; children: Sean, Pat, Kelly, Ryan, Casey. BA, Santa Clara U., 1964; JD, U. So. Calif., 1967. Bar: Calif., D.C., U.S. Supreme Ct. Judge advocate USMC, Vietnam, 1969-70; ptnr. O'Melveny & Myers, LA, 1971—. Assoc. editor U. So. Calif. Law Review, 1966—67. Capt. USMC, 1967-71, Vietnam. Mem.: DC Bar, LA County Bar Assn., Order of the Coif, ABA, State Bar Calif. (chmn., local disciplinary com.), Phi Delta Phi. Roman Catholic. Office: O'Melveny & Myers 400 S Hope St Ste 1321 Los Angeles CA 90071-2899 Office Phone: 213-430-6220. E-mail: mwood@omm.com.

WOOD, WILLIAM BARRY, III, biologist, educator; b. Balt., Feb. 19, 1938; s. William Barry, Jr. and Mary Lee (Hutchins) W.; m. Marie-Elisabeth Renate Hartisch, June 30, 1961; children: Oliver Hartisch, Christopher Barry. AB, Harvard U., 1959; PhD, Stanford U., 1963. Asst. prof. biology Calif. Inst. Tech., Pasadena, 1965-68, assoc. prof., 1968-69, prof. biology, 1970-77; prof. molecular, cellular and developmental biology U. Colo., Boulder, 1977—, chmn. dept., 1978-83, disting. prof., 2004—. Mem. panel for developmental biology NSF, 1970-72; physiol. chemistry study sect. NIH, 1974-78; mem. com. on sci. and public policy Nat. Acad. Scis., 1979-80; mem. NIH Cellular and Molecular Basis of Disease Rev. Com., 1984-88' mem. bd. sci. edn. Nat Acad. Scis., 2005- Author: (with J. H. Wilson, R.M. Benbow, L.E. Hood) Biochemistry: A Problems Approach, 2d edit., 1981, (with L.E. Hood and J.H. Wilson) Molecular Biology of Eucaryotic Cells, 1975, (with L.E. Hood and I.L. Weissman) Immunology, 1978, (with L.E. Hood, I.L. Weissman and J.H. Wilson) Immunology, 2d edit., 1984, (with L.E. Hood and I.L. Weissman) Concepts in Immunology, 1978; editl. rev. bd. Science, 1984-92; mem. editl. bd. Cell, 1984-87, Developmental Biology, 1995-1999; editor-in-chief, CBE Life Scis. Edn., 2005-; contbr. articles to profl. jours. Recipient U.S. Steel Molecular Biology award, 1969, Alexander von Humboldt Rsch prize, 2004; NIH Rsch. grantee, 1965—, Merit awardee, 1986-96; Guggenheim fellow, 1975-76. Fellow AAAS; mem. Nat. Acad. Scis., Am. Acad. Arts and Scis., Am. Soc. for Cell Biology, Genetics Soc. Am. Soc. for Developmental Biology. Office: Univ Colo Dept MCD Biology 347 UCB Boulder CO 80309

WOOD, WILLIAM BRAUCHER, ambassador; b. Aug. 7, 1950; BA, Bucknell U., 1973; MBA, George Washington U., 1975. Chief U.S. negotiator UN Security Coun.; prin. dep. asst. sec., acting asst. sec., Bur. Internat. Orgn. Affairs US Dept. State, Washington, 1998—2002, US amb. to Colombia Bogota, 2003—07, US amb. to Afghanistan Kabul, 2007—. Recipient James Clement Dunn Award for Excellence, 1998, Disting. Svc. award, US Dept. State, 2002. Office: DOS Amb 6180 Kabul Pl Dulles VA 20189 *

WOOD, WILLIAM C., surgeon, medical educator, academic chairman; b. Fairbury, Ill., May 3, 1940; s. William A. and Violet B. (Johnson) W.; m. Judith A. Lindsell, Aug. 15, 1964; children: Kristen Marie, William Andrew, Lindsay Ann. BS cum laude, Wheaton Coll., 1962; MD cum laude, Harvard U., 1966. Asst. resident Mass. Gen. Hosp., Boston, 1966-68, resident in surgery, 1970-74; clin. assoc. surg. br. immunology sect. Nat. Cancer Inst. NIH, Bethesda, Md., 1968-70; asst. prof. Harvard Med. Sch., Boston, 1975-82; asst. prof., chief surg. oncology Mass. Gen. Hosp., Harvard Med. Sch., Boston, 1982-90; prof., chmn. dept. surgery Sch. Medicine Emory U., Atlanta, 1991—. Chair breast com. Ea. Coop. Oncology Group, Boston, 1991-97; co-chmn. Early Breast Cancer Clin. Trialists Coop. Group, Oxford, Eng., 1995—, acting dir. Winship Cancer Inst., 1996-2000. Assoc. editor Am. Jour. Clin. Oncology, 1985-2003, CA: A Cancer Jour. for Clinicians, 2002-05; co-editor, Surgery of the Breast: Principles and Art and Advances in Breast Cancer Management, prin. editor, Anatomic Basis of Tumor Surgery, No. Am. editor, Oxford Textbook of Surgery (2nd edition). Bd. dirs., mem. exec. com. Gordon Conwell Theol. Sem., S. Hamilton, Mass., 1975—. Mem. Am. Soc. Clin. Oncology (bd. dirs. 1995—), Soc. Surg. Oncology (sec. 1995—. James Ewing award, 2005), Am. Coll. Surgeons (bd. gov. 1998-2005), SE Surg. Congress (pres. 2004-2005). Office: Emory U Dept Surgery 1364 Clifton Rd NE Dept Surgery Atlanta GA 30322-1061 *

WOOD, WILLIAM MCBRAYER, lawyer; b. Greenville, SC, Jan. 27, 1942; s. Oliver Gillan and Grace (McBrayer) W.; m. Nancy Cooper, 1973 (dec. 1993); children: Walter, Lewis; m. Jeanette Dobson Haney, June 25, 1994. BS in Acctg., U. S.C., Columbia, 1964, JD cum laude, 1972; LLM in Estate Planning (scholar), U. Miami, 1980. Bar: S.C. 1972, Fla. 1979, D.C. 1973, U.S. Tax Ct. 1972, U.S. Ct. Claims 1972, U.S. Supreme Ct. 1977; cert. mediator, SC, 2006. Intern ct. of claims sect., tax divsn. U.S. Dept. Justice, 1971; law clk. to chief judge U.S. Ct. Claims, Washington, 1972-74; ptnr. firm Edwards Wood, Duggan & Reese, Greer and Greenville, 1974-78; asst. prof. law Cumberland Law Sch., Samford U., Birmingham, Ala., 1978-79; faculty Nat. Inst. Trial Advocacy: N.E. Regional Inst., 1979, 83-90, 95-97, Fla. Regional Inst., 1989; teaching team 5th intensive trial techniques course Hofstra U., 1983; assoc. then capital ptnr. firm Shutts & Bowen, Miami, 1980-85; sole practice Miami, 1985—; also Rock Hill, S.C., 1994—; of counsel Griffin, Smith, Caldwell, Helder & Helms, Monroe, NC, 2001—. Lectr. Nat. Bus. Inst. Seminars, 2003—04. Contbg. editor: The Lawyers PC; Fla. editor: Drafting Wills and Trust Agreements; substantive com. editor ABA: The Tax Lawyer, 1983-2004 Pres. Piedmont Heritage Found., Inc. 1975-78; del. State Rep. Conv., 1985, 87, 90, Fla. State Rep. Conv., 1986, 88, 90, SC State Conv., 1978; exec. committeeman Miami-Dade County Republicans, 1985-94, Mecklenberg County, NC Rep. Party, 2005—; co-legal counsel, 1990-92; apptd. Miami-Dade County Indsl. Devel. Authority, 1990-94; mem. vestry Episc. Ch., 1993-94; committeeman, former cubmaster, Boy Scouts Am., Coral Gables, Fla.; With USAF, 1965-69, Vietnam. Decorated Air Force Commendation medal; recipient Am. Jurisprudence award in real property and tax I, 1971; winner Grand prize So. Living Mag. travel photo contest, 1968. Mem. ABA (taxation sect., tchg. law com., 1994-2000), Greer C. of C. (pres. 1977, Outstanding leadership award 1976), Greater Greenville C. of C. (dir. 1977), Order Wig and Robe, Estate Planning Council South Fla., Omicron Delta Kappa. Club: Bankers (bd. govs. 1989-94). Lodge: Masons, Scottish Rite, Rotary. Office: 5345 Wilgrove Mint Hill Rd Charlotte NC 28227-3467 Office Phone: 305-374-4441. E-mail: wmwood@bellsouth.net.

WOOD, WILLIAM PRESTON, writer, lawyer; b. Bronxville, NY, Apr. 23, 1951; s. Preston and Eleanor Catherine (Auby) W. BA, Middlebury Coll., 1973; JD, U. of the Pacific, 1976. Bar: Calif. 1976, U.S. Dist. Ct. (ea. dist.) Calif. 1976. Dep. dist. atty. Sacramento County District Atty., Sacramento, 1977—82; dir. publs. Calif. Dist. Attys. Assn., Sacramento, 1984—85; chief counsel Office Sec. State, Sacramento, 1999—2003; commr. Calif. Dept. Corps., 2003—05, Calif. Undersecretary of State, 2005—07; freelance writer, Sacramento, 1985—; commr. Author: (novels) Rampage, 1985, Gangland, 1988, Fugitive City, 1990, Court of Honor, 1991, Stay of Execution, 1994, The Bone Garden, 1994, Quicksand, 1998, Pressure Point, 2005, The Bribe, 2006, (motion picture) Rampage, 1992, Broken Trust, 1995; co-author (TV series) Kaz, 1978; contbr. articles to profl. jours. Pres. Citizens for a Better Sacramento, 1986. Mem. Writers Guild Am.-West. Republican. Episcopalian. Office Phone: 916-324-9011.

WOOD, WILLIS BOWNE, JR., retired utilities executive; b. Kansas City, Mo., Sept. 15, 1934; s. Willis Bowne Sr. and Mina (Henderson) W.; m. Dixie Gravel, Aug. 31, 1955; children: Bradley, William, Josh. BS in Petroleum Engring., U. Tulsa, 1957; grad. advanced mgmt. program, Harvard U., 1983. With So. Calif. Gas Co., LA, 1960-74, from v.p. to sr. v.p., 1975-80, exec. v.p., 1983-84; pres., CEO Pacific Lighting Gas Supply Co., LA, 1981-83; from sr. v.p. to chmn., pres., CEO, Pacific Enterprises, LA, 1984-93, chmn., CEO, 1993-98; ret., 1998. Bd. dirs. Automobile Club So. Calif., chmn. bd. dirs., 2005—07, vice chmn., 2007—. Past bd. dirs. LA World Affairs Coun.; past dir., past chmn. bus coun. for Sustainable Energy Future, 1994—; past dir. Pacific Coun. Internat. Affairs; trustee U. So. Calif.; past trustee, past vice-chmn. Harvey Mudd Coll., Claremont, Calif., 1984—2005; trustee emeritus, past chmn. Calif. Med. Ctr. Found., LA, 1983—2002; past trustee, past pres. SW Mus., LA; trustee John and Dora Haynes Found., 1998—. Recipient Disting. Alumni U. Tulsa, 1995; inductee U. Tulsa Engring. Hall of Fame, 2001. Mem. Soc. Petroleum Engrs., Calif. State C. of C. (past bd. dirs.), Am. Automobile Assn. (dir. 1999-, chmn. 2002-05), NAM (past bd. dirs.), Hacienda Golf Club, Calif. Club, Shady Canyon Golf Club. Republican.

WOODALL, BRIDGETTE A., archivist; d. Glen A. and Linda J. Woodall. BA, Adrian Coll., Mich., 1993; MDiv, Emory U., Atlanta, 1997; MS, Simmons Coll., Boston, 2005. Office adminstr. World Meth. Evangelism Inst., Atlanta, 1995—97; asst. archivist spl. collections Emory U., Woodruff Libr., 1995—96; asst. pastor Point Pl. United Ch. Christ, Toledo, 1998—99; substitute tchr. Monroe County Intermediate Sch. Dist., Mich., 1998—2000; sr. supr., head receiving B. Dalton Bookseller (divsn. Barnes & Noble Booksellers), Toledo, 1999—2000; dept. mgr. Barnes & Noble Booksellers, 2000—02; dept. supr. trade books MIT and Harvard Med. Coop. Collegiate Bookstores (divsn. Barnes & Noble Booksellers), Cambridge, 2002—04; archives intern New Eng. Hist. Genealogical Soc., Boston, 2002—03; records mgmt. intern Archdiocese Boston Archives, 2004—05, project archivist for reconfiguration, 2005—06, assoc. archivist, 2006—. Internship supr. archives program Simmons Coll., Boston, 2006—. Contbr. columns in newspapers. Pen pal, mentor Promising Pals Program, Boston, 2005—; reading tutor Helping One Student to Succeed, Bedford, Mich., 1997—98; vol. Village Players Theatrical Group, Toledo, 1997—2002; prison chaplain Ga. Justice Project, Atlanta, 1995—96. Mem.: Assn. Cath. Diocesan Archivists, New Eng. Archivists, Soc. Am. Archivists, Phi Eta Sigma, Phi Alpha Theta, Order Omega, Mortar Bd., Chi Omega. Avocations: reading, writing, travel, gardening. Office: Archdiocese Boston Archives 2121 Commonwealth Ave Brighton MA 02135

WOODALL, DAVID MONROE, engineer, researcher, dean; b. Perryville, Ark., Aug. 2, 1945; m. Linda Carol Page, June 6, 1966; 1 child, Zachary Page. BA, Hendrix Coll., 1967; MS, Columbia U., 1968; PhD, Cornell U., 1976. Registered profl. engr., Idaho. Nuc. engr. Westinghouse Corp., Pitts., 1968-70; asst. prof. U. Rochester, NYC, 1974-77, U. N.Mex., Albuquerque, 1977-79, assoc. prof., 1979-83, chair dept., 1980-83, prof., 1984-86; group physics mgr. Idaho Nat. Engring. Lab., Idaho Falls, 1986-92; assoc. dean, dir. rsch. U. Idaho, Moscow, 1992-99, acting dean, 1999; dean coll. sci., engring., math. U. Alaska, Fairbanks, 1999—2003; dir. Ctr. for Nanosensor Tech., 2001—03. Provost & v.p. for academic affairs, Oregon Inst. of Tech., 2003—, EAC commr. Accreditation Bd. Engring. Tech., 1990-95, bd. dir., 1997-2003; cons. in field. Contbr. articles to profl. jours. Grantee NSF, DOE, AFOSR, Office Naval Rsch., DMEA, others. Mem. Am. Nuc. Soc. (chpt. chair 1982-83), Am. Soc. Engring. Edn. (divsn. chair 1993, 95, chair engring. rsch. coun., v.p.). Office: Oregon Institute of Technology 3201 Campus Drive Klamath Falls OR 97601 E-mail: david.woodall@oit.edu.

WOODALL, JERRY M., research scientist, educator; b. Tacoma Park, Md., Sept. 5, 1938; m. Susan Woodall; children: Chandler B., Marshall O., Debra M., Sunny L., Serena J. BS, MIT, 1960; PhD in Elec. Engring., Cornell U., 1982. Various positions, Thomas J Watson Rsch. Ctr. IBM; prof. microelectronics Charles William Harrison Dist. Purdue U., West Lafayette, Ind., 1993—99; C. Baldwin Sawyer prof. of elec. engring. and prof. of applied physics Yale U., New Haven, 1999—; also co-founder and Chief Sci. Officer LightSpin Tech. Inc., Bethesda, Md. Dir. NSF Materials Rsch. Sci. and Engring. Ctr. Tech. Enabling Heterostructural Materials. Recipient Heinrich Welker Gold medal Inst. Physics, 1988. Fellow IEEE (Jack A. Morton award 1984), Am. Vacuum Soc. (pres.-elect 1996-97, Medard Welch award 1990), Electrochem. Soc. (Solid State Sci. and Tech. award 1985), Am. Phys. Soc.; mem. Nat. Acad. Engrs. Office: Chief Sci Officer LightSpin Tech Inc PO Box 30198 Bethesda MD 20824-0198 also: Becton Ctr Rm 507 Yale Univ PO Box 208284 New Haven CT 06520-8284 E-mail: jerry.woodall@yale.edu.

WOODALL, SAMUEL ROY, JR., lawyer; b. July 8, 1936; s. Samuel Roy Woodall; m. Jane Marvin Brock, Aug. 5, 1958; children: Samuel Roy III, Lawrence B., Claiborne A., George G. BA, U. Ky., 1958, LLB, 1962; postgrad., Yale U., 1959. Bar: Ky. 1962. Atty. Ky. Dept. Ins., 1962-64, gen. counsel, 1965-66; commr. ins. Commonwealth Ky., 1966-68; assoc. firm Wyatt, Grafton and Sloss, Louisville, 1968-69, ptnr., 1969-72; pres. Western Pioneer Life Ins. Co. (and predecessors), Louisville, 1972-76; asst. to pres. Am. Life & Accident Ins. Co., Louisville, 1976-80; pres. Nat. Assn. Life Cos., Washington, 1980-93; v.p. and chief counsel state rels. Am. Coun. Life Ins., Washington, 1993-98; with Morris, Manning & Martin (Atlanta-based firm), Washington, 1998—2001; ins. cons. Congl. Rsch. Svc., Libr. of Congres, Washington, 2001—; sr. ins. policy analyst U.S. Treasury Dept., 2002—. Guest instr. ins. law U. Louisville, 1968—69. Note editor: U. Ky. Law Rev., 1961—62. Pres. Citizen's Met. Planning coun., Louisville, 1970—71; chmn. City of Louisville Riverfront Commn., 1970—75, Ky. Heritage Commn., 1964—77; bd. dirs. Bingham Child Guidance Clinic, Louisville, 1969—76, Youth Performing Arts Coun., 1979—80. Named one of Ky.'s 3 Outstanding Young Men, Ky. Jr. C. of C., 1968; recipient Sullivan medallion, U. Ky., 1958; fellow Woodrow Wilson, Yale U., 1959. Mem.: ABA, Fedn. Ins. Counsel, D.C. Bar Assn., Ky. Bar Assn., Phi Beta Kappa, Phi Alpha Delta (pres. chpt. 1961—62). Home: 2851 29th St NW Washington DC 20008-4111 Office: US Dept Treasury 15th and Pennsylvania Ave NW Washington DC 20220

WOODALL, THOMAS A., state supreme court justice; b. Meridian, Miss., July 14, 1950; m. Debbie Bogan, 1972; children: Scott, Matthew, Claire. BA in History, Millsaps Coll., 1972; JD, U. Va., 1975. Former legal editor Michie Co.; with Rives and Peterson, Birmingham, Ala., 1975—91; ptnr. Woodall and Maddox, Birmingham, 1991—96; circuit judge Jefferson County, 1996—2001; assoc. justice Ala. Supreme Ct., 2001—. Mem. Ala. Pattern Jury Instrn.-Civil Com., 1985—2001, vice chmn., 1992—2001. Mem.: Birmingham Bar Assn. (chair com. on grievance, civil ct. procedures and membership). Republican. Methodist. Office: Ala State Supreme Ct 300 Dexter Ave Montgomery AL 36104-3741 *

WOODARD, ALFRE, actress; b. Tulsa, Nov. 8, 1953; m. Roderick Spencer, 1983; 2 children. Student, Boston U. Appeared in (films) Remember My Name, 1976, Health, Cross Creek, 1983 (Acad. award nomination), Extremities, 1986, Scrooged, 1988, Mandela, 1988, Miss Firecracker, 1989, Grand Canyon, 1991, The Gun in Betty Lou's Handbag, 1992, Passion Fish, 1992, Heart and Souls, 1993, Rich in Love, 1993, Bopha!, 1993, Blue Chips, 1994, Crooklyn, 1994, How to Make an American Quilt, 1995, Statistically Speaking, 1995, Primal Fear, 1996, A Step Toward Tomorrow, 1996, Stat Trek: First Contact, 1996, Follow Me Home, 1996, Down in the Delta, 1998, Brown Sugar, 1998, Mumford, 1999, What's Cooking, 2000, Love and Basketball, 2000, K-PAX, 2001, Baby of the Family, 2002, (voice) The Wild Thornberrys Movie, 2002, The Singing Detective, 2003, The Core, 2003, Radio, 2003, The Forgotten, 2004, Beauty Shop, 2005, Something New, 2006, (TV series) Tucker's Witch, 1982-83, Sara, 1985, St. Elsewhere, 1985-87, Hill Street Blues (Emmy award for guest appearance in drama series 1984), L.A. Law (Emmy award for guest appearance in drama series 1987), Desperate Housewives (Screen Actors Guild Award for outstanding performance by an ensemble in a comedy series, 2006), 2005-; (TV spls.) For Colored Girls Who Have Considered Suicide/When the Rainbow is Enuf, Trial of the Moke, Words by Heart, (TV films) A Mother's Courage: The Mary Thomas Story, Child Saver, Ambush Murder, Freedom Road, 1979, Sophisticated Gents, 1981, The Killing Floor, Unnatural Causes, 1986, Mandela, 1987, The Child Saver, Sweet Revenge, 1990, Blue Bayou, 1990, Race to Freedom: The Underground Railroad, 1994, Wizard of Oz in Concert, 1995, The Piano Lesson, 1995, Journey to Mars, 1996, Gulliver's Travels, 1996, Member of the Wedding, 1997, Miss Evers' Boys, 1997, Cadillac Desert (miniseries), 1997, Funny Valentines, 1999 (also exec. prodr.), Holiday Heart, 2000, A Wrinkle in Time (miniseries), 2003, The Water is Wide, 2005, others, (plays) For Colored Girls Who Have Considered Suicide, When the Rainbow is Enuf, (off-Broadway plays) A Map of the World, 1985, A Winter's Tale 1989, So Nice They Named Twice, Horatio, What's Cookin', 2000, Love and Basketball, 2000, Dinosaur, 2000. Recipient Emmy awards for guest appearance in drama series, Josephine Premice award for sustained excellence Classical Theatre of Harlem, 2006. Office: Touchstone TV 100 Universal Plz Bldg 2128 Ste G Universal City CA 91608

WOODARD, CAROL JANE, educational consultant; b. Buffalo, Jan. 19, 1929; d. Harold August and Violet Maybelle (Landsittel) Young; m. Ralph Arthur Woodard, Aug. 19, 1950; children: Camaron Jane, Carsen Jane, Cooper Ralph. BA, Hartwick Coll., 1950; MA, Syracuse U., 1952, PhD, SUNY, Buffalo, 1972; LHD (hon.), Hartwick Coll., 1991; postgrad., Bank St. Coll., Harvard U. Cert. tchr., NY State. Tchr., Orchard Park, NY, 1950-51, Danville, Ind., 1951-52, Akron, NY, 1952-54; dir. Garden Nursery Sch., Williamsville, NY, 1955-65; tchr. Amherst Coop. Nursery Sch., NY, 1967-69; asst. prof. early childhood edn. SUNY, Buffalo, 1969-72, lab. demonstration tchr. and student teaching supr., 1969-76, assoc. prof., 1972-79, prof., 1979-88, prof. emeritus, 1988—; dir. Consultants in Early Childhood, 1988—. Cons. Lutheran Ch. Am., Villa Maria Coll., Buffalo Pub. Sch., Buffalo Mus. Sci., Headstart Tng. Programs, Erie Cmty. Coll., NY State Dept. Edn., numerous workshops.; cons. sch. systems, indsl. firms, pub., civic orgns. in child devel.; vis. prof. The Netherlands and East China Univ., Shanghai, People's Republic of China; sci. trainer The Wright Group, 1995. Author 7 books for young children, 2 textbooks in field; co-author: Physical Science in Early Childhood, 1987; co-author nat. curriculum for ch. sch. for 3-yr.-olds; author: (booklet) You Can Help Your Baby Learn; author/coord. TAKE CARE child protection project, 1987; contbr. chpt. to books, articles to profl. jour. Trustee Hartwick Coll., Oneonta, NY, 1978-87, trustee emeritus, 2004-; cons. EPIC Birth to Three Program, 1992; design cons. indoor playground Noah's Ark Jewish Ctr., Buffalo, 1992; Sites Project coord., cons. Let's Talk project Buffalo Pub. Sch., 1994—2005; student tchg. supr. SUNY, Fredonia, 1994-2004. Mem. Nat. Assn. Edn. Young Children, Early Childhood Edn. Council Western NY, Assn. Childhood Edn. Internat., Phi Delta Kappa, Pi Lambda Theta. Home: 85 Ruskin Road East Aurora NY 14052-3028

WOODARD, CATHERINE, arts patron; m. Nelson Blitz Jr.; children: Perri Blitz, Allison Blitz. BA in History magna cum laude, Wake Forest Univ., 1981; MS in Journalism, Columbia Univ., 1982. Reporter Fort Worth Star-Telegram, Tex., 1982—84, NY Newsday, 1984—94; dep. editor Newsday Direct, 1994—95; news editor, iGuide News Corp., NYC, 1995—96. Named one of Top 200 Collectors, ARTnews Mag., 2004; recipient James Wright Brown Pub. Svc. award, Deadline Club, NY Newspaper Pub. award, Soc. of Silurians award. Mem.: Mus. Modern Art Print Associates, Artists Space (bd. dir., coord. new media), Phi Beta Kappa. Avocation: Collecting Viennese furniture, prints and works on paper, especially Much, Picasso, Kirchner and Johns. Home Phone: 212-879-8923.

WOODARD, DIANE E., music educator; d. Harry Moore and Mary Purdy Woodard; m. Bruce N. Wardrep, Sept. 12, 1998. B in Music Edn., Ga. Coll., 1970; MusM, Ga. State U., 1975, cert. in edn. specialist, 1985, PhD, 1994. Cert. tchg. Ga. Choral dir. Babb Jr. HS, Forest Park, Ga., 1970—79, Jonesboro HS, Ga., 1979—2001, chair music dept., 1981—91; asst. choral dir. Woodward Acad., College Park, Ga., 2001—02; choral dir. Galloway Sch., Atlanta, 2002—. Music tchr. Fountain Jr. H.S., Forest Park, 1971—72. Organist, choir dir. St. Timothy's Luth. Ch., Forest Park, 1983—87; mem. Atlanta Symphony Orch. Chorus, 1983—. Mem.: MENC (so. divsn. bd. dirs. 1995—97, nat. assembly state pres. 1995—97), Am. Choral Dirs. Assn. (treas. Ga. chpt. 1977—80), Ga. Music Educators Assn. (organizing chair all-state chorus event 1978, 1979, chair choral divsn. 1979—81, organizing chair all-state chorus event 1982, 1983, 1985, region chair all-state chorus auditions 1994, pres. 1995—97, so. divsn. bd. nat. conf. 1995—98, nat. assembly state pres. 1997, exec. com. 1997—98, bd. dirs. 1997—98, region chair all-state chorus auditions 1998, 1999, 2000, 2002—05, dist. chair all-state chorus auditions 1990, coun. 1975—87, Music Educator of Yr. 2004). Office: Galloway Sch 215 W Wieuca Rd NW Atlanta GA 30342

WOODARD, JON L., lawyer; b. Pa., Feb. 17, 1973; s. John B. and Eleanor F. Woodard. BS, AB, Miami U., Oxford, Ohio, 1996; JD, Pa. State U., Carlisle, 1999. Bar: Pa., U.S. Patent and Trademark Office. Assoc. MacDonald Illig Jones & Britton LLP, Erie, Pa., 1994—. Office: MacDonald Illig Jones & Britton LLP 100 State St Ste 700 Erie PA 16507 Office Phone: 814-870-7664.

WOODARD, JOSEPH LAMAR, law librarian, emeritus professor; b. Auburndale, Fla., Dec. 28, 1937; s. Wilbur Allen and Florence Virginia (Ladd) Woodard; m. Eleanor Eugenia Cummings, Aug. 7, 1964; children: Robert Edward, James Frederick. BA, U. Fla., 1959, JD, 1962; MLS, Columbia U., 1964. Bar: Fla. 1962, U.S. Dist. Ct. (mid. dist.) Fla. 1970. Asst. reference libr. Columbia U., NYC, 1962—64; asst. libr. Cahill, Gordon, Reindel and Ohl, NYC, 1964—65; law libr. Tulane U., 1965—69; ptnr. Schuh, Schuh and Woodard, St. Petersburg, Fla., 1969—71; law libr. Stetson U., 1971—2001, prof. law, 1979—2001, law libr., prof. emeritus, 2001—. Pres. Tampa Bay Libr. Consortium, 1981, 1988—89. Stated clk. Presbytery Tampa Bay, 2005—06. With USAR, 1957—63. Named to Hall of Fame, Stetson U. Coll. Law, 2006. Mem.: ABA, Pinellas Pub. Libr. Coop. (sec.-treas. 1993—94, pres. 1994—95), Am. Assn. Law Librs. (sec.-treas. SE chpt. 1975—78), Fla. Bar Assn. Republican. Personal E-mail: lamar@woodardfamily.org.

WOODBRIDGE, JOHN DUNNING, history professor; b. Salisbury, NC, May 24, 1941; s. Charles Jahleel and Ruth (Dunning) W.; m. Susan Jane Frerichs, June 28, 1970; children: Elisabeth Anne, Joshua, David. BA in History, Wheaton Coll., 1963; MA in History, Mich. State U., 1965; PhD de Troisième Cycle, U. Toulouse, France, 1969; MDiv, Trinity Evang. Div. Sch., Deerfield, Ill., 1971. Vis. prof. history U. Toulouse, 1968-69; asst. prof. history Trinity Coll., Deerfield, 1970-74; prof. ch. history Trinity Evang. Div. Sch., Deerfield, 1970—; vis. prof. history Northwestern U., Evanston, Ill., 1988-95. Vis. prof. religion Hautes Etudes, Sorbonne, U. Paris, 1996, 99. Author: Biblical Authority, 1982, Revolt in Prerevolutionary France, 1995; editor: Great Leaders of the Christian Church, 1988; co-editor: Historische Kritik und biblischer kanon, 1988; sr. editor Christianity Today, 1997-99. NEH fellow, 1973-74, Herzog August Bibliothek fellow, 1982, ACLS fellow, Paris, 1976-77; NEH summer grant, Chgo., 1995. Mem. Am. Soc. Eighteenth Century Studies, Soc. French History. Mem. Evangelical Free Ch. Avocation: composing music.

WOODBURN, NORMA DENMAN, biology educator, researcher; b. NYC, Nov. 19, 1921; d. George Griffin Denman and Rose Lillian Langtry; m. Robert P. Woodburn, July 21, 1946 (dec.); children: Lillian E., Pamela J., Preston M. Student in Biology, U. Mich., 1940—41; BA, Hunter Coll., NYC, 1943; degree in Biology, Bridgewater State Coll., Mass., 1980; student, U. Mass., Dartmouth, Mass., 1981—82. Cert. tchr. N.J., Mass. Jr. chemist Celanese Corp., Newark, 1943; tchr. botany Salem Coll., Winston-Salem, NC, 1943—44; tchr. sci. Gardner Sch., NYC, 1944—45, Leonard Sch., NYC, 1945—47, Fay Sch., Boston, 1948—50, Middleboro HS, 1950—87. Nat. biology tchr. methodology exch. People to People, China, 1987; aide rsch. expedition to South Pacific, Baja Mex. Dr. Eugenie Clark, 1988—2002. Author: Unwilling Captive, 1996. Vol. Burkland Elem. Sch., Middleboro, 2000—06, U.S. Agrl. Dept., Taunton, Mass., 1988—90. Recipient Recognition cert., Middleboro (Mass.) Conservation Commn., 1986, Ret. award, NEA, 1987, Accomplishment award, Plymouth County Edn. Assn., 1987, Recognition cert., Middleboro (Mass.) Pub. Libr., 2003; grantee Marine Sci., NSF, 1980. Mem.: Nat. Biology Tchr. Assn. (life), Nat. Fedn. Women's Clubs. Avocations: conservation, marine biology. Home: 4 Nook Rd Plymouth MA 02360

WOODBURN, RALPH ROBERT, JR., lawyer; b. Haverhill, Mass., Nov. 3, 1946; s. Ralph Robert and Josephine Marie (McClure) W.; m. Janet M. Smith, Sept. 15, 1985. BA, Mich. State U., 1967; JD, Harvard U., 1972; LLM, Boston U., 1981. Bar: Mass. 1972, U.S. Tax Ct. 1987. Assoc. Bowers, Fortier & Lakin, Boston, 1972-76; from assoc. to ptnr. Hausserman, Davison & Shattuck, Boston, 1976-83; ptnr. Palmer & Dodge, Boston, 1983—2005, Edwards Angell Palmer & Dodge, Boston, 2005—. Tchr. Harvard Ctr. for Lifelong Learning, Cambridge, Mass., 1986-89; chmn. Wellesley Cable Access Bd., 1993-95. Contbr. articles to Boston Bar Jour. and Estate Planning. Treas. Exeter Assn. of New Eng., Boston, 1985-89, v.p., 1989-91, pres., 1991-93. Fellow Am. Coll. Trust and Estate Counsel; mem. ABA, Boston Bar Assn. (chmn. probate legislation 1983-93), Boston Com. Fgn. Rels., Brae Burn Country Club (Newton, Mass.), Keokuk Country Club, Harvard Club of Boston, Boston Probate and Estate Planning Forum (program chair 1996-97, moderator 1997-98), Harvard Travellers Club. Home: 25 Cypress Rd Wellesley MA 02481-2918 Office: Edwards Angell Palmer & Dodge LLP 111 Huntington Ave Boston MA 02199-7613 Office Phone: 617-239-0123. Business E-mail: rwoodburn@eapdlaw.com.

WOODBURY, LARK KARIN, secondary school educator; b. Springfield, Vt., Dec. 18, 1950; d. William Henry Rogers Jr. and Dorothy Jeane Lett Rogers, Clayton M. Longhurst (Stepfather); m. Douglas Alma Woodbury, May 15, 1970; children: Susan Woodbury Dearden, Michael Douglas, Nathan Rogers, Jill Woodbury Johnson, Paulette Tom Toledo. BS, Weber State U., Ogden, Utah, 1995, MEd, 1999. Lic. cosmetologist Utah, cert. choice theory and reality therapy William Glasser Inst. Sales rep. Avon Products, Layton and Ogden, Utah, 1974—2000, stand-in mgr., 1978—90; tchr. specialist youth in custody Davis Sch. Dist., Farmington, Utah, 1995—97; tchr. Layton HS, Davis Sch. Dist., 1997—, coord. svc. learning program, 2001—04. Utah state coord. Dirksen Congl. Ctr., Pekin, Ill., 2001—02. Contbr. state curriculum and the Internet Connections Project; editor: (online lessons) Service Learning. Adult advisor and choices instr. Layton Youth Ct., 1998—2006; youth leader LDS Ch., Layton, 2000—06. Recipient Recognition award, Davis Sch. Bd., 1997, Legendary Lancer award, Layton High Student Assn., 2001, 2006; grantee, Citibank, 2006. Mem.: NEA, Nat. Coun. of Social Studies, Davis Ednl. Assn., Utah Edn. Assn., Layton Kiwanis (hon.; Layton HS Key Club advisor 1998—), Gold Key Honor Soc., Psi Chi, Phi Alpha Theta, Phi Kappa Phi. Avocations: travel, writing music, dining out. Home: 2186 North 2300 East Layton UT 84040 Office: Layton HS 440 Lancer Ln Layton UT 84041 Home Phone: 801-546-6701; Office Phone: 801-402-4961. Business E-Mail: lwoodbury@dsdmail.net.

WOODBURY, MARDA LIGGETT, librarian, writer; b. NYC, Sept. 20, 1925; d. Walter W. and Edith F. (Fleischer) Liggett; m. Philip J. Evans, Sept. 1948 (div. 1950); 1 child, Mark W. Evans; m. Mark Lee Woodbury, 1956 (div. 1969); children: Brian, Heather. Student, Bklyn. Coll., 1942-44; BA in Chemistry and Polit. Sci., Bard Coll., Annandale-on-Hudson, NY, 1946; BS in Libr. Studies, Columbia U., NYC, 1948; postgrad., U. Calif., Berkeley, 1955-56, 60-61, MJ, 1995. Cert. tchr. Libr. various spl., med. and pub. librs., San Francisco, 1948—60, Coll. Pk. H.S., Mt. Diablo, Calif., 1962-67; elem. sch. libr. Oakland and Berkeley, Calif., 1967-69; libr. dir. Far West Lab. Ednl. Rsch. & Devel., San Francisco, 1969-73; libr., editor Gifted Resource Ctr., San Mateo, Calif., 1973-75; libr. cons. Rsch. Ventures, Berkeley, Calif., 1975—2003; libr. dir. Life Chiropractic Coll., San Lorenzo, Calif., 1980-95. Author: A Guide to Sources of Educational Information, 1976, 2d edit., 1982, Selecting Instructional Materials, 1978, Selecting Materials for Instruction, Vol. I: Issues and Policies, 1979, Vol. II: Media and the Curriculum, 1980, Vol. III: Subject Areas and Implementation, 1980, Childhood Information Resources, 1985 (Outstanding Ref. Work, Assn. Ref. Librs. 1985), Youth Information Resources, 1987, Stopping the Presses: The Murder of Walter W. Liggett, 1998; mem. editorial bd. Ref. Libr., 1980-95. Home: 145 Monte Cresta Ave Apt 402 Oakland CA 94611-4809 Office Phone: 510-653-5876. Personal E-mail: mardawood@peoplepc.com.

WOODBURY, MAX ATKIN, mathematics professor; b. St. George, Utah, Apr. 30, 1917; s. Angus Munn and Grace (Atkin) W.; m. Lida Gottsch, May 30, 1947; children— Carolyn, Max TenEyck, Christopher, Gregory. BS, U. Utah, 1939; MS, U. Mich., 1941, PhD, 1948; M.P.H., U. N.C., Chapel Hill, 1977. Mem. faculty U. Mich., 1947-49; mem. Inst. for Adv. Study, Princeton, N.J., 1949-50; mem. faculty Princeton U., 1950-52, U. Pa., 1952-54; prin. investigator logistics research project Office Naval Research, George Washington U., 1954-56; faculty NYU, 1956-65; prof. computer sci. Duke U., prof. biomath. Med. Ctr., 1966-88, sr. fellow Ctr. for Study of Aging and Human Devel., 1975—, sr. fellow, sr. scientist Ctr. Demographic Studies, 1985—, prof. emeritus, 1987—. Pres. Biomed. Information-processing Orgn., 1961-62, Inst. for Biomed. Computer Research, 1961-71; cons. WHO, UNIVAC, CBS on computer election forecasts, 1952-62, sci. orgns., univs., govt. agys., corps. Contbr. articles to profl. jours. Served with USAAF, 1941-46, MTO. USPHS, NIH grantee, also other govt. agys., 1947—; recipient MERIT award Nat. Inst. on Aging, NIH, June 1, 1988-May 31, 1998. Fellow AAAS, Am. Statis. Assn., Inst. Math. Statistics; mem. numerous sci., profl. socs., Phi Beta Kappa, Sigma Xi, Phi Kappa Phi (inventor of GoM methodology). Home: 1901 Hoke Ave Birmingham AL 35217-3523

WOODBURY, RICHARD BENJAMIN, anthropologist, educator; b. West Lafayette, Ind., May 16, 1917; s. Charles Goodrich and Marion (Benjamin) W.; m. Nathalie Ferris Sampson, Sept. 18, 1948. Student, Oberlin Coll., 1934-36; BS in Anthropology cum laude, Harvard U., 1939, MA, 1942, PhD, 1949; postgrad., Columbia U., 1939-40. Archeol. research, Ariz., 1938, 39, Fla., 1940, Guatemala, 1947-49, El Morro Nat. Monument, N.Mex., 1953-56, Tehuacan, Mex., 1964; archaeologist United Fruit Co. Zaculeu Project, Guatemala, 1947-50; assoc. prof. anthropology U. Ky., 1950-52, Columbia U., 1952-58; rsch. assoc. prof. anthropology interdisciplinary arid lands program U. Ariz., 1959-63; curator archeology and anthropology U.S. Nat. Mus., Smithsonian Instn., Washington, 1963-69, acting. head office anthropology, 1965-66, chmn. office anthropology, 1966-67; prof., chmn. dept. anthropology U. Mass., Amherst, 1969-73, prof., 1973-81, prof. emeritus, 1981—, acting assoc. provost, dean grad. sch., 1973-74. Mem. divsn. anthropology and psychology NRC, 1954-57; bd. dirs. Archaeol. Conservancy, 1979-84, Valley Health Plan, Amherst, 1981-84, Mus. of No. Ariz., 1983-90; liason rep. for Smithsonian Instn., Com. for Recovery of Archeol. Remains, 1965-69; assoc. seminar on ecol. systems and cultural evolution Columbia U., 1964-73; mem. exec. com. bd. dirs. Human Relations Area Files, Inc., New Haven, Conn., 1968-70; cons. Conn. Hist. Commn., 1970-72. Author (with A.S. Trik) The Ruins of Zaculeu, Guatemala, 2 vols., 1953, Prehistoric Stone Implements of Northeastern Arizona, 1954, Alfred V. Kidder, 1973, Sixty Years of Southwestern Archaeology, 1993, (chpt.) (with James A. Neely) The Prehistory of the Tehuacan Valley, Vol. 4, 1972; editor: (with I.A. Sanders) Societies Around the World (2 vols.), 1953, (with others) The Excavation of Hawikuh, 1966, Am. Antiquity, 1954-58, Abstracts of New World Archaeology; editor-in-chief: Am. Anthropologist, 1975-78; mem. editorial bd.: Am. Jour. Archeology, 1957-72. Mem. sch. com., Shutesbury, Mass., 1979—82; chmn. fin. com. Friends of Amherst Stray Animals (Dakin Animal Shelter), 1983—85, trustee, 1991—; mem. Shutesbury Hist. Commn., 1998—2006, sec., 1999—2004. With USAF, 1942—45. Fellow, Mus. No. Ariz., 1985. Fellow AAAS (coun. rep. Am. Anthrop. Assn. 1961-63, com. on desert and arid zones rsch. Southwest and Rocky Mountains divsn. 1958-64, vice-chair 1962-64, com. arid lands 1969-74, sec. 1970-72), Am. Anthrop. Assn. (exec. bd. 1963-66, A.V. Kidder award 1989), Archeol. Inst. Am. (exec. com. 1965-67); mem. Soc. Am. Archeology (treas. 1953-54, pres. 1958-59, chmn. fin. com. 1987-89, Fiftieth Anniversary award 1985, Disting. Svc. award 1988), Ariz. Archeol. and Hist. Soc., Nature Conservancy, Archeol. Conservancy (life). Office: U Mass Dept Anthropology Machmer Hall Amherst MA 01003

WOODCOCK, DAVID GEOFFREY, architect, educator; b. Manchester, Eng., May 28, 1937; s. Herbert Edwin and Constance Mary (Bristol) Woodcock; m. Kathleen Mary Bishop, Oct. 1, 1960 (dec. 1964); 1 child, Jonathan Alfred; m. Valerie Frances Gubbins, July 4, 1964; children: Frances Mary, Penelope Jane. BA in Architecture with 1st class honors, U. Manchester, 1960, D in Town Planning, 1966. Arch. emeritus, Tex. Lectr. U. Manchester, 1961; asst. prof. Tex. A&M U., College Station, 1962-66; sr. lectr. Kent. Inst. Art & Design, Canterbury, England, 1966—70; assoc. prof. Tex. A&M U., College Station, 1970—76, prof., 1976—; dir. Ctr. Heritage Conservation, 1991—2007. Pvt. practice, Canterbury, 1966—70, College Station, 1980—. Bd. dirs. Opera and Performing Arts Soc., Tex. A&M U., 1980—83, 1988—91, pres., 1993—94; peer reviewer U.S. Gen. Svc. Adminstrn., 2004—; active Episc. Diocese Tex. Archtl. Commn., 1987—95; mem. adv. bd. Hammons Sch. Architecture Drury Coll., Mo., 1990—93, Savannah (Ga.) Coll. Arts and Design/Architecture, 1987—93. Recipient Rsch. Excellence award, Tex. Hist. Commn., 1991, Romieniec award for Archtl. Edn., Tex. Soc. Archs., 1995, Truett Latimer Profl. award, Preservation Tex., Inc., 1998. Fellow: AIA (hist. resource com. adv. group 2005—), Assn. Collegiate Schs. Architecture (regional dir. 1981—84, Disting. prof. 1991), Assn. Preservation Tech. Internat. (bd. dirs. 1990—, v.p. 1998—99, pres. 1999—2001, Harley J. McKee award 2003), Soc. Antiquaries London; mem.: Nat. Coun. Preservation Edn. Avocations: drawing, cross disciplinary education. Office: Tex A&M U Dept Architecture College Station TX 77843-3137 Office Phone: 979-845-7850. Business E-Mail: d-woodcock@tamu.edu.

WOODCOCK, JANET, federal official; b. Washington, Pa., Aug. 29, 1948; d. John and Frances (Crocker) W.; m. Roger Henry Miller, Nov. 16, 1981; children: Kathleen Miller, Susanne Miller. BS cum laude, Bucknell U., 1970; MD, Northwestern U., Chgo., 1977. Diplomate Am. Bd. Internal Medicine. Intern Hershey Med. Ctr./Pa. State U., 1977-78, resident in internal medicine, 1978-80, chief resident in medicine, 1980-81; fellow in rheumatology U. Calif./VA Med. Ctr., San Francisco, 1982-84; instr. medicine divsn. rheumatology and immunology VA Med. Ctr., San Francisco, 1984-85; med. officer divsn. biol. investigational new drugs Ctr. for Biologics Evaluation and Rsch./FDA, Rockville, Md., 1986-87, group leader divsn. biol. investigational new drugs, 1987-88, dep. dir. divsn. biol. investigational new drugs, 1988, dir. divsn. biol. investigational new drugs, 1988-90; dir. office of therapeutics rsch. and rev. Ctr. for Biologics Evaluation and Rsch., FDA, Rockville, Md., 1992-94, acting dep. dir., 1990-92; dir. Ctr. for Drug Evaluation and Rsch., FDA, Rockville, Md., 1994—2003; dep. commr. ops. FDA, Rockville, Md., 2003—. Instr. medicine, asst. prof. divsn. gen. internal medicine Hershey Med. Ctr./Pa. State U., 1981; analytical chemist rsch. divsn. A.B. Dick Co., Niles, Ill., 1971-73. Nat. Merit scholar Bucknell U., 1966, Pa. State scholar, 1966; Rsch. fellow Am. Rheumatism Assn.; VA Investigator grantee, 1985. Mem. Alpha Omega Alpha, Alpha Lambda Delta. Office: Ctr Drug Evaluation & Rsch US Food & Drug Admin 5600 Fishers Lane Rockville MD 20857

WOODEN, JOHN ROBERT, former college basketball coach; b. Martinsville, Ind., Oct. 14, 1910; s. Joshua Hugh and Roxie (Rothrock) W.; m. Nellie C. Riley, Aug. 8, 1932; children: Nancy Anne, James Hugh. BS, Purdue U., 1932; MS, Ind. State U., 1947. Athletic dir., basketball and baseball coach Ind. State Tchrs. Coll., 1946-48; head basketball coach UCLA, 1948-75. Lectr. to colls., coaches, business. Author: Practical Modern Basketball, 1966, They Call Me Coach, 1972; co-author: Wooden--a Lifetime of Reflections and Observations On and Off the Court, 1997, Inch and Miles--Pyramid to Success for Kids, 2004, One on One, 2004; contbr. articles to profl. jours. Served to lt. USNR, 1943-46. Named All-Am. basketball player Purdue U., 1930-32, Coll. Basketball Player Yr., 1932, to All-Time All-Am. Team Helms Athletic Found., 1943, Nat. Basketball Hall of Fame, Springfield (Mass.) Coll., as player, 1960, as coach, 1970, Ind. State Basketball Hall of Fame, 1962, Calif. Father of Yr., 1964, 75, Coach of Yr. U.S. Basketball Writers Assn., 1964, 67, 69, 70, 72, 73, Sportsman of Yr. Sports Illustrated, 1973, GTE Acad. All-Am., 1994, Nat. Collegiate Basketball Hall of Fame, 2006; recipient Whitney Young award Urban League, 1973, 1st ann. Velvet Covered Brick award Layman's Leadership Inst., 1974, 1st ann. Dr. James Naismith Peachbasket award, 1974, Medal of Excellence Bellarmine Coll., 1985, Sportslike Pathfinder award to Hoosier with extraordinary svc. on behalf of Am. youth, 1993, 40 for the Age award Sports Illustrated, 1994, the 1st Frank G. Wells Disney award for role model to youth, 1995, Disting. Am. award Pres. Reagan, 1995, Svc. to Mankind award Lexington Theol. Sem., 1995, NCAA Theodore Roosevelt Sportsman award, 1995, Vince Lombardi award for excellence, 2000, Ind. Legend award, 2000, Presdl. Medal of Freedom, 2003, Pres. Ford award NCAA, 2006; named Basketball Coach of Century, 2000. *I have tried to live the philosophy of my personal definition of success which I formulated in the middle thirties shortly after I entered the teaching profession. Not being satisfied that success was merely the accumulation of material possessions or the attainment of a position of power or prestige, I chose to define success as "peace of mind which can be attained only through the self-satisfaction that comes from knowing you did your best to become the best that you are capable of becoming.".*

WOODFORD, ARTHUR MACKINNON, retired library director, historian; b. Detroit, Nov. 23, 1940; s. Frank Bury and Mary-Kirk (MacKinnon) W.; m. Mary R. Woodford; children: Mark, Cristopher, Amy, Joyce, Kathleen, Lindsey. Student, U. Wis., 1958-60; BA in History, Wayne State U., 1963; AM in LS, U. Mich., 1964. Libr. Detroit Pub. Libr., 1964-74; asst. dir. Grosse Pointe (Mich.) Pub. Libr., 1974-77; dir. St. Clair Shores (Mich.) Pub. Libr., 1977—2005; ret., 2005—. Author: All Our Yesterdays, 1969, Detroit and Its Banks, 1974, Detroit: American Urban Renaissance, 1979, Charting The Inland Seas, 1991, Tonnancour, 1994, vol. 2, 1996, This Is Detroit: 1701-2001, 2001. With USNR, 1958-64. Mem. Mich. Libr. Assn. (v.p. 1988-89), Gt. Lakes Maritime Inst., Prismatic Club Detroit (pres. 1982), Algonquin Club of Detroit and Windsor (treas. 1983-93). Avocations: tennis, bridge, reading, model ship building. Home: 3284 S Channel Dr Harsens Island MI 48028

WOODFORD, PETER C., lawyer; BA, Dartmouth Coll., 1971; JD with honors, George Washington U., 1978. Bar: Ill. 1978, US Ct. Appeals (3rd, 5th, 7th cir.), US Dist. Ct. (no. dist.) Ill., US Dist. Ct. (ea. dist.) Mich., US Tax Ct. Ptnr., gen. counsel Seyfarth Shaw LLP, Chgo. Mem.: ABA. Office: Seyfarth Shaw LLP 131 S Dearborn Ste 2400 Chicago IL 60603-5577 Office Phone: 312-460-5908. Office Fax: 312-460-7908. Business E-Mail: pwoodford@seyfarth.com.

WOODHOUSE, GAY VANDERPOEL, former state attorney general, lawyer; b. Torrington, Wyo., Jan. 8, 1950; d. Wayne Gaylord and Sally (Rouse) Vanderpoel; m. Randy Woodhouse, Nov. 26, 1983; children: Dustin, Houston. BA with honors, U. Wyo., 1972, JD, 1977. Bar: Wyo. 1978, U.S. Dist. Ct. Wyo., U.S. Supreme Ct. Dir. student Legal Svcs., Laramie, Wyo., 1976—77; assoc. Donald Jones Law Offices, Torrington, 1977—78; asst. atty. gen. State of Wyo., Cheyenne, 1978—84, sr. asst. atty. gen., 1984—89, spl. U.S. atty., 1987—89, asst. U.S. atty., 1990—95, chief dept. atty. gen., 1995—98, atty. gen., 1998—2000. Chmn. Wyo. Tel. Consumer Panel, Casper, 1982—86; advisor Cheyenne Halfway House, 1984—93; chmn. Wyo. Silent Witness Initiative Zero Domestic Violence by 2010, 1997, Wyo. Domestic Violence Elimination Coun., 1999—2001; mem. State Bar Commn. First Dist., 2002—05; spl. projects cons. N.Am. Securities Adminstrs. Assn., 1987—89; Chmn. bd. Pathfinder, 1987; S.E. Wyo. Mental Health. Mem.: Wyo. State Bar (pres.-elect 2006—07, pres. 2007—08), Federalist Soc. for Law and Pub.Policy Studies (v.p., Wyo. chpt. 2003—04), Prevent Child Abuse Wyo. (pres. 2004—05), Laramie County Bar Assn., Cheyenne (Wyo.) C. of C., Cheyenne Rotary (bd. dirs.), Toastmasters, Rotary. Republican. Avocations: inline speed skating, stained glass. Office: 123 Capitol Bldg Cheyenne WY 82002-0001 Mailing: PO Box 1888 Cheyenne WY 82003 Office Phone: 307-432-9399. Fax: 307-638-1975. Personal E-mail: gaywoodhouselaw@aol.com. Business E-Mail: Gay@gaywoodhouselaw.com. *

WOODHOUSE, JOHN FREDERICK, retired wholesale distribution executive; b. Wilmington, Del., Nov. 30, 1930; s. John Crawford and Anna (Houth) W.; m. Marilyn Ruth Morrow, June 18, 1955; children: John Crawford II, Marjorie Ann Woodhouse Purdy. BA, Wesleyan U., 1953, DHL, 1997; MBA, Harvard U., 1955. Bus. devel. officer Can. Imperial Bank of Commerce, Toronto, Ont., Canada, 1955—59; various fin. positions Ford Motor Co., Dearborn, Mich., 1959—64, Cooper Industries, Inc., Mount Vernon, Ohio, 1964—67, treas. Houston, 1967—69, Crescent-Niagara Corp., Buffalo, 1968—69; exec. v.p., CFO Sysco Corp., Houston, 1969—71, pres., COO, 1972—83, pres., CEO, 1983—85, chmn., CEO, 1985—96, mem. exec. and fin. coms., 1996—98, chmn. bd. dirs., chmn. exec. com., 1998—2000, sr. chmn., 2000—01; ret. Bd. dirs., men. exec. com. Shell Oil Co., 1991-2002; bd. dirs. Harvard Bus. Sch. Assocs., 1995-2001. Chmn. Mich. 16th dist. rep. Club, 1962-64; treas. Cooper Industries Found., 1967-69; trustee Wesleyan U., 1976-92, vice-chmn., 1986-92, chmn. comprehensive capital campaign, 1998-05; ruling elder Presbyn. Ch.; trustee, chmn. audit com., mem. exec. com. Mt. Holyoke Coll., South Hadley, Mass., 1996-2006; bd. dirs. Winrock Internat. Inst. Agrl. Devel., 1993-2000, mem. fin. com., mem. exec. com., chmn. investment com.; bd. advisors The Retail Food Industry Ctr., U. Minn., 1998-2002; trustee The Am. Inst. Food Distbn., Elmwood Pk., N.J., 2001—, The Food Inst., 2001—, Presbyn. Mo-Ranch Assembly, Hunt, Tex., 2002—, Meml. Park Conservancy, Houston, 2004—. Diplomate recognition Nat. Restaurant Assn., 2001, Hall of Fame award Nat. Frozen Foods Assn., 2002, Raymond Baldwin award Wesleyan U., 2005. Mem. Nat. Am. Wholesale Grocers Assn. (bd. dirs. 1990-2002, vice chmn. 1992, chmn. 1994-96), Internat. Foodservice Distbrs. Assn. (Herbert Hoover award 2000), Fin. Execs. Inst., Harvard Bus. Sch. Club, Sigma Chi (Significant Sig 1992). Avocations: backpacking, canoeing, tennis. Office: CLW Group 11111 Katy Freeway Ste 870 Houston TX 77079 Home Phone: 281-497-6127; Office Phone: 832-358-1700. E-mail: john.f.woodhouse@sbcglobal.net.

WOODHOUSE, MICHAEL A., restaurant holdings company executive; BS in Natural Scis., MS in Natural Scis., Queen's Coll., Cambridge, Eng. Exec. v.p., CFO S&A Restaurant Corp.; pres., internat. divsn. Pearle Health Svcs., Inc.; exec. v.p., CFO T.G.I. Friday's Inc., 1987; CFO Tia's Inc., Dallas; v.p., fin. Daka Internat. Inc., 1993—94, sr. v.p., CFO, 1994—95; sr. v.p., fin., CFO CBRL Group, 1995—99, exec. v.p., COO, 1999—2000, pres., COO, 2000—01, pres., CEO, 2001—04, chmn., pres., CEO, 2004—. Bd. dirs. CBRL Group, 1999—. Office: CBRL Group 305 Hartmann Dr Lebanon TN 37088 *

WOODHOUSE, THOMAS EDWIN, lawyer, trust company administrator; b. Cedar Rapids, Iowa, Apr. 30, 1940; s. Keith Wallace and Elinor Julia (Cherny) W.; m. Kiyoko Fujiie, May 29, 1965; children: Miya, Keith, Leighton. AB cum laude, Amherst Coll., 1962; JD, Harvard U., 1965. Bar: N.Y. 1966, U.S. Supreme Ct. 1969, Calif. 1975. Assoc. Chadbourne, Parke, Whiteside & Wolff, NYC, 1965-68; atty./adviser AID, Washington, 1968-69; counsel Pvt. Investment Co. for Asia S.A., Tokyo, 1969-72; ptnr. Woodhouse Lee & Davis, Singapore, 1972-74; assoc. Graham & James, San Francisco, 1974-75; asst. gen. counsel Natomas Co., San Francisco, 1975-81; mem. Lasky, Haas, Cohler & Munter, San Francisco, 1982-90; trust adminstr. Ronald Family Trust A, 1989—, Gordon P. Getty Family Trust, 1994—; sole practice Berkeley, 1990—2001. Of counsel Wilson, Sonsini, Goodrich & Rosati, Palo Alto, Calif., 1992-95; instr. law faculty U. Singapore, 1972-74; CEO, Vallejo Investments, 1997—. chmn. Police Rev. Com. of Berkeley (Calif.), 1980-84; mem. Berkeley Police Res., 1986—; bd. dirs. Friends Assn. of Svcs. for Elderly, 1979-84; clk. fin. com. Am. Friends Svc. Com. of No. Calif., 1979-83; pres. Zyzzyva Inc., lit. quar., 1985-87. Trustee Freedom from Hunger, 1989-99, Coun. of Friends Bancroft Libr., 1997-2002, chmn. 2002-2003, Coun. of Friends Amherst Coll. Libr., 1990-97, 2005-, Mark Twain Luncheon Club, 2002—, Dominican Sch. of Philosophy and Theology, 1998-2003; chmn. Friends of Amherst Coll. Libr., 1990-97, 2005—. With U.S. Army, 1958. Fellow Am. Bar Found. (life); mem. Calif. Bar Assn., Assn. Internat. de Bibliophilie, Harvard Club, Univ. Club, Book Club Calif., Roxburghe Club, Travellers Club, Grolier Club, Faculty Club U. Calif.-Berkeley, Mira Vista Golf and Country Club. Republican. Roman Catholic. Home and Office: 1800 San Antonio Ave Berkeley CA 94707-1618 Personal E-mail: robert606@earthlink.net.

WOODHURST, ROBERT STANFORD, JR., architect; b. Abbeville, SC, July 12, 1921; s. Robert Stanford and Eva (Ferguson) W.; m. Dorothy Ann Carwile, Aug. 4, 1945; 1 son: Robert Stanford III. BS in Architecture, Clemson U., 1942. Registered arch., S.C., Ga., NCARB. Designer Harold Woodward, Arch., Spartanburg, SC, 1946-47; assoc. arch. F. Arthur Hazard, Arch., Augusta, Ga., 1947-54; ptnr. Woodhurst & O'Brien, Architects, Augusta, Ga., 1954-83, Woodhurst Partnership, Augusta, Ga., 1983—. V.p. Southeastern Architects and Engrs., Inc., Augusta, 1964-83; lectr. history architecture N. Augusta Community Coll.; mem. nat. exam. com. Nat. Council Arch tl. Regis. Bds.; pres. Ga. State Bd. Archs. Chmn. Augusta-richmond County Planning Commn., 1966-68; trustee Hist. Augusta, Inc., active Mayor's Adv. Com., 1965-68; mem. Augusta Bldg. Code Bd. Appeals, 1955-58. Served to capt. U.S. Army, 1942-45. Decorated Air medal with 7 oak leaf clusters; Croix de Guerre avec palms (France); prisoner of war, Germany. Fellow AIA (Bronze medal 1942); mem. Ga. Assn. AIA (pres. 1977, Bronze medal 1977, Rothchild Silver Medal 1987), Soc. Archtl. Historians, Nat. Coun. Archtl. Registration Bds., Augusta Country Club, Pinnacle Club. Democrat. Baptist. Achievements include designed and built: 1st Bapt. Ch., Augusta, Univ. Hosp. Med Ctr., Augusta, Peabody Apts. and Irvin Towers, Augusta, W. Lake Country Club, Augusta, Med. Libr., Med. Coll. Ga., Libr. Voorhees Coll., Denmark, S.C., Ambulatory Care Ctr. Univ. Hosp. Augusta, Married Students Apts., Med. Coll. Ga., Covenant Presbyn. Ch., Augusta, Student Ctr. Voorhees Coll., Pres.' Home Voorhees Coll., others. Home: 810 Dogwood Ln Augusta GA 30909-2704 Office: Woodhurst Partnership 607 15th St Augusta GA 30901-2601 Office Phone: 706-724-4343. Personal E-mail: twparch@aol.com.

WOODLAND, N. JOSEPH, retired optical engineer, retired mechanical engineer; b. Atlantic City, Sept. 6, 1921; BSME, Drexel U., 1947, DEng (hon.), 1998; MME, Syracuse U., 1956. Tech. asst. to unit chief, liquid thermal diffusion project for separating uranium isotopes Manhattan Project, Oak Ridge, Tenn., 1943—46; mech. designer Burlington Industries, 1947; lectr. in mech. engring. Drexel U., 1948—49, cons., 1987; cons. in aircraft hydraulics design, 1950; various positions at staff and sr. levels IBM Corp., 1951—87; cons., 1987—88. Named one of Drexel U.'s 100 Most Outstanding Alumni, 1992; recipient Nat. Medal Tech. for invention of bar code, 1992. Mem.: Anthony J. Drexel Soc. Achievements include patents in field.

WOODLEY, DAVID TIMOTHY, dermatology educator; b. Aug. 11, 1948; s. Raoul Ramos-Mimosa and Marian (Schlueter) W.; m. Christina Paschall Prentice, May 4, 1974; children; David Thatcher, Thomas Colgate, Peter paschall. AB, Washington U., St. Louis, 1968; MD, U. Mo., 1973. Diplomate Am. Bd. Internal Medicine, Am. Bd. Dermatology, Nat. Bd. Internal Medicine. Intern Beth Israel Med. Ctr., Mt. Sinai Sch. Medicine, N.Y. Hosp., Cornell U. Sch. Medicine, NYC, 1973-74; resident in internal medicine U. Nebr., Omaha, 1974-76; resident in dermatology U. N.C., Chapel Hill, 1976-78, asst. prof. dermatology, 1983-85, assoc. prof. dermatology, 1985-88; prof. medicine, co-chief divsn. dermatology Cornell U. Med. Ctr., NYC, 1988-89; prof., vice chair dept. dermatology Stanford (Calif.) U., 1989-93; prof., chair dept. dermatology Northwestern U., Chgo., 1993-99; co-chief dermatology U. So. Calif. Sch. Medicine, LA, 1999—. Research fellow U. Paris, 1978-80; expert NIH, Bethesda, Md., 1983-89; prof., assoc. chmn. dermatology Stanford U Sch. Medicine, 1989-93; chmn. dermatology Sch. Medicine Northwestern U., 1993-99; prof., chmn. dermatology U. So. Calif., 1999—; mem. study sect. NIH. Contbr. chpts. to books and articles in field to profl. jours. Mem. Potomac Albicore Fleet, Washington, 1982-83, Chapel Hill, 1983—, Jungian Soc. Triangle Area, Chapel Hill, 1983—. Fellow Am. Acad. Dermatology; co-owner, mem. ACS (assoc.), Dermatology Found., Am. Soc. for Clin. Rsch., Soc. Investigative Dermatology, Assn. Physician Poets, Am. Soc. for Clin. Investigation. Office: U So Calif Keck Sch Medicine Dept Dermatology UC Norris Cancer Ctr Topping Tower 3905 1441 Eastlake Ave Los Angeles CA 90033 Office Phone: 323-865-0983.

WOODLEY, JOHN PAUL, JR., civilian military employee, lawyer; b. Shreveport, La., Sept. 28, 1953; s. John Paul and Hazel Eugenia (Iles) W.; m. Priscilla Anne Ingersoll, June 6, 1981; children: Elizabeth Ingersoll, Cornelia Ingersoll. BA, Washington & Lee U., 1974, JD, 1977. Bar: Va. 1977, U.S. Ct. Appeals (4th cir.) 1978, U.S. Dist. Ct. (ea. dist.) Va. 1979, U.S. Ct. Mil. Appeals 1979, U.S. Supreme Ct. 1982, U.S. Ct. Appeals (5th cir.) 1984, U.S. Ct. Appeals (11th and fed. cirs.) 1985. Law clk. to judge U.S. Dist. Ct., Richmond, Va., 1977-79; pvt. practice Richmond, 1985-86; ptnr. Woodley Simon & Woodley, Richmond, 1986—90; asst. commonwealth atty. Henrico county State of Va., 1990—94, dep. atty. gen. (govt. ops) Richmond, 1994—98, sec. nat. resources, 1998—2001; asst. dep. under sec. for environment US Dept. Def., Washington, 2001—03; prin. dep. asst. sec. (civil works) Dept. Army, US Dept. Def., 2004—05, asst. sec. (civil works), 2003—04, 2005—. Treas. Richmond Rep. Com., 1988. Capt. JAGC, U.S. Army, 1979-85, maj. Res., 1986. Decorated Legion of Merit, Meritorious Svc. medal with 2 oak leaf clusters, Army Commendation medal with 1 oak leaf cluster, Army Achievement medal; recipient Sec. Def. medal for Outstanding Pub. Svc. Mem. ABA, Rep. Nat. Lawyers Assn. (bd. govs. 1988), Va. State Bar, Richmond Bar Assn., Assn. Trial Lawyers Am., Phi Beta Kappa, Assn. Va. Hearing Officers, Va. Trial Lawyers Assn., Va. Rep. Lawyers Assn. (chmn. 1987—), Richmond First Club. Roman Catholic. Avocation: skiing. Office: US Army 108 Army Pentagon Washington DC 20310 *

WOODLIFF, GEORGE FRANKLIN, III, priest; b. Jackson, Miss., June 16, 1948; s. George Franklin and Ann Morse Woodliff; m. Jill McLacrin Woodliff, Nov. 24, 1976; children: Lauren, Anna Rose, Elizabeth. BBA, U. Miss., Oxford, 1970; JD, U. Va., 1973; BTh, Oxford U., Eng., 1995. Assoc. Heddberg & Woodliff, Jackson, Miss., 1973—76, ptnr., 1976—91, mng. ptnr., 1986—89; chaplain Miss. State U., Starkville, 1995—98; rector Trinity Episcopal Ch., Yazoo City, 1998—. Founder, chmn. Yazoo City Ministers Assn., 2003, Stand Firm, Jackson, 2004—. Author: Rediscovering Christian Orthodoxy in Episcopal Anglicanism, 2004. Chaplain Boys and Girls Club Bd., Yazoo City, 2006—; mem. Gateway MAP Coalition, Yazoo City, 2006—. Mem.: Mensa. Avocations: music, movies, reading, walking. Home: 875 Crestview Dr Yazoo City MS 39194-2510 Office: Trinity Episcopal Ch 323 N Main St Yazoo City MS 39194 Office Phone: 662-746-5082.

WOODMAN, BETTY, sculptor; b. Norwalk, Conn., 1930; Attended, Alfred U., 1948—50. Exhibitions include Mus. Arts and Design, Boston Mus. Fine Arts, Carnegie-Mellon Inst., Cooper Hewitt Nat. Design Mus., Internat. Ceramic Mus., Faenza, LA County Mus. Art, Met. Mus. Art, Mint Mus. Craft and Design, Musee de Arts Decoratifs, Stejelijk Mus., Victoria and Albert Mus., World Ceramic Ctr., Ichon, Korea, others. Recipient Visionary award, Am. Crafts Mus., 1998; fellow Nat. Endowment for Arts, 1980, 1986, Rockefeller Found., 1995; hon. fellow, Nat. Coun. Educators in Ceramic Arts, 2000. Office: c/o Garth Clark Gallery 24 W 57th St Ste 305 New York NY 10019

WOODMAN, G. ROGER, management consultant; b. Point Pleasant, NJ, Feb. 25, 1953; s. George Emil and Emma (Stringham) W.; m. Jean Wilson; 1 child, Kevin Richard. AS, Ocean County Coll., 1981; student, Trenton State Coll., 1987. Sr. operator, night supr. Ocean County Nat. Bank, Point Pleasant, 1973—85; constrn. ofcl. N.J. Dept. Cmty. Affairs, Trenton, 1985—87; pres., sr. cons. Cynosure Cons., Inc., Lakewood, NJ, 1987—. Environ. cons. Environ Health Inspections, Lakewood, 1988, N.J. Dept. Cmty. Affairs, Trenton, 1989-95, BNK, Restorations, Clifton, N.J., 1989—. Author: (with others) Uniform Construction Code, 1985. County committeeman Ocean County Reps., Lakewood, 1989-98; life mem. Bay Head Vo. Fire Co., 1971—; mem. Lakewood Rep. Club, 1989-98; mem. Fishermen's Meml. Fund, 1998—, chmn., 2001. Mem. Nat. Fire Protection Assn., N.J. Fireman's Assn., Am. Mgmt. Assn., Masons (Durand lodge master 1980, treas. 2000, sec. 2001—, jr. grand steward 2002-03, DRI 2003-07). Avocations: gardening, hiking, travel, model trains, reading. Office: Cynosure Consultants 14 Marlow Dr Jackson NJ 08527-4678 Office Phone: 732-261-0288.

WOODMAN, GREY MUSGRAVE, psychiatrist; b. Birmingham, England, Jan. 26, 1922; came to U.S., 1959, naturalized 1963; s. Edward Musgrave and Ida (Cullen) W.; m. Irene Woodman; children: Sheila, Shonagh. BA, Oxford U., Eng., 1943, MA, BM, BChir, 1945; grad., Clinton Citizens Police Acad., 2001. Ship's surgeon Brit. Merchant Marines, 1946-48; intern Whipps Cross Hosp., London, 1949-50, med. registrar, 1951-53, Gen. Hosp., Newcastle-on-Tyne, England, 1953-54; gen. practice London, 1954-56; physician USAF Hosp., 1956-59; resident in psychiatry U. Okla. Med. Ctr., 1959-62; staff psychiatrist Western Mo. Mental Health Ctr., Kansas City, 1962-76; med. dir. Mental Health Ctr. Clinton County, Clinton, Iowa, 1976-87; pvt. practice Clinton, 1976—; founder, dir. Lincolnshire Clinic, The London Psychiat. Clinic, 1997—. Mem. staff Jane Lamb Health Ctr., Mercy Hosp., Comphealth; psychiat. cons. Mufon. Mem. Prevent Child Abuse Coun. Recipient Internat. Order of Merit, 1999, Claire Behr Meml. award, Pathway Living Ctr., 2006. Fellow Royal Soc. Medicine (London, life); mem. AMA (life), Am. Psychiat. Assn. (life), Am. Acad. Med. Hypoanalysts (clin.), Brit. Med. Assn., World Fedn. Mental Health, Iowa Med. Soc. (past chmn. hospice com.), Internat. Assn. Social Psychiatry, Clinton Co. Prevent Child Abuse Coun., Am. Red Cross (mental health specialist 1996—), Oxford Club (life), Moose. Republican. Episcopalian. Home: 515 N 13th St Clinton IA 52732-4816 Office: London Psychiat Clinic 212 Wilson Bldg 5th Ave Clinton IA 52732 Office Phone: 563-243-7721. Business E-Mail: greyufo@mchso.com.

WOODMAN, HAROLD DAVID, historian, educator; b. Chgo., Apr. 21, 1928; s. Joseph Benjamin and Helen Ruth (Sollo) W.; m. Leonora Becker; children— Allan James, David Edward. BA, Roosevelt U., 1957; MA, U. Chgo., 1959, PhD, 1964. Lectr. Roosevelt U., 1962-63; asst. prof. history U. Mo., Columbia, 1963-66, assoc. prof., 1966-69, prof., 1969-71, Purdue U., West Lafayette, Ind., 1971-97, Louis Martin Sears disting. prof., 1990-97, prof. emeritus, 1997—; chmn. Com. on Am. Studies, 1981-94. Author: Conflict and Consensus in American History, 1966, 9th rev. edit., 1996, Slavery and the Southern Economy, 1966, King Cotton and His Retainers, 1968, Legacy of the American Civil War, 1973, New South-New Law, 1995; mem. editl. bd. Jour. So. History, 1972-75, Wis. Hist. Soc., 1972-76, Bus. History Rev., 1971-77, Agrl. History, 1976-82, Am. Hist. Rev., 1981-84, Jour. Am. History, 1985-88. Served with U.S. Army, 1950-52. Recipient Otto Wirth award Roosevelt U., 1990; Woodrow Wilson Internat. Center for Scholars fellow, 1977; Faculty grant Social Sci. Rsch. Coun., 1969-70; Nat. Humanities Ctr. fellow, 1983-84 Mem. Am. Hist. Assn., Orgn. Am. Historians, Econ. History Assn., Agrl. History Soc. (pres. 1983-84, Everett E. Edwards award 1963), Soc. Am. Historians, Bus. History Conf. (pres. 1981-82), Ind. Assn. Historians (pres. 1983-84), So. Hist. Assn. (exec. coun. 1982-85, Ramsdell award 1965, pres. 1995-96). Home: 1100 N Grant St West Lafayette IN 47906-2460 Office: Purdue U Dept History West Lafayette IN 47907 Business E-Mail: hwoodman@purdue.edu.

WOODMAN, STEWART, chef; b. 1974; m. Heidi Woodman. Apprentice The Fairmont Banff Springs hotel, Alberta, Canada; sous chef Essex House, NYC, Le Bernardin, NYC; chef Mercer Kitchen, NYC, Jean Georges, NYC, Zoe, NYC, Restaurant Levain, Mpls.; co-owner, exec. chef Five Restaurant & Street Lounge, Mpls. Recipient Best New Chef award, Food and Wine Mag., 2006. Office: Five Restaurant & Street Lounge 2917 Bryant Ave S Minneapolis MN 55408 Office Phone: 612-827-5555.

WOODRESS, JAMES LESLIE, JR., language educator; b. Webster Groves, Mo., July 7, 1916; s. James Leslie and Jessie (Smith) W.; m. Roberta Wilson, Sept. 28, 1940. AB, Amherst Coll., 1938; A.M., NYU, 1943; PhD, Duke U., 1950; LittD, U. Nebr., 1995. News editor Sta. KWK, St. Louis, 1939-40; rewriteman, editor UPI, NYC, 1940-43; instr. English, Grinnell (Iowa) Coll., 1949-50; asst. prof. English, Butler U., Indpls., 1950-53, asso. prof., 1953-58; asso. prof. English, San Fernando Valley (Calif.) State Coll., 1958-61, prof., 1961-66, chmn. dept., 1959-63, dean letters and scis., 1963-65; prof. English, U. Calif.-Davis, 1966-87, chmn. dept., 1970-74; vis. prof. Sorbonne, Paris, 1974-75, 83. Author: Howells and Italy, 1952, Booth Tarkington: Gentleman from Indiana, 1955, A Yankee's Odyssey: The Life of Joel Barlow, 1958, Dissertations in American Literature, 1957, 3rd edit., 1968, Willa Cather: Her Life and Art, 1970, 3rd edit., 1981, American Fiction 1900-50, 1974, Willa Cather: A Literary Life, 1987; editor: Eight American Authors, 1971, American Literary Scholarship: An Annual, 1965-69, 75-77, 79, 81, 87, Critical Essays on Walt Whitman, 1983, Cather's The Troll Garden, 1983, (with Richard Morris) Voices from America's Past, anthology, 1961-62, 75. Served to lt. AUS, 1943-46. Ford Fund for Advancement Edn. fellow, 1952-53; Guggenheim fellow, 1957-58; Fulbright lectr. France, 1962-63; Fulbright lectr. Italy, 1965-66; recipient Hubbell medal, 1985 Mem. MLA (sec. Am. Lit. group 1962-63), AAUP, Phi Beta Kappa. Address: 892 Harrison Ave Claremont CA 91711-4128

WOODRICK, ROBERT, food products executive; Chmn. D&W Food Ctrs., Grand Rapids, Mich. Emeritus trustee Aquinas Coll.; trustee Grand Rapids CC. Office: D&W Food Ctrs 3001 Orchard Vista Dr SE Grand Rapids MI 49546-7078

WOODRIFF, LEE, company executive; s. Ray and Margaret; BS, Mont. State U., 1964; MS U. Wis.; PhD, Columbia Pacific U., 2002. Instr. Mont. State U., Bozeman, 1963—64, U. Wis., Milw., 1964—65, U. Calif., Berkley, 1991, Northeastern U., Boston, 1992; asst. prof. Middle East Tech. U., 1965—67, Humboldt State U., Arcata, Calif., 1967—70; prof. Menlo Coll., Menlo Park, Calif., 1970—96; CEO, pres. Naefels Ltd., Henderson, Nev., 1997—. Cons., founder Menlo Rsch. Assocs., Arcata, 1980—96; CEO Centro Ltd., Henderson, 1996—2005; pilot, flight instr. Recipient various tchg. awards. Mem.: AAUP, Am. Math. Assn., Math. Assn. Am. Avocations: sailing, skiing. Office: 12140 Big Davis Rd Three Forks MT 59752

WOODRING, DEWAYNE STANLEY, religious organization administrator; b. Gary, Ind., Nov. 10, 1931; s. J. Stanley and Vera Luella (Brown) Woodring; m. Donna Jean Wishart, June 15, 1957; children: Judith Lynn Bigelow, Beth Ellen Carey. BS in Speech with distinction, Northwestern U., Evanson, Ill., 1954; postgrad., Northwestern U., 1954—57; MDiv, Garrett Theol. Sem., 1957; LHD, Mt. Union Coll., 1967; DD, Salem Coll., 1970. Ordained to ministry Meth. Ch., 1955. Assoc. dir. youth Gary YMCA, 1950—55; min. edn. Griffith Meth. Ch., Ind., 1955—57; min. adminstrn. and program 1st Meth. Ch., Eugene, Oreg., 1957—59; dir. pub. rels. Dakotas area Meth. Ch., 1959—60, dir. pub. rels. Ohio area, 1960—64; adminstrv. exec. to bishop Ohio East area United Meth. Ch., Canton, 1964—77, asst. gen. sec. Gen. Coun. Fin. and Adminstr. Evanston, Ill., 1977—79, assoc. gen. sec., 1979—84; exec. dir., CEO Religious Conf. Mgmt. Assn., Indpls., 1982—. Staff dept. radio svcs. 2d Assembly World Coun. Chs., Evanston, 1954; vice-chmn. commn. entertainment and program North Ctrl. Jurisdictional Conf., 1968—72, chmn., 1972—76; mem. commn. gen. conf. United Meth. Ch., 1972—93, mgr., exec. dir., 1976—93, mem. divsn. interpretation, 1969—72; chmn. commn. Ohio Coun. Chs., 1961—65; exec. com. Nat. Assn. United Meth. Found., 1968—72, World Meth. Coun., 1986—2001; v.p. Ohio East Area United Meth. Found., 1967—76; chmn. bd. mgrs. United Meth. Bldg., Evanston, 1977—84; mem. adv. bd. Nassau/Paradise Island, 1997—99, Red Lion Hotels and Inns, PR Conv. Ctr., GMG Solutions; lectr., cons. in field. Creator (radio series) The Word and Music, prodr., dir. (TV series) Parables in Miniature, 1957—59. Adviser East Ohio Conf. Comm. Commn., 1968—76; bd. dirs. First Internat. Summit Edn., 1989; trustee, 1st v.p. Copeland Oaks Retirement Ctr., Sebring, Ohio, 1969—76; pres. Guild Assocs., 1971—. Named to, Ky. Cols., 1989, Hall of Leaders, Conv. Liaison Coun., 1994; recipient Cert. Meeting Profl. award, 1985, Cert. Expt. Mgr. award, 1988, Sagamore of Wabash award, State Ind., 2007. Mem.: Marriot Customer Leadership Forum (mem. customer adv. bd.), Found. Internat. Meetings (bd. dirs.), Cert. Meeting Profls. (bd. dirs. 1983—92), Ind. Conv. Visitors Assn. (bd. dirs. 1996—2000), Def. Orientation Conf. Assn. (chaplain), Conv. Industry Coun. (bd. dirs., past chmn.), Meeting Profl. Internat., Ind. Soc. Assn. Execs. (Meeting Planner of the Yr. award 1990), Am. Soc. Assn. Execs. Home: 7224 Chablis Ct Indianapolis IN 46278-1540 Office: 1 RCA Dome Ste 120 Indianapolis IN 46225-1023 Office Phone: 317-632-1888.

WOODRING, JOHN HOWELL, radiologist; b. Louisville, Sept. 10, 1951; s. Franklyn Howell and Dorothy Moore Woodring; m. Catherine Anne Martin, Aug. 27, 1977; children: Paul Martin, Mark Reynolds. BS, U. of Louisville, 1972; MD, U. of Ky., 1976. Lic. diagnostic radiology Am. Bd. of Radiology. Intern Louisville Gen. Hosp., 1976—77; resident physician U. of Ky. Med. Ctr., Lexington, 1977—80; asst. prof. of diagnostic radiology U. of Ky., Lexington, 1980—84, assoc. prof. of diagnostic radiology, 1984—92, prof. of diagnostic radiology, 1992—98; staff radiologist Lexington VA Med. Ctr., Lexington, 1999—. Chief of radiology svc. Lexington VA Med. Ctr., 2000—02. Contbr. articles to sci. jours. (Cert. of Merit Am. Roentgen Ray Soc., 1994). Asst. scoutmaster Boy Scouts of Am., Louisville, 1968—77; senior-high counselor 1st United Meth. Ch., Lexington, 1984—87, Sunday sch. tchr., 1992—2000. Fellow: Am. Coll. of Chest Physicians (hon.), Am. Coll. of Radiology (hon.); mem.: Soc. of Thoracic Radiology, Radiol. Soc. of N.Am. (life), So. Med. Assn. Liberal. Presbyterian. Achievements include first to demonstrate role of computed tomography in evaluation of coronary artery disease, and evaluation of cervical spine fractures; propose the use of endobronchial stents in the treatment of right pneumonectomy syndrome; role of computed tomography in the evaluation of congenital lobar emphysema; identify risk factors for the development of salicylate-induced pulmonary edema; demonstrate that there is no statistically significant difference in the distribution of pleural effusion between the right and left hemithorax in congestive heart failure; development of pulmonary artery-bronchus ratio as a means of diagnosing congestive heart failure. Avocations: model trains, antique cars, music, literature. Home: 336 Arcadia Park Lexington KY 40503 Office: Radiology Svc Lexington VA Med Ctr CDD-114 1101 Veterans Dr Lexington KY 40502

WOODROW, RANDALL MARK, lawyer; b. Anniston, Ala., June 17, 1956; s. Herbert Milisam and Rose (Marshall) W.; m. Carolyn Ann Jackson, Jan. 7, 1977; children: Amanda Lauren, Emily Claire, Taylor Jackson, Douglas Cockrell. BA in Polit. Sci., Jacksonville State U., Ala., 1978; JD, Samford U., 1981. Bar: Ala. 1981. Law clk. to judge U.S. Dist. Ct. (no. dist.) Ala., 1981-82; ptnr. Doster & Woodrow, Anniston, Ala., 1990—. Asst. dist. atty. 7th Jud. Cir., Anniston, 1983; adj. prof. Jacksonville State U., 1985-86; gen. counsel Jacksonville State Univs., 1985—. Chmn. crusade Calhoun County Cancer Soc., Anniston, 1983; pres. Boys Clubs of Anniston, Inc., 1985; mem. Calhoun County Econ. Devel. Coun., 1995—; mem. Jacksonville (Ala.) Planning Commn., 1995—; mem. City of Jacksonville Bd. Edn., 1996—. Mem. ABA, Ala. Bar Assn., Calhoun County Bar Assn., Calhoun County C. of C. Home: 509 6th St NE Jacksonville AL 36265-1617 Office: Doster & Woodrow PO Box 2286 Anniston AL 36202-2286 Office Phone: 256-238-6005. Personal E-mail: rmwoodrow@aol.com.

WOODRUFF, BOB (ROBERT WARREN WOODRUFF), newscaster; b. Bloomfield Hills, Mich., Aug. 18, 1961; m. Lee Woodruff, Sept. 11, 1988; children: Mack, Cathryn, Nora, Claire. BA, Colgate U., 1983; JD, U. Mich., 1987. Atty.; law tchr. Beijing; translator during Tiananmen Sq. uprising CBS News, Beijing, 1989; corr., Justice Dept. ABC News, Washington, fgn. corr. Belgrade, Kosovo, Europe, Middle East, London bur. corr., corr. NYC, 2002; interim anchor ABC World News Tonight, NYC, 2005, co-anchor, 2006. Co-author (with Lee Woodruff): In an Instant: A Family's Journey of Love and Healing, 2007. Recipient Alfred I. Dupont award for 9/11 reporting, George Foster Peabody award for 9/11 reporting, David Bloom award for excellence in enterprise reporting, Radio & TV Corr. Assn., 2006. Fluent in Mandarin Chinese. Office: ABC News Press Rels Fl 2 47 W 66th St New York NY 10023-6201 *

WOODRUFF, C(HARLES) ROY, retired professional association executive, consultant; b. Anniston, Ala., Sept. 27, 1938; m. Kay Carolyn Jernigan, June 26, 1962; children: Charles R. Jr., Earl David. BA, U. Ala., 1960; BD, So. Bapt. Theol. Sem., 1963, PhD in Psychology of Religion and Pastoral Care, 1966. Diplomate Am. Assn. Pastoral Counselors; lic. profl. counselor, Va. Asst. pastor Ft. Mitchell Bapt. Ch., South Ft. Mitchell, Ky., 1960-63; Protestant chaplain Silvercrest Hosp., New Albany, Ind., 1963-66; dir. dept. pastoral care and edn. Bryce State Hosp., Tuscaloosa, Ala., 1966-71; assoc. prof., chaplain supr. dept. patient counseling Med. Coll. Va., Richmond, 1971-76; assoc. prof., chmn. dept. psychology of religion and pastoral care Midwestern Bapt. Theol. Sem., Kansas City, Mo., 1976-78; exec. dir. Peninsula Pastoral Counseling Ctr., Newport News, Va., 1978-88, Am. Assn. Pastoral Counselors, Washington, 1988—2003; interim pastor Vienna (Va.) Bapt. Ch., 2004—06. Lecturing fellow Interpreter's House, Lake Junaluska, N.C., 1968-78; pastoral counselor, clin. supr. Psychol. Clinic, U. Ala., Tuscaloosa, 1969-71; adj. staff mem. The Counseling Inst., Kansas City, 1976-78, adj. prof., John Leland Ctr. for Theol. Studies, Fairfax, Va., vis. prof., Korea Profl. Inst. of Psychotherapy and Spirtuality, Seoul, Korea. Author: Alcoholism and Christian Experience, 1968, Spiritual Care for Addicted Persons and Families, 2006; (with others) Alcohol, In and Out of the Church, 1968, Work Adjustment: The Goal of Rehabilitation, 1973, Pastoral Theology and Ministry, Key Resources, 1983, The Dictionary of Pastoral Care and Counseling, 1990; also articles. Apptd. by Gov. of Va. to Bd. Profl. Counselors, Commonwealth of Va., 1987-95 (chmn. 1993-95); mem. Nat. Mental Health Leadership Forum, 1990-93; pres. Coalition on Ministry in Specialized Settings, 1996-2000. Recipient Disting. Contbns. award Am. Assn. Pastoral Counselors, 2003; United Meth. Ch. Gen. Bd. Christian Social Concerns grantee, 1965; So. Bapt. Theol. Sem. teaching fellow, 1965-66. Fellow Coll. Chaplains of Am. Protestant Hosp. Assn.; mem. Assn. for Clin. Pastoral Edn. (cert. supr.), Assn. Couples for Marriage Enrichment (cert.). Home: 10827 Burr Oak Way Burke VA 22015-2416

WOODRUFF, ELLEN LOUISE, chaplain; b. Bertha, Minn., Jan. 30, 1942; d. Harold Ernest and Ruth Eleanor (Olson) Klebs; m. John S. Woodruff, July 31, 1969; children: Ruth Ellen, Jonathan C. BA, U. Minn., 1969; Assoc. in Ministry, Luther Sem., St. Paul, 2000. Recreation therapist

St. Mary's Hosp., Mpls., 1969, Belgrade Nursing Home, Minn., 1971—73; dir. youth camp Elks Assn., Brainerd, Minn., 1976—95; student chaplain Regions Hosp., St. Paul, 1997—98, Good Samaritan Homes, Mpls. & St. Paul, 1998—99; conservator St. Paul, 2000—03; chaplain St. Gertrude's Health and Rehab. Ctr., 2003—05, Hurricane Katrina Relief, 2005—07. Mem. program com. Mid-States Camping Assn., Chgo., 1992—94; leader/spkr. Ch. Retreats, 1985—. Author (editor): Klebs Family History, 2001, Awesome Angels, 2002. Vol. chaplain Hurricane Katrina, 2005; active Shepherd of the Valley Luth. Ch. Recipient J.B. Fritzjerald award, Mpls. Park & Recreation, 1969; grantee, U. Minn., 1966—68. Mem.: Assn. Profl. Chaplains, Am. Camping Assn. (sec. newsletter 1983—95, bd. dirs. 1980—83, 1990—93, Sue Tinker award 1993). Home: 9391 Knighton Woodbury MN 55125-3721

WOODRUFF, FAY, paleoceanographer, geological researcher; b. Boston, Jan. 23, 1944; d. Lorande Mitchell and Anne (Fay) W.; m. Alexander Whitehill Clowes, May 20, 1972 (div. Oct. 1974); m. Robert G. Douglas, Jan. 27, 1980; children: Ellen, Katerina. RN, Mass. Gen. Hosp. Sch. Nursing, Boston, 1966; BA, Boston U., 1971; MS, U. So. Calif., 1979. Rsch. assoc. U. So. Calif., LA, 1978-81, rsch. faculty, 1981-96. Keynote spkr. 4th Internat. Symposium on Benthic Foraminifera, Sendai, Japan, 1990. Contbg. author: Geological Society of America Memoir, 1985; contbr. articles to profl. jours. Life mem. The Nature Conservancy, Washington, 1992; bd. dirs. Friends of Friendship Park, Inc., 1995-2001; co-founder, v.p. Resources Families Adopted Ea. European Children, Inc., L.A., 1996-2000. NSF grantee, 1986-94. Mem. Am. Geophys. Union, Geol. Soc. Am., Internat. Union Geol. Scis. (internat. commn. on stratigraphy, subcommn. on Neogene stratigraphy 1991-99), Soc. Woman Geographers (sec. So. Calif. chpt. 1990-96), Soc. Econ. Paleontologists and Mineralogists (sec., editor N.Am. Micropaleontology sect. 1988-90), Sigma Xi. Office: U So Calif Earth Scis Los Angeles CA 90089-0001 Office Phone: 310-544-2291.

WOODRUFF, JAY NOEL, editor, writer; b. Cooperstown, NY, Oct. 31, 1960; s. Robert Arnold Woodruff, Jr. and Marcia Shick Woodruff; m. Sarah Jean Carew, Oct. 1, 1988; children: Joseph Francis, Samuel Robert, Anne Elizabeth. BA in English, Harvard U., 1983; MFA, U. Iowa, 1987. Rsch. tchg. fellow Harvard U., Cambridge, Mass., 1987—91; mng. editor DoubleTake Mag., Durham, NC, 1993—96; sr. editor Esquire Mag., New York, 1998—2000; asst. mng. editor Entertainment Weekly, New York, 2000—06, mng. editor EW.com, 2006—. Editor: (book) A Piece of Work; contbr. essays; author: (short stories) various publications. Mem.: Am. Soc. Mag. Editors. Catholic. Office: Entertainment Weekly 1675 Broadway New York NY 10019 Personal E-mail: jnwoodruff@aol.com. Business E-Mail: jay_woodruff@ew.com.

WOODRUFF, JUDY CARLINE, broadcast journalist; b. Tulsa, Nov. 20, 1946; d. William Henry and Anna Lee (Payne) W.; m. Albert R. Hunt, Jr., Apr. 5, 1980; children: Jeffrey Woodruff, Benjamin Woodruff, Lauren Ann Lee. Student, Meredith Coll., 1964-66; BA, Duke U., 1968. News announcer, reporter Sta. WAGA-TV, Atlanta, 1970-75; news corr. NBC News, Atlanta, 1975-76, White House corr. Washington, 1977-83; anchor Frontline, PBS documentary series, 1984—90; corr. MacNeil-Lehrer News Hour, PBS, Washington, 1983-93; anchor, sr. corr. CNN, Washington, 1993—2005; moderator Vice Presidential Debate, 1988, America Votes, 2003, 2004; sr. corr., polit. editor The News Hour With Jim Lehrer, 2007—. Bd. advisors Henry Grady Sch. Journalism, U. Ga., 1979-82, Benton Fellowship in Broadcast Journalism, U. Chgo., 1984-90, Knight Fellowship in Journalism, Stanford U., 1985-99; bd. visitors Wake Forest U., 1982-89; trustee Duke U., 1985-97, emerita; founding bd. dirs. Internat. Women's Media Found.; vis. fellow, Joan Shorenstein Ctr.on the Press, Politics and Pub. Policy, Harvard U., 2005—; vis. prof. media and politics Duke U., 2006. Author: This is Judy Woodruff at the White House, 1982; corr: PBS Special Generation Next, 2006. Active Commn. on Women's Health, The Commonwealth Fund.; bd. trustee Freedom Forum, Urban Inst.; trustee Nat. Mus. Am. History, 2006—. Recipient award Leadership Atlanta, Class of 1974, Atlanta chpt. Women in Comms., 1975, Edward Weintal award for excellence in fgn. policy reporting, 1987, Joan Shorenstein Barone award for series on def. issues, 1987, Helen Bernstein award for excellence in journalism N.Y. Pub. Libr., 1989, Pres.'s 21st Century award Nat. Women's Hall of Fame, 1994, CableAce award for best newscaster, 1995, CableAce Best Anchor Team award, 1996, Allen H. Neuharth award for excellence in journalism, 1995, News and Documentary Emmy award, 1997, Internat. Matrix award, Assn. for Women in Comm., 2003, Leonard Zeidenberg First Amendment award, Radio-Television News Directors Assn. and Found., 2003; named to Ga. Assn. of Broadcasters Hall of Fame, 2003; grantee Pew Charitable Trusts, 2006—. Mem. NATAS (Atlanta chpt. Emmy award 1975), White House Corrs. Assn.

WOODRUFF, KAY HERRIN, pathologist, educator; b. Charlotte, NC, Sept. 22, 1942; d. Herman Keith and Helen Thelma (Tucker) Herrin; m. John T. Lyman, May 3, 1980; children: Robert, Geoffry, Carolyn. BA in Chemistry, Duke U., 1964; MD, Emory U., 1968. Diplomate Am. Bd. Pathology (trustee 1993—, sec. 1998-2000, v.p. 2000-2001, pres. 2001—). Medicine and pediat. intern U. N.C., Chapel Hill, 1968-69, resident in anatomic pathology, 1969-70; chief resident in anatomic pathology, instr. U. Okla., Oklahoma City, 1970-71, fellow in electron microscopy-pulmonary pathology, instr., 1971-72; chief resident in clin. pathology U. Calif., San Francisco, 1972-74, asst. clin. prof. dept. anatomic pathology, 1974-91, assoc. clin. prof., 1991—; chief electron microscopy VA Hosp., San Francisco, 1974-75; pvt. practice, San Pablo, Calif., 1981—. Pres. med. staff Brookside Hosp., San Pablo, 1994, med. dir. Regional Cancer Ctr., 1995-98; assoc. pathologist Children's Hosp., San Francisco, 1979-81, St. Joseph's Hosp., San Francisco, 1977-79; cons. pathologist Lawrence Berkeley (Calif.) Lab., 1974-93; med. dir. Bay Area Tumor Inst. Tissue Network, San Pablo, 1989—; asst. clin. prof. pathology health and med. scis. program U. Calif., Berkeley and U. Calif., San Francisco Joint Med. Program, 1985-91, assoc. clin. prof., 1991—, others. Contbr. articles and abstracts to med. jours. Mem. exec. bd. Richmond (Calif.) Quits Smoking, 1986-90, Bay Area Tumor Inst., Oakland, Calif., 1987—; mem. exec. bd. Contra Costa unit Am. Cancer Soc., Walanut Creek, Calif., 1985-87, mem. profl. edn. com., 1985-90, mem. pub. edn. com., 1985-86, mem. task force on breast health Calif. div., 1992-93; mem. transfusion adv. com. Irwin Meml. Blood Bank, San Francisco, 1977-83; chmn. transfusion adv. com. Alameda Contra Costa County Blood Bank, 1989-92; commr. Calif. Bd. Med. Quality Assurance, 1978-80; pres. Brookside Found., San Pablo, Calif., 1998-2000. Recipient young investigator award Am. Lung Assn., 1975-77; Outstanding Svc. awards Am. Cancer Soc., 1986, 87, Disting. Svc. award, 1988; Disting. Clin. Tchg. award U. Calif., San Francisco and Berkeley Joint Med. Program, 1987, Outstanding Tchg. award, 1988, Excellence in Basic Sci. Instrn. award, 1990, Excellence in Tchr. Clin. Scis. award, 1993; cert. of recognition Cmty. Svc. Richmond, 1989. Mem. AMA, Coll. Am. Pathologists (editl. bd. CAP Today 1986-90, bd. govs. 1990-96, chmn. coun. on practice mgmt. 1994, William Kuhn award for outstanding comm. 1996, Presdl. Medal of Honor 1995, 96), Am. Med. Women's Assn. (exec. bd. 1984-87, regional bd. govs. 1984-87), No. Calif. Women's Med. Assn. (pres. 1982-84), Calif. Soc. Pathologists (bd. dirs. 1988-90), No. Calif. Oncology Group, South Bay Pathology Soc. (pres. 1987), Am. Assn. Blood Banks, Calif. Med. Assn., Alameda-Contra Costa County Med. Soc., Am. Soc. Clin. Pathology, Calif. Pathology Soc. Avocations: classical music, music. Office: Doctors Med Ctr 2000 Vale Rd San Pablo CA 94806-3808

WOODRUFF, MARK REED, magazine editor; b. Roanoke, Va., Jan. 3, 1957; s. James Moses and Elizabeth (Reed) W. BFA, Va. Commonwealth U., 1981; postgrad., San Francisco State U., 1983-84. Freelance writer, NYC, 1984-88; features editor Taxi Mag., NYC, 1988-90; mng. editor Spin Mag., NYC, 1990-95; sr. editor Rolling Stone, NYC, 1995-97, asst. mng. editor, 1997-98; editor-in-chief Tennis mag., NYC, 1998—. Mem. Am. Soc. Mag. Editors. Democrat. Avocation: tennis. Home: 215 N Victoria Park Rd Fort Lauderdale FL 33301-3766 Office: Tennis Mag 79 Madison Ave 8th Fl New York NY 10016 E-mail: mwoodruff@tennismagazine.com.

WOODRUFF, NEAL, music educator; b. Kankakee, Ill., Apr. 18, 1969; s. William Jennings and Wanda L. Woodruff; m. Shannon L. Dunn, Apr. 24, 1974; children: Ryan Isaiah, Kayelyn Hope. BA in Music Edn., Olivet Nazarene U., Bourbonnais, Ill., 1991; MusM in Vocal Performance and Pedagogy, Choral Conducting, Stephen F. Austin State U., Nacogdoches, Tex., 1995; D in Musical Arts in Choral Conducting, U. Okla., Norman, 2002. Cert. Somatic Voicework Inst. for Contemporary Comml. Vocal Pedagogy, Shenandoah U., 2005. Chorus mem., understudy soloist Chgo. Symphony Orch. and Chorus, 1990—92; dir. choirs Herscher Jr. High, Ill., 1991—92; pastoral musician First Ch. of the Nazarene, Nacogdoches, 1992—95; assoc. prof. music So. Nazarene U., Bethany, Okla., 1995—99; pastoral musician First Ch. of the Nazarene, Canton, Ohio, 1999—2000; prof. music Olivet Nazarene U., Bourbonnais, 2000—. Adj. prof. voice Malone Coll., Canton, 1999—2000. Author, book reviewer: Choral Jour. Bd. mem. Kankakee Valley Symphony Orch. Assn., Ill., 2002—06. Mem.: Coll. Orch. Dirs. Assn., Christian Performing Artists Network, Music Educators Nat. Conf., Nat. Assn. Tchrs. Singing, Am. Choral Dirs. Assn. Home: 630 S Rosewood Ave Kankakee IL 60901 Office: Olivet Nazarene University One University Ave Bourbonnais IL 60914 Home Phone: 815-935-0760; Office Phone: 815-939-5202. Business E-Mail: nwoodruf@olivet.edu.

WOODRUFF, RANDALL LEE, lawyer; b. Anderson, Ind., July 31, 1954; s. Billy Max and Phyllis Joan (Helmick) W.; m. Lucetta Farnham, Aug. 15, 1976. BA, Ind. U., 1976, JD, 1985. Bar: Ind. 1985, U.S. Dist. Ct. (no. and so. dists.) Ind. 1985, U.S. Supreme Ct. 1989. Exec. dir Cmty. Justice Ctr., Anderson, 1979-85; assoc. Shearer, Schrock & Woodruff, Anderson, 1985-87; pvt. practice Anderson, 1987-97, Woodruff Law Offices, P.C., Anderson, 1997—. Bd. dirs. East Ctrl. Legal Svcs. Program, Anderson, 1986—89; trustee Chpt. 7 Bankruptcy Panel, So. Dist. Ind., 1991—. Bd. dirs. Offender Aid & Restoration of the U.S., 1988-93; chmn. Bd. Zoning Appeals, Town of Edgewood, Ind., 1998—. Mem. Ind. Assn. Criminal Def. Lawyers, Ct. Appointed Spl. Advocates (bd. dirs. 1988), Madison County Bar Assn. (sec./treas. 1990, v.p. 1991, pres. 1992). Mem. Christian Ch. (Disciples Of Christ). Office: 115-A E 9th St Anderson IN 46016 Office Phone: 765-644-6464. Business E-Mail: rlwtrustee@insightbb.com.

WOODRUFF, THOMAS ELLIS, electronics consulting executive; b. Stockton, Calif., Feb. 8, 1921; s. Ennis Casselberry and Gracella (Scotford) W.; m. Doris Elaine Walters, Jan. 14, 1947 (div. Aug. 1962); children: Mary Ann Woodruff Mahaffy, Patricia Lee; m. Ruth Elizabeth Craik, Feb. 25, 1964; 1 child, Robert Peter; stepchildren: Gordon Lee Vickers, Barbara Ann Vickers, Mary Jean Vickers. AA, Stockton Jr. Coll., 1941; BSEE, U. Calif., Berkeley, 1943. Registered profl. engr., Calif. Engr. GE, Syracuse, N.Y., 1944-47; staff engr. Hughes Aircraft Co., Culver City, Calif., 1947-56; mgr. electronics design Sanders Assocs., Nashua, N.H., 1956-58, chief engr. preliminary design, 1958-60, mgr. spl. programs div., 1960-62, corp. dir. systems, 1962-65, v.p., gen. mgr. corp. systems group, 1965-73, v.p. antisubmarine weapons and communications, 1966-72, dir., 1968-70, sr. dir., 1970-76, v.p. gen. mgr. ocean systems group, 1972-76, v.p. sci. and tech., 1976-88, corp. cons., 1989—; v.p. Sanders Nuclear Corp., Nashua, 1966-71. Mem. adv. com. Def. Intelligence Agy., Washington, 1978-83; joint adv. com. MIT Lincoln Lab., Bedford, Mass., 1988-89; cons. Superconductor Tech., Inc., Santa Barbara, Calif., 1988—, Oryx, Inc., Paramus, N.J., 1989—, Sanders/Lockheed, 1988-91, ret. 1992. Patentee, co-patentee 14 inventions in electronics for computers, control systems, video displays, submarine detection devices, others. Mem. IEEE (sr.). Republican. Avocations: skiing, photography, motorcycling, swimming. Home and Office: 8 Berkeley St Nashua NH 03064-2309 Office Phone: 603-882-5631. Personal E-mail: twuff@ieee.org.

WOODRUFF, TRUMAN O(WEN), physicist, emeritus educator; b. Salt Lake City, May 26, 1925; s. Wilford Owen and Evelyn (Ballif) W.; m. Ambrosina Lydia Solaroli, Sept. 14, 1948 (dec. June 1991); m. Patricia O'Keefe Vincent, Sept. 23, 1995. AB, Harvard U., 1947; BA, Oxford U., Eng., 1950; PhD, Calif. Inst. Tech., 1955. Nat. scholar Harvard, 1942-44, 46-47, Sheldon traveling fellow, 1947-48; Rhodes scholar Oxford U., 1948-50; Dow Chem. Co. fellow, Howard Hughes fellow Calif. Inst. Tech., 1950-54; research asso. physics U. Ill., 1954-55; physicist Gen. Elec. Research Lab., 1955-62; prof. physics Mich. State U., 1962-85, prof. emeritus, 1985—, chmn. dept., 1972-75; sr. scientist research labs. Hughes Aircraft Co., Malibu, Calif., 1986-87; cons. in physics Los Angeles, 1987-91. Vis. prof. Scuola Normale Superiore, Pisa, Italy, 1982—. Contbr. articles to sci. jours. Served with USNR, 1944-46. Fulbright fellow U. Pisa, 1968-69 Fellow Am. Phys. Soc.; mem. Assn. Harvard Chemists, Phi Beta Kappa, Sigma Xi.

WOODRUFF, VALERIE, school system administrator; m. Frank Woodruff; 1 child, Scott 1 stepchild, Sheri. BEd in Secondary Edn., Alderson Broaddus Coll., W. Va.; MA in guidance and counseling, U. Del.; postgrad. studies in vocat. edn. and curriculum devel., Temple U., 1999—. From tchr. to prin. New Castle County, Del., Cecil County Md.; assoc. sec. for curriculum and instructional improvement Del. Dept. Edn., Dover, Del., 1992—99, acting sec., 1999—2000, sec., 2000—. Bd. dir. Coun. of Chief State Sch. Officers, pres.; bd. dir. Del. Workforce Investment Bd., Youth Coun., State C. of C. Partnership; Del. repr. So. Regional Edn. Bd. Mem.: Coun Chief State Sch Officers (past pres). Office: Del Dept Edn John G Townsend Bldg 401 Federal St Ste 2 Dover DE 19901-3369 Office Phone: 302-739-4601, 302-735-4000. Office Fax: 302-739-4654. Business E-Mail: vwoodruff@doe.k12.de.us. *

WOODRUFF, VIRGINIA, broadcast journalist, writer; b. Morrisville, Pa. d. Edwin Nichols and Louise (Meredith) W.; m. Raymond F. Beagle Jr. (div.); m. Albert Plaut II (div.); 1 child, Elise Meredith. Student, Rutgers U. News corr. Sta. WNEW-TV Metromedia, NYC, 1967; nat., internat. critic-at-large Mut. Broadcasting System, 1968-75; lectr. Leigh Bur., 1969-71; byline columnist NY Daily Mirror, NYC, 1970-71; first Arts critic Teleprompter and Group W Cable TV, 1977-84; host/producer The First Nighter NY Times primetime cable highlight program, 1977-84; pres., chief exec. officer Starpower, Inc., 1984-91; affiliate news corr. ABC Radio Network, NYC, 1984-86; pres. Promarket People Inc., 1991-93; S.W. contbg. corr. Am. in the Morning, First Light, Mut. Broadcasting System, 1992; S.W. freelance corr. Voice of Am., USIA, 1992—. Perennial critic Off-Off Broadway Short Play Festival, NYC, 1984—; was 1st Woman on 10 O'Clock News, WNEW-TV, 1967. Contbg. feature writer Vis a Vis mag., 1988-91. Celebrity panel Arthritis Telethon, NYC, 1976. Selected episodes of First Nighter program in archives NY Pub. Libr., Billy Rose Theatre Collection, Rodgers and Hammerstein Collection, Performing Arts Rsch.Ctr. Mem. Drama Desk. Clubs: National Arts, Dutch Treat. Presbyterian. Personal E-mail: vwoodruff50@yahoo.com.

WOODRUM, CLIFTON A., III, lawyer, retired state legislator; b. Washington, July 23, 1938; s. Clifton A. Jr. and Margaret (Lanier) W.; m. Emily Abbitt, Aug. 10, 1963; children: Robert, Meredith W. Snowden, Anne. AB, U. N.C., 1961; LLB, U. Va., 1964. Bar: Va. 1964, U.S. Dist. Ct. (we. dist.) Va. 1964, U.S. Ct. Appeals (4th cir.) 1968, U.S. Supreme Ct. 1970. Assoc. Dodson, Pence & Coulter, Roanoke, Va., 1964-68; ptnr. Dodson, Pence, Viar, Woodrum & Mackey, 1968-95; counsel Dodson, Pence & Viar, 1995-98; mem. Va. Ho. of Dels., 1980—2004; ret., 2004—. Bd. dirs. Hometown Bank. Chmn. 6th Dist. Dem. Com., Va., 1972-76; mem. State Water Commn., 1981-2000, State Crime Commn., 1982-2000, chmn., 1995-98; chmn. Med. Malpractice Study, Va., 1984-85, Freedom of Info. Study, 1998-2000; mem. Electric Utility Restructing Com., 1997-2003, Freedom of Info. Adv. Coun., 2000-2002, chmn.; bd. dirs. Va. Coalition Open Govt., 2004—, We. Va. Land Trust, 2004—, Libr. of Va., 2004—. Recipient Freedom of Info. award, Va. Coalition on Govt., 1999, 2003, Outstanding Legislator award, Va. Assn. Chiefs of Police, 1999, Child Advocate award, Am. Acad. Pediats. (Va. chpt.), 1997, Profiles in Courage award, Coalition of Labor Union Women, 2002, Outstanding Svc. award, Va. Firefighters Assn., 2003, McCain Fellow Advocacy award, ACOG, 2006. Mem.: ABA, Roanoke Bar Assn., Va. Bar Assn. Episcopalian. Home: 2641 Cornwallis Ave SE Roanoke VA 24014-3339 Office: Clifton A Woodrum PO Box 990 Roanoke VA 24005-0990 Office Phone: 540-982-5547.

WOODRUM, PATRICIA ANN, librarian; b. Hutchinson, Kans., Oct. 11, 1941; d. Donald Jewell and Ruby Pauline (Shuman) Hoffman; m. Clayton Eugene Woodrum, Mar. 31, 1962; 1 child, Clayton Eugene, II. BA, Kans. State Coll., Pittsburg, 1963; MLS, U. Okla., 1966. Br. libr. Tulsa City-County Libr. System, 1964-65, head brs., 1965-66, head reference dept., 1966-67, chief extension, chief pub. svc., 1967-73, asst. dir., 1973-76, exec. dir., 1976-96; owner Paradigm Mgmt. Cons. Svcs., 1997—. Active Leadership Tulsa Alumni; exec. dir. Bot. Garden/Edn. and Rsch. Ctr.; bd. dirs. Tulsa Garden Ctr. Recipient Disting. Libr. award Okla. Libr. Assn., 1982, Leadership Tulsa Paragon award, 1987, Women in Comm. Newsmaker award, 1989, Outstanding Alumnus award U. Okla. Sch. Libr. Info. Studies, 1989, Headliner award Tulsa Press Club, 1996, Disting. Alumnus Coll. Arts and Scis., U. Okla., 2000; inducted into Tulsa City-County Libr. Hall of Fame, 1989, Okla. Womens Hall of Fame, 1993. Mem. ALA, Pub. Libr. Assn. (pres. 1993-94), Okla. Libr. Assn. (pres. 1978-79, Disting. Libr. award 1982, Meritorious Svc. award 1996), Tulsa Press Club. Democrat. Episcopalian. Avocations: swimming, gardening. Office Phone: 918-728-2700. Business E-Mail: pwoodrum@tulsaconnect.com.

WOODRUM, ROBERT LEE, executive search consultant; b. Merkel, Tex., Mar. 3, 1945; s. Bill and Norma (Shea) W.; m. Linda Mary Larkin, July 20, 1968; children: Jennifer, Michael. BA, Calif. State U., Northridge, 1967; postgrad., U. Okla., 1974. Press sec. U.S. Senate, Washington, 1977-78; dir. pub. affairs U.S. Office Personnel Mgmt., Washington, 1979-80; pres. Corp. Communications, Washington, 1980-82; v.p. Norton Simon Inc., NYC, 1982-83; spl. asst. to the commr. NFL, NYC, 1983-84; exec. dir. Ritz Paris Hemingway Award, 1984-87; pres. Ritz Paris Internat., 1984-86; sr. v.p. AmBase Corp., 1986-91; mng. dir. Korn/Ferry Internat., NYC, 1991—; dir. DataBuilt, Inc., 2000—. Advisor USIA, Washington, 1980-93, ARC, 1983, White House Vets. Com., 1979-80. Trustee N.Y.C. Meals on Wheels, Inc. Lt. comdr. USN, 1968-77. Mem.: Ocean Reef Club, S.C. Yacht Club. Office: 117 Harbour PSGE Hilton Head Island SC 29926-1265 Business E-Mail: woodrumr@kornferry.com.

WOODS, ALLAN P., information technology executive; B in History and Philosophy, St. John's Univ., NYC. Officer Bankers Trust of NY, 1970—72; pres. several subs. Fidata/Bradford Computer and Sys; exec. v.p. and head info. svc. dept Mellon Fin. Corp., 1986—99, vice chmn. & chief info. officer, 1999—. Adv. bd. mem. Banking Industry Tech. Secretariat; bd. dir. Holy Family Inst., Duquesne Uni. (exec. com.); mem. visitors' bd. Univ. Pitts. Sch. of Library and Info. Sci.; tech. com. mem. Univ. Pitts. Med. Ctr. Capt. USMC, Vietnam. Mem.: Fin. Svc. Roundtable. Office: Vice Chair & CIO Mellon Fin Corp One Mellon Ctr Pittsburgh PA 15258-0001

WOODS, CAROL SMITH, private school educator; d. David E. and Margaret (Ballinger) Smith; m. William Kent Woods, Apr. 1, 1980; children: Stephen, Todd. BA, U. Iowa, Iowa City, 1967; MEd, Xavier U., 1997. Tchg. coord. Montessori Ctr. Rm., Cin., 1975—2006; clin. dir. Cin. Masonic Children's Learning Ctr., 2006—. Cons. Am. Montessori Soc., Cin., 1982—99; adj. prof. Xavier U., Cin., 1992—2000; master tchr. Scottish Rite Learning Ctr., Cin., 1998—; presenter in field. Author: Wood's Words, 2002, Early Literacy Handbook, 2003, Woods' Words Advanced, 2006; contbr. articles to profl. jours. Mem.: ASCD, Acad. Orton-Gillingham Practitioners and Educators (cert. mem. 2001—), Am. Montessori Soc., Internat. Dyslexia Assn. Avocations: reading, exercise, crossword puzzles. Home: 3750 Broadview Dr Cincinnati OH 45208

WOODS, DALE, retired mathematics professor; b. Stone County, Mo., Nov. 1, 1922; s. Fielding J. Woods and N. Elizabeth Holt. BS, Mo. State U., 1943; MS, Okla. State U., 1950, EdD, 1960. Instr. ND State U., Fargo, 1946—50; geophysics rschr. Advanced Geophysics, Houston, 1950—51; asst. prof. U. So. Miss., Hattiesburg, 1951—52; rsch. asst. Halliburton, Houston, 1952—53; asst. prof. U. Memphis, 1953—57; assoc. prof. Idaho State U., Pocatello, 1957—59; prof., head divsn. math. Truman State U., Kirksville, Mo., 1959—82, prof. emeritus, 1982—; prof. U. Ctrl. Okla., 1982—93. Served with USN, 1944—45. Mem.: Am. Math. Soc., Math. Assn. Am., Masons. Democrat. Address: 2430 Holt Woods Rd Reeds Spring MO 65737

WOODS, DAN, information technology manager, consultant; BA in Computer Sci., U. Mich., 1982; MS in Journalism, Columbia U., 1989. Database editor The News and Observer/Nando.net, 1992—95; info. tech. cons. Time Inc. New Media, 1995—99, TheStreet.com, 1998—99; CTO CapitalThinking, 1999—2002. Mem. CTO adv. coun. InfoWorld; bd. mem. Big Star Entertainment; mem. policy adv. bd. on pub. key infrastructure Am. Bankers Assn. Author: The Education of a CTO, 2003; co-author: Developers Guide to the Java Web Server, 1999; contbr. articles to profl. jours.

WOODS, DANIEL JAMES, lawyer; b. Bklyn., Nov. 12, 1952; s. James J. and Elinor (Masten) W.; m. Kathryn Anne Morris, Dec. 27, 1974; children: Meghan M., Alexandra K., Shauna E. AB cum laude, U. So. Calif., 1974, JD, 1977. Bar: Calif. 1977, US Dist. Ct. (cen., ea., so., and no. dists.) Calif., US Ct. Appeals (9th cir.) 1978, US Supreme Ct. 1981. Law clk. to judge U.S. Dist. Ct. (ctrl. dist.), Calif., 1977-78; assoc. Brobeck, Phleger & Harrison, LA, 1978-84, ptnr., 1984-96, White & Case LLP, 1996—. Vol. pro tem LA Mcpl. Ct., 1985—, LA Superior Ct., 1989—. Roman Catholic. Avocations: tennis, bicycling, travel. Office: White & Case LLP 633 W 5th St Los Angeles CA 90071-2627 Office Phone: 213-620-7700. E-mail: dwoods@whitecase.com.

WOODS, DAVID G., dean; MusB, Washburn U.; MusM, Northwestern U., PhD in Philosophy; student, Aspen Inst., Copenhagen Conservatory Music. Dir. music Colo. Acad., 1966—73; chmn. div. music. edn. Iowa State U., Ames, 1974—84; dir. Sch. Music U. Ariz., 1985—91; dean Coll. Fine Arts U. Okla., 1991—97; dean Sch. Music. Ind. U., 1997—99; dean Sch. Fine Arts U. Conn., 2000—. Author: Phoebe in Her Petticoat, Congotay; co-author: Teaching Music in 21st Century, Jump Right In!; contbr. chapters to books, Handbook for Rsch. in Music Teaching & Learning, Second Handbook for Rsch. in Music Teaching & Learning. Fulbright scholar to Iceland, 1979, Fulbright scholar to Australia, 1986. Office: Office of the Dean U Conn Sch Fine Arts 830 Bolton Rd Rm 202 Unit 1128 Storrs Mansfield CT 06269 Home Phone: 860-429-5809; Office Phone: 860-486-3016. E-mail: david.woods@uconn.edu.

WOODS, DENNIS OLIVER, headmaster, market and political research analyst; b. Spirit Lake, Iowa, Mar. 11, 1947; s. Peter Ashton and Edna Elizabeth Woods; m. Jane Robertson; children: Miranda, Vijay, Catherine. BS in Agrl. Journalism, Iowa State U., 1970; MEd, Oreg. State U., 1973; postgrad., Multnomah Bible Coll., 1973—74, Computer Career Inst., 1974—75. Polit. rsch. asst., vol. several polit. and social action coms., Portland, 1976—79; market/polit. rsch. analyst Bardsley & Haslacher, Portland, 1980—84; market/statis. rsch. analyst Columbia Info. Sys., Portland, 1985—90; owner Target Market Strategies LLC, Clackamas, 1991—; founder, headmaster King's Way Classical Acad., Clackamas, 2001—. Lectr. in field. Author: Discipling the Nations, 1996, Keys to the Classics, 2001, Covenant & Crisis in American History, 2003; contbr. articles to profl. jours. Issues and strategy cons. Multnomah County Rep. Party, Portland, 1986—90, vice chmn., 1990; bd. mem. Oreg. Mktg. Assn., Portland, 1973—74. First lt. art. US Army, 1971—72. Mem.: Nat. Reform Assn. (adv. bd.), Interfaith Stewardship Alliance (adv. bd.). Presbyterian. Achievements include helped pioneer development of perception analyzer system for testing print and television advertising; one of the first to blend ancient trivium methodology (grammar, dialectic, rhetoric) and classical content with internet delivery technologies. Avocation: woodworking. Office: Kings Way Classical Acad PO Box 497 Clackamas OR 97015 Office Phone: 503-658-1755. Personal E-mail: tmarkets@netzero.org.

WOODS, DONALD E., healthcare executive; b. Memphis, Nov. 1, 1946; s. John Thomas and Hazel O. (Perry) W.; m. Shirlene M. Durutta, 1978 (div. 1992); children: Donald E. Jr., Lori Ann, Ryan Christopher; m. Joan M. Turley, 1995 (div. 2000); children: Kathryn Ashley, Lauren Rose. BS in Acctg., U. So. Calif., 1972, MBA, 1976. CPA, Calif. Audit supr. Ernst and Young, LA, 1972-76; asst. v.p. Am. Med. Internat., Beverly Hills, Calif., 1976-80; corp. contr. Safeco Title Ins. Co., Panorama City, Calif., 1980-82; sr. v.p. fin. Heritage divsn. Beverly Enterprises, Md., 1982-84; co-founder, CFO Hannover Health Care, Inc., Md., 1984-85; founder, pres., CEO Oakwood Living Ctrs., Inc., McLean, Va., 1985-91; owner, pres. HMS of Newport (R.I.), Inc., 1992—; owner, gen. mgr. Lizzie Borden Bed and Breakfast, LLC, Fall River, Mass. Sgt. USMC, 1964-68. Mem. AICPA, Newport C. of C. Avocations: sailing, skiing. Home: 173 Gideon Lawton Ln Portsmouth RI 02871 Office: HMS of Newport Inc PO Box 610 Newport RI 02840-0011

WOODS, DUANE C., waste management executive; b. Spokane, Wash., 1951; BA, U. Wash., Seattle, 1973; JD, U. Puget Sound, Tacoma, Wash., 1980. Bar: Wash. 1980. Asst. sec. State of Wash.; local and state policy and mgmt. positions City of Seattle; ptnr. Heller, Erhman White & McAuliffe and Summit Law Group; v.p., gen. counsel Western Group Waste Mgmt., Inc., Houston, sr. v.p. Western Group. Mem.: Phi Beta Kappa. Office: Waste Mgmt Inc 7025 N Scottsdale Rd Ste 200 Scottsdale AZ 85253 Office Fax: 480-624-8400, 866-863-7960. *

WOODS, GARY V., professional football team executive, former professional basketball team executive, automotive executive; b. Nov. 9, 1943; BBA, So. West Tex. State; MBA, SMU. Pres. San Antonio Spurs, 1988—93; ceo, pres., chair. McCombs Enterprises, San Antonio, 1979—; pres., ceo Minnesota Vikings, Eden Prairie, 1998—. Office: Minnesota Vikings 9520 Viking Dr Eden Prairie MN 55344-3898 also: Mark B Woods 755 E Mulberry Ave Ste 600 San Antonio TX 78212-6013

WOODS, HARRY ARTHUR, JR., lawyer; b. Hartford, Ark., Feb. 15, 1941; s. Harry Arthur and Viada (Young) W.; m. Carol Ann (Meschter), Jan. 21, 1967; children: Harry Arthur III, Elizabeth Ann. BA in Econs., Okla. State U., 1963; JD, NYU, 1966. Bar: Okla., 1970. Assoc. White and Case, NYC, 1966—67, Crowe and Dunlevy, Oklahoma City, 1971—75, ptnr., 1976—, dir. Councilman City of Edmond, 1975-79; mayor pro tem, 1977-79. Capt. JAGC, U.S. Army, 1967-71. Fellow Am. Bar Found., mem. ABA (ho. of dels. 2003-05, interim state del. 2004-05), Am. Law Inst., Internat. Assn. Def. Counsel, Okla. Bar Assn. (pres. 2004, bd. govs. 2001-05, profl. responsibility tribunal 1999-02; Outstanding Svc. award 1982, Golden Gavel award 1998, Neil Bogan Professionalism award 1998), Ruth Bader Ginsburg Inn of Ct. (pres. 1998-00), Okla. County Bar Assn. (bd. dirs. 2001-03). Democrat. Methodist. Avocations: rock climbing, flying, jogging, bicycling, photography. Office: Crowe and Dunlevy PC Ste 1800 20 N Broadway Oklahoma City OK 73102-8273 Office Phone: 405-235-7754. Office Fax: 405-272-5236. Business E-Mail: harry.woods@crowedunlevy.com. *

WOODS, J. P., religious organization administrator; b. Houston, June 22, 1950; s. William Oliver and Lilly Virginia (Hetherington) W. Student, Blinn Coll., 1968—69; BA, Ft. Lewis Coll., 1971; PhD in Bus. Adminstrn. Mktg., Trinity So. U., 2003. Ordained to ministry, Life Bible Coll., 1996. V.p. sales Bon Ton, Inc., Dallas, 1977-80; regional sales mgr. John O. Butler Co., Chgo., 1980-81; sales mgr. Fox Meyer, Inc., Oklahoma City, 1981-82; sales cons., trainer Rugby Labs., Inc., NYC, 1982-83; nat. dir. key accounts United Rsch. Labs., Inc., Mut. Pharm., Inc., Phila., 1983-88; v.p. Western div. Barr Labs., Pomona, NY, 1988-94; pres., CEO J. P. Woods Ministries, Inc., 1996—. Sr. pastor Aspen Christian World Outreach, Aspen, Colo., 1996—2006; elected to Tex. State Bd. Pharmacy, 1992. Author, editor: Sales and Marketing Techniques, 1984. Mem. Rep. Presdl. Task Force, Washington, 1982—, life membership honor roll; mem. Presdl. Commn., 1988; sustaining mem. Rep. Nat. Com., Washington, 1983—, cert. recognition, 1991-92; preferred mem. Nat. Conservative Polit. Action Com., Washington, 1983—; elected mem. Rep. Campaign Coun. Com., 1992—; elected del. State Tex. Rep. Party, 1992; founding mem. CBN Founders, Virginia Beach, Va., 1986—; active Christian Coalition, 1992—, Kenneth Copeland Prtns. Ministries, 1992. Recipient Medal of Merit, Ronald Reagan, Pres., Washington, 1985, Presdl. Commn. from Ronald Reagan, 1986, Cert. of Recognition Rep. Nat. Com., 1991-92; named to Rep. Presdl. Task Force Life Membership Honor Roll. Mem. Nat. Assn. Chain Druggists, Nat. Wholesale Drug Assn., Nat. Assn. Retail Druggists, Tex. Pharm. Assn. (com. mem. 1991-92), DAV Comdrs., U.S. Senatorial Club (founder). Mem. Full Gospel Ch. Avocations: collecting western art, golf, tennis, skiing, travel. Office Phone: 325-657-0420. Personal E-mail: TheRevJPW@aol.com, jpwminc@aol.com.

WOODS, JACQUELINE F., public relations executive; b. Oct. 22, 1947; BA, Muskingum Coll., 1969. Former v.p. of licensing and pricing Oracle Corp.; former pres. Ameritech Ill., Cleve., Ameritech Ohio subs. Ameritech Corp., Cleve.; sr. consultant Landau Public Relations, 2002—. Bd. dirs. Timken Co., Andersons Inc., School Specialty, Inc., 2006—. Exec. com. mem. Greater Cleve. Sports Commn.; trustee Playhouse Square, Muskingum Coll.; chair emeritus Cleve. Chapter of Am. Red Cross; bd. mem. Great Lakes Sci. Ctr., Cleve. Found., 1998—, Kent State U., 2004—, U. Hosp. Healthcare Sys., Columbus Met. Library. Named to OH Women Hall of Fame, 1998. Office: Landau Public Relations 700 W St Clair Ave Cleveland OH 44113 Fax: 312-207-1601. *

WOODS, JAMES, actor; b. Vernal, Utah, Apr. 18, 1947; m. Kathryn Morrison-Pahoa, 1980 (div. 1983); m. Sarah Owen, June 2, 1989 (div. 1990). Student, MIT, 1965-69. Performances include (Broadway prodns.) Borstal Boy, Trial of the Catonsville 9, Finishing Touches, Moonchildren (Theatre World award), off-Broadway prodn. Saved (Obie award, Clarence Derwent award); actor (films) The Visitors, 1971, Hickey and Boggs, 1972, The Way We Were, 1973, The Gambler, 1974, Night Moves, 1975, Distance, 1975, Alex & the Gypsy, 1976, The Choirboys, 1977, The Onion Field, 1979 (Golden Globe award nomination), The Black Marble, 1980, Eyewitness, 1981, Split Image, 1982, Fast-Walking, 1982, Videodrome, 1983, Against All Odds, 1984, Once Upon a Time in America, 1984, Cat's Eye, 1985, Joshua Then and Now, 1985, Salvador, 1986 (Acad. award nomination, 1987), Best Seller, 1987, Cop, 1988, The Boost, 1988, True Believer, 1989, Immediate Family, 1989, The Hard Way, 1991, Straight Talk, 1992, Diggstown, 1992, Chaplin, 1992, The Getaway, 1994, The Specialist, 1994, Curse of the Starving Class, 1994, Nixon, 1995, Casino, 1995, Ghosts of Mississippi, 1996 (Acad. award nomination, Golden Globe nomination), For Better or Worse, 1996, Killer: A Journal of Murder, 1996, (voice) Hercules, 1997, Contact, 1997, Vampires, 1998, Kicked in the Head, 1998, Another Day in Paradise, 1998, True Crime, 1999, The General's Daughter, 1998, Any Given Sunday, 1999, The Virgin Suicides, 2000, Race to Space, 2001, Scary Movie 2, 2001, Riding in Cars with Boys, 2001, John Q, 2002, (voice only) Stuart Little 2, 2002, Northfork, 2003, This Girl's Life, 2003, Ark, 2005, Pretty Persuasion, 2005, Be Cool, 2005, End Game, 2006; (TV films) All the Way Home, 1971, Footsteps, 1972, A Great American Tragedy, 1972, Foster and Laurie, 1975, F. Scott Fitzgerald in Hollywood, 1976, The Disappearance of Aimee, 1976, Raid on Entebbe, 1977, The Gift of Love, 1978, And Your Name is Jonah, 1979, The Incredible Journey of Doctor Meg Laurel, 1979, Badge of the Assassin, 1985, Promise, 1986 (Emmy award, Golden Apple award, Golden Globe award), In Love and War, 1987 (Golden Globe award nomination), My Name Is Bill W. (Emmy award 1989), Women & Men: Stories of Seduction, 1990, The Boys, 1991, Citizen Cohn, HBO, 1992 (Emmy nomination, Lead Actor - Miniseries, 1993), Jane's House, 1994, Indictment: The McMartin Trial, 1995 (Emmy nomination, Cable Ace nomination), The Summer of Ben Tyler, 1996 (Golden Globe nomination), Dirty Pictures, 2000, Showtime, 2000 (Best Actor in Mini-Series of Motion Picture Made for TV award Golden Satellite 2000), (voice only) Legend of the Lost Tribe, 2002, Rudy: The Rudy Giuliani Story, 2003; (TV miniseries) Holocaust, 1978; (TV series) Shark, 2006-; (TV appearances) Kojak, 1974, The Rockford Files, 1974, Welcome Back, Kotter, 1975, The Streets of San Francisco, 1975, The Rookies, 1975, Barnaby Jones, 1976, Police Story, 1976, Young Maverick, 1979, 80, (voice) The Simpsons, 1994, Fallen Angels, 1995, Clerks, 2002, Celebrity Poker Showdown 2004, 2005, (voice only) Family Guy, 2005, ER, 2005; dir., writer (films) Falling In Love in Pongo Ponga, 2002 Recipient Daytime Emmy for Outstanding Performer Animated Program for Disney's Hercules, 2000. Mem. Acad. Motion Picture Arts and Scis., Internat. Platform Assn., Players Club, Mountaingate Country Club. Avocations: golf, photography, cooking. Office: Guttman Assocs 118 S Beverly Dr Ste 201 Beverly Hills CA 90212-3016

WOODS, JAMES STERRETT, toxicologist; b. Lewistown, Pa., Feb. 26, 1940; s. James Sterrett and Jane Smith (Parker) W.; m. Nancy Fugate, Dec. 20, 1969; 1 dau., Erin Elizabeth. AB, Princeton U., 1962; MS, U. Wash., 1968, PhD, 1970; MPH, U. N.C., 1978. Diplomate Am. Bd. Toxicology. Rsch. assoc. dept. pharmacology Yale U. Sch. Medicine, New Haven, 1970-72; staff fellow environ. toxicology. Nat. Inst. Environ. Health Scis. br. NIH, Research Triangle Park, NC, 1972-75, head biochem. toxicology sect., 1975-77; sr. rsch. leader environ. occupl. health risk evaluation Battelle Ctrs. for Pub. Health Rsch. and Evaluation, Seattle, 1978—2006; prof. U. Wash., Seattle, 1979—. Pres. Am. Bd. Toxicology, 1997-98. Contbr. articles to profl. jours. With USN, 1962-66. Scholar USPHS, 1966-70; Fellow Am. Cancer Soc., 1970-72. Mem. AAAS, Am. Assn. Cancer Rsch., Am. Soc. Pharmacology and Exptl. Therapeutics, Pacific NW Assn. Toxicologists (founding pres.), Soc. Epidemiology Rsch., Soc. Toxicology, Am. Coll. of Epidemiology, Am. Bd. Toxicology (pres. 1997-98). Home: 4525 E Laurel Dr NE Seattle WA 98105-3838 Office: Univ Wash Ste 100 4225 Roosevelt Way NE Seattle WA 98105 Office Phone: 206-685-3443. Business E-Mail: jwoods@u.washington.edu.

WOODS, JOHN ELMER, plastic surgeon; b. Battle Creek, Mich., July 5, 1929; m. Janet Ruth; children: Sheryl, Mark, Jeffrey, Jennifer, Judson. BA, Asbury Coll., 1949, DHL, 1999; MD, Western Res. U., 1955; PhD, U. Minn., 1966. Intern Gorgas Hosp., Panama Canal Zone, 1955-56, resident in gen. surgery, 1956-57, Mayo Grad. Sch., Rochester, Minn., 1960-65, resident in plastic surgery, 1966-67, Brigham Hosp., Boston, Mass., 1968; fellow, transplant cons. Harvard Med. Sch., Cambridge, Mass., 1969; cons. in gen. and plastic surgery Mayo Clinic, Rochester, 1969-93, vice chmn. Dept. Surgery; asst. prof. Mayo Med. Sch., Rochester, 1973-76, assoc. prof., 1976-80, prof. plastic surgery, 1980-93, Stuart W. Harrington prof. surgery. Vis. prof. Yale Sch. Medicine, New Haven, 1984, Harvard Sch. Medicine, Cambridge, 1984. Contbr. over 200 articles to profl. jours.; also 26 book chpts. and 1 film. Recipient Disting. Mayo Clinician award, 1991, Disting. Mayo Alumnus award, 1999. Mem. AMA (coun. on sci. affairs 1985-87), ACS (grad edn. com. 1985-87), Am. Bd. Med. Specialties, Am. Bd. Plastic Surgery (sec.-treas. 1985-88, chmn. 1988-89), Am. Soc. Plastic Surgeons Ednl. Fedn. (pres. 1984-85). Avocations: skiing, sailing, reading, the arts. Office: Mayo Clinic Plummer N-10 Rochester MN 55905-0001 Business E-Mail: woods.john@mayo.edu.

WOODS, JOHN MAYNARD, lawyer; b. New Canaan, Conn., Jan. 14, 1955; s. John Eric and Margery (Maynard) W.; m. Elizabeth Anne Duff, Apr. 9, 1983; children: Avery Carson, Katherine McKercher, Abigail Elizabeth. AB, Middlebury Coll., 1976; JD with honors, Tulane U., 1980. Bar: N.Y. 1981, U.S. Dist. Ct. (ea. and so. dists.) N.Y. 1981, U.S. Ct. Appeals (5th cir.) 1984, U.S. Ct. Appeals (2d cir.) 1988, U.S. Ct. Appeals (4th cir.) 1992, U.S. Supreme Ct. 1998, U.S. Ct. Appeals (1st cir.) 2001, U.S. Ct. Appeals (11th cir.) 1999. Assoc. Thacher, Proffitt & Wood LLP, NYC, 1980-87, ptnr., maritime, admiralty internat. litig., ins., environ. law, 1987—, and head, litig., dispute resolution practice group. Chmn. Average Adjusters Assn. US. Contbg. editor Bus. Ins. Guide, 1989, Recreational Boating Law, 1992. Mem. ABA, Maritime Law Assn. U.S. (bd. dirs.), Assn. Bar City N.Y., Average Adjuster Assn. U.S. (chmn.). Office: Thacher Proffitt & Wood 2 World FinancialCtr New York NY 10281 Office Phone: 212-912-7672. Office Fax: 212-912-7751. Business E-Mail: jwoods@tpw.com.

WOODS, JOHN WILLIAM, electrical, computer and systems engineering educator, consultant; b. Washington, Dec. 5, 1943; s. John Gill and Margaret (McHugh) W.; m. Harriet Hemmerich, June 17, 1972; children: Anne, Christopher. BSEE, MIT, 1965, MSEE, 1967, PhD, 1970. Sr. rsch. engr. Lawrence Livermore (Calif.) Nat. Lab., 1973-76; asst. prof. Rensselaer Poly. Inst., Troy, NY, 1976-78, assoc. prof., 1978-84, prof., 1985—. Vis. prof. Delft Tech. U., The Netherlands, 1985, Heinrich-Hertz Inst., Berlin, 2000; program dir. NSF, Washington, 1987-88; assoc. dir. Ctr. for Image Processing Rsch., 1992—; cons. Kodak, Rochester, N.Y., 1985-86, Johns Hopkins Applied Physics Lab., Laurel, Md., 1987, Calian Comms. Ltd., 1990-91, Thomson Electronics, 2005; co-founder Focus Interactive Tech., Inc., 1993; assoc. dir. NSF I/U Ctr. for Next Generation Video, 1998-2001, dir. 2002-05; mem. compression com. Digital Cinema Initiatives, 2003-04. Author: Multidimensional Signal, Image, and Video Processing and Coding, 2006; co-author: Probability and Random Processes for Engineers, 1986, 3d edit., 2002; editor: Subband Image Coding, 1991; co-editor: Handbook of Visual Communications, 1995; mem. editl. bd. Graphical Models and Image Processing, 1989-93; contbg. author book chpts., articles to profl. jours. Mem. Com. Acad. Excellence, Clifton Park, N.Y., 1984. Capt. USAF, 1969-73. Grantee NSF, Army Rsch. Office, Advanced Rsch. Projects Agy., Ctr. Advanced TV Studies, 1978-2005. Fellow: IEEE (editl. bd. Trans. on Video Tech. 1990—2002, Third Millennium medal 2000); mem.: Nat. Com. for Info. Tech. Stds., Internat. Stds. Orgn. (mem. motion pictures expert group 2001—), IEEE Signal Processing Soc. (assoc. editor jour. 1979—82, com. chmn. 1983—85, ad. com. 1986—88, ednl. com. chmn. 1987—93, 1st IEEE Internat. Conf. on Image Processing 1994, co-chmn. tech. program com., Best Paper awards 1977, 1986, Meritorious Svc. award 1989, Tech. Achievement award 1993). Roman Catholic. Home: 43 Longview Dr Clifton Park NY 12065-2318 Office: Rensselaer Poly Inst ECSE Dept Troy NY 12180-3590 Home Phone: 518-383-3703; Office Phone: 518-276-6079. E-mail: woods@ecse.rpi.edu.

WOODS, KRYSTYNA JANINA, artist, pharmacist; b. Warwick, Queensland, Australia, Jan. 28, 1961; arrived in U.S., 1998; d. Jan and Janina Dzierzanowski; m. Ross Maxwell Woods, Aug. 28, 1993; children: Harrison George Maxwell, Jack Henry Alexander. BPharm, U. Queensland, Brisbane, 1980. Registered pharmacist Pharmacy Bd. Queensland. Pre-registration pharmacist, asst. mgr. Payless Chemists, Brisbane, Queensland, 1980—81; pharmacist, mgr. Benowa Pharmacy, Gold Coast, Australia, 1981—83; chief pharmacist, asst. mgr. Sorrento Pharmacy, Gold Coast, Australia, 1983—85; chief pharmacist, mgr. Moses Edward St. Pharmacy, Brisbane, 1986—88; chief pharmacist, part-time mgr. Aspley Day & Night Pharmacy, Brisbane, 1988—93; locum pharmacist mgr. Auchenflower Pharmacy, Brisbane, 1993—95, Terry White Pharmacy, Brisbane, 1993—95, Transit Ctr. Pharmacy, Brisbane, 1993—95; owner, mgr., chief pharmacist Indooroopilly Day & Night Pharmacy, Brisbane, 1995—2000. Model, actress Viviens Model Agy., Brisbane and Sydney, 1985—93; actress, model print, TV, radio and stage Margo Mott/Buckinghams, Gold Coast, 1985—93, Queensland Theatre Co., Brisbane, 1985—93, Javeenbah Little Theatre, Gold Coast, 1985—93, Gold Coast Little Theatre, 1982—84; mentor Young Australian Profls. in Am., NYC, 2003; represented Queensland, Australia in Miss World Pageant, 1985; lectr. Mt. Gravatt Tech. Coll. Further Edn., Brisbane, 1989; interviewed by mags. N.J. Monthly, 2001, Australian House and Garden Mag., 1999, Sunday Mail Mag., 1998, Matters Mag., 2005. One-woman shows include Natura Gallery, Heritage Hotel, Brisbane, 1995—97, Brisbane Herbsfest, 1995—97, Wentworth Gallery, Palm Beach, 1995—96, White Plains, 1995—96, Boston, 1995—96, Chgo., 1995—96, Madison Studio Gallery, 2001, The Show Gallery, Chatham, 2002—03, Internat. Art Expo, N.Y.C., 2003, Solange Rabello Art Gallery, Miami, 2003—04, Australian Consulate, N.Y.C., 2003, Arts Coun. of Morris Area, 2004, Happy Dog Gallery, Piermont, N.Y., 2004—06, Maplewood Open Studio Exhbn., 2005, South Orange and Maplewood Artist Studio Tour, 2005, exhibitions include Village Gallery, Laguna Beach, 2003, Maplewood/So. Orange Artist Study Tour, 2004—06, Artists Studio Tours, 2004—05, Happy Dog Gallery, Piermont, N.Y., 2004—06, Maplewood Open Studio Exhbn., 2006, executed murals, S. Orange/Maplewood, NJ, 2005. Rep. city for state visit by Queen Elizabeth II; asst. to pres. in presentation to MP regarding protection of pharmacy ownership Queensland Pharmacy Guild, Brisbane, 1997. Recipient Award of Merit for Outstanding Achievement, Manhattan Arts Internat., 1999, Art Show awards, city couns. and art assns., 1977—89, Adjudicator's Choice award, Warana Drama Festival and Arts, 1982. Mem.: Australian Am. Assn., Arts Coun. of Morris Area (invited spkr. art promotion 2002), Nat. Mus. Women in Arts, Maplewood Club, Internat. Friends Club, Catharine Lorillard Wolfe Art Club (assoc.). Episcopalian. Avocations: tennis, golf, interior decorating, reading, travel. Office: Krysia D Designs 422 Walton Rd Maplewood NJ 07040 E-mail: krysiadart@aol.com.

WOODS, LAWRENCE MILTON, airline company executive; b. Manderson, Wyo., Apr. 14, 1932; s. Ben Ray and Katherine (Youngman) Woods; m. Joan Frances Van Patten, June 10, 1952; 1 child, Laurie. B.Sc. with honors, U. Wyo., 1953; MA, N.Y. U., 1973, PhD, 1975; LL.D., Wagner Coll., 1973. CPA Colo., Mont.; bar: Mont. 1957. Acct. Peat, Marwick, Mitchell & Co. (C.P.A.'s), Billings, Mont., 1953; supervisory auditor Army Audit Agy., Denver, 1954-56; acct. Mobil Producing Co., Billings, Mont., 1956-59; planning analyst Socony Mobil Oil Co., NYC, 1959-63, planning mgr., 1963-65; v.p. N.Am. divsn. Mobil Oil Corp., NYC, 1966-67, gen. mgr. planning and econs. N.Am. divsn., 1967-69, v.p. N.Am. divsn., 1969-77, exec. v.p. N.Am. divsn., 1977-85, also dir. N.Am. divsn.; pres., CEO, dir. Centennial Airlines, Inc., 1985-87. Bd. dirs., chmn. The Heartland Funds, 2005. Author: Accounting for Capital, Construction and Maintenance Expeditures, 1967, The Wyoming Country Before Statehood, 1971, Sometimes the Books Froze, 1985, Moreton Frewen's Western Adventures, 1986, British Gentlemen in the Wild West, 1989; co-author: Takeover, 1980; editor: Wyoming Biographies, 1991, Wyoming's Big Horn Basin, 1996, Agent R, 2000, John Clay, Jr., 2001, Asa Shinn Mercer, 2003, A Material Witness, 2003, Alex Swan, 2006; contbr. Accountants' Encyclopedia, 1962; editor: Edward Shelley's Journal, 2005. With US Army, 1953—55. Mem.: AICPA, ABA, Mont. Bar Assn. Republican. Lutheran. Office: High Plains Pub Co PO Box 1860 Worland WY 82401-1860

WOODS, LEBBEUS, theoretical architect, educator; b. 1940; Student in Architecture, U. Ill.; student in Engring., Purdue U. Arch. Eero Saarinen Assocs., 1964—68; pvt. practice, 1968—; co-founder, sci. dir. Rsch. Inst. Exptl. Architecture, 1988—; prof. architecture Cooper Union, NYC. Vis. prof. The Bartlett, London, So. Calif. Inst. Architecture, LA, Columbia U., NYC, Harvard U. Prin. works include Centricity, 1987, Solohouse, 1988, Berlin Free-Zone, 1990, War and Architecture/Sarajevo Projects, 1993—94, Havana Projects, 1995, Terrain Projects, 1998—99, The Fall Installation, 2002; author: Radical Reconstruction, 1997, Lebbeus Woods: System Wien, 2005; co-author: The Storm and the Fall, 2004. Recipient Progressive Architecture award, Design Rsch., AIA Honors award, Chrysler award, Innovation in Design, 1994, Architecture award, AAAL, 2007. Office: Sch Architecture Cooper Union Cooper Sq New York NY 10003-7120 Office Phone: 212-353-4220. *

WOODS, MICHAEL LEE, lawyer; b. Denver, July 13, 1972; s. Robert Lee and Wai Chun Woods; m. Becky Turner Woods, Mar. 18, 2000; children: Fischer, Ella. BS in Mech. Engring., U. Colo., 1994; JD, George Washington U., 2002. Bar: Va. 2002, D.C. 2002, Ill. 2004. Atty. Finnegan Henderson, Washington, 2002—04, Caterpillar Inc., Peoria, Ill., 2004—. Editor: AIPLA Quarterly Jour., 2001. With USN, 1994—99. Office: Caterpillar 100 NE Adams St Peoria IL 61629 Office Phone: 309-675-4280. E-mail: woods.michael@insightbb.com.

WOODS, NANCY FUGATE, dean, women's health nurse, educator; BS, Wis. State U., 1968; MSN, U. Wash., 1969; PhD, U. N.C., 1978. Staff nurse Sacred Heart Hosp., Wis., 1968, Univ. Hosp., Wis., 1969-70, St. Francis Cabrini Hosp., 1970; nurse clinician Yale-New Haven Hosp., 1970-71; instr. nursing Duke U., Durham, N.C., 1971-72, from instr. to assoc. prof., 1972-78; assoc. prof. physiology U. Wash., Seattle, 1978-82, prof. physiology, 1982-84, chairperson dept. parent and child nursing, 1984-90, prof. dept. parent and child nursing, 1990—, dean Sch. Nursing, 1998—; dir. Ctr. Women's Health Rsch., U. Wash., Seattle, 1989—. Pres. scholar U. Calif., San Francisco, 1985-86. Contbr. articles to profl. jours. Fellow ANA, Am. Acad. Nursing, Inst. Medicare, N.A.S.; mem. AAUP, APHA, Am. Coll. Epidemiology, Soc. Menstrual Cycle Rsch. (v.p. 1981-82, pres. 1983-85), Soc. Advancement Women's Health Rsch. Office: U Wash Sch Nursing PO Box 357260 Seattle WA 98195-7260

WOODS, PENDLETON, college director, author; b. Ft. Smith, Ark., Dec. 18, 1923; s. John Powell and Mabel (Hon) W.; m. Lois Robin Freeman, Apr. 3, 1948; children: Margaret, Paul Pendleton, Nancy Cox. BA in Journalism, U. Ark., 1948; D (hon.), Okla. Christian U., Oklahoma City, 2005. Editor, asst. pub. mgr. Okla. Gas & Electric Co., Oklahoma City, 1948—69; dir. Living Legends of Okla., Okla. Christian U., Oklahoma City, 1969—82; dir. project, promotion Enterprise Sq. and Am. Citizenship Ctr., 1982—92, dir. Nat. Edn. Program and Am. Citizenship Ctr., 1992. Arbitrator BBB; leader youth seminars in field; state pub. affairs officer Employer Support Guard and Res. Author: You and Your Company Magazine, 1950, Church of Tomorrow, 1964, Myriad of Sports, 1971, This Was Oklahoma, 1979; recorded Sounds of Scouting, 1969, Born Grown,

1974 (We. Heritage award Nat. Cowboy Hall of Fame), One of a Kind, 1977, Countdown to Statehood, 1982, The Thunderbird Tradition, 1989, A Glimpse at Oklahoma, 1990, Historic Oklahoma County, 2002; editor Libertas. Vol. reader Okla. Libr. for the Blind; past pres. Okla. Assn. Epilepsy, Keep Okla. Beautiful, Okla. City Mental Health Clin.; past pres., hon. lifetime dir. Variety Health Ctr.; pub. rels. chmn. Okla. County chpt. ARC; past chmn. We. Heritage award Nat. Cowboy Hall of Fame; Am. Freedom Coun.; charter dir. Okla. Vets. Med. Rsch. Found.; cons. Exec. Svc. Corps.; ex-state comdr. Am. ex-Prisoners of War; vol. Okla. City VA Hosp.; state historian Okla. N.G.; chmn. Okla. City Independence Day Parade; exec. com. Okla. City Bicentennial Commn.; v.p. Okla. City chpt. Freedom Found.; bd. dirs. Campfire Girls Coun., Okla. Jr. Symphony, past pres.; bd. dirs. Zoo Amphitheater of Okla. City, Will Rogers Centennial Commn., Greater Okla. City Tree Bank Found., Boy Scout Am. (life); bd. dirs., co-founder Ctrl. Pk. Neighborhood Assn.; dir. Okla. for Resource Preservation; chmn. State Directional Signage Task Force. With US Army, WWII and Korean War, ret. col. Named Outstanding Young Man of Yr., Oklahoma City Jr. C. of C., 1953; recipient Silver Beaver award Boy Scouts Am., 1963, Wokan award Oklahoma City Coun. Camp Fire Girls, 1968, Silver medal Advt. Fedn. Am., Disting. Cmty. Svc. award Neighborhood Devel. and Conservation Ctr., 2 Commendation awards Am. Assn. for State and Local History, 4 honor medals Freedoms Found., Jefferson Davis medal United Daus. of Confederacy, Okla. Disting. Svc. medal (2), Outstanding Contbn. to Okla. Mus., Okla. Mus. Assn., 1987, Outstanding Contbn. to Okla. Tourism award Okla. Dept. Tourism, 1989, Cmty. Svc. award U. Ark. Alumni Assn., 1992, Citizenship and Patriot awards SAR, 1992, 5 Who Care award KOCO-TV, 1993, Jefferson award Am. Inst. for Pub. Svc., 1993, Mayor's award in Beautification, 1994, George Washington award Youth Leadership Found., St. Augustine, Fla., 1993, Golden Rule award J.C. Penney Found., 1999, Lifetime Achievement award Keep Okla. Beautiful, Pres.'s Vol. Svc. award, 2005; inducted into Okla. Journalism Hall of Fame, 2001, Okla. Mil. Hall of Fame, 2002, U. Ark. Journalism Hall of Fame, 2002, Okla. Historians Hall of Fame, 2007. Mem.: DAR (Medal of Honor 2005, Nation's Most Outstanding Ex-prisoner of War 2005, Outstanding Older Worker award for Okla. 2007), VFW, DAV, Okla. Distributive Edn., Okla. Jr. C. of C. (hon. life, past internat. dir.), Ctrl. Okla. Bus: Communicators (past pres., hon. life), Advt. Fedn. Am. (past dist. dir.), Soc. Assoc. Indsl. Editors (past v.p.), Okla. Vets. Coun. (chmn.), Okla. Heritage Assn., Okla. City Beautiful (publ. editor), Okla. Safety Coun. (publ. editor), Okla. County Hist. Soc. (dir., past pres.), 45th Inf. Divsn. Assn. (past pres.), Korean War Vets. Assn., Am. Legion, Mus. Unassigned Lands (chmn.), Mil. Order World Wars (regional comdr., Oklahoma City comdr., Okla. State comdr., nat. staff, Gold and Silver Patrick Henry Patriotism medals), Okla. Hist. Soc. (life; publ. editor,), Words of Jesus Found. (pres.), Okla. Zool. Soc. (past pres.), Okla. Geneal. Soc., Okla. County Sr. Nutrition Found. (sec., bd. dirs.), Freedom's Found. (v.p.), Nat. Eagle Scout Assn. (Okla. chmn.), U. Ark. Alumni Assn. (charter pres. Oklahoma City chpt.), Okla. Lung Assn. (pub. rels. com.), Am. Cancer Soc. (dir. Okla. County chpt.), Okla. Travel Industries Assn., Am. Ex-Prisoners of War (state comdr.), Okla. City Hist. Preservation Commn., Okla. City Clean and Green Coalition, Lincoln Park Country Club (pres.), Oklahoma City Advt. Club (past pres., hon. life), Kappa Sigma (nat. commr. publs.), Sigma Delta Chi. Home: 541 NW 31st St Oklahoma City OK 73118-7334 Office Phone: 405-425-5032. Personal E-mail: penwoods@cox.net.

WOODS, RANDALL BENNETT, history professor; b. Galveston, Tex., Oct. 10, 1944; s. Grady Bennett and Mary Dorothy Stokes Woods; m. Rhoda Margaret Lannen, June 18, 1966; children: Nicole Woods Olmstead, Jeffrey Randall. BA, U. Tex., Austin, 1967, MA, 1969, PhD, 1971—2001. Instr. U. Ark., Fayetteville, 1971, asst. prof., 1972, assoc. prof., 1979, prof., 1983, Cooper chair, 1988, disting. prof. history, 1994—, assoc. dean Fulbright coll. arts and scis., 1979—82, dean Fulbright coll. arts and scis., 1999—2002. Author: (history) A Changing of the Guard: Anglo-American Relations, 1941-1946, 1990, (history, biography) The Dawning of the Cold War, with Howard Jones, 1991, Fulbright: A Biography, 1995, Quest for Identity: America Since 1945, 2005, LBJ: Architect of American Ambition, 2006. Mem. Fayetteville Sch. Bd., 1982—86. E-6 staff sgt. US Army, 1969—75, 142 Artillery, Fayetteville, Ark. Recipient Alumni Disting. Faculty award, U. Ark., 1994, Ferrell Best Book in Pub. Rels. prize, Soc. Historians Am. Fgn. Rels., 1996, Outstanding Tchg. award, U. Ark. Tchg. Acad. Mem.: Soc. Historians Am. Fgn. Rels. (pres. 2006). Liberal. Episcopalian. Avocations: golf, travel, swimming. Home: 1781 Osage Bend Fayetteville AR 72701 Office: Univ Ark MAIN 416 Dept of History Fayetteville AR 72701 Office Phone: 479-575-5097. Office Fax: 479-575-2775. Business E-Mail: rwoods@uark.edu.

WOODS, REGINALD FOSTER, management consulting executive; b. Charleston, W.Va., Sept. 25, 1939; s. Reginald Foster and Jean Lee (Hill) W.; m. Katharine Terry Norden, May 11, 1963; children: Eric Arthur, Elizabeth Terry, Tracy Lee. BME, Cornell U., 1961, MME, 1962, MBA, 1963. Mktg. specialist Gen. Electric Co., NYC, 1963-64; dir. flight equipment and facilities planning Eastern Airlines, NYC, 1964-70; v.p. planning Butler Internat., Inc., Montvale, NJ, 1970, sr. v.p. fin., 1971-80, exec. v.p., 1980-86, pres., 1986-87; chmn. Mgmt. Resources Group, Inc., Saddle River, NJ, 1987-96; pres., CEO The Advantage Ptnrs., Chatham, NJ, 1992-94; pres. DCG Corp., 1994—2004; chmn. Dynamic Literacy LLC, Charlottesville, Va., 2006—. Bd. dirs. DCG Corp., Roseville, Calif., The Greenleaf Co., Cranford, NJ, Scitent, Inc., Charlottesville, Va.; chmn. Dynamic Literacy LLC, Charlottesville, Va. Mem. Keswick Club, Keswick Hunt Club. Home and Office: Fox Ridge Farm PO Box 490 Keswick VA 22947-0490

WOODS, RICHARD DALE, lawyer; b. Kans. City, Mo., May 20, 1950; s. Willard Dale and Betty Sue (Duncan) W.; m. Cecelia Ann Thompson, Aug. 11, 1973 (div. July 1996); children: Duncan Warren, Shannon Cecelia; m. Mary Linna Lash, June 6, 1999. BA with distinction, U. Kans., Lawrence, 1972; JD, U. Mo., 1975. Bar: Mo. 1975, Kans. 2000, US Dist. Ct. (we. dist.) Mo. 1975, US Tax Ct. 1999. Assoc. Shook, Hardy & Bacon L.L.P., Kansas City, Mo., 1975-79, ptnr., 1980-2000; shareholder Kirkland & Woods, P.C., Overland Park, Kans., 2001—. Gen. chmn. Estate Planning Symposium, Kansas City, 1985-86; chair Northland Coalition, 1993. Chmn. fin. com. North Woods Ch., Kansas City, 1986-88, 93-96; mem. sch. bd. N. Kansas City Sch. Dist., 1990-97, treas., 1992-97; mem. North Kansas City Ednl. Found., 1998-2002, pres., 1999-2002; mem. devel. com. Truman Med. Ctr., 1992—, chmn., 1992-98; mem. Clay County Tax Increment Fin. Commn., 1990-99; bd. dir. Heart of Am. Family Svcs., 1998-2004, sec., 2000-01, v.p. 2003-04, The Family Conservancy, 2005-07, v.p., 2005, chmn., 2006-07, Gilda's Club Kans. City, 2003—, sec., 2005-07. Named to Best Lawyers in Am., Trusts and Estates, 1993—. Fellow Am. Coll. Trust and Estate Counsel (Kans. state chair 2006-); mem. ABA, Mo. Bar Assn., Kans. Bar Assn., Johnson County Bar Assn., Kansas City Met. Bar Assn., Lawyers Assn. Kans. City (sec., v.p., pres. young lawyers sect. 1981-84), Kans. City Estate Planning Soc. (bd. dirs. 1985-88, 93-95), Ea. Kans. Estate Planning Coun. Democrat. Office: Kirkland & Woods PC 6201 College Blvd Ste 250 Overland Park KS 66211 Office Phone: 913-469-0900. E-mail: rwoods@kcnet.com.

WOODS, ROBERT EDWARD, lawyer; b. Albert Lea, Minn., Mar. 27, 1952; s. William Fabian and Maxine Elizabeth (Schmit) W.; m. Cynthia Anne Pratt, Dec. 26, 1975; children: Laura Marie Woods, Amy Elizabeth Woods. BA, U. Minn., 1974, JD, 1977; MBA, U. Pa., 1983. Bar: Minn. 1977, US Dist. Ct. Minn. 1980, US Ct. Appeals (8th cir.) 1980, Calif. 2000, US Ct. Appeals (9th cir.) 2000. Assoc. Moriarty & Janzen, Mpls., 1977-81, Berger & Montague, Phila., 1982-83, Briggs and Morgan, St. Paul and Mpls., 1983-84, ptnr., 1984-99; exec. v.p., gen. counsel InsWeb Corp., Redwood City, Calif., 1999-2000; gen. counsel BORN Info. Svcs., Inc., Mpls., 2000—04; pvt. practice Mpls., 2004—. Adj. prof. William Mitchell Coll. Law, St. Paul, 1985; exec. com., bd. dirs. LEX MUNDI, Ltd., Houston, 1989-93, chmn. bd. 1991-92; bd. dirs. Midwest Asia Ctr., 1993-95, chmn. bd., 1994-95. Co-author: (with others) Business Torts, 1989, (Carter G. Bishop) CCH Tax Research Consultant, Business Stages from Start-Up to Termination, 2005; sr. contbg. editor: Evidence in America: The Federal Rules in the States, 1987. Mem. ABA, Minn. State Bar Assn., State Bar of Calif., Hennepin County Bar Assn., Ramsey County Bar Assn. (chmn. corp., banking and bus. law sect. 1985-87), Assn. Trial Lawyers Am., Wharton Club of Minn., Phi Beta Kappa. Home: 28 N Deep Lake Rd North Oaks MN 55127-6506 Office: 110 Cheshire Ln Ste 300 Minneapolis MN 55305 Office Phone: 952-258-7919. Business E-Mail: rwoods@robertewoodspa.com.

WOODS, RONALD G., lawyer, former prosecutor; b. Moab, Utah, Jan. 1, 1938; LLB, U. Tex., 1964. Bar: Tex. 1964, US Supreme Ct. 1967, US Ct. Appeals (5th cir.) 1976, US Ct. Appeals (10th cir.), US Dist. Ct. (no., so., ea. and we. dists.) Tex. 1997. Spl. agent, legal advisor FBI, 1965—68; asst. dist. atty. Harris County Dist. Atty.'s Office, Tex., 1969—76, chief prosecutor Special Crimes Div. Tex., 1972—76; asst. US atty. (so. dist.) Tex. US Dept. Justice, 1976—85, US atty., 1990—93, chief Narcotics Div., 1976—78, chief Pub. Integrity Div., 1978—80, chief Fraud Div., 1980—85, sr. litig. counsel, 1980—85; pvt. practice Houston, 1993—. Adj. faculty mem. U. Tex. Law Sch. Trial Advocacy Seminars, 1985—94, 2002; chair merit selection panel US Magistrate Judge, So. Dist. Tex., 1990. Mem.: ABA, Nat. Assn. of Former US Attys., Coll. of State Bar of Tex., Nat. Criminal Defense Lawyers Assn., Tex. Criminal Defense Lawyers Assn., State Bar Tex., Fed. Bar Assn., Houston Bar Assn. (chair Fed. Practice Sect. 1992—93). Office: 5300 Memorial, Ste 1000 Houston TX 77077 Office Phone: 713-862-9600. Office Fax: 713-864-8738. E-mail: ron@ronwoodslaw.com.

WOODS, SANDRA KAY, real estate executive; b. Loveland, Colo., Oct. 11, 1944; d. Ivan H. and florence L. (Betz) Harris; m. Gary A. Woods, June 11, 1967; children: Stephanie Michelle, Michael Harris. BA, U. Colo., 1966, MA, 1967. Personnel mgmt. specialist CSC, Denver, 1967; asst. to regional dir. HEW, Denver, 1968-69; urban renewal rep. HUD, Denver, 1970-73, dir. program analysis, 1974-75, asst. regional dir. cmty. planning and devel., 1976-77, regional dir. fair housing, 1978-79; mgr. ea. facility project Adolph Coors Co., Golden, Colo., 1980, dir. real estate, 1981, v.p. chief environ. health and safety officer, 1982-96, v.p. strategic selling initiatives, 1996—2000; pres. Woods Properties LLP, Golden, 2000—. Mem. Exec. Exch., The White House, 1980. Bd. dirs. Golden Local Devel. Corp., 1981-82; fundraising dir. Coll. Arts and Scis., U. Colo., boulder, 1982-89, U. Colo.found.; mem. exec. bd. NCCJ, Denver, 1982-94; v.p. women in bus. Inc., Denver, 1982-83; mem. steering com. 1984 Yr. for All Denver Women, 1983-84; mem. 10th dist. Denver br. Fed. Res. Bd., 1990-96, chmn. bd., 1995-96; bd. dirs. Nat. Jewish Hosp., 1994—; chmn. Greater Denver Corp., 1991—. Named one of Outstanding Young Women Am., U.S. Jaycees, 1974, 78, Fifty Women to Watch, Businessweek, 1987, 92, Woman of Achievement YWCA, 1988. Mem. Indsl. Devel. Resources Coun. (bd. dirs. 1986-89), Am. Mgmt. Assn., Denver C. of C. (bd. dirs. 1988-96, Disting. Young Exec. award 1974, mem. Leadership Denver, 1976-77), Colo. Women's Forum, Nat. Assn. Office and Indsl. Park Developers (sec. 1988, treas. 1989), Committee of 200 (v.p. 1994-95), Phi Beta Kappa, Pi Alpha Alpha, PEO Club (Loveland). Republican. Presbyterian. E-mail: sandrawoods@qwest.net.

WOODS, STUART, writer; b. Manchester, Ga., Jan. 9, 1938; s. Stuart Franklin Lee and Dorothy Callaway Woods. BA, U. Ga., 1959. Writer, creative dir. various advt. agys., NYC and London, 1960-73; freelance writer, 1976—. Author: (memoir) Blue Water, Green Skipper, 1977, (travel book) A Romantic's Guide to the Country Inns of Britain and Ireland, 1979, 30 novels, including Chiefs (Edgar Allan Poe award 1982), Run Before the Wind, 1983, Deep Lie, 1986, Under the Lake, 1987, White Cargo, 1988, Grass Roots, 1989, Palindrome, 1991 (Edgar nomination, New York Dead, 1991, LA Times, 1993, Dead Eyes, 1994, Heat, 1994, Imperfect Strangers, 1995 (Grand Prix de Littérature Policière 1997), Choke, 1995, Dirt, 1996, Dead in the Water, 1997, Prince of Beverly Hills, 2004, Two Dollar Bill, 2005; contbr. articles to numerous publs. including Yachting, TV Guide, NY Times. Served as airman US N.G., 1961-62. Mem. Writers Guild Am., Authors Guild, Am. PEN, N.Y. Yacht Club, Century Assn. (N.Y.C.), Royal Yacht Squadron (Eng.). Democrat. Avocations: sailing, aviation. Office: Janklow & Nesbit care Anne Sibbald 445 Park Ave New York NY 10022 Address: 88 Parker Farm Rd Mount Desert ME 04660 Home: 570 Park Ave New York NY 10021-7370 Business E-Mail: stuart@stuartwoods.com.

WOODS, STUART HENRY, environmental scientist, educator; s. Morton C. and Anna Jean Woods. BS in Environ. Biology, Wash. State U., 1973; MS in Wildlife Ecology, Okla. State U., 1977; EdD, Okla. State U., Stillwater, 1991. Cert. endangered species rschr. Okla., 2007. Prof. Connors State Coll., Warner, Okla., 1980—. Rschr. Connors state coll. US Fish & Wildlife Svc., Muskogee, Okla. Chief judge Regional Sci. Fair, Muskogee, 1985—2007. Achievements include research in two endangered species in Oklahoma, the American Burying Beetle and the Red-Cockaded Woodpecker. Currently investigating why catfish in one Oklahoma lake has purple eggs instead of yellow. Office: Connors State Coll 2501N 41 East Muskogee OK 74403 Home Phone: 918-682-0002; Office Phone: 918-684-5475. Office Fax: 918-684-0420. Business E-Mail: swoods@connorsstate.edu.

WOODS, TIGER (ELDRICK WOODS), professional golfer; b. Cypress, Calif., Dec. 30, 1975; s. Earl (died May 5, 2006) and Kultida W., m. Elin Nordegren, Oct. 5, 2004; 1 child: Sam Alexis Woods. Student, Stanford U., Calif. Winner Optimist Internat. Jr. World Championship, 1984, 1985, 1988, 1989, 1990, 1991, Ins. Youth Golf Classic (youngest ever to win), 1990, 1992, CIF-So. Calif. HS Invitational Championship, 1991, So. Calif. Jr. Championship, 1991, PING/Phoenix Jr. Championship, 1991, 1992, Edgewood Tahoe Jr. Classic, 1991, LA City Jr. Championship, 1991, Orange Bowl Jr. Internat. Championship, 1991, US Jr. Amateur Championship (youngest ever to win), 1991, US Jr. Amateur Championship, 1992, US Jr. Amateur Championship (only golfer to win three times), 1993, Nabisco Mission Hills Desert Jr. Championship, 1992, Pro Gear San Antonio Shootout, 1992, So. Calif. Jr. Best Ball Championship, 1993, US Amateur Championship (youngest ever to win, also largest comeback ever), 1994, US Amateur Championship, 1995, 1996, Western Amateur Championship, 1994, So. Calif. Golf Assn. Amateur Championship, 1994, Pacific N.W. Amateur Championship, 1994, William Tucker Invitational, 1994, Jerry Pate Invitational, 1994, Stanford Invitational, 1995, Walt Disney World/Oldsmobile Classic, 1996, Las Vegas Invitational, 1996, NCAA Championship, 1996, John A. Burns Invitational, 1996, Cleve. Golf Championship, 1996, Tri-Match Championship (Stanford U., Ariz. State U., U. Ariz.), 1996, Cougar Classic, 1996, Pac-10 Championship (shot course record 61), 1996, NCAA West Regional, 1996, Masters Tournament, 1997, 2001, 2002, 2005, Mercedes Championships, 1997, 2000, Asian Honda Classic, 1997, GTE Byron Nelson Classic, 1997, Motorola Western Open, 1997, 1999, Johnnie Walker Classic, 1998, 2000, BellSouth Classic, 1998, PGA Grand Slam, 1998, 1999, 2000, 2001, 2002, 2005, 2006, Meml. Tournament, 1999, 2000, 2001, PGA Championship, 1999, 2000, 2006, Buick Invitational, 1999, 2003, 2005, 2006, 2007, Deutsche Bank-SAP Open, 1999, 2001, 2002, WGC NEC Invitational, 1999, 2000, 2001, 2005, Nat. Car Rental Classic, 1999, Tour Championship, 1999, WGC Am. Express Championship, 1999, 2002, 2003, 2005, 2006, WGC Am. CA Championship (formerly WGC Am. Express Championship), 2007, World Cup individual and team titles (with Mark O'Meara), 1999, AT&T Pebble Beach Pro-Am, 2000, Bay Hill Invitational, 2000, 2001, 2002, 2003, US Open Championship, 2000, 2002, Brit. Open Championship, 2000, 2005, 2006, Bell Can. Open, 2000, World Cup (with David Duval), 2000, The Players Championship, 2001, Williams World Challenge, 2001, Buick Open, 2002, 2006, WGC Accenture Match Play, 2003, Western Open, 2003, Ford Championship, 2005—06, WGC Bridgestone Invitational, 2006, 2007, Deutsche Bank Championship, 2006, Target World Challenge, 2006, Wachovia Championship, 2007. Mem. US Team World Amateur Team Championships, Versailles, France, 1994, Walker Cup Match, Porthcawl, Wales, 1995, Ryder Cup, 1997, 99, 2002, 04, 06, President's Cup, 1998, 2000, 03, 05, Dunhill Cup, 1998; founder, chmn. Tiger Woods Design, 2006—. Co-founder (with father, Earl) Tiger Woods Found. 1996-; With the Tiger Woods Foundation, initiated and supported community-based programs that promote the health, education and welfare to America's children (programs include: Tiger Woods Learning Center, Southern California, started in 2006, Start Something (partners with Target Corporation), started in 2000, Tiger Woods Foundation National Junior Golf Team, Target World Challenge (also host), Tiger Jam (AT&T-sponsored event) (also host) and various grant/scholarship programs). Named Player of Yr., Am. Jr. Golf Assn., 1991, Golf Digest, 1991, 1992, Golf World, 1993, 1994, LA Times, 1994, Orange County, 1994, Golf Writers Assn. Am., 2006, So. Calif. Player of Yr., 1991, 1992, 1993, Nat. Amateur of Yr., Titleist-Golfweek, 1991, 1992, Orange County League MVP, 1994, Pac-10 Player of Yr., 1995, 1996, First Team All-Am., 1995, 1996, Sportsman of Yr., Sports Illustrated, 1996, 2000, Reuters, 2000, PGA Tour Rookie of Yr., 1996, Fred Haskins Coll. Player of Yr., 1996, Jack Nicklaus Coll. Player of Yr., 1996, Male Athlete of Yr., AP, 1997, 1999, 2000, 2006, Male Athlete of Yr. (with Ken Griffey, Jr.), ESPN, 1997, Male Athlete of Yr., 1999—2001, World Sportsman of Yr., World Sports Acad., 1999, Most Powerful Person in Sports, Sporting News, 2000, World Champion of Champions, L'Equipe, France, 2000; named to First Team Rolex Jr. All Am., 1991, 1992; recipient Dial award, 1993, Jack Nicklaus Trophy, PGA Am., Golf Writers Assn. Am., 1997, 1999—2003, 2005—06, Byron Nelson award, PGA Tour, 1999—2003, Vardon Trophy, PGA of Am., 1999—2003, Mark H. McCormack award as No. 1 player on world ranking, 1999—2003, ESPY award, Best Golfer, 2005—07, Charlie Bartlett award, Golf Writers Assn. Am., 2007. Achievements include winning 13 maj. PGA Tour events including the Masters Tournament, 1997, 2001, 02, 05, PGA Championship, 1999, 2000, 06, 07, US Open Championship, 2000, 02, Brit. Open Championship, 2000, 05, 06; youngest player, first African Am., first Asian Am., and having largest margin of victory (12 strokes) to win Masters Tournament, 1997; first player ever to win US Open, Brit. Open and PGA Championship in same yr., 2000; first player ever to hold all 4 maj. golf championships at the same time, 2001; ranked number 1 player in world for a record 264 consecutive weeks, 1999-2004; youngest to win 50 PGA Tour titles with victory at Buick Open, 2006; 8 time PGA Tour Player Yr. Office: PGA PO Box 109601 100 Avenue Of Champions Palm Beach Gardens FL 33418-3665 *

WOODS, WILLIE E., information specialist; CEO, pres. Digital Sys. Internat. Corp., Arlington, Va., 1988—.

WOODSIDE, FRANK C., III, lawyer, educator, physician; b. Glen Ridge, NJ, Apr. 18, 1944; s. Frank C. and Dorothea (Poulin) W.; m. Julia K. Moses, Nov. 15, 1974; children: Patrick Michael, Christopher Ryan. BS, Ohio State U., Columbus, 1966, JD, 1969; MD, U. Cin., 1973. Diplomate Am. Bd. Legal Medicine, Am. Bd. Forensic Medicine, Am. Bd. Profl. Liability Attys. Mem. Dinsmore & Shohl, Cin.; clin. prof. pediats. emeritus U. Cin., 1992—. Adj. prof. law U. Cin., 1973—. Editor: Drug Product Liability, 1985—. Fellow Am. Coll. Legal Medicine, Am. Coll. Forensic Examiners, Am. Soc. Hosp. Attys., Soc. Ohio Hosp. Attys.; mem. ABA, FBA, Ohio Bar Assn., Internat. Assn. Def. Counsel, Def. Rsch. Inst. (chmn. drug and med. svc. com. 1988-91), Cin. Bar Assn. Office: Dinsmore & Shohl 1900 Chemed Ctr 255 E 5th St Cincinnati OH 45202-4700 Home Phone: 513-821-7889; Office Phone: 513-977-8266. Business E-Mail: frank.woodside@dinslaw.com.

WOODSIDE, LISA NICOLE, humanities educator; b. Portland, Oreg., Sept. 7, 1944; d. Lee and Emma (Wenstrom) W. Student, Reed Coll., Portland, Oreg., 1962—65; MA, U. Chgo., 1968; PhD, Bryn Mawr Coll., Pa., 1972; cert. Inst. Ednl. Mgmt., Harvard U., Cambridge, Mass., 1979; MA, West Chester U., Pa., 1994. Cert. tchr. ecstatic trance postures Cuyamungue Inst., N.Mex., 2003, wellness counseling, creative energy options. Mem. dean's staff Bryn Mawr Coll., 1970-72; asst. prof. Widener U., Chester, Pa., 1972-77, assoc. prof. humanities, 1978-83, asst. dean student svcs., 1972-76, assoc. dean, 1976-79, dean, 1979-83; acad. dean, prof. humanities Holy Family Coll., Phila., 1983—, v.p., dean acad. affairs, prof. humanities, 1990-98, prof. humanities, 1998—. Cons. State NJ Edn. Dept., 1990, Houghton-Mifflin for English reader, 2000; cons., reader Test of Spoken English Ednl. Testing Svc., 2002—04; accreditor Commn. on Higher Edn., Mid. States Assn., 1977—83, 1994. Co-author: New Age Spirituality: An Assessment. City commr. for cmty. rels., Chester, 1980-83; mem. Adult Edn. Coun. Phila. Recipient Crasilneck award for best paper Am. Soc. Clin. Hypnosis; Am. Assn. Papyrology grantee Bryn Mawr Coll., S. Maude Kaemmerling fellow. Mem.: MLA, AAUW (univ. rep. 1975—83), APA, Pa. Coll. Tchrs. Assn., Mid. States Classics Assn., Audubon Soc., Psi Chi, Alpha Sigma Lambda, Phi Eta Sigma. Office: Humanities Dept Holy Family U 9801 Frankford Ave Philadelphia PA 19114 Office Phone: 215-637-7700 x3441. Business E-Mail: woodside@holyfamily.edu.

WOOD-SMITH, DONALD, plastic surgeon; b. Sydney, June 30, 1937; s. William Frederick and Vera Mary; children: Christina Margaret, Donald William, Phillip Raynor. MB, BChir, Sydney U., 1954. Diplomate Am. Bd. Plastic Surgery. Surg. resident Lewisham Hosp., Sydney, 1954—57, Royal Marsden Hosp., 1957-58; resident plastic surgery NYU Hosp. Med. Ctr., 1960-64, asst., assoc. and attending surgeon, 1964-92; prof. plastic surgery Columbia Presbyn. Med. Ctr., 1991—. Vis. surgeon Bellevue Hosp., 1964-92, London Ind. Hosp., 1999-2005; chmn. plastic surgery Manhattan Eye Ear and Throat Hosp., 1975-77; assoc. prof. plastic surgery NYU, 1977-84, prof., 1984-92; surgeon, dir. plastic surgery Manhattan Eye Ear and Throat Hosp., 1977-84; cons. plastic surgeon NY Eye and Ear Infirmary, chmn. dept. plastic and reconstructive surgery, 1984— Author: Nursing Care of the Plastic Surgery Patient, 1967, Cosmetic Facial Surgery, 1973; contbr. articles to med. jours. Fellow ACS, Royal Coll. Surgeons of Edinburgh; mem. Am. Assn. Plastic Surgeons, Am. Soc. Plastic Surgeons, Am. Soc. Maxillofacial Surgeons, NY Acad. Medicine, Brit. Assn. Plastic Surgeons, NY Athletic Club. Office: 830 Park Ave New York NY 10021-2757 Address: 19 Wimpole St London W1G 8GE England Home Phone: 212-744-2225; Office Phone: 212-744-2224. Personal E-mail: dw830@aol.com.

WOODSOME, EDWIN VALENTINE, JR., lawyer; AB summa cum laude, Holy Cross Coll., 1968; JD magna cum laude, Harvard U., 1971. Bar: Mass. 1972, Calif. 1973, D.C. 1973. Law clk. to Hon. James R. Browning US Ct. Appeals (9th cir.), 1971—72; ptnr. Orrick, Herrington & Sutcliffe LLP, LA, 2003—. Mem.: State Bar Calif., D.C. Bar, ABA (litig. sect., environ. sect., employment sect.), L.A. County Bar Assn. Office: Orrick Herrington & Sutcliffe LLP 777 S Figueroa St Ste 3200 Los Angeles CA 90017 Office Phone: 213-612-2398. Business E-Mail: ewoodsome@orrick.com.

WOODSON, GAYLE ELLEN, otolaryngologist; b. Galveston, Tex., June 9, 1950; d. Clinton Eldon and Nancy Jean (Stephens) W.; m. Kevin Thomas Robbins; children: Nicholas, Gregory, Sarah. BA, Rice U., 1972; MD,

Baylor Coll. Medicine, 1975. Diplomate Am. Bd. Otolaryngology (bd. dirs., residency rev. com. for otolaryngology, exam. chair). Fellow Baylor Coll. Medicine, Houston, 1976, Inst. Laryngology & Otology, London, 1981-82; asst. prof. Baylor Coll. Medicine, 1982-87; asst. attending Harris County Hosp. Dist., Houston, 1982-86; with courtesy staff Saint Luke's Episcopal Hosp., Houston, 1982-87; assoc. attending The Methodist Hosp., Houston, 1982-87; asst. prof. U. Calif. Med. Sch., San Diego, 1987-89; chief otolaryngology VA Med. Ctr., San Diego, 1987-92; assoc. prof. U. Calif. Sch. Med., San Diego, 1989-92; prof. otolaryngology U. Tenn., Memphis, 1993—2000, So. Ill. U., 2003—. Numerous presentations and lectures in field. Contbr. numerous articles and abstracts to med. jours., also videotapes. Recipient deRoldes award, Am. Layrngol. Assn., 2003. Fellow ACS (bd. govs.), Royal Coll. Surgeons, Soc. Univ. Otolaryngologists (past pres.), Am. Soc. Head and Neck Surgery, Am. Laryngol. Assn. (pres.-elect de Roaldes award, 2003), Triological Soc.; mem. AMA, Am. Acad. Otolaryngology-Head and Neck Surgery (bd. dirs. 1993-96), Am. Med. Women's Assn. (past pres. Memphis br.), Soc. Head and Neck Oncologists Eng., Am. Physiol. Soc., Assn. Women Surgeons, Am. Soc. Head and Neck Surgeons, Johns Hopkins Soc. Scholars, Collegium OtoRhinolaryngolicum Amicus Sacrum. Office: Southern Illinois Univ PO Box 19662 Springfield IL 62794-9662 Home Phone: 217-726-0026. Business E-Mail: gwoodson@siumed.edu.

WOODSON, JACQUELINE, writer; b. Columbus, Ohio, Feb. 12, 1964; 1 child. Fellow MacDowell Colony and the Fine Arts Work Ctr., Provincetown, Mass. Author: (book) Last Summer With Maizon, 1990, Martin Luther King Jr., and His Birthday, 1990, The Dear One, 1991, Maizon at Blue Hill, 1992, I Hadn't Meant to Tell You This, 1994, Between Madison and Palmetto, 1995, Autobiography of a Family Photo, 1995, From the Notebooks of Melanin Sun, 1995, A Way Out of No Way, 1996, The House You Pass on the Way, 1997, We Had a Picnic this Past Sunday, 1997, If You Come Softly, 1998, Lena, 1998, Miracle's Boys, 2000, Sweet, Sweet Memory, 2000, The Other Side, 2001, Hush, 2002, Our Gracie Aunt, 2002, Visiting Day, 2002, Locomotion, 2003 (Nat. Book award nominee, 2003); author: (ill. by E.B. Lewis) Coming On Home Soon, 2004 (Caldecott award, 2005, Am. Libr. Assn. Notable Book, 2005, Child Mag. Best of 2004, Booklist Editor's Choice); author: (ill. by Hudson Talbott) Show Way, 2005 (Newbery Honor Book, 2006). Recipient Coretta Scott King Honors, 2001, Kenyon Review award for lit. excellence in fiction, 3 Am. Libr. Assn. awards, 2 Jane Adams Peace award honors, 3 Lambda Lit. awards.

WOODSON, MIKE, professional basketball coach; b. Indpls., Mar. 24, 1958; m. Terri Woodson; children: Alexis, Mariah. Grad., Ind. U., 1980. Profl. basketball player NY Knicks, 1981—82, NJ Nets, 1982, Kans. City Kings (now Sacramento Kings), 1982—86, LA Clippers, 1986—88, Houston Rockets, 1988—91, Cleve. Cavaliers, 1991, asst. coach, 1999—2001, Milw. Bucks, 1996—99, Phila. 76ers, 2001—03, Detroit Pistons, 2003—04; head coach Atlanta Hawks, 2004—. Office: Atlanta Hawks Centennial Tower 101 Marietta St NW Ste 1900 Atlanta GA 30303 *

WOODSON, RILEY DONALD, thoracic and cardiovascular surgeon, lawyer; b. Winfield, Kans., Dec. 24, 1931; s. Riley Delma and Virginia Marie Woodson (Stepmother), Ruth Benedict Woodson; married; children: Riley David, Wade Clinton. BA, U. Kans., 1953, MD, 1956; JD, U. Toledo, 1984. Bar: Ohio 1984, US Dist. Ct. (no. dist. Ohio) 1985; Med. Licensure Kans., 1956, Calif., 1961, Ariz., 1962, Ohio, 1968, diplomate Am. Bd. Surgery, 1964, Am. Bd. Thoracic Surgery, 1968, Am. Bd. Cardiothoracic Surgery, 1978. Intern Parkland Meml. Hosp., Southwestern Med. Sch., Dallas, 1956—57; resident in gen. surgery U. Minn. Hosps., Mpls., 1957—63; resident in thoracic and cardiovasc. surgery U. Oreg. Med. Sch., Portland, 1965—67; asst. prof. surgery, asst. chief, thoracic and cardiovasc. surgery U. Ill. Sch. Medicine, Chgo., 1967—69; assoc. prof. surgery, chief, thoracic and cardiovasc. surgery Med. U. Ohio, Toledo, 1969—78, clin. assoc. prof. surgery, 1979—; pvt. practice Toledo, 1978—92, Palm Springs, Calif., 1993—96; contract med. malpractice case analyst Jacobson, Maynard, Tuschman & Kalur, LLC, Toledo, 1997—98; ptnr. Sodeman, Kirkhope & Woodson, LLP, Toledo, 2001—. Pres. Ohio Coll. Chest Physicians, Columbus, 1971—72; medicolegal case cons., Toledo, Port Clinton, Ohio, 1975—2006; mem. jud. and profl. rels. Ohio State Med. Assn., Columbus, 1986—90; bd. dirs. Palm Springs Acad. Medicine, 1994—96. Author 29 works in nat. and internat. med. and legal publs. Nat. basic and advanced CPR faculty Am. Heart Assn., 1976—83; exec. com. mem., bd. trustees sec., med. dir. Regional Emergency Med. Svcs. NW Ohio, Toledo, 1975—79; trustee NW Ohio Heart Assn., Toledo, 1976—80. Capt. USNR, 1963—88. Recipient Owl Soc., U. Kans., 1952, Sachem Cir., Omicron Delta Kappa (Pres.), 1953, Russell Hayden Outstanding Med. Student Rsch. medal, 1956, Outstanding Resident Rsch. award, Portland Surg. Soc., 1967, Ann. Outstanding Med. Writing award, NW Medicine, 1967, Golden Apple for Tchg. Excellence, Med. U. Ohio, 1972, Outstanding Physician Vol., NW Ohio Heart Assn., 1980; Summerfield scholar, U. Kans., 1949, Nat. Honor Soc. scholar, 1949, Athletic scholarship Basketball and Track, 1949. Fellow: ACS (sr.), Soc. Vascular Surgery (disting. fellow), Am. Coll. Legal Medicine (sr.), Am. Coll. Angiology (sr.), Am. Coll. Chest Physicians (sr.; gov. 1972—78), Am. Coll. Cardiology (sr.); mem.: AMA, AAUP (sr.), ABA, Am. Soc. Law and Medicine, Soc. Internat. Surgery, Undersea Med. Soc., Assn. Academic Surgery, Assn. Mil. Surgeons of US, Toledo Surg. Soc. (founding mem.), Am. Thoracic Soc. (sr.), Soc. Thoracic Surgeons (sr.), Am. Assn. Surgery of Trauma (sr.), Am. Assn. Vascular Surgery (sr.), Toledo Acad. Med., Ohio Med. Assn., Ottawa County Bar Assn., Toledo Bar Assn. (mem. JD/MD and continuing legal edn. commns. 1985—), Ohio Bar Assn., U. Kans. Varsity K Club, Shrine, Scottish Rite, Knights Templar, Phi Kappa Phi, MENSA, Beta Theta Pi (U. Kans. chpt. pres. 1953). Office: 4445-E Marin Pines Port Clinton OH 43452 Office Phone: 419-797-7311. Office Fax: 419-797-7311. Personal E-mail: rd_woodson2@hotmail.com.

WOODSON, RUBY GARRARD, educational administrator, chemistry educator; b. Dothan, Ala., June 22, 1931; d. David and Ella Mae (McClendon) Garrard; m. William Dallas Woodson, Dec. 22, 1956 (div. May 1970); 1 child, William. B.S. in Chemistry, Fla. A&M U., 1951; M.A. in Edn., Am. U., 1959. Tchr. chemistry Moton High Sch., Brooksville, Fla., 1951-52; tchr. math. and sci. Pub. Sch. of D.C., 1953-66; tchr., chmn. dept. sci. Western High Sch., Washington, 1966-69; assoc. prof. chemistry. U. Md., College Park, 1970-71; tchr., chmn. sci. dept. Wilson High Sch., Washington, 1969-73; founder, dir. Cromwell Acad., Washington, 1973—; cons. Office of Edn., Washington, 1974-76. Author: Some Recent Advances in the Teaching of High School Chemistry, 1979. Attendee First Black Polit. Conv., Gary, Ind., 1971; participant Congl. Black Caucus Conv., Washington, 1981-84. Amos Lewis scholar, 1948; NSF grantee, 1957, 63, 67, 71; Mem. Nat. Assn. Secondary Sch. Prins., NEA, Black Child Devel. Assn., Parents Assn. Inc. (pres. 1977-85). Roman Catholic. Avocations: travel; theater; swimming. Home: 3202 Mckinley St NW Washington DC 20015-1635

WOODSON-GLENN, YOLANDA, social worker; b. LA, July 29, 1958; d. Lewie B. and Clareece Woodson; children: James Glenn, Kimberly Glenn. BA cum laude in journalism, Bowie State, 1995; MA in counseling psychology, Bowie State U.; postgrad., Calif. Grad. Inst. Social worker Dept. Children and Family Svcs., Baltimore, MD, 1994-95; victim advocate State's Atty's Office, Annapolis, MD, 1995-96; social worker Children of the Village, Carson, CA, 1997-99, Dept. of Children and Family Svcs., Lakewood, CA, 1999—. Counselor City of Refuge Ch., Gardena, Calif., 2000—. Author: Suffering for Righteousness, 2001. Pentecostal. Avocations: cooking, crafts, museums, concerts. Home: 17125 Stark Ave Cerritos CA 90703 E-mail: ywoodsonglenn@aol.com.

WOODSON-HOWARD, MARLENE ERDLEY, former state legislator; b. Ford City, Pa., Mar. 8, 1937; d. James and Susie (Lettrich) Erdley; m. Francis M. Howard; children: George Woodson, Bert Woodson, Robert Woodson, Daniel Woodson, David Woodson. BS, Ind. U. of Pa., 1958; MA, U. South Fla., 1968; EdD, Nova U., 1981. Prof. math. Manatee Community Coll., 1970-82, dir., Inst. Advancement, 1982-86; exec. dir. Manatee Community Coll. Foundation, 1982-86; pres. Pegasus Enterprises, Inc., 1986—; state senator Fla., 1986-90. Candidate for gov. of Fla., 1990; past pres. New Coll. Libr. Assn.; past pres. Manatee Symphony; bd. dirs. Manatee Red Cross; bd. dirs. Manatee Players, Inc., v.p.; trustee Fla. Kiwanis Found. Mem. Manatee C. of C., Sarasota C. of C., Sarasota Kiwanis (bd. dirs., v.p., pres.), Bradenton Kiwanis. Republican. Roman Catholic. Home: 12 Tidy Island Blvd Bradenton FL 34210-3301 E-mail: marlenewhoward@aol.com.

WOODS-TAYLOR, CLEORA LYNESIA, mathematics educator, consultant; d. Ray Clayton and Clara Lynn Woods; children: Lynesia Raychelle Taylor, Lanetria Taylor Christa. BS, Prairie View A&M U., Tex., 1991; MA, U. Mo., Kansas City, 2003. Cert. tchr. Mo., 2003. Adj. instr. algebra Houston C.C. (NW Campus), 1992; instr. algebra Houston Ind. Sch. Dist., 1992—93, Faith Acad., Kansas City, Mo., 1995—99, Lincoln Coll. Prep. Acad., Kansas City, Mo., 2001—; dir. math. Kansas City Sch. Dist., Mo. Math cons. Mo. Math Acad. Dir. of performing arts dept. Harvest Ch., Kansas City, Mo., 1995—2001. Mem.: Alpha Kappa Alpha. Office: Lincoln Coll Prep Acad 2012 E 23rd St Kansas City MO 64127 Home Phone: 816-797-0804; Office Phone: 816-418-7478. Office Fax: 816-418-3530. Business E-Mail: ctaylor@kcmsd.net.

WOODSWORTH, ANNE, retired academic administrator, librarian; came to U.S., 1983; d. Thorvald Ernst and Roma Yrsa Lindner; 1 child, Yrsa Anne. BFA, U. Man., 1962; BLS, U. Toronto, 1964, MLS, 1969; PhD, U. Pitts., 1987. Edn. libr. U. Man., 1964—65; reference libr. Winnipeg Pub. Libr., 1965—67; reference libr. sci. and medicine dept. U. Toronto, 1967—68; med. libr. Toronto We. Hosp., 1969—70; rsch. asst. to chief libr. U. Toronto, 1970—71, head reference dept., 1971—74; pers. dir. Toronto Pub. Libr., 1975—78; dir. librs. York U., Toronto, 1978—83; assoc. provost for librs. U. Pitts., 1983—88, assoc. prof., 1988—91; dean Palmer Sch. Libr. and Info. Sci., L.I. U., 1991—98; dean Sch. Edn. Dowling Coll., Oakdale, NY, 1999—2000; dean sch. info. and libr. sci. Pratt Inst., Bklyn., 2000—02, acting provost, 2002—03; provost Katherine Gibbs Sch., Melville, NY, 2003; learning sys. advisor Bklyn. Pub. Libr., 2004—06. Pres. Anne Lindner Ltd., 1974—83; rsch. libraries adv. coun. OCLC, 1984—87. Author: The Alternative Press in Canada, 1972, Leadership and Research Libraries, 1988, Patterns and Options for Managing Information Technology on Campus, 1990, Library Cooperation and Networks, 1991, Managing the Economics of Leasing and Contracting Out Information Services, 1993, Reinvesting in the Information Job Family, 1993, The Future of Education for Librarianship: Looking Forward from the Past, 1994. Sec., mem. bd. trustees Katharine Gibbs Sch., L.I., 2003-04; dir. Sr. Fellows Inst., 1995-98; trustee L.I. Librs. Resources Coun., 1993-96; bd. dirs. Population Rsch. Found., Toronto, 1980-83. Grantee Can. Coun., 1974, Ont. Arts Coun., 1974, Coun. on Libr. Resources, 1986, 88, 91, 93; UCLA sr. fellow, 1985. Mem. ALA (com. on accreditation 1990-94, councillor 1993-97), Can. Assn. Rsch. Librs. (pres. 1981-83), Assn. Rsch. Librs. (bd. dirs. 1981-84, v.p. 1984-85, pres. 1985-86), Assn. Coll. and Rsch. Librs. (chair K.G. Saur award com. 1991-93), Assn. for Libr. and Info. Sci. Edn. (chair honors and awards com. 1995, bd. dirs. 1998-99, v.p. 1998-99), Am. Soc. Higher Edn., Internet Soc., Am. Soc. Info. Sci. (convenor 1999-2000), Archons of Colophon. Personal E-mail: alwoods@intergate.com.

WOODWARD, BOB (ROBERT UPSHUR WOODWARD), newspaper reporter, writer; b. Geneva, Ill., Mar. 26, 1943; s. Alfred E. and Jane (Upshur) W.; m. Elsa Walsh, Nov. 25, 1989; children: Tali, Diana. BA, Yale U., 1965. Reporter Montgomery County (Md.) Sentinel, 1970-71; reporter Washington Post, 1971-78, met. editor, 1979-81, asst. mng. editor, 1981—. Author: Wired: The Short Life and Fast Times of John Belushi, 1984, Veil: The Secret Wars of the CIA, 1981-1987, 1987, The Commanders: The Pentagon and the First Gulf War, 1989-1991, 1991, The Agenda: Inside the Clinton White House, 1994, The Choice: How Bill Clinton Won, 1996, Shadow: Five Presidents and the Legacy of Watergate, 1974-1999, 1999, Maestro: Greenspan's Fed and the American Boom, 2000, Bush At War: Inside the Bush White House, 2002, Plan of Attack, 2004, State of Denial: Bush at War, Part III, 2006; Co-Author: (with Carl Bernstein) All the President's Men, 1974, The Final Days, 1976, The Secret Man: The Story of Watergate's Deep Throat, 2005, (with Scott Armstrong) The Brethren: Inside the Supreme Court, 1979. Served with USN, 1965-70. Office: Washington Post Co 1150 15th St NW Washington DC 20071-0002

WOODWARD, CLIFFORD EDWARD, chemical engineer; b. Richmond, Va, Jan. 17, 1941; s. Clifford Rawlings and Myrtis (Wilson) W.; m. Katherine Roberts, June 1, 1967; children: Ted, Robert, Christopher, John. BSChemE, Va. Poly. Inst. and State U., 1962, MS in Nuclear Sci. and Engr., 1963; MSChemE, U. Houston, 1975. Registered profl. engr., Tex. Devel. engr. Olin Corp., 1963-65; supervising engr. Monsanto Co., 1965-72; lead engr. Brown & Root Inc., Houston, 1972-74; process mgr. Kvaerner Process Inc., Houston, 1974-77, 1979-81, process dir., 1983-88, process mgr., 1992—2000; prin. engr. Jacobs Engring. Group, Inc., Houston, 1977-79; process mgr. M.W. Kellogg, Amsterdam, NC, 1981-83, sr. engr. mgr. Houston, 1988-89; process dept. mgr. BE&K, Houston, 1989-92; pres. Protective Environ. Engring. Svcs. Inc., Houston, 2000—. Mem. planning comm. City of Alvin, Tex., 1970-72; founder Cypress Creek Emergency Med. Svc. Assn., 1975; pres. Klein (Tex.) Sch. Bd., 1979-90. Mem. AIChE, Engrs. Coun. of Houston (v.p., sec. 1991). Achievements include electrodeposition of polymers from latex solutions and surface kinetics and direct contact heat transfer. Home: 4114 Oxhill Rd Spring TX 77388-9705 Home Phone: 281-353-2804; Office Phone: 281-353-8980. E-mail: cwoodward@peesiengineering.com.

WOODWARD, DANIEL HOLT, librarian, researcher; b. Ft. Worth, Oct. 17, 1931; s. Enos Paul and Jessie Grider (Butts) W.; m. Mary Jane Gerra, Aug. 27, 1954; children: Jeffrey, Peter. BA, U. Colo., 1951, MA, 1955; PhD, Yale, 1958; MSLS, Cath. U. Am., 1969. Mem. faculty Mary Washington Coll. of U. Va., 1957-72, prof. English, 1966-72, librarian, 1969-72, Huntington Library, Art Collections and Bot. Gardens, San Marino, Calif., 1972-90, sr. rsch. assoc., 1990-97; ind. scholar, 1997—. Editor: The Poems and Translations of Robert Fletcher, 1970, The Ellesmere Chaucer: A New Monochromatic Facsimile, 1997, Wallace Stevens, Vassar Viewed Veraciously, 1997; co-editor: New Ellesmere Chaucer Facsimile, Ellesmere Chaucer: Essays in Interpretation, 2 vols., 1995. Bd. dirs. Friends of the Princeton U. Libr. With US Army, 1952—54. Mem. Bibliog. Soc. Am., Phi Beta Kappa, Beta Phi Mu. Home: 80 Runyon Mill Rd Hopewell NJ 08525 Personal E-mail: danmjwood@yahoo.com.

WOODWARD, JAMES FRANKLIN, science educator; b. Boston, Dec. 22, 1941; s. William Redin and Edith Jones Woodward; life ptnr. Carole Schulze. BA, Middlebury Coll., 1964; MS, NYU, 1969; PhD, U. Denver, 1972. Prof. Calif. State U., Fullerton, 1972—2005, prof. emeritus, 2005—. Contbr. articles to profl. jours. Mem.: AIAA, NY Acad. Scis., History Sci. Soc., Internat. Soc. Gen. Relativity and Gravitation (life). Independent. Achievements include patents for propulsion based on transient inertial effects (Mach effects). Avocations: hiking, flamenco guitar. Office Phone: 714-278-3596. Office Fax: 714-278-5810. Business E-Mail: jwoodward@fullerton.edu.

WOODWARD, JAMES HOYT, retired academic administrator, engineering educator; b. Sanford, Fla., Nov. 24, 1939; s. James Hoyt and Edith Pearl (Breeden) Woodward; m. Martha Ruth Hill, Oct. 13, 1956; children: Connie, Tracey, Wade. BS in Aero. Engring. with honors, Ga. Tech. Inst., 1962, MS in Aero. Engring., 1963, PhD in Engring. Mechanics, 1967; MBA, U. Ala.-Birmingham, 1973. Asst. prof. engring. mechanics USAF Acad., Colo., 1965-67, assoc. prof. Colo., 1967-68; asst. prof. N.C. State U., 1968-69; assoc. prof. engring. U. Ala., Birmingham, 1969-70, assoc. prof., 1973-77, prof. civil engring., 1977-89, asst. v.p., 1973-78, dean engring., 1978-84, acad. v.p., 1984-89; chancellor U. N.C., Charlotte, 1989—2005. Dir. tech. devel. Rust Engring. Co., Birmingham, 1970—73; cons. in field. Contbr. articles to profl. jours. With USAF, 1965—68. Mem.: Am. Soc. Engring. Edn., Sigma Xi. Methodist. Office: U NC Charlotte Chancellors Emeriti Office 9201 Univ City Blvd Charlotte NC 28223-0002

WOODWARD, JOAN B., science association director; BS magna cum laude, U. Mo.; MS in engring. econ. systems, Stanford U.; PhD in mech. engring., U. Calif. With Sandia Nat. Labs., Albuquerque, 1974, dir., Environ. Progs. Ctr., leader material support group, nat. security and weapons progs., mgr., Neutron Generator and Explosives Component Ctr., v.p., Energy, Info., and Infrastructure Tech. Div., currently exec. v.p., dep. dir. Chair lab. mgmt. coun. for Mission and Risk Mgmt. Oversight Sandia Nat. Labs., responsible for ind. assessment of weapons' safety, security, and reliability; bd. mem. Intelligence Sci. Bd (ISB), Congl. Commn. to assess vulnerabilities of US infrastructure to Electromagnetic Pulse; mem. Army Sci. Bd (ASB) study on Force Protection, Defense Sci. Bd. (DSB) study on Homeland Security; co-chair Nat. Reconnaissance Office Bd. (NRO) for Nat. Space Security (NSS); served Nat. Acad. Study on S&T for countering Terrorism. Mem. adv. coun. Kirtland Hon. Comdrs.; mem. bd. adv. Family Security Group, Ctr. for Security Policy; bd. dirs. Bosque Sch., Greater Albuquerque C. of C. Mem.: U. N.Mex Sch. Engring. Bd. of Visitors, U. Mo.-Rolla Dean's Bd. Visitors, N.Mex Women's Forum, Soc. Women Engrs. (life), Phi Kappa Phi. Office: Sandia Nat Labs PO Box 5800, Mail Stop 0102 Albuquerque NM 87185-0102

WOODWARD, JOANNE GIGNILLIAT, actress; b. Thomasville, Ga., Feb. 27, 1930; d. Wade and Elinor (Trimmier) W.; m. Paul Newman, Jan. 29, 1958; children: Elinor Terese, Melissa Stewart, Clea Olivia. Student, La. State U., 1947-49; grad., Neighborhood Playhouse Dramatic Sch., NYC. First TV appearance in Penny, Robert Montgomery Presents, 1952; understudy broadway play Picnic, 1953; appeared in plays Baby Want a Kiss, 1964, Candida, 1982, The Glass Menagerie, Williamstown Theatré Festival, 1985, Sweet Bird of Youth, Toronto, 1988; motion pictures include Three Faces of Eve, 1957 (Acad. award Best Actress, Nat. Bd. Rev. award, Fgn. Press award), Count Three and Pray, 1955, Long Hot Summer, 1958, No Down Payment, 1957, Sound and the Fury, 1959, A Kiss Before Dying, 1956, Rally Round the Flag Boys, 1958, The Fugitive Kind, 1960, Paris Blues, 1961, The Stripper, 1963, A New Kind of Love, 1963, A Big Hand for the Little Lady, 1965, A Fine Madness, 1965, Rachel, Rachel, 1968, Winning, 1969, WUSA, 1970, They Might Be Giants, 1971, The Effect of Gamma Rays on Man-in-the-Moon Marigolds, 1972 (Cannes Film Festival award), Summer Wishes, Winter Dreams, 1973 (N.Y. Film Critics award), The Drowning Pool, 1975, The End, 1978, Harry and Son, 1984, Glass Menagerie, 1987, Mr. & Mrs. Bridge, 1990, Philadelphia, 1993, The Age of Innocence (voice), 1993, My Knees Were Jumping: Remembering the Kindertransports, (voice) 1998; TV appearances include All the Way Home; TV-film appearances in Sybil, 1976, Come Back, Little Sheba, 1977, See How She Runs, 1978 (Emmy award), Streets of L.A., 1979, The Shadow Box, 1980, Crisis at Central High, 1981, Do You Remember Love?, 1985 (Emmy award), Blind Spot, 1993 (Emmy nomination, Lead Actress - Miniseries, 1993), Breathing Lessons, 1994 (Emmy nomination, Lead Actress - Special, 1994, Golden Globe award, Best Actress), James Dean: A Portrait, 1996; narrator film documentary Angel Dust, TV documentary on Group Theatre, 1989. Co-recipient (with Paul Newman) Kennedy Ctr. Honors for Lifetime Achievement in the Performing Arts. Democrat. Episcopalian. Office: ICM 40 W 57th St Fl 16 New York NY 10019-4098

WOODWARD, KENNETH EMERSON, retired mechanical engineer; b. Washington, Oct. 30, 1927; s. George Washington and Mary Josephine (Compton) W.; m. Mary Margaret Eungard, Mar. 29, 1956; children: Stephen Mark, Kristi Lynn. BME, George Washington U., 1949, M Engring. Adminstrn., 1960; MS, U. Md., 1953; PhD, Am. U., 1973. Mech. engr. Naval Rsch. Lab., Washington, 1950-54; supr. med. engring. program, chief engring. support branch, chief reliability and assessment, value engring. program mgr. Harry Diamond Labs., Washington, 1955-74; sci. adviser U.S. Army Med. Bioengring. R & D Lab., Ft. Detrick, Md., 1974-75; mech. engr. Woolcott & Co., Washington, 1975-90; ret., 1990. Author: Solar Energy Applications for the Home, 1978; contbr. over 40 articles to profl. publs. With U.S. Army, 1946-47. Recipient Dept. of the Army Decoration for Exceptional Civilian Svc., Honors Achievement award Angiology Rsch. Found., Purdue Frederick Co., Engring. Alumni Achievement award George Washington U., Washington, 1987. Mem. ASME, Am. Soc. for Artificial Internal Organs. Republican. Baptist. Achievements include 12 U.S. and 2 foreign patents, development of artifical human heart. Home: 1701 Hunts End Ct Vienna VA 22182-1833

WOODWARD, KIRK, theater director; b. Louisville, Nov. 22, 1947; s. Ernest and Mary Hardin (Morris) W.; m. Patricia Ann Woodward, June 23, 1984; children: Erin, Heather, Craig. BA, Washington and Lee U., 1969. Acting instr. NYC Housing Authority, 1975; dir. acting studies Pushcart Players, Verona, NJ, 1979-82; dir. New Scripts Project, NYC, 1986; pres. The Attic Ensemble, Jersey City, 1982-85; programmer analyst Time Warner Inc., NYC, 1985—2001; mng. dir. Stage Left, Inc., NYC, 1986-95; instr. Adult Sch. Montclair, 1998—. Tech. writer Vis. Nurse Svc., NYC, 2001—; artistic dir. Troupe of Vagabonds Theatre, Bloomfield, NJ, 2002—; instr. Performers Theater Workshop, 1989—2004. Author: (play) Who's Who in Murder, 1990 (1st pl. award Hardin County Playwriting Competition). Elder Presbyn. Ch. Upper Montclair. 1st lt. USAR, 1970-72, Korea. Lt. US Army, 1970—73. Mem. Soc. for Tech. Comm., Dramatists Guild Am., Delta Upsilon. Presbyterian. Avocation: piano. Home: 25 Melrose Pl Montclair NJ 07042-2531 Office: VNSNY 5 Penn Plz New York NY 10001 Home Phone: 973-744-5755; Office Phone: 212-609-5509. Personal E-mail: kwdwd@aim.com.

WOODWARD, LESTER RAY, lawyer; b. Lincoln, Nebr., May 24, 1932; s. Wendell Smith and Mary Elizabeth (Theobald) W.; m. Marianne Martinson, Dec. 27, 1958; children: Victoria L. Woodward Eisele, Richard T., David M., Andrew E. BSBA, U. Nebr., 1953; LLB, Harvard U., 1957; LLD (hon.), Bethany Coll., 1974. Bar: Colo., 1957. Assoc. Davis, Graham & Stubbs, Denver, 1957-59, 60-62, ptnr., 1962—2004, sr. counsel, 2004—. Teaching fellow Sch. Law Harvard U., 1959-60. Bd. dirs. Bethany Coll., Lindsborg, Kans., 1966-74, 87-95, chmn., 1989-92; bd. dirs. Pub. Edn. Coalition, Denver, 1985-92, chmn., 1988-89; mem. Colo. Commn. Higher Edn., Denver, 1977-86, chmn., 1979-81; mem. bd. edn. Denver Pub. Schs., 1999-2005, pres., 2003-05. Mem. ABA, Colo. Bar Assn., Am. Law Inst. Republican. Lutheran. Home: 680 Bellaire St Denver CO 80220-4935 Home Phone: 303-322-8758; Office Phone: 303-892-7392. Business E-Mail: les.woodward@dgslaw.com.

WOODWARD, MARGARET NEWBERN, language educator; b. Jarvisburg, NC, Nov. 4, 1945; d. James Edward and Mary Willa (Bass) Newbern; m. Raymond Bross Caroom (dec.); children: Donna Sue Padilla, Richard Lee Fulcher, Michael Wayne Fulcher; m. Robert Whitmore Woodward, July 10, 2001. BS in Edn., Elizabeth City State U., NC, 1978; MEd, U. SC, Columbia, 1990. Sci. and health tchr. Currituck County Schs., Currituck, NC, 1978—81, Pasquatauk County Schs., Elizabeth City, 1981—84; English and social studies tchr. Sumter Sch. Dist., Sumter, SC, 1984—2006, English tchr., 2006—. Adj. prof. Embry Riddle Aero. U., Shaw AFB, SC, 1993—; tchr. cons. SC Geog. Alliance, U. SC, Columbia, 1998. Named Disting. Reading Tchr., Sumter Sch. Dist., Tchr. of Yr., 1992. Mem.: Internat. Reading Assn., Nat. Coun. Tchrs. English, Phi Delta Kappa. Mem. Lds Ch. Avocations: golf, reading, fitness, travel. Home: 3100 Hwy 261N Rembert SC 29128

WOODWARD, RALPH BARCLAY, music educator, small business owner; b. Blackfoot, Idaho, Nov. 11, 1944; s. H. Ralph and Margaret Barclay Woodward. Student, U. Ill., Urbana, 1962—64; BS in Music Edn., Brigham Young U., Salt Lake City, 1970; student, Folkwangschule, Essen, Germany, 1968—69, student, 1971. Student Am. Wind Symphony, 1963; tchr. music Elko County Sch. Dist., Carlin, Nev., 1972; tchr. Round Valley Consol. Sch. Dist., Eagar, Ariz., 1973; French horn Rheinische Philharmonie, Koblenz, Germany, 1974—75, Städtische Orchester, Wuppertal, 1976; salesman Daynes Music and Keyboard Showcase, Salt Lake City, 1977—82; founder and dir. Salt Lake Children's Choir, 1979—; prin. and owner Cherbourne Music, 1995—. Freelance musician, 1977—; composer and arranger. Prodr.: (albums) Beside Thy Cradle, 1995, A Day in Spring, 2000; musician: (plays) Fiddler on the Roof (European prodn.), 1968, Compania d'Opera Milano Touri Orchestra, 1971, Ruhrland Orchestra, 1969, Rheinische Philharimonie, 1975, (albums) Concerto Amsterdam, 1971, Columbia Symphony Orchestra, 1983, (ballets) Ballet West Orch., 1977. Missionary LDS Ch., Brazil, 1965—66. Recipient Spl. Recognition award, Gloden Gate Internat. Children's Choir Festival, 1999. Mem.: Am. Choral Dir.'s Assn. Mem. Lds Ch. Avocations: athletics, hiking, writing, languages.

WOODWARD, RALPH LEE, JR., retired historian, educator; b. New London, Conn., Dec. 2, 1934; s. Ralph Lee and Beulah Mae (Suter) W.; m. Sue Dawn McGrady, Dec. 30, 1958; children: Mark Lee, Laura Lynn, Matthew McGrady; m. Janice Chatelain, Aug. 8, 1996. AB cum laude, Central Coll., Mo., 1955; MA, Tulane U., 1959, PhD, 1962. Asst. prof. history Wichita U., Kans., 1961-62, U. S.W. La., Lafayette, 1962-63, U. NC, Chapel Hill, 1963-67, assoc. prof., 1967-70; prof. history Tulane U., New Orleans, 1970-99, head dept. history, 1973-75, chmn. dept. history, 1986-88; dir. Tulane Summer in C. Am., 1975-78; prof. in charge Tulane Jr. Year Abroad, Paris, 1975-76; Penrose prof. L.Am. studies Tex. Christian U., Ft. Worth, 1999—2003; ret., 2003. Fulbright lectr. U. Chile, U. Catolica de Valparaiso, Chile, 1965-66, U. del Salvador, Universidad Nacional, Buenos Aires, 1968; vis. prof. US Mil. Acad., West Point, NY, 1989; regional liaison officer Emergency Com. to Aid Latin Am. Scholars, 1974; Joe & Teresa Long prof. social studies Tarleton State U., Stephenville, Tex., 2007. Author: Class Privilege and Economic Development, 1966, Robinson Crusoe's Island, 1969, Positivism in Latin America, 1850-1900, 1971, Central America: A Nation Divided, 1976, 3d edit., 1999, Tribute to Don Bernardo de Galvez, 1979, Belize, 1980, Nicaragua, 1983, 2d edit., 1994, El Salvador, 1988, Guatemala, 1992, Rafael Carrera and the Emergence of the Republic of Guatemala, 1993 (Alfred B. Thomas Book award), A Short History of Guatemala, 2005; editor: Central America: Historical Perspectives on the Contemporary Crises, 1988, Here and There in Mexico: The Travel Writings of Mary Ashley Townsend, 2001; assoc. editor: Revista del Pensamiento Centroamericano, 1975, Research Guide to Central America and the Caribbean, 1985, Encyclopedia of Latin American History and Culture, 1996; contbg. editor: Handbook of Latin American Studies, 1987-90; series editor: World Bibliographical Series, 1987-2000; contbr. articles to profl. jours. Bd. dirs. Common Cause Miss., 2004—05. Capt. USMC, 1955—58. Recipient Alfred B. Thomas Book award Southeastern Coun. Latin Latin Am. Studies, 1994; Henry L. and Grace Doherty Found. fellow Tulane U., 1962; named La. Humanist of Yr. La. Endowment for Humanities, 1995, Disting. Svc. award, Conf. Latin Am. History, 2002. Mem. Am. Hist. Assn. (mem. Conf. L.Am. History, pres. 1989, mem. gen. com. 1974-76, com. on Andean studies 1972-77, chmn. com. on Ctrl. Am. studies 1996-98, Disting. Svc. award 2002), Southeastern Conf. L.Am. Studies (program chmn. 1975, pres. 1975-76), Geography and History Acad. Guatemala, Southern Hist. Assn. (mem. L.Am. and Caribben sect.). Democrat. Episcopalian. Home Phone: 660-248-9891. Personal E-mail: clioclio@sbcglobal.net.

WOODWARD, THOMAS MORGAN, actor; b. Ft. Worth, Sept. 16, 1925; s. Valin Ridge and Francis Louise (McKinley) W.; m. Enid Anne Loftis, Nov. 18, 1950; 1 child, Enid Anne. AA, Arlington State Coll., 1948; BBA, U. Tex., 1951. Motion picture and TV actor, 1955—; numerous TV appearances include Dallas; motion pictures include The Great Locomotive Chase, 1955, Slaughter on 10th Ave., 1957, The Gun Hawk, 1962, Cool Hand Luke, 1966, The Wild Country, 1973, Which Way Is Up, 1977, Speed Trap, 1978, Battle Beyond the Stars, 1980, Girls Just Want to Have Fun, 1985, Dark Before Dawn, 1987, Gunsmoke III, 1991. With USAAF, 1944-45; to capt. USAF, 1951-53. Recipient Golden Boot award Motion Picture and TV Fund, 1988, Golden Lariat award Nat. Western Film Festival, 1988, Lifetime Achievement award Arlington Tex. Arts Coun., 1994, Lifetime Achievement award Wild West Film Festival, 1995, Internat. Star award 1997, Silver Spur award, Hollywood, Calif., 2004, Hands Across History Western film award Sedona, Ariz., 2004, Spirit of the West award, 2006;, Golden Star Halo award So. Calif. Motion Picture Coun., 2006; named Disting. Alumnus of Arts U. Tex., 1969; named to Walk of Western Stars William S. Hart Mus., LA, 1990. Mem. Acad. Motion Picture Arts and Scis., SAR, Pi Kappa Alpha (Disting. Achievement award 1981, inducted into Order of West Range 1988).

WOOD-WARREN, MAXINE, artist, art educator; b. Ponca City, Oklahoma, Jan. 14, 1927; d. William Roy and Helen Enrica (Huffer) Wood; m. William Guy Warren, Jr., June 1, 1949; one child, Alison. BFA, Okla. State U., 1948, MS, 1971; student, Santa Fe Inst. Fine Arts, 1986, student, 1992. Art tchr. McKinley Elem. Sch., Ponca City, Okla., 1950, 1956—60; dir., initiator Pk. Bldg. Contemporary Art Gallery Conoco, Inc., Ponca City, Okla., 1962—65; art tchr. Trout Elem., Ponca City, Okla., 1967—70; chmn. art dept. Ponca City Sr. H.S., Okla., 1977—86; studio artist paintings and monotypes Riverbluff Studio, Ponca City, 1986—. Artist cons. Native Am. Found., Chief Standing Bear, Ponca City, Okla., 1994—; mem. art faculty Arts Adventure, Ponca City, 1993, 94; bd. dir. Okla. Visual Arts Coalition, Oklahoma City, 1992-2001, Arts Place, Ponca City, 2003; initiator artists survival kit, 1998—, Charter bd. dir., Arts Place, Ponca City, 2003, chmn. visual arts Marland Estate Commn., Ponca City, 1976-79, initiator Artists in Residence,1976. Represented in permanent collections Okla. Contemporary Art Mus., Oklahoma City, 1969, Philbrook Art Mus., Tulsa (honorable mention 1948, 66, 68). Recipient 2d prize Internat. Am. Greetings, 5th prize Internat. Ford Times Mag., 1963, 2d prize Internat. Golden Press Book Illustration, 1962. Mem. Individual Artists Okla.(I.O.A.), O.U.A.C., Tulsa Artists Coalition (T.A.C.) Ponca City Art Assn., Okla. Edn. Assn., Okla. Retired Educators Assn., Living Artists Soc., Nat. Mus. Women in Arts, Okla. Art Inst., Ind. Artists Okla., Tulsa Artists Coalition, Zeta Tau Alpha. Independent. Avocations: discussion group, books, dogs. Studio: 7182 River Ridge Dr Ponca City OK 74604-9103

WOODWELL, GEORGE MASTERS, ecologist, conservationist; b. Cambridge, Mass., Oct. 23, 1928; s. Philip McIntire and Virginia (Sellers) W.; m. Alice Katharine Rondthaler, June 23, 1955; children: Caroline Alice, Marjorie Virginia, Jane Katharine, John Christopher. AB, Dartmouth Coll., 1950; AM, Duke U., 1956, PhD, 1958; DSc (hon.), Williams Coll., 1977, Miami U., 1984, Carleton Coll., 1988, Muhlenberg Coll., 1990, Duke U., 1994, Dartmouth Coll., 1996. Mem. faculty U. Maine, 1957-61, assoc. prof. botany, 1960-61; vis. asst. ecologist, biology dept. Brookhaven Nat. Lab., Upton, NY, 1961-62, ecologist, 1965-67, sr. ecologist, 1967-75; founder, dir. Ecosystems Center, 1975-85; dep. and asst. dir. Marine Biol. Lab., Woods Hole, Mass., 1975-76; founder, pres. and dir. Woods Hole Research Ctr., 1985—2005, dir. emeritus, 2005—. Founder, chmn. Conf. on Long Term Biol. Consequences of Nuclear War, 1982-83. Editor: Ecological Effects of Nuclear War, 1965, Diversity and Stability in Ecological Systems, 1969, (with E.V. Pecan) Carbon and the Biosphere, 1973, The Role of Terrestrial Vegetation in the Global Carbon Cycle: Measurement by Remote Sensing, 1984, The Earth in Transition: Patterns and Processes of Biotic Impoverishment, 1990, (with K. Ramakrishna) Forests for the Future, 1993, (with F.T. Mackenzie) Biotic Feedbacks in the Warming of the Earth, 1995, Forests In A Full World, 2001 Founding trustee Environ. Def. Fund, 1967, Natural Resources Def. Coun., 1970, vice chmn., 1974-04, World Resources Inst., 1982-96; bd. dirs. Conservation Found., 1975-77, Ctr. for Marine Conservation, 1990-98, The Ocean Conservancy, 1999-2006, World Wildlife Fund, 1970-84, chmn., 1980-84, Ruth Mott Fund, 1984-91, chmn., 1989-91; bd. trustees Inst. Environ. Rsch. in Amazon, 1996—; adv. com. TMI Pub. Health Fund, 1980-94; bd. trustees Grand Canyon Nat. Pk. Found., 1999—. Recipient Joseph Priestley award Dickinson Coll., 1993, Hutchinson medal Garden Club of Am., 1993, Disting. Svc. award Am. Inst. Biol. Scis., 1982, Heinz Environ. prize, 1996, Volvo Environ. prize, 2001. Fellow AAAS, Am. Acad. Arts and Scis.; mem. NAS, Brit. Ecol. Soc., Ecol. Soc. Am. (v.p. 1966-67, pres. 1977-78), Sea Edn. Assn. (bd. dirs. 1980-85), World Comm. on Forests and Sustainable Development, 1994-98, Sigma Xi. Achievements include rsch., pub. on structure and function of natural communities, biotic impoverishment, especially ecological effects of ionizing radiation, effects of persistent toxins, world carbon cycle and warming of the earth, sci. and internat. environ. affairs. Office: Woods Hole Rsch Ctr 149 Woods Hole Rd Woods Hole MA 02543 Home Phone: 508-548-0680; Office Phone: 508-540-9900 x104. Business E-Mail: gmwoodwell@whrc.org.

WOODWORTH, RAMSEY LLOYD, lawyer; b. Syracuse, NY, Dec. 26, 1941; m. Diane Elizabeth McMillion, June 12, 1971; children: Scott, Ashley, Jeffrey. AB, Brown U., 1964; LLM cum laude, Syracuse U., NY, 1967. Bar: N.Y. 1967, D.C. 1968, U.S. Ct. Appeals (D.C. cir.) 1968. Atty., advisor FCC, Washington, 1967-68; from assoc. to ptnr. Hedrick & Lane, Washington, 1968-82; prin. Wilkes, Artis, Hedrick & Lane, Chartered, Washington, 1982-99; of counsel Shook, Hardy & Bacon LLP, Washington, 1999—2003, Irwin, Campbell & Tannenwald, PC, Washington, 2003—. Convenor Peace Luth. Ch., Alexandria, 1985-86; chair Libr. Am. Broadcasting Found., Inc., 1997—. Mem. Fed. Comm. Bar Assn. (exec. com. 1986-89, chair profl. responsibility com. 1984-86, treas. 1989-90, chmn. Fed. Commn. Bar Assn. Found. 1991-93, trustee 1991-94, Univ. Club Washington, Order of Coif. Avocation: swimming. Office: Irwin Campbell & Tannenwald PC 1730 Rhode Island Ave NW Washington DC 20036 Office Phone: 202-772-0013. E-mail: rwoodworth@ictpc.com.

WOODY, GEORGE EDWARD, psychiatrist, educator; s. Paul Richard Woody and Harriet McGaughey; m. Christina Demetrovits, Sept. 14, 1985; children: Christina Mary, Nicholas George. MD, Temple U., Phila.; D (hon.), Pavlov State Med. U., St. Petersburg, Russia. Diplomate Am. Bd. Psychiatry, 1974, Am. Bd. Psychiatry and Neurology, 1993. Chief substance abuse treatment unit Phila. VA Med. Ctr., 1982—2000; prof. dept. psychiatry U. Pa., 1994—. Prin. investigator Del. Valley node clin. trials network U. Pa., 1999—; bd. dirs. Treatment Rsch. Inst., Phila. Contbr. articles to profl. jours. Lt. USN, 1965—67. Recipient Nyswander-Dole award, Methadone Treatment Providers Assn., 1991, Excellence in Collaborative Rsch. award, Nat. Inst. Drug Abuse, 2006. Fellow: Am. Psychiat. Assn. (life). Achievements include research in treatment outcome studies in substance use disorders. Home: 4110 Timber Ln Philadelphia PA 19129 Office: 600 Public Ledger Bldg 150 S Independence Mall W Philadelphia PA 19106 Home Phone: 215-842-0767; Office Phone: 215-399-0980. Business E-Mail: woody@tresearch.org.

WOODY, JOHN FREDERICK, retired secondary school educator; b. Indpls., Apr. 27, 1941; s. Ralph Edwin and Crystal Oleta (Thomas) W.; m. Nancy Ann Henry, July 7, 1963; children: Michael, Laura. BS in Secondary Sch. Teaching, Butler U., 1963, MS in Edn., 1967, adminstrn. lic., 1979, postgrad., 1991—, UCLA, 1980-82, Ind. U., 1990, U. Amsterdam, The Netherlands, 1985, Mont. State U., 1993, Purdue U., 1994. Tchr. Pub. Sch. 90, Indpls., 1963-66, Broad Ripple High Sch., Indpls., 1966-89; tchr., head social studies dept. Arlington H.S., Indpls., 1989—2003; ret., 2003. Author: (resource kits for hist. events) Cram, Inc., 1976-81, (filmstrips) Lowe Sheldrew, 1976-81; contbr. articles to profl. jours. and sch. materials. Sponsor Rep. Nat. Com., 1982—; deacon North Star Bapt. Ch., 1983—, Oak Spring Ch., 2004—; mem. U.S. Congress German Bundestag Select Com. Ind., 1986-93; vol. Arlington HS Libr., 2005-06. Fulbright scholar U.S. Info. Agy., 1985. Mem. ASCD, Nat. Coun. Social Studies, Ind. Coun. Social Studies, Arlington Acad. Com. Baptist. Avocations: reading, writing, swimming, lifting weights. Home: 7362 Woodside Dr Indianapolis IN 46260-3137

WOODY, MARY FLORENCE, nursing educator, academic administrator; b. Chambers County, Ala., Mar. 31, 1926; d. Hugh Ernest and May Lillie (Gilliland) W. Diploma, Charity Hosp. Sch. Nursing, 1947; BS, Columbia U., 1953, MA, 1955. Staff nurse Wheeler Hosp., Lafayette, Ala., 1947-48; polio nurse Willard Parker Hosp., NYC, 1949; staff nurse, supr. VA Hosp., Montgomery, Ala., 1950-53; faculty, field supr. nursing dept. Columbia U. Tchrs. Coll., NYC, 1955-56; asst. dir. nursing Emory U. Hosp., Atlanta, assoc. dir., DON, 1984-93; clin. asst. prof. Emory U. Sch. Nursing, Atlanta, 1956-68, interim dean, 1992-93; asst. dir., DON Grady Meml. Hosp., Atlanta, 1968-79; founding dean, prof. Auburn U. Sch. Nursing, Ala., 1979-84; disting. emeritus prof. Emory U., 2003—. Chair Ga. Statewide Master Planning Com. for Nursing and Nursing Edn., 1971-75; faculty preceptor patient care adminstrn. Sch. Public Health, U. Minn., 1977-79; bd. dirs. Wesley Woods Found. & Long Term Hosp.; chair bd. dirs. Am. Jour. Nursing Co., 1978-83. Recipent Spl. Recognition award 5th Dist. and Ga. Nurses Assn., 1978, 93, Disting. Achievement in Nursing Svc. award Columbia U. Tchrs. Coll. Alumni Assn., 1992, Jane Van de Vrede Outstanding Svc. to Citizens Ga. award Ga. League Nursing, Cert. Spl. Recognition award Ga. Nurses Assn., 1993, Internat. Founders award Sigma Theta Tau, 1999, The Marie Hippensteel award, 1999, Disting. Prof. award Emeritus Coll. Emory U., 2003; named Ga. Women Pioneer in Health Care, Ga. Commn. on Women and Ga. Womens History Month Com., 1998, Hall of Fame Nursing, Tchrs. Coll., Columbia, U., N.Y Fellow Am. Acad. Nursing (charter, Living Legend 1997); mem. Am. Nurses Assn., Nat. League Nursing, Am. Heart Assn., Emory U. Nell Hodgson Woodruff Sch. Nursing Alumni Assn. (hon.), Sigma Theta Tau (Marie Hippensteel Lingemald award for excellence in nursing 1999); mem. Nursing Tchr.'s Coll. Columbia U. of Hall of Fame (charter). Democrat. Address: 19488 Veterans Memorial Pkwy Lafayette AL 36862

WOODY, TERESA ANN, lawyer; b. Littlefield, Tex., Jan. 8, 1960; d. Ronald L. and Shirley A. (Yates) Woody; m. Rik N. Siro, Aug. 9, 1980; children: Alexander L. Siro, Lia A. Siro. BA with high distinction, U. Calif., Berkeley, 1982; JD magna cum laude, U. Calif., Hastings, 1985. Bar: Mo. 1985, Calif. 1986, Kans. 1995, U.S. Ct. Internat. Trade 1998. Law clk. Hon. Ross T. Roberts, U.S. Dist. Ct. (we. dist.) Mo., Kansas City, 1985-86; assoc. Spencer Fane Britt & Browne, Kansas City, 1986-92; ptnr. Spencer Fane Britt & Browne, LLP, Kansas City, 1993—2004, chair litig. dept., 2001—04; ptnr. Stueve Siegel Hanson Woody LLP, Kansas City, 2004—07, Woody Law Firm PC, Kansas City, 2007—. Pres., bd. dirs. Westport Ballet Theatre, Kansas City, 1988—89, Mattie Rhodes Counseling and Arts Ctr., Kansas City, 1994—95; mem. steering com. Centurions Leadership Program, Kansas City, 1992—94. Mem.: ABA (chair com. environ. litig. techs. 1996—97), Assn. Women Lawyers Greater Kansas City (pres. 1992—93), Midwest Regional Conf. Women Law (co-chair 1997—98), Nat. Conf. Women's Bar Assns. (bd. dirs. 1994—97). Office: Woody Law Firm PC 1044 Main St Ste 500 Kansas City MO 64105 Office Phone: 816-421-4246. Business E-Mail: teresa@woodylawfirm.com.

WOOFTER, VIVIEN PERRINE, interior designer, consultant; d. Orie Ray and Hazel Lucille (Bostic) Perrine; m. Perry Wilson Woofter, Oct. 5, 1952; children: James Perry, Lori Evan Hugh. BS in Home Econ., W.Va. U., 1952, LHD (hon.), 1998. Lic. interior designer Va., 2003. Interior designer GSA, Washington, 1968—76; head interior design The White Ho., 1976—77, U.S. Dept. Health & Human Services, 1977—81; sr. interior designer U.S. Dept. of State, 1981—88; dir. interiors & furnishings divsn. Overseas Buildings Ops., U.S. Dept. of State, 1988—. Mem. W.Va. U. Alumni Bd., Morgantown, 1994—; vol. mem. designer renovation W.Va. U. President's Ho. Com., 1996—2003; mem. W.Va. U. Found. Bd., 1999—; pres. Coll. Creative Arts Vis. Com., 2001—. Author: Develop. Furniture Standards- Phys. Handicap (Written up in Congl. Record, 1977); interior design Interior Design Hdqs. Bldg. for HHS (Fed. Design Coun. of Excellence, 1979), Riyadh Embassy, Paris, Buenos Aires - (Meritorius Honor & Superior Honor, 1988). Restoration work Met. Theater, Morgantown, 2003. Mem.: Internat. Interior Design Assoc. Achievements include development of Art Programs for all new embassies; Culturally Significan Program for US State Dept. Overseas Ident; a Maintenance Manual for US State Dept. Culturally Significant Buildingsofp; Featured in Articles, in Architectural Digest, Southern Accents, Paris Match, Chicago Tribune, other newspapersnchi. Home: 4856 N 35th Rd Arlington VA 22207 Office: Interiors & Furnishings Div Overseas Buildings Ops US Dept State Washington DC 20520 Personal E-mail: vivienwoofter@erols.com. E-mail: woofterv p@state.gov.

WOO HO, DOREEN, investment banker; b. Australia; m. James Woo Ho; 3 children. B, Smith Coll.; MA in East Asian Studies & Chinese History, Columbia U. With Citibank, Taipei; corr. Time mag., Phnom Penh, Cambodia; with Citibank, 1972—98; pres. consumer credit group Wells Fargo, 1998—, pres. corp. trust services. Bd. dir. San Francisco Opera Assn., 2001—, v.p treas., exec. com. mem., chair audit com., vice chair dir. & officers com., fin. adv. com.; co-founder Asian Pacific Islander Scholarship Fund. Named one of 25 Most Powerful Women in Banking, US Banker, 2006; recipient Fin. Woman of Yr., San Francisco Fin. Women's Assn., 2004. Mailing: San Francisco Opera Assn 301 Van Ness Ave San Francisco CA 94102 Office: Wells Fargo 420 Montgomery St San Francisco CA 94163 *

WOOKEY, JOHN, computer software company executive; b. Seattle; married; 3 children. BS in Econs. and Math., U. Calif., Berkeley, MS in Engrng. Scis. Various mgmt. positions Anderson Consulting, Williams & Burrows, Inc.; v.p. devel. Ross Systems, 1987—95; v.p. fin. applications products Oracle Corp., Redwood Shores, Calif., 1995—99, sr. v.p. fin. applications products, 1999—2000, sr. v.p. applications devel., 2000—. Office: Oracle Corp 500 Oracle Pky Redwood City CA 94065 Office Phone: 650-506-0024. *

WOOKEY, SARA HASTINGS, artist; b. Columbus, Ohio, Jan. 13, 1972; d. Wayne Hastings and Barbara Ann Wookey; m. S. Sean Fox, Aug. 10, 2006. Student, U. Ill., 1990—93; studied with Nina Martin and Francis Becker, NY Dance Intensive, 1993—94; BFA with honors in Dance, Ohio State U., Columbus, 1996; postgrad., UCLA, 2004—. Artist dir. Wookey Works, 1996—. Mem. adv. bd. So. Calif. Dance Connection, L.A., Dance Camerawest, L.A.; guest artist Amsterdam Sch. for Arts, 1998, Duncan Ctr. Konzervator, Prague, Czech Republic, 1998, Dans Werkplaats Amsterdam, 1999, Henry Jurriens Stichting, Amsterdam, 1999, Ohio State U., 1999, 2003, ArtEZ, 2004, San Jacinto Coll., Houston, 2004; tchr. DV8 Pys. Theater, 1999, Kenyon Coll., 2003, Calif. State U., Fullerton, 2004; tchr., asst. Cirquit Esq Studio, Montreal, Canada, 2005; faculty Amsterdam Sch. for Arts, 1999—2005; tchg. assoc. UCLA, 2005—07. Dir.(performance): Surface, 2002, Love's Geography: Revisited, 2005; choreographer: Words Fly About, 1999; Manner, 2000; The Skirt, 2000; Fields on the 4th Floor, 2001; choregrapher: FACE, 2003. Mem. LA Conservancy, LA, LA Forum for Art and Urban Designh, LA. Recipient Choregraphic Incentive award, Job Coher, Mayor of Amsterdam, 2001; grantee, Netherlands Funds for Arts, 2001, Amsterdam Funds for Arts, 2001.

WOOL, ALAN D., mathematics educator; b. Plymouth, NH, May 29, 1950; s. Louis Thomas and Priscilla Ann Wool; m. Sally Marie Wentworth, Aug. 26, 1972; children: Amy Rebecca, Jason Alan. BS in Math, Plymouth State Coll., 1972, EdM in Math, 1976. Cert. track ofcl. N.H. Tchr. Daniel Hand H.S., Madison, Conn., 1972—74, Gilford (N.H.) Mid. Sch. and H.S., 1974—2003, Gilford H.S., 2003—05. Cross county coach. Named Girls Cross County Coach of Yr., Nat. Fedn. Interscholastic Coaches Assn., 1991; named to, Gilford H.S. Hall of Fame, 1999, N.H. Coaches Assn. Hall of Fame, 1999. Mem.: NEA, N.H. Track Officials Assn. (cross county com.), N.H. Interscholastic Athletic Assn., N.H. Edn. Assn., Gilford Edn. Assn., Belknap County Sportsmen's Assn. Baptist. Avocations: hunting, fishing, jogging. Office: Gilford High Sch 88 Alvah Wilson Rd Gilford NH 03249

WOOLARD, EDGAR S., JR., retired chemical company executive; b. Wash., NC, Apr. 15, 1934; s. Edgar Smith and Mamie (Boone) W.; m. Peggy Harrell, 1956; children: Annette, Lynda. BS, N.C. State U., 1956. Indsl. engr. DuPont, Kinston, NC, 1957-59, 1959-62, supr. mfg. sect., 1962-64, planning supr., 1964-65, staff asst to prodn. mgr. Wilmington, Del., 1965-66, product supr. Old Hickory, Tenn., 1966-69, engrng. supt., 1969-70, asst. plant mgr. Camden, SC, 1970-71, plant mgr. Kinston, SC, 1971-73, dir. products mktg. div. Wilmington, Del., 1973-75, mng. dir. textile mktg. div., 1975-76, mgr. corp. plans dept., 1976-77, gen. dir. products and planning div., 1977-78, gen. mgr. textile fibers, 1978-81, v.p. textile fibers, 1981-83, exec. v.p., 1983-85, vice chmn., 1985-87, pres., COO, 1987-89, chmn., CEO, 1989-96, chmn., 1997—98. Bd. dirs. NC Textile Found., Citicorp, Apple Computer Inc., Dupont, 1996-2000, NY Stock Exch., 2005-2006, NYSE Group, Inc., 2006-, Telex Comms. Inc. Trustee Med. Ctr. Del., N.C. State U., Winterthur Mus. Lt. U.S. Army. Recipient Internat. Palladium medal Soc. Chimie Industrille (Am. sect.), 1995. Office: NYSE Group Inc 11 Wall St New York NY 10005 Office Phone: 212-656-3000.

WOOLDRIDGE, PATRICE MARIE, marketing professional, personal trainer; b. Chgo., June 3, 1954; d. Charles E. and Marlys E. Reardon; m. Patrick Woolridge, June 27, 1981. AS, Moraine Valley Coll., 1974; BA, Govs. State U., 1976, MA, 1977; MBA, Loyola U., Chgo., 1983. Cmty. prof. Govs. State U., University Park, Ill., 1977-78; counselor, social worker Bloom Twp. HS, Chicago Heights, Ill., 1977-78; market analyst Dr. Scholl Footcare, Chgo., 1978-79; supr. consumer rsch. Unocal, Schaumburg, Ill., 1979-84; group rsch. dir. Tatham-Laird & Kudner, Chgo., 1984-87; v.p., assoc. dir. strategic planning & rsch. Bayer Bess Vanderwarker Advt., Chgo., 1987-90; v.p. dir. qualitative svcs. Goldring/MIL Rsch., 1990-91; pres. Wooldridge Assocs., Inc., Chgo., 1991—. Instr. dancing, 1969—89; instr. Arica Inst., NYC, 1978—, T'ai Chi Found.,

NYC, 1986—. Performer: Anawim Players, 1985—97. Participant White House Conf. Small Bus., 1996; treas. Karma Thegsum Choling, Chgo., 1987—97; bd. dirs. Illustrated Theatre Co., Chgo., 1987, Human Process, Chgo., 1992—2004, T'ai Chi Found., Inc., 1994—97, 2004, pres. bd. dirs., 2003—04; adv. bd. N.W. Suburban Boy Scouts Am., Schaumburg, 1984. Recipient Gold medallion, Ogilvy Awards, 2000. Mem.: Union Concerned Scietists, Qualitative Rsch. Cons. Assn., Am. Mktg. Assn., Planetary Soc. Home and Office: 1717 W Rascher Ave Chicago IL 60640-1117 Business E-Mail: patrice@wastrategy.com.

WOOLDRIDGE, SUE ELLEN, former federal agency administrator, lawyer; b. Riverside, Calif., Feb. 15, 1961; d. Robert and Patricia Wooldridge; m. J. Steven Griles, Mar. 26, 2007. BA, U. Calif. Davis, 1983; JD, Harvard U., 1987. Bar: Calif., U.S. Supreme Ct. Assoc. Diepenbrock, Wulff, Plant & Hannegan, Sacramento, 1987—94; spl. asst. atty. gen. State of Calif., Sacramento, 1994—98; founding ptnr. Riegles Campos & Kenyon LLP, Sacramento, 1999—2001; gen. counsel Calif. Fair Polit. Practices Com., 2000; dep. chief of staff US Dept. Interior, Washington, DC, 2001—04, solicitor, 2004—05; asst. atty. gen. environment & nat. resources US Dept. Justice, Washington, DC, 2005—07. *

WOOLDRIDGE, WILLIAM CHARLES, lawyer; b. Miami, Fla., Feb. 24, 1943; s. Clarence Edward and Easter Marguerite (Souders) W.; m. Joyce L. Norton, June 15, 1968; children: William Charles, John Michael. BA, Harvard U., 1965; LLB, U. Va., 1969. Bar: Va. 1969. Atty. Norfolk and Western Ry. Co., 1973-82; with Norfolk So. Corp., 1982-2000, v.p. dept. law, 1996-2000. Pres. John Marshall Found., Richmond, Va., 1992-94; pres. Norfolk Hist. Soc., 1995-96; chair Friends of Chrysler Mus. Hist. Houses, 1997-99; bd. dirs. Sta. WHRO (FM and TV), 1997-00, WHRO Found., 2003-05, Libr. Va. Found. Capt. JAGC, US Army, 1969-73. Republican.

WOOLER, JOHN WILLIAM, multi-media specialist; s. William James and Moira Nesbitt Wooler; m. Rosemary Bernadette Gorman, June 20, 1980; children: Lewis James, Roxanna Susan, Carla Louise. Student, Dundee Sch. Of Tech., Scotland, 1978—79. Dep. head of a&r Virgin Records Uk, London, 1984—94; sr. v.p. Virgin Records USA, LA, 1994—2002. Record prodr., LA. Prodr.: (music) various (grammys, 1993). Office: Sunset Strip Inc 1201 Alta Loma Los Angeles CA 90069 Home Phone: 310-989-3916; Office Phone: 310-360-4055. Business E-Mail: jwooler@sunsetstrip.com.

WOOLERY, JAMES C., lawyer; b. Louisville, May 8, 1969; BA cum laude, Wake Forest Univ., 1991; JD, Univ. Ky., 1994. Bar: NY 1995. Assoc. Cravath Swaine & Moore, NYC, 1994—95, 1997—2002, ptnr., corp., 2002—, assoc. London, 1995—97. Office: Cravath Swaine & Moore LLP Worldwide Plz 825 Eighth Ave New York NY 10019-7475 Office Phone: 212-474-1912. Office Fax: 212-474-3700. Business E-Mail: jwoolery@cravath.com.

WOOLEY, GERALDINE HAMILTON, poet, writer; b. Idlewild, Mich., Feb. 15, 1942; d. Charles Loren and Alice (Smith) Hamilton; m. David Wooley, June 11, 1961 (div. 1983); children: Vickie Wooley Houston, Monica Wooley Roberts, Deborah Wooley Williams. GED, Flint, Mich. Cosmetologist pvt. practice, Flint, Mich., 1967-70; tchr's. aide Flint Comty. Schs., 1969-71; nurse's aide Clara Barton Home, Flint, 1972; factory worker GM AC Plant, Flint, 1973-76; child care worker Beecher Cmty. Schs., Flint, 1987-89; poet, songwriter Flint, 1994—. Songwriter Hilltop Records, Hollywood, Calif., 1996—. Author: (poems) Between The Raindrops, 1995 (Editor's Choice 1995), At Water's Edge, 1995 (Editor's Choice 1995), Tapestry, 1996 (Editor's Choice 1996), Memories of Tomorrow, 1996 (Editor's Choice 1996), (poems) A Treasury of Famous Poets, 1997 (Editor's Choice award 1997). Mem. PTA Flint Sch. Dist., 1969-70. Named to Internat. Poetry Hall of Fame, 1996. Mem. Internat. Soc. Of Poets, Nat. Writers Assn., Internat. Black Writers. Democrat. Avocations: camping, playing organ, exploring old houses, writing. Home: 723 E Lansing Apt 611E Idlewild MI 49642 Office Phone: 810-423-2053. E-mail: ladyknight77@webtv.net.

WOOLF, KENNETH HOWARD, architect; b. NYC, Aug. 19, 1938; s. Howard Walter and Elizabeth Ann (Levy) W.; m. Elizabeth Adair Rainwater, July 3, 1965; children: Robert Gregg, Susan Adair, Jennifer Adair. BArch, Cornell U., 1961. Staff arch. Look & Morrison, Archs., Pensacola, Fla., 1965-72; pvt. practice arch. Pensacola, Fla., 1972—. Instr. architecture Pensacola Jr. Coll., part-time 1967-76; chmn. Pensacola Archtl. Rev. Bd., 1970-81; mem. Gulf Breeze Planning Bd., 1976-78; chmn. Pensacola City Bd. Adjustment and Appeals, 1995—. Prin. works include Coca-Cola Bottling Co. Plant, Pensacola, 1974, 3 profl. office bldgs. towers, Pensacola, 1976, 1984, 1992, Bapt. Hosp. addition, 1977, The Village, Housing for Elderly, 1978, 1981, 1998, 2006, Azalea Trace Ret. Cmty. Complex, 1980, 1999, Northview Cmty., 1981, Coca-Cola Bottling Plant, Beaumont, Tex., 1983, Episcopal Day Sch., Pensacola, 1993, 6 oncology ctrs., 1990, 1994, 1996, 1999, 2002, 2003, 2005. With USN, 1961-65. Named Jaycee of Yr., 1970. Mem. AIA (sec. N.W. Fla. chpt. 1976-77, 77-78, pres. 1979-81, Comml. Design Hon. award 1975), Rotary. Episcopalian. Home: 15 N Sunset Blvd Gulf Breeze FL 32561-4051 Office: 100 W Gadsden St Pensacola FL 32501-3910 Office Phone: 850-438-3653. Business E-Mail: khwarch@networktel.net.

WOOLF, STEVEN MICHAEL, artistic director; b. Milw., Dec. 23, 1947; s. Raleigh and Lenore (Shurman) W. BA in Theatre, U. Wis., 1968, MFA, 1971; D of Fine Arts (hon.), U. Mo., 1993. Prodn. stage mgr. The Juilliard Sch. Drama, NYC, 1973-75; project prodr. Musical Theatre Lab., NYC, 1974-75; prodn. stage mgr. Barter Theatre, Abingdon, Va., 1976-79, Stagewest, Springfield, Mass., 1976-79; prodn. mgr. Repertory Theatre of St. Louis, 1980-83, acting artistic dir., mng. dir., 1983-85, mng. dir., 1985-86, artistic dir., 1986—. Adj. faculty Webster U., St. Louis, 1982—; mem. nat. negotiating coms. League of Resident Theatres, N.Y.C., 1986—; on-site evaluator Nat. Endowment for the Arts, 1985. Dir. plays A Life in the Theatre, 1982, the Crucible, 1986, Company, 1987, The Voice of the Prairie, 1988, 90, The Boys Next Door, 1989, Dog Logic, 1990, Born Yesterday, 1990, Terra Nova, 1991, The Diary of Anne Frank, 1991, Other Peoples Money, 1991, Six Degrees of Separation, 1992, Sight Unseen, 1993, Lion in Winter, 1993, Death and the Maiden, 1993, The Living, 1994, Wait Until Dark, 1994, The Caine Mutiny Court Martial, 1994. The Life of Galileo, 1995, Death of a Salesman, 1995, Betrayal, 1996, As Bees in Honey Drown, 1997, Who's Afraid of Virginia Woolf, 1998, Closer, 1998, Dinner With Friends, 2000, The Dresser, 2001, The Shape of Things, 2002, Copenhagen, 2003, Two Rockin' Gents, 2003, The Goat, Or Who is Sylvia, 2003, Blue/Orange, 2004, The Crucible, 2004, The Retreat From Moscow, 2004, Henry IV & Humble Boy, 2006, others. Mem. ad hoc coms. for funding Mo. Arts Coun., St. Louis, 1988; chair citizen rev. panel Reg. Arts Commn., St. Louis, 1986; bd. dirs. Mo. Citizens for the Arts, 1990—; exec. com. League of Resident Theatres, 1990—. Recipient award Mo. Citizens for the Arts, 1992, Women's Polit. Caucus, 1993, award for Individual Excellence in the Arts, Arts Edn. Coun., 1993. Mem. AFTRA, Soc. of Stage Dirs. and Choreographers, Actors Equity Assn. Office: Repertory Theatre St Louis 130 Edgar Rd Saint Louis MO 63119-3228 Home Phone: 314-367-4401; Office Phone: 314-968-7340. Personal E-mail: swoolf@repstl.org.

WOOLF, WILLIAM BLAUVELT, retired association executive; b. New Rochelle, NY, Sept. 18, 1932; s. Douglas Gordon and Katharine Hutton (Blauvelt) W. AA, John Muir Jr. Coll., 1951; student, U. Calif., Berkeley, 1995; BA, Pomona Coll., 1953; MA, Claremont Grad. Sch., Calif., 1955; PhD, U. Mich., 1960. Instr., asst. prof., asso. prof. U. Wash., Seattle, 1959-68; assoc. sec., dir. adminstrn. AAUP, Washington, 1968-79; mng. editor Math. Revs., Am. Math. Soc., Ann Arbor, Mich., 1979-90, acting exec. editor, 1984-85; assoc. exec. dir. Am. Math. Soc., Providence, 1990-96. Bd. dirs. Nat. Child Rsch. Ctr., Washington, 1975-77; trustee Friends Sch., Detroit, 1985-90, treas., 1986-90; mem. Law and Justice Coun., Jefferson County, Wash., 1998—, chmn., 2001; mem. Wash. State U. Jefferson County Adv. Team, 1999-2003, chmn., 2002-2003, Jefferson County Edn. Com., 1998-2003, chmn., 1999-2001; bd. dirs. Jefferson County Farmers Market Assn., 2002-03. Fulbright Research fellow U. Helsinki, Finland, 1963-64 Fellow AAAS; mem. ACLU (life, treas. Washington 1966-68, bd. dirs. Washtenaw County and Mich. State 1989-90, bd. dirs. R.I. State 1993-95, treas. 1994-95, chmn. Jefferson County chpt. 2003-2005), Am. Math. Soc., Math. Assn. Am. Mem. Soc. Of Friends. Home: PO Box 235 Port Townsend WA 98368-0235

WOOLFENDEN, JAMES MANNING, nuclear medicine physician, educator; b. LA, Nov. 8, 1942; BA with distinction, Stanford U., 1964; MD, U. Wash., 1968. Diplomate Am. Bd. Nuclear Medicine (chmn. credentials com. 1993-94, vice chmn. exams. com. 1993-95, chmn. exam. com. 1995-96, sec. 1994-96, chmn. 1996-97, life mem.), Nat. Bd. Med. Examiners. Med. intern L.A. County-U. So. Calif. Med. Ctr., 1968-69; med. resident West L.A. VA Med. Ctr., 1969-70; nuclear medicine resident L.A. County-U. So. Calif. Med. Ctr., 1972-74; from asst. prof. radiology to assoc. prof. radiology U. Ariz., Tucson, 1974-84, prof. radiology, 1984—. Med. staff Univ. Med. Ctr., Tucson, 1974—; cons. VA Med. Ctr., 1974—; cons. med. staff Tucson Med. Ctr., 1975-2004, Carondelet St. Joseph's Hosp., 1974-98, St. Mary's Hosp., Tucson, 1976-90; mem. Nat. Cancer Inst. site visit team NIH, 1976, mem. NHLB Inst. site visit team NIH, 1976, mem. diagnostic radiology study sect., 1989-97, chmn., 1995-97; med. liaison officer network EPA, 1983-85; cons.-tchg. med. staff Kino Cmty. Hosp., 1984-94; med. officer Clin. Ctr., NIH, Bethesda, 1984-85; mem. Ariz. Cancer Ctr., U. Ariz., 1988—, sr. clin. scientist Univ. Heart Ctr., 1990—; Ariz. bd. regents U. Ariz. Presdl. Search Com., 1990-91; chmn. Ariz. Atomic Energy Commn., 1979-80, Ariz. Radiation Regulatory Hearing Bd., 1981—; bd. dirs. Calif. Radioactive Materials Mgmt. Forum, chmn., 1994-95, Western Forum Edn. in Safe Disposal of Low-Level Radioactive Waste, 1990-2000, vice chmn., 1991-92, chmn., 1992-94. Manuscript reviewer: Noninvasive Med. Imaging, 1983-84, Jour. Nuclear Medicine, 1985—, Investigative Radiology, 1989-94, Archives of Internal Medicine, 1990—; contbr. book chpts.: Diagnostic Nuclear Medicine, 2d edit., 1988, Adjuvant Therapy of Cancer, 1977, Fundamentals of Nuclear Medicine, 1988, others; contbr. articles to profl. jours. Mem. Am. Heart Assn. Coun. on Cardiovasc. Radiology. Maj. U.S. Army, 1970-72, Vietnam. Fellow Am. Coll. Nuc. Physicians (long range planning com. 1981-83, govt. affairs com. 1984-94, exec. com. 1987-91, sec. 1989-91, parliamentarian 1991-95, treas. 1996-98, publs. com. 1993-98, chmn. publs. com. 1993-94, pres.-elect 1998-99, pres. 1999-2000, others); mem. AMA (diagnostic and therapeutic tech. assessment reference panel 1982-98), Am. Nuc. Soc., Soc. Nuc. Medicine (com. on audit 1992-99, trustee 1992-96, ho. dels. 1996-2003, fin. com. 1996-99, bd. dirs. 1997-99, bronze medal for sci. exhibit 1984, bd. dirs., sec.-treas. So. Calif. chpt. 1993-95, pres.-elect 1995-96, pres. 1996-99), Assn. Univ. Radiologists, Ariz. Med. Assn., European Assn. Nuc. Medicine, Pima County Med. Soc., Radiol. Soc. N.Am., Acad. Molecular Imaging, Soc. for Molecular Imaging. Office: Ariz Health Scis Ctr Nuc Medicine 1501 N Campbell Ave Tucson AZ 85724-5068

WOOLFOLK, ROBERT LEE, psychologist, educator; b. Hot Springs, Ark., Oct. 5, 1947; s. Robert Lee Woolfolk and Jane Davis; m. Lesley Ann Allen, Nov. 24, 1995. BA, U. Tex., Austin, 1968, PhD, 1973. Lic. clin. psychologist NJ, 1977. Prof. Rutgers U., New Brunswick, NJ, 1974—. Vis. prof. Princeton U., NJ, 1982—2007. Author: (book) Stress, Sanity, and Survival, 1978, The Cure of Souls, 1998, Treating Somatization, 2007, Principles and Practice of Stress Management; editor: Jour. Theoretical and Philos. Psychology, 2002—05. Mem.: APA. Office: Princeton Univ Green Hall Princeton NJ 08544 Office Phone: 609-924-8362. Business E-Mail: woolfolk@princeton.edu.

WOOLHOUSE, MAUREEN ANN, mathematics professor; b. Somerville, Mass., Sept. 28, 1944; d. James Francis and Mary Margaret O'Brien; m. Jan Edward Woolhouse, June 24, 1973; children: Megan Short, Matthew Jason, Elizabeth Leslie. BA, Anna Maria Coll., Paxton, Mass, 1966; M in Edn., Worcester State Coll., Mass., 1972; M in Math., Worcester Poly. Inst., Mass., 1990. Asst. prof. math. Dean Jr. Coll., Franklin, Mass., 1988—92; assoc. prof., prof. math. Middlesex C.C., Lowell, 1992—2001; prof. math. Quinsigamond C.C., Worcester, 2001—. Cmty. v.p. United Way, Worcester, 1982—84; bd. mem. Instl. Rev. Bd. U. Mass. Med. Ctr., 1978—82; chmn. Worcester Cmty. Action Coun., 1980—82. Mem.: New England Assn. Two Yr. Coll. (pres. 2000—02). Democrat. Avocations: travel, golf, gardening, baking. Home: 84 Coolidge Road Worcester MA 01602 Office: Quinsigamond Community College 670 West Boylston Street Worcester MA 01606 Office Phone: 508-854-2731. Personal E-mail: mwoolhouse@qcc.mass.edu.

WOOLLAM, JOHN ARTHUR, electrical engineering educator, physics professor; b. Kalamazoo, Mich., Aug. 10, 1939; s. Arthur Edward and Mildred Edith (Hakes) W.; children: Catherine Jane, Susan June. BA in Physics, Kenyon Coll., 1961; MS in Physics, Mich. State U., 1963, PhD in Solid State Physics, 1967; MSEE, Case Western Res. U., 1978; Doctorate (hon.), Linköping (Sweden) U., 2004. Rsch. scientist NASA Lewis Rsch. Ctr., Cleve., 1967-80; prof. U. Nebr., Lincoln, 1979—, dir. Ctr. Microelectronic and Optical Materials Rsch., 1988—2000; pres. J.A. Woollam Co., Inc., Lincoln, 1987—. Editor Jour. Applied Physics Com., 1979-94. Trustee J.A. Woollam Found. Grantee NASA, NSF, USAF, Advanced Rsch. Projects Agy. Fellow Am. Phys. Soc., Am. Vacuum Soc. (chmn. thin film divsn. 1989-91). Office: U Nebr Dept Elec Engring 209NWSEC Lincoln NE 68588-0511 Personal E-mail: jwoollam@jawollam.com.

WOOLLEY, BRIAN N., lawyer; s. Stuart W. and Shirley S. Woolley; m. Patricia L. Martin, Oct. 26, 1985; children: Meredith, Philip. BS, Iowa State U., 1978; JD, Northwestern U., Chgo., 1982. Bar: Mo. 1982, U.S. Dist. Ct. Western Dist. Mo. 1982, Ill. 1984, No. Dist. Ill. 1984, U.S. Cts. Appeal for 7th, 8th and 10th Circuits. Assoc. Lathrop, Koontz, Kansas City, Mo., 1982—84, D'Ancona & Pflaum, Chgo., 1984—86; mem. Lathrop & Gage L.C., Kansas City, Mo., 1986—. Guest lectr. U. Mo., Kansas City, 2001—. Contbg. editor: The Developing Labor Law, 2003—07. Bd. dirs., pres. Wonderscope Children's Mus., Shawnee, Kans., 1996—2004; chmn., legal counsel com. Farmhouse Fraternity Bd. Dirs., Kansas City, Mo., 2000—; bd. dirs. Arthritis Found. of Greater Kansas City (Mo.), 2004—. Mem.: ABA, Am. Health Lawyers Assn., Soc. Human Resource Mgmt. Office: Lathrop & Gage LC 2345 Grand #2800 Kansas City MO 64108

WOOLLEY, DONNA PEARL, lumber company executive; b. Drain, Oreg., Jan. 3, 1926; d. Chester A. and Mona B. (Cheever) Rydell; m. Harold Woolley, Dec. 27, 1952 (dec. Sept. 1970); children: Daniel, Debra, Donald. Diploma, Drain High Sch. Sec. No. Life Ins. Co., Eugene, Oreg., 1943—44; sec., bookkeeper D & W Lumber Co., Sutherlin, Oreg., 1944, Woolley Logging Co. & Earl Harris Lumber Co., Drain, 1944—70; pres. Woolley Logging Co., 1970—, Smith River Lumber Co., 1970—, Mt. Baldy Mill, 1970—81, Drain Plywood Co., 1970—81, Woolley Enterprises, Inc., Drain, 1973—, Eagle's View Mgmt. Co., Inc., Eugene, 1981—. Bd. dirs. Wildlife Safari, Winston, 1991, Oreg. Cmty. Found., Portland, 1990-99, chair, 1997-99; bd. trustees Linfield Coll., McMinnville, U. Oreg. Found., Eugene, Oreg. Trl. coun. Boy Scouts Am., 1980—, World Forestry Ctr., Portland, 1990, Umpqua C.C. Fedn., 2001. Recipient Pioneer award, U. Oreg., 1982, Pres.'s medal, 2005, Econ. and Social Devel. award, Soroptimist Club, 1991, First Citizen of Eugene award, 2000, Aubrey Watzek award, Lewis & Clark Coll., 2001, Howard Vollum award, Associated Fund Raisers in Philanthropy Oreg. chpt., 2001, Pioneer award, Umpqua C.C., 2003, Hart Pioneer award, Wildlife Safari, 2003, Pres. medal, U. Oreg., 2005, Paul Harris fellow, Rotary, 2006. Mem. Oreg. Women's Forum, Pacific Internat. Trapshooting Assn., Amateur Trapshooting Assn., Eugene C. of C. (bd. dirs. 1989-92), Arlington Club, Town Club (bd. dirs., pres.), Sunnydale Grange, Cottage Grove/Eugene Rod & Gun Club. Republican. Avocations: golf, travel. Office: Eagle's View Mgmt Co Inc 1399 Franklin Blvd Eugene OR 97403-1979

WOOLLEY, MARY ELIZABETH, science administrator, advocate; b. Chgo., Mar. 16, 1947; John Joseph and Ellen Louise (Bakke) McEnerney; m. John Stuart Woolley, Dec. 6, 1969 (div. 1985); children: George Newsom, Nora Ellen; m. Michael Howland Campbell, Jan. 1, 1989 (div. 2004). BS, Stanford U., 1969; MA, San Francisco State U., 1972; postgrad., U. Calif., San Francisco and Berkeley, 1974-75. Assoc. dir. Inst. Epidemiology and Behavioral Medicine, San Francisco, 1979-81; adminstr. Med. Rsch. Inst. of San Francisco, 1981-82, v.p., adminstr., 1982-86, v.p., exec. dir., 1986-90; pres. Research! Am., Alexandria, Va., 1990—. Cons. in fin. and mgmt. NIH, Bethesda, Md., 1984—92; adj. faculty U. Calif. Sch. Pub. Health, Berkeley, 1983—92, mem. Dean's adv. coun., 1995—2002; founding mem. Whitehead Inst. Bd. Assocs., 1995—; bd. dirs. Lovelace Inst., Respiratory Rsch. Inst., vice chmn., 1999—2004; bd. dirs. Children's Rsch. Inst., Washington, 2003—07; lectr. to profl. assns.; mem. bd. visitors Harvard U. Sch. Pub. Health, Cambridge, 2002—; mem. dean's coun. Johns Hopkins Sch. of Nursing, 2002—; mem. bd. advisors IBM Life Scis., 2003—. Editor Jour. of Soc. Rsch. Adminstrs., 1986-89, mem. editl. rev. bd., 1989-95; mem. editl. bd. Jour. Women's Health, 1992-2003, Sci. Comm., 1994—; contbr. articles and editls. to profl. jours. Bd. dirs. Kensington (Calif.) Edn. Found., 1986-89, Enterprise for H.S. Students, 1990-92; mem. capital campaign com. Calif. Shakespeare Festival, 1989-91, v.p. Med. Rsch. Assns. Am., 1993-95; bd. advisors Friends of Cancer Rsch., 1996—; bd. dirs. Nat. Patient Safety Found., 1998-2000, Friends of Nat. Inst. of Nursing Rsch., 2001-07. Recipient Silver Touchstone award Am. Hosp. Assn., 1994, Disting. Svc. award Columbia Coll. Physicians and Surgeons, 1994, Advocacy award Fedn. Am. Socs. Exptl. Biology, 1998, Advocacy award Friends Nat. Inst. Nursing Rsch., 1999, Leadership award Coun. Scientific Soc. Pres.'s, 1999, Advocacy award Friends of Dental Rsch., 2002; honored Women of Vision Am. Com. Weizmann Inst. Sci., 2004, 05, 06, Advocacy award Am. Soc. Biochemistry and Molecular Biology, 2007. Fellow AAAS; mem. Assn. Ind. Rsch. Insts. (pres.-elect 1987-89, pres. 1989-90), Inst. Medicine (elected), Soc. Rsch. Adminstrs. (bd. dirs. 1986-90, bd. advisors 1990-93, Hartford-Nicholson Svc. award 1990, Disting. Contbn. to Rsch. Adminstrn. award, 1993), Calif. Biomed. Rsch. Assn. (bd. govs. 1986-90), Nat. Press Club. Democrat. Office: Research! Am 1101 King St Ste 520 Alexandria VA 22314-3067 Home Phone: 202-737-5998; Office Phone: 703-739-2577. Business E-Mail: mwoolley@researchamerica.org.

WOOLLEY, ROGER SWIRE, lawyer; b. Chgo., Nov. 18, 1924; s/ Anthony Walter and Agnes Louise (MacMurray) W.; m. Patricia Ann Jundt, 1951 (dec. 1978); children: Elliott Payne, Merrit Ann. BA, Coll. William & Mary, 1947; student, Exeter Coll., London, 1947-48; LLB, Columbia U., 1951. Bar: Calif., U.S. Supreme Ct. Legal counsel Solar Aircraft, San Diego, 1952-54; prin. Law Offices of Roger S. Woolley, Rancho Santa Fe, Calif., 1954—. Active Automobile Club So. Calif., L.A., dir. 1974-98, chmn. 1988-90; active Am. Automobile Assn., Falls Church, Va., Orlando, Fla., dir., 1986-97, chmn., 1991-93; founding dir., sec. Bank La Jolla, 1962-68; founding dir., sec. Rancho Santa Fe Savs. & Loan, 1972-78; founding dir., sec. Torrey Pines Bank, 1979-84; dir. Scripps Meml. Hosp. Found., La Jolla, Calif. 1984—; trustee emeritus The Endowment Assn. of Coll. William & Mary, Williamsburg, Va.; chmn., mem. Calif. State Hwy. Commn., 1958-67. Lt. jr. U.S. Navy, 1942-46, WW II. Mem. ABA, State Bar Calif., San Diego County Bar Assn., Rotary Club Rancho Santa Fe. Office: Law Offices of Roger S Woolley PO Box R 16903 Avenida de Acacias Rancho Santa Fe CA 92067 Office Phone: 858-756-1144.

WOOLLING, KENNETH RAU, vascular internist; b. Indpls., Mar. 6, 1918; m. Catherine Margaret McColl, Mar. 20, 1948; 2 children. BA magna cum laude, Butler U., 1939; postgrad., Harvard U., 1939-40; MD, Ind. U., 1943; MS in Medicine, U. Minn., 1951. Diplomate Nat. Bd. Med. Examiners, Am. Bd. Internal Medicine, Am. Bd. Cardiovascular Disease. Intern Indpls. City Hosp. (now Wishard Meml.), Indpls., 1943-44; resident in internal medicine Marion County Gen. Hosp., Indpls., 1947; fellow, first asst. internal medicine Mayo Found., Rochester, Minn., 1948-52; mem. med. staff, mem. tchg. staff postgrad. med. edn. Marion County Gen. Hosp. (name now Wishard Meml. Hosp.), Indpls., 1952—; founder, dir., peripheral vascular diseases clinic Indpls City & Marion County Gen. Hosp. (now Wishard Meml.), Indpls., 1952-68; pvt. practice internal medicine and cardiovascular diseases Indpls, 1952—; founder, dir. peripheral vascular diseases clinic Meth. Hosp., Indpls., 1967-72, founder, dir. vascular lab., 1970-73, mem. med. staff, tchr. staff postgrad. med. edn., 1952—. Mem. med. staff St. Vincent Hosp., St. Francis Hosp. and Winona Meml. Hosp., Indpls., 1952—; charter mem. med. staff Cmty. Hosp., Indpls., 1952—; charter mem. med. adv. com. Butler U., Indpls, 1956—. Contbr. articles to profl. jours., 1950—. Capt. Med. Corps U.S. Army, 1944-46. Fellow ACP, Am. Coll. Chest Physicians, Coun. on Cardiology Am. Heart Assn., Am. Coll. Angiology (gov. state of Ind. 1979-80); mem. AMA (50 Yr. award 1993), SAR, Internat. Union Angiology, Am. Soc. Internal Medicine, Am. Diabetes Assn., Ind. State Med. Soc., Ind. Diabetes Assn., Am. Fedn. for Clin. Rsch., N.Y. Acad. Med. Scis., North Ctrl. Clin. Soc., Mayo Cardiovascular Soc., Ind. Hist. Soc., Res. Officers Assn., Indpls. Med. Soc., Am. Legion, Shriners, Masons (Scottish Rite and Mystic Tie Lodge, 50 yr. award 1989), Contemporary Club of Indpls., Indpls. Athletic Club, Columbia Club, Highland Golf and Country Club, Phi Delta Theta (50 yr. award 1985), Phi Kappa Phi, Phi Chi. Presbyterian. Office: PO Box 80192 Indianapolis IN 46280-0192

WOOLLS, ESTHER BLANCHE, library science educator; b. Louisville, Mar. 30, 1935; d. Arthur William and Esther Lennie (Smith) Sutton; m. Donald Paul Woolls, Oct. 21, 1953 (div. Nov. 1982); 1 son, Arthur Paul AB in Fine Arts, Ind. U., 1958, MA in Libr. Sci., 1962, PhD in Libr. Sci., 1973. Elem. libr. Hammond (Ind.) Pub. Schs., 1958-65, libr. coord., 1965-67, Roswell (N.Mex.) Ind. Schs., 1967-70; prof. libr. sci. U. Pitts., 1973-97; prof., dir. Sch. Lib. and Info. Sci. San Jose (Calif.) State U., 1997—2005; consulting editor Librs. Unlimited, Glendale, Calif., 2005—. Exec. dir. Beta Phi Mu, 1981-95. Author: The School Library Media Manager, 1995, 3d edit., 2004, So You're Going to Run a Library, 1995, Ideas for School Library Media Centers, 1996, Whole School Library Handbook, 2004; co-author: Information Literacy, 1999; editor: Continuing Professional Education and IFLA: Past, Present, and a Vision for the Future, 1993, Delivering Lifelong Continuing Professional Education Across Space and Time, 2001. Fulbright scholar, 1995-96; recipient Disting. Svc. award Pa. Sch. Librs. Assn., 1993. Mem. ALA (mem. coun. 1985-89, 95—2003), Am. Assn. Sch. Librs. (bd. dirs. 1983-88, pres. 1993-94, Disting. Svc. award 1997), Pa. Learning Resources Assn. (pres. 1984-85), Internat. Assn. Sch. Librs. (pres. 1998-2001), Internat. Fedn. Libr. Assns. (mem. standing com. sch. librs. sect. 1991-99, sec. Continuing Profl. Edn. Round Table 2000—). Office: Libraries Unlimited 2040 Verdugo Blvd Glendale CA 91208

WOOLSEY, LYNN C., congresswoman; b. Seattle, Nov. 3, 1937; 4 children. BS, U. San Francisco, 1981. Mgr. human resources Harris Digital Telephone, 1969—80; owner Woolsey Personnel Svcs., 1980—92; mem. U.S. Congress from 6th Calif. dist., 1993—, ranking mem. edn. reform subcom. ho. com. edn. and the workforce. Mem. Petaluma City Coun., 1984-92 Mem.: NOW, LWV, Sierra Club. Democrat. Office: US Ho Reps 2263 Rayburn Ho Office Bldg Washington DC 20515-0506 Address: Santa Rosa Dist Office Ste 200 1101 College Ave Santa Rosa CA 95404 also: San Rafael Dist Office Ste 354 1050 Northgate Dr San Rafael CA 94903 *

WOOLSEY, R(OBERT) JAMES, lawyer, former CIA director; b. Tulsa, Sept. 21, 1941; s. Robert James and Clyde (Kirby) W.; m. Suzanne Haley, Aug. 15, 1965; children— Robert Nathaniel, Daniel James, Benjamin Haley. BA with great distinction, Stanford U., 1963; MA (Rhodes scholar), Oxford U., Eng., 1965; LLB, Yale U., 1968. Bar: Calif. bar 1969, D.C. bar 1970. Program analyst Office Sec. Def., Washington, 1968-70, NSC, Washington, 1970; gen. counsel Com. Armed Services, U.S. Senate, 1970-73; assoc. firm Shea & Gardner, Washington, 1973-77, ptnr., 1979-89, 1991-93; under sec. USN US Dept. Def., 1977—79; amb. & U.S. rep. to negotiation on conventional armed forces in Europe US Dept. State, 1989-91; dir. CIA, Washington, 1993-95; ptnr. Shea & Gardner, 1995—2002; v.p. Global Strategic Security Booz Allen Hamilton, McLean, Va., 2002—. Adv. U.S. del. SALT, Helsinki and Vienna, 1969-70 Mem. Pres.'s Commn. on Strategic Forces, 1983-84, Fed. Ethics Law Reform, 1989; Blue Ribbon Commn. on Defense Mgmt., 1985-86; del.-at-large Soviet Arms Talks, Geneva, 1983-86; mem. Rumsfeld Commn. to Assess Ballistic Missile Threat, 1998; mem. Nat. Commn. on Terrorism 1999-2000; trustee Stanford U., 1972-74, Regent Smithsonian Instution, 1989-93; bd. chmn. Freedom House; adv. bd. chmn. Clean Fuels Found., New Uses Council; vice-chmn. adv. bd. Global Options LLC; trustee Ctr. for Strategic & Internat. Studies; past mem. bd. gov. Phila. Stock Exch.; dir. Info. Sys. Lab., Linsang Ptnrs., Fibersense Tech. Corp., Invicta Networks, DIANA LLC, Agorics Inc.; mem. bd. adv. BioDefense Corp.; past bd. dir. Martin Marietta, British Aerospace, Fairchild Industries, Titan Corp., DynCorp, USF&G, Sun Healthcare Group, Inc., Yurie Systems, Inc. Served with U.S. Army, 1968-70. Mem. Council Fgn. Relations, Phi Beta Kappa. Presbyterian. Office: Booz Allen Hamilton 8283 Greensboro Dr Mc Lean VA 22102

WOOLSEY, ROBERT PAUL, church musician; s. Ralph Alzore and June Virginia (Hanneman) Woolsey. Student, Calif. Inst. Arts, Valencia, 1973—74. Assoc. musician St. Paul's Cathedral, LA, 1975—76; audio cons., engr. Skyline Recording, LA, 1979—80; co-founder, tech. dir. Woolsey Green Prodn., LA, 1981—93; freelance sound editor LA, 1994—98; prin. organist St. Andrew & St. Charles Episcopal Ch., LA, 1999—2006, St. James Episcopal Ch., S. Pasadena, Calif., 2006—; deputy organist Cathedral Our Lady Angels, LA, 2005—. Prodr.(dir.): (DVD) Ven Creator Spiritus, 2005; composer musical arrangements; featured guest performer with condr. Paul Salamanovich:. Recipient Grammy Nomination Best Jazz Vocal Group, Nat. Acad. Recording Arts and Scis., 1984. Mem.: Am. Guild Organists. Avocations: video photographer, scuba diving. Office: c/o Lawson Infinity LA Office N 3112 Sunset Ln Oxnard CA 93035

WOOLSEY, THOMAS ALLEN, neuroscientist, biologist; b. Balt., Apr. 17, 1943; s. Clinton Nathan and Harriet (Runion) W.; m. Cynthia Tull Ward, June 8, 1969; children: Alix, Timothy. BS, U. Wis., 1965; MD, Johns Hopkins, 1969. Asst. prof. anatomy Washington U. Sch. Medicine, St. Louis, 1971-75, asst. prof. anatomy, neurobiology, 1975-77, assoc. prof. anatomy, neurobiology, 1977-80, assoc. prof. anatomy, neurobiology, physiology biophysics, 1980-83, coord. neurosci. program, 1980-84, sr. neuroscientist, 1982—, prof. neurology, neurological surgery, 1984—, dir. experimental neurology, neurological surgery, 1984—. Chmn., Washington U. Teaching Space Evaluation, 1989-90. Contbr. articles to profl. jours. NIH Rsch. grantee, 1970—; George H. and Ethel R. Bishop scholar, 1984—; recipient McKnight Neurosci. Devel. award, 1982-85, Jacob Javits award NIH, 1993-2000; fellow John Simon Guggenheim Found., 2004. Fellow AAAS; mem. Am. Assn. Anatomists, Am. Acad. Neurology, St. Louis Acad. Sci., Soc. Neurosci., Johns Hopkins Med. Surgical Assn., Cajal Club. Avocations: hiking, history, woodworking. Office: Washington U Sch Medicine 660 S Euclid Ave # 8057 Saint Louis MO 63110-1010 Home Phone: 314-495-5791; Office Phone: 314-362-3601. E-mail: tom63105@yahoo.com.

WOOLSTON-CATLIN, MARIAN, retired psychiatrist; b. Seattle, Jan. 20, 1931; d. Howard Brown and Katharine Nichols (Dally) Woolston; m. Randolph Catlin Jr., July 5, 1959; children: Laura Louise, Jennifer Woolston, Randolph III. BA cum laude, Vassar Coll., 1951; MD, Harvard U., 1955. Diplomate Nat. Bd. Med. Examiners. Intern in pediatric medicine Children's Hosp., Boston, 1956, asst. resident in pediatric medicine, 1956; resident in psychiatry Mass. Mental Health Ctr., Boston, 1957-59; fellow in child psychiatry Tavistock Clin., London, 1960; Commonwealth fellow in child psychiatry Harvard U. at Gaebler Children's Unit, Waltham, Mass., 1975-78, clin. instr. psychiatry, 1978-79; pvt. practice Wellesley Hills, Mass., 1978-91, Medfield, Mass., 1991—2006; ret., 2006. Clin. instr. psychiatry Harvard U. at Mass. Mental Health Ctr., Boston, 1957-59, 78-82, Tufts U. at Mass. Mental Health Ctr., 1957-59; mem. exec. bd. Parents' and Children's Svcs., Boston, 1983-86. Designer H.H. Hunnewell Meml. Garden for New Eng. Flower Show Mass. Hort. Soc., 1975 (Ames Cup award). Exec. bd. Ext. Divsn. New Eng. Conservatory Music, 1972-75; charter mem. reuse com. Medfield State Hosp., 1992—; corporator Schepens Eye Rsch. Inst., 2005—, adv. bd., rsch. com. 2006—; adv. bd. Women's Eye Health Task Force, 2005—. Fellow Am. Acad. Child and Adolescent Psychiatry; mem. AMA, Am. Psychiat. Assn. (life), Mass. Psychiat. Assn., Mass. Med. Soc., New Eng. Coun. Child and Adolescent Psychiatry (hon.), Boston Vassar Club (exec. bd. 1963-75), Hills Garden Club Wellesley (exec. bd. and design chief 1973-75). Episcopalian. Avocations: landscape design, sculpting.

WOOLVERTON, DIANE MARIE, literature and language professor; d. Robert Paton, Jr. Marshall and Delores Mildred Merkling; m. Thomas Roy Woolverton, July 8, 2000; 1 child, Shawn Kirean Copeland. BS in Philosophy, Buffalo State Coll., NY, 1989; BS in Secondary Edn. English, Buffalo State Coll., 1999, MS in English Edn., 2003. Cert. Tchr. U. the State NY, 2004, Written English and English Vocabulary Brainbench, 2004, Content Editor/Proofreader Grammatika, 2004. English and reading tchr. St. Benedict's RC Sch., Amherst, NY, 1999—2005; owner, pres. Read-Write Resources, Buffalo, 2004—; adj. prof. Medaille Coll., Buffalo, 2004—; educator North Tonawanda City Sch. Dist., NY, 2004—, Williamsville Ctrl. Sch. Dist., NY, 2006—. Writer ReadWrite Resources, Buffalo, 2004—. Actor: (semi-profl. drama/theatre) Lend Me a Tenor (Kay award, 1993). Dir. St. Benedict Ann. Sch. Musicals; mem. Rep. Nat. Com., Buffalo, 2006—, NYS English Coun., Albany; vol. Project Flight: Books for Kids, Buffalo, 1997—98. Mem.: Nat. Coun. Tchrs. English (assoc.). Conservative. Avocations: painting, travel, reading. Office: ReadWrite Resources 1749 Hertel Ave Buffalo NY 14216-3001 Home Phone: 716-446-1346; Office Phone: 716-860-7352. Personal E-mail: dwoolverton@adelphia.net. Business E-Mail: dwoolverton@readwriteresources.com.

WOOLWORTH, ERIC S., professional sports team executive; m. Jocelyn Woolworth; 1 child, Cassidy. Grad. cum laude, Georgetown U.; grad., Georgetown U. Law Ctr. Gen. counsel Miami Heat, Fla., 1995—2001, interim pres., 2000—01, pres. bus. ops., 2001—. Bd. mem. Big Bros. Big Sisters, Children's Craniofacial Assn. Office: Miami Heat AmericanAirlines Arena 601 Biscayne Blvd Miami FL 33132 *

WOOLWORTH, SUSAN VALK, primary school educator; b. Toledo, Ohio, Apr. 24, 1954; d. Robert Earl and Alice (Melick) Valk; children: Alison Valk, Andrew Baker. BA, Pine Manor Jr. Coll., Chestnut Hill, Mass., 1974; BS, Boston U., 1976. Tchr. kindergarten Lancaster (Pa.) Country Day Sch., 1986—2007. Past bd. dirs. YWCA, Lancaster, Pa., Fulton Opera House, Planned Parenthood, Vis. Nurse Assn., Hands-On House. Mem.: Jr. League (sustainer), Sigma Gamma. Republican. Episcopalian. Avocations: walking, gardening, tennis, decorating.

WOOSLEY, STANFORD EARL, astrophysicist; b. Texarkana, Tex., Dec. 8, 1944; s. Homer Earl and Wanda Faye (Fisher) W.; m. Petra Berkemeyer; children William D., Amanda Faye. BA in Physics, Rice U., 1966, PhD in Astrophysics, 1971. Rsch. assoc. Rice U., Houston, 1971-73; rsch. fellow in physics Kellogg Radiation Lab. Calif. Inst. Tech., Pasadena, 1973-75; asst. prof. astronomy U. Calif., Santa Cruz, 1975-78, assoc. prof., 1978-83, prof. astronomy and astrophysics, 1983—. Cons. Lawrence Livermore Nat. Lab., 1974-; chair dept. astronomy and astrophysics, U. Calif. Santa Cruz, 1983-1987, 1989-1991, 1998-2003, 2006; dir. DOE-SciDAC Computational Astrophysics Consortium, 2006-. Editor: High Energy Transients, 1984, Supernova, 1991, Nuclear Astrophysics, 1993, Internat. Jour. Modern Physics, 1994-, New Astronomy, 1996-; contbr. over 400 articles to profl. jours. Named A. V. Humboldt Prof. 1995-97; Outstanding Faculty, Divsn. Biological and Phys. Sci., U. Calif. Santa Cruz, 2004, faculty rsch. lectr., 2007. Fellow Am. Phys. Soc. (H. A. Bethe prize 2005); mem. Am. Astron. Soc. (Bruno Rossi prize 2005), Internat. Astronomical Union, Am. Acad. Arts and Sci., Nat. Acad. Sci. (Physics Divsn.). Achievements include research into the lives and deaths of massive stars and supernova, nucleosynthesis and x-ray and gamma ray bursts. Home: 115 Auburn Ave Santa Cruz CA 95060-6231 Office: U Calif Dept Astronomy and Astrophysics Santa Cruz CA 95064

WOOSNAM, IAN HAROLD, professional golfer; b. St. Martins, Shropshire, UK, Mar. 2, 1958; s. Harold and Joan Woosnam; m. Glendryth Mervyn Pugh, Nov. 12, 1983; children: Daniel Ian, Rebecca Louise, Ami Victoria. Student, St. Martins Modern Sch. Profl. golfer, 1976—. Tournament winner News of the World under 23 match-play, 1979, Cacharel under 25 Championship, 1982, Swiss Open, 1982, Silk Cut Masters, 1983, Scandinavian Enterprise Open, 1984, Zambian Open, 1985, Lawrence Batley TPC, 1986, 555 Kenya Open, 1986, Hong Kong Open, 1987, Jersey Open, 1987, Cepsa Madrid Open, 1987, Bell's Scottish Open, 1987, 90, Lancome Trophy, 1987, 93, Suntory World Match-Play Championship, 1987, 90, World Cup (Wales) Team and Individual, 1987, Million Dollar Challenge, 1987, Welsh Pro Championship, 1988, Volvo PGA Championship, 1988, Panasonic European Open, 1988, Carrols Irish Open, 1988, 89, AmEx Med Open, 1990, Epson Grand Prix, 1990, Torras Monte Carlo Open, 1990, 91, Fujistu Mediterranean Open, 1991, US Masters, 1991, USF&G Classic, 1991, PGA Grand Slam of Golf, 1991, World Cup Individual, 1991, European Montecarlo Open, 1992, Murphy's English Open, 1993, Air France Cannes Open, 1994, Brit. Masters, 1994, Johnnie Walker Classic, 1996, Scottish Open, 1996, German Open, 1996, Heineken Classic, 1996, Volvo PGA Championship, 1997, Hyundai Motor Masters, 1997; ranked 1st Sony world rankings, 1991, Ryder Cup Team Mem., 1983, 85 (winners), 87 (winners), 89, 91, 93, 95 (winners), 97 (winners), Cisco World Match Play championship, 2001, vice-capt. Ryder Cup winners, 2001-02; capt. European Ryder Cup Team, 2006; named to Order Brit. Empire, 2007. Avocations: snooker, sports, water-skiing. Office Phone: 44 7768 862459. E-mail: dbarlow@imgworld.com.

WOOSNAM, RICHARD EDWARD, venture capitalist, lawyer; b. Anderson, Ind., June 27, 1942; s. Richard Wendell and Ruth (Cleveland) W.; m. Diane Dalto; children: Cynthia S., Elizabeth C. BS, Ind. U., 1964, JD, 1967, MBA, 1968. Bar: Ind. 1967, US Dist. Ct. (so. dist.) Ind. 1967. Instr. bus. law Ind. U., Bloomington, 1966-68; assoc. Ferguson, Ferguson & Lloyd, Bloomington, 1967-68; dep. pros. Monroe County, Bloomington, 1967-68; tax acct. Price Waterhouse, Phila., 1968-69; v.p., treas. Innovest Group, Inc., Phila., 1969-82, chmn., pres., 1983—. Bd. dirs. Capital Mgmt. Corp., NY Achievement, LLC, Innovest Talent Svcs., Inc., Ind. U. Found., Phila. Hospitality, Inc., Phila. Zoo, Pa. Acad. Fine Arts, Arts and Bus. Coun. Greater Phila.; vice chmn. World Affairs Coun. Phila.; chmn. Walnut St. Theatre. Mem. ABA, Ind. Bar Assn., Union League Phila., Sunday Breakfast Club, Pa Soc. Office: 1528 Walnut St Ste 1701 Philadelphia PA 19102 Business E-Mail: rwoosnam@innovestgrp.com.

WOOSTER, LARRY D., music educator; b. Tucson, Ariz., Aug. 1, 1960; s. Arthur Wayne Wooster and Barbara A McCastle; m. Lynette M Collingwood, June 18, 1983; 1 child, Elizabeth M. AA, Concordia Coll., 1980; BS in Edn., Concordia Teachers Coll., 1982; MA, U. N.Mex, 1985; Ednl. Specialist (EdS), Nova Southeastern U., 2005, ABD, 2006. Cert. profl. tchr. N.Mex, 1982, master tchr. Iowa, 1991. Tchr./music dir. Immanuel Luth. Ch. and Sch., Albuquerque, 1982—91; tchr. St. Paul Luth. Ch. and Sch., Fort Dodge, Iowa, 1991—97; music dir./tchr. Grace Luth. Ch. and Sch., Lancaster, Calif., 1997—. Gen. electric math fellow Albuquerque Cmty. Found., 1985—86. Mem.: Music Educators Nat. Conf. Lutheran Church - Missouri Synod. Avocations: hot air balloon pilot, travel. Office: Grace Lutheran Church and School 856 West Newgrove St Lancaster CA 93534 Home Phone: 661-946-6670; Office Phone: 661-948-1018. Business E-Mail: lwooster@gracelancaster.org.

WOOSTER, ROBERT, history professor; b. Beaumont, Tex., Aug. 27, 1956; s. Ralph Ancil and Edna Lee (Jones) W.; m. Catherine Cox, 1992. BA, Lamar U., 1977, MA, 1979; PhD, U. Tex., 1985. Scholar in residence Tex. State Hist. Assn., Liberty, 1985-86; asst. prof. Tex. A&M U., Corpus Christi, 1986-90, assoc. prof., 1990-95, prof., 1995—, chmn. dept. humanities, 1997—2000, Piper prof., 1998, Frantz prof. history, 2001—04. Author: Soldiers, Sutlers and Settlers (Bates award 1987), U.S. Military and Indian Policy, 1988, History of Fort Davis, 1990, Nelson A. Miles and The Twilight of the Frontier Army, 1993, The Civil War 100, 1998, The Civil War Bookshelf, 2001, Frontier Crossroads: Fort Davis and the West, 2006; editor: Soldier, Surgeon, Scholar: The Memoirs of William Henry Corbusier, 2003; co-editor: (with William Kessel) Encyclopedia of Native American Wars & Warfare, 2005; editl. adv. bd. Southwestern Hist. Quar., Austin, Tex., 1989—, Military History of the West, 1995—, Jour. of the West, 1996-2000. Dep. dir. U.S. Mil. Acad./ROTC fellowship U.S. Mil. Acad., West Point, N.Y., 1990. Fellow Tex. State Hist. Assn. (pres. 2005—06); mem. Orgn. Am. Historians. Democrat. Home: 4600 Ocean Dr Apt 708 Corpus Christi TX 78412-2543 Office: Texas A&M Univ 6300 Ocean Dr Corpus Christi TX 78412-5599 Office Phone: 361-825-2402. Business E-Mail: robert.wooster@tamucc.edu.

WOOSTER, STEPHANIE LYNNE, art historian, artist; b. Livonia, Mich., Dec. 7, 1975; d. Ronald J. and Patricia Lynne Wooster. BA magna cum laude, Kalamazoo Coll., Mich., 1998; MFA with distinction in Painting, Pratt Inst., Bklyn., 2003, MS with distinction in Art History, 2003. Tchr. English Sch. No. 160 Advanced English Study, St. Petersburg, Russia, 1996—97; grading asst. Pratt Inst., Art History Dept., Bklyn., 2000—02; instr. sch. art history U. St. Andrews, Scotland, 2004—05. Co-editor: INFERNO: Jour. Art History; exhibitions include Gov.'s Residence, Lansing, Mich., Pratt Inst., Bklyn., Internat. Mus.Horse, Lexington, KY, Muskegon Museum Art, Mich., Mt. Pleasant, Mich., Kalamazoo Coll., Mich., Fla. State U. Mus.Fine Arts, Tallahassee, Fla., Hammerstein Ballroom, Manhattan Ctr., NY, Grand Rapids, Mich., Michican Equine Artists Founders Exhbn., Grand Rapids, Mich. (First Pl. award, 1998), ARC Gallery, Chgo., Studio 23/The ARTS Ctr., Bay City, Mich., Preservation Trust Mus., St. Andrews, Scotland, Williamsburg Art and Hist. Ctr., Bklyn., Stephen F. Austin State U., Nacogdoches, 2007, Lowell Area Arts Coun., Mich., 2007. Recipient Brian Gougeon Art prize, Art Dept., Kalamazoo Coll., 1995, Michael Waskowsky Art prize, 1997, Sr. Exhbn. Paintings award, 1998, Cert. of Excellence award for outstanding merit in grad. fine arts, Fine Art Dept., Pratt Inst., 2003, Pratt Ctr. Outstanding Academic Achievement award, Pratt Inst., 2003; scholar, Art Dept., Kalamazoo Coll., 1994—98, 1998; Beatrice Cox Pratt in Venice scholarship, Art History Dept., Pratt Inst., 2001, Pratt Alumni Venice scholarship, 2001, scholarship, U. Pitts. Ctr. for Russian and East European Studies, Summer Lang. Inst., 2007. Mem.: Brit. Assn. Slavonic and East European Studies, Am. Assn. Advancement of Slavic Studies, Soc.Historians East European and Russian Art and Arch., Assn. of the Historians of Nineteenth-Century Art, Coll. Art Assn., Am. Acad. Equine Art (assoc.), Urban Inst. Contemporary Arts, Equine Art Guild, Alpha Lambda Delta, Phi Beta Kappa. Home: 5150 Meandering Creek Dr Belmont MI 49306-9000 Home Phone: 616-874-8813. Personal E-mail: steph_wooster@hotmail.com.

WOOTEN, CECIL AARON, retired religious organization administrator; b. Laurel, Miss., June 3, 1924; s. Cecil A. and Alice (Cox) W.; m. Helen Moss, Apr. 4, 1947; children: Michael, Margaret, Martin, Marsha, Mark. BS in Mech. Engring, U. Ala., 1949. With CBI Industries, 1941—83, bd. dirs., 1965-83, mng. dir. CBI Constructors Ltd., London, 1957-62, mgr. Houston sales dist., 1962-64, v.p. engring., 1964—68, v.p., mgr. corp. svcs. Oak Brook, Ill., 1968-69, sr. v.p.-gen. sales mgr., 1969-78; sr. v.p. comml. devel. Chgo. Bridge & Iron Co. (subs. CBI Industries), 1978-79; sr. v.p. corp. adminstrn. CBI Industries, Oak Brook, 1980-83; dir. devel. Christian Family Services, Gainesville, Fla., 1983-86, Denver Ch. of Christ, 1986-88, Boston Ch. of Christ, 1988-92; pres. Internat. Chs. of Christ, Inc., LA, 1994-99; chair Internat. Chs. Christ, LA, 1999—2000, retired, 2002. Bd. dirs. Oak Brook (Ill.) Bank. Former trustee Elmhurst (Ill.) Coll.; former bd. sponsors Good Samaritan Hosp., Downers Grove, Ill. Served to 1st lt. AUS, 1943-46. Mem. ASME, NSPE, Rotary. Personal E-mail: cecilwooten@hotmail.com.

WOOTEN, FRANK THOMAS, retired research facility executive; b. Fayetteville, NC, Sept. 24, 1935; s. Frank Thomas and Katherine (McRae) Wooten; m. Linda Walker, July 14, 1962; children: Laurin Walker, Patrick Thomas, Ashley Tripp. BSEE, Duke U., 1957, PhD, 1964. Engr. Corning Glass Works, Raleigh, NC, 1964—66; from engr. to pres. Rsch. Triangle Inst., Research Triangle Park, NC, 1966—89, pres., 1989—99; ret., 1999. Bd. dirs. N.C. Biotech. Ctr., Troxler Electronics Labs., N.C. Biosci. Investment Fund. Contbr. articles on semiconductors and biomedical engring. to profl. publs.; patentee semiconductors tech. Lt. (j.g.) USN, 1957—59. Recipient Disting. Engring. Alumnus award, Duke U., 1991; fellow, Shell, 1961. Mem.: IEEE, Nat. Inst. Statis. Scis. (corp. 1990—98), Ballistic Missile Def. Orgn. (tech. application rev. panel 1990—94), Assn. for Advancement Med. Instrumentation (chmn. com. on aerospace tech. 1971—77). Baptist.

WOOTEN, H. OMAR, systems engineer, researcher; s. John D. Wooten, Jr. and Anita Wooten. BS, Morehouse Coll., Atlanta, 2000; MS, Ga. Inst. Tech., Atlanta, 2002, PhD, 2005. Grad. rsch. asst. Los Alamos Nat. Lab., N.Mex., 2001—05, tech. staff mem., 2005—. Contbr. articles to profl. jours. Office: Los Alamos Nat Labs PO Box 1663 Los Alamos NM 87545 Home Phone: 505-577-1094; Office Phone: 505-665-3279. Office Fax: 505-667-1878. Personal E-mail: omarwooten@yahoo.com. Business E-Mail: hasani@lanl.gov.

WOOTEN, JAMES H., JR., lawyer, engineering executive; BA in Criminal Justice, U. Ill., 1978; JD, U. Chgo., 1982. Assoc. Gardner, Carton & Douglas, Chgo., 1982—88; assoc. gen. counsel, asst. sec. Ill. Tool Works Inc., Glenview, Ill., 1988—2005, v.p., gen. counsel, 2005, sr. v.p., gen. counsel, corp. sec., 2005—. Mem.: ABA, Cook County Bar Assn., Exec. Leadership Coun., Minority Corp. Counsel Assn., Soc. Corp. Secs. and Governance Profls., Am. Corp. Counsel Assn., Chgo. Bar Assn., Phi Delta Phi. Office: Illinois Tool Works 3600 W Lake Ave Glenview IL 60026 E-mail: jwooten@itw.com. *

WOOTEN, JAMES TERRELL, journalist; b. Detroit, July 13, 1937; s. J.R. and Clara Charlene (Richmond) W.; m. Katherine Joanne Richardson, Aug. 26, 1958 (dec. 1978); children: Karen, Kristen, Katie, Elizabeth; m. Patience Jean O'Connor, Sept. 27, 1980; 1 dau., Jacqueline DeLacie O'Connor. BA, Bethel Coll., McKenzie Tenn., 1958; B.D., Presbyn. Theol. Sem., Memphis, 1961. Reporter Huntsville Times, Ala., 1965-68, N.Y. Times, NYC, 1968-73, 74-78; columnist Phila. Inquirer, 1973-74; writer Esquire mag., NYC, 1978-79; nat. corr. ABC News, Washington, 1979—, now sr. corr. Author: Soldier, 1972, Dasher, 1978, We Are All the Same: A Story of a Boy's Courage and a Mother's Love, 2004 (25th Annual Robert F. Kennedy Book award, 2005). Recipient Ernie Pyle Meml. award Scripps-Howard, 1974; recipient Blue Pencil award Columbia U., 1979

WOOTEN, JOEL ORBA, JR., lawyer; b. Hazlehurst, Ga., June 4, 1950; s. Joel Orba and Mary Eleanor (Whitlock) W.; m. Sybrina G. Franklin; children: Joel III, Katherine, Frank. BBA, U. Ga., 1972, JD, 1975. Bar: Ga. 1975, U.S. Dist. Ct. (mid. dist.) Ga. 1976, U.S. Ct. Appeals (11th cir.) 1981. Ptnr. Kelly, Denney, Pease & Allison, Columbus, Ga., 1975-88, Butler, Wooten, Overby & Cheeley, Columbus, Ga., 1988—. Bd. regents Univ. Sys. of Ga., 1999-2006, chair, 2004-05. With U.S. Army, 1972. Mem. Am. Bar Assn., Fed. Bar Assn., Ga. Trial Lawyers Assn., State Bar Ga. (chmn. gen. practice & trial sect. 1990-91), Columbus Lawyers Club (pres 1988-89), Columbus Younger Lawyers (pres. 1983-84), Assn. Trial Lawyers Am., U. Ga. Alumni Soc. (bd. dirs. 1981-83, 89-91). Office: Butler, Wooten, & Fryhofer, LLP 105 Thirteenth St Columbus GA 31901 Office Phone: 706-322-1990.

WOOTEN, MARC, hospital administrator, medical educator; s. Marc and Mosie Wooten; m. Mary Wooten, July 15, 1995; children: Marc, Michael. MBA, UCLA, 1975; MD, U. of Tex. Southwestern Med. Sch., 1988. Asst. prof. of medicine Tulane U. Med. Ctr., New Orleans, 1995—97; assoc. prof. of medicine Jefferson Med. Coll., Wilmington, Del., 1997—2003; voluntary clin. assoc. prof. of medicine Ind. U. Sch. of Medicine, Ft. Wayne, Ind., 2003—; chief of staff VA No. Ind. Health Care Sys., Ft. Wayne, Ind., 2003—. Contbr. articles to med. jours. Capt. USAF, 1974—82. Decorated Air Force Commendation medal USAF; named Jr. Officer of the Quar., 1980. Fellow: ACP, Am. Coll. of Rheumatology, Am. Coll. of Physician Executives (cert. physician exec.). Office: Dept VA Affairs 2121 Lake Ave Fort Wayne IN 46805 Office Phone: 260-460-1311.

WOOTEN, MICHAEL ERIC, academic administrator; b. San Diego, June 12, 1959; s. James Willis and Elease (Lewis) W. AA, DeKalb C.C., 1981; BA in Psychology, Chapman U., 1986; MA in Leadership and Orgnl. Mgmt., Norwich U., 1996; MS in Acquisition and Contract Mgmt., Naval Postgrad. Sch., 1997. Air traffic controller, Tustin, Calif., 1983—86; commd. 2nd lt. USMC, 1987, advanced through grades to maj., 1997, supply officer, 1988—91; aide-de-camp Marine Corps Logistics Base, Albany, Ga., 1991-92; logistics officer Hdqs. Battalion, Albany, Ga., 1992-93; supply officer First Light Anti Aircraft Missile Battalion, Yuma, Ariz., 1993—96; student Naval Postgrad. Sch., 1996-97; contracting officer Hdqs. USMC, Washington, 1998—2001; dep. dir. Marine Corps Regional Contracting Office, 2001—02; contracting officer, chief of contracting Coalition Forces Landing Component Command, 2002; comdg. officer Tenant Activities Co. Hdqrs. Btn., Marine Corps Base, Quantico, 2002—03; deputy for contracting Defense Acquisition U., 2003, prof. contract mgmt., 2005—06, deputy dir. ops., 2006—. Nonresident dir. Navy Mut. Aid Assn., Arlington, Va., 1994; regional dir. NPS Taekwondo Assn. Schs., Va.; dir. contracting, Office of CFO, Govt. DC, 2004-05; adj. prof. U. DC, 2004-05. Vice chmn. Prince William County Republican com., 2004—06; vestry mem. Pohick Episcopal Ch.; mem. Am. Anglican Coun., Brotherhood of St. Andrews, Cmty. Criminal Justice Bd. Decorated Marine Combat Ribbon (Afghanistan), Navy Commendation medal, Joint Svc. Commendation medal, Meritorious Svc. medal, Army Commendation medal, Mil. Outstanding vol. Svc. medal, Superior Svc. award Outstanding Marine Corps student, 1997. Mem. NAACP, Nat. Contract Mgmt. Assn., Marine Corps Assn., Mensa, Phi Beta Sigma. Episcopalian. Avocations: politics, Tae Kwon Do (4th degree black belt). Office: Defense Acquisition Univ 9820 Belvoir Rd Fort Belvoir VA 22060 Office Phone: 703-805-2140. Business E-Mail: mike.wooten@dau.mil.

WOOTEN, ROSALIE (ROSALIE O'REILLY WOOTEN), automotive company executive; Exec. v.p. O'Reilly Automotive Inc., Springfield, Mo., also bd. dir., 1993—. Office: O'Reilly Automotive Inc 233 S Patterson Ave Springfield MO 65802-2298

WOOTTERS, WILLIAM K., physics professor; BS, Stanford U., Calif., 1973; PhD, U. Tex., Austin, 1980. Mem. faculty to Barclay Jermain prof. natural philos. Williams Coll., Williamstown, Mass., 1982—. Vis. rschr. Santa Fe Inst., 1989—90, U. Montreal, 1994; collaborator IBM Watson Rsch. Ctr., 1995, 98. Contbr. articles to sci. jours. Recipient Internat. Quantum Comm. award, Internat. Orgn. for Quantum Communication, Measurement and Computing and Tamagawa U., 2006. Fellow: Am. Phys. Soc. (Prize for a Faculty Mem. for Rsch. in an Undergraduate Instn. 2007). Achievements include proving the no cloning theorem, which forbids the creation of identical copies of an arbitrary unknown quantum state, along with Wojciech H. Zurek and Dennis Dieks in 1982. Office: Dept Physics Williams Coll Williamstown MA 01267 Office Phone: 413-597-2156. E-mail: william.wootters@williams.edu. *

WOOTTON, JOHN FRANCIS, physiology educator; b. Penn Yan, NY, May 31, 1929; s. John Edenden and Margaret Eliza (Smith) W.; m. Joyce Albertine Mac Mullen, Aug. 28, 1959; children: J. Timothy, David M., Barbara H., Bruce C. BS, Cornell U., 1951, MS, 1953, PhD, 1960. Grad. rsch. asst. Cornell U., Ithaca, NY, 1956-60, from asst. prof. to prof. emeritus, 1962—2004, prof. emeritus, 2004—, assoc. dean Grad. Sch., 1980-83; post doctoral fellow U. Coll., London, 1960-62. Grad. faculty rep. field of physiology Cornell U., 1990-92, 93-97, chmn. dept. physiology, 1997-98, co-chmn. dept. biomed. scis., 1998-99, chmn. 1999-2000; vis. scientist MRC Molecular Biology, Cambridge, Eng., 1969-70, Nat. Inst. Med. Rsch., London, 1985-86, 92-93, 2002; temporary sr. rsch. assoc. Stanford (Calif.) U., 1977-78. Contbr. articles to profl. jours. 1st lt. USAR, 1954-56. Rsch. and Travel grantee NIH, USDA Burroughs Wellcom Fund, Med. Rsch. Coun., Cornell Biotech. Program. Mem. AAAS, Am. Soc. Biochemistry and Molecular Biology, Am. Chem. Soc., Biophys. Soc., Protein Soc., Sigma Xi (v.p., pres. Cornell chpt.). Avocations: travel, choral singing, gardening, art, fishing. Office: Cornell U Dept Biomed Scis T8-014 Vet Rsch Tower Ithaca NY 14853-5908 Business E-Mail: jfw1@cornell.edu.

WORAM, BRIAN J., lawyer, construction executive; b. Perth Amboy, NJ, July 24, 1960; m. Allison M. Woram. BS in Mech. Engring., Tex. A&M U., College Station, 1981; JD, U. Tex., Austin, 1986. Bar: Tex. 1986. Reservoir engr. Exxon Co.; assoc. to shareholder Locke, Liddell & Sapp; regional gen. counsel Centex Homes (subs. of Centex Corp.), 1995—97, v.p., gen. counsel, 1997—98, sr. v.p., gen. counsel, 1998—2005; sr. v.p., chief legal officer Centex Corp., 2005—. Contbr. articles to profl. jours. Mem.: ABA, Tau Beta Pi, Pi Tau Sigma, Phi Delta Phi. Mailing: Centex Corp PO Box 199000 Dallas TX 75219-9000 *

WORBOYS, ROGER DICK, retired communications executive; b. Syracuse, NY, Sept. 1, 1947; s. Carl Stape and Dorothy Elsa (Dick) W.; m. Mary Lee Tasker, Nov. 27, 1971; children: Thomas, Elizabeth. Bachelors degree, Alfred U., 1969; M in Bus., U. N.H., 1971. Mgr.- regional mgr. Continental Cablevision, Boston, 1974-86; v.p. ops. Simmons Comm., Stamford, Conn., 1986-88, Insight Comm., Glasgow, Scotland, NYC, 1988-95, Bresnan Comms., White Plains, N.Y., 1996-98, sr. v.p., 1999-2000; ret., 2001. Adv. bd. ctr. venture rsch. U. NH. Bd. trustees Alfred U.; bd. dirs. Great Bay Svcs.; adv. bd. Newport Computer Svcs. Mem.: Rotary Internat., Portsmouth N.H. C. of C. (pres. 1983), Mechanics Fre Soc. Roman Catholic.

WORBY, DAVID E., lawyer; b. Nyack, NY, Feb. 11, 1951; s. Louis Lincoln and Diana (Zacharia) W.; m. Cynthia Worby, Oct. 1, 1983; children: Jess, Rebecca, Samuel. BA, Cornell U., Ithaca, NY, 1973; JD, Villanova U., Pa., 1976. Bar: NY 1977, US Dist. Ct. Southern Dist. NY, US Dist. Ct. Eastern Dist. NY 1978. Assoc. Clark, Gagliardi & Miller, White Plains, NY, 1977-81; founder, sr. ptnr. Worby Groner Edelman LLP, White Plains, NY, 1981—. Founder David E. Worby Scholarship Fund, David E. Worby Course in Advanced Trial Practice; co-founder Adv. for Safety and Accident Prevention. Host (radio talk shows) Worby's World, Worby's Law, guest appearances CBS, NBC, ABC, FOX, WOR TV, Court TV, CNN, Lawline. Bd. dirs. Victims Assitance Svcs., Westchester County, N.Y., 1987—; coun. mem. Constrn. Industry Coun., Westchester County, 1988—, Northern Westchester Ctr. for Arts, Avon Theatre Film Ctr. Named one of Top Personal Injury Attorneys, NY Mag.; recipient Cmty. Svc. award, Westchester Cmty. Opportunity Prog., Westchester Bus. and Leadership Ann. award, UJA Fedn., Ann. Cmty. Svc. award, Phoenix House, Yeshiva Ohr Hameir of Westchester Cmty. Ann. Svc. award. Mem. Internat. Acad. Trial Lawyers, Assn. Trial Lawyers Am., Westchester County Tort Reparations, Rockland County Bar Assn., Westchester County Bar Assn.,NY State Bar Assn., New Rochelle Bar Assn., White Plains Bar Assn., NY County Lawyers Assn., NY State Trial Lawyers Assn., Million Dollar Advocates Forum. Avocations: music, writing, art, sports. Office: Worby Groner Edelman LLP 11 Martine Ave Ph White Plains NY 10606-1934 *

WORCESTER, HOWARD LESTER, internist; b. Kansas City, Mo., Jan. 3, 1945; s. Howard Elmer and Alma Jane (Evans) W. div.; m. Tammy Worcester; children: Tiffany, Chase. BS, U. Oregon, 1967, MD, 1971. Diplomate Am. Bd. Internal Medicine, Am. Bd. Forensic Pathology. Intern Harbor Gen. Hosp. UCLA, 1971-72; med. officer U.S. Army, West Germany, 1972-75; resident U. Calif., Irvine, 1975-77, chief med. resident, 1977-78; pvt. practice internal medicine Meml. Hosp., Long Beach, Calif., 1978—. Dir. utilization rev. Long Beach Meml. Hosp., 1983—, trustee, 1983—, also bd. dirs.; cons. Sultanate of Oman, Muscat, Oman, 1984—. Patron L.A. County Mus. Major U.S. Army, 1972-75. Recipient Merck scholarship U. Oreg. Med. Sch., 1969 Mem. Long Beach Meml. Hosp. Med. Group (pres. 1983—), Long Beach Meml. Med. Svc. Orgn. (pres. 1993-96), Phi Beta Kappa, Alpha Omega Alpha. Episcopalian. Avocations: cooking, wine collecting, travel, sports. Home: 11042 Skyline Dr Santa Ana CA 92705-2473 Office: Meml Med Group 2650 Elm Ave Ste 309 Long Beach CA 90806-1600 Office Phone: 562-595-8549. Personal E-mail: rworcester@cox.net.

WORDEN, KATHARINE COLE, sculptor; b. NYC, May 4, 1925; d. Philip Gillette and Katharine (Pyle) Cole; m. Frederic G. Worden, Jan. 8, 1944; children: Fred, Dwight, Philip, Barbara, Katharine. Student, Potters Ch., Tucson, 1940-42, Sarah Lawrence Coll., 1942-44. Exhibited in group shows at Royce Galleries, Galerie Francoise Besnard, Paris, Cooling Gallery, London, Galerie Schumacher, Munich, Selected Artists Gallery, N.Y.C., Art Inst. Boston, Reid Gallery, Nashville, Weiner Gallery, N.Y.C., Boston Athanaeum, House of Humor and Satire, Gabrovo, Bulgaria, 1983, Newport Bay Club, 1984; pvt. collections Grand Palais, Paris, Dakar and Bathurst, Africa. Occupl. therapist psychopathic ward L.A. County Gen. Hosp., 1953-57; Headstart vol., Watts, Calif., 1965-67; tchr. sculpture Watts Towers Art Ctr., 1967-69; participant White House Women Doers Luncheon meeting, 1968; dir. Cambridgeport Problem Ctr., Cambridge, Mass., 1969-71; mem. Jud. Nominating Commn., 1976-79; bd. overseers Boston Mus. Fine Arts, 1980-83; bd. govs. Newport Seamens Ch. Inst., 1989-91; tustee Comm. Rsch., Miami, Fla., 1960-69, chmn. bd., 1966-69; trustee Newport Art Mus., 1984-86, 92-94, Jamestown Cmty. Theatre, 1994-97, 99-2005, 06—, Newport Health Found., 1986-91, Hawthorne Sea Fund, 1990-93; bd. dirs. Boston Ctr. for Arts, 1976-80, Child and Family Svcs. Newport County, 1983-97, 99-2005, 06—; mem. Nat. Com. for the Performing Arts, 2006-07. Mem. Common Cause (Mass adv. bd. 1971-72, dir. 1974-75), Mass. Civil Liberties Union (exec. bd. 1973-74, dir. 1976-77). Home: 9 Meadow Ln Jamestown RI 02835 Office Phone: 401-423-1758.

WORDEN, ROBERT L., government agency administrator, researcher; b. Olean, NY, June 5, 1945; s. John L. and Leone E. (Borer) W.; m. Norma Jean Chue; children: Maia, Peter, Nathaniel. BA cum laude, St. Bonaventure U., 1967; MA, Georgetown U., 1969, PhD, 1972. Applicant screener, coder U.S. Peace Corps, Washington, 1967-68, statis. analyst, 1968-70; rsch. analyst Fed. Rsch. Divsn. Libr. of Congress, Washington, 1973-81, sr. rsch. analyst Fed. Rsch. Divsn., 1981-82, unit supr. Fed. Rsch. Divsn., 1982-85, sect. head Fed. Rsch. Divsn., 1985-98, acting chief Fed. Rsch. Divsn., 1997-98, chief Fed. Rsch. Divsn., 1998—, acting chief Asian divsn., 2002—03, acting spl. asst. to the dir. for collections and svcs., 2004—06, COO office of scholarly programs, 2006—. Co-author, editor: The Veterans Benefits Administration: An Organizational History, 1776-1994, 1995, India: A Country Study, 1996; co-author, co-editor: China and the Third World - Champion or Challenger?, 1986, China: A Country Study, 1988. Sec.-treas. Annapolis (Md.) Preservation Trust, Inc., 1987-95, pres., 1995-97, sec., 2000—; chmn. Bd. Elections Suprs., Annapolis, 1983-86. 1st lt. U.S. Army, 1971-73. Georgetown U. fellow, 1970-71. Mem. Libr. of Congress Profl. Assn., Libr. of Congress Asian Am. Assn., Assn. Asian Am. Studies, Assn. Asian Studies, Annapolis History Consortium. Democrat. Roman Catholic. Avocations: genealogy, foreign travel, reading, hist. rsch. Home: 30 Murray Ave Annapolis MD 21401-2843 Office: Libr of Congress Fed Rsch Divsn 101 Independence Ave SE Washington DC 20540-4840 Office Phone: 202-707-3909. Fax: (202) 707-3920. Business E-Mail: rwor@loc.gov.

WORDEN, VIRGINIA HILL, academic administrator, lawyer; b. Florence, SC, Dec. 4, 1947; d. Albert Michael and Virginia Copeland Hill; m. Geoffrey Field Worden; children: Annette Field, Katherine Hill, Zachary Albert. BA in Econs., Randolph-Macon Woman's Coll., Lynchburg, Va., 1969; MA in Econs., Vanderbilt U., Nashville, Tenn., 1973; JD, NYU, NYC, 1975; postgrad., Union Theol. Sem., NYC, 1987—93. Assoc. Davis, Polk & Wardwell, NYC, 1975—80; co-founder, pres. Bridges, Inc., 1988—95; interim pres. Randolph Coll. (formerly Randolph-Macon Woman's Coll.), 2006—. Trustee Kent Pl. Sch., 1986—98, pres. bd. trustees, 1993—97, Randolph-Macon Woman's Coll., 1992—2002, 1997—2000; mem. poverty initiative Union Theol. Sem., 2005—; bd. dirs. NC Outward Bound Sch., 1983—94, vice-chmn., 1992—94; bd. dirs. Outward Bound USA, 2000—06, vice chmn. expeditionary learning, 1993—. Home: 3115 Rivermont Ave Lynchburg VA 24503

WORDSWORTH, JERRY L., wholesale distribution executive; b. Charlotte, NC, Sept. 22, 1945; BS, N.C. State U., 1963. With MBM, Rocky Mount, NC, 1966—, CEO, pres. & chmn. Co-owner Carolina Panthers. Office: MBM 2641 Mountainbrook Rd Rocky Mount NC 27802 Home: PO Box 800 Rocky Mount NC 27802-0800 Office Fax: 252-985-7241. *

WORELL, JUDITH P., psychologist, educator; b. NYC; d. Moses and Dorothy Goldfarb; m. Leonard Worell, Aug. 11, 1947 (div.); children: Amy, Beth, Wendy; m. H.A. Smith, Mar. 23, 1985 BS magna cum laude, Queens Coll., 1950; MA, Ohio State U., 1952, PhD in Clin. Psychology, 1954; DHL (hon.), Colby-Sawyer Coll., 1993. Research assoc. Iowa Psychopathic Hosp., Iowa City, 1957-59; research assoc. Okla. State U., 1960-66; asst. prof. U. Ky., Lexington, 1969-71, assoc. prof., 1971-75, prof. ednl. and counseling psychology, 1976—, dir. counseling psychology tng. program, 1980-93, chairperson dept. ednl. and counseling psychology, 1993-97, prof. emerita, 1999—. Author: (with C.M. Nelson) Managing Instructional Problems, 1974; (with W.E. Stilwell) Psychology for Teachers and Students, 1981; Psychological Development in the Elementary Years, 1982; (with Fred Danner) The Adolescent as Decision-maker: Applications to Development and Education, 1989; (with Pam Remer) Feminist Perspectives in Therapy: An Empowerment Model for Women, 1992; (with N. Johnson) Shaping the Future of Feminist Psychology: Education, Research, and Practice, 1997, (with Norine Johnson & Michael Roberts) Beyond Appearance: A New Look at Adolescent Girls, 1999, Encyclopedia of Women and Gender: Sex Similarities and Differences and the Impact of Society on Gender, 2001, (with Pam Remer) Feminist Perspectives in Therapy: Empowering Diverse Women, 2003, (with Carol Goodheart) Oxford Handbook of Girls' and Women's Psychological Health, 2006; assoc. editor Jour. Cons. and Clin. Psychology, 1976-79, mem. editl. bd., 1984-89; assoc. editor Psychol. Women Quar., 1984-89, editor, 1989-95; mem. editorial bd. Sex Roles, 1984-2000, Psychol. Assessment, 1991-97, Clin. Psychology Rev., 1991-97, Women and Therapy, 1992-2000; cons., reviewer 10 jours.; contbr. articles to profl. jours. Named U. Ky. Campus Woman of Yr., 1976, Outstanding Univ. Grad. prof., 1991, Disting. Ky. psychologist, 1990; USPHS fellow, 1953; NIMH rsch. grantee, 1962-69. Fellow APA (pres. Clin. Psychology of Women 1986-88, chmn. com. state assn. rels. 1982-83, fellow selection divsn. 35 com. 1983-84, policy and planning bd. 1989-92, publs. and comm. bd. 1992-99, chair 1996-98, chair jours. com., pres. divsn. psychology of women 1997-98, Disting. Leader for Women in Psychology 1990, Carolyn Wood Sherif award, 2001, Psychology of Women Heritage award 2004, coun. rep. 2000-02, chair women's caucus 2002) Soc. Psychol. Study of Social Issues (chmn. fellow com. 2005-), Ky. Psychol. Assn. (pres. 1981-82, rep. at large 1995-97), Southeastern Psychol. Assn. (exec. coun. mem.-at-large, pres.-elect 1993-94 pres. 1994-95), Am. Women in Psychology, Phi Beta Kappa. Home: 3892 Gloucester Dr Lexington KY 40510-9729 Office: U Ky Dept Ednl and Counseling Psychology 245 Dickey Hl Lexington KY 40506-0017 E-mail: jworell@alltel.net.

WORENKLEIN, JACOB JOSHUA, lawyer; b. NYC, Oct. 1, 1948; s. Abraham and Cela (Zyskind) W.; divorced; children: David, Daniel, Laura; m. Cindy Sternkler, Feb. 26, 1995; 1 child, Sasha Anne. BA, Columbia U., 1969; MBA, JD, NYU, 1973. Bar: N.Y. 1974. From assoc. to ptnr. Milbank, Tweed, Hadley & McCloy, NYC, 1973-93, chmn. firm planning com., 1988-90, exec. com., 1990-93, sr. advisor to exec. com., 1993-94; mng. dir., group head of global project fin. group Lehman Bros., NYC, 1993-96; mng. dir., head project fin, commodity fin., export fin. Soc. Gen., NYC, 1996-98, mng. dir., global head project and sector fin. Paris and NYC, 1998—2003; chmn., CEO U.S. Power Generating Co., NYC, 2003—, Astoria Generating Co., 2006—. Mem. investment banking mgmt. com. Lehman Bros., 1993-96; mem. adv. coun. Amoco Power Resources Corp., 1995-97; adj. prof. fin. NYU Stern Sch. of Bus.; bd. dirs., mem. audit com. CDC Globeleq, 2004—, Ormat Techs., Inc., 2004—. Mem. editl. bd. Jour. Structured and Project Fin., 1996—; contbr. articles to profl. jours. Chmn. bd. Old Broadway Synagogue, N.Y.C., 2001-, pres. 1978-2001; trustee Fedn. Jewish Philanthropies, N.Y.C., 1984-86; bd. overseers United Jewish Appeal-Fedn. Jewish Philanthropies, 1987, chmn. lawyers divsn. major gifts, 1989-91, chmn. lawyers divsn., 1991-93, bd. dirs., 1991-97; trustee Jewish Cmty. Rels. Coun. N.Y., 1995-98, Com. for Econ. Devel., 2001-. Mem. Coun. on Fgn. Rels. Office Phone: 212-792-0180. E-mail: worenklein@aol.com.

WORK, BRUCE VAN SYOC, small business owner, consultant; b. Monmouth, Ill., Mar. 20, 1942; s. Robert M. and Evelyn (Ruskin) W.; m. Janet Kay Brown, Nov. 12, 1966; children: Bruce, Terra. BA, Monmouth Coll., 1964; BS, U. Mo.-Rolla, 1966; postgrad., U. Chgo., 1978-79. Registered profl. engr., Ill. Various mgmt. positions Midcon Corp. (and subs.), 1966-79; pres. Indsl. Fuels Corp., Troy, Mich., 1979-85, Costain Coal Inc., Troy, Mich., 1985-89; pvt. practice small bus. cons., 1989-92; bus. cons. Wallis Oil Co., 1992-2000; small bus. cons., 2000—. Mem. various coms. Cuba United Meth. Ch. Mem. Detroit Athletic Club, Blue Key. Office: 2280 Hwy DD Cuba MO 65453-9684 Office Phone: 573-885-4724. *People are the key to our success. Treat each individual as you would like to be treated.*

WORK, CHARLES ROBERT, lawyer; b. Glendale, Calif., June 21, 1940; s. Raymond P. and Minna M. (Fricke) W.; m. Linda S. Smith, Oct. 4, 1965 (div.); children: Matthew Keehn, Mary Lucila Landis, Benjamin Reed; m. Veronica A. Haggart, Apr., 1985, 1 child, Andrew Haggart. BA, Wesleyan U., 1962; JD, U. Chgo., 1965; LLM, Georgetown U., 1966. Bar: D.C. 1965, Utah 1965. Asst. U.S. atty. D.C., 1966-73; dep. adminstr. law enforcement assistance adminstrn., U.S. Dept. Justice, 1973-75; ptnr. Peabody, Lambert & Meyers, Washington, 1975-82, McDermott, Will & Emery, Washington, 1982—. Recipient Rockefeller Pub. Service award 1978. Mem. D.C. Bar (pres. 1976-77). Office: McDermott Will & Emery 600 13th St NW Fl 12-8 Washington DC 20005-3005 Office Phone: 202-756-8030. E-mail: cwork@mwe.com.

WORKMAN, GEORGE HENRY, structural engineering consultant; b. Muskegon, Mich., Sept. 18, 1939; s. Harvey Merton and Bettie Jane (Meyers) W.; m. Vicki Sue Hanish, June 17, 1967; children: Mark, Larry. AS, Muskegon C.C., 1960; BS in Engring., MS in Engring., U. Mich., 1966, PhD, 1969. Registered profl. engr., Ohio. Prin. engr. Battelle Meml. Inst., Columbus, Ohio, 1969-76; pres. Applied Mechanics Inc., Longboat Key, Fla., 1976—. Instr. dept. civil engring. Ohio State U., 1973, 82. Contbr. tech. papers to nat. and internat. confs. With USN, 1961-64. Mem. ASME, Am. Acad. Mechanics, Sigma Xi, Chi Epsilon, Phi Kappa Phi, Phi Thea Kappa. Congregationalist. Home and Office: 3431 Bayou Ct Longboat Key FL 34228-3028 Office Phone: 941-383-0721. Business E-Mail: workman@appliedmechanicsincorporated.com.

WORKMAN, JEROME JAMES, JR., chemist; b. Northfield, Minn., Aug. 6, 1952; s. Jerome James and Louise Mae (Sladek) W.; m. Rebecca Marie Zittel, Aug. 3, 1974; children: Cristina Louise, Stephannie Michelle, Daniel Jerome, Sara Marie, Michael Timothy. BA with honors, St. Mary's U., Winona, Minn., 1976, MA with distinction, 1980; PhD, Columbia Pacific U., San Rafael, Calif., 1984; postgrad., MIT, 2001—; grad. in Sr. Exec. Program, Columbia U., 2004, postgrad., 2004—06. Cert. in bus. excellence Columbia U., 2006. Prin. Workman & Assocs., Mankato, Minn., 1980-82; pres. Biochem. Cons., Mankato, Minn., 1982-84; sr. chemist Technicon Instruments, Tarrytown, NY, 1984-87; sr. scientist Hitachi Instruments, Danbury, Conn., 1987-89; supervising scientist Bran & Luebbe/Technicon, Tarrytown, 1987; mgr. tech. support NIR Systems/Perstorp Analytical, Silver Spring, Md., 1989-90, mgr. mktg., 1990-92, dir. mktg., 1992-93; assoc. advisor Inst. Textile Tech., Charlottesville, Va., 1992—; prin. scientist Perkin Elmer Corp., Norwalk, Conn., 1993-96; sr. rsch. fellow Kimberly-Clark Corp., Analytical and Measurement Tech., Neenah, Wis., 1996—2002; chief tech. officer, v.p. rsch. and engring. Argose, Inc., Waltham, Mass., 2002—04; dir. rsch. and tech. Thermo Fisher Sci., Inc. (formerly Thermo Electron Corp.), Madison, Wis., 2004—07; dir. measurement sys. Luminous Med. Inc., Carlsbad, Calif., 2007—. Instr. Fedn. Analytical Chemistry and Spectroscopy Socs.; external examiner U. Guelph, Ont., Can., 1993-94, chair rep. indsl. adv. bd. Ctr. for Process Analytical Chemistry 1993—2002; apptd. mem. subcom. on process analytical techs. U.S. FDA, 2002, vis. prof., 2002; mem. Nat. Acads. nat. rsch. panel on assessment of NIST programs, 2003—; mem. NRC panel U.S. Nat. Acads., 2003—. Author: Handbook of Organic Compounds: NIR, IR, Raman, and UV-Vis Spectra Featuring Polymers and Surfactants, 3 vols., 2000; co-author: Statistics in Spectroscopy, 1991, 2d edit., 2003, Near-Infrared Spectroscopy in Agr., 2003, Chemometrics in Spectroscopy, 2007, Practical Guide to Interpretive Near-Infrared Spectroscopy, 2007, (jour. series) Chemometrics in Spectroscopy, UV-Vis Spectroscopy, 1993; editor: The Process Pages for NIRnews, Internat. Com. for Near Infrared Spectroscopy, 1993—97; co-editor: Applied Spectroscopy: A Compact Reference for Practitioners, 1998, Near-Infrared Reflectance Spectroscopy in Analysis of Agricultural Products, 2003, Spectroscopy Letters 1996-2002, 2003; contbg. editor: Spectroscopy Mag.; assoc. editor Wiley-Intersci. Series in Lab. Automation, 1993, Applied Spectroscopy Reviews, 1995—2000, Lab. Robotics and Automation, 1995—98, process editor Jour. Near Infrared Spectroscopy, 1995—97, mem. adv. editl. bd. Spectroscopy, 1995—; contbr. articles. Recipient Heart of Gold award Minn. affiliate Am. Heart Assn., 1984, Ea. Analytical Symposium award, 2002; Am. Heart Assn. H.N. and H.B. Shapira scholar, 1971-72; NSF grantee, 1977-78. Fellow: ASTM (exec. com., chair main com. on molecular spectroscopy, Award of Merit 2002, Appreciations award 2000, 2005), Am. Inst. Chemists, Royal Soc. Chemistry U.K. (chartered chemist, chartered scientist); mem.: Coblentz Soc. (bd. mgrs. 2002—06), Joint Com. Atomic and Molecular Phys. Data (chmn. UV-VIS, exec. coun.), Coun. Near-Infrared Spectroscopy (pres.), Soc. for Applied Spectroscopy (Nat. Tour spkr. 2006), Am. Chem. Soc. (instr. course on Practical Near-IR Analysis), Nat. Honor Soc., Sigma Xi, Delta Epsilon Sigma. Achievements include research in molecular spectroscopy, statistics and chemometrics; development and applications of spectroscopic methods and sensors to consumer products and processes; U.S. and international patents for analytical systems. Office: Luminous Med Inc 2461 Impala Dr Carlsbad CA 92010 Business E-Mail: jerry.workman@luminousmed.com.

WORKMAN, JOHN MITCHELL, chemist; b. Uniontown, Pa., Oct. 25, 1949; s. Hugh Lawrence and Mary Louise (Mitchell) W.; m. Gayle Sue Zappin, Nov. 20, 1987. BA in Psychology, Miami U., Oxford, Ohio, 1971; MS in Edn., Kans. State U., 1976; MS in Chemistry, U. Cin., 1985, PhD in Chemistry, 1987; MBA in Fin., Wright State U., 1995. Tchg. and rsch. asst. dept. chemistry Wright State U., Dayton, Ohio, 1977—81; grad. tchg. asst. U. Cin., 1982—83, grad. rsch. asst., 1983—86; sr. scientist Chemsys Inc., Fairborn, Ohio, 1986—89, dir. elemental analysis, 1989—, lab. dir., 1994—. Contbr. articles to jours. Analytical Chemistry, Applied Spectroscopy. With U.S. Army, 1972-75. Mem.: Soc. for Applied Spectroscopy, Am. Phys. Soc., Am. Chem. Soc., Sigma Iota Epsilon, Sigma Pi Sigma, Sigma Xi. Episcopalian. Personal E-mail: tacitfalcon@woh.rr.com.

WORKMAN, JOHN P., JR., marketing professor; b. Wilmington, NC, Sept. 26, 1958; s. John P. and Elinor A. Workman; m. Jeanne Marie Bertch, June 19, 1993; children: Justina Suzanne, Juliana Leigh. BS, NC State U., 1980; MBA, U. Va., 1984; PhD, MIT, 1991. Product mktg. engr. Tex. Instruments, Johnson City, Tenn., 1980—82, field sales engr. Fairfax, Va., 1984—85; asst. prof. mktg. U. NC, Chapel Hill, 1991—98; assoc. prof. mktg. Creighton U., Omaha, 1998—2002, prof. mktg., 2003—. Expert witness Kutak Rock, Omaha, 2000—02; vis. fellow Jesuit Inst. at Boston Coll., 2005—06. Music min. St. Stephen the Martyr Ch., Omaha, 1998—; bd. dirs. Colleagues in Jesuit Bus. Edn., 2002—04; dir. Ignatian Commons Initiative. Recipient Best Paper award in mktg. strategy track, Am. Mktg. Assn., 1997, Best Paper of Yr. award, Jour. of Acad. Sci., 2000, Teacher of Yr., Creighton U. Coll. Bus., 2002, Outstanding Faculty award, 2003; Rsch. grant, Mktg. Sci. Inst., 1995, 1998. Mem.: Acad. Mgmt., Acad. Mktg. Sci., Am. Mktg. Assn. (mem. academic coun. 2000—02). Roman Catholic. Avocations: piano, jogging, ice skating, Web surfing. Home Phone: 402-333-9708. Office Fax: 402-280-5565. Business E-Mail: workman@creighton.edu.

WORKMAN, SHARON JOY, journalist; b. Louisa, Ky., May 20, 1930; d. Charlie B. Workman and Jessie Virginia Beaire; children: Patrick Corsiglia, Joan Corsiglia, James Corsiglia, Cynthia Corsiglia. BA, Marshall Coll., 1952; MA in Lit., Oxford U., Eng., 1990; MA in Creative Writing, Dartmouth Coll., 1992; studied French at, U. Laval, Quebec, U. Lyon, France, Villefranche-sur-Mer and MonfLarquin, France, Spa, Belgium. Feature writer The Herald-Advertiser, Huntington, W.Va., 1951—52; mil. intelligence analyst Hdqrs. US Armed Forces Far East, Psychol. Warfare Sect., Japan, 1952—54; reporter Life Mag., NYC, 1954—59, People Mag., NYC, 1974—88. Mem.: DAR, TIME-LIFE Alumni Assn., Dartmouth Club, Overseas Press Club, The Coll. Club of Boston, The Tokeneke Club. Republican. Meth. Avocations: travel, swimming, opera, museums, concerts. Home: 9 Hale Ln Darien CT 06820 Personal E-mail: sharonworkman@aol.com.

WORKS, MARGARET ELIZABETH, retired art educator; b. Akron, Ohio, Mar. 28, 1931; d. William Paul and Florence E. Neal; m. Robert Lee Works (dec.). BFA, Carnegie Mellon U., Pitts., Pa., 1951; MS, U. So. Calif., LA, 1957. Cert. tchr. elem. and secondary art Pa., 1951, life credential in art Calif., 1953, secondary life credential Calif., 1960. Tchr. LA Unified Sch. Dist., 1953—91; supr. art edn. fieldwork Calif. State U. Dominguez Hills, Carson, Calif., 1993—2004, instr. art, 1993—2004; ret., 2004. Mem. new tchr. com. LA Unified Sch. Dist., 1965—66, mem. review and revision art com., 1984—85, 1992—93; mem. com. Eveinings for Edueators LA County Mus. Art, 1975—90; workshop leader in field; curatorial asst. Mingel Folk Art Mus., La Jolla, Calif., 1980, San Diego, 2002; judge advanced placement Ednl. Testing Svc., Princeton, NJ, 1989; tchr. mentor LA County Schs., 1993—2001. Exhibitions include Scaife House Gallery, 1952 (2d Pl. award, 1952), LA County Mcpl. Art Gallery, 1983. Judge art shows So. Calif., 1965—2006; ofcl. election poll LA County Election Bd., 1991—2006. Mem.: Calif. Art Edn. Assn. (historian 2004—06, chmn. 2004—06, named Retired Educator of Yr. 2005), PVAC Paleteers. Avocations: printmaking, drawing, painting, travel, cooking. Studio: 27850 Longhill Dr Rancho Palos Verdes CA 90274

WORLEY, APRIL COLE, artist, grant writer; b. Santa Barbara, Calif., Dec. 17, 1976; d. John E. Colgan and Susan Valerie Geoghegan; m. Peter Ryan Worley, June 10, 2001; 1 child, Gabriel Evan. BA in Humanities, New Coll. Calif., 2001. Grant writer Nimbus Grants, San Luis Obispo, Calif., 2004—. Editor: COLD mag.; contbr. articles to profl. jours.; contbg. writer Violet Mag., 2005, Ctrl. Coast Mag., 2006; author: Road, 2001, The Underling, 2003, Women and Their Bikes, 2005; Exhibited in group shows at The Retro Unfit, San Luis Obispo, Calif., 2005. Avocations: riding motorcycles, photography, silk screening, hiking, dancing. E-mail: apemayhem@hotmail.com.

WORLEY, CAROLYN ANN HINER, retired secondary school educator; b. May 1, 1944; m. James Edward Worley; children: James Edward Jr., Andrew Edmund. BA, Georgetown Coll., Ky., 1967; cert. languages, U. Paris, 1968; MA, U. Ky., Lexington, 1972. Cert. tchr. Ky., 1987. French tchr. Harrodsburg HS, Ky., 1968—70, 1976—77; dir. child care ctr. St. Philips Episc. Ch., Harrodsburg, 1981—86; French and social studies tchr. Mercer County HS, Harrodsburg, 1986—2003; ret., 2003. Organist, pianist St. Philip's Episc. Ch., 1974—86, Harrodsburg Christian Ch., 1986—2004. Mem.: Daus. of King, Harrodsburg Hist. Soc., Am. Guild Organists, Marcel Proust Reading Group, Delta Kappa Gamma. Home: 878 Warwick Rd Harrodsburg KY 40330

WORLEY, LLOYD DOUGLAS, language educator; b. Lafayette, La., Sept. 11, 1946; s. Albert Stiles and Doris (Christy) W.; m. Maydean Ann Mouton, Apr. 4, 1966; children: Erin Shawn, Albert Stiles II. BA, U. SW La., 1968, MA, 1972; PhD, So. Ill. U., 1979. Ordained priest, Liberal Cath. Ch., 1977, consecrated aux. bishop, 2005. Tchr. Lafayette H.S., 1969-74; vis. asst. prof. dept. English So. Ill. U., Carbondale, 1979-80; asst. prof. dept. English Pa. State U., DuBois, 1980-87; assoc. prof., assoc. dir. composition dept. English U. No. Colo., Greeley, 1987-88, prof. dept. English, 1988—, chair dept. English, 1988—90. Acting dir. Writing Component Ctr. Basic Skills, So. Ill. U., 1980. Editor: Ruthven Literary Bull., 1988-92; contbr. book chpts., articles. Rector Parish of St. Albertus Magnus The Liberal Cath. Ch., 1987-2001, sec-treas. Am. Province; provost Am. Clerical Synod Chpt. The Liberal Cath. Ch., 1991-2001; Sovereign Grand Master, Order of Holy Sepulchre, 1982-; vicar-gen. Decorated Knight Bachelor, 1996, Hereditary Knight of San Luigi, 1996, Knight Cmdr. Order of Merit St. Angilbert, 1993, Prelate Comdr. Order of Noble Companions of Swan, 1993, Grand Chamberlain, 1995, Knight Order of Guadalupe, 1995, Knight Comdr. Justice Sovereign Order St. John, Knight Grand Cross of Bear of Alabona, 1995, Knight Grand Cross Order St. Stanislaus, 1998, Knight Comp. Crown of Alabona, 1998, Knight Grand Cross Order St. John, 1998, Knight Grand Cross Order Sts. Constantine the Great and Helen, Knight Grand Cross of Justice Ordine dei Cavalieri Lauretani, Grand Cross with Collar of Order of Noble Companion of Swan, 2000 Grand Cross of Justice, Sovrano Ordine Militare ed Ospitaliero di S.Maria di Gerusalemme Teutonico di Svevia; created hereditary Baron, Royal and Serene House of Alabona-Ostrogojsk et de Garama, HRSH Prince William I, created Count Palatine of Maxalla, 1996, created Hereditary Duke of Maxalla, 2000. Fellow Philalethes Soc.; mem. ASCD, Internat. Assn. for Fantastic in Arts (divsn. head Am. Lit. 1987-93), Lord Ruthven Assembly (pres. 1988-94, founding pres. emeritus 1994), Conf. Coll. Composition and Commn., Nat. Coun. Tchrs. English, Am. Conf. Irish Studies, Sigma Tau Delta (bd. dirs. 1990-96, high plains regent various states 1992-96, 10-Yr. Outstanding Advisor award 1997), Masons (century lodge #190), Order of DeMolay (chevalier, cross of honor, legion of honor), Knights Holy Sepulchre (Sov. Grand Master), Rose Croix Martinist Order (pres. premier nat. coun.). Democrat. Office: 3620 W 10th B-150 Greeley CO 80634-9655 Home Phone: 970-356-3002; Office Phone: 970-357-2942. Office Fax: 206-350-2268. Business E-Mail: prof@profw.com.

WORLEY, RICHARD B., financial consultant; b. 1945; m. Leslie Anne Miller. Grad., U. Tenn. Chmn. Miller Anderson & Sherrerd; CEO, chief investment officer Morgan Stanley Investment Mgmt.; now mng. dir. Permit Capital Group LLC, 2002—. Bd. trustees Putnam Investments, 2004—. Trustee Med. Ctr. of U. Pa., Colonial Williamsburg Found., The Robert Wood Johnson Found., Princeton, NJ, 2000—; mem. investment com. Phila. Orchestra.

WORLEY, ROBERT BRUCE, JR., lawyer; b. Mobile, Ala., Mar. 9, 1960; s. Robert Bruce and Linda (Knight) Worley; m. Catherine Anna Steck, Nov. 14, 1987; children: Nancy Jane, Catherine Turner. BBA with honors and distinction, U. Ky., 1982; JD, Tulane U., 1985. Bar: La. 1985, Tex. 2003, U.S. Dist. Ct. (ea. dist. La.) 1985, U.S. Dist. Ct. (mid. dist. La.) 1986, U.S. Dist. Ct. (we. dist. La.) 1988, U.S. Dist. Ct. (ea. dist. Ark.) 1996, U.S. Dist. Ct. (we. dist. Ark.) 1996, U.S. Dist. Ct. (cen. dist. Ill.) 1997, U.S. Dist. Ct. (so. dist. Tex.) 2001, U.S. Dist. Ct. (ea. dist. Tex.) 2001, U.S. Ct. Appeals (5th cir.) 1990, U.S. Ct. Appeals (4th cir.) 1990, U.S. Ct. Appeals (6th cir.) 1996, U.S. Ct. Appeals (7th cir.) 1997, U.S. Ct. Appeals (11th cir.) 1998, U.S. Ct. Appeals (8th cir.) 1999, U.S. Supreme Ct. 1999. Assoc. Gelpi, Sullivan, Carroll and Laborde, New Orleans, 1985—88; ptnr. Kullman Firm, New Orleans, 1988—99, Jones, Walker, Waechter, Poitevent, Carrere & Denegre, New Orleans, 1999—. Chmn. profl. employment com. Jones Walker et al, New Orleans, 2001—04, chmn. United Way, 2000—, Mem., pres. New Orleans Area Habitat for Humanity Bd.; co-chair lawyers com. New Orleans United Way Campaign, 2003; chmn. La. Jr. Tennis Coun.; bd. dirs. La. Tennis Assn.; pres. ch. coun. Rayne Meml. United Meth. Ch. Named One of Best Labor and Employment Lawyers, New Orleans Mag., 2005; recipient, 2006, Leadership in Law award, City Business, 2006. Mem.: ABA, Am. Inns Ct., Coll. Master Adv. and Barristers, New Orleans Bar Assn., La. State Bar Assn. Avocations: tennis, swimming, fishing. Office: Jones Walker et al 201 St Charles Ave New Orleans LA 70170-5100 Office Phone: 504-582-8192. Business E-Mail: rworley@joneswalker.com.

WORMAN, HOWARD JAY, internist, educator; b. Paterson, NJ, May 21, 1959; s. Louis and Dora (Rubin) W. BA, Cornell U., 1981; MD, U. Chgo., 1985. Diplomate Am. Bd. Internal Medicine. Intern NY Hosp., NYC, 1985—86, resident, 1986—87; guest investigator Rockefeller U., NYC, 1987—90; asst. prof. Mt. Sinai Sch. Medicine, NYC, 1990—94; asst. attending physician Mt. Sinai Hosp., NYC, 1990—94; asst. prof. Columbia U. Coll. Physicians and Surgeons, NYC, 1995—98, assoc. prof., 1998—2007, prof., 2007—; asst. attending physician NY Presbyn. Hosp., Columbia-U. Med. Ctr., NYC, 1995—98, assoc. attending physician, 1998—2007, attending physician, 2007—; dir. divsn. digestive and liver diseases NY Presbyn. Hosp., NYC, 1999—2002. Mem. med. adv. com. Muscular Dystrophy Assn., 2000—05. Mem. editl. bd. Hepatology, Frontiers in Biosci., World Jour. Gastroenterology, Biomed. Ctrl. Cell Biology; mem. bd. reviewing editors Molecular Biology of the Cell; contbr. articles to profl. jours. Recipient Physician-Scientist award NIH, 1987-92; Charles E. Culpeper scholar in Med. Scis., 1994-95, Irma T. Hirschl scholar, 1997-2002. Mem. AAAS, ACP, Am. Chem. Soc., Am. Fedn. Med. Rsch. (Trainee award in clin. rsch. 1989, Henry Christian award 1990), Am. Soc. Cell Biology, Am. Assn. Study of Liver Diseases, Am. Gastroent. Assn., Am. Soc. Clin. Investigation, N.Y. Acad. Scis. (vice chmn. biol. scis. sect. 1992-93, chmn. 1993-94), Am. Diabetes Assn., Hon. Order Ky. Cols., Phi Beta Kappa. Democrat. Jewish. Avocations: music, reading. Office: Columbia U Coll Physicians-Surgeons 630 W 168th St New York NY 10032-3795 Business E-Mail: hjwl4@columbia.edu.

WORMER, THOMAS ANDREW, surgeon; b. Buffalo, Dec. 3, 1956; s. Donald Andrew and Elinor Ann (Bliss) W.; m. Melissa Jane Ertell, Apr. 11, 1988; children: Matthew Thomas, Margaret Elizabeth, Samuel James, Sarah Jane. BS, Allegheny Coll., 1978; MD, Albany Med. Coll., 1984. Diplomate Am. Bd. Surgery. Intern Millard Fillmore Hosp., Buffalo, 1984—85, resident in gen. surgery, 1985—89; attending surgeon F.F. Thompson Hosp., Canandaigua, NY, 1989—95, chief surgery, 1994—99. Fellow ACS; mem. Canandaigua Med. Soc. (pres. 1994), N.Y. State Med. Soc. Presbyterian. Office: Canandaigua Medical Group 335 Parrish St Canandaigua NY 14424-1794 E-mail: twormer@rochester.rr.com.

WORMLEY, DAVID NEAL, engineering educator; BSME, MIT, 1962, MSME, 1964, PhD in Mech. Engring., 1968. Mem. faculty MIT, 1967—92, head dept. mech. engring., 1982—91, assoc. dean engring., 1991—92; dean Coll. Engring., prof. mech. engring. Pa. State U., University Park, 1992—. Past chmn. exec. com. NRC Transp. Rsch. Bd.; past chair adv. com. NSF Engring. Directorate. Fellow: ASEE (pres. 2005), ASME (Lewis Moody award, Dynamic Sys. and Control Divsn. Edn. award 1997); mem.: Am. Soc. Engring. Edn., Pi Tau Sigma, Sigma Xi. Achievements include research in dynamic systems and control with application to transportation, energy production and conversion and fluid actuation systems. Office: Pa State U 101 Hammond Bldg University Park PA 16802

WORNER, THERESA MARIE, internist, educator; b. Breckenridge, Minn., Feb. 19, 1948; d. William Daniel and Elizabeth (Stelten) W.; m. Martin Herbst, Mar. 24, 1979. AB, St. Theresa Coll., 1970; MD, U. Minn., 1974. Diplomate Am. Bd. Internal Medicine. Rotating intern Kings County Hosp., Bklyn., 1974-75, resident medicine, 1975-77; fellow VA Med. Ctr., Bronx, NY, 1977-78, chief med. sect. Alcoholism treatment program, 1978-87; asst. prof. medicine Mt. Sinai Sch. Medicine, NYC, 1984-87; mem. faculty Postgrad. Ctr., 1985-90; physician in charge alcoholism svcs. L.I. Coll. Hosp., Bkyn., 1987-92; assoc. prof. clin. medicine SUNY, Health Sci. Ctr., Bkyn., 1988—; dir. rsch. 32BJ Health Fund, 1992-99; clin. assoc. prof. Pub. Health Cornell U. Med. Coll., 1996—; pres. Menachem Publ., Bethlehem, NH, 1999—. Pres./founder Alcohol. Info, 1995-97; advisor Patient Care Mag., 1984—; cons. REA, 1996—. Referee Hepatology, 1986, Jour. Study Alcohol, 1984—, Substance Abuse, 1992—, Alcoholism: Clinical and Exptl. Rsch., 1992—, Drug and Alcohol Dependence, 1993—, Drug Therapy, 1994—, Addiction, 1996—; contbr. numerous articles to profl. jours. Active Israel Mus., Israeli Opera, Israel Symphony. Grantee Child Welfare Adminstrn., 1991, 92, 93; recipient Physicians Recognition award AMA, 1984, 89, 91, 96, Cert. of Merit Govt. Employees Ins. Co., 1986, PACT Intern Site award, 1991, 92. Fellow ACP, N.Y. Acad. Medicine; mem. AAAS, Am. Med. Soc. on Alcoholism and Other Drug Dependence, Am. Soc. Internal Medicine, Am. Assn. for Study Liver Diseases (Travel award 1978), N.Y. Acad. Scis., Rsch. Soc. on Alcoholism, Internat. Soc. Biologic Rsch. in Alcoholism.

WORONOFF, ISRAEL, former psychology educator; b. Bklyn., Dec. 30, 1926; s. Samuel and Lena (Silberman) W.; m. Fay Goldberg, Feb. 11, 1950; 1 child, Gary. AB in Psychology, U. Mich., 1949, MA in Sociology, 1952, PhD in Edn., 1954. Lic. psychologist, Mich. Instr. Flint (Mich.) Jr. Coll., 1953-54; asst. prof. St. Cloud (Minn.) State Coll., 1954-56, Ea. Mich. U., Ypsilanti, 1956-59, assoc. prof., 1959-62, prof., 1962-92, prof. emeritus. Cons. psychologist Midwest Mental Health Clinic, Dearborn, Mich., 1978-83, Orchard Hills Psychiat. Ctr., Novi, Mich., 1983—; mem. Bd. Jewish Fedn. Washtenaw County, 1997-2003; co-chair Bd. Jewish Family Svc. of Ann Arbor, 1997. Author: Educator's Guide to Stress Management, 1986. Mem. bd. Jewish Family Svc. of Ann Arbor, 1996—; mem. cmty. rels. com. Jewish Cmty. Assn., Ann Arbor, Mich., 1990-92; v.p. edn. Beth Israel Congregation, Ann Arbor, 1985-87; mem. adv. bd. Mich. Anti-Defamation League of B'nai B'rith, 1958—. Mem. APA, Mich. Psychol. Assn. Democrat. Home: 2519 Londonderry Rd Ann Arbor MI 48104-4017

WORONOV, MARY PETER, actress; b. Bklyn., Dec. 8, 1946; d. Victor D. and Carol W.; m. Ted Gershuny, 1969 (div.); m. Ted Whitehead, 1979. Student, Cornell Univ., 1964—68. Actor: (films) The Chelsea Girls, 1967, Death Race 2000, 1975, Rock 'n' Roll High School, 1979, Eating Raoul, 1982, Black Widow, 1987, Warlock, 1989, Good Girls Don't, 1995, The Munster's Scary Little Christmas, 1996, Invisible Mom II, 1999, New Women, 2001; (TV series) Logan's Run, 1977, Sledge Hammer!, 1987; (TV films) Challenge of a Lifetime, 1985, (TV spl.) Cheech and Chong's Get Out of My Room, 1985, (stage prodns.) Kitchenette, 1968, Boom Boom Room, 1974; author: Wake for the Angels: Paintings and Stories, 1994, Swimming Underground: My Years in the Warhol Factory, 1995, Snake, 2000, Niagara, 2002, Eyewitness to Warhol, 2002, Blind Love, 2004; dir.: (TV show) Little Vampire, Blind Love, The Gigolo. Avocation: painting.

WORRALL, JOHN DENNIS, economics professor, consultant, writer; b. Wildwood, NJ, July 29, 1942; s. John and Adele Veronica (McKenna) W.; m. Suzanne Elizabeth Hopkins; children: Heather, John; m. Janet Priscilla Moran; 1 child, Kevin. BA, Rutgers U., 1969, MA, 1972, PhD, 1976. Asst. dir. Rutgers Bur. Econ. Rsch., New Brunswick, NJ, 1974-77; dir. rsch. Nat. Ctr. for Employment Handicapped-Human Resources Ctr., LI, NY, 1977-78; v.p., dir. econ. rsch. NCCI, NYC, 1979-83; prof. econs. Rutgers U., Camden, NJ, 1983—, asst. dir. Bur. Econ. Rsch. New Brunswick, NJ, 1983—. Advisor Courier Post newspaper, Camden, 1994-97; John R. Commons lectr. U. Wis. Bus. Sch., Madison, 1991. Co-author: An Evaluation of Policy Related Rehabilitation Research, 1975; co-editor: Placement in Rehabilitation, 1979, Benefit Issues in Workers' Compensation, 1985; editor: Safety and the Workforce, 1983; assoc. editor Jour. Ins.: Math. and Econs., 1990-2000, Jour. Risk and Ins., 1992—. Del. White House Conf. on Handicapped, Washington, 1977; pres. South Jersey Irish Am. Unity Conf., Fedn. Irish Am. Socs., Phila., 1996-98; bd. dirs. St. Patrick's Day Observance Com., Phila., 1996-98, Phila. Immigration Resource Ctr., 1999-2001. Sgt. U.S. Army, 1960-66. Named Outstanding Faculty Mem. Rutgers U. Alumni Assn., 1991; honoree Gaelic Ball, Ladies Ancient Order Hibernians, Phila., 1998. Fellow Risk Theory Soc. (sec. 1990, pres. 1991); mem. Nat. Acad. Social Ins., Am. Econs. Assn., Am. Risk and Ins. Assn. (Robert I. Mehr award 2001), Commodore John Barry Soc. (pres. 1996-98). Roman Catholic. Avocations: golf, fishing. Office: Rutgers U Armitage Hall Camden NJ 08102 Office Phone: 856-225-6290. Business E-Mail: jworrall@crab.rutgers.edu.

WORRELL, AUDREY MARTINY, geriatric psychiatrist; b. Phila, Aug. 12, 1935; d. Francis Aloysius and Dorothy (Rawley) Martiny; m. Richard Vernon Worrell, June 14, 1958; children: Philip Vernon, Amy Elizabeth. MD, Meharry Med. Coll., 1960. Diplomate Am. Bd. Psychiatry and Neurology. Intern Misericordia Hosp., Phila., 1960-61; resident SUNY-Buffalo Affiliated Hosp., NY, 1961-63, Buffaflo Psychiat. Ctr., NY, 1963-64; dir. capitol region Mental Health Ctr., Hartford, Conn., 1974-77; acting regional dir. Region IV State Dept. Mental Health, 1976-77; asst. chief psychiatry VA Med. Ctr., Newington, Conn., 1977-78, acting chief psychiatry, 1978-79, chief psychiatry, 1978-80; dir. Capitol Regional Mental Health Facilities, Hartford, Conn., 1980-87; clin. prof. psychiatry U. Conn., 1981-87; commr. State Dept. Mental Health, Hartford, 1981-86; CEO, med. dir. Vista Sandia Hosp., Albuquerque, 1986-88; dir. consultation liason Lovelace Med. Ctr., Albuquerque, 1988-89, geriatric psychiatry, 1989-93; dir. geriatric psychiatry Charter Hosp., Albuquerque, 1993-96, St. Joseph Med. Sys., Albuquerque, 1994—; pvt. practice, 1996—2003; part-time cons. Albuquerque VA Hosp., 2003—. Contbr. articles to profl. jour. Bd. dir. Transitional Svc., Buffalo, 1973-74, ARC, Buffalo, 1973-74, Child and Family Svc., Hartford, 1972-73; co-chmn. United Way/Combined Health Appeal, State of Conn., 1983, 84; active Child Welfare Inst. Adv. Bd., Hartford, 1983—, Conn. Prison Bd., Hartford, 1984-85; chmn. Gov. Task Force on Mental Health Policy, 1982-85; mem. Gov.Task Force on Homeless, 1983-85. Recipient Leadership award Conn. Coun. Mental Health Ctr., 1983, Outstanding Contbn. award to Health Svc., YWCA, Hartford, 1983. Mem. AMA, APHA, NASMHPD (sec., bd. dir. 1982-86), New Eng. Mental Health Commr. Assn., Am. Med. Women's Assn., Conn. Assn. Mental Health and Aging, Conn. Coalition for Homeless Inc., Conn. Rehab. Assn., Am. Assn. Psychiat. Adminstr., Am. Hosp. Assn., Am. Orthopsychiat. Assn., Assn. Mental Health Adminstr., Hosp. and Cmty. Psychiatry Svc., Corporators of Inst. of Living of Hartford, Am. Psychiat. Assn., Conn. Psychiat. Soc., Am. Coll. Psychiatrists, Am. Coll. Mental Health Adminstr. Office: Albuquerque VA Hosp Gibson & San Mateo Albuquerque NM 87107

WORRELL, CYNTHIA LEE, bank executive; b. Moncton, NB, Can., May 27, 1957; came to U.S., 1979; d. Ronald William and Audrey Helen (Crothers) Jones; m. Geoffrey H. Worrell, Sept. 1, 1979; children: Lindsay Andrea, Geoffrey Andrew, Ashley Taylor. BA in Edn. with honors, U. New Brunswick, Fredericton, 1979. Lic. real estate broker, Mass., Pa., Calif. Instr. New Brunswick C.C., Fredericton, N.B., Canada, 1978-79, Massasoit C.C., Brockton, Mass., 1981-82, Brockton Cmty. Schs., 1981-82; regional mgr. and instr. Worldwide Ednl. Svcs., Clifton, NJ, program dir. Taunton, Mass., 1995; procedures and documentation analyst Capital Blue Cross, Harrisburg, Pa., 1985; v.p., br. mgr. Comfed Mortgage Co., Inc., Mass., 1985-90; sr. residential loan officer Bank of Am., Santa Clara, Calif., 1990-92; regional sales mgr., asst. v.p. Shearson Lehman Mortgage, San Jose, Calif., 1992-93; br. mgr. Cypress Fin., San Jose, 1993-94; area and ops. br. mgr. PNC Mortgage Corp. Am., San Jose, 1994—; program dir. worldwide Ednl. Svcs., Taunton, Mass., 1995; area prodn. mgr. Plymouth Mortgage Co., Foxborough, Mass., 1995-96, Ameriquest Mortgage, Hingham, Mass., 1996-97; br. mgr. Bank United of Tex. Commonwealth United Mortgage, West Bridgewater, Mass., 1996—; br. mgr. Nat. City Mortgage-Commonwealth United Mortgage, 1997-98, Family Choice Mortgage, West Bridgewater, 1998—2000, Orchard Mortgage, Raynham, Mass., 2000—06; asst. v.p., br. mgr. Sallie Mae Home Loans, West Wareham, Mass., 2006—. Guest spkr. numerous trade shows, real estate bd. seminars, cmty. workshops, stress mgmt. personal profiles, motivational speaking and workshops; instr. mortgage banking Calif. State U., Hayward, 1994—; mem. adv. bd., instr., outside cons. Calif. State U. Ext. divsn., 1993-95; cert. trainer Carlson Learning Co., 1993—; trainer in diversity, conflict resolution, sexual harassment, and time mgmt.; cmty. trainer WCR, BPW, Old Colony Vocat. Sch., Wareham H.S., Wareham Mid. and Elem. Schs., Wareham Supts. Office, Fall River Sch. Dist., Old Rochester Jr. and Sr. H.S., Bristol County Tng. Consortium, and Transitional Assistance, Bridgewater Cmty., Wareham Foster Parents, Wareham Decas Sch., 1996—. Mem. editl. bd. Mortgage Originator, 1995; contbr. articles to profl. jours. Vol. Handi Kids, Bridgewater, Mass., 1985—90, Fremont/Newark YMCA youth basketball and soccer; active Forest Park PTA, Self-Def. Inst. Tau Kwon Do Club; donor Berwick Boys Club; mem. adv. com. Wareham H.S., mem. coun.; alumni dir. U. New Brunswick, 1998—; bd. dirs. Wareham Childcare; trustee Le Lycee Internat. de la Nouvelle Angleterre, Inc., Boston, 1997; trustee, chair Tabor Acad., Marion, Mass. Named to IBC 200 Women of Achievement, 1991-92, ABI 2000 Notable Women, 1991-92,ABI Personalities of Am., 1992, Internat. Order of Merit, 1992, The World Found. of Successful Women, 1992, Outstanding Young Women in Am., 1984, 88. Mem. NAFE, Mass. Mortgage Bankers Assn., Data Entry Mgmt. Assn., Middleboro C. of C., Chief Exec. Officer Club Boston, Wareham Bus. and Profl. Women's Club (v.p. program dir.), Taunton Area C. of C., Toastmasters, Plymouth Bd. Realtors, Bristol County Bd. Realtors, Women's Coun. of Realtors, Bristol County C. of C. Republican. Avocations: swimming, golf, horseback riding, curling. Home: 2 Peter Cooper Dr Wareham MA 02571-2209 Office: Pinnacle Fin Corp 2360 Cranberry Hwy PO 98 West Wareham MA 02570 Office Phone: 508-930-1792. Personal E-mail: clworrell@aol.com.

WORRELL, SHARYN DIANNE KELLEY, volunteer, retired flight attendant; b. Lynn, Mass., Feb. 23, 1948; d. Richard Allen Kelley and Norma Lovett (Gregory); m. Blaine Patten Worrell, Feb. 15, 1979 (div. Dec. 20, 1985); 1 child, Ryan Richard. Flight attendant United Airlines, Chgo., 1966—2002. Spkr. and co-founder Speakers' Bur. LA-based Flight Attendants; spkr. in field. Author: Ancestral Lines of Joseph Browne of Essex County, Massachusetts and Mary Brown (Joseph's wife) of Kensington, New Hampshire with Related Brown Lines, From Stewardess to Flight Attendant-The Changing Years; co-author: The History of the Auxiliary of Good Shepherd Hospital, Barrington, Illinois; compiler Illinois Court, National Society Women Descendants of the Ancient and Honorable Artillery Company, Celebrating 60 Years. Co-founder Young Women's League for Muscular Dystrophy Assn., LA, 1975; asst. supt. of Sunday sch.; summer Sunday sch. supt.; sch. bd. Immanuel Luth. Ch. and Sch., Palatine, Ill., 1990—93, pub. rels. chair, 1992—2002, bd. of human care ministry com. mem., 1999—2001, pres's. vol. svc. award chmn., 2000—04, bd. of trustees, sec. of congregation, 2001—03; bd. mem. Aux. Good Shepherd Hosp., Barrington, Ill., 2000—, pres., 2006, mem. chair, 2000—02, chef fest bd. mem., founder sch. artwork project, 2003—06; founding mem. Immanuel Luth. Sch. Edn. Found., Palatine, 1998—2003; program chair Art in the Barn, bd. mem.; reach for the stars event chairperson Immanuel Luth. Sch. Edn. Found., Palatine, Ill., 1998—2003. Recipient Vol. Recognition, YMCA, 1988, Servant of Youth award, Boy Scouts Am., Merit awards (3), United Air Lines, Pres.'s Vol. Svc. Lifetime award, George W. Bush, 2006. Mem.: DAR, Clipped Wings, Soc. Dau. Colonial Wars, Continental Soc. Daus. Indian Wars (charter mem., cradle roll), Nat. Soc. U.S. Daus. 1812, Nat. Soc. Daus. of Union, Soc. Desc. Washington's Army at Valley Forge (organizing Ill. brigade comdr.), Nat. Soc. Sons and Daus. Pilgrims (Ill. br. organizing gov.), Daus. Am. Colonists (state libr.), Hereditary Order Descs. Loyalists and Patriots Am.

Revolution (life), Order First Families Conn. (life; founding mem.), Nat. Soc. Descs. Early Quakers (life), Hereditary Order First Families Mass. (life; primary), Her. Ord. Desc. Colonial Govs. (life), Nat. Soc. Colonial Dames XVII Century (charter mem., chpt. historian, state chaplain, chpt. pres., chpt. chaplain, state 2d v.p., state chair heraldry and coat arms, chpt. libr.), Huguenot Soc. Ill. (registrar, dir.), Ill. State Soc. Dames Ct. of Honor (3d v.p.), Nat. Soc. Magna Carta Dames and Barons, Soc. Mayflower Descs. State of Ill. (life; chmn. jr. membership, elder), Soc. Descs. of Colonial Clergy (life), Nat. Soc. Women Descs. Ancient and Hon. Arty. Co. (life; first v.p., treas., hospitality chmn., chaplain), Assn. Daus. Early Am. Witches (life; nat. corr. sec. gen., guest spkr.), Daus. Union Vets. of Civil War 1861-1865 (life; chaplain), Nat. Sons and Daus. Antebellum Planters (life), Presdl. Families Am. (life), Order Crown of Charlemagne in U.S.A. (life), Soveriegn Soc. Ams. Royal Descent (life), Order Descs. Colonial Physicians and Chirugiens (life), Order First Families of Maine (life; corr. sec. gen., charter mem., 2d v.p.), Family of Bruce Soc. Am. (life), Guild Colonial Artists and Tradesmen (life; charter mem.), Sons and Daus. Colonial and Antebellum Bench and Bar (life), Order First Families R.I. and Providence Plantations, N.H. Hist. Soc., Essex Soc. Genealogists, New Eng. Historic Geneal. Soc., Order Merovingian Dynasty (life), Order Ams. Armorial Ancestry (life), Flagon and Trencher (life), Nat. Soc. New Eng. Women (life; 1st v.p. 2006, nat. yearbook chmn., Vol. Cmty. Svc. award 1995), Ill. Cameo Soc. (life), Piscataqua Pioneers (life). Lutheran. Achievements include Lobbied 3 years for exoneration of 6 women executed in 1692 as Salem witches during the Witch Hysteria. Acting Gov. Jane Swift signed the Bill on October 31, 2001 exonerating all 6. Avocations: genealogy, volunteering. Home: 269 Bluff Ct Lake Barrington IL 60010-7312 Personal E-mail: sdworrell@aol.com.

WORRELL, STEWART PHILLIP, lawyer, diversified financial services company executive; b. Montreal, Apr. 13, 1956; s. Arthur Agustus and Sybil Agatha (Jones) Worrell. Chmn. The Libr. Trust, Montreal, 1999—. Charter mem. Mbanx, Toronto, 1998—. Author: (poetry) Children Dressed in Black, 1999. Mem. Fed. Bar Assn., InterAm. Bar Assn., Conseil de Roi, US Ski Assn., Beaconsfield Yacht Club, Univ. Club. Avocations: skiing, sailing, chess, golf, photography. Personal E-mail: s.p.worrell@hotmail.com.

WORSFOLD, VICTOR LEONARD, retired social sciences educator; b. Glasgow, Scotland; s. Victor Leonard Worsfold and Mary MacMillan Thomson. MA, U. St. Andrews, Scotland, 1966; diploma in edn., U. Oxford, Eng., 1967; MA, U. Toronto, Can., 1970; PhD, Harvard U., Cambridge, Mass., 1975. Asst. prof. Antioch Grad. Sch. Edn., Cambridge, 1973—75; asst. to assoc. prof. U. Tex., Richardson, 1975—2001; ret., 2001; cons. U. Tex., Dallas, 2001—07. Contbr. articles to profl. jours. Founding mem. Dallas Symphony Chorus, 1970—86; bd. dirs. Suicide in Crisis Ctr., Dallas, 1975—82. Named Outstanding Tchr. award, Chancellor of U. Tex. Sys., 1988—89. Home: 2424 Winterstone Dr Plano TX 75023

WORSLEY, JAMES RANDOLPH, JR., lawyer; b. Rocky Mount, NC, July 28, 1924; s. James Randolph and Helen Marie (Killian) W.; m. Cornelia Cheston, Feb. 11, 1956; children: Cornelia Worsley Newell, Julia Worsley Neilson, Charlotte Cheston Worsley. BS, E. Carolina U., 1944; postgrad., Harvard U., 1944-45, LLB, 1949. Bar: N.C. 1949, D.C. 1949. Assoc. Klagsbrunn, Hanes & Irwin, Washington, 1949-54; ptnr. Ober, Kaler, Grimes & Shriver (and predecessor firm), Washington, 1955-94, coun., 1995—. Chmn. Md. Potomac Water Authority, 1969-71, Montgomery County (Md.) Charter Revision Commn., 1967; mem. pastoral coun. Archdiocese of Washington, 1975-78; bd. dirs. Madeira Sch., McLean, Va., 1975-81. Fellow Am. Bar Found.; mem. Chevy Chase Club, Met. Club, Knights of Malta. Democrat. Roman Catholic. Avocations: sailing, tennis. Home: 11 Quincy St Chevy Chase MD 20815-4226 Office: Ober Kaler Grimes & Shriver 1401 H St NW Ste 500 Washington DC 20005-2175 Home Phone: 301-656-3961; Office Phone: 202-408-8400.

WORTH, GARY JAMES, communications executive; b. Berkeley Township, NJ, Dec. 13, 1940; s. Melvin Raymond and Viola Vista (Landis) W. Student, Trenton State Coll., 1964, Palm Beach Jr. Coll., 1958-59. Dir. sta. relations MBS, Inc., NYC, 1972, v.p. sta. relations, 1972, exec. v.p. Washington, 1972-79, mem. exec. com., 1978-79; v.p. Mut. Reports, Inc., Washington, 1972-79, dir., 1972-79; v.p., dir. WCFL, Inc., Chgo., 1979, Mut. Radio N.Y., Inc., NYC, 1979; pres., dir. Robert Wold Co. Inc. and subs. Wold Communications, Inc., LA, 1980-85; pres., chief exec. officer, dir. WesternWorld Inc. and subs. WesternWorld TV, LA, 1986-93, The Video Tape Co., North Hollywood, Calif., 1987-93; sec. dir. WesternWorld Video Inc., LA, 1986-87; CEO Starcom Television Svcs., Inc., 1993—96; chmn., CEO Starcom Entertainment, Inc., 1993—; CEO Starcom Mgmt. Svcs. Inc., 1993—, New Age Conversions, Inc., 1996—. Producer, dir.: USAF movie Assignment McGuire. Served to capt. USAF, 1960-66, Vietnam. Decorated Air Force Commendation medal, Armed Forces Expeditionary medal.; recipient Chief Herbert H. Almers Meml. award Bergen County (N.J.) Police Acad., 1972 Mem. Nat. Assn. Broadcasters, Nat. Assn. TV Program Execs., Nat. Informercial Mktg. Assn. Methodist. Personal E-mail: star2874@msn.com.

WORTH, GEORGE JOHN, retired English literature educator; b. Vienna, June 11, 1929; arrived in U.S., 1940, naturalized, 1945; s. Adolph and Theresa (Schreier) W.; m. Carol Laverne Dinsdale, Mar. 17, 1951; children: Theresa Jean (Wilkinson), Paul Dinsdale. AB, U. Chgo., 1948, MA, 1951; PhD, U. Ill., 1954. Instr. English U. Ill., Urbana, 1954-55; faculty U. Kans., Lawrence, 1955—, assoc. prof., 1962-65, prof. English lit., 1965-95; prof. emeritus English, 1995—; asst. chmn. dept. U. Kans., Lawrence, 1961-62, assoc. chmn., 1962-63, acting chmn., 1963-64, chmn., 1964-79. Author: James Hannay: His Life and Work, 1964, William Harrison Ainsworth, 1972, Dickensian Melodrama, 1978, Thomas Hughes, 1984, Great Expectations: An Annotated Bibliography, 1986, (book) Macmillan's Magazine, 1859-1907, 2003; editor: (with Harold Orel) Six Studies in Nineteenth Century English Literature and Thought, 1962, The Nineteenth Century Writer and His Audience, 1969, (with Edwin Eigner) Victorian Criticism of the Novel, 1985. Mem. MLA, Dickens Fellowship, Dickens Soc., Midwest Victorian Studies Assn., Rsch. Soc. for Victorian Periodicals. Office: U Kans Dept English Wescoe Hall Lawrence KS 66045-7590 E-mail: GJWorth@aol.com.

WORTHAM, THOMAS RICHARD, literature and language professor; b. Liberal, Kans., Dec. 5, 1943; s. Tom and Ruth (Cavanaugh) W. AB, Marquette U., 1965; PhD, Ind. U., 1970. From asst. prof. to assoc. prof. UCLA, 1970-82, prof., 1982—, vice-chmn. and dir. undergrad. studies, 1993-97, chmn. dept., 1997—2007. Vis. prof. Am. lit. U. Warsaw, Poland, 1976-77; sr. rsch. fellow Am. Coun. of Learned Socs., 1983-84. Editor: James Russell Lowell's The Biglow Papers: A Critical Edition, 1977, Letters of W. D. Howells, vol. 4, 1892-1901, 1983, The Early Prose Writings of William Dean Howells, 1853-1861, 1990, William Dean Howells' My Mark Twain, 1996, Mark Twain's Chapters From My Autobiography, 1999; asst. editor Nineteenth-Century Fiction, 1971-75, mem. adv. bd., 1976-83, co-editor, 1983-86; co-editor Nineteenth-Century Literature, 1986-95, editor, 1995—; mem. editl. bd. The Collected Works of Ralph Waldo Emerson, 1996—, Am. Documentary Heritage Libr., 1999—. Regent's faculty fellow in the humanities U. Calif., 1971; travel grantee Nat. Endowment for the Humanities, 1985-86, 88-89; grants-in-aid of rsch. Am. Philos. Soc., 1976, 81. Mem. MLA Am. (Norman Foerster prize com. of Am. Lit. sect. 1973, chmn. Pacific coast region, com. on manuscript holdings of Am. Lit. sect. 1972-78, mem. Hubbell prize com. of Am. Lit. sect. 1989-91), Am. Studies Assn., Ralph Waldo Emerson Soc. (bd. dirs. 1992-95), Assn. for Document Editing, Internat. Assn. Univ. Profs. English, Soc. Textual Scholarship. Lutheran. Office: U Calif Dept English 405 Hilgard Ave Los Angeles CA 90095-1530 Office Phone: 310-825-1175. Business E-Mail: wortham@humnet.ucla.edu.

WORTHEN, KEVIN, dean, law educator; AS, Coll. Ea. Utah, 1978; BA summa cum laude, Brigham Young U., 1979, JD summa cum laude, 1982. Law clerk for Judge Malcolm R. Wilkey U.S. Ct. Appeals, Columbia Cir., 1982—83; Judge Byron R. White U.S. Supreme Ct., 1984; atty. Jennings, Strouss & Salmon, Phoenix, 1984—87; Fullbright scholar U. Chile Law Sch., 1994; prof. law Brigham Young U., J. Ruben Clark Law Sch., 1987—, assoc. dean, 1999—2004, dean, 2004—. Chmn. Utah State Constl. Revision Commn. Contbr. articles to law jours. Order of Coif. Mem.: Ariz. State Bar Assn. Office: Brigham Young U J Reuben Clark Sch Law 340 JRCB Provo UT 84602 Office Phone: 801-422-6383. E-mail: worthenk@lawgate.byu.edu. *

WORTHING, CAROL MARIE, retired minister; b. Duluth, Minn., Dec. 27, 1934; d. Truman James and Helga Maria (Bolander) W.; children: Gregory Alan Beatty, Graydon Ernest Beatty. BS, U. Minn., 1965; MDiv, Northwestern Theol. Seminary, 1982; DMin, Grad. Theol. Found., Notre Dame, Ind., 1988; MBA in Ch. Mgmt., Grad. Theol. Found., Donaldson, Ind., 1993; cert., Austin Presbyn. Theol. Sem., 2001; PhD, Grad. Theol. Found., 2002. Cert. Episcopal Diocese of Tex., 2003. Secondary educator Ind. (Minn.) Sch. Dist., 1965-78; teaching fellow U. Minn., 1968-70; contract counselor Luth. Social Svc., Duluth, 1976-78; media cons. Luth. Media Svcs., St. Paul, 1978-80; asst. pastor Messiah Luth. Ch., Fargo, ND, 1982-83, vice pastor, 1983-84; assoc. editor Luth. Ch. Am. Ptnrs., Phila., 1982-84; editorial assoc. Luth. Ptnrs. Evang. Luth. Ch. Am., Phila. and Mpls., 1984—2004; parish pastor Resurrection Luth. Ch., Pierre, SD, 1984-89; assoc. pastor Bethlehem Luth. Ch., Cedar Falls, Iowa, 1989-90; exec. dir. Ill. Conf. Chs., Springfield, 1990-96, Tex. Conf. of Chs., 1996—2003; ret., 2003. Asst. pastor Messiah Luth. Ch., Fargo, N.D., 1982-84; mem. pub. rels. and interpretation com. Red River Valley Synod, Fargo, 1984-86, mem. ch. devel., Pierre, 1986-87; mem. mgmt. com. office comm. Luth. Ch. in Am., N.Y.C., Phila., 1984-88; mem. mission ptnrs. S.D. Synod, 1988, chmn. assembly resolutions com., 1988; mem. pre-assembly planning com., ecumenics com., chmn. resolutions com. N.E. Iowa Synod, 1989-90; mem. ch. and society com., 1990-96; ecumenical com., 1995-96; Luth. Ecumenical Rep. Network, 1995—2003; mem. Cen. and So. Ill. Synod, 1996; mem. S.W. Tex. Synod, 1996—2003, mem. ecumenical com., 1998-2001; mem. ecumenical com. Mpls. Area synod and St. Paul Area synod ELCA, 2004—; nat. edn. cons. Am. Film Inst., Washington, 1967-70; chaplain state legis. bodies, Pierre, 1984-89; mem. exec. bd. Luth. Ecumenical Rep. Network for Region 4, Evang. Luth. Ch. in Am., 2002-03; preacher Nat. Cathedral, Washington, 2002. Author: Cinematics and English, 1967, Peer Counseling, 1977, Tischrede Lexegete, 1986, 88, 90, Way of the Cross, Way of Justice Walk, 1987, Introducing Collaboration as a Leadership Stance and Style in an Established Statewide Conference of Churches, 1993, The Anointing of Jesus--A Christological Necessity, 2001. Co-facilitator Parents of Retarded Children, 1985; bd. dirs. Countryside Hospice, 1985; cons. to adminstrv. bd. Mo. Shores Women's Ctr., 1986. Named John Macquarrie fellow, Grad. Theol. Found., 2002, homilist, Tex. Day, Washington Nat. Cathedral, 2002. Mem. NAFE, Nat. Assn. Ecumenical Staff (chair of site selection com. 1991-92, chair of scholarship com. 1993-94, mem. profl. devel. com. 1993-94, chair program planning com. 1996, bd. dirs. 1995-96), Pierre-Ft. Pierre Ministerium (v.p. 1986-87, pres. 1987-88). Democrat. Avocations: writing prose and poetry, concerts, theater, art, photography. Home: 5555 Dewey Hill Rd # 106 Edina MN 55439 Personal E-mail: cworthi@winternet.com. *Ecumenism is, I believe, about full coherence between our ecclesiology and our ethics. The Spirit of God calls the church to come together for a compassionate purpose: to respond to all who suffer, so that the world might be transformed into God's own vision of peace, justice, and love.*

WORTHING, LOUIE FABIAN, III, plastic surgeon; b. Wharton, Tex., Feb. 28, 1947; s. Louie Fabian Jr. and Imogene (Cogburn) W. BA in Biology, Baylor U., Waco, Tex., 1969; MD, U. Tex., Galveston, 1973. Diplomate Am. Bd. Plastic and Reconstructive Surgery. Owner Aesthetic Biotherapy Ctr., Houston, 1993-95, L. Fabian Worthing III MD PA, Houston, 1980—. Bd. trustees, pres. bd. Pallen Corp., Houston. Bd. trustees Houston Grand Opera, 1988-96. Fellow ACS; mem. AMA, Texas Medical Assn., Am. Bd. Plastic Surg., Am. Soc. Plastic and Reconstructive Surgeons, Am. Soc. Aesthetic Plastic Surgeons, Champions Golf Club, Bentwater Golf Club, Houstonian Club, Univ. Club. Office: 17070 Red Oak Dr Ste 307 Houston TX 77090-2616 Office Phone: 281-440-7797.

WORTHINGTON, BRUCE R., lawyer, energy executive; b. 1949; BA in Econs. cum laude, Claremont McKenna Coll.; JD, U. Calif., Davis. Bar: Calif. 1974. Joined law dept. Pacific Gas and Electric Co., 1974, sr. counsel, chief counsel corp., 1991—94, v.p., gen. counsel, 1994—95, sr. v.p., gen. counsel, 1995—97, PG&E Corp., San Francisco, 1997—. Corp. rep. Calif. Minority Counsel Prog. Mem.: ABA (vice chair Sect. Pub. Utility, Comm., and Transp. Law), Calif. Bar Assn., San Francisco Bar Assn. Office: PG&E Corp One Market Spear Tower Ste 2400 San Francisco CA 94105 Office Phone: 415-267-7133. E-mail: Bruce.Worthington@pge-corp.com. *

WORTHINGTON, DANIEL GLEN, lawyer, educator; b. Rexburg, Idaho, Aug. 15, 1957; BA magna cum laude, Brigham Young U., Provo, Utah, 1982, MEd, 1986, EdD, 1989, JD cum laude, 1989; LLM in Taxation, U. Fla., Gainesville, 2002. Bar: Utah 1990. Asst. to assoc. dean students Brigham Young U., 1986—88, cons., 1987—89, mgr. planned giving, tech. cons., 1989—90, adj. prof. law and edn., 1989—; asst. dean students Coll. Eastern Utah, 1985—86; assoc. dean, exec. dir. devel. Porterville Coll. Found., 1990—91; prin. Worthington & Assoc., Provo, Utah, 1991—93; mng. atty., ptnr. Walstad & Babcock, Provo; assoc. dean U. SD Sch. Law, 1994—95, exec. v.p. found., 1995—2001; pres. Wealth Mgmt. Group, WE Consulting. Assoc. v.p. gen. counsel U. Ctrl. Fla. Found., Orlando, adj. faculty Masters of Tax Program; sr. cons. Fla. Hosp. and the U. S.D. Bus. Sch., 1997—2001; cons. Citigroup Trust Svcs., 1997—2001; sr. cons. Fla. Hosp., 1997—99, v.p. gen. counsel, 1999—2003; bd. dirs. SD Trust Co. Editor-in-chief jour. Edn. and Law Perspectives, 1986-88, co-chair, exec. adv. bd., dir., 1988-91; mem. editl. bd. Planned Giving Design Ctr., 2002—, Endowment Devel. Svc., 1999—; contbr. articles to profl. jour. Exec. v.p. SD Planned Giving Coun., 1994-2001; nat. assembly del. Nat. Com. on Planned, 1994—; mem. Nat. Valuation Task Force, 2002-04; pres. Greater Orlando Planned Giving Round Table, 1999—2004; v.p., gen. counsel Fla. Hosp. Found., 1999-2003; pres. Wealth Mgmt. Group, 2003-06, Worthington Consulting Group, 2006—; sr. cons., maranatha vols. Internat., 1998—, Fla. conf. of Seventh-Day Adventists, 2000-03, Cmty. Found. of Ctrl. Fla. Boys & Girls Club of Ctrl. Fla., 2002—04, Robert Langford Family Found., 2003, Glenda Morgan Family Found., 2004—, Rocky Mountain Adventist Health Care Found., Denver, 2005-, Boca Raton Cmty. Hosp. Found., 2006-; pres. Family Bank Design Ctr., 2002—. With USAFR, 1982-88. Fellow Boy Scouts Am.; mem. Supreme Ct. Hist. Soc., Federalist Soc., mem., Am. Judicature Soc., 1994; Nat. Soc. Fund Raising Exec., Nat. Eagle Scout Assn., Scouting Heritage Soc. (life), Phi Kappa Phi. Personal E-mail: worthingtongroup@aol.com.

WORTHINGTON, GEORGE RHODES, retired naval officer; b. Louisville, July 11, 1937; s. William Bowman and Elizabeth (Frost) W.; m. Sydna Anne Alexander, Mar. 28, 1981 (div. Oct. 1990); children: Rhodes Ballard, Graham Rankins, Greer Anne. BS, U.S. Naval Acad., 1961; postgrad., USMC, Quantico, Va., 1975-76, Nat. War Coll., 1978-79. Commd. ensign USN, 1961, advanced through grades to rear adm., 1989, communications officer USS Halsey Powell San Diego, 1961-63, flag lt., aide comdr. cruiser-destroyer Flotilla Seven, 1963-65, exec. officer Underwater Demolition Team Eleven Coronado, Calif., 1965-68, ops. officer USS Strong Charleston, S.C., 1969-71, exec. officer Naval Spl. Warfare Group Saigon, Vietnam, 1971-72, comdg. officer SEAL Team One Coronado, 1972-74, naval attache Def. Attache Office Phnom Penh, Cambodia, 1974-75, comdg. officer Undersea Warfare Group One Coronado, 1976-78, program sponsor Office of Chief of Naval Ops. Washington, 1979-85; comdr. Naval Spl. Warfare Group One, Coronado, 1985-87; chief of staff Spl. Ops. Command Europe USN, Stuttgart, Fed. Republic Germany, 1987-88; dep. asst. sec. of def. (spl. ops.) Def. Dept., Washington, 1988-89; comdr. Naval Spl. Warfare Command, Coronado, 1989-92; mktg. agent, cons. PIDEAC Inc., Coronado, 1992-96. Naval adv. IFG Ltd.; with Burdeshaw Assoc., Inc.; former v.p. govt. rels. WarRoom Rsch., Inc.; bd. dirs. ZODIAC N.Am., WESCAM-Sonoma, Inc., Spl. Ops. Warrior Found. Decorated D.S.M., Legion of Merit (2), Def. Superior Svc. medal, Meritorious Svc. medal. Mem. Res. Officers Assn. (past chpt. pres.), U.S. Parachute Assn., Underwater Demolition Team-Seal Assn. (life), Mayflower Soc. D.C. (life), Naval Acad. Alumni Assn., Naval Inst., Navy League San Diego, Nat. Def. Indsl. Assn. (life), Army-Navy Club, Army-Navy Country Club. Republican. Episcopalian. Avocations: masters swimming, skiing, sport parachuting. Address: 1118 Pacifica Ave Chula Vista CA 91913-1550 Fax: 619-216-1712. E-mail: grw7@cox.net.

WORTHINGTON, JOHN M., retail executive; With Famous-Barr divsn. May Dept. Stores; with Kohl's Corp., Menomonee Falls, Wis., 1993—, sr. v.p., territory dir. NE region, exec. v.p., dir. stores, 2005—. Mem. retail adv. bd. Inst. Mktg. Brigham Young U. Marriott Sch. Mgmt. Office: Kohls Corp N56 W17000 Ridgewood Dr Menomonee Falls WI 53051-5660 Office Phone: 262-703-7000. *

WORTHINGTON, MELVIN LEROY, minister, writer; b. Greenville, NC, June 17, 1937; s. Wilbur Leroy and Alma Lee (Braxton) W.; m. Anne Katherine Wilson, Sept. 12, 1959; children: Daniel Edward, Lydia Anne. Diploma, Imperial Detective Acad., Cin., 1965; B.Bibl.Edn., Columbia Bible Coll., SC, 1959; B.Th., Luther Rice Sem., Jacksonville, Fla., 1967, B.Div., 1969, M.Th., 1970, D.Th., 1974; M.Ed., Ga. State U.-Atlanta, 1979; EdD, Vanderbilt U., 1998. Ordained to ministry, Central Conf. Free Will Baptists, 1957. Pastor Union Chapel Free Will Bapt. Ch., Chocowinity, NC, 1959-62, Palmetto Free Will Bapt. Ch., Vanceboro, NC, 1959-62, First Free Will Bapt. Ch., Darlington, SC, 1962-66, Wesconnett Free Will Bapt. Ch., Jacksonville, Fla., 1967, First Free Will Bapt. Ch., Amory, Miss., 1967-72, Albany, Ga., 1972-79; exec. sec. Nat. Assn. Free Will Bapt., Inc., Antioch, 1979—2002, chmn. Sunday Sch. bd., 1975-77, asst. moderator, 1977-79, chmn. grad. study com., 1976-77, exec. sec. emeritus, 2002—; pastor Liberty Free Will Bapt. Ch., Ayden, NC, 2003—. Clk. S.C. State Assn. Free Will Bapt., Florence, 1966-67; asst. moderator Ga. State Assn. Free Will Bapt., Moultrie, 1973-74, moderator, 1975-79; pres. Ga. Bible Inst., Albany, 1978 Editor in chief: Contact mag., 1979—2002, author editorial, 1980—2002; contbr. articles to profl. jours. Adv. bd. Nat. Fedn. Decency, 1985; nat. bd. dirs. Christian Leaders for Responsible TV, 1986 Mem. Evang. Press Assn., Religious Conf. Mgmt. Assn. (dir. 1983, v.p. 1986, pres. 1989-92), Nashville C. of C., Future Farmers Am. (N.C. Farmer degree 1955, Am. Farmer degree 1957). Democrat. Mem. Free Will Baptist Ch. Office: Nat Assn Free Will Bapt Inc 5233 Mount View Rd Antioch TN 37013-2306 Office Phone: 252-746-3132. *The basic principle which has guided, governed and guarded my life has been a burning desire to find, follow and finish the will of God.*

WORTHINGTON, ROBERT FLETCHER, JR., lawyer; b. Knoxville, Tenn., July 17, 1931; s. Robert Fletcher Worthington and Rachel Ann Boggs; m. Julie McCrary (dec.); children: Julia Elizabeth Worthington Farry, Katherine Louisa Worthington Kinnard; m. Carole Lynch Worthington; 1 child, Cassandra Lynch. LLD, U. Tenn., 1957. Bar: Tenn. 1957, DC 1977. Assoc. Baker & Baker, Knoxville, 1957—59; ptnr. Baker, Young, Young & Baker, Knoxville, 1959—63, Baker Worthington, Knoxville, 1963—94; of counsel Baker, Donelsen, Bearman, Caldwell & Berkowitz, Knoxville, 1994—. Gen. counsel Tenn. Valley indsl. com. Tenn. Gas Assn. and NeWire, Inc. Mem. past pres. coun. Tenn. Bus. Roundtable; past vice chmn. Tenn. Higher Edn. Commn.; gen. counsel World's Fair, Knoxville, 1982; mem. adv. bd. Cumberland trail conf. Cumberland Trail State Pk.; mem. adv. bd. Florence Crittenton Agy., Inc. Devel. Coun., Cmty. Sch. Arts; chmn. bd. govs. Club LeConte; bd. dirs. East Tenn. Intermodal Transp. Commerce Ctr., Inc., Boathouse Benevolent Soc., Inc., Knoxville Zool. Soc., East Tenn. Hist. Soc. 1st lt. inf. US Army, 1953—60. Named to Dean's Cir., U. Tenn. Coll. Law-, Best Lawyers in Am., 1991—. Mem.: ABA, D.C. Bar Assn., Knoxville Bar Assn., Tenn. Bar Assn., Phi Delta Phi. Office: Baker Donelson Bearman Caldwell & Berkowitz Ste 2200 900 S Gay St Knoxville TN 37902 Office Phone: 865-549-7000. Office Fax: 865-633-7200. Business E-Mail: rworthington@bakerdonelson.com.

WORTHINGTON, SANDRA BOULTON, lawyer; b. Phila., July 12, 1956; BA with high distinction, U. Va., 1978; JD, Temple U., 1983. Bar: Pa. 1983, US Dist. Ct. (ea. dist.) Pa. 1984. Summer clk. Ct. of Common Pleas Montgomery County, Pa., 1981; legal intern Peruto, Ryan & Vitullo, Phila., 1982-83; assoc. Michael D. Fioretti Law Office, Phila., 1983-84; founding ptnr. Stocker & Worthington Law Office, Jenkintown, Pa., 1984—2005; sr. atty. Worthington Law Group, Jenkintown, Pa., 2005—. Legal counsel Phila. Women's Squash Racquets Assn., 1985—. Mem. Pa. Trial Lawyers Assn., Pa. Bar Assn., Montgomery County Bar Assn. Avocations: small business consulting, squash, tennis. Office: Worthington Law Group The Rectory Ste 2 436 Old York Rd Jenkintown PA 19046-2840

WORTHINGTON, TRACY, retired operations research specialist; b. Wichita, Kans., Mar. 6, 1939; s. Maurice Glenn Worthington and Thelma Evelyn Mendenhall; m. Margaret Eloise Ward, May 20, 1961; 1 child, Kimberly Marie. BS, Wichita State U., 1972; M in Engring., Tex. A & M U., College Station, 1976. EIT Kans. State Bd., 1972. Machinist, toolmaker, draftsman, pvt. sector aviation industry, Wichita, 1956—72; ops. rsch. analyst, pub. sector Petersburg, Va., 1981—95; ret. Fed. Govt., 1995. With USAF, 1961—65. Mem.: Air Force Assn. (life). Home Phone: 251-575-7057. Personal E-mail: tmew@frontiernet.net.

WORTHINGTON, WILLIAM ALBERT, III, lawyer; b. June 26, 1950; s. William Albert Jr. and Patricia Lou (Reynolds) W.; children: Elizabeth Clark, Emily Robin, Katherine Anne, William Jackson. BS, U. Utah, 1972; JD, Washington and Lee U., 1976. Bar: Tex. 1976, U.S. Dist. Ct. (so. dist.) Tex. 1977, U.S. Ct. Appeals (5th cir.) 1977, U.S. Ct. Appeals (11th cir.) 1981, U.S. Supreme Ct. 1981, U.S. Dist. Ct. (we. dist.) Tex. 1982, U.S. Dist. Ct. (ea. dist.) Tex. 1986, U.S. Dist. Ct. (no. dist.) Tex. 1993. Assoc. Sewell & Riggs, Houston, 1976—82, ptnr., 1982—89, shareholder, 1990—94; ptnr. Strasburger & Price, LLP, Houston, 1994—. Exec. editor Washington and Lee Law Rev., 1976; contbr. articles to law jours. Active Houston YMCA, Amnesty Internat. U.S.A., ARC; del. state bar of Tex. to Rep. Cuba, 2001. Mem. Am. Law Inst., Def. Rsch. Inst., Product Liability Adv. Coun., Houston Bar Found., Tex. Bd. Legal Specialization (cert. civil trial lawyer, personal injury trial lawyer), U.S. Cycling Fedn., Sierra Club. Office: Strasburger & Price LLP 1401 Mckinney Ste 2200 Houston TX 77010-3033 Home Phone: 713-661-2977; Office Phone: 713-951-5600. Business E-Mail: william.worthington@strasburger.com.

WORTHLEY, HAROLD FIELD, retired minister, educator; b. Brewer, Maine, Nov. 3, 1928; s. Herbert Morrison and Aline May (Field) W.; m. Barbara Louise Bent, June 25, 1955; children: Susan Louise Field, Laura May, David Bruce. AB, Boston U., 1950, MA, 1951; STB, Harvard Div.

Sch., 1954, STM, 1956, ThD, 1970. Ordained to ministry United Ch. of Christ, 1954. Min. Congl. chs., Maine, N.H. and Mass., 1952-62; assoc. prof. religion, chaplain Wheaton Coll., Norton, Mass., 1963-77; exec. sec., archivist Congl. Christian Hist. Soc., Boston, 1971—2004; exec. dir. Am. Congl. Assn., 1999—2004; libr. Congl. Libr., Boston, 1977—2004, libr. emeritus, 2004—. Editor Bull. of Congl. Library, 1976—2004, Hist. Intelligencer, 1980-86. Author: Inventory of the Records of the Particular Churches of Massachusetts, 1620-1805, 1970; contbr. articles to profl. jours. Fellow Pilgrim Soc., Congl. Christian Hist. Soc. Home: 14 Mansfield Ave Norton MA 02766-2212 E-mail: blwhfw@msn.com.

WORTHY, K(ENNETH) MARTIN, retired lawyer; b. Dawson, Ga., Sept. 24, 1920; s. Kenneth Spencer and Jeffrie Pruett (Martin) W.; m. Eleanor Vreeland (Blewett), Feb. 15, 1947 (dec. July 26, 1981); children: Jeffrie Martin, William Blewett; m. Katherine Teasley (Jackson), June 17, 1983. Attended, The Citadel, 1937-39; PhB, Emory U., 1941; MBA cum laude, Harvard U., 1943; JD cum laude, Emory U., 1947. Bar: Ga., 1947; D.C., 1948. Assoc. Foley and Lardner (formerly Hopkins, Sutter, Hamel, and Park), Washington, 1948-51, ptnr., 1952-69, 72-90, sr. counsel, 1991—; chief counsel IRS, 1969—72; asst. gen. counsel Treasury Dept., 1969—72. Mem. Nat. Coun. Organized Crime, 1970-72; cons. Justice Dept., 1972-74. Co-author: (with John M. Appleman) Basic Estate Planning, 1957; contbg. articles to profl. jour. Del. Montgomery County Civic Fedn., 1951—61, D.C. Area Health and Welfare Coun., 1960—61; pres. Sea Island Property Owners Assn., 2004—05; chmn. dept. fin., mem. diocesan coun. Episc. Diocese, Washington, 1969—70; trustee Associated Marine Inst. Found., 1999—2002, Ga. Wilderness Inst., 1997—2003, emeritus, 2003—; trustee St. Simons Island Libr. Found., 2000—, chmn., 2001—05; fellow Aspen Inst., 1982—92; trustee St. John's Coll., Annapolis and Santa Fe, 1987—93, 1995—2001, Sherman Found., Newport Beach, Calif., 1991—; mem. coun. Emory U. Law Sch., 1976—2001, chmn., 1993—95, emeritus, 2001—; bd. dirs. Assn. Citadel Men, 1964—68; trustee Chelsea Sch., 1981—2001, trustee emeritus, 2001—. Capt. US Army, 1943—46, 1951—52. Recipient Army Commendation Ribbon, 1945; Treasury Exceptional Svc. Award and medal, 1972; IRS Commr. Award, 1972; Disting. Alumnus Award, Emory U., 1992. Fellow Am. Bar Found., Am. Coll. Tax Counsel (bd. regents 1980-88, chmn. 1985-87), Atlantic Coun. (counselor 1989-99); mem. ABA (coun. taxation sect. 1965-69, 72-75, chmn. 1973-74, del. Nat. Conf. Lawyers and CPAs 1981-87, ho. of dels. 1983-89, chmn. audit com. 1985-90; Disting. Svc. award taxation sect. 2004), Fed. Bar Assn. (nat. coun. 1969-74, 77-79), Ga. Bar Assn., D.C. Bar, Am. Law Inst., Am. Tax Policy Inst. (trustee 1989-98), Rotary, Chevy Chase Club, Met. Club, Sea Island Club, Ivy League Club (pres. 2002-03), Harvard Club N.Y.C., Phi Delta Theta, Phi Delta Phi, Omicron Delta Kappa. Office: Foley and Lardner 3000 K St NW Ste 500 Washington DC 20007-5143 Personal E-mail: kmartinworthy@aol.com. Business E-Mail: kworthy@foley.com.

WORTHY, PATRICIA MORRIS, lawyer, educator; b. Ft. Benning, Ga., May 28, 1944; d. Walter and Ruby Mae (Lovett) Morris. AA, Queensborough C.C., 1964; BA, Bklyn. Coll., 1966; JD, Howard U., 1969. Bar: DC 1971. Trial atty. NLRB, Washington, 1969—71; dep. gen. counsel ACTION, Washington, 1971—74; assoc. Dolphin, Branton, Stafford & Webber, Washington, 1974—77; dep. asst. sec. for regulatory functions HUD, Washington, 1977—80; adj. prof. Howard U. Sch. Law, 1979—82; chmn. D.C. Pub. Svc. Commn., 1980—91, Washington Met. Area Transit Commn., 1980—91; chief of staff Office of Mayor Sharon Pratt Kelly, Washington, 1991—92; prof. law Howard U., Washington, 1992—2001; dean acad. affairs Howard U. Law Sch., Washington, 2001—02, 2003—04, interim dean, 2002—03; prof. law Howard U., Washington, 2004—. Chmn. DC Jud. Nomination Commn., 1992-05, mem., 2005-06. Bd. dirs. Nat. Black Child Devel. Inst., 1975-80, Anacostia Econ. Devel. Corp., 1970-74; chmn. Occupl. Safety and Health Bd., Washington, 1979-80; trustee WETA-TV Channel 26, 1984-94. Mem. ABA, Nat. Conf. Black Lawyers, Nat. Conf. Bar Examiners (multistate profl. responsibility com. 1986-89), World Peace Through Law (chairperson young lawyers sect. 1973-75). Office: Howard U Sch Law Van Ness & Connecticut Ave NW Washington DC 20001 Office Phone: 202-806-8061.

WORTIS, AVI See AVI

WORTLEY, GEORGE CORNELIUS, congressman, consultant; b. Syracuse, NY, Dec. 8, 1926; s. George C. and Arlene (Hirsh) W.; m. Barbara Jane Hennessy, May 13, 1950; children: George C. IV, Ann Wortley Lavin, Elizabeth Wortley Ring. BS, Syracuse U., 1948. Newspaper pub., pres. Manlius Pub. Corp., Fayetteville, NY, 1950-92; pres. Nat. Editorial Found., 1968-73; mem. 97th-100th Congresses from 27th N.Y. Dist., 1981-89, mem. Banking, Fin. and Urban Affairs com., mem. Select Com. on Aging, Select Com. on Children, Youth and Family; pvt. bus. cons., investor Washington, 1989—. Pres. Am. Newspapers Reps., 1966—68; bd. dirs. Dierman, Wortley, Zola & Assocs., Washington Solutions. Pres. Hiawatha coun. Boy Scouts Am., 1972-75; mem. Nat. Commn. on Hist. Publs. and Records, 1977-80, Fayetteville Sr. Citizen Housing Commn., 1977-80; mem. allocations com. United Way of Ctrl. N.Y., 1979-81; mem. pub. rels. com. St. Camillus Health Care Ctr., 1971-78; mem. fed. legis. com. Am. Lung Assn., 1974-77; bd. dirs. Crouse-Irving Meml. Hosp. Found., 1975-87, pres. 1979-81; bd. dirs. Am. Heart Assn., Upstate N.Y., 1960-80, chmn. pub. rels. com., 1970-74, chmn. legis. com. 1977, mem. fund raising adv. com., 1974-79; trustee Cazenovia Coll., 1981-94; bd. dirs. Onondaga Hist. Assn., 1980-90; dir. Global Leadership Inst., 1987-2001. Served with MMR, USNR, WWII. Recipient Silver Beaver award Boy Scouts Am., 1973, Silver Antelope award, 1981 Mem. Nat. Newspaper Assn. (legis. com. 1976-80), Greater Syracuse C. of C. (dir. 1979-81), Upstate Coun. Indsl. Editors, LeMoyne Coll. Pres.'s Assocs., Syracuse U. Alumni Assn. (nat. treas. 1973-77), Former Mems. of U.S. Congress Assn., Navy League of U.S., Cosmos Club, Georgetown Club, Coral Ridge Yacht Club, Lions, KC, Kappa Sigma (pres. 1957-59). Republican. Roman Catholic. Office: 1750 K St NW Ste 325 Washington DC 20006-2326

WORTLEY, MICAHEL D., lawyer; b. Tulsa, June 9, 1947; BA with highest honors, So. Meth. U., 1970, JD with honors, 1978; MRP, U. NC, 1973. Bar: Tex. 1978. Shareholder Johnson & Wortley PC, 1985—93, mng. dir., 1993—93; ptnr., co-head Corp. Fin. & Securities Sect. Vinson & Elkins LLP, Dallas, 1993—. Mem.: ABA, Dallas Bar Assn. Office: Vinson & Elkins LLP Trammell Crow Center 2001 Ross Ave, Ste 3700 Dallas TX 75201 Office Phone: 214-220-7732. E-mail: mwortley@velaw.com.

WORTMAN, MARLENE STEIN, historian; b. Vienna; d. Leon and Pauline (Lindenbuam) Stein; m. Richard S. Wortman, June 14, 1960; 1 child, Leonie. AB, Syracuse U., 1958; PhD, U. Chgo., 1966; postgrad. in law, Bklyn. Law Sch., 1988-92. Asst. prof. in Am. history Ill. Inst. Tech., Chgo., 1969-77; ind. scholar Inst. for Rsch. in History, NYC, 1977-81, Princeton (N.J.) Rsch. Forum, 1981-87. Pres., v.p. Princeton Rsch. Forum, 1981-85; grants officer Inst. for Rsch. in History, N.Y.C., 1980; coord. Chgo. Met. Area Women's History Group, 1974-76. Editor: (book) Women in American Law, 1985; co-author: The Roads They Made: Women in Illinois History, 1977; contbr. articles to profl. jours; editor: (newsletter) Conf. Group in Women's History, 1975-77. Vice pres. ACLU, N.J., 1982-84, co-chair Women's Rights Com., 1983-87. Conf. grantee on housing N.J. Com. for Humanities, Princeton, 1983; grantee NEH, 1979-81; recipient travel fellowship Am. Philos. Soc., 1975, rsch. fellowship Ill. Inst. Tech., 1974. Mem. NOW, Planned Parenthood. Avocation: hiking. Home: 410 Riverside Dr Apt 91 New York NY 10025-7924

WORTMAN, RICHARD S., historian, educator; b. NYC, Mar. 24, 1938; s. Joseph R. and Ruth (Nacht) W.; m. Marlene Stein, June 14, 1960; 1 child, Leonie. BA, Cornell U., 1958; MA, U. Chgo., 1960, PhD, 1964. Instr. history U. Chgo., 1963-64, asst. prof., 1964-69, asso. prof., 1969-76, prof., 1976-77; prof. history Princeton U., 1977-88, dir. Russian studies, 1982-88; prof. history Columbia U., 1988—; Bryce prof. history, 2001—. Trustee Nat. Coun. for Soviet and Ea. European Rsch., 1983-89; sr. fellow Harriman Inst., 1985-86; bd. dirs. Soc. Ct. Studies, London, 2002—; mem. adv. bd. Kennan Inst., 2005—, Soc.Court Studies, Washington, 2002—. Author: The Crisis of Russian Populism, 1967, The Development of a Russian Legal Consciousness, 1976, (with Leopold Haimson and Ziva Galili) The Making of Three Russian Revolutionaries: Voices from the Menshevik Past, 1987, Scenarios of Power: Myth and Ceremony in Russian Monarchy, vol. I, 1995, vol. II (George L. Mosse prize Am. Hist. Assn., Efim Etkind prize), 2000, Scenario's of Power, 2006. Social Sci. Rsch. Coun. grantee, 1975-76; Guggenheim fellow. Mem. Am. Assn. Advancement Slavic Studies (pres. Mid-Atlantic Slavic Conf. 1982-83), AAUP., Am. Hist. Assn., Soc. for Court Studies. Home: 410 Riverside Dr Apt 91 New York NY 10025-7924 Business E-Mail: rsw3@columbia.edu.

WOSTAL, HOLLY ANN, music educator; b. New Braunfels, Tex., Dec. 22, 1960; d. Samuel Joseph and June Marie Wostal; 1 child, Richard Ross. BA in Music Edn., Houston Bapt. U., 1986; M.Applied Music in Conducting, U. of Houston, 1990. Cert. all level music tchr. Tex., 1986, Mo., 2005. Asst. h.s. dir. Alief Ind. Sch. Dist., Alief, Tex., 1986—88; asst. choral condr. Houston Symphony, 1988—90; cmty. choral/symphonic dir. Lee Coll., Baytown, Tex., 1990—93; elem. music tchr. Sheldon Ind. Sch. Dist., Houston, 1991—92, Pasadena Ind. Sch. Dist., Pasadena, Tex., 1992—93; head h.s. choral dir. Bastrop Ind. Sch. Dist., Bastrop, Tex., 1998—2004; jr./sr. h.s. choral dir. Carl Junction R-1 Sch. Dist., Carl Junction, Mo., 2004—06. Music coord. and condr. City of Baytown, Tex., 1992—93; choir dir. First United Meth., Bastrop, 2001—02, First Christian Ch., Ruidoso, N.Mex., 1997—98, St. John's United Meth., Baytown, 1992—93. Scholar Grad. scholar, MD Anderson, 1988, Dept. of Music scholar, Houston Bapt. U., 1984—86. Mem.: Mo. Choral Dirs. Assn. Avocations: travel, hiking, crossword puzzles, cooking. Home: 1709 Dogwood Dr Joplin MO 64801 Office: Freeman Health Sys 3201 McClellan Joplin MO 64801 Home Phone: 417-623-3164.

WOTEKI, CATHERINE ELLEN, nutritionist; b. Ft. Leavenworth, Kans., Oct. 7, 1947; d. Joseph Jeremiah and Catherine (Costello) O'Connor; m. Thomas Henry Woteki, June 7, 1969. BS, Mary Washington Coll., 1969; MS, Va. Poly. Inst. and State U., 1971, PhD, 1973. Registered dietitian. Asst. prof. Drexel U., Phila., 1975-77; project dir. Congl. Office of Tech. Assessment, Washington, 1977-80; group leader USDA, Washington, 1980-83; dep. dir. Nat. Ctr. for Health Stats., Washington, 1983-90; dir. Food and Nutrition Bd., Washington, 1990-93; dep. assoc. dir. for sci. Office of Sci. and Tech. Policy, Washington, 1994-95; undersec. food safety USDA Office of Food Safety, Washington, 1996—2001; dean agrl. Iowa State U., 2002—05; global dir. sci. affairs Macs, Inc., 2005—. Contbr. articles to profl. jours. Named Outstanding alumna Va. Poly. Inst. and State U., 1987; recipient Elijah White award Nat. Ctr. for Health Stats., 1987, Spl. Recognition award USPHS, 1987, Staff Achievement award Inst. of Medicine, 1991. Mem. Am. Inst. Nutrition, Am. Dietetic Assn. Coun. on Rsch., Inst. Food Technologists, Am. Pub. Health Assn., Inst. Medicine Office Phone: 703-821-4900.

WOTHERSPOON, MARY RUTH, artist, writer; b. Greenville, SC, Feb. 3, 1924; d. Sigmond and Margaret Heyn Sanger; m. William Wallace Wotherspoon, Dec. 28, 1985; m. Eugene Thomas Swigart, Jr. (dec.); children: Thomas John, Stephen Herrick, Margaret Elizabeth, Mary Catherine. BA, Toledo U., 1976. Bd. dirs. Conlon Svc. Ctr., Toledo, 1974—85, Child Daycare Ctr., Toledo, 1964—66. Editor (also illustrator): Poems and Prose by Margot Sanger, 1979; illustrator Johnny Bushytail, 1957; author (also publisher): So Here I Am: But Where Did I Come From?: An Adoptee's Search for Identity, 1994; one-man shows include Sanger Libr., Toledo, Ohio, 1994, The Scarab Club, Detroit, 1992, Monkey Tree Gallery, N. Mex., 2003. Founding sustainer emeritus Art Mus. Aides, Toledo, 1957—2006; mem. Jr. League of Toledo, 1946—2006; mem. women's com. Det. Inst. Arts, Mich., 1992—94. Mem.: Alliance Francaise of Toledo, Nat. Mus. Women Arts, N.Mex. Women in Arts, Garden Club Mich., Santa Fe Garden Club. Republican. Episcopalian. Avocations: art, skiing, golf, aerobics, reading. Home: 3101 Pecos Trail #691 Santa Fe NM 87505

WOTIPKA, CHRISTINE MIN, education educator; BA in Internat. Rels. and French, U. Minn., Twin Cities, 1993; MA in Sociology, Stanford U., 1999, PhD in Internat. Comparative Edn., 2001. Vol. U.S. Peace Corps, Thailand, 1993—95; econ. rschr., English editor 1st Econ. Rsch. Inst., 1995—96; rsch. asst. Comparative Sociology Workshop, 1996—2001; cons. MentorNet, 2001; asst. prof. edn., dir. master's program in internat. and comparative edn. Stanford (Calif.) U., 2001—03; global fellow, vis. asst. prof. internat. inst. UCLA, 2003—04; vis. scholar, acting asst. prof., sch. edn. Stanford Univ., 2004—. Faculty affiliate Expansion and Impact of World Human Rights Regime project, 2002—; MacArthur Consortium affiliate Ctr. for Internat. Security and Coop., 2000—; mem. adv. bd. sci. and tech. TV Digital Turbulence, 2002—. Office: Stanford U Sch Edn 485 Lasuen Mall Stanford CA 94305-3096

WOTT, JOHN ARTHUR, retired arboretum and botanical garden executive, horticulture educator; b. Fremont, Ohio, Apr. 10, 1939; s. Arthur Otto Louis and Esther Wilhelmina (Werth) W.; children: Christopher, Timothy, Holly. BS, Ohio State U., 1961; MS, Cornell U., 1966, PhD, 1968. Mem. staff Ohio State Coop. Extension Svc., Bowling Green, 1961-64; rsch. asst. Cornell U., Ithaca, NY, 1964-68; prof. Purdue U., West Lafayette, Ind., 1968-81; prof. Ctr. Urban Horticulture U. Wash., Seattle, 1981—2006, prof. emeritus, 2006—; assoc. dir. Ctr. Urban Horticulture U. Wash., Seattle, 1990-93, acting dir., 2004—05; dir. arboreta Washington Park Arboretum, Seattle, 1993—2005. Writer columns for Nursery Mgmt. Profession, Balls and Burlap, Am. Nurseryman, The Arboretum Found.; contbr. articles to profl. jours. and papers including Nursery Mgr. Profl., Balls and Burlap, Arboreteum Found. Bull., Am. Nurseryman. Mem. Am. Soc. Hort. Sci. (com. chmn. 1967-82), Am. Assn. Bot. Gardens and Arboreta, Internat. Plant Propagators Soc. (internat. pres. 1984, internat. sec.-treas. 1985—2006). Avocations: music, antiques. Office Phone: 206-543-8602. Personal E-mail: jwott10623@aol.com. Business E-Mail: jwott@u.washington.edu.

WOUK, HERMAN, writer; b. NYC, May 27, 1915; s. Abraham Isaac and Esther (Levine) W.; m. Betty Sarah Brown, Dec. 9, 1945; children: Abraham Isaac (dec.), Nathaniel, Joseph. AB with gen. honors, Columbia U., 1934; LHD (hon.), Yeshiva U., 1954; LLD (hon.), Clark U., 1960; LittD (hon.), Am. Internat. Coll., 1979; PhD (hon.), Bar-Ilan U., 1990, Hebrew U., 1997; DLitt (hon), George Washington U., 2001, Trinity Coll., 1998. Writer radio programs for various comedians, NYC, 1935; asst. writer weekly radio scripts comedian Fred Allen, 1936-41. Presdl. cons. to U.S. Treasury, 1941; vis. prof. English Yeshiva U., 1952-57; scholar-in-residence Aspen Inst. Humanistic Studies, 1973-74 Author: (novels) Aurora Dawn, 1947, The City Boy, 1948, Slattery's Hurricane, 1949, The Caine Mutiny, 1951 (Pulitzer Prize award for fiction, 1952), Marjorie Morningstar, 1955, Youngblood Hawke, 1962, Don't Stop the Carnival, 1965, The Winds of War, 1971, War and Remembrance, 1978, Inside, Outside, 1985 (Washingtonian Book award, 1986), The Hope, 1993, The Glory, 1994, A Hole in Texas, 2004, (dramas) The Traitor, 1949, The Caine Mutiny Court-Martial, 1953, (comedy) Nature's Way, 1957, (non-fiction) This is My God, 1959, The Will to Live On, 2000, (screenplays for TV serials) The Winds of War, 1983, War and Remembrance, 1986. Trustee Coll. of V.I., 1961-69; bd. dirs. Washington Nat. Symphony, 1969-71, Kennedy Ctr. Prodns., 1974-75. Exec. officer U.S.S. Southard USNR, 1942-46, PTO. Recipient Richard H. Fox prize, 1934, Columbia U. medal for Excellence, 1952, Alexander Hamilton medal, 1980, U. Calif.-Berkeley medal, 1984, Golden Plate award Am. Acad. Achievement, 1986, USN Meml. Found. 'Lone Sailor' award, 1987, Yad Vashem KaZetnik award, 1990, Bar Ilan U. Guardian of Zion award, 1998, USCD medal U. Calif.-San Diego, 1998. Mem. Naval Res. Assn., Dramatists Guild, Authors Guild, Internat. Platform Assn. (Ralph Waldo Emerson award 1981), PEN Clubs: Bohemian (San Francisco); Cosmos, Metropolitan (Washington); Century Assn. (N.Y.C.). Jewish. Office: care BSW Literary Agy 303 Crestview Dr Palm Springs CA 92264

WOVSANIKER, ALAN, lawyer, educator; b. Newark, Mar. 19, 1953; s. Harold and Sally (Gooen) Wovsaniker. AB, Brown U., 1974; JD, Harvard U., 1977. Bar: N.J. 1977. Law clk. to presiding judge U.S. Dist. Ct. N.J., Camden, 1977-78; ptnr. Lowenstein Sandler PC, Roseland, NJ, 1978—. Adj. prof. Seton Hall Law Sch., 1988—91, Rutgers U. Law Sch., 1989—95; chmn. dist. ethics com. Supreme Ct. Contbr. articles to profl. jours. Mem.: Essex County Bar Assn. (trustee 1996—99, chmn. banking law com. 1994—97, chmn. corp. law com. 1999—2003). Office: Lowenstein Sandler PC 65 Livingston Ave Roseland NJ 07068-1791 E-mail: awovsaniker@lowenstein.com.

WOYCZYNSKI, WOJBOR ANDRZEJ, mathematician, educator; b. Czestochowa, Poland, Oct. 24, 1943; came to U.S., 1970; s. Eugeniusz and Otylia Sabina (Borkiewicz) W.; m. Elizabeth W. Holbrook; children: Lauren Pike, Gregory Holbrook, Martin Wojbor. MSEE, Wroclaw Poly., 1966; PhD in Math., Wroclaw U., 1968. Asst. prof. Inst. Math. Wroclaw U., 1968-72, assoc. prof., 1972-77; prof. dept. math. Cleve. State U., 1977-82; prof., chmn. dept. math. and stats. Case Western Res. U., Cleve., 1982-91, dir. Ctr. for Stochastic and Chaotic Processes in Sci. and Tech., 1989—, chmn. dept. stats., 2002. Rsch. fellow Inst. Math. Polish Acad. Scis., Warsaw, 1969-76; postdoctoral fellow Carnegie-Mellon U., Pitts., 1970-72; vis. assoc. prof. Northwestern U., Evanston, Ill., 1976-77; vis. prof. Aarhus (Denmark) U., 1972, U. Paris, 1973, U. Wis., Madison, 1976, U. S.C., 1979, U. N.C., Chapel Hill, 1983-84, Gottingen (Germany) U., 1985, 91, 96, U. NSW, Sydney, Australia, 1988, Nagoya (Japan) U., 1992, 93, 94, U. Minn., Mpls., 1994, Tokyo U., 1997, Princeton U., 1998, U. Paris 6, 2003. Dep. editor in chief: Annals of the Polish Math. Soc., 1973-77; assoc. editor Chemometrics Jour., 1987-94, Probability and Math. Stats., 1988—, Annals of Applied Probability, 1989-96, Stochastic Processes and Their Applications, 1993-99; co-editor: Martingale Theory and Harmonic Analysis in Banach Spaces, 1982, Probability Theory and Harmonic Analysis, 1986, Nonlinear Waves and Weak Turbulence, 1993, Nonlinear Stochastic PDE's: Hydrodynamic Limit and Burgers' Turbulence, 1995, In a Reporter's Eye: The Life of Stefan Banach, 1996, Stochastic Models in Geosystems, 1997; author: (monograph) Martingales and Geometry in Banach Spaces I, 1975, part II, 1978, Burgers-KPZ Turbulence: Göttingen Lectures, 1998; co-author: Random Series and Stochastic Integrals: Single and Multiple, 1992, Distributions in the Physical and Engineering Sciences, vol. 1: Distributional and Fractal Calculus, Integral Transforms and Wavelets, 1997, Introductory Statistics and Random Phenomena. Uncertainty, Complexity and Chaotic Behavior in Engineering and Science, 1998, A First Course in Statistics for Signal Analysis, 2005. Rsch. grantee NSF, 1970, 71, 76, 77, 81, 87—, Office of Naval Rsch., 1985-96. Fellow Inst. Math. Stats.; mem. Am. Math. Soc., Am. Statis. Assn., Polish Math. Soc. (Gt. prize 1972), Polish Inst. Arts and Scis., Racquet Club East. Roman Catholic. Avocations: tennis, music, skiing, sailing, rare books collecting. Home: 3296 Grenway Rd Cleveland OH 44122-3412 Office: Case Western Res U Dept Statistics Cleveland OH 44106 E-mail: waw@po.cwru.edu.

WOYS, JAMES E., health and medical products executive; B in Acctg., Ariz. State U., Tempe; MBA, Golden Gate U., San Francisco. Cons. Arthur Andersen/PriceWaterhouse; dir. corp. tax Found. Health Corp., v.p. fin., CFO; interim CFO, pres. govt. and specialty svcs., mem. exec. oper. team Health Net, Inc. Office: Health Net Inc 21650 Oxnard St Woodland Hills CA 91367 Office Phone: 818-676-6000. *

WOYSKI, MARGARET SKILLMAN, retired geology educator; b. West Chester, Pa., July 26, 1921; d. Willis Rowland and Clara Louise (Howson) Skillman; m. Mark M. Woyski, June 19, 1948; children: Nancy Elizabeth, William Bruno, Ronald David, Wendelin Jane. BA in Chemistry, Wellesley Coll., Mass., 1943; MS in Geology, U. Minn., Mpls., 1945, PhD in Geology, 1946. Geologist Mo. Geol. Survey and Water Resources, Rolla, 1946-48; instr. U. Wis., Madison, 1948-52; lectr. Calif. State U., Long Beach, 1963-67, lectr. to prof. Fullerton, 1966-91, assoc. dean Sch. Natural Sci. and Math., 1981-91, emeritus prof., 1991—. Contbr. articles to profl. jours.; author lab. manuals; editor guidebooks. Fellow Geol. Soc. Am. (program chmn. 1982); mem. South Coast Geol. Soc. (hon. pres. 1974), Mineral Soc. Am. Home: 880 Morningside Dr Apt M-320 Fullerton CA 92835-3577

WOZENCRAFT, JOHN MCREYNOLDS, retired communications engineer; ScD, MIT, 1957. Head. comm. divsn. Lincoln Lab.; prof. elec. engrng. emeritus MIT, Cambridge, Mass. Co-author: Principles of Communication Engrng., 1965. Fellow: IEEE (Alexander Graham Bell medal 2006). Achievements include development of sequential decoding and the signal space approach to digital communication. *

WOZNIAK, STEVE (STEPHEN GARY WOZNIAK), computer scientist, philanthropist; b. San Jose, Calif., Aug. 11, 1950; s. Jerry; m. Alice Robertson, 1980 (div.); m. Candice Clark, 1987 (div.); 3 children; m. Suzanne Mulkern, 1990. BS in computer sci. and elec. engring., U. Calif., Berkeley, 1987; DSc (hon.), NC State U., 2004. Designer calculator chips Hewlett-Packard Co., 1976; co-founder Apple Computer, Inc., 1976, v.p. R&D, 1976—81, designer, 1979—81, re-joined as principal, v.p. engring., 1983—85, cons., 1985—; co-founder CL9 - Remote Control Co., pres., 1985—89; founder US Festivals, San Bernardino, Calif., 1983; co-chmn. Axlon, Inc., Sunnyvale, Calif., 1986—; co-founder Wheels of Zeus (wOz), Los Gatos, Calif., 2002, chmn., CEO, 2002—04, chief tech. officer, pres., 2004—06; co-founder, exec. v.p., chief tech. officer Acquicor Tech. Inc., Irvine, Calif., 2005—. Bd. dirs. Jacent, Danger, Inc., Acquicor Tech. Inc., 2005—; Dem. convention del. (Hart), 1984; former tchr. Co-author (with Gina Smith): iWoz: Computer Geek to Cult Icon: how I invented the personal computer, co-founded Apple, and had fun doing it, 2006. Founder Elec. Frontier Found.; founding sponsor Tech Museum, Silicon Valley Ballet, Children's Discovery Museum, San Jose, Calif. Named to Nat. Inventor's Hall of Fame, 2000, Consumer Electronics Hall of Fame, 2004; recipient Grace Murray Hopper award, Assn. Computing Machinery, 1979, Nat. Medal Tech., presented by Pres. Ronald Reagan, 1985, Fellow award, Computer History Mus., 1997, Heinz Award for Tech., 2000, numerous awards from tech. and cmty. groups. Mem.: Fremason, Charity Lodge (life). Achievements include invention of the first line of Apple products - the Apple I and II computers; influenced the popular Macintosh computer; supports the Los Gatos School Dist., providing students and teachers with hands-on teaching and donations of state-of-the-art tech. equip; sponsored computers for schs. in USSR through US/USSR Iniative, 1990; youngest Fortune 500 man in 1982 at age 27; involved in charitable activities in field of education. Avocation: pets (dogs). Office: Acquicor Tech Inc 4910 Birch St Ste 102 Newport Beach CA 92660 Office Phone: 408-358-6030.

WRAASE, DENNIS RICHARD, utilities executive, accountant; b. Washington, Mar. 15, 1944; s. Richard Harold and Esther Morelle (Cowan) W.;

m. Cecilia Anne Kirby, Dec. 30, 1987; children: Richard Reid, Elisabeth Kirby. BS, U. Md., 1966; MS, George Washington U., 1975. CPA, Md. Acct. Exxon Corp., Balt., 1966-70, fin. analyst Houston, 1970-74; mgr. fin. systems Potomac Electric Power Co., Washington, 1974-78, asst. comptr., 1978-81, dir. computer and gen. svcs., 1981-83, comptr., 1983-92, v.p., 1986-89, sr. v.p., 1989—, CFO, 1996—; exec. v.p. Potomac Capital Investment, Washington, 1999, pres., COO, 2000—; pres., CEO Pepco Holding Inc., 2002—, chmn., 2004—. Pres. Olney Jaycees, Md., 1978; bd. dirs., v.p. Nat. Capital area Boy Scouts Am., Washington, 1987—, Washington Bd. Trade, Federal City Coun., 2001—; bd. dirs. Washington Performing Arts Soc., 2002—, Washington Hosp. Ctr., 2002-, U. Md. Found., 2003-. With USAR, 1967-73; US C. of C., 2004. Mem. AICPA, Fin. Execs. Inst. Democrat. Lutheran. Office: Potomac Electric Power Co 701 NInth St NW Ste 1000 Washington DC 20068 Business E-Mail: drwraase@pepco.com.

WRAE, NATASHA, lawyer; b. 1971; BS in Molecular and Cell Biology, U. Ariz., 1992; JD, U. Balt., 1999. Lic.: Ariz. 1999, Md. 1999, bar: Ariz. Worked for Mayo Clinic, Rochester, Minn.; atty. Law Office of Natasha Wrae, Tucson, 1999—. Former coach Cholla High Sch. Mock Trial Prog.; head coach U. Ariz. Mock Trial Prog.; vol. judge Tucson 4-H. Named one of 40 Under 40, Tucson Bus. Edge, 2006. Mem.: Am. Mock Trial Assn., Am. Civil. Liberties Union, Nat. Assn. Women Bus. Owners, Nat. Assn. Criminal Def. Lawyers, Ariz. Attorneys for Criminal Justice, ABA, Pima County Bar Assn. Office: Law Office of Natasha Wrae 100 N Stone Ave Ste 512 Tucson AZ 85701 Office Phone: 520-624-4224.

WRAGA, WILLIAM GERARD, education educator; b. Teaneck, NJ, Mar. 21, 1957; s. William Francis and Maryjane M. (Conlon) W.; m. Amy Jeanne Schneider, June 26, 1982; children: William Frederic, Ian Thomas. AB, Rutgers U., 1979; MAT, U. Chgo., 1980; EdD, Rutgers U., 1991. Tchr. Hillsborough H.S., Belle Mead, N.J., 1980-81, Green Brook (N.J.) H.S., 1981-84, Mendham (N.J.) H.S., 1984-86; dept. supr. Freehold (N.J.) Twp. H.S., 1986-87; dist. supr. K-12 Bernards Twp. Pub. Schs., Basking Ridge, N.J., 1987-94; adj. asst. prof. Rider U., Lawrenceville, 1994; asst. prof. dept. edn. leadership U. Ga., Athens, 1995-99, assoc. prof., 1999—2004, interim founding head dept. ednl. adminstrn. and policy, 2002—04, prof. dept. ednl. adminstrn. and policy, 2004—05, prof. dept. lifelong edn., adminstrn. and policy, 2005—. Chmn. civics com. N.J. State Dept. Edn., 1988—90, mem. social studies core course proficiencies panel, 1989—91; bd. dirs. N.J. Coun. for Social Studies, 1988—90, chmn. publ. com., 1988—89; mem. exec. bd. N.J. ASCD, 1992—93; mem. adv. com. N.J. Vietnam Vets. Meml. Ednl. Ctr., 1993—94; cons. La. Bd. Regents, 2004—06, Coll. Edn., U. Iowa; presenter in field. Author: Democracy's High School, 1994; contbg. author: Readings in Middle School Curriculum, 1993, Curriculum Issues and the New Century, 1995, Handbook on Teaching Social Issues, 1996, We Gain More Than We Give, 1997, Historical Dictionary of American Education, 1999, Encyclopedia of Education, 2003, Explorations in Curriculum History, 2005, Experiencing Dewey, 2005; exec. editor Focus on Edn. Jour., N.J. ASCD, 1993; co-editor: Rsch. Rev. for Sch. Leaders, 1996, 1998, 2000; guest co-editor Social Edn., 1990, mem. editl. bd. History of Edn. Quar., 2004—, former mem. editl. bd. Jour. Curriculum and Supervision, The Ednl. Forum; contbr. articles and book revs. to profl. jours. Grad. Merit scholar Rutgers U., 1984-85, 85-86; recipient Excellence in Dissertation award Rutgers Grad. Sch. Edn. Alumni Assn., 1992, Russell H. Yeany, Jr. Rsch. award Coll. Edn. U. Ga., 2007. Fellow John Dewey Soc. (bd. dirs. 2000-02); mem. Am. Ednl. Rsch. Assn., Profs. of Curriculum (Factotum 1998-99), Soc. Study Curriculum History (pres. 2001—03), Soc. Profs. Edn. (exec. bd. 2003—05), Phi Delta Kappa, Pi Lambda Theta, Kappa Delta Pi. Office: U Ga Coll Edn Dept Lifelong Edn Adminstrn and Policy 850 College Station Rd Athens GA 30602-4808 Business E-Mail: wraga@uga.edu.

WRAGGE, CHRIS, newscaster; b. Hackensack, June 19, 1970; m. Victoria Silvstedt, June 2000. BA Comm., U. NH. Reporter WMUR-TV, Manchester, NH; sportscaster WVIT-TV, Hartford, Conn.; reporter NBC Sports; correspondent Entertainment Tonight, 1996—97; sports dir. KPRC-TV, Houston, 1998—2004; on-site correspondent PGA Tour Sunday, 2000—04; sportscaster WCBS-TV, NYC, 2004—06; co-anchor CBS2 News at Noon/5, 2006; main anchor WCBS-TV, NYC, 2006—. Avocation: golf. Office: CBS Broadcast Ctr 51 W 52nd St New York NY 10001 *

WRANCHER, ELIZABETH ANN, music educator, opera singer; b. Indpls., Oct. 19, 1930; d. Charles Edwin and Evelyn Louise (Helck) W. MusB, Ind. U., 1955. Opera singer, Europe, 1955-68; asst. prof. music U. South Fla., Tampa, 1968-74; pvt. practice Winter Park, Fla., 1974—; assoc. prof. music U. Ctrl. Fla., Orlando, 1974—2003. Cons. Disney World, Orlando, 1987—; summer tchr. Music Theatre Bavaria, Oberandorf, Germany, 2001. Actress in 3 German movies, 1963-67; opera concert singer, 1968-91; recorded music of Thomas Beversdorf. Past bd. dirs., adv. bd. Orlando Opera Co. Recipient Life Achievement award, 1993, T.I.P. award U. Ctrl. Fla., 1996; Fulbright scholar, Germany, 1955; U. Ctrl. Fla. grantee, 1987. Mem.: Fla. State Music Tchrs. Assn., Fla. Vocal Assn., Nat. Assn. Tchrs. Singing (pres. Ctrl. Fla. chpt. 1996—), Nat. Arts and Letters, Nat. Federated Music Clubs (life), Wed. Music Club (1st v.p. 2004—05, pres. 2005—06, bd. dirs. 2007), Phi Kappa Lambda, Mu Phi Epsilon (life). Republican. Baptist. Achievements include concert recordings in Mozarteum Archives, Salzburg, Austria, Augsburg Germany Archives. Avocations: art, pastels, philosophy, religions. Home: 2630 Amsden Rd Winter Park FL 32792-3513 Home Phone: 407-678-1916; Office Phone: 407-678-1916. Personal E-mail: ewrancher@yahoo.com.

WRATHALL, JAMES R., lawyer; b. Sept. 14, 1962; BS cum laude, Tulane Univ., 1984; JD cum laude, Georgetown Univ., 1987. Bar: Md. 1987, DC 1990. Ptnr., vice chmn. Bankruptcy & Comml. dept. Wilmer Cutler Pickering Hale & Dorr, Washington. Editor (articles): Georgetown Law Jour. Named one of Top Lawyers in Washington, Washingtonian mag., 2004. Mem.: ABA, Am. Bankruptcy Inst. Office: Wilmer Cutler Pickering Hale & Dorr Willard Office Bldg 1445 Pennsylvania Ave NW Washington DC 20004 Office Phone: 202-663-6895. Office Fax: 202-942-8484. Business E-Mail: james.wrathall@wilmerhale.com.

WRAY, BETTY BEASLEY, allergist, immunologist, pediatrician; b. Ga., 1935; MD, Med Coll. Ga., 1960. Diplomate Am. Bd. Allergy and Immunology, Am. Bd. Clin. Lab. Immunology. Intern Talmadge Meml. Hosp., Augusta, Ga., 1960-61, resident in pediatrics, 1962, 64-65, fellow in pediatric allergy, 1966-68; staff mem. Med. Coll. Ga., Augusta, 1979—, prof. pediat. medicine, interim dean Sch. Medicine, v.p. clin. activities, 2000—02, prof. emeritus, 2002—. Mem.: Am. Coll. Allergy, Asthma and Immunology, Am. Acad. Pediat., Am. Acad. Allergy and Immunology, Am. Pediatric Soc. Office: Med Coll Georgia BG 1009 Augusta GA 30912 Office Phone: 706-721-3531. E-mail: bettyw@mail.mcg.edu.

WRAY, CECIL, JR., lawyer; b. Memphis, Nov. 19, 1934; s. Thomas Cecil and Margaret (Malone) W.; m. Gilda Gates, Sept. 11, 1964; children: Christopher A., Kathleen Wray Baughman. Student, U. Va., 1952-53; BA magna cum laude, Vanderbilt U., 1956; LLB, Yale U., 1959. Bar: Tenn. 1959, N.Y. 1961, U.S. Supreme Ct. 1964. Registered counseil juridique, France, 1978-82. Law clk. to justice Tom C. Clark U.S. Supreme Ct., Washington, 1959-60; assoc. Debevoise & Plimpton, NYC, 1960-67, ptnr., 1968-96, of counsel, 1997-99, resident ptnr. Paris, 1976-79. Adj. prof. N.Y. Law Sch., 1997-2001. Co-author: Innovative Corporate Financing Techniques, 1986. Bd. dirs. Search & Care, Inc., N.Y.C., pres., 1981-87; bd. dirs. Episcopal Charities, N.Y., pres., 1995-2002; vestryman St. James' Ch., N.Y.C., 1982-87, warden, 1988-94; trustee Fondation des Etats-Unis, Paris, 1976-79, Ch. Pension Fund; bd. dirs. East Side Comty. Ctr., Inc.; bd. fgn. parishes Episcopal Ch., 1995—; bd. dirs. Hudson Highlands Land Trust; commr. Adirondack Park Agy.; chmn. bd. Ch. Ins. Co. Fellow Am. Coll. Investment Counsel (trustee 1981-86, pres. 1983-84); mem. Am. Law Inst., Assn. Bar City N.Y., Coun. Fgn. Rels., Ausable Club (St. Huberts, N.Y.), Union Club, Century Club, Order of Coif, Phi Beta Kappa. Episcopalian. Home: 47 E 88th St New York NY 10128-1152 Office: Debevoise & Plimpton 919 3rd Ave New York NY 10022-3902

WRAY, CHRISTOPHER ASHER, lawyer, former federal agency administrator; b. Dec. 1966; Grad. cum laude, Yale U., 1989, JD, 1989. Law clk. to Hon. J. Michael Luttig U.S. Ct. Appeals (4th Cir.), 1992—93; atty. King & Spaulding, LLP, Atlanta, 1993—97; asst. U.S. atty. criminal divsn. (No. dist.) Ga. US Dept. Justice, Atlanta, 1997—2001, assoc. dep. atty. gen. Washington, 2001, prin. assoc. atty. gen. criminal divsn., 2001—03, acting asst. atty. gen. criminal divsn., 2003, asst. atty. gen. criminal divsn., 2003—05; ptnr. King & Spalding LLP, Washington, 2005—. Office: King & Spalding LLP 1700 Pennsylvania Ave NW Washington DC 20006 E-mail: cwray@kslaw.com.

WRAY, GERALDINE SMITHERMAN (JERRY WRAY), artist; b. Shreveport, La., Dec. 15, 1925; d. David Ewart and Mary Virginia (Hoss) Smitherman; m. George Downing Wray, June 24, 1947; children: Mary Virginia Hill, Deanie Galloway, George D. Wray III, Nancy Armistead. BFA with honors, Newcomb Art Sch., Tulane U., 1946. Tchr. children's art. One woman shows include Don Batman Gallery, Kansas City, Mo., 1982, Gallery II, Baton Rouge, 1985, McNeese Coll., Lake Charles, La., 1987, Dragonfly Gallery, Shreveport, La., 1987, Barnwell Garden and Art Ctr., Shreveport, 1988, 95, Southdown Mus., Houma, La., 1989, La. State U., Shreveport, 1991, WTN Radio Station, Shreveport, 1993, The Cambridge Club, Shreveport, 1993, Centenary Coll., 1993, Northwestern State U., Natchitoches, La., 1995, Goddard Mus., Ardmore, Okla., 1996, Art Buyers Caravan, Atlanta, 1996, Lockhaven (Pa.) U., 1996, Billingsley Gallery, Pensacola, Fla., 1996, Casa D'Arte, Shreveport, La., 1996, N.E. State U., Monroe, La., 1997, Art Expo, N.Y.C., 1997, Palmer Gallery, Hot Springs Ark., 1998, Tower Art Gallery, Shreveport, La., 1999, Meadows Mus. Retrospective, Shreveport, 2003, Schumpert Hosp. Integrated Medicine, Shreveport, 2003, Midwestern Tex. U., 2003, Wichita Falls, Tex., 2003, Bistineau Art Gallery, Shreveport, La., 2004; group shows include Watercolor USA Springfield, Mo., 1988, Waddell's Gallery, Shreveport, 1988, 91, Water Works Gallery, Dallas, 1990, Southwestern Watercolor Show, 1991 (D'Arches award, Creative Artist award 1997), Masur Mus. Exhbn. (honorable mention 91, 92), Bossier Art Ctr., Bossier City, La., 1992, Irving Art Assn. (honorable mention), 1992, Leon Loard Gallery, Montgomery, Ala., 1993, Ward-Nasse Gallery, N.Y.C., 1993, 97, Soc. Experimental Artists Internat. (1st. place, honorable mention), 1993, Nat. Watercolor Soc. Ann., 1994-96, 98, 2003, Art Expo, N.Y.C., 1996, Casa D'Arte, Shreveport, 1996, Art Buyers Caravan, Atlanta, 1996, Off The Wall Gallery, Savannah, Ga., 1997, Art Effects Gallery, Merian, Pa., Boulevard Art Gallery, Macon, Ga., 1997, Visual Inspirations, Newton, N.J., 1997, Mossey Brake Gallery, Tex., 1997, Barnwell Ctr. (with children & grandchildren), Shreveport LA, 1998, Schumpert Imaging Ctr., 2000, Manhattan Arts Mag. Showcase Award, Nat. Assn. Women Artist Traveling Show, Northwestern U., La., 2004, Catherine Lollard Wolf Competitive Show, N.Y.C., 2005, Shreveport Regional Arts Coun. Show, 2005, 06, Meadows Mus., Shreveport, La., 2006; permanent collections include NAWA, Zimmerli Mus., Rutgers Univ., N.J.-Meir Mus., Lynchburg, Va., Goddard Mus. Ardmore, Okla., Bibl. Arts Ctr., Dallas, La. State Capitol Bldg., Lockhaven Mus., Pa., LSUS Med. Ctr., Shreveport, LA., Shacknow Mus., Plantation, Fla., Meadows Mus., Shreveport, La., Integrated Medicine Schumpert Wellness Ctr., Shreveport, Midwestern U., Tex., Northwestern U., Natchitoches, La., Catherine Lollard Wolfe Exhibit, N.Y.C. Art chmn. Jr. League, Shreveport, 1955-60; bd. dirs. Holiday-in-Dixie Cotillion, Shreveport, 1974-76. Inducted into Visual Artists Hall of Fame, Shreveport, La., 1998. Mem. Nat. Assn. Women Artists, Nat. Watercolor Soc. (signature mem. 1994, 96), Southwestern Watercolor Soc. (signature mem. 1991), La. Watercolor Soc. (signature mem. 1990), La. Artists Inc. (elected mem.), Internat. Soc. Exptl. Artists (signature mem.), We. Fedn. Soc. Artists (signature mem.), Watercolor Soc. Houston (signature mem.), Ga. Water Color Soc. (signature mem.). Episcopalian. Avocation: tennis. Home: 573 Spring Lake Dr Shreveport LA 71106-4603 Personal E-mail: jerrywray@bellsouth.net.

WRAY, KENT, academic administrator; m. Wanda Wray. BS in Physics, Washburn U.; BS in Civil Engring., Kans. State U.; MS in Civil Engring., Air Force Inst. Tech.; PhD in Civil Engring., Tex. A&M U. Engr. Kans. Hwy. Dept.; chmn. dept. civil engring. Tex. Tech. U.; dean engring. and tech. Ohio U.; provost and sr. v.p. for acad. and student affairs Mich. Technol. U., Houghton, 2000—05, prof. civil engring.; provost, exec. vice chancellor academic affairs U. Mo.-Rolla, 2006—. Chair Ohio Engring. Deans Coun., 1990. Contbr. articles to profl. jours. Served in USAF, 1968—76, served in USAFR, 1976—90. Recipient Coll.-level Halliburton Outstanding Rsch. award, Halliburton Outstanding Tchr. award. Fellow: ASCE. Office: U Missouri-Rolla 204 Parker Hall 1870 Miner Cir Rolla MO 65409 Office Phone: 573-341-4138. *

WRAY, ROBERT, lawyer; s. George and Ann (Moriarty) W.; m. Lila Keogh (dec.); children: Jennifer, Edward, Hillary. BS, Loyola U., 1957; JD, U. Mich., 1960. Bar: DC, Ill. 1960. Assoc. Hopkins & Sutter, Chgo., 1964—69; gen. counsel Agy. for Internat. Devel., 1969—71; sr. counsel TRW, Inc., 1972—73, Export-Import Bank of the U.S., 1974—79; prin. Robert Wray Assocs., 1979—86; internat. ptnr. Pierson, Ball & Dowd, 1986—87; prin. Robert Wray Assocs., 1988—; spec. counsel Graham & James, 1988—97; ptnr. Holland & Knight, Washington, 1997—2003; mng. mem. Robert Wray PLLC, Washington, 2003—. Recipient medal of superior honor Dept. of State. Mem.: Chevy Chase Club, Annapolis Yacht Club, Talbot Country Club, Met. Club, Bretton Woods Com. Office: 1150 Connecticut Ave NW Ste 350 Washington DC 20036

WRAY, THOMAS JEFFERSON, lawyer; b. Nashville, July 17, 1949; s. William Esker and Imogene (Cushman) W.; m. Susan Elizabeth Wells, Aug. 19, 1972; children: William Clark, Caroline Kell. BA, Emory U., 1971; JD, U. Va., 1974. Bar: Tex. 1974, U.S. Dist. Ct. (so., no. and ea. dists.) Tex. 1976, U.S. Ct. Appeals (5th and 11th cirs.) 1976, U.S. Supreme Ct. 1987. Assoc. Fulbright & Jaworski, L.L.P., Houston, 1974-82; ptnr. Fulbright & Jaworski, Houston, 1982—. Editor (assoc.): Tex. Employment Law Handbook, 2005—07; contbr. chapters to books. Mem. ABA, Coll. Labor and Employment Lawyers, Houston Bar Assn., Houston Mgmt. Lawyers Forum (chmn. 1981-82), Briar Club, Phi Beta Kappa. Republican. Episcopalian. Home: 3662 Ella Lee Ln Houston TX 77027-4105 Office: Fulbright & Jaworski 1301 Mckinney St Ste 5100 Houston TX 77010-3095 Office Phone: 713-651-5585. Business E-Mail: tjwray@fulbright.com.

WRAY, WILSON E., JR., lawyer; b. Buffalo, Mar. 6, 1971; BA in Polit. Sci. and Am. Hist. cum laude, U. Rochester, 1993; JD, Georgetown U., 1996. Bar: Tex. 1996, US Dist. Ct. (no. and ea. dists. Tex.). Sr. atty. Loewinsohn Flegle, L.L.P., Dallas. Bd. dirs. Hope Internat., Dallas. Named a Rising Star, Tex. Super Lawyers mag., 2006. Mem.: Dallas Bar Assn. *

WREGHITT, RANDALL L., theater producer; BS in Journalism, Iowa State U., 1978. Prodr.: (Broadway plays) The Beauty Queen of Leenane, 1998 (Drama Desk award outstanding new play, 1998), Electra, 1998, Band in Berlin, 1999, The Lonesome West, 1999, The Real Thing, 2000, One Flew Over the Cuckoo's Nest, 2001 (Tony award best revival of a play, 2001), Hedda Gabler, 2001, Metamorphoses, 2002 (Drama Desk award outstanding new play, 2002), Golda's Balcony, 2003, Little Women, 2005, The Lieutenant of Inishmore, 2006, Grey Gardens, 2006, (off-Broadway) Three Tall Women, 1994, Zombie Prom, 1996, As Bees in Honey Drown, 1997. Named one of People to Watch in 2007, Sunday Star Ledger. *

WREN, CHRISTOPHER R., computer scientist, researcher; s. Richard G. and Mary Louise Wren. PhD, MIT, Cambridge, Mass., 2000. Founder Perceptive Networks Inc., Waltham, Mass., 2000—01; rsch. scientist MERL, Cambridge, 2001—. Rsch. asst., similar MIT, 1989—2000. Mem.: IEEE, Assn. Computing Machinery. Achievements include research in science of artificial perception and the design of human computer interfaces. Office: MERL 8th Fl 201 Broadway Cambridge MA 02139 Office Phone: +1 617.621.7519. Office Fax: +1 617.621.7550. Business E-Mail: wren@merl.com.

WREN, GAYDEN, playwright, theater director; b. NYC, May 24, 1961; s. Gayden and Mary Alice Wren; m. Sara Holliday, July 7, 2001. BA, Oberlin Coll., 1983. Entertainment editor NY Times Syndicate, NYC, 1995—. Author: (book) A Most Ingenious Paradox: The Art of Gilbert & Sullivan, (theater) As If, Baseball, Sex and Other Facts of Life, Ernest, An Evening with Gilbert & Sullivan, A Gilbert & Sullivan Christmas Carol, ID, Moonlight and Midnight, A Night on the Tomb, Swords & Frenchmen, Tales from the Bible, Two for the Show, Very Truly Yours, Gilbert & Sullivan, The World According to Gilbert & Sullivan; dir.: (Operas) The Sorcerer, HMS Pinafore, The Pirates of Penzance, Patience, Iolanthe, Princess Ida, The Mikade, Ruddigore, The Gondoliers, Utopia, Limited. Dir. The Gilbert & Sullivan Light Opera Co. of LI, Merrick, NY, 1984—; artistic dir. The New Punctuation Army Inc., NYC, 1984—; chmn. Citizens for Classic Movies, NYC, 1992—; artistic dir. Troupers Light Opera, New Canaan, Conn., 2002—03. Home: 19-92 78th St East Elmhurst NY 11370 Office: New York Times Syndicate 500 Seventh Ave 8th Fl New York NY 10018 Office Phone: 212-556-4994. Business E-Mail: wreng@nytimes.com.

WREN, JOHN D., advertising executive; married; 2 children. BA, MBA, Adelphi U., 1975. Mgmt. cons. Arthur Anderson & Co.; with Norton Simon Inc., Needham Harper Worldwide; joined Diversified Agency Services (subs. Omnicom Group, Inc.), 1986, CFO, pres., 1990—93, chmn., CEO, 1993—95; pres. Omnicom Group, Inc., NYC, 1995—97, pres., CEO, 1997—. Office: Omnicom Group Inc 437 Madison Ave Fl 9 New York NY 10022-7001 *

WREN, ROBERT JAMES, aerospace engineering manager; b. Moline, Ill., May 12, 1935; m. Jordis Wren; children: James, Patrick, Kiley. BSCE, U. Tex., 1956; MSCE, So. Meth. U., 1962; doctoral candidate, U. Houston. Registered profl. engr. Tex. Engring. aide Ctrl. Power and Light Co., Corpus Christi, 1954; sta. clk. City of Austin (Tex.) Power Plant, 1954-55; assoc. engr., hydraulic engr. U.S. Bur. of Reclamation, Austin, 1955-57; structural test engr. Gen. Dynamics, Ft. Worth, 1957-62; sr. structural dynamics engr., mgr. vibration and acoustic test facility NASA-Manned Spacecraft Ctr., Houston, 1962-63, 63-66, head exptl. dynamics sect., 1965-70; mgr. Apollo Spacecraft 2TV-1 CSM Test Program, 1966-68, Apollo Lunar Module-2 Drop Test Program, 1968-70; mgr. structural design space sta., space base, lunar base, mars mission NASA-Manned Spacecraft Ctr., Houston, 1970-73; mgr. structural design and devel., space shuttle carrier aircraft-747 NASA Johnson Space Ctr., Houston, 1973-74, mgr. structural divsn. space shuttle payload systems, 1974-84; mgr. engring. directorate for space shuttle payload safety NASA-Johnson Space Ctr., Houston, 1984-94, mem. space shuttle payload safety rev. panel, 1984-2000, alternate chmn. space shuttle payload safety review panel, 1990-2000, mgr. engring. dir. vehicle and payload flight sys. safety, 1994-2000. Mem. NASA Internat. Space Sta. Flight sys. safety panel, 1994-2000, dir. safety and mission assurance Internat. Space Sta. Program Office, United Space Alliance Hdqs., Houston, 2000—. Pres. Friendswood Little League Baseball, 1980-83; bd. dirs. Bay Area YMCA, Houston, 1982—, chmn., 1983-84. Recipient Sustained Superior Performance award NASA, Personal Letter of Commendation, George Low NASA Apollo Program, Outstanding Svc. award NASA, Group Achievement awards NASA; Paul Harris fellow Rotary. Mem. Space Ctr. Rotary (dir., treas., sec., v.p. 1979-85, pres. 1985-86, Rotary dist. 5890/govt. rep. 1986-87, area coord. 1987-89, zone leader 1988-89, gov.'s aide 1989-90, chmn. dist. assembly 1989-90, 93-94, fin. com. 1989-91, Rotary Nat. award for Space Achievement Found./co-founder, bd. dirs. 1984—), Rotary World Health Found. Plastic Surgery for Children (co-founder, bd. dirs. 1985—), Rotary Space Meml. Found. (co-founder, bd. dirs. 1986—, co-founder, bd. dirs. Space Ctr. Rotary Endowment Found., 1987—). Methodist. Avocations: snow and water skiing, running, scuba diving, tennis, sailing. Home: PO Box 1466 Friendswood TX 77549-1466 Office: United Space Alliance Hdqrs 1150 Gemini Houston TX 77058 E-mail: robert.j.wren@usahq.unitedspacealliance.com.

WRENN, CHRISTOPHER JAY, physician; b. Margarita, Panama Canal Zone, July 16, 1947; s. Earl Walton and Maxine Elizabeth (Luther) Wrenn; m. Nancy Margaret Bowie, June 27, 1970; children: Kristina Elizabeth, Courtney Bowie. BS, Baylor U., 1969; MD, U. Nebr., 1973. Diplomate Am. Bd. Pediatrics, Am. Bd. Allergy and Immunology. Intern pediatrics Children's Med. Ctr., Dallas, 1973-74, resident pediatrics, 1974-76, chief resident pediatrics, 1976-77; staff pediatrician Los Barrios Unidos Community Clinic, Dallas, 1977-78; fellow allergy and immunology Med. Br. U. Tex., Galveston, Tex., 1978-80; practice medicine specializing in allergy Graves-Gilbert Clinic, Bowling Green, Ky., 1980-83, Wichita Clinic, 1983-84, Allergy Clinic, Tyler, Tex., 1984—. Staff pediatrician Dallas County Juvenile Detention Ctr., 1975—78, Buckner Bapt. Children's Home, 1977—78. Co-author: Pediatrics by Self Instruction, 1982. Fellow: Am. Coll. Allergists, Am. Acad. Pediat.; mem.: Am. Acad. Allergy and Immunology. Presbyterian. Avocation: writing fiction and poetry. Office: Allergy Clinic PA 1128 Medical Dr Tyler TX 75701 Office Phone: 903-593-8273.

WRENN, SUSAN STROUD, language educator; b. Memphis, Feb. 20, 1951; d. David Stroud Jr. and Mildred Harrison Stroud; m. Michael David Wrenn, July 19, 1980. Student, Miss. State Coll. Women, Columbus, 1969—70, Phillips County CC, Helena, Ark., 1970; BS in Edn., U. Ark., Fayetteville, 1973; MA, U. Tex., Arlington, 1979. Cert. tchr. Tex. Spanish tchr. DeSoto HS, Tex., 1974—98, Dallas County CCs, 1980—82, Lewisville Ind. Sch. Dist., Tex., 1998—2007, chmn. fgn. lang dept. Marcus HS, 2003—04, coord. langs. other than English Tex., 2004—. State sponsor, bd. dirs. Pan Am. Student Form, Tex., 1981—91; project dir. Mid. Sch. Spanish Advanced Placement Grant, Tex., 2005—06, Fgn. Lang. Assistance Program Grant, Washington, 2004—; Spanish instr. Mountain View campus Dallas County CC, Dallas, 1980—82, Spanish instr. Cedar Valley campus, 1982. Fellow, Am. Assn. Tchrs. French, 2006. Mem.: NEA, AAUW (officer), Metroplex Fgn. Lan. Suprs., Nat. Assn. Dist. Suprs. Fgn. Lang., Tex. Fgn. Lang. Assn., Am. Assn. Tchrs. Spanish and Portuguese, Lewisville Edn. Assn., Am. Coun. Tchrs. Fgn. Lang., Tex. State Tchrs. Assn., Sigma Delta Pi, Phi Sigma IOta, Alpha Delta Kappa, Alpha Delta Kappa (prs.). Methodist. Avocations: travel, reading. Home: 702 Laramie Dr Lewisville TX 75077-2846

WRIGHT, ALAN, lawyer; b. Ft. Worth, May 17, 1956; BA with high honors, U. Tex., 1978, MPA, 1982, JD with honors, 1982. Bar: N.Mex. 1982, Tex. 1985, admitted to practice: US Ct. Appeals (10th Cir.) 1982, US Dist. Ct. (Dist. N.Mex.) 1983, US Dist. Ct. (No. Dist.) Tex. 1984, US Ct. Appeals (5th Cir.) 1984, US Dist. Ct. (We. Dist.) Tex. 1986, US Supreme Ct. 1987, US Dist. Ct. (So. Dist.) Tex. 1992, US Dist. Ct. (Ea. Dist.) Tex. 1992, US Ct. Appeals (3rd Cir.) 1992, US Ct. Appeals (11rd Cir.) 1992, US Ct. Appeals (6th Cir.) 1993, US Ct. Appeals (8th Cir.) 1995, US Ct. Appeals

(Fed. Cir.) 2005. Ptnr., appellate law Haynes and Boone LLP, Dallas. Mem.: Dallas Bar Found., Dallas Bar Assn., ABA, State Bar N. Mex., Phi Beta Kappa. Office: Haynes and Boone LLP 901 Main St Ste 3100 Dallas TX 75202-3789 Office Phone: 214-651-5575. Office Fax: 214-200-0614. Business E-Mail: alan.wright@haynesboone.com.

WRIGHT, ANDREW, English literature educator; b. Columbus, Ohio, June 28, 1923; s. Francis Joseph and Katharine (Timberman) W.; m. Virginia Rosemary Banks, June 27, 1952; children: Matthew Leslie Francis, Emma Stanbery. AB, Harvard U., 1947; MA, Ohio State U., 1948, PhD, 1951. Prof. English lit. U. Calif., San Diego, 1963—, chmn. dept. lit., 1971-74; dir. U. Calif. Study Center, U.K. and Ireland, 1980-82. Vis. prof. U. Queensland, Australia, 1984, Colegio de la Frontera Norte, San Antonio del Mar, Baja, Calif., 1991-92. Author: Jane Austen's Novels: A Study In Structure, 1953, Joyce Cary: A Preface to His Novels, 1958, Henry Fielding: Mask and Feast, 1965, Blake's Job: A Commentary, 1972, Anthony Trollope: Dream and Art, 1983; Fictional Discourse and Historical Space, 1987; contbg. author numerous books, articles to profl. jours., numerous short stories to lit. mags.; editorial bd. Nineteenth Century Fiction, 1964-86. Bd. dirs. Calif. Coun. Humanities, 1983-87. Guggenheim fellow, 1960, 70; Fulbright Sr. Research fellow, 1960-61 Fellow Royal Soc. Lit.; mem. MLA, Jane Austen Soc., Athenaeum (London), Trollope Soc., Santayana Soc., Phi Beta Kappa. Home: 7227 Olivetas Ave La Jolla CA 92037-5335 Office: U Calif San Diego Dept Lit La Jolla CA 92093-0410 Business E-Mail: ahwright@ucsd.edu.

WRIGHT, BAGLEY, venture capitalist, entrepreneur, art collector; m. Virginia Bloedel; children: Merrill, Charles, Robin, Bing. BA, Princeton U., 1946. With Daily Mirror, Newsweek; real estate developer Pentagram Corp., Harbor Properties; chmn Physio Control Corp., 1968—80. Developer Space Needle, Seattle. Named one of Top 200 Collectors, ARTnews Mag., 2004, 2006. Avocation: Collector of Contemporary Art; Japanese Art. Office: 407 Dexter Ave Seattle WA 98109

WRIGHT, BARBARA CLARE, business librarian; b. Mt. Holly, NJ, Dec. 6, 1943; d. Charles Hodge and Charlotte Elizabeth (Brown) W. BA, Temple U., 1966; MS, Drexel U., 1972; MA, Temple U., 1985. Circulation asst. Temple U., Phila., 1967-72, asst. to dir., 1972-75, asst. to dir. of pub. svcs., 1975-77, reference libr., 1977-80, bus. libr., 1980—2007; ret. Mem. ALA, Pa. Libr. Assn., Spl. Librs. Assn., Assn. Coll. and Rsch. Librs., Drexel U. Libr. Sch. Alumni Assn. Democrat. Home Phone: 215-561-1391; Office Phone: 215-204-3189. Business E-Mail: bwright@temple.edu.

WRIGHT, BETTY REN, children's book writer; b. Wakefield, Mich., June 15, 1927; d. William and Revena Evelyn (Trezise) W.; m. George Albert Frederiksen, Oct. 9, 1976. BA, Milw.-Downer Coll., 1949. With Western Pub. Co., Inc., 1949-78, mng. editor Racine Editl., 1967-78. Author: The Doll House Murders, 1983, Christina's Ghost, 1985, The Summer of Mrs. MacGregor, 1986, A Ghost in the Window, 1987, The Pike River Phantom, 1988, Rosie and the Dance of the Dinosaurs, 1989, The Ghost of Ernie P., 1990, A Ghost in the House, 1991, The Scariest Night, 1991, The Ghosts of Mercy Manor, The Ghost of Popcorn Hill, 1993, The Ghost Witch, 1993, A Ghost Comes Calling, 1994, Out of the Dark, 1995, Haunted Summer, 1996, Too Many Secrets, 1997, The Ghost in Room 11, 1998, A Ghost in the Family, 1998, Pet Detectives, 1999, The Moonlight Man, 2000, The Wish Master, 2000, Crandalls' Castle, 2003, The Blizzard, 2003, Princess for a Week, 2006; contbr. articles to mags. Recipient Alumni Svc. award Lawrence U., 1973, Lynde and Harry Bradley Maj. Achievement award, 1997, numerous awards for books including Mo. Mark Twain award, 1986, 96, Tex. Bluebonnet award, 1986, 88, Young Readers award Pacific N.W. Libr. Assn., 1986, Reviewer's Choice Booklist, Ala. Young Readers award, 1987, Ga. Children's Choice award, 1988, Ind. Young Hoosier Book award, 1989, 96, Children's Choice Book/Internat. Reading Assn.—CBC, 1984, S.C. Children's Choice award, 1995, Okla. Sequoyah Children's Choice award, 1988, 95, award Fla. Sunshine State, 2001, Notable Wis. Author for Youth Lit. award, 2006. Mem.: Coun. Wis. Authors (Juvenile Book award 1985, 1996), Allied Authors, Phi Beta Kappa. Avocations: reading, travel. Home and Office: 6223 Hilltop Dr Racine WI 53406-3479

WRIGHT, BOB (ROBERT CHARLES WRIGHT), diversified technology and services company executive, former broadcast executive; b. Rockville Center, NY, Apr. 23, 1943; m. Suzanne Werner, Aug. 26, 1967; children: Kate, Christopher, Maggie. AB in History, Coll. Holy Cross, 1965; LLB, U. Va., 1968. Bar: N.Y. 1968, Va. 1968, Mass. 1970, N.J. 1971. With GE Co., 1969—70, 1973—80, gen. mgr. plastics sales dept., 1978—80; law sec. to chief judge U.S. Dist. Ct., NY, 1970—73; pres. Cox Cable Comm., Atlanta, 1980—83; exec. v.p. Cox Comm., 1980—83; v.p., gen. mgr. housewares, audio and cable TV ops. GE Co., 1983—84, vice chmn., exec. officer, 2000—; pres., CEO GE Fin. Svcs. Inc., 1984—86, NBC, NYC, 1986—2001, chmn., CEO, 2001—04, NBC Universal, 2004—07. Bd. dirs. GE Co., 2000—, Motion Picture & Television Fund Corp., Damon Runyon Cancer Res. Found.; bd. trustees Am. Film Inst., Mus. Television & Radio; hon. trustee Found. Am. Women in Radio & Television; bd. governors NY - Presbyterian Hosp.; mem. Soc. NY Hosp. Inc.; trustee Coll. Holy Cross; co-founder Autism Speaks, 2005—. Recipient Steven J. Ross Humanitarian of Yr. award, UJA Fedn. NY. Office: GE Co 3135 Easton Tpke Fairfield CT 06431-0001 *

WRIGHT, BONNIE H., middle school educator; b. Raleigh, NC, Sept. 30, 1960; d. William T. and Secunda P. Huxster; m. Tony T. Wright, Aug. 8, 1989 (dec.); 1 child, Josh Gordon. BA in Early Childhood Edn., U. NC, Charlotte, 1982, BA in Intermediate Edn., 1984, BA in Intermediate Edn., 2002. Cert. mentor N.C., 1989. Mid. sch. math tchr. Scotland County Schs., Laurinburg, NC, 1984—88; 5th grade tchr. Charlotte-Mecklenburg Schs., NC, 1988—89, 6th grade tchr., 1989—90, elem. and mid. sch. math tchr., 1992—2000; mid. sch. math tchr. Wake County Pub. Schs., Raleigh, NC, 1991—92; 7th and 8th grade sci. tchr. Charlotte Christian Sch., NC, 2000—07; 7th and 8th grade tchr. Providence Day Sch., NC, 2007—. Migrant edn. instr. Scotland County Schs., Laurinburg, NC, 1984—85; math tutor Charlotte Christian Sch., 2000—07. Vol. Operation Christmas Child Charlotte Christian Schs., 2000—07; Sunday sch. tchr. U. City United Meth. Ch., Charlotte, 1994—98; Bible svc. project Charlotte Christian Schs., 2002—07. Named to Nat. Honor Roll Outstanding Tchrs., 2006; recipient Tchr. of Yr. award, Sycamore Ln. Mid. Sch. in Scotland County, 1987, Unsung Am. Heroes award, ING, 2005. Fellow: N.C. Assn. Educators (assoc.), Internat. Reading Assn. (assoc.), Assn. Christian Schs. (assoc.), PTO (assoc.); mem.: Parent Tchr. Fellowship (assoc.), N.C. Coun. Tchrs. Math. (assoc.), N.C. Sci. Tchrs. Assn. (assoc.), Delta Zeta (life). Dc Statehood Party. Methodist. Avocations: travel, coin collector, piano, cross-stitching, scrapbooking. Office: Providence Day Sch 5800 Sardis Rd Charlotte NC 28270 Home Phone: 704-554-7228; Office Phone: 704-887-7026. Office Fax: 704-887-7042. Business E-Mail: bonnie.wright@providenceday.org.

WRIGHT, BONNIE SHANKLE, assistant principal, choir director; b. Jan. 16, 1960; d. Preston and Adeline Luttrell Shankle; m. James Barry Wright, June 9, 1984; children: Preston, David. B in Music Edn., Ind. U., 1983; MA in Tchg., Bethel Coll., 1990. Cert. ednl. specialist Union U., 2005. Tchr. Covington Elem., Tenn., 1986—99; chorus, drama tchr. Covington HS, 1999—2003; asst. prin. Covington Integrated Arts Acad., 2003—05. Instr. Red Cross, 1983—2004; pianist, bell choir dir. First United Methodist Ch., Covington, 1997—2005, choir dir., 2003—05. Mem.: Alpha Delta Kappa (pres. 2003). Republican. Methodist. Office: Covington Integrated Arts Acad 760 Bert Johnston Covington TN 38019

WRIGHT, BRADLEY ABBOTT, lawyer; b. Des Moines, Nov. 24, 1964; s. James Bradley and Carolyn (Abbott) W.; m. Alisa Labut, Aug. 24, 1993; children: Hannah, Alexandra, John James. BA, Miami U., Oxford, Ohio, 1987; JD, Ohio State U., 1990. Bar: Ohio 1990. Assoc. Roetzel & Andress, Akron, Ohio, 1990-97, ptnr., 1997—. Grad. Leadership Akron, 1998; active Big Bros. and Big Sisters, Inc., Akron, United Way of Summit County, Akron. Mem. Akron Bar Assn. (vice chmn./social chmn.), Transp. Lawyers Assn., Def. Rsch. Inst., Assn. for Transp. Law Logistics and Policy, Am. Trucking Assn., Nat. Assn. R.R. Trial Counsel, USLAW Network, Inc. (bd. dirs.). Home: 91 N Hayden Pkwy Hudson OH 44236-3157 Office: Roetzel & Andress 222 S Main St Akron OH 44308-1533 Business E-Mail: bwright@ralaw.com.

WRIGHT, BURTON, sociologist; b. Detroit, Jan. 31, 1917; s. Burton and Hazel Marie (Thomas) Wright; m. Marie Fidelis Gallivan, Jan. 26, 1942; children: Burton III(dec.), Catherine Margaret(dec.). AA, C.Z. Coll., 1944; BA, U. Wash., 1947, MA, 1949; PhD, Fla. State U., 1972. Enlisted USN, 1937, commd. and advanced through grades to comdr., 1957; dir. Naval Res. Recruiting, 1960-64; ret., 1964; mem. faculty U. Wash., 1947-49, George Washington U., Washington, 1954-60, Rollins Coll., Winter Park, Fla., 1966-69; prof. dept. sociology U. Ctrl. Fla., Orlando, 1972-82, prof. emeritus, 1982-89; ret., 1989; prof. sociology Troy State U., 1991—. Cons. Ford Found., 1951, Dept. Air Force, 1955, U.S. Army Chem. Corps, 1956; mem. faculty Northwestern U., summers 1956-59; vis. prof. sociology Troy U., Dothon; dir. Am. Sociol. Assn. Nat. Honors Program, 1981-89. Author: (with J.P. Weiss and C.M. Unkovic) Perspective: An Introduction to Sociology, 1975, (with V. Fox) Criminal Justice and the Social Sciences, 1978, (with J.P. Weiss) Social Problems, 1980; contbr. articles to publs. Decorated Navy Commendation medal. Fellow Am. Anthrop. Assn.; mem. AAUP, Am. Sociol. Assn. (membership com. 1983-86), Soc. Psychol. Study Social Problems, Am. Acad. Arts and Scis., Soc. Study Social Problems, So. Sociol. Soc., North Ctrl. Sociol. Soc., Univ. Club (Winter Park). Roman Catholic. Home: 502 Dunleith Blvd Dothan AL 36303-2936 Personal E-mail: bw7626@ala.net.

WRIGHT, C. T. ENUS, former academic administrator; b. Social Circle, Ga., Oct. 4, 1942; s. George and Carrie Mae (Enus) W.; m. Mary Stephens, Aug. 9, 1974. BS, Fort Valley State U., Ga., 1964; MA, Atlanta U., 1967; PhD, Boston U., 1977; LHD, Mary Holmes Coll., 2000. Tchr. Ga. Pub. Schs., Social Circle, 1965-67; mem. faculty Morris Brown Coll., Atlanta, 1967-73, divsn. chmn., 1973-77; program dir., asst. provost Eastern Wash. U., Cheney, 1977-81; v.p. acad. affairs Talladega Coll. (Ala.), 1981-82; pres. Cheyney U. Pa., Cheyney, 1982-85; v.p. and provost Fla. Meml. Coll., 1985-89; pres. Internat. Found. and Coord. African-African Am. Summit, 1989-2001; chmn., founder The Light of Hope Inst., 2000—; pres., CEO IFESH, 2001—04; pres. AZ Africa, 2004—. Cons. and lectr. in field; bd. dirs. Internat. Found. Edn. and Self Help, England, Leon Sullivan Trust, South Africa, People's Investment Fund for Africa, Fountain Hills Kiwanis Club, 2006—; chmn. adv. com. AMI Consultants, 2002—. Author: (booklet) The History of Black Historical Mythology, 1980; contbr. articles to profl. jours. Commr. Wash. Pub. Broadcasting, Olympia, 1980—84; exec. com. Boy Scouts Am., Phila., 1982—; Goodwill Amb. State of Ga., 1997—; chmn. com. World Children Relief, 2002—; bd. mem. Fountain Hills Sch., 2007—. Human Rels. scholar, 1969, Nat. Tchg. fellow, Boston U., 1971. Mem. NEA (coms. 1965—), Am. Assn. Colls. and Univs. (coms. 1982—), Am. Hist. Assn. (coms. 1970—), Assn. Study Afro-Am. Life and History (coms. 1965—), Nat. Assn. Equal Opportunity in Higher Edn. (coms. 1982—), Kiwanis Club Fountain Hills (bd. dirs. 2006—), Lions Club, Tuscan Club. Baptist. Address: 17420 E Dull Knife Dr Fountain Hills AZ 85268 Office Phone: 480-837-5534. E-mail: ctwright31@cox.net.

WRIGHT, CAROLYN D., language educator, poet; b. Mountain Home, Ark., 1949; BA, U. Memphis, 1971; MFA, U. Ark., 1976. Lectr. poetry San Francisco State U., 1979—81; prof. English Brown U., Providence, 1983—. Vis. faculty Burren Sch. Art., Ireland, 1996, U. Iowa., 1997, U. Cin., 2004. Author: Terrorism, 1979, Translations of the Gospel Back into Tongues, 1981, Further Adventures With You, 1986, String Light, 1991 (Poetry Ctr. Book award), Just Whistle, 1993, The Lost Roads Project: A Walk-in Book of Arkansas, 1994, The Reader's Map of Arkansas, 1994, Tremble, 1996, Deepstep Come Shining, 1998, Steal Away: Selected and New Poems, 2002, One Big Self, 2003, Cooling Time: An American Poetry Vigil, 2005, numerous poems. Named State Poet RI, 1994—99; recipient Witter Bynner prize for poetry, 1986, Whiting Writers award, 1989, Gov. Award for Arts, RI, 1990, Lila Wallace award, 1992; fellow, Nat. Endowment for Arts, 1981, 1987; Guggenheim fellow, 1987, MacArthur Fellow, 2004. Fellow: Am. Acad. Arts and Scis. Office: Brown U Box 1923 Providence RI 02912 Business E-Mail: Carolyn_Wright@Brown.edu.

WRIGHT, C(ARROLL) LEE, JR., architecture educator; m. Beverly Ann Carroll, 1980; children: Benjamin Carroll, Alexander Lee. BArch, U. Tex., 1963, MArch, 1969. With Hirsch and Cassetti, Elmira, NY, 1964—65, Claude Pendley, Austin, Brook, Barr, Graeber and White, Austin, Pierce/Lacey Assocs., Dallas, 1965; mem. faculty U. Tex., Arlington, 1968—, assoc. prof. arch., 1972—, assoc. dean, 1975—77, dir. arch. program, 1978—79, undergrad. advisor, 1989—99, interim dean Sch. Arch., 1999—2001, assoc. dean Sch. Arch., 1993—99, dir. arch., 2002—04; pvt. practice Lee Wright Assocs., 1968—. Mem. univ. curriculum com. U. Tex., Arlington; bd. dirs. Dallas Arch. Found., 1999—2002; acad. and career counselor Sch. Arch., 2004—. Named Outstanding Advisor, U. Tex. Arlington, 1993. Office: Univ Tex Arlington Sch Arch Rm 203 Box 19108 701 S Nedderman Dr Arlington TX 76019-0108

WRIGHT, CECILIA POWERS, gifted and talented educator; b. Phila., Sept. 30, 1946; d. Robert Francis and Rosemary (Redditt) Powers. BS, West Chester U., Pa., 1968; MS, Pa. State U., 1972; MA, Gratz Coll., Melrose Park, Pa., 1996; EdD, Immaculate U., 2006. Tchr. Haverford Twp. Sch. Dist., Havertown, Pa., 1968—73; author/editor and instr. McGraw Hill, Paoli, Pa., 1973—78; tchr. Lower Merion Sch. Dist., Wynnewood, Pa., 1987—90; gifted tchr. West Chester Area Sch. Dist., 1990—, tchr., 1999—2007; instr. Neumann Coll., Aston, Pa., 2006—. Assoc. prof., cons. Regional Tng. Ctr., Gratz Coll., Randolph, NJ, 1996—; seminar presenter Coll. NJ, Trenton, 1998—2000; adj. prof. Neumann Coll., 2006—. Author (and editor): Careers: A Multicultural View, 1977 (Excellence award, 1977). Leader Girl Scouts U.S., Havertown, 1983—87; chairperson good citizens DAR, Chester County, Pa., 1996—. Named to Leaders in Am. Elem. Edn., Haverford Twp. Sch. Dist., 1971; recipient award, Nat. Band Assn., 2000—01. Mem.: NEA, Band and Orch. Assn. (pres. 2000), Pa. State Edn. Assn. (rep. 1998—). Avocations: painting, travel, bicycling. Home: 15 E Wilmot Ave Havertown PA 19083 Business E-Mail: cwright@wcasd.net.

WRIGHT, CHARLES PENZEL, JR., writer, educator; b. Pickwick Dam, Tenn., Aug. 25, 1935; s. Charles Penzel and Mary Castleman (Winter) Wright; m. Holly McIntire, Apr. 6, 1969; 1 child, Luke Savin Herrick. BA, Davidson Coll., 1957; MFA, U. Iowa, 1963; postgrad., U. Rome, 1963—64. Mem. faculty U. Calif., Irvine, Calif., 1966—83, prof. English, 1976—83; Souder Family Prof. Poetry U. Va., Charlottesville, 1983—. Vis. prof. N.Am. Lit. U., Padua, Italy, 1968—69; disting. vis. prof. U. Degli Studi, Florence, Italy, 1992. Translator: The Storm and Other Poems (Eugenio Montale), 1978 (PEN Translation prize, 1979), Orphic Songs (Dino Campana), 1984; author: (books) The Grave of the Right Hand, 1970, Hard Freight, 1973, Bloodlines, 1975, China Trace, 1977, The Southern Cross, 1981, Country Music - Selected Early Poems, 1982, The Other Side of the River, 1984, Halflife, 1988, Zone Journals, 1988, Xionia, 1990, The World of the Ten Thousand Things, 1990, Quarter Notes, 1995, Chickamauga, 1995 (Lenore Marshall Poetry prize Acad. Am. Poets, 1996), Black Zodiac, 1997 (Pulitzer prize poetry, 1998), Appalachia, 1998, North American Bear, 1999, Negative Blue, 2000, A Short History of the Shadow, 2002, Buffalo Yoga, 2004, Scar Tissue, 2006 (Griffin Poetry prize (internat.), 2007), Littlefoot, 2007. With AUS, 1957—61. Recipient Nat Book award for Poetry, 1983, citation in poetry, Brandeis U. Creative Arts Awards, 1987, L.A. Times Book prize, 1997, award, Nat. Book Critics Circle, 1997, Ambassador Book award, 1998, Poetry prize, Griffen Internat., Can., 2007; fellow Guggenheim fellow, 1976, Ingram Merrill fellow, 1980, 1993; scholar, Fulbright Found., 1963—65. Mem.: Acad. Am. Poets (chancellor), Am. Acad. Arts and Sci., Am. Acad. Arts and Letters, Fellowship of So. Writers. Home: 940 Locust Ave Charlottesville VA 22901-4030 Office: English Dept Univ Va Charlottesville VA 22901

WRIGHT, CHATT GRANDISON, academic administrator; b. San Mateo, Calif., Sept. 17, 1941; s. Virgil Tandy and Louise (Jeschien) W.; children from previous marriage: Stephen Brook, Jon David, Shelley Adams; m. Janice Teply, Nov. 28, 1993. Student, U. Calif., Berkeley, 1960-62; BA in Polit. Sci., U. Calif., Davis, 1964; MA in Econs., U. Hawaii, 1968. Instr. econs. U. Hawaii, Honolulu, 1968-70; mgr. corp. planning Telecheck Internat., Inc., Honolulu, 1969—70; economist State of Hawaii, Honolulu, 1970—71; adminstr. manpower City & County of Honolulu, 1971-72; bus. adminstr., dean. Hawaii Pacific U., Honolulu, 1972-74, v.p., 1974-76, pres., 1976—. Mem. City and County of Honolulu Manpower Area Planning Commn., 1976—82; mem. Mayor's Salary Commn. City and County of Honolulu, 1977—80; mem. Honolulu City Ethics Commn., 1978—84, City and County of Honolulu Labor Market Adv. Coun., 1982—84; bd. dirs. Hawaii Econ. Devel. Corp., 1980—84; trustee Queen's Med. Ctr., Honolulu, 1986—92, Honolulu Armed Svcs. YMCA, 1984—86, Hawaii Maritime Ctr., 1990—92; chmn. bd. trustees Hist. Hawaii Found., 1995—96, trustee, 1990—96; mem. adv. bd. Cancer Rsch. Ctr. Hawaii, 1987; trustee St. Andrew's Priory Sch., 1994—98; bd. dirs. Hawaii Visitors Bur., 1995—97; bd. dir. Downtown Improvement Assn., 1988—96; bd. dirs. Outrigger Duke Kahanamoku Found., 1996—98, Hawaii Opera Theatre, 1997—99; bd. govs. Hawaii Coun. on Econ. Edn., 1998—; trustee Oceanic Inst., 1998—, chmn., 2003—; mem. Hawaii Execs. Coun., 1996—, chmn., 2002, Hawaii Exec. Conf., 2002; bd. govs. Hawaii Med. Libr., 1989—92; mem. adv. bd. Aloha coun. Boy Scouts Am., 1991—2002; trustee Molokai Gen. Hosp., 1991—92; mem. Pacific Asian Affairs Coun., 1998—2001; steering com. Asian Devel. Bank, 2000—. With USN, 1968—70. Recipient Pioneer award Pioneer Fed. Savs. Bank, 1982, Stephen J. Jackstadt award, Hawaii Coun. Econ. Edn., 1998; named Sales Person of Yr., Sales and Mktg. Execs. of Honolulu, 1998; Paul Harris fellow Rotary, 1986; named to Honolulu 100, Honolulu Mag., 2005. Mem.: Hawaii Assn. Ind. Colls. and Univs. (chmn. 1986), Western Coll. Assn. (exec. com. 1989—92), Hawaii Joint Coun. Econ. Edn. (bd. dirs. 1982—88), Nat. Assn. Intercollegiate Athletics (mem. 1985—98, vice chair NAIA coun. of pres. 1994), Assn. Governing Bds. Univs. and Colls., Am. Assn. Higher Edn., Soc. Sci. Assn. (mem. 1994—99), Japan-Am. Soc. Honolulu, Waialae Country Club, Plaza Club (bd. govs. 1992—97), Pacific Club (Honolulu), Outrigger Canoe Club. Republican. Episcopalian. Avocations: hunting, fishing, reading, travel. Office: Hawaii Pacific U Office of Pres 1166 Fort Street Mall Honolulu HI 96813-2708 E-mail: president@hpu.edu. *

WRIGHT, CHRIS, professional sports team executive; b. Eng. arrived in US, 1978; m. Walla Wright; children: Christy, Jeff, Ned. Grad., Carnegie Coll. Phys. Edn., Headingly Leeds, Yorkshire, Eng. Gen. mgr. Maj. Indoor Soccer League Pitts. Spirit, 1981—86, Maj. Indoor Soccer League Minn. Strikers, 1986—87; cons. State of Minn.; pres. Minn. Timberwolves, 2005—. Office: Minn Timberwolves 600 First Ave N Minneapolis MN 55403 *

WRIGHT, CLARK PHILLIPS, computer systems specialist; b. Orange, Tex., Aug. 30, 1942; s. Madison Brown and Mary Elizabeth (Phillips) W.; m. Stacy Charlotte Klutz, June 5, 1965 (div. Oct. 1979); m. Cora Lou Alexandria Schelling, Oct. 31, 1979; 1 child, Isaac Schelling. BA, U. Tex., 1965. Computer programmer Lockheed Electronics Co., Houston, 1965-67; prin. analyst Control Data Corp., St. Paul, 1967-76; computer scientist DBA Systems, Inc., Lanham, Md., 1976-79; engring. specialist Ford Aerospace Corp., Houston, 1979-90, Loral Aerospace Corp., 1990-97, Lockheed Martin Space Mission, 1997—. Precinct chmn. Rep. Party of Tex., 1982-86. Mem. IEEE, Math. Assn. Am., Assn. Computing Machinery, SAR (chartered, sec., treas.), Sons Republic Tex., Info. Sys. Security Assn., Masons, Rotary. Avocations: travel, photography. Home: 5000 Park Ave Dickinson TX 77539-7013 Office: Lockheed Martin Space Ops PO Box 58487 Houston TX 77258-8487 Office Phone: 281-853-3186. Personal E-mail: cpw@ghg.net. Business E-Mail: clark.p.wright@lmco.com.

WRIGHT, CONSTANCE STOREY, retired humanities educator; b. Boston, Mar. 3, 1928; d. Samuel Lame and Dorothy Storey Wright. BA, Scripps Coll., 1950; MA, U. Calif., Berkeley, 1959, PhD, 1965. Instr. English Grinnell Coll., Iowa, 1952—65; asst. prof. U. Colo., Boulder, 1965—69, assoc. prof., 1969—92, prof. emeritus, 1992—; ret., 1992. Adv. bd. Genders, Boulder, 1985—89, Medieval Assn., Rocky Mountain, Tempe, Ariz., 1987—92; rschr. Monterey (Calif.) Mus. Art, 1996—. Editor: Equally in God's Image, 1990; asst. editor: English Lang. Notes, 1965—2003; author (editor): Tales within Tales: Apuleius through Time, 2000. Sec., bd. dirs. Residents Assn., Carmel, Calif., 1993—2000, Preservation Found., Carmel, 2002—. Mem.: MLA, Dante Soc. Am., New Chaucer Soc. Avocations: Asian art, Asian antiques, Latin literature. Home: PO Box 2331 Carmel CA 93921

WRIGHT, CREIGHTON BOLTER, cardiovascular surgeon, educator; b. Washington, Jan. 29, 1939; s. Benjamin Washington and Catherine Adele (Bolter) W.; m. Carolyn Eleanor Craver, Jan. 29, 1966; children: Creighton Bolter, Benson, Kathryn, Elizabeth. BA, Duke U., 1961, MD, 1965; MBA, Xavier U., Cin., 1995. Diplomate Am. Bd. Surgery, Am. Bd. Thoracic Surgery, Am. Bd. Gen. Vascular Surgery. Intern Duke U., Durham, NC, 1965—66; resident in surgery U. Va., Charlottesville, 1966—71; asst. prof., then assoc. prof. George Washington U., Washington, 1974—76; assoc. prof., then prof. surgery U. Iowa, Iowa City, 1976—81; prof. clin. surgery, assoc. dean U. Cin., 1982—; prof. clin. surgery Uniformed Svcs. U., 1982—; dir. dept. surgery Jewish Hosp., Cin., 1989—2003; med. dir. cardiovasc. svcs. Health Alliance Cin., 1999—2003; chief of staff VA Med. Ctr., Cin., 2003—. Councilor Acad. Medicine, 2003—. Editor: Vascular Grafting, 1983, (with others) Venous Trauma, 1983; contbr. articles to med. jours., chpts. to books. Col. USAR, 1966-93. Decorated Bronze Star; recipient Kindred Resident Tchr. award, 1967, Golden Apple Tchg. award, 1975, Tchg. award Jewish Hosp., 2001. Mem.: Greater Cin. Vascular Soc. (pres. 1997—98), Cin. Surgery Soc. (pres. 1996), Midwestern Vascular Surgery Soc., So. Thoracic Surgery Assn., Muller Surg. Soc. (pres. 1985—87), Am. Heart Assn. S.W. Ohio (v.p. 1998—, pres. 2000, Kaplan award 1999, award of excellence 2003), Internat. Soc. Cardiovasc. Surgery, Ctrl. Surg. Assn., Soc. Thoracic Surgery, Am. Assn. Thoracic Surgery, Soc. Vascular Surgery, Soc. Univ. Surgeons, Assn. Acad. Surgery (pres. 1980), Comml. Club, Sigma Chi (Significant Sig award 1993, Hall of Fame 2005), Alpha Omega Alpha. Home: 312 E 2d St Covington KY 41011-1704 Office: Cardiovascular Vascular & Thoracic Surgeons 4030 Smith Rd Ste 300 Norwood OH 45209 Office Phone: 513-421-3494. Personal E-mail: cbw@one.net.

WRIGHT, DANIEL V., career military officer, judge; b. Birmingham, Ala., July 4, 1951; married; 4 children. Grad., US Mil Acad., West Point, NY, 1973; JD, U. Miami, 1980; grad., Army War Coll., Army Command and Gen. Staff Coll., JAG Grad. Course. Bar: Fla. Advanced through ranks to maj. gen. US Army, 1973—2005, with 25th Inf. Divsn. Schofield

Barracks, Hawaii, 1973—77, prosecutor Ft. Dix, NJ, 1980—82, chief adminstrv. law, 1982—85, regimental judge adv. 75th rancher regiment Ft. Benning, Ga., 1985—88, tchr. mil. law br. ctr. for army leadership Command and Gen. Staff Coll. Ft. Leavenworth, Kans., 1988—90, br. chief, 1990—92, dep. staff judge adv. XVIII Airborne Corps Ft. Bragg, 1992—93, legal adv. joint spl. ops. command, 1993—96, staff judge adv. so. European task force Vicenza, Italy, 1996—98, staff judge adv. XVIII airborne corps. Ft. Bragg, 1999—2001, comdr. legal svcs. agy., chief judge ct. criminal appeals, 2001—03, asst. JAG mil. law and ops., 2003—05, asst. JAG, 2005—. Decorated Def. Superior Svc. medal, Legion of Merit, Army Meritorious Svc. medal, Joint Svc. Commendation medal, Army Commendation medal, Army Achievement medal, Armed Forces Expeditionary medal, Humanitarian Svc. medal, Expert Infantryman's Badge, Master Parachutist Badge, Ranger Tab. Office: JAG 2700 Army Pentagon Washington DC 20310-2700 Office Phone: 703-693-5112. *

WRIGHT, DARCY LAUREEN, leadership educator, writer; b. Berkeley, Calif., Apr. 15, 1959; d. Larry Edward Mobraaten and Natalie Paula Wells; m. Kirby Michael Wright, Dec. 28, 1991. MBA, San Diego State U., 2003. Assoc. prodr. Golden Films, Menlo Park, Calif., 1995—2000; sr. prodr. Holiday Channel, San Jose, 2000—01; dir. profl. mentor program Tri-City Med. Ctr., Oceanside, Calif., 2004—. Founder SAT Success, Redwood City, Calif., 1998—2000. Recipient Best Feature award, Santa Clarita Internat. Film Festival, 1998, Peak Performance award, Am. Soc. Trainers and Developers, 2006. Democrat. Avocations: jogging, swimming, writing, travel, gardening. Home: 1604 Marbella Dr Vista CA 92081-5463 Office: Tri-City Medical Center 4002 Vista Way Oceanside CA 92056 Office Phone: 760-940-3170. Personal E-mail: wrightdl@tcmc.com. E-mail: dlwright@tcmc.com.

WRIGHT, DAVID ALAN, environmental toxicology professor, consultant; b. Crayford, Kent, Eng., June 4, 1948; s. Alan Frederick and Ivy May Wright; m. Lee Ann Morgan, Dec. 28, 1990; children: Frederick Casey Scharmen, Robert Francis Scharmen, Joanna Margaret, William David. BSc, Newcastle U., Eng., 1969, PhD, 1973, DSc, 1979. Sr. demonstrator U. Newcastle, England, 1974—79; prof. U. Md. Ctr. Environ. Sci., Chesapeake Biol. Lab., Solomons, Md., 1979—. Pres. Environ. Rsch. Svcs., Balt., 1995—. Author: (text-book) Environmental Toxicology, Environmental Toxicology, Chinese Edition; contbr. over 100 peer rev. articles to profl. jours. Numerous grants, NSF, EPA, NOAA, ACE, US Navy, Md. Port Adminstrn., Md. Dept. Natural Resources, 1979—. Fellow: Inst. Marine Engring. Sci. and Tech.; mem.: Soc. Naval Architects and Marine Engrs., Soc. Environ. Toxicology and Chemistry. Achievements include three patents on water sterilization and ballast water treatment technologies. Office: Univ Md Ctr Environ Sci CBL 1 Williams St Solomons MD 20688 Office Phone: 410-326-7240. Business E-Mail: wright@cbl.umces.edu.

WRIGHT, DAVID ALLEN, professional baseball player; b. Norfolk, Va., Dec. 20, 1982; Draft pick NY Mets, 2001, third baseman, 2004—. Endorsements Hickey Freeman, Nike spikes and batting gloves, Vitamin Water, Wilson David Wright signature glove. Founder David Wright Found., 2005—. Named Va. All-State Player of Yr., 2001, Gatorade Va. HS Player of Yr., 2001, Nat. League Rookie of Yr., NJ Sports Writers, 2004; named to Nat. League All-Star Team, Maj. League Baseball, 2006—07; recipient Most Outstanding Play of Yr. award, This Year in Baseball awards, 2005. Mailing: NY Mets Shea Stadium 123-01 Roosevelt Ave Flushing NY 11368-1699 *

WRIGHT, DAVID BURTON, retired newspaper publishing company executive; b. Fowler, Ind., Aug. 29, 1933; s. Claude Matthew and Rose Ellen (Lavelle) Wright; m. Geraldine F. Gray, May 9, 1964; children: David Andrew, Anne Kathleen. AB, Wabash Coll., 1955. CPA Ind. Audit staff George S. Olive Co. C.P.A.s, Indpls., 1958-63, mgmt. cons., 1963-65; controller Herff Jones Co., 1965-69, corp. controller, asst. sec., 1970-71; asst. bus. mgr. Indpls. Newspapers Inc., 1971-77; asst. sec., treas. Central Newspapers Inc., 1975-79, Muncie Newspapers Inc., 1975-93, Indpls. Newspapers Inc., 1975-93, bus. mgr., 1977-93; sec., treas. Central Newspapers Inc., 1979-89; v.p. Indpls. Newspapers Inc., 1982-93. Mem. St. Francis Hosp. Adv. Bd., Indpls., 1983—99. Sec. St. Francis Hosp. adv. Bd., Indpls., 1986—87, v.p., 1987—91, pres., 1991—93. Served US Army, 1956—58. Mem.: Ind. Assn. CPAs, Knights Columbus, Indpls. Econ. Club. Roman Cath. Home: 6713 Forrest Commons Blvd Indianapolis IN 46227-2396 E-mail: daviddavegerry@aol.com.

WRIGHT, DAVID C., school system administrator; b. Jan. 19, 1951; BS, Bloomsburg State Coll., Pa., 1972; MS in Edn., Bucknell U., Lewisburg, Pa., 2001. Cert. tchr. Pa. Sch. counselor Loyalsock Twp. Sch. Dist., Williamsport, Pa., 1993—2001, dir. student svcs., 2001—03, Williamsport Area Sch. Dist., 2003—. Mem.: ASCD, Pa. Assn. Pupil Svcs. Adminstrs., Nat. Assn. Pupil Svcs. Adminstrs. Office: Williamsport Area Sch Dist 201 W 3d St Williamsport PA 17701

WRIGHT, DAVID JOHN, telecommunications systems specialist, educator; b. London, June 20, 1947; arrived in Canada, 1981; m. Mina Wright; 2 children. BA with honors, Cambridge U., 1968, PhD, 1972. Sr. scientific officer Dept. Environment, London, 1972-76; lectr. Ahmadu Bello U., Zaria, Nigeria, 1976-78, Sussex U., Brighton, United Kingdom, 1978-81; assoc. prof. U. Ottawa, Canada, 1981-87, prof., 1987—. Vis. rschr. Nortel Networks, Ottawa, 1988-89; provider cons. and tng. for the telecomms. industry in wireless networks voice and video over networks, and MPLS. Author: Broadband: Business Services, Technologies and Strategic Impact, 1993 (translated into Japanese, 1994), Telelearning via the Internet, 1999, The Business Case for the Web Based Training, 2000, Voice Over Packet Networks, 2001; contbr. articles to profl. jours. and chpts. to books. Mem. IEEE, Assn. for Computing Machinery. Avocation: piano. Business E-Mail: dwright@uottawa.ca.

WRIGHT, DAVID L., food and beverage company executive; b. Wenatchee, Wash., Mar. 12, 1949; s. Franklin Sven and Mary Elizabeth (Collins) W.; m. Karen Sue Rice, Mar. 28, 1981; children: Kara, Erin, Jonathan, Anna Catherine. BA, U. Calif., Davis, 1971. Chief of rsch. dept. of benefit payments State of Calif., Sacramento, 1972-75; profl. staff mem. com. on agr. U.S. Ho. Reps., Washington, 1975-77; adminstrv. asst., chief of staff Rep. William C. Wampler, Washington, 1977-81; spl. asst. for legis. affairs to Pres. The White House, Washington, 1981-84; dir. govt. affairs PepsiCo Inc., Purchase, NY, 1984-87, v.p. worldwide govt. affairs, 1987—2005; ret. Mem. exec. com. U.S. Coun. for Internat. Bus., 1997-2005; bd. dirs. U.S. C. of C.; vice chair Harvard Ctr. on Media and Child Health, 2004-06. Capt. USAR, 1971-79. Mem Capitol Hill Club.

WRIGHT, DEBORAH C., bank executive; b. Bennetsville, SC, Jan. 30, 1958; BA, Radcliffe, 1979; MBA, JD, Harvard U., 1984. Assoc. corp. fin. First Boston Bank, 1984; dir. mktg. NYC Partnership, Harlem, 1987; apptd. Housing Authority Bd. NYC, 1992, commr., 1994—96; dir. Upper Manhattan Zone Devel. Corp., 1996—99; pres, CEO Carver Bancorp, Harlem, 1999—, chmn., 2005—. Bd. dirs. Carver Bancorp, Inc., Kraft Foods, Time Warner, 2005—. Bd. dirs. Harvard U., Meml. Sloan-Kettering Cancer Ctr., Partnership NYC, Ministers and Missionaries Benefit Bd. Am. Baptist Churches; founding mem. Lower Manhattan Develop. Corp. Named Community Banker of the Year, The Am. Banker, 2003. Office: Carver Bancorp 75 W 125th St New York NY 10027

WRIGHT, DEIL SPENCER, political science professor; b. Three Rivers, Mich., June 18, 1930; s. William Henry and Gertrude Louise (Buck) W.; m. Patricia Mae Jaffke, Aug. 22, 1953; children: David C., Mark W., Matthew D., Lois L. BA, U. Mich., 1952, M in Pub. Adminstrn., 1954, PhD, 1957. Asst. prof. polit. sci. Wayne State U., Detroit, 1956-59; from asst. to assoc. prof. U. Iowa, Iowa City, 1959-67; assoc. prof. U. Calif., Berkeley, 1965-66; prof. U. N.C., Chapel Hill, 1967-83, alumni disting. prof., 1983—; Carl Hatch vis. prof. U. N.Mex., Albuquerque, 1987. Lectr. USIA, Washington, various dates; cons. Office Mgmt. and Budget, Washington, 1979-80. Author: Understanding Intergovernmental Relations, 3d edit., 1988; editor: Federalism and Intergovernmental Relations, 1984, Globalization and Decentralization, 1996; contbr. over 100 articles to various polit. sci. and pub. adminstrn. jours. Mem. dir's. adv. com. NIH, Bethesda, Md., 1970-74, N.C. Coun. on State Goals and Policies, Raleigh, 1973-77, N.C. State Internship Coun., Raleigh, 1985-93. Internat. Inst. Mgmt. research fellow, Berlin, 1977. Fellow Nat. Acad. Pub. Adminstrn.; mem. AAAS, Am. Polit. Sci. Assn., Am. Soc. Pub. Adminstrn. (Waldo Lifetime Career Achievement award), Midwest Polit. Sci. Assn., Policy Studies Orgn., So. Polit. Sci. Assn. (pres. 1981-82). Lodges: Rotary (bd. dirs. Chapel Hill club 1981, 84, 90, v.p. 2000-01, pres. 2001-02). Republican. Methodist. Home: 204 Velma Rd Chapel Hill NC 27514-7641 Office: U North Carolina Dept Polit Sci CB 3265 Chapel Hill NC 27599-3265 Office Phone: 919-962-0414.

WRIGHT, DELL, residential care and treatment facility executive; b. Greenville, SC, Aug. 29, 1944; s. Thomas C. and Marie (Tate) W.; m. Ines R. Teran, Oct 22, 1977; children: Anthony, Andre, Fionna, Al-Jonn. Diploma in computer tech., Control Data Inst., 1969. Electronic tester RCA, Marlboro, Mass., 1970-71; customer svc. rep. Honeywell Info. Systems, Inc., Waltham, Mass., 1971-75; computer technician Bendix Field Engring., Columbia, Md., 1975-78; sr. field engr. Ford Aerospace and Comm. Corp., Palo Alto, Calif., 1978-79; systems integration engr. Kentron Internat./NASA/JPL, Pasadena, Calif., 1979-83; sr. fabrication technician Rockwell Internat., Anaheim, Calif., 1983-84; computer engr. Al-Johi Internat., Dhahran, Saudi Arabia, 1984-85; sr. test engr. Gen. Dynamics, San Diego, 1985-88; owner Wrights Food Vending Svc., 1988—90; pres., founder Residential Care and Treatment Facility for Youth, 1991—. Author: Inspirational, 1995, My Life's Journey, 2005; inventor mechanical multiple picture frame. Chair, utilities commr. City of Colton, Calif., 1996—. With U.S. Army, 1962-65. Democrat. Avocations: rv camping, fishing, motorcycling.

WRIGHT, DOUGLAS, playwright; b. Dallas, 1962; BA, Yale U., 1985; MFA, Tisch Sch. Arts, NYU, 1987. Author: (plays) The Stonewater Rapture, 1987, Buzzsaw Berkeley, 1989, Watbanaland, 1994, Quills, 1995 (OBIE award for Playwriting, 1996), I Am My Own Wife, 2003 (Pulitzer prize for Drama, 2004, Tony award best play, 2004, Drama Desk award best play, 2004), The Little Mermaid, 2005, Interrogating the Nude; author, dir.: Unwrap Your Candy, 2001 (Paul Selvin award, Writers Guild Am., 2001); author: (screenplays) Quills, 2000 (Golden Satellite for Best Motion Picture Screenplay, 2000, Phoenix Film Critics Soc. award for Best Screenplay, 2000). Office: Lyceum Theatre 149 W 45th St New York NY 10036

WRIGHT, DOUGLAS TYNDALL, former university administrator; b. Toronto, Ont., Can., Oct. 4, 1927; s. George C. and Etta (Tyndall) W. BASc. with honors in Civil Engring, U. Toronto, 1949; MS in Structural Engring, U. Ill., 1952; PhD in Engring, U. Cambridge, 1954; D.Eng. (hon.), Carleton U., 1967; LLD (hon.), Brock U., 1967, Concordia U., 1982; DSc (hon.), Meml. U. Nfld., 1969; DHL (hon.), Northeastern U., 1985, U. Waterloo, 1995; DUniv (hon.), Strathclyde U., Glasgow, 1989; D de L'Université, Compiegne U., France, 1991; D Univ. (hon.), Université de Sherbrooke, 1992; DSc, McMaster U., 1993, Queen's U., 1993; LLD (hon.), U. Waterloo, 1995; LLD, U. Toronto, Can., 2005. Lectr. dept. civil engring. Queen's U., 1954-55, asst. prof., 1955-58, assoc. prof., 1958; prof. civil engring. U. Waterloo, 1958-67, chmn. dept. civil engring., 1958-63, dean engring., 1959-66; chmn. Ont. Com. on Univ. Affairs Govt. of Ont., 1967-72, Ont. Commn. Post-Secondary Edn., Toronto, 1969-72, dep. provincial sec. for social devel., 1972-79; dep. minister culture and recreation, 1979-80; pres. U. Waterloo, Ont., 1981-93, prof. engring. Ont., 1981—, pres. emeritus Ont., 1995—. Vis. prof. U. Autónoma Mex., 1964, 66, U. Sherbrooke, 1966—67; cons. engr. Netherlands and Mexican Pavillions Expo, 1967, Olympic Sports Palace, Mexico City, 1968, Ont. Place Dome and Forum, 1971; tech. advisor Toronto Skydome, 1984—92; bd. dirs. Com Dev Ltd., Geometrica Inc., Perimeter Inst. for Theoretical Physics, RDM Corp.; mem. Premier's Coun. on Sci. and Tech., Ont., 1985—91; Can. rep. Coun. Internat. Inst. Applied Sys. Analysis, Laxenburg, Austria, 1986—97; prime min.'s personal rep. to Coun. Misn. of Edn., 1990—91. Contbr. articles to profl. jours. Bd. govs. Stratford Shakesperean Festival, 1984—86, mem. senate, 1987; bd. dirs. African Students Found., Toronto, 1961—66, Ont. Curriculum Inst., 1964—67, Ont. R&D Challenge Fund, 1998—2004, NB Innovation Found., 2001—05. Decorated Officer Order of Can., chevalier Ordre National du Mérite (France); recipient Gold medal Ont. Profl. Engrs., 1990, Gold Medal award Can. Coun. Profl. Engrs., 1992, Sir. John Kennedy Medal award Engring. Inst. Can., 1995, Can. Entrepreneur of Yr. award, 1997; Athlone fellow, 1952-54. Fellow ASCE, Can. Acad. Engring., Engring. Inst. Can. (del. Engrs. Coun. Profl. Devel., N.Y.C. 1961-70); mem. Assn. Profl. Engrs. Province Ont., Internat. Assn. Bridge and Structural Engring., Internat. Assn. Shell Structures, Royal Can. Yacht Club, Univ. Club (Toronto). Personal E-mail: dtwright@uwaterloo.ca.

WRIGHT, DOUGLASS BROWNELL, retired judge, lawyer; b. Hartford, Conn., May 30, 1912; s. Arthur Brownell and Sylvia (Stephens) W.; m. Jane Hamersley, Sept. 24, 1938 (dec. Feb. 1997); children: Jane C., Douglass B., Hamersley S., Elizabeth B., Arthur W.; m. Ann Hallowell Ferguson, Nov., 1999. AB, Yale U., 1933; LL.B., Hartford Coll. Law, 1937. Bar: Conn. 1937. Legal dept. Aetna Life Ins. Co., 1937-39; partner Davis, Lee, Howard & Wright, Hartford, 1939—; lectr. law U. Conn., 1946—; asst. state's atty. Conn., 1952-59; judge Conn. Circuit Court, 1959-65, Conn. Superior Ct., 1965—98; ret., 1998. Leader orch. Judge Wright and the Four Wrongs Author: Connecticut Law of Torts, 1956, Connecticut Legal Forms, 5 vols., 1958, Connecticut Jury Instructions, 3 vols., 1960, 76. Sec., dir. Captioned Films for the Deaf, Inc.; bd. dirs., pres. Am. Sch. for Deaf, 1942—; trustee Hartt Mus. Found., 1949—, Good Will Boys Club Hartford, 1950—; regent U. Hartford; bd. dirs. Vis. Nurse Assn., Newington Home for Crippled Children, Hartford Times Farm, Loomis Sch.; incorporator Conn. Inst. for Blind. Served as lt. USNR, 1942-45. Mem. Phi Beta Kappa, Psi Upsilon. Clubs: University (Hartford), Hartford Golf (Hartford), Hartford Tennis (Hartford), 20th Century (Hartford); Coral Beach and Tennis (Bermuda); Hillsboro (Pompano Beach, Fla.). Congregationalist. Home: 20 Loeffler Rd Apt T519 Bloomfield CT 06002-2273 Office: 95 Washington St Hartford CT 06106-4431

WRIGHT, EDWARD LEONARD, astronomy educator; b. Washington, Aug. 25, 1947; s. Rufus William and Gertrude (Leonard) W.; m. Patricia Jaskun, Mar. 18, 1978; children: William, Diana. AB summa cum laude, Harvard U., 1969, PhD, 1976. Asst. prof. physics MIT, Cambridge, 1976-80, assoc. prof., 1980-81; prof. astronomy UCLA, 1981—. Recipient Jr. Fellowship Harvard U. Soc. Fellows, 1973-76. Fellow Am. Acad. Arts & Scis. Achievements include co-investigation of the Cosmic Background Explorer (COBE); research on the Space Infra Red Telescope Facility (SIRTF). Office: UCLA Dept of Astronomy 405 Hilgard Ave Los Angeles CA 90095-9000 *

WRIGHT, ELEASE, insurance company executive; BS in Edn., U. Conn. Sr. v.p. human resources Aetna Inc., Hartford, Conn., 1999—. Mem.: advisory bd., Cornell Univ. Center for Advanced Human Resource Studies, bd. of advisors, Univ. Conn. School of Bus., Exec. Leadership Council. Office: 151 Farmington Ave Hartford CT 06156-0001

WRIGHT, ERNEST MARSHALL, physiologist, consultant; b. Belfast, Ireland, June 8, 1940; came to U.S., 1965; BSc, U. London, 1961, DSc, 1978; PhD, U. Sheffield, Eng., 1964. Research fellow Harvard U., Boston, 1965-66; from asst. prof. to full prof. physiology UCLA Med. Sch., 1967—, chmn. dept. physiology, 1987—2000. Cons. NIH, Bethesda, Md., 1982—, Senator Jacob K. Javits neurosci. investigator, 1985. Fellow: Royal Soc., Biophysical Soc. Office: UCLA Sch Med Dept Physiology 10833 Le Conte Ave Los Angeles CA 90095-1751

WRIGHT, FAITH-DORIAN, artist; b. Bklyn., Feb. 9, 1934; d. Abraham and Molly (Janoff) J.; children: Jordan Merritt, Igrid-beth. BS, NYU, 1955, MA, 1958; postgrad., Pratt and Parsons Sch. of Design. Works exhibited in Kathryn Markel Gallery, N.Y.C., 1981, 92, Cumberland Gallery, Nashville, 1981, 92, Barbara Gillman Gallery, Miami, 1982, Hand and Hand Gallery, 1985, 86, Suzanne Gross, Phila., 1986, 87, Gallery Four, Alexandria, Va., 1986, 87, 88, Henri Gallery, Washington, 1986, 87, 88, 89. 90. 91. 92. 93. 94, Benton Gallery, Southampton, 1986, 87, 88, 89, 91, 92, 93, King Stephen Mus., Hungary, 1987, Nat. Gallery Women in the Arts, 1987, 88, 90, 91, 92, Ruth Volid Gallery, Chgo., 1990, James Gallery, Pitts., 1990, Aart Vark Gallery, Phila., 1990, Merrill Chase Gallery, Chgo., 1990, 91, 92, Guild Hall Mus., East Hampton, N.Y., 1991, Joy Berman Gallery, Phila., 1992, Ctr. for Book Arts, N.Y.C., 1992, Barnard-Biederman Fine Arts, N.Y.C., 1994, Arlene Bujese Gallery, East Hampton, 1994, 95, 96, Stoney Brook U., 1994, Harper Collins Exhbn. Space, 1995, Ctr. for Book Arts, 1996, arlene bujese, 1997, Galerie Cargo, Paris, 1997, N.Y. State Mus., Albany, 1997, U. Mont., Missoula, 2002, Nat. Mus. Women in Arts, Washington, 2002, Arlene Bujese, East Hampton, N.Y., 1997-03, Seton Hall U., NJ, 2003, Arlene Bujese Gallery, East Hampton, N.Y. 2003—, Gayle Wilson Gallery, Southampton, N.Y., 2004-2005; permanent collections Nat. Postal Art Mus., Ottawa, Can., Nat. Inst. Design, Ahmedabad, India, Fine Arts Acad., New Delhi, India, Mus. Modern Art, N.Y.C., Nat. Mus. Women in the Arts, Washington, D.C., Israel Mus., Jerusalem, Brenau Coll., Grainsville, Ga. Blue Cross, Blue Shield, Phila., Mc Donald's, Oakbrook, Ill., The Hyatt Collection, Chgo., Guild Hall Mus., Saul, Ewing, Reineck & Saul, Phila., Shevick, Ravich, Koster, Tobin, Clark, N.J., Sidley & Austin, L.A., Catalano & Sparber, N.Y., Islip (N.Y.) Mus. of Art, NY Pet Rescue Orgn., Larchmont, Islip (NY) Mus.; contbr. critical essays to various periodicals. Mem. Women in Arts, Women's Caucus for Arts, Artists Equity, Visitation Bd. of Met. Mus.-Rockefeller Connection. Address: 300 E 74th St New York NY 10021-3712

WRIGHT, FELIX E., manufacturing executive; b. 1935; married Student, East Tex. State U., 1958. With Leggett & Platt, Inc., Carthage, Mo., 1959—, sr. v.p., from 1976, chief operating officer, exec. v.p., 1979, pres., COO, 1985-2000, vice chmn., 1999—2002, pres., CEO, 2000—02, chmn., CEO, 2002—06, chmn., 2006—. Office: Leggett & Platt Inc 1 Leggett Rd Carthage MO 64836-9649 *

WRIGHT, FRANCES JANE, educational psychologist; b. LA, Dec. 22, 1943; d. step-father John David and Evelyn Jane (Dale) Brinegar. BA, Long Beach State U., 1965; MA, Brigham Young U., 1968, EdD, 1980; postgrad., U. Nev., 1970, U. Utah, 1972-73; postdoctoral, Utah State U., 1985-86. Cert. secondary tchr., adminstr., Utah. Asst. dir. Teenpost Project, San Pedro, Calif., 1966; caseworker Los Angeles County, 1966-67; self-care inservice dir. Utah State Tng. Sch., American Fork, Utah, 1968, vocat. project designer, 1968; tchr. mentally handicapped Santa Ana Unified Schs., Calif., 1968-69; state specialist intellectually handicapped State Office Edn., Salt Lake City, 1969-70; vocat. counselor Manpower, Salt Lake City, 1970-71; tchr. severely handicapped Davis County Schs., Farmington, Utah, 1971-73, diagnostician, 1973-74, resource elem. tchr., 1974-78; instr. Brigham Young U., Salt Lake City, 1976-83; resource tchr. jr. high Davis County Schs., Farmington, 1978-90; ednl. cons. Murray, Utah, 1973-90; chief ednl. diagnostician Ctr. for Evaluation of Learning and Devel., Layton, Utah, 1989-90. Clin. dir. assessment and observation program Idaho Youth Ranch, 1990-95, clin. dir. intake program, 1992-94, supr. family preservation svc./aftercare teams, 1993-95, co-ranch treatment dir. and placement officer, 1995; cons. juvenile correctional dist. 5, 1996-2000; cons., counselor address issues with youth and families, 2001-06; program mgr. Libery Care Svcs. Mental Health Clinic, 2006—; clinician Region 5 Behavioral Health, 2006—; clin. cons. Magic Hot Springs Youth Camp, 1996-97; mem. cmty. accountability bd. McNeil Assn., 1996-2000, Dist. 5 Juvenile Justice Coun., 1997—, parent project facilitator, 1998-2000; trainer Detour prison prevention programfor adolescents, 1997-2000; cons. Northstar Family Preservation, 1997-2001; mem. Juvenile Justice Coun., 1996—; acting chmn. Dist. 5 Juvenile Justice Coun., 1998-99, chmn. 1999-2001; mem. Idaho Juvenile Justice Commn., 1999-2001; adv. bd. So. Central Learning Ctr., 1999-2001; mem. oversight bd., evaluator Status Offender prog. 1997-2000; program dir. Liberty Care Svc.; clin. program mgr. Liberty Care Svcs., 2002-06; clinician Adult Behavior Health Dept. Health/Welfare, 2006—; lectr. in field; pvt. cons./counselor lic. in juvenile justice, youth, edn. and other related concerns. Named Profl. of Yr. Utah Assn. for Children with Learning Disabilities, 1985, Prol. of the Yr., Idaho Youth Ranch Treatment Ctrs., 1992, 1993. Mem. Assn. Children/Adults with Learning Disabilities (del. 1979-85, 87, nat. nominating com., 1985-86, nat. bd. dirs. 1988-91), Am. Counseling Assn., Idaho Mental Health Counselors Assn., Utah Assn. Children/Adults with Learning Disabilities (exec. bd. 1978-84, profl. adv. bd. 1985-90, coord. LDA orgn. Idaho 1991-2000), Coun. Learning Disabilities, ASCD (regional adv.), Nat. Wildlife Found., World Wildlife Fedn., Best Friends Animal Sanctuary, Job's Daughters. Democrat. Mem. Lds Ch. Avocations: genealogy, horseback riding, sketching, crafts, reading. Home: 2176 Julie Ln Twin Falls ID 83301-8361 Office: Liberty Care Svc Pvt Mental Health Clin 460 Main Ave S Ste C Twin Falls ID 83301-7972 Office Phone: 208-736-2177. Business E-Mail: libertycare@onewest.net. *Personal philosophy: I dream of the day when man will value man and his surrounding world for their intrinsic value instead of what they can or could do for a specific person.*

WRIGHT, FRANCES MARY, principal; b. La Mesa, Calif., Aug. 9, 1958; d. Dominique and Joeann Ancona; m. James Randal Wright, Apr. 28, 2002; children: Melissa Sulser, John Sulser. AA, Grossmont Coll., El Cajon, Calif., 1978; BA in Liberal Studies, San Diego State U., 1980, Calif. tchg. credential, 1981; MA in Ednl. Adminstrn., Nat. U., San Diego, 2004. Basic skills instr. Ocean Beach Elem., Calif., 1981—83; tchr. 3rd and 2nd grades Holy Trinity Sch., El Cajun, Calif., 1983—92; tchr. 3rd grade St. Martin of Tours Acad., La Mesa, Calif., 1992—2000; jr. high tchr. St. Michael Acad., San Diego, 2000—04, vice prin., 2000—04; prin. St. Mary, Star of the Sea Sch., Oceanside, Calif., 2004—. Mem.: NCEA, ASCD. Roman Catholic.

WRIGHT, FRANZ PAUL, poet, writer, translator; b. Vienna, 1953; s. James Wright and Liberty Kardulis. Grad., Oberlin College, 1977; studied postgrad., U. Va. Translator, author of introduction Rainer Maria Rilke, The Unknown Rilke, 1990; translator modern and contemporary French and German poets; author: (poems) Tapping the White Cane of Solitude, 1976, The Earth Without You, 1980, Eight Poems, 1981, The One Whose Eyes Open When You Close Your Eyes, 1982, No Siege Is Absolute, 1983, Going North in Winter, 1986, Entry in an Unknown Hand, 1989, Midnight Postscript, 1990, And Still the Hand Will Sleep in Its Glass Ship, 1990, Rorschach Test, 1995, The Night World and the Word Night, 1993, Knell,

1998, ILL LIT: Selected and New Poems, 1998, The Beforelife, 2001, Walking to Martha's Vineyard, 2003 (Pulitzer Prize for poetry, 2004); represented in anthologies; contbr. articles to profl. publs. Recipient Witter Bynner prize for Poetry, 1995, PEN/Voelcker award, 1996, Pulitzer prize in Poetry, 2004; NEA fellow, 1985, 92, Guggenheim fellow, 1989, Whiting fellow, 1991.

WRIGHT, FREDERICK LEWIS, II, lawyer; b. Roanoke, Va., Sept. 17, 1951; s. Frederick Lewis and Dorothy Marie (Trent) W.; m. Margaret Suzanne Rey, Oct. 16, 1982; children: Lauren Elizabeth, Emily Trent. BA, Ga. State U., 1978; JD, U. Ga., 1981. Bar: Ga. 1982, US Dist. Ct. (no. dist.) Ga. 1984, US Ct. Appeals (11th, 8th and 4th cirs.) 1984, US Supreme Ct. 1990. Law clk. to presiding justice US Ct. Appeals, Atlanta, 1981-82; ptnr. Smith, Currie and Hancock, Atlanta, 1982-96, Vaughn, Wright and Boyer, Atlanta, 1997—. Articles editor Ga. Law Rev., 1980—81. Mem.: ABA (forum com. constrn. industry), Ga. Def. Lawyers Assn., Fed. Bar Assn., Def. Rsch. Inst., Order of Coif. Methodist. Office: One Paces West Ste 1740 2727 Paces Ferry Rd Atlanta GA 30339 Office Phone: 770-805-9889. Personal E-mail: fwright@mindspring.com.

WRIGHT, G. TODD, lab administrator, director; s. William Houghton and Betty Ritenour Wright; m. Colleen Rae Lebrum, June 22, 1974; children: Chris, Kellie, Matthew. BSME, Va. Poly. Inst. and State U., Blacksburg, VA, 1974, MSME, 1976, PhD, 1979. Lab. dir. Savannah River Nat. Lab., Aiken, SC, 2003—; rsch. mgr. River Protection Project, Hanford, Wash., 2001—02; dep. dir. Savannah River Tech. Ctr., Aiken, SC, 1997—2000; mgr., ops. Westinghouse Savannah River Site, Aiken, SC, 1989—97; rsch. mgr. E. I. duPont Savannah River Lab, Aiken, SC, 1983—89. Office: Savannah River Nat Lab Building 773-A A221 Aiken SC 29808 Home Phone: 803-507-0974; Office Phone: 803-725-3994. Office Fax: 803-725-1660; E-mail: todd.wright@srnl.doe.gov.

WRIGHT, GEORGE CULLEN, retired electronics company executive; b. Anderson, SC, June 28, 1923; s. Benjamin Norman and Essie Floride (Cole) W.; m. Kathleen Ashe, Oct. 19, 1947; children: Carol Ann (Mrs. John C. Marquardt), George Cullen, Florenda Jean, William Norman. BS, Clemson U., 1948. Asst. supt. Duke Power Co., 1949-56; city mgr. Gaffney, SC, 1956-60; v.p. mktg. Hubbard & Co., Chgo., 1960-65; dir. Methode Electronics, Inc., Rolling Meadows, Ill., 1956—; v.p., dir. Anchor Coupling Co., Inc., Libertyville, Ill., 1973-76. Pres., dir. Exec. Extension & Ventures, Inc., Barrington, Ill., 1976-78, White Marlin Marine, Inc., Anderson, S.C., 1976-86, Piedmont Corp., 1986-2001. Patentee in field. Pres. Barrington East Assn., 1968-70. Served with AUS, 1942-45. Mem. AIEE Electron Industry Assn., Am. Mgmt. Assn., Rotary, Sertoma (pres. 1963-65). Home: PO Box 130 Townville SC 29689-0130 Personal E-mail: wright_george@bellsouth.net.

WRIGHT, GLADYS STONE, music educator, writer, composer; b. Wasco, Oreg., Mar. 8, 1925; d. Murvel Stuart and Daisy Violet (Warren) Stone; m. Alfred George Wright, June 28, 1953. BS, U. Oreg., 1948, MS, 1953. Dir. bands Elmira (Oreg.) U-4 H.S., 1948-53, Otterbein (Ind.) H.S., 1954-61, Klondike H.S., West Lafayette, Ind., 1962-70, Harrison H.S., West Lafayette, 1970-84. Organizer, condr. Musical Friendship Tours, Ctrl. Am., 1967-79; v.p., condr. U.S. Collegiate Wind Band, 1975—; bd. dirs. John Philip Sousa Found., 1984—; chmn. Sudler Cup, 1986—, Sudler Flag, 1982; pres. Internat. Music Tours, 1984—, Key to the City, Taxco, Mex., 1975. Editor: Woman Conductor, 1986—; composer: marches Big Bowl and Trumpets and Tabards, 1987; contbg. editor: Informusica (Spain). Recipient Medal of the order John Philip Sousa Found., 1988, Star of Order, 1991, Internat. Contbrn. to Music award Phi Beta Mu, 2000; 1st woman guest condr. U.S. Navy Band, Washington, 1961, Goldman Band, NYC, 1958, Kneller Hall Band, London, 1975, Tri-State Music Festival Massed Orch., Band, Choir, 1985; elected to Women Bd. Dirs. Hall of Fame of Disting. Women Condrs., 1994; inductee Hall of Fame Disting. Condrs., Nat. Band Assn., 1999; named Ind.'s Sagamore of the Wabash, 2004. Mem. Am. Bandmasters Assn. (bd. dirs. 1993, 1st woman mem.), Women Band Dirs. Nat. Assn. (founding pres. 1967, sec. 1985, recipient Silver Baton 1974, Golden Rose 1990, Hall of Fame 1995), Am. Sch. Band Dirs. Assn., Nat. Band Assn. (Citation excellence 1970), Tippecanoe Arts Fedn. (bd. dirs. 1986-90), Tippecanoe Fife and Drum Corps. (bd. dirs. 1984), DAR, Col. Dames-Pre Quitanen Chpt., New Eng. Women, Tau Beta Sigma (Outstanding Svc. to Music award 1970), Phi Beta Mu (1st hon. woman mem. 1972), N.Am. Wildlife Park (Battleground, Ind., bd dirs. 1985, 1990—). Avocation: history.

WRIGHT, GREGORY A., oil industry executive; BBA, Ohio State U., 1971; MBA, U. Del., 1979. With Columbia Gas Systems Inc., 1972—81; positions through v.p. Valero Energy Corp., 1981—95; v.p. corp. comm. Tesoro Corp., San Antonio, 1995—2001, sr. v.p., CFO, 2001—03, exec. v.p., CFO, 2003—07, exec. v.p., Chief Adminstrv. Officer, 2007—. Office: Tesoro Petroleum 300 Concord Plz San Antonio TX 78216-6999 *

WRIGHT, GWENDOLYN, writer, architecture educator, historian; b. Chgo., May 14, 1946; d. William Kemp and Mary Ruth (Brown) W.; m. Paul Rabinow, Nov. 18, 1980 (div. 1982); m. Thomas Bender, Jan. 14, 1984; children: David, Sophia. BA, NYU, 1969; MArch, U. Calif., Berkeley, 1974, PhD, 1980. Assoc. prof. Columbia U., NYC, 1983—87, prof., 1988—; dir. Buell Ctr. for Study Am. Architecture, NYC, 1988—92. Cons. Fulbright Scholars, Coun. Internat. Exch. Scholars, Washington, 1988-91, ArchNet, 1999—, Nat. Bldg. Mus., Washington, 2001—. Author: Building the Dream: A Social History of Housing in America, 1980, Moralism and the Model Home, 1981, The History of History in American Schools of Architecture, 1990, The Politics of Design in French Colonial Urbanism, 1991, USA: Modern Architectures in History, 2007; writer N.Y. Times, 1999; presenter PBS TV series History Detectives, 2003—. Fellow, Ford Found., 1979—80, Stanford Inst. for Humanities, 1982—83, Mich. Inst. for Humanities, 1991, Getty Ctr. for History of Art and the Humanities, 1992—93, Guggenheim Found., 2004—05, Graham Found., 2004—05. Fellow: Soc. Am. Historians, NY Inst. for Humanities; mem.: Soc. Archtl. Historians, Coll. Art Assn., Am. Hist. Assn., Orgn. Am. Historians. Democrat. Home: 54 Washington Mews New York NY 10003-6608 Office: Columbia U Avery Hall New York NY 10027 Home Phone: 212-228-6454; Office Phone: 212-854-1587. Business E-Mail: gw8@columbia.edu.

WRIGHT, HARRISON MORRIS, historian, educator; b. Phila., Oct. 6, 1928; s. Sydney L. and Catharine W. (Morris) W.; m. Josephine Stearns Cole, July 20, 1957; children— Rebecca H., J. Rodman, Thomas F., Daniel H., James L. BA, Harvard U., Cambridge, Mass., 1950, MA, 1953, PhD, 1957. Teaching fellow Harvard, 1955-57; mem. faculty Swarthmore Coll., 1957—, prof. history, 1968-87, Isaac H. Clothier prof. history and internat. relations, 1987-93, chmn. dept., 1968-79, provost, 1979-84, Clothier prof. and provost emeritus, 1993—, acting pres., 1982. Bd. dir. Paul Cuffee Sch., 2001—. Author: New Zealand, 1769-1840: Early Years of Western Contact, 1959, The Burden of the Present: Liberal-Radical Controversy over Southern African History, 1977; Editor: The New Imperialism—Analysis of Late Nineteenth-Century Expansion, 1961, 2d edit., 1976, Sir James Rose Innes: Selected Correspondence (1884-1902), 1972. Mem. Jamestown Harbor Commn., RI, 2000—03. Fulbright scholar New Zealand, 1950-51; Ford Found. fgn. areas fellow Eng. and Ghana, 1961-62; grantee Am. Philos. Soc., S. Africa, 1966-67; grantee Old Dominion Fund, S. Africa, 1971 Mem.: Jamestown Hist. Soc. (bd. dirs. 1997—2003, 2004—, v.p. 2005—), RI Hist. Soc. (bd. dirs. 1998—2005), Hist. Soc. Pa. (coun. 1984—91, v.p. 1986—88, chmn. 1989—91, coun. emeritus 1992—), African Studies Assn., Sailing Inst. (bd. dirs. 1998—2007), Humanities Forum R.I. (bd. dirs. 1995—2000), Newport Hist. Soc. (bd. dirs. 1973—88, 2006—), Phi Beta Kappa. Home: PO Box 209 Jamestown RI 02835-0209

WRIGHT, HARRY HERCULES, psychiatrist; b. Charleston, SC, Jan. 4, 1948; s. Harry Vernon and Agnes Lucile (Simmons) W. BS, U. S.C., 1970; MD, MBA, U. Pa., 1976. Resident in psychiatry Wm. S. Hall Psychiat. Inst., Columbia, SC, 1977—79; adminstrv. fellow in psychiatry NIMH, Rockville, Md., 1979; fellow in child psychiatry William S. Hall Psychiat. Inst., 1979—81, instr. child psychiatrist, 1981—; instr. dept. neuropsychiatry and behavioral sci. U. S.C. Sch. Medicine, 1981—82, asst. prof., 1982—86, assoc. prof., 1986—90, prof., 1990—. Contbr. articles to profl. jours. Bd. dirs. Carolina Children's Home, 1992—, Zero to Three, 1997—; bd. trustees, First Steps to Sch. Readiness, 1999-2003; mem. landmarks commn. City of Columbia, 1986-98. Recipient Freed award, Hall Psychiat. Inst., 1978, Outstanding Svc. award, Sickle Cell Found., Clin. Sci. Rsch. award, 1998, Am.'s Top Doctors award, 2001—06, Rsch. Advancement award, U. SC, 2002, 2004, 2006; grantee Falk fellow, 1977—79, Laughlin fellow, 1979. Mem.: AAAS, Am. Coll. Psychiatrists, Am. Soc. Human Genetics, Soc. Study Psychiatry and Culture, Acad. Orgnl. and Occupl. Psychiatry, So. Med. Assn., Am. Soc. Adolescent Psychiatry, World Assn. Infant Mental Health, World Psychiat. Assn., Am. Acad. Child Psychiatry, Autism Soc. Am., Riverbank Zool. Soc., Sigma Xi, Omicron Delta Kappa. Methodist. Home: PO Box 12474 Columbia SC 29211-2474 Office: 3555 Harden St Ext Ste 104 Columbia SC 29203-6894 Home Phone: 803-765-1642; Office Phone: 803-434-4250.

WRIGHT, HERBERT E(DGAR), JR., geologist; b. Malden, Mass., Sept. 13, 1917; s. Herbert E. and Annie M. (Richardson) W.; m. Rhea Jane Hahn, June 21, 1943; children: Richard, Jonathan, Stephen, Andrew, Jeffrey. AB, Harvard U., 1939, MA, 1941, PhD, 1943; DSc (hon.), Trinity Coll., Dublin, Ireland, 1966, U. Minn., 1996; PhD (hon.), Lund U., Sweden, 1987. Instr. Brown U., 1946-47; asst. prof. geology U. Minn., Mpls., 1947-51, asso. prof., 1951-59, prof., 1959-74, Regents' prof. geology, ecology and botany, 1974-88, Regents' prof. geology, ecology & botany emeritus, 1988—; dir. Limnological Research Center, 1963-90. Served to maj. USAAF, 1942-45. Decorated D.F.C., Air medal with 6 oak leaf clusters; recipient Pomerance award Archeol. Inst. Am., 1985, Ann. award Sci. Mus. Minn., 1990; Guggenheim fellow, 1954-55, Wenner-Gren fellow, 1954-55. Fellow AAAS, Geol. Soc. Am. (Ann. award archeol. divsn. 1989, Disting. Career award geology and geomorphology divsn. 1992), Soc. Am. Archeology (Fryxell award 1993); mem. NAS, Ecol. Soc. Am., Internat. Quaternary Assn. (hon. pres. 16th Congress 2003), Am. Quaternary Assn. (Career award 1996). Achievements include research on Quaternary geology, paleoecology, paleolimnology and environ. archaeology in Minn., Wyo., Sweden, Yukon, Labrador, Peru, eastern Mediterranean. Home: 1426 Hythe St Saint Paul MN 55108-1423 Office: U of Minn 310 Pillsbury Dr SE Minneapolis MN 55455-0219 Business E-Mail: hew@umn.edu.

WRIGHT, JAMES DORSEY, lawyer; b. Easton, Md., July 11, 1944; s. M. Dorsey and Dorothy (Booker) W.; m. Christine Ulrich, May 17, 1980. BA, U. Del., 1966; JD, Harvard U., 1969. Bar: Md. 1969. Law clk. to presiding judge Frank A. Kaufman, U.S. Dist. Ct. (Md.) U.S. Dist. Ct. Md., Balt., 1969-70; assoc. Venable, Baetjer & Howard (now Venable LLP), Balt., 1970-75, ptnr., Real Estate practice, 1976—. Mem. ABA, Am. Coll. Real Estate Lawyers, Md. State Bar Assn., Bar Assn. Balt. City, Md. Club (Balt.). Office: Venable LLP 1800 Merc Bank & Trust Bldg 2 Hopkins Plz Baltimore MD 21201 Office Phone: 410-244-7422. Office Fax: 410-244-7742. Business E-Mail: jdwright@venable.com.

WRIGHT, JAMES EDWARD, academic administrator, historian, educator; b. Madison, Wis., Aug. 16, 1939; s. Donald J. and Myrtle (Hendricks) Wright; m. Joan Bussan, Sept. 3, 1962 (div.); children: James J., Ann Marie, Michael J.; m. Susan DeBevoise, Aug. 18, 1984. BS, Wis. State U., 1964; MS, U. Wis., 1966, PhD, 1969; MA (hon.), Dartmouth Coll., 1980. From asst. prof. to assoc. prof. history Dartmouth Coll., Hanover, NH, 1969—80, prof. history, 1980—, assoc. dean faculty, 1981—85, dean faculty, 1989—97, acting pres., 1995, provost, 1997—98, pres., 1998—. Sr. historian U. Mid Am., Lincoln, Nebr., 1976—77; humanist-in-residence Colo. Humanities Coun., Georgetown, 1975. Author: Galena Lead District, 1966, Politics of Populism, 1974, Progressive Yankees, 1987; author: (co-editor) Great Plains Experience, 1978. Trustee Kimball Union Acad., Meriden, NH, 1990—94; dir. Sherman Fairchild Found., Greenwich, Conn., 1991—; chair Hanover Dem. Town Com., 1970—74; bd. dirs. Divsn. 1 NCAA, 2001—03. Cpl. USMC, 1957—60. Danforth fellow, 1964—69, Guggenheim fellow, 1973—74, Charles Warren fellow, Harvard U., 1980—81. Fellow: Am. Acad. Arts and Scis.; mem.: Western History Assn. (chair Caughey prize 1986—87), The Century Assn., Orgn. Am. Historians (chair film, media com. 1983—85), Phi Beta Kappa. Home: 1 Tuck Dr Hanover NH 03755-3575 Office: Dartmouth Coll Office of the President 207 Parkhurst Hall Hanover NH 03755 Home Phone: 603-643-8230; Office Phone: 603-646-2223. Business E-Mail: james.wright@dartmouth.edu.

WRIGHT, JAMES F., agricultural products executive; Sr. level positions K-Mart Corp., 1974—88, Western Auto Supply Co., 1988—96; pres., CEO Tire Kingdom, 1997—2000; pres., COO Tractor Supply, Brentwood, Tenn., 2000—, pres., CEO, 2004—. Mem.: Automotive Parts and Accessories Assn. (past chmn.). Office: Tractor Supply Co 200 Powell Pl Brentwood TN 37027 *

WRIGHT, J(AMES) LAWRENCE, lawyer; b. Portland, Oreg., Apr. 12, 1943; s. William A. and Esther M. (Nelson) W.; m. Mary Aileene Roche, June 29, 1968; children: Rachel, Jonathan, Christopher. BBA, Gonzaga U., 1966, JD, 1972; LLM, NYU, 1977. Bar: Wash. 1972, U.S. Ct. Mil. Appeals 1974, U.S. Tax Ct. 1976, U.S. Supreme Ct. 1976. Prin. Halverson & Applegate, P.S., Yakima, Wash., 1972-74, 77—, pres., 1998—. Mem. St. Elizabeth Hosp. Found., Yakima, 1986-89, Yakima Meml. Hosp. Found., 1990—; pres. fin. bd. St. Paul's Cathedral, Yakima, 1979—; mem. fin. coun. Diocese of Yakima, 1994—; v.p. Apple Tree Racing Assn., 1986-87; bd. dirs. Capital Theatre, Yakima, 1985-95. Capt. U.S. Army, 1966-68, 74-76. Mem. ABA, Wash. Bar Assn., Yakima County Bar Assn., Rotary. Roman Catholic. Avocations: tennis, golf. Office: Halverson & Applegate PS PO Box 22730 1433 Lakeside Ct Ste 100 Yakima WA 98902-7354

WRIGHT, JAMES RALPH, retired lawyer; b. Pitts., Jan. 18, 1944; s. Paul J. and Gertrude M. (Stienecker) W.; m. Harriett Ann Howard, Sept. 7, 1968; children: Karen, Cathy. BS, Ohio State U., 1966; JD, George Washington U., 1969. Bar: D.C. 1973, U.S. Dist. Ct. D.C. 1975, U.S. Ct. Appeals (D.C. cir.) 1981. Dir. legal affairs Airport Operators Coun. Internat., Washington, 1969-70; with NAS, Washington, 1970—2006, staff officer, counsel com. on motor vehicles, 1973-74, staff counsel, 1974-80, gen. counsel, 1980—2006; ret. Exec. dir. Nat. Academies' Corp., a Calif. nonprofit pub. benefit corp., 1986—. Editor, pub. newsletter, 1985-90. Mem. ABA.

WRIGHT, JANE COOKE, oncologist, educator, consultant; b. NYC, Nov. 30, 1919; d. Louis T. and Corinne (Cooke) W.; m. David D. Jones. AB, Smith Coll., 1942; MD with honors, N.Y. Med. Coll., 1945; D in Med. Scis., Women's Med. Coll. Pa., 1965; ScD, Denison U., 1971. Intern Bellevue Hosp., NYC, 1945-46, resident, 1946, mem. staff, 1955-67; resident Harlem Hosp., 1947, chief resident, 1948; clin. Cancer Rsch. Found., Harlem Hosp., 1949-52; dir., 1952-55; mem. staff Harlem Hosp., 1949-55; practice medicine specializing in clin. cancer chemotherapy NYC; mem. faculty dept. surgery Med. Ctr., N.Y. U., NYC, 1955-67, adj. assoc. prof., 1961-67, also dir. cancer chemotherapy services research, 1955-67; prof. surgery N.Y. Med. Coll., NYC, 1967-87, prof. surgery emeritus, 1987—, assoc. dean, 1967-75; mem. staff Manhattan VA Hosp., 1955-67, Midtown, Met., Bird S. Color, Flower-Fifth Ave. Hosps., all NYC, 1967-79, Westchester County Med. Center, Valhalla, NY, 1971-87, Lincoln Hosp., Bronx, NY, 1979-87. Cons. Health Ins. Plan of Greater N.Y., 1962—94, Blvd. Hosp., 1963—, St. Luke's Hosp., Newburgh, NY, 1964—; pelvic malignancy rev. com. N.Y. Gynecol. Soc., 1965—66, St. Vincent's Hosp., NYC, 1966—, Dept. Health, Edn. and Welfare, 1968—70, Wyckoff Heights Hosp., NYC, 1969—, NIH, 1971—, others; adv. bd. Skin Cancer Found. Contbr. articles to profl. jours. Mem. Manhattan coun. State Commn. Human Rights, 1949—, Pres.'s Commn. Heart Disease, Cancer and Stroke, 1964-65, Nat. Adv. Cancer Coun. NIH, 1966-70, N.Y. State Women's Coun., 1970-72; bd. dirs. Medico-CARE, Health Svcs. Improvement Fund Inc.; trustee Smith Coll., Northampton, Mass., 1970-80. Recipient numerous awards, including; Mademoiselle mag. award, 1952; Lady Year award Harriet Beecher Stowe Jr. High Sch., 1958; Spirit Achievement award Albert Einstein Sch. Medicine, 1965; certificate Honor award George Gershwin Jr. High Sch., 1967; Myrtle Wreath award Hadassah, 1967; Smith medal Smith Coll., 1968; Outstanding Am. Women award Am. Mothers Com. Inc., 1970; honored as one of 150 Am. Women Physicians at exhbn. Changing the Face of Medicine at the Nat. Libr. Medicine, NIH, 2003; Golden Plate award Am. Acad. Achievement, 1971; Exceptional Black Scientists Poster Ciba Geigy, 1980. Fellow N.Y. Acad. Medicine; mem. Nat. Med. Assn. (edit. bd. jours.), Manhattan Ctrl. Med. Soc., N.Y. County Med. Soc. (nominating com.), AMA, AAAS, Am. Assn. Cancer Rsch. (dir. Rsch. Salute 1971-74, established Jane Cooke Wright lectureship 2006), N.Y. Acad. Scis., N.Y. Cancer Soc., Internat. Med. and Rsch. Found. (v.p.), Am. Cancer Soc. (dir. div.), N.Y. Cancer Soc. (pres. 1970-71), Am. Soc. Clin. Oncology (sec. treas. 1964-67, Spl. Appreciation award as a founding mem. 2004), Contin Soc., Sigma Xi, Lambda Kappa Mu, Alpha Omega Alpha. Clubs: The 400 (N.Y. Med. Coll.). Address: 7002 Kennedy Blvd East Apt 9C Guttenberg NJ 07093

WRIGHT, JASON HOWARD SEBASTIAN, communications executive; b. Waterbury, Conn., Nov. 2, 1960; s. Joseph Thomas and Lyda (Hawkins) W. AB, Georgetown U., 1982. With Aetna Life & Casualty Co., Hartford, Conn., 1982—87, mgr. corp. pub. rels., 1987-88, dir. corp. comms., 1988—90; v.p. comm. RJR Nabisco, 1990—93; sr. v.p. Nabisco Group Holdings Corp. (formerly RJR Nabisco), 1993—2000; prin. Geer Mountain Holdings, LLC, 2000—03; sr. v.p. comm. and pub. affairs Merrill Lynch & Co. Inc., 2003—. Bd. dirs. CCW Holdings Corp. Trustee Mus. for African Art, NYC, Cooper Union for the Advancement of Sci. and Art, James Beard Found. Democrat. Avocation: tennis. Office: Merrill Lynch & Co Inc 4 World Fin Ctr New York NY 10080 Home Phone: 860-927-1629; Office Phone: 212-449-3535. E-mail: jason_wright@ml.com.

WRIGHT, JAY, men's college basketball coach; b. Dec. 24, 1961; m. Patricia Reilly; children: Taylor, Colin, Reilly. Graduated with degrees in economics and sociology, Bucknell Univ., 1983. Adminstrv. asst. Phila. Stars Football, 1983; began career in coaching U. Rochester, 1984; various assignments including scouting, on-court coaching and recruiting, 1987—92; aide Drexel Univ., 1984, asst. coach, 1986—87, Villanova Univ., 1987—92, UNLV, 1992—94; head coach Univ. Rochester, 1984—86, Hofstra Univ., 1994—2001, Villanova Univ., 2001—. Asst. coach U.S.A. Basketball World Championship for Young Men Qualifying Team, 2000; head coach U.S.A. Basketball, 2005. Involved with Phila. Chpt. Coaches vs Cancer. Named Phila. Big Five Eastern College Coach of Yr., 2004—05. Office: Villanova Univ Dept Athletics 800 Lancaster Ln Villanova PA 19085-1603

WRIGHT, JEANNE ELIZABETH JASON, advertising executive; b. Washington, June 24, 1934; d. Robert Stewart and Elizabeth (Gaddis) Jason; m. Benjamin Hickman Wright, Oct. 30, 1965; stepchildren: Benjamin (dec.), Deborah, David, Patricia. BA, Radcliffe Coll., 1956; MA, U. Chgo., 1958. Psychiat. social worker Lake County Mental Health Clinic, Gary, Ind., Psychiat. and Psychosomatic Inst., Michael Reese Hosp., Chgo., Jewish Child Care Assn., NYC, 1958-70; gen. mgr. Black Media, Inc. (advt. rep. co.), NYC, 1970-74, pres., 1974-75; pres., exec. editor, syndicator weekly editorial features Black Resources, Inc., NYC, 1975-99; ret., 1999. Mem. planning com. First Black Power Conf., Newark, 1966, Second Black Power Conf., Phila., 1967, First Internat. Black Cultural & Bus. Expn., N.Y.C., 1971; nat. bd. dirs. Afro-Am. Family & Community Svcs., Inc., Chgo., 1971-75; founding coun. mem. Nat. Assault on Illiteracy Program, 1980-99; pres. Metro-N.Y. chpt. Nat. Assn. Media Women, Inc., 1986-89. Recipient Pres.' award Nat. Assn. Black Women Attys., 1977, 2d ann. Freedom's Jour. award Journalism Students and Faculty of U. D.C. Dept. Communicative and Performing Arts, 1979, Communication award Harlem Svc. Ctr., ARC, 1988, Spl. award Beta Omicron chpt. Phi Delta Kappa, 1982; named Disting. Black Woman in Industry, Nat. Coun. Negro Women, 1981. Mem. AAAS, Nat. Assn. Social Workers, Acad. Cert. Social Workers, Nat. Assn. Media Women (pres. Met. N.Y. chpt. 1986-89, Nat. Media Woman of Yr. award l984, 86, Founders award l986), Newswomen's Club N.Y., U. Chgo. Alumni Assn., NAACP, Radcliffe Club, Harvard Club, Alpha Kappa Alpha Sorority Inc. (Gamma Zeta Omega Chpt.). Democrat. Home and Office: 1800 NW 187th St Opa Locka FL 33056-3317

WRIGHT, JEFFREY, actor; b. Washington, Dec. 7, 1965; m. Carmen Ejogo, Aug. 2000; 1 child, Elijah. BA in polit. sci., Amherst Coll., 1987, degree (hon.), 2004. Actor: (plays) Les Blancs, 1989, She Stoops to Conquer, 1990—91, Juno and the Paycock, Search and Destroy, 1990—91, Playboy of the West Indies, Daylight in the Exile, Othello (NY Shakespeare Fest.), Angels in America: Millennium Approaches, 1993—94, Angels in America: Perestroika, 1993—94 (Outer Critics Circle award best sup. actor, 1994, Drama Desk award for featured actor, 1994, Tony award for featured actor, 1994), Bring in da Noise, Bring in da Funk, 1996, King Lear, 1996, This Is How It Goes, 2005; (films) Presumed Innocent, 1990, Jumpin' at the Boneyard, 1991, Basquiat, 1996, Critical Care, 1997, Celebrity, 1998, Ride With the Devil, 1999, Cement, 1999, Sin's Kitchen, 2000, Crime and Punishment in Suburbia, 2000, Hamlet, 2000, Shaft, 2000 (Toronto Film Critics Assoc. award for best sup. actor, 2000), Boycott, 2001, Ali, 2000, Eye See You, 2001, Intolerable Cruelty, 2002, The Manchurian Candidate, 2004, Broken Flowers, 2005, Syriana, 2005, Lady in the Water, 2006, Casino Royale, 2006; (TV films) Boycott, 2001, Lackawanna Blues, 2005; (TV miniseries) Angels in America, 2003 (Golden Globe for best supporting actor in a miniseries, 2004, Emmy award Outstanding Supporting Actor in a Miniseries or a Movie, 2004). Office: Creative Artists Agency 9830 Wilshire Blvd Beverly Hills CA 90211 *

WRIGHT, JEFFREY A., biology, physics educator; BA, Bellarmine Univ.; MA, Univ. Louisville. Cert. Nat. Bd. Tchg. Standards. Tchr. Trinity H.S., 1990—98; physics, biol. tchr. Louisville Male Traditional H.S., 1998—. Chmn. Physics Alliance; mentor tchr. Nat. Bd. Certification. Named Ky. H.S. Tchr. of Yr., 2005, Ky. Tchr. of Yr., 2006; recipient Disney Tchr. award, 2005. Mem.: LATTICE Tech. Alliance, Louisville Area Chemistry and Physics Alliances, Ky. Assn. Physics Tchrs., NEA, Ky. Edn. Assn., Nat. Sci. Tchr. Assn., Louisville Area Amateur Astronomers. Office: Louisville Male HS 4409 Preston Hwy Louisville KY 40213 Office Phone: 502-485-8292. Office Fax: 502-485-8770. Business E-Mail: JWright4@Jefferson.k12.ky.us. *

WRIGHT, JESSE HARTZELL, psychiatrist, educator; b. Altoona, Pa., Sept. 21, 1943; s. Jesse H. and Marion (Stone) W.; m. Susanne Judy Wright, July 9, 1967; children: Andrew, Laura. BS, Juniata Coll., 1965; MD, Jefferson Med. Coll., 1969; PhD, U. Louisville, 1976. Diplomate Am. Bd. Psychiatry and Neurology, Am. Bd. Med. Examiners; lic. psychiatrist, Ky. Asst. prof. U. Louisville, 1975-79, assoc. prof., 1979-87, prof., 1987—; clin. dir. Norton Psychiat. Clinic, Louisville, 1975-83, med. dir., 1983—; chief adult psychiatry U. Louisville, 2000—; resident in psychiatry U. Mich., Ann Arbor, 1970-73. Author: first multimedia computer program for psychotherapy, Good Days Ahead, chpts. to books; contbr. articles to prof. jours; author: (self help book for depression) Getting Your Life Back, (textbook with DVD) Learning Cognitive-Behavior Therapy, others. Fellow Am.Psychiat. Assn., Am. Coll. Psychiatrists; mem. Ky. Psychiat. Assn. (sec. 1979-80, v.p. 1980-81, pres. 1982-83), Acad. Cognitive Therapy (founding pres.), Alpha Omega Alpha. Avocations: gardening, running, theater, skiing. Home: 15 Indian Hills Trl Louisville KY 40207-1532 Office: Norton Psychiat Clinic 200 E Chestnut St Louisville KY 40202-1822

WRIGHT, JO ANNE, priest; b. Wichita, Kans., May 31, 1935; d. Everett Joseph and Agnes Josephine (Ketcham) Steinheimer; m. John Cook Wright, June 25, 1955 (div. June 1976); children: Elizabeth, Jennifer, Melanie, Kennedy Weston. AB, Oberlin Coll., 1955; MDiv, Ch. Divinity Sch. of Pacific, Berkeley, Calif., 1987. Ordained deacon Episcopal Ch., 1987, ordained priest, 1987. Pre-sch. tchr. Children's Hour Headstart, Lawrence, Kans., 1977-79; reference libr. Lawrence (Kans.) Pub. Libr., 1979-84; rector St. Luke's Episcopal Ch., Wamego, Kans., 1987-98, St. John's Episcopal Ch., Vinita, Okla., 1999—2005; mem. diocesan coun. Diocese of Okla., 2000—01, dean NE region, 2001—05; ret. Youth officer Diocese of Kans., Topeka, 1987-92, rural missioner, 1992-98, mem. standing com., mem. diocesan coun., 1997-98; pres. Vinita Minsterial Alliance, 2001, sec., 2003. Writer monthly column Plenteous Harvest, 1987-92. Chair Wamego Coun. Chs., 1998, CROP walk organizer, 1988, 92, 95; tour leader Ednl. Opportunities, Israel, 1998; mem. bishop search com. Diocese Okla., 2005-2007. Roanridge grantee Episcopal Ch. U.S.A., 1995. Mem. Phi Beta Kappa. Democrat. Avocations: reading, travel. Home: 821 N Foreman Apt 222 Vinita OK 74301-1432 E-mail: jowright@junct.com.

WRIGHT, JOAN L., artist; d. William Henry and Elsie Christina (Motzer) Harrison; m. Barry Duane Wright; children: Stephen Craig, Michael Alan, Jeffrey Lynn. Student, Art League LA, 1964-68, Valley Coll., 1966-69. Designer, sculpture, glazer Al Hardy, Burbank, Calif., 1951-53; budget coord. Los Angeles County, North Hollywood, Calif., 1953; writer Intermountain Contractor, Salt Lake City, 1954-56; artist, instr. Art League LA, Van Nuys, Calif., 1966—, Sylmar, Calif., 1966—; jewelry designer, artist, 1968—. Rep. for State of Calif. Presdl. Arts Program, Washington. Contbr. articles to art publs.; films, children's books, album covers; featured in many books and publs. western art; collector plates, Danbury Mint, Norwalk, Conn., 1995—, other pub. cos., installations of murals worldwide, exhibitions include Gene Autry Western Heritage Mus., LA, Lancaster Mus. Art, Ronald Reagan Libr., Simi, Calif., Las Vegas (Nev.) Art Mus., Chas Russell Mus., China, Learnin' Tree, Boulder, Colo., Scafa, other cos. Mem.: Wildlife Waystation, Oil Painters Am., Internat. Art and Culture Assn., Women Artists of West (bd. dirs. 1971—73, pres. 1974—77, v.p. 1978—), Audubon Soc. Avocations: birdwatching, environmental activities, sports, stained glass, stamp collecting/philately. Personal E-mail: jwartist1@aol.com.

WRIGHT, JOHN, classics educator; b. NYC, Mar. 9, 1941; s. Henry and Dorothy (Chaya) W.; m. Ellen Faber, June 16, 1962; children: Jennifer, Emily. BA, Swarthmore Coll., 1962; MA, Ind. U., 1964, PhD, 1971. Instr. classics U. Rochester, NY, 1968—72, asst. prof., 1972—75; assoc. prof. Northwestern U., Evanston, Ill., 1975-77, prof., 1977—83, dept. chmn., 1978—97, 2000—01, John Evans prof. Latin lang. and lit., 1983—2001, prof. emeritus in svc., 2002—05, prof. emeritus, 2005—. Author: The Play of Antichrist, 1967, Dancing in Chains: The Stylistic Unity of the Comoedia Palliata, 1974, The Life of Cola de Rienzo, 1975, Essays on the Iliad: Selected Modern Criticism, 1978, Plautus: Curculio, Introduction and Notes, 1981, rev. edit., 1993, Ralph Stanley and the Clinch Mountain Boys: A Discography, 1983, The Five-String Banjo Stanley Style, 1984, rev. edit. (Clyde Pharr) Homeric Greek: A Book for Beginners, 1985, It's the Hardest Music in the World to Play: The Ralph Stanley Story in His Own Words, 1987, Traveling the High Way Home: Ralph Stanley and the World of Traditional Bluegrass Music, 1993; albums Everything She Asks For, 1993, Traveling the High Way Home, 1995, Promises, 1996, Ellen and John Wright 1, Ellen and John Wright 2, 1998, I Shook Hands with Eleanor Roosevelt, 2004; contbr. articles to profl. jours. Fellow Am. Acad. Rome, 1966-68; Nat. Endowment Humanities Younger humanist fellow, 1973-74; named to Honorable Order of Ky. Colonels; recipient songwriting prize Santa Fe Bluegrass and Old Time Music Festival, 1996. Mem.: Am. Fedn. of Musicians, Local 1000, BMI, Nat. Acad. Recording Arts and Scis., Am. Acad. in Rome Soc. of Fellows, Internat. Bluegrass Music Assn. (Print Media Personality of Yr. 1994), Chgo. Area Bluegrass Assn. Home: 1137 Noyes St Evanston IL 60201-2633 Personal E-mail: jhwright@northwestern.edu.

WRIGHT, JOHN COLLINS, retired chemistry professor; b. Oak Hill, W.Va., Aug. 5, 1927; s. John C. and Irene (Collins) W.; m. Margaret Ann Cyphers, Sept. 11, 1949; children: Jeffrey Cyphers, John Timothy, Curtis Scott, Keith Alexander. BS, W.Va. Wesleyan Coll., 1948, LLD, 1974; PhD, U. Ill., 1951; DSc (hon.), U. Ala., 1979, W.Va. Inst. Tech., 1979. Research chemist Hercules, Inc., 1951-57; mem. faculty W.Va. Wesleyan Coll., 1957-64; asst. program dir. NSF, 1964-65; dean Coll. Arts and Scis., No. Ariz. U., 1966-70, W.Va. U., Morgantown, 1970-74; vice chancellor W.Va. Bd. Regents, Charleston, 1974-78; pres. U. Ala., Huntsville, 1978-88, prof. chemistry, 1988-95, prof. emeritus, 1995—; interim pres. W.Va. Coll. Grad. Studies, Institute, 1975-76. Hon. rsch. assoc. Univ. Coll., London, 1962-63; cons. NSF, 1965—, Army Sci. Bd., U.S. Army, 1979-82, Nat. Sci. Resources Ctr. Served with USNR, 1945-46. Mich. fellow Center Study Higher Edn., U. Mich., 1965-66 Mem. AAAS, NSTA. Office: 2312 Carlton Cove Blvd Huntsville AL 35802 Office Phone: 256-883-2272. E-mail: johnhasp@aol.com.

WRIGHT, JOHN COTTON, archivist, consultant; b. Sharon, Mass., July 27, 1928; s. George Carroll and Dorothy (Cotton) Wright; m. VerlieAnn Kapule Malina, May 23, 1978. Degree in philosophy, U. Hawaii, Manoa, 1955, MLS, 1987. Cert. archivist Acad. Archivists. Editl. asst. U. Hawaii Press, Honolulu, 1953—55; self employed Kona, Hawaii, 1956—57; adminstrv. asst. Oahu Rwy. and Land Co., Honolulu, 1958—61; asst. to chmn. Dillingham Corp., Honolulu, 1962—66; historian, archivist Bernice Pauahi Bishop Mus., Honolulu, 1966—81; pres. Wright Cons., Kailua, Hawaii, 1982—; prodn. editor Mechas Press, LLC, Honolulu, 1998—. Cons. Mariners Mus., Newport News, Va., 1967, JDR 3rd Fund, NYC, 1975, NYC, 77, Asia Found., San Francisco, 1979, San Francisco, 81. Mem.: Internat. Coun. Archives (hon.). Office: Wright Cons 361 Kaimake Loop Kailua HI 96734-2018 Office Phone: 808-261-3714.

WRIGHT, JOHN DANIEL, minister; b. Middletown, Ohio, July 30, 1984; s. Hargie and Ilene Wright. LittD (hon.), Christian Ministry Inst. Tex.; DD (hon.), St. Luke Evang. Sch. Bibl. Studies. Ordained minister 2001, lic. to preach 2003, evangelist 2003. Pres., CEO, Johnsboro Online, Richmond, Ky.; founder Am. Assoc. Wedding Officiants. Recipient Ky. Col., The Hon. Paul E. Patton, Gov. Ky., 2002. Mem.: Masons. Republican. Home: 217 Keystone Dr Apt 10 Richmond KY 40475-8573 Personal E-mail: jdw@jdwright.us.

WRIGHT, JOHN F., state supreme court justice; BS, U. Nebr., 1967, JD, 1970. Atty. Wright & Simmons, 1970-84, Wright, Sorensen & Brower, 1984-91; mem., coord. Commn. on Post Secondary Edn., 1991-92; judge Nebr. Ct. Appeals, 1992-94; assoc. justice Nebr. Supreme Ct., 1994—. Chmn. bd. dirs. Panhandle Legal Svcs., 1970. Mem. Scottsbluff Bd. Edn., 1980-87, pres., 1984, 86. Served with U.S. Army, 1970, Nebr. N.G., 1970-76. Recipient Friend of Edn. award Scottsbluff Edn. Assn., 1992. Office: Nebr Supreme Ct 2207 State Capitol PO Box 98910 Lincoln NE 68509-8910 *

WRIGHT, JOHN ROBERT, retired pathologist, educator; b. Winnipeg, Man., Can., Aug. 18, 1935; came to U.S., 1961, naturalized, 1968; s. Ross Grant and Anna Marie (Crispin) W.; m. Deanna Pauline Johnson, June 25, 1960 (dec. May 24, 2004); children— Carolyn Deanna, David John. MD with honors, U. Man., 1959. Diplomate: Am. Bd. Pathology. Intern Winnipeg Gen. Hosp., 1959-60, resident, 1960-61, Balt. City Hosp., 1961-63, Buffalo Gen. Hosp., 1963-64; teaching fellow in medicine U. Man., 1960-61; instr. in pathology, Buswell fellow SUNY-Buffalo, 1965-67, prof. pathology, chmn. dept. pathology, 1974-96, interim dean medicine, v.p. clin. affairs, 1997-98, dean medicine, 1998—2001; asst. chief pathology Balt. City Hosps. and; asst. prof. Johns Hopkins U., 1967-74; cons. Roswell Park Meml. Inst., 1975—2005, bd. visitors, 1981-97, interim dir., 1985-86, chmn. bd. visitors, 1987-97; ret., 2005. Recipient Louis A. and Ruth Siegel Disting. Teaching award SUNY-Buffalo, 1977, 78, 88, Deans award SUNY, 1987. Fellow Assn. Pathology Chairs (sr., pres. 1994-96); mem. AMA, AAAS, Coll. Am. Pathologists, Am. Soc. Investigative Pathologists, Am. Soc. Clin. Pathologists, U.S. and Can. Acad. Pathology, Alpha Omega Alpha. Achievements include research in amyloidosis and aging. Home: 46 Wynngate Ln Williamsville NY 14221-1840 Office: 206 Farber Hall SUNY Buffalo NY 14214 Personal E-mail: jrwright@buffalo.edu.

WRIGHT, JOSEPH ROBERT, JR., corporate executive; b. Tulsa, Sept. 24, 1938; s. Joe Robert and Ann Helen (Cech) W. BS, Colo. Sch. Mines, 1961; M.I.A., Yale U., 1964. V.p. Booz, Allen & Hamilton, 1965-71; dep. dir. Bur. Census, Dept. Commerce, 1971-72; dep. adminstr. Social and Econ. Statis. Adminstrn., 1972-73, acting asst. sec. econ. affairs, 1973; asst. sec. adminstr. Dept. Agr., 1973-76; pres. Citicorp Retail Inc. and Retail Consumer Svcs. Inc., NYC; v.p. Citicorp, Inc., NYC, 1976—81; dep. sec. Dept. Commerce, Washington, 1981-82; dep. dir. Office Mgmt. and Budget, Washington, 1982-88; chmn. Pres.'s Coun. on Integrity and Efficiency, 1982-89, Pres.'s Coun. on Mgmt. Improvement, 1984-89; dir. Office Mgmt. and Budget, 1988-89; exec. v.p., vice chmn., bd. dirs. W.R. Grace & Co., NYC, 1989-94; chmn. Grace Energy, Inc., 1989—94, Grace Environ,. Inc., 1989—94; chmn., CEO, dir. AmTec, Inc., NYC, 1994—2000; vice chmn. Terremark Worldwide, 2000—. Fed. co-chmn. Coastal Plains Regional Commn., 1981-82, Four Corners Regional Commn., 1981-82, New Eng. Regional Commn., 1981-82, Old West Regional Commn., 1981-82, Pacific N.W. Regional Commn., 1981-82, S.W. Border Regional Commn., 1981-82; co-chmn. Baker & Taylor, 1996-2002; chmn. GRC Internat., 1997-2000; vice chmn. Jefferson Consulting, 1998-2004; pres., CEO, dir. PanAmSat Inc., 2001-06; bd. dirs. Travelers, 1990-99, Harcourt Bruce Janovich, 1990-92, GRC Internat., 1994-99, Baker & Taylor, 1995-2002, PanAmSat Inc., 1995-2006, Verso-Tech, 1998-2004, Titan Corp., 2000-05, AT&T Govt. Markets, 2000-05, Terremark Worldwide, 2000—, Sci. Games Inc., 2004—, Intelsat Ltd., 2006—; chmn., dir. Intelsat, Ltd., Bermuda, NYC, 2006—. Mem. Pres. Export Coun., 1989-93, adv. bd. Coun. for Excellence in Govt., 1988-96; trustee Hampton U., 1990-98; mem. Pres.'s Commn. on Postal Reform, 2004-05; mem. Pres.'s Nat. Security Telecomm. Adv. Coun., 2005—; mem. FCC Network Reliability and Interoperability Coun., FCC Media Security and Reliability Coun.; mem. Def. Bus. Bd., 2007—. 1st lt. AUS, 1963—65. Recipient Disting. Achievement medal Colo. Sch. Mines, 1985, Pres.'s Citizens award and medal, 1989; named Govt. Exec. of Yr. Govt. Computer News Mag., 1988. Mem. Nat. Acad. Pub. Adminstrn. (mem. com. for responsible fed. budget), Colo. Sch. Mines Alumni Assn., Chief Execs. Orgn., World Bus. Coun., Coun. on Fgn. Rels., Reagan Alumni Assn., NY Econ. Club, Bridge Golf Club (NY), Lost Tree Country Club (Fla.). Home: 10 Gracie Sq Apt 7G New York NY 10028-8031 Office: Intelsat Ltd 405 Lexington Ave 53rd Fl New York NY 10174 Office Phone: 212-839-1806. Business E-Mail: joe.wright@intelsat.com.

WRIGHT, JOSEPHINE ROSA BEATRICE, musicologist; b. Detroit, Sept. 5, 1942; d. Joseph Le Vander and Eva Lee Garrison W.; Mus.B., U. Mo., Columbia, 1963, M.A., 1967; Mus.M., Pius XII Acad., Florence, Italy, 1964; Ph.D., N.Y.U., 1975. Instr. music York Coll., CUNY, 1972-75, asst. prof., 1975; asst. prof. Afro-Am. studies in musicology Harvard U., Cambridge, Mass., 1976-81; assoc. dir. integration of Afro-Am. folk arts with music project, Nat. Endowment Humanities, 1979-82; assoc. prof. music and Black studies Coll. of Wooster, 1981-90, prof. music and Black studies, 1991-2000, prof. Music and The Josephine Lincoln Morris prof. Black studies, 2000-, chair Africana studies, 2002—; panelist, cons. on music Mass. Coun. of Arts and Humanities, 1978-80; cons. Nat. Endowment Humanities, 1982-83, 87, 89, 90, Ohio Humanities Coun., 1986; apptd. mem. Nat. Artistic Directorate, Am. Classical Music Hall of Fame, Cin. Author: Ignatius Sancho (1729-1780), An Early African Composer in England: The Collected Edition of His Music in Facsimile, 1981; editor: Am. Music, 1993-97, Music in African Am. Culture series, 1995—2000; editor of new music: The Black Perspective in Music, 1979-91, (with Sam Floyd) New Perspectives on Music: Essays in Honor of Eileen Southern, 1992; co-editor: The Bicentennial Issue of The Black Perspective in Music, 1976, (with Eileen Southern) African-American Traditions in Song, Sermon, Tale and Dance, 1991, (with Eileen Southern) Images: Iconography of Music in African-American Culture, 2000; mem. editl. bd. Jour. Am. Musicol. Soc., 2003, Am. Music, 2004, Jour. Soc. for Am. Music, 2006—; contbr. articles to profl. jours. Mem. Am. Musicol. Soc. (dir.-at-large 1998-2000), Soc. Am. Music (bd. dirs.), Nat. Coun. for black studies, U. Mo. Faculty of Arts and Sci. Alumni Assn. (trustee 1982-85), Pi Kappa Lambda. Democrat. Anglican. Office Phone: 330-263-2044. Business E-Mail: jwright@wooster.edu.

WRIGHT, JUDITH ANN, elementary school educator; d. Harold Eugene Donzé and Glenna Mae Van Hise; m. Kurt Ornell Wright, Sept. 4, 1965 (dec.); children: Tyson, Karin Paul, Jennifer. BA, Calif. State U., Northridge, 1964, MA in Spl. Edn., 1995. Spl. edn. tchr., Malabar St. Elem. Sch. L.A. Unified Sch. Dist., 1988—93, spl. edn. tchr., Leo Politi Elem. Sch., 1993—97, resource specialist tchr., 1997—. Office: Sylvan Park Elem Sch 6238 Noble Ave Van Nuys CA 91411 Home Phone: 818-767-5037; Office Phone: 818-988-9816. Personal E-mail: jwright916@aol.com.

WRIGHT, JUDITH MARGARET, law librarian, educator, dean; b. Jackson, Tenn., Aug. 16, 1944; d. Joseph Clarence and Mary Catherine (Key) Wright; m. Mark A. Johnson, Apr. 17, 1976; children: Paul, Michael. BS, U. Memphis, 1966; MA, U. Chgo., 1971; JD, DePaul U., 1980. Bar: Ill. 1980. Librarian Oceanway Sch., Jacksonville, Fla., 1966-67; program dir. ARC, South Vietnam, 1967-68; documents and reference librarian D'Angelo Law Library, U. Chgo., 1970-74, reference librarian, 1974-77, dir., lectr. in law, 1980—2000, law libr., assoc. dean for libr. and info. svcs., lectr. in law, 2000—. Mem. adv. bd. Legal Reference Svcs. Quar., 1981—. Mem.: Chgo. Assn. Law Libraries, Am. Assn. Law Libraries, ABA. Democrat. Methodist. Office: U Chgo Law Sch D'Angelo Law Libr 1111 E 60th St Chicago IL 60637-2745 Home Phone: 773-947-0282; Office Phone: 773-702-9616. Office Fax: 773-702-2889. Business E-Mail: jm-wright@uchicago.edu.

WRIGHT, KATIE HARPER, educational administrator, journalist; b. Crawfordsville, Ark., Oct. 5, 1923; d. James Hale and Connie Mary (Locke) Harper; m. Marvin Wright, Mar. 21, 1952; 1 child, Virginia K. Jordan. BA, U. Ill., 1944, MEd, 1959; EdD, St. Louis U., 1979. Elem. and spl. edn. tchr. East St. Louis (Ill.) Pub. Schs., 1944-65, dir. Dist. 189 Instrnl. Materials Program, 1965-71, dir. spl. edn. Dists. 188, 189, 1971-77, asst. supt. programs, 1977-79; interim supt. East St. Louis Sch. Dist. 189, 1993-94. Adj. faculty Harris/Stowe State Coll., 1980, adj. prof. edn. emeritus; mem. staff St. Louis U., 1989—; interim supt. Dist. 189 Schs., 1994—; mem. Pres.'s Commn. on Excellence in Spl. Edn. Author: Delta Sigma Theta/East St. Louis Chapter History, 1992; contbr. articles to profl. jours.; feature writer St. Louis Argus Newspaper, 1979—. Mem. Ill. Commn. on Children, 1973-85, East St. Louis Bd. Election Comms., East St. Louis Fin. Adv. Authority, 1999—; pres. bd. dirs. St. Clair County Mental Health Ctr., 1970-72, 87—; bd. dirs. River Bluff coun. Girl Scouts USA, 1979—, nat. bd. dirs., 1981-84; bd. dirs. Jackie Joyner-Kersee Youth Ctr. Found., 1991—, United Way, 1979—, Urban League, 1979—, Provident Counseling Ctr., 1995-98; pres. bd. trustees East St. Louis Pub. Libr., 1972-77; pres., bd. dirs. St. Clair County Mental Health Ctrs., 1987; mem. adv. bd. Magna Bank; charter mem. Coalition of 100 Black Women; mem. coord. coun. ethnic affairs Synod of Mid-Am., Presbyn. Ch. U.S.A.; mem. Ill. Dept. Corrections Sch. Bd., 1995—; charter mem. Metro East Links Group, Gateway chpt. The Links, Inc.; mem. Ill. Minority/Female Bus. Coun., 1991—; mem. Pres.'s Commn. on Excellence in Spl. Edn., 2001--. Recipient of more than 150 awards including Lamp of Learning award East St. Louis Jr. Wednesday Club, 1965, Outstanding Working Woman award Downtown St. Louis, Inc., 1967, Ill. State citation for ednl. document Love is Not Enough, 1974, Delta Sigma Theta citation for document Good Works, 1979, Girl Scout Thanks badge, 1982, award Nat. Coun. Negro Women, 1983, Cmty. Svc. award Met. East Bar Assn., 1983, Journalist award Sigma Gamma Rho, Spelman Coll. Alumni award, 1990, A World of Difference award, 1990, 92, Edn. award St. Louis, YWCA, 1991, SIU-E-Kimmel award, 1991, St. Clair County Mental Health award, 1992, Gateway East Met. Ministry Dr. M.L. King award, 1993, Nat. Coun. Negro Women Black Leader of Yr., 1995, Disting. Alumni award U. Ill., 1996, Pioneer award Mosque 28B, 2000, Tri Del Globe award, 2001, Urban League Merit award, 2002, Ill. Office of Edn. award, 2002, Eugene B. Redmond Writers Club award, 2002, NFPW Quest award, 2004, Liberty Bell award St. Clair County Bar Assocs., 2005, St. Clair County Bar Assn. award, 2005; named Woman of Achievement, St. Louis Globe Democrat, 1974, Outstanding Adminstr. So. Region III Office Edn., 1975, Woman of Yr. in Edn. St. Clair County YWCA, 1987, Nat. Top Lady of Yr., 1988, Disting. Alumnus U. Ill., 1996, Citizen Amb., South Africa, 1996, sch. named after her East St. Louis Sch., 2005; named to Vashon H.S. Hall of Fame, 1989, Sr. Illinoisan Hall of Fame, 1997; East St. Louis Elem. Sch. named for Dr. Katie Harper Wright, 2005. Mem. Am. Librs. Trustees Assn. (regional v.p. 1978-79, 92, nat. sec. 1979-80), Ill. Commn. on Children, Mensa, Coun. for Exceptional Children (mem. pres.'s commn. excellence spl. edn.), Top Ladies of Distinction (pres. 1987-91, nat. editor 1991—, Journalism award 1992, Media award 1992), Delta Sigma Theta (chpt. pres. 1960-62, Letters award 2000), Kappa Delta Pi (pres. So. Ill. U. chpt. 1973-74), Phi Delta Kappa (Svc. Key award 1984, chpt. pres. 1984-85), Iota Phi Lambda, Phi Lambda Theta (chpt. pres. 1985-87), East St. Louis Women's Club (pres. 1973-75). Republican. Home: 733 N 40th St East Saint Louis IL 62205-2138

WRIGHT, KENNETH BROOKS, lawyer; b. Whittier, Calif., June 5, 1934; s. Albert Harold and Marian (Schwey) W.; m. Sandra Beryl Smith, June 20, 1959; children: Margo Teresa, Daniel Brooks, John Waugh. BA cum laude, Pomona Coll., 1956; JD, Stanford U., 1960. Bar: Calif. 1961, U.S. Supreme Ct. 1979. Assoc., then ptnr. Lawler, Felix & Hall, 1961—77; ptnr. Morgan, Lewis & Bockius, LA, 1978—99, counsel, 1999—2003, ret. ptnr., 2004. Tchg. team leader Nat. Inst. Trial Advocacy, 1978-80; governing com. Calif. Continuing Edn. Bar, 1973-77, chmn., 1975-76; nat. panel arbitrators Am. Arbitration Assn., 1970-91; lectr. ABA Sect. Litig. Nat. Inst., 1979-86; bd. dirs. L.A. Internat. Comml. Arbitration Ctr. Chmn. bd. editors: Am. Bar Jour, 1977-81. Pres. Pomona Coll. Alumni Assn., 1970-71; pres. parent tchr. com. Campbell Hall Sch., 1973-74, bd. dirs., vice chmn., 1994—; counsel Vol. League San Fernando Valley, 1979-81; chmn. sect. adminstrn. justice Town Hall of Calif., 1970-71; sr. warden Episcopal Ch., 1973-74. Served with U.S. Army, 1956-57. Mem. ABA (dir. programs litig. sect. 1977-81, coun. 1982-88, standing com on comm. 1978-88, chmn. 1987-88, chmn. sect. book pub. com. 1986-89, pres. fellows young lawyers 1985-86, bd. dirs. 1980-89), Internat. Bar Assn., Assn. Bus. Trial Lawyers (chair com. alt. dispute resolution 1991-93, bd. dirs. 1993-96), Am. Law Inst., Am. Bar Found., State Bar Calif. (gov. com. continuing edn. bar 1972-77, chmn. 1975-76), Conf. Barristers (exec. com. 1966-69, 1st v.p. 1969), L.A. County Bar Assn. (com. judiciary 1981-83, chmn. CLE adv. com. 1989-91, vice-chmn. CLE com. 1991-93, bd. dirs. L.A. Lawyers 1989-94), L.A. County Bar Found. (bd. dirs., trustee 1993-99, exec. com. internat. sect. 1996-99), Jonathan Club, Phi Beta Kappa. Republican. Avocations: skiing, tennis. Home: 3610 Longridge Ave Sherman Oaks CA 91423-4918 Office: Morgan Lewis & Bockius 300 S Grand Ave Los Angeles CA 90071-3109

WRIGHT, KEVIN DALE, medical researcher; b. Wichita, Kans., Aug. 13, 1978; s. Dale Howard and Patricia Ethel Wright; m. Sasha Naomi Fureman, July 2, 2005. BA in Biology and Religion with honors, Augustana Coll., Rock Island, Ill., 2000; MPA, No. Ill. U., DeKalb, 2002. Adminstrv. intern Village of Deerfield, Ill., 2000—02; preds. mgmt. fellow Nat. Cancer Inst., Bethesda, Md., 2002—04, health sci. analyst, 2004—. Analyst Def. Intelligence Agy. USNR, 2003—06. Mem.: ASPA, Mensa, Pi Alpha Alpha. Avocations: golf, exercise, woodworking, softball.

WRIGHT, KRISTOPHER, biology professor; b. St. Paul; m. Angela Schaefer, Sept. 6, 1998; children: Quinn children: Caleb. PhD, Oreg. State U. Prof. biology U. Wis., Platteville, 2001—. Pres. Platteville Cmty. Arboretum, 2005—06. Office Phone: 608-342-1689.

WRIGHT, LARRY JAN, epidemiologist; s. J. Evan and Mary Bluemel Wright; m. LaVonda Eddington, June 17, 1960; children: Deborah Hamilton, Karl Larry, Tana Lynn. BS, U. Utah, Salt Lake City, 1960, MD, 1964. Diplomate Am. Bd. Internal Medicine, 1972. Intern, resident on ward medicine Barnes Hosp. Wash. U., St. Louis, 1964—66; clin. assoc. Nat. Inst. Allergy and Infectious Diseases, Bethesda, Md., 1966—68; sr. med. resident U. Wash. Hosps., Seattle, 1968—69; clin. infectious disease fellow U. Wash., Seattle, 1969—71; pvt. practice Inter-Mountain Clinic, Salt Lake City, 1971—89; clin. dir. microbiology, virology, and molecular laboratories LDS Hosp. and Urban Ctrl. Region, Salt Lake City, 1989—2000, infectious disease cons., epidemiology rschr., 1989—. Pres. InterMountain Clinic, Inc, Salt Lake City, 1981—86; vice chmn. dept. medicine LDS Hosp., Salt Lake City, 1988—89, pres. med. staff, 1989—90; bd. govs. IHC Corp., Salt Lake City, 1989—91. Contbr. articles to profl. jours. Governing bd. Work Activity Ctr. for Adults with Disabilities, Salt Lake City, 1992—98. Lt. comdr. USPHS, 1966—68. Nat. Found. scholar, March of Dimes, 1960—64. Fellow: ACP, Infectious Disease Soc. Am.; mem.: Am. Soc. for Internal Medicine, Am. Soc. for Microbiology, Alpha Omega Alpha, Phi Beta Kappa. Achievements include research in infectious diseases. Avocations: sailing, skiing, golf, hiking, travel. Office: LDS Hosp 370 9th Ave Salt Lake City UT 84103 Home Phone: 801-277-7179; Office Phone: 801-408-1006.

WRIGHT, LAURA L., air transportation executive; m. Randy Wright; children: Lindsay, Jeffrey. BSA, MSA, Univ. No. Tex., 1982. CPA Tex. Tax mgr. Arthur Young & Co., Dallas; dir. corp. taxation Southwest Airlines, Dallas, 1988—90, dir. corp. fin., 1990—95, asst. treas., 1995—98, treas.,

1998—2001, v.p. fin. & treas., 2001—04, sr. v.p. fin. & CFO, 2004—. Named one of 50 Women to Watch, Wall St. Journal, 2005. Office: Southwest Airlines 2702 Love Field Dr PO Box 36611 Dallas TX 75235-1611 Office Phone: 214-792-7784. Office Fax: 214-792-4011.

WRIGHT, LAWRENCE GEORGE, writer; b. Oklahoma City, Aug. 2, 1947; s. John Donald and Dorothy (Peacock) W.; m. Roberta Murphy, Jan. 22, 1970; children: Gordon, Caroline. BA, Tulane U., 1969; MA in Linguistics, Am. U., Cairo, 1971. English tchr. Am. U., Cairo; writer Southern Voices, So. Regional Coun., Atlanta, 1973—80, Texas Monthly Mag., Austin, 1980; founder Tex. Writers' Month. Mem. Coun. on Fgn. Rels. Author: Saints & Sinners, 1993, Remembering Satan, 1994, Twins: Genes, Environment, and the Mystery of Identity, 1997, The Looming Tower, 2006 (Pulitzer Prize for General Nonfiction, 2007, Helen Bernstein Book award, NY Pub. Libr., 2007, J. Anthony Lukas Book prize, 2007), (novels) God's Favorite, 2000, (children's books) City Children, Country Summer, 1979, (memoir) In the New World, 1988, (screenplays) Noriega: God's Favorite, 2000, (with Ed Zwick, Menno Meyjes) The Siege, 1998, (plays) Sonny's Last Shot; contributing writer, The New Yorker, 1992-. Recipient NYU Olive Branch award for internat. reporting, Nat. Magazine award for reporting, John Bartlow Martin award for Public Interest Magazine Journalism, Overseas Press Club's Ed Cunningham award for best magazine reporting, O'Henry award for Best Work of Magazine Journalism, Tex. Inst. Letters, 2005. Fluent in Arabic. *

WRIGHT, LEONARD DOUGLAS, protective services official, retired military officer; b. Ft. Bragg, NC, July 9, 1951; s. Willie Beckom and Margaret Velna (Parker) Wright; m. Dorothy LaVerne Hicks, July 17, 1987; children: Tammi Endy, Laura Holt, Blinda Dubeor. Grad., 71st HS, Fayetteville NC, 1970. Cert. state correctional officer FDLE Tng./Stds., Fla., 1994. Quartermaster USN, Norfolk, Va., 1970—94; correctional officer Dept. of Correction, Avon Park, Fla., 1994—. Decorated Navy Achievment award. Fellow: Fleet Res. (assoc.). Republican. Home: 4600 Mundell Ave Sebring FL 33870 Office: Dept Corrections State of Fla County Rd 64 E Sebring FL 33872 Home Phone: 863-382-6768; Office Phone: 863-453-3174. Personal E-mail: qmclst1181@earthlink.net.

WRIGHT, LORI DUNKLE, musician, educator; b. Kettering, Ohio, Sept. 17, 1967; d. Robert Kean and Elaine Mary Dunkle; m. Douglas Allan Wright, Aug. 1, 1992; 1 child, Rebecca Ann. MusB in Edn., Ohio State U., 1989, MA, 2001. Tchg. Cert., K12 Music Ohio Dept. of Edn., 1989. Orch. dir. Kent City Schs., Ohio, 1990—91, Worthington City Schs., Columbus, Ohio, 1991—. Clinician Ministry of Edn., Santiago, Chile, 2002; cellist, asst. prin. Springfield Symphony Orch., Ohio, 1991—; state treas. Ohio Music Edn. Assn., 2004—. Mem.: NEA (assoc.), Am. Fedn. of Musicians (assoc.), Music Edn. Nat. Conf. (assoc.; treas., state of ohio 2004—), Am. String Tchrs. Assn. (assoc.), Ohio State U. Alumni Assn. (life), Phi Kappa Phi (life), Delta Omicron (life). Conservative-R. Christian. Avocations: travel, golf, camping, hiking, backpacking. Home Phone: 614-786-7148; Office Phone: 614-883-2617.

WRIGHT, MARGARET HAGEN, computer scientist, administrator; b. San Francisco, Feb. 18, 1944; m. 1965; 1 child. BS in Mat., Stanford U., 1964, MS in Computer Sci., 1965, PhD in Computer Sci., 1976. Devel. engr. Sylvania Electronic System, 1965-71; sr. rsch. assoc., Systems Optimization Lab., Dept. Ops. Rsch. Stanford U., Palo Alto, Calif., 1976-88; with Computing Sci. Rsch. Ctr. Bell Lab., Lucent Tech., 1988, disting. mem. tech. staff, 1993, head Sci. Computing Rsch. Dept., 1997; prof. Dept. Computer Sci. Courant Inst. Math. Sci., NYU, 2005—, chair, Dept. Computer Sci., 2005—. Adv. com. Directorate Math. and Physical Sci., Nat. Sci. Found., 1994—98, chair., 1997—98; sci. adv. com. Math. Sciences Rsch. Inst., Berkeley, Calif. Assoc. editor Jour. Sci. Stats. Computer Programming, Math. Programming, Soc. Indsl. and Applied Math. Jour. on Sci. Computing, editor-in-chief Soc. Indsl. and Applied Math. Rev., Soc. Indsl. and Applied Math. Jour. on Optmization. Mem. Am. Acad. Arts and Sciences, NAE, NAS, Assn. Computing Machinery (bd. dirs. numerical analysis assn. spl. interest group), Soc. Indsl. and Applied Math. (pres. 1995-96, Award for Disting. Svc. to Profession 2001), Math. Programming Soc. Achievements include research contributing to enlarged knowledge of methods for nonlinear programming, particularly unconstrained; linearly constrained and nonlinearly constrained optimization; mathematical software, numerical linear algebra; software library development. Office: Computer Sci Dept Warren Wearver Hall Rm 405 251 Mercer St New York NY 10012 Office Fax: 212-995-4124. E-mail: mhw@cs.nyu.edu.

WRIGHT, MARGARET TAYLOR, marketing consultant, publisher; b. Wilmington, NC, Nov. 8, 1949; d. Thomas Henry and Margaret (Taylor) W. BA, U. N.C., 1972; MBA, Wake Forest U., 1978. Child advocacy specialist Child Advocacy Council Dept. Human Resources, Raleigh, NC, 1973-74; region dir. N.C. Office for Children Dept. Human Resources, Winston-Salem, 1974-76; product mgr. food div. Am. Home Products, NYC, 1978-80; account exec. Ted Bates Advt., NYC, 1981; product mgr. C.F. Mueller div. McKesson, Inc., Jersey City, 1981-83; mgr. new products Popsicle div. Sara Lee Corp., Englewood, NJ, 1983-86; pres. Wright Mktg. Blueprint, Old Chatham, NY, 1987—; chmn. Equatorial Group, Ltd., Old Chatham, NY, 1994—; pub. Grey Play Round Table Mag. on African Grey Parrots, Old Chatham, NY, 1994—, Nature's Corner Mag., 2005—. Author: African Grey Parrots, A Complete Owner's Manual, 2001; co-author: (pamphlets) Children--Helping Them Grow, 1973; pub.: Grey Play Round Table mag., 1994—; pub., creator Nature's Corner Mag., 2005. Youth coord. Jim Holshouser Gubernatorial Campaign, New Hanover County, N.C., 1972; mem. Jr. League, N.Y. and N.C., 1972-84. Episcopalian. Avocations: tennis, sailing, golf, travel. Home: # 9-609 13835 N Tatum Blvd Phoenix AZ 85032 Personal E-mail: merlin@africangreys.com.

WRIGHT, MARK A., lawyer; b. Manchester, NH, Oct. 23, 1965; s. Laurence Gary Wright and Sophia Mary Abuod; m. Paula M. Venne; children: Michael, Matthew. BS, U. N.H., 1987; JD, 1991, MS in Intellectual Property, 1997. Bar: N.H. 1991, Mass. 1998. Ptnr. McLane, Graf, Anderson & Middleton, Manchester, NH, 1991—. Chmn. Auburn (N.H.) Zoning Bd., 1995—. Named one of Best Lawyers in Am., 2003, 2004, 2005, N.H.'s Forty Under 40, Manchester (N.H.) Union Leader, 2005. Mem.: ABA, Internat. Trademark Assn., N.H. Bar Assn. (chmn. corp. bus. and banking sect.). Office: McLane Law Firm 900 Elm St Manchester NH 03101

WRIGHT, MARSHALL, manufacturing executive, diplomat; b. El Dorado, Ark., July 14, 1926; s. John Harvey and Helen Vaughan (Williams) W.; m. Mable Olean Johnson, Sept. 12, 1950 (dec. June 1989); children: William Marshall, Jefferson Vaughan; m. Lind Groseclose Vaughan, Mar. 31, 1990. Student, U. Ark., 1946-48, Cornell U., 1957-58; BS in Fgn. Service, Georgetown U., 1951. Joined U.S. Fgn. Service, 1953; vice consul Egypt, 1953-55; adminstrv. officer Can., 1956; econ. officer Burma, 1958-60; polit. officer Thailand, 1966-67; spokesman for State Dept., 1964-66; country dir. for Philippines, 1969; sr. mem. NSC, 1967-68, dir. long range planning, 1970-72; asst. sec. state for congl. relations, 1972-74; sr. fellow Nat. War Coll., 1969-70; v.p. govt. affairs Eaton Corp., 1974-76, v.p. pub. affairs, 1976-80, v.p. corp. affairs, 1980-91. Chmn. Cleve. ARC; trustee Cleve. Orch., Cleve. Inst. Music; chmn. Cleve. Com. Fgn. Rels.; vice chmn. Govtl. Rsch. Inst.; mem. Conf. Bd. Pub. Affairs Rsch. Coun., MAPI, Pub. Affairs Coun.; bd. dirs. Cleveland Town Hall, Bus. Industry Polit. action Com. With USMC, 1944-46. Recipient Meritorious Service award State Dept., 1966, Distinguished Service award, 1972 Mem. Am. Fgn. Svc. Assn., Met. Club, Dacor, Mayfield Country, Union, Moss Creek Golf Club, Berkeley Hall Golf Club. Home: 22 Cedar Ln Hilton Head Island SC 29926-1025 Home Phone: 843-837-7474; Office Phone: 843-837-7474.

WRIGHT, MARY ELLEN, theater educator; b. Commerce, Tex. d. Joseph Perry and Ora Berniece Gentry; m. James Hatfield; children: Christopher Collin, Sarah Allison Wright Metzger. BA summa cum laude, U. Tex., Tyler, 1988, MAIS, 1991—91; PhD, Tex. Tech U., Lubbock, 2001. Lectr. U. Tex. at Tyler, 1994—95, 1996—2001, asst. prof., 2002—. Adjudicator Tex. U. Interscholastic League, 1993—, St. Gregory's Sch., Tyler, 1999—; conf. planner Assn. for Theatre in Higher Edn., 1994—98; presenter in field. Costume designer (musical) Annie, (play) The Mandrake; dir.: (play) A Small Family Business, Eleemosynary; costume designer (play) Oleanna (Citation for Excellence in Costume Design, 1992); author: (play) Maggie and Mac; author: (presenter) (workshop) Creative Drama in the Classroom; costume designer (play) Othello; dir.: (play) The King Stag; costume designer (musical) The Fantasticks; dir.: (play) Art; costume designer (musical) Sound of Music, (play) Comic Potential (Citation of Excellence for Costume Design, 2001); dir.: (play) Beauty Queen of Leenane, Pygmalion; contbr. articles to profl. publs. Recipient award, Assn. for Theatre in Higher Edn., 2002, Citation of Excellence for Festival Hosting, Kennedy Ctr./Am. Coll. Theatre Festival, 1999—2000; grantee Adrian Hall Del. Project, Tex. Commn. on the Arts, 2003. Mem.: Tex. Ednl. Theatre Assn., Assn. for Theatre in Higher Edn. (conf. planner 1994—98), Alpha Chi, Phi Kappa Phi, Alpha Psi Omega (advisor 1996—2003), Gamma Phi Beta (life). Home: 5404 Briar Cove Dr Tyler TX 75703 Office: U Tex at Tyler 3900 University Blvd Tyler TX 75799 E-mail: mwright@mail.uttyl.edu.

WRIGHT, MINTURN TATUM, III, retired lawyer; b. Phila., Aug. 7, 1925; s. Minturn T. and Anna (Moss) Wright; m. Nonya R. Stevens, May 11, 1957; children: Minturn T., Richard S., Robert M., Marian F. BA, Yale U., 1949; LLB, U. Pa., 1952. Bar: Pa. 1953, U.S. Ct. Appeals (3d cir.) 1953, U.S. Supreme Ct. 1962. Law clk. US Ct. Appeals (3d cir.), 1952-53; assoc. Dechert LLP, Phila., 1953-61, ptnr., 1961-95, chmn., 1982-84; ret. Vis. prof. U. Pa. Law Sch., 1965—69, 1993—97; bd. dirs. Cotiga Devel. Co. Contbr. articles to profl. jours. Trustee Acad. Natural Scis., Phila., 1958—, chmn., 1976—81; trustee Marshall-Reynolds Found., Hawk Mountain Sanctuary Assn., chmn. bd. dirs., 1992—97. With US Army, 1943—46. Mem.: ABA, Phila. Bar Assn., Pa. Bar Assn., Milldam Club. Episcopalian. Office: Dechert LLP Cira Ctr 2929 Arch St Philadelphia PA 19104-2808 Office Phone: 215-994-2689.

WRIGHT, OTIS DALINO, II, judge; b. Tuskegee, Ala., July 7, 1944; BA, Calif. State U., 1976; JD, Southwestern Sch. Law, 1980. Bar: Calif. 1980. Dep. sheriff LA County Sheriff's Dept., 1969—80; dep. dist. atty. Office Atty. Gen., Calif. Dept. Justice, 1980—83; ptnr. Wilson, Elser, Moskowitz, Edelman & Dicker LLP, 1983—2005; judge Superior Ct. Calif., County LA, 2005—07, U.S. Dist. Ct. (ctrl. dist.) Calif., 2007—. With USMC, 1963—69. Office: US Dist Ct 255 E Temple St Los Angeles CA 90012 *

WRIGHT, PAUL KENNETH, mechanical engineer, educator; b. Watford, Eng., Aug. 24, 1947; came to US, 1979; s. Kenneth Browett and Violet Anne (Woodland) W.; m. Frances June Ody, Oct. 24, 1970 (div. June 1984); children: Samuel, Joseph, Thomas; m. Terry Lee Naylor Schuster, Jan. 1, 1996; stepchildren: Jesse, Jennifer. BSc in Indsl. Metallurgy, U. Birmingham, Eng., 1968, MSc, 1970, PhD in Indsl. Metallurgy, 1971. Consulting engr. dept. sci. and indsl. rsch. Govt. New Zealand, Auckland, 1972—74; sr. lectr. dept. mech. engring. U. Auckland, New Zealand, 1975—79; rsch. assoc. physics Cavendish Lab. U. Cambridge, England, 1978—79; prof. mech. engring. Carnegie Mellon U., Pitts., 1979-87; prof. computer sci., dir. robotics and mfg. rsch. lab. NYU Courant Inst. Math. Scis., NYC, 1987-91; prof. mech. engring. U. Calif., Berkeley, 1991—, A. Martin Berlin prof. and chair mech. engring., 1996—. Mem. mfg. studies bd. NRC, Washington, 1988; co-chair Mgt. Tech. prog. U. Calif., Berkeley, 1995—2005, assoc. dean Coll. Engring., 1999—2005, co-dir. Berkeley Mfg. Inst. and Berkeley Wireless Rsch. Ctr., 1999—, chief scientist Ctr. Info. Tech. Rsch. in Interests of Soc., 2006—. Contbr. articles to sci. jours.; co-author: Manufacturing Intelligence, 1988, Energy Scavenging for Wireless Sensor Networks with Special Focus on Vibrations, 2004; author: 21st Century Manufacturing, 2001. Recipient Bursary award Royal Soc., London, 1978. Mem. ASME (Blackall award 1984), N.Am. Mfg. Rsch. Inst., Am. Computing, NAE. Mem. Ch. Eng. Achievements include patents in field. Avocations: singing jazz, skiing, sports. Office: UC Berkeley 5133 Etcheverry Hall Mailstop 1740 Berkeley CA 94720-1740 Office Phone: 510-642-2527. Office Fax: 510-643-5599. E-mail: pwright@me.berkeley.edu. *

WRIGHT, PETER MELDRIM, lawyer; b. Charlottesville, Va., Apr. 10, 1946; s. David McCord and Caroline Wallace (Jones) W.; m. Astrid Gabriella Mercedes Sandberg, June 4, 1972; children: David Habersham, Christian Langdon. AB, U. Ga., 1967, JD, 1972. Bar: Ga. 1972, US Dist. Ct. (no. dist.) Ga. 1972. Assoc. Jones, Bird & Howell, Atlanta, 1972-77, ptnr., 1977-82, Alston & Bird, Atlanta, 1982-2001; gen. counsel Resource Healthcare of Am., Inc., 2001—. Sec. Atlanta coun. Soc. Colonial Wars in Ga., 1985-88, dep. gov., 1989-91, mem. coun., 2003-06; mem. Soc. Cin. Ga., Savannah, historian, 1996—, v.p., 1998-2004, pres., 2004-07, v.p., 2007-. Mem. Ga. Bar Assn., Ga. Hist. Soc. (bd. curators 1993-2000, sec. 1994-98; v.p. Atlanta chpt. 1998-2000), Skidway Health and Living Svs., Inc. (pres., dir. 2003-), Oglethorpe Club (Savannah, Ga.), St. Andrew's Soc. Savannah. Office: Resource Healthcare Am One Buckhead Plz Ste 900 3060 Peachtree Rd NW Atlanta GA 30305

WRIGHT, PHILIP B., lawyer; BS, U. Mo., Columbia, 1979; JD, Georgetown U., 1982; LLM, NYU, 1985. Ptnr., group co-leader Tax Advice and Controversy Bryan Cave LLP, St. Louis. Office: Bryan Cave LLP One Metropolitan Square 211 N Broadway, Ste 3600 Saint Louis MO 63102 Office Phone: 314-259-2499. Business E-Mail: pbwright@bryancave.com.

WRIGHT, RANDOLPH EARLE, retired petroleum company executive; b. Brownsville, Tex., Dec. 22, 1920; s. William Randolph and Nelle Mae (Earle) W.; m. Elaine Marie Harris, May 9, 1943; 1 son, Randolph Earle. BS, U. Tex., 1942. With Texaco Inc., 1946-82, mgr. gas div. Houston, 1968-70, gen. mgr. producing dept., 1970-71, v.p. gas dept., 1971-82, v.p., sr. officer Houston, 1972-80; past pres., dir. Sabine Pipe Line Co.; v.p., asst. to pres. Texaco U.S.A., 1980-82, ret., 1982; past v.p. Texaco Mineral Co. Past chmn. engring. found. adv. council U. Tex., Austin. Past mem. exec. bd. Sam Houston Area coun. Boy Scouts Am.; past bd. dirs., past pres. Jr. Achievement S.E. Tex.; past bd. dirs. Houston Symphony Soc., Tex. Research League, Houston C. of C.; past trustee U. St. Thomas, S.W. Rsch. Inst. Served with USNR, World War II.

WRIGHT, RAYFIELD, professional football player; b. Griffin, Georgia, Aug. 23, 1945; Attended, Fort Valley St. Univ. Offensive tackle Dallas Cowboys, 1967—79. Named to NFL All-Decade Team, 1970s, NFL Pro Football Hall of Fame, 2006; recipient Dallas Cowboys Ring of Honor. Achievements include six NFL Pro-Bowl appearances; being member two-time Super Bowl Champions. Office: Pro Football Hall of Fame 2121 George Halas Dr NW Canton OH 44708 Office Phone: 330-456-8207.

WRIGHT, RICHARD NEWPORT, III, retired engineering executive, engineering educator; b. Syracuse, NY, May 17, 1932; s. Richard Newport and Carolyn (Baker) Wright; m. Teresa Rios, Aug. 23, 1959; children: John Stannard, Carolyn Maria, Maria, Elizabeth Rebecca, Edward Newport. BCE, Syracuse U., 1953, MCE (Parcel fellow), 1955; PhD, U. Ill., 1962. Jr. engr. Pa. R.R., Phila., 1953-55; instr. civil engring. U. Ill., Urbana, 1957-62, asst. prof., 1962-65, assoc. prof., 1965-70, prof., 1970-74, adj. prof., 1974-79; chief structures sect. Bldg. Rsch. divsn. U.S. Bur. Stds., Washington, 1971—72; dep. dir. Ctr. Bldg. Tech., 1972—73, dir., 1974—91; dir. Bldg. and Fire Rsch. Lab. Nat. Inst. Stds. and Tech., 1991—99; chmn. Bd. Infrastructure and Constructed Environment, 1999—2002; ret., 2002. Pres. Internat. Coun. Bldg. Rsch., Studies and Documentation, 1983—86. Contbr. articles to profl. jours. Govt. ofcl., Gaithersburg, Md., 1971—99; pres. Montgomery Village Found., 1989—90, 2001—03, bd. dirs., 1985—. With AUS, 1955—57. Named Fed. Engr. of the Yr., Nat. Soc. Profl. Engrs.; recipient Henry L. Michel award Industry Advancement Rsch., Civil Engring. Rsch. Found., 1999, Internat. Award, Japan Soc. Civil Engrs., 2003. Fellow: AAAS; mem.: NAE, ASCE (hon.). Home: 20081 Doolittle St Montgomery Village MD 20886-1354 Office: Dept of Commerce Nat Inst Standards & Tech Bldg And Fire Research Labs Gaithersburg MD 20899-0001 Personal E-mail: richard.n.wright@verizon.net.

WRIGHT, RICHARD STEVENS, film producer; b. Phila., Aug. 1, 1960; s. Minturn Tatum III and Nonya Rhodes (Stevens) W. BA, Brown U., 1982. Producer Metzner, Bruce, Mitchell, NYC, 1983-86; pres. Prodn. Softworks Co., Hollywood, Calif. Prodr.: (films) Underworld, 2003, The Cave, 2005, Underworld: Evolution, 2006, Crank, 2006, Blood and Chocolate, 2007; exec. prodr.: Going All the Way, 1997, The Real Blonde, 1997, 200 Cigarettes, 1999, Autumn in New York, 2000, The Mothman Prophecies, 2002. *

WRIGHT, RICK (RICHARD A. WRIGHT), lawyer; b. Las Vegas, Apr. 4, 1947; AA, N.Mex Mil. Acad., 1967; BS, U. Nev., 1969; JD, U. So. Calif., 1972. Bar: Nev. 1972, US Dist. Ct., Nev., US Ct. Appeals (9th cir.), US Supreme Ct. Law clk. for Judge Roger D. Foley US Dist. Ct., 1972—73; asst. US atty. Dist. of Nev. US Dept. Justice, 1973—78; mem. Wright Judd & Winckler, Las Vegas. Mem. 9th Cir. Judicial Conf., 1980—83, Nev. Supreme Ct. Com. to Study Profl. Misconduct, 1987—90. Named Best Criminal Defense Atty., Las Vegas Review-Jour., 1999. Master: Nev. Am. Inns of Ct.; fellow: Am. Coll. Trial Lawyers; mem.: ABA, Nev. Attys. for Criminal Justice, Nev. Trial Lawyers Assn., Calif. Attys. for Criminal Justice, Nat. Assn. Criminal Defense Lawyers, Clark County Bar Assn., So. Calif. Law Review, Order of the Coif, Phi Kappa Phi. Office: Wright Judd & Winckler 300 S Fourth St, Ste 701 Las Vegas NV 89101 Office Phone: 702-382-4004. Office Fax: 702-382-4800. *

WRIGHT, ROBERT PAYTON, lawyer; b. Beaumont, Tex., Feb. 15, 1951; s. Vernon Gerald and Huberta Read (Nunn) W.; m. Sallie Chesnutt Smith, July 16, 1977; children: Payton Cullen, Elizabeth Risher. AB, Princeton U., 1972; JD, Columbia U., 1975. Bar: Tex. 1975. Ptnr. Baker Botts L.L.P., Houston, 1975—. Author: The Texas Homebuyer's Manual, 1986. Mem. Am. Coll. Real Estate Lawyers (bd. govs. 2002-05), State Bar Tex. (chmn. coun. real estate, probate, trust law sect. 1994-95), Houston Bar Assn. (chmn. real estate sect. 1989-90), Tex. Coll. Real Estate Lawyers, Houston Real Estate Lawyers Coun., Houston Club. Episcopalian. Office Phone: 713-229-1237.

WRIGHT, SABRA DELL, music educator; b. Abilene, Tex., Nov. 4, 1953; d. Clead Elman Stark and Dottie Dell Quickel Stark; m. Richard Patrick Wright, Nov. 13, 1987; children: Richard Steven, Jerrod Sterling. B in Music Edn., Tarleton State U., Stephenville, Tex., 1975; M in Elem. Edn., Ariz. State U., Flagstaff, 1993. Cert. all-level music edn. Tex. Bd. Edn., 1975, K-12 music edn. Ariz. State Bd. Edn., 1992. Owner/tchr. Pirouette Dancers Studio, Stephenville, Tex., 1971—75; elem. music tchr. Irving Ind. Sch. Dist., Tex., 1975—80; mgr., horse trainer Bar Nothing Quarter Horse and Thoroughbred Ranch, Arthur City, Tex., 1980—85; mgr. brood mare farm Karho Arabians, Scottsdale, Ariz., 1985—86; elem. music tchr. Paradise Valley Ind. Sch. Dist., Phoenix, 1986—96; jr. high choral dir. Wichita Falls Ind. Sch. Dist., Tex., 1996—97; elem. music tchr. Iowa Pk. Consol. Ind. Sch. Dist., Tex., 1997—. Dance, choreography cons. U.S. Bi-Centennial Celebration, Irving, Tex., 1975—76; adult leader/ mgr. Wichita Count 4-H Horse Club, Iowa Park, Tex., 1998—2004; horse trainer, riding instr. Ridin' Right Tng. Facility, Iowa Park, 1998—. Student aide Teens Aid the Retarded, Irving, 1968—71, STARS: Teens Aid the Retarded, Stephenville, Tex., 1971—75; adult den leader Boy Scouts Am., Wichita Falls, 1996—97, Iowa Park, Tex., 1997—2004; instr. Whispers of Hope Riding Facility, Wichita Falls, 1998—2004. Recipient Outstanding Leadership award, Wichita County 4-H Orgn., 2000—01; scholar, Tarleton State U., 1971—75, Tex. State Teens Aid the Retarded, 1975. Mem.: Ariz. State Tchrs. Assn. (site rep., tchr. adv. 1993—96), Tex. Assn.Choral Dir. (assoc.), Tex. Music Educators Assn. (assoc.), Assn. Tex. Profl. Educators (assoc.), Am. Quarter Horse Assn. (assoc.), Am. Paint Horse Assn. (assoc.). Non-Partisan. Christian. Avocations: reading, community theater, horseback riding. Office: Bradford Elem 809 Texowa Rd Iowa Park TX 76367 Home Phone: 940-592-8525; Office Phone: 940-592-5841. Business E-Mail: swright@ipcisd.net, sweight@ipcid.net.

WRIGHT, SCOTT OLIN, federal judge; b. Haigler, Nebr., Jan. 15, 1923; s. Jesse H. and Martha I. Wright; m. Shirley Frances Young, Aug. 25, 1972. Student, Central Coll., Fayette, Mo., 1940-42; LLB, U. Mo., Columbia, 1950. Bar: Mo. 1950. City atty., Columbia, 1951-53; pros. atty. Boone County, Mo., 1954-58; practice of law Columbia, 1958-79; U.S. dist. judge Western Dist. Mo., Kansas City, from 1979. Pres. Young Democrats Boone County, 1950, United Fund Columbia, 1965. Served with USN, 1942-43; as aviator USMC, 1943-46. Decorated Air medal. Mem. ABA, Am. Trial Lawyers Assn., Mo. Bar Assn., Mo. Trial Lawyers Assn., Boone County Bar Assn. Clubs: Rockhill Tennis, Woodside Racquet. Lodges: Rotary (pres. Columbia 1965). Unitarian Universalist. Office: Charles E Whitaker Courthouse 400 E 9th St Ste 8662 Kansas City MO 64106-2684 Office Phone: 816-512-5700.

WRIGHT, SHEENA, not-for-profit developer; b. Bronx, NY; m. Gregg Walker; 2 children. BA, Columbia Coll., 1990; JD, Columbia Law, 1994. Former editl. asst., Washington Bureau NY Times; assoc. atty. Wachtell, Lipton, Rosen and Katz, 1994—99; sr. assoc. Reboul, MacMurray, Hewitt, Maynard and Kristol, 1999—2000; gen. coun., exec. v.p. bus. devel. Crave Technologies, 2000—02; pres., CEO Abyssinian Development Corp., 2002—. Spkr. in field; mem. Neighborhood Investment Advisory Panel, Fed. Reserve Bank of New York Advisory Bd.; bd. dir. Citizens Union Found.; chmn. SEA Corp. Named one of The Women Shaping the World, Essence Mag., 2006, 40 Under 40, Crain's NY Bus. Mag., 2006. Office: Abyssinian Devel Corp 4 W 125th St New York NY 10027

WRIGHT, STUART I., materials scientist, materials engineer; b. Murray, Utah, Sept. 22, 1962; BS, Brigham Young U., Provo, Utah, 1987, MS, 1988; PhD, Yale U., New Haven, 1992. Staff mem. Los Alamos Nat. Lab., N.Mex., 1992—95; scientist EDAX-TSL, Draper, Utah, 1995—. Mem.: ASM Internat. (Henry Marion Howe medal 1994), Microscopy Soc. Am., Minerals, Metals and Materials Soc. Achievements include development of fully automated electron backscatter diffraction system. Office: EDAX-TSL Ste H 392 E 12300 S Draper UT 84020

WRIGHT, SUSAN WEBBER, federal judge; b. Texarkana, Ark., Aug. 22, 1948; d. Thomas Edward and Betty Jane (Gary) Webber; m. Robert Ross Wright, III, May 21, 1983; 1 child, Robin Elizabeth. BA, Randolph-Macon Woman's Coll., 1970; MPA, U. Ark., 1972, JD with high honors, 1975. Bar: Ark. 1975. Law clk. U.S. Ct. Appeals (8th Cir.), 1975-76; from asst. prof. to assoc. prof. law U. Ark., Little Rock, 1976—83, prof., 1983-90, asst. dean, 1976-78; dist. judge U.S. Dist. Ct. (ea. dist.) Ark., Little Rock, 1990—, chief judge, 1998—2005. Vis. assoc. prof. Ohio State U., Columbus, 1981, La. State U., Baton Rouge, 1982—83; mem. adv. com. U.S. Ct. Appeals (8th cir.), St. Louis, 1983—88. Author (with R. Wright): Land Use in a Nutshell, 1978, Land Use in a Nutshell, 2d edit., 1985; editor-in-chief: Ark. Law Rev., 1975; contbr. articles to profl. jours. Mem.: Am. Law Inst., Pulaski County Bar Assn., Ark. Bar Assn., Am. Judicature Soc., Ark. Women's Forum. Anglican. Office: US District Court 600 W Capitol Ave Ste 522 Little Rock AR 72201-3329 Office Phone: 501-604-5100. Business E-Mail: susan_wright@ared.uscourts.gov.

WRIGHT, SYLVIA, government agency administrator; b. Balt. BA, Temple U., 1963, MA, 1965. Group leader Sch. Improvement Program Office U.S. Dept. Edn., Washington, dir. Sch. Support and Tech. Programs, Office Elementary and Secondary Edn., 2001—.

WRIGHT, TAMI LADONNA, pre-school educator; d. Joseph Edward and Eva LaVerne Wright; 1 child, William Marcus Reynolds. MusB, Bethany Coll., 1984; BS in Family & Child Devel., U. Ctrl. Okla., 2000, MS in Family & Child Svcs., 2002; MS in Reading, Okla. State U., 2004. Literacy mentor New Zealand Presch. Project, Auckland, 1986—90; lab. tchr. U. Va., Charlottesville, Va., 1990—92; lead tchr. Kinder Care, Okla. City, 1994; head start head tchr. Cmty. Action Program, Okla. City, 1994—2001; head start dir. CDI Temp. Grantee, Denver, 2002—03, Ponca Tribe Okla., 2003—05; child care tchr. Independence CC, Kans.; pre-sch. asst. St. Andrew's Catholic Sch., Independence, Kans. Mem. Success By Early Childhood Coun., Ponca City, 2003—; N.W. rep. Spirits Hope Domestic Violence Coalition, Okla. City, 2005—. Contbr. articles to profl. jours. Mem. troop coun. Boy Scout Am., Independence, 2006—. Mem.: Tri-State Indian Head Start Dirs. Assn., Nat. Assn. Edn. Young Children, Early Childhood Assn. Okla. (conf. co-chair 2000), Phi Kappa Phi. Democrat. Catholic. Avocations: cross stitch, reading. Home: 725 N 13th St Independence KS 67301-2740 Home Phone: 620-719-0397. Personal E-mail: ecteacher1@yahoo.com.

WRIGHT, THEODORE OTIS, forensic engineer; b. Gillette, Wyo., Jan. 17, 1921; s. James Otis and Gladys Mary (Marquiss) Wright; m. Phyllis Mae Reeves, June 21, 1942 (div. 1968); children: Mary Suzanne, Theodore Otis Jr., Barbara Joan; m. Edith Marjorie Jewett, May 22, 1968; children: Marjorie Jane, Elizabeth Carter. BSEE, U. Ill., 1951, MS in Engring., 1952; postgrad., Air Command and Staff Coll., 1956—57, UCLA, 1958. Registered profl. engr., Wash. Commd. 2d lt. USAF, 1942-65, advanced through grades to lt. col., 1957, ret., 1965; dep. for engring. Titan SPO, USAF Sys. Command, LA, 1957-65; rsch. engr. Boeing Co., Seattle, 1965-81; pres. Pretzelwich, Inc., Seattle, 1981—2002; cons., forensic engr. in pvt. practice Bellevue, Wash., 1988—. Adj. prof. U. Wash., 1967—68, Greenriver Jr. Coll., 1967—68; internat. presenter in field. Contbr. articles to profl. jours. Decorated Purple Heart, Air medal. Fellow: NSPE (life; v.p. western region 1985—87); mem.: ASTM (mem. com. E-43 metric practice 1988—, chmn. 2004—), Am. Nat. Metric Coun. (bd. dirs. 1978—94), Wash. Soc. Profl. Engrs. (state pres. 1981—82, Disting. Svc. award 1980, Engr. of the Yr. 1996, Columbia award 1996), Nat. Coun. Weights and Measures, U.S. Metric Assn. (life cert. advanced metrication specialist), Air Force Assn. (life; state pres. 1974—76, 1990—91, Jimmy Doolittle fellow 1975), Order of Daedalians (life), Tau Beta Pi, Pi Mu Epsilon, Eta Kappa Nu. Democrat. Presbyterian. Avocations: flying, photography, classical music, archaeology. Home: Apt 423 22975 SE Black Nugget Rd Issaquah WA 98029 Personal E-mail: towright1969@msn.com.

WRIGHT, THEODORE PAUL, JR., political science professor; b. Pt. Washington, NY, Apr. 12, 1926; s. Theodore Paul and Margaret (McCarl) W.; m. Susan Jane Standfast, Feb. 18, 1967; children: Henry Sewall, Margaret Standfast, Catherine Berrian (Mrs. Matthew H. Smith). BA magna cum laude, Swarthmore Coll., 1949; MA, Yale U., 1951, PhD, 1957. Instr. govt. Bates Coll., Lewiston, Maine, 1955-57; asst. prof., 1957-64; assoc. prof., 1964-65; assoc. prof. polit. sci. Grad. Sch. Public Affairs, SUNY, Albany, 1965-71, prof., 1971-95; prof. emeritus SUNY, Albany, 1995—. Mem. Columbia U. Faculty seminar on South Asia, 1967—. Author: American Support of Free Elections Abroad, 1964; contbr. chapters to books, articles to profl. jours. Trustee Am. Inst. Pakistan Studies, 1973-82; bd. dirs. Am. Coun. Study of Islamic Societies, 1998—, European Conf. on Modern South Asian Studies, 1974-. Served with USNR, 1944-46. Carnegie intern Indian civilization U. Chgo., 1961-62; Fulbright rsch. prof. India, 1963-64; Am. Inst. Indian Studies rsch. fellow India, 1969-70; Am. Coun. Learned Socs. grantee on South Asia in London, 1974-75; Am. Inst. Pakistan Studies/Fulbright rsch. fellow, Pakistan, 1983-84, Fulbright lectr., 1990-91. Mem. South Asian Muslim Studies Assn. (pres. 1988-2000, newsletter editor 2000—), Assn. Asian Studies (chmn. NY Conf. on Asian Studies 1988-89), Coun. for Study of Islam and Democracy, Dutch Settlers Soc. of Albany (pres. 1988-90, 98-2001, 1st v.p. 2002-), The New Netherland Inst. (bd. dirs. 2000—, sec. 2007—), Adirondack Mountain Club, Phi Beta Kappa (chpt. pres. 1992-93), Phi Delta Theta. Unitarian Universalist. Home: 17 Wellington Way Niskayuna NY 12309 Personal E-mail: wright15@juno.com.

WRIGHT, THEODORE ROBERT FAIRBANK, biologist, educator; b. Kodaikanal, Tamil Nadu, India, Apr. 10, 1928; s. Horace Kepler and Adelaide Caskey (Fairbank) Wright; m. Eileen Marie Yongen, Jan. 6, 1951 (dec. Jan. 2002). AB in Biology, Princeton U., 1949; MA in Biology, Wesleyan U., 1954; PhD in Zoology, Yale U., 1959. Asst. professor biology Johns Hopkins U., Balt., 1959-65; assoc. prof. biology U. Va., Charlottesville, 1965-75, prof. biology, 1975-95; prof. emeritus, 1995—. Vis. scientist Max Planck Inst. for Biology, Tubingen, 1975-76, Devel. Biology Ctr., U. Calif., Irvine, 1982. Editor: The Genetics and Biology of Drosophila, vol. 2a-c, 1978, vol. 2d, 1980, Genetic Regulatory Hierarchies in Development, 1990; co-editor: Advances in Genetics, 1988-92. With U.S. Army, 1950-52. NIH postdoctoral fellow Max Planck Inst. for Biology, Tubingen, Fed. Republic Germany, 1958-59; NSF grantee, 1967-72, 90-93; NIH grantee, 1972-93; Am. Cancer Soc. grantee, 1988-90. Fellow AAAS; mem. AAUP, Genetics Soc. Am., Soc. for Devel. Biology, Va. Acad. Sci., Sigma Xi.

WRIGHT, THOMAS PARKER, artist; b. Springfield, Mo., July 3, 1924; s. James Lewis and Vesta Marie (Parker) Wright; m. Elizabeth Jane Smith; children from previous marriage: Jeffrey, Kathleen, Thomas, Ramona, Karen. BA in Math., Henderson State U., 1948; MA in Math., La. State U., 1962. Math., sci. tchr. Hondo (N.Mex.) Union H.S., 1950-53; prin. Westridge (Ark.) H.S., 1954-55; math. tchr. Santa Ana (Calif.) Unified Sch. Dist., 1955-63; math., computer instr. Santa Ana Coll., 1963-71; adminstrv. dean Rancho Santiago CC., Santa Ana, 1971-79; art gallery mgr. Lahaina (Hawaii) Galleries, Inc., 1979-80; pres. Maui Fine Arts, Inc., Kihei, 1981—2006; computer sci. instr. Maui C.C., Kahului, Hawaii, 1983-94. Multi-media and internet software developer NSF. One-man shows include Maui C.C., 1989, exhibited in group shows at Art Maui, 1984, 1986, 1989. Pres. Santa Ana Tchrs. Assn., 1960, Santa Ana Coll. Faculty Assn., 1965. 2d lt. USMCR, 1944—46, 1st lt. USMCR, 1950—52. Mem.: NEA, U. Hawaii Profl. Assembly. Republican. Presbyterian. Avocations: painting, computer art, ocean fishing, photography. Home: 902 Wilshire Ct Mc Kinney TX 75070 Home Phone: 972-547-0295. Business E-Mail: wrightt@hawaii.edu. E-mail: liztomw@netscape.net.

WRIGHT, TONY, advertising executive; b. London, United Kingdom; Student, l'universite Paris-Sorbonne, Freie Universitat Berlin. With Saatchi & Saatchi, London, Chiat/Day, LA & Toronto; co-founder McElligott Wright Morrison White (sold to Omnicom), Mpls., 1989; founding ptnr. (with Omnicom) Berlin Wright Cameron, NYC; worldwide chief strategy officer Ogilvy & Mather, 1995—2004; CEO, pres. Lowe Worldwide (divsn. Interpublic), NYC, 2004—06, chmn., 2006—. Named to Advt. Hall of Fame, Am. Advt. Fedn., 2001. Office: Lowe Worldwide 150 East 42nd St New York NY 10017 Office Phone: 212-605-8000. *

WRIGHT, VIRGINIA, art collector, curator; m. Bagley Wright; children: Merrill, Charles, Robin, Bing. BA, Barnard Coll., 1951. Asst. Sidney Janis Gallery; trustee Virginia Wright Fund, Seattle Art Mus. Curator Color Field Paintings and Related Abstractions, 2005. Named one of Top 200 Collectors, ARTnews Mag., 2004, 2006. Avocation: Collector of Contemporary Art; Japanese Art.

WRIGHT, WAYNE E., education educator; b. Bellflower, Calif., May 1, 1967; s. James L. and Janet Wright; m. Phal Mao Wright, May 28, 1994; children: Jeffrey Sovan, Michael Sopat, Catherine Sophaline. BA in Liberal Studies, Calif. State U., Long Beach, 1992, MA in Lang., Literacy and Learning, 1998; PhD in Ednl. Leadership and Policy Studies, Ariz. State U., Tempe, 2004. Humanitarian vol. Cambodian Am. Nat. Devel. Orgn., Phnom Penh, 1993—94; tchr. bilingual Khmer (Cambodian) Long Beach Unified Sch. Dist., Calif., 1994—2000; rschr. Lang. Policy Rsch. Unit Edn. Policy Studies Lab., Tempe, Ariz., 2000—04; asst. prof. U. Tex., San Antonio, 2004—. Co-dir. Lang. Policy Rsch. Unit Edn. Policy Studies Lab., Tempe, 2004—; book rev. editor Internat. Multilingual Rsch. Jour., Washington, 2006—. Co-editor: Ebonics in the Urban Education Debate; editor: Jour. Southeast Asian Am. Edn. and Advancement, 2006—; contbr. articles to profl. jours. Preparing Future Faculty fellow, Ariz. State U., 2001—04, Grad. Scholars Program scholar, 2000—04, Noel Chadwick Gray fellow, 2001, dean's fellow, 2003, dissertation grantee, Grad. Student Assn., Ariz. State U., 2002. Mem.: TESOL, Nat. Assn. for the Edn. and Advancement of Cambodian, Laotian, and Vietnamese Ams. (v.p. for publs. 2005—), Am. Assn. for Applied Linguistics, Nat. Assn. for Bilingual Edn. (co-chair lang. policy spl. interest group 2002—06), Am. Edn. Rsch. Assn. Mem. Lds Ch. Avocation: music. Office: U Tex San Antonio One UTSA Cir San Antonio TX 78249 Office Phone: 210-458-2024. Office Fax: 210-458-5962. Business E-Mail: wayne.wright@utsa.edu.

WRIGHT, WAYNE KENNETH, federal agency statistician; b. Chelsea, Mass., Jan. 26, 1944; s. Wayne K. and Louise Annette (Olson) W.; m. Sharon Kay Brown, Aug. 30, 1964 (div. 1974); 1 child, Trent Edward; m. Linda Susan Berkel, Mar. 15, 1975 (div. 1979); 1 child, Stacey Danielle; m. Bonnie Sue Oberhelman, Apr. 3, 1982; 1 child, Forrest Kenneth. BS in Sociology, U. Iowa, 1971; postgrad., U. North Iowa, 1971-72; cert. in marketing, Atlanta U., 1988. Survey asst. Shive-Hall-Hattery Engring., Cedar Rapids, Iowa, 1962-66; chem. lab technician Wilson Packing Plant, Cedar Rapids, 1966-71; grad. rsch. asst. U. No. Iowa, Cedar Falls, 1971-72, grad. tchg. asst., demographic and econ. stats., 1972-73; survey statistician U.S. Bur. Census, Kansas City, Kans., 1973-74, info. specialist, 1974-83, Charlotte, NC, 1983—; data specialist U.S. Bur. of Census, Charlotte, NC, 1991—. Named Ky. Col., 1987; named Hon. Citizen, City of Beloit (Wis.), 1974. Fellow Alpha Kappa Delta. Lutheran. Avocations: fishing, camping, hiking, alpine skiing and racing. Home: 1417 Morrocroft Trl Gastonia NC 28054-6499 Office: US Bur Census 901 Center Park Dr Ste 106 Charlotte NC 28217-2935 Office Phone: 704-424-6431. Personal E-mail: wrghtgmp@aol.com. Business E-Mail: w.kenneth.wright@census.gov.

WRIGHT, WILEY REED, JR., lawyer, retired judge, mediator; b. Seattle, Jan. 31, 1932; s. Wiley Reed and Gertrude Ellen (Datson) W.; m. Sally Harrison Clarke, 1955 (div. 1963); children: Wiley III, Margaret, Andrew; m. Roberta Hostinsky, Oct. 18, 1963; children: Cathryn, Amy, Susan. BS in Commerce, Washington and Lee U., 1954, LLB, 1956. Bar: Va. 1956, U.S. Dist. Ct. (ea. dist.) Va. 1956, U.S. Ct. Appeals (4th cir.) 1956, U.S. Supreme Ct. 1993. Law clk. to hon. judge U.S. Dist. Ct., Alexandria, Va., 1958-59; ptnr. Clarke, Richard, Moncure & Whitehead, Alexandria, 1959-68; judge corp. and cir. cts. Alexandria, 1968-79; chief judge cir. ct., 1979-84; ptnr. Hazel & Thomas P.C., Alexandria, 1984-96; mediator McCammon Mediation Group Ltd., Richmond, Va., 1996—. Mem. at large Va. State Bar Coun., 1984-90; mem. Jud. Coun. Va., 1982-84, vice chmn. jud. conf. Va., 1980-82. Assoc. editor: Virginia Circuit Judges Benchbook, 1987. Legal counsel to Alexandria C. of C., 1984-88. 1st lt. U.S. Army, 1956-58. Fellow: Va. Law Found., Am. Bar Found.; mem.: Va. Bar Assn., Omicron Delta Kappa, Phi Delta Phi. Avocations: boating, fishing. Home: 579 Lovers Ln Lancaster VA 22503 Office: McCammon Group Bank of Am Ctr 1111 E Main St Ste 1700 Richmond VA 23219 Office Phone: 804-343-0922. Business E-Mail: bwright@kaballero.com.

WRIGHT, WILL, computer game designer; b. Atlanta, Jan. 20, 1960; s. Will Wright, Sr. and Beverlye (Edwards) Wright; m. Joell Jones. Attended, La. State U., La. Tech., The New Sch., Manhattan. Co-founder Maxis Software, Inc.(purchased by Electronic Arts, Inc. in 1997), 1987—97. Designer (computer game) Raid on Bungeling Bay, Broderbund Software, Inc., 1984, SimCity, 1989, SimCity Terrain Editor, Infogrames, 1989, SimCity Enhanced CD ROM, Interplay Entertainment Corp., Maxis Software Inc., 1993, Empire Deluxe Scenarios, New World Computing, Inc., 1993, SimIsle:Missions in the Rainforest, Maxis UK, Ltd., 1995, Seaman, Vivarium Inc., 1999, Psychonauts, Majesco Entertainment Co., 2005, Re-Mission, HopeLab, 2006, The Sims, 2000, The Sims Livin' Large, 2000, Sims Coaster, 2001, Sim Golf, 2001, SimEarth: The Living Planet, Maxis Software, Inc., 1990, SimAnt: The Electronic Art Colony, 1991, RoboSport, 1991, SimLife, 1992, A-Train, 1992, SimCity Classic, 1994, SimFarm, 1993, SimCity 2000 Urban Renewal Kit, 1994, SimTown, 1995, SimTower: The Vertical Empire, 1995, Marble Drop, 1997, SimPark, 1996, SimCopter, 1996, Sim Tunes, 1996, Full Tilt! Pinball, 1996, A-Train Construction Set, Maxis Software Inc., Ocean Software Inc., 1992, SimCity 3000, Electronic Arts, Inc., 1999, The Sims, 2000, SimCity 3000 Unlimited, 2000, The Sims: House Party Expansion Pack, 2001, The Sims: Hot Date Expansion Pack, 2001, The Sims: Unleashed, 2002, The Sims Online, 2002, The Sims (Deluxe Edition), 2002, The Sims: Vacation Expansion Pack, 2002, The Sims: Superstar, 2003, The Sims: Makin Magic, 2003, The Sims: Bustin' Out, 2003, The Sims: Makin Magic Expansion Pack, 2003, Sim City 4 Expansion Pack, 2003, Sim City 4 Rush Hour, 2003, The Urbz: Sims in the City, 2004, SimCity 4, 2004, The Sims: Mega Deluxe, 2004, The Sims 2 University, 2004, The Sims 2: Nightlife, 2005, The Sims 2: Open for Business, 2006, The Sims 2, Electronic Arts, Inc., Maxis Software Inc., 2005, co-designer with Fred Haslam SimCity2000, Maxis Software Inc., 1993. Named one of the most important people in gaming, technology, and entertainment by publications such as, Entertainment Weekly, Time, PC Gamer, Discover and Game Spy; named to Acad. of Interactive Arts and Sciences' Hall of Fame, 2002; recipient Lifetime Achievement award, Game Developers Choice awards, 2001, PC Mag., 2005, Vanguard award, Producers Guild of Am., 2007. *

WRIGHT, WILLIAM COOK, archivist, director; b. Jersey City, July 11, 1939; s. Harry Cook and Edna Marguerite Tompkins) W. BA, Gettysburg Coll., 1961; MA, U. Del., 1965, PhD, 1971. Tchr. Salem (N.J.) High Sch., 1961-65; adj. instr. U. Del., Newark, 1968-70; assoc. dir. N.J. Hist. Commn., Trenton, 1970-76; head Bur. Archives and History N.J. State Libr., Trenton, 1976-83; dir. Div. Archives and Records Mgmt., N.J. State Dept., Trenton, 1983-85; chief Bur. Records Mgmt., Trenton, 1985-89, ret., 1989. Coord. state hist. records adv. bd. Nat. Hist. Publs. and Records Commn. 1976-87; mem. adv. com. for papers of William Livingston; sec. N.J. State Records Com., 1976-85, chmn., 1985; mem. adv. bd. dirs. N.J. Archives Series, 1971-86; mem. region 2 adv. coun. Nat. Archives and Records Svc., 1976-77; mem. adv. com. N.J. Newspaper Project, 1983-85, state rev. com. for hist. sites, 1976-79; mem. implementation and planning com. N.J. Supreme Ct., 1982 Author monograph: The Secession Movement in the Middle Atlantic States, 1972; compiler Directory of N.J. Newspapers, 1765-1970; contbr. articles and book revs to profl. jours. Mem. Lawrence Twp. Cultural and Heritage Adv. Com., 1989-92, chmn., 1991. Recipient Award of Recognition N.J. Hist. Comm., 1992. Mem. Acad. Cert. Achivists (cert.). Home: 7 Redwood Ct Glassboro NJ 08028-2934 Personal E-mail: wcwright@comcast.net.

WRIGHT, WILLIAM EVAN, physician, consultant; b. NYC, Aug. 1, 1946; s. Samuel and Frances Elnora (Perpente) W.; m. Diana Claire Dryer, Aug. 15, 1970; children: Jason William, Elizabeth Garland, Edwin Samuel. BA in Music, U. Rochester, 1968; MD, U. Pa., 1972; MSPH, U. Utah, 1979; MS in Physiology, Harvard U., 1980. Diplomate Am. Bd Internal Medicine, Am. Bd. Preventive Medicine, Occupl. Medicine, Am. Bd. Ind. Med. Examiners; ACOEM cert. med. rev. officer; cert. FAA med. examiner. Intern LDS Hosp., Salt Lake City, 1972-73, resident, 1973-75, U. Utah Med. Ctr., Salt Lake City, 1978-79, Harvard Sch. Pub. Health, Boston, 1979-80; asst. prof. U. So. Calif., LA, 1980-86; med. dir. U.S. DEA, Arlington, Va., 1986-96; program mgr., site med. dir. DynCorp, Reston, Va., 1991-96; med. dir. Md. Office, CORE, Inc., Irvine, Calif., 1996—2003; cons. Office of Worker Advocacy, U.S. Dept. Energy, Washington, 2003—05; pres. WorkWright, Inc., 2005—. Cons. Westwood Group, 2003—05; dist. med. cons. U.S. Dept. Labor, 2006—. Contbr. articles to profl. jours. Maj. M.C., U.S. Army, 1975-77. Fellow ACP, Am. Coll. Occupl. and Environ. Medicine, mem. Cosmos Club (Washington), Alpha Omega Alpha. Avocation: music. Home: 6801 Wemberly Way Mc Lean VA 22101-1532 Office Phone: 703-556-0092. E-mail: ww4ohs@cox.net.

WRIGHT CARRIER, J. T., business owner; b. McKenzie, Tenn., July 31, 1952; d. Gilbert M. and Mildred B. Wright; m. William W. Carrier III, July 28, 1973; 1 child, Morgan Bailey. BA in Psychology cum laude, Memphis State U., 1974, MA in Ednl. Counseling, Pers. Svcs., 1976, EdD, 1992. Sales rep. API Inc., Memphis, 1980—; casting dir. Theatrics Etc., Memphis, 1980—. Profl. model; casting dir., crew svcs. staff for nat. feature and advt. accts. including Warner Bros., Disney, Phillips 66, Exxon, KC Masterpiece BBQ Sauce, Northwest Airlines; scriptwriter for corp. videos, including Fed. Express, Memphis Bus. Jour.; developer Careers 2000 ednl. video series for adolescents. Pub. Crisis Intervention Studies for Memphis Police Dept.; crew svcs. for U.S. Def. Dept. tng. videos. Co-founder Memphis and Shelby County Film, Tape and Music Commn. Named Miss Memphis, 1972, Top Casting Co. Adweek Mag., 1986. Avocations: environmentalism, ballet, modern dance, theater. Office: Theatrics Etc PO Box 11862 Memphis TN 38111-0862 Home Phone: 901-753-9366; Office Phone: 901-278-7454.

WRIGHTON, MARK STEPHEN, academic administrator, chemistry professor; b. Jacksonville, Fla., June 11, 1949; s. Robert D. and Doris (Cutler) Wrighton; children: James Joseph, Rebecca Ann. BS, Fla. State U., 1969; PhD, Calif. Inst. Tech., 1972; DSc (hon.), U. West Fla., 1983. From asst. prof. chemistry to provost MIT, Cambridge, 1972—90, Frederick G. Keys prof in chemistry, 1981, head dept. chemistry, 1987—90, provost, 1990—95; prof., chancellor Washington U., St. Louis, 1995—. Bd. dirs. A.G. Edwards, Inc., Brooks Automation, Danforth Plant Sci. Ctr., Nidus Ctr. for Sci. Enterprise, Barnes Jewish Hosp., BJC HealthCare, Assn. Am. Univs., St. Louis Regional Chamber and Growth Assn., Bus. Higher Edn. Forum., Univs. Rsch. Assn., Global Climate and Energy Project, Cabot Corp. Author: Organometallic Photochemistry, 1979. Trustee St. Louis Art Mus., Mo. Bot. Garden, St. Louis Symphony Orch., St. Louis Sci. Ctr.; bd. dirs. United Way Greater St. Louis; trustee St. Louis Sci. Ctr. Recipient Herbert Newby McCoy award, Calif. Inst. Tech., 1972, Disting. Alumni award, 1992, E.O. Lawrence award, Dept. Energy, 1983, Halpern award in photochemistry, N.Y. Acad. Scis., 1983, Fresenius award, Phi Lambda Upsilon, 1984, Dreyfus tchr.-scholar, 1975—80; fellow, Alfred P. Sloan, 1974—76, MacArthur fellow, 1983—88. Fellow: AAAS; mem.: Acad. of Sci. of St. Louis, Electrochem. Soc., Am. Chem. Soc. (award in pure chemistry 1981, award in inorganic chemistry 1988), Am. Philos. Soc., Am. Acad. Arts and Scis., Sigma Xi. Office: Washington Univ Office of Chancellor One Brookings Dr Campus Box 1192 Saint Louis MO 63130-4899 Office Phone: 314-935-5100. Business E-Mail: wrighton@wustl.edu.

WRIGHT PENN, ROBIN, actress; b. Dallas, Apr. 8, 1966; d. Fred Wright; m. Sean Penn, Apr. 27, 1996; children: Dylan Frances, Hopper Jack. Television appearances include The Yellow Rose, 1983-84, Santa Barbara, 1984-87 (Emmy awards Best Ingenue in a Daytime Drama series 1985-87); films include Hollywood Vice Squad, 1986, The Princess Bride, 1987, State of Grace, 1990, Denial, 1991, The Playboys, 1992, Toys, 1992, Forrest Gump, 1994, The Crossing Guard, 1995, Moll Flanders, 1995, Loved, 1996, She's so Lovely, 1997, Loved, 1997 (Seattle Film Festival Award for best actress, 1997), Hurly-Burly, 1998, Just to Be Together, 1999, Message in a Bottle, 1999, Unbreakable, 2000, The Pledge, 2001, The Last Castle, 2001, White Oleander, 2002, The Singing Detective, 2003, A Home at the End of the World, 2004, Nine Lives, 2005, Sorry Haters, 2005; actor, exec. prodr. (films) Virgin, 2003; (TV miniseries) Empire Falls, 2005. Office: United Talent Agy 9560 Wilshire Blvd Beverly Hills CA 90212

WRIGLEY, DREW H., prosecutor, lawyer; b. Fargo, ND, Oct. 1965; BA, U. N.D., 1988; JD, Am. U., 1991. Pros. atty. City of Fargo, 1992—93; asst. dist. atty. Phila. Dist. Atty.'s Office, 1993—98; gen. counsel for pub. policy N.D. Workers Compensation Bur., 1998—99; exec. dir., legal counsel ND Rep. Party, 1999—2000; dep. chief of staff Office of Gov. of ND, 2000—01; US atty. ND US Dept. Justice, 2001—. Office: US Attys Office 655 First Ave N Ste 250 Fargo ND 58102 *

WRIGLEY, WILLIAM, JR., (BILL WRIGLEY JR.), candy company executive; b. 1964; Asst. to pres. William Wrigley Jr. Co., Chgo., 1985—92, v.p., 1991—98, sr. v.p., 1999, pres., CEO, 1999—2006, chmn. bd., 2004—, exec. chmn., 2006—. Bd. dirs. William Wrigley Jr. Co., 1988—. Named one of Forbes' Richest Americans, 2006; recipient Hunt-Scanlon Human Capitol Advantage award, 2003, Golden Plate award, Acad. Achievement, 2006. Office: William Wrigley Jr Inc 410 N Michigan Ave Chicago IL 60611 *

WRINKLE, JOHN NEWTON, lawyer; b. Chattanooga, July 31, 1929; s. John Stuart and Anne (Ownbey) W.; m. Louise Rucker Agee, Feb. 1, 1958; children: Anne Blair, Margaret Rucker. BA, Vanderbilt U., 1951; LLB, Yale U., 1955. Bar: Ala. 1955, U.S. Dist. Ct. (no. dist.) Ala. 1956, U.S. Ct. Appeals (5th cir.) 1958, U.S. Ct. Appeals (11th cir.) 1981, U.S. Tax Ct. 1957. Assoc. White, Bradley, Arant, All & Rose, Birmingham, Ala., 1955-63; ptnr. Bradley Arant Rose & White LLP, 1963-92, counsel, 1993—. Coord. pre-law students Birmingham So. Coll., 1989—. Trustee Birmingham Symphony Assn., 1970-79, 80-83, Episcopal Found. Jefferson County, 1994-2000; mem. bd. advisors St. Andrew's Sewanee Sch., 1985—; bd. dirs. Yale Law Sch. Fund, 2005—. With USAF, 1951-52. Disting. fellow Birmingham-Southern Coll., 1995—. Fellow Am. Coll. Trust and Estate Counsel; mem. ABA, So. Employee Benefits Conf. (steering com. 1970-73), Birmingham Bar Assn., Assn. of Bar of City of N.Y., Birmingham Com. Fgn. Rels., Redstone Club, Mountain Brook Club, Summit Club, Knickerbocker Club (N.Y.C.), Yale Club (N.Y.C.), Phi Beta Kappa, Phi Alpha Delta. Episcopalian. Home: 2 Beechwood Rd Birmingham AL 35213-3914 Office: Bradley Arant Rose & White LLP 1819 5 Ave N Birmingham AL 35203 Office Phone: 205-521-8000. Business E-Mail: jwrinkle@bradleyarant.com.

WRISTON, KATHRYN DINEEN, corporate director, consultant; b. Syracuse, NY; d. Robert Emmet and Carolyn (Bareham) Dineen; m. Walter B. Wriston, Mar. 14, 1968; 1 stepchild. Student, U. Geneva, 1958-59; BA cum laude, Smith Coll., 1960; LLB, U. Mich., 1963. Bar: N.Y. 1964, U.S. Ct. Appeals (2d cir.) 1964, U.S. Supreme Ct. 1968. Assoc. Shearman & Sterling, NYC, 1963-68. Mem. audit com., corp. responsibility com., fin. com., 2003, Goodyear Tire and Rubber Co., 2002-03, mem. fin. com., 2003; bd. dirs. Northwestern Mut. Life Ins. Co., mem. ins. products and mktg. com., 1986-89, audit com., 1989-, chmn. audit com., 2001-05, investment and fin. policy com., 1989-95; dir. Santa Fe Snyder Corp., 1990-00, mem. audit com. 1990-93, 95-00, nominating com., 1990-99, compensation com., 1998-99, conceptual framework task force Indep. Standards Bd., 1998-00, dir. 1990-00; trustee Fin. Acctg. Found., 1992-97, selection com., 1992-97, audit com., 1992-96, chair, 1993-96, chair devel. com., 1996-97, fin. com., 1994-97. exec. com., 1996-97; task force on timely fin. reporting guidanace Fin. Acctg. Stds. Bd., 1982-83, mem. bd. agenda adv. com., 1981-85, process and structure com., 1981-85, chair, 1983-85, adv. coun., 1981-85; exec. com. CPR Inst. for Dispute Resolution, 1994-99; dir. The Stanley Works, 1996—, mem. fin. and pension coms., 1996-97, 02—, chair audit com., 1997-02, exec. com., 1997-05, mem. compensation com., 2004-. Mem. vis. com. U. Mich. Law Sch., 1973-2006; trustee Fordham U., Bronx, N.Y., 1971-81, vice-chair bd. trustees, 1980-81, student affairs com., 1971-77, chair, 1974-77, faculty affairs com., com. on law sch., 1978-81, grievance com., 1971-81; ea. region selection panel Pres. Commn. on White House Fellowships, 1981-83, chair, 1982-83; bus. com. Nat. Ctr. for State Cts., 1982-88; bd. overseers Rand Inst. for Civil Justice, 1985-93; trustee John A. Hartford Found., 1991—, pres., 2002-, grant com., 1991—, vice-chair, 1992—, chair evaluation com., 1998—, audit com., 1992-2002, chair, 1993-2002, sec., 1996-2002, ex-officio, 2002-; mem. Gov. Wilson's NY Little Hoover Commn., 1974; trustee Cath. Health Care Sys., NYC, 1999—2003. Mem. ABA, Nat. Assn. Accts., Practicing Law Inst. (exec. 1976—, programs and publs. com., chair 1979-04, membership com. 1976-79, chair 1977-79, nominating com. 1978, 81-85, v.p., 1985-05, mem. bar rev. courses 1978-79, fin. com. 1989—, mem. Am. Law Inst./ABA subcom. on Am. law network 1989-91), Fin. Women's Assn. N.Y., N.Y. County Lawyers Assn. (legal aid com. 1972-76), N.Y. State Bar Assn., Assn. of Bar of City of N.Y.

WROBBEL, KAREN, education educator, consultant; b. Phila., Nov. 14, 1956; d. Raymond and Lillian Sauter; m. Paul H Wrobbel, Aug. 20, 1977; children: Elizabeth Gorden, Rebekah Stathakis. BA, Biola U., 1981; MA, Wheaton Coll., 1988; EdD, U. Minn., 2005. Cert. elem. tchr. Assn. Christian Schs. Internat., 2003, Bible specialist Assn. Christian Schs. Internat., 2003. Tchr. Christiansen Acad., Rubio, Venezuela, 1982—83; asst. head and tchr. Evang. Christian Acad., Madrid, 1983—97; children's edn. coord. Evang. Alliance Mission, Wheaton, Ill., 1997—2003; asst. prof. Trinity Internat. U., Deerfield, Ill., 2003—, dir. Sch. Edn., 2006—. Children's edn. cons. Evang. Alliance Mission, Wheaton, Ill., 2003—; sch. bd. mem. Hinkson Christian Acad., Moscow; co-chair Intermission Missionary Kid Edn. Consultation, Colorado Springs, Colo., 1999—2001. Contbg. editor (newsletter) World Pulse, 2002—04; contbr. articles to profl. jours. Recipient Mary LeBar award in Christian Edn., Wheaton Coll., 1988. Mem.: ASCD, Nat. Coun. Tchrs. Math., Am. Ednl. Rsch. Assn., Phi Delta Kappa. Evangelical Christian. Office: Trinity Internat Univ 2065 Half Day Rd Deerfield IL 60015 Office Phone: 847-317-7178. Office Fax: 847-317-4786. Business E-Mail: kwrobbel@tiu.edu.

WROBEL, BRUCE J., energy and utilities company executive; Degree in Econs. and Mgmt. Sci., MIT, 1980. Co-founder US power co. (acquried by Sithe Energies Inc., 1986), 1981; exec. v.p. worldwide bus. devel. and fin. Sithe Energies Inc., 1986—99; founder EnCom, Japan, 1999, Guinea Aluminum Products Corp. (GAPCO); CEO, pres. Herakles Capital Corp., NYC; CEO Sithe Energies Inc., NYC, 2003—.

WROBLE, ARTHUR GERARD, judge; s. Arthur Stanley and Sophia P. Wroble; m. Mary Ellen Sheehan, Nov. 19, 1977; children: Sophia Ann, Sarah Jean, Stacey Margaret. BSBA with honors, U. Fla., Gainesville, 1970, MBA, 1971, JD, 1973. Bar: Fla. 1973, US Ct. Appeals (5th cir.) 1974, US Dist. Ct. (so. dist.) Fla. 1974, US Supreme Ct. 1976, US Ct. Appeals (11th cir.) 1981, US Dist. Ct. (mid. dist.) 1982, US Dist. Ct. (no. dist.) Fla. 1986, US Army Ct. Mil. Rev. 1989, US Ct. Mil. Appeals 1990. Ptnr. Burns, Middleton, Farrell & Faust, West Palm Beach, Fla., 1973—82, Wolf, Block, Schorr & Solis-Cohen, Phila. & West Palm Beach, 1982-87, Scott, Royce, Harris & Bryan, PA, Palm Beach, Fla., 1987-89, Grantham and Wroble, PA, Lake Worth, Fla., 1989-92; prin. Arthur G. Wroble, PA, West Palm Beach, 1992-2000; cir. judge 15th Jud. Ct. Fla., Palm Beach, 2001—07. Mem. 15th Jud. Cir. Ct. Nominating Commn., 1979-83; mem. U. Fla. Law Ctr. Coun., 1981-84, 99—, US Magistrate Merit Selection Panel, so. dist. Fla., 1987; adv. bd. alternative sentencing program Palm Beach County Pub. Defender's Office; adj. instr. bus. law Coll. Boca Raton (now Lynn U.), 1988; 16th dist. screening com. US Svc. Acad., Fla., 2001-07. Contbr. articles to profl. jours. Bd. dirs. Palm Glades Girl Scout Coun., 1996—2006, 2006—; co-chmn. profl. devel. United Way, 1984—85; dir. Leadership Palm Beach County, 1990—92. Served to lt. col. JAG, USAR. Named Eagle Scout, Boy Scouts Am., 1962; named to Athletic Hall Fame, Biship Moore H.S., Orlando, 1997. Mem. ABA, Fla. Bar (bd. govs. young lawyers sect. 1979-83, bd. govs. 1985-89), Palm Beach County Bar Assn. (pres. young lawyers sect. 1978-79, bd. dirs. 1979-81, sec.-treas. 1981-83, pres. 1984-85), Fla. Bar Found. (bd. dirs. 1986-93), Fla. Assn. Women Lawyers, Fla. Coun. Bar Assn. Pres. (bd. dirs. 1986-92), Hispanic Bar Assn. of Palm Beach County, M.F. Cunningham Bar Assn., Guild Cath. Lawyers Diocese Palm Beach, Inc. (pres. 1980-81, bd. dirs. 1981-2001, Monsignor Jeremiah P. O'Mahoney Outstanding Lawyer award 1993), Legal Aid Soc. Palm Beach County, Inc. (bd. dirs. 1981-2000), Univ. Fla. Alumni Assn., Palm Beach County Club (pres. 1983-84), Kiwanis (pres. 1980-81, pres. West Palm Beach found. 1989-2000, dir. 1991—, Citizen of Yr. 1994, George F. Hixon fellowship 1999), KC (grand knight 1978-79), Am. Inns of Ct LIV (West Palm Beach chpt. pres. 1999-2000, bd. dirs. 1995-2000), Am. Legion. Roman Catholic.

WROE, THOMAS, JR., semiconductor company executive; BS in Engring., U. RI, 1972. Mfg. engr. materials and controls Tex. Instruments Inc., Attleboro, Mass., 1972—95, pres. materials and controls, 1995—98, sr. v.p., 1998—, pres. sensors and controls, 2000—. Mem. exec. com. Mass. Bus. Roundtable; mem. bd. advisors Carroll Sch. Mgmt., Boston Coll.; chmn. bd. United Way Greater Attleboro/Taunton, gen. campaign chmn., 1997; vice chmn. Assoc. Industries Mass., mem. bd.; mem. bd. trustees Mass. Taxpayers Found.; mem. bd. dirs. Cape Cod Healthcare. Office: Tex Instruments 34 Forest St Attleboro MA 02703 also: Tex Instruments Inc 12500 TI Blvd Dallas TX 75243 Office Phone: 972-995-2011. Office Fax: 972-995-4360.

WRONG, DENNIS HUME, retired sociologist, educator; b. Toronto, Nov. 22, 1923; s. Humphrey Hume and Mary Joyce (Hutton) W.; m. Elaine L. Gale, Nov. 24, 1949 (div. Oct. 1965); 1 child, Terence Hume; m. Jacqueline Conrath, Mar. 26, 1966; stepchildren: Jaya, Sheila. BA, U. Toronto, 1945; PhD, Columbia U., 1956. Tchr. Princeton U., 1949-50, Rutgers U., 1950-51, U. Toronto, 1954-56, Brown U., 1956-61; mem. grad. faculty New Sch. Social Research, 1961-63; prof. sociology, chmn. dept. Univ. Coll., NYU, 1963-65; prof. sociology NYU, 1966-94, prof. emeritus, 1994—; retired. Vis. prof. U. Nev., 1965-66; vis. fellow Oxford (Eng.) U., 1978, European U. Inst., 1996-97; Simon vis. prof. U. Manchester, Eng., 1978. Author: American and Canadian Viewpoints, 1955, Population, 1956, 2d edit., 1959, Population and Society, 1961, 3rd edit., 1977, Skeptical Sociology, 1976, Power: Its Forms, Bases and Uses, 1979, 3rd edit., 1995, Class Fertility Trends in Western Nations, 1980, The Problem of Order: What Unites and Divides Society, 1994, 2d edit., 1995, The Modern Condition: Essays at Century's End, 1998, The Oversocialized Conception of Man (reissue of Skeptical Sociology), 1999, Reflections on a Politically Skeptical Era, 2003, 2d edit. 2005, The Persistence of the Particular, 2005; editor: Social Research, 1961-64, (with Harry L. Gracey) Readings in Introductory Sociology, 1967, 3rd edit., 1977, Contemporary Sociology: A Journal of Reviews, 1972-74, Max Weber, 1970; mem. editl. bd. Dissent, 1966—; contbg. editor Partisan Rev., 1981-87. Guggenheim fellow, 1984-85, Woodrow Wilson Internat. Ctr. for Scholars fellow, 1991-92. Mem.: Soc. for Advancement of Socio-Econs., Eastern Sociol. Soc., Am. Sociol. Assn. Personal E-mail: dhwrong@voicenet.com.

WROTH, JAMES MELVIN, retired military officer; b. Lincoln, Nebr., Feb. 2, 1929; s. Charles M. and Reba (Sharp) Wroth; m. Donna Mae Benson, June 4, 1951 (dec.); children: Mark, David S., Mary E. Bannon; m. Molly B. Mullan, June 15, 1975; stepchildren: Edward H. Mullan(dec.), Philip C. Mullan. BS, U. Nebr., 1951; postgrad., F.A. Sch., 1955—56, Command and Gen. Staff Coll., 1962—63; MBA, Syracuse U., 1963; postgrad., Armed Forces Staff Coll., 1967, Army War Coll., 1968, Harvard U., 1972. Commd. 2d lt. US Army, 1951, advanced through grades to brig. gen., 1973, U.S. Army, Republic of Korea, 1952-53; instr. A.A.A. Sch., Ft. Bliss, Tex., 1954-56; with 3d Inf. Div., Ft. Benning, Ga., also Germany, 1957-61; with Office Chief of Staff US Army, 1963-66; comdg. officer 1st Bn. 31st Arty., Republic of Korea, 1967; exec. asst. to asst. sec. Army US Army, 1968-70; exec. officer I Field Force Vietnam Arty., 1970; comdg. officer 52d Arty. Group, Vietnam, 1971; with Office Dep. Chief Staff for Personnel, Dept. Army, 1972-75; comdg. gen. VII Corps Arty. and Augsburg Germany Mil. Community, 1975-77; comdr. 2d ROTC region, Ft. Knox, Ky., 1977-79; ret., 1979; v.p., dir. mgmt. scis. ops. Gen. Research Corp., McLean, Va., 1979-82; group v.p Info. Systems & Network Corp., Bethesda, Md., 1982-93; pres. J-Tech, Inc., 1993—96. Trustee Washington Adventist Hosp. Found., 1989—93. Decorated D.S.M., Legion of Merit, Bronze Star, Air Medal with V device, Army Commendation medal, Vietnamese Gallantry Cross with palm; recipient F. A. Assn. award, 1950, John J. Pershing award, 1951, 40 and 8 award, 1951, Presdl. Unit Citation, US Coast Guard, 2005. Mem.: U.S. Coast Guard Aux. (past flotilla comdr.), Ret. Officers Assn. (past chpt. pres.), Nat Soc. Pershing Rifles (past nat. comdr.), Indian Creek Yacht and Country Club (dir. 2000—03), Indian Creek Yacht Club (past commodore), Beta Gamma Sigma, Alpha Kappa Psi. Personal E-mail: jim.wroth@us.army.mil.

WROTH, L(AWRENCE) KINVIN, law educator; b. Providence, July 9, 1932; s. Lawrence Counselman and Barbara (Pease) W.; m. Susan Collins, May 2, 1958 (div. 1972); children: Ann K., Caroline D., Eliza H.; m. Deborah Bethell, Aug. 10, 1972; 1 dau., Katharine L.; stepchildren— John H., David H., Elizabeth T. and Sarah B. Zobel. BA, Yale U., 1954; LLB, Harvard U., 1960. Bar: Mass. 1960, Maine 1974. Teaching fellow, asst. prof. law Dickinson Sch. Law, 1960-62; rsch. assoc. Harvard U., 1962-64; assoc. prof. law U. Maine Sch. Law, Portland, 1964-66, prof., 1966-96; assoc. dean Sch. Law U. Maine, 1977-78, acting dean, 1978-80, dean, 1980-90; prof. Vt. Law Sch., 1996—, dean, 1996—2004, pres., 2003—04; dir. Land Use Inst. Vt. Law Sch., Royalton, 2005—. Rsch. fellow Charles Warren Center Studies in Am. History, Harvard U., 1968-74; cons. civil and probate procedure, profl. and jud. responsibility, and ct.-bar rels. Maine Supreme Jud. Ct., 1967-96; cons. civil, probate, family ct. and criminal procedure and evidence Vt. Supreme Ct., 1969— Author: (with R.H. Field and V.L. McKusick) Maine Civil Practice, 2d edit., 1970; editor-in-chief: Province in Rebellion, 1975; editor: (with H.B. Zobel) Legal papers of John Adams, 1965; reporter: Vermont Rules of Civil Procedure, 1971, Vermont Rules of Criminal Procedure, 1974, Maine Rules of Probate Procedure, 1980, (with J. Dooley) Vermont Rules of Evidence, 1982, Maine Code of Judicial Conduct, 1993, Vermont Code of Judicial Conduct, 1994. Pres. Greater Portland Landmarks, Inc., 1966—69, adv. trustee, 1969—85; adv. coun. Nat. Trust Hist. Preservation, 1967—70; mem. Maine Commn. on Legal Needs, 1989—90, Commn. to Study Future of Maine's Cts., 1991—93, Commn. on Future of Vt.'s Judiciary, 1998—99, Vt. Bus. Roundtable, 1998—2004; bd. dirs. Maine Bar Found., 1983—89, sec., 1983—86, v.p., 1987, pres., 1988, fellow, 1991; bd. dirs. Pine Tree Legal Assistance Inc., 1985—96, Nat. Assn. IOLTA Programs, Inc., 1988—90, Portland Symphony Orch., 1990—98, v.p. ops. and resources, 1991—95, pres., 1995—96. Recipient Littleton-Griswold prize Am. Hist. Assn., 1966, Howard H. Dana award Maine Bar Found., 1991, Justice Louis Scolnik award Maine Civil Liberties Union, 1992, Herbert Harley award Am. Judicature Soc., 1994. Fellow Am. Bar Found.; mem. ABA, Maine Bar Assn. (Disting. Svc. award 1990), Am. Law Inst., Vermont Bar Assn., Colonial Soc. Mass., Mass. Hist. Soc. Office: Vt Law Sch PO Box 96 South Royalton VT 05068-0096 Office Phone: 802-831-1268. E-mail: kwroth@vermontlaw.edu.

WROTTEN, MARYLEAN, medical coordinator, counselor; d. Evelyn Saxton and Perry Elmore; 1 child, Evelyn DeShawn Wroten. Student, Audrey Cohn Coll., 1984. Approved med. authorized pers. Fedn. Puerto Rican Orgns., 1991; strategist crisis intervention pers. Fedn. Puerto Rican Orgns., 1991, cert. CPR-First Aid Fedn. Puerto Rican Orgns., 2004. Resident therapist Audrey Cohen Coll., 1991—; med. coord. Agy. Fedn. Multicultural Orgns., NY, 1991—. Author: (poetry) I Love God (Editor's Choice award, 2004), Hope, 2004. Youth coord. Jackson Dem. Club, Bronx, 1995—99; Sunday sch. tchr. Praying Band of Faith, Bronx, 1985—89; proposal rev. com. Neighborhood Adv. Bd., Bronx, 1995—96; del. 1199 Nat. Health & Human Employees Union, NYC, 1996—2004. Mem.: Internat. Soc. Poets (disting.). Democrat. Pentecostal. Avocations: hiking, reading, volunteering, singing. Office: Federation Multicultural Organization 2 VanSinderen Ave Brooklyn NY 11207 Office Phone: 212-234-2268. Personal E-mail: Lynnmary10@yahoo.com.

WRUBLE, BERNHARDT KARP, lawyer; b. Wilkes-Barre, Pa., Mar. 21, 1942; s. Maurice and Ruth Yvonne (Karp) W.; m. Judith Marilyn (Eyges), Nov. 16, 1968 (div. 1987); children: Justine, Vanessa, Alexis; m. Jill (Diamond), Nov. 24, 1990; children: Mattia, Austin. BA in Polit. Sci., Williams Coll., Williamstown, Mass., 1963; JD, U. Pa., 1966; postgrad., N.Y. Univ., 1972—74, Harvard U., 1978. Bar: Conn., 2003, U.S. Dist. Ct. (so. dist.) N.Y., 1969, U.S. Dist. Ct. (ea. dist.) N.Y., 1972, U.S. Ct. Appeals (2d cir.), 1972, U.S. Supreme Ct., 1972, U.S. Ct. Appeals (7th cir.), 1974, U.S. Ct. Appeals (D.C. and 4th cir.), 1984, U.S. Ct. Appeals (5th cir.), 1985, U.S. Ct. Appeals (11th cir.) 1986. Law clk. to presiding judge U.S. Ct. Appeals (3d cir.), 1966—67; assoc. Simpson, Thacher, and Bartlet, NYC, 1968—73, ptnr., 1974—77; prin. dep. gen. counsel U.S. Dept. Army, Washington, 1977—79; dir. Office Govt. Ethics, Washington, 1979; exec. asst. to sec. and dep. sec. U.S. Dept. Energy, Washington, 1979—81; dir. President's Interagy. Coal Export Task Force, Washington, 1980—81; ptnr. Verner, Liipfert, Bernhard, McPherson, and Hand, Washington, 1981—99; sr. v.p. legal affairs N.W. Airlines, St. Paul, 1999—2001. Bd. dir. Epilepsy Found. Am., 1983, chmn., 1991. Hartford County Pro Bono Award, 2004. Mem. ABA, D.C. Bar Assn., N.Y. State Bar Assn., Williams Coll. Alumni Assn. (pres. Washington chpt. 1986-91), Williams Coll. Soc. Alumni Assn. (exec. com. 1988-91). Democrat. Office Phone: 860-521-3543. Personal E-mail: bkwruble@yahoo.com.

WRUBLE, BRIAN FREDERICK, investor; b. Kalamazoo, Apr. 18, 1943; s. Milton and Rose Muriel (Nathanson) W.; m. Susan Roberta Shifrin, June 23, 1968 (div. Oct. 1984); children: Amy Carolyn, Jordan Todd; m. Kathleen Wilson Bratton, Apr. 20, 1985; 1 child, Henrietta Zane Bratton. BEE, Cornell U., 1965, MEE, 1966; MBA with distinction, NYU, 1976. Field engr. Sperry Gyroscope Corp., Lake Success, NY, 1966—70; v.p. Alliance One Instl. Svcs., Inc., NYC, 1970—76, H. C. Wainwright and Co., Inc., NYC, 1976-77, Wainwright Securities, Inc., NYC, 1977; v.p., co-mgr. fundamental equities rsch. Smith Barney, Harris Upham & Co., NYC, 1977-79; exec. v.p. chief fin. ops. Equitable Life Assurance Soc. U.S., NYC, 1979-92; chmn., pres., CEO Equitable Capital Mgmt. Corp., NYC, 1985-92; chief investment officer Equitable Life Assurance Soc. U.S., NYC, 1991-92; pres., COO, dir. Delaware Mgmt. Holdings, Inc., 1992-95; pres., CEO The Delaware Group, 1992-95; pres., COO Delaware Mgmt. Co., 1992-95; chmn. Delaware Distributors, Inc., 1992-95; chmn., CEO Delaware Svc. Co., Inc., 1992—95; gen. ptnr. Odyssey Ptnrs., L.P., NYC, 1995—; mng. prin. Odyssey Investment Ptnrs., LLC, NYC, 1997—98, spl. ltd. ptnr., 1999—2004; pvt. investor, 2004—. Chmn., pres. Equitable Realty Assets Corp., Atlanta, 1983—92; v.p., dir. TELMARI, Inc., NYC, 1982—83, Equitable Variable Life Ins. Co., 1987—92; chmn. Equico Capital Corp., NYC, 1984—92; CEO Equitable Gen. of Okla., Oklahoma City, 1985—86; trustee Equitable Retirement Plans, NYC, 1980—86; trustee bd. III Oppenheimer Funds, 2001—, trustee bd. I, 2005—, chmn. bd. I, 2006—; pres. Hudson River Trust, 1991—92, Equitable Funds, 1991—92; mem. investment adv. bd. Zurich Fin. Svc. Group, 2004—; dir. Spl. Value Opportunities Fund LLC, 2004—. Vice-chmn. Boys Choir of Harlem, NYC, 1984—92; vice chmn. Corp. Ptnrs. Phila. Art Mus., 1993—95; bd. govs. Jerome Levy Econ. Inst., 1990—2001; bd. dirs. Harlem Youth Devel. Found., 1989—92, Corp. Ptnrs. Phila. Art Mus., 1992—95, The Jackson Lab., Inc., 1990—, Inst. for Advanced Study, 1992—, treas., 2006—. Recipient Heroes award Boys Choir Harlem, 1990, Founders award, 1993. Mem.: IEEE, Phila. C. of C. (bd. dirs. 1992—95, mem. exec. com. 1993—95), Inst. CFAs (CFA, bd. trustees 1992—98, vice chmn. 1993—94, chmn. 1994—95, bd. trustees rsch. found. 1994—95, 2000—02, assoc. editor CFA Digest 1983—), N.Y. Soc. Security Analysts, Assn. Investment Mgmt. and Rsch. (gov. 1992—98, C. Steward Sheppard award 2000). Republican. Jewish. Avocations: skiing, amateur radio.

WRUCK, ERICH-OSKAR, retired foreign language educator, administrator; b. Gross-Kroessin/Pomerania, Germany, Oct. 29, 1928; came to U.S., 1952, naturalized, 1954; s. Erich Albert and Erna (Kroening) W.; m. Esther Emmy Schmidt, Oct. 3, 1953; children: Eric Gordon, Karin Esther (dec.), Krista Elisabeth. BA magna cum laude, Rutgers U., 1959; MA, 1961, PhD, 1969. Asst. instr. Rutgers U., New Brunswick, NJ, 1959-62; asst. prof. Davidson (N.C.) Coll., 1962-69, assoc. prof., 1969-73, prof., chmn. dept. German, 1983-87; established exch. program Marburg (Germany) U., 1963; with U. Würzburg, Germany, 1985; dir. Davidson abroad program Marburg, 1966-67, 71-72; jr. yr. abroad program Würzburg, 1986-87, 89-92; ret., 1994. Cons. faculty U.S. Army Command and Gen. Staff Coll., 1974-85. 1st lt. U.S. Army, 1953-57, to col. USAR, 1986. Recipient Julius Maximilians medal U. Wuerzburg, 1987; named to Arty. OCS Hall of Fame, 1996; Henry Rutgers scholar. Mem. Goethe Assn., Freies Deutsches Hochstift, Schiller Assn., Goethe Soc. of N. Am. (charter), Soc. German Am. Studies. Lutheran. Avocations: painting, photography, soaring, skiing, running.

WRUCKE-NELSON, ANN C., elementary school educator; b. Mankato, Minn., Nov. 5, 1939; d. G.F. and Dorothy (Thomas) Wrucke; children: Chris, Dor-Ella. BS, Mankato State U., 1961; MLA, So. Meth. U., 1974; postgrad., U. Minn., 1963, Tex. Woman's U., EdD in Early Childhood Edn., 1992. Cert. elem., kindergarten, ESL, history tchr., Tex., adminstrn., 2000. Tchr. Rochester (Minn.) Pub. Schs., Christ the King Sch., Dallas; dir., tchr. Norway Christian Presch., Dallas; Every Student Learns Lang. program kindergarten tchr. Dallas Ind. Sch. Dist., 1971—. Tchr. summer session Tex. Woman's U., 1991; tchr. PreK Rosemont Primary, 2005-; presenter in field. Prodr.: (video) A Year of Language Learning, 1990. Sunday sch. tchr. Holy Trinity Ch. Recipient Tchr. of Yr. award, 1989; Tex. TESOL scholar, 1994; Bill Martin Literacy Conf. scholar; named ESL Tchr. of Yr., 1991. Mem. Kindergarten Tchrs. Tex., Phi Delta Kappa. Mailing: Rosemont 1919 Steven Forest Dr Dallas TX 75208

WU, BENJAMIN H., federal agency administrator, lawyer; BA, NYU, 1985; JD, U. Pittsburgh, 1988. Former counsel Office of Congresswoman Constance A. Morella; former counsel, sci. com. US Ho. of Reps., mem., investigations and oversight subcom., 1993—94, mem., tech. subcom., 1995—2001; dep. under sec. for tech. US Dept. Commerce, Washington, 2001—04, exec. sec., NSTC com. on tech., asst. sec. for tech. policy, 2004—.

WU, CARL, medical researcher; PhD, Harvard U., 1979. Postdoctoral fellow Harvard U., 1979—82; joined Lab. Biochemistry Nat. Cancer Inst., 1982; chief Lab. Molecular Cell Biology Ctr. Cancer Rsch., Nat. Cancer Inst., 1996—, also head Chromosome Structure and Gene Regulation Sect., Lab. Molecular Cell Biology. Contbr. articles to sci. jours. Recipient Outstanding Young Scientist Award, Md. Acad. Sciences, 1987, Young Investigator Award, Am. Soc. Biochemistry and Molecular Biology, 1992. Mem.: NAS, Am. Acad. Arts and Sciences. Office: Lab Molecular Cell Biology Nat Cancer Inst Ctr Cancer Rsch 37 Convent Dr Bldg 37 Rm 6068 Bethesda MD 20892-4255 Office Phone: 301-496-3029. Office Fax: 301-435-3697. E-mail: carlwu@helix.nih.gov.

WU, CHWAN-HWA JOHN, adult education educator; arrived in US, 1983; BS, Nat. Chiao Tung U., Taiwan, 1980; PhD, Poly. U., NY, 1987. Prof. Auburn U., Ala., 1987—. Contbr. articles to profl. jours. Network Security Rsch. grantee, Dept. of Def., 1987—2007. Fellow: IEEE. Achievements include patents pending for network security. Office: Auburn University Electrical and Computer Eng Dept Auburn University AL 36849-5201 Office Phone: 334-844-1851. Business E-Mail: wu@eng.auburn.edu.

WU, DANIEL, actor; b. San Francisco, Sept. 30, 1974; BA in Achitecture, U. Oreg., 1997. Vocalist Alive, Hong Kong. Founder, instructor Wushu Club, U. Oreg. Actor: (films) Young & Dangerous: The Prequel, 1998, Bishonen, 1998, City of Glass, 1998, Gorgeous, 1999, Gen-X Cops, 1999, Purple Storm, 1999, 2000 AD, 2000, Headlines, 2001, Hit Team, 2001, Peony Pavilion, 2001, Cop on a Mission, 2001, Born Wild, 2001, Beijing Rocks, 2001, The Peeping, 2002, Beauty and the Breast, 2002, Princess D, 2002, Love Undercover, 2002, Devil Face, Angel Heart, 2002, Naked Weapon, 2002, Love Undercover 2, 2003, Hidden Track, 2003, Miss Du Shi Niang, 2003, Magic Kitchen, 2004, Enter the Phoenix, 2004, One Night in Mongkok, 2004, Around the World in 80 Days, 2004, The Huadu Chronicles: Blade of the Rose, 2004, New Police Story, 2004 (Best Supporting Actor award, Golden Horse Awards, 2004), Beyond Our Ken, 2004, House of Fury, 2005, Divergence, 2005, Chin bui but dzui, 2005, Everlasting Regret, 2005, (voice) Dragon Blade, 2005; actor, prodr.: (films) Night Corridor, 2003; actor(guest appearances): (TV series) MTV Whatever Things, 2003, Getaway, 2005,: (documentaries) Hong Kong Superstars, 2001. Avocations: Kung Fu, travel, photography, swimming, wakeboarding, fitness. Office: c/o The JC Grp 145 Waterloo Rd Kowloon Hong Kong

WU, DAVID, congressman; b. Taiwan, Apr. 8, 1955; came to US, 1961; m. Michelle Wu; children: Matthew, Sarah. BS, Stanford U., Calif., 1977; student, Harvard Med. Sch.; JD, Yale U., New Haven, 1982. Clk. to fed. judge, Portland, Oreg.; ptnr. Cohen & Wu, Oreg., 1988-98; mem. US Congress from 1st Oreg. dist., 1999—, mem. edn. and labor com., mem. sci. & tech. com., chmn. subcommittee on tech. and innovation, mem. fgn. affairs com., mem. exec. bd. Congl. Asian Pacific Am. Caucus, mem. New Dem. Coalition. Democrat. Office: 620 SW Main Ste 606 Portland OR 97205 Office Phone: 202-225-0855, 503-326-2901. Office Fax: 503-326-5066. *

WU, DE TING, mathematics professor, researcher, writer; b. Shanghai, Jan. 9, 1938; came to U.S., 1981; s. Bing Huo and Wei Fen (Zhang) W.; m. Pei Hua Zhang, July 16, 1974; 1 child, Yin. BA, Peking U., China, 1962; MA, U. Ga., 1983, PhD, 1988. Instr. Shanghai Textile Coll., 1963-71; worker Shanghai # 12 Textile Factory, 1971-78; sr. lectr. Shanghai Textile Coll., 1978-81; tchg. asst. U. Ga., Athens, 1981-88; assoc. prof. Morehouse Coll., Atlanta, 1989—. Editor: Selected Problems from Theoretical Mechanics, 1981. Bd. dirs. Orgn. Chinese Ams., 1992-96, Asian-Pacific Ams. of Coun. of Ga., 1994. Mem. AAUP, Shanghai Mechanics Assn., Am. Math. Soc., Math. Assn. Am. Avocations: photography, travel, playing contract bridge. Office: Morehouse Coll Dept Math 830 Westview Dr SW Dept Math Atlanta GA 30314-3773 Office Phone: 404-681-2800 2459. E-mail: dtwu@morehouse.edu.

WU, ERIC, entrepreneur; b. 1982; Grad., U. Ariz., 2005. Co-founder JobDoggy.com, 2002; founder LiveByCampus LLC, Scottsdale, Ariz., 2006—. Named one of Best Entrepreneurs Under 25, BusinessWeek, 2006; recipient Polaris Sr. award, U. Ariz., 2005. Office: LiveByCampus LLC Ste 110 10245 E Via Linda Scottsdale AZ 85258 Office Phone: 800-796-1733. Office Fax: 800-796-1659. E-mail: info@livebycampus.com.

WU, FRANK H., law educator, journalist; b. Cleve., Aug. 20, 1967; s. Hai and Grace (Ma) Wu. BA, Johns Hopkins U., 1988; JD, U. Mich., 1991. Bar: Calif. 1992, DC 1995. Law clerk to Honorable Frank Battisti, Cleve., 1991—92; assoc. Morrison & Foerster, San Francisco, 1992-94; fellow Stanford U. Law Sch., Palo Alto, Calif., 1994-95; asst. prof. Howard U. Law Sch., Washington, 1995—98, assoc. prof., 1998—2001, prof., 2002—04, clinic dir., 2000—02; dean, prof. law Wayne State U. Law Sch., Detroit, 2004—. Scholar-in-residence Deep Springs Coll., 2001—03; vis. prof. U. Mich., 2002—03; adj. prof. Columbia U., 2002—04. Co-author: (book) Beyond Self Interest, 1996, Race, Rights and Reparation: Law and the Japanese American Internment, 2001; contbg. author: book The Affirmative Action Debate, 1996, Illegal Immigration Viewpoints, 1996; author: Yellow: Race in Amercia Beyond Black and White, 2001. Chmn. DC Human Rights Commn., 2001—03, DC Ct. Appeals Bd. Profl. Responsibility, 2003—04; bd. dirs. Leadership Conf. on Civil Rights Edn. Fund, 2004—; trustee Gallaudet U., 2000—. Named one of Best Lawyers Under 40, Nat. Asian Pacific Am. Bar Assn., 2004. Fellow: Am. Bar Found.; mem.: Com. of 100, Am. Law Inst., Asian Pacific ABA (dir. ednl. fund 1995—98). Office: Wayne State Univ Law Sch 471 W Palmer St Detroit MI 48202 Home Phone: 202-487-5775; Office Phone: 313-577-3933. Business E-Mail: frankhwu@wayne.edu.

WU, FUMING, computer science educator; s. L. Wu and H. Shen; m. Y. Fang, June 11, 1992; 1 child, Wenbo. PhD in Math. and Theoretical Computer Sci., U. Haifa, Isreal, 1998. Sr. mem. sci. staff Nortel Networks, Richardson, Tex., 2000; rsch. scientist Alcatel USA Resources, Inc., Plano, Tex., 2001—06; asst. prof. of computer sci. Tex. A&M Internat. U., Laredo, 2006—. Contbr. scientific papers to profl. jours. Mem.: ACM, IEEE (sr.). Achievements include patents pending for. Office: Tex A&M Internat U CH302C 5201 University Blvd Laredo TX 78041-1900 Home Phone: 214-387-9355; Office Phone: 956-326-2600. Personal E-mail: fwu@ieee.org. Business E-Mail: fwu@tamiu.edu.

WU, GEORGE H., federal judge; b. NYC, 1950; BA, Pomona Coll., 1972; JD, U. Chgo. Law Sch., 1975. Bar: Calif. 1975. Assoc. Latham & Watkins, 1975—79, LeBoeuf, Lamb, Leiby & MacRae, 1989—91; law clk. Hon. Stanley N. Barnes, US Ct. Appeals (9th cir.), 1976—77, 1979; asst. US atty. US Atty's Office (Ctrl. dist.) Calif., 1982—89, 1991—93; judge LA Mcpl. Ct., 1993—96, LA Superior Ct., 1996—2007, US Dist. Ct. (Ctrl. dist.) Calif., 2007—. Asst. prof. law U. Tenn. Coll. Law, 1979—82. Office: US Dist Ct 312 N Spring St Los Angeles CA 90012 *

WU, HARRY PAO-TUNG, retired librarian; b. Jinan, Shandong, China, May 1, 1932; arrived in U.S., 1960; s. James Ching-Mei and Elizabeth Hsiao (Lu) Wu; m. Irene I-Len Sun, June 23, 1961; children: Eva Pei-Chen, Walter Pei-Liang. BA, Nat. Taiwan U., Taipei, 1959; postgrad., Ohio State U., 1962; MLS, Kent State U., 1966. Archive and libr. asst. Taiwan Handicraft Promotion Ctr., Taipei, 1959-60; student asst. Kent State U. Libr., 1960-61; reference libr. Massillon (Ohio) Pub. Libr., 1964-65, acting asst. dir., 1965, asst. dir., head adult svcs., 1966; dir. Flesh Pub. Libr., Piqua, Ohio, 1966-68, St. Clair County Libr. Sys., Port Huron, Mich., 1968-96; founder, dir. Blue Water Libr. Fedn., Port Huron, 1974-96; ret., 1996. Pres. Mich. Libr. Film Cir., Lansing, 1977—79; mem. St. Clair County Literacy Project Com., 1986—96. Cmty. mem. editl. bd. Times Herald, 1998—99. Bd. dirs. Mich. Waterways Coun. Girl Scouts U.S., Port Huron, 1985—86, Blue Water Reading Coun., 1987—88, United Way St. Clair County, Mich., 1990—91; trustee Libr. Mich., 1992—95; mem. sister city com. City of Port Huron, 2002—04. Mem.: ALA, Chinese-Am. Librs. Assn., Detroit Suburban Librs. Roundtable, Assn. Ednl. Comm. and Tech., Am. Mgmt. Assn., Mich. Libr. Assn., Port Huron Internat. Club (pres. 1988), Rotary (dir. 1972—74, 1988—90, grand marshall Internat. Day Parade 2005, Paul Harris fellow 1988). Home: 1518 Holland Ave Port Huron MI 48060-1511

WU, HENRY H., urologist, surgeon; s. Kenneth C. and Mei F. Wu; m. Catherine H. Hsueh, May 26, 2001; children: Amelia H., Alexander H. BA magna cum laude, U. Rochester, NY; MD, NYU, NYC. Diplomate Am. Bd. Urology, 2000. Urologist, CERO So. Calif. Urology, Inc., Los Alamitos, Calif., 2005—. Fellow: ACS; mem.: Am. Urol. Assn. (life), Phi Beta Kappa. Office: So Calif Urology Inc 3801 Katella Ave Suite 320 Los Alamitos CA 90720 Office Phone: 562-598-0200. Office Fax: 562-598-0222.

WU, HONG, pathologist; arrived in U.S., 1988; d. Xing-Yu Wu and Xu-Zhi Xu; m. Lance Mark Wiseman, Nov. 24, 1999. MD, Peking Union Med. Coll., Beijing, 1986; PhD, U. Va., 1992. Diplomate in surg. and clin. pathology and in dermatopathology Am. Bd. Pathology. Rsch. asst. dept. med. genetics Inst. Basic Med. Scis., Chinese Acad. Med. Scis., Beijing, 1987—88; rsch. assoc. dept. microbiology U. Va. Sch. Medicine, Charlottesville, 1993—94; resident dept. pathology and lab. medicne U. Pa., 1994—99, fellow dept. dermatology, 1999—2000; assoc. mem., staff pathologist dept. pathology Fox Chase Cancer Ctr., Phila., 2000—. Contbr. articles to profl. jours. Mem.: Am. Soc. Clin. Pathologists, Coll. Am. Pathologists, Am. Soc. Dermatopathology. Office: Fox Chase Cancer Ctr 7701 Burholme Ave Philadelphia PA 19111 Office Phone: 215-728-6900. E-mail: hong.wu@fccc.edu.

WU, HSIU KWANG, economist, educator; b. Hankow, China, Dec. 14, 1935; came to U.S., 1952, naturalized, 1963; s. Kao Cheng and Edith (Huang) W.; m. Kathleen Gibbs Johnson, Aug. 17, 1968. Grad., Lawrenceville Sch., 1954; AB, Princeton U., 1958; MBA, U. Pa., 1960, PhD, 1963. Prof., group coordinator fin., econs. and internat. bus. Boston U., 1968-72; prof., chmn. fin., econs. and legal studies faculty U. Ala., 1972-81, Lee Bidgood prof. fin. and econs., 1978-97, Ala. Banker Edn. Found. Banking Chair prof., 1973-78, prof. emeritus fin., 1997—; econ. adviser Office of Comptroller of Currency, U.S. Treasury, 1966-69, 75-80; dir. Ala. Fed., 1984-88, SECOR Bank FSB, 1988-93, chmn. bd., 1992-93. Cons. instl. investor study SEC, 1969-70; mem. com. examiners undergrad. program for counseling and evaluation test in bus. Ednl. Testing Service, 1971, 77 Co-editor: Elements of Investments, 2d rev. edit, 1972; Contbr. articles to law and econ. jours. Sloan Faculty fellow Sloan Sch. Mgmt., Mass. Inst. Tech., 1965-66 Mem. Am. Fin. Assn., Fin. Mgmt. Assn. Home: 3201 Old Barn Ct Ponte Vedra Beach FL 32082-3713

WU, HUI, language educator; b. Nanchang, Jiangxi, China; arrived in US, 1993; d. Minsheng Wu and Taozi Yu; m. Daoming Chen, Jan. 1, 1982; 1 child, T. Donna Chen. BA in English Edn., Nanchang Vocat. Tchrs. Coll., 1980; MA in English, Jiangxi U., Nanchang, 1983; PhD in English, Tex. Christian U., Ft. Worth, 1998. Assoc. prof. Jiangxi U., 1982—92, 1992—93, assoc. chmn. fgn. lang. dept., 1987—93; lectr. U. Ctrl. Ark., Conway, 1997—2001, asst. prof., 2001—06, assoc. prof., 2006—. Translator: (into Chinese) Rhetoric and Irony (by Jan Swearingen), 2004. Mem.: MLA, Coll. Composition and Commn. Assn. Office: U Ctrl Ark 201 Donaghey Ave Conway AR 72035

WU, JAMES CHEN-YUAN, aerospace engineering educator; b. Nanking, China, Oct. 5, 1931; came to U.S., 1953, naturalized, 1963; s. Chien Lieh and Cheng-Ling Wu; m. Mei-Ying Chang, Sept. 7, 1957; children—Alberta Yee-Hwa, Norbert Mao-Hwa. Student, Nat. Taiwan U., 1949-52; BS, Gonzaga U., 1954; postgrad., Columbia U., 1954; MS (univ. fellow), U. Ill., 1955, PhD, 1957. Engr. Wah Chang Corp., NYC, 1954; researcher Mass. Inst. Tech. at Cambridge, 1957; asst. prof. Gonzaga U., Spokane, Wash., 1957-59; research specialist Douglas Aircraft Co., 1959-65, group leader, 1960-61, supr., 1961-62, br. chief, 1963-65; prof. aerospace engring. Ga. Inst. Tech., 1965-96; pres. Applied Aero, LLC, 1996—. Cons. N.Am. Aviation Co., Geophys. Tech. Corp., European Atomic Energy Commn., Ispra, Italy, European Atomic Energy Commn. (research center), U.S. Army Research Office, Durham, S.C. Contbr. articles to profl. jours. Chmn. bd. dirs. Chinese-Am. Inst. Recipient profl. achievement award Douglas Aricraft Co., 1963, Outstanding Tchrs. award Gonzaga U., 1959; Asso. fellow Am. Inst. Aeros. and Astronautics Mem. Am. Soc. Engring. Sci. (founding), Soc. Indsl. and Applied Math. (vice-chmn. Pacific N.W. 1958-59), Am. Astron. Soc. (sr.), Am. Phys. Soc., Nat. Assn. Chinese Ams. (pres. Atlanta chpt.), Sigma Xi, Tau Beta Pi, Sigma Alpha Nu. Office: Sch Aerospace Engring Georgia Inst Tech 48365 Avalon Heights Ter Fremont CA 94539-8005

WU, JEFF (CHIEN-FU WU), engineering educator; BS, Nat. Taiwan U., 1971; PhD in Statistics, U. Calif., Berkeley, 1976. Mem. Statistics Dept. U. Wis., 1977—88; GM/NSERC chair in quality and productivity U. Waterloo, 1988—93; H.C. Carver prof. statistics, prof. industrial and ops. engring. U. Mich., Ann Arbor, 1993—2003; prof., Coca-Cola chair in engring. statistics Sch. Industrial Sys. Engring., Ga. Inst. Tech., Atlanta, 2003—. P.C. Mahalanobis Meml. Indian Statistical Insts., 1998. Contbr. articles to profl. jours. Recipient Wilcoxon Prize, 1990, Jerome Sacks Award for Outstanding Cross-Disciplinary Rsch., Nat. Inst. Statistical Scis., 2005. Fellow: Am. Statistical Assn. (Jack Youden Prize 1997, 2005), Inst. Math. Statistics, Am. Soc. for Quality (Brumbaugh Award 1992); mem.: NAE, Academia Sinica. Office: Sch Industrial and Sys Engring Ga Inst Tech 765 Ferst Dr, NW Atlanta GA 30332-0205 Office Phone: 404-385-4262. Office Fax: 404-894-2301. E-mail: jeff.wu@isye.gatech.edu.

WU, JIAN, operations research specialist; BS, Zhejiang U., Hangzhou, China, 1998, MS, 2001; PhD, Rutgers U., Piscataway, NJ, 2002—. Rsch. assoc. Zhejiang U., Hangzhou, 1998—2001, Rutgers U., Piscataway, 2002—. Recipient 3d prize Contest Computer Aided Instrn. Software Design, Zhejiang U., 1999; fellow Undergraduate Fellowship, 1994—98. Mem.: Materials Rsch. Soc., IEEE, Sigma Xi. Achievements include development of 4H-SiC merged PiN Schottky (MPS) power rectifiers with record high figure-of-merit; 4H-SiC lateral MOSFETs with high mobility; novel MOSFET structure: MOS controlled vertical field effect transistors. Office: Rutgers U Dept ECE 94 Brett Rd Piscataway NJ 08854 Home Phone: 201-233-9670; Office Phone: 732-445-0601. Business E-Mail: jianwu@rci.rutgers.edu.

WU, JIE, electronics engineer, educator; d. Fu Chen Wu and Zheng Chen Yu; life ptnr. Michael Heinz Stoiber. B in Engring., Hefei U. Tech., Hefei, Anhui Prov., China, 1993; MS in Engring., Hefei U. Tech., 1996; PhD, Chinese Acad. of Scis., Shanghai, P.R. China, 1999, U. Notre Dame, Notre Dame, Ind., 2004. Rsch. assoc. U. Notre Dame, Ind., 2003—04; asst. prof. U. Tenn., Knoxville, 2004—. Contbr. articles to profl. jour. Recipient Faculty Early Career Devel. Award, NSF, 2005, Ralph E. Powe Jr. Faculty Award, Oak Ridge Associated Univ., 2006; grantee Rate-Based Sensor Devel. for Advancing Heat Transfer Measurements, NSF. Achievements include patents pending for Method and apparatus for AC micropump; Method and apparatus for enhancing microbial detection; parallel plate electrodes for particle concentrate or removal; rate-based sensors for advanced real-time analysis and diagnosis; patents for AC electrothermal techniques for microfluidies maniplulation. Office: U Tenn 1508 Middle Dr Knoxville TN 37996 Home Phone: 865-573-1712, 865-573-1712; Office Phone: 865-974-5494. Office Fax: 865-974-5483. Personal E-mail: jaynewu@utk.edu.

WU, JONATHAN T. H., science educator; PhD, Purdue U., West Lafayette, Ind., 1980. Prof. U. Colo., Denver, 1981—.

WU, JULIAN K., neurosurgeon; b. China, Mar. 9, 1956; ScB, Brown U., Providence, 1977; MD, U. Conn., Farmington, 1981. Diplomate Am. Bd. Neurol. Sugery, 1990. Intern Boston City Hosp., 1981—82; resident Tufts New Eng. Med. Ctr., Boston, 1982—87; chief neurosurgery Beth Israel Deconess Med. Ctr., Boston, 1997—2005; assoc. prof. neurosurgery Harvard U. Med. Sch., Boston, 2000—05; assoc. chmn. neurosurgery Tufts New England Med. Ctr., 2005—; prof. neurosurgery Tufts New England Med. Sch., 2007—. Bd. mem. Brain Tumor Soc., 1994—. Contbg. author (books) The Practice of Neurosurgery, 1996, Cancer Of The Nervous System, 2004. Recipient Charlton Fund award, Tufts U. Med. Sch., Boston, 1991. Master: Neursurgeons Soc. Am.; fellow: Am. Coll. Surgeons; mem.: Am. Assn. Neurol. Surgeons, Sigma Xi. Office: Tufts New England Med Ctr 750 Washington St Boston MA 02111

WU, JUNXIAN, chemist, researcher; b. JingDeZhen City, JiangXi, China, Feb. 1, 1976; arrived in US, 2005, permanent resident; d. Zuqian Wu and ZhaoDi Luo; m. Shan Guan, June 12, 2000; 1 child, Alyssa Guan. BS in Materials Sci. with honors, BeiHan U., Beijing, 1997; MS in Materials Sci., BeiHan U., 2000; PhD in Materials Sci., U. Minn., Mpls., 2005. Rsch. asst. U. Minn., 2000—05; sr. rsch. chemist Ashland Splty. Chem., Dublin, Ohio, 2005—. Contbr. articles to profl. jours. Mem.: Materials Rsch. Soc. Achievements include research in diblock copolymers, specialty polymers and adhesives. Office: Ashland Specialty Chem 5200 Blazer Pky Dublin OH 43017 Home: 4381 Camden Cir Dublin OH 43016 Office Fax: 614-790-6106. Business E-Mail: jwu@ashland.com.

WU, KATHLEEN J., lawyer; b. Great Neck, NY, 1960; BA, Columbia U., 1982; JD, George Washington U., 1985. Bar: NY 1986, Conn. 1986, Tex. 1987. Ptnr., Real Estate, Fin., Bus. Transactions Andrews Kurth LLP, Dallas, mem. mgmt. com. Contbr. articles to profl. jour.; lectr. in field. Mem. Dallas Assembly; bd. dir. Women's Leadership Exchange (Southwest), Tex. Cultural Trust Coun.; adv. bd. Turtle Creek Manor; bd. trustees Greenhill Sch. Named a Texas "super lawyer", Tex. Monthly Mag., 2003, 2004; named one of top 6 "go to" real estate lawyers in Tex., Tex. Lawyer Mag., 2003, best lawyers in Dallas, DMagazine, 2003. Mem.: Attys. Serving Cmty. (co-hon. chmn. 2003), Nat. Asian Pacific ABA, State Bar Tex., ABA, Conn. Bar Assn., NY State Bar Assn., Dallas Bar Assn. Office: Andrews Kurth LLP 1717 Main St Ste 3700 Dallas TX 75201 Office Phone: 214-659-4448. Office Fax: 214-659-4401. Business E-Mail: kwu@andrewskurth.com.

WU, LI-TZY, alcohol/drug abuse services professional, researcher; d. Yu-Tsai and Yu-Chi Wu; m. Hsin-Hsong Tseng, Apr. 20, 1992; children: Jonathan Tseng, Harrison Tseng. DSc, Johns Hopkins U., 1998. RN N.J., 1993. Psychiat. epidemiologist RTI Internat., Research Triangle Park, NC, 1999—2005; assoc. prof. Sch. Medicine Duke U., Durham, NC, 2005—. Recipient Nat. Inst. on Drug Abuse Women and Gender Jr. Investigator Travel award, 2001; fellow, NIH, 1997—99; grantee, Nat. Inst. Drug Abuse, 2000—02, 2003—06, Nat. Inst. Alcohol Abuse and Alcoholism, 2001—03. Mem.: APHA, Coll. on Problems of Drug Dependence, Delta Omega (Alpha chpt.).

WU, MARGARET, research scientist; Sr. scientific advisor ExxonMobil Rsch. & Engring. Co. Recipient Thomas Alva Edison Patent award, 2005. Mem.: Am. Chem. Soc. (award in indsl. chemistry 2007), Chinese Am. Chem. Soc. Office: ExxonMobil Rsch & Engring Co Rt 22 East Annandale NJ 08801 Office Phone: 908-730-2157. Office Fax: 908-730-3314. Business E-Mail: margaret.m.wu@exxonmobil.com. *

WU, MAW-KUEN, physicist; b. Hualien, Taiwan, Dec. 6, 1949; married; 2 children. BS in Physics, Tamkang U., Taiwan, 1973, MS in Physics, 1975; PhD in Physics, U. Houston, 1981. Rsch. scientist physics U. Houston, 1982—84; asst. prof. physics U. Ala., Huntsville, 1982—86, prof. physics, 1987—88; prof. applied physics Columbia U., 1988—94; prof. Nat. Tsing Hua U., 1994—. Vis. chair prof. Nat. Tsing Hua U., 1990—94, dir. materials sci. ctr., 1992—95, chmn. rsch. and devel. coun., 1995—98; vice chmn. Nat. Sci. Coun., 2000—02, min, 2004, 05; dir. inst. physics Academia Sinica, Taipei, Taiwan, 2002—04. Contbr. articles to sci. jours. Recipient Spl. award, NASA, 1988, U.S.A. Chinese Assn. Engring. Annual award, 1988, Tamkang Golden Eagle award, 1989, Bernd. T. Matthias prize, 1994, Y.T. Lee Outstanding Scientist award, 1995. Fellow: Chinese Phys. Soc., Third World Acad. Scis.; mem.: Asia-Pacific Acad. Material, NAS (fgn. assoc. 2004, Comstock prize 1988). Achievements include patents in field. Office: Inst Physics Academia Sinica Taipei 11529 Taiwan E-mail: mkwu@phys.sinica.edu.tw.

WU, MIN, computer and electrical engineer; b. China; BA in Econs., Tshinghua U., 1996; BSE in Elec. Engring., Tsinghua U., 1996; MA in Elec. Engring., Princeton U., 1998, PhD in Elec. Engring., 2001. Asst. prof. dept. elec. and computer engring. U. Md., 2001—06, assoc. prof., 2006—. Author: Multimedia Fingerprinting Forensics for Traitor Tracing, 2005; co-author: Multimedia Data Hiding, 2003; contbr. articles to profl. jour. Named one of Top 100 Young Innovators, MIT Tech. Review, 2004; recipient Career award, NSF, 2002, Young Investigator award, US Dept. Defense, Office Naval Rsch., 2005, Best Paper award, IEEE, European Signal Processing Soc. Achievements include co-holder of 5 US patents. Business E-Mail: minwu@eng.umd.edu.

WU, SHI TSAN, science research administrator, educator; b. Nanchang, Kiangxi, Peoples' Republic of China, July 31, 1933; came to US, 1957; s. Shu Zee and Duan Ming (Pao) Wu; m. Mai San Kao, Sept. 4, 1964; children: Cheyenne, Roselind, Patricia. BS in Mech. Engring., Nat. Taiwan U., 1955; MS in Mech. Engring., Ill. Inst. Tech., 1959; PhD in Aerospace Engring., U. Colo., 1967. Various tchg. positions, 1955-64; asst. rsch. prof. Rsch. Inst., Huntsville, Ala., 1967-69, assoc. prof. mech. engring., 1969-72, prof. mech. engring., 1972—, founder, dir. Ctr. Space Plasma and Aeronomic Rsch., 1986—, disting. prof. to disting. prof. emeritus, 1990—. Vis. scientist High Altitude Obs. Nat. Ctr. Atmospheric Rsch., summers 1969, 72, 73, rsch. asst., 1964-67; vis. prof. U. Sci. & Tech. China, 1982—, Wu-Han U., 1982—, LaTrobe U., Melbourne, Australia, 1975-76; PhD thesis examiner Tel Aviv U., 1982; cons. Battelle Rsch. Lab., 1978—, various labs. Dept. Commerce, 1974—, Wyle Labs., Huntsville, Ala., 1970-75, Northrup Corp., Huntsville, 1969-74; project specialist Chinese Provincial U. Devel. Project, World Bank, 1989—, others; founder, 1st dir. Inst. Space Physics, Astrophysics and Edn., U. Ala., Huntsville, 1995—; participant Solar Maximum Yr. Workshops in Australia, People's Republic of China, Ireland, USSR (chmn. various coms.). Corr. editor Acta Astrophysica Sinica, 1985; contbr. articles to profl. jours. Recipient Wright Gardner award Ala. Acad. Sci., 1986, Sixth Nat. Natural Sci. award Chinese Sci. Coun., 1994, Disting. Rschr. award Rsch. Inst. Alumni Assn., 1997; Fulbright-Hays scholar Australia, 1975-76; NSF fellow U. Colo., 1971. Fellow AIAA (dir. Miss. sect. 1980-82, 1987, chmn. various local and nat. coms. and confs., Herman Orberth award 1983, Martin Schilling award 1987, award for disting. leadership and svc. 1993, Plasmadynamics and Lasers award 1996, James Van Allen Space Environments award 2006); mem. Ctr. Space Sci. and Applied Tech., Chinese Acad. Sci (hon. 1990, Sci. and Tech. Achievement award 1992), NASA (sec. Adv. Solar Obs. Sci. Working Grp. 1981, chmn. various coms. and confs.), ASME (modeling & simulation com. Solar Energy divsn. 1979), Internat. Coun. Sci. Unions (various coms.), Sigma Xi (pres. 1974-76, sec. 1972-74, named Rschr. of Yr. 1979, Outstanding Svc. award 1977). Office: Dept Mech and Aerospace Engring U Ala Huntsville N272B Tech Hall Huntsville AL 35899 Office Phone: 256-824-6413. E-mail: wus@cspar.uah.edu.

WU, SHI-QI (SAMUEL WU), medical geneticist; b. Anhuei, China, Oct. 14, 1945; s. Wu Qi-Qiang and Xu Yi-Fang. MD, Shanghai First Med. Coll., China, 1971. Diplomate Am. Bd. Med. Genetics. Internist Xian 52 Hosp., China, 1972-73, res. gen. surgery, 1973-78; res. hematololgy Zhongshang Hosp., Shanghai, 1979-84; fellowship clin. cytogenetics U. Wis., 1985-88; fellowship cytogenetics U. B.C., Vancouver, Canada, 1988-90; co-dir. cytogenetics. rsch. lab Comp. Cancer Ctr. U. Wis., Madison, Wis., 1993-98; cons. cytogenetics Wis. State Lab Hygiene, Madison, Wis., 1993-98; assoc. scientist human oncol. U. Wis. Med. Sch., Madison, 1990-92, sr. scientist human oncology, 1992-98; assoc. prof. dept pediat. U. So. Calif., 1998—2005; dir. cytogenetics lab Children's Hosp., LA, 1998—; program dir. Am. Bd. Med. Genetics program in CHLA Med. Sch. Children's Hosp. U. So. Calif., 1999—, prof. Depts. Pediat. and Pathology Keck Sch. Medicine, 2005—. Mem. ACMG, Am. Assn. Cancer Rsch., Am. Soc. Med. Gene. Office: Children's Hosp Cytogenetics Lab Mailstop 43 4650 W Sunset Blvd Los Angeles CA 90027-6062 Business E-Mail: SWU@chla.usc.edu.

WU, SHUO-SHENG, director; b. Taipei, Taiwan, Taiwan, July 5, 1971; s. Wu-Tien Wu and Su-Lan Wang; m. Xiaomin Qiu, Feb. 10, 2003; 1 child, Fiona. BS in Geology, Nat. Taiwan U., Taipei, 1993; MS in Cmty. and Regional Planning, U. Tex., Austin, 1996; PhD in Geog. Info. Sci., Tex. State U., San Marcos, 2006. Planning dept. intern City Pflugerville Planning Dept., Tex., 1998—99; natural resources specialist Alamo Area Coun. Govts., San Antonio, 1999—2000; sys. support specialist Tex. Dept. Transp., Austin, 2000—01; GIS redistricting specialist Bickerstaff, Heath, Smiley, Pollan, Kever & McDaniel LLP, 2001—02; doctoral instrnl. asst. Tex. State U., San Marcos, 2002—06, program faculty, 2006—. Contbr. articles profl. jours. Mem.: APA, Internat. Assn. Chinese Profl. in Geographic Info. Sys., Urban and Regional Info. Sys. Assn., Am. Congress on Surverying and Mapping, Am. Soc. Photogrammetry and Remote Sensing, Geographic Info. Sci. and Sys., Assn. Am. Geographers (3d Pl. Student Paper Competition 2005, 2006, 1st Pl. Student Post Competition 2003). Home: 2303 Vienna Rd Apt C Rolla MO 65401 Office: US Geological Survey 1400 Independence Rd Rolla MO 65401 Home Phone: 573-426-6323; Office Phone: 573-308-3879. Personal E-mail: sw1020@txstate.edu. Business E-Mail: swu@usgs.gov.

WU, SING-YUNG, physician, researcher; b. China, 1939; MB, Nat. Taiwan U., 1963; PhD, U. Wash., 1969; MD, Johns Hopkins U., 1971. Staff physician VA Med. Ctr., Long Beach, Calif., 1977—; asst. prof. U. Calif., Irvine, 1977—84, assoc. prof., 1985—90, prof. dept. radiol. scis. and medicine, 1990—. Editor: Thyroid Hormone Metabolism, 1991, 1994.

Office: Thyroid Rsch Lab 5901 E 7th St Long Beach CA 90822 Office Phone: 562-826-5808. Business E-Mail: sing.wu@va.gov.

WU, TAI TE, biological sciences and engineering educator; b. Shanghai, Aug. 2, 1935; m. Anna Fang, Apr. 16, 1966; 1 child, Richard. MB, BS, U. Hong Kong, 1956; BSMechE, U. Ill., Urbana, 1958; SM in Applied Physics, Harvard U., Cambridge, Mass., 1959; PhD in Engring. (Gordon McKay fellow), Harvard U., 1961. Rsch. fellow in structural mechanics Harvard U., 1961-63; rsch. fellow in biol. chemistry Harvard U. (Med. Sch.), 1964, rsch. assoc., 1965-66; rsch. scientist Hydronautics, Inc., Rockville, Md., 1962; asst. prof. engring. Brown U., Providence, 1963-65; asst. prof. biomath. Grad. Sch. Med. Scis., Cornell U. Med. Coll., NYC, 1967-68, assoc. prof., 1968-70; assoc. prof. physics and engring. scis. Northwestern U., Evanston, Ill., 1970-73, prof., 1973-74, prof. biochemistry and molecular biology and engring. scis., 1973-85, acting chmn. dept. engring. scis., 1974, prof. biochem., molecular biology, cell biology and biomed. engring., engring. scis., applied math., 1985-94, prof. biochemistry, molecular biology, cell biology, biomed. engring., 1994—. Author (with E.A. Kabat and others): Variable Regions of Immunoglobulin Chains, 1976, Sequences of Immunoglobulin Chains, 1979, Sequences of Proteins of Immunological Importance, 1983, Sequences of Proteins of Immunological Interest, 1987, 5th edit., 1991; editor: New Methodologies in Studies of Protein Configuration, 1985, Analytical Molecular Biology, 2001, Best Scientific Discovery or Worst Scientific Fraud of the 20th Century, 2006; contbr. articles to profl. jours. Recipient Progress award Chinese Engrs. and Scientists Assn. So. Calif., LA, 1971, Rsch. Career Devel. award NIH, 1974-79; C.T. Loo scholar, 1959-60. Mem. Am. Soc. Biochem. and Molecular Biology, Sigma Xi, Tau Beta Pi, Pi Mu Epsilon Office: Northwestern U Dept Biochem Molecular and Cell Biology Evanston IL 60208-3500 Office Phone: 847-491-7849. Business E-Mail: t-wu@northwestern.edu.

WU, TAI TSUN, physicist, researcher; b. Shanghai, Dec. 1, 1933; came to U.S., 1950, naturalized, 1964; s. King Ching and Wei Van (Tsang) W.; m. Sau Lan Yu, June 18, 1967. BS, U. Minn., 1953; S.M., Harvard U., 1954, PhD, 1956. Jr. fellow Soc. Fellows Harvard U., 1956-59, asst. prof., 1959-63, assoc. prof., 1963-66, Gordon McKay prof. applied physics, 1966—, prof. physics, 1994—. Mem. Inst. Advanced Study, Princeton, 1958-59, 60-61, 62-63; vis. prof. Rockefeller U., 1966-67; sci. assoc. Deutsches Elektronen-Synchrotron, Hamburg, Ger., 1970-71, 82-83; Kramers prof. U. Utrecht, Netherlands, 1977-78; sci. assoc. CERN, Geneva, Switzerland, 1977-78, 86—. Author: (with Ronold W.P. King) Scattering and Diffraction of Waves, 1959, (with Barry M. McCoy) Two-Dimensional Ising Model, 1973, (with Ronold W.P. King, Glenn S. Smith and Margaret Owens) Antennas in Matter: Fundamentals, Theory and Applications, 1981, (with Hung Cheng) Expanding Protons: Scattering at High Energies, 1987, (with Raymond Gastmans) The Ubiquitous Photon: Helicity Method for QED and QCD, 1990, (with Ronold W.P. King and Margaret Owens) Lateral Electromagnetic Waves: Theory and Applications to Communications, Geophysical Exploration, and Remote Sensing, 1992. Putnam scholar, 1953; fellow A.P. Sloan Found., 1960-66, NSF, 1966-67, Guggenheim Found., 1970-71; recipient Alexander von Humboldt award, 1985, Dannie Heineman prize math. physics, Am. Inst. Physics, 1999; named Lee Kuan Yew Disting. visitor, Singapore, 2006. Mem. Am. Acad. Arts and Scis., Sigma Xi, Eta Kappa Nu, Tau Beta Pi. Office: Harvard U 204B Pierce Hall Cambridge MA 02138-2901 *A person's strength is, simultaneously, his weakness.*

WU, TIEN HSING, civil engineering educator, consultant; b. Shanghai, Mar. 2, 1923; arrived in U.S., 1947, naturalized, 1957; s. Chong-Yung and Ying Mei (Pih) Woo; m. Pei-Hsing Lin, Aug. 14, 1952; children: Mei, Anne. BS, St. John's U., Shanghai, 1947; MS, U. Ill., 1948, PhD, 1951. Registered profl. engr., Ohio, Ill. Civil engr. DeLeuw Cather & Co., Chgo., 1951—52, Ill. Divsn. Hwys., Springfield, 1952—53; from asst. prof. to prof. Mich. State U., East Lansing, 1953—65; prof. civil engring. Ohio State U., Columbus, 1965—. Vis. prof. Norwegian Geotech. Inst., Oslo, 1959, 70, 76, Nat. U. Mex., Mexico City, 1964, Royal Inst. Tech., Stockholm, 1980, S.W. Jiaotung U., Chengdu, China, 1986; UN cons. Punjab Agrl. U., Ludhiana, India, 1981. Author: Soil Dynamics, 1970, Soil Mechanics, 2d. rev. edit., 1976; contbr. articles to profl. jours. Recipient Antarctica Svc. medal, 1967, Lichtenstein award, Ohio State U., 1973, Rsch. award, 1984. Mem.: ASCE (hon. State of the Art award 1990, Ernest award 2000), Sigma Xi. Home: 100 Brookside Oval Worthington OH 43085-3638 Office Phone: 614-292-1071. Business E-Mail: wu.26@osu.edu.

WU, TSE CHENG, chemist, researcher; b. Hong Kong, Aug. 21, 1923; came to U.S., 1947, naturalized, 1962; s. Shau Chuan and Shui (Chan) W.; m. Janet Ling, June 14, 1963; children: Alan, Anna, Bernard. BS, Yenching U., 1946; MS, U. Ill., 1948; PhD, Iowa State U., 1952. Prodn. chemist Yungli Industries, Tangku, China, 1946-47; rsch. assoc. Iowa State U., Ames, 1952-53; rsch. chemist duPont Co., Waynesboro, Va., 1953-60, GE, Waterford, NY, 1960-71; sr. rsch. chemist Abcor, Inc., Wilmington, Mass., 1971-77; rsch. assoc. Allied-Signal, Inc., Morristown, NJ, 1977-88; cons., 1989—. Contbr. articles to profl. jours; patentee in polymer chemistry and organosilicon chemistry. Mem. Troy Arts Guild, 1968-71, Morris County Art Assn., 1981, Rossmoor Art Assn., 1999. Recipient Gold medallion award for inventions GE, 1967; Allied Corp. patent award, 1983; Eastman Kodak Rsch. fellow, 1951-52. Mem. Am. Chem. Soc., Sigma Xi, Phi Kappa Phi, Phi Lambda Upsilon, Alpha Chi Sigma. Home: 601 Red Wing Ct Walnut Creek CA 94595-3927

WU, TUNG, curator, artist, art historian, educator; b. Fuzhou, Fukien, China, Dec. 10, 1940; came to U.S., 1965; s. Chin-Wen and Jingrong (Chen) W.; m. Ying Chin, July 16, 1974. BA, Normal U., Taipei, Taiwan, 1962; postgrad., U. Mich., 1967-70, Harvard U., 1979—. Rsch. asst. Nat. Palace Mus., Taichung, Taiwan, 1962-65; with visual art archive U. Mich., 1966-68; rsch. asst. Cleve. Mus. Art, 1968; Ford Found. curatorial intern Nelson-Atkins Mus. Art, Kansas City, Mo., 1969; rsch. fellow Mus. Fine Arts, Boston, 1971-79, asst. curator, 1980-84, assoc. curator, 1984—85, curator Asian art, 1985—91, Matsutaro Shoriki curator Asian art, 1992—2004, emeritus Matsutaro Shoriki curator Asian art, 2005—, head dept. art of Asia, Oceania and Africa, 1999—2004. Guest rsch. fellow The Palace Mus., Beijing; tchg. asst. U. Kans., Lawrence, 1969, Harvard U., 1978, vis. lectr., 75, Emmanuel Coll., Boston, 1992; assoc. prof. Simmons Coll., Boston, 1993; advisor Chinese Inst. Am., NYC, 1985—, Chinese Cultural Found., San Francisco, 1985—87, Nat. Mus. History, Taipei, 1984—; cons. Project Emperor-One, Boston, 1983—86; panelist mus. program NEA, 1995; panelist Korea Found. Workshop on Korean painting, Seoul, 2000, Workshop Korean Buddhist art, Gyeongju, Republic of Korea, 2002, Workshop Korean crafts, 2003, Workshop Korean archaeology, 2004, Korean architecture, Gyeongju, 2005. Mem. Nat. Com. on U.S.-China Rels., Washington, 1985—, Nat. Devel. Seminar Taipei, 1989, 92, Nat. Edn. Reform, Taipei, 1994; The Ink Soc. of Hong Kong (advisor 2003—), dept. Asian trade art Peabody Mus., Salem. Mass., 1991—; trustee W.A. Compton Found. Oriental Arts, 1988-2004 Grantee Freer Found. U. Mich., 1968, Ford Found., Kansas City, 1969, Smithsonian Instn., Washington, 1978; recipient Outstanding Alumnus award Taiwan Normal U., 1997, Best Exhibition Catalogue, Independent Publ. Assn, 1997 Mem. Taoist Soc. Japan, Soc. Chinese Kunqu Opera, Soc. Chinese Calligraphy. Office: Mus Fine Arts Asiatic Dept 465 Huntington Ave Boston MA 02115-5597 Office Phone: 617-492-1829. Personal E-mail: wutungart@yahoo.com.

WU, XIN, electrical engineer, researcher, educator; s. Jizhou Wu and Lingling Liu. B of Engring., Tsinghua U., Beijing, 1996; MS, Chinese Acad. Scis., Beijing, 1999; M of Engring., Johns Hopkins U., Balt., 2001; PhD, U. Md., College Park, 2004. Rsch. asst Johns Hopkins, Balt., 1999—2001, U. Md., College Park, 2001—03; rsch. engr. Etenna Corp, Laurel, Md., 2003—04; spl. operation engr. Ansys/Fluent Inc., Austin, Tex., 2004—05; product mgr. Fluent Inc., 2005—. Contbr. articles to profl. jours. Scholarship, Tsinghua U., 1998, Chinese Acad. Scis., 1998, Johns Hopkins U., 1999, U. Md., 2001—03. Mem.: IEEE. Independent Thinkers. Achievements include patents pending for mesh fencing technique for PCB edge radiated emission suppression; research in computational electromagnetics, radiated EMI noise reduction technologies, electromagnetic bandgap materials, high-speed eletronic packaging performance and signal integrity analysis, electromagnetic modeling and EMC. Avocations: travel, soccer, reading, photography, history. Home Phone: 512-784-8835.

WU, YIDER, research scientist; b. Taipei, Taiwan, Jan. 11, 1968; arrived in US, 1992, permanent resident; s. Jui-han and Hsiu-yu Wu. BS, Nat. Tsing-Hua U., Taiwan, 1990; MS, U. Mass., Lowell, 1994; PhD, N.C. State, Raleigh, 1999. Rsch. asst. NC State, Raleigh, 1994—99; mem. of tech. staff Advanced Micro Devices, Sunnyvale, Calif., 1999—2004; dept. mgr. Macronix, 2004—; dir. Eon Silicon Solution Inc., Taiwan, 2005—. Patent adv. Advanced Micro Devices, Sunnyvale, Calif., 2000—04; presenter at profl. confs. Contbr. scientific papers, articles to profl. jours. (introductory invited paper, 2000). Mem. Taiwanese Assn. of N.C., Raleigh, 1995—98; v.p. Taiwanese Student Assn., N.C. State, Raleigh, 1995—96. With Taiwan Army, 1990—92. Scholar Outstanding Rschr., Semiconductor Rsch. Corp., 1998. Mem.: IEEE, Semiconductor Rsch. Corp. Buddhist. Achievements include patents in field. Avocations: jogging, swimming, travel, hiking. Personal E-mail: yider_wu@yahoo.com.

WU, YING, telecommunications industry executive; b. Beijing, 1961; BS in Engring., Beijing Indsl. U., 1982; MS, NJ Inst. Tech., 1987. Rschr. Bell Labs and Bellcore Lab, 1987—91; founder, pres. Starcom Inc., 1991—95; pres. UTStarcom China Co., Ltd., 1995—; vice-chmn., exec. v.p. UTStarcom Inc., 1995—. Office: UTStarcom 10th Fl 2d Bldg Oriental Trading City Oriental Sq No 1 E Chang An St Beijing 100738 China Office Phone: 86-10-85205588. Office Fax: 86-10-85205599.

WU, YUSEN (JOHN WOO), film director; b. Guangzhou, Canton, China, May 1, 1946; Asst. dir. Shaw Bros. Studios, 1969. Dir. (films) A Better Tomorrow, 1986, The Killer, 1989, Bullet in the Head, Hard Boiled, Hard Target, 1993, Broken Arrow, 1996, Face/Off, 1997 (Acad. Sci. Fiction, Horror and Fantasy Films Saturn award Best Dir.), Black Jack, 1998, Kings Ransom, 1998, Hong Kong Face-Off, 1998, Mission Impossible 2, 1999, Windtalkers, 2002, Hire: The Hostage, 2002, Paycheck, 2003, The Red Circle, 2006; writer, prodr., dir. (TV) Once a Thief: Brother Against Brother, 1996; exec. prodr. The Replacement Killers, 1998. Recipient CineAsia Lifetime Achievement award, 1996. Office: William Morris Agency c/o Mike Simpson 151 S El Camino Dr Beverly Hills CA 90212-2775

WUBBENA, JAN HELMUT, music professor; b. Dover, Del., July 11, 1947; s. Wyatt Jan and Erika Luise Wubbena; m. Teresa Lee Roper, May 17, 1980; children: Robert, Mary. BA, Lebanon Valley Coll., Annville, Pa., 1969; MusM, U. Colo., Boulder, 1970, D of Mus. Arts, 1975. Asst. prof. music Ferrum Coll., Va., 1975—77; prof. music John Brown U., Siloam Springs, Ark., 1977—. Organist, choirmaster Grace Episcopal Ch., Siloam Springs, 1977—. Composer: (choral work) With Every Power for Good, 1980, There is a Land of Pure Delight, 1999, Guide Us Waking Lord, 2002. Fellow: Am. Guild Organists (assoc.; chpt. dean 1982—84, coord. for edn. in Region VII 1984—88, chair nat. com. on ednl. resources 1988—90, dist. convenor for Ark. 2006—); mem.: Assn. Anglican Musicians. Episcopalian. Home: 410 E Jefferson St Siloam Springs AR 72761 Office: John Brown Univ 2000 W University Ave Siloam Springs AR 72761 Office Phone: 479-524-7159. Personal E-mail: wubbenark@cox.net. Business E-Mail: jwubbena@jbu.edu.

WUDUNN, SHERYL, journalist, correspondent; b. NYC, Nov. 16, 1959; d. David and Alice (Mark) WuDunn; m. Nicholas D. Kristof, Oct. 8, 1988. BA, Cornell U., Ithaca, NY, 1981; MBA, Harvard U., 1986; MPA, Princeton U., 1988. Lending officer Bankers Trust Co., NYC, 1981—84; intern reporter Wall St. Jour., LA, 1986; bus. reporter South China Morning Post, Hong Kong, 1987; corr. NY Times, Beijing, 1989—93, Tokyo, 1995—99, exec. dir. Nexgen group NYC, 1999—; anchor, prin. writer PAGE ONE Discovery Times Channel, 2003. Co-author: China Wakes, 1994, Thunder From the East, 2000. Recipient Pulitzer Prize for fgn. reporting, 1990, George Polk award, L.I. U., N.Y., 1990, Hal Boyle award, Overseas Press Club, 1990. Avocations: aerobics, singing. Office: NY Times 229 W 43rd St New York NY 10036

WUEBBLING, DONALD J., lawyer, insurance company executive; b. Nov. 29, 1945; m. Carol Wuebbling; children: Matthew, Monica. Chief compliance officer Legends Fund Inc.; sr. v.p. & gen. counsel Broadwing Comms., LLC, Western & Southern Fin. Group, Cin. Bd. mem. Server-Vault Corp. Bd. dirs. Cin. Symphony Orchestra, 2006—; bd. trustees May Festival. Office: Western and Southern Fin Group 400 Broadway Cincinnati OH 45202 *

WUEBKER, COLLEEN MARIE, retired librarian; b. LaCrosse, Wis., June 22, 1943; d. Harris M. and Mary Frances (Collins) Gruber; m. William Joseph Wuebker, Aug. 14, 1965; children: Jon Paul, Timothy William, Maree Jean. BA, Mt. Mercy Coll., 1965; MS, Mankato State U., 1975. Cert. permanent profl. media specialist, tchr. Iowa. Secondary tchr. Luverne Cmty. Sch., Minn., 1965-66; tchr. St. Mary's Sch., Larchwood, Iowa, 1966; secondary tchr. SEMCO Community Sch., Gilman, Iowa, 1966-67; substitute tchr. West Bend-Mallard (Iowa) Cmty. Schs., 1968-74, sch. media specialist, 1974—2002, 1975—2002; ret., 2002. Mem. selection com. Lakeland Area Edn. Agy., Cylinder, Iowa, 1977—; mem. Gov.'s Sch. Efficiency Task Force, West Bend, 1987; mem. sch. evaluation team Dept. Pub. Instrn., Des Moines, 1986. Spkr. Marriage Encounter Movement, Sioux City Diocese, 1985—, Pre-Cana Workshops, Emmetsburg, 1985—; mem., liturgy and music coord., song leader Sts. Peter and Paul Parish Coun., West Bend, 1987—; chmn. Parish Liturgy Com., West Bend, 1987—. Mem.: Iowa Ednl. Media Assn., Cath. Daus. Am. (past v.p. West Bend). Roman Catholic. Avocations: genealogy, music. Home: Box 426 11 1st Ave NE West Bend IA 50597-0426

WUENSCH, BERNHARDT JOHN, ceramic engineering educator; b. Paterson, NJ, Sept. 17, 1933; s. Bernhardt and Ruth Hannah (Slack) W.; m. Mary Jane Harriman, June 4, 1960; children: Stefan Raymond, Katrina Ruth. SB in Physics, MIT, 1955, SM in Physics, 1957, PhD in Crystallography, 1963; DEng (hon.), Hanyang U., Seoul, 2003. Rsch. fellow U. Bern, Switzerland, 1963-64; asst. prof. ceramics MIT, Cambridge, 1964-69, assoc. prof. ceramics, 1969-74, prof., 1974—, TDK chair materials sci. and engring., 1985-90, dir. Ctr. Materials Sci. and Engring., 1988-93, acting dept. head dept. materials sci. and engring., 1980. Vis. prof. Crystallographic Inst., U. Saarland, Fed. Republic Germany, 1973; physicist Max Planck Institut für Festkorperforschung, Stuttgart, Fed. Republic Germany, 1981; mem. US nat. com. for crystallography NRC, NAS, 1980-82, 89-94; mem. NE regional com. for selection of Marshall Scholars, 1970-73, chmn., 1974-80. Co-editor: Modulated Structures, 1979, Neutron Scattering in Materials Science, 1995; adv. editor: Physics and Chemistry of Minerals, 1976—85; assoc. editor Can. Mineralogist, 1978—80; editor: Zeitschrift fuer Kristallographie, 1981—88, Jour. Ceramic Processing Rsch., 2000—. Ford Found. postdoctoral fellow, 1964-66. Fellow Am. Ceramic Soc. (Outstanding Educator award 1987), Mineral. Soc. Am.; mem. AAAS, Am. Crystallographic Assn., Mineral. Assn. Can., Materials Rsch. Soc. Episcopalian. Home: 190 Southfield Rd Concord MA 01742-3432 Office: MIT 77 Massachusetts Ave Rm 13-4037 Cambridge MA 02139-4307 Office Phone: 617-253-6889. Business E-Mail: wuensch@mit.edu.

WUENSCHE, VERNON EDGAR, construction company executive; b. Elgin, Tex., Nov. 25, 1945; s. Harry Edwin Jacob and Emma Martha (Dube) W. BBA, U. Tex., 1967, MBA, 1968. CPA, Tex. Audit asst. Arthur Andersen & Co., Houston, 1968-70; tax cons. Peat Marwick Mitchell & Co., Houston, 1970; cost acct. Bemis Bros. Bag Co., Houston, 1970-71; asst. controller Prodn. Systems Internat., Inc., Houston, 1971-72; controller Am. Housing Guild, Inc., Houston, 1972-73, Wood Bros. Homes, Inc., Houston, Dallas, 1973-74, Oklahoma City, 1975; pres., founder, custom home builder Woodmark Homes, Inc., Houston, Dallas, Austin, Tex., 1975—; founder, kitchen and bath renovator Woodmark Kitchen & Bath, Inc., 1994—. Election judge Harris County, Houston, 1978, Rep. state del., Tex., 1978, 80, 94, 96, 98, 2000, 02, 04, 06; elder Meml. Luth. Ch., Houston, 1982-2002, elder emeritus, 2003; founder Texans for Efficiency in Govt., 1991, Bus. Consensus, 1999, Legal Reform Now, 2004; bd. dirs. Houston Entrepreneurs Forum. With USAR, 1968—74. Recipient Builder of Tex. Design award Tex. Arch. Mag., 1994. Mem. Alley Theater Guild, Tex. Wendish Heritage Soc., U. Tex. Ex-Students Assn., Rice Design Alliance, Mus. of Fine Arts, Arts Symposium of Houston, Phi Kappa Phi, Beta Gamma Sigma. Avocation: running. Office Phone: 713-468-3300. Business E-Mail: vern@woodmarkkitchens.com, vern@legalreformnow.org.

WUERL, DONALD WILLIAM, archbishop; b. Pitts., Nov. 12, 1940; s. Francis J. and Mary A. (Schiffhauer) W. BA, Cath. U. Am., 1962; MA, Cath. U. Am., Rome, 1963; ThM, Pontifical Gregorian U., Rome, 1967; ThD, Pontifical U. St. Thomas, Rome, 1974; DD (hon.), Duquesne U., 1989, Washington and Jefferson Coll., 1990; HLD (hon.), La Roche Coll., 1990; LHD (hon.), St. Vincent Coll., 1992. Ordained priest Roman Cath. Ch., 1966. Asst. pastor, parochial vicar St. Rosalia Ch., Pitts., 1967-69; sec. to Cardinal John Wright Congregation for Clergy, Rome, 1969-79; vice-rector St. Paul Sem., Pitts., 1980-81, rector, 1981-85; apptd. aux. bishop Archdiocese of Seattle, Wash., 1985, aux. bishop Wash., 1985—87; apptd. titular bishop of Rossmarkaeum, 1985; titular bishop of Rossmarkaeum, 1986—87; apptd. bishop Diocese of Pitts., Pa., 1988, bishop Pa., 1988—2006; archbishop Archdiocese of Washington, Washington, 2006—. Sec. to Bishop of Pitts., 1967-69; lectr. Duquesne U., Pitts., 1968-69, 80-85, Pontifical U. St. Thomas, 1975-79; lectr. adult theology program Diocese of Pitts., 1967-69, dir. Inst. Continuing Edn. for Priests, 1982-84, assoc. gen. sec., 1985; ofcl. Congregation for Clergy, Rome, 1969-79; mem. alumni bd. govs. Cath. U. Am., 1977-84, vice-pres. for religious, 1981-82; exec. sec. to Papal rep. for Study of Sems. in U.S., 1982-85. Author: The Forty Martyrs, 1971, Fathers of the Church, 1975, The Catholic Priesthood Today, 1976, A Visit to the Vatican, 1981, The Church and Her Sacraments: Making Christ Visible, 1990; co-author: The Teaching of Christ: A Catholic Catechism for Adults, 1976, rev., 1984, 91, abridged, 1979, study guide, 1977, A Catholic Catechism, 1986; contbg. author: New Catholic Ency.; contbr. articles to religion publs.; author religious cassette programs. Recipient Disting. Pennsylvanian award Gannon U., 1989, Brotherhood award NCCJ, 1991, Treee of Life award Jewish Nat. Fund, 1992, Disting. Alumni award Cath. U. Am., 1992; named Vectors/Pitts. Man of Yr. in religion, 1988. Mem. Am. Cath. Hist. Assn., Cath. Theol. Soc. Am., Fellowship Cath. Scholars, Acad. Romana Universale, Phi Kappa Theta (Man of Achievement award 1988). Office: Archdiocesan Pastoral Ctr 5001 Eastern Ave Hyattsville MD 20782-3447 Mailing: PO Box 29260 Washington DC 20017-0260

WUHL, CHARLES MICHAEL, psychiatrist; b. N.Y.C., Sept. 24, 1943; s. Isadore and Sali (Ackner) W.; m. Gail; children— Elise, Amy. M.D., U. Bologna, 1973. Diplomate Am. Bd. Psychiatry and Neurology. Intern, N.Y. Med. Coll., 1975-76, resident in psychiatry, 1976-77; fellow in child psychiatry Columbia Presbyn. Med. Center, 1977-78; practice medicine specializing in psychiatry and child psychiatry, Englewood, N.J., 1978—; attending staff, mem. faculty N.Y. Med. Coll.; psychiatrist NYU, also asst. clin. prof. psychiatry NYU Sch. Medicine. Contbr. to Psychosocial Aspects of Pediatric Care, 1978, World Book Ency., 1980—. Mem. Am. Psychiat Assn., AMA, Am. Acad. Child Psychiatry. Office: 163 Engle St Englewood NJ 07631-2530 Office Phone: 201-569-2228. Business E-Mail: cw3@nyu.edu.

WUJCIK, THEO FRANK, artist; b. Detroit, Jan. 29, 1936; s. Stanley and Anna Wujcik; children: Anna, Kathryn Tenney, Frankie. Diploma, Ctr. for Creative Studies, Detroit, 1962; Master Printer, Tamarind Inst. Lithography, LA, 1968. Instr. printmaking Ctr. for Creative Studies, Detroit, 1962—70; shop dir. graphic studio U. South Fla., Tampa, 1970—72, assoc. prof., 1972—2003, prof. emeritus, 2003—. Exhibitions include Gulf Coast Mus. Art, Largo, Fla., 2000, Lowe Art Mus., U. Miami, Coral Gables, Fla., 2001, Polk Mus. Art, Lakeland, Fla., 2001—02, Tampa Mus. Art, 2006—07, Nobel Peace Ctr., Oslo, 2007, Bozar Mus., Brussels, 2007, Represented in permanent collections Mus. Modern Art, N.Y., Whitney Mus. Am. Art, Bklyn. Mus., L.A. County Mus. Art, Yale U. Art Gallery, New Haven, Conn., Mus. Fine Arts, Boston, Chgo. Inst. Art, Detroit Inst. Arts, Pasadena Art Mus., Calif., Libr. Congress, Washington. With US Army, 1954—56. Printmakingfellowship, Nat. Endowment for Arts, 1977—78, Ind. Artist fellowship, Fla. Dept. State, Cultural Affairs, 2001—02, fellowship, Edwin Austin Abbey Meml. Fund for Mural Painting in Am., 2004. Home: 1507 E Ninth Ave Tampa FL 33605-3711 Office Phone: 813-242-8241.

WULBERT, DANIEL ELIOT, mathematician, educator; s. Morris and Anna (Greenberg) W.; children: Kera, Noah. BA, Knox Coll., 1963; MA, U. Tex., Austin, 1964, PhD, 1966. Rsch. assoc. U. Lund, Sweden, 1966-67; asst. prof. U. Wash., Seattle, 1967-73; prof. U. Calif.-San Diego, La Jolla, 1973—, provost Revelle Coll., 2003—. Vis. prof. Northwestern U., Evanston, Ill., 1977. Contbr. articles in field. Office: Provost Bldg Revelle Coll 0321 U Calif San Diego La Jolla CA 92093-0321 Business E-Mail: dwulbert@ucsd.edu.

WULF, WILLIAM ALLAN, foundation administrator, information scientist, educator; b. Chgo., Dec. 8, 1939; s. Otto H. and Helen W. (Westermeier) Wulf; m. Anita K. Jones, July 1, 1977; children: Karin, Ellen. BS, U. Ill., 1961, MSEE, 1963; PhD in Computer Sci., U. Va., 1968. Prof. computer sci. Carnegie-Mellon Univ., Pitts., 1968—81; chmn., CEO Tartan Labs., Pitts., 1981—87; univ. prof., AT&T prof. engring. U. Va., Charlottesville, Va., 1988—. Bd. dir. Nat. Action Coun. Minorities Engring., Inst. Women and Tech., Biblioteque Alexandrina; asst. dir. NSF, Washington, 1988—90; cons. various computer mfrs. Author: Fundamental Structures of Computer Science, 1981. Bd. dirs. Pitts. High Tech. Coun., 1982—88. Recipient Kenneth Andrew Roe award, Am. Assn. Engring. Socs., 2001, Chair's award, 2007. Fellow: AAAS, IEEE, Assn. Women in Sci., Assn. Computing Machinery, Am. Philos. Soc.; mem.: NAE (pres. 1996—2007), NRC (vice chair), Chinese Acad. Engring., Japanese Acad. Engring., Russian Acad. Sci., Spanish Acad. Engring., Am. Acad. Arts and Scis. Avocations: woodworking, photography. Office: Dept Computer Sci Univ Va Thornton Hall Charlottesville VA 22901 Office Phone: 434-982-2223. E-mail: wwulf@nae.edu.

WULKER, LAURENCE JOSEPH, portfolio manager, educator, financial planner; b. Cin., Apr. 6, 1945; s. Joseph Laurence and Dorothea Clare

(Link) W. BS, Xavier U., Cin., 1967, MA, 1971; cert. fin. planner, Coll. Fin. Planner, 1985. Instr. Lloyd HS, Erlanger, Ky., 1967-68, Elder HS, Cin., 1968-73, Peoples HS, Cin., 1973-74, Regina HS, Cin. Tech. U., Cin., 1974-75; stockbroker Harrison-Bache, Cin., 1976-78; portfolio mgr., fin. planner, v.p. investments UBS, Cin., 1978—; formed Wulker/Cummins Group Paine Webber/UBS, Cin., 1997—2006; instr. U. Cin., 1981-98, Nat. Inst. Fin., South Plainfield, NJ, 1986-88; sys. operator investor forum Compuserve, Ohio, 1985—86; sys. operator fin. planning forum Tristate Online, Cin., 1991—93. Spkr. numerous seminars 1984-. Author column Japanese-Am. League Newsletter, 1985-96; contbr. articles to Cin. Enquirer, Cin. Post, Cin. Bus. Courier. Bd. dirs., v.p., pres. No. Ky. Symphony, 1993-99; treas. Friends of Findlay Market, Findlay Market Assn., 1999—; bd. dirs. Riverwinds Condo Assn., Behringer- Crawford Mus., 2003—. Named one of the best stockbrokers in the country Money Mag., 1987; Fulbright scholar HEW, 1972. Mem. Internat. Assn. Fin. Planners (bd. dirs. Cin. chpt. 1980-87), Fulbright Soc., Order Ky. Cols. Roman Catholic. Avocations: computers, tennis, golf, volleyball, reading. Home: Riverwinds Condos 558 Davenport Ave No 11 Cincinnati OH 45204-1362 Home Phone: 513-921-2966; Office Phone: 513-369-4181. Office Fax: 513-369-4020. Business E-Mail: laurence.wulker@ubs.com.

WUNDER, CHARLES C(OOPER), physiologist, biophysicist, educator; b. Pitts., Oct. 2, 1928; s. Edgar Douglas and Annabel (Cooper) W.; m. Marcia Lynn Barnes, Apr. 4, 1962; children: E(dgar) Douglas, David Barnes, Donald Charles. AB in Biology, Washington and Jefferson Coll., 1949; MS in Biophysics, U. Pitts., 1952, PhD in Biophysics, 1954. Assoc. U. Iowa, Iowa City, 1954-56, asst. prof. physiology and biophysics, 1956-63, assoc. prof. physiology and biophysics, 1963-71, prof. physiology and biophysics, 1971-98, prof. emeritus, 1998—. Cons. for biol. simulation of weightlessness U.S. Air Force, 1964; vis. scientist Mayo Found., Rochester, Minn., 1966-67. Author: Life into Space: An Introduction to Space Biology, 1966; also chpts., numerous articles, abstracts Recipient Research Career Devel. award NIH, 1961-66; AEC predoctoral fellow U. Pitts., 1951-53; NIH spl. fellow, 1966-67; grantee NIH, NASA Mem. Am. Physiol. Soc., The Biophys. Soc. (charter), Aerospace Med. Assn., Iowa Acad. Sci. (chmn. physiology sect. 1971-72, 83-84, 96-97), Am. Soc. Biomechanics (founding), Aerospace Physiologist Soc., Iowa Physiol. Soc. (pres. 1996-97), Am. Soc. for Gravitational and Space Biology (Founders award 2000). Presbyterian. Achievements include the establishment of chronic centrifugation as an approach for investigating gravity's role as a biological determinant. Home: 702 W Park Rd Iowa City IA 52246-2425 Office: U Iowa BSB Iowa City IA 52242 Business E-Mail: charles-wunder@uiowa.edu.

WUNDERLICH, ALFRED LEON, artist, educator; b. Salem, Oreg., June 26, 1939; s. Joseph Anthony and Anna Margaret (Meyer) W.; children: Annelise, Jonathan Resor. Cert., Cooper Union, 1961; BFA, Yale U., 1962, MFA, 1968. Dir. visual studies program Hopkins Ctr., Dartmouth Coll., Hanover, NH, 1965-66; asst. prof. art Hopkins Ctr., Darmouth Coll., Hanover, NH, 1966-74; assoc. prof. R.I. Sch. of Design, Providence, 1983-94; prof. R.I. Sch. of Design, Providence, 1994—2005, prof. emeritus, 2005—. Adj. lectr. Hunter Coll. CUNY, 1973, adj. prof., vis. artist Pahlavi U., Shiraz Iran, 1978, vis. artist U. Edinburgh, Scotland, Edinburgh Internat. Arts Festival, 1973, Kansas City Art Inst., Art Inst. Chgo., Ohio State U., 1986, Carnegie Mellon U., 1987, Moscow State U., 1991, Ariz. State U., 1995; fine arts advisor Inst. for Internat. Edn.; mem. US Art in Space team, met with Soviet Artists Union team, Moscow, 1990; owner, artistic dir. GAS-523 project to fly aboard NASA Space Shuttle; executor first bacteria based living paintings, Rich Biology Labs. M.I.T., 2001. One-man shows include Dartmouth Coll., 1969, Kyoto, Japan, 1969, Pahlavi U., 1978, Kwanghow Mus., Canton, China, 1979, Chang-tu Mus., Szechwan, China, 1978, MIT, 1981, Swarthmore Coll., 1985, Knoerdler Gallery, NYC, 1995, 97, Alfonz Ver Gallery, San Francisco, 1997, 98; group exhbns. Harvard U. 1995, MIT 1996, also group exhbns.; represented in permanent collections Mus. Modern Art, NYC, Art Inst. Chgo., Yale U. Art Gallery, Nat. Gallery Scotland, 1st Nat. Bank Boston, Dartmouth Coll., Smithsonian-Cooper Hewitt Mus., Stanford U. Art Mus., others. Recipient Bocour Color award, 1960; Yale ALumni fellow, 1962-63, Yaddo fellow, 1973, Dartmouth Faculty fellow, 1968; Fulbright grantee to India, 1963-64; Rsch. grantee Dartmouth Coll., 1970-72, SUNY, 1983. Home: 1850 Big Ridge Rd Healdsburg CA 95448

WUNDERLICH, BERNHARD, retired physical chemistry professor; b. Brandenburg, Germany, May 28, 1931; came to U.S., 1954, naturalized, 1960; s. Richard O. and Johanne (Wohlgefahrt) W.; m. Adelheid Felix, Dec. 28, 1953; children: Caryn Cornelia, Brent Bernhard. Student, Humboldt U., Berlin, Germany, 1949-53, Goethe U., Frankfurt, Germany, 1953-54, Hastings Coll., 1954-55; PhD, Northwestern U., 1957. Instr. chemistry Northwestern U., Evanston, Ill., 1957-58, Cornell U., Ithaca, NY, 1958-60, asst. prof., 1960-63; assoc. prof. phys. chemistry Rensselaer Poly. Inst., Troy, NY, 1963-65, prof. phys. chemistry, 1965-88, prof. emeritus, 1988—; prof. chemistry U. Tenn., Knoxville, 1988-2001, prof. emeritus, 2001—; Disting. scientist div. chemistry Oak Ridge Nat. Lab., 1988-2001. Cons. E.I. duPont de Nemours Co., 1963-88; dir. Lab. for Advanced Thermal Analysis; rsch. in solid state of linear high polymers and thermal analysis, 1980-2001. Author: Macromolecular Physics, Vol. 1, 1973, Vol. 2, 1976, Vol. 3, 1980, Thermal Analysis, 1990, Thermal Analysis of Polymeric Materials, 2005; author computer and audio courses on Crystals of Linear Macromolecules, and Thermal Analysis of Materials; contbr. over 575 articles to profl. jours.; mem. editl. bd. Chemistry, 1965-68, Makromolekulare Chemie, 1966-96; mem. editl. bd. Jour. Thermal Analysis and Calorimetry, 1963-2001, mem. hon. bd., 2004—; mem. adv. bd. Jour. Polymer Sci., 1963-2001, Macromolecules, 1984-88, Polymers for Advanced Tech., 1988-2001, Macromolecular Sci. and Physics, 1995-2001, Thermochim. Acta, 1996-2001. Recipient Humboldt award, 1987-88, award for applied chem. thermodynamics Swiss Soc. for Thermal Analysis and Calorimetry, 1993, TA Instruments award Internat. Conf. Thermal Analysis and Calorimetry, 1996. Fellow Am. Phys. Soc., N.Am., Thermal Analysis Soc. (Mettler award in thermal analysis 1971, Disting. Svc. award 2002); mem. Am. Chem. Soc. Home: 200 Baltusrol Rd Knoxville TN 37934-3707 Personal E-mail: wunderlich@chartertn.net.

WUNDERLICH, DOROTHY ANASTASIA, superintendent; b. Evergreen Pk., Ill., Apr. 30, 1952; d. Raymond William and Dorothy Patricia Gavin; m. Russell Jay Wunderlich, June 15, 1974; children: Colleen Wunderlich Ciarlette, Meghan Gavin. BA, U. St. Francis, Joliet, Ill., 1973; MEd, Ill. State U., Normal, 1991; MA, Lewis U., Romeoville, Ill., 1998, CAS, 2001. Tchr. Joliet Township Dist., Ill., 1985—96; tchr., curriculum dir. Will County Sch. Dist., Lockport, Ill., 1997—2002; curriculum dir. Cicero Pub. Sch. Dist., 2002—05; asst. superintendent Berwyn North Sch. Dist., Berwyn, Ill., 2005—. Tchr. Power Luncheon, 2001. Mem. pres. coun. Purdue U.; mem. ednl. found. Berwyn Dist. Mem.: Purdue Music Org. Home: 1040 N Lakeshore Dr Apt 20B Chicago IL 60611 Office: Berwyn North Sch Dist 98 6633 W 16th St Berwyn IL 60402

WUNDERMAN, JAN DARCOURT, artist; b. Winnipeg, Man., Can., Jan. 22, 1921; d. Rene Paul and Georgette Marie (Guionet) Darcourt; m. Frank Joseph Malina, 1938 (div. 1945); m. Lester Wunderman (div. 1967); children: Marc, Geroge, Karen Renee. BFA, Otis Art Inst., LA, 1942. One man shows include Easthampton Guild Hall, LI, 1977, Denise Bibro Fine Art Gallery, NYC, 1992-94, 1996-2002, 04, 06-07, Roko Gallery, 1963, 66, 68, 71, 73, 76, Bibro Show: Painting Survey, 1950-2006, 2006-07; represented in numerous permanent pub., corp. and pvt. collections including Zimmerli Mus., NYU Loeb Collection, Norfolk Mus., Health and Sci. Ctr., Salt Lake City, Alfred Kouri Collection, Skidmore Coll. Print Collection, Nat. Assn. of Women Artists, Rutgers U., 1994, Albright Knox Mus., 1998-99, Daimler Chrysler Coll., Germany, 2002, Northwest Airlines, Detroit, 2003, abstract-nonrepresentational. Recipient Ohashi award Pan Pacific Exhbn., Tokyo and Osaka, 1962, Emily Lowe award 1965, J.J. Akston Found. prize, 1965, Canaday Meml. prize, 1979, Marian De Solo Mendes prize, 1981, Charles Horman Meml. prize, 1983, Amelia Peabody award Nat. Assn. Women, 1991, Grumbacher Gold medal of honor, 1992, Doris Kreindler award 1992. Mem. Nat. Assn. Women Artists (medal of honor 1966, Marcia Brady Tucker award 1965, E. Holzinger prize 1966, Jane C. Stanley prize 1977, Marge Greenblatt award 1990, Amelia Peabody award 1991, Solveig Stomsoe Palmer prize 1997), Am. Soc. Contemporary Artists (corr. sec. 1977-78, Bocour award 1980, Elizabeth Erlanger Meml. award 1990, Kreindler award 1992, N. Ransom award 2002), Contemporary Artists Guild (Irwin Zlowe Meml. award 1998). Avocations: history, travel. Address: Denise Bibro Fine Art Gallery 529 West 20th St New York NY 10011

WUNNICKE, BROOKE, lawyer; b. Dallas, May 9, 1918; d. Rudolph von Falkenstein and Lulu Lenore Brooke; m. James M. Wunnicke, Apr. 11, 1940; (dec. 1977); 1 child, Diane B. BA, Stanford U., 1939; JD, U. Colo., 1945. Bar: Wyo. 1946, Colo. 1969, U.S. Dist. Ct. Wyo. 1947, U.S. Dist. Ct. Colo. 1970, U.S. Supreme Ct. 1958, U.S. Ct. Appeals (10th cir.) 1958. Pvt. practice law, 1946—56; ptnr. Williams & Wunnicke, Cheyenne, Wyo., 1956—69; counsel Calkins, Kramer, Grimshaw & Harring, Denver, 1969—73; chief appellate dep. atty. Dist. Atty's Office, Denver, 1973—86; counsel Hall & Evans L.L.C., Denver, 1986—. Adj. prof. law U. Denver Coll. Law, 1978-97, 1st Frank H. Ricketson Jr. adj. prof., 2003; lectr. Internat. Practicum Inst. Denver, 1978-2003 Author: Ethics Compliance for Business Lawyers, 1987; co-author: Standby Letters of Credit, 1989, Corporate Financial Risk Management, 1992, UCP 500 and Standby Letters of Credit-Special Report, 1994, Standby and Commercial Letters of Credit, 2000, 2007, Legal Opinion Letters Formbook, 2002, 2007; contbr. articles to profl. jours. Pres. Laramie County Bar Assn., Cheyenne, 1967-68; Dir. Cheyenne C. of C., 1965-68 Recipient Outstanding Svc. award, Colo. Dist. Attys. Coun., 1979, 1982, 1986, Disting. Alumni awards, U. Colo. Sch. Law, 1986, 1993, William Lee Knous award, 1997, Lathrop Trailblazer award, Colo. Women's Bar Assn., 1992, Eleanor P. Williams award for Disting. Svc. to Legal Profession, 1997, Potter Lifetime Profl. Svc. award, 1999, Nat. award, Def. Rsch. Inst., 1999, Law Star award, Denver Coll. Law, 2003. Fellow Colo. Bar Found. (hon.), Am. Bar Found.; mem. ABA, Wyo. State Bar, Denver Bar Assn. (hon. life; trustee 1977-80, award of merit 2004), Colo. Bar Assn. (hon., life, Award of Merit 1999), Am. Arbitration Assn. (comml. panel), William E. Doyle Inn of Ct. (hon.), Order of Coif, Phi Beta Kappa. Republican. Avocations: reading, writing. Office: Hall & Evans LLC 1125 17th St Ste 600 Denver CO 80202-2037 Office Phone: 303-628-3363. Business E-Mail: wunnickeb@hallevans.com.

WUNNING, STEVEN H., manufacturing executive; B engring., Univ. Mo.; MBA, Univ. Ill. Mfg. mgmt. positions Caterpillar Inc., Peoria, Ill., 1973—87; mgmt. positions Caterpillar Logistics Services Inc., 1987—90, v.p., 1990—94, pres., 1994—98; corp. v.p. logistics & prod. services Caterpillar Inc., Peoria, Ill., 1998—2000, corp. v.p. logistics div., 2000—04, group pres., 2004—. Bd. dir. Black & Veatch Holding Co. Chmn. Ctrl. Ill. chpt. Am. Red Cross; trustee Proctor Hosp., Peoria, Ill., Manufacturers Alliance MAPI, Arlington, Va. Office: Caterpillar Inc 100 NE Adams St Peoria IL 61629 *

WUNSCH, HANNAH, anesthesiologist, researcher; b. Boston, July 29, 1975; d. Carl Isaac and Marjory Wunsch. BA, Harvard U., Cambridge, 1997; MSc, London Sch. Hygiene and Tropical Medicine, 2002; MD, Wash. U., St Louis, 2003. Lic. NY, 2004. Rsch. fellow Intensive Care Nat Audit and Rsch. Centre, London, 2003; resident physician Columbia U., NYC, 2003—. Freelance sci. writer, 1997—2003. Asst. editor: Jour. Evidence-based Health Policy and Mgmt., 1998—99. Recipient Young Investigator award, Am. Soc. Critical Care Anesthesiology, 2007; Va. Apgar scholar, Columbia U., Dept. Anesthesiology, 2003—. Mem.: Am. Soc. Critical Care Anesthesiologists, Am. Soc. Anesthesiologists, Soc. Critical Care Medicine. Office: Columbia Univ Dept Anesthesia 622 W 168th St PH5-505 New York NY 10032 Office Phone: 212-749-1016. Business E-Mail: hw2125@columbia.edu.

WUNSCH, JAMES STEVENSON, political science professor; b. Detroit, Sept. 27, 1946; s. Richard Ellis and Jane Rolston (Kershaw) W.; m. Lillian C. Richards, Mar. 29, 1969 (div. Feb. 1983), 1 child, Kathryn; m. Mary Gayle Gundlach, Aug. 19, 1983; children: Hallie, Hannah. BA, Duke U., 1968; MA, Ind. U., 1971, PhD, 1974. Rsch. fellow U. Ghana, Accra, 1971-72; asst. prof. Creighton U., Omaha, 1974-78, assoc. prof., 1978-86, prof. polit. sci., 1986—, chmn. dept., 1983-93, 96—, dir. African studies program, 1998—. Social sci. analyst and cons., Ghana, Liberia, Kenya, Sudan, Thailand, Philippines, Joint African Inst., African Devel. Bank, USAID, Washington, 1978-80; vis. assoc. prof. Ind. U., Bloomington, 1985-86; sr. project mgr. Assocs. in Rural Devel., Burlington, Vt., 1987-88, cons., Bangladesh, Zambia, Nigeria, South Africa, Swaziland, Botswana, Uganda, 1985—; USIA Disting. lectr., South Africa, 1993. Author: The Failure of the Centralized State, 1990, Local Governance in Africa, 2004 (monograph) Rural Development, Decentralization and Administrative Reform, 1988; mem. bd. editors Pub. Adminstrn. and Devel., 1998—; contbr. more than 40 articles to profl. jours., chpts. to books. Bd. dirs. Omaha Symphony Chorus, 1977-78, Nebr. Choral Arts Soc., 1982-96, Voices of Omaha, 1982-85, Trinity Cathedral, Omaha, 1980-83; participant Leadership Omaha, 1982-83; mem. Omaha Com. Fgn. Rels., 1975-95; mem. govt. affairs com. Greater Omaha C. of C., 1980-85; mem. issues and interests com. Nebr. Rep. party, 1984-88. Recipient R.F. Kennedy Quality Tchg. award Creighton U., 1985, Burlington No. award, 1992, Dean's award for excellence in tchg., 1994, Dean's award for excellence in scholarship, 2000, Dean's award for excellence insvc., 2006, Student Senate award for excellence in advising, 1989; rsch. award NSF, NEH, USAID, Am. Philos. Soc.; Fulbright-Hays fellow in Ghana, 1971-72, Internat. Affairs fellow N.Y. Coun. Fgn. Rels., 1978-79. Mem. Am. Polit. Sci. Assn., Midwest Polit. Sci. Assn., African Studies Assn., Internat. Studies Assn., Phi Beta Kappa, Pi Sigma Alpha, Phi Beta Delta. Episcopalian. Avocations: vocal music, camping, cross country skiing, bicycling. Home: 1631 N 53rd St Omaha NE 68104-4947 Office: Creighton U Dept Polit Sci 30th And California Omaha NE 68178-0001 Office Phone: 402-280-2568. Business E-Mail: jwunsch@creighton.edu.

WUNSCH COX, KATHRYN SUTHERLAND, retired lawyer; b. Tipton, Mo., Jan. 30, 1935; d. Lewis Benjamin and Norene Marie (Wolf) Sutherland; m. Charles Martin Wunsch, Dec. 22, 1956 (div. May 1988); children: Debra Kay Wolff, Laura Ellen Stubberud; m. John E. Cox, Apr. 2, 2005. AB, Ind. U., 1958, JD summa cum laude, 1977; postgrad., Stanford U., Calif., 1977. Founder Wunsch and George, San Francisco, 1989-93, Kathryn Wunsch and Assoc. Counsel, San Francisco, 1993-99; ret., 1999. Articles editor Ind. U. Law Rev., 1975—76. Trustee Minuteman Found., 2002—03; founder, pres. Sun City Anthem Lifelong Learning Ctr., 2004—06. Mem. Sun City Anthem Garden Club (founder, pres. 2001—), Phi Beta Kappa. Republican. Avocations: collecting fine art and antiques, theater, opera, gardening, hiking.

WUORI, STEPHEN J., energy executive; BS in Civil Engring., Mich. Technol. U., Houghton. Pres. Enbridge Pipelines Inc. and Enbridge Energy Ptnrs., L.P. Enbridge, Inc., 1997—2000, group v.p. planning and devel., group v.p., CFO, exec. v.p., CFO & corp. devel. Office: Enbridge Energy Ptnrs LP 1100 Louisiana Ste 3300 Houston TX 77002 Office Phone: 713-821-2000. *

WUORINEN, CHARLES PETER, composer; b. NYC, June 9, 1938; s. John Henry and Alfhild (Kalijarvi) W. BA, Columbia U., 1961, MA, 1963; DMus (hon.), Jersey City State Coll., 1971. Lectr. Columbia U., 1964-65, instr., 1965-69, asst. prof., 1969-71, co-dir. Group Contemporary Music, 1962—; prof. music Rutgers U., 1984—2005. Vis. lectr. Princeton U., 1967-68, New England Conservatory, 1968-71, Yale U., 1983; adj. lectr. U. South Fla., 1971-72; faculty Manhattan Sch. Music, 1972-79, U. So. Calif., 1981; artistic dir., chmn. Am. Composers Orch., 1973-87; composer-in-residence Ojai Festival, 1975, Santa Fe Chamber Music Festival, 1993, 2001, Tanglewood Music Festival, 2001; San Francisco Symphony, 1984-89; condr. Cleve. Orch., 1976, Finnish Radio Orch., 1979, Helsinki Philharm., 1979; disting. prof. Rutgers U., 1984—; vis. prof. SUNY, Buffalo, 1989-94, NYU, 1990 Author: Simple Composition; mem. editorial bd. Perspectives of New Music; bd. mem. Composers Recs. Inc., 1962-89; composer numerous works including Music for Orchestra, 1956, Be Mery All That Be Present, mixed chorus, 1957, Concert for Four Trombones, 1960, Madrigale Spirituale, 1960, Turetzky Pieces, 1960, Evolutio: organ, 1961, Evolution Transcripta for chamber orch., 1961, Tiento Sobre Cabezon, 1961, Concert for Double Bass Alone, 1961, Trio No. 1 for flute, cello and piano, 1961, Invention for percussion quintet, 1962, Octet, 1962, Duuiensela for cello and piano, 1962, Bearbeitungen über das Glogauer Liederbuch, 1962, The Prayer of Jonah, 1962, 2d Flute Trio: Piece for Stefan Wolpe, 1962, Chamber Concerto for cello and 10 players, 1963, Piano Variations, 1963, Flute Variations, 1963, Composition for violin and 10 instruments, 1964, Chamber Concerto for flute and 10 players, 1964, Orchestral and Electronic Exchanges, 1965, Composition for oboe and piano, 1965, Chamber Concerto for oboe and 10 players, 1965, Super Salutem for male voices and instruments, 1964, Piano Concerto, 1966, The Bells for carillon, 1966 (revised 1997), Bicinium, 2 oboes, 1966, Janissary Music for 1 percussionist, 1966, Harpsichord Divisions, 1966, Making Ends Meet for piano four-hands, 1966, John Bull: Salve Regina Versus Septem, 1966, Duo for violin and piano, 1967, The Politics of Harmony: A Masque, 1967, String Trio, 1968, Flute Variations II, 1968, Time's Encomium (electronic), 1969, Adapting to the Times for cello and piano, 1969, The Long and the Short for violin, 1969, Nature's Concord trumpet and piano, 1969, Piano Sonata, 1969, Ringing Changes for percussion, 1970, A Song, 1970, Tuba Concerto, 1970, A Message to Denmark Hill, 1970, Cello Variations, 1970, String Quartet, 1971, Canzona for 12 instruments, 1971, Grand Bamboula for string orch., 1971, Amplified Violin Concerto, 1972, Harp Variations, 1972, Bassoon Variations, 1972, Violin Variations, 1972, On Alligators for 8 instruments, 1972, Speculum Speculi for 6 players, 1972, Third Trio for flute, cello and piano, 1973, 12 Short Pieces for piano, 1973, Grand Union for cello and drums, 1973, Arabia Felix for 6 Instruments, 1973, Second Piano Concerto, 1974, Fantasia for violin and piano, 1974, The W. of Babylon (opera), 1975, TASHI, 1975, Hyperion for 12 instruments, 1975, Cello Variations 2, 1975, 2d Piano Sonata, 1976, Percussion Symphony, 1976, The Winds, 1977, Fast Fantasy for cello and piano, 1977, Archangel for trombone and string quartet, 1977, Six Pieces for violin and piano, 1977, Six Songs for two voices, Wind Quintet, Self Similar Waltz for piano, Ancestors for chamber ensemble, 1978, Two-Part Symphony, 1978, Archaeopteryx for bass trombone and chamber ensemble, 1978, The Magic Art, A Masque for chamber orch, 1979, Fortune for 4 instruments, 1979, 2d String Quartet, 1979, The Celestial Sphere for chorus and orch., 1979, Psalm 39 for baritone and guitar, 1979, Percussion Duo, 1979, Joan's for 5 instruments, 1979, Blue Bamboula for piano, 1980, Capriccio for piano, 1981, Horn Trio, 1981, Trio for bass instruments, 1981, New York Notes for 6 players, 1982, Mass, 1982, Divertimento, 1982 (string quartet), Divertimento for alto sax and piano, 1982, Spinoff for violin, double bass and congas, 1983, Trio for violin, cello and piano, 1983, Third Piano Concerto, 1983, Rhapsody for violin and orch., 1984, Concertino, 1984, Natural Fantasy for organ, 1985, Horn Trio Continued, 1985, Trombone Trio, 1985, Prelude to Kullervo for tuba and orch., 1985, Double Solo for Horn Trio, 1985, Fanfare for the Houston Symphony, 1986, The Golden Dance for orch., 1986, Third Piano Sonata, 1986, Third String Quartet, 1987, Galliard for chamber orch., 1987, Bamboula Beach for orch., 1987, FIVE: Concerto for amplified cello and orch., 1987, Sonata for violin and piano, 1988; (piano) Bagatelle, 1988, Ave Christe, 1988; Contrafactum, 1969 (orch.), Reliquary for Igor Stravinsky, 1975, Short Suite, 1981, Crossfire, 1984, Movers and Shakers, 1984, Bamboula Squared, 1984, Another Happy Birthday, 1988, Machault Mon Chou, 1988, String Sextet, 1989, A Solis Ortu, 1989, Astra, 1990, Delight of the Muses, 1991, Missa Brevis, 1991, The Mission of Virgil, 1993; (soprano and piano) Twang, 1989; Genesis, 1989 (chorus and orch.), A Winter's Tale for Soprano and Six Instruments, 1992, Microsymphony, 1992, Missa Renovata, 1992, Saxophone Quartet, 1992, Concerto for Saxophone Quartet and Orch., 1993, Percussion Quartet, 1994, Piano Quintet, 1994, Christes Crosse, 1994, Lightenings VIII, 1994, Guitar Variations, 1994, Sonata for Guitar and Piano, 1995, The Great Procession, 1995, Katz Fugue for piano, 1995, Windfall (band), 1994, Schoenberg Op. 31 Variations, 1996 (remade for two pianos), The River of Light, 1996 (string orch. and percussion), Epithalamium, 1997 (two instruments), Symphony Seven, 1997, Fenton Songs, 1997, Cello Variations III, 1997, Lepton trio for celeste, piano and harp, 1998; An Orbicle of Jasp, 1999 (cello and piano); Brass Quintet, 2000, Fourth String Quartet, 2000; Cyclops 2000 (chamber orch.); Haroun and the Sea of Stories, 1997-2001 (opera); Stanzas Before Time, 2001 (tenor and harp); Buttons and Bows, 2001 (cello and accordion); Alap, 2001, Josquiniana (string quartet), 2001; Two Machine Portraits, September 11, 2001, 2001 (tenor and piano); Fifty Fifty, 2001 (two pianos); The Haroun Songbook, 2002 (4 vocal soloists and piano); Hexadactyl, 2002 (guitar); Pentecost, 2002 (tenor and harp), 4th Piano Concerto, 2003, Fenton Songs II (soprano and piano trio), 2002, The Long Boat (mezzo, English horn), 2003, The Haroun Piano Book (solo piano), 2003, Dodecadactyl (two guitars), 2003, Visible (mezzo and violin), 2004, Ashberyana (baritone and ensemble), 2004, Duo Sonata (flute, piano), 2004, Theologoumenon (orchestra), 2005, Flying to Kahani (piano and orchestra), 2005, Heart Shadow (piano), 2005, Praegustatum (piano), 2006, Never Again the Same (bass-baritone and tuba), 2006, Spin 5 (for violin and 18 players), 2006, Eighth Symphony, 2006, Iridule (oboe & six players), 2006, Eleven Short Pieces (violin, vibes), 2006, Scherzo (piano), 2007, Synaxis (4 soli and chamber orchestra), 2007. Recipient Philharmonic Young Composers award, 1954; Bennington Composers Conf. scholar, 1956-60; Bearns prize, 1958-59, 61; MacDowell Colony fellow, 1958; Alice M. Ditson fellow, 1959; Arthur Rose teaching fellow, 1960; Broadcast Music-Student Composers award, 1959, 61, 62, 63; Lili Boulanger Meml. award, 1963; Festival fellow Santa Fe Opera, 1962; Festival fellow World's Fair Music and Sound, 1962; commd. by Koussevitzky Found., 1964, Berkshire Music Center, 1963, Fromm Found., 1963-71, Ford Found., 1962, Orch. of Am., 1958, Columbia U., 1956, Washington and Lee U., 1964, Fine Arts Quartet, 1969, Naumberg Found., 1971, U. South Fla., 1972, Nat. Opera Inst., 1973, Light Fantastic Players, 1973, N.Y. State Council on the Arts, 1974, N.Y. Philharm., 1974, Balt. Chamber Music Soc., 1974, Buffalo Philharm., 1974, Ojai Festival, 1974, Contemporary Chamber Ensemble, 1974, TASHI, 1974, Beethoven Festival, Bonn, 1978, Albany Symphony, 1981, San Francisco Symphony, 1984, 86, 88, 89, Cleve. Orch., 1984, Balt. Symphony, 1984, Houston Symphony, 1986, N.Y.C. Ballet, 1987, 90, Libr. of Congress, 1988, New World Symphony, 1987, Chamber Music Soc. Lincoln Ctr., 1989, 92, Am./ Soviet Youth Orch., 1990, Phila. Orch., 1992, Beethorenhalle Orch., Bonn Mönchengladbach and Ludwig Forum, Germany; grantee Nat. Inst. Arts and Letters, 1967, Nat. Endowment Arts, 1974, 76; Guggenheim fellow, 1968, 72; Ingraham Merrill fellow, 1972, Rockefeller Found. fellow, 1979, 80, 81, John D. and Catherine T. MacArthur fellow, 1986-91; recipient Pulitzer prize, 1970, Brandeis U. creative arts award, 1970, Creative Artists Pub. Svc. award, 1976; Arts and Letters award Finlandia Found., 1976, Koussevitzky Internat. Rec. award, 1970, 72. Mem. AAAS, AAAL, Am. Soc. Univ. Composers, Am. Composers Alliance (former bd. dirs.), Am. Music Ctr. (bd. dirs.), Internat. Soc. Contemporary Music (bd. dirs.), Am.

Acad. Arts and Scis., Phi Beta Kappa. Office: care Howard Stokar Mgmt 870 W End Ave New York NY 10025-4918 Office Phone: 212-866-5798. Business E-Mail: hstokar@stokar.com.

WURDEMAN, LEW EDWARD, Internet company executive, consultant; b. Colorado Springs, Colo., Oct. 31, 1949; s. Robert Martin and Shirley Gladys (Reetz) W. Student, U. Tex., 1967-69, U. Minn., 1969-72. Adminstr. Control Data Corp., Bloomington, Minn., 1969-81; product splst., 1981-83; sys. mgr., 1983-84; cons., 1984-89; mgr. The Roach Orgn., Inc., Mpls., 1989-90; computer cons. Wurdeman Enterprises, Inc., Farmington, Minn., 1991-93; sr. cons. Norstan Consulting, Minnetonka, Minn., 1993-2001; photographer Vividere Glamour Photography, 1996—; tree farm owner Golden Pond Farm, 2003—. Freelance photographer; virtual tour photographer 360 Minn., 2003—. Commr. Parks and Recreation Dept., City of Farmington, Minn., 2001-03. Mem. Internat. Freelance Photographers Orgn., Internat. Glamour Photographers Assn., Photog. Soc. Am. Profl. Photographers Am., German Shepherd Dog Club Mpls., German Shepherd Dog Club Am. Republican. Lutheran. Avocations: dog breeding and training, computers, photography. Office: Link Up Hosting PO Box 332 Farmington MN 55024-0332 Office Phone: 612-327-6178. Business E-Mail: lew@wurdeman.org. E-mail: lew@linkuphosting.com.

WURGAFT, JACK, lawyer; b. Newark, Oct. 15, 1943; BA, Rutgers U., 1965; JD, NY Law Sch., 1968; LLM, NYU, 1974. Admitted: NJ 1968, US Dist. Ct. Dist. NJ, cert.: Civil Trial Atty., Supreme Ct. NJ. Founding ptnr. Javerbaum & Wurgaft (now Javerbaum, Wurgaft, Hicks Kahn Wikstrom & Sinins), Springfield, NJ, 1978—. Capt. US Army, 1969—71. Named Profl. Lawyer of Yr., Union County, NJ Commn. on Professionalism, 2005. Master: Richard J. Hughes Inns of Ct.; mem.: ABA, Million Dollar Advocates Forum, Union County Adv. Com., Essex County Bench Bar Com., Am. Bd. Trial Advocates (pres. 1999—2001), Assn. Trial Lawyers Am., Assn. Trial Lawyers Am.-NJ, NJ State Bar Assn., Union County Bar Assn., Essex County Bar Assn. Office: Park Place Legal Ctr 959 S Springfield Ave Springfield NJ 07081-3555 Office Phone: 973-379-4200. Office Fax: 973-379-7872. Business E-Mail: jackw@whz.com.

WURM, JAN, artist, educator; BA in Pictorial Arts, UCLA, 1972; MA in Painting, Royal Coll. Art, London, 1975. Instr. U. Calif. Berkeley Ext., 1996—. Bd. mem. Achenbach graphic arts coun. Fine Arts Museums San Francisco, 2003—, chair liaison com., 2003—; judge Redwood Art Assn., 2001; juror Ctrl. Calif. Art League Annual Exhbn., 1997; lectr. in field. Artist: (group exhbns.): Grunwald Gallery, LA, 1972, Brunel U., London, 1974, Royal Coll. Art, 1975, 2006, Commonwealth Inst., London, 1975, LA County Mus. Art, 1976, 79, Triad Gallery, North Hollywood, Calif., 1977, Band Libr. Art Gallery, Glendale, Calif., 1978, LA Mcpl. Art Gallery, 1978, Newport Harbor Art Mus., 1979, Saddleback Coll., Mission Viejo, 1979, 83, Internat. Pavilion of Humour, Montreal, 1980, San Jose Inst. Contemporary Art, 1984, LA County Vets. Meml. Park, 1984, Calif. State U., Hayward, 1984, Berkeley Arts Ctr., 1984, 88, San Mateo County Ctr. for the Arts, 1985, Adlen Arts, Santa Rosa, 1986, Vorpal Gallery, 1987, 89, 91,92, 93, Matrix Gallery, Sacramento, 1988, Soco Gallery, Napa, Calif., 1990, Main St. Gallery, Napa Coll., 1996, U. Calif. San Francisco, 1997, 2003, 05, Joseph Chowning Gallery, 1997, Artworks/Bookarts, Santa Monica, 1999, Napa Coll. Art Gallery, 2000, 01, 02, ProArts, Oakland, 2004, Studio Gallery, San Francisco, 2005, 06, Mus. Fur Kommunikation, Berlin, 2006, San Mateo City Hall Gallery, 2006, Galerie Nering + Stern, Berlin, 2006; (one-woman shows): UCLA, 1972, Cupertino Libr., Calif., 1978, So. Exposure Gallery, San Francisco, 1978, 80, LA Mcpl. Art Gallery, 1978, Foothill Coll., Los Altos Hills, Calif., 1979, Saddleback Coll., 1980, Ariz. State U., 1981, New Coll. Calif., 1983, Reed Whipple Cultural Ctr., Las Vegas, 1985, Main St. Gallery Napa Valley Coll., 1987, Chabot Coll., 1987, Vorpal Gallery, 1989, Pence Gallery, Davis, Calif., 1997, Morris Graves Mus. Art, Eureka, Calif., 2000, Art in City Hall, 2001, Grad. Theol. Union, Berkeley, 2002, Addison St. Windows Gallery, Berkeley, 2004, Miller-Weitzel Gallery, Cleve., 2005, Springer-Croke Fine Art, San Francisco, 2006, 50 Calif., San Francisco, 2006; (permanent collections): Fine Arts Mus., San Francisco, Oakland Mus., NY Pub. Libr., Children's Hosp. Oakland, Stiftung von Donnersmarck, Berlin, Archive Verein der Berliner Kuenstlerinnen, Berlin, Girl Scouts Am. Oakland Hdqrs., Mansour Travel, Shoemaker & Hoard, Wash., DC, Robert Flynn Johnson, Dr. Peter Selz, Heide Durr, Berlin, many others. Docent Julia Morgan's Berkeley City Club, 1996—99; bd. mem. Achenbach Graphic Arts Coun., Fine Arts Mus., San Francisco, 2004—06. Clifton Webb scholar, UCLA, 1971, 1972. Mem.: Artists Space, ProArts, Coll. Art Assn., Berkeley Arts Club, Berkeley City Club, Berkeley Breakfast Group. Avocations: swimming, travel. E-mail: wurm@berkeley.edu.

WURMFELD, SANFORD, artist, educator; b. NYC, Dec. 6, 1942; s. Charles Jacob and Esther W.; m. Rella Stuart-Hunt, Dec. 11, 1971; children: Jeremy Philip, Treva. BA in Art with honors, Dartmouth Coll., 1964; ind. study, Rome, 1964—65. Lectr. Hunter Coll., NYC, 1967—72, asst. prof., 1972—77, assoc. prof., 1977—80, chmn. dept. art, 1978—2006, prof. art, 1980—, Caroff prof., 2000—. Vis. artist lectr. Calif. State Coll., Hayward, Cooper Union, NY, Bard Coll., Anondale-on-Hudson, NY, Drexel U., Phila., 1970, SUNY, Fredonia, 1971, Livingston Coll., New Brunswick, NJ, 1973, Whitney Mus., 1982, Met. Mus. Art, 1987, Princeton U., 1990, The Slade Sch. U. Coll., London, 1991, Chelsea Coll. Art, London, 1991, Whitney Mus., 1992, Hochschule der Kurst, Berlin, 1995, Simon Fraser U., Vancouver, 1996, U. Victoria, B.C., 1996, Acad. Minerva, The Netherlands, Glasgow Sch. of Art, Scotland, 1997, external examiner, 1999—2003. One-man shows include Talbot Rice Gallery, Edinburgh, 2004, Altötting, Germany, 2003, Karl Ernst Osthaus Mus., Hagen, Germany, 2000, Susan Caldwell Gallery, Inc., N.Y., 1978, Bard Coll. Invitational Exhibit, 1977, Susan Caldwell Gallery, 1976-77, Galarie Denise Rene, 1974, Rockefeller Meml. Gallery, Fredonia, N.Y., 1971, Tibor de Nagy Gallery, 1968, Bryant Park, N.Y., Fischbach Gallery, 1969; group shows include Mus. Modern Art, N.Y., 1968, Grank Palais, Paris, 1968, Kunsthaus, Zurich, 1968, Tate Gallery, London, 1968, Ft. Worth Art Ctr., 1969, Galerie de Gestlo, Kunstfair, Basel Switzerland, 1970, 72, Columbia Film Festival, 1973, Galerie Denise Rene, 1974, Hopkins Ctr. Galleries, 1974, Lehigh U., 1976, Susan Caldwell Gallery, 1977-79, Toni Birckhard Gallery, Cin., 1980, Carnegie Internat., 1983, Shanghai Exhbn. Hall Shanghai, China, 1986, Long Beach Mus. of Art, Calif., 1989, William Paterson Coll. of N.J., 1990, Hallwells Contemporary Arts Ctr., Buffalo, 1991, Louis Stern Fine Arts, L.A., 1995, Andre Zarre Gallery, N.Y., 1996, 2003, Condeso-Lawcer Gallery, N.Y., 1997, Karl Ost Haus-Mus., Hagen, Germany, Mucsarnok, Budapest, 1999, 02, Am. Acad. Arts and Letters, 2000, Hunter Coll. Times Sq. Gallery, 2003, 04, Concordia Coll., Ann Arbor, 2006, Panorama Mesdag, The Hague, 2006, Pratt Manhattan Gallery, 2007, Wooster Art Space, 2007; represented in permanent collections at Espace de l'Art Conret, Mouans-Sartoux, France, Karl Ernst Osthaus Mus., Hagen, Germany, Met. Mus. Art, N.Y., Guggenheim Mus., N.Y., SUNY, Fredonia, Ctrl. Trust Co., Cin., AT&T, N.Y., Baxter Travenol Labs., Deerfield, Ill., GE Corp., Fairfield, Conn., Sprengler Mus., Hannover, Germany, City of Hannover, Shreve, Lamb & Harmon Corp., N.Y., Silkscreeners Guild, Germany, Warner Nat. Corp., Cin., U. N.C., William Hayes Ackland Meml. Art Ctr., Chapel Hill, others; contbr. articles to profl. jour. Recipient Ames award Dartmouth Coll., 1964; fellow Guggenheim Found., 1974, Nat. Endowments for the Arts Individual Artist's, 1987-88; CUNY faculty rsch. grantee. Home: 18 Warren St New York NY 10007-1066 Office: Hunter Coll Dept Art 695 Park Ave New York NY 10021-5024 Office Phone: 212-772-5051. Business E-Mail: swurmfel@hunter.cuny.edu.

WÜRSIG, BERND GERHARD, marine biology educator; b. Barsinghausen, Germany, Nov. 9, 1948; s. Gerhard Paul and Charlotte Annemarie (Yorkowski) Würsig; m. Melany Anne Carballeira, Nov. 19, 1969; children: Kim Carballeira, Paul Carballeira. BS, Ohio State U., 1971; PhD, SUNY, Stony Brook, 1978. Postdoct. rschr. U. Calif., Santa Cruz, 1978-81; prof. Moss Landing (Calif.) Marine Labs., 1981-89; prof. marine biology, dir. Marine Mammal Lab. Tex. A&M U., Galveston, 1989—, Regents prof., 2006—, dir. The Inst. of Marine Life Scis., 1996—. Govt. cons. Minerals Mgmt. Svc., Washington, 1980—. Contbr. articles to profl. jours., 7-part miniseries to TV on lives of dolphins, dolphin problems induced by humans, also Discovery Channel show on Life of B Würsig; co-author: The Hawaiian Spinner Dolphin, 1994, Whales, Dolphins and Porpoises, 1995; sr. advisor (IMAX film) Dolphins, 2000 (nominee Acad. award best spl. category nature movie), sr. author The Marine Mammals of the Gulf of Mexico, 2000; co-editor: The Encyclopedia of Marine Mammals, 2002. Recipient Chmn.'s award for rsch. and exploration, Nat. Geog. Soc., 1998, Alban-Heiser award for excellence in Tex. conservation rsch., Zool. Soc. Houston, 1991; Fulbright Found. scholar, 2001—03. Mem. Marine Mammal Soc. (pres. 1991-93), N.Y. Acad. Scis., Soc. Cryptozoology, Am. Behavior Soc., Am. Mus. Natural History, Soc. Archimedes. Clubs: Explorers (N.Y.C.) (fellow of research). Avocations: photography, diving, airplane piloting, skiing, hiking. Home: 2402 Creekridge Pearland TX 77581- also: 2402 Creekridge Dr Pearland TX 77581-5728 Office Phone: 409-740-4413. Business E-Mail: wursigb@tamug.edu.

WURSTER, ABIGAIL MICHELLE, theater educator, costume designer; b. St. Louis, Nov. 1, 1977; d. David and Ruth Wurster. BA, Valparaiso U., Ind., 1999; MFA, Ill. State U., Normal, 2003. Theatre costume designer Francis Marion U., Florence, SC, 2003—, prof. theatre, 2003—. Mem. .choir St. Luke Luth. Ch., Florence, 2006. Scholar, Traditional Theatre Tng., Kyoto, Japan, 2005. Mem.: U.S. Inst. Theatre Tech., SC. Theatre Assn., Alpha Psi Omega. Office: Francis Marion Univ 4822 E Palmetto St Florence SC 29506 Home Phone: 843-618-1733; Office Phone: 843-661-1685. Business E-Mail: awurster@fmarion.edu.

WURSTER, CHARLES FREDERICK, environmental scientist, educator; b. Phila., Aug. 1, 1930; s. Charles Frederick and Helen B. Wurster; children: Steven Hadley, Nina F., Erik Frederick. SB, Haverford Coll., 1952; MS, U. Del., 1954; PhD, Stanford U., 1957. Tchg. asst. U. Del., 1952-54; rsch. asst. Stanford U., 1954-57; Fulbright fellow Innsbruck, Austria, 1957-58; rsch. chemist Monsanto Rsch. Corp., 1959-62; rsch. assoc. biol. scis. Dartmouth Coll., 1962-65; asst. prof. biol. scis. SUNY, Stony Brook, 1965-70; assoc. prof. environ. scis. Marine Scis. Rsch. Ctr., 1970-94, prof. emeritus, 1994—. Founding trustee, sec., mem. exec. com. Environ. Def., 1967—; vis. prof. Macquarie U., Sydney, 1988; mem. adminstr.'s pesticide policy adv. com. EPA, 1975—78; leader ecol. tours worldwide. Contbr. articles to profl. publs. Scholar, U. Wash., Seattle. Fellow: AAAS; mem.: Nat. Pks. Conservation Assn. (trustee 1970—79), Defenders Wildlife (dir. 1975—84, 1987—96). Achievements include research on DDT, PCBs, other chlorinated hydrocarbon effects on phytoplankton, birds; relationship between environmental sciences and public policy; seabird protection; instrumental in banning several insecticides, including DDT, Dieldrin and Aldrin. Address: 644 Hillside Dr E Seattle WA 98112 Personal E-mail: cfwurster@yahoo.com.

WURSTER, DALE ERWIN, pharmacist, educator, retired dean; b. Sparta, Wis., Apr. 10, 1918; s. Edward Emil and Emma Sophia (Steingraeber) W.; m. June Margaret Peterson, June 16, 1944; children: Dale Eric, Susan Gay. BS, U. Wis., 1942, PhD, 1947. U. Wis. Sch. Pharmacy, Madison, 1958-71, mem. faculty, 1947-71; prof., dean N.D. State U. Coll. Pharmacy, 1971-72; prof. Dale E. Wurster Ctr. Pharm. Tech., Iowa City, 2003, dean, 1972-84, dean emeritus, 1984—. George B. Kaufman Meml. lectr. Ohio State U., 1968; Hancher Finkbine Medallion prof. U. Iowa, 1984; Joseph V. Swintosky disting. lectr. U. Ky., 2000; cons. in field; phys. sci. adminstr. USN, 1960-63; sci. advisor U. Wis. Alumni Rsch. Found., 1968-72; mem. revision com. U.S. Pharmacopoeia, 1961-70; mem. pharmacy rev. com. USPHS, 1966-72; mem. tech. adv. com. contraceptive R&D program Ea. Va. Med. Sch., 1987-2002, rsch., U. Wis. Contbr. articles to profl. jours., chpts. to books; patentee in field. With USNR, 1944-46. Recipient Superior Achievement citation Navy Dept., 1964, merit citation U. Wis., 1976, Disting. Alumni award U. Wis. Sch. Pharmacy, 1984, Takeru Higuchi Rsch. award Acad. Pharm. Scis., 2007; Dale E. Wurster Ctr. Pharm. Tech. at U. Iowa named in his honor. Fellow Am. Assn. Pharm. Scientists (founder, sponsor Dale E. Wurster rsch. award 1990—, Disting. Pharm. Scientist award 1991); mem. Am. Assn. Colls. Pharmacy (exec. com. 1964-66, chmn. conf. tchrs. 1960-61, vis. scientist 1963-70, Disting. Educator award 1983), Acad. Pharm. Scis. (exec. com. 1967-70, chmn. basic pharmaceutics sect. 1965-67, pres. 1975, Indsl. Pharm. Tech. award 1980), Am. Pharm. Assn. (chmn. sci. sect. 1964-65, rsch. achievement award 1965, Wis. Disting. Svc. award 1971), Iowa Pharmacists Assn. (Robert G. Gibbs award 1983), Wis. Acad. Scis., Arts and Letters, Soc. Investigative Dermatology, Rumanian Soc. Med. Sci. (hon.), Am. Found. Pharm. Edn. (bd. grants 1987-92), Sigma Xi, Kappa Psi (past officer), Rho Chi, Phi Lambda Upsilon, Phi Sigma. Home: 16 Brickwood Cir NE Iowa City IA 52240-9129 Office Phone: 319-335-8799.

WURTELE, CHRISTOPHER ANGUS, paint and coatings company executive; b. Mpls., Aug. 25, 1934; Valentine and Charlotte (Lindley) W.; m. Heather Campbell (div. Feb. 1977); children: Christopher, Andrew, Heidi; m. Margaret Von Blon, Aug. 21, 1977. BA, Yale U., 1956; MBA, Stanford U., 1961. V.p. Minn. Paints, Inc., Mpls., 1962—65; exec. v.p. Minn. Paints, Inc. (merged with Valspar Corp. 1970), Mpls., 1965—73, pres., CEO, 1973-96, chmn., 1973-98. With USN, 1956—59. Mem.: Mpls. Club. Episcopalian. Home: 2970 Gale Rd Wayzata MN 55391 Office: 4900 IDS Ctr 80 S 8th St Minneapolis MN 55402

WURTMAN, RICHARD JAY, neuroscientist, educator; b. Phila., Mar. 9, 1936; s. Samuel Richard and Hilda (Schreiber) W.; m. Judith Joy Hirschhorn, Nov. 15, 1959; children: Rachael Elisabeth, David Franklin. AB, U. Pa., 1956; MD, Harvard U., 1960. Intern Mass. Gen. Hosp., 1960-61, resident, 1961-62, fellow medicine, 1965-66, clin. assoc. in medicine, 1985—; research assoc., med. research officer NIMH, 1962-67; mem. faculty MIT, Cambridge, 1967—, prof. endocrinology and metabolism, 1970-80, prof. neuroendocrine regulation, 1980-94, Cecil H. Green disting. prof., 1994—; dir. Clin. Rsch. Ctr., MIT, Cambridge, 1985—2005; prof. neurosci. MIT, 1984-94. Lectr. medicine Harvard Med. Sch., 1969—; prof. Harvard-MIT Divsn. Health Scis. and Tech., 1978—; Smithies lectr. Oxford U., 2002; sci. dir. Ctr. for Brain Scis. and Metabolism Charitable Trust, 1981—; invited prof. U. Geneva, 1981; Sterling vis. prof. Boston U., 1981; vis. fellow Balliol Coll., Oxford U., 1997; mem. small grants study sect. NIMH, 1967-69, preclin. psychopharmacology study sect., 1971-75; behavioral biology adv. panel NASA, 1969-72; coun. basic sci. Am. Heart Assn., 1969-74; rsch. adv. bd. Parkinson's Disease Found., 1972-80, Am. Parkinson's Disease Assn., 1978—; com. phototherapy in newborns NRC-Nat. Acad. Scis., 1972-74, com. nutrition, brain devel. and behavior, 1976, mem. space applications bd., 1976-82; mem. task force on drug devel. Muscular Dystrophy Assn., 1980-87; chmn. life scis. adv. com. NASA, 1979-82; chmn. adv. bd. Alzheimer's Disease Assn., 1981-84; assoc. neurosci. rsch. program MIT, 1974-82; chmn. life scis. adv. bd. USAF, 1985—94; founder, chmn. sci. adv. bd. Interneuron Pharms., Inc., 1989-99; co-founder Wurtco, 1999, Back Bay Sci., 1999. Author: Catecholamines, 1966; (with others) The Pineal, 1968; editor: (with Judith Wurtman) Nutrition and the Brain, Vols. I and II, 1977, Vols. III, IV, V., 1979, Vol. VI, 1983, Vol. VII, 1986, Vol. VIII, 1990, contbr. articles to profl. jours.; chpts. to books. Mem. bd. overseers Boston Symphony Orch., 1997—; bd. dirs. Fenway Cmty. Health Ctr., Boston, 1998—2003, Provincetown Art Assn. and Mus., 2000—, pres., 2005—. Recipient various awards and lectureships. Mem. Endocrine Soc. (Ernst Oppenheim award 1972), Am. Physiol. Soc., Am. Soc. Biol. Chemists, Am. Soc. Pharmacology and Exptl. Therapeutics (John Jacob Abel award 1968), Am. Soc. Neurochemistry, Soc. Neuroscis., Am. Soc. Clin. Nutrition, Am. Inst. Nutrition (Osborne & Mendel award 1982), Harvard Club (Boston), St. Botolph Club. Achievements include some 80 U.S. patents on new treatments for diseases and conditions; invention of melatonin for promoting sleep, of dexfenfluramine for treating obesity, of citicoline for treating stroke and of Sarafem for the treatment of premenstrual syndrome. Home: 300 Boylston St Boston MA 02116-3923 Office: Mass Inst Tech 77 Massachusetts Ave, 46-5023 Cambridge MA 02139-1323 Office Phone: 617-253-6731. Business E-Mail: dick@mit.edu.

WURTZ, THOMAS J., bank executive; BS, W.Va. U.; MBA, Ariz. State U. V.p. asset liability mgmt. Calif. Fed. Bank; mgr. capital markets U.S. Office of Thrift Supervision Western Region; dir. forecasting, asst. treas. Wachovia Corp., Charlotte, NC, 1994—99, sr. v.p., treas., head treas. and planning divsn., 1999—2002, exec. v.p., treas., 2002—06, exec. v.p., CFO, 2006—. Office: Wachovia Corp 1 Wachovia Ctr Charlotte NC 28288-0013 *

WURZBACH, LINDA, educational consultant; b. San Antonio, Jan. 21, 1954; d. Delmar Earl Wurzbach, Dorothy Lang Wurzbach; m. Mark Allison Tatom. BS, U. Tex., 1975, MEd, 1978. Lic. tchr. Tex. Tchr. Austin Ind. Sch. Dist., Tex., 1976—81; project mgr. Tex. Sch. for the Blind and Visually Impaired, Austin, 1981—82, tchr., 1982—89; project dir. The Psychol. Corp., San Antonio, 1989—90; planner Tex. Edn. Agy., Austin, 1990—96; sr. project assoc. Coun. Chief State Sch. Officers, Washington, 1996—98; pres. Resources for Learning, LLC, Austin, 1998—. Cons. in field. Editor: TxBESS Toolkit, 2005, TxBESS Activity Profile, 2001, Fine Arts Curriculum Frameworks, 2000; author: Works in Progress, 1997, Portfolio Assessment for Beginning Teachers, 1999, Performance Assessment System, 2000; prodr.: (video) If You Love It, Teach It., 2000, Express Yourself, 2001, Fine Arts for All Students, 2003, Beginning Teacher Induction Toolkit: A Systems Approach, 2004; contbr. articles to profl. jours. Mem.: ASCD, Women Pres.' Orgn., U.S. Women's C. of C., Nat. Coun. Measurement in Edn., Am. Ednl. Rsch. Assn., Nat. Staff Devel. Coun. Home: 4504 Moose Dr Austin TX 78749 Home Phone: 512-282-7882. Personal E-mail: lindaw@resourcesforlearning.net.

WURZEL, LEONARD, retired candy manufacturing company executive; b. Phila., Feb. 4, 1918; s. Maurice L. and Dora (Goldberg) W.; m. Elaine Cohen, Aug. 18, 1949; children— Mark L., Lawrence J. BS, Washington and Jefferson Coll., 1939; MBA, Harvard, 1941. With Loft Candy Corp., Long Island City, NY, 1946-64, v.p., 1949-56, exec. v.p., 1956-57, pres., 1957-64, dir., 1949-64; chmn., dir. Calico Cottage Candies, Inc., 1964-94; ret., 1994; mayor Village of Sands Point, NY 1989—. Capt. US Army, 1941—46. Decorated Bronze Star. Mem. Assn. Mfrs. Confectionery and Chocolate (bd. dirs., past pres., chmn.), Candy Chocolate and Confectionery Inst. (bd. dirs., treas.), Retail Confectioners Internat. (bd. dirs., past pres.) Home: 25 Woodland Dr Sands Point NY 11050-1136 Office: 26 Tibbits Ln Sands Point NY 11050-1135

WUSINICH, JOSEPH F., III, lawyer, educator; b. Phila., Pa., Oct. 30, 1946; s. Joseph F. Wusinich Jr. and Mary M. (Madden) Wusinich; m. Catherine T. Consalvi, Sept. 7, 1968; children: Nicole, Lisa, Dana, Maria, Christa, Joanna, Catherine. BSc in Mgmt. Mktg., St. Joseph's U., Phila., 1968; JD, DePaul U., Chgo., 1974; LLM in Trial Advocacy, Temple U., Phila., 1995. Bar: Pa. 1974, U.S. Dist. Ct. (ea. dist.) Pa. 1976, U.S. Circuit Ct. Appeals Third Circuit 1976, U.S. Supreme Ct. 1984. Assoc. house counsel Liberty Mut. Ins. Co., Phila., 1974—76; law ptnr. Landis & Wusinich, West Chester, Pa., 1976—80, Wusinich & McCarthy, West Chester, Pa., 1980—85, Wusinich & Brogan, West Chester, Pa., 1993—2000, Wusinich, Brogan & Stanzione, Downington, Pa., 2000—; sr., mng. atty. Law Offices Joseph F. Wusinich, III, West Chester, Pa., 1985—93. Pres. coun., bd. trustees Immaculata U., Pa., 1997—; chair, vice chair med. health related issues PA. Bar Assn., Harrisburg, 2000—. Contbr. bull. and articles in field. Lt., chief tng. ops. officer, combat engr. US Army, 1968—71, Vietnam. Decorated Army Commendation medal US Army, Bronze Star medal; recipient Defender of Life award, Pro-Life of Chester County, West Chester, Pa., 1998, St. Thomas More award, Pro-Life Union of S.E. Pa., Phila., 2002. Master: Hon. John E. Stively, Jr. Am. Inn Ct. (pres. elect 2002—03, pres. 2003—06); mem.: KC, Downington Pa. chpt. (3rd degree Knight 1987—). Republican. Roman Catholic. Avocation: basketball. Office: Wusinich Brogan Stanzione 537 W Uwchlan Ave Ste 200 Downingtown PA 19335 Office Phone: 610-594-1600. Office Fax: 610-594-6518. Business E-Mail: info@wusinichbrogan.com.

WUSSLER, ROBERT JOSEPH, broadcast executive, media consultant; b. Newark, Sept. 8, 1936; s. William and Anna (MacDonald) Wussler; children: Robert Joseph, Rosemary, Sally, Stefanie, Christopher, Jeanne. BA in Comm. Arts, Seton Hall U., South Orange, NJ, 1957, LLD (hon.), 1976, Emerson Coll., Boston, 1976. With CBS News, NYC, 1957-72; v.p., gen. mgr. Sta. WBBM-TV, Chgo., 1972-74; v.p. CBS Sports, NYC, 1974-76, pres., 1977-78, Sta. CBS-TV, NYC, 1976-77, Pyramid Enterprises Ltd., NYC, 1979—80; exec. v.p. Turner Broadcasting System Inc., Atlanta, 1979—89, sr. exec. v.p., from 1987, bd. dirs.; pres. Atlanta Sports Teams, Inc., 1981-87; pres., chief exec. officer COMSAT Video Enterprises, Inc., Washington, 1989-92; pres. Wussler Group, 1992—. Chmn. bd. dirs. NATAS, 1980—84, 1986—90; co-owner Denver Nuggets, 1989—92; bd. dirs. Atlanta Hawks Ltd., Atlanta Braves Nat. League Baseball Club, Inc. Trustee Marymount Manhattan Coll., 1977—81; bd. regents Seton Hall U., 1978—84. Recipient Emmy awards, numerous other nat. and internat. news and sports awards. Mem.: European Broadcasting Union, Nat. Cable TV Assn. (mem. satellite network com.), Cable Advt. Bur., Ariz. Heart Inst., Internat. Radio and TV Soc., Dirs. Guild Am. Roman Catholic. Home and Office: Unit 4630 75 Fourteenth St Atlanta GA 30309 Personal E-mail: rjwtv@aol.com.

WÜTHRICH, KURT, molecular biologist, biophysicist, educator; b. Oct. 4, 1938; MS in Chemistry, Physics and Maths., U. Bern, Switzerland, 1962; Eidgenössisches Turn-und Sportlehrerdiplom, U. Basel, Switzerland, 1964, PhD in Chemistry, 1964; D in Chemistry (hon.), U. Siena, Italy, 1997; PhD (hon.), U. Zürich, Switzerland, 1997, Ecole Polytechnique Fédérale, Lausanne, Switzerland, 2001, U. Sheffield, Eng., 2004, U. Valencia, Spain, 2004, King George's Med. U., Lucknow, India, 2005, U. Pecs, Hungary, 2005, Lomonosov State U., Russia, 2006. Postdoctoral tng. U. Basel, U. Calif., Berkeley, Bell Telephone Labs., Murray Hill, N.J., 1964-69; prof. biophysics ETH Zurich, Zürich, Switzerland, 1972—, chmn. dept. biology, 1995-2000; prof. structural biology The Scripps Rsch Inst., La Jolla, 2001—. Mem. coun. Internat. Union Pure and Applied Biophysics, 1975-78, 87-90, sec. gen., 1978-84, v.p., 1984-87; mem. gen. com. Internat. Coun. Sci. Unions, 1980-86, standing com. on free circulation of scientists, 1982-90. Editor Jour. Biomolecular NMR, Quar. Rev. Biophysics, Macromolecular Structures; contbr. articles to profl. jours. Recipient Friedrich Miescher prize Schweizerische Biochemische Gesellschaft, 1974, shield of faculty of medicine Tokyo U., 1983, P. Bruylants medal Cath. U. Louvain, 1986, Stein and Moore award Protein Soc., U.S., 1990, Louisa Gross Horwitz prize Columbia U., 1991, Gilbert N. Lewis medal U. Calif., Berkeley, 1991, Marcel Benoist prize Swiss Confederation, 1992, Disting. Svc. award Miami Winter Symposia, 1993, Prix Louis Jeantet de Médecine, Geneva, 1993, Kaj Linderstrøm-Lang prize Kaj Linderstrøm-Lang Found., Copenhagen, 1996, Eminent Scientist of RIKEN (Tokyo), 1997, Kyoto prize in Advanced Tech., 1998, Guenther Laukien prize Exptl. Nuclear Magnetic Resonance Conf., 1999, Otto Warburg medal Soc. for

Biochemistry and Molecular Biology, Germany, 1999, World award M. Gorbatschow Found., 2002, Nobel Prize in Chemistry, 2002; Swiss award, 2002; Fgn. fellow Indian Nat. Sci. Acad.; hon. fellow NAS India. Fellow: AAAS; mem.: U.S. Nat. Acad., World Innovation Found., Schweizerische Akademie der Medizinischen Wissenschaften, Schweizerische Akademie der Technischen Wissenschaften, Acad. Scis. Inst. France, Academia Europea, European Molecular Biology Orgn., Deutsche Akad. der Naturforscher Leopoldina, Indian Biophys. Soc. (hon.), Nuc. Magnetic Resonance Soc. Japan (hon.), Groupement Ampère (hon.), Latvian Acad. Sci. (hon.), European Acad. Arts and Humanities (hon.), Hungarian Acad. Sci. (hon.), Internat. Soc. Magnetic Resonance in Medicine (hon.), Royal Soc. Edinburgh (hon.), Royal Soc. Chemistry (hon.), Swiss Chem. Soc. (hon.), Nat. Magnetic Resonance Soc. India (hon.), Japanese Biochem. Soc. (hon.), Am. Acad. Arts and Scis. (hon.). Office: ETH Zurich Inst Molecular Biology Biophysics 8093 Zurich Switzerland also: Scripps Rsch Inst Dept Molecular Biology 10550 N Torrey Pines Rd La Jolla CA 92037 Office Phone: +41-44-633-2475.

WUZOR, GEOFFREY ONYEMA, psychotherapist; b. Port Harcourt, Nigeria, Dec. 22, 1954; s. Amadioha and Epelle Grace Wuzor; m. Florence E. Wuzor, Oct. 29, 2004; children: Beatrice, Chelem, Ugwechi, Sunday, Prince stepchildren: Imani, Ikpoki, Ologhi. BS, U. England, Oxford, 1982, Southeastern U., 1986, MBA, 1988, AS, 1990; postgrad., Howard U., 1993—96; PhD, La Salle U., 1998. Adminstrv. asst. to dean Howard U., Sch. Divinity, Washington, 1991—96; asst. tchr. behavior mgmt. Edgemead-Raymond A. Rogers Jr. Sch., Upper Marlboro, Md., 1997—98; residential counselor Cmty. Residences - Queen Elizabeth Ho., Annandale, Va., 1997—98; adminstrv. asst. Md.-Nat. Capital Pk. and Planning Commn., Upper Marlboro, 1998—2001; program coord. Psychotherapeutic Outreach Svcs., Washington, 2000—03, program mgr., 2002—03; cons., cmty. support counselor Life Stride, Inc., 2004—05; residential program counselor Loudoun County Govt., Dept. Mental Health/Mental Retardation and Substance Abuse, Leesburg, Va., 2005—. Author: Essential Assessments in Behavioral Psychology, 2001, Management Pyramid, 1995. Gen. sec. Ogbakor Ikwerre USA, Wash., DC, pres. Mem.: Am. Psychological Assn. Democrat. Avocations: tennis, sports. Home: 6630 Ga Ave NW 204 Washington DC 20012 Office: Primary Care Support Svc PO Box 56698 Washington DC 20040 Office Phone: 202-251-5606. Office Fax: 202-723-9144. E-mail: geowuzor1@juno.com.

WYANT, CLYDE W., JR., manufacturing executive; b. Ada, Okla., Sept. 20, 1938; s. Clyde W. and Geneva Pauline (George) W.; m. Anne L. Edgerton, Nov. 23, 1984; children: Lynn, John, James, Markham, Carolyn BA in History, Stanford U., 1960; MBA, Harvard U., 1965. Asst. to pres. Helmerich & Payne, Inc., Tulsa, 1965-68, fin. v.p., 1968-85; exec. v.p., chief fin. officer Purolator Products Co. (formerly Facet Enterprises, Inc.), Tulsa, 1985-90; exec. v.p., CFO, treas. Lennox Internat., Inc., 1990-2001. Dir. Am. Nursery Products, Tahlequah, Okla., Hawkins Energy Co., Tulsa. Vice pres., trustee Holland Hall Sch., Tulsa, 1978-86; trustee Hillcrest Med. Ctr., Tulsa; vice chmn. admissions com. Tulsa Area United Way, 1979-86, chmn. allocations com., 1987, pres.-elect 1989, pres., 1990; fin. com. chmn. Community Network for Public Edn., Tulsa, 1983-85, Okla. Profl. Affairs Tribunal, 1989—; pres., treas., dir. Jr. Achievement of Greater Tulsa, 1978-86; community advisor Jr. League of Tulsa, 1979-82. Served to lt. U.S. Army, 1960-62 Recipient Bronze Leadership award Jr. Achievement, 1983 Mem. Fin. Execs. Inst. (pres. 1979-80), Am. Petroleum Inst., Mid-Continent Harvard Bus. Sch. Assn. (pres. 1980-82) Clubs: Tulsa Tennis (pres. 1985). Avocations: fishing, cooking, tennis. Office: Lennox Internat Inc PO Box 799900 Dallas TX 75379-9900 also: Two Warren Pl E 61st St Ste 1100 Tulsa OK 74136-0523 Home: 2140 Lake Park Blvd Richardson TX 75080-2252

WYANT, JAMES CLAIR, engineering company executive, educator; b. Morenci, Mich., July 31, 1943; s. Clair William and Idah May (Burroughs) W.; m. Louise Doherty, Nov. 20, 1971; 1 child, Clair Frederick. BS, Case Inst. Tech. (now Case Western Res. U.), 1965; MS in Optics, U. Rochester, 1967, PhD in Optics, 1968. Optical engr. Itek Corp., Lexington, Mass., 1968-74, mgr. optical engring., 1974; lectr. physics Lowell Technol. Inst., Mass., 1969—72, instr. math. and physics, 1970—74; asst. prof. optical scis. U. Ariz., Tucson, 1974—76, assoc. prof., 1976—79, prof., 1979—, prof. elec. and computer engring., 1985—, dir. optical scis., 1999—2005, dean Coll. Optical Scis., 2005—; pres., chmn. bd. dirs. WYKO Corp., Tucson, 1984—97. Vis. prof. U. Rochester, NY, 1983; chmn. Gordon Conf. Holography Plymouth State Coll., NH, 1984; bd. dirs. ILX Lightwave, 1988—, Veeco, 1997—99, Optics 1, 1999—, DMetrix, 2001—; bd. chmn. 4D Tech. Corp., 2002—; vis. prof. Changchun U., 2005—. Editor: Applied Optics and Optical Engineering, vols. VII-X, 1979-80, 83, 87. Fellow Internat. Soc. Optical Engring. (pres. 1986, Gold medal 2003), Optical Soc. Am. (bd. dirs. 1979-81, Tech. Achievement award 1988, Joseph Fraunhofer award 1992, R&D 100 award 1993, Gold medal 2003); mem. Am. Inst. Physics, NAE. Office: Coll Optical Scis U Ariz 1630 E University Blvd Tucson AZ 85721 Office Phone: 520-621-2448. E-mail: Jim.Wyant@Optics.Arizona.Edu. *

WYARD, VICKI SHAW, investment and insurance company executive; b. LA, Oct. 29, 1945; d. Clinton Gilbert and Lois (Griswold) Shaw; m. Gary Edwin Wyard, July 1, 1966; children: Brett, Lori, Lisa. Student, Carleton Coll., 1963-65; BS, U. Minn., 1967. Cert. fin. planner. Systems analyst Univac Fed. Systems Div., Mpls., 1967-69, Internat. Timesharing Corp., Chaska, Minn., 1973-76; dir. Minnetonka Bd. of Edn., Excelsior, Minn., 1978-81, vice chairperson, 1981-84; fin. planner IDS Fin. Svcs., Mpls., 1986-89, trainer of planners, 1988-89; fin. planner, rep. Fin. Network Investment Corp., Torrance, Calif., 1989-91, Multi-Fin. Securities Corp., Mpls., 1991—2007. Bd. dirs. Westerlund Products Corp., Homescape Systems; seminar presenter in field. Contbr. articles to profl. jours. Trustee Washburn Child Guidance Ctr., Mpls., 1986-89; bd. dirs. Perspectives, Inc., St. Louis Park, Minn., 1988-2007, pres. bd., 1989-96; chmn. stewardship campaign Wayzata Cmty. Ch., 1996-98, pres. com., 1999-2005; mem. Heritage Found. com., 2006-07, WCC Heritage Found. Mem. Internat. Assn. Fin. Planners, Fin. Profls. Assn. (bd. dir., v.p. legis. and regulatory task force Mpls. chpt. 1990-92). Avocations: skiing, writing, reading, music, golf. Home and Office: 3630 Northome Rd Wayzata MN 55391-3021 Business E-Mail: vswyard@aol.com.

WYATT, EDITH ELIZABETH, elementary school educator; b. San Diego, Aug. 13, 1914; d. Jesse Wellington and Elizabeth (Fultz) Carne; m. Lee Ora Wyatt, Mar. 30, 1947 (dec. Jan. 1966); children: Glenn Stanley (dec.), David Allen. BA, San Diego State Coll., 1936. Elem. tchr. Nat. Sch. Dist., National City, Calif., 1938-76. Sec. San Diego County Parks Soc., 1986-96, sec.-treas., 1998—; librarian Congl. Ch. Women's Fellowship, Chula Vista, Calif., 1980—; active Boy Scouts Am, 1959—. Recipient Who award San Diego County Tchrs. Assn., 1968, Silver Fawn award Boy Scouts Am. Mem. AAUW (sec. 1978-80, pub. rels. 1985—), Calif. Ret. Tchrs. Assn. (scholarship com. 1985-90, 92-95, treas. South Shores divsn. # 60 1996-2004), Starlite Hiking Club (sec.-treas. 1979—). Avocation: hiking. Home: 165 E Millan St Chula Vista CA 91910-6255

WYATT, EDWARD AVERY, V, city manager; b. Petersburg, Va., Nov. 1, 1941; s. Edward Avery IV and Martha Vaughan (Seabury) W.; m. Regina Helen Stec, Aug. 23, 1969; children: Edward Avery VI, Stephen Alexander, Kent Seabury. AS in Bus., Bluefield Coll.; BS in Bus., Pub. Adminstrn., Va. Poly. Inst. and State U., 1964; M.Commerce, U. Richmond, 1969; MA in Polit. Sci., Appalachian State U., 1977. Chief gen. svc. City of Petersburg, Va., 1966-67, asst. to city mgr. Va., 1967-70; city mgr. City of Washington, NC, 1970-73, City of Morganton, NC, 1973-78, City of Greenville, NC, 1978-82, City of Fairfax, Va., 1982-91, City of Wilson, NC, 1991—2004, interim town mgr., adminstr. Adj. lectr. George E. Mason U. Bus. Sch., 1985-86, 1995-2003; bd. dir. Electricities of NC, sec. 2000; commr. NC Ea. Mcpl. Power Agy., 1996-2004. Contbr. numerous articles to profl. jour. and newsletters. Chmn. NC Code Ofcl. Qualification Bd., 1980-82; mem. adv. bd. Wilson Salvation Army, 1992—, vice chair, 2007; chmn. adv. coun. Wilson Boys and Girls Club, 2005-06; bd. dirs. Flynn Home, Diversified Opportunites, Wilson United Way; chmn. Wilson Bd. Elections, Wilson Hist. Assn., Preservation Wilson. With USN, 1964—70, with USAR, 1964—70. Recipient Dennis Duffey Meml. award Fairfax Police Youth Club, Red Barrett Spl. Achievement award Wilson Baseball Hot Stove chpt., 2004; named GEM of Yr., Wilson Downtown Devel. Corp., 2004; Paul Harris fellow Rotary Internat. Mem. Internat. City Mgmt. Assn. (endowment com. 1985-2000, chair 1991-92, city mgr. plan task force 1993-94), Va. Local Govt. Mgmt. Assn. (pres. 1989-90), NC City/County Mgmt. Assn. (pres.2000-01), Soc. Cincinnati in Va., Rotary Dist. 7720 (asst. dist. gov. 2003-07, dist. gov. nominee 2007). Home: 1307 Waverly Rd NW Wilson NC 27896-1483 Office Phone: 252-314-9658.

WYATT, GERARD ROBERT, biology professor, researcher; b. Palo Alto, Calif., Sept. 3, 1925; came to Can., 1935; s. Horace Graham and Mary Aimee (Strickland) W.; m. Sarah Silver Morton, Dec. 19, 1951 (dec. Mar. 1981); children— Eve Morton, Graham Strickland, Diana Silver; m. Mary Evelyn Rogers, Mar. 16, 1985 BA, U. B.C., Can., 1945; postgrad., U. Calif.-Berkeley, 1946-47; PhD, Cambridge U., 1950. Research scientist Can. Dept. Agr., Sault Ste. Marie, Ont., 1950-54; asst. prof. biochemistry Yale U., New Haven, 1954-60, assoc. prof., prof. biology, 1960-73; prof. biology Queen's U., Kingston, Ont., 1973-94, prof. emeritus, 1994—; sci. dir. Insect Biotech Can., 1990-93. Contbr. articles to profl. jours. Guggenheim fellow, 1956; Killam Research fellow, 1985 Fellow Royal Soc. Can. Avocation: natural history. Home: 114 Earl St Kingston ON Canada K7L 2H1 E-mail: meandj@kus.net.

WYATT, HELEN J., special education educator; b. Fayette, Miss., Jan. 1, 1948; d. Milton Louis and Hazel James; m. Dewitt Wyatt, Aug. 26, 1973; children: Derrick Dewayne, Carla Amaris. BS in Bus. Edn., Alcorn A & M Coll., Lorman, Miss., 1969; MS in Spl. Edn., Alcorn State U., Miss., 1979, MEd in Adminstrn and Supervision, 1994; EdD in Spl. Svcs. and Exceptional Edn., Nova Southeastern U., 2000. Lic. bus. edn. tchr. Miss. State Dept. Edn., spl. edn. tchr. La. Dept. Edn., child search coord. La. Dept. Edn., parish or city sch. supr. instrn. La. Dept. Edn., parish or city sch. supr.dir. spl. edn. La. Dept. Edn., supr. student tchg. La. Dept. Edn. Tchr. St. Joachim Cath. Elem. Sch., Chgo., 1970—71; counselor, employment and tng. instr. Fayette Pub. Svc. Careers Program, 1971—74; exec. sec. Alcorn State Admission Office, Lorman, 1975—78; spl. edn. tchr. Tensas Parish Sch. Dist., St. Joseph, La., 1978—86, Concordia Parish Sch. Dist., Vidalia, La., 1987—89, facilitator individual edn. plan, 1989—2000; assoc. prof., dir. Am. Reads-Miss. Alcorn State U., 2000—. Parish monitor Concordia Parish Spl. Edn. Dept., Vidalia, 1989—2000; state monitor La. State Dept of Edn., Baton Rouge, 1995—2000; cons. automated individual edn. plan Region 6 parishes, Alexandria, La., 1998—2000; presenter for spl. edn. tngs. Concordia Spl. Edn. Dept., Vidalia, 1989—2000; adminstr. Alcorn State U., 2000—; trainer Americorps members Am. Reads-Miss., Alcorn State, 2000—; workshop presenter Multi-State Cross Program Tng. Conf., Nashville, 2005. Author: (practicum) Assisting Newly Hired Special Education Teachers to Function More Effectively Through Inservice Training and Mentoring; contbr., workshop presenter: 10th Nat. Svc. Orientation Life After AmeriCorps (Commendation, Gov. of Miss., 2003); writer (handbook) Guidebook for New Special Education Teachers (Commendation, Spl. Edn. Supr., 2000). Mentor for youth Zion Hill #1 Bapt. Ch., Natchez, Miss., 1995—2005. Recipient Cmty.-Based Tutorial Program grant, La. Dept. of Edn., 2000—07, Conf. commendations, Miss. Commn. Vol. Svc., 2000—07, sci. fair judge commendations, Natchez-Adams Sch. Dist., 2001—04, Cert. of Excellence, SW Miss. Ctr. Ednl. Tech., 2003, Read Across Am. Appreciation cert., NEA, 2006. Mem.: NAACP, CEC (assoc.), Alcorn Alumni Assn. (life), Phi Delta Kappa (assoc.; historian 1996—97, Cert. Appreciation 1997), Delta Sigma Theta (pres., v.p., treas. Vidalia Alumnae chpt. 1966—2007, Pres.'s award Vidalia Alumnae chpt. 2006). Democrat. Baptist. Avocations: travel, reading, completing puzzles, playing computer games. Home: 401 S Spruce St Vidalia LA 71373 Office: Alcorn State U 1000 ASU Dr 480 Alcorn State MS 39096 Office Phone: 601-877-6215. Office Fax: 601-877-6213. Personal E-mail: hjwyatt@bellsouth.net. E-mail: hwyatt@alcorn.edu.

WYATT, JAMES FRANK, JR., lawyer; b. Talladega, Ala., Dec. 1, 1922; s. James Frank and Nannie Lee (Heaslett) W.; m. Rosemary Barbara Slone, Dec. 21, 1951; children: Martha Lee, James Frank III. BS, Auburn U., 1943; JD, Georgetown U., 1949, postgrad., 1950. Bar: D.C. 1949, Ala. 1950, Ill. 1953, U.S. Supreme Ct 1953. Atty. Office Chief Counsel, IRS, 1949-51; tax counsel Universal Oil Products Co., Des Plaines, Ill., 1951-63, asst. treas., 1963-66, v.p. fin., treas., 1966-75; treas. CF Industries, Inc., Long Grove, Ill., 1976-78, v.p. fin., treas., 1978-82; assoc. Tenney & Bentley, 1983-85, Arnstein, Gluck, Lehr, Barron & Milligan, 1985-88; pvt. practice, 1989—. Dir. 1st Nat. Bank, Des Plaines. Village trustee, Barrington, Ill., 1963-75; bd. dirs. Buehler YMCA, Barrington Twp. Republican Orgn., 1963—; pres. Barrington Area Rep. Workshops, 1962-63. Served to capt., Judge Adv. Gen. Corps AUS, 1944-47. Mem. Tax Execs. Inst. (v.p. 1965-66, chpt. pres. 1961-62), Fed., Am., Chgo. bar assns., Barrington Home Owners Assn. (pres. 1960-61), Newcomen Soc., Assn. U.S. Army, Scabbard and Blade, Phi Delta Phi, Sigma Chi. Clubs: Barrington Hills Country; Economics, University (Chgo.). Episcopalian. Home: 625 Concord Pl Barrington IL 60010-4508 Office: 200 Applebee St Barrington IL 60010-3060

WYATT, JAMES LUTHER, drapery hardware company executive; b. Williamsburg, Ky., May 13, 1924; s. Jesse Luther and Grace Edwina (Little) W.; m. Barbara Christman, Aug. 28, 1946; children— Linda Lou, William Charles Christman (dec.). BS, U. Ky., 1947, MS, 1948; Sc.D., Mass. Inst. Tech., 1952. Registered profl. engr., Ohio, Pa. Devel. engr. titanium div. Nat. Lead Co., Sayreville, NJ, 1948-50; tech. mgr., head, dept. metall. engring., mgr. new products Horizons, Inc., Cleve., 1953-57; cons., asso. Booz, Allen & Hamilton, NYC, 1957-61; v.p. program devel. Armour Research Found., Chgo., 1961-63; v.p. new product devel. Joy Mfg. Co., Pitts., 1963-67; v.p. corp. devel. Nat. Gypsum Co., Buffalo, 1967-69, Max Factor & Co., Hollywood, Calif., 1969-71; pres. Wyatt & Co., 1971—, Jimbabs, Inc., 1983—, Ambassador Industries, Inc., Los Angeles, 1988—. U.S. del. 1st World Metall. Congress. Contbr. tech., mgmt. papers to profl. lit.; patentee in field. Mem. Pompano Beach Power Squadron, adminstr. officer, 1991, exec. officer, 1992, comdr., 1993; chmn. bd. trustees Meth. Ch., 1992, mem. fin. com., 1993, mem. adminstrv. bd.; chmn. bd. trustees 1st United Meth. Ch., Boca Raton; bd. dirs., v.p. Golden Harbour Homeowners Assn., 1997—. Lt. col. USAAF, 1942-46. Elected to U. Ky. Hall of Distinction, 2001. Mem. AIME, Am. Soc. Metals, Econ. Club (Chgo.), Execs. Club (Chgo.), Univ. Club (N.Y.C.), Calif. Yacht Club, Pompano Beach Power Squadron (comdr.), Sigma Phi Epsilon, Alpha Chi Sigma. Clubs: Econs. (Chgo.), Execs. (Chgo.); Univ. (N.Y.C.); Calif. Yacht. Home: 510 Golden Harbour Dr Boca Raton FL 33432-2942 Office: 510 Golden Harbour Dr Boca Raton FL 33432-2942 Office Phone: 561-395-9148. Personal E-mail: jim_wyatt@juno.com.

WYATT, JOSEPH LUCIAN, JR., lawyer, writer; b. Chgo., Feb. 21, 1924; s. Joseph Lucian and Cecile Gertrude (Zadico) W.; m. Marjorie Kathryn Simmons, Apr. 9, 1954; children: Daniel, Linn, Jonathan. AB in English Lit. with honors, Northwestern U., 1947; LLB, Harvard U., 1949. Bar: Calif. 1950, U.S. Dist. Ct. (cen. dist.) Calif. 1950, U.S. Ct. Appeals (9th cir.) 1950, U.S. Tax Ct., U.S. Supreme Ct. 1965. Assoc. firm Brady, Nossaman & Walker, Los Angeles, 1950-58, ptnr. LA, 1958-61; pvt. practice LA, 1961-71; sr. mem. Cooper, Wyatt, Tepper & Plant, P.C., LA, 1971-79; of counsel Beardsley, Hufstedler & Kemble, LA, 1979-81; ptnr. Hufstedler & Kaus, LA, 1981-95; sr. of counsel Morrison & Foerster, LA, 1995—. Mem. faculty Pacific Coast Banking Sch., Seattle, 1963-92, Southwestern Grad. Sch. Banking, 1988-89; advisor Restatement, Trusts 3d, 1988—. Author: Trust Administration and Taxation, 4 vols., 1964—; editor: Trusts and Estates, 1962-74. Lectr. continuing legal edn. programs, Calif. and Tex.; trustee Pacific Oaks Coll. and Children's Sch., 1969-97; counsel, parliamentarian Calif. Democratic party and presdl. conv. dels., 1971—; mem. Calif. State Personnel Bd., 1961-71, v.p., 1963-65, pres., 1965-67; bd trustees Calif. Pub. Employees Retirement System, 1963-71. 1st sgt. USAAF, 1943-45. Fellow Am. Coll. of Trust and Estate Counsel; mem. ABA, Internat. Acad. Estate and Trust Law (treas. 1990-96), Am. Law Inst., Calif. State Bar Assn. (del. state conf. 1956, 62-67), L.A. Bar Assn. (trustee 1956). Democrat. Christian Scientist. Avocations: fishing, composing doggerel. Home: 1119 Armada Dr Pasadena CA 91103-2805 Office Phone: 213-892-5200. E-mail: jwyatt@mofo.com, jwyatt3@charter.net.

WYATT, KYLE K., curator, historian; b. Salinas, Calif., 1952; s. Kenneth R. and Denoya Petty Wyatt; m. Diane E. Williams, 1999 (div. 2005); 1 child, Kailen Williams Wyatt. BA, U. Pacific, Stockton, Calif., 1974, MA, 1984; postgrad., U. Calif., Davis, 1986—90. Self-employed cons., Sacramento, 1977—; curator history Nev. State RR Mus., Carson City, 1990—99; curator history and tech. Calif. State RR Mus., Sacramento, 1999—. Bd. dirs. Knight Foundry Corp., Sutter Creek, Calif., 2000, now chmn. Holt-Atherton Pacific Ctr. Western Studies fellow, U. Pacific, 1979, History Dept. fellow, 1980. Mem.: Tourist RR Assn., Assn. Rlwy. Museums, Soc. Indsl. Archeology, Lexington Group Transp. History, Rlwy. and Locomotive Hist. Soc. (Fred Stindt fellow in RR history Pacific Coast chpt. 1987). Avocations: natural history, music, historical study, hiking, photography. Office: Calif State RR Mus 111 I St Sacramento CA 95814 Office Phone: 916-324-7660.

WYATT, OSCAR SHERMAN, JR., energy company executive; b. Beaumont, Tex., July 11, 1924; s. Oscar Sherman Sr. and Eva (Coday) Wyatt; m. Lynn Sakowitz; children: Steven, Douglas, Oscar Sherman III, Brad. BS in Mech. Engring., Tex. A&M U., 1949. With Kerr-McGee Co., 1949, Reed Roller Bit Co., 1949—51; ptnr. Wymore Oil Co., 1951—55; founder Coastal Corp., Corpus Christi, Tex., 1955—2001, chmn. exec. com. Houston. Trustee DeBakey Med. Found., 1987—; founding mem., bd. stewards Tex. Aviation Hall of Fame, 1997—. With USAF, WWII. Office: 3355 W Alabama Ste 500 Houston TX 77098 Office Phone: 713-877-6700. E-mail: ow@nucoastal.com.

WYATT, ROBERT LEE, IV, lawyer; s. Robert Lee III and Louise Carole (Bard) W.; m. Vicki Harris Wyatt. BS, Southeastern Okla. State U., Durant, 1986; JD, U. Okla., Norman, 1989. Bar: Okla. 1989, US Dist. Ct. (we. dist.) Okla. 1990, US Ct. Appeals (10th cir.) 1990, US Dist. Ct. (no. dist.) Okla. 1991, US Ct. Appeals (8th cir.) 1991, US Supreme Ct. 1993, US Dist. Ct. (Ea. Dist.) 2004. Intern Okla. State Bur. Investigation, Oklahoma City, 1988-89, guest lectr., 1989; dep. spl. counsel Gov. of Okla., 1995; atty. Jones & Wyatt, Enid, Okla., 1989-2000. Criminal justice panel atty. We. Dist. Okla., Wyatt Law Office, 2000—. Contbr. Vernon's Forms Oklahoma, Criminal Law and Procedure, 1999. Counsel to Fire Civil Svc. Commn. City of Enid, 1998-2000. Named an Okla. Super Lawyer, 2006; named one of Best Lawyers in Am., 2007. Mem. Okla. Bar Assn. (mem. criminal law com., guest lectr. 2003-06), Oklahoma County Bar Assn., Okla. Criminal Def. Lawyers Assn. (Internet Champion of Liberty award, 2003), Nat. Inst. for Trial Advocacy, Nat. Assn. Criminal Defense Lawyers (life mem.), Luther Bohanon Am. Inn of Ct. (barrister), Phi Delta Phi, Alpha Chi. Democrat. Baptist. Office Phone: 405-234-5500. Business E-Mail: bobwyatt@wyattlaw.com.

WYATT, ROBERT ODELL, journalism educator; b. Jackson, Tenn., Feb. 7, 1946; s. Odell and Sera Mae (Mebane) Wyatt. BA, U. of the South, 1968; MA, Northwestern U., Evanston, Ill., 1970, PhD, 1973; MS, U. Tenn., 1977; Cert. in Theology, Seabury-Western Theol. Sem., 2002; MTS, Vanderbilt U., Nashville, 2004. Ordained priest Episcopal Ch., 2004. From asst. to assoc. prof. U. Tenn., Nashville, 1973-79; assoc. prof. Mid. Tenn. State U., Murfreesboro, 1979-84, prof., 1984—, dir. Office Comm. Rsch., 1989—. Vis. prof. comm. U. Caen, France, 1994; cons. in comm.; mem. Pulitzer Prize Jury, 1980, 85, 91, 93, 99, chair jury, 1985, 91, 93, 99; bd. trustees Seabury-Western Theol. Sem., Evanston, Ill., 1996-2001. Author: Free Expression and the American Public, 1991 (Sigma Delta Chi award for rsch. on journalism 1992); co-author, Free Expression in 5 Cultures, 2004; editor book sect. The Nashville Tennessean, 1978-93; contbr. articles to profl. jours. Worcester prize World Assn. for Pub. Opinion Rsch., 1996, Vanderbilt U. Founder's medal, 2004. Mem. Assn. for Edn. in Journalism and Mass Comm., Internat. Comm. Assn., Am. Assn. Pub. Opinion Rsch. Democrat. Episcopalian. Home: 3526 Maple Ave Berwyn IL 60402 Office: St Helena's Episcopal Ch Burr Ridge IL 60527

WYATT, THOMAS CSABA, lawyer; b. Toronto, Ont., Can., Mar. 19, 1952; arrived in U.S., 1979; s. Charles Wojatsek and Marietta Marcinkova; m. Helen A. Johnson, Dec. 24, 1979; children: J.P. Max, Stephen M. BCL, McGill U., 1974; BA, Bishop's U., 1975; LLM, U. Montréal, 1980; JD, U. San Francisco, 1981. Bar: Que. 1975, Calif. 1982, U.S. Dist. Ct. (no. dist.) Calif. 1982, U.S. Ct. Appeals (9th cir.) 1982. Assoc. counsel Can. Gen. Electric, Montreal, 1975—77; solicitor Du Pont Can., Inc., Montreal, 1977—79; internat. counsel Computerland Corp., Oakland, Calif., 1982—85; sr. counsel Bank of Am., San Francisco, 1985—87, Intel Corp., Santa Clara, Calif., 1987—90; gen. counsel Philips Semiconductors, Sunnyvale, Calif., 1990—2001; ptnr. Sapiential Prime, 2001—06. Arbitrator Am. Arbitration Assn., San Francisco, 1985-2005; founder, dir. Actineon, Inc., Sunnyvale, Calif., 2001-05. Bd. dirs. Silicon Valley Law Found., 2000—02. Mem. Silicon Valley Assn. Gen. Counsel (chmn. 1998-2000), Santa Clara County Bar Assn. (trustee 2001-02), Knightly Order of Vitez, Knights of Malta. Roman Catholic. Personal E-mail: tcwyatt@comcast.net.

WYATT, WILSON WATKINS, JR., communications executive, writer; b. Louisville, Dec. 3, 1943; s. Wilson Watkins Sr. and Anne (Duncan) W.; m. Jane Clay, Aug. 15, 1964 (dec. 1975); children: Carol, Wilson III, Sarah Wyatt; m. Kathleen Valonis, June 14, 1998. Student, U. of the South, 1961-65. Reporter The Courier-Jour., Louisville, 1965-67; pub. rels. account exec. Doe-Anderson Advt., Louisville, 1967-68; account exec. Zimmer-McClaskey-Lewis (McCann-Ericksn Advtsg.), Louisville, 1968-70; ptnr. Bennett & Wyatt Pub. Rels., Louisville, 1970-71; state rep., vice chair appropriations and revenue com. Ky. Gen. Assembly, Frankfort, 1969-71; exec. dir. Louisville Cen. Area Inc., 1971-77; dir. corp. affairs and communications Brown & Williamson Tobacco Corp., Louisville, 1977-82; v.p. pub. policy BATUS Inc., Washington, 1982-86, v.p. corp. affairs Louisville, 1986-90; sr. v.p. corp. affairs PNC Fin. Corp., Pitts., 1990-92; sr. v.p. corp. comm. and govt. rels. The Travelers Cos., Hartford, 1992-94; exec. dir., CEO Am. Acad. of Actuaries, Washington, 1995-98; CEO Wyatt Comm. Cons., 1998—. Lead U.S. def. pub. rels. activities against hostile takeover for B.A.T. Industries, U.K., 1989-90; chmn. Travelers Found., 1991-94; moderator Working Writers Forum, Md., 2006-. Mem. youth adv. com. Atlantic Inst., 1967-68; del. North Atlantic Treaty Assn. Young Leaders Conf., 1967; chmn. Leadership Effort for All Dems., Ky., 1967-68; regional campaign coord. for Robert F. Kennedy, Ky.-Ind., 1968; mem. Pres.'s Forum, Washington, 1988-91; trustee Conn. Policy Econ. Commn., 1992-95; mem. exec. com. Hartford Downtown Coun., 1992-94; mem. adv. bd. Dem. Leadership Coun., Washington; mem. Am. Savings Edn. Campaign U.S. Dept. Labor, 1996. Named one of Outstanding Young Men in Am., Ky. Jaycees, 1973. Mem. The Pres.'s Forum, Pub. Affairs Rsch.

Coun. (conf. bd. 1986-95), Forum I, Assn. Chief Execs. Coun., Pub. Affairs Coun. (bd. dirs. 1982—, exec. com. 1982-86), Speakers Club (Washington), Greater Hartford C. of C. (exec. com. 1992-94), Hartford Stage (bd. dirs. 1993-95), Md. Writers Assn., Eastern Shore Writers Assn. (v.p. 2006—), Working Writers Forum (moderator), Bay to Ocean Writers Conf. (mem. steering com., chmn. editl. rev. bd. The Delmarva Rev.). Avocations: boating, photography, writing. Home and Office: PO Box 298 Bozman MD 21612 Personal E-mail: wwwtwo@earthlink.net.

WYCHE, CYRIL THOMAS, lawyer; b. Greenville, SC, Jan. 28, 1926; C. Granville and Mary (Wheeler) W.; m. Harriet Smith, June 19, 1948; children: Sara McCall, Bradford Wheeler, Mary Frances. BE, Yale U., 1946; LLB, U. Va., 1949; LLD (hon.), Clemson U., 1997, Furman U., 1997; HLD (hon.), Wofford Coll. Bar: S.C. 1948, U.S. Dist. Ct. S.C. 1950, U.S. Ct. Appeals (4th cir.) 1952, U.S. Ct. Claims 1964, U.S. Supreme Ct. 1970. Ptnr. Wyche, Burgess, Freeman & Parham, P.A., Greenville, SC, 1948—. Pres., bd. dirs. YMCA, Greenville, 1960; pres. Greenville Little Theatre, 1965, Arts Festival Assn., Greenville, 1970, Greenville Community Corp., 1976—; bd. dirs. Greater Greenville C. of C., 1980. Served with USN, 1943-46. Named Environmentalist of Yr., State of S.C., 1979; recipient Conservation award Gulf Oil Corp., 1983, Alexander Calder award, 1996, Garden Clubs Am., 1999, Oak Leaf award The Nature Conservancy, 1996, Order of the Palmetto award S.C. Gov., 1996. Mem. ABA (Environ. award 2002), S.C. Bar Assn., Greenville County Bar Assn., Am. Judicature Soc., Nat. Wildlife Fedn. (Spl. Conservation Achievement award 2003). Presbyterian. Avocations: skiing, scuba diving, piano, tennis, white water canoeing. Office: Wyche Burgess Freeman & Parham 44 E Camperdown Way PO Box 728 Greenville SC 29602-0728 Home Phone: 864-288-6049; Office Phone: 864-242-8213. E-mail: twyche@wyche.com.

WYCHE, JAMES RAMAGE, lawyer; s. Madison Baker Wyche III and Marguerite Ramage Wyche; m. Sally B. Hubbard. BS magna cum laude in Fin., Clemson U., 2000; JD cum laude, Duke U., 2003. Bar: NC 2003, US Dist. Ct. (mid. dist.) NC 2003. Intern Sen. J. Strom Thurmond, 1997; atty. Kennedy Covington Lobdell & Hickman, Charlotte, NC, 2003—. Bd. dirs. young leaders United Way, Charlotte; bd. dirs. Camp Sea Gull, Camp Seafarer. Scholar, Wachovia Bank Nat. Assn., 1998—2000. Mem.: Phi Kappa Phi, Beta Gamma Sigma, Omicron Delta Kappa. Office: Kennedy Covington 214 N Tryon St 47th Flr Charlotte NC 28202 Office Phone: 704-331-7400.

WYCHE, MADISON BAKER, III, lawyer; b. Albany, Ga., Aug. 11, 1947; s. Madison Baker Jr. and Merle (McKemie) W.; m. Marguerite Jernigan Ramage, Aug. 7, 1971; children: Madison Baker IV, James Ramage. BA, Vanderbilt U., 1969, JD, 1972. Bar: Ga. 1972, U.S. Dist. Ct. (mid. dist.) Ga. 1972, U.S. Ct. Appeals (5th cir.) 1973, S.C. 1976, U.S. Dist. Ct. S.C. 1977, U.S. Ct. Appeals (4th cir.) 1977, U.S. Supreme Ct. 1980, U.S. Ct. Appeals (11th cir.) 1981, U.S. Dist. Ct. (no. dist.) Ga. 1995. Assoc. Perry, Walters, Lippitt & Custer, Albany, 1972-76, Thompson, Ogletree & Deakins, Greenville, SC, 1976-77, Ogletree, Deakins, Smoak & Stewart, Greenville, 1977-80; shareholder Ogletree, Deakins, Nash, Smoak & Stewart P.C., Greenville, 1980—. Bd. dirs. Happy Ho., Inc., Albany. Co-editor Labor and Employment Law for South Carolina Lawyers, 1999, 3d edit., 2004. Co-incorporator, sec. State of Tenn. Intercollegiate State Legislature, Nashville, 1967-69; mem. employer and employee rels. com., legal issues & workplace policy com. N.C. Citizens for Bus. and Industry, Raleigh, 1984—; mem. Greenville C. of C., gen. counsel, 2003-06, bd. dirs., 2003-06; mem. Advantage Greenville, Greenville Chamber Found., 2003-06; United Way Greenville; bd. dirs. Palmetto Soc. of the United Way, 1992-2004; mem. vestry Christ Episcopal Ch., Greenville, 1981-85; treas. All Saints Episcopal Ch., Linville, NC 2001-05; mem. bd. visitors Clemson U., 1998-2001, mem. profl. advancement and continuing edn. bd., 2003—; bd. dirs. Blue Ridge coun. Boy Scouts Am., 1999-2000; bd. dirs. Internat. Arts Festival, ARTISPHERE, Greenville, 2003—, gen. counsel, 2006—. Capt. US Army, 1969—77. Recipient Eagle Scouts award Boy Scouts Am., 1961, God and Country award, 1961. Mem. ABA, Coll. Labor and Employment Lawyers, SC Bar Assn. (unauthorized practice of law com. 1977-95, chmn. 1982-92, ho. of dels. 1991-98, 2004—, nominating com. 1992-95, CLE divsn., chmn., 1997-98, exec. com. 1995-99, chmn. seminars subcom. 1995-97), Ga. Bar Assn., Atlanta Bar Assn., S.C. Def. Trial Lawyers Assn., St. Andrews Soc. Upper S.C. (bd. dirs. 1979-81, v.p. 1986-87, pres. 1988-90, scholarship chmn. 1998—), Vanderbilt U. Alumni Assn. (pres. S.C. chpt. 1990-95, bd. dirs. 1994—), The Poinsett Club (v.p., bd. dirs.) (Greenville, S.C.), Rotary (bd. dirs. 1982-84, Paul Harris fellow 1986), Commerce Club of Greenville (bd. dirs. 1990-2007), Phi Delta Phi. Office: Ogletree Deakins Nash Smoak & Stewart PO Box 2757 Greenville SC 29602-2757 Office Phone: 864-271-1300.

WYCKOFF, SYLVIA SPENCER, art educator, artist; b. Pitts., Nov. 14, 1915; d. Lynn Boyd Wyckoff and Bess Jeannette Hohes. BFA, Syracuse U., NY, 1937, MFA, 1944. Cert. art tchr. NY, 1987. Art tchr. various pub. schs., Homer and Cobleskill, NY, 1937—42; instr. Coll. Visual Arts, Syracuse U., 1942—81, asst. to full prof., chmn. freshman core program, 1971—72, chmn. London art program; ret., 1981. Adj. art instr. Cazenovia Coll.; judge arts recognition and talent search Nat. Found. Arts, Princeton, NJ, 1983. Exhibited in group shows, Cortland, NY, 1938, Syracuse Regional Show, 1942—45 (1st prize for watercolor, 1943), with Rick Wolff, Oneida, NY, exhibitions include Nat. League Am. Pen Women, NYC and Washington, DC, 1968 (1st prize for watercolor, 1945), Chancellor's Office, Syracuse U., 1976, St. Lawrence U., Munson William Proctor Mus. Art, Utica, NY, 1980—81, Cazenovia Watercolor Soc., 1981—95, Core Faculty-Wells Coll., one-woman shows include Coleman Hall, Cazenovia, NY, 1975, New Coll. Art Bldg., Cazenovia Coll., 2004. Dispatcher CAVAC (Cazenovia Area Vol. Corps., NY, 1974—91; vol. Stone Quarry Art Pk. Recipient 1st prize for watercolor, Onondaga Hist. Soc., 1945, Gordon Steele award for painting, Assoc. Artists of Syracuse, 1968, spl. award, NY State Tchrs. Assn., 1981. Mem.: Nat. Mus. Women in Arts (charter mem.), Stone Quarry Art Pk., Manson Williams Proctor Mus., Cazenovia Watercolor Soc. (founder 1976, first recipient Priscilla Hancock award 1992), Sigma Chi Alpha, Eta Phi Upsilon (hon.), Alpha Xi Delta (award to 10% Top Alumnae 1967). Presbyterian. Achievements include first woman on athletic bd., Syracuse U., 1974; named in honor of Spl. Sylvia Wyckoff Book award, Alpha Sigma Lambda, U. Coll. Syracuse, NY, 1981. Avocations: painting, drawing, bridge, knitting. Home: 4 Liberty St Cazenovia NY 13035

WYCOFF, CHARLES COLEMAN, writer, retired anesthesiologist; b. Glazier, Tex., Sept. 2, 1918; s. James Garfield and Ada Sharpe (Braden) W.; m. Gene Marie Henry, May 16, 1942 (dec.); children: Michelle, Geoffrey, Brian, Roger, Daniel, Norman, Irene, Teresa. AB, U. Calif., Berkeley, 1941; MD, U. Calif., San Francisco, 1943; postgrad., U. London, 1954-55. Diplomate Am. Bd. Anesthesiology. Intern San Francisco County Hosp., 1943-44; resident in anesthesiology U. Calif. Hosp., San Francisco, 1944-45; tng. in anesthesiology Walter Reed Gen. Hosp., 1945; founder The Wycoff Group of Anesthesiology, San Francisco, 1947-53; chief of anesthesia St. Joseph's Hosp., San Francisco, 1947-52, organizer residency tng. program in anesthesiology, 1950, San Francisco County Hosp., 1954, chief anesthesia, 1953-54; tchr. practice anesthesiology Presbyn. Med. Ctr., NYC, 1955-63; asst. prof. anesthesiology Columbia U., NYC, 1955-63; clin. practice anesthesiology St. Francis Meml. Hosp., San Francisco, 1963-84. Prodr., dir. films on regional anesthesia; contbr. articles to sci. jours. Scoutmaster Boy Scouts Am., San Francisco, 1953-55. Capt. MC, US Army, 1945-47. Mem. Alumni Faculty Assn. Sch. Medicine U. Calif.-San Francisco (councilor-at-large 1979-80). Democrat. Avocations: researching origins of human behavior, writing, gardening. Home: 3875 Castro Valley Blvd Spc 55 Castro Valley CA 94546-4584

WYCOFF, WILLIAM MORTIMER, lawyer; b. Pitts., Jan. 1, 1941; s. William Clyde and Margaret (Shaffer) W.; m. Deborah Seyl, Jan. 25, 1963; children: Ann Richardson, Pieter Claesen. AB, Cornell U., 1963; JD, Northwestern U., 1966. Bar: Pa. 1967, U.S. Ct. Appeals (3d cir.) 1967), U.S. Dist. Ct. (we. dist.) Pa. 1967. Assoc., now ptnr. Thorp Reed and Armstrong, Pitts., 1966—. Pres. Children's Home Pitts., 1976-78, 86-88, 2004-; pres. Pressley Ridge Schs., Pitts., 1988-90, now bd. dirs.; pres. Pressley Ridge Found., 1998-2004, no bd. dirs.; pres., bd. dirs. Pitts. Dance Coun., 1991-94; trustee Pitts. Cultural Trust, 1991-94. Fellow Internat. Acad. Trial Lawyers, Am. Coll. Trial Lawyers; mem. Acad. Trial Lawyers Allegheny County. Avocations: photography, skiing, biking, hiking, golf. Office: Thorp Reed & Armstrong LLP One Oxford Ctr 14th Fl 301 Grant St Pittsburgh PA 15219 Office Phone: 412-394-7782. Business E-Mail: wwycoff@thorpreed.com.

WYDEN, RON(ALD) (LEE), senator; b. Wichita, Kans., May 3, 1949; s. Peter and Edith W.; m. Laurie Oseran, Sept. 5, 1978 (div. 1999); 2 children; m. Nancy Bass, Sept. 2005. Student, U. Santa Barbara, 1967-69; AB in Polit. Sci., with distinction, Stanford U., 1971; JD, U. Oreg., 1974. Bar: Oreg. 1975. Campaign aide Senator Wayne Morse, 1972, 74; co-founder, co-dir. Oreg. Gray Panthers, 1974-80; dir. Oreg. Legal Services for Elderly, 1977-79; instr. gerontology U. Oreg., 1976, U. Portland, 1980, Portland State U., 1979; mem. 97th-104th Congresses from 3d Oreg. dist., Washington, 1981-96; US Senator form Oreg., 1996—. Mem. com. fin. US Senate, com. intelligence, com. energy and natural resources, com. budget, spl. com. on aging. Contbr. articles to profl. journals. Mem. Oreg. Environmental Coun. Recipient Service to Oreg. Consumers award Oreg. Consumers League, 1978, Citizen of Yr. award Oreg. Assn. Social Workers, 1979, Significant Service award Multnomah County Area Agy. on Aging, 1980, Philip A. Hart Pubilc Svc. award Consumer Fedn. Am., 1999, Champion of Sci. award, U. Oreg./The Sci. Coalition, 2003; named Young Man of Yr. Oreg. Jr. C. of C., 1980, Senator of Yr. Nat. Assn. Police Orgn., 1997, People of Yr (with Rep. Christopher Cox) PC Computing mag., 1999, Legis. of Yr. Info. Tech. Coun., 2000; named to Legis. Hall of Fame Am. Electronics Assn. Mem. ABA, Iowa Bar Assn., Oreg. Bar Assn. Democrat. Jewish. Office: US Senate 230 Dirksen Senate Office Bldg Washington DC 20510-0001 also: District Office Ste 585 1220 SW 3rd Ave Portland OR 97204 Office Phone: 202-224-5244, 503-326-7525. Office Fax: 202-228-2717. *

WYDICK, RICHARD CREWS, lawyer, educator; b. Pueblo, Colo., Nov. 1, 1937; s. Charles Richard and Alice Wydick; m. Judith Brandli James, 1961; children: William Bruce, Derrick Cameron. BA, Williams Coll., 1959; LL.B., Stanford U., 1962. Bar: Calif. bar 1962. Asso. firm Brobeck, Phleger & Harrison, San Francisco, 1966-71; mem. faculty U. Calif. Law Sch., Davis, 1971—, prof. law, 1975—2003, dean, 1978-80, prof. emeritus, 2003—. Author: Plain English for Lawyers, 5th edit., 2005 Served to capt. USAR, 1962-66. Office: Sch Law U Calif Davis CA 95616

WYDRA, FRANK THOMAS, healthcare executive; b. Republic, Pa., May 11, 1939; s. Frank T. and Anne M. (Kois) W.; m. Karen Branch, June 24, 1961; children: Denise Lee, Sheryl Lynn, Frank Thomas III. BS in Mgmt., U. Ill., 1961. V.p. Allied Supermarkets, Inc., Detroit, 1967-75; sr. v.p. HGH Health System, Detroit, 1975-85; pres. Radius Health Care Sysytems, Inc., Detroit, 1983-85; cons. Birmingham, Mich., 1985-88; exec. v.p. The Chi Group, Ann Arbor, Mich., 1988-91; mng. ptnr., CEO, owner IRI, Mgmt. Cons., Detroit, 1991—. Lectr. various profl. groups; bd. dirs. Mich. Health Systems Inc., Saber-Salisbury Assocs. Inc., Midwestern Health Ctr., MultiCare Med. Inc., RHS Inc. Author: Learner Controlled Instruction, 1980, (with others) Hospital Survival Guide, 1984, The Cure, 1992; creator 2 mgmt. games Performulations, 1978, The Dynamics of Power and Authority, 1981; contbr. articles to profl. jours. Personnel program advisor Mich. State U. Sch. Labor Relations, 1979-83; chmn. new programs Wayne County Community Coll., Detroit, 1979-80; bd. dirs. Detroit Metro Youth Found., 1980-83, State Mich. Health Occupations Council, Lansing, 1982-85. Capt. U.S. Army, 1961-63. Recipient numerous awards ASTD, Nat. Soc. Performance and Instrn., Mich. SOc. Instructional Tech., Supermarket Inst. Mem. Am. Hosp. Assn., Planning Soc. of Am. Hosp. Assn., Hosp. Personnel Adminstrs. Assn. (pres. 1981-82, numerous awards), Am. Mgmt. Assn., Am. Soc. Hosp. Pers.Adminstrs. (bd. dirs. 1981-83), Mich. Soc. Instrnl. Tech. (life, pres. 1973-74), Mich. Hosp. Assn., Employers Assn. Detroit (bd. dirs. 1982-85), Detroit Athletic Club. Avocations: writing, sailing. Home: 8945 Reese Rd Clarkston MI 48348

WYETH, JAMES BROWNING, artist; b. Wilmington, Del., July 6, 1946; s. Andrew and Betsy (James) W.; m. Phyllis Overton Mills, Dec. 12, 1968. Privately tutored. One-man shows include M. Knoedler & Co., N.Y.C., 1966, William A. Farnsworth Mus., Rockland, Maine, 1969, 1992, 1995, Coe Kerr Gallery, N.Y.C., 1974, 1990, Brandywine River Mus., Chadds Ford, Pa., 1974, 1994, 1995, 1999, Joslyn Art Mus., Omaha, 1976, Pa. Acad. Fine Arts, 1980, Greenville County Art Mus., Greenville, N.C., 1981, Amon Carter Mus., Ft. Worth, 1981, Anchorage Fine Arts Mus., 1983, James Graham and Sons, N.Y.C., 1993, 1995, 1999, 2000, Decatur House, 1995, Double Door Gallery, Isleboro, Maine, 1996, Butler Art Inst., Youngstown, Ohio, 1999, Russell Rotunda, Washington, 2000, Ringling Mus. Art, Sarasota, Fla., New Britain (Conn.) Mus. Am. Art, one-man shows include touring exhibn. An American Vision: Three Generations of Wyeth Art, various mus. worldwide, 1987—, Farnsworth Art Mus., 1988—2000, Terra Mus. Am. Art, Chgo., 1997—, (illustrator) childrens books, The Stray, 1979, Cabbages and Kings, 1997. Mem. NEA, 1972; mem. stamp adv. com. U.S. Postal Svc., 1969; bd. govs. Nat. Space Inst., 1975. With Del. Air N.G., 1966—71. Mem.: NAD (assoc. 1969—80, academician 1980—). Office: care Priscilla Vail Caldwell James Graham & Sons 1014 Madison Ave New York NY 10021-0103 Fax: (212) 794-2454. E-mail: jgsgal@aol.com.

WYGANT, FOSTER LAURANCE, art educator; b. Dayton, Ohio, Oct. 30, 1920; s. Harold F. and M. Esther (Weber) W.; m. Rae E. Hoyt, 1 child, Nancy Laura Profl. diploma, Juilliard Sch. Music, 1942; BA, Columbia U., 1949, MA, 1956, Ed.D., 1959; postgrad., Am. Art Sch., Art Students League, 1951-53. Clarinetist Dallas Symphony and free-lance clarinetist, NYC, 1945-47; publicity, fund-raising positions, and free-lance artist, 1952-56; tchr. art, pub. schs., 1956-59; asst. prof. Montclair State Coll., NJ, 1959-63, assoc. prof. NJ, 1963-68; prof. art edn. U. Cin., 1968-87, chmn. dept., 1968-84, dir. Sch. Art Edn. and Art History, 1984-86, emeritus prof., 1987—. Pub., owner Interwood Press, 1987—; vis. sr. lectr. Leeds Coll. Art, Eng., 1966; regional chmn. Scholastic Awards Program, 1968-84; chmn. Action for Arts in Ohio Schs., 1974-75. Author: Art in American Schools in the Nineteenth Century, 1983, School Art in American Culture 1820-1970, 1993, School Art in American Culture Supplement: 1900-1915, 1997; editor, prin. author: Standards for Art Teacher Preparation Programs, 1979, Principles, Purposes and Standards for School Art Programs, 1982; contbr. numerous articles to profl. jours. Pres. Tri-State Chamber Players, Inc., 2002—. With US Army, 1941—45. N.Y. State and Juilliard Sch. Music scholar, 1939-41; Kellogg Found. fellow Columbia U., 1955-56 Nat. Art Edn. Assn. (V. Pres., nat. dir. higher edn. divsn. 1975-79, Recognition award 1980, Disting. Svc. award 1982, Disting. fellow 1995), Ohio Art Edn. Assn. (pres. 1972-74, Disting. fellow 2000), Seminar for Rsch. in Art Edn., Coun. for Policy Studies in Art Edn., Am. Fedn. Musicians, Phi Beta Kappa. Home: 3562 Interwood Ave Cincinnati OH 45220-1824 Office Phone: 513-751-5239. Business E-Mail: wygantfl@ucmail.uc.edu.

WYGANT, PATRICIA BRYANS, artist; b. Marion, Ohio, Nov. 10, 1926; d. Ralph Armond and Frances Annetta (Kilbury) Bryans. BFA, Syracuse U., 1950. Resident Millay Colony for Arts, Austerlitz, N.Y., 1979. Exhibited in 62 nat. juried exhbns. including Watercolor USA, Nat. Watercolor Soc., Watercolor Workshop Greek Islands Sifnos Amorgos, Paros, 1988; paintings publ. in A Gallery of Marine Art, 1988, 98, The Best of Watercolor, 1995 (1st Pl. award). Recipient Winsor Newton award Rochester Art Club, 1994. Mem. Am. Artists Profl. League, Ga. Watercolor Soc. (signature mem.), Niagara Frontier Watercolor Soc. (signature mem.). Avocation: travel. Office: Anderson Alley Artists 250 N Goodman St Rochester NY 14607

WYKER, KENNETH E., lawyer; b. NYC, Apr. 1, 1961; s. Robert Harris and Elin Barbara (Eisner) W. BA, Trinity Coll., 1983; JD, George Washington U., 1986. Bar: Pa. 1987, D.C. 1988. Staff atty. Securities & Exch. Commn., Washington, 1986-87; assoc. gen. counsel Infotech., Fairfax, Va., 1988-90; sr. v.p. legal affairs Clear Channel Comms., San Antonio, 1993—; corp. counsel Greater Media, East Brunswick, N.J., 1990-93; gen. counsel Clear Channel Comms., 2001—06. Bd. charitable giving Children;s Shelter, San Antonio, 1993-95. Mem. Am. Corp. Coun. Assn. (bd. dirs. San Antonio chpt. 1998—). *

WYKLE, MAY L., dean, educator, researcher; BSN, Case Western Res. U., 1956, MSN Psychiat. Nursing, PhD Edn. Dean, Cellar prof. gerontological nursing Frances Payne Bolton Sch. Nursing, Ohio, 1988—; dean, dir. u. ctr. aging and health Case Western Res. U. Established ednl. programs, Europe, Africa, Asia; vis. prof. U. Mich., U. Tex.-Houston, U. Zimbabwe-Africa; del., served on planning com. White Ho. Conf. on Aging, 1993. Contbr. articles, chapters to books; author: Decision Making in Long-Term Care, Practicing Rehabilitation with Geriatric Clients, Stress and Health Among the Elderly, Family Caregiving Across the Lifespan, Service Minority Elders in the 21st Century (AJN Book of Yr. award, 2000). Dir. Robert Wood Johnson Tchg. Nursing Home Project; project dir. several tng. grants; cons. nursing homes, psychiat. hosps.; mem. bd. dirs. numerous cmty. orgns., nursing homes, profl. assns. Named first Pope Eminent scholar, Rosalynn Carter Inst. Human Devel. Southwestern State U., Americus, Ga., Outstanding Rschr. in State of Ohio, Ohio Rsch. Coun. on Aging, Ohio Network Edn. Cons. in field of Aging, 1992; recipient Humanitarian award, Outstanding Contbns. to Nursing Profession, 1999, Acad. award, NIMH Geriatric Mental Health, Merit award, Cleve. Coun. Black Nurses, Gerontological Doris Schwartz Nursing Rsch. award, Gerontological Soc. Am., Belle Sherwin award, Cleve. Vis. Nurse Assn., Leadership award excellence in geriatric care, Midwest Alliance in Nursing, Disting. nurse-scholar lectr. award, Nat. Coun. Nursing Rsch., Nursing Educator award, New Cleve. Woman mag. Fellow: Gerontological Soc. Am., Am. Acad. Nursing; mem.: NIA, NIMH, NINR, Vets Adminstrn. (geriatric/gerontology adv. com.), Sigma Theta Tau Internat. (pres.-elect 1999). Office: 10900 Euclid Ave Cleveland OH 44106

WYKOFF, GARY LEE, writer; b. Erie, Pa., Apr. 27, 1953; s. Donald Lloyd Wykoff and Thelma Jean Anderson. BA, Pa. State U., State College, 1976. Founder, editor, pub., writer, artist Ind. Press, Erie, 1991—2006. Founder, educator, editor Word Factory, Erie. Contbr. articles to publs.; author: Sounding the Madness, 2005, Street #4, 2006, Hit Singles, 2007. Recipient Stairways Outstanding Cmty. Svc. award, Student Achievement award, Pa. State U. Mem.: Mensa, Pax Christyi. Avocation: poetry. Home: 1120 W 4th St Apt 1A Erie PA 16507-1093

WYLAM, MARK EDWARD, medical educator, researcher; b. Muncie, Ind., Sept. 15, 1958; s. William Bruce and Barbara Ann Wylam; m. Jill Hughel, July 5, 1980; children: Michelle Lynn, Michael John, Nicholas Edward. B., U. Notre Dame, Ind., 1980; MD, Georgetown U., Washington, DC, 1984. Asst. prof. medicine and pediat. U. Chgo., 1992—98; assoc. prof. medicine and pediat. Mayo Clinic Coll. of Medicine, Rochester, Minn., 1998—. Sect. chmn. critical care Mayo Clinic Coll. of Medicine, 2005—. Fellow: Am. Thoracic Soc. Achievements include research in effects of endotoxin on endothelial cell nitric oxide activity. Office: Mayo Clinic Coll Medicine 200 First St SW Rochester MN 55905 Office Phone: 507-284-2957. Business E-Mail: wylam.mark@mayo.edu.

WYLAN, BARBARA, artist; b. Providence, 1933; divorced; children: Andrea, Brock. BFA, R.I. Sch. of Design, Providence, 1955; studied with Donald Stoltenberg, Claude Croney, Murray Wentworth, Ruth Wynn, Charles Movalli, Dong Kingman. Tchr. watercolor workshops; juror various exhbns. One-woman shows include Sturgis Libr., Mass., 1974, 77, 83, Falmouth Artists' Guild, Mass., 1977, Skylight Gallery, Colo., 1979, Market Barn Gallery, Falmouth, Mass., 1981, 89, 91, Dom's Restaurant, Mass., 1981, Spectrum Am. Artists and Craftsmen, Brewster, Mass., 1983-88, 90, 92-93, 95, 2000, 03, Cape Cod Conservatory, Mass., 1984, 86, Cape Cod Mus. Nat. History, Brewster, Mass., 1987, Old Selectmens' Gallery, West Barnstable, Mass., 1995, Cahoon Mus. Am. Art, Cotuit, Mass., 1998; exhibited in group shows at Watercolor USA (Springfield award 1982), Nat. Soc. Painters in Casein and Acrylic 38th Ann., Nat. Arts club, NYC (Dr. David Soloway award 1991), Cahoon Mus. Art, Coteit, Mass., 1991, 97, 2003, 04, 06, Cape Cod Mus. Art, Dennis, Mass., 2002, 06; represented in permanent and pvt. collections Mobile (Ala.) Mus. Art, Cahoon Mus. Am. Art, Cotuit, Mass., Cape Cod Mus. of Art, Dennis, Mass., Springfield, Mo. Art Mus. Mem. Nat. Soc. Painters in Casein and Acrylic, Watercolor USA Honor Soc., New Eng. Watercolor Soc., Copley Soc. Art, and Twenty-one in Truro.

WYLAND, MARK, state official; b. Escondido, Calif. 1 child, Nicole. BA in Internat. Rels., Pomona Coll.; MA in Polit. sci., Columbia U. Co-owner family bus.; state assembly mem. Dist. 74 Calif. State Assembly, 2000—. Mem. bus. and professions com.; mem. edn. com.; mem. govtl. orgn. com.; vice-chair revenue and taxation com.; mem. VA com.; mem. Escondido Union Sch. Bd.; trustee Pomona Coll. Mem.: YMCA, Encinitis. Republican. Mailing: Rm 4130 PO Box 942849 Sacramento CA 94249 Home: 1800 Thibodo Rd Ste 300 Vista CA 92081-7515

WYLDE, KATHRYN S., business organization executive; BA, St. Olaf Coll., 1968. With Lutheran Med. Ctr., 1968—79; pres., CEO, N.Y.C. Housing Partnership, 1982—96; founding pres., CEO, N.Y.C. Investment Fund, 1996—; pres., CEO Partnership for N.Y.C., 2000—. Chair Luth. Med. Ctr., Bklyn.; mem. bus. adv. bd. CUNY; bd. dirs. NYC Econ. Devel. Corp., Biomed. Rsch. Alliance N.Y., NYC Leadership Acad., Manhattan Inst. Policy Rsch. Recipient HBSCNY Bus. Statesman award. Office: Partnership for NYC One Battery Pk Plz 5th Fl New York NY 10004 Business E-Mail: kwylde@nycp.org.

WYLE, FREDERICK S., lawyer; b. Berlin, May 9, 1928; came to U.S., 1939, naturalized, 1944; s. Norbert and Malwina (Mauer) W.; m. Katinka Franz, June 29, 1969; children: Susan Kim, Christopher Anthony, Katherine Anne. BA magna cum laude, Harvard U., 1951, LL.B., 1954. Bar: Mass. 1954, Calif. 1955, N.Y. 1958. Teaching fellow Harvard Law Sch., 1954-55; law clk. U.S. Dist. Ct., No. Dist. Calif., 1955-57; assoc. firm Paul, Weiss, Rifkind, Wharton & Garrison, NYC, 1957-58; pvt. practice San Francisco, 1958-62; spl. asst. def. rep. U.S. del. to NATO, Paris, 1962-63; mem. Policy Planning Council, Dept. State, Washington, 1963-65; dep. asst. sec. def. for European and NATO affairs Dept. Def., Washington, 1966-69; v.p. devel., gen. counsel Schroders, Inc., NYC, 1969-71, atty., cons., 1971-72; chief exec. officer Saturday Rev. Industries, Inc., San Francisco, 1972-76; individual practice law San Francisco, 1976—82. Internat. counsel to Fed. States Micronesia, 1974-82; cons. Rand Corp., Dept. Def., Nuclear Regulatory Commn. Contbr. to: Ency. Brit, 1972, also articles in profl. publs., newspapers. Trustee US Interest Bicycle Club Casino, 1996-99; trustee in bankruptcy Garden City, Inc., 2000-07; liquidating trustee Synthetic Industries, 2000—, Biosurg. Industries, 2000—; negotiator for Gov. of Calif. with Indian tribes re gambling,

2003. With AUS, 1946-47. Mem. Internat. Inst. Strategic Studies, Phi Beta Kappa. Office: 3 Embarcadero Ctr Fl 7 San Francisco CA 94111-4065 Personal E-mail: fwyle@earthlink.net.

WYLE, NOAH, actor; b. Hollywood, Calif., June 4, 1971; m. Tracy Warbin, 2000; children: Owen Strausser, Auden. Artistic prodr. The Blank Theatre Co., LA. Actor: (films) Crooked Hearts, 1991, A Few Good Men, 1992, Swing Kids, 1993, There Goes My Baby, 1994, The Myth of Fingerprints, 1997, Can't Stop Dancing, 1999, Scenes of the Crime, 2001, Enough, 2002, White Oleander, 2002, The Californians, 2004; (TV films) Blind Faith, 1990, Guinevere, 1994, Pirates of Silicon Valley, 1999, Fail Safe, 2000, The Librarian: Quest for the Spear, 2004; (TV series) ER, 1994—2005 (SAG award for outstanding performance by ensemble in drama series, 1998, 1999, TV Guide award for supporting actor of yr. in drama series, 2001); assoc. prodr. Myth of Fingerprints, 1997. Office: The Blank Theatre Co 1301 Lucile Ave Los Angeles CA 90026

WYLIE, GUY STEPHEN, psychologist, educator; s. Henry John and Shirley Elizabeth Wylie; m. Janiese Arends, May 17, 1981. BA, Bucknell U., Lewisburg, Pa., 1973; MS, Kans. State Coll. at Pittsburg, 1976; PhD in Counseling, Kans. State U., 1989. Cert. counselor Nat. Bd. for Cert. Counselors, Inc., 1983. Human svc. program coord./psychology instr. Western Nebr. C.C., Scottsbluff, Nebr., 1977—. Bd. mem. Panhandle Partnership for Health and Human Svcs., Panhandle of Nebraska, Nebr., 1997—2003; chmn. region i behavioral health adv. bd. Panhandle Mental Health Ctr., Scottsbluff, Nebr., 1985—; co-chairperson State of Nebr. Substance Abuse Adv. Bd., Lincoln, Nebr., 1994—96; bd. mem. Nebr. State Mental Health Adv. Bd., Lincoln, 1986—90. Pottery and sculpture. Pres. and dir. Scottsbluff-Gering Duplicate Bridge Club, Scottsbluff, Nebr., 1990—2007. Recipient Excellence in Tchg. award, WNCC Phi Theta Kappa, 1999—2000, Outstanding Faculty Mem. award, 1981—82, UNMC Coll. of Nursing Tchr. award, U. of Nebr. Med. Ctr. Coll. of Nursing, 1991. Mem.: Nat. Orgn. for Human Svcs., APA, ACA, Am. Contract Bridge League (unit bd. mem. 1990—2007, Bronze Life Master 2003), Elks (scholarship com. chmn. 1988—2007, Elk of the Yr. 2001-2002). Avocations: potter, bridge. Office: Western Nebraska Community College 1601 East 27th St Scottsbluff NE 69361 Home Phone: 308-635-0562; Office Phone: 308-635-6129. Office Fax: 308-635-6100. Personal E-mail: gwylie@wncc.net.

WYLIE, JAMES MALCOLM, adult education educator; b. NYC, Mar. 16, 1938; s. James M. and Nancy Beatrice (Worthy) Wylie. BS, Boston U., 1960. Columnist Mexico City Times, 1964; prof. Cooper Union Coll., NYC, 1986—. Author: The Lost Rebellion, 1971, The Homestead Grays, 1977, The Sign of Dawn, 1981; participant Spoleto Festival U.S.A., 2001. Office: 51 Astor Pl New York NY 10003-7132

WYLIE, PAUL RICHTER, JR., lawyer; b. Dec. 25, 1936; s. Paul Richter and Alice (Dredge) W.; m. Arlene Marie Klem, Mar. 6, 1982; children: Lynne Catherine, John Michael, Thomas Robert. BSChemE, Mont. State U., 1959; JD, Am. U., 1965. Bar: Utah 1978, Calif. 1970, U.S. Supreme Ct. 1971, Mont. 1990. Patent examiner U.S. Patent and Trademark Office, Washington, 1962-64; asst. gen. patent counsel Dart Industries Inc., LA, 1967-81; pvt. practice LA, 1981-86, Pacific Palisades, Calif., 1986—2006, Bozeman, Mont., 1990—. Author: The Irish General, 2007. Mem. ABA, AIChE, Am. Intellectual Property Law Assn., L.a. Intellectual Property Law Assn., Am. Chem. Soc., Licensing Execs. Soc., Tech. Transfer Soc. Home: 106 Silverwood Dr Bozeman MT 59715-9255 Office: 1805 W Dickerson St Ste 3 Bozeman MT 59715-4131

WYLLIE, STANLEY CLARKE, retired librarian; b. Clearwater, Fla., Nov. 19, 1935; s. Stanley Clarke and Euginia Lee (Tison) W.; m. Martha Ann Thomason, June 14, 1963; children: Stanley Clarke Jr., Susan Lynne DeHerder, Patricia Anne. BS in History and Social Scis., Fla. So. Coll., 1958; MS in Libr. Sci., Fla. State U., 1963. Tchr. civics and English Lakeland (Fla.) Jr. H.S., 1960-61; libr. I Tampa (Fla.) Pub. Libr., 1962; dir. Chestatee Reg. Libr. Sys., Gainesville, Ga., 1963-64; ind. and sci. ref. libr. Dayton and Montgomery County Pub. Libr., Dayton, Ohio, 1964-66, collection libr., 1967-73, social scis. and genealogy ref. libr., 1973-90; ret. Adv. bd. Sinclair C.C. Srs., recording sec., 2005—. Editor Mad River Currents newsletter, 1996-97, Bits, 1964-66. Corr. sec. Montgomery County Geneal. Soc., 1990-91, rec. sec., 1997-98; pres. Men's Rep. Club, Lakeland, 1960-61; mem. TV cable commn. City of Riverside, Ohio, 1997-98; presiding judge Riverside, Montgomery County Bd. Elections, 1992—; mem. exec. com. Montgomery County Rep. Party, 2004—, ctrl. com., 2004—; lay reader All Sts. Angelican Cath. Ch., 1978-2007, lay reader emeritus, 2007—. Recipient Edward M. Selby award Ohio Lodge Rsch., 1991-92, R. Marion Snyder award Ohio chpt. Rsch., 2005, Alumnus Disting. svc. award Fla. So. Coll., 1991; Knight York Cross of Honor, Ohio Priory #18, KYCH, 1983; named Ky. Col. Mem.: AARP (dist. coord. 1997—99), Dayton and Montgomery County Pub. Libr. Staff Assn. (past pres.), Mensa, Pub. Employee Retirees Inc. (chpt. pres. 1998, dist. 3 rep. 1999—2002), Civitan of Dayton (pres.-elect 2007—), Knights of Khorassan, Pres.'s Club of Dayton (pres. 2000—01), Fla. Geneal. Soc., Far Hills High Twelve Club, Odd Fellows (Noble Grand Steuben Rebekah Lodge 1997, chief patriarch Mad River Encampment # 16 1998—99, grand lodge rep. 1998—2000, Noble grand 1998—2001, Noble Grand Steuben Rebekah Lodge 2000, pres. S.W. Boosters Assn. 2001—04, pres. S.W. Promotional Assn. 2001—06, Marion lodge #18 Noble Grand 2003—04, grand patriarch Grand Encampment Ohio 2003—04, maj. occidental Canton patriarchs militant 2003—07, deptl. adjuntant 2007), Grand Monarch, El Aliman Sanctorum, Ancient Mystic Order of Samaritans, Toastmasters (area 3 gov. 1995, v.p. edn. 1997), Audubon Soc., Order of DeMolay (adv. bd. 3d dist. 1996—2002, Cross of Honor, Legion of Honor), Order Rainbow for Girls (Grand Cross of Color), Dayton High Twelve (pres. 1994), SAR (pres. Richard Montgomery chpt. 1990—91, Silver Good Citizenship medal 1997), Fla. State Geneal. Soc., United Ancient Order of Druids (noble arch Franklin Grove #2), United Ancient Order of Druids (grand grove midwest chpt. 2004—05, grand herald, grand dir. ceremonies nat. grand grove chpt.), Am. Fedn. State, County, Mcpl. Employees (v.p. 2004—05, 2006—, treas. 2007—), Lions (pres. 1996—97, zone chmn. 1996—98, Pres. Excellence award 1997), Jr. Order Mechanics (counsellor 2005—06), Grange, Marion Lodge, Orange Order (worthy master Gideons Hope 802 2002—03), Improved Order of Redmen (Sachem Lone Eagle Lodge 2004—05), Elks (Exalted ruler 2005—06), KP (chancellor comdr. Red Star Lodge 2000—01, Grand Lodge rep. 2002—, dist. dep. 2004—06), Shriners, Masons. Anglican Catholic. Avocations: reading, stamp collecting/philately. Home: 4960 Franlou Ave Dayton OH 45432-3120 Personal E-mail: scwyllie@msn.com. E-mail: stanleycwyllie@yahoo.com.

WYLLY, BARBARA BENTLEY, volunteer; b. Bala-Cynwyd, Pa., June 10, 1924; d. William Henry and Virginia (Barclay) Bentley; m. William Beck Wylly, Apr. 26, 1947; children: Virginia Wylly Johnson, Barbara Wylly Klausman, Thomas C. II. A, Briarcliff Jr. Coll., 1943. Pres. bd. dirs. Hillside Hosp. Inc., Atlanta, 1982, mem. adv. coun., 1982—; pres. Atlanta Symphony Assocs., 1975—76, mem. adv. bd., 1976—; chmn. bd. dirs. Ctr. Puppetry Arts, Atlanta, 1988—2004, mem. exec. com., 1988—. Bd. dirs. Mountain Conservation Trust, Atlanta Opera Guild, 1999—; mem. bd. sponsors Georgian Chamber Players, 2000—. Republican. Episcopalian. Avocations: walking, reading, music. Home: 940 Foxcroft Rd NW Atlanta GA 30327-2622 Office: Ctr Puppetry Arts 1404 Spring St NW Atlanta GA 30309-2820

WYLY, CHARLES JOSEPH, JR., entrepreneur; b. Lake Providence, La., Oct. 13, 1933; s. Charles Joseph and Flora (Evans) W.; m. Caroline Denmon; children: Martha, Charles Joseph III, Emily, Jennifer. BS, La. Tech. U., 1956. Sales rep. IBM Service Bur. Corp., 1956-64; v.p. Wyly Corp., Dallas, 1964-65, exec. v.p., 1965-69, pres., 1969-73, chmn. exec. com., 1973-76, dir., 1964-76; chmn. bd. Earth Resources Co., 1968-80. Vice chmn. bd. dirs. USACafes, Inc. (Bonanza Internat., Inc.), 1968-89, Sterling Software, Inc.; chmn. Tex. High-Speed Rail Authority, 1990-91, Maverick Capital, 1990-96; ret. chmn. Michaels Stores, Inc. Mem. Pres.'s Advisory Council on Mgmt. Improvement, 1970-73; vice-chmn. Devel. Council So. Methodist U. Found. Sci. and Engring., 1970-71; Mem. Republican Nat. Fin. Com., 1970—; Bd. dirs. Dallas County United Way Fund; pres. Dallas Theater Center., 1972-79. Mem. Am. Mgmt. Assn., Pi Kappa Alpha, Omicron Delta Kappa, Delta Sigma Pi, Beta Gamma Sigma. Clubs: City, Crescent, Park City, Brookhollow (Dallas). Office: Ste 1000 300 Crescent Ct Dallas TX 75201-7852

WYLY, SAMUEL E., retail executive; Founder Univ. Computing Co., 1963-79; co-owner, chmn. Bonanza Steakhouse, 1967-89; founder Datran, Inc., 1968; co-founder, mem. exec. com. Earth Resources Co., 1968-80; co-founder, chmn. Sterling Software, Inc., 1981—; chmn. Michaels Stores Inc., Irving, Tex., 1984—. Named one of Forbes' Richest Americans, 2006. Office: Michaels Stores Inc 8000 Bent Branch Dr Irving TX 75063

WYMAN, DAVID SWORD, retired historian, educator; b. Weymouth, Mass., Mar. 6, 1929; s. Hollis Judson and Ruth (Sword) W.; m. Mildred Louise Smith, Sept. 13, 1950; children: James Nayler, Teresa Carol. AB, Boston U., 1951; EdM, Plymouth State Coll., 1961; AM, Harvard U., 1962, PhD, 1966; DHL (hon.), Hebrew Union Coll. Jewish Inst. Religion, 1986, Yeshiva U., 1988. Various positions, 1951-57; tchr. pub. schs. Tilton, NH, 1957-60; tchr. pub. high sch. Penacook, NH, 1960-61; prof. history U. Mass., Amherst, 1966-91, Josiah DuBois prof. history, 1986-91, Josiah DuBois prof. emeritus, 1991—, chmn. Judaic Studies Program, 1977-78, 82-84, chmn. David S. Wyman Inst. for Holocaust Studies, 2003—. Acad. advisor Simon Wiesenthal Ctr., L.A., 1983—; nat. coun. Nat. Christian Leadership Conf. for Israel, 1986, numerous radio and TV appearances; historian advisor to films. Author: Paper Walls: America and the Refugee Crisis, 1938-41, 1968, The Abandonment of the Jews: America and the Holocaust, 1941-45, 1984 (Anisfield-Wolf award 1984, Stuart Bernath award 1984, Theodore Saloutos book award 1984, Present Tense Lit. award 1984, Boston Hadassah Myrtle Wreath award 1985, Nat. Jewish Book award 1985), new edit., 2007; co-author: A Race Against Death: Peter Bergson, America, and the Holocaust, 2002; editor: America and the Holocaust, 13 vols. documents, 1989-90, The World Reacts to the Holocaust, 1996; contbr. articles to profl. jours., chpts. to books. Recipient Chancellor's medal, U. Mass., 1986, Achievement award Isaac M. Wise Temple, Cin. 1986, Humanitarian award Bklyn. Holocaust Meml. Com., 1986, Herbert Katzki award Am. Jewish Joint Distbn. Com., 1999; elected to Boston U. Collegium Disting. Alumni, 1986; Woodrow Wilson fellow, 1961-62, 65-66; grantee Social Sci. Rsch. Coun., 1969-70, Am. Coun. Learned Socs., 1969-70, Charles Warren Ctr. at Harvard U., 1969-70. Mem. Soc. for Am. Baseball Rsch., N.H. Hist. Soc., Friends Hist. Assn., Phi Beta Kappa. Avocations: baseball, local history. Home: 61 Columbia Dr Amherst MA 01002-3105

WYMAN, JAMES VERNON, retired publishing executive; b. Brockton, Mass., Nov. 17, 1923; s. George Dewey and Christine Laverne (Skinner) W.; m. Viola Marie Bousquet, June 24, 1950; children: J. Vernon, Douglas Phillip, Carolyn Anne. Student, Northeastern U., Boston, 1946—48; BS in Journalism, Boston U., 1951. From staff to dep. exec. editor Providence Jour.-Bull., 1951-88, v.p., exec. editor, 1989-95, ret., 1995. Dean's adv. bd. Boston U. Coll. Comm. With AUS, 1942-46, PTO. Recipient Yankee Quill award, 1989, Disting. Alumni award Boston U. Coll. of Comm. Alumni Bd., 1996; named to RI Journalism Hall of Fame, 1999. Mem. New Eng. AP News Execs. Assn. (past pres.), AP Mng. Editors Assn., New Eng. Soc. Newspaper Editors, Acad. New Eng. Journalists (past dir.), New Eng. Newspaper Assn., Sigma Delta Chi (past pres. New Eng. chpt.), Roman Catholic. Home: 44 Starflower Ct Wakefield RI 02879-5475 Personal E-mail: foxtango44@cox.net.

WYMAN, RALPH MARK, multifamily office firm executive; b. Usti, Czechoslovakia, Feb. 7, 1926; arrived in U.S., 1941, naturalized, 1946; s. Hans and Stella (Parnas) Wyman; m. Lotte Ann Novak, Oct. 25, 1947; 1 child, Leslie Andrea Wyman Cooper. Student, Upper Can. Coll., 1942, Bucknell U., 1942-43; BSBA, NYU, 1945; postgrad., Columbia U., 1945-46. Asst. mgr. export dept. Liebermann Waelchi & Co., Inc., NYC, 1946-47; trainee White Weld Co., 1947-48; v.p. H. O. Canfield Co., 1948-65, vice chmn. bd. dirs., 1965-79, bd. dirs., 1953-79, Pantasote Inc., 1960-89, vice chmn. bd. dirs., 1967-89; mng. partner United Eagle Mgmt. Co., Eagle Mgmt. Co., 1960-95; pres. Veritas, Inc., 1960—2005; bd. dirs., chmn. Eagle Capital Internat. LLC, 1985—; bd. dirs., vice chmn. Affiliate Artists, Inc., 1971-88; chmn. AMA Eagle LLC, 2003—. Pres. Panwy Found.; bd. dirs. United Way Greenwich, Conn., 1980—86, Kids in Crisis, Greenwich, 1993—2001, sec., 1995—2001; trustee Greenwich Acad., 1963—71, chmn., 1968—70; elder, trustee Synod New Eng., 1974—76; trustee Princeton Theol. Sem., 1976—2001, vice chmn., 1997—2001, trustee emeritus, 2001—; trustee Ctr. Theol. Inquiry, 1997—. Mem.: Indian Harbor Yacht Club, Greenwich Country Club, Lambda Chi Alpha. Home: 34 Baldwin Farms N Greenwich CT 06831-3307 Office: # 4 Greenwich Office Park IV Greenwich CT 06831-5246 Home Phone: 203-869-1821; Office Phone: 203-661-6616. Business E-Mail: ralph.wyman@amaglobal.com.

WYMAN, RICHARD THOMAS, information technology manager, researcher; b. Wilmington, Del., June 4, 1951; s. William Harper and Marian Kathryn (Bode) W., Pa. State U., 1969-71, Def. Language Inst., 1974-75, Control Data Inst., Dallas, 1979. Enlisted U.S. Army, 1971, served to staff sgt., 1979; data ctr. mgr. thrift svcs. divsn. ADP Inc., Dallas, 1979-80; support mgr. Electronic Data Sys., Inc., Dallas, 1980-85, info. modeling analyst, 1985-90; pres. Strategic InfoSource, Plano, Tex., 1991-93; sr. cons. The SABRE Group, Ft. Worth, 1993-97; assoc. Perot Sys. Corp., Richardson, Tex., 1997-98; info. architect The Technical Resource Connection, Inc., Tampa, Fla., 1998—2005; enterprise architect Perot Sys. Corp., Plano, Tex., 2005—. Rep. 101st Airborne Divsn. Nat. Conf. Skill Maintenance, Ft. Meade, Md., 1977. Author: (spl. course) U.S. Army Intelligence, 1978-79. Co-chmn. sub-com. City Bond Referendum Com., Plano, 1990; mem. City of Plano Historic Landmark Com., 1993-97, vice chmn. 1996, chmn. 1996-97. Recipient Army Commendation medal, 1978, 79, Vol. Svc. award, Office of Mayor, Plano, 1990. Achievements include patents pending for computer system and process for aiding in an outsourcing environment. Home: 3608 Trailview Dr Plano TX 75074 Office: Perot Systems Corp 2300 W Plano Pkwy Plano TX 75075 Business E-Mail: richard.wyman@ps.net.

WYMAN, RICHARD VAUGHN, engineering educator, company executive; b. Painesville, Ohio, Feb. 22, 1927; s. Vaughn Ely and Melinda (Ward) W.; m. Anne Fenton, Dec. 27, 1947; 1 son, William Fenton. BS, Case Western Res. U., 1948; MS, U. Mich., 1949; PhD, U. Ariz., 1974. Registered profl. engr., Nev., Ariz.; registered geologist, Ariz., Calif.; lic. water right surveyor, Nev. Geologist N.J. Zinc Co., 1949, 52-53, Cerro de Pasco Corp., 1950-52; chief geologist Western Gold & Uranium, Inc., St. George, Utah, 1953-55, gen. supt., 1955-57, v.p., 1957-59; pres. Intermountain Exploration Co., Boulder City, Nev., 1959-93; tunnel supt. Reynolds Electric & Engring. Co., 1961-63, mining engr., 1965-67; asst. mgr. ops. Reynolds Electric and & Engring. Co., 1967-69; constrn. supt. engr. Sunshine Mining Co., 1963-65; lectr. U. Nev., Las Vegas, 1969-73, assoc. prof., 1973-80, dept. chmn., 1976-80, prof., 1980-92, prof. emeritus, 1992—, chmn. dept. civil and mech. engring., 1984-90, chmn. dept. civil and environ. engring., 1990-91. Mineral rep. Ariz. Strip Adv. Bd., 1976-80, U.S.B.L.M.; mem. peer rev. com. Nuclear Waste Site, Dept. Energy, Las Vegas, 1978-82; pres. Ariz. Juno Resources, Boulder City, 1980-87, v.p., 1990-97; pres. Wyman Engring. Cons., 1987—; cons. Corp. Andina de Fomento, Caracas, Venezuela, 1977-78; v.p. Comstock Gold, Inc., 1984-93; program evaluator Accreditation Bd. for Engring. and Tech., 1995-2001. Contbr. articles to profl. jours. Sec. Washington County Republican Party, Utah, 1958-60; del. Utah Rep. Conv., 1958-60; scoutmaster Boy Scouts Am., 1959-69; mem. citizens adv. com., tech. adv. com. Clark County Regional Flood Control Dist., 1998-2004. Served with USN, 1944-46. Recipient Order of Engr. award, 2000. Fellow ASCE (life; edn. divsn. 1990, local rep. nat. conv. Las Vegas), Soc. Econ. Geologists (life); mem. AIME/SME (life, chmn. So. Nev. sect. 1971-72, dir. 1968-2002, sec.-treas. 1974-92, chmn. Pacific S.W. Minerals Conf. 1972, gen. chmn. nat. conv. 1980, Disting. Mem. award 1989, Legion of Honor 1999), Assn. Engring. Geologists (dir. S.W. sect. 1989-91), Am. Inst. Minerals Appraisers, Am. Water Works Assn., Nev. Mining Assn. (assoc.), Northwest Mining Assn., Geological Soc. Nev., Assn. Ground Water Scientists and Engrs., Arctic Inst. N.Am. (life), Am. Soc. Engring. Edn., Soc. for History of Discoveries, Am. Philatelic Soc., SAR, Am. Legion, Sigma Xi (pres. Las Vegas sect. 1986-91), Phi Kappa Phi (pres. U. Nev. Las Vegas chpt. 100 1982-83), Sigma Gamma Epsilon, Tau Beta Pi. Congregationalist. Home: 610 Bryant Ct Boulder City NV 89005-3017 Office: Wyman Engring PO Box 60473 Boulder City NV 89006-0473 Home Phone: 702-293-4178; Office Phone: 702-293-1098.

WYNALDA, ERIC, professional soccer player; b. Fullerton, June 9, 1969; m. Amy. Student, San Diego State U. Forward FC Saarbruecken, Vfl Bochum Football Club, San Jose Clash, Calif., 1996-99; with U.S. Nat. Team, 1990—2002; forward Miami Fusion, 1999—2003; soccer analyst, World Cup commentator ESPN, 2006. Named to All-Copa Am. Team, 1995; named U.S. Soccer Male Athlete of Yr., 1996. Achievements include being all-time leading scorer on US World Cup Soccer team.

WYNAR, BOHDAN STEPHEN, retired librarian, writer, editor; b. Lviv, Ukraine, Sept. 7, 1926; came to U.S., 1950, naturalized, 1957; s. John I. and Euphrosina (Doryk) W.; children: Taras, Michael, Roxolana. Diplom-Volkswirt Econs., U. Munich, Germany, 1949, PhD, 1950; MA, U. Denver, 1958. Methods analyst, statistician Tramco Corp., Cleve., 1951-53; freelance journalist Soviet Econs., Cleve., 1954-56; adminstrv. asst. U. Denver Librs., 1958-59, head tech. svcs. div., 1959-62; assoc. prof. Sch. Librarianship, U. Denver, 1962-66; dir. div. libr. edn. State U. Coll., Geneseo, NY, 1966-67, dean Sch. Libr. Sci., prof., 1967-69; pres. Libraries Unlimited Inc., 1969—2002. Author: Soviet Light Industry, 1956, Economic Colonialism, 1958, Ukrainian Industry, 1964, Introduction to Bibliography and Reference Work, 4th edit, 1967, Introduction to Cataloging and Classification, 8th edit, 1992, Major Writings on Soviet Economy, 1966, Library Acquisitions, 2d edit, 1971, Research Methods in Library Science, 1971, Economic Thought in Kievan Rus', 1974; co-author: Comprehensive Bibliography of Cataloging and Classification, 2 vols., 1973, Ukraine: A Bibliographic Guide to English Language Publications, 1990, Independent Ukraine: A Bibliographic Guide to English Language Publications, 1989-99, 2000, Wynar's Introduction to Cataloging and Classification, 2000; editor Ukrainian Quar., 1953-58, Preliminary Checklist of Colorado Bibliography, 1963, Studies in Librarianship, 1963-66, Research Studies in Library Science, 1970—, Best Reference Books, 3d edit., 1985, 4th edit., 1992, Colorado Bibliography, 1980; gen. editor: American Reference Books Ann., 1969-2001; editor: ARBA Guide to Subject Encyclopedias and Dictionaries, 1985, ARBA Guide To Biographical Dictionaries, Reference Books in Paperback, An Annotated Guide, 2d edit., 1976, 3rd edit., 1991, Dictionary of Am. Library Biography, 1978, Ukraine-A Bibliographic Guide to English-Language Publications, 1990, 99, International Writings of Bohdan S. Wynar 1949-1992, 1993, Independent Ukraine, Bibliographic Guide, 2000, My Life-Memoirs-, 2003, Recommended Reference Books for Medium-Sized and Small Libraries, 1981-2001; co-editor, contbr. Ency. Ukraine, 1955—; editor Library Sci. Ann., 1984-90, 98, Libr. Info. Sci. Annual 1984-90, 98—. Bd. dirs., mem. exec. bd. ZAREVO, Inc. Mem. ALA (pres. Ukrainian Congress com. br., Denver 1976), Colo. Library Assn., N.Y. Library Assn., Am. Assn. Advancement Slavic Studies (pres. Ukrainian Research Found. 1976-90), AAUP, Ukranian Hist. Assn. (exec. bd.), Sevčenko Societe Scientifique (Paris), Ukrainian Acad. Arts and Scis. (N.Y.C.).

WYNDRUM, RALPH WILLIAM, JR., communications consultant; b. NYC, Apr. 20, 1937; s. Ralph W. and Virginia M. (Woolley) W.; m. Meta Schmidt, Apr. 23, 1960; children: Dorothy, Jeanne, Ralph, Joan BS, Columbia U., 1959, MSEE, 1960, MS Bus. Adminstrn., 1978; DSc, NYU, 1963. Mem. tech. staff Bell Labs., Murray Hill, NJ, 1963—65, supr. exploratory circuit design, 1965—69, head loop transmission tech. dept. Holmdel and Whippany, NJ, 1969—79, head advanced loop transmission sys. dept. Whippany, 1979—87, head internat. loop sys. dept., 1987, dir. sys. analysis ctr., 1987—90, dir. quality process ctr., 1990—92, dir. quality, engring., software and techs., 1993—94; v.p. AT&T World Svcs., 1994—, dir. process engr. ctr., 1995—96; tech. v.p. AT&T Labs., 1996—99, v.p. program mgmt., 1999—2000, exec. cons., 2000—; CEO Exec. Engring. Cons., 2000—; staff exec. SmartOrg, Inc., Menlo Park, Calif., 2001—04. Adj. prof. N.J. Inst. Tech., 1965, Rutgers U., 2004—, Stevens Inst. Tech., 1980—88, mem. industry adv. bd., 2000—; pres. The Innovation Inst., Washington, 2007—. Contbr. articles to profl. jours.; patentee in field Fellow: IEEE (bd. dirs. 1988—90, v.p. publs. 1990—91, bd. dirs. 2000—01, 2003—04, v.p. tech. activities 2003—04, exec. com. 2004, bd. dirs. 2006, Pres.'s Leadership award 1991); mem.: IEEE-USA (v.p. tech. policy 2002—03, bd. dirs. 2002—, pres. 2006, CEO, Innovation Inst. 2006—), IEEE Components, Packaging and Mfg. Tech. Soc. (pres. 1992—95), IEEE Comm. Soc. (chmn. conf. bd. 1981—87), Shrewsbury River Yacht Club, Sigma Xi, Beta Gamma Sigma, Eta Kappa Nu. Republican. Roman Catholic. Office: 35 Cooney Ter Fair Haven NJ 07704-3001 Office Phone: 732-219-0005. Personal E-mail: rwyndrum@comcast.net. Business E-Mail: r.wyndrum@ieee.com.

WYNER, YEHUDI, composer, pianist, conductor, educator; b. Calgary, Alta., Can., June 1, 1929; s. Lazar and Sarah Naomi (Shumiatcher) Weiner; m. Nancy Joan Braverman, Sept. 16, 1951 (div. 1967); children: Isaiah, Adam, Cassia; m. Susan M. Davenny, June 15, 1967. Diploma, Juilliard Sch. Music, 1946; AB, Yale U., 1950, B.Mus., 1951, M.Mus., 1953; MA, Harvard U., 1952. Vis. assoc. prof. Hofstra Coll., 1959; lectr. Queens Coll., NYC, 1959-60; instr. Hebrew Union Coll., NYC, 1957-59; music dir. Westchester Reform Temple, NYC, 1959-68; asst. prof. theory Yale U., 1963-69, assoc. prof. theory, 1969-77, chmn. composition dept., 1969-73; prof. music SUNY, Purchase, 1978-89, dean music, 1978-82. Faculty Tanglewood Music Ctr. (formerly Berkshire Music Ctr.), 1975-97; vis. prof. composition Cornell U., 1987, Ziskind vis. prof. composition Brandeis U., 1987-88, Walter Naumburg prof. composition, dir. contemporary ensemble, 1989-2005, prof. emeritus, 2005-; vis. prof. Harvard U., 1991-93, 96-98, 2003-04, 07—; Mary Duke Biddle Disting. composer Duke U., 1995; master composer Atlantic Ctr. for the Arts, 2005. Mus. dir. Turnau Opera Assn., 1961—64, New Haven Opera Soc., 1968—77, mem. Bach Aria group, 1968—, composer, condr. Tanglewood, 1961, composer-in-residence Santa Fe Chamber Music Festival, 1982, Am. Acad. Rome, 1991; composer-in-residence: Atlantic Ctr. Arts, 2005; composer: Easy Suite for Piano, 1949, Songs, 1950—2004, Two Chorale Preludes for Organ, 1951, Partita for piano, 1952, Dance Variations for wind octet, 1953, rev., 1959, Psalm 143, chorus, 1952, Sonata for piano, 1954, Concert Duo for violin and piano, 1955—57, Dedication Anthem, 1957, Serenade for Seven Instruments, 1958, Passover Offering for Flute, Clarinet, Cello and

Trombone, 1959, Three Informal Pieces for violin and piano, 1961, Friday Evening Service for Cantor, Chorus, Organ, 1963, orchestrated, 1992, (incidental music for play) The Old Glory, 1964, Torah Service with Instruments, 1966, Da Camera for piano and orch., 1967, Cadenza! for clarinet and harpsichord (or piano), 1969, De Novo for cello and small ensemble, 1971, Liturgical Fragments for the High Holidays, 1971, Three Short Fantasies for piano, 1963—71, Canto Cantabile for soprano and concert band, 1972, (music for play) The Mirror, 1972—73, Memorial Music for soprano and 3 flutes, 1971—73, Intermedio for soprano and string orchestra, 1974, Wedding Music, 1976, Dances of Atonement for violin and piano, 1976, Fragments from Antiquity: 5 songs for soprano and symphony orch., 1978, Romances for Piano Quartet, 1980, All the Rage for flute and piano, 1980, Processionals and Marches, 1979, 1980, Tanz and Maissele for clarinet, violin, cello, piano, 1981, On This Most Voluptuous Night for soprano and 7 instruments, 1982, Wind Quintet, 1984, String Quartet, 1985, Composition for Viola and piano, 1987, Toward the Center for piano, 1988, Sweet Consort for flute and piano, 1988, Leonardo Vincitore for 2 sopranos, string bass and piano, 1988, O To Be a Dragon, four songs for women's chorus and piano, 1989, Trapunto Junction for brass trio and percussion, 1991, Changing Time for small ensemble, 1991, New Fantasies for piano, 1991, Amadeus' Billiard for small ensemble, 1991, Il Cane Minore for 2 clarinets and bassoon, 1992, Wedding Dances: From the Notebook of Suzanne de Venné, 1993, Post Fantasies for piano, 1993, Prologue and Narrative for cello and orch., 1994, Song Cycle for soprano, baritone and piano: Restaurants, Wines-Bistros, Shrines, 1994, More Fantasies for piano, 1994—2002, Lyric Harmony for orch., 1995, Praise Ye the Lord for soprano and ensemble, 1996, Brandeis Sunday for string quartet, 1996, A Mad Tea Party for soprano, tenor, baritones, flute, violin, cello and piano, 1996, Epilogue for orch., 1996, Horntrio, 1997, Madrigal for string quartet, 1999, The Second Madrigal: Voices of Women for soprano and eleven players, 1999, Capriccio for oboe and string trio, 1999, Commedia for clarinet and piano, 2002, Tuscan Triptych: Echoes of Hannibal (string orch. version of String Quartet 1985), 2002, (piano concerto) Chiavi in mano, 2004 (Pulitzer Prize for music, 2006), (com-mns.) Yale U., 1958, Mich. U., 1959, Fromm Found., 1960, Koussevitzky Found. at Lib. Congress, 1960, 1991, Ford Found., 1971, Yale Band, Yale Repertory Theater, Cantilena Chamber Players, Aeolian Chamber Players, Santa Fe Chamber Music Festival, Collage of Boston, N.Y. Woodwind Quintet, Frank Taplin project, NEA Consortium, Boston Symphony Chamber Players, Atlantic Symphonietta, Carnegie Hall Am. Composers Orch., RNCM Mancester Internat. Cello Festival, Boston Symphony; pub. Associated Music Pub., Inc.; recs.: Bridge, New World, Albany, Naxos, Pro Arte & Columbia Records. Recipient Elise Stoeger prize, Lincoln Ctr. Chamber Music Soc., 1998; Rome Prize fellow, 1953—56, Alfred E. Hertz fellow, U. Calif., 1953—54, Guggenheim fellow, 1960, 1977, Rockefeller Found. fellow, Bellagio, 1998, Inst. Arts and Letters grant, 1961, grantee, NEA, 1976. Mem. Am. Music Ctr. (v.p.), Am. Acad. Arts and Letters (elected). Office: Music Dept Brandeis U Waltham MA 02454

WYNGAARDEN, JAMES BARNES, retired physician; b. East Grand Rapids, Mich., Oct. 19, 1924; s. Martin Jacob and Johanna (Kempers) W.; m. Ethel Vredevoogd, June 20, 1946 (div. 1977); children: Patricia Wyngaarden Fitzpatrick, Joanna Wyngaarden Gandy, Martha Wyngaarden Krauss, Lisa Wyngaarden, James Barnes Jr. Student, Calvin Coll., 1942—43, Western Mich. U., 1943—44; MD, U. Mich., 1948; DSc (hon.), U. Mich., Med. Coll. of Ohio, 1984, U. Ill., 1985, George Washington U., 1986, U. SC, West Mich. U., 1989, Duke U., 2006; PhD (hon.), Tel Aviv U., 1987. Diplomate Am. Bd. Internal Medicine. Intern Mass. Gen. Hosp., Boston, 1948-49, resident, 1949-51; vis. investigator Pub. Health Rsch. Inst., NYC, 1952-53; investigator NIH, USPHS, Bethesda, Md., 1953-56; asso. prof. medicine and biochemistry Duke U. Med. Sch., 1956-61, prof., 1961-65; vis. scientist Inst. Biologie-Physiochemique, Paris, 1963-64; prof., chmn. U. Pa. Med. Sch., 1965-67; physician-in-chief Med. Svc. Hosp. U. PA., Phila., 1965-67; Frederic M. Hanes prof., chmn. dept. medicine Duke U. Sch. of Medicine, Durham, NC, 1967-82; physician-in-chief Med. Svc. Duke U. Hosp., Durham, 1967-82; chief of staff Duke U. Hosp., Durham, 1981-82; dir. NIH, Bethesda, MD, 1982-89; assoc. dir. life scis. Office of Sci. and Tech. Policy, Exec. Office of Pres., The White House, 1989-90; dir. Human Genome Orgn., 1990-91; fgn. sec. NAS, 1990-94; prof. medicine, assoc. vice chancellor for health affairs Duke U., Durham, NC, 1990-94, ret., 1994; mem. staff VA, Durham County Hosps.; sr. assoc. dean internat. med. programs U. Pa., Phila., 1995-97. Cons. Office Sci. and Tech. Exec. Office of Pres., 1966-72; Mem. Pres.'s Sci. Adv. Com., 1972-73; mem. Pres.'s Com. for Nat. Medal of Sci., 1977-80; mem. adv. com. biology and medicine AEC, 1966-68; mem. bd. sci. counselors NIH, 1971-74; mem. adv. bd. Howard Hughes Med. Inst., 1969-82; mem. adv. council Life Ins. Med. Research Fund, 1967-70; adv. bd. Sci. Yr., 1977-81; vice-chmn. Com. on Study Nat. Needs for Biomed. and Behavioral Rsch. Personnel, NRC, 1977-81; bd. dirs. Idera Pharm., Genaera Pharm., Van Andel Rsch. Inst.; prin. Wash. Adv. Group, 1995-02. Author: (with W.N. Kelley) Gout and Hyperuricemia, 1976; mem. editorial bd. Jour. Biol. Chemistry, 1971-74, Arthritis and Rheumatism, 1959-66, Jour. Clin. Investigation, 1962-66, Ann. Internal Medicine, 1964-74, Medicine, 1963-90; editor: (with J.B. Stanbury, D.S. Fredrickson) The Metabolic Basis of Inherited Disease, 1960, 66, 72, 78, 83, (with O. Sperling and A. DeVries) Purine Metabolism in Man, 1974, (with L.H. Smith, Jr.) Cecil Textbook of Medicine, 16th edit., 1982, 19th edit., 1992. Bd. dirs. Royal Soc. Medicine Found., 1971-76, The Robert Wood Johnson Found. Clin. Scholar Program, 1973-78. Ensign USNR, 1943-46; sr. surgeon USPHS, 1951-56, rear adm. USPHS, 1982-90. Recipient Borden Undergrad. Research award, U. Mich., 1948, NC Gov.'s award for sci., 1974, Disting. Alumnus award We. Mich. U., 1984, Robert Williams award Assn. Profs. Medicine, 1985, Dalton scholar in medicine, Mass. Gen. Hosp., 1950, Richard Schweiker Excellence in Govt. award, 1985, Fedn. of Am. Socs. of Exptl. Biology Pub. Svc. award, 1989, Humanitarian award Nat. Orgn. for Rare Diseases, 1990; Royal Coll. Physicians fellow, 1984. Mem. Am. Rheumatism Assn., Am. Fedn. Clin. Rsch.; So. Soc. Clin. Investigation (pres. 1974, founder's medal 1978), ACP (John Phillips Meml. award 1980), Am. Soc. Clin. Investigation, AAAS, Am. Soc. Biol. Chemists, Assn. Am. Physicians (councillor 1973-77, pres. 1978, Kober medal 1991), Endocrine Soc., Nat. Acad. Scis., Royal Acad. Scis. Sweden, Am. Acad. Arts and Sci., Inst. Medicine, Sigma Xi. Clubs: Interurban Clinical (Balt.). Democrat. Presbyterian. Avocations: tennis, skiing, painting. Office Phone: 919-383-0921. Personal E-mail: jwyngaarden@nc.rr.com.

WYN-JONES, ALUN (WILLIAM WYN-JONES), software developer, mathematician; b. Tremadoc, Gwynedd, Wales, Aug. 15, 1946; arrived in U.S., 1976; s. Goronwy Wyn and Mai Jones; m. Jocelyn Ripley, July 29, 1977; 1 stepchild, Electra Truman BSc honors, U. Manchester, UK, 1968; MSc, U. Coll. London, 1970. Rsch. engr. Marconi-Elliott Computer Labs., Borehamwood, England, 1970—71; asst. tutor math. Poly. North London, 1971—72; programmer CRC Info. Sys., Ltd., London, 1972—76; mgr. devel. Warner Computer (now Warner Ins.), NYC, 1976—80; pres., owner, developer Wallsoft Sys., Inc., NYC, 1982—92, Integrity Sys. Corp., NYC, 1980—94. Cons. investment banking divsn. Goldman, Sachs & Co., N.Y.C., 1994-2000, FirstRain, Inc., N.Y.C., 2000-02, Thomson Fin., 2002-04, XL2Web, 2005—; invited spkr. profl. confs Author, co-author computer software Recipient Byte Award Distinction Byte Editors and Columnists, 1988, Readers Choice award Data Based Advisor Readers, 1990, 91 Mem. AAAS, Am. Math. Soc., Math. Assn. Am Achievements include development of template programming in automatic code generation. Home: 3241 Enola Rd Carlisle PA 17015 Personal E-mail: awynjones@comcast.net.

WYNN, ALBERT RUSSELL, congressman; b. Phila., Sept. 10, 1951; m. Jessie Jackson, Jan. 14, 1994 (sep.); 1 child, Gabrielle; m. Gaines Clore Wynn. BS, U. Pitts., 1973; student, Howard U.; JD, Georgetown U., 1977. Intern African Regional Affairs, U.S. State Dept., 1972-73; exec. dir. consumer protection divsn. Prince George's County, 1977-81; mem. Md. Ho. of Dels., 1983-86; lawyer Albert R. Wynn & Assocs., 1982-86; mem. Md. State Senate from Dist. 25, 1987-92, U.S. Congress from 4th Md. Dist., Washington, 1993—; dep. Dem. whip; mem. commerce com. Mem. banking & fin. svcs com., internat. rels. com., Patuxent Inst. reform task force, 1988-92, joint com. econ. devel. strategy, 1989-92; del. Dem. Nat. Conv. 1984, 88,96; pres. Metro. Washington coun. consumer agencies. Mem. NAACP legal assistance program, coalition on black affairs, voter registration, edn. coalition, gov.'s task force drunk & drugged driving; 1st vice chmn. legis. black caucus; chmn. Prince George's County black elected officials alliance. Recipient 100 Most Influential Black Americans, Ebony mag., 2006. Mem. J. Franklin Bourne Bar Assn., Kappa Alpha Psi (past pres.). Democrat. Baptist. Office: US Ho of Reps 434 Cannon House Ofc Bldg Washington DC 20515-0001 Office Phone: 202-225-8699. *

WYNN, BOBBYE FAYE, music educator; b. Morton, Miss., Nov. 11, 1950; d. Albert Wilson and Lucy Bob Winstead; m. Daniel Arthur Wynn; children: Daniel Ashley, Melody Joy. BS in Edn., Miss. Coll., 1977. Cert. tchr. Miss. Tchr. Powell Elem. Sch., Jackson, Miss., 1979, Woodville Heights Elem. Sch., Jackson, 1979—80; 6th grade tchr. West Elem. Sch., Natchez, Miss., 1981—84; tchr. West Primary Sch., Natchez, 1984—86, music tchr., 1990—; tchr. Northside Elem. Sch., Natchez, 1987—89; elem. music tchr. Northside Primary Sch., Natchez, Miss., 1989—90. Named Tchr. of Yr., Natchez-Adams Sch. Dist., 1997; recipient Cochran Disting. Arts Educator award, 2005; grantee Internat. Paper Co., 2000, Entergy, 2003—05. Mem.: Miss. Music Educators Assn. (dist. chmn. 1989—90, pres. elect 1990—91, pres. elem. divsn. 1991—92, past pres. elem. divsn. 1992—93, honor choir chmn. 1992—95, bd. mem. 2002—05), Music Educators Nat. Assn. Baptist. Office: West Primary Sch 161 Lewis Dr Natchez MS 39120 Home Phone: 601-445-2295; Office Phone: 601-445-2891. Fax: 601-445-3010. E-mail: cidom@natchez.k12.ms.us.

WYNN, BRENDA RENEAU, former trade association executive; b. Ft. Hood, Tex. d. Norman L. and Marjorie L. (Shaffer) Fallen; 1 child from previous marriage, Jennifer G. Houghton. Student, U. Okla. Dir. edn. Associated Builders and Contractors Western Okla., Oklahoma City, exec. dir.; commr. of labor OK, Okla. City, 1994—2006. Contbr. articles to trade publs. Mem. Okla. Soc. Execs., Okla. State C. of C., Oklahoma City C. of C. Achievements include 1st female exec. dir. of Assoc. Builders and Contractors Western Okla. Address: 200 W Wilshire Blvd Ste A-12 Oklahoma City OK 73116-7756 Office Phone: 405-528-1500. Business E-Mail: reneau_wynn@oklaosf.state.ok.us.

WYNN, JOHN CHARLES, clergyman, retired theology studies educator; b. Akron, Ohio, Apr. 11, 1920; s. John Francis and Martha Esther (Griffith) W.; m. Rachel Linnell, Aug. 27, 1943; children: Mark Edward, Martha Lois Borland, Maryan Kay Ainsworth. BA, Coll. Wooster, 1941; BD, Yale U., 1944; MA, Columbia U., 1963, EdD, 1965; DD, Davis and Elkins Coll., 1958. Ordained to ministry Presbyn. Ch. (U.S.A.), 1944. Student asst. pastor Trinity Luth. Ch., New Haven, 1943-44; assoc. minister First Presbyn. Ch., Evanston, Ill., 1944-47; pastor Presbyn. Ch. El Dorado, Kans., 1947-50; dir. family edn. and research United Presbyn. Bd. Christian Edn., Phila., 1950-59; prof. Colgate Rochester/Bexley Hall/Crozer Divinity Sch., 1959-85; prof. emeritus Colgate Rochester/Bexley Hall/Crozer Theol. Sem., 1985—; pvt. practice family therapy; vis. prof. U. Rochester, San Francisco Theol. Sem., St. Bernard's Sem., Wesley Theol. Sem., Hartford Theol. Found.; postdoctoral fellow Cornell U., 1973-74, St. John's U., 1980. Mem. summer faculty Union Theol. Sem., N.Y.C., San Francisco Theol. Sem.; del. study conf. World Coun. Chs., 1953, 57, 64, 65, 67, 75, 80; lectr. 5 univs., Republic of South Africa, 1968; chmn. com. on sexuality in human cmty. U.P. Ch.; vol. mem. chaplaincy staff Charlestown Care Ctr., Balt. Author: How Christian Parents Face Family Problems, 1955, Pastoral Ministry to Families, 1957, Families in the Church, A Protestant Survey, 1961, Christian Education for Liberation and Other Upsetting Ideas, 1977, Family Therapy in Pastoral Ministry, 1982 (rev. and expanded as Family Therapy in Pastoral Ministry: Counseling for the Nineties, 1991), The Family Therapist, 1987; Editor: Sermons on Marriage and Family Life, 1956, Sex, Family and Society in Theological Focus, 1966, Sexual Ethics and Christian Responsibility, 1970; Contbr. articles to mags. and religious jours. Bd. dir. Presbyn. Life, Planned Parenthood League Rochester and Monroe County, Family Service Rochester, Samaritan Pastoral Counseling Ctr. Fellow Am. Assn. Marriage and Family Therapy (approved supr.); mem. Religious Edn. Assn., Nat. Coun. Chs. of Christ in U.S.A. (chmn. com. family life 1957-60), Nat. Coun. Family Rels., Family Svc. Assn. Am., Rochester Coun. Chs. (dir.) Address: 717 Maiden Choice Ln Apt 523 Catonsville MD 21228-6173 E-mail: rlwynn1@verizon.net.

WYNN, JOHN THOMAS, retired academic administrator, farming executive, economic consultant, oil and gas producer; b. Corsicana, Tex., May 4, 1938; s. Sam Grady and Marjorie (Reese) W.; m. Sally Ruth Adams, Mar. 19, 1958 (div. 1975); children: Martha Maria, Catherine Clarissa, Lorraine Lemae; m. Myra Louise Alexander, Oct. 30, 1976; 1 child, John Thomas. AA, Wharton County Jr. Coll., 1960; BBA in Gen. Bus., Agrl. and Mech. Coll. Tex., 1962; MBA, Tex. A&M U., 1965; PhD in Higher Edn. Mgmt., U. So. Miss., 1973. Asst. registrar, then. instr. Tex. A&M U., College Station, 1962—67; exec. dean Delgado C.C., New Orleans, 1967—74, program dir., 1977—78; asst. exec. sec. So. Assn. Colls and Schs., Atlanta, 1974—77; pres. emeritus Williamsburg Tech. Coll., Kingstree, SC, 1978—94; pres., CEO econ. cons. M&W Farm & Ranch, Egypt, Tex., 1994—. Cons. AID, Dominican Republic, 1966; bd. govs. Coastal Edn. Consortium, Conway, S.C., 1982-90; mem. exec. com. pres.'s coun. S.C. Tech. Edn. Coll., Columbia, 1985-86. Vestryman St. Thomas Episc. Ch., College Station, 1962-67, St. George Episc. Ch., New Orleans, 1969-72; vestryman St. Thomas' Episc. Ch., Wharton, Tex., 1998-2001, 06—, sr. warden, 1999-2000; Rep. precinct 2 chmn., Wharton County, Tex., 1998-2000. Served as sgt. USAR, 1955-62. Recipient Order of the Palmetto S.C. Gen. Assembly, 1994; named Hon. Order of Ky. Cols.; col. Aide-de-Camp, La., col. Aide-de-Camp, Ala.; col. Aide-de-Camp, N.Mex. Mem. Future Farmers Assn. (hon.), S.C. Tech. Edn. Assn. (bd. dirs. 1985-88), Kingstree C. of C. (bd. dirs. 1981-84), Kiwanis, Masons (32 degree), Shriners (hon.), Phi Delta Kappa, Kappa Delta Pi. Avocations: chess, camping, music composition, reading. Home and Office: PO Box 307 Egypt TX 77436 Office Phone: 979-677-3572. Personal E-mail: johnwynn@agristar.net. Business E-Mail: egypttexas@agristar.net.

WYNN, KAREN, psychologist, educator, researcher; b. Austin, Tex., Dec. 18, 1962; d. Lucy Shombert and William "Buddy" Wynn; m. Paul Bloom; children: Max Bloom, Zachary Bloom. BA, McGill U., Montreal, Que., Can., 1985; PhD, MIT, 1990. Asst. prof. psychology, asst. rsch. scientist in cognitive sci. U. Ariz., Tucson, 1990—96, assoc. prof. psychology, assoc. rsch. scientist in cognitive sci., dir. developmental psychology program, 1996—99; prof. psychology and cognitive sci. Yale U., New Haven, 1999—. Vis. assoc. rsch scientist, med. rsch. coun. cognitive develop. unit U. Coll. London, 1997—98; lectr. in field. Contbr. articles to profl. jours. and newspapers; participated in radio interviews. Recipient James McKeen Cattell Found. Sabbatical award, 1997, Disting. Sci. award for Early Career Contbn. to Psychology, APA, 2000, Troland Rsch. award, NAS, 2001; grantee, NIH, NSF, 1987—90. Mem.: Cognition (editl. bd. mem.), Trends in Cognitive Scis. (adv. editl. bd. mem. 1998), Soc. for Rsch. in Child Devel., Internat. Soc. Infant Studies. Avocation: dressage. Office: 2 Hillhouse Ave Yale Univ Dept Psychology Box 208205 New Haven CT 06520-8205 Office Phone: 203-436-1406. Office Fax: 203-436-1915. Business E-Mail: karen.wynn@yale.edu.

WYNN, ROBERT E., electronics executive, retired military officer; b. Dallas, Jan. 31, 1942; s. Wendell W. and Thelma (Smart) W.; m. Lavenia K. Davis, Mar. 25, 1972; children: Leslie, Lauren. Bachelors degree, West Point Mil. Acad., 1964; MEE, U. Tenn., 1971. Commd. 2d lt. U.S. Army, 1964, advanced through grades to commdg. gen., 1990; chief comm. Ops. Divsn. 5th Signal Command, Heidelberg, Germany, 1979-81, chief of staff Worms, Germany, 1984-85; chief plans and programs, dep. chief staff Ops. and Plans DCS for OPS and PLANS, Washington, 1981-84; comdr. 2d Signal Brigade, Mannheim, Germany, 1986-88, U.S. Army Info. Systems Command/Tng. Doctrine Command, Ft. Monroe, Va., 1988-90; commdg. gen. 7th Signal Command, Ft. Ritchie, Md., 1990-92, U.S. Army Info. Systems Engrng. Command, Ft. Huachuca, Ariz., 1992-95; ret., 1995; mgr. C3 sys. Raytheon E-Systems Inc., Richardson, Tex., 1995-97; v.p. Harris Corp., Alexandria, Va., 1997—. Decorated Bronze Star, Legion of Merit, Silver Order of Mercury. Mem. Assn. U.S. Army Assn. Grads. (life), Armed Forces Comm. and Electronics Assn. (life, bd. dirs.), Sky Soldier (life, 173d airborne brigade), Signal Corps Regiment (life). Avocations: golf, tennis. Office: Harris Corp 1201 E Abingdon Dr Ste 300 Alexandria VA 22314-1487 Home: 355 Baytree Dr Melbourne FL 32940-2106

WYNN, STANFORD ALAN, lawyer; b. Milw., May 9, 1950; s. Sherburn and Marjory (Tarrant) Wynn. BBA, U. Wis., Milw., 1972; JD, Case Western Res. U., 1975; LLM in Taxation, U. Miami, 1976. Bar: Wis. 1975, Fla. 1976. Assoc. Walsh and Simon, Milw., 1976-78; dir. advanced planning Northwestern Mut. Life Ins. Co., Milw., 1978—. Author: The Insurance Counselor-Split Dollar Life Insurance, 1991; cons. editor: The Insurance Counselor-The Irrevocable Life Insurance Trust, 1995. Bd. dirs. Waukesha Estate Planning Coun., 1985—86. Office: Northwestern Mut Life Ins Co 720 E Wisconsin Ave Milwaukee WI 53202-4703

WYNN, STEVE ALAN (STEPHEN A. WYNN), hotel and gaming company executive; b. New Haven, Conn., Jan. 27, 1942; m. Elaine Paschal, 1963; children: Kevyn, Gillian. BA, U. Pa, 1963. Pres., CEO Best Brands, Inc., 1969-72; chmn., pres., CEO Mirage Resorts Inc. (formerly Golden Nugget Inc.), 1973—2000; mng. mem. Valvino Lamore, LLC, 2000—02; chmn., CEO Wynn Resorts Ltd., 2002—; owner Wynn Las Vegas Resort, 2005—, Wynn Macau, 2006—. Bd. trustees John F. Kennedy Ctr. for Performing Arts, 2006—. Named one of Top 200 Collectors, ARTnews Mag., 2004, 2006, 100 Most Influential People, Time Mag., 2006, Forbes' Richest Americans, 2003—, World's Richest People, Forbes mag., 2004—, People to Watch in 2007, Sunday Star Ledger. Jewish. Avocation: Collector of French Impressionism; Modern and Contemporary Art. Office: Wynn Resorts Ltd 3145 Las Vegas Blvd S Las Vegas NV 89109 *

WYNN, THOMAS JOSEPH, judge, educator; b. Chgo., Aug. 30, 1918; s. Phillip H. and Delia B (Madden) W.; m. Bernadette L. Lavelle, Apr. 17, 1948; children: Thomas Joseph, John P. AB, DePaul U., 1941, JD, 1942. Bar: Ill. 1942. Spl. investigator Phoenix & Murphy, Chgo., 1942; pvt. practice law Chgo., 1946-59; ptnr. Wynn & Ryan, Chgo., 1959-79; assoc. judge Cir. Ct. Cook County, Ill., 1979-83, judge chancery div. mechanic's lien sect. Ill., 1983-96, retired Ill., 1996. Lectr. bus. law Latin Am. Inst., Chgo., 1946-47; mem. faculty Coll. Commerce, DePaul U., Chgo., 1947-98, assoc. dean Evening div., 1957-73, prof., 1972-79, part-time faculty, 1979-83, adj. prof. bus. law, 1983-98; asst. atty. gen. Ill., 1957-58; bd. dirs., gen. counsel Suburbanite Bowl, Inc., 1958-79; gen. legal counsel Chgo. Consortium Colls. and Univs., GM Tool Corp.; pres., bd. dirs. Metroplex Leasing and Financing, Inc. Candidate for alderman Chgo. City Coun., 1951; candidate for judge Mcpl. Ct. Chgo., 1956; exec. sec., bd. dirs. Ill. Good Govt. Inst., 1958-79; mem. adv. bd. to dean Coll Law DePaul U., 1992—. Ensign-lt. (S.G.) USNR, 1942-46. Mem. Ill. Bar Assn., Chgo. Bar Assn. (mem. arbitration and alternative dispute resolution com., civil practice coms., mem. internat. law com., mem. judiciary com., mem. cir. ct. com.), Ill. Judges Assn. (com. mandatory arbitration alt. dispute resolution, com. pubs.), Assn. Univ. Evening Colls. (past chmn.), Am. Bus. Law Assn. (pres. 1972-73), Am. Real Estate and Urban Econs. Assn., Chgo. Area Evening Deans and Dirs. Assn., U.S. Adult Edn. Assn., Ill. Adult Edn. Assn., Am. Right-of-Way Assn. (advisor chmn., nat. ednl. com., 1963-64), St. Vincent DePaul Soc., DePaul Law Alumni Assn. (past pres.), Smithsonian Inst., Pres.'s Club, (DePaul U. 1986—), Blue Key, Gamma Eta Gamma, Beta Gamma Sigma, Delta Mu Delta. Home: 27592 W Cuba Rd Barrington IL 60010-2770

WYNN, WILL, mayor; b. Beaumont, Tex. m. Anne Elizabeth Wynn, 1992; 2 children. B in Environ. Design cum laude, Tex. A&M U., 1984. Founder CIVITAS Investments, Inc., 1997; mayor City of Austin, Tex., 2003—. With Hill Country Conservancy, St. David's Found., Women and their Work, KLRU, Blanton Mus., Austin Poetry Slam, Austin Film Soc.; chmn. Downtown Austin Alliance; dir. Children's Mus. and Heritage Soc. Named Austinite of Yr., Austin Under Forty; recipient Scenic Hero award, Scenic Austin. Mem.: Urban Land Inst. Avocations: listening to music, canoeing, bicycling. Mailing: PO Box 1088 Austin TX 78767 Office: Mcpl Bldg 124 West 8th St #103 Austin TX 78701 *

WYNNE, BRIAN JAMES, retired professional society administrator; b. NYC, Dec. 2, 1950; s. Bernard and Dolores (Doyle) W. Student, Institute des Sciences Politiques, Paris, 1970-71; BA, Coll. Holy Cross, 1972; MA, U. So. Calif., 1974. Staff Exec. Cons., Inc., McLean, Va., 1974-76; prin., 1976-78; exec. dir. Indsl. Designers Soc. Am., Washington, 1978-88. Cons. to various non-profit orgns.; dir. Worldesign 85, founder Worldesign Found. Mem. Am. Soc. Assn. Execs., Indsl. Designers Soc. Am. (hon.), Phi Sigma Iota. Home: 5200 N Ocean Blvd Apt 1004 Lauderdale By The Sea FL 33308-3019

WYNNE, JAMES J., research scientist; B in Physics, M in Physics, PhD in Physics, Harvard U. Mgr. Laser Physics and Chemistry Group IBM T.J. Watson Rsch. Ctr.; rsch. scientist IBM Watson Rsch. Ctr., 1971—. Contbr. articles, scientific papers. Co-recipient R.W. Wood prize, Optical Soc. Am., 2004; named one of Inventors of the Yr., Ea. NY Intellectual Property Law Assn., 2001; named to National Inventors Hall of Fame, 2002. Achievements include patents in field; development of Lasik eye surgery. Office: Watson Rsch Ctr 1101 Kithawan Rd Ste 134 Yorktown Heights NY 10598

WYNNE, JOHN CARLTON, lawyer; b. Oklahoma City, 1961; BS in Economics, magna cum laude, U. Okla., 1983, JD cum laude, 1986. Bar: Tex. 1986. Ptnr., Banking /Fin. Andrews Kurth LLP, Houston, chmn. pro bono com. Mem.: Fifth Cir. Bar Assn., State Bar Tex., Houston Bar Assn., Phi Beta Kappa. Office: Andrews Kurth LLP 600 Travis St Ste 4200 Houston TX 77002-3090 Office Phone: 713-220-4088. Office Fax: 713-238-7234. Business E-Mail: jwynne@andrewskurth.com.

WYNNE, JOHNNY CALVIN, dean, plant pathologist, researcher; b. Williamston, NC, May 17, 1943; s. James Harry and Rachel Loraine (Ayers) Wynne; m. Diane Louise Sawyer, 1961 (div. Feb. 1989); m. Jacqueline Crawford Creech, Nov. 25, 1989; children: Debbie Ann, Donna Carol, John Christopher, James Alexander. BS, N.C. State U., 1965, MS, 1968, PhD, 1974. Instr. crop sci. dept. N.C. State U., Raleigh, 1968-74, from asst. prof. to assoc. prof., 1974—83, prof., 1983-91, acting tchg. adminstr., 1987-89, head dept., 1989-91, assoc. dean, dir. N.C. agr. rsch. svc., 1992—2003, dean, exec. dir. Coll. Agr. & Life Scis., 2003—. Recipient Rsch. award, Nat. Peanut Coun., 1992. Fellow: AAAS, Am. Soc.

Agron, Crop Sci. Soc. Am., Am. Peanut Rsch. and Edn. Soc. (pres. 1990, Bailey award 1977); mem.: So. Assn. Exptl. Sta. Dirs. (chmn. 1994), Coun. Agrl. Sci. and Tech., Sigma Iota Rho. Office: NC State Univ PO Box 7643 Raleigh NC 27695-0001 E-mail: johnny_wynne@ncsu.edu.

WYNNE, MICHAEL WALTER, civilian military employee; b. Hillsborough County, Fla., Sept. 4, 1944; s. Edward P. and Dorothy T. Wynne; m. Barbara Ann Hill, July 23, 1966; children: Lisa, Collene, Karen, Laura. BS in Gen. Engring., U.S. Mil. Acad., 1966; MSEE, Air Force Inst. Tech., 1970; MBA in Fin., U. Colo., 1975. Commd. lt. USAF, 1966, advanced through grades to capt., 1969; project engr. Electronics Systems Div., Bedford, Mass., 1966-68; asst. prof. astronautics USAF Acad., Colorado Springs, 1970-73; sec.-treas., v.p. R.A.D. Inc., Colorado Springs, 1973-75; mgr. estimating dept. Ft. Worth div. Gen. Dynamics, 1975-78, mgr. pricing, corp. hdqrs., St. Louis, 1978-82; v.p. contracts, estimating Land Systems div. Gen. Dynamics, Sterling Heights, Mich., 1982-87, v.p. bus. devel., 1987-91; corp.v.p., gen. mgr. Space Systems Div. Gen. Dynamics, San Diego, 1991-92, pres., corp. v.p. Space Systems Div., 1992—94; v.p., gen. mgr. space launch systems Lockheed Martin Astronautics, 1994—97; sr. v.p. for internat. planning & bus. devel. Gen. Dynamics, 1997—99; prin. under sec. acquisition, tech. & logistics US Dept. Def., Washington, 2001—05, under sec. for acquisition, tech. & logistics, 2005, sec. Dept. of Air Force, 2005—. Fellow Nat. Contract Mgmt. Assn. (pres. Detroit chpt. 1983-86), Assn. U.S. Army (pres. Detroit chpt. 1987-89), Am. Def. Preparedness Assn. (pres. Mich. chpt. 1986-87). Roman Catholic. Avocations: golf, skiing. Office: USAF 1670 Air Force Pentagon Washington DC 20330 *

WYNNE, WILLIAM FRANCIS, lawyer; b. NYC, Sept. 21, 1952; s. William F. and Catherine Wynne; m. Barbara Brizzi Wynne; children: William, Andrew, Emily. AB in Econs., Rutgers U., 1973; JD, U. Pa., 1976. Bar: N.Y. 1977. From assoc. to ptnr. White & Case LLP, NYC, 1976—. Law chmn. mgmt. bd. White & Case LLP, NYC, 2004—. Office: White & Case LLP 1155 Avenue of the Americas New York NY 10036-2787 Business E-Mail: wwynne@whitecase.com.

WYNNE-EDWARDS, HUGH ROBERT, geologist, educator, entrepreneur; b. Montreal, Que., Can., Jan. 19, 1934; s. Vero Copner and Jeannie Campbell (Morris) W.-E.; married Janet Elizabeth McGregor; children from previous marriages: Robin Alexander, Katherine Elizabeth, Renée Elizabeth Lortie, Krista Smyth, Jeannie Elizabeth, Alexander Vernon. BSc with 1st class honors, U. Aberdeen, Scotland, 1955; MA, Queen's U., Kingston, Ont., Can., 1957, PhD, 1959; DSc (hon.), Meml. U., 1975. Registered profl. engr., B.C., 1995. With Geol. Survey Can., 1958-59; lectr. Queen's U., 1968-72, asst. prof., then assoc. prof., 1961-68, prof., head dept. geol. scis., 1968-72; prof., then Cominco prof., head dept. geol. scis. U. B.C., Vancouver, Canada, 1972-77; asst. sec. univ. br. Ministry of State for Sci. and Tech., Ottawa, Canada, 1977-79; sci. dir. Alcan Internat. Ltd., Montreal, 1979-80, v.p. R & D, chief sci. officer, 1980-89; CEO Moli Energy Ltd., Vancouver, 1989-90; pres. Terracy Inc., Vancouver, 1989—; sci. advisor Teck Corp., Vancouver, 1989-91; pres., CEO B.C. Rsch. Inc., Vancouver, 1993-97, exec. chmn., pres., 1997-2000. Chmn. Silvagen Inc., 1996-99; advisor Directorate Mining and Geology, Uttar Pradesh, India, 1964, Grenville project Que. Dept. Natural Resources, 1968-72; vis. prof. U. Aberdeen, 1965-66, U. Witwatersrand, Johannesburg, South Africa, 1972; UN cons., India, 1974; pres. SCITEC, 1977-78; mem. sci. adv. com. CBC, 1980-84; mem. Sci. Coun. Can., 1983-89, Nat. Adv. Bd. on Sci. and Tech., 1987-90 indsl. liaison com. UN Ctr. for Sci. and Tech. in Devel., 1982-84; vice chmn. tech. adv. group Bus. Coun. for Sustainable Devel., Geneva, 1991; mem. Nat. Biotech. Adv. Coun., 1995-98; chmn. Neurosci. Can. Partnership, 1999-2003, Azure Dynamics Inc., 2000-01; pres. Silvagen Holdings Inc., 1999-2000; bd. dirs. Welichem Biotech Inc., chmn., 2000-, bd. dirs. Photon Control Inc. Bd. dirs. Royal Victoria Hosp., Montreal, 1984-89. Decorated officer Order of Can., 1991; recipient Spendiarov prize 24th Internat. Geol. Congress, Montreal, 1972. Fellow Can. Acad. Engring., Royal Soc. Can., World Acad. Arts and Scis.; mem. Can. Rsch. Mgmt. Assn. (vice chmn. 1982-84, chmn. 1984-85, Assn. medal 1987), Univ. Club (Montreal). Mem. United Ch. Canada. Avocations: tennis, skiing, carpentry. Office: Terracy Inc 2030 27th St West Vancouver BC Canada V7V 4L4 Office Phone: 604-926-1191. Business E-Mail: hughwynn@terracy.com.

WYRICK, CHARLES LLOYD, JR., editor, writer; b. Greensboro, NC, May 5, 1939; s. Charles Lloyd and Edythe Ellen (Ellis) W.; m. Constance Michelle Hooper, Aug. 22, 1964; 1 child, Charles Lloyd, III; m. Katherine Harrison, Apr. 26, 1997; 1 child, Christopher Conrad. BA, Davidson Coll., NC, 1961; MFA, U. NC, 1967. Instr. Stephens Coll., Columbia, Mo., 1964-66; asst. head programs div. Va. Museum, Richmond, 1966-68; exec. dir. Assn. Preservation Va. Antiquities, Richmond, 1968-70; pres. Research & Restoration, Inc., Richmond, 1970-73; dir. Del. Art Mus., Wilmington, 1973-79, Gibbes Mus. Art, Charleston, S.C., 1980-86; pres. Wyrick & Co., Charleston, 1986—, Dixie Media, Inc., Charleston, 1989—; editl. dir. Gibbes Smith, Pub., 2005—; editor, pub. "Omnibus", 1989-94. Mem. Richmond Commn. Archt. Rev., 1969-72, New Castle County (Del.) Hist. Rev. Bd., 1975-88, also vice chmn.; mem. Bd. Archtl. Rev. City of Charleston, 1988-94, chmn., 1992-94; mem. Charleston Consortium on Higher Edn.; cons. in field. Author: "The 17th Street Market", 1972; contbr. articles to profl. jours. Bd. visitors Davison Coll., 1974-77; chmn. Econs. of Amenities City of Charleston, 1978; chmn. bd. dirs. S.C. Coastal Conservation League, 1989-94, Charleston Area Arts Coun., 1989-91, Friends of Charleston County Courthouse, 1989-94, Pub. Art Trust, 1988-90; adv. com. S.C. Dept. Natural Resources, 1992-2004. 1st lt. US Army, 1961—63. Recipient 1st award spl. column writing Va. Press Assn., 1973 Mem. Assn. Am. Pubs., Pubs. Assn. of South (bd. dirs. 1990-92, pres. 1991-92), S.C. Acad. Authors (bd. dirs. 1990-92), Carolina Yacht Club, Yeamans Hall Club. Office: PO Box 89 Charleston SC 29402-0089 Home: 3 Chisolm St Unit 201 Charleston SC 29401-1838 Office Phone: 843-795-9946.

WYRICK, JERMAINE ALBERT, lawyer; b. Detroit, Oct. 19, 1971; s. Albert and Loretta Wyrick. BA in Polit. Sci., U. Mich., 1993; JD, Wayne State U., 1996. Bar: Mich., US Dist. Ct. (ea. dist.) Mich., 1997, US Ct. Appeals (6th cir.), 1997, US Supreme Ct., 2001. Pvt. practice, Detroit, 1997—. Bd. dirs. Coalition Affirmative Action Preservation NAACP, Legal Redress, Detroit; lectr. in field. Bd. dirs. Coleman A. Young Scholarship Found.; with Angels Night Wayne County Juvenile Ct., 1998. Coun. on Legal Edu. Opportunity fellow, Ohio, 1993; recipient Achievement award Coleman A. Young Found., 1989-92, Disting. Grad. award, 1993, Pro Bono Project award FBA ea. dist. Mich., 1997, Fed Bar Assn. award, 1997, 2001, Trailblazer award Jordan Ednl. Svcs., 2004, Civil Rights and Edn. award U.S. Attys. Office, 2005, Five Under Ten award U. Mich. African Am. Alumni Coun. Mem. ABA, ATLA, Nat. Bar Assn. (region IV bd. dirs.), Mich. Trial Lawyers Assn., Wolverine Bar Assn.(bd. dirs.). Democrat. Mem. Hartford Meml. Bapt. Ch. Avocations: basketball, golf. Home: PO Box 44646 Detroit MI 48244 Office: Law Offices Jermaine A Wyrick P L C Ste 1610 615 Griswold Detroit MI 48226-3319 Home Phone: 313-850-6647; Office Phone: 313-964-8950. E-mail: attyjaw1@ameritech.net.

WYRSCH, JAMES ROBERT, lawyer, educator, writer; b. Springfield, Mo., Feb. 23, 1942; s. Louis Joseph and Jane Elizabeth (Welsh) W.; m. B. Darlene Wyrsch, Oct. 18, 1975; children: Scott, Keith, Mark, Brian, Marcia. BA, U. Notre Dame, Ind., 1963; JD, Georgetown U., Washington, DC, 1966; LLM, U. Mo., Kansas City, 1972. Bar: Mo. 1966, US Ct. Appeals (8th cir.) 1971, US Ct. Appeals (10th cir.) 1974, US Ct. Appeals (5th cir.) 1974, US Ct. Appeals (6th cir.) 1982, US Ct. Appeals (11th cir.) 1984, US Ct. Appeals (7th cir.) 1986, US Ct. Appeals (4th cir.) 1990, US Ct. Appeals (9th cir.) 1998, US Ct. Mil. Appeals 1978, US Tax Ct. 1983, US Supreme Ct. 1972. Assoc. Wyrsch, Hobbs & Mirakian P.C., Kansas City, Mo., 1970-71, of counsel, 1972-77, ptnr., 1978—, pres., shareholder, 1988—. Adj. prof. U. Mo., Kansas City, 1981—; mem. Mo. Supreme Ct. Procedures Com., 1983—; mem. adv. coun. legal assts. program U. Mo. at Kansas City, 1985-88; mem. cir. ct. adv. com. Jackson County, Mo., 1998—; mem. jud. selection com. U.S. Magistrate US Dist. Ct. Mo., 1985; mem. fed. practice com. US Dist. Ct. Mo., 1985-88; mem. subcom. to draft model criminal instrns.for dist. cts. of 8th cir., 1986—; bd. dirs. Kansas City Bar Found.; Mo. membership co-chmn., 2002-06; nat. membership vice chair US Supreme Ct. Hist. Soc., 2006-07, chair, 2007—. Contbr. articles to profl. jours.; co-author: Missouri Criminal Trial Practice, 1994. Capt. US Army, 1966—69. Recipient Joint Svcs. Commendation medal, 1969, U. Mo. Kansas City Svc. award Law Found., 1991-92, Lawyer of Yr. award Mo. Lawyers Weekly, 2001, Practitioner of Yr. award U. Mo. Kans. City Law Sch. Alumni Assn., 2002; named Best of the Bar, Kansas City Bus. Jour., 2002-06, Dean of Trial Bar award Kans. City Met. Bar Assn., 2002, Lifetime Achievement award Kansas City Bar Assn., 2004, Charles Shaw Trial Advocacy award Mo. Assn. Crminal Def. Lawyers, 2004; named a KC Legal Leader of Yr., Daily Record, 2005. Fellow: Mo. Bar Found., Am. Coll. Trial Lawyers (access to justice com. 2002—, Mo. State chair 2004—06), Am. Bar Found. (life); mem.: ATLA, ABA, US Supreme Ct. Hist. Soc. (nat. mem. chair. 2007—), Nat. Lawyers Assn. (chmn. criminal law com. 2003), Coll. Master Advs. and Barristers (sr. counsel), Mo. Assn. Criminal Def. Attys. (dir. 1978, sec. 1982), Nat. Assn. Criminal Def. Attys., Am. Bd. Trial Advs. (adv.), Kansas City Met. Bar Assn. (chmn. anti-trust com. 1981, chmn. bus. tort, anti-trust, franchise com. 1998), Mo. Bar Assn. (vice chmn. criminal law com. 1978—79), Am. Arbitration Assn. (panel arbitrators 1976—2000), Country Club of Blue Springs, Kansas City Club, Phi Delta Phi. Democrat. Roman Catholic. Home: 1501 NE Sunny Creek Ln Blue Springs MO 64014-2044 Office: Wyrsch Hobbs & Mirakian PC 1000 Walnut St Ste 1600 Kansas City MO 64106-2140 Office Phone: 816-221-0080. Business E-Mail: jimwyrsch@whmlaw.net.

WYRSCH, MARTHA B., lawyer, energy executive; b. Laramie, Wyo., 1958; m. Gerry Wyrsch; 2 children. BA in Lit., U. Wyo., 1980; JD, George Washington U., 1986; graduate, Harvard Bus. Sch. Advanced Mgmt. Program, 2002. Legis. asst. to Sen. Alan K. Simpson of Wyo., 1980—83; assoc. Davis, Graham & Stubbs, 1986—91; v.p., gen. counsel and sec. KN Energy Inc. (now Kinder Morgan, Inc.), 1991—99; sr. v.p., gen. counsel, sec., Duke Energy Field Svcs. Duke Energy Corp., Charlotte, NC, 1999—2001, sr. v.p., gen. counsel, energy transmission and distbn., 2001—03, sr. v.p., legal affairs, 2003—04, group v.p., gen. counsel, sec., 2004—05; pres., CEO Duke Energy Gas Transmission, Houston, 2005—. Bd. advisors George Washington Law Sch.; bd. dirs. Inst. and Sch. for Environ. and Natural Resources, U. Wyo. Mem.: ABA (vice chair, pub. utility, comm. and transp. law sect.), Interstate Natural Gas Assn. Am., Edison Elec. Inst., Am. Gas Assn., Am. Corp. Counsel Assn., Colo. Bar Assn. Office: Duke Energy Gas Transmission 5400 Westheimer Ct Houston TX 77056 *

WYRTKI, KLAUS, oceanography educator; b. Tarnowitz, Germany, Feb. 7, 1925; came to U.S., 1961; s. Wilhelm and Margarete (Pacharzina) W.; m. Helga Kocher, June 6, 1954 (div. 1970); children: Undine, Oliver; m. Erika Maassen. PhD magna cum laude, U. Kiel, Germany, 1950. With German Hydrographic Inst., Hamburg, 1950-51; German Rsch. Coun. postdoctoral rsch. fellow U. Kiel, 1951-54; head Inst. Marine Rsch., Djakarta, Indonesia, 1954-57; sr. rsch. officer, then prin. rsch. officer div. fisheries and oceanography Commonwealth Sci. and Indsl. Rsch. Orgn., Sydney, Australia, 1958-61; assoc. rsch. oceanographer, then rsch. oceanographer Scripps Instn. Oceanography, U. Calif., 1961-64; prof. oceanography U. Hawaii, Honolulu, 1964—, prof. emeritus, 1993. Chmn. North Pacific Expt., 1974-80, com. on climate changes and ocean internat. Assn. Phys. Scis. of the Oceans; mem. Spl. Com. on Ocean Rsch. Working Group on Prediction of El Nino, Sci. Working Group on Topography Expt., panel on climate and global change NOAA. Author: El Nino—The Dynamic Response of the Equatorial Pacific Ocean to Atmospheric Forcing, 1975; editor: Oceanographic Atlas of the International Indian Ocean Expedition, 1971; mem. editl. bd. Jour. Phys. Oceanography, 1971-79. Recipient Excellence in Rsch. award U. Hawaii, 1980, Rosenstiel award U. Miami, 1981, Prince Albert I medal Internat. Assn. Phys. Scis. Ocean, 2003, Alexander Agassiz medal NAS, 2004 Fellow Am. Geophys. Union (Maurice Ewing medal 1989), Am. Meteorol. Soc. (Harald Ulrick Sverdrup Gold medal 1991), Deutsche Meteorologische Gesellschaft (Albert Defant medal 1992), Am. Acad. Arts & Scis. E-mail: wyrtki@aloha.net. *

WYSCHOGROD, EDITH, philosophy educator; b. NYC; d. Morris and Selma Shurer; m. Michael Wyschogrod, Mar. 6, 1955; children: Daniel, Tamar. AB, Hunter Coll., 1957; PhD, Columbia U., 1970. Prof. philosophy Queens Coll., Flushing, NY, 1967-92; J. Newton Rayzor prof. philosophy and religious thought Rice U., Houston, 1992—2003, emerita, 2003—. Vis. prof. philosophy Villanova U. 2003; Croghan vis. prof. religion Williams Coll. 2004. Author: Emmanuel Levinas: The Problem of Ethical Metaphysics, 1974, 2d edit., 2000, Spirit in Ashes, 1985, Saints and Postmodernism, 1990, An Ethics of Remembering: History, Heterology and the Nameless Others; co-editor: Lacan and Theological Discourse, 1989, The Enigma of Gift and Sacrifice, 2002, The Ethical, 2003, Crossover Queries: Dwelling with Negatives, Embodying Philosophy's Others, 2006. Nat. Humanities Ctr. fellow, 1981, Woodrow Wilson Ctr. fellow, 1987-88, Guggenheim fellow, 1995-96. Fellow Am. Acad. Arts and Scis.; mem. Am. Acad. Religion (pres. 1992-93). Home: Apt 9C 522 West End Ave New York NY 10024 E-mail: stedith@rice.edu.

WYSE, JASON LAMAR, music educator, director; b. Bellefonaine, Ohio, Sept. 20, 1978; s. LaMar LaRay and Karon Eve Wyse; m. Julie Marie Unkefer, Nov. 6, 2004. MusB, Grove City Coll., Pa., 2001; MusM, The Ohio State U., Columbus, 2003. Dir. bands Punxsutawney (Pa.) Area H.S., 2003—; asst. dir. bands Brecksville-Broadview Heights H.S., Broadview Heights, Ohio, 2006—. Mem.: Ohio Music Educators Assn.

WYSE, ROGER EARL, physiologist, department chairman; b. Wauseon, Ohio, Apr. 22, 1943; BS in Agr., Ohio State U., 1965; MS, Mich. State U., 1967, PhD in Crop Sci., 1969. Fellow Mich. State U., 1969-70; plant physiologist Agr. Rsch. Svc. USDA, 1970-86; dean of rsch. Cook Coll. Rutgers U., 1986-92; dean, dir. Coll. Agr. and Life Sci. U. Wis., Madison, 1992-98; mng. dir. Burrill & Co., San Francisco, 1998—. Recipient Arthur Flemming award, 1982. Fellow Am. Soc. Agronomy, Crop Sci. Soc. Am.; mem. AAAS, Am. Soc. Plant Physiol. Office: Burrill & Co 1 Embarcadero Ctr Ste 2700 San Francisco CA 94111-3744

WYSK, RICHARD A., engineering educator, researcher; b. Holyoke, Mass., Sept. 22, 1948; s. Stanley and Sophia Dorothy (Mazurowski) W.; m. Caryl Lynne Ray, Jan. 18, 1969; children: Richard Patrick, Rebecca Jeanne, Robyn Caryl. BS in Indsl. Engring. & Ops. Rsch., U. Mass., 1972, MS in Indsl. Engring. & Ops. Rsch., 1973; PhD in Indsl. Engring., Purdue U., 1977. Prodn. control mgr. Gen. Electric, Erie, Pa., 1973-75; rsch. analyst Caterpillar Tractor, Inc., Peoria, Ill., 1975-76; assoc. prof. Va. Polytechnic Inst., Blacksburg, 1977-83; prof. Pa. State U., State College, 1983-90, William Lionhard chair in engring., 1995—; dir. Inst. Mfg. Systems, College Station, 1990-94; Royce Wisenbaker chair Tex. A&M U., College Station, 1990-94; William Lionhard chair in engring. William Leonhard chair in engring., State College, 1995—. Co-author: A Study Guide for the P.E. in I.E., 1982, An Intro to Automated Proc. Plan., 1985, Modern Manufacturing Process Engineering, 1989, Computer-aided Manufacturing, 1991 (Book-of-the-Yr. award Inst. Indsl. Engrs. 1992, E. Eugene Merchant Mfg. Textbook award Soc. Mfg. Engrs. 1992). Pks. commr. Montgomery County Pks. & Recreation, Blacksburg, 1982-83; adv. mem. Inst. Systems Rsch. U. Md., 1991-95. With U.S. Army, 1969-71, Vietnam. Decorated Army Commendation medal with 2 oak leaf clusters. Fellow Inst. Indsl. Engrs. (chpt. pres. 1990—, Region III Award of Excellence 1982, D. Baker award 1993), Soc. Mfg. Engrs. (sr., Outstanding Young Mfg. Engr. 1981), Engring. Accreditation Commn. (commr. 1990-92), Sigma Xi. Avocations: racquetball, basketball. Office: Pa State U 310 Leonard Bldg University Park PA 16802 Home Phone: 814-466-7046; Office Phone: 814-863-1001. Business E-Mail: rwysk@psu.edu.

WYSOCKI, CHARLES JOSEPH, neuroscientist; b. Utica, NY, May 4, 1947; s. Charles C. and Helen T. (Szczesna) W.; m. Linda Lorraine Moore, Dec. 21, 1968; children: Tracy Lynn, Theresa Marie, Alexandra Charlene. BA, SUNY, Oswego, 1973; MS, Fla. State U., 1976, PhD in Psychobiology, 1978. Grass Found. fellow The Jackson Lab., Bar Harbor, Maine, 1973; postdoctoral tng. Monell Chem. Senses Ctr., Phila., 1978-81, asst. mem., 1980-83, assoc. mem., 1983-90, mem., 1990--; adj. prof. anatomy U. Pa., Phila., 1985--. Sci. advisor Olfactory Rsch. Fund, N.Y.C., 1989—; chmn. of tng. Monell Chem. Senses Ctr., Phila., 1989—; project officer, coord. U.S. Russia Sci. Esch. Program in the Chem. Senses, Washington, 1990—. Editor: Chemical Senses Vol. 3: Genetics of Perception and Communication, 1991; contbr. editor: (newsletter) The Armoa-Chology Rev., 1986--; contbr. articles to profl. jours. With U.S. Army, 1968-70, Vietnam. NIH grantee 1985--; recipient Kenji Nakanishi Rsch. award Takasago Internat. Corp., 1988. Mem. Assn. for Chemoreception Scis. (membership chmn. 1989-91), N.Y. Acad. Scis., Soc. Neurosci., Internat. Brain Rsch. Orgn., Sigma Xi (Best Student Rsch. award 1976). Office: Monell Chem Senses Ctr 3500 Market St Philadelphia PA 19104-3308 Office Phone: 215-898-6666. Office Fax: 215-898-2084. Business E-Mail: wysocki@monell.org. *

WYSOCKI, SUSAN, women's health nurse practitioner; Grad., Boston Coll. Sch. Nursing; cert. as nurse practitioner, NJ Coll. Medicine and Dentistry and Planned Parenthood Fedn. Am. Cert. Women's Health nurse practitioner Nat. Certification Corp. Pres., CEO Nat. Assn. Nurse Practitioners in Women's Health. Spkr. and opinion leader in the field of women's health; mem. adv. bd., spkr. bur. Ortho-McNeil, Berlex, Pfizer (Parke-Davis), Wyeth, Pharmacia, Organon; mem. adv. bd. 3M Corp., Solvay, Novavax, Merck, Barr. Editor: Clinical Challenges in Women's Health: A Handbook for Nurse Practitioners, Women's Health Care: A Practical Journal for Nurse Practitioners, Conversations in Couseling; contbg. editor (and Washington DC bur. chief): Nurse Practitioner World News; mem. editl. bd. Am. Journal of Nurse Practitioners, Dialogues in Contraception, Contraceptive Tech. Update, Medscape Nurses, mem. adv. panel mem. Contraception Online; contbr. articles to nursing publications. Recipient Lifetime Achievement award, 2000, award for polit. activism, Nurse Practitioner Jour., 2003. Mem.: Am. Coll. Nurse Practitioners (founding pres., Cutting Edge award 2003), Nat. Alliance Nurse Practitioners (chair), Am. Acad. Nurse Practitioners (charter fellow). Office: Nat Assn Nurse Practitioners in Women's Health 505 C St NE Washington DC 20002 Office Phone: 202-543-9693. Office Fax: 202-543-9858.

WYSONG, EARL EDWARD, sociologist, educator; b. Kokomo, Ind., June 25, 1944; s. Earl Wysong and June Maxine Talbert; m. Janet Sue Myers, Aug. 30, 1966; children: Kristi Lynn, Heather Sue. BS in Edn., Ind. U., 1968; MA in Sociology, Ball State U., Muncie, Ind., 1971; PhD in Sociology, Purdue U., 1990. Cert. secondary edn. Ind. Dept. Pub. Instrn., 1968. Asst. prof. sociology Ind. U., Kokomo, 1991—95, assoc. prof. sociology, 1995—98, prof. sociology, 1998—. Author: (books) High Risk and High Stakes: Health Professionals, Politics, and Policy, 1992; co-author: The New Class Society, 1999, The New Class Society: Goodbye American Dream, 2d edit., 2003; mem. editl. bd.: Jour. Contemporary Sociology, 2001—05; contbr. chapters to books, articles to profl. jours. Doctoral Dissertation Improvement grantee, NSF, 1990, Faculty Fellowship Rsch. grantee, Ind. U. Kokomo, 1992. Mem.: Am. Fedn. Tchrs., Am. Sociol. Assn., Ind. Acad. Social Scis. (dir. sociology and anthropology 1993—96, exec. v.p. 1997—98, pres. 1998—99), North Ctrl. Sociol. Assn., Midwest Sociol. Soc., Soc. for the Study Social Problems (program co-chair 1999—2000). Home: 2850 East Southway Blvd Kokomo IN 46902 Office: Ind Univ Kokomo 2300 South Washington St Kokomo IN 46904-9003 Office Phone: 765-455-9394. Business E-Mail: ewysong@iuk.edu.

WYSS, DAVID ALEN, diversified financial services company executive; b. Ft. Wayne, Ind., Nov. 14, 1944; s. Alen G. and Anne W. (Winicker) W.; m. Grace H. Hawes, June 11, 1966; children: Sarah J., Alen D. BS, MIT, 1966; PhD, Harvard U., 1971. Economist Fed. Res., Washington, 1970-74, sr. economist, 1975-77; advisor Bank Eng., London, 1974-75; sr. staff economist Council Econ. Advisers, Washington, 1977-79; v.p. DRI Ltd., London, 1979-83; rsch. dir. DRI/McGraw Hill, Lexington, Mass., 1983-97; chief economist Std. & Poor's/DRI, Lexington, 1997-99, Std. & Poor's, NYC, 1999—. Bd. dirs. NY Collegium. Contbr. numerous articles to profl. jours. Mem. Am. Econ. Assn., Nat. Assn. Bus. Office: Standard & Poors 55 Water St Ste 39th Fl New York NY 10041-0003 Home Phone: 646-840-0343; Office Phone: 212-438-4952. Business E-Mail: david_wyss@sandp.com.

WYSS, JOHN BENEDICT, lawyer; b. Evanston, Ill., Nov. 23, 1947; s. Walther Erwin and Caroline Nettie (Benedict) W.; m. Joanne P. Comstock, Oct. 22, 1994; children: John Christian, Kirsten Dunlop. BS in Physics summa cum laude, Stanford U., 1969; JD, Yale U., 1972. Bar: Calif. 1972, D.C. 1974, U.S. Supreme Ct. 1976. Trial atty. antitrust div. U.S. Dept. Justice, Washington, 1972-74; assoc. Kirkland & Ellis, Washington, 1974-78, ptnr., 1978-83, Wiley Rein LLP, Washington, 1983—. Mem. ABA, Phi Beta Kappa. Office: Wiley Rein LLP 1776 K St NW Washington DC 20006-2304 Office Phone: 202-719-7038. Business E-Mail: jwyss@wileyrein.com.

WYSZYNSKI, DIEGO FEDERICO, epidemiologist, educator; b. Buenos Aires, May 19, 1967; m. Caroline Panhuysen, Sept. 7, 1963; children: Shoshana Basia, Sara Yentl, Daniel Yehoshua, Rena Michal. MD, U. Buenos Aires Sch. of Medicine, Argentina, 1991; MHS, Johns Hopkins Sch. of Pub. Health, 1994, PhD, 1996. MD Min. of Health, Argentina, 1991. Asst. prof. medicine and epidemiology Boston U. Sch. Medicine, 1999—. Editor: (reference books) Cleft Lip and Palate: From Origin to Treatment, Neural Tube Defects: From Origin to Treatment; genetics sect. editor: Cleft Palata-Craniofacial Jour. Recipient NIH FARE fellow, NIH, 2000, Rsch. award, Cleft Palate Found., 2002. Achievements include research in the etiology of birth defects; patent pending for use of genetic markers for the identification of metabolic syndrome. Office: Boston Univ Sch of Medicine 715 Albany Str L-320 Boston MA 02118 E-mail: dfw@bu.edu.

WYZNER, EUGENIUSZ, diplomat; s. Henryk and Janina Wyzner; m. Elzbieta Laudanska, June 27, 1961; 1 child, Jaroslaw. LLM, U. Warsaw, 1954; postgrad., Hague Acad. Internat. Law, Netherlands, 1958. Mem. staff Ministry Fgn. Affairs, 1956—71, dir. legal dept., 1971—73; ambassador to Geneva, 1973-78; dir. dept. internat. orgns. Ministry Fgn. Affairs, Warsaw, 1978-81; chmn. UN Disarmament Commn., 1982; undersec. gen. conf. services and spl. assignments UN, NYC, 1982-92, undersec. gen. pub. info., 1992-94; dep. min. for fgn. affairs Republic of Poland, Warsaw, 1994-95, 1st dep. min. for fgn. affairs, sec. of state, 1996-97; permanent rep. amb. to UN NYC, 1998-99; vice-chmn. Internat. Civil Svc. Commn., NYC, 1999—. Vice-chmn. preparatory com. Internat. Conf. on Human Rights, chmn. com. on periodic reports on human rights, 1965-68; chmn. sub-com. of UN Com. on Peaceful Uses of Outer Space, 1967-82; pres.

Rev. Conf. of Parties to Treaty on Prohibition of Nuclear Weapons, 1977; mem. Polish del. of UN Gen. Assembly, UN Programme Planing and Budgeting Bd., 1984-93; chmn. UN Publs. Bd., 1982-93; chmn. com. for 2000 review conf. of the parties to the treaty on the non-proliferation of nuclear weapons, 1998-99. Decorated Cross of Polonia Restituta Polish Council of State, 1969, 77, Golden Cross of Merit, 1964, Comdr.'s Cross with a star Order of Polonia Restituta, 1996, Comdr. of the Legion d'Honneur, Pres. of France and Grand Comdr.'s Cross of the Order of the Phoenix, Pres. of Greece, 1996. Mem. Internat. Inst. Outer Space Law (bd. dirs. 1974—, Citation 1977), Internat. Peace Acad. (bd. dirs. 1983-91), Internat. Congress Inst. (bd. dirs. 1987-90), Internat. Congress Acad. (mem. senate 1990-95). Office: Internat Civil Svc Commn Rm 1050 2 United Nations Plz New York NY 10017-4403 Business E-Mail: wyzner@un.org.

XI, CECILIA Q., research scientist; PhD, Northwestern U., 2003. Cert. NASPExAM Testamur Heart Rhythm Soc. Contbr. articles to profl. jours. Finalist Rosanna Degani Young Investigators Competition, 2002; recipient 2d prize poster contest, 2003, Jos. Willems Young Investigator presenter, Jour. Electrocardiology, 2003, Spl. Performance award, 2005; fellow, Northwestern U., 2000; Ou Yangzao scholar, Nanjing U., 1994, People scholar, 1995, Wu Jianxiong and Yuan Jialiu scholar, 1995, Bao Gang scholar, 1996. Achievements include patents pending for method to monitor progression of atrial fibrillation; methods and devices for determining exercise compliance diagnostics; research in new features for modern pacemakers and ICDs; development of remote monitoring system for patients with heart diseases; design of protocols to evaluate new features/products; invention of methods and improvement for existing algorithms for pacemakers and ICDs; publications in cardiovascular research. Office Phone: 408-522-6619.

XI, LEI, medical educator; b. Chengdu, China, Dec. 4, 1962; arrived in US, 1990; s. Ning Xi and Meiling Zhao; m. Thuy Nguyen Ho; children: Lillian Shee, Luke Shee. MD, Chengdu Inst. of Phys. Culture, China, 1983; postgrad., U. of Geneva, Switzerland, 1990; postdoctoral, U. of Wis., Madison, 1992, Va. Commonwealth U., Richmond, 2000. Team physician Chinese Nat. Athletes Tng. Ctr., Beijing, 1983—87; instr. of medicine Va. Commonwealth U., Richmond, 2000—05, asst. prof. of medicine, 2005—. Contbr. articles to biomed. jours.; reviewer: sci. jours. Mem.: Am. Heart Assn. (Scientist Devel. grant 2005—08), Am. Physiol. Soc. (Rsch. Career Enhancement award 2002). Office: Va Commonwealth Univ Rm 7042 1101 E Marshall St Richmond VA 23298-0281 Office Phone: 804-475-9589. Business E-Mail: lxi@vcu.edu.

XIA, GUOHUA, scientist, psychiatrist, psychologist; married; 1 child, M-Y. MB in Clinical Medicine, Beijing Med. U., 1986; PhD in Psychology, U. Nebr., Lincoln, 2002. Lic. Calif., Ohio. Physician The 2nd Hosp. of Hebei Med. U., Shijiazhuang, China, 1986—93; tchr. ZhongGuanCun Software Coll., Beijing, 1993—95; counselor Counseling and Psychotherapy Ctr. Peking U., Beijing, 1993—95; database analyst, info. specialist and grad. asst. U. Nebr., Lincoln, 1995—2001; physician U. Texas, Houston, 2001—02, U. Tex. Southwestern Med. Ctr., Dallas, 2002—05; asst. prof. Case Western Reserve U., 2005—, head, Transcranial Magnetic Stimulation program, 2005—. Sec. Hebei Mental Health Orgn., Shijiazhuang, 1990—93. Contbr. articles to profl. jours., chapters to books. Recipient Young Investigator award, Nat. Alliance for Rsch. on Schizophrenia and Depression, 2005, NCDEU New Investigator award, NIMH, 2006. Mem.: Am. Psychology Assn., Psychol. Assn. China, Chinese Med. Assn. (Excellent Acad. Paper award 1993), Chinese Mental Health Assn., Am. Psychiatry Assn., Kappa Omicron Nu.

XIA, JIDING, chemical engineering educator; b. Jiangyin, Jiangsu, China, Mar. 23, 1921; arrived in US, 1993; s. Baogen Xia; m. Ming Yu, Oct. 1, 1958; children: Wei, Men. BS, Zhejiang U., Hangzhou, China, 1945, MS, 1948. Assoc. prof. Haijiang U., Fujian, China, 1949-50, Nanjing Normal U., China, 1953-54; dir. tchg. and rsch. divsn. Southeast U., China, 1954-58; assoc. prof. and dir. teaching/rsch. divsn. So. Yangtze U. (formerly Wuxi U. Light Industry), China, 1958-85, prof. chem. engring., 1985-92; rsch. chemist U. Wis., Madison, 1995-96. Vis. prof. Wayne State U., Detroit, 1993-95; mem. expert group synthetic detergents and fatty acids, Ministry of Light Industry China, 1979-86; vis. prof. The VI Univ. of Paris, 1986;, evaluation com. acad. degree Authorized U., 1980-84, Jiangsu Light Industry Sr. Engrs., 1982-92; project evaluator China Nat. Natural Sci. Found. Surface Chemistry, 1985—; cons. Chemithon Co., Seattle, 1990-93, Aging Toilet Soap Factory, China, 1991—, Tianjin Rsch. Inst. Interface and Colloid Scis., 1993, Stepan Co., Chgo., 1994, Proctor & Gamble Co., Cin., 1994-95, Vista Chem. Co., Houston, 1994—; mem. adv. com. Internat. Symposium on Surfactants in Solution, 1993. Author: Synthetic Detergents, 1976, Chemistry and Technology of Surfactants and Detergents, 1997; author and editor: Protein-Based Surfactants, 2001, Gemini Surfactants-Synthesis Interface Behavior and Applications, 2004; editor: Composite Soaps, 1987; translator: Comprehensive Refining of Sunflower Seed Oil, 1956, Chemistry of Oil and Fats, 1958, Manufacture of Detergents, 1986; mem. editl. bd. Jour. Surfactant Industry, 1982-90, Jour. Petro-Finechemicals, 1982, Chinese Ency. LIght Industry, 1987-91; contbr. more than 120 articles to acad. jours. Recipient award Ministry of Petroleum Industry for EOR Project, 1992, Outstanding Contbn. to Chinese Higher Edn. award State Coun., 1992, Ministry of Light Industry for rsch. on composite soaps, 1983, Remarkable Achievement in Sci. and Tech. Invention and Innovation, UN, 1994; Excellent Advanced Sci. Rsch. fellow Wuxi, 1990, 93. Mem. China Assn. Surfactants and Detergent Industry (hon. dir. 1992, standing dir. 1983-92), Jiangsu Soc. of Daily Chem. Industry (chmn. 1978-85), Am. Chem. Soc. Home: 500 E Irving Ave Apt 620 Madison Heights MI 48071-1957 Office Phone: 248-577-1453. Personal E-mail: xiajiding@aol.com.

XIA, KAIMING, mechanical engineer; s. Lanying Xia; m. Xiaojuan Hu; children: Jiajie, Claire, Andrew. PhD, U. Ill., Chgo., 2003. Bridge engr. Shanghai Rlwy. Bur., Bengbu, China, 1992—94; lectr. SW Jiaotong U., Chengdu, China, 1997—98; postdoctoral fellow U. Ill., Chgo., 2003—04; sr. rsch. and devel. engr. Caterpillar, Peoria, Ill., 2004—. Contbr. research (Fellowship of 7th US Nat. Congress on Compuational Mechanics, 2003). Mem.: Am. Acad. Mechanics, US Assn. Computational Mechanics (fellow 7th nat. conf. 2003). Achievements include development of two kinds of three dimensional infinite elements for fluid flow in porous media; a superelasticity material model for shape memory alloys; derived second derivative of shape function in finite elements; multiscale/stabilized finite element for solid mechanics; a medium resoultion blade/soil model for earhmoving system; a foam type viscoplasticity model for asphalt compaction. Office: TC-E 852 Machine Rsch Caterpilar PO Box 1875 Peoria IL 61656-1875 Home Phone: 309-689-0768; Office Phone: 309-578-4145.

XIA, YUNKAI, engineer; PhD, W.Va. U., Morgantown, 2004. Engr. China U. Mining & Tech., Beijing, 1991—94; project mgr. Golden State Grp., Beijing, 1994—99; sr. process engr. Taggart, LLC, Pitts., 2004—. Contbr. articles to profl. jours. Mem.: Sigma Xi. Achievements include patents for the fluidized-bed reactor for fine natural flake graphite purification by chlorination, process and equipment, SiC wiskers and particles separation technology; development of computational fluid dynamics application in mineral processing; research in fine coal gravity separation process design; design of coal preparation plant process simulation, flowsheet design, engineering, plant start-up and testing. Office: Taggart LLC 2090 Greentree Rd Pittsburgh PA PA 15 Office Phone: 412-253-8062. Personal E-mail: ykxia@yahoo.com.

XIA, YUSEN, education educator; s. Tianying and Aiying (Liu) Xia. BA, Xi'Dian U., Xi'an, China, 1996; MA, Chinese Acad. Sci., Beijing, 1999; PhD, U. Tex., Austin, 2004. Asst. prof. Ga. State U., Atlanta, 2004—. Recipient Tex. Excellence Tchg. award, U. Tex., Austin, 2003. Mem.: Inst. Ops. Rsch. Mgmt. Sci.

XIANG, HUI, biochemist, researcher; b. Wanxian, Sichuan, China, Sept. 6, 1968; arrived in U.S., 2001; s. Jun Xiang and Yuhua Wen; m. Yu Zhu, Dec. 25, 1995; 1 child, Angela. BSc, Sichuan U., Chengdu, China, 1989; MSc, Dalhousie U., Halifax, Can., 1993. Quality insp. Shuyang Pharm. Co., Chengdu, 1989—92; tech. officer Biotech. Rsch. Inst. Nat. Rsch. Coun., Montreal, Canada, 1995—99; assoc. scientist DSM Biologics, Montreal, 1999—2001; staff scientist DuPont Pharm., Wilmington, Del., 2001, Bristol-Myers Squibb, Wilmington, 2001—02; sr. scientist Allergan, Inc., Irvine, Calif., 2002—. Contbr. articles to profl. jours. F.C. Harrison fellow, McGill U., Montreal, 1994—95, grad. fellow, Dalhousie U., 1992—93. Mem.: Am. Soc. Quality (cert. quality auditor), Regulatory Affairs Profl. Soc. (cert. regulatory affairs), Am. Chem. Soc., European Fedn. Biotechnology. Home Phone: 949-251-8952; Office Phone: 714-246-5330. E-mail: hxgmtlqc@yahoo.com.

XIAO, ZHOUSHENG, pharmacologist, bone biologist; permanent resident, 2005; s. Yunfei Xiao; m. Changhong Jiang, Feb. 2, 1992; 1 child, Zheng. MD, Nanhua U., Hengyang, China, 1987; PhD in Molecular Pharmacology, Ctrl. S. Univ., Changsha, China, 2003. Postdoctoral staff human metabolic sect. NIEHS, 1995—96; rsch. assoc. nephrology and medicine Duke U. Med. Ctr., 1996—99; rsch. asst. prof. nephrology and medicine Duke U. Med. Ctr., 2001—04; assoc. prof. pharmacology Clin. Pharmacology Inst. Ctrl. S. Univ., Changsha, 1999—2001, prof. pharmacology Clin. Pharmacology Inst., 2003—07; rsch. asst. prof. Kidney Inst./Internal Medicine U. Kans. Med. Ctr., Kansas City, 2004—. Vice-dir. molecular pharmacology lab., Xiangya Sch. Medicine Ctrl. S. Univ., Changsha, 1999—2001, PhD mentor Clin. Pharmacology Inst., 2003—07. Recipient Young Investigator award, Nature Sci. Found. Commn. Hunan, 1996, Excellent Young Tchr. & Rschr. award, Edn. Commn. China, 1999, 1st Prize of Sci. & Tech. Progress award, U. Commn. China, 2001, Young Investigator award of 25th ASBMR, Am. Soc. Bone & Mineral Rsch., 2003, 3d Prize of Sci. & Tech. Progress award, State Edn. Commn. China, 1999; Rsch. grant for Runx2 isoforms function in osteoblastic differentiation of Bone marrow derived mesenchymal stem cells, 1999, Rsch. grant for phytoestrogens regulating osteoblastic differentiation in bone marrow-derived mesenchymal stem cells, Nat. Nature Sci. Found. China, 2001, Rsch. grant. for differential function & regulation of Runx2 isoforms, NIH & Nat. Inst. Arthritis & Musculoskeletal & Skin Diseases, 2003, Rsch. grant for P&F Project, NIH & Nat. Inst. Diabetes, 2006. Mem.: Chinese Pharmacological Soc., Am. Soc. Bone & Mineral Rsch. Achievements include discovery of how phytoestrogens regulate osteoblastic differentiation in bone marrow-derived mesenchymal stem cells; how runx2 isoforms play a different role in bone formation; how primary cilia and polycystin -1 have an important role in bone development and bone formation; a new mutation of CYP2C19 gene in Chinese bai population. Home: 12761 Mackey St Overland Park KS 66213 Office: Kidney Inst/Univ Kans Med Ctr 3901 Rainbow Blvd Kansas City KS 66160 Office Fax: 913-588-9251. Business E-Mail: zxiao@kumc.edu.

XIE, CHI, transportation engineer, researcher; b. Leng Shui Jiang, China, Oct. 16, 1975; arrived in US, 2000; s. Yisheng Xie and Ping Yang; m. Li Sheng, June 27, 2004. B in Engring., Tsinghua U., Beijing, China, 1998; M in Engring., Nat. U. Singapore, 2000; MS, U. Mass., Amerst, 2005; PhD, Cornell U., Ithaca, NY, 2007. Rsch. scholar Nat. U. Singapore, 1998—2000; rsch. asst. U. Mass., Amherst, 2001—03; tchg. asst. Cornell U., Ithaca, 2003—07; vis. scholar U. Tex., Austin, 2007—. Contbr. articles to profl. jours. Recipient Student Competition winner, Mil. Ops. Rsch. Soc., 2004, John E. Perry Tchg. award, Cornell U., 2005; grantee, 2004, 2007; scholar, Nat. U. Singapore, 1998. Mem.: ASCE, IEEE, Inst. Transp. Engrs., Transp. Rsch. Bd., Inst. Ops. Rsch. and Mgmt. Scis. Achievements include for the first time, developed and published an evacuation network optimization model integrating roadway contraflow and intersection control. Avocations: swimming, skiing, golf. Office: 55 Railroad Row White River Junction VT 05001

XIE, HUIKAI, engineering educator; s. Chengmai Xie and Fuqing Du; m. Yuxiao Tong, Sept. 19, 1968; children: Yutong, Brian. PhD, Carnegie Mellon U., Pitts., 2002. Dir. engring. Akustica, Inc., Pitts., 2002—02; asst. prof. U. Fla., Gainesville, 2002—. Tech. cons. Robert Bosch Corp., Palo Alto, Calif., 2000—02; presenter and com. mem. tech. confs. Contbr. chapters to books (Best paper of the yr., 1996). Recipient Excellent Tchg. award, Tsinghua U., 1996; grantee, NSF, 2004, 2006. Mem.: IEEE (v.p. Gainesville chpt. 2005—). Achievements include patents for vertical displacement device; method of fabricating microstructures and devices made therefrom. Office: University of Florida 221 Benton Hall Gainesville FL 32611 Home Phone: 352-331-9589; Office Phone: 352-846-0441. Business E-Mail: hkx@ufl.edu.

XIE, JEFF ZHENGQUAN, lawyer; b. Hubei, China, Mar. 18, 1963; m. Bin Wu; 1 child, Maylene. JD, Ga. State U., 1999. Bar: Ga. 2000, U.S. Dist. Ct. (no. dist.) Ga. 2000, U.S. Ct. Internat. Trade 2001. Asst. counsel Ga. Dept. Corrections, Atlanta, 1999—2000; mng. mem. Xie Law Offices, LLC, Norcross, Ga., 2000—. Mem.: ABA, Am. Immigration Lawyers Assn. Office: Xie Law Offices Llc 1770 Indian Trail Lilburn Rd Ste 450 Norcross GA 30093-2676 Office Phone: 678-421-9668. Business E-Mail: jeffxie@uslawnet.com.

XIE, KEN, software company executive; b. China; BS, MS Computer Sci., Tsinghua U.; MEE, U. Stanford. Founder, CEO, pres. NetScreen, 1997—2004, Stanford Infosystems, Fortinet Inc., 2000—. Mng. partner Jedi Venture; security architect Healtheon. Named a Technology Pioneer, World Econ. Forum, 2006; recipient Top 15 Technology Innovator, Computer Reseller News magazine, 2004, Northern California Entrepreneur of the Year, Ernst & Young, 2006. Office: Fortinet Inc 1090 Kifer Rd Sunnyvale CA 94086 Office Phone: +1-408-235-7700. Office Fax: +1-408-235-7737.

XIE, RUI-HUA, physicist, researcher; b. Ganxian, Jiangxi, China, Sept. 21, 1969; arrived in Can., 1997; s. Xiangan Xie and Yuying Yang; m. Qin Rao, Dec. 28, 1995; children: Jianing, Calvin. BS, Wuhan U., 1991, M of Engring., 1993; PhD, Nanjing U., 1996. Rsch. asst. Wuhan (China) U., 1991-93, Nanjing (China) U., 1993-96; rschr. CCAST, Beijing, 1996-97, U. Toronto, Ont., Can., 1997-98; Alexander von Humboldt fellow Max-Planck Inst. Ströngsforschung, Göttingen, Germany, 1998-2000; tchg., rsch. asst. Queen's U., Ont., 2000—01; guest rschr. NIST, Gaithersburg, Md., 2001—04; rsch. scientist Tex. A&M U., Coll. Sta., 2004—. Contbr. articles to profl. jours.; mem. editl. bd. Jour. Computational and Theoretical Nanusci. Mem.: Am. Chem. Soc., Am. Phys. Soc., Sigma Xi. Avocation: stamp collecting/philately. Office: Tex A&M U Inst Quantum Studies College Station TX 77843-4242 Home: 4-415 College Main College Station TX 77840 Personal E-mail: johnxie2006@hotmail.com. Business E-Mail: rhxie04@tamu.edu.

XIE, XIAOLIANG SUNNEY, chemist, educator; arrived in U.S., 1985; PhD in Chemistry, U. Calif., 1990. Postdoctoral fellow U. Chgo., 1990—92; sr. rsch. scientist Environ. Molecular Scis. Lab. Pacific N.W. Nat. Lab., Richland, Wash., 1992—95, chief scientist Environ. Molecular Scis. Lab., 1995—98; prof. chemistry and chem. biology Harvard U., Cambridge, Mass., 1999—. Recipient Coblentz award, Coblentz Soc., 1996, Raymond and Beverly Sackler Prize in Phys. Scis., Israel, 2003, Pioneer award, NIH, 2004. Mem.: Biophysical Soc., Optical Soc. Am., Am. Chem. Soc. Achievements include research in single molecule spectroscopy at room temperature, single molecule enzymology, conformational dynamics of proteins, and near-field optical microscopy; patents for Coherent Anti-Stokes Raman Scattering Microscopy, a noninvasive method for imaging live cells and tissues. Office: Harvard U Conant Chemistry Lab 12 Oxford St M026 Cambridge MA 02138 Home Phone: 781-674-1385; Office Phone: 617-496-6501. E-mail: xie@chemistry.harvard.edu.

XIE, YU, adult education educator; b. Zhenjiang, Jiangsu, China, Oct. 12, 1959; s. Liangyao Xie and Huazhen Zhao; m. Yijun Helen Gu, Dec. 1985; children: Raissa, Kevin. BA in Metallurgical Engring., Shanghai U. of Tech., China, 1982; MA in History of Sci., MS in Sociology, U. Wis., Madison, 1984, PhD in Sociology, 1989. From asst. to assoc. prof. U. Mich., Ann Arbor, 1989-96, John Stephenson Perrin prof. sociology, 1996, now Frederick G.L. Huetwell prof. sociology. Mem. adv. panel sociology program NSF, 1995-97; bd. dirs. Bd. Overseers of Gen. Social Survey. Dep. editor Am. Sociol. Review, 1996—; mem. editl. bd. Sociol. Methods and Rsch., 1989—, Am. Jour. Sociology, 1994-96, Sociol. Methodology, 1994-97; presenter in field; contbr. articles to profl. jours. Spencer fellow Nat. Acad. Edn., 1991-92; recipient Young Investigator award NSF, 1992-97, Faculty Scholar award William T. Grant Found., 1994-99. Fellow: Am. Acad. Arts & Sci., Academia Sinica (academician); mem. Am. Stat. Assn., Am. Sociol. Assn., Sociol. Rsch. Assn. (elected mem.), Population Assn. of Am. Office: U Mich Population Studies Ctr 426 Thompson St Ann Arbor MI 48104-2321 Business E-Mail: yuxie@umich.edu.

XIN, JACK, mathematician, educator; BS in Math., Peking U., 1985; MS in Math., NYU, 1988, PhD in Math., 1990. Postdoctoral fellow Math. Scis. Rsch. Inst., Berkeley, Calif., 1990—91, Inst. for Advanced Study, Princeton, NJ, 1991—92; asst. prof. math. U. Ariz., 1991—97, assoc. prof., 1997—99; prof. math. U. Tex., Austin, 1999—. Invited prof. Math. Inst. Stuttgart (Germany) U., 1998; invited prof. Multimedia Lab. Hokkaido (Japan) U., 2000; invited prof. Inst. de Henri Poincaré, Paris, 2002. Contbr. articles to profl. jours. Fellow, John Simon Guggenheim Meml. Found., 2003; grantee, NSF, 1993—96, 1996—99, Army Rsch. Office, 1999—2000, 2000—02, 2002—03, Info. Tech. Rsch., NSF, 2002—; NFR Rsch. fellow, Swedish Natural Sci. Rsch. Coun., Inst. Mittag-Leffler, Sweden, 1994. Office: Dept Math Univ Tex Austin Austin TX 78712 Office Phone: 512-471-3149.

XIN, YAN PING, special education educator; d. Huifu Xin and Yueying Shi; m. Xiaodong Wang, May 12, 1990; 1 child, Yixin Wang. BS in Psychology, East China Normal U., Shanghai, 1984, MS in Psychology, 1987; MEd in Spl. Edn., Lehigh U., 1995, PhD in Spl. Edn., 2002. Instr., rschr. East China Normal U., 1987—92; program mgr., instr. Lehigh U., Bethlehem, Pa., 1992—95, rsch. asst., 1996—2002; asst. prof. Purdue U., West Lafayette, Ind., 2002—. Recipient Outstanding Achievement award, East China Normal U., 1983, Donald T. Campbell Social Sci. Rsch. award, Lehigh U., 1997, Outstanding Student Rsch. award, Am. Edn. Rsch. Assn., Spl. Edn. Research-Special Interest Group, 2003. Mem.: Coun. Learning Disabilities, Coun. Exceptional Children, Am. Edn. Rsch. Assn., Phi Beta Delta. Office: Purdue U 100 North University St West Lafayette IN 47906 Office Phone: 765-494-0870. Office Fax: 765-496-1228. Business E-Mail: yxin@purdue.edu.

XING, YIPING, electrical engineer, researcher; PhD, Stevens Inst. Tech., Hoboken, NJ, 2006. Sys. engr. China Unicom, Chengdu, 2001—02; rsch. asst. dept. elec. and computer engring. Stevens Inst. Tech., 2002—. Contbr. articles to profl. jours. Named Outstanding Rsch. Asst. dept. elec. and computer engring., Stevens Inst. Tech., 2005; recipient Grad. Fellowship award Sch. Engring., 2005, Best Ph.D thesis award in elec. engring., 2006. Mem.: IEEE (CCNC Best Student Paper award 2006, DySPAN Student Travel Grant award 2005). Achievements include research in next generation wireless communication networks. Office: Stevens Inst Tech Dept Elec and Computer Engring 1 Castle Point Hoboken NJ 07030 Home Phone: 551-655-5777; Office Phone: 201-216-8312. Personal E-mail: yipingxing@gmail.com. E-mail: yxing@stevens.edu.

XIONG, LIUFENG, research scientist; 1 child, Jasmine Shone. PhD, U. Tex., Austin. Sr. scientist Honda Rsch. Inst., Columbus, Ohio, 2004—. Mem.: Electrochem. Soc., Am. Chem. Soc., Materials Rsch. Soc., Sigma Xi (Sci. Soc.). Achievements include research in fuel cell.

XIONG, NING, computer scientist; b. Shanghai, Nov. 11, 1964; arrived in Sweden, 2000; s. Dezheng and Guiling (Li) Xiong; m. Xiaoyu Wang, Oct. 10, 1968. BS, Dong Hua U., Shanghai, 1986, MS, 1989; PhD with Excellent Distinction, U. Kaiserslautern, Germany, 2000. Asst. lectr. Dong Hua U., Shanghai, 1989—92, lectr., 1992—95; rsch. asst. U. Kaiserlautern, Germany, 1996—2000; guest rschr. Swedish Defence Rsch. Agy., Stockholm, 2000—01; rschr. Royal Inst. Tech., Stockholm, 2001—02; sr. lectr. Mid Sweden U., 2003—04; sr. lectr. dept. computer sci. and electronics Mälardalen U., 2004—. Project leader in intelligent robotics Dong Hua U., Shanghai, 1990—95; key rschr. in fuzzy systems U. Kaiserslautern, Kaiserslautern, Germany, 1996—2000; cons. feature selection Schott Glass Co., Mainz, Germany, 2000; prin. investigator in sensor management Swedish Defence Rsch. Agy., Stockholm, 2000—01; co-chair Swedish Artificial Intelligence and Learning Sys. Conf., 2005. Author: (book) Designing Compact and Comprehensible Fuzzy Controllers Usng Genetic Algorithms., 2001; mem. editl. bd.: Internat. Jour. Hybrid Intelligent Sys., 2007—; contbr. articles to profl. jours, papers to sci. confs. and convs., 2000, chapters to books. Named an Outstanding Young Tchr., Dong Hua U., 1993; recipient Outstanding Paper award, Sci. and Tech. Com., Shanghai, 1995; grantee Doctoral Fellowship, German Academic Exchange Service, 1995-2000. Mem.: IEEE. Avocations: travel, ping pong/table tennis. Office: Mälardalen U Dept Computer Science and Electronics SE-721 23 Västerås Sweden Office Phone: 0046 21 151716. Personal E-mail: n.xiong@ieee.org. Business E-Mail: ning.xiong@mdh.se.

XIONG, TOUSU SAYDANGNMVANG, minister, theology studies educator; b. Hmong Long Cheng, June 23, 1966; arrived in U.S., 1976, naturalized, 1996; s. Nhialue Saydang and May (Vang) X.; m. Zoua Pahoua Moua, Sept. 14, 1993; children: Chivkeeb Genesis Toupa, Naamonunas Ruth, Nujsimloob Hebrews, Nkaujzuapaaj Esther. BA in Bibl. Studies, Simpson Coll., San Francisco, 1989; MA in Theology, Mennonite Brethren Bibl. Sem., Fresno, Calif., 1991; AS in Computerized Acctg., Phillips Jr. Coll., Fresno, Calif., 1993. Ordained to ministry Christian and Missionary Alliance, 1991. Assoc. min. Hmong San Raphael (Calif.) Bapt. Ch., 1986-88; youth min. Hmong Alliance Ch. of Santa Barbara, Goleta, Calif., 1984-85, Hmong Alliance Ch. of Fresno, 1989—; med. record acct. Dr. Suchat Jariangprasert Med. Clinic, Fresno, Calif., 1993—96; assoc., shareholder Wal-Mart Stores, Inc., Bentonville, Ark., 1998—. Mission coun., Santa Barbara, Calif.; scoutmaster Boy Scouts Am., 1984—85. Avocations: hiking, camping, computers. Office: Hmong Alliance Ch Fresno 8234 E Belmont Ave Fresno CA 93727-9725 Mailing: PO Box 8764 Fresno CA 93747 Personal E-mail: xteagle76@yahoo.com. *In my life as I have experienced both the world of the Hmong Animistic Religion in the East and the Christian faith from the West, I have come to realize that Jesus Christ is superior, for Jesus is the way, the truth and the life pointing us towards the Supreme and Creator Being.*

XIU, FAXIAN, research scientist; b. Lai Zhou, China, Aug. 20, 1978; m. Yantong Liu, Apr. 11, 2006. PhD, U. Calif., Riverside, 2006. Rsch. asst. UCLA, 2001—02, U. Calif., Riverside, 2003—06; rsch. scientist ZN Tech., Inc., Brea, Calif., 2007—. Recipient Indsl. award, U. Calif. Riverside, 2006; Student fellow, UCLA, 2002, U. Calif. Riverside, 2003—06. Mem.: IEEE (assoc.), Materials Rsch. Soc. (assoc.), Sigma Xi (assoc.). Achievements include patents for innovative ZnO doping by Sb and P. Office: ZN Technology Inc 910 Columbia St Brea CA 92821 Home Phone: 951-231-7880; Office Phone: 951-231-7880.

XIU, LIMING, electrical engineer; m. Zhihong You; children: Katherine, Helen. BS, TsingHua U., Beijing, 1981—86, MS, 1986—88; MS in Elec. Engring., Tex. A&M U., College Station, 1993—95. Project mgr. China Radiation Tech. Corp., Beijing, 1989—90; rsch. scientist U. Houston, 1990—93; sr. mem. tech. staff Tex. Instruments Inc., Dallas, 1995—. Contbr. articles to profl. jours. Mem.: IEEE (mem. chair, circuit and sys. soc., Dallas chpt. 2003—04, vice chair 2004—), Cir. and Sys. Soc. (gen. chmn. Dallas chpt. 2006). Achievements include patents for precision frequency and phase synthesis; scalable high-speed precision frequency and phase synthesis; patents pending for precision jitter-free frequency synthesis; scalable high-speed precision frequency and phase synthesis; flying-adder frequency synthesizer-based digital-controlled oscillator and video decoder including the same. Avocations: soccer, tennis, travel. Office: Texas Instruments Inc 12500 TI Blvd Dallas TX 75243 Home Phone: 214-480-4930; Office Phone: 214-480-4930.

XOUBI, NED, nuclear engineer; b. 1959; s. S. and N. Xoubi; m. Suzan Xoubi; children: Vivian, Yahya, Lisa. BSc in Nuc. Engring., U. Wis., Madison, 1984; PhD in Nuc. Engring., U. Cin. Registered profl. engr., Ohio. Instr. nuc. engring. U. Cin., 2002—06; nuc. rschr. Oak Ridge Nat. Lab., Tenn., 2004—. Contbr. articles to prof. jours. Recipient Nuc. Engring. Student Lab. Synthesis award, Oak Ridge Nat. Lab., 2004; fellow, Nat. Acad. Nuc. Tng., 2003—04, U. Cin., 2005. Mem.: IEEE, Am. Nuc. Soc. (pres. U. Cin. chpt. 2002—05).

XU, CHRIS, physicist, educator; b. Shanghai; PhD, Cornell U., Ithaca, NY, 1996. Mem. tech. staff Bell Labs., Holmdel, NJ, 1997—2002; prof. Cornell U., 2002—. Contbr. chapters to books, over 100 articles to profl. jours. Achievements include 20 patents in field. Office: Cornell Univ 276 Clark Hall Ithaca NY 14853

XU, DONG, biophysicist, researcher; b. Beijing, Mar. 5, 1965; came to U.S., 1990; s. Hong-qing Xu and Dexia Hu; m. Jingxi Chu, July 27, 1991. BS, Peking U., Beijing, 1987, MS, 1990. Rsch. asst. dept. physics Peking U., 1988-90; teaching asst. dept. physics NYU, 1990, U. Ill., Urbana, 1991, rsch. asst. Beckman Inst., 1991—. Contbr. articles to prof. jours. Recipient scholarship Peking U., 1983-87. Mem. Am. Physics Soc. Achievements include development (with Prof. Klaus Schulten) of the spin-boson model for the electron transfer in the photosynthetic reaction center. Office: Univ Ill Beckman Inst 405 N Mathews Ave Rm 3141 Urbana IL 61801-2325

XU, DONGMING, engineer, researcher; b. Wuhan, Hubei, China, Apr. 28, 1978; BS, Xi'an Jiaotong U., China, 1999; MS, U. Fla., Gainesville, 2001, PhD, 2005. Postdoctoral rsch. asst. U. Fla., 1999—2006; integrated circuit designer Linear Tech., Cary, NC, 2006—. Contbr. articles to profl. publs., procs. in field. Recipient Meritorious prize, Consortium Math. and Applications, First Place award, Nat. Math. Contest Modeling, China. Mem.: IEEE. Home Phone: 352-871-0202; Office Phone: 919-535-0076. Personal E-mail: dmxu@cnel.ufl.edu.

XU, FENG, research scientist, educator; b. Xiaoshan, Zhejiang, China, Feb. 20, 1964; s. Rupeng Xu and Aiqing Chai; m. Ling Ying, Oct. 6, 1963; 1 child, Duo. PhD, Dalian Inst. Chem. Physics, China, 1999. Assoc. prof. Dalian Inst. of Chem. Physics, Dalian, Liaoning, China, 1999—2001; postdoctoral rschr. analytical instruments divsn. Shimadzu Corp, Kyoto, 2001—03; postdoctoral rschr. U. Tokushima Dept Medicinal Chemistry, Tokushima, Japan, 2003—05; rsch. assoc. La. State U. Chemistry Dept., Baton Rouge, 2005—. Mem. internat. adv. bd. analytical abstracts Royal Soc. of Chemistry, London, 2004—. Author: Electrophoresis, Analytical Chemistry; contbr. articles to profl. jours. Office: La State U 8000 GSRI Rd Bldg 3100 Baton Rouge LA 70820 Office Phone: 225-578-5248. E-mail: fengxu22@gmail.com.

XU, HAIPING, application developer, educator; arrived in US, 1996; s. Nianxiang Zheng and Ming Xu; m. Cindy Liu, 2004; 1 child, Angelia. BS, Zhejiang U., Hanghou, China, 1989; MS, Wright State U., Dayton, Ohio, 1998; PhD, U. Ill., Chgo., 2003. Software engr. Shen-Yan Sys. Tech. Inc., Beijing, 1992—95, Hewlett-Packard Co., Beijing, 1995—96; asst. prof. U. Mass., North Dartmouth, 2004—. Co-dir. Concurrent Software Sys. Lab., North Dartmouth, 2004—. Recipient Outstanding Thesis award, U. Ill., 2004; scholar, Dayton Area Grad. Studies Inst., 1998. Mem.: IEEE, Assn. Computing Machinery. Office: Univ Mass Dartmouth 285 Old Westport Rd North Dartmouth MA 02747 Office Phone: 508-910-6427.

XU, JIAQIONG, research scientist, statistician; m. Siyong Zhang, Jan. 23, 1989; children: Amy Yiran Zhang, Katie Xinran Zhang. PhD, U. Waterloo, Ontario, Can., 2003. Lectr., asst. rschr. SW Petroleum U., Nanchong, Sichuan, China, 1989—98; rsch. asst. York U., Toronto, Ontario, Canada, 1998—99, U. Waterloo, 1999—2003; asst. prof. rsch. U. Okla. Health Scis. Ctr., Oklahoma City, 2003—. Author; contbr. articles to profl. jours. Mem.: Am. Heat Assn. (Sandra A. Daugherty award 2006), Am. Statis. Assn. (Mary G. Natrella scholar 2001). Office: Univ Okla Health Scis 801 NE 13th St Rm CHB100 Oklahoma City OK 73104 Home Phone: 405-286-5818; Office Phone: 405-271-3090.

XU, JINCHAO, mathematics professor; m. Jenny Li; children: Lillian, Marissa. BA, Xiangtan U., Xiangtan, Hunan, China, 1982; MA, Peking U., Beijing, 1984; PhD, Cornell U., Ithaca, NY, 1988. Asst. prof. Pa. State U., State College, 1989—91, assoc. prof., 1991—95, prof., 1995—, dir. Ctr. Computational Math. and Applications, 1997—; dir. Inst. Computational and Applied Math., Xiangtan U., Hunan, China, 1996—. Co-editor: Numerical Methods in Applied Sciences, 1996; mem. editl. bd.: SIAM Jour. Numerical Analysis, 1993—2002, Jour. Computational Math., 1993—, Jour. Computational Methods Applied Scis. and Engring., 2000—, Advances Computational Math., 2000—, Math. Computation, 2001—, Math. Modeling and Numerical Analysis, 2002—, Numerische Mathematik, 2003—, Chinese Jour. Computational Physics, 2003—, Internat. Jour. Numerical Analysis & Modeling, 2003—, Math. Models and Methods Applied Sci., 2004—; contbr. articles to profl. jours. Recipient Liu Meml. award, Cornell U., 1988, Natural Sci. award, Academia Sinica, 1989, Schlumberger Found. award, 1993, First Feng Kang prize Sci. Computing, 1995, Outstanding Achievement award, Xiangtan U., China, 1995, Rsch. award Nat. Outstanding Youth (Class B), 2005; fellow, Chinese Ministry Edn., Peking U., 1999—2004, Hunan Province China, Xiangtan U., 2003—; grantee, NSF, 2000—03, 2002—05, 2002—04, Indsl. funds, Honda, 2003—04, NSF, 2005—06, Pa. State U., 2006. Mem.: Am. Math. Soc. (assoc.), Soc. Indsl. and Applied Math. (assoc.). Office: Department of Mathematics Penn State University Park State College PA 16802 Business E-Mail: xu@math.psu.edu.

XU, JINHUI, engineering educator; b. Yuanjiang, China, Jan. 7, 1970; arrived in US, 1995; s. Changlin Xu and Shuzhen Yang; m. Binhin Wang, July 1, 1995; 1 child, Nicole Wang. BS, U. Sci. Tech. China, Hefei, 1992, MS, 1995; PhD, U. Notre Dame, South Bend, Ind., 2000. Rsch. asst. Fla. Internat. U., Miami, 1995—96; tchg. asst., rsch. asst. U. Notre Dame, South Bend, Ind., 1996—99, grad. fellow, 1999—2000; asst. prof. U. Buffalo SUNY, 2000—06, assoc. prof., 2006—. Cons. Brilliant Optical Network LLC, Buffalo, 2002; spkr. in field. Contbr. scientific papers to profl. jours. Recipient Faculty Partnership award, IBM, 2001, Faculty Early Career Devel. award, NSF, 2005. Mem.: Spl. Interest Group Automata and Computability Theory, Am. Soc. Engring. Edn., Assn. Computing Machinery. Office: Dept Computer Sci Engring SUNY Buffalo Buffalo NY 14260

XU, MINGXIN, mathematics professor; b. Shanghai, Jan. 3, 1974; d. Weiding and Ximei Xu; m. Andrea Micheletti Xu, Mar. 24, 2006. BS, Shanghai Jiao Tong U., China, 1996; MS, Syracuse U., NY, 1998; PhD, Caregie Mellon U., Pa., 2004. Asst. prof. U. NC, Charlotte, 2004—. Contbr. articles various profl. jours. Rsch. grant, Nat. Sci. Found., 2005—07. Office: U NC 9201 U City Blvd Charlotte NC 28223 Business E-Mail: mxu2@uncc.edu.

XU, PING, chemist; b. Shanghai, Apr. 29, 1957; came to U.S., 1985; s. Yuan Xu and Changfu Zhu; m. Shuhong Wang, Feb. 17, 1987; children: Helen W., Olivia W. BS, East China U. Chem. Tech., Shanghai, 1982, MS, 1984, U. Cin., 1987, PhD, 1991. Asst. prof. East China U. Chem. Tech., 1984-85; Paul J. Flory meml. fellow U. Cin., 1990-92; sr. rsch. chemist Quantum Chem. Corp., Cin., 1991-94; polymer scientist W.L. Gore & Assocs., Inc., Elkton, Md., 1994—. Vis. scientist Oak Ridge (Tenn.) Nat. Lab., 1998—; vis. scientist Nat. Inst. Stds. and Tech., Gaithersburg, Md., 1999—. Contbr. numerous articles to sci. jours. Mem. AAAS, Am. Chem. Soc., Material Rsch. Soc. Achievements include research in engineering, rubber elasticity, polymer morphology and polymer physics. Home: 22 Piersons Rdg Hockessin DE 19707-9291 Office: WL Gore & Assocs Inc 2401 Singerly Rd Elkton MD 21921-2733 E-mail: pxu@aol.com.

XUE, YIBIN, metallurgist, educator; d. Guangyu Xue and Caiyun Wang; m. Dahui Qi, May 2, 1988. PhD, Ga. Tech, Atlanta, 1998. Sr. rsch. scientist MicroCoating Techs., Inc, Chamblee, Ga., 1999—2002; asst. rsch. prof. Miss. State U., 2004—. Mem.: AIAA, ASME, Am. Soc. Testing and Materials. Achievements include development of a microstructure-based multistage fatigue model for metals; research in rsch. understanding the fatigue failure in metallic alloys. Office Phone: 662-325-5450.

XUE, YONGKANG, science educator; m. Su Q. Liu, Jan. 10, 1973; children: Fransis, Cathleen. PhD, U. Utah, 1987. Rsch. scientist Ctr. for Oean-Land-Atmosphre Studies, Bletsville, Md., 1993—97, U. Md., College Park, 1997—99; assoc. prof. UCLA, 1999—2003, prof., 2003—. Mem.: Am. Assn. Geography, Am. Geophys. Union, Am. Meteorol. Soc. Office: UCLA 1255 Bunche Hall Los Angeles CA 90094-1524 Business E-Mail: yxue@geog.ucla.edu.

YABLON, HEATHER D., lawyer; b. LI, Jan. 14, 1970; BA, U. Mich., 1992; JD, St. John's U., 1995. Bar: NY 1996. Ptnr. Wilson, Elser, Moskowitz, Edelman & Dicker LLP, NYC. Mem.: Assn. of the Bar of the City of NY, NY State Bar Assn. Office: Wilson Elser Moskowitz Edelman & Dicker LLP 150 E 42nd St 23rd Fl New York NY 10017-5639 Office Phone: 212-490-3000 ext. 2578. Office Fax: 212-490-3038. Business E-Mail: yablonh@wemed.com.

YABLON, JEFFERY LEE, lawyer; b. Chgo., June 28, 1948; s. Robert R. and Faye I. (Goldberg) Y.; m. Jean C. LaPrade, Apr. 17, 1983. BA with honors, U. Wis., 1970; JD, Stanford U., 1973. Bar: Calif. 1974, D.C. 1975. Law clk. to Judge Cynthia Holcomb Hall U.S. Tax Ct., Washington, 1973-75; Fulbright scholar U. Florence, Italy, 1975-76; assoc. Covington & Burling, Washington, 1976-80, Lee, Toomey & Kent, Washington, 1980-82, Pillsbury Winthrop Shaw Pittman LLP, Washington, 1982-84, ptnr., 1984—. Mem. bd. advisors Taxation of Exempts Jour., 1998—. Contbr. articles to legal jours.; editl. adv. bd. Moment Mag., 2000—. Mem. ABA, State Bar Calif., D.C. Bar, Cosmos Club. Jewish. Office: Pillsbury Winthrop Shaw Pittman LLP 2300 N St NW Washington DC 20037-1172 Office Phone: 202-663-8441. Business E-mail: jeffery.yablon@pillsburylaw.com.

YABLON, LEONARD HAROLD, publishing executive; b. NYC, June 3, 1929; s. Philip A. and Sarah (Herman) Y.; m. Carolyn Sydney Torgan (dec. Aug. 1995); children: Scott Richard, Bonnie Michelle; m. Pamela Gallin; children: Laura, Abigail, Hilary, Peter. BS, L.I. U., 1950; MBA, CCNY, 1969. CPA, N.Y. Acct., 1950-63; emeritus dir. Forbes Inc., NYC; chmn. emeritus Forbes Family Holdings Inc.; pres. Sangre de Cristo Ranches; pres. emeritus Fiji Forbes; v.p. emeritus Forbes Investors Adv. Inst.; pres. emeritus Forbes Trinchera, Forbes Europe. Sec.-treas. Forbes Found.; bd. dirs. Yablon Found., Mack Goldner Found. Home and Office: 2 Fargo Ln Irvington NY 10533-1202 Office Phone: 914-591-8387. Business E-Mail: lyablon@forbes.com.

YABLONOVITCH, ELI, electrical engineering educator; b. Puch, Austria, Dec. 15, 1946; BSc, McGill U., 1967; AM, Harvard U., 1969, PhD in Applied Physics, 1972. Tchg. fellow Harvard U., 1971—72, asst. prof. applied physics, 1974-76, assoc. prof. applied physics, 1976-79; mem. tech. staff Bell Labs., 1972-74; rsch. assoc., group head Exxon Rsch. Ctr., 1979-84; mem. tech. staff Bellcore, 1984-90, disting. mem. staff, 1990-93, dir. solid state physics rsch., 1991-93; prof. elec. engring. UCLA, 1993—. Chmn. Gordon Conf. on Nonlinear Optics and Lasers, 1979; founder W/PECS Series of Photonic Crystal Internat. Workshops, 1999; Clifford Paterson lectr. Royal Soc. London, 2000; Edison lectr. Notre Dame U., 2004; Anson L. Clark Meml. lectr. U. Tex., 2004; Morris Loeb lectr. Harvard U., 2005; co-founder Eelctronics Inc., Luxtem, Inc., Luminoscent., Inc. A.P. Sloan fellow, 1978-79; recipient Julius Springer prize in applied physics, 2001. Fellow: IEEE (W. Streifer Sci. Achievement award 1993), Optical Soc. Am. (Adolph Lomb medal 1978, R.W. Wood prize 1996), Am. Physics Soc.; mem.: NAS, NAE. Achievements include research in solar cells, strained-semiconductor lasers, photonic band structure. Office: UCLA Dept Elec Engring 66-147K Engring Bldg IV Los Angeles CA 90095-1594 Business E-Mail: eliy@ee.ucla.edu.

YABUKI, JEFFREY W., data processing company executive, former accounting company executive; BBA, Calif. State U. Cert. CPA Calif., Minn., lic. Nat. Assn. Securities Dealers. With Am. Express Co., 1987—99; v.p., mergers & acquisitions Am. Express Tax Bus. Svcs., Mpls., 1996—98, pres., CEO NYC, 1998—99; pres. H&R Block Internat., 1999—2002; exec. v.p., COO H&R Block Inc., Kans. City, 2002—05; pres., CEO Fiserv, Inc., Brookfield, Wis., 2005—. Bd. dir. PetSmart, Inc., 2004—, Fiserv Inc., 2005—, MBIA. Former mem. Minn. Bd. Accountancy. Office: Fiserv Inc 255 Fiserv Dr Brookfield WI 53045 *

YACANTE, MARIA LUCY, music educator, researcher; b. San Juan, Argentina, July 4, 1941; arrived in U.S., 1978; d. Carlos Alberto Yacante and Maria Elena Cuello. Maestra Normal Nacional, Sarmiento Normal Sch., San Juan, Argentina, 1966; MusB in piano, Tex. Wesleyan U., Ft. Worth, 1982; MusM in piano pedagogy, Tex. Christian U., Ft. Worth, 1984, post grad., 1989. Prof. of music Sarmiento Normal Sch., San Juan, Argentina, 1975—76, Nat. U. of San Juan, Argentina, 1975—78; piano accompanist Tex. Wesleyan U., 1978—82; piano instr. piano prep. divsn. Tex. Christian U., 1983—88; piano tchr. Our Lady of Victory, Ft. Worth, 1985—86, Ft. Worth Music and Arts Sch., 1986—87, independent piano studio, Ft. Worth, 1983—2006, Ray Rich Music Edn., Ft. Worth, 2006—. Piano tchr. Inst. Superior de Artes, San Juan, Argentina, 1963—64; adjudicator piano festivals, 1989, 92, 2000; spkr. Reflections on Learning and Tchng., 2001—; adjudicator Ft. Worth Piano Tchrs. Forum, 2002, 04, 07; student in tchrs. program Plano Tex. Internat. Acad. and Festival (formerly Tex. Christian U./Cliburn Piano Inst.), 2005, 06, 07. Performer solo recitals. Mem.: Ind. Piano Tchrs. Forum (chair 2002—), Tex. Fedn. of Music Clubs, Tex. Music Tchrs. Assn., Music Tchrs. Nat. Assn., Ft. Worth Piano Tchrs. Forum (first v.p., piano recitals 2004—), Ft. Worth Music Tchrs. Assn. Forum (chair 2002—06), Ft. Worth Music Tchrs. Assn. (chmn. piano recitals 2001—, bd. dirs. 2007), Pi Kappa Lambda. Avocations: reading, writing, drawing. Home: PO Box 100912 Fort Worth TX 76185-0912

YACCARINO, LINDA, marketing executive; m. Claude Yaccarino; children: Matthew, Christian. V.p. advt. and program sales Select Media Comms.; mem. syndication div. Turner Entertainment, 1993, v.p., sales mgr. sales, 1997—99, sr. v.p., 1999—2004, exec. v.p., gen. mgr. ad sales and mktg., 2004—; v.p. sales CNBC. Named a Woman to Watch, Advt. Age, 2007. Office: Turner Entertainment 1050 Techwood Dr Atlanta GA 30318 Office Phone: 404-827-1717. Office Fax: 404-885-4947. *

YACK, PATRICK ASHLEY, editor; b. Little Rock, Oct. 25, 1951; s. Leo Patrick and Sarah Ann (Dew) Y.; m. Suzanne (Burnett) Y.; children: Alexander Ryan, Kendall Elizabeth. BFA, So. Meth. U., 1974. Staff asst. U.S. Rep. Alan Steelman, Washington, 1975-76; press aide U.S. Senator Charles Percy, Chgo., 1977-78; reporter Fla. Times-Union, Jacksonville, 1979-80, regional reporter Atlanta, 1981-82; reporter The Denver Post, 1983-85, Washington bur. chief, 1985-87; nat. editor Atlanta Constitution, 1987-89; mng. editor The Register-Guard, Eugene, Oreg., 1989-94; editor News & Record, Greensboro, NC, 1994-98, Fla. Times-Union, Jacksonville, 1998—. Journalism coun. So. Meth. U.; journalism adv. coun. U. Fla., Gainesville, 2003—; mem. com. protect journalists Investigative Reporters and Editors; bd. dirs. First Amendment Found. Mem. news/editl. adv. bd. Am. Press Inst.; active First Amendment Found.; bd. dirs. Leadership Jacksonville, 2004—05; co-chair Freedom of Info. Com. Mem.: Am. Soc. Newspaper Editors (past membership com. chair, co-chair Freedom of Info.), Fla. Soc. Newspaper Editors (former pres., bd. dirs.).

YACKEL, JAMES WILLIAM, mathematician, academic administrator; b. Sanborn, Minn., Mar. 6, 1936; s. Ewald W. and Marie E. (Heydlauff) Y.; m. Erna Beth Seecamp, Aug. 20, 1960; children: Jonathan, Juliet, Carolyn. BA, U. Minn., 1958, MA, 1960, PhD, 1964. Rsch. instr. dept. math. Dartmouth Coll., Hanover, NH, 1964-66; asst. prof. dept. stats. Purdue U., West Lafayette, Ind., 1966-69, from assoc. prof. to prof., 1969-76, assoc. dean sci., 1976-87; vice chancellor acad. affairs Purdue U. Calumet, Hammond, Ind., 1987-90, chancellor, 1990-2001, chancellor emeritus, 2001—. Rsch. mathematician Inst. Def. Analysis, Washington, 1969. Author: Applicable Finite Mathematics, 1974; editor Statistical Decision Theory, 1971; contbr. articles to profl. jours. Fellow AAAS; mem. Am. Math. Soc., Math. Assn. Am., Inst. Math. Stats. Achievements include research on Ramsey's theorem and finite graphs. E-mail: yackelj@calumet.Purdue.edu.

YACKIRA, MICHAEL WILLIAM, electric power industry executive; b. NYC, Aug. 14, 1951; s. Alan Israel and Lillian (Landau) Y.; m. Roberta Guido, July 24, 1977; 3 children BS in Acctg., Herbert H. Lehman Coll., CUNY, 1972. CPA. Sr. acct. Arthur Andersen, NYC, 1972-75; v.p. St. Joe Petroleum, Houston, 1975-83; mgr. fin. analysis U.S. Industries, Stamford, Conn., 1983-84; dir. bus. analysis and research GTE Svc. Corp., Stamford, 1984-85, dir. bus. devel. and analysis, 1985-86, asst. controller budget planning and analysis, 1986-87; v.p. fin. and revenues GTE Fla., Tampa, 1987-88; v.p. fin. and info. mgmt. GTE Info. Svcs., Tampa, 1988-89; v.p. corp. devel. and planning FPL Group, Inc., Juno Beach, Fla., 1989-91; chief planning officer Fla. Power and Light Co., 1990-91; sr. v.p. market and regulatory services, then sr. v.p. CFO Fla. Power & Light Co., Juno Beach, 1991—98; pres. FPL Energy Inc., 1998—2000; v.p., CFO Mars Inc., 2001—02; exec. v.p. strategy & policy Sierra Pacific Resources, Las Vegas, Nev., 2003, corp. exec. v.p., CFO, 2003—07, pres., COO, 2007, pres., CEO, 2007—. Bd. dir. Am. Heart Assn., United Way So. Nev. Office: Sierra Pacific Resources 6226 W Sahara Ave Las Vegas NV 89146 *

YACOUB, IGNATIUS I., dean; b. Dwar Taha, Syria, Jan. 5, 1937; came to U.S. 1978; s. Immanuel and Martha (Kharma) Y.; m. Mary Haddad, Sept. 14, 1961; children: Hilda, Lena, Emile. AB, Mid. East Coll., Beirut, Lebanon, 1960; MA, Pacific Union Coll., Angwin, Calif., 1964; PhD, Claremont Grad. Sch., Calif., 1976. Dean studies Mid. East Coll., Beirut, 1967-73, 75-78; dir. dept. edn. Afro-Mideast divsn. Seventh-Day Adventist Ch., 1970-73, dir. dept. pub. affairs, 1975-78; prof., chmn. dept. bus. econs. Southwestern Union Coll., Keene, Tex., 1978-80; prof., chmn. dept. bus. and econs. Loma Linda U., Riverside, Calif., 1980-86, founding dean Sch. of Bus. and Mgmt., 1986-90, prof. mgmt., 1995—; founding dean Sch. Bus. and Mgmt., La Sierra U., Riverside, 1990—95; prof. adminstrn. and mgmt. Loma Linda U., Loma Linda, Calif., 1995—. Bd. dirs. Riverside Nat. Bank; bd. advisors City Nat. Bank, 1997—2003. Mem. Exec. 2000 Coun. Riverside Cmty. Hosp. Found., 1991-95. Recipient Gov.'s Appreciation award, Lions Club, Lions Club award, Beirut, cert. Appreciation Exec. 2000 Coun., 1994, 95, Cert. of Appreciation Claremont Grad. Sch. Alumni Coun., 1996, Mentemoreles Univ. Mex., 1992, 94. Mem. Am. Mgmt. Assn., Acad. Mgmt., Soc. for Advancement Mgmt., Greater Riverside C. of C. (Svc. award 1995), Corona C. of C. Seventh-Day Adventist. Home: 2722 Litchfield Dr Riverside CA 92503-6213 Office Phone: 909-558-7148. Personal E-mail: iyacoub@charter.net. Business E-Mail: iyacoub@univ.llu.edu.

YACOVONE, ELLEN ELAINE, banker; b. Aug. 4, 1951; d. Wilfred Elliott and Charlotte Frances (Fox) Drew; m. Richard Daniel Yacovone, June 2, 1979; stepchildren: Christopher Daniel, Kimberly Marie. Student, Broome C.C., 1973-80; cert., Inst. Fin. Edn., Chgo., 1974. Sec. to exec. v.p. Ithaca Savs., NYC, 1968; mortgage clk. Citizens Savs. Bank, 1968-69; with Lincoln Bank, Van Nuys, Calif., 1970-71; asst. bookkeeper Henry's Jewelers, Binghamton, N.Y., 1971-74; teller, br. supt., br. mgr. 1st Fed. Savs., Binghamton, 1974-82, v.p., ctrl. regional sales mgr., 1982-86, dist. sales mgr., 1986-88; br. mgr. Gt. Western Bank, Pensacola, Fla., 1988-89, v.p., regional mgr. San Diego, 1989-95; br. v.p. Washington Mut. Bank (formerly Gateway Ctr.), San Diego, 1995—, Northpark, Calif., 1996—, fin. ctr. mgr. San Diego, Northpark; consumer lending mgr. Calif. Coast Credit Union, 2003. V.p., owner, operator EYE Shirts, 1995—. Vol. Sta. WSKG Pub. TV, Conklin, N.Y., 1974-88, United Way Broome County, Binghamton, 1976-88; mem. Gov.'s Commn. Domestic Violence, Albany, N.Y., 1983-87; mem. Found. State U. Ctr. Binghamton; bd. dirs. Interfaith Shelter Network, San Dieog, 1992-2002, Schs. Success and the San Diego Innovative Preschool Project, 1995-2000, San Diego Urban League, 1995—, Black Econ. Task Force, 1995—. Named Woman of Achievement Broome County Status Women Coun., 1981. Mem. Triple Cities Bus. and Prol. Women (pres. 1979-81, Young Careerist award 1977), Sales and Mktg. Execs., Inst. Fin. Edn. (bd. dirs. 1976-88, pres. 1984-85, winner N.Y. state speech contest 1984), Broome County C. of C., Broome County Bankers Assn. (bd. dirs. 1979-88, pres. 1983-84), Watercolor Soc., Catfish Club. Republican. Methodist. Avocations: exercise, hand painting wearables, woodworking, gardening, needlecrafts. Office: Calif Coast Credit Union PO Box 502080 San Diego CA 92150 Home: 11761 N Joi Dr Oro Valley AZ 85737-8871

YACOWITZ, HAROLD, biochemist, nutritionist; b. NYC, Feb. 17, 1922; s. Louis and Clara (Kurtzberg) Yacowitz; m. Ann Ruth Barnett, Dec. 31, 1941; children: Caryn R., Richard S., Suzanne Yacowitz Dragan. BS, Cornell U., Ithaca, NY, 1948, M in Nutritional Sci., 1948, PhD, 1950. Rsch. biochemist Parke-Davis Inc., Detroit, 1950-51; assoc. prof. Ohio State U., Columbus, 1951-55; head nutrition rsch. dept. Squibb Inst. for Med. Rsch., New Brunswick, NJ, 1955-59; dir. rsch. Nopco Chem. Co. Inc., Harrison,

NJ, 1959-61, Amburgo Co. Inc., Phila., 1961-80; rsch. assoc. Fairleigh Dickinson U., Madison, NJ, 1961-80; pres., dir. rsch. Dr. H. Yacowitz & Co., Piscataway, NJ, 1961—, Animal Identification & Marking Systems Inc., Piscataway, 1982-97. Pres. Peninsula Investment & Devel. Inc., Cambridge, Md., 1961—; pres. bd. dirs. rsch. Drug Delivery Devices Inc., Piscataway, 1991—. Contbr. articles to profl. jours. Leader Boy Scouts Am., Ithaca, NY, 1946—50, Piscataway, 1955—59. With US Army, 1943—46, ETO, PTO. Grange League Fedn. fellow, Cornell U., 1949—50, Coun. Arteriosclerosis fellow, Am. Heart Assn., 1970. Fellow: NY Acad. Scis. (chmn. sect. biology and medicine 1972—76); mem.: Am. Assn. Lab. Animal Scientists, Am. Inst. Nutrition, Am. Chem. Soc., Exptl. Investors Club (New Brunswick pres. 1955—59). Jewish. Achievements include patents in field. Avocations: gardening, sailing, fishing, swimming. Office: Drug Delivery Devices Inc 221 2nd Ave Piscataway NJ 08854-3519 Office Phone: 732-356-9366.

YADAV, OM PRAKASH, reliability engineer, educator; b. Naghore, India, July 7, 1964; s. Matadeen and Chiriya Yadav; m. Uma Yadav, Dec. 15, 2005. B of Engring., U. Rajasthan, Jaiper, India, 1986; MS, Nat. Inst. Indsl. Engring., Bombay, 1992; PhD, Wayne State U., Detroit, Mich., 2002. Asst. prof. M.R. Engring. Coll., Jaiper, India, 1987—96, assoc. prof., 1996—99; grad. rsch. asst. Wayne State U., Detroit, 1999—2002; reliability engr. Rapid Global Solution Inc. (based at Ford Motor Co.), Detroit, 2002—04; asst. prof. ND State U., Fargo, 2004—. Contbr. articles to profl. jours. Founding mem. (non-govtl. orgn.) Sahyog-Rashms, India, 1992—. Mem.: Am. Soc. Quality, Inst. Indsl. Engrs., Soc. Mfg. Engrs. Office: ND State Univ GECIE 202 1410 14th Ave N Fargo ND 58105 Office Phone: 701-231-7285. Office Fax: 701-231-7195. Business E-Mail: Om.Yadav@ndsu.edu.

YADAV, PRASHANT, economics educator; arrived in Spain, 2004, permanent resident; s. Surendra and Usha Yadav. BS in Chemical Engring., Indian Inst. Tech., Roorkee, 1995; PhD, U. Ala., Tuscaloosa, 2004. Prof. supply chain mgmt. MIT, Spain, 2004—. Office: MIT-Zaragoza International Logistics Pro Avenida Gomez Laguna 25 Zaragoza 50009 Spain Office Phone: + 34 976077615.

YADEKA, THEOPHILUS ADENIYI, hospital administrator; b. Ibadan, Nigeria, Apr. 16, 1939; came to U.S., 1971; s. Joshua A. and Alice (Opawole) Y.; m. Julianah M., Aug. 23, 1965; children: Olatunde, Mofoluke, Ayoola, Mobolaji, Adedoja. Diploma, S.D.A. Nursing Sch., 1965, SUNY, 1972; BS in Healthcare Adminstrn., St. Francis Coll., 1976; MS in Healthcare & Hosp. Adminstrn., L.I. U., 1977. Lic. pvt. sch. tchr. clin. instr. Charge and staff nurse Met. City Hosp., NYC, 1971—74, Barnabas Hosps., NYC, 1974—77; prin. hosp. adminstr. Ministry of Health/State Hosp. Mgmt. Bd., Ibadan, Nigeria, 1978-85; asst. chief hosp. adminstr. State Hosps. Mgmt. Bd., Ibadan, Nigeria, 1985-89; asst. DON Lincoln Hosp., Bronx, NY, 1977—78, 1989-90; asst. dir. Bronx Lebanon Hosp. Ctr., 1990—95; clin. instr., healthcare cons., 1999—. Fellow Internat. Biog. Ctr. Eng.; mem. Am. Coll. Hosp. Adminstrs., Am. Coll. Nursing Home Adminstrs., Inst. Health Svc. Adminstrs. Nigeria. Office Phone: 212-564-0500.

YADRICK, ROBERT MARTIN, occupational analyst; b. Kansas City, Mo., Oct. 24, 1949; s. John George and Joanne Jean Yadrick; m. Patricia Eileen (Koelzer), May 30, 1986 (div. 2004); children: Lauren Nicole, John Nicholas. BA, Rockhurst Coll., 1971; MA, U. Mo., 1973, PhD, 1975. Cert. profl. ergonomist Bd. Certification in Profl. Ergonomics, Inc. Asst. prof. psychology Columbia (Mo.) Coll., 1975-78; rsch. assoc. U. Mo., Columbia, 1978-79; sr. rsch. assoc. Ctrl.-N.E. Colo. Health Sys. Agy., Inc., Denver, 1979-82; sr. human factors engr. McDonnell Douglas Corp., St. Louis, 1982-90; rsch. scientist Metrica, Inc., San Antonio, 1991; pers. rsch. psychologist USAF Rsch. Lab., Brooks AFB, Tex., 1991-99; occupl. analyst USAF, Randolph AFB, Tex., 1999—, quality assurance mgr., 2001—. Adj. lectr. U. Tex. San Antonio, Our Lady of the Lake U., St. Mary's U., Wayland Bapt. Univ.; editor newsletter Insight, Human Factors and Ergonomics Soc., Santa Monica, Calif., 1994-96, reviewer visual performance tech. group, 1995-97; reviewer jour. Behavior Rsch. Methods, Instruments and Computers, 1996. Contbr. articles to profl. jours. Recipient Lab. Dir.'s award Armstrong Lab., 1996. Mem.: Sigma Xi. Avocations: flying, hiking, water sports. Personal E-mail: sloper52@aol.com. Business E-Mail: robert.yadrick@randolph.af.mil.

YADUSH, JOHN G, musician, real estate investor, educator; b. Allentown, Pa., Oct. 20, 1968; s. William Jacob and Mary Mamie Yadush; m. Chantel Lynn Rupert, July 2, 2006. BA in Music Edn., Temple U., Phila., 2002. Cert. profl. music Musician's Inst., Hollywood, Calif., 1990, tchr. K-12 Pa. Pvt. music instr., Whitehall, Pa., 1990—99, Phila., 1990—99, Balt., 1990—99; performing musician Chico's Vibe, Phila., 2000—. Music tchr. Balt. County Pub. Schs., 2002—; owner, real estate investor Acorn Properties, Fogelsville, Pa., 2005—. Avocations: music, reading. Office: Acorn Properties PO Box 351 Fogelsville PA 18051

YAEGER, DOUGLAS HARRISON, gas industry executive; b. St. Louis, Mar. 3, 1949; s. Walter Earl and Mary Eloise (Drinkwater) Y.; m. Lynn Mary Halloran, June 24, 1951; children: Lauren Harrison, Drew Halloran. BS, Miami U., Oxford, Ohio, 1971; MBA, St. Louis U., 1976. Sales asst. Miss. River Transmission Corp., St. Louis, 1974-75, coordinator mktg. and regulatory supply, 1975-78, coordinator mktg. and supply, 1978, mgr. mktg. and supply coordination, 1978-81, asst. v.p. mktg., 1981-82, v.p. mktg., 1982-86, sr. v.p. mktg., 1986-88, exec. v.p., 1988-90; v.p. Laclede Gas Co., St. Louis, 1990—97, pres., 1997—2000, chmn., CEO, 1999—2000; chmn., pres., CEO Laclede Group Inc., St. Louis, 2000—. Bd. dir. Am. Gas Assn., First Banks Inc., St. Louis. Dir. Barnes Jewish Hosp., St. Louis; bd. commr. St. Louis Sci. Ctr. Mem. Am. Gas Assn., So. Gass Assn., Interstate Natural Gas Assn., Assn. Corp. Growth, Sunset Country, Media, Strathalbyn Farm, The Planning Forum, St. Louis Club. Avocations: golf, fishing, hunting. Office: LACLEDE GAS COMPANY 720 Olive St Saint Louis MO 63101 *

YAEGER, EVELYN ANN, lawyer; b. Balt., May 7, 1965; d. Ronald James and Anne Kathryn Yaeger. BA in Econs., Am. U., Washington, 1987; JD, Loyola U., LA, 1993. Bar: Calif. 1993, Tex. 1994. With ops. divsn. Toyo Trust & Banking Co., Ltd., LA, 1987—90; atty. Law Offices Charles M. Bradshaw, Dallas, 1995—98, Gibson, McClure, Wallace & Daniels, Dallas, 1998—. Named Rising Star Super Lawyer, Tex. Monthly/Law & Politics Mag., 2005. Mem.: ASHRAE, Tex. Women's Lawyer Assn., Dallas Bar Assn. (mem. e-mentoring program, judge mock trial HS championship 2007). Avocation: softball. Home: 4172 Beechwood Ln Dallas TX 75220 Office: Gibson McClure Wallace and Daniels LLP Ste 1300 8080 N Central Expy Dallas TX 75206

YAFFE, BARBARA MARLENE, journalist; b. Montreal, Que., Can., Mar. 4, 1953; d. Allan and Anne (Freedman) Yaffe; Student, McGill U., 1970-73; BA, U. Toronto, 1974; B in Journalism, Carleton U., 1975. Reporter Montreal Gazette, 1975-76, Toronto Globe and Mail, 1976-79, reporter, columnist Halifax, N.S., 1979-81; chief nat. TV news bur. CBC, St. Johns, Nfld., Canada, 1981-84, Edmonton, Alta., Canada, 1983; reporter Toronto Globe and Mail, St. John's, 1984-86; editor Sunday Express, St. John's, 1987-88, Vancouver Sun, 1988-93, columnist, edit. bd. adv., 1993—. Recipient Gov. Gen.'s award, Roland Michener Found., 1977, Commentary award, Jack Webster Found., 2004, Animal Action award, Internat. Fund for Animal Welfare, 2004. Office: c/o Vancouver Sun Ste 1 200 Granville St Vancouver BC Canada V6C 3N3 Office Phone: 604-605-2189. Business E-Mail: byaffe@png.canwest.com.

YAFFE, JAMES, writer; b. Chgo., Mar. 31, 1927; s. Samuel and Florence (Scheinman) Y.; m. Elaine Gordon, Mar. 1, 1964; children: Deborah Ann, Rebecca Elizabeth, Gideon Daniel. Grad., Fieldston Sch., 1944; BA summa cum laude, Yale U., 1948. Prof. Colo. Coll., Colo. Springs, 1968—2002, prof. emeritus, 2002—. Author: Poor Cousin Evelyn, 1951, The Good-for-Nothing, 1953, What's the Big Hurry?, 1954, Nothing But the Night, 1959, Mister Margolies, 1962, Nobody Does You Any Favors, 1966, The American Jews, 1968, The Voyage of the Franz Joseph, 1970, So Sue Me!, 1972, Saul and Morris, Worlds Apart, 1982, A Nice Murder for Mom, 1988, Mom Meets Her Maker, 1990, Mom Doth Murder Sleep, 1991, Mom Among the Liars, 1992, My Mother the Detective, 1997; play The Deadly Game, 1960, (with Jerome Weidman) Ivory Tower, 1967, Cliffhanger, 1985; also TV plays, stories, essays, revs. Served with USNR, 1945-46. Recipient Nat. Arts Found award, 1968 Mem. P.E.N., Authors League, Writers Guild of Am., Dramatists Guild, A.A.U.P., Mystery Writers of Am., Phi Beta Kappa. Clubs: Elizabethan (Yale). Jewish. Avocations: music, bridge, movies. Home: 12 W 72 St New York NY 10023

YAFFE, STUART ALLEN, physician; b. Springfield, Ill., July 6, 1927; m. Natalie, 1952; children: Scott, Kim Yaffe Schoenburg. BS cum laude, U. Alaska, 1951; MD, St. Louis U., 1956. Diplomate Am. Bd. Family Practice. Intern St. Louis CIty Hosp., 1956-57, resident, 1957-58; physician pvt. practice, 1958—; clin. assoc. prof. So. Ill. U. Sch. Medicine., Springfield, 1971—; ptnr. Springfield Clinic, 1989—. With U.S. Army, 1945-47. Mem. AMA, Am. Acad. Family Physicians, Ill. Acad. Family Physicians, Ill. State Med. Soc., Sangamon County Med. Soc. Office: 1100 Centre West Dr Springfield IL 62704-2100 Home Phone: 217-546-3604; Office Phone: 217-793-9960.

YAFFE, SUMNER JASON, pediatrician, educator, science administrator; b. Boston, May 9, 1923; s. Henry H. and Ida E. (Fisher) Yaffe; m. Susanne Hecht Goldstein, 2005; children: Steven, Kristine, Jason, Noah, Ian, Zachary. AB, Harvard U., 1945, MA, 1950; MD, U. Vt., 1954. Diplomate Am. Bd. Pediatrics. Rsch. fellow in pharmacology U. Vt. Coll. Medicine, Burlington, 1950—52; intern in pediat. Children's Hosp., Boston, 1954—55, resident, 1955-56; resident in pediatrics St. Mary's Hosp., London, 1956-57; instr. pediatrics Stanford U., Palo Alto, Calif., 1959-60, asst. prof., 1960-63; assoc. prof. pediatrics SUNY-Buffalo, 1963-66, prof., 1966-75, adj. prof. biochem. pharmacology, 1968-75, acting chmn. dept. pediatrics, 1974-75; prof. pediatrics and pharmacology U. Pa., Phila., 1975-81; clin. prof. pediat. Johns Hopkins Hosp., 1986—2001; vis. prof. pediat. UCLA Sch. Medicine, 2001—06; cons. prof. Stanford Med. Ctr., 2006—. Vis. prof. pharmacology Karolinska Inst., Stockholm, 1969—70; dir. Pediat. Renal Clinic, Stanford Med. Ctr., 1960—63; dir. newborn nursery svc. Palo Alto-Stanford Hosp., 1960—63, program dir. Clin. Rsch. Ctr. for Premature Infants, 1962—63; dir. Clin. Rsch. Ctr. for Children Children's Hosp., Buffalo, 1963—70, dir. Poison Control Ctr., 1967—75, dir. divsn. clin. pharmacology, Phila., 1975—81; dir. Ctr. for Rsch. for Mothers and Children Nat. Inst. Child Health and Human Devel., NIH, 1981—2001, program cons., 1963—71, mem. tng. grant com., 1963—65, mem. reproductive biology com., 1965—67; mem. adv. panel on maternal and child health WHO, Geneva, 1970—; liaison rep. drug rsch. bd. NRC, 1971—75, com. on drug dependence, 1972—75, mem. com. on problems of drug safety, 1972—75; mem. adv. panel in pediat. U.S. Pharmacopeia, 1970—, mem. adv. panel in toxicology, 1974—75; cons. Am. Found. for Maternal and Child Health, Inc., 1973—; pres. Maternal and Child Health Rsch. Found., Children's Hosp., 1974—75; Wall Meml. lectr. Children's Hosp., Washington, 1968—; Dr. W.E. Upjohn lectr. Can. Med. Assn., 1974; Louisville pediat. lectr. Sch. Medicine U. Louisville, 1974; William N. Creasy vis. prof. clin. pharmacology SUNY, 1976; advisor Internat. Childbirth Assn. Greater Phila., 1979—83; guest lectr. dept. pediat. Georgetown U. Hosp., Washington, 1988—2001; lectr. in pediat. Johns Hopkins Sch. Medicine, Balt., 1988—2001; mem. Roundtable on Drug Devel., Inst. of Medicine. Author: (book) Clinics in Perinatology, 1974, Drug Assessment: Criteria and Methods, 1979, Pediatric Pharmacology, 1980, Pediatric Pharmacology, 2d edit., 1992; author: (with R. Galinsky) Clinical Therapeutics, 1978; editor (with R. H. Schwartz): Drug and Chemical Risks to the Fetus and Newborn, 1980; editor: (with G. G. Briggs, T. w. Bodendorfer, R. K. Freeman) Drugs in Pregnancy and Lactatin, A Reference Guide to Fetal and Neonatal Risk, 1983, Drugs in Pregnancy and Lactatin, A Reference Guide to Fetal and Neonatal Risk, 2d, edit., 1986, Drugs in Pregnancy and Lactatin, A Reference Guide to Fetal and Neonatal Risk, 4th edit., 1994, Drugs in Pregnancy and Lactatin, A Reference Guide to Fetal and Neonatal Risk, 5th edit., 1998; editor: (with J. V. Aranda) Pediatric Phyarmacology, 2d edit., 1993, Neonatal and Pediatric Pharmacology, 3d edit., 2004; mem. editl. bd.: Pediatric Alert, 1977—, Pharmacology, 1977—, Devel. Pharmacology and Therapeutics, 1979—95, mem. editl. adv. bd.: Drug Therapy, 1979—, cons. editor: Clin. Pharacokinetics, 1977; co-editor: Developmental Pharmacology, 1979—94; contbr. articles to profl. jours. With US Army, 1943—44. Recipient Oscar Hunter award, ASCPT, 2002, Sumner J. Yaffe award, PPAG, 2002; scholar Fulbright, 1956—57. Fellow: Acad. Pharm. Scis.; mem.: AAUP, AMA (com. on drugs 1963—68), Soc. Pediat. Rsch., Perinatal Rsch. Soc., Fedn. Am. Socs. Exptl. Biology, Am. Soc. Pharmacology and Exptl. Therapeutics, Am. Soc. Clin. Pharmacology and Therapeutics (chmn. sect. pediatric pharmacology 1977—83), Am. Pub. Health Assn., Soc. Maternal Fetal Medicine (hon.), Am. Pharmaceutics Assn., Am. Pediat. Soc., Am. Fedn. for Clin. Rsch., Am. Coll. Clin. Pharmacology and Chemotherapy, Am. Acad. Pediat. (chmn. com. drugs 1967—76), Alpha Omega Alpha, Sigma Xi. Personal E-mail: sjyatla@yahoo.com.

YAGAMI, KAZUO, historian; s. Iko and Tomeko Yagami; m. Frances Tay; children: Michelle, Michael. BA in English, Daito Bunka U., Tokyo, 1981; PhD, Fla. State U., Tallahassee, 2002. Vis. asst. prof. U. North Fla., Jacksonville, 2002—03; lectr. U. No. Colo., Greeley, 2004—06; asst. prof. Savannah State U., Ga., 2006—. Author: Konoe Fumimaro and the Failure of Peace in Japan, 1931-1941: A Critical Appraisal of Three-time Prime Minister. Faculty and Rsch. and Publ. grantee, U. No. Colo., 2004, Japan-United States Friendship Commn. grantee, NE Asia Coun., Assn. Asian Studies, Inc., 2000, dissertation rsch. grantee, Fla. State U. Mem.: Am. Hist. Assn. (assoc.). Home: 2748 Oak Park Ct Tallahassee FL 32308 Office: Savannah State Univ 3219 College St Savannah GA 31404 Home Phone: 850-385-8323; Office Phone: 912-356-2461. Personal E-mail: kazuoyagami@yahoo.com. Business E-Mail: yagamik@savstate.edu.

YAGER, JOSEPH ARTHUR, JR., economist, consultant; b. Owensville, Ind., Apr. 14, 1916; s. Joseph Arthur and Edna (Pratt) Y.; m. Virginia Estella Beroset, Sept. 2, 1938; children: Thomas, Martha. AB, U. Mich., 1937, JD, 1939, MA, 1940; grad., Nat. War Coll., 1955. Economist OPA, 1942-44; economist State Dept., 1946-47, chief China research br., 1949-50, chief div. rsch. for Far East, 1952—57; attaché U.S. consulate gen., Canton, China, 1947-48, consul Hong Kong, 1950-51; econ. counselor Taipei, 1957-59; dep. chief of mission, 1959-61; dir. Office Chinese Affairs, 1961, Office East Asian Affairs, 1961-63; mem. Policy Planning Council, 1963-66, vice chmn., 1966-68; dep. dir. internat. and social studies div. Inst. Def. Analyses, 1968-72; sr. fellow Brookings Instn., 1972-83, guest scholar, 1983-86; resident cons. Sci. Applications Internat. Corp., 1986-89, sr. fellow, 1989-96; cons., 1996—. Author: Transforming Agriculture in Taiwan, 1988, Prospects for Nuclear Weapons Proliferation in a Changing Europe, 1992; co-author: Energy and U.S. Foreign Policy, 1974, New Means of Financing International Needs, 1978, Military Equation in Northeast Asia, 1979, Nonproliferation and U.S. Foreign Policy, 1980, International Cooperation in Nuclear Energy, 1981, Energy Balance in Northeast Asia, 1984, Energy Policy Experience of Asian Countries, 1987. Served in AUS, 1944-45. Mem. Phi Delta Phi, Delta Tau Delta. Home: 10450 Lottsford Rd #5109 Bowie MD 20721 Office Phone: 301-541-5094. Personal E-mail: hoosierjoe@earthlink.net.

YAGER, THOMAS C., retired judge; b. LA, Feb. 16, 1918; s. Thomas C. and May M. (McGowan) Yager; m. Antonia M. Gussenhoven, Nov. 2, 2000. AB in pol. sci., UCLA, 1939, gen. secondary lifetime tchg. credential, 1940; JD, USC, 1948; LLD, Western State U., Calif., 1972. Reader UCLA Philosophy Dept., 1940; atty., 1949-57; legal advisor Gov. Calif., 1957, 58; superior ct. sr. judge Calif., 1959-78; founder Cmty. Betterment Svc., LA. Author: numerous legal and religious books; contbr. articles to profl. jours. Founder Judge Thomas C. Yager and Antonia M. Yager Found., LA. Maj. US Army, 1942—46. Office: The Cmty Betterment Svc 108 N Gower St Los Angeles CA 90004-3828 Personal E-mail: pvtsecty@aol.com, tonilsngls@sbcglobal.net.

YAGGI, W. TIMOTHY, manufacturing executive; B, Princeton U., NJ; MBA in Mktg., Mich. State U. Direct mktg. position J. Crew, NYC; various sales and mktg. positions including mktg. mgr. personal care divsn. Norelco Consumer Products Co., Stamford, Conn.; with Whirlpool Corp., 1994—, various positions including v.p. global growth and brand mktg., gen. mgr. brand merchandising, gen. mgr. laundry mktg. strategy, various positions including gen. mgr. Roper and Estate, dir. mktg. Whirlpool cooking products, dir. mktg. Whirlpool brand dishwashers and compactors, v.p. ops. and strategy, 2000, v.p. KitchenAid, 2001—02, v.p. Whirlpool Brand N.Am., 2002, sr. v.p., gen. mgr. Brand Portfolio Group N.Am., 2002—06, exec. v.p. market ops., 2006—. Office: Whirlpool Corp 2000 N M-63 Benton Harbor MI 49022-2692

YAGUDIN, ALEXEI, Olympic athlete, ice skater; b. St. Petersburg, Russia, Mar. 18, 1980; s. Zoya. Attended, Acad. Sports and Physical Culture, 2001. Winner World Jr. Skating Championships, World Championships, 1999, 2001, 2002, Olympic Championship (Mens), 2002, European Figure Skating Champion (Mens), 2002. Tours with Smucker's Stars on Ice, Can. HSBC Stars on Ice. Finalist Athlete Yr., ABC Wide World Sports, 1999. Achievements include second youngest men's world champion in history; first Russian man to win world championship. Avocations: tennis, bowling, fishing, travel, computers, soccer, golf. Office: c/o Internat Skating Ctr Conn PO Box 577 Simsbury CT 06070

YAKU, TAKEO T., computer scientist, educator; b. Tokyo, Oct. 21, 1947; s. Masao and Teru (Nagashima) Yaku. BSc, Jiyu Gakuen Coll., Tokyo, 1970; MSc, Waseda U., Tokyo, 1972, DSc, 1977. Rschr. Rsch. Inst. Sci. and Engring. Waseda U., Japan, 1975—76; vis. lectr. Tokai U., Hiratsuka, Japan, 1975—76, 1985—90, asst. prof., 1976—79, assoc. prof., 1979—85; prof. Nihon U., Setagaya-Tokyo, 1992—. Rsch. assoc. Inst. Sci. and Tech. Waseda U., 1975—76, vis. lectr., 1979—92; Toyo U., Kawagoe, Japan, 1991—94, Tokyo Denki U., 1992—94, assoc. prof., Japan, 1985—92, chmn. curriculum bd. Sch. Sci. and Engring., 1991—92; vis. lectr. Tsuru U., 1994—95, Hitotsubashi U., 1995—96, Nigata U., 1996, 98, Shimane U., 2002, Musashino Art U., 2006—07; vice dir. Inst. Info. Sci. Coll. Humanities and Scis. Nihon U., Setagaya-Tokyo, 1994—98, chmn. dept. applied math., 1997—98, advisor dean student job placement, 1998—2001, vice advisor dean rsch. activities, 2004—05, chmn. earth info. math. scis. Grad. Sch. Integrated Basic Scis., 2004—05, vice advisor dean job placement, 2005—, chmn. earth info. math. scis. Grad. Sch. Integrated Basic Scis., 2007—. Author: (with others) Micro Computer Handbook, 1985, (with others) Structured Editors, 1987; editorial bd. mem: Transac. Inst. Electronics, Information and Communication Engrs., 1993-98; contbr. articles to profl. jours. Mem. examination com. Nat. Pers. Authority, Japan, 1994-96; trustee Japan Assn. Devel. Info. Edn., 2005-. Fellow, IBM, 1978; grantee, Sakkokai Fund, 1978—81. Fellow Tokau U. Ski Alpine Club; mem. Am. Math. Soc., Assn. Computing Machinery, Japan Soc. Computer Assisted Instrn. (mem. com. 1987—). Home: 3-4-4-405 Yagisawa Nishi-Tokyo 202-0022 Japan Office: Nihon U 3-25-40 Sakura-Josui Setagaya Tokyo 156-8550 Japan Personal E-mail: yaku@acm.org. Business E-Mail: yaku@cs.chs.nihon-u.ac.jp.

YALAM, ARNOLD ROBERT, allergist, immunologist, consultant; b. NYC, Apr. 11, 1940; s. Herman and Sylvia (Taber) Y.; m. Carol Ann Strocker, June 16, 1964; children: John, Matthew. AB, Johns Hopkins U., 1960; MD, U. Md., Balt., 1964. Diplomate Am. Bd. Internal Medicine, Am. Bd. Allergy and Immunology. Intern Jackson Meml. Hosp., Miami, Fla., 1964-65; resident in internal medicine SUNY Downstate Med. Ctr., Bklyn., 1965-67; fellow Scripps Clinic and Rsch. Found., La Jolla, Calif., 1967-68; cons. allergist and immunologist San Diego, 1970—. Maj. US Army, 1968—70. Fellow Am. Acad. Allergy and Immunoloy; mem. Am. Soc. Addiction Medicine (cert.), San Diego Allergy Soc.

YALAMANCHILI, SURYA, advertising executive; b. Norristown, PA, 1982; BS Fin. and Psychology, Rutgers U., 2003. CEO (self employed) Surreal Publications, 1996—2000; mktg. dir. Allegiant Media, 1999—2001; brand mgr. Procter & Gamble, 2003—. Named one of 40 Under 40, Advt. Age, 2007. Achievements include starting a successful e-commerce strategy co. at age 15. Office: Proctor & Gamble One Procter & Gamble Plz Cincinnati OH 45202 Office Phone: 513-983-1100. *

YALAVARTHI, RAMARAJA, physician; MD, Guntur Med. Coll., India, 1975. Diplomate Am. Bd. Internal Medicine, Am. Bd. Gerontology. Intern Govt. Gen. Hosp., 1974—75, India Ellis Hosp., 1975—76; resident psychiatry SUNY, Stony Brook, 1976—78; resident internal medicine Weiss Meml. Hosp., Chgo., 1978—80; chmn. dept. medicine, pres. med. staff St. James Hosp. and Health Ctrs., Chgo. Heights and Olympia Fields, 2004—05, pres. med. staff, 2004—05; chmn. quality improvement com. South Suburban Hosp.; physician WellGroup Health Partners, Chgo. Heights. Recipient Leadership award (Internat. Med. Grad. Physician), AMA Assn., 2005. Mem.: AMA, Indian Am. Med. Assn., Am. Assn. Physicians from India. Office: WellGroup Health Partners 333 Dixie Hwy Chicago Heights IL 60411 Business E-Mail: rajayalavarthi@pol.net.

YALDEN, MAXWELL FREEMAN, Canadian diplomat; b. Toronto, Ont., Can., Apr. 12, 1930; s. Frederick and Marie (Smith) Y.; m. Janice Shaw, Jan. 28, 1952; children: Robert, Cicely (dec.). BA, Victoria Coll., U. Toronto, 1952; MA, U. Mich., 1954, PhD, 1956; D.U. (hon.), U. Ottawa; LLD (hon.), Carleton U. With Can. Dept. External Affairs, 1956-69, asst. undersec. state, 1969-73, dep. minister communications, 1973-77, commr. ofcl. langs., 1977-84; Can. amb. to Belgium and Luxembourg, 1984-87; chief commr. Can. Human Rights Commn., Ottawa, 1987—96; mem. UN Human Rights Com., 1996—2004. Decorated companion Order of Can. Office: 201 31 Durham Pvt Ottawa ON Canada K1M 2J1

YALE, JOHN PAUL, computer systems developer; b. Uhrichsville, Ohio, Sept. 4, 1945; s. Vernon Elna and Joan (Papworth) Y.; m. Mary Anne Hinkley, Feb. 9, 1966 (dec. May 2001); children: John Vernon, Eric Kendall; m. Ann M. Willey, Oct. 2006. AAS, Orange County C.C., 1968; BS, Ohio U., 1971; MS in Engring., U. New Haven, 2006. Dir. Pub. Broadcasting, Athens, Ohio, 1969-71; freelance prodr./dir. GGT, Niantic, Conn., 1971-79; dir. media svcs. L & M Hosps., New London, Conn., 1979-96; dir. sys. devel. C&E group MPTN, Ledyard, Conn., 1996—. Mem. Internat. TV Assn., Internat. Teleconf. Assn., Assn. fo Multimedia Internat., Toastmasters Internat., Project Mgmt. Inst. Home: Westgate Farm 299 Pond Hill Rd Chatham NY 12037 Office: 110 Pequot Trail PO Box 3180 Mashantucket CT 06339-3180 Business E-Mail: john@jpyale.net.

YALE (YELEYENIDE-YALE), MELPOMENE FOTINE, researcher, anthropologist, archaeologist, art historian, conservator; b. NYC, Mar. 31, 1963; d. John P. and Serina Yale (Yeleyenide-Yale). BA in Art History, Columbia U., 1985, MA in Art History and Arch., 1998, MA in Anthropology, 2001; studied lithics and flint knapping with Prof. William Parry, CUNY Grad. Ctr., 2001; studied, Art Students League N.Y., 1987; studied fine art, Nat. Acad. Sch. Fine Arts, 1997—98; studied art history, painting, drawing, inorganic and organic chemistry, Lehman Coll., 1980—81, studied, 1987—88, studied, 1995, studied, 1996, Hunter Coll., 1983; studied with renowned iconographer Constantine Youssis, 1996—98. Sci. asst. dept. anthropology The Am. Mus. Natural History, NYC, 1987—89, collections mgmt. asst. dept. anthropology, 1989—90; fieldwork archeologist (excavations) Brit. Sch. Arch., Palaikastro, Crete, 1990, 1991; fieldwork archeologist Fordham U., Rose Hill Excavations, NY, 2000; conservator The Benaki Mus., Athens, Greece, 1991, 1992, The Monastery of St. John the Theologian, Patmos, Greece, 1992, The Hispanic Soc. Am., NYC, 1989—93, Brit. Sch. Archeol. Excavations, Palaikastro, Crete, 1990, 1991, Nat. Acad., 1997, Lilly Hollander Conservation Studio, NY, 1998—99, N.Y. Acad. Medicine, NY, 1999, Sherman Fairchild Ctr. Objects Conservation, Met. Mus. Art, NY, 2000; pvt. conservator, 1993—; rsch. asst. Ani project Columbia U.-World Monuments Found., NY, 1997; curatorial asst. Nat. Acad. N.Y., 1997; rsch. asst. to prof. emeritus Ralph Solecki and Dr. Rose Solecki Shanidar project Columbia U., 2001—03, coord. Ralph Holloway Endocast collection preservation and rsch. project, 2002—04, ind. rschr. prehistoric collection, 2003—. Designer (group fashion show) Chinese New Yr. Festival, Columbia Univ., 1984. Vol. Greek Orthodox Clergy Laity Congress, Greek Orthodox Archdiocese N.Am. and S.Am., NYC, 1984, NY Convocation for Peace in the Middle East, US Interreligious Com. for Peace in the Middle East, 1990. Recipient Cert. of merit Bd. Edn. Art Exhbn., N.Y. Daily News, Lever Ho., N.Y.C., 1981, Cert. of Achievement, N.Y. Acad. Medicine, 1999, Mcpl. hon., Moudros Lemnos Greece, 2004, Mcpl. award, 2005. Mem.: N.Y. State Archaeol. Assn., Archeol. Inst. Am., Registered Profl. Archaeologists, Am. Inst. Conservation (profl.), Am. Anthrop. Assn., The Prehistoric Soc. Achievements include research in emergence of human cognition in the Palaeolithic as indicated by stone tools and art; research on brain casting techniques; independent research towards a PhD on emergence of human cognition in Palaeolithic Period of Greece and Aegean based on Palaeontological-Palaeoanthropological data, stone tools, art, & their relation; to and their influence throughout the Palaeoanthropogeographic region of Europe and the World. Avocations: flintknapping, mosaics, painting, collecting art, archel. material, and stone tools for study. Personal E-mail: mfy2@columbia.edu.

YALE (YELEYENIDE-YALE), SERINA, philanthropist, apparel designer; b. Moudros, Lemnos, Greece, Oct. 16, 1924; d. Adam and Fotika Chiros; m. John P. Yale (Yeleyenide-Yale); children: Mary Anne, Andrew Chris, Melpomene Fotine. Grad., Washington Irving HS, NYC, 1941. Draper haute couture dept. Henri Bendel, NYC, 1941—46, Bergdorf Goodman, NYC, 1946—53; asst. designer R&K Originals, NYC, 1953—56. Pres., mem. bd. dirs. Jr. Philoptochos Philanthropic Soc., Ch. of Holy Trinity, Greek Orthodox Cath. Ch. NYC, 1942—49, mem. bd., 1949—91; pres. bd. dirs. Philoptochos Philanthropic Soc., Ch. St. Spyridon, NYC, 1971—72, 1977—78; chair supervisory com. St. Michael's Home for the Aged, Yonkers, NY, 1982—84; hospitality chair 27th Greek Orthodox Clergy Laity Congress, Greek Orthodox Archdiocese N.Am. and S.Am., NYC, 1984; pres. NY Diocese Philptochos Philanthropic Soc., Greek Orthodox Archdiocese of North and South Am., NYC, 1986—88; Greek sec., mem. exec. bd. Nat. Philoptochos Philanthropic Soc., NYC, 1986—88, cardiac chmn., 1986—88; coord. benefit luncheon Greek Children's Fund, Meml. Hosp. Sloan-Kettering Cancer Ctr., NYC, 1988—90; mem. organizing com. NY Convocation for Peace in the Mid. East, US Interreligious Com. for Peace in the Mid. East, 1990, del. Ch. Women United, 1990; treas., bd. dirs. Ch. St. Spyridon, NYC, 1990—91; hon. amb. of hospitality and goodwill Greek Orthodox Archdiocese of N. and S.Am., 1933—54, Greek war relief organizer, 1941—54; hon. amb. hospitality and goodwill Consulate Gen. Greece, NYC, 1944—54; Sunday sch. tchr. Ch. of Holy Trinity, Greek Orthodox Cath. of NYC, 1938—54; asst. treas., bd. dirs. Ch. Women United, NYC, 1986—92, NGO rep. UN, 1991—92. Recipient Mcpl. honor, Moudros Lemnos Greece, 2004, Mcpl. award, 2005, Title of Archon, Order of St. Andrew of Ecumenical Patriarchate in Constantinople, 1966, Archdiocesan Medal of St. Paul, Archbishop Iakovos of N.Am. and S.Am., 1972. Home: 4555 Henry Hudson Pky Bronx NY 10471

YALE, SEYMOUR HERSHEL, dental radiologist, educator, gerontologist, dean; b. Chgo., Nov. 27, 1920; s. Henry and Dorothy (Kulwin) Y.; m. Muriel Jane Cohen, Nov. 6, 1943; children: Russell Steven, Patricia Ruth. BS, U. Ill., 1944, D.D.S., 1945, postgrad., 1947-48, Spertus Inst. Jewish Studies, 1995—. Pvt. practice of dentistry, 1945-54, 56—; asst. clin. dentistry U. Ill., 1948-49, instr. clin. dentistry, 1949-53, asst. prof. clin. dentistry, 1953-54, assoc. prof. dept. radiology Coll. Dentistry, 1956, prof., head dept. Coll. Dentistry, 1957-65, adminstrv. asst. to dean Coll. Dentistry, 1961-63, asst. dean Coll. Dentistry, 1963-64, acting dean Coll. Dentistry, 1964-65, dean, 1965-87, dean emeritus, 1987—, also mem. grad. faculty dept. radiology Coll. Medicine Chgo., prof. dentistry and health resources mgmt. Sch. Pub. Health, 1987—. Sr. dental dir. Dental Care Plus Mgmt. Corp., Chgo.; pres., dir. dental edn. Dental Care Plus Mgmt. Ednl. Svcs., Ltd.; health care facilities planner; dir. tng. Dental Technicians Sch., U.S. Naval Tng. Ctr., Bainbridge, md., 1954-56; mem. subcom. 16 Nat. Com. on Radiation Protection; mem. Radiation Protection Adv. Bd., State of Ill., 1971, City of Chgo. Health Sys. Agy.; founder Ctr. for Rsch. in Periodontal Disease and Oral Molecular Biology, 1977; organizer, chmn. Nat. Conf. on Hepatitis-B in Dentistry, 1982; organizer, dir. Univ. Taskforce Primary Health Care Project, U. Ill., Chgo.; chmn. U. Ill.-U. Stockholm-U. Gothenberg Conf. on Geriatrics, 1985; dir. planning AMVETS/UIC Tchg. Nursing Home Project, 1987-91; co-sponsor 1st Egyptian Dental Congress, 1984; adj. prof. Ctr. for Exercise Sci. and Cardiovasc. Rsch., Northeastern Ill. U., Chgo., 1991, Northwestern U. Sch. Dentistry Divsn. Behavioural Scis., Evanston, Ill., 1996—. Editor-in-chief Dental Care Plus Mgmt. Digest, 1995—. Bd. dirs., co-benefactor (with wife) World Heritage Mus., U. Ill., Urbana, 1985; mem. Hillel Bd., U. Ill.-Chgo.; life mem. (with wife) Bronze Circle of Coll. Liberal Arts, U. Ill., Urbana; mem. (with wife) Pres.' Council, U. Ill. Recipient centennial research award Chgo. Dental Soc., 1959; Distinguished Alumnus award U. Ill., 1973; Harry Sicher Meml. Lecture award Am. Coll. Stomologic Surgeons, 1983 Fellow Acad. Gen. Dentistry (hon.), Am. Coll. Dentists; mem. Ill. Dental Soc. (mem. com. on radiology), Chgo. Dental Soc., Internat. Assn. Dental Rsch., Am. Acad. Oral Roentgenology, Am. Dental Assn., Odontographic Soc. Chgo. (Award of Merit 1982), Council Dental Deans State Ill. (chmn.), N.Y. Acad. Scis., Gerontol. Soc. Am., Pierre Fauchard Acad. (Man of Yr. award Ill. sect. 1988), Am. Pub. Health Assn., Gerontol. Soc. Am., Omicron Kappa Upsilon, Sigma Xi, Alpha Omega (hon.) Achievements include established (with wife) collection of Coins of Ottoman Empire and Related Mohammedan States and supplemental antique map collection at World Heritage Mus., U of Ill.; established Muriel C. Yale Collection, antique maps of Holy Land collection at Spertus Inst. Jewish Studies. Home: 155 N Harbor Dr Chicago IL 60601-7364 Office: 30 N Michigan Ave Chicago IL 60602-3402 E-mail: ddssy@uic.edu.

YALEN, GARY N., retired insurance company executive; b. NYC, May 17, 1942; s. Sidney Leo and Mildred (Epstein) Y.; m. Rena Lynn Gear, Nov. 3, 1968; children— Robert, Lesley BEE, Rensselaer Poly. Inst., 1964; MBA, U. Chgo., 1965. Chartered fin. analyst. Mktg. engr. N.Y. Telephone Co., NYC, 1965-69; security analyst Merrill Lynch, NYC, 1969-74; from security analyst to exec. v.p. Irving Trust Co., NYC, 1974—89; exec. v.p. Bank of N.Y., 1989-90; chief investment officer, exec. v.p. Fortis Asset Mgmt. (formerly Amev), 1990-95; pres., chief investment officer Fortis Advisers, 1995-2001, Fortis Asset Mgmt., 2001—02; ret., 2002. Served with U.S. Army, 1966-68, Vietnam. Mem.: Beta Gamma Sigma. Avocations: chess, golf, bridge. Home: 360 E 88th St Apt 36B New York NY 10128

YALMAN, ANN, judge, lawyer; b. Boston, June 9, 1948; d. Richard George and Joan (Osterman) Yalman. BA, Antioch Coll., 1970; JD, NYU, 1973. Trial atty. Fla. Rural Legal Svcs., Immokalee, Fla., 1973-74; staff atty. EEO, Atlanta, 1974-76; pvt. practice Santa Fe, 1976—2005; probate judge Santa Fe County, 1999—2005; mcpl. judge Santa Fe, 2006—. Part time U.S. magistrate, N.Mex., 1988—96. Commr. Met. Water Bd., Santa Fe, 1986-88. Mem. N.Mex. Bar Assn. (commr. Santa Fe chpt. 1983-86). Home: 441 Calle La Paz Santa Fe NM 87505-2821 Office: 2511 Camino Entrada Santa Fe NM 87507 Home Phone: 505-983-2615; Office Phone: 505-955-5133. Business E-Mail: ayalman@santa-fenm.gov.

YALOW, ROSALYN SUSSMAN, biophysicist; b. NYC, July 19, 1921; d. Simon and Clara (Zipper) Sussman; m. Aaron Yalow, June 6, 1943; children: Benjamin, Elanna. AB, Hunter Coll., 1941; MS, U. Ill., Urbana, 1942, PhD, 1945; DSc (hon.), U. Ill., Chgo., 1974, Phila. Coll. Pharmacy and Sci., 1976, NY Med. Coll., 1976, Med. Coll. Wis., Milw., 1977, Yeshiva U., 1977, Southampton Coll., NY, 1978, Bucknell U., 1978, Princeton U., 1978, Jersey City State Coll., 1979, Med. Coll. Pa., 1979, Manhattan Coll., 1979, U. Vt., 1980, U. Hartford, 1980, Rutgers U., 1980, Rensselaer Poly. Inst., 1980, Colgate U., 1981, U. So. Calif., 1981, Clarkson Coll., 1982, U. Miami, 1983, Washington U., St. Louis, 1983, Adelphi U., 1983, U. Alta., 1983, SUNY, 1984, Tel Aviv U., 1985, Claremont U., Calif., 1986, Mills Coll., Oakland, Calif., 1986, Cedar Crest Coll., Allentown, Pa., 1988, Drew U., Madison, NJ, 1988, Lehigh U., 1988; LHD (hon.), Hunter Coll., 1978; DSc (hon.), San Francisco State U., 1989, Technion-Israel Inst. Tech., Haifa, 1989, Med. Coll. Ohio Toledo, 1991; LHD (hon.), Sacred Heart U., Conn., 1978, St. Michael's Coll., Winooski Park, Vt., 1979, Johns Hopkins U., 1979, Coll. St. Rose, 1988, Spertus Coll. Judaica, Chgo., 1988; DHC (hon.), U. Rosario, Argentina, 1980, U. Ghent, Belgium, 1984; D. Humanities and Letters (hon.), Columbia U., 1984; DSc (hon.), Fairleigh Dickinson U., 1992, Conn. Coll., 1992, Smith Coll., Northampton, Mass., 1994, Union Coll., Schenectady, 1994. Diplomate Am. Bd. Scis. Lectr., asst. prof. physics Hunter Coll., 1946-50; physicist, asst. chief radioisotope service VA Med. Ctr., Bronx, NY, 1950-70, chief nuclear medicine, 1970-80, acting chief radioisotope service, 1968-70, sr. med. investigator emeritus; research prof. Mt. Sinai Sch. Med., CUNY, 1968-74, Disting. Service prof., 1974-79, Solomon A. Berson Disting. prof.-at-large, 1986—; chmn. dept. clin. scis. Montefiore Med. Ctr., Bronx, 1980-85; Disting. prof.-at-large Albert Einstein Coll. Med., Yeshiva U., 1979-85, prof. emeritus, 1986. Cons. Lenox Hill Hosp., NYC, 1956—62, WHO, Bombay, 1978; sec. U.S. Nat. Com. on Med. Physics, 1963—67; mem. nat. com. Radiation Protection, subcom. 13, 1957, Pres.'s Study Group on Careers for Women, 1966—72; sr. med. investigator VA, 1972—92, sr. med. investigator emeritus, 1992—. Co-editor: Hormone and Metabolic Research, 1973—79; editl. adv. coun. Acta Diabetologica Latina, 1975—77, Ency. Universalis, 1978—, editl. bd. Mt. Sinai Jour. Medicine, 1976—79, Diabetes, 1976, Endocrinology, 1967—72, contbr. numerous articles to profl. jours. Bd. dirs. NY Diabetes Assn., 1974. Recipient VA William S. Middleton Med. Rsch. award, 1960, Eli Lilly award, Am. Diabetes Assn., 1961, Van Slyke award, NY met. sect. Am. Assn. Clin. Chemists, 1968, ACP award, 1971, Dickson prize, U. Pitts., 1971, Howard Taylor Ricketts award, U. Chgo., 1971, Gairdner Found. Internat. award, 1971, Commemorative medallion, Am. Diabetes Assn., 1972, Bernstein award, Med. Soc. State NY, 1974, Boehringer-Mannheim Corp. award, Am. Assn. Clin. Chemists, 1975, Sci. achievement award, AMA, 1975, Exceptional Svc. award, VA, 1975, A. Cressy Morrison award, NY Acad. Scis., 1975, sustaining membership award, Assn. Mil. Surgeons, 1975, Disting. Achievement award, Modern Medicine, 1976, Albert Lasker Basic Med. Rsch. award, 1976, La Madonnina Internat. prize, Milan, 1977, Golden Plate award, Am. Acad. Achievement, 1977, Nobel prize in physiology or medicine, 1977, citation of esteem, St. John's U., 1979, G. von Hevesy medal, 1978, Rosalyn S. Yalow R&D award established, Am. Diabetes Assn., 1978, Banting medal, 1978, Torch of Learning award, Am. Friends Hebrew U., 1978, Virchow Gold medal, Virchow-Pirquet Med. Soc., 1978, Gratum Genus Humanum Gold medal, World Fedn. Nuc. Medicine or Biology, 1978, Jacobi medallion, Assoc. Alumni Mt. Sinai Sch. Med., 1978, Jubilee medal, Coll. of New Rochelle, 1978, VA Exceptional Svc. award, 1978, Fed. Woman's award, 1961, Harvey lectr., 1966, Am. Gastroenterol. Assn. Meml. lectr., 1972, Joslin lectr., New Eng. Diabetes Assn., 1972, 1st Hagedorn Meml. lectr., Acta Endocrinologica Congress, 1973, Franklin I. Harris Meml. lectr., 1973, Sarasota Med. award for achievement and excellence, 1979, Gold medal, Phi Lambda Kappa, 1980, Achievement in Life award, Ency. Britannica, 1980, Theobald Smith award, 1982, Pres.'s Cabinet award, U. Detroit, 1982, John and Samuel Bard award in med. and sci., Bard Coll., 1982, Disting. Rsch. award, Dallas Assn. Retarded Citizens, 1982, Nat. medal of Sci., 1988, Abram L. Sachar Silver medallion, Brandeis U., 1989, Disting. Scientist of Yr. award, ARCS, NYC, 1989, Golden Scroll award, The Jewish Advocate, Boston, 1989, spl. award, Clin. Ligand Assay Soc., Washington, 1988, numerous others. Fellow: Clin. Soc. N.Y. Diabetes Assn., Am. Coll. Radiology (assoc. in physics), N.Y. Acad. Scis. (chmn. biophysics divsn. 1964—65); mem.: NAS, Am. Physiol. Soc., Endocrine Soc. (pres. 1978, Kocn award 1972), Soc. Nuc. Medicine, Soc. Nuc. Medicine (hon.), Am. Gastroenterol. Assn. (hon.), Am. Coll. Nuc. Physicians (hon.), Harvey soc. (hon.), Med. Assn. Argentina (hon.), Diabetes Soc. Argentina (hon.), The N.Y. Acad. Medicine (hon.), N.Y. Roentgen Soc. (hon.), Biophys. Soc., Am. Assn. Physicists in Medicine, Radiation Rsch. Soc., Am. Phys. Soc., Am. Acad. Arts and Scis., Tau Beta Pi, Sigma Delta Epsilon, Pi Mu Epsilon, Sigma Pi Sigma, Sigma Xi, Phi Beta Kappa. Office: Vet Affairs Med Ctr 130 W Kingsbridge Rd Bronx NY 10468-3904

YAMADA, KENNETH MANAO, cell biologist; s. Paul Manao and Masaye Yamada; m. Susan Jane Sleeper, July 1, 1973. BA in Biol. Scis., Stanford U., 1966, PhD in Biol. Scis., 1971, MD, 1972. Intern Seton Med. Ctr., Daly City, Calif., 1972-73; commd. lt. USPHS, 1974, advanced through grades to capt., 1982—2003, ret., 2003; sect. chief Nat. Cancer Inst., Bethesda, Md., 1980-90; lab. chief Nat. Inst. Dental and Craniofacial Rsch., NIH, Bethesda, 1990-96, br. chief, 1996—. Mem. Cell Biology Study sect. NIH, 1979—83; mem. external adv. com. Cancer Rsch. Ctr. Howard U., 1979—88; co-chmn. Gordon Conf. on Fibronectin, 1982; Stadtler lectr. U. Tex. Sys. Cancer Ctr. M.D. Anderson Hosp., 1988; Swerling lectr. Dana-Farber Cancer Inst. Harvard Med. Sch., 1988; Retzius lectr. Karolinska Inst., 2005. Editor: Jour. Cell Biology, 1999—; contbr. more than 350 publs. to biomed. lit. Recipient Eli Luke and Jacob David Rsch. award, 1972, Sr. Lectureship award, Am. Soc. Matrix Bio., 2004. Fellow: AAAS; mem.: Soc. Devel. Biology, Southeastern Cancer Rsch. Assn. (bd. dirs. 1980—83), Am. Soc. Matrix Biology (coun. 2003—), Internat. Soc. Matrix Biology (coun. 1994—2006), Am. Soc. Biochemistry and Molecular Biology, Am. Soc. Cell Biology (coun. 1992—95), Sigma Xi, Phi Beta Kappa. Office: NIDCR Nat Inst Health 30 Convent Dr Bldg 30 Rm 426 Bethesda MD 20892-4370 Office Phone: 301-496-9124. Business E-Mail: kenneth.yamada@nih.gov.

YAMADA, TETSUJI, health economist, educator; M of Internat. Affairs, Columbia U., 1978; MPhil, Grad. Ctr. of CUNY, 1983, PhD in Econs., 1987. Instr. CUNY, NYC, 1982—86; postdoctoral fellow Grad. Ctr. of CUNY, NYC, 1987; asst. prof. dept. econs. Rutgers U., Camden, NJ, 1987—91, assoc. prof., 1993—2002, chair dept. econs., 1996-99, faculty assoc., Walter Rand Inst., 1999—, ctr. assoc., faculty ctr. children and childhood studies, 2000—, prof., 2003—, assoc. mem. Inst. Health, Health Care Policy and Aging Rsch., 2004—; rsch. fellow NBER, 1987-90, rsch. assoc., 1991-94, Ctr. Pacific Basin Fed. Res. Bank, San Francisco, 1990—; assoc. prof. Ritsumeikan U., Kyoto, 1991-92; health economist Internat. Leadership Ctr. Longevity and Soc., 1993-94; exec. bd. China East Inst. Soc. Ins., China, 1998—2004. Rep. Japan Econ. Fedn., Ditchley, Oxford, England, 1994; vis. rsch. scholar Inst. Policy and Planning Scis., Tsukuba U., Japan, 1997—2007; vis. rsch. scholar dept. health econs. and mgmt. Peking U. Sch. Mgmt., China, 2005; vis. rsch. scholar Hosei inst. aging Hosei U., Japan, 2005—; vis. rsch. scholar dept. cmty. health and preventive medicine sch. medicine Hamamatsu U., Japan, 2006—; temp. adviser WHO, 1999; cons. Japan Found., 2001, 03, 2005—07; adviser Japanese Am. Assn. N.Y., 2006—. Mem. editl. bd.: Internat. Jour. Applied Econs., 2004—, Sci. Jours. Internat., 2006—, reviewer, referee: profl. jours., books, rsch. grants; contbr. articles to profl. jours. Grantee, Ministry Edn., Japan, 1991, Iryo Kagaku Kenkyu Jo, Japan, 1991—92, Pfizer Health Rsch. Found., 1992—93, 21st Century Cultural Rsch. Found., 1993, Ministry Health and Welfare, Japan, 1993—94, Nomura Found., Japan, 1995—96, Iryo Kagaku Kenkyu Jo, Japan, 1996—97, Iryo Keizai Kenkyu Kiko, Japan, 1997—98, Ctr. for Children and Childhood Studies, 2000—01, 2002—03, Ministry of Edn., Sci., Sports and Culture of Japan, 2002—03, 2005—, Inst. Statis. Rsch., Labor Marjet Rsch. Com., 2003—04, Pfizer Health Rsch. Found., 2003—05; OSRP grant, Rutgers U., 1992—, Dialogues grant, 2002—03, Internat. Health Econ. Rsch. grant, Eli Lilly, 2005—06. Mem. Am. Econ. Assn., Internat. Health Econs. Assn. (sci. com. 2006—), So. Econs. Assn., We. Econ. Assn., Am. Soc. Health Econs. (sci. com. 2005—), Internat. Soc. for Pharmacoeconomics and Outcome Rsch. (mem. rev. com. 2005-06), Japan Econ. Seminar, Inst. Statis. Rsch. (labor market rsch. com. 2003-04), Omicron Delta Epsilon (award). Home: 300 East 40th St #4M New York NY 10016 Office: Dept Econs-CCAS Rutgers Univ State Univ NJ Camden NJ 08102 Office Phone: 856-225-6136, 856-225-6136. Personal E-mail: ytetsuji@aol.com. Business E-Mail: tyamada@crab.rutgers.edu.

YAMADA, TOHRU, biologist, educator, researcher, director; b. Hadano, Kanagawa, Japan, June 30, 1975; s. Yoshio and Tamiko Yamada; m. Kaori Horiguchi, Sept. 13, 2005. Bachelor's degree, Tokyo Inst. Tech., 1999, Master's degree, 2001, PhD, 2003. Post-doctoral fellow dept. microbiology/immunology U. Ill. Coll. Medicine, Chgo., 2003—04, vis. rsch. asst. prof. dept. surg. oncology, 2004—06; dir drug devel. CDG Therapeutics Inc., 2006—. Contbr. articles to profl. jours. First Class scholar, Japan Student Svcs. Orgn., 1999. Mem.: Am. Soc. Gene Therapy, Am. Assn. Cancer Rsch., Am. Soc. Microbiology. Office: U Ill Coll Medicine Chgo 840 South Wood St Chicago IL 60612 Personal E-mail: tohru630@gmail.com. Business E-Mail: tohru@uic.edu.

YAMAGUCHI, DEAN TAKAO, medical educator, researcher; s. Jiro and Elaine Chizuru Yamaguchi; m. Susan Sueko Hondo, June 19, 1977; children: Dean Jared Norio, Tory Jordan Emi, Eden Jami Miki. MD, Tulane U., New Orleans, 1977, PhD, 1978. Diplomate Am. Bd. Internal Medicine, 1982, subspecialty nephrology Am. Bd. Internal Medicine, 1986. Intern ob-gyn Charity Hosp. La., New Orleans, 1978—79; intern internal medicine Tulane U. Affiliated Program in Internal Medicine, New Orleans, 1979, resident internal medicine, 1980—82; fellow nephrology UCLA-Wadsworth VA Med. Ctr. Program, 1982—84; assoc. investigator VA Med. Ctr. West LA, 1984—86, rsch. assoc., 1986—90, clin. investigator, 1990—95, assoc. dir. for rsch., geriat. rsch., edn., and clin. ctr., 1995—2000; assoc. chief of staff R&D VA Greater LA Healthcare Sys., 2000—. Adj. instr. anatomy Tulane U. Sch. Medicine, New Orleans, 1978—81; asst. prof. medicine in residence UCLA Sch. Medicine, 1984—91, assoc. prof. medicine in residence, 1991—2000; prof. medicine in residence David Geffen Sch. Medicine, UCLA, 2000—; sci. adv. coun. Am. Fedn. for Aging Rsch., NYC, 2005—; merit rev. bd. endocrinology B VHA, Washington, 2006—; bd. dirs. Brentwood Biomedical Rsch. Inst., LA, Sepulveda Rsch. Corp., Calif. Asst. baseball coach Taft H.S., Woodland Hills, Calif., 2003. Recipient Merck Manual award, Tulane U., 1977, Owl Club Tchg. award, 1978, 1979, Arthur Cherkin award, UCLA Multicampus Program in Geriat. and Gerontology, 2000; fellow, Nat. Kidney Found., 1984—85, Hiroshima Internat. Coun. for Med. Care of the Radiation Exposed, HICARE, 1992; grantee, VHA, 1986—. Mem.: Soc. for Exptl. Biology and Medicine, Am. Physiol. Soc., Endocrine Soc., Internat. Bone and Mineral Soc., Am. Soc. for Bone and Mineral Rsch. (Fuller-Albright Young Investigator award 1991), Internat. Soc. Nephrology, Alpha Omega Alpha, Phi Lambda Upsilon, Phi Beta Kappa. Avocation: coaching baseball and softball. Office: VA Greater Los Angeles Healthcare System 11301 Wilshire Blvd Los Angeles CA 90073 Home Phone: 818-347-1094; Office Phone: 310-268-4437. Office Fax: 310-268-4856. Business E-Mail: dean.yamaguchi@va.gov.

YAMAGUCHI, KEN, surgeon, educator; b. LA, Nov. 8, 1960; s. Hiroshi and Yoshiko Yamaguchi; m. Kathy Taeko Yamaguchi; children: Kelli Emiko, Kyle Kiyoshi. BS, UCLA, 1983, MA, 1985; MD, George Washington U., 1989. Diplomate Am. Bd. Orthopedic Surgery. Intern George Washington U., resident in orthopedic surgery; fellow shoulder and elbow surgery Columbia U.; assoc. prof. Washington U., St. Louis, 1995—; staff physician John Cochran VA Hosp., St. Louis, 1996—. Reviewer Am. Jour. Sports Medicine, 1996—; cons. reviewer Jour. Shoulder and Elbow Surgery, 1998—; assoc. editor Techniques in Shoulder and Elbow Surgery, 1999—, Jour. Bone and Joint Surgery, 1997—; contbr. articles to profl. jours. Recipient Emanual B. Kaplan award, 1997, Rsch. award Soc. Radiologists, 1998; N.Am. Travelling fellow, 1997. Mem. AMA, Am. Acad. Orthop. Surgeons, Mid.-Am. Orthop. Assn., St. Louis Orthop. Soc. Avocations: rollerblading, tennis, swimming. Office: Washington U Dept Orthop Surgery 1 Barnes Jewish Hosp Plz Saint Louis MO 63110 Office Phone: 314-742-2534. Business E-Mail: yamaguchik@wustl.edu. *

YAMAGUCHI, KENNETH STEVEN, chemistry professor; b. Pasadena, Calif., Sept. 5, 1957; s. Ken and Charlotte Yamaguchi; m. Karin Bartels. BS in Chemistry, Calif. State U., Long Beach, 1979, MS in Organic Chemistry, 1981; PhD in Analytical Chemistry, U. Calif., Riverside, 1985. Rsch. chemist L'Air Liquide, Paris, 1985—94; prof. chemistry NJ City U., Jersey City, 1995—. Contbr. articles to profl. jours. Grantee, NSF, 2003, Dept. Def., 2004, 2006. Mem.: Am. Chem. Soc.

YAMAGUCHI, MASAYA, musician, educator; b. Japan, July 18, 1970; s. Shigenori and Mieko Yamaguchi. BA in English, Meikai U., 1994; MA in Jazz Performance, CCNY, 1999. Author: The Complete Thesaurus of Musical Scales, 1999, Symmetrical Scales for Jazz Improvisation, 2001, Pentatonicism in Jazz: Creative Aspects & Practice, 2002;: 2d edit., 2006, John Coltrane Plays Coltrane Changes, 2003, A Creative Approach to Multi-Tonic Changes: Beyond Coltrane's Harmonic Formula, 2004, Charlie Parker "Yardbird" Originals, 2005; contbr. articles to profl. jours. Home: 321 W 54th St Apt 305 New York NY 10019 Personal E-mail: masayayamaguchi@hotmail.com.

YAMAGUCHI, YURIKO FUJITA, artist; b. Japan, Jan. 25, 1948; came to the U.S., 1971; d. Alexander and Michi (Hirose) Fujita; m. Hiroyuki Yamaguchi, Mar. 25, 1975; children: Seiji, Mariko. BA, U. Calif., Berkeley, 1975; MFA, U. Md., 1979. Instr. U. Md., College Park, 1988—97; adj. faculty Corcoran Sch. Art, Washington, 1988-97; asst. prof. George Washington U., 2003—. Vis. artist Md. Inst. Art, Balt., 1991, Balt., 95, Mass. Coll. Art, Boston, 1994. One-woman shows include Columbia U., NY, Howard Scott Gallery, N.Y.C., 2005, Mus. Contemporary Art, Ise, Japan, 2005, exhibited in group shows at Hirshhorn Mus., 1984, L.A. County Mus., 1987, Koplin Gallery, L.A., 1991, 1994, 1996, 1999, 2002, 2007, Gallery Emon, Japan, 1997, 2000, Numark Gallery, 1999, 2003,

2005, Del. Ctr. for Contemporary Arts, 2001, Suyama Space, Seattle, 2002, Mus. Modern Art, Kanagawa, Japan, 2004, Represented in permanent collections Atlanta Internat. Airport, Hirshhorn Mus., Nat. Mus. Women in Arts, Nat. Mus. Am. Art, Smith Coll. Art Mus., Corcoran Gallery of Art. Recipient Benesse award, 2005, Joan Mitchell award, 2005, Am. Acad. Arts & Letter award, 2006; Va. Mus. Fine Arts fellow, 1988, 85, 2001; Mid-Atlantic Found. fellow, 1995; Va. Commn. Arts grantee, 1994, 2000, Salzburg Kunstlerhaus Residency grantee, 1993; Franz and Virginia Bauer grantee, 2004. Home: 1517 Snughill Ct Vienna VA 22182-1724 E-mail: yuriko414@aol.com.

YAMAKOV, VESSELIN IVANOV, aerospace scientist, researcher; b. Sofia, Bulgaria, Sept. 1, 1965; arrived in U.S., 1999; s. Ivan Yakov and Anna Borisova Yamakov; m. Milena Momcheva Marinova, Dec. 20, 2002; children: Ioan Vesselinov, Miroslava Marinova Marinova. PhD, Inst. Phys. Chemistry, Sofia, 1999. Rsch. scientist Argonne Nat. Lab., Ill. Rsch. scientist Inst. of Applied Mineralogy, Bulgarian Acad. of Scis., Sofia, 1991—95, Inst. for Phys. Chemistry, Bulgarian Acad. of Scis., Sofia, 1995—99, Argonne Nat. Lab., 1999—2003; staff scientist Nat. Inst. of Aerospace, Hampton, Va., 2003—. Office: Nat Inst of Aerospace 100 Exploration Way Hampton VA 23666 Office Phone: 757-864-2850. Personal E-mail: vyamakov@mail.com. Business E-Mail: yamakov@nianet.org.

YAMAMOTO, ALICE M., secondary school educator; b. Phoenix, Sept. 8, 1958; d. Frank and Kumiko Yamamoto. BA in Journalism, U Ariz., 1981; MEd in Curiculum and Instrn., Ariz. State U., 1997. Cert. cmty. coll. tchr. Ariz. English tchr. Mountain Pointe H.S., Phoenix, 1993—96, Desert Vista H.S., Phoenix, 1996—99, 1999—; tchr. Rio Salado Coll., Tempe, 1999—. Acad. decathlon coach Desert Vista H.S., Phoenix, 1996—2001, Asian Student Union co-sponsor, 1999—. Recipient Most Improved Coach award, Ariz. Acad. Decathlon, 1999. Mem.: MLA (assoc.), NEA (assoc.). Home: 779 E Park Ave Chandler AZ 85225-1757 Office: Desert Vista HS 16440 S 32nd St Phoenix AZ 85048-7807

YAMAMOTO, DONALD YUKIO, ambassador; b. Seattle, Mar. 13, 1953; s. Hideo and Lillian Yamamoto; m. Margaret Darling, Dec. 11, 1982; 2 children. BA, Columbia Coll., 1975; East Asian cert., Columbia U., 1978; M in Internat. Affairs, Columbia U., NYC, 1978. With Fgn. Svc. US Dept. State, 1980—, staff aide to amb. Beijing, human rights officer, 1989, prin. officer Fukuoka Consulate Japan, charge d'Affaires US Embassy Asmara Eritrea, dep. dir. East African Affairs, 1998—2000, US amb. to Republic of Djibouti, 2000—03, dep. asst. sec. of state Bur. African Affairs, 2003—06, US amb. to Ethiopia Addis Ababa, 2006—. Office: DOS Amb 2030 Addis Ababa Pl Washington DC 20521-2030 *

YAMAMOTO, HISASHI, chemistry professor; b. Kobe, Japan, July 16, 1943; s. Taro and Junko (Harima) Yamamoto. BS, Kyoto U., Japan, 1967; PhD, Harvard U., 1971. With Toray Industries, Inc., 1971—72; instr. Kyoto U., 1972-76, lectr., 1976-77; assoc. prof. U. Hawaii, Honolulu, 1977-80, Nagoya U., Japan, 1980-83, prof. applied chemistry, 1983—2002, councilor, 1997—99; Arthur Holly Compton disting. svc. prof. chemistry U. Chgo., 2002—. Contbr. articles to sci. jours.; mem. editl. bd.: Organic Syntheses, 1988—93, mem. adv. bd.:, 1993—, Organic Letters, 1999—, European Jour. Organic Chemistry, 1999—, Advanced Synthesis & Catalysis, 2001—, mem. editl. bd.: Synlett, 1989—, Ctrl. European Sci. Jours., 2002—, consulting editor: Tetrahedron: Asymmetry, 1990—, Tetrahedron and Tetrahedron Letters, 2003—, mem. internat. adv. bd.: Ency. Reagents for Organic Synthesis, 1992—95, Bull. Korean Chem. Soc., 1998—, mem. editl. adv. bd.: Jour. Am. Chem. Soc., 1994—99, Bull. Chem. Soc. Japan, 2005—, Trends in Organic Chemistry, 2005—. Recipient Chem. Soc. Japan Award for Young Chemist, 1977, IBM Sci. award, 1988, Houkou award, Hattori Houkou, Japan, 1991, Chunichi Culture award, Chunichi Newspaper, Japan, 1992, Prelog medal, 1993, Chem. Soc. Japan award, 1995, Toray Sci. and Tech. award, 1997, Max-Tishler prize, 1998, Le Grand Prix de la Fondation Maison de la Chimie, 2002, Nat. Prize of Purple medal, Japan, 2002, Molecular Chirality award, Molecular Chirality Rsch. Assn., 2003, Yamada prize, 2004, Humboldt Rsch. award, Alexander von Humboldt Found., Germany, 2007, Japan Acad. prize, 2007. Fellow: AAAS; mem.: Soc. Synthetic Organic Chemistry, Japan, Pharm. Soc. Japan, Royal Soc. Chemistry, Am. Chem. Soc. (2006 Tetrahedron Prize for Creativity in Organic Chemistry 2006). Office: Dept Chemistry U Chgo SCL 317 5725 S Ellis Ave Chicago IL 60637 Office Phone: 773-702-5059. Office Fax: 773-702-0805. E-mail: yamamoto@uchicago.edu. *

YAMAMOTO, IRWIN TORAKI, editor, publishing executive; b. Wailuku, Maui, Hawaii, Apr. 5, 1955; s. Torao and Yukie (Urata) Yamamoto. BBA in Mktg., Chaminade U., Honolulu, 1977. Pres., editor, pub. Yamamoto Forecast, Kahului, Hawaii, 1977—. Author: Profit Making in the Stock Market, 1983; columnist: Hawaii Herald, 1978—. Named Top Market Timer, Timer Digest, Top Gold Timer, Top Bond Timer, Timer Digest Honor Roll; named to Select Info. Exch. and Rating Stock Selectors. Avocations: exercise, music, reading, philosophy. Home and Office: PO Box 573 Kahului HI 96733-7073 Office Phone: 808-877-2690.

YAMAMOTO, JANET KAZUKO, science educator; d. Shunta and Chizuko Catherine Yamamoto. BA, U. Calif., Davis, 1976; PhD, U. Tex. Med. Br., 1981. Rsch. assoc. scientist Okla. Med. Rsch. Found., Oklahoma City, 1982—83; rschr. U. Calif., Davis, 1983—85; asst. rsch. immunologist U. Calif. Sch. Vet. Medicine, 1985—91, adj. assoc. prof., 1991—93; assoc. prof. U. Fla. Coll. Vet. Medicine, Gainesville, 1993—2001, prof., 2001—. Cons. Ft. Dodge Animal Health, Iowa, 2000—. Bd. dirs. Creating Hope Internat. (Afghanistan Projects), Mich., 1996—. Recipient Pfizer Animal Health award, U. Fla., 1996; fellow, U. Tex. Med. Br., Galveston, 1979—81, U. Calif., San Diego, 1981—82. Mem.: Clin. Immunology Soc., Internat. AIDS Soc., Am. Assn. Immunologists, Phi Zeta Upsilon. Achievements include discovery of FIV (feline immunodeficiency virus) and vaccine. Avocation: music. Office: U Fla Coll Vet Medicine PO Box 110880 Gainesville FL 32611 E-mail: yamamotoj@mail.vetmed.ufl.edu.

YAMAMOTO, JOE, retired psychiatrist, educator; b. LA, Apr. 18, 1924; s. Zenzaburo and Tomie (Yamada) Y.; m. Maria Fujitomi, Sept. 5, 1947; children: Eric Robert, Andrew Jolyon. Student, Los Angeles City Coll., 1941-42, Hamline U., 1943-45; BS, U. Minn., 1946, M.B., 1948, MD, 1949. Asst. prof. dept. psychiatry, neurology, behavioral sci. U. Okla. Med. Center, 1955-58, asst. prof., 1958-60; assoc. prof. dept. psychiatry U. So. Calif. Sch. Medicine, Los Angeles, 1961-69, prof., 1969-77, co-dir. grad. edn. psychiatry, 1963-70; prof. UCLA, 1977-94, emeritus prof., 1994—; dir. Psychiat. Outpatient Clinic, Los Angeles County-U. So. Calif. Med. Center, 1958-77; dir. adult ambulatory care services UCLA Neuropsychiat. Inst., 1977-88, chief Lab. for Cross Cultural Studies; ret. Contbr. articles in field to profl. jours. Served to capt., M.C. U.S. Army, 1953-55. Fellow Am. Psychiat. Assn. (life), Pacific Rim Coll. Psychiatrists, Am. Acad. Psychoanalysis (trustee, mem. exec. com., pres. 1978-79), Am. Coll. Psychiatrists, Am. Orthopsychiat. Assn. (pres.-elect 1993-94, pres. 1994-95, past pres.), Am. Assn. for Social Psychiatry (trustee 1981-84, v.p. 1984-86); mem. So. Calif. Psychoanalytic Inst. and Soc. (pres. 1972-73), Soc. for Study of Culture and Psychiatry, Group for Advancement Psychiatry (bd. dirs. 1992-94), Kappa Phi, Alpha Omega Alpha. *Learning about the diverse peoples of America, I have been fascinated with how we can be Asian, Hispanic, Black, European, and Native American and still identify with our national values. We value our freedom, individual rights and our ability to be someone different but equal. In mental health also there is a need for recognition of cultural differences and the need of treatment response to the individual.*

YAMAMOTO, KAORU, retired psychology professor; b. Tokyo, Mar. 28, 1932; arrived in U.S., 1959; s. Saburo and Hideko (Watanabe) Y.; m. Etsuko Hamazaki, Apr. 6, 1959 (div. 1986); m. Carol-Lynne Moore, Oct. 4, 1986; children: Keita Carey Moore, Kiyomi Lynne Moore. BS in Engring., U. Tokyo, 1953; MA, U. Minn., 1960, PhD, 1962. Engr. Toppan Printing Co., Tokyo, 1953; engr., rsch. chemist Japan Oxygen Co., Tokyo, 1954-57, 58-59; asst. prof. Kent (Ohio) State U., 1962-65; from asst. to assoc. prof. U. Iowa, Iowa City, 1965-68; prof. Pa. State U., University Park, 1968-72, Ariz. State U., Tempe, 1972-87, U. Colo., Denver, 1987-99, prof. emeritus, 1999—. Vis. prof. U. Minn., Mpls., 1974, Simon Fraser U., Burnaby, B.C., Can., 1984, U.Victoria, B.C., 1985, 86, U. Wash., Seattle, 1987, Zhejiang Normal U., Jinhua, China, 1991; Fulbright lectr. U. Iceland, 1985. Author: The Child and His Image, 1972, Their World, Our World, 1993; author, editor 10 books, including Children and Stress, 2001, Too Clever for Our Own Good, 2007; co-author: Beyond Words, 1988; editor Am. Ednl. Rsch. Jour., 1972-75, Ednl. Forum, 1984-92; contbr. chpts. to books and articles to profl. jours. Recipient Disting. Tchr. award Ariz. State U., 1980; Landsdowne scholar U. Victoria, 1985, Ctr. scholar Ctr. for Rsch. on Ethics and Values Azusa Pacific U., 1998-2000. Fellow: APA; mem.: Motus Humanus. Avocations: winter sports, travel, classical music, reading. Office: 13651 W 54th Ave Arvada CO 80002

YAMAMOTO, KEITH ROBERT, molecular biologist, educator; b. Des Moines, Feb. 4, 1946; BS, Iowa State U., 1968; PhD, Princeton U., 1973. Asst. prof. biochemistry U. Calif., San Francisco, 1976-79, assoc. prof., 1979-83, prof. biochemistry, 1983—2003, vice chmn. dept. biochemistry & biophysics, 1985—94, dir. biochemistry and molecular biology program, 1988—2001, chmn. dept. cellular & molecular pharmacology, 1994—2003, prof. dept. cellular & molecular pharmacology, 1994—; vice dean for rsch. UCSF Sch. Medicine, 2002—03, exec. vice dean, 2002—. Co-author: Gene Wars: Military Control Over the New Genetic Technologies, 1988; co-editor: Transcriptional Regulation, 1992; assoc. editor: Jour. Molecular Biology, 1988—2001; editor: Molecular Biology of the Cell, 1991—2001; editor-in-chief:, 2002—. Testifier hearings on biol. warfare com. on govtl. affairs U.S. Senate, Washington, 1989. Recipient Career Devel. award, NIH, 1977-82, UCSF Disting. Teaching award, 1979-80, Dreyfus Teacher-Scholar award, 1982-86, Gregory Pincus medal Worchester Found. for Exptl. Biology, 1990, Vanderbilt U. Medal of Merit, 1999. Fellow: AAAS; mem.: IOM (elected 2003), NAS, Am. Acad. Arts & Sciences, Am. Acad. Microbiology. Office: UCSF Box 2280 San Francisco CA 94143-2280 Office Phone: 415-476-3128. Office Fax: 415-476-6129. E-mail: yamamoto@cgl.ucsf.edu.

YAMAMOTO, MASAHIRO, adult education educator; b. Iwamizawa, Japan, Dec. 22, 1959; s. Kazuo and Tsuyako Yamamoto. PhD, U. Ala., Tuscaloosa, 1998. Vis. asst. prof. Randolph-Macon Coll., Ashland, Va., 1994—2001; asst. prof. U. Wyo., Laramie, 2003. Author: (history monograph) Nanking: Anatomy of an Atrocity (History Book Club selection, 2000); contbr. articles to profl. jours. Mem.: Mil. History Soc. Japan, Soc. for Mil. History, Assn. Asian Studies. Office: University of Wyoming PO Box 3603 University Station Laramie WY 82071 Home Phone: 307-745-4463; Office Phone: 307-766-2802. Office Fax: 307-766-2727. Personal E-mail: stonewallmy@yahoo.com. Business E-Mail: yamamoto@uwyo.edu.

YAMAMOTO, MASAKO, music educator, director; b. Okayama, Japan; d. Yoshio and Satoko Ogawa; m. Tadashi Yamamoto, Nov. 23, 1985; children: Ayae, Yoshie. MusB in Voice Performance, Elisabeth U. Music, Japan, 1979; MS in Music Edn., U. Ill., 1997, EdD in Music Edn., 2002. Cert. tchr. Music for Young Children, Can., Harmony Rd., Oreg., music tchr. Yamaguchi prefecture Bd. Edn., Japan. Music educator Bd. Edn., Japan, 1979—89, Melody Acad. Music, San Jose, Calif., 2003—07; Japanese lang., culture tchr. Urbana Sch. Dist., 1994—95; dir. Masako's Music Studio, Fremont, 2007—. Brass band dir. Kumage Mid. Sch., Japan, 1983—84; dance club dir. Tabuse Spl. Edn. Sch., Japan, 1980—83, rsch. dir., 1981—83. Recipient Verdell Frazier Young awards, U. Ill., 2001, 2002; Marilyn Pflederer Zimmerman Music Edn. Doctoral fellowship, 1998. Mem.: Am. Coll. of Musicians (assoc.), Kappa Delta Pi (assoc.), Pi Kappa Lambda (assoc.). Achievements include research in multicultural music education. Avocations: running, piano. Studio: 39977 Mission Blvd Fremont CA 94539 Office Phone: 510-565-6230.

YAMANOUCHI, MIDORI, social sciences educator; b. Osaka City, Japan, Jan. 8, 1928; permanent resident, 1957; d. Shin'ichi and Fumiko (Urai) Yamanouchi; m. Edward J. Rynn, Oct. 10, 1975 (dec. July 29, 1987). Diploma, Tokyo Kasei U., 1948; student, U. Tampa, 1950—51; AB, Sophia U. Internat. Divsn., 1956; MA, Mich. State U., 1958, PhD, 1972; MA in LS, U. Mich., 1959. Chief rsch. assoc. Internat. Divsn. Sophia U., Tokyo, 1952—56; libr., bibliographer Mich. State U., East Lansing, 1959—63, 1964—67; asst. dir. R&D Sperry & Hutchinson Co., NYC, 1963—64; asst. prof. sociology and anthropology Marshall U., Huntington, W.Va., 1967—70, Fisk U., Nashville, 1970—72; assoc. prof. Livingston Coll., Salisbury, NC, 1972—74; vis. prof. Frostburg State U., 1974—75; prof. U. Scranton, Pa., 1975—2006; v.p. acad. affairs Lackawanna Coll., 2006—. Translator: Listen to the Voices from the Sea, 2000, In The Far Away Mountains and Rivers, 2005; editor: Sociol. Viewpoint, 1989—91, 2004—05; assoc. editor Comparative Civilizations Rev., 1996—2001. Trustee Lacawac Sanctuary, Lake Ariel, Pa., 1993—, Lackawanna Coll., 1995—2001, 2002—06, Tokyo Kasei U., 1997—; mem. pres. coun. Cedar Crest Coll., 1996—2002; mem. adv. bd. Northeastern Intermediate Unit Sch. Bd., Scranton, Pa., 1998—, Diversity Inst. Coll. Misericordia, Dallas, Pa., 1999—; bd. mem. Northeastern Pa. Philharmonic, 2006—, Everhart Mus., 2003—. Recipient Seeley Svc. medal, Lackawanna Coll., 2001, Ednl. Svc. award, Wilkes Barre (Pa.) Bd. Edn., 2002. Mem.: Assn. for Gen. and Liberal Studies (mem. exec. bd. 1975—78), Internat. Orgn. for Unification of Terminological Neologisms (del. UN, non-govt. orgn. 1995—, Disting. Contbn. award 2000), Internat. Soc. for Comparative Study of Civilizations (mem. exec. bd. 1978—2005, editor newsletter 1990—93), Pa. Sociol. Soc. (editor newsletter 1986—89, pres. 1990—91). Home: 220 Salem Pk Ln Lake Ariel PA 18436 Office: Lackawanna Coll 501 Vine St Scranton PA 18509 Office Phone: 570-504-1593. Business E-Mail: yamanouchim@lackawanna.edu.

YAMASHINA, TADASHI (GEORGE), transportation executive; arrived in U.S., 1993; m. Hiromi Yamashina; children: Kae, Kaki. BME, Waseda U., 1977. From engr. to project mgr. Toyota Motor Corp., Aichi, Japan, 1977—93; from exec. coord. to pres. Toyota Tech. Ctr., Ann Arbor, Mich., 1993—2001, pres., 2001—. Office: Toyota Technical Ctr USA Inc 1555 Woodridge Ave RR 7 Ann Arbor MI 48105

YAMASHITA, KENNETH AKIRA, library administrator, librarian; b. Topaz, Utah, Sept. 11, 1945; s. Susumu and Kiyoko (Kitano) Y. BA, Rutgers U., 1967, MLS, 1972; ArtsD, Simmons Coll., 1982. Reference libr. Montclair Free Pub. Libr., NJ, 1970-73; ext. svcs. libr. Decatur (Ill.) Pub. Libr., 1973-75; asst. to commr. Chgo. Pub. Libr., 1975-78; mktg. rep. Computer Libr. Sys., Inc., Newtonville, Mass., 1978-79; asst. to dir. Mass. Bd. Libr. Commrs., Boston, 1979-81; supervising libr. Stockton (Calif.)-San Joaquin County Pub. Libr., 1982-90, libr. divsn. mgr., 1990—. Guest lectr. Sch. Libr. Sci., U. Mich., Ann Arbor, 1978; bldg. program cons. Lakeland (Fla.) Pub. Libr., Calaveras County (Calif.) Pub. Libr., 1982—; advisor to prof. publs. U. Wis., Madison, Calif. State Libr., Sacramento, Gale Pub., Detroit, 1989—; state, fed. grant writer Calaveras County Libr., San Andreas, Calif., 1991; mem. rev. com. multi-ethnic recruitment scholarship program Calif. State Libr., 1990, 95; mem. design com. Libr. Edn. Funding Program Calif. State Libr., 1988. Assoc. editor: (reference book) Guide to Multicultural Resources, 1995-97; contbr.: Problems in Library Management, 1981, chpts. to books. Sec., bd. dirs. Stockton Shelter for Homeless, 1993-96; mem. diversity awareness team City of Stockton, 1994-98; mem. citizen rev. team United Way San Joaquin County, 1994, 95; participant Leadership Stockton, 1995; co-chair Joint Conf. Librs. of Color, 2006. Asian Studies Com. fellow Ind. U., 1967-69, Carnegie Grant fellow Ind. U., 1969-70, Friends of the Montclair Free Pub. Libr. fellow Rutgers U., 1971, HEA Title II B fellow Simmons Coll., 1979-80. Mem. ALA (chair, adv. com. Office for Libr. Outreach Svcs. 1987-90, councilor 1995-98, 99—, nominating com. 1995, com. on coms. 1997-98, spectrum initiative steering com. 1997—, Equality award, 2007), Asian/Pacific ALA (pres. 1996-97), Calif. Libr. Assn. (coun., assembly mem. 1987-93, pres. pub. libr. sect. 1998), Pub. Libr. Assn. (bd. dirs. & exec. com. 2000-03), Beta Phi Mu. Democrat. Avocations: videos/films, music, aerobics, cooking, travel. Office: Stockton San Joaquin County Pub Libr 605 N El Dorado St Stockton CA 95202-1907

YAMAUCHI, EDWIN MASAO, history professor; b. Hilo, Hawaii, Feb. 1, 1937; s. Shokyo Yamauchi and Haruko (Owan) Yamauchi Higa; m. Kimie Honda, Aug. 31, 1962; children: Brian, Gail. Student, U. Hawaii, 1957-58; BA, Shelton Coll., 1960; MA, Brandeis U., 1962, PhD, 1964. Instr. Greek lang. Shelton Coll., Ringwood, NJ, 1960-61; grad. asst. Brandeis U., Waltham, Mass., 1962-63; asst. prof. Rutgers U., New Brunswick, NJ, 1964-69; assoc. prof. Miami U., Oxford, Ohio, 1969-73, prof. dept. history, 1973—, dir. grad. studies, 1978-82. Author: Pre-Christian Gnosticism, 1973, World of the First Christians, 1981, Foes from the North Frontier, 1982, Persia and the Bible, 1990, Africa and the Bible, 2004, others; sr. editor Christianity Today, 1992-94; editor: Africa and Africans in Antiquity, 2001 Fellow NEH, 1968, Inst. for Holy Land Studies, Jerusalem, 1968, Inst. for Advanced Christian Studies, 1974-75; grantee Am. Philos. Soc., 1970. Fellow Am. Sci. Affiliation (pres. 1983), Inst. Bibl. Rsch. (chair 1984-86, pres. 1987-89); mem. Conf. on Faith and History (pres. 1974-76), Near East Archaeol. Soc. (v.p. 1978-79), Archaeol. Inst. Am. (chpt. pres. 1973-74), Evang. Theol. Soc. (pres. 2005-06) Office: Miami Univ Dept History Oxford OH 45056 Home Phone: 513-523-2819; Office Phone: 513-529-5141. Business E-Mail: yamauce@muohio.edu.

YAMAWAKI, NOBUYUKI, engineering educator, biomedical engineer, researcher; b. Engring., Utsunomiya U., Tochigi, Japan, 1990, M in Engring., 1992; PhD in Engring., Osaka U., Toyonaka, Japan, 1995. Cert. tchg. Tochigi, Japan, 1992. Rsch. assoc. Kinki U., Kinokawa, Wakayania, Japan, 1995—2001, lectr., 2001—07, assoc. prof., 2007—. Rsch. assoc. U. Minn., Mpls., 2004—05. Author: System Signal Processing and Programming, 2003; contbr. articles to profl. jours. Mem.: IEEE, Soc. Neurosci. Achievements include research in enhanced time-trequency spatial approach for motor imagery classification. Office: Kinki Univ 930 Nishimitani Kinokawa-shi 649-6493 Japan Office Phone: 81-736-77-0345 ext. 4206. Business E-Mail: yamawaki@waka.kindai.ac.jp.

YAMBRUSIC, EDWARD SLAVKO, lawyer, consultant; b. Conway, Pa., Mar. 9, 1933; s. Michael Misko and Slavica Sylvia (Yambrusic) Y.; m. Natalie Visniak, 1990. BA, Duquesne U., 1957; postgrad., Georgetown U. Law Ctr., 1959-61; JD, U. Balt., 1966; cert., The Hague Acad. Internat. Law, Netherlands, 1967-69; diploma, Ctr. Study and Rsch. Internat. Law and Internat. Rels., 1970; PhD in Pub. Internat. Law, Cath. U. Am., 1984. Bar: Md. 1969, US Ct. Customs and Patent Appeals 1972, US Supreme Ct. 1972, US. Ct Internat. Trade 1988. Copyright examiner US Copyright Office, Libr. of Congress, Washington, 1960-69; atty. adviser Office Register of Copyrights, 1969-98; pvt. practice internat. and immigration law, 1969—. Legal counsel Nat. Ethnic Studies Assembly, 1976—, Soc. Fed. Linguists, 1980; pres. AMCRO Internat. Consulting, Inc., 1995—. Author: Treat Interpretation: Theory and Reality, 1987, The Trade-Based Approaches to the Protection of Intellectual Property, 1990; contbr. articles to ofcl. newsletter Nat. Confedn. Am. Ethnic Groups, also legal jours. Pres. Nat. Confedn. Am. Ethnic Groups, Washington; nat. chmn. Croatian-Am. Bicentennial Com. nat. chmn. Nat. Pilgrimage of Croatian-Ams. to Nat. Shrine of Immaculate Conception, Washington; v.p. Croatian Acad. Am. Served to capt. US Army, 1957-59. Duquesne U. Tamburitzans scholar, 1953-57; Hague Acad. Internat. Law fellow, 1970. Mem. ABA, Md. Bar Assn., Internat. Law Assn., Internat. Fiscal Assn., Am. Soc. Internat. Law, Croatian Cath. Union Am., Croatian Frat. Union Am. Republican. Roman Catholic. Certificate issued by the Librarian of Congress in recognition of 40 years of distinguished service to the people of the United States of America, 1957-98. Home and Office: 4720 Massachusetts Ave NW Washington DC 20016-2346 Office Phone: 202-244-1626.

YAMIN, MICHAEL GEOFFREY, lawyer; b. NYC, Nov. 10, 1931; s. Michael and Ethel Yamin; m. Martina Schaap, Apr. 16, 1961; children: Michael Jeremy, Katrina. AB magna cum laude, Harvard U., 1953, LLB, 1958. Bar: NY 1959, U.S. Dist. Ct. (so. and ea. dists.) NY, U.S. Ct. Appeals (2d cir.) 1966, U.S. Supreme Ct. 1967. Assoc. Weil, Gotshal & Manges, NYC, 1958-65; sr. ptnr. Colton, Hartnick, Yamin & Sheresky, NYC, 1966-93, Kaufmann, Feiner, Yamin, Gildin & Robbins, LLP, NYC, 1993—. Trustee Gov.'s Com. Scholastic Achievement, 1976—; mem. Manhattan Cmty. Bd. 6, 1974—88, Manhattan Borough Bd., 1986—88; trustee Project Sail, Inc., 2005—. Mem.: ABA, Internat. Bar Assn., Soc. de Legis. Comparee, Internat. Law Assn., Am. Fgn. Law Assn. (Am. br.), Fed. Bar Coun., Assn. Bar City of NY, NY State Bar Assn., Harvard Alumni Assn. (bd. dirs. 1995—98, 2005—), Harvard Club of NYC (sub-chmn. schs. and scholarships com. 1972—93, trustee NY Found. 1981—, bd. mgrs. 1985—88, chair ho. com. 1992—95, bd. mgrs. 1993—98, v.p. 1995—98, chair comm. com. 1997—99, chair membership svcs. com. 1999—2000, pres. NY found. 1999—2006, chair cmty. svc. com. 2006—), Harvard Faculty Club (Cambridge, Mass.). Office: Kaufmann Feiner Yamin Gildin & Robbins LLP 777 3rd Ave New York NY 10017-1401 Office Phone: 212-755-3100. Business E-Mail: myamin@kaufmannfeiner.com.

YAMIN, ROBERT JOSEPH, lawyer; b. Waterbury, Conn., May 31, 1949; s. Joseph George and Elizabeth Mary (Bouharoun) Y.; m. Dianne Elizabeth Yamin, Sept. 3, 1988; children: Samantha Blythe, Rebecca Anne. Student, Yale U., 1978; AB summa cum laude, Western Conn. State U., Danbury, 1979; JD, Harvard U., 1982. Bar: Conn. 1982, U.S. Dist. Ct. Conn. 1983, U.S. Tax Ct. 1983, N.Y. 1984, U.S. Supreme Ct. 1986. Mng. ptnr. Yamin & Yamin LLP, Danbury, Conn., 1990—; corp. counsel, chief legal officer City of Danbury, Conn., 2002—. Conferee Am. Soc. Writers on Legal Subjects, 1985. Bd. editors Conn. Bar Jour., 1991—. Pres. Greater Danbury Young Republicans, 1973-75; del. White House Conf. on Libr. and Info. Svcs., 1978; mem. state ctrl. com. Conn. Rep. party, 1992—; councilman, minority leader Danbury City Coun., 1993—; corp. counsel, chief legal officer City of Danbury, 2002—. Fellow Acad. Continuing Legal Edn., 1985. Mem. ABA (mem. forum com. on health law 1986—), Fed. Bar Assn., N.Y. Bar Assn., Danbury Bar Assn., Conn. Bar Assn. (profl. discipline com. 1983-93, chmn. young lawyers com. on corp. and bus. law 1985-86), Conn. Health Lawyers Assn., Lions Club of Danbury (dir. 1993-94), Phi Alpha Delta. Roman Catholic. Avocations: political consultant, outdoor activities, travel. Home: 66 Barnum Rd Danbury CT 06811-2938 Office: Yamin & Yamin LLP 4 Moss Ave Danbury CT 06810-6818 Office Phone: 203-744-7090. Personal E-mail: ryamin5567@aol.com. Business E-Mail: lawyers@yaminlaw.com.

YAMIN, SONYA, music educator, voice educator; b. San Antonio, Feb. 4, 1970; d. Robert Rangel Ochoa and Maria Martha Garcia; m. Leslie Neil Yamin, Jan. 14, 1995; children: Joshua Ochoa, Kaisar Jonas. Grad., John Marshall H.S., San Antonio, Texas, 1984—88; student in Vocal Performance, U. Tex., 1988—94. Co. mem. Little Opera Co., San Antonio, 1993—94; voice faculty John Marshall H.S., San Antonio, 1998—, Earl

Warren H.S., San Antonio, 2004—, William Taft H.S., San Antonio, 2005—, Ronald Reagan H.S., San Antonio, 2005—. Vocal cons./coach Guadalupe Cultural Arts Theater, San Antonio, 2003—04. Singer (vocalist/instrumentalist): (CD) Ancient Echoes:Music from the time of Jesus and the second temple (#2 in NPR's New Sounds Ann. Listener's Poll, 2002), La Noche Buena (NPR's Weekend Edit. Best Year's Music by Ned Wharton, 2005). Named one of, Outstanding Coll. Students of Am., 1989; Music scholarship, U. Tex., 1988-1992. Mem.: Tex. Music Educators Assn., Nat. Assn. of Tchrs. of Singing (1st place winner Sophomore divsn. 1989, 1st place winner Jr. divsn. 1990, 1st place winner Sr. divsn. 1991), Golden Key Nat. Honor Soc., Sigma Alpha Iota. Achievements include Role: 1st Spirit in The Magic Flute with the San Antonio Music Festival 1991; Vocalist/SAVAE-representing the USA at the International Baroque Music Festival of Bolivia; Vocalist/SAVAE has been featured on national radio shows including NPR's Performance Today, Sound & Spirit, Latino USA, The Savvy Traveler, and Weekend Edition; Vocalist/SAVAE-Director Ridley Scott included a track from that recording in his 2005 feature film, The Kingdom of Heaven; Vocalist/SAVAE-the groups music is required listening in many university music programs; Role: Maria in West Side Story at the Josephine Theater 1999; Role: Rizzo in Grease at the Josephine Theater 1999; Role: Consuela in World Premiere of Liberty at the Josephine Theater 1999; Role: Maid in The Devil take Her with the University of Texas at San Antonio Opera Department 1990; vocalist for Internationally known ancient/early music group, SAVAE; Virgen de los Indios CD charted #11 in Billboard Charts World Music in 1999; Vocalist/SAVAE-recorded original compositions for PBS Award Winning Documentary Discovering Dominga by Academy Award Winning Composer Todd Boekelheide. Avocations: vocal recording, performing in musical theater, ballet. Office: Sonya Yamin's Voice Studio 11844 Bandera Rd # 206 Helotes TX 78023 Home Phone: 210-639-4736; Office Phone: 210-639-4736. Personal E-mail: s_yamin@hotmail.com.

YAMMINE, RIAD NASSIF, retired oil industry executive; b. Hammana, Lebanon, Apr. 12, 1934; came to US, 1952, naturalized, 1963; s. Nassib Nassif and Emilie (Daou) Yammine; m. Beverly Ann Hosack, Sept. 14, 1954; children: Kathleen Gross, Cynthia Rotman, Michael. BS in Petroleum Engring., Pa. State U., 1956; postgrad. advanced mgmt. program, Harvard U., 1977. Registered profl. engr., Ohio. Engr. Trans-Arabian Pipe Line Co., Saudia Arabia, 1956-61; with Marathon Pipe Line Co., 1961-75, mgr. we. divsn. Casper, Wyo., 1971-74, mgr. Ea. divsn. Martinsville, Ill., 1974-75; mktg. ops. divsn. mgr. Marathon Oil Co., 1975-83, pres., 1983-84; v.p. supply and transp. Marathon Petroleum Co., 1984-88, dir., 1984-90; pres. EMRO Mktg. Co., 1988-98; exec. v.p. Marathon Ashland Petroleum, 1998-99; ret. Bd. dirs. Marathon Oil Co., Centracomm Comm. Ltd., Thermo Fan LLC; vice chmn. bd. Findlay Devel. LLC.; chmn. bd. dirs. YHY Group, Inc. Patentee in field. Past trustee Wright State U. Found., Fisk U; bd. dirs. Findlay C. of C., bd. mgrs. Findlay Devel. LLC. Mem. ASME, Am. Petroleum Inst. (bd. dir.), Springfield and Clark C. of C. (bd. dirs.), Findlay C. of C. (bd. dirs.), Findlay Country Club. Republican. Home: 200 Penbrooke Dr Findlay OH 45840-8301

YAMNIK, DALE ARTHUR, quality assurance professional, food products executive; b. Milw. s. Arthur Herman Yamnik and Audrey Mary Dickson; m. Kristine Astin Yamnik. BS, U. Wis., Milw., 1973. Registered environ. health scientist Utah, 1978, sanitarian Ariz., 1992. Food and dairy compliance officer III Utah Dept. Agr., Salt Lake City, 1978—89; environ. health specialist III Utah Dept. Health, Salt Lake City, 1989—91; quality assurance dir. Smith's Food & Drug Ctrs., Inc, Tolleson, Ariz., 1991—99; food safety mgr. Albertsons, Inc, Denver, 1999—2004; quality assurance mgr. Yum! Brands, Inc., Denver, 2004—. Scout master Boy Scouts Am., Denver, 2002—06. Republican. Mem. Lds Ch. Avocations: reading, hiking, swimming, bicycling. Home: 542 Eaglestone Dr Castle Rock CO 80104 Office: Yum! Brands Inc 542 Eaglestone Dr Castle Rock CO 80104 Home Phone: 303-792-9987; Office Phone: 303-708-1536. Business E-Mail: dale.yamnik@yum.com.

YAMPOLSKY, PHYLLIS, artist; b. Phila. d. Louis Jacob Yampolsky and Bassia Yampolsky Green; m. Peter Forakis, June 12, 1959 (div. 1964); children: Gia, Jozeph Peter. Student, Phila. Mus. Sch. Arts, 1950-52, Inst. Allende, San Miguel de Allende, Mex., 1954-55, Ecole Beaux Arts, Fontainbleau, France, 1956, Hans Hofmann Atelier, NYC, 1956-58. Founder, dir., tchr. Workshop Yampolsky, NYC, 1956-66; art instr. 92d St. YMHA, NYC, 1958-60; founder, dir. Hall of Issues, NYC, 1960-61; 1st artist-in-residence NYC, 1966-67; creator, dir. Portrait of Ten Towns NY State Coun. Arts, 1967-70; founder, officer Northeast Windham Coun. Arts, Vt., 1978-79; instr. Vt. Acad., Saxton's River, 1979-81, Vt. C.C., Springfield, 1979-81; co-founder, instr. New Vt. Sch. Arts, 1981; founder, pres. Ind. Friends McCarren Pk., Inc., NYC, 1988—. Creator, dir., prodr. Hoving Happenings, 1966, 67; cons. Model Cities, Columbus, Ohio, 1968, Province Ont. Coun. Arts, 1968-70, Phila. Bicentennial Commn., Smithsonian Inst. Bicentennial Travelling Festival Kit; cons., panelist, performance artists Arcosanti, Ariz., 1977-78, 80, 81; facilitator NEA, 1970-75; cons., organizer, program dir. Habitat II CBO Host Com., NYC, 1995-96; spl. events dir. Youth Pavilion, World's Fair, San Antonio, 1968; writer, dir. art curriculum Marylerose Acad., Albany, 1969, Bennett Coll., 1970; presenter Habitat II, UN conf., Istanbul, Turkey, 1996. One-woman shows include Phila. Art Alliance, 1953, Judson Gallery, NYC, 1960, 62, Walker Gallery, NYC, 1974, Kulicke Gallery, NYC, 1975, Graham Gallery, NYC, 1977, O.K. Harris and Susan Caldwell Galleries, NYC, 1978, Stryke Gallery, NYC, Windam Coll., Vt., 1978, Marlboro Coll., Vt., 1981, A Place Apart, NYC, 1984, City Bank Gallery, Bklyn., 1986, Loft Lawyers, NYC, 1987, 479 Gallery, NYC, 1996, Stephan Gang, 1999, The Cave, 2000; exhibited in group shows at Park Place Gallery, NYC, Brata Gallery, Cornell U., Dallas Mus. Fine Arts, Mus. Erotic Art, San Francisco, Mus. Erotic Art, Stockholm, Whitney Mus., Weisner Gallery, NYC, City Without Walls Gallery, Newark, Green Gallery, NYC, Leo Castelli Gallery, NYC, Allan Stone Gallery, NYC, Franklin Furnace, NYC, Dorsky Gallery, NYC, Bklyn. Terminal Show, NYC, Food Stamp Gallery, NYC, ABC No Rio, NYC, Blue Mountain Gallery, NYC, Boriqua Coll., NYC, Phila. Mus. Art, Holland-Goldowsky, Chgo., Peter David, Mpls., Mc Nay Inst., San Antonio, Tex., Stephen Gang Gallery, NYC, The Cave, Bklyn., Bklyn. Brewery; represented in permenant collections Am. Town Hall Wall Sys. used in Robert Kennedy Presdl. Primary, 1968, Clinton Presdl. Campaign and Inaugural Festivities, 1993, 97, UN Women's Conf., Beijing, 1995, UN 50th Celebration, NYC, 1995, V.P. Gore's Reinvention Revolution Conf., Washington, 1996-97, March Against Cancer, Washington, 1998, W.A.F.E. Festival/Conf. on the Environment, Bklyn., 1998, The Hague (The Netherlands) Appeal Peace Conf., 1999, Main St. Millennium, Washington, Dallas Mus. Fine Arts, Mus. Erotic Art, Pres. Clinton Libr.; contbr. articles to profl. jours. Recipient Cue Mag., 1967, Betsy Barlow Rogers award Ind. Friends McCarren Pk., 1995; Ecole Beaux Arts scholar, Hans Hofmann Atelier scholar; grantee Ind. Friends McCarren Pk., J.M. Kaplan Fund, Andy Warhol Found., NY Found., Vincent Astor Found., Citizen's Com. NYC Inc., 1990—. Personal E-mail: partage@earthlink.net.

YAN, MARTIN, celebrity chef; b. Guangzhou, China, 1948; m. Susan Yan; 2 children. Grad., Overseas Inst. Cookery, Hong Kong; BS Food Sci., MS Food Sci., U. Calif., Davis; PhD Culinary Arts (hon.), Johnson & Wales U.; PhD Humane Letters (hon.), Colo. Inst. Art. Product mgr. canning corp., Hong Kong, 1976; mgr. head chef Lee's Garden Restaurant, Alberta, 1977; tchr., Chinese Cooking U. Calif.; founder Yan Can Cook Inc., 1997—, Yan Can Internat. Cooking School, San Francisco. Guest chef-instr. Calif. Culinary Acad., Johnson & Wales U., Culinary Inst. Am., U. San Francisco. Host (TV series) Yan Can Cook, 1978—, Martin Yan's Chinatowns, 2002—, Martin Yan Quick & Easy, 2004—; author: Yan Can Cookbook, 1981, The Joy of Wokking, 1982, Martin Yan, the Chinese Chef, 1985, A Wok For All Seasons, 1988, Everybody's Wokking, 1991, The Well-Seasoned Wok, 1992, Simply Delicious, 1993, A Simple Guide to Chinese Ingredients, 1994, Martin Yan's Culinary Journey Through China, 1995, Martin Yan's Asia, 1997, Martin Yan's Feast, 1998, Chinese Cooking for Dummies, 2000, Martin Yan's Invitation to Chinese Cooking, 2000, Martin Yan's Asian Favorites, 2001, Martin Yan's Chinatown Cooking, 2002, Martin Yan's Quick and Easy, 2004; guest appearances (TV series) The Today Show, A&E: Top Ten Television Chefs, Cooking Live with Sara Moulton, The Tonight Show, Good Morning America, Q&A Asia, Lo & Co., Howie Mandell Show, Donnie & Marie Show, Mornings on Two, Live with Regis and Kelly, The Dennis Miller Show, Talk Asia (CNN Asia), The Martin Short Show. Named Culinary Diplomat, Am. Culinary Fedn.; recipient Best TV Cooking Show, James Beard Found., 1994, Best TV Food Journalism award, 1996, D'Artagnan Cervena Who's Who of Food and Beverage award, 2001, Single Camera Photography award, Daytime Emmy Awards, 1998, Antonin Careme award, Chef's Assoc. of the Pacific Coast, Courvoisier Leadership award. Achievements include design of cookware and kitchen tools; owner of several pan-Asian restaurants. Office: Yan Can Cook Inc PO Box 4755 Foster City CA 94404 Office Phone: 650-341-0701. Business E-Mail: martin@yancancook.com. *

YANAGISAWA, MASASHI, geneticist, educator, researcher; b. Tokyo, 1960; MD summa cum laude, U. Tsukuba, Japan, 1985; PhD in Med. Scis., U. Tsukuba, 1988. Postdoct. fellow dept. pharmacology Inst. Basic Med. Scis. U. Tsukuba, Japan, 1988-89, asst. prof. pharmacology dept. pharmacology Inst. Basic Med., 1989-91; asst. prof. pharmacology dept. pharmacology Kyoto U., Japan, 1991; assoc. prof. dept. molecular genetics U. Tex. Southwestern Med. Ctr. Dallas, 1991-96, prof. dept. molecular genetics, 1996—, assoc. investigator Howard Hughes Med. Inst., 1991-96, investigator Howard Hughes Med. Ctr., 1996—, George L. MacGregor Disting. Chair in Biomed. Scis., 1998—. Invited lectr. The Arthur C. Corcoran Meml. Lectr. Coun. for High Blood Pressure Rsch. AHA, 1995; State-of-the-Art lectr. HHMI-NIH Rsch. Scholar Program 1995; keynote lectr. Keystone Symposium on the Molecular Biology of the Cardiovasc. Sys., 1996; invited spkr. opening symposium Harvard Inst. Human Genetics, 1997, Nature Conf., 1996, others. Contbr. numerous articles to profl. jours. Fellow Fellowships of Japan Soc. Promotion of Sci., 1988-89; recipient Donal Seldin award Internat. Congr. Nephrology, 1997, Takamine Young Investigator award Japanese Soc. Cardiovasc. Endocrinolgy and Metabolism, 1997, J.J. Abel award Am. Soc. Pharmacology and Exptl. Therapeutics, 1998, Med. Rsch award Robert J. and Claire Pasarow Found., 1998, Novartis award AHA, 1998, Kilby award Kilby Awards Found., 1998, Amgen award Am. Soc. Biochemistry and Molecular Biology, 1999, Gold Medal award Tokyo Techno-Forum, 2000, Jacobaeus award Nordisk Insulin Found., 2001. Mem. Am. Soc. Biochemistry and Molecular Biology (Amgen award 1995), NAS. Office: U Tex Southwestern Med Ctr Room Y5210 5323 Harry Hines Blvd Rm Y5210 Dallas TX 75390-7208 Fax: 214-648-5068. E-mail: afcsushi@aol.com.

YANAS, JOHN JOSEPH, lawyer; b. Albany, NY, July 18, 1929; m. Mary Faith Casey; children: John J., Joseph J., Kathleen Ann, Mary Patricia. Student Russell Sage Coll., 1947-50; LLB, Albany Law Sch., 1953, LLD, 1989. Bar: NY 1954, U.S. Ct. Appeals (2d cir.) 1962. Assoc. Casey, Honikel and Wisely, Albany, 1954-60; ptnr. Dugan, Casey, Burke & Lyons, Albany, 1960-69; ptnr. Casey, Yanas, Mitchell & Amerling, Albany, 1969-84, Casey, Yanas, Clyne, Mitchell & Amerling, Albany, 1984-88; ptnr. Degraff, Foy, Kunz & Devine LLP, 1989—; counsel Albany County Pub. Welfare Dist., 1959-60; mem. Albany City CSC, 1970-73, Albany County CSC, 1970-73; justice Albany City Ct., 1973-77; Bank. Trustee Christian Bros. Acad., Albany, 1972-2002, chair, 1992, Albany Law Sch., 1975-2001, chair, 1993. Fellow Am. Bar Found., NY Bar Found., ABA; mem. Am. Coll. Real Estate Lawyers, NY State Bar Assn. (chmn. real property law sect. 1974-75, (chmn. com. to confer with N.Y. State Realty Bd. 1975-77, chmn. com. continuing legal edn. 1977-80, treas. 1980-86, chmn. fin. com. 1987, pres.-elect 1988, pres. 1989), Albany County Bar Assn. (pres. 1978). Office: 90 State St Albany NY 12207 Office Phone: 518-462-5300.

YANCEY, ASA GREENWOOD, SR., physician, educator; b. Atlanta, Aug. 19, 1916; s. Arthur H. and Daisy L. (Sherard) Yancey; m. Carolyn E. Dunbar, Dec. 28, 1944; children: Arthur H. II, Carolyn L., Caren L., Asa Greenwood Jr. BS, Morehouse Coll., Atlanta, 1937, ScD (hon.), 1991; MD, U. Mich., 1941; ScD (hon.), Howard U., Cambridge, Mass., 1991. Diplomate Am. Bd. Surgery. Intern City Hosp., Cleve., 1941-42; resident Freedmen's Hosp., Washington, 1942-45, U.S. Marine Hosp., Boston, 1945; instr. surgery Meharry Med. Coll., 1946-48; chief surgery VA Hosp., Tuskegee, Ala., 1948-58; chief surgery of Hughes Spalding Pavilion, 1958-72; pvt. practice specializing in surgery Atlanta, 1958-86; from asst. prof. to assoc. prof. surgery Emory U., 1958—75, prof., 1975-86, prof. emeritus, 1986—, assoc. dean Sch. Medicine, 1972-89; med. dir. Grady Meml. Hosp., Atlanta, 1972-89, trustee, 1989—93; clin. prof. surgery Morehouse Sch. Medicine, 1985—; mem. staff Hughes Spalding Hosp., St. Joseph Hosp., Emory U. Hosp., 1986—88. Contbr. articles to profl. jours. Mem. Atlanta Bd. Edn., 1967—77, Fulton-De Kalb Hosp. Authority. 1st lt. M.C. US Army, 1942. Fellow: ACS, Am. Surg. Assn.; mem.: So. Surg. Assn., Inst. Medicine of NAS, Nat. Med. Assn. (1st v.p. 1988—89, trustee 1960—66, mem. editl. bd. jour. 1964—80). Baptist. Home and Office: 2845 Engle Rd NW Atlanta GA 30318-7216 Office Phone: 404-799-5045.

YANCEY, CAROLYN DUNBAR, retired education policymaker; b. Detroit, Feb. 10, 1921; d. Henry Steward and Annie Louise (Dye) Dunbar; m. Asa Greenwood Yancey, Sr., Dec. 28, 1944; children: Arthur H. II, Carolyn L., Caren L., Asa Greenwood Jr. BA, Wayne State U., Detroit, 1941. Cert. tchr. Mich. Mem. Bd. Edn. Atlanta Pub. Schs., 1982-97, v.p. Bd. Edn., 1993. Mem. bd. regents Univ. Sys. Ga., 1985—92; trustee Spellman Coll., Atlanta, 1972—2001; bd. dirs. Women's C. of C., Atlanta, 1972—74. Pres. PTA Frank L. Stanton Sch., Atlanta, 1960; active voter registration Atlanta Voters League, 1963. Recipient Leadership award, NAACP, 1981, Achievement award, Atlanta Med. Assn., 1982, Daniel James Gen. Edn. award, Tuskegee Airmen, Inc., 1993. Mem.: Links Inc. (pres. 1968), Delta Sigma Theta. Congregationalist. Avocations: sewing, homemaking. Home and Office: 2845 Engle Rd NW Atlanta GA 30318-7216

YANCEY, CHERYL LYNN, apparel designer, educator; b. Gary, Ind., Sept. 5, 1956; d. Ralph Eugene and Rachel M Neeley; m. Quinton Earl Yancey, Jan. 29, 1950. BS, Ind. State U., Terre Haute, 1983; MFA, George Wash. U., Washington, 1988. Asst. prof. Allentown Coll. St. Francis deSales, Centerville, Pa., 1989—95; assoc. prof. Shenandoah U., Winchester, Va., 1995—. Costume design art exhibit, Costume Design in the Shenandoah Valley, costume design, Shenandoah Summer Music Theatre, Pennsylvania Shakespeare Theatre. Women's min. Amazing Grace Fellowship Ch., Winchester, Va., 2006—07. Recipient Meritorious Achievement award, Am. Coll. Theatre Festival, 1988, 1990, 1993; fellow, George Wash. U., 1985—88. Mem.: US Inst. Tech. Theatre. Independent. Avocations: Bible study, reading, travel, history. Home: 108 Southdown Cir Stephens City VA 22655 Office: Shenandoah U 1460 University Dr Winchester VA 22601 Home Phone: 540-868-2844; Office Phone: 540-545-7247. Home Fax: 540-868-0046. Personal E-mail: clyancey1@comcast.net. E-mail: cyancey@su.edu.

YANCEY, KIM BRUCE, dermatology researcher; b. Atlanta, Nov. 25, 1952; s. Andrew Jackson and Edrie (Johnson) Yancey. BS, U. Ga., Athens, 1974; MD, Med. Coll. Ga., 1978. Diplomate Am. Bd. Dermatology. Intern dept. internal medicine Med. Coll. Ga., Augusta, 1978-79, resident dept. dermatology, 1979-81; med. staff fellow dermatology br. NIH, Bethesda, Md., 1981-84, sr. staff fellow dermatology br., 1984-85, sr. investigator dermatology br., 1993—2000; asst. prof. dept. dermatology Uniformed Svcs. U. Health Scis., Bethesda, 1985-87, assoc. prof. dept. dermatology, 1987-93, acting chmn. dept. dermatology, 1990-93; prof., chair dept. dermatology Med. Coll. Wis., Milw., 2001—. Cons. Walter Reed Army Med. Ctr., Washington, 1985—2000. Author monographs and sci. manuscripts; mem. various editl. bds.; contbr. articles to profl. jours. Grantee NIH, 1986—, NATO, 1988-93. Fellow: Am. Acad. Dermatology (editl. bd. 1986—93, 2004—); mem.: AMA, Med. Coll. Physicians (mem. exec. com. 2004—, chmn. 2004—05), Assn. Profs. Dermatology (chmn. program com. 2004), Wis. Dermatol. Assn., Dermatology Found., Am. Fedn. Med. Rsch., Soc. Investigative Dermatology (bd. dirs. 1982—84, co-chmn. ea. region 1990—92, co-chmn. program com. 2004, bd. dir. 2004—), Am. Dermatol. Assn. (Young Leadership award 1986), Am. Bd. Dermatology (v.p. 2005), Am. Soc. Clin. Investigation. Methodist. Office: Med Coll Wis Dept Dermatology 8701 Watertown Plank Rd Milwaukee WI 53226 Office Phone: 414-456-4081. Business E-Mail: kyancey@mcw.edu.

YANCEY, PHILIP DAVID, editor, author; b. Atlanta, Nov. 4, 1949; s. Marshall Watts and Mildred Sylvania (Diem) Y.; m. Janet Elenor Norwood, June 2, 1970. BA magna cum laude, Columbia Bible Coll., SC, 1970; MA with highest honors, Wheaton Coll., Ill., 1972; MA, U. Chgo., 1990. Writer, then mng. editor Campus Life mag., Wheaton, 1970-75, editor, 1974-80; editor-at-large Christianity Today, 1980—. Author: After The Wedding, 1976, Where Is God When It Hurts?, 1977 (Gold medallion award Evang. Christian Pubs. Assn. 1978), Growing Places, 1978, Unhappy Secrets of the Christian Life, 1979, Fearfully and Wonderfully Made, 1980 (Gold Medallion award), Insight, 1982, In His Image (Gold Medallion award), 1984, Open Windows, 1984, The Student Bible, 1986 (Gold Medallion award), Disappointment with God, 1988 (Gold Medallion award), I Was Just Wondering, 1989, Reality and the Vision, 1990, Praying with the KGB, 1992, Pain: The Gift Nobody Wants, 1993 (Gold Medallion award); also articles. Mem. Evang. Press Assn. (Periodical of Year award 1975) Office: Campus Life Mag Christianity Today 465 Gundersen Dr Carol Stream IL 60188-2415

YANCEY, RICHARD CHARLES, investment banker; b. Spokane, Wash., May 28, 1926; s. George R. and M. Ruth (Yenney) Y.; m. Mary Anne Shaffer, Feb. 5, 1956; children: Leslie, Jennifer, Richard C. Jr. BA in Econs., Whitman Coll., Walla Walla, Wash., 1949; MBA with distinction, Harvard U., 1952. Assoc. Dillon, Read & Co. Inc., NYC, 1952—63; v.p. Dillon, Read & Co., Inc., NYC, 1963-75, mng. dir., 1975-89, dir., 1990; sr. adv., 1992; ret. Dillon, Read & Co., Inc., NYC, 1992. Sr. advisor Ad Media Ptnrs., Inc., NYC; vice chmn., dir. Czech and Slovak Am. Enterprise Fund, Massapequa, NY; past partnership bd. Whittle Comms. L.P., Knoxville, Tenn.; bd. dirs. Prin. Funds, Des Moines. Former chmn. bd. dirs. Win Group of Funds, Seattle; former bd. overseers Whitman Coll.; former trustee, former pres. Plymouth Ch. of Pilgrims, Bklyn.; former trustee NY Infirmary-Beekman Downtown Hosp.; bd. dirs. Bklyn. Chamber Music Soc. With USNR, 1944-46, PTO. Recipient Pres.'s USA Freedom ECups Call to Svc. award. Mem. N.Y. Soc. Security Analysts, Assn. for Investment Mgmt. and Rsch., Harvard Club, Met. Club, N.Y.C., Pilgrims of the U.S. Republican. Home: 42 Monroe Pl Brooklyn NY 11201-2603 Office: Ad Media Ptnrs Inc 19th Fl 444 Madison Ave Fl 19 New York NY 10022-6903 Home Phone: 718-852-1729; Office Phone: 212-759-1870. Personal E-mail: rc1yancey@earthlink.net. Business E-Mail: ryancey@admediapartners.com.

YANCIK, JOSEPH JOHN, retired government official; b. Mt. Olive, Ill., Dec. 1, 1930; s. Joseph John and Anna (Gubach) Y., m. Rosemary Panich, Feb. 19, 1955; children— Geri Anne, Ellen Marie. BS, U. Ill., 1954; MS in Mining Engring., Mo. Sch. Mines, 1956; PhD, U. Mo., Rolla, 1960. Mining research engr. St. Joe Lead Co., Bonne Terre, Mo., 1955-58; mgr. research and devel. Monsanto Co., St. Louis, 1960-70; asst. dir. mining U.S. Bur. Mines, Washington, 1970-77; v.p. research Nat. Coal Assn., Washington, 1977-82; pres. Bituminous Coal Research, Inc., Washington, 1980-82; dir. Coal Export Office U.S. Dept. Commerce, Washington, 1982-84; dir. Office of Energy Internat. Trade Adminstrn., Washington, 1984-95; pvt. practice Mc Lean, Va., 1995—2003; ret., 2003. Cons. energy in internat. trade and investment; dir. energy affairs U.S.-Russia Bus. Coun., Washington, 1996—2002. Contbr. articles to profl. jours. Served with C.E. U.S. Army, 1950-52. Recipient Alumni Achievement award U. Mo.-Rolla, 1975, Silver Medal award U.S. Dept. Commerce, 1986, Gold Medal award Dept. Commerce, 1992. Roman Catholic. Home and Office: 1703 James Payne Cir Mc Lean VA 22101-4223 Home Phone: 703-532-7464. E-mail: joeyan12@msn.com.

YANCOPOULOS, GEORGE D., pharmaceutical executive; BA, Columbia U., 1980, PhD in Biochemistry and Molecular Biophysics, 1986, MD, 1987. Sr. staff scientist Regeneron Labs., Tarrytown, NY, 1989—91, head of discovery, 1991—92, v.p. discovery, 1992—97, chief scientific officer, 1998—, sr. v.p. rsch., 1997—2000; exec. v.p., pres. Regeneron Rsch. Labs., Regeneron Pharm., 2000—. Adj. prof. Columbia U., 1990—; bd. dirs. The Planetary Soc. Recipient Univ. medal for excellence, Columbia U., 2002; Howard Hughes fellow, 1987, Lucille P. Markey scholar, 1988—89. Fellow: Am. Acad. Arts & Sciences; mem.: NAS. Office: Regeneron Labs 777 Old Saw Mill River Rd Tarrytown NY 10591

YANDELL, CATHY MARLEEN, language educator; b. Anadarko, Okla., Dec. 27, 1949; d. Lloyd O. and Maurine (Dunn) Y.; m. Mark S. McNeil, Sept. 7, 1974; children: Elizabeth Yandell McNeil, Laura Yandell McNeil. Student, Inst. des Professeurs de Français à l'Etranger U. Sorbonne, Paris, 1969—70; BA, U. N.Mex., 1971; MA, U. Calif., Berkeley, 1973, PhD, 1977. Tchg. asst. U. Calif., Berkeley, 1971, acting instr., 1976—77; asst. prof. Carleton Coll., Northfield, Minn., 1977—83, assoc. prof., 1983—89, prof. French, 1989—. Chair commn. on the status of women Carleton Coll., Northfield, 1983-85, ednl. policy com., 1985-86, 96-97, romance langs. and lits., 1990-94, chair faculty affairs com., 2000-02, pres. of faculty, 1991-94, Bryn-Jones disting. tchg. prof. humanities, 1996-99, mentor to jr. faculty, 1996—, W.I. and Hulda F. Daniell prof. French lit., lang. and culture, 1999—; dir. Paris French Studies Program, 1998, 2004. Author: Carpe Corpus: Time and Gender in Early Modern France, 2000; co-author: Vagabondages: Initiation ã la litt. d'expression française, 1996, 1996; contbr. to Art & Argumentation: The Sixteenth Century Dialogue, 1993, French Texts/American Contexts: French Women Writers, 1994, Montaigne: A Collection of Essays, Vol. 4, Language and Meaning, 1995, Reflexivity in Women Writeres of the Ancien Régime, 1998, High Anxiety, 2002, Ronsard, figure de la variété, 2002, Lectrices d'Ancien Régime, 2003, Reflections on Teaching, 2004, Ecriture courante: Critical Perspectives on French and Francophone Women, 2005, Masculinites in Sixteenth-Century France, 2006, Paysage et nature a La Renaissance, 2007, Approaches to Teaching the Heptameron, 2007; editor: Pontus de Tyard's Solitaire Second, ou prose de la musique, 1980; contbr. articles to profl. jours. Active exec. com., then mem. Amnesty Internat., Northfield, 1980—. Grantee Faculty Devel., Carleton Coll., 1988, 1991; Regents' Travelling fellow, U. Calif. Berkeley, 1975—76, NEH Rsch. fellow., 1994—95, Mellon Faculty fellow, 2003, Roth Faculty Rsch. fellow, 2007, Mellon New Directions grantee, 2006. Mem.: MLA (del. 1989—92, chair exec. com. French 16th Century lit. 2001—05), Sixteenth Century Soc. (program chmn. French lit. 2007—), Phi Beta Kappa (pres. 2004—05). Democrat. Home: 514 5th St E Northfield MN 55057-2220 Office: Carleton College 1 N College St Northfield MN 55057-4044 Office Phone: 507-222-4245. Business E-Mail: cyandell@carleton.edu.

YANDERS, ARMON FREDERICK, biological sciences educator, science administrator; b. Lincoln, Nebr., Apr. 12, 1928; s. Fred W. and Beatrice (Pate) Yanders; m. Evelyn Louise Gatz, Aug. 1, 1948; children: Mark Frederick, Kent Michael. AB, Nebr. State Coll., Peru, 1948; MS, U. Nebr., 1950, PhD, 1953. Rsch. asso. Oak Ridge Nat. Lab. and Northwestern U., 1953-54; biophysicist US Naval Radiol. Def. Lab., San Francisco, 1955-58; asso. geneticist Argonne Nat. Lab., Ill., 1958-59; with dept. zoology Mich. State U., 1959-69; prof., asst. dean Mich. State U. (Coll. Natural Sci.), 1963-69; prof. biol. scis. U. Mo., Columbia, 1969—, dean Coll. Arts and Scis., 1969-82, rsch. prof., dir. Environ. Trace Substances Rsch. Ctr., 1983-93, dir. Alzheimer's Disease and Related Disorders Program, 1994—, dir. Spinal Cord Injury Rsch. Program, 2002—, rsch. prof., dir. Environ. Trace Substances Rsch. Ctr. and Sinclair Comparative Medicine Rsch. Farm, 1984-94, prof. emeritus, 1994—; dean emeritus, 2007—. Trustee Argonne Univs. Assn., 1965-77, v.p., 1969-73, pres., 1973, 76-77, chmn. bd., 1973-75; bd. dirs. Coun. Colls. Arts and Scis., 1981-82; mem. adv. com. environ. hazards VA, Washington, 1985-2002, chmn. sci. coun., 1988-2000, chmn. of com., 1990-2002. Contbr. articles to profl. jours. Trustee Peru State Coll., 1992-2001. Served from ensign to lt. USNR, 1954-58. Recipient Disting. Svc. award Peru State Coll., 1989, U. Mo., 2007. Fellow AAAS; mem. AAUP (Robert W. Martin acad. freedom award 1971), Environ. Mutagen Soc., Genetics Soc. Am., Radiation Rsch. Soc., Soc. Environ. Toxicology and Chemistry. Home: 1204 Castle Bay Pl Columbia MO 65203-6257 Office: U Mo 521 Clark Hall Columbia MO 65211-4420 Office Phone: 573-882-1640. Business E-Mail: YandersA@umsystem.edu.

YANDLE, STEPHEN THOMAS, dean; b. Oakland, Calif., Mar. 7, 1947; s. Clyde Thomas and Jane Walker (Hess) Y.; m. Martha Anne Welch, June 26, 1971. BA, U. Va., 1969, JD, 1972. Bar: Va. 1972. Asst. dir. admissions U. Va. Law Sch., Charlottesville, 1972-76; from asst. to assoc. dean Northwestern U. Sch. Law, Chgo., 1976-85; assoc. dean Yale U. Law Sch., New Haven, 1985—2002; exec. dir. Housing Authority of New Haven, 2002—04; dep. cons. on legal edn. ABA, 2004—06; v.p. global law sch. programs LexisNexis, 2007—. Bd. dirs. The Access Group, 1996-2004; lectr. in law Yale Law Sch., 2002-04; vis. scholar Am. Bar Found., 2006. Commr. New Haven Housing Authority, 1998-02; trustee Nat. Assoc. for Law Placement Found. for Rsch. and Edn., 2000-04. Capt. U.S. Army, 1972. Mem. Law Sch. Admission Coun. (programs, edn. and prelaw com. 1978-84), Assn. Am. Law Schs. (chmn. legal edn. and admissions sect. 1979, nominations com. 1987, chmn. adminstrn. of law schs. sect. 1991), Nat. Assn. for Law Placement (pres. 1984-85, co-chmn. Joint Nat. Assn. com. on placement 1986-88), New Haven Legal Assistance Assn. (bd. dirs., treas. 1992-98). Home Phone: 312-587-3147; Office Phone: 312-606-3526. Business E-Mail: stephen.yandle@lexisnexis.com.

YANEY, GEORGE, retired history professor; b. Teaneck, NJ, Oct. 30, 1930; s. Arthur J. and Frances (Levings) Y.; m. Ann Hinrichs, June 7, 1952; children: Brian, Dale, Carolyn, Tara. B in Mgmt. Engring., Rensselaer Poly. Inst., 1952; MA in History, U. Colo., 1956; PhD, Princeton U., 1961. Instr. Coll. Wooster, Ohio, 1957-58; prof. history U. Md., College Park, 1960-92, prof. emeritus, 1992—; ret., 1992. Author: Systematization of Russian Government, 1973, Urge to Mobilize, 1982, World of the Manager, 1994. Served to capt. USMC, 1952-54. Rsch. fellow Harvard U., 1969-70, fellow Slavic Rsch. Ctr., U. Hokkaido, Japan, 1990-91; Fulbright grantee, 1975, 77, 85, Internat. Rsch. Exchanges Bd. grantee 1965, 75, 77, 85, 89. Home: 1831 Pine Mesa Grove Colorado Springs CO 80918 Personal E-mail: georgeyaney@msn.com.

YANG, BINGEN, mechanical engineering educator; PhD, U. Calif., Berkeley. Prof. U. So. Calif. Author, Stress, Strain and Structural Dynamics: And Interactive Handbook of Formulas, Solutions and MATLAB Toolboxes, 2005; contbr. over 150 sci. papers to profl. jours., confs. Fellow: ASME. Achievements include pioneering the Distributed Transfer Function Method, a technique for modeling, analysis and control of complex distributed parameter systems; creation of miniature Piezoelectric forceps integrated with fiber optics camera for minimally invasive surgery; development of innovative time-delay approach for non-colocated and robust control of flexible mech. sys.; development of integrated reference and computer software for engineering education and distance learning; development of high-precision algorithms for modeling and analysis of inflatable/deployable/expendable space structures. Office: USC Dept Aerospace & Mech Engring Los Angeles CA 90089-1453 Business E-Mail: bingen@usc.edu.

YANG, BING-SHIANG, engineering educator; BME (hon.), Nat. Taiwan U., 1994, MME, 1996; PhD in Mech. Engring, Biomechanics, U. Mich., 2004. Cert. nat. refrigeration and air-conditioning profl. engr., ROC, 1995. Rsch. asst. Nat. Taiwan U., Taipei, 1993—96; engr. Tenkey Refrigeration MFG. Co. Ltd., Taipei, 1994; lectr. Tjing-Ling Indsl. Rsch. Ctr., Taipei, 1995—96; tchg. asst. Nat. Taiwan U., 1998—99; rsch. asst. U. Mich., 1999—2004; rsch. assoc. Rehab. Inst. of Chgo., 2005—06; postdoctoral fellow Northwestern U., Chgo., 2005—06; asst. prof. Nat. Chiao U., 2006—; dir. Movement Biomechanics and Med. Application Lab. Nat. Chiao Tung U., 2006—. Mem. com. Internat. Conf. on Rehab. Robotics, Chgo., 2005; mem. award com. Nat. Sci. Coun., Taiwan, 2006, external grant reviewer, Taiwan, 07, Nat. Med. Rsch. Coun., Singapore, 2007; rsch. affiliate Brain Rsch. Ctr. Nat. Chiao Tung U., 2006—; organizer Internat. Conf. Mech. in Medicine and Biology, Singapore, 2006; spkr. in field. Contbr. articles to profl. pubs. Second lt. Armor, Army, 1996—98, Taiwan. Decorated Best Trainee award ROC Army Pre-Mil. Tng. Ctr., ranked 1st/250 second lt. ROC Army Armor Officer Tng. Ctr.; finalist Young Investigator award, Internat. Soc. Biomech., 2006; recipient Academic, Personal, Profl., and Leadership Devel. Cert., U. Mich., 2004, Sarah Baskin Rsch. Excellence award, Rehab. Inst. Chgo., 2006; Tchg. Fellow, U. Mich., 2004, Advanced Rehab. Rsch. Tng. Postdoctoral fellowship, US Nat. Inst. on Disability and Rehab. Rsch., 2005—, Travel grant, Neural Control of Movement Soc. and Nat. Inst. on Disability and Rehab. Rsch., 2006, U Mich. Internat. Inst., 2002, U Mich. Rackham Grad. Sch., 2002, 2003, 2004. Mem.: Taiwanese Soc. Biomechanics, Soc. for Neurosci., Soc. for Neural Control of Movement, Internat. Soc. of Biomechanics, Am. Soc. of Biomechanics, Am. Soc. for Mech. Engineers. Achievements include patents for self-guided drill jib for equal-distance holes, ROC utility model; research in simulation study of human balance control on raised rigid structures; experimental study of age and gender differences on stepping and balancing behavior on laterally-compliant raised structures; modelling of human balance control on raised structures with lateral structural compliance; sensory input-enhanced stroke rehabilitation; task-specific modulation arm/hand posture and stiffness. Avocations: martial arts (3d Dan-black belt), swimming, ping pong/table tennis, bicycling, travel. Business E-Mail: bsyang@umich.edu.

YANG, CHARLES QI-XIANG, chemistry educator, researcher, consultant; b. Sanchang, Jiangsu, China, Jan. 30, 1944; came to U.S., 1982; s. Weizhu and Zhiyin (Zhou) Yang; 1 child, Chen. BS, Peking U., China, 1969; MS, Nanking U., China, 1981; PhD, Kans. State U., 1987. Rsch. scientist Henan Rsch. Inst. of Chemistry, Zhenzhou, Honan, China, 1975-78, 82; intern lab. scientist Perkin-Elmer Corp., Eden Prairie, Minn., 1986; asst. prof. Marshall U., Huntington, W.Va., 1987-90; assoc. prof. U. Ga., Athens, 1990-95, prof., 1995—. Cons. in field. Contbg. author: Adhesion Science, 1984, The Structures of Cellulose, 1987, Adhesives, Sealants, and Coatings for Space and Harsh Environment, 1988, Structure-Property Relations in Polymers, 1993; contbr. articles to profl. jours. Mem. Am. Chem. Soc. (treas. Cen. Ohio Valley sect. 1989, chmn.-elect Cen. Ohio Valley sect. 1990, chmn-elect N.E. Ga. sect. 1991, chmn. N.E. Ga. sect. 1992), Am. Assn. Textile Chemists and Colorists, Fiber Soc. Achievements include patents in field; development of new durable press finishing and flame retardant finishing systems. Avocations: swimming, hiking, classical music. Home: 189 Elderberry Cir Athens GA 30605-4954 Office: U Ga 305 Dawson Hall Athens GA 30602 Office Phone: 706-542-4912. Business E-Mail: cyang@fcs.uga.edu.

YANG, CHEN NING FRANKLIN, physicist, educator; b. Hofei, Anhui, Anhwei, China, Oct. 1, 1922; naturalized, 1964; s. Ke Chuan and Meng Hwa Loh Yang; m. Chih Li Tu, Aug. 26, 1950 (dec. 2003); children: Franklin, Gilbert, Eulee; m. Weng Fan Yang, 2005. BSC, Nat. SW Associated U., Kunming, China, 1942; MSc, Tsinghua U., 1944; PhD, U. Chgo., 1948; DSc (hon.), Princeton U., 1958, Bklyn. Polytechnic Inst., 1965, U. Wroclaw, Poland, 1974, Gustavus Adolphus Coll., Minn., 1975, U. Md., 1979, U. Durham, Eng., 1979, Fudan U., China, 1984, Eidg. Technische Hochschule, Switzerland, 1987, Moscow State U., 1992, Drexel U., 1995, Tsinghua U., Taiwan, 1996, Chiao Tung U., 1996, Chinese U., Hong Kong, 1997, U. Mich., 1998, SUNY, Stony Brook, 1999, Washington Coll., 1999, Baptist U., Hong Kong, 1999, Chung-Cheng U., Taiwan, 2000, U. Sci. and Tech., Hong Kong, 2002, Ecole Normale Superioeure, Paris, France, 2003. Instr. U. Chgo., 1948—49; postdoctoral position Inst. Adv. Study, Princeton, NJ, 1949—53, prof., 1955—66; position at Brookhaven Lab., 1953—54; Albert Einstein prof. physics SUNY, Stony Brook, 1966—99, prof. emeritus, 1999—; dir. Inst. Theoretical Physics, 1966—99; dir. emeritus C.N. Yang Inst. Theoretical Physics; disting. prof.-at-large Chinese U. Hong Kong, 1986—; prof. Tsinghua U., Beijing, 1998, Ji-Bei Hoang and Kai-Qun Lu prof., 2005—. Chmn., divsn. particles and fields Internat. Union Pure and Applied Physics, 1972—76; chmn. Fachbeirat, Max Planck Inst. Physics, 1980—83; established the found. Ctr. for Advanced Rsch., Zhongshan U., 1983, chmn.; organized a theoretical physics divsn. Nankai Inst. Math., 1986; coun. mem. Shaw Prize, mem. bd. adjudicators, 2005—; invited lectr. Contbr. articles to profl. jours.; author: Elementary Particles: a short history of some discoveries in atomic physics, 1961. Mem. governing coun. Courant Inst. Math. Sci., 1963—; mem. sci. adv. com. IBM, 1966—71; mem. High Energy Physics Adv. Panel, 1968—70; bd. trustee Rockefeller U., 1970—76, Stony Brook Found., 1981—99, Salk Inst., 1978—89, Ben Gurion U., 1981—, Brookhaven Sci. Associates, 1998—99; mem. Woods Hole Oceangraphic Institution, 1962—78; mem. coun. scholars The Libr. Congress, 1990—; bd. dir. Neuroscience Inst., 1983—88, Scientific American Inc., 1983—90. Co-recipient Nobel Prize in Physics, 1957; recipient Albert Einstein Commemorative award, 1957, Rumford prize, 1980, US Nat. Medal Sci., 1986, Benjamin Franklin medal, 1993, Bower award, 1994, N. Bogoliubov prize, 1996, Lars Onsager prize, 1999, King Faisal prize, 2001. Fellow: Am. Phys. Soc. (chmn., divsn. particles and fields 1970—71), Academia Sinica (Taiwan); mem.: AAAS (bd. dir. 1975—79), Brazilian Acad. Sciences, Asia Pacific Ctr. Theoretical Physics (pres. 1996), Assn. Asia Pacific Phys. Societies (pres. 1989—94), Nat. Assn. Chinese Americans (pres. 1977—80), Pontifical Acad. Sciences, Korean Acad. Sci. and Tech., Royal Spanish Acad. Sci., Polish Acad. Sciences, Venezuelan Acad. Sciences, Am. Philos. Soc., Russian Acad. Sciences, Royal Soc. London (fgn. mem.), NAS (chmn. panel of theoretical physics, physics survey com. 1965), Chinese Acad. Sciences. Achievements include being best known for the Yang-Mills Theory, the Yang-Baxter equation, and work with Tsung-dao Lee on parity nonconservation in weak interactions. Office: Tsinghua U Ctr for Advanced Study 1 Qinghuayuan Beijing 100084 China

YANG, CHENGHAI, agricultural engineer, researcher; b. Chengcheng, China, Sept. 25, 1962; s. Jianming Yang and Chunai Liu; m. Yueting Wang, Mar. 17, 1987; children: Ying, Michael Jiale, Melissa Mengying. BS in Agrl. Engring., NW Agrl. U., 1983, MS in Agrl. Engring., 1986; PhD in Agrl. Engring., U. Idaho, 1994. Instr. NW Agrl. U., 1986—90; vis. scholar U. Idaho, Moscow, 1990—91, grad. asst., 1991—94; rsch. scientist Tex. A&M U. Sys., Weslaco, 1995—2005; agrl. engr. USDA Agrl. Rsch. Svc., Weslaco, 2005—. Contbr. articles to profl. jours. Treas., sec. Chinese-Am. Assn. in Rio Grande Valley of Tex., Weslaco, 2000—01. Named Disting. Young Faculty Mem., NW Agrl. U., 1990. Mem.: Am. Soc. Photogrametry and Remote Sensing (co-chair 20th biennial workshop on aerial photography, videography 2005), Assn. Chinese Am. Agrl., Biol., and Food Engrs. (newsletter editor, at-large bd. dirs., sec., v.p., pres. 2007, Outstanding Svc. awards 2003, 2004), Am. Soc. Agrl. and Biol. Engrs. (com., sec., vice-chair, chair 1993—), Phi Kappa Phi. Achievements include research in integrating remote sensing technology for precision agriculture and mapping invasive weeds. Home: 2210 Northgate Dr Weslaco TX 78596 Office: USDA Agricultural Research Service 2413 E Hwy 83 Weslaco TX 78596 Home Phone: 956-973-2911; Office Phone: 956-969-4837. Office Fax: 956-969-4893. Business E-Mail: cyang@weslaco.ars.usda.gov.

YANG, DAGANG, mathematician, educator; PhD, SUNY, Stony Brook, 1986; BS, Zhe Jiang U., 1982. Vis. asst. prof. Purdue U., West Lafayette, Ind., 1987—89; assoc. prof. Tulane U., New Orleans, 1989—. Contbr. articles to profl. publs. Fellow, Sloan Found., 1984—85; grantee, NSF, 1987—. Mem.: Am. Math. Soc. Achievements include research in differential geometry, Einstein Manifolds. Office: Tulane U Dept Math New Orleans LA 70118 E-mail: dgy@tulane.edu.

YANG, DEBRA WONG, lawyer, former prosecutor; b. LA, 1959; 3 children. B, Pitzer Coll., 1981; JD, Boston Coll., 1985. Assoc. Haight Dickson Brown & Bonesteel, Santa Monica, Calif., 1985—87, Wildman Harrold Allen & Dixon, Chgo., 1987; law clk. to Dist. Judge Ronald Lew LA, 1988—89; atty. Greenberg Glusker, 1989; judge L.A. Mcpl. Ct., 1997—2000, L.A. Superior Ct., 2000—02; US atty. (ctrl. dist.) Calif. US Dept. Justice, LA, 2002—06; ptnr., co-chair crisis mgmt. practice group Gibson, Dunn & Crutcher LLP, LA, 2007—. Adj. prof. U. So. Calif. Law Sch. Mem.: Asian Pacific Bar Assn. (Pub. Svc. award 2003), Asian Am. Bar Assn., So. Calif. Chinese Lawyer Assn. Republican. Achievements include first to being the first Asian-American woman to serve as a US Attorney, 2002. Office: Gibson Dunn & Crutcher LLP 333 S Grand Ave Los Angeles CA 90071-3197 *

YANG, EMELINE, lawyer; b. Oxford, Miss., Oct. 17, 1970; BA in Econs. and Managerial Studies, Rice U., Houston, 1992; JD, U. Pa. Law Sch., 1995. Bar: Tex. 1995. Assoc. Hughes & Luce, LLP, Tex., 1995—97, Winstead, Sechrest & Minick, P.C., Dallas, 1997—2002, shareholder, 2003—. Mem. Atty. Serving Cmty., Dallas; co-worker Formosan Christian Ch. Dallas, 1997—2004; bd. dir. Asian Am. Forum, Inc., Dallas, 2001—06, Women's Fin. Exch. Inc., Dallas, 2001—02. Named a Tex. Rising Star, Tex. Monthly, 2004; named one of Best Lawyers in Dallas, D Mag., 2005. Fellow: Dallas Assn. Young Lawyers Found., Dallas Bar Assn. (bd. dir. 2000), Tex. Bar Found. (life); mem.: ABA, Tex. Assn. Bank Counsel, Dallas Asian Am. Bar Assn. (pres. and bd. dir. 2000), Dallas Women Lawyers Assn. (historian 2001, bd. dir. 2001—02), Nat. Asian Pacific Am. Bar Assn. (S.W. regional gov. 2004—05). Office: Winstead Sechrest & Minick PC 5400 Renaissance Tower 1201 Elm St Dallas TX 75270 Office Phone: 214-745-5687. Office Fax: 214-745-5390. E-mail: eyang@winstead.com. *

YANG, GRACE H., lawyer; d. Tai-cheng and Alice Yang; m. James T. Huang; 2 children. BA, Yale U., New Haven, Conn., 1994; JD, Cornell Law Sch., Ithaca, NY, 1997. Bar: Fla. Bar 1997, DC Bar 1997. Assoc. Holland & Knight LLP, Tampa, Fla., 1997—2005; shareholder GrayRobinson, P.A., Tampa, 2005—. Bd. mem. Yale Club of Tampa Bay, 2001—; steering com. mem. Bay Area Legal Services; v.p. membership Hillsborough Assn. for Women Lawyers, 2004—06. Home: 319 Columbia Dr Tampa FL 33606-3724 Office: GrayRobinson PA 201 N Franklin St Ste 2200 Tampa FL 33602 Office Phone: 813-273-5043. Business E-Mail: gyang@gray-robinson.com.

YANG, GUANGBIN, engineer; s. Xitan and Meirong Y.; m. Ling Jin, Nov. 19, 1991; children: Benjamin, Laurence. BS, Hangzhou Inst. Elec. Engring., China, 1986, M of Engring., 1989; MS, Wayne State U., Detroit, 1998, DPhil, 2000. Engr., team leader China Elec. Product Reliability & Environ. Testing, Guangzhou, China, 1989-95; rsch. asst. Wayne State U., Detroit, 1995-96; rschr. Ford Motor Co., Dearborn, Mich., 1996-98; reliability engr. Yazaki N.Am., Inc., Canton, Mich., 1998-2000; tech. expert Ford Motor Co., Dearborn, Mich., 2000—. Mem. tech. com. Fault-Tolerance Computation Soc., Beijing, 1994-95; cons. in field. Author: Life Cycle Reliability Engineering, 2007; mem. editl. bd. Internat. Jour. Reliability, Quality and Safety Engring.; contbr. articles to profl. jours.; referee various tech. jours. and internat. confs. Recipient Engr. of Yr. award, IEEE Reliability Soc., 2002. Mem. IEEE (sr.), Internat. Soc. Sci. and Applied Tech. (organizer and chair invited sessions, mem. program com. Internat. Conf. on Reliability and Quality in Design), Am. Soc. Quality (sr.), IEEE Reliability Soc. (chair automotive sys. com., internat. program com. chair, Engr. of the Yr. award 2002), Reliability Conf. France. Avocations: poetry, classical music. Office: Ford Motor Co 2000 Rotunda Dr MD 1258 Dearborn MI 48124

YANG, HENRY S. (HONG YANG), metallurgist, materials engineer; b. Tai Xin, Jiang Su, China, Oct. 27, 1964; came to U.S., 1989; s. Xiao-Wen and Yan-Hua (Li) Y.; m. Xiao-Ping (Susan) Su, May 1, 1992; children: Jenny Su, Rachel Su. BS, Harbin Inst. Tech., China, 1984; MPhil, U. Birmingham, Eng., 1987, PhD, 1989. Postdoctoral rsch. fellow U. Calif., Davis, 1989-92, staff rsch. assoc., 1992-93; staff rsch. metallurgist Kaiser Aluminum & Chem. Corp., Pleasanton, Calif., 1994-98; sr. metall. Kaiser Aluminum Engineered Products, LA, 1999—. Instr. Laney Coll., Oakland, Calif., 1994-95. Contbr. articles to internat. sci. jours. Recipient Emsley award Inst. Materials, London, 1988, Pfeil medal and prize Inst. of Materials, London, 1993, Buehler Tch. Paper Merit award Internat. Metallographic Soc., 1997. Mem. The Minerals, Metals and Materials Soc., Materials Rsch. Soc. Christian. Achievements include contributions to the understanding of superplasticity in aluminum alloys, titanium alloys, and intermetallics; study of physical and mechanical metallurgy problems of aluminum alloys. Office: Kaiser Aluminum Engrd Products 6250 Bandini Blvd Los Angeles CA 90040-3168

YANG, HENRY T.Y., chancellor, educator; b. Chungking, China, Nov. 29, 1940; s. Chen Pei and Wei Gen Yang; m. Dilling Tsui, Sept. 2, 1966; children: Maria, Martha. BS, Nat. Taiwan U., 1962, D, 2004; MS, W.Va. U., 1965; PhD, Cornell U., 1968; D (hon.), Purdue U., 1996, Hong Kong U. Sci. and Tech., 2002, City U. Hong Kong, 2005. Structural engr. Gilbert Assocs., Reading, Pa., 1968—69; asst. prof. Sch. Aeros. and Astronautics, Purdue U., West Lafayette, Ind., 1969, assoc. prof., 1972, prof., 1976—94, Neil A. Armstrong Disting. prof. aero. and astronautical engring., 1988—94, sch. head, 1979—84; dean engring. Purdue U., 1984—94; chancellor U. Calif., Santa Barbara, 1994—. Mem. sci. adv. bd. USAF, 1985—89, mem. sci. adv. group aero. sys. divsn., 1986—89; mem. aero. adv. com. NASA, 1985—89; mem. engring. adv. com. NSF, 1988—91; def. sci. bd. DoD (merged with Def. Mfg. Bd.), 1988—91, mem. def. mfg. bd., 1998—99; mem. mechanics bd. vis. ONR, 1990—93; mem. tech. adv. com. Pratt & Whitney, 1993—95; mem. Naval Rsch. Adv. Com., 1996—98; bd. dirs. AlliedSignal, 1996—99, Calif. Coun. Sci. and Technology, 1997—2004; rschr. in field. Contbr. over 160 articles in engring. to profl. jours. Bd. trustees Univs. Rsch. Assn., 2002—; bd. dirs. Axle and Mfg., 2004—. Named Hon. alumnus, U. Calif. Santa Barbara, 2001, Exec. of Yr., South Coast Bus. and Tech. Awards Dinner, 2004; recipient Twelve Outstanding Tchg. awards, Purdue U., 1970—94, Outstanding Aerospace Engr. award, 1999, Educator of Yr. award, Goleta C. of C., 2002, Pierre Claeyssens award disting. svc., Emmaus Santa Barbara, 2004. Fellow: AIAA, Am. Soc. Engring. Edn. (Centennial medal 1993, Benjamin Garver Lamme award, Gold medal 1998); mem.: ASCE, NAE (mem. acad. adv. bd. 1991—94), ASME, Univs. Rsch. Assn., Academia Sinica, Tau Beta Pi. Office: U Calif Santa Barbara Chancellors Office 5221 Cheadle Hall Santa Barbara CA 93106-2030

YANG, JERRY, Internet company executive; b. Taiwan, Nov. 6, 1968; married; 1 child. BSEE, MSEE, Stanford U., 1990, PhD studies in Elec. Engring. Co-creator Yahoo! Navigational Guide to the Internet, 1994; co-founder Yahoo!, Inc., Sunnyvale, Calif., 1995—, CEO, 2007—. Bd. dir. Yahoo! Inc., Yahoo! Japan, Alibaba, Cisco Systems, Inc., 2000—. Co-author (with David Filo, Karen Heyman): (books) Yahoo! Unplugged: your Discovery Guide to the Web, 1995; co-author: (with David Filo, Richard Raucci, Elizabeth Crane) Yahooligans!: Way Cool Web Sites, 1996. Trustee Stanford Univ. Named one of 400 Richest Ams., Forbes mag., 2004, 2005, 2006. Mem.: Com. 100, Phi Kappa Psi. Named company YAHOO!(acronym for Yet Another Hierarchical Officious Oracle). Office: Yahoo! Inc 701 First Ave Sunnyvale CA 94089-1019 *

YANG, JOSEPH, lawyer; s. Tony Tien-Sheng and Hsiu-Ying Tsai Yang; m. Roxana H. Hwu, 1999; children: Jacqueline O., Russell A. BS, Calif. Inst. Tech., 1986, MS, 1987, PhD, 1991; JD, Stanford U., 1996. Bar: U.S. Patent and Trademark Office 1996, Calif. 1996, U.S. Ct. Appeals (Fed. Cir.) 2002. Engr. TRW Corp., Redondo Beach, Calif., 1986—87; Office Naval Rsch. fellow Calif. Inst. Tech., Pasadena, Calif., 1987—91; rsch. engr. Shell Devel. Co., Houston, 1991—93; tech. advisor Weil, Gotshal & Manges LLP, Menlo Park, Calif., 1994—95; atty. McCutchen, Doyle, Brown & Enersen LLP, Palo Alto, 1995—98; counsel Skadden, Arps, Slate, Meagher & Flom LLP, Palo Alto, 1998—2005; v.p., gen. counsel Cryptography Rsch. Inc., San Francisco, 2005—; founding ptnr. PatentEsque Law Group, LLP, Menlo Park, 2005—. Adj. prof. Sch. Law U. Calif., Berkeley, 1998—99; program chair Practicing Law Inst., NY, 2002—; co-founder intellectual property transactions practice Skadden Arps LLP, Palo Alto; ednl. patron The Assocs. of Calif. Inst. Tech., Pasadena, 1999—; spkr. on intellectual property law. Editor: Advanced Licensing Agreements, 2003—; contbr. chapters to books, articles to jours. including The Practical Lawyer, The Licensing Jour., others. Active Assocs. Calif. Inst. Tech., Pasadena, 1999—. Named Outstanding Student in Engring. at Caltech, Inst. for Advancement of Engring., 1986; fellow, US Office Naval Rsch., 1987—91; scholar, Gen. Motors Corp., 1983—86. Mem.: Licensing Execs. Soc., Am. Intellectual Property Law Assn., Calif. Inst. Tech. Alumni Assn. (dir. 1999—2003), Caltech Alumni Assn. (pres. San Francisco chpt. 1999—2003). Office: PatentEsque Law Group LLP 2460 Sand Hill Rd Ste 101 Menlo Park CA 94025 Home Phone: 650-917-9002; Office Phone: 650-233-0822. Business E-Mail: joe@patentesque.com.

YANG, KAI, engineering educator; b. Beijing, June 18, 1965; s. Guanghua Yang and Yishi Sun; m. Qian Yu, Sept. 15, 2003; children: Fan, Kevin J., Arthur E., Nina. BS, China Petroleum U., Dongying, Shandong, 1982; MS, U. Mich., Ann Arbor, 1985; PhD, U. Mich., 1990. Asst. prof. Wayne State U., Detroit, 1990—95, assoc. prof., 1995—2002, prof., 2002—. Pres. Enterprise Excellence Inst., LLC, West Bloomfield, Mich., 2003—. Author: (books) Design for Six Sigma: A Roadmap for Product Development, Multivariate Statistical Methods for Quality Management, Design for Six Sigma for Service, Voice of the Customer Capturing and Analysis. Grantee Rsch. grant, Gen. Motors, 1991—2000, NSF, 1995, Ford Motor, 1995—2002, DaimlerChrysler, 1997—2003, Siemens, 2005—. Mem.: Am. Soc. Quality (chmn. Edward award com. 2006—), Inst. Indsl. Engrs.

Home: 1880 Poppleton Dr West Bloomfield MI 48324 Office: Wayne State Univ 4815 Fourth St #2151 Detroit MI 48201 Office Fax: 313-577-8833; Home Fax: 313-577-8833. Personal E-mail: kyang777@yahoo.com. Business E-Mail: kyang1@wayne.edu.

YANG, KEY PAIK, librarian, archivist; b. Naju, Cholla Namdo, Korea, Jan. 8, 1920; s. Yunmuk and Yunhui Yang; m. Hazel K. Yang; children: Won Kyung, A Kyung, Mal Kyung. Diploma, Soong Sil Acad., Pyongyang, Korea, 1939; diploma in Commerce, Nihon U., Tokyo, 1943; BA in Polit. Sci., Monmouth Coll., 1949; MA in Pub. Adminstrn., Am. U., 1958; MSLS, Cath. U. Am., 1960; PhD (hon.), Dongguk U., Seoul, Korea, 1975. With Chosen Kinyu Kumiai, Seoul, 1939, Chosen Kinsoku Butshi Eidan, Seoul, 1943—45; chief Property Custodian Office, Seoul, 1945—46; head of sect. Pub. Works Divsn., Seoul, Kyonggi Province, 1947—48, Pub. Info., Seoul, 1948—49; head Korean sect. Libr. of Congress, Washington, 1950—94, chief, Asian divsn., 1994—95; advisor Korean Embassy Archives, Washington. Mem. panel Bd. of U.S. Civil Svc. Examiners, 1955—55; chmn. Subcom. on East Asian Librs., 1980—80. Author: Physiology of Korean Culture, Art and Civilization: Facts and Thoughts, Introduction to Koreanology, Quotations to Ponder: Medley of Quotations on Traditional Society of Korea, China and Japan, Collected Works of Key P. Yang, 6 vols., 2005, Nationhood, Culture and Koreanology: A Polemic, rev. edit., 2006, Korean Book Lexicon, Korea, Japan, China: Their Traditional Social Molds, Quotations to Ponder: An Anthology; co-author: The School of Yi Confucianism; contbr. articles to profl. jours. Recipient Meritorious award, The Libr. of Congress, 1984; U.S. State Dept. sr. fellow, Korea, 1965, Fulbright Lectr., Korean U., Seoul, 1983, Harvard U. grantee in Korean Ecology, 1960. Mem.: Assn. of Asian Studies. Democrat-Npl. Home: 5104 Marlyn Drive Bethesda MD 20816

YANG, LIJIAN, educator; s. Zhenchuan Yang and Qiaoyun Yan; m. Yuliya Zyryanova, Dec. 27, 2002. BS, Peking U., Beijing, 1987; MS, U. NC, Chapel Hill, 1993, PhD, 1995. Asst. prof. Mich. State U., East Lansing, 1997—2001, assoc. prof., 2001—06, prof., 2006—. Judith C. & William G. Bollinger vis. prof. U. Pa., Phila., 2001—02; vis. prof. Peking U., 2004; vis. assoc. prof. Nat. U. Singapore, 2005. Assoc. editor: Computational Stats., 2000—06, Statistica Sinica, 2006—, Jour. Data Sci., 2007—. Fellow: Royal Statis. Soc.; mem.: Internat. Statis. Inst. (elected), Inst. Math. Stats., Am. Statis. Assn. (fellow 2003—04). Office: Michigan State University Department of Statistics and Probability East Lansing MI 48824 Business E-Mail: yang@stt.msu.edu.

YANG, PEIDONG, material science researcher; b. Suzhou, Jiangsu, China, Aug. 22, 1971; came to US, 1993; s. Xueli and Amei Yang; m. Mei Wang, May 15, 1996. BS in Chemistry, U. Sci. and Tech. of China, Hefei, 1993; MS, Harvard U., 1995, PhD in Chemistry, 1997. Rsch. asst. U. Sci. and Tech. of China, 1989-93, Harvard U., Cambridge, Mass., 1993—99; postdoctoral fellow U. Calif., Santa Barbara, 1997—99, assoc. prof. dept. chemistry, materials sci. and engring. Berkeley, 1999—, dep. dir. Ctr. Integrated Nanomechanical Systems. Chevron Texaco chair chemistry U. Calif., Berkeley, 2003. Assoc. editor: Jour. Am. Chem. Soc. Named to TR100, MIT Tech. Rev., 2003; recipient Zhongzhi Zhang prize, 1992, Presdl. prize, U. Sci. and Tech. of China, 1993, Camille and Henry Dreyfus New Faculty award, 1999, 3M Untenured Faculty award, 2000, Rsch. Innovation award, 2001, Hellman Family Faculty award, 2001, CAREER award, NSF, 2001, Young Investigator award, Alan T. Waterman award, 2007, Arnold and Mabel Beckman Young Investigator award, 2002, Camille Dreyfus Tchr.-Scholar award, 2004, Dupont Young Prof. award, 2004, Julius Springer prize for Applied Physics, 2004; grantee Alfred P. Sloan Rsch. fellowship, 2001. Mem. Am. Chem. Soc. (chmn. nanoscience subdivision, 2003, ExxonMobil Solid State Chemistry award, 2001, Pure Chemistry award, 2005), Materials Rsch. Soc. (Outstanding Young Investigator award, 2004), Am. Phys. Soc. Achievements include invention of metal oxide nanorods and their incorporation into the high temperature superconductor, thus enhancing the critical current density. Office: Dept Chemistry U Calif Berkeley B68 Hildebrand Hall Berkeley CA 94720-1460 Office Phone: 510-643-1545. Office Fax: 510-642-7301. E-mail: p_yang@berkeley.edu. *

YANG, PHILIP Q., sociologist; arrived in US, 1986, naturalized, 2005; m. Jianling Li, Dec. 20, 1984; children: Ming, William Zeus. PhB, Zhongshan U., Guangzhou, China, 1982; MA, UCLA, 1988, PhD, 1993. Asst. prof. Zhongshan U., Guangzhou, 1982—86; lectr. UCLA, 1994—95; from asst. prof. to assoc. prof. Calif. Poly. State U., San Luis Obispo, 1995—2001; from assoc. prof. to prof. Tex. Woman's U., Denton, 1999—. Author: Post-1965 Immigration to the United States: Structural Determinants, 1995, Ethnic Studies: Issues and Approaches, 2000; editor: Introduction to Ethnic Studies: A Reader, 1999; contbr. articles to profl. jours., chapters to books. Fellow, UN, 1986—87; grantee, NSF, 2002—04; Chancellor's Rsch. fellow, Tex. Woman's U., 2001—02, 2002—03. Mem.: Population Assn. Am., N.Am. Chinese Sociologists' Assn. (bd. dirs. 2001—03), Nat. Assn. for Ethnic Studies, Assn. for Asian Am. Studies (bd. dirs. 2001—03), Southwestern Social Sci. Assn., Assn. Chinese Profs. Social Scis. in the US, Am. Sociol. Assn. (Book award Internat. Migration Sect. 1998). Office: Texas Womans Univ PO Box 425887 Denton TX 76204 Office Phone: 940-898-2054. Office Fax: 940-898-2067. Business E-Mail: pyang@mail.twu.edu.

YANG, RALPH TZU-BOW, chemical engineer, educator; b. Chung King, China, Sept. 18, 1942; came to U.S., 1965, naturalized, 1976; s. Chen Pei and Wei (Gee) Y.; m. Frances H. Chang, Dec. 23, 1972; children: Michael, Robert. BS, Nat. Taiwan U., 1964; MS, Yale U., 1968, PhD, 1971. Rsch. assoc. Argonne (Ill.) Nat. Lab., 1972-73; scientist Aluminum Co. Am., Pitts., 1973-74; group leader Brookhaven Nat. Lab., Upton, N.Y., 1974-78; assoc. prof. chem. engring. SUNY, Buffalo, 1978-82, prof., 1982-95, chmn. chem. engring. dept., 1990-95, Praxair prof. chem. engring., chmn. dept., 1993-95; prof. chem. engring., chmn. dept. U. Mich., Ann Arbor, 1995—2000. Cons. in field. Author: Gas Separation by Adsorption Processes, 1987, Adsorbents: Fundamentals & Applications, 2003; editor Chem. Engring. Series Imperial Coll. Press, 1996—; contbr. articles to profl. jours. Rsch. grantee NSF, 1980—, Dept. Energy, 1980—, Alcoa Found., 1979-81; recipient Clarence Gerhold award for separations, 1997. Fellow AIChE (William H. Walker award for excellence in contbn. to chem. engring. lit. 1991, Inst. award for excellence in gases tech. 1996, Clarence Gerhold award separation divsn. 1997); mem. NAE, Am. Chem. Soc. (adv. bd. Ind. Engring. Chem. Rsch. Jour. 1991-93, award in seperations sci. and tech., 2003), Am. Carbon Soc. (adv. bd. 1985—, Sigri award for overall contbn. to sci. or tech. of carbon materials 1999), Am. Soc. Engring. Edn., Internat. Adsorption Soc. (adv. bd. Jour. Adsorption 1993—, bd. dirs. 1998—, adv. bd. Adsorption Sci. and Tech. 1986—, Separation and Purification Methods 1997—, Applied Catalysis, 2000—). Achievements include patents in field. Office: U Mich Dept Chem Engring Ann Arbor MI 48109 Business E-Mail: yang@umich.edu.

YANG, ROXANA HWU, lawyer, investor; d. Sen-Yao and Guey-Dan Liaw Hwu; m. Joseph Yang; children: Jacqueline, Russell. BSEE, U. Calif., LA, 0199; JD, U. Calif., Berkeley, 1997. Bar: Calif., US Patent and Trademark Office, US Dist. Ct. (no dist.) Calif., US Ct. Appeals (fed. cir.); lic. real estate broker Calif. Atty. Pennie & Edmonds, LLP, Palo Alto, Calif., 1997—2001; prin. Law Office Roxana H. Yang, Los Altos, 2001—05; mng. ptnr. PatentEsque Law Group, LLP, 2005—. Faculty Practising Law Inst., San Francisco, 2002—. Contbr. articles to profl. jours. Ednl. patron Assocs. Calif. Inst. Tech., Pasadena, 1999—2006. Recipient Am. Jury award Torts, Pepperdine U. Sch. Law, Am. Jury award Real Property. Office: PatentEsque Law Group LLP PO Box 400 Los Altos CA 94023 Home Phone: 650-917-9002; Office Phone: 650-948-0822. Office Fax: 650-948-0833. Business E-Mail: roxana@patentesque.com.

YANG, SCHUMAN CHUO, music educator; b. Canton, Kwongtung, China, Dec. 28, 1924; d. Yen Chuo and Shao-Keu Lee; m. Johann Y. Yang, Jan. 1, 1949; 1 child, Johann Y. Jr. MusB, Wheaton Coll., Ill., 1953; MusM, Am. Conservatory Music, Chgo., 1958; EdS, George Peabody Coll., Nashville, 1966; PhD in Music, Vanderbilt U., Nashville, 1973. Voice instr. Georgetown Coll., Ky., 1960—61; music tchr. Ohio County Sch. Sys., Hartford, Ky., 1962—64; asst. prof. music East Tex. Bapt. Coll., Marshall, 1966—68, La. Tech. U., Ruston, 1968—70, assoc. prof. music, 1971—73, prof. music, 1973—93; vis. prof. Hong Kong Bapt. Seminary, 1994—2000. Singer (dir., prodr.) Operas. Helping Asian refugees adjust to living in the US First Bapt. Ch., Shevreport, La., 1980—92. Recipient Outstanding Woman Faculty award, La. Tech Assn. Women Students, 1977; fellow Summer Seminar Fellowship award, Nat. Endowment for the Humanities, 1979; grantee Coll. Faculty Program award, AAUW Edn. Found., 1964—66. Mem.: Nat. Assn. Tchrs. Singing (life), La. State Arts Coun. (assoc.; adv. panel 1986—92). Home Phone: 469-241-0507.

YANG, SHU, materials scientist; b. China; BS in Material Sci., Fudan U., 1992; MS in Chemistry and Chem. Biology, Cornell U., 1997, PhD in Chemistry and Chem. Biology, 1999. Skirkanich asst. prof. in materials sci. and engring. U. Pa. Contbr. articles to profl. jour. Named one of Top 100 Young Innovators, MIT Tech. Review, 2004; recipient ICI award in applied polymer sci., ACS, 1999, Unilever award in polymer sci. and enring., 2001. Office: U Pa Dept Materials Sci and Engring 203 LRSM 3231 Walnut St Philadelphia PA 19104-6272

YANG, SONG-YU, medical biochemist; b. Wu-Xi, Jiangsu, China, Oct. 27, 1938; came to U.S., 1981; s. Rong-Geng Zhong and Su-Fei Yang; m. Xue-Ying He, Jan. 1965; children: Ying-Zi, Yu-Xiao. *Grandparents Xue-Ying Chu and Si-Zeng (Debao) Yang were teacher and principle, respectively, at Fu-Rein High School in Wu-Xi and Shanghai. Debao was also clergyman of the Wu-Xi Episcopal Church. Jin and Zi-Fan Zhong were grandmother and grandfather respectively. Father Rong-Geng Zhong was a pediatrician and president of Wu-Xi County Hospital. Mother Su-Fei Yang raised six children. Wife Xue-Ying is a research scientist of NYS OMRDD. Son Yu-Xiao is father of Lauren, Adrew and Marcus, and is an associate editor of Annals of Internal Medicine and a gastroenterologist at the University of Pennsylvania Medical Center. Daughter Ying-Zi is a patent specialist of Regeneron Pharmaceuticals.* MD, Peking U. Med. Ctr., China, 1960; MS, CCNY, 1982; PhD, CUNY, 1984. Instr. Peking U. Med. Coll., 1960—75; asst. prof. Shanghai Inst. Biochem. and Cell Biology, Chinese Acad. Sci., 1975—80; tchg. asst. CCNY, NYC, 1981—84, rsch. assoc., rsch. found., 1984—88; rsch. scientist NY State Office Mental Retardation and Devel. Disabilities, 1988—; head med. biochem. lab. Inst. for Basic Rsch. in Devel. Disabilities, 1994—. Contbr. chpts. to books and numerous articles to profl. jours. Investigator Am. Heart Assn., N.Y.C., 1991-94. Recipient L.J. Curtman prize CCNY, 1984, Wall Street Run Fellowship award, 1991, NIH Rsch. award, 1994, Alzheimer's Assn. Rsch. award, 1999. Mem. Am. Soc. Biochemistry and Molecular Biology. Research in fatty acid oxidation and the steroid hormone metabolism, neurological disorders; enzymes and related genes HSD17B10. Office: NYS Inst Basic Rsch Devel Disabilities Dept Neurochemistry 1050 Forest Hill Rd Staten Island NY 10314-6356 Personal E-mail: yang_songyu@yahoo.com.

YANG, TSONG-TOH (T.T.), pharmacist, researcher; b. Taiwan, Mar. 1, 1949; s. Yen-Leng and Chhai-Shia Lin Yang; m. Lee-Ju Wu Yang, Aug. 26, 1951; children: Benson Pin-Sheng, Steven Shih-E. BS in Pharmacy, Kaohsiung Med. Coll., Taiwan, 1971; MS in Pharmacy, U. R.I., 1979; PhD in Pharm. Sci., U. So. Calif., 1984. Registered pharmacist Taiwan, 1971. Med. supply officer Chinese Army in Taiwan, 1971—73; prodn. supr. Sterling Products Internat. Inc., Taiwan, Taipei, 1973—77; tchg. asst. U. R.I., Kingston, 1977—79, U. So. Calif., LA, 1979—81, U. N.C., Chapel Hill, 1982—83; rsch. pharmacist Am. Cyanamid Co., Pearl River, NY, 1984—85; devel. fellow Schering-Plough Rsch. Inst., Kenilworth, NJ, 1985—2006; pharm. cons., 2007—. Recipient Pres.'s award for Devel., Schering-Plough Rsch. Inst., 1994, 2002, 2005, DuPont Gold award for dry powder inhaler, 1998, Thomas Alva Edison Patent award, R&D Coun. NJ, 2005. Mem.: Am. Chinese Pharm. Assn., Controlled Release Soc., Am. Assn. for Pharm. Scientists. Achievements include patents for Preparation of powder agglomerates; inhaler for powdered medications; invention of Twisthaler dry powder inhaler- device and formulation. Home: 9 Old Farm Rd Warren NJ 07059 Personal E-mail: ttyangphd@yahoo.com.

YANG, WEN-CHING, chemical engineer; b. Taipei, Taiwan, Nov. 11, 1939; came to U.S., 1964; s. Ting-Lien and Ho (Lee) Y.; m. Rae Tien, Aug. 24, 1968; children: Evonne R., Peter T. BSChemE, Nat. Taiwan U., Taipei, 1962; MSChemE, U. Calif., Berkeley, 1965; PhD in Chem. Engring., Carnegie Mellon U., 1968. Sr. engr. rsch. and devel. ctr. Westinghouse Electric Co., Pitts., 1968-76, fellow engr., 1976-93, adv. engr. sci. and tech. ctr., 1993-98, Siemens Westinghouse Power Corp., Pitts., 1998—2005; sr. energy advisor Sci. Applications Internat. Corp., 2006—. Instr. U. Pitts., 1980, 83; cons., adj. prof., 2004-; chmn. rsch. rev. panel Office Fossil Energy, Dept. Energy, Washington, 1990; hon. guest prof. Tsinghua U., Beijing, 1996—; co-chair 10th Internat. Conf. on Fluidization, Beijing, 2001; spkr. in field. Author: (with others) Encyclopedia of Fluid Mechanics, 1986, 92; editor spl. vol. Powder Tech. jour., 1987, 98; editor: Fluidization, Solids Handling, and Processing, 1999, Handbook of Fluidization and Fluid-Particle Systems, 2003; contbr. over 100 papers to sci. jours. Fellow AIChE (programming chair and sec. group 3, editor 9 symposium series vols. 1987-88, 92-93, sec. particle tech. forum 1993-95, Fluidized Processes Recognition award 1993, George Westinghouse Signature award of excellence 1995. Fluidization Lectureship award 2000); mem. Am. Chem. Soc., Chinese Am. Chem. Soc. (pres. Pitts. chpt. 1994), Orgn. Chinese Am. (pres. Pitts. chpt. 2006-). Achievements include patents in field; development of widely-used correlations and design equations in pneumatic transport and fluidization areas. Home: 3117 Treeline Dr Murrysville PA 15668-1569 Home Phone: 724-327-3011. Personal E-mail: yangwc1139@gmail.com.

YANG, WESLEY, lawyer; b. Canton, China, Nov. 12, 1949; came to US, 1951; s. C.K. and Louise (Chin) Y.; m. Mary Ann McDunn, May 31, 1975; children: Margaret, Thomas Michael. Student, Chinese U. Hong Kong, 1969-71; grad. chef, South China Inst. Catering, Hong Kong, 1970; BA cum laude in East Asian Hist., U. Pitts., 1972, JD, 1975. Bar: Pa. 1975, US Tax Ct. 1984; CPA, Pa. Supervising tax specialist Coopers & Lybrand, Pitts., 1975-79; mgr. internat. taxes Dravo Corp., Pitts., 1979-84; pvt. practice atty. Pitts., 1984-88; of counsel Babst, Calland, Clements & Zomnir, Pitts., 1988; ptnr. Klett, Rooney, Lieber & Schorling, Pitts., Leech, Tishman, Fuscaldo & Lampl, LLC, Pitts, 2007—. Adj. prof. grad. prog. in taxation Robert Morris Coll., Pitts., 1982-84; asst. prof. taxation and acctg. Duquesne U. Sch. Bus. and Adminstrn., Pitts., 1984-90. Contbr. articles to profl. jours.; co-author: Representing Physicians, Estate Planning and Adminstrn. in Pa., The Tools and Techniques of Charitable Giving. Named one of Top 100 Attys., Worth mag., 2005—06. Mem. ABA, Allegheny County Bar Assn., Pa. Inst. CPA, Pitts. Tax Club. Office: Leech Tishman Fuscaldo & Lampl LLC Citizens Bank Bldg 30th Fl 525 William Penn Pl Pittsburgh PA 15219 Office Phone: 412-261-1600 ext. 269. E-mail: wyang@leechtishman.com. *

YANIKOSKI, RICHARD ALAN, educational association and academic administrator; b. Chgo. Heights, Ill., Nov. 30, 1946; s. Florian Felix and Julia Gertrude (Smith) Y.; m. Wendy Kay Towner, June 25, 1977; children: Laura, Catherine, Kristin. BA, Stonehill Coll., 1968; PhD, U. Chgo., 1987. Evaluation coord. DePaul U., Chgo., 1975—77, dir. inst. planning and rsch., 1978—82, assoc. v.p. academic affairs, 1983—91; rsch. asst. Spencer Found., Chgo., 1977—78; assoc. prof., dir. Mgmt. Pub. Svcs. Prog., 1991—94; dir. Chaddick Inst., 1993—94; pres. St. Xavier U., Chgo., 1994—2003, pres. emeritus, 2003—; pres., CEO Assn. Cath. Colls. and Univs., Washington, 2003—. Lectr. Sch. Edn. Loyola U., Chgo. Contbg. author: Values in Conflict, 1986, Education in Massachusetts, 1989, Survey of Social Sciences: Government and Politics, 1995; mem. editl. bd. Jour. Mktg. in Higher Edn.; contbr. articles to profl. jours. Mem. Univ.-City Edn. Group, Chgo., 1986-87, Ill. Export Devel. Internship Com., 1985-88; mem. exec. com. Ill. Consortium Ednl. Opportunity, 1986-88, Fedn. Ind. Ill. Colls. and Univs., 1995-; mem. adv. bd. St. Joseph Sch., La Porte, Ind., 1990-93; trustee Stonehill Coll., North Easton, Mass., 1995—; chmn. Metro S.W. Alliance, 1996—; bd. dirs. Washington Higher Edn. Secretariate, Ch. Exec. in Higher Edn., Internat. Fedn. Cath. Univs., Assn. Mercy Higher Edn.; founder, Harry F. and Elaine M. Chaddick Inst. Met. Devel. Rsch. grantee Exxon Edn. Found., 1985. Mem. Assn. Instl. Rsch., Assn. Study Higher Edn., Am. Ednl. Rsch. Assn. Roman Catholic. Office: Assn Cath Colls and Univs 1 Dupont Cir Ste 650 Washington DC 20036 Office Phone: 773-298-3309. E-mail: ryanikoski@accunet.org. *

YANKWITT, GEORGE B(RUCE), lawyer; b. Bklyn. Feb. 4, 1943; s. Irvin and Roslyn (Smith) Y.; m. Adrienne G. Schwartz, Nov. 24, 1966; children— Ian, Russell, Craig. B.S., N.Y. State Sch. Indsl. and Labor Relations, Cornell U., 1964, LL.B. with distinction, 1967. Bar: N.Y. 1967, U.S. Dist. Ct. (so. and ea. dists.) N.Y. 1968, U.S. Tax Ct. 1982, U.S. Ct. Appeals (2d cir.) 1968. Assoc. law clk. to judge U.S. Ct. Appeals (2d cir.), 1967-68; assoc. Graubard, Moskovitz, McGoldrick, Dannett & Horowitz, N.Y.C., 1968-72; assoc. Finley, Kumble, Heine, Underberg & Grutman, N.Y.C., 1972-74; assoc. Robinson, Silverman, Pearce, Aronsohn & Berman, N.Y.C., 1974-76, ptnr., 1976, ptnr., group co-head Comml. Litig., Bryan Cave LLP. Mem. Fed. Bar Council (treas., chmn. com. on 2d cir. cts.), ABA, N.Y. State Bar Assn., N.Y. State Trial Lawyers Assn., N.Y. County Lawyers Assn., Order of Coif. Editor, Cornell Law Rev. Office: Bryan Cave LLP 1290 Ave of the Americas New York NY 10104 Office Phone: 212-541-2220. E-mail: gbyankwitt@bryancave.com.

YANNAS, IOANNIS VASSILIOS, polymer science educator; b. Athens, Apr. 14, 1935; s. Vassilios Pavlos and Thalia (Sarafoglou) Yannas; m. Stamatia Frondistou (div. Oct. 1984); children: Tania, Alexis. AB, Harvard U., 1957; SM, MIT, 1959; MS, Princeton U., 1965, PhD, 1966. Asst. prof. mech. engring. MIT, Cambridge, 1966-68, duPont asst. prof., 1968-69, assoc. prof., 1969-78, prof. polymer sci. and engring. dept. mech. engring., 1978—, prof. dept. materials sci. and engring., 1983—; prof. Harvard-MIT Div. Health Scis. and Tech., Cambridge, 1978—. Vis. prof. Royal Inst. Tech., Stockholm, 1974. Author: Tissue and Organ Regeneration in Adults, 2001; editor: Regenerative Medicine, 2 vols., 2005; mem. editl. bd. Jour. Biomed. Materials Rsch., 1986—, Jour. Materials Sci. Materials Medicine, 1990—, Tissue Engring., 1994—, Interface, 2004, Biomed. Materials (China); contbr. articles to profl. jours. Recipient Founders award, Soc. Biomaterials, 1982, Clemson award, 1992, Fred O. Conley award, Soc. Plastics Engrs., 1982, award in medicine and genetics, Sci. Digest/Cutty Sark, 1982, Doolittle award, Am. Chem. Soc., 1988; fellow, Shriners Burns Inst., Mass. Gen. Hosp., 1980—81; Pub. Health Svc. fellow, Princeton U., 1963. Fellow: Biomaterials Sci. and Engring., Am. Inst. Med. and Biol. Engrs. (founding mem.), Am. Inst. Chemists; mem.: Inst. Medicine Nat. Acad Scis. Achievements include patents in field. Office: MIT Bldg 3-332 77 Mass Ave Cambridge MA 02139-4307

YANNELLA, DONALD, literature and language professor; b. NYC, May 12, 1934; s. Donald Joseph and Johanna (Meehan) Y.; m. Kathleen Malone, May 23, 1959; children: Susan Y. Harrigan, Katherine Y. Jennings, Donald III, Christopher, Clare. BS, Fordham U., 1956, MA, 1963, PhD, 1971. Tchg. asst. dept. English Auburn U., 1956-57; prof. dept. English U. So. Miss., 1981-83, Rowan U. (formerly Glassboro State Coll.), 1964-81, 83-91, prof. emeritus, 1991—; prof. dept. English Barat Coll., 1991-94, disting prof. Am. lit., 1995—2000. Dir. grad. studies English Rowan U., 1973-81, co-dir. Am. studies program, 1974-81; chair dept. English U. So. Miss., 1981-83; v.p. acad. affairs, dean coll. Barat Coll., 1991-94; cons. in field. Author: American Prose to 1820, 1979, Ralph Waldo Emerson, 1982, The Perfect Prodigy: Melville on the Birth of Malcolm, 1986, Herman Melville's Malcolm Letter: "Man's Final Lore", 1992, New Essays on Billy Budd, 2002, 2d edit., 2007; contbr. articles to profl. jours. With U.S. Army, 1957-58. Recipient Merit awards Rowan U., 1979-80, 85-86; NEH fellow, 1978-79. Mem. AAUP (chpt. pres. 1968-69, mem. cons. group Coll. and Univ. Govt. 1969, v.p. NJ State Conf. 1969-71, founding editor NJ Conf. newsletter 1969-71, nat. spl. com. non-tenured faculty 1971-72, chair 1973-79), Modern Lang. Assn. (Am. lit. sect., sec.-treas. 1982-85, exec. com. 1982-86, 88, adv. coun. 1986-88, nominating com. 1987-89, chair 1989, award 1988), Melville Soc. (program chair 1972-73, acting sec.-treas. 1973-74, acting editor 1973-74, sec.-treas. 1975-89, editor 1976-89, pres. 1990), Nat. Project Ctr. Film & Humanities (adv. com. 1974-75). Office Phone: 609-978-6443. Business E-Mail: yannellakd@aol.com.

YANNEY, PATRICK STEVEN, human resources specialist; b. Denver, Sept. 9, 1952; s. Merle Philip and Madeline Veronica Yanney; m. Stephanie Ann Robinson, Aug. 15, 1981; children: Mark Phillip, Luke Steven. BA, Colo. State U., 1974. Gatekeeper Glen Eyrie Conf. Ctr., 1974—76, reception ctr./bookstore mgr., 1977—78; adminstrv. asst. to dir. of adminstrv. svcs. The Navigators, 1978—79, pers. and facilities mgr., 1980—82, dir. adminstrv. svcs., 1983—91, pers. svcs. dir., 1992—2006, corp. human resources dir., 2000—. Chmn. supervisory com. Mountain Bell Credit Union, Colorado Springs, 1984—86; guest lectr. Webster U., Colorado Springs, 2003—04. Editor: ASTD newsletter, 1988—89; contbr. articles to profl. jours.; actor: (TV). Vol. mediator BBB, Colorado Springs, 1995—, 4th Jud. Dist. Small Claims Ct., Colorado Springs, 1997—. Named Outstanding Young Bus. and Profl. Person, Rotary Internat., 1986. Mem.: ASTD, Toastmasters (area gov. 1988—89). Avocations: Porsche racing, aviation, photography, camping, commercial acting. Office: The Navigators 3820 N 30th St Colorado Springs CO 80904 Home Phone: 719-531-0361; Office Phone: 719-594-2362. E-mail: pat.yanney@navigators.org.

YANNI, JOHN MICHAEL, pharmacologist; b. St. Mary's, Pa., Nov. 3, 1952; s. John Paul and Regina (Emmert) Y.; m. Nancy Jane Reedy, Sept. 22, 1979; children: Susan Elizabeth, Jennifer Ruth, Steven Reedy. BS, Allegheny Coll., 1974; MS, Va. Commonwealth U., 1979, PhD, 1982; AMP, Harvard U., 2000. Biologist A.H. Robins Co., Richmond, Va., 1980-82, sr. rsch. biologist, 1982-86, rsch. assoc., 1986-88; group leader Eastman Kodak Co., Rochester, N.Y., 1988-90; asst. dir. Alcon Labs., Inc., Ft. Worth, 1990-92, dir., 1992-93, sr. dir., 1993-2000, v.p. pharm rsch. R & D, 2001—. Contbr. articles to profl. jours.; patentee in field. Alden scholar Allegheny Coll., 1974. Mem. Am. Soc. Pharmacology and Exptl. Therapeutics, N.Y. Acad. Sci., Assn. for Rsch. in Vision and Ophthalmology, Soc. for Leukocyte Biology, Am. Acad. Allergy, Asthma and Immunology. Achievements include patents in area of allergy; description of thromboxane A2's muco-secretory effect; identification of antiallergic potential of Arylalkly-heterocyclic amines; discovery of drugs Patanol and Emadine for treatment of ocular allergy; description of secretory response of human conjunctival and choroidal mast cells; discovery of drug Nevanac for inflammation and pain. Office: Alcon Labs Inc 6201 South Fwy Fort Worth TX 76134-2099 Business E-Mail: john.yanni@alconlabs.com.

YANNONE, RONALD MATTHEW, systems engineer, researcher; s. Fanny Kalamira Yannone. BSEE, Stevens Inst. Tech., 1976; MSEE, Syracuse U., 1979. Elec. engr. GE, Utica, NY, 1976—91; math tutor Asbury Pk. Mid. Sch., NJ, 1992—95, Brookdale CC, 1992—95; engring. fellow BAE Electronics & Integrated Solutions, Nashua, NH, 1996—. Editor: BAE Systems Fellows Periodical, 2004—05; contbr. chapters to books, articles to profl. jours. Med. missionary Missionary, Edn. Evangelistic Tng., Huntingdon, Tenn., 1992—95; math problem developer Am. Math. Competitions, Lincoln, Nebr., 1994—. Named to, Electronic Warfare Tech. Hall of Fame, 2005. Mem.: Internat. Acad. Sci., Assn. of Old Crows, Mega Soc. (editor Noesis 2004). Achievements include patents for passive 360-degree target ranging; Commander's Decision Aid (CDA) for U.S. Army ground combat vehicles; passive single-aircraft air-to-air ranging; passive missile time-to-go estimation; patents pending in field. Avocations: reading, puzzles, swimming, rowing, exercise. Home: 189 Ash St 2 Nashua NH 03060 Office: BAE Sys Electronics and Integrated Solutions 95 Canal St Nashua NH 03064 Home Phone: 603-886-0098; Office Phone: 603-885-0454. Office Fax: 603-885-0698. Business E-Mail: ronald.m.yannone@baesystems.com.

YANNUCCI, THOMAS DAVID, lawyer; b. Springfield, Ohio, Mar. 30, 1950; s. David Marion and Patricia (Wilson) Y.; m. Lisa Marie Copeland, June 30, 1972; children: Teresa, Andrea, Thomas D. Jr. AB summa cum laude, U. Notre Dame, 1972, JD cum laude, 1976. Bar: Ohio 1977, U.S. Ct. Appeals (D.C., 1st, 2d, 3d, 4th, 5th, 6th, 7th, 8th, 11th and 10th cirs.) 1980, U.S. Supreme Ct. 1980, D.C. 1981. Law clk. to Judge John Danaher US Ct. Appeals (DC cir.), Washington, 1976-77; trial atty. US Dept. Justice, 1977-80; ptnr. Kirkland & Ellis, 1980—, chair firm mgmt. com., 2001—. Editor-in-chief U. Notre Dame Law Rev., 1975-76. Roman Catholic. Office: Kirkland & Ellis LLP 655 15th St NW Ste 1200 Washington DC 20005-5793 Office Phone: 202-879-5000. Office Fax: 202-879-5200. Business E-Mail: tyannucci@kirkland.com.

YANNUL, EDWARD, chemical engineer, writer; s. Edward Thomas Yannul and Lucille Ann Marie Yeager; m. Roxanne Marrandino, July 15, 1994. AS in Engring., Camden County Coll., Blackwood, NJ, 1984; BSChemE, U. Pa., Phila., 1986. Process engr. Rohm and Haas Co., Bristol, Pa., 1987—94, sr. process engr., 1994—99; sr. process devel. engr. J. M. Huber Corp. Engineered Materials, Havre de Grace, Md., 1999—2003; engring. assoc. process engring. Clorox Svcs. Corp., Pleasanton, Calif., 2003—06; product engr. Rohm and Haas Co. CMPT Inc., Newark, Del., 2006—. Author: Quick Hit TRIZ Assessment: User's and Facilitator's Guide, 2005; contbr. articles to profl. jours. Recipient R&D Achievement award, Clorox Svcs. Corp., 2004, Engring. Excellence award, 2005. Mem.: NRA, AIChE, Mensa. Republican. Roman Catholic. Achievements include patents in field. Avocations: martial arts, politics, hiking, fishing, history. Home: 29 Yosemite Dr Bear DE 19701

YANO, ELIZABETH MARTIN, epidemiologist, researcher; d. William Oliver Martin and Marjorie Ann Turner; m. Grant Akira Yano, May 3, 1986; children: Michael, David, Steven. BS in Psychobiology, UCLA, 1983, MSPH in Epidemiology, 1986, PhD in Epidemiology, 1995. Rsch. analyst med. outcomes study RAND Corp., Santa Monica, Calif., 1984—86, rsch. epidemiologist, 1986—95; project mgr. dept. medicine UCLA, 1986—88, assoc. prof. health svcs. Sch. Pub. Health, 1997—; sr. assoc. Arlene Fink Assocs., Inc., Pacific Palisades, Calif., 1986—95; assoc. chief pace evaluation Sepulveda (Calif.) VA Med. Ctr., 1989—94, assoc. chief evaluation and decision support, 1994—97; rsch. health scientist VA Health Svcs. R & D Ctr. Excellence, Sepulveda, 1993—97, asst. dir., 1997—99, assoc. dir., 1999—2002, sr. social scientist, 2002—, co-dir. VA associated health postdoctoral tng. program, 2002—04, deputy dir., 2004—. Mem. sci. rev. bd. VA Greater LA Healthcare Sys., 2002—; exec. com. mem. colorectal cancer quality enhancement rsch. initiative Ctr. for Chronic Disease Outcomes Rsch., Mpls., 2001—; mem. nat. ethics task force on gender disparities Dept. Vets., Washington, 2001—; presenter in field. Contbr. articles to profl. jours. Chair VA Women's Health Rsch. Agenda Conf., 2004. Recipient Achievement awards, UCLA Alumni Assn., 1980, 1981, Nat. Psychology Honors award, Psi Chi, 1982; grantee, VA HSR&D Svc., 1997—99, 1998—2002, VHA Survey of Women Veterans Health Programs and Practices, Dept. Vets. Affairs, 2001; Regents scholar, UCLA, 1979—83, Alumni scholar, UCLA Alumni Assn., 1979—83, UCLA Coll. Honors Meeker scholar, UCLA Coll. Honors Program, 1981—82, UCLA Marhoefer Med. scholar, UCLA, 1982—83, Health Policy fellow, RAND-UCLA, Inst. Medicine, Pew Meml. Trusts, 1986—89. Mem.: Acad. Health, Soc. for Gen. Internal Medicine. Office: VA Health Svcs R&D Ctr Excellence 16111 Plummer St 152 Sepulveda CA 91343 Business E-Mail: elizabeth.yano@va.gov.

YANOFF, MYRON, ophthalmologist; b. Phila., Dec. 21, 1936; s. Jacob and Lillian S. (Fishman) Yanoff; m. Karin Michelle Lindblad, Aug. 8, 1980; 1 child, Alexis A.;children from previous marriage: Steven L., David A., Joanne M. AB, U. Pa., 1957, MD, 1961. Prof. ophthalmology and pathology U. Pa. Med. Sch., Phila.; William F. Norris and George E. de Schweinitz prof. ophthalmology, chmn. dept., dir. Scheie Eye Inst., 1977-86; chmn., prof. ophthalmology Drexel U., Phila., 1988—. 1st exch. vis. prof. U. Vienna, 1992. Author: Ocular Pathology, Textbook of Ophthalmology; contbr. articles to profl. jours. Served to maj. M.C. USAR. Recipient Humboldt award, 1988. Mem.: Am. Acad. Ophthalmology (Sr. Honor award 1995), Am. Ophthalmic Soc., Verhoeff Soc. Office: 219 N Broad St Fl 3 Philadelphia PA 19107 Mailing: PO Box 0254 Gwynedd Valley PA 19437-0254 Office Phone: 215-762-3937. Business E-Mail: myanoff@drexelmed.edu.

YANOFSKY, CHARLES, retired biology professor; b. NYC, Apr. 17, 1925; s. Frank and Jennie (Kopatz) Y.; m. Carol Cohen, June 19, 1949, (dec. Dec. 1990); children: Stephen David, Robert Howard, Martin Fred; m. Edna Crawford, Jan. 4, 1992. BS, CCNY, 1948; MS, Yale U., 1950, PhD, 1951, DSc (hon.), 1981, U. Chgo., 1980. Rsch. asst. Yale U., 1951-54; asst. prof. microbiology Western Res. U. Med. Sch., 1954-57; mem. faculty Stanford U., 1958—2000, prof. biology, 1961—2000, Herzstein prof. biology, 1966—2000, prof. emeritus, 2000—; ret. Career investigator Am. Heart Assn., 1969-95. Served with AUS, 1944-46. Recipient Lederle Med. Faculty award, 1957, Eli Lilly award bacteriology, 1959, U.S. Steel Co. award molecular biology, 1964, Howard Taylor Ricketts award U. Chgo., 1966, Albert and Mary Lasker award, 1971, Townsend Harris medal Coll. City N.Y., 1973, Louisa Gross Horwitz prize in biology and biochemistry Columbia U., 1976, V.D. Mattia award Roche Inst., 1982, medal Genetics Soc. Am., 1983, Internat. award Gairdner Found., 1985, named Passano Laureate, Passano Found., 1992; recipient William C. Rose award in biochemistry and molecular biology, 1997, Abbott Lifetime Achievement award Am. Soc. Microbiology, 1998, Nat. medal of Sci., 2003. Mem. NAS (Selman A. Waksman award in microbiology 1972), Am. Acad. Arts and Scis., Genetics Soc. Am. (pres. 1969, Thomas Hunt Morgan medal 1990), Am. Soc. Biol. Chemists (pres. 1984), Royal Soc. (fgn. mem.), Japanese Biochem. Soc. (hon.) Home: 725 Mayfield Ave Stanford CA 94305-1016 Office: Stanford U Dept Of Biological Sci Stanford CA 94305

YANOTI, TIMOTHY, bank executive; B in Physics, Clarkson U., Potsdam, NY; MBA, Cornell U., Ithaca, NY. Aerospace engr.; dir. asset backed securities Greenwich Capital Markets; investment banking positions Drexel Burnham Lambert; mng. dir. GE Capital; with structured products group Nat. City Corp., Cleve., 2006, sr. mng. dir. capital markets, sr. v.p. Office: Nat City Corp Nat City Ctr 1900 E Ninth St Cleveland OH 44114-3484 Office Phone: 216-222-2000. *

YANTIS, STEVEN GEORGE, psychology educator; b. Oct. 24, 1955; BS in Psychology with honors, U. Wash., 1978; PhD in Exptl. Psychology, U. Mich., 1985. Postdoctoral fellow dept. psychology Stanford U., 1985-86; asst. prof. psychology Johns Hopkins U., Balt., 1986-92, assoc. prof. psychology and cognitive sci., 1992-95, prof. psychology, cognitive sci., 1995—. Mem. perception and cognition rsch. rev. com. NIMH, 1993-97, chair, 1996-97, spl. reviewer psychobiology and behavior rsch. rev. com. Mem. editl. bd. Jour. Exptl. Psychology: Human Perception and Performance, 1991—, Perception & Psychophysics, 1991—, Psychol. Bull., 1994-1999, Psychological Science, 1999-2003, Psychonomic Bulletin & Review, 2006-; contbr. articles to profl. jours. Recipient Troland Rsch. award NAS, 1996; NSF grad. fellow, 1981-84; Rackham Dissertation fellow, 1984-85. Mem. APA (Disting. Sci. award for Early Career Contbn. to Psychology 1994), Am. Psychol. Soc., Ea. Psychol. Assn., Psychonomic Soc. Office: Dept Psychology Ames 139 Johns Hopkins Univ Baltimore MD 21218-2686

YAO, ANDREW CHI-CHIH, engineering educator; b. Shanghai, Dec. 24, 1946; BS in Physics, Nat. Taiwan U., 1967; AM in Physics, Harvard U., 1969, PhD in Physics, 1972; PhD in Computer Sci., U. Ill., 1975; DSc (hon.), City U. Hong Kong, 2003; DEng (hon.), Hong Kong U. Sci. and Tech., 2004. Rsch. assoc. physics dept. U. Calif., Santa Barbara, 1972—73; asst. prof. math. MIT, 1975—76; asst. prof. computer sci. Stanford U., 1976—81, prof., 1982—86, U. Calif., Berkeley, 1981—82; William and Edna Macaleer prof. engring. and applied sci. Princeton U., 1986—2004; prof. Ctr. Advanced Study Tsinghua U., 2004—; disting. prof.-at-large Chinese U. Hong Kong, 2005—. Vis. scientist IBM Rsch. Ctr., Yorktown Heights, NY, 1975, San Jose, Calif., 1980—81, San Jose, 1982—83, Bell Labs., Murray Hill, NJ, 1978, Xerox Palo Alto Rsch. Ctr., Calif., 1979; cons. DEC Systems Rsch. Ctr., Palo Alto, Calif., 1986, AT&T Bell Labs., Murray Hill, NJ, 1991, Microsoft Rsch. Asia, Beijing, 2003—04. Contbr. articles to profl. jours.; mem. editl. bd.: Jour. Algorithms, 1980—91, SIAM Jour. Computing, 1981—87, mng. editor:, 1989—91, mem. editl. bd.: Jour. Assn. Computing Machinery, 1982—83, Info. and Control, 1982—85, Algorithmica, 1985—, Random Structures & Algorithms, 1990—2002, Jour. Cryptology, 1991—96, mem. adv. bd.: Internat. Jour. Founds. of Computer Sci., 1994—, adv. editor: Jour. Combinatorial Optimization, 1997—, assoc. editor-in-chief: Jour. Software, 2001—. 2nd lt. Taiwan Air Force, 1967—68. Recipient Donald E. Knuth Prize, 1996, Pan Weh-Yuan Rsch. award, 2003. Fellow: AAAS; mem.: Soc. Indsl. and Applied Math. (George Polya prize 1987), IEEE, Assn. Computing Machinery (A.M. Turing award 2000), Am. Math Soc., Chinese Acad. Scis. (fgn. mem.), Am. Acad. Arts and Scis., Academia Sinica, NAS. Office: Ctr Advanced Study Tsinghua U Beijing 100084 China E-mail: yao@cs.princeton.edu.

YAO, BIN, mechanical engineering educator; b. Shaanxi, China, Dec. 23, 1968; came to U.S., 1992; s. Weikuan Yao and Qingrong Liu; m. Ying Xie, July 14, 1999 (div. 2003). PhD, U. Calif., Berkeley, 1996. Postdoctoral rschr. mech. engring. dept. U. Calif., Berkeley, 1996; asst. prof. Sch. Mech. Engring. Purdue U., West Lafayette, Ind., 1996—2002, assoc. prof. Sch. Mech. Engring., 2002—. Summer faculty sabbatical leave Advanced Hydraulics Group, Joliet (Ill.) plant, Caterpillar Inc., 1997. Contbr. numerous tech. articles to profl. publs. (NSF Career award 1998). Recipient O. Hugo Schuck Best Paper award Am. Automatic Control Coun., 2004; Regents fellow U. Calif., 1992. Mem. IEEE, ASME. Avocations: sports, travel, art, music. Office: Purdue U Sch Mech Engring West Lafayette IN 47907 Office Phone: 765-494-7746. Office Fax: 765-494-0539. Business E-Mail: byao@ieee.org.

YAO, DAVID DA-WEI, engineering educator; b. Shanghai, July 14, 1950; came to U.S., 1983, naturalized, 1990; s. William Kang-Fu and Nancy Yun-Lan (Lu) Y.; m. Helen Zhi-Heng Chen, Jan. 31, 1979; children: Henry, John. MASc, U. Toronto, Ont., Can., 1981, PhD, 1983. Assoc. prof. systems engring. Harvard U., Cambridge, Mass., 1986-88; asst. prof. indsl. engring. and ops. rsch. Columbia U., NYC, 1983-86, prof., 1988—, Thomas Alva Edison prof., 1992—. Acad. visitor AT&T Bell Labs., Holmdel, N.J., 1989, T.J. Watson Rsch. Ctr., IBM, Yorktown, N.Y., 1990—. Co-author: Monotone Structure in Discrete-Event Systems, 1994, Fundamentals of Queueing Networks, 2001, Dynamic Control of Quality in Production-Inventory Systems, 2002; contbr. over 160 articles to profl. jours. including Maths. Ops. Rsch., Jour. of Assn. Computing Machinery, Advances in Applied Probability. Recipient Presdl. Young Investigator award NSF, Washington, 1987-92, Guggenheim fellow John Simon Guggenheim Meml. Found., N.Y.C., 1991-92. Fellow IEEE, Inst. Ops. Rsch. Mgmt. Scis.; mem. Soc. Indsl. and Applied Math. (Outstanding Paper prize 2003), Ops. Rsch. Soc. Am. (George Nicholson prize 1983, Franz Edelman award 1999). Achievements include development of theory of algebraic structures in discrete-event systems, theory of stochastic convexity and its applications in queuing networks, stochastic network models for manufacturing systems and supply chains, methodologies in the optimization and control of stochastic discrete-event systems. Home: 1261 Underhill Ave Yorktown Heights NY 10598-5718 Office: Columbia U IEOR Dept 302 Mudd Bldg New York NY 10027-6699 Business E-Mail: yao@columbia.edu.

YAO, FRANCES, music educator, small business owner; arrived in U.S., 1976; d. Ted Yao and Phuong Hue Chi; children: Christopher Y. Shi, Daniel H. Shi. BA, Nat. Conservatory, Saigon, Vietnam, 1973. Cert. tchr. Suzuki and piano performance Ga., 1973. Pianist Chinese Alliance Ch., Saigon, Vietnam, 1970—75; tchr. piano Hai Quang Music Sch., Saigon, Vietnam, 1973—75, Sandy Springs Music Sch., Roswell, Ga., 1976—78, Ephrata (Pa.) Music Acad., 1975—77, Frances Yao's Piano Studio, Alpharetta, Ga., 1980—. Mem. choir, leader sect. Johns Creek Bapt. Ch., Alpharetta, Ga., 2001—. Recipient Beethoven 200-yr. Piano Competition award, German Culture Inst., 1970. Mem.: Music Tchr. Nat. Assn., North Fulton Music Tchr. Assn., N.D. Music Tchrs. Assn. (chmn. auditions 1983—, v.p. 1992), Ga. Music Educators Assn. (assoc.), Ga. Music Teachers Assn. (assoc.). Avocations: swimming, travel, music, photography, reading. Home Phone: 770-410-1988.

YAO, JOHN SEN, physician; b. Honolulu, Aug. 28, 1954; s. Hsin-Hung and Dorothy W. Yao; m. Pauline A. Mysliwiec, Oct. 16, 1993. MPH, Columbia U., 1978, MD, 1983; MBA, UCLA, 1998; MPA, Harvard U., 1999. Diplomate Am. Bd. Internal Medicine, Nat. Bd. Med. Examiners. Resident in internal medicine U. Calif.-San Francisco Med. Ctr., 1983-86, asst. clin. prof., 1988-94; chief med. officer USPHS, Calif., 1990-98; med. dir. Cigna Healthcare, inc., 1997-98; fellow in policy studies Harvard U., Cambridge, Mass., 1998—. Mem. exec. com. State of Calif. TB Control, 1994—; mem. steering com. Breast and Cervical Cancer Prevention, Stte of Calif., 1991-94; med. advisor State of Calif. Medicaid Reform com., 1994-95. Contbr. articles to profl. jours. Med. advisor Gov.'s Coun. on Exercise and Health, Calif., 19945; mem. Calif. HIV-AIDS Commn., 1990-93. Fellow ACP. Avocations: golf, tennis, skiing, classical music, opera. Office: PO Box 191202 San Francisco CA 94119 E-mail: jyaomd@jyaomd.com.

YAO, LIHUA, research scientist, statistician; PhD, Ohio State U., Columbus, 1997. Sr. rsch. scientist CTB/McGraw-Hill, Monterey, Calif., 1999—. Achievements include development of software BMIRT LinkMIRT. Office: CTB/McGraw-Hill 20 Ryan Ranch Rd Monterey CA 93940 Office Phone: 831-393-7731.

YAO, TITO GO, pediatrician; b. Manila, May 30, 1943; arrived in U.S., 1970, naturalized, 1984; s. Vincente and Sin Keng (Go) Yao; m. Lilia Ytem, July 3, 1976; children: Robert, James, Richard. MD, Far Eastern U., Manila, 1969. Diplomate Am. Bd. Pediatrics, Am. Bd. Quality Assurance. Intern Evang. Deaconess Hosp., Milw., 1970-71; resident in pediatrics T.C. Thompson Children's Hosp., Chattanooga, 1971-72, Meth. Hosp., Bklyn., 1972-73; fellow St. Christopher Hosp. Children, Phila., 1973-74, Cook County Children's Hosp., Chgo., 1974-75; dir. GSK Med. Ctr., Chgo., 1976—; preceptor Rush Med. Coll., 2003—. Chmn. dept. pediat. St. Anne's Hosp., Chgo., 1986—88, Loretto Hosp., Chgo., 1988—; dir. RJ Med. Ctr., Chgo., 1980—; mem. staff Norwegian Am. Hosp., St. Anthony's Hosp., St. Mary Nazareth Hosp. Fellow: Am. Coll. Utilization Rev. Physicians, Am. Acad. Pediat. (life); mem.: AMA (life Physician Recognition award 1973—), Chgo. Pediatric Soc., Chgo. Med. Soc., Am. Assn. Individual Investors, Ill. Med. Assn., Assn. Philippine Physicians Practicing in Am. Home: 5140 W Chicago Ave Chicago IL 60651-2903 Office Phone: 773-287-0751, 773-287-0752. Personal E-mail: titogyao@aol.com.

YAO, YONGXUE, immunologist; b. Hengshui, China, Oct. 23, 1971; s. Yusheng Yao and Shuhui Wang; m. Zhuo Wang, Aug. 30, 1997; 1 child, Daniel. MD, China Med. U., Shenyang, 1996; PhD, Fukui Med. U., Japan, 2003. Diplomate China Med. U., Shenyang, 1996. Resident China Med. U., Shenyang, China, 1996—97; postdoctoral fellow Ind. U. Sch. of Medicine, Indpls., 2003—05, rsch. assoc. Grantee Postdoctoral Fellowship, AHA, 2004, 2005—06; Monbosho Scholarship, Japanese Gov., 1997—2003. Communist. Achievements include research in role of interleukine-4 indendritic cell-mediated immunity. Avocations: swimming, reading. Home: 3735 Wishbone Blvd Indianapolis IN 46268 Office: Indiana Univ Sch of Medicine Wells Ctr Pediat Rsch 702 Barnhill Dr RI-2659 Indianapolis IN 46202 Home Phone: 317-471-8395; Office Phone: 317-274-8805. Business E-Mail: yonyao@iupui.edu.

YAOI, TAKURO, biochemist; b. Sakai, Osaka, Japan, Sept. 3, 1966; s. Yoshihito and Masako Yaoi; m. Harumi Mizukami, Apr. 3, 2001. BS, Tokyo U. Agrl. Tech., 1991; MS, Tokyo Inst. Tech., Yokohama, 1993, PhD, 1996. Postdocoral rschr. U. Chgo. Argonne Nat. Lab., Argonne, Ill., 1996—98; vis. rschr. NASA Ames Rsch. Ctr., Moffett Field, Calif., 1998—2000; asst. rsch. specialist U. Calif., Berkeley, 2001—02; rsch. scientist FreshGene, Inc., Concord, Calif., 2002—03; scientist Panomics, Inc., Redwood City, Calif., 2003—06, sr. scientist Fremont, Calif., 2006—. Contbr. articles to profl. jours. Mem.: NY Acad. Scis., Am. Soc. for Biochemistry and Molecular Biology. Achievements include patents in field. Office: Panomics Inc 6519 Dumbarton Cir Fremont CA 94555 Office Fax: 510-818-2610. Business E-Mail: tyaoi@panomics.com.

YAP, GEORGE S., immunologist, educator; b. Lucena City, Quezon Province, Philippines, Oct. 13, 1967; s. Leonardo Yap and Mary So. PhD, McGill U., Montreal, Can., 1994. Fogarty fellow and assoc. NIH, Bethesda, Md., 1994—2000; Manning asst. prof. Brown U., Providence, 2000—. Grantee, NIH, 2002—. Mem.: Am. Soc. Microbiology (mem. editl. bd. Infection and Immunity jour. 2000—), Faculty of 1000. Independent. Achievements include discovery of gene mutation in Tyk2 kinase linked to resistance to autoimmunity and susceptibility to infection; autophagic destruction of apicomplexan parasites. Avocations: cooking, baking. Office: Brown U 171 Meeting St Providence RI 02912 Office Phone: 401-863-3483. Office Fax: 401-863-171. Business E-Mail: george_yap@brown.edu.

YAPIJAKIS, CONSTANTINE, environmental engineer, educator, consultant; b. Drama, Macedonia, Greece, July 18, 1948; arrived in U.S., 1971; s. Nikos and Stella (Voyagi) Yapijakis; m. Lily Huang, July 10, 1993; 1 child, Nicole Isako. MS in Civil Engring., Nat. Tech. U., Athens, Greece, 1971; MS in Environ. Engring., NYU, 1973; PhD in Environ. Engring., Poly. U., NYC, 1981. Registered profl. engr., N.Y., civil engr., Tech. Chamber of Greece. Jr. engr. Dr. Panaghiotakis' Cons. Group, Athens, 1969-71; intern engr. Dutch Pub. Wks. Dept., Amsterdam, 1970; environ. lab. asst. NYU, NYC, 1971-73; environ. engr. City Planning Dept., NYC, 1972, John J. Kassner & Co., NYC, 1973, Hazen and Sawyer, P.C., NYC, 1973-78; adj. prof. CCNY/Polytechnic U., 1977—; assoc. prof. Pratt Inst., NYC, 1980-86; prof. environ. engring., environ. rsch. lab dir. The Cooper Union, NYC, 1986—. Founding ptnr. Hellenic EnvironTech, Inc., Athens, Greece, 1991—; cons., presenter in field. Co-author: (book) Scale-up of Treatment Processes, 1983, Industrial Wastes Treatment Handbook, 1993, Hazardous Waste Site Remediation Mgmt., 1999, Water Quality-Reflection of Land Use, 1999, Environmental Engineering and Pollution Control, 2001, Handbook of Industrial and Hazardous Waste Treatment, 2004, Waste Treatment in the Food Processing Industry, 2005, Waste Treatment in the Process Industries, 2005, Hazardous Industrial Waste Management, 2006; contbr. articles to profl. jours. Recipient Earth Day award and medallion, City Club N.Y., 1995, Intern Egnr. award, Inst. Internat. Edn., 1972; grantee, NSF, 1988, 1992; scholar Intern. Engr., Internat. Assn. Students Tech. Edn., 1970, Sr. scholar, Fulbright Program, Greece, 1993—94, Fulbright Program, Aegean Initiative, 2002. Mem.: Assn. Environ. Engring. and Sci. Profs., Environ. Law Inst., N.Y. Water Environment Assn. (Met. chpt. bd. dirs. 1992—94, 2001—03, chmn. edn. com., Svc. award 1995, Membership award 1996—99, Svc. award 2004, Membership award 2004), N.Y. Acad. Scis. (judge h.s. sci. projects ann. competition 1994—), Internat. Assn. Water Quality, Am. Water Wks. Assn. (hon. life), Water Environment Fedn. (VIP Cir. 1994, Recruiters Recognition Club 1996). Achievements include development of design of preozonation - D.E. filtration process for New York City's water supply, design for rotating biological contractors for application to industrial and hazardous wastes; research in extensive lead, arsenic, TPH, pesticides contamination in surface soil of parks and playgrounds in New York City, perc pollution prevention study for 2000 drycleaners in N.Y.C; fast-rate bioremediation for protection of groundwater, enhanced solar evaporation and photo-oxidation for treatment of hazardous wastes; pollution prevention in the construction industry and brownfields development in N.Y.C. metro area. Avocations: travel, photography, reading, movies. Office: The Cooper Union Sch of Engring 51 Astor Pl New York NY 10003-7185 Office Phone: 212-353-4292. E-mail: yapi@cooper.edu.

YARAGUDRI, VINOD K., neuroscientist, researcher; b. Belgaum, Karanataka, India, July 11, 1973; s. Kallappa V. and Ratna K. Yaragudri; m. Shilpa Sulebhavi, Apr. 3, 2003; 1 child, Nathan. BS, Karanatak U., Dharwad, India, 1994, MS, 1996; PhD, NIMH and Neuroscience, Bangalore, India, 2002. Rsch. scholar NIMH and Neuroscis., Banglore, India, 1996—97, sr. rsch. scholar, 1997—2001; rsch. project mgr. Nathan S. Kline Inst. Psychiat. Rsch., Orangeburg, NY, 2002—03, asst. rsch. scientist, 2003—05, assoc. rsch. scientist, 2005—; rsch. project mgr. N.Y. State Psychiat. Inst., NYC, 2002—03, asst. rsch. scientist, 2003—05, assoc. rsch. scientist, 2005—. Contbr. articles to profl. jours. Founder Narayana Rural Devel. Soc., Mudhol, India, 2003. Recipient Academic Excellence Gold medal, Karnatak U., Dharwad, India, 1997, Burswood Rsch. Poster award, Asian Pacific Congress Clin. Biochemistry, 2004; fellow, Lady Tata Meml. Trust, India, 1998, Indian Coun. Med. Rsch., 1999—2001, Internat. Brain Rsch. Orgn., 2001, Rsch. Found. Mental Hygeine, 2002—; grantee, Am. Found. Suicide Prevention, 2004—06; scholar, Karnataka State Tchr.'s Assn., Bangalore, India, 1991, Jindal Aluminium Trust, Bangalore, India, 1994—96. Mem.: Am. Found. Suicide Prevention (hon.), Soc. Biol. Psychiatry (assoc.), Internat. Cannabinoid Rsch. Soc. (assoc.), Rsch. Soc. Alcoholism (assoc.), Schizophrenia Rsch. Forum (life), Indian Acad. Neurosci. (life), Internat. Brain Rsch. Orgn. (life). Achievements include research in the implication of the role of the brain endocannabinoid system in major depressive disorder and suicide. Home: 120 Nottingham Ct Montvale NJ 07645 Office: Nathan Kline Inst 140 Old Orangeburg Rd Orangeburg NY 10962 Home Phone: 201-746-0634; Office Phone: 845-398-5454. Office Fax: 845-398-5451. Personal E-mail: ky_vinod@yahoo.com. Business E-Mail: vyaragudri@nki.rfmh.org.

YARASHESKI, KEVIN EDWARD, medical educator; s. Edward and Elsie Yarasheski; m. Jill Andrea Campbell, July 7, 1995; 1 child, Curtis Alexander. PhD, Kent State U., 1986. Assoc. prof. Washington U. Sch. Medicine, St. Louis, 1999—2007, prof., 2007—. Grantee, NIH, 1989—. Mem.: Am. Physiol. Soc. (assoc.). Achievements include research in Pathogenesis and treatments for metabolic syndromes. Office: Washington U Sch Medicine 660 S Euclid Ave Metabolism Box 8127 Saint Louis MO 63110 Home Phone: 314-849-8209; Office Phone: 314-362-8173.

YARBOROUGH, WILLIAM GLENN, JR., military officer, forester, international business executive; b. Rock Hill, SC, June 21, 1940; s. William Glenn and Bessie (Rainsford) Y.; m. Betsy Gibson, Jan. 24, 1969; children: Bill, Clinton, Frank, Elizabeth. BS, U. S.C., 1961, MBA, 1969; postgrad., Command and Gen. Staff Coll., 1970, Naval War Coll., 1979, U. Va., 1983. Commd. to U.S. Army, advanced through grades to col., 1980, co. and troop comdr., squadron staff officer Vietnam and Europe, 1961-71, strategist Washington, 1971-73; chief of assignments Office Pers. Mgmt. Mil. Pers. Ctr., Washington, 1973-76; comdr. 1st Squadron 1st Cavalry, Europe, 1976-78; chief of staff, spl. asst. to chief of staff 1st Armored Divsn., Europe, 1978; br. chief Office of Chief of Staff, Washington, 1979-80; exec. to dep. comdg. gen. Material Devel. and Readiness Command, Washington, 1980-81; mil. dep. for asst. sec. for rsch., devel. and acquisition Washington, 1981-85; dir. ops. Ford Aerospace, Washington, 1986—89; army mktg. dir. Grumman Corp., Bethpage, NY, 1990-93; pres., CEO Allied Rsch. Corp., Vienna, Va., 1993—2001; founder & prin. WGY & Assocs. Bd. dirs. Carleton Techs., Eads N.Am. Def. Co., Valentec Inc. Trustee Patton Mus.; treas. US Cavalry Assn.; bd. dirs. So Others Might Eat (Some), Easter Seals; bd. dirs. Moore Sch. Bus. U. S.C. Decorated Silver Star, Bronze Star medal with 4 oak leaf clusters and V device, Purple Heart, Legion of Merit. Mem. VFW, SAR, KC, Assn. U.S. Army (George Washington chpt., v.p. membership), Am. Legion, Armed Forces Comms. and Electronics Assn., U.S. Army Armor Assn., Nat. Def. Indsl. Assn. (bd. dirs. N.Y. chpt.), Rotary Internat., Mil. Order of the World Wars, N.G. Assn., Res. Officers Assn., Soc. of the Purple Heart, Army-Navy Club, Army Navy Country Club, Belle-Meade Country Club, Tower Club. Republican. Roman Catholic. Home: Box 115 Thomson GA 30824-0115 Office: Box 828 Mc Lean VA 22101 Office Phone: 703-748-1717. Office Fax: 928-222-5742. Personal E-mail: wgyarc@aol.com.

YARBROUGH, ALLYSON DEBRA, electrical engineer; b. Peterborough, England, Feb. 14, 1958; d. Freddy Dekhoma and Rosalind Mavis Y.; m. John Russell Scarpulla, May. 8, 1990. BSEE, N.Mex. State U., 1979; MSEE, Cornell U., 1985, PhD in Elec. Engring., 1988. Rsch. asst. Nat. Atmospheric and Ionospheric Ctr., Arecibo, P.R., 1979; microwave applications engr. Hewlett-Packard Co., Santa Rosa, Calif., 1979-82; assoc. prof. Calif. State U., LA, 1988-89; tech. staff Aerospace Corp., El Segundo, Calif., 1989-93, sect. mgr., 1993-99, dept. dir., 1999—. Mem. IEEE, Microwave Theory and Techniques Soc., Alpha Kappa Alpha, Eta Kappa Nu. Democrat. Roman Catholic. Avocations: woodworking, sewing, collecting vintage radios. Home: 26821 Grays Lake Rd Palos Verdes Estates CA 90275 Home Phone: 310-594-9841; Office Phone: 310-375-9695. Personal E-mail: blue.onyx@verizon.net.

YARBROUGH, KATHRYN DAVIS, public health nurse; b. Montrose, Colo., Aug. 31, 1947; d. L.O. and V. Jean (Dunn) Davis; m. James H. Yarbrough, Aug. 8, 1970; children: James, Jason. Diploma, Good Samaritan Hosp. Sch. Nursing, Phoenix, 1971; BSN, Kennesaw State Coll., 1996. RN, Ga.; cert. NAACOG. Supr. Cherokee County Health Dept., Canton, Ga., 1976-97. Den mother Boy Scouts Am., Canton, 1986-87; bd. dirs. Cancer soc., Canton, 1987—, Cherokee County Violence Ctr., 1990, First Steps Bd., 1993-97, Cherokee County Advocacy Ctr., 1994-97; HIV cons. ARC, Canton, 1988—, disaster vol., Cherokee County, 1993-99; co-chair Early Intervention Coun., Canton, 1991-93; mem. Leadership Cherokee, 1994, Interagy Coun., 1994; mem. Blue Ridge Jud. Cir. Domestic Violence Task Force, 1995. Mem.: ANA, Ga. Nurses Assn., Svc. League Cherokee County (hon.). Methodist. E-mail: Kyarbro216@aol.com.

YARBROUGH, MARTHA CORNELIA, music educator; b. Waycross, Ga., Feb. 8, 1940; d. Henry Elliott and Jessie (Sirmans) Y. BME, Stetson U., 1962; MME, Fla. State U., 1968, PhD, 1973. Choral dir. Ware County H.S., Waycross, 1962-64, Glynn Acad., Brunswick, Ga., 1964—70; asst. choral dir. Fla. State U., 1970-72; cons. in music Muscogee County Sch. Dist., Columbus, Ga., 1972-73; cons. in tchr. edn. Psycho-Edno. Cons., Inc., Tallahassee, 1972-73; asst. prof. music edn., dir. choruses and oratorio socs. Syracuse (NY) U., 1973-76; assoc. prof. music edn. Syracuse U., 1976-83, prof., 1983-86, acting asst. dean Coll. Visual and Performing Arts, 1980-82, acting dir. Sch. Music, 1980-82, chmn. music edn., 1982-86; prof. music La. State U., Baton Rouge, 1986—, coord. music edn., 1986—2000, Haymon prof. of music, 1995—, disting. rsch. master arts, humanities, social scis., 2004. Artist-in-residence Sch. Music U. Ala., Tuscaloosa, 1989-90, 98, 2002; chair exec. com. Music Edn. Rsch. Coun., 1992-94. Co-author: Competency-Based Music Education, 1980; mem. editl. com.: Jour. Rsch. in Music Edn., editor-in-chief:, 2000—; contbr. chapters to books, articles to profl. jours. Recipient Disting. Rsch. Master of Arts, Humanities and Social Scis. award, La. State U., 2004. Mem. Music Educators Nat. Conf. (Sr. Rschr. award 1996), La. State Music Assn., Am. Ednl. Rsch. Assn., Soc. Rsch. Music Edn. (mem. exec. com. 1988-90, program chair 1990-92, chair 1992-94), AAUP, Coll. Music Soc., Pi Kappa Lambda, Phi Beta, Kappa Delta Pi. Office: Sch Music La State U Baton Rouge LA 70803-2504 Office Phone: 225-578-2481. Business E-Mail: cyarbro@lsu.edu.

YARBROUGH, MATTHEW E., lawyer; b. Dallas, Oct. 12, 1966; s. Fletcher L. and Harriet S. Yarbrough; m. Gina Scalise Yarbrough, July 22, 1989; children: Madeleine, Jack. BA, Tex. Christian U., 1989; JD, So. Meth. U., 1993. Bar: Tex. 1994, US Dist. Ct. (all dists. Tex.) 1994, US Ct. Appeals (5th cir.) 1994. Assoc. McKool Smith, Dallas, 1993—95; asst. US atty. US Atty.'s Office, Dallas, 1995—2000; spl. counsel Vinson & Elkins, Dallas, 2000—01; ptnr. Fish & Richardson, P.C., Dallas, 2001. Spl. counsel Internet Bur., Dallas; adj. prof. trial advocacy So. Meth. U., Dallas, adj. prof. computer litig. Contbr. articles Articles in field. Bd. dirs. S.W. Advocacy Sch., Dallas, Leadership Dallas. Named Tex. Super Lawyer in Litig., One of Dallas' Best Lawyers, D Mag.; named one of NLJ Top 40 Under 40; recipient Pro Bono award, DBA, 1994, award for outstanding prosecutor, INS, 1999, Outstanding prosecutor award, FBI, 2000. Mem.: ABA, Am. Intellectual Property Law Assn., Dallas Bar Assn.

YARBROUGH, TERRY PINCKNEY, physician; b. Columbia, SC, Apr. 2, 1940; s. Dabney Randolph and Frances Horton (Colcock) Y.; m. Alexandra Mayo, Aug. 28, 1965; children: Alexandra, Laurens. MD, Med. Coll. Va., 1965. Intern U. Tex. Med. Br., Galveston, 1965—66; resident in internal medicine Med. Coll. Va., Richmond, 1968—71; pvt. practice Internal Medicine of Portsmouth Ltd., 1971—. Capt. USAR, 1966-68. Mem. ACP, Am. Coll. of Cardiology, Coun. Clin. Cardiology, Am. Heart Assn., Am. Soc. of Internal Medicine, Med. Soc. of Va. Episcopalian. Office: Internal Medicine Portsmouth Ltd 3300 High St Portsmouth VA 23707-3321 Home Phone: 757-483-6360.

YARCHOAN, ROBERT, clinical immunologist, researcher; b. NYC, July 21, 1950; s. Zachary and Anne Mae (Veneroso) Y.; m. Giovana Tosato; children: Mark, John. BA magna cum laude, Amherst Coll., 1971; MD, U. Pa., 1975. Diplomate Am. Bd. Internal Medicine, Am. Bd. Allergy and Immunology. Resident in medicine U. Minn. Hosps., Mpls., 1975-78; clin. assoc. metabolism br. Nat. Cancer Inst., Bethesda, Md., 1978-80, investigator metabolism br., 1980-83, investigator clin. oncology program, 1983-87, sr. investigator clin. oncology program, 1988-91, chief retroviral diseases sect. medicine br., 1991-96, chief HIV and AIDS malignancy br., 1996—, AIDS coord., 2006—. Assoc. editor Jour. Immunology, 1985-89, AIDS Rsch. and Human Retroviruses, 1986-2004, AIDS, 1990-2000, Jour. AIDS, 2000-06, Jour. Human Virology, 2002-04, Infectious Agents and Cancer, 2006-; sect. editor Thymus, 1992-97; contbr. articles to sci. jours., chpts. to textbooks; patentee in field. Capt. USPHS, 1978—. Recipient Commendation medal USPHS, 1991, Asst. Sec. Health award US govt. Dept. Health & Human Svcs., 1989, Inventors award US Dept. Commerce, 1986, 87, Fed. Tech. Transfer Act award, 1999, 2000, 01, Outstanding Svc. medal USPHS, 2002, awarded NIH First World AIDS Day award, 2006. Fellow AAAS; mem. Am. Soc. Hematology, Am. Assn. Immunologists, Clin. Immunology Soc., Am. Soc. for Clin. Investigation, Phi Beta Kappa, Sigma Xi. Achievements include co-inventor of therapies for AIDS and AIDS malignancies including ddI (didanosine) and ddC (zalcitabine) for AIDS and IL-12 for Kaposi's sarcoma; co-developer of therapies for AIDS and AIDS malignancies including AZT (zidovudine) for AIDS and paclitaxel for Kaposi's sarcoma; research in interactions between viruses and the immune system, therapy of AIDS and virally induced tumors; pathogenesis of AIDS and viral-induced tumors.

YARDE, RICHARD FOSTER, art educator; b. Boston, Oct. 29, 1939; s. Edgar St. Clair and Enid (Foster) Y.; m. Susan Donovan, July 8, 1967; children: Marcus, Owen. BFA in Painting cum laude, Boston U., 1962, MFA, 1964; DFA (hon., Mass. Coll. Arts, Boston, 1998. Asst. prof. art Boston U., 1965-71; assoc. prof. art Wellesley Coll., 1971-76; vis. assoc. prof. Amherst Coll., 1976-77, Mt. Holyoke Coll., 1980-81; vis. artist Mass. Coll. Art, 1977-80; prof. art U. Mass., Boston, 1981-90, Amherst, 1990—. Visual arts panelist Mass. Coun. Art and Humanities, 1976-78; bd. overseers Inst. Contemporary Art, Boston, 1991-2003; panelist Painting Mass. Cultural Coun. One-man shows include Studio Mus. in Harlem, San Diego Mus., Balt. Mus., Smith Coll. Mus. Art, Northampton, Mass., 1977, Mass. Coll. Art, 1996—99, Worcester Mus. Art, Mass., 2003, exhibited in group shows at Newport (RI) Art Mus., Nat. Acad. Design, N.Y.C. and Mass., Smithsonian Inst., Washington, 1999, New Mus. Contemporary Art, N.Y.C., 1999, Mus. Fine Arts, Boston, 1999, Master Drawings from the Smith Coll. Art Mus., Lacaixa and Madrid, 2002, DeCordova Mus., Lincoln, Mass., 2002, Inst. Contemporary Art, Boston, 2003, Heckscher Mus. Art, Huntington, NY, 2003, NAS, Washington, 2004—05, Sheldon Meml. Art Gallery U. Nebr., Lincoln, Nat. Acad. Design, 2005, Boston U. Art Gallery, 2005—06, Danforth Mus. Art, Framingham, Mass., 2005. Recipient Alumni award for disting. contbn. to arts Boston U., 1987, Chancellor's award disting. scholarship U. Mass., Boston, 1984, Acad. award in art Am. Acad. Arts and Letters, 1995, Disting. Tchg. award U. Mass. Amherst, 1997, Works on Paper award New Eng. Found. Arts, Boston, 1998, honoree Studio Mus. in Harlem Gala, N.Y.C., 2001; Nat. Endowment Arts fellow, 1976, Samuel F. Conti faculty fellow U. Mass., 2000, When the Spirit Moves Group Exhib., Spelman Coll. Mus., 2000, Charles Wright Mus., 2000, Commonwealth Award, Artist Category, Mass. Cultural Council, 2001, William P. and Gertrude Schweitzer prize Nat. Acad. Design, N.Y., others. Mem.: NAD (academician 1994—). Office: U Mass Amherst Fine Arts Ctr Dept Art and Art History 151 Pres Dr Office1 Amherst MA 01003-4330 E-mail: rfyarde@art.u.mass.edu.

YARDENI, EDWARD, economist, investment advisor; b. Haifa, Israel; BA magna cum laude, Cornell Univ.; MA, PhD, Yale Univ. Economist Fed. Reserve Bank of New York, Fed. Reserve Bd. Governors, U.S. Treasury Dept.; taught Grad. Sch. Bus. Columbia Univ.; chief economist C.J. Lawrence, Prudential Securities, E.F. Hutton; mng. dir., chief investment strategist Deutsche Bank; chief investment strategist Oak Associates Ltd., Akron, Ohio, 2004—. Contbr. articles to Wall St Jour., NY Times, Barron's; commentator Wall St. Week, CNBC, CNN's Moneyline. Office: Oak Associates Ste 250 3875 Embassy Pkwy Akron OH 44333 *

YARDLEY, BILL, journalist; Reporter New York Times. Office: The New York Times Hartfor Bur 210 Capitol Ave Rm 409 A Hartford CT 06106

YARDLEY, JIM, journalist; b. NYC, June 18, 1964; married; 3 children. BA in hist., U. NC at Chapel Hill, 1986. With Times Cmty. Newspapers, Fairfax County, Va., Anniston Star, Ala.; nat. desk reporter Atlanta Journal-Constitution, 1990—97; met. reporter NY Times, NYC, 1997—99, bur. chief Houston, 1999—2003, fgn. corr. Beijing, 2003—. Recipient Pulitzer Prize for internat. reporting (with James Kahn), 2006. Office: NY Times 229 W 43rd St New York NY 10036

YARDLEY, JONATHAN, journalist; b. Pitts., Oct. 27, 1939; s. William Woolsey and Helen (Gregory) Y.; m. Rosemary Roberts, June 14, 1961 (div. 1975); children: James Barrett, William W. II.; m. Susan L. Hartt, Mar. 23, 1975 (div. 1998); m. Marie Arana, Mar. 21, 1999. AB, U. N.C., 1961; DHL (hon.), George Washington U., 1987. Writer N.Y. Times, 1961—64; editl. writer, book editor Greensboro (N.C.) Daily News, 1964—74; book editor Miami (Fla.) Herald, 1974—78, Washington Star, 1978—81; book critic Washington Post, 1981—. Author: Ring: A Biography of Ring Lardner, 1977, Our Kind of People: The Story of an American Family, 1989, Out of Step: Notes from a Purple Decade, 1991, States of Mind: A Personal Journey Through the Mid-Atlantic, 1993, Misfit: The Strange Life of Frederick Exley, 1997, Monday Morning Quarterback, 1998; editor: My Life as Author and Editor (H.L. Mencken), 1993, Selected Stories (Ring Lardner), 1997. Recipient Pulitzer prize for criticism, 1981, Disting. Alumnus award U. N.C., 1989; Nieman fellow in journalism Harvard U., 1968-69. Address: Malecon de la Reserva 801 Miaflores Lima 18 Peru Home and Office: 1500 Vermont Ave NW 1 Washington DC 20005 Office Phone: 202-544-7779. Business E-Mail: yardleyj@washpost.com.

YARETT, JORDAN ELIOT, lawyer; b. NYC, Feb. 26, 1953; s. J.W. and Eva A. (Adler) Y.; m. Susan Ann Robbins, Oct. 9, 1983. BA, Yale U., 1975; JD, U. Pa., 1978. Bar: Pa. 1978, US Dist. Ct. (ea. dist.) Pa. 1980, NY 1984. Law clk. to presiding justice, Phila., 1978-80; assoc. Ballard, Spahr, Andrews & Ingersoll, Phila., 1980-84; mng. ptnr. structured fin. group Battle, Fowler, Jaffin & Kheel, NYC, 1985—99; ptnr. corp. dept. Paul, Weiss, Rifkind, Wharton & Garrison LLP, NYC, 1999—, co-head fin. group. Assoc. editor U. Pa. Law Rev., 1976-77, comment editor, 1977-78. Named a Dealmaker of Yr., Am. Lawyer mag., 2007. Mem. ABA (subcom. on securitization of assets), Nat. Assn. Bond Lawyers, Phi Beta Kappa. Office: Paul Weiss Rifkind Wharton & Garrison 1285 Ave of the Americas New York NY 10019-6064 Office Phone: 212-373-3126. Office Fax: 212-373-2124. E-mail: jyarett@paulweiss.com. *

YARI, BOB, film company executive, producer; b. 1962; Diploma in Cinematography. Owner El Camino Pictures, Bull's Eye Entertainment, Syndicate Films Internat., Bob Yari Prodns., Stratus Film Co., LA. Dir., exec. prodr.: (films) Mind Games, 1989; prodr.: Perfect Fit, 1999, Where the Red Fern Grows, 2003, Employee of the Month, 2004, Agent Cody Banks 2: Destination London, 2004, House of D, 2004, A Love Song for Bobby Long, 2004, Crash, 2004 (Best First Feature, Independent Spirit award, 2006), Haven, 2004, Hostage, 2005; prodr.: (films) Find Me Guilty, 2006; prodr.: (films) Block Party, 2005, The Illusionist, 2006, First Snow, 2006, The Hoax, 2006, Resurrecting the Champ, 2007, Kickin It Old Skool, 2007; exec. prodr.: Agent Cody Banks, 2003, Devil's Pond, 2003, Sueno, 2004, In Enemy Hands, 2004, Laws of Attraction, 2004, Around the Bend, 2004, Thumbsucker, 2005, The Matador, 2005, The Chumscrubber, 2005, The LA Riot Spectacular, 2005, Prime, 2005, Sueno, 2005, Even Money, 2006; exec. prodr.: (films) The Painted Veil, 2006. Named one of 50 Most Powerful People in Hollywood, Premiere mag., 2005. Office: Stratus Film Co 10850 Wilshire Blvd 6th Fl Los Angeles CA 90024 Office Phone: 310-234-8970. Office Fax: 310-234-8975. *

YARINGTON, CHARLES THOMAS, JR., surgeon, educator, health facility administrator; b. Sayre, Pa., Apr. 26, 1934; s. C.T. and Florence (Hutchinson) Yarington; m. Barbara Taylor Johnson, Sept. 28, 1963; children: Leslie Anne, Jennifer Lynne, Barbara Jane. AB, Princeton U., 1956; MD, Hahnemann Med. Coll., 1960; grad., Army Command and Gen. Staff Coll., 1969, Air War Coll., 1973, Indsl. Coll. Armed Forces, 1974. Intern Rochester Gen. Hosp., NY, 1960-61; resident Dartmouth Hosp., 1961-62, U. Rochester Strong Meml. Hosp., 1962-65; instr. otolaryngology U. Rochester Sch. Medicine, 1962-65; chief ENT US Army Hosp., Ft. Carson, Colo., 1965—67; asst. prof. surgery W.Va. U. Sch. Medicine, 1967-68; assoc. prof., chmn. dept. otorhinolarygology U. Nebr. Med. Ctr., 1968-69, prof., chmn. dept. otorhinolarygology, 1969-74; clin. prof. otolaryngology U. Wash., Seattle, 1974—; clin. prof. surgery Uniformed Svcs. U. Health Scis., Bethesda, Md., 1985—; chief otolaryngology Virginia Mason Med. Ctr., Seattle, 1978-88, 92-95, chief dept. surgery, 1988-91; surgeon Mason Clinic, Seattle, 1974-97. Cons. Surg. Gen. USAF, Hunter Group Med. Mgmt. Cons., 1996-98, Seattle Multispecialty Panel, 1998—; pres. Virginia Mason Rsch. Ctr., Seattle, 1983-85; trustee Mason Clinic, 1988-91; adv. coun. Nat. Inst. Neurol. Diseases, Communicative Diseases, Stroke of NIH, Bethesda, Md., 1986-90; bd. dirs. Virginia Mason Hosp., Virginia Mason Med. Ctr., bd. govs., 1989-98; bd. regents Uniformed Svcs. U. Health Scis., Bethesda, 2006—. Mem. editl. bd. Aviation, Space, Environ. Med. Jour., Otol. Clinics of N.Am., Mil. Medicine, Otolaryngology-Head and Neck Surgery; contbr. articles to profl. jours. Trustee Seattle Opera Assn., 1983-89. Served to lt. col. USAR, 56-70, to brig. gen. USAF, 1970-86. Decorated D.S.M., Legion of Merit, comdr. Venerable Order St. John (Gt. Britain), companion with star Order Orthodox Hospitallers (Republic of Cypress), knight grand cross Mil. and Hospitaller Order of St. Lazarus; recipient Sir Henry Wellcome medal, 1984. Fellow ACS, Royal Soc. Medicine, Am. Acad. Otolaryngology (Barraquer Meml. award 1968, mem. standing com., bd. govs. 1982-88, Honor award 1974); mem. AMA, Am. Broncho-Esophagological Assn. (coun., treas. 1982-86, pres. 1987-88), Am. Laryngol. Assn., Pacific Coast Soc. Ophthalmology and Otolaryngology (coun., pres. 1987-88), Soc. Med. Cons. to Armed Forces, Am. Soc. Head and Neck Surgery, N.W. Acad. Head and Neck Surgery (pres. 1984-86), Am. Soc. Otology, Rhinology and Laryngology (v.p. 1992-93, coun. 1997-2000), Res. Officers Assn. (past pres. Seattle chpt., nat. officer), Soc. Colonial Wars, Sons Revolution (pres. Wash. 1985-87), Internat. Power Boat Assn. (comdr. 1999-2000), Seattle Yacht Club (trustee 2001-05), Princeton Quadrangle Club, Broadmoor Golf Club, RAF Club (London), Sigma Xi. Home and Office: 2136 38th Ave E Seattle WA 98112

YARIV, AMNON, electrical engineering educator, research scientist; b. Tel Aviv, Apr. 13, 1930; arrived in U.S., 1951, naturalized, 1964; s. Shraga and Henya (Davidson) Y.; m. Frances Pokras, Apr. 10, 1972; children: Elizabeth, Dana, Gabriela. BS, U. Calif., Berkeley, 1954, MS, 1956, PhD, 1958. Mem. tech. staff Bell Telephone Labs., 1959-63; dir. laser research Watkins-Johnson Co., 1963-64; mem. faculty Calif. Inst. Tech., 1964—, Martin Summerfield prof. applied physics, 1966—. Co-founder Xponent, Orbits Corp., Teleris Corp., Inc. Author: Quantum Electronics, 1967, 75, 85, Introduction to Optical Electronics, 1971, 77, 89, Theory and Applications of Quantum Mechanics, Propagation of Light in Crystals. With Israeli Army, 1948—50. Recipient Pender award U. Pa., Harvey prize Technion, Israel, 1992. Fellow IEEE (Quantum Electronics award 1980), Am. Optical Soc. (Ives medal 1986, Esther Beller medal 1998), Am. Acad. Arts and Scis.; mem. NAS, NAE, Am. Phys. Soc. Office: 1201 E California Blvd Pasadena CA 91125-0001 Business E-Mail: ziemer@eas.uccs.edu.

YARKONY, GARY MICHAEL, physician, researcher; b. NYC, May 22, 1953; m. Kirsten Kohlmeyer; children: Judith, Rachel, Seth, Lauren. BA in Biology, SUNY, Buffalo, 1974; MD, SUNY, Syracuse, 1978; Master in Mgmt., Northwestern U., 1994. Intern, then resident in physical medicine, rehab. Northwestern U., Chgo., 1978—81, chief resident dept. rehab. medicine, 1980; asst. dir. head trauma program Rehab. Inc. Chgo., 1981—84, attending staff, 1981—94; chief of rehab. svcs. U. Chgo. Hosps. Rehab. Ctr., 1994—2000; clin. prof. sect. orthopaedic surgery and rehab. medicine U. Chgo. Med. Ctr., 1995—2000, clin. prof. dept. surgery and neurology, 1995—2000; clin. prof. dept. rehab. medicine Chgo. Med. Sch., 2000—. Attending physician Northwestern Meml. Hosp., Chgo., 1984-94, Provera St. Joseph's Hosp., Elgin, Ill., 2000—; assoc. prof. dept. rehab. medicine Northwestern U. Med. Sch., 1985-94; adj. prof. Pritzker Inst. for Med. Engring., Ill. Inst. Tech., 1991-97; dir. rehab. Midwest Regional Spinal Cord Injury Care Sys., Chgo., 1984-94; dir. rsch. Schwab Rehab. Hosp., 1997-2000. Contbr. articles to profl. jours. and chpts. to book. Fellow Am. Acad. Physical Medicine and Rehab.; mem. Assn. Academic Physiatrists, Am. Spinal Injury Assn., Internat. Med. Soc. Paraplegia, Internal Rehab. Medicine Assn., Phi Beta Kappa, Phi Eta Sigma. Office: Rehabilitation Medicine Spec 1990 Larkin Ave Ste 3 Elgin IL 60123-5827

YARMEY, RICHARD ANDREW, investment manager; b. Kingston, Pa., Aug. 23, 1948; s. Stanley Richard and Rose Mary (Rees) Y.; m. Jeanne Marie Cappelli, Aug. 5, 1972; children: Lynn Rees, Jessica Brett, Kristen Alexandra. BS, U. Scranton, 1970; JD, Cath. U., 1975. Bar: D.C. (inactive) 1976, U.S. Ct. Appeals (5th cir.) 1976, U.S. Tax Ct. 1978, U.S. Ct. Appeals (D.C. cir.) 1980. Contract adjudicator GAO, Washington, 1970-73; program asst. EPA, Washington, 1973; assoc. Sharon, Pierson, et al, Washington, 1975-82; of counsel Pierson, Semmes et al, Washington, 1982-93; prin. Yarmey Capital Mgmt., 1989-95; sr. portfolio mgr. PNC Advisors, 1995—2000; mng. dir. Instl. Investment Group, 2000—02; portfolio mgr. Pvt. Investment Adv. Program Merrill Lynch, Wilkes-Barre, Pa., 2002—. Fin. cons. various pension plans, individuals and bus. concerns, 1976-95; TV panelist, speaker, writer on portfolio mgmt.; instr. fin. mgmt. and investments continuing edn. Wilkes U., Wilkes-Barre. Mem.: CFA Inst., Phila. Analysts Soc., Alpha Sigma Nu. Democrat. Avocation: cabinetmaking. Office: 600 Balt Dr Wilkes Barre PA 18702 Home Phone: 570-587-2240; Office Phone: 570-829-8052. Business E-Mail: richard_yarmey@ml.com.

YARMUTH, JOHN ALLAN, congressman; b. Louisville, Nov. 4, 1947; s. Stanley Robert and Edna Elaine (Klein) Y.; m. Catherine Elizabeth Creedon, 1981; 1 child, Stanley Aaron. BA in Am. Studies, Yale U., 1969; postgrad. in law, Georgetown U., 1971-73. Stockbroker Stein Bros. & Boyce, Louisville, 1969-70; legis. asst. to Senator Marlow Cook US Senate, Washington, 1971-75; pub. Louisville Today mag., 1976-82; asst. v.p. univ. rels. U. Louisville, 1983-86; worked in pub. rels. and mktg. Caretenders Healthcorp, 1986—90; founder, exec. editor Louisville Eccentric Observer Newsweekly, 1990—2003; mem. US Congress from 3rd Ky. dist., 2007—, mem. edn. & labor com., oversight & govt. reform com. Founder, pres. Ctr. for Ky. Progress. Host (radio talk shows) Yarmuth & Ziegler, WAVE 3 TV, 2003, guest appearances Hot Button, 2004—05, editor, owner (publications) Kentucky Golfer. Bd. dirs. Better Bus. Bur., Louisville, 1979-85, Louisville Sch. Art, 1980-83, Sta. WKPC-TV, pub. TV, Louisville, 1983-88; bd. regents No. Ky. U., Highland Heights, 1980-83, Jewish Cmty. Ctr., Planned Parenthoodm Louisvill Forum. Named Person of Yr., Louisville Chpt. Alzheimer's Assn., 2004; named to Atherton High Sch. Hall of Fame, 2002; recipient editorial and column writing awards, Metro Louisville Journalism. Mem. Valhalla Golf Club, Melrose Club (Daufuskie, S.C.), Ky. Golf Assn., dir. Soc. Profl. Journalists. Democrat. Jewish. Avocation: golf. Office: 319 Cannon House Office Bldg Washington DC 20515 also: Romano Mazzoli Fed Bldg Ste 216 600 Martin Luther King Dr Louisville KY 40202 *

YARNELL, MICHAEL ALLAN, mediator, arbitrator, law educator; b. Chgo., Sept. 10, 1944; s. Howard Winfred and Mary Elizabeth (Card) Y.; m. Karen Alice Hockenyos, June 12, 1971 (div. Mar. 1994); children: Sarah

Munro, Jacob Rainey; m. Kristina Louise Renshaw, July 17, 1996. BS, Ariz. State U., 1967; JD with honors, U. Ill., 1971; MA, U. Phoenix, 2004. Bar: Ariz. 1971. Ptnr. Streich, Lang, Weeks & Cardon, Phoenix, 1971-91, also bd. dirs.; mem. Myers, Barnes & Jenkins, Phoenix, 1991; judge Maricopa County Superior Ct., Phoenix, 1991—2005, mediator, arbitrator, spl. master, 2005—; mem. faculty U. Phoenix; adj. prof. U. Canberra Law Sch., Australia, 2004—; asst. clin. prof. law Phoenix Sch. Law, 2006—. Author: Ins and Outs of Foreclosure, 1981, 12th edit., 2005; projects editor Law Rev. U. Ill. Law Forum, 1970; contbr. articles to profl. jours. Chairperson Phoenix Children's Theatre, 1987; vol. Habitat for Humanity, Adopt-a-Home sponsor; chmn. Legal Cmty. Builds, 1999. 1st lt. US Army, 1971-72, Korea. Fellow Ariz. Bar Found.; mem. ABA, Am. Arbitration Assn. (Roster Neutrals, Comml. Panel), Maricopa Bar Assn., State Bar Ariz. (Outstanding Contbn. to Continuing Legal Edn. award 1988, Com. on Profl. Conduct award 2000), Order of Coif, Lorna Lockwood Inn of Ct. (co-pres. 2000-01), Ariz. Yacht Club (vice comdr. 2000, comdr. 2001-02, staff comdr. 2002-03), Phi Kappa Phi. Republican. Avocations: computers, sailing, white-water rafting. Office: Esplanade Ctr 2415 E Camelback Rd Ste 700 Phoenix AZ 85016 Office Phone: 602-791-3364. Personal E-mail: michael@michaelyarnell.com.

YARNO, WENDY, pharmaceutical executive; BS, Portland State U., 1982; MBA, Temple U., 1988. Profl. rep. U.S. Human Health, 1983—85, mktg. analyst, 1985—87, product mgr. pediatric vaccines, 1988, assoc. dir. econ. affaris, 1989, sr. dir. mktg. planning, 1990—91, nat. account exec., 1991, sr. dir. managed health care affairs, 1992, project leader for U.S. Health Care Reform, 1992—93; v.p. ctrl. region Merck-Medco, 1994; v.p. hypertension and heart failure therapeutic bus. group U.S. Human Health, 1994—97; v.p. Ortho McNeil Pharm., Johnson & Johnson, 1997—98; v.p. worldwide human health Merck & Co., Inc., Whitehouse Station, NJ, 1999, v.p. human resources, 1999, sr. v.p. human resources, 2000—02, exec. v.p. worldwide human health mktg., 2002—05, gen. mgr., bus. unit, 2005—06, chief mktg. officer, 2006—. Bd. dir. St. Jude Med. Inc., 2002—. Bd. dirs. St. Jude Med. Ctr.; pres. bd. trustees Women's Health and Counseling Ctr., Somerville. Office: Merck and Co Inc One Merck Dr Whitehouse Station NJ 08889-0100 Office Phone: 908-423-6525. *

YAROS, CONSTANCE GREENBERG, painter, sculptor; b. Phila., Aug. 03; d. Harry William and Dorothy (Hofberg) Greenberg; m. Irvin Yaros, June 17, 1950 (dec. Nov. 1983); children: Michael J., Aimee Y. Silverman, Nancy S. Student, Temple U., Tyler Sch. of Art, Phila., 1957—60, Blai Studio, 1976—81, Pa. Acad. Fine Arts, 1987, student, 1978—79, Schuler Sch. of Art, 1990. One-woman shows include Tyler Alumni Gallery, 1992; exhibited in group shows icluding History Mus., Phila., 1984-88, Woodmere Art Mus., Phila., 1995, Am. Artists Profl. League, N.Y., 1993, Oil Painters Am., 1994, Art at the Armory, Phila., 1990-92, Artists Equity Assn. Triennial, 1984, 88, 91, Allied Artists of Am., 1988, Catherine Loriliard Wolfe Art Club, 1988, Salmagundi Art Club, 1988, Tyler Alumni Gallery-Diamond Club, Temple U., 1988-92, Phila. Sketch Club, 1987, Old York Rd. Art Guild, 1975; public collections at Temple U., Jefferson Park Hosp., Bd. City Trusts, Fed. Dist. Ct. House, Bd. City Trusts; numerous pvt. collections. Mem. Portrait Soc. Am., Am. Technion Assn., Greenpeace, Phila. Mus. Art, Allied Artists Am., Am. Soc. Classical Realism, Am. Soc. Portrait Artists, Am. Artist Profl. League, Pa. Acad. Fine Arts, Oil Painters Am., Artists Equity Assn., Woodmere Art Mus., Phila. Art Alliance, Archives of Women's Mus. of Art, Alumni Pa. Acad. Fine Arts, Alumni Tyler Sch. Art., Plastic Art Club. Avocations: music, ballet, exercise, photography. Home and Office: 2401 Pennsylvania Ave Ste 4a5 Philadelphia PA 19130-3002

YAROSLAVSKY, ANNA, biophysicist, educator; b. Saratov, Russia, Sept. 11, 1968; arrived in U.S., 1998; d. Nikita Petrovich Mityashin and Lubov Mikhailovna Mityashina; m. Ilya Vladimirovich Yaroslavsky, Oct. 23, 1987; 1 child, Anastasia Ilinichna Yaroslavksy. MS in Physics summa cum laude, Saratov State U., Russia, 1990, PhD in Physics, 1999. Engr. Russian Acad. Sci., Saratov, 1989—90, rsch. fellow, 1990—91, U. Twente, Enschede, Netherlands, 1992—93; scientist Heinrich Heine U., Dusseldorf, Germany, 1994—98; rsch. assoc. La. State U., Shreveport, La., 1998—2000; asst. physicist Wellman Ctr. Photomedicine, Boston, 2000—, instr., 2000—05; asst. prof. dept. dermatology Harvard Med. Sch., 2005—. Reviewer NIH, Bethesda, Md., 2004—, Optics Letters, Lasers in Surgery & Medicine; presenter in field. Co-author: Optics of Blood, 2002; contbr. articles to profl. jours. Fellow: Am. Soc. Lasers in Medicine and Surgery; mem.: Optical Soc. Am., Internat. Soc. Optical Engring., Animal Rescue League Boston. Avocations: music, history, art, sports. Home: 12 Farnum St North Andover MA 01845 Office: Wellman Ctr Photomedicine BHX 314B 55 Fruit St Boston MA 02114 Office Phone: 617-726-1590. Business E-Mail: yaroslav@helix.mgh.harvard.edu.

YARRINGTON, PATRICIA E., oil industry executive; b. Apr. 1956; B Polit. Sci., Pomona Coll., 1977; MBA, Northwestern U. With Chevron Corp., 1980—; sr. fin. analyst Chevron U.S.A. Inc., 1984—86, mgr. investor relations, 1986; various supervisory positions Chevron Products Co., Chevron U.S.A. Prodn. Co., Chevron Rsch. and Tech. Co.; mgr. credit card enterprises Chevron Products Co., 1995—97, comptr., 1997—98; pres. Chevron Can. Ltd., Vancouver, B.C., Canada, 1998—2000; v.p. strategic planning Chevron Corp., San Ramon, Calif., 2000—01, corp. v.p. policy, govt. & pub. affairs, 2002—07, corp. v.p., treas., 2007—. Bd. dirs. Chevron Phillips Chem. Co., ChevronTexaco Found. Bd. dirs. Chevron-Texaco Found. Office: Chevron Corp 6001 Bollinger Canyon Rd San Ramon CA 94583-2324

YARROW, PETER, folksinger; b. NYC, May 31, 1938; BA, Cornell U.; D (hon.), Nat. Lewis U., 2002, San Francisco State U., 2003. Mem. group: Peter, Paul, and Mary, 1962—, also solo performer, recording artist, Warner Bros.: albums with Peter, Paul, and Mary include: Peter, Paul, and Mary, Moving, In the Wind, In Concert, A Song Will Rise, See What Tomorrow Brings, Peter, Paul, and Mary Album, Album 1700, Late Again, Peter, Paul & Mommy, 10 Years Together: The Best Of, Reunion, Peter, Paul & Mommy, Too (Emmy nominee 1993), No Easy Walk to Freedom, Lifelines, Songs of Concience and Concern, In These Times, Carry It On; solo album: Peter, 1972, That's Enough for Me, 1973, Hard Times, 1975, Love Songs, 1975; on Broadway appearance: Peter, Paul, and Mary "From Bleecker to Broadway", 1986; TV spls. include: Reunion, Holiday Concert, Peter, Paul & Mommy, Too, Lifelines (PBS), Carry It On (PBS). Bd. dirs. Newport Folk Festival Found., Kerrville (Tex.) Folk Festival, 1971, Ctr. for Global Edn., Augsberg Coll.; chmn. bd. trustees Telluride Inst., 1997; founder, co-chair Oper. Respect, "Don't Laugh At Me", 1999 Recipient Emmy nominee for "Puff the Magic Dragon", 1979, Citizen Action Leadership award, Vista, 1979, Alfred Lowenstein award, 1982, Hospice Care of R.I. award, 1987, Nat. Emergency Civil Liberties Com. award, 1988, Interlochen Disting. Alumnus Arts award, 1992, Conn. Hospice award, 1993, Grammy award for prodr. Peter Paul & Mommy, Too, 1994, Kate Wolf Meml. award for the World Folk Music Assn., 1994, Tikkum Plam award, Ctrl. Synogogue, 1995, People for th Am. Way Defenders Democracy award, 1999, Ctrl. Sunagogue Shofar award, 1999, Spirit Crazy Horse award, 2000, AASC Sch. Counselor of Yr. award, 2001, Gandhi World Peace Flame, 2001,Rescuer of Humanity award, 2001, Starr Commonwealth Bd. Trustees Child Advocacy award, 2001, Good Neighbor award, 2002, N.Y. STate ASCS Educator of Yr. award, 2002, Jewish Leadership award, Panim, 2004, Wheel award Wheelock Family Theatre, 2006; Congressional hon., 1999.

YARUSS, HOWARD SETH, lawyer; b. NYC, Aug. 12, 1958; s. Ben and Bernice (Saltzman) Y. BS magna cumlaude, Brown U., 1980; student, London Sch. Econs., 1978-79; JD, U. Pa., 1983. Bar: N.Y. 1984, Pa. Assoc. Willkie, Farr & Gallagher, NYC, 1983-84, Baker & McKenzie, 1984-90; v.p. asst. gen. counsel Capital Reinsurance Co., NYC, 1991—97; exec. v.p., gen. counsel, sec. Radian Group Inc., 1997—. NY State Dem. Committeeman for 80th Assembly Dist. Office: Radian Group 1601 Market St Philadelphia PA 19103 Office Phone: 215-231-1388.

YARWOOD, BRUCE, health science association administrator; b. Sacramento, Calif. 2 children; 2 stepchildren. Mgr. MediCal program Calif. Dept. Health; exec. v.p. Calif. Assn. Health Facilities; CEO Crestwood Hospitals, Inc.; legis. counsel Am. Health Care Assn., Washington, acting pres., CEO, 2005, pres., 2005—. Office: Am Health Care Assn 1201 L St NW Washington DC 20005-4014 Office Phone: 202-842-4444. Office Fax: 202-842-3860. E-mail: byarwood@ahca.org.

YARYMOVYCH, MICHAEL IHOR, retired manufacturing company executive; b. Bialystok, Poland, Oct. 13, 1933; came to US, 1951, naturalized, 1956; s. Nicholas Joseph and Olga (Kruczowy) Y.; m. Roxolana Abramiuk, Nov. 21, 1951; children: Tatiana, Nicholas BS in Aerospace Engring., NYU, 1955; MS in Engring. Mechanics, Columbia U., 1956, D in Engring. Sci., 1969. Dep. asst. sec. rsch. and devel. USAF, Washington, 1967-70, chief scientist, 1973-75; dir. AGARD, NATO, Paris, 1970-73; asst. adminstr. field ops. ERDA, 1975-77; v.p. engring. N.Am. aerospace ops. Rockwell Internat. Corp., Seal beach, Calif., 1977-81, v.p. advanced systems devel. El Segundo, Calif., 1981-86, v.p., assoc. dir. Sys. Devel. Ctr., 1986-96, ret., 1996; v.p. internat. tech. The Boeing Co., 1996-98; chief scientist ANSER Corp., 1998—2003; ret. The Boeing Co., 1998; pres. Sarasota Space Assocs., 2003—. Mem. Air Force Sci. Adv. Bd., 1990-94; chmn. NATO Adv. Group for Aerospace R&D, 1994-97; chmn. NATO R&T Orgn., 1997-2000; cons. in field. Author papers in field. Recipient Exceptional Civilian Svc. award Dept. Air Force, 1968, 73, 75, 94, Disting. Svc. award ERDA, 1977; Guggenheim fellow, 1956-58. Fellow AIAA (dir., pres., gen. chmn. ann. meeting 1978); mem. Air Force Assn., Am. Astronautical Soc., Internat. Acad. Astronautics (v.p. sci. programs, pres., Theodore Von Karman award 2006). *

YASHER, MICHAEL, retired accountant; b. United, Pa., Aug. 17, 1928; s. Michael and Mary (Sasik) Y.; m. Margaret Jean Wallace, June 23, 1956 (dec. July 12, 1987); 1 child, Michael. BS, Pa. State U., University Park, 1956; diploma, Air Command & Staff Coll., 1972, Nat. Def. U., 1977; MA, Ctrl. Mich. U., Mt. Pleasant, 1983. CPA, D.C.; cert. profl. contract mgr., D.C. Enlisted USAF, 1948—52; commd. 1st lt. U.S. GAO, Washington, 1956—83, advanced through grades to col., 1982; officer USAF, 1961—88, ret., 1988; mem. appropriations com. U.S. House of Reps., 1978-79; acct. to the comptroller U.S. Air Materials Command, 1979-83; acct., cons. E. K. Williams Co., Silver Spring, Md., 1985-98. Contbr. numerous papers and articles to profl. publs. Treas. Boy Scouts Am., Rockville, Md., 1970; bd. dirs. Sr. Softball Assn., Montgomery County, Md., 1993—94, Montgomery County Sr. Sports Assn., 1999—2001; pres. Leisure World (Md.) Billiards Club, 1994—96, treas., 1997, 1999, pres., 2004—06, news corr., 2000—; commr., organizer Sr. Softball League, Montgomery County, 1994; participant Nat. Sr. Olympics, 1995—2007. Decorated with 14 mil. decorations; recipient Bronze medal softball, Md. Sr. Olympics, 1992—93, 1996—98, Silver medal softball, 1995, 2000—02, 2003, 2006, Gold medal softball, 1994, 1998—99, 2004, 2005, Bronze medal volleyball, 1993, 1995—97, 2005, Silver medal volleyball, 1998, 2000, 2002—03, 2006, Gold medal volleyball, 1999, 2005, 2001, Gold medal Volleyball, 2007, Bronze medal Billards, 1998, Bronze medal softball, Nat. Sr. Olympics, 1999, 2005, Gold medal Billiards, 2000, 2005, Silver medal Billiards, 2006, Meritorious Svc. award, U.S.G.A.O., 1975, USAF Outstanding Officer, Data Sys. Design Ctr., 1978, Silver medal 10 pin bowling doubles, 2003, Gold medal 10 pin bowling doubles, 2006, Gold medal Softball, Md. Sr. Olympics, 2007. Mem. AICPA, US Bowling Congress, Nat. Capital Area Bowling Assn., Res. Officers Assn., Disabled Am. Vets. Comdrs. Club, Leisure World Billiards Club, Nat. Sr. Games Assn. (charter mem.), Montgomery County Sr. Sports Assn., Am. Legion, VFW. Democrat. Roman Catholic. Avocations: coin collecting/numismatics, sports. Home: 15107 Interlachen Dr Apt 318 Silver Spring MD 20906-5629

YASHIMA, MUTSUO, language educator; b. Iwanai, Hokkaido, Japan, July 21, 1955; s. Mura Yashima; m. Gabriela Rodriguez de Yashima; children: Naomi Yashima Rodriguez, Sadami Yashima Rodriguez, Satomi Yashima Rodriguez. BS in Chem. Engring., Tokyo U. Agr. and Tech., 1978; MS in Stats., Kasas State U., Manhattan, 1991, MS in Elec. Engring., 1996; DEng, Osaka Prefecture U., Japan, 2000. Cert. environ. mgr., Japan, 1979. Environ. engr. Toyokuni Co., Osaka, Japan, 1978—80; rsch. asst. dept. chem. engring. Tokyo U. Agr. and Tech., 1980—86; grad. rsch. asst. dept. chem. engring. Kans. State U., 1989—91, rsch. asst. dept. chem. engring., 1992; chemist chromatography lab. Continental Analytical Svcs., Inc., Salina, Kans., 1992; grad. rsch. asst. dept. chem. engring. Kans. State U., 1993—96; operation mgr. Computer World Inc., Guadalajara, Mexico, 1996—97; tech. and sales asso. Cypress Systems, Inc., Lawrence, Kans., 1997; instr. English, Harvard 2000, Guadalajara, 1997—98; instr. U. Autonoma, Guadalajara, 1998; programmer, salesman AdLink Digital, Guadalajara, 1998—2001; instr. U. Autonoma, Guadalajara, 2003; instr. Japanese, Inst. Intercambio Cultural Mes.-Japones, Guadalajara, 2000—03; programmer, salesman Azamian Galleries, Guadalajara, 2001—04; instr. math. Etiquetas y empaques, Guadalajara, 2005; affiliate rsch. assoc. dept. chem. engring. Kans. State U., 1996—; instr. Japanese and English, Linguatec, 2005—. Grad. rsch. asst. Kans. State U., Manhattan, 1989—96. Mem.: IEEE, IEEE Signal Processing Soc., Sigma Xi (corr.). Avocations: reading, jogging, swimming. Home: Av Bahia de Todos los Santos #2743 Jalisco Tlaquipaque 45608 Mexico Office: Centro Tecnologico de Lenguas AC Av Tepeyac #225 Jalisco Guadalajara Mexico Home Phone: +52-33-3694-1470; Office Phone: +52-33-3587-4444. Personal E-mail: mutsuo_yashima@yahoo.com.mx.

YASHON, DAVID, neurosurgeon, educator; b. Chgo., May 13, 1935; s. Samuel and Dorothy (Cutler) Y.; children— Jaclyn, Lisa, Steven. BS in Medicine, U. Ill., 1958, MD, 1960. Diplomate Am. Bd. Neurol. Surgery. Intern U. Ill., 1961, resident, 1961-64, asst. in neuroanatomy, 1960; clin. instr. neurosurgery U. Chgo., 1965-66; asst. prof. neurosurgery Case Western Res U., Cleve., 1966-69; assoc. prof. neurosurgery Ohio State U., Columbus, 1969-74, prof., 1974-89, prof. emeritus, 1989—; mem. staff St. Ann's Hosp., Children's Hosp., Grant Med. Ctr., Ohio State U. East Med. Ctr. Cons. Med. Research and Devel. Command, U.S. Army; mem. Neurology B Study Sect NIH. Author: Spinal Injury; contbr. articles to med. jours. Served as capt. U.S. Army, 1960-68. Fellow Royal Coll. Surgeons Can. (cert.), A.C.S.; mem. AMA, Am. Physiol. Soc., Congress Neurol. Surgeons, Am. Assn. Anatomists, Canadian, Ohio neurosurg. socs., Am. Assn. Neurol. Surgeons, Research Soc. Neurol. Surgeons, Acad. Medicine Columbus and Franklin County, Soc. for Neurosci., Soc. Univ. Surgeons, Am. Acad. Neurology, Assn. for Acad. Surgery, Am. Acad. Neurol. Surgery, Am. Assn. for Surgery of Trauma, Central Surg. Soc., Ohio Med. Soc., Columbus Surg. Soc., Sigma Xi, Alpha Omega Alpha. Address: 500 Columbia Pl Bexley OH 43209-1677 E-mail: dyashon@columbus.rr.com.

YASNYI, ALLAN DAVID, communications company executive; b. New Orleans, June 22, 1942; s. Ben Z. and Bertha R. (Michalove) Y.; m. Susan K. Manders; children: Benjamin Charles, Evelyn Judith, Brian Mallut. BBA, Tulane U., 1964. Free-lance exec. producer, producer, writer, actor, designer TV, motion picture and theatre, 1961-73; producer, performer the Second City; dir. fin. and adminstrn. Quinn Martin Prodns., Hollywood, Calif., 1973-76, v.p. fin., 1976-77, exec. v.p. fin. & corp. planning, 1977; vice chmn., CEO QM Prodn., Beverly Hills, Calif., 1977-78, chmn. bd., CEO, 1978-80; exec. dir. Susan Manders Fine Art, 2002—; pres., CEO The Synapse Comm. Group, Inc., 1981—, ASI Entertainment, 1998-99. Mng. dir. Susan Mandears Fine Art, 2001—; exec. dir., adj. prof. U. So. Calif. Entertainment Tech. Ctr., 1994-99, exec. dir. emeritus, 1999—; participant IC IS Forum, 1990-95; exec. prodr. first live broadcast combining Intelsat, Intersputnik, The Voice of Am., and The Moscow World Radio Svc., 1990; resource guest Aspen Inst. Exec. Seminars, 1990; chmn. bd. dirs. Found. of Global Broadcasting, Washington, 1987-93; nat. adv. bd. DeSantis Ctr. Fla. Atlantic U., 1998-. Trustee Hollywood Arts Coun., 1980-83; exec. v.p., trustee Hollywood Hist. Trust, 1981-91; bd. dirs. Internat. Ctr. Intergative Studies, NYC, 1988-92; bd. dirs. Asthma and Allergy Found. Am., 1981-85. With US Army, 1964-66, Vietnam. Named to Tulane U. Hall of Fame. Mem. Acad. TV Arts and Sci., Inst. Noetic Sci., Hollywood Radio and TV Soc., Hollywood C. of C. (dir., vice chmn. 1978-93), Screen Actors Guild, Assn. Transpersonal Psychology (keynote spkr. 1988). Office: 4132 Fulton Ave Sherman Oaks CA 91423-4340 Office Phone: 818-995-0009. Personal E-mail: yasnyi@aol.com.

YASSIN, ROBERT ALAN, museum director, curator; b. Malden, Mass., May 22, 1941; s. Harold Benjamin and Florence Gertrude (Hoffman) Y.; m. Marilyn Kramer, June 9, 1963; children: Fredric Giles, Aaron David. BA, Dartmouth Coll., 1962; postgrad., Boston U., 1962—63; MA, U. Mich., 1965, postgrad., 1968—70, PhD candidate, 1970; postgrad., Yale U., 1966—68. Asst. to dir. Mus. Art U. Mich., 1965-66, asst. dir., 1970-72, assoc. dir., 1972-73, acting dir., 1973, instr. dept. history of art, 1970-73; co-dir. Joint Program in Mus. Tng., 1970-73; chief curator Indpls. Mus. Art, 1973-75, 87-89, acting dir., 1975, dir., 1975-89; exec. dir. Tucson Mus. Art, 1990—2001, Palos Verdes (Calif.) Art Ctr., 2002—. Adj. prof. Herron Sch. Art Ind. U./Purdue U., 1975-89. Contbr. to mus. publs. Rufus Choate scholar, 1962, Samuel H. Kress Found. fellow, 1968—70, Ford Found. fellow, 1966—68. Mem.: Calif. Assn. Museums, Western Mus. Assn., Nat. Trust Hist. Preservation, Coll. Art Assn. Am., Am. Assn. Museums (bd. dirs. Internat. Coun. Mus. 1986—89). Jewish. Office: Palos Verdes Art Ctr 5504 W Crestridge Rd Rancho Palos Verdes CA 90275 Home: 7321 Marina Pacifica Dr N Long Beach CA 90803-3808 Home Phone: 562-755-0681; Office Phone: 310-541-2479. Personal E-mail: rayassin@charter.net. Business E-Mail: byassin@pvartcenter.org.

YASSKY, ALAN, real estate company executive; Founder and pres. Rockland Realty, NY, 1964—. Dir. Rockland Cancer Soc., Rockland Housing Coalition, Clarkstown Indsl. Commn.; mem. bank adv. com. M&T. Named Realtor of Yr. in NY State, 1987; named one of Real Estate's 25 Most Influential Thought Leaders, Realtor Mag., 2006. Mem.: Rockland County Bd. Realtors (pres. 1976, chmn. membership com., chmn. legis. com., chmn. edn. com., chmn. nominating com., Realtor of Yr. 1980, 1987), NY State Assn. Realtors (bd. dirs. 1980, sec.-treas. 1984, chmn. budget and fin. com. 1984, v.p. 1985, pres.-elect 1986, pres. 1987, chmn. exec. com. 1988), Nat. Assn. Realtors (vice chmn. edn. com. 1988, 1990, chmn. housing needs com. 1992, v.p. and liaison to committees 1996, chmn. fin. com. 1998—2000, treas. 1997—2000, mem. strategic planning com., bd. dirs., Disting. Svc. Award 2003), Spring Valley Rotary Club (pres.). Office: Nat Assn Realtors 30700 Russell Ranch Rd Westlake Village CA 91362 Office Phone: 805-557-2300. Office Fax: 805-557-2680. *

YASTINE, BARBARA A., former diversified financial services company executive; BA in Journalism, NYU, 1981, MBA in Finance, 1987. Various communications and investor-relations positions W.R. Grace & Co.; dir. investor relations, Primerica Citigroup, 1987—91, v.p. investor relations and fin. planning & analysis, Traveler's Group, 1991, exec. v.p. fin. and insurance, CitiFinancial, chief admin. officer, global consumer group, 1998, chief auditor, CFO, global corp. and investment bank, 2000—02; CFO Credit Suisse First Boston, 2002—04. Bd. dirs. Symphony Services, Palo Alto, Calif., 2006—. Bd. dirs. Phoenix House.

YASUTAKE, NORIAKI, chef; Sushi chef Matsuba, Bethesda, Md., Inagiku Restaurant, NYC, Bond Street Sushi, NYC; head sushi chef Perry's, Washington, 2006—. Named one of Washington DC's Rising Stars, StarChefs.com, 2006; recipient 2nd place, Creative Sushi category, Nat. Sushi Soc., Washington, DC, 2002, 1st place, Creative Sushi category, 2006, Nat. Sushi Soc., NYC, 2003, 2nd place, World Sushi Olympics, 2006. Office: Perrys 1811 Columbia Rd NW Washington DC 20009 Office Phone: 202-234-6218. *

YATES, ALLISON A., medical association administrator; BS, MS, Univ. of Calif.; PhD, Univ. of Calif. at Berkley, 1974. Dean Univ. of Southern Miss., 1988—97, dir. emeritus food and nutrition bd. Washington, 1997—2003; sr. prog. officer food and nutrition bd. Inst. of Medicine, Washington; dir. nutritional sciences Environ Found., Arlington, Va.; dir. Beltsville (Md.) Human Nutrition Rsch. Ctr. US Dept. Agr. Office: Environ Ste 300 4350 N Fairfax Dr Arlington VA 22203 also: Beltsville Human Nutrition Rsch Ctr Bldg 307-C Barc-East 10300 Baltimore Ave Beltsville MD 20705-2350 Office Phone: 703-516-2349. Office Fax: 703-516-2304. E-mail: yatesa@ba.ars.usda.gov.

YATES, C. DANIEL, lawyer; b. Indpls., Sept. 27, 1947; AB, Ind. U., 1969, MBA, 1973; JD, Ind. U., Bloomington, 1973. Bar: Ind. 1973. Ptnr. estate planning and bus. succession planning grp. Bose, McKinney & Evans, LLP, Indpls. Mem. adv. bd., mem. planned giving com. Indpls. Zoo; bd. trustees Children's Mus. Indpls.; chmn. asset devel. com. Ctrl. Ind. Cmty. Found., Inc.; bd. govs. Legacy Fund Cmty. Found.; mem. planned giving com. Ind. U. Sch. Medicine; mem. planned giving adv. bd. Indpls.-Marion County Pub. Libr. Found., Inc., Noble of Ind.; elder Second Presbyn. Ch.; counsel Second Presbyn. Ch. Endowment Fund; bd. dirs., chmn. planned giving coun. Eiteljorg Mus. Am. Indians and Western Art; bd. dirs., mem. planned giving com. Indpls. Symphony Orch.; bd. dirs., sec. St. Vincent Hosp. Found.; bd. dirs. D.J. Angus-Scientech Ednl. Found., Inc. Named one of Top 100 Attys., Worth mag., 2006. Fellow: Am. Coll. Trust and Estate Counsel, Ind. Bar Found.; mem.: Planned Giving Grp. Ind., Estate Planning Coun. Indpls., ABA, Ind. State Bar Assn., Indpls. Bar Assn., Hillcrest Country Club, Rotary Club Indpls., Maxinkuckee Yacht Club, Contemporary Club Indpls. (bd. dirs.), Scientech Club Indpls., Inc., Econ. Club Indpls., Ind. Soc. Chgo., Phi Alpha Delta. Office: Bose McKinney & Evans LLP 2700 First Indiana Plz 135 N Pennsylvania St Indianapolis IN 46204 Office Phone: 317-684-5143. Office Fax: 317-223-0143. E-mail: dyates@boselaw.com. *

YATES, COLEEN DENISE, special education educator; b. Sacramento, Calif., Dec. 28, 1956; d. Kenneth Walter Brown and Edna Viola Pundt; children: James Jedidiah, Trista Denice, Devona Caryn. BS, Calif. State U., 1995. Substitute tchr. Roseville Union HS Dist., Roseville City Sch. Dist., Western Placer Unified Sch. Dist., Placer Union HS Dist., Eureka Union Sch. Dist., Calif., 1997; spl. edn. tchr. El Dorado HS, 1997, Chavez Elem. Sch., Davis Sr. HS, Calif., 1997—98, El Dorado HS, 1998, Mitchell Mid. Sch., Rancho Cordova, 1998—2000, Miles P. Richmond Sch., North Highlands, 2000—05, Rio Tierra Jr. HS, Sacramento, 2005—. Co-leader Girl Scouts Am., 1990—92, 1995—2000, parent vol., 1992—95; com. mem., parent vol. Boy Scouts Am., 1992—95; asst. biddy basketball coach Rocklin Parks & Recreation Dept., 1993—96; art docent vol. Rock Creek Elem. Sch., Auburn, 1990—92, Antelope Creek Elem. Sch., Rocklin, 1992—96; vol. classroom aide Rock Creek Elem. Sch., 1990—92, Antelope Creek Elem. Sch., 1992—96. Mem.: Calif. Assn. Health, Phys. Recreation, and Dance, Am. Alliance Health, Phys. Edn., Recreation and Dance, Golden Key. Home: 4900 2nd St Rocklin CA 95677

YATES, DAVID JOHN C., chemist, researcher; b. Stoke-on-Trent, Staffordshire, Eng., Feb. 13, 1927; arrived in US, 1958; s. Eric John and Beatrice Victoria Y.; m. Natalie Chmelnitsky, June 22, 1983 BS with honors, U. Birmingham, UK, 1949; PhD, U. Cambridge, Eng., 1955, Sc.D., 1968. Rsch. physicist Kodak Labs., Wealdstone, London, 1949-50; rsch. chemist Brit. Ceramic Rsch. Assn., Stoke-on-Trent, 1950-51; rsch. assoc. dept. colloid sci. U. Cambridge, 1951-58; lectr. Sch. Mines and dept. chemistry Columbia U., NYC, 1958-60; sr. rsch. fellow Nat. Phys. Lab., Teddington, England, 1960-61; rsch. assoc. corp. labs. Exxon Rsch. and Engring., Annandale, NJ, 1961-86; rsch. prof. dept. of chem. engring. Lafayette Coll., Easton, Pa., 1986-87; rsch. prof. dept. materials sci. Rutgers U., Piscataway, NJ, 1987-88; cons. San Diego, 1988—. Contbr. over 70 articles to profl. jours., chpts. to books; 13 U.S. patents, numerous fgn. patents. Fellow Inst. of Physics (U.K.), Royal Soc. Chemistry (U.K.), N.Y. Catalysis Club (chmn. 1966-67). Clubs: N.Y. Catalysis (chmn. 1965-66). Avocations: photography, bicycling, gliding, travel, sports cars.

YATES, ELLA GAINES, librarian, consultant; b. Atlanta, June 14, 1927; d. Fred Douglas and Laura (Moore) Gaines; m. Joseph L. Sydnor (dec.); 1 child, Jerri Gaines Sydnor Lee; m. Clayton R. Yates (dec.). AB, Spelman Coll., Atlanta, 1949; MS in L.S, Atlanta U., 1951; JD, Atlanta Law Sch., 1979. 1954Asst. br. librarian Bklyn. Pub. Library, 1951; head children's dept. Orange (N.J.) Pub. Library, 1956—59; br. librarian East Orange (N.J.) Pub. Library, 1960—69; med. librarian Orange Meml. Hosp., 1967—69; asst. dir. Montclair (N.J.) Pub. Library, 1970—72, Atlanta-Fulton Pub. Library, 1972—76, dir., 1976—81; dir. learning resource ctr. Seattle Opportunities Industrialization Ctr., 1982—84; asst. dir. adminstrn. Friendship Force, Atlanta, 1984—86; state librarian Commonwealth of Va., 1986—90; library cons. Price Waterhouse, 1991; adv. bd. Library of Congress Center for the Book, 1977—85; interim dir. Atlanta-Fulton Pub. Libr., 1998—99; cons., dir. Woodruff Libr., Atlanta, 2000—02. Cons. in field; vis. lectr. U. Wash., Seattle, 1981-83; mem. Va. Records Adv. Bd., 1986-90; mem. Nagara Exec. Bd., 1987-91. Contbr. to profl. jours. Vice chmn. N.J. Women's Coun. on Human Rels., 1957-59; chmn. Friends Fulton County Jail, 1973-81; bd. dirs. United Cerebral Palsy Greater Atlanta, Inc., 1979-81 Coalition Against Censorship, Washington, 1981-84, YMCA Met. Atlanta, 1979-81, Exec. Women's Network, 1979-82, Freedom To Read Found., 1979-85, Va. Black History Mus., Richmond, 1990-91; sec., exec. dir. Va. Libr. Found. Bd., 1986-90; founder Coretta Scott King Book Award, Ala., 1968—. Recipient meritorious svc. award Atlanta U., 1977, Phoenix award City of Atlanta, 1980, Serwa award Nat. Coalition 100 Black Women, 1989, Black Caucus award, 1989, disting. svc. award Clark-Atlanta U., 1991, ednl. support svc. award Tuskegee Airmen, 1993, Alumnae Achievement award Spelman Coll., 1998, Annie McPheters award Atlanta-Fulton Pub. Libr., 1998, Disting. Alumnae award Clark Atlanta U., 2001; named profl. woman of yr. NAACP N.J., 1972, outstanding chum of yr., 1976; named outstanding alumni Spelman Coll., 1977, named to alumni hall of fame, 1995. Mem. ALA (exec. bd. 1977-83, commn. freedom of access to info., founder Coretta Scott King Book Award 1968), NAACP, Southeastern Libr. Assn., Nat. Assn. Govt. Archives and Records Adminstrn. (exec. bd. 1987-91), Delta Sigma Theta (Pinnacle leadership award 2001). Baptist. Home and Office: 1171 Oriole Dr SW Atlanta GA 30311-2424 E-mail: ellayates4@aol.com.

YATES, GARY L., marriage and family therapist; b. Washington, Aug. 16, 1944; s. Lewis Edward and Norma Jean (Andruss) Y.; m. Cynthia Ann Pagay, Aug. 16, 1974; children: David, Jonathan, Daniel, Matthew, Nathan. BA, Am. U., 1967; MA, U. No. Colo., 1978. Tchr. St. Anthony's, Kailua, Hawaii, 1970-74, Acad. of Pacific, Honolulu, 1974-79; adminstr. Dept. Pub. Health, San Bernardino, Calif., 1979-81, Charles Drew Sch. of Medicine, LA, 1981-82; assoc. dir. Divsn. of Adolescent Medicine/Children's Hosp., LA, 1982-92; sr. program officer Calif. Wellness Found., Woodland Hills, Calif., 1992-93, program dir., 1993-94, pres., CEO, 1995—. Asst. clin. prof. U. So. Calif., 1988—; bd. dirs. Calif. Wellness Found., Grantmaker in Health, Hispanics in Philanthropy, So. Calif. Assn. Philanthropy, Coun. Found. Contbr. articles to profl. jours.; contbg. author: Multi Agency System of Care, 1990. Mem. L.A. Roundtable for Children, 1988-92, United Way Task Force on AIDS, L.A., 1988-92, San Bernardino Comm. Coun., 1980-82; chmn. Hawaii Sch. Counseling Assn., Honolulu, 1978-79. S(gt.) U.S. Army, 1968-70. Recipient NACO Achievement award Nat. Assn. U.S. Counties, 1980, 3rd Century award Hollywood Coord. Coun., 1989, Gov.'s Victim's Svc. award Gov. of Calif., 1990, Commendation award Calif. State Senate, 1992, Hispanic Health Leadership award, 1999, L.A. Free Clinic Lenny Somberg award, 1998. Mem. Am. Assn. Humanistic Psychologists, Soc. for Adolescent Medicine, Calif. Assn. Marriage and Family Therapists, Am. Pub. Health Assn. Democrat. Methodist. Avocations: reading, walking. Office: Calif Wellness Found 6320 Canoga Ave Ste 1700 Woodland Hills CA 91367-2565

YATES, JAMES ARTHUR, plastic surgeon; b. Butler, Pa., June 5, 1935; s. Adolph Walter and Laura Marie (De Foggie) Y.; m. Debra Lynne Stringer, June 19, 1983; 1 child, Jamie Dale Yates Reynolds. BA, Cornell U., 1956; MD, U. Md., 1960. Diplomate Am. Bd. Plastic Surgery, Nat. Bd. Med. Examiners, Am. Bd. Surgery; lic. physician, Pa., Ohio, R.I. Intern Cleve. Clinic Hosp., 1960—61, resident in gen. surgery, 1961—62, U. Pitts. Med. Ctr., 1963—65; resident in plastic surgery R.I. Hosp., 1966—67, chief resident, 1967—68; pvt. practice Plastic Surgery Ctr. Ltd., Camp Hill, Pa., 1968—; med. dir. Grandview Surgery Ctr., Camp Hill, Pa. Tchg. fellow gen. surgery U. Pitts. Med. Ctr., 1963-65, instr. gen. surgery, 1965-66; clin. instr. plastic surgery Milton S. Hershey (Pa.) Med. Ctr., 1968—; staff maxillofacial and plastic surgery dept. Harrisburg (Pa.) Hosp., 1968—; chief plastic and aesthetic surgery dept. Holy Spirit Hosp., Camp Hill, 1968—; staff Mechanicsburg Rehab. Hosp., Carlisle (Pa.) Hosp., Pinnacle Health Sys. Hosps.; med. dir. Grandview Surgery and Laser Ctr., Camp Hill; cons. Harrisburg State Hosp.; physician surveyor Am. Assn. Ambulatory Health Care; physician trainer plastic surgery residency program Am. Coll. Osteo. Surgery; bd. dirs., pres. Am. Assn. Accreditattion of Ambulatory Surgery Facilities. Contbr. articles to profl. jours.; adv. bd. Town and Country Mag. Police commr. West Shore Regional Police Dept.; pres. Boro Coun. Lemoyne Boro; mem. credentialling com. Keystone Health Plan; mem. task force on ambulatory surgery Pa. Dept. Health; mem. coun. Lemoyne (Pa.) Borough Coun., pres.; credentialing officer Freedom Health Care HMO; commr. West Shore Regional Police. Fellow ACS; mem. AMA, Pa. Med. Soc., Am. Burn Assn., Am. Soc. Plastic and Reconstructive Surgeons, Am. Burn Victim Found., Am. Soc. Aesthetic Plastic Surgery, Vail Cosmetic Surgery Soc., Pa. Plastic Surgery Soc. (past pres.), Am. Soc. Automobile Medicine, Northeastern Soc. Plastic Surgeons, Royal Soc. Medicine, Lipolysis Soc. N.Am., Internat. Soc. Clin. Plastic Surgeons, South Ctrl. Pa. Regional Med. Dirs., Am. Coll. Physician Execs. Republican. Roman Catholic. Avocations: bicycling, skiing, model building, sports cars. Home: 833 Kiehl Dr Lemoyne PA 17043-1201 Office: Plastic Surgery Ctr Ltd 205 Grandview Ave Camp Hill PA 17011-1708 Home Phone: 717-761-1281; Office Phone: 717-763-7814. Personal E-mail: jay5plas@msn.com.

YATES, JEROME WILLIAM, scientific administrator, researcher; b. Rockford, Ill., Nov. 9, 1936; s. Frank and Eily Yates; m. Mary Elizabeth McAuley, June 1, 1979; children: Elizabeth Ann, Sarah Eily. AB, Lawrence U., Appleton, Wis., 1961; MD, U. Ill., Chgo., 1965; MPH, Harvard Sch. of Pub. Health, Boston, 1981. Diplomate Nat. Bd. of Med. Examiners, 1966, Am. Coll. of Med. Executives, 2002. Rsch. scientist ii Roswell Pk. Cancer Inst., Buffalo, 1970—74; prof. of medicine U. Vt., Burlington, Vt., 1974—82; assoc. dir. for centers and cmty. oncology Nat. Cancer Inst., Bethesda, Md., 1982—87; sr. v.p. for clin. affairs Roswell Pk. Cancer Inst., Buffalo, 1987—2001; nat. v.p., rsch. Am. Cancer Soc., Atlanta, 2002—. Dir. Sheehan Meml. Hosp., Buffalo, 2003—; intermittent cons. and reviewer Nat. Cancer Inst., Bethesda, NY, 1971—. Contbr. scientific papers. Cancer ctr. adv. com. NCI Designated Cancer Ctr., 1982—2006; dir. Sheehan Meml. Hosp., Buffalo, 2003—06. Sp3 AMEDS US Army, 1955—57, Landstuhl, Germany. Recipient Outstanding Leadership and Svc. award, Assn. of Am. Cancer Ctr., 2002, Award of Merit, NIH, 1983, Outstanding Work Performance award, Nat. Cancer Inst., 1983, 1984, 1985. Mem.: Assn. of Am. Cancer Inst (assoc.; pres. 1991—92). Independent. Achievements include research in leukemia treatment, standard for 30 years; initiated community clinical oncology program. Avocations: aviation, golf. Home: 240 Independence Dr Orchard Park NY 14127 Office: Am Cancer Soc 1599 Clifton Rd Atlanta GA 30333 Home Phone: 716-662-3253; Office Phone: 404-798-7938.

YATES, JOHN MELVIN, ambassador; b. Superior, Mont., Nov. 25, 1939; s. Leon Glen and Violet May (McPheeters) Y.; m. Peggy Maureen Simpson, Mar. 26, 1961 (dec. Apr. 1986); children: Catherine Diener, John Simpson, Maureen Cole, Paul Marion, Leon Gregory; m. Mary Barbara Carlin, Jan. 30, 1988. AB, Stanford U., 1961; MA, Fletcher Sch. Law and Diplomacy, 1962, MALD, 1963, PhD, 1972. Fgn. service officer US Dept. State, Washington, 1964—2002, Algiers, Algeria, 1964-66, Blantyre, Malawi, 1967-68, Bamako, Mali, 1969-71, New Delhi, 1973-75, Ankara, Turkey, 1975-77, Libreville, Gabon, 1977-80, Washington, 1971-73, 80-82; amb. to Republic of Cape Verde, Am. Embassy, 1983-86, counselor for polit. affairs Manila, 1986-89, dep. chief of mission Lagos, Nigeria, 1989-91, Kinshasa, Zaire, 1991-93, chief of mission, 1993-95, amb. to Republic of Benin, Cotonou, 1995-98, amb. to Republic of Cameroon and Republic Equatorial Guinea, Yaounde, 1998—2001, ret., 2001; sr. US advisor Somalia Reconciliation Talks, 2004; sr. advisor Darfur (Sudan) Polit. Negotiations, 2005—06; spl. envoy for Somalia, 2007. Recipient Presdl. award for sustained superior accomplishment in conduct of fgn. policy. Mem. Am. Fgn. Service Assn. Home: CMR 480 Box 2317 APO AE 09128 Personal E-mail: johnnymontana@gmail.com.

YATES, JOHN THOMAS, JR., chemistry professor, research scientist; b. Winchester, Va., Aug. 3, 1935; s. John Thomas and Kathryn (Barnett) Y.; m. Kerin Joyce Narbut, Oct. 18, 1958; children: Geoffrey, Nathan. BS, Juniata Coll., 1956; PhD, MIT, 1960. Asst. prof. chemistry Antioch Coll., Yellow Springs, Ohio, 1960-63; NRC fellow, rsch. chemist Nat. Bur. Standards (now Nat. Inst. Standards and Tech.), Washington, 1963—65, rsch. staff, sect. chief, surface chemistry, 1965—82; R.K. Mellon prof. chemistry and physics U. Pitts., 1982—2006, founding dir., Surface Sci. Ctr., 1982—2006; prof. chem. U. Va., 2007—, Shannon fellow, 2007—. Sr. vis. scholar, U. East Anglia, 1970-71; Gwathmey vis. prof. U. Va., 2002-03 Author: Experimental Innovations in Surface Science, 1997; co-author: The Surface Scientist's Guide to Organometallic Chemistry, 1987, Molecular Physical Chemistry for Engineers, 2007; co-editor: Vibrational Spectroscopy of Molecules on Surfaces, 1987, Chemical Perspectives of Microelectronic Materials, Vol. 131; assoc. editor: Studies in Surface Science and Catalysis, 1986; series editor: Methods of Surface Characterization, 1987; bd. editors Ann. Rev. Phys. Chemistry, 1983-85, Jour. Phys. Chemistry, 1983-88, Jour. Chem. Physics, 1984-87, Jour. Catalysis, 1987-91, Chem. Revs., Langmuir, Surface Sci., Applications of Surface Sci., Accounts Chem. Rsch., Chem. Phys. letters, 1997-; assoc. editor Langmuir, 1991-98; mem. adv. bd. Chemical & Engineering News, 2001-2003; contbr. revs. and articles to profl. jours.; inventor desorption spectrometer, 1981. Sherman Fairchild Disting. scholar Calif. Inst. Tech., 1977-78; recipient Silver medal Dept. Commerce-Nat. Bur. Stds., 1973, Stratton award for Disting. Rsch., 1978, Gold medal Dept. Commerce Nat. Bur. Stds., 1981, Pres.'s Disting. Rsch. award U. Pitts., 1989, Procter & Gamble award, 1989, Alexander von Humboldt Sr. Rsch. award, 1995, 1997, Pitts.-Cleve. Catalysis Soc. award, 1998, J.W. Linnett lectr. Cambridge U., 2000, Outstanding Alumnus Juniata Coll., 2000, named Among 100 Most Highly Cited Chemists in World 1984—, G.N. Lewis lectr. U. Calif.-Berkeley, 2002; fellow Sidney Sussex Coll., 2000, Japan Soc. Promotion of Sci., 2002, Inst. Physics, 2004 Fellow Am. Phys. Soc. (bd. dirs. divsn. chem. physics 1991—, chmn. divsn. chem. physics 1989), Am. Vacuum Soc. (chmn. surface sci. divsn. 1973, 92, trustee 1975, bd. dirs. 1982-85, Medard Welch award 1994, fellow 1994); mem. NAS, Am. Chem. Soc. (chmn. divsn. colloid and surface chemistry, Langmuir lectr. 1979, Kendall award in colloid of surface chemistry 1986, E.W. Morley prize Cleve. chpt. 1990, Peter Debye lectr. Cornell U. 1993, Pitts. award 1998, Arthur W. Adamson award for Disting. Svc. in the Advancement of Surface Chemistry, 1999, Peter Debye Phys. Chemistry award, 2007), Pitts.-Cleve. Catalysis Soc. Office: Univ Va Dept Chemistry Charlottesville VA 22904-4319 Home: Po Box 124 Free Union VA 22940 Business E-Mail: johnt@virginia.edu.

YATES, LEIGHTON DELEVAN, JR., lawyer; b. Atlanta, Sept. 4, 1946; s. Leighton Delevan and Stella Louise (Hill) Y.; m. Phyllis Jeanne Hummer, Dec. 22, 1968; children: Leighton Delevan III, Lauren Jeanne. BA, Hampden-Sydney Coll., Va., 1968; JD with high honors, U. Fla., 1973. Bar: Fla. 1974, U.S. Dist. Ct. (middle dist.) Fla. 1975. Assoc. Maguire, Voorhis & Wells, P.A., Orlando, Fla., 1974-77, shareholder, 1978-98, dept. chmn., 1985-90; ptnr. Holland & Knight LLP, Orlando, Fla., 1998—, nat. practice group leader, 2005—. Bd. dirs. Hubbard Constrn. Co., Winter Park, Fla., 1985—2004, Blythe Constrn., Inc., Charlotte, NC, 1999—2004; adminstrv, dir. SunTrust Bank, Orlando, Fla., 1990—. Exec. editor U. Fla. Law Rev., 1973. Mem. Fla. Bd. Bar Examiners, 1992-97, 2002-05, vice chmn., 1995-96, chmn. 1996-97; chmn. Fla.'s Blood Ctrs., 1995—, vice chmn., 1980-95; chmn. Orlando Opera Co., 1994, pres., 1993; bd. dirs. Metro Orlando Econ. Devel. Commn., 2007-. Fellow Am. Bar Found.; mem. ABA, Fla. Bar Assn., Orange County Bar Assn., Univ. Club of Orlando, Country Club of Orlando, Order of the Coif, Omicron Delta Kappa, Phi Kappa Phi. Republican. Presbyterian. Avocations: scuba diving, bicycling, music, reading. Home: 3218 S Osceola Ave Orlando FL 32806-6251 Office: Holland & Knight LLP 200 S Orange Ave Ste 2600 Orlando FL 32801-3453 Office Phone: 407-425-8500. Personal E-mail: lyates@cfl.rr.com. Business E-Mail: leighton.yates@hklaw.com.

YATES, MARY CARLIN, civilian military employee, former ambassador; b. Portland, Oreg., Dec. 1946; m. John Melvin Yates. BA in English, Oreg. State U.; M in Comparative East West Humanities, NYU, postgrad. Joined fgn. svc., 1980; press attaché for Amb. Pamela Harriman US Dept. State, sr. cultural attaché Am. Embassy Paris, US amb. to Burundi Washington, 1999—2002, US amb. to Ghana, 2002—05; polit. adv. to the comdr. US European Command, 2005—. Mailing: HQ USEUCOM/ECPLAD Unit 30400 APO AE 09131 E-mail: Yates@eucom.mil. *

YATES, NORRIS WILLIAM, JR., lawyer; b. Alamo Heights, Tex., July 6, 1926; s. Norris William and Maggie Barkley (Curry) Y.; m. Mary Hutchings Spencer, Dec. 30, 1947 (div. Aug. 1949); 1 child, William Spencer; m. Jimmie Carolyn Cook, Sept. 17, 1955; children: Victoria Carolyn Marullo (dec.), Rebecca Elizabeth Yates Bird. BA in Econs., Tex. A&M U., 1950; JD, U. Tex., 1957. Bar: Tex. 1957, U.S. Ct. Mil. Appeals 1963, U.S. Supreme Ct. 1964. Asst. to mgr. rates and tariffs Slick Airways, Inc., San Antonio, 1950; assoc. Beckmann, Stanard, Wood, Barrow & Vance, San Antonio, 1957-60; pvt. practice San Antonio, 1960-67, 83—; asst. criminal dist. atty., chief civil sect. Bexar County Dist. Atty.'s Office, San Antonio, 1967-82. Mcpl. ct. judge City of San Antonio, 1966-67. Editor The Subpoena, 1958-59. Exec. com. Bexar County Dem. Party, San Antonio. Cpl. U.S. Army, Airborne Inf., 1944-46, ETO; 1st lt. USAF, 1951-55, B-29 Bomber Pilot, Korea, JAG lt. col. USAFR, ret. 1978. Decorated Bronze Star medal, combat inf. badge, glider badge, pilot's wings, three battle stars. Mem. Daedalians, Mil. Officer Assn. Am. (sec. Alamo chpt.), USAF Pilot Class 52-George Assn. (rec. sec.), 307th Bomb Group/Wing Inc. (past pres.), Toastmasters (past pres., Disting. Dist. Gov. 1969-70, Disting. Toastmaster 1984, Presdl. citation 1992), Masons (past master, 32 degree), San Antonio A&M Club (dir.), Oak Park Neighborhood Assn. (dir., past pres.), Sam Houston Club (mem. coun.) Democrat. Presbyterian. Avocations: travel, photography. Home: 2118 Kenilworth Blvd San Antonio TX 78209-2329 Personal E-mail: nyates@satx.rr.com.

YATES, PATRICIA LAWRENCE, elementary school educator; b. Rockland, Maine, Feb. 5, 1947; d. Edward Mark and Helen Mattson Lawrence; m. George Radford Yates, Dec. 30, 1966; children: Michelle Thomas, Matthew, Amy Lally, Jeremy. BA in Edn., U. South Fla., 1969. Kindergarten tchr. Forest Heights Sch., Lakeland, Fla., 1972—81; sub.,tutor Strongsville City Sch., Ohio, 1982—85; fourth grade tchr. St. Joseph and John Sch., Strongsville, Ohio, 1985—. Sr. tchr. cons. Geographic Alliance, 1992—; mem. handbell ensemble Renaissance Ringers; dir. children's bell choirs St. Joseph Ch. Author: (CD timeline) Timeline of Northeast Ohio 1620-1861, 2003. Mem.: Am. Guild of English Handbell Ringers, Nat. Coun. for Geog. Edn., Nat. Coun. Social Studies. Republican. Cath. Avocations: piano, needlecrafts, travel, handbells. Home: 17045 Shurmer Rd Strongsville OH 44136 Office Phone: 440-238-4877. Business E-Mail: pyates@ameritech.net.

YATES, RICHARD L., multi-industry company executive; BS in Acctg., Northeastern U., Boston. CPA. Ptnr. Arthur Young & Co.; treas. Paul Revere Ins. Group, 1985—95, v.p., 1985—91, contr., 1985—87, CFO, 1987—95, sr. v.p., 1991—93, exec. v.p., 1993—95; v.p., contr. Textron, Inc., Providence, 1995—2004, sr. v.p., corp. contr., 2004—. Mem. Corp. Exec. Bd. Contr.'s Leadership Roundtable. Mem.: AICPA, Mfrs. Alliance Fin. Coun. II, Fin. Execs. Inst., Mass. Soc. CPAs. Office: Textron Inc 40 Westminster St Providence RI 02903 Office Phone: 401-421-2800. *

YATES, RONALD EUGENE, newspaper editor, educator, author, journalist; b. Kansas City, Mo., Feb. 19, 1941; s. Guy Raymond and Willadene (Peterson) Y.; m. Ingeborg Zoelss, May 7, 1966; children: Jennifer Christina, Nicole Brigitte. BS (Gannett Newspapers scholar 1968-69, Angelo C. Scott Meml. scholar 1969), U. Kans., 1969. Reporter Kansas City (Kans.) Star, 1968; editor Univ. Daily Kansan, 1969; reporter, asst. city editor, fgn. corr. Chgo. Tribune, Chgo. and Tokyo, 1969-76, Asia and Latin Am. corr., 1976-82, met. editor, 1983—, nat. editor, 1984—, chief Asia corr., 1985—, sr. writer, 1992—; prof., chmn. dept. journalism U. Ill., Champaign, 1997—, dean Coll. Comm., 2003—. Contbr. articles to mags. Served with U.S. Army Intelligence, 1962-66. Recipient award for excellence in staff leadership William Allen White Sch. Journalism, 1968, Edward Scott Beck award for best fgn. reporting, 1975, 87, 89, Inter-Am. Press Assn. award for reporting on Latin Am., 1979, Peter Lisagor award for bus. and fin. reporting, 1993; named Outstanding Sr. U. Kans., 1969 Mem. Fgn. Corrs. Club of Japan (v.p. 1989—), Los Angeles Press, Sigma Delta Chi. Lutheran. Office Phone: 217-333-2350. Business E-Mail: ryates@uiuc.edu.

YATES, STEVEN A., curator, artist; b. Chgo., Nov. 14, 1949; s. Thomas A. and Phyllis E. (Wilson) Y.; m. Lynne A. Smith, Aug. 5, 1972; children: Kelsey Victoria, Mackenzie Phyllis. BFA, U. Nebr., 1972; MA, U. N.Mex., 1975, MFA, 1978. Curatorial asst. Sheldon Meml. Art Gallery, 1972-73, U. Art Mus., U. N.Mex., 1973-75; faculty dept. art Claremont (Calif.) Colls. and Pomona, 1976; part-time faculty U. N.Mex., Albuquerque, 1976—, assoc. adj. prof. dept. art and art history, 1994—; curator prints, drawings and photographs Mus. of N.Mex., Santa Fe, 1980-84; curator of photography Mus. Fine Arts, 1985—. Vis. prof. 19th and 20th century photography Santa Fe C.C., 1998-02; vis. specialist in field; instr. U. N.Mex., 1975-78; frequent lectr. and essayist on contemporary and early modern history of photography and rsch. internationally; guest artist Tamarind Inst., Albuquerque, 1988; vis. instr. Pomona Coll., Claremont Coll., Calif., 1976, U. Calif. LA, 1976; lectr., rschr., curator exhbns. internationally. One-man shows include Sheldon Meml. Art Gallery, Lincoln, Nebr., 1978, Gallery A-3, Moscow, 1996, Up and Down Gallery, Kharkov, Ukraine, 1997, U. Nebr., 1997, Mus. Photography, Riga, Latvia, 1998, Gallery A-3 Moscow, 2002; collaborative installation Ctr. for Contemprary Arts, Irving, Tex., 2000; group shows include San Francisco Mus. Modern Art, 1980, 81, 84, 86, 96, Cinema Ctr., Moscow, 1991, St. Petersburg, Russia, 1997, Photographic Icons: Film Form and Montage, A homage to Sergei Eisenstein adn Gustav Klucis, Latvia, 1998, Empires: Russia Past and Present, 1998; represented in permanent collections San Francisco Mus. Modern Art, Sheldon Art Gallery, Mint Mus., Art Mus. U. N.Mex., Ctr. for Creative Photography, Tucson; editor: The Essential Landscape, The New Mexico Photographic Survey, 1985; guest editor spl. issue Contemporary Photography, 1987, El Palacio, 1987, Poetics of Space: A Critical Photographic Anthology, 1995, Betty Hahn: Photography or Maybe Not, 1995, Theatre as Memory: L. Millet, 1999, The Avant-garde Document: A. Macijauskas, 2001, Idea Photographic: After Modernism, 2002, Poéticas del espacia, 2002, Alexander Rodchenko, Modern Photography, Film, and Photomontage, 2003; contbr. essays in field; numerous mus. catalogs and pubs. nationally and internationally. Ford Found. fellow, 1977, Nat. Endowment Arts fellow, 1980; recipient Vreeland award U. Nebr., 1972, Outstanding Alumni Achievement award U. Nebr., 1994; Sr. Fulbright Scholars award USSR, 1991, Russian Fedn., 1995. E-mail: steve.yates@state.nm.us.

YATES, YORK J., plastic surgeon; b. Utah; BS magna cum laude, U. Utah, MD. Diplomate Am. Bd. Plastic Surgery. Resident in plastic & reconstructive surgery U. Mo., Columbia, fellow in microsurgery; pvt. practice Tanner Clinic, Layton, Utah. Mem.: Alpha Omega Alpha. Office: Tanner Clinic 2121 N 1700 W Layton UT 84041 Office Phone: 801-773-4840. E-mail: yorkyates@msn.com. *

YATES-WILLIAMS, LINDA SNOW, real estate broker; b. St. Louis, July 20, 1938; d. Robert Anthony Jernue and June Alberta (Crowder) Armstrong; m. Charles Russell Snow, Nov. 26, 1958 (div. 1979); children: Cathryn Louise, Christopher Armstrong, Heather Highstone, Sean Webster; m. Alan Porter Yates, July 22, 1983 (dec.); m. John S. Williams, Mar. 10, 2006. BBA, Auburn U., 1973, MEd, 1975, EdD, 1998. Cert. profl. sec. Div. head placement div. Solutions Group, Atlanta, 1981-83; employment coord. Fulton Fed. Savs., Atlanta, 1983-84; owner, recruiter Data One, Inc., Atlanta, 1984-85; ops. mgr. Talent Tree Temporaries, Atlanta, 1985-87; legal asst., sec. Rice & Keene, Atlanta, 1987-90; legal word processing asst. Kilpatrick & Cody, Atlanta, 1990-94; pres., owner Power Comm., Cashiers, N.C., 1994-98; regional coord. S.E. region, regional mktg. rep. WorldConnect Comms., Tulsa; dir. mktg. electronic collection divsn. Am. Fin. and Credit Svcs., Inc.; area v.p., loan agent Enterprise Lenders, LLC; bd. dirs., corp. sec. The Hilltop Assocs. Inc., 1999—; real estate sales Exit Realty Beaufort; broker-in-charge Exit Island Realty, Bluffton, SC, 2006—. Adj. instr. DeKalb Coll., Atlanta, 1980-84, Mercer U., Atlanta, 1981-82; instr. bus. So. Union State Jr. Coll., Valley, Ala., 1974-75; radio advt. WAUD, Auburn, Ala., 1970-75, radio announcer Meet the Public; exec. legal sec. Swift, Currie, McGhee & Hiers, Atlanta, 1979-80, Samford, Torbert, Denson & Horsley, Opelika, Ala., 1969-71; dir. acad. planning, chmn. edn. divsn., mem. part-time faculty in ednl. adminstrn. CEU Grad. Coll., Nuevo Leon, Mex. Columnist Neon News Flash, 1995. Named Top Prodr., 2006; recipient Top Sales, 2006. Mem. Paralegal Assn. Beaufort County (charter mem., sec. 1993-94), Women Bus. Owners, Nat. Assn. Pers. Cons., Internat. Soc. Poets (Disting. mem., founding laureate mem. 2006, Internat. Poet of Merit 1996, Internat. Poetry Hall of Fame 1996), Cashiers Writers Group, 90-10 Club, Sunscribers, Phi Delta Kappa,

Alpha Xi Delta. Republican. Episcopalian. Avocations: golf, writing poetry, international travel. Office: 91 N Boone Rd Saint Helena Island SC 29920 Personal E-mail: linday1000@yahoo.com.

YATSENKO, YURI PETROVICH, economics professor, mathematician; b. Kiev, Ukraine, Oct. 15, 1955; arrived in US, 2000, permanent resident, 2001; s. Petr Yatsenko and Nadiya Betina; m. Natali Hritonenko; children: Oleg, Victoria, Olga. BS in Physics, Kiev State U., Ukraine, 1977, MS, 1977, PhD, 1981; DSc, Presidium Acad. Scis. USSR, 1988. Lic. prof. Edn. Ministry Ukraine, 1995. Sr. rschr., dept. head Cybernetics Inst. Ukrainian Acad. Scis., Kiev, 1983—96; prof. Kiev State U., 1991—93, Acad. Tech. & Agr., Bydgoszcz, Poland, 1993—95; sr. analyst Electric Submersible Pumps, Inc., Okla. City, Okla., 1997—99; adj. prof. U. Alta., Edmonton, Alberta, Canada, 1999—99; sr. sys. analyst Netherland, Sewell & Assoc., Inc., Dallas, 2000—01; prof. Houston Bapt. U., 2002—. Owner Cybernetics Cons. Inc., Edmonton, Alberta, Canada, 1996—2000; lectr. in field; mem. editl. bd. Internat. Jour. Applications and Applied Maths., United States, 2005—, Internat. Jour. Ecology and Devel., India, 2006—, Jour. Computational and Applied Maths., Ukraine, 2006—; assoc. editor Internat. Jour. Ecological Econs. and Stats., India, 2006—; mem. program & organizing coms. at confs. in field. Author: 5 Books; contbr. scientific papers to profl. jours. Rsch. grants, Sorros Internat. Sci. Found. & Edn. Ministry Ukraine, 1992—95, Rsch. grant, NATO, 2006—. Russian Orthodox. Achievements include research in mathematical modeling and optimization of economic and industrial development, technological change, innovation processes, and technology replacement. Home: 15434 Tysor Park Ln Houston TX 77095 Office: Houston Bapt Univ 7502 Fondren Houston TX 77074 Home Phone: 832-593-0037. Office Fax: 281-649-3436. Business E-Mail: yyatsenko@hbu.edu.

YAU, EDWARD TINTAI, toxicologist, pharmacologist; b. Canton, China, Dec. 29, 1944; came to U.S., 1967; s. Wing S. and Fong K. (Wong) Y.; m. Assumpta Koo, July 3, 1979; 1 child, Jonathan C. BS in Biology, Bapt. Coll., Hong Kong, 1967; PhD in Pharmacology, U. Miss., 1974. Diplomate Am. Bd. Toxicology. Postdoctoral fellow, then asst. prof. Purdue U., West Lafayette, Ind., 1974-77; toxicology supr. Wyeth Labs., Great Valley, Pa., 1977-79; sr. toxicologist CIBA-GEIGY Corp., Summit, N.J., 1979-82, mgr., 1982-86, asst. dir., 1986-88, dir., 1988-92, exec. dir., 1993-96; exec. dir. of toxicology and pathology Novartis Pharm. U.S., 1997-98; dir. toxicology Roberts Pharm. Corp., Eatontown, N.J., 1998-99, Forest Labs., NYC, 1999-2000, Vertex Pharm. Inc., Cambridge, Mass., 2000—. Adj. prof. U. Miss., Oxford, 1989-92, 95—. Contbr. articles to sci. publs. Recipient NSF award, 1970. Mem. Am. Chem. Soc., Am. Coll. Toxicology, Soc. Toxicology, Teratology Soc., Sigma Xi. Republican. Baptist. Home: 67 Grant Ave Clifton NJ 07011-3522 Office Phone: 617-444-6706. E-mail: edward_yau@vrtx.com, yauedwardt@aol.com.

YAU, SHING-TUNG, mathematics professor; b. Swatow, China, Apr. 4, 1949; arrived in U.S., 1969; m. Yu-Yun Kuo; children: Isaac, Michael. PhD, U. Calif., Berkeley, 1971; PhD (hon.), Chinese U. Hong Kong, 1980, Harvard U., 1987, Chao Tung U., 1997, Nat. Tsing Hua U., 2000, Macau U., 2002. Mem. Inst. Advanced Study, Princeton, NJ, 1971-72; asst. prof. math. SUNY, Stony Brook, 1972-73; prof. math. Stanford U., Ark., 1974-79; hon. prof. Chinese Acad. Scis, 1983; prof. math. Inst. Advanced Study, Princeton, 1979-84, U.Calif.-San Diego, La Jolla, 1984-87; hon. prof. Hangzhou U., 1987—, Tsinghau U., 1987—; prof. math. Harvard U., Cambridge, Mass., 1987—, William Casper Graustein Prof., 2000—; Fairchild Disting. Scholar Caltech, 1990; disting. vis. prof. SUNY, Stony Brook, 1990; hon. prof. Nankai U., 1993—; Higgins Prof., 1997—2000; hon. prof. Beijing U., 1998—, U. Sci. & Tech., China, 1999—, Zhejian U., 2002—; disting. prof.-at-large Chinese U. of Hong Kong, 2003. Vis. prof., chair math. dept. U. Tex., Austin, 1986; spl. chair Nat. Tsing Hua U., Hsinchu, Taiwan, 1991—92; Wilson T.S. Wang Disting. vis. prof. Chinese U., Hong Kong, 1991—92; adj. prof. math. Chinese U. of Hong Kong, 1994—2003, dir. Inst. Math. Scis., 1994—. Contbr. articles to profl. publs. Named Honorable prof., Fudan U. China, Academia Sinica China, Sci. Digest, Am. 100 brightest scientists under 40, 1984; recipient Calif. Scientist of Yr., 1979, Sr. Scientist award, Humboldt Found. fellow, 1985, Crafoord prize, 1994, Veblen prize, 1981, Fields medal, 1982, Certy prize, 1980, Nat. Medal Sci. (USA), 1997, China International Sci. and Tech. Cooperation award, 2003; grantee Sloan Fellow, 1975—76, Guggenheim Fellowship, 1982, MacArthur Fellow, 1985. Fellow: Russian Acad. Scis. (fgn. mem.); mem.: AAAS, Nat. Acad. Scis. (bd. mem. math. scis.), Scientific Adv. Coun., Chinese Acad. Sci. (hon. mem. academic com. 1980—, fgn. mem.), Acad. Sinica (Taiwan), Soc. Indsl. Applied Math., Am. Phys. Soc., Am. Math. Soc., Acad. Arts and Scis. Boston, N.Y. Acad. Scis. Office: Harvard U Dept Math 3d Fl Sci Ctr 1 Oxford St Cambridge MA 02138-2901 also: Inst Math Scis Chinese U Hong Kong Unit 601, 6/F Academic Bldg #1 Shatin Hong Kong E-mail: yau@math.harvard.edu, yau@ims.cuhk.edu.hk. *

YAU, SIU-TUNG, physics professor; BS, U. So. Calif., 1983; PhD, U. Ill. Urbana-Champaign, 1990. Assoc. prof. physics Hunter Coll. CUNY, NYC, 2001—06; assoc. prof. elec. engring. Cleve. State U., 2006—. Prodr.: (classical music CD) Haydn Mozart Beethoven. Mem.: Am. Chem. Soc. Achievements include discovery of the first sequence of molecular-scale images of the very earliest stages of crystal growth; invention of the first prototype field-effect transistor using protein as the active material. Business E-Mail: s.yau@csuohio.edu.

YAU, STEPHEN SIK-SANG, computer and information scientist, educator; b. Wusei, Kiangsu, China, Aug. 6, 1935; arrived in US, 1958, naturalized, 1968; BSEE, Nat. Taiwan U., Taipei, 1958; MSEE, U. Ill., Urbana, 1959, PhD, 1961. Asst. prof. elec. engring. Northwestern U., Evanston, Ill., 1961-64, assoc. prof., 1964-68, prof., 1968-88, prof. computer scis., 1970-88, Walter P. Murphy prof. Elec. Engring. and Computer Sci., 1986-88, also chmn. dept. computer scis., 1972-77, chmn. dept. elec. engring. and computer sci., 1977-88; prof. computer and info. sci., chmn. dept. U. Fla., Gainesville, 1988-94; prof. computer sci. and engring. Ariz. State U., Tempe, 1994—, chmn. dept. computer sci. and engring., 1994—2001, dir. Info. Assurance Ctr., 2006—. Conf. chmn. IEEE Computer Conf., Chgo., 1967; gen. chmn. Nat. Computer Conf., Chgo., 1974, First Internat. Computer Software and Applications Conf., Chgo., 1977; Trustee Nat. Electronics Conf., Inc., 1965-68; chmn. organizing com. 11th World Computer Congress, Internat. Fedn. Info. Processing, San Francisco, 1989; gen. co-chmn. Internat. Symposium on Autonomous Decentralized Systems, Japan, 1993, gen. chmn., Phoenix, 1995; conf. co-chair 24th Ann. Internat. Computer Software and Applications Conf., Taipei, 2000. Editor-in-chief Computer mag., 1981-84; assoc. editor Jour. Info. Sci., 1983-99; editor IEEE Trans. on Software Engring., 1988-91; contbr. numerous articles on software engring., distributed and parallel processing systems, computer sci., elec. engring. and related fields to profl. publs.; patentee in field. Recipient Louis E. Levy medal Franklin Inst., 1963, Golden Plate award Am. Acad. Achievement, 1964, The Silver Core award Internat. Fedn. Info. Processing, 1989, Spl. award, 1989, Overseas Outstanding Contributions award, Chinese Computer Fedn., 2006. Fellow IEEE (mem. governing bd. Computer Soc. 1967-76, pres. 1974-75, dir. Inst. 1976-77, chmn. awards com., 1996-97; Richard E. Merwin award Computer Soc. 1981, Centennial medal 1984, Extraordinary Achievement award 1985, Outstanding Contbn. award Computer Sci. Soc. 1985, The Third Millennium medal 2000, Tsutomu Kanai award 2002), AAAS, Franklin Inst.; mem. Assn. for Computing Machinery, Am. Fedn. Info.-Processing Soc. (mem. exec. com. 1974-76, 79-82, dir. 1972-82, chmn. awards com. 1979-82, v.p. 1982-84, pres. 1984-86; chmn. Nat. Computer Conf. Bd. 1982-83, spl. award 1990), Am. Soc. Engring. Edn., Sigma Xi, Tau Beta Pi, Eta Kappa Nu, Pi Mu Epsilon. Office: Ariz State U PO Box 878809 Tempe AZ 85287-8809 Business E-Mail: yau@asu.edu.

YAUCH, ADAM NATHANIEL (MCA), recording artist; b. Bklyn., Aug. 5, 1964; m. Dechen Wangdu, May 1998; 1 child, Tenzin Lowell. Founder, mem. The Beastie Boys, 1981—. Owner Grand Royal, Grand Royal mag., 1984—. Albums include Licensed to Ill, 1986, Paul's Boutique, 1989, Check Your Head, 1992, 94, Ill Communication, 1994, Some Old Bullshit, 1994, In Sound from Way Out, 1996, Def & Dumb, 1996, Hello Nasty, 1998, To the 5 Boroughs, 2004, The Mix Up, 2007, (extended play singles) Pollywog Stew, 1982, Cooky Puss, 1983, Rock Hard, 1984, Tour Shot, 1994, Sure Shot, 1994, Get It Together, 1994, Root Down, 1995, (singles) Jimmy James, 1992, Gratitude, 1992, Sabotage, 1994, Hey Ladies, 1997, (video) Skills to Pay the Bills, 1992; contbg. rap artists Heart to Soul, 1988, Rap Rap Rap, 1996, Rap: Most Valuable Players, 1996; vocalist Rap's Biggest Hits, 1990; prodr. Rap Declares War, 1992, Cb4, 1993, Rebirth of Cool (vol. 3), 1995, Music for Our Mother Ocean; dir. Beastie Boys music videos; prodr. (albums) Build a Nation, for Bad Brains, 2007. Office: care Capitol Records 1750 N Vine St Hollywood CA 90028-5209 *

YAUCK, F. ALAN, biology educator; s. Frank and Esper Yauck; m. Roberta N. Yauck; 1 child, Al; 1 child, Mary. BS in Edn., Valdosta State Coll., Ga., 1972; MS in Edn., Ga. Coll., Milledgeville, 1972. Cert. State Dept. Edn. Tchr., coach Dublin City Bd. Edn., Ga., 1972—2004. Biology instr. Mid. Ga. Coll., Dublin Ctr., 1990, adj. instr., 1990—2004, part-time instr., 2004—. Co-chmn. toys Helping Hand, Dublin. With USAR, 1973—79. Named Man of Yr., St. Patrick's Com., 2003. Mem.: Nat. Assn. Tchrs. (life), Nat. Biology Tchrs. (life), Adopt A Stream Trainer. D-Liberal. Baptist. Office: Mid Ga Coll Dublin Ctr 1900 Bellevue Rd Dublin GA 31021 Office Phone: 478-275-6643. Business E-Mail: ayauck@mgc.edu.

YAVARI, ARASH, engineering educator; b. Tehran, Iran, Feb. 11, 1974; s. Mansour Yavari and Batoul Mahmoudi. BS in Civil Engring., Sharif U. Tech., Iran, 1997; MS in Mech. Engring., George Wash. U., Washington, DC, 2000; PhD in Mech. Engring., Calif. Inst. Tech., Pasadena, 2005. Grad. asst. George Wash. U., 1998—2000, Calif. Inst. Tech., 2000—05; asst. prof. Ga. Inst. Tech., Atlanta, 2005—. Contbr. scientific papers more than 25 articles to profl. jours. Mem.: Am. Acad. Mechanics. Achievements include research in theoretical solid mechanics. Office: Georgia Inst Tech 790 Atlantic Dr Atlanta GA 30332 Office Phone: 404-894-2436.

YAVARKOVSKY, JEROME HAROLD, library director; b. NYC, May 12, 1940; B Mech. Engring., Rensselaer Poly. Inst., 1960; MS in Mgmt., MIT, 1962; M Libr. Sci., Columbia U., 1971. Lic. pub. libr. Adminstrv. specialist Bell Labs., Murray Hill, NJ, 1963-64; systems analyst J.C. Penney Co., NYC, 1965-67; tech. cons. Auerbach Assocs., NYC, 1967-68; head programming Columbia U., NYC, 1969-71, chief systems, 1971-72, asst. univ. libr., 1972-83; dean librs. Adelphi U., Garden City, NY, 1983-85; dir. NY State Libr., Albany, 1985-95; univ. libr. Boston Coll., Chestnut Hill, 1995—. Office: Thomas P O'Neill Libr Boston Coll Chestnut Hill MA 02467

YAVORNIK, BARBARA ANN, pre-school educator; b. Olympia, Wash., July 12, 1957; d. Eugene Earl and Betty Ann Brown; m. Edward J. Yavornik, II, Jan. 11, 1980. BA, Cen. Wash. U., Ellensburg, 1981; MEd, West Tex. A&M U., 1990. Cert. adminstrn. Dir., tchr. Fifth Ave. Pres-Sch., Ellensburg, 1981—82; tchr. Coronado Acad., Albuquerque, 1985—86, N.W. Primary, Hereford, Tex., 1987—. Presenter I-Teach K West Tex. A&M U. Sci. Conf., 2000, 01, 05; presenter HISD Sci. Inservice, 2005. Greeter coord. St. Anthony's Parish Coun., 2004—, eucharistic minister, 2004—; bd. dirs. Campfire, Hereford, 1988—90. Named Tchr. of Yr., N.W. Primary, 2002; recipient Excel in Sci. Tchg. award, Tex. Sci. Assn., 2001, Golden Apple award, Hereford Ind. Sch. Dist., 2004. Mem.: Hereford C. of C. (v.p. women's divsn. 1987—89), Delta Kappa Gamma (pres. 2002—04, v.p., Achievement award 1999—2004). Republican. Roman Catholic. Avocations: gardening, reading, collecting bears, travel. Home: 201 N Texas Ave Hereford TX 79045 Office: NW Primary Sch 400 Moreman Ave Hereford TX 79045 Office Phone: 806-363-7660. E-mail: barbarayavornik@herefordisd.net.

YAVORSKY, WILLIAM D., semiconductor company executive; BS in Bus. Adminstrn., Bowling Green State U.; postgrad., Stanford U., U. Va. With Xerox Corp., Genicom, Tektronix; dir. internat. sales InFocus Corp., 1993—96, v.p. worldwide sales, 1996—2000, sr. v.p., gen. mgr., 2000—03; v.p. worldwide sales Pixelworks, Inc., Tualatin, Oreg., 2004—. Office: Pixelworks Inc 8100 SW Nyberg Rd Tualatin OR 97062 Personal E-mail: billy@pixelworks.com.

YAVUZ, A. KADIR, aerospace engineer, researcher; PhD, Istanbul Tech. U., Turkey, 1999. Post-doctoral fellow dept. tech. Cornell U., Ithaca, NY, 2001—04, rsch. assoc. dept. tech., 2004—. Contbr. articles to profl. jours. Recipient Sci. Rsch. Encouragement award, Tubitak, 1991. Mem.: ASME (assoc.), AIAA (assoc.). Office: Cornell Univ TH111 Thurston Hall Ithaca NY 14850 Office Phone: 607-255-4077. Business E-Mail: ay47@cornell.edu.

YAWNEY, TRENT, former professional hockey coach, retired professional hockey player; b. Hudson Bay, Sask., Can., Sept. 29, 1965; m. Charlane Yawney; children: Ashley, Conor. Defenceman Can. Nat. Team, 1985—88, Chgo. Blackhawks, 1987—91, 1997—99, Calgary Flames, 1991—96, St. Louis Blues, 1996—97; asst. coach Chgo. Blackhawks, 1999—2000, head coach, 2005—06, Norfolk Admirals, 2000—05. Mem. Team Can., Olympic Games, Calgary, 1988. Named Minor Pro Coach of Yr., The Hockey News, 2003—04.

YAWORSKI, JAMES JOHN, III, elementary school educator; b. Conn., July 20, 1960; s. James John Yaworski, Jr. and Joyce Graham; m. Jeanette Anne Kotowski, July 28, 1990; children: Jordan Taylor, Blake Frances, Hunter James, Bo Michael. BS in Edn., U. Conn., Storrs, 1982; MEd, Ea. Conn. State U., Willimantic, 1989. Middle sch. math and history tchr. Canterbury Bd. Edn., 1983—. Girls soccer coach Baldwin Middle Sch., Canterbury, 1983—94, girls softball coach, 1984—94, mem. social studies curriculum com., 2002—06. Umpire Little League Baseball Canterbury Athletic Assn., 1978—94, soccer referee, 1990—94; instr. Ams. Game Baseball Camp, Norwich, Conn., 2006. Recipient 20th Yr. Tchg. award, Canterbury Bd. Edn., 2003. Mem.: Canterbury Edn. Assn. Office: Canterbury Bd Edn 45 Westminster Rd Canterbury CT 06331 Office Phone: 860-546-9421. E-mail: nettebo@juno.com.

YAWORSKY, BOHDAN, criminal justice educator; s. Dmytro and Cornelia Yaworsky; m. Tedra L. Buckmaster, Sept. 19, 2000; children: Amy Gravett, Samantha Wall. BA, Rutgers U., New Brunswick, 1969; MA, Rutgers U., Newark, 1981, PhD, 1994. Drug counselor U.S. Army, Long Binh, Vietnam, 1970—71; tng. coord. Middlesex County Probation Dept., New Brunswick, 1973—78; dir. criminal justice planning Union County, Elizabeth, NJ, 1978—80, acting dir dept. pub. safety, 1980, asst. county adminstr., 1980—81; prof., chair dept. criminal justice New Jersey City U., Jersey City, 1981—. Disting. faculty mem. Nat. Coun. Juvenile & Family Ct. Judges, Reno; sr. cons. Office Internat. Criminal Justice, Chgo., Rutgers Ctr. Mgmt. Devel., Piscataway, NJ; cons., Hamburg, NJ, 1978—, Nat. Inst. Corrections, Longmont, Colo.; charter mem. N.J. Supreme Ct. Mcpl. Ct. Certification Bd., Trenton; charter mem. exec. com. N.J. Supreme Ct. State Adv. Bd. for Probation, Trenton; charter mem. N.J. Juvenile Intensive Supervision Program Adv. Bd., Trenton. Author: 100 criminal justice studies. Mem.: Am. Correctional Assn., Am. Probation and Parole Assn. (cons.), Acad. Criminal Justice Scis. Office: New Jersey City U Dept Criminal Justice Jersey City NJ 07305

YAZDANPANAH, MEHDI MOHAMMAD, research scientist; arrived in U.S., 2001; s. Mohammad Hossein Yazdanpanah and Baygom Rezaie; m. Romaneh Jalilian. Degree in Applied Physics, Sharif U. Tech., Teheran, 1998; MS in Applied Physics, U. Beheshti, Tehran, 2001; PhD with honors, U. Louisville, 2006. Rsch. asst. U. Louisville, 2001—. Contbr. articles to profl. jours. Recipient Outstanding grad. student for U. of Louisville, 2005, Promotional Sect. Second Pl. award, Internat. Material Nanotechnology Workshop, 2004. Mem.: AAAS, Am. Phys. Soc. (assoc.). Achievements include discovery of room temperature self-assembly of metal alloy nanostructures through Ga reaction with metal; invention of selective growth of Ag2Ga nanoneedles on AFM tips. Home: 3143 Doreen way Louisville KY 40220 Office: University of Louisville Room 253 BRB University of Louisville Louisville KY Home Phone: 502-290-7324; Office Phone: 502-852-1551. Personal E-mail: mmyazd01@gwise.louisville.edu. E-mail: yazdaanpanah@yahoo.com.

YAZDI, AHMAD, computer scientist, researcher; b. Tehran, Iran, Apr. 8, 1978; s. Kazem Yazdi and Minoo Mapar. BS, Sharif U. of Tech., Tehran, 2000; MS, U. So. Calif., 2003; postgrad., U. Calif., Irvine, 2003—. Rsch. asst. U. Calif., Irvine, 2003—. Contbr. articles to profl. jours., confs. Fellow Ctr. for Pervasive Comm. and Computing, 2003—05. Mem.: IEEE, Eta Kappa Nu. Achievements include patents for a novel silicon-based differential non-uniform downsized distributed amplifier; ultra-wideband CMOS distributed mixer. Office: U Calif Irvine Dept Elec Engring and Computer Sci ET 521 Irvine CA 92697-2625 Home Phone: 949-735-7356. Personal E-mail: yazdi75a@yahoo.com. E-mail: yazdia@uci.edu.

YAZDI, MAHVASH, utilities executive; BS in Indsl. Mgmt., Poly. U., Pomona, Calif.; MBA, U. So. Calif., LA; grad. Mgmt. of Info. Tech. program, Harvard Bus. Sch. With IBM World Trade Corp.; v.p., chief info. officer Hughes Aircraft, 1994; with Edison Internat., Rosemead, Calif., 1997—, sr. v.p. bus. integration, chief info. officer So. Calif. Edison subs., sr. v.p. bus. integration, chief info. officer. Bd. dirs. Columbus Newport Corp.; adv. dir. Lotus Corp., IBM Corp.; mem. So. Calif. Forum of the Trusteeship of the Internat. Women's Forum, 2003. Mem. adv. bd. U. So. Calif. Marshall Sch. Bus.; bd. dirs. Claremont U. Consortium. Office: Edison Internat 2244 Walnut Grove Ave Rosemead CA 91770 Office Phone: 626-302-1212. *

YAZZIE, AARON FRANKLIN, events laborer; b. Ft. Defiance, Az., Apr. 30, 1962; s. Robert Franklin Yazzie Sr. and Sadie Mildred (Williams) Yazzie; life ptnr. Linda James, Jan. 20, 1965 (dec.). Mechanic Ft. Sill, Lawton, Okla., 1985—87; parts washer Embassy Suites, Phoenix, 1996—98; staff rug racker Baker Bros., Super Floors, Phoenix, 1997—99; events set up crew Ariz. State U., West Phoenix, 2002—04. V.p. Native Am. Student Orgn., Phoenix, 2002—03, pres., 2006—. Pvt. US Army, Korea. Recipient Mil. Svc. award, Dept. of Def., 1987. Mem.: Nat. Scholars Honor Soc. Democrat. Avocations: painting, bicycling, naturalist, pow wows. Home: Rancho Santa fe Apts #2134 10201N 44th D Glendale AZ 85302 Personal E-mail: aaronfyazzie62@hotmail.com. Business E-Mail: aaronfyazzie@asu.edu.

YE, JUN, physicist, researcher; b. Shanghai, Nov. 7, 1967; s. Shanxiang Ye and Changhong Fan; m. Ying Zhang, June 22, 1993; 1 child, Shirley Eileen. BS in Applied Physics, U. N.Mex., 1991, MS in Physics, 1991; PhD in Physics, U. Colo., 1997. Postdoctoral rschr. Calif. Inst. Tech., 1997—99; physicist Nat. Inst. Stds. and Tech., 1999—2004, fellow, 2004—; asst. prof. adjoint dept. physics U. Colo., 1999—2003, assoc. prof. adjoint dept. physics, 2004—; assoc. fellow JILA, Nat. Inst. Stds. and Tech., U. Colo., Boulder, 1999—2001, fellow, 2001—. Vis. prof. Inst. Exptl. Physics U. Innsbruck, Austria, 2004; guest prof. East China Normal U., Shanghai, 2004—, Shanghai Jiao Tong U., 2006—. Contbr. articles to sci. jours. Recipient Selection to Frontiers of Engring. Symposium, NAE, 2000, Tech. Rev. Mag.'s TR100 Young Innovator, Tech. Rev. Mag., 2002, Presdl. Early Career award for Scientists and Engrs., US Pres., 2003, Arthur S. Flemming award, US Fed. Govt., 2005, I.I. Ravi prize in Atomic, Molecular and Optical Physics, 2007; grantee Univ. fellowship, U. Colo. Boulder, 1993 - 1994, R.A. Millikan Prize fellowship, Calif. Inst. Tech., 1997 - 1999. Fellow: Optical Soc. Am. (Adolph Lomb medal 1999, William F. Meggers award 2006), Am. Phys. Soc. Achievements include invention of Cavity based ultrasensitive absorption spectroscopy; Phase locking independent ultrafast lasers; research in Highly stabilized lasers for precision measurements; Precision, wide bandwidth optical frequency comb; Cooling and trapping of alkaline earth atoms; Manipulation of cold molecules; patents for Comb generating optical cavity that includes an optical amplifier and an optical modulator; A novel cavity ringdown heterodyne spectroscopy: 1 x 10-10 sensitivity with microwatt light power; patents pending for Sub 10 - femtosecond active synchronization of two passively mode-locked Ti:sapphire oscillators. Office: JILA Nat Inst Standards & Tech U Colo Campus Box 440 Boulder CO 80309-0440 E-mail: ye@jila.colorado.edu. *

YE, XIAOFEI, education educator; s. Yulan Yang and Tiyu Ye; m. Qiuyu Julie Chen, 1996; 1 child, Meryl A. B in Engring., Northwestern Agrl. U., China, 1990; MS, South Dakota State U., 1998; PhD, U. Minn., 2004. Asst. prof. U. Tenn., Knoxville, 2004—. Author: (book chpt.) The Nutrition Handbook for Food Processors, Improving Thermal Processing of Foods, Thermal Technologies in Food Processing, (jour. paper) Lebensmittel-Wissenschaft und Technologie, Jour. of Food Engring. Grant, USDA, 2004. Mem.: Inst. Food Technologists, Am. Soc. Agrl. and Biol. Engrs., Alpha Epsilon (life). Office: The Univ of Tenn 2506 E J Chapman Dr Knoxville TN 37996 Business E-Mail: xye2@utk.edu.

YEADON, TAMMY PAMELA, information specialist; b. Bayonne, NJ, Feb. 3, 1967; d. Tom and Betty Yeadon. BS in Polymer and Plastics Engring., U. Detroit, 1989; MLS, Rutgers U., 1994. Engr. Whirlpool Corp., Benton Harbor, Mich., 1988, Ford Motor Co., Detroit, 1989-90, MedTech Group, South Plainfield, NJ, 1991; quality assurance analyst Block Drug, Jersey City, 1992-93; info. mgr. John Brown, Bridgewater, NJ, 1994-97; tech. knowledge specialist A.T. Kearney, NYC, 1998-99; sys. mgr. Berkshire Capital Corp., 2000—. Computer cons. Tyrell the Collection, Linden, N.J., 1991—; libr. cons. The Penn of N.Y., 1998-99. Tutor Literacy Vols. of Am., Elizabeth, N.J., 1993; vol. Gay Men's Health Crisis, N.Y.C., 1993. Mem. ALA, Am. Soc. of Info. Scis., Spl. Libr. Assn.

YEAGER, CAROLINE HALE, writer, retired radiologist, consultant; b. Little Rock, Sept. 5, 1946; d. George Glenn and Crenor Burnelle (Hale) Y.; m. William Berg Singer, July 8, 1978; children: Adina Atkinson Singer, Sarah Rose Singer. BA, Ind. U., Bloomington, 1968; MD, Ind. U., Indpls., 1971. Diplomate Am. Bd. Radiology; med. lic. State of Calif. Intern Good Samaritan Hosp., Los Angeles, 1971-72; resident in radiology King Drew Med. Ctr. UCLA, Los Angeles, 1972-76; dir. radiology Hubert Humphrey Health Ctr., Los Angeles, 1976-77; asst. prof. radiology UCLA, Los Angeles, 1977-84, King Drew Med. Ctr. UCLA, Los Angeles, 1977-85, dir. ultrasound, 1977-84; ptnr. pvt. practice Beverly Breast Ctr., Beverly Hills, Calif., 1984-87; cons. Clarity Communications, Pasadena, Calif., 1981—; pvt. practice radiology Claude Humphrey Health Ctr., 1991-93; dir. sonograms and mammograms Rancho Los Amigos Med. Ctr., 1993-94, ret., 1994. Trustee Assn. Teaching Physicians, L.A., 1976-81; cons. King Drew Med. Ctr., 1984, Gibraltar Savs., 1987, Cal Fed. Inc., 1986, Medical Faculty At Home Professions, 1989—, Mobil Diagnostics, 1991-92, Xerox

Corp., 1990-91, Frozen Leopard, Inc., 1990-91; writer gen. med. answers pub. on internet, 1994-. Author: (with others) Infectious Disease, 1978, Anatomy and Physiology for Medical Transcriptionists, 1992; contbr. articles to profl. jours. Trustee U. Synagogue, Los Angeles, 1975-79; mem. Friends of Pasadena Playhouse, 1987-90. Grantee for innovative tng. Nat. Fund for Med. Edn., 1980-81. Mem. Am. Inst. Ultrasound in Medicine, L.A. Radiology Soc. (ultrasound sect.), Nat. Soc. Performance and Instrn. (chmn. conf. Database 1991, publs. L.A. chpt. 1990, info. systems L.A. chpt. 1991, dir. adminstrn. L.A. chpt. 1992, Outstanding Achievement in Performance Improvement award L.A. chpt. 1990, bd. dirs. 1990-93, Pres. award for Outstanding Chpt. 1992, v.p. programs 1993), Stanford Profl. Women L.A. Jewish. Avocations: writing, humor, design. Home and Office: 3520 Yorkshire Rd Pasadena CA 91107-5440 Personal E-mail: doccarrie@earthlink.net.

YEAGER, DAVID P., transportation executive; b. 1953; BA, U. Dayton, 1975; MBA, Univ. Chgo., 1987. With affiliated cos. Hub Group, Inc., 1975—, vice chmn. bd. Lombard, Ill., 1992—, CEO, 1995—. Bd. dir. SPR Inc., Thrall Car Mfg. Co. Bd. dir. Children's Memorial Hospital-Chgo., Fenwick High School; mem. adv. council Univ. Dayton. Office: Hub Group 3050 Highland Pkwy Downers Grove IL 60515 *

YEAGER, DEBRA LYN, science educator; b. St. Paul, Mar. 20, 1957; d. Lyle Milton and Grace Jeanette (Mitchell) Yeager, adopted d. Wilma Mitchell; life ptnr. Christopher Charles Pfannes. AS in Computer Sci., Mesa C.C., Ariz., 1982; student, Scottsdale C.C., Ariz., 1979—80. Ordained minister Order of Melchizedek, 1991. Investigator - profiler Elk River Sheriff's Dept., Minn., 1992—94; sensor sci. tchr. Open U. of Minn., Mpls., 1994—99; sensory sci. tchr. Yeager Consulting / Into the Mystic, Minnetonka, Minn., 1998—2005, Wis. Indianhead Tech. Coll., New Richmond, 2003—, West Ctrl. Cancer Symposium, Willmar, Minn., 2003, U. Alaska-Sitka, 2003—, U. Manitoba, 2004—, U. Coll. Dublin, Ireland, 2004—, Queens U.-Belfast, Ireland, 2004—; on the air talent, lectr. Kare 11 - NBC TV Mpls, 2002—03, WCCO 4 - CBS TV. Mpls., 2002, NW Mag. Cable Show, New Hope, Minn., 1996; sensory sci. specialist, prof. spirituality Park Hill, Okla., 2005—. Criminologist and profiler Crema Law Offices, Mpls., 1999—. Author: (novel) Encounters with the Sixth Dimension (Book in print), Intervention across time, Medium, Rare - the Bio of Debra Yeager, Karman from MU. Mem.: Delta Zeta (hon.). Achievements include research in Metaphysical Studies; development of Programs of Metaphysical Studies. Avocations: motorcycling, designing jewelry, horse training, running, travel. Home and Office: PO Box 310 Park Hill OK 74451 Personal E-mail: century30@aol.com.

YEAGER, DENNIS RANDALL, lawyer; b. Dallas, Jan. 10, 1941; s. William C. and Katherine (Payne) Y.; m. Jere Jones, Aug. 31, 1963; children: Stephanie Ann O'Donnell, Karen Elizabeth Kimball, Brenda Marie. BSS, Loyola U. of South, 1964; LLB, Columbia U., 1967. Bar: N.Y. 1967, D.C. 1979, Tex. 2006, U.S. Supreme Ct., 1971, U.S. Ct. Appeals (2d cir.) 1972. Assoc. Willkie Farr & Gallagher, NYC, 1967-69; dir., chief exec. officer Nat. Employment Law Project, NYC, 1969-75; from assoc. to ptnr. Tufo, Johnston & Allegaert, NYC, 1975-80; ptnr. Yeager & Barrett, NYC, 1980-93; pvt. practice NYC, 1993—2005, San Antonio, 2005—. Chmn. program on bus. errors and omissions ins. Practicing Law Inst., 1983, program on role of outside counsel in bus. investigation, 1985; panelist program on dirs. and officers liabilities, 1988. Mem. Am. Coun. on Germany, N.Y.C., 1995—. Mem.: Alpha Sigma Nu, Blue Key. Roman Catholic. Office Phone: 210-824-1217. Business E-Mail: dryeagerlaw@cs.com.

YEAGER, JOSEPH HEIZER, JR., lawyer; b. Indpls., Jan. 8, 1957; s. Joseph Heizer and Marilyn Virginia (Hillyard) Y.; m. Candance A. Grass, June 2, 1984; children: Samuel, Henry. AB cum laude, Harvard U., 1979; JD cum laude, Ind. U., 1983. Bar: Ind. 1983, U.S. Dist. Ct. (so. and no. dist.) Ind. 1983, U.S. Ct. Appeals (7th cir.) 1986, (5th cir.) 1999, U.S. Supreme Ct. 1996. Dir. ops. Penn and Schoen Assocs., NYC, 1979-80; assoc. Baker & Daniels, Indpls., 1983-89, ptnr., 1990—, mem. mgmt. com., 2001—04. Bd. dirs. Indpls. Legal Aid Soc., 1990-99, pres. 1992-94; chmn. Indpls. Com. for UNICEF, 1986-91; mem. Indpls. Com. for Fgn. Affairs, 1986-91, Ind. Comm. for Continuing Legal Edn., 2003—. Mem. Ind. Bar Assn., Indpls. Bar Assn. (litigation sect. exec. com. 1985-86, 1996-2000, chair 1999), Cen. Ind. Regional Citizens League (bd. dirs. 1997-99). Democrat. Avocation: commercial pilot. Office: Baker & Daniels 300 N Meridian St Ste 2700 Indianapolis IN 46204-1782 Home Phone: 317-873-3984; Office Phone: 317-237-0300. Business E-Mail: jhyeager@bakerd.com.

YEAGER, KURT ERIC, research and development company executive; b. Cleve., Sept. 11, 1939; s. Joseph Ellsworth and Karolyn Kristine (Pedersen) Y.; m. Rosalie Ann McMillan, Feb. 5, 1960; children: Geoffrey, Phillip; m. Regina Ursula Querfurt, May 12, 1970; 1 dau., Victoria. BA in Chemistry, Kenyon Coll., 1961; postgrad., Ohio State U., 1961-62; MS in Physics, U. Calif., Davis, 1964; MS Wharton Sch. Bus., U. Pa., 1995. Tchg. asst. Ohio State U., 1961-62; officer, program mgr. Air Force Tech. Applications Ctr., Alexandria, Va., 1962-68; assoc. dept. dir. Mitre Corp., McLean, Va., 1968-72; dir. energy rsch. and devel. planning EPA, Washington, 1972-74; dir. fossil power plants dept. Electric Power Rsch. Inst., Palo Alto, Calif., 1974-79, dir. coal combustion systems, 1979-83, v.p. coal combustion systems, 1983-88, v.p. generation and storage, 1988-96, pres., CEO, 1996—2004; founder, pres., CEO, Keyworks, Aptos, Calif., 2004—. Chmn. World Energy Coun. Climate Change Study; dir. Galvin Elec. Initiative; Oak Ridge fossil energy adv. bd. Nat. Acad. Engring.; mem. exec. bd. Nat. Coal Coun.; bd. dirs. nat. coalition advanced mfg. US Energy Assn.; bd. dirs. APX Corp., Microfield Corp. Contbr. articles to profl. jours. Pres. No. Va. Youth Football Assn., 1973-74. Capt. USAF, 1962-68. Decorated Air Force Commendation medals (2); recipient Outstanding Svc. award EPA, 1974; named Energy Policy Leader, Sci. Am., 2003. Fellow ASME (rsch. policy bd., trustee com. econ. devel.); mem. AAAS, Am. Chem. Soc., Palo Alto C. of C. Republican. Episcopalian. Office Phone: 831-786-9832. Business E-Mail: kyeager@epri.com.

YEAGER, MARK LEONARD, lawyer; b. Chgo., Apr. 7, 1950; BA, U. Mich., 1972; JD cum laude, Northwestern U., 1975. Bar: Ill. 1975, Fla. 1985, US Supreme Ct. Ptnr. McDermott, Will & Emery LLP, Chgo., 1981—; mem. Trial Dept. McDermott, Will & Emery, Chgo. Dir. Taylor Capital Group, Inc., Rosemont, Ill., 1997—. Mem. alumni adv. bd. U. Mich. Dept. Econs. Mem.: ABA. Office: McDermott Will & Emery LLP 227 W Monroe St Ste 3100 Chicago IL 60606-5096 also: Taylor Capital Group 9550 W Higgins Rd Rosemont IL 60018 Office Phone: 312-984-7696. Office Fax: 312-984-7700. E-mail: myeager@mwe.com.

YEAGER, PETER CLEARY, sociologist, educator; b. Terre Haute, Ind., Nov. 29, 1949; s. Ralph Oscar and Dorothy (Cleary) Y.; m. Kathy Ellen Kram, Aug. 9, 1981; 1 child, Jason Kram Yeager. BA in Journalism, U. Minn., 1971; MS in Sociology, U. Wis., 1976, PhD in Sociology, 1981. Writer, photographer Sun Newspapers, Mpls., 1971-72; from lectr. to asst. prof. sociology Yale U., New Haven, 1979-82; from asst. to assoc. prof. sociology Boston U., 1982—. Rsch. fellow ethics and the professions program Harvard U., Cambridge, Mass., 1989-90. Co-author: Illegal Corporate Behavior, 1979, Corporate Crime, 1980 (named one of Choice's outstanding acad. books 1981), republished 2006; author: The Limits of Law, 1991. Bd. assessors 1st Parish in Framingham, Mass., 1992-94. Managerial Ethics Rsch. grantee Amerindam Found., 1989-92, Human Resources Policy Inst. Boston U., 1986-87, 93-94. Mem. Am. Sociol. Assn., Am. Soc. Criminology, Law and Soc. Assn., Soc. for Study of Social Problems, US Office of Rsch. Integrity (rsch. integrity adv. com., 1999-2004), Phi Beta Kappa, Kappa Tau Alpha. Avocations: hiking, reading, creative writing, tennis, travel. Office: Dept Sociology Boston U 96-100 Cummington St Boston MA 02215 Home Phone: 508-875-6204. Business E-Mail: pcyeager@bu.edu.

YEAGER, PHILLIP CHARLES, transportation company executive; b. Bellevue, Ky., Nov. 15, 1927; s. Ferd A. and Helen (Koehler) Y.; m. Joyce E. Ruebusch, June 2, 1951; children: David P., Debra A. Yeager Jensen, Mark A. BA, U. Cin., 1951. Warehouse mgr. Pure Carbonic Co., Cin., 1950-52; trace clk., rate clk., asst. office mgr. Pa. R.R., Chgo., 1952-56, salesman Kansas City, Mo., 1956-59, asst. dir. Trailvan Phila., 1959-65, div. sales mgr. Milw., 1965-68; dir. Trailvan Penn-Ctrl. R.R., NYC, 1968-71; pres. Hub City Terminals, Chgo., 1971-85; chmn. The Hub Group, Chgo., 1985—; also bd. dirs. Bd. dirs. 30 Hubcity terminals. Cpl. U.S. Army, 1946-47. Recipient Achievement award Intermodal Transp. Assn., 1991, Harry E. Salzberg medallion for outstanding achievement in transp.; named Chgo. Transp. Man of Yr., Chgo. Transp. Assn., 1990. Mem. N.Y. Traffic Club, Chgo. Traffic Club. Republican. Lutheran. Avocations: golf, biking, swimming.

YEAMANS, GEORGE THOMAS, librarian, educator; b. Nov. 7, 1929; s. James Norman and Dolphine Sophia (Manhart) Yeamans; m. Mary Ann Seng, Feb. 1, 1958; children: Debra, Susan, Julia. AB, U. Va., 1950; MLS, U. Ky., 1955; EdD, Ind. U., 1965. Asst. audio-visual dir. Ind. State U., Terre Haute, 1957—58; asst. film libr. Ball State U., Muncie, Ind., 1958—61, film libr., 1961—69, assoc. prof. libr. sci., 1969—72, prof., 1972—95, prof. emeritus, 1995—. Cons. Pendleton (Ind.) Sch. Corp., 1962, 67, Captioned Films for the Deaf Workshop, Muncie, 1963—65, Decatur (Ind.) Sch. Sys., 1978; adjudicator Ind. Media Fair, 1979—93, David Letterman Scholarship Program, 1993. Author: Projectionists' Programmed Primer, 1969, rev. edit., 1982, Mounting and Preserving Pictorial Materials, 1976, Tape Recording, 1978, Transparency Making, 1977, Photographic Principles, 1981, Computer Literacy-A Programmed Primer, 1985, Designing Dynamic Media Presentations, 1996, Robert F. Kennedy Archival Project, 1968—2004, Building Effective Creative Project Teams, 2000, Building Effective Creative Project Teams, rev. ed., 2007; songwriter: Branson Bound, 1996; contbr. articles to profl. jours. Campaign worker Wilson for Mayor, Muncie, 1979. With USMC, 1950—52. Recipient Citations of Achievement, Internat. Biog. Assn., Cambridge, Eng., 1973, Am. Biog. Assn., 1976, Mayor James P. Carey award for achievement for disting. contbns. to Ball State U. and City of Muncie, 1988; Video Info. Sys. grant, Ball State U., 1993. Mem.: ALA, NEA (del. assembly dept. audiovisual instrn. 1967), Audio-Visual Instrn. Dirs. Ind. (exec. bd. 1962—68, pres. 1966—67), Thomas Jefferson Soc. Alumni U. Va., Ind. Pub. Libr. Assn., Ind. Acad. Libr. Assn., Ind. Corp. and Network Libr. Assn., Ind. Libr. Fedn., Assn. Ednl. Comm. and Tech., Autisim Soc. Am., Assn. Ind. Media Educators (chmn. auditing com. 1979—81), Ind. Assn. Ednl. Comms. and Tech. (dist. dir. 1972—76), Am. Assn. Sch. Librs., Phi Delta Kappa. Republican. Unitarian-Universalist. Avocations: photography, stamp collecting/philately, coin collecting/numismatics, genealogy. Home: 4507 W Burton Dr Muncie IN 47304-3575

YEARGAN, MICHAEL, scenic designer; MFA, Yale U., 1973. Assoc. prof. design Yale Sch. Drama, New Haven; resident designer Yale Repertory Theatre. Scenic designer Becket, London's West End, Cyrano de Bergerac, Napoleon, Present Laughter, Stratford Festival, Can., Noises Off!, (Operas) Otello, Met. Opera, Ariadne auf Naxos, Cosi Fan Tutti, Don Giovanni, Susanna, The Great Gatsby, Norma, NYC Opera, Madama Butterfly, Tosca, La Finta, Giardiniera, Central Park, Previn's A Streetcar Named Desire, San Francisco Opera, Luisa Miller, Dead Man Walking, Simon Boccanegra, Cold Sassy Tree, Houston Grand Opera, Royal Opera House, London, Australian Opera, La Scala, Staatsoper, Vienna, The Nutcracker, San Francisco Ballet, The Rainmaker, 2006, (Off-Broadway) Dinah Was, Juvenalia, (Broadway Shows) Terrence McNally's The Ritz, Bad Habits, Hay Fever, Ah, Wilderness!, Athol Fugard's A Lesson From Aloes, The Light in the Piazza, Lincoln Ctr. Theater, 2005— (Tony Award for best scenic design of a musical, 2005, Drama Desk award outstanding set design of a musical, 2005), Awake and Sing!, 2006 (Drama Desk award outstanding set design of a play, 2006). Office: Yale Sch Drama PO Box 208325 New Haven CT 06520 also: Lincoln Ctr Theater 150 W 65th St New York NY 10023

YEARLEY, BARBARA ELLEN, music educator; b. Lorain, Ohio, May 5, 1950; d. Quentin Fred and June Louise Linger; m. Craig E. Yearley, Apr. 19, 1978; children: Eric Jason, Jay Alan. BSc in Edn., OH State U., 1973; student, Cleve. State U., 1989—90; M in Curriculum and Instrn., Ashland U., 2006. Cert. Elem. Music Tchr. (grades one through eight) Ohio, 1985, Elem. Edn. Tchr. Ohio, 1975. Music tchr. St. Mary Elem. Sch., Vermilion, Ohio, 1985—2000, St. Jude Sch., Elyria, Ohio, 1990—2000, Copopa Elem. Sch., Columbia Station, Ohio, 2000—. Reading tutor Columbia Station Sch. Dist., Ohio, 2000—04, music program prodr., 2000—, mentor, 2004—. Author, prodr.: music program Ohio Sings, 2003, Scientific Music, 2004. Organist First Bapt. Ch., Lorain, 1995—. Recipient Pursuit of Excellence award, Columbia Schs. Bd. Edn., 2001, Most Valuable Educator, Applebees Restaurant, Strongsville, OH, 2003. Mem.: Music Educators Nat. Conf., Ohio Edn. Assn., Nat. Educators Assn., Ohio Music Edn. Assn., Firelands Lions Club (publicity chmn. 2000—03, v.p. 2005—). Avocations: skiing, boating, gardening. Home: 8038 Claus Rd Amherst OH 44001 Office: Copopa Elem Sch 14168 SW River Columbia Station OH 44028

YEARWOOD, TRISHA, country music singer, songwriter; b. Monticello, Ga., 1964; m. Chris Latham (div.); m. Robert Reynolds, May 21, 1994 (div.); m. Garth Brooks, Dec. 10, 2005. Degree in Music Bus., Belmont U. Intern MTM Records, demo singer, commercial jingles singer; recording artist MCA Records. Albums include Trisha Yearwood, 1991 (double platinum), Hearts in Armor, 1992 (Grammy nomination: Best Country Female Vocal, 1994 for "Walkaway Joe"), The Song Remembers When, 1993, Thinkin' About You, 1995, Everybody Knows, 1996, (songbook) A Collection of Hits, 1997, Where Your Road Leads, 1998, Real Live Woman, 2000, Inside Out, 2001, Jasper County, 2005; back-up vocalist Garth Brooks albums; opening act Garth Brooks Tour, 1991; TV appearances on TNN American Music Shop, The Tonight Show, Late Night with David Letterman, Good Morning America, A&E Live By Request, 1998 Academy Awards, 1996 Summer Olympic Closing Ceremonies. Named Best New Country Artist by Am. Music Awards, 1992, Top New Female Vocalist by Acad. Country Music, 1992, Top Female Vocalist of Yr., 1998; Top Female Vocalist of Yr., Country Mus. Assn., 1997, 98; first female in country music history to have debut single reach #1 on charts with She's in Love with the Love, 1991; recipient Grammy awards for best female country vocal, 1998, best country vocal collaboration (with Aaron Neville) 1994, (with Garth Brooks), 1998.

YEATER, KATHLEEN WECKER, musician, educator; b. York, Pa., Oct. 2, 1947; d. Philip Emanuel and Kathryn Diehl Wecker; m. Robert Alan Yeater, Mar. 20, 1982; children: Amy Tomassone, Jennifer Diehl; stepchildren: Laurie Bryant, Jennifer Dorrough. BSc in Music Edn., Indiana U. of Pa., 1969. Orch. dir., string instr. Susquehannock H.S. So. York County Sch. Dist., Glen Rock, Pa., 1974—2006; ret., 2006. Violinist York Symphony Orch., 1974—, Salem String Quartet, York, 1983—; dir. York Jr. Symphony Orch., 1993—, condr., 1993—2005; guest condr. instrumental ensembles. Bd. mem. York Youth Symphony, 1985—2001. Named Outstanding Dir. Pa., Sch. Band & Orch. Mag., 1999; recipient Outstanding Tchr. award, South Ctrl. Pa. Joint Coun. Sch. Improvement, Shippensburg U., 1989. Mem.: NEA, Nat. Sch. Orch. Assn. (past pres. Pa. chpt. 1988—89, named Orch. Dir. of Yr. Pa. chpt. 2004, named Nat. Dir. of Yr. 1996), Am. Fedn. Musicians, Pa. Sch. Educators Assn., Am. String Tchr Assn., Music Educators Nat. Conf., Pa. Music Educators Assn. (Citation of Excellence 1986). Lutheran. Avocations: music, reading, gardening, cooking. Home: 4032 Robin Hood Dr York PA 17408 Personal E-mail: bobkathyyeater@comcast.net.

YEATES, MARIE R., lawyer; b. New Orleans, Feb. 24, 1956; BS summa cum laude, La. State U., 1977, JD, 1980. Bar: La. 1980, U.S. Ct. Appeals (5th cir.) 1981, U.S. Ct. Appeals (11th cir.) 1981, Tex. 1982, Tex. Supreme Ct. 1982, U.S. Dist. Ct. (so. dist.) Tex. 1985, U.S. Supreme Ct. 1986, U.S. Ct. Appeals (9th cir.) 1998, U.S. Dist. Ct. (no. dist.) Tex. 2001, U.S. Ct. Appeals (10th cir.) 2002, U.S. Ct. Appeals (7th cir.) 2004. Ptnr., co-head Appellate Sect. Vinson & Elkins LLP, Houston, 1990—. Office: Vinson & Elkins LLP First City Tower 1001 Fannin St, Ste 2300 Houston TX 77002 Office Phone: 713-758-4576. E-mail: myeates@velaw.com.

YEATMAN, HARRY CLAY, biologist, educator; b. Ashwood, Tenn., June 22, 1916; s. Trezevant Player and Mary (Wharton) Y.; m. Jean Hansford Anderson, Nov. 24, 1949; children— Henry Clay, Jean Hansford. AB, U. NC, Chapel Hill, 1939, MA, 1942, PhD, 1953; student, Cornell U., Ithaca, NY, summer 1937. Asst. prof. biology U. of South, Sewanee, Tenn., 1950-54, asso. prof., 1954-60, prof., 1960—, Kenan prof., 1980—, chmn. dept., 1972-76, elderhostel tchr., 1987-88. Vis. prof. marine biology Va. Inst. Marine Sci., Gloucester Point, summer 1967; cons. Smithsonian Instn., Sci. Applications, Inc., La Jolla, Calif., Ctrs. for Disease Control, Atlanta, WHO, Ecol. Analysts, Inc., Balt., Duke Power Co., Charlotte, N.C., Helminthic Disease Branch. Contbr. articles to profl. jours. Served with AUS, 1942-46. Gen. Edn. Bd. fellow, 1941-42; Brown Found. fellow, 1984 Fellow AAAS; mem. Soc. Systematic Biology (charter), Soc. Limnology and Oceanography (charter), Soc. Ichthyology and Herpetology, Tenn. Acad. Sci., Am. Micros. Soc., Am. Ornithologists Union, Tenn. Ornithol. Soc., Tenn. Archeol. Soc., Nat. Speleological Soc., Blue Key, Phi Beta Kappa, Sigma Xi, Omicron Delta Kappa, Sigma Nu. Republican. Episcopalian. Home: PO Box 356 Jumpoff Rd Sewanee TN 37375 Office: 735 University Ave Sewanee TN 37383-1000 Office Phone: 931-598-1000. Office Fax: 931-598-1145.

YEATMAN, HENRY CLAY, mechanical engineer; b. Sewanee, Tenn., July 13, 1957; s. Harry and Jean Yeatman; m. Paula Ann Hess, Oct. 7, 2000. BA in Math., U. South, Sewanee, Tenn., 1976—79; B of Mech. Engring., Ga. Inst. Tech., Atlanta, 1979—81. Tire devel. engr. B. F. Goodrich, Akron, Ohio, 1981—85; rsch. engr. Honda R&D Americas, Torrance, Calif., 1985—89; sr. engr. Am. Honda, Alpharetta, Ga., 1989—. Mem.: Soc. Automotive Entrs., Sports Car Club Am. Unitarian. Office: American Honda 4900 Marconi Dr Alpharetta GA 30005 Home Phone: 770-717-9568; Office Phone: 678-339-2567.

YEATS, ROBERT SHEPPARD, geologist, educator; b. Miami, Fla., Mar. 30, 1931; s. Robert Sheppard and Carolyn Elizabeth (Rountree) Y.; m. Lillian Eugenia Bowie, Dec. 30, 1952 (dec. Apr. 1991); children: Robert Bowie, David Claude, Stephen Paul, Kenneth James, Sara Elizabeth; m. Angela M. Hayes, Jan. 7, 1993. BA, U. Fla., 1952; MS, U. Wash., 1956, PhD, 1958. Registered geologist, Oreg., Calif., Wash. Geologist, petroleum exploration and prodn. Shell Oil Co., Ventura and L.A., Calif., 1958-67, Shell Devel. Co., Houston, 1967; assoc. prof. geology Ohio U., Athens, 1967-70, prof., 1970-77; prof. geology Oreg. State U., Corvallis, 1977-97, prof. oceanography, 1991-97, prof. emeritus, 1997—, chmn. dept., 1977-85; geologist U.S. Geol. Survey, 1968, 69, 75, Glomar Challenger scientist, 1971, co-chief scientist, 1973-74, 78; mem. Oreg. Bd. Geologist Examiners, 1981-83; chmn. Working Group I Internat. Lithosphere Program, 1987-90, chmn. task force group on paleoseismology, 1990-98; chmn. subcom. on Himalayan active faults Internat. Geol. Correlation Program, Project 206, 1984-92; mem. geophysics study com. NRC, 1987-94. Rschr. on Cenozoic tectonics of So. Calif., Oreg., Wash., New Zealand and Himalaya; active faults of Calif. Transverse Ranges, deep-sea drilling in Ea. Pacific; vis. scientist New Zealand Geol. Survey, 1983-84, 99, Geol. Survey of Japan, 1992, Inst. de Phys. du Globe de Paris, 1993, So. Calif. Earthquake Ctr.; sr. cons. Earth Cons. Internat., 1997—, ptnr., 2001—. Author: The Geology of Earthquakes, 1997, Living with Earthquakes in the Pacific Northwest, 1998, 2d edit., 2004, Living with Earthquakes in California-A Survivor's Guide, 2001. Mem. Ojai (Calif.) City Planning Commn., 1961-62, Ojai City Coun., 1962-65. 1st lt. U.S. Army, 1952-54. Named Richard H. Jahns Disting. Lectr. in Engring. Geology, 1995; Ohio U. rsch. fellow, 1973-74; grantee NSF, U.S. Geol. Survey. Fellow AAAS, Geol. Soc. Am. (chmn. structural geology and tectonics divsn. 1984-85, Cordilleran sect. 1988-89, assoc. editor bull. 1987-89); mem. Am. Assn. Petroleum Geologists (Outstanding Educator award Pacific sect. 1991, Michel T. Halbouty human needs award 1998), Am. Geophys. Union, Seismol. Soc. Am., Earthquake Engring. Rsch. Inst. Home: 1654 NW Crest Pl Corvallis OR 97330-1812 Office: Oreg State U Dept Geoscis Corvallis OR 97331-5506 Office Phone: 541-737-1226. E-mail: yeatsr@geo.oregonstate.edu.

YEATTS, KARIN BEATRICE, epidemiologist; b. Alexandria, Va., May 11, 1966; d. Fredrick Stuart and Ines Emilia Yeatts. MS in Environ. Sci. & Engring., VPI&SU, Blacksburg, Va., 1990; MS in Epidemiology, U. Mass., Amherst, 1994; PhD, U. NC, Chapel Hill, 1997. Rsch. asst. prof., sch. pub. health, dept. epidemiology U. NC, Chapel Hill, 2002—. Co-chmn. Asthma Alliance NC, Raleigh, 2005—07. Mem.: Soc. Epidemiologic Rsch., Internat. Soc. Environ. Epidemiology, Am. Thoracic Soc. Office: Univ NC Sch Pub Health Campus Box #7435 Mcgavran Greenberg Hall Chapel Hill NC 27599-7435 Office Fax: 919-966-2089. Business E-Mail: karin_yeatts@unc.edu.

YEAZEL, KEITH ARTHUR, lawyer; b. Fayetteville, NC, Feb. 14, 1956; s. Russell E. and Barbara E. (Weaver) Y.; m. Deborah M. MacDonald, Aug. 30, 1986. BA, Ohio State U., 1983; JD, Capital U., 1989. Bar: Ohio 1989, U.S. Dist. Ct. (so. dist.) Ohio 1989, U.S. Ct. Appeals (6th cir.) 1990, U.S. Supreme Ct. 1992. Law clk. to judge George C. Smith US Dist. Ct., Columbus, Ohio, 1988-89; pvt. practice Columbus, 1989—. Mem. Ohio Bar Assn., Columbus Bar Assn., Nat. Assn. Criminal Def. Lawyers, Ohio Assn. Criminal Def. Lawyers, Sixth Cir. Jud. Conf. (life), Order of Curia. Republican. Lutheran. Office: 5354 N High St Columbus OH 43214 Office Phone: 614-885-2900. Business E-Mail: yeazel@netwalk.com.

YEAZELL, RUTH BERNARD, English language educator; b. NYC, Apr. 4, 1947; d. Walter and Annabelle (Reich) Bernard; m. Stephen C. Yeazell, Aug. 14, 1969 (div. 1980). BA with high honors, Swarthmore Coll., 1967; MPhil, Yale U., 1970, PhD, 1971. Asst. prof. English Boston U., 1971-74, UCLA, 1975-77, assoc. prof., 1977-80, prof., 1980-91, Yale U., New Haven, 1991—, dir. grad. studies, 1993-98, 2007, Chace family prof., 1995—, chair, 2000—05. Author: Language and Knowledge in the Late Novels of Henry James, 1976, Death and Letters of Alice James, 1981, Fictions of Modesty: Women and Courtship in the English Novel, 1991, Harems of the Mind: Passages of Western Art and Literature, 2000; assoc. editor Nineteenth-Century Fiction, 1977-80; editor: Sex, Politics and Science in the 19th Century Novel, 1986, Henry James: A Collection of Critical Essays, 1994. Dir. Lewis Walpole Libr., 1996—. Woodrow Wilson fellow, 1967-68, Guggenheim fellow, 1979-80, NEH fellow, 1988-89, Pres.'s rsch. fellow U. Calif., 1988-89, Getty scholar, 2003-04 (declined), Bellagio Ctr. Residency scholar, 2005. Mem. MLA (exec. coun. 1985-88), English Inst. (supervising com. 1983-86). Office: Yale U Dept English New Haven CT 06520-8302 Business E-Mail: ruth.yeazell@yale.edu.

YECKE, CHERI PIERSON, educational researcher, administrator, policymaker, writer; b. St. Paul, Feb. 5, 1955; d. Leo Sylvester and Marceline Mae (Intihar) Pierson; m. Dennis Joseph Yecke, Dec. 22, 1973; children: Anastasia, Tiffany. BA, U. Hawaii, 1975; MST, U. Wis., River Falls, 1984; PhD, U. Va., 2001. Apptd. mem. State Bd. Edn., State of Va., 1995—98, dep. sec. edn., 1998—2001, sec. edn., 2001—02; dir. tchr. quality and pub. sch. choice US Dept. Edn., 2002—03; sr. adv. to White House on USA Freedom Corps., 2003; commr. edn. State of Minn., 2003—04; disting. sr. fellow for edn. and social policy Ctr. of the Am. Experiment, 2004—05; chancellor for K-12 edn. State of Fla., Tallahassee, 2005—. Author: The War Against Excellence: The Rising Tide of Mediocrity in America's Middle Schools, 2003, Mayhem in the Middle: How Middle Schools Have Failed America and How to Make Them Work, 2005. Mem.: Am. Coun. Trustees & Alumni, Nat. Assn. Scholars. Republican. Home: 1315 Peacefield Pl Tallahassee FL 32308-0844 Office Phone: 850-245-0509.

YEE, ALBERT HOY, writer, retired psychologist, educator; b. Santa Barbara, Calif., June 14, 1929; children: Lisa Diane, Hoyt Brian. BA, U. Calif., Berkeley, 1952; MA, San Francisco State U., 1959; Ed.D., Stanford U., 1965. Post-doctoral research fellow U. Oreg., Eugene, 1966-67; assoc. prof. edn. U. Wis., Madison, 1967-70, prof., 1970-73; prof. ednl. psychology, dean grad. studies and research Calif. State U., Long Beach, 1973-79, originating founder Grad. Ctr., 1974; prof. edn. U. Mont., 1979-83, dean Sch. Edn., 1979-82; sr. lectr. psychology Chinese U. of Hong Kong, 1985-89; dean, prof. psychology Am. Coll., Singapore; sr. lectr. psychology Nat. U., Singapore, 1989-90; dir. program U. Md., Hongkong, 1990; disting. vis. prof. ednl. psychology spl. adviser coll. grad. studies and internat. programs Marist Coll., 1990-92; prof. ednl. psychology Fla. Internat. U., Miami, 1992-94, rsch. scholar, 1994-95. Chmn. 1st Fed. Adv. Com. for Asian and Pacific Island Ams., Bur. Census, 1976-81; bd. dirs. Sino-Judaie Inst., 2004-. Author: Man, Society and the World, 1968; co-author: Comprehensive Spelling Instruction: Theory, Research and Application, 1971; editor: Social Interaction in Educational Settings, 1971, Perspectives on Management Systems Approaches to Education: A Symposium, 1973, Search for Meaning, 1984, A Study on Possible Future Developments for Hong Kong: Strategic Planning and Innovations, 1985, A People Misruled: Hong Kong and the Chinese Stepping-Stone Syndrome, 1989, 2d edit., 1992; editor: East Asian Higher Education: Traditions and Transformations, 1994, Whither Hong Kong: China's Shadow or Visionary Gleam?, 1999, Yeee-Hah!: Remembrances and Longing, 2005. With AUS, 1952-55, Korea, Japan. Recipient Civic Commendation Madison, 1973; sr. Fulbright lectr. Tokyo and Tamagawa Univs., Japan; also 1st Fulbright scholar to People's Republic China, 1972. Fellow AAAS, Nat. Conf. Research in English, Am. Psychol. Assn., Am. Psychol. Soc.; mem. Calif. Coll. and Univ. Faculty Assn. (founder 1961), Chinese Hist. Soc. Am. and Orgn. of Chinese Americans (Bicentennial speaker), Asian-Am. Psychol. Assn. (pres. 1979-82, jour. editor 1981-82), Western Mont. Stanford Alumni Club (founding pres. 1997—). Home: 3822 Lincoln Rd Missoula MT 59802-3039 E-mail: alyee@montana.com.

YEE, BENNIE SENE, construction manager, electrical engineer; b. Jersey City, Apr. 29, 1955; s. Kwok-Huie Sene and Chung-Sin Sene Yee. AAS in Elec. Tech., CUNY, Bklyn., 1985; B in Elec. Engring., Pratt Inst., Bklyn., 1990; MSEE, Columbia U., NYC, 1993. Libr. asst. Jersey City Pub. Libr., 1981—84; tutor math., computer CUNY, 1985—86; elec. tech. Con Edison NY, NYC, 1986—90, sr. telecom engr., 1991—99, LI, 2000—03; project mgr. Mazet Realty, NYC, 2004—. Cons. in field. Mem.: IEEE, Geospatial Info. and Tech. Assn., Tau Beta Pi. Avocations: photography, reading, history, woodworking. Home: 526 Jersey Ave Jersey City NJ 07302-2721 Office: Mazet Realty 21 Pell St New York NY 10013

YEE, FLORENCE, library director; Mgr. Pearl City Bookmobile, Hawaii Kai Pub. Libr.; br. mgr. Kaimuki Pub. Libr.; acting dir. Hawaii State Libr., Honolulu, 2003—04, dir., 2004—, Hawaii State Libr. for Blind and Physically Handicapped, Honolulu, 2004—. Mem. Congresswoman Patsy T. Mink Commn. Mem.: Hawaii Libr. Assn. Office: Hawaii State Libr 478 S King St Honolulu HI 96813-2901 Office Phone: 808-586-3555. Office Fax: 808-733-8426.

YEE, HENRY CHAN MYINT, cardiologist; b. Kyaukme, Burma, Dec. 26, 1961; s. Shaw Sing Yee and Kwan Yee Cho; m. Angela Dong Li Lii; 1 child, Stephanie. Diploma in biology, Mandalay Gen. Hosp., 1986; MBBS, Inst. Medicine, Mandalay, 1985. Intern Mandalay Gen. Hosp., 1985-86; pvt. practice Mandalay, 1986-92; rschr. in cardiology Albert Einstein Coll. Medicine, Bronx, NY, 1993-94; resident in internal medicine Seton Hall U. Grad. Sch. Med. Edn., Elizabeth, NJ, 1994-97; fellow in cardiology Kasier Permanente, LA, 1997-2000. Mem. Am. Coll. Physicians, Am. Coll. Cardiology.

YEE, LELAND Y., state senator; b. China; 4 children. Grad., U. Calif., Berkeley; MA, San Francisco State U.; PhD in Child Psychology, U. Hawaii. Pres. Bd. Edn. City of San Francisco, 1988-96, mem. Bd. Suprs., 1996—2002; mem. Calif. State Assembly, 2002—06, speaker pro tempore, 2004—, Calif. State Senate, 2006—. Pres. Nat. Asian Pacific Am. Caucus of State Legislators, 2004—. Address: San Francisco Stae Bldg 455 Golden Gate Ave Ste 14200 San Francisco CA 94102 Office: State Capitol Rm 4098 Sacramento CA 95814 Address: 400 S El Camino Rd Ste 630 San Mateo CA 94402 Office Phone: 916-319-2012. Business E-Mail: senator.yee@senate.ca.gov.

YEE, ROBERT DONALD, ophthalmologist; b. Beijing, Feb. 21, 1945; came to U.S., 1947, naturalized, 1947; s. James and Marian Y.M. (Li) Y.; m. Linda Margaret Neil, June 28, 1968; children: Jillian Neil, Allison Betram. AB in biology summa cum laude, Harvard U., 1966; MD in medicine cum laude, Harvard Med. Sch., 1970. Diplomate Am. Bd. Ophthalmology. Fullbright scholar, 1966; intern in internal medicine U. Rochester, NY, 1970-71; resident in ophthalmology Jules Stein Eye Inst. UCLA, 1971-74; fellow in neuro-ophthalmology Nat. Eye Inst., NIH, Bethesda, Md., 1974-76; chief ophthalmology Harbor-UCLA Med. Ctr., Torrance, Calif., 1976-78; asst. prof. ophthalmology Sch. Medicine UCLA, 1976-78, assoc. prof., 1978-82, prof., 1982-87; prof., dept. chmn. ophthalmology Ind. U. Sch. Medicine, Indpls., 1987—. Mem. residency rev. com. for ophthalmology Accrediation Coun. for Grad. Med. Edn., 1995-2002, vice-chmn., 1998-2000, chmn., 2000-2002. Mem. editorial bd. Investigative Ophthalmology and Visual Sci., 1982—, von Graefe's Archives of Ophthalmology, 1983-89; Feldman endowed chair ophthalmology UCLA, 1984-87; Grayson endowed chair ophthalmology Ind. U., 2003—. Author numerous med. research papers. Lt. comdr. USPHS, 1974—76. Grantee, NIH, 1976—84; scholar Dolly Green Rsch. scholar, 1984—86. Fellow: ACS, Am. Acad. Ophthalmology; mem.: AMA, Accreditation Cou. for Grad. Med. Edn. (residency rev. com., chair 2000—02), Indpls. Ophthal. Soc., Ind. Med. Soc., Chinese Am. Ophthal. Soc. (pres. 1996—98), Ind. Acad. Ophthalmology, Am. Ophthal Soc., Assn. Rsch. in Vision and Ophthalmology (chmn. eye movement sect. 1981, 1987, trustee 1996—2001, v.p. 2000—01), Phi Beta Kappa, Alpha Omega Alpha. Office: Ind U Med Ctr 702 Rotary Cir Indianapolis IN 46202-5133 Office Phone: 317-274-7101. E-mail: ryee@iupui.edu.

YEE, SANDRA GAYLE BROWN, library director, dean; b. Benzonia, Mich., July 17, 1949; d. Al Powell and Maxine G. (Wallace) Brown; m. D. Johnny Yee, June 29, 1974; 1 child, Melissa Ann. BA, Western Mich. U., 1970, MLS, 1973; EdD, U. Mich., 1979. Libr., coord. libr. svcs. Muskegon CC, Mich., 1973—82; coord. access svcs. Univ. Libr. Ea. Mich. U., Ypsilanti, 1982—90, assoc. dean learning resources and tech., 1990—2001; dean univ. libr. sys. Wayne State U., Detroit, 2001—. Author: (with M. Boone and R. Bullard) Training Student Library Assistants, 1991. Mem. ALA, Assn. Coll. and Rsch. Librs. (past chair univ. libr. sect. 2005), Mich. Libr. Assn. (treas. 1989-91, pres.-elect 1992-93, pres. 1993-94, past pres. 1994-95, Mich. libr. consortium bd. chair 1997-98, OCLC mem. coun. v.p., pres.-elect, 2006—). Office: Wayne State U Univ Libraries Detroit MI 48202 Office Phone: 313-577-4020. Office Fax: 313-577-5525. E-mail: sandra.yee@wayne.edu. *

YEE, SIENHO, law educator; b. Zhanjiang, Guangdong, China, July 9, 1965; BA, Brandeis U., 1989; JD, Columbia U., 1993. Bar: U.S. Ct. Appeals (3rd cir.) 1994, N.Y. 1994, U.S. Supreme Ct. 2004. Law clk. Judge Robert Cowen, US Ct. Appeals (3rd cir.), Trenton, NJ, 1993—94, Appeals Chamber, UN Internat. Criminal Tribunal for Former Yugoslavia, The Hague, Netherlands, 1995—96; counsel legal dept. Internat. Monetary Fund, Washington, 1996—97; tutor internat. law St Hugh's Coll., Oxford U., England, 1999—2000; vis. asst. prof. Northwestern U. Law Sch., Chgo., 2000; lectr. law Queen Mary, U. London, 2001; assoc. prof. law U. Colo. Law Sch., Boulder, 2001—06; prof., dir. Silk Rd. Inst. Internat. Law Xi'an Jiaotong U., China, 2006—. Assoc. Sullivan & Cromwell, NYC. Author: Towards an International Law of Co-progressiveness, 2004; editor-in-chief: Chinese Jour. Internat. Law, 2003; editor: International Law in the Post-Cold War World, 2001, International Crime and Punishment, vol. 1, 2003, International Crime and Punishment, vol. 2, 2004; contbr. articles to profl. jours. Wien Internat. scholar, Brandeis U., 1987—89, Harlan Fiske Stone scholar, Columbia Law Sch., 1990—92. Mem.: Phi Beta Kappa. Office: U Colo Law Sch 401 UCB Boulder CO 80309-0401 Home Phone: 720-273-0357; Office Phone: 303-735-0205. Office Fax: 707-788-4178; Home Fax: 707-788-4178. Personal E-mail: yee@sienhoyee.org.

YEFFETH, GLENN BARRY, publishing executive, management consultant; b. Bklyn., Dec. 3, 1961; s. Amnon and Millie Yeffeth; m. Jean Grant, Sept. 9, 1990 (div. Nov. 2, 2006); children: Benjamin Grant, Isabella Anne. BA in History, Oberlin Coll., Ohio, 1983; MBA, U. Chgo., 1986. Prin. Nolan Norton, Chgo., 1986—90; mng. dir. CSC Index, London, 1990—98; CEO, pub. BenBella Books, Inc., Dallas, 2001—. Author: The Da Vinci Mole. Office: BenBella Books Inc 6440 N Central Expressway #617 Dallas TX 75206 Office Phone: 214-750-3628. Office Fax: 214-750-3645. Business E-Mail: glenn@benbellabooks.com.

YEGULALP, TUNCEL M., mining engineer, educator; b. Konya, Turkey, Nov. 5, 1937; came to U.S., 1963; s. Faik Suleyman and Selma Safiye (Karatay) Y.; m. Sevinc Guneri, July 5, 1963; children: Ali, Serdar. BS, Tech. U., Istanbul, 1961; DEngring. Sci., Columbia U., 1968. Mining engr. M.T.A., Ankara, Turkey, 1961-63, chief feasibility studies group, 1971; rsch. engr. Mobil Rsch., Paulsboro, NJ, 1967-69; chief sys. cons. Sisag Ltd., Ankara, 1971-72; asst. prof. Columbia U., NYC, 1972-75; assoc. prof. Henry Krumb Sch. Mines, 1975-85, prof., 1985—. Dir. N.Y. Mining and Mineral Resources Inst. Rsch., 1987—; elected permanent mem. U.S. del. World Mining Congress, 1993. Author articles in field. Served to 2d lt. C.E. Turkish Army, 1969-71. Internat. AEC fellow, Vienna, 1963; Krumb fellow, Columbia U., 1964, Campbell fellow, 1965. Mem. AIME, Internat. Higher Edn. Acad. Scis., Turkish Studies Assn., Inst. for Ops. Rsch. and the Mgmt. Scis., Sigma Chi. Muslim. Office: Columbia U 926B SWM MC4711 500 W 120th St New York NY 10027 Home Phone: 201-836-2099; Office Phone: 212-854-2984. Business E-Mail: yegulalp@columbia.edu.

YEH, CHIA-CHOU, electrical engineer, researcher; b. Taipei, Taiwan, Oct. 10, 1978; arrived in US, 1996; s. Kuo Xsing and Hsu Pao Chai Yeh. BSEE with hons., Marquette U., Milw., Wis., 2000, MSEE, 2003, student in Elec. Engring., 2003—. Registered profl. engr., Dept. of Regulation and Licensing, Wis., 2000. Elec. engr. R. R. Donnelley & Sons Co., Dwight, Ill., 1998—99; power electronics engr. (intern) Eaton Corp., Milw., 2003—; grad. rsch. asst. Marquette U., Milw., 2003—07. Contbr. articles to profl. jours. Fellow, U.S. Dept. Edn., 2000—01; grantee, NSF, 2003—; scholar, Marquette U., 2001—02. Mem.: IEEE, Sigma Xi, Phi Mu Epsilon, Eta Kappa Nu, Tau Beta Pi. Avocations: travel, computer, music, movies. Home: 610 N 17th Street 309 Milwaukee WI 53233 Office: Marquette University 1515 W Wisconsin Ave Milwaukee WI 53233 Office Phone: 414-288-1593. Office Fax: 414-288-5579. Personal E-mail: cyeh@ieee.org. Business E-Mail: chiachou.yeh@marquette.edu.

YEH, EDWARD TU-HSING, cardiologist, educator, medical researcher; arrived in U.S., 1971; s. Jack and Pi-Lien Yeh; m. Hui-Ming Chang, Nov. 6, 1982; 1 child, Andrew Allen. MD, U. Calif., Davis, 1980. Diplomate Am. Bd. Cardiovascular Diseases. Asst. prof. Harvard Med. Sch., Boston, 1987—92; assoc. prof. U. Tex. Med. Sch., Houston, 1992—97, prof., 1997—2000; prof., chmn. cardiology MD Anderson Cancer Ctr., Houston, 2000—. Named Established Investigator, Am. Heart Assn., 1992. Mem.: Am. Heart Assn. (pres. Houston chpt. 2004—05), Assn. Am. Physicians (life). Achievements include patents in field; patents pending in field. Office: MD Anderson Cancer Ctr 1515 Holcombe 449 Houston TX 77030 Office Phone: 713-792-6242.

YEH, RAYMOND WEI-HWA, architect, educator; b. Shanghai, Feb. 25, 1942; came to U.S., 1958, naturalized, 1976; s. Herbert Hwan-Ching and Joyce Bo-Ding (Kwan) Y.; m. Hsiao-Yen Chen, Sept. 16, 1967; children—Bryant Po Yung, Clement Chung-Yung, Emily Su-Yung. BA, U. Oreg., 1965, B.Arch., 1967; M.Arch., U. Minn., 1969. Cert. Nat. Coun. Archtl. Registration Bds.; registered architect, Tex., Okla., Calif., Hawaii. Draftsman, designer various archtl. firms, 1965-68; design architect Ellerbe Architects, St. Paul, 1968-70; v.p., dir. design Sorey, Hill, Binnicker, Oklahoma City, 1973-74; prin. architect Raymond W.H. Yeh & Assos., Norman, Okla., 1974-80; asst. prof. to prof. U. Okla., Norman, 1970-79; head dept. architecture, prof. Calif. Poly. State U., San Luis Obispo, 1979-83; dean Coll. Architecture U. Okla., Norman, 1983-92; prin. architect W.H. Raymond Yeh, Norman, 1983-93; dean sch. architecture U. Hawaii at Manoa, Honolulu, 1993—. Profl. adviser Neighborhood Conservation and Devel. Center, Oklahoma City, 1977 79 Works include: St. Thomas More U. Parish and Student Center, Norman, Summit Ridge Center Retirement Community, Harrah, Okla., (recipient Nat. Design award Guild Religious Architecture 1978). Nat. Endowment for Arts fellow, 1978-79 Fellow AIA (dir., pres. Okla. chpt. 1986, design awards, nat. com. chmn. 1989); mem. Calif. Coun. Archtl. Edn. (dir., pres. 1982-83), Okla. Found. for Architecture (founding chair bd. 1989-90), Asian Soc. Okla. (award of Excellence 1992), Asia Pacific Ctr. for Arch. (founding bd. dirs. 1996). Presbyterian. Office: U Hawaii Manoa Sch Architecture Honolulu HI 96822 Business E-Mail: yeh@hawaii.edu.

YEH, YING-YU EMILY, music educator; permanent resident, 2004; d. Jing-Chao Yeh and Show-Chu Chu; m. Joseph Sanford Myers, July 26, 2003. MusB, Shenandoah U., 1998; MusM, U. Mo., 2001; MA, Ctrl. Bapt. Theol. Sem., 2004. Cert. tchr. Musikgarten, S.C., 2004, music tchr. in piano Mo. Music Tchr. Assn., 2006, music tchr. Am. Coll. Musicians, 2006. Pianist Eagle Heights Presbyn. Ch., Winchester, Va., 1997—98; dir. music, accompanist United Campus Ministry, Kansas City, Mo., 1999—2002; organist, accompanist Wornall Rd. Bapt. Ch., Kansas City, 2002—03; tchr. piano Toon Shop Sch. Music, Overland Pk., Kans., 2003—; instr. musikgarten Schmitt Music Ctr., Overland Pk., 2005—. Organist, accompyanist Bristol Hill United Meth. Ch., Kans. City, 2004—. Grantee, U. Mo., 1999—2002; scholar, Ctrl. Bapt. Theol. Sem., 2002—03, U. Mo., 2001—02; Rudolph C. Evans Piano scholarship, 1997. Mem.: Mid-Am. Music Assn., Am. Coll. Musicians (named to Nat. Honor Roll Guild Tchrs. 2004, 2005, 2006, 2007), Music Tchr. Nat. Assn. (cert. music tchr. in piano 2006—). Personal E-mail: musicblossom@yahoo.com.

YELENICK, MARY THERESE, lawyer; b. Denver, May 17, 1954; d. John Andrew and Maesel Joyce (Reed) Y. BA magna cum laude, Colo. Coll., 1976; JD cum laude, Georgetown U., 1979. Bar: DC 1979, NY 1982, US Dist. Ct. DC 1980, US Dist. Ct. (so. and ea. dists.) NY 1982, US Ct. Appeals (DC cir.) 1981, US Ct. Appeals (5th cir.) 1995, US Ct. Appeals (4th cir.) 2006, US Supreme Ct. 1992. Law clk. to presiding justices Superior Ct. DC, 1979-81; ptnr. Chadbourne & Parke, LLP, NYC, 1981—. Editor: Jour. Law and Policy Internat. Bus., 1978-79.; mem. NETWORK, Nat. Cath. Soc. Justice Lobby (bd. dirs. 2004—, bd. chair 2006-) Mem. Phi Beta Kappa. Democrat. Roman Catholic. Home: 310 E 46th St New York NY 10017-3002 Office: Chadbourne & Parke LLP 30 Rockefeller Plz Fl 31 Ste 3550 New York NY 10112-0129

YELICH, LYNNE, member of parliament; b. Mar. 24, 1953; m. Matt Yelich; 2 children. Grad., Kenaston HS, 1971. Farmer, Kenaston; mem. House of Commons, Ottawa, Ont., Canada, parliamentary sec. to minister human rels. and social devel., 2006—. Address: Unit #71 Market Mall 2325 Preston Ave Saskatoon SK S7J 2G2 Canada Office: House of Commons 715 Confederation Bldg Ottawa ON K1A 0A6 Canada Business E-Mail: yelicl@parl.gc.ca.

YELICH, NOLAN T., library director; b. Wis. BS, U. Wis., Oshkosh; MS, U. Wis., Madison. Dir. pub. svcs. Earl Gregg Swem Libr., Coll. William & Mary, Williamsburg, Va., 1968—73; dir. libr. svcs. Libr. Va., Richmond, 1973—94, acting state libr., 1994—95, state libr., 1994—. Recipient John Phillip Immroth Meml. award for Intellectual Freedom, ALA Intellectual Freedom Round Table, 2005. Mem.: Va. Sch. Boards Assn., Va. Libr. Assn. (past pres.), Chief Officers of State Libr. Agys. (Libr. of Congress liason 2004—06). Office: Libr of Va 800 E Broad St Richmond VA 23219 Office Phone: 804-692-3535. Office Fax: 804-692-3594. E-mail: nyelich@lva.lib.va.us. *

YELISEEV, ALEXEI ARKADIEVICH, biochemist, researcher; b. Moscow, Nov. 3, 1959; s. Arkadil Aleksandrovich and Tatiana Georgievna (Sokolova) Yeliseev; m. Elena Dmitrievna Polonnikova, Aug. 20, 1985; children: Ekaterina, Tatiana. MS in Chemistry, Moscow State U., 1981; PhD in Biochemistry, Russian Acad. Scis., 1987. From trainee rschr. to sr. rschr. A.N. Bakh Inst. Biochemistry, Russian Acad. Scis., Moscow, 1981-92, sr. rschr., 1992—. Vis. rsch. scientist U. Tex., Houston, 1993—99; sr. rsch. scientist Roche Vitamins, Inc., 1999—2001; staff scientist NIH, 2003—; sr. scientist Kosan Bioscis., Inc., 2001—03; mem. editl. bd. Protein Expression and Purificaltion, 2007—. Contbr. chapters to books, articles to profl. jours. Grantee, Internat. Sci. Found., 1994—95; Rsch. fellow, Alexander von Humboldt Stiftung, 1989—92, Internat. Union Biochemistry, 1992, Royal Soc. London, 1993. Mem.: AAAS, Russian Biochem. Soc. (lecturship 1987), Am. Soc. Microbiology. Avocations: travel, music, books. Office Phone: 301-443-0552. Business E-Mail: yeliseeva@mail.nih.gov.

YELLEN, JANET LOUISE, bank executive; b. Bklyn., Aug. 13, 1946; d. Julius and Anna Ruth (Blumenthal) Y.; m. George Arthur Akerlof, July 8, 1978; 1 child, Robert Joseph. BA in Econs. summa cum laude, Brown U., 1967; PhD, Yale U., 1971; LLD (hon.), Brown U., 1998; LHD (hon.), Bard Coll., 2000. Asst. prof. econs. Harvard U., Cambridge, Mass., 1971-76; lectr. London Sch. Econs. and Polit. Sci., Washington, 1978-80; asst. prof. econs. Sch. Bus. Adminstrn., U. Calif., Berkeley, 1980-82, assoc. prof., 1982-85, prof. Haas Sch. Bus., 1985—, Bernard T. Rocca Jr. prof. internat. bus. and trade, 1992—, Eugene E. and Catherine M. Trefethem prof. bus., 1999—; cons. div. internat. fin., Fed. Res. Sys., Washington, 1974-75, economist trade and fin. studies sect., 1977-78, mem., 1994-97; chair, Coun. Econ. Advisors Exec. Office of the Pres., Washington, 1997-99; pres., CEO Fed. Res. Bank San Francisco, 2004—. Mem. adv. panel in economics NSF, 1977—78, 1991—92, com. visitors, economics program, 1996, 2004; adv. bd. Women's Econ. Round Table, 1999—, Ctr. Internat. Polit. Economy, 1999—, Jerome Levy Economics Inst., 2002—, Calif. Assembly Select Com. on Asian Trade, 2003; bd. dirs. Economists Allied for Arms Reduction, 2002—, Delta Dental of Calif., 2003—; mem. amb. adv. coun. for Marshall Scholarships, 1996—, OECD, High-Level Sustainable Devel. Group, 1999—2001, NAS Panel, Ensuring Best Presidential Sci. and Tech. Appointments, 2000; chair Pres. Interagency Com. on Women's Bus. Enterprise, 1997—99, Econ. Policy Com. Orgn. for Econ. Coop. and Devel., 1997—99; rsch. fellow MIT, Cambridge, 1974; cons. Congl. Budget Office, 1975—76, mem. panel econ. advisers, 1993—94; rsch. affiliate Yale U., 1976; fellow Yale Corp., 2000—; rsch. assoc. Nat. Bureau Econ. Rsch., 1999—; prin. investigator Russell Sage Found. Grant on Sustainable Employment, 2000; sr. adviser Macroeconomic Advisers, 2003—; mem. Brookings Panel on Econ. Activity, 1987—88, 1990—91, sr. adviser, 1989—94, adv. bd., 1999—; Yrjö Jahnsson Found. lectr. on macroecon. theory, Helsinki, 1977—78; mem. Coun. on Fgn. Rels, 1976—81. Author: (monograph) (with Arrow and Shavell) The Limits of the Market in Resource Allocation, 1977; assoc. editor Jour. Econ. Perspectives, 1987-91; contbr. articles to profl. jours. Hon. Woodrow Wilson fellow, 1967, grad. fellow NSF, 1967-71, Guggenheim fellow, 1986-87, fellow, Am. Academy Arts and Sciences, 2001; grantee NSF, 1975-77, 90-94; Maria and Sidney Rolfe award for Nat. Econ. Svc., Women's Econ. Round Table, 1997, Wilbur Lucius Cross Medal, Yale U., 1997; named one of 50 Women to Watch, Wall St. Journal, 2005. Mem. Am. Econ. Assn. (adv. com. to Pres. 1986-87, nominating com. 1988-90, v.p. 2004-), Western Econ. Assn. (pres., 2003-04), Phi Beta Kappa. Office: Fed Res Bank San Francisco PO Box 7702 San Francisco CA 94105-7702 Office Phone: 415-974-2000. *

YELLON, ROBERT FORREST, surgeon, medical educator; b. NYC, June 26, 1956; s. Pauline Yellon; m. Keely Ann Cofano, June 24, 2003; children: Jeremy Marc, Nathaniel Benjamin. AB in Biology, Princeton U., NJ, 1978; MD, SUNY Stony Brook, 1986. Diplomate Am. Bd. of Otolaryngolgoy, 1993. Dir. of clin. svcs. dept. otolaryngology Children's Hosp. of Pitts., 1997—; assoc. prof. dept. otolaryngology U. Pitts., 2000—. Dir. pediat. ear ctr. Children's Hosp. of Pitts., 2006—. Editor: (textbook) Pediatric Otolaryngology. Named to Best Doctors in Am., 2006. Fellow: Am. Soc. of Pediat. Otolaryngology, Am. Acad. of Otolaryngology Head and Neck Surgery; mem.: Alpha Omega Alpha. Achievements include microtia surgery, aural atresia surgery, laryngotracheal reconstruction. Office: Children's Hospital of Pittsburgh 3705 5th Ave Pittsburgh PA 15213 Home Phone: 412-692-5902; Office Phone: 412-692-5902. Office Fax: 412-692-6074; Home Fax: 412-692-6974. E-mail: yellra@chp.edu.

YELTON, DIANNE BURGESS, secondary school educator; b. Albuquerque, Nov. 23, 1954; d. Robert Allen and Elizabeth (Donnelly) B.; m. Steven John Yelton, Aug. 13, 1988. BS in Edn., Miami U., 1977, MEd, 1983; degree in Tchr. Leadership, No. Ky. U., 2003. Tchr. Defiance (Ohio) City Schs., 1977-78; jr. high devel. handicapped tchr. Princeton City Schs., Cin., 1978-79, Oak Hills Local Schs., Cin., 1979-82, tchr. primary developmentally handicapped, 1982-88; tchr. Ft. Thomas (Ky.) Ind. Schs., 1988—. Supr. student tchrs. various sch. dists., 1980—; spkr. convs. and inservice workshops, 1979—. Recipient Outstanding Woman of No. Ky., 1998, Golden Apple Achiever award Ashland Oil, 1998, Ky. Post Golden Apple award, 1997, Tchg. Excellence award Jiffy Lube, 1997. Mem. NEA, Internat. Reading Assn., Nat. Coun. Tchrs. English, PTA, Ky. Col. (hon.). Methodist. Avocations: aerobics, spectator sports, dining out. Office: Highlands Mid Sch 2350 Memorial Pkwy Fort Thomas KY 41075-1111 Office Phone: 859-441-5222 15303. E-mail: dbyelton@yahoo.com.

YEN, ANDREW W., internal medicine physician; s. Ching S. and Lisa C. Yen. BS magna cum laude in Biol. Engring., Cornell U., Ithaca, NY, 1996—2000; MD, Loyola U., Chgo., 2000—04. Lic. Calif. Internal medicine physician U. Calif. Davis Med. Ctr., Sacramento, 2004—05, resident, 2005—07, tchr. physician tng. pathway, 2006—. Contbr. articles to profl. jours. Mem.: AMA, ACP, Am. Soc. Gastrointestinal Endoscopy, Am. Gastroent. Assn., Am. Coll. Gastroenterology, Chgo. Med. Soc., Moving Mountains, Alpha Epsilon, Tau Beta Pi. Office: Univ Calif Davis Med Ctr 4150 V St #3116 Sacramento CA 95817 Office Fax: 916-734-1150.

YEN, DAVID WEI-LUEN, information technology executive; b. Changhwa, Republic of China, Sept. 24, 1951; came to US, 1975. s. Te-Maw and Shoon-hwa (Luh) Y.; m. Grace Shau-Ling Jen, Jan. 9, 1977; children: Irene, Christine. BSEE, Nat. Taiwan U., Taipei, 1973; MS in Elec. and Computer Engring., U. Ill., Urbana-Champaign, 1977, PhD in Elec. and Computer Engring., 1980. Sr. mem. tech. staff TRW, Inc., Sunnyvale, Calif., 1980-82; mfg. automation position IBM Rsch., San Jose, Calif., 1982-84; co-founder, dir. hardware devel. Cydrome, Inc., Milpitas, Calif., 1984—88; with Sun Microsystems, Inc., Santa Clara, Calif., 1988—, v.p., gen. mgr. enterprise systems, integrated products, enterprise server products and enterprise server engring., exec. v.p. processor and network products, exec. v.p. scalable systems, head storage group, exec. v.p. microelectronics. Mem. IEEE (sec. computer standards com. 1983-84), Eta Kappa Nu, Phi Kappa Phi. Achievements include patents in field. Office: Sun Microsystems Inc 4150 Network Cir Santa Clara CA 95054 Office Phone: 650-960-1300. *

YEN, HENRY CHIN-YUAN, computer systems programmer, software engineer, consulting company executive; b. Mpls., Apr. 18, 1958; s. James and Elizabeth Y.; m. Michele Calen, Oct. 8, 1988; children: Andrew, Matthew. Sr. systems programmer Grumman Data Systems Corp., Bethpage, N.Y., 1978-83; mgr. Data Ctr. On-Line Software Internat., Inc., Ft. Lee, N.J., 1983-85, lead systems programmer, 1985-88; v.p. The Galamery Co., Inc., Del., 1988—, Aegis Info. Systems, Inc., Del., 1989—. Bd. dirs. Personal Computer Systems Corp. Bd. trustees Syosset Pub. Libr., NY, 2001—05. Mem. IEEE, Assn. Computing Machinery, Network and Sys. Profls. Assn., Mensa (bd. dirs. greater N.Y. chpt. 2002-), Intertel. Avocations: bicycling, profl. musician. Home: PO Box 1 Hicksville NY 11802-0001 Office: Aegis Info Systems Inc PO Box 730 Hicksville NY 11802-0730 Office Phone: 516-937-3700. Business E-Mail: henry@AegisInfoSys.com.

YEN, TEH FU, civil and environmental engineering educator; b. Kun-Ming, China, Jan. 9, 1927; came to U.S., 1949; s. Kwang Pu and Ren (Liu) Y.; m. Shiao-Ping Siao, May 30, 1959 BS, Cen. China U., 1947; MS, W.Va. U., 1953; PhD, Va. Poly. Inst. and State U., 1956; PhD (hon.), Pepperdine U., 1982, Internat. U. Dubna, Russia, 1996, All Russian Petroleum Exploration Inst., St. Petersburg, Russia, 1999. Sr. research chemist Good Yr. Tire & Rubber Co., Akron, 1955-59; fellow Mellon Inst., Pitts., 1959-65; sr. fellow Carnegie-Mellon U., Pitts., 1965-68; assoc. prof. Calif. State U., Los Angeles, 1968-69, U. So. Calif., 1969-80, prof. civil engring. and environ. engring., 1980—. Hon. prof. Shanghai U. Sci. and Tech., 1986, U. Petroleum, Beijing, 1987, Daqing Petroleum Inst., 1992; cons. Universal Oil Products, 1968-76, Chevron Oil Field Rsch. Co., 1968-75, Finnigan Corp., 1976-77, GE, 1977-80, United Techs., 1978-79, TRW Inc., 1982-83, Exxon, 1981-82, DuPont, 1985-88, Min. Petroleum, Beijing, 1982—, Biogas Rsch. Inst.-UN, Chengdu, 1991. Author: numerous tech. books; contbr. articles articles to profl. jours. Recipient Disting. Svc. award Tau Beta Pi, 1974, Imperial Crown Gold medal, Iran, 1976, Achievement award Chinese Engring. and Sci. Assocs. So. Calif., 1977, award Phi Kappa Phi, 1982, Outstanding Contbn. honor Pi Epsilon Tau, 1984, Svc. award Republic of Honduras, 1989, award in Petroleum Chem. Am. Chem. Soc., 1994, Kapitsa Gold medal Russian Fedn., 1995. Fellow Chem. Soc., Inst. Petroleum, Am. Inst. Chemists; mem. Am. Chem. Soc. (bd. dirs. 1993, councillor, founder and chmn. geochemistry divsn. 1979-81, Chinese Acad. Scis. (standing com.), Acad. Scis. Russian Fedn. (academician, fgn. mem.). Office: U So Calif KAP 224A Viterby Sch Engring 3620 S Vermont Ave Los Angeles CA 90089-2531 Office Phone: 213-740-0586. Business E-Mail: tfyen@usc.edu.

YEN, WEN-HSIUNG, language and music professional, educator; b. Tainan, Taiwan, June 26, 1934; came to U.S., 1969; m. Yuan-yuan Yen, Jan. 6, 1961; children: Tin-ju, Tin-jen, Tin-Tao. BA, Nat. Taiwan Normal U., 1960; MA, UCLA, 1971; PhD in Music, World U., 1988; Candidate Philosophy in Ethnomusicology, UCLA, 1995; cultural doctorate philosophy of music, The World Univ., 1988. Instr. Nat. Taichung Tchr. Coll., 1961-62; prof. Chinese Culture U., Taipei, 1964-69; lectr. West L.A. C.C., 1978-82; founder Chinese Culture Sch. L.A., 1976—. Grad. tchg. asst. U. Md., 1982-83; instr. L.A. City Coll., 1983—, Calif. State U. L.A., 1984—, Pasadena City Coll., 1989—; prof. Chinese Santa Monica (Calif.) Coll., 1986—, Calif. State U. Northridge, 1986—; founder Wen Yen Piano Studio, 1972—; founder, dir. Chinese Mus. Orch. So. Calif., 1974—; founder, pres. Chinese- Amer. Musicians Assn. of So. Calif., 1990—; co-chair Conf. Students of Chinese Lang. and Culture; Chinese lang. instrn. course designer, instr. All Seasons Children's Learning Ctr., 2001—; music dir. Soc. Confucian Studies Am., 2004—; dir. bd. Chinese Studies Ctr., Calif. State U., LA. Musician: musical compositions include Collection of Works by Mr. Yen, 1969, (recordings) Art Songs and Chinese Folk Songs, 1982, Ode To My Home Land, 1992, Mother Earth-Found-Season: Spring, Summer, Autumn and Winter, 1997, Song of 911; author: Taiwan Folk Songs, 1967, vol. 2, 1969, A Collection of Wen-hsiung Yen's Songs, 1968, vol. 2, 1987, vol. 3, 2000 (award Fedn. Overseas Assns., 2000, 2002); translator: Achievement and Methodology for Comparative Musicology, 1968, Chinese Musical Culture and Folk Songs, 1989, Silk and Bamboo Expresses Emotion and Meaning, 2000, Ethnomusicology Series, 2002; composer: 100 songs and instrumental music; exhibitor traditional Chinese musical instruments and publs., Chinese Culture Ctr., 1995, 1996, Arcadia Pub. Libr., 1999; musician: East and West Music Concert, 2004, Concert for Traditional Music and New Performing Arts, 2006; organizer concerts, contbr. articles to profl. jours. Bd. dirs. So. Calif. Coun. Chinese Sch., 1998—; bd. dirs. Chinese Studies Ctr., Calif. State U., L.A., 1990—; conductor Chinese Music Orch. So. Calif., 1974-; prodr. Chinese Art and Culture Festival, 1990-2003; sustaining mem. Rep. Nat. Com., 2002; advisor Lu Mei Tong Xin Hui Taiwanese Am. Assn., 2003—. Recipient 30 Yrs. Outstanding Tchr. award, Overseas Chinese Affairs Commn., Taiwan, 2006. Mem.: Chinese Writers Assn. So. Calif. (v.p. 2000), Fedn. Overseas Chinese Assns. (bd. dirs. (hon.) 2002), So. Calif. Coun. Chinese Schs. (v.p. 2000—, chmn. exec. com.), Chinese Am. PTA So. Calif. (supr. 1985—), Taiwan Benevloent Assn. Calif. (v.p. 1986, pres. 1987—89, bd. dirs.), Taiwan Benevolent Assn. Am. (bd. dirs.), Alumni Assn. Chinese Culture U. So. Calif., Soc. Asian Music (founder, pres.), Internat. Coun. Traditional Music, Coll. Music Soc., Soc. Ethnomusicology, Chinese Performing Arts Assn. of Am. (bd. dirs.), Chinese Choral Soc. So. Calif. (music dir.), Chinese-Am. Musicians Assn. So Calif. (pres.). Avocations: walking, ping pong/table tennis, tai chi chuan. Office: Chinese Culture Sch 615 Las Tunas Dr Ste B Arcadia CA 91007-8469 Office Phone: 626-447-3823. Personal E-mail: wenhyen2000@yahoo.com.

YENKIN, BERNARD KALMAN, coatings and resins company executive; b. Columbus, Ohio, Dec. 2, 1930; s. Abe I. and Eleanore G. Yenkin; m. Miriam Schottenstein, Mar. 31, 1957; children: Leslie Mara, Jonathan, Allison Katsev, Amy. BA, Yale U., 1952; MBA, Harvard U., 1954. V.p. Yenkin-Majestic Paint Corp., Columbus, 1968-77, pres., 1977-85, chmn. bd., 1985—. Pres. Columbus Jewish Fedn., 1980-82, Pro Musica Chamber Orch., Columbus, 1983-85, Columbus Torah Acad., 1977-79; bd. v.p. Jewish Ednl. Svc. N.Am., N.Y.C., 1991-95. Recipient Mayor's award for Vol. Svc. City of Columbus, 1984, Young Leadership award Columbus Jewish Fedn., 1965. Mem. Yale Club of Cen. Ohio (pres. 1979-81), Yale Club of N.Y., Athletic Club (Columbus). Office: Yenkin-Majestic Industries 1920 Leonard Ave Columbus OH 43219-2514

YEO, KIM ENG, artist; b. Singapore, Apr. 24, 1947; arrived in US, 1978, permanent resident, 2002; d. Cheng Chye and Seok Kim (Chew) Lee; m. Bock Cheng Yeo; children: Beng Lin, Beng Jene. Student, Nanyang Acad. Fine Arts, Singapore, 1963; BSc with honors, U. Singapore, 1968. Watercolor demonstrator Flushing Art League, NYC, 1980-84; art instr. Poppenhusen Inst., NYC, 1984; substitute art tchr. UN Internat. Sch., NYC, 1984-85; freelance paper product designer, 1981-87; textile designer J. Brown Designs, NYC, 1987-91; tchg. artist Flushing (N.Y.) Town Hall, 1995—2002; artist-in-residence Pub. Sch. 214, 165, Francis Lewis H.S., Flushing, 1997-2001. Visual arts panelist, Flushing Coun., 1985-87, Queen's Coun., 1998-99, 2001-04; watercolor workshop demonstrator Singapore Art Mus., 2000. One person shows at Alliance Francais, 1975-77, Bhirasri Inst. Modern Art, Bangkok, Thailand, 1975-77, Flushing Coun. on Arts, 1995, 2000, Adirondack Lakes Ctr. for the Arts, NY, 2005, Synagogue For Arts Gallery, NY, 2006; exhibitions include Mallette Gallery, LI, NY, 1998, 99, Artfolio Gallery, Singapore, 2000, Langston Hughes Cmty. Libr. and Cultural Ctr., NY, 2004; exhibited in group shows at Womanart Gallery, NYC, 1979-80, Nat. Art League, Douglastown, NY, 1979-86, Flushing Coun. on Arts, 1984-88, 96-2004, Postcrypt Art Gallery, NYC, 1997, Singapore Watercolor Soc., 1997-99, 2001-03, Queens Coun. on Arts, NY, 2002-05; represented in corp. and pvt. collections; artist greeting cards UNICEF, 1997-98; featured on QPATV Artists Series, 1993, QPTV Queens Jour., 2000; featured in Watercolor Mag., 1997, Internat. Artist Mag., 2004. Benefit show UN Devel. Fund for Women Singapore, 1999. Mem. Flushing Art League (bd. dirs., treas. 1979-85, award 1986), Flushing Coun. on Arts, Queens Coun. on Arts. Buddhist. Avocations: gardening, bookmaking. Home: 16202 77th Ave Flushing NY 11366-1022 Business E-Mail: artist@kimengyeo.com.

YEO, MARK ANDREWS, diversified financial services company executive; b. Lewistown, Pa., July 17, 1969; s. Herbert Presley and Cheryl Louise Yeo; m. Kathleen Marie Gordon. BS in Acctg., Pa. State U., State College, 1992. Stock broker F.N. Wolf, Inc., Alexandra, Va., 1992; sr. project analyst, trust officer NationBank Trust Co., NA, Silver Spring, Md., 1992—95; trust operation mgr. F&M Nat. Bank, Frederick, Md., 1995—96; dir. equity clearing BNP Paribas Securities Corp., King of Prussia, Pa., 1996—. With USMC, 1987—93, Desert Shield, Desert Storm. Mem.: Options Clearing Corp. Operational Round Table. Home: 321 Winding Way King Of Prussia PA 19406 Office: BNP Paribas Securities Corp 555 Croton Road 4th Fl King Of Prussia PA 19406 Home Phone: 610-212-9228; Office Phone: 610-491-1400. Office Fax: 610-491-1838. Personal E-mail: andyyeo@comcast.net. Business E-Mail: andy.yeo@americas.bnpparibas.com.

YEO, PATRICIA, chef; Degree in Biochemistry, Princeton U. Line cook Miracle Grill, NYC; sous chef Mesa Grill, NYC, 1991, Bolo, NYC, 1993—95; chef China Moon; opened Hawthorne Lane, Calif.; owner, exec. chef AZ, NYC, 2000—, Pazo, NYC, Sapa, NYC. Author: Cooking from A to Z with Patricia Yeo, 2002. Office: Sapa 43 W 24th St New York NY 10010 Office Phone: 212-929-1800. Office Fax: 212-929-7070.

YEO, RON, architect; b. LA, June 17, 1933; s. Clayton Erik and Rose G. (Westman) Y.; m. Birgitta S. Bergkvist, Sept. 29, 1962; children: Erik Elov, Katarina Kristina. B.Arch., U. So. Calif., 1959. Draftsman Montierth & Strickland (Architects), Long Beach, Calif., 1958-61; designer Gosta Edberg S.A.R. Arkitekt, Stockholm, 1962; partner Strickland & Yeo, Architects, Garden Grove, Calif., 1962-63, pres. Ron Yeo, Architect, Inc., Corona del Mar, Calif., 1963—. Cons., lectr. in field. Archtl. works include Garden Grove Civic and Cmty. Ctr., 1966, Hall Sculpture Studio, 1966, Garden Grove Cultural Ctr., 1978, Gem Theater, 1979, Festival Amphitheatre, 1983, Los Coyotes Paleontol. Interpretive Ctr., 1986, Calif. State U. Fullerton Alumni House, 1997, O'Neill Regional Pk. Nature Ctr., 1998, Upper Newport Bay Interpretive Ctr., 2000, Stough Canyon Nature Ctr., 2000, Quon residence, 2005. Mem. Orange County Planning Commn., 1972-73, 1975-76; chmn. Housing and Community Devel. Task Force, 1978, Orange County Fire Protection Planning Task Force, City of Newport Beach City Arts Commn., 1970-72; pres. Orange County Arts Alliance, 1980-81; gen. plan advisory com. Newport Beach, 2002-06. Fellow AIA; mem. Green Bldg. Coun., Internat. Conf. Bldg. Ofcls., Nat. Assn. for Interpretation (founding), Constrn. Specification Inst. Democrat. Office: Ron Yeo FAIA Architect Inc 500 Jasmine Ave Corona Del Mar CA 92625-2308

YEOMAN, LYNN CHALMERS, medical educator; b. Evanston, Ill., May 17, 1943; m. Carol J. Yeoman; children: Caroline, Christopher, Sarah. BA, DePauw U., Greencastle, 1965; PhD, U. Ill., Urbana, 1970. Instr. Baylor Coll. Medicine, Houston, 1972-73, asst. prof., 1973-76, assoc. prof., 1976-84, prof., 1984—; assoc. dir. Bristol-Baylor Lab, Houston, 1989-90; assoc. dir. anti-cancer drug discovery and cell and molecular biology Bristol-Myers Co., Wallingford, Conn., 1989—90; dir. curriculum database program Baylor Coll. Medicine, Houston, 1995—, dir. integrated problem solving program, 1997—, dir. ednl. resource ctr., 2001—, sr. dir. acad. computing, 2004—. Cons. Litton Bionetics, Ft. Detrick, Md., 1977-78, Colon Cancer Working Group, Houston, 1985-86, Oncos, Ltd., Houston, 1985-87, Bristol-Myers Co., Wallingford, Conn., 1985-89, Ubiquitex Techs. Corp., 1995-96, U. Tex. Med. Br., Galveston, 1998, ProteEx, Inc., 2001-03, Feedback Techs., Inc., 2004-; mem. com. revision U.S. Pharmacopeial Conv., 1985-90, 1995—, chmn. expert com. on biols. and biotech.: proteins and polysaccharides, 2000—, com. of experts exec. com., 2004—, chmn. content devel. task force, CATCHUM Project, Galveston, 2004—. Editor: Methods in Cancer Research, Vols. 19 and 20, 1982; mem. editl. bd. Frontiers in Biosci., Med. Edn. Online; contbr. articles to profl. jours. V.p. Marilyn Estates Assn., Houston, 2004-2005, chapel organist, St. Luke's United Meth. Ch., Houston, 1996-. NCI grantee, 1987-2003. Mem. Am. Chem. Soc., Am. Soc. Biochem. and Molecular Biology, Group on Ednl. Affairs. Methodist. Achievements include patent for detection of antigen gp650 in sera and other specimens from cancer patients with anti-gp650 monoclonal antibody. Home: 5434 Rutherglenn Dr Houston TX 77096-4032 Office: 1 Baylor Plz Houston TX 77030-3411 Office Phone: 713-798-7336. Business E-Mail: lyeoman@bcm.edu.

YEOMANS, DONALD KEITH, astronomer; b. Rochester, NY, May 3, 1942; s. George E. and Jessie Y.; m. Laurie Robyn Ernst, June 20, 1970; children: Sarah, Keith. BA, Middlebury Coll., Vt., 1964; MS, U. Md., 1967, PhD, 1970. Supr. Computer Scis. Corp., Silver Spring, Md., 1973-76; sr. rsch. astronomer Jet Propulsion Lab., Pasadena, Calif., 1976-92, supr., 1992—. Discipline specialist Internat. Halley Watch, 1982-89; sci. investigator NASA Comet Mission, 1987-91, Near-Earth Asteroid Rendezvous Mission, 1994-2001, Multi-Comet Flyby Mission, 1997-2002, Comet Impact Mission, 1999-2006; project scientist for asteroid sample return mission, 1998—; mgr. NASA Near-Earth Object Program Office, 1998-. Author: Comet Halley: Once in a Lifetime, 1985, The Distant Planets, 1989, Comets: A Chronological History of Observation, Science, Myth, and Folklore, 1991. Recipient Space Achievement award AIAA, 1985, Exceptional Svc. medal NASA, 1986, Achievement award Middlebury Coll. Alumni, 1987; named NASA/JPL Sr. Rsch. Scientist, 1993. Mem.: Am. Astron. Soc. (chair divsn. planetary scis. 1999—2000, chair hist. astronomy divsn. 2005—06). Democrat. Presbyterian. Avocations: tennis, history of astronomy. Office: Jet Propulsion Lab #301-150 4800 Oak Grove Dr Pasadena CA 91109-8001 Office Phone: 818-354-2127. Business E-Mail: donald.k.yeomans@jpl.nasa.gov.

YEOMANS, DONALD RALPH, Canadian government official, consultant; b. Toronto, Ont., Can., Mar. 25, 1925; s. Ralph and Louise (Weismiller) Y.; m. Catherine Simpson Williams, May 13, 1950; children: Patricia Ann, Nancy Louise, Jane Elizabeth. BASc, U. Toronto, 1947. Registered profl. engr., Ont., cert. mgmt. acct. Mem. Bur. of Govt. Orgns., Ottawa, Ont., 1962-64; dep. sec. Treasury Bd., Ottawa, 1964-69; asst. dep. minister Dept. Supply and Services, Ottawa, 1969-75; assoc. exec. dir. Anti-Inflation Bd., Ottawa, 1975-76; asst. dep. minister Dept. Nat. Health-Welfare, Ottawa, 1976-77; commr. Correctional Services of Can., Ottawa, 1977-85; chmn. Tariff Bd., 1985-89; spl. advisor Can. Jud. Centre, 1989-92; mem. bd. govs. Carleton U., 1980-93, chmn., 1989-91. Spl. advisor Royal Com. Govt. Orgns., 1961, Royal Com. Fin. Accountability, 1977; assoc. Cons. and Audit Can., 1992-97; exec. counsellor Pub. Svc. Commn., 1990-95; cons. to govt. and industry, 1990-97, bd. dirs. Corrections Corp. Can.; mem. bd. govs. Can. Comprehensive Audit Found., 1989-94; mem. ind. adv. com. Auditor Gen. Can., 1989-95; chmn. Coun. Adminstrv. Tribunals, 1986; chmn. Coun. Chairs Ont. Univs., 1991-93; mem. Expert Com. on AIDS in Prisons, 1992-94; chmn. awards com. Am. Correctional Assn., 1992-97; bd. dirs. Corrections Corp. Can., Baker Group Internat., Inc. Recipient Centennial medal Govt. Can., 1967, Jubilee medal Govt. Can., 1977, E.R. Cass award Am. Corr. Assn., 1991, Corr. Svc. of Can. Exemplary Svc. medal, 2000, Founder's award Carleton U., 2000; Australian Commonwealth fellow, 1985. Fellow: Soc. Mgmt. Accts. Can. (pres. 1977); mem.: Fed. Superannuates Nat. Assn. (pres. Ottawa br. 1998—2000, bd. dirs., nat. regional dir. 2002—), Inst. Pub. Adminstrn. Can. (pres. 1974), Assn. State Correctional Adminstrs. (pres. 1983, Spl. Founders award 2006), Ottawa Heart Inst. Alumni Assn. (v.p.), Five Lakes (pres. 1975); Canadian (Ottawa, pres. 1978), Canadian Club (Ottawa, pres. 1978), Five Lakes Club (pres. 1975). Home and Office: 205-211 Second Ave Ottawa ON Canada K1S 2H8 Office Phone: 613-232-5022. Fax: 613-231-4557. E-mail: kdyeom@cyberus.ca.

YEOSOCK, MICHAEL MICHAEL, funeral director, civil engineer; b. Wilkes-Barre, Pa., July 28, 1962; s. Michael J. and Patricia A. (Sauerwein) Y.; m. Mary Jacqueline Clemente; children: Adriana Grace, Christopher Michael. Student, Pa. State U., 1980-82; BS, W.Va. U., 1984; diploma in mortuary sci., New Eng. Inst., 1985; MS in Environ. Engring., U. New Haven, 1993. Cert. engr.-in-tng.; lic. profl. engr., Pa., Conn., NY. Project mgr. M.J. Pasonick, Jr., Inc., Wilkes-Barre, 1986-89; asst. civil engr. in tng. City of Norwalk (Conn.) Dept. of Pub. Works, 1989—, sr. engr., 1994—; supr. Jan Fabian Funeral Chapel, Hanover, Pa., 1990-91. Bd. dirs. Norwalk (Conn.) Tree Alliance. Mem. IEEE, AIME, ASCE, AAAS, Soc. Mining Engrs., Can. Mining and Metallurgy, NY Acad. Scis., Am. Rock Mechanics Assn., Internat. Soc. Rock Mechanics, Geospatial Info. and Tech. Assn., Inst. Traffic Engrs., Internat. Mcpl. Signal Assn. Republican. Russian Orthodox. Avocations: flying, white-water rafting. Home: 5 Country Club Dr White Plains NY 10607 Office: City of Norwalk 125 East Ave Norwalk CT 06851-5702 Home Phone: 914-345-7157; Office Phone: 203-854-7791. Personal E-mail: mmyeosock@optonline.net.

YEP, LAURENCE MICHAEL, author; b. San Francisco, June 14, 1948; s. Thomas Kim and Franche (Lee) Yep; m. Joanne Ryder, 1984. BA, U. Calif., Santa Cruz, 1970; PhD, SUNY, Buffalo, 1975. Tchr. San Jose (Calif.) City Coll., part-time 1975-76, Foothill Coll., Mountain View, Calif., 1975, U. Calif., Berkeley, 1987-89, writer in residence Santa Barbara, 1990. Book-of-the-Month writing fellow, 1970; teaching fellow SUNY, Buffalo, 1970-73, research fellow, 1973-74 Author sci. fiction stories, children's stories, 1968—: Sweetwater, 1973, reissue, 2004, Dragonwings (Newbery Honor Book award ALA 1976, Children's Book award Internat. Reading Assn. 1976), (Carter G. Woodson award Nat. Coun. Social Studies 1976), 1975, Child of the Owl, 1977, Seademons, 1977, Sea Glass, (Commonwealth Club lit. award 1979), 1979, Kind Hearts and Gentle Monsters, 1982, The Mark Twain Murders, 1982, Dragon of the Lost Sea, 1982, Liar, Liar, 1983, Tom Sawyer Fires, 1984, Dragon Steel, 1985, Mountain Light, 1985, Shadow Lord, 1985, Monster Makers, Inc., 1986, Curse of the Squirrel, 1987, The Rainbow People, 1989; author one-act plays Pay the Chinaman, 1987, FairyBones, 1987, Dragon Cauldron, 1991, The Lost Garden, 1991, The Star Fisher, 1991 (Christopher award 1992, W.Va. Literary award 1995), Tongues of Jade, 1991, Lion Dance, 1998, Cook's Family, 1998, The Imp Ate My Homework, 1998, Firecrackers, 1999, Amah, 1999, Cockroach Cooties, 2000,Dream Soul, 2000, Diary of Wong Ming Chin, 2000, The Magic Paintbrush, 2000, Angel Fish, 2000, The Diary of the Lady of Chiao Kuo, 2002, The Tiger's Apprentice, 2003, Tiger's Blood, 2005; theatrical adaption of Dragonwings, 1991, Dragon War, 1992, American Dragons, 1992, also editor, Butterfly Boy, 1993, Dragon's Gate, (Newbery Honor Book award ALA 1994), 1993, The Ghost Fox, 1993, The Man Who Tricked a Ghost, 1993 (Am. Book award 1995), The Shell Woman and the King, 1993, The Boy Who Swallowed Snakes, 1994, The Junior Thunder Lord, 1994, The Tiger Woman, 1994, Thief of Hearts, 1995, Ribbons, 1996, Goblin Pearls, 1996, The Khan's Daughter, 1996, The Traitor: Golden Mountain Chronicles: 1885, 2003. Literature fellow Nat. Endowment for Arts, 1990; recipient, Laura Ingalls Wilder award for contribution to children's literature, 2005. Mailing: 244 Crocker Ave Pacific Grove CA 93950

YERG, BEVERLY JOHNSON, retired physical education educator, researcher; b. Warren, Pa., Nov. 11, 1938; d. C. Walter and Emma Josephine Erickson Johnson; m. Robert Robison Yerg, June 24, 1961; 1 child, David Robert. BS, Temple U., 1960, EdM, 1973; PhD, U. Pitts., 1977. Tchr., coach Manheim Ctrl. Schs., Pa., 1961—64; tchr. Lancaster City Schs., 1960—61; substitute and homebound tchr. Warren Area Schs., 1964—73; lectr. LaRoche Coll., 1973—74; tchg. fellow U. Pitts., 1974—77; asst. prof. Fla. State U., Tallahassee, 1977—82, assoc. prof., 1982—2001, dept. head, 1982—85, dir. acad. support programs student athletes, 1986—93, chair pres.'s com. intercollegiate athletics; ret., 2001. Editl. bd., reviewer Jour. Tchg. Physical Edn., Nat. Assn. Athletic Acad. Advisors Jour., reviewer Rsch. Quar. Exercise and Sport, Merrill Pub. Co., Mosby Book Co.; contbr. chapters to books, articles to profl. jours. Bd. dirs. Neighborhood Health Clinic, Tallahassee, 1986—88; bd. mem. North Fla. Fellow Christian Athletes, 1987—90; chair Fla. Cabinet for Campus Ministry, Presbyn. Ch. USA, Fla., 1996—; treas., interim bd. of dirs. Presbyn. Assn. for Collegiate and Higher Edn. Ministries, 2004—06, treas., bd. dirs., 2006—; leadership team Higher Edn. Ministries Presbyn. Ch. USA, Louisville, 2001—; mem., pres., com. chair Presbyn. U. Ctr., 1984—2000; elder Fellowship Presbyn. Ch., 1987—90, Christ Presbyn. Ch, 1994—97; permanent jud. commn. Fla. Presbyn., Panama City, Fla., 2002—05, com. on preparation for ministry, 1991—97; bd. mem. YWCA, Warren, Pa., 1965—67. Named honoree, Assn. Internat. des Ecoles Supérieures d'Edn. Physique; recipient Peter W. Everett Honor award, Fla. Assn. for Health, Phys. Edn., Recreation, and Dance, 2002; Rsch. Consortium fellow, Am. Alliance for Health, Phys. Edn., Recreation, and Dance, 1986—. Mem.: Am. Ednl. Rsch. Assn., Fla. Assn. for Health, Phys. Edn., Recreation, and Dance, Am. Alliance for Health, Phys. Edn., Recreation, and Dance (life), Delta Psi Kappa (life; pres. 1984—86, bd. dir.). Presbyterian. Avocations: reading, handwork, gardening, woodworking. Home: 4121 Tralee Rd Tallahassee FL 32309-2822 Personal E-mail: yerg@coe.fsu.edu.

YERGIN, DANIEL HOWARD, writer, consultant; b. LA, Feb. 6, 1947; s. Irving H. and Naomi Y.; m. Angela Stent, Aug. 10, 1975; children: Alexander George, Rebecca Isabella. BA, Yale U., Eng., 1968; MA with first class honors, Cambridge U., Eng., 1970, PhD, 1974; PhD (hon.), U. Mo., 1980, U. Houston, 1994. Contbg. editor New York mag., 1968-70; research fellow Harvard U., Cambridge, Mass., 1974-76, lectr. bus. sch., 1976-79, lectr. Kennedy Sch. Govt., 1979-83, research assoc. Cambridge, 1983-90; chmn. Cambridge Energy Research Assoc., Cambridge, 1982-98, also chmn., sec. energy task force on strategic energy R&D, 1998—. Mem. policy adv. com. Program on U.S.-Japan Rels., Harvard U.; mem. bd. energy experts Dallas Morning News; mem. internat. panel advisors Asia-Pacific Petroleum Conf.; fellow World Econ. Forum, Davos. Author: Shattered Peace: The Origins of the Cold War and the National Security State, 1977, rev. edit., 1990, The Prize: Epic Quest for Oil, Money and Power, 1991 (Pulitzer Prize for non-fiction 1992, Eccle prize 1992); co-author: Cold War, 1977, Energy Future, 1979, Global Insecurity, 1982, Future of Oil Prices: Perils of Prophecy, 1984, Russia 2010: And What It Means for the World, 1993, the Commanding Heights, 1998; contbg. editor Atlantic Monthly, 1977-83. Mem. adv. bd. Solar Energy Rsch. Inst., Golden, Colo., 1979-81; sec. Energy Adv. Bd. Fellow Univ. Consortium for World Order Studies, 1974-75, Rockefeller Found., 1975-79, German Marshall Fund, 1980-81, Harvard U., Ctr. for Bus. and Govt., 1997—; Marshall scholar Cambridge U., 1974; recipient U.S. Energy award, 1997. Mem. PEN, Coun. on Fgn. Rels. (com. on studies), Nat. Petroleum Coun., Internat. Assn. for Energy Econs., Am. Hist. Assn., Am. Polit. Assn., Royal Inst. Internat. Affairs, Assn. Marshall Scholars (bd. dirs. 1988-91), U.S. Energy Assn. (bd. dirs.), Nat. Petroleum Coun., Yale Club (N.Y.C.), Harvard Club (N.Y.C.). Office: Cambridge Energy Research Assoc 55 Cambridge Pkwy Cambridge MA 02142-1234

YERKES, DAVID NORTON, architect; b. Cambridge, Mass., Nov. 5, 1911; s. Robert Mearns and Ada (Watterson) Y.; m. Catharine Noyes, Oct. 7, 1939 (dec. 1969); 1 dau., Catharine; m. Sarah Hitchcock Satterlee, July 9, 1972. BA, Harvard U., 1933; M.F.A., Yale U., 1935. Draftsman, designer, Chgo. and Washington, 1937-39, Deigert & Yerkes and Assos., Washington, 1945—65, David N. Yerkes & Assos., Washington, 1965—69, Yerkes, Pappas and Parker, 1980-83. Mem. panel archtl. advisers Nat. Commn. Fine Arts, 1961-63, 79-82; vice chmn. Presdl. Inaugural Parade Com., 1965 Prin. works include Voice of America Studios, Washington, 1958, Nat. Arboretum Hdqrs. Bldg. Am. Embassy, Somalia, also Madeira Sch. Auditorium, 1969; 4 stas. Washington subway sys., 1971-81, hdqrs., Nat. Trust Historic Preservation, Washington, 1977, suite, Time, Inc., Washington, 1980, also various schs., labs; paintings exhibited in New Eng. and Washington. Served to capt. AUS, 1943-45. Firm recipient numerous regional and nat. awards; recipient Kemper award AIA, 1972 Fellow AIA (bd. dirs. 1965-68, v.p. 1968-69, chmn. nat. honor awards jury 1966, chmn. Reynolds Meml. award jury 1969, pres. found. 1974-76) Home: 3050 Military Rd NW #449 Washington DC 20015

YERMAN, FREDRIC WARREN, lawyer; b. NYC, Jan. 8, 1943; s. Nat W. and Tina (Barotz) Y.; m. Ann R. Rochlin, May 31, 1965; children: Emily, Deborah. BA, CUNY, 1963; LLB, Columbia U., 1966. Bar: N.Y. 1967. Assoc. Kaye Scholer LLP, NYC, 1966—74, ptnr., 1974—, chmn. exec. com., 1990—92. Bd. dirs. United Way Tri-State, Jewish Bd. Family and Children Svcs., N.Y.C. Fellow Am. Coll. Trial Lawyers. Home: 31 Sheridan Rd Scarsdale NY 10583-1523 Office: Kaye Scholer LLP 425 Park Ave New York NY 10022-3506 Business E-Mail: fyerman@kayescholer.com.

YERRICK, RANDY KREGG, science educator; b. Owosso, Mich., Feb. 19, 1963; s. Rand Lee Yerrick and Sally Vernon; m. Metra Lynn Moghadam, June 6, 1986; children: Taylor James, Jackson David. PhD, Mich. State U., 1993. Tchr. Calif., Mich., NC, 1986. Assoc. prof. East Carolina U., Greenville, NC, 1993—99; prof. San Diego State U., 1999—. Disting. educator Apple, Cupertino, Calif., 1999—. Vol. Poway Unified Sch. Dist., San Diego, 1999—2005, Green Valley Ch., San Diego, 1999—2005. Recipient John Keating Award, Omicron Delta Kappan, 1998—99, Coll. Edn. Outstanding Faculty Award, San Diego State U., 2002—03, U. President's Top 25, 2003—04; NPACI Edn. Supercomputing fellow, Nat. Partnership for Advanced Computational Infrastructure, San Diego Supercomputer Ctr., 2001—02, Tchr. Scholar fellow, Ctr. for Tchg. and Learning, San Diego State U., 2002. Mem.: Nat. Assn. for Rsch. in Sci. Tchg. (life; leadership team 1994—2005). Republican. Protestant. Avocations: computers, tennis. Home Phone: 858-451-2298; Office Phone: 619-594-5090.

YERRID, C. STEVEN, lawyer; b. Charleston, W.Va., Sept. 30, 1949; s. Charles George and Audrey Faye Yerrid. BA in History and Polit. Sci., La. State U., 1971; JD, Georgetown U., 1975. Bar: Fla. 1975, Va. 1975, U.S. Supreme Ct. 1979, D.C. 1984; cert. civil trial advocate Nat. Bd. Trial Advocacy. Aide U.S. Senator Ellender, Washington, 1971-73; ptnr. Holland & Knight, Tampa, Fla., 1975-86; pres. Stagg, Hardy & Yerrid, Tampa, 1986-89, Yerrid, Knopik & Krieger PA, Tampa, 1990-2000, The Yerrid Law Firm, Tampa, 2000—. Mediator and Cir. Ct. arbitrator Fla. and Fed. Cts. Mem. ABA, Va. Bar Assn., D.C. Bar Assn., Fla. Bar Assn. (chmn. admiralty law com. 1984-85, bd. cert. com. 1988-91, vice chmn. 1990-91, chmn. 1994-95, bd. cert. civil trial lawyer), Southeastern Admiralty Law Inst., Am. Judicature Soc., ATLA (sustaining), Am. Bd. Trial Advocates (advocate), Maritime Law Assn. (proctor), Tex. Trial Lawyers Assn., Acad. Fla. Trial Lawyer (designated continuing legal edn. speaker 1982—, bd. dirs. 1989-97, 2000-01), Inner Cir. Advocates, Internat. Soc. Barristers, Am. Inns. of Ct. (supporting fellow), Cousteau Soc., Centre Club, Tampa Club, Univ. Club, Grand Havana Club, Old Memorial Golf Club. Democrat. Avocations: fishing, tennis, boxing. Office: The Yerrid Law Firm Bank of America Plz Ste 3910 101 E Kennedy Blvd Tampa FL 33602-5192 Office Phone: 813-222-8222. E-mail: syerrid@yerridlaw.com.

YERSIZ, HASAN, medical educator; b. Ankara, Turkey, Aug. 30, 1957; s. Hamdi and Mediha Yersiz; m. Sehnaz Alansatan, Mar. 18, 1983; 1 child, Melike. MD, Istanbul U., Turkey, 1981. Asst. prof. UCLA, 1998—2004, assoc. prof., 2004—. Dir. organ procurement UCLA Liver/Pancreas Transplant Ctr., 1995—. Mem. adv. bd. OneLegacy, LA. Scholar, Am. Field Svc., 1974—75. Mem.: Am. Soc. Transplant Surgeons (mem. of membership commitee 2003—). Achievements include development of In-Situ Split Liver Transplantation. Office: UCLA 10833 LeConte Ave Los Angeles CA 90095 Home Phone: 1-310-804-0902; Office Phone: 1-310-825-5318. Office Fax: 1-310-267-0392; Home Fax: 1-310-267-0392. Personal E-mail: hyersiz@ucla.edu.

YERUSHALMI, YOSEF HAYIM, historian, educator; b. NYC, May 20, 1932; s. Leon and Eva (Kaplan) Y.; m. Ophra Pearly, Jan. 4, 1959; 1 child, Ariel. BA, Yeshiva U., 1953; M in Hebrew Lit., Jewish Theol. Sem. Am., 1957; MA, Columbia U., 1961, PhD, 1966; MA (hon.), Harvard, 1970; DHL (hon.), Jewish Theol. Sem. Am., 1987; LHD (hon.), Hebrew Union Coll., 1996; PhD (hon.), U. Haifa, 1997, Ludwig Maximilians U., Munich, 1997; DHL (hon.), Spertus Inst., 2002; PhD (hon.), Ecole Pratique des Hautes Etudes Sorbonne Paris, 2003. Instr. Jewish history Rutgers U., New Brunswick, NJ, 1963-66; asst. prof. Hebrew and Jewish History Harvard U., 1966-70, prof., 1970-78, Jacob E. Safra prof. Jewish history and Sephardic civilization, 1978-80, chmn. dept. near eastern langs. and civilizations, 1978-80, Salo Wittmayer Baron Prof. of Jewish History, Culture, Soc.; dir. Columbia U. Inst. Israel and Jewish Studies, NYC, 1980—. Author: From Spanish Court to Italian Ghetto: Isaac Cardoso, A Study in Seventeenth-Century Marranism and Jewish Apologetics, 1971, Haggadah and History, 1975, The Lisbon Massacre of 1506, 1976, Zakhor: Jewish History and Jewish Memory, 1982, Freud's Moses: Judaism Terminable and Interminable, 1991, A Field in Anatot: Essays on Jewish History (in German), 1993, Servants of Kings and Not Servants of Servants: Some Aspects of the Political History of the Jews (in German), 1995, Sefardica: Essays on the History of the Jews, Marranos and New Christians of Hispano-Portuguese Origin (in French), 1998; author (in Hebrew): Spinoza on the Survival of the Jews, 1983; contbr. articles to profl. publs. on Spanish and Portuguese Jewry and history of psychoanalysis; chmn. publs. com. Jewish Publ. Soc., 1972-84; pres. Leo Baeck Inst., 1986-91. Bd. dirs. Conf. Jewish Social Studies, Psycho analytic Research and Devel. Fund, Editorial Bd., History and Memory. Recipient Newman medal CUNY, 1975, Nat. Jewish Book award, 1983, 92, Ansley award Columbia U. Press, 1968, Achievement medal Nat. Found. Jewish Culture, 1995, Leopold Lucas prize U. Tübingen, Germany, 2005; Kent fellow, 1963, Nat. Found. Jewish Culture, 1964, NEH, 1976-77, Rockefeller Found., 1983-84, Guggenheim Found., 1989-90, Carl Friedrich von Siemens Stiftung fellow, 1996-97, fellow Inst. Advanced Studies Tel Aviv U., 2004. Fellow Am. Acad. Jewish Research, Am. Acad. Arts and Scis., Acad. Portuguesa da História Lisbon (hon.), Acad. Sci. Lisboa (hon.). Office: Columbia U 511 Fayerweather Hall 1180 Amsterdam Ave New York NY 10027-7039

YERVES, KEN, information technology executive; B, Dowling Coll., NY; MBA, Jacksonville Univ., Fla. With Todd Travel Promotions, Micro Cons. Co. Inc.; asst. v.p., remarketing applications devel. JM Family Enterprises, Deerfield Beach, Fla., asst. v.p., tech. arch., planning and control, v.p. tech. delivery, 2001, sr. v.p. & chief info. officer. Office: SVP & CIO JM Family Enterp 100 Jim Moran Blvd Deerfield Beach FL 33442

YERXA, RON, film producer; Grad., Stanford U., Calif. Journalist, HS tchr., East LA; story analyst Time-Life Films; exec. CBS, Sovereign Films; co-founder Bona Fide Prodns., 1993—. Exec. prodr.: (films) Jack the Bear, 1993, I Am Trying to Break Your Heart, 2002; (TV films) The Spree, 1998; prodr.: (films) King of the Hill, 1993, Election, 1999, The Wood, 1999, Pumpkin, 2002, Cold Mountain, 2003, The Ice Harvest, 2005, Bee Season, 2005, Little Miss Sunshine, 2006, Little Children, 2006. Office: Bona Fide Prodns Ste 804 8899 Beverly Blvd Los Angeles CA 90048 *

YESAWICH, PETER CHARLES, advertising executive; b. Ithaca, NY, Oct. 28, 1950; s. Paul Joseph Jr. and Elizabeth (Larkin) Y.; m. Paris Pyne; children: Peter Charles, Paul Christopher, Logan Baker. BS, Cornell U., 1972, MS, 1974, PhD, 1976; AMP, Yale U., 1994. Dir. rsch. Robinsons, Inc., Orlando, Fla., 1976-78, v.p., 1978-81, exec. v.p., 1981-83; pres., CEO Ypartnership, Orlando, 1983—. Vis. assoc. prof. Cornell U., Ithaca, 1977—, U. Ctrl. Fla., Orlando, 1988—; chmn. Pope Tourism Inst., Orlando, 1988-90. Co-author: Marketing, Leadership in Hospitality, 2006; contbr. articles to profl. jours. Recipient World Travel award Am. Assn. Travel Editors, 1985, Silver Medal award Am. Assn. Advt. Agys., 1992, Adrian award Hospitality Sales and Mktg. Assn. Internat., 1993; named Author of Yr. Cornell Quar., 1986. Mem. Cornell Hotel Soc., Am. Hotel & Motel Assn., Caribbean Hotel Assn., Hotel Sales Mktg. Assn., Am. Mktg. Assn. Avocations: jogging, writing. Office: Ypartnership 423 S Keller Rd # 100 Orlando FL 32810-6102 Office Phone: 407-875-1111. Business E-Mail: peter.yesawich@ypartnership.com.

YESHION, THEODORE ELLIOT, crime laboratory director; b. NYC, Mar. 18, 1951; s. Norman Joseph and Selma (Schoenberg) Y.; m. Beverly Joy Post, July 18, 1976; children: Sarah Rochelle, Michael Jared. BS in Pre-Med. Biology, CUNY, Jamaica, NY, 1973; MS in Forensic Sci., George Washington U., 1975. Forensic serologist, spl. agt. N.C. Bur. Investigation, Raleigh, 1975-79; crime lab. analyst supr. Fla. Dept. Law Enforcement Tampa Regional Crime Lab., Tampa, 1979-83, chief, 1983—. Instr. Tampa Police Acad., 1980—, inst. govtl. svcs. Valencia C.C., Orlando, Fla., 1981—; forensic sci. cons. and expert witness, 1983—. Contbr. articles to profl. jours. Advisor Dept. Pub. Health Com. on Sexual Battery, Pinellas County, Fla., 1985—; bd. dirs. Hillsborough County Crisis Ctr., Tampa, 1980—; chmn. Fla. Dept. Law Enforcement AIDS Task Force, 1987-90; chmn. div. crime labs. and staff svcs. safety com., 1987-90; mem. Hillsborough County Task Force on Sexual Assault, 1980-82; mem. N.C. Rape Crisis Assn., 1978-79, N.C. Law Enforcement, 1975-79. Fellow Am. Acad. Forensic Scis.; mem. Am. Soc. Crime Lab. Dirs., So. Assn. Forensic Scientists, Ariz. Homicide Investigators Assn. (hon.), Bloodstain Evidence Specialists and Technicians Assn. Jewish. Avocation: black belt in shorin-ryu karate. Office: 4211A N Lois Ave Tampa FL 33614-7774

YETERIAN, EDWARD HARRY, psychologist, educator, administrator; b. New Britain, Conn., 1948; s. Arthur and Mary Yeterian; m. Margaret Emily Wellock; children— Robert, Julie. BS, Trinity Coll., 1970; MA, U. Conn., 1974, PhD, 1975. Rsch. fellow Harvard Med. Sch., Boston, 1975-78, postdoctoral fellow, 1975-78; cons. Maine State Bur. Mental Retardation, Augusta, 1982—88; v.p. for acad. affairs, dean of faculty, dept. psychology Colby Coll., Waterville, Maine. Author book chpts.; contbr. articles to profl. jours. Mem. bd. fellows Trinity Coll., Hartford, Conn., 1986—93. NIMH fellow, 1977-78. Mem. Soc. for Neurosci., Eastern Psychol. Assn., Nat. Assn. for Armenian Studies and Rsch. Avocations: automobile repair and rebuilding; short-wave radio. Home: 86 Lake Ridge Dr Sidney ME 04330-2103 Office: VP Acad Affairs Dept Psychology Colby Coll Waterville ME 04901

YETMAN, GARY, investment company executive; BBA, Adelphi Univ.; JD, Bklyn. Law Sch.; completed advanced study in taxation, NYU Law Sch. Bar: NY State 1975. Mgr., tax dept. Oppenheim, Appel, Dixon & Co.; pres., COO Wagner Stott Clearing Corp., NYC; pres., chmn. Merrill Lynch Prof. Clearing.; joined Merrill Lynch Prof. Clearing, 1980—; pres., CEO Merril Lynch Clearing Corp., New York, 1997—; mng. dir., co-head, global equity fin., global markets & investment banking divsn. Merrill Lynch. Bd. dir. Options Clearing Corp., Merrill Lynch. Mem.: Wall Street Tax Assn. (mem. 1983—93), Phila. Stock Exchange Option Com. (mem. 1986—88). Office: Merrill Lynch Pro 222 Broadway 6 New York NY 10038-2510

YETMAN, LEITH ELEANOR, academic administrator; b. Kellits, Clarendon, Jamaica, West Indies; came to US, 1967; d. 2nd child of 12 children of Percival Augustus and Grace Elizabeth (Anderson) Y.; m. Noel W. Miller, Apr. 8, 1961 (div. 1977); children: Donovan, Jo-Ann, Kirk, Lori-Anne; adopted children: LaFara, Samantha, Brandon Ryan. Attended, Bethlehem Teachers Coll., St. Elizabeth, Jamaica, 1960; BSc, Baruch Coll., 1976; MA, Columbia U., 1979. Cert. tchr., NY; accredited Bklyn. Inst. Bus. Tech., 1998. Legal sec. various law firms, NYC, 1969-76; instr. Taylor Bus. Inst., NYC, 1977-79; founder, pres., dir. NY Inst. English and Bus. (formerly NY Inst. Bus. Tech., NYC, 1981—; founder Bklyn. Inst. Bus. Tech. (formerly Grace Inst. Bus. Tech.), 1996. Recipient award, Prime Min. Jamaica P.J. Peterson, 2003, citations Hon. Virginia Fields, Gov. NY State, Hon. George E. Pataki, City Coun. NY, 2004, letters of recognition and praise Ex-First Ladies Barbara Bush, Hillary Clinton, Ex-Pres. Bill Clinton, Senator Charles Rangel, Ex-Mayor David Dinkins, others, award Prime of Jamaica, 2003, NYC Coun. citation The Emigrant Awards Found., 2004; Leith E. Yetman Day proclaimed June 1, 1994 by Manhattan Borough Pres. Office: NY Inst English and Bus 248 W 35th St New York NY 10001 Office Phone: 212-725-9400. Personal E-mail: eleany@aol.com. Business E-Mail: nyieb02@aol.com.

YETMAN, RANDALL JOHN, plastic surgeon; b. Casper, Wyo., Nov. 1, 1948; s. Jack Eugene and Mary Yetman; m. Nancy Lynn Devins, Apr. 29, 1969; children: Koren Dodson, Jamie Finnicum. Degree, SUNY, Buffalo, 1970; MD, U. Miami, 1975. Diplomate Am. Bd. Plastic Surgery, 1984. Intern in gen. surgery Albert Einstein Sch. Medicine, 1975—79, residency in gen. surgery, 1975—79; residency in plastic surgery Cornell Sch. Medicine, NYC, 1979—81, asst. prof. surgery, 1981—83; staff surgeon Cleve. Clinic, 1983—. Residency program dir. in plastic surgery Cleve. Clinic, 1995—. Fellow: ACS; mem.: Am. Soc. Plastic Surgeons, Am. Assn. Plastic Surgeons. Republican. Roman Catholic. Avocations: golf, fly fishing. Home: 2603 Fairmount Blvd Cleveland Heights OH 44106 Office: Cleveland Clinic 9500 Euclid Ave Cleveland OH 44106 Home Phone: 216-371-7721; Office Phone: 216-444-6908. Business E-Mail: yetmanr@ccf.org.

YETTER, R. PAUL, lawyer; b. Milw., Aug. 5, 1958; s. Richard and Lobelia (Gutierrez) Y.; m. Patricia D. Yetter, May 6, 1983; children: Chris, Mark, Michael, Joseph, Thomas, Andrew, Daniel. BA in Bus., U. Tex., El Paso, 1980; JD, Columbia U., 1983. Bar: Tex. 1983, US Dist. Ct. (all dists. Tex.), US Ct. Appeals (5th cir.); bd. cert. in civil trial law and personal injury trial law Tex. Bd. Legal Specialization. Law clk. to Hon. John R. Brown US Ct. Appeals (5th cir.), Houston, 1983-84; assoc. Baker & Botts, LLP, Houston, 1984-89, ptnr., 1990-97, Yetter & Warden, LLP, Houston, 1997—. Chair state judiciary rels. com. State Bar, 1995-96; mem. Funding Parity Task Force, 1995-97; mem. ex officio Jud. Selection Task Force, 1995-97; chair Alliance for Jud. Funding, Inc., 1996—; mem. ex officio contbns. com. Tex. Ctr. for the Judiciary, mem. com. on admissions, So. Dist., Tex., 2000—. Contbr. articles to profl. jours. Recipient Presdl. citation State Bar Tex., 1996; rsch. fellow Southwestern Legal Found.; named one of Top 10 Trial Lawyers in Am., Nat. Law Jour., 2004, Tex. Super Lawyer Bus. Litig., Tex. Monthly, 2003-06, One of Best Lawyers, H Tex. Mag., 2005, 06. Fellow Tex. Bar Foun., Houston Bar Found. Office: Yetter & Warden LLP 2 Houston Ctr 909 Fannin Ste 3600 Houston TX 77010 Office Phone: 713-632-8000. Business E-Mail: pyetter@yetterwarden.com.

YETTER, RICHARD, lawyer; b. Phila., Mar. 14, 1929; s. Frederick Jacob and Marie (Kircher) Y.; m. Lobelia Gutierrez, Feb. 4, 1955; children: Bruce, Tina Marie, Richard Paul, Erich David. BS, Pa. State U., 1951; JD, Marquette U., 1960. Bar: Wis. 1960, US Dist. Ct. (ea. dist.) Wis. 1960, Tex. 1961, US Dist. Ct. (we. dist.) Tex. 1971, US Ct. Appeals (5th cir.) 1972. Adjuster Md. Casualty Co., El Paso, Tex., 1960-62; pres. Richard Yetter & Assocs. Inc., El Paso, 1970-90; sole practitioner, El Paso, 1962-70, 90—. Assoc. judge Mcpl. Ct., El Paso, 1967-71; adj. prof. law Webster U., St. Louis. Pres. Pleasantview Home for Sr. Citizens, Inc., 1968-76; state committeeman Tex. Rep. Com., El Paso, 1968-70; chmn. adv. bd. SBA, Lubbock, Tex., Salvation Army, El Paso; active El Paso County Civil Svc. Commn., 1992-96. With USAF, 1951-60. Recipient William Booth award Salvation Army, 1997. Mem. Wis. State Bar, Tex. State Bar, El Paso Bar Assn., Coll. of the State Bar of Tex., El Paso Trial Lawyers Assn. (past bd. dirs.), El Paso Probate Bar Assn. (past bd. dirs.), Optimist (life, pres. El Paso), Mil. Order World Wars (life), Phi Delta Phi. Methodist. Avocation: walking. Office: 6070 Gateway Blvd E Ste 501 El Paso TX 79905-2031 Office Phone: 915-772-8999, 915-772-9062. E-mail: yetterlaw@bdmsl.net.

YEUDALL, WILLIAM ANDREW, biochemist, molecular oncologist; BSc with honors, U. Glasgow, Scotland, 1983; BDS, U. Glasgow, 1986, PhD, 1990. Rsch. fellow Beatson Inst. Cancer Rsch., Glasgow, 1987—90; lectr. U. Bristol, England, 1990—93; vis. assoc. Nat. Inst. Dental and Craniofacial Rsch., Bethesda, Md., 1993—97; vis. lectr. Eastman Dental Inst., London, 1995—98; clin. sr. lectr. King's Coll. London, 1999—2002; assoc. prof. Va. Commonwealth U., Richmond, 2002—. Mem. editl. bd. Oral Oncology, 1996—. Fellow: Internat. Acad. Oral Oncology (founding); mem.: Internat. Assn. Dental Rsch. Office: Va Commonwealth U 521 N 11th St Richmond VA 23298 Office Phone: 804-828-6415.

YEUN, PAUL LORENZO, clergy member; b. Hong Kong, Apr. 14, 1944; came to U.S., 1960; s. Kaki Yeun and Carmen (Flores) Pio; m. Elisabeth Wendy Chan, June 19, 1971; children: Evangeline, Abigail. BA, Azusa Pacific U., 1968; MDiv, Asbury Sem., 1971, MA, 1974; DMin, Lexington Sem., 1977. Ordained to ministry United Meth. Ch., 1973; lic. marriage and family therapist; lic. profl. counselor; cert. mental health clergy, profl. chaplain, parish pastor, Ohio, 1971-1981. Parish pastor Aberdeen (Ohio) United Meth. Ch., 1971-72, Morrow (Ohio) United Meth. Ch., 1972-76, Albany (Ohio) United Meth. Ch., 1976-78, Oakland Park United Meth. Ch., Columbus, Ohio, 1978-81; reserve chaplain USAF, Rickenbacker AFB, Ohio, 1980-81, protestant chaplain George Air Force Base, Calif., 1981-84, installation chaplain Clark Air Base, Philippines, 1984-87; sr. protestant chaplain USAF, Davis Monthan AFB, Tucson, 1987—92; sr. chaplain Lajas Field, Azore, Portugal, 1992—94; chief edn. and tng. Wilford Hall Medical Ctr., Tex., 1994—97; sr. regional chaplain Ramsrein AB, Germany, 1997—99; dir. pastoral svcs. Chambersburg Hosp., Pa., 1999—. Bd. dirs. Ariz. Marriage and Family Therapy, Tucson Met. Ministries, v.p. Letterkenny chapel com. Author: Dealing with the Psychological Needs of Aged, 1985, Meaning of our Membership Vows, 1987. Mem. Mil. Officers Am., 2002. Chaplain USAF, 1980—87, maj. USAF, 1987—94, lt. col. USAF, 1994—, served in Operation Desert Shield, served in Operation So. Watch, Saudi Arabia, served in Operation Allied Force, Europe, served in NATO exercise, Greece. Decorated Air Force Commendation medal with 3 oak leaf clusters, Air Force Meritorious Svc. medal with 4 oak leaf clusters, Air Force Outstanding Unit award with 4 oak leaf clusters, SW Asia medal, Expeditonary medal, Nat. Defense medal; named to Ky. Col., 1978; recipient Air Force Best Sermons, 1985, Man of Achievement award, 1989, Achievement award, Hosp. & Health Sys. Assn. Pa., 2003. Mem.: Assn. Profl. Chaplains (nominating com. 2003), Am. Legion (mem. state chaplain mental health task force 2004). Democrat. Office: 128 Buckingham Dr Chambersburg PA 17201 Home Phone: 717-709-1590; Office Phone: 717-267-7749. Business E-Mail: pyeun@summithealth.org. *Mutual respect is the basis for solving world's conflicts.*

YEUNG, BERNARD YIN, finance educator; b. Hong Kong, Sept. 29, 1953; s. Kwai Din and Kin Ling Yeung; m. Jean Jun Wei, Aug. 19, 1982; children: Michael B., Anne Y. BBA, U. B.C., Can., 1979; MBA, U. Chgo., 1981, PhD, 1984. Asst., assoc. prof. U. Alta., Edmondson, Canada, 1983—88; asst., assoc., prof. Internat. Bus. U. Mich. Bus. Sch., Ann Arbor, 1988—99, area rsch. dir. William Davidson Inst., 1997—2004; Abraham Krasnoff prof. Global Bus., prof. econs., strategy Stern Sch. Bus., NYU, 1999—, interim di. Global Bus. Inst., 2006—. Hon. co-chair strategy dept. Guanghua Sch. Mgmt., Peking U., 2004—; chair external evaluation com., IB dept. Nat. Taiwan U. Sch. Mgmt., 2004; external examiner, exec. MBA program Chinese U. Hong Kong, 2004—07; adv. prof. East China Normal U., 2006; dir. NYU China House, 2007—. Editor (assoc.): Jour. Internat. Studies, 2002—05; editor: (sr. consulting), 2007; editor: (assoc.) Mgmt. Sci., 2005, 2006; contbr. Founder Bus. Scholar Network, Aspen Corp. Soc. Responsibility, China, 2006—. Named Lim Kim San Disting. visitor, Nat. Singapore U., 2005; recipient Eugene Power award, 1993, Tchr. Excellence award, U. Mich. Bus. Sch., 1997, Moskowitz prize, 2001, Excellence in Tchg. award, Exec. Edn. Program, Stern Sch. Bus., NYU, 2002; NTT Rsch. Fellowship, U. Mich. Bus. Sch., 1996. Fellow: Acad. Internat. Bus. (elected v.p. 2000—02); mem.: Acad. Mgmt., Am. Fin. Assn., Am. Econ. Assn., Acad. Mgmt. Review (mem. editl. bd. 2005—). Avocations: reading, swimming. Home: Apt 11-O 1 Washington Sq Village New York NY 10012 Office: NYU Stern Bus Sch KMC Bldg 7-87 44 W 4th St New York NY 10012

YEUNG, EDWARD SZESHING, chemist; b. Hong Kong, Feb. 17, 1948; arrived in U.S., 1965; s. King Mai Luk and Yu Long Yeung; m. Anna Kunkwok Seto, Sept. 18, 1971; children: Rebecca Tze-Mai, Amanda Tze-Wen AB magna cum laude, Cornell U., 1968; PhD, U. Calif., Berkeley, 1972. Instr. chemistry Iowa State U., Ames, 1972-74, asst prof., 1974-77, assoc. prof, 1977-81, prof. chemistry, 1981-89, disting. prof., 1989—. Contbr. articles to profl. jours. Alfred P. Sloan fellow, 1974-76; recipient Am. Chem Soc. award in Analytical Chemistry, 1994. Fellow AAAS; mem. Soc. Applied Spectrosci. (Lester Strock award 1990), Am. Chem. Soc.

(award in chem. instrumentation 1987, award in analytical chemistry 1994, award in chromatography 2002). Home: 1005 Jarrett Cir Ames IA 50014-3937 Office: Iowa State U Gilman Hall Ames IA 50011

YEUNG, RONALD WAI-CHUN, engineering educator, researcher; s. Foo and Pui Fong Yeung; m. Grace Y. Chow, Sept. 5, 1970; 1 child, Brian H. BSME, U. Calif., Berkeley, 1968, MS Naval Architecture, 1970, PhD Engring., 1973. Naval arch. Advanced Marine Tech. Divsn., Litton Ship Sys., Culver City, Calif., 1970—71; instr. U. Calif. L.A. ext., Long Beach Naval Shipyard, 1970—71; asst., assoc. prof. MIT, Cambridge, 1974—82; prof. hydromechanics & ocean engring. U. Calif., Berkeley, 1982—, chair dept. naval architecture & offshore engring., 1989—96, prof., 1994—. Prin. R. W. Yeung - Consulting Naval Architect & Ocean Engr., Moraga, Calif., 1976—; Humboldt prof. U. Hamburg, Germany, 1988, Mercator U., Duisburg, Germany, 1998—99; vis. prof. Kyushu U. Inst. Applied Mech., Japan, 1988, Nat. Tech. U. Norway, CESOS, Trondheim, 2007. Editor: (spl. edition on Ocean Mechanics) Jour. Engring. Math., 1999; assoc. editor: Jour. Ship Rsch., 1975—95, Jour. Computers & Fluids, 1983—, Jour. Engring. Math., 1986—, Jour. Marine Systems & Offshore Tech., 2004—, Jour. Marine Sci. & Tech., 2006—, Ocean Engring Jour., 2006—; contbr. articles to profl. jours. Recipient Univ. Gold medal, U. Calif., 1968, Disting. Scientist award, Alexander von Humboldt Found., 1988, 1998, Best Paper award, ASME, Offshore Mechanics and Arctic Engring., 1991, ASME, Offshore Mech. and Arctic Engring., 2002, Georg Weinblum lectr., Naval Studies Bd., Soc. Naval Architects and Marine Engrs. and Schiffbautechnische Gesellschaft, 2002—03, Kenneth Davidson medal, Soc. Naval Architects and Marine Engrs., 2004; scholar Fulbright-Hayes Sr. scholar, U. Adelaide, Australian-Am. Edn. Found., 1981. Fellow: Soc. Naval Architects & Marine Engrs. (No. Calif. exec. com. and acad. liaison 1989—); mem.: Japanese Soc. Naval Architects, Am. Soc. Engring. Edn., Internat. Soc. Offshore and Polar Engrs. (chair hydrodynamics com. 2002—03), Phi Beta Kappa, Pi Tau Sigma, Tau Beta Pi. Home: 27 Indian Wells Moraga CA 94556-1020 Office: U Calif 6135 Etcheverry Hall Berkeley CA 94720-1740 Office Phone: 510-642-8347. E-mail: rwyeung@berkeley.edu.

YEUTTER, CLAYTON KEITH, lawyer, former secretary of agriculture; b. Eustis, Nebr., Dec. 10, 1930; s. Reinhold F. and Laura P. Y.; m. Cristena Bach; children: Victoria, Elena, Olivia. BS, Nebr. U., 1952, JD, 1963, PhD in Agrl. Econs., 1966; doctorate (hon.), Ariz. U., Clemson U., Georgetown U., Santa Clara U., Nebr. U., Nebr. Wesleyan U., U. Md., DePaul U. Bar: Nebr. 1963, D.C. 1977. Farmer, rancher, Nebr., 1957-75; mem. faculty dept. agrl. econs. U. Nebr., Lincoln, 1960-66; dir. U. Nebr. Mission in Colombia, South Am., 1968-70; exec. asst. to Gov. State of Nebr., Lincoln, 1966-68; regional dir. Com. for Reelection of Pres., 1972; adminstr. for consumer and mktg. services. USDA, Washington, 1970-71, asst. sec. for mktg. & consumer services, 1973-74, asst. sec. for internat. affairs & commodity programs, 1974-75; dep. spl. trade rep. Exec. Office of the Pres., Washington, 1975-77; sr. ptnr. Nelson, Harding, Yeutter & Leonard, Lincoln, Nebr., 1977-78; pres., chief exec. officer Chgo. Mercantile Exchange, 1978-85; U.S. trade rep. Exec. Office of the Pres., Washington, 1985-89; sec. USDA, Washington, 1989-91; chmn. Rep. Nat. Com., Washington, 1991-92; counsellor to the Pres. for domestic policy The White House, Washington, 1992; of counsel Hogan & Hartson LLP, Washington, 1993—. Contbr. numerous articles to profl. jours. Bd. dir. Am. Comml. Lines, Burlington Capital Group; bd. dirs. Coranta Holding Corp.; former dir. Caterpillar, Tex. Instruments, Weyerhaeuser, B.A.T. Industries, UK, Zurich Fin. Svcs., Switzerland, FMC, Con Agra Foods, Oppenheimer Funds. With USAF, 1952—57, with USAFR, 1957—87. Recipient Israel Prime Minister's medal, Master Builder of Men award FarmHouse, Leadership award Fowler-McCracken Commn., Consumers for World Trade award. Mem. Nebr. Bar Assn. Republican. Presbyterian. Avocations: skiing, water-skiing, weightlifting. Office: Hogan & Hartson LLP 555 Thirteenth St NW Washington DC 20004

YEVZLIN, ALEXANDER SASHA, nephrologist, medical products executive; b. Odessa, Ukraine, Jan. 10, 1972; s. Anatoly and Larissa Yevzlin; m. Paola Joanna Fliman, May 30, 1999; children: Alana Shoshana, Margarita Naomi. BA magna cum laude, Dartmouth Coll., Hanover, NH, 1994; MD, Ohio State U., Columbus, 1998. Diplomate Am. Bd. Internal Medicine, 1998, Am. Bd. Internal Medicine-Nephrology, 2002. Clin. asst. prof. U. Wis., Madison, 2004—07, dir. interventional nephrology, 2005—. V.p. new product devel. r4 Vascular, Inc., Mpls., 2007—07. Contbr. articles to profl. jours. Fellow Roessler fellowship in bioethics, Ohio State U. Coll. Medicine, 1995; John Marshall Raible Meml. scholar, Dartmouth Coll., 1990—94, Presdl. scholar in logic and lang. rsch., 1994, Bioethics Rsch. scholar, Cleve. Clinic Found., 1996. Mem.: ASDIN (cert.), ASN. Home: 9209 Bear Claw Way Madison WI 53717 Home Phone: 608-658-9657. Personal E-mail: asy@medicine.wisc.edu.

YEW, DAVID, physician, director; b. NYC, Oct. 5, 1970; MD, SUNY, 1996—99. Cert. Am. Bd. Emergency Medicine, 2003. Emergency medicine physician St. Luke's-Roosevelt Hosp., Columbia U., NYC, 1999—2001, Kaiser Permamente, Honolulu, 2002—03, Tripler Army Med. Ctr., Honolulu, 2003—; ship dr. Norwegian Cruise Line, Honolulu, 2005—; med. dir. AirMed Hawaii, Honolulu, 2006—. Disaster medicine physician Dept. Homeland Security FEMA/DMAT, Honolulu, 2003—; mcht. mariner US Coast Guard, Honolulu, 2004—; asst. clin. prof. dept. surgery U. Hawaii Med. Sch., Honolulu, 2005—. Contbr. chapters to books. Recipient Outstanding Staff Tchr. award/Jeffrey P. Kavolius award, Tripler Army Med. Ctr., 2005. Mem.: Fed. Physicians Assn. (assoc.), Air Med. Physicians Assn. (assoc.), Mensa (life). Achievements include development of virtual simulation education. Office: AirMed Hawaii 90 Nakolo Pl Ste 203 Honolulu HI 96817 Home Phone: 808-371-0244. Personal E-mail: yewdave@hotmail.com. Business E-Mail: dyew@airmed.com.

YGLESIAS, HELEN BASSINE, author, educator; b. NYC, Mar. 29, 1915; d. Solomon and Kate (Goldstein) Bassine; m. Bernard Cole, 1938 (div. 1950); children: Tamar Cole, Lewis Cole; m. Jose Yglesias, Aug. 19, 1950 (div. 1992); 1 child, Rafael. Student pub. schs.; LHD (hon.), U. Maine, 1996. Literary editor Nation Mag., 1965-70; adj. assoc. prof. writing Columbia Sch. Arts, NYC, 1973. Vis. prof. creative writing Writers Workshop, U. Iowa, Iowa City, 1980. Author: (novels) How She Died (Houghton Mifflin award), 1972, Family Feeling, 1976, Sweetsir, 1981, The Saviors, 1987, The Girls, 1999; (non-fiction) Starting: Early, Anew, Over and Late, 1978, Isabel Bishop, 1989. Home: Apt 1303 1261 5th Ave New York NY 10029-3866

YGLESIAS, KENNETH DALE, college president; b. Tampa, Fla. s. Jose and Julia Yglesias; m. Donna Carmen Belli, Nov., 1977. BA, U. South Fla., 1969; MA, Western Carolina U., 1973; EdD, U. So. Calif., 1977. Cert. tchr., Calif., Fla. Tchr., coach pub. schs., Tampa, 1969-73; tchr., dept. chmn. Am. Sch. Madrid, 1973-76; fgn. svc. officer USIA, Washington and Tel Aviv, 1977-79; assoc. prof. Pepperdine U., LA, 1979-83; prof., dir. El Camino Coll., Torrance, Calif., 1981-83; adminstrv. dean Coastline Coll., Fountain Valley, Calif., 1983-88; v.p. Coast C.C. Dist., Costa Mesa, Calif., 1988-95; pres. Golden West Coll., Huntington Beach, Calif., 1995—2004; chancellor Coast Cmty. Coll. Dist., Costa Mesa, Calif., 2004—. Contbr. articles to profl. jours. Bd. dirs. C.C.'s for Internat. Devel., 1988-94, Orange County Marine Inst., Costa Mesa, 1990-93, United Way Orange County, Santa Ana, Calif., 1991-94. Mem. Am. Assn. for Higher Edn. (Hispanic caucus), Assn. Calif. C.C. Adminstrs., Phi Delta Kappa. Democrat. Roman Catholic. Avocations: basketball fan, walking. Office: Golden West Coll PO Box 2748 Huntington Beach CA 92647-0748

YGLESIAS, RAFAEL JOSE, novelist; b. NYC, May 12, 1954; s. Jose and Helen (Bassine) Y.; m. Margaret Joskow, Oct. 15, 1977 (dec. June. 2004); children: Matthew, Nicholas. Author: Dr. Neruda's Cure for Evil, 1996, The Murderer Next Door, 1990, Only Children, 1988; screenwriter, author (film) Fearless, 1993; screenwriter (films) Death and the Maiden, 1995, Les Miserables, 1998, From Hell, 2001, Dark Water, 2005. Mem. The Author's Guild, Writer's Guild of Am., Acad. Motion Picture Arts and Scis.

YI, JIANLIAN, professional basketball player; b. Shenzhen, China, Oct. 27; Student, Sports Acad. Shenzhen; grad., Guangdong U. Tech. Player Guangdong Hongyuan So. Tigers Chinese Basketball Assn., Dongguan City, Guangdong, 2002—; forward Milw. Bucks, 2007—. Mem. Chinese Olympic Basketball Team, Athens, 2004. Achievements include being youngest player to ever play in highest league China Basketball Assn. (CBA), 2002; two-time CBA All-Star, 2004-2005. Office: Milw Bucks 1001 N Fourth St Milwaukee WI 53203 *

YI, MICHAEL, internist, pediatrician; Cert. internal medicine and pediatrics Ohio. Asst. prof. clin. medicine and pediat. U. Cin. Med. Ctr., 1999—2007. Asst. prof. Office: Divsn Gen Internal Medicine 231 Albert Sabin Way Rm 6603 Cincinnati OH 45267 Office Phone: 513-558-7581.

YI, MYONGHO, library and information scientist; b. Seoul, July 15, 1970; s. Sungsoo Yi and Imsoon Yoo; m. Jungeun Oh, Sept. 8, 2001; children: Hannah, Joshua. BA, U. North Tex., 1995, MS, 1996; PhD, Fla. State U., 2006. Adj. faculty Myongj Coll., Seoul, Republic of Korea, 2002—03; asst. prof. U. Okla., Norman, 2006—. Cons. SecureSoft, Seoul, 2000—02, IBM Korea, 2002—03. Webmaster Tallahasse Bapt. Ch., Fla., 2003. Recipient 1st Place Rsch. Poster, Fla. State U., 2004. Mem.: Am. Libr. and Info. Sci. Edn., Am. Soc. for Info. Sci. Office: U Okla 401 West Brooks Rm 120 Norman OK 73019 Home Phone: 405-217-3055; Office Phone: 405-325-3921. E-mail: josephmyi@gmail.com.

YI, TAEIL, mathematician, educator; b. Seoul, Republic of Korea, Dec. 16, 1962; s. Beomyoung and Bongwol Yi; m. Moonsil Kim, Nov. 20, 1962; children: Hanyong David, Changyong Peter. BS, Dankook U., Seoul, 1988, MS, 1990, U. Ill., 1994; MEd, U. Fla., 1997, PhD, 2000. Math. tchr. Yongmoon H.S., Seoul, South Korea, 1988—90; tchg. asst. U. Fla., Fla., 1995—2000, instr. Gainesville, 2000—01; asst. prof. U. Tex., Brownsville, 2001—. Advisor Pi Mu Epsilon U. Tex., Brownsville, 2002—. Prodr.: (instructional video) Name That Move (Jim Harbin Award / Fla. Assn. for Media in Edn., 1995); contbr. articles to profl. jours. Condr. choir Korean Ch., Urbana/Champaign, Ill., 1993—94; chief editor Korean Bapt. Ch., Gainesville, Fla., 1996—2001, dir. gen. affair, 1997—2000; leader youth group Open Door Ch., Brownsville, Tex., 2001, sec. bd., 2002. Recipient Jim Harbin award, Fla. Assn. Media Edn., 1995, Spl. Merit award, U. Tex. Brownsville, 2006. Mem.: Scientific Rsch. Soc., Soc. Indsl. and Applied Math., Math. Assn. Am., Am. Math. Soc., Sigma Xi, Phi Kappa Phi (life), Phi Mu Epsilon. Achievements include development of an automated stereotactic radiosurgery algorithm for brain tumor treatment planning, which has been developed by a software company for broad usage. Avocations: golf, studying theology. Home: 5 Deer Haven Ct Brownsville TX 78520 Office: Univ Tex Brownsville 80 Fort Brown Brownsville TX 78520 Office Phone: 956-882-6621. E-mail: Taeil.Yi@utb.edu.

YI, WEI, physicist; BEcons., Tsinghua U., Beijing, 1996; PhD, Harvard U., Cambridge, Mass., 2005. Rsch. asst. Inst. Physics, Chinese Acad. Scis., Beijing, 1996—99; rsch. asst., sch. engring. and applied scis., Harvard U., Cambridge, 1999—2005, postdoctoral fellow Sch. Engring. and Applied Scis., 2005—. Recipient Wei Hua Sci. and Tech. award, Chinese Acad. Scis., 1999; fellow, Harvard U., 1999—2000. Mem.: Am. Phys. Soc., Materials Rsch. Soc. Achievements include development of 3-Omega method for specific heat and thermal conductivity measurements of a filament-like specimen, and measured those thermal quantities of carbon nanotube bundles with only nanogram in mass; a three-terminal spectroscopy that probes both subsurface energy barriers and interband optical transitions in a semiconductor heterostructure; co-development of avalanche spin-valve transistor; observation of coulomb blockade and fano resonance in the tunneling spectroscopy between multiwalled carbon nanotubes and normal metals; demonstrated the potential of using a dual-probe scanning tunneling microscope to study nanoscale metal-semiconductor interfaces; research in measured temperature dependence of thermoelectric power in multiwalled carbon nanotubes; electron diffraction characterizations of spinel iron-oxide nanocrystals grown on iron whiskers; ballistic electron emission luminescence spectroscopy measurements of an InAs quantum dot heterostructure; vertically developed integrated optics for ballistic electron emission luminescence microscopy. Office: Harvard University 9 Oxford St Cambridge MA 02138 Office Phone: 617-496-5471. Business E-Mail: wyi@fas.harvard.edu.

YI, XIAOBIN, anesthesiologist, pain management specialist; arrived in US, 1993, naturalized, 2001; MD, Hunan Med. U., Changsha, China, 1985; PhD, Chinese Acad. Med. Scis., Beijing, China, 1990. Diplomate Am. Bd. Anesthesiology, 2004, Am. Bd. Pain Medicine, 2005. Medicine resident, 5th clinical coll. Beijing U., 1990—93; GI fellow, rsch. assoc. Sch. Medicine, U. Va., 1993—96, anesthesiology rsch. fellow, 1996—99; intern Wayne State U., Detroit Med. Ctr., 1999—2000; resident, anesthesiology SUNY Health Sci. Ctr., Syracuse, 2003—04; asst. prof. Sch. Medicine Wash. U., St. Louis, 2004—. Mem.: Biophysical Soc., Am. Soc. Regional Anesthesia and Pain Medicine, Am. Soc. Anesthesiologists. Office: Washington University School of Medicine Campus Box 8054 660 S Euclid Avenue Saint Louis MO 63110 Office Phone: 314-362-1630. Home Fax: 314-286-2675. Personal E-mail: yix@wustl.edu.

YIANNES, (IORDANIDES), sculptor, ceramist, educator; b. Athens, Greece, Dec. 16, 1943; came to U.S., 1967; 1 child, Joshua. Cert., Bklyn. Mus. Arts Sch., 1972; student, New Sch. Social Rsch., 1970-71. Instr. Bklyn. Mus. Art Sch., 1971-78, Bklyn. Coll. CUNY, 1972—82, Greenwich House Pottery, NYC, 1984-85, Queens Coll. CUNY, 1985-88, 1995—, Bklyn. Coll. CUNY, 1994—. Recipient 1st prize in ceramics Alfred Parker award, 1972, Lucile Blanch award for sculpture Woodstock Artist Assn., 1989; Max Beckman scholar Bklyn. Mus. N.Y., 1971-72; City Endowment for Arts grant visual arts program Queens Coun. Arts, 1980. Mem. Am. Crafts Coun. Avocation: sports. Home and Office: 20-41 Shore Blvd Long Island City NY 11105-3831

YIE, JUNMING, research scientist; m. Wei Chen, 2001; 1 child, Maya. BS, U. Sci. & Tech. China, Hefei, Anhui, 1994; PhD (hon.), Columbia U., NYC, 1999. Principle scientist Pfizer Global Rsch. & Devel., San Diego, 2001—. Recipient Achievement award, Pfizer La Jolla Oncology & Diabetes Therapeutic Zone, 2005. Mem.: NY Acad. Scis., Am. Diabetes Assn. Achievements include invention of antibodies to myostatin. Office: Pfizer Inc 10724 Science Center Dr San Diego CA 92121 Office Phone: 858-526-4790. Business E-Mail: junming.yie@pfizer.com.

YIELDING, K. LEMONE, physician; b. Auburn, Ala., Mar. 25, 1931; s. Riley Lafayette and Bertie (Dees) Y.; m. Lerena Wade Hauge, Dec. 7, 1973; children: K. Lemone, Michael Lafon, Teresa Louise, Riley Lafayette, Katrina Elizabeth, Elaine Louise Blodgett, Laura Carlen Blodgett. BS, Ala. Poly. Inst., 1949; MS, U. Ala., 1952, MD, 1954. Intern U. Ala. Med. Center, 1954-55; clin. assoc. Nat. Inst. Arthritis and Metabolic Diseases, NIH, 1955-57, sr. investigator, 1958-64; resident med. service USPHS Hosp., Balt., 1957-58; physician in practice of oncology and emergency medicine, 1995—. Adj. asst. prof. medicine Georgetown U. Med. Sch., 1958-64; cons. USPHS, 1964-68, 75—; prof. biochemistry, assoc. prof. medicine, chief lab. molecular biology U. Ala. Med. Ctr., Birmingham, 1964-80; prof., chmn. dept. anatomy, prof. medicine U. So. Ala. Coll. Medicine, Mobile, 1980-87; dean grad. sch. U. Tex. Med. Br., Galveston, 1987-95, dean emeritus, 1995—, v.p. for rsch., 1987-94; cons. Am. Heart Assn., Arthritis Found., NIH, NASA. Contbr. to profl. jours., books. Served with USPHS, 1955-64. Grantee USPHS, Am. Cancer Soc., Nat. Found.-March of Dimes, U.S. Army, Am. Inst. Cancer Research. Mem. Am. Soc. Biol. Chemistry, Am. Assn. Cancer Research, Am. Assn. Photobiology, Assn. Research Vision and Ophthalmology, Soc. Exptl. Biology and Medicine, Am. Soc. Pharm. and Exptl. Therapeutics, Am. Assn. Pathologists, So. Soc. Clin. Investigation, Am. Assn. Anatomy, Soc. Toxicology, Sigma Xi. Personal E-mail: lemoneyielding@hughes.net. E-mail: yielding@hiway.net.

YIH, MAE DUNN, state legislator; b. Shanghai, May 24, 1928; d. Chung Woo and Fung Wen (Feng) Dunn; m. Stephen W.H. Yih, 1953; children: Donald, Daniel. BA, Barnard Coll., 1951; postgrad., Columbia U., 1951-52. Asst. to bursar Barnard Coll., NYC, 1952-54; mem. Oreg. Ho. Reps. from 36th dist., 1977-83, Oreg. Senate from 19th dist., 1983—. Mem. Clover Ridge Elem. Sch. Bd., Albany, Oreg., 1969-78, Albany Union H.S. Bd., 1975-79; mem. Joint Legis. Ways and Means Com., Senate Transp. Com., 1999, Senate pres. pro-temore, 1993. Episcopalian. Home: 34465 Yih Ln NE Albany OR 97322-9557 Office: Oreg Senate S 307 State Capitol Salem OR 97310-0001

YILMA, TILAHUN DANIEL, virologist, veterinarian, educator, researcher; b. Bulki, Gemugofa, Ethiopia, Dec. 15, 1943; parents Wolde-Ab Yilma and Getenesh Negewo. BS in Vet. Sci., U. Calif., Davis, 1968, DVM, 1970, PhD in Microbiology, 1977. Head vet. scv. Min. Agr., Harar, Ethiopia, 1970-71; lectr. UNDP/FAO of the UN Sch. for Animal Health Assts., DebreZeit, Ethiopia, 1971-72; rsch. assoc. USDA, Greenport, N.Y., 1977-79; asst. prof. vet. microbiology, pathology Wash. State U., Pullman, 1980-85, assoc. prof. vet. microbiology, pathology, 1985-86; prof. virology U. Calif., Davis, 1986—, dir. Internat. Lab. Molecular Biology for Tropical Disease Agents. Patentee in field. Recipient Ciba-Geigy prize Ciba-Geigy Ltd., 1990, Beecham award, 1988. Mem.: NAS. Office: U Calif Sch Vet Medicine 2079A Haring Hall Davis CA 95616 Business E-Mail: tdyilma@ucdavis.edu.

YIM, MAN BIN, neurosurgeon, educator; b. Hong Seung, Chung Nam, Republic of Korea, Feb. 29, 1948; s. Byung Soon Yim and Jeung Ok Kang; m. In Sook Kim, Dec. 4, 1974; children: Chang Ok, Chang Baek. PhD, KyungPook Nat. U., Daegu, Republic of Korea, 1988. Lic. med. practitioner Ministry Health and Welfare, Republic of Korea, 1973, cert. Korean Bd. of Neurosurgery, 1981. Instr. Keimyung U. Sch. of Medicine, Daegu, Republic of Korea, 1981—83, asst. prof., 1983—87, assoc. prof., 1988—93, head neurosurgery Dong San Med. Ctr., 1991—99, chmn. neurosurgery, 1993—99, prof. neurosurgery, 1993—; dir. brain rsch. inst. Keimyung U., 2000—05; dean Keimjung U. Sch. Medicine, 2005—. Sec. gen. 5th Japanese and Korean Friendship Conf. on Surgery for Cerebral Stroke, Cheju, Republic of Korea, 1996—99; v.p. 7th Japanese and Korean Friendship Conf. on Surgery for Cerebral Stroke, KyungJu, 2002—; sci. trustee The Korean Soc. of Cerebrovascular Surgery, Seoul, 1996—98, sec. gen., 1998—, mem. arrangement com. 6th internat. workshop, 2000, pres., 2003—04. Author: Text Book of Neurosurgery; contbr. articles to profl. jours. including Jour. Korean Neurosurg. Soc. (Best Sci. Article, Korean Soc. of Cerebrovascular Surgery, 2003, Best Sci. Article, Korean Soc. of Neurosurgery, 2003). Capt. Army, 1973—76, Republic of Korea. Named Best Dr. in Cerebrovascular Disease, Shin Dong Ah monthly mag., 1999, Best Dr. in Cerebovascular Disease, Dong Ah Daily News, 2003; recipient Encouragement award of Han-Mi Essay Lit., The Korean Doctors' Weekly, 2003. Mem.: Korean Neurosurgical Soc. (licentiate; bd. trustees 1995—99, pres. (Daegu and Kyung Pook local chapt.) 1996—97, mem. bd. exam. com. 1996—99, mem. scientific com. 2000—02, bd. trustees 2003—), Korean Med. Assn. (licentiate), World Fedn. of Neurosurgical Societies (assoc.). Avocations: tennis, essay writing. Home: 1502 202 Dong Man-Chon WooBang 2 Cha Ap Daegu 706-759 Republic of Korea Office: Neurosurgery Keimyung Univ 194 DongSan Dong Jung-Gu Daegu 700-712 Republic of Korea Home Phone: 82-53-743-6975; Office Phone: 82-53-250-7700. Office Fax: 82-53-250-7356. Business E-Mail: y760111@dsmc.or.kr.

YIM, MAN-SUNG, engineering educator, consultant; arrived in US, 1983, naturalized, 2004; s. Hong-Kyu Yim and Hyun-Soon Kim; m. Soyoung Chang, Mar. 18, 1988; children: Eunji Allison, Minjie. BS, Seoul Nat. U., 1981, MS, 1983; PhD, U. Cin., 1987; SM, Harvard U., Cambridge, Mass., 1991, ScD, 1994. Cert. profl. engr., Korean Profl. Engineers' Assn., 1988. Rschr. Korea Advanced Energy Rsch. Inst., Daeduk, Republic of Korea, 1981—82; sr. rschr. Korea Atomic Energy Rsch. Inst., 1987—90; instr. Seoul Nat. U., 1989; lectr. MIT, Cambridge, Mass., 1994; asst. prof. NC State U., Raleigh, 1995—2001, assoc. prof., 2001—. Cons. Electric Power Rsch. Inst., Palo Alto, Calif., 1993—2001; dir. grad. programs nuc. engring. NC State U., Raleigh, 2001—07; mem. NC Sci. Adv. Bd. Air Toxic Emissions, 2004—; external steering com. mem. on nuc. nonproliferation Idaho Nat. Lab., Idaho Falls, 2005—. Author: A Guide to Personnel Monitoring for Radiation in the Hospital Environment, 1993; author: (with Petr Vaganov) Ecological Risk (in Russian), 1999; editl. adv. bd. mem.: Jour. Progress in Nuc. Energy, 2003—. Bd. mem. Christian Worldview Network, Clairemont, Calif., 2003—07; elder DuRaleigh Presbyn. Ch., Raleigh, NC, 2001—; chmn. Triangle Korean Sch., Raleigh, NC, 2005—07. Named Senior Research Ethics fellow, NC State U., 2005—; fellow, Health Physics Soc., 1992—93, Adv. Com. Nuc. Waste Nuc. Regulatory Commn., 1992—93, Sam Nunn Sch. Internat. Affairs Ga. Inst. Tech., 2003—04; scholar, Korean Sci. and Engring. Found., 1982; Fulbright scholar, Korean Am. Ednl. Commn., 1983—87, Jong Ha Lee scholar, Harvard U., 1991—93, Calvin and Lucy Ellis scholar, 1993—94. Mem.: Inst. Nuc. Materials Mgmt., Health Physics Soc., Am. Nuc. Soc. (exec. com. mem. 2005—07), Korean Nuc. Soc. (life), Alpha Nu Sigma Soc. Office: NC State Univ Box 7909 2500 Stinson Dr Raleigh NC 27695 Office Phone: 919-515-1466. Office Fax: 919-515-5115.

YING, JINFA, chemist; PhD, U. Ariz., Tucson, 1999—2004. Rsch. fellow NIH, Bethesda, Md., 2004—. Mem.: Am. Chem. Soc. Achievements include research in the development of NMR methods for biomolecular structures.

YING, JOHN L., manufacturing executive; b. Shanghai, People's Republic of China, June 15, 1948; came to U.S., 1970; s. D.C. and W.T. (Ma) Y.; m. Cynthia C. Chen, Apr. 6, 1981; children: Janice, Jonathan. BS, Tatung Inst. Tech., Taipei, Taiwan, 1969; MS, Poly. Inst. Bklyn., 1972; Profl. Engrs. Degree, Columbia U., NYC, 1974. Application engr. Summit Engring Co., Taipei, 1969-70; asst. to pres. James Betesh Import Co., NYC, 1972-73; strategic planner GM, Detroit, 1973-79; asst. to pres. Lawless Detroit Diesel Corp., City of Industry, Calif., 1979-81; pres., chief exec. officer Cen. Power Products, Inc., Grandview, Mo., 1981—, also bd. dirs. Bd. dirs. Ctrl. Mfg., Inc., Grandview, Mo., USA-China C. of C. Adv. bd. Enterprise Bank, Overland Park, Kans. Recipient Outstanding Minority Bus. Enterprise award Minority Bus. Devel. Agy., Kansas City/Washington, 1986. Mem. USA-China C. of C., Hallbrook Country Club. Republican. E-mail: JY@shuttlewagon.net.

YING, WEIHAI, biomedical researcher, educator; b. Shanghai, Aug. 18, 1963; arrived in US, 1991; s. Guoyuan Ying and Shuzhu Huang; m. Fan Wu, Feb. 14, 1991; 1 child, Ming Yin. BS, Shanghai Med. U., 1985; PhD, U. N.Mex, 1998. Postdoctoral fellow U. Calif., San Francisco,

1998—2002, asst. prof. dept. neurology, 2002—, asst. neurologist, 2002—03, asst. prof., 2003—; rsch. biologist San Francisco VA Med. Ctr., 2002—; full rsch. scientist No. Calif. Inst. Rsch. and Edn., San Francisco, 2003—. Mng. editor Frontiers in Biosci., Albertson, NY, 2005—; grant reviewer Am. Heart Assn. Nat. Ctr., Dallas, 2006—. Contbr. over 40 abstracts and 20 articles to profl. jours. and confs. Voting mem. safety subcom. VA Med. Ctr., San Francisco, 2004; mem. original com. 4th Sino-US Forum for Medicine in 21st Century, San Francisco, 2004—05. Recipient Nat. Rsch. Svc. award, NIH, 2000, Merit Rev. award, Dept. Veterans Affairs, U.S., 2004; grantee, NIH, 2005—, Am. Heart Assn. Western States Affiliate, 2003, 2005. Mem.: Am. Soc. Neuroscis., N.Y. Acad. Scis. Democrat. Achievements include research in elucidating the major mechanisms underlying the cell death induced by PARP-1-a key protein in stroke damage; discovery of NADH and NAD can be transported across the plasma membranes of astrocytes through P2X7 receptors; NAD, nobotanin B and pyruvate may be powerful drugs for treating ischemic stroke; acidosis can promote oxidative neuronal death. Avocations: music, travel, writing, sports, crabbing. Home: 3653 Lake Ontario Dr Fremont CA 94555 Office: San Francisco VA Med Ctr Dept Neurology San Francisco CA 94121 Home Phone: 510-324-3610; Office Phone: 415-221-4810 ext. 2487. Office Fax: 415-750-2273; Home Fax: 415-750-2273. Business E-Mail: weihai.ying@ucsf.edu.

YINGLING, PHYLLIS STUCKEY, writer; b. Martinsburg, W.Va., May 22, 1931; d. Carlton Bennett and Virginia DeHaven Stuckey; m. Lewis Carroll Yingling, Jr., June 26, 1954; children: Deborah Beth, Lewis Carroll III. BA in Edn., Shepherd Coll. (now Shepherd U.), Shepherdstown, W.Va., 1952; MEd in Edn. of Deaf, Western Md. Coll., Westminster, 1979. Cert. tchr. of deaf State of Md., 1979. Tchr. of the deaf and hard of hearing Prince George's County Pub. Schools, Oxen Hill, Md., 1971—73, Balt. City Pub. Schs., 1973—86, Parkville, Md., 1986—92; ret., 1992. Author: (children's book) My Best Friend, Elena Pappas, 1986, My Best Friend, Tony Santos, 1988; co-author: (children's book for dyslexic learners) Adventures of Dan and Sam, 1997, The Fantastic Fan and 7 More Fantastic Stories, 1999, Dan and Sam and the RV Trip, 2000; contbr. articles and stories to mags. (Best Story Award, 1984). Docent Md. Hist. Soc. Mus.; pres. Women's Internat. League for Peace and Freedom, U.S. Sect., Phila., 1999—2002; co-chair Women's Internat. League for Peace and Freedom, Catonsville, Md., 1995—99. Mem.: United Meth. Women. United Methodist. Avocations: watercolor and oil painting, travel, hiking, poetry.

YIOTIS, GAYLE, archivist, researcher, anthropologist, writer; d. Pedro and Margarette Rionda; m. Christos Fotios Yiotis; children: Fotios Christos, Peter Wesley. MA, George Washington U., Washington, 1992. Mus. specialist anthropology Smithsonian Instn., Washington, 1995—2003, archivist Nat. Mus. of Am. Indian, 2003—. Student career alumni network Marquette U., Milw., 2000—; presenter in field. Contbr. articles to profl. jours. Mem.: Acad. Certified Archivists, Soc. of Am. Archivists. Avocations: historical research, writing, martial arts, collecting.

YIOTIS, KRISTIN, librarian, educator; d. Florence Alonso and Constantine John Yiotis; life ptnr. Douglas S. Ronald. BA, SUNY, Albany, 1970—75; MA, San Francisco State U., Calif., 1986—88, MA, 1992—96; MLS, San Jose State U., Calif., 2004—. Writing instr. San Jose City Coll., San Jose, Calif., 1999—2000; reading instr. De Anza Coll., Cupertino, Calif., 2001—05. Author: (jour. article) Information Technology and Libraries (LITA/Endeavor Student Writing award, 2005). Recipient Jo Ann Clifton Student Writing award, Spl. Libr. Assn., 2005; grantee scholarship, Friends of the Mountain View Libr., 2003—06, San Jose Grad. Equity fellow, San Jose State U., 2005—. Mem.: ALA (chair, student chpt., San Jose State U. 2006—), Calif. Academic and Rsch. Libraries, Calif. Libr. Assn. Mem. Christian Science Ch. Avocations: lap swimming, road biking. Home: 539 Dawn Dr Sunnyvale CA 94087 Office: Sch Library and Info Science San Jose State One Washington Sq San Jose CA 95192-0029 Home Phone: 408-749-8522; Office Phone: 408-924-2490. Personal E-mail: kyiotis@yahoo.com. Business E-Mail: kyiotis@gmail.com.

YIP, KWOK LEUNG, physicist, researcher; b. Canton, China, Sept. 23, 1944; came to U.S., 1968; s. Tong and Ho (Mok) Y.; m. Gee-Ying Chao, Mar. 25, 1972; children: Nora Loey, Dana Tsing. BS, Chinese U. Hong Kong, 1965; MS, Providence Coll., 1970; PhD, Lehigh U., 1973. Rsch. assoc. U. Ill., Urbana, 1973-75; sr. tech. specialist, project mgr. Xerox Corp., Webster, NY, 1975-84; sr. prin. scientist Eastman Kodak Co., Rochester, NY, 1984—2007, Carestream Health, Inc., Rochester, 2007—. Contbr. articles to profl. jours. Mem. Am. Phys. Soc., Soc. for Imaging Sci. and Tech., Internat. Soc. for Optical Engring. Achievements include patents in digital printing and medical imaging technologies. Home: 1112 Everwild Vw Webster NY 14580-8740 Office: Carestream Health Inc 1049 Ridge Rd W Rochester NY 14615 Office Phone: 585-722-7150. Business E-Mail: kwok.yip@carestreamhealth.com.

YIP, WINNIE, health economics educator; arrived in U.S., 1984; BA, U. Calif., Berkeley, 1988; PhD, MIT, 1994. Asst. prof. econs., Sch. Pub. Health Harvard U., Cambridge, Mass., 1994—2001, assoc. prof. internat. health econs., Sch. Pub. Health, 2001—. Cons. World Bank, Washington, 1995—96, Washington, 1999—2000, Govt. Hong Kong, 1997—99. Mem.: Internat. Health Econs. Assn., Am. Econ. Assn., Phi Beta Kappa. Office: Harvard Sch Pub Health 124 Mt Auburn St Ste 410 S Cambridge MA 02138 E-mail: wyip@hsph.harvard.edu.

YLVISAKER, JAMES WILLIAM, insurance executive; b. Mpls., Minn., Feb. 26, 1938; s. Johannas Wilhelm and Lucille Elizabeth (Torgeson) Y.; m. Judith Diane Stevens, May 19, 1943 (div. Aug. 1980). BA, Luther Coll., 1960. Assoc. actuary North Am. Life & Casualty, Mpls., 1961-76; actuary IDS Life Ins. Co., Mpls., 1976-80; exec. v.p., chief operating officer Cologne Life Reinsurance Co., Stamford, Conn., 1980-89; pres., chief exec. officer IdeaLife Ins. Co., Stamford, 1989-90, also bd. dirs.; pres., COO, Horizons LLC, Hartford, Conn., 1997-99, U.S. Living Benefits, LLC, Hartford, Conn., 1999—. Bd. dirs. Reassurance Corp. of Del., Stamford, Stamford Life Ins. Co., 1983-90, cons. actuary, 1991—. Dist. chmn. United Way of Mpls., 1966; regional coord. Carlson for Mayor Campaign, Mpls., 1968; state chmn. Head for Gov. Campaign, Mpls., 1970; mem. bd. regents Luther Coll., Decorah, Iowa, 1990. Fellow Soc. Actuaries; mem. Am. Acad. Actuaries, Internat. Actuarial Assn. Avocations: reading, music, golf, travel. Home and Office: 40 Prides Crossing 312 Elm St New Canaan CT 06840-5305 Home Phone: 203-966-5154; Office Phone: 203-966-5154. E-mail: jimuslb@optonline.net.

YOAKAM, DWIGHT, country western musician; b. Pikeville, Ky., Oct. 23, 1956; Ph.D (hon.), Ohio Valley Coll., 2005. Albums include Guitars, Cadillacs, Etc. Etc., 1985, Hillbilly Deluxe, 1987, Buenas Noches From A Lonely Room, 1988, Just Lookin' for a Hit, 1989, If There Was a Way, 1990, This Time, 1993, Dwight Live, 1995, Gone, 1996; duet with Buck Owens Streets of Bakersfield, 1988 (No. 1 single); co-prodr. stage appearance Southern Rapture, 1993; appeared in Roswell, Showtime cable feature, 1994, Sling Blade, feature film, 1996, (films) Painted Hero aka Shadow of the Past, 1996, The Newton Boys, 1998, Ozzie and Harriet: The Adventures of America's Favorite Family, 1998, The Minus Man, 1999, South of Heaven, West of Hell, 2000, Panic Room, 2002, Hollywood Homicide, 2003, 3-Way, 2004, The Three Burials of Melquiades Estrada, 2005, Wedding Crashers, 2005, Bandidas, 2006, Crank, 2006, (TV) When Trumpets Fade, 1998; discs include Under the Covers, 1997, Come on Christmas, 1997, A Long Way Home, 1998, Last Chance Greatest Hits from the 90's, 1999, Dwightyoakam.net (Justguitar@dogbone), 2000. Named Top Male Vocalist by Acad. Country Music, 1986; recipient Grammy award for best country vocal performance by male for Ain't That Lonely Yet, 1993, 41st ann. Grammy award for best country collaboration with vocals for Same Old Train, 1998, also 14 nominations; Premiere Performance acting award Motion Picture Club, 1996. Address: Dwight Yoakam Tours 7920 W Sunset Blvd Ste 460 Los Angeles CA 90046-3300

YOAKAM, KELLY LYNN, harpist, educator; b. Little Rock, July 5, 1957; d. Vance Leonard and Donna Jo (Criner) Broadaway; m. Robert William Yoakam, Aug. 11, 1979; children: Amy Louise, Ryan William. BA, Harding U, 1979; A in Applied Music summa cum laude, Lansing Cmty. Coll., 2004. Tchr. of arts East Lansing Cmty. Edn., Holt Cmty. Edn., East Lansing, Mich., 1989—95; sec. The Bug Man Pest Control, Mason, 1987—; music tchr. pvt. practice, Mason, Mich., 1990—; tai chi instr. Lansing (Mich.) Cmty. Coll., 2002—. Cert. in Duchess Lace Jusith de Kreijer, Etten Leur, Netherlands, 1999. CD, Shantih-Lost in Time, 1995, Shantih-Winds of Change, 2004. Fellow, Mich. State U., 2004, 2005. Master: Capitol Area Music Tchrs. Assn. (chmn.dist. ensemble 2000—); mem.: Music Nat. Tchrs. Assn., Am. String Tchrs. Assn., Mich. Music Tchrs. Assn. (state chmn. non-competitive activities), Capitol Area Lace Makers (pres. 1992—97), Phi Theta Kappa. Office: Ms Yoakam 120 W Sycamore Street Mason MI 48854 Business E-Mail: kyoakam@sbcglobal.net.

YOCAM, DELBERT WAYNE, retired software products company executive; b. Long Beach, Calif., Dec. 24, 1943; s. Royal Delbert and Mary Rose (Gross) Y.; m. Janet McVeigh, June 13, 1965; children— Eric Wayne, Christian Jeremy, Elizabeth Janelle. BA in Bus. Adminstrn., Calif. State U.-Fullerton, 1966; MBA, Calif. State U., Long Beach, 1971. Mktg.-supply changeover coordinator Automotive Assembly div. Ford Motor Co., Dearborn, Mich., 1966-72; prodn. control mgr. Control Data Corp., Hawthorne, Calif., 1972-74; prodn. and material control mgr. Bourns Inc., Riverside, Calif., 1974-76; corp. material mgr. Computer Automation Inc., Irvine, Calif., 1976-78; prodn. planning mgr. central staff Cannon Electric div. ITT, World hdqrs., Santa Ana, Calif., 1978-79; exec. v.p., COO Apple Computer, Inc., Cupertino, Calif., 1979-91; pres., COO, dir. Textronix Inc., Wilsonville, Oreg., 1992-95; chmn., CEO Borland Internat., Inc./Inprise Corp., Scotts Valley, Calif., 1996-2000, ret., 2000. Mem. faculty Cypress Coll., Calif., 1972-79; bd. dirs. Adobe Sys Inc., San Jose, Calif., Softricity, Inc., Boston; vice chmn. Tech. Ctr. Innovation, San Jose, Calif., 1989-90. Mem. Am. Electronics Assn. (nat. bd. dirs. 1988-89), Control Data Corp. Mgmt. Assn. (co-founder 1974), L.A. County Heart Assn. (active 1966). E-mail: yocam@aol.com.

YOCAM, ERIC WAYNE, engineer; b. Garden Grove, Calif., Aug. 23, 1966; s. Delbert Wayne and Janet Yocam; m. Siu Kuen Annie Choi, Nov. 5, 2000; children: Hailey Jasmine, Nathan Connor. BS in Computer Engring., U. Pacific, Stockton, Calif., 1990; MBA, U. San Diego, 1997; MS in Fin., Seattle U., 2002; MS in Computer Sci., Calif. State U., Chico, 2004. Cert. software devel. profl., IEEE-Computer Soc., 2002, project mgmt. profl., PMI, 2002, E-commerce cons., tech. specialist, ICECC, 2002. Mem. of tech. staff Apple Computer/Claris Corp., Santa Clara, Calif., 1991—93, Media Vision Corp., Fremont, Calif., 1993—94; tech. mgr. Ray Dream Corp., Mountain View, Calif., 1994—96, Hewlett-Packard Co., Cupertino, Calif., 1997—97; data ctr. project mgr. Intuit Corp., San Diego, 1998—99; sr. program mgr. Microsoft Corp., Redmond, Wash., 1999—. Grad. fellowship, U. San Diego, 1997. Mem.: Sigma Xi. R-Consevative. Methodist. Avocations: private pilot, scuba diving, golf, skiing, surfing. Home: 213 259th Ave NE Sammamish WA 98074 Office Phone: 425-705-3390. Personal E-mail: eyocam@hotmail.com.

YOCHELSON, ELLIS L(EON), paleontologist; b. Washington, Nov. 14, 1928; s. Morris Wolf and Fannie (Botkin) Y.; m. Sally Witt, June 10, 1950; children: Jeffrey, Abby, Charles. BS, U. Kans., Lawrence, 1949, MS, 1950; PhD, Columbia U., NYC, 1955. Paleontologist U.S. Geol. Survey, 1952-85, scientist emeritus, 1991—; biostratigrapher, specializing in Paleozoic gastropods and minor classes of extinct mollusks; lectr. night sch. George Washington U., 1962-65; lectr. Univ. Coll., U. Md., 1966-74; rsch. assoc. Smithsonian Instn., Washington, 1967—; lectr. U. Del., 1981; vis. prof. U. Md., 1986-87; organizer N.Am. Paleontol. Conv., 1969, 1996, editor proc., 1970-71. Co-editor: Essays in Paleontology and Stratigraphy, 1967; editor: Scientific Ideas of G.K. Gilbert, 1980; editorial bd. Nat. Geog. Rsch. and Exploration; contbr. numerous articles to profl. jours.; sec. Internat. Congress Carb. Stratigraphy, 1979. Author: Charles Doolittle Walcott, Paleontologist, 1998, Smithsonian Institution Secretary Charles Doolittle Walcott, 2001. Fellow AAAS (chmn. sect. E 1971), Geol. Soc. Am. (History Geology Divsn. award 2003); mem. Soc. Systematic Zoology (sec. 1961-66, councilor 1973), Internat. Paleontol. Assn. (treas. 1972-76), Paleontol. Soc. (pres. 1976, Centennial fellow 2006), History of Earth Sci. Soc. (hon. life; sec.-treas. 1982-85, sec. 1986-87, pres. 1989), N.Am. Paleontol. Conv. (hon. life; sec.), Smithsonian Instn. (150th Anniversary com.), Sigma Xi. Office: Smithsonian Instn E-305A Mus Natural History Washington DC 20013-7012 Home Phone: 202-439-6229; Office Phone: 202-633-1363. Business E-Mail: yochelse@si.edu.

YOCHES, EDWARD ROBERT, lawyer; b. Denver, Jan. 23, 1953; s. Marvin and Ruth Devorah (Spiegleman) Y.; m. Karen Ruth Droller, Aug. 20, 1978; children: Aaron Stuart, Meryl Laura. BEE in Computer Sci., U. Colo., 1974; JD, U. Pa., 1980. Bar: D.C. 1980. Engr. Goddard Space Flight Ctr. NASA, Greenbelt, Md., 1974-77; assoc. Finnegan, Henderson, Farabow, Garrett & Dunner, Washington, 1980-88, ptnr., 1988—. Named one of best lawyers in intellectual property law, Best Lawyers in Am., 2005—06. Mem. ABA (chmn. computer law subcom. on trade secrets and internat. protection 1982-86), D.C. Bar Assn. (vice chmn. computer law div. 1985, chmn. 1986-87), Am. Intellectual Property Assn. Office: Finnegan Henderson Farabow Garrett & Dunner LLP 901 New York Ave NW Washington DC 20001-3315 Office Phone: 202-408-4000. Office Fax: 202-408-4400. Business E-Mail: bob.yoches@finnegan.com.

YOCK, ROBERT JOHN, federal judge; b. St. James, Minn., Jan. 11, 1938; s. William Julius and Erma Idella (Fritz) Y.; m. Carla Marie Moen, June 13, 1964; children: Signe Kara, Torunn Ingrid. BA, St. Olaf Coll., 1959; JD, U. Mich., 1962; postgraduate student, U. Strasbourg, France, 1961, Old Dominion Coll., 1964-65, U. Minn., 1966-67. Bar: Minn. 1962, US Supreme Ct. 1965, DC 1972. Assoc. Thomas, King, Swenson & Collatz, St. Paul, 1966-69; chief counsel Nat. Archives, Office Gen Counsel GSA, Washington, 1969-70, exec. asst. to adminstr., 1970-72, asst. gen. counsel, 1972-77; trial judge US Ct. Claims, Washington, 1977-82; judge US Ct. Fed. Claims, Washington, 1982—98, sr. judge, 1998—. Served with JAGC USN, 1962-66. Mem. ABA, Minn., Fed., DC Bar Assns. Office: US Ct Fed Claims 717 Madison Pl NW Washington DC 20439-0002 *

YOCKIM, JAMES CRAIG, foundation administrator; b. Williston, ND, Feb. 13, 1953; s. Daniel and Doris (Erickson) Y.; children: Jenna, Ericka. BSW, Pacific Luth. U., 1975; MSW, San Diego State U., 1979. Caseworker Dyslin Boys Ranch, Tacoma, 1975-77, head caseworker, program dir., 1979-80; landman Fayette Oil & Gas, Williston, 1980-82; owner Hy-Plains Energy, Williston, 1982-87; city fin. commr. City of Williston, 1984—88, 1998—2002; therapist Williston, 1983; senator N.D. State Senate, 1986-98; owner James C. Yockim Resources, Williston, 1987—. Dir. Bethel Luth. Found., 1993—; del. N.D. Dem. Conv., 1984, 86, 88, 90, 92, 94, 96, 98, 2000, 02, 04; dist. chmn. Dem. Party, Williston, 1988; caucus chmn. Dem. Caucus N.D. State Senate; mem. N.D. Legis. Coun., 1997-98; coun. pres. 1st Luth. Ch. Recipient Ruth Meiers award N.D. Mental Health Assn., 1989, Legislator of Yr. award N.D. Children's Caucus, 1989; named Outstanding Young North Dakotan N.D. Jaycees, 1988. Mem. NASW. Avocations: racquetball, golf. Home: 1123 2nd Ave E Williston ND 58801-4302 Office: PO Box 2344 Williston ND 58802-2344 Business E-Mail: JamesYoc@dia.net.

YOCUM, LEWIS ALBERT, orthopedist, surgeon; b. Chgo., Ill., 1947; MD, U. Ill. Coll. Medicine, 1973. Diplomate Am. Bd. Orthop. Surgery, Nat. Bd. Med. Examiners. Surgery intern McGaw Med. Ctr., Northwestern U., Ill., 1973—74, resident Ill., 1974—77; sports medicine fellow Kerlan-Jobe Orthop. Clinic, Inglewood, Calif., 1977; clin. asst. prof. U. Southern Calif. Sch. Medicine, LA; assoc. clin. prof. U. Calif., Irvine; orthop. surgeon Kerlan-Jobe Orthop. Clinic, LA. Bd. trustee Centinela Hosp. Med. Ctr.; asst. med. dir. Profl. Golf Assn., 1997—; team physician Anaheim Angels Profl. Baseball Team; orthop. cons. several dance companies. Panel reviewer American Journal of Sports Medicine; contbr. sevaral articles to profl. jours. Fellow: Am. Acad. Orthop. Surgeons, ACS. Office: Kerlan-Jobe Orthop Clinic 2400 E Katella Ave Ste 400 Anaheim CA 92806 *

YODAIKEN, RALPH E., pathologist, occupational health physician, educator; b. Johannesburg, Aug. 22, 1928; arrived in US, 1964, naturalized, 1970; m. Naomi Baumslag Yodaiken; children: Victor, Barry D., Ruth T. MD, U. Witwatersrand, Republic of South Africa, 1956; MPH, Johns Hopkins U., 1976. Diplomate Am. Bd. Pathology, Am. Bd. Forensic Medicine. Intern Coronation Hosp., Johannesburg, 1956-57; resident U. Witwatersrand Med. Ctr., 1957-58, Johannesburg Gen. Hosp., 1958; assoc. pathologist Buffalo Gen. Hosp., 1965-67; mem. staff Cin. Gen. Hosp., 1968-71; rsch. assoc. Johns Hopkins U. Sch. Hygiene and Pub. Health, Balt., 1976—; sr. staff mem. Nat. Inst. Occupational Safety and Health, Washington, 1977—, chmn. sr. adv. staff, 1983; dir. office occupational medicine Occupational Safety and Health Adminstrn., U.S. Dept. Labor, Washington, 1983-91, sr. med. advisor, 1991—98; clin. prof. preventive medicine U. Health Scis., Washington, 1983—. Lectr. U. Witwatersrand, 1958-63; asst. prof. pathology, SUNY Buffalo, 1963-67; assoc. prof. pathology U. Cin., 1968-71; prof. pathology, assoc. prof. medicine Emory U., Atlanta, 1971-75; adj. clin. prof. George Washington U., 1975—; sr. assoc. Johns Hopkins Sch. Hygiene and Pub. Health; clin. prof. preventive medicine uniformed svcs. U. Health Scis. Bd. mem. Am. Jewish Com., Bradley Blvd. Citizens Assn. With Israeli Commandos Israeli Army, 1948—50. Fellow Coll. Am. Pathologists, Am. Coll. Occupl. and Environ. Health, Am. Coll. Forensic Medicine. Democrat. Jewish. Office Phone: 301-728-4041. Personal E-mail: ryodaiken@aol.com.

YODER, BRUCE ALAN, chemist; b. Seward, Nebr., Apr. 29, 1962; s. Elwood John and Elda Raye (Stutzman) Y. BS in Chemistry, Wayne State Coll., 1983. Lab. technician Wayne (Nebr.) State Coll., 1982-83, Harris Labs., Lincoln, Nebr., 1984, chemist, 1984; scientist Dorsey Labs., Lincoln, 1984-86, scientist A, 1986-88; product stability analyst Sandoz Pharms., Lincoln, 1988-89, Sandoz Rsch. Inst., Lincoln, 1989-91; mgr. lab. computer ops. Sandoz Pharms., Lincoln, 1991-97; pres., CEO Data Mgmt. Svcs., Inc., Lincoln, 1997—. Active Lancaster County Young Reps., Lincoln, 1988—, co-chmn., 1990-91, pres., 1991-93; mem. Nebr. Fedn. Young Reps., 1988—, exec. com., 1990—, chmn., 1998-99; exec. com. Lancaster County Rep. Party, 1990-97; mem. Def. Adv. Com. Lancaster County, 1992-00; active Lincoln Mayor's Cmty. Cabinet, 1992-93, Lincoln City Charter Revision Commn., 1994-2002, co-chmn., 1998-2000, chmn., 2000-2002; trustee Wayne State Coll. Found., 1991—; advisor Jr. Achievement, 1993-97; bd. dirs. Lincoln Meadows Assn., 1998-99. Recipient Dwight M. Frost, MD award for overcoming a phys. disability Immanuel Rehab. Ctr., 1993, Verdi Smith Outstanding Voluntary Contbns. award Lancaster County Rep. Party, 1995-96, First Dist. Outstanding Vol. award Nebr. Reps., 1996-97, Daniel D. Fahrnbruch Leadership award Lancaster County GOP, 2000, Alumni Svc. award Wayne State Coll., 2006. Mem. Internat. Soc. for Pharm. Engrs., Am. Inst. Chemists, Am. Chem. Soc., Am. Assn. Pharm. Scientists, Lincoln Ind. Bus. Assn., Jaycees, Elephant Club. Mennonite. Achievements include design of a sample holder for solid dosage forms when using a hunter color instrument, design of a new computer system for Sandoz Pharmaceuticals laboratory computer operations, design of a new computer system for Novartis Consumer Health, Inc. Home and Office: 2240 Winding Way Lincoln NE 68506-2846 Office Phone: 402-483-1532. Personal E-mail: yoderb@aol.com.

YODER, DALE ROY, history educator; b. Sturgis, Mich., Dec. 20, 1955; s. Ernest Roy and Willa Mae (Parker) Yoder; m. Denise Kathleen Sivits, Apr. 12, 1985; 1 child, Daniel Parker. BS, Grand Valley State Coll., Allendale Mich., 1978, BS in Phys. Edn., 1981; MA in Phys. Edn. and Athletic Tng., Western Mich. U., Kalamazoo, 1983. Head athletic trainer Holland Pub. Schs., Mich., 1981—82; tchr. and athletic trainer South Dade H.S., Homestead, Fla., 1984—87; athletic trainer U. Mich. Medsport, Ann Arbor, 1987—90, Ypsilanti HS, 1991—92; soc. studies tchr. Benton Harbor Area Schs., 1992—. Adj. faculty Lake Mich. Coll., 1994—. Baseball umpire Mich. H.S. Athletic Assn., 1992—; vol. Midwest Boston Terrier Rescue, 2001—. Mem.: Amateur Baseball Umpires Assn., Fruitbelt Officials Assn., Nat. Coun. Social Studies. Office: Fair Plain NW Learning Acad 1452 Learning Ln Benton Harbor MI 49022

YODER, EDWIN MILTON, JR., columnist, educator, editor, writer; b. Greensboro, NC, July 18, 1934; s. Edwin M. and Mytrice M. (Logue) Y.; m. Mary Jane Warwick, Nov. 1, 1958; children: Anne Daphne, Edwin Warwick. BA, U. N.C., 1956; BA, MA (Rhodes scholar), Oxford U., Eng., 1958; D.H.L. (hon.), Grinnell Coll., 1980, Elon Coll., 1986; DLitt (hon.), U. N.C., 1993, Richmond Coll., London. Editorial writer Charlotte (N.C.) News, 1958-61; editorial writer Greensboro Daily News, 1961-64, assoc. editor, 1965-75; asst. prof. history U. N.C., Greensboro, 1964-65; editorial page editor Washington Star, 1975-81; syndicated columnist Washington Post Writers Group, 1982-97; prof. journalism and humanities Washington and Lee U., 1992—2002, prof. emeritus, 2002—. Hon. fellow Jesus Coll., Oxford, Eng., 1998—. Author: Night of the Old South Ball, 1984, The Unmaking of a Whig, 1990, Joe Alsop's Cold War, 1995, The Historical Present, 1997, Telling Others What to Think: Recollections of a Pundit, 2004, Lions at Lamb House, 2007; contbr. articles to periodicals. Trustee Inst. Early Am. History and Culture, Nat. Humanities Ctr. U. NC, 1990-96. Recipient awards editorial writing N.C. Press Assn., 1958, 61, 66, Walker Stone award Scripps-Howard Found., 1978, Pulitzer prize editorial writing, 1979; Disting. Alumnus award U. N.C., Chapel Hill, 1980 Mem. Nat. Conf. Editorial Writers, Am. Soc. Newspaper Editors. Democrat. Episcopalian. Home: 4001 Harris Pl Alexandria VA 22304-1720 Office Phone: 703-751-9022. E-mail: yoderem@aol.com.

YODER, KRISTINE E., molecular biologist, educator; b. Pa. PhD, U. Calif., San Diego, 2000. Rsch. asst. prof. Ohio State U., Columbus, 2006—.

YODER, PATRICIA DOHERTY, public relations executive; b. Pitts., Oct. 30, 1939; d. John Addison and Camella Grace (Conti) Doherty; children: Shari Lynn, Wendy Ann; m. James Ronald Wolfe, Oct. 30, 1999. BA, Duquesne U., 1961. Press sec. U.S. Ho. of Reps., 1965-69; dir. Office of Pub. Info., City of Ft. Wayne, 1973-76; asst. mgr. pub. and corp. comm. Mellon Bank N.A., Pitts., 1977-79; v.p. pub. affairs Am. Waterways Operators Inc., Washington, 1980-83, sr. v.p., gen. mgr., 1983-86, exec. v.p., dir. banking, 1989-91; exec. v.p., dir. internat. banking Hill and Knowlton Inc., Pitts.; sr. v.p. corp. and pub. affairs PNC Fin. Svcs. Group, Pitts., 1987-89; v.p., corp. pub. rels. and advt. GE Capital Svcs. Corp., Stamford, Conn., 1991-95; corp. v.p. pub. affairs and comm. GTE Corp., Stamford, 1995-96; sr. v.p. corp. comm. Avis Group Holdings, Garden City, NY, 1996-99; prin. PDY Assocs., 1999—. Trustee, exec. com. Duquesne U., Shadyside Hosp., Pressley Ridge Sch., Pitts., Ellis Sch.; bd. dirs.

Children's Mus., Civic Light Opera, Pitts. Ballet Theatre, Jr. League of City of N.Y. Recipient Outstanding Woman Bus. and Industry, 1988, Disting. Alumni award Duquesne U., 1996, McAnulty Svc. award, 2006. Mem. Pitts. Field Club, Duquesne Club, Indian Harbor Yacht Club, Boca Raton (Fla.) Resort and Country Club, Fox Hill Golf and Country Club, Gardener's Bay Country Club. Roman Catholic. Home and Office: 500 SE 5th Ave Apt 601 Boca Raton FL 33432-5510 Address: 23 Wireless Way Southampton NY 10028 Personal E-mail: pdyoder@mac.com.

YODER, RANDALL D., music educator; b. Lancaster, Pa., Jan. 21, 1949; s. David J. and Mary Lou Yoder; m. Leslee Ann Brenneman, Jan. 24, 1992; stepchildren: Dustin M. Kemper, Jelee Elizabeth Kemper. BS in Music Edn., Susquehanna U., 1971; MusM in Choral Conducting, Westminster Choir Coll., 1978. Tchr., choral dir. Northeastern Sch. Dist., Manchester, Pa., 1971—88, York City Schs., Pa., 1997—2006; music dir. Eastminster Presbyn. Ch., York, 2006—; choral dir. European Concert Tour Sound of Am., 2002, 2004, 2006—07. Dir. York County Honors Choir, 1998—; choral dir. Pa. Ambs. of Music, European Concert Tour, 2001; choral dir. European concert tour Sound of Am. Honor Choir, 2002, 04, 06. Composer: (original music for documentary) Historic Pennsylvania, 1996 (Emmy award, 1997), Hershey Park Memories, 1998, (CD) Christmas Rose, 2000, April Rose, 2004. Mem.: Music Educators Nat. Conf., Am. Choral Dirs. Assn. Avocation: travel.

YODER, RONNIE A., judge; b. Knoxville, Tenn., July 10, 1937; s. Raymond Abraham and Veryl Hope (Hostetler) Y.; m. Shirley Mae Grimes, June 28, 1961; children: Susan Elizabeth Torres, Mary Amanda Anderson, Elizabeth Anne Lee, John Anthony Gerhard. BA in Polit. Sci. with honors, U. Va., 1958, JD, 1961. Bar: Va. 1961, N.Y. 1963, D.C. 1965, U.S. Dist. Ct. D.C. 1965, U.S. Dist. Ct. (so. dist.) N.Y. 1969, U.S. Ct. Claims 1964, U.S. Supreme Ct. 1968. Assoc. Mudge Rose Guthrie & Alexander, NYC and Washington, 1962-70; of counsel Zuckert Scoutt & Rasenberger, Washington, 1970-72, ptnr., 1972-75; adminstrv. law judge U.S. Dept. Labor, Washington, 1976, CAB, Washington, 1976-84, U.S. Dept. Transp., Washington, 1985-98, acting chief adminstrv. law judge, 1999-2001, chief adminstv. law judge, 2001—. Adminstrv. law judge Nat. Transp. Safety Bd., 1979-80, Maritime Adminstrn., 1983, 86-88, FDIC, 1982-83, SBA, 1983, FAA, 1985—, Fed. Hwy. Adminstrn., 1985-2000, Fed. R.R. Adminstrn., 1993-95, Rsch. and Spl. Programs Adminstrn., 1991-2005, Surface Transp. Bd., 1996-97, Fed. Motor Carrier Safety Adminstrn., 2000—; Fed. Transp. Security Adminstrn., 2002-04, Pipeline and Hazardous Materials Safety Adminstrn., 2005—; mem. Adminstrv. Conf. of U.S., 1994-95. Mem. editorial bd. U. Va. Law Rev., 1959-61; contbr. articles to profl. jours. Sec., co-counsel Capital Headstart, 1966-68; narrator Lincoln Commn., 1985, 86; founder Ronnie A. Yoder Scholarship Va. Theol. Sem., 2007; mem. permanent jud. commn. Nat. Capital Presbytery, 1985-91. Rockefeller fellow Yale Divinity Sch., 1961-62. Fellow: Fed. Bar Found., Am. Bar Found.; mem.: SAR, FBA (jud. divsn. leadership coun. 1999—, bd. dirs. D.C. chpt. 1999—, pres. D.C. chpt. 2003—05), ABA (sec. nat. conf. adminstrv. law judges 1991—92, vice chmn. 1992—93, chmn.-elect 1993—94, chmn. 1994—95, vice chmn. social security com. sr. lawyers sect. 1996—2000, exec. com. nat. conf. adminstrv. law judges 1997—2001, judges adv. com. on ethics and profl. responsibility 2001—04, exec. com. nat. conf. adminstrv. law judges 2002—04, adminstrv. law sect., sec. sect. officers, chmn. task force govt. employees' participation profl. assns., jud. divsn. coun. 1994—95), Prettyman Leventhal Am. Inn of Ct., Am. Guild Musical Artists, D.C. Bar Assn., Va. Bar Assn., Nat. Assn. Adminstrv. Law Judges (jour. bd. advisors 2004—), Fed. Adminstrv. Law Judges Conf. (exec. com. 1976—81, 1985, 1987, 1999—), Am. Judicature Soc. (nat. adv. coun. 2005—), Phi Eta Sigma, Phi Beta Kappa. Home: 1400 Summit Ave Alexandria VA 22302-2735 Office: US Dept Transp E12-320 1200 New Jersey Ave SE Washington DC 20590 Office Phone: 202-366-2137. Personal E-mail: honron@aol.com. Business E-Mail: ronnie.yoder@dot.gov.

YODER, STEPHEN ALAN, lawyer; b. Wilmington, Del., Aug. 9, 1953; s. Richard Esser and Jane Frances (Whitby) Y.; m. Louise Lea Whitney, Sept. 3, 1977; children: Salle Lea, Katharine Anne, Caroline Whitney. AB, Duke U., 1975; JD, Northwestern U., 1978. Bar: Pa. 1978, Calif. 1983. Assoc. Reed Smith Shaw McClay, Pitts., 1978-83, Pettit & Martin, San Francisco, 1983-84, Reed Smith, Pitts., 1984-86, ptnr., 1987-90; mng. counsel Mellon Bank, Pitts., 1990-92, asst. gen. counsel, 1992-95; gen. counsel Am. South Bancorp., Birmingham, Ala., 1995—2002, sr. exec. v.p., gen. counsel, 2002; now ptnr. Balch & Bingham LLP, Birmingham, Ala. Trustee Birmingham Hist. Soc., 1996—, Ala. Eye Inst., Birmingham, 1996—. Office: Balch & Bingham Ste 2600 1901 Sixth Ave N Birmingham AL 35203-4644 Office Phone: 205-226-8791. Office Fax: 205-448-5645. E-mail: syoder@balch.com. *

YODER-WISE, PATRICIA SNYDER, nursing educator; d. Belford Grant and Leona Cora (Mohler) Snyder; m. Robert Thomas Wise, Feb. 17, 1973; children: Doreen Ellen Wise, Deborah Ann Wise. BSN, Ohio State U., 1963; MSN, Wayne State U., 1968; EdD, Tex. Tech. U., 1984. RN Tex., CNAA. Interim assoc. dean practice program Tex. Tech. U. Health Sci. Ctr. Sch. Nursing, Lubbock, 1979—, interim dean, prof., 1991-93, dean, prof., 1993-2000; clin. prof. U. Tex. Health Sci. Ctr., San Antonio, 1993—2000; prof. Tex. Woman's U., 2004—. Mem. rev. panel Nursing Outlook, 1993—; mem. adv. com. GlaxoWellcome, 1996—2000; mem. Nat. Quality Forum Health Profls. Provide and Health Plans Panel, 2001—06. Author, editor: Leading and Managing in Nursing, 1994 (Book of Yr. award, 1996, 2003), 1998, 2002; co-author: Beyond Leading and Managing, 2006 (Book of Yr. award, 2007); peer reviewer Jour. Profl. Nursing, 1984—2003, mem. editl. bd. Jour. Continuing Edn. Nursing, 1978—; editor: Jour. Continuing Edn. Nursing, 1988—. Mem. Leadership Am., 1999—2000; participant Leadership Tex.-Found. Women's Resources, 1997—98; mem. Leadership Tex., 1998—99. Recipient Women of Excellence in Medicine, YWCA, Lubbock, 1996, Woman of Excellence in Medicine, 1996, Nurse of Yr. Fellow: Am. Acad. Nursing (chair Inst. for Nursing Leadership 1999—2002, mem. planning com. 2004); mem.: ANCC (pres. 2005—07), ANA (del. 1995—2000, chair constituent assembly 1998—2000, sec. 2000—02, 1st v.p. 2002—05), Wise Group (pres.), Tex. Nurses Assn. (pres. 1995—99). Home: 7309 93d St Lubbock TX 79424 Office Phone: 806-866-9403, 806-790-4600. Personal E-mail: psywrn@aol.com.

YODOWITZ, EDWARD JAY, lawyer; b. NYC, 1943; BS, LI U., 1965; JD, U. Balt., 1969. Bar: NY 1972. With Skadden, Arps, Slate, Meagher & Flom LLP, NYC, 1969—, now sr. ptnr. securities and bus. fraud and accountants' liability. Co-chmn. Practicing Law Inst. seminars, 1985-95. Contbr. articles in publs.;, co-author several publs.; co-editor: Securities Class Actions: Abuses and Remedies, Nat. Legal Ctr. for the Pub. Interest, 1994. Bd. trustee LI U., 1990—99. Mem.: ABA, Planning Bd. of Village of Lawrence NY. Home: 105 Ocean Ave Lawrence NY 11559-2006 Office: Skadden Arps Slate Meagher & Flom LLP Four Times Sq New York NY 10036 Office Phone: 212-735-3450. Office Fax: 917-777-3450. Business E-Mail: eyodowit@skadden.com.

YOFFA, ELLEN J., information technology executive; BS, PhD, MIT. Tech. asst. to dir. IBM Rsch. Divsn.; with IBM Microelectronics Divsn.; dir., emerging sys. technologies IBM T.J. Watson Rsch. Ctr., Hawthorne, NY, dir., next generation web. Gen. chair IEEE/Assn. Computing Machinery Design Automation Conf., 1997. Mem. external adv. bd. U. So. Calif. Electrical Engring. Dept., U. Mass Electrical and Computer Engring. Dept. Recipient Marie R. Pistilli Women in Electronic Design Automation award, Design Automation Conf., 2006. Fellow: IEEE (pres., circuits and systems soc. 2006—, mem. exec. com. and bd. gov., circuits and systems soc., editl. adv. bd., Spectrum mag.); mem.: Assn. for Computing Machinery, Sigma Xi, Phi Beta Kappa. Office: IBM TJ Watson Rsch Ctr Room 3N-C26 19 Skyline Dr Hawthorne NY 10532 Office Phone: 914-784-5222. Office Fax: 914-784-6324. Business E-Mail: yoffa@us.ibm.com.

YOFFIE, ERICH H., religious organization administrator; m. Amy Jacobson; 2 children. Grad., Brandeis U., Hebrew Union Coll., NYC, 1974. Ordained rabbi 74. Rabbi, Lynbrook, NJ; rabbi Durham, NC; dir. Midwest Coun. Union Am. Hebrew Congregations, NYC, 1980—92, v.p., dir. Commn. on Social Action, 1992—96, pres., 1996—; exec. dir. Assn. Reform Zionists of Am., 1983—; pres. Union Reformed Judaism. Exec. editor: Reform Judaism mag., 1992—96; contbr. articles to profl. jours. Religious leader Million Mom March, 2000; regional pres., nat. v.p. NAm. Fedn. Temple Youth; bd. dirs. many Jewish orgns. including Mazon: A Jewish Response to Hunger and the Jewish Agy. for Israel. Named one of The Top 50 Rabbis in America, Newsweek Mag., 2007; named to Top Fifty List of Leadership, Forward Annual. Office: UAHC Hdqs 633 3rd Ave New York NY 10017-6706 *

YOGANATHAN, AJIT PRITHIVIRAJ, biomedical engineer, educator; b. Colombo, Sri Lanka, Dec. 6, 1951; came to U.S., 1973; s. Ponniah and Mangay (Navaratnam) Y.; m. Tripti Yoganathan. BSChemE with honors, Univ. Coll., U. London, 1973; PhDChemE, Calif. Inst. Tech., 1978. Engring. asst. Shell Oil Refinery, Stanlow, Eng., 1972; tchg. asst. Calif. Inst. Tech., 1973-74, 1976, rsch. fellow, 1977-79; asst. prof. Ga. Inst. Tech., 1979-83, assoc. prof., 1983-88, chmn. bioengring. com., 1984-88, prof. chem. engring., 1988-94, dir. Bioengring. Ctr., 1989—, prof. mech. engring., 1989-94, co-dir. Emory U.-Ga. Tech. Biomed. Tech. Ctr., 1992—, Regents prof., 1994—, assoc. chair biomed. engring., 1998—; Wallace H. Coulter disting. faculty chair, 2004—. Adj. assoc. prof. U. Ala., 1985. Founding fellow Am. Inst. Med. & Biol. Engring., 1992; recipient Edwin Walker prize Brit. Inst. Mech. Engrs., 1988, Humboldt fellowship, 1985, Am. Heart Assn.-Ga. Affiliate Rsch. Investigatorship award, 1980-83, Calif. Inst. Tech. fellowship, 1973-77, Goldsmid Medal and prize Univ. Coll., 1972-73, Brit. Coun. scholarship, 1971-73, Sigma Xi Rsch. award, 1995, HR Lissner award, ASME, 1997. Mem. AIChE, ASME (Bioengring. div., H.R. Lissner award 1997), Biomed. Engring. Soc., Am. Soc. Echocardiography (dir. 1987-91). Office: Sch Biomed Engring Ga Tech/Emory Atlanta GA 30332-0535 E-mail: ajit.yoganathan@bme.gatech.edu.

YOH, WILLIAM C., outsourcing company executive; BA, Duke U.; MBA, U. Pa. Engr. CSC Index; sr. v.p. bus. devel. Day & Zimmermann, sr. v.p. corp. strategy & fin.; regional pres. N.W. Region Yoh, Phila., 2002—03, pres., CEO, 2003—. Named one of 40 Under 40, Phila. Bus. Jour., 2006. Office: Yoh 1818 Market St Philadelphia PA 19103 Office Phone: 215-616-2650. Office Fax: 215-656-2687.

YOH, WILLIAM HARRY, JR., music educator; b. Reading, Pa., June 10, 1964; s. William Harry Yoh Sr. and Sylvia Mae (Boyer) Yoh; m. Colleen Mary Ryan, June 11, 1994; 1 child, Olivia Elaine. B of Music Edn., U. Mich., 1986. Educator band, chorus Millington Cmty. Schs., Mich., 1986—88, Glades County Schs., Moore Haven, Fla., 1988—89; educator, orch., band, chorus Madison Mid. Sch., Titusville, 1989—2000, Robert Louis Stevenson Elem. Sch. Arts, Merritt Osland, 2000—. Lead tchr. arts dept. Stevenson Elem. Sch., 2000—, mem. sch. adv. coun., 2002—04. Contbr. articles to profl. jours.; performer: (trombonist, music dir.) Historic Coca Village Playhouse, 1997—, (trombonist) Keystone Band, 1982—88, Perserverance Band, 1985—87, 76ers, 1983—84. Mem.: Fla. Music Educators Assn. (editl. com. 1997—99), Music Educators Nat. Conf., Windjammers Inltd. (trustee 1989—, trombonist, condr.). Republican. Mem. United Ch. Christ. Avocations: stamp collecting/philately, travel, theater. Home: 1112 Brumpton Pl Rockledge FL 32955 Office: Robert Louis Stevenson Elem Sch 1450 Martin Blvd Merritt Island FL 32952

YOHALEM, HARRY MORTON, lawyer; b. Phila., Jan. 21, 1943; s. Morton Eugene and Florence (Mishnun) Y.; m. Martha Caroline Remy, June 9, 1967; children: Seth, Mark. BA with honors, U. Wis., 1965; JD cum laude, Columbia U., 1969, M in Internat. Affairs, 1969. Bar: NY 1969, DC 1981, Calif. 1992, U.S. Supreme Ct. 1985. Assoc. Shearman & Sterling, NYC, 1969-71; asst. counsel to gov. State of NY, Albany, 1971-73, counsel office planning svcs., 1973-75; asst. gen. counsel FEA, Washington, 1975-77; mem. staff White House Energy Policy and Planning Office, Washington, 1977; dep. gen. counsel for legal svcs. Dept. Energy, Washington, 1978-80, dep. under sec., 1980-81; ptnr. Rogers & Wells, Washington, 1981-91; gen. counsel Calif. Inst. Tech., Pasadena, 1991—. Editor comments Columbia Jour. Transnat. Law, 1967-68, rsch. editor, 1968-69. Prin. Coun. for Excellence in Govt., Washington, 1990—; pres. Opera Bel Canto, Washington, 1984-87; mem. Lawyers Com. for Arts, Washington, 1981-88; bd. visitors dept. English U. Wis., 1999—. Harlan Fiske Stone scholar Columbia U., 1967, 69. Mem.: Athenaeum, Phi Kappa Phi. Home: 702 E California Blvd Pasadena CA 91106 Office: Calif Inst Tech Mail Code 109-31 1200 E California Blvd Pasadena CA 91125 Business E-Mail: harry.yohalem@caltech.edu.

YOHE, HARRY EDWARD, JR., special education educator; b. Columbia, Pa., July 20, 1950; s. Harry Edward Yohe and Doris Ruth McComsey; children: William Barris, Jordan Michele. BS in Elem. Edn., Jacksonville State U., Ala., 1977, MS in Spl. Edn., 1978, EdS in Spl. Edn., 1990. Lifetime tchg. cert. Dept. Elem. and Secondary Edn., Mo., 2007. Commd. lt. US Army, 1967, advanced through grades to command sgt. maj., ret., 1997; spl. educator Spl. Sch. Dist., Town and Country, Mo., 1999—. Decorated numerous medals US Army. Mem.: NEA, DAV (life), Coun. Exceptional Children, 173rd Airborne Brigade Soc. (life), Vietnam Vets. Am. (life), Jacksonville State U. Alumni Assn. (life), Eagle Scouts (life), Order of the Arrow (life), Sigma Nu (life). Roman Catholic. Avocations: boating, fishing, jogging, travel. Office Phone: 314-989-8100.

YOHN, WILLIAM H(ENDRICKS), JR., federal judge; b. Pottstown, Pa., Nov. 20, 1935; s. William H. and Dorothy C. (Cornelius) Y.; m. Jean Louise Kochel, Mar. 16, 1963; children: William H. III, Bradley G., Elizabeth Y. Lemmon. AB, Princeton U., 1957; JD, Yale U., 1960. Bar: Pa. 1961, U.S. Dist. Ct. D.C. 1961. Ptnr. Wells Campbell Reynier & Yohn, Pottstown, 1961-71; mem., chmn. coms. Pa. House of Reps., Harrisburg, 1968-80; ptnr. Binder Yohn & Kalis, Pottstown, 1971-81; judge Montgomery County Ct. of Common Pleas, Norristown, Pa., 1981-91, U.S. Dist. Ct. (ea. dist.), Pa., 1991—. Asst. dist. atty., Montgomery County Dist. Atty. Office, 1962-65; instr. Am. Inst. of Banking, 1963-66; bd. dirs. Fed. Jud. Ctr., 1999-2003; chair Third Cir. Com. on Model Criminal Jury Instrns, 2004-. Bd. dirs. Greater Pottstown Drug Abuse Prevention Program, 1970-76, Pottstown Meml. Med. Ctr., 1974-95, chmn., 1984-95; mem. exec. com. Yale Law Sch. Alumni Assn., 1998—. Cpl. USMCR, 1960-66. Mem. Pa. Bar Assn., Montgomery Bar Assn. (bd. dirs. 1967-70), Fed. Judge Assn. Republican. Office: US Dist Ct 14613 US Courthouse 601 Market St Philadelphia PA 19106-1713 Office Phone: 215-597-4361.

YOHO, BILLY LEE, lawyer; b. Huntington, W.Va., Oct. 24, 1925; s. Wilbert Wiley Yoho Sr. and Nellie Pansy (Bryan) Hawkins; m. Martha Sue Carroll; children: Kevin Richard, Karen Lee; m. Shirley Ann Stone Morris. BA, U. Md., 1950; LLD, U. Md., Balt., 1953. Bar: Md. 1953. Ptnr. Hoyert & Yoho Chartered, Lanham, Md., 1953—; gen. counsel City of College Park, Md., 1959-62; town atty. Town of Colmar Manor, Md., 1956-72; gen. counsel Prince George's Gen. Hosp., Cheverly, Md., 1955-74, MD22 Lions Rsch. Found., Balt., 1988—; ptnr. Hoyert & Yoho Chartered, Lanham, Md., 1987—. Mem. College Park airport program in saving the oldest airport in the world, 1968. With USN, 1943-47. Mem. ABA, Prince George's County Bar Assn. (pres. 1976-77), Md. Assn. Trial Attys., Lions Clubs Internat. (dist. gov. 1989-90, life mem.), NRA, U. Md. Alumni Assn. Republican. Baptist. Avocations: computing, genealogy, Christian studies. Home: 2262 Culp Rd Berkeley Springs WV 25411-4344 Office Phone: 301-459-4200. Business E-Mail: lee_yoho@mac.com.

YOKEN, MEL B(ARTON), language educator, writer, radio personality; b. Fall River, Mass., June 25, 1939; s. Albert Benjamin and Sylvia Sarah (White) Y.; m. Cynthia Stein, June 20, 1976; children: Andrew Brett, David Ryan, Jonathan Barry. BA, U. Mass., 1960; MAT, Brown U., Providence, 1961, PhD, 1972. Instr. French U. Mass., Dartmouth, 1966-72, asst. prof., 1976-81, prof., 1981—2000, chancellor prof., 2000. Dir. French summer study program French Inst., 1981-88; radio commentator, 1956-, Am. Field Svc., 1971—, pres., 1984-86, v.p., 2001—; vis. prof. Wheaton Coll., 1987, U. of Montreal, 1981-88; translator New Bedford Superior Ct., New Bedford, Mass., 1985—, Fall River Superior Ct., Fall River, Mass., 1985—; reader, cons. AP Exams in French, 1997—; nominating com. Nobel Prize for lit., 1972—, Acad. Am. Poets, 1999—. Author: Claude Tillier, 1976, Speech is Plurality, 1978, Claude Tillier (1801-44): Fame and Fortune in His Novelistic Work, 1978, Entretiens Quebecois I, 1986, Entretiens Quebecois II, 1989, Letters of Robert Molloy, 1989, Festschrift in Honor of Stowell Goding, 1993, Entretiens Quebecois III, 1999, Essays and Vignettes in Honor of John A. Rassias, 2007; contbr. articles to profl. jours. Pres. Friends of Fall River Pub. Libr., 1972-80, pres., bd. dirs., 1972-80; pres. New Bedford Pub. Libr., 1980-82; bd. dirs. Am. Field Svc., 1980—, pres., 1984-86, v.p., 2001—; v.p. Friends of U. Mass. Libr., 1998—, pres., 1999—; dir. Boivin Ctr., 1999—; hon. mem. adv. bd. The Irena Sendler Project. Decorated officier Ordre des Palmes académiques, Acad. Française, 2001, Order Nat. du Que., 2005; recipient Disting. Svc. award City Fall River, 1974, 80, Excellence in Tchg. French award, 1984-85, Gov.'s citation, 1986, Nat. Disting. Leadership award, 1990, Dist. Svc. award Mass. Fgn. Lang. Assn., 1992, Medaille de Vermeil du Rayonnement de la Langue Française, L'Academie Française, 1993, Outstanding Cmty. Svc. award, 1997, Disting. Alumni award, Durfee H.S., 1998, Golden Apple award Fall River Herald News, 1998; Govt. of Que. grantee, 1981-85, 87-89, Can. Embassy grantee, 1986, 87, Southeastern Mass. U. grantee, 1985, 89, 90; named Hon. Life Mem., Fall River Pub. Libr., 2003; named Mel Yoken Day in his honor by Mayor of New Bedford, 1990; named Real Hero in Edn., ARC, 2005. Mem. MLA (life), Am. Assn. Tchrs. French (life, hon. 2005), Am. Coun. Tchrs. Fgn. Langs., Middlebury Amicale (life), N.E. MLA (coord. 1987-91), New Eng. Fgn. Lang. Assn., Mass. Fgn. Lang. Assn. (bd. dirs. 1985-90, disting. svc. award 1992), NY State Assn. Fgn. Lang. Tchrs., Internat. Platform Assn., Francophone Assn. (v.p. 1990-98), Assn. Literary Scholars and Critics, Fall River C. of C., Brown U. Alumni Assn. (rep.), Richelieu Internat., Universal Manuscript Soc. (v.p. 1993-95). Avocations: travel, languages, baseball, postcards, meteorology. Home: 261 Carroll St New Bedford MA 02740-1412 Office: U Mass Dartmouth Lang Dept Old Westport Rd North Dartmouth MA 02747-2512 Business E-Mail: myoken@umassd.edu.

YOKOYAMA, WAYNE MAKOTO, medical educator, researcher, internist; b. WailukuMaui, Hawaii, July 1, 1952; BA, U. Rochester, NY, 1974; MD, U. Hawaii JA Burns Sch. Medicine, Manoa, Honolulu, 1978. Cert. Internal Medicine, Pediatric Rheumatology. Intern, internal medicine U. Iowa Hosp., Iowa City, 1978—79, resident, internal medicine, 1979—81, fellow, clin. rheumatology, 1982, fellow, rsch. rheumatology, 1985; fellow, rsch. immunology Nat. Inst. Allergy and Infectious Diseases/NIH, Bethesda, Md., 1989; asst. prof. medicine and rheumatology U. Calif., San Francisco, 1989—92; assoc. prof. medicine and microbiology Mt. Sinai Med. Sch., NYC; Sam and Audrey Lowe Levin chair for rsch. in arthritis Wash. U. Sch. Medicine, St. Louis, chief, rheumatology, divsn. dept. medicine, prof. medicine and pathology and immunology, dir., Ctr. for Arthritis and Related Diseases, dir., med. scientist trng. program. Investigator Howard Hughes Med. Inst., 1997—. Contbr. articles to profl. jours.; chair, editl. review group in rheumatology Doody Publishing, mem. adv. bd. Jour. Exptl. Medicine, mem. editl. bd. Jour. Clin. Immunology, assoc. editor Jour. Immunology, reviewer of severel peer-reviewed jours. Recipient Novartis prize for basic immunology, 2001. Mem.: Am. Soc. Clin. Investigation, Assn. Am. Physicians, Am. Acad. Microbiology, NAS. Address: Wash U Sch Medicine Dept Medicine Dept Pathology 10058 Clinical Sciences Research Bldg Saint Louis MO 63110 Mailing: Wash U Sch Medicine Divsn Rheumatology 666 S Euclid Ave Campus Box 8045 Saint Louis MO 63110 Office: Ctr for Advanced Medicine Medicine Multispecialty Ctr 4921 Parkview Pl Ste C Fl 5 Saint Louis MO 63110 Office Phone: 314-362-9075, 314-285-6263. Office Fax: 314-362-9257, 314-362-9257. Business E-Mail: yokoyama@imgate.wustl.edu. *

YOKUBAITIS, ROGER T., lawyer; b. Wharton, Tex., Jan. 9, 1945; Student, St. Louis U.; BA, JD, U. Houston, 1969. Bar: Tex. 1969, U.S. Dist. Ct. (so., we., ea. and no. dists.) Tex., U.S. Ct. Appeals (5th, 9th, 11 cirs.), U.S. Supreme Ct. Ptnr. Carmody & Yokubaitis, L.L.P., Houston, 1995—2000; prin. Roger T. Yokubaitis, P.L.L.C., Houston, 2000—. Mem. ABA, Houston Bar Assn., State Bar of Tex., Am. Bankruptcy Inst., Fed. Bar Assn., Federalist Soc. Office: Roger T Yokubaitis PLLC 1177 W Loop S Ste 1650 Houston TX 77027-9034 Personal E-mail: Yokubaitis@msn.com.

YOLEN, JANE, writer; b. NYC, Feb. 11, 1939; d. Will Hyatt and Isabelle (Berlin) Y.; m. David Wilber Stemple, Sept. 2, 1962; children: Heidi Elisabet, Adam Douglas, Jason Frederic. BA, Smith Coll., 1960; EdM, U. Mass., 1978, LLD (hon.), 2006, Coll. Our Lady of Elms, 1980, Smith Coll., Baypath Coll., Keene State Coll. Asst. editor This Week mag., 1960; mem. staff Saturday Rev., 1960; asst. editor Gold Medal Books, 1961, Rutledge Press, 1961—63; asst. juvenile editor A.A. Knopf, Inc., 1963—65; freelance writer, 1965—; lectr. dept. edn. Smith Coll., 1979—84; editor Jane Yolen books, imprint Harcourt Brace Jovanovich, 1988—97. Tchr. writers confs. Centrum, Cape Cod Writers Conf., Soc. Children's Book Writers, U. Mass.; mem. Mass. Coun. on Arts, 1974. Author: Pirates in Petticoats, 1963, The Witch Who Wasn't, 1964, The Emperor and the Kite, 1968, Writing Books for Children, 1973, The Girl Who Cried Flowers, 1974, The Hundredth Dove, 1978, The Dream Weaver, 1979, Commander Toad in Space, 1980, The Gift of Sarah Barker, 1981, Touch Magic, 1981, Dragon's Blood, 1982, Tales of Wonder, 1983, Heart's Blood, 1984, Cards of Grief, 1984, Dragonfield, 1985, Merlin's Booke, 1986, The Lullabye Songbook, 1986, Ring of Earth, 1986, Favorite Folktales From Around the World, 1986, Piggins, 1987, Owl Moon, 1987, Three Bears, 1987, A Sending of Dragons, 1987, The Devil's Arithmetic, 1988, Sister Light/Sister Dark, 1988, White Jenna, 1989, Dove Isabeau, 1989, Baby Bear's Bedtime Book, 1990, Tam Lin, 1990, Bird Watch, 1990, Sky Dogs, 1990, Wizard's Hall, 1991, All those Secrets of the World, 1991, Wings, 1991, Hark! A Christmas Sampler, 1991, Encounter, 1992, Briar Rose, 1992, Letting Swift River Go, 1992, What Rhymes with Moon, 1993, Welcome to the Greenhouse, 1993, Honkers, 1993, Here There Be Dragons, 1993, Grandad Bill's Song, 1994, Good Griselle, 1994, The Girl in the Golden Bower, 1994, Old Dame Counterpane, 1994, Old Macdonald's Songbook, 1994, Here There Be Unicorns, 1994, Beneath the Ghost Moon, 1994, The Wild Hunt, 1995, Ballad of the Pirate Queens, 1995, And Twelve Chinese Acrobats, 1995, Water Music, 1995, Among Angels, 1995, Here They Be Witches, 1995, O. Jerusalem, 1996, Welcome to the Sea of Sand, 1996, Passager, 1996, Hobby, 1996, Sacred Places, 1996, Here There Be Angels, 1996, Milk and Honey, 1996, Meet The Monsters, 1996, Once Upon Ice, 1997, Merlin, 1997, Child of Faerie, 1997, Twelve Impossible Things Before Breakfast, 1997, Miz Berlin Walks, 1997, Nocturne, 1997, Armageddon Summer, 1998, House/House, 1998, Prince of Egypt, 1998, Raising Yoder's Barn, 1998, The Wizard's Map, 1999, The Pictish Child, 1999, The Fairies' Ring, 1999, Moonball, 1999, Gray Heroes: Elder Tales From Around the World, 1999, How Does a

Dinosaur Say Goodnight, 2000, Off We Go, 2000, Queen's Own Fool, 2000, Not One Damsel in Distress, 2000, Mirror/Mirror, 2000, Color Me a Rhyme, 2000, Welcome to the River of Grass, 2001, The Fish Prince and Other Merman Stories, 2001, Odysseus in the Serpent's Maze, 2001, Dear Mother/Dear Daughter, 2001, Hippolyta and the Curse of the Amazons, 2002, Wild Wings, 2002, Firebird, 2002, Horizons, 2002, Animal Train, 2002, Harvest Home, 2002, Girl in a Cage, 2002, Sword of the Rightful King, 2003, How Do Dinosaurs Get Well Soon, 2003, Take Joy, 2003, My Brothers' Flying Machine, 2003, Hoptoad, 2003, Mightier than the Sword, 2003, The Radiation Sonnets, 2003, The Flying Witch, 2003, Jason and the Gorgon's Blood, 2004, How Do Dinosaurs Clean their Rooms?, 2004, The Barefoot Book of Ballet Stories, 2004, Prince Across the Water, 2004, Grandma's Hurrying Child, 2005, Perfect Wizard, 2005, Pay the Piper, 2005, Apple for the Teacher, 2005, Meow, 2005, How Do Dinosaurs Eat Their Food?, 2005, Fairy Tale Feast, 2006, Troll Bridge, 2006, This Little Piggy, 2006, Dimity Duck, 2006, Baby Bear's Books, 2006, Count Me a Rhyme, 2006, over 200 others. Mass. del. Dem. Nat. Conv., 1972; town coord. Robert Drinan's campaign, 1970; chmn. bd. trustees Hatfield (Mass.) Libr., 1978-83. Mem. Soc. Children's Book Writers (bd. dirs. 1974—), Children's Lit. Assn. (bd. dirs. 1977-79), Sci. Fiction Writers Am. (pres. 1986-88), Mystery Writers Am., Authors Guild. Democrat. Jewish/Quaker. Home: PO Box 27 Hatfield MA 01038-0027 E-mail: janeyolen@aol.com.

YOLLICK, BERNARD LAWRENCE, otolaryngologist, surgeon; b. Toronto, Mar. 24, 1922; came to U.S., 1949; s. Samuel and Beatrice (Roth) Y.; m. Liny L. Pajgin, 1947; children: Ingrid, Eric Lyf. Sr. Matriculation, Harbord Collegiate Inst., Toronto, 1939; MD, U. Toronto, 1945. Diplomate Am. Bd. Surgery, Am. Bd. Otolaryngology. Intern Sunnybrook Hosp., Toronto, 1945-46; resident D.C. Gen. Hosp., Washington, 1950, St. Louis County Hosp., Clayton, Mo., 1952-53; Am. Cancer Soc. fellow M.D. Anderson Cancer Hosp., Houston, 1953-54; resident in pathology Cook County Hosp., Chgo., 1949; surgeon Houston, 1953-59; fellowship in otolaryngology VA Hosp., Dallas, 1960-63; asst. prof. anatomy Baylor Med. Sch., Houston, 1953-59; assoc. prof. anatomy U. Tex. Dental Sch., Houston, 1953-59, Baylor Coll. Dentistry, Dallas, 1987-90; mem. staff Children's Med. Ctr., Dallas, 1990—; mem. staff, chief dept. otolaryngology St. Paul Med. Ctr., Dallas, 1990-98. Cons. Tex. Workers Compensation Ins. Fund, 1996—. Dept. Defense, Dallas, 1997—; mem. otolaryngology staff Vets. Adminstrn. Hosp., Dallas, 1990—. Contbr. articles to profl. jours. Served to capt. Royal Can. Army Med. Corps, 1942-45. Recipient fellowship Am. Cancer Soc., 1953. Fellow Am. Coll. Surgeons; mem. Tex. Otolaryn. Assn. (pres. 1979).

YONDA, ALFRED WILLIAM, mathematician; b. Cambridge, Mass., Aug. 10, 1919; s. Walter and Theophelia (Naruscewicz) Y.; m. Mary Jane McManus, Dec. 19, 1949 (dec.); children: Nancy, Kathryn, Elizabeth, John; m. Peggy A. Terrel, June 22, 1975. BS, U. Ala., 1952, MA in Math., 1954. Registered profl. engr. Mathematician rocket rsch. Redstone Arsenal, Huntsville, Ala., 1953, U.S. Army Ballistic Rsch. Labs., Aberdeen, Md., 1954-56; instr. math. U. Ala., Tuscaloosa, 1954, Temple U., Phila., 1956-57; assoc. scientist, rsch. & devel. divsn. Avco Corp., Wilmington, Mass., 1957-59; sr. mem. tech. staff RCA, Camden, NJ, 1959-66; mgr. computer analysis and programming dept. Raytheon Co. Space and Info. Systems Divsn., Sudbury, Mass., 1966-70, mgr. software systems lab., 1969-70, prin. engr. missiles systems divsn., 1970-73; mgr. sys. analysis & programming GTE Govt. Systems Corp., 1973-77, mgr. software engring. Atlantic ops., 1977-82, sr. mem. tech. staff Command Control & Comm. Sector, 1983-91; software systems engr. Yonda Software Systems Cons., 1991—. Contbr. articles to profl. jours. Pres. Milford Area Assn. Retarded Children, 1970-74, vice chmn. fin. com. Town of Medway, 1973; bd. dirs. Blackstone Valley Mental Health and Retardation Area, 1970-76; trustee Medway Librs., 1973-82, chmn., 1974-81. With USAAF, 1943-46. Hon. fellow Advanced Level Telecomm. Tng. Ctr., Ghaziabad, India, 1981. Mem. AAAS, IEEE, Math. Assn. Am., N.Y. Acad. Scis., Sigma Xi, Phi Eta Sigma, Pi Mu Epsilon (pres. Ala. chpt. 1953-54), Sigma Pi Sigma. Office: Cordiss Mills 65 Canal St Apt 122 Millbury MA 01527-3272 Home Phone: 508-865-4338. E-mail: awyonda@aol.com.

YONG, GUO, chemist, educator; MBA, Fairleigh Dickinson U., Madison, NJ, 2005; PhD, SUNY, Buffalo, 1996. Prin. scientist J&J Pharm R & D, Raritan, NJ, 1999—. Adj. prof. Fairleigh Dickinson U., Madison, 2005—. Office: J&J Pharm Rsch and Devel 1000 Rte 202 Raritan NJ 08869 Home Phone: 973-426-9649; Office Phone: 908-704-4309.

YONG, RAYMOND NEN-YIU, civil engineering educator; b. Singapore, Apr. 10, 1929; naturalized, 1966; s. Ngim Djin and Lucy (Loh) Y.; m. Florence Lechensky, July 8, 1961; children: Raymond T.M., Christopher T.K. BA in Math. and Physics, Washington and Jefferson Coll., 1950; BS, MIT, 1952; MS, Purdue U., 1954; MEngring., McGill U., Montreal, Que., Can., 1958, PhD, 1960. Chartered engr., Great Britain. Mem. faculty McGill U., 1959-95, prof. civil engring., 1965-72, William Scott prof. civil engring. and applied mechanics, 1972-95; dir. Geotech Rsch. Ctr., 1973-95; assoc. mem. Ctr. for Medicine, Ethics and Law McGill U., 1991-95. Adj. prof. civil engring. U. Fla., Gainesville, 1984—; adj. rsch. prof. civil engring. Carleton U., Ottawa, 1990; disting. rsch. prof. U. Wales, Cardiff, 1995-2002, emeritus prof., sr. sci. advisor, 2002-04; sr. sci. dir. Geoenviron. Engring. Rsch. Ctr., Cardiff Sch. Engring., U. Wales, 1995, prof. emeritus, 2002—. Author: Soil Properties and Behavior, 1975 (Japanese edit. 1977), Introduction to Soil Behavior, 1966 (Japanese edit. 1974), Vehicle Traction Mechanics, 1985, Principles of Contaminant Transport in Soils, 1992 (Japanese edit. 1995), Geoenvironmental Engineering: Contaminated Soils, Pollutant Fate and Mitigation, 2001, Natural Attenuation of Contaminants in Soils, 2004, Microstructure of Smectite Clays and Engineering Performance, 2006, Geoenvironmental Sustainability, 2006. Decorated chevalier Ordre National du Que.; recipient Killam prize Can. Coun., 1985, ASTM Charles B. Dudley award, 1988, Can. Environ. Achievement award, Lifetime Achievement Environment Can., 1991. Fellow Royal Soc. Can., Engring. Inst. Can., Can. Soc. for Civil Engring.; mem. ASCE, Inst. Civil Engrs., Soc. Rheology, Clay Minerals Soc., Internat. Soc. Terrain-Vehicle Systems (pres. 1993—), Can. Geotech. Soc. (R.F. Legget award 1993). Achievements include 52 patents in field. Office Phone: 250-655-3787. Personal E-mail: r.nyong@shaw.ca.

YONKMAN, FREDRICK ALBERS, lawyer, management consultant; b. Holland, Mich., Aug. 22, 1930; s. Fredrick Francis and Janet Dorothy (Albers) Y.; m. Kathleen VerMeulen, June 9, 1953 (div. Sept. 22, 1980); children: Sara, Margriet, Nina.; m. Barbara Anne Sullivan, Aug. 22, 1981 (div. Mar. 31, 1994); 1 child, Fredrick Ryan; m. Jewel Marie Humphrey, July 4, 1998. BA, Hope Coll., Holland, 1952; JD, U. Chgo., 1957. Bar: NY 1958, Mass. 1968, DC 1984. With Winthrop, Stimson, Putnam & Roberts, NYC, 1957-64; sec., gen. counsel Reuben H. Donnelley Corp., NYC, 1964-66, Dun & Bradstreet, Inc., NYC, 1966-68; ptnr. Sullivan & Worcester, Boston, 1968-72; gen. counsel Am. Express Co., NYC, 1972-78, exec. v.p., 1975-80; pres. Buck Cons., NYC, 1980-81; mgmt. cons., psychoanalyst, 1981—, NYU Graduate Sch. Clin. Social Work, 1982—83; counsel Peabody, Lambert & Myers, Washington, 1983-84; exec. dir. Asian Bus. Ctr., Rutgers U. Bus. Sch., Piscataway, NJ, 2003—05; night mgr. St. Francis Ho., St. Augustine, Fla., 2006—. Mem. bd., chmn. audit com. Kennecott Corp., 1978—81; adj. prof. law Georgetown U., 1976—78; chmn. Georgetown Internat. Law Inst., 1980—81; vis. com. U. Chgo. Law Sch., 1980—82; mem. exec. com. Warner-Amex, 1978—80; bd. dirs. and advisors Sageworks Inc., Raleigh, NC, 1998—2004. Chmn. Outward Bound, Inc., Garrison, NY, 1980—81, mem. nat. adv. bd., 2005—; bd. dirs. Washington Campus Program, 1976—81, Young Audiences, 1978—83. With CIC US Army, 1952—54. Recipient Silver Anniversary award NCAA, 1977. Mem.: ABA, NY State Bar Assn. Methodist. Home and Office: 3960 AIA South Unit 502 Saint Augustine FL 32080 Office Phone: 904-461-4449. Personal E-mail: fyonkman@optonline.net.

YONKMAN, MARK WILLIAM, lawyer; b. Traverse City, Mich., Sept. 22, 1960; s. Harry William and Thelma (Hoadly) Y. BA, Kalamazoo Coll., 1982; JD cum laude, Wayne State U., 1985. Bar: Mich. 1985, U.S. Dist. Ct. (we. and ea. dists.) Mich. 1986, U.S. Ct. Appeals (6th cir.) 1986. Assoc. Pepper, Hamilton & Scheetz, Detroit, 1984-88, Phila., 1988—; sr. v.p., asst. gen. counsel, asst. sec. Comerica Inc.; now sr. v.p., gen. counsel M&T Bank Corp., Buffalo. Mem. Mich. Bar Assn., Fed. Bar Assn., Detroit Bar Assn., Order of the Coif. Avocations: French and Portuguese langs., skiing, tennis, rowing. Office: M&T Bank Corp 1 M&T Plaza Buffalo NY 14203 Office Phone: 716-842-5445. *

YONTZ, KENNETH FREDRIC, medical and chemical company executive; b. Sandusky, Ohio, July 21, 1944; s. Kenneth Willard and Dorothy (Kromer) Y.; m. Jean Ann Marshall, July 21, 1962 (div. Aug. 1982); children: Terri, Christine, Michael, Jennifer; m. Karen Glojek, July 7, 1984 (wid. Dec. 1994); m. Karen Mc Diarmid, Jan. 10, 1997. BSBA, Bowling Green State U., 1971; MBA, Eastern Mich. U., 1979. Fin. planning mgr. Ford Motor Co., Rawsonville, Mich., 1970-74; fin. mgr. Chemetron Corp., Chgo., 1974-76, pres. fire systems div., 1976-80; pres. electronics div. Allen Bradley Co., Milw., 1980-83, group. pres. electronics, 1983-85, exec. v.p., 1985-86; chmn. bd. Apogent Techs., Milw., 1986—2003, Sybron Dental Specialities, Milw., 1986—2006. Bd. dirs. Rockwell Int., Milw. Founder Karen Yontz Womens Cardiac Awareness Ctr. Mem. Muirfield Village Golf Club, Vintage Club (Indian Wells, Calif.), Tradition Golf Club (La Quinta, Calif.), Chenequa Country Club (Hartford, Wis.), Flint Hills Country Club (Wichita), Milw. Country Club, Farmington Country Club (Charlottesville, Va.). Roman Catholic. *Positive results are seldom achieved from negative thoughts.*

YOO, JIN-HYEONG, research scientist; b. Seoul, Republic Of Korea, Dec. 28, 1964; s. Byung-Pil and Young-Ja (Jo) Yoo; m. Hae-Jeong Lee, Nov. 9, 1991; children: Seong-Min, Seong-Joon. PhD, Yonsei U., Seoul, 1999. Sr. rschr. Samsung Electro-mechanics Co., Suwon, Republic of Korea, 1990—95; rsch. scientist U. Md., College Park, 1999—. Office: Univ Md 3181 Glenn L Martin Hall College Park MD 20742 Office Phone: 301-405-1112. Business E-Mail: jhyoo@eng.umd.edu.

YOO, JOHN CHOON, law educator, former federal agency administrator; b. Seoul, South Korea, June 10, 1967; s. John H. and Sook (Hee) Y. BA in History, Harvard U., 1989; JD, Yale U., 1992. Bar: Pa. 1993, U.S. Dist. Ct. (9th cir.) 1997. Law clk. to Judge Laurence Silberman US Ct. Appeals (D.C. cir.), Washington, 1992-93; law clk. to Justice Clarence Thomas US Supreme Ct., Washington, 1994-95; gen. counsel US Senate Judiciary Com., Washington, 1995-96; prof. law Boalt Hall Sch. Law, Berkeley, Calif., 1993-94, 96—; dir. Internat. Legal Studies Program, Boalt Hall Sch. Law, Berkeley, Calif., 1999—2001; dep. asst. atty. gen., Office of Legal Counsel US Dept. Justice, Washington, 2001—03. Visiting prof. U. Chgo., Free U. of Amsterdam, 1998; visiting scholar Am. Enterprise Inst.; chair, sect. on scholarship Assn. of Am. Law Schools, 2000. Author: The Powers of War and Peace: The Constitution and Fgn. Affairs After 9/11, 2005, (novels) War by Other Means: An Insider's Account of the War on Terror, 2006. Recipient Paul M. Bator award, Federalist Soc. for Law & Pub. Policy. Fellow: Soc. of Historians of Am. Foreign Relations, Rockefeller Found., Coun. on Fgn. Rels.; mem.: Berkeley Jour. of Internat. Law, Nat. Constitution Ctr., The Federalist Soc. Office: Boalt Hall Sch Law U Calif Berkeley 890 Simon Hall Berkeley CA 94720-0001 E-mail: yoo@law.berkeley.edu.

YOO, VAK YEONG, health facility administrator; b. Seoul, Republic of Korea, June 28, 1947; d. Jang Mun Yoo and So Ran Choi. MA, Ewha Women's U., Seoul, 1974, MD, 1980. Med. diplomate internal medicine. Founder pvt. med. exam. ctr., Seoul, 1981—; dir. Yoovakyeong Internal Medicine, Seoul, 1981-92; head Med. Exam. Ctr., Seoul, 1981—; dir. Cheong-Vak P.B. Hosp., Seoul, 1992—; head Women's Health Dx & Climacteric, Seoul, 1992—. Mem. menopause and osteoporosis unit, 1992—, YVY-QOL Inst., 1997, YVY-QOL osteoporosis leader NOF-PPN, 1997; mem. sci. com. Koran Soc. Menopause, 1997-99; creator, organizer YVY-QOL support group for meno/osteoporosis Nat. Osteoporosis Found., 1997. Author: Phytoestrogens, 1995, Quality of Midbeyond Womens Life, 1996, Aging and Gender Specific Quality of Life, 1997; editor Jour. Meno/Osteoporosis, 1998—; co-editor Jour. Menopause Soc. Korea, 1999—; inventor in field. Mem. N.Am. Menopause Soc., Internat. Menopause Soc., Korean Soc. Endoscopy, Christian Med. Assn. (planning dir. 1993-96), Am. Assn. Clin. Endocrinologists, AAAS, Am. Soc. for Microbiology, Korean Soc. Endocrinology, Korean Diabetes Assn., Korean Soc. Menopause (sci. com. 1996-98, editing com. 1999—), Korean Soc. Circulation, The Endocrine Soc., NY Acad. Scis., NOF-Profl. Ptnr. Network, Am. Soc. Bone and Mineral Rsch. Avocations: travel, listening to music, opera music. Home: 138-60 Yongdu Dong Dongdaemun Ku Seoul 130-072 Republic of Korea Office: Cheongvak Antiaging Hosp 582 Shinsa Dong Kangnam Ku Seoul 135-120 Republic of Korea

YOON, BOGUM, literacy educator; b. Donghae, Kangwon, Republic of Korea, Apr. 22, 1961; d. Jundae Yoon and Oksoon Kim; m. Yongchan Ahn, Dec. 9, 1989; children: Junhyuck Ahn, Junsuk Ahn. BA in English Edn., Hongik U., Seoul, 1984; MA in English Edn. with distinction, SUNY, Potsdam, 2001; PhD in English Edn., U. Buffalo, 2004. Cert. secondary tchr. Min. Edn., 1984, TESOL, 1998. Rschr. for cultural & social affairs Asian & Pacific Council, Seoul, 1985—92; grad. asst. U. Buffalo, 2001—04; asst. prof. Tex. Woman's U., Denton, 2004—. Chair 41st rose spicola reading forum Tex. Woman's U., 2006—07; mem. editl. review bd. Mid. Grades Rsch. Jour., 2006—. Contbr. articles to profl. jours. Mem.: Nat. Reading Conf., Am. Ednl. Rsch. Assn.

YOON, E. YUL, retired career officer; b. Pyungyang, Korea, Feb. 10, 1927; s. Jung Soon and Jung Duk (Lee) Y.; m. Sun Sam Lee Yoon, Nov. 29, 1931; children: Kyung Ran, Kyung Im, Kwang Ho. Grad., Mil. Acad. Seoul, 1948; BS in Politics and Fgn. Policy, Dangook U., Seoul, Korea, 1955; grad., U.S. Air U., Montgomery, Ala., 1957. Squadron comdr. The 12th Fighter SQ F-51, Korea, 1952-53; armed force attache Korean Embassy, Paris, 1959-61; wing comdr. The 1st Combat Wing, The 10th Fighter Wing, Seoul, 1961-63; pres. Korean Air Force Coll., Seoul, 1963-64; supt. Korean Air Acad., Seoul, 1964-66; commanding gen. Combat Air Command, Korea, 1968-70; minister plenipotentiary Korean Embassy, France, Mexico, 1966-68; vice minister for def. devel. Ministry of Def., Seoul, 1970-73; pres., CEO Korea Tacoma Shipbuilding Indsl. Co., Korea, 1973-76, Buyeon Co., Ltd., Seoul, 1976-86; cons. United Tech./Martin Marieta, 1976-85. Mem. Korean Heavy Industrialization Com., Seoul, 1970-73. Decorated Eulchi and three Gold Stars, Chungmoo Meritorious Svc. medals, Korea, 1952, 53, Korean Disting. Svc. medal, 1955, U.S. Disting. Flying Cross, U.S. Air medal, Repub. of China Disting. Svc. medal. Mem. The Disting. Flying Cross Soc. (life), Ministry of Nat. Def. of Korea (rsch. assoc.). Avocations: photography, art collecting, golf. Personal E-mail: yulyoon@hotmail.com.

YOON, HYUNG-DOO, publisher, educator; b. Kobe, Japan, Dec. 27, 1935; s. Min-sik Yoon and Cheo-rye Kim; m. Shin Young-sook; three children. Grad., Grad. Sch. Mass. Comms., Seoul, 1984, Grad. Sch. Bus. Adminstrn., 1975; LLM, Dongkuk U., 1963, PhD in Pub. Sci., 2002. Pres. Bumwoo Publ. co., Seoul, 1966—. Vis. prof. Grad. Sch. Mass. Comm., 1991—. Author: Passing By, Passing It Away, 1979, At the Seashore of Vastitude, 1987, The Theory of Publishing Currency, 1989, The Way of Book and Mine, 1994, The Deceit and Truth of Korean Publication, 2002, Love of Mountains, Books and Country; editor: The History of Books In a Glance, 1997. Mem. Korean Publ. Assn. (bd. dirs. 1978—, v.p. 1992-94), Publ. Sci. Soc. (pres. 1989-95, 1999-2003), Korean Publ. Sci. Soc. (adv. 1996—), Korean Soc. Journalism & Comm. Studies (bd. dirs. 1990-92). Office: Bumwoo Publ Co 525-2 Moonbal-ri Gyoha-eup Pajursi Gyunggi-do 413-756 Republic of Korea Home Phone: 02-877-0676; Office Phone: 031-955-6900. Business E-Mail: bumwoosa@chol.com.

YOON, JAY MYOUNG, oncologist, hematologist, internist; b. Korea, Sept. 30, 1946; married. BA Coll. Liberal Arts & Sci. summa cum laude, Seoul Nat. U., 1967, MD summa cum laude, 1971. Diplomate Am. Bd. Internal Medicine, 1978, Am. Bd. Oncology, 1979, Am. Bd. Hematology, 1980. Intern Bklyn. Hosp. Ctr.-Cornell U., NYC, 1974—75; resident in medicine Bronx-Lebanon Hosp.-Albert Einstein Coll. Medicine, NYC, 1975—76; fellow in hematol. oncology Baystate Med. Ctr. Tufts U. Sch. Medicine, Springfield, Mass., 1976—78; fellow in oncology Roswell Park Cancer Inst. SUNY, Buffalo, 1978—79, rsch. clinician in oncology dept. Roswell Park Cancer Inst., 1979—80, rsch. instr. medicine, 1978—80; attending physician, med. oncologist St. Francis Hosp. and Health Ctr., Clarian Health Ptnrs., Beech Grove and Indpls., 1980—98; rsch. instr. medicine SUNY, 1978—80; prof. medicine Ulsan U. Med. Sch., 1997—98; CEO, pres. Yoon Clinic, P.C., Edmonds, Wash., 1999—; mem. med. staff Stevens Meml. Hosp., Edmonds, 1999—, Northwest Hosp., Seattle, 1999—, Swedish Med. Ctr., Seattle, 2000. Contbr. articles to profl. jours. Mem. AAAS, AMA, ADA, AACR, Am. Assn. Blood Banks, Am. Soc. Clin. Oncology, Am. Soc. Hematology, N.Y. Acad. Sci. Home: 11901 59th Ave W Mukilteo WA 98275-5569 Office: Yoon Clinic PC Edmonds Med and Profl Ctr 7631 212th St SW Ste 106 B Edmonds WA 98026-7565 Home Phone: 425-493-9999; Office Phone: 425-778-5551. Office Fax: 425-697-6222. Personal E-mail: yoonclinic@comcast.net.

YOON, JEONG WHAN, research scientist, educator; s. Guee-Young Yoon and Bunsun Kim; m. Younhee Cheon, Feb. 5, 1995; children: Junu, Hannah. PhD, KAIST, Republic of Korea, 1997. Sr. engr. LG Electronics, Seoul, 1998—2000; staff scientist Alcoa Tech. Ctr., Alcoa Center, Pa., 2001—07. Lead developer MSC Software Corp., Palo Alto, Calif., 2001—03. Editor: (spl. issue) Internat. Jour. Plasticity; editor, co-chair: NUMISHEET2005 Conf. Proceeding, 2005; contbr. articles to profl. jours. Home Phone: 1-724-325-1670; Office Phone: 1-724-337-1938.

YOON, JEONG-YEOL, biological engineer, educator; BS, Yonsei U., 1992; PhD, UCLA, 2004. Asst. prof. dept. agrl. and biosystems engring. U. Ariz., Tucson, 2004—, asst. prof. biomed. engring. program, 2005—. Mem. editl. bd. Jour. Biol. Engring., 2006—, Open Biotech. Jour., 2007—. Grantee, Biomedical Diagnostics S.A., 2005, U. Ariz. Found., 2005, NIH, 2006—, NSF, 2006—, Nat. Vet. Rsch. and Quarantine Svc., 2007—. Mem.: Soc. Photo-Optical Instrumentation Engrs., Am. Soc. Agrl. and Biol. Engrs., Inst. Biol. Engring. Office: U Ariz ABE Dept 1177 E 4th St Rm 403 Tucson AZ 85721-0038 Office Phone: 520-621-3587.

YOPCONKA, NATALIE ANN CATHERINE, secretary officer, computer specialist, educator, entrepreneur, small business owner; b. Taylor, Pa., July 21, 1942; d. Michael Joseph and Natalie Ann Lucille (Panek) Yopconka. BS in Bus. Adminstrn., Pers. and Indsl. Rels. with high honors, U. Md., 1965; MBA in Info. Tech., George Washington U., 1976, MA in Edn. and Human Devel. Higher Edn., 1988; postgrad. in Venture Capital and Entrepreneurship, U. Md., 1990—96. Mgmt. analyst, adminstrv. trainee, computer programmer U.S. Dept. Commerce, Maritime Adminstrn., Washington, 1965-67; computer programmer, computer specialist U.S. Dept. Labor, Washington, 1967-78; instr. computer sci. Assn. for Computing Machinery, Washington, 1978; instr. computer sci. and mgmt. tech. Montgomery Coll., Takoma Park and Rockville, Md., 1979; sr. programmer analyst Dynamic Data Processing, Inc., Silver Spring, Md., 1979; instr. Nat. Bus. Sch., Inc., Alexandria, Va., 1980; cons. McLeod Corp., Washington, 1980; lectr. computer sci., coop. coord. U. Md., College Park, 1980-81; sr. adminstrv. applications analyst programmer Data Transformation Corp., Washington, 1981; sr. sys. analyst Singer Link Simulation Sys. Divsn., Silver Spring, 1981-82; accessory designer Transart Corp., 1982-83; market rschr. Washington Fin. Svc., 1982-83; lectr. computer info. and sys. sci. U. D.C., Rockville, Md., 1983; prof. computer programming and mgmt. info. sys. Benjamin Franklin U., Washington, 1983; rschr. Info. U.S.A., Potomac, Md., 1983-85; admissions rep. Brook-Wein Bus. Inst., Washington, 1985; pvt. distbr. Hyattsville, Md., 1979—86; distbr. AMWAY Corp., 1979—93. Course developer, instr. Grad. Sch. USDA, Balt., 1986-87; field interviewer Nat. Drug Abuse Bur., 1989-90; chmn. Cert. for Computing Profls. Exam. Review Course for Balt. Washington, D.C. corridor, 1994-95; agent Kivex, Inc., 1996-97, 3COM Corp., 1997-99, Information Builders, Inc., 1997-2000; bus. owner, cons., computer specialist, application developer, educator, salesperson Sys. and Edn. Enterprises, 1979—. Mem. disability com. Takoma Pk., com. energy, housing and planning, Mayor, 1980-81; mem. Vision 2030 Balt./Howard County, 2002-03; mem. Missionary Oblates of Immaculate Mary; choir Our Lady of Sorrows Cath. Ch., 1977-82, St. John the Evangelist Cath. Ch., eucharistic min. 1990-2003, internet com., 1996-97, lector, 2003-05, echaristic minister and lector, 2007-; mem. Balt. Washington Corridor C. of C., 1996-97, citizens adv. com. to Bd. Edn. Howard County, 1991-92, computer adv. com., 1993-95; chair Leukemia Soc. Md., 1996; active Suburban Md. High Tech. Coun., 1994-95, Howard County High Tech. Coun., 1994-95; sec., mem. T.R.I.A.D./S.A.L.T. for Howard County, sec. 2003-07; patron, nominator Howard County Coun. for the Arts. Recipient chmn./woman of the yr., Leukemia Soc. of Md., 1996. Mem. AARP, NAFE, IEEE (Balt. sect., earlier Washington sect., computer soc., commn. soc., tech. com. on software engring., stds. coms. and groups, software standards assn.), ASCD, ASTD, IEEE, IEEE Computer Soc. (tech. com. on software engring., software engring. stds. coms. and groups), Software Stds. Assn., Info. Sys. Audit and Control Assn., Assn. Computing Machinery (DC chpt., edn. com., instr. 1978-79, edn. com. 1980-81, profl. devel. com. 1982-83), Data Processing Mgmt. Assn. (chmn. cert. for computing profls. exam. rev. course for Balt.-Washington corridor 1994-95), Balt. Washington Info. Sys. Educators (consortium com. 1984-85, program com. for 1986 regional tng. conf. 1985-86, vendor com. 1988-89), Fed. Automatic Data Processing Users Group (com. mem. 1976-1983), Armed Forces Comm. and Electronics Assn., Balt. Coun. Fgn. Affairs, Nat. Active and Ret. Fed. Employees Assn. (sec. Howard County chpt.), Nat. Bus. Edn. Assn., U. Md. Howard County Alumni Club (scholarship com. 1989), Columbia (Md.) Assn., Phi Delta Gamma (scholarship com. 1977-78, social com. 1980-81, hospitality com. 1982-83, sec. 1989-90). Achievements include first to write software engineering standards.

YORE, JOSEPH N., communications executive; b. Emporium, Pa., Feb. 5, 1934; s. Joseph Yore and Jennie Grouanz. Cert., Hollywood Ctr. Drama Sch., Calif., 1961. Ground keeper LA County Parks and Recreation, 1960—63; rschr. Walter E. Hurst Law Firm, Hollywood, Calif., 1963—89; pres. Seven Arts Press, Hollywood, 1989—. Prodr.(director, scriptwriter): Diary of A Hippie, 1968 (Telly bronze award, 2007). Mem. environ. rehab. adv. bd. plant 42 Air Force Base Wright Patterson, Ohio, 2000—06. Corp. USMC, 1953—56, Korea. Fellow: VFW, Am. Legion; mem.: AFTRA, Screen Actots Guild, Actor's Fund Am. (life). Avocations: painting, sculpting. Home: 38753-26th St E Palmdale CA 93550

YORIKAWA, HIROHARU, physicist, researcher; b. Hyogo, Japan, Aug. 4, 1958; s. Mineo and Yaeko (Kobayashi) Y. BS, Sci. U. Tokyo, 1983, MS, 1985, DSc, 1989. Rsch. asst. Utsunomiya (Japan) U., 1989—. Contbr. articles to Phys. Rev. B, Solid State Comms., Synthetic Metals, Appl. Phys.

Lett., others. Mem. Phys. Soc. Japan. Avocation: painting. Office: Utsunomiya U Faculty of Engring 7-1-2 Youtou Utsunomiya 321-8585 Japan E-mail: yorikawa@cc.utsunomiya-u.ac.jp.

YORIO, KIMBERLY, public relations executive; married; 1 child. With Children's Television Workshop; dir. mktg. Tihany Internat.; account exec. Kratz & Co. Pub. Relations; dir. cookbook mktg., spl. sales mgr. William Morrow; dir. mktg. Artisan Books; publicity cons. Workman Publishing; cofounder (with Caitlin Friedman), prin. YC Media. Guest spkr. Cornell U., Harvard U., Warton Coll., The Mass. Governors Conf. for Women, The Phila. Conf. for Women. Co-author (with Caitlin Friedman): The Girl's Guide to Being the Boss (Without Being a Bitch): Valuable Lessons, Smart Suggestions and True Stories for Succeeding as the Chick-in-Charge, 2006 (Quills award business The Quills Literacy Found., 2006). Office: YC Media Ste 310 547 West 27th St New York NY 10001 Office Phone: 212-609-5009 ext. 1. Office Fax: 212-684-0059.

YORK, CANDACE A., marketing professional, writer; b. Lubbock, Tex., Mar. 7, 1954; d. Billy John and Francis Ann York; m. James R. Callahan, Feb. 23, 1947. BFA in Art History, U. Tex., 1976. Archival asst. S.W. collection Tex. Tech. U., Lubbock, 1976—77; claims analyst Met. Life, Austin, Tex., 1977—78; mktg. software engr., info. devel. IBM Corp., Austin, Tex., 1978—. Author: 155 Tips to Protect Your Home and Wealth From Fire, 2003, numerous poems, short stories; contbr. articles to profl. jours. Vol. Austin (Tex.) Cmty. Gardens, 2003—04, Tex. Sch. Blind, 2003. Named Internat. Poet of Merit, Internat. Libr. Poetry, 2001; recipient Excellence award, Soc. Tech. Comm., 1980, Honorable Mention award, Iliad Press, 2001, 1st pl. poetry in motion competition, 2001, 2nd place, Sol poet laureate competition, 2002. Mem.: Assn. Interactive Media, Pub. Rels. Soc. Am. (programs com. Austin chpt. 2003), Acad. Am. Poets, Internat. High IQ Soc. Avocations: poetry, photography, guitar, painting, tai chi. Home: 8210 Bent Tree Rd #213 Austin TX 78759 Personal E-mail: canyork@aol.com.

YORK, DAVID P., former prosecutor; b. 1963; m. Annie York; 3 children. BA, Birmingham So. Coll.; JD, Samford U. Asst. dist. atty. Douglas Jud. Cir., 1990—91; assoc. atty. Johnston, Wilkins, Druhan & Holz, 1991—92; asst. dist. atty. 13th Jud. Cir., 1992—97; atty. Pierce, Ledyard, Latta, Wasden & Bowron, Mobile; US atty. (so. dist.) Ala. US Dept. Justice, 2001—05. *

YORK, E. TRAVIS, retired academic administrator; b. Mentone, Ala., July 4, 1922; s. E.T. and Leila (Hixon) Y.; m. Vermelle Cardwell, Dec. 26, 1946; children: Lisa Carol, Travis Loften. BS, Auburn U., 1942, MS, 1946, DSc (hon.), 1982; PhD, Cornell U., 1949; postgrad., George Washington U., 1957-59; DSc (hon.), U. Fla., 1984, Ohio State U., 1996, NC State U., 2003. Rsch. fellow Cornell U., Ithaca, 1946-49; Assoc. prof. N.C. State Coll., 1949-52, prof., 1952-56, head dept. agronomy, 1953-56; Eastern dir. Am. Potash Inst., 1956-59; dir. Ala. Extension Service, Auburn U., 1959-61; adminstr. Fed. Extension Service, U.S. Dept. Agr., 1961-63; provost for agr. U. Fla., 1963-67, v.p. agrl. affairs, 1967-73, exec. v.p., interim pres., 1973-74, Disting. Svc. prof., 1988-96. Chancellor State U. System of Fla., 1975—80, chancellor emeritus, 1980—. Mem. Am. Food for Peace Coun., 1961-62, Freedom from Hunger Com., 1961-62, Pres.'s. Panel Vocat. Edn., 1961-62; chmn. coun. grad. edn. in agrl. scis. So. Regional Edn. Bd., 1964-66, mem., 1975-80, exec. com., 1978-80, mem. pres. coun., Pres.' Sci. Adv. Coun. Task Force on World Food Problems, 1966-67; senate, exec. com. Nat. Assn. State Univs. and Land Grant Colls., 1967-70; mem. Edn. Commn. of States, 1975-79, steering com., 1977-79, treas., exec. com., 1978-79; bd. dirs. Nat. 4-H Svc. Com., 1963-75, AV Med. Corp., Sante Fe, 1987-96; trustee, bd. dirs Hlth Improvement Inc mem., 1996-98, exec. com. Nat. 4-H Found., 1968-73; mem.-at-large nat. coun. Boy Scouts Am., 1962-75; dir., pres. Alpha Gamma Rho Edn. Found., 1965-72; bd. dirs. Nat. Ctr. for Voluntary Action, 1970-74; mem. Bd. for Internat. Food and Agrl. Devel., 1980-86, chmn., 1983-86; trustee Escuela Agrícola Panamericana, 1980-88, Found. for Agronomic Rsch., 1980-92; tech. adv. com., cons. Group for Internat. Agrl. Rsch., 1983-89; trustee Agronomic Sci. Found., 1989-92; chmn. bd. Internat. Fertilizer Devel. Ctr., 1999-2004. Officer AUS, 1943-45. Recipient B.B. Comer award excellence natural sci. Auburn U., 1942; disting. svc. award Fla. Vet. Med. Assn., 1966; Nat. 4-H Alumni award, 1967; George Washington honor medal award Freedoms Found., 1967; nat. ptnr. in 4-H award, 1970; disting. faculty award U. Fla., Fla. Blue Key, 1972; E.T. York, Jr. disting. svc. award U. Fla., 1973; honors medal U. Fla. Acad. Scis., 1974; E.T. York svc. award Fla. Bd. Regents, 1983, disting. svc. award Am. Farm Bur., 1991, Svc. Above Self award Rotary Internat., 1994, Medal of Honor, DAR, 1998, Lifetime Achievement award Auburn U., 2006, Lifetime Achievement award, Fla. Student Assn., 2007; named to Fla. Agrl. Hall of Fame, 1990, Ala. Agrl. Hall of Honor, 1995, Internat. Adult and Continuing Edn. Hall of Fame, 1996; designated as Great Floridian, Fla. History Mus., 1997. Fellow AAAS, Am. Soc. Agronomy, Soil Sci. Soc. Am., AM. Crop Sci. Soc.; mem. Am. Soc. Hort. Sci. (hon.), Assn. So. Agrl. Scientists (pres. 1968), Blue Key, Rotary (dist. gov. 1981-82), Sigma Xi, Phi Kappa Phi, Alpha Zeta, Gamma Sigma Delta (Internat. Disting. Svc. award 1973), Omicron Delta Kappa, Phi Delta Kappa, Epsilon Sigma Phi, Alpha Gamma Rho (named to Hall of Fame 1982). Methodist. Home: 5200 SW 25th Blvd # 4216 Gainesville FL 32608-8925 Business E-Mail: etyork@ufl.edu.

YORK, GARY ALAN, lawyer; b. Glendale, Calif., Aug. 29, 1943; m. Lois York, 1987; 1 child, Jonathan Alan. BA, Pomona Coll., 1965; LLB, Stanford U., 1968. Bar: Calif. 1969. Ptnr. Dewey Ballantine, LA, 1985-95, Buchalter, Nemer, Fields & Younger, LA, 1995-98, Le Boeuf, Lamb, Greene & MacRae, LA, 1998—2002. Instr. law sch. UCLA, 1968-69. Bd. editors Stanford Law review, 1966-68. Mem. ABA (chmn. real estate fin. com., real property probate and trust sect. 1987-89, chmn. usury com. 1992-93), L.A. County Bar Assn. (chmn. real estate fin. sect. 1993-96, exec. com. 1995—), State Bar of Calif., Am. Coll. Real Estate Lawyers, Am. Coll. Mortgage Attys. Office: Baker & Hostetler LLP 333 S Grand Ave Ste 1800 Los Angeles CA 90071 E-mail: GYork@Bakerlaw.com.

YORK, HERBERT FRANK, university official; b. Rochester, NY, Nov. 24, 1921; s. Herbert Frank and Nellie Elizabeth (Lang) Y.; m. Sybil Dunford, Sept. 28, 1947; children: David Winters, Rachel, Cynthia. AB, U. Rochester, 1942, MS, 1943; PhD, U. Calif., Berkeley, 1949; DSc (hon.), Case Inst. Tech., 1960; LL.D., U. San Diego, 1964, Claremont Grad. Sch., 1974. Physicist Radiation Lab., U. Calif., Berkeley, 1943-58, assoc. dir., 1954-58; asst. prof. physics dept. U. Calif., Berkeley, 1951-54, assoc. prof., 1954-59, prof., 1959-61; dir. Lawrence Radiation Lab., Livermore, 1952-58; chief scientist Advanced Rsch. Project Agy., U.S. Dept. Def., 1958; dir. advanced rsch. projects divsn. Inst. for Def. Analyses, 1958; dir. def. rsch. and engring. Office Sec. Def., 1958-61; chancellor U. Calif.-San Diego, 1961—64, acting chancellor, 1970—72, prof. physics, 1964—88, prof. emeritus, 1988—, chmn. dept. physics, 1968-69, dean grad. studies, 1969-70, dir. program on sci., tech. and pub. affairs, 1972-88; dir. Inst. Global Conflict and Cooperation, 1983-88, dir. emeritus, 1988—. Amb. Comprehensive Test Ban Negotiations, 1979-81; trustee Aerospace Corp., Inglewood, Calif., 1961-87; mem. Pres.'s Sci. Adv. Com., 1957-58, 64-68, vice chmn., 1965-67; trustee Inst. def. Analysis, 1963-96; gen. adv. com. ACDA, 1962-69; mem. Def. Sci. Bd., 1977-81; spl. rep. of sec. def. at space arms control talks, 1978-79; mem. task force future nat. labs. Sec. Emergy, 1994-95; cons. Stockholm Internat. Peach Rsch. Inst.; rschr. in application atomic energy to nat. def. problems of arms control and disarmament, elem. particles. Author: Race to Oblivion, 1970, Arms Control, 1973, The Advisors, 1976, Making Weapons, Talking Peace, 1987, Does Strategic Defense Breed Offense?, 1987, (with Sanford Lakoff) A Shield in the Sky, 1989, Arms and the Physicist, 1994; also numerous articles on arms or disarmament; bd. dirs. Bull. Atomic Scientists. Trustee Bishop's Sch., La Jolla, Calif., 1963-65. Recipient E.O. Lawrence award AEC, 1962, Vannevan Bush award, 2000, Clark Kerr award, 2000, Enrico Fermi award, 2000; Guggenheim fellow, 1972. Fellow AAAS, Am. Phys. Soc. (forum on physics and soc. award 1976, Leo Szilard award 1994), Am. Acad. Arts and Sci.; mem. Fedn. Am. Scientists (chmn. 1970-71, exec. com. 1969-76, 95-2000, pub. svc. award 1992), Pugwash Movement 1969—, Phi Beta Kappa, Sigma Xi. Office Phone: 858-459-1776. Business E-Mail: hyork@uscd.edu.

YORK, JAMES ORISON, real estate executive; b. Brush, Colo., June 27, 1927; s. M. Orison and Marie L. (Kibble) Y.; m. Janice Marie Sjoberg, Aug. 1, 1959; children: Douglas James, Robert Orison. Student, U. Calif., Berkeley, 1945—46; BA cum laude, U. Wash., 1949. Tchg. fellow U. Wash., Seattle, 1950-52; econ. rsch. analyst Larry Smith & Co. Real Estate, Seattle, 1953-60, ptnr., 1960-66, pres. San Francisco, 1966-71; pres., chief exec. officer R.H. Macy Properties, NYC, also sr. v.p. planning and devel., dir. R.H. Macy & Co., Inc., 1971-88; chmn. James York Assocs. (real estate and venture capital), 1988—. Dir. emeritus UBP Properties, Inc.; chmn., N.Y.C. retail div. Am. Cancer Soc. Contbg. author: Shopping Towns-USA, 1960. Trustee ICSC Ednl. and Rsch. Found. With USNR, 1945-47. Recipient Disting. Alumnus award Econs. U. Wash., 1989. Fellow Phi Beta Kappa; mem. Am. Soc. Real Estate Counselors, Urban Land Inst., Internat. Real Estate Fedn., Internat. Coun. Shopping Ctrs., Olympic Club (San Francisco); Am. Yacht Club (Rye, N.Y.), Corinthian Yacht Club (Seattle), Union League (N.Y.C.), KM, Order St. John, Wash. Athletic Club (Seattle), Royal Victoria (B.C.) Yacht Club, Lambda Alpha. Home and Office: 4 Riverstone Laguna Niguel CA 92677-5309 also: Sunrise Country Club 6 Malaga Dr Rancho Mirage CA 92270-3820 Personal E-mail: jysail@aol.com.

YORK, JAMES WESLEY, JR., theoretical physicist, educator; b. Raleigh, NC, July 3, 1939; s. James Wesley and Mary Smedes (Poyner) York; m. Betty Louise Mattern, Aug. 19, 1961 (div. Apr. 2002); m. Sarah Williams Walt, June 13, 2002; children: Virginia York Setzer, Guilford Mattern. BS with high honors in Physics, N.C. State U., Raleigh, 1962, PhD in Physics, 1966. Asst. prof. N.C. State U., Raleigh, 1965-68; rsch. assoc. Princeton U., 1968-69, lectr., 1969-70, asst. prof., 1970-73; assoc. prof. U. N.C., Chapel Hill, 1973-77, prof. dept. physics, 1977-89, Agnew H. Bahnson, Jr. disting. prof. physics, 1989—2001, dir. Inst. Field Physics, 1984-90; vis. asst. prof. U. Md., College Park, 1972; prof. associe U. Paris, 1976; vis. scientist ctr. astrophysics Harvard, Smithsonian, Cambridge, 1977; vis. prof. U. Tex., Austin, 1979, 87; prof. physics Cornell U., 2002—07. Spkr. Internat. Symposium on Methods of Differential Geometry in Physics and Mechanics, Warsaw, 1976; spr. in field; Alfred Schild Meml. lectr. U. Tex., 1979; del. Seventh Internat. Congress on Math. Physics, Boulder, Colo., 1983, Tex. Symposium on Relativistic Astrophysics, Jerusalem, 1984, Marcel Grossman Meeting, Rome, 1985, Jerusalem, 97, Rio de Janeiro, 2003, NATO Advanced Study Inst., Les Houches, France, 1982, Huelva, Spain, 92, Paris, 92, Banff, Canada, 92, other internat. and nat. meetings; co-organizer sci. meetings including Neutron stars and pulsars, Princeton, 1969; Spacetime dynamics Aspen Ctr. for Theoretical Physics, 1981, Classical Problems in Gravitation, 1990, Cosmic Censorship, 1992; coord. lectr. Inst. Theoretical Physics U. Calif., Santa Barbara, 2000; mem. com. of visitors physics divsn NSF, 1991; plenary lectr. Fifth Can. Conf. on Gen. Relativity and Astrophysics, Waterloo, 1993, Directions in Gen. Relativity, College Park, Md., 1993, Pacific Coast Gravity Mtg., Salt Lake City, 1996, 2d Samos meeting, Greece, 1998; plenary lectr. 50 Years of the Cauchy Problem, Cargese, Corsica, 2002; hon. physics chmn. Cornelius Lanczos Internat. Centenary, Raleigh, NC, 1993; vis. prof. dept. physics N.C. State U., 1998—99, Inter-Instl. Disting. prof. physics, 2001—02. Mem. editl. bd. Jour. Math. Physics, 1989-92, contbr. chpts. to books, articles to sci. jours. Decorated Companion of St. Patrick, 1960; Ford Found. fellow, 1962-65, NSF postdoctoral fellow, 1969-70; Battelle Found. grantee, 1967, Nat. Rsch. Com. France grantee, 1976, NSF grantee, 1974—, travel grantee, 1971, 76, 83, 84; U.S.A.-Israel Binat. Sci. Found. grantee, 1987-90, 90-93, Kenan Found. grantee, 1990, W.N. Reynolds Found. grantee, 1998; recipient Disting. Alumnus award, 1997, Marcel Grossmann prize, Rio de Janeiro, 2003; co-winner Dannie Heineman prize for math. physics Am. Phys. Soc., 2003. Fellow Am. Phys. Soc.; mem. AAAS, Internat. Soc. Gen. Relativity and Gravitation, Phi Beta Kappa, Sigma Xi, Phi Kappa Phi, Tau Beta Pi, Sigma Pi Sigma, Pi Mu Epsilon, Phi Eta Sigma. Avocations: literature, reading. E-mail: jaswyork1@mac.com.

YORK, JANET BREWSTER, nurse, family and sex therapist, artist; b. NYC, Mar. 5, 1941; d. Edward Cox and Janet Stone Brewster; m. Albert Thompson York, Mar. 31, 1962 (dec.); children: Clifton Gaston, Torrance Brewster, 1 adopted child, Justin Brigham. AA with honors, Briarcliff Coll., 1961; RN with highest honors, U. Iowa, 1965; BA summa cum laude, Marymount Manhattan Coll., 1975; MA with honors, NYU, 1978. Nurse Manhattan Eye, Ear and Throat Hosp., NYC, 1966-74; nurse, counselor Washington Free Clinic, 1969-71; family therapist Ackerman Family Inst., NYC, 1976-80; sex therapist N.Y. Med. Coll., Flower Fifth Ave. Hosp., NYC, 1976-80; pvt. practice NYC, 1978—. Supervisory staff grad. edn. program in human sexuality N.Y.U. Med. Ctr., 1982-89, sculptor, 1988—, operator Piccadil Kennel, breeder Cavalier King Charles Spaniels and Chinese Cresteds; bd. dirs. Animal Med. Ctr. Represented in permanent collection The Dog Mus. of Am., St. Louis; author: Corneel the Cavalier, Corneel at the Plaza, Fredrik Goes to Hollywood; contbr. articles to profl. jours; author: (videotape) Death as a Part of Life. Named Vita fellow Internat. Coun. Sex Edn. and Parenthood, Am. U., 1981; recipient Evelyn Monte Sculpture award, 1988, 94, Ellsworth Howell Art Sculpture award Pen & Brush Club, 1991, 93, 96, 99, 2000, 02, Dog Fanciers Club, 1999. Mem. Nat. Assn. Women Artists, Am. Medallic Soc., Nantucket Art Assn., Walker Art Ctr., Nat. Sculpture Soc., Am. Kennel Club (art adv. com.), Nat. Mus. Women in Arts, Lawrence Beach Club, Millbrook Club, Progressive Toy Dog Club/L.I. Kennel Club (bd. dirs.), Morris & Essex Kennel Club. Home: 155 E 72nd St New York NY 10021-4371 Personal E-mail: Piccadiljy@aol.com.

YORK, JEROME B., investment company executive, former computer retail executive; b. Memphis, June 22, 1938; BS, U.S. Mil. Acad., 1960; MS, MIT, 1961; MBA, U. Mich., 1966. Various engring. positions GM Corp., Pontiac, Mich., 1962-67; various managerial positions Ford Motor Co., Deerborn, Mich., 1967-70; dir. strategic planning RCA Corp., Hertz Corp. (subs.), 1970-72, v.p., 1972-75; group v.p. Baker Industries, Inc., Parsippany, NJ, 1976-78; pres. Delta Truck Body Co., Inc., Montgomeryville, Pa., 1978-79; asst. contr. Chrysler de Mex. Chrysler Corp., Highland Park, Mich., 1979-82, mng. dir. Chrysler de Mex., 1982-85, v.p., gen. mgr. Dodge divsn., 1986-90, v.p., contr., 1989-90, exec. v.p., CFO, 1990-93; sr. v.p., CFO IBM Corp., Armonk, NY, 1993—95; vice chmn. Tracinda Corp., 1995—99; also bd. dirs. IBM Corp., Armonk, NY; chmn., pres., CEO Micro Warehouse, Inc., Norwalk, 2000—03; founder, CEO Harwinton Capital Corp., 2000—. Bd. dirs. Apple Computer, Inc., 1997—, Tyco Internat. Ltd., 2002—, Exide Technologies, 2005—, Metro Goldwyn Mayer, Inc., GM Corp., 2006.

YORK, JOAN ELIZABETH SMITH, psychologist; b. Englewood, N.J., Jan. 18, 1940; s. Julius Freeman and Lottie Winfred (Mays) Smith; B.A., W.Va. State Coll., 1962; M.Ed., Trenton State Coll., 1980; postgrad. in counseling psychology Union Grad. Lic. drug and alcohol counselor. Sch. Counselor, Portsmouth (Va.) Child-Family Service, 1972-73; dir. Richmond (Va.) City Jail-Work Release Program, 1974-75; counselor Employee Adv. Service, Trenton, 1975—2002; part-time counselor Trenton State Prison Evening Sch., 1981-82; pvt. counselor Delaware Valley Psychol. Clinic, part-time 1982—; pvt. therapist Mercer Consultation Assn., 1986—; drug and alcoholism counselor, 1987—; pvt. practice 1980-. First v.p., mem. exec. bd. N.J. Task Force on Women and Alcohol. Mem. Assn. of Black Psychologists, Am. Assn. Counseling and Devel., Nat. Black Alcoholism Counselors, N.J. Alcoholism Assn. Democrat. Baptist. Home Phone: 609-396-4887; Office Phone: 609-396-4887. Personal E-mail: jesy138@comcast.net.

YORK, MICHAEL (MICHAEL YORK-JOHNSON), actor; b. Fulmer, Eng., Mar. 27, 1942; s. Joseph Gwynne and Florence Edith (Chown) Johnson; m. Patricia McCallum, Mar. 27, 1968. MA, Oxford U., Eng., 1964; DFA (hon.), U. SC. Profl. debut with Dundee Repertory Theatre, Scotland, 1964; mem. Nat. Theatre Co., London, 1965-66; TV film or miniseries appearances include: Much Ado About Nothing, The Forsyte Saga, Rebel in the Grave, True Patriot, Jesus of Nazareth, 1977, A Man Called Intrepid, 1979, The Phantom of the Opera, 1983, The Master of Ballantrae, 1984, Space, 1985, The Far Country, 1985, Are You My Mother, 1986, Ponce de Leon, 1987, Till We Meet Again, 1989, The Road to Avonlea, 1991, Gardens of the World, 1993; The Four Minute Mile, The Lady and the Highway Man, 1988, The Heat of the Day, 1988, The Hunt for Stolen War Treasure, 1989, The Night of the Fox, 1990, The Magic Paintbrush, 1993, David Copperfield's Christmas, 1994, Teklab, 1994, Fall From Grace, 1994, Not of This Earth, 1995, Duel of Hearts, September, 1995, A Young Connecticut Yankee in King Arthur's Court, 1995, A Knight in Camelot, (TV series) Knots Landing, 1987, SeaQuest, 1995, The Naked Truth, 1995, Babylon 5, 1995, The Ring, 1996, Un Coup De Baguette Magique, True Women, 1997, Sliders, 1997, The Magnificat, 1997, the Long way home, 1997, A Christmas Carol, 1997, The Search for Nazi Gold, 1998, The Ripper 1998, Dead Man's Gun, 1998, Perfect Little Angels, 1998, The Haunting of Hell House, 2000, The Lot, 2000, Founding Fathers, 2002, Liberty's Kids, 2002, Curb Your Enthusiasm, 2002, Founding Brothers, 2002, La Femme Musketeer, 2004, Icon, 2005, The Simpsons, 2006, Law and Order: Criminal Intent, 2006; stage appearances include: Any Just Cause, 1967, Hamlet, 1970, Broadway prodns. of Outcry, 1973, Ring Round the Moon, 1975, Bent, 1980, Cyrano de Bergerac, 1981, Whisper in the Mind, 1990, The Crucible, 1991, Someone Who'll Watch Over Me, 1993, Nora, 1993, Ira Gershwin at 100, 1996, Enoch Arden, 2003, Russian David...Soviet Goliath, 2004, Peer Gynt, 2005, Shadows and Voices, 2005, Camelot, 2006; appeared in motion pictures including: The Taming of the Shrew, 1966, Accident, 1966, Red and Blue, 1967, Smashing Time, 1967, Romeo and Juliet, 1967, The Strange Affair, 1967, The Guru, 1968, Alfred the Great, 1968, Justine, 1969, Something for Everyone, 1969, Zeppelin, 1970, La Poudre D'Escampette, 1971, Cabaret, 1971, England Made Me, 1971, Lost Horizon, 1972, The Three Musketeers, 1973, Murder on the Orient Express, 1974, Great Expectations, 1974, Conduct Unbecoming, 1974, The Four Musketeers, 1975, Logan's Run, 1976, Seven Nights in Japan, The Last Remake of Beau Geste, 1977, The Island of Dr. Moreau, 1977, Fedora, 1977, The Riddle of the Sands, 1978, Final Assignment, 1980, The White Lions, Success is the Best Revenge, Perfect Little Angels, 1998, Dawn, 1985, Vengeance, 1986, The Secret of the Sahara, 1987, Imbalances, 1987, Lethal Obsession, 1987, Midnight Cop, 1988, The Return of the Musketeers, 1989, The Long Shadow, 1991, Eline Vere, 1991, Wide Sargasso Sea, 1991, Rochade, 1991, Discretion Assured, Shadow of a Kiss, 1993, Gospa, 1994, Goodbye America, Austin Powers, Dark Planet, The Treat, 1997, Wrongfully Accused, 1998, One Hell of a Guy, 1998, Lovers and Liars, 1998, The Ghostly Rental, 1999, Austin Powers: The Spy Who Shagged Me, 1999, The Omega Code, 1999, Borstal Boy, 2000, Megiddo, 2001, Austin Powers in Goldmember, 2002, Moscow Heat, 2004; radio performances The Dark Tower, 1977, (Peabody award), A Matter of Honor, 1986, Babbitt, 1987, The Crucible, 1988, Are You Now, UTZ, 1989, McTeague, 1992, Make and Break, 1993; recs. include: Mere Christianity, 1982, Anna Karenina, 1985, Don Quixote, 1986, The King Must Die, 1988, British Rock: The First Wave, UTZ, 1989, The Modigliani Scandal, 1989, The Mummy, 1989, Candide, 1989, The Vampire Lestat, 1989, The Berlin Stories, 1990, The Remains of the Day, 1990, City of Joy, 1991, Beyond Love, 1991, Memories, Dreams, Reflections, 1991, A Poet's Bible, 1992, Einstein's Dreams, 1993, Accidentally on Purpose, 1993, The English Patient, 1993, Fortune's Favorite, 1993, The Three Musketeers, 1993, Paradise Lost, 1993, The Book of Psalms, 1994, The Book of Virtues, 1994, The MagicPaw-Paw, 1994; (recs.) The Rubaiyat of Omar Khayyam, 1995, Aesop's Fables, 1995, The Poetry of Edgar Allen Poe, 1995, The Hunting of the Snark, Caesar's Women, 1996, Treasure Island, 1996, (Grammy nomination) The Wind in the Willows, 1996, Rose, 1996, Daily Word, 1997, Les Miserables, 1998, Caesar, 1998, Brave New World, 1998, Titanic Hearings, 1998, The Fencing Master, 1999 (Audie award), Rikki Tikki Tavi, 1999, King Rat, 1999, Going Home: Jesus and Buddha, 2000, The Lion, The Witch and The Wardrobe, 2000, A Shakespearean Actor Prepares, 2002, The Theory of Everything, 2003, Creating True Peace, 2003, The Bounty, 2003, Goodbye to Berlin, 2004, The Final Solution, 2004, For the Time Being: Advent, 2005, Jane Goodall's Message of Peace, How Do I Love Thee?, 2006; author: The Courage of Conviction, 1985, Voices of Survival, 1987; author: Accidentally on Purpose, 1992, A Shakespearean Actor Prepares, 2000, Dispatches From Armageddon, 2002, Are My Blinkers Showing?, 2005. Chmn. Calif. Youth Theatre. Decorated officer Order Brit. Empire, chevalier Nat. Order Arts and Letters (France). Avocations: travel, music, art. Office: Metropolitan Talent Agency 4500 Wilshire Blvd Fl 2 Los Angeles CA 90010-3858 Office Phone: 323-857-4500.

YORK, MICHAEL CHAREST, librarian; b. Newton, Mass., Jan. 2, 1947; s. Richard Francis and Frances Winship (Thibaut) Y.; m. Carol Roberts, June 26, 1982; 1 child, Michael Bradley. BA, U. N.H., 1971; MS, La. State U., 1972; MBA, Plymouth State Coll., 1990. Reference libr. Ithaca (N.Y.) Coll., 1973-77; asst. dir. libr. Castleton (Vt.) State Coll., 1977-81; libr. dir. Merrimack Valley Coll., Manchester, N.H., 1981-85, U. N.H., Manchester, 1985-91, univ. libr. Durham, 1991-95; libr. dir. Colby-Sawyer Coll., New London, N.H., 1996-98; dir. The Libr. and Archives of N.H. Polit. Tradition, Concord, 1998-99; libr. N.H. State Libr., Concord, 1999—. Mem. ALA, New Eng. Libr. Assn. (pres. 1988-89), N.H. Libr. Assn. (pres. 1999—), N.H. State Libr. Adv. Coun. Avocations: sailing, skiing, woodworking, politics. Office: NH State Libr 20 Park St Concord NH 03301-6316 Office Phone: 603-271-2397. Office Fax: 603-271-2082. Business E-Mail: myork@library.state.nh.us.

YORK, NEIL LONGLEY, history professor; b. San Luis Obispo, Calif., Apr. 21, 1951; s. Eric Kingsmill and Joel Barlow York; m. Carole Jean Mikita, Aug. 29, 1981; children: Jennifer Carole, Caitlin Kingsmill. BA, Brigham Young U., Provo, Utah, 1973, MA, 1975; PhD, U. Calif., Santa Barbara, 1978. Prof. history Brigham Young U., Provo, 1977—. Author: (history book) Mechanical Metamorphosis, 1985, Neither Kingdom Nor Nation, 1994, Fiction as Fact, 2001, Turning the World Upside Down, 2003, Portrait of a Patriot, 2005. Democrat-Npl. Church Of Jesus Christ Of Latter-Day Saints. Home: 2519 Cliff Swallow Dr Sandy UT 84093 Office: Brigham Young Univ Dept History Provo UT 84602 Home Phone: 801-943-5399; Office Phone: 801-422-3485. Business E-Mail: neil_york@byu.edu.

YORK, TINA, painter; b. Germany, Feb. 9, 1951; Student, Sch. Mus. Fine Arts, Boston, 1967-71; studied with, George Dergalis, Wayland, Mass., 1967-75; BA cum laude, Brandeis U., 1978; postgrad., N.Y. Med. Coll., 1980-83. Contbr. works to numerous publs., 1987-2003; one woman shows include Gallery Contemporary Art, Provincetown, Mass., 1969, Springfield (Mass.) Art Assn., 1971, Copley Soc., Boston, 1972-73, Boston U., 1974, Mendler Gallery, Rockport, Mass., 1974, Cambridge (Mass.) Art Assn., 1975, Ames Gallery, N.Y.C., 1976, Gallery Seven, Boston, 1977, Brandeis U., Waltham, Mass., 1978, Rue Oker Gallery of Art, Sturbridge, Mass.,

1979, Art Collectors Gallery, N.Y.C., 1981, 153 Gallery, Inc., N.Y.C., 1982, Creative Concepts, L.A., 1984, Alpha Contemporary Exhibits, L.A., 1985, Darraby Gallery, L.A., 1986, 8th St. Gallery, L.A., 1986, Koplin Gallery, L.A., 1987, Galerie Beverly Hills, Calif., 1988, Conv. Ctr., Rome, 1988, Merck, Sharpe & Dohme, Rahway, N.J., 1988, Erlgangen Kultur Borse, Germany, 1989, Arwell Gallery, Laguna, Calif., 1989, Deutsch-Amerikanisches Inst., Regensburg, Germany, 1990, Art in Pub. Bldgs., Nuremberg, Germany, 1990, Art Expo, N.Y.C., 1990, Amerikahaus, Nuremberg, 1990, Art 5, Nuremberg, 1990, Dresdner Bank, Nuremberg, 1990, Amer. Hosp. Assn., Washington, 1990, So. Med. Assn., Nashville, 1990, 94-95, Studio Gallery, North Hollywood, Calif., 1991-92, Galerie Lehman, Germany, Galerie Sud, Studio la Citta, Italy, Studio Gallery, Calif., 1991 La Foire Internat. d'Art Contemporain, Paris, 1992, 94, Med. Heritage Gall., Waco, Tex., 1991, Herbstmesse, Frankfurt, Germany, 1992-93, Kunstforum Internat., Aachen, Germany, 1993, Kunstlerhaus, Germany, 1993, Ambiente, Frankfurt, 1993-98, 2000-03, ART/LA, 1993-95, Internat. Art Fair, Czechoslovakia, 1993-2003, Art Fair, Seattle, 1993-94, Art Expo, Chgo., 1993-94, Frankfurter Buchmesse, Frankfurt, Germany, 1993, Art Expo, N.Y.C., 1993-96, Chgo. Trade Show, 1993, 95, 97, Toronto Trade Show, 1993, Art Cologne, Germany, 1993-94, 96, Centre d'Art Contemporain, Switzerland, Dresdner Bank, Germany, Galerie Littmann, Switzerland, Galerie Fischer, 1994, Art Asia, Hong Kong, 1994-96, Art Expo, Calif., 1994, 96, PPFA Toronto Trade Show, 1994-95, Limited Edit. Expo, New Orleans, 1994-95, Frankfurt Book Fair, 1994, 97-98, 2000, 03, Internat. Spring Fair, Birmingham, Eng., 1994, 95, Art Miami, 1994-95, Exposition of Art, Sydney, Australia, 1993, Art Taipei, Taiwan, 1993, 94, 95, Art Santa Fe, 1993-95, NASA Ames Rsch. Ctr., Moffett Field, Calif., 1994, NASA Johnson Space Ctr., Houston, 1995, Galerie Rudelko, Germany, Scheffler Galerie, Germany, 1995, Studio Gall., Ariz., 1996, Jahns House, Germany, 1996, Internat. Contemporary Art Fair, Madrid, 1995, West Valley Mus. Art, Phoenix, 1998, Las Vegas Art Mus., 2000, Paul Joseph Galleries, Las Vegas, 2002, Rio Decor, 2003, Tina York Studio, Naples, Fla., 2003, Marco Island Art Assn., Fla. 2004, Studio Gallery, Naples, 2004, 06, Area Arts Gallery, Naples, Fla., 2005, I.C. Fine Art 2000 Gallery, Las Vegas, 2005; group shows include Area Arts Gallery, Naples, NASA Art Programs, Washington, Mus. Fine Arts, Salt Lake City, Mus. Art, Las Vegas, Regional Mus. Art, Bautzen, Germany, Mus. Art, Downey, Calif., Carter Ctr., Atlanta; represented in permanent collections, Paul Joseph Galleries, Las Vegas, Rio Decor, Mus. of Art, Las Vegas, Downey (Calif.) Mus. Art, Mus. Fine Arts, Salt Lake City, Mcpl. Art Mus., Osaka, Japan, Regional Mus. Art, Bautzen, Germany, Carter Ctr., Atlanta, Kennedy Space Ctr., Fla., New Zealand Space Adminstrn., Auckland, NASA, Internat. Peace Acad., NY, USIA, BBC (Brit. Broadcasting Co.), Lagan Jute, Ltd., India, NIH, Universitet Kliment Orchridski, Bulgaria, Hiatt Internat., Beverly Hills, Calif., Paris, Gallery Dmovrosek, Yugoslavia, Columbia U., Nat. Cancer Inst., Md., Kulturamt der Stadt Nurnberg, Germany, Planetary Soc., Calif., Mayo Clin., Ariz., Nat. Air and Space Mus., Washington, Nat. Air and Space Mus., others; represented on Artrain USA; pub. NASA/Exploration of Space, 2004. First prize painting Arts Fest., Scituate, MA, 1969, Internatl. Show, Fall River, MA, 1971; third prize mixed media painting, De Cordova Mus., Lincoln, MA, 1972; second prize painting, Amer. Artists in Paris, Paris, 1975; first prize mixed media painting Inst. Contemporary Art, 1979; Gold medal painting, Spring Arts Fest., LA, 1985; first prize mixed media painting, One Fifty Three Gall., Inc., 1987. Mem.: Internat. High IQ Soc. Studio: Tina York Studio 754 Waterloo Ct Naples FL 34120 Office Phone: 239-659-2941. Business E-Mail: tinayorkstudio@aol.com.

YORK, VERMELLE CARDWELL, retired real estate broker and developer; b. Evergreen, Ala., Jan. 30, 1925; d. Frederick Lofton and Emmie Mildred (Pitts) Cardwell; m. E. Travis York, Jr., Dec. 26, 1946; children: Lisa, Travis. BS, Auburn U., Ala., 1946. Pres. Tralisa Corp., Gainesville, Fla., 1966—87, sec., treas., 1988—94, Caret Corp., Gainesville, Fla., 1979—86, pres., 1987—2004; ret., 2004. Mem. devel. com. Harn Mus., Gainesville, 1990-96, Hospice House, Gainesville, 1992-96; co-chair March of Dimes, Gainesville, 1995, Red Ribbon Campaign, 1989, 90; bd. dirs. Keep Alachua County Beautiful, Phillips Ctr. Performing Arts U. Fla.; bd. Gainesville Cmty. Found. Recipient Pres.'s Medallion, U. Fla., 1980; named Woman of Distinction, Santa Fe C.C., Gainesville, Fla., 1988, Vam York Theatre at Gainesville Cmty. Playhouse 05 dedicated in her honor; named one of Women Who Make a Difference, Girl Scouts Am., 2005 Mem. Gainesville Builders Assn. (bd. dirs. 1997—), The Heritage Club (mem. amb. com. 1991-96), P.E.O. (pres. 1989-90), Surfside N. Club, (dir. 1988-91), Gainesville Women's Forum (membership chair 1994-96), Altrusa, Rotary, DAR, Phi Kappa Phi. Avocation: genealogy. Home: 5200 SW 25th Blvd #4216 Gainesville FL 32608-8925 Personal E-mail: cvcyork@gru.net.

YORKE, JOHN BUNDY, lawyer; b. Rock Hill, SC, Aug. 5, 1954; s. N. Felix and Lane Knox Yorke; children: H. Spencer, N. Greer. BA, Wofford Coll., 1976; JD, Wake Forest U., 1979. Bar: N.C. 1979, S.C. 1987. Assoc. Wardlow, Knox, Knox, Freeman & Scofield, Charlotte, NC, 1979—87; v.p., gen. counsel World Way Corp., 1987—96; gen. counsel Integon Corp., Winston-Salem, NC, 1996—98; mem. Helms Mulliss & Wicker, PLLC, Charlotte, NC, 1998—. Dir. New South Pizza, Inc, Charlotte, NC. Trustee Thompson Child & Family Focus, Charlotte, NC, 2001. Mem.: Wake Forest Law Alumni Bd., N.C. Bar Assn. (chmn. corp. counsel sect. 1991—92), ABA, Wofford Coll. Nat. Alumni Assn. (pres. 2001), Phi Beta Kappa. Avocation: golf. Office: Helms Mulliss & Wicker PLLC 201 North Tryon Street Suite 3000 Charlotte NC 28202 Office Phone: 704-343-2167. Office Fax: 704-343-2000. Business E-Mail: john.yorke@hmw.com.

YORKE, MARIANNE, lawyer, real estate executive; b. Nov. 4, 1948; d. Joseph George and Catherine Veronica (Friel) Y. BA, West Chester U., 1971; JD, Temple U., 1980; MS in Ognl. Dynamics, U. Pa., 1987; M in Corp. Real Estate, Internat. Assn. Corp. Real Estate Execs., 1996. Bar: Pa. 1981, N.Y. 1992. Mgr. CIGNA Corp., Phila., 1982-85, asst. dir., 1985-90; v.p. Chase Manhattan Bank, NYC, 1990-92; real estate dir. Johnson & Johnson, 1992—. Real estate atty. Garfinkel & Volpicelli, Phila., 1980-82; prin., mng. ptnr. Yorke & Eisenman, Real Estate, Phila., 1976-89, prin., mng. ptnr. Yorke & Mac Lachlin Real Estate, Phila., 1989-02; lectr. Women in the Arts, 1982-90; guest spkr. Wharton Sch. Bus. Class of 1989, U. Pa., grad. sch. arts and sci. Class of 1988; asst. prof. bus. law Rider U. Grad Sch., 2002-03, asst. prof. real estate law and real estate transactions Rutgers U. Grad. Sch., 2003—. Contbr. articles to profl. jours. Solicitor Pa. Ballet, Phila., 1983-90, United Way, Phila., 1983-90; mem. steering com. U. Pa., 1986-90, dir. alumni assn., 1987-90; mem. adv. com. for econ. devel. Luth. Settlement House Adv., 1986-88; mem. Ctr. Adv. Bd., 2000—; bd. dirs. Hamilton Townhouse Assn., Phila., 1988-90, chmn. ins. com., 1989-90, 718 Broadway Inc., NYC, 1990-94, Johnson Health Care Svcs. Recipient Live for Life Mgmt., Johnson Health Mgmt., 1995, Pres. Quality Process Excellence award, EthiconEndo Surgery, 2000, Process Excellence award, Ethicon, Inc., 2001. Mem. ABA (forum on constrn. 1982-90), Pa. Bar Assn. (condominium and zoning com. 1982-90), Assn. of Bar of City of NY (sects. on internat. law and real property law 1992-94), Phila. Bar Assn., Phila. Women Real Estate Atty., CORENET, Nat. Assn. Corp. Real Estate Exec. (internat. coun. 1984-2002), comml. coun. 1984-2002), Internat. Atty., Roundtable, Women's Law Caucus, Phi Alpha Delta. Independent. Roman Catholic. Home: The Admiralty 55 Ocean Ave Monmouth Beach NJ 07750-1366 Office: Johnson & Johnson W H 7135 1 Johnson & Johnson Plz New Brunswick NJ 08933-0002 Office Phone: 732-524-3881. Business E-Mail: myorke@corus.jnj.com.

YORKE, THOMAS EDWARD, musician, vocalist; b. Wellingborough, England, Oct. 7, 1968; children: Noah, Agnes. Student in English and Art, Exeter U., Eng. Guitarist Flickernoise; orderly; vocalist, guitarist Radiohead, 1992—. Musician & vocalist (Radiohead albums) Pablo Honey, 1993, The Bends, 1995, Ok Computer, 1997 (Grammy award, Best Alternative Music Performance, 1998), Kid A, 2000 (Grammy award, Best Alternative Music Performance, 2001), Amnesiac, 2001, I Might Be Wrong: Live Recordings, 2001, Hail to the Thief, 2003, (solo albums) The Eraser, 2006. Office: Capital Records 1750 North Vine St 10th Floor Hollywood CA 90028 also: Chrysalis Music Group The Chrysalis Building Bramley Rd London W10 6SP England

YORKE-VINEY, SALLY ANNE, elementary school educator; b. Williamsport, Pa., Dec. 8, 1953; d. H. Allen and Mary Ellen Yearick; m. Malcolm Christopher Stanley Viney, Nov. 26, 1988; 1 child, Colin Patrick Allen Viney. BS in Edn., Shippensburg U., 1975; MEd, East Stroudsburg U., 1993; PhD, Marywood U., 2007—. Tchr. elem. sch. Selinsgrove Sch. Dist., Pa., 1975—76, Shikellamy Sch. Dist., Sunbury, 1976—82; tech. editor Lambda Techs., NYC, 1983—85; singer/actress AFTRA, SAG Actor's Equity, 1978—85; profl. singer/cabaret artist various Cruise Lines, 1985—91; tchr. elem. sch. East Stroudsburg Sch. Dist., Pa., 1991—2007. Adj. prof. East Stroudsburg U., 1999—2005; chair Arts in Edn. Com., 2003—06. Dir. choir Luth. Ch. of Savior, Mt. Pocono, Pa., 1989—99. Mem.: ASCD, Internat. Reading Assn., Phi Delta Kappa. Avocations: singing, theater. Home: HC89 Box 831 Pocono Summit PA 18346 Personal E-mail: malnsal@verizon.net.

YORMARK, BRETT D., professional sports team executive; s. Arlene Sloan; m. Amy Yormark; children: Madison, Drake. Student in Mgmt., Ind. U. Thrift plan adminstr. Banker's Trust, NYC, 1988—89; account exec. NJ Nets, East Rutherford, 1989—91, v.p. corp. mktg., 1994, sr. v.p. corp. mktg., 1995—98, pres., CEO, 2005—; account exec. Sports TV Katz Comm., Chgo., 1991—92; sr. account exec. Detroit Pistons, Auburn Hills, Mich., 1992—94; mng. dir. corp. mktg. NASCAR, NYC, 1998—2000, v.p. corp. mktg., 2000—05. Named one of 40 Under Forty, Crain's NY Bus., 2006, 40 Under 40, Sports Bus. Jour., 2006. Mem.: North Jersey Young Presidents Assn. Office: Nets Sports and Entertainment LLC 390 Murray Hill Pky East Rutherford NJ 07073 Office Phone: 201-935-8888. Office Fax: 201-935-1088. *

YORN, RICK, talent agent; b. 1968; Ptnr. Artists Mgmt. Group (acquired by The Firm), Beverly Hills, Calif., 2000—02; co-chmn. The Firm, Beverly Hills, Calif., 2002—. Prodr.: (films) Sidewalks of New York, 2001, You Stupid Man, 2002; exec. prodr.: Gangs of New York, 2002, The Aviator, 2004; exec. cons. (TV series) The Fighting Fitzgeralds, 2001. Office: The Firm 6th Fl 9465 Wilshire Blvd Beverly Hills CA 90212 Office Phone: 310-860-8000. Office Fax: 310-860-8100. *

YORSZ, STANLEY, lawyer; b. Norwich, Conn., June 5, 1953; s. Stanley and Helen (Chimilewski) Y.; m. Margaret A. McLean, June 14, 1986. BA, Colgate U., 1975; JD cum laude, Dickinson Sch. Law, Carlisle, Pa., 1978. Bar: Pa. 1978, U.S. Dist. Ct. (we. dist.) Pa. 1978, U.S. Ct. Appeals (3d cir.) 1980, U.S. Supreme Ct. 1980. Law clk. to judge Pa. Superior Ct., Pitts., 1978-80; assoc. Buchanan Ingersoll & Rooney PC, Pitts., 1980-86, ptnr., 1986—, chair securities litigation group. Editor comments Dickinson Law Rev., 1978. Mem. ABA, Allegheny County Bar Assn., Pa. Bar Assn., Rivers Club. Roman Catholic. Avocations: tennis, squash, golf. Office: Buchanan Ingersoll & Rooney PC 1 Oxford Ct Pittsburgh PA 15219-1407 Office Phone: 412-562-8841. Business E-Mail: stanley.yorsz@bipc.com.

YOSELOFF, JULIEN DAVID, publishing company executive; b. NYC, June 25, 1941; s. Thomas and Sara (Rothfuss) Y.; m. Darlene Starr Carbone, Aug. 6, 1967; children: Michael Ian, Anthony Alexander. BA, U. Pa., 1962; student, London Sch. Econs., 1962—63; MA, Rutgers U., 1994. With A.S. Barnes and Co., Inc., Cranbury, NJ, 1963-80; dir. Associated Univ. Presses, Inc., 1966—; pres. Rosemont Pub. and Printing Corp., 1985—. Served with AUS, 1964. Mem. Phi Beta Kappa Assocs., Phi Beta Kappa, Pi Sigma Alpha. Avocations: amateur radio, photography, bicycling. Office: 2010 Eastpark Blvd Cranbury NJ 08512-3518 Office Phone: 609-655-4770.

YOSELOFF, THOMAS, publisher; b. Sioux City, Iowa, Sept. 8, 1913; s. Morris and Sarah (Rabinowitz) Y.; m. Sara Rothfuss, Apr. 30, 1938 (div. 1964); children: Julien David, Mark Laurence; m. Lauretta Sellitti, Apr. 23, 1964; 1 dau., Tamar Rachel. AB, U. Iowa, 1934; LittD (hon.), Bucknell U., 1982; LHD (hon.), Fairleigh Dickinson U., 1982. Chmn. Rosemont Pub. & Printing Corp., 1969—, Associated Univ. Presses, 1969, Golden Cockerel Press, London, 1979—. Author: A Fellow of Infinite Jest, 1946, (with Lillian Stuckey) Merry Adventures of Till Eulenspiegel, 1944, Further Adventures of Till Eulenspiegel, 1957, The Time of My Life, 1979; Editor: Seven Poets in Search of an Answer, 1944, Voyage to America, 1961, Comic Almanac, 1963, The Man from the Mercury, 1986. Pres. Ctr. for War/Peace Studies, 1977-91. Recipient award of merit Bucknell U., 1975, award of merit U. Del., 1987. Mem. Phi Beta Kappa, Sigma Delta Chi, Delta Sigma Rho. Home: 27 Globeflower Ln West Windsor NJ 08550 Personal E-mail: lissie21@aol.com.

YOSHIDA, GLEN YOSHIO, otolaryngologist; b. Honolulu, Feb. 20, 1955; s. Charles K. and Yoshiko Yoshida; m. Nancy Marie Gustafson, Apr. 22, 1989; 1 child, Michael B. BA, Lawrence U., Appleton, Wis., 1977; MD, Uniformed Svcs. U. Health Scis., Bethesda, Md., 1982. Diplomate Am. Bd. Otolaryngology, 1987. Commd. 2d lt. US Army, 1982, advanced through grades to lt. col., 1994; intern otolaryn.-head and neck surgery Tripler Army Med. Ctr., Honolulu, 1982—83, resident otolaryn.-head and neck surgery, 1983—87; chief otolaryn.-head and neck surgery 121 Evac Hosp., Seoul, Republic of Korea, 1987—88; fellow head and neck surgery Meth. Hosp., Indpls., 1988—89; asst. chief otolaryn.-head and neck surgery Fitzsimons Army Med. Ctr., Aurora, Colo., 1989—96; mem. otolaryngology staff Altru Health Sys., Grand Forks, ND, 1996—. Mem. adv. bd. Grand Forks Pharmacy, 2000—; cons. in field; asst. clin. prof., co-program dir. otolaryngology residency U. Colo. Health Scis. Ctr., 1990—96; asst. clin. prof. Uniformed Svcs. U. Health Scis., 1995—96, U. ND Sch. Medicine, 1998—; presenter in field. Contbr. articles to med. jours. Otolaryngologist med. mission trip SW Med. Teams, Romania, 1995, Internat. Relief Teams, Honduras, 2006; med. vol. mission trip Calvary Luth. Ch., Honduras, 2004; bd. dirs. Greater Grand Forks Symphony Orch., 2001—. Decorated Army Commendation medal, Nat. Def. medal, Meritorious Svc. medal; recipient Tchr. of Yr. award, U. Colo. otolaryngology-head and neck surgery dept., 1996. Fellow: ACS, Am. Acad. Facial Plastic and Reconstructive Surgery, Am. Head and Neck Soc., Am. Acad. Otolaryngology-Head and Neck Surgery (Honor award 1998); mem.: Am. Acad. Sleep Medicine, Fighting Souix Club. Lutheran. Avocations: running, horseback riding, sled dogs, photography, golf. Office: Altru Health Sys 1000 S Columbia Rd 4D Grand Forks ND 58201

YOSHIDA, HIROYUKI, mathematician, computer scientist, educator, medical science educator; b. Yokote, Akita, Japan, Mar. 16, 1961; s. Tadashi Yoshida; m. Shinobu Muto. PhD, U. Tokyo, 1989. Asst. prof. Tokyo Inst. Polytechnics, Atsugi, Kanagawa, Japan, 1989—93; from vis. rsch. assoc. to asst. prof. U. Chgo., 1993—97, asst. prof., assoc. prof., 1997—2005; assoc. prof. Harvard Med. Sch., Boston, 2005—. Author: Windows Magic, 1992, The Best Guide to NeXT Computers, 1992; editor: Introduction to the BASIC Programming Language, 1992, Essential LAN Terminology 100, 1993, The Best Guide to the World Wide Web, 1996, Essential Network Terminology 100, 1997, The Internet Dictionary, 1997; contbr. chapters to books, articles to profl. publs. Recipient Cum Laude award Edn. Exhibit, Radiol. Soc. N.Am., 2000, Cert. Merit award Edn. Exhibit, 2004, Excellence in Design award Edn. Exhibit, 2002, Hon. Mention award, Internat. Soc. Optical Engring., 2002, Merit award, InfoRAD, 2006; grantee, Whitaker Found., 1995, Lewis Block Fund grant, U. Chgo., 1999, Am. Cancer Soc., 2000, 2005, NIH, 2000, Cancer Rsch. Found. Am., 2001, 2005, Nat. Cancer Inst., 2003. Mem.: IEEE, Assn. for Computing Machinery, Inst. Electronics, Info. and Comm. Engrs., Info. Processing Soc. Japan, Internat. Soc.Optical Engring., Am. Assn. Physicists Medicine. Office: Mass Gen Hosp Harvard Med Sch Dept Radiology 25 New Cardon St Boston MA 02114 Home: 4 Summit Rd Watertown MA 02472-3537 Office Phone: 617-643-2326. Business E-Mail: yoshida.hiro@mgh.harvard.edu.

YOSHIDA, STEPHEN P., lawyer; b. Honolulu, Nov. 6, 1978; BA, U. Portland, 2001; JD, U. Oreg., Eugene, 2004. Bar: Oreg. 2004. Atty. Martin Bischoff, Portland, 2004—. Recipient Order Coif award, U. Oreg. Sch. Law, 2004. Office: Martin Bischoff 888 SW Fifth Ave #900 Portland OR 97204 Home Phone: 503-970-1459; Office Phone: 503-224-3113. Office Fax: 503-224-9471. Business E-Mail: syoshida@martinbischoff.com.

YOSHIKAWA, HIROMI, pharmaceutical executive; b. Tokyo; B in Bus., Waseda Univ. Computer sys. sect., fin. dept. Otsuka Pharm. Co. Ltd., 1976—77; acctg. mgr. Japan Immunoresearch Lab. (after acquisition by OPC), 1977—80; in charge of installation, integrated mgmt. sys. China Otsuka (OPC subs.), 1980; fin. dept., Tokyo office Otsuka, 1994—97, developer, bus. sys., Europe London, 1997—2000; chmn., CEO Otsuka Am. Pharm. Inc. (OAPI), Rockville, Md., 2000—; also, chmn., CEO Otsuka Am. Inc. (OAI) holding co. Bd. dir. Pharm. Rsch. Mfr. Am. Office: Otsuka Am Pharm Inc 2440 Research Blvd Rockville MD 20850 Office Phone: 301-990-0030. Office Fax: 301-212-8647.

YOSHIMURA, YOSHIKO, librarian; b. Tokyo, Oct. 21, 1933; arrived in U.S., 1958; d. Shigeru and Jun Yoshimura. BA, Tsuda Coll., Tokyo, Japan, 1956; MSLS, Syracuse U, 1961; AM, Harvard U, 1971. Libr. asst. Toyo Bunko Libr., Tokyo, 1956—58; cadet, intern Syacuse (NY) U Libr., 1958—61; sr. cataloger Harvard-Yenching Libr., Cambridge, Mass., 1961—71; sr. Japanese cataloger Libr. of Congress, Washington, 1971—81, area specialist Japan, 1981—98. Author (compiler): Japanese Govt. Documents and Censored Pub., 1992, Censored Japanese Serials of the Pre-1946 Period, 1994, Pre 1956 Japanese Documents and Censored Materials, 2002—06. Home: 2311 Pimmit Dr No 1215 Falls Church VA 22043

YOSHIUCHI, ELLEN HAVEN, healthcare educator, clinical counselor; b. Newark, Apr. 15, 1949; d. Michael Joseph and Adeline V. (Lindblom) Haven; m. Takeshi Yoshiuchi, Dec. 1, 1973; children: Teri Takumi, Niki Noboru. BA summa cum laude, CUNY, 1980; M Profl. Studies in Human Rels., N.Y. Inst. Tech., 1991. Cert. bereavement svcs. counselor, cert. kidney early evaluation program. Pvt. practice childbirth edn., 1983—89; program asst. parent/family edn. St. Luke's/Roosevelt Hosp. Ctr., NYC, 1989—93, mem. faculty parent/family edn. program, 1990—2002; mem. faculty Family Ctr. at Riverdale Neighborhood House, Bronx, 1991—96; faculty mem. The Greater N.Y. March of Dimes, NYC, 1996—2001; mgr. patient svcs. N.Y.C. chpt. The Leukemia and Lymphoma Soc., 1998—2004; program dir. Nat. Kidney Found. of Greater N.Y., 2004—. Mem. perinatal bereavement com. St. Luke's/Roosevelt Hosp. Ctr., N.Y.C., 1989-95. Editor ASPO/N.Y.C. News, 1983-86; contbr. articles to profl. jours. Trustee Pan Asian Repertory Theatre, N.Y.C., 1996-2001. Fellow: Am. Coll. Childbirth Educators; mem.: NY Citizens' Com. on Health Care Decisions, Coun. Nephrology Social Workers, C.G. Jung Found. for Analytical Psychology, Lamaze Internat. (cert. tchr., pres. N.Y.C. chpt. 1987—91, nominating com. 1991—93, dir. ednl. program 1991—93). Office: 30 E 33d St New York NY 10016-6901 Office Phone: 212-889-2210 228.

YOSHIZU, JERI, public relations executive; b. 1969; BA Mgmt. Info. Systems, Calif. State U. Procurement analyst Toyota Motor Sales USA Inc., 1995—2000, interactive marketer, Genesis Grp., 2000—03, sales and promotion mgr., Scion Grp., 2003—. Named one of 40 Under 40, Advt. Age, 2007. Office: Toyota Scion Inc 300 El Cajon Blvd El Cajon CA 92020 Office Phone: 866-719-6892. Office Fax: 619-447-9123. *

YOSHIZUMI, DONALD TETSURO, dentist; b. Honolulu, Feb. 18, 1930; s. Richard Kiyoshi and Hatsue (Tanouye) Yoshizumi; m. Barbara Fujiko Iwashita, June 25, 1955 (dec. Feb. 1998); children: Beth Ann E., Cara Leigh S., Erin Yuri. BS, U. Hawaii, 1952; DDS, U. Mo., 1960, grad. cert. prosthodontics, 1962, MS, 1963. Clin. instr. U. Mo. Sch. Dentistry, Kansas City, 1960—63; pvt. practice Santa Clara, Calif., 1963—70, San Jose, Calif., 1970—. Contbr. articles to profl. jours. With USAF, 1952—56. Mem.: ADA, Santa Clara County Dental Soc., Calif. Dental Assn., Delta Sigma Delta, Omicron Kappa Upsilon. Home: 5054 Parkfield Ave San Jose CA 95129-3225 Office: 2011 Forest Ave Ste 1 San Jose CA 95128-4813

YOSHIZUMI, MARC O., ophthalmologist, educator; s. Richard K. and Hatsue Yoshizumi. MD, Yale U., 1970. Neuropathology fellow Oxford U., England, 1970—71; intern John Hopkins Hosp., Balt., 1971—72; neurology fellow U. Calif., San Francisco, 1972—74; resident ophthalmology Harvard Med. Sch., Boston, 1974—77, retina fellow, 1977—78; prof. UCLA Sch. Med., Jules Stein Eye Inst., 1978—; dir. eye trauma UCLA Med. Ctr., 1985—; dir. med. student edn. in ophthalmology UCLA Sch. Medicine, 1985—. Guest lectr, vis. prof. various nat. and internat. schs. Contbr. articles to profl. jours. Fellow: Am. Acad. Ophthalmology, Retina Soc. Office Phone: 310-825-4749. E-mail: yoshizumi@jsei.ucla.edu.

YOSKIN, JON WILLIAM, II, insurance company executive; b. Phila., Oct. 16, 1939; s. Lewis William and Louise (Houck) Y.; m. Dorothea James, Sept. 25, 1961 (div. Mar. 1992); children: Nicholas, Dorothea, Maurice P.; m. Elizabeth Anne Groves, Sept 26, 1992. Pvt. practice, Phila., 1959-74; sr. v.p. Mid. Atlantic Gen. Investment Co., Phila., 1974-80; exec. v.p. Transatlantic Life Assurance Co., Phila., 1980-85, Meritor Life Ins. Co., Phila., 1985-88; owner, CEO Tri-Arc Fin. Svcs., Phila., 1988—; chmn., CEO Magellan Ins. Co. Ltd., Bermuda, 1996—. Bd. dirs. Concerto Soloist, Phila., 1990-92, Nat. Media Corp., 1994-98, Phila. Commn. to End. Homelessness, 1995—; mem. Spl. Olympics Adv. Com. Mem. Nat. Assn. Life Underwriters, Coun. Ins. Agts. and Brokers (bd. dirs.), Profl. Assn. Ins. Agts., Sons of Am. Revolution, Mil. Order Loyal Legion of U.S. Republican. Episcopalian. Avocation: big game hunting. Office: Tri-Arc Fin Svcs 983 Old Eagle School Rd Ste 616 Wayne PA 19087-1711 Home: 1 Brightview Ave Hobe Sound FL 33455-2123 E-mail: jyoskin@triarcfs.com.

YOSKOWITZ, IRVING BENJAMIN, lawyer, energy executive; b. Bklyn., Dec. 2, 1945; s. Rubin and Jennie Y.; m. Carol L. Magil, Feb. 11, 1973; children: Stephen M., Robert J. BBA, CCNY, 1966; JD, Harvard U., 1969; postgraduate student, London Sch. Econs., 1971—72. Bar: NY 1970, DC 1972, Conn. 1982. Programmer IBM, East Fishkill, NY, 1966; sys. analyst Office Sec. Def., Washington, 1969—71; assoc. Arnold & Porter, Washington, 1972—73; atty. IBM, 1973—79, regional counsel Bethesda, Md., 1979; dep. gen. counsel United Technologies Corp., Hartford, Conn., 1979—81, v.p. and gen. counsel, 1981—86, sr. v.p., gen. counsel, 1986—90, exec. v.p., gen. counsel, 1990—98; sr. ptnr. Global Tech. Ptnrs., L.L.C., Washington, 1998—2005; sr. counsel Crowell & Moring, Washington, 2001—05; exec. v.p., gen. counsel Constellation Energy, Balt., 2005—. Bd. dirs. Wyle Corp., Darwin Profl. Underwriters, Inc. Mem. editl.

bd. Harvard Law Rev., 1968-69. With US Army, 1969-71. Knox fellow, 1971-72 Mem. ABA, Am. Corp. Counsel Assn. (bd. dirs. 1982-85), Assn. Gen. Counsel. Office: Constellation Energy 750 E Pratt St Baltimore MD 21202

YOST, BYRON A., retired physician; b. New Colombia, Pa., June 29, 1917; s. Oliver and Sarah Viola (Gehris) Yost; m. Ruth Marion Germann; children: Rebecca, Sally, Penny, Trudy. AB, U. Kans., Lawrence, 1939, MA in History, 1940, MD, 1949. Pvt. practice, Erie, Conn., 1951—53, Longmont, Colo., 1953—2003; ret., 2003. Pres., chief of staff Longmont Cmty. Hosp. Pres. Tiny Tim Youth Svc., Longmont. Sgt., 1943—44. Mem.: Boulder County Med. Soc. (pres.), Barber Shop Club, St. Vrain Round up Club (founder), Lions Club, Longmont Saddle Club, Masons. Republican. Avocations: training horses, hunting, skiing. Home: 13538 WCR1 Longmont CO 80504

YOST, DAN, telecommunications industry executive; BSEE, MBA, So. Meth. U., Dallas. Sr. mgmt. position NETCOM Online Comm., MetroCel Cellular, Inc., McCaw Cellular Comm., AT&T Wireless; pres., COO Allegiance Telecom, Inc., Dallas; exec. v.p. product and mktg. Qwest Comm. Internat., Inc., Denver, 2004—. Bd. dirs. ACE Cash Express. Office: Qwest Comm Internat Inc 1801 California St Denver CO 80202 Office Phone: 303-992-1400. Office Fax: 303-896-8515. *

YOST, GERALD B., lawyer; b. Harvey, Ill., Dec. 21, 1954; s. Richard Dennis and Marilyn Patricia (Moore) Y.; m. Kay Lynn Benton, Apr. 16, 1977; children: Matthew Brian, Benjamin Gerald, Andrew Richard. BA in Journalism, Drake U., 1976; student, Purdue U., 1975; JD, Hamline U., 1980. Bar: Minn. 1980, U.S. Dist. Ct. Minn. 1980, Wis. 1987. Assoc. Bergman, Street & Ulmen, Mpls., 1980—84; ptnr. Wasserman and Baill, Mpls., 1984—90, Yost, Stephenson & Sanford, Mpls., 1990—95, Yost & Baill LLP, Mpls., 1996—, Milw., 2005—. Editor: Student Osteo. Med. Assn. Publ. mag., 1976; mem. Law Review Hamline U., 1978-80. Active YMCA, St. Paul. Recipient Am. Jurisprudence award, Lawyers Coop. Pub. Co., St. Paul, 1979. Mem. ABA, Minn. State Bar Assn., Wis. Bar Assn., Phi Alpha Delta, Sigma Delta Chi. Avocations: tennis, racquetball, boating and water skiing, jogging. Home: 422 Mt Curve Blvd Saint Paul MN 55105 Office: Yost & Baill LLP 2050 US Bank Plaza South 220 S 6th St Minneapolis MN 55402-1803 also: Yost & Baill LLP 2300 N Mayfair Rd Ste 290 Milwaukee WI 53206 Office Phone: 612-338-6000, 414-259-0600. Business E-Mail: gyost@yostbaill.com.

YOST, NED, professional baseball player; b. Eureka, Calif., Aug. 19, 1954; m. Deborah Yost; children: Jenny, Ned, Josh, Andrew. Attended, Chabot Jr. Coll. With Milwaukee Brewers, 1980—83, Tex. Rangers, 1984, Montreal Expos, 1985; mgr. Milwaukee Brewers, 2003—; coaching staff Atlanta Braves, 1991—2002. Office: Miller Park 46th St Milwaukee WI 53214-3691

YOST, NICHOLAS CHURCHILL, lawyer; b. Washington, Aug. 15, 1938; s. Charles Woodruff and Irene Ravitch (Oldakowska) Yost; m. Sandra Moore Rennie; children: Robert, Scott, Daniel. AB in Pub. & Internat. Affairs, Princeton U., 1960; LLB, U. Calif., Berkeley, 1963. Bar: Calif., 1964, US Supreme Ct., 1972, DC, 1978. Dep. atty. gen. adminstrv. law Calif. Dept. Justice, 1965-69; counsel Calif. State Environ. Quality Study Coun., 1969-71; dep. atty. gen. in charge environ. unit Calif. Dept. Justice, 1971-77; gen. counsel Coun. Environ. Quality, Exec. Office of Pres., Washington, 1977-81; vis. scholar Environ. Law Inst., Washington, 1981-82; sr. atty. Ctr. for Law in Pub. Interest, Washington, 1982-85; ptnr. Dickstein, Shapiro & Morin, Washington, 1985-94, Sonnenschein Nath & Rosenthal, San Francisco, 1994—. US dir. Law and Adminstrn. Project under US USSR environ. agreement, 1977—81; dir. Pres.'s Task Force on Global Resources and Environment, 1980—81; mem US Del. to UN Conf. on Environment and Devel., Rio de Janeiro, 1992; mem. & subcom. chair Calif. EPA Blue Ribbon Commn. on a Unified Environ. Statute, 1994; NEPA counsel Presidio Trust. Contbr. articles to profl. journals Capt. US Army, 1963—65. Recipient Nat. Environ. Quality Award, Natural Resources Coun. Am., 1996. Mem. ABA (chmn. standing com. on environ. law 1989-91), State Bar Calif. (chmn. com. on environ. 1975-76), DC Bar Assn. (co-chmn. environ., energy and natural resources sect. 1985-86, 88-89), Environ. Law Inst. (bd. dirs. 1986-92), UN Assn. LA (v.p. 1969-71), UN Assn. Wash. (bd. dirs. 1987-93). Office: Sonnenschein Nath & Rosenthal LLP 26th Fl 525 Market St San Francisco CA 94105 Home Phone: 415-543-1031; Office Phone: 415-882-2440. Office Fax: 415-882-0300. Business E-Mail: nyost@sonnenschein.com.

YOST, PAUL ALEXANDER, JR., foundation executive, retired military officer; b. Phila., Jan. 3, 1929; s. Paul Alexander Sr. and Jeanne Moore (Bailey) Y.; m. Jan Worth, June 2, 1951; children: Linda L., Paul Alexander III, David J., Lisa L., Christopher J. BS, USCG Acad., 1951; MS, U. Conn., 1959; MA, George Washington U., 1964; grad., Naval War Coll., 1964. Commd. ensign USCG, 1951, advanced through grades to adm., 1986, comdr. 8th dist. New Orleans, 1978-81, chief staff hdqrs. Washington, 1981-84, comdr. 3d dist., maritime Atlantic def. zone, and Atlantic area NYC, 1984-86, commandant Washington, 1986-90, ret., 1990; pres. James Madison Found., Washington, 1990—. Decorated D.S.M. with gold star, Silver Star, Legion of Merit combat "V" with gold star, Meritorious Service Medal. Office: James Madison Meml Fellowship Found 2000 K St NW Washington DC 20006-1809

YOST, R. DAVID (DAVID YOST), pharmaceutical executive; b. 1947; married. BS, USAF Acad., 1969; MBA, UCLA, 1970. From v.p. to pres. Kauffman-Lattimer Co., Columbus, Ohio, 1969-74; from group v.p. to group pres. cen. region Alco Health Systems Corp., Malvern, Pa., 1989-97; pres., CEO, chmn. AmeriSource Health Corp., Malvern, Pa., 1997—2001; pres. Amerisource Bergen Corp., 2001—02, CEO, dir., 2002—. Capt. USAF, 1969—74. Office: AmerisourceBergen Corp 1300 Morris Dr Ste 100 Wayne PA 19087-5594

YOST, WILLIAM ALBERT, psychology professor; b. Dallas, Sept. 21, 1944; s. William Jacque and Gladys (Funk) Yost; m. Lee Prater, June 15, 1969; children: Kelley Ann, Alyson Leigh. BA, Colo. Coll., Colorado Springs, 1966, DSc (hon.), 1997; PhD, Ind. U., Bloomington, 1970. Assoc. prof. psychology U. Fla., Gainesville, 1971-77; dir. sensory physiology and perception program NSF, Washington, 1982-83; prof. psychology Loyola U., Chgo., 1979—, dir. Parmly Hearing Inst., 1977—2001, dir. interdisciplinary neurosci. minor, 1977—2001, prof. hearing scis., 1990—. Prof. psychology, adj. prof. otolaryngology Loyola U., Chgo., 1990—, acting v.p. rsch., 1999—2001, assoc. v.p. rsch., dean Grad. Sch., 2001—04; individual expert bio-acoustics Am. Nat. Stds. Inst., 1983—; mem. study sect. Nat. Inst. Deafness and Other Communication Disorders, 1990—94; chair hearing bioacoustics and biomechanics com. NRC, 1992—2001, mem. bd. on behavioral cognitive and sensory scis., 1998—2004. Author: Fundamentals of Hearing, 1977, 4th edit., 2000; editor (with others) New Directions in Hearing Science, 1985, Directional Hearing, 1987, Auditory Processing of Complex Sounds, 1987, Classification of Complex Sounds, 1989, Psychoacoustics, 1993; assoc. editor Auditory Neurosci., 1994-97; ad hoc reviewer NSF, Air Force Office Sci. Rsch., Office Naval Rsch., 1981—; contbr. chpts. to books, articles to profl. jours. Pres. Evanston Tennis Assn., Ill., 1984, 90. Grantee NSF, 1974—, NIH, 1975—, AFOSR, 1983—, ONR, 1989-90. Fellow AAAS, Am. Phys. Soc., Acoustical Soc. Am. (assoc. editor jour. 1984-91, chair tech. com. 1990-94, exec. com. 1999—, v.p. 2002-04, pres. 2004—, Silver medal 2006), Am. Speech-Lang.-Hearing Assn.; mem. NAS (exec. com. on hearing bioacoustics, biomechanics 1981-87, chmn. 1993-97), Assn. Rsch. in Otolaryngology (sec.-treas. 1984-87, pres.-elect 1987-88, pres. 1988-89), Nat. Inst. Deafness and Other Comm. Disorders (task force, rev. panel 1990-94, chmn. 1994), Am. Auditory Soc. (exec. bd. 1993-98). Office Phone: 773-508-2713. Business E-Mail: wyost@luc.edu. *I am fortunate that I am in an occupation that is so much fun. Teaching and research are very enjoyable. Most days for me are fun.*

YOU, YALI, music educator; b. Xian, Shaanxi Province, China, July 31, 1962; d. Damin You and Fang Lin; m. Paul Steven Knuth, Aug. 9, 2002. D of Musical Arts, U. of Cin., Cin., Ohio, 1989—96; MusM, Northwestern U., Evanston, Ill., 1986—87; BA, Shanghai Conservatory of Music, Shanghai, China, 1980—84. Cert. cello performance Northwestern U., 1988. Assoc. prof. music Hamline U., St. Paul, 1996—; adj. prof. music Concordia U., St. Paul, 1997—2001. Hon. prof. cello Xian Conservatory Music, China, 2005. Musician concert performances in various venues. Recipient Excellent Performance, 4th Chinese Nat. Chamber Music competition, 1985. Mem.: Am. Assoc. of Univ. Professors. Buddhism. Avocations: folk dancing, gardening, travel. Office: Hamline Univ 1536 Hewitt Ave Saint Paul MN 55104 Office Phone: 651-523-2439. E-mail: yyou@gw.hamline.edu.

YOUD, T. LESLIE, retired civil engineer; b. Spanish Fork, Utah, Apr. 2, 1938; s. Thomas Leslie and Mary (Evans) Y.; m. Denice Porter, June 26, 1962; children: Verlin, Lance, Melinda, Thomas, Emily. BS, Brigham Young U., 1964; PhD, Iowa State U., 1967. Rsch. civil engr. U.S. Geological Survey, Menlo Park, Calif., 1967-84; prof. Brigham Young U., Provo, Utah, 1984—2003; ret., 2003. Recipient Maeser Rsch. award Brigham Young U., 1991, Utah Engring. Educator of Yr., 1995, ASCE H. Bolton Seed medal, 2002. Mem. NAE, ASCE (hon.), Internat. Soc. for Soil Mechanics and Fnd. Engring., Earthquake Engring. Rsch. Inst. Mem. Lds Ch. Achievements include development of techniques for mapping earthquake induced liquefaction hazard and techniques for estimating earthquake induced lateral spread displacements; inventor system for coupling accelerometers into bore hole casings. Home: 1132 E 1010 N Orem UT 84097-4306 Office: Brigham Young U Dept Civil Engring Provo UT 84602 Office Phone: 801-422-6327. E-mail: tyoud@byu.edu.

YOUKER, JAMES EDWARD, radiologist; b. Cooperstown, NY, Nov. 13, 1928; s. Bliss Jacob and Marian (Ostrander) Y.; children— Elizabeth Ann, James David. AB, Colgate U., 1950; MD, U. Buffalo, 1954. Diplomate: Am. Bd. Radiology. Intern U. Minn., Mpls., 1954-55, resident in radiology, 1955-56, 58-60; resident in pathology Georgetown U., Washington, 1958; pvt. practice medicine, specializing in radiology Corpus Christi, Tex., 1956-58; asst. prof. radiology Med. Coll. Va., Richmond, 1961-63; research fellow U. Lund, Malmo, Sweden, 1963-64; asst. prof. radiology U. Calif., San Francisco, 1964-67; asso. prof. U. Clif., 1967-68; prof., chmn. dept. radiology Med. Coll. Wis., Milw., 1968—; dir. dept. radiology Milwaukee County Gen. Hosp., Milw., 1968-96; chmn. dept. radiology Froedtert Meml. Luth. Hosp., 1979—. Served with Project Hope, Indonesia, 1961; cons./lectr. VA Hosp., Richmond, 1961-63, San Francisco, 1964-68, Martinez, Calif., 1964-68; cons./lectr. Letterman Army Med. Center, San Francisco, 1964-68, Oakknoll Naval Hosp., Oakladn, Calif., 1964-68, VA Hosp., Milwaukee, Wis., 1968—; vis. prof. U. Calif. Sch. Medicine, San Francisco, 1974, Stanford U. Sch. Medicine, Palo Alto, Calif., 1976; vis. physician dept. cardiology St. Vincent's Hosp., Melbourne, Australia, 1974-75; mem. com. diagnosis breast cancer task force NIH, 1975-79; Head Physicians for Ford; chmn. health and med. sci. tech. com. for program planning com. North Div. High Sch., 1979; bd. dirs. Med. Coll. Wis., 1986-88, mem. residency rev. commn. for radiology, 1985-90. Contbr. numerous articles to profl. jours. Served with M.C. USN, 1956-58. N.Y. State Regents scholar, 1946; Buffalo Found. scholar, 1952; grantee USPHS; grantee Squibb Pharms.; grantee Nat. Cancer Inst.; grantee others. Fellow Am. Coll. Radiology (bd. chancellors 1978—84, vice-chmn. commn. on cancer 1972-74, chmn./mem. numerous coms., v.p. 1983-84); mem. Am. Bd. Med. Specialties (pres. 2000), AMA, Am. Roentgen Ray Soc. (adv. com. research and edn.), Assn. Univ. Radiologists (chmn. govt. affairs com. 1978-79), Med. Soc. Milwaukee County (hosp. med. staff liaison com. 1978-79), Milw. Acad. Medicine, Milw. Roentgen Ray Soc., Soc. Chairmen Acad. Radiolgy Depts. (pres. 1972, coms.), Vail Creative Concepts Conf. (co-founder), Wis. Med. Soc., Wis. Radiol. Soc., Clubs: Univ. (Milw.); Chenequa Country. Republican. Office: Froedtert Meml Luth Hosp 9200 W Wisconsin Ave Milwaukee WI 53226-3522 E-mail: jyouker@mcw.edu.

YOUMANS, JULIAN RAY, neurosurgeon, educator; b. Baxley, Ga., Jan. 2, 1928; s. John Edward and Jennie Lou (Milton) Y.; children— Reed Nesbit, John Edward, Julian Milton. BS, Emory U., 1949, MD, 1952; MS, U. Mich., 1955, PhD, 1957. Diplomate: Am. Bd. Neurol. Surgery. Intern U. Mich. Hosp., Ann Arbor, 1952-53, resident in neurol. surgery, 1953-55, 56-58; fellow in neurology U. London, 1955-56; asst. prof. neurosurgery U. Miss., 1959-62, assoc. prof., 1962-63, Med. U. S.C., 1963-65, prof., 1965-67, chief div. neurosurgery, 1963-67; prof. U. Calif., Davis, 1967-91; prof. emeritus, 1991—; chmn. dept. neurosurgery U. Calif., 1967-82. Cons. USAF, U.S. VA, NRC. Editor: Neurological Surgery, 1973; contbr. articles to profl. jours. No. vice chmn. Republican State Central Com. of Calif., 1979-81. Served with U.S. Navy, 1944-46. Mem. ACS (bd. govs. 1972-78), Congress of Neurol. Surgeons (exec. com. 1967-70), Am. Acad. Neurology, Am. Assn. Neurol. Surgeons, Am. Assn. Surgery of Trauma, Pan-Pacific Surg. Assn., Western Neurosurg. Soc., Neurosurg. Soc. Am., Soc. Neurol. Surgeons, Soc. Univ. Neurosurgeons, N. Pacific Soc. Neurology and Psychiatry, Royal Soc. Medicine, Am. Trauma Soc., U.S. C. of C., Bohemian Club, Sutter Club, Rotary. Republican. Episcopalian. Office Phone: 530-756-6018.

YOUN, ANTHONY SUNGJIN, plastic surgeon; b. Greenville, Mich., Oct. 31, 1972; Grad. with high honors, Kalamazoo Coll.; MD, Mich. State U., 1998. Cert. Am. Bd. Plastic Surgery, 2005. Resident gen. surgery Mich. State U., Grand Rapids, 1998—2001, resident plastic surgery, 2001—03; advanced aesthetic surgery fellowship Dr. Richard Ellenbogen, LA, 2003—04; founder, surgeon Hills Plastic Surgery and Laser Centre, Rochester Hills, Mich. Ptnr. Eye Place, Bloomfield Hills, Mich.; hosp. affiliations include William Beaumont Hosp. of Troy, Crittenton Hosp. and Unasource Surgery Ctr.; cons. plastic surgeon for US Weekly, In Touch, Life and Style, OK! Mag., Pink, Jane, Plastic Surgery Products Mag., Hour Detroit, Troy Somerset Gazette, Suburban Lifestyles, Baltimore Sun, Women's Lifestyle Mag., Plastic & Reconstructive Surgery, Aesthetic Surgery Jour., Women's Healthy Style Mag., and Metro Parent Mag., among others; spkr. in field. Authored and co-authored (numerous papers and scientific manuscripts), featured on Dr. 90210, guest appearances (radio) Motor City Midday on Live 97.1 FM, 96.3 FM WDVD. Named Top Doctors, Hour Detroit. Mem.: AMA, Am. Soc. Plastic Surgeons, Oakland County Med. Soc., Mich. State Med. Soc. Office: Beverly Hills Plastic Surgery Centre 1349 S Rochester Rd Ste 100B Rochester MI 48307 Office Phone: 248-650-1900. Office Fax: 248-650-1967. *

YOUNG, AARON, conceptual artist; BFA, San Francisco Art Inst., 2001; MFA, Yale Univ., New Haven, Conn., 2004. Represented in permanent collections Mus. Contemporary Art, Kansas City, Kans., Mus. Modern Art, NYC, one-man shows include Tender Buttons, Midway Contemporary Art, Minneapolis, Minn., 2004, exhibited in group shows at Paladar, 7th Havana Bienal, Havana, Cuba, 2000, Strictly Ballroom, Stanford University Museum, Palo Alto, CA, 2001, New Orleans Performance Festival, 2001, Circus, 8th Havana Bienal, 2002, From Here On, Guild & Greyshkul Gallery, NYC, 2003, Miami Heat, Miami Pacemaker Gallery, Miami, Fla., 2004, Let the Bullshit Run a Marathon, Nicole Klagsbrun Gallery NYC, 2004, Some Exhaust, Lehmann Maupin Gallery, NYC, 2004, Curatorial Choices: Drawing, Univ. Minn. Mus., 2005, Mus. Modern Art, NYC, 2005, Absolute Summer Show, Kirkhoff Contemporary Art, 2005, Day LABOR, P.S.1/MOMA, Long Island City, 2005, Whitney Biennial, Whitney Mus. Art, NYC, 2006. Office: c/o PS1 Contemporary Art Ctr 22-25 Jackson Ave Long Island City NY 11101

YOUNG, ALFRED BYRON, neurosurgeon; b. Nov. 6, 1939; s. Carlos Young and Margaret Louise (Rayburn) Stout; m. Judith Floy Gaines, Aug. 26, 1961; children: John Kevin, Alexander Bryce. BA, Transylvania U., 1961, D (hon.), 2006; MD, U. Ky., 1965. Diplomate Am. Bd. Neurol. Surgery (guest examiner 1980, 84, 94, 2005). Intern Vanderbilt U., Nashville, 1965-66, asst. resident in surgery, 1966-67, resident in neurosurgery, 1967-71; clin. instr. U. Ky., Lexington, Ky., 1973-74; pvt. practice Lexington, Ky., 1973-74; asst. prof. divsn. neurosurgery, dept. surgery U. Ky. Med. Ctr., Lexington, Ky., 1974—, prof., 1982—, acting chief, 1974-75, chief neurosurgery, 1977—; chief of staff U. Hosp., 2000—05, assoc. dean clin. affairs, 2000—05, sr. assoc. dean for clin. affairs, 2005—. Chmn. dept. surgery U. Ky., 1986-96, chmn. operating rm. comm. 1986-96, hosp. clin. bd., 1986-96, VA dean's comm. 1986-96, press comm., 1991-96, hosp. bd. elected faculty rep., 1994-96, chmn. managed care comm., 1994-96, coun. clin. chair, 1995-96; vis. prof. U. Cin., 1981, U. Louisville, 1988, Vanderbilt U., 1988; chmn. Johnston-Wright Endowed chair, 1988—, interim chair dept. neurosurg., 2007-; dir. Ky. Neuroscience Orthopadic Inst., 2004—; bd. dirs. Ky. Organ Donor Affiliates; mem. exec. com., bd. trustees Transylvania U.; presenter in field. Contbr. articles to profl. jours. Adv. bd. Ctrl. Bank & Trust; mem. liaison com. Shriner's Hosp. Maj. US Army, 1971—73, Korea. Named Am. Best Doctor award, Am. Top Doctors.; named one of Am.'s Best Drs., 2005, Am.'s Top Drs. for Cancer, 2005, 2006; recipient Disting. Alumnus award, Transylvania U., 2001, U. Ky. Coll. of Medicine, 2001, Morrison Medallion awards, 2001; grantee NIH, 1987—95, 1988—99, Bowman Gray/Pfizer, 1992—96, Upjohn Pharm., 1992—94, Sterling Winthrop, 1992—95, Ciba-Geigy, 1993—97. Mem. ACS, AMA, NIH (advisory comm. 1991-95, monitoring comm. 1994—, com. mem.), Nat. Inst. Neurol. Disorders, Acad. Neurological Surgeons, Am. Surgical Assn., Soc. Neurological Surgeons (fiscal resources and practice planning comm. 1992—), Neurosurgical Soc. Am., Am. Assn. Neurological Surgeons (cerebrovascular sect., joint sect. neurotrauma and critical care, joint sect. spinal disorders, joint sect. tumors, bylaws comm. 1979-83, chmn. bylaws comm. 1982-83, rep. to Nat. Inst. Neurol and Comm. Disorders and Stroke 1987-89), Congress Neurological Surgeons (rep. to NIH 1987—, Mahaley Clin. Rsch. award 1998), Ky. Med. Assn., Fayette County Med. Soc., Southern Neurosurgical Soc. (pres. 1991-92, pres.-elect 1990, exec. coun. 1986-94, treas. 1986-89, chmn. fin. comm. 1986-89, long range planning comm. 1990—, chmn. long range planning comm. 1992-93, constn. and bylaws comm. 1989-90, comm. disting. practioner award, 1992—, chmn. comm. disting. practioner award, 1992-93, nominating comm. 1992—, chmn. nominating comm. 1992-93, residents award comm. 1981-82), Am. Soc. Stereotactic and Functional Neurosurgery, Ky. Neurosurgical Soc. (pres. 1990-91), Soc. Internat. Surgery, Internat. Stereotactic Radiosurgery Soc., Leksell Gamma Knife Soc., Neurotrauma Soc., Am. Cancer Soc.-Ky. Divsn. (bd. dir. 1990—, prof. edn. comm. 1990-91), Am. Heart Assn. (stroke coun.). Achievements include patent (with others) in Multiple Function Intubation Apparatus and Method, 5,836,935 Implantable refillable controlled release device to deliver drugs directly to an internal portion of the body; research in zinc supplementation associated with improved neurologic recovery rate and visceral protein levels of patients with severe closed head-injury, nutritional and metabolic mgmt. of the head-injury patient, demographics of brain metastasis, neurosurgical diseases of aging patients, brain metastases, nutritional and metabolic variables correlate with amino acid forearm flux in patients with severe head injury, effect of lovastatin on early carotid atherosclerosis and cardiovascular events, and numerous others.

YOUNG, ALICE, lawyer; d. John and Elizabeth Y.; m. Thomas L. Shortall; children: Amanda, Stephen. AB magna cum laude, Yale U., 1971; JD, Harvard U., 1974. Bar: NY 1975, Washington 1991. Assoc. Coudert Bros., NYC, 1974-81; mng. ptnr. Graham & James, NYC, 1981-87; ptnr. Milbank, Tweed, Hadley & McCloy, NYC, 1987—94; ptnr., chair Asia Pacific Practice Kaye, Scholer LLP, NYC, 1994—. Bd. dirs. Mizuho Trust and Banking Co., mem. examining com., 2003—; spkr. Traphagen Distinguished Alumni Speakers Forum, Harvard Law Sch., 2004; bd. dirs. Deloitte & Touche, adv. bd. diversity, 2005—. Contbr. articles to profl. jours. Bus. com. Nat. Com. on U.S.-China Rels., 1993—, U.S.-China Bus. Coun., 1993—, Com. of 100, 1993—, vice-chmn., 1999—; bd. overseers visitation com. to Law Sch. Harvard U., 1994—99, chair subcomm. on grad. program, 1996; trustee Lingnan Found., NYC, 1984—91, Pan-Asian Repertory Theatre, NYC, 1987—90, Aspen Inst., Colo., 1988—, Am. Assembly, 2000—; bus. com. Met. Mus. Art, NYC, 1989—94; active Coun. on Fgn. Rels., 1977—, Chmn.'s Forum, 2000—; trustee Asia Found., 2002—. Named one of Top 100 Minority Leaders, 1998, one of 40 Under 40 Crain's Bus., NYC, 1989; Bates fellow Yale U., 1970, NDFL fellow Harvard U., 1967-68; recipient Star award NY Women's Agenda, 1992, Justice in Action award, Asia Am. Legal Defense and Edn. Fund, 2004. Mem. ABA, NY State Bar Assn. (fgn. investment com.), Assn. Bar City NY (spl. com. on rels. with Japanese bar, Union Internat. des Avocats), Nat. Asian Pacific Am. Bar Assn., Asian Am. Bar Assn. NY, Harvard Law Sch. Assn. NYC (trustee 1990-94), Japan Soc. (sec. 1989-97), Asia Soc. (pres.'s coun. 1984-2002). Office: Kaye Scholer LLP 425 Park Ave New York NY 10022-3506 Office Phone: 212-836-8047. Business E-Mail: ayoung@kayescholer.com.

YOUNG, ANDRE See DR. DRE

YOUNG, ANDREW JACKSON, JR., civil rights leader, pastor, retired mayor, ambassador, congressman; b. New Orleans, Mar. 12, 1932; s. Andrew J. and Daisy (Fuller) Y.; m. Jean Childs, June 7, 1954 (dec. 1994); children: Andrea, Lisa Dru, Paula Jean, Andrew J. III; m. Carolyn M. 1996. Student, Dillard U., 1947-48; BS, Howard U., 1951; B.D., Hartford Theol. Sem., 1955; D.D. (hon.), Wesleyan U., 1970, United Theol. Sem. Twin Cities, 1970; LL.D. (hon.), Wilberforce U., 1971, Clark Coll., 1973, Yale U., 1973, Swarthmore Coll., Atlanta U., Dartmouth U., 2005; numerous other hon. degrees. Ordained to ministry Congl. Ch., 1955; pastor Thomasville, Ga., 1955-57; assoc. dir. dept. youth work Nat. Council Chs., 1957-61; mem. staff So. Christian Leadership Conf., 1961-70, adminstr. citizen edn. program, 1961-64, exec. dir., 1964-70, exec. v.p., 1967-70; mem. US Congress from 5th Ga. Dist., 1973—77; permanent US rep. UN, NYC, 1977-79; mayor City of Atlanta, 1982—90; co-chmn. Atlanta Com. for the Olympic Games, 1996; prof. pub. affairs Ga. State U., Atlanta. Pres. Nat. Coun. Churches, 2000—01; chmn. nat. steering com. Working Families for Wal-Mart, 2006. Author: A Way Out of No Way: The Spiritual Memoirs of Andrew Young, 1994, An Easy Burden: The Civil Rights Movement and the Transformation of America, 1996. Chmn. Atlanta Community Relations Commn., 1970-72; chmn. bd. Delta Ministry of Miss.; bd. dirs. Martin Luther King, Jr. Center for Social Change, Robert F. Kennedy Meml. Found., Field Found., So. Christian Leadership Conf. Recipient Pax-Christi award St. John's U., 1970; Springarn medal.; Presdl. Medal of Freedom, 1980, French Legion of Honor medal, 1982; co-recipient, Martin Luther King, Jr., Award for Public Svc. (Ebony mag.), 1990. Mem. Ams. Dem. Action, Alpha Phi Alpha

YOUNG, ANNE B., neurologist, educator; AB, Vassar Coll., 1969; MD, Johns Hopkins U., 1973, PhD in Pharmacology, 1974. From asst. prof. to prof. chemistry Dept. Neurology, U. Mich., 1978-91; Julieanne Dorn prof. neurology Harvard Med. Sch., 1991—; chief neurology Mass. Gen. Hosp., 1991—. Fellow Scottish Rite Found., Lexington, 1973; med. intern Mt. Zion Hosp. & Med. Ctr., San Francisco; neurological resident Dept.

Neurology U. Calif., San Francisco.; David Segal vis. prof. Columbia U., 1996; presdl. lectr. Am. Acad. Neurology, 1996. Contbr. numerous articles to profl. jours. Recipient Tchr./Investor Devel. award NIH, 1979-84, Facility Devel. award Merck, 1987-89, Milton Wexler award for Huntington's Rsch. Huntington's Dis. Soc. Am., 1989, Weinstein-Goldenson award United Cerebral Palsy Assn., Inc., 1990. Mem. Inst. Medicine-Nat. Acad. Science. Office: Dept Neurology Mass Gen 15 Parkman St Ste 835 Boston MA 02114-3117

YOUNG, BARBARA, psychiatrist, psychotherapist, educator, photographer; b. Chgo., Oct. 27, 1920; d. William Harvey and Blanche (DeBra) Y. AB, Knox Coll., 1942; MD, Johns Hopkins U., 1945; grad., Balt. Psychoanalytic Inst., 1953. Intern Univ. Hosps., Iowa City, 1945-46, asst. resident in neurology, 1946—47; asst. resident in psychiatry Phipps Clinic, Johns Hopkins U. Hosp., Balt., 1947-49; staff psychiatrist Perry Point (Md.) VA Hosp., 1949-51; practice medicine specializing in psychiatry/psychoanalysis Balt., 1951—; instr. Johns Hopkins U., 1953-69, asst. prof. psychiatry, 1969—, prof. emeritus, 1997—; freelance photographer, 1958—. Lectr. dept. psychiatry Johns Hopkins U.; lectr. Lucy Daniels Found., Carey, N.C., dept. humanities Yale U. Med. Sch., Boston Inst. for Psychotherapy, local psychiat. and social orgns. Works represented in Mus. Modern Art, N.Y.C., Balt. Mus. Art, Santa Barbara (Calif.) Mus. Art, Eastman House, Rochester, N.Y., Yale U. Gallery of Art; photographer: The Plop-A-Lop Tree, 1995, Tales of Courage: Recovering LIfe After Catastrophe, 2003; contbr. articles to profl. jours. Mem.: Am. Psychoanlytic Assn., Am. Psychiat. Assn., Balt.-Washington Ctr. for Psychoanalysis. Democrat. Address: 5307 Herring Run Dr Baltimore MD 21214-1937 Office Phone: 410-426-3583. Personal E-mail: barbarayoungmd@mac.com.

YOUNG, BARNEY THORNTON, lawyer; b. Chillicothe, Tex., Aug. 10, 1934; s. Bayne and Helen Irene (Thornton) Y.; m. Sarah Elizabeth Taylor, Aug. 31, 1957; children: Jay Thornton, Sarah Elizabeth, Serena Taylor. BA, Yale U., 1955; LLB, U. Tex., 1958. Bar: Tex. 1958. Assoc. Thompson, Knight, Wright & Simmons, Dallas, 1958-65; ptnr. Rain, Harrell, Emery, Young & Doke, Dallas, 1965-87; mem. firm Locke Purnell Rain Harrell (A Profl. Corp.), 1987-98; of counsel Locke, Liddell & Sapp LLP, 1999—. Mem. adv. coun. Dallas Cmty. Chest Trust Fund, Inc., 1964-66; bd. dirs. Mental Health Assn. Dallas County, Inc., 1969-72, Trammell Crow Family Found., 1984-87; trustee Hockaday Sch., Dallas, 1971-77, 90—, chmn., 1994-96, Dallas Zool. Soc., 1986-92, Lamplighter Sch., Dallas, 1976-99, 2006—, chmn., 1983-86, St. Mark's Sch., Dallas, 1970—, pres., 1976-78, The Found. for Callier Ctr. and Comm. Disorders, 1988-99, Friends of Ctr. for Human Nutrition, 1988-2005, Dallas Hist. Soc., 1993-2001; bd. dirs. Susan G. Komen Breast Cancer Found., 2000-06, Nat. Assn. Ind. Schs., 2000-04; mem. Yale Devel. Bd., 1984-91, 98—. Fellow Tex. Bar Found., Dallas Bar Found.; mem. ABA, Tex. Bar Assn., Dallas Bar Assn., Am. Judicature Soc., Order of Coif, Phi Beta Kappa, Pi Sigma Alpha, Phi Gamma Delta, Phi Delta Phi, Dallas Country Club., Petroleum Club (Dallas), Yale Club (Dallas, N.Y.C.). Office: Locke Liddell & Sapp LLP 2200 Ross Ave Ste 2200 Dallas TX 75201-6776 Office Phone: 214-740-8402. Business E-Mail: byoung3@mindspring.com.

YOUNG, BARRY HARRISON, retired mathematician, mechanical engineer; b. Dallas, Dec. 9, 1948; s. Philip Haine and Dorothy Belle Young. BSME, So. Meth. U., Dallas, Tex., 1971; MS in Math., N.Mex. State U., Las Cruces, N.Mex., 1982. Mech. engr. Safsea, White Sands Missile Range, N.Mex., 1972—73; from mech. engr. to mathematician Calibration Lab. Instrumentation Directorate, White Sands Missile Range, 1973—2005, mathematician, 1986—2005, ret., 2005.

YOUNG, BETTE ANN, writer; b. Columbus, Ohio, Jan. 9, 1937; d. Richard Jack Abel and Gussie Ruth Dean Seiden; m. robert David Roth Mar. 17, 1957 (div. Dec. 1980); children: Deborah Anne Fay, Diane Hope Helbig, Robert David Roth Jr.; m. Sheldon Mike Young, Nov. 11, 1988. BA in Sociology, Oakland U., 1971; MA in Am. Culture, U. Mich., 1974, postgrad., 1977. Dir. libr. Jewish Cmty. Ctr., Detroit, 1980-82; edn. dir. Jewish Parents' Inst., Detroit, 1980-82; lectr. Adult Coll. Jewish Studies, Columbus, Ohio, 1985-87; adminstrv. sec. Nat. Coun. Jewish Women, Columbus, 1985-90; cons., membership dir., grant writer Columbus Jewish Hist. Soc., Columbus, 1987-90, oral historian, 1990—. Author: Congregation Shaarey Zedek, 1981, The History of the Association of Jewish Community Organization Personnel, 1969-87, 1987, The Columbus Jewish Foundation, 1994, Emma Lazarus in Her World, 1995; book critic Jewish News, 1980-82, Ohio Jewish Chronicle, 1991—, Columbus Dispatch, 1992—. Cmty. cons. Anti-Defamation League, Detroit, 1982-83. Democrat. Home: 4776 Smoketalk Ln Westerville OH 43081-7838

YOUNG, BILL (CHARLES WILLIAM YOUNG), congressman; b. Harmarville, Pa., Dec. 16, 1930; m. Beverly Young; children: Robert, Billy, Patrick. Mem. Fla. State Senate, 1961—71, minority leader, 1967—71; mem. US Congress from 10th dist. Fla., 1971—; former chmn. ho. appropriations/intelligence coms.; mem. Fla. Constn. Revision Commn., 1965-67; chmn. So. Hwy. Policy Com., 1966-68; mem. Electoral Coll., 1968. Appropriations com., chmn. subcom. Def., Labor, HHS and Edn. Fla. Legislature. With Nat. Guard USAR, 1948—57. Named Most Valuable Senator, Capitol Press Corps, 1969. Republican. Methodist. Office: US Ho Reps 2407 Rayburn Ho Office Bldg Washington DC 20515-0910 E-mail: bill.young@mail.house.gov. *

YOUNG, BRIAN, chef; b. Vancouver, BC, 1968; married; 3 children. Attended, Le Cordon Bleu, Paris. Cook Le Laurent, Quilted Giraffe; line cook Le Bernardin, chef de cuisine; exec. chef POP, Citarella, Harvest in Hudson, Hastings, NY; exec. chef, ptnr. Mainland, 2006; exec. chef Tavern on the Green, NYC, 2007—. Avocation: target shooting. Office: Tavern on the Green Central Park W at 67the St New York NY 10023 Office Phone: 212-873-3200. Office Fax: 212-580-4265. *

YOUNG, BRIANNE LAMONICA, rehabilitation services professional; b. Jackson, Miss., July 28, 1980; d. Leroy Laws and Jacqueline Denise Young. BS, Jackson State U., Miss., 2002, MS, 2005. Therapist intern Cares Behavioral Health Sys., Jackson, Miss., 2004; counselor youth svcs. Dept. Human Svcs., Jackson, 2005; counselor vocat. rehab. Dept. Rehab. Svcs., Jackson, 2006—. Mem.: ACA, Order Ea. Star (treas. 2006). Home: 113B Briarmeade Dr Clinton MS 39056 Office: Department Rehabilitation Svcs 3895 Beasley Rd Jackson MS 39213 Home Phone: 601-720-4452; Office Phone: 601-898-7078. Office Fax: 601-898-7064. Personal E-mail: oes2002@aol.com.

YOUNG, BRUCE KENNETH, obstetrician, gynecologist, educator; b. NYC, Aug. 11, 1938; s. Morton David and Cecile Barbara (Lebenson) Y.; m. Phyllis Ann Lipsius, Dec. 16, 1962; children: Kathryn Rachel, Caroline Sue. AB, Princeton U., 1959; MD, NYU, 1963. Diplomate Nat. Bd. Med. Examiners, Am. Bd. Ob-gyn.; cert. spl. competence in maternal-fetal medicine Am. Bd. Ob-gyn. Intern Montefiore Hosp., Bronx, NY, 1963-64; resident ob-gyn. Bellevue Hosp. Ctr., NYC, 1964-68, NYU Hosp., 1964-68, rsch. fellow reproductive endocrinology, 1966—67; chief obstetrics Bellevue Hosp., NYC, 1970-95; dir. obstet. svcs. NYU Hosps. Network, 1995—2005. Cons. N.J. Health Sys. Agy., Hoffman LaRoche Co., Kimberly Clark, Litton Ind., Revlon Corp., 1975—; dir. maternal and fetal medicine NYU Sch. Medicine Med. Ctr., N.Y.C., 1975—2005; prof. ob-gyn. NYU Sch. Medicine, 1980—, Silverman prof. ob-gyn., 1996—. Editor: Perinatal Medicine Today, 1980, Problems in Perinatal Medicine, 1986, Jour. Maternal-Fetal Neonatal Medicine; mem. editl. bd. Diagnostic Gynecology and Obstetrics, Jour. Perinatal Medicine; contbr. chpts. to books and articles to profl. jours. Bd. dirs. N.Y. State Prenatal Diagnostic Ctr., N.Y.C., 1977-87; chair health professions bd. Greater N.Y. March of Dimes, N.Y.C., 1995—2005, v.p., dir., 1995-2005. Recipient Disting. Svc. in Med. Edn. award March of Dimes, 1985, Voluntary Svc. award March of Dimes, 1990, Program Excellence award March of Dimes, 1991, Outstanding Achievement award, Solomon A. Berson Med. Alumni Achievement award, NYU, 2005. Fellow ACOG, Am. Fertility Soc., Am. Gynecol. and Obstet. Soc., Am. Assn. Gynecol. Laparoscopists, Soc. Laparoendoscopic Surgeons, N.Y. Perinatal Soc. (pres. 1997-99), N.Y. Obstet. Soc. (pres. 2001-02); mem. AMA, Soc. Maternal-Fetal Medicine, NYU Sch. Medicine Alumni Assn. (pres. 1995-96, citation 1996), Mar-a-Lago Club. Home: 530 1st Ave, Ste 5G New York NY 10016-6402 Home Phone: 212-249-0099; Office Phone: 212-263-6359. E-mail: youngbo1@nyumc.org.

YOUNG, BRUCE WILSON, language educator; b. Roosevelt, Utah, Nov. 3, 1950; s. Daren Curtis and Ruth Wilson Young; m. Margaret Blair Young, May 17, 1985; children: Kaila Corinne Lifferth, Robert Daren, Julia Ruth, Michael Bruce. BA summa cum laude, Brigham Young U., Provo, Utah, 1975; MA, Columbia U., NYC, 1976; PhD, Harvard U., Cambridge, Mass., 1983. Tchg. fellow Harvard U., 1978—81, instr., 1981—83; asst. prof. Brigham Young U., 1983—88, assoc. prof., 1988—. Dramaturg prodn. winter's tale Brigham Young U. Theatre and Media Arts Dept., 1989—90; assoc. dir. Brigham Young U., London Centre, London, 1996. Assoc. editor: Jour. Rocky Mountain Medieval and Renaissance Assn., 1986; contbr. chapters to books, articles to profl. jours. Various positions Ch. of Jesus Christ of Latter-Day Saints, 1958—. Huntington Libr. fellow, Rocky Mountain MLA, 1990, Alcuin fellow, Brigham Young U., 2002—04. Mem.: Internat. Shakespeare Assn., Shakespeare Assn. Am. Mem. Lds Ch. Avocations: travel, languages, music. Home: 561 N 700 W Provo UT 84601 Office: Brigham Young Univ English Depart Provo UT 84602 Office Phone: 801-422-2977. Office Fax: 801-422-0221. E-mail: bruce_young@byu.edu.

YOUNG, BRYANT LLEWELLYN, lawyer; b. Rockford, Ill., Mar. 9, 1948; s. Llewellyn Anker and Florence Ruth Y. AB, Cornell U., 1970; JD, Stanford U., 1974. Bar: Calif. 1974, Nev. 1975, D.C. 1979. Law clk. U.S. Dist. Ct. (no. dist.) Calif., San Francisco, 1974-75; assoc. Dinkelspiel, Pelavin, Steefel & Levitt, San Francisco, 1975-77; White House fellow, spl. asst. to sec. HUD, Washington, 1977-78, spl. asst. to sec., 1978-79; gen. mgr. to acting gen. mgr. New Cmty. Devel. Corp., 1979-80; mgmt. cons. AVCO Corp., 1980; spl. asst. to chmn. bd., CEO U.S. Synthetic Fuels Corp., Washington, 1980-81, project dir., 1981; pres. Trident Mgmt. Corp., San Francisco, 1981-87; of counsel Pelavin, Norberg, Harlick & Beck, San Francisco, 1981-82, ptnr., 1982-87; mng. ptnr. bus. sect. Carroll, Burdick & McDonough, San Francisco, 1987-90; founding ptnr. Young, Vogl & Harlick, San Francisco, 1990-93, Young, Vogl, Harlick, Wilson & Simpson, LLP, San Francisco, 1993-99; pres. Young Enterprises, Inc., 1995—2004; mgr. SRY Industries LLC, 1997—, KML Hospitality Industries LLC, 1997—, Nev. Nugget LLC, 2004—; ptnr. Young Vogl LLP, 1999—2001; prin. Law Offices of Bryant L. Young, 2002—. Dir. The Whitman Inst. Pub. affairs com. San Francisco Aid Retarded Citizens, Inc., 1977; U.S. co-chmn. New Towns Working Group, U.S.-USSR Agreement on Cooperation in Field of Housing and Other Constrn., 1979-80; treas., bd. dirs. White House Fellows Found., 1980-84; prin. Coun. Excellence in Govt., Washington, 1986-94; adv. com. Nat. Multi-Housing Coun., 1987-92; mem. Ross Sch. Found., 1994-97, sec., 1995-97; bd. dirs. Marin AIDS Project, 1996-97, sec., 1997; trustee Ross Sch., 1997-2003, pres. 2002-2003. Mem. ABA (real property, trust and probate law sects. 1975-96), White House Fellows Assn. (chmn. ann. meeting 1979, del. China 1980), Marin County Sch. Bds. Assn., Am. Field Svc. Returnees Assn., Can.-Am. C. of C. No. Calif. (v.p., bd. dirs. 1992), Chile-Calif. Found. (exec. com., bd. dirs. 1993-96). Office: 44 Montgomery St ste 4020 San Francisco CA 94104-4602 Office Phone: 415-291-1970. E-mail: bly@ebzlaw.net.

YOUNG, BURT, actor; b. NYC, Apr. 30, 1940; s. Michael and Josephine Y.; m. May 20, 1961 (dec.); children: Richard (dec.), Anne Susan. Student public, pvt. schs., NYC. Pres. White Crown Carpet Cleaners, 1964-67, Aurura Carpet Installation Co., 1966-69; owner, operator Burts Blues Tapes-Records, 1978. Author: book Uncle Joe Shannon, 1978; films include The Gang That Couldn't Shoot Straight, 1971, Acrosss 110th Street, 1972, Cinderella Liberty, 1973, Chinatown, 1973, The Gambler, 1974, The Killer Elite, 1975, Harry and Walter Go To New York, 1976, Chinatown, Rocky, 1976 (Acad. award nominee best supporting actor), Twilight's Last Gleaming, 1977, The Choirboys, 1977, Convoy, 1978, Rocky II, 1979, Blood Beach, 1980, All the Marbles, 1981, Rocky III, 1982, Lookin' to Get Out, 1982, Amittyville: The Possession, 1982, Once Upon a Time in America, 1984, Over the Brooklyn Bridge, 1984, The Pope of Greenwich Village, 1984, Rocky IV, 1985, Back to School, 1986, Last Exit to Brooklyn, 1990, Tashunga, 1995, Red Blooded American Girl, 1995, Kicked in the Head, 1997, Heaven Before I Die, 1997, The Undertaker's Wedding, 1997, She's So Lovely, 1997, Firehouse, 1997, The Deli, 1997, The Mouse, 1997, Mickey Blue Eyes, 1999, Terra bruciata, 1999, Table One, 2000, Never Look Back, 2000, Blue Moon, 2000, The Day the Ponies Come Back, 2000, Cugini, 2001, The Boys of Sunset Ridge, 2001, Plan B, 2001, And She Was, 2002, Checkout, 2002, The Adventures of Pluto Nash, 2002, Kiss the Bride, 2002, Crooked Lines, 2003, Shut Up and Kiss Me!, 2004, The Wager, 2004, Land of Plenty, 2004, Downtown: A Street Tale, 2004, Transamerica, 2005, Nicky's Game, 2005, Rocky Balboa, 2006; author and star of films: Daddy, I Don't Like It Like This, CBS-TV, 1977, Uncle Joe Shanon, 1978; TV films The Great Niagara, 1974, Hustling, 1975, Serpico: The Deadly Game, 1976, Murder Can Hurt You, 1980, Before Women Had Wings, 1997, Firehouse, 1997, Greener Fields, 1998, Gioco di specchi, 2000, (TV series) You and Me Kid, 1983, Roomies, 1987, Alternate Realities, 2002; dir., Sunshine Film Co. Served with USMC, 1957-59. Mem. Acad. Motion Picture Arts and Scis., Writers Guild Am., Hole in the Wall Gang of Corona. Roman Catholic. *

YOUNG, CHARLES EDWARD, former academic administrator; b. San Bernardino, Calif., Dec. 30, 1931; s. Clayton Charles and Eula May (Walters) Young. AA, San Bernardino Coll., 1954; AB, U. Calif., Riverside, 1955; MA, UCLA, 1957, PhD, 1960; DHL (hon.), U. Judaism, LA, 1969; DHL (hon.), Occidental Coll., LA, 1997. Congl. fellow, Washington, 1958—59; adminstrv. analyst Office of the Pres., U. Calif., Berkeley, 1959—60; asst. prof. polit. sci. U. Calif., Davis, 1960, UCLA, 1960—66, assoc. prof., 1966—69, prof., 1969—97, asst. to chancellor, 1960—62, asst. chancellor, 1962—63, vice chancellor, adminstrn., 1963—68, chancellor, 1968—97, chancellor emeritus, 1997—; pres. U. Fla., Gainesville, 1999—2004. Bd. dirs. Intel Corp., Acad. TV Arts and Sci. Found., L.A. Met. Project; cons. Peace Corps., 1961—62, Ford Found. on Latin Am. Activities, 1964—66. Mem. Nat. Com. on U.S.-China Rels.; adminstrv. bd. Internat. Assn. Univs; mem. Knight Found. Commn. on Intercollegiate Athletics, Calif. Coun. on Sci. and Tech., Town Hall of Calif., Carnegie Comm. Task Force on Sci. and Tech. and the States, Pacific Coun. on Internat. Policy, NCAA Pres.'s Comm., Coun. for Govt.-Univ.-Industry Rsch. Roundtable and the Nat. Rsch. Coun. Adv. Bd.-Issues in Sci. and Tech.; chancellor's assocs. UCLA; coun. trustees L.A. Ednl. Alliance for Restructuring Now; past chair. Assn. Am. Univs., Nat. Assn. State Univs. and Land-Grant Colls.; past co-chair Calif. Campus Compact; trustee UCLA Found.; bd. dirs. Found. Internat. Exchange Sci. and Cultural Info. by Telecom., L.A. Internat. Visitors Coun., Greater L.A. Energy Coalition, L.A. World Affairs Coun. With USAF, 1951—52. Named Young Man of Year, Westwood Jr. C. of C., 1962; recipient Inter-Am. U. Cooperaton award, Inter-Am. Orgn. Higher Edn., Neil H. Jacoby Internat. award, UCLA Student Ctr., 1987, Edward A. Dickson Alumnus of Yr. award, UCLA Alumni Assn., 1994, Disting. Svc. award, U. Calif. Riverside Alumni Assn., 1996, Treasure of L.A. award, L.A. Ctrl. City Assn., 1996, Albert Schweitzer Leadership award, Hugh O'Brien Youth Found., 1996; fellow, UCLA Coll. Letters and Sci., 1996. Fellow: AAAS; mem.: Nat. Collegiate Athletic Assn. Pres. Commn.

YOUNG, CHRISTOPHER, composer; b. Red Bank, NJ, Apr. 28, 1957; m. Anne Atkins. Scores include (films) The Dorm That Dripped Blood, 1982, Robbie, 1982, The Power, 1983, Savage Hunter, 1984, Highpoint, 1984, Wheels of Fire, 1984, Avenging Angel, 1984, Def-Con 4, 1985, Wizards of the Lost Kingdom, 1985, Barbarian Queen, 1985, Nightmare on Elm Street Part II: Freddy's Revenge, 1985, Godzilla 1985, 1985, Torment, 1986, Getting Even, 1986, Invaders from Mars, 1986, Trick or Treat, 1986, Hellraiser, 1987, Flowers in the Attic, 1987, The Telephone, 1987, Bat-21, 1988, Haunted Summer, 1988, Hellbound: Hellraiser II, 1988, The Fly II, 1989, Hider in the House, 1989, Bright Angel, 1991, The Five Heartbeats, 1991, The Vagrant, 1992, The Dark Half, 1992, Rapid Fire, 1992, Jennifer Eight, 1992, Sliver, 1993, Dream Lover, 1994, Murder in the First, 1995, (TV movies) American Harvest, 1987, Last Flight Out, 1990, Max and Helen, 1990, Murder in the First, 1994, Judicial Consent, 1995, Tales From the Hood, 1995, Species, 1995, Virtuosity, 1995, Copycate, 1995, Unforgettable, 1996, Norma Jean and Marilyn, 1996, Head Above Water, 1996, Set it Off, 1996, Murder at 1600, 1997, Hard Rain, 1998, Rounders, 1998, Urban Legend, 1998, Entrapment, 1999 (BMI Film Music award, 2000), Wonder Boys, 2000, Bless the Child, 2000, The Gift, 2000, Sweet November, 2001, Swordfish, 2001 (BMI Film Music award, 2002), Bandits, 2001, The Shipping News, 2001, The Tower, 2002, The Country Bears, 2002, The Core, 2003, The Devil & Daniel Webster, 2003, Runaway Jury, 2003, The Grudge, 2004 (BMI Film Music award, 2005), The Exorcism of Emily Rose, 2005, The Grudge 2, 2006, Ghost Rider, 2007, Spider-Man 3, 2007. Office: Costa Communications 8265 Sunset Blvd #101 Los Angeles CA 90046 *

YOUNG, CHRISTOPHER AARON, lawyer; BA magna cum laude in Bus., Buena Vista Coll., 1995; JD with honors, U. Iowa Sch. Law, 1998. Bar: Minn. 1998, US Dist. Ct. (dist. Minn.), US Ct. Appeals (8th cir.). Sr. assoc. Fulbright & Jaworski, L.L.P., Mpls. Contbr. articles to profl. publs. Named a Rising Star, Minn. Super Lawyers mag., 2006. Mem.: Hennepin County Bar Assn., Minn. State Bar Assn. Avocations: fishing, hunting, racquetball. Office: Fulbright & Jaworski LLP 2100 IDS Ctr 80 S 8th St Minneapolis MN 55402 Office Phone: 612-321-2816. E-mail: cayoung@fulbright.com. *

YOUNG, DAVID, anesthesiologist, educator; b. Miami, Fla. BS in Biochemistry, Fla. State U., Tallahassee, 1990; MD, U. Miami Sch. Medicine, Fla., 1990—94. Maj., anesthesiologist U.S. Army, Fort Hood, Tex., 1999—2002; pediatric anesthesiologist Baylor Coll. Medicine, Houston, 2002—06. Maj. US Army, 1999—2002, Fort Hood, TX. Office: Tex Children's Hosp 6621 Fannin St Ste A-200 Houston TX 77030 Office Phone: 832-824-5800. Office Fax: 832-825-5801.

YOUNG, DAVID L., entrepreneur, retail executive; b. Plainfield, NJ, Nov. 10, 1960; s. William L. and Anne V. Young. Pres., CEO Boca Micro Tech., Inc., Boca Raton, Fla., 1991—2001; chmn., CEO BMI Gaming, Inc., Boca Raton, 2002—. Named one of Top 500 Internet Retailer In Am., Internet Retailer Mag., 2006, 2007, Top 500 Fastest growing Firms, INC Mag., 2007; named to Hot 100 List of the Fastest Growing Firms In Am., PriceWaterhouseCoopers / Entrepreneur Mag., 2006, 2007; recipient AAWM Golden Web award. Independent. Office: BMI Gaming Inc 3500 NW Boca Raton Blvd Boca Raton FL 33431 Office Phone: 561-391-7200. Office Fax: 561-391-8040. Business E-Mail: david@bmigaming.com.

YOUNG, DAVID MICHAEL, biochemist, molecular biologist, internist, educator; b. Bluffton, Ind., Oct. 11, 1935; s. Eli and Ruth (Comer) Y.; m. Diane Tangeman, Dec. 28, 1957 (div. 1971); children: Peter Michael, Amy Katherine; m. Lucia Virginia Patat, Sept. 2, 1972; children: David Michael II, Allison Amelia. BS, Duke U., 1957, MD, 1959. Diplomate: Nat. Bd. Med. Examiners. Intern pediatrics dept. Duke U. Med. Ctr., Durham, NC, 1958-60; staff scientist Lab Cellular Physiology and Metabolism Nat. Heart Inst., NIH, 1960-62; vis. scientist McCollum-Pratt Inst., Johns Hopkins U., Balt., 1962-63, asst. prof. biology, 1963-64; asst. prof. Harvard U. Med. Sch., Boston, 1965-72, assoc. prof. Biol. chemistry, 1972-79, tutor biochem. scis., 1966-76, mem. grad. program for advanced study in immunology, 1971-76, assoc. chmn. div. med. scis., chmn. program for cell biology, 1972-76; head Lab Phys. Biochemistry Mass. Gen. Hosp., Boston, 1965-79; prof. biochemistry U. Fla. Coll. Medicine, Gainesville, 1979—, prof. medicine, 1979-86, chmn. dept. biochemistry and molecular biology, 1979-81, prof. molecular biology, 1981-86, prof. pediatrics, 1986—. Mem. cell physiology study sect. NIH, Bethesda, Md., 1978-82, sect. chmn., 1980; acad. assoc. Nichols Inst., San Juan Capistrano, Calif., 1976—; vis. prof. biology Johns Hopkins U., 1994, 95. Editor-in-chief: Jour. Molecular and Cellular Biochemistry, 1983—; patentee nerve growth factor, nerve growth factor antibody. Served to sr. surgeon USPHS, 1959-63. USPHS spl. fellow, 1962; recipient career devel. award USPHS, 1967-72; NI-Hresearch grantee, 1964—; grantee John A. Hartford Found., 1968-73 Fellow AAAS; mem. Am. Soc. Biol. Chemists, Am. Chem. Soc., Biophys. Soc., Am. Soc. for Clin. Investigation, Am. Heart Assn. (research allocations com. 1976-79), Am. Soc. for Cell Biology, Alpha Omega Alpha

YOUNG, DAVID P., physics professor; Asst. prof. La. State U., Baton Rouge. Contbr. articles to profl. jours. Recipient CAREER award, NSF, 2005. Office: Dept Physics La State U Baton Rouge LA 70803 Office Phone: 225-578-2490. Office Fax: 225-578-5855. E-mail: dyoung1@lsu.edu.

YOUNG, DAVID WILLIAM, retired management educator; b. LA, Feb. 8, 1942; s. William Albert and Hilda Mary (Cook) Y.; m. Ernestine M.L. Van Schaik, Oct. 4, 1968 (div. 1975); m. Francesca Michela Larson, Jan. 28, 1984; children: Christian William, Anthony Edwin. BA, Occidental Coll., 1963; MA, UCLA, 1966; D in Bus. Adminstrn., Harvard U., 1977. Systems engr. IBM, Glendale, Calif., 1963-64; asst. to pres. Lundberg Survey, Inc., Hollywood, Calif., 1964-66; program economist U.S. AID, El Salvador, 1966-69; cons. Thomas Goldsmith & Assoc., Cambridge, Mass., 1969-71; mng. dir. Commonwealth Mgmt. Sys., Cambridge, 1971—; assoc. prof. mgmt. Harvard U. Sch. Pub. Health, Boston, 1976-85, adj. faculty mem., 1985—; prof. mgmt. Boston U. Sch. Mgmt., 1985—2006, chmn. dept. acctg., 1986-91, dir. acctg. MBA program, 1989-93, dir. inst. acctg. rsch. and edn., 1989-93, dir. health care mgmt. program, 1991-94, prof. emeritus, 2006—; prin. The Crimson Group, Cambridge, 1994—. Vis. prof. mgmt. control Instituto de Estudios Superiores de la Empresa, Barcelona, Spain, 1984, 2004; vis. prof. U. Bologna, Italy, 2005—, CEIBS, Shanghai, 2004, Esade Bus. Sch., Barcelona, 2007. Author: The Managerial Process in Human Service Agencies, 1979, Financial Control in Health Care, 1984, The Hospital Power Equilibrium, 1985, Management Control in Nonprofit Organizations, 1984, 7th edit., 2003, Introduction to Financial and Management Accounting: A User Perspective, 1994, Primer on Financial Accounting, 1998, Primer on Management Accounting, 1999, Managing Integrated Delivery Systems: A Framework for Action, 1999, The Manager's Guide to Creative Cost Cutting: 181 Ways to Build the Bottom Line, 2003, Techniques of Management Accounting,: An Essential Guide for Managers and Financial Professionals 2003, Management Accounting in Health Care Organizations, 2003; contbr. articles to profl. jours. Trustee Roxbury Comprehensive Cmty. Health Ctr., 1983-86, Art Inst., Boston, 1990-96, Mass. Eye and Ear Infirmary, Boston, 1990-92, Symmes Hosp., Arlington, 1993-94, The Atrium Sch., 1995-97, Youville Hosp., 1997-2000, Coolidge Corner Theatre Found., 2000—, Spaulding Rehab. Hosp., 2001-05; commr., chair Mass. Hosp. Payment Sys., 1992-

95. Milton Fund fellow Harvard Med. Sch., 1984. Mem.: Am. Acctg. Assn. Democrat. Office: Boston U Sch Mgmt 595 Commonwealth Ave Boston MA 02215-1704 Office Phone: 781-648-8417. E-mail: davidyoung204@cs.com.

YOUNG, DELANO VICTOR, cell biologist, pharmaceutical scientist, biochemist, educator; b. Honolulu, Nov. 17, 1945; s. Lum Fai and Gladys Sau Pung (Wong) Y.; m. Chin-Yi Caroline Yang, Jan. 31, 1970; 1 child, Heather Tien. BS, Stanford U., 1967; PhD, Columbia U., 1973. Postdoctoral fellow Salk Inst. for Biol. Studies, San Diego, 1973-75; asst. prof. dept. chemistry Boston U., 1975-83; asst. dir. Bioassay Systems Rsch. Corp., Woburn, Mass., 1984-86; sr. scientist Damon Biotech, Inc., Needham Heights, Mass., 1986-88, dir., 1988-90; head cell biology Abbott Biotech, Inc. (formerly Damon Biotech, Inc.), Needham Heights, 1990-92; group leader tissue culture Transkaryotic Therapies, Inc., Cambridge, Mass., 1992-94; sect. head, cell culture NitroMed, Inc., Boston, 1994—2006. Cons. D. Van Nostrand Pub., Boston, 1975-83, Allyn and Bacon Pub., Boston, 1975-83; vis. scholar in biochemistry and molecular biology Harvard U., 1982-83; reviewer Sci. Jour. in Biochemistry, 1973—; initial scientist several biotech. start-up cos., Boston area; adj. faculty mem. Mass. Bay CC, Wellesley, 2007-. Author: (chpt.) Inverted Microcarriers: Using Microencapsulation to Grow Anchorage-Dependent Cells, 1992, Culture of Anchorage Dependent Cells, 1999; contbr. over 30 articles to profl. jours. Eugene Higgins fellow Columbia U., 1967-68, Jane Coffin Childs fellow Salk Inst., 1973-75; GM scholar Stanford U., 1963-67. Mem. AAAS, Sigma Xi, Phi Beta Kappa, Phi Lambda Upsilon. Roman Catholic. Achievements include significant contributions to understanding of the nutritional requirements of cancer cells, to devel. of recombinant protein prodn. in biotechnology and cultivation of anchorage dependent cells and to nitric oxide pharmaceuticals. Home: 12 Dennis Rd Wellesley MA 02481 Home Phone: 781-235-9208. Personal E-mail: delyoung@verizon.net.

YOUNG, DELMON DAMARCUS, professional baseball player; b. Montgomery, Ala., Sept. 14, 1985; s. Larry and Bonnie Young. Outfielder Tampa Bay Devil Rays, 2006—. Named Minor League Player of Yr., Baseball Am., 2005, #1 Prospect, 2006. Achievements include being the second youngest player in the major leagues in 2006; 31 hits in his first 20 major league games, only six players in the last 50 years have matched or exceeded that total. Mailing: Tropicana Field One Tropicana Dr Saint Petersburg FL 33705 Office Phone: 727-825-3137. *

YOUNG, DONA DAVIS GAGLIANO, insurance company executive, lawyer; b. Bklyn., Jan. 8, 1954; BA and MA in Polit. Sci., Drew U., 1976; JD, U. Conn., 1980. Bar: Conn. 1980, U.S. Dist. Ct. Conn. 1980. Joined The Phoenix Cos., Hartford, Conn., 1980, asst. counsel, 1981—83, assoc. counsel, 1983, dir. reinsurance adminstrn., 1983—84, dir. and asst. v.p. reinsurance adminstrn., 1984—85, 2nd v.p., ins. counsel, 1985-87, v.p., asst. gen. counsel, 1987-89, sr. v.p. individual sales and mktg., gen. counsel, 1989-94, exec. v.p., gen. counsel, 1994—2000, pres., COO, 2000—02, pres., CEO, chmn., 2003—. Bd. dirs. Sonoco Products Co., 1995—, Wachovia Corp., 2000—, Foot Locker Inc. Chair United Way Capital Area Cmty. Campaign, 2003; bd. dirs. Hartford Hosp.; bd. trustees Goodspeed Opera House Found. Inc. Named Laura A. Johnson Woman of Yr., Hartford Coll. for Women, 2002; recipient Leadership Award for Women in Bus., New England Coun., 1994, Antoinette Bascetta Women's Career Devel. Award, Trust House, Hartford, Conn., 2000, Outstanding Alumni Award, Drew U., 2001, Disting. Grad. Award, U. Conn. Sch. Law, 2002, Human Rels. Award, Nat. Conf. Cmty. and Justice, 2002. Mem. ABA, Hartford County Bar Assn., Conn. Bar Assn., N.Y. Bar Assn. *

YOUNG, DONALD ALAN, federal agency administrator; b. Oakland, Calif., Feb. 8, 1939; s. Leo Alan and Pearl Anita (Walker) Y.; children: Jennifer, Karen BA, U. Calif., Berkeley, 1960, MD, 1964. Diplomate Am. Bd. Internal Medicine. Intern, then resident in internal medicine U. Calif. Hosp., San Francisco, 1964-66; resident in internal medicine Parkland Hosp., Dallas, 1966-67; fellow chest diseases U. Calif. Hosp., San Francisco, 1967-68; mem. staff Palo Alto (Calif.) Med. Clinic, 1970-75; med. dir. Am. Lung Assn., 1975-77; scholar adminstrv. scholars program VA, Washington, 1977-80; dep. dir. policy Bur. Program Policy Health Care Financing Adminstrn., HHS, Washington, 1980—84; exec. dir. Prospective Payment Assessment Commn., Washington, 1984—97; sr. v.p. Am. Assn. Health Plans, 1997—99; COO, med. dir., pres. Health Ins. Associates Am., 1999—2003; now acting asst. sec. planning and evaluation HHS, Washington. Clin. instr. U. Calif. Med. Sch., San Francisco, 1968—70, Stanford U. Med. Sch., 1970—75. Bd. visitors Ind. U. Served with M.C. AUS, 1968-70. Decorated Commendation medal.; Recipient Borden award, 1964 Home: 6109 Trotter Ridge Ct Columbia MD 21044-4919 Office: Ste 500 1201 F St NW Washington DC 20004

YOUNG, DONALD E., congressman; b. Meridian, Calif., June 9, 1933; m. Lula Fredson; children: Joni, Dawn. AA, Yuba Jr. Coll., 1952; BA., Chico State Coll., Calif., 1958. Former educator, river boat capt.; mem. Fort Yukon City Council, 6 years, mayor, 4 years; mem. Alaska Ho. of Reps., 1966-70, Alaska Senate, 1970-73, U.S. Congress from Alaska, 1973—; now ranking mem. transp. & infrastructure com., chmn. resources com., steering com., homeland sec. com. Served in 41st Tank bn. US Army, 1955—57. Republican. Episcopalian. Office: US Ho Reps 2111 Rayburn Ho Office Bldg Washington DC 20515 Office Phone: 202-225-5765. Office Fax: 202-225-0425. *

YOUNG, DONALD STIRLING, clinical pathology educator; b. Belfast, N. Ireland, Dec. 17, 1933; s. John Stirling and Ruth Muir (Whipple) Y.; m. Silja Meret; children: Gordon, Robert, Peter. MB, ChB, U. Aberdeen, Scotland, 1957; PhD in Chem. Pathology, U. London, 1962. Terminable lectr. materia medica U. Aberdeen, 1958-59; fellow Postgrad. Med. Sch., U. London, 1959-62, registrar, 1962-64; vis. scientist NIH, Bethesda, Md., 1965-66, chief clin. chemistry service, 1966-77; head clin. chemistry sect. Mayo Clinic, Rochester, Minn., 1977-84; prof. pathology and lab. medicine U. Pa., 1984—, vice chmn. lab. medicine dept. pathology and lab. medicine, 1994—; dir. William Pepper Lab. Hosp. of U. Pa., 1984—. Past bd. dirs. Nat. Com. Clin. Lab. Standards. Co-editor: Drug Interference and Drug Metabolism in Clinical Chemistry, 1976, Clinician and Chemist, 1979, Chemical Diagnosis of Disease, 1979, Drug Measurement and Drug Effects in Laboratory Health Science, 1980, Interpretation of Clinical Laboratory Tests, 1985, Effects of Preanalytical Variables on Clinical Laboratory Tests, 1997, Effects of Drugs on Clinical Laboratory Tests, 2000, Effects of Disease on Clinical Laboratory Tests, 2001. Recipient Dir.'s award NIH, 1977, Gerard B. Lambert award, 1974-75, MDS Health Group award Can. Soc. Clin. Chemists, 1978; Roman lectr. Australian Assn. Clin. Biochemists, 1979; Jendrassik award Hungarian Soc. Clin. Pathologists, 1985, ATB award Italian Soc. Clin. Biochemistry, 1987. Mem. Am. Assn. Clin. Chemistry (J.H. Roe award Capital sect. 1973, Bernard Gerulat award N.J. sect. 1977, Ames award 1977, Van Slyke award N.Y. met. sect. 1985, J.G. Reinhold award Phila. sect. 1993, past pres.), Internat. Fedn. Clin. Chemists (past pres.), Acad. Clin. Lab. Physicians and Scientists (past exec. com.), Assn. Clin. Biochemists (Ciba-Corning lectr. 1985). Achievements include research in clinical chemistry, optimized use of the clinical laboratory. Office: Hosp U Pa 3400 Spruce St Philadelphia PA 19104-4283 Business E-Mail: donaldyo@mail.med.upenn.edu.

YOUNG, DOUGLAS HOWARD, lawyer; b. Bronxville, NY, Oct. 16, 1948; s. Joseph Paul and Frances (Lally) Y.; m. Betsy Baker, Apr. 24, 1971; children: Jeffrey D., Kevin C. BA, Gettysburg Coll., 1970; JD magna cum laude, Syracuse U., 1978. Bar: N.Y. 1979, U.S. Dist. Ct. (no. dist.) N.Y. 1979, U.S. Claims Ct. 1992, NC, 2000. Ptnr. Melvin & Melvin, Syracuse, N.Y., 1978—. Pres. Onondaga County Legal Svcs. Corp., Syracuse, 1995-96; village atty. Village of Jordan, N.Y., 1980—. Editor Syracuse Law Rev., 1977-78; contbr. articles to profl. jours. Cub scout leader Boy Scouts Am., Syracuse, 1980-81; umpire Liverpool (N.Y.) Little League, Babe Ruth League, 1981-90, Optimists Basketball, Liverpool, 1985-87; coach Babe Ruth Baseball, Liverpool, 1989-90; vol. ARC, 2007, Habitat for Humanity, 2007, DAU Chpt. 11, Wilmington, 2007. Capt. USAF, 1971-76. Named Eagle Scout Boy Scouts Am., 1965. Episcopalian. Avocations: gardening, golf, hiking. Office: Melvin & Melvin PLLC 217 S Salina St Syracuse NY 13202-1390 Home: 10164 Whispering Cove Ct Leland NC 28451 Office Phone: 315-422-1311.

YOUNG, DOUGLAS REA, lawyer; b. LA, July 21, 1948; s. James Douglas and Dorothy Belle (Rea) Y.; m. Terry Forrest, Jan. 19, 1974; 1 child, Megann Forrest BA cum laude, Yale U., 1971; JD, U. Calif., Berkeley, 1976. Bar: Calif., 1976, US Dist. Ct. (no. dist.) Calif. 1976, US Ct. Appeals (6th and 9th cirs.) 1977, US Dist. Ct. (ctrl. dist.) Calif. 1979, US Dist. Ct. Hawaii, US Dist. Ct. (so. dist.) Calif., US Supreme Ct. 1982; cert. specialist in appellate law. Law clk. U.S. Dist. Ct. (no. dist.) Calif., San Francisco, 1976—77; assoc. Farella, Braun & Martel LLP, San Francisco, 1977—82, ptnr., 1983—. Spl. master US Dist. Ct. (no. dist.) Calif., 1977-78, 88, 96, 2000; mem. Criminal Justice Act Def. Panel no. dist. Calif.; mem. faculty Calif. Continuing Edn. of Bar, Berkeley, 1982—, Nat. Inst. Trial Advocacy, Berkeley, 1984—, Practicing Law Inst., 1988—; adj. prof. Hastings Coll. Advocacy, 1985—; vis. lectr. law Boalt Hall/U. Calif., Berkeley, 1986; judge pro tem San Francisco Mcpl. Ct., 1984-05, San Francisco Superior Ct., 1990—. Author: (with Purver and Davis) California Trial Handbook, ed edit., (with Hon. Richard Byrne, Purver and Davis), 3d edit., (with Purver, Davis and Kerper) The Trial Lawyers Book, (with Hon. Eugene Lynch, Taylor, Purver and Davis) California Negotiation and Settlement Handbook; contbr. articles to profl. jours Bd. dirs. Berkeley Law Found., 1977-78, chmn., 1978-79; bd. dirs. San Francisco Legal Aid Soc., pres., 1993—; bd. dirs. Pub. Interest Clearinghouse, San Francisco, chmn., 1987—, treas., 1988—; chmn. Attys. Task Force for Children, Legal Svcs. for Children, 1987—; mem. State Bar Appellate Law Adv. Commn., 1994— Recipient Appreciation award Berkeley Law Found., 1983, Criminal Justice Achievement award Criminal Trial Lawyers Assn. No. Calif., 2002; named a No. Calif. Super Lawyer San Francisco mag., 2004-05, Top Ten Super Lawyer San Francisco mag., 2005-06. Fellow ABA (Pro Bono Pub. award 1992), Am. Coll. Trial Lawyers, Am. Acad. Appellate Lawyers; mem. San Francisco Bar Assn. (founding chmn. litig. sect. 1988-89, award of appreciation 1989, bd. dirs. 1990-91, pres. 2001), Calif. Acad. Appellate Lawyers, McFetridge Am. Inn of Ct. (master), Lawyers Club San Francisco. Democrat. Office: Farella Braun & Martel 235 Montgomery St Ste 3000 San Francisco CA 94104-2902 Office Phone: 415-954-4438. Business E-Mail: dyoung@fbm.com.

YOUNG, EDWIN HAROLD, chemical and metallurgical engineering educator; b. Detroit, Nov. 4, 1918; s. William George and Alice Pearl (Hicks) Y.; m. Ida Signe Suma, June 25, 1944; children: David Harold, Barbara Ellen. BS in Chem. Engring, U. Detroit, 1942; MS in Chem. Engring, U. Mich., 1949, MS in Metall. Engring, 1952. Chem. engr. Wright Air Devel. Center, Dayton, Ohio, 1942-43; instr. U. Mich., Ann Arbor, 1946-52, asst. prof., 1952-56, assoc. prof., 1956-59, prof. chem. and metall. engring., 1959-89, prof. emeritus chem. and metall. engring., 1989—. Mem. Mich. Bd. Registration for Profl. Engrs., 1963-78, chmn., 1969-70, 72-73, 75-76; mem. Mich. Bd. Registration for Architects, 1963-78 Author: (with L.E. Brownell) Process Equipment Design, 1959; contbr. articles to profl. jours. Dist. commr. Boy Scouts Am., 1961-64; mem. Wolverine coun., 1965-68. With USNR, 1943-46, to capt. Res. ret., 1978. Fellow ASME, ASHRAE, AIChE (Donald Q Kern award 1979), Am. Inst. Chemists, Engring. Soc. Detroit; mem. Am. Chem. Soc., Am. Soc. Engring. Edn., Nat. Soc. Profl. Engrs. (pres. 1968-69, award 1977), Mich. Soc. Profl. Engrs. (pres. 1962-63, Engr. of Year award 1976), Mich. Assn. of Professions (pres. 1966, Distinguished award 1970), Nat. Council Engring. Examiners, Naval Res. Assn., Res. Officers Assn., Sigma Xi, Tau Beta Pi, Phi Kappa Phi, Phi Lambda Upsilon, Alpha Chi Sigma. Republican. Baptist. Home: 609 Dartmoor Rd Ann Arbor MI 48103-4513 Personal E-mail: ehyoung@engin.umich.edu.

YOUNG, EDWIN S. W., federal agency official; b. Honolulu, Nov. 13, 1943; s. Hoon Kwan and Clara (Lee) Y.; m. Joan Tay, May 19, 1978. BA, U. Hawaii, Honolulu, 1966; MBA, U. Utah, Salt Lake City, 1975; MS, U. So. Calif., LA, 1983. Asst. gen. mgr. Royal Men's Shops, Inc., Honolulu, 1973-75; mgmt. analyst U.S. Gen. Acctg. Office, Denver and Honolulu, 1976-83; audit mgr. USAF Audit Agy., LA, 1983-84, 87-90; fgn. svc. officer Dept. State, 1984-87; with Office of Insp. Gen., Office Policy & Program Rev., Washington, 1984-87; divsn. dir., asst. dir., dir. prodn. Naval Audit Svc. Western Region, Vallejo, Calif., 1990-95; desk officer, planning and policy dir. Naval Audit Svc., Washington, 1995; regional inspector gen. for auditing, audit mgr. U.S. Small Bus. Adminstrn., LA, 1995-2000; dir. internal audit Calif. State U., Fullerton, 2000—01; dep. city auditor City of Palo Alto, Calif., 2001—. U.S. govt. rep. Pacific and Asian Affairs Coun., Honolulu, 1978—83; USN audit svc. rep. World Affairs Coun. No. Calif., 1990—95; exec. dir. The Asian-Am. Found. Phoenix, 1990—; SBA rep. World Affairs Coun. So. Calif., 1995—2000; Calif. State Fullerton rep. World Affairs Coun., 2000—01; City of Palo Alto rep. World Affairs Coun. No. Calif., 2001—. Community coord. Kailua Neighborhood Bd., Honolulu, 1978-83; area rep. Urban Mass Transit Authority, Honolulu, 1978-83. Capt. USAF, 1966-72. Recipient Commendation awards U.S. Gen. Acctg. Office, 1980, USAF Audit Agy., 1983, 88, 90, USAF Acctg. and Fin. Ctr., 1984, U.S. Naval Audit Svc. award 1992, 94, 95, Assn. Local Auditors award/winner nat. award for best audit, 2004, 05, 06, 07. Mem. Assn. Govt. Accts., Inst. Internal Auditors, Chinese C. of C., World Affairs Coun. Roman Catholic. Avocations: photography, skiing, swimming, tennis, snorkeling. E-mail: eswyoung@aol.com.

YOUNG, ELIZABETH BELL, organization consultant; b. Franklinton, NC, July 2, 1929; d. Joseph H. and Eulalia V. Bell; m. Charles A. Young, Nov. 27, 1964. BA, N.C. Cen. U., 1948, MA, 1950; PhD, Ohio State U., 1959. Cert. speech pathologist; cert. audiologist. Chairperson dept. English Barber Scotia Coll., Concord, NC, 1949-52; dir. speech area, prof. Talladega (Ala.) Coll., 1954-56; dir. speech clinic, prof. Va. State U., Petersburg, 1956-57; prof. Fla. A&M U., Tallahassee, 1959; chmn. dept. English Fayetteville (N.C.) State U., 1959-63; speech pathologist, rsch. assoc. Howard U. Sch. Dentistry, Washington, 1963-64; prof., chairperson dept. English U. Md.-East Shore, Princess Anne, Md., 1965-66; prof., supr. Speech Clinic Cath. U. Am., Washington, 1966-79; congl. staff aide U.S. Ho. of Reps., Washington, 1981-82, 88-90; prof. speech U. D.C., Washington, 1983-84; cons. nat. and local orgns. Washington, 1985-88, 90—. Lectr. over 250 speeches, seminars and workshops; speechwriter, cons. Nat. Assn. Equal Opportunity in Higher Edn., Washington, 1990. Contbr. articles to profl. jours. Fundraiser, pub. rels. polit. candidates, 1963-90; bd. dirs. United Negro Coll. Fund, 1970-80, D.C. Gen. Hosp. Handicapped Intervention Program, 1970-91. Recipient Citations and Certs. of Achievement community and nat. orgns., 1959-90. Fellow Am. Speech-Lang.-Hearing Assn.; mem. Pub. Mems. Assn. (bd. mem. 1980-91, 97-2003, 2003-04), Ohio State U. Alumni Assn., N.C. Cen. U. Alumni Assn. Democrat. Baptist. Avocations: reading, collecting sculpture of foreign countries, travel, writing, public speaking.

YOUNG, ESTELLE IRENE, dermatologist, educator; b. NYC, Nov. 2, 1945; d. Sidney D. and Blanche (Krosney) Young. BA magna cum laude, Mt. Holyoke Coll., 1967; MD, Downstate Med. Ctr., 1971. Intern Lenox Hill Hosp., NYC, 1971—72, resident in medicine, 1972—73; resident in dermatology Columbia Presbyn. Hosp., 1973—74, NYU Hosp., 1974—75, Boston U. Hosp., 1975—76; asst. dermatologist Harvard U. Health Svcs., Cambridge, 1975—76; assoc. staff mem. dermatology Boston U. Med. Ctr., 1975—76, 1976—77; pvt. practice medicine specializing in dermatology Petersburg, Va., 1976—97; mem. staff Poplar Springs Hosp., 1976—2002, Southside Regional Med. Ctr. (formerly Petersburg Gen. Hosp.), 1976—2002, Ctrl. State Hosp., 1984—2007. Clin. instr. dept. dermatology Med. Coll. Va., 1976-87, asst. clinic prof., 1988-94, assoc. clin. prof., 1994-2002; sec. med. staff Petersburg Gen. Hosp., 1982; dermatology cons. Cerebral Palsy Assn. N.Y. State, 1999-2005, 2007—. Author: Visions of Mauna Kea; contbr. articles to profl. jours. Fellow: Am. Acad. Dermatology; mem.: Hawaii Dermatology Soc., Tidewater Dermatology Soc. (pres. 1982—83), Va. Dermatology Soc., Amateur Astronomers ASsn., Physicians Social Responsibility Soc., Tidewater Physicians Social Responsibility (pres. 1990), Internat. Physicians Prevention of Nuclear War, Sigma Xi. Home and Office: PO Box 20182 New York NY 10021-0063 Office Fax: 212-249-5948. Personal E-mail: eiy112@aol.com.

YOUNG, EVERETT J., management consultant, agricultural economist; b. Webberville, Mich., Mar. 14, 1913; s. J.P. and Ullie Josephine (Sigourney) Y.; m. Irene Elizabeth Olick, June 18, 1949. BS in Agrl. Econs., Mich. State U., 1939, MBA, 1960. Field rep. Mich. Fam Bur., Lansing, Mich., 1940-45; asst. exec. sec. Mich. Assn. Farmer Coops., Lansing., 1945-55; fin., mktg. advisor US State Dept., Thailand, 1955-57; mktg. specialist Mich. Dept. Agrl., Lansing, 1957-58; mgr. Dairy Assn. Retail Inds., Detroit, 1961-63; ast. dir. Agrl. Coop. Devel. Internat., Washington, 1968-70; appraiser County of Eaton, Charlotte, Mich., 1974-83; farm mgr. 2 farms pvt. practice, Charlotte, 1972-96. Cons. E. Jay Young Mktg., Detroit, 1962-68, Experience, Inc., Mnpls., 1969-71, Africa, Asia Internat. Devel. Svcs., Washington, 1971-73; chief of party Internat. Coop. Devel. Assn., Uruguay, 1969-70. Author: Agricultural Cooperative, 1952; (USDA Aid Pub.) Food Mktg. in Developing Countries, 1970. Bd. dirs. Episc. Westrn Diocese Mich., Kalamzaoo, 1978-82; exec. com. Eaton County Rep. Club, Charlotte, 1983. Recipient Bishop's cross Episc. Ch., Kalamazoo, 1978. Mem. Internat. Assn. Agrl. Economists, Am. Fgn. Svc. Assn., Internat. Platform Assn., Circumnavigators Club (life), Shriners, Patriarch Mich. State U., Knights Templar, Lansing Farmers Club, Bangkok Econ. Club, Detroit Kiwanis Club. Republican. Methodist. Avocations: travel, organ, languages. Home: 1797 Packard Hwy Charlotte MI 48813-9717

YOUNG, FRANK EDWARD, retired federal agency and religious organization administrator; b. Mineola, NY, Sept. 1, 1931; s. Frank E. and Erma F. Y.; m. Leanne Hutchinson, Oct. 20, 1956; children: Lorrie, Debora, Peggy, Frank, Jonathan. MD, SUNY, 1956; PhD, Case Western Res. U., 1962; DSc (hon.), Roberts Wesleyan Coll., 1983, Houghton Coll., 1984, SUNY, 1986, L.I. U., 1986, Western Bapt. Coll., 1988. Asst. prof. pathology Western Res. U., Cleve., 1962-65; assoc. mem. microbiology Scripps Clinic & Rsch. Found., LaJolla, Calif., 1965-68; assoc. prof. biology U. Calif., San Diego, 1967-70; mem. microbiology & exptl. pathology Scripps Clinic & Rsch. Found., LaJolla, Calif., 1968-70; prof. microbiology and chmn. dept., prof. pathology and radiation biology and biophysics U. Rochester, N.Y., 1970-79, dir. Med. Ctr., N.Y., 1979-81, dean Sch. Medicine and Dentistry, N.Y., 1979-84, v.p. for health affairs N.Y., 1981-84; commr. FDA, Rockville, Md., 1984-89, dep. asst. sec. for health sci. and environ., 1989-93; dir. office emergency preparedness, 1993-96; pastor adult ministries 4th Presbyn. Ch., Bethesda, Md., 1996—2002; exec. dir. Reformed Theol. Sem. Met. Washington, Bethesda, 1996-99; v.p. Reformed Theol. Sem., Bethesda, Md., 1999—; chmn., CEO, Cosmos Alliance, 2002—; ptnr. Essex Woodlands Health Ventures, 2006—. U.S. rep. WHO exec. bd., Geneva, 1985-88; bd. dirs. High Tech., Rochester, N.Y., 1983-84. Contbr. numerous articles on cloning, gene mapping, gene shuttle vectors, 1970-84; initiator Fed. Regulations rules to increase access to exptl. drugs to desperately ill, 1987-88. Lectr. Christian orgns., 1970—; mem. United Way, Rochester, N.Y., 1982-84, N.Y. State Statutory Adv. Com. on DNA, Albany, N.Y., 1978. Recipient sec.'s spl. citation Dept. Health and Human Svcs., 1989, Surgeon Gen.'s Exemplary Svc. medal, 1988, Disting. Svc. medal Pub. Health Svc., 1986, Edward Mott award, 1985, Surgeon Gen.'s Medallion, 1992. Mem. Inst. Medicine of NAS, AAAS, Am. Acad. Microbiology (bd. govs.). Avocations: fishing, boating. Office Phone: 301-908-3182. Personal E-mail: FrankCosmos@aol.com.

YOUNG, FREDERIC HISGEN, information systems executive, data processing consultant; b. Boston, Sept. 7, 1936; s. Ralph Randel Jr. and Wilhelmina Amalia (Imberger) Y.; m. Carol Joan Costello, Sept. 7, 1963 (div. Dec. 1971); children: Tracy Jean, Jodi Ann; m. Kathleen Paula Thorne, Dec. 1, 1984. BBA, U. Mass., 1961; JD, Suffolk U., 1966; AAS in Acctg., Ivy Tech. State Coll., 2005. Mgr. systems and programs Matrix Corp., Burlington, Mass., 1968-69; sr. cons. Programming Dimensions, Inc., Burlington, 1969-70; bus. mgr. JTB Rehab. Ctr., North Reding, Mass., 1970-75; regional bus. mgr. Mass. Dept. Mental Health, Waltham, 1975-78, dir. personnel mgmt. Boston, 1978-81; prin. cons. Lafayette Assocs., Chelsea, Mass., 1980-81; asst. regional dir. Corp. for Applied Systems, Indpls., 1982-84; v.p. cons. svcs. HAS, Inc., Carmel, Ind., 1984-88; v.p. info. sytems Ind. Fed. Credit Union, Anderson, Ind., 1988-95; sys. cons. AIC, Inc., Indpls., 1995-96; sr. cons. Whittman-Hart, Inc., 1996-98; pres. FHY Assocs., Inc., Rio Rancho, N.Mex., 1999-2000; sr. cons. March-FIRST, Spencer, Ind., 2000-01; divsn. mgr. PACE, 2001—. With USN, 1954-56. Republican. Avocation: woodworking. Home and Office: FHY Assocs Inc 623 Antter Ct Ellettsville IN 47429 Office Phone: 812-935-5139. Personal E-mail: fredericyoung@earthlink.net.

YOUNG, GAIL DIANE, secondary school educator; d. Melvin D Maze and Dorothy L (Evers) Maze; m. Kurt W. Young, Oct. 2, 1982; children: Amy, Kaylynn. BS in family and consumer sci., Miami U., 1982; MS in edn., U. of Dayton, 1999. Family and consumer sci. tchr. West Carrollton Sr. High, Ohio, 1982—. Family and consumer sci. dept. chair West Carrollton Sr. High, Ohio, 1997—; career tech. planning dist. tchr. liaison to the miami valley career tech. ctr. West Carrollton Sr. H.S., Ohio, 2002—; bldg. lead mentor - entry yr. tchg. program West Carrollton Sr. High, 2001—02; career devel. course mentor Miamisburg Sr. H.S., Ohio, 1999, Fairborn Sr. H.S., Ohio, 2000; career devel. adv. mem. Miami Valley Career Tech. Ctr., Clayton, Ohio, 2004—; owner/moderator - fcs work&family list serve The first nationwide E-mail group list for FCS teachers, 1997—. Co-founder, former v.p. Milton-Union Early Childhood Ctr., Inc. (non-profit), West Milton, Ohio, 2003; 4-h advisor Miami County 4H Program, Troy, Ohio, 2000. Recipient I Dare You award for Qualities of Leadership, William H. Danforth Found., 1978, Significant Educator award, West Carrollton Edn. Recognition Assn., 1987—, Dickinson T. Guiler award for excellence in edn., 2005. Mem.: NEA, West Carrollton Fellowship Educators, Phi Upsilon Omicron, Kappa Delta Pi. Avocations: travel, boating, gardening, painting. Home Phone: 937-698-3008; Office Phone: 937-859-5121.

YOUNG, GARY WILLIAM, minister, educator, retired military officer; b. Boscobel, Wis., Aug. 8, 1939; s. Howard Austin and Gladys Marie Young; m. Carole Jane Goldsmith-Reynolds, June 2, 1990; children: Cary J., Stacey D. Reynolds, Lisa M., Lauren R. King, Garret S. Reynolds, Lesley J. Reynolds. BS in Secondary Edn., Wis. State Coll & Inst. Tech., Platteville, 1962; BS in Bus. Adminstrn., U. Wis., Platteville, 1992, MS in Adult Edn., 1993. Lic. reverend United Fellowship of Christ Internat., 2004. English tchr. East HS, Green Bay, Wis., 1962—63; seaman apprentice, ensign, capt. USN, 1963—88; English, history tchr. Boothville-Venice, Plaquemines Parish, 1989; adj. faculty bus., gen edn. SW Wis. Tech. Coll., Fennimore, 1990—93; CEO, chief trainer Young Sys., Boscobel, 1992—2002; mission min. United Fellowship of Christ Internat., Boscobel, 2004—. Advisor, ship rider Vietnamese Navy, Saigon, 1967; OIC PTF divsns. 12 and 13 Cosrivron One, Coronado, Calif., 1974—75, chief staff officer, 1975—76; commdg. officer Naval and Marine Corps

Res. Ctr., Des Moines, 1976—79; dir. recruiting Chief of Naval Res., New Orleans, 1979—82; chair Dept. Def. Joint Advt. Com., Washington, 1981—82; English instr. U. Wis., Platteville, 1991—92; field trainer NE Iowa CC, Calmar, 1993—97. Author, editor: training manual Total Quality Leadership. Religious, grief counseling World Christianship Ministries, Boscobel, 2004—07. Capt. USN, 1963—88. Decorated Bronze star US Pres., Staff Svc. Honor medal first class Republic of Vietnam, Meritorious Svc. medal USN, Commendation medal. Mem.: Vietnam Veterans Am. (life), Free and Accepted Masons (assoc.), 40 & 8 (assoc.), Game Wardens of Vietnam (life), VFW (life; post comdr. 2007), Am. Legion (life), Fleet Res. Assn. (life), 9th Va. Cav. Co B (sec. 1997—98), 1st Wis. Cav. Co D (sec. 1999—2001). Protestant. Avocations: golf, history. Home: 1004 Chestnut St Boscobel WI 53280

YOUNG, GENEVIEVE LEMAN, publishing executive, editor; b. Geneva, Sept. 25, 1930; came to U.S., 1945, naturalized, 1968; d. Clarence Kuangson and Juliana Helen (Yen) Y.; m. Cedric Sun, 1955 (div. 1972); m. Gordon Parks, Aug. 26, 1973 (div. 1979). BA (Wellesley Coll. scholar), Wellesley Coll., 1952. Asst. editor Harper & Row (pubs.), NYC, 1960-62, editor, 1962-64, asst. mng. editor, 1964-66, mng. editor, 1966-70; exec. editor J.B. Lippincott Co., NYC, 1970-77, v.p., 1972-77; sr. editor Little, Brown & Co., NYC, 1977-85; editor-in-chief Lit. Guild Am., NYC, 1985-88; v.p., editorial dir. Bantam Books, NYC, 1988-92. Alumna trustee Phillips Acad., Andover, Mass., 1975-78, class agt., 1979-85; mem. Wellesley Bus. Leadership Coun., 1989-98; mem. Youth Counseling League, 1986-98, pres., 1989-96, mem. com. of 100, 1991-93; mem. Literacy Ptnrs., Inc., NYC, 1992-2001, sec., 1996-2001; mem. Andover Devel. Bd., 1993-98; trustee Jewish Bd. Family and Children's Svcs., 1996-98, Meserve-Kunhardt Found., 2006—. Recipient Alumna Achievement award Wellesley Coll., 1982, Matrix award, 1988. Mem. Assn. Am. Pubs. (exec. coun. gen. pub. div. 1975-78, 85-87, freedom to read com. 1972-75), Women's Media Group (pres. 1981-82, 2d v.p. 1994-95), Century Assn. Home: 30 Park Ave New York NY 10016-3801

YOUNG, GEORGE CRESSLER, federal judge; b. Cin., Aug. 4, 1916; s. George Philip and Gladys (Cressler) Y.; m. Iris June Hart, Oct. 6, 1951; children: George Cressler, Barbara Ann. AB, U. Fla., 1938, LLB, 1940; postgrad., Harvard Law Sch., 1947. Bar: Fla. 1940. Practice in, Winter Haven, 1940-41; asso. firm Smathers, Thompson, Maxwell & Dyer, Miami, 1947; adminstrv., legislative asst. to Senator Smathers of Fla., 1948-52; asst. U.S. atty. Jacksonville, 1952; partner firm Knight, Kincaid, Young & Harris, Jacksonville, 1953-61; U.S. dist. judge No., Middle and So. dists. Fla., 1961-73; chief judge Middle Dist., 1973-81, sr. judge, 1981—. Mem. com. on adminstrn. fed. magistrates system Jud. Conf. U.S., 1973-80 Bd. dirs. Jacksonville United Cerebral Palsy Assn., 1953-60. Served to lt. (s.g.) USNR, 1942-46. Mem. Rollins Coll. Alumni Assn. (pres. 1968-69), ABA (spl. com. for adminstrn. criminal justice), Fla. Bar Assn. (gov. 1960-61), Jacksonville Bar Assn. (past pres.), Order of Coif, Fla. Blue Key, Phi Beta Kappa, Phi Kappa Phi, Phi Delta Phi, Sigma Alpha Epsilon. Home: 2424 Shrewsbury Rd Orlando FL 32803-1334 Office: George C Young US Courthouse and Fed Bldg 80 N Hughey Ave Orlando FL 32801-2278

YOUNG, GEORGE HAYWOOD, III, investment banker; b. Washington, Feb. 10, 1959; s. George H. Jr. and Jeanne Marie (Collins) Y.; m. Adina Chouequet, Oct. 12, 1996; children: Nathalie Haywood, George Haywood IV. BA in Internat. Rels. with honors, Brown U., 1982; MPhil in Internat. Rels., Magdalene Coll., U. Cambridge, Eng., 1983; M in Pub. and Pvt. Mgmt., Yale U., 1987. Assoc. cons. Bain & Co., Boston, 1983-85; assoc. mergers and acquisitions dept. CS First Boston, NYC, 1987-90, v.p., 1990-91, dir., 1992-94; White House fellow U.S. Dept. Treasury, Washington, 1991-92; sr. v.p. Lehman Bros., NYC, 1994-96, mng. dir., 1996—2007, head global communications group, 2000—07. Chmn. sr. client coun. Lehman Bros., NYC, 2004-07, mem. global investment banking exec. com., 2004-07, mem. firm strategy com., 2005-07; spkr. in field Application reader White House Fellows Commn., NYC, 1993—; mem. alumni coun. exec. com. Phillips Acad., Andover, Mass., 1994—98, vis. mem. fin. and investment com. bd. trustees, 1998—2004; mem. regional selection panel White House Fellows Commn., NYC, 2002—04; vol. Ch. of the Holy Trinity, NYC, 1990—97. Mem. Coun. Fgn. Rels. (term membership selection com.), Assn. U.S. Army, Harrow Sch. Assn., Army and Navy Club, Yale Golf Club, Union Club NYC, Metedeconk Nat. Golf Club, Misquamicut Club. Roman Catholic.

YOUNG, GWYNNE A., lawyer; b. Durham, NC, 1950; AB, Duke U., 1971; JD, U. Fla., 1974. Bar: Fla. 1974. Asst. state atty. 13th Judicial Cir., Fla.; mem. Carlton, Fields P.A., Tampa, Fla. Instr. U. Fla. Coll. Law, 1974. Exec. editor U. Fla. Law Review, 1973-74. Pres. Jr. League Tampa, Inc., 1985-86; bd. dirs. Assn. Jr. Leagues, Inc., 1987-89, Duke U. Nat. Alumni Assn., 1993—, pres., 1999-2000; trustee Duke U., 1999—2001, Tampa Bar Performing Arts Ctr. Fellow: Am. Bar Found.; mem.: U. Fla. Law Ctr. Assn. (trustee), Fla. Bar (bd. govs.). Office: Carlton Fields Corp Ctr Three at Internat Plaza 4221 W Boy Scout Blvd Tampa FL 33607-5736 Business E-Mail: gyoung@carltonfields.com.

YOUNG, HARRISON, II, software development and marketing executive; b. Bklyn., Feb. 11, 1944; s. Harrison and Bobbie Aline (King) Y.; m. Shirley Gene Stanfield, Aug. 31, 1967 (div. Sept. 21, 1992); children: Melanie Marie, Tracy Lea; m. Emelie Martha Mannweiler, Dec. 18, 1993. BBA, Pacific Western U., LA, 1990; MBA, U. Leicester, Eng., 1993. Cert. computer profl. Sr. systems rep. Info. Systems divsn. RCA, Houston, 1967-70; sr. scientist and program mgr. Tetra Tech Inc., San Diego, 1970-74; co-founder, dir., exec. v.p. and sr. program mgr. Atlantic Analysis Corp., Norfolk, Va., 1974-85; program mgr. Comarco Inc., Anaheim, Calif., 1985-86, v.p., divsn. gen. mgr., 1986-87, pres. Washington-based subs., 1987-88, pres., CEO, dir. Anaheim, 1985-90; pres., CEO Tetra Tech Systems Integration subsidiary Honeywell, San Diego, 1990-92; pres., COO JWK Internat. Corp., Annandale, Va., 1992-94; pres., CEO, chmn. Advanced Programming Concepts, Austin, Tex., 1994—. Bd. dirs. Blue Cross Blue Shield of Va., 1976-81. With USN, 1961-67. Mem. Am. Mgmt. Assn., Armed Forces Comms. and Electronics Assn., Nat. Contract Mgmt. Assn., Data Processing Mgmt. Assn., Instrumentation Soc. Am. Avocations: boating, computers, foreign travel. Home: 1753 Stonebridge Dr S Ann Arbor MI 48108-8511 Office: Advanced Programming Concepts Inc 3300 Duval Rd Ste 200 Austin TX 78759-3544

YOUNG, HAYS WILSON JORDEN, research scientist; b. Memphis, Dec. 14, 1975; s. Dianne and Don Wayne Berryhill (Stepfather); m. Linda Isabel Castellanos, July 19, 2003. BS in Biochemistry and Biology, Fla. State U., Tallahassee, 1999; PhD in Biochemistry and Immunology, U. Tex., Houston, 2004. Postdoctoral fellow Baylor Coll. Medicine, Houston, 2003—04, MD Anderson Cancer Ctr., Houston, 2004—07; DNA Tech. Sect. Adminstr. Ark. State Crime Lab., Little Rock, 2007—. Recipient NIH Loan Repayment award, NIH, 2006—, Outstanding Rsch. award, U. Tex., 2002, 2003; F32 - NRSA Fellowship grantee, NIH, 2006—. Mem.: Am. Thoracic Soc., Am. Mensa, Alpha Chi Sigma (Detar scholar 1999). Office: Ark State Crime Lab 3 Natural Resources Dr Little Rock AR 72215 Personal E-mail: hayswj@yahoo.com.

YOUNG, HENRY E., tissue engineering medical educator; b. Dayton, Ohio, Dec. 5, 1951; s. Henry O. and Lucille M. Y.; m. Valerie E. Achorn, May 16, 1976; 1 child, Katherine. BS in Biology, Ohio State U., 1974; MS in Zoology, U. Ark., 1977; PhD, Tex. Tech. U., 1983. Instr.biochemistry Rush-Presbyn.-St. Luke's Med. Ctr., Chgo., 1987—88; asst. prof. anatomy Mercer U. Sch. Medicine, Macon, Ga., 1988—95, asst. prof. surgery, 1988—94, assoc. prof. anatomy, pediat., 1995—2004, prof. anatomy, pediat., 2004—. Inventor in field. Recipient Hooding award for excellence in tchg. and rsch., Mercer U. Med. Sch., 1993, 1994, Gender Equity award, Am. Med. Women's Assn., 1997, Humanism in Medicine award, Arnold P. Gold Found., 2005; NIH Postdoctoral fellow in biochemistry, Case We. Res. U., Cleve., 1983—85, postdoctoral fellow, Muscular Dystrophy Assn., 1985—87. Mem.: Am. Soc. Cell Biology, Stem Cells and Regen Medicine, Tissue Culture Soc., Am. Assn. Anatomists, Arnold P. Gold Found., Humanism Hon. Soc. Achievements include discovery of adult germ layer lineage stem cells, adult pluripotent stem cells, and adult near totipotent stem cells; invention of muscle morphogenetic protein and scar inhibitory factor. Avocation: reading. Office: Mercer U Sch Medicine 1550 College St Macon GA 31207-1500 Office Phone: 478-301-4034. Business E-Mail: young_he@mercer.edu.

YOUNG, HOWARD J., lawyer; b. Derby, Conn., Aug. 19, 1967; BA in Polit. Sci., magna cum laude, Tufts U., 1989; JD, Duke U., 1993. Bar: Md. 1993, DC 1994. Sr. counsel Office of Counsel to the Insp. Gen., US Dept HHS, 1997—99, dep. chief civil recoveries branch, 1999—2002; ptnr., health care practice group Sonnenschein Nath & Rosenthal LLP, Washington. Editl. bd. mem. Healthcare Exec.; contbr. articles to profl. jours. Named AHLA Self Disclosure Task Force Mem.; recipient several OIG Exceptional Achievement awards and other govt. awards. Mem.: ABA (health law sect.), Gerson Lehrman Coun. Advisors, DC Bar Assn., Health Care Compliance Assn., Am. Health Lawyers Assn. Office: Sonnenschein Nath & Rosenthal LLP Ste 600, E Tower 1301 K St NW Washington DC 20005-3364 Office Phone: 202-408-9210. Office Fax: 202-408-6399. Business E-Mail: hyoung@sonnenschein.com. *

YOUNG, HUGH DAVID, physics professor, writer; b. Ames, Iowa, Nov. 3, 1930; s. Hugh Surber and Nellie Sibella (Peters) Y.; m. Alice Carroll, June 25, 1960; children: Gretchen Carroll, Rebecca Susan BS in Physics, Carnegie-Mellon U., 1952, MS in Physics, 1953, PhD in Physics, 1959, BFA in Music, 1972. From instr. to assoc. prof. physics Carnegie-Mellon U., Pitts., 1956-77, prof., 1977—; head dept. natural scis. Margaret Morrison Carnegie Coll., Carnegie-Mellon U., 1962-67, acad. coordinator, lectr. modern engring. mgrs. program, 1966-82. Vis. assoc. prof. physics U. Calif., Berkeley, 1967-68, vis. prof. physics, 1974; asst. organist St. Paul's Cathedral, Pitts., 1978-82 Author: Statistical Treatment of Experimental Data, 1962, Fundamentals of Mechanics and Heat, 2d edit., 1974, Fundamentals of Optics and Modern Physics, 2d edit., 1976; (with Sears and Zemansky) College Physics, 7th edit., 1990, University Physics, 9th edit., 1996. Bd. dirs. Renaissance and Baroque Soc., 1980-86. Recipient Ryan Tchg. award Carnegie Inst. Tech., 1965, Doherty award Carnegie Mellon U., 1997. Mem. Am. Assn. Physics Tchrs., Am. Phys. Soc., Am. Guild Organists (assoc.) Democrat. Avocations: organ, rock climbing. Home: 5746 Aylesboro Ave Pittsburgh PA 15217-1412 Office: Carnegie-Mellon Univ Dept Physics Pittsburgh PA 15213 Home Phone: 412-422-5772; Office Phone: 412-268-2759. Business E-Mail: hdy@andrew.cmu.edu.

YOUNG, J. WARREN, magazine publisher; Pub. Boys' Life and Scouting Mag., Irving, Tex. Office: Boys' Life PO Box 152079 Irving TX 75015-2079

YOUNG, JACK ALLISON, financial executive; b. Aurora, Ill., Dec. 31, 1931; s. Neal A. and Gladys Young; m. Virginia Dawson, Jan. 24, 1959; children: Amy D., Andrew A. BS in Journalism, U. Ill., 1954. CLU; chartered fin. cons.; registered security rep. Advt. writer Caterpillar Tractor Co., 1956-58; inst. agent Equitable Life Assurance Soc., St. Geneva, Ill., 1958—, ins. broker, 1972—; pres. Jack A. Young and Assocs., 1978—, Creative Brokerage, Inc., 1982-95. Past pres., gen. securities prin. Chartered Planning, Ltd., 1984-2000; past trustee Equitable CLU Assn.; past chmn. Equitable Nat. Agents Forum. Bd. dirs. Tri-City Famiy Services, 1975-83, pres., 1979-81; trustee Delnor-Community Health System, 1985-97, chmn., 1988-91; bd. dirs. St. Charles Ctr. Phys. Rehab., 1991-97; chmn., pres. Delnor-Cmty. Health Care Found., 1986-88; dir. Kane County Bar Found., Inc., 1997-2000. Lt. (j.g.) USN, 1956. Named to Equitable Hall of Fame, 1978. Mem. Million Dollar Round Table (life), Am. Soc. C.L.U.s, Am. Coll. C.L.U. Golden Key Soc., Fox Valley Estate Planning Council, Internat. Assn. for Fin. Planning, Inc., Aurora Assn. Life Underwriters (past pres., nat. committeeman), Nat. Assn. Securities Dealers (registered prin.), Geneva Golf Club (pres. 1994). Home: 18 Campbell St Geneva IL 60134-2732 Office: 28 N Bennett St Geneva IL 60134-2207 Office Phone: 630-232-4141. Personal E-mail: jayassoc@aol.com. Business E-Mail: yjackayoung@aol.com.

YOUNG, JACQUELINE EURN HAI, former state legislator, consultant; b. Honolulu, May 20, 1934; d. Paul Bai and Martha (Cho) Y.; m. Harry Valentine Daniels, Dec. 25, 1954 (div. 1978); children: Paula, Harry, Nani, Laura; m. Daniel Anderson, Sept. 25, 1978 (div. 1984); m. Everett Kleinjans, Sept. 4, 1988 (div. 1998). BS in Speech Pathology, Audiology, U. Hawaii, 1969; MS in Edn., Spl. Edn., Old Dominion U., 1972; advanced cert., Loyola Coll., 1977; PhD in Communication, Women's Studies, Union Inst., 1989. Dir. dept. speech and hearing Md. Sch. for the Blind, Balt., 1975-77; dir. deaf-blind project Easter Seal Soc. Oahu, Hawaii, 1977-78; project dir. equal ednl. opportunity programs Hawaii State Dept. Edn., Honolulu, 1978-85, state ednl. specialist, 1978-90; state rep. dist. 20 Hawaii State Legislature, Honolulu, 1990-92, state rep. dist. 51, 1992-94; vice-speaker Hawaii Ho. of Reps., Honolulu. Apptd. to U.S. Dept. Def. Adv. Commn. on Women in the Svc.; cons. spl. edn. U.S. Dept. Edn., dept. edn. Guam, Am. Samoa, Ponape, Palau, Marshall Islands, 1977-85; cons. to orgns. on issues relating to workplace diversity; adj. prof. commn., anthopology, mgmt. Hawaii Pacific U.; chief staff officer Am. Cancer Soc. Hawaii Pacific, 2004—. TV writer, host, producer, 1992—. 1st v.p. Nat. Women's Polit. Caucus, 1988-90; chair Hawaii Women's Polit. Caucus, 1987-89; bd. dirs. YWCA Oahu, Kalihi Palama Immigrant Svc. Ctr., Hawaii Dem. Movement, Family Peace Ctr.; appointee Honolulu County Com. on the Status of Women, 1986-87; founding bd. dirs. Windward Spouse Abuse Shelter, 1993—; campaign dir. Protect Our Constn., 1998; trustee St. Louis Sch., 1997-99; mem. nat. adv. coun. ACLU, 2004; nat. bd. dirs. Hawaiian Am. Coalition; mem. Asian and Pacific Islander Am. Health Assn.; mem. Hawaii State Adv. Com. on Civil Rights. Recipient Outstanding Woman Leader award YWCA of Oahu, 1994, Pres.'s award Union Inst., 1993, Fellow of the Pacific award Hawaii-Pacific U., 1993, Headliner award Honolulu chpt. Women in Commn., 1993, Korean Am. Alliance Washington Spl. Recognition award, 1998, Hawaii Women Lawyers Disting. Svc. award, 1999, Disting. Equity Adv. award Hawaii chpt. Nat. Coalition for Sex Equity in Edn., 1998, NEA Mary Hatwood Futrell for advancing women's rights award, 1999, Friend of Social Work award Hawaii chpt. NASW, 1998, Allan Saunders award Hawaii chpt. ACLU, 1999, Light of the Orient award Korean Am. Found., 2006; named one of Extraordinary Women Hawaii, Found. Hawaii Women's History, 2001.

YOUNG, JAMES E., real estate company executive, consultant, engineer; b. Celina, Ohio, Sept. 1, 1941; s. Thomas D. and Margaret E. (Flora) Y.; m. Patricia C. Teare, June 13, 1964; children: Kathleen M., Peter C. BSME, Rose-Hulman Inst. Tech., 1963; MBA, Ind. U., 1965; EdS, Ind. State U., 1998. V.p. Citicorp, NYC, 1965-73; pres. James E. Young & Assoc., Inc., Indpls., 1974-91, The Young Group, Naples, Fla., 1991—. Vis. prof. guest lectr. Purdue U., Lafayette, Ind., 1986—; adv. bd. Purdue-Anderson, Inc., 1985—, Rsch. Inst. for Devel. of Interactive Learning Sys., Terre Haute, Ind., 1986—; pres. Remote Equipment Corp., Indpls., 1988-90; pres. Forum for Internat. Profl. Svcs., Inc., 1988-91, bd. dirs.; chmn. bd. WKJM, Inc., 1989-90; chmn. World Competitiveness Conf., 1990—; pres. G & G Angola, Inc., 1991-98, Ramco of Ind., 1992-98, Jaymer, Inc., 1996—. Author: Industrial Communications Networks, 1987, Load Rating Analysis For Steel Manhole Covers, 1995; Load Rating Analysis for Composite Manhole Covers, 1996, What Makes Steel Manhole Covers Unsafe?, 1999; Smart Choices for Composite Manhole Covers, 2000; patentee in field. Co-founder, chmn. bd. Ind. Amateur Baseball Assn., Inc., 1982—; mktg. chmn. Ind. Major League Baseball Commn., Indpls., 1982-86. Mem. ASME, Soc. Mfg. Engrs., Bus. Modernization and Tech. Corp. (chmn. telecom. 1984—), Rotary, Beta Gamma Sigma. Avocations: reading, boating, golf. E-mail: jyoungnaples@aol.com.

YOUNG, JAMES EDWARD, lawyer; b. Painesville, Ohio, Apr. 20, 1946; s. James M. and Isabel P. (Rogers) Y. BBA, Ohio U., 1968; JD, Ohio State U., 1972. Bar: Ohio 1972. Law clk. to chief judge U.S. Ct. Appeals, Nashville, 1972-73; chief counsel City of Cleve., 1980-81, law dir., 1981-82; assoc. Jones, Day, Reavis & Pogue (now Jones Day), Cleve., 1973—79, ptnr., 1983—. Office: Jones Day 901 Lakeside Ave E Cleveland OH 44114-1190 Office Phone: 216-586-7259. Business E-Mail: jameseyoung@jonesday.com.

YOUNG, JAMES JULIUS, academic administrator, retired military officer; b. Ft. Ringgold, Tex., Nov. 28, 1926; s. John Cooper and Violet Thelma (Ohl) Y.; m. June Agnes Hillstead, Dec. 17, 1948; children: Robert Michael, Steven Andrew, Patrick James, Mary Frances. BS, U. Md., 1960; M.H.A., Baylor U., 1962; PhD in Hosp. and Health Adminstrn, U. Iowa, 1969. Commd. 2d lt. U.S. Army, 1947, advanced through grades to brig. gen., 1977, comdr., med. ops. officer, dir. tng. field med. units in European Command, 1949-53; comdr. Mil. Med. Leadership Sch., 1953-54; med. advisor (Nationalist Army of China), 1955-57; asst. adminstr. Fitzsimons Army Med. Center, 1957-60; med. plans and ops. officer (US Forces), Korea, 1962-63; sr. field med. instr., chief field med. service Med. Field Service Sch., 1963-66; dir. health care orgn. and mgmt. analysis Office of Surgeon Gen., 1969-71; dir. med. plans and ops. directorate Office of the Surgeon, Military Assistance Command, Vietnam, 1971-72; exec. officer, chief adminstrv. services Silas Hays Army Hosp., 1973-74; military health analyst, military health care study OMB, Exec. Office of Pres., 1974-76; dep. dir. resources mgmt. and cons. for health care adminstrn. Office of Surgeon Gen., 1976-77; chief med. svcs. corps U.S. Army, 1977-81; dir. resources mgmt. Office of Surgeon Gen., 1977-81; ret., 1981; instr. U. Iowa, 1967-69; asst. prof., preceptor Baylor U., 1973-74; vice chancellor for health affairs W.Va. Bd. Regents, Charleston, 1982-87; dean sch. of allied health scis. U. Tex. Health Sci. Ctr., San Antonio, 1987-90, interim dean Sch. Medicine, 1988-89, dean Sch. Medicine, 1989—, dean emeritus, 2000—. Cons. to Min. of Health, Republic of Vietnam, 1971-72, 1989-2000; adj. prof. Baylor U., 1977-81, George Washington U., 1975-76, W.Va. U., 1986; prof. U. Tex. health Sci. Ctr., San Antonio, 1989-2000. Contbr. articles to profl. jours. Decorated D.S.M., Legion of Merit, Meritorious Service medal, others; recipient Walter Reed medal, 1981; Army Med. Dept. medal for contbn. to health service, 1981, Order of Mil. Med. Merit, 1981, U. Tex. Health Scis. Ctr. Hon. medallion Fountains of Progress, 2000; recipient Humanism in Medicine medallion Health Care Foun. NJ, 2000. Roman Catholic. Home: 1610 Anchor Dr San Antonio TX 78213-1943 Personal E-mail: jyoung51@satx.rr.com.

YOUNG, JAMES MORNINGSTAR, internist, military officer; b. Massillon, Ohio, Oct. 28, 1929; s. Ralph Louis and Pauline Louise (Morningstar) Y.; m. Bettylu Jones, July 3, 1952; children: Anne Christine, Mark Andrew, Patricia Jane, Elizabeth Lynne, Judith Pamela, Claudia Dianne; m. Mariette M. Aubuchon, Oct. 11, 1970; children: Gretchen Camille, Jason Paul. AB, Duke U., 1951, MD, 1955. Diplomate Am. Bd. Internal Medicine. Intern Bethesda Naval Hosp., 1955-56, asst. dir. tissue bank, 1956-58, resident, 1958-61; commd. lt. (j.g.) USN, 1955, advanced through grades to lt. comdr., 1961, promoted to temporary rank capt., 1963; White House physician to Presidents Kennedy and Johnson, Washington, 1963-66. Asst. chief medicine and dir. of interns, Oakland (Calif.) Naval Hosp., 1966-69; chief medicine Naval Hosp. Boston, Chelsea, Mass., 1969-74; med. officer Naval Air Sta., South Weymouth, Mass., 1974-75; assoc. clin. prof. medicine Boston U. Sch. Medicine, 1969-75; v.p. med. affairs Mass. Blue Shield/Blue Cross, 1975-87; lectr. Harvard Sch. Pub. Health, 1987-90; sr. advisor Beijing Coll. Traditional Chinese Medicine, 1987-88; med. advisor U.S.-China People's Friendship Assn., Washington, 1988-90; cons. USPHS, Office Asst. Sec. for Health, Nat. Ctr. for Health Svcs., Rsch. and Health Care Tech. Assessment, HHS, 1985-90; v.p. for med. affairs Greenery Rehab. Group, Inc., 1988-90; assoc. med. dir. New. Eng. Rehab. Hosp., 1992-95, chief medicine, 1992-95. Contbr. articles to med. publs. Decorated knight comdr. with star Equestrian Order of the Holy Sepulchre of Jerusalem; named Disting. Citizen of Washington H.S., Massillon, Ohio, 1993. Fellow ACP, AMA, Alpha Omega Alpha, Omicron Delta Kappa, Beta Omega Sigma, Sigma Alpha Epsilon. Home: 77 Harvey Mill Rd Lee NH 03824-6302 Personal E-mail: jmyoung9@hotmail.com.

YOUNG, JAMES R., rail transportation executive; m. Shirley Young; 3 children. Grad., U. Nebr., Omaha. With Union Pacific Corp., 1978—, mgmt. fin. and ops., asst. v.p. re-engring. Union Pacific RR Co., 1994—95, v.p. re-engring. and design, 1995, v.p. customer svc. planning & quality, 1997, v.p. fin. & quality, sr. v.p., corp. treas., 1998—99, sr. v.p. fin., corp. contr., 1999, exec. v.p., CFO, 1999—2004, pres. & COO Union Pacific RR Co., 2004—05, bd. dirs., 2005—, pres., CEO, 2005—, chmn., 2007—. Bd. mem. Grupo Ferroviario Mexicano, Assn. Am. RRs. Bd. mem. Creighton U., Omaha, Joslyn Art Mus., U. Nebr. Med. Ctr. Office: Union Pacific Corp 1400 Douglas St Omaha NE 68179-1001 Office Phone: 402-544-5000. *

YOUNG, JAY ALFRED, chemical safety and health consultant, editor, writer; b. Huntington, Ind., Sept. 8, 1920; s. Jacob Phillip and Marie (Skully) Y.; m. Anne Elizabeth Neff, June 29, 1942 (dec. June 1962); children: John, Paul, Cecelia, Michael, Joseph, Andrea, Therese, Gregory, Thomas, Lucy, Margaret, Antonia; m. Mary Ann Owens, Aug. 15, 1962; children: James, Laurence; 4 stepchildren. BS, Ind. U., Bloomington, 1939; AM, Oberlin Coll., Ohio, 1940; PhD, U. Notre Dame, South Bend, Ind., 1950. Chief chemist Asbestos Mfg. Co., Huntington, Ind., 1941-42; ordnance engr. U.S. War Dept., Washington, 1942-44; from instr. to prof. chemistry King's Coll., Wilkes-Barre, Pa., 1949-69; vis. prof. Carleton U., Ottawa, Ont., Canada, 1969-70, Fla. State U., Tallahassee, 1975-77; Hudson prof. Auburn (Ala.) U., 1970-75; mgr. tech. publs. Chem. Mfrs. Assn., Washington, 1977-80; chem. safety and health cons. Silver Spring, Md., 1980—. Pro bono cons. OSHA, EPA, Consumer Product Safety Commn., Washington, 1980—; contributor Ency. Britannica, 1974-; lectr. in field. Author: Practice in Thinking, 1958, Elements of General Chemistry, 1960, Chemical Concepts, 1963, Selected Principles of Chemistry, 1963, Arithmetic for Students of Science, 1968, Instructor's Guide for Chemistry, a Cultural Approach, 1971, Study Guide for General Chemistry, 1974, Fire!, 1977, Actions and Reactions, 1978, Chemistry, A Human Concern, 1978, Kitchen Chemistry, 1980, Electron Microscopy Safety Handbook, 1985, Introduction to Toxicology, 2004; co-author: Study Guide for Continental Classroom Chemistry, NBC/TV, vols. I and II, 1959, 60, Keys to Chemistry, 1973, Chemistry Preparation Laboratory, 1973, Keys to Oxidation-Reduction, 1974, Things that Last, 1977, Principles of Laboratory Safety (with videotape), 1980, OSHA Hazard Communication Regulations, 1984, Chemical Safety Manual for Small Businesses, 1989, 2d edit., 1992, Developing a Chemical Hygiene Plan, 1990; editor: Guidelines and Recommendations for the Preparation and Continuing Education of Secondary School Teachers of Chemistry, 1977, Improving Safety in the Chemical Laboratory: A Practical Guide, 1989, 2d edit., 1992 (also contbr.), Safety in Academic Chemistry Laboratories, Vols. 1 and 2, 7th edit., 2002, Chemical Safety for Teachers and Their Supervisors, Grades 7-12, 2001; co-editor: Heath Chemistry Laboratory Experiments, 1987, Handbook of Chemical Health and Safety, 2001 (also contbr.), Chem. Lab. Info. Profiles, 2001—; contbr. articles to profl. jours. Tech. resource person to media and expert witness regarding chem. hazards, precautions, transp. incidents involving chems.; mem. NSF Coll. Chemistry Commn., 1962-68. Lt. USNR, 1944-46. Recipient Disting. Chemistry Alumnus award U. Notre Dame, 1968, Excellence in Chemistry Tchg. award Mfg. Chemists Assn., 1970. Fellow AAAS; mem. Am. Chem. Soc. (councilor 1963-87, policy com. 1970-81, sec. divsn. chem. edn. 1969-78, chmn. divsn. chem. health and safety 1979-80, mem. chem. safety com. 1982-2003, Chem. Health and Safety award 1991, Outstanding Svc. award 2003). Roman Catholic. Avocations: wood and metalworking, gardening. Home and Office: 12916 Allerton Ln Silver Spring MD 20904-3105 Office Phone: 301-384-1768. Personal E-mail: chemsafety@verizon.net.

YOUNG, JAY MAITLAND, health products executive, consultant; b. Louisville, Nov. 26, 1944; s. Clyde Dudley and Olive May (Tyas) Y. BA in Chemistry and Math. magna cum laude, Vanderbilt U., 1966; MS in Biochemistry, Yale U., 1967, MPhil in Phys. Chemistry, 1968, PhD in Chemistry, 1971. Cert. Am. Med. Writers Assn. Multi-disciplinary Core, 1999. Asst. prof. chemistry Bryn Mawr (Pa.) Coll., 1970-76; rsch. biochemist Abbott Labs., Ill., 1977-78, project mgr. physiol. diagnostics Abbott Park, 1978-80, project mgr. cancer product devel., 1980-82, internat. clin. specialist sci. affairs, 1982-85, clin. project mgr. physiol. diagnostic quality and sci. support, 1986-90, staff quality assurance and sci. support, 1990-93, fertility, pregnancy, thyroid mgr., quality and sci. support, 1993-95, fertility, pregnancy, thyroid, cancer mgr., product quality assurance, 1995-97, staff noninfectious disease diagnostics sci. affairs, 1997—2001; cons. and med. writer diagnostic and pharm. areas, 2002—. Cons. Inst. for Cancer Rsch., Fox Chase, Phila., 1974, vis. scientist, 1975-76; honors examiner Swarthmore Coll., 1973, 74, mem. vis. evaluation com., 1975; presenter to med. groups on cancer markers, viral hepatitis and epidemiology of AIDS, 1982-84. Contbr. articles to profl. jours. Vol. Episcopal Ch. Outreach Commn. Named to Hon. Order Ky. Cols.; predoctoral fellow NSF, Yale U., 1966-70; postdoctoral fellow, NIH, U. Oxford, 1971-72; travel grantee NATO, 1974. Mem. Am. Med. Writers Assn. (Del. Valley chpt. program chair 2002-03, treas. 2003-06, cert mem. Multi-disciplinary Core 1999). Home Phone: 773-728-1386; Office Phone: 610-322-4444. E-mail: maitland@mailbug.com.

YOUNG, JEREMY EDWARD, systems engineer; b. Pocatella, Idaho, Dec. 10, 1971; s. Roger Chris and Janet Malanie Young; m. Mandy Kaye Gyger, May 27, 2000 (div. July 29, 2007); 1 child, Aiden William. BS in Physics, Wash. State U., Pullman, 1998, MS in Physics. Sr. optical engr. Corvis Corp, Columbia, Md., 2000—03; sys. engr. QSS Group, NASA Contractor, Cleve., 2003—04; laser sys. scientist, engr. Fibertek Inc., Herndon, Va., 2004—. Mem.: Mensa. Home Phone: 703-349-6319; Office Phone: 703-956-3666.

YOUNG, JESS RAY, retired internist; b. Fairfield, Ill., Feb. 4, 1928; s. Edgar S. and Clara B. (Musgrave) Y.; m. Gloria Wynn, July 10, 1953; children— James C., Patricia A. BS, Franciscan U., 1951; MD, St. Louis U., 1955. Intern Highland Alameda County Hosp., Oakland, Calif., 1955-56; resident in internal medicine Cleve. Clinic Hosp., 1956-59, mem. staff dept. vascular medicine, 1959-97, chmn. dept., 1976-97; ret., 1998. Co-author: Leg Ulcer, 1975, Peripheral Vascular Diseases, 1991, 1996; contbr. articles to profl. jours., chpts. to books. Served with AUS, 1946-47. Mem. AMA, Am. Heart Assn. (stroke council), Am. Coll. Cardiology, Internat. Cardiovascular Soc., ACP, Am. Fedn. Clic. Research, Ohio Soc. Internal Medicine, Soc. for Vascular Medicine and Rsch., Inter-Urban Club. Methodist. Home: 1503 Burlington Rd Cleveland OH 44118-1216 Personal E-mail: jesyoung@adelphia.net.

YOUNG, JESSICA S.E., secondary school educator; b. Phila., Apr. 5, 1951; d. Frank Henry and Shirley Ruth (Rosen) Edelman; m. Michael Andrew Young, Dec. 19, 1971; children: Shana Claire, Paula Ruth, Henry David. AB, U. Chgo., 1971; MA, Columbia U., NYC, 1973, MPhil, 1975, PhD, 1988. Tchr. The Harvard Sch., Chgo., 1990—94, Oak Park (Ill.) and River Forest H.S., 1994—. Reader AP European History Exam., 1997—. Co-author: (book) The New Teacher's Guide to AP European History, 2005. Mem. AP European History Test Devel. Com., Princeton, NJ, 2003—. Finalist Golden Apple award, Golden Apple Found., Ill., 2001. Mem.: Nat. Coun. Social Studies, Am. Hist. Assn. (Beveridge Family Tchg. Prize 2001), World History Assn. (Nat. Tchg. Prize 2002, 2001, 2003). Office: Oak Park & River Forest HS 201 N Scoville Oak Park IL 60302 Office Phone: 708-383-0700 ext. 3360. Business E-Mail: jyoung@oprfhs.org.

YOUNG, JOHN F., utilities executive; m. Julie Young; children: Jack, Will. B in Mech. Engring., US Naval Acad., Annapolis, Md., 1978. Positions including comml. sales rep., position in wholesale and retail mktg. fuel planning and procurement, head fin. and investor rels. office So. Co., 1983—2000, exec. v.p. So. Generation; sr. v.p. Sierra Pacific Resources Corp.; COO Exelon Power Exelon Corp., 2003, pres. Exelon Power, 2003—04, pres. Exelon Generation, 2004—05, exec. v.p. fin. and markets, 2005—, CFO, 2005—. Bd. dirs. Assn. Edison Illuminating Cos., Utility Bus. Edn. Coalition. Engring. officer USS Ticonderoga USN. Office: Exelon Corp 10 S Dearborn St 37th Fl PO Box 805398 Chicago IL 60680-5398 Office Phone: 800-483-3220. *

YOUNG, JOHN HARDIN, lawyer; b. Washington, Apr. 25, 1948; s. John D. and Laura Virginia (Gwathmey) Y.; m. Mary Frances (Farley) Crosby. JD, U. Va., 1973; BCL, Oxford U., Eng., 1976. Bar: Va. 1973, DC 1974, Pa. 1979, U.S. Dist. Ct. Va. 1974, U.S. Dist. Ct. DC 1974, U.S. Dist. Ct. Md. 1989, U.S. Ct. Fed. Claims 1974, U.S. Ct. Appeals (4th, 5th, Fed. and DC cirs.), Internat. Trade Ct. 1974, U.S. Supreme Ct. 1977. Ptnr., counsel Porter Wright Morris & Arthur, Washington, 1988—99; with Exec. Office of the Pres., Washington, 2000; counsel Sandler, Reiff & Young, PC, 2001—; exec. v.p. external affairs SECORIX, Inc., Washington, 2004—. Mem. adv. bd. Antitrust Bull., 1980-1994; mem. U.S. Sec. State's adv. com. Pvt. internat. Law, 1987-95; chmn. Va. Retirement Sys. Rev. Bd., 1990-94; asst. atty. gen. Commonwealth of Va., 1976-78; mem. Delmarva Interstate Compact, 2004-06; moderator Alexandria Forum, 1993-98, Fedn. Forum/TV Channel 10, 1989-91; sr. v.p., gen. counsel various tech. cos.; adj. prof. George Mason U. Sch. Law, 2003—05 Author: Young's Federal Rules of Evidence, Mastering Written Discovery; contbr. articles to profl. jours. Spl. counsel Dem. Nat. Com., 1998—99, chair nat. lawyers coun., 1998—2004; lead recount counsel for V.P. Gore Fla., 2000; organizer promote the vote Dem. Nat. Com., 2001—. Fellow: Am. Bar Found. (life); mem.: ABA (chmn. adminstrv. law and regulatory practice sect. 1999—2000, standing com. on continuing edn. of the bar 2002—04, standing com. on election law 2005—07, bd. govs. 2007—, fellow adminstrv. law 2001—), Am. Inns of Ct. Found. (trustee 2004—, chair rule of law conf. 2007), Temple Bar Found. (bd. dirs., founder), Comml. Bar Assn. U.K., George Mason Am. Inn of Ct. (master 1990—, pres. 2002—03, Best Spl. Projects award 2003), Am. Law Inst. (life), Cosmos Club, Phi Alpha Theta (history honors). Episcopalian. Office Phone: 202-479-1111. Business E-Mail: young@sandlerreiff.com.

YOUNG, JOHN JACOB, JR., federal agency administrator; b. Moreland, Ga., May 29, 1962; s. John Jacob and Gloria Jewell (Wheelus) Young; m. Barbara Joan Schleihauf, Oct. 22, 1988; children: Nathan Jacob, William Joseph. BS in Aerospace Engring., Ga. Inst. Tech., 1985; MS in Aeronautics and Astronautics, Stanford U., 1987. Engr. in Tng., Ga. Intern US Senator Sam Nunn Intern Prog., Washington, 1984; engring. coop. Gen. Dynamics Ft. Worth Divsn., 1980-84; mem. tech. staff The BDM Corp., Huntsville, Ala., 1985-86, Rockwell Internat. Missile Systems Divsn., Duluth, Ga., 1987-88, Sandia Nat. Labs., Albuquerque, 1988-93; AIAA Congl. fellow profl. staff subcommittee on def. US Senate Appropriations Com., Washington, 1991-93, profl. staff subcommittee on def.; asst. sec. rsch. devel. & acquisition, USN US Dept. Def., Washington, 2001—05, dir. def. rsch. & engring., acquisition, tech. & logistics, 2005—. Organizer, coach BDM Co-ed. Softball team, Huntsville, Ala., 1986; big brother Big Bros., Big Sisters, Huntsville, Ala., 1986; tutor El Dorado HS, Albuquerque, 1989-90. Recipient AIAA Gen. Dynamics scholarship, 1984; fellow Coll. Engring, Stanford U., 1985; named Outstanding Young Engr., AIAA Atlanta Section, 1988. Fellow AIAA; mem. Briaerean Soc., Phi Kappa Phi, Tau Beta Pi, Sigma Gamma Tau, Phi Eta Sigma. Presbyterian. Office: US Dept Def 3030 Def Pentagon Rm 3C638 Washington DC 20301 *

YOUNG, JOHN LLOYD, actor; b. July 04; BA in Drama, Brown U. Actor: (Broadway plays) Jersey Boys, 2005 (Theatre World award, 2006, Outer Critics Cir. award, outstanding actor in a musical, 2006, Drama Desk award outstanding actor in a musical, 2006, Tony award, best performance by leading actor in a musical, 2006), (Off-Broadway) Spring Awakening, 2000, The Five Hysterical Girls Theorem, 2001, Sarah, Plain & Tall, 2002, The Summer of the Swans, 2003, (regional theatre) A Christmas Carol, Ferdinand, 2002, Spare Change, 2004, The Chosen, 2004 (named best featured actor in a play, NJ Star-Ledger, 2004), A Bronx Tale, 2005, The Drawer Boy, 2005; (TV series) Law & Order, 2002; (films) The Belligerents, The Roman Soldier, 2001, Moon River, 2001. Adv. bd. William Inge Festival. Mailing: c/o Nina Shreiber ACME NY 875 Avenue of the Americas New York NY 10001 Office Phone: 212-328-0386. Office Fax: 646-472-5203. E-mail: jlynyc@johnlloydyoung.com.

YOUNG, JOHN PAUL, accountant; s. Robert Emmet and Virginia Ann Young; m. Kelli Flanagan Flanagan; children: Emmet Flanagan, Beckett Flanagan. BS, King's Coll., Wilkes-Barre, Pa., 1989; JD, U. NC, Chapel Hill, 1994; LLM, Case Western Res. U., Clev., 1999. CPA Pa., 1991; bar: Pa. 2000, NY 1995, NJ 1994. Auditor Coopers & Lybrand, NYC, 1989—91; tax assoc. Deloitte & Touche, NYC, 1994—97; tax mgr. PriceWaterhouseCoopers, Clev., 1997—99; assoc. Duane Morris, Philadelphia, Pa., 1999—2005, Schnader, Harrison, Segal & Lewis, Phila., 2005—06; v.p., tax counsel ACE-INA, Phila., 2006—. Editor: Important Developments in Tax Aspects of Bankruptcy; contbr. articles to profl. jours. With Vols. for Indigent Program, Phila., 2000—06. Recipient Order of the Barristers, U. NC, Sch. Law, 1994; Moreau scholar, King's Coll., 1985—89. Mem.: FBA (tax sect.), ABA (tax sect.), Phila. Bar Assn. (tax sect.). Office: Ace-Ina 510 Walnut St Philadelphia PA 19106 Home Phone: 610-544-2366; Office Phone: 215-640-1566. Business E-Mail: john.young@ace-ina.com.

YOUNG, JOHN WATTS, retired astronaut; b. San Francisco, Sept. 24, 1930; s. William H. Y.; m. Susy Feldman; children by previous marriage: Sandra, John. BS in Aero. Engring, Ga. Inst. Tech., 1952; LLD (hon.), Western State U., 1969; D Applied Sci. (hon.), Fla. Technol. U., 1970; DSc (hon.), U. S.C., 1981, Brown U., 1983; DEng (hon.), Glasgow U., 2001; PhD (hon.), Ga. Tech. U., 2003. Joined USN, 1952, advanced through grades to capt.; test pilot, program mgr. F4 weapons systems projects, 1959-62; then maintenance officer Fighter Squadron 143, Naval Air Sta., Miramar, Calif.; chief astronaut office Flight Ops. Directorate NASA, 1974-87, spl. asst. dir. JSC for engring. ops., safety, 1987-96, assoc. dir. (tech.) JSC, 1996—2004; ret., 2004. Cons. NASA. Decorated DFC (3), D.S.M. (2); recipient NASA Disting. Svc. medal (4), NASA Exceptional Svc. medal (2), NASA Engring. Achievement medal, 1988, NASA Outstanding Leadership medal, 1992, NASA Outstanding Achievement medal, 1994, AIAA Goddard Astronautics award, 2000, Congl. Space medal of honor, 1981; named Disting. Young Alumni Svc. award Ga. Tech. Acad. Disting. Engrs., 1994; named to Nat. Aviation Hall of Fame, 1988, Ga. Aviation Hall of Fame, 1998, Tex. Aviation Hall of Fame, 2003, Ga. Tech. Engring. Hall of Fame, 2005. Fellow Am. Astronautical Soc. (Flight Achievement award 1972, 81, 83, Space Flight award 1993), Soc. Exptl. Test Pilots (Iven Kincheloe award 1972, 81), AIAA (Haley Astronautics award 1973, 82, 84, NASA Disting. Exec. 1998, 2001, Rotary Space Trophy 2000, Houston Hall of Fame 2002); mem. Sigma Chi. Achievements include being an astronaut NASA, made 1st two-man 3 orbit flight, Gemini 3, Mar. 1965, Gemini 10 3 day flight, 1966, Apollo 10 8-day flight lunar landing dress rehearsal, 1969, Apollo 16 11 day lunar landing and surface exploration, 1972; comdr. 54 hour, 36 orbit 1st flight of Space Shuttle, 1981, and 10-day orbital flight 1st flight Space Lab, 1983; dir. space shuttle br., astronaut office, 1973-75.

YOUNG, JON NATHAN, archaeologist; b. Hibbing, Minn., May 30, 1938; s. Robert Nathan Young and Mary Elizabeth (Barrows) Roy; m. Karen Sue Johnson, June 5, 1961 (div. May 1980); children: Shawn Nathan, Kevin Leigh; m. Tucker Heitman, June 18, 1988 (div. Apr. 1996). BA magna cum laude, U. Ariz., 1960, PhD, 1967; MA, U. Ky., 1962. Archeologist Nat. Park Svc. Southwest Archeol. Ctr., Globe and Tucson, Ariz., 1967-75; exec., camp dir. YMCA of Metro. Tucson, 1976-77; asst. dir. Kit Carson Meml. Found., Taos, N.Mex., 1978; co-dir. Las Palomas de Taos, 1979; archeologist Nat. Forest Svc., Carson Nat. Forest, Taos, 1980-99, Taos Ski Valley, 2000—05. Exec. order cons. U.S. Sec. Interior, 1973-75. Author: The Salado Culture in Southwestern Prehistory, 1967; co-author: Excavation of Mound 7, 1981, First-Day Road Log in Tectonic Development of the Southern Sangre de Cristo Mountains, 1990, The Gila Pueblo Salado, 1997. Active YMCA White Rag Soc. Grantee NEH, 1978; Ariz. Wilson Found., NSF, Ky. Rsch. Found. fellow, 1960-62; Baird Found., Bausch and Lomb, Elks; recipient cert. merit USDA, 1987, 89. Fellow AAAS, Am. Anthrop. Assn., Explorers Club, Royal Anthrop. Inst.; mem. Am. Com. for Preservation of Archaeological Collection, Current Anthropology Ariz. Archaeol. and Hist. Soc., Ariz. Hist. Soc., Friends of Taos Pub. Libr., New Mex. Heritage Preservation Alliance, Soc. Hist. Archaeology, Soc. Am. Archaeology, Southwest Forest Svc. Amigos, Millicent Rogers Mus., Pinal County Hist. Soc. (life), Taos Archaeol. Soc., Taos County Hist. Soc. (bd. dirs.), Taos Hist. Mus., Sigma Xi, Phi Beta Kappa, Alpha Kappa Delta, Phi Kappa Phi, Delta Chi. Home: HCR 74 Box 24826 El Prado NM 87529-9549 Home Phone: 505-776-8336.

YOUNG, JONATHAN, lawyer; BA in Govt. magna cum laude, U. Va., 1979; JD, Georgetown U., 1983. Law clk. to Hon. Caleb M. Wright US Dist. Ct. of Del.; trial atty. civil divsn. US Dept. Justice, Washington; atty. Anderson Kill & Olick PC, Shea & Gould, 1994—98; ptnr. Reed Smith LLP, NYC, 1998—, mem. exec. com. Office: Reed Smith 599 Lexington Ave 29th Fl New York NY 10022 Office Phone: 212-521-5414. Fax: 212-521-5450. Business E-Mail: jyoung@reedsmith.com.

YOUNG, JUDITH ANNE, animal conservationist; b. LA, Feb. 11, 1953; d. John Mahlstedt Young and Cynthia Sheilds Tunnicciff. CEO Otter Conservation Ctr., Statesboro, Ga., 1983—. Copyright U.S. Govt., 1995. Avocations: gardening, agriculture. Office Phone: 912-839-2100. Personal E-mail: judy@g-net.net.

YOUNG, JULIA ANNE, librarian, elementary school educator; b. El Campo, Tex., July 25, 1958; d. Harold Lane and Marcella Jeanne (Payne) Y. BA in English and French, Sam Houston State U., Huntsville, Tex., 1979; MBA, Sam Houston State U., 1982; M in Libr. and Info. Sci., U. Tex., 1986. Cert. tchr. secondary bus., elem. and secondary English 1-12, talented and gifted K-12, PK-12 learning resource ctrs., K-8 elem. gen., Tex., spl. tng. Libr. Media Specialist, Dallas, 2003-05. Cataloguer Sam Houston State U., 1976-85; mem. acquisitions and serials staff Tex. State Libr., Austin, 1985-86; cataloguer PCL Grad. Libr. U. Tex., Austin, 1985-86; libr., tchr. Dallas Ind. Sch. Dist., 1986—. Vol. voter registration, Huntsville, 1982—83; active Common Cause, Dallas, 1976, 2000; leader Girl Scouts U.S., Huntsville, 1976, Dallas, 1987—88; sec. PTA, 1998—2000; fin. com. adminstrv. bd. Highland Park United Meth. Ch., 1995—97; ch. choir Oak Lawn United Meth. Ch., 2001—02, mem. handbell choir, 2001—05. Recipient Books for Libr. award, 2004; grantee, Jr. League, Dallas, 1994, 1996, 2002, 2003, Spanish Embassy, 2002, NEH, 2005—06, NEA, 2005—06;, Tex. Edn. Agy. scholar, 2002. Mem. AAUW, Tex. Libr. Assn., Tex. Computer Educators' Assn., Dallas Emmaus Cmty., Dallas Assn. Sch. Librs. (chmn. interest group, area rep. 2005-06, scholarship com. chair 2006-07). Democrat. Avocations: swimming, reading, walking, needlecrafts, writing. Home: PO Box 190403 Dallas TX 75219-0403

YOUNG, JUNE HURLEY, elementary school educator, writer; b. Cleve., Jan. 30, 1932; d. Albrd C. Ching and Helen M. Walker; m. John Robert Young, Feb. 17, 1977 (dec.); children: Sean K. Hurley, Kathleen Hurley Coker. BA in Edn. cum laude, Fla. State U., 1953; Master's, U. So. Fla., 1979. Cert. tchr. Fla. Tchr. grade 5 Norwood Elem. Sch.; tchr. grades 5 and 6 Pasadena Elem. Sch., tchr. grade 1; tchr. kindergarten Romper Room TV, Kindergarten Corners', WEDU-TV, 1985, Baypoint Elem. Sch.; tchr. gifted and talented 16th St. Mid. Sch., 1987; realtor Frank T. Hurley Assocs., Realtor, Inc., 1950—. Mktg. dir., adminstrv. asst. Cohutta Lodge, Chatsorth, Ga., 2007. Author: The Don CeSar Story, 1975, How to Be Your Child's Best Teacher, 1980, Florida's Pinellas Peninsula, 1985, rev. edit., 1998, The Vinoy-Faded Glory Renewed, 1999; contbr. articles to newspapers. Pres. St. Petersburg Coterie, 1953—61, Pan Hellenic, St. Petersburg, 1965—67; chmn. Save the Don CeSar Hotel Com., St. Petersburg, 1971—72. Nominee Outstanding Tchr., 1957; recipient Outstanding Woman Vol. award, Eckerd Drug Co., 2000; grantee, Fla. Endowment of Arts, 1980—83. Mem.: Suntan Art Assn., Camp Farthest Out (sec.-leader 1980—2006), Pass-a-Grille Woman's Club (chorus mem. 1999—2005), Phi Kappa Phi. Republican. Methodist. Avocations: watercolor painting, designing glass jewelry. Home: 362 89th Ave NE Saint Petersburg FL 33702 Office Phone: 706-695-9601.

YOUNG, KENNETH WAYNE, environmental health specialist; b. Woodstock, Va., Feb. 12, 1947; s. Kenneth Woodrow and Florence Eleanor (Schmidt) Young; m. Sandra Lynn Sweet (div.); 1 child, James Ira. BS, East Tenn. State U., 1969. Social worker Surry County Social Svcs., Surry, Va., 1972—73; sanitarian Richmond City Health Dept., Richmond, Va., 1974—84, Caroline County Health Dept., Bowling Green, Va., 1984—86; sr. environ. health specialist Chesterfield (Va) Health Dept., 1986—. Editor: (Newsletter) Coalition Report, 1976—92. Comm. dir. Richmond Human Rights, Richmond, Va., 1973—93; pres. RHRC Found., Inc., Richmond, 1978—84. With US Army, 1970. Recipient Human Rights award, Richmond Human Rights Coalition, 1986. Mem.: ACLU, Va. Organizing Project, Richmond Peace Ctr., Richmond Friends Mtg. Democrat. Achievements include founder of Va. Ctrl. Am. Network, 1982. Home: 1942 N Junaluska Dr Richmond VA 23225-2322 Office: Chesterfield Health Dept PO Box 100 Chesterfield VA 23832 Office Phone: 804-751-4456. Office Fax: 804-717-6106. Business E-Mail: Wayne.Young@vdh.virginia.gov.

YOUNG, LAURA, choreographer, educator; b. Boston, Aug. 5, 1947; d. James Vincent and Adelaide Janet Young; m. Anthony Charles Catanzaro, Sept. 26, 1970 (div. Nov. 1981); m. Christopher Edward Mehl, Aug. 23, 1987. Grad. H.S., Cohasset, Mass. Dancer Met. Opera Ballet, NYC, 1971-73, Boston Ballet Co., 1963-65, prin. dancer, 1965-71, 73-89, ballet mistress, 1989-91. Guest tchr. Dance Tchrs. Club Boston, 1978—82, Dance Masters Assn., 1979, 90, 92, 93, Walnut Hill Sch., Natick, Mass., 1984—87, Natick, 1990—91, Granite State Ballet, 1993, Portland Ballet, Maine, Nat. Dance Theatre Bermuda, 1993, Worcester Performing Arts Sch., Mass., 1994, Alwin Sch. Dance Summer Intensive, Albuquerque, 1994—95, Ashland Youth Ballet, Ky., 1995, N.E. Regional Festival, 1996, Okla. Summer Arts Inst., 2000, Pitts. Ballet Theater Summer Program, 2000; asst. dir. Boston Ballet II, 1984—86, tchr., dir., 1986—96, dir. Summer Dance Program, 1986—94; dir. DanceLab, 2001—; 1st hon. mem. Dance Masters Assn., Chpt. 5, 1992; mem. faculty Boston Conservatory, 1990—94, Boston Ballet Sch., 2004—, prin., 1993—2004. Choreographer (ballets) Occasional Waltzes, 1984, Albinoni Suite, 1986, Champ Dances, 1987, A Place of Sound and Mind, 1988, Deadlock, 1989, Rumpelstiltskin, 1989. Recipient Leadership award Greater Boston C. of C., 1987; named Disting. Bostonian Boston's 350th Jubilee Com., 1980. Mem. Am. Guild Mus. Artists, Dance Masters Am. (hon.). Office: Boston Ballet Co 19 Clarendon St Boston MA 02116-6100 Office Phone: 617-456-6250. Business E-Mail: lyoung@bostonballet.com.

YOUNG, LAUREN SUE JONES, education educator; b. San Diego, July 21, 1947; d. Warren Calvin and Lola Esther Jones; 1 child, Forest McRay Young. AB, Occidental Coll., 1969; MS, San Diego State U., 1971; EdM, Harvard U., 1979, EdD, 1984. Adminstrv. asst. Child Devel. Research Unit, Nairobi, Kenya, 1969-70; asst. prof. San Diego State U., 1974—78, assoc. dir. Tchr. Corps., 1971—78; co-chmn. and mem. Harvard Ednl. Review, Cambridge, Mass., 1979-81; research assoc. The Huron Inst., Cambridge, 1980-82, Atari Cambridge Research Lab., Cambridge, 1982-84; policy analyst N.Y. State Dept. Social Services, Albany, 1984-85, spl. asst. to commr., 1985-87; assoc. prof. Mich. State U., East Lansing, 1987-2001; sr. program officer, dir. The Spencer Found., Chgo., 1998—; bd. dirs. Josephinum Acad., 1999—, bd. chair, 2005—. Cons. Am. Insts. for Rsch., Cambridge, 1980, Tchr. Corps, Boston area, 1978-80, instr., Pago Pago, Am. Samoa, 1979; rsch. assoc. A Study of H.S.'s, Cambridge, 1980-82; disting. visitor John D. and Catherine T. MacArthur Found., 1995-96. Co-editor: Too Little, Too Late, 1988; mem. editorial bd. Evaluation Rev. Jour., L.A., 1984-88, Jour. Negro Edn. Team mem. Operation Crossroads Africa, Morogoro, Tanzania, 1968; mem. program adv. bd. Spencer Found., 1992; chair bd. dirs. Josephinum Acad., Chgo., 2005-07. Recipient Danforth Found. fellow, St. Louis, 1978-84, tchr. scholar award, M.S.U., 1993. Mem. Am. Ednl. Research Assn. Office: The Spencer Foundation 625 N Michigan Ave Ste 1600 Chicago IL 60611-3109

YOUNG, LAURENCE RETMAN, biomedical engineer, educator; b. NYC, Dec. 19, 1935; s. Benjamin and Bess (Retman) Y.; m. Joan Marie Fisher, June 12, 1960; children: Eliot Fisher, Leslie Ann, Robert Retman. AB, Amherst Coll., 1957; SB, MIT, 1957, SM, 1959, ScD, 1962; Certificat de License (French Govt. fellow), Faculty of Sci. U. of Paris, France, 1958. Registered profl. engr., Mass. Engr. Sperry Gyroscope Co., Great Neck, NY, 1957; engr. NASA Instrumentation Lab., MIT, 1958-60, asst. prof. aero. and astronautics, 1962-67, assoc. prof., 1967-70, prof., 1970—, payload specialist spacelab life sci., 1991-93; Apollo Program prof., chair in astronautics MIT, Cambridge, 1995—; prof. Baylor Coll. Medicine, Houston, 1996—2003; prof. of health sci. and tech. Harvard MIT, 2003—. Dir. Nat. Space Biomed. Rsch. Inst., 1997-01; summer lectr. U. Ala., Huntsville, 1966-68; lectr. Med. Sch. Harvard U., 1970-78; mem. tng. com. biomed. engring. NIH, 1971-73; mem. com. space medicine and biology Space Sci. Bd., NAS, 1974-77, chmn. vestibular panel summer study of life scis. in space, 1977; mem. com. engring. and clin. care NAE, 1970; mem. Air Force Sci. Adv. Bd., 1979-85; mem. Air Force Studies Bd., NRC, 1982, Aeros. and Space Engrs. Bd., 1982-87; mem. NRC Com. on Space Sta., 1987, 1991—, Com. on Human Exploration Space, 1990, Com. on Human Factors, 1990—; CHABA coun. NASA Task Force on Sci. Uses of Space Sta., 1982-85; vis. prof. Swiss Fed. Inst. Tech., Zurich, 1972-73, Conservatoire Nationale des Arts and Metiers, Paris, 1972-73, Stanford U., 1987-88; vis. scientist Kantonsspital Zurich, 1972-73; prin. investigator vestibular expts. on Spacelabs— 1, SLS-1, 2 and D-1, 1977—; cons. Applied Sci. Lab., NASA, Gulf & Western, Link div. Singer Co., Boeing, Lockheed, others; payload specialist Space Shuttle STS-58 (Spacelab SLS-2), NASA Johnson Space Ctr., 1992—; vis. prof. Coll. de France, Paris, 2003. Contbg. author: chpt. on vestibular system Medical Physiology, 1974, Handbook of Physiology, 1983, Encyclopedia of Neuroscience, 1987; editorial bd. chpt. on vestibular system Internat. Jour. Man-Machine

Studies, 1966-75, Neurosci., 1976-92; contbr. numerous articles to profl. jours. Recipient Pub. Svc. Group Achievement award NASA, 1984, Exceptional Civilian Svc. award USAR, 1985, Koetser Found. prize, 1998. Fellow IEEE (Franklin V. Taylor award 1963, First Ann. Space Life Sci. lectr. 1990), AIAA (Dryden lectr. 1981), Aerospace Medical Assn. (Jeffries Medical Rsch. award 1992), Aerospace Human Factor Assn. (Paul Hensen award 1995), Am. Inst. Med. and Biol. Engring., US Ski Assn. (award of merit 1976), Explorers Club; mem. NAE, Inst. Medicine, Am. Physiol. Soc. (1st lectr. in aerospace life scis. 1990), Biomed. Engring. Soc. (founding/charter mem., dir. 1972-75, pres. 1979-80, Alza lectr. 1984), Aerospace Med. Assn., ASTM (com. on snow skiing 1975—, chmn. 1988-93), Internat. Soc. Skiing Safety (bd. dirs. 1977-85), Internat. Fedn. Automatic Control (tech. com. biomed. engring. 1975-85), AIAA (working group for simulator facilities 1976-80), Nat. Acad. Engrs., Inst. Medicine, Internat. Acad. Astronautics (corr.), Barany Soc., Cosmos Club, Tau Beta Pi. Achievements include research in instrumentation and basic and applied research in field of vestibular function; psychophysical work on semicircular canal and otolith function led to models which are applied to flight simulator motion control and are being extended to include visually-induced motion effects; ski injurys. Home: 217 Thorndike St Apt 108 Cambridge MA 02141-1504 Office: MIT Man-Vehicle Lab Rm 37-219 Cambridge MA 02139 Business E-Mail: lry@mit.edu.

YOUNG, LAWRENCE, electrical engineering educator; b. Hull, Eng., July 5, 1925; arrived in Can., 1955; naturalized, 1972; s. Herbert and Dora Y.; m. Margaret Elisabeth Jane, Jan. 5, 1951. BA, Cambridge U., Eng., 1946, PhD, 1950, DSc, 1963. Asst. lectr. Imperial Coll., London, 1952-55; mem. research staff B.C. Research Council, 1955-63; assoc. prof. U. B.C., Vancouver, 1963-65, prof. dept. elec. engring., 1965-90, prof. emeritus, 1990—. Author: Anodic Oxide Films, 1961; contbr. articles to profl. jours. Recipient Callinan award Dielectrics div. Electrochemical Soc., 1983, Can. Electrochem. Gold medal, 1990. Fellow IEEE, Royal Soc. Can., Electrochem. Soc. Office: U BC Dept Elec and Computer Engring Vancouver BC Canada V6T 1W5 Business E-Mail: youngl@interchange.ubc.ca.

YOUNG, LOWELL SUNG-YI, health facility administrator, medical educator; b. Honolulu, Dec. 5, 1938; AB, Princeton U., 1960; MD, Harvard U., 1964. Di;omate Am. Bd. Internal Medicine with subspecialty in infectious diseases. Intern, jr. asst. resident, sr. asst. resident med. divsn. Bellevue Hosp. and Meml. Hosp., NYC, 1964-67; fellow in medicine Cornell U. Med. Coll., 1965-67; epidemic intelligence officer bacterial diseases br. Nat. Communicable Disease Ctr., Atlanta, 1967-69, chief spl. pathogens sect., 1968-69; spl. postdoctoral rsch. fellow Nat. Inst. Allergy and Infectious Diseases, 1969-70; rsch. fellow in medicine Meml. Hosp./Cornell U. Med. Coll., 1969-70; clin. asst. physicisn infectious disease svc. dept. medicine Meml. Hosp., 1970-72, assoc. dir. microbiology lab., 1971-72; instr. in medicine Cornell U. Med. Coll., 1970-72; chief divsn. infectious disease Calif. Pacific Med. Ctr., San Francisco, 1985-99; asst. clinician Sloan-Kettering Inst. for Cancer Rsch., 1971-72; dir. Kuzell Inst., San Francisco, 1985—; asst., assoc. prof. med. UCLA, 1972—85. Adj. prof. pharmacy U. of Pacific, San Francisco, 1989-95; mem. microbiology and invectious diseases adv. com. Nat. Inst. Allergy and Infectious Diseases, 1981-85, mem. allergy and immunology rsch. com., 1975-79; mem. adv. coun. Nat. Infectious diseases, 1996-2000; mem. staff Calif. Pacific Med. Ctr., Mt. Zion Hosp. and Med. Ctr., U. Calif., San Francisco. Mem. editl. bd. Antimicrobial Agts. and Chemotherapy, Infection and Immunity; contbr. numerous articles to profl. jours., chpts. to books. Recipient Alexander D. Langmuir prize Epidemic Intelligence Svc., 1970, Garrod medal Brit. Soc., 1992. Fellow ACP (mem. med. self-assessment com.), Infectious Diseases Soc. Am. (councillor 1983-85); mem. Am. Soc. for Clin. Investigation, Am. Fedn. for Clin. Rsch., Am. Soc. for Microbiology, Western Soc. for Clin. Rsch., Internat. Immunocompromised Host Soc., Brit. Soc. Antimicrobial Chemotherapy. Office: Kuzell Inst 2200 Webster St Ste 305 San Francisco CA 94115-1821 Office Phone: 415-600-1734. Business E-Mail: younglx@sutterhealth.org.

YOUNG, LUCIA PATAT, psychotherapist; b. Charleston, SC, Aug. 19, 1947; d. Leon Philip and Amelia (Wallace) P.; m. David Michael Young, Sept. 2, 1972; children: David Michael II, Allison Amelia. BS, U. S.C., 1969; MEd, EdS, U. Fla., 1991, PhD, 1996. Lic. mental health counselor Nat. Bd. Cert. Counselors. Mental health assoc. Med. U. S.C., Charleston, 1969; exec. sec. Mass. Gen. Hosp., Boston, 1969-73, sr. biol. and biochem. technician dept. neurology, summer 1974; adminstrv. asst. Harvard U., Cambridge, Mass., 1973-74; tchr. biology, anatomy and physiology Brimmer & May Sch., Chestnut Hill, Mass., 1974-76; mng. editl. asst. Molecular and Cellular Biochemistry, Gainesville, Fla., 1982-86; adminstrv. asst. U. Fla. Found., Gainesville, Fla., 1986-89; addictions counselor Bridge House Residential Ctr., Gainesville, 1990-91; sch. guidance counselor Trenton (Fla.) Middle and H.S., 1991-92; mental health counselor, children's outpatient dept. Mental Health Svcs., Gainesville, 1992-93; children's bereavement counselor, family counselor Hospice of N. Ctrl. Fla., Gainesville, 1993-96; pvt. practice Gainesville, 1996—2000, Gloucester, Mass., 2000—01, Ellsworth, Maine, 2001—; trauma therapist Arbour Trauma Counseling Ctr., Allston, Mass., 2000—01. Mem. AAAS, Am. Assn. Marriage and Family Therapy, Internat. Assn. Eating Disorders Profls., Kappa Delta Pi, Chi Sigma Iota. Office: 114 State St Ellsworth ME 04605 Home: Po Box 408 Sullivan ME 04664-0408 Office Phone: 207-667-4334. Personal E-mail: luciayoungly@yahoo.com.

YOUNG, LUCY CLEAVER, retired physician; b. Aug. 8, 1943; d. Oliver B. and Ada (Smith) Cleaver; m. Lynn H. Young, Feb. 4, 1968 (div. 1977); m. Lynn H. Young, Apr. 2, 1986; 1 child, Clinton Oliver. BS in Chemistry, Wheaton Coll., Ill., 1965; MD, Ohio State U., 1969. Diplomate Am. Bd. Family Practice, Bd. Ins. Medicine. Rotating intern Riverside Meth. Hosp., Columbus, Ohio, 1969—70; resident Trumbull Meml. Hosp., Warren, Ohio, 1970—71; practice medicine specializing in family practice West Chicago, Ill., 1971—73, Paw Paw and Mendota, Ill., 1973—78; co-founder, med. dir. Wholistic Health Ctr. of Mendota, 1976—78; asst. med. dir. Gt. Lakes head office Met. Life Ins. Co., Aurora, Ill., 1979—80; med. dir. Commonwealth Life Ins. Co., Louisville, 1980—85; locum tenens family practice Kron Med. Corp. of Chapel Hill, NC, 1986—89; physician Red Bird Mission & Med. Ctr., Beverly, Ky., 1989—90; family practice floater Ochsner Clinic satellites, New Orleans, 1990—2006; ret. Assoc. prof. U. Ill. Abraham Lincoln Sch. Medicine, 1976-79; faculty monitor MacNeal Meml. Hosp. Family Practice Ctr. (Ill.), 1979-80; faculty preceptor U. Louisville Family Practice Dept., 1981-85; clin. faculty preceptor La. State U. Sch. Medicine, 1992-2006; mem. staffs Ctrl. DuPage Hosp., Winfield, Ill., 1971-73, Mendota Cmty. Hosp., 1973-80, Ochsner Found. Hosp., New Orleans, 1991-2006; musician La. Via de Cristo, 2003-05. Vol. Red Bird Med. Ctr., 1985—; part-time worship coord. Hosanna Luth. Ch., Mandeville, La., 1996-97; musician, lay preacher, nursing home visitor, 1990—. Fellow Am. Acad. Family Practice; mem. Christian Med. and Dental Assns. (del. to Ho. 1995-2000). Lutheran. Home: PO Box 0730 Madisonville LA 70447-0730

YOUNG, MARGARET LABASH, librarian, information consultant, editor; b. Bridgeport, Conn., Aug. 17, 1926; d. George and Mary (Feltovic) Labash; m. Harold Chester Young, June 7, 1958 (div. July 1991); children: Jeffery Avery, Amy Margaret. BA, Cornell U., 1948; AMLS, U. Mich., 1959. Mktg. grader Harvard Bus. Sch., Boston, 1949-52; ops. rsch. sales asst. Arthur D. Little, Inc., Boston, 1953-57; reference libr. U. Mich., Dearborn, 1959-62; editor Gale Rsch., Detroit, 1964-74, Mpls., 1977-88; libr. Salzburg (Austria) Seminar, 1981-83; editor, info. cons. self employed, Hopkins, Minn., 1989—. Tax libr. cons. KPMG Peat Marwick, LLP, Mpls., 1991—; indexer Small Bus. Innovation Rsch., Minn. Project Innovation, Mpls., 1990-97. Co-editor: Directory of Special Libraries and Information Centers, edits. 3-6, 1974-81, Life Sciences Organizations and Agencies Directory, 1988; editor: Scientific and Technical Organizations and Agencies Directory, 1985, 2d edit., 1987. Host family Am. Field Svcs., 1979-80, 80-81; mem. steering com. Twin Cities Internat. Citizens Award, 1996-99. Mem. Spl. Librs. Assn. (internat. rels. chair Minn. chpt. 1994—2003, Quality in Action award, Minn. Chpt. Spl. Librs. Assn., 2003, Fannie Simon award Pub. divsn. 1989), Am. Soc. Indexers, Beta Phi Mu. Democrat. Episcopalian. Avocations: travel, gardening, classical music, dance, aerobics. Home: 313 Farmdale Rd W Hopkins MN 55343-7111

YOUNG, MARK V., sports association executive; With Smith Hulsey and Busey; sr. atty. The Charter Co.; gen. counsel Assn. Tennis Profls., Ponte Vedra Beach, Fla., 1990—, exec. v.p., CEO Ams., 2006—. Office: Assn Tennis Profls 201 ATP Tour Blvd Ponte Vedra Beach FL 32082 Office Phone: 904-285-8000. Office Fax: 904-285-5966. *

YOUNG, MARLENE ANNETTE, lawyer; b. Portland, Oreg., Mar. 3, 1946; d. Hardy Shelby and Eunice Jean (Gregory) Y.; m. Abdullah Samir Rifai, June 3, 1973 (div. May 1981); m. John Hollister Stein, Jan. 1, 1986. BS, Portland State U., 1967; PhD, Georgetown U., 1973; JD, Willamette U., 1975. Bar: Oreg. 1975. Dir. research Multnomah County Sheriff's Office, Portland, 1975-77; sole practice Wilsonville, Oreg., 1975-81; exec. dir. Applied Systems Research & Data, Wilsonville, 1976-81, Nat. Orgn. Victim Assistance, Washington, 1981—. Instr. Essex Community Coll., 1971-73, U. Utah, 1976-78, Portland State U., 1979; cons. U. Research Corp., Washington, 1979-83, ABT Assocs., Boston, 1984—. Author: Victim Service System, 1983; (manuals) Patrol Officers and Crime Victims, 1984, Prosecutors: Attorneys for the People, Advocates for the Victims, 1984; editor: Justice and Older Americans, 1977; contbr. articles to profl. jours. Mem. Ways and Means Com., Wilsonville City, 1977-79, planning commn., 1979-81; Bd. visitors Willamette Coll. Law, Salem, Oreg., 1981-83; bd. dirs. Chemeketa Community Coll., Salem, 1979. Recipient Presdl. award Nat. Orgn. Victim Assistance, Washington, 1981, 92, Pub.Policy award World Fedn. Mental Health, Washington, 1983, Found. for Improvementof Justice award, 1988. Mem. ABA (criminal justice sect., adv. bd. 1981-90), Am. Profl. Soc. Abuse of Children (bd. dirs. 1986—), Soc. Traumatic Stress Studies (bd. dirs. 1985—, treas.), World Soc. Victimology (adv. bd. 1979—, exec. com. 1986—, v.p., Hans Von Hentig award 1985). Democrat. Methodist. Avocations: piano, running, gardening, pets.

YOUNG, MARVIN OSCAR, lawyer; b. Union, Mo., Apr. 4, 1929; s. Otto Christopher and Irene Adelheide (Barlage) Y.; m. Sue Carol Mathews, Aug. 23, 1952; children: Victoria Leigh, Kendall Marvin. AB, Westminster Coll., 1951; JD, U. Mich., 1954, LLD, 1989. Bar: Mo. 1954. Practice law firm Thompson, Mitchell, Thompson Douglas, St. Louis, 1954-55, 57-58; atty. Mo. Farmers Assn., Columbia, 1958-67; exec. v.p. First Mo. Corp., Columbia, 1965-68; v.p. ops. MFA-Central Coop., Columbia, 1967-68; v.p., gen. counsel, sec. Peabody Coal Co., St. Louis, 1968-82; gen. counsel Peabody Holding Co., Inc., St. Louis, 1983-85; also dir., sec. subs. and affiliates Peabody Coal Co.; ptnr. Gallop, Johnson & Neuman, St. Louis, 1986—, chmn. corp. dept., 1988-90, chmn. energy dept., 1990—. City atty., Warson Woods, Mo., 1990—; spkr. in field. Contbr. articles to profl. jours. Pres. Warson Woods PTA, 1974-75; trustee Met. Sewer Dist. St. Louis, 1974-80, chmn. 1978-80; mem. Mo. Energy Coun., 1973-77, Mo. Environ. Improvement and Energy Resources Authority, 1983-87, vice-chmn. 1986-87; trustee Eastern Mineral Law Found., 1983-98; pres. Alumni Assn. Westminster Coll., Fulton, Mo., 1978-80, trustee coll., 1977—, exec. com., 1978-2003, chmn. 1986-90, chmn. investment com., 1998-2002; chmn. Churchill Meml. and Libr., Fulton, 1992-2000; mem. chancellor's coun. adv. bd. U. Mo., St. Louis, 1992—; trustee Stages—St. Louis, 2001—; lawyers adv. coun. Gt. Plains Legal Found., Kansas City, Mo., 1976-84; mem. Rep. Com. Boone County, Mo., 1962-68, chmn. legis. dist. com., 1962-64, 66-68; alt. del. Rep. Nat. Conv., 1968; pres. Clayton Twp. Rep. Club, 1973-77; mem. St. Lucas United Ch. of Christ, 2004—. Capt. USAF, 1955-57. Churchill fellow Churchill Meml. and Libr., Fulton, Mo.; recipient Alumni Merit award Westminster Coll., 1972; named Coal Lawyer of Yr., Nat. Coal Assn., 1994 Mem. ABA, Mo. Bar Assn., Bar Assn. Met. St. Louis, Round Table Club St. Louis, John Marshall Rep. Lawyers Club (pres. 1977), Mo. Athletic Club, Shamrock Club St. Louis County, Rotary (bd. dirs. St. Louis club 1993-95), Barristers Soc. (life), Order of Coif (life), Masons, Shriners. Home: 555 Flanders Dr Saint Louis MO 63122-1617 Office: Gallop Johnson & Neuman LC 101 S Hanley Rd Ste 1700 Saint Louis MO 63105-3489 Office Phone: 314-615-6210. E-mail: moyoung@gjn.com.

YOUNG, MARY ELIZABETH, history professor; b. Utica, NY, Dec. 16, 1929; d. Clarence Whitford and Mary Tippit Y. BA, Oberlin Coll., 1950; PhD, Cornell U., 1955. Instr. dept. history Ohio State U., Columbus, 1955-58, asst. prof., 1958-63, assoc. prof., 1963-69, prof., 1969-73; prof. history U. Rochester, NY, 1973—2000, prof. emeritus, 2000—. Cons. in field. Author: Redskins, Ruffleshirts, and Rednecks: Indian Allotments in Alabama and Mississippi, 1830-1860, 1961; co-editor, contbr.: The Frontier in American Development: Essays in Honor of Paul Wallace Gates, 1969. Recipient Pelzer award Miss. Valley Hist. Assn., 1955, award Am. Studies Assn., 1982, Ray A. Billington award, 1982; Shalkenbach Found. grantee, 1951-55, Social Sci. Rsch. Coun. grantee, 1968-69; Ezra Cornell fellow Cornell U., 1951-55. Mem. Am. Hist. Assn., Orgn. Am. Historians, Soc. for Historians of the Early Am. Republic, Am. Antiquarian Soc. Home: 2230 Clover St Rochester NY 14618-4124 Office: U Rochester Dept History Rochester NY 14627 Office Phone: 585-275-2054. Business E-Mail: yngm@mail.rochester.edu.

YOUNG, MERWIN CRAWFORD, political science professor; b. Phila., Nov. 7, 1931; s. Ralph Aubrey and Louise (Merwin) Y.; m. Rebecca Conrad, Aug. 17, 1957; children: Eva Colcord, Louise Conrad, Estelle Merwin, Emily Harriet. BA, U. Mich., 1953; postgrad., Inst. Hist. Rsch. U. London, 1955-56, Inst d'Etudes Politiques, U. Paris, 1956-57; PhD, Harvard U., 1964; DSc (hon.), Fla. Internat. U., 1998. Asst. prof. polit. sci. U. Wis., Madison, 1963-66, assoc. prof., 1966-69, prof., 1969—2001, emeritus, 2001—, Rupert Emerson prof., 1983; H. Edwin Young prof., 1994; chmn. African Studies Program U. Wis., Madison, 1964-68, chmn. dept. polit. sci., 1969-72, 84-87, assoc. dean Grad. Sch., 1968-71, acting dean Coll. Letters and Sci., 1992-93. Vis. prof. Makerere U. Coll., Kampala, Uganda, 1965-66; dean Faculty of Social Sci. Nat. U., Lubumbashi, Zaire, 1973-75; Fulbright prof. U. Dakar, Senegal, 1987-88. Author: Politics in the Congo, 1965, The Politics of Cultural Pluralism, 1976 (Herskovits prize 1977, Ralph Bunche prize 1979), Ideology and Development in Africa, 1982, The African Colonial State in Comparative Perspective, 1994 (Gregory Luebbert prize 1995); co-author: Cooperatives and Development, 1981, The Rise and Decline of the Zairian State, 1985; editor: The Rising Tide of Cultural Pluralism: The Nation-State at Bay?, 1993, Ethnic Diversity and Public Policy, 1998, The Accommodation of Cultural Diversity, 1999; co-editor: Dilemmas of Democracy in Nigeria, 1995, Beyond State Crisis? Postcolonial Africa and Post-Soviet Eurasia in Comparative Perspective, 2002. Served to 1st lt. U.S. Army, 1953-55. Fellow Woodrow Wilson Internat. Ctr. for Scholars, 1983—84; Social Sci. Rsch. fellow, 1967—68, Ford Faculty fellow, 1972—73, Guggenheim Found. fellow, 1977—78, vis. fellow, Inst. for Advanced Study, Princeton, 1980—81. Mem. AAAS, Am. Acad. Arts and Scis., Am. Polit. Sci. Assn., African Studies Assn. (pres. 1982-83, Disting. Africanist award 1991), Coun. Fgn. Rels. Home: 639 Crandall St Madison WI 53711-1836 Office: U Wis Dept Polit Sci North Hall 1050 Bascom Mall Madison WI 53706-1389 Business E-Mail: young@polisci.wisc.edu.

YOUNG, MICHAEL ANTHONY, lawyer; b. Lima, Ohio, Sept. 3, 1960; s. William John and Bettye Jean (Day) Y. BS magna cum laude, U. Cen. Fla., 1981; JD with honors, Fla. State U., 1984. Bar: Ga. 1984, Fla. 1985. Assoc. Kilpatrick & Cody, Atlanta, 1984-86, Stokes, Lazarus & Carmichael, Atlanta, 1986-89; pvt. practice, Atlanta, 1989—. Jud. intern U.S. Dist. Ct. (no. dist.) Fla., 1984; weekend atty. Atlanta Legal Aid Soc., 1985-86. Rsch. editor Fla. State U. Law Rev., 1982-84; contbr. articles to legal jours. Dir., pres. ChildKind Found. Mem. ABA, Assn. Trial Lawyers of Am., Fla. Bar Assn., Ga. Bar Assn., Atlanta Bar Assn. Avocations: scuba diving, golf, weightlifting. Home: 5275 S Trimble Rd NE Atlanta GA 30342-2174 Office: 1050 Crown Pointe Pkwy Ste 330 Atlanta GA 30338 Office Phone: 770-698-5700.

YOUNG, MICHAEL BRIAN, professional baseball player; b. Covina, Calif., Oct. 19, 1976; m. Cristina Barbosa, Nov. 25, 2000. Student, U. Calif., Santa Barbara. Draft pick Toronto Blue Jays, 1997; infielder Tex. Rangers, 2000—. Mem. US Team World Baseball Classic, 2006. Named All-Star Game MVP, 2006; named to Am. League All-Star Team, 2004—07; recipient Harold McKinney Good Guy award, Dallas-Ft. Worth Baseball Writers' Assn. of Am., 2003. Achievements include winning batting title, Am. League of Maj. League Baseball, 2005; led Am. League in hits (221), 2005. Avocations: golf, billiards. Office: Texas Rangers Baseball Club 1000 Ballpark Way Arlington TX 76011 *

YOUNG, MICHAEL CHUNG-EN, allergist, immunologist, pediatrician; b. Chgo., July 10, 1953; s. Koon C. and Siu Fun (Hui) Y.; m. Karen Lee Young, Apr. 7, 1979; 1 child, Liane. AB cum laude, Harvard Coll., 1975; MD, Yale U., 1979. Diplomate Am. Bd. Allergy and Immunology, Am. Bd. Pediatrics, Nat. Bd. Med. Examiners. Resident pediat. Children's Hosp., Boston, 1979—82, fellow in allergy and immunology, 1982—84, asst. in medicine (immunology), attending physician, 1984—; clin. instr. pediat. Harvard Med. Sch., Boston, 1985—2001, asst. clin. prof. pediat., 2002—. Mem. active staff South Shore Hosp., South Weymouth, Mass., 1985—. Author: Peanut Allergy Answer Book, 2001, 2d edit., 2006; contbr. articles to profl. jours. Named physician honoree, Asthma and Allergy Found. Am., 2001; named to Guide to Top Doctors, Ctr. for the Study of Svcs.; recipient Nat. Rsch. Svc. award, NIH, 1982—84, Mariel C. Furlong award for Making a Difference, Food Allergy & Anaphylaxis Network, 2005. Fellow Am. Coll. Allergy and Immunology (Parke Davis Allergy Fellows award 1983), Am. Acad. Allergy and Immunology, Am. Coll. Chest Physicians, Am. Acad. Pediatrics; mem. New Eng. Soc. Allergy, Mass. Allergy Soc. (pres. 1992-94), Mass. Med. Soc. Office: South Shore Allergy & Asthma Specialists 851 Main St South Weymouth MA 02190-1612

YOUNG, MICHAEL KENT, academic administrator, law educator; b. Sacramento, Nov. 4, 1949; s. Vance Lynn and Ethelyn M. (Sowards) Young; m. Suzan Kay Stewart, June 1, 1972; children: Stewart, Kathryn, Andrew. BA summa cum laude, Brigham Young U., Provo, Utah, 1973; JD magna cum laude, Harvard U., Cambridge, Mass., 1976. Bar: Calif. 1976, NY 1985. Law clk. to Justice Benjamin Kaplan, Supreme Jud. Ct. Mass., Boston, 1976—77; law clk. to Justice William H. Rehnquist U.S. Supreme Ct., Washington, 1977—78; assoc. prof., prof., Fuyo prof. Japanese law Columbia U., NYC, 1978—98, dir. Program Internat. Human Rights and Religious Liberties, 1995—98; dir. Ctr. Japanese Legal Studies Ctr. for Korean Legal Studies, NYC, 1985—98; dean, Lobingier prof. comparative law and jurisprudence George Washington U. Sch. of Law, Washington, 1998—2004; dep. legal advisor U.S. Dept. State, Washington, 1989—91, dep. under sec. for econ. affairs, 1991—93, amb. for trade and environ. affairs, 1992—93; pres. U. Utah, Salt Lake City, 2004—. Mem. US Commn. on Internat. Religious Freedom, 1998—2005, chair, 2001—02, 2002—03, vice chair, 2002—03; vis. scholar law faculty U. Tokyo, 1978—80, 1983; vis. prof. Waseda U., 1989; chmn. bd. advisors Japan Soc., 1996—98; counsel select subcom. on arms transfers to Bosnia US Ho. of Reps., 1996; mem. steering com. Law Profs. for Dole, 1996; mem. com. on internat. jud. rels. US Jud. Conf., 1999—2005; mem. Brown v. Bd. Edn. 50th Anniversary Commemoration Com.; chair NAFTA labor agreement adv. com. Dept. of Labor; mem. trade and environ. policy adv. com. US Trade Rep. Office, 2003—. Author: Fundamentals of U.S. Trade Law, 2001, Japanese Law in Context, 2001. Bd. visitors USAF Acad., 2000—02; bd. dirs. Salt Lake C. of C., Envision Utah, Alliance for Unity, Herbert I. and Elsa B. Michael Found., The Craig H. Neilsen Found., Magnet Bank. Named Communicator of Yr., Publs. Soc. Am. and Internat. Assn. Bus. Communicators; recipient Disting. Contbns. to Human Rights award, Ctr. for Internat. Religious Freedom, Brigham Young U., 2004, Excellence in Edn. award, Utah Hispanic C. of C., Excellence in Ethics award, Utah Valley State U., 2005, Internat. Humanitarian award, Pub. Affairs Office, LDS Ch., 2006, Disting. Svc. award, J. Reuben Clark Soc., 2006, The Helping Hand award, Utah Youth Village, 2006; POSCO Rsch. Inst. fellow, 1995—98, Japan Found. fellow, 1979—80, Fulbright fellow, 1983—84. Fellow: Am. Bar Found.; mem.: Coun. Fgn. Rels. Mem. Lds Ch. Avocations: skiing, scuba diving, photography. Home: 1480 Military Way Salt Lake City UT 84103 Office: U Utah 201 S President's Cir Rm 203 Salt Lake City UT 84112 Office Phone: 801-581-5701. Business E-Mail: president@utah.edu.

YOUNG, MICHAEL KENT, physics professor; b. Arcadia, Calif., Aug. 12, 1965; s. Howard Kent and Barbara Loiuse Young; m. Renee Ann Ellison, July 22, 1989; children: Ryan Michael, Tyler Kent, Dylan Lee. BS, Point Loma Nazarene U., San Diego, 1987; MS, UCLA, 1989, PhD, 1993. Engr. McDonnell Douglas Corp., Monrovia, Calif., 1984—87; prof. physics Antelope Valley Coll., Lancaster, Calif., 1991—95, Pasadena City Coll., Calif., 1992—95, Santa Barbara City Coll., Calif., 1995—. Advisor Natural Philosophers, Santa Barbara, 1995—99, Gaming Club, Santa Barbara, 2003—, Engring. and Sci. Club, Santa Barbara, 2007—; chair Instrnl. Tech., Santa Barbara, 1997—99; senator Santa Barbara City Coll., Calif., 1997—2000, chair dept. physics, engring., 2000—. Mem.: AAPT (assoc.). Office: Santa Barbara City Coll 721 Cliff Dr Santa Barbara CA 93109 Home Phone: 805-642-4430. Business E-mail: young@sbcc.edu.

YOUNG, MICHAEL PHILLIP, orthopedist, surgeon; b. Oak Park, Ill., Jan. 14, 1952; s. James William and Irene Olga Young; m. Kristine Marie Curran, Sept. 7, 1974; children: Vanessa, Stephen, Allison Elizabeth. BS cum laude, U. Ill., 1974, MD, 1978. Diplomate Am. Bd. Orthop. Surgery, 1985. Intern Loyola U. Med. Ctr., Maywood, Ill., 1978—79, orthop. surgery resident, 1979—83; clin. instr. Hines Veterans Adminstr., 1983—85; ptrn. Lake Cook Orthop. Assoc., Barrington, Ill., 1983—. Bd. dirs. Tricounty Physicians Assn., Barrington, 1996—2000; gov. coun. Good Shepherd Hosp., Barrington, 1992—2002. Adult leadership Boy Scouts of Am., 1992—94; coach Barrington Youth Soccer, 1994—95. Fellow: Am. Acad. Orthop. Surgery, Am. Coll. Surgeons. Office: Lake Cook Orthop Assoc 27401 W Highway 22 Ste 125 Barrington IL 60010 Office Phone: 847-381-0388.

YOUNG, MICHAEL WARREN, geneticist, educator; b. Miami, Fla., Mar. 28, 1949; s. Lloyd George and Mildred (Tillery) Y.; m. Laurel Ann Eckhardt, Dec. 27, 1978; children: Natalie, Arissa. BA, U. Tex., 1971, PhD, 1975. NIH postdoctoral fellow Stanford (Calif.) U. Med. Sch., 1975-77; asst. prof. genetics Rockefeller U., NYC, 1976—83, assoc. prof., 1984—88, prof., 1988—, Richard and Jeanne Fisher prof., 2004—. Investigator Howard Hughes Med. Inst., N.Y.C., 1987-96; adv. panel on genetic biology NSF, Washington, 1983-87; spl. advisor Am. Cancer Soc., N.Y.C., 1985—; spl. reviewer genetics study sect. NIH, Bethesda, Md., 1990—, cell biology study sect., 1993-97; head Rockefeller unit NSF Sci. and Tech. Ctr. Biol. Timing, 1991-2001; dir. Levy/White Ctr. Mind, Brain and Behavioral Studies Rockefeller U., N.Y.C., 2000-2002, v.p. academic affairs, 2004-. Contbr. articles to profl. jours. Meyer Found. fellow, N.Y.C.,

1978-83. Fellow N.Y. Soc. Fellows; mem. AAAS, Genetics Soc. Am., Am. Soc. Microbiologists, N.Y. Acad. Scis., Harvey Soc. (treas. 2001-04). Achievements include research on transposable DNA elements, molecular genetics of nerve and muscle development, biological clocks, molecular control of circadian rhythms. Home: 51 Greenwoods Rd Old Tappan NJ 07675-7018 Office: The Rockefeller Univ 1230 York Ave New York NY 10021-6399

YOUNG, PATRICIA JANEAN, speech pathology/audiology services professional; b. San Diego, Nov. 30, 1953; d. Bernarr E. and Janean Romig Young. AA, Palomar C.C., San Marcos, Calif., 1974; BA, Calif. State U., Chico, 1976; MA, Calif. State U., Long Beach, 1981. Cert. clin. competence Am. Speech-Lang.-Hearing Assn., lic. speech pathologist Calif., cert. tchr. Calif. Mgmt. trainee Robinson's Dept. Store, LA, 1976—78; speech and hearing screening coord. Riverview Hearing, Speech, Lang. Ctrs., Long Beach, 1978—81, speech pathologist, 1981—84, Lake Elsinore Unified Sch. Dist., Calif., 1998—; speech pathologist, dir. Speech Pathology Svcs., Carlsbad and Temecula, Calif., 1984—. Prodr. TV shows on comm. disorders Long Beach Cable TV, 1983; coord. pub. svc. announcement and interviewee for Disabilities Awareness Week ABC TV, San Diego, 1986, San Diego, 88. Game inventor: Match This!, 1995; author: (children's book) Bird Boy, 2006; contbr. poetry to lit. publs.;, author. Named to Outstanding Young Women Am. Mem.: Calif. Speech-Lang-Hearing Assn. (region rep., Outstanding Achievement award 1987), Am. Speech-Lang-Hearing Assn., Zeta Tau Alpha. Avocations: writing, theater, decorating. Home: 31935 Calle Espinoza Temecula CA 92592 Office: Lake Elsinore Unified Sch Dist 545 Chaney St Lake Elsinore CA 92530 Home Phone: 951-303-9422; Office Phone: 951-253-7000 x5390. Personal E-mail: pjyoung2000@aol.com.

YOUNG, PATRICK, editor, writer; b. Ladysmith, Wis., Oct. 19, 1937; s. Rodney and Janice (Wolf) Y.; m. Leah Ruth Figelman, Oct. 8, 1966; 1 child, Justine Young Gottshall. BA, U. Colo., 1960. Reporter UPI, Washington, 1961-62; journalist USN, 1963-64; staff writer Nat. Observer, Silver Spring, Md., 1965-77; free-lance writer Laurel, Md., 1977-79; mem. sr. staff Pres.'s Commn. on the Accident at Three Mile Island, Washington, 1979; chief sci. and med. writer Newhouse News Svc., Washington, 1980-88; editor Sci. News, Washington, 1988-95; ind. writer, editor, cons., 1995—. Sci. writer in residence U. Wis., 1986. Author: Asthma and Allergies, 1980, Drugs and Pregnancy, 1987, Schizophrenia, 1988; co-author: Keeping Young Athletes Healthy, 1991. With USN, 1963-64. Recipient Howard W. Blakeslee award Am. Heart Assn., 1971, Sci. Writing award in physics and astronomy Am. Inst. Physics, 1974, James T. Grady award Am. Chem. Soc., 1977. Mem. Nat. Assn. Sci. Writers, Nat. Press Club, Am. Assn. Adv. Sci. Home Phone: 301-498-4251; Office Phone: 301-498-4251. Business E-Mail: young@nasw.org.

YOUNG, PAUL, graphic designer, edcator; m. Bonnie K. Burgund. BFA in Graphic Design, U. Ill., Urbana, 1983, EdM in Curriculum and Instrn., 2006. Art dir. Advt. Studios Inc, Milw., 1983—86; graphic designer Arnell Bickford Assoc, NYC, 1986—87; art dir. Muscular Dystrophy Assoc, NYC, 1987—90, The Creative Black Book, NYC, 1990—93; pub. The Octopus, Champaign, Ill., 1994—98; assoc. prof. Parkland Coll., Champaign, 1998—; ptnr. Electric Pictures, Champaign, 1992—. Mem.: Ad Club Champaign-Urbana (bd. mem. 2002—05). Office: Parkland Coll 2400 W Bradley Ave Champaign IL 61821 Office Phone: 217-351-2403, 217-398-1923. Business E-Mail: pyoung@parkland.edu, paul@electric-pictures.com.

YOUNG, PAUL ANDREW, anatomist; b. St. Louis, Oct. 3, 1926; s. Nicholas A. and Olive A. (Langford) Y.; m. Catherine Ann Hofmeister, May 14, 1949; children— Paul, Robert, David, Ann, Carol, Richard, James, Steven, Kevin, Michael. BS, St. Louis U., 1947, MS, 1953; PhD, U. Buffalo, 1957. Asst. in anatomy U. Buffalo, 1953, instr. anatomy, 1957; asst. prof. anatomy St. Louis U., 1957, assoc. prof., 1966, prof., 1972—, chmn. dept., 1973—2004, prof. anatomy in surgery, 2004, prof. and chair emeritus, dept. anatomy and neurobiology, 2006. Author: (with B.D. Bhagat and D.E. Biggerstaff) Fundamentals of Visceral Innervation, 1977, (with P.H. Young) Basic Clinical Neuroanatomy, 1996, (with P.H.Young and D.L.Tolbert) Basic Clinical Neuroscience, 2007, also computer assisted neurological anatomy tutorials; contbr. articles to profl. publs. Recipient Preclinical Golden Apple Tchg. award, St. Louis U. Sch. Medicine, 1974, 2000, Outstanding Preclinical, 1981, 1985, 1986, 1991, 1992, St. Louis Acad. Sci., 1993, Emerson Excellence for St. Louis U. faculty, 2001. Mem. Am. Assn. Anatomists, Am. Assn. Clin. Anatomists, Soc. Neurosci., Sigma Xi, Alpha Omega Alpha. Office: St Louis Univ Ctr for Anatomical Science and Education 1402 S Grand Blvd Saint Louis MO 63104-1004 Home Phone: 636-225-1437; Office Phone: 314-977-8025. Personal E-mail: dutchess1003@sbcglobal.net. Business E-Mail: youngpa@slu.edu.

YOUNG, PAUL RAY, medical association administrator, physician; b. Fairfield, Nebr., June 27, 1932; s. Earl Edward and Louisa May (Saunders) Young; m. Irene Marie Gray (div. 1971); children: Michael, Susan, Jean, James; m. Faye Elizabeth Hall, Oct. 28, 1972. BA, U. Nebr., Lincoln, 1953; MD, U. Nebr., Omaha, 1958. Diplomate Am. Bd. Family Practice. Intern Rsch. Hosp., Kansas City, Mo., 1958—59, dir. continuing med. edn., 1967—71; pvt. practice Raytown, Mo., 1961—67; assoc. prof. family practice U. Mo. Coll. Medicine, Columbia, 1971—75; chmn. dept. U. Nebr. Coll. Medicine, 1975—80, U. Tex. Med. Br., Galveston, 1980—88; dep. dir. Am. Bd. Family Practice, Lexington, Ky., 1988—90, exec. dir., 1990—97, sr. exec., 1998—2003, emeritus exec. dir., 2003—. Chmn. RRC for Family Practice, Chgo., 1979—87. Founding editor: Family Practice Recert, 1979, Jour. Am. Bd. Family Practice, 1987. Pres. Nicholas J. Piscano Meml. Found., 1990—97. Capt. M.C. USAF, 1959—61. Fellow: Am. Acad. Family Physicians; mem.: Soc. Tchrs. Family Medicine (bd. dirs. 1970—72), Alpha Omega Alpha. Office: Am Bd Family Medicine Inc 2228 Young Dr Lexington KY 40505-4219 Office Phone: 859-269-5626. Business E-Mail: pyoung@theabfm.org.

YOUNG, PAULA EVA, animal shelter director; b. Caracas, Venezuela, May 11, 1958; arrived in U.S., 1962; d. James Francis and Fulvia (Guzzaloni) Y.; 1 child, Jonas Borra. Cert., Am. Acad. Dramatic Arts, NYC, 1979; BA, CUNY, 1997. Lobbyist, facilitator East Bronx Coun. on Aging, NYC, 1989—90; journalist N.Y. Newsday, NYC, 1990—94; mng. editor, journalist City News, NYC, 1994—95; dir. Office Comm. N.Y.C. Dept. Citywide Adminstrv. Svcs., 1995—98; asst. commr. pub. affairs N.Y.C. Dept. Sanitation, 1998—2001; owner, mgr. Between the Lines Restaurant, Westchester County, NY, 2001—03; dir. Mt. Vernon (NY) Animal Shelter, 2003—. Mem. animal cruelty task force Office of Dist. Atty., Westchester County, 2005—; bd. dirs. NY State Wildlife Rehab. Coun., 2003—. Democrat. Avocation: wildlife and animal rescue. Office: 600 Garden Ave Mount Vernon NY 10550 Home: 28 Colabaugh Pond Rd Croton On Hudson NY 10520-3313 Office Phone: 914-522-5945.

YOUNG, PETER ROBERT, library director; b. Washington, Aug. 13, 1944; s. Ju Chin and Jane Kathrine (Lybrand) Y.; m. Mary Sue Townsend, Mar. 25, 1978; children: Kathryn, Timothy; children from previous marriage: Robert, Jonathan. AB Philosophy, Coll. Wooster, Ohio, 1966; MSLS Libr. Svc., Columbia U., 1968. Adminstrv. libr. Am. U. Libr., Washington, 1968; head cataloger, reference libr. Franklin & Marshall Coll. Libr., Lancaster, Pa., 1971-74; asst. libr. pub. svcs. Rice U. Librs., Houston, 1974-76; asst. dir. Grand Rapids (Mich.) Pub. Libr., 1978; sales support libr. CL Systems Inc., Newtonville, Mass., 1976-78, libr. systems analyst, 1978-80; customer svcs. officer Cataloging Distbn. Svc. Libr. Congress, Washington, 1980-84, asst. chief Marc edit. divsn., 1984-85, chief Copyright Cataloging divsn., 1985-88; dir. acad. info. svcs. The Faxon Co., Westwood, Mass., 1988-89, dir. Faxon Inst. Advanced Studies Scholarly and Sci. Communication, 1989-90; exec. dir. U.S. Nat. Commn. Librs. and Info. Sci., Washington, 1990-97; chief cataloguing distbn. svc. Libr. of Congress, Washington, 1997—2001, acting chief Asian div., 2001—02; dir. Nat. Agrl. Libr., Beltsville, Md., 2002—. Exec. bd. Fed. Libr. and Info. Ctr. com., 1993-96; adv. bd. Highsmith Press, 1991-99; co chair libr. stats. standard revision com. Nat. Standards Info. Office, 1989-93; libr. adminstrs. devel. program U. Md., 1984; implementation task force libr. data Nat. Ctr. Edn. Stats. U.S. Office Edn., 1988, adv. coun. edn. stats. Office Edn. Rsch. and Improvement, 1990; head U.S. deleg. to FAO consultation on agrl. info. mgmt., Rome, 2002; lectr. in field. Mem. edit. bd. Serials Review; contbr. articles to profl. jours. With U.S. Army, 1968-70, Vietnam, 3 Bronze Stars. Mem. ALA (pub. policy for pub. librs. com., com. rsch. and stats., council, various coms., assns.), Internat. Stds. Orgn. (libr. stats. and libr. performance indicators stds.), Chinese Am. Libr. Assn. (chair pub. rels. com. 1987-88, pres. 1989-90), U.S. Nat. Commn. Librs. and Info. Sci. (stats. task force 1988-89). Office: Nat Agrl Library Abraham Lincoln Bldg 10301 Baltimore Ave Beltsville MD 20705-2351

YOUNG, PHILIP HOWARD, library director; b. Ithaca, NY, Oct. 7, 1953; s. Charles Robert and Betty Irene (Osborne) Young; m. Nancy Ann Stutsman, Aug. 18, 1979. BA, U. Va., 1975; PhD, U. Pa., 1980; MLS, Ind. U., 1983. Asst. prof. history Appalachian State U., Boone, NC, 1980-82; reference asst. Lilly Libr. Ind. U., Bloomington, 1982-83; adminstr., info. specialist Ind. Corp. Sci. & Tech., Indpls., 1983-85; dir. Krannert Meml. Libr. U. Indpls., 1985—. Mem.: Archeol. Inst. Am., Am. Libr. Assn., Phi Beta Kappa, Beta Phi Mu, Phi Alpha Theta. Democrat. Home: 4332 Silver Springs Dr Greenwood IN 46142-9623 Office: U Indpls Krannert Meml Libr 1400 E Hanna Ave Indianapolis IN 46227-3630 Office Phone: 317-788-3399. E-mail: pyoung@uindy.edu.

YOUNG, PHYLLIS CASSELMAN, music educator; b. Milan, Kans., Oct. 20, 1925; d. Phillip James and Velma (Stewart) Casselman; m. James M. Young, July 14, 1945 (dec. Sept. 1991). MusB with high honors, U. Tex., 1949, MusM, 1950. Tchr. string instruments Kansas City (Kans.) Pub. Schs., 1951-52; prof. cello and string pedagogy U. Tex., Austin, 1953—; dir. U. Tex. String Project, Austin, 1958-93; Parker C. Fielder Regents prof. music U. Tex., Austin, 1991—. Presenter numerous workshops and master classes, 1976—. Author: Playing the String Game, 1978, The String Play, 1986; also articles. Mem. Am. String Tchrs. Assn. (state pres. 1972-74, nat. pres. 1978-80, Nat. citation 1974, 82, Disting. Svc. award 1984, Paul Rolland Lifetime Achievement award 2002), European String Tchrs. Assn. (hon. mem. Brit. br.), Music Educators Nat. Conf., Suzuki Assn. Ams., Tex. Music Educators Assn. Home: 7304 W Rim Dr Austin TX 78731-2043 Office: Sch Music Univ Tex Austin TX 78712 Business E-Mail: phyllis@mail.utexas.edu.

YOUNG, RAYMOND HENRY, lawyer; b. Boston, Sept. 28, 1927; s. Raymond H. and Clara Elms (Oakman) Y.; m. Louisa Breda, Sept. 1, 1951; children: Christopher, Pamela, Amy. AB, Yale U., 1947, LLB, 1950. Bar: Mass. 1951. Assoc. Warner, Stackpole, Stetson & Bradlee, Boston, 1950-52; pvt. practice Boston, 1952-64; ptnr. Young & Bayle, Boston, 1964—. Mem. ABA (past sec. sect. real property, probate and trust law, mem. commn. legal problems of the elderly), Am. Coll. Trust and Estate Counsel (mem. joint editorial bd. for trust and estate acts, 1988-2007), Am. Law Inst. (advisor for restatement property 3d donative transfers, cons. restatement trusts 3d), Nat. Commn. on Nat. Probate Ct. Standards, Internat. Acad. Trust and Estate Law (past pres.), Mass. Bar Assn., Boston Bar Assn. (past pres.), Boston Estate Planning Coun. (past pres., Estate Planner of Yr. award 1991), Boston Probate and Estate Planning Forum. Home: 122 Garfield St Watertown MA 02472-4916 Office: Young & Bayle 150 Federal St Boston MA 02110-1713

YOUNG, REBECCA MARY CONRAD, retired state legislator; b. Clairton, Pa., Feb. 28, 1934; d. Walter Emerson and Harriet Averill (Colcord) Conrad; m. Merwin Crawford Young, Aug. 17, 1957; children: Eve, Louise, Estelle, Emily. BA, U. Mich., 1955; MA in Teaching, Harvard U., 1963; JD, U. Wis., 1983. Bar: Wis. 1983. Commr. State Hwy. Commn., Madison, Wis., 1974-76; dep. sec. Wis. Dept. of Adminstrn., Madison, 1976-77; assoc. Wadsack, Julian & Lawton, Madison, 1983-84; elected rep. Wis. State Assembly, Madison, 1985-99. Translator: Katanga Secession, 1966. Supr. Dane County Bd., Madison, 1970-74; mem. Madison Sch. Bd., 1979-85. Recipient Wis. NOW Feminist of Yr. award, 1996, Eunice Zoghlin Edgar Lifetime Achievement award ACLU, 1997, Outstanding Legislator award Wis. Counties Assn., 1998, Voice for Choice award Planned Parenthood Wis., 1998, Luan Gilbert award for outstanding activities in domestic violence intervention and prevention Domestic Violence Intervention Svc., 1998. Mem. LWV. Democrat. Avocations: board games, hiking. Home: 639 Crandall St Madison WI 53711-1836

YOUNG, RICHARD ALAN, association executive; b. Oak Park, Ill., Mar. 17, 1935; m. Carol Ann Schellinger, June 28, 1958; children: Steven, Karen, Christopher. BA, U. Iowa, 1958; MS, PhD, Western State U., 2000. Chief engr. Cardox Corp., Chgo., 1958-61; asst. chief engr. Goodman Mfg. Co., Chgo., 1961-63; plant and environ. engr. Signode Corp., Glenview, Ill., 1963-68; editor Pollution Engring. Tech. Pub. Co., Barrington, Ill., 1968-81; exec. dir. Nat. Registry of Environ. Profls., 1988—; pub. Cahners Pub. Co., Des Plaines, Ill., 1990-95; exec. dir. Office Infrastructure Preparedness, 2004—. Adj. prof. George Williams Coll., Ea. Ky. U., 2004-; mcpl. pollution control adviser and enforcement officer for 24 cities and fed govts; ofcl rep. and pollution control expert U.S. Govt. at tech. transfer meetings; exec. dir. Internat. Certification Accreditation Bd., 1999—, Office of Infrastructure Preparedness, 2004-, Nat. Assn. Environ. Risk Auditors, 2004-, African Inst. Environ. Profl., 2005. Editor 26 books on environ. engring.; pollution engring.; series editor, Marcel Dekker Inc., N.Y.C.; contbr. articles to profl. jours.; patentee in field. Recipient Jesse H. Neal certificate for outstanding editorial writing Am. Bus. Press, Inc., 1971, Outstanding Service award Western Soc. Engrs., Charles Ellet award as Most Outstanding Engr. of Yr. 1970; Environ. Quality award EPA, 1976 Mem. Internat. Assn. for Pollution Control (dir.), Am. Soc. Bus. Press Editors (Editl. Excellence award 1980, Design Excellence award 1982), Am. Inst. Plant Engrs. (past nat. chmn. environ. quality), Internat. Congress Environ. Profls. (mng. dir.), Nat. Inst. Hazardous Materials Mgmts. (dir. 1984-88, cert. hazardous materials mgr.).

YOUNG, RICHARD WILLIAM, chemicals executive; b. Ridgewood, NY, Oct. 17, 1926; s. Charles Michael and Louise Margaret (Baust) Y.; m. Sheila deLisser, Sept. 11, 1949; children: Christine, Noreen, Brian, Eileen. AB, Dartmouth Coll., 1946, A.M., 1947; PhD, Columbia U., 1950; DSc (hon.), Regis Coll., 2002. Sr. rsch. chemist Chemotherapy div. Am. Cyanamid Co., Conn., 1950-56, group leader pesticide chems. Agrl. div. Conn., 1956-58, dir. chem. Agrl. div. Conn., 1958-60, dir. chem. rsch. cen. rsch. div. Conn., 1960-62; asst. dir. rsch. Polaroid Corp., Cambridge, Mass., 1962-69, v.p., 1963-69, sr. v.p. rsch. and devel., 1969-72, sr. v.p., pres. Internat. div., 1972-80, exec. v.p., dir. worldwide mktg., 1980-82; pres. Houghton Mifflin Co., Boston, 1982-85; chmn., CEO Mentor O & O, Inc., Norwell, Mass., 1985-92. Bd. dirs. Bay State Milling Corp., Quincy, Mass., Instron Corp., Canton, Mass., Oceantrawl Inc., Seattle, Mentor Corp., Santa Barbara, Calif. Patentee in field. Chmn. bd. trustees Regis Coll., Weston, Mass.; trustee Mass. Eye and Ear Infirmary, Boston, 1963-90, Trinitas Found., Quincy; mem. corp. Northeastern U., Boston, 1960-92; bd. dirs. Martin Meml. Hosp. Found., 2002—. Mem. Am. Chem. Soc. Home: 4 Scotch Pine Cir Wellesley Hills MA 02481-1222 Office: Trinitas Found 100 Congress St Quincy MA 02169-0906 E-mail: rwy1926@aol.com.

YOUNG, RICK (RICHARD ALLEN), molecular biologist, educator; b. Pitts., Mar. 12, 1954; s. Allen Young and Jane (Moore) Stockhausen. BS in Biol. Sci., Ind. U., 1975; PhD in Molecular Biology, Biochemistry, Yale U., 1979. Postdoctoral fellow Swiss Inst. Exptl. Cancer Research, Lausanne, Switzerland, 1979-80, Stanford (Calif.) U., 1981-84; assoc. prof. biology MIT, Cambridge, 1984—, now prof.; mem. Whitehead Inst. Biomed. Research, Cambridge, 1984—, now prin. investigator. Cons., com. mem. WHO, Geneva, Switzerland, 1983-89, chmn. biology subcom., 1987-90. Grantee WHO, NIH, 1984—; recipient Molecular Parasitology award Burroughs Wellcome Co., 1987, Chiron Corp. Biotechnology award Am. Society for Microbiology, 1994 Fellow Molecular Medicine Soc. (charter); mem. AAAS, Am. Acad. Microbiology, Genetics Soc. Am. Avocations: skiing, mountain climbing. Office: Whitehead Inst Biomed Research 9 Cambridge Ctr Cambridge MA 02142-1479 E-mail: young@wi.mit.edu.

YOUNG, ROBERT A., III, freight systems executive; b. Ft. Smith, Ark., Sept. 23, 1940; s. Robert A. and Vivian (Curtis) Y.; m. Mary Carleton McRae; children: Tracy, Christy, Robert A. IV (dec.), Stephen BA in Econs., Washington and Lee U., 1963. Supr. terminal ops. Ark. Best Freight, Ft. Smith, 1964-65; pres. Data-Tronics Inc, Ft. Smith, 1965-67; sr. v.p. Nat. Bank of Commerce, Dallas, 1967-70; v.p. fin. Ark. Best Corp., Ft. Smith, 1970-73, exec. v.p., 1973, chief operating officer, 1973-88, pres., 1973—2004, chief exec. officer, 1988—, chmn., 2004—; pres. ABF Freight Systems, Inc., Ft. Smith, 1979-94. Bd. dirs. First Nat. Bank, Ft. Smith. Pres. United Way, Ft. Smith, 1981; bd. dirs. ATA Found., Inc., Ft. Smith Boys and Girls Club; chmn. bd. trustees Lyon Coll., Sparks Regional Med. Ctr., Ft. Smith, 1995-2004. Recipient Silver Beaver award Boy Scouts Am. Mem. Am. Trucking Assn. (v.p. at large), Phi Delta Theta. Presbyterian. Office: Ark Best Corp PO Box 10048 Fort Smith AR 72917-0048 also: Arkansas Best Corp PO Box 10048 Fort Smith AR 72917-0048

YOUNG, ROBERT BOND, lawyer; b. Phila., May 18, 1943; s. Robert A. and Anna Battelle (Bond) Y.; m. Karen Alexander, June 17, 1966; children: Jeffrey A., Randall C. BA, Denison U., 1965; JD, Ohio State U., 1969. Bar: Ohio 1969, U.S. Dist. Ct. (so. dist.) Ohio 1970, Del. 1975, U.S. Dist. Ct. Del. 1976, U.S. Supreme Ct. 1978, U.S. Ct. Appeals (3d cir.) 1986. Assoc. Young & Alexander, Dayton, Ohio, 1969-72, ptnr., 1973-75; pvt. practice Dover, Del., 1975-84, 1992—; sr. ptnr. Young & Sherlock, Dover, 1985-92. Adj. prof. bus. law Del. Community Coll., Dover, 1975-79; adj. prof. ins. law Wesley Coll., Dover, 1993—; pres. Overseas Fiber Export Corp., Dover, 1978—. Author: (light verse/text book) Grappling With Grammar, 1976, (musical comedies) To The Revolution, 1976, MacBeth: A Family Musical, 1977, O, 1978, Swarthmore Fight Song, 1979, Calibants Rage. Mgr. Dover Little League, 1978-87, Sr. League All-Star mgr., 1984, 86, bd. dirs. 1982, 84; bd. dirs. Del. Soc. Prevention Cruelty to Animals, 1980. Mem. ABA, Am. Bd. Trial Lawyers (Del. chpt. pres. elect 1991-93, pres. 1993-95), Def. Rsch. Inst., Del. State Bar Assn. (pres. 2004), Assn. Def. Trial Advocates, Terry Carey Am. Inn of Ct. (master 1991—, counselor 1994-95). Avocations: youth sports, creative writing. *

YOUNG, ROBERT CRABILL, medical researcher, science administrator, internist; b. Columbus, Ohio, 1940; BS in zoology, Ohio State U., 1960; MD, Cornell U., 1965. Diplomate Am. Bd. Internal Medicine, subspecialty bds. hematology and med. oncology. Intern N.Y. Hosp., NYC, 1965-66, resident, 1966-67; sr. resident Yale-New Haven Med. Ctr., 1969-70; sr. investigator, attending physician med. br. Nat. Cancer Inst., Bethesda, Md., 1971—, chief med. br., 1974-88; pres. Fox Chase Cancer Ctr., Phila., 1988—. Clin. prof. medicine Georgetown U., from 1974, assoc. prof., 1976-84; clin. prof. medicine George Washington U., 1984—; bd. Sci. Advisors, Nat. Cancer Inst., 1996—; bd. Nat. Cancer Policy, 1997-99; chmn. bd. Nat. Comprehensive Cancer Network. Assoc. editor Jour. Clin. Oncology; chmn. editl. bd. Oncology Times. Sr. surgeon USPHS, 1967-69. Fellow ACP; mem. Am. Soc. Hematology, Am. Assn. Cancer Rsch., Am. Soc. Clin. Oncology (pres. 1990), Am. Cancer Soc. (bd. dir. 1995-99, 1st v.p. 1999-2000, pres. 2002), Internat. Gynecol. Cancer Soc. (pres.-elect 1998, pres. 2000). Office: Fox Chase Cancer Ctr 333 Cottman Ave Philadelphia PA 19111

YOUNG, ROBERT CRAIG, banker; b. NYC, Mar. 15, 1960; s. Robert J. and Gloria L. (Sandhop) Y.; m. Anke Ott, Dec. 2, 2000. BS cum laude, NYU, 1982, MBA, 1985. Asst. v.p. Chem. Bank, NYC, 1982-86; project mgr. GE Credit Corp., Stamford, Conn., 1986-87; dir. Merrill Lynch & Co., NYC, 1987-94; sr. v.p. Greenwich (Conn.) Capital Markets, Inc., 1994-97; mng. dir. Nomura Securities, NYC, 1997-2001; divsn. dir. Macquarie, NYC, 2001—. Home: 98 Revere Rd Manhasset NY 11030-2733 Office: Macquarie 125 W 55th St New York NY 10019 Office Phone: 212-231-1707. E-mail: rcyoung@optonline.net.

YOUNG, ROBERT P., JR., state supreme court justice; B cum laude, Harvard U., 1974, JD, 1977. Atty. Dickinson, Wright, Moon, Van Dusen & Freeman, 1977-1992; v.p., corp. sec., gen. counsel AAA Mich., 1992; judge Mich. Ct. Appeals 1st Dist., 1995—98; justice Mich. Supreme Ct., 1999—. Mem. Mich. Civil Svc. Commn.; bd. trustees Cen. Mich. U. Mem.: ABA, Mich. State Bar Assn., Mich. Supreme Ct. Historical Soc. Office: Mich Supreme Ct PO Box 30052 Lansing MI 48909-7552 *

YOUNG, ROLAND FREDERIC, III, lawyer; b. Norway, Maine, Apr. 8, 1954; s. Roland Frederic Jr. and Marylyn May (Bartlett) Y.; m. Dona Davis Gagliano, Aug. 18, 1979; children: Meghan, Wesley, Taylor. AB, Cornell U., 1976; JD, U. Conn., 1979. Bar: Conn. 1979, U.S. Dist. Ct. Conn., U.S. Tax Ct., U.S. Ct. Appeals (2d cir.). Ptnr. Howard, Kohn, Sprague & FitzGerald, Hartford, Conn., 1984-91, O'Brien, Tanski & Young, Hartford, Conn., 1991—. Lectr. Hartford Grad. Ctr., 1991-98. Author (seminar booklet) Confidentiality of Med. Records, 1989, Limiting Damages, 1990; co-author (seminar booklet) Med. Malpractice in Conn., 1992; editor Conn. Risk Mgmt. Assn., 1986-98. Trustee Mooreland Mill Sch.; vice chmn. Conn. Nat. Kideny Found. Mem. Conn. Hosp. Assn., Hartford County Bar Assn. (chmn. medico-legal liaison com.). Avocation: golf. Office: O'Brien Tanski & Young City Place II 16th Fl Hartford CT 06103 Office Phone: 860-525-2700. Business E-Mail: rfy@otylaw.com.

YOUNG, RONALD FARIS, commodities trader; b. Schenectady, Dec. 17, 1939; s. James Vernon and Dorothy (Girod) Y.; m. Anne Randolph Kendig, Feb. 23, 1963; children: Margaret Randolph Reynolds, Anne Corbin Gray. BA, U. Va., 1962; MBA, Harvard U., 1966. Grain trader Continental Grain Co., 1966-70; pres. Conti-Commodities, Chgo., 1970; v.p. commodity sales DuPont, Glore Forgan, Chgo., 1971-72; self-employed commodity trader Chgo. Bd. Trade, 1972-78; ind. trader Va. Trading Co., 1978-90, pres., 1978-84, dep. chmn., 1984-89; pres. Randolph Ptnrs., Ltd., 1983-91. Chmn. bd. Chgo. Bd. Trade, 1978, dir., 1975—77, 1980, 2003. Bd. dirs. Princeton Fund, 1981-82, Lake Forest Hosp., 1981-84, Lake Forest Country Day Sch., 1981-86. Served with USMCR, 1959-65. Mem. Racquet Club (bd. dirs. 1989-97), Onwentsia Club (Lake Forest, Ill., bd. dirs. 1981-90, pres. 1991-93), Everglades Club (Palm Beach, Fla.), Bath and Tennis Club of Palm Beach (bd. dirs. 2007—). Republican. Episcopalian. Home: 531 N Mayflower Rd Lake Forest IL 60045

YOUNG, ROY ALTON, university administrator, educator; b. McAlister, N.Mex., Mar. 1, 1921; s. John Arthur and Etta Julia (Sprinkle) Y.; m. Marilyn Ruth Sandman, May 22, 1950; children: Janet Elizabeth, Randall Owen. BS, N.Mex. A&M Coll., 1941; MS, Iowa State U., Ames, 1942, PhD, 1948; LLD (hon.), N.Mex. State U., Las Cruces, 1978. Tchg. fellow Iowa State U., 1941-42, instr., 1946-47, Indsl. fellow, 1947-48; asst. prof. Oreg. State U., 1948-50, assoc. prof., 1950-53, prof., 1953—, head dept.

botany and plant pathology, 1958-66, dean rsch., 1966-70, acting pres., 1969-70, v.p. rsch. and grad. studies, 1970-76, dir. Office for Natural Resources Policy, 1986-90; chancellor U. Nebr., Lincoln, 1976-80; mng. dir., pres. Boyce Thompson Inst. Plant Rsch., Cornell U., Ithaca, NY, 1980-86. Mem. Commn. on Undergrad. Edn. in Biol. Scis., 1963-68; mem. Gov.'s Sci. Coun., 1987-90; cons. State Exptl. Stas. divsn. USDA; chmn. subcom. plant pathogens, agriculture bd. NAS-NRC, 1965-68; mem. exec. com. study on problems of pest control, 1972-75; mem. exec. com. Nat. Govs.' Coun. on Sci. and Tech., 1970-74; mem. US com. man and biosphere UNESCO, 1973-82; mem. com. to rev. US component Internat. Biol. Program, NAS, 1974-76; mem. adv. panel on postdoctoral fellowships in environ. sci. Rockefeller Found., 1974-78; bd. dirs. Pacific Power & Light Co., 1974-91, PacifiCorp., 1984-91, Boyce Thompson Inst. for Plant Rsch., 1975-93, Boyce Thompson Southwestern Arboretum, 1981-92, Oreg. Grad. Inst., 1987-94; mem. adv. com. Directorate for Engring. and Applied Sci., NSF, 1977-81; mem. sea grant adv. panel, 1978-80; mem. policy adv. com. Office of Grants, USDA, 1985-86. Trustee Ithaca Coll., 1982-89. Lt. USNR, 1943-46. Recipient Disting. Svc. award Oreg. State U., 1978. Fellow AAAS (exec. com. Pacific div. 1963-67, pres. div. 1971), Am. Phytopathology Soc. (pres. Pacific div. 1957, chmn. spl. com. to develop plans for endowment 1984-86, bd. dirs. 1986-88); mem. Oreg. Acad. Sci., Nat. Assn. State Univs. and Land Grant Colls. (chmn. coun. for rsch. policy and adminstrn. 1970, chmn. standing com. on environment and energy 1974-82, chmn. com. on environment 1984-86), Sigma Xi, Phi Kappa Phi, Phi Sigma, Sigma Alpha Epsilon. Home: 3605 NW Van Buren Ave Corvallis OR 97330-4950

YOUNG, RUSSELL DAWSON, physicist, consultant; b. Huntington, NY, Aug. 17, 1923; s. C. Halsey and Edna (Dawson) Young; m. Carol Vaughn Jones, Aug. 14, 1954; children: Bessmarie, Gale, Janet, Shari. BS in Physics, Rensselaer Poly. Inst., Troy, NY, 1953; PhD in Physics, Pa. State U., 1959. Rsch. assoc. Pa. State U., State College, 1959-61; project leader Nat. Bur. Stds., Gaithersburg, Md., 1961-73, chief optics and micrometrology, 1973-78, chief mech. processing div., 1975-80, ind. sys. div. chief, 1980-81, chief mech. prodn. div., 1980-81; pres. R.D. Young Cons., Pasadena, Md., 1981—. Contbr. articles to profl. jours.; inventor in field of instrumentation. 1st lt. Signal Corps, U.S. Army, 1943-46. Recipient Edward V. Condon award Dept. Commerce, 1974, Silver medal 1979, Gaede-Langmuir award 1994, Presdl. citation 1986, Washington Acad. Scis. award 1988. Fellow Internat. Inst. Prodn. Engring. Rsch., Nat. Inst. Standards and Tech. Avocation: boating. Home: 10586 Edwardian Ln New Market MD 21774-3219 Personal E-mail: cryoung2@aol.com.

YOUNG, RUTH BROOKS, retired elementary school educator; b. Balt., Aug. 30, 1933; d. Benjamin Franklin and Ora Estelle Brooks; m. David Donald Young Sr., 1952 (dec.); children: David Donald Jr. (dec.), Gerard Brooks Sr., Mark Douglas (dec.), Elizabeth Allyson Mack. BS, Coppin State Tchrs. Coll., 1958; MS, Morgan State Coll., 1975. Cert. tchr., Md. Tchr. Balt. City Pub. Schs., 1958-98, supervising tchr., 1968-72, sch. test coord., 1990-96; ret., 1998. Mem. Phi Delta Kappa. Democrat. Lutheran.

YOUNG, SANDRA COOPER, retired librarian; b. Schenectady, NY, Jan. 18, 1939; d. John Remington and Esther May (Carl) Cooper; m. Charles William Young Jr.; children: Charles W. III, Kimberly Anderson, Kathryn Whalen, Karen. BA in Anthropology, Syracuse U., 1961; MSLS, U. Ky., 1980. Info. resources asst. Council of State Govts., Lexington, Ky., 1981-82; sr. tech. info. rsch. analyst Ashland Oil Co., Lexington, 1983—94; ret., 1994. Co-author: Directory of Special Libraries in the Bluegrass, 1991. Chmn. libr. com. LWV, Lexington, 1985, bd. dirs., 1990; bd. dirs., sec. Friends Lexington Pub. Libr., 1998—; vol. Friends Book Cellar, 1998—; RSVP vol. Lexington in Bloom, 2002, judge; active Mayor's Tree Bd., 2003— Named to Hon. Order of Ky. Cols., 1979. Mem. AAUW (pres. Ky. chpt. 1980-82), ALA, Spl. Librs. Assn. (pres. Ky. chpt. 1987), Cen. Ky. Online User's Group, Ky. Libr. Assn., Evergreen Garden Club (pres. 1989-91), Lexington Coun. Garden Clubs (v.p., sec.), Landscape Design Cons., Garden Club Ky. (pres. 2004-06), Kappa Kappa Gamma. Democrat. Roman Catholic. Avocations: reading, golf, needlecrafts. Home: 209 Clinton Rd Lexington KY 40502-1923

YOUNG, SHELDON MIKE, lawyer, author; b. Cleve., Aug. 27, 1926; s. Jack and Ray Y.; m. Margery Ann Polster, Dec. 25, 1948 (div. 1988); children: Jeffrey, Martin, Janet; m. Bette Abel Roth, Nov. 11, 1988. BA, Ohio State U., 1948, JD, 1951; LLM, Case Western Res. U., 1962. Bar: Ohio 1951, U.S. Dist. Ct. (no. dist.) Ohio. Gen. counsel Eugene M. Klein & Assocs., Actuaries, Cleve., 1952-72; assoc. Shapiro, Persky & Marken, Cleve., 1972-74; counsel pension tech. svcs. dept. CNA Ins., Chgo., 1974-76; ptnr. Weiss & Young, Cleve., 1976; of counsel Arter & Hadden, Cleve., 1977-85, Squire, Sanders & Dempsey, Cleve., 1985-87; pvt. practice Columbus, 1987-91; of counsel Schwartz, Kelm, Warren & Rubenstein, Columbus, 1991—93, Walter & Haverfield, Columbus, 1993—. Instr. Case Western Res. U. Law Sch., 1962-82, 85, U. Akron Law Sch., 1984, 88. Author: Pension and Profit Sharing Plans, 7 vols., 1977-93, (novel) Toledoth-City of Generations, 2003; freelance writer for newspapers and mags.; contbr. articles to pension jours. Served with USN, WWII. Recipient award Nathan Burkan Meml. Copyright Competition, 1951. Fellow Am. Coll. Employee Benefits Counsel (charter); mem. ABA (chair obsolete pension rev. rule task force), Cleve. Bar Assn., Columbus Bar Assn., Masons. Jewish. Home and Office: Walter & Haverfield 4776 Smoketalk Ln Westerville OH 43081-7838 Home Phone: 614-890-3018; Office Phone: 614-898-1096. Office Fax: 614-898-7190. Personal E-mail: yomike@earthlink.net.

YOUNG, SHERILYN BURNETT, lawyer; b. Providence, Nov. 7, 1953; d. Archie C. III and Hope (Westcott) Burnett; m. Gary Richard Young, Oct. 9, 1977; 3 children. BA, Cornell U., Ithaca, NY, 1975; JD, Franklin Pierce Law Ctr., 1982. Bar: N.H. 1982, U.S. Dist. Ct. N.H. 1982, U.S. Tax Ct. 1983. Assoc. Orr & Reno, P.A., Concord, N.H., 1982-87; founder Rath, Young and Pignatelli, P.C., Concord, 1987—96. Trustee U. Sys. N.H., Concord Hosp., 1991-98; bd. dirs. N.H. Hist. Soc., Franklin Pierce Law Ctr.; legis. counsel to Gov. Gregg, Concord, 1989-90; mem. adv. coun. to ins. commr., 1989-93; spkr. in field. Legal counsel Rudman for U.S. Senate campaign, Concord, 1984-93; bd. dirs. Concord chpt. ARC, 1988-91; mem. N.H. adv. bd. New Eng. Legal Found., 1991-97; pres. Concord Hosp. Assn., 1991-97, bd. dirs. Mem. ABA, NH Bar Assn., New Eng. Coun., Concord C. of C. (bd. dirs. 1988-91), NH Bus. and Industry Assn. (bd. dirs. 2004-), Cornell Club NH. Republican. Avocations: skiing, tennis. Office Phone: 603-226-2600.

YOUNG, STACY A., information technology manager; Knowledge officer Global Engine Manufacturing Alliance, DaimlerChrysler, Auburn Hills, Mich. Recipient Women of Color Tech. award, 2005. Office: Chrysler Group 1000 Chrysler Dr Auburn Hills MI 48326-2766

YOUNG, STEPHEN BERNARD, urogynecologist, surgeon; b. Bklyn., Apr. 21, 1943; s. Alice Dora (Klein) and Louis Wolf Young; m. Martha Anne Abeles, June 25, 1995; children: Sarah Chi, Ezekiel Elye, Ray Malka. BA, Columbia U., NYC, 1964; MD, George Washington U., 1968. Diplomate Nat. Bd. Med. Examiners, Am. Bd. Ob/Gyn. Fellow vaginal surgery Women and Infants Hosp., Brown U., Providence, 1986—89; prof., ob-gyn., chief urogynecology and reconstructive pelvic surgery U. Mass. Med. Sch., Worcester, 1990—. Tchr. in field, Guatemala, 1994, Beijing, 2005, Beijing, 07, Chennai, India, 06, Chennai, 07. Contbr. articles to profl. jours., chapters to books. Recipient Women and Infants Excellence in Tchg. award, 1984, Clin. Tchg. award, U. Mass., 1994, Faculty Tchg. award, 1996, 2005, Golden Apple Med. Student Tchg. award, 2005—06, 2006—07. Mem.: ACOG, Soc. Gynecologic Surgeons (pres. 2007—), Am. Urogynecologic Soc. (pres. 2004—05, chair sci. program com. 2004, Prize Paper award 2000). Avocations: music, meditation. Office: Univ Mass 119 Belmont St Worcester MA 01605 Home Phone: 978-464-5987; Office Phone: 508-334-9842.

YOUNG, STEPHEN K., dean, academic administrator; DDS, U. Mo., 1971; MS in Oral Pathology, U. Mich., 1974. Diplomate Am. Bd. Oral Pathology. Asst. prof., oral and maxillofacial surgery U. Okla. Coll. Dentistry, David Ross Boyd prof., adj. prof., pathology, assoc. dean, dean, 1999—. Contbr. articles to profl. jours. Chair Nat. Cancer Inst.'s Ad Hoc Cancer Edn. Grant Review Com. Recipient President award, Okla. Dental Assn., 1988. Office: 1001 Stanton L Young Blvd Rm 507 Oklahoma City OK 73190 Office Phone: 405-271-5444. Home Fax: 405-271-3423. Business E-Mail: stephen-young@ouhsc.edu.

YOUNG, STEVEN, retired professional football player; b. Salt Lake City, Oct. 11, 1961; JD, Brigham Young, 1993. With L.A. Express, USFL, 1984—85, Tampa Bay Buccaneers, 1985—87; quarterback San Francisco 49ers, 1987—2000; panelist ESPN Sunday NFL Countdown, 2001—. Founder, mgr. Forever Young Found. benefitting Bay Area and Utah youth-oriented charities, 1993—. Named MVP, NFL, 1992, Player of Yr., 1994, All-Am. team quarterback, The Sporting News, 1983, Top-rated quarterback, NFL, 1991, NFL MVP, The Sporting News, 1992, NFL All-Pro team quarterback, 1992, Bay Area Sports Hall of Fame Profl. Athlete of Yr., 1992, Superbowl MVP, 1994; recipient Davey O'Brien award, 1983. Achievements include played in Pro Bowl, 1992, 93; highest rate passer NFL, 1991-93; inducted to the Pro Football Hall of Fame, 2005. Mailing: Forever Young Foundation PO Box 527 Park City UT 84060

YOUNG, STEVEN L., lawyer; b. Bklyn., Mar. 8, 1954; BA, SUNY, Binghamton, 1975; JD, St. John's U., 1978. Bar: NY 1979, US Dist. Ct. So. Dist. NY, US Dist. Ct. Ea. Dist. NY, US Dist. Ct. No. Dist. NY. Ptnr. Wilson, Elser, Moskowitz, Edelman & Dicker LLP, White Plains, NYC. Mem.: ABA, Westchester County Bar Assn., NY State Bar Assn. Office: Wilson Elser Moskowitz Edelman & Dicker LLP 3 Gannett Dr White Plains NY 10604 Office Phone: 914-323-7000 ext. 4252. Office Fax: 914-323-7001. Business E-Mail: youngs@wemed.com.

YOUNG, TERESA GAIL HILGER, retired adult education educator; b. Modesto, Calif., Mar. 4, 1948; d. Richard George and Jessie Dennie (Dennis) Long; m. Charles Ray Young, June 22, 1974; 1 child, Gregory Paul. BS in Edn., Abilene Christian U., Tex., 1970; MEd in Curriculum, Tarleton State U., Stephenville, Tex., 1976; postgrad., Tex. Tech U., 1990-92. Cert. supr., mid-mgmt., supt., Tex. Tchr. sci. Tex. Youth Coun., Gatesville, 1970-73, Gatesville Ind. Sch. Dist., 1973-81; coord. Edn. and Tng. Ctr., Cen. Tex. Coll., Gatesville, 1983; tchr. Tex. Dept. of Criminal Justice-ID, 1984—2002; ret., 2003. Conf. presenter. Trustee Jonesboro (Tex.) Ind. Sch. Dist., 1988-96. Teacher of the Year for Region II of Tex. Dept. of Criminal Justice, 1997-98. Mem. Am. Fedn. Tchrs., Assn. Tex. Profl. Educators. E-mail: tyoung@htcomp.net.

YOUNG, TERRI L., ophthalmologist; b. Sacramento, 1959; AB in BioChemistry and Sociology, Bowdoin Coll., Brunswick, Maine, 1981; MD in Medicine, Harvard U., 1986. Postdoctoral in pediat. Children's Hosp. Boston, 1986—87; resident in ophthalmology U. Ill., Chgo., 1987—90; clin. instr. ophthalmology U. Ill. Sch. Medicine, Chgo., 1989—90; extern in strabismus and adult motility disorders U. Iowa, 1991; fellow in pediatric ophthalmology, strabismus and adult motility disorders U. Pa. and Children's Hosp. Phila., 1990—92; clin. instr. opthalmology U. Pa., 1990—92; instr. neurobiology and ophthalmology Harvard Med. Sch., 1992—94; asst. prof. ophthalmology U. Minn., 1994—2000, asst. prof. pediat., 1998—2000, assoc. prof. pediat., 2000; dir.Ophthalmic Genetics Rsch. Ctr., Children's Hosp. Phila., 2000—; assoc. prof. ophthalmology and pediat. U. Pa., 2001—. Recipient Surdna Undergrad. Rsch. fellowship, Bowdoin Coll., 1980—81, Stanley J. Sarnoff Soc. Cardiovascular Rsch. award and fellowship, Harvard Med. Sch., 1983—84, Commonwealth Fund Rsch. fellowship, 1985, George and Mary Knox Harvaard Med. Grad. award, 1984, Grad. Kaiser Merit award, Nat. Med. Fellowship, 1986, Keeshin Prize Rsch. award, Inst. Medicine Chgo., 1990, Honor award, Am. Acad. Ophthalmology, 1998, Robert Wood Johnson Faculty Devel. award, 1992—97, Honor award, Am. Acad. Ophthalmology, 1998, Am. Assn. Pediatric Ophthalmology and Strabismus, 2002; selected as part of, NIH's "Changing the Face of Medicine" exhbn., 2003. Fellow: Am. Ophthalmol. Soc. Office: Duke U Eye Ctr Box 3082 2351 Erwin Rd Durham NC 27705 Office Phone: 919-684-0584. Business E-Mail: terri.young@duke.edu.

YOUNG, THOMAS LEE, lawyer; b. Los Angeles, Feb. 21, 1944; s. J. Donald and Nancy M. Young; m. Kathleen Grace Jacob, Sept. 10, 1967; children: Barbara, Deborah, Amy. Student, Marquette U., 1963; BA, St. John's Coll., 1966; JD, Notre Dame U., 1972; postgrad., Harvard U., 1984—85. Bar: Ohio 1972. Assoc. Fuller, Henry, Hodge & Snyder, Toledo, 1972—75; assoc. counsel Scott Paper Co., Phila., 1975—76; joined legal dept. Owens-Ill., Inc., Toledo, 1976—, asst. gen. counsel, 1983—88, v.p., gen. counsel oper., 1988—90, gen. counsel, sec., 1990—93, exec. v.p., admin & genl. counsel, 1993—2003, chief fin. officer, 2003—05. Bd. dirs. Manor Care Inc., Rocky Mountain Bottle Co., Gen. Chem. Ptnrs., GMP Employers Retirement Trust, Owens-Ill., Inc., Franklin Electric Co. Inc. 1st lt. US Army, 1966—69, Vietnam. Mem.: ABA, Toledo Bar Assn., Ohio State Bar Assn. Roman Catholic. Avocation: tennis.

YOUNG, THOMAS WILLIAM, medical examiner; b. La Mesa, Calif., June 12, 1956; s. William Lowell and Mary Carolyn Young; m. Yara Cerna Cerna, Aug. 7, 1977; children: Michael Thomas, Miriam Elaine, Richard Thomas. BS, Loma Linda U., Calif., MD, 1980. Lic. anatomic & clinical pathology Am. Bd. Pathology, Fla., 1985, forensic pathology Am. Bd. Pathology, Fla., 1989. Chief anatomic pathology Ehrling Bergquist Strategic Hosp., Offutt Air Force Base, Nebr., 1985—88; assoc. med. examiner Office of Med. Examiner, Fulton County, Atlanta, 1989—95; med. examiner Jackson County, Kansas City, 1996—2006; forensic pathologist Heartland Forensic Pathology LLC, Kansas City, 2007—. Clin. asst. prof. pathology Emory U. Sch. Medicine, Atlanta, 1991—94, asst. prof. pathology, 1994—95; clin. assoc. prof. U. Mo., Kans. City, 1995—; dir. Office of Jackson County Med. Examiner Forensic Pathology Tng. Program, 2002—06. Contbr. articles to profl. jours. Maj. USAF, 1985—88, Offutt AFB. Fellow: Am. Soc. Clin. Pathologists, Coll. Am. Pathologists, Am. Acad. Forensic Scis.; mem.: Alpha Omega Alpha. Achievements include leading construction of 10,000 sqare-foot medical examiner facility in Kansas City. Office: Jackson County Med Examiners 660 E 24th St Kansas City MO 64108 Home: 12717 Oakmont Dr Kansas City MO 64145 Office Fax: 816-404-1345. Personal E-mail: tyoung532@kc.rr.com.

YOUNG, TZAY Y., electrical and computer engineering educator; b. Shanghai, Jan. 11, 1933; came to U.S., 1958; s. Chao-Hsiung and Chiu-Ming (Chu) Y.; m. Lily Liu, Dec. 27, 1965; children: Debbie Chia-Pei, Arthur Chia-Kai. BS, Nat. Taiwan U., Taipei, 1955; MS, U. Vt., 1959; DEng, Johns Hopkins U., 1962. Rsch. assoc. Johns Hopkins U., Balt., 1962-63; mem. tech. staff Bell Labs., Murray Hill, NJ, 1963-64; asst. prof. Carnegie-Mellon U., Pitts., 1964-68, assoc. prof., 1968-74; prof. elec. and computer engring. U. Miami, Coral Gables, Fla., 1974—2003, acting chmn. dept., 1988-91, chmn. dept., 1991-2000, prof. emeritus, 2004—. Sr. postdoctoral rsch. assoc. NAS, NASA, Goddard Space Flight Ctr., Md., 1972-73. Author: (with T.W. Calvert) Classification, Estimation and Pattern Recognition, 1974; editor: (with K.S. Fu) Handbook of Pattern Recognition and Image Processing, 1986; editor: Handbook of Pattern Recognition and Image Processing, vol. 2, Computer Vision, 1994; also numerous articles. Rsch. grantee NSF, NASA, FHTIC, also indsl. grants. Fellow IEEE (assoc. editor Trans. Computers 1974-76; editorial bd. Trans. Pattern Analysis and Machine Intelligence 1979-84, adv. bd. 1984-90); mem. Sigma Xi, Eta Kappa Nu, Omicron Delta Kappa. E-mail: tyoung@miami.edu.

YOUNG, VERA LEE HALL, academic administrator, director; b. Natchitoches, La., Jan. 9, 1944; d. Sidney and Gertrude (Bell) H.; m. Willie L. Young, Aug. 21, 1965 (div. June 1971). BS, Grambling State U., 1967; MS, Bank St. Coll., 1977; PhD with distinction, Century U., 1985. Cert. tchr., La., N.J., N.Y. Ednl. cons. family day care program N.Y.C. Community Sch. Dist. 6; ednl. dir. Leslie Freeman Daycare Ctr., Bklyn., 1973-74; tchr. West N.Y. Bd. of Edn., 1978—; exec. dir., founder Operation Super Inst., Ft. Lee, NJ, 1986—. Lectr., tchr., panelist and cons. in field; participant Statewide Child Care Adv. Coun. Conf., N.J., 1980, State Ill. Tchrs. Conf., 1987, U. S.C. Tchrs. Conf., Georgetown, 1989; discussant Speaking for Schools radio program, N.J., N.Y.; program developer N.Y. Pub. Schs., 1996; del. 24th Internat. Congree Arts and Comms., 1997; instr. Funda C.C., Soweto, South Africa, 1998. Author: A Day Care Solution in America: The Learning Center, 1985; contbr. articles to field. Recipient Internat. Order of Merit award (# 320 of 500 world-wide), Internat. Biog. Ctr., Cambridge, Eng.; named Educator or Yr., Black Achievement and Awards, 1988; Dept. Labor grantee, Jerusalem, 1982-83 Mem. NEA, Nat. Alliance Bus., N.J. Edn. Assn. (conf. participant 1987), N.J. Women Bus. Ownership Orgn., Internat. Platform Assn., Internat. Reading Assn., Minority & Women Owned Bus. N.Y., Bank St. Coll. Alumni Assn., Gambling Coll. Alumni Assn. Mem. Dutch Reform Ch. Avocations: reading, travel, sports. Office: Operation Super 229 Main St # 1834 Fort Lee NJ 07024-5709

YOUNG, VERNON LEROY, plastic surgeon, researcher; b. Oneida, Ky., Oct. 14, 1945; s. Roy Young and Susie Lou; m. Jill Marie Meyer, Mar. 12, 1988; children: Ann Elizabeth, Hunter, Chase, Hampton. BA, U. Ky., Lexington, 1966, MD, 1970. Prof. plastic surgery Washington U., St. Louis, 1979—2002; pres. Body Aesthetic Plastic Surgery, St. Louis, 2002—. Cons. Cook Biotech, Indpls., 2000—06, Ethicon, NJ, 2003—06; mem. adv. bd. Renovo, Manchester, England, 2006, Aovtech, Sydney, 2006. Capt. US Army, 1971—73. Mem.: Am. Assn. Plastic Surgery, Am. Soc. for Aesthetic Surgery, Am. Soc. Plastic Surgeons. Episcopalian. Avocation: gardening. Home: 18229 Melrose Rd Wildwood MO 63069 Office: Body Aesthetic Plastic Surgery 969 Mason Rd Saint Louis MO 63141

YOUNG, VERNON LEWIS, retired lawyer; b. Seaman, Ohio, Oct. 13, 1919; s. Ezra S. and Anna (Bloom) Y.; m. Eileen Humble, 1941; children: Robert, Loretta, Bettie Jo, Jon W., Denise L. Student, Alfred Holbrook Coll., Manchester, Ohio, 1938—39; JD, Ohio No. U., Ada, 1942. Bar: Ohio 1942. Employee War Dept., 1942; sole practice West Union, Ohio, 1942-50, 78-81; ptnr. Young & Young, West Union, 1959—78, Young & Caldwell, 1978—81, 1995—2003, ret., 2003; ptnr. Young-Caldwell & BUBP, West Union, 1981-95; ret. Spl. counsel Office of Atty. Gen., State of Ohio, West Union, solicitor Cities of Jamestown, Seaman, Winchester, Manchester, Ohio; pros. atty. Adams County, Ohio, 1952-56, acting county judge, 1968-79. Mayor City of Seaman, 1944-46; mem. Adams County Health Bd., West Union, 1968-75; chmn. membership com. Eastern Shore Inst. Lifelong Learning, Fairhope, Ala., 1983-84; mem. Rep. Presdl. Task Force, 1980-94. Mem.: Adams County Bar Assn. (former pres.), Jr. Bar (pres. Ohio No. U. 1941—42), Ohio State Bar Assn., Ohio No. Univ., Lions (pres. 1950—51, dist. gov. 1951—52), Masons (32 degrees), Sigma Delta Kappa (chancellor 1940). Avocations: fishing, hunting, gardening. Home: 10 Hickory Dr Seaman OH 45679-9762

YOUNG, VICTORIA E., occupational health nurse, lawyer; b. Concord, Mich., Apr. 20, 1933; d. Arthur Raymond and Edith Louise (Hands) Y. Diploma, Mercy Sch. Nursing, Jackson, Mich., 1954; BSN, UCLA, 1960, MPH in Adminstrn., 1966; JD, U. West LA, Culver City, 1973. Bar: Calif., U.S. Dist. Ct., Calif.; RN, Calif.; cert. pub. health nurse, pediatric nurse practitioner. Pub. health nurse L.A. City and Los Angeles County Health Dept.; exec. dir. Santa Monica (Calif.) Vis. Nurse Assn.; sch. nurse practitioner L.A. Unified Schs.; relief nurse L.A. Times. Vol. Moorpark City Hall, Moorpark Sr. Ctr; mem. Disaster Assistance Response Team, Moorpark. Ret. capt. USNR, Desert Storm. Mem. Nat. Assn. Pediatric Nurse Assocs. and Practitioners, Calif. Bar Assn., Fleet Res. Assn., Moorpark Woman's Fortnightly Club (treas. 1998-99). Home: 4359 Brookdale Ln Moorpark CA 93021-2302

YOUNG, VINCE PAUL, JR., professional football player; b. Houston, June 18, 1983; Student, U. Tex., 2002—06. Quarterback Tenn. Titans, Nashville, 2006—. Named Rose Bowl MVP, 2005, 2006, ESPY award, Best Male Coll. Athlete, 2006, NFL Offensive Rookie of Yr., AP, 2006; recipient Davey O'Brien Nat. Quarterback Award, 2005, Manning award, 2005. Achievements include being the quarterback in NCAA div.1 National Champion for Texas Longhorns, 2006; being the only player in NCAA div. 1 history to pass for 2,500 yards and rush for 1,000 yards in the same season, 2005; the third overall selection in the 2006 NFL Draft. Office: Tenn Titans One Titans Way Nashville TN 37213

YOUNG, WAYNE C., lawyer; b. Camden, NJ, July 8, 1970; BS, Ind. State U., 1993; JD, South Tex. Coll. Law, Houston, 1997. Bar: Tex. 1997, Tex. Supreme Ct., US Dist. Ct. (so. dist. Tex.). Sr. assoc. Powers & Frost, L.L.P., Houston. Named a Rising Star, Tex. Super Lawyers mag., 2006. Mem.: Houston Bar Assn. Office: Powers & Frost LLP 2400 One Houston Ctr 1221 McKinney St Houston TX 77010 Office Phone: 713-767-1555. E-mail: wyoung@powersfrost.com. *

YOUNG, WILLIAM BENJAMIN, retired special education educator; b. Wichita, Kans., Jan. 30, 1929; s. Ernest William and Florence Belle (McCann) Y.; m. La Vona P., Feb., 1949 (div. 1973); children: Lynda, David, Timothy; m. Patricia Sue Reber, Aug., 1974. Student, Southwestern Coll., Winfield, Kans., 1947-48; B in Gen. Edn., U. Omaha, 1961; MS in Pers. Counseling, Miami U., Oxford, Ohio, 1965; PhD in Exceptional Edn., Adminstrn. and Counseling, Ohio State U., 1972. Cert. elem. and secondary adminstr., tchr., counselor, psychologist, psychometrist, spl. edn., mental retardation, learning disabled/behavior disordered, emotionally handicapped, Ind.; cert. K-12 guidance counselor and edn. leadership, Fla.; lic sexologist, flight instr.; lic. Coast Guard capt. Enlisted USAF, 1948, commd. 2nd lt., 1955, advanced through grades to capt., 1960, ret., 1966; numerous teaching and counseling positions as civilian, 1966-91; co-owner, instr. Ft. Wayne Ground Schs., Ind., 1984-88; marriage and family counselor, pvt. practice, 1966-91; tchr., counselor, behavior specialist Broward County Schs., Ft. Lauderdale, Fla., 1989-99; ret., 1999. Cons., internat. presenter/lectr. learning and behavior problems. Mem. 32 degree Masons. Avocations: travel, swimming. Home and Office: 1101 SW 70th Ter Plantation FL 33317-4135 E-mail: wby130@aol.com.

YOUNG, WILLIAM D., lawyer; b. Aug. 26, 1960; BBA, U. Miss., 1982, JD, 1984. Bar: Tex. 1985. Ptnr. Vinson & Elkins LLP, Dallas, 1998—, co-head Bus. & Internat. Sect. Mem.: ABA. Office: Vinson & Elkins Trammell Crow Ctr 2001 Ross Ave, Ste 3700 Dallas TX 75201 Office Phone: 214-220-7994. E-mail: byoung@velaw.com.

YOUNG, WILLIAM GLOVER, federal judge; b. Huntington, NY, Sept. 23, 1940; s. Woodhull Benjamin and Margaret Jean (Wilkes) Young; m. Beverly June Bigelow, Aug. 5, 1967; children: Mark Edward, Jeffrey Woodhull, Todd Russell. AB, Harvard U., 1962, LLB, 1967; LLD, New Eng. Sch. Law, 2001. Bar: Mass. 1967, admitted to practice: US Supreme

Ct. 1970. Law clk. to chief justice Supreme Jud. Ct., Mass., 1967-68; spl. asst. atty. gen. Mass., 1969-72; chief legal counsel to gov. Mass., 1972-74; assoc. Bingham, Dana and Gould, Boston, 1968-72, ptnr., 1975-78; assoc. justice Superior Ct., Commonwealth of Mass., Boston, 1978-85; judge US Dist. Ct. Mass., Boston, 1985—, chief judge, 1999—2005. Mem. budget com. US Jud. Conf., 1987—2001, chmn. economy subcom., 1991—2001; lectr. Boston Coll. Law Sch., 1968—90, Boston U. Law Sch., 1979—, Harvard Law Sch., 1979—90. Author: Evidence, Massachusetts Practice Series, 1998, Reflections of a Trial Judge, 2002, Massachusetts Evidentiary Standards, 2006, Vanishing Trials, Vanishing Juries, Vanishing Constitution, 2007; co-author: Daubert's Gatekeeper: The Role of the District Judge in Admitting Expert Testimony. Capt. US Army, 1962—64. Mem.: Boston Bar Assn., Mass. Bar Assn., Am. Law Inst., Harvard Alumni (pres. 1976—77). Office: US Courthouse Rm 5710 Boston MA 02210 Office Phone: 617-748-9138. Business E-Mail: william_young@mad.uscourts.gov.

YOUNG, WILLIAM H., labor union administrator; b. 1947; m. Debbie Young; 4 children. Mem., Ctrl. Calif. Coast Br. 52 Nat. Assn. Letter Carriers, San Luis Obispo, 1965, pres., Ctrl. Calif. Coast Br. 52, 1971—78, regional adminstrv. asst., 1978—86, nat. bus. agent San Francisco region, 1986—90, asst. sec.-treas. Washington, 1990—94, dir. city devel., v.p., 1994—98, exec. v.p., 1998—2002, nat. pres., 2002—. Officer Calif. State Assn., 1972—; v.p. Am. Fedn. Labor, Coun. Indsl. Orgn. (AFL-CIO). Nat. v.p. Muscular Dystrophy Assn. (MDA); mem. adv. bd. Walter P. Reuther Libr. Labor and Urban Affairs, Wayne State U., Detroit. Served with US Army. Office: Nat Assn Letter Carriers 100 Ind Ave NW Washington DC 20001-2144 Office Phone: 202-393-4695. *

YOUNG, WILLIAM WEBB, military officer, aire warfare specialist, poet; b. St. Louis, Aug. 4, 1967; s. Raymond Andrew and Betty Rosella (Myers) Young; children: Jamie Elizabeth, Christen Lee, Sara Rayan. Commd. ensign USN, 1987; Persian Gulf War/Cold War vet. Svc. officer Three Rivers Serenity Group, Poplar Bluff, Mo., 1989—2002, dist. 8 spl. needs com. chmn., 2001—. Author numerous poems. Local stream team coord. Mo. Dept. Conservation, Butler County, Mo., 1997—, frontiers program leader, 1998—; water quality monitoring vol. Mo. Dept. Natural Resources, Butler County, Mo., 1999—2002. Decorated Battle "E" Award Persian Excursion US Navy, Order of the Spanish Main, Joint Meritorious Unit award, Nat. Def. medal, Overseas Deployment Ribbon, Good Conduct medal, Kuwait Liberation medal, Saudi Arabia Liberation Medal, Disting. Expert Pistol medal, Expert Rifle medal, Meritorious Unit Commendation for Bravery and Heroism, Russian Cold War Star, Navy Achievement medal, Silver Life Saving medal; recipient Iliad Lit. award, Internat. Poet of Merit, 1996, Editors Choice award, 1996, Americanism award, Grande Voiture of NJ Navy, 1990, Loyalty Day award, VFW, 1990. Fellow: K.C. (1st degree crusader, Altar Server award 1981); mem.: Internat. Soc. Poets, Disabled Am. Vets. (life Golden Anchor award 1988), Amherst Soc., Iraqi Desert Yacht Club, Gulf of Oman Yacht Club, Gulf of Sidra Yacht Club, Persian Gulf Yacht Club, Persian Gulf Health Club (life; adminstr.), Am. Legion (honor guard). Roman Catholic. Avocation: art. Home: 201 W Lexington Ave Poplar Bluff MO 63901

YOUNG, WISE, neurosurgeon, educator, medical researcher; b. Hong Kong, Jan. 1, 1950; BS in Chemistry and Biology, Reed U., 1971; PhD in Physiology and Biophysics, U. Iowa, 1975; MD, Stanford U., 1977. Cert. Na. Bd. of Med. Examiners, 1977, NY State Med. Lic., 1977. Residency tng., surgery and neurosurgery NYU Med. Ctr., 1977—79; rschr. NYU Neurosurgery Rsch. Labs., 1979—84, assoc. prof., 1984—89, dir., 1984—, prof., 1989—97; head, founding dir., prof. W.M. Keck Ctr. for Collaborative Neuroscience, Rutgers U., Piscataway, NJ, 1997—. Elected Richard H. Schindell Chair in Neuroscience, Rutgers U., 2006—. Contbr. articles to profl. jours.; founder, former editor-in-chief Journal of Neurotrama, has appeared 20/20 with Barbara Walters, with Christopher Reeve on Today Show, 48 Hours, Eye-to-Eye, Fox News and CNN news mag. with Jeff Greenfield, work featured in Life, USA Today and others. Named Tall Texan of Yr., 1997, 'America's Best' in the field of spinal cord injury rsch., TIME Mag., 2001; named to Spinal Cord Injury Hall of Fame (first researcher), 2005; recipient Jacob Javitz Neuroscience award, NIH Nat. Inst. Neurol. Disorders and Stroke, 1985—92, Wakeman award for rsch. in Neuroscis., 1991, Disting. Svc. award, Neurotrauma Soc., 1994, 'Cure' Award, 1998, Trustees Award for Excellence in Rsch., 2001, Asian Am. Achievement Award, 2002, Douglass Medal, 2003, Elizabeth M. Boggs Award, 2004. Mem.: NAS. Office: Rutgers Univ Divsn Life Scis Nelson Biol Labs 604 Allison Rd Piscataway NJ 08854 E-mail: wisey@pipeline.com, young@biology.rutgers.edu. *

YOUNGBLOOD, BETTY J., academic administrator; b. Detroit; m. Ralph P. Youngblood; 1 child. BA in Political Sci., Oakland U., Rochester, Mich.; MA in South Asian Studies, U. Minn., PhD in Political Sci. Formerly mem. faculty State U. West Ga., Tex. Tech. U.; various adminstrv. positions Kennesaw State U., Marietta, Ga.; v.p. acad. affairs MacMurray Coll., Jacksonville, Ill., Wesley Coll., Dover, Del.; vice chancellor acad. affairs, dean faculty, prof. polit. sci. U. Wis.-Superior, 1990-91, acting chancellor, 1991-92, chancellor, 1992—95; pres. We. Oreg. U., 1995—2002, Lake Superior State U., Mich., 2002—. Cons., evaluator North Ctrl. Assn. Colls. and Schs. Contbr. articles to profl. jours. Bd. dirs. United Way, Sault Ste. Marie. Rsch. grantee for study in N.W. India. Mem. Sault Ste. Marie C. of C., War Meml. Hosp., Rotary. Office: Lake Superior State Univ 650 W Easterday Ave Sault Sainte Marie MI 49783

YOUNGBLOOD, SANDRA LEA, retired secondary school educator; b. St. Joseph, Mich., Apr. 16, 1939; d. Franklin Alba and Mary Elizabeth (Flaradean) Youngblood. AA, Benton Harbor C.C., Mich., 1959; BA, Western Mich. U., Kalamazoo, 1961; MA, Mich. State U., Lansing, 1970. Tchr. social studies Muskegon Heights Jr. High, Mich., 1961—64; tchr. English and reading Reeths-Puffer Sch. Dist., Muskegon, Mich., 1964—90; ret., 1990. Pvt. reading tchr., Muskegon, 1964—91; reading tutor Benona Elem. Sch., Shelby, Mich., 1993—. Author: (poetry book) Random. Mem. treatment com. Substance Abuse Collaborative Muskegon County Health Project, 2003—. Named Outstanding Polit. Sci. Student, Benton Harbor C.C., 1959, Outstanding History Student, DAR, 1957; recipient Peacekeeper award, Open Peace Edn. Network, 2002. Mem.: NAACP, Mich. Assn. Ret. Sch. Pers. (sec. Oceana County chpt. 1992—2004), Nat. Pub. Radio and TV, Truthout, Physicians Com. for Responsible Medicine, Spl. Olympics, Habitat for Humanity, Am. Soc. for the Prevention of Cruelty to Animals, Nat. Pks. Conservation Assn., Pets Best Friends (sec. 1998—2005), World Wildlife Fedn., Humane Soc. US, Defenders of Wildlife, Audubon Soc., Frederic Meijer Gardens, Interfaith Alliance, Women's History Mus., Muskegan Mus. Art. Democrat. Avocations: writing poetry, needlecrafts.

YOUNGBLOOD, SYLVIA T., counselor; b. Phila., July 9, 1970; d. David and Shirley Lee Fields; m. Anthony W. Youngblood, May 7, 1994; children: Zachariah E., Chloe S. BS, Lincoln U., Phila., 1992, M of Human Sci., 1999. Dist. coord. Big Bro. Big Sister, Phila., 1992—94; violence prevention facilitator PSSC, Phila., 1995; case mgr., supr. Crime Prevention Assn., Phila., 1995—2001; therapist, cons. Carson Valley Sch., Flourtown, Pa., 2002—. Facilitator sex edn. Harambee Charter Sch., Phila., 1999—2000; facilitator peer pressure edn. Bapt. Ch., Phila., 2007—. Author: (book) God Is Watching Over You, 2007, (parent devotion book) 31 Days Of Victorious Parenting Devotion, 2007. Telephone operator WHYY Channel 12/91FM, Phila., 1999—2001; candy striper Pa. Hosp., Phila., 1985; Sunday sch. tchr. Mt. Airy Ch., Phila., 2004—, vacation bible sch. tchr., 1995—. Mem.: Pi Gamma Mu. Avocations: cooking, writing.

YOUNG-CAMPBELL, LAURA L., speech pathology/audiology services professional; b. Alaska; d. Ken and Alice Young; m. Donald Campbell; 1 child, Jennifer. BE in Comm. Disorders & Spl. Edn., Gonzaga U., Spokane, Wash., 1979—83; MS in Speech & Hearing Scis., U. Ariz., Tucson, 1990—93. Cert. spl. svcs. in speech pathology Alaska Dept. Edn., 1983, cert. of clin. competence in speech pathology Am. Speech-Hearing Assn., 1994, advanced cert. speech pathology Alaska Dept. Edn., 2002. Speech-lang. pathologist Matanuska-Susitna Borough Sch. Dist., Palmer, Alaska, 1983—. Mem. editl. bd. Perpspectives on Sch. Based Issues, Am. Speech-Hearing Assn., Md. Del., amb. to China People to People Internat., 2006—; vol. Alaska Health Fair, 1998—; healthy hearing vol. Spl. Olympics, Alaska, 2002—. Recipient award for continuing edn., Am. Speech-Hearing Assn., 1994—2006, Friend of Assn. award, Alaska Speech-Hearing Assn., 2004. Mem.: Mat-Su Speech-Hearing Assn., Coun. Exceptional Children, Alaska Speech Hearing Assn. (exec. bd. 1995—), Am. Speech-Hearing Assn. (licentiate; legislative councilor 2005—), Mat-Su Alaska Edn. Assn. (life; del. assembly 1999—). Avocations: travel, gardening, reading, movies. Office: Matanuska-Susitna Borough Schs 501 N Gulkana St Palmer AK 99645 Home Phone: 907-376-2261.

YOUNGDAHL, JAY THOMAS, lawyer; b. St. Louis, May 29, 1952; s. James Edward and Patricia Ruth (Lucy) Y.; m. Mary Ellen Vogler, Dec. 12, 1981; children: Benjamin Douglass, Colleen Alexandra. BS, U. Houston, 1978; JD, U. Tex., 1980; MA, St. John's Coll., 2004; MDiv, Harvard U., 2007. Bar: Ark. 1981, Tex., 1992, D.C. 1993, U.S. Dist. Ct. (ea. and we. dists.) Ark. 1981, U.S. Ct. Appeals (8th, 10th and 11th cirs.) 1981, U.S. Claims Ct. 1992, U.S. Tax Ct. 1981, Tex. 1994. Mng. ptnr. Youngdahl Law Firms, 1981—. Gen. counsel Vox.com, East Bay Pub., L.P.; adj. instr. Webster Coll., Little Rock, 1983-95; adj. prof. U. Ark., Little Rock Sch. of Law, 1988-90; mem. Ark. Employment Security Div. Adv. Coun., Little Rock, 1980-97, Gov.'s Workers Compensation Study Com., Little Rock, 1985-86. With U.S. Army, 1972-74. Mem. ABA, Ark. Bar Assn. (chmn. labor law sect. 1983-84), ATLA, Ark. Trial Lawyers Assn., AFL-CIO Lawyers Coordinating Com. (adv. bd.), Acad. Rail Labor Attys., Tex. Trial Lawyers Assn., State Bar Tex. (Pro Bono Coll. 1996). Avocations: triathlons, art, culinary arts. Office: Youngdahl Law Firm 1414 S Friendswood Friendswood TX 77546 Office Phone: 281-996-0750. Business E-Mail: jyoungdahl@youngdahl.com.

YOUNGDAHL, PAUL FREDERICK, mechanical engineer; b. Brockway, Pa., Oct. 8, 1921; s. Harry Ludwig and Esther Marie (Carlson) Y.; m. Elinor Louise Jensen, Nov. 27, 1943; children: Mark Erik, Marcia Linnea, Melinda Louise. Student Pa. State U., 1938-40; BS in Engring., U. Mich., 1942, MS in Engring., 1949, PhD, 1962. Indsl. and devel. engr. DuPont, Bridgeport, Conn., 1942-43, Carneys Point, N.J., 1946-48; dir. research Mech. Handling Systems, Detroit, 1953-62; prof. U. Mich., Ann Arbor, 1962-74; cons. mech. engr., Palo Alto, Calif., 1974—; dir. Liquid Drive Corp., Holly, Mich. Contbr. articles to profl. jours. With USNR, 1943-46. Mem. Mich. Soc. Profl. Engrs., Nat. Soc. Profl. Engrs., ASME, Am. Soc. Engring. Edn., Mich. Assn. Professions, Sigma Xi, Tau Beta Pi, Phi Kappa Phi, Pi Tau Sigma. Methodist. Address: 151 Del Mesa Carmel Carmel CA 93923 Office Phone: 831-622-9965.

YOUNGEN, GREGORY KEITH, medical librarian; b. Terre Haute, Ind., Dec. 8, 1955; s. Calvin Keith and Barbara Joan Youngen; m. Valerie Ann Lashbrook, Sept. 16, 1978; children: Angela Rene Cameron, Anthony Keith. BS, Ind. State U., Terre Haute, 1982; MLS, Ind. U., Bloomington, 1983. Reference libr. Tex. Dept. Water Resources, Austin, 1983—85; asst. engring. libr. Purdue U., West Lafayette, Ind., 1985—88; engring. libr. Argonne Nat. Lab., Chgo., 1988—90; supr. libr. Oak Ridge Nat. Lab., Ill., 1990—95; physics/astronomy libr. U. Ill., Urbana, 1995—2003, vet. medicine libr., 2004—. With USN, 1974—78. Mem.: Med. Libr. Assn. (chair vet. med. libr. sect. 2006—). Home: 2201 Wyld Dr Urbana IL 61801 Office: Univ Ill 2201 S Lincoln Ave Urbana IL 61802 Home Phone: 217-344-8140; Office Phone: 217-333-8778.

YOUNGER, JENNIFER A., university librarian; BA in history, U. Wis.-Madison, MLA, PhD in info. studies. Various positions in libr. sys. U. Wis.-Madison, 1977—91; asst. dir. tech. svc. Ohio State U. libr., 1991—97; Edward H. Arnold dir. univ. libraries U. Notre Dame, 1997—. Editor: (jour.) Library Resources & Technical Services. Mem.: ALA, Assn. Libr. Collections & Tech. Svc. (pres. 1993—94), Beta Phi Mu. Office: Univ Notre Dame 221 Hesburgh Library Notre Dame IN 46556 Office Phone: 574-631-7790. Office Fax: 574-631-6772. E-mail: Jennifer.A.Younger@nd.edu. *

YOUNGER, JUDITH TESS, law educator; b. NYC, Dec. 20, 1933; d. Sidney and Kate (Greenbaum) Weintraub; m. Irving Younger, Jan. 21, 1955; children: Rebecca, Abigail M. BS, Cornell U., 1954; JD, NYU, 1958; LLD (hon.), Hofstra U., 1974. Bar: N.Y. 1958, U.S. Supreme Ct 1962, D.C. 1983, Minn. 1985. Law clk. to judge U.S. Dist. Ct., 1958-60; assoc. firm Chadbourne, Parke, Whiteside & Wolff, NYC, 1960-62; mem. firm Younger and Younger, and (successors), 1962-67; adj. asst. prof. NYU Sch. Law, 1967-69; asst. atty. gen. State of N.Y., 1969-70; assoc. prof. Hofstra U. Sch. Law, 1970-72, prof., assoc. dean, 1972-74; dean, prof. Syracuse Coll. Law, 1974-75; dep. dean, prof. law Cornell Law Sch., 1975-78, prof. law, 1975-85; vis. prof. U. Minn. Law Sch., Mpls., 1984-85, prof., 1985-91, Joseph E. Wargo Anoka County Bar Assn. prof. family law, 1991—. Of counsel Popham, Haik, Schnobrich & Kaufman, Ltd., Mpls., 1989-95; cons. NOW, 1972-74, Suffolk County for Revision of Its Real Property Tax Act, 1972-73; mem. N.Y. Gov.'s Panel To Screen Candidates of Ct. of Claims Judges, 1973-74; mem. Minn. Lawyers' Profl. Responsibility Bd., 1991-93. Contbr. articles to profl. jours. Trustee Cornell U., 1973-78. Mem.: AAUP (v.p. Cornell U. chpt. 1978—79), ABA (council legal edn. 1975—79), Minn. Bar Assn., Assn. of Bar of City of N.Y., Am. Law Inst. (adv. restatement property 1982—84). Home: 3520 W Calhoun Pkwy Minneapolis MN 55416-4657 Office: U Minn Law Sch Minneapolis MN 55455 Home Phone: 612-925-5894; Office Phone: 612-625-5844. Business E-Mail: young001@umn.edu.

YOUNGER, LAURIE, broadcast executive; BA in Comm., Queens Coll.; MBA, UCLA, 1983. Former dir. bus. affairs 20th Century Fox; dir. bus. affairs network TV divsn. The Walt Disney Co., 1985—86, v.p. bus. affairs, 1986—90; sr. v.p. bus. affairs and adminstrn. Walt Disney TV and Telecomm.; sr. v.p. ABC Inc., 1996—98, sr. v.p., CFO, 1998—2003, exec. v.p., CFO, 2003—; exec. v.p. ABC TV Distbn., 2000—03; pres. Buena Vista Worldwide TV, 2003—. Named one of 100 Most Powerful Women in Hollywood, Hollywood Reporter, 2003, 2004, 2005, 2006. Office: ABC Inc 500 S Buena Vista St Burbank CA 91521-4775 *

YOUNGLOVE, GEORGIA A., agricultural studies educator; d. Bill Ollan and Helen Carolyn (Person) Younglove; 1 child, Brooke Lynn Howard. BS, Okla. State U., Stillwater, 1991; MS, Tex. A&M U., College Station, 1993; PhD, U. Wyo., Laramie, 1998. Grad. asst. U. Wyo., Laramie, 1994—98; assoc. prof. agr. Chadron State Coll., Chadron, Nebr., 1998—. Contbr. articles to profl. jours. Nat. adv. Am. Pre-Vet Med. Assn., 2005—06; youth dir. Colo. Pinto Horse Assn., 2006; treas. Whitney (Nebr.) Sch. Bd., 2001—04. Named Outstanding Prof., Chadron State Coll. Sch. Profl. Studies, 2003—04. Mem.: Midwest Soc. Animal Scientists (quadrathlon com. 2004—), Am. Soc. Animal Scientists, Soc. for Range Mgmt. (assoc.), Am. Paint Horse Assn., Am. Pinto Horse Assn. (life). Office: Chadron State Coll 1000 Main Chadron NE 69337 Office Phone: 308-432-6237. Office Fax: 308-432-6369. Business E-Mail: gyounglove@csc.edu.

YOUNGMAN, LOLA JEANNE, music educator; b. Royal Oak, Mich., Mar. 18, 1951; d. Robert Edward Grant and Elaine Margaret Eddy; m. David Frederick Youngman, June 22, 2002; m. Richard Vincent Lewis, Apr. 9, 1977 (div. Sept. 30, 2001); children: Adam Ryan Lewis, Jessica Marie Lewis. BS in Edn., Ctrl. Mich. U., Mt. Pleasant, 1973; student, Wayne State U., Detroit, 1975—76. Cert. tchr. Yamaha Music Sch., Atlanta & L.A., lic. Real Estate N.C., 1987, cert. tchr. K-8, tchr. K-9 music. Elem. vocal music tchr. Lamphere Sch. Dist., Madison Heights, Mich., 1974—78; dir., tchr. Yamaha Music Sch., Raleigh, NC, 1985—95; pvt. piano tchr. Raleigh, 1985—97; real estate agent Doreen Silber & Co., Raleigh, 1987; elem. vocal music tchr. Wake County Schs., Raleigh, 1997—. Musician (pianist); singer: Dave Youngman Band, 2002—. Mem.: N.C. Assn. Educators, Black Horse Run Women's Club (pres. 1988, v.p.). Avocations: tennis, singing. Home: 4908 Boulder Creek Ln Raleigh NC 27613

YOUNGMAN, OWEN RALPH, newspaper executive; b. Chgo., Apr. 24, 1953; s. Ralph Elmer and Charlotte Earldine (Ottoson) Y.; m. Linda Ann Erlandson, Aug. 24, 1975. DSc, LHD, North Park U., 2005. Sportswriter Ashtabula (Ohio) Star-Beacon, 1969-71; office clk. Chgo. Tribune, 1971-73, transcriber, 1973-75, copy editor, slotman, 1976-79, copy chief, news editor, 1979-83, dep. sports editor, 1984-86, assoc. met. editor, 1986-88, assoc. features editor, 1988-90, dep. fin. editor, 1990-91, assoc. mng. editor, 1991-93, features editor, 1993-95, mng. editor, features, 1995, dir. interactive media, 1996-99, dir. planning and devel., 1999, v.p. devel., 2000—06, sr. v.p. strategy and devel., 2007—. Bd. dirs. Swedish Covenant Hosp., Legacy website, Solti Found. USA; nat. exec. bd. Evang. Covenant Ch. Named to Ashtabula HS Alumni Hall of Fame, Ohio, 2005. Mem. Newspaper Assn. Am. New Media Fedn., Am. Soc. Newspaper Editors, Presidents Club North Park U., Arts Club Chgo. Avocation: vocal and instrumental music. Home: 40 Kenmore Ave Deerfield IL 60015-4750 Office: Chicago Tribune 435 N Michigan Ave Chicago IL 60611-4066 Home Phone: 847-940-1191; Office Phone: 312-222-4179. Business E-Mail: oyoungman@tribune.com.

YOUNG-POHLMAN, COLETTE LISA, music educator; b. Honolulu, July 20, 1952; d. Richard Ah On and Winifred Oi Chin Chang Young; m. Kurt I. Pohlman, Oct. 5, 1985; 1 child, Vinson Sterling Pohlman. EdB, U. Hawaii-Manoa, Honolulu, 1974, postgrad., 1975. Part-time tchr. dept. edn. Kalani High, Honolulu, 1978—79; chpt. 1 reading tchr. McKinley High, Honolulu, 1979—80, basic skills tchr., 1980—81; part-time tchg. asst. pvt. preschs., Honolulu, 1981—82; part-time tchr. dept. edn., chpt. 1 reading Ala Wai Elem. and Palolo Elem., 1982—83; classroom tchr. Heeia Elem., Kaneohe, Hawaii, 1990; part-time tchr. dept. edn. Wailupe Valley Elem., Honolulu, 1990—91; instrnl. resource augmentation tchr. Maemae Elem., Honolulu, 1991—92; project tchr. Title I reading Washington Intermediate, Honolulu, 1992—94; instrnl. resource augmentation tchr. Accelerated Gifted & Talented Performing Arts, Kailua, Hawaii, 1994—97; classroom tchr. Mokapu Elem., Kailua, 1997—2002, instrnl. resource augmentation music tchr., 2002—07, Ann. Winter Concert and Talent Showcase, 2002—07; music specialist Aica Elem., 2007—. Dir., choreographer, scripting/editing of musical play productions in elem. settings Windward Dist., Kalaheo Complex. Dir.(choreographer, writer): (multicultural musical plays) Little Firefly, the Rough-face Girl, Double Happiness, Souled Out; composer: There's Something About a Pet, 1998 (2d Pl. award, 1998); composer: (choreographer) (new sch. song dance) Enchantment of Mokapu, 2000, Reading Rap, 2003, (music video) Enchantment of Mokapu, 2006, (plays) Petite Rouge, 2006—07 (Hawaii Student Digital Showcase grant award, 2007); prodr. (dir.): (weekly TV program Olelo Cablevision) Na Keiki Hauoli o Mokapu, The Happy Children of Mokapu. Mem., tchr. Boy Scouts Am. Troop 113, 1999—. Mem.: Hawaii State Tchrs. Assn., Hawaii Music Educators Assn., Hawaii Orff Schulwerk Assn. (bd. dirs. 2005—), Am. Orff Schulwerk Assn., Music Educators Nat. Conf., Nat. Educators Assn. Avocations: composing songs, poetry, singing, keyboard, storytelling. Home: 45-427 Loli'i St Kaneohe HI 96744-5911 Office Phone: 808-483-7200 ext. 246. Business E-Mail: colette-youngpohlman@notes.k12.hi.us.

YOUNGQUIST, WALTER LEWELLYN, geologist, consultant; b. Mpls., May 5, 1921; s. Walter Raymond and Selma Regina (Knock) Y.; m. Elizabeth Salome Pearson, Dec. 11, 1943; children: John, Karen, Louise, Robert. BA, Gustavus Adolphus Coll., St. Peter, Minn., 1942; MSc, U. Iowa, 1943, PhD, 1948. Registered profl. geologist, Oreg. Jr. geologist U.S. Geol. Survey, 1943-44; rsch. assoc. U. Iowa, Iowa City, 1945-48; asst. prof. geology U. Idaho, Moscow, 1948-51; sr. geologist Internat. Petroleum Co., Talara, Peru, 1951-54; prof. geology U. Kans., Lawrence, 1954-57, U. Oreg., Eugene, 1957-66; cons. geologist Minerals dept. Exxon Corp., Houston, 1968-73; geothermal cons. Eugene Water & Electric Bd., 1973-92; ind. cons. Eugene, 1992—. Author: Investing in Natural Resources, 1980, Mineral Resources and the Destinies of Nations, 1990, GeoDestinies, 1997; co-author: Ordovician Cephalopod Fauna of Baffin Island, 1954. Ensign, USNR, 1944-45. Recipient Lowden Prize in Geology, U. Iowa, 1943, Journalist award, Am. Assn. Petroleum Geology, 2000, Disting. Alumni award Gustavus Adolphus Coll., 2002. Fellow AAAS, Geol. Soc. Am.; mem. Am. Assn. Petroleum Geologists, Internat. Assn. Math. Geology, Soc. Exploration Geophysicists, Geothermal Resources Coun., N.W. Energy Assn., N.Y. Acad. Scis., Sigma Xi. Lutheran. Avocations: fly-tying, photography, fishing. Office: PO Box 5501 Eugene OR 97405-0501 Personal E-mail: wyoungst@mindspring.com.

YOUNGREN, DELVANA HOPE, secondary school educator; b. LA, Apr. 13, 1941; d. Herman Melvin and Betty Floy (England) Ferguson; m. Allan Morse Youngren, June 17, 1961; children: Erik Allan, Deanna Marie. BA, Calif. State Coll., Long Beach, 1963; MA, Calif. State Coll., 1968. Cert. secondary tchr., Calif. Tchr. Long Beach (Calif.) Unified Sch. Dist., 1963-70, Faith Christian Acad., Pasadena, Tex., 1975-80, Cherry Valley (Calif.) Brethren Christian Sch., 1980-86, Arrowhead Christian Acad., Redlands, Calif., 1984—87, New Life Christian Acad., San Bernardino, Calif., 1987-90, Mt. View Jr. H.S., Beaumont, Calif., 1990—2002, Mt. View Mid. Sch., Beaumont, 2002—. Chmn. GATE, Gifted and Talented, Calif.; educator Drug, Alcohol & Tobacco Edn.; tech. computer tchr. On-Line Learning, Novanet. Head computer dept. San Gorgonio Pass Geneal. Soc., Banning, Calif., 1992-95; mem. Yucaipa Geneal. Soc., 1992-95. Mem. NEA, Calif. Tchrs. Assn., Beaumont Tchrs. Assn., Calif. Inland Area Math. Project, Soroptomists (Beaumont chpt.). Republican. Avocations: sports, cats. Home: 10640 Jonathan Ave Cherry Valley CA 92223-4974 Office: Beaumont United Sch Dist PO Box 187 Beaumont CA 92223-0187 Office Phone: 951-845-1627. E-mail: delvana@aol.com.

YOUNGS, DIANE CAMPFIELD, learning disabilities specialist, educator; b. Margaretville, NY, Feb. 16, 1954; d. Richard Maxwell and Charlotte June (Rickard) Campfield; m. William H. Youngs, June 30, 1984. BS in Edn., SUNY, Geneseo, 1976, MS in Edn., 1977. Professionally recognized spl. educator. Tchr. educable mentally retarded Tompkins-Seneca-Tioga Bd. Coop. Edni. Svcs., Ithaca, NY, 1978-80; tchr. learning disabled Joint Svc. for Spl. Edn., Mishawaka, Ind., 1980-97; assoc. faculty Ind. U.-South Bend Grad. Sch. Edn., 1996-98. Vis. lectr. dept. edn. Ind. U., South Bend, 1998-2002, lectr., 2002—; mem. Task Force for Reorgn. Spl. Edn., Mishawaka, 1990-91; coord. Tiny Talkers Summer Speech/Lang. Camp, 1994—. Recipient Tchg. award, Ind. U. Trustees, 2005, 2006. Mem. AAUP, Coun. for Exceptional Children, Learning Disabilities Assn., Coun. for Learning Disabilities, Ind. Prof. Reading, Internat. Reading Assn., Nat. Coun. Tchrs. English, Kappa Delta Pi. E-mail: dyoungs@iusb.edu.

YOUNGS, MICHAEL THERON, JR., non-commissioned officer; b. Binghamton, NY, Nov. 30, 1973; s. Michael Theron Youngs, Sr. and Diane Marie Sykes; m. Marianne Jeanette Viren, Apr. 17, 1992; children:

Mychelle Leigh, Lauren Nicole, Michael Theron III. Student, Ctrl. Tex. Coll., 2003. Enlisted US Army, 1992, advanced through grades to sgt. first class, 2003, gens. enlisted aide Ft. Drum, NY, 1997—98, 2001—03, asst. dining facility mgr. Ft. Drum, NY, 2003—05. Task force mayor U.S. Army, Iraq, 2004—05. Fellow: 1000 Islands 700 Club. Avocations: bowling, softball, golf. Home: 9116 B General Pike Loop Fort Drum NY 13603 Office: E Company 210th BSB Bldg 10182 4th Armored Divsn Fort Drum NY 13602 Business E-Mail: michael.youngs@us.army.mil.

YOUNGS, WILLIAM ELLIS, photographer, electronics engineer; b. Miami, Fla., Apr. 30, 1916; s. Edward Ray and Maude Myrtle (Burd) Y.; m. Mary Helen Still, Aug. 28, 1948; 1 child, Renee Helen. Student, Nat. Radio Inst., 1952. Film technician Washington Motion Picture Co., 1934-35, U.S. Dept. State, Washington, 1948-53; night service mgr. MGM Film Exchange, Washington, 1936-41; mgr., projectionist Calvert Theatre, Prince Frederick, Md., 1941-42; research asst. Exec. Office of the President, Washington, 1942; photo lab technician Office War Info., Washington, 1942-43; br. chief, advisor film and equipment USIA, Washington, 1953-78; engr., projectionist Motion Picture Assn. Am., Washington, 1979-94; photographer, chaplain Vets. Commn., Falls Church, Va., 1997—. Advisor Stephens Coll., Columbia, Mo., 1973-75. Columnist Falls Church (Va.) Sun-Echo, 1953-55. Pres. Greenway Downs Civic Assn., Falls Church, 1953-54; pres. Second (Indian Head) Div. Assn. DC br., 1953-57; hon. recruiter USN, 1984; chaplain, photographer Vets. Common, USA, Arlington/Falls Church, Va., 1997—. With US Army, 1943-45, ETO. Fellow Soc. Motion Picture and TV Engrs. (life; nat. membership chmn. 1969, Outstanding Svc. award 1979); mem. Washington Film and Video Coun. (life; pres. 1967-68), Univ. Film and Video Assn., SAR (pres. Fairfax Resolves 1991-92, chaplain emeritus 2002, Va. ofcl. photographer, nat. mem. mag. adv. com. SAR/DAR liaison com. 1990—, historian 1993-94, editor 1994—, Meritorious Svc. medal 1991, Va. medal, 1994, Pres. Gen.'s citation for Disting. Svc. and Silver Good Citizenship medal 1994, Patriot medal 1996), People To People (hon.). Presbyterian. Avocations: photography, historical and technical writing. Home: 1436 Mayflower Dr Mc Lean VA 22101-5614

YOUNGWOOD, ALFRED DONALD, lawyer; b. NYC, Apr. 27, 1938; s. Milton and Lillian (Ginsburg) Y.; m. Judith Goldfarb, June 24, 1963; children: Jonathan David, Stephen Michael. BA magna cum laude, Yale U., 1959; LLB magna cum laude, Harvard U., 1962. Bar: NY 1962, DC 1970, US Tax Ct. 1964, US Ct. Appeals (2d cir.) 1969. Law clk. to judge US Dist. Ct. NY, 1962-63; assoc. Paul, Weiss, Rifkind, Wharton & Garrison LLP, NYC, 1964-70, ptnr., 1970—, chair, 1999—. Pres. Ctrl. Synagogue, NYC, 2003—06, trustee; bd. dirs. The Legal Aid Soc., NYC. Fulbright scholar, London, 1963-64. Fellow Am. Coll. Tax Counsel; mem. ABA, NY State Bar Assn. (chmn. tax sect. 1978-79, exec. com. 1971—, ho. of dels. 1979-80), Assn. of Bar of City of NY, Coun. on Fgn. Rels. Home: 1125 Park Ave New York NY 10128-1243 Office: Paul Weiss Rifkind Wharton & Garrison LLP 1285 Avenue Of The Americas New York NY 10019-6064 Home Phone: 212-860-8848. Business E-Mail: ayoungwood@paulweiss.com.

YOUNKER, KATHLEEN TEUBER, pianist, music educator; b. St. Cloud, Minn., Jan. 22, 1947; d. Hans Richard and Philomena (Hortsch) T.; m. Daniel William Younker, July 19, 1968; children: Laura, Jonathan. BA in History and Philosophy, St. Cloud State U., 1968; ARCT in Piano Performance, Royal Conservatory Toronto, Ont., Can., 1983; BA in Music, Bishop's U., Lennoxville, Que., Can., 1984; pvt. piano student, Rose Goldblatt, Montreal, 1985-95; MA in Spl. Studies, St. Cloud State U., 2002. Self-employed piano tchr., Lennoxville, 1978—97, St. Cloud, 1997—; sch. music tchr. Eastern Twps. Regional Sch. Bd., Lennoxville, 1982-86; ch. organist Peace United Ch. of Christ, St. Cloud, 1998-99; accompanist Sauk Rapids (Minn.) Rice HS, 1999—2000. Mem Music Tchrs. Nat Assn., Nat. Guild Piano Tchrs., Can. Fedn. Music Tcrs. Assns. (com. mem., ex officio nat. conv. 1997), Minn. Music Tchrs. Assn. (com. mem. state conv. 1999-01, com. mem. piano exam devel. com. 2002—), Eastern Twps. Music Tchrs. Assn. (pres. 1989-91), Que. Music Tchrs. Assn. (pres. provincial coun. 1993-97). Avocations: home restoration, pets, reading, gardening, cooking, entertaining.

YOUNT, GEORGE STUART, paper company executive; b. LA, Mar. 4, 1949; s. Stanley George and Agnes (Pratt) Y.; m. Geraldine Marie Silvio, July 18, 1970; children: Trisha Marie, Christopher George. Postgrad., Harvard U., 1983-86. Mgmt. trainee Fortifiber Corp., LA, 1969-71, asst. to v.p. ops., 1971-75, adminstrv. v.p., treas., sec., 1975-85, exec. v.p., sec., CFO, bd. dirs., 1985-90, chmn., CEO, 1991—2006; pres., dir. Fonzia Corp., 1993—2006. Bd. dirs. Stanwall Corp., pres., 1989—, Thompson & Co. Ins. Svcs., Pasadena, Calif., 1996—, Parasol Found., 1999—, Tracerton Enterprises, Inc., 2001-2004; past pres. Hollister Ranch Cattle Coop., Gaviota, Calif., 1986-88; trustee Sierra Nev. Coll., 1999-07, vice chair, 2002; adv. bd. Med. Tech. Internat., Inc., 2004-. Team leader LA United Way, 1981-86; bd. dirs. Big Bros. Greater LA, 1984-87, LA coun. Boy Scouts Am., 1992-2001; mem. Young Pres. Orgn., 1991, forum moderator, 1993-95, 2005—, chpt. forum officer, 1997-99; presdl. appointee Tahoe Regional Planning Agy. Governing Bd., 2002—; mem. adv. bd. Incline Village Cmty. Hosp., 2005-06; trustee Sierra Nev. Coll. Found., 2007-. Named Humanitarian of Yr., Incline Village, Nev., 2003. Mem.: Am. Paper Inst. (dir. 1993—95, splty. coaters and extrusion sect. 1990—2000), Washoe County Hon. Chief Dep. Sheriff's Assn., Newcomen Soc. (life), Conferie des Chevaliers du Tastevin Wine and Food Soc., Wine and Food Soc., Chaine des Rotisseurs Food and Wine Soc., Internat. Wine and Food Soc., Rotary (bd. dirs. LA club 1992—94), Jonathan Club (LA), U. Nev. Alumni Assn. (life), USN League Club (life). Avocations: scuba diving, electronics, cattle ranching, computers. Office: Fortifiber Corp 913 Tahoe Blvd Incline Village NV 89451-9309

YOUNT, GWENDOLYN AUDREY, humanities educator; b. Indpls., July 24, 1957; d. August de Alba and Hena Yount; 1 child, Clark. AA, L.A. City Coll., 1977; BA, UCLA, 1979, MA, 1982, Candidate in Philosophy, 1987. Cert. C.C. lifetime credential Calif., bilingual cert. competence. Ednl. aide Alexander Hamilton H.S., LA, 1975—76; tchg. fellow UCLA, 1981—88; instr. L.A. Unified Sch. Dist., 1982—90; prof. Institut Franco-Americain de Mgmt., Paris, 1983—84; instr. Santa Monica Coll., Calif., 1987—88; lectr. U. Calif., Riverside, 1988—91; instr. Beverly Hills Adult Sch., Calif., 1986—88; assoc. prof. Riverside C.C., Calif., 1990—. Dir. RCC Study Abroad Program in Spain, Salamanca, Spain, 1998—2002, RCC Study Abroad Program in Costa Rica, San Jose, Costa Rica, 1993, UCLA Spanish Program in Mex., Guadalajara, Mexico, 1987. Dancer (ballet performance) Celebrate Dance, 2000; actor: (mus. theater) La Cage Aux Folles, 1998; singer: (vocal performance) Montreux Jazz Festival, 1993. Adminstr. G. Yount scholarship Riverside County Found., 1998—2003; sen. Acad. Senate, Riverside, 1997—2003; mem. Spanish lang. steering com. Riverside Pub. Libr., 1989—91; charter mem. Mus. of Tolerance, LA, 1994—2003. Named Most Influential Instr., RCC Disabled Student Svcs., 1993, 1998, Tchr. of Distinction, LDS Ch., 1998, 2000, 2001, 2002, Tchr. of the Yr., Riverside C.C., 1999—2000, 2000—01, 2002—03; grantee Univ. grantee for grad. study, UCLA, 1979. Mem.: Philol Soc. of the Pacific Coast, Assn. for Tchrs. of Spanish, Sigma Tau Sigma, Alpha Mu Gamma (pres. 1977—78), Sigma Delta Pi (v.p. 1985—86). Liberal. Avocations: travel, reading, studying. Office: Riverside C C 4800 Magnolia Ave Riverside CA 92506 Home Phone: 951-243-9858. Business E-Mail: gwen.yount@rcc.edu.

YOURZAK, ROBERT JOSEPH, management consultant, educator, engineer; b. Mpls., Aug. 27, 1947; s. Ruth Phyllis Sorenson. BCE, U. Minn., 1969; MSCE, U. Wash., 1971, MBA, 1975. Registered profl. engr., Wash., Minn. Surveyor N.C. Hoium & Assocs., Mpls., 1965-68, Lot Surveys Co., Mpls., 1968-69; site layout engr. Sheehy Constrn. Co., St. Paul, 1968; structural engring. aide Dunham Assocs., Mpls., 1969; aircraft and aerospace structural engr., program rep. Boeing Co., Seattle, 1969-75; engr., estimator Howard S. Wright Constrn. Co., Seattle, 1976-77; dir. project devel. and adminstrn. DeLeuw Cather & Co., Seattle, 1977-78; sr. mgmt. cons. Alexander Grant & Co., Mpls., 1978-79; mgr. project sys. dept., project mgr. Henningson, Durham & Richardson, Mpls., 1979-80; dir. project mgmt., regional offices Ellerbe Assocs., Inc., Mpls., 1980-81; pres. Robert Yourzak & Assocs., Inc., Mpls., 1982—. Lectr. engring. mgmt. U. Wash., 1977-78; lectr., adj. asst. prof. dept. civil and mineral engring. and mech./indsl. engring. Ctr. for Devel. of Tech. Leadership, Inst. Tech.; mem. strategic mgmt. and orgn. dept., mgmt. scis. dept. Sch. Mgmt., U. Minn., 1979-90, 96—; bd. adv. inst. tech., 1989-93; founding mem., membership com., mem. U. of Minn. com. Minn. High Tech. Coun., 1983-95; instr. principles mgmt. dept. bus. and pub. policy Concordia U., 1997, instr. constrn. mgmt., constrn. estimating and scheduling, bldg. orgn. and tech., project mgmt. and planning skills, project mgmt. software, supervision and applied leadership, and supervisory techniques for bus. Inver Hills C.C., 1998—; instr. introduction to engring. and design, statics, mechanics of materials, ops. mgmt. North Hennepin C.C., 2002—; adj. instr. ops. mgmt. Hamline U., St. Paul, 2001; spkr. in field. Author: Project Management and Motivating and Managing the Project Team, 1984, (with others) Field Guide to Project Management, 1998, 2004 (sec. edition). Chmn. regional art group experience Seattle Art Mus., 1975-78; mem. Pacific N.W. Arts Coun., 1977-78, ex-officio adviser Mus. Week, 1976; bd. dirs. Friends of the Rep. Seattle Repertory Theatre, 1973-77; mem. Symphonics Seattle Symphony Orch., 1975-78. Named Outstanding Young Man of Am., U.S. Jaycees, 1978; scholar Boeing Co., 1967-68, Sheehy Constrn. Co., summer 1967. Fellow ASCE (chmn. continuing edn. subcom. Seattle chpt. 1976-79, chmn. program com. 1978, mem. transp. and urban planning tech. group 1978, Edmund Friedman Young Engr. award 1979, chmn. continuing edn. subcom. 1979-80, chmn. energy com. Minn. chpt. 1980-81, bd. dirs. 1981-89, sec. 1981-83, v.p. profl. svcs. 1983-84, v.p. info. svcs. 1984-85, pres. 1986-87, past pres. 1987-89, spkr.), PMI Project Mgmt. Inst. (cert. project mgmt. prof., spkr., founding pres. 1985, chmn., adv. com. 1987-89, bd. dirs. 1984-86, program com. chmn. and organizing com. mem. Minn. chpt. 1984, spkr., project mgr. internat. mktg. program 1985-86, chmn. internat. mktg. standing com. 1986, long range and strategic planning com. 1988-93, chmn. 1992, v.p. pub. rels. 1987-88, ex-officio dir. 1989, 92, internat. pres. 1990, chmn. bd. 1991, ex-officio chmn. 1992, internat. bd. dirs., chmn. nominating com. 1992, PMI fellow 1995, chmn. exec. dir. selection com. 1996-97, Robert J. Yourzak Scholarship Award established Minn. chpt. 1998—), Inst. Indsl. Engrs. (pres. Twin Cities chpt. 1985-86, chmn. program com. 1983-84, bd. dirs. 1985-88, awards com., chmn. 1984-89, fellow 1999, spkr.); mem. ASTD (So. Minn. chpt.), Am. Cons. Engrs. Coun. (peer reviewer 1986-89), Am. Arbitration Assn. (mem. Mpls. panel of constrn. arbitrators), Minn. Surveyors and Engrs. Soc., Cons. Engrs. Coun. Minn. (chmn. pub. rels. com. 1983-85, vice chmn. 1988, chmn. 1989, program com. chmn. Midwest engrs. conf. and exposition 1985-90, spkr., Honor award 1992), Inst. Mgmt. Cons. (cert. mgmt. cons.), Mpls. Soc. Fine Arts, Internat. Facility Mgmt. Assn., Am. Soc. Engring. Edn., Rainer Club (co-chmn. Oktoberfest), Sierra club, Chowder Soc., Mountaineers, North Star Ski Touring, Chi Epsilon (life). Office: 7320 Gallagher Dr Ste 325 Minneapolis MN 55435-4510

YOUSEF, FATHI SALAAMA, communications educator, management consultant; b. Cairo, Jan. 2, 1934; arrived in U.S., 1968, naturalized, 1973; s. Salaama and Rose (Tadros) Yousef; m. Marjan Lowies El-Faizy, June 24, 1994. BA, Ain Shams U., Cairo, 1955; MA, U. Minn., 1970, PhD, 1972. Svc. ctr. supt. Shell Oil Co., Cairo, 1955-61; indsl., mgmt. tng. instr. ARAMCO, Dhahran, Saudi Arabia, 1961-68; tchg. assoc. U. Minn., Mpls., 1968-72; comm. studies prof. emeritus Calif. State U., Long Beach, 1972—. With orgn. and indsl. engring. dept. ARAMCO, 1978—80. Co-author: An Introduction to Intercultural Communication, 1975, 1985; contbr. Grantee, NSF, 1981, 1982, 1983. Mem.: Assn. Egyptian Am. Scholars. Democrat. Office: Calif State U Dept Comm Studies Long Beach CA 90840-2407 Business E-Mail: fyousef@csulb.edu.

YOUSEF, MAHMOUD, mathematics professor, computer scientist, educator; s. Abdullah and Haniefa (Abu Mukh) Yousef; m. Gamileh Abu Mukh, June 29, 1993; children: Ahmed, Abdala, Janna, Mohammed. BS, Yarmouk U., Irbid, Jordan, 1986; MA, Kent State U., Ohio, 1992; MS, PhD, La. Tech U., Ruston, 2001. Tchr. Ministry of Edn., Tulkarem, Jordan, 1986—88; grad. asst. Kent State U., Kent, Ohio, 1989—92, adj. faculty, 1992—94, 1996—97; instr. United Arab Emirates U., Al-Ain, 1994—96; grad. asst. La. Tech U., Ruston, 1997—2000; vis. prof. Grambling State U., La., 2000—01; asst. prof. U. Ctrl. Mo., Warrensburg, 2001—05, assoc. prof., 2005—. Adj. prof. Kent State U., 1988—89. Contbr. articles to profl. jours. Panel judge Assn. for Computing Machinery, 2004. Named Tchr. of Distinction, United Arab Emirates U., 1994—96; grantee, U. Ctrl. Mo., 2001—07, Ednl. Advancement Found., 2004. Mem.: Math. Assn. Am., Consortium for Computing Sciences in Colls. (steering com. 2003—07), Phi Kappa Phi. Avocations: reading, soccer, travel. Office: Univ Ctrl Mo Dept Math & Computer Sci Warrensburg MO 64093 Home Phone: 660-747-1664; Office Phone: 660-543-8892. Office Fax: 660-543-8013. Business E-Mail: yousef@ucmo.edu.

YOUST, DAVID BENNETT, career development educator; b. May 14, 1938; s. Howard Page and Agnes (Bennett) Y.; m. Faye Phillips; children: Stacy Sillen, Shawna Sannier, Liesl Berger, Genny Rankin, Elizabeth Curley. BS, SUNY-Albany, 1959; MS, Syracuse U., NY, 1961; PhD, Mich. State U., 1969. Cert. career counselor Nat. Bd. Counselor Cert. Tchr. sci. North Syracuse schs., 1959-61; adminstr. student pers. Mich. State U., 1961-63; counselor, prin., program dir. Rochester (N.Y.) schs., 1963-70; sr. rsch. technologist Eastman Kodak Co., Rochester, 1970-72; asst. dean Nat. Tech. Inst. for the Deaf, Rochester Inst. Tech., 1972-74; mem. faculty Empire State Coll., SUNY, Rochester, 1974-78; exec. dir. Career Devel. Coun., Corning, N.Y., 1978-84; mgr. engring. tng. Corning Inc., N.Y., 1984-90; ptnr. Phillips Tng. Sys., Inc., 1989—. Former adj. faculty Corning C.C., Elmira Coll., C.W. Post Coll.; mediator cmty. dispute resolution, former bd. dirs. Cmty. Dispute Resolution Ctr., Ithaca, NY; instr. MSF motorcycle safety; EEO mediator U.S. Postal Svc. Author guide, articles in field; former mem. editl. bd. Career Devel. Quar. Former bd. dirs. 171 Cedar Arts Ctr. Mem. ACA, Nat. Career Devel. Assn. (Merit award 1970, 84), Am. Ednl. Rsch. Assn., Assn. Measurement and Evaluation in Guidance. Republican. E-mail: dyoust@gmail.com.

YOUTCHEFF, JOHN SHELDON, physicist; b. Newark, Apr. 16, 1925; s. Slav Joseph and Florence Catherine (Davidson) Y.; m. Elsie Marianne, June 17, 1950; children: Karen Janette, John Sheldon, Mark Allen, Heidi Mary Anne, Lisa Ellen AB, Columbia U., 1949, BS, 1950; PhD, UCLA, 1953. Registered profl. engr., Calif., DC. Ops. analyst GE Co., Ithaca, NY, 1953—56, cons., engr. missile & space divsn. Phila., 1956—64, mgr. advanced reliability programs, 1964—72; mgr. reliability and maintainability Litton Industries, College Park, Md., 1972—73; program mgr. U.S. Postal Svc. Hdqrs., Washington, 1973—. Instr. U. Pa., 1965-66, Villanova U., 1957— Lt. USAAF, 1943-46; to comdr. USNR, 1946— Fellow AAAS, Br. Interplanetary Soc., AIAA, Explorers Club; mem. IEEE (sr.), Ops. Rsch. Soc., Rsch. Soc. Am., Am. Math. Soc., Am. Physics Soc., Am. Chem. Soc., Am. Astron. Soc., Am. Geol. Soc., NSPE, Engring. and Tech. Socs., Coun. Del. Valley (spkrs. bur.), USCG Aux. (flotilla comdr.), Res. Officers Assn., Am. Legion, Optimists Internat. (pres. Valley Forge chpt. 1970-71) Roman Catholic. Office: L'Enfant Plz Washington DC 20260

YOVANOF, SILVANA, physician; b. Lubojno, Macedonia, Jan. 14, 1956; came to U.S., 1961; d. Peter and Nuna Yovanof. BS in Biology and Psychology, Loyola U., Chgo., 1978; MS, U. Ill., 1982; MD, Am. U. Caribbean, Montserrat, 1985. Diplomate Am. Bd. Internal Medicine. Intern Deaconess Hosp., St. Louis, 1986-87; resident in internal medicine St. Joseph Mercy Hosp., Pontiac, Mich., 1987-89, chief resident in medicine, 1989-90; fellow U. Ill. Med. Ctr., Chgo., 1990-92; chmn. dept. medicine Monongahela Valley Hosp., 2002—. Mem. adv. panel Internal Medicine for the Specialist, 1988—; affiliated with hosps. Jefferson Hosp., Pitts., 1991, MonValley Hosp., Monongahela, Pa., 1993, Mercy Hosp., Pitts., 1995. Contbr. articles to profl. jours. including Neurosci. Letters. Mem.: ACP, Am. Assn. Clin. Endocrinologists, Allegheny County Med. Soc. (med. legal com. 1996—), Pa. State Med. Soc., Am. Diabetes Assn. Office: Med and Endocrinology Assoc 420 W Main St Monongahela PA 15063-2552 Home Phone: 412-887-3237; Office Phone: 724-258-8680. E-mail: syovanof@peoplepc.com.

YOVANOVICH, ROBYN DOBSON, theater educator, department chairman; d. Robert Vernon and Gwendolyn Armstrong Dobson; m. Donald Yovanovich, Nov. 10, 1990; 1 child, Anna Clancey. BA, Cath. U. Am., Washington, DC, 1971—75. Editor Middleburg Life, Middleburg, Va., 1989—91; fine arts dept. chmn. Foxcroft Sch., Middleburg, 1997—. Chmn. of volunteers Va. Gold Cup/Internat. Gold Cup, The Plains, 1989—2006. Editor: (book) Middleburg and Nearby; contbr. color commentator; actor: (TV commercials) Soft and Dri/ Mountain Dew, (musical revue- ford's theatre) Uncle Funky's Mistletoe Revue; (Broadway plays, and Off Broadway), 1977—80. Com. mem. Am. Cancer Soc. Charity Polo Classic, The Plains, 1996, Range Rover Internat. Polo Classic, The Plains, 2002; bd. mem. The Middleburg Players, 1998—2002. Grantee Kenan Grant for Profl. Devel., Foxcroft Sch., 2006. Republican. Episcopalian. Avocation: interior design. Home: PO Box 1877 Middleburg VA 20118 Office: Foxcroft Sch PO Box 5555 Middleburg VA 20118 Office Phone: 540-687-4373. Personal E-mail: dony13@aol.com. Business E-Mail: ryovanovich@foxcroft.org.

YOVICH, DANIEL JOHN, chemist, educator; b. Chgo., Mar. 5, 1930; s. Milan D. and Sophie (Dorociak) Y.; m. Anita Barbara Moreland, Feb. 7, 1959; children: Daniel, Amy, David, Julie Ann. Ph.B., DePaul U., 1952; MA, Governors State U., 1975, MS, 1976. Cert. reality therapist, profl. mgr. Formulator Nat. Lead Co., 1950-52, 56-59; researcher Montgomery Ward, Chgo., 1959-62; tech. dir. Riley Bros., Inc., Burlington, Iowa, 1962-66, Mortell Co., Kankakee, Ill., 1966-70; exec. dir. Dan Yovich Assos., 1970-79; asst. prof. Purdue U., Hammond, Ind., 1979-84, assoc. prof., 1984-90, prof., 1990-2000, prof. emeritus, 2000—. Instr. Army Security Agy. Sch., 1954—56, Napoleon Hill Acad., 1965—66; cons. Learning House, 1964—; assoc. Hill, Zediker & Assocs. Psychologists, Kankakee, 1975—79; mem. adv. bd. Nat. Congress Inventor Orgns., 1984; vis. prof. Grand Valley State U., 2000—, Northwood U., 2001—. Author: Applied Creativity; prdr., moderator: (program) Careers Unlimited, Sta. WCIU-TV, Chgo., 1967; contbr. articles to profl. jours.; patentee game Krypto, coating Sanitane. Mem. cmty. adv. coun. Governors State U., 1978; mem. Hammond (Ind.) Hist. Soc. Served to 1st lt. AUS, 1952-56. Recipient Outstanding Citizen Award News Pub. Co. Am., 1971, Outstanding Tchr. award Purdue U., 1980, 82, 83, Faculty Service award Nat. U. Continuing Edn. Assn., 1984, Disting. Service award Purdue U.-Calumet Alumni Assn., 1988, Arthur Young award Venture Mag., 1988, Entrepreneurial Edn. award Inc. Mag., 1990, Indiana Spirit of Innovation award, 1996. Mem. World Future Soc., Am. Soc. Profl. Supervision (exec. sec. 1986), Inventors and Entrepreneurs Soc. Am. (founder, exec. dir. 1984, prodr. Salute Vet. Recognition Programs 1999—), Global Intuition Network, Internat. Creativity Network, Infantry Officer Cand. Sch. Alumni Assn. (life), Napoleon Hill Found., Inst. Reality Therapy, Inst. Contemporary Living, Soc. Am. Inventors (life), Am. Legion, Vets. of the Battle of the Bulge (historian), Army and Navy Club of Grand Rapids Home: 3527 Whispering Brook Dr SE Kentwood MI 49508-3733 Personal E-mail: danyovich@sbcglobal.net.

YOVITS, MARSHALL CLINTON, information scientist, educator, dean; b. Bklyn., May 16, 1923; s. Louis Frederick and Rebecca (Gerber) Y.; m. Anita S. Friedman, Aug. 2, 1952; children: Bruce J., Mara F., Steven. BS, Union Coll., Schenectady, 1944, MS, 1948, Yale U., 1949, PhD, 1951. Sr. physicist Johns Hopkins U., 1951—56; physicist electronics br. Office Naval Rsch., Washington, 1956, head info. sys. br., 1956—62; dir. Naval Analysis Group, 1962—66; prof., chmn. dept. computer and info. sci. Ohio State U., 1966—78, prof., 1978—79; prof. computer and info. sci. Sch. of Sci., Ind. U., Purdue U., Indpls., 1980—, dean, 1980—88; prof. emeritus Ind. U., Purdue U., Indpls., 1993—. Gen. chmn. Computer Sci. Conf. NSF, 1973. Editor: (with Scott Cameron) Self-Organizing Systems, Proc. Interdisciplinary Conf., 1960, Large-Capacity Memory Techniques for Computing Systems, 1961 (with George T. Jacobi, Gordon D. Goldstein) Self-Organizing Systems, 1962, (with D.M. Gilford, R.H. Wilcox, E. Staveley, H.D. Lerner) Research Program Effectiveness, 1966, Advances in Computers, Vol. 11, 1971; editor: series Advances in Computers, Vols. 13-40; contbr. rsch. articles to profl. jours. Recipient Superior Civilian Svc. award, U.S. Navy, 1964, Outstanding Performance award, 1961; fellow AEC fellow, 1950—51, Indpls. Ctr. Advanced Rsch., 1988—89. Fellow AAAS (chmn. coun. sect. T 1985-88, chmn. 1996-98), IEEE (computer soc. chmn. awards com. 1989, bd. govs. 1988-89, computer pioneer award 1990), Assn. for Computing Machinery (coun., gen. chmn. computer sci. conf. 1982), EDUCOM (nominating com.), Sigma Xi. Home: 9016 Dewberry Ct Indianapolis IN 46260-1527 Office Phone: 317-274-9737. E-mail: myovits@iupui.edu.

YOW, KAY (SANDRA KAY YOW), women's college basketball coach; Grad. in English, East Carolina Coll., Greenville, NC, 1964. Head coach Allen Jay HS, 1960, Gibsonville HS, Elon Coll., NC State U., Raleigh, 1975—. Head coach USA Basketball Women's Team World Univ. Games, 1981; asst. coach US Women's Olympic Team, LA, 1984, head coach, Seoul, Republic of Korea, 88. Co-recipient Bob Bradley Spirit & Courage award, 2007; named to Guilford County Sports Hall of Fame, Elon Coll. Hall of Fame, Women's Sports Hall of Fame, NC Sports Hall of Fame, Fellowship of Christian Athletes Hall of Fame, Women's Basketball Hall of Fame, Naismith Basketball Hall of Fame; recipient Laurel Wreath award, State of NC, 2007, Naismith award, Outstanding Contbn. to Women's Basketball, 2007, Jimmy V ESPY award for Perseverance, 2007. Achievements include coaching her teams to five ACC (Atlantic Coast Conf.) Championships. Office: NC State U Womens Basketball Reynolds Coliseum 114 Box 8501 Raleigh NC 27695-8501 Office Phone: 919-515-2880. Office Fax: 919-513-0326. E-mail: kay_yow@ncsu.edu. *

YOW, VALERIE RALEIGH, historian, writer, counselor; d. Fletcher Raleigh Yow and Mae Moore Wyatt; m. Richard Quinney, June 14, 1958 (div. 1989); children: Laura Ellen Quinney, Anne Holloway Quinney. AB, U. NC, Greensboro, 1956; PhD in History, U. Wis., Madison, 1967; postgrad., Harvard U., Cambridge, Mass., 1980—81; MA in Counseling Psychology, Boston Coll., 1983. Nat. cert. psychologist N.Am. Masters Psychology, 1994. Faculty Bklyn Coll., 1966—70; instr. history dept. U. RI, Kingston, 1974—80; asst. prof. No. Ill. U., DeKalb, 1984—91; psychol. counselor Counseling Couples and Individuals, Chapel Hill, NC, 1994—. Author: (plays) In the Service of Others (1st pl. Gt. Chgo. Playwrights Expn., 1987), Past Tense/Present Tense, Betty Smith Meets Carl Jung: Some Memories, Dreams, Reflections, Recording Oral History: A Guide to the Humanities and Social Sciences, 1994, 2005, Bernice Kelly Harris: A Good Life Was Writing, 1999, Betty Smith and A Tree Grows in Brooklyn, 2007; co-author: Biography and Oral History Handbook of Oral History, 2006. Mem. Eno River Assn., Durham, NC, 1995—2007. Recipient Harvey Kantor award in Recognition of Outstanding Achievement in Oral History, New Eng. Oral History Assn., 2005, Outstanding Acad. Texts, ALA's Choice for book Rec. Oral History, 2007. Mem.: C. G. Jung Soc. Rsch. Triangle (bd. dirs. 2002—04), Orgn. Am. Historians, Oral History Assn. (mem. governing coun. 2006—, book rev. editor oral history rev. 2000—07). Democrat. Unitarian. Avocations: art, painting. Home and Office: 12 Davie Cir Chapel Hill NC 27514 Home Phone: 919-929-2384.

YRIGOYEN, CHARLES, JR., retired church denomination executive; b. Phila., Dec. 9, 1937; s. Charles and Erma Mae (Suters) Y.; m. Jeanette Alice Brittingham, Dec. 13, 1958; children: Debra Jean, Charles III. BS in Econs., U. Pa., 1959; BD, Lancaster Theol. Sem., Pa., 1962; ThM, Ea. Bapt. Theol. Sem., Phila., 1964; PhD, Temple U., 1973; DD (hon.), Albright Coll., 1987. Ordained to ministry United Meth. Ch., 1960. Pastor various chs. Meth. Ch., Pa., 1958-66, campus min. Phila., 1966-68; chaplain, prof. religion Albright Coll., Reading, Pa., 1968-82; gen. sec. Gen. Com. on Archives and History, United Meth. Ch., Madison, NJ, 1982—2005; dir. United Methodist Studies Evangelical Theol. Sem., 2006—, Lancaster Theol. Sem., 2007—. Vis. scholar Union Theol. Sem., N.Y.C., 1980, adj. prof., 1982-93, 2000-02; adj. prof. ch. history Drew U., Madison, 1982-2005; adj. prof. Moravian Theol. Sem., Bethlehem, Pa., 1994-02; exec. com. World Meth. Coun., 1986-2006; bd. dir. Wesley Works Editl. Project, 1982-2006; adj. prof. Luth. Theol. Sem., Phila., 1999. Author: Acts for Our Time, 1987, John Wesley: Holiness of Heart and Life, 1996, Belief Matters: United Methodism's Doctrinal Standards, 2001; editor: Reformed and Catholic, 1978, Catholic and Reformed, 1979, Historical Dictionary of Methodism, 1996, 2d edit., 2005, The Global Impact of the Wesleyan Traditions and Their Related Movements, 2002, Praising The God of Grace: The Theology of Charles Westey's Hymns, 2005; United Methodism@Forty: A History of The United Methodist Church, 2007; editor Methodist History Jour., 1982-2006. Mem. alumni coun. Lancaster Theol. Sem., 2002—. Masland fellow Union Theol. Sem., 1975, 80; disting. svc. award, United Methodist Ch., 2005. Mem. World Meth. Hist. Soc. (gen. sec. 1987-2006), Wesley Hist. Soc., Wesleyan Theol. Soc., Charles Wesley Soc., Oxford Inst. Meth. Theol. Studies, Mercersburg Soc. (bd. dirs.), United Meth. Hist. Soc. Republican. Methodist. Avocation: model railroads. Home: I 106 950 Willow Valley Lakes Dr Willow Street PA 17584-9663 Home Phone: 717-464-3276. E-mail: cyrigoyen@evangelical.edu, jyrigoyen@cs.com.

YSASI-DIAZ, GLORIA, wholesale distribution executive; BS in Chem. Engring., Univ. Rochester; MBA, Coll. William & Mary. Ops. positions GE Co., 1978—84; ops. positions to sr. v.p., process mgmt. R.R. Donnelley, Chgo., 1984—2005; v.p. operational excellence, US branch-based businesses WW Grainger Co., Chgo., 2005—. Named one of 50 Most Important Hispanics in Tech., Bus., Hispanic Engineer and Info. Tech. mag., 2005. Office: 100 Grainger Pkwy Lake Forest IL 60045-5201 Office Phone: 847-535-1000. Office Fax: 847-535-0878.

YSIKES, JUANITA LOU, art educator; b. Belen, N.Mex., Dec. 22, 1951; d. Melvin Vernette and Doris Marie (McArthur) Lovelady; m. James Carroll Fulcher, May 30, 1970 (div. Aug. 1988); children: Lee Collins Fulcher, Amy Laura Fulcher; m. Robert Harry Sikes, Dec. 26, 1990. BS in Edn., Ea. N.Mex. U., 1983. Cert. tchr., N.Mex. Bookkeeper J & L Auto Salvage, Socorro, N.Mex., 1970-72, Navajo Mobil, Truth or Consequences, N.Mex., 1972-75; subs. tchr. Portales (N.Mex.) Schs., 1977-78, art aide, 1988-91; tchr., aide spl. edn. Ft. Summer (N.Mex.) High Sch., 1978-83, tchr. spl. edn., 1983-86; tutor ESL and GED Ea. N.Mex. U. Clovis Campus, Ft. Summer, 1986-87; fashion illustrator Slyduds Clothing, Roswell and Ft. Summer, N.Mex., 1987-88; instr. drawing Ea. N.Mex. U., Portales, 1989-90; tchr. art Portales Jr. High Sch., 1991—. Supt. art dept. DeBaca County Fair Bd., Ft. Summer, 1979-87; advisor Portales Elem. Spl. Art Program, Portales, 1989-91; coord. Portales Jr. High Spl. Art Program, Portales, 1991-2001; sponsor art club Portales HS, 2001—; judge arts and crafts dept. Roosevelt County Fair, Portales, 1992. Exhibited in group shows Crafter's Crossing Gallery, Ft. Worth, numerous art fairs. Vol. Sierra County Rescue Squad, Truth or Consequences, 1973-75, Mayors Christmas Tree, Portales, 1989-90; coord., 1991—. Recipient Outstanding Citizenship award Sierra County Rescue Squad, 1974, 75; named Artist of Month Ft. Sumner Pub. Libr., 1987. Mem. NEA (pres. local chpt. 1992—), Nat. Art Edn. Assn., Gamma Zeta (pres. Beta Sigma Phi chpt. 1984-88). Democrat. Mem. Ch. of Christ. Avocations: painting, sewing, bowling, archery. Home: 2108 W Beech St Portales NM 88130-9303 Office: Portales Jr High Sch 300 E 5th St Portales NM 88130-6082

YSSELDYKE, JAMES EDWARD, psychology professor; b. Grand Rapids, Mich., Jan. 1, 1944; 2 children. Student in psychology, Calvin Coll., 1962-65; BA in Psychology and Biology, Western Mich. U., 1966; MA in Sch. Psychology, U. Ill., 1968, PhD, 1971. Lic. cons. psychologist, Minn. Tchr. spl. edn. Kent County Juvenile Ct. Ctr., Grand Rapids, 1966-67; rsch. asst. U. Ill. Inst. Rsch. on Exceptional Children, 1969-70, tchg. asst. dept. ednl. psychology, 1970; sch. psychology intern Oakland County Schs., Pontiac, Mich., 1970-71; asst. prof. sch. psychology Pa. State U., 1971-75, assoc. prof., 1975, U. Minn., Mpls., 1975-79, prof., 1979-91, dir. Inst. Rsch. on Learning Disabilities, 1977-83, dir. Nat. Sch. Psychology Insvc. Tng. Network, 1977-83, dir. sch. psychology program, 1987-93, dir. Nat. Ctr. on Ednl. Outcomes, 1991-99, assoc. dean for rsch., 2000—05. Emma Birkmaier endowed prof. U. Minn., 1998-2000; advisor, cons. and researcher in field. Author: (with J. Salvia) Assessment in Special and Remedial Education, 2007, 10th edit., (with B. Algozzine and M. Thurlow) Critical Issues in Special and Remedial Education, 1992, 3d edit., 2000, Strategies and Tactics for Effective Instruction, 1997, (with S.L. Christenson) Functional Assessment of Academic Behavior, 2003, (with B. Algozzine) Every Teachers Guide to Special Education, 2007; editor: Exceptional Children, 1984-90; assoc. editor: The School Psychologist, 1972-75, mem. editorial bd., cons. editor numerous jours.; contbr. chpts. to books and articles to jours. Recipient Disting. Tchg. award U. Minn., 1988, Disting. Alumni award U. Ill. Coll. Edn., 1998; fellow NIMH, 1967-69; grantee in field. Fellow APA (Lightner Witmer award 1973); mem. APA, NASP, Am. Ednl. Rsch. Assn., Coun. for Exceptional Children (Rsch. award 1995), Coun. for Ednl. Diagnostic Svcs. Office: Univ Minn Coll Edn Human Devel 350 Elliott Hall 75 E River Rd Minneapolis MN 55455-0296 Business E-Mail: jim@umn.edu.

YSURSA, BEN T., state official; b. Boise, Idaho, June 10, 1949; m. Penny Ysursa; children: Shawn Del, Matthew, Andrew. BA, Gonzaga U., 1971; JD, St. Louis U. Law Sch., 1974. Bar: Idaho 1974. Dep. sec. state State of Idaho, Boise, 1974—76, chief dep., 1976—2002, sec. state, 2002—. Mem. Basque Ctr., St. John's Parish; pres. Adh County Lincoln Day, 1990. Recipient Boyd Martin award, Assn. Idaho Cities, Outstanding Adminstr., Idaho Rep. Party, 1992. Mem.: Reagan-Bush Idaho Com. (treas. 1984), NHSS (secs. state 2003), Idaho State Bar Assn. Republican. Roman Catholic. Office: Office Sec State Rm 203 700 W Jefferson Boise ID 83720-0080 Office Phone: 208-334-2300. Office Fax: 208-334-2282. E-mail: bysursa@idsos.state.id.us. *

YU, ANDREW, minister; b. Fu-Yang, Chekian, China, Feb. 28, 1927; came to the U.S., 1972; s. Kung-Chu Yu and Mei-Chen Liu; m. Julie Yu, July 13, 1957; children: Peter, Ruth. BTh, Taiwan Bapt. Theol. Sem., Taipei, 1957; postgrad., Tanghai U., Taichung, Taiwan, 1965; MA in Ministry Studies, Moody Bible Inst., 1991; postgrad., Bibl. Archaeology Soc., 1993, Fuller Theol. Sem., 1996, Fuqua Internat. Sch. Christian Comm., 1998. Cert. pastoral counseling. Jour. clk. Bankers Trust Co., NYC, 1972-80; pastoral coounselor Am. Assn. Christian Counseling, Forest, Va., 1991—; minister Manhattan Chinese Bapt. Ch., NYC, 1980—, sr. pastor, 1986—. Author: Rekinling the Fires of Revial, 1993, A Master Piece of Spirituality, 1995, The Poem of Draw Wings, 2001; editor Chinese Christian Workers, 1999—; editor: Chinese Newsletter, N.Y., 1999-2002. Mem. positive thinking divsn. Guideposts Norman Vincent Peal Ctr. for Positive Thinking, Paulling, NY, 2003; mem. Bapt. World Alliance 100th Anniversary Congress, Bermingham, England, 2005. Recipient Lifetime Royal Patronage status Kevin, Prince Regent Princepality of Hutt River Province, Australia, 1994, Cert. of Appreciation, Ronald Reagan Presdl. Found., 2003. Mem.: Poetry Soc. Am. Avocations: reading, writing, music, travel, collecting. Home: Apt 20E 675 Water St New York NY 10002 Office: Manhattan Chinese Bapt Ch 236 W 72nd St New York NY 10023 Office Phone: 212-496-1486. Personal E-mail: andreweyu@gmail.com.

YU, ANTHONY C., religion and literature educator; b. Hong Kong, Oct. 6, 1938; came to U.S., 1956, naturalized, 1976; s. P.C. and Norma (Au) Y.; m. Priscilla Tang, Sept. 18, 1963; 1 son, Christopher Dietrich. BA, Houghton Coll., 1960; STB, Fuller Theol. Sem., 1963; PhD, U. Chgo., 1969, DLitt, 1996. Instr. U. Ill., Chgo., 1967-68; asst. prof. U. Chgo., 1968-74, assoc. prof., 1974-78, prof., 1978—2005, prof. emeritus, 2005—. Assoc. vis. prof. Ind. U., Bloomington, 1975; Whitney J. Oates short-term vis. fellow Princeton U., 1986; disting. vis. prof. Faculty of Arts, U. Alta., Can., 1992; mem. joint com. on study Chinese civilization Am. Coun. Learned Socs., 1980-86, bd. dirs., 1986-94; regional chmn. Mellon Fellowship in Humanities, 1982-92; bd. dirs. Ill. Humanities Coun., 1995-97; vis. prof. dept. religion Chinese U. Hong Kong, 1997; mem. com. social thought U. Chgo., 2004—. Asst. editor Jour. Asian Studies, 1975-78; co-editor Jour. Religion, 1980—; author, editor: Parnassus Revisited, 1973; editor, translator: The Journey to the West, 4 vols., 1977-83, Essays on The Journey to the West and Other Studies (in Chinese), 1989, The Monkey and the Monk, An Abridgment of the Journey to the West, 2006; co-editor (with Mary Gerhart) Morphologies of Faith: Essays on Religion and Culture in Honor of Nathan A. Scott, Jr., 1990, Rereading the Stone: Desire and the Making of Fiction in Dream of the Red Chamber, 1997, State and Religion in China: Historical and Textual Perspectives, 2005, Dream of the Red Chamber, Journey to the West, and Other Studies, Chinese edit., 2006. Recipient Gordon J. Laing prize, 1983; Danforth fellow, 1960-67; Guggenheim fellow, 1976-77; NEH translation grantee, 1977-82; Am. Coun. Learned Socs. sr. fellow, 1986-87, Mellon Emeriti fellow, 2006—; Masterworks Study grant NEH Seminar for Pub. Sch. Tchrs., 1992; elected academician Academia Sinica, 1998; Phi Beta Kappa vis. scholar 2001-02. Fellow Am. Acad. Arts and Scis.; mem. MLA (exec. coun. 1998—2001), Assn. for Asian Studies, Am. Acad. Religion (bd. dirs. 1995-97), Am. Comparative Lit. Assn., Milton Soc. Am., Arts Club. Home: 950 N Clark St Unit G Chicago IL 60610-8702 Office: U Chicago 1025 E 58th St Chicago IL 60637-1509 Office Phone: 773-702-8245. Business E-Mail: acyu@midway.uchicago.edu.

YU, BIN, statistician, educator; b. Harbin, China, Mar. 18, 1963; arrived in U.S., 1985; d. Dibei Yu, Xiaomin Yu; m. Ke-ning Shen, June 15, 1987; children: Maya Yu Shen, Matthew Yan Shen. BS in Math, Peking U., 1984; MA in Stats., U. Calif. Berkeley, 1987, PhD of Stats., 1990. Asst. prof. U. Wis. Madison, 1990—92; asst. prof., assoc. prof. U. Calif. Berkeley, 1993—2000, prof., 2001—. Postdoctoral fellow MSRI, Berkeley, 1991; vis. asst. prof. Yale U., New Haven, 1993; mem. tech. staff Bell Labs. Lucent, Murray Hill, NJ, 1997—2000. Guest editor spl. issue Statistica Sinica, 2001; contbr. articles to profl. jours. Grantee, Academic Rsch. Orgn., 1991, 1994, 1998, 2001, 2004, NSF, 1994, 1998, 2001, 2004; Guggenheim fellow, 2006. Fellow: IEEE, Am. Stats. Assn., Inst. Math. Stats. Achievements include patents for lossless coding and data network tomography. Avocations: reading, walking, swimming, movies. Office: Univ Calif Berkeley 367 Evans Hall #3860 Berkeley CA 94720

YU, BING, researcher; s. Zhicheng Yu and Guilin Wang; m. Xuerong Liu, Sept. 28, 1998; children: Ruthie, Cynthia. BS, U. Electronic Sci. & Tech. China, Chengdu, 1989, MS, 1994; PhD in Elec. Engring., Va. Tech, Blacksburg, 2005. Rsch. engr. Chinese Acad. Engring. Physics, Mianyang, Sichuan, China, 1989—91; lectr. U. Electronic Sci. & Tech. China, Chengdu, 1994—99; engr. Chang Tong Mobile Telecomm. Eng. Co., Ltd., Chengdu, 1995—97; engring. supr. Alcatel Telecomm. Sys. Co., Ltd., Chengdu, 1997—98; rsch. asst. Nanyang Technol. U. Singapore, 1999—2000, Va. Tech, 2000—05; postdoctoral rsch. assoc. Duke U., Durham, 2005—; scientist Endls Optics Corp., Raleigh, NC, 2006—. Contbr. articles to profl. jours. and patent disclosures. Recipient Excellent Young Rschr. award, Chinese Acad. Engring Physics, 1991, Travel Fund, Grad. Student Assn., Va. Tech, 2003—04, Super Grad. Rsch. Asst. award, Va. Tech, Ctr. Photonics Tech., 2005; fellowship, U. Louisville, 2000. Mem.: Nat. Postdoctoral Assn., Optical Soc. Am. Achievements include research in minimally invasive optical technology to monitor tumor oxygenation and vascularity for breast cancer diagnostics and miniature imaging system for tumor margin assessment; invention of thermally tunable extrinsic fabry—pérot filter; tunable optical filter based white light interferometry; development of grating-assisted demodulation of interferometric sensors; fiber fabry—perot sensors for detection of partial discharges in power transformers. Avocations: soccer, ping pong/table tennis, fishing. Office: Duke Univ 136 Hudson Hall Box 90281 Durham NC 27708 Office Phone: 919-660-5032. Office Fax: 919-684-4488. Business E-Mail: bing.yu@duke.edu.

YU, CHACK YUNG, pediatrics educator, molecular biologist; b. Guangdong, People Republic of China, Dec. 24, 1957; s. Hung Ho and Shui-Wo (Kwok) Y.; m. Lai-Chu, Apr. 23, 1987; children: Gayang Heidi, Gakit Richard. BS, Chinese U. Hong Kong, 1981, MPhil, 1983; DPhil, Oxford U., England, 1988. Asst. prof. Ohio State U., Columbus, 1990-96, assoc. prof., 1996—. Contbr. articles to profl. jours. Grantee NIH, Bethesda, Md., 1994—, March of Dimes, 1992-94; postdoctoral fellow Med. Rsch. Coun. Lab. Molecular Biology, Cambridge, England, 1987-90. Mem. AAAS, Am. Assn. Immunologists, Am. Soc. Human Genetics, Am. Soc. Microbiology, Am. Soc. Biochemistry and Molecular Biology, Soc. for Pediat. Rsch. Office: Children's Rsch Inst 700 Childrens Dr Columbus OH 43205-2664 E-mail: cyu@chi.osu.edu.

YU, CHUANZHAO, electrical engineer, researcher; b. Shuangcheng, China, Apr. 30, 1975; s. Zhifu Yu and Lizhi Wang; m. Yanhua Chen, Sept. 23, 1999; 1 child, Savannah J. Bachelors, Shanghai Jiaotong U., 1997; PhD, U. Ctrl. Fla., 2006. Rsch. asst. Tsinghua U., Beijing, 1997—2000, Nanoelectronic Reliability Lab., U. Ctrl. Fla., Orlando, Fla., 2003—; engr. Huawei Technologies, Beijing, 2000—03. Intern engr. Advanced Micro Devices, Sunnydale, Calif., 2005. Author: IEEE Transactions on Electron Devices, IEEE Trans. Dev. and Mater. Rel., Microelectronics Reliability. Recipient Self-funded Student award, China Govt., 2006; fellow Travel fellowship, Univ. Ctrl. Fla., 2006; Provost fellowship, 2003, Merit fellowship, 2004. Mem.: Phi Kappa Phi (hon.). Achievements include research in improved models and extraction method for nanoscale MOSFETs; reliability of novel MOSFETs (nanoscale devices, high-k dielectrics, silicon-on-insulator devices, and 1 nm ultra-thin oxide) for microelectronic applications - from device level to circuit level; equivalent circuit models for predicting the reliability of performance for new silicon transistor designs was developed; development of a methodology to predict the reliability effects on the RFIC with these novel devices, which provides guidance for the reliability consideration of the circuit design; research in interface circuit design for MEMS sensors; design of CMOS voltage-control oscillator (VCO), power amplifier (PA), low noise amplifier (LNA), mixer, output buffer and PLL: Analysis of circuit performance; Equivalent circuit modeling for devices; development of board support packet (BSP) system and low-layer drivers for router NetEngine16/NetEngine08. Office: Nano-Electronic Reliability Lab Rsch Park U Ctrl Fla Orlando FL 32816 Personal E-mail: chuanzhaoyu@yahoo.com.

YU, CLEMENT TAK, educator, researcher, consultant; b. Hong Kong, Aug. 31, 1948; came to U.S., 1967; s. Ching Hang and Chen-Chun (Sheit) Y.; m. Teresa Yuen-Ling Chan; children: Victor Kar-Yun, Christine Mei-Yun. BSc, Columbia U., 1970; PhD, Cornell U., 1973. Asst. prof. U. Alberta, Edmunton, Can., 1973-77, assoc. prof., 1977-78, U. Ill., Chgo., 1978-84, prof., 1984—. Cons. System Devel. Corp., MCC, Shell Oil, Amoco Oil, Argonne Nat. Lab., Trilogy, Info. Arts., Fla. Internat. U. Contbr. more than 200 article to profl. confs. and jours. Mem. IEEE (assoc. editor 1994-98), Assn. for Computing Machinery (spl. interest group on info. retrieval, chmn. 1985-87, chmn. conf. 2006), Distributed and Parallel Databases (mem. editl. bd. 1992—). Office: U Ill Dept Computer Sci Chicago IL 60607-7053 Office Phone: 312-996-2318. Business E-Mail: yu@cs.uic.edu.

YU, FEI, internist; b. Beijing, Mar. 12, 1956; came to U.S., 1990; d. Longshan and Dan (Zheng) Y.; m. Xiangqun Fu, Jan. 7, 1984; 1 child, Danni. MD, Beijing Med. U., 1982; PhD in Med. Sci., Beijing Union Med. Coll., 1989. Diplomate Am. Bd. Internal Medicine, Am. Bd. Med. Acupuncture. Intern The People's Hosp., Beijing Med. U., 1981-82; resident in internal medicine Jishuitan Hosp., Beijing, 1983-84, Beijing Union Med. Coll. Hosp., 1984-87; clin. fellow hematology dept. internal medicine Beijing Union Med. Coll., Chinese Acad. Med. Scis., 1987-89; rsch. fellow dept. devel. cell biology Sloan-Ketterng Inst. Cancer Rsch., NYC, 1991-93; rsch. fellow dept. internal medicine Columbia U. Coll. Physicians and Surgeons, NYC, 1993—95; resident in medicine N.Y. Meth. Hosp., Bklyn., 1996-99; physician Regal Med. PC, Clifton, NJ, 2000—02, Clifton Med. & Rehab. Ctr., 2003; pvt. practice Englewood Cliffs, NJ, 2003—. Contbr. articles to profl. jours. Mem. AMA. Avocations: music, swimming, novel reading, travel, stamp collecting. Office: 385 Sylvan Ave 25 Englewood Cliffs NJ 07632 Office Phone: 201-567-0686. Personal E-mail: dnffy@aol.com.

YU, GEORGE TZUCHIAO, political science professor; b. London, May 16, 1931; s. Wangteh and Ying (Ho) Y.; m. Priscilla Chang, Aug. 11, 1957; children: Anthony, Phillip. AB, U. Calif., Berkeley, 1954, MA, 1957, PhD, 1961. Asst. prof. polit. sci. U. N.C., Chapel Hill, 1961-65; assoc. prof. polit. sci. U. Ill., Urbana, 1965-70, prof., 1970—, head dept., 1987-92, dir. Ctr. for East Asian and Pacific Studies, 1992—, dir. grad. studies, 1981-85, chair Asian Am. studies com., 1997—2002. Vis. sr. lectr. polit. sci. Univ. Coll., Nairobi, 1968. Author: The Chinese Anarchist Movement, 1961, 65, Party Politics in Republican China, 1966, China and Tanzania, 1970, China's African Policy, 1975, Intra-Asian International Relations, 1977, Modern China and Its Revolutionary Process, 1985, American Studies in China, 1993, China in Transition, 1994, Asia's New World Order, 1997, Mongolia and Northeast Asia, 1999. Grantee, Social Sci. Rsch. Coun., 1967—68, 1970—71, NEH, 1978—81, 1984—86, Earhart Found., 1976—77, 1981—83, 1988, Ford Found., 1985—87, 1989, 1992, Freeman Found., 1996, 1997, 1999, 2001—03. Mem. Assn. Asian Studies. Office: 702 S Wright St Urbana IL 61801-3631 Business E-Mail: g-yu@uiuc.edu.

YU, HONG, humanities educator; d. ChangMao Yu and QingJu Ju; m. Andrew Bennett; children: Alexander Yu Bennett, Olivia Hong Bennett. BS, Huazhong U. Sci. & Tech., WuHan, China, 1990; MS, Beijing U., 1993; MPhil, Columbia U., NYC, 1997; PhD, Columbia U., 2002. Postdoctoral rsch. scientist Columbia U., 2002—04, assoc. rsch. scientist, 2004—06; asst. prof. U. Wis., Milw., 2006—. Contbr. articles to profl. jours. Grantee Rsch. grant, Juvenile Diabetes Rsch. Found., 2004—06, U. Wis., 2007—. Achievements include invention of algorithms for identifying texts that summarize image content. Office: Univ Wis 2400 Hartford Ave Enderris Hall 939 Milwaukee WI 53201 Business E-Mail: hongyu@uwm.edu.

YU, HYUK, chemist, educator; b. Kapsan, Korea, Jan. 20, 1933; s. Namjik and Keedong (Shin) Y.; m. Gail Emmens, Jan. 20, 1964; children: Jeffrey, Steven, Douglas. BSChemE, Seoul Nat. U., 1955; MS in Organic Chemistry, U. So. Calif., 1958; PhD in Phys. Chemistry, Princeton U., 1962. Rsch. assoc. Dartmouth Coll., Hanover, NH, 1962-63; rsch. chemist Nat. Inst. Sci. and Tech., Washington, 1963-67; asst. prof. U. Wis., Madison, 1967-69, assoc. prof., 1969-78, prof. chemistry, 1978—, Evan P. Helfaer chair chemistry, 1991—95, Eastman-Kodak prof. emeritus, W.H. Stockmayer prof. emeritus. Fulbright-Hays lectr. Inha U., Inchon, Korea,1972; chmn. Gordon Rsch. Conf. Polymer Physics, 1986, 93; cons. LG Chem., Daejeon. Contbr. articles to profl. jours. John Simon Guggenheim Found. fellow, 1984; recipient Alexander von Humboldt award Humboldt Found., 1992. Fellow Am. Phys. Soc. (High-Polymer Physics prize, 1994); mem. Am. Chem. Soc. (exec. com. polymer chemistry divsn., editorial adv. bd. 1988-91, Ho-Am Basic Sci. prize, 1997, Colloid and Surface Chemistry Langmuir Lectr. award 1999), N.Y. Acad. Scis., Biophys. Soc., Materials Rsch. Soc., Korean Chem. Soc. (life), Polymer Soc. Korea (life), Sigma Xi (chpt. pres. 1987-88). Office: Univ Wis 1101 University Ave Madison WI 53706-1396 Home Phone: 608-437-4862. Business E-Mail: yu@chem.wisc.edu.

YU, JAE-HYUK, geneticist, educator; Degree cum laude, Seoul Nat. U., Republic of Korea, 1986; PhD in Genetics, U. Wis., Madison, 1995. Post-doc. rsch. assoc. Tex. A&M U., Tex., 1995—98; investigator Cereon Genomics, LLC, Cambridge, Mass., 1998—2000; asst. prof. U. Wis., Madison, Wis., 2000—06, assoc. prof., 2006—. With South Korean Army, 1986—89. Mem.: Genetics Soc. Am. Achievements include research in fungal signal transduction and development. Office: Univ Wisconsin Dept Bacteriology Madison WI 53706

YU, JEN, medical educator; b. Taipei, Taiwan, Jan. 23, 1943; came to U.S., 1969; s. Chin Chuan and Shiu Lan (Lin) Y.; m. Janet Chen, June 16, 1973; children: Benjamin, Christopher. MD, Nat. Taiwan U., 1968; PhD in Physiology, U. Pa., 1972. Diplomate Am. Bd. Phys. Medicine and Rehab. Intern Phila. Gen. Hosp., 1972-73; resident in phys. medicine and rehab. Hosps. of U. Pa., 1973-75; asst. prof. dept. phys. medicine and rehab. U. Pa. Sch. Medicine, Phila., 1975-76, U. Tex. Health Sci. Ctr., San Antonio, 1976-79, assoc. prof., 1979-81; prof. dept. phys. medicine and rehab. U. Calif. Irvine Coll. Medicine, 1981-82, prof., chmn. dept. phys. medicine and rehab., 1982—. Contbr. articles to profl. jours. Mem. Am. Acad. Phys. Medicine and Rehab., Am. Congress Rehab. Medicine, Assn. Acad. Physiatrists, Am. Assn. Anatomists, Soc. for Neurosci. Office: U Calif Irvine Med Ctr Dept Phys Medicine & Rehab 101 The City Dr Orange CA 92868-3201 Home Phone: 949-856-3264; Office Phone: 714-456-6504. Business E-Mail: jyu@uci.edu.

YU, JESSICA, director, producer, writer, editor; b. 1966; BA in English with honors, Yale U. Bd. dirs. Internat. Documentary Assn. Prodr.(dir.): Home Base: A Chinatown Callen Heinlenville, Sour Death Balls, 1992, Breathing Lessons: The Life and Work of Mark O'Brien, 1996 (Acad. award for best documentary short subject, 1997), Better Late, 1997, In the Realms of the Unreal, 2004; (TV films) Men of Re-enaction, 1998; dir.: The Cake Eaters, 2005; (documentaries, feature) The Living Museum, 1998; contbr. articles. Recipient Edward R. Murrow award, Skeptics Soc., 1995, 24 film festival awards. Fellow: Yaddo, MacDowell Colony; mem.: Phi Beta Kappa.

YU, JIU-KANG, mathematics professor; BS in Math., Nat. Taiwain Univ., Taipei, 1989; PhD, Harvard Univ., 1994. Instr. Princeton Univ., 1994—96, asst. prof., 1996—2000; assoc. prof. Purdue Univ., 2003—; asst. prof. Univ. Md., 2000—03, assoc. prof., 2003—. Recipient Chern prize, Internat. Congress of Chinese Mathematicians, 2001; fellow, Alfred P. Sloan Found., 1994, 2001—03. Achievements include being one of 18 top mathematicians and computer scientists (Atlas of Lie Groups Project) from the US to successfully map E8, one of the largest and most complicated structures in mathematics. Office: Dept Math Purdue Univ West Lafayette IN 47907 Office Phone: 765-494-1946. Business E-Mail: jyu@math.purdue.edu. *

YU, KITSON SZEWAI, computer science educator; b. Toishan, Kwangtung, China, Apr. 4, 1950; came to U.S., 1969; s. Ho Yee and Yin Sang (Chan) Y.; m. Mabel Griseldis Wong, July 15, 1972; 1 child, Robin Roberta Emily. BS, Troy State U., 1974, MS, 1977, BS, 1980. Cert. systems profl.; cert. data processing educator. V.p. Troy (Ala.) Computer Ctr., 1976-81; computer instr. Tory State U., 1980-81, Linn Benton Community Coll., Albany, Oreg., 1981—, dir. real estate program, 1985—. Mng. broker Kitson Realty, Corvallis, Oreg., 1975—. Vice pres. econ. devel. Daleville C. of C., Ala., 1976; dir. Corvalis Youth Symphony, 1990-93. Mem. Data Processing Mgmt. Assn. (bd. dirs. at large 1982-93, v.p. 1984-85, pres. 1985-86), Greater Albany Rotary (treas. 1985—), Corvallis Multiple Listing Exch. (bd. dirs. 1990-94), Gamma Beta Phi. Office: Linn Benton C C 6500 Pacific Blvd SW Albany OR 97321-3774 *Personal philosophy: Ask, when appropriate; Aid, when appreciated.*

YU, MING, engineering educator, researcher; s. Chongguang Yu and Zhongying Su; m. Tian Xing, Aug. 28, 1992; children: Ellen Tian, Karen Tian, Tim Tian. BEE, Hubei Inst. Auto Tech., 1984; MEE, Huazhong U. Sci. and Tech., 1987; D of Engring., Tsinghua U., China, 1994; PhD, Rutgers U., New Brunswick, NJ, 2002. Sr. tech. staff mem. AT&T Labs, Middletown, NJ, 1997—2000; asst. prof. SUNY, Binghamton, NY, 2003—06, Fla. State U., Tallahassee, 2006—. Sr. software engr. Jedai Broadband Networks, Red Bank, 2000; sys. engr. AT&T Labs, Middletown, 2002—03. Contbr. articles to profl. jours. Fin. chair IEEE Iwat, NYC, 2005—; cyber trust panelist NSF, Washington, 2004—05, it rsch. panelist, 2004; tech. program com. IEEE Wireless Comm. and Network Conf., Piscataway, NJ, 2005—, Internat. Workshop on Antennas Tech., 2005, Internat. Conf. Networking Sensing and Control, 2005, Internat. Conf. Circuits and Systems, 2003, Systems Man and Cybernetics Sys. Assurance, 2005; reviewer IEEE Trans on Comm., Antennas and Propagations, Piscataway, 2005—; guest editor Int. J. of Wireless and Mobile Computing, Piscataway, 2003—. Recipient Third Millenium medal, IEEE, 2000. Mem.: IEEE (sr. regional 1 award 2006). Achievements include development of novel routing protocols and traffic models. Home: 294 Cardiff Dr Morganville NJ 07751 Office: Fla State U Dept ECE 2525 Pottsdamer St Tallahassee FL 32310 Home Phone: 732-817-1886; Office Phone: 850-410-6263. Office Fax: 850-410-6479. Personal E-mail: mingyu@ieee.org. Business E-Mail: mingyu@eng.fsu.edu.

YU, PAULINE RUTH, former dean, educational association administrator; b. Rochester, NY, Mar. 5, 1949; d. Paul N. and Irene (Tang) Y.; m. Theodore D. Huters, Aug. 23, 1975 (div. Feb. 2000); children: Emily Elizabeth, Matthew Charles, Alexander David. BA in History and Lit. magna cum laude, Harvard U., 1971; MA in Comparative Lit., Stanford U., 1973, PhD in Comparative Lit., 1976. Asst. prof., then assoc. prof. U. Minn., Mpls., 1976-85; assoc. prof., then prof. Columbia U., NYC, 1985-89; prof., founding chair dept. East Asian langs. and lit. U. Calif., Irvine, 1989-94; dean humanities UCLA, 1994—2003, prof. East Asian langs. and culture, 1994—2003; pres. Am. Coun. Learned Socs., NYC, 2003—. Author: The Poetry of Wang Wei, 1980, The Reading of Imagery in the Chinese Poetic Tradition, 1987; editor and contbg. author: Voices of the Song Lyric in China, 1994, Culture and State in Chinese History: Conventions, Accommodations, and Critiques, 1997, Ways with Words: Writing about Reading Texts from Early China, 2000; editor, contbr.: The Longman Anthology of World Literature; mem. editl. bd. Tang Studies, Chinese Lit., Comparative Lit. Studies, 1993—; mem. Scholars' Coun., Libr. of Congress, 2006—. Mem. nat. adv. bd. Woodrow Wilson Found., 2004—07; mem. internat. adv. bd. Asia Rsch. Inst., Nat. U. Singapore, 2002—; mem. western ctr. exec. coun. Am. Acad. Arts and Scis., 2000—03; bd. dirs. Am. Coun. Learned Socs., 1998—; trustee Nat. Humanities Ctr., 2000—, Asian Cultural Coun., 2006—, mem. exec. com., 2006—; bd. dirs. The Teagle Found., 2003—, mem. exec. com., 2005—; mem. adv. coun. dept. East Asian studies Princeton U., 2003—; bd. overseers Harvard U., 2003—, mem. exec. com., 2006—; mem. adv. bd. Coun. for Internat. Exch. of Scholars, 2001—05. Guggenheim fellow, 1983-84, ACLS fellow, 1983-84; recipient Profl. Achievement award U. Calif. at Irvine Alumni Assn., 1993. Fellow Am. Acad. Arts and Scis., Am. Philos. Soc.; mem. MLA, Assn. Asian Studies (mem. China and Inner Asia coun. 1982-85), Am. Comparative Lit. Assn., Am. Oriental Soc., Phi Beta Kappa Soc. (senator 1997—, exec. com. 2001—). Office: Am Coun Learned Societies 633 Third Ave New York NY 10017-6795 Home Phone: 212-260-3375; Office Phone: 212-697-1505 x 121. E-mail: paulineyu@acls.org.

YU, PETER LEGASPI, rehabilitation physician; b. Jan. 31, 1957; BS, U. Santo Tomas, Manila, 1975, MD, 1979. Diplomate Am. Bd. Ind. Med. Examiners, U.S. Ednl. Coun. Fgn. Med. Grads., 1980, U.S. Fed. Lic. Examination, 1982, Philippine Med. Bd. Examination, 1980. Intern Vets. Meml. Med. Ctr., Quezon City, The Philippines, 1979-80; resident in gen. surgery St. Clare's Hosp., NYC, 1982-84; resident in phys. medicine U. Ala., Birmingham, 1984—87; pvt. practice South Bend, Ind., 1988—. Attending physiatrist Meth. Hosp., Gary, Ind., 1989—, Merrillville, 1989—, Porter Meml. Hosp., Ind., 1994-2000, Meml. Hosp., South Bend, 1988—, Lakeland Med. Ctr., Niles, 1995-2002, St. Anthony Med. Ctr., Crown Point, Ind., 1992—, St. Mary's Med. Ctr., Hobart, Ind., 1994—, St. Catherines Hosp., East Chicago, Ind., 1994—; rehab. dir. Healthwin Hosp., South Bend, 1999-2002, Cardinal Nursing and Rehab. Ctr., South Bend, 1999-2001, 07—, Silverbrook Manor, Niles, Mich., 1997-2001, Ironwood Health and Rehab. Ctr., 2004—; rehab. dir. Hamilton Cmtys., New Carlisle, Ind., 2006—. Contbg. editor: US Thomasian Mag., 2006—. Vol., chmn. Philippine Centennial Celebration for South Bend, Ind., 1998, Philippine Centennial Celebration SW Mich.; lector St. Pius X Cath. Ch., Granger, Ind., 2006—07. Mem. AMA, No. Ind. Rehab. Med. (pres.), Philippine Am. Physiatry Assn., (pres. 1999-2001), Asian Am. Med. Soc. (bd. dirs. 1999-02, 2006—), Am. Acad. Phys. Medicine and Rehab., Am. Congress Rehab. Medicine, Am. Acad. Electrodiagnostic Medicine, Am. Acad. Exec. Physicians, Ind. State Med. Assn., Ind. Soc. Phys. Medicine and Rehab., Ind. Philippine Med. Assn. (pres. 2007—, chmn. med. and surg. mission to Aklan Province, Philippines 2007), St. Joseph County Med. Soc., U. Santo Tomas Med. Alumni Assn. Am. (auditor 2006—), U. Santo Tomas Medicine Class 1979 (sec. USA chpt. 2003—, editor-in-chief newsletter). Address: 8127 Merrillville Rd Merrillville IN 46410-6158 Personal E-mail: nirm-mvl@sbcglobal.net.

YU, ROBERT KUAN-JEN, biochemistry professor; b. Chungking, China, Jan. 27, 1938; came to U.S., 1962; m. Helen Chow, July 1, 1972; children: David S., Jennifer S. BS, Tunghai U., Taiwan, 1960; PhD, U. Ill., 1967; Med.ScD. (hon.), Tokyo, 1980; MA (hon.), Yale U., 1985. Rsch. assoc., instr. Albert Einstein Coll. Medicine, Bronx, 1967-72; asst. prof. Yale U., New Haven, 1973-75, assoc. prof., 1975-82, prof., 1983-88; prof. biochemistry, chmn. dept. Med. Coll. Va. Va. Commonwealth U., Richmond, 1988-2000; dir. Inst. Mol. Med. Genetics Med. Coll., Augusta, Ga., 2000—; dir. Inst. Neurosci. Med. Coll. Ga., Augusta, 2005—. Mem. study sect. NIH, Washington, 1980-84, 96—; mem. Bd. Lab. Svcs., Va., 1994-98. Editor: Gangioside Structure Function and Biomedical Potential, 1984, New Trends in Ganglioside Research, 1988; contbr. over 500 articles to profl. publs. Josiah Macy scholar, 1979; grantee NIH, 1975—, 84-91; recipient Va. Outstanding Scientist of Yr. award, 1995, Alexander von Humboldt award, 1990, GRA Eminent scholar, 2000, Dist. Alumnus award Tunghai U., 2003, Achievement award Chinese Assn. Engrs. and Scientists So. Calif., 2004, Outstanding Faculty award Sch. Medicine, Med. Coll. Ga., 2006. Mem. AAAS, Am. Soc. Cell Biology, Am. Soc. Neurochemistry (mem. coun. 1983-86, 91-95, pres. 2001-03), Internat. Soc. Neurochemistry, Soc. Neurosci., Am. Soc. Biochemistry and Molecular Biology, Am. Chem. Soc., N.Y. Acad. Sci., Academia Sinica (academician). Business E-Mail: ryu@mcg.edu.

YU, SHAN PING, neuroscientist, educator; s. Yong-niang Yu; m. Ling Wei; 1 child, Steven S. MS, Inst. of Pharmacology and Toxicology, Beijing, China, 1982; MD, Capital Inst. of Medicine, Beijing, China, 1982; PhD, SUNY, 1990. Rsch. asst. neuropharmacology Inst. Pharmacology and Toxicology, Beijing, 1982—84; vis. rschr. Lund U., Sweden, 1985—86; postdoctoral rschr. Howard Hughes Med. Inst., Stony Brook, NY, 1990—92; asst. prof. Wash. U., St. Louis, 1992—98, assoc. prof., 1998—2002, Med. U. S.C., Charleston, 2002—. Contbr. articles to profl. jours. Recipient Grant-in-Aid award, Am. Heart Assn., 1999, Am. Heart Assn. and Bugher award, 2001; Oversea fellow, WHO, 1985, Rsch. grantee, NSF, 1999, NIH, 2001. Mem.: Soc. for Neuroscience. Achievements include discovery of Potassium channel regulation in neuronal apoptosis and novel regulations of glutamate receptors. Home: 1214 Waterfront Dr Mount Pleasant SC 29464 Office: Med Univ of SC 280 Calhoun St Charleston SC 29425 Office Phone: 843-792-2992. Personal E-mail: yusp@musc.edu.

YU, SIMON SHYI-JIAN, entomologist, educator; b. Ilan, Taiwan, Republic of China, Sept. 11, 1935; arrived in Can. 1963, U.S. in 1968; s. Son-Wei and Ah-So (Liao) Yu; m. Rachel R.C. Yeh, Setp. 16, 1967; children: Robert Yu, Edmund Yu. BS, Nat. Taiwan U., 1959; MS, McGill U., Montreal, Can., 1965, PhD, 1968; postdoctoral, Cornell U. and Oreg. State U., 1968-74. Rsch. entomologist Taiwan Sugar Co., Kuohsiung, Taiwan, 1961-62; rsch. asst. McGill U., Montreal, 1963-68; postdoctoral fellow Cornell U., Ithaca, N.Y., 1968-69; rsch. assoc. Oreg. State U., Corvallis, 1969-74, asst. prof., 1974-79; asst. prof. U. Fla., Gainesville, 1980-82, assoc. prof., 1982-86, prof., 1986—2006, prof. emeritus, 2006—. Contbr. articles to profl. jours., chapters to books. 2nd lt. Chinese infantry, 1959-61. Rsch. grantee NIH, 1979, USDA, 1980, 82, 85, 90, 91, EPA, 1981, NSF, 1988, 90. Mem. Entomol. Soc. Am., AAAS, Am. Chem. Soc., The Soc. Sigma Xi, Fla. Entomol. Soc. Avocations: classical music, fishing, bicycling. Office: U Fla Dept Entomology And NE Gainesville FL 32611 Home: 5205 NW 43rd Rd Gainesville FL 32606-4323 Office Phone: 352-392-1901. Business E-Mail: yusj@ufl.edu.

YU, TIAN-EN, musician, music educator; d. Hong Liang Yu and Junyia Xu; m. Nicholas Stephen Isaacs, July 26, 1990. Student, Shanghai Conservatory, 1961—69; Artist Diploma, Oberlin Conservatory, 1989. Pianist Shanghai Ballet, 1970—80, Shanghai Philharmonic, 1980—86; accompanist Oberlin Conservatory, Ohio, 1988—89; instr. Cmty. Sch. Music and Arts, Mountain View, Calif., 1990—95; lectr. in piano Santa Clara U., Calif., 1993—; tutor, accompanist Interlochen (Mich.) Music Camp, 1987. Judge U.S. Open Piano Competition, 1993, 96, 99, 2004—06. Musician: Shanghai Philharmonic, Santa Clara U. Orch., Oberlin Conservatory. Scholar, Oberlin Conservatory, 1986—88. Mem.: Am. Coll. Musicians. Avocations: knitting, sewing, flower arranging, cats. Personal E-mail: tianenyuxu77@yahoo.com.

YU, WEI-WEN, retired engineering educator; b. Shandong, China, July 10, 1924; arrived in U.S., 1954; s. Chi-tung and Mong-shih Yu; m. Yueh-hsin Wang, Sept. 6, 1953; children: Julie H.H., Dorothy H.L., Gordon H.I. BS, Nat. Taiwan U., 1950; MS, Okla. State U., 1955; PhD, Cornell U., 1960. Registered profl. engr., Mo. Structural engr. T.H. McKaig & Assocs., Buffalo, 1955—56, 1959—60; rsch. engr. Am. Iron and Steel Inst., NYC, 1960—67; staff engr. TRW Sys., Redondo Beach, Calif., 1967—68; assoc. prof. U. Mo., Rolla, 1968—72, prof., 1972—82, Curator's prof., 1982—92, Curator's prof. emeritus, 1992—. Dir. Ctr. for Cold-Formed Steel Structures, Rolla, 1990—2000; founding dir. Wei-Wen Yu Ctr. for Cold-Formed Steel Structures, Rolla, 2001—. Author: Cold-Formed Steel Structures, 1973, Cold-Formed Steel Design, 1985, 1991, 2000; guest editor: Spl. Issue on Recent Devels. in Thin-Walled Structures, 1998; editor (and co-editor): Recent Rsch. and Devel. in Cold-Formed Steel Design and Constrn., 1971—; guest editor Spl. issue on Cold-Formed Steel Structures, 1993. Recipient Alumni Merit award, U. Mo. Sch. of Mines and Metallurgy/U. Mo.-Rolla Alumni Assn., 1979, Arch T. Colwell Merit award, Soc. Automotive Engrs., 1988. Fellow: ASCE (Shortridge Hardesty award 2001); mem.: U. Mo.-Rolla Acad. Civil Engrs. (hon.), Chi-Epsilon (chpt. honor). Achievements include research in Cold-formed steel structures. Avocations: reading, gardening. Office: U Mo Rolla Dept Civil Engring Rolla MO 65409

YU, YI-HAO, endocrinologist, educator, physician, research scientist; s. Shi-Qing Yu, Hui-Ling Gan; m. Yiying Zhang; 1 child, Irene. BS, Fudan U., Shanghai, China; MS, PhD, MD, NYU. Diplomate Am. Bd. Internal Medicine. Rsch. asst. prof. NYU Sch. Medicine, NYC; resident physician Columbia Presbyn. Hosp., NYC, 1996—98, physician, endocrine fellow, 1998—2001; Markey rsch. fellow Columbia U. Coll. Physicians and Surgeons, NYC, 1998—2001; staff physician Columbia Presbyn. Med. Ctr., 2001—, dir. adult nutrition and TPN svc.; asst. prof. medicine Columbia U. Coll. Physicians and Surgeons. Cons. Physicians Cons. Network, Mt. Arlington, NJ; mem. com. Nat. Bd. Nutrition Support Certification, Inc., CNSP. Contbr. articles, sci. papers, books in field. Fellow, China-U.S. Biochemistry Exam. and Application/Ray Wu Soc., in Atherosclerosis, NIH, 1998—2001; grantee NIH, 2001—, Pfizer, 2002—; rsch. grantee, Endocrine Fellows Found., 1999. Fellow: Am. Coll. Endocrinology; mem.: ACP, AAAS, AMA, Am. Soc. Parenteral and Enteral Nutrition, Am.-Chinese Med. Assn. (med. cons. 2001—), Am. Assn. Clin. Endocrinologists, Am. Soc. Cell Biology, N.Y. U. Alumni, Fudan Alumnin U.S. Avocations: Chinese calligraphy, travel, hiking, swimming. Office: Columbia Univ P&S 630 West 168th St PH10-305J New York NY 10032 Home Phone: 212-865-6681. Office Fax: 212-305-3213. Business E-Mail: yy102@columbia.edu.

YU, YING-SHIH, retired history professor, writer; b. Tientsin, China, Jan. 22, 1930; s. Hsieh-chung and Ya-yen (Yew) Y.; m. Monica Shu-ping Chen, June 6, 1964; children: Sylvia, Judy. BA, New Asia Coll., Chinese U., Hong Kong, 1952; PhD in History, Harvard U., 1962; LL.D. (hon.), Chinese U. Hong Kong, 1977; LittD, Middlebury Coll., 1984. Asst. prof. history U. Mich., Ann Arbor, 1962-66; assoc. prof. Chinese history Harvard U., Cambridge, 1966-69, prof., 1969-77; pres. New Asia Coll., 1973-75; Charles Seymour prof. history Yale U., New Haven, 1977-87; Michael Henry Strater univ. prof. Princeton U., NJ, 1987—2001, emeritus prof. Ea. Asian studies & history NJ, 2001—; sr. disting. scholar John W. Kluge Ctr., Library of Congress, Washington, 2005—. Overseas cons. Project of Confucian Ethics, Singapore, 1983-88. Author: Trade and Expansion in Han China: A Study in the Structure of Sino-Barbarian Economic Relations, 1967, History and Thought, 1976, The Two Worlds of the Red Chamber Dream, 1978, Religious Ethic and Merchant Class in Early Modern China, 1986; co-author: (with Robert Irick and Kwang-ching Liu) American-Chinese Relations, 1784-1941, 1960. (with Willard J. Peterson and Andrew Plaks) The Power of Culture: Studies in Chinese Cultural History, 1994; author, editor: Early Chinese History in People's Republic of China, 1981; co-editor Asia Major, 1987—. Co-recipient John W. Kluge prize for Study of Humanity, Libr. Congress, 2006. Mem. Academia Sinica, Am. Philosophical Soc. Avocation: reading. Office: Princeton U 211 Jones Dr Princeton NJ 08540 *

YUAN, JUNYING, medical educator, researcher; b. Shanghai; BS, Fudan U., Shanghai, 1982; PhD in Neuroscience, Harvard U., 1989. Postdoctoral trainee in devel. biology MIT, 1989—90; instr. medicine Harvard U., 1990—91, asst. prof. medicine and program in neuroscience, 1992—96, asst. prof. cell biology and program in neuroscience, 1996—2000, prof., 2000—; asst. geneticist Cardiovasc. Rsch. Ctr. Mass. Gen. Hosp., 1990—96. Mem. editl. bd.: Current Biology, 1996, ad hoc reviewer: NIH Human Embryology and Devel. 2 Study Sect., 1995, regular reviewer:, 1996—; patentee in field, —; contbr. articles to profl. jours.; presenter in field, —. Recipient Wilson S. Stone Meml. award, MD Anderson Cancer Ctr. U. Tex., 1994, Established Investigator award, Am. Heart Assn., 1996—, Dir.'s Pioneer Award, NIH, 2005; fellow Ryan, Harvard Med. Sch., 1985—89. Fellow: Am. Acad. Arts & Scis. Office: Harvard Med Sch Dept Cell Biology 240 Longwood Ave Boston MA 02115-5701 Office Phone: 617-432-4170. Office Fax: 617-432-4177. E-mail: jyuan@hms.harvard.edu. *

YUAN, LONGPING, agronomist; b. Jiangxi, China, 1930; Grad., Southwest Agriculture Inst., 1953. Rsch. prof. Hunan Acad. Agrl. Scis., 1971; tech. advisor Internat. Rice Inst., 1980—81; academician Chinese Acad. Engring., 1995—; dir. gen. China Hybrid Rice Rsch. and Devel. Ctr., Hunan. Internat. chief cons. UN Food and Agriculture Orgn., 1991—. Recipient Sci. award, UNESCO, 1987, China State Preeminent Sci. and Tech. award, 2001, Ramon Magasaysay award, 2001, Medal Honor, United Nat. FAO, Wolf prize in agr., Wolf Found., Israel, 2004, World Food Prize, World Food Found., USA, 2004. Mem.: NAS. Achievements include development of indica hybrid rice in 1973; first scientist to successfully alter the self-pollinating characteristic of rice, which lead to large-scale farming of hybrid rice; known as "Father of Hybrid Rice". Office: Chinese Acad Engrng 3 Fuxing Rd Beijing 100038 China E-mail: lpyuan@public.cs.hn.cn.

YUAN, NANCI, pediatrician, pulmonologist, educator; MD, Hahnemann U., 1996. Diplomate Am. Bd. Pediat., 1999, Am. Bd. Sleep Medicine, 2005. Clin. asst. prof. LPCH Stanford, Palo Alto, Calif., 2003—. Home and Office: 770 Welch Rd Ste 350 Palo Alto CA 94304-5786 Home Phone: 650-723-5191; Office Phone: 650-723-5191.

YUAN, NICOLE PATRICIA, healthcare educator; m. Jerel Eric Slaughter. BA, Oberlin Coll., 1995; PhD, Bowling Green State U., 2002. Psychology lic. Ariz. Bd. Psychologist Examiners. Dir. substance abuse rsch. Mel and Enid Zuckerman Coll. Pub. Health U. Ariz., Tucson, 2002—06, asst. prof., 2006—. Mem.: APHA, APA, Internat. Soc. Traumatic Stress Studies, Soc. Cmty. Rsch. and Action, Ariz. Psychol. Assn., So. Ariz. Psychol. Assn. (chair profl. outreach com. 2006—). Office: U Ariz Bldg 202 1295 N Martin Ave Tucson AZ 85724 Home Phone: 520-319-8689; Office Phone: 520-626-7215. Office Fax: 520-626-8716. Business E-Mail: nyuan@email.arizona.edu.

YUAN, ROBIN TSU-WANG, plastic surgeon; b. Boston, July 2, 1954; s. Robert Hsun-Piao and Grace I. (Chen) Y. AB, Harvard U., 1974, MD, 1978. Diplomate Am. Bd. Plastic Surgery. Resident in gen. surgery UCLA Med. Ctr., 1978-80, Cedars-Sinai Med. Ctr., LA, 1980-81, 83-84; resident in plastic surgery U. Miami (Fla.)-Jackson Meml. Hosp., 1985-87; pvt. practice LA, 1987—. Clin. instr. divsn. plastic surgery UCLA, 1987-98, asst. clin. prof., 1998—; vice-chief divsn. plastic surgery Cedars-Sinai Med. Ctr., LA, 1991—; pres., CEO, founder Family of Independent Reconstructive Surgery Teams, 1990—, pres. Millard Soc., 2003. Author: Cheer Up...You're Only Half Dead!, Reflections at Mid-Life, 1996; contbr. numerous articles to med. jours. Mem. Am. Soc. Plastic and Reconstructive Surgery, Am. Cleft Palate Assn., Calif. Med. Assn. (del.), LA County Med. Assn. (bd. govs. dist. 1), Phi Lambda (co-mgr. 1991—). Avocations: tennis, skiing, golf, creative writing, violin. Office: 462 N Linden Dr Ste 236 Beverly Hills CA 90212 Office Phone: 310-385-8425. Personal E-mail: robinpbhps@aol.com.

YUAN, ZHEN, biomedical researcher; b. Zibo City, Shandong, China, Dec. 16, 1972; s. Changgong Yuan and Guifen Yin; m. Lu Yin; 1 child, Anzhe. PhD, U. Sci. & Tech., Hefei, China, 2002. Engineering, U. Sci. and Tech., China, 2002. Rsch. asst. dept. modern mechanics U. Sci. and Tech., Hefei, 1996—2002; postdoctoral rsch. fellow Inst. High Performance Computing, Nat. U. Singapore, Singapore City, 2002—04; postdoctoral rsch. assoc. physics dept. Clemson Univ., 2004—05; postdoctoral rsch. scientist biomedical engring. dept. U. Fla., Gainesville, 2005—. Fellow, Nat. U. Singapore, 2003; scholar Lixue Pandeng, Chiense Acad. Scis., 2002. Mem.: SPIE (hon.), OSA (hon.). Achievements include research in biomedical imaging of cancer-related diseases; invention of finite-elment-based photoacoustic imaging; electric-sensitive BIOMEMS; first to hydrogel biomaterials development. Home: 1001 SW 16th Ave Apt 77 Gainesville FL 32601 Office: U Fla Biomed Engring Dept 130 BME Bldg PO Box 116131 Gainesville FL 32611 Home Phone: 352-374-4571; Office Phone: 352-392-0965. Office Fax: 352-392-9791. Business E-Mail: yzhen@bme.ufl.edu.

YUDELL, BUZZ (ROBERT YUDELL), architect; BA, Yale Coll., New Haven, 1969, MArch, 1973. Founding ptnr., ptnr.-in-charge Moore Ruble Yudell, Santa Monica, Calif., 1977—. Co-recipient Gold medal, AIA LA, 2007. Fellow: AIA. Office: Moore Ruble Yudell 933 Pico Blvd Santa Monica CA 90405 Office Phone: 310-450-1400. Office Fax: 310-450-1403. *

YUDKOWSKY, RACHEL, medical educator; b. NY, 1955; m. Moshe Yudkowsky; children: Eliezer, Channah. MD, Northwestern U., Evanston, Ill., 1979. Cert. psychiatry Am. Bd. Psychiatry and Neurology. Faculty dept. psychiatry Evanston Northwestern Healthcare, Ill., 1985—99; asst. prof. dept. med. edn. U. Ill. Coll. Medicine, Chgo., 1999—. Clerkship dir., residency program dir. and dir. edn., dept. psychiatry Evanston Northwestern Healthcare, Chgo., 1990; dir. clin. performance ctr. U. Ill. Coll. Medicine, 2001—. Office: U Ill Chgo Coll Medicine Dept Med Edn MC 591 808 S Wood St Chicago IL 60612 Office Phone: 312-996-3598. Business E-Mail: rachely@uic.edu.

YUDOF, MARK GEORGE, academic and federal agency administrator, law educator; b. Phila., Oct. 30, 1944; s. Jack and Eleanor (Parris) Y.; m. Judith Lynn Gomel, July 11, 1965; children: Seth Adam, Samara Lisa. BA, U. Pa., 1965, LLB, 1968. Bar: Pa. 1970, U.S. Supreme Ct. 1974, U.S. Dist. Ct. (we. dist.) Tex. 1975, U.S. Ct. Appeals (5th cir.) 1976, Tex. 1980. Law clk. to judge US Ct. Appeals (5th cir.), 1968-69; assoc. gen. counsel to ABA study FTC, 1969; rsch. assoc. Harvard Ctr. Law and Edn., 1969-70, sr. staff atty., 1970-71; lectr. Harvard Grad. Sch. Edn., 1970-71; asst. prof. law U. Tex., Austin, 1971-74, prof., 1974—97, 2002—, assoc. dean, 1979-84, James A. Elkins Cent. chair in law, 1983-97, dean, 1984-94, exec. v.p., provost, 1994-97, John Jeffers rsch. chair in law, 1991-94; pres. U. Minn., 1997—2002; chancellor U. Tex. Sys., 2002—, Jamail regents chair higher edn. leadership, 2002—, Wright chair fed. courts, 2002—. Of counsel Penzoil vs. Texaco, 1987. Author: When Government Speaks, 1983 (Scribes Book award 1983, cert. merit ABA 1983), (with others) Educational Policy and the Law, 1992, (with others) Gender Justice, 1986. Mem. Tex. Gov.'s Task Force on Sch. Fin., 1989-90, Tex. Gov.'s Select Com. on Edn., 1988; bd. dirs. Freedom to Read Found., 1989-91; mem. Austin Cable Commn., 1981-84, chmn., 1982; mem. nat. panel on sch. desegregation rsch. Ford Found., 1977-80; mem. state exec. com. Univ. Interscholastic League, 1983-86; bd. dirs. Jewish Children's Regional Svc., 1980-86; mem. Gov.'s Select Task Force on Pub. Edn., 1995; mem. Telecomms. Infrastructure Fund Bd., State of Tex., 1995-97; adv. bd. Nat. Inst. for Literacy, 2002-06, Pres. Coun. on Svc. and Civic Participation, 2006—; chmn. Coun. Pub. Univ. Pres. and Chancellors, 2006—. Recipient

Tchg. Excellence award, 1975, Most Meritorious Book award Scribes, 1983, Humanitarian award Austin region NCCJ, 1988, Antidefamation League Jurisprudence award, 1991, James Wilson award U. Pa. Law Sch., 2004; hon. fellow Queen Mary and Westfield Coll., U. London. Fellow: Am. Acad. Arts & Sci., Am. Bar Found., Tex. Bar Found.; mem.: Edn. Testing Svc. (mem. bd. dirs. 2000—02), Am. Coun. Edn. (mem. com. on leadership and instl. effectiveness 2000), Assn. Am. Law Schs. (chmn. law and edn. sect. 1983—84, exec. com. 1988—90), Tex. Bar Found., Am. Law Inst. Avocation: collecting antique maps. Office: U Texas System 601 Colorado St Austin TX 78701-2904 Office Phone: 512-499-4201. E-mail: myudof@utsystem.edu.

YUE, AGNES KAU-WAH, otolaryngologist; b. Shanghai, Peoples Republic China, Dec. 1, 1947; arrived in US, 1967; d. Chen Kia and Nee Yuan; m. Gerald Kumata, Sept. 25, 1982; children: Julie, Allison, Benjamin. BA, Wellesley Coll., 1970; MD, Med. Coll. Pa., 1974; postgrad., Yale U., 1974-78. Intern Yale-New Haven Hosp., 1974-75, resident, 1975-78; fellow U. Tex. M.D. Anderson Cancer Ctr., Houston, 1978-79; asst. prof. U. Wash., Seattle, 1979-82; physician Pacific Med. Ctr., Seattle, 1979-90; pvt. practice Seattle, 1991—. Fellow Am. Acad. Otolaryngology; mem. Northwest Acad. Otolaryngology. Avocations: sailing, opera, cooking. Office: 1801 NW Market St Ste 410 Seattle WA 98107-3909 Office Phone: 206-782-1090.

YUE, ALFRED SHUI-CHOH, metallurgical engineer, consultant; b. China, Nov. 12, 1920; s. Choy Noon-woo and Sze Man-hun (Tom) Yue; m. Virginia Chin-wen Tang, May 21, 1944; children: Mary, Raymond Yuan, John, Ling Tsao, David, Nancy Chang. BS, Chao-tung U., 1942; MS, Ill. Inst. Tech., 1950; PhD, Purdue U., 1956. Assoc. engr. Taiwan Aluminum Co., 1942-47; instr. Purdue U., 1952-56; research engr. Dow Chem. Co., Midland, Mich., 1956-62; sr. mem. Lockheed, Palo Alto Rsch. Lab., 1962-69; from prof. engring. and applied sci. to cons. UCLA, LA, 1969—. Hon. prof. Xian Jiao-tong U., China, 1980. Sec.-gen. Chinese Culture Assn. U.S., 1967; bd. dirs. Chinese scholar to U.S. Fellow: AIAA (assoc.); mem.: AIME, Materials Rsch. Soc., Am. Soc. Metals, Sigma Xi, Phi Tau Phi (pres. 1978—82), Tau Beta Pia, Sigma Pi Sigma. Personal E-mail: asyue@yahoo.com.

YUE, WUSI, mechanical engineer, researcher; arrived in US, 1999; s. Xianjin Yue and Congying Hu; m. Yuhong Zhao, May 1993. BS in Engring, Huazhong U. Sci. and Tech., Wuhan, Hubei Province, People's Republic of China, 1988; PhD, U. Iowa, Iowa City, 2003. Asst. rsch. engr. Beijing Inst. of Applied Physics and Computational Math., 1992—98; postdoctoral fellow Johns Hopkins U., Balt., 2003—. Mem.: ASME, APS, Sigma Xi. Achievements include development of Computational Method For Simulating Turbulent Free Surface Flows; Numerical Model For Plant Canopy To Study Structures Of Turbulence Within And Above Canopies. Office: Johns Hopkins U 313 Ames Hall 3400 N Charles St Baltimore MD 21218 Home Phone: 410-243-3187; Office Phone: 443-825-5321. Personal E-mail: wusiyue@gmail.com.

YUE, XIAOHANG, finance educator; BS in Mgmt. Engring., Beijing U. Aeornautics; MS in Engring., Asian Inst. Tech.; PhD, U. Tex., Richardson, 1999—2002. Cert. ops. mgmt. U. Tex., 2002. Asst. prof. ops. mgmt. U. Wis., Milw., 2003—. Home: 4851 N Anita Ave Whitefish Bay WI 53217 Office: Univ Wis PO Box 742 Milwaukee WI 53201 Business E-Mail: xyue@uwm.edu.

YUECHIMING, ROGER YUE YUEN SHING, mathematics professor; b. Mauritius, Feb. 25, 1937; s. James and Marie Yuechiming; m. Renée Bethery, Nov. 9, 1963; children: Francoise, Marianne, Isabelle. BSc with 1st class honours, U. Manchester, Eng., 1964, PhD, 1967. Asst. U. Strasbourg, France, 1967-69; lectr. math. U. Paris VII, 1970—. Participant math. confs. and seminars in numerous countries; referee various math. jours. Contbr. over 100 articles to profl. jours. Mem. French Math. Soc., Am. Math. Soc., London Math. Soc., Belgian Math. Soc., Japan Math. Soc. Achievements include introduction of concept of p-injective modules and the more generalized notion of YJ-injectivity, new approaches in ring and module theory leading to a better understanding of von Neumann regular rings, V-rings, self-injective rings and generalizations. Home: 38 rue du Surmelin 75020 Paris France Office: U Paris VII Unité Mixte de Rsch 9994 CNRS 2 Pl Jussieu 75251 Paris France

YUEN, BENSON BOLDEN, air transportation and software executive, consultant; b. Hong Kong, Nov. 20, 1960; arrived in U.S., 1968; s. Eugene Howard and Janet Yuen. BSBA in Fin. summa cum laude, U. Cen. Fla., 1983. Mgr. market planning and automation Fla. Express, Inc., Orlando, 1983-85, dir. pricing, 1986-87; dir. customer svc. Seabrook Mktg., Inc., Houston, 1988-91, v.p. customer svc., 1992-94; v.p. consulting svcs. PROS Strategic Solutions, Inc., Houston, 1994-96, sr. v.p. mktg. and consulting svcs., 1996-99; sr. v.p. PROS Revenue Mgmt., Inc., Houston, 2000, pres. travel and transp., 2000—. Cons. airline revenue mgmt., mktg. automation, bus. mgmt., sys. devel. and bus. process engring. to more than 100 transp. cos. worldwide; pres. travel and transp. divsn. PROS Revenue Mgmt., Inc., 2000—. Designer (software) Passenger Revenue Forecast and Optimization System, 1989, Group Revenue Optimization and Management System Version 3, 1990-94, Version 4, 1995—, Holiday Mgmt. Module, Network Pricing Analysis Sys., Hub Complex Optimization; mem. editl. bd. Jour. Revenue and Pricing Mgmt.; contbr. articles to profl. jours. Avocations: travel, music. Office: PROS Revenue Mgmt Inc 3100 Main St Ste 900 Houston TX 77002-9312 Office Phone: 713-335-5202. E-mail: boldenhou@yahoo.com.

YUEN, STANLEY MANFUNG, engineering company executive, electrical engineer; arrived in US, 1998; s. Shu Wang and Han Fun Yuen; m. Eileen DeeAng Ang; children: Elyssa Day, Ariana Day. PhD, U. Pa., Phila., 1987. Prin. engr. GE Aerospace, Moorestown, NJ, 1983—92; head dept. The Hong Kong Poly. U., China, 1993—97; COO CompuSensor Tech. Corp., Gaithersbrug, Md., 1998—. V.p. Phila. Chinatown Devel. Corp., 1985—89, pres., 1990—91. Finalist Young Leader Phila. award, Phila. Jr. C. of C., 1983. Mem.: IEEE (pres. local aerospace & electronic sys. chpt. 1989—91, recipient Outstanding Young Mem. award 1992, named Radar Engr. of Yr. 1992), Eta Kappa Nu (named Outstanding Young Elec. Engr. 1990). Achievements include development of Developed a new spectral analysis technique for detecting close-in missile threats involving minimal radar dwell time for the AEGIS environment; design of the very first 3-dimensional cylindrical systolic array for multi-input/multi-output applications; patents in field; patents pending for. Home Phone: 267-992-8873; Office Phone: 301-990-1100.

YUFEROV, VADIM, research scientist; b. Ivanovo city, Russia, Jan. 9, 1938; s. Petr Yuferov and Anna Yuferova; m. Svetlana Shteynberg, Sept. 7, 1939; children: Anna Tolstikova, Anastasia Yuferova. DSc in Biology, Russian Acad. of Med. Sci., Moscow, 1992. Rsch. fellow Ivanovsky Inst. of Virology, Moscow, 1968—92; WHO fellow Nat. Inst. for Med. Rsch., London, 1972—73; guest rsch. fellow Karolinska Inst., Stockholm, 1992; sr. rsch. assoc. Rockefeller U., NYC, 1993—. Author: (research) Pharmacogenetics; author (research) Synapse; author: (research) Addiction Biology. Recipient award, State Coun. of Ministries, Moscow, 1986. Mem.: Soc. for Neurosci. Achievements include development of Technology for production of reverse transcriptase in commercial scale. Home: 2942 W 5th St Apt 7L Brooklyn NY 11224 Office: Rockefeller Univ 1230 York Ave New York NY 10021 Home Phone: 718-996-3788; Office Phone: 212-327-8234. Business E-Mail: yuferov@rracefeller.edu.

YUGLER, RICHARD S., lawyer; b. Passaic, NJ, Sept. 5, 1955; s. Abram and Audrey (DuBester) Y.; m. A. Christine Tarpey, Mar. 8, 1986; children Simon and Susannah. BA, Syracuse U., 1977; JD, Lewis & Clark Coll., Portland, 1980. Bar: Oreg. 1980, Washington 2002, Oreg. Supreme Ct., Washington Supreme Ct., US Supreme Ct. (Dist. Oreg.) 1981, US Ct. Appeals (9th Cir.) 1982, US Ct. Appeals (Fed. Cir.) 1985, US Supreme Ct. 1983. Assoc. Merten & Saltveit, Portland, 1980-83, Merten & Fink, Portland, 1983-85; pvt. practice, Portland, 1985-86, 89—; ptnr. Redden, McGaughey, Yugler & Jack, Portland, 1986-87, Merten & Yugler, Portland, 1987-89; barrister Am. Inn at Ct., Portland, 1987—; ptnr. Landye Bennett Blumstein LLP, Portland, Oreg. Arbitrator, settlement panelist Multnomah County Cts. & Pvt. UMI Panels. Author: Child Care Task Force Committee Report, 1987. Bd. dirs., officer New Rose Theatre, 1986-89; mem. Dizziness & Balance Disorder Assn., Family Head Injury support Group, 1989, child care task force City Club of Portland, 1985-87, author com. report, 1987. Mem. ABA (young lawyers sect.), Nat. Bar Assn., Oreg. Trial Lawyers Assn. (membership com.), Assn. Trial Lawyers Am., Multnomah Bar Assn. (sec. 1990, continuing legal edn. com. 1988, bd. dirs. reorgn. task force 1989, chmn. com. Bicentennial of U.S. Constn. 1987, award of merit 1986-87), Oreg. State Bar Assn. (local profl. responsibility com. 1989, pres.-elect 2006), Lewis and Clark Alumni Assn. (pub. rels. com. 1987), City Club of Portland (child care task force 1985-87). Avocations: squash, golf, running, skiing. Office: Landye Bennett Blumstein LLP Ste 3500 1300 SW 5th Ave Portland OR 97201 Office Phone: 503-224-4100. Office Fax: 503-224-4133. E-mail: ryugler@landye-bennett.com.

YUKSEL, MURAT, computer scientist, educator; arrived in US, 1998; s. Ali and Zeynep Yuksel; m. Bahar Sumbul; children: Ibrahim Selim children: Abdullah Yusuf, Meryem. BS, Ege U., 1996; MS, Rensselaer Poly. Inst., 1999, PhD, 2002. Instr., sys. adminstr. Internat. Turkmen Turkish U., Ashgabat, Turkmenistan, 1996—98; grad. tchg. and rsch. asst. Rensselaer Poly. Inst., Troy, NY, 1999—2002, postdoctoral rsch. assoc., 2002—06; asst. prof. U. Nev.-Reno, 2006—. Sr. rsch. engr. Omega Advanced Solutions, Inc., Troy, 2002—. Contbr. articles to profl. jours. Recipient Achievement award, Sun Microsystems Labs, Burlington, MA, 2001; scholar, Turkish Govt., 1998. Mem.: IEEE (nominated Best Paper award 2003), IEEE Computer Soc., Sigma Xi. Muslim. Achievements include patents for calculation of layered routes in a distributed manner; efficient system and method of node and link insertion for deadlock-free routing on arbitrary topologies; patents pending for method of optimizing network capacity and fault tolerance in deadlock-free routing. Home Phone: 518-273-1057.

YULE, CAROLL JANE, real estate broker; b. Owatonna, Minn., Feb. 19, 1948; d. Leland R and Jean L Heiden; m. Dennis F Yule, June 6, 1969; 1 child, Tara K. Attended, Macalester Coll., 1966—68, U. Minn., 1968—69. Broker Calif., 1996. Owner All-U-Med, Temple, Tex., 1994—96; broker owner Shear Realty, Apple Valley, Calif., 1996—. Dir. Victor Valley Assn. of Realtors, Victorville, Calif., 2004—, Desert Cmty. Bank. Contbr. monthly column. Program com. Rotary Internat., Victorville, Calif., 2000—05; pres. Victorville C. of C., 2003—04; chmn. for ann. fundraiser Victor Valley Coll. Found., 2000—05; mem. chmn. Victor Valley Bd. of Realtors, 2004—05. Recipient Realtor of the Yr., Victor Valley Assn. of Realtors, 2003, Dir. of the Yr., Victorville C. of C., 2000—01, 2001—02, 2002—03. Avocations: golf, book club. Home: 13253 Country Club Dr Spring Valley Lake CA 92395 Office: Shear Realty 18564 Highway 18 Ste 205 Apple Valley CA 92307 Home Phone: 760-243-3803; Office Phone: 760-243-3803. Office Fax: 760-243-3804; Home Fax: 760-243-3804. Personal E-mail: cyule@mscomm.com.

YULE, JOE See ROONEY, MICKEY

YULISH, CHARLES BARRY, retired public relations executive; b. Cleve., Oct. 24, 1936; s. Isadore and Shirley Yulish; m. Barbara Pearlman, Aug. 22, 1973 (div. 1995); 1 child, Alexi Jules-Nicholas; m. Cynthia Brown Fleek, Oct. 28, 1995. AA in Govt., U. Fla., 1957; BS in Polit. Sci., Kent State U., 1959; MPA, Maxwell Sch., Syracuse U., 1963; postgrad., NYU, 1961-63, New Sch. Social Rsch., 1963-64. Spl. projects officer U.S. AEC, Washington and NYC, 1961-63; pub. affairs mgr. Atomic Indsl. Forum, NYC, 1963-66; pres., chief exec. officer Charles Yulish Assocs. Inc., NYC, 1966-83; exec. v.p. Wesley, Brown & Bartle Inc., NYC, 1984-87; vice chmn., ptnr. Holt, Ross & Yulish, Edison, NJ, 1988-92; exec. v.p., mng. dir. E. Bruce Harrison Co., Washington, 1993-95; v.p. corp. comm. USEC Inc., Bethesda, Md., 1995—2005; ret., 2005. Writer, dir. (film) Energy: We Have the Choices, 1978 (Golden Eagle award); editor: Hard vs. Soft Energy Paths, 1980; author over 60 articles on classical music. Founder, bd. dirs. Serge Koussevitsky Archives Soc., N.Y.C., 1977; bd. dirs. Imperial Russia Hist. Soc., 1986, U.K. and U.S. Friends of Benjamin Franklin. Maxwell fellow Syracuse U., 1960. Mem. Internat. Assn. Pub. Participation Practitioners, Soc. Profl. Mgmt. Cons. (cert.). Home: 1438 Q St NW Washington DC 20009-3808

YULMETYEV, RENAT MUZIPOVICH, physicist, educator; b. Kazan, Tatarstan, USSR, Dec. 14, 1940; s. Muzip Garipovich and Zainab Khairullovna (Davletshina) Yulmetyev; m. Dinara Gabidullovna Bulgakova, Oct. 30, 1965; 1 child, Timur. MS, Kazan State U., 1962, PhD, 1967; D in Physics, Ukranian Inst. Physics, Kyiv, 1981. Theoretical physicist. Sr. lectr. Kazan State Pedagog. Inst., 1965-70; assoc. prof. Kazan State Pedagog. U., 1970-83, prof., 1983—, dean phys.-math. faculty, 1971-72, 78-86, mem. faculty, 1978—, head chair theoretical physics, physicist, 1984—94, leading scientific collaborator, dept. physics, 1994—. Sr. sci. collaborator, chief sci. group Kazan State U., 1993—; Soros prof. Kazan Pedagogical U., 1994—. Author: An Introduction to Statistical Physics of Liquids, 1972, Microscopic Dynamics of Liquids, 2006; contbr. articles to internat. profl. jours. Named Honored Scientist, Tatarstan Republic and Russian Fedn., 1990, Russian Fedn., 2000, Hon. Man of Higher Prof. Edn., 2001—; grantee, Internat. Soros Sci. Edn. Programme Fund, 1994—2001, Russian Fund Fundamental Rsch., 1994—96, 2002—, Russian Humanitarian Sci. Found., 1997—2005, DAAD, 1999—2000, NOIKR Found. Tatarstan Republic, 2000—, Ministry Higher Edn. and Sci., 2005; Competitive Ctr. Fundamental Rsch. grantee, St. Petersburg U., 1992—98. Mem.: NY Acad. Scis., Acad. Nature Russian Fedn. (academician). Avocations: painting, classical music, travel, literature. Office: Tatar State U of Pedagogical and Humanities Sci Tatarstan St 2 420021 Kazan Russia Business E-Mail: rmy@theory.kazan-spu.ru.

YUN, JAMES KYOON, electrical engineer; b. Andong, South Korea, Oct. 26, 1965; came to U.S., 1973; s. Joh Kyong and Karen Suk (Kim) Y. BSEE, U. Ill., 1987, MSEE, 1989. System engr. GE Co., Syracuse, NY, 1989-91, software engr., 1991-93, Martin Marietta Corp., Syracuse, 1993-95; sr. mem. engring. staff Lockheed Martin Corp., Moorestown, NJ, 1995—. Cons. Silver Knight Co., Liverpool, N.Y., 1994—. Inventor seal indicator. Mem. IEEE, Assn. for Computing Machinery, Tau Beta Pi, Eta Kappa Nu.

YUN, LIANG, marine engineer, educator; b. Shanghai, July 15, 1932; s. KunLin and Yun Ya (Sun) Y.; m. Li-Hui Qiu, Jan. 1, 1962; children: Gang, Xiao. Grad., Dalian U. Tech., China, 1953. Asst. prof. Mil. Engring. Acad. China, Harbin, 1953-56, lectr., 1956-66, Harbin Shipbldg. Engring. Inst., 1966-73; dir. air cushion vehicle divsn. Marine Design & Rsch. Inst. China, Shanghai, 1973-85, dep. chief engr., prof., sr. engr., cons., 1980—; tech. dir. China Air Cushion Tech. Corp., Shanghai, 1984-86, Flying Dragon Sci. and Tech. Ltd., Hong Kong, 2000—, Engain Tech Ltd., Hong Kong, 2000—. Prof. Harbin Shipbldg. Engring. U., 1988—, Wu Han Transport Engring. U., China, 1990—; dir. Advanced Marine Vessel, Internat. Advanced Vehicles Assocs., Inc. Author: Theory and Design of Air Cushion Vehicle (in Chinese), 1990, 2000, (in English), 1993, 98. Recipient 2nd Class Nat. award Nat. Def. Com. China, Beijing, 1980, 2nd Class Nat. award China State Shipbldg. Corp., Beijing, 1992, 1st Class Nat. award Kwang-Hua Sci. and Tech. Found., Beijing, 1994., 1st Class Nat. award China State Shipbuilding Corp., 2002. Fellow Royal Instn. Naval Architects; mem. China Soc. Naval Architects and Marine Engrs. (standing dir. 1993-97, chmn. high performance vehicle subcom. 1984—, vice chmn. cons. ship design com. 1992-2002, cons. ship design com. 2002—). Home: 439 Huan Long R Bldg 7 Apt 1401 Shanghai 200127 China Office: Marine Design & Rsch Inst 1688 Xi Zang Nan Rd 200011 Shanghai China Personal E-mail: liangyunb@yahoo.com.

YUNDT, BETTY BRANDENBURG, elementary school educator; b. Corydon, Ind., Sept. 23, 1957; d. Melvin Marion and Lena Beatrice (Blake) Brandenburg; m. Randall Gene Yundt, Apr. 2, 1978; 1 child, Cameron Blake. BS, Ind. U. SE, New Albany, 1981, MS with highest distinction, 1989. Cert. elem. tchr. Rank I, Ind., Ky; lic. prin. Ind. Western U. Tchr. pre-kindergarten Keneseth Israel Sch., Louisville, 1981—82; tchr. Dept. Def. Dependent Sch., Goppingen, Germany, 1983—86; curriculum coord. Iroquois and West End Child Devel. Ctr., Louisville; elem. tchr. Ft. Knox (Ky.) Sch. Dist., 1986—87; curriculum facilitator Walker Intermediate Sch., 1987—. KERA Fellows II cohort. Named Tchr. of Yr., Ft. Knox, Ky., 2003; named to, USA Today All Star Tchr. Team, 2003; recipient Campbellsville Coll. Excellence in Edn. award, 2003. Mem. NEA, ASCD, Internat. Reading Assn., Ind. Coun. Tchrs. Math., Louisville Assn. for Children Under Six, Kappa Delta Pi, Phi Lambda Theta, Alpha Chi. Home: 40 Springdale Rd Guston KY 40142-7151 Office Phone: 502-624-7835. Business E-Mail: betty.yundt@am.dodea.edu. E-mail: teechyundt@bbtel.com.

YUNE, MARC E., surgeon; b. Republic of Korea, Feb. 1, 1965; s. H. Y. and Kay Yune; children: Sydney, Chloe, Gabby. MD, Ind. U., Indpls., 1991. Resident Ind. U., Indpls., 1991—93, 1993—96; surgeon pvt. practice, Atlanta, 1997—. Fellow, Atlanta, 1996—97. Mem.: Alpha Omega Alpha. Office: ASC 1625 Pld Alabama Rd Ste 201 Roswell GA 30076

YUNG, CHI-WAH RUDY, ophthalmologist, educator; b. Hong Kong, Mar. 12, 1956; arrived in US, 1976; s. Ching-Fai Yung and Yuk-Ying Ngai; m. Diana Lee Yung, May 14, 1984; children: Ella Amanda, Phillip Thomas. BS, Ind. State U., Terre Haute, 1980; MD, Ind. U., Indpls., 1984. Diplomate Am. Bd. Ophthalmology. Asst. clin. prof. Ind. U. Sch. Medicine, Indpls., 1988—90, asst. prof. ophthalmology, 1990—96, assoc. prof. ophthalmology, 1996—. Dir. Regenstrief Eye Clinic Wishard Health Svcs., Indpls., 1988—, chief ophthalmology, 1990—; chmn. Ind. Eye Injury Registry, Indpls., 2002—; assoc. examiner Am. Bd. Ophthalmology. Mem. editl. bd.: Comprehensive Ophthalmology Update, 2000—. Named Outstanding Prof. in Clin. Sci., Ind. U., 2004; recipient Outstanding Rsch. Publ. award, Am. Soc. Ophthalmic Plastic and Reconstructive Surgery, 1995, Trustee Tchg. award, Ind. U., 2000, 2001, 2003. Fellow: ACS, Am. Acad. Ophthalmology; mem.: AMA, Indpls. Ophthalmological Soc. (pres. 2002—04), Ind. Am. Chinese Assn. (pres. 2000). Avocations: fishing, hiking. Office: Ind Univ Sch Medicine 702 Rotary Cir Indianapolis IN 46202

YUNG, PATSY P., lawyer; Grad., U. Tex., Austin; JD cum laude, South Tex. Coll. Law. Cert.: Tex. Bd. Legal Specialization (immigration and nationality law), bar: Tex. 1997. Ptnr., dir. Immigration Practice Grp. Lynn, Pham & Ross, L.L.P., Dallas. Named a Rising Star, Tex. Super Lawyers mag., 2006. Mem.: Dallas Asian Am. Bar Assn. (sec., exec. com. mem.), Tex. Young Lawyers Assn. (Pres.'s Award of Merit 2003, 2004), Am. Immigration Lawyers Assn. *

YUNIS, AMIRA, real estate company officer; b. Richfield, Minn., 1971; 1 child. Exec. v.p. & prin. Nat. Retail group Newmark Knight Frank Retail, NYC, 2000—. Named one of 40 Under 40, Crain's NY Bus., 2007. Mem.: Comml. Industrial Brokerage Soc., Internat. Coun. Shopping Ctrs., Real Estate Bd. NY (Retail Deal of Yr. award 2006). Office: Newmark Knight Frank Retail 110 E 42nd St New York NY 10017 Office Phone: 212-372-2397. E-mail: AYunis@newmarkkf.com.

YUNIS, JORGE JOSE, anatomy, pathology, and microbiology educator; b. Sincelejo, Colombia, Oct. 5, 1933; s. José and Victoria (Turbay) Yunis. MD, Complutense U., Madrid, 1956, PhD, 1957; D (hon.), UCLA, 1997. Gen. practice medicine, Barranquilla, Colombia, 1957-59; resident in clin. pathology U. Minn., Mpls., 1959-62, resident in anat. pathology, 1962-64, mem. faculty, 1965-89, prof., 1969-89, dir. grad. studies of lab. medicine, 1969-74, dir. grad. studies of pathology, 1972-74, chmn. human genetics com. for health scis., 1972-77; mem. faculty Hahnemann U., Phila., 1989-92, prof. dept. neoplastic diseases, 1989-92, vice chmn., assoc. dir. Inst. for Cancer and Blood Diseases, 1989-92, dir. Human Genetics and Molecular Biology Div., 1989-92, prof. dept. pathology, 1991-92; prof. depts. anatomy, pathology, microbiology & immunology Thomas Jefferson U. Med. Coll., Phila., 1993—; dir. cancer biol., dept. anatomy, pathology, cell biology Thomas Jefferson U. Med. Col., Phila., 1993—. Vis. prof. numerous univs. Author: Human Chromosome Method, 1965, 1975, Biochemical Methods in Red Cell Genetics, 1969, Molecular Pathology, 1975, New Chromosomal Syndromes, 1977, Molecular Structure Human Chromosomes, 1995, Esencia Humana, 1995, Así es la Vida, 1997, The Myth of God, 2002; contbr. more than 250 articles to profl. jours. Named Clin. Prof. of Yr. Harvard Med. Sch., 1987; honored by Colombian Parliament, Bogota, 1986, 93, Colombian Med. Schs. Assn., 1993. Mem. Leukemia Soc. Am. (trustee 1983-88), Colombian Acad. Medicine. Avocations: poetry, literature, photography.

YURASKO, FRANK NOEL, judge; b. Rahway, NJ, Dec. 22, 1938; s. Frank H. and Estelle (Yurasko) m. Mary Byrd, July 23, 1966 (dec. 1991); children: Elizabeth Anne, Suzanne, Frank; m. Rosalee Yurasko, May 1997. BA, Brown U., 1960; cert., London Sch. Econs., 1961; student, Gray's Inn., London, 1960—61; JD, Yale U., 1964. Bar: NJ 1964, U.S. Dist. Ct. NJ 1965, U.S. Supreme Ct. 1969, Fla. 1979, U.S. Ct. Appeals 1980, cert.: NJ (civil trial atty.). Judge's law clk. NJ Dept. Judiciary, Trenton, 1964-66; ptnr. Graham, Yurasko, Golden, Lintner & Rothchild, Somerville, NJ, 1966-80; pvt. practice Somerville, 1980—. Judge Montgomery Twp. Mcpl. Ct., NJ, 1973-84; twp. atty. Hillsborough Twp., NJ, 1973-2000; atty. Green Brook Bd. Adjustment, NJ, 1973-2001. Trustee Gill/St. Bernard Sch., Bernardsville, NJ; mem. alumni bd. trustees Peddie Sch., Hightstown, NJ. Mem. ABA, Am. Jud. Soc., NJ Bar Assn., Fla. Bar Assn., Somerset County Bar Assn., Mercer County Bar Assn., Assn. Trial Lawyers Am., Trial Attys. NJ, NJ Fedn. Planning Ofcls., Fed. Bar Assn. Home Phone: 908-218-9068. E-mail: fyurasko@compuserve.com.

YURCHENCO, HENRIETTA WEISS, musicologist, writer; b. New Haven, Mar. 22, 1916; d. Edward and Rebecca (Bernblum) Weiss; m. Basil Yurchenco, June 1936 (div. 1955); 1 child, Peter; m. Irving Levine, 1965 (div. 1979). Student, Yale U., 1935-36; student piano scholarship, Mannes Coll. Music, 1936-38. Radio prodr. Sta. WNYC, Sta. WBAI, others, 1939-69; writer, critic, tchr., folk music editor Am. Record Guide and Musical Am., 1959-70; radio prodr. Air Am., 2006. Prof. music CCNY, 1962—86, Bklyn. Coll., 1966—69, New Sch. Social Rsch., 1961—68; co-dir. project study women in music Grad. Ctr. CUNY; mem. exec. com. Panamerican Musical Rsch. Arts. Author: A Fiesta of Folk Songs from Spain and Latin America, 1967, A Mighty Hard Road: A Biography of Woody Guthrie, 1970, Hablamos! Puerto Ricans Speak, 1971, Around the World in 80 Years: A Memoir, 2003, in Spanish, 2004, In Their Own Voices: Judeo-Hispanic Song and Story, 2006; contbr. articles to profl.

jours.; field recs. issued by Libr. Congress, Folkways, Nonesuch, Folkways/Smithsonian, Global Village, Rounder Records, collections in Libr. Congress, Discoteca Hebrew U., Jerusalem, Arias Montana Inst., Madrid, Inst. Nacional Indigenista, Mexico City, Am. Sephardic Found., Instituto Cervantes (Spanish Cultural Inst.). Recipient award, Nat. Inst. Fine Arts, Mex., 2003; grants-in-aid, Am. Philos. Soc., 1954, 1956, 1957, 1965, 1967, 1989, CUNY Faculty Rsch. Fund, 1970, 1983, 1987, NEH grantee, 1964. Mem.: Am. Musicologists Soc., Internat. Assn. Study Popular Music, Soc. Am. Music, Soc. Asian Music, Internat. Coun. Traditional Music (mem. com. women's studies), Soc. Ethnomusicology (hon.). Home: 360 W 22d St New York NY 10011-2600 Office: 139th St And Convent Ave New York NY 10031 Personal E-mail: hyurchenco@verizon.net.

YURECHKO, JOHN JOSEPH, federal agency administrator, director; b. Hazleton, Pa., Apr. 12, 1948; s. Andrew Joseph and Helen Theresa Yurechko; m. Jane Teresa Haltmaier, Sept. 25, 1982; children: Christine, Alice, Janie. BA in History, Wesleyan U., Middletown, Conn., 1970; MA, U. Calif., Berkeley, 1973, PhD in History, 1980. Intelligence analyst Def. Intelligence Agy. (DIA), Washington, 1981—88, senior analyst, command, control, comm. program mgr., 1988—94, spl. planning office chief, 1994—96, info. warfare office chief, 1996—98, def. intelligence sr. level officer (DISL), def. intelligence officer (DIO), 1998—2004; nat. counter-intelligence officer for sci. and tech, dir. strategy and policy Nat. Counter-intelligence Exec. (NCIX), Washington, 2004; dir. analysis and collection, sr. exec. svc. NCIX, 2005; dep. nat. intelligence officer for warning, 2007. Adj. prof. nat. security studies program Georgetown U., Washington, 1986—92; prof. Inst. World Politics, 2007. Author, editor: poetry jour. Gallery Works, 1972—80; contbr. articles to jours. and books in field. Recipient Nat. Intelligence Achievement award, Dir. Central Intelligence, Washington, 1992. Avocations: poetry, martial arts, swimming, weightlifting.

YURIKO, (YURIKO KIKUCHI), dancer, choreographer; b. San Jose, Calif., 1920; m. Charles Kikuchi, 1946. Student, UCLA, Martha Graham Sch.; Doctor Honoris Causa (hon.), La Fedn. Francaise De Danse, 1987; Doctorate (hon.), Boston Conservatory, 2006. Mem. Martha Graham Dance Co., 1944-67; dance tchr. NYC, 1945—; dir., founder Yuriko Dance Co., 1960—78; assoc. artistic dir. Martha Graham Dance Co., 1991—. Artistic dir. dance company Time and Talents Club, Bombay, 1974; organizer Modern Dance Sch., Ctr. Internat. de la Danse, Paris, 1975; resident guest tchr., modern dance cons. Ballet Nacional de Cuba, 1976; ind. modern dance choreographer Warsaw Weiklki Classic Ballet Co., 1977, 78, Australian Dance Theater's Concert at Adelaide Festival of the Arts, 1978; guest tchr., choreographer Akar Modern Dance Co., Switzerland, 1981; guest tchr. Nat. U. Costa Rica, Nat. Ballet of Mexico, Martha Graham Sch. Contemporary Dance; guest artist and tchr. various cities including London, Paris, Mexico City, Zurich, Tokyo and Cologne, Germany; founder & dir., The Arigato Project; founder Martha Graham Ensemble, 1983. Dancer premiere prodns. Appalachian Spring, Cave of the Heart, Dark Meadow, Embattled Garden, Clytemnestra; appeared on Broadway as Eliza in The King and I, 1951; performed feature role The Small House of Uncle Thomas, Sandhog, Flower Drug Song; dir., re-staged Broadway prodn. of The King and I with Yul Bryner, 1977, London prodn., 1979, dir. Toyko prodn., 1978; dir. Madame Butterfly. Recipient Bessie award NY Dance and Performance, 1991; Tribute NY/Japan Soc., 2004; Honor Saeko Ichinohe Dance Co., 2005; grantee NY State Arts Coun., Nat. Endowment for the Arts; Guggenheim fellow for choreography, 1968; commissioned to choreograph and perform Judith Symphony.

YURIST, SVETLAN JOSEPH, mechanical engineer; b. Kharkov, USSR, Nov. 20, 1931; came to U.S., 1979, naturalized, 1985; s. Joseph A. and Rosalia S. (Zoilman) Y.; m. Imma Lea Erlikh, Oct. 11, 1960; 1 child, Eugene. MSME with honors, Poly. Inst. Odessa, USSR, 1954. Engr., designer Welding Equipment Plant, Novaya Utka, USSR, 1954-56; sr. tech. engr. Heavy Duty Automotive Crane Plant, Odessa, USSR, 1956-60, asst. chief metallugist, 1971-78; supr. rsch. lab. Inst. Spl. Methods in Foundry Industry, Odessa, 1960-66, project engr. sci. rsch., 1966-70; engr. designer Teledyne Cast Product, Pomona, Calif., 1979-81; sr. mech. engr. Walt Elliot Disney Enterprises, Glendale, Calif., 1981-83; foundry liaison engr. Pacific Pumps divsn. Dresser Industries, Inc., Huntington Park, Calif., 1984-86; casting engr. Superior Industries Internat., Inc., Van Nuys, Calif., 1986-89; mech. engr. TAMCO Steel, Rancho Cucamonga, Calif., 1989-96. Contbr. articles to profl. jours. Recipient award for design of automatic lines for casting electric motor parts USSR Ministry Machine Bldg. and Handtools Mfr., 1966, for equipment for permanent mold casting All Union Exhbn. of Nat. Econ. Achievements, 1966-70. Achievements include patents for permanent mold casting. Home: 1718 Downs St Oceanside CA 92054-6191 Personal E-mail: siyurist@netzero.com.

YURK, TODD MICHAEL, retired health products executive; b. Sheboygan, Wis., Feb. 21, 1956; s. Harold Robert and Barbara Ann Jurk; 1 child, Natasha Mary Michaela. BS, U. Wis., Madison, 1990. Registered med. supplier Health Care Fin. Adminstrn., 1999, initial med. device distributor FDA, 1992. Grant reviewer Health Resources Svc. Adminstrn., Washington, 2006—. Petty officier 3d class USN, 1984—88. Mem.: Am. Acad. Med. Adminstrs., Am. Coll. Med. Practice Execs., Mensa. Home: 540 Petra Ln Sheboygan WI 53081 Home Phone: 920-694-0540.

YURKANIN, J. PAUL, surgeon, educator; b. Cleve., July 20, 1970; s. Michael and Halena Yurkanin; m. Lisa Marie Oberg, Apr. 26, 2003; children: John Paul Jr., Isabella Grace. BS, St. Lawrence U., Canton, NY, 1992; MD, Georgetown U. Sch. Medicine, Washington, 1996. Diplomate Am. Bd. Urology, 2005. Pres. AZ Minimally Invasive Urologic Surgery, Tucson, 2003—. Clin. asst. prof. surgery U. Ariz. Coll. Medicine, Tucson, 2003—. Mem.: Endourology Soc., Am. Urol. Assn. (assoc.). Office: AZ Minimally Invasive Urologic Surgery 5240 E Knight Dr #108 Tucson AZ 85712 Office Phone: 520-321-4266. Office Fax: 520-321-4048.

YUROW, MICHAEL JAY, lawyer; b. Washington, July 11, 1954; s. John Jesse and Bette Hilary (Troshinsky) Y.; m. Rita B. Abraham, Jan. 11, 1987; children: Mathew, Samuel, Sarah Elizabeth. BA, U. Calif., Santa Cruz, 1976; M in Regional Planning, Cornell U., 1980; JD, Tulane U., 1985. Bar: Va. 1986, U.S. Ct. Appeals (4th cir.) 1986, D.C. 1993. Ptnr., Real Estate practice Venable LLP, Vienna, Va., 1997—, ptnr. in charge, No. Va. Office, 2004—. Cornell U. fellow, 1978-80, HUD fellow, 1978-80. Mem. ABA, Va. Bar Assn., D.C. Bar Assn. Office: Venable LLP Suite 300 8010 Towers Crescent Dr Vienna VA 22182 Office Phone: 703-760-1640. Office Fax: 703-821-8949. Business E-Mail: mjyurow@venable.com.

YURT, ROGER WILLIAM, surgeon, educator; b. Louisville, June 8, 1945; s. Albert William and Mary Louise (McGrath) Y.; m. Joan A. Terry, Sept. 3, 1971; children: Jennifer, Daniel, Gregory. BS in Biology, Loyola U., New Orleans, 1967; MS, U. Miami, 1972. Diplomate Nat. Bd. Med. Examiners. Intern. Parkland Meml. Hosp.-Southwestern Med. Sch., U. Tex., Dallas, 1972-73, resident, 1973-74; postdoctoral trainee NIH, 1975-77; resident, chief resident N.Y. Hosp.-Cornell Med. Ctr., NYC, 1977-79, acting dir. Burn Ctr., dir. rsch., 1982-83, dir. Trauma Ctr., 1992-99, prof. surgery, 1982-92, 92—, The Johnson & Johnson disting. prof. surgery, 1995—; vice chmn. dept. surgery Cornell U. Med. Coll., NYC, 1987—, acting chmn., 1991-93, dir. Burn Ctr., 1995—. Acting surgeon-in-chief The N.Y. Hosp., 1991-93; clin. asst. prof. surgery Uniformed Svcs. U. Health Sci., Bethesda, Md., 1980-82; clin. asst. prof. gen. surgery Health Sci. Ctr., U. Tex., San Antonio, 1981-82; chmn. burn com., Regional Emer. Med. Svcs. N.Y., 1982-84, mem. trauma ctr. adv. com., 1984-89, chmn., 1995-98, mem. burn ctr. adv. com., chmn., 1996-2000, mem. sp. ref. ctr. com., chmn., 1996-98, N.Y. Bklyn. ACS Com. Trauma, 1994-96; dir. Mulhearn Rsch.Lab., N.Y.C., 1982—. Editor: Infections in Surgery, 1981-88; contbr. articles to med. jours. Maj. M.C., U.S. Army, 1979-82. Recipient Hewitt award, Royal Soc. medicine, 2003, Irma Hirschl Trust Career Scientist award, 1984-88; grantee United Health Found., 1968-69, NIH, 1984-87; fellow Sch. Medicine, U. Miami, summer, 1969-71, USPHS, 1973-75, postdoctoral fellow medicine Robert B. Brigham Hosp.-Harvard U. Med. Sch., Boston, 1974-77. Mem. Am. Surg. Infection Soc. (charter, chmn. membership com., sec. 1987-90, pres. 1991-92), Am. Surg. Assn., Assn. Acad. Surgery, Soc. U. Surgeons, Internat. Surg. Soc., Am. Assn. Surgery Trauma, Alpha Omega Alpha, Omicron Delta Kappa. Roman Catholic. Office: NY Hosp Cornell Med Ctr Dir The Burn Ctr 525 E 68th St Rm L-706 New York NY 10021-4885

YUSPEH, ALAN RALPH, lawyer, health company executive; b. New Orleans, June 13, 1949; s. Michel and Rose Fay (Rabenovitz) Y.; m. Janet Horn, June 8, 1975. BA, Yale U., 1971; MBA, Harvard U., 1973; JD, Georgetown U., 1978. Bar: DC 1978. Mgmt. cons. McKinsey & Co., Washington, 1973-74; adminstrv. asst., legis. asst. Office of U.S. Senator J. Bennett Johnston, Washington, 1974-78; atty. Shaw, Pittman, Potts & Trowbridge, Washington, 1978-79, Ginsburg, Feldman, Weil and Bress, Washington, 1979-82; gen. counsel Com. on Armed Svcs.-U.S. Senate, Washington, 1982-85; ptnr. Preston, Thorgrimson, Ellis & Holman, Washington, 1985-88, Miller & Chevalier, Washington, 1988-91, Howrey & Simon, Washington, 1991-97; sr. v.p. ethics, compliance and corp. responsibility HCA, Nashville, 1997—. Coord. Def. Industry Initiative on Bus., Ethics and Conduct, 1987-97; pres. Health Care Compliance Assn., 2002. Editor Law and Policy in Internat. Bus. Jour., 1978-79, Nat. Contract Mgmt. Jour., 1988-92; assoc. editor Pub. Contract Law Jour., 1987-91. Chmn. bd. ethics, City of Balt., 1988-96, planning commn., 1996-97; chmn. bd. dirs. Tenn. Repertory Theater, 2002-05; bd. dirs. Balt. Housing Authority, 1996-97, Ethics Officer Assn., 2001-04, YMCA Mid. Tenn. Camp, 2002-, Tenn. Performing Arts Ctr., 2003-, Nashville Pub. Libr. Found., 2005-. 1st lt. USAR, 1971-77. Office: HCA One Park Plaza Nashville TN 37203 Home: 126 Third Ave N Franklin TN 37064 Office Phone: 615-344-1005. Business E-Mail: alan.yuspeh@hcahealthcare.com.

YUSSUF IZZUDDIM, SHAH GHAFRAULLAH SULTAN, Sultan of Perak; b. Batu Gajah, Perak, Malaysia, Apr. 19, 1928; s. Sultan Yussuff Izzuddin Shah; m. Tuanku Bainun binti Mohd. Ali, 1955; children: Raja Nazrin, Raja Azureen, Raja Ashman, Raja Eleen, Raja Yong Sofia. Student, Malay Coll., Nottingham U. and Lincoln Inn.; DLitt (hon.), U. Malaya, 1979, U. Sains Malaysia, 1980. Bar: Eng. 1954. Asst. sec. state, Perak, 1954-55; magistrate Kuala Lumpur, 1955-56; session court pres., 1957-59; fed. counsel and Dy pub. prosecutor Perak, 1959; state legal advisor Perak, 1959-62; registrar high ct. Kuala Lumpur, Malaysia, 1962-63; chief registrar Fed. Ct., Kuala Lumpur, 1963-65, high ct. judge, 1965, fed. judge, 1973, chief justice, 1979; Lord Pres., 1982-83; 34th Sultan of Perak, 1984—; named King of Malaysia, 1989-94. Author: The Role of Constitutional Rulers. Co-chancellor U. Sains Malaysia, 1971, chancellor U. Malay, 1986—; chmn. Higher Edn. Adv. Council, 1974; v.p. Olympic Coun., Malayisa. Decorated PMN, 1979, SSM, 1983. Mem. Internat. Hockey Fedn., Malaysian Hockey Fedn. (pres.). Office: Istama Iskandarish 33000 Kuala Kangsar Perak Malaysia

YZAGUIRRE, RAUL HUMBERTO, civil rights leader; b. San Juan, Tex., July 22, 1939; s. Ruben Antonio and Eva Linda (Morin) Y.; m. Audrey H. Bristow, Jan. 2, 1965; children: Regina Dolores, Raul Humberto, Elisa Almalinda, Roberto Hayse, Rebecca Morin, Benjamin Ruben. Student, U. Md., 1963-64; BS, George Washington U., 1968. Registered med. technologist. Student and community activist, 1963-65; active War on Poverty, 1969-74; founder, exec. dir. Interstate Research Assocs (Hispanic cons. firm), Washington, 1969-73; v.p. Center for Community Change, Washington, 1974; community organizer in S.Tex., 1974; pres. Nat. Council of La Raza, Washington, 1974—2004. Lectr. Harvard U., U. Notre Dame, U. Tex., others.; commr. U.S. Nat. Commn. for UNESCO, 1983—; chmn. bd. dirs. Associated SW Investors, 1976—. Co-chmn. Nat. Urban Coalition, 1975-83; co-chmn. Working Com. on Concerns of Hispanics and Blacks, 1979—, sec. ind. sector, 1983-84; sec., chmn. Forum of Nat. Hispanic Orgns., 1976-79; chmn. adv. com. I.N.S.; former trustee Common Cause; co-founder, chmn. Nat. Neighborhood Coalition, 1977—; immediate past chair Ind. Sector; bd. dirs. Enterprise Found., Nat. Dem. Insts. Served with USAF, 1959-62. Recipient Rockefeller Public Service award, 1979, Common Cause Pub. Service award, 1986; fellow Inst. Politics John F. Kennedy Sch. Govt. Mem. Am. GI Forum, Hispanic Assn. Corp. Responsibility (co-founder, chmn. bd. dirs.). Democrat. Roman Catholic. *The civil rights struggle of the 80's will be the transformation of America to a truly pluralistic society where cultural differences will not only be tolerated, but indeed valued.*

YZERMAN, STEVE (STEPHEN GREGORY YZERMAN), professional sports team executive, retired professional hockey player; b. Cranbrook, BC, Can., May 9, 1965; married; 3 children. Center Detroit Red Wings, 1983—2006, captain, 1986—2006, v.p., 2006—. Player NHL All-Star Game, 1984, 1988—93, 1997, 99, 2000; mem. Team Can., Olympic Games, Nagano, Japan, 1998, Salt Lake City, 2002. Named Sporting News NHL Rookie of Yr., 1984; named to All-Rookie Team, NHL, 1984, First All-Star Team, 2000; recipient Lester B. Pearson award, 1989, Conn Smythe Trophy, 1998, Frank J. Selke Trophy, 2000, Bill Masterton Trophy, 2003, Lester Patrick Award, 2006. Achievements include being the youngest person ever to play in the NHL All-Star game, 1984; being a member of Stanley Cup Champion Detroit Red Wings, 1997, 1998, 2002; being a member of gold medal Canadian Hockey team, Salt Lake City Olympic Games, 2002; being the longest serving captain in NHL history; having his number, 19, retired by Detroit Red Wings, 2007. Office: Detroit Red Wings Joe Louis Arena 600 Civic Center Dr Detroit MI 48226-4419

ZAAGE, HERMAN, printmaker, educator; b. Jersey City, Apr. 2, 1927; s. Henry and Anna Zaage; m. Sylvia Beal, Feb. 12, 1949; children: Valeda, Peter. Black and white finisher Walker Engraving Corp., N.Y.C., 1955—94; printmaking instr. The New Sch., N.Y.C., 1964—2007, The Art Lab, Staten Island, 1974—. Abraxas Multiple Modern Gods, 1964, Seasons of the Mind Unconscious Victories, 1969, Mezzotint Print, 1988. Print donation Protectors of Pine Oak Woods, Staten Island, 2001, The Art Lab, Staten Island, 2000. With US Army, 1948—50, Tex. Recipient Jomiller award, Nat. Acad., 1989, Audubon Artists Gold medal, Audubon Artists, 1997, Commission, Print Club Albany, 1999. Mem.: Audubon Artists, Soc. Am. Graphic Artists. Avocations: hiking, classical music, jazz. Office: Art Lab At Snug Harbor 1000 Richmond Terr Staten Island NY 10301 Personal E-mail: sylhz@earthlink.net.

ZABANAL, EDUARDO OLEGARIO, lawyer; b. Legazpi City, Albay, The Philippines, Aug. 8, 1952; came to U.S., 1986; s. Jose Agas and Maria Soledad (Olegario) Z.; m. Leorosie Rebodos Nabor, June 18, 1983; children: Shalimar Rosary, Angelica Almira, Regina Tatiana, Lorelei Blossom, Eduardo Olegario, Jr. BA, Aquinas U., The Philippines, 1972; BL, U. The Philippines, 1978. Bar: Hawaii 1990, The Philippines 1979, U.S. Dist. Ct. Hawaii 1990, U.S. Ct. Appeals (9th cir.) 2002. Assoc. Pacis & Reyes, Manila, 1979-86; pvt. practice Honolulu, 1990—. Contbr. articles to profl. jours. Bd. dirs. Kahaluu Neighborhood Bd., Honolulu, 1991-93; active Filipino Coalition for Solidarity, Honolulu, 1991—. Recipient recognition among Disting. Filipinos in Oahu, FIL-AM Courier, 1995, Outstanding Vol. award HSBA, 2003. Mem. ABA, ATLA, Hawaii State Bar Assn., Am. Civil Immigration Lawyers Assn., Hawaii Filipino Lawyers Assn., Integrated Bar The Philippines, Philippine Bar Assn., Filipino C. of C. Hawaii. Roman Catholic. Avocations: jogging, travel, reading. Home: 91-1146 Lanakoi St Kapolei HI 96707-2907 Personal E-mail: e.zabanal@worldnet.att.net.

ZABARANKIN, MICHAEL, operations research specialist, educator; s. Yurii Zabarankin and Anna Zabarankina; m. Ilona Zabarankin. MS in Applied Math., Kiev Taras Shevchenko U., Ukraine, 1996; MS in Engring., U. Fla., Gainesville, 2001; PhD in Mechanics of Solids (hon.), Kiev Taras Shevchenko U., Ukraine, 1999; PhD in Ops. Rsch., U. Fla., Gainesville, 2003. Vis. asst. prof. Grad. Engring. and Rsch. Ctr., U. Fla., Shalimar, 2003—04; asst. prof. Stevens Inst. Tech., Hoboken, NJ, 2004. Author: (book) Convex Functional Analysis, Series: Systems and Control: Foundations and Applications, 2005; co-editor: Robust Optimization Design, 2006. Achievements include research in the theory of generalized deviation measures and it's applications; the theory of generalized analytic functions and its application in fluid dynamics; risk analysis in military applications. Office: Stevens Inst Tech Castle Point on Hudson Hoboken NJ 07030 Office Phone: 201-216-5434.

ZABECKI, DAVID TADEUSZ, engineer, educator, military historian, military officer; b. Springfield, Mass., Aug. 8, 1947; s. Julian Tadeusz and Virginia Charlotte (Luthgren) Z.; m. Marlies Schweigler, 1991; children: Konrad Josef, Jonathan Tadeusz. BA, Xavier U., 1972, MA, 1973; MS, Fla. Inst. Tech., 1976; PhD in Engring., Calif. Coast U., 1987; diploma, U.S. Army War Coll., 1995; PhD in Mil. Sci., Royal Mil. Coll. Sci., 2004; grad. exec. program Russian and Am. gen. officers, Harvard U., 2002. Patrolman Xavier U. Campus Police, Cin., 1972—74; quality assurance specialist Rock Island Arsenal, Ill., 1974—77; quality engr. Deere & Co., Moline, Ill., 1977—84, Zweibruecken, Germany, 1985—93; adj. instr. Fla. Inst. Tech., Fla., 1977—79; adj. lectr. European program City Colls. Chgo., 1986—89; asst. prof. Am. Mil. U., 1993—2003; dep. chief of staff for ops. 7th Army Res. Command, Schwetzingen, Germany, 1997—98, chief of staff, 1998—2000; dep. chief USAR, Washington, 2000—02; comdg. gen. 7th Army Res. Command, Schwetzingen, Germany, 2002—03; dep. chief of staff for mobilization and res. affairs US Army Europe, 2003—07; sr. security advisor US Coord. and Monitoring Mission (Roadmap to Peace in the Mid. East), 2003. Comdr. Task Force Normandy-60, U.S. Army Europe, 2004; exec. dir. Europe, Dept. Def. World War II 60th Anniversary Observance Com., 2004—05; comdg. gdn. US So. Europe Task Force Rear Airborne, 2005-06; lectr. in field. Author: Karl Doenitz: A Defense, 1972, Field Artillery in the 1980's, 1983, Steel Wind: Colonel Georg Bruchmueller and The Birth of Modern Artillery, 1994, The German 1918 Offensives: A Case Study in the Operational Level of War, 2006; editor in chief: WWII in Europe: An Ency., 1998, translator, editor: On the German Art of War: Truppenfuhrung, 2001, contbg. editor: Mil. History mag., 1987—99, World War II mag., 1987—99; editor: Vietnam mag., 2000—; series editor: The Art of War, 2000—03; editor: Vietnam: A Reader, 2002; book reviewer: Mil. Rev., Jour. of Royal Arty., —; developer contbn. margin differential concept of quality cost analysis, —. Served to maj. gen. US Army, 1966—69, 1996—97, 2002—06 USAR, 1969—2007. Decorated DSM, Combat Infantryman's Badge, Bronze Star, Army Commendation medal, Meritorious Svc. medal with 5 oak leaf clusters, Legion of Merit with 2 oak leaf clusters, Def. Superior Svc. medal, US Army Gen. Staff Identification badge, German Army Proficiency badge in gold; Knight Comdr. Order St. John Jerusalem, Knight Sovereign Mil. Order Temple Jerusalem, Knight Comdr. Order of St. Michael of the Wing (Portugal), Gen. John J. Pershing award U.S. Army Command and Staff Coll., 1988, George Washington Honor medal Freedoms Found., 1988, Wm. Hornaday Dist. Svc. in Conservation award, 1963, Knowlton award Mil. Intelligence Corps Assn. Fellow: Ermine Soc.; mem.: Polish Inst. Arts and Scis. in Am., Assn. US Army, NY Acad. Scis., Royal Arty. Assn., Co. Mil. Historians, German Philatelic Socs., Res. Officers Assn., Ancient Order of St. Barbara, US Field Arty. Assn., Am. Soc. Quality Control (cert. quality engr., cert. reliability engr.), Soc. 173d Airborne Brigade (hon.), VFW, Nat. Eagle Scouts Assn., Army and Navy Club Washington, Nat. Sojourners, York Rite, Scottish Rite, Masons, Alpha Sigma Nu. Address: Guenterstal Strasse 86 79100 Freiberg Germany Office Phone: 49-761-3848281. Personal E-mail: david.zabecki@gmx.de.

ZABEL, DIANE MARION, school librarian; b. Antigo, Wis., Mar. 20, 1957; d. Frank and Nina Wilcenski; m. Craig Robert Zabel, May 17, 1980; 1 child, Zachary. BS, U. Wis., 1978; M, U. Ill., Urbana-Champaign, 1980, MS, 1982. Libr., dir. Fluvanna County Libr., Palmyra, Va., 1983—84; cataloger Bosler Free Libr., Carlisle, Pa., 1984—85; asst. libr. Pa. State U., Univeristy Park, 1985—86, social sci. ref. libr., 1986—98, bus. libr., 1998—2000, endowed libr. for bus., 2001—. Co-editor: Bridging the Gap: Examining Polarity in America, 1995, The Quality Management Sourcebook, 1994, The Flexible Workplace: A Sourcebook of Information and Research, 2001; editor: Reference and User Svcs. Quar., 2006—. Mem.: ALA (chair collection devel. and evaluation sect. 1999—2000), Reference and User Svcs. Assn. (pres. 2005—06), Internat. Coun. Hotel, Restaurant and Internat. Edn., Assn. Coll. and Rsch. Librs. (sec. instrn. sect. 1995—96). Avocations: reading, travel. Office: Schreyer Bus Libr Pa State Univ 309 Paterno Libr University Park PA 16802-1810 Office Phone: 814-865-1013. Business E-Mail: dxz2@psu.edu.

ZABEL, DIANNE DONNELLY, retired elementary school educator; b. Woodburn, Oreg., Jan. 11, 1944; d. Joseph Emmett Donnelly and Beatrice Anna Bailey, Walter Eugene Bailey (Stepfather); m. Alfred Anthony Zabel, June 11, 1972; children: Shane Allen, Jill Anne. BA in Elem. Edn., Mt. Marty Coll., Yankton, SD, 1966. Cert. elem. edn. tchr. Fla., Mentally Handicapped (0-21 years) Fla. Tchr. 3d grade St. Joseph Sch., Pierre, SD, 1967—68, St. Anthony Parish, Tigard, Oreg., 1968—70; tchr. 2d gade Mohave County Sch. Dist., Peach Springs, Ariz., 1970—71; tchr. varying exceptionalities Brevard County Sch. Sys., Melbourne, Fla., 1986—2005. Editor: (exceptional children's cookbook) Cooking With Class (Achievement Excellence award, 2001). Vol. Habitat For Humanity, Melbourne, 2000—05. Mem.: Coun. Exceptional Children. Roman Catholic. Avocations: travel, crocheting. Home: 7730 Pine Lake Dr Melbourne FL 32904 Office: Croton Elem Sch 1449 Croton Rd Melbourne FL 32935 Home Phone: 321-724-8789. Personal E-mail: ajsz5260@earthlink.net.

ZABEL, SHELDON ALTER, lawyer, educator; b. Omaha, Apr. 25, 1941; s. Louis Julius and Anne (Rothenberg) Z.; m. Roberta Jean Butz, May 10, 1975; children: Andrew Louis, Douglas Patrick, Robert Stewart Warren. AB cum laude, Princeton U., 1963; JD cum laude, Northwestern U., 1966. Bar: Ill. 1966, U.S. Supreme Ct. 1976. Law clk. to presiding justice Ill. Supreme Ct., 1966-67; assoc. Schiff, Hardin LLP, Chgo., 1967-73, ptnr., 1973—. Instr. environ. law Loyola U., Chgo. Mem. ABA, Chgo. Bar Assn., Chgo. Coun. Lawyers, Order of Coif, Union League Club, Met. Club (Chgo.) Jewish. Avocations: skiing, bicycling. Office: Schiff Hardin LLP Sears Tower 233 S Wacker Dr Ste 6600 Chicago IL 60606-6473 Home Phone: 312-642-7824; Office Phone: 312-258-5540. Business E-Mail: szabel@schiffhardin.com.

ZABEL, WILLIAM DAVID, lawyer; b. Omaha, Dec. 14, 1936; s. Louis J. and Anne I. Z.; m. Deborah M. Miller, Oct. 31, 1979; children by previous marriage: Richard, David. AB summa cum laude, Princeton U., 1958; LLB cum laude, Harvard U., 1961. Bar: N.Y. 1961, U.S. Supreme Ct. 1966, Fla. 1975. Ptnr. Schulte Roth & Zabel, NYC, 1969—. Lectr. Cornell Law Sch., So. Fed. Tax Inst., U. Miami Inst. Estate Planning, Great Plains Tax Inst., Assn. of Bar of City of N.Y., Practising Law Inst., profl. orgns.; N.Y. State adv. com. U.S. Civil Rights Commn., 1969-73; vol. civil rights litigator Lawyers Constl. Def. Com., Miss., summer 1965; bd. dirs. Del. Mgmt. Holdings Inc.; chmn., Human Rights First, 2000- Author: Estate

Planning for the Large Estate, 1976, Domicile, Wills and Tax Problems of Migrating Clients Transplanted to Florida, 1976, Income, Estate and Gift Tax Consequences of Marital Settlements, 1979, Estate Planning for Interests in a Closely Held Business, 1981, Use of Trusts in Connection with Marital Dissolutions, 1983, Thy Will Be Done?, 1991, The Rich Die Richer -- and You Can Too, 1995; Am. editor: The Lawyer, Eng., 1963-66; mem. editl. adv. bd. Trusts and Estates Mag.; contbr. articles to profl. jours. Pres. Merlin Found.; mem. Lymphoma Found., Soros Founds. (Newly Ind. States and the Baltic Republics, Hungary, Romania, Bulgaria and Ctrl. European U.), Open Soc. Fund, Inc., Human Rights Watch/Helsinki, Doctors of World, Winston Found. World Peace, Ottinger Found., David H. Cogan Found., The Picower Med. Rsch. Inst., Lawson Valentine Found., Am. Friends of the Israel Mus., Am. Com. for Weizmann Inst. Sci.; legal counsel Internat. Confedn. Art Dealers; bd. dirs. Tauber Inst., Sakharov Archives, Brandeis U., Population Action Internat., 1996-2004, Lincoln Ctr. Theater, 1996-, Acad. Am. Poets, 1977-; trustee The New Sch. for Social Rsch., 1994—; adv. bd. Project on Death in Am.; chmn. Princeton U. Planned Giving Com., 1991—. Recipient Disting. Cmty. Svc. award Brandeis U., 1986, U.S. Masters Squash Team Bronze medal 14th Maccabiah Games, 1993, Disting. Svc award, New Sch. U., Extraordinary Leader award, Lawyers Com. for Human Rights, 2003, Lifetime Achievement award, Am. Lawyer mag., 2006; fellow Brandeis U., 1987—. Fellow Am. Coll. Trust and Estate Coun., Internat. Acad. Estate and Trust Law, N.Y. Bar Found., Am. Bar Found.; mem. ABA, Am. Law Inst., N.Y. State Bar Assn., Assn. of Bar of City of N.Y. (internat. human rights com.), Human Rights First (formerly Lawyers Com. for Human Rights) (bd. dirs., chmn., 2005), Vol. Lawyers for Arts (bd. dirs.), Estate Planning Coun. N.Y.C. (bd. dirs. 1975-79), Fla. Bar Assn., Harmonie Club (pres. 1989-91), Phi Beta Kappa. Office: Schulte Roth & Zabel 919 Third Ave New York NY 10022-4774 also: Phillips Point W Tower 10th Fl 777 S Flagler Dr West Palm Beach FL 33401-6161 Office Phone: 212-758-2351. Office Fax: 212-592-5955. Business E-Mail: william.zabel@srz.com.

ZABETAKIS, PAUL MICHAEL, nephrologist, educator; b. Washington, Pa., July 30, 1947; s. Michael G. and Rebecca A. (Banakas) Z.; m. Martha Robinson, Oct. 3, 1970; 1 child, Amy Shannon. BA, Washington & Jefferson Coll., 1969; mD, U. Tenn., 1972. Diplomate Am. Bd. Internal Medicine, Am. Bd. Nephrology. Intern in medicine U. Pitts., 1972-73, resident in medicine, 1973-75; fellow in nephrology Yale U., New Haven, 1975-77; asst. chief nephrology-hypertension Lenox Hill Hosp., NYC, 1977-82, assoc. chief nephrology-hypertension, 1978-99, dir. home peritoneal dialysis, 1985-99; asst. prof. clin. medicine NY Med. Coll., Valhalla, 1980-88, assoc. prof. clin. medicine, 1988-92; clin. asst. prof. medicine Cornell U., NYC, 1992-93; clin. assoc. prof. medicine NYU, 1993-99; exec. v.p., COO Everest Healthcare Svc., Oak Park, Ill., 1999-2001; CEO Extracorporeal Alliance Fresenius Med. Care, N.Am., 2001—06; pres. Renal Rsch. Inst., 2006—. Mem. editl. bd. Clinical Nephrology, 1979—, Clinical and Experimental Dialysis and Apheresis, 1983-86, Geriatric Nephrology and Urology, 1995—, Advances in Renal Replacement Therapy, 1999—; nephrology cons. Nicholas Inst. Sports Medicine and Athletic Trauma Lenox Hill Hosp., N.Y.C., 1978-99, rsch. physician, 1982-99; mem. hypertension svc. adv. com. ARC, N.Y.C., 1981-99; mem. exec. com. End Stage Renal Disease Network N.Y. Inc., 1986-99, treas., 1992-93, chmn. long-range planning com., 1994; bd. dirs. Physician Hosp. Orgn. Lenox Hill Hosp., chmn. bd. dirs., 1996-99, v.p. med. bd., 1997-99; vice-chmn. quality improvement, med. dir. Everest Healthcare Svcs., Chgo., 1996-99. Contbr. numerous chpts. to books; patentee in field; lectr. in field; contbr. articles to profl. jours. Fellow ACP, Am. Coll. Preventive Medicine, Am. Coll. Sports Medicine; mem. N.Y. County Med. Soc., Med. Soc. of State of N.Y., Am. Heart Assn., Westchester Heart Assn., N.Y. Soc. Nephrology, Am. Soc. Nephrology, Internat. Soc. Nephrology, N.Y. Acad. Scis., N.Y. State Fedn. Profl. Health Educators, Am. Fedn. Clin. Sch., Internat. Soc. Peritoneal Dialysis, Am. Soc. Artificial Internal Organs (program com. 1995-99), Soc. Critical Care Medicine, Am. Coll. Nutrition, Internat. Soc. for Renal Nutrition and Metabolism, Internat. Soc. Geriatric Nephrology and Urology (founding mem., sec-treas. 1994-99). Avocation: sailboat racing. Office Phone: 708-498-9114. Business E-Mail: paul.zabetakis@fmc-na.com.

ZABLE, JACK LOUIS, mechanical engineer, educator; b. Bklyn., Feb. 24, 1942; s. Phillip David and Gertrude Zable; m. Barbara Zable; children: Brian, Ilyse, Robert. BSME, CCNY, 1963; MSME, Purdue U., 1965, PhD, 1969. Sr. tech. staff IBM, Endicott, NY and Boulder, Colo., 1964—97; prof. attendant, dept. mech. engring. U. Colo., Boulder, 1997—. Dir. Industry/Univ. Coop. Projects Ctr. U. Colo., Boulder, 1999—; mem. IBM Acad. Tech., Armonk, NY, 1990—97. Contbr. chapters to books, articles to profl. jours. Pres. Temple Concord, Binghamton, NY, 1982—84; bd. mem. Jewish Fedn., Binghamton, NY, 1984—88. Fellow: ASME; mem.: Sigma Xi, Pi Tau Sigma. Republican. Jewish. Achievements include patents in field of printer technologies. Avocations: hiking, reading, golf, bridge. Home: 6798 Snead Ct Niwot CO 80503 Office: U Colo ME Dept Campus Box 427 Boulder CO 80309 E-mail: zable@spot.colorado.edu.

ZABORSZKY, LASZLO, neuroscientist; b. Budapest, Hungary, Oct. 9, 1944; s. Ilona Hegedus and Geza Zaborszky; 1 child, Sarah. MD, Semmelweis Med. Sch., Budapest, Hungary, 1969, PhD, 1981, DSc, 1999. Assoc. prof. U. Va., Charlottesville, 1981—93; prof. Rutgers U., Newark, 1993—. Author: (monograph) Afferent Connection of the Medial Basal Hypothalamus, 1982; editor: (text book) Neuroanatomical Tract-Tracing Methods 2: Plenum, 1989, Neuroanatomical Tract-Tracing 3: Molecules-Neurons-Systems, 2005. Grantee, NIH/NINDS, 1986—. Mem.: Soc. for Neurosci. Achievements include research in Basal Forebrain. Home: 2 Green Acres Dr Verona NJ 07044 Office: Rutgers Univ 197 University Ave Newark NJ 07102 Home Phone: 973-353-1080; Office Phone: 973-353-1080. Business E-Mail: zaborszky@axon.rutgers.edu.

ZACARÍAS, FERNANDO R. K., physician; b. Sept. 9, 1944; MD, U. Mexico, Mexico City, 1969; DPH, Harvard U., 1986. Intern St. Francis Gen. Hosp., Pitts.; resident in family medicine U. Miami; resident in internal medicine, infectious diseases Grady Meml. Hosp. Emory U., Atlanta; assoc. researcher Mexican Social Security Inst., 1975-79; prof. cmty. medicine U. Mex., 1978-79; prof. microbiology and parasitology U. Anáhuac, Mexico City, 1976-79; vis. scientist Ctrs. for Disease Control, Atlanta, 1982-84; regional advisor on STD and AIDS Pan Am. Health Orgn., Washington, 1984-89, sr. regional advisor on AIDS/STD, 1989-93, coord. AIDS/STD program, 1993—.

ZACARÍAS, KAREN, playwright; m. Rett Zacarías; children: Nico, Kati. BA, Stanford U.; MA in Playwriting, Boston U., 1995. Cert. tchr. grades K-12 Washington, DC. Founding artistic dir. Young Playwrights Theater, Washington. Author: (plays) Blue Buick in My Driveway, The Thirteenth Summer of William and Pilar, The Barechested Man, 1995, The Sins of Sor Juana, 1998 (Hispanic Playwrights Project winner, 1998, Charles MacArthur award outstanding new play Helen Hayes awards, 2000), The Book Club Play, Mariela in the Desert, 2005 (AT&T First Stages award, 2004), (for children) Cinderella Eats Rice and Beans: A Salsa Musical, Ferdinand: The Bull, The Magical Pióata, Einstein Is A Dummy, 2004. Recipient Francesca Primus prize, The Francesca Ronnie Primus Found. and Am. Theatre Critics' Assn., 2006. Office: Young Playwrights Theatre 2437 15th St NW Washington DC 20009 Office Phone: 202-387-9173. Office Fax: 202-387-9176.

ZACCAGNINI, ANTHONY JACKSON, lawyer; b. Princeton, W.Va., July 26, 1960; BA cum laude, Washington & Lee U., 1983; JD, U. Balt. Law Sch., 1986. Bar: Md. 1987, US Dist. Ct. (dist. Md.) 1995, DC 1997, US Supreme Ct. 1998. Prin. Semmes, Bowen & Semmes. Major JAGC USAR. Mem.: Md. Criminal Def. Attys. Assn., Def. Rsch. Inst., Md. Assn. Def. Counsel, Risk Mgmt. Soc. (assoc.), Omicron Delta Kappa. Office: Semmes Bowen & Semmes 250 West Pratt St 16 Fl Baltimore MD 21201 also: Semmes Bowen & Semmes Ste 1100 1001 Connecticut Ave NW Washington DC 20036 Office Phone: 410-576-4781, 202-822-8250. E-mail: azaccagnini@semmes.com. *

ZACCARIA, ADRIAN, utilities executive; b. 1944; BS, US Mcht. Marine Acad., 1966. Engr. Raytheon Co., Lexington, Mass., 1967-68, Gen. Dynamics Corp., Falls Ch., Va., 1968-71; with Bechtel Grp., Inc., San Francisco, 1974—, pres., COO, 1996—. Bd. trustees US Mcht. Marine Acad. Mem.: NAE. Office: Bechtel Grp Inc 50 Beale St San Francisco CA 94105-1895 Office Phone: 415-768-1234. *

ZACCHINO, NARDA, newspaper editor; b. San Diego, 1947; BA in english lit., UCLA. Assoc. editor L.A. Times, Calif. Office: Los Angeles Times Times Mirror Sq Los Angeles CA 90053

ZACCONE, SUZANNE MARIA, sales executive; b. Chgo., Oct. 23, 1957; d. Dominic Robert and Lorretta F. (Urban) Zaccone. Sales sec. Brookeridge Realty, Downers Grove, 1975—76; sales cons. Kafka Estates Inc., Downers Grove, 1975—76; adminstrv. asst. Chem. Dist., Inc., Oak Brook, Ill., 1976—77; sales rep., mgr. Anographics Corp., Burr Ridge, Ill., 1977—85; pres., owner Graphic Solutions, Inc., Burr Ridge, 1985—. Bd. dirs. Di Trolio Flexigraphic Inst. Curriculum adv. bd. mem. Sch. Dist. 99, 1997, 1998, 1999, 2000, 2001. Named Supplier of Yr. Through Preferred Supplied, Gen. Binding Corp., 1988—99; recipient Supplier Mem. award, Internat. Bottled Water Assn., 1987—88, Supplier award, SBA, 1990, Top Performer Supplier award, Cutler Hammer Westinghouse Divsn., 1993—99, Blue Chip Enterprise Initiative award, 1994, Converter of Yr., RMI, 2006. Mem.: NAFE, Ditrolio Flexographic Inst. (bd. dirs.), World Label Assn. (1st pl. in World Championship 1994—96, 2002—04), Women in Packaging (exec. bd.), Inst. Packaging Profls., Women Entrepreneurs DuPage County (past pres.), Tag and Label Mfrs. Inst. (chmn. pub. rels. and mktg. com., bd. dirs., pres. 1998—2000, Best Managed Co. award 1992, 1st place award in US for Screen Printing 1994—97, 1999—2001, Best Managed Co. award 2001—03). Avocations: reading, sailing, cooking, needlepoint, scuba diving. Office: Graphic Solutions Inc 311 Shore Dr Burr Ridge IL 60521-5859 Office Phone: 630-325-8181. Personal E-mail: szaccone@gsitech.com. Business E-Mail: suzanne.zaccone@graphicsolutionsinc.com.

ZACEK, JOSEPH FREDERICK, historian, educator; b. Stickney, Ill., Dec. 18, 1930; s. Joseph and Emilie (Dvorak) Z.; m. Judith Ellen Cohen (div. 1975); 1 child, Natalie Ann; m. Jane Perlberg Shapiro; stepchildren: Leslie Helen, Peter Carl. BA summa cum laude, U. Ill., Champaign-Urbana, 1952, MA in History, 1953, PhD in History, 1962; cert., Columbia U. Inst. on East Cen. Europe, 1962. Asst. prof. history Occidental Coll., LA, 1962-65; asst. prof., dir. Russian & East European Programs UCLA, 1965-68; assoc. prof. SUNY at Albany, 1968-71, dir. Russian and East European Programs, 1968-77, 91-92, prof., 1971—2001, chair dept. history, 1974-77, prof. emeritus, 2001—. Selection com. for East Europe Internat. Rsch. and Exch. Bd., Princeton, NJ, 1978-81; nat. bd. cons. NEH, Washington, 1975—; vis. scholar IREX Comenius U., Bratislava, and Charles U., Prague, Czechoslovakia, 1973, Columbia U., 1977-78, U. Ill, Champaign-Urbana, 1987. Author: Palacky: The Historian as Scholar and Nationalist, 1970; editor, co-author: Frantisek Palacky, 1798-1876: A Centennial Appreciation, 1981, The Enlightenment and the National Revivals in Eastern Europe, 1983, The Intimate Palacky, 1984; also numerous periodical articles and chpts. in multi-authored books. With M.I., U.S. Army, 1954-57. Fgn. Area Tng. fellow Ford Found., Columbia U., 1960-62, Sr. Humanities fellow Rockefeller Found., 1977-78, fellow Russian Rsch. Ctr. Harvard U., 1986-91; Rsch. grantee Am. Coun. Learned Soc./Soc. Sci. Rsch. Coun., 1965, Am. Philos. Soc., 1968; recipient Comenius medal Govt. of Czech and Slovak Fed. Republic, 1992, Medal of Comenius Pedagogical Inst. in Prague, 1992, Josef Hlávka medal of Czechoslovak Acad. of Scis. in Prague, 1992, others. Mem. Am. Hist. Assn., Am. Assn. for Advancement Slavic Studies, Western Slavic Conf., Czechoslovak History Conf., Slovak Studies Assn., Consortium on Revolutionary Europe, Assn. for Study of Ethnicity and Nationalism, Phi Beta Kappa. Avocations: travel, gardening, music. Home: 22 Sandhurst Dr Slingerlands NY 12159-9418 Office Phone: 518-482-7478. Business E-Mail: zacekj@union.edu.

ZACHARIAS, DONALD WAYNE, retired academic administrator; b. Salem, Ind., Sept. 28, 1935; s. William Otto and Estelle Mae (Newlon) Z.; m. Tommie Kline Dekle, Aug. 16, 1959; children: Alan, Eric, Leslie. BA, Georgetown Coll., Ky., 1957, LLD (hon.), 1983; MA, Ind. U., 1959, PhD, 1963. Asst. prof. communication and theatre Ind. U., 1963-69; assoc. prof. U. Tex., Austin, 1969-72, prof., 1972-79, asst. to pres., 1974-77; exec. asst. to chancellor U. Tex. System, 1978-79; pres. Western Ky. U., 1979-85, Miss. State U., Starkville, 1985-97, pres. emeritus, 1998—. Bd. dirs. First Fed. Savs. & Loan Assn., Bowling Green, Ky., Inst. for Tech. Devel., Sanderson Farms, Inc., Miss. Econ. Coun.; dir. John Grisham Libr., Starkville, 1998-2003. Author: In Pursuit of Peace: Speeches of the Sixties, 1970. Bd. dirs. Greenview Hosp.; pres. Southeastern Conf., 1989-91. With U.S. Army, 1959-60. Named Mississippian of Yr. Data Processing Mgmt. Assn.; recipient Teaching award Ind. U. Found., 1963, Cactus Teaching award U. Tex., 1971, Justin Smith Morrill award U.S. Dept. Agriculture, 1992, Disting. Teaching award Honors Program, 2000. Mem. Inst. Tech. Devel. (bd. dirs. 1985-92), Nat. Assn. State Univs. and Land-Grant Colls. (exec. com. 1990-92), Phi Kappa Phi (pres. 1978). Democrat. Episcopalian. E-mail: dwz2@msstate.edu.

ZACHARIAS, NIKOLAOS MARIOS, obstetrician, gynecologist, perinatologist; b. Athens, Greece; s. Marios Nikolaos and Constantoula Marios Zacharias; m. Ioanna Dimitrios Athanassaki, May 12, 2000. MD, Nat. and Kapodistrian U., Athens, 1995. Gen. practitioner Greek Nat. Health Svc., Vassiliki, Greece, 1996-97; gen. surgery intern Laikon Gen. Hosp., Athens, 1997-98; chief resident in ob-gyn. Baylor Coll. Medicine, Houston, 1998—2002; fellow in maternal-fetal medicine U. Tex. Med. Br., Galveston, 2002—05; asst. prof. ob-gyn Baylor Coll. Medicine, Houston, 2005—; program dir. dist. prenatal ultrasound maternal fetal medicine Harris County Hosp., Houston, 2005—. Undergrad. Ann. scholar Found. State Scholarships, 1990-94; Papadakis grantee Nat. and Kapodistrian U. Athens, 1990-95, Kontoleon grantee, 1998-2002, Acad. fellow U. Tex. Med. Br., 2002-. Fellow ACOG; mem. AMA, Athens Med. Assn., Gen. Med. Coun., Tex. Med. Assn., Soc. for Maternal-Fetal Medicine. Avocations: swimming, basketball, travel. Home: 125 White Dr Bellaire TX 77401 Office: Baylor Coll Medicine 1709 Dryden Ste 1100 Houston TX 77030-2400 Business E-Mail: nmz@bcm.edu, zachan@hchd.tmc.edu.

ZACHARIAS, NORBERT, astronomer; b. Beckum, Westfalen, Germany, June 7, 1957; arrived in U.S., 1993; s. Wilhelm and Maria Zacharias; m. Marion Ingrid Eichler, June 23, 1983. BA in Physics, U. Kiel, Germany, 1979; MS in Physics, U. Hamburg, Germany, 1982, PhD in Physics and Astronomy, 1987. Cert. postgrad. studies Inst. Astronomy, Cambridge, Eng., 1983. Chief cataloging and requirements divsn. U.S. Naval Obs., Washington, 2005—. Recipient Newcomb award, U.S. Naval Obs., 2005. Mem.: Astronomische Gesellschaft, Astron. Soc. of the Pacific, Am. Astron. Soc., Internat. Astron. Union, Sierra Club (life). Independent. Achievements include research in first astrometric all-sky survey with electronic detector UCAC. Avocations: sailing, travel, bicycling. Office: US Naval Observatory 3450 Mass Ave NW Washington DC 20392 Office Phone: 202-762-1423. Office Fax: 202-762-1516. Business E-Mail: nz@usno.navy.mil.

ZACHAROULIS, DIMITRIS, surgeon, researcher; b. Larisa, Greece, Nov. 8, 1967; s. Christos Zacharoulis and Anastasia Tsita. Grad. Diploma (hon.), 5th Gen. Lyceum, Greece, 1985; PhD, U. Athens, 2000. Cert. Ptychion Iatrikes Aristotelian U. Thessaloniki, Greece, 1991, Gen. Surgery Boards Com., 2000. Rsch. fellow U. Athens, 1991—92; surgery intern Greek Army, Alexandroupolis, Greece, 1992—93; gen. practitioner Greek Ministry of Health, Larisa, Greece, 1993—94; rsch. fellow Harvard Med., Boston, 1994—95; resident gen. surgery SUNY, Syracuse, 1995—2000; clin. fellow, registrar, cons. of hpb surgery Hammersmith Hosp., London, 2000—03; sr. lectr. U. of Thessaly, Larisa, Greece, 2003—06. Mem. Med. Assn. of LARISA, Larisa, Greece, 2005—06, Greek Med. Assn., 2005—06. Mil. dr. US Army, 1992—93, Greece. Achievements include research in Investigation of New Technology in Liver Surgery.The use of Radiofrequency Energy in bloodless resection of solid organs and endoscopy. Home: Kalliarhou Larisa 41221 Greece Office: Univ of Thessaly Univ Hosp Larisa 41222 Greece Home Phone: +1030-2410-232-931; Office Phone: +1030-2410-682-730. Office Fax: +1030-2410-670-100; Home Fax: +1030-2410-670-100. Personal E-mail: zachadim@yahoo.com.

ZACHARSKI, DENNIS EDWARD, lawyer; b. Detroit, Feb. 25, 1951; s. Edward J. and Margaret R. (Cendrowski) Z.; m. Susan G. Foster, Aug. 8, 1975; children: Jeffrey Alan, Lauren Michelle. BBA, U. Mich., 1973; JD, Mich. State U., 1977. Bar: Mich. 1977, U.S. Dist. Ct. (ea. dist.) Mich. 1977, U.S. Dist. Ct. (we. dist.) Mich. 1982, U.S. Supreme Ct. 1988, U.S. Ct. Appeals (6th cir.) 1990, Ohio, 1993. Atty. Lacey & Jones, Birmingham, Mich., 1977—. Case evaluator Mediation Tribunal Assn., Detroit; arbitrator Am. Arbitration Assn., Southfield, Mich. Mem. Oakland County Bar Assn., Assn. Trial Def. Counsel, Mich. Trial Def. Counsel, Defense Rsch. Inst. Avocations: golf, skiing, soccer, tennis, bicycling. Office: Lacey & Jones 600 S Adams Rd Ste 300 Birmingham MI 48009-6827 Office Phone: 248-433-1414. Business E-Mail: dzacharski@laceyjones.com.

ZACHARY, JE'QUITA YVETTE, elementary school educator, singer; d. Jesse B. and Sharon Yvonne Zachary. AA in Music, Gordon Coll., 1997; BA in Music & Bus., Clayton Coll. and State U., 2000. Tchr. music Victory Charter Sch., East Point, Ga., 2002—04; music promoter Atlanta International Records, Atlanta, 1999—2001; tchr. Odyssey Charter Sch., Newnan, 2004—05; tchr. 5th grade reading tchr. KIPP WAYS Acad., New Birth South, Ga., 2004—05. Tchr. after sch. chorus Odyssey Charter Sch., Newnan, Ga., 2005—; children's choir helper New Birth South, New Birth South, Jonesboro, 2005—. Singer: (songs, plays and dances) Martin's Dream and Mine and Songs from His Heart. Ch. mem. New Birth South, New Birth South, Ga., 2004. Home Phone: 678-469-6435. Personal E-mail: jequitaz@yahoo.com.

ZACHARY, LOUIS GEORGE, chemical company consultant; b. Aug. 14, 1927; s. George E. and Angelike (Hantsis) Zacharakis; m. Lillie Vletas, Apr. 20, 1955; children: Leslie A., Louis George. Prodn. supr. Dewey & Almy Co., Acton, Mass., 1951-52; salesman chem. divsn. Union Camp Corp., Wayne, NJ, 1952-59, sales mgr. chem. divsn., 1959-62, gen. mgr. chem. ops., 1962-66, gen. mgr. chem. divsn., 1970-78, v.p., 1974-78, Drake Mgmt. Co., NYC, 1966-70; sr. v.p. GAF Corp., NYC, 1978-82, mem. office of chmn., 1981-82; cons., 1983-84; chmn., CEO Universal Die Casting, Inc., Saline, Mich., 1984—90; acting pres. chem. divsn. Church & Dwight Inc., 1990—91; v.p. Nat. Exec. Svc. Corp., NYC, 1993—96. Vis. com. chem. engring. dept. Johns Hopkins U., Balt., 1981-83. Co-editor: Tall Oil and Its Uses, 1965. With USN, 1945—46. Mem. Chem. Mfrs. Assn. (dir. 1979-83), Synthetic Organic Chem. Mfrs. Assn., Soc. Chem. Industry, Harvard Club NJ (exec. com., trustee 2000—). Home: 227 Oak Ridge Ave Summit NJ 07901-3258 Personal E-mail: louiszachary@aol.com.

ZACHERT, MARTHA JANE, retired librarian; b. York, Pa., Feb. 7, 1920; d. Paul Rodes and Elizabeth Agnes (Lau) Koontz; m. Edward G. Zachert, Aug. 25, 1946; 1 child, Lillian Elizabeth. AB, Lebanon Valley Coll., 1941; MLS, Emory U., 1953; DLS, Columbia U., 1968. Asst. Enoch Pratt Free Library, Balt., 1941-46; head librarian Wood Research Inst., Atlanta, 1947; sch. librarian DeKalb (Ga.) County Schs., 1950-52; head librarian, prof. history of pharmacy So. Coll. Pharmacy, Mercer U., Atlanta, 1952-63; instr. Ga. State Coll., 1962-63, Emory U., summers 1955-59, 1956-57, 59-60; mem. faculty Library Sch., Fla. State U., 1963-78, prof., 1973-78, Coll. Librarianship U. S.C., Columbia, 1973-74, 78-84. Vis. fellow Brit. Library, 1980; cons. So. Regional Med. Library, Emory U., 1976-77, Nat. Library Medicine, 1977, others. Author: Fine Printing in Georgia, 1950s-1990, 1994; assoc. editor Jour. Libr. History, 1966-71, 73-76; mng. editor, 1971-73; cons. editor Jour. Libr. Adminstrn., 1979-86; contbr. numerous articles to profl. jours. Fellow Med. Libr. Assn. (named among 100 Most Notables 1998); mem. ALA, Spl. Libs. Assn. (past pres. Fla. chpt., spl. citation 1977, Hall of Fame 1985), Am. Printing History Assn., Beta Phi Mu (pres. 1974-75). Home and Office: 4436 Meandering Way #108AG Tallahassee FL 32308-8705

ZACHERT, VIRGINIA, retired psychologist; b. Jacksonville, Ala., Mar. 1, 1920; d. R.E. and Cora H. (Massee) Z. Student, Norman Jr. Coll., 1937; AB, Ga. State Woman's Coll., 1940; MA, Emory U., 1947; PhD, Purdue U., 1949. Diplomate Am. Bd. Profl. Psychologists. Statistician Davison-Paxon Co., Atlanta, 1941-44; research psychologist Mil. Contracts, Auburn Research Found., Ala. Poly. Inst.; indsl. and research psychologist Sturm & O'Brien (cons. engrs.), 1958-59; research project dir. Western Design, Biloxi, Miss., 1960-61; self-employed cons. psychologist Norman Park, Ga., 1961-71, Good Hope, Ga., 1971-99; ret. Rsch. assoc. med. edn. Med. Coll. Ga., Augusta, 1963-65, assoc. prof., 1965-70, rsch. prof., 1970-84, rsch. prof. emeritus, 1984—, chief learning materials divsn., 1973-84, faculty senate, 1976-84, acad. coun., 1976-82, pres. acad. coun., 1983, sec., 1978; mem. Ga. Bd. Examiners Psychologists, 1974-79, v.p., 1977, pres. 1978; adv. bd. Comdr. Gen. ATC USAF, 1967-70; cons. Ga. Silver Haired Legislature, 1980-86, senator, 1987-93, pres. protem, 1987-88, pres., 1989-93, rep., spkr. protem, 1993-96, spkr., 1997-98, Nat. Silver-Haired Congress rep., 1995—, spkr. 1997-99; govs. appointee White House Conf. on Aging, 1971, 96, Ga. Coun. on Aging, 1988-96; U.S. Senate mem. Fed. Coun. on the Aging, 1990-93; senator appointee White House Conf. on Aging, 1995; Ga. Health Decision's appointee to Ga. Coalition for Health, 1996-98. Author: (with P.L. Wilds) Essentials of Gynecology-Oncology, 1967, Applications of Gynecology-Oncology, 1967. Del. White House Conf. on Aging, 1981, 95. Served as aerologist USN, 1944-46; aviation psychologist, Lackland Air Force, San Antonio, USAF, 1949-55. Recipient Jane Kennedy Excellence Aging award, 1999. Fellow AAAS, Am. Psychol. Assn.; mem. AAUP (chpt. pres. 1977-80), Sigma Xi. (chpt. pres. 1980-81) Baptist. Home: 4275 Owens Rd # 403 Evans GA 30809 *It's really quite simple-I find, if I wish to be understood or heard, that simplicity is necessary but not ever easy. Simplicity is basic, essential and always the major factor in my search for truth.*

ZACHMANN, WILLIAM FRANCIS, computer and communications industry market research company executive; b. Cleve., Oct. 19, 1942; s. Kurt Wilhelm and Jean (O'Konski) Z.; m. Elizabeth Ann Loftus, June 7, 1980. BA, Harvard U., 1966. Programmer, analyst Cambridge (Mass.) Computer Assocs., 1967-69; sys. rsch. officer 1st Nat. Bank, Boston, 1969-74; dir. rsch. Forum Corp., Boston, 1974-75; coord. personnel adminstrn. Harvard U., Cambridge, 1976-77; mgr. tech. support CallData Sys., Boston, 1977-79; v.p. tech. assessment Internat. Data Corp., Framingham, Mass., 1979-83, v.p. corp. rsch., 1983-87, sr. v.p., 1987-88; pres. Canopus Rsch., Duxbury, Mass., 1988—, editor, pub. Canopus report, 1992—, host Canopus rsch. forum, 1992-99; v.p. Meta Group, Stamford, Conn., 2000—02; chmn., CEO Canopus Rsch. Inc., Duxbury, 2002—; pres., CEO Agility, 2004—. Mem. Harvard (Boston), Harvard Faculty (Cambridge), Compuserve. Author: Keys to Application Development

Productivity, 1981; contbg. editor Computer Industry Report, 1982-88, Communications and Distributed Resources Report, 1983-87, PC World mag., 1987-88; columnist On Communications mag., 1984-86, Software News mag., 1984-86, Computerworld mag., 1986-88, Infoworld mag., 1987-88, Micromarketworld mag., 1985-87, PC Mag., 1988-92, PC Week mag., 1988-92, MacUser mag., 1988-89, Windows World, 1992-95, Ad Week's Marketing Computers, 1993-95, Computing Pro, 1996-99, CIO mag., 1999-2002, Redmond Developer News, 2006—; columnist, sr. contbg. editor OS/2 Professional, 1992-94, Real Estate Jour., 2004—, Duxbury Clipper, 2004—. Mem. City Mgrs. Adv. Com. on Cable TV, Cambridge, 1979-93; mem. Duxbury Econ. Devel. Com., 1992-95, 2004—; mem. Planning Bd., Duxbury, 1995-2001, vice chmn., 1996-2000. Home: 160 Standish St Duxbury MA 02332-5065 Office: Canopus Rsch Inc PO Box 2805 Duxbury MA 02331-2805 Office Phone: 781-934-9800. Business E-Mail: wfz@canopusresearch.com.

ZACHRY, HENRY BARTELL, JR., construction executive; b. Laredo, Texas; m. Mollie Zachry; children: John, David, Anne Rochelle, Ellen Carrie. BS in Civil Engring., Texas A&M, 1954. Joined H.B. Zachry Co. (now Zachry Constrn. Corp.), 1957; pres. Zachry Constrn. Corp., 1965, CEO San Antonio, 1984—2004, chmn., 1984—. Pilot USAF, 1954—57. Named a Texas Bus. Hall of Fame inductee; recipient Texas A&M Disting. Alumnus, 1997, Texas A&M Engineering's Outstanding Alumni Honor award, 2005. Office: Zachry Constrn Corp 527 Logwood San Antonio TX 78221 *

ZACK, ARNOLD MARSHALL, lawyer, mediator, arbitrator, judge; b. Lynn, Mass., Oct. 7, 1931; s. Samuel George and Bess Ethel (Freedman) Z.; m. Norma Eta Wilner, Aug. 10, 1969; children: Jonathan Samuel, Rachel Ann. AB, Tufts Coll., 1953; LLB, Yale U., 1956; MPA, Harvard U., 1961. Asst. to Saul Wallen (arbitrator), 1956-63; cons. govt. South Africa UN Mission to Congo, 1960; cons. U.S. Peace Corps, 1961-63, Labor Dept., 1962-79, Pres.'s Study Commn. on Nat. Service Corps, 1962-63, U.S. AID, 1963—, Friedrich Ebert Stiftung, 1963-64, Nat. Center for Dispute Settlement, 1968-76; v.p. adminstrn. tribunal Asian Development Bank, 2004—. Cons. IMF, 2000—02, Govt. Italy, 2002—, Internat. Labor Orgn., 1961—; chmn. steering com. Permanent Ct. Arbitration, 2002—; vis. Fulbright lectr. Haile Selassie U., Addis Ababa, Ethiopia, 1963—64; referee Nat. R.R. Adjustment Bd., 1964—; mem. faculty Labor and Worklife Program Harvard Law Sch., 1985—; full time mediator/arbitrator, Boston, 1968—; bd. dirs. Ctr. for Socio-Legal Studies faculty of law U. Natal, South Africa, 1986—92; mem. Fgn. Svc. Labor Rels. Bd., 1982—84, Presdl. Emergency Bds. 221 and 222; chair Presdl. Emergency Bd. 232, 234; chmn. Essential Industries Dispute Settlement Bd. Bermuda, 1993—2000; chair Essential Svcs. Dispute Settlement Bd. Bermuda, 1996—2000; vis. lectr. Yale Law Sch., 1995—96; permanent arbitrator Am. Airlines & APA, IRS & NTEU, Commonwealth Mass., Overseas Fedn. Tchrs., Def. Dept. Author: Labor Training in Developing Countries, 1964, Ethiopia's High Level Manpower-Analysis and Projections, 1964, Handbook on Grievance Arbitration in the Public Sector, 1974, Handbook on Fact Finding and Arbitration in the Public Sector, 1974, Grievance Arbitration, A Practical Guide, 1977; (with R. Bloch) Arbitration of Discipline and Discharge Cases, 1979, (with R. Bloch) The Agreement in Negotiation and Arbitration, 1983, 2d edition, 1995, Arbitration in Practice, 1984, Mediation in the Public Sector, 1985, Grievance Arbitration: Cases on the Merits in Discipline Discharge and Contract Interpretation, 1989, Handbook on Grievance Arbitration: Issues on Procedure and Ethics, 1992, (with J. Dunlop) Mediation and Arbitration of Employment Disputes, 1997, Arbitration Discipline and Discharge Cases, 2000; contbr. articles to profl. jours. Bd. visitors Harvard U. Recipient Whitney North Seymour medal for oustanding contbn. to arbitration, 1980, Cushing Gavin award, 1986, Mildred Spaulding award, 1987, Disting. Svc. award for arbitration of labor-mgmt. disputes, 1989, Pioneer award Assn. Conflict Resolution, 2003, Willoughby Abner award, Assn. for Conflict Resolution, 2004; Wertheim fellow Harvard U., 1996-97. Fellow: African Studies Assn.; mem.: ABA (mem. coun. labor and employment law sect. 2000—06), Coll. Labor and Employment Lawyers, Internat. Soc. for Labor Law and Social Security (bd. dirs.), Indsl. Rels. Rsch. Assn. (bd. dirs.), Am. Arbitration Assn. (dir. Labor-Mgmt. Inst. 1966—68), Nat. Acad. Arbitrators (treas. 1972—75, bd. govs. 1977—79, v.p. 1980—82, pres. Rsch. and Edn. Found. 1989—91, pres. 1994—95), Yale Law Sch. Assn., Yale Club (N.Y.C.), Harvard Club ((Boston)). Address: 170 W Canton St Boston MA 02118-1216 Home Phone: 617-262-0478.

ZACK, DANIEL GERARD, library consultant; b. Waukegan, Ill., Oct. 1, 1943; s. Raymond Gerard and Rosanna Marie (Atkinson) Z.; m. Mary Frances Anthony, Aug. 25, 1966; children: Jennifer Lee, Rebecca Jane. BA in Psychology, Western Ill. U., 1967; MS in Libr. Sci., U. Ill., 1975. Editor IBM Corp., Rochester, Minn., 1968-70, Memorex Corp., Mpls., 1970-74; rsch. assoc. Libr. Rsch. Ctr. U. Ill., Urbana, 1974-75; asst. dir. Portage County Pub. Libr., Stevens Point, Wis., 1976-78; dir. Burlington Pub. Libr., Iowa, 1978-87, Gail Borden Pub. Libr., Elgin, Ill., 1987—2004, Beloit Pub. Libr., Wis., 2007—; with Libr. Cons. Svcs., 2004—. Trustee Batavia Pub. Libr., Ill., 1997-2003; founder Friends of Ill. Libr., 1990, bd. dirs. 1990-97. Mem. ALA, ACLU, Ill. Libr. Assn. (mgr. pub. libr. forum 1991-92, 2002-03, exec. bd. dirs. 1992-95, pub. policy com. 1995-98), Pub. Libr. Assn. (intellectual freedom com. 1993-96), Kiwanis.

ZACK, ROBERT G., lawyer, investment company executive; JD, Univ. Va., 1975. Assoc. gen. counsel Oppenheimer Funds, NYC, 1981—85, sr. v.p. & assoc. gen. counsel, 1985—2001, sr. v.p., acting gen. counsel, 2001—02, sr. v.p., gen. counsel, 2002—03, exec. v.p., gen. counsel, 2004—. Office: Oppenheimer Funds 2 World Financial Ctr 225 Liberty St New York NY 10281 also: Oppenheimer Funds 498 7th Ave New York NY 10018 Office Phone: 212-323-0250. Office Fax: 212-323-0558.

ZACK, STEPHEN NEAL, lawyer; b. Detroit, Dec. 2, 1947; s. Benn Zack and Anita (Rabinovich) Petluck; children: Jason, Tracey. BA, U. Fla., 1969, JD, 1971. Bar: Fla. 1972, NY 1982, DC 1986, US Dist. Ct. (no. and so. dists.) Fla. 1986, U.S. Ct. Appeals (5th and 11th cirs.)1986. Sr. ptnr. Floyd, Pearson, Richman, Greer, Weil, Zack & Brumbaugh P.A., Miami, Fla., 1972-91, Zack, Hanzman & Ponce P.A., Miami, 1991—95, Zack Kosnitzky P.A., 1995—2002, Boies, Schiller & Flexner LLP, Miami, 2002—. Legis. aide to Congressman Claude Pepper, 1971-72; chmn. environ. rev. bd. City of Miami, 1978-79, Fla. law ctr. coun. U. Fla., 1982; mem. Speakers Adv. Com. on Future, Jud. Nomination Commn. for 11th Cir.; spl. counsel to Gov. Bob Graham, 1986; bd. dirs. Jewish Family Services, 1984-; chmn. State Fla. Ethics Comm.; former pres. Nat. Conf. Bar Presidents. Named to Hall of Fame, U. Fla. Mem. ABA (life fellow, chmn. House Del. 2004—2006, mem. bd. govs.), ALTA, Fla. Bar Assn. (pres. young lawyers sect. 1975-76, bd. govs. 1977-88, chmn. internat. law sect. 1981-82, pres. 1989-90), Acad. Fla. Trial Lawyers (bd. dirs. 1982-86), Dade County Bar Assn. (bd. dirs. & pres. young lawyers sect. 1975-76), Cuban-Am. Lawyers Assn., Federacion Interamericana de Abogados, Blue Key (pres. Fla. chpt.), Omicron Delta Kappa. Office: Boies Schiller & Flexner LLP Bank of Amer Tower 100 SE 2nd St Ste 2800 Miami FL 33131-2115 Office Phone: 305-539-8400. E-mail: szack@bsfllp.com.

ZACKHEOS, H.E. SOTIRIOS, ambassador; b. Nicosia, Cyprus, Jan. 24, 1950; 2 children. BA in Law, U. Athens, 1972, BA in Econs. and Polit. Sci., 1976; MA in Polit. Sci., Stanford U., 1977. Corp. leader, credit control mgr. N.P. Lanitis Group of Cos.; attache in econ. divsn. and protocol dept. Ministry Fgn. Affairs, 1974—75, dir. Dir.-Gens. Office, 1975—76, sec. polit. affairs divsn., 1977—79, clk. Cyprus Embassy in Moscow, 1979—85, agrl. dir. econ. and cultural dept., 1985—87, dir. dept. coordination, enlightenment and planning, 1987—89, first Cyprus resident amb. to China with concurrent accreditations to Japan, Pakistan, Philippines and Mongolia, 1989—93, dir. econ. affairs divsn., non-resident amb. of Cyprus to Lebanon, 1993, dir. polit. affairs divsn., 1995, permanent rep. to UN Office Geneva, 1996—97, NYC, 1997—. Office: 13 E 40th St New York NY 10016

ZACKS, DAVID M., lawyer; b. NYC, Mar. 2, 1942; s. Ken and Lucille Zacks; m. Barbara Zacks, Apr. 2, 1989; children: Taylor, Ben;children from previous marriage: Toby, Leslie. BA in Polit. Sci. with honors, Wake Forest U., Winston-Salem, NC, 1964, JD with honors, 1967. Ptnr. Hull, Towell, Norman, Augusta, Ga., 1971—76, Knox & Zacks PC, Augusta, 1976—94, Kilpatrick Stockton LLP, Atlanta, 1994—. Nat. chmn. Am. Cancer Soc., Atlanta, 2002—03; trustee Leadership Ga., Atlanta, 1990—93; mem. dean's adv. bd. Emory U. Med. Sch., Atlanta, 2004—; bd. visitors Wake Forest U. Sch. Law, 2007—. Capt. JAGC US Army, 1967—71. Recipient Justice Robert Benham award for cmty. svc., State Bar Ga., Atlanta, 2003. Mem.: Ga. Bar Assn. Avocations: golf, hiking, boating. Office: Kilpatrick Stockton LLP 1100 Peachtree St Ste 2800 Atlanta GA 30309

ZADEH, JAVAD HAMADANI, mathematics professor; b. Kerman, Iran, Oct. 2, 1940; arrived in U.S., 1964; s. Bagher Hamadani Zadeh and Fatemeh Asadi; children: Neda, Mina. BA, The Am. U. Beirut, Lebanon, 1963; MS, Purdue U., West Lafayette, Ind., 1966; PhD, MPhil, Columbia U., NYC, 1976. Cert. tchr. Ga. Profl. Standards Commn., 1988. Instr. math. Shiraz U., Iran, 1963—64, Ctr. Coll. Ky., Danville, Ky., 1966—67, Bowling Green State U., Ohio, 1969—70; from instr. to asst. prof. Sharif U. Tech., Tehran, Iran, 1970—82, chmn. dept. math. and computer sci., 1979—81, assoc. prof., 1982—86; vis. prof. math. U. Ga., Athens, 1986—87; tchr. math. Ga. Pub. Schs., Atlanta, 1990—92; asst. prof. math. Mid. Ga. Coll., Cochran, Ga., 1992—93; assoc. prof. Brewton-Parker Coll., Mt. Vernon, Ga., 1993—97, prof., 1997—2006; asst. prof. math. Dalton State Coll., Ga., 2006—. Postdoctoral rsch. fellow dept. math. U. Calif., 1976—77. Author: Shenidi Che-Gaft, 1970, 2d edit., 2000; editor: Bull. Iranian Math. Soc., 1979—81; contbr. articles to profl. jours. Home: 8740 Roswell Rd 9D Atlanta GA 30350 Office Phone: 706-272-2580. Personal E-mail: javadhz@yahoo.com.

ZADEH, MANSOUR T., food products executive; Sr. info. tech. leader PepsiCo; head info. tech. Miller Brewing Co.; chief tech. officer Kraft Foods; chief info. officer Smithfield Foods, Inc., Va., 2002—. Named one of 25 Most Influential Consumer Goods Execs. That Make a Difference, Consumer Goods Tech. mag., 2004. Office: Smithfield Foods Inc 200 Commerce St Smithfield VA 23430 Office Phone: 757-365-3000. *

ZAENTZ, SAUL, film producer, former record company executive; b. Passaic, NJ, Feb. 28, 1921; Owner Fantasy Records, 1975—2005. Founder Saul Zaentz Film Ctr., 1980. Producer films: One Flew Over the Cuckoo's Nest, 1975 (Oscar for Best Picture, 1975), Three Warriors, 1977, Lord of the Rings, 1978, Amadeus, 1984 (Oscar for Best Picture, 1984), The Unbearable Lightness of Being, 1988, At Play in the Fields of the Lord, 1991, The English Patient, 1996 (Academy Award for Producer Best Picture, Irving G. Thalberg award, 1996); exec. producer The Mosquito Coast, 1986. Recipient Prodr. of Yr. Award, Nat. Bd. Review, 2005; fellow Acad. Fellowship, British Acad. Film Award (BAFTA), 2003. Office: Saul Zaentz Co 2600 10th St Berkeley CA 94710-2522

ZAFERSON, WILLIAM S., philosophy educator, publisher; b. Kalavrita, Greece, Feb. 10, 1925; came to U.S., 1953; s. Steven A. and Katharine (Michael) Z.; m. Toni Adelgunde Humberg, Oct. 15, 1955. BA in Lit. cum laude, U. Athens, Greece, 1952; MA in Classical Lang. and Lit., U. Chgo., 1965; DPhil magna cum laude, U. Athens, 1976; postgrad., Truman Coll., 2000; Internat. Scholar in Tr origin. classical texts. Asst. prof. U. Upper Iowa, Fayette, 1966-68, Marymount Coll., Salina, Kans., 1968-70; prof. philosophy St. Mary's U., San Antonio, Tex., 1970-72. Internat. scholar translating original classical texts and Greek, Latin, German and French. Author: The Meaning of Metempsychosis, 1965, The Universe, Its Elements and Justice, 1974, A Hymn to Health, 1975, The Platonic View of Moral Law and the Influence of the Tragedians on Plato's Thoughts, 1976, The Perfect Family, 1986, The Heraclitean Logos, 1996; author, pub.: The Songs of the Muses for Gods and Men, 1999, (70 philos. poems set to music) Hephaestus, 2000, (poem set to music) Hermes to King Odysseus, 2001, (lyrics and music) Mother Gaea's Reprobation, 2001, (lyrics and music) Pluto and Persephone (A Look into the Elusinian Mysteries Verifying Every Soul's Immortality), 2002, (poem set to music) Hymn to the Earth: Mother of All, 2002, (music) The Throne of Virtue, 2002, The Titans (War of Ideologies. Vice versus Virtue, words & music), 2003, The Virtuous Woman, 2006, others. A. Daniel L. Shorey fellow, U. Chgo., 1955. Mem. NRTA, AAUP, Am. Philos. Assn. (ctrl. divsn. emeritus), U. Chgo. Alumni Assn., Am. Assn. Learned Socs., Goethe-Institut Chgo., Nat. Assn. Scholars, Am.-Swedish Cultural Assn., Chgo. Avocations: poetry, classical music, opera, hiking, swimming.

ZAFFINO, MICHAEL J., social studies educator; BS, So. Conn. State U., New Haven, 1988, MS, 1992. Dir. admissions Notre Dame HS, West Haven, Conn., 1998—2001; prin. Our Lady of Victory Sch., West Haven, 2001—02; tchr. social studies Thurgood Marshall Mid. Sch., Bridgeport, Conn., 2002—. Named 1998 Alumnus of Yr., Our Lady of Victory Sch., 1998. Mem.: NEA, Conn. Edn. Assn.

ZAFFIRINI, JUDITH, state legislator, small business owner; b. Laredo, Tex., Feb. 13, 1946; d. George and Nieves Pappas; m. Carlos Zaffirini, 1965; 1 child, Carlos Jr. BS, U. Tex., 1967, MA, 1970, PhD, 1978. Committeewoman Tex. State Dem. Exec. Com., 1978-84; mem. Tex. State Senate, 1987—, pres. pro tempore, 1997; owner Zaffirini Comms., Laredo, 1998—. Del. Dem. Nat. Conv., 1980, 84. Recipient Medal of Excellence Nat. League United Latin Am. Citizens, 1987, Jose Maria Morelos y Pavon Medal of Merit for leadership in strengthening U.S.-Mex. rels., 1987; named Woman of Achievement Tex. Press Women, 1980, Gov. of Tex. for a Day, Apr. 19, 1997, Ten Best Legislators Tex. Monthly Mag., 1997, 2001, Disting. Alumnus U. Tex., 2003; inductee Nat. Hispanic Hal of Fame, 1987. Democrat. Roman Catholic. Home: PO Box 627 Laredo TX 78042-0627 Office: 1407 Washington St Laredo TX 78040-4411 Office Phone: 956-724-8379. E-mail: judith.zaffirini@senate.state.tx.us.

ZAFONTE, ROSS D., physiatrist; b. Freeport, NY, Nov. 30, 1960; BS, U. Ga., 1981; DO, Nova Southeastern/Southeastern Coll. Osteopathic Medicine, Ft. Lauderdale, Fla., 1985; completed, Leadership Program for Physicians in Academic Health Ctrs., Harvard U. Sch. Pub. Health, 1998. Resident Mt. Sinai Sch. Medicine, NYC, 1986—89, chief resident; resident, phys. medicine rehabilitation Detroit Osteopathic Hosp., 1985—86; instr. Thomas Jefferson U., Phila., 1989-90; asst. prof. U. Mo., Columbia, 1991-92; asst. prof. to assoc. prof. Wayne State U., Detroit, 1992—, interim chmn. physical med and rehab.; med. dir. tramatic brain injury unit Rehab. Inst. of Mich., Detroit, co-dir. residency tng. program, 1994-96, v.p., med. affairs, chief of staff, interim pres., 1999—2000; sr. v.p., rehabilitation svcs. Detroit Med. Ctr., physiatrist-in-chief; chief phys. medicine Detroit Receiving Hosp., 1992; chmn., dept. phys. medicine and rehabilitation U. Pitts. Sch. Medicine, prof., dept. phys. medicine and rehabilitation; v.p., clin. rehabilitation svcs. U. Pitts. Med. Ctr.; bd. dir. U. Pitts. Med. Ctr. Rehabilitation Hosp.; med. dir., phys. medicine and rehabilitation inpatient and outpatient svcs. U. Pitts. Med. Ctr., South Side. Spkr. in field; cons. Nat. Hwy. Traffic Safety Bd., Ronald Reagan Inst. Emergency Medicine, George Washington U., U. Lund, Sweden. Contbr. articles to profl. jours.; jour. reviewer Archives Phys. Medicine and Rehabilitation, Am. jour. Phys. Medicine and Rehabilitation, jour. reviewer, mem. editl. bd. Jour. Head Trauma Rehabilitation. Recipient Frank Blumenthal award for tchg. excellence Wayne State/Rehab. Inst., 1994, Appled award for tchg. excellence U. Mo., 1991, Excellence in Scientific Presentation award, Am. Psychological Assn., Nat. Excellence in Tchg. award, NJ Med. Sch., 2004; Prince Fellow Lectureship, Rehabilitation Inst. Chgo./Northwestern U., 2003; named one of Best Doctors in Am. (Midwest) Honor Roll, 1996-2006, Best Doctors in Pitts., Pitts. Mag., 2002-2006. Fellow Am. Acad. Phys. Medicine and Rehab.(President's Citation Presentation award, 2005, Walter J. Zeiter Lectureship, 2006), Am. Bd. Electrodiagnostic Medicine; mem. Am. Spinal Injury Assn., Brain Injury Assn. (program com. chmn. 1995-96, Young Investigator award 1996, Pioneer in TBI Rsch., 2006), Am. Assn. Acad. Physiatrists (program com. mem.), Am. Acad. Phys. Medicine Clin. Practice Guidelines Com., Am. Assn. Electrodiagnostic Medicine, Internat. Assn. for the Study of Traumatic Brain Injury. Avocations: baseball, running. Office: U Pitts Med Ctr Rehab Medicine Ctr 3471 Fifth Ave Ste 1103 Pittsburgh PA 15213 Office Phone: 412-648-6979. Business E-Mail: zafonterd@upmc.edu. *

ZAGANO, PHYLLIS, religious studies educator; BA in English, Marymount Coll., Tarrytown, NY, 1969; MS in Pub. Rels., Boston U., 1970; MA in English, L.I.U., 1972; PhD in English, SUNY, Stony Brook, 1979; MA in Theology, St. John's U., Jamaica, NY, 1990. Program officer Nat. Humanities Ctr., NYC, 1979—80; asst. prof. comms. Fordham U., Bronx, NY, 1980—84; rschr. Archdiocese of NY, 1984—86; ind. rschr. NYC, 1986—88; assoc. prof. Boston U., 1988—98, adj. assoc. prof. theology, 1988—98, dir. inst. for democratic comm., 1988—98; sr. rsch. assoc. in residence, spl. assoc. prof. religious studies Hofstra U., Hempstead, NY, 2002—. Vis. Aquinas chair St. Thomas Aquinas Coll., 2005; vis. assoc. prof. Cath. studies Yale Div. Sch., 2005. Author: Religion and Public Affairs, 1987, Social Impact of the Mass Media, 1991, Woman to Woman, 1993, On Prayer, 1994, Ita Ford: Missionary Martyr, 1996, Twentieth Century Apostles, 1999, Things New and Old, 1999, Holy Saturday: An Argument for the Restoration of the Formale Diaconate in the Catholic Church, 2000 (Book award Catholic Press Assn. 2001, Coll. Theology Soc. 2002), Dorothy Day: In My Own Words, 2003, Called to Serve: A Spirituality for Deacons, 2004, The Dominican Tradition, 2006, Acerca de la Oracion: Una Carta a Mi Amijado (Book award Cath. Press Assn. 2003); monthly radio host Boston U. World of Ideas, 1992-97; series editor Spirituality in History, 2006-. Lector, lay min. Ch. St. Vincent Ferrer, NYC, 1980—92, Our Lady of the Miraculous Medal Ch., 1996—, Newman Ctr., Boston U., 1992—96. Comdr. USNR, 1976—. Faculty Rsch. grantee Fordham U., 1983, Rsch. grantee Nat. Inst. Peace, 1989, Rsch. grantee Wabash Ctr., 2003; Coolidge fellow Episcopal Divinity Sch., 1987; recipient citation for heroism Nassau County (N.Y.) Fire Commn., 1995. Mem. Am. Acad. Religion (co-chair Roman Cath. Studies, 1991-2001), Am. Cath. Philos. Assn., Coll. Theology Soc., Cath. Theol. Soc. Am., Naval Res. Assn., Soc. for Study of Christian Spirituality. Roman Catholic. Office: 115 Hofstra Univ Hempstead NY 11549 Office Phone: 516-463-5612. Business E-Mail: phyllis.zagano@hofstra.edu.

ZAGAR, ROBERT JOHN, psychologist, researcher; b. Great Lakes, Ill., Nov. 26, 1948; s. Anthony John and Helen Gertrude (Kurzynowski) Z.; m. Agata. MS in Psychology, Ill. Inst. Tech., Chgo., 1975; PhD in Psychology, Northwestern U., 1981; MPH in Pub. Health, U. Ill. Med. Ctr., Chgo., 1982; postgrad., DePaul U., 1982-83, Barry U., 1984-85. Clin. psychologist, Ill.; sch. psychologist, Ill. Sch. psychologist Chgo. Pub. Schs., 1991-93; asst. prof. Nat. Louis U., Evanston, Ill., 1991-93; psychologist Juvenile Divsn. Cir. Ct., Chgo., 1985-91; economist Ill. Dept. Labor, 1986-87; pvt. practice Chgo., 1992—. Cons. psychologist But. Disability Determination, Chgo., 1992—, Dept. Children and Family Svcs., 1992—, Juvenile Divsn. Cir. Ct., 1992—; asst. prof. Ill. Sch. Profl. Psychology, 1989—2006, Argosy U., 1992—2006; sch. psychologist Aurora Pub. Schs., Ill., 1989—91; asst. prof. Forest Sch. Profl. Psychology, Wheeling, 1988—89; sch. psychology Chgo. Pub. Schs., 1999—, Woodstock, 2000—01; invited spkr. Nat. Summit Youth Violence, U.S. Dept. Dept. Corrections, others; asst prof. Lewis U., 1998—, Chgo. Sch. Profl. Psychology, 2007—. Contbr. articles to profl. jours. in field of neuropsychol. tests, forensic exams. and aggress. Mem. APA, APHA, Am. Psychol. Soc., Fla. Psychol. Assn., Ill. Psychol. Assn., Nat. Assn. Sch. Psychologists, Ill. Sch. Psychology Assn. Roman Catholic. Achievements include development of the first cradle to jail actuarial empirical and objective measures of dangerousness. Office: 233 E Erie St Ste 610 Chicago IL 60611 Office Phone: 312-266-3411. Personal E-mail: drzagar@hotmail.com.

ZAGARIS, BRUCE, lawyer; b. Modesto, Calif., Sept. 4, 1947; s. Nickolas M. and Dorothy (Chicoine) Zagaris. BA, George Washington U., 1969; JD, 1972, LLM, 1973, Stockholm U., 1975; student, Free U., Brussels, 1976. Bar: Oreg. 1973, Idaho 1976, Calif. 1978, US Ct. Appeals (10th cir.) 1978, US Ct. Appeals (4th cir.) 1979, US Supreme Ct. 1982. Law clk. US Dist. Ct., Charleston, W.Va., 1972—73; asst. atty. gen. State of Idaho, Boise, 1973—74; atty., cons. Ada Coun. Govt., Boise, 1974; assoc. Nordic Law Cons., Brussels and Stockholm, 1974—76, Glad Tuttle & White, San Francisco, 1976—77; lectr. U. W.I., Bridgetown, Barbados, 1977—78; ptnr Berliner & Maloney, Washington, 1978—90; adj. prof. Antioch Sch. Law, Washington, 1983—84; counsel Oppenheimer, Wolff & Donnelly, 1990—92; adj. prof. Fordham U. Sch. law, 1990—; assoc. Cameron & Hombostel, 1992—; cons. 13 nat. govt. UN; adj. prof. Washington Coll. Sch. Law Am. U., 1993, U. Montana Law Sch., 2004—06; editor in chief, reporter Internat. Enforcement Law; editor Internat. Criminal Law Casebook, 2006. Author: (book) Internat. Tax Law, 1978, Fgn. Investment in US, 1980; editor: Internat. Hanbook on Drug Control, 1992. Mem.: Internat. Penal Law Assn. (rep. to orgn. of Am. states), Internat. Fiscal Assn., Washington Fgn. Law Soc. (pres. 1990—91), Am. Soc. Internat. Law (exec. coun. 1990—92), ABA (chmn. com. internat. tax law, sect. internat. tax law 1989—92, chmn. com. internat. criminal law, criminal justice sect. 1990—93, Union Internationales des Avocats, coordinating com. immigration), Epsilon Housing Trust (mem. Washington 1984), Sigma Chi. Office: Berliner Corcoran & Rowe LLP 1101 Seventeenth St NW Ste 1100 Washington DC 20036 Office Phone: 202-293-5555.

ZAGAT, NINA, publishing executive; m. Tim Zagat, 1965; children: Ted, John. AB, Vassar Coll., 1963; LLB, Yale U.; attended, Le Cordon Bleu Ecole de Cuisine. Atty. Sherman and Sterling, NYC, 1966—90; co-founder, co-pub. Zagat Survey, NYC, 1979—; co-chair, co-founder Zagat.com, 1999—. Served on White House Conference on Travel and Tourism; mem. Who's Who of Food and Beverage in Am.; mem. of the corp. Culinary Institute of Am., 1994—, established lecture series, 2001. Office: Zagat Survey 4 Columbus Circle New York NY 10019

ZAGAT, TIM, publishing executive; m. Nina Zagat, 1965; children: Ted, John. BA, Harvard U., 1961; LLB, Yale U., 1966. Assoc. Hughes, Hubbard & Reed; ptnr. Pomerantz, Levy, Haudek & Block, 1976—82; chief litigation counsel Gulf & Western Industries Inc., 1980—87; co-founder, publisher Zagat Survey, 1979—. Office: Zagat Survey 4 Columbus Circle New York NY 10019

ZAGEL, JAMES BLOCK, federal judge; b. Chgo., Mar. 4, 1941; s. Samuel and Ethel (Samuels) Z.; m. Margaret Maxwell, May 27, 1979. BA, U. Chgo., 1962, MA in Philosophy, 1962; JD, Harvard U., 1965. Bar: Ill. 1965, U.S. Dist. Ct. (no. dist.) Ill. 1965, U.S. Supreme Ct. 1970, U.S. Ct. Appeals (7th cir.) 1972. Asst. state atty. Cook County, 1965—69; asst. atty. gen. criminal justice divsn. State of Ill., Springfield, 1970-77; chief prosecuting atty. Ill. Jud. Inquiry Bd., Springfield, 1973-75; exec. dir. Ill. Law Enforcement Commn., Springfield, 1977-79; dir. Ill. Dept. Revenue, Springfield, 1979-80, Ill. Dept. State Police, Springfield, 1980-87; judge U.S. Dist. Ct. (no. dist.) Ill., Chgo., 1987—. Co-author: Criminal Law and

Its Administration, 1989, Cases and Comments on Criminal Procedure, 1992, Author's Money to Burn, 2002. Named Outstanding Young Citizen, Chgo. Jaycees, 1977; recipient Disting. Svc. Merit award Assn. Commerce and Industry, 1983. Mem. Chgo. Bar Assn., Jud. Conf. of U.S. (codes of conduct com. 1987-92). Office: US Dist Ct 219 S Dearborn St Ste 2588 Chicago IL 60604-1801

ZAGEL, MARGARET MAXWELL, lawyer; b. Centralia, Ill., Jan. 17, 1949; d. Francis Edgar and Joan (Beckmeyer) Maxwell; m. James Block Zagel, May 27, 1979. BA, Tulane U., 1970; JD, U. Ill., 1973. Bar: Ill. 1973, U.S. Ct. Appeals (7th cir.), U.S. Supreme Ct. Atty. Ill. Appellate Defender's Office, Chgo., 1973-75, law clk. to Hon. Seymour Simon, 1975-76; assoc., then ptnr. Schuyler Roche & Zwirner, Chgo., 1976-84; gen. counsel Grant Thornton LLP, Chgo., 1984-98, mng. prin. risk, regulatory & legal affairs, gen counsel, 2003; v.p., gen. counsel Tellabs, Inc., Lisle, Ill., 1998—99; sr. v.p., chief legal and admin. officer Organic, Inc., San Francisco, 1999—2001; spec. coun. litigation transactions Arthur Andersen LLP, 2002; practice lead, corp. governance, risk and crisis mgmt., co-gen. coun. Altheimer & Gray, 2002—03. Mem. planning com. Securities Inst. Northwestern U., Chgo., 1993—, mem. corp. counsel planning com., 1994-2000; mem. civil justice reform adv. com. U.S. Cir. Ct. (no. dist.) Ill., Chgo., 1994-95; mem. Ill. Commn. Regulatory Issues, mem. ACCA 1986, Nat. Assoc. Corp. Dir., 2002-2004, Economic Club Chgo. 2003-, Women Corp. Dirs. 2003-; mem. vis. com. Coll. Law U. Ill., 1997-2001.; bd. dirs. Atrion Corp. 2002-2003. Office: Grant Thornton LLP 175 W Jackson 20th Fl Chicago IL 60604

ZAGER, BERNARD SOLOMON, physician, consultant; b. Detroit, Nov. 3, 1926; s. Philip and Lena Zager; m. Denise Acheson, Sept. 11, 1953; children: Robert, Gerald, Martin. BA with distinction, Wayne State U., 1946; MD, Northwestern U., 1950. Diplomate Am. Bd. Preventive Medicine and Occpl. Medicine. Intern Detroit Grace Hosp., 1949-50, resident in surgery, 1952-56; chief physician AAD Ford Motor Co., Utica, Mich., 1964-68; med. dir. Nuc. Energy Divsn. GE, San Jose, Calif., 1968-87; occupl. medicine cons. Reno, 1987—. Capt. US Army, 1950—51, Korea. Mem.: Alpha Omega Alpha. Home and Office: 1210 Bridlewood Way Reno NV 89509-7116 Home Phone: 775-329-8940; Office Phone: 775-329-8940. Personal E-mail: bernzag@aol.com.

ZAGER, RONALD, chemist, consultant; s. Joseph and Theodora Zager; m. Anne Coykendall Chase, 1995. BS, Bklyn. Coll., 1955; MS in Chemistry, Stevens Inst. Tech., 1969. Chemist Charles Pfizer & Co., NYC, Halocarbon Products, Hackensack, NJ; devel. chemist Tenneco Chems., Garfield, NJ; sr. chemist Givaudan Corp., Clifton, NJ; tech. dir. Internat. Flavors and Fragrances, Union Beach, NJ; cons., pres. Ronald Zager Assocs. LLC. Overseas tech. cons. Unistar Program, UN, 1992. Mem. Am. Chem. Soc., Assn. Cons. Chemists and Chem. Engrs. (v.p. 1990-92, pres. 1993-94). Achievements include research in aroma chemicals and organic fluorocarbons. Office: Ronald Zager Assocs LLC Box 1200 408 Glen Ledge Rd Glen NH 03838 Office Phone: 603-383-4166. Business E-Mail: rzager@chemconsultants.com.

ZAGER, STEVEN MARK, lawyer; b. Memphis, Nov. 16, 1958; s. Jack and Sylvia (Bloomfield) Z.; m. Debra D'Angelo; children: Samantha, Amanda, Kathryn, Jackson. BA, Vanderbilt U., 1979, JD, 1983. Bar: Tex. 1984, U.S. Dist. Ct. (all dists.) Tex. 1984, U.S. Dist. Ct. Ariz. 1992, U.S. Dist. Ct. (D.C.) 1998, U.S. Ct. Appeals (5th, 6th, and 11th cirs.) 1983, U.S. Ct. Appeals (D.C. cir.) 1991, U.S. Ct. Appeals (Fed. cir.) 1997, U.S. Supreme Ct. 1991. Assoc. Fulbright & Jaworski, Houston, 1983-86, Weil, Gotshal & Manges, Houston, 1986-90, ptnr., 1990-98, head Houston office litigation sect., 1994-96; mng. ptnr. Tex. offices Brobeck, Phleger & Harrison, Austin, 1999—2001, firm ops. com., 1999—2003, head nat. litigation group, 2001—03; firm ops. com. Akin, Gump, Strauss, Hauer & Feld, LLP, Houston, 2003—. Adj. prof. U. Houston Sch. Law, 1990—95; nat. adv. bd. NALP, 1996—99. Contbr. articles to Tex. Bar Jour., Texas Lawyer, Houston Lawyer. Bd. dirs., exec. com. Alley Theatre, Houston, 1988-96, Tex. Accts. and Lawyers for the Arts, Houston, 1984-88; adv. bd. Montgomery Bell Acad., 1996-2004, chmn., 2004-05; bd. dirs. Vol. Legal Svcs. Ctrl. Tex., 2000-01 (bd. trustees 2004-), TV Sta. KLRU, 2001-03, M.D. Anderson Cancer Ctr., 2005-, Houston Arboredum, 2005- Named Outstanding Young Man in Am., U.S. Jaycees, 1983, Best Civil Def. Trial Lawyer in Tex., Tex. Lawyer, 2003; named one of 45 Best Lawyers Under 45 in Am., Tex. Super Lawyers, Tex. Monthly Mag., 2003, 2004, The Nation's Top Litigators, Nat. Law Jour., 2007; recipient Frank J. Scurlock award, State Bar Tex., 1991, Outstanding Pro Bono Svc., Professionalism award, Tex. Ctr. for Legal Ethics, 2002. Mem. ABA (litigation sect.), State Bar Tex. (dir. 1997-98, Frank J. Scurlock award 1991), Houston Bar Assn. (sec. 1996-97, v.p. 1997-98, bd. dirs. 1993-96, 2004-06, chair law and arts com. 1994, chair adminstrn. of justice com. 1995, rodeo com. 1997, chair law and media com. 2004, chair cmty. svc. task force 2004, Outstanding Young Lawyer in Houston 1991, Pres.'s award 1996-98), Houston Vol. Lawyers Program (bd. dirs. 1997-98, chair 1998), Travis County Bar Assn. (bd. dirs. 2001-03, chair bench bar program 2000, chair, 2003, jud. affairs com. 1999-2000), Fed. Bar Assn. Office: Akin Gump Strauss Hauer & Feld 1111 Louisiana 44th Flr Houston TX 77002 Office Phone: 713-220-8109. Business E-Mail: szager@akingump.com.

ZAGHLOUL, DINA AMAL, quality assurance professional, consultant; b. Omaha, Oct. 6, 1975; d. F. Omar and Hoda Z. BS in Biochemistry, U. Nebr., 1996; postgrad., Concord Law Sch., Calif., 2003. Quality assurance chemist Cargill, Blair, Nebr., 1996—97; validation specialist PharmTech, Libertyville, Ill., 1997—98; cons. Interim Tech., Oak Brook, Ill., 1998—99; sr. cons. Whittman-Hart, Chgo., 1999; quality assurance mgr. U.S. Office Products IT, Des Plaines, Ill., 1999—2000; cons. Interim Tech. Cons., Scottsdale, Ariz., 2000—; ind. cons. Scottsdale, 2000—. Mem. Am. Chem. Soc., Alpha Lambda Delta, Phi Lambda Upsilon, Phi Eta Sigma. Avocations: sports, reading. Personal E-mail: dzaghloul@msn.com.

ZAGON, IAN STUART, neuroscience and anatomy educator, researcher, inventor; s. Benjamin and Beatrice (Shaffer) Z.; m. Eileen Kostel, Nov. 26, 1964. BS, U. Wis., 1965; MS, U. Ill., Urbana, 1969; PhD, U. Colo., Denver, 1972. Asst. prof. biol. structure U. Miami, Fla., 1972-74; asst. prof. anatomy Pa. State U., Hershey, 1974-78, prof. genetics, 1975—, assoc. prof. anatomy, 1978-85, prof., 1985-91, prof. cell and molecular biology and neurosci., 1984—, prof. neurosci. and anatomy, 1991—2003, prof. neural and behavioral scis., 2003—, disting. educator, 2002—, disting. univ. prof., 2005—, program dir. on edn. in human structure, 2005—. Cons. Nat. Inst. on Drug Abuse, Rockville, Md., 1980—; cons., reviewer NIH, Bethesda, Md., 1984—; grant reviewer Am. Heart Assn. of Pa., 1985—, mem. rsch. com., 1988—, bd. dirs., 1992-97, v.p., 1993-96; founder ZoeGenics LLC. Author: Maternal Substance Abuse and the Developing Nervous System, 1992, Receptors in the Developing Nervous System, 1993; mem. editl. bd. Brain Rsch. Bull., 1980—, sect. editor for cellular and molecular neurobiology, 1994—; mem. editl. bd. Physiology and Behavior, 1987-97, Pharmacology, Biochemistry and Behavior, 1989—, Internat. Jour. Oncology, 1998—, Advances in Neuroimmunology, 1990, Internat. Jour. Devel. Neurosci., 1987-89, Brain Rsch., 1992-2005, Devel. Brain Rsch., 1992-2006, Cancer Therapy, 2003—, Exptl. Biology and Medicine, 2006—; contbr. numerous articles to med. and profl. jours.; patentee on growth factors, receptors, devel., cancer, wound healing. Recipient Entrepreneurial Achievement award, Kutztown U., The John Marshall Soc., Franklin and Marshall Coll.; grantee NIH, Am. Cancer Soc., Nat. Inst. Drug Abuse, Philip Morris, Nat. Multiple Sclerosis Soc. Mem.: Am. Assn. Cancer Rsch., Am. Diabetes Assn., Assn. for Rsch. in Vision and Ophthalmology, Soc. for Neurosci., Am. Soc. Cell Biology. Achievements include discovery of low-dose naltrexone, topical naltrexone and insulin, opioid growth factor therapies, non-erythroid spectrin, CCK-C receptor, and opioid growth factor receptor gene. Office: Pa State U Coll Medicine PO Box 850 H109 500 University Dr Hershey PA 17033-0850 E-mail: isz1@psu.edu.

ZAGOREN, JOY CARROLL, health facility director, researcher; b. NYC, Oct. 31, 1933; d. Murray Morris and Celia (Donner) Rossman; m. Robert H. Zagoren, June 29, 1958 (div. 1988); children: Glenn, Robin; m. Robert Henry Chester, Apr. 1, 1988 (dec. Mar. 1998); children: Peter Chester, Lisabeth Chester, Melinda Chester, Cecily Chester, Kate Chester. BS, NYU, 1957; MS, Adelphi U., Garden City, NY, 1969; PhD with distinction, NYU, 1981. Sec. sch. faculty Great Neck Pub. Schs., NY, 1957-71; rsch. scientist Inst. Psychobiol. Studies, Queens Village, NY, 1968-71; rsch. assoc. Albert Einstein Coll. Medicine, Bronx, NY, 1971-84; asst. prof. SUNY Sch. Medicine, Stony Brook, 1984-86; dir. Seriatum, NYC, 1991—. Ptnr. Winter Tree Collection; chmn. Esrath Nashim Hosp., 1986—; med. bd. dir. Sarah Herzog Meml. Hosp.; lectr. in field. Editor: The Node of Ranvier, 1984; contbr. articles to profl. jours. Chair Peace Corps Svc. Coun., Tri-State, 1965-75; chair Homeland Security Upper East Side of Manhattan, OEM CERT program, 2004—; pres. Kidney Found. LI, NY, 1965-77; v.p. United Cmty. Fund LI, 1970-83; bd. dirs. Jerusalem Mental Health Ctr., NYC, 1986—; mem. med. bd. dirs. Sarah Herzog Meml. Hosp., hon. chair dinner, 1995, chair dinner, 1996, med. chair, 1998, chair membership cocktail party, 2000, chair bd. dirs., 2000—; chmn. mem. NY Acad. Scis., 2000, vice chair Lyceum Club, NY Acad. Scis., 2001; mem. med. adv. bd. www.hipforkids.org. Named Disting. Alumnus of Yr., Adelphi U., 1986; recipient Svc. awards, Kidney Found., Kiwanis, others, 1970—87; fellow NIH fellow, 1982-84, Svc. awards Kidney Found., Kiwanis, others, 1970-87, NIH, 1982—84; hon. lectr., N.Y. Acad. Scis., 2006. Mem. AAAS, Nat. Acad. Sci., Am. Assn. Neuropathology, NY Acad. Scis. (lectr. 2003, 06, v.p. Lyceum Soc. 2001—). Democrat. Jewish. Avocations: art, literature, piano, swimming, gardening. Home: 405 E 82nd St New York NY 10028-6038 Office: Seriatum 405 East 82d St New York NY 10028

ZAGORIA, SAM D(AVID), reporter, educator, federal agency administrator; b. Somerville, NJ, Apr. 9, 1919; s. Nathan and Rebecca (Shapiro) Z.; m. Sylvia Bomse, Dec. 21, 1941; children: Paul, Marjorie Zagoria Isacks, Ronald. BL in Journalism, Rutgers U., 1941. With New Brunswick (N.J.) Daily Home News, 1940-41, N.J. Def. Coun., Trenton, 1941-42, Fed. Office Govt. Reports, Newark, 1942; reporter Washington Post, 1946-55; adminstrv. asst. to Senator Clifford P. Case, Washington, 1955-65; pres. Washington Newspaper Guild, 1953; mem. NLRB, Washington, 1965-69; dir. Labor-Mgmt. Rels. Svc. U.S. Conf. of Mayors, Washington, 1970-78; mem. U.S. Consumer Product Safety Commn., 1978-84; ombudsman Washington Post, 1984-86; arbitrator, 1986—. Fulbright lectr., Copenhagen, 1987; vis. prof. Fla. Atlantic U., Boca Raton, 1988—91; adj. prof. Wake Forest U., Winston-Salem, NC, 1993—2001. Author: Public Workers, Public Unions, 1972, The Ombudsman: How Good Governments Handle Citizens' Grievances, 1988. Campaign mgr. reelection Senator Case, 1960; campaign mgr. race for gov., former Sec. of Labor James P. Mitchell, 1961. With USAAF, 1942-45. Nieman fellow Harvard U., 1954. Mem. Common Cause, Nat. Consumers League, Rutgers U. Alumni Assn. Jewish. also: 2864 Wynfield Crossing Ln Winston Salem NC 27103-6597 Address: 3101 S Ocean Blvd 622 Boca Raton FL 33487 Office Phone: 561-274-6376.

ZAGORIN, JANET SUSAN, legal firm administrator, marketing professional; b. Lakewood, NJ; d. Irving C. and Dorothy (Tarshish) Zagorin. BA, Douglass Coll., 1975; MLS, Rutgers U., 1977. Asst. law libr. N.J. Atty. Gen., Trenton, 1977-78; head of reference sect. Cardozo U. Law Sch., NYC, 1978-79; law and legis. svcs. libr. FTC, Washington, 1979-81; dir. of reference Paul Weiss Rifkind, NYC, 1981-82; libr. dir. Riker Danzig Scherer & Hyland, Morristown, NJ, 1982; libr., profl. devel. dir. Baker & McKenzie, NYC, 1982-96; dir. practice devel. and info. svcs. Stroock & Stroock & Lavan LLP, NYC, 1996-98; dir. practice devel. Cadwalader, Wickersham & Taft, NYC, 1998-99, Gibson, Dunn & Crutcher, NYC, 1999—2001; dir. mktg. Sidley Austin Brown & Wood, NYC, 2001—04; dir. practice devel. Sidley Austin LLP, NYC, 2004—. Bd. dirs. N.Y. Cares, 1998—, audit com., 2007—. Mem.: ABA (vice chmn. standing com. Law Libr. Congress 1995—96, chmn. 1996—2001, law 2000 steering com. Libr. Congress), Am. Assn. Law Librs. (chair fgn. comparative internat. law com. 1990—91, vice chair pvt. law librs. 1990—91, chair com. on recruitment 1991, chair 1991—), Fin. Women's Assn. (bd. dirs. 1993—95, 1999—2000), Hadassah. Office: Sidley Austin LLP 787 Seventh Ave New York NY 10019-6018 Office Phone: 212-839-8797. Business E-Mail: jzagorin@sidley.com.

ZAGORIN, PEREZ, historian, educator; b. Chgo., May 29, 1920; s. Solomon Novitz and Mildred (Ginsburg) Z.; m. Honoré Desmond Sharrer, May 29, 1947; 1 son, Adam. AB, U. Chgo., 1941; A.M., Harvard U., 1947, PhD, 1952. Various positions OWI, U.S. Govt., U.P. Syndicate, CIO, 1942-46; instr. Amherst Coll., 1947-49; lectr. Vassar Coll., 1951-53; from asst. prof. to prof. history McGill U., 1955-65; prof. U. Rochester, 1965—, Joseph C. Wilson prof. history, 1982-90, Joseph C. Wilson prof. history emeritus, 1990—, chmn. dept., 1968-69, acting chmn. dept., 1988-89; vis. prof. Johns Hopkins, 1964-65; Amundsen vis. prof. U. Pitts., 1964; William Andrews Clark Meml. Library prof. UCLA, 1975-76. Thompson lectr. history Vassar Coll., 1987. Author: A History of Political Thought in the English Revolution, 1954, 2d edit., 2000, The Court and the Country, 1969, Culture and Politics from Puritanism to the Enlightenment, 1980, Rebels and Rulers 1500-1660, 2 vols., 1982, 2d edit., 2003, Ways of Lying: Dissimulation, Persecution, and Conformity in Early Modern Europe, 1990, Milton Aristocrat and Rebel: The Poet and His Politics, 1992, Francis Bacon, 1998 (named one of Best Academic Books, Choice, 1998), The English Revolution: Politics, Events, Ideas, 1998, How the Idea of Religious Toleration Came to the West, 2003 (named one of Best Books, LA Times, 2003), Thycydides: An Introduction for the Common Reader, 2005; co-editor: Philosophy Science and Religion in England 1640-1700, 1991, Guide to Historical Literature, 1994; contbr. numerous articles to hist. jours.; mem. editl. bd. Jour. of the History of Ideas. Sheldon travel fellow Harvard U., 1949-50, Fulbright fellow 1949-50, faculty rsch. fellow Social Sci. Rsch. Coun., 1958-59, 61-62, sr. rsch. fellow Folger Shakespeare Libr., 1964-65, fellow Inst. Advanced Study, Princeton, N.J., 1972-73, sr. fellow Nat. Humanities Ctr., 1978-79, fellow Ctr. Advanced Study in Behavioral Scis., 1983-84, Guggenheim fellow, 1983-84, Edgar F. Shannon Ctr. for Advanced Studies fellow U. Va., 1994—, Fellow Royal Hist. Soc., Am. Acad. Arts and Scis.; mem. Am. Hist. Assn. (chmn. Gershoy and Schuyler prize com. 1982-84). Home: 2990 Beaumont Farm Rd Charlottesville VA 22901-8717 Office: U Rochester Dept History Rochester NY 14627

ZAHN, CARL FREDERICK, museum program director, photographer, graphics designer; b. Louisville, Mar. 9, 1928; s. Fred Joseph and Myrtle (Fulks) Z.; m. Betty Jane Woodrow, Nov. 18, 1950 (div. July 1977); children: Lisa, Karen, Richard; m. Felicitas Magdalena Fuhlrott, July 30, 1979 (dec. Mar. 1999). BA, Harvard Coll., 1948. Asst. in conservation Fogg Art Mus., Cambridge, Mass., 1949-50; with art dept. Benton & Bowles Inc., NYC, 1950-51; design asst. Inst. Contemporary Art, Boston, 1951-56; dir. publs. Mus. Fine Arts, Boston, 1956—; also dir. exhbns., 1995-96; ret., 1997; co-founder Mus. Pub. Ptnrs., 2000. Exhibitions include: Addison Gallery Am. Art, Andover, Mass., 1959, Am. Inst. Graphic Arts, N.Y.C., 1960—, Rose Art Mus. Brandeis U., Waltham, Mass., 1969; author: Introduction to Hermann Zapf and His Design Philosophy, 1987, Books and Such Designed by Carl Zahn at the Museum of Fine Arts, Boston, 1956-97, 1997; co-author Weston's Westons: Portraits and Nudes, 1989; co-editor: Eye of the Beholder: Masterpieces from the Isabella Stewart Gardner Museum, 2003. Mem. Soc. Printers, Bund Deutscher Buchkünstler, East Chop Tennis Club (bd. dirs. 1970-72), Longwood Cricket Club. also: 1808 Par Pl Sarasota FL 34240-9689 E-mail: czbird@comcast.net.

ZAHN, DONALD JACK, lawyer; b. Oct. 24, 1941; s. Jerome and Clara (Zinsher) Z.; m. Laurie R. Hyman, Aug. 19, 1966; children: Lawrence, Melissa. AB, NYU, 1963; LLB, Union U., 1966; LLM in Taxation, NYU, 1967. Bar: N.Y. 1966, U.S. Dist. Ct. (no. dist.) N.Y. 1966, U.S. Tax Ct. 1969, U.S. Ct. Appeals (2d cir. 1970), Tex. 1972, U.S. Ct. Appeals (5th and 11th cirs.). Assoc. Bond, Schoeneck and King, Syracuse, NY, 1967-71; ptnr. Haynes and Boone, Dallas, 1971-82, Akin, Gump, Strauss, Hauer & Feld, Dallas, 1982-92; assoc. prof. internat. taxation, fed. income taxation, entities taxation, business associations Tex. Wesleyan Sch. Law, Ft. Worth, 1992-99. Vis. prof. fed. income taxation Baylor U. Sch. Law, 1995, prof. fed. income taxation and bus. orgns. II, 2000; grad. taxation program U. San Diego Sch. Law, 1996—98, fed. income taxation, corp. taxation, current income tax problems, tax ethics; adj. prof. Sch. Law So. Meth U., Dallas, 1972—87, 1990—91. Trustee, sec. mem. exec. and fin. com., nominating com. Greenhill Sch., Addison, Tex., 1980-90; trustee, chmn. budget com., mem. fin. com. Jewish Fedn. Greater Dallas, 1978-89; trustee, chmn. Found. Jewish Fedn., Dallas, 1980-89; trustee, v.p., pres. Dallas chpt. Am. Jewish Com., 1980-92; mem. Tex. World Trade Coun., 1986-87, Dallas Mayor's Internat. Com. Mem. State Bar Tex. (sec. 1982-83, chmn. tax sect. 1984-85, newsletter taxation sect. editor 1980-81), Internat. Bar Assn., Internat. Comte (N.Tex. commn.), Ctr. for Am. and Internat. Law (adv. bd., treas. Internat. and Comparative Law Ctr., lectr. Acad. in Internat. Law), N.Y. State Bar Assn. Address: 11218 Hillcrest Rd Dallas TX 75230-3501 Office Phone: 214-769-9712. Office Fax: 214-368-5301. E-mail: donzahn@flash.net.

ZAHN, PAULA, newscaster; b. Omaha, Feb. 24, 1956; m. Richard Cohen; children: Haley Brynne, Jared Brandon, Austin Bryce. BA in journalism, Stephens Coll., Columbia, Mo., 1978. With Sta. WFAA-TV, Dallas, 1978, Sta. KFMB-TV, San Diego, 1979—81, Sta. KPRC-TV, Houston, 1981—83, Sta. WHDH-TV, Boston, 1983—85; anchor, reporter Sta. KCBS-TV, LA, 1985—87; anchor The Health Show ABC News, NYC, 1987—88, co-anchor World News This Morning, 1988—90; co-anchor CBS This Morning CBS News, NYC, 1990—96, anchor CBS Evening News Sat. edit., 1996—99; anchor The Fox Report with Paula Zahn Fox News Network, NYC, 1999, anchor The Edge with Paula Zahn, 1999—2001; co-anchor American Morning CNN, 2001—03, co-anchor People in the News, 2002—07, anchor Paula Zahn Now, 2003—07. Primetime co-host Olympic Winter Games, Albertville, France, 1992; co-anchor Olympic Winter Games, Lillehammer, Norway, 94. Musician (Cellist): Carnegie Hall Debut, 1992. Named Newscaster of Yr., Am. Women in Radio and TV, 1983; recipient Broadcasting Award, Nat. Commn. Working Women, 1982, Spirit Achievement Award, Albert Einstein Coll. Medicine, 1993, Cancer Awareness Award, Congl. Families Action for Cancer Awareness, 1994, Emmy award for outstanding coverage of a continuing news story, 1994, Spirit of Life Award, City of Hope Cancer Ctr., 2003. *

ZAHND, RICHARD H., sports association executive, lawyer; b. NYC, July 22, 1946; s. Hugo and Rose (Genovese) Z.; m. Phyllis Beth Workman, Aug. 13, 1978; children: Andrew Richard, Melissa Dawn. AB, NYU, 1968, JD, 1971. Bar: N.Y. 1972. Assoc. Paul, Weiss, Rifkind, Wharton & Garrison, NYC, 1971-74; staff atty. Madison Square Garden Corp., NYC, 1974-75; v.p. legal affairs Madison Square Garden Center, Inc., NYC, 1975-79; v.p., gen. counsel Madison Square Garden Corp., NYC, 1979-86; v.p. N.Y. Knickerbockers Basketball Club, NYC, 1979-86, N.Y. Rangers Hockey Club, NYC, 1979-86; ptnr. Morrison & Foerster, NYC, 1986-91; exec. v.p., gen. counsel NHL Enterprises, L.P., NYC, 1992—. Served to capt. U.S. Army, 1972. John Norton Pomeroy scholar NYU Law Sch., 1969; Mortimer Bishop scholar NYU Law Sch., 1969; Judge Jacob Markowitz scholar NYU Law Sch., 1970; recipient Am. Jurisprudence prize NYU Law Sch., 1969 Episcopalian. Office: NHL Enterprises LP Fl 46 1251 Ave of the Americas New York NY 10020-1104 Office Phone: 212-789-2023. Business E-Mail: rzahnd@nhl.com.

ZAHNEIS, LEONA BETH, lawyer; b. Louisville, Ky., Oct. 22, 1971; BS in Nursing, Eastern Ky. U., 1993; JD, Salmon P. Chase Coll. Law, 2001. Bar: Ohio 2001; lic. Ky., 1993. Assoc. White, Getgey & Meyer Co., LPA, Cin. Named one of Ohio's Rising Stars, Super Lawyers, 2006. Mem.: Northern Ky. Bar Assn. (Judge West award), Ohio State Bar Assn., Cin. Bar Assn., Order of Curia. Office: White Getgey & Meyer Co LPA 1700 Fourth & Vine Tower 1 W Fourth St Cincinnati OH 45202-3621 Office Phone: 513-241-3685. Office Fax: 513-241-2399.

ZAHNER, MARY ANNE, art educator; b. Dover, Ohio, Mar. 30, 1938; d. Alfred James and Anna Elizabeth (Stewart) Riggle; m. Gordon Dean Zahner, Aug. 27, 1960 (dec. Mar. 1967); 1 child, Anne Colette Krach; m. John Charles Opalek, Aug. 21, 1982. BFA, Ohio U., 1960, MA, 1969; PhD, Ohio State U., 1987. Lic. tchr. Ohio. Instr. art Springfield Twp. Schs., Akron, Ohio, 1960-61, Logan H.S., Ohio, 1961-62, Dover H.S., 1967-68, chair art dept., 1969-71; teaching asst. Ohio State U., Columbus, 1980-82; from instr. art edn. to asst. prof. U. Dayton, 1971-74, asst. prof., 1974-91, assoc. prof., 1991-2000, prof., 2000—. Mem. faculty rights, governance and svc. com. U. Dayton, 1992—93, mem. arts series com., 1995—98; reviewer Harcourt, Brace, 1993—98, Prentice Hall, Inc., 1996—98; mem. higher edn. steering com. Ohio Dept. Edn., 1995, mem. adv. com., tchr. preparation programs, 97; exec. bd. Western Regional Profl. Devel. Ctr., 1996—2004. Author: Barkan, 2003; contbr. chapters to books; Exhibited in group shows at Westbeth Gallery, N.Y., 1995, exhibitions include Univ. Coun. for Art Edn., Pleiades Gallery Contemporary Art, 2006, Pleiades Gallery Contemporary Art, NY, 2006—07. Mem. Kettering (Ohio) Arts Coun., 1988—93, sec., 1990; mem. discretionary support com. Miami Valley Arts Coun., Dayton, 1992; coord. 3d congl. art contest sponsored by Tony P. Hall Dayton, 1993—95; mem.-at-large edn. com. Culture Works: Arts and Culture Alliance Miami Valley, 1996. Recipient Best of Show award, Canton Art Inst., 1969, Inst. Faculty award, Ohio Partnership for Visual Arts, 1989. Fellow: Ohio Art Edn. Assn. (mem. editl. bd. Ohio Art Edn. Jour. 1986—2005, editor newsletter Artline 1988, workshop coord. 1992, cons. tchr. insvc. for Dayton Pub. Schs. 1995, workshop coord. 1997, Outstanding Art Tchr. we. dist. 1992, 1996); mem.: ASCD, Univ. Coun. Art Edn., Ohio Alliance Arts Edn., Assn. Tchr. Educators, Nat. Art Edn. Assn., Phi Kappa Phi, Phi Delta Kappa. Democrat. Avocations: music, theater, physical fitness. Office: U Dayton 300 College Park Dayton OH 45469-0001 Home Phone: 937-374-1905; Office Phone: 937-229-3207. Business E-Mail: mary.zahner@notes.udayton.edu.

ZAHNER KRAEFT, DOROTHY SIMKIN, retired elementary school educator, school librarian; arrived in US, 1931; d. Robert Louis and Margaret Isadore (Timberlake) Simkin; m. Henry Zahner (div.); children: Mary De Avilan, Robert Louis; m. Norman John Kraeft, May 28, 2005 (div. Jan. 2007). BA in Sociology, Whittier Coll., 1948; MLS, U. So. Calif., LA, 1952. Cert. tchr. Calif., Ariz. Tchr. LA and Pasadena Sch., Calif., 1969-93; dir., owner Betty Ingram Sch., North Hollywood, Calif., 1976-79; dir. Foothill Nursery Sch., La Crescenta, Calif., 1970s; tchr. L.A. Unified Sch. Dist., 1980s; guest tchr. Washington Unified Sch. Dist., Phoenix, 1994-97; ret., 2002. Guest tchr. Osborn Sch. Dist., 1998-2000, Madison Sch. Dist., Phoenix, 1999-2001. Author: poems pub. in U.S., Europe and China. Bd. dirs. Ariz. Tenants Assn., Phoenix, 1994, 95; vol. Am. Friends Svc. Com., Phila., Calif., 1985-, Common Cause, LA, 1990, Internat. Rescue Com.; domestic violence vol., Phoeniz, 1999-2000; vol. Dem. candidates, LA and

Phoenix; poll marshall Election Bd., Phoenix. Recipient cert. appreciation, Project Hope, 2005. Mem.: Ariz. State Poetry Soc. (pres. 2002—03, chmn. 2004), Alameda Writers Group, Phoenix Poetry Soc. (pres. 1998, anthology editl. co. 2001, featured Tucson reader 2005, com. mem., Poet of Yr. 2000, poetry awards 1995, 2000), Am. Assn. Ret. Persons, Phoenix Writers Club (sec. 1998, featured reader 2007). Democrat. Avocations: theater, films, music, swimming, reading.

ZAHNISER, RACHEL S., lawyer; b. Campbellsville, Ky., Dec. 12, 1972; BA in Eng., Centre Coll. Ky, 1994; MSLS, U. Ky., 1995, JD, 1999. Bar: Ky. 1999, Ohio 2003. Law clerk Chief US Dist. Judge, Eastern Dist. Ky., US Cir. Judge, Sixth Cir. Ct. of Appeals; assoc. Taft, Stettinius & Hollister LLP, Cin., mem., Profl. Women's Resource Grp. Named one of Ohio's Rising Stars, Super Lawyers, 2006. Mem.: Order of Coif. Office: Taft Stettinius & Hollister LLP 425 Walnut St Ste 1800 Cincinnati OH 45202-3957 Office Phone: 513-381-2838. Office Fax: 513-381-0205.

ZAHORCHAK, GERALD LEE, school system administrator; b. Johnstown, Pa., June 12, 1957; s. John Cyril and Ruth (Cale) Z. BS, St. Francis Coll., 1980; MEd, Ind. U. of Pa., 1987; EdD, Pa. State U. Cert. elem. and secondary prin., reading specialist, supt. Elem. tchr., asst. football coach Greater Johnstown Sch. Dist., Pa., 1980-83, parent coord., reading specialist, 1989; instr. middle sch. reading, head football coach North Star Sch. Dist., Boswell, Pa., 1985-89; prin. Stonycreek Sch. Dist., Shanksville, Pa., 1989-92, North Star Sch. Dist., Boswell, Pa., 1992; dist. supt., programs coord. Greater Johnstown, Pa.; dep. sec. for elem. & secondary edn. Pa. Dept. Edn., 2003—05, acting sec. edn., 2005—06, sec. edn., 2006—, established child devel. and early learning office. Study skills cons., Mass., 1989—; presenter to univ. couns.; nat. ednl. leader, prin. spkr., Coun. of Chief State Sch. Officials Sch. Improvement Conf., 2005; presenter in field Author: Footreading, 1986, Transition to a Middle School, 1994. Chmn. Greater Johnstown Vo-Tech Bd., 1986-89; mem. Greater Johnstown Sch. Bd., 1986-89, Johnstown City Coun., dep. mayor. Named one of Outstanding Young Men in Am., 1988-89, Outstanding Young Citizen of Greater Johnstown Area, 1990, Pa.'s Outstanding Young Citizen, 1990; recipient Humanitarian Svc. award United Cerebral Palsy, 1982, Pa. State Sch. Study Council's Caldwell award for Excellence in Administrn. and Supervision, Disting. Alumnus in Edn. President's award, St. Francis Univ., 2002, Pa. League of Urban Sch. Leadership award, 2004, Pa. Assn. Fed. Programs Disting. Educator award, 2005 Mem. Nat. Assn. Secondary Sch. Prins., Assn. for Supervision and Curriculum Devel.(Pa. Outstanding Rsch. and Publication award, 1996), NEA, Johnstown Jaycees (Pa. Outstanding Young Citizen, 1991, 1996), Johnstown Rotary (pres., 2003), Johnstown Oldtimers Baseball (bd. dirs.), K.C. (4th degree), Pa. Assn. of Secondary Sch. Prins.(Ednl. Excellence award, 2005) Democrat. Roman Catholic. Avocations: reading, strength training. Home: 2000 Young St Johnstown PA 15902-3365 Office: Pa Dept Edn 333 Market St Harrisburg PA 17126-5820 Office Phone: 717-787-5820. *

ZAHRAN, MOHAMED MOSTAFA, electrical engineer, educator; b. Cairo; arrived in US, 1999; BS in Computer Engring., Cairo U., 1997, MS in Computer Engring., 1999; PhD, U. Md., College Park, 2003. Rsch. scientist George Washington U., Washington, 2003—04; asst. prof. CUNY, NYC, 2004—. Reviewer: profl. jours., confs., workshops. Recipient Best Talk award, Grad. Rsch. Interaction Day U. Md., 2002, Best Sci. Talk award, Elec. and Computer Engring. Grad. Student Assn. U. Md., 2002, Best Paper award, Internat. Conf. on Computer Design, 2003; grantee, Assn. Computing Machinery, 2003, 2004; PSC-CUNY Fund grantee, CUNY, 2005—06, Collaborative Rsch Experience for Undergraduates fund grantee, Computer Rsch. Assn., 2006—. Mem.: IEEE, Assn. Computing Machinery, Sigma Xi. Achievements include research in computer architecture. Personal E-mail: mzahran@ieee.org.

ZAIDI, ASAD R., medical products executive, biomedical engineer; b. Karachi, Pakistan, Jan. 25, 1954; MS in Biomedical Engring., U. Calif., Irvine. CEO Epinex Diagnostics, Irvine, Calif., 2002—. Sec. S. Asian Network, Cypress, Calif. Achievements include patents for Rapid Immunoassays. Home Phone: 949-660-7770; Office Phone: 949-660-7770. Office Fax: 949-660-7772; Home Fax: 949-660-7772. Business E-Mail: asad@epinex.com.

ZAIDI, EMILY LOUISE, retired elementary school educator; b. Hoquiam, Wash., Apr. 20, 1924; d. Burdick Newton and Emily Caroline (Williams) Johnston; m. M. Baqar Abbas Zaidi, June 12, 1949 (dec. Dec. 1983). BA in Edn. and Social Studies, Ea. Wash. State U., 1948; MEd, U. Wash., 1964, EdD, 1974. Tchr. 4th grade Hoquiam Schs., 1948—49; tchr. grades 5-6 Lake Washington Sch. Dist., Kirkland, Wash., 1949—51; tchr. grades 2-3 Port Angeles Schs., Wash., 1951—54; tchr. grade 2 Seattle Schs., 1954—55; tchr., reading specialist Northshore Sch. Dist., Bothell, Wash., 1955—69, Sacramento City Schs., 1969—87; ret., 1987. Mem. Calif. State Instrnl. Materials Panel, Sacramento, 1975. Mem. Sacramento Opera Assn., 1986—, Sacramento Ballet Assn., 1987—2000. Fulbright Commn. Exch. Tchr., 1961—62. Democrat. Avocations: writing, children's literature, reading, travel. Home: 4230 N River Way Sacramento CA 95864-6055 Personal E-mail: e.zaidi@sbcglobal.net.

ZAIDI, IQBAL MEHDI, biochemist, research scientist; b. Bijnor, India, June 30, 1957; s. Iqbal Haider and Habib (Zehra) Z.; m. Nuzhat Shikoh, Jan. 2, 1993; 1 child, Shan Zehra. BS in Chemistry with honors, Aligarh Med. U., 1976, MS in Biochemistry, 1978, PhD in Biochemistry, 1984. Rsch. fellow Indsl. Toxicology Rsch. Ctr., Lucknow, India, 1979-83; rsch. affiliate NY State Health Dept., Albany, 1984-91; scientist, project mgr., program mgr., group mgr. Applied Biosystems, Applera Corp., Foster City, Calif., 1991—. Contbr. articles to profl. jours. Mem. AAAS, Am. Chem. Soc. (biochem. tech. divsn. 1992-98), Shia Assn. Bay Area, NY Acad. Scis., Am. Soc. Quality, Project Mgmt. Inst. Avocations: photography, swimming, travel, natural history. Office: Applied Biosystems 850 Lincoln Centre Dr Foster City CA 94404-1128 Personal E-mail: zaidins22@yahoo.com.

ZAIDI, MOHAMMAD A., metal products executive; Grad. in Metall. Engring., Indian Inst. Tech., Kanpur, India, 1975; M in Materials Tech., Imperial Coll., London, 1977, PhD in Mech. Metallurgy, 1980. Sr. engr. Alcoa, Inc., Alcoa Center, Pa., 1985, mgr. tech. devel. and transfer for aluminum-intensive vehicle, 1991—92, with Automotive GmbH plant Soest, Germany, 1992—95, dir. product strategy, 1995—97, v.p. tech. devel. Automotive bus., 1997—98, dir. tech. worldwide automotive and extrusions Alcoa Center, 1998—2001, pres. Alcoa Automotive Fabrication and Assembly bus., COO Automotive Castings bus., 2001—03, v.p., chief tech. officer, 2003—06, exec. v.p. market strategy, tech. and quality, 2006—. Contbr. articles to sci. jours. Office: Alcoa Inc Alcoa Tech Ctr 100 Technical Dr New Kensington PA 15069 *

ZAIMAN, K(OICHI) ROBERT, dentist; b. Cin., Oct. 19, 1944; s. Noboru Gary and Toshiko (Matsuyama) Zaiman; m. Kimberly Ann Sass, Nov. 6, 1976; children: Kara Jean, Matthew Robert. Student, Creighton U., Omaha, 1962-64, DDS, 1968. Asst. prof. Creighton U. Sch. Dentistry, Omaha, 1971-73, assoc. prof., 1973-75; pvt. practice dentistry Omaha, 1971—. Dir. Chicano and Native-Am. Free Clinic Creighton U., Omaha, 1970—75. Mem. bd. elders King of Kings Luth. Ch., 1990—95, deacon, 1995—; past v.p., bd. dirs. Japanese-Am. Citizens League, Omaha, 1977—86. Fellow: Internat. Coll. Dentistry, Acad. Continuing Edn., Acad. Gen. Dentistry (nat. del. 1971—76, pres. 1976—77), Pierre Fauchard Internat. Hon. Acad.; mem.: ADA, Omaha Dental Study Club (pres. 1999—2001), Nebr. Dental Assn. (del. 1971—94, 1996—), Omaha Dist. Dental Soc. (bd. dirs. 1968, treas. 1980—85, peer rev. 1996—), Delta Sigma Delta (pres. 1973—74). Office: 10841 Q St Ste 109 Omaha NE 68137-3741 Office Phone: 402-339-4999.

ZAIS, MITCHELL M., career military officer; b. Ft. Bragg, NC; Grad. in Engring., US Mil. Acad., West Point, NY; MS, PhD, U. Wash. Commd. infantry U.S. Army, advanced through grades to brigadier gen.; infantry svc. airborne, air assault, mechanized, ceremonial standard, Bradley, light infantry, other, Vietnam, Korea, U.S.; comdr. 2 rifle cos., infantry battalion, light infantry brigade; chief war plans Chmn. Joint Chiefs of Staff; social aide The White House, Washington; exec. officer to comdr. in chief U.S. So. Command, Panama; commanding gen. Coalition Joint Task Force, Kuwait, Joint Task Force Provide Refuge for Kosovar Refugees in U.S.; dep. comdg. gen. maneuvers Ft. Riley, Kans.; chief of staff USAR Command, Ft. McPherson, Ga. Asst. prof. U.S. Mil. Acad.

ZAISER, KENT AMES, lawyer; b. St. Petersburg, Fla., June 10, 1945; s. Robert Alan and Marion (Brown) Z. AB, Duke U., 1967; postgrad., U. Calif., Berkeley, 1971; JD, U. Fla., 1972. Bar: Fla. 1973, U.S. Dist. Ct. (no. dist.) Fla. 1974, U.S. Supreme Ct. 1978, U.S. Dist. Ct. (so. dist.) Fla. 1980, U.S. Dist. Ct. (mid. dist.) Fla. 1981, U.S. Ct. Appeals (11th cir.) 1981. Rsch. aide Fla. Supreme Ct., Tallahassee, 1973-75, adminstrv. asst. to chief justice, 1975-76; asst. gen. counsel Fla. Dept. Natural Resources, Tallahassee, 1976-80; asst. atty. gen. Fla. Dept. Legal Affairs, Tallahassee, 1980-85; dep. gen. counsel S.W. Fla. Water Mgmt. Dist., Brooksville, 1985-89, gen. counsel, 1989-92; ptnr. Foley and Lardner, Tallahassee, 1992-93; prin. Kent A. Zaiser, P.A., Tallahassee, 1994—. Cons. Fla. State Cts. Adminstr., Tallahassee, 1975; mem. Fla. New Motor Vehicle Arbitration Bd., 1998-99. Contbg. author: Environmental Regulation and Litigation in Florida, 1980-84. Campaign chmn. Vince Fechtel for State Rep. of Fla., Leesburg, 1972. Mem. Jefferson County Bar Assn., Govs. Club. Democrat. Episcopalian. Home: 3286 Longleaf Rd Tallahassee FL 32310-6406 Office: PO Box 6045 Tallahassee FL 32314-6045 Home Phone: 850-576-2464; Office Phone: 850-576-7600.

ZAITZ, LESLIE LEE, reporter; b. St. Helens, Oreg., June 23, 1955; s. Clarence and Joanne (Kness) Z.; m. Julie Grenz, Feb. 24, 1981 (div. Aug. 1986); children: Grant, Dain; m. Scotta Callister, Oct. 16, 1987. Student, U. Oreg., 1974-75, Portland State U., Oreg., 1975-76. Reporter Springfield News, Oreg., 1974-76, The Oregonian, Portland, Oreg., 1976-87, now sr. investigative reporter; pres. Wheatland Pub. Corp., Keizer, Oreg., 1987; pub. Keizertimes, Keizer, Oreg., 1987. Author: (reference book) Paper Trail, 1981; pub. South Salem Times, Salem, Oreg., 1988. Mem. Keizer Bus. Retention and Devel. Commn., 1988; bd. dirs. Salem (Oreg.) chpt. ARC, 1989. Co-recipient George Polk award for Nat. Reporting, 2006; recipient Bruce Baer Award, 1978, 1981, 1999, 2001. Mem. Investigative Reporters and Editors, Oreg. Newspaper Pubs. Assn., Salem C. of C. (bd. dirs. 1989). Democrat. Office: The Oregonian 1320 SW Broadway Portland OR 97201 Office Phone: 503-585-0985. E-mail: leszaitz@news.oregonian.com. *

ZAITZEFF, ROGER MICHAEL, lawyer; b. Detroit, June 25, 1940; s. Peter and Mary (Fedchenia) Z.; children: Zachary, Natasha, Zoe, Peter. BA with high honors and high distinction, U. Mich., 1962; MA with distinction, U. Calif., Berkeley, 1963, JD, 1969. Bar: NY 1970, US Dist. Ct. (so. dist.) NY 1975, US Ct. Appeals (2d cir.) 1975, DC 1985. Assoc. Seward & Kissel, NYC, 1969-77, ptnr., 1977-94, Latham & Wakins, NYC, 1994-2000, LeBoeuf Lamb Greene & MacRae, NYC, 2000—02, Swidler Berlin LLP, NYC, 2002—05, Sheppard Mullin Richter & Hampton LLP, NYC, 2005—. Contbr. articles to profl. jours. Mem. Tribar Opinion Com., 1990-93. Heller grantee U. Mich., 1962; recipient William Jennings Bryan Prize. Fellow: Am. Bar Found. (life); mem.: Phi Beta Kappa Assocs. Office: Sheppard Mullin Richter & Hampton LLP 30 Rockefeller Plz 24th Fl New York NY 10112 Office Phone: 212-332-3837.

ZAJAC, JOHN, semiconductor equipment company executive; b. NYC, July 21, 1946; s. John Andrew and Catherine (Canepa) Z.; m. Vera Barbagallo, Jan. 13, 1973; children: Jennifer, Michelle. AAS, NYU, 1966; BEE, U. Ky., Lawrence, 1968. Project engr. B.C.D. Computing, NYC, 1968-70; v.p. Beacon Systems, Commack, N.Y., 1970-73, E.T. Systems, Santa Clara, Calif., 1973-77; v.p. research and devel. Eaton Corp., Sunnyvale, Calif., 1977-81; pres. Semitech/Gen. Signal, Los Gatos, Calif., 1981-83; mgr. advanced product div. Tegal/Motorola Inc., Novato, Calif., 1983-86; v.p. research and devel. U.S. Alcohol Inc., San Jose, Calif., 1986—2002; staff scientist Mattson Tech., Fremont, Calif., 1994—2002; dir. R&D Silicon Etch Tech., 2003—04; v.p. R&D Zajac Optimum Output Motors, Inc., San Jose, 2004—. Author: The Delicate Balance, 1988, A Thief's Way to Heaven, 1999, Pyramids, Prophecy and 666, 2000; guest TV and radio. Achievements include patents in field.

ZAJICEK, JERONYM, retired music educator; b. Krasne Brezno, Czechoslovakia, Nov. 10, 1926; came to U.S., 1952; s. Frantisek Zajicek and Emilie (Lauterkranz) Zajickova. Studied with, Otakar Jeremias, Prague, Czechoslovakia, 1946—49; student, Charles U., Prague, Czechoslovakia, 1946-49; MusB, Roosevelt U., 1957, MusM, 1958; studied with, K.B. Jirak, Paul A. Pisk; PhD, Charles U., Prague, 1990. Music program dir. for Czechoslovak sect. Radio Free Europe, Munich, 1950-52; prof. theory and composition Loop Coll., Chgo., 1964-96; ret. Composer Clarinet Sonata, 1958, Sinfonietta for large orch., 1958, Cello Sonata, 1975; recorded Concertino for flute and string orch., 1973, Willie Schwegler Flute and Cologne Radio Orch., String Quartet, 1963, Sonatina for flute, clarinet and bassoon, 1966, Pater Noster for mixed chorus, 1990, Twenty Czech Carols, 2001, Twenty Moravian Carols for four part children chorus, 2002, Twenty Carols From Slovakia, 2004. Oliver Ditson fellow, 1956, 57; 1st prize Violin Sonata Internat. Soc. for Contemporary Music (Chgo. chpt. 1964); named hon. citizen Hrochuv Tynec, Czech Republic, 1998. Roman Catholic. Home: 4230 Prescott Ave Lyons IL 60534-1537 Office: Harold Washington Coll 30 E Lake St Chicago IL 60601-2403

ZAK, ROBERT JOSEPH, lawyer; b. Steubenville, Ohio, July 29, 1946; s. Joseph and Pearl (Munyas) Zak; m. Kristy Hubbard Winkler, Sept. 13, 1980; children: Elizabeth Adele, Robert Joseph Jr, Barbara Ann. BS, W.Va. U., 1968, JD, 1975. Bar: WVa 1975, US Dist Ct (so dist) WVa 1975, US Dist Ct (no dist) WVa 1989, US Ct Appeals (4th cir) 1990. Staff atty. Pub. Svc. Commn. of W.Va., Charleston, 1975-76; assoc. Preiser & Wilson L.C., Charleston, 1976-81, ptnr., 1981-85; sr. ptnr. Zak & Assocs., Charleston, 1985—. Hearing examiner W.Va. Bd. Regents, Charleston, 1987—90; spl. asst. atty. gen. State of W.Va., 1987—90; mem. Workers Compensation Appeals Bd., 1991—97, 2001—04. Chmn. West Va. Support Enforcement Commn., 2003—. With US Army, 1969—71, Vietnam. Fellow: Am Acad Matrimonial Lawyers; mem.: Order Barristers. Republican. Presbyterian. Office: Zak & Assocs 607 Ohio Ave Charleston WV 25302-2228 Office Phone: 304-345-0745. E-mail: zakslaw@hotmail.com.

ZAKANITCH, ROBERT RAHWAY, artist; b. Elizabeth, NJ; s. Andrew and Mary Z. Student, Newark Sch. Fine and Indsl. Art, NJ, 1954-57. Vis. artist, lectr. Sch. Art Inst. Chgo., 1976, U. Calif., San Diego, 1974; lectr. in field. One-man shows include Henri Gallery, Alexandria, Va., 1965, Reese Palley Gallery, NYC, 1970—71, Cunningham Ward, 1973—74, Holly Solomon Gallery, 1977, exhibited in group shows at Franklin Gallery, Cornell U., 1978, Va. Mus. Fine Arts, 1979, Palais des Beaux-Arts, Brussels, 1979, Inst. Contemporary Art, U. Pa., 1979, New Mus., NY, 1979, Galerie Daniel Templon, Paris, 1980, Nat. Gallery Art, Washington, 1980, Indpls. Mus. Art, 1980, San Francisco Art Inst., 1980, Whitney Mus. Am. Art, NYC, 1981, Jacksonville Art Mus., 1981, Galeria Civica, Italy, 1982, Mus. Fine Arts, Boston, 1982, Fay Gold Gallery, Atlanta, 1982, High Mus. Art, 1983, Meml. Art Gallery, Rochester, NY, 1983, Kunstmuseum, Luzern, 1983, Robert Miller Gallery, 1978—79, 1981, 1984—85, 1988, Galerie Liatowitsch, Basel, Switzerland, 1978, Galerie Rudolf Zwirner, Cologne, Germany, 1979, Daniel Templon Gallery, NYC, 1980, Bruno Bischofberger Gallery, Zurich, 1980, James Mayor Gallery, London, 1981, Marcus Gallery, 1984, Inst. Contemporary Art, Phila., 1981, Akira Ikeda Gallery, Nagoya, Japan, 1981, Daniel Templon Gallery, Paris, 1982, 1987, 1991, McIntosh-Drysdale Gallery, Washington, 1983, Harcus Gallery, Boston, 1984, 1987, 1989, Delahunty Gallery, Dallas, 1984, Helander/Rubinstein Gallery, Palm Beach, Fla., 1985, 1989, Asher Faure Gallery, LA, 1985, Yares Gallery, Scottsdale, Ariz., 1987, Sidney Janis Gallery, NYC, 1990, Jason McCoy Gallery, 1994—95, Guild Hall, East Hampton, NY, 1995, Hirschl & Adler, NYC, 1995, Patricia Faure Gallery, LA, 1997, Santa Monica, Calif., 2003, Locks Gallery, Phila., 1997, 1999, Patricia Faure Gallery, LA, 2003, Spike Gallery, NYC, 2003, 2005, 2006. With U.S. Army, 1958-60. John Simon Guggenheim fellow, 1995. Studio: 119 N 11th St Brooklyn NY 11211-1163 Office Phone: 718-486-7735. Personal E-mail: robertraw@earthlink.net. E-mail: robert@zakanitch.com.

ZAKHEIM, DOV SOLOMON, economist, former federal agency administrator; b. Dec. 18, 1948; s. Zvi Hirsh and Bella (Rabinowitz) Zakheim; m. Barbara Jane Portnoi, Aug. 20, 1972 (div. 1990); children: Keith Samuel, Roger Israel, Scott Elisha; m. Deborah Bing Lowy, May 26, 1991. Student, London Sch. Econs., 1968—69; BA summa cum laude, Columbia U., N.Y.C., 1970; DPhil, Oxford U., Eng., 1974. Rsch. fellow St. Antony's Coll. Oxford U., 1974; asst. to mng. dir. U.K. br. Internat. Credit Bank Geneva, 1974-75; assoc. analyst Nat. Security and Internat. Affairs Congl. Budget Office, Washington, 1975-78, prin. analyst, 1978-81; spl. asst. to asst. sec. for internat. security policy US Dept. Def., Washington, 1981-82, spl. asst. to under sec., 1982-83, asst. under sec. for policy & resources), 1983-85, dep. under sec. for planning & resources, 1985-87; exec. v.p. Sys. Planning Corp., Arlington, Va., 1987-90, corp. v.p., 1990-2001; CEO SPC Int Inc, 1998—2001; under-sec. (comptr.) & CFO US Dept. Def., Washington, 2001—04; v.p. Booz Allen Hamilton, McLean, Va., 2004—. Cons. to sec. def. and undersec. def., 1987—2000, 2004—; adj. prof. Nat. Def. U., 1992, Columbia U., 1995—96, Yeshiva U., 1995—96; adj prof., presdl. fellow Trinity Coll., Conn., 1998; guest lectr. War Coll. Author: (book) Flight of the Lavi; contbr. articles to profl jours. Mem US Comn Preservation Am's Heritage Abroad, 1991—95; mem. bd. visitors Dept. Def. Overseas Regulatory Ctrs., 1998; mem. Dept. Def. Bus. Bd., 2004—, Chief Naval Ops. Exec. Panel, 2004—; mem Secy Def Task Force Def Reform; mem bd deps Brit Jews, 1971—72; mem Chief Rabbi's Chaplaincy Bd, England, 1971—72; bd dirs Friends of Jewish Chapel, US Naval Acad, 1997—. Fellow, NSF, 1970—73, Kellet, Columbia Col, 1974. Mem.: Royal Inst Int Affairs (UK), Int Inst Strategic Studies, Coun Foreign Relations, Cosmos Club, Columbia Club, United Oxford and Cambridge Univ Club, Phi Beta Kappa. Home: 817 Lamberton Dr Silver Spring MD 20902-3038 Office: Booz Allen Hamilton 8283 Greensboro Dr Mc Lean VA 22102 Office Phone: 703-902-7000. Business E-Mail: zakheim_dov@bah.com.

ZAKIM, DAVID, biochemist; b. Paterson, NJ, July 10, 1935; s. Sam and Ruth (Sorokin) Zakim; m. Nancy Jane Levine, June 12, 1957 (div. 1976); children: Michael, Eric, Thomas; m. Dagmar Aurelia Stanke, July 30, 1978; children: Tamara, Robert. AB in Chemistry, Cornell U., 1956; MD summa cum laude, SUNY, Bklyn., 1961. Diplomate Am Bd Internal Med. Intern N.Y. Hosp., NYC, 1961-62, asst. resident, 1962-63, fellow, 1963-65; asst. prof. to prof. medicine and pharmacology U. Calif., San Francisco, 1968-83; Vincent Astor Disting. prof. medicine Cornell U. Med. Coll., NYC, 1983-2000; prof. biochemistry Cornell U. Grad. Sch. Med. Sci., NYC, 1983-2000, prof. emeritus, 2000—; chief scientist, chmn. Zmedix Corp., San Francisco. Editor: Hepatology: A Textbook of Liver Disease, 1982, 4th edit., 2002, Disorders of Acid Secretion, 1991, (series) Current Topics in Gastroenterology, 1985, Gastroenterology Medicine Today, 1992—95; contbr. articles to profl. jours. Capt US Army, 1965—68. Named Distinguished Alumnus, SUNY-Brooklyn, 1986. Mem.: Am. Soc. Clin. Investigation, Am. Soc. Biol. Chemists, Am. Assn. Physicians. Personal E-mail: dzakim@pacbell.net, david@zmedix.net.

ZAKIM, TOM EDWARD, history professor; s. David and Nancy Zakim; m. Jill Diane Foley; 1 child, Arielle Maia. PhD, U. So. Calif., 2004. Lectr. U. Calif., San Diego, 2003—04, vis. scholar Berkeley, Calif., 2004—. Mem.: Am. Hist. Assn. Achievements include patents pending for medical diagnosis software.

ZAKIN, JACQUES LOUIS, chemical engineering educator; b. NYC, Jan. 28, 1927; s. Mordecai and Ada Davies (Fishbein) Z.; m. Laura Pienkny, June 11, 1950; children: Richard Joseph, David Fredric, Barbara Ellen, Emily Anne, Susan Beth. BSChemE, Cornell U., 1949; MChemE, Columbia U., 1950; DEng. Sci., NYU, 1959. Chem. engr. Flintkote Research Labs., Whippany, NJ, 1950-51; research technologist, research dept. Socony-Mobil, Bklyn., 1951-53, sr. research technologist, 1953-56, supervising technologist, 1959-62; assoc. prof. chem. engring. U. Mo., Rolla, 1962-65, prof., 1965-77, dir. minority engring. program, 1974-77, dir. women in engring. program, 1975-77; chmn. dept. chem. engring. Ohio State U., Columbus, 1977-94, Helen C. Kurtz prof. chem. engring., 1994-2000, Helen C. Kurtz prof. emeritus, 2000—. Chmn. sci. manpower and resources com. Coun. Chem. Rsch., 1984-86, governing bd., 1986-89; exec. com., 1988-89; adv. bd. State of Ohio Alternative Fuels, 1992-93; vis. prof. Technion, 1968-69, 94-95, Hebrew U., 1987; disting. vis. prof. Mex. Acad. Scis. and Mex.-USA Found. for Scis., 1999. Co-editor: Proc. Turbulence Symposium, 1969, 71, 73, 75, 77, 79, 81, 83; contbr. articles to profl. jours Bd. dirs. Rolla Cmty. Concert Assn., 1966-77, 2d v.p., 1975-77; bd. dirs. Ozark Mental Health Assn., 1976-77; trustee Ohio State Hillel Found., 1981-84, treas., 1984-89, pres., 1989-92; trustee Congregation Beth Tikvah, 1983; bd. trustees Columbus Jewish Fedn., 1989-92; co-chmn. Academics and Scientists for Soviet Refuseniks. With USNR, 1945-46. Recipient Outstanding Rsch. award U. Mo., 1970, Josef Hlavka Meml. medal Czechoslovakian Acad. Sci., 1992, Clara M. and Peter L. Scott Faculty award, 1996, Rsch. award Japanese Govt., 2001; named Outstanding Educator of Yr., Ohio Soc. Profl. Engrs., 1994, Tech. Person of Yr., Columbus Tech. Coun., 1987; Am. Chem. Soc. Petroleum Rsch. Fund Internat. fellow, 1968-69, Socony-Mobil Employee Incentive fellow NYU, 1956-59, Sr. Fulbright Rsch. fellow Technion, 1994-95. Fellow Am. Inst. Chem. Engrs.; mem. Am. Chem. Soc., Soc. of Rheology, Am. Soc. Engring. Edn., U. Mo. Acad. Chem. Engrs., Sigma Xi, Phi Lambda Upsilon, Phi Eta Sigma, Alpha Chi Sigma, Tau Beta Pi, Phi Kappa Phi. Jewish. Achievements include patents in field. Office: Ohio State U 140 W 19th Ave Columbus OH 43210-1110 Business E-Mail: zakin.1@osu.edu.

ZAKTSMAN, YONA R., business owner; b. Laguna Beach, Calif., Apr. 2, 1971; d. Alfred Neil and Lily Katherine (Nguyen) Gelberg; m. Michael Robert Zaktsman, May 12, 1999; children: Lucas Scott, Lani Mae. BFA, Lagune Coll. Art and Design, Calif., 1993; BA in Art History and Bus., Calif. State U., Irvine, 1997. Assoc. Marshall Galleries, Laguna Beach, Calif., 1997—2000; asst. designer Bryan Michael Gallery, 2000—02, head designer, 2002—05; co-owner Meriks and Zaktsman Studios, San Diego, 2005—. Mem., sec. San Diego Inter-Mus. Promotion Coun., 2006—. Sunday sch. tchr. St. Edward's Cath. Ch., Dana Point, Calif., 2000—04. Mem.: Omicron Delta Kappa, Kappa Kappa Gamma. Independent. Roman Catholic. Avocations: painting, travel, photography.

ZALAVRAS, CHARALAMPOS, orthopedic surgeon; arrived in U.S., 2000; s. Georgios Zalavras and Maria Zalavra. Attended, Aristoteleion U. Med. Sch., Greece, 1991; PhD, U. Ioannina, Greece, 2000. Cert. orthop.

surgeon Ministry of Health, Greece, European Union, physician's cert. of registration Med. Bd. Calif. Resident dept. orthop. surgery U. Ioannina, Ioannina, Greece, 1996—2000; from clin. rsch. fellow to assoc. prof. Dept. Orthop. Surgery U. So. Calif., LA, 2000—06, assoc. prof. Dept. Orthop. Surgery, 2006—. Recipient Best Scientific Work award, Balkan Congress Orthops., 1997, Best Resident, Fellow Paper award, Arthroscopy Assn. No. Am., 2002, Marshall Urist Young Investigator award, Assn. Bone and Joint Surgeons, 2003. Mem.: Hellenic Soc. for Reconstructive Microsurgery, Hellenic Soc. for Surgery of Hand, Hellenic Assn. Orthop. Surgery and Traumatology, European Soc. Sports Traumatology, Knee Surgery and Arthroscopy, Western Orthop. Assn. Office: USC Med Ctr 1200 N State St GNH 3900 Los Angeles CA 90033 Office Phone: 323-226-7346. Office Fax: 323-226-4051. Business E-Mail: zalavras@usc.edu.

ZALAZNICK, LAUREN, broadcast executive; married; 3 children. Grad., Brown U. With MTV Networks, USA Cable; sr. v.p. original programming & devel. VH1; exec. v.p. network enterprises NBC Universal Television Networks, pres. Trio Networks, 2002—05, pres. Bravo Network, 2004—. Named one of 100 Most Powerful Women in Entertainment, Hollywood Reporter, 2006. Office: NBC Universal Television Group 30 Rockefeller Plz New York NY 10112 Office Phone: 212-664-4444. Office Fax: 212-664-3720. *

ZALAZNICK, SHELDON, retired editor, journalist; b. Bronx, Aug. 6, 1928; s. Samuel and Esther Leah (Schneiderman) Z.; m. Vera Altobelli, Apr. 4, 1953; 1 dau., Andrea. BA, NYU, 1948; MA, Tchrs. Coll. Columbia, 1950. Tchr. English Benjamin Franklin H.S., NYC, 1950-52; assoc. editor Newsweek mag., 1952-56; v.p. Manning Pub. Relations Co., 1956-59; sr. editor Forbes mag., 1959-63, mng. editor, 1976-89; founding editor New York mag. sect. NY Herald Tribune, NYC, 1963-64; Sunday editor NY Herald Tribune, 1964-66; staff writer Gen. Learning Corp., 1966-67; assoc. editor Fortune mag., 1967-69; v.p., editl. dir. New York mag., 1969-76. Home: 458 W 246th St Bronx NY 10471-3330 E-mail: zalaznick@optonline.net.

ZALDARRIAGA, MATIAS, cosmologist, physics professor; b. Buenos Aires, 1971; Degree in Phys. Sci., U. Buenos Aires, 1994; PhD., MIT, 1998. Keck vis. prof. Inst. Adv. Study, Princeton, NJ, 2001—02; asst. prof. NYU, 2001—02; assoc. prof. Dept. Physics, Harvard U., 2003, prof.; assoc. prof. Dept. Astronomy, Harvard U., 2003, prof. Packard Fellow, David and Lucile Packard Found., 2001, MacArthur Fellow, John D. and Catherine T. MacArthur Found, 2006. Achievements include design of CMBFAST computer software tool for astronomy research. Office: Harvard-Smithsonian Center for Astrophysics 60 Garden St MS 51 Cambridge MA 02138 Office Phone: 617-384-9665. Office Fax: 617-495-7093.

ZALES, MARY CLARE, library director; Adminstr. state aid to pub. librs. Pa. Dept. Edn., Harrisburg, exec. asst. to dep. sec. librs., dep. sec. for librs. & commr. librs., 2004—. Mem.: Chief Officers of State Libr. Agencies. Office: Office of Commonwealth Librs 333 Market St Harrisburg PA 17126-1745 Office Phone: 717-787-2646. Office Fax: 717-772-3265. E-mail: mzales@state.pa.us. *

ZALESKE, DAVID JOSEPH, surgeon, research scientist, health facility administrator; b. Feb. 9, 1950; BS, Yale U., 1971; MD, Harvard U., 1975. Diplomate Nat. Bd. Med. Examiners, Am. Bd. Orthop. Surgery. Intern, resident Mass. Gen. Hosp., Boston, 1975-77; orthop. resident Combined Harvard Orthop. Program, Boston, 1977-81; chief pediat. orthopedics Mass. Gen. Hosp., Boston, 1981—2001; assoc. prof. orthopedics Harvard Med. Sch., Boston, 1981—2001; prof. orthopedics George Washington U./Children's Nat. Med. Ctr., Washington, 2001—04; surg. dir. orthop. Children's Hosp. and Clinics, 2004—. Grantee, NIH, 1998—2001. Office: Childrens Hosp and Clinics of Minn 2525 Chicago Ave S Minneapolis MN 55404

ZALESKI, JAN FRANCISZEK, biochemist; b. Bytom, Poland, Feb. 3, 1949; came to U.S., 1979; s. Stanislaw and Maria (Fliska) Z.; m. Margaret M. Toczkowska, Dec. 28, 1971; children: Marta, Monika. MS in Biochemistry, U. Warsaw, Poland, 1971, PhD in Biochemistry, 1978. Rsch. assoc., asst. prof., assoc. prof. U. Warsaw Inst. Biochemistry, 1971-82; vis. scientist Roswell Park Meml. Inst., Buffalo, 1979-82; assoc. scientist Okla. Med. Rsch. Found., Oklahoma City, 1982-85; rsch. assoc. U. Pa. Med. Sch., Phila., 1985-88; vis. scientist Great Lakes Lab., Buffalo, 1988; rsch. assoc. prof. Rutgers U. Sch. Pharmacy, New Brunswick, NJ, 1989-97. Cons. J.A. Haley Vets. Hosp., Tampa, 1985, Great Lakes Lab., Buffalo, 1988, Wyeth-Ayerst Rsch., Princeton, 1994. Contbr. articles to profl. jours., chpts. to books. Mem. Am. Soc. Biochemistry and Molecular Biology. Avocations: antique and modern prints collecting, interior decorating, gardening, photography, basketball. Personal E-mail: jmzaleski@comcast.net.

ZALESKI, JEAN, artist; b. Birkirkara, Malta; d. John M. and Carolina (Micallef) Busuttil; children: Jeffrey, Philip, Susan. Student, Art Students League, NYC, 1955—58, New Sch., 1967—69, Moore Coll. Art, Phila., 1970—71, Parsons Sch. Design, NYC, 1974—75, Pratt Inst., 1976—77. Dir. art Studio 733, Great Neck, NY, 1963-67; sr. art instr. Hussian Coll. Art, Phila., 1970-71; dir. Naples (Italy) Art Studio, 1972-74; corp. sec. Women in The Arts, NYC, 1974-75, exec. coord., 1976-78. Adj. lectr. Bklyn. Coll., 1974-75, Hofstra U., 1977-82, Cooper Union, 1986. One-woman shows include Neikrug Gallery, NYC, 1970, Wallnuts Gallery, Phila., 1971, Il Gabbiano Gallery, Naples, Italy, 1973, Adelphi U., Garden City, NY, 1975, Women in Arts Gallery, NYC, 1975, Alonzo Gallery, 1979—80, Va. Ctr. for Creative Arts, Sweet Briar, 1981, Hodgell Galleries, Sarasota, Fla., 1982—83, Elaine Starkman Gallery, NYC, 1986, Romano Gallery, Barnegat Light, N.J., 1987—88, Citicorp Ctr., NYC, 1988—89, Z Gallery, 1991, Sweet Briar Coll., Va., 1993, Trinity Coll., Hartford, Conn., 1996, Myungsook Lee Gallery, NYC, 1997—98, Slater Mus., Norwich, Conn., 1999, Four Decades of Painting, Retrospective Westbeth Gallery, NYC, 2000, St. James Cavalier Contemporary Art Ctr., Valletta, Malta, 2002, exhibited in group shows at Art U.S.A., NYC, 1969, Internat. Art Exhbn., Cannes, France, 1969, Frick Mus., Pitts., 1970, NAD, NYC, 1970—71, Phila. Mus. Art, 1971, Am. Women Artists, Palazzo Vecchio, Florence, Italy, 1972, Internat. Women's Arts Festival, Milan, 1973 (Gold medal), Bklyn. Mus., 1975, Sweet Briar Coll., Va., 1977, CUNY, 1978, Va. Ctr., 1988, Mus. Hudson Highlands, 1982, Pace U. Gallery, NYC, 1982, Bayly Mus., Charlottesville, Va., 1986, Allbright Knox Mus., Buffalo, 1986, E. Starkman Gallery, NYC, 1987, Nabisco, 1989, Queens Coll., NY, 1991—92, Mus. City of NY, 1993, Nat. Mus. Fine Arts, Malta, 2000, Mediterranean Conf. Ctr., 2001, Westbeth Gallery, NYC, 2002—07, Represented in permanent collections NY Pub. Libr., Met. Mus. Art, NYC, Va. Ctr. for Creative Arts, Nat. Mus. Women in Arts, Mus. City of NY, Nat. Mus. Malta; author: Winged Spirits, 1995; co-author: COW/LINES, 1983. Recipient Susan B. Anthony award NOW, 1986; MacDowell fellow, 1971—, Ragdale fellow, 1986—, Va. Ctr. for Creative Arts fellow, 1976—, Tyrone Guthrie Ctr. fellow, 1991; grantee NEA/Brown U., 1982, Artists Space, 1988; invited to White House by Pres. Carter, 1977. Mem. Artists Equity, Women in the Arts. Democrat. Roman Catholic. Achievements include represented Malta in UN art exhibition celebrating entry of 25 countries to E.U. 2004. Avocations: music, opera, writing. Office Phone: 212-929-4194. Personal E-mail: zaleskijean@aol.com.

ZALESKI, JOHN R., medical researcher; b. N.Y.C., Aug. 20, 1964; s. Henry Julian and Gretchen Victoria (Anderson) Zaleski; m. Cheryl Ann Giangiulio, May 26, 1986; children: Matthew Gregory, Andrew John. BS, Boston U., Mass., 1986, MS, 1987; PhD, U. Pa., Phila., 1996. Tech. staff Nichols Rsch., McLean, Va., 1986—90; sr. analyst Lockheed Martin, Phila., 1990—96, mgr., 1996—97, chief arch., 1997—2001; advisor Siemens Med., Malvern, Pa., 2001—06, dir., 2006—. Contbr. articles various profl. jours. Sch. dir., pres. Coatesville Area Sch. Bd., Pa., 2005—06. Recipient Prin. Key Expert dist., 2007, 5th Spirit of Innovation award, Siemens Med., 2005—06, 2d Innovation award, 2003—04, Critical Care MVP award, 2003, 1st Spirit of Innovation award, 2002—03, Pres. award, Lockheed Martin, 2000. Mem.: IEEE. Achievements include patents for patient medical parameter user interface system; system for processing image represtative data. Avocations: sailing, bicycling, weight-lifting, music. Office: Siemens Med 51 Valley Stream Pkwy Malvern PA 19355 Business E-Mail: john.zaleski@siemens.com.

ZALESKI-VEGAZO, ILENE, librarian; b. Worcester, Mass., Sept. 26, 1946; d. John Dominic and Emily Viola (Jarvais) Z. BS in Zoology cum laude, U. Mass., 1968; MLS, U. R.I., 1973. Biology tchr. Northampton (Mass.) Sch. for Girls, 1968-69; asst. circulation libr. U. R.I. Libr., Kingston, 1972-73, audiovisual cataloger computerized cataloging libr., 1973-75; asst. editor Deep Sea Rsch/Oceanographic Abstracts and Bibliography, Woods Hole, Mass., 1977; scientific book reviewer Small Press Rev., Vt., 1977-78; assoc. editor Oceanographic Lit. Rev., Woods Hole, 1978-83; cons. editor RP Record in Natural Resources and Environ. Mgmt., Woods Hole, 1983-84; sr. editor Woods Hole Data Base, 1983-84; asst. to dir. North Miami Pub. Libr., 1984—2002, dir., 2002—06. Ofcl. del. Gov.'s Conf. on Librs. and Info. Svcs., 1990; judge Benjamin Franklin Awards Competition, 1996-2006. Named Vol. of Yr. Learn to Read Vols. of Miami, 1989; Ilene Zaleski Day named in City of North Miami, 1991, 94, 2006; recipient Key to City of North Miami, 2006. Mem. ALA, Fla. Pub. Libr. Assn. (dir.-at large 1994—, sec. 1993, Libr. Employee of Yr. 1989-90), North Miami Woman's Club (pres. 1993-95, v.p. 1991-93, treas. 1989-91), Fla. Libr. Assn. (chair awards com. 2005-06), Dade County LIbr. Assn. (scholarship chair 2004-05), Assn. Fla. Laubach Orgns. (pres. 1990-91), Train Collectors Assn. Avocations: reading, bicycling, aerobics, travel, toy trains. Office: North Miami Pub Libr 835 NE 132nd St Miami FL 33161-4116 Home Phone: 386-740-1293; Office Phone: 305-891-5535. Business E-Mail: izbabycar@aol.com.

ZALEZNIK, ABRAHAM, psychoanalyst, management specialist, educator; b. Phila., Jan. 30, 1924; s. Isadore and Anna (Appelbaum) Z.; m. Elizabeth Ann Aron, June 24, 1945; children: Dori Faith, Ira Harry. AB in Econs., Alma Coll., 1945, DLitt (hon.), 1992; MBA, Harvard U., 1947, DCS, 1951; grad., Boston Psychoanalytic Soc. and Inst., 1965; D (hon.), U. Montreal, 1999; prof. (hon.), Haute Etude Commercial, France, 2001. Research asst. Harvard U. Grad. Sch. Bus. Adminstrn., 1947-48, instr., 1948-51, asst. prof., 1951-56, assoc. prof., 1956-61, prof., 1961—, Cahners-Rabb prof. social psychology of mgmt., 1967-83, Konosuke Matsushita prof. leadership, 1983-90, Konosuke Matsushita prof. leadership emeritus, 1990—; research fellow Boston Psychoanalytic Soc. and Inst., 1965-68, mem. faculty, 1972—; pvt. practice psychoanalysis Boston, 1968—. Cons. in field. Author: Human Dilemmas of Leadership, 1966, (with Manfred F.R. Kets de Vries) Power and the Corporate Mind, 1975, The Managerial Mystique, 1989, An Executive Guide to Motivating People, 1990, Learning Leadership, 1992; contbr. articles to profl. jours. Bd. overseers Beth Israel Hosp., Boston, 1968—. With USN, 1942-46. Mem. Boston Psychoanalytic Soc., Am. Psychoanalytic Assn. (cert.), Am. Sociol. Assn., Tavern Club (Boston), Belmont Country Club (Mass.). Home: 170 N Ocean Blvd Palm Beach FL 33480-3946 Office: Harvard University Business School Boston MA 02163 Home Phone: 561-832-5270; Office Phone: 617-495-6285. E-mail: azaleznik@hbs.edu.

ZALIAPIN, ILYA, statistician; b. Chelyabinsk, Russia, Mar. 6, 1973; s. Vladimir Zalyapin and Nelly Zalyapina; m. Elena Tchigriaeva, Apr. 30, 1999; 1 child, Vladimir. MSc, Lomonosov Moscow State U., 1995; PhD, Russian Acad. Sci., 1999. Rsch. scientist MITPAN, Russian Acad. Sci., Moscow, 1994—2001; postdoctoral fellow U. Calif. Inst. Geophys. and Planet. Phys., LA, 1999—2001, rschr., 2001—06; asst. prof. dept. math. and stats. U. Nev., Reno, 2006—. Mem.: So. Calif. Earthquake Ctr., Inst. of Math. Stats., Am. Geophys. Union. Office: U Nevada Dept Math and Stat 084 Reno NV 89557 Home: 2433 Crestone Dr Reno NV 89523 Office Phone: 775-784-6077. Personal E-mail: zal@unr.edu.

ZALK, DAVID MARK, industrial hygienist, occupational health researcher; b. Boston, Sept. 21, 1964; s. Bertram Marcus and Sophia Abrams Zalk; m. Janice Kirsh; children: Joshua Aaron, Jacob Benjamin, Jesse Hirsh. BA in Environ. Studies and Chemistry, U. Calif., Santa Barbara, 1987; MPH in Indsl. Hygiene, U. Calif., Berkeley, 1994; student, Delft U. Tech., Netherlands, 2006—. Cert. indsl. hygienist Am. Bd. of Indsl. Hygiene. Br. mgr. P.W. Stephens Environ., Health & Safety, Santa Clara, Calif., 1988—90; indsl. hygienist U. Calif., Lawrence Livermore Nat. Lab., 1993—. Co-chair, task force 10 preventive techs. Collaborating Centres on Occupl. Health WHO, Geneva, 2001—, expert indsl. hygiene, 2005—; US rep. Internat. Control Banding Working Group, 2002—; co-chair US Nat. Control Banding Workshop, Washington, 2003—04, 2004—05, 2d Internat. Control Banding Workshop, Cin., 2003—04; chair 3d Internat. Control Banding Workshop, Johannesburg, 2004—; v.p. Found. for Occupl. Health and Safety, Cin. Author: Control Banding; A Literature Review and Critical Analysis; co-author: Guidance for Conduction Control Banding Analyses; dir.: (tng. video) The Adventures of Ergoman; contbr. articles to profl. jours. Classroom vol. Schallenberger Elem., San Jose, Calif., 2000—05. Named Jeff Lee lectr., Found. for Occupl. Health and Safety, 2003; recipient award of distinction, U. Calif. Santa Barbara, 1987, John J. Bloomfield award, Am. Conf. Govtl. Indsl. Hygienists, 1996, award of excellence, Nat. Nuc. Security Adminstrn., 2003; U.C. Berkeley scholar, Pub. Health Alumni, 1993. Mem.: Internat. Occupl. Hygiene Assn. (bd. dirs. 1999—2005, pres. 2002—03), Internat. Ergonomics Assn. (corr.; Internat. Occupl. Hygiene Assn. liaison 2001—05), Am. Indsl. Hygiene Assn. (assoc.; internat. affairs com. liaison 1999—2005), Am. Conf. Govtl. Indsl. Hygienists (assoc.; task force chair 1996—97, chair internat. com. 1998—2006, mem. internat. com. 2006—), Brit. Occupl. Hygiene Assn. (assoc.), Internat. Congress Occupl. Health (assoc.; Internat. Occupl. Hygiene Assn. liason 2002—05). Jewish. Achievements include research in metals analysis and detection methods relating to explosive events; patents for ergonomic material-handling device; patents pending for particle glue, airborne small-particle binder and reaerosolization inhibitor; creator and expert of post-detonation sciences. Avocation: soccer. Office: U Calif Lawrence Livermore Nat Lab 7000 East Ave L 871 Livermore CA 94550 Home Phone: 408-267-1413; Office Phone: 925-422-8904. Business E-Mail: zalk1@llnl.gov.

ZALL, PAUL MAXWELL, language educator, consultant; m. Elisabeth Weisz, June 21, 1948; children: Jonathan, Barnaby, Andrew. BA, Swarthmore Coll., 1948; AM, Harvard U., 1950, PhD, 1951. Teaching fellow Harvard U., 1950-51; instr. Cornell U., 1951-55, U. Oreg., 1955-56; research editor Boeing Co., 1956-57; asst. prof. Calif. State Coll., Los Angeles, 1957-61, asso. prof., 1961-64, prof. English, 1964-86; research scholar, cons. to library docents Huntington Library, San Marino, Calif., 1986-96; acting chmn. dept. Calif. State Coll., 1969-71. Cons. in report writing, proposal preparation and brochures to industry and govt. agys., 1957-99. Author: Elements of Technical Report Writing, 1962, Hundred Merry Tales, 1963, Nest of Ninnies, 1970, Weakly Blast, 1960-85, Literary Criticism of William Wordsworth, 1966, (with John Durham) Plain Style, 1967, Simple Cobler of Aggawam in America, 1969; (with J.R. Trevor) Proverb to Poem, 1970, Selected Satires of Peter Pindar, 1971, Comical Spirit of Seventy Six, 1976, (with Leonard Franco) Practical Writing, 1978, Ben Franklin Laughing, 1980; (with J.A.L. Lemay) Autobiography of Benjamin Franklin, 1981; Norton Critical Edition of Franklin's Autobiography, 1986, Abe Lincoln Laughing, 1983, 95; (with E. Birdsall) Descriptive Sketches, 1984, Mark Twain Laughing, 1985, Being Here, 1987, George Washington Laughing, 1989, Franklin's Autobiography: Model Life, 1989, Founding Mothers, 1991, Becoming American, 1993, 98, Lincoln's Legacy, 1994, Wit and Wisdom of the Founding Fathers, 1996, Blue and Gray Laughing, 1996, Lincoln on Lincoln, 1999, 2003, Dolley Madison, 2001, Franklin on Franklin, 2001, Jefferson on Jefferson, 2002, Washington on Washington, 2003, Adams on Adams, 2004, Benjamin Franklin's Humor, 2005, Lincoln's Legacy of Laughter, 2007, Thirteen Essays From the Wordsworth Circle, 2007. Pres. Friends of South Pasadena Library, 1967-70. Served with USAAF, 1942-45, ETO. Recipient Outstanding Prof. award, 1965; fellow, Am. Philos. Soc., 1964, 1966, Huntington Libr., 1993; grantee, John Carter Brown Libr., Huntington Libr., 1993. Home: 2040 Amherst Dr South Pasadena CA 91030-3906 Office: Huntington Libr San Marino CA 91108 Fax: 626-449-5720. E-mail: pzall9@hotmail.com.

ZALLEN, HAROLD, academic administrator, chemist; b. Boston, Apr. 7, 1926; s. Joseph and Lillian L. (Stahl) Z.; m. Eugenia Malone, Aug. 23, 1959. BS in Pharmacy, Northeastern U., Boston, 1951; EdM in Sci. and Math., Boston U., 1954; MS in Organic Synthetic Medicinal Chemistry and Biochemistry, Purdue U., West Lafayette, Ind., 1959; PhD in Analytical Medicinal Chemistry and Nucleonics, Purdue U., 1960. Registered pharmacist, Mass., Ind. With USAAF, 1943-46, combat flier, sgt. 487th bomb group H, 839th bomb squadron; commd. 1st lt. U.S. Army, 1955, advanced through grades to col., 1986; ret.; mgr. Shoppers World Pharmacy, Inc., Framingham, Mass., 1951-53; asst. prof. phys. sci. Portia Law Sch. Calvin Coolidge Coll., Boston, 1952-54; tchr. physics and chemistry Natick (Mass.) High Sch., 1955-56; asst. prof. microbiology Lowell Gen. Hosp. Sch. Nursing, Mass., 1955-56; grad. instr., asst. radiol. control officer Purdue U., West Lafayette, Ind., 1957-58; assoc. prof. chemistry Coll. Pharmacy Mercer U., Atlanta, 1960-61; assoc. prof. to prof., head dept. radiol. scis., dir. Office Radiol. Safety Auburn U., Ala., 1961-66; specialist phys. sci. rsch. div. higher edn. rsch. Bur. Rsch., U.S. Office Edn., 1966-67, head curriculum higher edn. rsch., 1967; head instructional sci. equipment program, assoc. program dir., then dir. spl. projects program NSF, Washington, 1967-72; asst. dean, dir. rsch. and grad. studies Okla. State U., Stillwater, 1972-73, prof. chemistry, 1972-73, rsch. prof. biochemistry and molecular biology, 1973-75; assoc. v.p. for adminstrn. and fin., CEO Health Scis. Ctr. Campus U. Okla., Oklahoma City and Tulsa, 1973-75, assoc. v.p. for systems planning, procedure devel. and spl. projects, cen. adminstrn. Norman, 1975—; exec. v.p. Acad. World Inc., 1975—; pres., CEO Malone, Zallen & Assocs. div. AcaWorld Corp., Greenville, NC; v.p., dir. nuclear divsn. Vachon, Nix & Assocs., Atlanta; pres., CEO Computer Profls. Inc., Computer Distbrs. Corp., Malone Group Internat., Columbus, Ga.; sci. advisor Litton Corp./Army Rsch. Inst., 1991, Omega Tng. Group Inc./GIAT Industries, France, 1992—, Wetzel Internat., Inc., 1994—; chmn. bd. dirs. Cons. Unltd., Columbus, Ga. Asst. dean, dir. rsch. and grad. studies Okla. State U., Stillwater, 1972-73; analytical chemist Communicable Diseases Ctr. USPHS, Atlanta, 1962; spl. lectr. NSF Radiobiology Inst., Tuskegee U., 1963-64, head instrnl. sci. equipment program, assoc. program dir., dir. spl. projects program, 1967-72; pres. Pres.'s Sci. and Technol. Adv. Commn., Washington; v.p. Okla. Coll. Osteo. Medicine and Surgery, Tulsa; Gov. NC primary alt. to So. States Energy Bd., 1984-90, exec. com. bd., 1986; bd. vis. Tex. Christian U., Ft. Worth, 1973-76; adv. coun. Coll. Sci. and Math. Auburn U., 2003—; cons. in field. Editor, pub. Jour. Internat 6800 Computer Ctr.; contbr. articles to profl. jours. Hon. chmn. bus. adv. coun., Ala., 2003; rep. candidate NC Gen. Assembly, 1986; mem. nat. rep. congl. com. Recipient Mayoralty cert. of merit and Key to City, City of New Orleans, 1973, Most Outstanding Alumni award Northeastern U., 1996, Comdg. Gen. award U.S. Army Inf. Ctr., 1998; GE sci. fellow Union U., Schenectady, NY., 1955, fellow Purdue Rsch. Found., 1958, Elks Cancer Soc., 1959, Am. Cancer Soc., 1960. Mem. Am. Chem. Soc. (bd. dirs., chmn. Auburn sect. 1966), Am. Soc. Engring. Edn. (long range planning com.), Nat. Coun. Univ. Adminstrs., Soc. Rsch. Adminstrs. (pres. So. sect. from 1974, chmn. publs. com.), Health Physics Soc., Greenville (NC) Area C. of C. (chmn. rsch.), Columbus Club, Rotary (chmn. bull. com. Auburn 1963, bd. dirs. Auburn 1964, bd. dirs. Stillwater 1972-73, Greenville 1981-86, charter pres. Greenville, N.C. Morning Club 1986, 91, 94, Paul Harris fellow, R.I. Svc. Above Self award 1986), Masons (32 degree), Shriners, Sigma Xi, Phi Lambda Upsilon, Rho Chi, Phi Delta Kappa, Delta Sigma Theta, Beta Phi (past nat. sec.) Baptist. Office: Malone Group International PO Box 3682 Auburn AL 36831-3682 Office Phone: 334-887-2085. Personal E-mail: zallen1780@hotmail.com.

ZALOZNIK, ARLENE JOYCE, retired oncologist, military officer; b. Pitts., Jan. 30, 1948; d. Ernest and Frances Elizabeth (Augustin) Z. BS, Carlow Coll., 1969; MS, Duquesne U., 1972; MD, Med. Coll. Pa., 1976. Diplomate Am. Bd. Internal Medicine, Am. Bd. Oncology. Commd. U.S. Army, 1976, advanced through grades to col.; intern then resident in internal medicine Madigan Army Med. Ctr., Tacoma, 1976-77; fellow in hematology and oncology Fitzsimons Army Med. Ctr., Aurora, Colo., 1979-81, staff oncology, 1981-82, asst. chief med. oncology, 1982-84, chief hematology and oncology, 1984-86, Brooke Army Med. Ctr., Ft. Sam Houston, Tex., 1986-90; assoc. prof., chief divsn. hematology/oncology divsn. Tex. Tech. U. Health Scis., El Paso, 1997—2005; ret., 2005. Clin. instr. dept. medicine U. Colo. Health Sci. Ctr., 1982-86. Contbr. articles to books and profl. jours. Active profl. edn. com. Aurora-Adams Unit Am. Cancer Soc., 1983-86, pres., 1983-86, active Colo. divsn., 1984-86. Fellow ACP; mem. Am. Soc. Clin. Oncology. Home: 324 Sharondale Dr El Paso TX 79912-4250

ZALTA, EDWARD, otolaryngologist, physician; b. Houston, Mar. 2, 1930; s. Nouri Louis and Marie Zahde (Lizmi) Zalta; m. Carolyn Mary Gordon, Oct. 8, 1971; 1 child, Ryan David;children from previous marriage: Nouri Allan, Lori Ann, Barry Thomas, Marci Louise. BS, Tulane U., 1952, MD, 1956. Diplomate Am. Bd. Quality Assurance and Utilization Rev. Physicians. Intern Brooke Army Hosp., San Antonio, 1956—57; resident otolaryngology U.S. Army Hosp., Ft. Campbell, Ky., 1957—60; practice medicine specializing in otolaryngology Glendora, West Covina and San Dimas, Calif., 1960—82. ENT cons. City of Hope Med. Ctr., 1961—76; mem. staff Foothill Presbyn.; past pres. L.A. Found. Cmty. Svc., L.A. Poison Info. Ctr., So. Calif. Physicians Coun., Inc.; founder, chmn. bd. dirs., CEO Health Solutions Internat.; founder, chmn. bd. dirs. CAPP CARE, Inc.; founder Inter-Hosp. Coun. Continuing Med. Edn.; trustee U.S. Pharmacopeial Conv., Inc.; mem. adv. bd. Global Health Sys., Inc. Author (with others): Medicine and Your Money; mem. editl. staff Jour. Assn. Managed Healthcare Orgns., Managed Care Interface, Mng. Employee Health Benefits, mem. editl. adv. bd. Inside Medicaid Managed Care, Disease Mgmt. News, Managed Care Outlook; contbr. articles to profl. jours. Pres. bd. govts. Glendora Unified Sch. Dist., 1965—71; mem. Calif. Cancer Adv. Coun., 1967—71, Commn. Californias, Los Angeles County Commn. Economy and Efficiency. Served to capt. Med. Corps US Army, 1957—60. Recipient award of Merit, Order St. Lazarus, 1981. Mem.: AMA, Los Angeles County Med. Assn., Am. Coll. Med. Quality, Am. Assn. Preferred Provider Orgns., Am. Coun. Otolaryngology, Am. Acad. Otolaryngology, Calif. Med. Assn., Pacific Golf Club (San Juan Capistrano), Glendora Country Club, Ctr. Club (Costa Mesa, Calif.), Sea Bluff Beach and Racquet Club, Centurion Club, Phi Delta Epsilon, Kappa Nu. Republican. Jewish. Home: 3 Morning Dove Laguna Niguel CA 92677 Office: Ste 1123 27136 B Paseo Espada San Juan Capistrano CA 92675 Office Phone: 949-292-1951. Personal E-mail: edzalta@cox.net.

ZALTMAN, MARK ALLEN, federal agency administrator; b. Revere, Mass., Apr. 27, 1948; s. Isadore and Ethel Zaltman; m. Donna Jean Matthews, Jan. 13, 1974; 1 child, Rebecca. BA magna cum laude, U. Mass., 1970; MA, Binghamton U., 1974, PhD, 1995. Claims examiner Social Security Adminstrn., Chgo., 1974-90; labor rels. specialist Dept. Housing Urban Devel., Chgo., 1990-98, Region V human resources coord., 1998—. Tchg. asst. U. Wis., Milw., 1971-72, Binghamton (N.Y.) U., 1972-74; del. Milw. County Labor Coun., 1971-72. Author: Suburban/Rural Conflict in Late 19th Century Chicago, 1998; contbr. articles to profl. jours. Chief steward Am. Fedn. Govt. Employees Local 1395, Chgo., 1974—75, v.p., 1975—79, exec. v.p., 1979—83; mem. adv. bd. fed. sector labor rels. and labor law program Chgo.-Kent Coll. Law, 1998—; bd. dirs. Temple Menorah, Chgo., 2000—. Recipient Achievement award Am. Fedn. Govt. Employees Local 1395, 1976. Mem. Phi Beta Kappa, Phi Eta Sigma. Avocations: reading, travel. Office Phone: 312-353-5950 x2557. Business E-Mail: mark_zaltman@hud.gov.

ZALUTSKY, MORTON HERMAN, lawyer; b. Schenectady, Mar. 8, 1935; s. Albert and Gertrude (Daffner) Z.; m. Audrey Englebardt, June 16, 1957; children: Jane, Diane, Samuel BA, Yale U., 1957; JD, U. Chgo., 1960. Bar: Oreg. 1961. Law clk. to presiding judge Oreg. Supreme Ct., 1960-61; assoc. Hart, Davidson, Veazie & Hanlon, 1961-63, Veatch & Lovett, 1963-64, Morrison, Bailey, Dunn, Cohen & Miller, 1964-69; prin. Morton H. Zalutsky, P.C., 1970-76; ptnr. Dahl, Zalutsky, Nichols & Hinson, 1977-79, Zalutsky & Klarquist, P.C., Portland, Oreg., 1980-85, Zalutsky, Klarquist & Johnson, Inc., Portland, 1985-94; Zalutsky & Klarquist, P.C., Portland, 1994—. Instr. Portland State U., 1961-64, Northwestern Sch. of Law, 1969-70; assoc. prof. U. Miami Law Sch.; lectr. Practising Law Inst., 1971—, Oreg. State Bar Continuing Legal Edn. Program, 1970, Am. Law Inst.-ABA Continuing Legal Edn. Program, 1973—, 34th, 37th NYU ann. insts. fed. taxation, So. Fed. Tax Inst., U. Miami Inst. Estate Planning, Southwestern Legal Found., Internat. Foun. Employee Benefit Plans, others; dir. A-E-F-C Pension Plan, 1994-99, chmn., 1989-99. Author: (with others) The Professional Corporation in Oregon, 1970, 82; contbg. author: The Dentist and the Law, 3d edit.; editor-in-chief: Matthew Bender's Federal Tax Service, 1987-90; contbr. articles to profl. jours. Mem. vis. com. U. Chgo. Law Sch., 1986-88. Mem. ABA (vice chair profl. svcs. 1987-89, mem. coun. tax sect. 1985-87, spl. coord. 1980-85), Am. Law Inst., Am. Bar Retirement Assn. (trustee, bd. dirs., vice chair 1990-91, chair 1991-92), Am. Coll. Employee Benefits Coun. (charter mem.), Am. Coll. Tax Coun. (charter mem.), Multnomah County Bar Assn., Am. Tax Lawyers (charter mem.), Oreg. Estate Planning Coun. Jewish. Home: 3118 SW Fairmount Blvd Portland OR 97201-1466 Office: 215 SW Washington St Fl 3 Portland OR 97204-2636 Office Phone: 503-248-0300. E-mail: mort@erisalaw.com.

ZAMARIN, RONALD GEORGE, lawyer; b. NYC, May 2, 1946; s. Leonard Leon and Laura Aileen (Gargus) Z.; m. Kathleen Veronica Durkin, July 20, 1968; children: Ryan, Chad, Jennifer. BA, UCLA, 1969, JD, 1972. Bar: Ill. 1972, U.S. Ct. Appeals (7th cir.) 1972, Fed. Trial Bar. Assoc. Isham, Lincoln & Beale, Chgo., 1972-79, ptnr., 1980-88; pvt. practice Des Plaines, Ill., 1988—2003, Palatine, Ill., 2003—. Coop. atty. ACLU, Chgo., 1982—; litigating mem. Lawyers Com. for Civil Rights under Law, Chgo., 1974-78. Co-author: Media Law Handbook, 1982. Trustee, treas. Palatine Pub. Libr. Dist. (Ill.), 1980-89; co-chair Citizens Com. for the Palatine Libr., 1990-95, Citizens Com. for the Palatine Park Dist., 1994—; co-founder Palatine Pub. Libr. Found.; mem. Palatine Adv. Bd., 1978-79; mem. bd. commrs. Palatine Boys' Baseball, 1983-98, sec., 1986-98. Mem.: ABA (forum on comm. law), First Amendment Lawyers Assn. Office: Suite 700 800 E Northwest Hwy Palatine IL 60074 Home: 200 White Branch Ct Buffalo Grove IL 60089 Home Phone: 847-883-9454; Office Phone: 847-705-3895. Personal E-mail: rgzlaw@comcast.net.

ZAMARRA, GALEN, chef; b. Switzerland; Grad., Culinary Inst. Am. Garde mgr. Bouley, NYC; cook Michel Bras, France, Georges Blanc, France, L'Arpege, France, Union Pacific, NYC; chef de cuisine Bouley Bakery, NYC, 2000—01; co-owner, chef Mas (farmhouse), NYC, 2004—. Named Grey Poupon Rising Star Chef of Yr., James Beard Found., 2001, Best New Restaurant, NYC, Esquire Mag., 2004; named one of NYC's Rising Stars, StarChefs.com, 2006. Office: Mas (farmhouse) 39 Downing St New York NY 10014 Office Phone: 212-255-1790.

ZAMARRIPA, VICTOR MANUEL, sound recording engineer, purchasing agent; b. Matamoros, Tamaulipas, Mexico, Sept. 27, 1959; s. Preston Lee Jobe and Elidia Zamarripa Jobe. Grad., C.E. Vail H.S., La Feria, Texas, 1977. Cert. audio rec. engr., Tex., 2000. Mem. com. La Fiesta De La Feria, Tex., 1999—; chief audio engr. Valley Internat. Christian Ctr., San Benito, Tex., 1999—2005. Cons., installer, engr. Missing Lynck Prodns., La Feria, Tex., 1974—. Prodr.(rec. and mixing engr.): rec. studios. Leader Valley Internat. Christian Ctr., San Benito, Tex., 1999—2005. Recipient Tejano award, Tex. Conjunto Assn., 2002. Home: Box 6906 1008 S Chelo Dr La Feria TX 78559 Office: Missing Lynck Prodns 1008 S Chelo Dr La Feria TX 78559 Home Phone: 956-797-4718; Office Phone: 956-797-4718. Personal E-mail: vzamarripa@aol.com.

ZAMARY, KIMBERLY KYLE, lawyer; b. Lexington, Ky., June 27, 1975; BA in Hist., Ohio State U., 1997, BA in Polit. Sci., 1997; JD, U. Cin., 2000. Bar: Ohio 2000, Ky. 2001, US Dist. Ct. Southern Dist. Ohio 2001, US Dist. Ct. Eastern Dist. Ky. 2001, US Ct. of Appeals Sixth Cir. 2002. Assoc. Kohnen & Patton LLP, Cin. Named one of Ohio's Rising Stars, Super Lawyers, 2006. Mem.: Ky. Bar Assn., Ohio State Bar Assn., Cin. Bar Assn. Office: Kohnen & Patton LLP PNC Ctr Ste 800 201 E Fifth St Cincinnati OH 45202 Office Phone: 513-381-0656. Office Fax: 513-381-5823.

ZAMBELLO, FRANCESCA, opera and theater director; b. NYC, Aug. 24, 1956; BA, Colgate U., 1978. Asst. dir. Lyric Opera of Chgo., 1981-82, San Francisco Opera, 1983-84. Guest dir. San Francisco Opera, Teatro La Fenice, Houston Grand Opera, Met. Opera, Seattle Opera, Royal Opera House, Covent Garden, Bastille, Opera de Paris, Teatro alla Scalla, Royal Nat. Theater, London; recent operatic works include Les Troyens, 2003, William Tell, 2003, Fiery Angel, 2004, Salome, 2004, An American Tragedy, 2005, Porgy & Bess, 2005, La Bohème, 2006, Die Walküre, 2007; dir. stage prodn. Napoleon, 2000, West Side Story, 2004, Aladdin, The Little Prince, 2004, Prairie, 2006, Rebecca, 2006, Showboat, 2006, Disney's The Little Mermaid, 2007. Recipient Chevalier des Arts et des Lettres, Russian Fedn. medal for Svc. to Culture, 3 Olivier awards, London Soc. Theaters; Grantee Nat. Opera Inst. Office: ICM 40 W 57th St Fl 16 New York NY 10019-4098 *

ZAMBIE, ALLAN JOHN, lawyer; b. Cleve., June 9, 1935; s. Anton J. and Martha (Adamski) Z.; m. Nancy Hall, Sept. 22, 1973. Student, Ohio U., 1953-54; BA, Denison U., 1957; LL.B., Western Res. U. (now Case Western Res. U.), 1960. Bar: Ohio 1960. Asso. firm Hribar and Conway, Euclid, Ohio, 1961-63; staff atty. The Higbee Co., Cleve., 1963-67, asst. sec., 1967-69, sec., 1969-74, v.p.-sec., 1974-88, gen. counsel, 1978-88; v.p., sec., gen. counsel The Lamson & Sessions Co., Cleve., 1989-94; of counsel Conway, Marken, Wyner, Kurant & Kern Co., LPA, Cleve., 1994-95; v.p.-sec. John P. Murphy Found., Cleve., 1996-2000, exec. v.p., 2001—. V.p., sec. Kulas Found., 2001—06, v.p., sec., treas. Kulas Found., 2006-. Trustee Cleve. Music Sch. Settlement, pres. bd. trustees, 1980—82, treas., 1996—2001; trustee N.E. Ohio affiliate Am. Heart Assn., 1989—96. With US Army, 1960—61. Mem.: Am. Soc. Corporate Secs. (nat. v.p. 1977—), Cleve. Bar Assn., Ohio Bar Assn. Office: 50 Pub Sq Ste 924 Cleveland OH 44113-2203 Home: 25243 Bryden Rd Beachwood OH 44122 Office Phone: 216-623-4772. Business E-Mail: azambie@murphykulas.org.

ZAMBOLDI, RICHARD HENRY, lawyer; b. Kittanning, Pa., Nov. 22, 1941; s. Henry F. and Florence E. (Colligan) Z.; m. Maria Therese Reiser, Aug. 12, 1967; children: Elizabeth M., Richard H. Jr., Margaret B. BBA, St. Bonaventure U., 1963; JD, Villanova U., 1966. Bar: U.S. Dist. Ct. (we. dist.) Pa. 1966, Pa. 1968, U.S. Ct. Appeals (3d cir.) 1970, U.S. Supreme Ct. 1981. Law clk. U.S. Dist. Ct. (we. dist.) Pa., Pitts., 1966-67; atty. Nat. Labor Rels. Bd., Pitts., 1967-68; assoc. Kanehann & McDonald, Allentown, Pa., 1968-69; ptnr. Elderkin Martin Kelly Messina & Zamboldi, Erie, Pa., 1969-90, Knox McLaughlin Gornall & Sennett, Erie, 1990—, pres., 1997—2006. Author (student articles) Villanova Law Rev., 1964-65, editor, 1965-66. Mem. Pa. Bar Assn., Erie County Bar Assn. Republican. Roman Catholic. Home: 6206 Lake Shore Dr Erie PA 16505-1013 Office: Knox McLaughlin Gornall & Sennett 120 W 10th St Erie PA 16501-1410 Office Phone: 814-459-2800. Business E-Mail: rzamboldi@kmgslaw.com.

ZAMBONE, ALANA MARIA, special education educator, consultant; b. Vineland, NJ, Sept. 17, 1952; d. L. Alan and Joyce (Bernero) Z. AB in Spl. Edn. and Elem. Edn., U. N.C., Chapel Hill, 1974; MS in Human Devel. Liaison, George Peabody Coll. Tchrs., 1978; PhD in Spl. Edn., Vanderbilt U., 1984. Cert. spl. edn., elem. edn., visual impairments, mental retardation, N.C. Tchr., counselor Orange County Assn. for Retarded Citizens, Chapel Hill, N.C., 1973-74; lead tchr. Shelbyville-Bedford (Tenn.) County Adult Svc. Ctr., 1974; program coord. Dickson (Tenn.) County Adult Svcs., 1974-75; dept. head, habilitative svcs. CloverBottom Devel. Ctr., Nashville, Tenn., 1975-76; exec. dir. Waves, Inc. Adult Svcs., Fairview, Tenn., 1976-77; from vocat. cons. to liaison, Peabody Tchrs. Coll. Vanderbilt U., 1977-80; chairperson, bd. dirs. Residential Svcs., Inc., Nashville, 1976-80; asst. prof., coord., dept. curriculum N.C. State U., Raleigh, N.C., 1981-84; coord. and asst. prof., div. spl. edn. Minot (N.D.) State U., 1984-86; coord. internat. outreach svcs. Hilton-Perkins Internat. Program Perkins Sch. for the Blind, Watertown, Mass., 1989-94; assoc. prof., dir. Inst. for Visually Impaired Pa. Coll. Optometry, Phila., 1994—. Co-founder, sr. rsch. fellow Walker-Wheelock Inst. for Equity in Edn.; sr. project dir. exceptional needs assessment devel. lab. Edn. Devel. Corp., Newton, Mass., 1998—; co-coord. grad. program tchrs. of students with spl. needs, grad. faculty infant toddler program evaluator Danforth cmty. devel. project Wheelock Coll., 1995-98; nat. cons. Am. Found. for the Blind, NYC, 1986-89; adj. asst. prof. div. spl. edn., Columbia U., 1987—; co-dir. model infant/toddler program, sch. medicine, U. N.C., Chapel Hill, 1983-84; project dir., mem. grad. faculty severe and multiple disabilities Simmons Coll., 1990—; bd. dirs. ND Coun. for the Arts, Specialized Svcs. for Children, Inc.; adv. bd. Blind Babies Found.; adv. com. Robert E. Miller, Inc., Community Residential Svcs. for Disabled Children; sch. edn. rep. to fac. N.C. State U., sch. edn. fac. senate, others; dir. visual impairment tng. programs N.C. Ctrl. U., 2002-05; affiliate dept. curriculum and instrn. East Carolina U. Greenville, N.C. Grantee Busch Found., N.D. Coun. Arts, Nat. Coun. on the Arts, Dean's Grant Program, Burlington/No. Found., Kate B. Reynolds Found., Nat. Rural Spl. Edn. Consortium, U.S. Office Human Devel. Svcs., U.S. Office of Spl. Edn. Mem. Coun. for Exceptional Children (past dir. div. visual handicaps), Assn. for Retarded Citizens, Assn. for Persons with Severe Handicaps, Am. Assn. Mental Deficiency, Am. Assn. for Applied Behavior Analysis, Nat. Assn. for Parents of the Visually Impaired, Internat. Assn. for the Edn. of the Deaf-Blind, Assn. for the Edn. and Rehab. of the Blind and Visually Impaired (pre-sch. div., multihandicaps div., chairperson multiple disabilities div.), Internat. Coun. Educators of Children and Youth Who Are Blinded or Visually Impaired (co-coord. functions curriculum devel. project 1993—) Avocation: scuba diving. Office: Inst for Equity in Schs Affiliate Walker Home & Sch 1968 Central Ave Needham MA 02492-1410 also: Edn Devel Corp 35 Chapel St Newton MA 02458-1010 also: East Carolina Univ Sch Edn 307 Speight Hall Greenville NC 27858 Office Phone: 919-530-5346. Personal E-mail: azambone@earthlink.net.

ZAMBONI, WILLIAM ARNOLD, plastic and reconstructive surgeon, lab director; b. Reno, Nev., Dec. 10, 1958; s. Roger and Judy (Young) Z.; m. Karen Burke, Apr. 9, 1988. BS, U. Nev., 1980, MD, 1984. Diplomate Am. Bd. Surgery, Am. Bd. Plastic Surgery. Intern So. Ill. U. Sch. Medicine, Springfield, 1984-85, gen. surg. resident, 1985-89, resident in plastic surgery, 1989-91; asst. prof. surgery So. Ill. U., Springfield, 1991-94, chief sect. hyperbaric medicine, dir. hyperbaric rsch. lab., 1991-94; prof., chief divsn. plastic surgery U. Nev., Las Vegas, 1994—, dir. microsurgical and hyperbaric rsch. lab., 1994—; chmn., dept. surgery Univ. Nev. Sch. Medicine, Las Vegas, 2002—; adj. prof., biol. sci. Univ. Nev. Las Vegas, 2002—; adj. faculty Nev. Cancer Ctr., 2003—. Author: (textbook) Applications of Hyperbaric Oxygen Therapy in Plastic Surgery, 1995, Hyperbaric Medicine Practice, 1994, Plastic Surgery: The Requisites, 1993, Orthopedic Clinics of North America, 1993; contbr. numerous articles to profl. pubs. including Surgical Forum vol. XLVI, Plastic Reconstructive Surgery, others. Recipient Jr. Faculty Rsch. award U. Nev., 1994-95, Rudolf W. Gunnerman Silver State award for Excellence in Sci. & Tech., Desert Rsch. Inst., 2000; named one of Top Forty Under Forty, Las Vegas Bus. Press, 1998, Disting. Physician of Yr. award, Nev. State Med. Assn., 2005; named Alumnus of Yr. Univ. Nev. Sch. Medicine, 2003, Top Plastic Surgeon, Las Vegas Life, 2004; NIH grantee, 1994-99, Ctrl. Rsch. Com. grantee, 1993-94, more than 20 other grants. Fellow ACS; mem. AMA, Am. Soc. Plastic and Reconstructive Surgery (plastic surgery edn. found. DATA com. 1994—, breast reconstruction advocacy project 1995-96), Am. Soc. Aesthetic Plastic Surgery, Am. Soc. Reconstructive Microsurgery, Plastic Surgery Rsch. Coun., Undersea and Hyperbaric Med. Soc. (exec. com. sec. 1991-92, clin. trials com. 1993-94, Paul Bert award for outstanding rsch. contributions, 2000), Am. Assn. Univ. Professors, Am. Burn Assn. Roman Catholic. Avocations: skiing, golf, fishing, football. Office: U Nev Sch Med 2040 W Charleston Blvd Ste 601 Las Vegas NV 89102-2245 Address: 3150 N Tenaya Way Las Vegas NV 89128-0443 also: 1707 W Charleston Blvd Las Vegas NV 89102-2351 Business E-Mail: wzamboni@unr.edu. *

ZAMBRANO, CARLOS ALBERTO, professional baseball player; b. Puerto Cabello, Venezuela, June 1, 1981; m. Ismary Zambrano; 2 children. Pitcher Chgo. Cubs, 2002—. Named to Nat. League All-Star Game, 2004. Achievements include allowing only 9 home runs in the 2003 season, making him the second big league starter since Pedro Martinez to allow fewer than 10 home runs in a full season; becoming the youngest Cub in franchise history to start on Opening Day and pitch in an All-Star game, 2004. Mailing: Wrigley Field 1060 W Addison Chicago IL 60613-4397 Office Phone: 773-404-2827. *

ZAMBRI, MELISSA MARIE, lawyer, educator; b. Albany, NY, Dec. 16, 1971; d. Zachary Edward and Donna Marie Zambri; life ptnr. Gina Marie Moran; children: Anthony, Sofia. BS in Fin., Siena Coll., 1994; MBA in Health Sys., Union Coll., 1998; JD, Albany Law Sch., 1998. Bar: NY 1999, US Dist. Ct. (no. dist.) NY 1999. Atty. Sherrin & Glasel, LLP, Albany, 1998—99, Hiscock & Barclay, LLP, Albany, 1999—. Adj. prof. mgmt. Grad. Coll. Union U., 2005—; lectr. in field. Contbg. editor Health Care Law Guide, 2003—; exec. editor: Albany Law Jour. Sci. Tech., 1997—98. Mentor grad. program Union Coll., 2000—05; vol. coach Miss Shen Softball, Clifton Park, NY, 1990—2001. Recipient Student Achievement award, The Wall St. Jour., 1994; Merit scholar, Albany Law Sch., 1994—97, Union Coll., 1995—96. Mem.: ABA, NY State Bar Assn., Am. Health Lawyers Assn. Office: Hiscock & Barclay LLP 50 Beaver St Albany NY 12207 Office Phone: 518-434-2163. Office Fax: 518-434-2621. Business E-Mail: mzambri@hiscockbarclay.com.

ZAME, WILLIAM R., economist, mathematician, educator; b. Long Beach, NY, Nov. 4, 1945; s. Herbert and Miriam Zame; m. Linda Susan Goettina, Nov. 24, 1997; m. Elaine Bennett, 1989 (dec. 1995). BS, Calif. Inst. Tech., Pasadena, 1965; MS, Tulane U., 1967, PhD, 1970. Instr. Rice U., Houston, 1970—72; asst prof. math. SUNY, Buffalo, 1972—76; assoc. prof. math. Tulane U., New Orleans, 1975—78, SUNY, Buffalo, 1976—81, prof. math., 1981—91; prof. math. and econs. Johns Hopkins U., Balt., 1991—94, UCLA, 1994—. Assoc. editor Jour. Math. Econs., 1988—, Jour. Econ. Theory, 1990—, Econometrica, 1998—; mem. com. on status of women in the econs. profn., 1997—99; co-organizer profl. confs. including Exptl. Econs., Calif. Inst. Tech./UCLA, 1999, Econometric Soc. Summer Mtgs., 2002; vis. prof. Inst. Advanced Study, U. Wash., Inst. Math. and its Applications, Math. Scis. Rsch. Inst., Inst. Mittag-Leffler, U. Copenhagen, Va. Poly. Inst., U. Calif., Berkeley. Contbr. articles to profl. jours., chapters to books. Grantee NSF, 1970—88, 1988—; Guggenheim fellow, 2004—05. Fellow: Econometric Soc. (program com. summer mtgs. 1991, 1997, program co-chair summer mtgs. 2002). Office: UCLA Dept Econs 405 Hilgard Ave Los Angeles CA 90095-9000

ZAMECNIK, PAUL CHARLES, oncologist, medical researcher; b. Cleve., Nov. 22, 1912; married; 3 children. AB, Dartmouth Coll., 1933; MD, Harvard U., 1936; DSc (hon.), U. Utrecht, 1966, Columbia U., 1971, Harvard U., 1982, Roger Williams Coll., 1983, Dartmouth Coll., 1988, U. Mass., 1994. Resident Huntington Meml. Hosp. Harvard U., Boston, 1936—37; intern U. Hosps., Cleve., 1938—39; Moseley traveling fellow Carlsberg Labs. Harvard U., Copenhagen, 1939—40; Finney-Howell fellow Rockefeller Inst., 1941—42; instr., assoc. prof. medicine Harvard U., 1942—56, Collis P. Huntington prof. oncologic medicine, 1956—79; dir. J.C. Warren Labs., 1956—79; chmn. exec. com. Dept. Medicine Harvard U., 1956—61; emeritus prof. oncological medicine Sch. Medicine, 1979—; prin. sci. Worcester Found. Experimental Biology, 1979—97; physician Mass. Gen. Hosp., 1956—79, hon. physician, 1979—, sr. scientist, 1998—. Vis. fellow dept. chemistry Calif. Tech. U., 1952; vis. Commonwealth scholar in chemistry U. Cambridge, 1962. Recipient Warren Triennial prize, Mass. Gen. Hosp., 1946, 1950, 1999, James Ewing award, 1962, Borden award, 1965, Am. Cancer Soc. Nat. award, 1968, Passano award, 1970, Nat. medal of sci., NSF, 1991, Hudson Hoagland award, 1992, City of Medicine award, Durham, N.C., 1995, Enterprize 2000 award, City of Worcester, Mass., 1996, Lasker award for Special Achievement in Medicine, Lasker Found., 1996, Lifetime Achievement award, Inst. Human Virology, 2004. Mem.: NAS, Nat. Acad. Medicine, Am. Philosophy Soc., Am. Soc. Biol. Chemists (Merck award 1997), Mass. Med. Soc. (Ann. Orator 1998), Nat. Acad. Scis., Assn. Am. Physicians, Am. Assn. Cancer Rsch. (pres. 1964—65), Am. Soc. Biol. Chemists, Am. Acad. Arts and Scis., Interurban Club. Office: Mass Gen Hosp Charlestown 149 13th St Rm 1494005 Charlestown MA 02129-2020 Office Fax: 671-724-9627.

ZAMFIR, NICOLAE VICTOR, physicist, researcher; b. Brasov, Romania, Mar. 24, 1952; arrived in U.S., 1992; s. Nicolae Zamfir, Livia Zamfir; m. Ecaterina Edita Petre; children: Radu Bogdan, Ioana Livia. Masters Degree (magna cum laude), U. Bucharest, Romania, 1976; PhD, Ctrl. Inst. Physics, Bucharest, Romania, 1984. Physicist Inst. Physics and Nuc. Engring., Magurele, Bucharest, Romania, 1978—84, sr. rschr. Bucharest, 1984—; physicist Brookhaven Nat. Lab., Upton, NY, 1994—97; sr. rsch. scientist Yale U., New Haven, 1997—2004; dir. Nat. Inst. Physics and Nuc. Engring., Bucharest, 2004—; plenipotentiary rep. Romania Joint Inst. Nuc. Rsch., Dubna. Cons. Clark U., Worcester, Mass., 1992—2003; mem. adv. com. 10 Internat. Confs. Contbr. over 190 articles to profl. jours.;, co-editor 7 internat. conf. proceedings. Recipient Hurmuzescu award in physics, Romanian Acad., 1984. Mem.: AAAS, European Phys. Soc., Am. Phys. Soc. Achievements include research in evolution of nuclear collectivity, phase/shape transition and phase co-existence in nuclei, octupole collectivity in nuclear structure. Office: Nat Inst Physics and Nuc Engring PO Box MG6 Bucharest Romania Business E-Mail: zamfir@tandem.nipne.ro.

ZAMKA, GEORGE D., astronaut; b. Jersey City, June 29, 1962; s. Conrad P. and Sofia Zamka; m. Elisa P. Walker; 2 children. BS in Math., U.S. Naval Acad., 1984; MS in Engring. Mgmt., Fla. Inst. Tech., 1997. Commd. 2d lt. USMC, 1984, advanced through grades to lt. col.; with Navy Attack Squadron, Marine All Weather Attacki Squadron, VMA, El Toro, Calif.; squadron weapons and tactics instr.; with Marine All Weather Fighter Attack Squadron VMFA, El Toro; forward air contr. 1st Bn., 5th Marines, Camp Pendleton, Calif.; with 31st Marine Expeditionary Unit, USS Belleau Wood, Western Pacific; test pilot/project officer Naval Strike Aircraft Test Squadron; aircraft maintenance officer VMFA, 1998; astronaut (pilot) NASA, Houston, 1998—, various duties with Astronaut Office. Pilot STS-120 Mission to Internat. Space Station, 2006. Decorated 6 Navy Strike Air medals, Navy Commendation medal with Combat V. Mem.: Soc. Exptl. Test Pilots, Marine Corps Assn., U.S. Naval Acad. Alumni Assn. Achievements include logged over 3,000 flight hours in over 30 different aircraft. Avocations: weightlifting, running, bicycling, scuba diving, boating. Office: Astronaut Office /CB NASA Johnson Space Ctr Houston TX 77058

ZAMMIT, JOSEPH PAUL, lawyer; b. NYC, May 19, 1948; s. John and Farla (Rudolph) Z.; m. Dorothy Therese O'Neill, June 6, 1970; children: Michael, Paul, Brian. AB, Fordham U., 1968; JD, Harvard U., 1971; LLM, NYU, 1974. Bar: N.Y. 1972, U.S. Dist. Ct. (so. and ea. dists.) N.Y. 1973, U.S. Dist. Ct. (no. dist.) Ala. 1989, U.S. Dist. Ct. (we. dist.) N.Y., 1991, U.S. Dist. Ct. (no. dist.) N.Y. 1983, US Dist. Ct. Colo., 2007, U.S. Ct. Appeals (2d cir.) 1973, U.S. Ct. Appeals (11th cir.) 1987, U.S. Ct. Appeals (fed. cir.) 1995, U.S. Supreme Ct. 1978. Assoc. Reavis & McGrath, NYC, 1971-74; asst. prof. law St. John's U., Jamaica, NY, 1974-76, assoc. prof., 1976-78; assoc. Reavis & McGrath, NYC, 1978-79, ptnr., 1979-88, Fulbright & Jaworski L.L.P. (formerly Fulbright Jaworski & Reavis McGrath), NYC, 1989—. Adj. assoc. prof. St. John's U., Jamaica, 1979-83, adj. prof., 1984—; mem. panel comml. arbitrators tech. panel Am. Arbitration Assn., N.Y.C., 1977—. Bd. editors E-commerce Law and Strategy, 1987—; contbr. articles to profl. jours. Mem.: ABA, Computer Law Assn., Assn. Bar City of N.Y. (chmn. comml. liability subcom. 1981—87, chmn. com. on computer law 1995—98, fed. cts. com. 1998—2001, info. tech. law com. 2004—06, internat. comml. disputes com. 2007), N.Y. State Bar Assn., Phi Beta Kappa. Office: Fulbright & Jaworski LLP 666 5th Ave Fl 31 New York NY 10103-0001 Office Phone: 212-318-3000. Personal E-mail: jzammit@fulbright.com.

ZAMORA, MARJORIE DIXON, retired political science professor; b. Farm Randolph, NY, Nov. 8, 1933; d. Wendell Hadley and Jessie (Mercer) Dixon; m. Cornelio Raul Zamora, Dec. 20, 1969; 1 child, Daniel Cornelio. BA, Earlham Coll., 1956; MA, U. Ill., 1968; postgrad., U. Ill., Chgo., 1989—. Tchr. Ridge, Sch., Godsman Sch., Stenson Sch., various cities, 1956-62; with U.S. Peace Corps, tchr. Palmares High Sch., Costa Rica, 1963-64; reporter Lerner Newspaper, Chgo., 1965; dormitory counselor U. Ill., Urbana, 1966-68, 86; instr. Chgo. City Coll., 1968-69; prof. polit. sci. Moraine Valley C.C., Palos Hills, Ill., 1969-94, prof. emerita. Rschr. U. Ill., Chgo., 1985-88. Author short stories; contbr. articles on Costa Rican polit. bus. cycle and economy, land reform to publs. in U.S., Cen. Am.; contbr. short stories to mags. Dir., founder Dept. of Peace Coalition, 2000—05; rep. Beijing Plus Five Regional Steering Com., 1999; appointed to planning com. for a dept. of peace bill Rep. D. Kucinich; pub. speaker Dept. of Peace and Nonviolence & Peace in Space Bills in Congress,

2005—06; active Peace Alliance Orgn. Mem. AAUW (Western Spring area chpt. 1999, Ill. congressional liaison 2000—), Western Springs Band and Orch. Assn. (pres. 1990-91), Am. Assn. Ret. Persons, State Cmty. Coll. Retirees Assn. Mem. Soc. Of Friends. Avocations: skiing, swimming, writing fiction, nonfiction and filmscripts, symphonic music, scuba. Home: 3820 Lawn Ave Western Springs IL 60558-1141 Office Phone: 708-246-7363. E-mail: marjoriez@aol.com.

ZAMOS, JEROME, lawyer, real estate consultant; b. Rochester, NY, Nov. 6, 1938; s. Morris and Anna Zamos; m. Patricia Kay Crampton, Aug. 24, 1962 (div. Mar. 1982); m. Judith Eleanore Fenwick, Oct. 9, 1983; children: Elizabeth, Margaret, Susan. AB, U. Rochester, NY, 1961; JD, Northwestern U., Chgo., 1964; MBA, Claremont Grad. Sch., Calif., 1988. Bar: Calif. 1965, US Supreme Ct. 1969; lic. real estate broker Calif., 1972. Dep. county counsel County of LA, LA, 1967—68; atty. First Charter Fin., Beverly Hills, Calif., 1968—70; gen. counsel Pacific Am. Real Estate Funds, Santa Barbara, Calif., 1971—73, Am. Devel. Co., Costa Mesa, Calif., 1982—85; pvt. practice law Santa Barbara, 1973—82, Woodland Hills, Calif., 1989—; exec. v.p. gen. counsel Mercury Savs. & Loan Assn., Huntington Beach, Calif., 1985—88; ptnr. Zamos & Okojie, LA and Woodland Hills; counsel Butler Century 21 Realty, Santa Barbara, 2002—. Candidate US Ho. Reps., Santa Barbara, 1978. Mem.: ABA. Democrat. Jewish. Home: 5228 Campo Rd Woodland Hills CA 91364 Office: Zamos & Okojie 880 West First St Ste 313 Los Angeles CA 90012 Home Phone: 818-348-7151.

ZAMVIL, LINDA SUSAN, psychiatrist, educator; d. Louis and Stella Savage Zamvil; m. John Mott-Smith; m. John McNeil Angier II, Aug. 26, 1990; children: Lucas Angier, Robin Tucker Angier stepchildren: Katrina Meadville Angier, Judith Tegan Angier, John McNeil Angier III. BA cum laude, U. Calif., Berkeley, 1973; MD, U. Cinn., 1983. Lic. Mass., 1984, Calif., 1988, NH, 1990, Nat. Bd. Examiners, 1984, Am. Soc. Addiction Medicine, 1992, diplomate Am. Bd. of Psychiatry and Neurology, 1988, Am. Bd. of Psychiatry and Neurology, Am. Bd. Child and Adolescent Psychiatry, 1991, Am. Bd. of Adult Psychiatry. Counselor, med. asst. Santa Cruz Women's Health Ctr., Calif., 1977—78, Yolo County Rape Crisis and Womankind Health Ctr., Santa Cruz, 1978—79; clin. fellow in pediat. Harvard Med. Sch., 1983—84, clin. fellow in psychiatry, 1984—90, clin. instr. in psychiatry, 1990—98, asst. clin. prof. psychiatry, 1999—; intern, resident, psychiatrist Mass. Gen. Hosp., 1983—, intern in pediat., 1983—84, intern, resident Chelsea, 1983—85, resident in psychiatry Dept. Psychiatry, 1984—87, psychiatrist Revere Health Ctr. Mass., 1985—86, mem. women's com. Dept. Psychiatry, 1986—90, resident in child psychiatry, 1987—90, clin. assoc. in psychiatry, 1990—, psychiatrist, 2001; intern Med. Sch. Harvard U., Boston, 1983—84, resident Med. Sch., 1984—87, fellow child and adolescent psychiatry Med. Sch., 1987—90; with Pembroke Hosp., Mass., 1985—90, Westwood Lodge, Mass., 1985—90, Lynn and Union Hosps., Mass., 1988—90, The Cambridge (Mass.) Hosp., 1988—90, psychiatrist, 1988—90, 1997—, psychiatrist Ctr. St. Clinic Somerville, 1999—2002, dir. mental health and addictions, 1999—2000; with New Eng. Meml., Stoneham, Mass., 1989—90; staff psychiatrist Cath. Med. Ctr., Manchester, NH, 1990—94, with, 1990—95; staff psychiatrist Meml. Hosp., Nashua, 1990—94, with, 1990—96, McLean Hosp., Belmont, Mass., 1993—, attending child psychiatrist Child and Adolescent Program Dept. Psychiatry, 2002—; with Sts. Meml. Med. Ctr., Lowell, Mass., 1996—99, psychiatrist Teen Health/Pediatric Counseling Svcs., 1997—99; with St. Joseph Hosp., Nashua, 1997—99, Somerville Hosp., Mass., 1997—, Mt. Auburn Hosp., Cambridge, 1997—; med. dir. adolescent chem. dependency svcs. Brookside Hosp., Nashua, 1990—91, med. dir. child and adolescent psychiatry, 1990—94, mem. instnl. rev. bd. N.E. Psychiat. Assocs., 1990—94, mem. med. record and rev./utilization rev. com., 1990—94, with, 1990—99, med. dir. child and adolescent program svcs., 1991—94; intern, resident Chelsea Health Ctr., 1983—85, psychiatrist, 2001; psychiat. cons. STRAIGHT, Outpatient Adolescent Substance Abuse Treatment, Stoughton, Mass., 1986—87, McLean Hosp., Belmont, Mass., 1992—; psychiatrist Human Resource Inst., Malden and Franklin, Mass., 1986—87, Family Svc. Assn., Boston, 1988—90, Ctr. Mental Health and Retardation Svcs., Waltham, Mass., 1989—90, Stoneybrook Counseling Ctr., Chelmsford, Mass., 1989—90; staff psychiatrist Lahey Hitchcock Clinic, Nashua, 1994—96; med. dir. Northeast Psychiat. Assoc., Lowell, Mass., 1996—99, Charter Behavioral Health Sys. Brookside/New Eng., Lowell, 1996—99, Cambridge Psychiat. Svcs., Inc., Psychiat. Recruitment and Placement Svcs. (sub. North Charles, Inc.-affiliation with Harvard Med. Sch. Dept. Psychiatry Cambridge Hosp.), 1996—2000, Mass. Behavioral Health Partnership, Boston, 2000—01; dir. Ambulatory Psychiatry Svcs. The Cambridge Health Alliance, 1999—2000, Somerville, 1999—2000; mem. instnl. rev. bd. Dept. Psychiatry The Cambridge Health Alliance Cambridge Hosp., 1999—2000; dir. Child and Adolescent Psychiatry, Advs., Inc., Framingham, 2001—, Framingham/Marlborough, Mass., 2002—. Bd. dirs. New Eng. Coun. Psychiatrists, Waltham; mem. com. youth and children NH Coun. Child and Adolescent Psychiatry, 1992—94; mem. Psychiat. Adv. Panel Patient Care Assessment Com. Bd. Registration in Medicine Commonwealth Mass., 1997—; with New Eng. States Partnership Divsn. Med. Assistance Pediatric Psychoactive Medication Prescribing Workgroup Commonwealth Mass., 2001—; mem. adv. bd. Families Depression Awareness, Waltham, 2004—; invited spkr. in field; rschr. in field. Expert reviewer Bipolar Disorder and Depression, 1999; contbr. chapters to books, monographs in books, articles in newsletters. Organizer continuing edn. Ednl. Programs, N.E.; chair N.E. coms. Calif. Gov.'s scholar, Gov. Ronald Reagan, 1969. Mem.: Internat. Soc. Bipolar Disorders, Am. Soc. Addiction Medicine (spkr.), Am. Acad. Psychiatrists Alcoholism and Addictions, Am. Acad. Child and Adolescent Psychiatry, Mass. Med. Soc., Mass. Psychiat. Assn., New Eng. Coun. Child and Adolescent Psychiatry (mental health task force 2001—, mem. consortium New Eng. Coun. Child Psychiatry 2001—, mass. chpt. acad. pediat. com. access to mental health 2001—, mem. bd. 2002—05, spkr.), Am. Acad. Child and Adolescent Psychiatry (presenter 1992), Am. Psychiat. Assn. (mem. nat. com. psychiatrists 1985—86, leader pub. mental health programs 1985—86, spkr. 1986, 1991, Mead Johnson fellow 1985—86). Achievements include worked with Depakote/Valproate as both a principal investigator and as a co-investigator studying the effects of lithium on Bipolar Mood Disorder in adults, adolescents and children; contributed to neuroimaging studies with children and adolescents who are on the mood stabilizer lithium. Office: Advs Inc 27 Hollis St Framingham MA 01702 Office Phone: 508-935-0769.

ZANARDELLI, JOHN JOSEPH, healthcare organization executive; b. Monongahela, Pa., July 27, 1950; s. John and Linda (Lazzari) Z.; m. Suzanne King, Jan. 29, 1972; children: Brandon John, Stephen William, Robyn Lynn. Student, Davis & Elkins Coll., 1968; AA, C.C. Allegheny Cty, Pitts., 1970; AS in Acctg., C.C. Allegheny Cty., Pitts., 1991; BS in Edn., California State Coll. Pa., 1972; MPH, U. Pitts., 1979, cert. acct., 1994; cert. non-profit mgmt., Harvard U., 1998; cert. gen. mgmt., Carnegie Mellon U., 1999. Rsch. asst. grad. sch. pub. health U. Pitts., 1973-78; adminstrv. resident Ctrl. Med. Ctr. and Hosp., Pitts., 1978-79; vice-chmn., sec., dir. Allegheny Mountain Health Enterprises, Inc., Oil City, Pa., 1985-88; exec. v.p. Oil City Area Health Ctr., Inc., 1979-88; exec. v.p., COO Grane Healthcare, Inc., Pitts., 1988-90; adminstr., COO Southwood Psychiat. Hosp., Inc., Pitts., 1990-91; exec. dir. Allegheny divsn. Presbyn. Sr.Care, Pitts., Pa., 1991-92; exec. dir., CEO United Meth. Svcs. for Aging, 1993—. Preceptor, mentor health adminstrn. program U. Pitts. Grad. Sch. Pub. Health, 1980—, vis. faculty, 1997—98; adj. asst. prof. health svcs. adminstrn. Grad. Sch. Pub. Health, 1998—2001, adj. assoc. prof. health policy and mgmt., 2001—05, adj. assoc. prof. behavioral and cmty. health scis., 2005—; pres. HCCP, Inc., Pitts., 1983—; bd. dirs. Faith-Based Network, Inc., 1998—; co-chair pub. rels. and mktg. com. Davis and Elkins Coll., 2000—02; co-chair exec.-in-residence com. U. Pitts. Grad. Sch. Pub. Health, 2001—02, exec. in residence, health adminstrn. program, 2001—03, fellow evaluation sci., dept. behavioral and cmty. health scis., 2004—; preceptor, Initiative on Social Enterprise, Harvard Bus. Sch., 2001—; mem. planning com. and faculty longterm care program U. Pitts. Inst. Aging, 2002—05; mem. evidence based mgmt. collaborative Acad. Mgmt. and Carnegie Mellon U., 2007—. Fellow: Am. Coll. Healthcare Execs.; mem.: Delta Omega (Omicron chpt., pres. 2000—01). Home: 2997 Greenwald Rd Bethel Park PA 15102-1615 Office: Asbury Heights 700 Bower Hill Rd Pittsburgh PA 15243-2040 Office Phone: 412-571-5134. Business E-Mail: johnzan@alumni.pitt.edu, jzanardelli@asburyheights.org.

ZAND, DALE EZRA, business management educator; b. NYC, July 22, 1926; m. Charlotte Edith Rosenfeld, Oct. 16, 1949; children: Fern, Mark, Karen, Jonathan, Matthew. BEE, Cooper Union, 1945; MBA, NYU, 1949, PhD, 1954. Asst. to v.p. Spectator Bags, 1947-49; v.p. Glo-Cold Co., 1949-50; mem. faculty Stern Sch. Bus., NYU, NYC, 1950—, prof. mgmt., 1963—, chmn. dept., 1968—, sr. faculty fellow, 1999—. Cons. to industry, 1951—; bd. dirs. Newfield Exploration Co., Inst. Applied Behavioral Sci. Author: Information, Organization, and Power, 1981, The Leadership Triad, 1997, also articles. Served with USNR, 1945. Ford Found. fellow, 1959-60 Mem. Am. Psychol. Soc., Inst. Mgmt. Sci., Acad. Mgmt., Internat. Assn. Applied Social Scientists. Office: NYU 40 W 4th St KMC890 New York NY 10012-0157

ZANDER, EDWARD J., communications executive; b. Bklyn., Jan. 12, 1947; m. Mona Zander; 2 children. BSEE, Rensselaer Poly. Inst., 1968; MBA, Boston U., 1975. Formerly with Apollo Computer, Data Gen., Raytheon; with Sun Microsystems Inc., Palo Alto, Calif., 1987—2002, COO, 1998—2002, pres., COO, 1999—2002; mng. dir. Silver Lake Ptnrs., 2002—03; chmn., CEO Motorola Inc., Schaumburg, Ill., 2004—. Bd. dirs. Documentum, Inc., Portal Software, Inc., Rhythms Netconnections, inc., Seagate Tech., Time Warner Inc., 2007—. Mem. sci. adv. bd. Rensselaer Poly. Inst., Troy, NY, presdl. advisor; mem. dean's adv. bd., sch. of mgmt. Boston U.; bd. dirs. Jason Found. for Edn.; mem. Economics Club Chgo., Exec. Club Chgo.; mem. civic com. Comml. Club Chgo. Named one of 50 Who Matter Now, CNNMoney.com Bus. 2.0, 2006. Office: Motorola Inc 1303 E Algonquin Rd Schaumburg IL 60196 *

ZANDER, GAILLIENNE GLASHOW, psychologist; b. Bklyn., Apr. 7, 1932; d. Saul and Anna (Karasik) G.; m. A.J. Zander, Aug. 5, 1952; children: Elizabeth L., Caroline M., Catherine A. MusB, U. Wis., 1953, MS, 1970; PhD, Marquette U., 1984. Diplomate Am. Bd. Forensic Examiners, Am. Acad. Pain Mgmt.; cert. Am. Soc. Clin. Hypnosis. Music tchr. Wis. Sch. Systems, 1953-65; psychol. asst. Vernon Psychol. Labs., Chgo., 1965-70; psychologist Milw. Pub. Schs., 1970-92, CESA 19, Kenosha, Wis., 1977-78; pvt. practice psychology Milw., 1980—. Fellow Am. Orthopsychiat. Assn.; mem. APA, Wis. Psychol. Assn. Home: 13750 Carson Ct Brookfield WI 53005-4989 also: A Healing Ctr 20860 Watertown Rd Waukesha WI 53186-1872 Office Phone: 262-821-6117. Personal E-mail: zanderga@aol.com.

ZANDI, IRAJ, plastic surgeon; MD, U. Tehran, 1965. Intern Monmouth Med. Ctr., Long Branch, NJ, 1966—67; resident LI Hosp., Bklyn., 1967—72, Allentown, Pa., 1972—74. Office: 2557 Mowry Ave Ste 20 Fremont CA 94538-1614

ZANDMAN, FELIX, electronics executive; b. Grodno, Poland, 1928; MS, U. Nancy, France, 1953; PhD, U. Paris The Sorbonne; doctorate (hon.), Univ. Beer Sheva, Israel Inst. Tech. (Technion). With French Nat. Ctr. Sci. Rsch., Paris, 1950-53; with engring. and consulting SNECMA, 1953-57; dir. basic rsch. Tatnall Measuring Systems Co., Phoenixville, Pa., 1957-62; founder, dir., chmn. bd. Vishay Intertechnology, Malvern, Pa., 1962—, pres., 1962—98, CEO, 1962—2004, chief tech. officer, 2004—. Author: Never the Last Journey, 3 textbooks in electronics; contbr. articles to profl. jours. Recipient Medal of Honor, Electronic Industries Alliance, 2001. Achievements include 39 patents in electronics. Office: Vishay Intertechnology 63 Lincoln Hwy Malvern PA 19355 *

ZANE, BILLY, actor; b. Chgo., Feb. 24, 1966; m. Lisa Collins, 1988 (div. 1995). Appeared in films Back To The Future, 1985, Critters, 1986, Dead Calm, 1989, The Case of the Hillside Strangler, 1989, Back To The Future Part II, 1989, Memphis Belle, 1990, Blood and Concrete I.R.S., 1991, Orlando, 1992, Sniper, 1993, Tombstone, 1993, Only You, 1994, Tales From The Crypt Presents Demon Knight, 1995, Danger Zone, 1995, Head Above Water, 1996, The Phantom, 1996, Titanic, 1997, Susan's Plan, 1998, (voice) Pocahontas II: Journey to a New World, 1998, Taxman, 1999, Morgan's Ferry, 1999, The Believer, 2001, CQ, 2001, Landspeed, 2001, Claim, 2002, Starving Hysterical Naked, 2003, Imaginary Grace, 2003, Vlad, 2003, Three, 2004, Dead Fish, 2004, Silver City, 2004, The Pleasure Drivers, 2005, The Last Drop, 2005, BloodRayne, 2005, Mem-o-re, 2005, (TV miniseries) Cleopatra, 1999, Sole Survivor, 2000, (TV movies) Hendrix, 2000, The Diamond of Jeru, 2001, Invincible, 2001, Bet Your Life, 2004; actor, prodr.: I Woke Up Early the Day I Died, 1998, Sea Devils, 2002; actor, exec. prodr: This World, Then the Fireworks, 1997; actor, exec. prodr., dir.: Big Kiss, 2004; dir.: (TV series) Stop for a Minute, 2001; appeared in Broadway prodn.: Chicago, 2002. Office: Creative Artists Agy 9830 Wilshire Blvd Beverly Hills CA 90212-1825

ZANE, JEFFREY P., lawyer; s. Irving and Pearl Zane; m. Deborah Vicki Balik, 1990; children: Gabrielle B., Alexander B. BS in Econs. and Bus., Hofstra U., Hempstead, NY, 1972; JD, NY Law Sch., NYC, 1977. Bar: Fla. 1979, NY 1983, US Tax Ct. 1983, US Tax Ct. 1993. Tax acct. Seidman & Seidman, CPA, NYC, 1977—78, Ernst & Whinney, NYC, 1978—79; mgr. tax dept. Tennenbaum, Topping & Weitz, CPA, Ft.Lauderdale, 1979—81; vice pres., fin. planning UST Corp., Boston, 1981—84; vice pres., trust dept. UST Corp, 1981—84; pres., shareholder Jeffrey P. Zane, P.A., Palm Beach Gardens, Fla., 1984—. Pres. Attys.Real Estate Coun. Palm Beach County, Inc., Palm Beach Gardens, 2005—. Officer, bd. mem. Temple Beth David, Palm Beach Gardens, 2001—, Diabetes Rsch. Inst., Miami, Fla., 1985—2005. Avocations: golf, tennis, sailing, skiing, cooking. Office: Jeffrey P Zane PA 4800 Riverside Dr Ste 101 Palm Beach Gardens FL 33410 Home Phone: 561-691-3359; Office Phone: 561-627-1277. Business E-Mail: jeff@zanelaw.com.

ZANE, PHILLIP CRAIG, lawyer; b. NYC, Sept. 25, 1961; s. Martin I.L. and Rosalind Carol (Siegler) Z.; m. Denise Janine Wydra; 1 child, Christopher Abelard. BA, Pomona Coll., 1983; postgrad., U. Mich., 1985-88; JD cum laude, NYU, 1991. Bar: Ill. 1991, D.C. 1996, U.S. Dist. Ct. (no. dist.) Ill. 1991, U.S. Ct. Appeals (7th cir.) 1994, U.S. Ct. Appeals (8th cir.) 1993, U.S. Ct. Appeals (9th cir.) 1996, U.S. Fed. Cir. Ct. 1994, U.S. Dist. Ct. D.C. 2000, U.S. Supreme Ct. 2004. Assoc. Mayer, Brown & Platt, Chgo., 1991-93; judicial law clerk to Hon. Morris S. Arnold 8th Cir. Ct. Appeals, Little Rock, 1993-94; assoc. Mayer, Brown & Platt, Chgo., 1994-95, Morgan, Lewis & Bockius, Washington, 1996-2000, of counsel, 2000—04; solo practice, 2004—05; of counsel Baker, Donelson, Bearman, Caldwell & Berkowitz, PC, 2005—. Staff editor NYU Rev. of Law and Social Change, 1989-90, critical legal studies editor, 1990-91; editor Sherman Act Almanac, 1998; contbr. articles to profl. jours. Sec. gen. coun. Arthur F. Burns Fellowship Program, Inc., 1998—. Fellow Thomas J. Watson Found., 1983-84; fgn. lang. area studies fellow U. Mich., Ann Arbor, 1986, 87-88. Mem. ABA (vice chair Sherman Act sect. one com. 1999-2001), Ill. State Bar Assn. (spl. com. on Law Day in Moscow and Kiev 1992). Democrat. Avocation: legal history. Office: Baker Donelson Bearman Caldwell & Berkowitz PC 555 11th St NW Fl 6 Washington DC 20004-1314 Office Phone: 202-508-3490. E-mail: pzane@bakerdonelson.com.

ZANE, writer, publishing executive; Pub. Strebor Books Internat. LLC, Largo, Md., 1999—. Author: (novels) Addicted, 2001, Skyscraper, 2003, Nervous, 2003, The Heat Seekers, 2003, Afterburn, 2005; co-author Shame on it All, 2005; author: (short stories) (collection) The Sex Chronicles: Shattering the Myth, 2002, Gettin' Buck Wild: The Sex Chronicles, 2002; editor: Chocolate Flava, 2004, Breaking the Cycle, 2005 (NAACP Image award for outstanding lit. work-fiction, 2006). Office: Strebor Books PO Box 6505 Upper Marlboro MD 20792 Office Phone: 301-583-0616. Business E-Mail: zane@eroticanoir.com.

ZANETTI, TERESA A., state representative; b. Columbus, Ga., Jan. 20, 1958; m. Gregory Zanetti; children: Daniel, Michael. BA, Harvard U., 1979; MA, St. John's Coll., 1987. Test adminstr. Army Edn. Ctrs., Augsburg, Germany, 1982—85; bur. chief N.Mex. State Dept. Regulation and Licensing, 1989—90; faculty Albuquerque Acad., 1990—97; columnist Albuquerque Tribune, 2000—02; state rep. dist. 15 N.Mex. Ho. of Reps., Santa Fe, 2002—. Mem. N.Mex. State. Bd. Edn., 2001—02. Named Rookie of the Yr., Greater Albuquerque C. of C., 2002; Coe fellow, Stanford U., 1995. Republican.

ZANI, FREDERICK CAESAR, retired financial consultant; b. Medford, Mass., June 9, 1929; s. John and Catherine (Voluletti) Zani; m. Dorothy Ann Menezes, Feb. 20, 1960; children: Gregory Robert, Elizabeth Ruth. BS, Salem State Coll., 1954; M.Ed., Boston U., 1959, cert. in advanced grad. studies, 1967; PhD (hon.), World U., 1986. Lic. sch. psychologist. Tchr., 1954—60; tchr. pub. schs. Gloucester, Mass., 1960—65; guidance counselor Attleboro, Mass. public schs., 1965—90; ret. Former owner, exec. dir. Zani Group Internat. Consulting Co., 1990—. Contbr. articles to profl. jours. Recipient Outstanding Svc. award, Bristol County Tchrs. Assn. Mem.: Ret. State, County and Mcpl. Employees Assn., Boston Children's Hosp. Med. Center Parent Orgn. for Exceptional Children, Mass. Sch. Psychologists Assn., Mass. Ret. Tchrs. Assn., Mass. Tchrs. Assn., Attleboro Tchrs. Assn., Mass. Assn. Children with Learning Disabilities (v.p. Attleboro chpt. 1969—70), Ret. Nat. Educators Assn., Christian Edn. Assn., Internat. Platform Assn. Mem. Assembly Of God. Ch. Home: 45 Washington St Unit 210 Plainville MA 02762-2686 Personal E-mail: fcz1@comcast.com.

ZANIC, MICHAEL G., lawyer; b. 1964; BA, U. Pitts., 1986, JD, 1989. Bar: Pa. 1989. Assoc. K&L Gates, Pitts., 1989—97, ptnr., 1997—, vice-chair, Hiring Com., 1999—2002, practice area leader-litig., Mgmt. Com., 2000—04, co-adminstrv. ptnr., Mgmt. Com., 2005—. Named a Fast Tracker, Pitts. Bus. Times, 2004; named Pa. Super Lawyer, Law and Politics mag., 2004—06; named one of Best Lawyers in Am. for bus. litig., 2003—06, Best Lawyers in Am. for comml. litig., 2006, Best Lawyers in Am. for ins. law, 2006, Litigation's Rising Stars, The Am. Lawyer, 2007; named to Chambers USA Client's Guide, 2006, Guide to the World's Leading Ins. and Reinsurance Lawyers, 2006, Lawdragon 500: New Stars, New Worlds, 2006. Mem.: Pa. Bar Assn., Allegheny County Bar Assn., ABA. Office: Kirkpatrick & Lockhart Preston Gates Ellis LLP Henry W Oliver Bldg 535 Smithfield St Pittsburgh PA 15222 Office Phone: 412-355-6500. Office Fax: 412-355-6501. *

ZANJACOMO, PAULO REGIS, engineering executive; s. Expedicto and Alzira Zanjacomo; m. Hilda Hortensia Valero Tonone, Mar. 27, 1999. BSc in Computer Scis., U. Sao Paulo, 1990, MSc in Applied Math., 1992; PhD in Indsl. Engring., Ga. Inst. Tech., 1998. Asst. prof. U. Sao Paulo, 1992—94; sr. engr. for rsch. and product design Energy Imperium, Atlanta, 1999—99; dir. rsch. and design Altra Energy Technologies, Houston, 1999—2000; chief tech. officer Delfin Energy, Atlanta, 2000—04, Stats. and Research Autom. Trading Desk Charleston, SC, 2002—. Contbr. articles to profl. jours. Mem.: INFORMS.

ZANJANI, ESMAIL D., medical educator, research scientist; b. Rasht, Iran, Dec. 23, 1938; came to U.S., 1959; s. Hussayn D. and Sakineh (Shadkan) Z.; m. Sally Springmeyer, 1963; children: Don, Mariah, George. BA, NYU, 1964, MS, 1966, PhD in Exptl. Hematology, 1969. Asst. prof. medicine Mt. Sinai Sch. Medicine, NYC, 1970-72, asst. prof. physics, 1970-77; organizing chmn. dept. physics Imperial Med. Ctr. Iran, 1976-79, organizing dean basic scis., 1976-79; dir. bone marrow tissue culture diagnostic unit, rsch. physics VA Med. Ctr., Mpls., 1977-87, rsch. career scientist to sr. rsch. career scientist Reno, 1979—; prof. dept. physics, dept. medicine U. Minn. Sch. Medicine, Mpls., 1977-87; adj. prof. medicine and physiology U. Nev. Sch. Medicine, Reno, 1987—2002, prof. dept. animal biotechnology, Coll. Agr., Biotechnology and Natural Resources, 2002—, dir., Stem Cell and Exptl. Hematology Lab., chair, dept. animal biotechnology. Mem., hematology study sect. NIH, 1998—2002. Author: (with M. Tavassoli and J.L. Ascensao) Regulation of Erythropoiesis, 1988, (with M. Tavassoli, J.L. Ascensao, N.G. Abraham and A.S. Levine) Molecular Biology of Hemopoiesis, 1988, (with J.L. Ascensao, M. Tavassoli, F.R. MacKintosh and A.S. Levine) Molecular Biology of Erythropoiesis, 1989; mem. editl. bd. Stem Cell, 1980-83, Blood, 1983-88, Jour. Cell Cloning, 1983-91, Jour. Pathobiology, 1991-; mem. editl. bd. Exptl. Hematology, 1984-87, assoc. editor, 1998, editor-in-chief, 2003; assoc. editor, Jour. of Hematology and Stem Cell Rsch., 2000; bd. reviewers Jour. Lab. Clin. Medicine, 1991—; contbr. chpts. to over 40 books; contbr. several articles to profl. jours.; contbr. chapters to books. Recipient Jay F. Krakaur award, Gladys Mateyko award for excellence in biology; grants NIH, M.E.R.I.T. award, Nat. Heart, Lung, and Blood Inst., NIH, 1997. Mem. Internat. Soc. Exptl. Hematology (coun., pres., 2001, editor), Am. Soc. Hematology, Am. Fedn. Clin. Rsch., Ctrl. Soc. Clin. Rsch., European Hematology Soc., Am. Soc. of Gene Therapy, Sigma Xi (award). Achievements include leading a team of scientists that have created the first human-sheep chimera, which has the body of a sheep and half human organs. Home: 4360 Slide Mountain Cir Reno NV 89511-9530 Office: VA Med Ctr 151B 1000 Locust St Reno NV 89502-2597 also: Dept Animal Biotechnology Univ Nev Mail Stop 202 Fleischmann Agr Office 103 1664 N Virginia St Reno NV 89557 Office Phone: 775-784-7737. Office Fax: 775-784-7736. Business E-Mail: ezanjani@cabnr.unr.edu, Zanjani@scs.unr.edu. *

ZANK, VIRGINIA, literature and language professor; b. Plainview, Ark., Apr. 29, 1942; d. Hayes Dale and Imogene Bridges; m. Martin J. Kugel (dec.); children: Cynthia Gail Kugel, Melissa Gene Kugel-Couch; m. Dale M. Zank, Nov. 25, 1995. BS in Secondary Edn., John Brown U., 1963; MA in English, Ctrl. Mo. State U., 1978. Lifetime cert. tchr. English Mo. Tchr. Higbee (Mo.) H.S., 1963—64; tchr. English Hallsville (Mo.) H.S., 1964—67, Marshall (Mo.) H.S., 1967—93; assoc. prof. English Mo. Valley Coll., Marshall, 1993—. Named Disting. Educator, Optimist Club, Marshall, 1997; recipient Gov.'s award for tchg. excellence, State of Mo., 1996. Mem.: Mo. State Tchrs. Assn., Nat. Coun. Tchrs. English, Mo. Assn. Tchrs. English (pres.). Home: PO Box 658 Marshall MO 65340 Office: Mo Valley Coll 500 E College Marshall MO 65340 Business E-Mail: zankv@moval.edu.

ZANNIERI, NINA, museum director; b. Summit, NJ, Feb. 1, 1955; d. Angelo Joseph and Louise Mary (Brumm) Z.; m. Douglas M. Vogel, Oct. 29, 1994. BA, Boston Coll., 1977; postgrad., Coll. of William & Mary, 1977-78; MA, Brown U., 1980. Curatorial asst. R.I. Hist. Soc., Providence, 1980-81, asst. curator, 1981-83, curator, 1983-86; dir. Paul Revere Meml. Assn., Boston, 1986—. Gen. editor: (exhbn. catalog) Paul Revere: The

Man Behind the Myth, 1988; collaborator: A Most Magnificent Mansion; project dir.: (exhbn. catalog) Let Virtue Be A Guide To Thee, 1983 Mem. Am. Assn. Mus.'s (bd. dirs. 1999-02, vice-chair 2002-03), New Eng. Mus. Assn. (pres. 1998-02), Am. Assn. State and Local History (gov. coun. 2004-), Phi Beta Kappa. Office: Paul Revere Meml Assn The Paul Revere House 19 North Sq Boston MA 02113-2405

ZANNINO, RICHARD F., publishing executive; b. Oct. 26, 1958; m. Anna Zannino; 4 children. BS in Fin. and Economics, Bentley Coll., 1980; MBA, Pace U., 1983. With Continental Group, Inc., Stamford, Conn.; various fin. positions Emery Worldwide, 1984—86, Peter Kiewit Sons, Inc., 1986—91, JWP, 1992; v.p., CFO Saks Fifth Ave., 1993—98; CFO Gen. Signal Corp., 1998; various sr. level positions including exec. v.p. Liz Claiborne, Inc., 1998—2001; CFO Dow Jones & Co., NYC, 2001—02, exec. v.p., COO, 2002—06, CEO, 2006—. Vice chmn. Advt. Edn. Found.; mem. dean's adv. coun.coll. commerce and fin. Villanova U.; mem. Columbia Bus. Sch. Media Forum. Office: Dow Jones & Co 1 World Fin Ctr 200 Liberty St New York NY 10281 Office Phone: 212-416-2000. *

ZANOT, CRAIG ALLEN, lawyer; b. Wyandotte, Mich., Nov. 15, 1955; s. Thomas and Faye Blanch (Sperry) Zanot. AB with distinction, U. Mich., 1977; JD cum laude, Ind. U., 1980. U.S. Ct. Appeals (6th cir.) 1985, U.S. Dist. Ct. (ea. dist.) Mich. 1987, U.S. Dist. Ct. (we. dist.) Mich. 1990. Law clk. to presiding justice Allen County Superior Ct, Ft. Wayne, 1980-81; ptnr. Davidson, Breen & Doud P.C., Saginaw, Mich., 1981—. Mem.: ABA, Genesee County Bar Assn., Bay County Bar Assn., Saginaw County Bar Assn., Mich. Bar Assn. Roman Catholic. Home: 547 S Linwood Beach Rd Linwood MI 48634-9432 Office: Davidson Breen & Doud PC 1121 N Michigan Ave Saginaw MI 48602-4762 Office Phone: 989-752-9595. E-mail: umchiphi@aol.com.

ZANSKY, MICHAEL, artist, production designer; b. NYC, Sept. 30, 1947; s. Louis and Jeanette Zansky; m. Jill DeVanyar (div.). BFA, Boston U., 1969. Exhibitions include Opus Gallery, Coral Gables, Fla., 1990, Berry-Hill Galleries, NYC, 1991, 1993, 1996, Rockland Ctr. Arts, West Nyack, NY, 1998, Calvin Morris Gallery, 1998, Gallery Camino Real, Boca Raton, Fla., 1999, Universal Concepts Unltd., NYC, 2000, 2002, Briggs-Robinson Gallery, 2003, 2006, Gigantic Art Space/ARCO, Black Box, Madrid, 2005, Gigantic Art Space, NYC, 2006, Nassau County Mus., 2007, Silvermine Art Guild, 2007, Fieldgate Gallery, London, 2007; engineer: Edsvik Konsthalles, 2006; performance installation, Manhattan Sch. Music, NYC, 2005, Juilliard Sch. Music, 2005, Cal Arts, 2005, numerous group exhbns., Represented in permanent collections Berkeley Art Mus., Calif., Brooklyn Mus. Art, Kranert Art Mus., Champaign, Ill., Nenberger Mus., Purchase, NY, Whitney Mus. Art, Mus. Modern Art, NYC; Something to Talk About, 1995; prodn. designer, prodn. designer: (films) Kiss of Death, 1995; The Juror, 1996; First Wives Club, 1996; Donnie Brasco, 1997; Great Expectations, 1998; Out of Towners, 1999; Gloria, 1999; Godzilla, 2000; Flawless, 2001; Heart of Gold, 2006; prodn. designer: numerous others; master set painter: (numerous TV programs, including) Law and Order Spl. Victims Unit, 2005; The Sopranos, 1999—2005; scenic charge, set painter (numerous commls., theater prodns.). Mem.: Rockland Found. Arts (bd. dirs.), Sculpture Guild NY (bd. dirs.). Home: PO Box 42 West Nyack NY 10994 Personal E-mail: zansky@optonline.net.

ZANUCK, RICHARD DARRYL, motion picture company executive; b. Beverly Hills, Calif., Dec. 13, 1934; s. Darryl F. and Virginia (Fox) Z.; m. Lili Gentle; children: Virginia, Janet; m. Linda Harrison, Oct. 26, 1969; children: Harrison Richard, Dean Francis; m. Lili Fini, Sept. 23, 1978. Grad., Harvard Mil. Acad., 1952; BA, Stanford, 1956. Story, prodn. asst. Darryl F. Zanuck Prodns., 1956, v.p., 1956-62; president's prodn. rep. 20th Century-Fox Studios, Beverly Hills, 1962-63, v.p. charge prodn., 1963-69, pres., 1969-71, dir., 1966-71; founder, pres., owner Zanuck Co., Beverly Hills, 1989—. Chmn. 20th Century-Fox Television, Inc.; sr. exec. v.p. Warner Bros., Inc., 1971-72; co-founder, pres. Zanuck/Brown Co., 1972-88. Producer: The Sting, 1973 (Acad. award), The Sugarland Express, 1974, Jaws, 1975, Jaws 2, 1978, The Island, 1980, Neighbors, 1982, The Verdict, 1983, Cocoon, 1985, Cocoon, the Return, 1988, Driving Miss Daisy, 1989 (Acad. award, Irving G. Thalberg award 1991), Rush, 1991, Rich in Love, 1992, Mulholland Falls, 1996, Deep Impact, 1998, True Crime, 1999, Rules of Engagement, 1999, Planet of the Apes, 2000, Road to Perdition, 2001, Big Fish, 2003; prodr. Acad. Award Show, 2000. Nat. chmn. Fibrosis Assn., 1966-68; mem. organizing com. 1984 Olympics; trustee Harvard Sch. 2d lt. U.S. Army. Named Producer of Yr., Nat. Assn. Theatre Owners, 1974, '85, Producers Guild Am., 1989; recipient Irving Thalberg award, 1991, Lifetime Achievement award, Producers Guild Am., 1993. Mem. Acad. Motion Picture Arts and Scis. (bd. govs.), Screen Producers Guild, Phi Gamma Delta. Office: Zanuck Co 9465 Wilshire Blvd Ste 930 Beverly Hills CA 90212-2608

ZAPATA, ANGEL, pastor; b. Mayaguez, PR, Mar. 23, 1950; s. Jorge Zapata and Isabel Velez; m. Rosita Zapata, Aug. 16, 2003; children: Angel, Michael, CeLina, Angie, Sarah, Arianna, Natalie Roman, Shaila Salliant. BA in Sociology, magna cum laude, Mercy Coll., 1984; MSW magna cum laude, Yeshiva U., NY, 1995. Chaplain United Chaplains, NY State, 2006, Ordained Pastor NY State, 2006; LCSW NY, 1995; cert. social studies and history tchr. NY State Higher Edn., 1989. Cons. Fed. Govt., 1970—2000. Pastor Promised Land Ch., Bronx, 2007. Sgt. US Army, 1968—71, Vietnam, Japan, Europe. Decorated Combat Inf. Badge US Army, Purple Heart, Bronze Star, Vietnamese Cross of Gallantry. Mem.: Phi Gamma Mu. Home: Radio City Sta PO Box 241 New York NY 10101-0241

ZAPEL, ARTHUR LEWIS, book publishing executive; b. Chgo., 1921; m. Janet Michel (dec.); children: Linda (dec.), Mark, Theodore, Michelle; m. Cynthia Rogers Pisor, 1986; stepchildren: Dawn, Anthony. BA in English, U. Wis., 1946. Writer, prodr. Westinghouse Radio Stas.; film writer Galbreath Studios, Ft. Wayne; creative dir. Kling Studios, Chgo., 1952-54; writer, prodr. TV commls. J. Walter Thompson Advt., Chgo., 1954-73, v.p. TV and radio prodn., 1954-73; founder, pres. Arthur Meriwether, Inc., 1973-83; pres. Meriwether Pub. Ltd., 1969-90, chmn., 1990-97. Pres. Westcliffe (Colo.) Ctr. for the Arts. Author: Sweet Uncertainty, 2001; illustrator: 'Twas the Night Before, The Jabberwock mystery; created game A Can of Squirms; wrote plays and musical comedy scripts for ednl. use in schs. and chs.; supr. editing and prodn. 2500 plays and musicals, 1970-99; exec. editor 210 books on theater skills for secular and religious use. Founding pres. Art Students League of Colorado Springs, 1992; past pres. Colo. Springs Symphony Coun.; past bd. dirs. Colorado Springs Opera Festival. Recipient numerous awards Freedoms Found., Valley Forge, Art Dirs. Club N.Y., Art Dirs. Chgo., Hollywood Advt., 1960-67, Gold Records Radio Ad Bur., 1959-60, XV Festival Internat. Du Film Publicitaire Venise, 1968, Gold Camera award U.S. Indsl. Film Festival, 1983, Dukane award, 1983, Gold award Houston Internat. Film Festival, 1984, 2d pl. award Best New Fiction, Colo. Ind. Publishers Assoc., 2002. Office: Meriwether Pub Ltd 885 Elkton Dr Colorado Springs CO 80907-3576

ZAPF, HERMANN, book and type designer; b. Nuremberg, Germany, Nov. 8, 1918; s. Hermann and Magdalene (Schlamp) Zapf; m. Gudrun von Hesse, Aug. 18, 1951; 1 child, Christian Ludwig. D in Fine Arts (hon.), U. Ill., 2003. Freelance designer, 1938—; type dir. D. Stempel AG, type foundry, Frankfurt, Fed. Republic of Germany, 1947-56; design cons. Mergenthaler Linotype Co. (NYC and Frankfurt), 1957-74; cons. Hallmark Internat., Kansas City, Mo., 1966-73; v.p. Design Processing Internat. Inc., NYC, 1977—87; prof. typographic computer programs Rochester (N.Y.) Inst. Tech., 1977-87; chmn. Zapf, Burns & Co., NYC, 1987-91. Instr. lettering Werkkunstschule, Offenbach, Fed. Republic Germany., 1948-50; prof. graphic design Carnegie Inst. Tech., 1960; instr. typography Technische Hochschule, Darmstadt, Fed. Republic Germany, 1972-81. Author: William Morris, 1948, Pen and Graver, 1952, Manuale Typographicum, 1954, 1968, About Alphabets, 1960, 1970, Typographic Variations, 1964, Orbis Typographicus, 1980, Hora fugit/Carpe diem, 1984, Hermann Zapf and His Design Philosophy, 1987, ABC-XYZapf, 1989, Poetry Through Typography, 1993, August Rosenberger, 1996, (film) The Art of Hermann Zapf, German version Die Welt der Buchstaben von Hermann Zapf, (CD-ROM) The World of Alphabets, 2001, Alphabet Stories: A Chronicle of Technical Developments, 2007; designer types Palatino, Melior, Optima, ITC Zapf Chancery, ITC Zapf Internat., Digiset Marconi, Digiset Edison, Digiset Aurelia, Pan-Nigerian, Sequoyah, URW-Roman and San Serif, Renaissance Roman, Linotype, Zapfino Extra, Optima nova, ITC Dingbats, Zapf Essentials, Palatino Sans, Palatino Arabic. Hon. pres. Edward Johnston Found., Ditchling, England. Named hon. citizen, State of Tex., 1970, hon. Royal Designer for Industry, London, 1985; recipient Silver medal, Brussels, 1962, 1st prize typography, Biennale Brno, Czechoslovakia, 1966, Gold medal, Type Dirs. Club, N.Y., Frederic W. Goudy award, Inst. Tech. Rochester, 1969, Silver medal, Internat. Book Exhbn., Leipzig, 1971, Gold medal, 1989, Johannes Gutenberg prize, Mainz, Fed. German Republic, 1974, Gold medal, Museo Bodoniano, Parma, Italy, 1975, J.H. Merck award, Darmstadt, 1978, Robert Hunter Middleton award, Chgo., 1987, Euro Design award, Oostende, 1994, Wadim Lazursky award, Acad. of Graphic Arts, Moscow, 1996, SOTA Typography award, Chgo., 2003. Mem.: Internat. Gutenberg Gesellschaft, Bund Deutscher Grafik Designer, Alliance Graphique Internat., Am. Math. Soc., Royal Soc. Arts, Dante e.V. (German TEX Group) (hon.), Soc. Scribes N.Y. (hon.), Brno Biennale Assn. (hon.), Goudy Internat. Ctr. (hon.), Alcuin Soc. Can. (hon.), Typographers Internat. Assn. (hon.), Chgo. Calligraphy Collective (hon.), Eesti Kalligraafide Koondis (hon.; Tallinn, Estonia), Wynkyn de Worde Soc. (hon.), Soc. Calligraphy (hon.), Grafiska Inst. (hon.), Bund Deutscher Buchkünstler (hon.), Soc. Graphic Designers Can. (hon.), Soc. Printers (hon.), Soc. Typographic Arts (hon.), Soc. Typographique de France (hon.), Assocs. of Stanford Univ. Librs., Art Dirs. Club Kansas City (hon.), Alpha Beta Club (hon.; Hong Kong), Friends of Calligraphy (hon.), Double Crown Club (hon.), Type Dirs. Club N.Y.C. (hon.), Soc. Scribes and Illuminators (hon.), Typophiles (hon.), Letter Exch. (hon.), Washington Calligrapher's Guild (hon.), Monterey Calligrapher's Guild (hon.), Caxton Club (hon.), Gamma Epsilon Tau (hon.).

ZAPFFE, NINA BYROM, retired elementary school educator; b. Independence, Mo., Aug. 17, 1925; d. Richmond Douglas and Nina Belle (Howell) Byrom; m. Robert Glenn Fessler, June 25, 1946 (dec. June 1947); 1 child, Robert Glenn Fessler Zapffe; m. Fred Zapffe, July 1, 1952 (dec. Dec. 1999); children: Paul Douglas, Carl Raymond. BA, So. Meth. U., Dallas, 1946. Fin. sec. Tyler St. Meth. Ch., Dallas, 1948-49; tchr. Dallas Ind. Sch. Dist., 1949-52, Norman (Okla.) Pub. Schs., 1966-74; chief reader for GED Writing Skills Test Part II GED Testing Svc., Am. Coun. on Edn., Washington, 1990—98; ret., 1998. Adv. com. Acad. Resource Ctr. Moore-Norman Tech. Ctr., 1988-2004. Adv. bd. Norman Salvation Army, 1978-90, chmn., 1986; organizer, historian Norman Salvation Army Womens Aux., 1983-2000, pres., 1985; organizer, past pres. Norman Literacy Coun., 1976—; organizing com., past pres. Norman Interfaith Coun., 1974-93; organizing com., past treas. Friends of the Norman Libr., 1979—; mem. McFarlin Meml. United Meth. Ch., historian 2-in-1 Sunday Sch. class, 1990-2002, lay leader, 1980-81, adminstrv. bd., 2001-2004; pres. Two At Summit Class, 2007. Named Woman of Yr., Norman Bus. and Profl. Women, 1999; named to Literacy Hall of Fame, Pioneer Libr. Sys., Norman, 1995; recipient medal of appreciation, SAR, 2002. Mem. DAR (regent Black Beaver chpt. 1998-2000, state literacy chmn. 2000-02, chpt. sec. 2003—), Nat. Soc. Daus. 1812 (pres. 1889er chpt. 1991-93, state treas. 1996-2000, chpt. sec. 2002—), Old Regime Study Club (pres. 1998-99), Coterie Club (pres. 1996, 2002), Delta Delta Delta Alumnae. Independent. Avocation: genealogy. Home: 2717 Walnut Rd Norman OK 73072-6940

ZAPHIRIOU, GEORGE ARISTOTLE, lawyer, educator; b. July 10, 1919; came to U.S., 1973, naturalized, 1977; s. Aristotle George and Callie Constantine (Economou) Z.; m. Peaches J. Griffin, June 1, 1973; children: Ari, Marie. JD, U. Athens, 1940; LLM, U. London, 1950. Bar: Supreme Ct. Greece 1946, Eng. 1956, Ill. 1975, Va. 1983. Gen. counsel Counties Ship Mgmt. and R & K Ltd., London, 1951-61; practicing barrister, lectr. City of London Poly., 1961-73; vis. prof. Ill. Inst. Tech.-Chgo. Kent Coll. Law, 1973-76; pvt. practice Northbrook, Ill., 1976-78; prof. law George Mason U. Sch. Law, 1978-94, prof. law emeritus, adj. prof., 1994—. Prof. internat. transactions George Mason U. Internat. Inst., 1992-94; mem. Odin, Feldman & Pittelman P.C., Fairfax, Va., 1994-96; mem. study group on internat. elec. commerce conv. and other pvt. internat. law convs. U.S. Dept. of State. Author: Transfer of Chattels in Private International Law, 1956, U.S. edit., 1981, European Business Law, 1970; co-author: Declining Jurisdiction in Private International Law, 1995; joint editor: Jour. Bus. Law, London, 1962-73; bd. dirs. and bd. editors Am. Jour. Comp. Law of Am. Soc. Comparative Law, 1980-94; contbr. articles to profl. jours. Mem.: ABA, George Mason Am. Inn of Ct. (founder, master, emeritus), Am. Arbitration Assn. (panel comml. arbitrators), Chgo. Bar Assn., Ill. Bar Assn. Home: 400 Green Pasture Dr Rockville MD 20852-4233 Business E-Mail: gzaphiri@gmu.edu.

ZAPOLSKY, DAVID A., lawyer; JD, Boalt Hall Sch. Law, Berkeley, Calif. Former litig. ptnr. Dorsey & Whitney and Bogle & Gates Law Firm; v.p., assoc. gen. counsel litig. and regulatory matters Amazon.com, Seattle, 1999—2006, exec. v.p., gen. counsel, 2006—. Office: Amazon.com Ste 1200 1200 12th Ave So Seattle WA 98144-2734

ZAPPA, GAIL, record producer; m. Frank Zappa (dec.); children: Moon, Dweezil, Ahmet, Diva. Recipient (with Frank Zappa) Best Recording Package-Boxed Grammy award for Frank Zappa's Civilization, Phaze III, 1996.

ZAPPALA, STEPHEN A., state supreme court justice; b. 1932; s. Frank and Josephine Zappala. BA, Duquesne U.; LL.B., Georgetown U., 1958. Bar: Pa. 1958. Solicitor Allegheny County, Pitts., 1974-76; judge Ct. of Common Pleas-Allegheny County, 1980-82; assoc. justice Pa. Supreme Ct., 1982—2003, judge. Served with U.S. Army. Office: Gladys Zappa LLC 14 McKelvey Ave Pittsburgh PA 15218-1454

ZAPPE, JOHN PAUL, city editor, newspaper executive, educator; b. NYC, July 30, 1952; s. John Paul and Carolyn (Pikor) Z. BA, Marist Coll., 1978; JD, Syracuse U., NY, 1978. Reporter Poughkeepsie Jour., 1973-75, Nev. State Jour., Reno, 1979-80; prin. Am. Media Bold, Oakland, Calif., 1981-83; reporter Press-Telegram, Long Beach, Calif., 1983-88, city editor, 1988-97, webmaster PT Connect, 1995-97, mgr. new media, 1997-98; dir. new media Riverside (Calif.) Press-Enterprise, 1998-2000; v.p. new media L.A. Newspaper Group, Woodland Hills, Calif., 2000—03; sr. cons. Zappe Media Svcs., 2003—; dir. bus. devel. Classified Intelligence, sr. analyst. Tchr. Syracuse U., 1976-78, Calif. State U., 1985-87, U. So. Calif., 2003—04; prin. Am. Media Bold, 1981-83. Chmn. Local 69 Newspaper Guild, Long Beach, 1984-87. Mem. NAA New Media Fedn., Sierra Club (mem. exec. com. Long Beach group, LA chpt.). Office Phone: 562-252-0686. Business E-Mail: zappemedia@gmail.com.

ZARATE, JUAN CARLOS, federal official; b. Santa Ana, Calif., 1971; AB magna cum laude, Harvard U., JD cum laude. Bar: 1997. Law clerk US Dist. Ct. (So. dist.) Calif.; atty. appellate sect. criminal divsn. U.S. Dept. Justice, Washington, prosecutor terrorism and violent crime sect.; asst. sec. treas. counter-terrorist financing U.S. Dept. Treasury, Washington, 2004—05; dep. asst. to the Pres. The White House, Washington, 2005—; dep. nat. security advisor for combating terrorism NSC, Washington, 2005—. Head Fin. Crimes Enforcement Network (FinCEN), Office Fgn. Assets Control (OFAC), Tri-Border conf., Brazil, U.S. delegation to UAE; head treas. delegation G-8 Counter-Terrorism conf., Florence, Italy; policy advisor criminal investigation divsn. IRS; policy advisor Fin. Action Task Force (FATF). Author: (book) Forging Democracy, 1994; contbr. articles to profl. jours. Rotary internat. fellow, U. Salamanca, Spain. Mem.: Calif. Bar Assn. Office: Nat Security Coun 1600 Pennsylvania Ave Washington DC 20500

ZARB, FRANK GUSTAVE, investment company executive; b. NYC, Feb. 17, 1935; s. Gustave and Rosemary (Antinoro) Z.; m. Patricia Koster, Mar. 31, 1957; children: Krista Anne, Frank, Jr. BBA, Hofstra U., 1957, MBA, 1962, L.H.D., 1975. Trainee Cities Service Oil Co., NYC, 1957-62; gen. partner Goodbody & Co., NYC, 1962-69; exec. v.p. CBWL-Hayden Stone, Inc. (investment banking), NYC, 1969-71; asst. sec. US Dept. Labor, Washington, 1971-72; exec. v.p. Hayden Stone, Inc., NYC, 1972-73; assoc. dir., Office Mgmt. & Budget Exec. Office of the Pres., Washington, 1973-74; asst. to Pres. for energy affairs The White House, Washington, 1974-77; adminstr. Fed. Energy Adminstrn., Washington, 1974-77; adv. U.S. Congress, Washington, 1977-78; gen. ptnr. Lazard Freres & Co., NYC, 1977-88; chmn., pres., CEO Smith, Barney, Harris, Upham & Co., Inc., NYC, 1988-93; vice chmn., group chief exec. The Travelers Inc., NYC, 1993-94; chmn., pres., CEO, Alexander & Alexander Svcs. Inc., NYC, 1994-97; pres. Nat. Assn. Securities Dealers, 1997-98, chmn., CEO, 1997—2000, Nasdaq Stock Market, Inc, 1997—2001; chmn. Frank Zarb Associates; sr. adv., mng. dir. Hellman & Friedman LLC, San Francisco, 2002—; interim chmn. Am. Internat. Group (AIG), NYC, 2005—06. Bd. dirs. CS First Boston, Inc., Coun. on Fgn. Rels., FPL Group, Inc., 2002-; chmn. L.I. Power Authority, 1996-97; bd. dirs., mem. exec. com. Am. Internat. Group (AIG), 2001-; co-chair, Promontory Fin. Group, 2006- Author: The Stockmarket Handbook, 1969, Handbook of Financial Markets, The Municipal Bond Handbook Mem. bd. trustees Gerald R. Ford Found.; mem. and former chmn. bd. trustees Hofstra U, bd. dirs. Lower Manhattan Develop. Corp. Recipient Disting. Scholar award Hofstra U., 1974; bus. sch. named in his honor Hofstra U. Mem. Coun. Fgn. Rels. *

ZARE, RICHARD NEIL, chemistry professor; b. Cleve., Nov. 19, 1939; s. Milton and Dorothy (Amdur) Zare; m. Susan Leigh (Shively), Apr. 20, 1963; children: Bethany Jean, Bonnie Sue, Rachel Amdur. BA, Harvard U., 1961, PhD (hon.), 1964; post grad., U. Calif., Berkeley, 1961—63; DS (hon.), U. Ariz., 1990, Northwestern U., 1993, ETH, Zürich, 1993, Columbia U., 2000, State U. West Ga., 2001; DP (hon.), Uppsala U., Sweden, 2000; PhD (hon.), U. York, 2001, Hunan U., 2002, U. Paul Sabatier, 2003. Postdoctoral fellow Harvard U., 1964; rsch. assoc. Joint Inst. for Lab. Astrophysics, 1964—65; asst. prof., chemistry MIT, 1965—66; asst. prof., dept. physics and astrophysics U. Colo., 1966—68, assoc. prof. physics, astrophysics, chemistry, 1968—69; prof. chemistry Columbia U., 1969—77, Higgins prof. natural sci., 1975—77; prof. Stanford U., 1977—, Shell, disting. prof. chemistry, 1980—85, Marguerite Blake Wilbur prof., natural sci., 1987—, prof., physics, 1992—, Howard Hughes Med. Inst. prof., 2006—. Cons. Aeronomy Lab, NOAA, 1966—77; radio standards physics divsn. Nat. Bur. Std., 1968—77, Lawrence Livermore Lab., U. Calif., 1974—, SRI, Internat., 1974—, Los Alamos Sci. Lab., U. Calif., 1975—; fellow adj. Joint Inst. Lab. Astrophysics, U. Colo.; sci. adv. com. IBM, 1977—92; chmn. commn. on phys., scis., and math applications Nat. Rsch. Coun., 1992—95; chmn. bd. dir. Ann. Rev., Inc., 1995—. Contbr. articles to profl. jour.; editor: Chem. Physics Letters, 1982—85. Named Calif. Scientist of Yr., 1997; recipient Fresenius Award, Phi Lambda Upsilon, 1974, Michael Polanyi Medal, 1979, Nat. Medal Sci., 1983, Spectroscopy Soc. Pitts. Award, 1983, Michelson-Morley Award, Case Inst. Tech., Case We. Res. U., 1986, ISCO Award for significant contbn. to instrumentation for biochemical separations, 1990, Bing Fellowship Tchg. Award, 1996, Ea. Analytical Symposium Award, 1997, Exceptional Sci. Achievement Award, NASA, 1997, Space award Aviation Week and Space Tech., 1997, Disting. Svc. Award, Nat. Sci. Bd., 1998, Centennial Medal, Harvard U., The Welch Award, 1999, Faraday Medal, Royal Soc. Chemistry, 2001, Wolf prize in chemistry, Wolf Found., Israel, 2005; fellow Alfred P. Sloan fellow, 1967—69, Non-resident fellow, Joint Inst. for Lab. Astrophysics, 1970—, Christensen fellow, St. Catherine's Coll. Oxford U., 1982, Stanford U., 1984—86. Fellow: AAAS, Inst. of Physics, Royal Soc. Chemistry (hon.), Calif. Acad. Sci. (hon.); mem.: NAS (coun. mem., Chem. Sci. Award 1991), European Acad. Scis., Chinese Acad. Scis. (fgn.), Swedish Acad. Engring. Sci. (fgn.), Royal Soc. London, Chem. Soc. London, World Jewish Acad. Scis. (hon.), Am. Philos. Soc., Am. Chem. Soc. (Harrison Howe Award 1985, Remsen Award 1985, Kirkwood Award 1986, Willard Gibbs Medal 1990, Peter Debye Award in phys. chemistry 1991, Linus Pauling Medal 1993, Dannie-Heineman Prize 1993, The Harvey Prize 1993, Analytical Chemistry Divsn. Award in chem. instrumentation 1995, Analytical Chemistry Award 1998, G.M. Kosalapoff Award 1998, E. Bright Wilson award in spectroscopy 1999, Nobel Laureate Signature Award 2000, Charles Lathrop Parsons award 2001, Madison Marshall award 2001, James Flack Norris award for outstanding achievement in the tchg. of chemistry 2004, Nichols medal NY sect. 2005), Am. Phys. Soc. (Earle K. Plyler prize 1981, Irving Langmuir Prize 1985, Arthur L. Schawlow prize in laser sci. 2000), Am. Acad. Arts and Scis., Phi Beta Delta. Achievements include research in laser chemistry and chem. physics. Office: Stanford U Dept Chemistry Stanford CA 94305-5080 Office Phone: 650-723-3062. Business E-Mail: zare@stanford.edu.

ZARELLA, PETER T., state supreme court justice; b. Boston; BS, Northeastern U., 1972; JD, Suffolk U., 1975. Bar: Mass. 1975, Conn. 1977, U.S. Dist. Ct. Mass. 1976, U.S. Dist. Ct. Conn. 1977, U.S. Supreme Ct. 1985, U.S. Ct. Appeals (2d cir.) 1985, U.S. Dist. Ct., So. Dist. N.Y. 1990. Pvt. practice, 1977—96; ptnr. Brown, Paindiris & Zarella, Hartford, Conn., 1978—96; judge Superior Ct., 1996—99, Appellate Ct., 1999—2001; assoc. justice Conn. Supreme Ct., 2001—. Chmn. Criminal Justice Commn., 2001—; chmn. rules com. Superior Ct., 2001—. Mem.Ethics Commn., Town of West Hartford, Conn., 1992—95, mem. Charter Revision Commn., 1995—96. Mem.: Conn. Bar Assn. (mem. exec. com. coml. law and bankruptcy sect. 1985—90, mem. banking law com. 1990—94). Office: Conn Supreme Ct 231 Capitol Ave Hartford CT 06106

ZAREM, ABE MORDECAI, management consulting executive; b. Chgo., Mar. 7, 1917; s. I.H. and Lea (Kaufman) Z.; m. Esther Mariam Moskovitz, Oct. 4, 1941; children: Janet Ruth, David Michael, Mark Charles. BS in Elec. Engring, Ill. Inst. Tech., 1939, LL.D. (hon.), 1968; MS in Elec. Engring, Calif. Inst. Tech., 1940, PhD, 1944; LL.D., U. Calif. at Santa Cruz, 1967. Design engr. very high voltage power transmission system Allis Chalmers Rsch. div., 1944; group leader Ultra Micro Time Program Manhattan Dist. Project/CalTech, 1944—45; initiator, group mgr. Microtime & Electro Optical Phys. Rsch., U.S. Naval Test Sta., 1945-48; assoc. dir., mgr. L.A. div. Stanford Rsch. Inst., 1948-56; mem. faculty UCLA, 1956-61; founder, chmn., pres. Electro-Optical Systems, Inc., Pasadena, Calif., 1956-67; v.p. Xerox Corp., LA, 1963-67, sr. v.p., dir. corp. devel., bd. dirs., 1967-69; mgmt. and engring. cons., 1969-79; founder, chmn. Xerox Devel. Corp., LA, 1975-80; chmn. strategic bus. planning, techno-econ. and venture capital, pres., owner Abe M. Zarem & Co., 1981—; founder, mng. dir., Frontier Assoc., 1980—. Mem. adv. com. competitive tech. program State of Calif., 1989; mem. Calif. Coun. Sci. and Tech., chmn. advanced sci. & tech. programs com., 1989-97, disting. fellow 1997—; cons., disting. vis. exec. in sci. and tech., sr. advisor on tech. transfer and commercialization and strategic planning studies Jet Propulsion Lab./Calif. Inst. of Tech., 1997—; cons., advisor, chair of sr.

adv. bd. UCLA Brain Rsch. Inst., 1997—; mem. adv. bd. dept. urology UCLA, 1994—. Author: Utilization of Solar Energy, 1963. Traffic and parking commr. City of Beverly Hills, 1971-72, planning commr., 1972-73; Bd. dirs. Music Center Opera Assn., Los Angeles, 1968—; nat. trustee City of Hope; trustee Calif. Inst. Arts, 1973-76. Named Outstanding Young Elec. Engr. in U.S. Eta Kappa Nu, 1948; One of America's Ten Outstanding Young Men U.S. Jr. C. of C., 1950; recipient Elmer F. Sperry medal Instrument Soc. Am., 1969 Fellow AIAA, IEEE; sci. mem. (a founder) Solar Energy Soc.; mem. Nat. Acad. Engring. Achievements include inventing World's fastest high-speed camera, automatic oscillograph. Home: 9640 Lomitas Ave Beverly Hills CA 90210-3333 Personal E-mail: azarem@mednet.ucla.edu. *I have always had a Vision, Mission & Series of Strategic Objectives - The principal one having been instilled by loving parents & family who encouraged me. I was born to identify talent and to challenge it to do more and better than it would have done if it had not met me. In stretching and challenging people, I fulfill the role of mentor and tormentor.*

ZAREM, HARVEY ALAN, plastic surgeon; b. Savannah, Ga., Feb. 13, 1932; s. Harry A. and Rose (Gold) Z.; m. Beth McCanghey, July 11, 1981; children: Harold, Allison, Melissa, Kathryn, Michael, Robert. BA, Yale U., 1953; MD, Columbia U. Coll. Physicians and Surgeons, 1957. Diplomate Am. Bd. Surgery, Am. Bd. Plastic Surgery; lic. physician, Md., Ill., Calif. Intern, surgery Johns Hopkins Hosp., Balt., 1957-58, resident, plastic surgery, 1964-66; rsch. fellow Peter Bent Brigham Hosp., Boston, 1958-59, asst. resident, surgery, 1959-61; resident, surgery then chief resident Boston City Hosp., 1961-63; postdoctoral fellow NYU, NYC, 1963-64; from asst. prof. to assoc. prof. surgery U. Chgo., 1966-73; head, sect. plastic surgery U. Chgo. Hosp. and Clinics; prof. surgery U. Calif., LA, 1973-87, prof. emeritus, 1987—, chief, divsn. plastic and reconstructive surgery, 1973—87; mem. med. staff Pacific Surgicenter, Santa Monica, Calif., 1987—. Physician Sepulveda (Calif.) VA Hosp., 1974—; mem. med. staff St. Johns Hosp., Santa Monica, Calif., 1987—, Santa Monica Hosp., 1988—; vis. prof. So. Ill. U., 1983, Lackaland AFB, 1986, Creighton U., 1987, Comesa, Milan, 1989, Baylor Coll. Medicine, 1990; Kazanjian vis. prof. Mass. Gen. Hosp., 1986, 88; cons. and presenter in field; cons. plastic surgery, Wadsworth VA Hosp., LA; surgeon, Extreme Makeover, ABC TV, 2003-. Contbr. numerous articles to profl. jours. Grantee NIH, 1964-75, NIH, 1967-72, Sheldon and Carol Appel Family Found., 1982—, Chantal Pharms., 1983-84, Mentor Corp./Heyer-Schulte Products, 1985—, Michael Jackson Burn Found., 1986-87. Fellow ACS; mem. AMA, Am. Soc. Plastic Reconstructive Sugeons, Inc., Am. Burn Assn., Am. Cleft Palat Assn., Am. Assn. Plastic Surgeons (trustee 1987, 1989), Am. Soc. Aesthetic Plastic Surgery, Inc., Am. Assn. Hand Surgery, Am. Assn. Surgery of Trauma, Calif. Med. Asssn., Calif. Soc. Plastic Surgeons, New Eng. Soc. Plastic Surgeons (hon.), L.A. County Med. Assn., Johns Hopkins Med. and Surg. Soc., Plastic Surgery Rsch. Coun., Soc. Head and Neck Surgeons (sr.), Soc. U. Surgeons, Lipoplasty Soc. N.Am., Bay Surgical Soc., N.W. Soc. Plastic Surgeons (hon.), Calif. Plastic Surgeon Assn. (pres.), Calif. Yacht Club, Beverly Hills Country Club, (bd. dirs.). Office: Pacific Surgicenter 1301 20th St Ste 470 Santa Monica CA 90404-2082 Home Phone: 310-474-3904; Office Phone: 310-315-0222. Business E-Mail: hzarem@ucla.edu, drzarem@drzarem.com. *

ZAREMSKI, MILES JAY, lawyer; b. Chgo., Aug. 16, 1948; s. Samuel and Ann (Levine) Z.; m. Elena Cinthia Resnik, July 19, 1970; children: Jason Lane, Lauren Devra. BS, U. Ill., 1970; JD, Case Western Res. U., 1973. Bar: Ill. 1973, Pa. 2000, Ind. 2000, U.S. Dist. Ct. (no. dist.) Ill. 1973, U.S. Dist. Ct. Nebr. 1996, U.S. Dist. Ct. (ea. dist.) Tenn. 1997, U.S. Dist. Ct. (no. dist.) Ind. 2005, U.S. Ct. Appeals (7th cir.) 1973, U.S. Ct. Appeals (8th cir.) 1988, U.S. Ct. Appeals (6th cir.) 1998, U.S. Ct. Appeals (9th cir.) 2002, U.S. Supreme Ct. 1977. Spl. asst. state's atty. Lake County, Ill., 1980-82, ptnr. Kamensky, Rubinstein, Hochman, & DeLott, Lincolnwood, Chgo., Ill., 2000—06; ptnr., founder Kamensky Law Group, Northbrook, Ill., 2007—. Arbitrator, mandatory arbitration programs Cook and Lake Counties, Ill., 1990—; asst. prof. med. jurisprudence Rosalind Franklin U. Medicine and Sci., 1991—; adj. faculty U. Chgo. Law Sch., 1999—2001; advisor to congressman and staffs on patient rights, 1999—2003; adj. prof. Case We. Res. Law Sch., 2002—03; vis. prof. divsn. of law Macquarie U., Sydney, 2004; cons. Gerson-Lehmon, Washington, NY, 2005—; clin. advisors, NYC, 2007—; lectr. nat. and internat. healthcare, medical jurisprudence. Editor: Medical and Hospital Negligence, 4 vols., 1988, supplement, 1993, 95-99; contbr. chpts. in books and articles to profl. jours.; author: Reengineering Healthcare Liability Litigation, 1997, supplement, 1999; mem. editl. bd. Medicine and Law, Haita, Israel, 2004—; patentee in field Oversight com. law sch. Case Western Res. U., Cleve., 1999, alumni bd. dirs., 1996-99; mem. exec. com. law sch. ctr for health care Loyola U., Chgo., 1987-89; mem. lakefront commn. City of Highland Park, Ill., 1982-84; bd. dirs., coun., officer Regional Organ Bank Ill., Chgo., 1986-91, The Lambs, Libertyville, Ill., 1982-84, Jocelyn Ctr. for Mental Health, 1994-96; field play marshall U.S. Olympics Baseball, Atlanta, 1996. Named one of Outstanding Young Men in Am., U.S. Jaycees, 1979; named Superlawyer, Health Care-Ill., 2005, 06, Leading Lawyer, 2005, 06. Fellow: Am. Bar Found., Am. Coll. Legal Medicine (assoc. in law 1973—91, editl. bd. Jour. Legal Medicine 1981—, chair legal com. 1996—98, chair Amicus com. 1997—, bd. govs., sec. 1999—2000, treas. 2000—01, pres.-elect 2001—02, pres. 2002—03); mem.: ABA (editor-in-chief Forum 1979—81, vice chmn. 1979—90, chmn. med. and law com. 1984—85, editl. bd. Forum on Health Law 1989—91, spl. com. on med. profl. liability 1991—95, 1998—, chmn. spl. com. on med. profl. liability 2000—03, chmn. std. com. med. profl. liability 2003—05, chmn. emeritus std. commn. on med. profl. liability 2005—, chmn. med. and law com. 2005—, various coms. tort, trial and ins. practice sect.), Medicine and Law (mem. editl. bd.), Am. Arbitration Assn. (arbitrator 2002—, comml. arbitration panel 2006—), World Congress Med. Law (mem. editl. bd. Medicine and Law 2004—), Ill. Assn. Healthcare Attys., Quality Mgmt. Health Care (editl. bd.), Am. Soc. Writers on Legal Subjects (scribes), Am. Health Law Assn. (vice chair hosp. liability com. 1999—2001), Am. Soc. Law and Medicine (editor-in-chief 1981—83, bd. editors 1983—86), Lake County Bar Assn., Ill. Bar Assn. (1st and 3d prizes 1978—79). Jewish. Avocations: baseball, soccer, coaching athletic teams. Office: Kamensky Rubinstein Hochman DeLott 7250 N Cicero Ave Ste 200 Lincolnwood IL 60712 Office Phone: 847-982-1776, 847-418-3830. Business E-Mail: mzaremski@kr-law.com. *"Success is a journey; not a destination." "A man may make many mistakes but he isn't a failure until he starts blaming someone else." John R. Wooden.*

ZARET, BARRY LEWIS, cardiologist, medical educator; b. NYC, Oct. 3, 1940; s. Irving Z. and Beatrice (Fader) Zaret; m. Myrna Zimmerman, June 23, 1963; children: Adam L., Elliot C., Owen M. BS, Queens Coll., Flushing, NY, 1962; MD, NYU, 1966; MA, Yale U., New Haven, Conn., 1982. Diplomate Am. Bd. Internal Medicine. Intern Bellevue Hosp., NYC, 1966-67, resident, 1967-79; rsch. fellow John Hopkins U., Balt., 1969-71; asst. prof. medicine Yale U., New Haven, 1973-76, assoc. prof. medicine and diagnostic radiology, 1976, chief sect. cardiology, 1978—2004, assoc. prof. medicine and diagnostic radiology, 1980-82, prof. medicine and diagnostic radiology, 1982-84, Robert W. Berliner prof. medicine, 1984—, assoc. chair clin. affairs dept. internal medicine, 1994—2004; mem. staff Yale-New Haven Med. Ctr.; med. dir. Yale-New Haven Med. Hosp. Heart Ctr., 1999—2004. Mem. cardiovasc. subsplty. bd. Am Bd. Internal Medicine, 2002—. Mem. editl. bd. Am. Jour. Cardiology, 1977—, Jour. Am. Coll. Cardiology, 1986-91, 92-97, Jour. Cardiac Imaging, 1986—, Circulation, 1993; assoc. editor: Yearbook of Nuc. Medicine, 1980-95; editor-in-chief Jour. Nuc. Cardiology, 1993-2004; contbr. articles to profl. jours. Recipient Casimir Funk award Soc. Mil. Surgeons, 1973; recipient Herrman Blumgart Pioneer award New Eng. chpt. Soc. Nuc. Medicine, 1978, Solomon Berson Alumni Achievement award in clin. sci. NYU Sch. Medicine, 1998, Ellis Island medal Honor, 2004. Fellow Am. Coll. Cardiology, Coun. Clin. Cardiology, Am. Heart Assn., Coun. Circulation, Am. Heart Assn., Am. Physiology Soc.; mem. Am. Soc. Clin. Investigation, Am. Fedn. Clin. Rsch., Assn. Am. Physicians, Soc. Nuc. Medicine, Am. Soc. Nuc. Cardiology (Disting. Svc. award 2006), Assn. Univ. Cardiologists, Assn. Profs. Cardiology (pres. 1992), Phi Beta Kappa, Alpha Omega Alpha, Interurban Clin. Club. Jewish. Home: 15 Cassway Rd Woodbridge CT 06525-1214 Office: 333 Cedar St # 3 New Haven CT 06520-8017 Office Phone: 203-785-4127.

ZARGES, THOMAS H., engineering executive; Degree in Engring., Va. Mil. Inst. V.p. bus. devel. United Engrs. & Constructors, 1990; pres., CEO power and indsl./mfg. divsns. Washington Group, 1991; sr. exec. v.p. ops. Washington Group Internat., Boise, Idaho, 2002—. Office: Washington Group Internat PO Box 73 Boise ID 83729

ZARGHAMI, CYMA, broadcast executive; b. Iran, 1962; d. Gorham and Catherine; m. George Obergfoll, 1994; children: Liam, Ethan. BA, U. of Vt., Burlington, 2000. Scheduling clerk, scheduling exec., programming exec. Nickelodeon, 1985—96, exec. v.p., gen. mgr., 1996—2004, pres., 2004—. Directs co. initiatives Big Help and Kids Pick the Pres. Campaign; launched Nick Jr., SNICK, Nicktoons. Named one of 100 Most Powerful Women in Entertainment, Hollywood Reporter, 2006. Office: Nickelodeon 1515 Broadway New York NY 10036 *

ZARIF, FARID, internist, nutritionist; s. James Little and Eddie Ruth Fife. Of Nnaturopathy, Am. Holistic Coll., 1989; PhD in Human Nutrition, Am. Holistic Coll. Nutrition, 1991; MPH, Glendale U., 2003, MS in Sports Medicine, 2006. Founder, owner Expressions Self Protection Ctr., LA, 1981—90; fitness trainer, sports medicine and nutrition therapist Zarif Fitness, Ingelwood, Calif., 1990—2004; clin. rschr. Fedder Orthopedic Group, Manhattan Beach, Calif., 2004, Cedars-Sinai Inst. Spine Disorders, LA, 2004; instr., prof. dept. sco. Star Edn. Prep Acad., Culver City, Calif., 2004—05; dir., activity specialist Ctr. Surg. Treatment Obesity, Hawaiian Gardens, Calif., 2002—06; dir. sports nutrition and medicine Porter Ranch Med. Ctr., Calif., 2006—. Careers counselor West Blvd. Edn. Ctr., 1993—96; tchr. Star Edn. Prep Acad., 2004—05, Prins. Faith Coll. Prep Acad., 2005—06, Ctr. Surg. Treatment Obesity, 2003—. Contbr. articles to profl. jours. Mem.: AMA, Am. Dietetic Assn., Am. Soc. Baariatric Physicians, Soc. Internat. Nutrition, Soc. Clin. Nutrition, Am. Soc. Nutritional Scis., Am. Coll. Sports Medicine. Office: 211 Med Wellness Inglewood CA 90301

ZARING, ALLEN G., homebuilding company executive; Student, Babson Coll. Founder, chmn., CEO Zaring Homes, 1964—. With U.S. Army. Recipient High Achievement award Profl. Builders Mag.; named Builder of Yr., Home Builders Assn. Greater Cin., 1995, Ams. Best Builder. Office: 625 Eden Park Dr #1250 Cincinnati OH 45202-6024 Fax: 513-247-2667.

ZARINS, BERTRAM, orthopedic surgeon; b. Latvia, June 22, 1942; came to U.S., 1946, naturalized, 1956; s. Richard Arthur and Maria (Rozenbergs) Z. AB in Chemistry, Lafayette Coll., 1963; MD, SUNY, Syracuse, 1967. Diplomate Am. Bd. Orthop. Surgery. Clin. instr. orthop. surgery Harvard Med. Sch., Boston, 1976—, asst. clin. prof., 1982—, assoc. clin. prof., 1996—, Harvard Thorndike prof. orthopaedic surgery, 2007—; orthop. surgeon Mass. Gen. Hosp., Boston, 1982-95, chief sports medicine svc., 1982—; team physician Boston Bruins Hockey Team, 1976—. Chmn. edn. com. Sports Medicine Coun., U.S. Olympic Com., 1980-92; team physician New England Patriots football team, 1982—; head physician USA Olympic teams XIV Winter Olympic Games, Sarajevo, Yugoslavia, 1984, cons. editor for sports medicine Jour. of Bone and Joint Surgery, 1999—. Contbr. articles to profl. jours. Team physician N.E. Revolution profl. soccer team, 1996—. Lt. comdr. M.C., USNR, 1973-75. Fellow ACS, Am. Acad. Orthop. Surgeons (chmn. com. on sports medicine 1993-97), Am. Coll. Sports Medicine; mem. AMA, Internat. Arthroscopy Assn. (bd. dirs. 1991-95), Arthroscopy Assn. N.Am., N.Am. Trauma Assn. (pres. 1977), Internat. Soc. of Arthroscopy, Knee Surgery and Orthopaedic Sports Medicine, Am. Shoulder and Elbow Surgeons, Herodicus Soc., Brookline (Mass.) Country Club, Somerset Club. Office Phone: 617-726-3421. Business E-Mail: bzarins@partners.org.

ZARINS, CHRISTOPHER KRISTAPS, surgeon, educator; b. Tukums, Latvia, Dec. 2, 1943; came to U.S., 1946; s. Richard A. and Maria (Rozenbergs) Z.; m. Zinta Zarins, July 8, 1967; children: Daina, Sascha, Karina. BA, Lehigh U., 1964; MD, Johns Hopkins U., 1968. Surgery residency U. Mich., Ann Arbor, 1968-74; asst. prof. surgery U. Chgo., 1976-79, assoc. prof. surgery, 1979-82, prof. surgery, 1983-93, chief of vascular surgery, 1978-93; prof. surgery Stanford (Calif.) U., 1993—, chmn. divsn. vascular surgery, 1993—2005, acting chmn. dept. of surgery, 1995-97. Author: Essays In Surgery, 1986, Atlas of Vascular Surgery, 1988; editor Jour. of Surg. Rsch., 1982-95; contbr. articles to profl. jours. Pres. Latvian Med. Found., Boston, 1991. Lt. comdr. USN, 1974-76. Grantee NIH, NSF. Mem. Am. Surg. Soc., Soc. for Clin. Surgery, Soc. for Vascular Surgery (pres. 1998-99), Internat. Soc. for Cardiovascular Surgery, Soc. of Univ. Surgeons, Latvian Nat. Acad. of Scis., Latvian Vascular Surg. Soc. (pres. 1989), Soc. for Vascular Surgery (pres. 1998-99). Avocations: triathlons, skiing. Office: Stanford U Med Ctr Divsn Vascular Surgery 300 Pasteur Dr # H3642 Stanford CA 94304-2203 Office Phone: 650-725-7830.

ZARKIN, HERBERT J., wholesale distribution executive; b. 1938; m. Susan Zarkin; children: Amy, Ann. Attended, U. Pa. Exec. vice-pres. Zayre Corp., Framingham, Mass., until 1986; pres. Zayre Corp., HomeClub subs., Framingham, Mass., 1986-88; chmn. Zayre Corp., Zayre Stores div., Framingham, Mass., 1988; pres., CEO Waban Inc, Natick, 1988-95, chmn. bd., 1997-98; chmn. HomeBase, Irvine, Calif., 1999—2001, BJ's Wholesale Club, Inc., Natick, Mass., 1997—2006, chmn., interim CEO, 2006—07, chmn., CEO, 2007—. Office: BJs Wholesale Club Inc 1 Mercer Rd Natick MA 01760-2400 *

ZARO, BRAD A., research and development company executive, biologist; b. San Jose, Calif., Dec. 4, 1949; s. Raymond J. and Irene R. Z.; children: Amy C., Kristen E. BA in Zoology, San Jose State U., 1974, MA in Biology, 1981. Chemist, Dept. Drug Metabolism Syntex Rsch., Inc., Palo Alto, Calif., 1976-78, chemist II, Dept. Drug Metabolism, 1978-81, chemist III, Dept. Drug Metabolism, 1981-84, clin. rsch. assoc. I, Inst. of Clin. Medicine, 1984-85, clin. rsch. assoc. II, Inst. of Clin. Medicine, 1985-87, sen. clin. rsch. assoc., Inst. of Clin. Medicine, 1985-87; sen. clin. rsch. assoc. Triton Biosciences, Inc., Alameda, Calif., 1988, mgr. clin. trials, 1988; pres., CEO Clinimetrics Rsch. Assoc., Inc., San Jose, 1988—. Contbr. articles to scholarly jours. Mem. AAAS, Am. Coll. Clin. Pharmacology, Am. Soc. Pharmacognosy, Assn. Clin. Rsch. Profls., Drug Info. Assn. Democrat. Roman Catholic. Avocations: scuba diving, skiing, flying. Office: Clinimetrics Rsch Assocs 5285 Hellyer Ave San Jose CA 95138

ZAROS, WENDY CECILIA, soprano, educator; d. Leonard and Doris Zaros; m. Ben Harrison, July 13, 2002. BS in Music Edn., Roberts Wesleyan Coll., 1999; MusM in Vocal Performance, New England Conservatory, 2001. Lic. tchr. music N.Y., 1995, S.C., 2002. Pvt. practice voice instr., Mass., 1995—2001, NY, 2001—02; tchg. asst. music history New Eng. Conservatory, Boston, 1999, rschr., 2000—01; tchr. music Dows Lane Elem. Sch. Irvington (N.Y.) Pub. Schs., 2001—02; instr. voice Anderson (S.C.) Acad. Music, 2002—03; mem. faculty voice Clemson (S.C.) U., 2003—05. Singer numerous ch. choirs. Singer: (albums) Peaceable Kingdom, 1998, (Operas) numerous shows including, NEC Opera, 1999—2001, Rome Festival Orch., 2000, New Eng. Conservatory Opera, 2001, Spartanburg Repertory Co., 2002, 2003, Harrower Opera Studio, 2003, Crittenden Opera Studio, 2004, Brooks Performing Arts Theater, 2004, NY Opera Forum, 2005—07, Westminster Choir Coll., 2005, Touring Concert Opera Co., 2005—07, Operesque Classical Concerts, 2006. Coord., dir., performer Opera in Armonk, NY, 2005; vol. Pivot Ministries, Darien, Conn., 1992—95. Finalist Miss Teen USA, 1991—94; recipient Nat. Talent award, Miss Am. Pre-teen, 1989, 3d Runner Up award, Miss Am. Teen N.Y., 1993, 1st Runner Up award, Roberts Wesleyan Coll. Concerto Competition, 1998, Achievement award, Di Capo Opera Theater, 1995, award, Palmetto Opera Competition, 2003; scholar, New Eng. Conservatory, Roberts Wesleyan Coll., Byram Hills Coll.; Touring Concert Opera grant of study, 2006—07. Mem.: Nat. Assn. Tchg. Soc., Alpha Kappa Sigma, Phi Kappa Lambda. Avocations: skiing, travel.

ZARR, MELVYN, lawyer, educator; b. Worcester, Mass., Aug. 29, 1936; m. Gail Sclar, Aug. 29, 1971. AB, Clark U., 1958; LL.B., Harvard U., 1963. Bar: Mass. bar 1964, Maine bar 1973. Staff atty. NAACP Legal Def. & Edn. Fund, Inc., NYC, 1963-69; co-dir. Mass. Law Reform Inst., Boston, 1970-73; prof. law U. Maine, 1973—; U.S. magistrate, Portland, Maine, 1977-82. Mem.: Am. Law Inst. Home: 19 Mckinley Rd Falmouth ME 04105-1913 Office: U Maine Sch Law 246 Deering Ave Portland ME 04102-2837 Office Phone: 207-780-4359. Business E-Mail: mzarr@usm.maine.edu.

ZARRA, ERNEST JOSEPH, III, secondary school educator, researcher; b. Montclair, NJ, Dec. 14, 1955; s. Ernest Joseph Jr. and Faith Zarra; m. Susan Sembrat, May 29, 1976; children: Elya Joelle, Jonathan Joseph. BA, Northeastern Bible Coll., 1978; MA, Simon Greenleaf U., 1981; MABS, Grace Grad. Sch., Long Beach, Calif., 1986; MEd, Calif. State U., Bakersfield, 1988; PhD, U. So. Calif., 1999. Cert. tchr., N.J., Calif. Pvt. sch. tchr., 1978-89; pastor Millington Bapt. Ch., Basking Ridge, NJ, 1994-95; tchr., GATE coord. Fruitvale Sch. Dist. Pub. Sch., Bakersfield, Calif., 1989-94, 95-00; tchr. govt. and econs. Centennial H.S., Bakersfield, Calif., 2000—, girls varsity soccer coach, 2000—. Adj. faculty Calif. State U., Bakersfield, 1998—, Pt. Loma Nazarene U.; lectr. U. Pa., Bakersfield Coll., Fresno Pacific U., U. San Diego, others; presenter in field. Author: It Should Never Happen Here, 1997; contbr. articles to profl. jours. Youth coach Am. Youth Soccer Orgn., Kern County, Calif., 1993—; youth and adults tchr. Laurelglen Bible Ch., Bakersfield, 1984—; presenter to law enforcement officers Kern County Sheriffs Dept., 1988. Named All-Am. Soccer Player Nat. Christian Coll. Athletic Assn., 1978, All-State. All Dist., All Conf.; drafted Dallas Tornado (NASL), 1978. Mem. ASCD, Am. Ednl. Rsch. Assn., Evang. Theol. Soc., Link Inst., Kappa Delta Pi (Character Edn. Partnership). Republican. Mennonite Brethren. Avocations: athletics, writing, travel, ministry, debate. Home: 400 Sinaloa Ave Bakersfield CA 93312-9334

ZARRELLA, RONALD L., pharmaceutical executive; b. Waterbury, CT, 1949; BS electrical engineering, Worcester Polytechnic Institute, Worcester, MA, 1971; student, NYU Graduate School of Business. With Bristol Myers Co., Esmark Corp.; executive Bausch & Lomb, 1985—94; v.p., No. Am. Vehicle Sales General Motors, 1994—98; exec. v.p. General Motors, North America, 1998—2001; chmn., CEO Bausch & Lomb, 2001—. Bd. dir. Avaya, Inc., FIRST (For Inspiration and Recognition of Science and Technology), Univ. of Rochester Medical Center. Mem.: Rochester Institute of Technology, Comm. for Economic Development, Nat. Italian Found. Office: c/o Bausch & Lomb One Bausch & Lomb Place Rochester NY 14604

ZARRES, SHARON L., marriage and family therapist, health facility administrator; b. Altadena, Calif., June 11, 1947; d. Verne Ivan and Ruth Elizabeth Hatfield; m. Michael Paul Zarres, 1977; adopted children: Rebecca, Philip, Victor, Amber, James MacKenzie. BA, Azusa Pacific U., 2000, MA in Clin. Psychology, 2002, MA in Marriage and Family Therapy, 2003. Ordained to ministry Western Evang. Orgn. Dir. Jack & Jill Pre-Sch./Grade Sch., La Puente, Calif.; office mgr. World Vision Internat., Monrovia, Calif., 1985—95; owner, mgr. Zarres Family Day Care, Covina, Calif., 1995—2005; adminstr., marriage and family therapist Father's Heart Ranch, Desert Hot Springs, Calif., 2003—. Mem. integration com. Azusa (Calif.) Pacific U., 2000—, tchg. and rsch. asst., 2001—02. Foster parent Koinonia Foster Homes, San Bernardino, Calif.; v.p., founder Lighthouse Prayer, Covina, lay counselor, 1980—90; bd. dirs. Prevailing Word, Azusa. Avocations: reading, travel, movies. Home and Office: 71-175 Aurora Rd Desert Hot Springs CA 92241

ZARRO, JANICE ANNE, lawyer; b. Newark, June 30, 1947; BA, Rutgers U., 1969; JD, IIT-Chgo.-Kent Coll. Law, 1973. Bar: Pa. 1974. Counsel jud. com. U.S. Ho. Reps., Washington, 1973-77; profl. staff mem. counsel labor and human resources com. U.S. Senate, Washington, 1977-80; dir. Avon Products, Inc., NYC, 1980-81, Washington, 1982-86, v.p., 1986-90; pres. The Novus Group, Inc., 1990-92; dir. fed. affairs Mallinckrodt Med., 1992—, v.p., 1993-94; v.p. govt. affairs Worldwide Mallinckrodt Inc., 1994-2000; exec. dir. Women's Resource Ctr. Sarasota County, 2003—. Gen. counsel Nat. Italian-Am. Found., 1989-96, chair bd. trustees, 1996-99; mem. Bus. Govt. Rels. Coun., Washington, 1987—; past chair Women's Fgn. Policy Group. Past chmn. Nat. Capital chpt. Multiple Sclerosis Soc. Recipient Leadership Recognition award Nat. Women's Econ. Alliance, 1984. Office Phone: 341-366-1700. Business E-Mail: jzarro@thewomensresourcecenter.org.

ZARTMAN, DAVID LESTER, retired zoology educator, researcher; b. Albuquerque, July 6, 1940; s. Lester Grant and Mary Elizabeth (Kitchel) Z.; m. Micheal Aline Plemmons, July 6, 1963; children: Kami Renee, Dalan Lee. BS cum laude in Dairy Husbandry, N.Mex. State U., 1962; MS in Genetics, Ohio State U., 1966, PhD in Genetics, 1968. Cert. dairy cattle specialist, Am. Registry Profl. Animal Scientists. Jr. ptnr. Marlea Guernsey Farm, Albuquerque, 1962-64; grad. rsch. assoc. Ohio State U., Columbus, 1964-68; asst. prof. dairy sci. N.Mex. State U., Las Cruces, 1968-71, assoc. prof., 1971-79, prof., 1979-84, Ohio State U., Columbus, 1984—2006, emeritus prof., 2006—. Chmn. dept. Ohio State U., Columbus, 1984-99; pres. Mary K. Zartman, Inc., Albuquerque, 1976-84; cons. Bio-Med. Electronics, Inc., San Diego, 1984-89, Zartemp, Inc., Northbrook, Ill., 1990, Recom Applied Solutions, 1993-2000, Am. Registry of Profl. Animal Scientists, 1996—, Midwest Univs. Consortium for Internat. Assistance, 2004. Contbr. articles to profl. jours.; patentee in field. Recipient State Regional Outstanding Young Farmer award Jaycees, 1963, Disting. Rsch. award N.Mex. State U. Coll. Agr. and Home Econs., 1983, Outstanding Svc. award Ohio Poultry Assn., 1999, Grazier of Yr. award Gt. Lakes Internat. Grazing Conf., 2001, hon. state degree Ohio FFA, 2000, The Jack Tucker Disting. Svc. award Ohio Forage and Grassland Coun., 2004; course acclaimed by Humane Soc. of U.S.; named one of Top 100 Agr. Alumni, N.Mex. State U. Centennial, 1987; spl. postdoctoral fellow NIH, New Zealand, 1973; Fulbright-Hayes lectr., Malaysia, 1976. Fellow AAAS; mem. Am. Dairy Sci. Assn., Am. Soc. Animal Sci., Dairy Shrine Club, Ohio Farm Bur., Sigma Xi, Gamma Sigma Delta, Alpha Gamma Rho (1st Outstanding Alumnus N.Mex. chpt. 1985), Alpha Zeta, Phi Kappa Phi. Home: 7671 Deer Creek Dr Worthington OH 43085-1551 Office: Ohio State U 2027 Coffey Rd Columbus OH 43210-1043 Home Phone: 614-431-3479; Office Phone: 614-292-1387. Business E-Mail: zartman.3@osu.edu.

ZARTMAN, PATRICK JOSEPH, secondary school educator; b. San Pedro, Calif., Mar. 12, 1942; s. Charles George and Agnes Christina Zartman; m. Charleen Therese Sharkie, July 31, 1976; children: Therese Ann, Christine Marie. BA, Loyola U., LA, 1964, MA, 1965. Tchr., coach

San Gabriel Mission HS, 1965—67, Bishop Montgomery HS, Torrance, 1967—71, Torrance HS, 1971—. Pres., CEO Spoilers Enterprizes, 1970—; coach USA Volleyball, Colorado Springs, 1970, 74, 2000—04; head coach Major League Volleyball LA Starlites, 1987; Am. coach Brazilian Women's Beach Volleyball Olympic Gold medalists, 1996; coach U.S. Women's FISU Beach Volleyball Univ. World Champions & Gold Medalists, 2002. Author: (book) Youth Volleyball, 1997; contbr. articles to profl. jours.; coach/writer: instrnl. videos. Roman Catholic. Home: 37 4th St Hermosa Beach CA 90254 Office: Spoilers Enterprizes 37 4th St Hermosa Beach CA 90254 Office Phone: 310-379-1869. Business E-Mail: pzartman@teacher.tusd.org.

ZARWYN, BERTHOLD, physicist, consultant; b. Vienna, Aug. 22, 1921; came to US, 1949, naturalized, 1955; s. Joseph and Bronislawa Regina (Unger) Zarwyn. ME, Gliwice, Poland, 1946; ScD, UN Univ., Munich, 1947; PhD, NYU, 1954; ScD in Engring., Columbia U., NYC, 1963. Project engr. Curtiss-Wright Corp., Woodridge, NJ, 1951-55; staff scientist AMF Corp., NYC, 1955-57; chief scientist Link Aviation Co., Binghamton, NY, 1957-58; head rsch. staff Am. Bosch-Arma Corp., Garden City, NY, 1958-63; corp. cons. Cutler-Hammer Corp., Deer Park, NY, 1963-65; chief engr. Bell Aerosystems Corp., Niagara Falls, NY, 1965-66; sr. cons. Mitre Corp., Bedford, Mass., 1966-68; spl. asst. to commdg. gen., acting chief engr. Hdqs. US Army Materiel Command, Arlington, Va., 1968-71; chief phys. scis. br. US Army Devel. and Readiness Command, Alexandria, Va., 1971-75; phys. scientist US Army Harry Diamond Labs., Washington, 1975-78; chief sys. analysis br. US Army Elec. Rsch. and Devel. Command, Adelphi, Md., 1978-79, chief tech. divsn., 1979-81, asst. tech. dir., 1981-85; spl. asst. to dep. chief of staff for tech. & program mgmt. US Army Lab. Command, Adelphi, Md., 1985-87; pres. Pan-Tech. Corp., Delray Beach, Fla., 1987—. Adj. faculty, lectr., cons. in field; dir. Film Microelectronics Co. Inc., Burlington, Mass., 1965-67. Mem. editl. bd. Bavarian Soc. Engrs., 1947-49, transl. panel Russian Jour. Applied Math. and Mechanics with Pergamon Inst., 1956-57; inventor nuc. gyroscope, microwave holography, other items. Mem. IEEE, Am. Phys. Soc., NY Acad. Scis., Sigma Xi. Home and Office: Pan-Tech Corp 7589 Mansfield Hollow Rd Delray Beach FL 33446-3314 Office Phone: 561-637-9387. Personal E-mail: zarwyn22@comcast.net.

ZARYCHTA, WILLIAM ALEX, medical officer, physician assistant; BS in Health, West Chester U., 1996; AAS in Nursing, Gloucester County Coll., 1999; BS in Physician Asst. Studies, Hahnemann U., 2001; M in Physician Asst. Studies, U. Nebr., 2002. Cert. physician asst. Nat. Commn. Certification Physician Assts., paramedic Nat. Registry Emergency Med. Technicians, lic. physician asst.; RN, Pa. Paramedic Mercy Health Sys., Darby, Pa., 1993—99, emergency RN, 1999—2000; emergency medicine physician asst. Brandywine Emergency Physician Assocs., Coatesville, Pa., 2001—06; mil. medicine physician asst. US Army, Afghanistan, 2004—05; med. officer dept. homeland security USPHS, DC, 2006—. Clin. instr. Arcadia U., Glenside, Pa., 2001—06, Drexel U., Phila., 2001—06, clin. asst. prof., 2006—. Contbr. articles to profl. jours. Med. screening Spl. Olympics, Phila., 2000, Mid-Atlantic Boating Assn., Ocean City, Md., 2001. With US Army, 1990—2006, with USPHS, 2006—. Decorated Bronze Star medal, 3 Army Commendation medals, 3 Army Achievement medals, Humanitarian Svc. medal, Mil. Outstanding Vol. Svc. medal, Global War on Terrorism Expeditionary and Svc. medals, Combat Action ribbon, Combat Med. badge, Excellence in Competition Pistol badge, Physician Asst. badge USCG, State of NJ Disting. Svc. medal; recipient Presdl. Academic Fitness award. Fellow: Pub. Health Svc. Acad. Physician Assts. (bd. dirs.), Pa. Soc. Physician Assts., Soc. Emergency Medicine Physician Assts., Am. Acad. Physician Assts., Soc. Army Physician Assts.; mem.: Commissioned Officer Assn., Res. Officers Assn., EMT Hist. Soc. (disting.), Assn. Mil. Surgeons US (life), Am. Coll. Clinicians (charter), Phi Theta Kappa. Office: USCG HQ HSC k 2100 Second St SW Washington DC 20593-0001

ZASADA, MARY EILEEN, nursing administrator; b. Waterbury, Conn., July 23, 1957; d. Walter Francis and Elizabeth Ann (Doyle) Lewis; m. Peter Pilkington Zasada, Sept. 8, 1984; children: Kathleen, Andrew. Diploma in nursing, St. Vincent's Med. Ctr., 1978; BS in Mgmt., Tiekyo Post U., 1983; MSN, Sacred Heart U., 1997. RN, Conn. Staff New Britian (Conn.) Gen. Hosp., 1978-79, St. Mary's Hosp., Waterbury, Conn., 1980-84, nurse analyst, 1984-98, project leader clin. applications, 1998—. Bd. dirs. Conn. Healthcare Informatics Network. Mem. Rotary Internat. (bd. dirs. 1990-98, Paul Harris fellow), Girls Inc. of Waterbury (bd. dirs. 1996-2001), Sigma Theta Tau (Mu Delta chpt.). Home: 122 Terrell Farm Rd Bethlehem CT 06751-1408 Office: St Marys Hosp 56 Franklin St Waterbury CT 06706-1238

ZASLAV, DAVID M., broadcast executive; b. Brooklyn, NY, Jan. 15, 1960; m. Pam Zaslav, 1987; 3 children. Student, Cornell U., 1978—79; BS, SUNY, Binghamton, 1981; JD cum laude, Boston U., 1985. Corp. entertainment atty. LeBouef, Lamb, Leiby & MacRae; gen. counsel, NBC Cable NBC, 1988, v.p. bus. affairs CNBC, 1990, v.p. bus. devel., 1992, sr. v.p. affiliate mktg. & sales, 1993, exec. v.p. bus. devel. and affiliate sales mktg. NBC Cable Networks, 1995, pres. NBC Cable Distribution, 1996, pres. NBC Universal Cable, 1999—2006, pres. Domestic TV and New Media Distribution, 2006; pres., CEO Discovery Comm. Inc., 2007—. Bd. dirs. A&E Network, Nat. Geographic TV, TiVo, 2000—, Nat. Cable Ctr., Cable in the Classroom, NYC Ctr. Communications; adj. prof. Fordham U. Mem.: Nat. Assn. TV Program Execs. (bd. mem.), Nat. Cable & Telecommunications Assn. (bd. mem.). Office: Discovery Comm 1 Discovery Pl Silver Spring MD 20910 *

ZASLAW, NEAL, musicologist; b. NYC, June 28, 1939; s. Alexander and Bertha Lampert Zaslaw; m. Ellen Faust, June 10, 1962; children: Sarah, Diana. BA, Harvard U., Cambridge, Mass., 1961; MS, Juilliard Sch., NY, 1963; MA, Columbia U., NY, 1965, PhD, 1970. Herbert Gussman prof. music Cornell U., Ithaca, NY, 1970—. Musicological advisor Lincoln Ctr., NYC, 1988—92; instr. Juilliard Grad. Sch., NYC, 1988—92; musicological supr. Decca Records Ltd., London, 1978—82; instr. City Coll., CUNY, NYC; musical adv. St. Paul Chamber Orch., 2003—06. Author: Mozart's Symphonies: Context, Performance Practice, Reception, 1989, The Classical Era from the 1740s to the End of the 18th Century, 1989, The Compleast Mozart, 1990, W.A. Mozart: Portfolio of a Genius, 1991, Mozart's Piano Concertos: Text, Context, Interpretation, 1996, The Birth of the Orchestra: History of an Institution 1650-1815, 2004; editor-in-chief: Current Musicology, 1967—70; contbr. articles to profl. jours. Book review editor Music Libr. Assn. Notes, 1970—75. Recipient Österreichische Ehrenkreuz für Wissenschaft und Kunst award, Austrian Ministry Culture, 1991; fellow, Am. Coun. Learned Soc., 1983—84; Dissertation Yr. fellow, Martha Baird Rockefeller Fund for Music, 1968—69, Sr. fellow, NEH, 1976—77. Fellow: Am. Acad. Arts & Sci.; mem.: Soc. France Musicology, Soc. der Musikforschung, Royal Musical Assn., Am. Musicol. Soc. (v.p. 1992—94). Office: Cornell Univ Lincoln Hall Ithaca NY 14853-4101 Home Phone: 607-257-1052; Office Phone: 607-255-4279. Business E-Mail: naz2@cornell.edu.

ZASLOWSKY, DAVID PAUL, lawyer; b. NYC, Dec. 30, 1960; s. Daniel N. and Rhoda Z.; m. Lisa Ann Freudenberger, Aug. 26, 1982; children: Amanda Lauren, Michael Joel, Steven Ira. BS in Computer/Info. Sci. summa cum laude, Bklyn. Coll., 1981; JD, Yale U., 1984. Bar: N.Y. 1984, N.J. 1984, U.S. Dist. Ct. (so. and ea. dist.) N.Y. 1985, U.S. Dist. Ct. N.J. 1985, U.S. Cir. Ct. (2d cir.) 1992. Assoc. Baker & McKenzie, NYC, 1984-94, ptnr., 1994—. Author: (with others) Federal Civil Practice, 1989, Transnational Litigation in U.S. Federal Courts, 1991, Litigating International Commercial Disputes, 1996; editor: International Litigation and Arbitration Alert, 2001-. Mem. ABA (litigation sect.), N.Y. State Bar Assn. (comml. and fed. litigation sect.), Assn. Bar City N.Y. Office: Baker & McKenzie 1114 Ave of the Americas New York NY 10036 E-mail: david.zaslowsky@bakernet.com.

ZATALAVA, CHRISTINE MICHELLE, science educator; d. Michael and Mary Lou Hare; m. Mark Zatalava, Aug. 0, 1997; children: Elizabeth, Thomas, Joshua. BS, Shippensburg U., Pa., 1995, U. Pitts., Johnstown, Pa., 1999; Masters in Sch. Leadership, Wilmington Coll., New Castle, Del., 2006—. Cert. level 2 tchr. biology and gen. sci. Pa., 2003, std. profl. edn. Md., 2005. Sci. educator Greater Johnstown Sch. Dist., Pa., 2000—04, Shanksville-Stonycreek Sch. Dist., Pa., 2004—05; biology educator Harford County Pub. Schs., Aberdeen, Md., 2005—. Precana marriage counselor St. Peter's Cath. Ch., Somerset, Pa., 2000—05. Recipient Tchr. with the Most Positive Influence award, Greater Johnstown High Student Body, 2000—01. Mem.: Pi Lambda Theta, Alpha Phi Internat. Frat. (life Order of Omega award 1995). Conservative. Roman Catholic. Avocation: home and garden party designer. Home: 73 Billy Goss Loop North East MD 21901 Home Phone: 410-287-9317. Personal E-mail: czathgp@hotmail.com.

ZATSIORSKY, VLADIMIR MOISEEVICH (MICHAILOVICH), biomechanics educator, researcher; b. Leningrad, Russia, Dec. 26, 1932; came to U.S., 1990; s. Moisey T. and Berta L. (Bardenstein) Z.; m. Rita Y. Zatsiorsky, Oct. 27, 1960; children: Betty V. Ulitsky, Michael V. PhD, Lesgaft Inst. Phys. Culture, Leningrad, 1961; DSc, Ctrl. Inst. Phys. Culture, Moscow, 1969; D honoris causa, Acad. Phys. Culture, Wroclaw, Poland, 1999, Russian State U. Phys. Culture, 2003. Asst. prof. Lvov Inst. Phys. Culture, Ukraine, 1954—57; asst. prof., assoc. prof., prof. Ctrl. Inst. Phys. Culture, Moscow, 1959—90; vis. prof. UCLA, 1990, U. Calgary, Canada, 1991; prof. kinesiology Pa. State U., University Park, 1991—2003. Med. commn. Internat. Olympic Com., 1982—. Author (15 books including): Science and Practice of Strength Training, 1995—2006, Kinematics of Human Motion, 1998, Kinetics of Human Motion, 2002; editor: Biomechanics in Sport, 2000, Classics in Movement Science, 2001 (all books published in English, Russian, German, Italian, Spanish, Portuguese, Chinese, Japanese, Polish, Romanian, Czech, Serbo-Croatian & Bulgarian); contbr. more than 380 rsch. papers. Recipient J. Dyson award Internat. Soc. of Sport Biomechanics, 1992. Fellow: Am. Acad. Kinesiology; mem.: Internat. Soc. Sport Kinetics (hon.). Avocations: reading, music.

ZAUBLER, THOMAS SCOT, psychiatrist, educator; b. NY, June 13, 1963; s. Leland and Lynn Zaubler; m. Katharine L. Sonnenberg, Sept. 11, 1993; children: William Sonnenberg, Elizabeth Dale Sonnenberg. BA, Columbia U., 1986; MD, Albert Einstein Coll. of Medicine, 1991; MPH, U. Wash., 1997. Diplomate Nat. Bd. Med. Examiners, 1992, lic. gen. psychiatry Am. Bd. Psychiatry and Neurology, 1997, cert. subspecialty in psychosomatic medicine Am. Bd. Psychiatry and Neurology, 2005. Resident gen. psychiatry Cornell Med. Ctr. N.Y. Hosp., 1991—95; fellow psychosomatic medicine U. Wash., Seattle, 1995—97; dir. residency tng., asst. prof. Dept. Psychiatry Med. Ctr. Georgetown U., Washington, 1997—2000; chmn. Dept. Psychiatry Morristown (N.J.) Meml. Hosp., 2000—, med. dir. Dept. Psychiatry, 2000—; clin. assoc. prof. Dept. Psychiatry U. of Medicine and Dentistry N.J. Med. Sch., Newark, 2002—. Contbr. chapters to books, articles to profl. jours. Named Top Psychiatrist, Consumers' Checkbook, Guide to Top Doctors, 2002—05; recipient Tchr. of the Yr. award, Dept. Psychiatry, U. of Medicine and Dentistry, N.J. Med. Sch., 2002; grantee, NIH, 1995—97. Fellow: Am. Psychiat. Assn. (life); mem.: Am. Coll. Physician Execs., Am. Coll. Psychiatry, Acad. Psychosomatic Medicine. Office: Morristown Meml Hosp 100 Madison Ave Morristown NJ 07960 Office Phone: 973-971-5366. Office Fax: 973-290-7166. Business E-Mail: thomas.zaubler@atlantichealth.org.

ZAUCHA, JEROME J., lawyer; b. Uniontown, Pa. AB summa cum laude, Univ. Notre Dame, 1974; JD, Yale Univ., 1977. Bar: Pa. 1977, DC 1978. Ptnr., Internat. Trade practice Venable LLP, Washington. Mem.: Phi Beta Kappa. Office: Venable LLP 575 7th St NW Washington DC 20004 Office Phone: 202-344-4710. Office Fax: 202-344-8300. Business E-Mail: jjzaucha@venable.com.

ZAUDER, GAIL S., investment banker; b. 1957; AB cum laude, Smith Coll.; MBA, Yale U. With Lehman Brothers Kuhn Loeb; joined Credit Suisse First Boston, NYC, 1985, mng. dir., head, Mergers & Acquisitions, Retail and Apparel Investment Banking Group, 1992—98, mng. dir., worldwide head, Luxury Goods Investment Banking Group, 1998—2001; founder, mng. dir. Elixir Advisors, NYC, 2002—. Bd. dir. GAR Found. Named a Top Dealmaker, Dealmaker mag., 2006. *

ZAUDERER, MARK CARL, lawyer; b. Jan. 26, 1946; BA, Union Coll., 1967; JD, NYU, 1971. Bar: N.Y. 1972, US Dist. Ct. (So. & Ea. dist. NY) 1974, US Ct. Appeals (2d, 5th, Fed. cir.), US Supreme Ct. 1993. Law clk. U.S. Dist. Ct., Newark, 1971—72; founding ptnr. Solomon Zauderer Ellenhorn Frischer & Sharp, NYC, 1981—2003; ptnr., litigation practice DLA Piper Rudnick Gray Cary, NYC, 2003—05; ptnr. Flemming Zulack Williamson Zauderer LLP, NYC, 2005—. Faculty chmn. Practicing Law Inst. Program., Litigating Comml. Cases up to Trial, N.Y.C. and San Francisco, 1986, faculty mem. Deposition Skills Tng. Program, N.Y., 1986, 88-90; adv. com. on civil practice to Chief Adminstrn. Judge N.Y. State Ctrs., 1992—; trustee bd. advisors Union Coll., 1993—; chief Judge's Task Force on Comml. Cts., 1995—; chmn. Chief Judge's Commn. on Jury, 2003—. Author, moderator practising law inst. satellite TV program Deposition Strategy and Tactics, 1989; contbr. articles to profl. jours. Life fellow N.Y. Bar Found.; mem. ABA, N.Y. State Bar Assn. (exec. com. 1991—, chmn. exec. com. 1996-97, comml. and fed. litigation sect., chmn. complex civil litigation com.), Assn. of Bar of City of N.Y. (chmn. com. complex civil litigation, comml. and fed. litigation sect., mem. exec. com. 1991—, chair 1996-97), Fed. Bar Coun. (trustee 1998-2004, treas. 1998—, pres.-elect 2004-2006, pres. 2006—). Office: Flemming Zulack Williamson Zauderer LLP One Liberty Plz 35th Fl New York NY 10006-1404 Home Phone: 914-833-2542; Office Phone: 212-412-9562. Office Fax: 212-964-9200. Business E-Mail: mzauderer@fzwz.com.

ZAVACKY, SUSAN KLINE, law librarian; b. Doylestown, Pa., May 5, 1953; d. Percy H. and Helen C. K.; m. Stephen C. Zavacky, Sept. 12, 1981. BS in Libr. Edn., Millersville U., Pa., 1971-75. Asst. libr. Legis. Reference Bureau, Harrisburg, Pa., 1975-79, libr., 1979—. Vice chair. legis. rsch. librs. staff sect. Nat. Conf. of State Legis., Denver, 1987-88, chair, 1988-89; mem. Dauphin County Libr. Sys. Mem.: Greater Phila. Law Libr. Assn., Easter Seal Soc., Chesapeake Bay Found. Office: Legis Reference Bur Main Capitol Building Rm 641 Harrisburg PA 17120-0033

ZAVADA, BARBARA JOHANNA, artist, educator; b. Jena, Thueringia, Germany, June 20, 1938; arrived in U.S., 1953; d. Paul Egon Weber and Johanna-Helene Kuehlich; m. Gerhard Manfred Grote (div.); 1 child, Erika Barbara Grote. Studied with Karl Bobeck, Berlin, 1962; AA in Fine Art Print Making, Rochester Inst. Tech., NY, 1966; postgrad., Art Students League, NYC, 1970—71. Cert. Traphagen Sch. Fashions, NYC, 1960. Painter, 1960—; fashion designer H & U Schmidt, Berlin, 1961—62, Dave Goldberg, NYC, 1967—71; graphic designer Zavada Assocs., Stamford, Conn., 1974—90. Lectr. in field. One-woman shows include Mus. Art, Sci. and Industry, Bridgeport, Conn., 1974, Bruce Mus., Conn., 1976, Conn. Women's Bank, 1985, Stamford Landmark Tower Rotunda, Conn., 1985, So. Conn. State U., 1990, John Wesley Powell Meml. Mus., Page, Ariz., 1996, Edge of Cedars Mus., Blanding, Utah, 1996, 1999, Western Colo. Arts Ctr., Grand Junction, 1998, Zavada Fine Art Studio-Gallery Arroyo, Seco, N.Mex., 1998—2005, Iron Mission State Pk., Utah, 2000, Beaver St. Gallery, Flagstaff, Ariz., 2005, Represented in permanent collections Concordia Hist. Soc., St. Louis, pmwgallery.com, artprice.com, Saint-Romain-au-Mont-d'Or, France. Search and rescue pilot CAP, Rochester, NY, 1964—68, SI, NY, 1969—70; v.p. German Lang. Sch., Westport, Conn., 1981—83; graphics, scholarship fund Greenwich Acad., 1985—90. Recipient 1st prize, NYC Fashion Competition, 1960, Faber Birren Color award, Stamford, 1981. Mem.: CAP, Nat. Women's History Mus. Avocations: travel, winemaking, hiking, golf. Home: HC 64 Box 3001 Castle Valley UT 84532-9614 Personal E-mail: bjzavada@yahoo.com.

ZAVALIN, ANDREY I., optics scientist, educator; BS, MS, Moscow Engring. Physics Inst., Russia, 1982, PhD, 1990. Sr. rsch. assoc. Russian Acad. Scis., Moscow, 1989—99; rsch. prof. NASA Ctr. Photonic Materials and Devices, Nashville, 1999—2003, Vanderbilt U., Nashville, 2003—. Adj. prof. Conservative Optical Logic Devices Program Fisk U., Nashville, 2004—. Mem.: Soc. Sci. Exploration, Optical Soc. Am., Am. Phys. Soc. Achievements include research in multipolar electromagnetic and acoustic waves; development of effect of a self-assembly in one-beam optical trap; optical logic devices; ionoluminescence in nano-particles. Home: 104 Glenway Ct Nashville TN 37221-3021 Office: Vanderbilt University VU Sta B 351807 2301 Vanderbilt Pl Nashville TN 37235-1807 Office Phone: 615-397-6743. Office Fax: 615-329-8634. E-mail: andrey.zavalin@vanderbilt.edu.

ZAVATSKY, MICHAEL JOSEPH, lawyer; b. Wheeling, W.Va., Dec. 15, 1948; s. Mike and Mary (Mirich) Z.; m. Kathleen Hanson, May 28, 1983; children: David, Emily. BA in Internat. Studies, Ohio State U., 1970; MA in Polit. Sci., U. Hawaii, 1972; JD, U. Cin., 1980. Bar: Ohio 1980, U.S. Dist. Ct. (so. dist.) Ohio 1981, U.S. Ct. Appeals (6th cir.) 1985, U.S. Supreme Ct. 1989. Ptnr. Taft, Stettinius & Hollister, Cin., 1980—. Adj. prof. in trial practice and immigration law U. Cin., 1986— Trustee Internat. Visitors Ctr., Cin., 1984-86; bd. dirs. Cin. Charter Com., 1988-91; bd. dirs., mem. steering com. Leadership Cin., 1994-96. Capt. USAF, 1973-77. William Graham fellow U. Cin., 1979, East West Ctr. fellow U. Hawaii, 1970; named Best Lawyers in Am., 1995—, Ohio Super Lawyers, 2003—, Cin. Leading Lawyers, 2004—. Mem ABA, Ohio Bar Assn., Cin. Bar Assn., Am. Immigration Lawyers Assn. (chmn. Ohio chpt. 1987-88, 90-93), Potter Stewart Inn of Ct., Order of Coif. Home: 3820 Eileen Dr Cincinnati OH 45209-2013 Office: 1800 US Bank Tower Cincinnati OH 45202 Office Phone: 513-357-9393.

ZAVON, MITCHELL RALPH, occupational medicine physician; b. NYC, May 9, 1923; s. Irving and Claire (Gutterman) Z.; m. Betty Berthold, June 24, 1976; children by previous marriage: Peter, Dan, Juliet, Barbara. Student, Cornell U., 1940-43, Harvard U., 1943-44; MD, Boston U., 1949; postgrad., Duke U., 1951-52, U. Cin., 1956-58. Diplomate Am. Bd. Med. Examiners, Am. Bd. Preventive Medicine, Am. Bd. Indsl. Hygiene. Intern Wilson Meml. Hosp., Johnson City, NY, 1949-50; surgeon USPHS, Washington, 1950-56; from instr. to asst. clin. prof. U. Cin., 1952-74, from asst. prof. to clin. prof. indsl. medicine, 1956-71; asst. health commr. Cin. Health Dept., 1956-74; med. dir. Ethyl Corp., Baton Rouge, 1974-76; dir. health Occidental Chem. Corp., Niagara Falls, NY, 1976-86; pres., med. dir. Agatha Corp., Sarasota, Fla., 1968—. Mem., cons., del. Threshold Limits Com., 1962-87; mem., cons. Biol. Indices Com., 1982-96; pres. Place-to-Be, 1978-83; mem. cons. staff Mt. St. Mary's Hosp., 1980-94; med. dir. Buffalo Union Occupl. Health Ctr., 1996-98; mem. sci. adv. bd. Internat. Joint Commn. (U.S./Can.), 1977-80; pres. Am. Assn. Poison Control Ctrs., 1962-64. Contbr. articles to profl. jours. Bd. dirs. HART; mem. Cincinnatus Assocs., 1969-77; mem. Niagara County (N.Y.) Bd. Health, 1994-00, pres., 1997; chair Sarasota/Manatee Common Cause. Fellow APHA, Am. Coll. Occupl. and Environ. Medicine, Am. Indsl. Hygiene Assn.; mem. AMA, AAAS, N.Y. State Med. Soc., Niagara County Med. Soc., Am. Conf. Govtl. Indsl. Hygienists. Unitarian Universalist. Home and Office: 4559 Trails Dr Sarasota FL 34232-3450 Office Phone: 941-378-7015. Personal E-mail: zavonm@cs.com.

ZAWACKI, BRUCE EDWIN, surgeon, educator, ethicist; b. Northampton, Mass., Dec. 6, 1935; BS, Coll. of Holy Cross, 1957; MD, Harvard U., 1961; MA, U. So. Calif., 1986. Diplomate Am. Bd. Surgery. Intern in surgery Mass. Gen. Hosp., 1961—62, resident in surgery, 1962—65; vis. scholar in trauma surgery Birmingham Accident Hosp., Birmingham, England, 1966; resident in surgery Mass. Gen. Hosp., 1967; gen. surgeon So. Calif. Permanente Med. Group, Panorama City, 1969-71; dir. burn ctr. L.A. County and U. So. Calif. Med. Ctr., LA, 1971-98; assoc. prof. surgery U. So. Calif. Sch. Medicine, LA, 1975-98, assoc. prof. emeritus, 1998—; assoc. prof. religion U. So. Calif. Sch. Religion, LA, 1992-98; assoc. for edn. Pacific Ctr. for Health Policy and Ethics, 1997—; adj. assoc. prof. religion U. So. Calif., 2001—02. Contbr. articles to profl. jours. Served to maj. U.S. Army, 1967-68. Mem. Am. Burn Assn. (2d v.p., bd. trustees 1992-93; Harvey Stuart Allen Disting. Svc. award 1996), Am. Soc. Bioethics and Humanities, L.A. Surg. Soc., Internat. Soc. for Burn Injuries. Achievements include first to describe the natural history of reversible burn injury, the independence of burn hypermetabolism from evaporative water loss and an autonomous role for burn patients without precedent for survival.

ZAWADA, EDWARD THADDEUS, JR., physician, educator; b. Chgo., Oct. 3, 1947; s. Edward Thaddeus and Evelyn Mary (Kovarek) Z.; m. Nancy Ann Stephen, Mar. 26, 1977; children: Elizabeth, Nicholas, Victoria, Alexandra. BS summa cum laude, Loyola U., Chgo., 1969; MD summa cum laude, Loyola-Stritch Sch. Medicine, 1973. Diplomate Am. Bd. Internal Medicine, Am. Bd. Nephrology, Am. Bd. Nutrition, Am. Bd. Critical Care, Am. Bd. Geriatrics, Am. Bd. Clin. Pharm., Am. Bd. Forensic Examiners, Am. Bd. Forensic Medicine; specialist Hypertension, Am. Soc. Hypertension. Intern UCLA Hosp., 1973, resident, 1974-76; asst. prof. medicine UCLA, 1978-79, U. Utah, Salt Lake City, 1979-81; assoc. prof. medicine Med. Coll. Va., Richmond, 1981-83; assoc. prof. medicine, physiology & pharmacology U. SD Sch. Medicine, Sioux Falls, 1983-86, Freeman prof., chmn. dept. Internal Medicine, 1987—2002, prof. emeritus, 2002—, chief div. nephrology and hypertension, 1983-88, pres. univ. physician's practice plan, 1992—95; v.p. sci. affairs, dir. dialysis, critical care Avera Health Sys., 2002—04, dir. e-icu, 2004—. Chief renal sect. Salt Lake VA Med. Ctr., 1980-81; asst. chief med. service McGuire VA Med. Ctr., Richmond, 1981-83. Editor: Geriatric Nephrology and Urology, 1984; contbr. articles to profl. publs. Pres. Minnehaha div. Am. Heart Assn., 1984-87, pres. Dakota affiliate Am. Heart Assn., 1989-91. VA Hosp. System grantee, 1981-85, 85-88; Health and Human Svcs. grantee Pub. Health Scvs. Rsch. Adminstrn. Bureau Health Profl., 1993—. Master ACP; fellow Am. Coll. Chest Physicians, Am. Coll. Nutrition, Am. Coll. Clin. Pharmacology, Internat. Coll. Angiology, Am. Coll. Angiology, Am. Coll. Clin. Pharmacology, Am. Coll. Forensic Examiners, Royal Soc. Medicine, Soc. for Vascular Medicine and Biology, Am. Soc. Nephrology; mem. Internat. Soc. Nephrology, Am. Soc. Pharmacology and Exptl. Therapeutics, Am. Physiol. Soc., Am. Inst. Nutrition, Am. Soc. Clin. Nutrition, Am. Geriatric Soc., Am. Soc. Transplant Physicians, Westward Ho Country Club. Democrat. Roman Catholic. Avocations: golf, tennis, skiing, cinema, music. Home: 2908 S Duchess Ave Sioux Falls SD 57103-4826 Office: North Central Kidney Inst 1001 E 21st St Ste 300 Sioux Falls SD 57105-1017 Office Phone: 605-322-5800. E-mail: ezawada@sio.micko.net, edward.zawada@mckennan.org.

ZAWADZKI-JANUSZ, STACY LYNN, music educator, performing arts educator; b. Buffalo, June 13, 1974; d. Michael Thomas and Diane Theresa Zawadzki; m. Robert Paul Janusz, Aug. 13. BA magna cum laude, U. Buffalo, NYC, 1996, MA and Humanities magna cum laude, 2004. CPR,

ARC; cert. tchr. N.Y. Substitute tchr. P.S. 139 Elem. Sch., 1999—2000; dance tchr. I.S. 232 Winthrop Intermediate Sch., 2000—00; choreographer, workshop tchr. West Seneca East H.S., NY, 2002—, Cheektowaga Ctrl. H.S., NY, 2002; tchr. art Arts in Edn., West Seneca, NY, 2002—; choreographer Walh's Performing Arts Studios, Orchard Park, NY, 2004—, Royal Acad. Ballet and Dance, Kenmore, NY, 2005—, Irish Classical Theatre, Buffalo, 2005—; prof. mus. theatre and dance Niagara U., Niagara Falls, NY, 2005—; co-founder, artistic dir., choreographer Youth for Truth Performing Arts Co., Inc., 2005—. Mem. Buffalo Contemporary Dance Co., Marie-Christine Giordano Dance Co., Alpha Omega Dance Co., New Dance Collective Dance Co., Zodiaque Dance Co.; dir. and founder ECNAD Dance Co.; dance educator, choreographer St. Margaret's Cath. Sch.; adjudicator dance competitions throughout U.S.; artistic dir., co-founder, choreographer Youth for Truth Performing Arts Co.; summer dance educator U. Buffalo. Choreographer Music is Art Festival and Elmwood Art Festival, Zodiaque Dance Co., Am. Coll. Dance Festival, various musicals including Gypsy, Once on This Island, Pippin, Singin' the the Rain, High Society, 42nd Street, Guys and Dolls, Hello Dolly, My Fair Lady, West Side Story, Oklahoma, Damn Yankees, Bye Bye Birdie, Anything Goes, Jesus Christ Superstar and Grease; choreographer A Man of No Importance, — (Artie award), Sound of Music, —, Godspell, —; choreographer MTC Prodns., Lancaster Opera House, NYC, 2003—, dancer performer NYC, Can., Conn., Mex., Brit. Virgin Islands. Recipient Choreogaphy award, NY State TANYS Theatre Assn. Home: 145 Pierce St Buffalo NY 14206-3328 Office Phone: 716-704-9969. Personal E-mail: dancestace@roadrunner.com.

ZAWICKI, JOSEPH LEO, science educator; b. Batavia, NY, Sept. 24, 1958; s. Leo Stanley Zawicki, Rita Zawicki; m. Ann Marie Hartley, July 27, 1984; children: Richard John, Erin Kathleen, Lee Joseph, Sean Michael. BA, Canisius Coll., 1980; MSEd, U. Rochester, 1989; PhD in Sci. Edn., SUNY, Buffalo, 2002. Cert. tchr. certificate N.Y. Lab technologist Strong Meml. Hosp., Rochester, NY, 1984—89; tchr., dept. chair Elba Ctrl. Sch., Elba, NY, 1989—2002; asst. prof. Buffalo State Coll., Buffalo, 2002—. Lectr. Buffalo State Coll., NY, 2001—02, U. Buffalo, 2002; item writer, cons. N.Y. State Edn. Dept., Albany, 1995—; physics mentor N.Y. State Mentor Network, Oneonta, 1996—; bd. dirs. N.Y. Sci. Edn. Leadership Assn. Developer Optic Bench Sci., 2001. Bd. dirs. Cornell Coop. Ext., Batavia, 1996—98; dir. religious edn. Our Lady of Fatima, Elba, 1999—. Recipient St. Joseph the Worker award, Diocese of Buffalo, 2001; grantee Environ. Empowerment, N.Y. State, 1998. Mem.: Nat. Assn. Rsch. in Sci. Tchg., N.Y. State Edn. Leadership Assn., Sci. Tchrs. Assn. N.Y., Am. Assn. Physics Tchrs., Am. Chem. Soc. Avocations: youth programs, reading. Home: PO Box 172 7 S Main St Elba NY 14058-0172 Office: Buffalo State Coll Sci 130 Dept Earth Scis and Sci Edn 1300 Elmwood Ave Buffalo NY 14222 Office Phone: 716-878-3800. Business E-Mail: zawickjl@buffalostate.edu.

ZAWISTOWSKI, STEPHEN LOUIS, psychologist, educator; b. Lackawanna, NY, July 28, 1955; s. Louis Henry and Alice Theresa (Bartus) Z.; m. Jane Elaine Clark, May 26, 1979; 1 child, Matthew. BA, Canisius Coll., 1977; AM, U. Ill., 1979, PhD, 1983. Cert. tech. animal rescue specialist, Am. Humane Assn./Rescue 3. Vis. asst. prof. Ind. U., Bloomington, 1983-84, postdoctoral fellow, 1984-85; asst. prof. St. John's U., NYC, 1985-88; exec. sr. v.p. ASPCA, NYC, 1988—. Adj. prof. U. Ill. Vet. Coll., 2004; nat. rsch. coun. panel for rev. of the nat. zoo Nat. Rsch. Coun., 2003—04. Author: Animal Shelter Medicine for Veterinarians and Staff, 2004, co-editor, 2004; co-author: Animal Rights Handbook, 1990; editor Animal Behavior Cons. Newsletter, 2001; co-editor: For Kids Who Love Animals, 1991; contbg. editor Animal Watch Mag., 1990-2004; co-exec. prodr. (film) Question of Respect, 1990 (Silver Apple award 1990); writer, host ASPCA pet check segments, PBS; mem. bd. editors Psychologists for the Ethical Treatment of Animals, 1988-95; founding co-editor Jour. Applied Animal Welfare Sci.; contbg. editor, sci. advisor Animaland Mag., 1998-2000; script cons. Animal Rescue Kid, 1997; contbr. articles to profl. jours. Scoutmaster Boy Scouts Am., SI, 1988-98; asst. coach SI Youth Soccer, 1986-95; bd. dirs. Nat. Coun. on Pet Population Study and Policy, v.p., 1995-96, 99-2000, pres., 1996-97, advisor, 2004—; mem. steering com. NY State Watchable Wildlife Program; mem. Nat. Humane Dog Tng. Task Force; bd. dirs. United for Wildlife, 1999-2001, Harmony Inst. Cmty. Adv. Bd.; mem. sci. adv. com. Humane Farm Animal Care, 2003—; bd. dirs., vice chair Alliance for the Contraception of Cats and Dogs, 2005, chmn. 2006-07. Recipient Stan Lesny scholarship Kosciuszki Found., 1977, U. Ill. Grad. fellowship, 1977, Postdoctoral fellowship NSF, 1984, Patrick Daley award for contbns. to edn. St. John's U.; named Psychologist of Yr., Psychologists for Ethical Treatment of Animals, 1989. Mem. World Soc. for Protection of Animals (sci. adv. panel 2003—), Animal Behavior Soc. (cert. applied animal behaviorist, chmn. bd. profl. cert. 1998—, devel. com. 1995-98, animal welfare com. 1989-95), Order of Arrow (mem. exec. bd. 1996-98), Sigma Xi. Achievements include research in genetics and animal learning, animal behavior and welfare. Office: ASPCA 110 5th Ave 2d Fl New York NY 10010 Office Phone: 212-876-7700 ext. 4401. Business E-Mail: SteveZ@aspca.org.

ZAWODNY, LARAE JEAN, artist, secondary school educator; b. Chgo., Feb. 9, 1949; d. Raymond William and Dorothy (Hammersmith) Koppit; m. Janusz Kazimierz Zawodny, Sept. 18, 1971; 1 child, Roman Janusz. BA magna cum laude, U. Nebr., Omaha, 1970; MFA, Claremont Grad. U., Calif., 1982. Artist Color on Edge, Vancouver, Wash., 1985—; secondary tchr. dept. visual and performing arts Vancouver Sch. Dist., 1992-99; artist, instr. Vancouver Sch. Arts and Acads., 1996-99. One-woman shows include Claremont Grad. U., 1982, U. Portland, 1984, Columbia Arts Ctr., Vancouver, 1985, City Hall, Beaverton, Oreg., 1989, Royal Durst Theatre, Vancouver, 1997, exhibited in group shows at Lang Gallery Scripps Coll., Claremont, 1978, Libra Gallery, 1981, 1982, Factory Pl., L.A., 1982, U. Calif., Irvine, 1982, Portland Ctr. Visual Arts, 1983, Elizabeth Leach Gallery, 1983, 1984, Coos Bay (Oreg.) Art Mus., 1985, Marianne Partlow Gallery, Olympia, Wash., 1986—87, Pacific N.W. Art Expo, Seattle, 1986, U. Portland, 1986, Abbot Hall Gallery, Portland, 1990, Vancouver Sch. Arts and Acads., Wash., 1997, 1998, 2006, North Bank Gallery, Vancouver, Wash., 2005, 2006, Represented in permanent collections Mercedes Benz Corp., Frankfurt, Germany, Pomona Coll., Claremont. Home: 23703 NE Margaret Rd Brush Prairie WA 98606-5602

ZAX, LEONARD A., lawyer; b. Paterson, NJ, July 16, 1950; s. Harry and Shirley Jeanne (Hollander) Z.; m. Helen Kemp, May 25, 1980; children: David Hollander, Laura Alexandra. BA, U. Chgo., 1971; M of City Planning, Harvard U., 1975, JD, 1975. Bar: N.J. 1978, D.C. 1978. Spl. asst. to gen. counsel HUD, 1975-76, spl. asst. to sec., 1976-77; lectr., mem. faculty Harvard U., Cambridge, Mass., 1977-78; assoc. Fried, Frank, Harris, Shriver & Kampelman, Washington, 1977-82, ptnr., 1982-95, Latham & Watkins, Washington, 1995—, also chmn. real estate group. Co-chmn. Mayor's Downtown Housing Commn., Washington, 1986-89, D.C. Enterprise Zones Study Commn., 1986-89; D.C. Downtown Interactive Retail Task Force, 1996-98; co-chmn. Washington adv. com. Asian Real Estate Assn., Washington, 1991-92. Contbg. author Nat. Law Jour., N.Y. Times, L.A. Times, Harvard Law Bull., Real Estate Fin. Jour., Urban Land, Washington Business Jour., Washington Post; editor: Real Estate and the RTC: A Guide to Asset Purchases and Contracting, Urban Land Inst., 1990. Trustee Nat. Bldg. Mus., D.C. Preservation League, 1988-95; mem. Fannie Mae Nat. Adv. Coun., 1994-95; mem. vis. com. Harvard Design Sch., 2000—. Mem. ABA (chmn. com. on housing and urban devel. law 1986-89, steering com. representation of the Homeless Project 1988-91, governing bd. forum com. affordable housing and community devel. 1991-94), D.C. Bar Assn., Urban Land Inst., Nat. Multi Housing Coun. Home: 4511 28th St NW Washington DC 20008-1035 Office: Latham & Watkins 555 11thSt NW Ste 1000 Washington DC 20004-1304

ZAX, MELVIN, psychologist, educator; b. Cambridge, Mass., Apr. 14, 1928; s. Joseph and Sadie (Kirshner) Z.; m. Ruth Leah Vogel, Apr. 23, 1977; children: Jeffrey S., David B., Jonathan B. AB, Boston U., 1951, A.M., 1952; PhD, U. Tenn., 1955. Clin. psychologist U. Tenn., Knoxville, 1955-56; staff psychologist St. Elizabeths Hosp., Washington, 1956-57; asst. prof. psychology U. Rochester, NY, 1957-62, assoc. prof. psychology NY, 1962-67, prof. NY, 1967-93, prof. emeritus NY, 1993—; pvt. practice, 1973—. Chmn. exptl. and spl. tng. rev. com. NIMH, 1970-71. Author: (with G. Stricker) Patterns of Psychopathology, 1963, (with E.L. Cowen) Abnormal Psychology: Changing Conceptions, 1972, (with G.A. Specter) An Introduction to Community Psychology, 1974, (with M. Nichols) Catharsis in Psychotherapy, 1977; editor: (with Stricker) The Study of Abnormal Behavior: Selected Readings, 1964, (with Cowen and E.A. Gardner) Emergent Approaches to Mental Health Problems, 1967, (with D. Dorr and J. Bonner) The Psychology of Discipline, 1983; adv. editor Jour. Cons. and Clin. Psychology, 1965-81; contbr. articles to profl. jours. Served with AUS, 1946-47. NIMH spl. research fellow Psykologisk Inst., Copenhagen, 1966-67 Fellow Am. Psychol. Assn.; mem. Eastern Psychol. Assn., AAUP, Phi Beta Kappa, Sigma Xi, Phi Kappa Phi. Home: 27 Sky Ridge Dr Rochester NY 14625-2167

ZAYAC, LINDA MARY, sociologist, educator; d. Ernest F. and Barbara T. Dauplaise; m. Paul Edward Zayac, Nov. 3, 1976; children: Nicholas Alexander, Alexander Joseph. BA in Sociology and Psychology, Am. Internat. Coll., Springfield, Mass., 1972, MA in Edn., 1973. Instr. of social studies Southwick H.S., Mass., 1975—79; project dir. visual edn. lab. Southwick Pub. H.S., 1978—85; co-owner sr. cons. and svcs. Pvt. Geriatric Care Mgmt. Firm, West Springfield, Mass., 1999—2002; instr. sociology Westfield State Coll., Westfield, 1994—, dir. ctr. for instrnl. tech., 2003—07. Mem. Town Meeting, West Springfield, 1983—2002; traffic safety com. chair Town of West Springfield, 1989—2002; chair Master Plan Commn., 1994—2002; mem. Planning Bd., 1983—2002, Traffic Adv. Commn., 1989—2002, Pioneer Valley Planning Commn. Joint Study Com., West Springfield, 1990—2002, Holyyoke, Mass., 1990—2002; chair Corridor Bus. Assn., Riverdale, Mass., 1993—2002; mem. Pioneer Valley Planning Commn. Study Group, 1989—2002, Mass. Sr. Action Coun., 1995—2002, Dem. Town Com., 1983—2002; lacrosse dir. Youth League, 1992—98; pres. Lacrosse Booster Club, 1998—2002; it steering com. Westfield State Coll., 2003—. Mem.: Mass. Coun. Aging Affairs, Nat. Assn. Profl. Geriatric Care Mgrs., Children Aging Parents, Native Am. Inst., Mass. Women in Pub. Higher Edn., Mass. Coll. Online (liason 2003—06), Mass. Teachers Assn., NERCOMP (assoc.). Home: 79 Highmeadow Dr West Springfield MA 01089 Office: Westfield State Coll 577 Western Ave Westfield MA 01086 Home Phone: 413-737-3872; Office Phone: 413-572-8142. Office Fax: 413-572-8048. Business E-Mail: lzayac@wsc.ma.edu.

ZAYAS-BAZAN, EDUARDO, foreign language educator; b. Camagüey, Cuba, Nov. 17, 1935; came to US, 1962, naturalized, 1969; s. Manuel Eduardo and Aida Modesta (Loret de Mola); m. Lourdes Abascal; children: Eduardo, Elena María. Dr. en Derecho, U. Nacional José Martí, 1958; MS, Kans. State Tchrs.' Coll., 1966. Social worker Cuban Refugee Asst. Program, 1962-64; Spanish tchr. Plattsmouth High Sch., 1964-65, Topeka West High Sch., 1965-66; Spanish instr. Appalachian State U., 1966-68; asst. prof. East Tenn. State U., Johnson City, 1968-73, assoc. prof., 1973-79, prof., 1979-99, chmn. fgn. lang. dept., 1973-93, prof. emeritus, 1999—. Author (with P. Ferreiro): Cómo dominar la redacción, 1989; author: (with G. Fernández de la Torriente) Cómo aumentar su vocabulario 3; author: Cómo escribir cartas eficaces, 1989; author: (with N.A. Humbach and José B. Fernández) Nuestro mundo, 1990; author: (with José Fernández) iArriba!, 1993, 1997; author: (with Carolyn M. Novak) No se equivoque con el inglés, 1993; author: El inglés que usted no sabe que sabe, Primera y Segunda Serie, 1993; author: (with Susan Bacon and Dulce García) Conexiones, 1999, 2002, 2006; editor (with Anthony G. Lozano): Del amor a la revolución, 1975; editor: (with L. Suárez) De aquí y de allá, 1980; editor: (with G. J. Fernández) Así somos, 1983; translator: Secret Report on Cuban Revolution, 1981; author (with Susan Bacon): iArriba!, 2001, 2004. Pres. Sister Cities Internat., Johnson City, 1971-76. Recipient Disting. Faculty award E. Tenn. State U., 1978 Mem.: Cuban Cultural Heritage Assn. (bd. dirs. 2000—02, sec. 2003—06, v.p. 2006—07), Nat. Assn. Cuban-Am. Educators (pres. 1991—93, chair bd. dirs. 1994—2002, pres. 2002—04, treas. 2004—), Tenn. Fgn. Lang. Teaching Assn. (pres. 1980, Jacqueline Elliott award 1989), Am. Assn. Tchrs. Spanish and Portuguese (pres. 1985, assoc. editor Hispania 1994—98), Am. Coun. Tchrs. Fgn. Langs., Municipality of Camagüey in Exile (pres. 2000—02, editor El Camagüeyano Libre 2002—), Sigma Delta Pi (Premio Martel 1984). Home: 7540 SW 52 Ct Miami FL 33143 Office Phone: 305-495-5436. Personal E-mail: ezbazan@aol.com.

ZAYDON, JEMILLE ANN, language educator, communications educator; b. Peckville, Pa., Feb. 21; d. Joseph and Catherine Ann (Hazzouri) Zaydon. Student, Barry Coll. for Women, 1957—58; BS, Marywood U., 1963; MS in Edn., Wilkes U., 1978; postgrad., Temple U. Tchr. St. Hugh Elem. Sch., Coconut Grove, Fla., Allapattah Elem. Sch., Miami, Columbus Elem. Sch., Westfield, NJ; comm. instr. Keystone Job Corps, Drums, Pa.; vol. instr. Keystone Rehab. Ctr., Scranton, Pa.; curriculum cons. for mentally retarded Vienna; prof. English and reading Lackawanna Jr. Coll., Scranton, head dept. English, speech and reading, chmn. dept. arts, humanities and social studies; assoc. prof. Marywood U., Wilkes U. Adj. prof. English U. Scranton; comm. instr. Lackawanna County Vocat. Tech. Sch. Editor: Lebanese Am. Jour. Supr. recreation program, Hazleton, Pa.; founder, adviser Keystone Kourier; sec. Fedn. Youth, Willim W. Scranton; coord. annual Christmas for Mentally Retarded Keystone City Residence; supr. students Heart Fund campaign; developer program mentally retarded Allied Svcs. Handicapped Scranton; class rep. Marywood U. Fund Dr.; gen. faculty coord. Am. Cancer Soc.; active ARC, March of Dimes, Heart Fund, Leukemia and United Fund drs., Sickle Cell Anemia Found.; exec. bd. Northeastern Pa. Environ. Coun., co-chmn. pub. edn. and funding; bd. v.p. Lackawanna County Commr., 2003—; bd. dirs. Lackawanna County Commn. for Women, 2003—07, v.p. exec. bd., 2003—07, 2d v.p., 2004—06, seminar chair, 2005, mem. April seminar exec. com., 2007; exec. bd. Lackawanna County Commr., 2004—; chmn. seminar Lackawanna County Commn.; instr. Confraternity Christian Doctrine; chairperson St. Joseph's Melkite Cath. Ch., 2003—04; bd. dirs. Michael F. Harrity Meml. Fund. Named Tchr. of the Yr., Tchr. We Will Never Forget, Dade County Allpattah Elem. Students, 1991, N.E. Woman, Scranton Sunday Times, 1993; recipient Faculty Mem. of the Yr. award, Keystone Job Corps, Humanitarian award, Outstanding Educators award, 1992, Educators award, Dade County; Svc. scholar, Barry Coll. Mem.: NEA, Pa. State Edn. Assn., Theta Chi Beta (charter pres.), Sigma Tau Delta, Beta Lambda Tau, Lambda Iota Tau (life). Home: 608 N Main Ave Scranton PA 18504-1870 Personal E-mail: jemillez@webtv.net.

ZAYDON, THOMAS JOHN, JR., plastic surgeon; b. Phila., Apr. 3, 1952; s. Thomas J. and Helen (Joseph) Z. BS, Fla. State U., 1974; MD with spl. honors, Hahnemann Med. U., 1978. Cert. Am. Bd. Plastic Surgery, 1982; diplomate Am. Bd. Surgery, 1991. Intern in gen. surgery Eastern Va. Med. Sch., Norfolk, 1978—79, resident in gen. surgery, 1979—80; jr. resident in gen. surgery Monmouth Med. Ctr., Long Beach, NJ, 1980-81, sr. resident in gen. surgery, 1981-82; resident in plastic surgery La. State U., New Orleans, 1982-83, chief resident in plastic surgery, 1983-84, clin. instr.; pvt. practice surgery Cosmetic Surgery Inst., Miami, 1984—; assoc. chief plastic surgery Miami Heart Inst., Fla., 1984—85; assoc. chief, plastic surgery Mercy Hosp., 2004—05; pvt. practice. Vol. clin. instr. plastic surgery U. Miami, Fla. 1986—. Author articles and book chpts. in field. Fellow ACS; mem. Dade County Med. Assn., John Rives Surg. Soc., Aesculapian Soc. Miami, Fla. Med. Assn., Fla. Soc. Plastic and Reconstructive Surgeons, Fla. Soc. Plastic Surgeons, Greater Miami Soc. Plastic Surgeons, Am. Soc. Plastic Surgeons, Am. Soc. Aesthetic Plastic Surgery, Southeastern Soc. Plastic Surgeons. Office: Cosmetic Surgery Inst Miami Mercy Hosp Profl Bldg 3661 S Miami Ave Ste 509 Miami FL 33133-4206 also: Dadeland Med Ctr 7400 N Kendall Dr Ste 502 Miami FL 33156 Office Phone: 305-856-3030. E-mail: tzaydon@pol.net.

ZAYHOWSKI, JOHN J., electrical engineer, researcher; b. Troy, NY, 1958; s. John J. and Carole E. J. Zayhowski; m. Lien N. Zayhowski, 1982; children: Justine A., Kimberly M. BS, MS, MIT, Cambridge, Mass., 1982, PhD, 1986. Engr. Tex. Instruments, Dallas, 1979-82; mem. tech. staff Lincoln Lab. MIT, Lexington, Mass., 1986—2000, sr. staff Lincoln Lab., 2000—. Chmn. Advanced Concepts Com., Lincoln Lab., 1998-99; vis. prof. Tufts U., Medford, Mass., 1997; chmn. various meetings in field; cons. in field. Author: (chpt.) Handbook of Photonics, 1997, 2d edit., 2007, Encyclopedia of Applied Physics, 1994, LIA Handbook of Laser Materials Processing, 1999, The Optics Encyclopedia, Basic Foundations and Practical Applications, 2003, Encyclopedia of Physics, 3d edit., 2005, Solid-State Lasers and Applications, 2007; topical editor Optics Letters, 2005—; contbr. over 70 articles to profl. jours. Pres. Sherwood Forest Homeowners Assn., 1997-98. Recipient fellowship Hertz Found., 1981, scholarship Edith Craig Reynolds, 1977, 1998 R&D 100 award R&D Magazine, commendation for Excellence in Tech. Communications Laser Focus World, 1996, 99, Appreciation cert. NBC, 2004, Team award MIT, 2002, 03, Tech. Excellence award, MIT, 2005. Mem. Optical Soc. Am., Sigma Xi, Tau Beta Pi, Eta Kappa Nu. Achievements include development of microchip laser technology resulting in four start-up companies; 16 patents in field. Office: MIT Lincoln Lab L-142 244 Wood St Lexington MA 02420-9108

ZAZULIA, ALLYSON ROBYN, neurologist, educator; b. Perth Amboy, NJ, Dec. 19, 1967; d. Irwin Zazulia and Nina Foer; m. Michael Neil Diringer, June 3, 2001; 1 child, Daniel Diringer. BS in Psychology, U. Md., College Park, 1990; MD, Georgetown U., DC, 1994. Lic. dr. Nat. Bd. Med. Examiners, 1995, diplomate neurology Am. Bd. Psychiatry & Neurology, 1999, vascular neurology Am. Bd. Psychiatry & Neurology, 2006. Rsch. asst. NIH, Bethesda, Md., 1988—90; resident internal medicine Wash. U., St. Louis, 1994—95, resident neurology, 1995—98, fellow cerebrovascular disease, 1998—2000, instr. neurology, 1998—2001, asst. prof. neurology & radiology, 2001—; attending neurologist Barnes-Jewish Hosp., St. Louis, 1998—. Dir. pre-clinical neurol. edn. Wash. U., 2001—, mem. editl. bd. Internet Stroke Ctr., 2005—. Recipient Coursemaster of Yr. award, Wash. U. Sch. Medicine, 2005, Samuel R. Goldstein Leadership award in med. student edn., 2006; grantee Patient-Oriented Rsch. Career Devel. award, NIH, 2003. Mem.: Am. Heart Assn. (assoc.), Am. Acad. Neurology (assoc.), Alpha Omega Alpha, Phi Beta Kappa. Office: Wash Univ Sch Medicine 660 S Euclid Ave Campus Box 8111 Saint Louis MO 63110 Home Phone: 314-567-8545.

ZAZZALI, JAMES R., retired state supreme court justice; b. Newark, June 17, 1937; s. Andrew F. Zazzali; m. Eileen Fitzsimmons; children: Mara, James Jr., Robert, Courtney, Kevin. BA, Georgetown U., 1958, JD, 1962. Bar: NJ, NY, DC. Law clk. to Hon. Lawrence A. Whipple U.S. Dist. Ct. NJ, 1964—65; from asst. prosecutor to chief appellate sect. Essex County Prosecutor's Office, 1965—68; ptnr. Zazzali, Zazzali, Fagella, & Nowak, Newark; gen. counsel NJ Sports and Exposition Authority, 1973—81; atty. gen. State of NJ, Trenton, 1981—82; assoc. justice NJ Supreme Ct., Trenton, 2000—06, chief justice, 2006—07. Adj. prof. Seton Hall Law Sch., 1984—; commr. NJ State Commn. of Investigation, 1984—94, chmn., 1990—94; vice-chair Disciplinary Rev Bd., 1984—2000. Democrat. *

ZBAR, LLOYD IRWIN STANLEY, otolaryngologist, educator; b. Jersey City, June 2, 1939; m. Margo Wally, Mar. 25, 1965; children: Ross I.S., Brett I.W. MD, Queen's U., Kingston, Ont., Can., 1964. Cert. otolaryngologist. Intern Beth Israel/Harvard, Boston, 1964; resident surgery French Hosp., NYC, 1965—66; resident otolaryngology Bellevue Hosp. Ctr.-NYU, NYC, 1966—69, fellow otolaryngology, 1969—70; chmn. med. edn. com. Mountainside Hosp., Montclair, NJ, 1979—89, dir. otolaryngology, 1990—97, 1999—. Sec. med. bd. Mountainside Hosp., Glen Ridge, N.J., 1986-90, clin. assoc. prof. otolaryngology NYU Sch. Medicine Contbr. rev. to New Eng. Jour. Medicine, 1988 Mem. exec. bd. Boy Scouts Am., Essex County, N.J., 1984-95; pres. Mountainside Physicians Scholarship Loan Fund, 1972-85 With USAF. Named a Top Dr. NY Metro Area, 1998—2007. Fellow ACS, Am. Acad. Otolaryngology-Head and Neck Surgery, Royal Soc. Medicine Office: 200 Highland Ave Glen Ridge NJ 07028-1528 Office Phone: 973-744-2424. Office Fax: 973-743-3111. Personal E-mail: liszmd@yahoo.com.

ZBORNAK, KENT, television producer; Actor: (TV series) The Golden Palace, The Larry Sanders Show; stage mgr. (TV series) The Mommies, The Golden Girls, 1991—92, The Golden Palace, The Five Mrs. Buchanans, Blossom; prodr.: (TV series) Newsradio, 1996—99, Oh Grow Up, Go Fish, The O'Keefes, 2003, The Office, 2005—06, (co-exec. prodr.), 2006— (Danny Thomas Prodr. of Yr. award in Episodic TV - Comedy, Producers Guild of Am., 2007). Office: c/o NBC Television Network 30 Rockefeller Plz New York NY 10112 *

ZDANIS, RICHARD ALBERT, academic administrator; b. Balt., July 15, 1935; s. Albert Francis and Elsie (Kral) Z.; m. Barbara Rosenberger, June 5, 1955; children: Michael Richard, Carole Lynn. BA, Johns Hopkins U., 1957, PhD in Physics, 1960. Rsch. assoc. Princeton (N.J.) U., 1960-61, instr., 1961-62; asst. prof., then assoc. prof. Johns Hopkins U., Balt., 1962-69, prof., 1969-88, assoc. provost, 1975-79, v.p. for adminstrv. svcs., 1977-79, vice provost, 1979-88; provost Case Western Res. U., Cleve., 1988-2000, retired, 2000. Cons. Naval Ordnance Lab., 1967-68, 69-74. Bd. dirs. Great Lakes Sci. Mus., 1990-2004, Cleve. Edn. Found., 1990-96; mem. governing coun. Ohio LINK, 1994-2000; mem. Cleve. Initiative for Edn., 1999-2004. Mem.: Associated Univs. Inc. (bd. dirs.), Am. Phys. Soc.

ZDERIC, STEPHEN ANTHONY, urologist, surgeon; b. Detroit, July 2, 1956; s. John Anthony and Marie Alice Zderic; m. Kathleen (Kate) Marie Cronan, Dec. 6, 1953; children: Olivia Cronan, Colin Cronan, Natalie Sang Me. BS Chemistry and BioChemistry, U. Calif. Riverside, 1979; MD, UCLA, 1983. Cert. Urologist Am. Bd. of Urology, 1993. Asst. prof. surgery in urology Sch. Medicine U. Pa., Phila., 1991—99; attending surgeon Children's Hosp. Phila., 1991—; assoc. prof. surgery in urology Sch. Medicine Sch. Medicine U. Pa., 1999—2006, prof. surgery in urology, 2006—. Editor: (sci. mongraph) Muscle Matrix and Bladder Function, Pediatric Gender Assignment A Critical Reappraisal; cons. reviewer Jour. Urology, Brit. Jour. Urology; contbr. articles to profl. jours. Grantee, NIH, 1993—98, 1994—95, 2003—05, 1998—; Rsch. Grant, Am. Found. Urologic Disease, 1989—90. Avocations: tennis, skiing, swimming. Office: Children's Hosp Philadelphia 34th & Civic Center Blvd Philadelphia PA 19104 Home Phone: 610-793-4644; Office Phone: 215-590-3766. Office Fax: 215-590-3985. Personal E-mail: zderic@email.chop.edu.

ZEAGER, LLOYD, librarian; b. Elizabethtown, Pa., Sept. 19, 1942; s. Russel S. and Anna Mae (Givens) Z. BA, Goshen Coll., 1976; MS, Drexel U., 1983. Sec., adminstrv. asst. Mennonite Brotherly Aid, Salunga, Pa.,

1967-72; asst. libr. Lancaster (Pa.) Mennonite Hist. Soc., 1976-82, libr., 1983—2006, asst. libr., 2007—. Author: A York County Givens Family, 1980, Master Alphabetical Compilation of Hymns Appearing in Mennonite Hymn Books, 1980, Mission in the City, 1997. Mem. ALA, Hymn Soc. U.S. and Can. Democrat. Mennonite. Avocations: hymnology, genealogy. Office: Lancaster Mennonite Hist Soc 2215 Millstream Rd Lancaster PA 17602-1429

ZEALEY, SHARON JANINE, lawyer; b. St. Paul, Aug. 30, 1959; d. Marion Edward and Freddie Zealey. BS, Xavier U. of La., 1981; JD, U. Cin., 1984. Bar: Ohio 1984; U.S. Dist. Ct. (so. dist.) Ohio 1985; U.S. Ct. Appeals (6th cir.) 1990; U.S. Supreme Ct. 1990. Law clk. U.S. Atty. for S. Dist. of Ohio, Cin., 1982; trust adminstr. U.S. Bank (formerly First Nat. Bank), Cin., 1984-86; atty. UAW Legal Svcs., Cin., 1986-88; assoc. Manley, Burke, Lipton & Fischer, Cin., 1988-91; mng. atty. and dep. atty. gen. Ohio Atty. Gen. Office, Cin., 1991-95; asst. U.S. atty. criminal div. for So. Dist. Ohio U.S. Attys. Office, Cin., 1995-97; United States atty. So. Dist. Ohio, Cin., 1997—2001; ptnr. Blank Rome LLP, 2001—06; sr. counsel Coca-Cola Co., Atlanta, 2006—. Adj. instr. Coll. Law U. Cin., 1997—; mem. U.S. Atty. Gen.'s Adv. Com., 1999—2001, chair civil rights subcom., 2001; mem. merit selection com. Sixth Cir. Ct. of Appeals Bankruptcy Ct., 1992—96, 2003. Mem. commn. Cin. Cmty. Action Now, 2001—; commr. Tall Stacks Commn., City of Cin., 1990—94, Mayor's Commn. on Children, City of Cin., 1992—94; mem. equal employment adv. rev. panel City of Cin., 1989—91; bd. dirs. Nat. Inst. for Law and Equity, 2002—; trustee, bd. visitors U. Cin. Coll. Law, 1992—; trustee Legal Aid Soc. Cin., 1987—92; bd. dirs. Freestore Foodbank, 2003—, Playhouse in the Park, 2002—; co-chair Greater Cin. Minority Counsel Program, 2005—; mem. exec. bd. Cin. Youth Collaborative, 2005—. Named Career Woman of Achievement, Cin. YWCA, 1988; named one of Top Ten Women Attys., Women's Bus. Cin., 2005; named to Super Lawyers, Ohio, 2006; recipient Disting. Alumni award, Friends of Women's Studies, U. Cin., 2001, Theodore M. Berry award for outstanding achievement in politics and in svc. to cmty., Cin. chpt. NACCP, 1998, Nicholas Longworth III Alumni Achievement award for disting. pub. svc., U. Cin. Coll. Law, 1997. Mem. Black Lawyers Assn. of Cin. (pres. 1989-91, round table 1988-), Legal Aid Soc. (sec. 1991-92), ABA, Fed. Bar Assn., Ohio Bar Assn., Nat. Bar Assn. (bd. govs. 1988-1990, Mem. of Yr. region VI 1990), Cin. Bar Assn. (trustee 1989-94), Cin. CAN Commn. Democrat. Episcopalian. Office: Coca-Cola Co One Coca-Cola Plz NAT 2062 PO Box 1734 Atlanta GA 30301 Office Phone: 513-362-8700, 404-676-2121. Business E-Mail: zealey@blankRome.com.

ZEARFOSS, HERBERT KEYSER, retired lawyer; b. Montandon, Pa., Oct. 13, 1929; s. Dean Wilson and Susan Lesher (Keyser) Z.; m. Thelma Mary McCarthy, Dec. 19, 1953 (dec. 1984); children: Timothy McCarthy, Jonathan Andrew, Sarah Creighton; m. Suzanne VanderVeer, Nov. 14, 1992. AB, Bucknell U., 1951; postgrad., Yale U., 1951-53; JD, Am. U., 1958. Bar: Pa. 1959, US Dist. Ct. (mid. dist.) Pa. 1959, US Dist. Ct. (ea. dist.) Pa. 1975, US Supreme Ct. 1975. Ptnr. Fetter & Zearfoss, Lewisburg, Pa., 1959-60; asst. counsel Fidelity Mut. Life Ins. Co., Phila., 1960-67, sr. v.p., gen. counsel, 1978-82; sec., mgr. Ins. Fedn. of Pa. Inc., 1967-68; ptnr. Zearfoss & Campbell, 1968-78; sr. v.p., sec., gen. counsel Provident Indemmity Life Ins. Co. and parent co. Provident Am. Corp., Norristown, Pa., 1982-87; sole practice Radnor, Pa., 1987-91; adj. faculty Cabrini Coll., 1988-90; asst. gen. counsel, asst. sec. Teleflex Inc., Limerick, Pa., 1991-2001. Author: The Life Insurance Law of Pennsylvania, 1983; book rev. editor Am. U. Law Rev., 1956-58. Rep. Pa. Gen. Assembly from 167th dist., 1968-78; Justice of Peace, Radnor Twp., Delaware County, Pa., 1966-67; v.p. Valley Forge coun. Boy Scouts Am., 1982-86; treas. Netherlands-Am. Amity Trust, Inc., 1981-86; treas. Civil War Mus., Phila., 2003—; bd. dirs. Am. Revolution Patriots Fund, 2002-06. Lt. comdr. USNR, 1954—58. Decorated officer Order of Orange-Nassau (Netherlands); recipient Silver Beaver award Boy Scouts Am., 1989. Mem. ABA, Pa. Bar Assn., Assn. Life Ins. Counsel, Netherlands Soc. Phila. (pres. 1979-83), SAR (pres. Phila. Continental chpt. 1986-87), Colonial Soc. Pa. (gov. 1988-91), Del. Soc. Cin. (pres. 1996-99), Soc. Colonial Wars in the Commonwealth Pa. (gov. 2004-07), Pa. Geneal. Soc. (counsel 1987-91, pres. 1995—), Soc. War 1812 (pres. gen. 1996-99), Mil. Order Loyal Legion US (comdr., Pa. comdr. 1999-2001, judge adv.-in-chief 2001-05), Sovereign Mil. Order Temple Jerusalem (grand officer), Priory of Phila. (prior 1994-98), Yale Club Phila., Phila. Club, Penn Club, Merion Cricket Club, Omicron Delta Kappa, Phi Alpha Delta, Phi Alpha Theta, Tau Kappa Alpha, Pi Sigma Alpha. Republican. Presbyterian. Home: 532 Candace Ln Villanova PA 19085-1702 Personal E-mail: hzearfoss@aol.com.

ZEBROSKI, EDWIN LEOPOLD, risk management consultant; b. Chgo., Apr. 1, 1921; s. Peter Paul and Sophie (Rydz) Z.; m. Gisela Karin Rudolph, Sept. 6, 1969; children: Lars, Zoe, Susan, Peggy. BS, U. Chgo., 1941; PhD, U. Calif., Berkeley, 1947. Registered prof. engr., Calif. Project engr. Gen. Electric Co., Schenectady, N.Y., 1947-53, mgr. devel. engring. San Jose, Calif., 1958-73; mgr. engring. SRI Internat., Menlo Park, Calif., 1954-58, dir. systems and materials dept., 1974-79; dir. nuclear safety analysis ctr. EPRI, Palo Alto, Calif., 1979-81; v.p. engring. INPO, Atlanta, 1981-83; chief nuclear scientist EPRI, 1982—88; dir. risk mgmt. svcs. APTECH Engring. Svcs., Sunnyvale, Calif., 1988-97; safety and risk mgmt. advisor DOE-Sandia Nat. Lab., 2000—04. Vis. prof. Purdue U., Lafayette, Ind., 1977-78; cons. OTA, Washington, 1980, 82-83, Dept. Energy, Washington, 1985-90, panels Nat. Rsch. Coun., 1990—, Electricite de France, 1986-87, Dept. Interior, Washington, 1987-89, EPRI, Palo Alto, 1988-98, Acad. Sci., USSR, 1987, Karlsruhe Lab., Germany, 1988; mem. commn. engring. edn. NRC, Washington, 1970-73; mem. NAS-NRC Panel on Decision-Making in Govt. Agy., 1997-98; mem. NAS-NRC Panel on High Level Waste R&D, 2001; mem. NAE Panel on Countering Terrorism, 2002—03. Contbr. chpts. to books, numerous articles to profl. jours.; patentee in field. Pres. bd. dirs. Unitarian Ch., Palo Alto, 2005—06; bd. dirs. Stevenson House, Palo Alto, 2003—07. Recipient Charles A. Coffin award Gen. Electric Co., Schenectady, 1954, Edward Teller award, 2002. Fellow AAAS, Am. Nuclear Soc. (bd. exec. com. 1969-71), Am. Inst. Chemists; mem. NAE (chmn. energy com. 1984-86, chmn. mem. com. 1986-87, policy com. 1995-96), Am. Phys. Soc., Soc. for Risk Analysis. Avocations: safety and risk management, public sector decision processes, music, writing. Business E-Mail: edzeb1@comcast.net.

ZECK, VAN, federal agency administrator; b. Morgantown, W.Va. BS, W.Va. U., 1970. With U.S. Dept. Treas., 1971—, various positions in data processing, marketable securities ops., adminstrn., with bur. internal audit staff; asst. commr. financing Bur. Pub. Debt U.S. Dept. Treas., 1982—87, dep. commr., 1987—98, commr., 1998—. Office: US Dept Treas Bur Pub Debt PO Box 7015 Parkersburg WV 26106 *

ZECKHAUSER, RICHARD JAY, economist, educator; b. Phila., Nov. 1, 1940; s. Julius Nathaniel and Estelle (Borgenicht) Zeckhauser; m. Nancy Mackell Hoover, Sept. 9, 1967; children: Bryn Gordon, Benjamin Rennell. AB, Harvard U., 1962, PhD, 1969. Jr. fellow Soc. Fellows Harvard U., Cambridge, Mass., 1965-68, mem. faculty, 1968—, prof. polit. econ. Kennedy Sch., 1972—, Frank P. Ramsey prof. polit. economy. Founder, bd. dirs. Niederhoffer, Cross & Zeckhauser, 1968—84; sr. advisor, prin. Equity Resource Investments, 2005—; bus. adv. bd. Tengion, Inc., 2006—; bd. dirs. Comm. Group Ins., Mass., Digi-Block, Inc. Co-author: A Primer for Policy Analysis, 1978, Demographic Dimensions of the New Republic, 1981, The Early Admissions Game: Joining the Elite, 2003; editor or co-editor: Benefit-Cost and Policy Analysis, 1974, What Role for Government, 1982, Principals and Agents: The Structure of Business, 1985, Am. Soc. Pub. and Pvt. Responsibilities, 1986, Privatization and State-Owned Enterprise: Lessons from the United Kingdom, Canada and the United States, 1988, Strategy and Choice, 1991, Wise Choices, Games, Decisions, and Negotiations, 1996, Targeting in Social Programs: Avoiding Bad Beta, Removing Bad Apples, 2006; contbr. articles to profl. jours., chapters to books; rsch. on fin., coll. admissions and healthcare. Bd. dirs. Commonwealth Sch. Finalist, World Paris Championship, 1998; named winner, numerous regional and nat. contract brige competitions; recipient 2d pl., US Mixed-Teams Championship, 2003, 3d pl., US Open Pairs Championship, 2004. Fellow: AAAS, Inst. Medicine/NAS, Assn. Pub. Policy and Mgmt., Econometric Soc. Office: Harvard U John F Kennedy Sch Govt 79 JFK St Cambridge MA 02138-5801 Business E-Mail: richard-zeckhauser@harvard.edu.

ZEDILLO PONCE DE LEÓN, ERNESTO, former president of Mexico; b. Mexico City, Apr. 27, 1951; s. Rodolfo Zedillo Castillo and Martha Alicia Ponce de Leon; m. Nilda Patricia Velasco Nuñez; children: Ernesto, Emiliano, Carlos, Nild Patricia, Rodrigo. Student, Instituto Politécnico Nacional, Bradford U., U. Colo.; MA, Yale U., 1977, PhD, 1981, LLD (hon.), 2001. With Partido Revolucionario Institucional, 1971—, Instituto de Estudios Políticos, Económicos y Sociales; econ. rschr. Dirreción Gen. de Programación Económica y Social; lectr. Colegio de Mex., 1978-80; dep. mgr. finance and econ. rsch., advisor to bd. dirs. Banco de Mex.; dep. sec. for planning and budget Govt. Mex., Mexico City, 1985-88, sec. for planning and budget, 1988-92, sec. public edn., 1992-93; campaign mgr. presdl. nominee Luis Donald Colosio Partido Revolucionario Institucional, 1993-94; pres. Govt. Mex., Mexico City, 1994—2000; chair, high level panel financing for devel. UN; prof., internat. economics, politics Yale U.; dir. Yale Ctr. Study of Globalization, 2002—; co-chmn. Internat. Task Force on Global Public Goods, UN Commn. on Private Sector and Devel.; chair Global Devel. Network. Mem. Trilateral Commn.; mem. internat. adv. bd. Coun. Fgn. Rels.; bd. dirs. Inst. Internat. Economics. Recipient Wilbur Cross Medal, Yale U., 2001, Franklin D. Roosevelt Freedom from Fear award, Gold Insigne, Coun. Americas, Tribuna Americana award, Casa de America, Madrid, Berkeley medal, U. Calif. Office: Yale U Ctr Study of Globalization Betts Hall New Haven CT 06520

ZEDROSSER, JOSEPH JOHN, lawyer; b. Milw., Jan. 24, 1938; s. Joseph and Rose (Zollner) Z.; m. Antonina Krass, Sept. 6, 1997. AB, Marquette U., 1959; LLB, Harvard U., 1963. Bar: N.Y. 1964, U.S. Dist. Ct. (so. dist.) N.Y. 1966, U.S. Dist. Ct. (ea. dist.) N.Y. 1971, U.S. Ct. Appeals (2d cir.) 1971, U.S. Ct. Appeals (D.C. Cir.) 1975, U.S. Supreme Ct. 1975. Assoc. William G. Mulligan, NYC, 1964-67, Christy, Bauman, Frey and Christy and successors, NYC, 1967-71; dir. cmty. devel. unit Bedford-Stuyvesant Cmty. Legal Svcs. Corp., NYC, 1971-73; assoc. atty. fed. defender svcs. unit Legal Aid Soc., NYC, 1973-74; asst. atty. gen. Environ. Protection Bur., N.Y. State Dept. Law, NYC, 1974-80; regional counsel EPA, NYC, 1980-82; assoc. prof. St. John's U. Sch. Law, NYC, 1982-86; ptnr. Rivkin, Radler, Dunne & Bayh, Uniondale, N.Y., 1986-89, Breed, Abbott & Morgan, NYC, 1989-93, Whitman Breed Abbott & Morgan, NYC, 1993-95; v.p. CPR Inst. for Dispute Resolution, NYC, 1996; sr. investigative counsel com. on investigations, taxation, and gov. ops. N.Y. State Senate, 1998-99; asst. atty. gen. Environ. Protection Bur. N.Y. State Office Atty. Gen., NYC, 1999—. Lectr., contbr. to course handbooks for courses sponsored by Practicing Law Inst. and other assns. Lt. USNR, 1965-74, USAR, 1963-65. Mem. ABA, Assn. Bar City N.Y., N.Y. State Bar Assn., Alpha Sigma Nu. Roman Catholic. Home: 1520 York Ave Apt 15B New York NY 10028-7982

ZEE, PHYLLIS C., physician, educator, researcher; b. Hong Kong, June 27, 1954; came to U.S., 1973; d. William and King Di (Wong) Cheung; m. Benjamin Zee; children: David, Caroline, Alex. BA, Mills Coll., 1976; PhD, Chgo. Med. Sch., 1980, MD, 1983. Diplomate Am. Bd. Psychiatry and Neurology, Am. Bd. Med. Examiners, Am. Bd. Sleep Medicine. NIH postdoctoral fellow Northwestern U., Evanston, Ill., 1987-89, asst. prof. neurobiology and neurology Chgo., 1989-95, assoc. prof., 1996—2000, prof., 2001—; dir. Sleep Ctr. Northwestern Meml. Hosp., Chgo., 1991—. Mem. bd. advisors Jour. Biol. Rhythms, 1994—; bd. dirs. Nat. Sleep Found., 2003—; mem. NIH study sect. Contbr. articles to profl. jours. Fellow Buelher Ctr. on Aging, 1995—, Brookdale Found., 1994; grantee NIH, 1994—. Fellow: Am. Sleep Disorders Assn.; mem.: Am. Neurol. Assn., Soc. Biol. Rhythms, Soc. for Neuroscience, Am. Acad. Neurology. Office: Northwestern U 710 N Lake Shore Dr Chicago IL 60611-3006 Office Phone: 312-908-8549. Business E-Mail: p-zee@northwestern.edu.

ZEECK, DAVID A., newspaper editor; m. Valarie S. Zeeck; children: Phillip, Michael. BJ, U. Mo., 1973; MBA, Rockhurst Coll. Various positions The Kans. City Star, 1974—94; exec. editor The News Tribune, Tacoma, 1994—. Instr. in field. Mem.: Am. Assn. Newspaper Editors (bd. dirs., pres. 2006—07). Presbyn. Office: The News Tribune 1950 South St Tacoma WA 98405 Mailing: PO Box 11000 Tacoma WA 98411 E-mail: david.zeeck@mail.tribnet.com. *

ZEEVI, ADRIANA, microbiologist, immunologist; BA in Microbiology, MA in Microbiology, Ilan Univ., Ramat-Gan, Israel, PhD in Immunology; postdoctoral study, Blood Ctr., Southeastern Wis. Rsch. investigator Blood Ctr., Southeastern Wis.; prof., pathology, surgery Univ. Pitts. Med. Ctr. Bd. dir. United Network for Organ Sharing (UNOS). Sect. editor Clin. Immunology. Recipient New Investigator award, NIH, 1994, Astellas Clin. Sci. Established Investigator award (Prof. Level), Am. Soc. Transplantation, 2007. Mem.: Am. Soc.Histocompatibility & Immunogenetics (pres.-elect, chair, sci. affairs). Office: McGowan Inst Regenerative Medicine Univ Pitts--Ste 200 100 Technology Dr Pittsburgh PA 15219-3110 Office Phone: 412-235-5100, 412-624-1073. Office Fax: 412-235-5110. Business E-Mail: zeevia@upmc.edu. *

ZEFFREN, EUGENE, cosmetics executive; b. St. Louis, Nov. 21, 1941; s. Harry Morris and Bess (Dennis) Z.; m. Steccia Leigh Stern, Feb. 2, 1964; children: Maryl Renee, Bradley Cruvant. AB, Washington U., 1963; MS, U. Chgo., 1965, PhD, 1967. Research chemist Procter & Gamble Co., Cin., 1967-75, sect. head, 1975-77, assoc. dir., 1977-79; v.p. R & D, Helene Curtis, Inc., Chgo., 1979-95; pres. Helene Curtis USA, Chgo., 1995-96; sr. v.p. Helene Curtis bus. unit Unilever Home and Personal Care USA, Chgo., 1996-98, exec. v.p., COO hair and deodorant bus. unit, 1998-2000; sr. v.p. brand devel. Unilever Home and Personal Care N.Am., 2000—02; chmn. NFG Stuff, LLC, 2002—; CEO AG Brands, LLC, 2005—. Mem. vis. com. for phys. scis. U. Chgo., 1995—; active Wash. U. Nat. Coun. for Arts and Scis., 1997—; pres. bd. dirs. River North Dance Co., 1998-2000, chmn. 2000-04. Co-author: The Study of Enzyme Mechanisms, 1973; contbr. articles to profl. jours. Bd. dirs. Goodman Theatre, 1999—, Children's Meml. Rsch. Ctr., 2002—05; trustee Spertus Inst. Jewish Studies, 2002—. Recipient award, Cosmetic Ingredient Buyers and Suppliers, 1990. Mem. AAAS, Am. Chem. Soc., Soc. Cosmetic Chemists, Cosmetic Toiletry and Fragrance Assn. (sci. adv. com. 1979-95, vice chmn. 1984-88, chmn. 1988-90, bd. dirs. 1996-02), Soap and Detergent Assn. (bd. dirs., exec. com. bd. 2000-02), Indsl. Rsch. Inst., Omicron Delta Kappa. Democrat. Jewish. Achievements include patents in field of enzymes and hair care. Avocations: tennis, skiing, reading adventure and espionage novels.

ZEGAS, ALAN LEE, lawyer; b. Newark, Oct. 28, 1952; s. Norman and Harriet (Lava) Z.; m. Tina Hannah Burk, Aug. 22, 1976; children: Rachel Sarah, Leah Ariel, Joelle Shira. BS, U. Pa., 1974; MBA, Harvard U., 1978; JD, Rutgers U., 1981. Bar: N.J. 1981, U.S. Dist. Ct. N.J. 1981, N.Y. 1982, U.S. Ct. Appeals (3d cir.) 1982. Law clk. to Hon. H. Lee Sarokin U.S. Dist. Ct. N.J., Newark, 1981-83; assoc. Robinson, Wayne, Levin, Riccio & La Sala, Newark, 1983-84; pvt. practice Chatham, NJ, 1984—. Adj. prof. law Rutgers U., Newark, 1983-88; reader N.J. Bd. Bar Examiners, Trenton, 1985; pres. Assn. Criminal Def. Lawyers N.J., 1998-99. Editor-in-chief Rutgers U. Law Rev., 1980-81; editor (pamphlet) Law Tips for the Elderly, 1983. Mem. N.J. Bar Assn. (dist. rep. young lawyers div. 1983-85, vice chmn. 1985-86, trustee 1986-88, chmn. criminal law sect. 1996-97), Essex County Bar Assn. (chmn. lawyers referral service 1986—), Rutgers U. Law Sch. Alumni Assn. (rep. 1983—), U. Pa. Alumni Assn. (sec. 1986-87), Harvard U. Bus. Sch. Alumni Assn., Assn. Criminal Def. Lawyers of N.J. (pres. 1998-99). Home: 476 South St New Providence NJ 07974-2132 Office: 552 Main St Chatham NJ 07928-2120

ZEGURA, STEPHEN LUKE, biologist, anthropologist, educator; b. San Francisco, Calif., July 2, 1943; s. Dragomir Božo Zegura and Adele Eugenia-Cecilia Perelli-Minetti; m. Elizabeth Ann Chesney, Jan. 23, 1983; children: Daniel Dragomir, Krista Elise. BA, Stanford U., Calif., 1965; MS, U. Wis., Madison, 1969, PhD, 1971. Asst. prof. NYU, NYC, 1971—72; from asst. prof. to prof. U. Ariz., Tucson, 1972—92, prof., 1992—. Contbr. articles to profl. jours., to mags.; co-editor, contg. author: Eskimos of Northwestern Alaska: A Biological Perspective, 1978. Fellow, Woodrow Wilson Found., 1965—66; grantee, Internat. Demokritos Found., 1985, NRC, 1990, IREX, 1988. Fellow: Human Biology Coun., Am. Anthrop. Assn.; mem.: Am. Assn. Phys. Anthropologists. Avocation: golf. Home: 1580 N Rachel Pl Tucson AZ 85721 Office: Anthrop Dept Univ Ariz Haury 310E Tucson AZ 85721

ZEHNER, LEE RANDALL, entrepreneur, chemist; b. Darby, Pa., Mar. 15, 1947; s. Warren L. and Alycia G. (Van Riper) Z.; m. Susan D. Hovland, June 23, 1973; children: Adam, Erica. BS in Chemistry, U. Pa., Phila., 1968; PhD in Organic Chemistry, U. Minn., Mpls., 1973. Sr. rsch. chemist ARCO Chem. Co., Glenolden, Pa., 1973—78; rsch. group leader Ashland Chem. Co., Dublin, Ohio, 1978-82; mgr. organic rsch. W.R. Grace & Co., Clarksville, Md., 1982-85; dir. biotech. divsn. Biospherics Inc., Beltsville, Md., 1985—91, v.p. sci. svcs., 1991—98; founder, pres. VivaLac Inc., Ashton, 1998—. Contbr. scientific papers to profl. jours. Mem.: Am. Diabetes Assn., Inst. Food Technologists, Am. Chem. Soc. Achievements include patents in field; research in food ingredients and chemical processing; invention of Whey Low sugar substitute; D-tagatose as low-calorie sweetener; D-tagatose as anti-hyperglycemic drug; development of chemical processes for manufacture of ethylene glycol from coal, methacrylate intermediate, adipic acid from coal and butadiene. Avocations: swimming, opera, chess. Home: 131 Brinkwood Rd Brookeville MD 20833-2304 Office: VivaLac Inc PO Box 264 Ashton MD 20861 Personal E-mail: lzehner@wheylow.com.

ZEHR, CONNIE, sculptor, art educator; b. Ohio, 1938; BFA, Ohio State U. Artist Occidental Coll., 1977; visiting artist Calif. State U. Fullerton, 1978—80, Claremont Grad. Sch., 1981, UCLA, 1981, U. Calif. Irvine, 1981—82; prof. Claremont Grad. Sch., 1982—, chairperson dept. art. One-woman shows include Newspace, L.A., Calif., 2002, Harris Art Gallery, U. LaVerne, Calif., 1998, Weingart Gallery, Occidental Coll., 1991, Santa Monica (Calif.) Coll. Art Gallery Santa Monica (Calif.) Coll., 1989, West Gallery, Claremont Coll. Grad. Sch., 1988, Taipei (Taiwan) Fine Arts Mus., 1987, Calif. State U., Fullterton, Calif., Barnsdall Mcpl. Art Gallery, L.A., Calif. Mural Project Claremont Cmty. Found., 1999; Transit Ctr. Art Com. City Claremont, 1992; Visual Art Com. Claremont Cmty. Found., 1991—; Art Selection Panel for Grand Hope Park Cmty. Redevel. Agency, LA, 1986; Process Oriented Design Santa Ana Calif., 1987. Grantee Individual Artist Grant, Nat. Endowment Arts, 1975, Landmark Project, Art Collaboration, 1984, Individual Artist Grant, 1986, Mentor Grant, Lorser Feitelson & Helen Lundeberg-Feitelson Arts Found., 1987. Office: Art Dept Claremont Grad U 251 East 10th St Claremont CA 91711 Office Phone: 909-607-9292.

ZEHR, NORMAN ROBERT, retired association administrator; b. Niagara Falls, May 19, 1930; s. George Andrew and Ina kate (Morrell) Zehr; m. Janet Hutchinson, Apr. 24, 1976; children: Jeannette Ann, Leslie. Engr. of mines, Colo. Sch. Mines, 1952, MS, 1956. Sales trainee Ingersoll-Rand Co., NYC, 1955—56, sales engr. Lima, Peru, 1956—64, regional mgr. mining and constrn. sales, 1964—68, gen. sales mgr. Latin Am. NYC, 1968—69, gen. mgr. Latin Am. ops., 1969—71, v.p., 1975—83, Ingersoll Rand Internat., Woodcliff Lake, NJ, 1971—72, pres., 1972—83; exec. dir. Colo. Sch. Mines Alumni Assn., 1984—95; ret., 1995. Mem. editl. bd. Encyclopedia of the Korean War, 2000. With US Army, 1952—54. Recipient Disting. Achievement medal, Colo. Sch. Mines, 1977. Mem.: AIME, Nat. Soc. Pershing Rifles, Scabbard and Blade, Mining Club, Sigma Nu.

ZEIDENSTEIN, GEORGE, population educator; b. Pitts., July 29, 1929; s. Max and Sophia (Cohen) Z.; m. Sondra F. Auerbach, Jan. 25, 1953; children: Laura, Louis Peter. BA, U. Pitts., 1951; JD cum laude, Harvard U., 1954. Bar: N.Y. 1954. Pvt. practice, NYC, 1954—65; vol. lawyer Lawyers Constl. Def. Com., Holly Springs, Miss., 1965; ptnr. Spear and Hill, 1962—65; country dir. Kathmandu, Nepal, Peace Corps, Nepal, 1965—68; regional dir. designate Office E. Asia and Pacific, Washington, 1968; pres. Bklyn. Linear City Devel. Corp., NYC, 1968—69; sr. program officer Asia and Pacific Ford Found., 1969—71, dep. head Asia and Pacific, 1971—72, rep. Bangladesh, 1972—76; pres., trustee Population Coun., NYC, 1976—93; disting. fellow Harvard Ctr. Population and Devel. Studies, Cambridge, Mass., 1993—. Chmn. Himalayas coun. Asia Soc., 1970-72; assoc. seminar tradition and change in South and S.E. Asia, Columbia U., 1971-73, assoc. seminar on tech. and pub. issues, 1981-85; coun. Overseas Devel. Coun., 1979-93; chmn. Appraisal Group Global Com. Parliamentarians on Population and Devel., 1985-86; bd. visitors Grad. Sch. Pub. Health, U. Pitts., 1988—; advisor to chair Ind. Commn. on Population and Quality of Life, 1993-95. Vice chmn. bd. trustees, chmn. program com. Save the Children Fedn., 1991-95, Internat. Ctr. Rsch. on Women, 1993—; chmn. Internat. HIV/AIDS Alliance, 1993—; bd. dirs. Earthforce, 1993-95; active Britton Woods Com., 1992—. Decorated knight comdr. Order of Lion (Finland, Senegal). Home: 795 East St N Goshen CT 06756-1130 Office: Harvard Ctr Population Devel Studies 9 Bow St Cambridge MA 02138-5103

ZEIDMAN, PHILIP FISHER, lawyer; b. Birmingham, Ala., May 2, 1934; s. Eugene Morris and Ida (Fisher) Z.; m. Nancy Levy, Aug. 19, 1956; children: Elizabeth Miriam, John Fisher (dec.), Jennifer Kahn. BA cum laude, Yale U., 1955; LLB, Harvard U., 1958; postgrad., Grad. Sch. Bus. Adminstrn., 1957-58. Bar: Ala. 1958, Fla. 1960, U.S. Supreme Ct. 1961, D.C. 1968, N.Y. 1981. Trial atty. FTC, 1960-61; staff asst. White House Com. Small Bus., 1961-63; spl. asst. to adminstr. SBA, 1961-63, asst. gen. counsel, 1963-65, gen. counsel, 1965-68; spl. asst. to Vice Pres. of U.S., 1968; govt. rels. mgr. Nat. Alliance Businessmen, 1968; founding prin. Brownstein & Zeidman P.C., Washington, 1968-96; sr. ptnr. Rudnick, Wolfe, Epstien & Zeidman, Washington, 1996-99; ptnr. Piper Marbury Rudnick & Wolfe, Washington, 1999—2004; ptnr., co-chmn. Franchise & Distribution practice group DLA Piper Rudnick Gray Cary, Washington, 2005—. Chmn. grants and benefits com. Adminstrv. Conf. U.S., 1968; chmn. food industry adv. com. Dept. Energy, 1979-81; chmn. distbn. and food merchandising subcom. Alliance to Save Energy, 1978; mem. Pres.'s Commn. on Exec. Exch., 1978-81; gen. counsel Internat. Franchise Assn., Am. Bus. Conf.; spl. counsel Japanese Franchise Assn.; advisor to govts. and internat. orgns.; founder EastEuropeLaw, Ltd., Budapest, Hungary. Editor, author: Survey of Laws and Regulations Affecting International Franchising, 1982, 2nd edit., 1990, Regulation of Buying and Selling a Franchise, 1983, Legal Aspects of Selling and Buying, 1983, 2nd edit., 1991; cons. editor Global Franchising Alert; assoc. editor Jour. of International Franchising Law and Distribution; contbg. editor Legal Times of Washington, 1978-85; mem. adv. bd. Antitrust and Trade Regulation Report for Bur. Nat. Affairs, 1978-85. Mem. young leadership coun. Dem.

Nat. Com.; exec. dir. Dem. platform com., 1972; adviser Nat. Presdl. Campaign of Jimmy Carter, 1976; mem. pres.'s adv. com. John F. Kennedy Ctr. for Performing Arts, 1981; mem. adv. bd. Yale U. Sch. Mgmt.; trustee Yale-China Assn., 1983-89; dir. & mem. exec. com. Appleseed Found. 1994—; mem. adv. bd. DeWitt Wallace Ctr. for Comm., Terry Sanford Inst. Pub. Policy, Duke U., 1994-98; mem. Council for Excellence in Govt., Adminstrv. Conf. U.S.; gen. counsel Internat. Franchise Assn., Am. Bus. Conf.; spl. counsel Japan Franchise Assn.. With USAF, 1958-60. Recipient Younger Fed. Lawyer award Fed. Bar Assn., 1965; Jonathan Davenport Oratorical award, 1954; William Houston McKim award, 1955 Mem. ABA (chmn. com. on franchising 1977-81), D.C. Bar Assn., Ala. Bar Assn., Fla. Bar Assn., Fed. Bar Assn., Bar Assn. D.C., Internat. Bar Assn. (chmn. internat. franchising com. 1986-90, mem. coun. sect. bus. law 1996—), Am. Intellectual Property Law Assn. (chmn. franchising com. 1987-90), Assn. Yale U. Alumni (class rep.). Office: DLA Piper Rudnick Gray Cary 1200 19th St NW Washington DC 20036-2412 Office Phone: 202-861-6676. Office Fax: 202-223-2085. Business E-Mail: philip.zeidman@dlapiper.com.

ZEIGER, LARRY See KING, LARRY

ZEIGER, MIKHAIL, composer, concert pianist; b. Moscow, Jan. 7, 1949; s. Isaak and Elena Zeiger, Rachel Zeiger (Stepmother); m. Olga Makarova, Mar. 15, 2004. MusB, Simferopol Music Coll., Russia, 1968; MusM, Gorky Conservatory, Nizhny Novgorod, Russia, 1973; PhD in Music Composition, Moscow Conservatory, 1983. Resident piano soloist Voronezh Philharm., Voronezh, Russia, 1974—95; prof. music LI Conservatory, SUNY, Old Westbury, NY, 1997—. Pres. Voronezh Brunch All-Russia Composer's Union, Voronezh, 1989—93. Composer: (opera) Magic Kolobok, (ballet) Harlequinade, (concerto for orchestra) The Tyger, (choral) Hymns to St. Tikhon of Zadonsk, (cantata) Poet-Prophet. Home Phone: 212-942-8667. Personal E-mail: mzeiger@nyc.rr.com.

ZEIGLER, ANN DEPENDER, lawyer; b. Spokane, June 7, 1947; d. F. Norman and Dorothy dePender; m. Paul Stewart Zeigler, June 20, 1970; 1 child, Kate Elizabeth. BA magna cum laude, Ft. Wright Coll. Holy Names, 1969; MFA in Creative Writing, U. Mont., Missoula, 1975; JD, U. Houston, 1984. Bar: Tex. 1984. Course adminstr. legal comm. U. Houston, 1982—84; assoc. Dula, Shields & Egbert, 1984—87; ind. project atty., 1987; assoc. Dow, Cogburn & Friedman, 1987—90; assoc. bankruptcy sect., chpt. 7 trustee rep. Hughes, Watters & Askanase, Houston, 1990—. Spkr. in field. Co-editor: Insurance Guide-Arts Nonprofits, 1993, Basic Issues in Estate Planning-Representing the Artist, 1994, Leading the Arts Nonprofit: Duties of Officers and Directors, 1999; mem. editl. bd. Houston Lawyer, 1999— (award Best Series of Articles for 2-part series on bankruptcy amendments); guest editor spl. hist. issue: Houston Lawyer, 2000, 2001, guest editor 40th ann. issue:, 2003, assoc. editor: Keeping Up With, 2002—05, 2007—; contbr. articles to profl. jours. Mem.: ABA, Can. Bar Assn., Houston Bar Assn. (chair law and arts com. 1996—97, co-chair ann. fiction contest), State Bar Tex. (bankruptcy sect.), Phi Alpha Delta. Democrat. Home: 4038 Cheena Dr Houston TX 77025-4702 Office: Hughes Watters & Askanase Three Allen Ctr 333 Clay St 29th Fl Houston TX 77002-4168 Home Phone: 713-661-9204; Office Phone: 713-328-2816. Business E-Mail: azeigler@hwa.com.

ZEIGLER, GEORGE GAVIN, painter, sculptor; b. Nashville, Aug. 20, 1962; s. George Zeigler and Sandy Lawrence. BA, Fordham U., NYC. Cert. programmer Pratt Inst.; furniture craftsman Ctr. Furniture Crafsmanship, Rockport, Maine. Mem.: Illustrators Club.

ZEILBERGER, DORON, mathematics professor, researcher; b. Haifa, Israel, July 2, 1950; s. Yehuda Heinz and Ruth (Alexander) Z.; m. Jane Deborah LeGrange, June 3, 1979; children: Celia, Tamar, Hadas. BS with first class hons., U. London, 1972; PhD, Weizmann Inst., Rehovot, Israel, 1976. Mem. Inst. for Advanced Study, Princeton, NJ, 1977-78, 93; vis. asst. prof. Ga. Inst. Tech., Atlanta, 1978-79; lectr. U. Ill., Urbana, 1979-80; sr. scientist Weizmann Inst., Rehovot, Israel, 1980-82; lectr. U. Pa., Phila., 1982-83; assoc. prof. Drexel U., Phila., 1983-88, prof., 1988-90, Temple U., Phila., 1990-99, Laura H. Carnell prof., 1999-2001; bd. govs. prof. Rutgers U., New Brunswick, NJ, 2001—. Mem. editl. bd. Elec. Jour. of Combinations, others, editor-in-chief Advances in Applied Math.; contbr. numerous articles to profl. jours. Mem. Am. Math. Soc. (Leroy P. Steele prize 1998), Math. Assn. Am. (Lester R. Ford award 1990), Inst. for Combinatorics and Its Applications (Euler medal, 2004). Business E-Mail: zeilberg@math.rutgers.edu.

ZEILIG, NANCY MEEKS, writer, editor; b. Nashville, Apr. 28, 1943; d. Edward Harvey and Nancy Evelyn (Self) Meeks; m. Lanny Kenneth Fielder, Aug. 20, 1964 (div. Dec. 1970); m. Charles Elliot Zeilig, Jan. 6, 1974 (div. Dec. 1989); 1 child, Sasha Rebecca; m. Kenn Lively, Apr. 22, 2006. BA, Birmingham-So. Coll., 1964; postgrad., Vanderbilt U., 1971-73. Editorial asst. Reuben H. Donnelley, NYC, 1969-70; asst. editor Vanderbilt U., Nashville, 1970-74; editor U. Minn., St. Paul, 1975; asst. editor McGraw-Hill Inc., Mpls., 1975-76; mng. editor Denver mag., 1976-80; editor Jour. Am. Water Works Assn., Denver, 1981—99; owner Nancy Zeilig Writing & Editing, Denver, 2000—. Editor, co-pub.: WomanSource, 1982, rev. edit., 1984; contbr. articles to trade and consumer mags. Co-chair arts adv. com. Denver Sch. Arts, 1994-96. Avocations: travel, reading, cooking. Home Phone: 303-758-8846; Office Phone: 303-758-7750. E-mail: nzeilig@earthlink.net.

ZEINE, RANA RAMSEY, neuropathologist, research professor; b. Beirut, May 13, 1962; arrived in US, 1998, permanent resident, 2005; d. Ramsey and Omayma Zeine; m. Hinhark Gan, July 1, 1989. BS in Biology, Am. U. Beirut, 1983, MD, 1987; PhD, McGill U., Montreal, Can., 1993. Rsch. fellow Ottawa (Can.) U., 1995—98; rsch. assoc. Albert Einstein Coll., NY, 1998—2000, resident in neuropathology NY, 2002—04; resident in pathology Montefiore Med. Ctr./Albert Einstein Coll. Medicine, Bronx, NY, 2000—04; rsch. scientist Ctr. for Dementia Rsch. Nathan Kline Inst., NY, 2004—05; rsch. asst. prof. Cancer Ctr. Northwestern U., Chgo., 2006—07; rsch. assoc., asst. prof. Inst. Molecular Pediat. Scis. U. Chgo., 2007—. Presenter in field. Author abstracts in field; contbr. articles to profl. jours. Fellow, Multiple Sclerosis Soc. Can., 1996—98. Mem.: AMA (fellow 2003—), U.S. and Can. Assn. Pathologists, Internat. Soc. Neuropathology, Coll. Am. Pathologists, NY Acad. Scis. Mem. Baha'I Faith. Avocations: ballet, piano, swimming. Office: U Chgo Inst for Molecular Pediat Sci 5841 S Maryland Ave MC 4060 Rm N144 Chicago IL 60637 Office Phone: 773-834-0815. Personal E-mail: harkzen@aol.com. Business E-Mail: rzeine@peds.bsd.uchicago.edu.

ZEIS, JOANNE A., medical writer; BS in Psychology, Tufts Univ.; continuing edn. student, Harvard Med. Sch.; continuing edn. student, Ctr. Spirituality, Theology and Health, Duke Univ. Med. Ctr. Author: (books) You Are Not Alone: 15 People with Behçet's, 1997, Essential Guide to Behçet's Disease, 2003, Basic Information on Behçet's Disease, Behçet's Disease: Medical Research Studies; profiled (TV spl.) Discovery Health Channel's Mystery Diagnosis documentary on patients with Behçet's Disease, 2005. Recipient Citation for Disting. Svc., AMA, 2006. Mem.: Am. Med. Writers Assn., Internat. Soc. for Behçet's Disease. Office: PO Box 255 Uxbridge MA 01569 Office Fax: 508-278-5145. E-mail: joanne@behcetsdisease.com. *

ZEISEL, STEVEN H., nutritionist, scientist, educator; b. NYC, July 16, 1950; BS in Life Sci., MIT, 1971; MD, Harvard Med. Sch., 1975; PhD in Nutrition, MIT, 1980. Asst. in medicine Children's Hosp., Boston, 1980-81; asst. prof. pathology and pediatrics Boston U. Sch. Medicine, 1982—90, assoc. prof., 1987-90, prof., 1990; prof. dept. pediatrics U. N.C., Chapel Hill, 1990—, prof. dept. nutrition, 1990—, chair dept. nutrition, 1990—2005; chair med. edn. com. Am. Soc. Clin. Nutrition, 1995—97. Chair joint membership com. AIN/ASCN, 1992-94; chmn. adv. bd. Gen. Clin. Rsch. Ctr., U. N.C., 1990-2000; mem. Inst. of Medicine panel on folate and B Vitamins, 1997-99; mem. sci. adv. bd. Monsanto Corp., 1998-2000; mem. sci. coun. Dannon Inst.; bd. dirs. Interactive Info. Editor-in-chief Jour. Nutritional Biochemistry. Mem. Internat. Soc. for Rsch. on Human Milk and Lactation, Am. Soc. Nutritional Scis., Am. Soc. Clin. Nutrition (councilor 1991-94, chmn. residency edn. and subspecialty tng. com. 1995—), Am. Soc. Parenteral and Enteral Nutrition, Am. Coll. Nutrition, Am. Pub. Health Assn., Soc. Pediatric Rsch. Office: UNC Dept Nutrition #7461 Sch Pub Health/Sch Medicine 2115A Michael Hooker Rsch Ctr Chapel Hill NC 27599-7461 Office Phone: 919-843-4731. Office Fax: 919-843-8555. E-mail: steven_zeisel@unc.edu.

ZEITHAMMER, ROBERT, adult education educator; m. Colette Wiseman. PhD, MIT, Cambridge, Mass., 2003. Asst. prof. U. Chgo. GSB, 2003—07, UCLA Anderson Sch. Mgmt., 2007—. Office: Anderson School of Management 110 Westwood Plaza Los Angeles CA 90095

ZEITLER, WILLIAM M., information technology executive; BS, Gannon Univ., 1969. Mgmt. positions through v.p. mktg. AS/400 IBM, 1969—96, gen. mgr. AS/400, server brand mgmt., & worldwide software sales & mktg., 1996—2000, gen. mgr. enterprise servers, 2000, sr. v.p., group exec. server group, 2000—03, sr. v.p., group exec systems & tech. group, 2003—. Office: IBM 1 New Orchard Rd Armonk NY 10504 *

ZEITLIN, EUGENIA PAWLIK, librarian, educator, writer; b. NYC, Jan. 29; d. Charles and Pauline (Klimowski) Pawlik; m. Herbert Zakary Zeitlin, July 3, 1949; children: Mark Clyde, Joyce Therese Zeitlin Harris, Ann Victoria, Clare Katherine. BA in English, Bklyn. Coll., 1945; MA in English, NYU, NYC, 1951; MALS, Rosary Coll., 1968. Teaching credential N.Y., Ariz., Calif., Ill. English tchr., Sea Cliff, L.I., NY, 1945—47; English, math. tchr. Merrick (N.Y.) Sch. Dist., 1948—49; English tchr. Wilson Sch. Dist., Phoenix, 1949—50; counselor West Phoenix (Ariz.) High Sch., 1953—56; asst. prof. English Wright Coll., Chgo., 1965—66; asst. prof. English, asst. to v.p. curriculum and instrn. Oakton C.C., Des Plaines, Ill., 1970—76; libr. Pasadena City Coll., LA, 1979—84, L.A. Pub. Libr., 1984—2004; ret., 2004. Contbr. articles to profl. jours. Named Northridge City Employee of Yr., 1986. Mem. AAUW (br. pres. Lancaster, Calif. 1959-60), Thoreau Soc. (life), Beta Phi Mu. Avocations: writing and editing, book collecting. Home: 20124 Phaeton Dr Woodland Hills CA 91364-5633

ZEITLIN, HERBERT ZAKARY, college administrator, real estate consultant, writer; b. NYC, Jan. 14; s. Leonard and Martha Josephine (Soff) Zeitlin; m. Eugenia F. Pawlik, July 3, 1949; children: Mark Clyde, Joyce Therese Zeitlin Harris, Ann Victoria, Clare Katherine. BS, NYU, 1947, MA, 1949; EdD, Stanford U., 1956. Tchr. Mepham HS, Bellmore, NY, 1946—47, Nassau County Vocat. Edn. Extension Bd., Mineola, NY; electronics instr., adj. faculty Mephan CC; tchr., counselor, dir. testing Phoenix Union HS and Coll. Dist.; dean eve. coll., prin. high sch. Antelope Valley Union HS and Coll. Dist., Lancaster, Calif.; dean instrn. Southwestern Coll., Chula Vista, Calif.; pres., supt., cons. Triton Coll., River Grove, Ill., 1964—79; dean, pres. West LA Coll., 1976-80; pres. Trident Cons., LA, mgmt. cons., 1976—; adj. faculty Ariz. State U., Flagstaff, No. Ill. U., DeKalb, U. Calif., Santa Barbara. Author: Turbulent Birth of Triton College, 2001, Corruption: How to Fight It and Win, 2004, What Makes A Teacher Great?, 2005; editor: in field. Pres. Antelope Valley Breeze & Sage, Bon Vivant Homeowners Assn.; mayor Upper Woodland Hills, Calif. With USAAF, 1942—46. Named Adminstr. of the Yr., Triton Coll. Faculty Assn., 1974, Most Influential Educator in Ill., Chgo. Sun Times; recipient Spl. commendation, Chgo. Tribune, Richard Ogilvie, former Gov. Ill., Spl. Achievement award for visionary accomplishment, Ill. Sch. Adminstrs. Assn. Mem.: Ariz. State Vocat. Assn. (pres.), Ariz. Vocat. Guidance Assn. (pres.), Maywood Ill. Rotary (pres.), Antelope Valley Rotary (pres.). Mailing: Trident Cons PO Box 571412 Tarzana CA 91357 Home: 20124 Phacton Dr Woodland Hills CA 91364 Home Phone: 818-884-7819; Office Phone: 818-999-2030, 818-884-7819. Personal E-mail: herbertzzeitlin@aol.com. *I always felt that being the president of an organization, having held many presidencies in my lifetime, was like being the quarterback on the football team. You had a choice of running with the ball and taking some bruises or passing it to someone who should score. I was lucky most of the time in selecting some very fine receivers.*

ZEITLIN, JIDE JAMES, investor; b. Ibadan, Nigeria; came to U.S., 1976; s. Arnold S. and Marian F. Z. BA, Amherst Coll., 1985; MBA, Harvard U., 1987. Mng. dir. Goldman, Sachs & Co., NYC, 1987—2005, The Keffi Group Ltd., 2006—. Bd. dirs. Affiliated Mgr. Group, Coach, Inc. Trustee Amherst Coll., Common Ground Cmty., Milton Acad., Montefiore Med. Ctr., Playwrights Horizons, Teach for Am. Office: 590 Madison Ave 37th Fl New York NY 10022

ZEITLIN, LAURIE, printing company and information technology executive; BA in Econs., Duke U., 1984; MBA in Fin., U. Pa., 1989. Rsch. asst. Touche Ross & Co., 1985—87; sr. mng. consulting Deloitte & Touche LLP, 1989—95; dir. info. tech., sr. mgr. application devel., v.p. info. tech. Home Depot, Inc., Atllanta, 1995—2003; sr. v.p., chief info. officer Kinko's Inc., Dallas, 2003—. Named one of Premier 100 IT Leaders, Computerworld, 2006. Office: Kinkos 13155 Noel Rd Ste 1600 Dallas TX 75240 Office Phone: 214-550-7020. E-mail: laurie.zeitlin@fedexkinkos.com.

ZEITLIN, LOUISE R., music educator; arrived in U.S., 1965; d. Gerald Leon and Aideen Natalie Zeitlin; m. James Wilfred Howsmon, Aug. 21, 1988; children: Rachel Elizabeth, Andrew Stuart. MusB, Eastman Sch. Music, 1985; MusM, Yale U., 1987. Mem. faculty Suzuki-Orff Sch., Chgo., 1995—98, Brevard (N.C.) Music Ctr., 1998—2004; tchr. Baldwin Wallace Coll., Berea, Ohio, 2004—. Faculty MacPhail Ctr. Arts, Mpls., 1990—93, Cleve. (Ohio) Inst. Music, 1994—2004, Oberlin (Ohio) Cmty. Music Sch., 2003—04; adj. faculty Carleton Coll., Northfield, Minn., 1991—93; lectr. in field. Musician: Chgo. (Ill.) String Ensemble, Chgo. (Ill.) Philharmonic, Brevard (N.C.) Music Ctr. Orch., Brevard Music Ctr., 1999—, Oberlin Coll. Cmty. Music Sch., 2003. Recipient Tchr. Recognition award, Nat. Found. Advancement Arts, 2003. Mem.: Ohio Viola Soc. (pres. 2000—02), Am. Viola Soc. (sec. 2002—04, bd. dirs. 2001—04). Avocation: figure skating. Office: Baldwin Wallace College 275 Eastland Rd Berea OH 44017

ZEITLIN, MARILYN AUDREY, museum director; b. Newark, July 14, 1941; d. Sidney M. and Theresa Feigenblatt) Litchfield; widowed; children: Charles C. Sweedler, Milo Sweedler. Student, Vanderbilt U., 1963-65; AB in Humanities, Harvard U., 1966, MA in Teaching of English, 1967; postgrad., Cornell U., 1971-74. Dir. Ctr. Gallery, Bucknell U., Lewisburg, Pa., 1975-78; Freedman Gallery, Albright Coll., Reading, Pa., 1978-81; Anderson Gallery, Va. Commonwealth U., Richmond, 1981-87; curator, acting co-dir. Contemporary Arts Mus., Houston, 1987-90; exec. dir. Washington Projects for the Arts, 1990-92; dir. Univ. Art Mus., Ariz. State U., Tempe, 1992—. Juror Dallas Mus. of Arts, McKnight Awards, Mpls.; grant evaluator IMS; grant evaluator, panelist NEH; lectr., cons. in field. Editor, contbr. essays to art publs. Bd. dirs. Cultural Alliance Washington; curator, commr. for U.S. for 1995 Venice Biennale. Samuel H. Kress fellow, 1972-73. Mem. Assn. Coll. and Univ. Mus. and Galleries (v.p. 1986-88), Am. Assn. Mus., Coll. Art Assn. (U.S. commr. Venice Biennale 1995). Office: Ariz State U Art Mus PO Box 872911 Tempe AZ 85287-2911

ZEITLIN, MAURICE, sociology educator; b. Detroit, Feb. 24, 1935; s. Albert J. and Rose (Goldberg) Zeitlin; m. Marilyn Geller, Mar. 1, 1959; children: Michelle, Carla, Erica. BA cum laude, Wayne State U., 1957; MA, U. Calif., Berkeley, 1960, PhD, 1964. Instr. anthropology and sociology Princeton (N.J.) U., 1961-64; rsch. assoc. Ctr. Internat. Studies, 1962-64; from asst. prof. to assoc. prof. sociology U. Wis., Madison, 1964—70, prof., 1970-77; dir. Ctr. Social Orgn., 1974-76; disting. prof. sociology UCLA, 1977—, rsch. assoc. Inst. Inds. Rels. Vis. prof. polit. sci. and sociology Hebrew U., Jerusalem, 1971—72. Author (with R. Scheer): Cuba: An American Tragedy, 1963, 1964, Revolutionary Politics and the Cuban Working Class, 1967, 1970, The Civil Wars in Chile, 1984; author: (with R. E. Ratcliff) Landlords and Capitalists, 1988, The Large Corporation and Contemporary Classes, 1989; author: (with J. Stepan-Norris) Talking Union, 1996, Left Out: Reds and America's Industrial Unions, 2003; Latin Am. editor: Ramparts mag., 1967—73, editor-in-chief: Political Power and Social Theory, 1980—90; mem. editl. adv. bd. Progressive mag., 1985—96; editor (with J. Petras): Latin America: Reform or Revolution?, 1968, American Society, Inc., 1970, 1977, Father Camilo Torres: Revolutionary Writings, 1972, Classes Class Conflict, and the State, 1980, How Mighty a Force?, 1983, Insurgent Workers: The Origins of Industrial Unionism, 1987. Chmn. Madison Citizens for a Vote on Vietnam, 1967—68, Am. Com. for Chile, 1973—75; mem. exec. bd. U.S. Com. Justice to Latin Am. Polit. Prisoners, 1977—84; mem. exec. com. Calif. Campaign for Econ. Democracy, 1983—86. Co-recipient Inaugural Disting. Publ. award in Labor Studies, Soc. for Study Social Problems, 1996; named to Ten Best Censored Stories list, 1978; recipient Project Censored award, Top Censored Story, 1981; Ford Found. fellow, 1965—67, 1970—71, Guggenheim fellow, 1981—82, NSF grantee, 1981, 1982, 1998. Mem.: Internat. Sociol. Assn. (mem. editl. bd. 1977—81), Am. Sociol. Assn. (mem. governing coun. 1977—80, co-recipient Disting. Contbn. Scholarship award in Polit. Sociology 1992, 1996, 2002, The 2004 Max Weber award for an Outstanding Book Published Over the Past Three Years in Orgns., Occupations and Work). Democrat. Jewish. Office: UCLA Dept Sociology 264 Haines Hall Los Angeles CA 90095-1551 Office Phone: 310-825-3968. Business E-Mail: zeitlin@soc.ucla.edu. *Personal philosophy: "If I am not for myself who will be? And when I am for myself, what am I?" Hillel, the Elder.*

ZEKMAN, TERRI MARGARET, graphic designer; b. Chgo., Sept. 13, 1950; d. Theodore Nathan and Lois (Bernstein) Z.; m. Alan Daniels, Apr. 12, 1980; children: Jesse Logan, Dakota Caitlin. BFA, Washington U., St. Louis, 1971; postgrad, Art Inst. Chgo., 1974-75. Graphic designer (on retainer) greeting cards and related products Recycled Paper Products Co., Chgo., 1970—, Jillson Roberts, Inc., Calif.; apprenticed graphic designer Helmuth, Obata & Kassabaum, St. Louis, 1970-71; graphic designer Container Corp., Chgo., 1971; graphic designer, art dir., photographer Cuerden Advt. Design, Denver, 1971-74; art dir. D'Arcy, McManus & Masius Advt., Chgo., 1975-76; freelance graphic designer Chgo., 1976-77; art dir. Garfield Linn Advt., Chgo., 1977-78; graphic designer Keiser Design Group, Van Noy & Co., Los Angeles, 1978-79; owner and operator graphic design studio Los Angeles, 1979—. Art and photography tchr. Ctr. for Early Edn., L.A., 1996—, Buckley Sch., Sherman Oaks, 1996—; 3d grade tchr. asst., 1999—. Recipient cert. of merit St. Louis Outdoor Poster Contest, 1970, Denver Art Dirs. Club, 1973 Personal E-mail: redzek50@aol.com.

ZELANTE, THOMAS ANDREW, lawyer; b. NYC, Nov. 30, 1954; s. Sabino and Rae Zelante; m. Maureen Connors; children: Thomas Andrew Jr., Christopher William. BA, LaSalle Coll., 1976; JD, Seton Hall U., 1979. Bar: NJ 1980. Assoc. atty. Ribis, McCluskey, Short Hills, NJ, 1982—83, Bowkley & Zelante, Randolph, NJ, 1986—. Mem. ethics com. Morris and Sussex counties Supreme Ct. of NJ Dist. X, 1996—2000; town atty. Borough of Victory Gardens, NJ, 2005—; atty. Morristown Zoning Bd. Adjustment, 2006—. Mem. govtl. affairs com. Morris County C. of C., Morristown, mem. infrastructure adv. group, 2004—06; mem. NJ Health Care Facilities Financing Authority, 2002—04; chmn. Morris County Dem. Com., Morristown, 2002—04; mem. Head Start of Morris County, 1998—2003, pres., 2003—04; trustee Ramapo Coll., Mahwah, NJ, 2004—, chmn. bd. trustees, 2005—; commr. Morris County Bd. Taxation, Morristown, 2005—. Mem.: Morris County Bar Assn. (trustee, Cmty. Svc./Pro Bono award (lifetime achievement) 2004). Avocations: golf, travel, ice hockey. Home: 7 Stoneybrook Way Morristown NJ 07960 Office: Bowkley & Zelante 390 Rte 10 West Randolph NJ 07869 Home Phone: 973-267-5045; Office Phone: 973-361-1500. Office Fax: 973-366-0191.

ZELAYA, IAN A., biologist, consultant; BS in Engring., Escuela Agrícola Panamericana, Zamorano, Honduras, 1994; MSc, Iowa State U., Ames, 1997, PhD, 2002. Rsch. asst. Escuela Agrícola Panamericana, El Zamorano, Honduras, 1989—94, Iowa State U., Ames, 1994—2002, rsch. assoc., 2002—04; team leader Syngenta Ltd., Bracknell, Berkshire, England, 2005—. David W. Staniforth scholarship, Iowa State U., 1997—2002. Mem.: Escuela Agrícola Panamericana Alumni Assn. (assoc.; v.p. 2000—02), Agronomy Grad. Club (assoc.; pres. 1996—97), Gamma Sigma Delta. Office Phone: 44 (0) 1344-413916. Business E-Mail: iazelaya@iastate.edu.

ZELAZNY, CATHERINE, retired elementary school educator; d. Edward and Irene R. Zelazny. BS in Edn., Edinboro U., 1971, postgrad. in Sch. Adminstrn., 1987; MEd in Guidance and Counseling, Gannon U., 1974, postgrad. small bus., 2005; postgrad. pre-law, Pa. State U., 1985. Counselor, math. tchr. Gannondale Home for Girls, Erie, Pa., 1972; tchr. Ft. LeBoeuf Sch. Dist., Waterford, Pa., 1972—77, 1979—86, 1987—2006, counselor, 1977—78; spl. edn. coord. Edinboro Intermediate Unit # 5, 1978—79; ret., 2006. Pvt. practice counselor, Erie, Pa.; mentor to educators, probationary boys, Erie. Author: Teacher Handbook and Parent Handbook, 1987. Logistics/project mgr., coord. Summer Arts Festival, Erie, 1980—85; mem. County Com. for Abuse Prevention, Erie; vice chmn. Erie County Dem. Party, Erie, 2002—06; chmn. Erie County Dem. Party State Com., 2006—. Recipient Project GIVE award, Pa. Dept. Edn., 1972. Mem.: NEA, Pa. Edn. Assn., Ft. LeBoeuf Edn. Assn. (treas., v.p., pres., mem. grievance com., membership com.), Erie County Hist. Soc., Phi Delta Kappa (v.p.). Avocations: antiques, piano, jewelry collecting. Home: 903 W Grandview Blvd Erie PA 16509

ZELAZNY, GARY A., dermatologist; b. Dallas, Nov. 13, 1941; BA, U. Tex., Austin, 1959—63; MD, U. Tex., Dallas, 1963—67. Residency Skin & Cancer Hosp. Phila., 1968—71. Maj. US Army, 1971—73. Fellow: Am. Acad. Dermatology.

ZELBY, LEON WOLF, electrical engineer, educator, consultant; b. Sosnowiec, Poland, Mar. 26, 1925; came to U.S., 1946, naturalized, 1951; s. Herszel and Helen (Wajnryb) Zylberberg; m. Rachel Kupfermintz, Dec. 28, 1954; children: Laurie Susan, Andrew Stephen. BSEE, Moore Sch. Elec. Engring., 1956; MS, Calif. Inst. Tech., 1957; PhD, U. Pa., 1961. Registered profl. engr., Pa., Okla. Mem. staff RCA, Hughes R & D Labs., Lincoln Lab., MIT, Sandia Corp., Argonne (Ill.) Nat. Labs., Inst. for Energy Analysis; mem. faculty U. Pa., 1959-67, assoc. prof., 1964-67; assoc. dir. plasma engring. Inst. Direct Energy Conversion, 1962-67; prof. U. Okla., Norman, 1967-95, dir. Sch. Elec. Engring., 1967-71; ret., 1995. Cons. RCA, 1961-67, Moore Sch. Elec. Engring., 1967-68, also pvt. firms. Editor

Tech. and Soc. mag., 1990-93; contbr. articles on energy-associated problems and issues to profl. jours. With AUS, 1946-47. Cons. Electrodynamic Corp. fellow Calif. Inst. Tech., 1957, Mpls.-Honeywell fellow U. Pa., 1957-58, Harrison fellow, 1958. Mem. IEEE, Franklin Inst., Sigma Xi, Tau Beta Pi, Eta Kappa Nu, Pi Mu Epsilon, Sigma Tau, Phi Kappa Phi. Home: 1009 Whispering Pines Dr Norman OK 73072-6912 Personal E-mail: zelby@ou.edu. *To learn as much, and to experience as much as possible, without harm to others; read, study, vary professional and recreational activities within constraints of the system.*

ZELDES, ILYA M., forensic scientist, lawyer; b. Baku, Azerbaidjan, Mar. 15, 1933; came to U.S., 1976; s. Michael B. and Pauline L. (Ainbinder) Z.; m. Emma S. Kryss, Nov. 5, 1957; 1 child, Irina Zeldes Rieser. JD, U. Azerbaidjan, Baku, 1955; PhD in Forensic Scis., U. Moscow, 1969. Expert-criminalist Med. Examiner's Bur., Baku, 1954-57; rsch. assoc. Criminalistics Lab., Moscow, 1958-62; sr. rsch. assoc. All-Union Sci. Rsch. Inst. Forensic Expertise, Moscow, 1962-75; chief forensic scientist S.D. Forensic Lab., Pierre, 1977-93. Owner Forensic Scientist's Svcs., Pierre, 1977-93. Author: Physical-Technical Examination, 1968, Complex Examination, 1971, The Problems of Crime, 1981, A Geneological History, 2002; contbr. numerous articles to profl. publs. in Australia, Austria, Bulgaria, Can., Eng., Germany, Holland, Hungary, India, Ireland, Israel, Rep. of China, Russia, U.S. and USSR. Mem. Internat. Assn. Identification (rep. S.D. chpt. 1979-93, chmn. forensic lab. analysis subcom. 1991-98, firearm and toolmark identification subcom. 2001-05), Am. Soc. Crime Lab. Dirs., Am. Assn. Firearm and Toolmark Examiners (emeritus). Avocations: travel, genealogy. Home: 5735 Foxlake Dr Apt 1 Fort Myers FL 33917-5661 Personal E-mail: ilyaz33@hotmail.com.

ZELDIN, KIM S., lawyer; b. Springfield, Pa., Nov. 24, 1961; d. Michael Herman and Saydean Zeldin. BA with highest honors, U. Calif., Santa Cruz, 1985; JD cum laude, U. Calif. Hastings Coll. Law, San Francisco, 1988. Bar: Calif. 1988, US Dist. Ct. (no. dist. Calif.) 1988, US Dist. Ct. (ctrl. and ea. dists. Calif.) 1990, US Dist. Ct. (so. dist. Calif.) 2000, Calif. Supreme Ct. 1988. Assoc., sr. counsel Pillsbury Winthrop LLP, San Francisco, 1988—2002; ptnr. Liner Yankelevitz, Sunshine & Regenstreif LLP, 2002—. Bd. mem. San Francisco Women Lawyers, 1994—97. Bd. mem. Pets are Wonderful Support, 2001—02, Breathe Calif., 2006—. Recipient Fair Housing Leadership award, Fair Housing of Marin, Calif., 2003, No. Calif. Super Lawyers award, Super Lawyers Mag., 2004—06. Mem.: ABA, Western Pension and Benefits Conf., French-Am. C. of C., Nat. Assn. Women Bus. Owners, Assn. Trial Lawyers Am., San Francisco Bar Assn., Order of the Coif. Office: Liner Yankelevitz Sunshine Regenstreif LLP 199 Fremont St 20th Fl San Francisco CA 94105 Office Phone: 415-489-7755. Office Fax: 415-489-7701.

ZELDIN, RICHARD PACKER, publisher; b. Worcester, Mass., Aug. 7, 1918; s. M. and Virginia (Gealt) Z.; m. Virginia Graves, Nov. 25, 1950; children— Elizabeth Ann, Richard Shepherd. BS, West Chester U., Pa., 1942; grad. exec. program bus. adminstrn., Columbia U., 1966. Gen. mgr. profl. and reference book div. McGraw-Hill Book Co., Inc., 1948-68; v.p., publishing dir. Litton Ednl. Pub. Co., Inc., 1968-70; pres. R.R. Bowker Co., 1970-76, Xerox Coll. Pub., Xerox Individualized Pub., 1970-76; pub. John Wiley & Sons, Inc., 1976-83; v.p. Moseley Assocs. Inc., NYC, 1983—. Sec.-treas. sci., tech. and med. book pubs. group Assn. Am. Pubs., 1966-70; mem. adv. com. comml. publs. AEC, 1966-70 Author: A Tennis Guide to the USA, 1980, Business Forms on File, 1984, Personal Forms on File, 1984; contbr. Scholarly Publishing, Books, Journals, Publishers and Libraries in the 20th Century, 2002. Served to lt. USNR, 1942-46. Recipient Disting. Alumni award West Chester U., 1974. Mem. Info. Industry Assn. (sec. 1973—), IEEE, Am. Soc. Info. Sci., Soc. for Scholarly Pub. Clubs: Dutch Treat (N.Y.C.), Pubs. Lunch (N.Y.C.). Home: 20 Fairfield Dr Eatontown NJ 07724-3114 Office: Moseley Assocs Inc 342 Madison Ave Rm 1414 New York NY 10173-1423

ZELIAZKOVA, MARIONA GEORGIEVA V., music educator; b. Pleven, Bulgaria, Sept. 19, 1964; arrived in US, 2002; d. Georgi Vasileva Stanchev and Ekaterina Vasileva Stancheva; m. Georgi Zhelyazkov Zhelyazkov, Aug. 16, 1986; children: Deyan, Kris. M Music Edn., Acad. Musical and Dance Arts, Plovdiv, Bulgaria, 1987; cert. German as Fgn. Lang., Goether Inst., Sofia, Bulgaria, 1994, cert. intermediate knowledge German lang., 1995; BS in Commn., Sofia U. St. Kliment Ohriaski, 1997. Music tchr. Brookhaven Meth. Child Devel. Ctr., Atlanta, 2002—, Peachtree Luth. Presch., Atlanta, 2003—05. Piano tchr. Gwinnett Sch. Music, Grayson, Ga., 2003—; substitute tchr. Gwinnett County Pub. Schs., Lawrenceville, Ga., 2005—; substitute organist, pianist various chs., Atlanta, 2003—. Mem.: Ga. Presch. Assn. Office: Brookhaven Meth Child Devel Ctr 1366 N Druid Hills Rd NE Atlanta GA 30319

ZELIKOW, PHILIP DAVID, public policy educator, former federal official; b. NYC, Sept. 21, 1954; s. Nate and Lee (Landsman) Z.; m. Paige Ellen Partain, May 30, 1982; children: Alexander, Carolyn. BA, U. Redlands, 1977; JD, U. Houston, 1981; MA, Tufts U., 1984, PhD, 1995. Bar: Tex. 1979. Briefing atty. Tex. Ct. Criminal Appeals, Austin, 1979-80; assoc. David Berg and Assocs., P.C., Houston, 1980-84; adj. prof. Naval Postgrad. Sch., Monterey, Calif., 1984-85; fgn. svc. officer US Dept. State, Washington and overseas, 1985-89; dir. European security NSC, Washington, 1989-91; assoc. prof. pub. policy John F. Kennedy Sch. Govt. Harvard U., Cambridge, Mass., 1991-98; Burkett Miller prof. history U. Va., Charlottesville, 1998—, dir. Miller Ctr. Pub. Affairs, 1998—2005; counselor US Dept. State, Washington, 2005—07. Mem. Presdl. Fgn. Intelligence Advisory Bd., 2001—03; exec. dir. Nat. Commn. on Terrorist Attacks Upon U.S. (The 9-11 Commn.), 2003—04. Author: American Military Strategy: Memos to a President, 2001; co-author: (with Condoleeza Rice) Germany United and Europe Transformed: A Study in Statecraft, 1995, (with Ernest R. May) The Kennedy Tapes: Inside the White House During the Cuban Missile Crisis, 1997, (with Graham T. Allison) Essence of Decision: Explaiing the Cuban Missile Crisis, 1999; editor: Why People Don't Trust Government, 1997; commentator newspapers, TV and radio programs, 1991—. Recipient 1st Pl. in Nation award Moot Ct. Competition, ABA, 1979. Mem. Internat. Inst. for Strategic Studies, Coun. Fgn. Rels., State Bar Tex., Soc. for Historians of Am. Fgn. Rels., Am. Polit. Sci. Assn. Avocations: hiking, skiing, tennis. Office: Corcoran Dept History U Va PO Box 400180 Randall Hall Charlottesville VA 22904 E-mail: pdz6n@Virginia.edu.

ZELIN, JEROME, retired retail executive; b. Bklyn., Dec. 24, 1930; s. Isidore and Ida (Roffman) Z.; m. Muriel Altsher, Dec. 18, 1955; children— Dorothy, Michael, Steven. BS magna cum laude, N.Y.U., 1952. Acct. Seymour Schwartz CPA, 1954-57; partner firm Schwartz, Zelin & Weiss CPAs, NYC, 1958-61; vice chmn., pres., exec. v.p., treas., financial v.p., dir. Unishops, Inc. (retail co.), Jersey City, 1961-74; exec. v.p. Masters, Inc., Westbury, NY, 1974-97; cons. Master's, Inc., Westbury, NY, 1997-2000; ret. Served with AUS, 1952-54. Mem. N.Y. Soc. CPAs, Am. Inst. CPAs, Beta Gamma Sigma, Tau Alpha Omega. Jewish. Home: 6 Maiden Stone Lane Monroe Township NJ 08831 Personal E-mail: jzelin1000@aol.com.

ZELINSKI, JOSEPH JOHN, engineering educator, consultant; b. Glen Lyon, Pa., Dec. 30, 1922; s. John Joseph and Lottie Mary (Oshinski) Z.; m. Mildred G. Sirois, July 22, 1946; children: Douglas John, Peter David. BS, Pa. State U., University Park, 1944; PhD, Pa. State U., 1950. Grad. fellow Pa. State U., University Park, 1946—50; project supr. applied physics lab. Johns Hopkins U., Silver Spring, Md., 1950—58; staff scientist Space Tech. Labs. (now TRW, Inc.), Redondo Beach, Calif., 1958—60; head chem. tech. divsn. Ops. Evaluation Group MIT, Cambridge, 1960—62; prin. rsch. scientist Avco Everett Rsch. Lab., Mass., 1962—64; prof. mech. engring. Northeastern U., Boston, 1964—85, prof. emeritus, 1985—; pres. World Edn. Resources, Ltd., Tampa, Fla., 1984—. Cons. Avco Everett Rsch. Lab., 1964-71, Pratt & Whitney Aircraft, East Hartford, Conn., 1966-70, Modern Electric Products and Phys. Scis. Co., Inc., Boston, 1980-82, Morrison, Mahoney and Miller, Boston, 1984; vice-chmn., chmn. exec. com. Univ. Grad. Coun., Northeastern U., Boston, 1980-84, dir. mech. engring. grad. program, 1982-85; del. 4th World Conf. Continuing Engring. Edn., Beijing China People to People, Spokane, Wash., 1989. Contbr. articles to profl. jours. Prin. Confraternity Christian Doctrine, Andover, Mass., 1961-64; pres. Andover Edn. Coun., 1962-64; vice chmn. Dem. Town Com., Boxford, Mass., 1980-84. Lt. (j.g.) USNR, 1943-46, PTO. Mem. AAAS, ASME, Am. Chem. Soc. Democrat. Roman Catholic. Achievements include foreign and domestic patents for coal combustion system for magnetohydrodynamic power generation, for fuel-cooled combustion systems for jet engines flying at high Mach numbers; prediction of optical observables of re-entry vehicles from analysis of decomposition mechanisms of heat-shield materials; invention of high-temperature furnace for production of crystalline graphite; development of a design method for ramjet combustors, liquid fuel-oxygen combustion system for Avco Mark 5 MHD power generator, carbon-air combustion system for lasers. E-mail: jjzelin@bellsouth.net.

ZELINSKY, DANIEL, mathematics professor; b. Chgo., Nov. 22, 1922; s. Isaac and Ann (Ruttenberg) Z.; m. Zelda Oser, Sept. 23, 1945; children: Mara Sachs, Paul O., David. BS, U. Chgo., 1941, MS, 1943, PhD, 1946. Rsch. mathematician applied math group Columbia U., NYC, 1944-45; instr. U. Chgo., 1943-44, 46-47; Nat. Rsch. Coun. fellow Inst. Advanced Study, Princeton, NJ, 1947-49; from asst. to assoc. prof. dept. math. Northwestern U., Evanston, Ill., 1949-60, prof., 1960-93, prof. emeritus, 1993—, acting chmn. math. dept., 1959-60, chmn., 1975-78. Vis. prof. U. Calif. Berkeley, 1960, Fla. State U., Tallahassee, 1963, Hebrew U., Jerusalem, 1970-71, 85, others; vis. scholar Tata Inst., 1979; mem. various coms. Northwestern U.; lectr. in field. Author: A First Course in Linear Algebra, 1968, rev. edit., 1973; contbr. articles to profl. jours. Fulbright grantee Kyoto U., 1955-56, grantee NSF, 1958-80; Guggenheim fellow Inst. Advanced Study, 1956-57, Indo-Am. fellow, 1978-79. Fellow AAAS (mem. nominating com. sect. A 1977-80, chmn. elect sect. A 1984-85, chmn. 1985-86, retiring chmn. 1986-87), Am. Math. Soc. (mem. coun. 1961-67, editor Transactions of A.M.S. 1961-67, mem. various coms., mem. editorial bd. Notices of A.M.S. 1983-86, chmn. editorial bds. com. 1989, chmn. ad hoc com. 1991-92). Jewish. Home: 613 Hunter Rd Wilmette IL 60091-2213 Office: Northwestern U Dept Math Evanston IL 60208-0001 Business E-Mail: dz@northwestern.edu.

ZELINSKY, PAUL O., illustrator, artist, writer; b. Evanston, Ill., Feb. 14, 1953; s. Daniel and Zelda B. (Oser) Z.; m. Deborah M. Hallen, Dec. 31, 1981; children: Anna H., Rachel L. BA summa cum laude, Yale U., 1974; MFA in Painting, Tyler Sch. Art, 1976. Art instr. San Diego State U., 1976; freelance illustrator/author, 1977—. Illustrator: Emily Upham's Revenge, 1978, How I Hunted the Little Fellows, 1979, The History of Helpless Harry, 1980, What Amanda Saw, 1981, Ralph S. Mouse, 1982, The Song in the Walnut Grove, 1982, The Sun's Asleep Behind the Hill, 1982, Zoo Doings, 1983, Hansel and Gretel, 1984 (Caldecott Honor 1985), The Story of Mrs. Lovewright and Purrless her Cat, 1985, The Random House Book of Humor for Children, 1988, Strider, 1991, The Enchanted Castle, 1992, Dear Mr. Henshaw, 1993, More Rootabagas, 1993, Swamp Angel, 1994 (Caldecott honor 1995), Five Children and It, 1999, Awful Ogre's Awful Day, 2001, Doodler Doodling, 2004, Toys Got Out, 2006, The Shivers in the Fridge, 2006; illustrator, adapter: The Maid and the Mouse and the Odd-shaped House, 1981, Rumpelstiltskin 1986 (Caldecott medal 1987), Rapunzel, 1997 (Caldecott medal 1998); illustrator, author: The Lion and the Stoat, 1984; illustrator, adapter, designer: The Wheels on the Bus, 1990, Knick-Knack Paddywhack!, 2002. Recipient Boston Globe/Horn Book Honor, 1994, Best Illustrated Book N.Y. Times Book Rev., 1981, 85, 94, 2001, 02, Reading Magic award Parenting Mag., 1990, 94, 2002; runner-up Bologna Ragazzi award 2005, Mazza medallion, 2006. Mem. PEN, Graphic Artists Guild, Author's Guild, Soc. Children's Book Writers and Illustrators, Phi Beta Kappa.

ZELIS, ROBERT FELIX, cardiologist, educator; b. Perth Amboy, NJ, Aug. 5, 1939; s. Felix Andrew and Rita Marie (Jurasz) Z.; m. Gail Ann Heelon, Sept. 10, 1960; children: Robert Felix, Kathleen, Karen, David. BS cum laude, U. Mass., 1960; MD with honors, U. Chgo., 1964. Diplomate: Am. Bd. Internal Medicine (cardiovascular disease). Intern, then asst. resident in medicine Beth Israel Hosp., Harvard U. Med. Sch., 1964-66; clin. assoc. (lt. comdr. USPHS) cardiology br. Nat. Heart Inst., NIH, Bethesda, Md., 1966-68; mem. faculty U. Calif. Med. Sch., Davis, 1968-74, asst. assoc. prof. medicine, 1972-74, chief lab. clin. physiology, 1968-74, asst. chief sect. cardiovasc. medicine, 1970-74; prof. medicine and cellular/molecular physiology Milton S. Hershey (Pa.) Med. Ctr., Pa. State U. Coll. Medicine, 1974—, chief divsn. cardiology, 1974-84, dir. cardiology rsch., 1984—2002. Editor: The Peripheral Circulations, 1975; co-editor: Calcium Blockers, 1982; mem. editorial bd. Annals Internal Medicine, 1976-79, Am. Jour. Physiology, 1976-79, Circulation, 1979-82, Am. Heart Jour., 1980-90, Am. Jour. Cardiology, 1983-86, Jour. Cardiovasc. Pharmacology, 1991-2001, Jour. Am. Coll. Cardiology, 1994-99; contbr. articles to profl. jours. Walter S. Barr fellow, 1960-64; recipient Borden Rsch. award, 1964, Palmer award for Faculty Mentoring Pa. State U., 1997, Disting. Educator award Pa. State U. Coll. Medicine, 2003, Disting. Svc. award U. Chgo. Med. and Biol. Scis. Alumni Assn., 2004. Fellow A.C.P., Am. Coll. Chest Physicians, Am. Coll. Cardiology (gov. Eastern Pa. 1977-80); mem. Am. Fedn. Clin. Research (pres. 1977-78), Am. Soc. Clin. Investigation (nat. council 1981-85, v.p. 1984-85), Am. Physiol. Soc., Assn. Am. Physicians, Assn. Univ. Cardiologists, Am. Soc. Pharmacology and Exptl. Therapeutics, Am. Heart Assn. (nat. fellow councils circulation, arteriosclerosis, clin. cardiology and epidemiology, v.p. for community programs 1979-81, award of merit 1983 v.p., exec. com. Pa. 1976-79, pres. Pa. affiliate 1979-80, Charles T. Mears Humanitarian award 1984), Western Soc. Clin. Research, Sigma Xi, Alpha Omega Alpha, Phi Eta Sigma. Roman Catholic. Home: 815 Verden Dr Hummelstown PA 17036-9700 Office: MS Hershey Med Ctr Cardiology Divsn HO-47 PO Box 850 Hershey PA 17033-0850 Home Phone: 717-533-7512.

ZELITCH, ISRAEL, retired scientist; b. Phila., June 18, 1924; s. Judah and Helen (Sherman) Z.; m. Ruth Helen Goldman, June 30, 1945; children: Helen, Bernard, Deborah. BS, Pa. State U., 1947; PhD, U. Wis., 1951. Nat. research coun. postdoctoral fellow NYU Coll. Medicine, NYC, 1951-52; asst. biochemist Conn. Agrl. Experiment Sta., New Haven, 1952-54, assoc. biochemist, 1954-60, biochemist, 1960-63, head dept. biochemistry, 1963-79, Samuel W. Johnson Disting. scientist, 1974—, head dept. biochemistry and genetics, 1980—94, now disting. scientist emeritus. Adj. prof. Dept. molecular biophysics and biochemistry Yale U., New Haven, 1958—, dept. biology, 1979—; chmn. Gordon Research Conf., 1979. Editorial bd. Plant Physiology, 1964-78, Archives of Biochemistry and Biophysics, 1969-77; editorial com. Annual Rev. of Plant Physiology, 1969-74; bd. editors Am. Scientist, 1984-90; author: Photosynthesis, Photorespiration, and Plant Productivity, 1971; contbr. articles to profl. jours. 1st lt. U.S. Army, 1944-46. Guggenheim fellow Guggenheim Found., U. Oxford, 1960, Am. Acad. Arts and Scis., 1980; recipient Fulbright Disting. Prof. award, Yugoslavia, 1981. Fellow AAAS; mem. Am. Soc. Plant Physiologists (exec. com. 1973-76, pres. 1977-78), Am. Soc. for Biochemistry and Molecular Biology, Am. Chem. Soc., Phi Beta Kappa. Jewish. Home: 70 Hall St Hamden CT 06517-3419 Office: Conn Agrl Experiment Sta 123 Huntington St PO Box 1106 New Haven CT 06504-1106 Office Phone: 203-974-8465.

ZELIZER, JULIAN E., historian, educator; b. Union, NJ, Dec. 6, 1969; s. Gerald Lee and Viviana Adela Zelizer; m. Nora K. Zelizer. BA, Brandeis U., 1991; MA, Johns Hopkins U., 1993, PhD, 1996. Asst. prof. SUNY Albany, 1996-99, assoc. prof., 1999—. Polit. expert WRGB TV-6, Albany, 1998—; commn. mem. New Yorkers for Pub. Affairs TV, Albany, 1999—. Author: Taxing America, 1998 (OAH Hawley prize 2000, D.B. Hardeman prize 1998); editl. bd. mem. Jour. for Multimedia History, 1998-2000; contbr. articles to profl. jours. Dirksen fellow Dirksen Ctr., 1999, rsch. fellow Brookings Instn., 1995-96; grantee NEH, 2000. Jewish.

ZELIZER, VIVIANA, sociologist, educator; BA, Rutgers Univ., 1971; MA in Sociology, Columbia Univ., 1974, MPhil, 1974, PhD, 1977. Vis. instr. Columbia Univ., 1976; asst. prof. sociology Rutgers Univ., 1976—78, Barnard Coll., 1978—82, acting chair, dept. sociology, 1978—80, assoc. prof., 1982—85, prof., 1985—88; grad. faculty Columbia Univ., 1978—82; prof. Princeton Univ., 1988—2002, Lloyd Cotsen '50 prof. sociology, 2002—. Recipient Elizur Wright award, Am. Risk and Ins. Assn., 1985, C.W. Mills award, Soc. Study of Social Problems, 1985; grantee John Simon Guggenheim Mem. Found. Fellowship, 1996—97. Fellow: Am. Acad. Arts & Scis.; mem.: Sociol. Rsch. Assn., Phi Beta Kappa. Reads, speaks, writes English, Spanish, French, Italian. Office: Dept Sociology 120 Wallace Hall Princeton Univ Princeton NJ 08544 Office Phone: 609-258-4557. Business E-Mail: vzelizer@princeton.edu. *

ZELL, JOSEPHINE MAY, retired language educator; b. Harwood, Lancashire, England, Apr. 26, 1934; d. Joseph Henry Howe and Emily Emma Herod; m. Robert Zell, Apr. 17, 1968 (div. Oct. 2002); children: Rosemary, Philip. BA Honors English Lang. and Lit., U. Manchester, Eng., 1955; MA in Latin, U. Wis., 1989. Chair dept. English, Milham Ford Sch., Oxford, England, 1964—68; lectr. English, U. Wis., Milw., 1968—71; tchr. English, Madison (Wis) Met. Sch. Dist., 1977—97; tchr. Latin, West H.S., Madison Sch. Dist., 1992—97. Author: (poetry) The Curtain Rises, 1993. Mem.: AAUW. Methodist. Home: 7001 Havenswood Dr Madison WI 53718

ZELL, SAMUEL, real estate company executive; b. Chgo., Sept. 28, 1941; s. Bernard Zell; m. Helen Zell; 3 children. BA, U. Mich., 1963, JD, 1966, LLD (hon.), 2005. With Yates Holleb and Michelson, 1966-68; co-founder, pres. Equity Fin. & Mgmt. Co., Chgo., 1968—76; pres., chmn. Equity Group Investments, LLC (formerly Equity Fin. & Mgmt. Co.), Chgo., 1976—; chmn. Great Am. Mgmt. and Investment Inc., 1981—; co-chmn. Revco D.S.; owner Tribune Co., 2007—, Chgo. Cubs, 2007—. Chmn. Delta Queen Steamboat Co., New Orleans, 1984—, Eagle Industries Inc.; chmn. Itel Corp., 1985—, Nat. Assn. Real Estate Investment Trusts, 1998-2000; bd. dirs. The Tribune Co., 2007- Named one of Forbes' Richest Americans, 2006, World's Richest People, Forbes Mag., 2005—, 50 Who Matter Now, Business 2.0, 2007. Republican. Avocations: racquetball, skiing. Office: Equity International Two N Riverside Plz Ste 700 Chicago IL 60606 *

ZELLER, CHRISTOPHER LEE, preservation archaeologist; b. Northampton, Pa., Nov. 25, 1956; s. Karl Fredrich and Joan Veron (Hagenbuch) Zeller; m. Christi Joanne Wiggins, Apr. 24, 1982 (div. Mar. 11, 2004); 1 child, Kaeti Grace. BA in Anthropology, Ft. Lewis Coll., 1980. Fireline archaeologist US Forest Svc., cert. ski patroller Nat. Ski Patrol and Assn. Profl. Patrollers, EMT Colo. Preservation tech., foreman San Juan Stabilization, Mancos, Colo., 1977—81; archaeologist Bur. Land Mgmt., Durango, Colo., 1982; preservation specialist Paul Nickens and Assocs., Montrose, Colo., 1983; ind. contractor, preservation specialist Woods Canyon Archaeol. Cons., Yellow Jacket, Colo., 1985—87; ind. contractor, project dir. Four Corners Rsch. Inst., Durango, 1986—87; owner, operator Petro Graphics, Durango, 1987—. Ski patroller Durango Mountain Resort, 1974—83, patrol foreman, 1984—2002, asst. patrol dir., 2003—. Achievements include invention of toboggan platform; conducted over 80 major preservation projects involving over 70 archaeological and historic sites in American Southwest. Avocations: fine art, trout fishing, motorcycle touring. Office: Petro Graphics Po Box 745 Durango CO 81302 Office Phone: 970-799-5146.

ZELLER, JOSEPH PAUL, advertising executive; b. Crestline, Ohio, Mar. 19, 1940; s. Paul Edward and Grace Beatrice (Kinstle) Z.; m. Nancy Jane Schmidt, June 17, 1961; children: Laurie, Joe. BA, U. Notre Dame, 1962; MFA, Ohio U., 1963. Mgr.radio/television Drewrys Ltd. USA, Inc., South Bend, Ind., 1963-64; media supr. Tatham-Laird & Kudner, Chgo., 1964-67; v.p. assoc. media dir. J. Walter Thompson Co., Chgo., 1967-77; v.p. media dir. v.p. Campbell-Mithun, Chgo., 1977-80; sr. v.p., dir. media, fin., chmn. media coun. D'Arcy Masius Benton & Bowles, Chgo., 1980-96, sr. v.p., 1996-2000; pres. Fox River Trading Co., East Dundee, Ill., 2000—. Chmn. Z Prop, 1986—; dir. circle Desert Caballeros Mus., 1994-96; founder Native Am. Images web mag., 1999. Pres. Amateur Hockey Assn. Ill., 1985. Named to Ill. Hockey Hall of Fame, 2005. Mem. Broadcast Pioneers, Chgo. Advt. Club, Moose. Roman Catholic. Avocations: hockey, photography, music. Business E-Mail: trader@rivertradingpost.com.

ZELLER, KURT-ALEXANDER, vocalist, actor, stage director, voice educator; b. Portland, Oreg.; s. Norman K. and Johanna (Beckham) Z. BFA, MusB, So. Meth. U.; MusM, U. Cin., D in Musical Arts, 1990. Asst. prof. voice Willamette U., Salem, Oreg., 1993—. Vocal performances with orgns. including Salem (Oreg.) Chamber Orch., Opera Theatre South Bend, Ind., Portland Chamber Orch., at Brevard (N.C.) Music Ctr., Rogue Valley (Oreg.) Opera, Oreg. Shakespeare Festival, Ashland; editor jour. Cantus Firmus, Internat. Soc. Early Music singers, 1992-97; contbr. articles to mus. publs. Mabel Henderson grantee Mu Phi Epsilon Found., 1987, Merle Montgomery doctoral grantee, 1989. Mem. Nat. Assn. Tchrs. of Singing (treas. Cascade chpt. 1993-97, v.p. 1999—, Oreg. dist. winner artist awards 1996), Early Music Guild Oreg. (bd. dirs. 1993—), Mu Phi Epsilon (dir. Pacific N.W. dist 3 1992-96, chmn. internat. standing rules 1995—). Methodist. Office: Willamette Univ Dept Music 900 State St Salem OR 97301-3931

ZELLER, MARILYNN KAY, retired librarian; b. Scottsbluff, Nebr., Mar. 1, 1940; d. William Harold and Dorothy Elizabeth (Wilkins) Richards; m. Robert Jerome Zeller, May 21, 1966; children: Kevin Jerome and Renae Kay. BS, Calvary Bible Coll., 1985; MLS, U. Mo., Columbia, 1989. Cert. libr. File clk. Waddell & Reed, Kansas City, Mo., 1962-65; payroll clk. Century Fin. Co., Kansas City, Mo., 1965-67, Percy Kent Bag Co., Independence, Mo., 1968-70; accounts receivable Swansons on the Plaza, Kansas City, 1971-73; clk. casualty ins. Mill Mutuals, Kansas City, 1977-80; registrar's asst. Calvary Bible Coll., Kansas City, 1980-85, libr. asst., 1985-88, asst. libr., 1988-89, head libr., 1990—96. Chairperson libr. com. Calvary Bible Coll., Kansas City, 1990-96; libr. rep. Friends of the Hilda Kroeker Libr., Kansas City, 1990-96. Author: History of the Christian Librarian's Association, 1989. Mem. Christian Librs. Assn. Avocations: walking, reading, crocheting, sewing, swimming. Home: 401 13th Ave N Greenwood MO 64034-9750

ZELLER, MICHAEL EDWARD, physicist, researcher; b. San Francisco, Oct. 8, 1939; s. Edward Michael and Marie (Eschen) Z.; m. Linda Marie Smith, June 12, 1960; children: Jeffrey, Daniel. BS, Stanford U., 1961; MS, UCLA, 1964, PhD, 1968. Rsch. assoc. UCLA, 1968-69; instr. physics Yale U., New Haven, 1969-70, asst. prof., 1970-76, assoc. prof., 1976-82, prof., 1982—, chmn., 1989-95, Henry Ford II prof., 1996—. Recipient DeVane medal Phi Beta Kappa, 1980. Fellow Am. Phys. Soc.; mem. N.Y. Acad.

Sci., Sigma Xi, Sigma Pi Sigma. Democrat. Jewish. Home: 135 Newton Rd Woodbridge CT 06525-1534 Office: Yale U Physics Dept 260 Whitney Ave New Haven CT 06511-8903 Business E-Mail: michael.zeller@yale.edu.

ZELLER, MICHAEL EUGENE, lawyer; b. Queens, NY, June 19, 1967; s. Hans Ludwig and Geri Ann (Schottenstein) Z. BA, Union Coll., 1989; JD, Temple Law Sch., 1992; LLM magna cum laude, U. Hamburg, Germany, 1994. Bar: N.Y. 1992, U.S. Dist. Ct. (so. and ea. dists.) N.Y. 1995, N.C. 1996. Fgn. intern Bryan Gonzalez Vargas y Gonzalez Baz, Mexico City, 1990; student law clk. Hon. Jane Cutler Greenspan, Phila., 1990-91; fgn. clk. DROSTE, Hamburg, 1991, fgn. assoc., translator, 1992-94; freelance translator Charlotte, N.C., 1995—; mem. Internat. and Corp. Law Group of Moore & Van Allen PLLC, Charlotte, 1995—; coun. CIT Small Business Lending Corp., 1997; owner, restaurateur Salad Garden, LLC. and Salad Garden Café, LLC, 1998—2001; owner Nighttime Entertainment LLC, 1999—2001, BGZ Properties LLC; mem. Moore & VanAllen, Charlotte, NC. Active Charlotte World Affairs Coun., Charlotte Mayor's Internat. Cabinet; bd. dirs. Alemannia Soc., 1996-2000, Young Affiliates of Mint Mus., 1999-2000; bd. dirs., pres. Southgate Commons Homeowners Assn., 1998-2002; vol. atty. counsel Children's Rights, 1995-, bd. dirs., 2003-06. Named Vol. Lawyer of Yr., Children's Law Ctr., 1998, 2003; scholar, Fedn. German/Am. Clubs, 1987. Mem.: ABA, So. Poverty Law Ctr., European Am. Bus. Forum, Gewerblicher Rechtsschultz und Urheberrecht e.V., Nat. Ctr. for Employee Ownership, ESOP Assn., Mecklenburg County Bar Assn., NC Bar Assn., NY State Bar Assn. Avocations: singing, theater, golf, cooking, hiking.

ZELLER, RONALD JOHN, lawyer; b. Phila., Jan. 28, 1940; m. Lucille Bell; children: John, Kevin, Suzanne. BSBA, LaSalle Univ., 1964; JD, Ohio State U., 1967. Bar: Mich. 1968, Fla. 1971. Ptnr. Patton & Kanner, Miami, Fla., 1973-80, of counsel, 1980-89; dir., pres., CEO Norwegian Cruise Lines, 1980-86; pres. Twenty First Century Mgmt. Group, Inc., Coconut Grove, Fla., 1986-90, Miami Voice Corp., 1990-92; gen. counsel Splty. Mgmt. Co., Delray Beach, Fla., 1992-93, pres., 1994-96; ptnr. Zeller & Assocs., LLC, Palm Beach, Fla., 1996—; of counsel Koeppel Gottleib Mesches, 2000—06, Gottleib Mesches, L.P., 2007—. Dep. chmn. Cruise Lines Internat. Assoc., NYC, 1981-85, chmn., 1986. Trustee United Way Dade County, 1981-86; pres. Cath. Charities, Archdiocese of Miami 1976-78, Broward County, 1975-76, Excalibur Devel. Ctrs., Inc., 1973-75; mem. citizens bd. U. Miami, 1980-92; mem. exec. bd. New World Sch. Arts, 1986-87; mem. centennial campaign com. Ohio State U. Coll. Law, 1982-92; mem. nat. coun. Moritz Coll. Law; mem. coun. Pres.'s Assocs., LaSalle U., 1982-87; mem. Fla. Postsecondary Edn. Planning Commn., 1986-87; mem. Cmty. Assns. Inst., 1995-2000; chmn. exec. com. Maritime Inst., 1997-99; mem. utility rev. bd. Village of Wellington, 1997-98; mem. gen. counsel Palm Beach Maritime Mus., 1997-2005; mem. Fla. com. Affirm Thy Friendship Campaign, Ohio State U., 1997-2000; mem. cruise line incentive com. Port of Palm Beach, 1997-2000; mem. ecumenical rev. bd. Diocese Palm Beach, 2002—03, mem. comm. adv. bd., 2002—. Mem. ABA (sect. taxation, closely held businesses. com.), Fla. Bar Assn. (lawyers and CPA's com. 2003-04, long range planning com. 2001-04), Maritime Law Assn. (proctor in admiralty), Pres.' Club Ohio State U. Office: Zeller & Assocs LLC Trump Plz Office Ctr 525 S Flagler Dr Ste 200 West Palm Beach FL 33401 Home Phone: 561-792-1272; Office Phone: 561-802-4480. Office Fax: 561-802-4387.

ZELLER, SCOTT L., psychiatrist; b. Macomb, Ill., Dec. 4, 1960; s. Gerald L. and Marilyn Zeller; m. Susan Brydges Winchester, Jan. 19, 1996; 1 child, Douglas Winchester. BA, Ill. Wesleyan U., Bloomington, 1982; MD, Northwestern U., Chgo., 1986. Diplomate Nat. Bd. Med. Examiners, 1987. Resident U. Calif., San Francisco, 1986—89; attending physician psychiat. emergency svcs. Alameda County Med. Ctr., San Leandro, Calif., 1988—97; chief psychiat. emergency svcs. Alamda County Med. Ctr., 1997—; ptnr. JSA Health Mgmt., Houston, 2006—. Bd. dirs. Psychiat. Emergency Solutions, Inc, Houston; chmn. We. Emergency Psychiatry Conf., Oakland, Calif., 2001—. Editor: Emergency Psychiatry: Principles and Practice; editor: (pub.) Harpoon Mag., 1989—93; contbr. chapters to books, columns in newspapers, articles to profl. jours. Physician, asst. clinic dir. Katrina relief efforts Astrodome, Houston, 2005; spkr., writer and planner Ctrl. Fwy., San Francisco, 1996—99; bd. dirs. San Francisco Symphony Symphonix, 1991—95, San Francisco Press Club, 1992—94. Mem.: Am. Assn. Emergency Psychiatry (v.p. 1999—), Sigma Pi (life). Avocations: hiking, travel. Office: Alameda County Med Ctr 2060 Fairmont Dr San Leandro CA 94578 Office Phone: 510-346-1363. Business E-Mail: szeller@acmedctr.org.

ZELLERBACH, WILLIAM JOSEPH, retired paper company executive; b. San Francisco, Sept. 15, 1920; s. Harold Lionel and Doris (Joseph) Z.; m. Margery Haber, Feb. 25, 1946; children: John William, Thomas Harold, Charles Ralph, Nancy. BS, Wharton Sch., U. Pa., 1942; grad., Advanced Mgmt. Program, Harvard U., 1958. With Crown Zellerbach Corp. and subs., 1946-85; officer, dir. Crown Zellerbach Corp., 1960-85. Mem gen. adv. com. fgn. assistance programs AID, 1965-68; chmn. bd. Zellerbach Family Found. Served as lt. USNR, 1942-46. Mem. Nat. Paper trade Assn. (pres. 1970) Clubs: Villa Taverna (San Francisco), Presidio Golf (San Francisco), Pacific Union (San Francisco), Commonwealth (San Francisco); Peninsula Country (San Mateo, Calif.). Office: 120 Montgomery St Ste 1960 San Francisco CA 94104-4323

ZELLERS, ROBERT CHARLES, materials engineer, consultant, speaker; b. Youngstown, Ohio, June 13, 1943; s. Charles Newton and Beatrice Eleanor (Snavely) Z.; m. Patricia Ann Ockerman, Nov. 27, 1965; children: Derek, Shannon, Robyn. BEng in Civil Engring., Youngstown State U., 1967. Registered profl. engr., Pa., Ohio; registered profl. land surveyor, Pa. Materials engr. Standard Slag Co., Youngstown, 1966-72; asst. chief engr. The Duquesne Slag Co., Pitts., 1972-81; exec. sec. Pa. Slag Assn., Pitts., 1972-81; v.p. engring. Forta Corp., Grove City, Pa., 1978-82, exec. v.p., 1983-97; owner, mgr. Zellers Design Group, Mercer, Pa., 1982—; owner Zellers Galleries, Mercer, 1979—; prin. IMTEK, Grove City, Pa., 1988-91; pres. ICEMS, Toledo, 1992-99; v.p. MIZEL, Crowley, Tex., 1994-97; pres. ZELLCO, Crowley, Tex., 1994-97; v.p. mktg. Fibercon Internat. Inc., 1998-99; dir. tech. and engring. Nycon, Inc., Mercer, 1999—2001, v.p. tech. and engring., 2002—06; v.p. engring. and tech. sales, ptnr. NMW, Inc., Mercer, 2006—. Presenter, spkr., reviewer in field. Contbr. articles to profl. jours. Dir. pub. rels. Greenville Symphony Orch. Mem. ASCE, ASTM (various coms.), Constrn. Specifications Inst., Internat. Code Coun., Nat. Ready Mixed Concrete Assn., Fiber Reinforced Concrete Assn. (co-founder, pres. 2004-), Transp. Rsch. Bd., Am. Concrete Inst. (various coms.), Lions. Home Phone: 724-475-2171; Office Phone: 724-475-1177. Personal E-mail: zzzman13@hotmail.com.

ZELLNER, ARNOLD, economics, econometrics and statistics professor; b. Bklyn., Jan. 2, 1927; s. Israel and Doris (Kleiman) Z.; m. Agnes Marie Sumares, June 20, 1953; children— David S., Philip A., Samuel N., Daniel A., Michael A. AB in Physics, Harvard U., Cambridge, Mass., 1949; PhD in Econs., U. Calif., Berkeley, 1957; D (hon.), U. Autonoma de Madrid, 1986, Tecnia de Lisboa, Portugal, 1991, U. Kiel, Germany, 1998, Erasmus U., Rotterdam, Netherlands, 2006. Asst., then assoc. prof. econs. U. Wash., 1955-60; Fulbright vis. prof. Netherlands Sch. Econs., Rotterdam, 1960-61; assoc. prof., then prof. econs. U. Wis., 1961-66; H.G.B. Alexander disting. service prof. econs. and statistics U. Chgo., 1966-96, prof. emeritus, 1996—; dir. H.G.B. Alexander Rsch. Found., 1973—. Cons. Battelle Meml. Inst., 1964—71; vis. rsch. prof. U. Calif., Berkeley, 1971, vis. prof., 1997—2006, Am. U., Cairo, 1997, Hebrew U., 1997; trustee Nat. Opinion Rsch. Corp., 1973—80; bd. dirs. Nat. Bur. Econ. Rsch., 1980—; seminar leader NSF-NBER Seminar on Bayesian Inference in Econometrics and Stats., 1970—95. Co-author: Systems Simulation for Regional Analysis, 1969, Estimating the Parameters of the Markov Probability Model, 1970; author: Bayesian Inference in Econometrics, 1971, Basic Issues in Econometrics, 1984, Bayesian Analysis in Econometrics and Statistics: The Zellner View and Papers, 1997, Statistics, Econometrics and Forecasting, 2004; editor: Economic Statistics and Econometrics, 1968, Seasonal Analysis of Economic Time Series, 1978, Simplicity, Inference and Modelling, 2001; assoc. editor: Econometrica, 1962-68; founding co-editor: Jour. Econometrics, 1972—; co-editor Studies in Bayesian Econometrics and Statistics, 1975, The Economics of Marine Resources, 2001, The Structural Econometrics, Time Series Analysis Approach, 2004; founding editor ASA Jour. Bus. and Econ. Stats., 1983; contbr. articles to profl. jours. Pres. Leonard J. Savage Meml. Trust Fund, Chgo., 1977-2000. Fellow AAAS, Am. Acad. Arts and Scis., Am. Econ. Assn., Internat. Inst. Forecasters, Econometric Soc., Am. Statis. Assn. (pres. elect 1990—, pres. 1991—, chmn. bus. and econs. sect. 1980, chmn. Bayesian statis. sci. sect. 1993); mem. Internat. Statis. Inst., Internat. Soc. Bayesian Analysis (co-pres. 1993, pres. 1994-96, Founders award 1998), Soc. Actuaries (trustee, rsch. found., 1994-98). Avocations: golf, tennis, travel, theater, music. Home: 5628 S Dorchester Ave Chicago IL 60637-1722 Office: U Chgo Grad Sch Bus 5807 S Woodlawn Ave Chicago IL 60637-1511 Office Phone: 773-702-7145. Business E-Mail: arnold.zellner@chicagogsb.edu.

ZELLWEGER, RENEE, actress; b. Katy, Tex., Apr. 25, 1969; d. Emil Erich Zellweger and Kjellfrid Irene Andreassen; m. Kenny Chesney, May 9, 2005 (annulled Dec. 20, 2005). BA in English, U. Tex., 1991. Actress: (films) Reality Bites, 1994, Love and a .45, 1994, 8 Seconds, 1994, The Low Life, 1995, Empire Records, 1995, The Whole Wide World, 1996, Jerry Maguire, 1996, Texas Chainsaw Massacre: The Next Generation, 1997, Deceiver, 1997, One True Thing, 1998, A Price Above Rubies, 1998, The Bachelor, 1999, Nurse Betty, 2000 (Golden Globe award for best actress in a comedy or musical 2000), Me, Myself & Irene, 2000, Bridget Jones's Diary, 2001 (nominee Best Actress SAG award, Broadcast Film Critics Assn. award, Brit. Acad. Award and Acad. award 2001; Golden Globe award nominee best actress in a comedy or musical, 2001), White Oleander, 2002, Chicago, 2002 (Golden Globe award for best supporting actress in a comedy or musical, 2002, SAG award for Best Actress, 2003, Academy award nominee Best Actress, 2003), Down With Love, 2003, Cold Mountain, 2003 (Golden Globe for best supporting actress, 2004, Screen Actors Guild Award for best supporting actress, 2004, Acad. Award for best supporting actress, 2004), (voice) Shark Tale, 2004, Bridget Jones: The Edge of Reason, 2004, Cinderella Man, 2005; (TV films) A Taste for Killing, 1992, Murder in the Heartland, 1993, Shake, Rattle and Rock 1994. Recipient Crystal award, Women in Film Crystal + Lucy awards, 2007. Office: Byant Joel Creative Artists Agy 9830 Wilshire Blvd Beverly Hills CA 90212

ZELMAN, SUSAN TAVE, school system administrator; m. Allan Zelman; 3 children. DEd, U. Mich.; D in Pub. Edn. (hon.), U. Rio Grande, Ohio; D in Humanities (hon.), Youngstown U. Assoc. prof. edn. Emmanuel Coll., Boston, chair dept. edn.; assoc commr. ednl. dept. personnel Mass. Dept. Edn., 1988—94; dep. commr. Mo. Dept. Elem. and Secondary Edn., Jefferson City, 1994—99; supt. pub. instrn. Ohio Dept Edn., Columbus, 1999—. Rschr. Edn. Tech. Ctr. Harvard Grad. Sch. Edn. Recipient Nat, Sci. Rsch. Opportunity award, Columbus Tchrs. Coll. Office: Ohio Dept Edn 25 S Front St Columbus OH 43215-4183 *

ZELMANOWITZ, JULIUS MARTIN, mathematics professor, academic administrator; b. NYC, Feb. 20, 1941; s. Morris and Tillie (Holtz) Z.; m. Joan R. Traubel, June 24, 1962; 1 child, Dawn Michèle. AB, Harvard U., 1962; MS, U. Wis., 1963, PhD, 1966. From asst. prof. to assoc. prof. U. Calif., Santa Barbara, 1966—77, prof. math., 1977—2006, assoc. vice chancellor acad. affairs, 1985-87, assoc. vice chancellor acad. personnel, 1988-98; assoc. prof. Carnegie-Mellon U., Pitts., 1970-71; interim vice provost acad. initiatives U. Calif., 1999-2000, v.p. acad. initiatives, 2000—06, sr. vice provost acad. programs, 2005; dep. dir. Math. Sci. Rsch. Inst., Berkeley, Calif., 2006—. Vis. asst. prof. UCLA, 1969—70, vis. assoc. prof., 1973—74; vis. prof. U. Rome, 1977, McGill U., Montreal, Que., Canada, 1982—83, 1987—88, U. Munich, 1983, 88, U. Calif., Berkeley, 2006—. Contbr. articles to profl. jours. Sr. rsch. grantee Italian Nat. Rsch. Coun., Rome, 1977, Palermo, 1988; named Milw. Prof. of Maths. The Technion, Haifa, Israel, 1979; Fulbright sr. fellow, Munich, 1983. Mem. Am. Math. Soc., Math. Assn. Am. Home: 2040 Franklin St # 1407 San Francisco CA 94109-2982 Office: 17 Gauss Way Berkeley CA 94720-5070 Office Phone: 510-643-6040. Business E-Mail: julius@math.ucsb.edu, jz@msri.org.

ZELNAK, STEPHEN P., JR., construction materials company executive; BS, Ga. Inst. Tech.; M Adminstrv. Sci. and Bus. Adminstrn., U. Ala. With Martin Marietta Corp., Raleigh, NC, 1981—, head aggregates ops., 1982-92, pres. materials group, 1992-93; pres. Martin Marietta Materials, Raleigh, NC, 1993, CEO, 1993—, chmn. bd. dirs., 1997—. Bd. dir. Beazer Homes USA Inc. Former chmn. NC Citizens for Bus. and Industry. Office: Martin Marietta Materials Inc 2710 Wycliff Rd Raleigh NC 27607 *

ZELNER, KYLE FORBES, historian, educator; b. Highland Park, Mich., Mar. 3, 1968; s. Harry Lee and Sheila B. Zelner; m. Tisha Mae Montanaro, July 10, 1993. BA with honors, U. Mich., Dearborn, 1990; MA, Wayne State U., Detroit, 1993; PhD, Coll. William & Mary, Williamsburg, Va., 2003. Adj. asst. prof. history Thomas Nelson C.C., Hampton, Va., 1997—2004; asst. prof. history U. So. Miss., Hattiesburg, Miss., 2004—. Vis. asst. prof. history Coll. of William & Mary, 2003—04. Author: (web site) Colonial Warfare-The United States at War: Understanding Conflict and Society; book rev. editor: The So. Quar., 2005—; contbr. chapters to books. Scholar, Wayne State U., 1991—93, Coll. William & Mary, 1993—98, 1999—2001, Sons and Daughters Pilgrims, 1996—97. Mem.: Soc. Mil. History, New Eng. Hist. and Geneal. Soc., Am. Hist. Assn., Orgn. Am. Historians (chmn. state membership 2006), Omohundro Inst. Early Am. History and Culture (assoc.), Phi Alpha Theta (life). Avocations: reading, cooking. Office: Univ So Miss History Dept 118 Coll Dr 5047 Hattiesburg MS 39406-0001 Home Phone: 601-297-7967; Office Phone: 601-266-6196. Office Fax: 601-266-4334. Business E-Mail: kyle.zelner@usm.edu.

ZELNICK, CARL ROBERT, writer, educator; b. NYC, Aug. 9, 1940; s. David Isadore and Lillian (Ostrow) Z.; m. Pamela Margaret Sharp, Dec. 30, 1967; children: Eva Michal, Dara Yael, Marni Ruth. BS, Cornell U., 1961; LLB, U. Va., 1964. Bar: NY 1965, DC 1966. Law assoc. H. Charles Ephraim, Washington, 1966-67; corr./columnist Anchorage Daily News, 1968-76; assoc. editor Environ. Law Reporter, 1971-72; spl. corr. Christian Sci. Monitor, 1973-77; corr./bur. chief Nat. Pub. Radio, Washington, 1972-76; exec. editor Frost/Nixon Interviews, Washington, 1976-77; dir. news coverage ABC-TV, Washington, 1977-81; dep. bur. chief ABC News, Washington, 1981-82, Moscow bur. chief, corr., 1982-84, Israel corr., 1984-86; ABC News Pentagon corr. Washington, 1986-94; media fellow Hoover Instn., Stanford U., 1998. Mem. Citizens Commn. on Race, 1998—2003; vis. prof. Boston U., 1998—2000, prof., 2000—, chmn. dept. journalism, 2002—; rsch. fellow Hoover Instn., 2002—. Author: Backfire--A Reporter Looks at Affirmative Action, 1996, Gore--A Political Life, 1999, Winning Florida: How the Bush Team Fought the Battle, 2000, Swing Dance: Justice O'Connor and the Michigan Muddle, 2004, After Gaza, 2006; contbr. articles to newspapers and mags. Served with USMC, 1964-65. Recipient Gavel awards Am. Bar Assn., 1969, 74, Du Pont award Columbia U. Sch. Journalism, 1984, Emmy award, 1984, 92; rsch. fellow Hooer Inst., 2001—. Mem. Council on Fgn. Relations, Phi Epsilon Pi, Pi Delta Phi. Jewish. Office: Boston U Coll Comm 640 Commonwealth Ave Boston MA 02215-2422 Business E-Mail: bzelnick@bu.edu.

ZELNICK, RONALD STUART, surgeon; b. NYC, Dec. 6, 1958; BS, George Washington U., 1980; MD, Albany Med. Coll., 1984. Diplomate Am. Bd. Surgery, Am. Bd. Colon Rectal Surgery. Resident gen. surgery L.I. Jewish Hosp., New Hyde Park, N.Y., 1984-89; fellowship colon and rectal surgery Henry Ford Hosp., Detroit, 1989-90; pvt. practice Jupiter, Fla., 1991—. Fellow ACS, Am. Soc. Colon Rectal Surgeons; mem. Fla. Surg. Soc., Fla. Colon Rectal Surgery Soc. Office: Ste 105 210 Jupiter Lakes Blvd #3105 Jupiter FL 33458 Office Phone: 561-575-7875.

ZELNICK, STRAUSS, entertainment company executive; b. Boston, June 26, 1957; s. Allan Zelnick and Elsa Lee Strauss; m. Wendy Belzberg, 1990; children: Cooper, Lucas, Leigh. BA summa cum laude, Wesleyan U., Middletown, Ct., 1979; MBA, Harvard U., 1983, JD cum laude, 1983. Bar: N.Y. 1984. Dir. internat. TV Columbia Pictures Internat. Corp., NYC, 1983-85, v.p. internat. TV, 1985-86; sr. v.p. corp. devel. Vestron Inc., Stamford, Conn., 1986-87, exec. v.p., 1987, pres., chief oper. officer, 1988-89, Twentieth Century Fox, LA, 1989-93; pres., CEO Crystal Dynamics, Palo Alto, Calif., 1993-95, BMG Entertainment N.Am., NYC, 1994—98, BMG Entertainment, NYC, 1998—2001; founder, ptnr. ZelnickMedia, 2001—. Non-exec. dir. Reed Elsevier PLC, 2005—, Reed Elsevier NV, 2005—, Reed Elsevier Group PLC, 2005—; chmn. Columbia Music Entertainment of Japan, OTX and ITN Networks, Take-Two Interactive Software, 2007—; bd. dir. Carver Bancorp, Inc., Blockbuster Inc., UGO Networks, Naylor Inc.; former exec. chmn. Direct Holdings (sold to Reader's Digest in 2007). Trustee Wesleyan U., 1992—; mem. contemporary arts coun. Mus. Modern Art, 1989, Young Pres. Orgn.; chmn. Covenant House Calif., 1992-95; bd. dirs. Covenant House, N.Y.C., 1995-2000. Mem. N.Y. State Bar Assn.., Nat. Acad. Recording Arts and Sciences (assoc. mem.), Harvard Club, Recording Industry Assn. Am. (bd. dir.), Motion Picture Assn. Am. (bd. dir.), Phi Beta Kappa. Avocations: squash, sailing, skiing. Office: ZelnickMedia 650 5th Ave New York NY 10019 Office Phone: 212-223-1383. Office Fax: 212-223-1384. *

ZELON, LAURIE DEE, judge; b. Durham, NC, Nov. 15, 1952; d. Irving and Doris Miriam (Baker) Z.; m. David L. George, Dec. 30, 1979; children: Jeremy, Daniel. BA in English with distinction, Cornell U., 1974; JD, Harvard U., 1977. Bar: Calif. 1977, US Ct. Appeals (9th cir.) 1978, US Supreme Ct. 1989. Assoc. Beardsley, Hufstedler & Kemble, LA, 1977-81, Hufstedler, Miller, Carlson & Beardsley, LA, 1981-82, ptnr., 1983-88, Hufstedler, Miller, Kaus & Beardsley, LA, 1988-90, Hufstedler, Kaus & Ettinger, LA, 1990-91, Morrison & Foerster, LA, 1991-2000; judge LA Superior Ct., 2000—03; assoc. justice Calif. Ct. Appeal, LA, 2003—. Contbg. author: West's California Litigation Forms: Civil Procedure Before Trial, 1996; editor-in-chief Harvard Civil Rights and Civil Liberties Law Rev., 1976-77 Bd. dirs. NY Civil Liberties Union, 1973-74. Mem. ABA (chmn. young lawyers divsn. pro bono project 1981-83, delivery and pro bono projects com. 1983-85, subgrant competition-subgrant monitoring project 1985-86, chair standing com. on lawyers pub. svc. responsibility 1987-90, chair law firm pro bono project 1989-91, standing com. legal aid and indigent defendants 1991-97, chmn. 1993-97, mem. ho. dels. 1993—, state del. 1998-2006, commn. on ethics 2000 1997-2002, bd. govs. 2006—), Calif. Bar Assn. (bd. dirs. appellate project 1995-2000, chair commn. on access to justice 1997-99), LA County Bar Assn. (trustee 1989-91, v.p. 1992-93, sr. v.p. 1993-94, pres.-elect 1994-95, pres. 1995-96, fed. cts. and practices com. 1984-93, vice chmn. 1987-88, chmn. 1988-89, chmn. judiciary com. 1991-92, chmn. real estate litigation subsect. 1991-92), Women Lawyers Assn. LA, Calif. Women Lawyers Assn. Democrat. Office: Calif Ct of Appeal 2d Appellate Dist 300 S Spring St Los Angeles CA 90013 Home Phone: 213-999-5478. Business E-Mail: laurie.zelon@jud.ca.gov.

ZEMANIAN, ARMEN HUMPARTSOUM, electrical engineer, mathematician; b. Bridgewater, Mass., Apr. 16, 1925; s. Parsegh and Filor (Paparian) Z.; m. Edna Odell Williamson Zemanian, July 12, 1958; children: Peter, Thomas, Lewis, Susan. BEE, CCNY, 1947; ScD in Engring., NYU, 1953; prof. (hon.), Dubna U., Russia, 1996. Registered profl. engr., N.Y. Tutor CCNY, 1947-48; engr. The Maintenance Co., NYC, 1948-52; from asst. to assoc. prof. NYU, 1952-62; prof. SUNY, Stony Brook, 1962-83, leading prof., 1983-98, distinguished prof., 1998—. Author: Distribution Theory and Transform Analysis, 1965, Generalized Integral Transformations, 1968, Realizability Theory for Continuous Linear Systems, 1972, Infinite Electrical Networks, 1991, Transfiniteness for Graphs, Electrical Networks and Random Walks, 1996; Pristine Transfinite Graphs and Permissive Electrical Networks, 2001, Graphs and Networks: Transfinite and NonStandard, 2004; co-author: Electronics, 1961; co-founder, editor-in-chief emeritus Circuits, Systems and Signal Processing, 1982—. Sr. Faculty fellow NSF, 1975-76; recipient Sci. award Armenian Students Assns. Am., 1982. Fellow IEEE, IEEE Circuits and Systems Soc. (Golden Jubilee medal 2000), Am. Math. Soc., Russian Acad. Natural Scis. (fgn.; Kapitsa Gold medal 1996), Armenian Acad. Scis. (fgn.), Armenian Acad. Engrs. (fgn.), Sigma Xi, Tau Beta Pi, Eta Kappa Nu. Democrat. Presbyterian. Office: SUNY Electrical Engring Dept Stony Brook NY 11794-0001 Personal E-mail: aezem@optonline.net. Business E-Mail: zeman@ee.sunysb.edu.

ZEMECKIS, ROBERT L., film director; b. Chgo., May 14, 1952; m. Mary Ellen Trainor July 26, 1980 (div. 2000), 1 child, Alexander; m. Leslie Harter, Dec. 4, 2001. Student, U. So. Calif. Cinema Sch. Co-owner ImageMovers prodn. co., DarkCastle Entertainment. Dir. (films) I Wanna Hold Your Hand (also writer), 1978, Used Cars, 1980, Romancing the Stone, 1984, Back to the Future (also writer), 1985, Who Framed Roger Rabbit?, 1988, Back to the Future Part II (also writer), 1989, Back to the Future Part III (also writer), 1990, Death Becomes Her (also prodr.), 1992, Forrest Gump, 1994 (Best Dir. Acad. award), Contact, 1996 (TV series episode) Amazing Stories; co-screenwriter 1941, 1979, Trespass (also exec. prodr.), 1992; prodr. (films) Contact, 1997, (TV series) Johnny Bago, 1993, The House on Haunted Hill, 1999, Thirteen Ghosts, 2001, Ritual, 2001, Ghost Ship, 2002, Gothika, 2003, House of Wax, 2005, The Prize Winner of Defiance, Ohio, 2005, The Reaping, 2007; exec. prodr. (films) The Public Eye, 1992, Tales from the Crypt Presents: Demon Knight, 1995, The Frighteners, 1996, Tales from the Crypt Presents: Bordello of Blood, 1996 (also writer), The 20th Century: The Pursuit of Happiness, 1999 (TV), Matchstick Men, 2003, Last Holiday, 2006, Monster House, 2006, (TV series) Tales from the Crypt, 1989, W.E.I.R.D. World, 1995, Perversions of Science, 1997; writer (films) 1941, 1979, Used Cars, 1980; TV guest appearances include Parker Lewis Can't Lose, 1990; prodr., dir. What Lies Beneath, 2000, Cast Away, 2000, The Polar Express, 2004. Mem. bd. councilors U. So. Calif. Sch. Cinema-TV. Mem. Dirs. Guild Am. Office: care Gelfand Rennert & Feldman 1880 Century Park E Ste 900 Los Angeles CA 90067-1609 also: Creative Artists Agy c/o Karen Sage 9830 Wilshire Blvd Beverly Hills CA 90212-1804 also: South Side Amusement Bugalow 127 100 Universal City Plz Universal City CA 91608-1002 *

ZEMM, SANDRA PHYLLIS, lawyer; b. Chgo., Aug. 18, 1947; d. Walter Stanley and Bernice Phyllis (Churas) Z. BS, U. Ill., 1969; JD, Fla. State U., Tallahassee, 1974. Bar: Fla. 74, Ill. 75. With fin. dept. Sinclair Oil, Chgo., 1969-70; indsl. rels. advisor Conco Inc., Mendota, Ill., 1970-72; assoc. Seyfarth, Shaw, Fairweather & Geraldson, Chgo., 1975-82, ptnr., 1982—. Mem. Art Inst. Alliance, Chgo., 1993—97, 2006—; bd. dirs. Chgo. Residential Inc., 1995—97, pres., 1995—97. Mem. Ill. State Bar Assn.,

Fla. State Bar Assn., Univ. Club Chgo. (bd. dirs. 1991-94); Nat. Coll. of Labor and Employment Lawyers. Office: Seyfarth Shaw LLP 831 S Dearborn St Ste 2400 Chicago IL 60603-5577

ZEN, E-AN, research geologist, educator; b. Peking, China, May 31, 1928; came to U.S., 1946, naturalized, 1963; s. Hung-chun and Heng-chi'h (Chen) Z. AB, Cornell U., 1951; MA, Harvard U., 1952, PhD, 1955. Rsch. fellow Woods Hole Oceanographic Inst., 1955-56, rsch. assoc., 1956-58; asst. prof. U. N.C., 1958-59; geologist U.S. Geol. Survey, 1959-80, rsch. geologist, 1981-89, scientist emeritus, 1990—; sr. scientist Va. Mus. Natural History. Adj. prof. geology U. Md., 1990—; vis. assoc. prof. Calif. Inst. Tech., 1962; Crosby vis. prof. MIT, 1973; Harry H. Hess sr. vis. fellow Princeton U., 1981; counselor 28th Internat. Geol. Congress. 1986-89. Contbr. articles to profl. jours. Recipient Maj. John Coke medal Geol. Soc. London, 1992, Outstanding Contbn. to Pub. Understanding of Geology award Am. Geol. Inst., 1994, Thomas Jefferson medal Va. Mus. Natural History Found., 1996. Fellow: AAAS, Mineral Soc. Am. (coun. 1975—77, pres. 1975—76, Roebling medal 1991), Geol. Soc. Am. (councillor 1985—88, v.p. 1991, ores. 1992, Day medal 1986), Am. Acad. Arts and Scis.; mem.: NAS, Geol. Soc. Washington (pres. 1973), Va. Mus. Natural History (sr. scientist). Office: U Md Dept Geology College Park MD 20742-0001

ZENDLE, HOWARD MARK, systems engineer, researcher; b. Binghamton, NY, June 8, 1949; s. Abraham and Evelyn (Hershowitz) Z. BA in Physics summa cum laude, SUNY, Binghamton, 1972, MA in Physics, 1976; MSEE, Syracuse U., 1987. With IBM, Owego, NY, 1974—94, staff programmer, 1978-83, mgr. microprocessor application software, 1979-81, mgr. tactical avionics software, 1981-82, adv. programmer, 1983-86, sr. programmer, 1986-94, Loral, Owego, NY, 1994-96, Lockheed Martin, Owego, NY, 1996—2005, sys. engr. sr. staff, 2005—. Sec. Men's Club Beth David Synagogue, Binghamton, 1984-85, v.p., 1986-88; bd. dirs. Jewish Cmty. Ctr., Binghamton, 1983-86. Recipient SPOT award, Lockheed Martin, 2006, 2007. Mem. IEEE, AIAA, Ctrl. Electric Railfan's Assn., Masons, Phi Beta Kappa, Sigma Pi Sigma. Republican. Avocations: railfanning, history. Home: 5 Leigh St Johnson City NY 13790-1608 Office: Lockheed Martin 1801 State Route 17C Owego NY 13827-3998 Office Phone: 607-751-2625. Personal E-mail: hzendle@stny.rr.com.

ZENG, DONGSONG, computer scientist; PhD, Va. Tech, 2005. Engr. Glocom Inc., Germantown, Md., 2000—04; scientist Honeywell Advanced Tech. Ctr., Columbia, Md., 2004—. Mem.: IEEE. Office: Honeywell 7000 Columbia Gateway Dr Columbia MD 21046 Home Phone: 301-972-4023. Business E-Mail: dongsong.zeng@honeywell.com.

ZENG, EDDY YONGPING, chemist; b. Guangzhou, China, Jan. 11, 1960; came to U.S., 1986; s. Li and Qiuzhen (Zhou) Zeng. BS, U. Sci. and Tech. of China, Heifei, 1982; MS, Zhongshan U., Guangzhou, China, 1985; MA, U. So. Calif., LA, 1989, PhD, 1991. Rsch./tchg. asst. dept. chemistry U. So. Calif., LA, 1986-90; chemist Enviropro, Inc., Chatsworth, Calif., 1990-92; prin. scientist So. Calif. Coastal Water Rsch. Project, Westminster, 1992—. Lectr. dept. chemistry Zhongshen U., 1985-86; adj. prof. State Key Lab. of Organic Geochemistry, Guangzhou, 1998—. Contbr. articles to profl. jours. Mem. Am. Chem. Soc., So. Calif. Environ. Chemist Soc. (pres. 1997-98), Soc. of Environ. Texicology and Chemistry (bd. dirs. So. Calif. chpt. 1999—). Office: So Calif Coastal Water Rsch Project 7171 Fenwick Ln Westminster CA 92683-5218 E-mail: ypzeng@yahoo.com.

ZENG, HONG, audio system architect, researcher; b. Changchun, Jilin, China, Feb. 20, 1958; arrived in France, 1990; s. Peiwei Zeng and Shige Chen; m. Yuzhi Guo, Jan. 14, 1983 (div. Nov. 2000); 1 child, Yu; m. Jie Li, Aug. 8, 2001; 2 children: Aisling, Elaine. B in Elec. Engring., Jilin U; M in Elec. Engring., U. Pierre & Marie Curie, Paris, 1991, D in Physics, 1996. Asst. engr. Hangzhou (China) Applied Acoustics Rsch. Inst., 1982-85, rsch. engr., dir. magnetic signal processing sect., 1985-90; rsch. engr. French Nat. Sci. Rsch. Ctr., Paris, 1990-95; sys. engr. O1dB Co., Lyon, France, 1995-98; sr. software engr., project team leader ATI Technologies, Inc., Toronto, 1998-2001; audio sys. arch. ViXS Sys. Inc., Toronto, 2001—. Contbr. articles to profl. jours.; inventor in field. Recipient Sci. and Tech. award China Shipbuilding Industry Corp., Beijing, 1989. Mem. IEEE. Home: 815 Grandview Way Toronto ON Canada M2N 6V5 Office: VIXS Sys Pkwy Pl 245 Consumers Rd M2J 1R3 Toronto ON Canada Personal E-mail: hongzeng@hotmail.com.

ZENG, HONGLIU HENRY, geophysicist, geologist; b. Ningdu, Jiangxi, China, Jan. 5, 1957; arrived in U.S., 1989; s. Zhikang Zeng and Lianrong Chen; m. Yan Phoebe Yang, Feb. 4, 1986; children: Luying, Leo. BA, U. Petroleum, Dongying, 1982, MA, 1985; PhD, U. Tex., 1994. Advanced geoscientist Texaco Inc., New Orleans, 1994—96; rsch. scientist Bur. Econ. Geology, Jackson Sch. Geosci., U. Tex., Austin, 1997—. Lectr. U. Petroleum, Beijing, 1995—99. Contbr. articles to profl. jours. Mem.: Soc. Exploration Geophysicists, Am. Assn. Petroleum Geologists (Wallace E. Pratt Meml. award 2005). Achievements include invention of stratal slicing, a 3-D seismic data interpretation technique; Seismic frequency control on seismic stratigraphy, a seimic data interpretation therory; research in seismic sedimentology, seismic stratigraphy, reservoir characterization, and special seismic processing, as applied to petroleum prospecting. Office: Bur Econ Geology Bldg 130 10100 Burnet Rd Austin TX 78758-4445 Office Phone: 512-475-6382. Business E-Mail: hongliu.zeng@beg.utexas.edu.

ZENG, MING, molecular biologist, researcher; b. Dajishan, China, Sept. 8, 1968; arrived in US, 1993, naturalized; s. Guangjun Zeng and Jinyu Liao; m. Elena O. Martsen; children: Katherine, Andrew. BS, Beijing Normal U., 1990; grad., Chinese Acad. Med. Sci, Peking Uion Med. Coll., Beijing, 1990. Rschr. Duke U. Med. Ctr./Howard Hughes Med. Inst., NC, 1997—2001; scientist Schering Plough Rsch. Inst., Kenilworth, NJ, 2001—05, Attagene Inc., NC, 2005—. Vis. scientist Tampa Bay Rsch. Inst., Fla., 1993—96; rschr. Salem Teikyo U., 1996—97. Contbr. articles to profl. jours. First rank scholar, Beijing Normal U./Beijing Tchg. U., 1998. Achievements include research in drug target identification; nitric oxide biology; pathway profiling and new biotechnology development. Home: 304 New Parkside Dr Chapel Hill NC 27516-1162 Office: Attagene Inc Ste 270 PO Box 12054 Research Triangle Park NC 27709 Office Phone: 919-313-0167. Personal E-mail: mzen2000@hotmail.com.

ZENGER, JOHN HANCOCK, training company executive; b. Salt Lake City, Nov. 13, 1931; s. John H. and L. (Hancock) Z.; m. Dixie Robison, June 1, 1955 (div. 1978); children: Mark R., Robin, Todd R., Blake R., Mitchell R., Drew R.; m. Holly Olsen, June 29, 1979; stepchildren: Roger, Kirk, Lori, Michael. BS, Brigham Young U., 1955; MBA, UCLA, 1957; DBA, U. So. Calif., 1963; Doctorate (hon.), Utah Valley State Coll., 2006. Asst. prof. Grad Sch. Bus. U. So. Calif., LA, 1966—67; exec. v.p. Blanfield-Smith and Co., Pasadena, Calif., 1965—67; v.p. human resources Syntex Corp., Palo Alto, Calif., 1967—77; pres. Zenger-Miller Inc., Cupertino, Calif., 1977—92; group v.p. Times Mirror Co., San Jose, 1992—97; pres., CEO Provant, Inc.; CEO Zenger Folkman Corp., 2003—. Chmn. Palo Alto Human Rels. Coun., 1961-66; trustee Utah Valley State Coll., chmn., 2003-04; pres. Midway Boosters, Inc. Ford Found. fellow, 1962-63; recipient Disting. Svc. award Brigham Young U., 1983; named to Human Resources Devel. Hall of Fame, 1994. Mem. Brigham Young U. Alumni Assn. (pres. 1981). Independent. Mem. Lds Ch. Avocation: magic. Home: 275 Luzern Rd Midway UT 84049-1268 Office Phone: 801-705-9494. E-mail: jzenger@zfco.com.

ZENKOVSKY, BETTY JEAN, modern languages educator; b. Mankato, Minn., Mar. 6, 1927; d. William and Sarah (Cloyd) Bubbers; m. Serge A. Zenkovsky, May 10, 1952. AB in Russian, U. Mich., Ann Arbor, 1950; AM in Slavic Studies, Ind. U., Bloomington, 1954; postgrad., Radcliffe U., Cambridge, Mass., 1956—58. Instr. modern langs. Stetson U., DeLand, Fla., 1958—60, asst. prof., 1962—65; instr. fgn. langs. U. Colo., Boulder, 1960—62; vis. lectr. Russian, Vanderbilt U., Nashville, 1967—68; rsch. assoc., translator NEH, DeLand, 1978—82. Co-translator: The Nikonian Chronicle, (5 vols.), 1984, 86, 88, 89. Grace Hill fellow, Radcliffe Grad. Sch., Cambridge, Mass., 1957—58. Mem. AAUW (pres. DeLand chpt. 1982-84, sec. Daytona Beach chpt. 1984-86), DAR (chpt. James Ormond br., vice regent, 1988-89), Am. Assn. Advancement Slavic Studies, Am. Assn. Tchrs. Slavic and Ea. European Langs., UN Assn., So. Conf. Slavic Studies, Tiger Bay Club of Volusia County, St. Barbara's Philoptochos. Democrat. Greek Orthodox. Home: 1224 S Peninsula Dr Apt 507 Daytona Beach FL 32118-4861 Home Fax: 386-253-3540. Personal E-mail: bjzenk@aol.com.

ZENN, MICHAEL ROBERT, plastic and reconstructive surgeon; b. NYC, Feb. 28, 1962; s. Renee Schwam; m. Susan Speer; children: Andrew, Erica. BA, U. Pa., 1984; MD, Cornell U., 1988. Diplomate Am. Bd. Gen. Surgery, Am. Bd. Plastic Surgery. Resident in gen. surgery N.Y. Hosp., NYC, 1988-93; resident in plastic surgery Mass. Gen. Hosp., Boston, 1993-95; fellow in microsurgery Meml. Sloan-Kettering Cancer Ctr., NYC, 1995; asst. prof. plastic surgery U. N.C., Chapel Hill, 1996-2000, Duke U. Med. Ctr., Durham, NC, 2000—05, assoc. prof. plastic surgery, 2005—. Contbr. articles to profl. jours. Named a Best Doctor for Women-Southeast Region, Ladies Home Jour., 2002, Best Doctor, Redbook mag., 2001; recipient NC Med. Soc. Tobacco Control award, 1999; named Best Cosmetic Surgeon in the Triangle, News and Observer, 1997. Fellow ACS (assoc.); mem. AMA, Am. Soc. Plastic Surgeons, Am. Soc. Reconstructive Microsurgery, World Soc. Reconstrictive Microsurgery, Plastic Surgery Rsch. Coun., NC Med. Soc., NC Soc. Plastic and Reconstructive Surgeons (v.p., 2001-02, pres., 2002-03), Nathan A. Womack Surg. Soc., Alpha Omega Alpha Avocations: painting, golf. Office: Plastic Surgery 3358 Duke Univ Med Ctr Durham NC 27710 E-mail: michael.zenn@duke.edu. *

ZENNER, SHELDON TOBY, lawyer; b. Chgo., Jan. 11, 1953; s. Max and Clara (Goldner) Z.; m. Ellen June Morgan, Sept. 2, 1984; children: Elie, Nathaniel. BA, Northwestern U., 1974, JD, 1978. Bar: U.S. Dist. Ct. (no. dist.) Ill. 1978. Assoc. Shadur, Krupp & Miller, Chgo., 1978-80; law clk. to judge U.S. Dist. Ct. (no. dist.) Ill., Chgo., 1980-81; asst. U.S. atty., dep. chief spl. prosecutions div. No. Dist. of Ill., Chgo., 1981-89; ptnr. Katten Muchin Rosenman LLP, Chgo., 1989—. Adj. faculty Medill Sch. Journalism, Northwestern U., 1982-89, Sch. of Law, 1986—; mem. practitioners adv. com. U.S. Sentencing Commn.; mem. editl. adv. bd. Northwestern U. Magazine. Mem. Phi Beta Kappa. Office: Katten Muchin Rosenman LLP 525 W Monroe St Chicago IL 60661-3693 Office Phone: 312-902-5476. Business E-Mail: sheldon.zenner@kattenlaw.com.

ZENTAY, JOHN H., lawyer; AB cum laude, Harvard U., 1953, LLB, 1958. Bar: Mo. 1958, DC 1966, US Supreme Ct. 1962. Legis. asst. to U.S. Senator Stuart Symington, Mo., 1958—62; mem. legis. staff AID, U.S. Dept. of State, 1963—66; cons. Bureau of the Budget, Washington, 1967—68; ptnr. Verner Liipfert Bernhard McPherson & Hand, Washington; ptnr., chmn. Fed. Affairs & Legis. practice group DLA Piper US LLP, Washington, 2002—. Mem. adv. com. on revision of rules of practice & procedure FERC, Washington, 1979—81. Bd. dir. Found. for Nat. Archives; trustee George C. Marshall Found.; chmn. fin. com. Nat. Protestant Episcopal Cathedral; bd. mem. Beauvoir Sch.; mem. long range planning com. St. Albans Sch.; mem. bd. mgr. Historical Soc. of Washington; bd. mem. Children's Hosp. Nat. Med. Ctr. Served US Army, 1953—55. Office: DLA Piper US LLP 1200 19th St NW Washington DC 20036-2412 Office Phone: 202-861-6449. Office Fax: 202-689-8563. Business E-Mail: john.zentay@dlapiper.com.

ZENTMYER, HUGH J., engineering executive; BS, U. Cin.; MBA, Xavier U., Cin. Various acctg. positions including v.p. fin. Strapping Divsn. Signode Corp. (acquired by Ill. Tool Works), 1968—86; ops. mgmt. position Ill. Tool Works (ITW), Glenview, 1986, exec. v.p. Bd. dirs. Marmon Group. Bd. mem. St. Patrick's HS. Office: Ill Tool Works 3600 W Lake Ave Glenview IL 60026-1215 Office Phone: 847-724-7500. Office Fax: 847-657-4572. *

ZEOLLA, KIM ANNE, minister; b. Pitts., Jan. 21, 1961; d. Edward William Logue and Melody Joy Long; m. Allen Lee Zeolla, Sept. 8, 1984; children: April Nicole, Daniel Nicholas, Jonathan Michael. Student, Dayspring Bible Sch., 1982—84; grad., Greater Works Outreach Bible Sch., Monroeville, Pa., 2007. Ordained Greater Works Outreach Bible Sch., 2007. Min. women's groups, retreats, outreach, families, 1998—. Founder, min. Expressions of Love, Pitts., 1998—; v.p. min. develop., exec. bd. Murrysville Aglow Lighthouse, Murrysville, Pa., 2003—05; coord. Cornerstone Min., Drug Awareness Seminar, Export, Pa., 2004; team leader Murrysville Aglow Cmty. Outreach, 2004; prayer chairperson Pure Freedom (abstinence retreat), 2004; ministry team chair Healing and Prophetic Conf., Latter Glory Ministries, Pa., 2005—06; prayer chairperson Capital Stewardship Campaign, Cornerstone Ministries Pa., 2005—07, prayer co-chair, 2005—07; mem. pastors gathering Harmony Zelionople United Meth. Ch., 2005; prophetic evangelistic leader Expressions of Love Outreach, Pitts., 2005; min. Peek 'N Peak Resort Aglow Conf., NYC, 2006; asst. to worship and drama leader Peek'N Peak Resort and Conf. Ctr., Findley Lake, NY, 2006; prophetic proclamations leader Harp n Bowi, St. Martins Episcopal Ch., Monroeville, Pa.; AM intercession participant 25th Holy Spirit Seminar, Greater Works Outreach, Monroeville, Pa., 2006; MC, ministry team chair LAtter Glory Ministries, Monroeville, Pa., 2007; prophetic intercessor Northeast Glory Conf. Aglow Internat., 2007; spkr. in field. Judge fine arts Assemblies of God, Pa. and Del., 2001—06; deaf interpreter Our Lady of Joy C.C.D. Class, Plum Boro, Pa., 2002—04; vol. ARC, Pitts., 2004; team leader Murrysville Aglow Cmty. Outreach, 2004; vol. ARC Disaster Relief, 2004; bd. dir. Latter Glory Ministries, India and USA, 2005—; choreographer March for Jesus, Pitts., 1997—98; leadership United for Christ Marriage Ministry, Pitts., 1988—94, Dayspring Christian Ctr., Pitts., 1988—99; jr./sr. high new life bible study tchr. Pitts., 1995—2003; fin. sec. Murrysville Aglow Lighthouse, 2002—03; group leader VIP visually inspired people Cornerstone Ministries, Export, Pa., 2004, leader beginners' sign class Pa., 2004, elder lead prayer and ministry team, 2005—06, mem. women's connection ministry team, 2006—07; dance ministry with Daus. of Judah, New Life Assembly Women's Conf., Pitts., 2005; evangelistic outreach Washington, Pa., 2005; active Expressions of Love Outreach Three Rivers Regatta, Pitts., 2006; mem. ministry team Pitts. healing crusade 1st Presbyn. Ch. Pitts., 2006—; spkr. Murrysville Bible Study, Pa., Monroeville Aglow Lighthouse, Pa.; intercessor Extreme Prophetic Media Dept., 2007—; ministry team mem. sexual wholeness seminar Bakerstown United Meth. Ch., Gibsonia, Pa., 2007; intercessor XP Media, Extreme Prophetic Media Dept., Ariz., 2007—; prophetic proclamation leader Harpnbowl@Cornerstone TeleVision, Wall, Pa., 2007. Mem. Full Gospel Ch. Home: 128 Alcan Dr Pittsburgh PA 15239 Personal E-mail: kimmwaone@yahoo.com.

ZEPEDA, SUSAN GHOZEIL, foundation administrator; b. NYC, Aug. 8, 1946; d. Harry S. and Anne (Golden) Kantor; m. Isaac Ghozeil, Jan. 29, 1967 (div. Oct. 1979); children: Daniel Jacob Ghozeil, Adam Leo Ghozeil; m. Fernando Zepeda, Jan. 2, 1983 (div. Feb. 1998); children: Paloma Andrea, Sofia Elisa. BA, Brown U., 1967; MA, U. Ariz., 1971, postgrad., 1971-75; PhD, Internat. Coll., 1985. Rsch. assoc. div. bus. and econ. rsch. U. Ariz., Tucson, 1971-73, rsch. assoc. Coll. Medicine, 1975-76; assoc. dir. Pima Alcoholism Consortium, Tucson, 1976-79, exec. dir., 1979-80; dep. dir. pub. health Orange County Health Care Agy., Santa Ana, Calif., 1980-89, dir. policy, planning, 1989-90; dir. pub. fin. Orange County, 1990-92; dir. San Luis Obispo County Health Agy., 1993-99; CEO Healthcare Found. Orange County, Santa Ana, Calif., 1999—2005; exec. dir. Found. for Healthy Ky., 2005—. Cons. Tucson Sch. Dist., 1973—75, U.S. Dept. Labor, Washington, 1976—79, Indian Health Svc., Rockville, Md., 1984—85; ptnr. Zepeda Assocs., Fullerton, Calif., 1987—93; presenter in field. Mem. Fullerton Planning Commn., 1984—91, chmn., 1990—91; mem. Calif. Task Force Comparable Worth, 1984—85, Calif. Dist. Appeal Bd. No. 510, LA, 1986—. Recipient Women of Achievement award, Orange County Bd. Suprs., 1988, Disting. Achievement awards, Nat. Assn. Counties, 1985—87, 1989. Mem.: APHA, Grantmakers in Health (bd. dirs. 2004—), So. Calif. Grantmakers (bd. dirs. 2002—05), County Alcohol Program Adminstrs. Assn. Calif. (v.p. 1983, pres. 1984—85), Ctrl. Coast Hosp. Coun. (chair 1996), Nat. Assn. County and City Health Ofcls. (bd. dirs.), County Health Execs. Assn. (v.p. 1998—99), Health Funders Partnership Orange County (chair 2000—02), Rotary Club (pres. 2001—02). Avocation: fiber arts. Office: Found for a Healthy Ky 9300 Shelbyville Rd Ste 1305 Louisville KY 40222 Home: 10203 Springhurst Gardens Cir Louisville KY 40241 Home Phone: 502-326-5966; Office Phone: 502-326-2583. Business E-Mail: szepeda@healthyky.org.

ZEPF, THOMAS HERMAN, retired physics professor; b. Cin., Feb. 13, 1935; s. Paul A. and Agnes J. (Schulz) Z. BS summa cum laude, Xavier U., 1957; MS, St. Louis U., 1960, PhD, 1963. Asst. prof. physics Creighton U., Omaha, 1962-67, assoc. prof., 1967-75, prof., 1975—2002, prof. emeritus, 2002—, acting chmn. dept. physics, 1963-66, chmn., 1966-73, 81-93, coord. allied health programs, 1975-76, coord. pre-health scis. advising, 1976-81. Cons. physicist VA Hosp., Omaha, 1966-71; vis. prof. physics St. Louis U., 1973-74; program evaluator Am. Coun. on Edn., 1988-2002. Contbr. articles and abstracts to Surface Sci., Bull. Am. Phys. Soc., Proceedings Nebr. Acad. Sci., The Physics Tchr. Jour., others. Recipient Cert. Recognition award, Phi Beta Kappa U. Cin. chpt., 1953. Mem. Am. Phys. Soc., Am. Assn. Physics Tchrs. (pres. Nebr. sect. 1978), Nebr. Acad. Sci. (life, chmn. physics sect. 1985-05), Internat. Brotherhood Magicians, Soc. Am. Magicians (pres. assembly #7, 1964-65), KC, Sigma Xi (Achievement award for rsch. St. Louis chpt. 1963, pres. Omaha chpt. 1993-94), Sigma Pi Sigma. Roman Catholic. Office: Creighton U Dept Physics Omaha NE 68178-0001 Home Phone: 402-558-3125. Business E-Mail: thzepf@creighton.edu. *The real magic we all have at our disposal is the ability to comprehend our world, to understand how things behave. This understanding, which we gain through science, enables us to predict outcomes and exert a measure of control over nature. It's a sacred trust. It makes the scientist a kind of modern day magician.*

ZEPPOS, NICHOLAS S., academic administrator; BA, U. Wis., 1976, JD, 1979. Atty., Washington; joined faculty Vanderbilt U., Nashville, 1987, assoc. dean rsch. Law Sch., assoc. provost, 1999, vice chancellor for instnl. planning and advancement, 2000, provost, vice chancellor for acad. affairs, prof. law, 2001—, interim chancellor, 2007—. Contbr. articles to publs. Office: Vanderbilt U Interim Chancellor's Office 211 Kirkland Hall Nashville TN 37240 Office Phone: 615-322-2615, 615-322-4219. Office Fax: 615-343-8340. Business E-Mail: nick.zeppos@vanderbilt.edu. E-mail: ichancellor@vanderbilt.edu. *

ZERBE, KATHRYN JANE, psychiatrist; b. Harrisburg, Pa., Oct. 17, 1951; d. Grover Franklin and Ethel (Schreckengaust) Z. BS with BA equivalent cum laude, Duke U., Durham, NC, 1973; MD, Temple U., Phila., 1978. Diplomate Am. Bd. Psychiatry. Resident Karl Menninger Sch. Psychiatry, Topeka, 1982, dean, dir. edn. and rsch., 1992-97; staff psychiatrist Menninger Found., Topeka, 1982-2001; v.p. edn. and rsch. The Menninger Clinic, Topeka, 1993-97, prof., 1997-2001, Jack Aron chair in psychiat. edn., 1997-2001, apptd. tng. and supr. analyst, 1995—; prof. psychiatry, prof. ob-gyn. Oreg. Health Scis. Univ., Portland, 2001—; dir. behavioral medicine dept. Oreg. Health Scis. U., Portland, 2001—06; dir. outpatient clinic Oreg. Health Scis. Univ., Portland, 2003—, vice chair for psychotherapy, 2003—; tng. and supr. analyst Oreg. Psychoanalytic Inst., 2002—. Instr. numerous seminars and courses. Author: The Body Betrayed: Women, Eating Disorders and Treatment, 1993, Women's Mental Health in Primary Care, 1999, Eating Disorders for Ob-Gyns, 2007, numerous articles profl. rsch. papers; editor: Womens Mental Health: Primary Care Clinics, 2001; assoc. editor:, 1996—98; editor: Bull. of Menninger Clinic, 1998;; mem. editl. bd.: Eating Disorders Rev., Eating Disorders: The Jour. of Treatment and Prevention Postgrad. Medicine; editor (sect.): Current Women's Health; contbr. book revs. and articles to profl. jours. Probation officer Juvenile divsn. Dauphin County, Pa., 1973. Recipient Ann. Laughlin Merit award The Nat. Psychiat. Endowment Fund, 1982, Outstanding Paper of Profl. Programs award The Menninger Found. Alumni Assn., 1982, Writing award Topeka Inst. for Psychoanalysis, 1985, 90, Mentorship award, 1997, Women Helping Women award, 1995, Tchr. of Yr. award Psychiatry Residents, 1988, 96, 99, 03, 05, 06; named one of Outstanding Young Women in Am., 1986, 88, Portland's Top Drs., 2007; Seeley fellow, 1979-82; Hilde Bruch lectureship, 1996. Fellow Am. Psychiat. Assn. (Alexandra Symonds award 2005, Edith Sabshin award); mem. AMA, Am. Coll. Psychiatrists, Am. Med. Women's Assn., Oreg. Med. Assn., Oreg. Psychiat. Assn., Sigma Xi, Alpha Omega Alpha. Avocations: writing, reading, art history, travel. Office: Oreg Health and Scis U Adult Psychiatry 3181 SW Sam Jackson Park Rd Portland OR 97239-3098 Office Phone: 503-494-1009. Personal E-mail: kzbone@comcast.net. Business E-Mail: zerbek@ohsu.edu.

ZERELLA, JOSEPH T., retired pediatric surgeon; b. Youngstown, Ohio, Mar. 7, 1941; s. Atilio and Ann (Capuzello) Z.; m. Diana Isabelle Talbot, Aug. 5, 1967; children: Ann, Michael, Mark. BS, Northwestern U., 1962, MD, 1966. Diplomate Am. Bd. Surgery, Am. Bd. Pediatric Surgery. Intern Med. Coll. Wis., Milw., 1966-67, resident in surgery, 1967-68, 70-73; tng. fellow in pediatric surgery Children's Hosp. Med. Ctr., Cin., 1973-75; staff pediatric surgeon Phoenix Children's Hosp., 1975—; pvt. practice medicine, specializing in pediatric surgery Phoenix, 1975—. Mem. staff Good Samaritan Hosp., Phoenix, 1975—, sect. chief pediatric surgery, 1979—; mem. staff St. Joseph's Hosp., Phoenix, 1975—, sect. chief pediatric surgery, 1980—. Contbr. articles to profl. jours. Capt. USAR, 1968—70. Fellow ACS, Am. Acad. Pediatrics, Am. Pediatric Surg. Assn., Pacific Assn. Pediatric Surgeons. Roman Catholic. Mailing: 8426 N 15th Dr Phoenix AZ 85021 E-mail: dzerella@aol.com.

ZEREN, KARL JOSEPH, dentist, educator; children: Sarah, Lindsey, Kurt. BS in Psychology, U. Md., College Park, 1969; DDS, U. Md., Balt., 1975. Diplomate Am. Bd. Periodontology, 1986. Attending in periodontics Johns Hopkins Med. Instn., Balt., 1980—. Asst. clin. prof. U. Md., Sch. Dentistry, Balt., 1987—. Contbr. scientific papers. Lay chaliscist Trinity Episcopal Ch., Towson, Md., 2005—07. Lt. U.S. Navy, 1976—77. Named one of, Top Dentists in the Am., 2005. Mem.: Am. Coll. Dentists, Internat. Coll. Dentists, Md. Soc. Periodontists (pres. 1988—90), Am. Acad. Periodontology. Independent-Republican. Episcopalian. Achievements include research in human allograft block gtafting in dento-alveolar ridge augmentation. Avocations: golf, skiing, travel. Office: Karl J Zeren DDS LLC 9515 Deereco Rd Ste 308 Timonium MD 21093 Home Phone: 410-252-8335; Office Phone: 410-252-0871. Personal E-mail: zeren@comcast.net. E-mail: kjzeren@verizon.net.

ZERGER, KIRSTEN LOUISE, mediator, lawyer; b. Newton, Kans., Oct. 15, 1950; d. Homer Joshua and Karolyn Louise (Kaufman) Z.; m. Edward Peters Dick, Mar. 28, 1969 (div. 1978); 1 child, Daagya Shanti; m. Sanford Norman Nathan, June 14, 1980; children: Jesse Zerger, Jonathan Kaufman, Joshua Zev. BA with highest distinction, Bethel Coll., 1973; JD, U. Calif., Berkeley, 1977. Bar: Calif. 1977, US Dist. Ct. (no. dist.) Calif. 1977, US Ct. Appeals (9th cir.) 1987, US Supreme Ct. 1985. Staff atty. United Farm Workers, AFL-CIO, Salinas, Calif., 1977-79; staff atty. Calif. Tchrs. Assn., Burlingame, 1979-85, chief counsel, 1985-88; pvt. practice, Berkeley, 1988-93; dir. edn. and training, Kans. Inst. Peace and Conflict Resolution, Bethel Coll., North Newton, Kans., 2006—; mediation co-trainer, Bridge Builders, London Mennonite Centre, 2003-05; of counsel Leonard Carder, LLP, Oakland, Calif., 2005-07; instr. Bethel Coll., North Newton, 1997-2002; approved mediator, trainer Kans. Supreme Ct., 1998-; speaker edn., profl. confs. Writer on mediation, facilitation and tng. and public sector labor law issues; co-editor: California Public Sector Labor Law, 1989; contbr. articles to profl. jours. Founding mgr. Cmty. Mediation Ctr., 1999-2000, sr. tng. assoc., 2002-06. Mem. Heartland Mediators Assn., Calif. Bar Assn. (labor and employment law sects., chmn. pub. sector com. 1983-85, membership com. 1982-83, exec. com., 1985-89, treas. 1986-87, vice-chair 1987-88, advisor 1988-89). Office Phone: 316-284-5217. Business E-Mail: kzerger@bethelks.edu.

ZERHOUNI, ELIAS ADAM, federal agency administrator; b. Algeria, Apr. 12, 1951; s. Mohamed and Yamna (Raahmouni) Z.; m. Nadia Azza, Oct. 25, 1975; children: Djillali, Yasmin, Adam. MD, U. Algiers, 1975. Diplomate Am. Bd. Radiology. Asst. dir. body CT Johns Hopkins Hospital, Balt., 1978—81; vice chmn., dir. body imaging De Paul Hospital, Norfolk, Va., 1982—85; co-dir. MRI and body CT, coord. clinical research Johns Hopkins Med. Institutions, Balt., 1985—88, dir. thoracic imaging and MRI, 1988—96; dir. Advanced Med. Imaging Inst., Norfolk, Va., 1991—92; radiologist-in-chief Johns Hopkins Hospital, Balt., 1996—; dir. NIH, Bethesda, Md., 2002—. Resident in diagnostic radiology Johns Hopkins U., Balt., 1975—79, instr., 1978—79, asst. prof. radiology, 1979—81, Ea. Va. Med. Sch., Norfolk, Va., 1981—83, assoc. prof. radiology, 1983—85; cons. Nat. Cancer Inst., NHLBI, 1985—88; assoc. prof. radiology Johns Hopkins U., Balt., 1985—92, prof. radiology, 1992; centennial lectr. Swedish Royal Acad. Radiology, Stockholm, 1994; prof. biomed. engring. Johns Hopkins U., Balt., 1995, chmn. radiology, 1996—, exec. vice dean, vice dean clinical affairs, 1996—99, vice dean research, 1999—2000, exec. vice dean, 2000—02; assoc. editor, mem. of the editorial bd. Journal of Surgical and Radiological Anatomy, 1980—86; assoc. editor Radiology, 1983—90; mem. editorial bd. Topics in Clinical MRI, 1990—96; assoc. editor, mem. of the editorial bd. Journal of Thoracic Imaging, 1990—97. Patentee in field. Recipient Lauterbur award for MRI research, 1989, 93, Hounsfield award for CT Imaging, 1991. Mem.: Inst. of Med., NAS, Soc. for Chmn. of Academic Radiology Dept., Soc. for Cardiovascular Magnetic Resonance, N. Am. Soc. for Cardiac Imaging, Balt. City Med. Soc., Am. Assn. for the Advancement of Sci., Am. Coll. of Radiology, Am. Heart Assn., Internat. Soc. for Magnetic Resonance in Med. (bd. of trustees 1995—98), Fleischner Soc. (Fleischner Soc. medal 1997), Assn. of U. Radiologists, Soc.of Computed Body Tomography, Soc. of Thoracic Radiology (founding member), Radiological Soc. of N.Am., Am. Roentgen Ray Soc. Avocations: swimming, windsurfing, music. Office: NIH 9000 Rockville Pike Bethesda MD 20892 Office Phone: 301-496-2433. Office Fax: 301-402-2700. E-mail: ez26y@nih.gov.

ZERIN, STEVEN DAVID, lawyer; b. NYC, Oct. 1, 1953; s. Stanley Robert and Cecilie Paula (Goldberg) Z.; children: Alexander James, J. Oliver. BS, Syracuse U., 1974; JD, St. Johns U., 1977. Bar: N.Y. 1978, U.S. Dist. Ct. (so. dist.) N.Y. 1985, U.S. Supreme Ct. 1986. Of coun. Sperry, Weinberg, Wels, Waldman & Rubenstein, NYC, 1982-85; ptnr. Wels & Zerin, NYC, 1985—. Trustee, mem. bd. govs. Daytop Village. Mem. ABA (exec. mem. and lectr. family law sect.), N.Y. State Bar Assn. (exec. com. family law sect.), Assn. of Bar of City of N.Y. Democrat. Home: 12 E 88th St New York NY 10128-0535 Office: Wels & Zerin 600 Madison Ave Fl 22 New York NY 10022-1615 Office Phone: 212-838-8608. Business E-Mail: szerin@welsandzerin.com.

ZERMAN, ALLAN H., lawyer; b. St. Louis, Feb. 3, 1937; s. Jay and Rose (Fadem) Z.; m. Marilyn Sandra Schear, Aug. 24, 1958 (div. 1980); children: Lisa, Laura, Leslie; m. Marilyn Rose House, May 28, 1982. AB, Washington U., St. Louis, 1958, JD, 1960. Bar: Mo. 1960, U.S. Ct. Appeals (8th cir.) 1961, U.S. Supreme Ct. 1972; diplomate Am. Coll. Family Trial Lawyers. Pvt. practice, Clayton, Mo., 1961—. Capt. USAR, 1960-67. Fellow Am. Acad. Matrimonial Lawyers; diplomate Am. Coll. Family & Trial Lawyers; mem. Mo. Bar Assn. (contbg. editor jour. 1988—), St. Louis Met. Bar Assn., St. Louis County Bar Assn. Republican. Jewish. Office: 100 S Brentwood Blvd Ste 325 Saint Louis MO 63105-1691 E-mail: ahz3@aol.com.

ZERMAN, MELVYN BERNARD, retired publishing executive, writer; b. NYC, July 10, 1930; s. Abraham and Ida (Belsky) Zirman; m. Miriam Baron, Jan. 2, 1985 (dec.); children: Andrew, Jared, Lenore. BA, U. Mich., 1952; MA, Columbia U., 1953. With Oxford Book Co., NYC, 1953-55; asst. editor Abelard-Schuman, Pubs., NYC, 1955-57; office mgr., salesman Harper & Row, NYC, 1957-61, sales rep., 1961-69, sales mgr., 1969-79, Random House, Inc., NYC, 1979-83, sales cons., 1983-87; pres., pub. Limelight Edits., NYC, 1983—2004. Mem. exec. com. N.Y. Is Book Country, N.Y.C., 1985-2004. Author: Call the Final Witness, 1977, Beyond a Reasonable Doubt, 1981 (Freedoms Found. medal 1981), Taking on the Press, 1986. Mem.: Phi Beta Kappa. Democrat. Avocations: book collecting, travel.

ZERUBAVEL, EVIATAR, sociologist, educator; BA in Sociology, Anthropology and Polit. Sci., Tel-Aviv U., 1971; MA in Sociology, U. Pa., 1973, PhD, 1976. Asst. prof. psychiatry and sociology U. Pitts., 1976—80; assoc. prof. sociology Columbia U., 1980—84, Queens Coll., 1984—85; prof. sociology SUNY, Stony Brook, 1985—88, Rutgers U., 1988—, dir. sociology grad. program, 1992—2001. Author: Patterns of Time in Hospital Life: A Sociological Perspective, 1979, Hidden Rhythms: Schedules and Calendars in Social Life, 1981, The Seven-Day Circle: The History and Meaning of the Week, 1985, The Fine Line: Making Distinctions in Everyday Life, 1991, 1993, Terra Cognita: The Mental Discovery of America, 1992, Social Mindscapes: An Invitation to Cognitive Sociology, 1997, 1999, The Clockwork Muse: A Practical Guide to Writing Theses, Dissertations, and Books, 1999, Time Maps: Collective Memory and the Social Shape of the Past, 2003. Fellow, John Simon Guggenheim Meml. Found., 2003. Mem.: Am. Sociol. Assn. (chair culture sect. 2000—01). Office: Rutgers Univ Dept Sociology 54 Joyce Kilmer Ave Piscataway NJ 08854

ZERUNYAN, FRANK VRAM, lawyer, councilman; b. Istanbul, Turkey, Sept. 17, 1959; came to U.S., 1978; s. Jack Hagop and Ayda (Yagupyan) Z.; m. Jody Lynn Forman, May 18, 1986; children: Daniel, Nicole. French Bacalaureat, Coll. Samuel Moorat, Paris, 1978; BA, Calif. State U., Long Beach, 1982; JD, Western State U., Fullerton, Calif., 1985; postgrad., U. Southern Calif., 1988. Bar: Calif. 1989, D.C. 1995, U.S. Dist. Ct. (ctrl. dist.) Calif. 1989, U.S. Dist. Ct. (no. dist.) Calif. 2001, U.S. Ct. Internat. Trade 1994, U. S. Supreme Ct. 2000. V.p. law Internat. Mktg. Alliance, Torrance, Calif., 1985-89; pvt. practice LA, 1989-92; mng. mem. Yacoubian & Zerunyan, P.C., LA, 1992-95; shareholder Sulmeyer Kupetz, LA, 1995—2005; mng. mem., gen. counsel Pub.-Private Cmty. Devel. LLC, 2005—. Instr. law Alex Pilibos Sch., L.A., 1993-99; judge pro tem, L.A. Superior Ct.; mem. adv. com. Bus. Tech. Ctr. of L.A., 2003—. Editor: SKB&R Newsletter, 1995-2005. Chmn. scholarship com. Orgn. Istanbul Armenians, Van Nuys, Calif., 1992—94; legal counsel and policy adv. com. Armenian Nat. Com. of Am., Armenian Nat. Com. of Am., Washington, 1993—; planning commr., past chmn. City of Rolling Hills Estates, 2000; policy svc. task force Little Company of Mary Hosp., 2003—05; mem. Rolling Hills Estates City Coun., 2003—; mem. energy and environ. com. and water policy task force So. Calif. Assn. Govt.; chair legis. com. Contract Cities Calif.; gov. apptd. mem. Med. Bd. Calif.; bd. dirs. Am. Youth Soccer Orgn., Palos Verdes, Calif., 1995—2005, referee adminstr., 1995—2004; bd. dirs., vice-chmn. Daniel Freeman Hosps. Found., 1998—2003, chmn., 2002—03. Mem.: So. Calif. Assn. Govt. (mem. water policy task force, mem. energy and environment com.), Fin. Lawyers Conf., Armenian Bar Assn. (bd. govs. 2003—, exec. com., chmn. bd.). Avocations: golf, soccer. Office: Pub Private Cmty Devel LLC 608 Silver Spur Rd Ste 290 Rolling Hills Estates CA 90274 Business E-Mail: fzerunyan@publicprivatecd.com.

ZERVAS, NICHOLAS THEMISTOCLES, neurosurgeon; b. Lynn, Mass., Mar. 9, 1929; s. Themistocles and Demetra P. (Stasinopoulos) Z.; m. Thalia Poleway, Feb. 15, 1959; children: T. Nicholas, Christopher Louis, Rhea. AB, Harvard U., 1950; MD, U. Chgo., 1954. Intern N.Y. Hosp., 1955; resident in neurology Montreal Neurol. Inst., 1956; resident in neurosurgery Mass. Gen. Hosp., Boston, 1958-62; fellow in stereotaxic cerebral surgery U. Paris, 1960-61; asst. attending surgeon, asso. neurosurgery Jefferson Med. Coll., Phila., 1962-67; asso. prof. surgery Harvard U., 1971-77; also chief neurosurg. service Beth Israel Hosp., Boston, 1967-77; prof. surgery Harvard U., 1977-200; also chief neurosurg. service Mass. Gen. Hosp., 1977-2000; Higgins prof. neurosurgery Harvard U., 1986-2000. Contbr. numerous articles to sci. jours. Chmn. Mass. Coun. Arts and Humanities, 1983-91; trustee Boston Symphony Orch., 1990—, vice chmn., 1993—, pres., 1994-2002; bd. dirs. Medical Edn. South African Blacks, 2004-. Capt. M.C. AUS, 1956-58, 87-2002. Fellow Am. Acad. Arts and Scis.; mem. Am. Acad. Neurol. Surgery (pres. 1990-91), Am. Assn. Neurol. Surgeons, Soc. Neurol. Surgeons, Am. Neurol. Assn., Am. Bd. Neurol. Surgery (chmn. 1990-91), Inst. Medicine Nat. Acad. Scis., Sigma Xi. Home: 100 Canton Ave Milton MA 02186-3507 Business E-Mail: nzervas@partners.org.

ZESCH, HAL, energy executive; BBA in Acctg., U. Tex., Austin. CPA. Audit and consulting mgr. Deloitte & Touche; various positions including v.p. best bus. practices, asst. corp. contr., contr. natural gas ops., and dir. corp. acctg. Valero Energy Corp., San Antonio, v.p. SAP systems integration, v.p., chief info. officer, 2003. Office: Valero Energy Corpn PO Box 696000 San Antonio TX 78269-6000

ZETCHER, ARNOLD B., apparel executive; b. 1940; m. Ellen Zetcher. BA, Washington U., 1962. With Federated Dept. Stores, NYC, 1962-76; chmn. bd., CEO Bonwit Teller, NYC, 1976-80; with Kohl's Corp., NYC, 1980-83; chmn., CEO Kohl's Food Stores, NYC, John Breuner Co., San Ramon, Calif., 1983-86; pres. The Talbots, Inc., Hingham, Mass., 1987—2007, CEO, 1988—2007, chmn., 2000—. Trustee Wash. U.; bd. mem. Celebrity Series of Boston. Named CEO of Year for Retail, Apparel and Accessories, Financial World mag., 1995; named one of Top 25 Managers, BusinessWeek, 2000. Mem.: Nat. Retail Fedn. (exec. com., chmn. 2004—05). Office: The Talbots Inc 1 Talbots Dr Hingham MA 02043-1501 *

ZETHMAYR-LOLAKOS, ELLEN, music educator, writer; b. Chgo., Dec. 1943; d. Anthony Paul and Helen Catherine Mishur; m. David Zethmayr (div.); children: Sylvia Zethmayr, Noël Zethmayr, Benjamin Zethmayr, K. Aurencz Zethmayr, Miriam Zethmayr; m. Thomas Christ Lolakos, June 8, 2003. AA, Mt. St. Clare Coll., Clinton, Iowa, 1964; BA, Marycrest Coll., Davenport, Iowa, 1967; postgrad., U. Ill., Chgo., 1984—86, Am. Conservatory of Music, 1968—74. Cert. tchr. Mo., Ill. Tchr. 1st and 2d grades Sisters of St. Francis, 1967—73; tchr., rschr., dir. St. Stephens Acad., La Grange, Ill., 1986—90; tchr. programs for gifted Louis U., Wheaton, Ill., 1986—93; piano tchr. Music Makers, Western Springs, Ill., 1996—; tchr., arranger, co-composer, performer, 2003—; co-prodr. Prospect Players, 2003—. Home schooling cons. St. Stephens Acad., 1987—90; mem. staff, asst. Prospect Players, Des Plaines, Ill., 2003—05; choir dir. Arlington HS, 2004—. Author: (poetry) Poems of a Dreamer, 1973; sculpture, Madonna & Child, wood mosaic, Hands on Piano Keyboard; singer Grant Park Chorus, Chgo., 1989, Opera La Traviata, Glen Ellyn, Ill., 1990; playwright, prodr., actress, musician: Butter Without a Bagel, 2006; More or Less Butter Without a Bagel, 2006; prodr.: Peanut Butter and Jelly, 2007. Recipient Outstanding award, 1st pl. paper divsn., Am. Jr. Acad. Sci., 1961. Mem.: Internat. Dyslexia Assn., Nat. Assn. Tchrs. of Singing, Nat. Guild Piano Tchrs. Eastern Orthodox. Avocations: art, woodcarving, writing, music. Home and Office: 413 S 8th Ave La Grange IL 60525

ZETSCHE, DIETER, automotive executive; b. Istanbul, Turkey, May 5, 1953; m. Gisela Zetsche. Grad., U. Karisuhe, 1971—76; DEng, Tech. U. Paderborn, 1982. Joined rsch. dept. Daimier-Benz AG, 1976—81, asst. to chief engr. comml. vehicle divsn., 1981—84, coord. comml. vehicle devel. activities, 1984—86, sr. mgr., chief engr. cross-country vehicle unit, 1986—87; head devel. dept., chief engr. Mercedes-Benz do Brazil, 1987—88, mem. mgmt., 1988—89; pres. Mercedes-Benz, Argentina, 1989—91, Freightliner Corp., Portland, Oreg., 1991—92; dep. mem. bd. mgmt. Mercedes-Benz AG, 1992, chief engr. devel. divsn. passenger cars bus. unit, 1992, mem. bd. mgmt. sales divsn., 1995, Daimier-Benz AG, 1997—98, DaimlerChrysler AG, 1998—99, mem. bd. mgmt. comml. vehicle divsn., 1999—2000, chmn. bd. mgmt., 2006—, mem. bd. mgmt., Mercedes Car Group, 2005—; mem. bd. mgmt., CEO Chrysler Group Divsn., 2000—05. Spokesperson for TV commercials DaimlerChrysler, 2006. Named one of 100 Most Influential People, Time Mag., 2006. Office: DaimierChrysler AG Epplestrasse 225 D-70546 Stuttgart Germany Office Phone: +49-711-17-0. Office Fax: +49-711-17-94022. *

ZETTEL, LAURA A., psychology professor, researcher; b. Warren, Mich., Feb. 29, 1976; d. Richard J. and Donna Zettel. BA, U. Mich., Ann Arbor, 1997; PhD, U. Calif., Irvine, 2004. Rschr. U. Mich., Ann Arbor, 1997—98; instr. and rschr. U. Calif., Irvine, 1998—2005; prof. Calif. State U., Fullerton, Calif., 2005—. Tchg. asst. cons. U. Calif., Irvine, 2002—04; adj. faculty Soka U. Am., Aliso Viejo, Calif., 2004. Named Most Promising Future Faculty Mem., U. Calif. Irvine, 2004; fellow, 2004; grantee, Anthony Marchionne Found., 2003. Mem.: APA, Gerontol. Soc. Am. Avocations: travel, reading, tennis. Office: Psychology Dept CSUF PO Box 6846 Fullerton CA 92834-6846 Home Phone: 714-547-4057; Office Phone: 714-278-3898. Business E-Mail: lzettel@fullerton.edu.

ZEUGNER, JOHN FINN, historian, educator, writer; b. NYC, Oct. 7, 1938; s. Orland Kump and Ethel (Finn) Z.; m. Alice Chatfield Valentine, Sept. 7, 1968; children: Emily Valentine, Maxwell Finn, Laura Ruth. AB, Harvard U., 1959; MA, Fla. State U., 1968, PhD, 1971. Night mgr. Beach Cart, Sarasota, Fla., 1960-67; asst. prof. history Worcester Poly. Inst., Mass., 1971-74, assoc. prof., 1974-82, prof., 1982—; Fulbright lectr. Osaka U., Kobe U., Japan, 1976-78. Vis. prof. Keio U., Tokyo, 1981-83; Bryant Drake guest prof. Kobe Coll., Japan, 1994-95. Contbr. articles to profl. jours. With USCG, 1961—62. Named Paris Fletcher Disting. Prof. Humanities, Worcester Poly. Inst., 1985; grantee NEA, 1970 Mem.: Soc. Historians Am. Fgn. Rels., Orgn. Am. Historians. Avocations: tennis, chess. Home: 31 William St Worcester MA 01609-2313 Office: Worcester Poly Inst Humanities & Arts Dept Worcester MA 01609 Office Phone: 508-831-5246. Business E-Mail: jzeugner@wpi.edu.

ZEUSCHNER, ERWIN ARNOLD, brokerage house executive; b. Freiburg, Germany, Nov. 17, 1935; came to U.S., 1936; s. Reinhold Hermann and Helene Barbara (Maas) Z.; m. Christa Elfreide Ellmers, June 20, 1959 (dec. Aug., 1971); children— Peter Erwin, Suzanne Christina, Andrea Ellmers; m. Margaret Anne Finn, Mar. 25, 1972; 1 dau., Elizabeth Nora. BA in Econs., Queens Coll., 1957; MBA in Fin, NYU, 1964. Sr. v.p. Chase Manhattan Bank, NYC, 1970-72; sr. v.p., dir. Chase Investors Mgmt. Corp., 1972-80; sr. v.p. Chase Manhattan Corp., 1970-80; ptnr. David J. Greene & Co. (investment advs.), NYC, 1980—. Trustee Marymount Manhattan Coll., 1997. Served to capt. USAF, 1958-60. Mem. N.Y. Soc. Security Analysts (dir.) Home: 1 Middle Dr Manhasset NY 11030-1414 Office: 599 Lexington Ave New York NY 10022-6030

ZEVGOLIS, IOANNIS, geotechnical engineer, researcher; b. Athens, Greece, May 6, 1977; arrived in U.S., 2002; s. Emmanouil Zevgolis and Aikaterini Zevgolis - Protonotarios. Diploma in Mining and Metall. Engring., Nat. Tech. U. Athens, Greece, 2002; MS in Engring., Sch. Civil Engring. Purdue U., West Lafayette, Ind., 2003, PhD, 2007. Lic. profl. engr., Tech. Chamber Greece, EU, 2002. Rsch. and tchg. asst. Purdue U., West Lafayette, Ind., 2002—07. Named to Chancellor's List, 2004—06; recipient Thomaidio award, Nat. Tech. U. Athens, 2002, Best Diploma Thesis, Tech. Chamber Greece, 2002, Outstanding Civil Engring. Grad. Student award, Purdue U., 2007, Nellie Munson Tchg. Asst. award in civil engring., 2007; scholar, Gerondelis Found., 2004, Empeirikion Found., 2004—07. Mem.: ASCE, Geo-Inst. of ASCE, Tech. Chamber of Greece, Soc. Mining, Metallurgy and Exploration, Bd. European Students Tech. (v.p. pub. rels. and mktg. 2000—01), Internat. Geosynthetics Soc., Internat. Soc. Soil Mechanics and Geotechnical Engring. Achievements include research in soil reinforcement methods; reliability and risk analysis in geotechnical engineering; underground space development. Home: 7-9 Gavriilidou St 11141 Athens Greece E-mail: i.zevgolis@alumni.purdue.edu.

ZEVON, SCOTT J., plastic surgeon; BA in Philosophy, State U. of New York, Binghampton, 1974; MD in Medicine, Boston U. School of Medicine, 1979. Cert. American Bd. of Plastic Surgery, 1989, American Bd. of Surgery, 1987, fellow American Coll. of Surgeons. Gen. stud. residency St. Luke's-Roosevelt Hosp. Ctr., NY, 1979—84; plastic surgery resident Nassau County Med. Ctr., NY, 1984—86; visiting physician Fellowship, Craniofacial Surgery, Mayo Clinic, Rochester, Minn., 1986—87; Attending Physician Plastic Surgery, St. Luke's-Roosevelt Hosp. Ctr., NY; chief Divsn. of Plastic Surgery, Long Island Coll. Hosp., NY. Clinical Instructor in Surgery Columbia U. Coll. of Physicians and Surgeons, New York, 1987—. Named one of the Best Doctors in New York, Castle Connolly Directory, New York Magazine; recipient Best Website to www.drzevon-.com, Plastic Surgery Network. Mem.: American Soc. of Plastic Surgeons (ASPS), American Soc. for Aesthetic Plastic Surgery (ASAPS), Lipoplasty Soc. of North America, Northeastern Regional Soc. of Plastic and Reconstructive Surgeons (NRSPRS), New York County Med. Soc. (NY-CMS). Office: Central Park Plastic Surgery 75 Ctr Park West New York NY 10023 Office Phone: 212-496-6600. E-mail: surgery@drzevon.com. *

ZEWAIL, AHMED HASSAN, chemistry and physics educator, consultant, editor; b. Damanhour, Egypt, Feb. 26, 1946; arrived in U.S., 1969, 1982; s. Hassan A. Zewail and Rawhia Dar; m. Dema Zewail; children: Maha, Amani, Nabeel, Hani. BS, Alexandria U., Egypt, 1967, MS, 1969; PhD, U. Pa., 1974; MA (hon.), Oxford U., 1991; DSc (hon.), Am. U., Cairo, 1993, Katholieke U., Leuven, Belgium, U. Pa., U. Lausanne, Switzerland, 1997; DU (hon.), Swinburne U., Australia, 1999; HDA Sc (hon.), Arab Acad. for Sci. and Tech., Egypt, 1999, Alexandria U., 1999; DSc (hon.), U. New Brunswick, Canada, 2000; DHC (hon.), U. Rome, Italy, 2000, U. de Liège, Belgium, 2000. Teaching asst. U. Pa., Phila., 1969—70; IBM fellow U. Calif., Berkeley, 1974—76; asst. prof. chem. physics Calif. Inst. Tech., Pasadena, 1976—78, assoc. prof., 1978—82, prof., 1982—89, Linus Pauling prof. chem. physics, 1990—94, Linus Pauling prof. chemistry and prof. physics, 1995—, dir. NSF Lab. for Molecular Scis., 1996—. Cons. Xerox Corp., Webster, NY, 1977—80, ARCO Solar, Inc., Calif., 1978—81. Editor Laser Chemistry, 1980—85, Jour. Phys. Chemistry, 1985—90, Chem. Physics Letters, 1991—; editor: International Series Monographs on Chemistry, 1992—, Advances in Laser Spectroscopy, 1977—, 1978—, Photochemistry and Photobiology, 1983—, Ultrafast Phenomena, 1990—, 1993—, 1994—, The Chemical Bond: Structure and Dynamics, 1992, Femtochemistry-Ultrafast Dynamics of the Chemical Bond, 1994; contbr. numerous articles to sci. jours., patentee in solar energy field. Recipient Tchr.-Scholar award, Dreyfus Found., 1979—85, Alexander von Humboldt Sr. U.S. Scientist award, 1983, John Simon Guggenheim Meml. Found. award, 1987, King Faisal Internat. prize in sci., 1989, NASA award, 1991, 1st AMM Achievement award, 1991, Nobel Laureate Signature award, 1992, Carl Zeiss award, Cairo U. Medal and Shield of Honor, 1992, U. Qatar medal, 1993, Wolf prize in chemistry, Wolf Found., Israel, 1993, Niles award of honor Bonner Chemiepreis, Germany, 1994, Order of Merit first class, Egypt, 1995, Coll. de France medal Leonardo Da Vinci award of excellence, France, 1995, J.G. Kirwood medal, Yale U., 1996, Beijing U. medal, 1996, Robert A. Welch award in chemistry, 1997, Pitts. Spectroscopy award, 1997, Benjamin Franklin medal, 1999, Paul Karrer Gold medal, Zurich, 1999, Roentgen prize, Germany, 1999, E.O. Lawrence award, U.S. Govt., 1999, Merski award, U. Nebr., 1999, Nobel prize in Chemistry, 1999, Egypt Postage Stamp with portrait issued, 1999, Grand Collar of the Nile, Highest Award, 2000, Order of Zayed, United Arab Emirates, 2000, Ahmed Zewail fellow established, U. Pa., 2000, Order of Cedar, Lebanon, 2000, Order of ISESCO 1st class, Saudi Arabia, 2000, Order of merit, Tunisia, 2000, Insignia Pontifical Acad., Vatican, 2000, Albert Einstein World Award of Sci., 2006. Mem.: NAS (Chem. Scis. award 1996), AAAS, Third World Acad. Scis., European Acad. Arts, Scis. and Humanities, Royal Danish Acad. Scis. and Letters, Pontifical Acad. Sci., Am. Phys. Soc. (Herbert P. Broida prize 1995), Am. Philos. Soc., Am. Chem. Soc. (Buck-Whitney medal 1985, Harrison-Howe award 1989, Hoechst prize 1990, Peter Debye award 1997, Linus Pauling medal 1997, 1st E.B. Wilson award 1997, William H. Nichols award 1998, Richard C. Tolman medal 1998), Am. Acad. Arts and Scis. (Royal Netherlands Acad. Arts and Scis. medal 1993), Sigma Xi (Earle K. Plyler prize 1993, Wolf prize 1993). Office: Arthur Amos Noyes Lab of Chem Physics Mail Code 127-72 Pasadena CA 91125

ZEX, DAMON, artist; b. Columbus, Ohio, July 11, 1963; s. Arnold Hobart Zaner, Rhoda Lee Zaner. BA, Ohio State U., 1985, MFA, 1991. Sales rep. FAZ Art Products, Columbus, Ohio, 1984—86; dir. gallery Artreach Gallery, Columbus, 1986—87; designer Contemporary Glass, Columbus, 1987—88; comml. designer Columbus Arts & Entertainment Mag., Columbus, 1988—89, Ohio Transmission Corp., Columbus, 1989—91; videographer, tech. dir. Cmty. 21 TV, Columbus, 1992—2001; co-owner Damon Zex Ltd., Columbus, 2001—. Expert art witness U.S. Fed. Ct., Columbus, 1999. Video artist Zex Invasion, 1992—2001 (Innovation award, 2000); Zex Cards, 1991; actor: Zex TV, 1993—2001 (Comedy award, 1994, 1997, 1998). Avocations: chess, yoga, dance, astrology, weight training. Home: Apt 361A 2913 Neil Ave Columbus OH 43202-2043 Office Phone: 614-262-0274. E-mail: zex@zexart.com.

ZGALJARDIC, DENNIS JOSEPH, clinical neuropsychologist; b. Flushing, NY, Mar. 11, 1975; s. Joseph and Maria Zgaljardic; m. Heather Ann Zgaljardic, July 13, 2002; 1 child, Isabella Jean. PhD, CUNY, 2004; degree, SUNY, Buffalo. License in Psychology NYS Licensing Bd. in Psychology, 2005. Clin. neuropsychology fellow North Shore U. Hosp., Manhasset, NY, 2003—05; clin. neuropsychologist Transitional Learning Ctr. at Galveston, Tex., 2005—. Adj. prof. Queens Coll., Flushing, NY,

1998—2005. Contbr. articles to profl. jours. Scholar, CUNY, 1998. Mem.: APA (assoc.), Internat. Neuropsychologiclal Soc. (life), Golden Key. Home Phone: 917-757-3164; Office Phone: 409-797-1472. Personal E-mail: neurodjz2@yahoo.com.

ZHANG, CHARLES C., financial planner; MA in Econs., Western Mich. U., 1991; MBA, Northwestern U., 2004. ChFC; CFP; CLU; chartered mutual fund counselor; cert. fund specialist. Sr. fin. advisor Am. Express Fin. Advisors, Inc., Kalamazoo, 1991—. Adj. prof. finance Western Mich. U. Mem. Am. Soc. CLU and ChFC, Inst. cert. Fin. Planners, Internat. Assn. Fin. Planning. Office: Am Express Fin Advisors Inc 1302 W Milham Portage MI 49024 E-mail: charles.c.zhang@aexp.com. *

ZHANG, CYNTHIA HONGBING, lawyer; b. Linshui, Sichuan Province, China, Apr. 24, 1966; d. Xintian Zhang and Zaifeng Guo. BS, Tsinghua U., Beijing, 1987, MS, 1990—90; PhD, Ind. U., 1995; JD, U. Houston, 2001. Bar: Md. 2002, DC 2003, U.S. Patent and Trademark Office 2002, Mass. 2004. Postdoctoral rschr. Dana Farber Cancer Inst. and Harvard Med. Sch., Boston, 1995—97, Boston U., 1998; jud. intern US Dist. Ct. (so. dist.) Tex., Houston, 2000; assoc. Shanks & Herbert, Alexandria, Va., 2001—03, Palmer & Dodge LLP, Boston, 2003—05; patent atty. Novartis Corp. Intellectual Property, Cambridge, Mass., 2005—. Mem.: ABA, Am. Intellectual Property Law Assn. Achievements include research in functional analysis of an intron 3' splice site in Caenorhabditis elegans. Office: Novartis Pharm Corp 1 Health Plaza Bldg 430/204 East Hanover NJ 07936 Office Phone: 617-871-3096, 617-871-3096. Office Fax: 617-871-3392.

ZHANG, DAJUN, biomedical engineering educator; BS, Beijing U., 1987, MS, 1990; PhD, CUNY, NYC, 1997. Postdoctoral rschr. CCNY, NYC, 1997—98; rsch. engr. U. Chgo., 1998—2000; asst. prof. Rutgers, State U. NJ, Piscataway, 2000—. Dir. Bone Mechanics Lab. Rutgers State U., Piscataway, 2000—, undergrad. student rsch, supervision, 2000—06; proposal reviewer NSF, 2003—06. Reviewer: Annals Biomed. Engring. Busch Biomedical grantee, Rutgers State U. NJ, 2002, 2004. Mem.: AAAS. Achievements include design of multiple experimental setups; development of novel research on multiple interdisciplinary fronts. Office: Rutgers State University of New Jersey 98 Brett Rd Piscataway NJ 08854 Home Phone: 732-301-2813; Office Phone: 732-445-3797.

ZHANG, DA-LIN D., meteorologist, educator; b. Yangzhou, Jiangsu, China, Mar. 25, 1952; s. Daoquan D. and Wanzheng W. (Liu) Z.; m. Xiao-Ning X. Zhao, Oct. 18, 1978; children: Jie Jay, Ping Nina. BS in Engring. Mechanics, U. Sci. and Tech. of China, Hefei, 1976; MS in Meteorology, Pa. State U., 1981, PhD in Meteorology, 1985. Rsch. asst. Inst. Atmospheric Physics, Academia Sinica, 1976-80; grad. rsch. asst., rsch. assoc. dept. meteorology Pa. State U., 1980-86; postdoctoral fellow Nat. Ctr. for Atmospheric Rsch., 1986-88; asst. prof. McGill U., Montreal, 1989-94, assoc. prof., 1994-96, U. Md., College Park, 1996-99, prof. meteorology, 1999—; rsch. assoc. dept. physics Univ. of Toronto, Ont., Canada, 1988—89. Overseas expert assessor Chinese Acad. Scis., Beijing, 1999—; guest prof. Nanjing U., 1999—; guest sr. scientist Chinese Acad. Meteorol. Scis., 2000—; overseas dir. State key Lab. Severe Weather, China Meteor Adminstrn.; sci. adv. China Meteorol. Adminstrn., 2005—; dean Atmospheric Scis. Coll., Nanjing U. Info. Sci. and Tech. Assoc. editor Monthly Weather Rev., 1998-2001, Weather and Forecasting, 1992-98, editor 2006—; mem. editl. bd. Acta Meteorologica Sinica, 1995—; co-chief editor Advances in Atmospheric Sci., 1999; contbr. over 90 articles to profl. jour., chpts. to books. Fellow Royal Meteorol. Soc., Am. Meteorol. Soc. (Meisinger award 1991). Avocations: ping pong/table tennis, music. Office: Univ of Maryland Dept Meteorology College Park MD 20742 Office Phone: 301-405-2018. Business E-Mail: dalin@atmos.umd.edu.

ZHANG, DAN, engineering educator, researcher; arrived in Can., 1997, naturalized, 2001; s. Hongtao Zhang and Yu Li; m. Junmei Guo, Aug. 8, 1990; children: Mengjia, James William. BS in Mech. Engring., Dong Hua U., Shanghai, 1986, MS in Mech. Engring., 1994; PhD, Laval U., Quebec City, Can., 2000. Rsch. scientist NRC Can., London, Ontario, 2000—04; asst. prof. U. Ont. Inst. Tech., Oshawa, 2004—, assoc. prof., 2006—07, assoc. prof., programs dir., 2007—. Dir. Durham Region Mfrs. Assn., Oshawa, 2004; bd. dirs. Lake Ontario chpt. Profl. Engrs. Ontario, 2007—. Recipient Tchg. Excellence award, Faculty Engring. and Applied Sci., U. Ont. Inst. Tech., 2006; Discovery grantee, Natural Scis. and Engring. Rsch. Coun. Can., 2006—. Mem.: IEEE, ASME (Cert. Appreciation, Computers and Info. in Engring. Conf. 2004, 2006), Soc. Mfg. Engrs., Can. Soc. for Mech. Engring., Materials and Mfg. Ont. (Indsl. fellow 2001—03). Achievements include patents pending for high accuracy parallel kinematic machine. Office: Univ Ontario Inst Tech 2000 Simcoe St North Oshawa ON Canada L1H 7K4 Office Phone: 9057218668 ext. 2965. Office Fax: 9057213370. Personal E-mail: dan_zhang99@hotmail.com. Business E-Mail: dan.zhang@uoit.ca.

ZHANG, DONNA D., toxicologist, educator; d. Ningyuan Zhou and Jifen Yu; m. Shufeng Zhang; children: Shirley, Vivian, Mae. PhD, NYU, NYC, 1997. Rsch. asst. prof. U. Mo., Columbia, 1999—2005; asst. prof. U. Ariz., Tucson, 2005—. Grantee, NIH, Am. Cancer Soc. Mem.: AACR, Soc. Toxicology. Achievements include research in anti-cancer drug discovery. Office: Univ Arizona 1703 E Mabel St Tucson AZ 85721

ZHANG, EUGENE, engineering educator; b. Beijing; s. Tiezheng Zhang and Zhimin Liu; m. Yue Zhang; 1 child, Andrew. Student, Peking U., Beijing, 1988—91; PhD, Ga. Tech, Atlanta, 2004. Asst. prof. Oreg. State U., Corvallis, 2004—. Grantee, NSF, 2006. Mem.: Assn. for Computing Machinery, IEEE Computer Soc. Office: Oreg State Univ 2111 Kelley Engring Ctr Corvallis OR 97330 Office Phone: 541-737-8599. Business E-Mail: zhange@eecs.oregonstate.edu.

ZHANG, GUILI, statistician, educator; d. Zhaonan Zhang and Cuihua Jia. PhD, U. Fla., Gainesville, 2005. Grad. instr. U. Fla., 1997—2003, statis. rschr., 1999—2005, rsch. scientist, 2005—06; asst. prof. East Carolina U., Greenville, NC, 2006—. Recipient Best Paper award, Frontiers in Edn., 2004. Mem.: APA, Nat. Coun. Measurement in Edn., Am. Soc. Engring. Edn. (Best Paper award), Am. Ednl. Rsch. Assn., Phi Kappa Phi. Office Phone: 252-328-4989. Business E-Mail: zhangg@ecu.edu.

ZHANG, GUOLONG, immunologist, educator; b. Quanjiao, Anhui, China, Aug. 25, 1971; s. Liren Zhang and Yulan Dong; m. Yan Song, Dec. 15, 1972; children: Alex Shijie, Andrew Shixuan. BS, China Agrl. U., Beijing, 1993, MS, 1995; PhD, Kans. State U., Manhattan, 1999. Postdoctoral fellow Yale U. Sch. of Medicine, New Haven, 2000—01; asst. prof. of molecular biology Okla. State U., Stillwater, 2002—07, assoc. prof. molecular biology, 2007—. Contbr. articles to profl. jours. (Pres.'s award China Agrl. U., 1992, Travel Fellowship Grant award for young investigators Soc. for Exptl. Biology and Medicine, 1998, Big XII Faculty Fellowship award Okla. State U., 2005). Mem.: AAAS, Conf. of Rsch. Workers in Animal Diseases, Am. Assn. Vet. Immunologists, Am. Assn. Immunologists (Jr. Faculty Travel award 2004). Achievements include patents pending for Fowlicidins and Methods of Their Use. Office: Okla State Univ 212 Animal Sci Bldg Stillwater OK 74078 Office Phone: 405-744-6619. Business E-Mail: glenn.zhang@okstate.edu.

ZHANG, HENG, research scientist, educator; s. Qixiu Zhang and Quanlu He; m. Ying Huang; 1 child, Jiyu. B in Engring., Ctrl. South U., 1982, M in Engring., 1986; PhD, U. NSW, 1999. Asst. to assoc. prof. Hunan U., Changsha, China, 1986—93, prof., 1999—; rschr. U. Newcastle, Australia, 1993—95; rsch. scholar U. NSW, Australia, 1995—99; postdoctoral rsch. fellow U. Conn., 1999—2001; sr. scientist NanoGroup Inc., Willington, Conn., 2001—. Contbr. over 100 sci. publs. in field. Recipient Second prize, Nat. Edn. Bd. of People's Republic of China, 1988, Third prize, Ministry of Mech. and Electronic Industry of People's Republic of China, 1992, Disting. Young Scientist, Ministry of Mech. Industry of People's Republic of China, 1992, Second prize for Sci. and Tech., 1996, 1998, Third prize for Sci. and Tech., 1996, Second prize, Bur. of Mech. Industry of People's Republic of China., 1999; Overseas Postgraduate Rsch. Scholarship, Dept. Edn. of Australia, 1993, scholarship, Australian Rsch. Coun., 1995, Postdoctoral fellowship, Australian Nat. U., 1999, Oversea Scholar fellowship, Ministry of Edn. of People's Republic of China, 2001. Mem.: Materials Rsch. Soc. (assoc.). Achievements include discovery of a large group (about 78) of novel rare-earth compounds R3T29M4B10, a few hundred of pseudo-compounds, determination of the crystalline structure and magnetic structure of R3T29M4B10; invention of nanostructured magnetic ceramic and soft magnet composites with ultrafine components and high performance; design and development of exchange-spring coupled nanostructured hard and soft magnetic composite with high energy density at ambient and elevated temperatures; design and development of nanostructured ceramic coating technique for orthopedic and dental implants with various complicated surface profiles and geometries with high bioactivity; strong bonding and fast healing after implantation, innovation of doped nanocrystal hydroxypatite coating for orthopedic and dental implants with antibacterial function; which can significantly reduce the infection caused by implantation surgery; patents pending for plasma thermal spray making integrated oxide fuel cell and electrodes; innovation of nanostructured Sr1-1.5xYxTiO3 anode material for solid oxide fuel cell using a wet chemical method; invention of a novel nanostructured Pd-TM oxide ceramic catalyst system with higher stability for low-temperature methane combustion; achieving hydrogenization for titanium at low temperature; creation of mullite-insulating coating on the surface of silicon carbide whiskers with exceptional electrical insulating feature and mechanical property; discovery of ternary Cu-Ti-Zr and binary Zn-M (M = Nb, V, Ti, Zr) amorphous solids; development of innovation of novel Cu-Ni-Sn-P-Ce series glass films with super mechanical property; establishment of a modeling system to describe the formation and stability of Cu-P based glasses; and predict the amorphization by solid-state phase transition. Office: NanoGroup 156 J River Rd Willington CT 06279 Home Phone: 860-423-6757; Office Phone: 860-487-3838. Personal E-mail: hgzh@yahoo.com.

ZHANG, HONG (RICK), design engineer, researcher; b. Hancheng, Shaanxi, China, May 28, 1960; s. Runmin Zhang and Mingzhu Ma; m. Li Qu, Apr. 1, 1995; 1 child, Chi (Jim). PhD, Beijing U. Aero & Astro, 1992. Assoc. prof. Beijing Inst. Machinery Industry, 1992—95; post doctoral rschr. U. Minn., Mpls., 1998—2001; design engr. ADC Telecomm., Inc., 2001—02; sr. design engr. Princetel, Inc., Lawrenceville, NJ, 2002—. Presenter in field. Contbr. articles to profl. jours. Fellow, Nanyang Technol. U., Singapore, 1995—97. Achievements include patents for Apparatus and method for sensing switching positions of a MEMS optical switch; Latching apparatus for a MEMS optical switch; MEMS optical switch on a single chip and method. Pub; A new type of load balancing mechanisms for planetary gearing; scanning apparatus; patents pending for optic rotary joint using rotatable fiber; anti-backlash planetary gearing for optic rotary joint; two-channel, dual-mode fiber optic rotary joint; off-axis optic slip ring. Office: 1595 Reed Rd Pennington NJ 08534 Home Phone: 732-331-5984. Office Fax: 609-895-9552. Personal E-mail: mr_hongzhang@yahoo.com.

ZHANG, JIAWEI, finance educator; s. Chuanfu Zhang and Yongzhen Zeng; m. Yu Shi, Aug. 2004. BS in Applied Math., Tsinghua U., 1996; PhD, Stanford U., Calif., 2004. Asst. prof. NYU, 2004—. Mem.: INFORMS (Optimization prize for young rschrs. 2004). Achievements include research in algorithm design for NP-hard combinatorial optimization problems. Office Phone: 212-998-0811. Business E-Mail: jzhang@stern.nyu.edu.

ZHANG, KEHONG, pharmacologist, educator; b. Tumen, Jilin Province, China, Nov. 4, 1964; married. PhD, La. State U., 1997. Asst. prof. psychiatry and neurosci. Harvard Med. Sch./McLean Hosp., Belmont, Mass., 1999—. Contbr. articles to profl. jours. Recipient Branfman Found. award, Branfman Found., 2002, Livingston award, Harvard Med. Sch., 2000, Alfred Pope Young Investigator award, 2001, Travel award, Am. Coll. Neuropharmacology, 2002; fellow, Pharm. Rsch,. and Mfrs. Am/ion, 1995. Mem.: ASPET, Soc. Neuroscis. Office: Harvard Med Sch McLean Hosp 115 Mill St Belmont MA 02478 Home: 346 Lincoln St Apt 3 Waltham MA 02451-2141 Home Phone: 718-894-5182; Office Phone: 617-855-3222. Business E-Mail: kz@mclean.harvard.edu.

ZHANG, LEI, physics professor; b. Shanghai, June 11, 1966; s. Guo Rui Zhang and Gua Zhen Dong; m. Qiuhong Zhao. MS, Fla. Internat. U., Miami, 1995, La. Tech U., Ruston, 1995; PhD, U. Tex., Arlington, 2000. Vis. asst. prof. physics Elizabeth City State U., NC, 2002—05; asst. prof. physics Winston-Salem State U., NC, 2005—. Mem. U. Tex. Sys. Student Adv. Coun., 1999—2000; pres. Grad. Student Coun. U. Tex., Arlington, 1999—2000. Mem.: Am. Phys. Soc. Achievements include development of novel nuclear methods to detect and analyze the change of electric density in polymer-dispersed liquid crystal (PDLC) materials. Home: 2112 Fiddlers Ct # G Winston Salem NC 27107 Home Phone: 336-650-0942; Office Phone: 336-750-2919. Personal E-mail: zhanglei90@hotmail.com. E-mail: zhangl@wssu.edu.

ZHANG, LI, engineer, researcher, educator; b. Beijing, Nov. 8, 1969; s. Qicheng Zhang and Liuying. MS in Nuclear Engring., MIT, 1996, MS in Elec. Engring and Computer Sci., 1996, PhD in Radiol. Scis., 1998. Tchg. asst. MIT, Cambridge, 1993-94, rsch. asst., 1994-98; sys. engr. Robotic Vision Sys., Inc., Hauppauge, NY, 1998; tech. mgr. Youngtech Inc., Edison, NJ, 1998—2001; project leader ADP Inc., Parsippany, NJ, 2001—03; pres. Internat. Innovative Imaging Sys., LLC, Piscataway, NJ, 2003—; prof. DeVry U., Westminster, Colo., 2005—. Dir. electronics Beijing Perfect Electronics Engring. Corp., Beijing, 1992-93; project mgr. AT&T, Bedminster, N.J., 1998-99. Mem. AAAS, IEEE, SPIE, Assn. for Computing Machinery, Health Physics Soc., Am. Nuclear Soc., N.Y. Acad. Scis., Sigma Xi. Achievements include creation and research for explosive detection and nuclear medicine imaging. Avocations: hiking, travel, movies, Broadway shows, computer/internet surfing. Office Phone: 732-801-4508. E-mail: lizhang@alum.mit.edu.

ZHANG, LI, neurologist; b. Dalian, China, July 3, 1957; arrived in US, 1989; d. Zhi Xin Zhang and Yun Chui Liu; m. Xiaoqi Gruan, Apr. 25, 1983; 1 child, Rui Gruan. MD, China Med. U., Shen Yang, 1982. Resident in surgery Dalian Med. Sch., 1983—88; attending surgeon Dalian Third Hosp., 1988—89; rsch. scholar Washington U., St. Louis, 1989—94; intern in medicine St. Louis Med. Ctr., 1994—95; resident in neurology U. Chgo., 1995—98, neurophysiology fellow, 1998—99; attending neurologist West Suburban Hosp., Oak Park, Ill., 1999—2002, Neuromed Clinic, Naperville, Ill., 2002—, Edward Hosp., Naperville, 2002—, Ctrl. DuPage Hosp., Naperville, 2002—. Recipient Sir Charles Scott Sheridon award for excellence in electromyography, U. Chgo., 1999. Fellow: Am. Electrodiagonstic Medicine; mem.: Am. Acad. Neurology. Avocations: dance, piano, reading, interior decorating. Office: Neuromed LLC 38517 Winfield Rd Warrenville IL 60555

ZHANG, LIANG, research scientist; s. Jianmin Zhang and Xiuying Zeng; m. Qin Yang. PhD, U. Okla., Norman, 2006. Rsch. asst. U. Okla., Norman, 2002—06, rsch. assoc., 2006—. Reviewer: Chem. Engring. Jour., 2007—, Jour. Catalysis; contbr. articles to profl. jours. Recipient Timpano award Best Paper Competition, OSA and OMS, 2006; SWNT scholar for Internat. Workshop on Nucleation and Growth Mechanism of Carbon Nanotube, NASA and Rice U., 2007, Rsch. Assistantship, U. Okla., 2002—06. Mem.: AAAS, AIChE, Am. Chemistry Soc., Sigma Xi Soc. Achievements include patents pending for novel method for growing and harvesting single-walled carbon nanotubes. Home: 829 E Lindsey Norman OK 73071 Office: CBME University of Oklahoma 100 E Boyd T-335 Norman OK 73019 Home Phone: 405-370-4696; Office Phone: 405-325-9178. Business E-Mail: lyon17@ou.edu.

ZHANG, MING, business and management consultant; b. Jiangsu, China, 1962; arrived in U.S., 1988; m. Jiping Wu, 1993; children: Oak, Sky. BA, Nanjing U., China, 1983, MA, 1986; cert., Johns Hopkins U.-Nanjing U., 1987; PhD, Purdue U., West Lafayette, Ind., 1994. Rsch. fellow Nat. Def. U., Washington, 1994—97; rsch. analyst Libr. Congress, Washington, 1995—97; cons. Carnegie Endowment, Washington, 1998—99; non-resident sr fellow Atlantic Coun. US, Washington, 2000—; dir. rsch. IHS Internat., Arlington, Va., 1998—2004; owner, pres. Crossroads Initiative LLC, Va., 2002—. Spkr. in field. Author: Major Powers at a Crossroads, 1995, China's Changing Nuclear Posture, 1999, A Triad of Another Kind, 1999. Grantee Tchg. grant, Rockefeller Bros. Fund, 1991, Travel grant, Am. Polit. Sci. Assn., 1993, Rsch. grant, NDU Found., 1994—97. Avocations: basketball, travel. Office Phone: 703-264-9080. Personal E-mail: mingzhang28@aol.com.

ZHANG, MINGZHI, nephrologist, educator; s. Wende and Lee Zhang; m. Suwang Wang; children: Xiao-xiao, Cathy. MD, Xuzhou Med. Coll., 1985. Instr. Xuzhou Med. Coll., 1990—92, assoc. prof., 1992—94; rsch. assoc. Vanderbilt U., Nashville, 1994, rsch. instr., 1997—99, rsch. asst. prof., 1999—2006, asst. prof., 2006—. Achievements include patents for colorectal cancer chemoprevention; development of application of tissue microarray in nephrology; discovery of intrarenal dopamine regulates renin angiotensin system. Office: Vanderbilt University School of Medicine MCN S3206 Nashville TN 37232 Home Phone: 615-383-5658; Office Phone: 615-343-1548. Office Fax: 615-343-1548. Business E-Mail: mingzhi.zhang@vanderbilt.edu.

ZHANG, NENGLI, research scientist; b. Sichuan, China, Jan. 8, 1940; arrived in US, 1989; s. Sunxian Zhang and Huirong Xiong; m. Xiaohui Sun, Jan. 29, 1968; 1 child, Chi. BS equivalent in thermophysics, Tsinghua U., Beijing, 1962; PhD equivalent in thermophysics, Tsinghua U., 1984. Rsch. asst. Tsinghua U., Beijing, 1962—78, asst. prof., 1978—80; vis. scholar U. Mich., Ann Arbor, 1981—83; assoc. prof. Tsinghua U., 1984—89; rsch. assoc. U. Mich., 1989—93; sr. rsch. assoc. NRC at NASA Lewis Rsch. Ctr., Cleve., 1994—98; sr. scientist Ohio Aerospace Inst. at NASA Glenn Rsch. Ctr., Cleve., 1998—. Concurrent deputy chief engr. Hai Hua New Tech. Devel. Ctr., Beijing, 1984—88; cons. Beijing Inst. of Rubber Industry, 1984—86, Da peng Sci.-Tech. Industry Ltd., Co., 1987—89. Author: Process System Engineering (in Chinese), 1982; contbr. articles various profl. jours. Recipient Achievements in Sci. award, Beijing Sci.-Tech. Com., 1983, Nat. Sci-Tech. Progress award, Nat. Sci.-Tech. Com., 1985, Achievement in Sci. award, China State Edn. Com., 1988, Achievement in Natural Sci. award, Nat. Sci-Tech. Com., 1989, 3 NASA Tech Innovations awards, NASA, 1998. Mem.: Am. Assn. for Advancement of Sci., Am. Soc. of Mech. Engrs. Achievements include patents for innovative heat pipe systems using new working fluids; shadowgraphic method to measure contact angles with flow visualization in a sessile drop; research in thermal instability in evaporating sessile drops; identifying the profiles near three-phase contact line through caustic-diffraction of wave; convective instability in transient evaporating thin liquid layer; catastrophe optics applying to study of spreading of liquid drops. Avocations: music, gardening, sports. Home: 34671 Plantation Pl North Ridgeville OH 44039 Office: Ohio Aerospace Inst NASA Glenn Rsch Ctr 21000 Brookpark Rd Cleveland OH 44135 Office Phone: 216-433-8750. Business E-Mail: nzhang@grc.nasa.gov.

ZHANG, QIMING, engineering educator, researcher; arrived in US, 1981; s. Hui and Baoqin (Baoqin) Zhang; m. Ailan Cheng, Nov. 17, 1963; children: Andrew, Michelle. BS, Nanjiang U., 1981; PhD, Pa. State U., 1986. Rschr. Brookhaven Nat. Lab., LI, NY, 1988—91; faculty Pa. State U., University Park, 1991—. Mem. bd. dirs. Electropolymer Tech., Inc., Palo Alto, Calif., 1999—2002; cons. Thin Film Electronics, Linkoping, Sweden, 2000—01, Bridge Semiconductor, Inc., Pitts., 2004; keynote spkr. in field. Editor: Electroactive Polymers, 1999. Mem. adv. com. Knowledge Found. Conf., Calif., 2000. Recipient David Rank award, Pa. State U. physics dept., 1982, Outstanding Rsch. award, Pa. State Engring. Soc., 1999. Mem.: IEEE (sr.; mem. tech. program com. internat. ultrasonic symposium 1994—, assoc. editor IEEE, ultrasounics, ferroelectrics and frequency control 2002—), Am. Phys. Soc., Materials Rsch. Soc. (organizer fall meeting symposium 2003). Achievements include patents for relaxor ferroelectric polymers; polyvinylidene fluoride/tri-fluoroethylene (PVDF-TrFE) based terpolymers. Office: Pa State U 187 MRL University Park PA 16802 Office Phone: 814-863-8994. Business E-Mail: qxz1@psu.edu.

ZHANG, RUICHONG, civil and mechanical engineer, educator; b. Shanghai, Dec. 6, 1962; s. Xiangting Zhang and Shoumei Wang; m. Min Zhou, July 1, 1987; children: Vincent, Vivian (Cynthia). BS, Tongji U., 1984, MS, 1987; PhD, Fla. Atlantic U., 1992. Asst. prof. Tongji U., Shanghai, 1987; rsch. asst. U. Colo., Boulder, 1987-88, Fla. Atlantic U., Boca Raton, 1988-92; rsch. assoc. Princeton (N.J.) U., 1992-95; rsch. asst. prof. U. So. Calif., LA, 1995-97; asst. prof. Colo. Sch. Mines, Golden, 1997-2000, assoc. prof., 2001—. Mem. ASCE, Earthquake Engring. Rsch. Inst., Internat. Assn. Structural Safety Reliability (Jr. Rsch. prize 1997). Home: 16501 W Ellsworth Ave Golden CO 80401-6540 Office: Colo Sch Mines Divsn Engring Golden CO 80401 Office Phone: 303-273-3671. Business E-Mail: rzhang@mines.edu.

ZHANG, SHIBAO, electrical engineer; BS, Tsinghua U., Beijing, 1994, MS, 1997; PhD, Kans. State U., Manhattan, 2001. Sr. engr. PCORE Electric Co., Inc., LeRoy, NY, 2002—. High-voltage bushing expert. Contbr. scientific papers to profl. jours. Mem.: IEEE (sr.). Home Phone: 585-292-5529; Office Phone: 585-768-1273. E-mail: shibao.zhang@ieee.org.

ZHANG, SHUGUANG, biomedical engineer; b. Chongqing, Sichuan, China, Feb. 9, 1953; came to US, 1980; s. Zenming and Xingdi (Zhao) Z.; m. Kathleen R. Schaefer, June 12, 1982; 1 child, Niklas. BS in Biochemistry, Sichuan U., China, 1980; PhD in Genetics, Biochemistry and Molecular Biology, U. Calif., Santa Barbara, 1988. Am. Cancer Soc. postdoctoral fellow structural and molecular biology MIT, Cambridge, Mass., 1988—91, rsch. scientist dept. biology, 1992-96, prin. rsch. scientist, 1997—, assoc. dir. Ctr. Biomedical Engring., 1998—. Cons. Acorda Therapeutics, NYC, 1996; sci. adv. Mitsubishi Chem. Corpn., Tokyo, 1997; vis. prof. Qinghua U., Beijing, 1998—, Chinese Acad. Med. Sci., Beijing, China U. Petroleum, Qingdao; hon. prof., disting. Changjiang scholar Sichuan U., Chengdu, China. Contbr. articles to profl. jours. Recipient R & D 100 award, R & D Magazine, 2004, Wilhelm Exner medal, Austria, 2006; grantee, Whitaker Found., 1997, NIH, 1997, Japan Soc. for Promotion of Sci., 2003, Japan Advancement for Med. Instrument, 2005, John Simon Guggenheim fellowship, 2006. Mem.: Internat. Soc. Study of Origin of Life, NY Acad. Scis., Protein Soc., Human Genome Orgn., Am. Soc.

Biochemistry and Molecular Biology, AAAS, Sigma Xi. Achievements include a patent on a discovery of self-assembling peptide systems. Office: Lab Molecular Self-Assembly MIT 77 Mass Ave Bldg 56-341 Cambridge MA 02139 E-mail: shuguang@mit.edu.

ZHANG, WENXIAN, librarian; came to U.S., 1988; s. Jiatai Zhang and Sufen Cao; m. Qun Du, Oct. 12, 1987; children: Michelle, Nathan. BA, Beijing U., 1985; MLS, So. Conn. State U., 1989, MS in Bus., 1993. Libr. Yellow River U., Zhengzhou, 1985-86, acting dir. libr., 1986-88; grad. asst. So. Conn. State U., New Haven, 1988-89; asst. dir. Ansonia (Conn.) Libr., 1990-91, libr. dir., 1991—95; head pub. svcs. Rollins Coll., Winter Park, Fla., 1995—2001, assoc. prof., head archives and spl. collections, 2001—. Reference libr. Ctrl. Conn. State U., New Britain, 1993—95. Grantee Christian Higher Edn. in Asia, N.Y., 1988-89; H. W. Wilson scholar, 1989-90. Mem. Soc. Am. Archivists, Soc. Fla. Archivists, Chinese Am. Librs. Assn., Winter Park Hist. Assn., Orlando Chinese Profl. Assn. (treas., mem. bd. dir.), Beta Phi Mu. Avocations: archival management, Chinese librarianship, Asian American affairs. Home: 2226 Wembley Pl Oviedo FL 32765-7360 Office: Rollins Coll Box 2768 Winter Park FL 32789 Business E-Mail: wzhang@rollins.edu.

ZHANG, XINWEN, computer scientist, researcher; b. Niangxiang, China, Jan. 1, 1974; s. Qiqiu Zhang and Meizhi Xiao; m. Wei Xiong. BA, Huazhong U., Wuhan, China, 1995; PhD, George Mason U., Fairfax, Va., 2006. Software devel. engr. CE-Infosys Pte. Ltd., 1998—2000; rsch. asst. George Mason U., 2001—. Achievements include research in access control models, application in trusted computing systems, high assurance systems. Home: 1351 Lassen Ave Milpitas CA 95035 Office: 75 W Plumeria Dr San Jose CA 95134 Office Phone: 408-544-5642. Personal E-mail: xinwenzhang@hotmail.com. Business E-Mail: xinwen.z@samsung.com.

ZHANG, YANWEN, physicist; MS, Beijing Normal U., 1990—93, PhD in Sci., 1993—99; PhD in Engring. Physics, Lund U., Sweden, 1995—98. Asst. prof., divsn. ion physics Uppsala U., Sweden, 2000—02; sr. rsch. scientist Pacific NW Nat. Lab., Richland, Wash., 2003—. Recipient Outstanding Young Alumnae award, Beijing Normal U., 1990, Hon. Docent award, Lund U., Sweden, 2004, Presdl. Early Career award for scientists & engrs., US Govt., 2005, Early Career Scientist and Engr. award, Office Sci., Dept. Edn., 2005, EMSL Dir. award, Pacific NW Nat. Lab., 2006. Mem.: Materials Rsch. Soc. Avocations: skiing, camping, hiking, hunting. Office Phone: 509-376-3429. Business E-Mail: yanwen.zhang@pnl.gov.

ZHANG, YAWEI, epidemiologist; m. Kaiyong Zou, May 15, 1994; 1 child, Zhihan Zou. MD, West China U., Chengdu, 1993; PhD, Yale U., New Haven, Conn., 2004. Postdoctoral fellow Nat. Cancer Inst., Rockville, Md., 2004—05; asst. prof. Yale U., 2005—. Rsch. asst. Yale U., 2001—04. Editor: Encyclopedia of Global Health. Mem.: APHA (assoc.), InterLymph (assoc.), Internat. Genetic Epidemiology Soc. (assoc.), Am. Assn. Cancer Rsch. (assoc. Scholar in Tng. award 2005). Achievements include research in personal hair dye use and risk of non-hodgkin lymphoma; genetic susceptibility and risk of non-hodgkin lymphoma; PCBs and CYP1A1 and risk of breast cancer. Office: Yale Univ 60 College St New Haven CT 06520 Office Phone: 203-785-6210. Business E-Mail: yawei.zhang@yale.edu.

ZHANG, YOUXUE, geology educator; b. Huarong County, Hunan, China, Sept. 17, 1957; came to U.S., 1983; s. Zaiyi Zhang and Dezhen Wu; m. Zhengjiu Xu; children: Dan, Ray. BS in Geol. Scis., Peking U., Beijing, 1982; MA in Geol. Scis., Columbia U., 1985, MPhil, 1987, PhD in Geol. Scis., 1989. Grad. rsch. asst. Columbia U., NYC, 1983-88; postdoctoral fellow Calif. Inst. Tech., 1988-91; asst. prof. geology U. Mich., Ann Arbor, 1991-97, assoc. prof., 1997—2004, prof., 2004—. Contbr. articles to profl. jours. Named Young Investigator, NSF, 1994. Fellow: AAAS, Geol. Soc. Am.; mem.: Am. Geophys. Union, Geochem. Soc. (F.W. Clarke medal 1993), Mineral. Soc. Am., Sigma Xi. Office: Dept Geol Sci U Mich Ann Arbor MI 48109-1005 E-mail: youxue@umich.edu.

ZHANG, YUWEN, mechanical engineer, researcher, educator; b. Xiaoyi, Shanxi, China, Jan. 7, 1965; came to US, 1994; s. Zengwei and Linmei (Zhao) Z.; m. Jianfeng Guo, Jan. 1, 1988; children: Angela, Joanna. BS, Xian U., China, 1985, MS, 1988, PhD, 1998. Asst. prof. Xi'an Jiaotong U., 1991-92, assoc. prof., 1992-94; rsch. assoc. Wright State U., Dayton, Ohio, 1994-95, U. Conn., Storrs, 1995-98, rsch. scientist, 1999—2000; sr. engr. Thermoflow, Inc., 2000; asst. prof. N.Mex. State U., 2001—03; assoc. prof. U. Mo., Columbia, 2003—. Author book; contbr. over 100 articles to profl. jours. Recipient Young Investigator award, Office of Naval Rsch. Mem. AIAA (sr.), ASME. Achievements include research in microscale heat transfer and heat transfer in manufacturing and materials processing. Office: Univ Mo Columbia Dept Engring Columbia MO 65211 Home Phone: 573-446-2590; Office Phone: 573-884-6936. Business E-Mail: zhangyu@missouri.edu.

ZHANG, ZHIWEI, research scientist; b. Wuhan City, China, Oct. 5, 1964; s. Lian Wen and Guang Ming (Tang) Z.; m. Mei X. Zhang, June 18, 1991; children: Jenny, Olivia, Megan, Victoria. BS, Huangzhong U. Sci. and Tech., Wuhan, China, 1985; MS, Va. Commonwealth U., 1994; PhD, Va. Tech., 1999. Sr. rsch. analyst Nat. Opinion Rsch. Ctr., Washington, 1997-98; rsch. scientist Nat. Opinion Rsch. Ctr. U. Chgo., Washington, 1999—2001, sr. rsch. scientist Nat. Opinion Rsch. Ctr., 2002—. Author drug use and workplace programs and policies, 1999; chief analystic leader ADAM project Nat. Inst. Justice, U.S. Dept. Justice, 2001-04. Sci. corr.: Sci. and Tech. Daily, 1988—90; contbr. articles to profl. jours. Recipient Bur. of Justice Stats. award, 1997; Bur. Labor Stats./Dept. Labor grantee, 1999, NIDA/U.S. Dept. HHS grantee, 2001-03, Appalachian Regional Commn. grantee, 2006—. Mem. AAAS, APHA, Am. Sociol. Assn. (Clifford C. Clogg award 1996), Am. Stats. Assn., Phi Kappa Phi. Avocations: reading, tennis. Office: Nat Opinion Rsch Ctr 1350 Connecticut Ave NW Ste 500 Washington DC 20036-1736

ZHANG, ZHONGQI, chemist; arrived in U.S., 1989, naturalized, 2003; m. Rong Wang, Dec. 25, 1990; children: Justin R., Wesley S. PhD, Purdue U., 1990—95. Postdoctoral rsch. assoc. Nat. High Magnetic Field Lab., Tallahassee, 1995—97; scientist Amgen, Thousand Oaks, Calif., 1997—. Mem.: Am. Chem. Soc., Am. Soc. for Mass Spectrometry. Achievements include invention of techniques in mass spectrometry based peptide sequencing; research in quantitative prediction of peptide tandem mass spectrum; invention of method for gradient elution in micro-flow liquid chromatography; first to new technique for studying protein structure using hydrogen exchange and mass spectrometry; invention of new method for charge state deconvolution in electrospray mass spectrometry; development of software for automated mining of mass spectrometric data; research in peptide conformation by collision-induced dissociation. Office: Amgen One Amgen Ctr Dr Thousand Oaks CA 91320 Home Phone: 805-241-3963. Personal E-mail: zzhang@amgen.com.

ZHAO, CHONGHAO, neurologist, educator; MD, Guangzhou Med. Coll., China, 1986; PhD, Med. Coll. Va., 1994. Diplomate Am. Bd. Neurology, Ill., 2004, Am. Bd. Med. Acupuncture, Calif., 2002. Sr. lectr. UCLA, LA, 2001—; pres. Calif. Headache and Pain Ctr., Burbank; staff physician Providence St. Joseph Med. Ctr. Contbr. articles to profl. jours. Hon. chmn. physicians' adv. bd. Nat. Rep. Congl. Com., Washington, 2005—05; pres. So-Sue-Fang Ednl. Found., Guangzhou, China, 2003—05. Recipient Ronald Reagan Rep. Gold medal, Nat. Rep. Congl. Com., 2005; fellow, Cleve. Clinic Found., 2003. Mem.: Am. Acad. Pain Medicine, Am. Pain Soc., Am. Acad. Neurology, Am. Headache Soc. Achievements include research in Superficial cervical plexus block as an acute abortive therapy for intractable headache. Office: Calif Headache and Pain Ctr 201 S Buena Vista St Ste 238 Burbank CA 91505 Office Phone: 818-842-1688. Office Fax: 818-842-1638. E-mail: drzhao@chpci.com.

ZHAO, FENG-QI, endocrinologist, educator; PhD, U. Alta., Edmonton, Can., 1995. Asst. prof. U. Vt., Burlington, 2001—. Contbr. articles to profl. jours. Mem.: Endocrine Assn. (assoc.). Office: Univ Vt 570 Main St Burlington VT 05405 Office Phone: 802-656-0786. Office Fax: 802-656-8196.

ZHAO, HONG, biomedical engineer, educator; b. Beijing, Dec. 10, 1959; d. Yongkai Zhao and Hengyun Liu; m. Weijian Guo; 1 child, Jiannan. MD (hon.), Beijing Med. U., 1983; Master (hon.), Inst. Nat. Polytechnique de Lorraine, Nancy, France, 1998; PhD in Biomed. Engring. (hon.), U. Henri Poincaré, Nancy, France, 2002. Asst. prof. Beijing Heart, Lung, Blood Vessel Med. Ctr., He Bei, 1986—92; assoc. prof. Inst. Clin. Med. Sci., China-Japan Friendship Hosp., Beijing, 1993—2002; scientist BioChain Inst., Inc., Calif., 2002—. Contbr. articles to profl. jours. Recipient Young Investigator award, 4th Asian Congress for Microcirculation, 2000. Mem.: Soc. Française Biorhéologie Fondamentale et Clinique. Personal E-mail: hongzhao_email@yahoo.com.

ZHAO, KEZHONG, electrical engineer; b. Fujian, China, Apr. 8, 1978; s. Cheng Qi Zhao and Yue Ying Wang; m. Xi Lin, Dec. 28, 2003; 1 child, Yi-Fei. BS, Ohio State U., Columbus, 2001, MS, 2003, PhD, 2007. Grad. rsch. assoc. ElectroSci. Lab., Columbus, Ohio, 2001—. Fellow, Northrop Grumman Corp., 2003—04. E-mail: zhao.u4@osu.edu.

ZHAO, WENMING, retired biochemistry and molecular biology educator; b. Xi-Xiang County, China, Jan. 24, 1938; s. Fa-Ke Zhao and Yuan-Hui Yu; m. Zhi-Hui Hu, Jan. 19, 1963; 2 children: Meng, Yuan. BS, Northwestern Coll. Agrl., 1960, MSc, 1964. Asst. Northwestern Coll. Agrl., Yang-Ling, China, 1960-61, tchr., 1974-93, Shanxi Labour U., Dai-Yuan, China, 1965-70, Zhou-Zhi Middle Sch., China, 1971-73, Xi'an (China) Jiaotong U., 1994—2003; ret. Vice dean of studies Shanxi Labour U., 1965-66; dir. tchg. Northwestern Agrl. U., 1990-93; dir. inst. Xi'an Jiaotong U., 1994-98; vice-dir. Shaanxi Biochem. Soc., 1995-2005; vis. scholar dept. botany U. Durham, Eng., 1981-83; vis. prof. dept. biol. sci. U. Calgary, Can., 1991. Author: Gene Engineering of Seed Proteins, 1995; editor: Teaching Material of Biochemistry, 1979, Teaching Material for Plant Molecular Biology, 1986; translator Introduction of Plant Biochemistry, 1988; contbr. over 167 articles to profl. jours. Mem. alliance Shaanxi Province, 1985. Recipient Prize State Coun. of China, 1992. Fellow Chinese Soc. of Biochemistry and Molecular Biology (dir. agrl. com. 1993), Chinese Soc. of Cell Biology. Achievements include research in gene engineering of seed proteins and plant molecular biology. Avocation: reading. Home: PO Box 065 3 Cun 34 Bldg Xi'an Jiaotong Univ Xi'an 710048 China Office: Dept Biosci & Engring Sch Life Scis & Tech Xi'an Jiaotong U Xi'an 710049 China Home: 144 Sunrise Pl Vestal NY 13850 E-mail: wmzhao2004@yahoo.com, wmzhao@mail.xjtu.edu.cn.

ZHAO, XIANFENG FRANK, pathologist, educator; s. Chuanzhong Zhao and Chuanyu Dong; m. Min Yu, Jan. 27, 1992; children: Helen, Walter. MD, Shandong U., Jinan, China, 1985; PhD, U. We. Ont., London, Can., 1996. Lic. Ind., 2002, Pa., 2003, Mo., 2004, Md., 2005. Postdoctoral fellow Roswell Park Cancer Inst., Buffalo, 1996—99; pathology resident SUNY, Buffalo, 1999—2003; clin. fellow U. Pa., Phila., 2003—04; asst. prof. pathology and immunology sch. medicine Wash. U., St. Louis, 2004—05; asst. prof. pathology sch. medicine U. Md., Balt., 2005—. Dir. hematopathology fellowship med. ctr. U. Md., Balt., 2006—. Mem.: US and Can. Acad. Pathologists, Am. Soc. Hematology, Soc. Hematopathology. Office: Univ Maryland Sch Med 22 S Greene St NBW78 Baltimore MD 21201 Office Phone: 410-328-5555.

ZHAO, XUEHENG, research scientist; s. Dishun Zhao and Shouzhen Wang; m. Tang Yarong, May 1, 1999. BE, Beijing Inst. Clothing Tech., 1994; PhD, U. Ga., Athens, 2004. Instr. Dept. Applied Chemistry, Beijing U. Chem. Tech., 1997—99; rsch. asst. U. Ga., Athens, 1999—2004; postdoctoral rsch. scientist Dept. Biology, Jackson State U., Miss., 2004—. Reviewer (jour.) Jour. of Hazardous Materials. Student Rsch. grantee, Am. Assn. of Textile Chemists and Colorists, 2001. Mem.: Am. Chem. Soc. (assoc.), Miss. Acad. of Sci. (assoc.). Home Phone: 601-979-1226; Office Phone: 601-979-1226. E-mail: xueheng.zhao@jsums.edu.

ZHAO, ZHEN, music educator; b. Tian Jin, China, Aug. 27, 1947; arrived in U.S., 1985; parents Tian Qi Zhao and Pei Ying Gong; m. Yang Zhong Zhang, Apr. 29, 1976; 1 child, William Wen Wei Zhang. *Husband Yang Zhong Zhang earned his physics PhD from the University of Texas at Austin in 1988. Son William Wen Wei Zhang received his Bachelor of Science degree in Electrical Engineering from the University of Texas at Austin in 2002. After graduating, he established a web site design company under the name of Star 16 Studios. He has launched numerous web sites for clients in many fields.* MusB, U. Tex., 1991, MusM, 1994. Pvt. piano tchr., Austin, Tex., 1995—. Contbr. articles to profl. jours. Mem.: Nat. Guild Piano Tchrs., Music Tchrs. Nat. Assn., Tex. Music Tchrs. Assn., Austin Dist. Music Tchrs. Assn. Achievements include established the Zhen Zhao piano studio; her students have won numerous piano competitions. Avocations: ping pong/table tennis, tai chi, travel, photography. Personal E-mail: zhaozhen@austin.rr.com.

ZHARIKOV, ALEXANDER NIKOLAEVICH, trade union federation executive; b. Michailov, Rjazan, Russia, Jan. 2, 1945; s. Nikolaj Philippovich and Claudia Egorovna (Gorodnicheva) Z.; m. Eva Svachova; children: Michail, Anette. Student, Shipbldg. Inst., Leningrad, Russia, 1969. Sec. Student Orgn. Shipbldg. Inst., Leningrad, 1967-70; dir. student dept. Leningrad City Youth Orgn., Leningrad, 1970-71, sec., 1971-74; vice chmn. Com. Youth Orgns. USSR, Moscow, 1974-76; chmn. Student Coun. USSR, Moscow, 1976-78; v.p. Internat. Union Students, Prague, Czechoslovakia, 1978-84; officer Internat. Dept. Ctrl. Com. CPSU, Moscow, 1984-88; dir. internat. dept. All Union Ctrl. Coun. Trade Unions, Moscow, 1988-90; gen. sec. World Fedn. Trade Unions, Prague, 1990—. Co-author: International Union of Students, 1978. Mem. City Com. Leningrad Youth Orgn., 1970-71, sec., 1971-74; mem. Ctrl. Com. Youth Orgn. USSR, Moscow, 1978-84. Capt. Russian mil., 1962-66. Personal E-mail: evaanete@seznam.cz.

ZHDANOV, BORIS, research scientist; MSc in Physics, Moscow State U., 1970, PhD, 1975. Assoc. prof. Moscow State U., 1988—99; vis. prof. USAF Acad., Colo., 1998—2000, sr. scientist, 2004—; prin. scientist Directed Energy Solutions, Inc., Colorado Springs, 2000—04. Office Phone: 719-333-2109. Business E-Mail: boris.zhdanov@usafa.edu.

ZHEN, JUAN, medical researcher; arrived in US, 2001; d. Zhizhong Zhen and Suzhen Yuan; m. Ke Zhang, Mar. 28, 2000; children: Michael Zhang, Claire Zhang. PhD, Ill. State U., Normal, 2005. Rsch. asst. Ill. State U., Normal, 2001, U. Ill., Chgo. Med. Sch., Peoria, 2001—03; asst. rsch. scientist NYU Med. Ctr., 2005—. Office: NYU Med Ctr 550 First Ave New York NY 10016

ZHEN, LI, systems analyst, researcher; d. Shumin Li and Lingqin Zhao; m. Xiangpeng Jing, May 20, 2006. BS, Zhengzhou U., 1999; MS, Beijing U. Posts and Telecom., 2002; PhD, Rutgers U., New Brunswick, NJ, 2007. Tchg. asst., dept. elec. and computer engring. Rutgers U., Piscataway, NJ, 2002—05, rsch. asst., dept. elec. and computer engring., 2005—. Summer lectr. Rutgers Engring. Sch., Piscataway, NJ, 2005. Contbr. articles to profl. jours. Scholar, Zhengzhou U., 1995—99. Achievements include development of comet coordination infrastructure; rudder agent framework; cometG computational infrastructure; cometG/GARE asynchronous replica exchange engine. Office: Rutgers Univ Piscataway NJ 08854 Home Phone: 732-445-3807; Office Phone: 732-445-3807. Personal E-mail: zhljenny@gmail.com.

ZHENG, GANG, mathematician, statistician, researcher; arrived in U.S., 1994; s. Chang-Gen Zheng; m. Liu Ling-Xian. BS in Applied Math., Fudan U., Shanghai, 1987; MS in Math., Mich. Technol. U., 1996; PhD in Stats., George Washington U., 2000. Lectr. Shanghai Second Poly. U., 1987—94; math. statistician Nat. Heart, Lung and Blood Inst., Bethesda, Md., 2000—. Contbr. articles to profl. jours. Fellow: The Royal Statis. Soc.; mem.: Internat. Statis Inst., Internat. Biometrics Soc., Internat. Indian Statis. Assn. (life), Internat. Chinese Statis. Assn. (life), Inst. Math. Stats., Am. Statis. Assn. Office: National Heart Lung and Blood Institute 6701 Rockledge Dr MSC 7938 Room 8223 Bethesda MD 20892-7938 Office Phone: 301-435-1287.

ZHENG, JAMES, architectural firm executive; b. 1970; BA in Arch., Univ. Ill. Chgo., 1995; MBA student, Northwestern Univ. Kellogg Sch. Bus. Assoc. prin. Goettsch Ptnrs., Chgo., 1995—2005, dir. Asian ops., 1995—, ptnr., 2005—. Named one of 40 Under Forty, Crain's Chgo. Bus., 2005. Office: Goettsch Ptnrs Inc Floor 17 224 S Michigan Ave Chicago IL 60604 Office Phone: 312-356-0600. Office Fax: 312-356-0601. *

ZHENG, LINGYI ALBERT, materials scientist, materials engineer, researcher; s. Cheng and Yuhe Zheng; m. Zhenwan Jennifer Xu; 1 child, Albert D. PhD, Rice U., Houston, 1999. Sr. engr. Micron Tech., Boise, Idaho, 1999—2004, Micron Tech. Inc, Manassas, Va., 2004—. Contbr. articles to profl. jours. Scholar, Rice U., 1995. Mem.: IEEE. Achievements include patents in field. Home Phone: 571-278-3678; Office Phone: 703-396-1452. Personal E-mail: albertzheng@yahoo.com.

ZHENG, MIN, engineer; d. ZiYing Zhao and Shuzhong Zheng; m. Xiangdong Bi, Apr. 19, 1995. PhD, Inst. Physics, Chinese Acad. Scis., 1997. Postdoc. rsch. assoc. Ctr. Materials Rsch. and Analysis, Dept. Physics, U. Nebr., Lincoln, 1998—2000; staff R&D engr. Maxtor Corp./MMC Tech., San Jose, Calif., 2000—. Postdoc. fellow Max-Planck-Instt. Mikrostrucktur, Halle/Saale, Germany, 1997—98. Contbr. articles to profl. jours., The Royal Fellowship fellow, 1997. Mem.: Sigma Xi. Achievements include patents pending for. Home: 284 Rio Verde Pl #3 Milpitas CA 95035 Office: MMC Technology 2001 Fortune Dr San Jose CA 95131 E-mail: zhengmin70@hotmail.com.

ZHENG, QI, statistician, biomathematician; b. Lanxi, Zhejiang, China, July 8, 1958; arrived in U.S., 1988; s. Huanming Zheng and Sulan Zhuge; m. Huiping Hu, May 12, 1987; children: Yan, Eric Hugh. BS in math., Zhejiang U., 1978—82; PhD in stats., Tex. A&M U., 1988—93, postgrad., 1993. Cert. independent Mathematica trainer. Post-doc Nat. Ctr. Toxicological Rsch., Jefferson, Ark., 1994—96, staff fellow, 1996—2002; rsch. scientist Tex. A&M U., College Station, 2002—03, assoc. prof. dept. epidemiology and biostats. Sch. Rural Pub. Health, 2003—. Contbr. articles to jour. (Commendable Svc. award, FDA, 1997). Grantee Mathematica Vis. Scholar Grant, Wolfram Rsch. Inc., 1995, 1997. Mem.: Am. Statis. Assn., Phi Kappa Phi. Achievements include research in directed mutation hypothesis; irrelevancy of dispersion index in the molecular clock controversy; stochastic modeling of carcinogenesis: development of algorithms and first comprehensive computer software SALVADOR for estimating mutation rates using data from fluctuation experiments. Avocations: reading, mountain hiking, music. Office: Tex A&M U Sys Health Sci Ctr Sch Rural Pub Health Dept Epidemiology and Biostats College Station TX 77843 E-mail: qzheng@srph.tamhsc.edu.

ZHENG, WENXIN, gynecologist, pathologist; MD, Shanghai Med. U., China, 1983. Diplomate Am. Bd. Pathology, 1996. Asst. prof. pathology and gynecology U. So. Calif., LA, 1996—2000; assoc. prof. pathology and gynecology Yale U., New Haven, 2000—05; tenured prof. pathology and gynecology U. Ariz., Tucson, 2005—. Funding pres. Assn. Chinese Physicians - Calif., LA, 1997—2001. Achievements include research in precursor lesions of gynecologic cancers. Office: Univ Ariz 1501 N Campbell Ave Tucson AZ 85718

ZHITNIK, ALEXEI, professional hockey player; b. Kiev, Russia, Oct. 10, 1972; m. Luda Zhitnik. Defenseman La Kings, 1992—95, Buffalo Sabres, 1995—2005, NY Islanders, 2005—06, Phila. Flyers, 2006—07, Atlanta Thrashers, 2007—. Mem. def. team Russia World Championships, Austria, 1996, World Cup Tournament, 1996, World Championships, Italy, 1993—94; rep. Gold medal unified team Albertville Winter Olympics, France, 1992. Office: Atlanta Thrashers Centennial Tower, Ste 1900 101 Marietta Street NW Atlanta GA 30303 Office Phone: 516-501-6700. Office Fax: 516-501-6762.

ZHONG, QIXIN, physical chemist, chemistry professor; B of Engring., Wuhan Poly. U., 1993; PhD, NC State U., Raleigh, 2003. Engr. Chinese Acad. Agrl. Scis., Beijing, 1993—98; rsch. asst. NC State U., Raleigh, 1999—2003; post-doctoral rsch. assoc. Iowa State U., Ames, 2003—05; asst. prof. U. Tenn., Knoxville, 2005—. Panelist USDA Coop. State Rsch. and Extension Svc., Washington; presenter in field. Contbr. articles to profl. jours. Recipient Third Pl. award Math. Competition, Wuhan Food Industry Coll., 1993, Outstanding Contbr. award, U. Tex. Food Sci. Club, 2006, Profl. Devel. award, U. Tenn.; grantee, So. Region Fruits Rsch. Consortium, 2007; scholar, Wuhan Food Industry Coll., 1989—93; Idea grantee, U. Tenn. Inst. Agr., 2006. Mem.: AIChE, Chinese Am. Food Soc., Am. Chem. Soc., Inst. Food Technologists. Achievements include patents pending for method for purifying nisin and sustained release encapsulated microbials such as nisin; invention of non-thermal pasteurization of prouce; modification of protein functionalities with supercritical fluids; cellulose particle stabilizer. Office: Univ Tenn 2509 River Dr Knoxville TN 37996-4539 Business E-Mail: qzhong@utk.edu.

ZHONG, SHENG, computer scientist; b. Nanjing, Jiangsu, China, May 25, 1974; arrived in US, 1999; s. Quisheng Zhong and Ying Long; m. Yue Ji, July 5, 2005. BS, Nanjing U., China, 1996, MEd, 1999; PhD, Yale U., New Haven, Conn., 2004. Rschr. DIMACS Ctr., Stevens Tech., NJ, 2004—05; asst. prof. SUNY, Buffalo, 2005—. Office: SUNY Computer Sci & Engring 201 Bell Hall Buffalo NY 14260

ZHOU, BANG RONG, physicist, researcher; b. Chengdu, Sichuan, China, Apr. 18, 1941; s. Fu Cheng and Ying Juan (Wang) Z.; m. Yong Pu Kang, Feb. 2, 1981; 1 child, Xiao Zhi. Grad., U. Sci. and Tech. China, Beijing, 1963, degree, 1966. Tchg. asst. U. Sci. and Tech. of China, Hefei, 1973-78, lectr., 1979-85, assoc. prof. Grad. Sch., Chinese Acad. Scis. Beijing, 1985-87, 87-90, prof., 1990—. Vis. scholar Fermi Nat. Accelerator Lab., Batavia, 1981-83, Stanford Linear Accelerator Ctr., Calif., 1983; assoc. vis. prof. Internat. Centre for Theoretical Physics, Trieste, Italy, 1992, 94, 98; judging specialist Nat. Natural Sci. award of China in Physics and Astronomy, 2002-. Author: Quantum Field Theory; contbr. articles to profl. jours. including Atomic Energy, Nuclear Physics B, Physics Letters B, Phys. Rev. D, others. Recipient award Chinese Nat. Sci. Conf., 1978, Sci. Achievements award Chinese Acad. Scis., 1981, award Nat. Natural Sci. of China, 1982, Spl. Allowance Upon Contbn. to Chinese Advanced

Edn. award The State Coun. of China, 1992. Mem. Chinese Assn. High Energy Physics, Chinese Assn. Physics, Western Returned Scholars' Assn. Achievements include participating in work on straton (quark) model of hadrons; creative research on asymptotic freedom in heavy quark potential, dynamical chiral and electroweak symmetry breaking, finite temperature field theory and phase transitions. Avocations: collecting stamps and coins, swimming, ping-pong, classical music, athletic competition, detective films on television. Office: Chinese Acad Scis Grad Sch Beijing 100049 China Home Phone: 0086-010-62620024. E-mail: zhoubr@163bj.com, zhoubr@gucas.ac.cn.

ZHOU, DAZHUANG, aerospace scientist, researcher; s. Xianghuan Zhou and Gulan Deng; m. Beibei Xu; 1 child, Yi. PhD in Physics, Nat. U. Ireland, Dublin, 1999. Assoc. rschr. Fermi Inst., U. Chgo., 1983—85; assoc. prof. U. Sci. and Tech. China, Hefei, 1990—96; rschr. Nat. Agy. for Radiation Protection, Rome, 1992—94, Dublin Inst. for Advanced Studies, 1996—2004, NASA-Johnson Space Ctr., Houston, 2004—. Master: NASA-Johnson Space Ctr. Home Phone: 281-333-0431; Office Phone: 281-244-6196. Business E-Mail: dzhou@ems.jsc.nasa.gov.

ZHOU, DESHENG, petroleum engineer; b. Wusheng, Sichuan, China, Nov. 1963; s. L. Zhou and H. Luong; m. Xiaoping Zhang, Sept. 1988; children: Ruoyao, Jennifer Aileen. BS, Beijing U., Aeronautics and Astronautics, China, 1985; MS, S.W. Petroleum Inst., China, 1988; D in Engring., S.W. Petroleum Inst., 1992; PhD, La. State U., 2000. Cert. petroleum engineer, China. Engr. China Nat. Petroleum Corp., Nanchong, Sichuan, China, 1988—94, vice chmn. petroleum-mech. engring. dept., 1994—96; from rsch. assoc. to rsch. asst. La. State U., Baton Rouge, 1996—2000; sr. petroleum engr. IHS Energy, Dallas, 2000—. Contbr. articles to profl. jours. Recipient 2d Class award, Tech. and Sci. Progress. Mem.: China Soc. Petroleum Engrs. (dir. Nanchong divsn. 1994—96), Nat. Petroleum Engring. Honor Soc. Achievements include patents for parabolic tooth of roller cone bit; design of three types of roller cone bits: XHP1s, XHP2s, and XHP3s; research in computer simulation of rock-bit interaction, leak-off tests in shallow marine sediments. Home: 7510 David Dr Frisco TX 75034 Office: Ihs Energy 17177 Preston Rd # 200 Dallas TX 75248-1235 Personal E-mail: deshzhou@yahoo.com. Business E-Mail: desheng.zhou@ihsenergy.com.

ZHOU, HONG, engineering educator; s. Deyong and Huayue Zhou; m. Yufang Wang. PhD, U. So. Miss., 2004. Asst. prof. St. Joseph Coll., West Hartford, Conn., 2004—. Mem. editl. bd.: IJCSIS, IJCITP. Recipient Best Sports Svc. award, U. So. Miss., 2000. Mem.: IEEE, Assn. Computing Machines, Simsbury Badminton Club. Achievements include patents for Sword2.0. Office: Saint Joseph Coll 1678 Asylum Ave West Hartford CT 06117 Office Phone: 860-231-5826.

ZHOU, LIMING, environmental scientist; m. Ying Zhang, Apr. 5, 2006. BS, Tsinghua U., Beijing, China, 1998; MS, Dalian Inst. Chem. Physics, China, 2001; PhD, Clarkson U., Potsdam, NY, 2004. Rsch. asst. Clarkson U., 2001—04; environ. scientist Providence Engring., Baton Rouge, 2004—05, sr. environ. scientist Batron Rouge, 2005—. Designer (atmospheric environment) Intelligent Air Monitor System (Albert Einstein Award by Providence Engring., 2004). Chmn. Chinese Students and Scholar Assn., Potsdam, 2003. Mem.: Am. Chem. Soc., Am. Assn. Aerosol Rsch. Achievements include development of advanced receptor model methods and cheometric tools to further our understanding of the origin and characteristics of atmospheric pollutants; environment algorithm software and information system; air quality monitoring insrumentation. Office: Providence Engring and Environ 1201 Main St Baton Rouge LA 70802 Office Phone: 225-766-7400. Office Fax: 225-766-7440. Business E-Mail: limingzhou@providenceeng.com.

ZHOU, MIN, geophysicist; s. Zhongxian Zhou and Qinfang Jiang; m. Chunyu Xu, Nov. 21, 1996; 1 child, Joshua J. BS, Peking U., Beijing, China, 1991, MS, 1994; PhD, U. Utah, Salt Lake City, 2005. Instr. Peking U., 1994—98; rsch. asst. U. Utah, Salt Lake City, 1999—2005; geophysicist BP Am., Inc., Houston, 2005—. Dean asst. dept. geophys. Peking U., 1994—96; intern INCO, Sudbury, Ontario, 2001, Veritas DGC Inc, Houston, 2003, Bp Am., Houston, 2005; geophysicist GX Tech., Houston, 2005. Guanghua scholar, Peking U., 1992—93. Mem.: Soc. Exploration Geophysicist (assoc.). Achievements include research in multiple elimination: 2D and 3D primary only imaging condition, radon domain multiple elimination, and wave equation based multiple elimination; wave equation modeling, inversion and migration: 2D/3D acoustic/elastic wave equation modeling, wave equation waveform inversion, reverse-time migration and wave equation wavefront migration; interferometric imaging: Interferometric migration and datuming of CDP data, and reduced-time migration; traveltime tomography: refraction traveltime tomography and interferometric traveltime tomography. Office: BP America Inc 501 Westlake Park Blvd 14 114B Houston TX 77079 Home Phone: 281-531-5015; Office Phone: 281-366-7017. Personal E-mail: mzhou04@hotmail.com.

ZHOU, NAN, finance educator; BA, Tsinghua U., Beijing, 1989; M, So. Ill. U., Carbondale, 1993; PhD, U. Minn., Mpls., 2000. Lectr. SUNY, Binghamton, 1999—2000, asst. prof., 2000—06, assoc. prof., 2006—. Vis. scholar NYU, 2005, Zhejiang U., China, 2006; rsch. assoc. Inst. Fin. and Acctg. Studies, Xiamen U., China, 2006—. Contbr. articles to profl. jours. and pubs. Office: SUNY Sch Mgmt Binghamton NY 13902-6000 Home Phone: 607-729-2511; Office Phone: 607-777-2401. Business E-Mail: nzhou@binghamton.edu.

ZHOU, PENGBO, medical educator; b. Beijing; PhD, U. Mich. Med. Sch., Ann Arbor, 1993. Instr. Harvard Med. Sch., Boston, 1999—99, postdoctoral fellow, 1996—99, U. Chgo., Chgo., 1994—96; asst. prof. Cornell U. Weill Med. Coll., NYC, 1999—2005, assoc. prof., 2006—. Cons. Rigel Pharm., South San Francisco, 2001—02. Contbr. articles to profl. jours. Recipient Rsch. award, Dorothy Rodbell Cohen Found., 2000—01, 2003—04, award, Mary Kay Ash Charitable Found., 2000—02, Acad. award, Beijing U., 1986—87, Irmat Hirschl Career Scientist award, 2007—, Young Investigator award, AMDeC Found., 2000—03, Lee Murphy Meml. award, U. Mich. Dept. Biology, 1992; fellow, Horace H. Rackham Sch. Grad. Studies, U. Mich., 1991—92; grantee Travel grant, Am. Assn. Cancer Rsch., 1994, various grants, NIH; scholar, Leukemia and Lymphoma Soc., 2000—01, Sidney Kimmel Found. Cancer Rsch., 2000—02. Mem.: Am. Soc. Hematology. Achievements include patents for developed the protein knockout technology. Office Phone: 212-746-6415.

ZHOU, QIUPING, nursing educator, director; d. Xiaohu Zhou and Qynqin Mao; m. Shenbao Qiu, Dec. 31, 1985; children: Jessica W. Qiu, Christopher W. Qiu. MSN, U. Alta., Edmonton, Can., 1994; PhD, U. Md., Balt., 2001. Asst. prof. George Mason U., Fairfax, Va., 2006—. Dir. program Avon-Inova Cares Breast Cancer Network, Falls Church, Va., 2002—; health rschr. Inova Fairfax Hosp., Falls Church, 1998—. Contbr. articles to profl. jours. Fundraiser Avon Walk Breast Cancer, Washington, 2005—07. Recipient Dissertation award, 2001. Mem.: Sigma Theta Tau (hon.). Office: George Mason Univ 4400 Univ Dr Fairfax VA 22030 Home Phone: 703-426-5769; Office Phone: 703-993-9167. Business E-Mail: qzhou3@gmu.edu.

ZHOU, SHAO MAN, chemist, researcher; arrived in US, 2000; s. Xingde Zhou and Huixiu Yi; m. Yi Huang, Mar. 1, 2000. BA, Jiangxi Normal U., 1994; PhD, Shanghai Inst. Organic Chemistry, Chinese Acad. Sci., 2000. Postdoctoral fellow Wayne State U., Detroit, 2000—03, rsch. assoc., 2003—. Recipient award, BASF, 2000, Chinese Acad. Scis., 2000. Mem.: Am. Chem. Soc. Achievements include patents for 2, 2-BIS(hydroxymethyl) cyclopropylidenemethyl -purines, -pyrimidines as antiviral agents; research in synthesis of stereodefined (chiral) cyclopropylboronic acids and their application. Home Phone: 313-832-8784. Personal E-mail: shaomanzhou@yahoo.com.

ZHOU, SOPHIA HUAI, biomedical engineering scientist; b. Huaiyin, Jiangsu, China, Dec. 6, 1953; MS, Dalhousie U., Halifax, Can., 1987, PhD, 1991. Profl. engr., Nova Scotia. Rsch. assoc. U. Alta., Edmonton, Canada, 1991-93, asst. prof., 1993-94, St. Louis U., 1994—95; engring. scientist Hewlett-Packard Co., Andover, Mass., 1995-99; prin. scientist Agilent Techs. Inc., Andover, Mass., 1999—2001; sr. rsch. mgr. Advanced Algorithm Rsch. Ctr.; prin. scientist Philips Med Sys., Thousand Oaks, Calif., 2001—. Contbr. articles to profl. jours.; editor: Jour. of Electrocardiology. Mem. editl. bd. Journ. of Electro Cardiology. Fellow Am. Coll. Cardiology; mem. NY Acad. Sci., Soc. Women Engrs., Internat. Soc. Electrocardiology, Internat. Soc. Computerized Electrocardiology, Am. Heart Assn., Assn. for Advancement of Med. Instrumentation, Internat. Electromagnetic Commn. (convener). Achievements include design of automated ECG interpretations. Office: Philips Med Sys 1525 Rancho Conejo Blvd Ste 100 Thousand Oaks CA 91320 Business E-Mail: sophia.zhou@philips.com.

ZHOU, YIQUN, humanities educator; b. Yongxin, China, 1971; d. Yuanbiao Zhou and Peiqiong Liu. PhD, U. Chgo., 2004. Asst. prof. Asian langs. Stanford U., Calif., 2006—. Home Phone: 219-241-3331. Business E-Mail: yzhou1@stanford.edu.

ZHOU, YONG-PIN, finance educator; 1 child, Aidan J. MA, Johns Hopkins U., Balt., 1995; PhD, U. Pa., Phila., 2000. Asst. prof. U. Wash. Bus. Sch., Seattle, 2000—. Mem.: Inst. Ops. Rsch. and Mgmt. Sci. Office: U Wash Bus Sch Box 353200 Seattle WA 98195-3200 Office Phone: 206-221-5324.

ZHU, LIE, physics professor; BS in Space Physics, U. Sci. and Tech. of China, Hefei, 1982, MS in Space Sci., 1985; PhD in Space Physics, U. Alaska, Fairbanks, 1990. Contbr. articles to profl. jours., chapters to books. Mem.: Am. Geophys. Union (guest editor Radio Sci. 1994—98), Com. on Space Rsch. (assoc.). Office: Utah State U Old Main Hill Logan UT 84322-4405 Office Phone: 435-797-2967. Business E-Mail: zhu@cc.usu.edu.

ZHU, MINGZHAO, immunologist, microbiologist; b. Baodi, Tianjin, China, June 27, 1976; arrived in US, 2004; s. Guohui Zhu and Guifang Zhao; m. Xiaojuan Liu, Oct. 2, 2002; 1 child, Candice Jinning. BS, Peking U., Beijing, 1998; PhD, Chinese Acad. Med. Scis., Beijing, 2003. Rsch. assoc. U. Chgo., 2004—. Editor: English-Chinese Dictionary of Medicine, 1999; contbr. articles to profl. jours. Recipient Outstanding Grad. award, Peking U., 1998, Excellent PhD Student award, Chinese Acad. Med. Scis., 1999—2002; scholar, Aetna Inc., 1997; Orient Overseas Container Line Ltd. scholar, Hong Kong's Tung Found., 1995, Conf. fellow, NY Acad. Scis., 2006. Mem.: Am. Assn. Immunologists, Sigma Xi. Achievements include research in NF-kappaB2 is required for the establishment of central tolerance through an Aire-dependent pathway; co-immunization with B7-1 costimulatory gene enhanced HPV16 E6E7 DNA vaccine-induced specific immune responses; study on HSV-1gD DNA vaccine to protect mice cornea from primary viral challenge; prophylactic and therapeutic vaccines for human papillomavirus infections and associated neoplasia; mutations and sequencing of HPV16E6E7 gene of human papillomavirus from patients with HPV infection in Beijing; lymphotoxin pathway-directed, autoimmune regulator-independent central tolerance to arthritogenic collagen; enhancement of DNA vaccine potency against herpes simplex virus 1 by co-administration of an interleukin-18 expression plasmid as a genetic adjuvant; enhancement of herpes simplex virus-1 glycoprotein-D DNA vaccine induced specific immune responses by coimmunization with interleukin-2 genetic adjuvant; construction of herpes simplex virus type I glycoprotein D DNA vaccine and its preliminary study; enhancement of human papillomavirus type 16E6E7 vaccine-induced specific immune response by coimmunization with B7-1 co-stimulatory gene; recent development of herpes simplex virus vaccine; immunogenicity of human papillomavirus 16 E6E7 fusion genes was increased by gene modification; AIRE or not: the role of LTbR(TNFRSF3) in negative selection. Office: University of Chicago 5841 S Maryland Ave Chicago IL 60637

ZHU, QIANG, education educator; s. Tingyi Zhu and Jingqin Xu; m. Yanping Zhang; children: Han, Kayla Jie. BSc, S.E. U., China, 1978—82, MEng, 1982—84; MSc, McMaster U., Can., 1988—90; PhD, U. Waterloo, Can., 1990—95. Lectr. SE U., 1984—88; vis. scientist IBM Centre for Advanced Studies, Toronto, Canada, 1998—2005, faculty fellow, 2003—; asst. prof. U. Mich., Dearborn, 1995—2001, assoc. prof., 2001—07, prof., 2007—. Assoc. editor Internat. Jour. Computers and Their Applications, 2005—; program com. mem., numerous internat. confs., 1998—2007; workshop/track/session/publicity chair, numerous internat. confs., 1985—2007. Contbr. articles to profl. jours. and pubs. Recipient Partnership Rsch. award, IBM U. Rels., 1999, Faculty award, 2003, 2004; Rsch. grant, NSF, 1998, IBM Toronto Lab., 1998, 2002, 2007, NSF, 2005. Mem.: IEEE, Assn. Computing Machinery. Achievements include research in techniques for multidatabase cost modeling, multidimensional non-ordered discrete data space indexing, etc. Office: Univ Mich 4901 Evergreen Rd Dearborn MI 48128-1491

ZHU, YINGWU, application developer, educator; BS, Huazhong U. Sci. & Tech., Wuhan, 1994, MS, 1997; PhD, U. Cin., Ohio, 2005. Cert. Mcse Microsoft, 1999, Mcp Miscrosoft, 1999. Software engr. and project mgr. J&A Securities Co. Ltd., Shenzheng, Guangdong, China, 1997—2000; asst. prof. Seattle U., 2005—. Program com. mem., registration co-chair Internat. Conf. Networking, Arch., and Storage, Guilin, China, 2007—; program com. mem. IFIP Internat. Conf., Taipei, 2007—, Internat. Workshop on File Sys. and Storage Technol., Beijing, 2007—, 4th Middleware Doctoral Symposium, Newport Beach, Calif., 2007—; reviewer IEEE Comm. Letters, Internat. Jour. Network Security, Jour. Parallel and Distributed Computing, IEEE Transactions Computer, IEEE Transactions Parallel and Distributed Sys., and numerious conferences. Contbr. articles various profl. jours.

ZHU, YONG, research scientist; b. Shanghai, Oct. 30, 1947; s. Shuping Chu and Zhiping Wang; m. Shaokui Wang, Apr. 22, 1977; 1 child, Shenke. B of Engr., East China Inst. Chem. Tech., Shanghai, 1981; postgrad., Tianhin Inst. Textile Engring., 1982; PhD in Organic Chemistry, U. Ill., 1992. Laborer Qingdao (China) Cigarette Manufacture, 1968-72; rsch. asst. Qingdao Inst. Light Industry, 1972-77; asst. prof., head dept. Shandong Inst. Textile Engring., China, 1983-87; vis. scientist U. Ill., Urbana, 1987-88, tchg./rsch. asst., 1988-92, postdoctoral rsch. assoc., 1992-93; scientist Procter and Gamble Far East, Kobe, Japan, 1993-95; sr. staff scientist Procter and Gamble Co., Cin., 1995—. Cons. Qingdao Manufacture of Dyeing Auxiliaries, 1983-87, Jiaonan Manufacture of Fragrances, China, 1984-87; hon. prof. Qingolao U., China, 2004. Patentee in field; contbr. chpts. to books and articles to profl. jours. Recipient Edn. scholarship Chinese Edn. Assn., 1987. Mem. Am. Chem. Soc. (vol. in pub. outreach 1991-95), Inter-Am. Photochem. Soc., Chinese Color-Optical Soc., Shandong Textile Engring. Assn. Achievements include patent in field. Avocations: volleyball, swimming, violin, travel, ballroom dancing.

ZHUANG, XIAOWEI, biophysicist, educator; BS in Physics, U. of Sci. and Tech., China, 1991; MS in Physics, U. Calif., Berkeley, 1993, PhD., 1996. Post doc. fellow Stanford U. Dept. of Physics, Stanford, Calif., 1997—2001; asst. prof., dept. chemistry and chemical biology Harvard U., Cambridge, Mass., 2001—05, asst. prof., dept. physics, 2001—05, assoc. prof. chem. and chemical biology, 2005—, assoc. prof. physics, 2005—. Mem. standing com., biophysics program Harvard U., 2002—, mem. exec. com., Ctr. for Imaging and Mesoscopic Sci., 2002—04; mem. steering com. Broad Inst., 2003—, Harvard U., 2003—, MIT, 2003—; Howard Hughes Med. Inst. Investigator, 2005; Gunnar and Gunnel Kallén Lectr. Lund U., Sweden, 2004; Jean-François Lefèvre Lectr. Ecole Supérieure de Biotechnologie de Stansbourg, France, 2004. Named to Worlds Top 100 Young Innovators award, Technology Review, 2004; recipient Bernice Teuteberg Mem. Scholarship, U. Calif., 1991, George C. and Helen N. Pardee Scholarship, 1992, Victor F. Lenzen Mem. Scholarship, 1993, Chodorow Postdoctoral Fellowship, Stanford U., 1997, Individual Nat. Rsch. Svc. award, Nat. Inst. of Health, 2000, Young Investigator award, Office Naval Rsch., 2002, Beckman Young Investigator award, 2003, Searle Scholarship, 2003, CAREER award, Nat. Sci. Found., 2003, Camille Dreyfus Teacher-Scholar award, 2005; Packard Fellowship for Sci. and Engring., 2003, MacArthur Fellowship, 2003, Alfred P. Sloan Rsch. Fellowship, 2004. Mem.: Am. Biophysical Soc., Am. Soc. Cell Biology, Am. Chemical Soc. (award in pure chemistry 2007), Am. Physical Soc. Office: Dept Chemistry and Chemical Biology Harvard U 12 Oxford St Cambridge MA 02138 Office Phone: 617-496-9558. Office Fax: 617-496-9559. Business E-Mail: zhuang@chemistry.harvard.edu.

ZHUK, SERGEI IVANOVICH, history professor, researcher; b. Vatutino, Ukraine, Dec. 18, 1958; s. Ivan Grigorovich Zhuk and Valentina Fedorovan Kochetkova; m. Irina Mikhailovna Kozintseva, Sept. 27, 1959; 1 child, Andrey Sergeievich. Kandidat istoricheskikh nauk, Inst. World History, Soviet Acad. Scis., 1987; Doktor istoricheskikh nauk, Dnipropetrovsk State U., Ukraine, 1996; PhD, Johns Hopkins U., 2002. Assoc. prof. Dnipropetrovs'k State U., Dnipropetrovs'k, 1989—97; asst. prof. Ball State U., Muncie, Ind., 2003—. Author: Russia's Lost Reformation, 2004. Recipient Mellon Fellowship, Am. Coun. of Learnes Socs., 2003—04; fellow Kennan Inst., Woodrow Wilson Internat. Ctr. for Scholars, 2002—03; grantee IARO, Internat. Exchage Bd., 1999—2000, Bellagio Ctr., Rockefeller Found., 1996, Fulbright, U.S. Govt., 1994—95. Mem.: Am. Assn. Advanced Slavic Studies, Am. Hist. Assn. Home: 2530 W White River Blvd Apt 6 Muncie IN 47303 Office: Ball State Univ Department of History Muncie IN 47306 Home Phone: 765-287-1203; Office Phone: 765-285-8735. Office Fax: 765-285-5612; Home Fax: 765-285-5612. Personal E-mail: zhuks@mail.ru. Business E-Mail: sizhuk@bsu.edu.

ZHUKOVSKY, ALEXANDER, mechanical engineer; b. St. Petersburg, Russia, Sept. 26, 1936; arrived in US, 1988; s. Valentin Zhukovsky and Valentina Zhukovsky - Guchman; m. Faina Margolin, Jan. 14, 1958; 1 child, Eugene. MS in Mech. Engring., Leningrad Poly. Inst., St. Petersburg, 1959, PhD in Mech. Engring., 1967. Mech. engr. Turbine Constrn. Corp., St. Petersburg, 1959—63; staff rschr. Boiler & Turbine Sci. Inst., St. Petersburg, 1966—71; sr. engr., sr. staff rschr. Electromashinery Corp. Electrosila, St. Petersburg, 1971—88; design engr. Plasma Fusion Ctr., MIT, Cambridge, Mass., 1988—89; sr. design engr. Francis Bitter Nat. Magnet Lab., MIT, Cambridge, 1990—96; rsch. engr. Plasma Sci. and Fusion Ctr., MIT, Cambridge, 1996—. Contbr. scientific papers in field cryogenics and applied superconductivity to profl. jours. Recipient Infinite Mile award for outstanding achievement as a rsch. engr., MIT, 2004. Achievements include patents for superconducting joint with niobium-tin; removable coil form for superconducting nmr magnets; device for checking an electrical machine cooling system; design of cryogenic equipment and superconducting magnets for nmr and plasma fusion research. Avocations: travel, skiing. Office: MIT Plasma Science and Fusion Center 190 Albany St NW22-209 Cambridge MA 02139 Office Phone: 617-258-5291.

ZHUKOVSKY, MIKHAIL ANDREYEVICH, biophysicist; b. Leningrad, Russia, Jan. 12, 1970; s. Andrey Pavlovich Zhukovsky and Valeria Grigoryevna Zhukovskaya. MSc, St. Petersburg State U., Russia, 1993, PhD, 1997. Rschr. St. Petersburg State U., 1997—98; post-doctoral fellow NIH, Bethesda, Md., 1998—2002, Dana-Farber Cancer Inst., Boston, 2002—. Scholar, Swedish Inst., Stockholm, 1995. Mem.: AAAS, Biophys. Soc. Avocations: chess, travel. Office: Dand Farber Cancer Inst 44 Binney St Boston MA 02115

ZI, GOANGSEUP, engineering educator; b. Suncheon, Jenlanam Do, Apr. 5, 1969; s. Gyu-Yul Zi and Myung-Ja Kim; m. Soo Yun Cho, Jan. 29, 1994; children: Haeun, Evelyn Hayoon, Hawon. BSc, Hanyang U., Korea, 1994, MSc, 1996; PhD, Northwestern U., 2002. 1st Grade Civil Engineer, KSCE / Seoul, Korea, 1994. Engr. Korea Infrastructure Safety and Tech., Anyang, Kyungki Do, Republic of Korea, 1996—97; postdoctoral fellow Northwestern U., Evanston, Ill., 2002—04; asst. prof. Korea U., Seoul, Republic of Korea, 2004—. Rsch., edn. Korea U., Seoul, Korea (South), 2004—. V.p. Korean Student Assn., Northwestern U., Evanston, Ill., 1998—99. Sgt. Korean Army, 1989—91, South Korea. Recipient Industry Stipend of Excellence, Larfarge and EDF, 2001, Best Lectr. award, Korea U., 2004—05; Walter P. Murphy hon. fellowship, Northwestern U., McCormick Sch. Engring., 1998-1999. Presbyterian. Achievements include research in size effect of negative-positive geometries, development of constitutive models, analysis of radionuclide decontamination using microwaves, computational mechanics; development of GFRP bridge deck system. Office: Korea U Anam Dong 5Ga 1 South Korea Seoul 136-701 Republic of Korea Home Phone: 82-2-948-3909; Office Phone: 82-2-3290-3324. Personal E-mail: g-zi@korea.ac.kr.

ZIBART, MICHAEL ALAN, wholesale book company executive; b. Nashville, Mar. 12, 1947; s. Alan Walter and Joy (Hughes) Z.; m. Margaret Anne Boyd, Dec. 27, 1976; children: Emily Joy, Mary Claire. BA, Vanderbilt U., 1969. Mgmt. trainee Zibart Bros. Books, Nashville, 1961-69; property mgr. Pollack Co., Nashville, 1966-69; buyer Ingram Book Co., Nashville, 1970-75, mgr. trade dept., 1976, v.p., 1976-85, exec. v.p., 1985-88; founder, pres. ProMotion, Inc., Nashville, 1988—. Author: Almanac on Bookselling, 3d edit., 1980; pub. (monthly book review) BookPage, 1988—. Office: ProMotion Inc 2143 Belcourt Ave Nashville TN 37212-3503 Office Phone: 615-292-8926.

ZIBELL, DONALD FREDRICK, lawyer; b. St. Paul, Feb. 13, 1937; s. Otto Ernst and Anna Emma Zibell; m. Luella Louise Lepisto, Oct. 14, 1967; 1 child, Deanne. BA, U. Minn., 1959; JD, William Mitchell Coll. Law, 1962. Bar: Minn.; cert. public acct. Minn. Mng. tax ptnr. Boulay, Heutmaker, Zibell and Co., PLLP, Mpls., 1959—90; real estate devel., 1965—; pvt. practice Roseville, Minn., 1990—. Dir. Cmty. Resource Bank, N.A., Northfield, Minn., 1999—; dir., treas. Poly-Cam, Inc., Blaine, Minn., 1992—; dir. Roseville (Minn.) Cmty. Bank, 1983—91. Trustee, treas. North Suburban Cmty. Found., Roseville, 1982—; dir., asst. treas. Donald and Luella Zibell Family Found., Shoreview, Minn., 1999—; trustee, exec. com. William Mitchell Coll. Law, St. Paul, 2002—; mem. various other charitable bds. and adv. coms. Named one of Ten Outstanding Young Men of Minn., Minn. Jaycees, 1971, 100 Who Made a Difference, William Mitchell Coll. Law, 2001. Mem.: ABA, Roseville Rotary Club (former pres. 1970—, Paul Harris fellow 1980), Minn. Soc. CPAs and AICPA (life; former com. chair 1964—). Republican. Luth. Avocations: gardening, reading, boating, golf, spectator sports. Home: 3422 Chandler Rd Saint Paul MN 55126-3914 Office: 2233 N Hamline Ave 511 Saint Paul MN 55113

ZIDICH, JOHN M., publishing executive; b. San Francisco, 1954; m. Pam Zidich; children: Katie, Ali. Circulation dist. mgr. to advt. and sales mgmt. positions The Record (Gannett Newspapers), Stockton, Calif., 1977—90; retail advt. mgr. Reno Gazette-Jour., Nev., 1990—2000, pres., pub., 2000—01; exec. v.p. Ariz. Republic, Phoenix, 2001—04, pres., COO, 2004—05, CEO, pub., 2005—. Bd. dir. Banner Health Found., Greater Phoenix C. of C., Phoenix Suns Charities. Mem.: Ariz. Sports Found. Avocations: cooking, golf, entertaining. Office: Arizona Republic 200 E Van Buren St PO Box 1950 Phoenix AZ 85001 Office Phone: 602-444-8000. *

ZIEBARTH, ROBERT CHARLES, management consultant; b. Evanston, Ill., Sept. 12, 1936; s. Charles A. and Marian (Miller) Z.; m. Patience Arnold Kirkpatrick, Aug. 28, 1971; children— Dana Kirkpatrick, Scott Kirkpatrick, Christopher, Nicholas. AB, Princeton, 1958; MBA, Harvard, 1964. With Bell & Howell Co., Chgo., 1964-73, treas., chief fin. officer, 1969-73; mgmt. cons. Ziebarth Co., 1973—. Mem. dirs. adv. bd. Arkwright Boston Ins. Co., devel. com. Nat. Assn. Ind. Schs.; bd. dirs. M.B.A. Resources, Inc., Telemedia, Inc., Corp. Resources, Inc., Nordemann Grimm Inc. Assoc. Community Renewal Soc., Citizens Coun. Gateway House; mem. Ill. Bd. Higher Edn., Ill. Joint Edn. Commn.; trustee Choate Sch.; trustee, pres. Latin Sch.Chgo., Chgo. Maternity Ctr.; bd. dirs. Harvard Bus. Sch. Fund, U.S.O., Inc., Prentice Women's Hosp., Northwestern Meml. Corp., Found. for Reproductive Rsch. and Edn., Endowments Inc., Bond Portfolio Endowments Inc. Served to lt. USNR, 1958-62. Mem. Naval Hist. Found., Art Inst. Chgo., Chgo. Hist. Soc., Mus. Modern Art. Clubs: Mid-Am. (Chgo.), Racquet (Chgo.), Saddle and Cycle (Chgo.), Economic (Chgo.), Executives (Chgo.). Presbyterian. Office: PO Box 4569 Ketchum ID 83340-4569

ZIEBOLD, ERIC, chef; Grad., Culinary Inst. Am. Cook Vidalia, Washington; chef de partie Spago Restaurant, Washington; chef The French Laundry; exec. chef City Zen, Mandarin Oriental, Washington. Named one of America's Best New Chefs, Food & Wine Mag., 2005, Washington DC's Rising Stars, StarChefs.com, 2006. Office: City Zen 1330 Marland Ave SW Washington DC 20004 Office Phone: 202-554-8588. *

ZIEFF, SUSAN GAIL, healthcare educator; BS, Boston U., 1980; MA, U. Calif., Berkeley, 1985, PhD, 1993. Prof. kinesiology San Francisco State U., 1997—. Lab. dir. for sociocultural & psychol. studies of phys. activity San Francisco State U., 1997—. Grantee Rsch. grant, Calif. Policy Rsch. Ctr., U. Calif., 2007. Achievements include research in the relationship between knowledge acquisition and lifestyle changes associated with health-related physical activity. Avocations: travel, yoga, bass guitar, music. Office: San Francisco State Univ 1600 Holloway Ave San Francisco CA 94132-4161 Office Fax: 415-338-7566.

ZIEGLER, ANNETTE KINGSLAND, state supreme court justice; b. Grand Rapids, Mich., Mar. 6, 1964; d. Rex Raymond and Joyce Wanda (Wirth) Kingsland; m. Jeffrey John Ziegler, July 1, 1994; 3 children. B in Psychology and Bus. Adminstrn., Hope Coll., Holland, Mich., 1986; JD, Marquette U., Milw., 1989. Bar: Wis. 1989. Assoc. O'Neil, Cannon & Hollman S.C., Milw., 1989-95; pro bono spl. asst. dist. atty. Milw. County, 1992, 1996; asst. US atty. Ea. Dist. Wis., Milw., 1995—97; judge Washington County Cir. Ct., 1997—2007; Ct. Appeals Judge Dist. II Ct. Appeals Jud. Exch. Program, 1999; assoc. justice Wis. Supreme Ct., 2007—. Faculty mem. Wis. Jud. Coll. Staff editor jour. Marquette U. Law Sch., 1987-89; contbr. articles to profl. jours. Mem. ABA, ATLA, Wis. State Bar, Wis. Acad. Trial Lawyers, Washington County Bar Assn., Milw. Bar Assn., Assn. Women Lawyers. Office: Wis Supreme Ct 16 E State Capitol PO Box 1688 Madison WI 53701-1688 *

ZIEGLER, ARTHUR P., JR., foundation executive; b. Pitts., June 20, 1937; s. Arthur P. and Vinnie (DeWinter) Ziegler. BA, U. Pitts., 1958, MA, 1959; postgrad., Union Theol. Sem., NYC, 1960, Western Res. U., 1961. Instr. Carnegie Mellon U., Pitts., 1961-64, Pa. State U., 1961-63; pres. Pitts. History, Landmarks, 1964—, Cranston Devel. Corp., 1980-87. Trustee Allegheny Found., Pitts., 1975—, Walden Trust, 1990—, Sarah Scaife Found., 2000—; trustee emeritus Nat. Trust, Washington; chmn. Allegheny County Hist. Properties Commn., Pa. Editor: (novels) A Critical Edition of Lord of the Flies, 1964; author: (book) Historic Preservation of Inner City Areas, 1971, Revolving Funds for Historic Preservation, 1975; co-author: Allegheny, 1975, Historic Preservation for Small Towns, 1980, Landmark Architecture of Allegheny County, 1987. Mem. N.E. regional, Pitts. adv. coun. Fannie Mae; advisor 10,000 Friends of Pa.; dir. Riverlife Task Force, Pitts.; advisor, sustainable architecture program Carnegie Mellon U.; mem. Market Sq. Leadership Com., New Granada Theatre Restoration Com.; mem. bd. advisors Waterfront Ctr. Recipient Crowninshield award, Nat. Trust, Nat. Recognition award, Ptnrs. for a livable Cmty., Pvt. Sector award, Pres. of the US, Otto Haas award, Preservation, Pa., Pa. Man of Yr. in Arts award, Pitts., Jaycees, Golden Quill award, Remax Renaissance award. Mem.: Internat. Urban Devel. Assn. (dir.), Allegheny HYP Club. Avocation: gardening. Office: One Station Sq Ste 450 Pittsburgh PA 15219

ZIEGLER, DEWEY KIPER, neurologist, educator; b. Omaha, May 31, 1920; s. Isidor and Pearl (Kiper) Z.; Mar. 30, 1954; children: Amy, Laura, Sara. BA, Harvard U., 1941, MD, 1945. Diplomate Am. Bd. Psychiatry and Neurology (bd. dirs. 1974-83, exec. com. 1978-82). Intern in medicine Boston City Hosp., 1945-46; asst. resident then chief resident in neurology N.Y. Neurol. Inst.-Columbia U. Coll. Physicians and Surgeons, 1948-51; resident in psychiatry Boston Psychopathic Hosp., 1951-53; asst. chief neurol. service Montefiore Hosp., NYC; and asst. prof. neurology Columbia U., 1953-55; asst. prof. U. Minn., 1955-56; asso. clin. prof. U. Kans. Med. Sch., 1956-64, chief dept. neurology, 1968-85; prof. U. Kans. Med. Center, 1964-89, prof. emeritus, 1989—. Cons. Social Security Adminstrn., 1975—; mem. com. on certification and co-certification Am. Bd. Med. Specialties, 1979-82 Author: In Divided and Distinguished Worlds, 1942; Contbr. numerous articles to profl. jours. Served to lt., j.g., M.C. USNR, 1946-48. Fellow Am. Acad. Neurology (pres. 1979-81); mem. AMA, Am. Neurol. Assn. (v.p. 1972-73), Am. Headache Assn. Jewish. Home: 8347 Delmar Ln Shawnee Mission KS 66207-1821 Office: Kans U Med Ctr 3900 Rainbow Blvd Kansas City KS 66103-2918 Home Phone: 913-648-7244.

ZIEGLER, DHYANA, broadcasting educator, academic administrator; b. NYC, May 5, 1949; d. Ernest and Alberta Allie (Guy) Z. BS cum laude, CUNY, 1981; MA in Radio and TV, So. Ill. U., 1983, PhD in Higher Edn., 1985. Freelance researcher Essence Mag., NYC, 1972-75; copywriter, radio producer Rosenfeld, Sirowitz & Lawson Advt. Agy., NYC, 1974-75; exec. v.p. Patten & Guest Prodns., NYC, 1976-79; prodn. intern Sta. WNEW TV, NYC, 1979-80; upward bound counselor Seton Hall U., South Orange, NY, 1979-81; prodn. intern Sta. WCBS TV, NYC, 1980-81; asst. prof. Jackson (Miss.) State U., 1984-85; assoc. dir. Diversity Resources and Ednl. Svcs. U. Tenn., Knoxville, 1995, prof. broadcasting, pres., faculty senate; Garth C. Reeves Eminent Scholar Chair of Excellence in Journalism Fla. A&M U., 1997, asst. v.p., instructional tech., asst. v.p. academic affairs, acting v.p. sponsored rsch., mem. Innovation Park bd., dir. U. planning, 2002. Bd. dirs. Knoxville Women's Ctr., 1989-92; bd. trustees East Tenn. Discovery Ctr., Knoxville, 1989-92; adv. bd. Bethel Love Kitchen, Knoxville, 1990-93; subject matter expert Gov.'s Digital Divide Coun. Author books; contbr. articles to profl. jours.; producer, dir. (video documentary) Single Parenting, 1988 (2d Pl. award), Rape is a Reality, 1982 (UPI Outstanding Achievement award 1982). Chmn. comms. Knoxville chpt. NAACP, 1990-91, chpt. advisor U. Tenn. student chpt., 1989—, chmn. chancellor's commn. for blacks, 1990-95, pres. faculty senate, 1995—; chmn. social action com. Delta Sigma Theta, Knoxville, 1986-89, mem. commn. on arts and letters, 1990-91; bd. dirs. East Tenn. regional Am. Heart Assn., 1990—; mem. athletics bd. U. Tenn., 1990—; regional devel. edn. coord. Delta Rsch. and Ednl. Found. (chairperson Rsch. and resource com.), v.p., bd. dirs.; mem. allocations com. United Way, Knoxville, 1990-91; bd. trustee Florida Virtual HS, 2002-04, 2004-; bd. dirs. Fla. Virtual Sch. So. Scholarship Found. Named one of Top 50 African-Ams. in Tech., U.S. Black Engring. Info. Tech. Mag. and Black-money.com, 2002, 2003, 2004; recipient Gov.'s Outstanding Faculty Mem. of the Yr., 1987—88, Rsch. award, 1992, Coll. of Comms., Outstanding Faculty award, Interfraternity Coun., 1992, YWCA Finalist in Edn., 1990, Consortium of Dr.'s award, 1991; fellow, Poynter Inst., 1992; grantee, FISPE, US Dept. of Edn., 1989—, Delta Rsch. & Ednl. Found., 1987, 1990; inductee, U. Tenn. African Am. Hall of Fame, 1994, Leadership Devel. Initiative scholar, Grad. Sch. Edn., Mgmt. and Leadership in Edn. Inst., Harvard U., 2000, Chosen Fulbright-Hays Spl. Seminar Participant, US Dept. Edn. and the Nat. Com. on US-China Rels., China, 2004. Mem. NAFE, Women in Comm. (pres. Knoxville chpt. 1990—), Broadcast Edn. Assn. (chair multicultural div. 1989-92, chair gender divsn. 1996—), Speech Comm. Assn., Soc. Profl. Journalists (Jane Pauley task force on mass comm. edn. 1995-96, co-author Jane Pauley Task Force Report 1996), Golden Key Nat. Honor Soc., Kappa Tau Alpha, Phi Delta Kappa, Delta Sigma Theta (Post-secondary Educators award 1992, Black Achievement award 1993), Phi Kappa Phi. Office: U Tenn 295 Communications Bldg Knoxville TN 37996-0001 also: Fla A&M U Academic Affairs I&R Program FHAC 301 Tallahassee FL 32307 Office Phone: 850-599-3460, 850-599-3461. Business E-Mail: dhyz@aol.com.

ZIEGLER, DONALD EMIL, retired federal judge; b. Pitts., Oct. 1, 1936; s. Emil Nicholas and Elizabeth Ziegler; m. Claudia J. Chermak, May 1, 1965; 1 son, Scott Emil. BA, Duquesne U., 1958; LL.B., Georgetown U., 1961. Bar: Pa. 1962, U.S. Supreme Ct. 1967. Practice law, Pitts., 1962-74; judge Ct. of Common Pleas of Allegheny County, Pa., 1974-78, U.S. Dist. Ct. (we. dist.) Pa., Pitts., 1978—2003, chief judge, 1994-2001. Mem. Jud. Conf. U.S., 1997-2000. Treas. Big Bros. of Allegheny County, 1969-74. Mem. ABA, Pa. Bar Assn., Allegheny County Bar Assn., Am. Judicature Soc., St. Thomas More Soc. Clubs: Oakmont Country. Democrat. Roman Catholic. Office: 100 Ross St Ste 105 Pittsburgh PA 15219-2013 Office Phone: 412-281-6770. E-mail: coopzieg@aol.com.

ZIEGLER, DONALD ROBERT, accountant; b. Lancaster, Pa., Nov. 15, 1932; s. John Jacob and Esther Mae (McKelly) Z.; m. Suzanne Foster; children: D. Rand, Scott F., Kurt J. BS in Econ. Acctg., Franklin and Marshall Coll., 1954. CPA, Pa. Mgr., sr. staff mem. Price Waterhouse, Phila., 1954-67, ptnr., 1967-92, sr. practice ptnr., 1978-92, mng. ptnr. Mid-Atlantic area, 1985-88, vice chmn. S.E. region, 1988-92, mem. policy bd. NYC, 1980-88, mem. mgmt. com., 1986-92. Author: (with others) Managing and Accounting for Inventories, 1980; contbg. author various books in field. Trustee Franklin and Marshall Coll., 1983—, mem. alumni exec. coun., 1979—83, mem. exec. com., 1995—, chmn. audit com., 1989—2003, vice-chmn. bd. trustees, 2002—, mem. Phila. alumni coun.; trustee Pa. Ballet, 1988—92, 1994—95, mem. devel. and fin. coms., vice chmn. bd. trustees, 1989—92, chmn. exec. com., 1989—91; chmn. audit com., budget and fin. com., ethics com., bd. of adjustment Town of Dewey Beach; bd. dirs. Beebe Med. Ctr., 2000—06, Beebe Med. Found., 2001—06, So. Del. Surgery Ctr., 2003—06. With US Army, 1955—57. Recipient Outstanding Soldier award U.S. Army, 1955, Disting. Svc. Alumni medal Franklin and Marshall Coll., 1991. Mem. AICPA (auditing stds. com. 1973-76, chmn. subcom. fraud 1976-80), Pa. Inst. CPAs (Phila. chpt. exec. coun.), Rehoboth Beach Country Club (bd. govs. 2000—, treas. 2003—), Phila. Aviation Club (bd. govs. and treas. 1969-90), Franklin and Marshall Soc. Disting. Alumni. Home: One West St Dewey Beach DE 19971 Office: PricewaterhouseCoopers LLP Two Commerce Sq 2001 Market St Ste 1700 Philadelphia PA 19103-7042 Personal E-mail: drsfzig@comcast.net.

ZIEGLER, EKHARD ERICH, pediatrics educator; b. Saalfelden, Austria, Apr. 12, 1940; children: Stefan, Gabriele, Lena. MD, U. Innsbruck, Austria, 1964. Diplomate: Am. Bd. Pediatrics. Intern U. Innsbruck, 1966-67, resident in pediatrics, 1967-68 70-71, resident in pharmacology, 1964-66, asst. dept. pediatrics, 1970-73; vis. instr. pediatrics U. Iowa, Iowa City, 1968-70, asst. prof. pediatrics, 1973-76, assoc. prof., 1976-81, prof., 1981—. Mem. nutrition study sect. NIH, 1988-92. Recipient Nutrition award Am. Acad. Pediactrics, 1988. Mem. Am. Soc. Clin. Nutrition, Soc. Pediatric Research, Soc. Exptl. Biology and Medicine, N.Am. Soc. Pediatric Gastroenterology, Midwest Soc. Pediatric Research, Am. Pediatric Soc., The Nutrition Soc., N.Y. Acad. Scis., Am. Acad. Pediatrics., Am. Dietetic Assn. (hon.). Clubs: Univ. Athletic (Iowa City). Office: U Iowa Dept Pediatrics Iowa City IA 52242 Office Phone: 319-335-4570. Business E-Mail: ekhard-ziegler@uiowa.edu.

ZIEGLER, GWENDOLYN WOODS, minister, consultant; d. William Darnell and Christine Anna Woods; children: Geraldine, Tonia Elaine, Faith Evangeline, Charity Elise. BTh, United Bible Coll., Orlando, Fla., 1988, EdM, 1990; DMin, Howard U., 2006. Pastoral lic. Deliverance Evangelistic Ctrs., Inc./N.J., 1970, Evangelistic lic. Deliverance Evangelistic Ctrs., Inc./N.J., 1967. Pres./cons. G. Chafto Industries, Washington, 1990—; v.p. In The Midst, Inc., Severn, Md., 1999—2002. Spl. asst. to the pres. We Can Do Ministries, Inc., Newark, 1990—92; tchr./radio broadcaster Positive Proof Ministries, Orange, NJ, 1995—97; cons./radio broadcaster Global Ministries, South Orange, NJ, 1997—98. Author: (non-fiction book) Judgment Work - A Conclusion To The Matter, 2003. Mem.: N.Am. Bookdealers Exch. Independent. Office Phone: 301-758-5386. E-mail: gwen_ziegler@hotmail.com.

ZIEGLER, HENRY STEINWAY, retired lawyer; b. Utica, NY, June 21, 1933; s. Frederick J. and Alice (Cantwell) Z.; m. Patricia Blackmore (div.); children: Frederick S., Alicia P., Timothy O.; m. Jourdan Arpelle, Apr. 6, 1991. AB, Harvard U., 1955; LLB, Columbia U., 1958. Bar: N.Y. 1961, U.S. Dist. Ct. (ea. and so. dists.) N.Y. 1962, U.S. Ct. Appeals (2d cir.) 1963, U.S. Tax Ct. 1972. Assoc. Shearman & Sterling, NYC, 1958-67, ptnr., 1967-92; chmn. CEO Deutsche Bank Trust Co., 1995-97, trust estate planning dir., 1998—99; sr. v.p. Fiduciary Trust Co. Internat., NYC, 1999—2003; pres., cons., governance and transfer of family wealth HSZ Cons. LLC, 2003—06; of counsel Withers Beigman LLP, 2006—07. Pres. Chamber Music Soc. of Lincoln Ctr., Inc., 1983-89, bd. dirs., 2004—; pres. Lincoln Ctr. for Performing Arts, N.Y.C., 1985-89; hon. trustee St. Lukes-Roosevelt Hosp. Ctr.; bd. regents Am. Coll. Trust Estate Counsel, 1988-94. With U.S. Army, 1958-60, 61-62. Mem. ABA (former vice chmn. internat. com. on property probate and trust law), Acad. internat. Trust and Estate Law (mem. exec. coun., v.p.), N.Y. State Bar Assn., Assn. Bar City of N.Y., Century Assn., Order St. John of Jerusalem. Clubs: Racquet and Tennis, Knickerbocker. Republican. Avocation: music. Home: 55 Liberty St Apt # 7A New York NY 10005 Office Phone: 212-848-9842. Personal E-mail: hsziegler@earthlink.net.

ZIEGLER, JACK (JACK DENMORE), cartoonist; b. NYC, July 13, 1942; s. John Denmore and Kathleen Miriam (Clark) Z.; m. Jean Ann Rice, Apr. 20, 1968 (div. 1995); children: Jessica, Benjamin, Maxwell; m. Kelli Joseph, Aug. 1996. BA in Comm. Arts, Fordham U., 1964. Free-lance cartoonist, NYC, 1972—; cartoonist The New Yorker, NYC, 1974—. Author: Hamburger Madness, 1978, Filthy Little Things, 1981, Marital Blitz, 1987, Celebrity Cartoons of the Rich and Famous, 1987, Worst Case Scenarios, 1990, Mr. Knocky, 1993, The Essential Jack Ziegler, 2000, How's The Squid?, 2004, Olive Or Twist?, 2005, You Had Me at Bow Wow, 2006; illustrator: (children's books) Lily of the Forest, 1987, Flying Boy, 1988, Annie's Pet, 1989, Eli and the Dimplemeyers, 1994 (adult books) Waiting Games, 1983, The Joy of Stress, 1984, That's Incurable!, 1984, Modern Superstitions, 1985, The No-Sex Handbook, 1990, There'll Be a Slight Delay, 1991, Byte Me!, 1996, Fictoids, 2005. Democrat. Personal E-mail: jkziegler@sbcglobal.net.

ZIEGLER, JAMES L., marketing executive; b. Fort Benning, Ga., Sept. 10, 1965; s. Gordon L. and Kum S. Ziegler. BS, US Mil. Acad., 1989; MBA, U. Chgo., 1998. Sales Pfizer, Inc, Dallas, 1993—96; biotech. exec. Amgen, Inc., Thousand Oaks, Calif., 2000—. Bd. mem. West Point Soc. LA, 2000—03. Capt. US Army, 1989—93. Decorated Army Achievement Medal U.S. Army, Army Commendation Medal; recipient Disting. Contbn., Nat. Hispanic Med. Assn., 2003, President's award, Nat. Med. Assn., 2004, Significant Achievement award, Assn. of Am. Indian Physicians, 2002. Personal E-mail: jziegle@gsb.uchicago.edu.

ZIEGLER, JANICE H., lawyer; b. Bklyn., Jan. 25, 1962; m. Karl Groskaufmanis. BS in Indsl. & Labor Rels., with honors, Cornell U., 1984; JD magna cum laude, Harvard U., 1987. Bar: Mass. 1987, DC 1989. Law clk. to Hon. John H. Pratt US Dist. Ct DC; assoc. to ptnr. Shaw Pittman LLP, Washington; ptnr., health care practice group Sonnenschein Nath & Rosenthal LLP, Washington, 2003—. Mem.: ABA (health law sect.), Am. Health Lawyers Assn., DC Bar Assn. (health law sect.). Office: Sonnenschein Nath & Rosenthal LLP Ste 600, E Tower 1301 K St NW Washington DC 20015 Office Phone: 202-408-9158. Office Fax: 202-408-6399. Business E-Mail: jziegler@sonnenschein.com.

ZIEGLER, JOHN ALAN, historian, political scientist, educator; b. Belleville, Ill., Jan. 28, 1933; s. John Wendell and Georgia Elizabeth (Reppel) Z.; m. Carol Ruth Alcorn, June 15, 1963; children: Mimi, Robin. BS, So. Ill. U., 1955, MS, 1956; Rotary Found. fellow, St. Andrews U., Scotland, 1956-57; PhD, Syracuse U., 1970. Asst. prof. polit. sci. and social sci. Calif. State U., Hayward, 1966-72; lectr. Am. civilization Calif. State Poly. U., Pomona, 1972-74; assoc. prof. polit. sci. Hendrix Coll., Conway, Ark., 1974-84, prof., 1984-91, Harold and Lucy Cabe Disting. prof. history and politics, 1991-98, emeritus prof., 1998—, legendary lectr., 1998. Coord. and founder Hendrix-Oxford program, 1979-98, head social sci. area, 1978-82, chmn. dept. polit. sci. and history, 1974-83; guest lectr. St. Peter's Coll., Oxford U., 1983, 90, 94, Clare Coll., Cambridge U., 1988, 89, Dundee U., 1994; Churchill life fellow Westminster Coll., Fulton, Mo.; participant Wilton Pk. Confs., Wiston House Internat. Conf. Ctr., Sussex, England, 1979—. Author: Experimentalism and Institutional Change, 1994, In Search of the Special Relationship with Britain, 2000. With AUS, 1957-60. Mem. AAUP, Friends Churchill Meml. (life), Am. Friends Wilton Park, ACLU, Royal Oak Found., South Downs Soc. (life), Dundee (Scotland) Curling Club. Mem. United Ch. of Christ. Home: PO Box 1045 Conway AR 72033-1045 Office: Hendrix Coll Conway AR 72032 E-mail: johnziegler@webtv.net.

ZIEGLER, JOHN AUGUSTUS, JR., lawyer; b. Grosse Pointe, Mich., Feb. 9, 1934; s. John Augustus and Monnabell M. Ziegler; m. G. Kay Brubeck; children: John Augustus III, Laura, Lisa, Adeline. AB, U. Mich., JD, 1957. Bar: Mich. 1957. Since practiced in, Detroit; assoc. Dickinson, Wright, McKean & Cudlip, 1957-65, ptnr., 1965-68, Parsons, Tennent, Hammond, Hardig & Ziegelman, 1969-70, Ziegler, Dykhouse & Wise, 1970-77; pres., CEO Nat. Hockey League, 1977-92, chmn. bd. govs., 1976-78; of counsel Dickinson, Wright, PLLC, Bloomfield Hills, 1992—99. Personal E-mail: jzee@adelphia.net.

ZIEGLER, R. W., JR., lawyer, consultant; b. Pitts. children: Caroline, Gretchen, Jeremy, Benjamin, Phoebe, Polly. Student, Carnegie Mellon, U. Pitts.; JD, Duquesne U., 1972. Bar: Pa. 1972, Calif. 1981, U.S. Ct. Appeals (3d cir.) 1977, U.S. Dist. Ct. (we. dist.) Pa. 1972, U.S. Supreme Ct. 1977, U.S. Tax Ct. 1978, Calif. 1982, U.S. Dist. Ct. (no. dist.) Calif. 1982, U.S. Ct. Appeals (9th cir.) 1982. Ptnr. Ziegler & Ombres, Pitts., 1973-79; pres. Ziegler Ross Inc., San Francisco, 1979—. Lectr. for Bar Assns. Author: Law Practice Management; editor: Law Office Guide in Computing. Mem. ABA, Am. Mgmt. Assn., Pa. State Bar Assn., Calif. State Bar Assn., Assn. of Legal Admin., Young Presidents' Org., Am. Assn. of Law Librarians., San Francisco Bar Assn. Office: 1559B Sloat Blvd Ste 200 San Francisco CA 94132 Office Phone: 415-682-4944.

ZIEGLER, RICHARD FERDINAND, lawyer; b. Elizabeth, NJ, Aug. 1, 1949; m. Carolyn Lewis; children: Anna B., David A., Andrew P. D-J. BA summa cum laude in Hist., Yale U., 1971; JD magna cum laude, Harvard U., 1975. Bar: NY 1976, US Dist. Ct. (so. and ea. dists. NY) 1976, US Dist. Ct. (ea. dist. Mich.) 1982, US Supreme Ct. 1984, US Dist. Ct. (no. dist. NY) 1987. Law clk. to judge US Dist. Ct. (so. dist.), NYC, 1975-76; assoc. Paul, Weiss, Rifkind, Wharton & Garrison, NYC, 1976-77; asst. US atty. US Dept. Justice (so. dist. NY), NYC, 1977-80; assoc. Cleary, Gottlieb, Steen & Hamilton, NYC, 1980-83, ptnr., 1983—2002; sr. v.p. legal affairs, gen. counsel 3M Co., St. Paul, 2003—. Lectr. law Columbia Law Sch., 1997—. Mem. ABA, Assn. Bar City of NY, Fed. Bar Coun., NY State Bar Assn. (chmn. com. on profl. ethics, 1995-98). Office: 3M Ctr Bldg 220 14W 07 Saint Paul MN 55144

ZIEGLER, RICHARD J., dean, educator; BS in biology, Muhlenberg Coll., 1965; PhD in microbiology, Temple U., 1970. Rsch. assoc. in microbiology Rockefeller U., 1970—71; asst. prof. microbiology U. Minn.-Duluth, 1971—77, assoc. prof. microbiology, 1977—89; prof. microbiology Sch. Medicine, U. Minn.-Duluth, 1989—, interim dean, 1997—98, dean, 1998—. Recipient James H. Sova award, Minn. Med. Found., 2000. Office: UMD Sch Medicine 1035 Univ Dr Duluth MN 55812 Office Phone: 218-726-7572. Fax: 218-726-7383. Business E-Mail: rziegler@d.umn.edu.

ZIEGLER, ROCHELLE ELIZABETH, special education educator; b. Virginia Beach, Va., Dec. 21, 1974; d. Robert Herman and Elizabeth Ethiel Ziegler. BS in Interdisciplinary Studies /Mental Retardation, Norfolk State U., Norfolk, Va., 2003; M in Severe Disabilities, Norfolk State U., 2005. Tchr. asst. Southeastern Coop. Ednl. Programs, Virginia Beach, Va., 1995—2004; tchr. spl. edn. Portsmouth Pub. Schs., 2005—. Mentor Young Sister's In Christ, Virginia Beach, Va., 1996. Recipient Nat. Collegiate Edn. Awards, US Achievement Acad., 2000; scholar All-Am. Scholar at Large Divsn., 2000. Mem.: Coun. of Exceptional Children (assoc.). Democrat-Npl. Bapt. Avocations: reading, helping in the community/church, exercise. Home: 834 Tuition Dr Virginia Beach VA 23462 Home Phone: 757-962-5812. Personal E-mail: rez1221@msn.com.

ZIEGLER, WILLIAM ALEXANDER, lawyer; b. NYC, July 15, 1924; s. William Alexander and Sally (Cootes) Z.; m. Glenn Crawley, Feb. 10, 1950; children: Richard S., Daryl A. Henning, Susan G. Barrows, W. Thomas. AB, Harvard U., 1944, JD, 1949. Bar: NY 1949, US Tax Ct. 1950, US Dist. Ct. (so. dist.) NY 1949, US Dist. Ct. (ea. dist.) NY 1957, US Dist. Ct. (no. dist.) Ohio 1973, US Dist. Ct. (ea. dist.) Mich. 1983, US Ct. Apppeals (1st cir.) 1963, US Ct. Appeals (2d cir.) 1957, US Ct. Appeals (3d cir.) 1986, US Ct. Appeals (4th cir.) 1979, US Ct. Appeals (5th cir.) 1987, US Ct. Appeals (6th cir.) 1984, US Ct. Appeals (7th cir.) 1992, US Ct. Appeals (8th cir.) 1981, US Ct. Appeals (9th cir.) 1973, US Ct. Appeals (10th and 11th cirs.) 1983, US Ct. Appeals (DC cir.) 1972, US Supreme Ct. 1972. Assoc. Sullivan & Cromwell, NYC, 1949-56, ptnr., 1957-89. Cons. in field, 1989—. Bd. dir. Wilton Land Conservation Trust, Conn., Friends of Canterbury Cathedral in US; former bd. drs. Harvard Law Sch. Assn. NYC, St. Mark's Sch., Salisbury Sch., Am. Dressage Inst., St. Paul's Ch. (Norwalk, Conn.), Std. Comml. Corp.; chair exec. com. Engring. Info., Inc., The H.W. Wilson Co.; sec. The H. W. Wilson Found., Big Brothers of NYC, Fgn. Policy Assn.; v.p. Manhattan Coun. Boy Scouts of Am., Ox

Ridge Hunt Club; pres. Land Trust of Darien, Conn. Served with USN, 1943—46. Mem. Assn. Bar City NY, Riverside Country Club (Mont.), Harvard Club of Fairfield Country (bd. dir.), Harvard Club Mont. Episcopalian. Avocations: music, golf, literature.

ZIEHLER, TONY JOSEPH, insurance agent; b. Anderson, Ind., June 20, 1936; s. Joseph Anthony and Julie Ann (Kette) Z.; m. Alice Mae Pattison, Apr. 2, 1956 (div. 1972); children: Susan Z. Brown, Kathryn Z. Dwyer, Jane Z. Bee, Patricia Z. Koty, Michael; m. Barbara Buys Wood, Feb. 28, 1981; stepchildren: David Wayne Wood, Brent Douglas Wood. BSBA, U. Ariz., Tucson, 1958. CLU. Prin. mng. ptnr. Ziehler Ins. Group, LLC, Tucson, 1958—. Mem. Fed. Jud. Magistrate Selection Com., 1998—. Employee edn. chmn. So. Ariz. Div. Am. Cancer Soc.; co-chmn. Medic-Alert Found., Pima County, Ariz.; chmn. Tucson Festival Soc.; mem. Salpointe High Sch. Found., others. Recipient William Wisdom award U. Ariz., Tucson, 1958. Mem. Nat. Assn. of Ins. & Fin. Advisors (pres. 1963-64, Agt. of Yr. 1975), Ariz. Nat. Assn. of Life Underwriters (pres. 1970-71, Agt. of Yr. 1980), So. Ariz. CLU Soc. (pres. 1968-69), Salvation Army (pres. adv. bd. 1984-85), Univ. of Ariz. Found. (mem. planned giving com.), Rotary, (com. chmn.), Tucson Conquistadores (pres. 1985-86), Los Charros del Desierto, Golden Key Soc., Million Dollar Round Table, Tucson Country Club, White Mountain Country Club (Pinetop, Ariz.). Republican. Avocations: travel, horseback riding, hiking, sports. Home: 4845 N Camino Escuela Tucson AZ 85718-5913 Office: 6992 E Broadway Blvd Tucson AZ 85710-2803 Home Phone: 520-577-4554; Office Phone: 520-747-8787. E-mail: tony-ziehler@leavitt.com.

ZIELINSKI, MICHAEL EDMUND, osteopath; b. Highland Park, Mich., Aug. 10, 1958; s. Edmund Donald and Rosemary Stella Zielinski; m. Michelle Ann Craig, Aug. 19, 1989; children: Paige, Payton, Carter. BA cum laude, Oakland U., Rochester, Mich., 1980; DO, Mich. State U., East Lansing, 1984. Med. dir. emergency dept. Lapeer Med. Hosp., Mich., 1994—98; staff physician Knollwood Clinic, Lapeer, 1998—2000; med. dir. Waterford Ambulatory Care, Waterford, Mich., 2000—; owner Lapeer Family and Urgent Care, Lapeer, 2004—. Columnist: Oakland Press, 2005—. Fellow: Am. Coll. Emergency Medicine, Am. Acad. Emergency Medicine; mem.: Am. Osteo. Assn. Office: Waterford Ambulartory Care Ctr Waterford MI 48327

ZIELINSKI, PAUL BERNARD, grant program administrator, civil engineer; b. West Allis, Wis., Sept. 9, 1932; s. Stanley Charles and Lottie Charlotte (Pliszkiewicz) Z.; m. Monica Theresa Beres, July 13, 1957; children: Daniel Paul, Gregory John, Robert Mathias, Sarah Ann. BSCE, Marquette U., 1956; MS, U. Wis., 1961, PhD, 1965. Registered profl. engr., Wis., S.C. Asst. instr. engring. mechanics Marquette U., Milw., 1956-59, asst. prof., 1964-67; instr. civil engring. U. Wis., Madison, 1959-64; from asst. prof. to prof. Clemson (S.C.) U., 1967-78, prof. environ. and systems engring., 1978-82, prof. civil engring., 1982-90, prof. emeritus, 1991—; dir. S.C. Water Resources Rsch. Inst., Clemson, 1978-90; assoc. dir. associateship grant program Nat. Rsch. Coun., Washington, 1990—2006; ret., 2006. Cons. swirl devices for storm water separation Am. Pub. Works Assn., Chgo., 1973-76, Nat. Coun. Examiners of Engring. and Surveying, Clemson, 1973-. Author numerous publs. on hydraulics and water resources rsch. Chmn. Clemson City Planning Commn., 1971-74; ex-officio mem. S.C. Water Resources Commn., Columbia, 1978-90. Mem. ASCE, Sigma Xi. Roman Catholic. Home: 508 Shorecrest Dr Clemson SC 29631 Home Phone: 864-654-2891.

ZIELINSKI, THOMAS C., lawyer, insurance company executive; Various positions Cozen & O'Connor, P.C., 1982—2001; sr. v.p., gen. counsel Coventry Health Care Inc., Bethesda, Md., 2001—. Office: Coventry Health Care Inc 6705 Rockledge Dr Ste 900 Bethesda MD 20817 Office Phone: 301-581-0600. Office Fax: 301-493-0731. Business E-Mail: tielinski@cvty.com. *

ZIEMAN, MARK, newspaper editor; b. El Dorado, Kan., Jan. 17, 1945; m. Kristi Zieman (div.); m. Rhonda Chriss Lokeman; 4 children. Degree in Journalism, Kans. U., 1983. Mem. staff Houston bur. The Wall St. Jour., 1984—86; columnist Kans. City (Mo.) Star, 1986—89, editor projects desk, 1989—92, mng. editor, 1992—97, v.p, editor, 1997—. Recipient Pulitzer prize, 1992. Office: The Kansas City Star 1729 Grand Blvd Kansas City MO 64108-1458 Office Phone: 816-234-4878. E-mail: zieman@kcstar.com. *

ZIEMBA, KAREN, actress; Appeared in Broadway plays A Chorus Line, Teddy & Alice, 42nd Street, Crazy for You, Chicago, Contact (Drama Desk award, Outer Critics Cir. award, Tony award, 2000), Never Gonna Dance (Tony nom. best featured actress in a play, 2004); (off-Broadway) And the World Goes 'Round (Drama Desk award) I Do! I Do!; (musical) Steel Pier (Tony award nominee), The Pajama Game, Allegro, Leading Ladies, 2005; (tour) Crazy for You (Joseph Jefferson award), Chicago (1998-99); (regional plays) Much Ado About Nothing, House and Garden, The Foreigner, Fifth of July, Curtains, 2006 (Outer Critics Cir. award outstanding featured actress in a musical, 2007); (opera) The Most Happy Fella, 110 in the Shade; singer Allegro, Grand Night for Singing; (TV show) Sondheim: A Celebration at Carnegie Hall, Evening at Pops, My Favorite Broadway: The Leading Ladies, Law and Order; (film) The Devil and Daniel Webster; (albums) And the World Goes 'Round, Fifty Million Frenchmen, Lost in Boston II, Shakespeare on Broadway, 110 In The Shade, The Most Happy Fella, Ziegfeld Follies of 1936. *

ZIEMER, JAMES L., motorcycle company executive; BBA, MBA, U. Wis., Milw. CPA Wis. With Harley-Davidson, Inc., Milw., 1969—, v.p., CFO, 1990—2005, pres., CEO, 2005—; pres. Harley-Davidson Found., 1993—. Bd. dirs. Harley-Davidson, Inc. Office: Harley-Davidson Inc PO Box 653 3700 W Juneau Ave Milwaukee WI 53201-0653 *

ZIEMER, RODGER EDMUND, electrical engineering educator, consultant; b. Sargeant, Minn., Aug. 22, 1937; s. Arnold Edmund and Ruth Ann (Rush) Z.; m. Sandra Lorann Person, June 23, 1960; children: Mark Edmund, Amy Lorann, Norma Jean, Sandra Lynn. BS, U. Minn., 1960, MS, 1962, PhD, 1965. Registered profl. engr., Mo. Research asst. U. Minn., Mpls., 1960-62, research assoc., 1962; prof. elec. engring. U. Mo., Rolla, 1968-83, U. Colo., Colorado Springs, 1984—, chmn. dept. elec. engring., 1984-93; program dir. comms. rsch. NSF, 1998-2001. Cons. Emerson Electric Co., St. Louis, 1972-84, Mid-Am. Regional Coun., Kansas City, Mo., 1974, Motorola, Inc., Scottsdale, Ariz., 1980-84, Martin Marietta, Orlando, 1980-81, TRW, Colorado Springs, summer, 1985, Sperry, Phoenix, 1986, Pericle Communications, summer, 1994, Motorola, Schaumburg, 1995, Scottsdale, 1996, Arlington Heights, 1997. Author: Principles of Communications, 1976, Principles of Communications, 2d edit., 1985, Principles of Communications, 3d edit., 1990, Principles of Communications, 4th edit., 1995, Principles of Communications, 5th edit., 2002, Signals and Systems, 1983, Signals and Systems, 2d edit., 1989, Signals and Systems, 3d edit., 1993, Signals and Systems, 4th edit., 1998, Digital Communications and Spread Spectrum Systems, 1985, Introduction to Digital Communication, 1992, Introduction to Digital Communication, 2d edit., 2001, Introduction to Spread Spectrum Communications, 1995, Elements of Engineering Probability and Statistics, 1997; editor: IEEE Jour. on Selected Areas in Comms., 1989, 1992, 1995, IEEE Comm. Mag., 1991. Served to capt. USAF, 1965-68. Scholar Western Electric, 1957-59; trainee NASA, 1962-65. Fellow IEEE (life; Third Millenium award 2000); mem. Am. Soc. Engring. Edn., Armed Forces Comms. and Electronics Assn., Sigma Xi, Tau Beta Pi, Eta Kappa Nu. Lutheran. Home: 8315 Pilot Ct Colorado Springs CO 80920-4412 Office: Univ Colo PO Box 7150 Colorado Springs CO 80933-7150 Home Phone: 719-590-7859; Office Phone: 719-262-3350. Business E-Mail: ziemer@eas.uccs.edu.

ZIEN, CHIP, actor; b. Milwaukee, Wis., Mar. 20, 1947; BA, U. Pa. Actor: (Broadway plays) Ride the Winds, 1974, The Suicide, 1980, Into the Woods, 1987, Grand Hotel, 1989, Falsettos, 1992, The Boys from Syracuse, 2002, Chitty Chitty Bang Bang, 2005, Les Miserables, 2007, (Off-Broadway) How to Succeed in Business Without Really Trying, 1972, Smile, Smile, Smile, 1973, Tuscaloosa's Calling Me... But I'm Not Going, 1975, Dear Mr. G, 1975, In Trousers, 1979, Split, 1980, March of the Falsettos, 1981, Isn't It Romantic, 1983, Hot L Baltimore, 1984, Diamonds, 1984, An Imaginary Life, 1993, A New Brain, 1998, They're Playing Our Song, 2004; (films) Mrs. Parker and the Vicious Circle, 1994, Die Schelme von Schelm, 1995, Snake Eyes, 1998, The Siege, 1998, Brooklyn Thrill Killers, 1999, Breakfast of Champions, 1999, United 93, 2006; (TV films) Quiet Killer, 1994, Cagney & Lacey: The View Through the Glass Ceiling, 1995, Cagney & Lacey: True Convictions, 1996, Inseparable, 2006. *

ZIENTZ, MICHAEL WAYNE, lawyer; BA in Govt., U. Tex., Austin, 1994; JD, U. Miami, 1997. Bar: Tex. 1997, Fla. 1998. Assoc. Barrett, Burke, Wilson, Castle, Daffin & Frappier, L.L.P., Addison, 1998—. Named a Rising Star, Tex. Super Lawyers mag., 2006. Mem.: Dallas Bar Assn., ABA. Office: Barrett Burke Wilson Castle Daffin & Frappier LLP 15000 Surveyor Blvd Ste 100 Addison TX 75001 Office Phone: 972-386-5040 ext. 0642. E-mail: michaelz@bbwcdf.com. *

ZIERDEN, DON, professional basketball coach; m. Anne Zierden; children: Isaiah, Rachel. Student, Mt. Senario Coll. Coach De La Salle HS, U. Tulsa, 1986—88, Continental Basketball Assn. La Crosse Catbirds, 1990—94; head coach Continental Basketball Assn. Pitts. Piranhas, 1995, Continental Basketball Assn. La Crosse Bobcats, 1996; video coord. NBA Minn. Timberwolves, 1999—2000, asst. coach, dir. player devel., 2000—05; asst. coach NBA Detroit Pistons, 2005—07; head coach WNBA Minn. Lynx, 2007—. Office: Minn Lynx 600 First Ave N Minneapolis MN 55403 *

ZIERES, CAROL LYNNE, military officer; b. Mar. 1, 1960; BA in Biology, SUNY, Oswego, 1982; MA in Human Resources Mgmt., Chapman U., Orange, Calif., 1999. Commd. 2d lt. USAR, advanced through grades to col., 1982—2006, project officer Office of Chief Arlington, Va., 2003—04; sec. gen. staff AR-MEDcom, Pinellas Park, Fla., 2004—06; med. brigade tng. comdr. 3d Med. Tng. Bridgade, Ft. Sam Houston, Tex., 2006—. Decorated Meritorious Svc. medal. Mem.: Assn. Mil. Surgeons US, Order Mil. Med. Merit. Home: 340 Treeline Park Apt 1223 San Antonio TX 78208 Personal E-mail: czieres906@aol.com.

ZIERING, WILLIAM MARK, lawyer; b. New Britain, Conn., Feb. 4, 1931; s. Jacob Max and Esther (Freedman) Z.; m. Harriet Koskoff, Aug. 20, 1958 (div. Sept. 1993); 1 son, Benjamin. BA, Yale U., 1952; JD, Harvard U., 1955. Bar: Conn. 1955, Calif. 1962. Assoc. Koskoff & McMahon, Plainville, Conn., 1959-60; sr. trial atty. SEC, San Francisco, 1960-65; pvt. practice law San Francisco, 1965—; ptnr. Bremer & Ziering, 1972-77. Instr. Golden Gate U. Law Sch., San Francisco, 1968-75 Vice pres., bd. dirs. Calif. League Handicapped, 1972—. Served to comdr. USNR, 1955-58. Mem. ABA, Calif. Bar Assn., San Francisco Bar Assn. (past chmn. securities, corps. and banking), Navy League (dir.) Clubs: Commonwealth. Home: 440 Davis Ct Apt 620 San Francisco CA 94111-2418 Office Phone: 415-982-4581. Personal E-mail: wmziering@sbcglobal.net.

ZIERLER, NEAL, retired mathematician; b. Balt., Sept. 17, 1926; children: Robert Eugene, Joan Mariye, Ann Michie. AB, Johns Hopkins U., 1945; AM, Harvard U., 1949, PhD, 1959. Mathematician, physicist Ballistic Rsch. Labs., Aberdeen, Md., 1951; mem. tech. staff instrumentation lab. MIT, Cambridge, Mass., 1952-54, mem. tech. staff Lincoln Lab. Lexington, Mass., 1954-60; supr. info. processing group of jet propulsion lab. Calif. Inst. Tech., Pasadena, 1960-61; sr. scientist ARCON Corp., Lexington, 1961-62; head sub-dept. process analysis MITRE Corp., Bedford, Mass., 1962-65; tech. staff Ctr. for Comm. Rsch. Inst. Def. Analysis, Princeton, N.J., 1965-96. Patentee error-detecting and -correcting devices; contbr. articles to profl. jours. Lt. USN, 1944-46. Fellow IEEE; mem. Am. Math. Soc., Math. Assn. Am., Am. Physics Soc. Avocations: tennis, skiing, photography. Business E-Mail: nzierler@ieee.org.

ZIEROLF, MARY LOUISE, nurse anesthetist; b. Lima, Ohio, Dec. 12, 1946; d. Charles Peter and Agatha Cecilia (Jackman) Z. Diploma in nursing, St. Rita's Sch. Nursing, Lima, Ohio, 1967; diploma in anesthesia, Cin. Gen. Hosp., 1971; BS in Edn., U. Cin., 1974. RN, Ohio; cert. nurse anesthetist; cert. CPR instr., neonatal resuscitation. Staff nurse operating rm. St. Rita's Hosp., Lima, 1967-69; staff anesthetist, insvc. coord. Mercy Anesthesia Assocs Inc/Anesthesia & Intensive Care Cons, Cin., 1971—; staff anesthetist, specialist in obstet. anesthesia McCullough-Hype Hosp., Oxford, Ohio, 1993-96; staff anesthetist, specializing in obstet. anesthesia Mercy Fairfield, 1996—; staff anesthetist Intensive Care Consultants, Inc. Vis. lectr. Coll. Nursing, U. Cin., 1990-92; lectr. anesthesia in 3d world countries, 1992. Author papers. Mem. anniversary program to Russia, People to People/Citizen Amb. Program, Seattle, 1991, participant in 1st CRNA anesthesia exch. of tech. and sci. info. in China, 1989; active taking monthly blood pressures Fairfax (Ohio) Sr. Citizens, 1988—. Named one of Outstanding Young Women of Am., 1976. Mem. Am. Assn. Nurse Anesthetists, Ohio State Assn. Nurse Anesthetists (bd. dirs. 1981-83, 92—, pres. Greater Cin. Ednl. Dist. 1991—, chair fall Osana meeting 1995—, co-chair fall meeting 1997, sec. 1996-97), Am. Bus. Woman's Assn. (pres. 7 Hills chpt. 1982—, Woman of Yr. 1982), U. Cin. Alumni Assn., Gen. Hosp. Sch. Nurse Anesthesia Alumni, U. Cin. Sch. Nurse Anesthesia Alumni (treas. 1997—). Roman Catholic. Avocations: reading, travel, volunteer work for needy and elderly. Home: 6 W Knoll Ct Fairfield OH 45014-3637 Office: Mercy Hosp Fairfield 3000 Mack Rd Fairfield OH 45014-5335

ZIESE, NANCYLEE HANSON, social worker; m. J. A. Ziese; 1 child, G. Graham. BA in Sociology, Morningside Coll., Sioux City, 1960; MSW, U. Iowa, Iowa City, 1982, cert. in aging studies, 1986; Edn. for Minister, U. of South, Cedar Rapids, Iowa, 1996. Social worker Florence Crittenton Home, Sioux City, 1960—65, L.A. County, 1965; social worker, supr. Polk County Dept. Social Welfare, Des Moines, 1966—69; social worker, cmty. liaison Tommy Dale Meml., Sioux City, 1977—79; dir. internships Briar Cliff Coll., Sioux City, 1981—83; dir. continuing edn. Coe Coll., Cedar Rapids, Iowa, 1983—85; exec. dir. Profl. Women's Network, Cedar Rapids, 1985—87; pvt. practice counselor, cons., spkr., writer WoMan-place Counseling, Cedar Rapids, 1985—87, 1999—; coord. adoption Hillcrest Family Svcs., Cedar Rapids, 1987—99. Bd. dirs. Young Parent's Network M.E.L.D., Cedar Rapids, pres., 1994—96; cons. cmty. improvement, recycling; spkr. in field; gov. apptd. mem. Iowa State Child Advocacy Bd., 2002—. Contbr. articles to newspapers. Steering bd. Iowa Women's Polit. Caucus, 1987—93, pres., 1992—93; dep. gen. conv. Episcopal Ch. USA, 1997—2006; past chair Iowa Birth Defects Inst. Adv. Com., Iowa Assn. Adoption Agys.; bd. dirs. Linn County Adolescent Pregnancy Prevention Coalition, treas., 1992—96; steering com. mem. ERA Iowa 1992, 1991—93; gov.'s com. Adoption Reform in Iowa, 1993—94; lt. gov.'s com. spl. needs Adoption in Iowa, 1994; co-founder, pres. Iowa Breast Cancer Action Found., 1998—; mem. to chmn. Cedar Rapids Civil Rights Commn., 2000—04, 2007—; clinic advisor Cmty. Health Free Clinic, 2005—; bd. dirs. commn. mem. Human Needs, commn. on ministry Episcopal Diocese Iowa, 1996—99, standing com., 2000—06, dep. gen. conv., 2000—06; v.p. Sioux City Sch. Bd., 1978—83; bd. dirs., pres. Friends of Iowa Pub. TV, 1978—88; bd. dirs., pres. Family Svc. Boys and Girls Home, Sioux City, 1973—81; bd. dirs. Goodwill Industries S.E. Iowa, 2003—. Named Woman of Yr., Linn County, Cedar Rapids, 1995; recipient Outstanding Svc. awards, Sioux City C. of C., 1976, Siouxland Arts Coun., 1977, Child Advocate-Children's Voice award, 2004; Paul Harris fellow, Rotary, 2005. Mem.: AAUW (bd. dirs., pub. policy chair 1995—2001, pres. 2000—01), Profl. Women's Network Cedar Rapids (bd. mem., Woman of Yr. 1997), NASW, Rotary Internat. Avocations: community service, social justice advocate, reading. Home and Office: 1759 Applewood Pl NE Cedar Rapids IA 52402-3321 E-mail: ziesenancylee@hotmail.com.

ZIESENHENNE, JOHN WILLIAM, insurance agent; b. Richmond, Calif., Apr. 15, 1957; s. Henry George and Lucille Clara (Floring) Z. Student, Contra Costa Jr. Coll., San Pablo, Calif., 1977; BA in U.S. History, U. Calif., Berkeley, 1980. Mgr. Melins Refrigeration Co., Richmond, 1980-83; broker, ptnr. M.A. Hays Ins. Co., Richmond, 1983—. Councilman City of Richmond, 1981—; pres. Mt. Olive Luth. Ch. Mem. Nat. Inst. Art and Disabilities (bd. pres.), Am. Cancer Soc. (vice-chair West Contra Costa chpt.), West Contra Costa YMCA (bd. dirs., past pres.), Youth Svc. Bur. (v.p.), West Contra Costa Salesian Boys and Girls Club (vice-chair). Democrat. Office: MA Hays Ins Co 232 Broadway Richmond CA 94804 Office Phone: 510-235-0353.

ZIETZ, KARYL LYNN KOPELMAN See LYNN, KARYL

ZIFCHAK, WILLIAM C., lawyer; b. 1948; BA, Harvard U., 1970; JD, Columbia U., 1973. Bar: N.Y. 1974, U.S. Ct. Appeals (2d cir.) 1975, U.S. Ct. Appeals (3d cir., D.C. cir.) 1983, U.S. Dist. Ct. (so. dist.) N.Y. 1984. Ptnr., co-chair labor and employment law dept. Kaye, Scholer, Fierman, Hays & Handler, NYC. Planning com. NYU Ann. Nat. Conf. Labor, 1991-97. Contbr. articles to profl. jours. Named a Super Lawyer, NY, 2006, 2007. Mem. ABA (sect. labor and employment law 1975—, subcom. antitrust, RICO and labor rels. law), Assn. Bar City of N.Y. (sec. com. labor and employment law 1984-87), N.Y. State Bar (comml.-fed. litig. sect. co-chair labor and employment law com. 1995-97). Office: Kaye Scholer LLP 425 Park Ave New York NY 10022-3506 Business E-Mail: wzifchak@kayescholer.com.

ZIFF, LARZER, literature and language professor; b. Holyoke, Mass., Oct. 2, 1927; s. Isadore Menden and Sara (Rosenbloom) Z.; m. Ruth Rosalind Geisenberger; children— Joshua, Oliver, Joel, Abigail. Student, Middlebury Coll., 1945-47; MA, U. Chgo., 1951, PhD, 1955; MA (hon.), U. Oxford, Eng., U. Pa. Prof. English U. Calif., Berkeley, 1956-73; univ. lectr. Oxford U., Eng., 1973-78; prof. English U. Pa., 1978-81; Caroline Donovan prof. English Johns Hopkins U., Balt., 1981—, chair dept., 1991-95. Dir. U. Calif. Edn. Abroad Program, U.K., Ireland, 1969-71; cons. and lectr. in field. Author: The Career of John Cotton, 1962; The American 1890's, 1968; Puritanism in America, 1973; Literary Democracy, 1981; Writing in the New Nation, 1991, Return Passages, 2000, Mark Twain: Life and Legacy, 2004; also articles, essays in profl. jours.; mem. editl. bds. including ELH, 1981—94. Recipient numerous awards for excellence in English including Christian Gauss award, the American 1890's, 1967; Fulbright fellow, 1959-60, fellow Am. Coun. Learned Socs., 1963-64, Newberry Libr., 1964, NEH, 1967-68, Guggenheim fellow, 1977-78, Woodrow Wilson Internat. Ctr. for Scholars, 1986-87; Fulbright Disting. Sr. Lectr., 1993. Fellow Am. Acad. Arts and Scis., Am. Philos. Soc., Am. Antiquarian Soc., Soc. Am. Historians. Office: Johns Hopkins U Dept English Baltimore MD 21218 Office Phone: 410-516-4172. Personal E-mail: lziff@attglobal.net.

ZIFFREN, KENNETH, lawyer; b. Chgo., June 24, 1940; BA, Northwestern U., 1962; JD, UCLA, 1965. Bar: Calif. 1967. Law clerk to Chief Justice Warren, 1965—66; ptnr. Ziffren, Brittenham, Branca & Fischer, LA. Mem.: ABA, L.A. Copyright Soc., Beverly Hills Bar Assn., L.A. County Bar Assn. (pres. 1977—78), State Bar Calif. Office: Ziffren Brittenham Branca & Fischer 1801 Century Park W Los Angeles CA 90067-6406

ZIGLAR, JAMES W., biometrics industry executive, lawyer, educator; b. Pascagoula, Miss., Dec. 8, 1945; married; 3 children. BA, George Washington U., 1968, JD, 1972. Bar: Va. 1972, D.C. 1973, N.Y. 1975, Ariz. 1977. Staff asst. Senator James Eastland, Washington, 1964-71; spl. asst. Dept. of Justice, Washington, 1971-72; law clk. to assoc. justice Harry Blackmun U.S. Supreme Ct., Washington, 1972-73; assoc. Mudge, Rose, Guthrie et al, NYC, 1973-77; ptnr. O'Connor, Cavanagh, Anderson et al, Phoenix, 1977-80; sr. v.p. Dillon, Read & Co., NYC, 1980-84; mng. dir. UBS Fin. Svcs., NYC, 1984—87, 1990—98, 2004—05; asst. sec. Dept. of Interior, Washington, 1987-88; mng. dir. Drexel Burnham Lambert Inc., NYC, 1989-90; sgt. at arms U.S. Senate, Washington, 1998—2001; commr. immigration and naturalization serv. U.S. Dept. Justice, Washington, 2001—02; resident fellow Inst. of Politics Harvard U., Cambridge, Mass., 2003; pres. and CEO Cross Match Tech., Inc., Palm Beach Gardens, Fla., 2005—. Disting. vis. prof. Law Sch. George Washington U., 2003—04. Office: 3950 RCA Blvd Ste 5001 Palm Beach Gardens FL 33410 Office Phone: 561-622-1650. Business E-Mail: james.ziglar@crossmatch.com.

ZIGLER, EDWARD FRANK, psychologist, educator; b. Kansas City, Mo., Mar. 1, 1930; s. Louis and Gertrude (Gleitman) Z.; m. Bernice Gorelick, Aug. 28, 1955; 1 child, Scott. BA, U. Mo.-Kansas City, 1954; PhD, U. Tex., 1958; MA (hon.), Yale, 1967; DSc (hon.), Boston Coll., 1985; LHD (hon.), Bank St. Coll. Edn., 1989, U. New Haven, 1991, St. Joseph Coll., 1991; PhD (hon.), U. Mo., 1993, CUNY, 1995, degree (hon.), 1995, Wheelock Coll., 2005; LLD (hon.), Gonzaga U., 1995; HHD, Park U., 2000; LHD, McGill U., 2001. Psychol. intern Worcester (Mass.) State Hosp., 1957-59; asst. prof. psychology U. Mo., 1958-59; mem. faculty Yale U., 1959—, prof. psychology and child study center, 1967—, Sterling prof., 1976—, dir. child devel. program, 1961-76, chmn. dept. psychology, 1973-74; head psychology sect. Yale Child Study Center, 1967—; dir. Bush Center in Child Devel. and Social Policy, 1977—. Chief Children's Bur. NEW, Washington, 1970-72; cons. in field, 1962—; mem. nat. steering com. Project Head Start, 1965-70, chmn. 15th anniversary Head Start com., 1980; mem. nat. adv. com. Nat. Lab. Early Childhood Edn., 1967-70; nat. rsch. adv. bd. Nat. Assn. Retarded Children, 1968-73; nat. rsch. coun. Project Follow-Through, 1968-70; chmn. adv. com. Vietnamese Children's Resettlement, 1975; mem. Pres.'s Com. on Mental Retardation, 1980; joint appointee Yale U. Sch. Medicine, 1982—, chmn. Yale Infant Care Leave Commn., 1983-85, Parents as Tchrs., 1986—; mem. adv. com. Head Start Quality and Expansion, 1993; mem. adv. com. on svcs. for families with infants and toddlers HHS, 1994; mem. 25th Anniversary hon. com. Children's Def. Fund, 1997; mem. program com. Head Start's 5th Nat. Rsch. Conf., 1998—; mem. nat. adv. panel hon. chair, hist. mentor Nat. Head Start Assn.: Fulfilling the Promise 2010 Project 1998-00; mem. adv. com. Head Start Rsch. and Evaluation for Adminstrn. for Children and Families, 1999—, Nat. Partnership's Family Leave Income Initiative, 1999—; mem. program com. Head Start Nat. Rsch. Conf., 2005. Author, co-author, editor books and monographs; contbr. articles to profl. jours. With AUS, 1951-53. Recipient Gunnar Dybwad Disting. scholar in behavioral and social sci. award Nat. Assn. Retarded Children, 1964, 69, Social Sci. Aux. award, 1962, Alumni Achievement award U. Mo., 1965, Alumnus of Yr. award, 1972, C. Anderson Aldrich award Am. Acad. Pediatrics, 1985, Nat. Achievement award Assn. for Advancement of Psychology, 1985, Dorothea Lynde Dix Humanitarian award for svc. to handicapped Elwyn Inst., 1987, Sci. Leadership award Joseph P. Kennedy Jr. Found., 1990, Mensa Edn. and Rsch. Found. award for excellence, 1990,

Nat. Head Start Assn. award, 1990 Founders award, 1995, Bldg. dedication Edward Zigler Head Start Ctr., 1990, As They Grow award in edn. Parents mag., 1990, Excellence in Edn. award Pi Lambda Theta, 1991, Friend of Edn. award Conn. Edn. Assn., 1991, Loyola-Mellon Social Sci. award 1991, Pres.'s award Conn. Assn. Human Svcs., 1991, Harold W. McGraw, Jr. prize in edn., 1992, Disting. Achievement in Rsch. award Internat. Assn. Sci. Study of Mental Deficiency, 1992, Disting. Svc. award Coun. Chief State Sch. Officers, 1993, Outstanding Fed. Leadership in Support of Head Start Rsch., Adminstrn. on Children, Youth and Families, 1993, Child and Family Advocacy award Parents as Tchrs. Nat. Ctr., 1994, Nat. Distinction award U. Pa. Edn. Alumni Assn., 1994, Disting. Fellow award So. Conn. State U. chpt. Phi Delta Kappa, 1997, Lifetime Achievement award in Applied and Preventive Psychology Am Assn. Applied and Preventive Psychology, 1998, Recognition award Coun. for Early Childhood Profls., Child Devel. Assocs., 1999, Heinz award pub. policy, 1999, Nat. Head Start Assn. award appreciation, 2000, Disting. Svc. medal Tchrs. Coll. Columbia U., 2000, Disting. Alumnus U. Tex., 2000, Key to the City, Independence, Mo., 2000, Nat. Head Start Assn. award appreciation, 2000, Disting. Svc. medal Tchrs. Coll. Columbia U., 2000, Lifetime Mentoring award, ACYF, 2000, Lifetime Contbn. psychology award CT Psychol. Assn., 2000, Lifetime Commitment to comty. svc. award Ct dept. higher edn. and CT commn. on nat. and comty. svc., 2001, Florence Halpern award disting. profl. contbns. in clin. psychology APA, 2001, Bridges Over Barrtiers awrd, Family REsources Youth Svcs. Coalition Ky., 2002, others; named Hon. Commr. Internat. Yr. of Child, 1979. Fellow Am. Orthopsychiat. Assn. (Blanche F. Ittleson award 1989, pres. 1993-94), APA (pres. divsn. 7, 1974-75, G. Stanley Hall award 1979, award for disting. contbns. to psychology in pub. interest 1982, Nicholas Hobbs award 1985, award for disting. profl. contbns. to knowledge 1986, Edgar A. Doll award 1986, award for disting. contbn. to cmty. psychology and cmty. mental health 1989, pres.-elect divsn. 37 1997, pres. 1998, past pres. 1999, Bronfenbrenner Lifetime Contbn. award divsn. 7 1998, Florence Halpern award for disting. profl. contbns. in clin. psychology divsn. 12 2001); mem. Inst. Medicine of NAS, AAAS, Am. Acad. Mental Retardation (Career Rsch. award 1982), Soc. Psychol. Study Social Issues (Kurt Lewin meml. award 1995), Zero to Three (Dolley Madison award 1995), P.R. Head Start Assn. (Outstanding Leadership award 1995, True Father of Headstart recognition award 1996, award of appreciation for lifelong support and participation 1997), Am. Psychol. Found. (gold medal for life contbn. 1997, Parents Child Care award for advocacy 1998, Heinz award in pub. policy, 1999). Home: 177 Ridgewood Ave North Haven CT 06473-4442 Office: Edward Zigler Ctr Child Devel and Social Policy 310 Prospect St New Haven CT 06511 E-mail: edward.zigler@yale.edu.

ZIGO, PAUL EDWARD, historian, educator; b. Newark, July 14, 1942; s. Edward and Jeannette Zigo; m. Kim Irene Schmerler; children: Paul Jr., Drew, Travis, Marc, Kristen. BA in History, Rutgers U., New Brunswick, NJ, 1964; M in Pers. and Guidance, Rider U., Lawrenceville, NJ, 1973; diploma, US Army War Coll., Carlisle Barracks, Pa., 1989; M in Recent Am. Diplomatic and Mil. History, Temple U., Phila., 2000. Lic. radio broadcaster FCC. Asst. dir. cmty. rels. Monmouth U., West Long Branch, NJ, 1966—75, dir. cmty. rels., 1975—77; dir. off campus svcs. Brookdale CC, Lincroft, NJ, 1977—2003, asst. prof. history, 2003—, dir. Ctr. World War II Studies and Conflict Resolution, 2003—. Exec. prodr. cable series Triumphant Spirit: America's World War II Generation Speaks, 2002—; bd. dirs. Eastern CC Social Sci. Assn., Arlington, Va.; adv. coun. Brookdale CC Internat. Ctr. Policy adv. bd. mem. NJ Profl. Devel. Ctr. Early Childhood Edn., Union, 2001—03; mem., exec. com. Monmouth U., Monmouth Jr. Sci. Symposium, West Long Branch, NJ, 1979—2005; bd. dirs. Western Monmouth C. of C., Freehold, NJ, 1999—2005; mem. edn. adv. coun. Battleship NJ (BB 62) History Mus., Camden; mem. allocations com. Monmouth County United Way, Farmingdale; founder ann. study abroad program Brookdale CC, 2000, chair adv. coun. Ctr. for WWII Studies and Conflict Resolution; mem. Ft. Monmouth Retiree Coun., Eatontown, NJ; founder Ctr. for WWII Studies and Conflict Resolution, Brookdale CC, 2000. Col. USAR, 1964—94. Decorated Def. Meritorious Svc. medal US Dept. of Def., Legion of Merit medal US Army; named to Point Pleasant Beach HS Hall of Fame, Point Pleasant Beach Pub. Edn. Found., 2002; recipient Cert. of Recognition for Svc. to Monmouth County, Monmouth County Bd. of Chosen Freeholders, 1994, Excellence award for Outstanding Contbns. to Tchg., Leadership and Learning, Nat. Inst. for Staff and Orgnl. Devel., 2005, George Washington Honor medal, Freedoms Found. at Valley Forge, 2006. Mem.: Eastern Cmty. Colls. Social Sci. Assn. (assoc.), Brookdale CC Faculty Assn. (assoc.), Mil. History Soc. (assoc.), Assn. of US Army (assoc.), Monmouth chpt. Vets. Battle of Bulge (assoc.). Roman Catholic. Avocations: military history, overseas and national travel, photography. Home: 15 Beach Rd Neptune NJ 07753 Office: Brookdale CC 765 Newman Springs Rd Lincroft NJ 07738 Home Phone: 732-775-2146; Office Phone: 732-224-2029. Office Fax: 732-224-2444. Personal E-mail: pzigo@optonline.net. Business E-Mail: pzigo@brookdalecc.edu.

ZIGWEID, RICHARD NEIL, music educator; b. Buffalo, Wyo., May 29, 1977; s. Robert E. and Peggy J. Zigweid; m. Christy Anne Davis, June 16, 2001; 1 child, Whitney Christine. B in Music Edn., U. Wyo., 2000. Cert. tchr. Nebr. Dept. Edn., 2001. Band/choir tchr. Limon (Colo.) Pub. Schs., 2000—01; band tchr. Sidney (Nebr.) Pub. Schs., 2001—. Sponsor Nat. Jr. Honor Soc., Sidney, 2003—04. Mem.: Music Educator Nat. Conf. (assoc.). Democrat. Office: Sidney Public Schools 2103 King St Sidney NE 69162 Home Phone: 308-254-3412; Office Phone: 308-254-5853. Office Fax: 308-254-5992.

ZIKMUND, BARBARA BROWN, minister, religious organization administrator, educator; b. Ann Arbor, Mich., Oct. 16, 1939; d. Henry Daniels and Helen Langworthy Brown; m. Joseph Zikmund II, Aug. 26, 1961; 1 child, Brian Joseph. BA, Beloit Coll., 1961; BDiv, Duke U., 1964, PhD, 1969; D in Div (hon.), Doane Coll., 1984, Chgo. Theol. Sem., 1985, Ursinus Coll., 1989; LHD, U. Hartford, 1998. Ordained to ministry United Ch. of Christ, 1964. Instr. Albright Coll., Reading, Pa., 1966-67, Temple U., Phila., 1967-68, Ursinus Coll., Collegeville, Pa., 1968-69; asst. prof. religious studies Albion Coll., Mich., 1970-75; asst. prof. ch. history, dir. studies Chgo. Theol. Sem., 1975-80; dean and assoc. prof. ch. history Pacific Sch. Religion, Berkeley, Calif., 1981-85, dean and prof. ch. history, 1985-90; pres. Hartford (Conn.) Sem., 1990-2000; vis. scholar Wesley Theol. Sem., Washington. Prof. grad. sch. am. studies Doshisha U., Kyoto, Japan, 2000-05; vis. Life Cycle Inst. scholar Cath. U. Am., 2005-07; chmn. United Ch. of Christ Hist. Coun., 1983-85, mem. coun. for ecumenism, 1983-89; mem. Nat. Coun. Chs. Commn. on Faith and Order, 1979-87, World Coun. of Chs. Programme Theol. Edn., 1984-91, Nat. Coun. Chs. Working Group on Inter-Faith Rels., 1992-96, Nat. Coun. Chs. Commn. on Inter-faith Rels., 1996-2007, chair Commn. on Inter-faith Rels., 2000-07, World Conf. Assns. for Theol. Instns., sec. treas., 1992-96, pres., 1996-2000. Author: Discovering the Church, 1983, Clergy Women: An Uphill Calling, 1998; editor: Hidden Histories in the UCC, 1984, vol. 2, 1987; (with Manschreck) American Religous Experiment, 1976; mem. editl. bd. Jour. Ecumenical Studies, 1987—, Mid-Stream, 1991—; series editor: Living Theological Heritage of the United Church of Christ, co-editor Vol. 7 United and Uniting, 2005; contbr. articles to profl. jours. Mem. City Coun., Albion, Mich., 1972-75; elector Wadsworth Atheneum, 1994-2000; corporator St. Francis Hosp., 1994-2000, Hartford Hosp., 1996-2000; pres. Greater Hartford Consortium for Higher Edn., 1994-96. NEH grantee, 1974-75; Woodrow Wilson fellow, 1964-66; vis. scholar Schlesinger Libr. Women's History, Radcliffe Coll., 1988-89, Disting. Alumna, Duke Divinity Sch., 1994; recipient Disting. Svc. Citation Beloit Coll., 1986; Antoinette Brown award, United Ch. of Christ, 2005. Mem. Assn. Theol. Schs. (v.p. 1984-86, pres. 1986-88, issues implementation grantee 1983-84, Disting. Svc. award 2004), Am. Soc. Ch. History (coun. 1983-85, pres. elect 1996-97, pres. 1997-98), Internat. Assn. Women Ministers (v.p. 1977-79), AAUW (v.p. 1973-75), Greater Hartford C. of C. (bd. dirs. 1992-95). Democrat. Home: 4545 Connecticut Ave NW Apt 510 Washington DC 20008-6018 Office: Wesley Theol Sem 4500 Massachusetts Ave Washington DC 20016 Office Phone: 202-885-8600. Business E-Mail: beebeezee@verizon.net. E-mail: zikmund@cua.edu.

ZILBERT, ALLEN BRUCE, education educator, computer scientist, consultant; b. Bronx, NY, May 26, 1957; s. Murray and Perla Z.; m. Barbara Dale Palley, July 1, 1984; children: Heather Robynne, Jared Lee. BA in Econ., CUNY, 1978; MBA, St. Johns U., 1980, advanced profl. cert., 1982; MEd in Adminstrv. Computer Systems Edn., Columbia U., 1986, EdD, 1988; postgrad., Kennedy-Western U., 1995—. Instr. bus. computer info. systems & quantitative methods Hofstra U., Hempstead, NY, 1981-83; asst. prof. info. systems Pace U. Sch. Computer Sci. and Info. Systems, NYC, 1983-89; dir. ancillary sys. Advanced Med. Sys., Rockville Centre, 1989—90; asst. prof. mgmt. Coll. Mgmt. LI U. Sch. Bus., Brookville, NJ, 1990—94; asst. prof. mgmt. info. sys. Sy Syms Sch. Bus., David Zysman prof. of mgmt. info. sys. Yeshiva U., NYC, 1994-2000; assoc. prof. math./computer sci. Molloy Coll., Rockville Centre, 2000—03, dir. computer sci. and computer info. sys. programs, 2000—03; assoc. prof. computer info. sys. Briarcliffe Coll., Patchogue/ Bethpage, 2003—, chair computer info. sys. dept., 2003—04, dir. acad. portal and web sys., 2003—07, dir. acad. tech., 2007—, v.p. acad. senate. Mem. acad. affairs com. Pace U. Sch. Computer Sci. and Info. Sys., 2003—, v.p. academic senate, 2003-; chmn. personal computer resources com. Advanced Med. Sys., 1989-90; campuswide computer com. LI U., 1991-94, chmn., 1993-94, chmn. scholarship awards com., 1990-91; assembly collegiate schs. bus. curriculum planning com. Coll. Mgmt., 1993-94, chmn. computer needs, usage and stds. com., 1990-93, chmn. mgmt. dept. computer com., chmn. scholar awards com., 1992-93; book and software reviewer. Contbr. articles to profl. jours. Mem. IEEE, Assn. for Computer Tng. and Support, Assn. for Computing Machinery, Assn. of Info. Tech. Profls., Internat. Assn. for Computer Info. Sys., Internat. Assn. Mgmt., Info. Resources Mgmt. Assn Business E-Mail: azilbert@bcl.edu.

ZILKHA, EZRA KHEDOURI, banker; b. Baghdad, Iraq, July 31, 1925; arrived in U.S., 1941, naturalized, 1950; s. Khedouri A. and Louise (Bashi) Z.; m. Cecile Iny, Feb. 6, 1950; children: Elias Donald, Donna, Bettina Louise. Grad., Hill Sch., Pottstown, Pa., 1943; AB, Wesleyan U., Middletown, Conn., 1947, LLD (hon.), 1987. Dir. Zilkha & Sons, Inc., NYC, 1946—, chmn., pres., 1956—. Dir. Cigna Corp., Phila., 1968—96, former chmn. investment com.; dir. Mothercare, Ltd., England, 1970—82, INA Life Ins. Co. of NY, 1973—87, Blyth Eastman Dillon & Co., 1976—79, Newhall Land & Farming Co., Calif., 1977—2004, Revlon, Inc., 1981—95, Chgo. Milw. Corp., 1981—96, Cambridge Assocs., Boston, 1988—2000; vice chmn. bd. Fortune Bancorp, 1990—94, Handy & Harman, 1969—88; chmn. bd. Fidelity Internat. Bank., 1968—79; chmn. Union Holdings, 1984—90. Trustee emeritus, former chmn. investment com. Wesleyan U.; hon. trustee, former chmn. investment com. Brookings Inst., Washington; former trustee Spence Sch., NYC, French Inst., NYC, Lycee Francais de NY; trustee Am. Soc. French Legion of Honor; former mem. exec. com., former chmn. bd. Internat. Ctr. for Disabled, NYC. Decorated comdr. Legion d'Honneur, officer Ordre Nat. du Merite (France); recipient Freedom of Human Spirit award Internat. Ctr. for Disabled, 1989, Pilier d'Or award French Inst./Alliance Francaise, 1995, Charles de Ferry de Fontnouvelle award Lycee Francais de N.Y., 2003. Mem.: Coun. Fgn. Rels., The Brook Club, Travellers Club, Meadow Club, Knickerbocker Club, Racquet & Tennis Club. Office Phone: 212-758-7750.

ZILLMER, JOHN J., waste management administrator; MBA, Kellogg Graduate School Northwestern Univ. Mgmt. Aramark Corp., pres. food and support services group, exec. vice-pres.; chmn. bd. and CEO Allied Waste Industries, 2005—. Mem. bd. dir. United Stations Directors, Inc. Office: Allied Waste Management Ste 100 15880 N Greenway Hayden Loop Scottsdale AZ 85260 Office Phone: 480-627-2700. *

ZILLY, THOMAS SAMUEL, federal judge; b. Detroit, Jan. 1, 1935; s. George Samuel and Bernice M. (McWhinney) Z.; divorced; children: John, Peter, Paul, Luke; m. Jane Greller Noland, Oct. 8, 1988; stepchildren: Allison Noland, Jennifer Noland. BA, U. Mich., 1956; LLD, Cornell U., 1962. Bar: Wash. 1962, U.S. Ct. Appeals (9th cir.) 1962, U.S. Supreme Ct. 1976. Ptnr. Lane, Powell, Moss & Miller, Seattle, 1962-88; dist. judge U.S. Dist. Ct. (we. dist.) Wash., Seattle, 1988—. Judge pro tem Seattle Mcpl. Ct., 1972-80; mem. adv. com. bankruptcy rules U.S. Judicial Conf., 1998—; chair adv. com. U.S. Jud. Conf., 2004—. Contbr. articles to profl. jours. Mem. Cen. Area Sch. Council, Seattle, 1969-70; scoutmaster Thunderbird Dist. council Boy Scouts Am. Seattle, 1976-84; bd. dirs. East Madison YMCA. Served to lt. (j.g.) USN, 1956-59. Recipient Tuahku Dist. Service to Youth award Boy Scouts Am., 1983. Mem. ABA, Wash. State Bar Assn., Seattle-King County Bar Assn. (treas. 1979-80, trustee 1980-83, sec. 1983-84, 2d v.p. 1984-85, 1st v.p. 1985-86, pres. 1986-87). Office: US Dist Ct 700 Stewart St Ste 15229 Seattle WA 98101

ZILTZ, BOB, publishing executive; Account mgr. Prevention mag. Rodale Inc., Chgo., 1993—2001, nat. advt. dir., 2001—03, assoc. pub. nat. advt. sales, 2003, v.p., pub. Prevention mag., 2006—. Office: Prevention mag 733 3rd Ave #15 New York NY 10017 Office Phone: 212-573-0217. E-mail: Bob.Ziltz@Rodale.com. *

ZILVETI, CARLOS BENJAMIN, preventive medicine physician, pediatrician; b. Sucre, Bolivia, June 14, 1928; came to U.S., 1956; s. Carlos and Marina (De La Reza) Z.; m. Halina J. Daszewski, Sept. 8, 1957 (div. Sept. 1976); 1 child: Carlos Joseph III; m. Vita Palazzolo, Sept. 5, 1987. BS, Sacred Heart Coll., Sucre, Bolivia, 1946; MD, U. San Francisco Xavier, Sucre, Bolivia, 1954; MPH, Yale U., New Haven, Conn., 1966. Physician in rural medicine Bolivian Power Co., La Paz, 1955; intern Hosp. Obrero Victor Paz Estenssoro, La Paz, 1956; asst. resident in pediats. St. Luke's Hosp., Meml. Cancer Ctr., Woman's Hosp., NYC, 1957-58; resident and chief resident in pediats. Hosp. of St. Raphael, New Haven, 1958-59; pvt. practice New Haven and Branford, Conn., 1960-63; dir. maternal-child health New Haven Dept. Health, 1964-74; regional med. officer South and Ctrl. Am. Peace Corps, Bogota, Colombia, 1975-76; regional med. officer, sci. attache in West Africa U.S. Dept. of State, Liberia, Ghana, Togo, Sierra Leone, 1976-79; reserve appt. of maj., advanced to col. USAF, San Antonio, 1979-91, chief environ. medicine Wilford Hall Med. Ctr., 1979-83, cons. preventive and occupl. medicine, 1983-91, cons. aerospace-preventive medicine Wilford Hall Med. Ctr. Lackland AFB, Tex., 1984-91, ret. col., 1991. Cons. FDA, HEW, Washington, 1966-75; cons. to Headstart Am. Acad. Pediats., Stanford-Norwalk, Conn., 1968-75; regional med. officer, sci. attache West Africa U.S. Dept. State. Contbr. articles to profl. jours. Chmn. gov.'s task force Conn. State Dept. Health, Hartford, 1969-75. Fellow Am. Acad. Pediats. (emeritus), Am. Coll. Preventive Medicine (emeritus); mem. APHA, AMA, New Eng. Pub. Health Assn., Conn. Acad. Preventive Medicine, Am. Occupl. Med. Assn. Avocations: swimming, tennis, golf, travel, classical music. Home: 9222 Dover Rdg San Antonio TX 78250-3557

ZIMAN, BARRY RUSSELL, government relations executive; s. Arthur Ziman and Eileen Ziman Ravin. BA, SUNY, 1980—84. Legislative dir. NY State Assembly, 1988—89; dir. of legislation and commn. NY State Assemblyman Larry Seabrook, Albany, 1985—89; dir. of govt. and pub. affairs NY and NJ. Printing Industry Assn., 1989—92; dir. of strategic advocacy Consumer Splty. Products Assn., Washington, 1992—2001; dir. state affairs Coll. of Am. Pathologists, Washington, 2001—. Polit. analyst Manila Broadcasting Co., Washington, 2003—05; cons. Gerson Lehman Group, NYC, 2004. Dep. mayor's econ. adv. com., NYC, 1991—92; state student coord. NY State Dem. Com., Mondale-Ferraro Presdl. Campaign, 1984; campaign adviser State Senator Larry Seabrook For U.S. Congress, NYC, 2000—01; bd. mem. Oneonta Ancillary Services Corp., 1983—84, Binding Together Inc. (Non-Profit), NYC, 1991—92. Recipient President's award, Coll. of Am. Pathologists, 2003, 2004; scholar NY State Regents scholar, NY State Regents, 1979. Office: Coll of Am Pathologists 1350 I Street NW Ste 590 Washington DC 20005 Home Phone: 703-271-6260; Office Phone: 202-354-7117.

ZIMAND, HARVEY FOLKS, lawyer; b. NYC, Aug. 28, 1928; s. Savel and Gertrude (Folks) Z.; m. Ingeborg Rockosch, 1963 (div. 1980); children: Patricia Folks Carpenter, Stephanie Folks Plexico; m. Noel French, Apr. 30, 1983 (dec. 2006). BA, Colgate U., 1950; postgrad., Oxford U., Eng., 1950; MA, U. Chgo., 1951; postgrad., Columbia U., 1952-53; LL.B., Yale U., 1957. Bar: N.Y. 1957. Rapporteur Council for Fgn. Relations, NYC, 1952-53; atty. Dept. Navy, Washington, 1956-70; ptnr. Kelley Drye & Warren, NYC, 1970—. Dir. Toronto-Dominion Trust Co., N.Y.C., 1975-83. Bd. editors The Chase Jour. Bd. dirs. Virginia Day Nursery, N.Y.C., 1980-84. Served to cpl. U.S. Army, 1951-53 Named to The Best Lawyers in Am., 1996—, Best Lawyers in NY, 1996—. Fellow NY Bar Found., Am. Coll. Trust and Estate Counsel; mem. ABA, NY State Bar Assn., Assn. Bar City of NY, Estate Planning Coun., Univ. Club, Yale Club (NYC), Randolph Mountain Club (NH). Republican. Episcopalian. Home: 120 E 81st St New York NY 10028-1428 Office: Kelley Drye & Warren LLP 101 Park Ave New York NY 10178-0002 Business E-Mail: hzimand@kelleydrye.com.

ZIMBALIST, MICHAEL, publishing executive; m. Melissa Zimbalist; children: Lila, Peri, Quentin. BA in Chemistry and Philosophy, Brown U., 1979. Mgmt. positions AT&T Downtown Digital; dir. production Capital Cities/ABC, 1995—97; gen. mgr., online svcs. United Media, Divsn. E.W. Scripps Co., 1997—99; exec. v.p., mktg. and bus. develop. ePod Corp. (sold to Star Media Network), 1999—2001; exec. dir. Online Publishers Assn., 2001—04, pres., 2004—06; v.p., R&D ops. NY Times Co., 2006—. Disney imagineer, wrote and produced a number of i; frequent commentator on issues affecting the online media and advertising bus.; regular spkr. at industry conf. and events. Exec. prodr. (Disney imagineer, wrote & produced): a number of interactive exhibits at Epcot Ctr. and Euro Disneyland for sponsors such as AT&T and IBM; contbr. TV shows for Hanna Barbara and interactive games for MCA/Universal Studios; guest appearances NBC News and CNN; contbr. to NY Times, Wall Street Jour., and USA Today. Office: NY Times Co 229 W 43rd St New York NY 10036

ZIMBARDO, PHILIP GEORGE, psychologist, educator, writer; b. NYC, Mar. 23, 1933; s. George and Margaret (Bisicchia) Z.; m. Christina Maslach, Aug. 10, 1972; children: Zara, Tanya; 1 son by previous marriage, Adam. AB, Bklyn. Coll., 1954; MS, Yale U., 1955, PhD, 1959; D (hon.), U. Peru, 1996; LHD in Clin. Psychology, Pacific Grad. Sch. Psychology, 1996, D (hon.), 1997, Nat. U. of San Martin, 1996, Nat. U. Peru, Thessalonoki, Greece, 1997, Aristotle U., 1998. Asst. prof. psychology Yale U., New Haven, 1959-61, NYU, NYC, 1961-67; vis. assoc. prof. psychology Columbia U., NYC, 1967-68; prof. psychology Stanford (Calif.) U., 1968—. Pres. P.G. Zimbardo, Inc., San Francisco; sr. project advisor Exploratorium, 1993; host, writer, gen. acad. advisor PBS-TV series Discovering Psychology, 1987, 2001; cons. NBC. Author: Cognitive Control of Motivation, 1969, Canvassing for Peace, 1970, Psychology and Life, 18th edit., 2005, Shyness, What It Is, What To Do About It, 1977, Influencing Attitudes and Changing Behavior, rev. edit., 1977, The Shyness Workbook, 1979, A Parent's Guide to the Shy Child, 1981, reprinted, 1999, The Psychology of Attitude Change and Social Influence, 1991, Core Concepts in Psychology, 5th edit., 2005, The Lucifer Effect, 2007. Ctr. for Advanced Study of Behavioral Scis. fellow, 1971; recipient Peace medal Tokyo Police Dept., 1972, City Medal of Honor, Salamanca, Spain, Disting. Tchr. award Am. Psychol. Found., 1975, award Havel Found., 2005. Fellow APA (pres. 2002, Presdl. citation Discovery Psychology series 1994, Tchg. award 1999); mem. Am. Psychol. Soc., AAUP, Internat. Congress Psychology, Western Psychol. Assn. (pres. 1985, 2001), Ea. Psychol. Assn., Calif. Psychol. Assn. (Disting. Contbn. to Rsch. award 1978), Soc. for Psychol. Study of Social Issues, Coun. Sci. Soc. Pres. (chair 2005), Sigma Xi, Phi Beta Kappa, Psi Chi. Roman Catholic. Office: Stanford U Psychology Dept Stanford CA 94305 Office Phone: 415-776-4748. Office Fax: 415-673-2294. Business E-Mail: zim@stanford.edu. *One of the few virtues of growing up in a poor urban ghetto is the realization that people are the most important resource we have— to be used wisely, well and as often as possible. The second is the tempering of book learning by street wits. The third is to value a career that allows me to contribute to improving the quality of our lives through research and teaching.*

ZIMET, CARL NORMAN, psychologist, educator; b. Vienna, June 3, 1925; came to U.S., 1943, naturalized, 1945; s. Leon and Gisela (Kosser) Z.; m. Sara F. Goodman, June 4, 1950; children: Andrew, Gregory. BA, Cornell U., 1949; PhD, Syracuse U., 1953; postdoctoral fellow, Stanford U., 1953-55. Diplomate in clin. psychology Am. Bd. Profl. Psychology (trustee 1966-74). Instr., then asst. prof. psychology and psychiatry Yale U., 1955-63; mem. faculty U. Colo. Med. Center, 1963—, prof. clin. psychology, 1965—2007, head div., 1963—2006, prof. emeritus, 2007—. Mem. Colo. Bd. Psychol. Examiners, 1966-72, Colo. Mental Health Planning Commn., 1964-66; mem. acad. adv. com. John F. Kennedy Child Devel. Center, U. Colo., 1966-68; chmn. Council for Nat. Register of Health Service Providers in Psychology, 1975-85, pres., mem. exec. bd. div. psychotherapy, 1970-89; chair exec. com. Assn. Psychol. Internship Ctrs., 1988-91. Bd. editors: Jour. Clin. Psychology, 1962-91, Jour. Clin. and Cons. Psychology, 1964-73, Psychotherapy, 1967—, Profl. Psychology, 1969-75. With USNR, 1943-46. Recipient Disting. Service award Colo. Psychol. Assn., 1976 Fellow: APA (coun. reps. 1969—72, 1973—76, bd. dirs. 1985—88, Disting. award for profl. contbn., div. psychotherapy and div. clin. psychology 1987), Soc. Personality Assessment (pres. 1975—76, 1975—76, chair gen. psychol. svcs. 1987—97, bd. dirs.); mem.: Med. Sch. Profs. Psychology (pres. 1992—94, bd. dirs. 2004—06), Denver Psychoanalytic (trustee 1968—71), Am. Acad. Clin. Psychology (pres. 1993—2001). Home: 400 E 3rd Ave # 901 Denver CO 80203 Office Phone: 303-315-8611. Business E-Mail: carl.zimet@uchsc.edu.

ZIMET, LLOYD, sport psychologist, health educator, program planner and administrator; b. Bklyn., 1951; s. Victor R. and Marcia Z. BA, Whittier Coll., Calif., 1973; MA, U. Md., 1983, PhD, 1984; MPH, NYU, 1989. Ordained min. Universal Life Ch., 2007. Head basketball coach Aarhus U., Denmark, 1973—78, 1980—82, 1985—86; resident dir. U. Md., College Park, 1978—80; sports supr. Montgomery County Dept. Recreation, Md., 1978, 1982—84; dir. health promotion Optimal Fitness Inc., NYC, 1986—91; internat. cons. cmty. and occupational health, 1984—; dir. World of Discovery Day Camp, Bklyn., 1997—2000. Dir. edn. AIDS Ctr. of Queens County, NY, 1989-90; bd. dirs. Patricia Manning Meml. Fund childhood cancer Am. Cancer Soc., Queens, 1988-95; mem. AIDS med. adv. com. NYC Bd. Edn., 1989-90; mem. adv. bd. Adolescent Health Network, Queens, 1989-90; keynote speaker NYU Health Edn. Alumni, 1990, USPHS Region II Conf., 1991; prevention specialist Hillsborough County Sch. Dist., Fla., 2004, mem. sch. health adv. com., 2004, staff & program developer, 2005; program dir. HIV/STD/Pregnancy Prevention Program, Youth Risk Behavior Survery, Fla. Youth Surveys, 2005; mem. AIDS adv. com. Dept. Edn., State of Fla., 2004, Dist. Wellness Task Force. Bd. govs. US Amateur Boxing Fedn., Colorado Springs, Colo., 1988-91; bd. dirs. Met. Amateur Boxing Fedn., NYC, 1988-91; mem. USA Boxing Nat. Scholarship com., 1984-88. Fellow: Soc. Pub. Health Educators; mem.: AAHPERD, APHA, APA.

ZIMMAN STETSON, NANCY See STUART, NANCY

ZIMMATORE, JOHN JOSEPH, information technology manager; s. John J. and Rose M. Zimmatore; m. Emily L. D'Alessio, Dec. 4, 2001. BA, SUNY, Stony Brook, 1977, MA, 1979. Program mgr. usability Internat. Bus. Machines Corp, Atlanta, 1985—94; sr. user interface arch. Sales Technologies, Inc., Atlanta, 1994—97; sr. human factors engr. Delta Air Lines, Atlanta, 1997—99; exec. dir. of info. architecture iXL, Inc., Atlanta, 1999—2001; mgr. user experience InterContinental Hotels Group, Atlanta, 2002—05; sr. mgr. usabilty Staples, Inc., Framingham, Mass., 2006—07. Pres., prin. cons. Effortless Tech., Inc., Atlanta, 1999—2000; presenter in field. Disaster comm., radio operator Worcester Emergency Comm. Team, Mass., 2006—07. Recipient Interface Design Achievement award, Internat. Bus. Machines Corp., 1986, First Invention Publ. award, 1989, Process Quality award, 1994; grantee, Sigma Xi, 1979; scholar, NY State Bd. Regents, 1973—77. Mem.: Usability Profls. Assn., Assn. Computing Machinery, Am. Radio Relay League. Achievements include invention of multiple-item clipboard; rapid prototyping tool; graphic symbol to indicate immediate actions from a menu bar; design of first Common User Access compliant application; graphical user interface for aircraft boarding process. Avocations: amateur radio, music, photography. Home Phone: 508-799-9125; Office Phone: 508-253-3848. Business E-Mail: john.zimmatore@staples.com.

ZIMMER, DONALD WILLIAM, former professional baseball coach, professional baseball manager, retired professional baseball player; b. Cin., Jan. 17, 1931; s. Harold Lesley and Lorraine Bertha (Ernst) Z.; m. Jean Carol Bauerle, Aug. 16, 1951; children: Thomas Jeffrey, Donna Jean. Student Pub. Schs., Cin. Baseball player Dodger Farm Clubs, 1949-54, Bklyn. Dodgers, 1954-57, L.A. Dodgers, 1958-59, 1963, Chgo. Cubs, 1960-61, N.Y. Mets, 1962, Cin. Reds, 1962, Washington Senators, 1963-65, Toei Flyers, Tokyo, 1966; mgr. Cin. Reds Farm Clubs, Knoxville and Buffalo, 1967, Indpls., 1968, San Diego Padre Farm Clubs, Key West, Fla., 1969, Padre Farm Club, Salt Lake City, 1970; coach Montreal Expos, Que., Canada, 1971; mgr. San Diego Padres, 1972-73; coach Boston Red Sox, 1974-76, 1992, mgr., 1976-80, Tex. Rangers, 1981-82; coach Chgo. Cubs, 1984, 85, 86, mgr., 1988-91; coach San Francisco Giants, 1987, Colo. Rockies, Denver, 1993-95, N.Y. Yankees, 1983, 1986, 1996—2003; sr. baseball advisor Tampa Bay Devil Rays, 2004—07. Mem. minor league All-Star Teams, Hornell, N.Y., 1950, Elmira, N.Y., 1951, Mobile, Ala., 1952, St. Paul, 1953; player World Series teams 1955, 56, 59; coach World Series teams 1975, 96, 98, 99, 2000, 01, 03; mem. adv. bd. Baseball Assistance Team. Recipient Bill Stern award NBC, 1949; named St. Paul Rookie of Yr., 1953, All Star Team Player, 1961, All Star Coach, 1978, 81, 90, 97, 99, 2000, 01, 02, 03; named Nat. League Mgr. of Yr. 1989. Mem. Profl. Baseball Players Assn. (life), Maj. League Baseball Players Alumni Assn., Old Time Ball Players Wis. Office: c/o Tampa Bay Devil Rays 1 Tropicana Drive Saint Petersburg FL 33705 Office Phone: 727-825-3137.

ZIMMER, GEORGE A., men's apparel executive; b. NYC, Nov. 21, 1948; s. Robert Zimmer; m. Lorri Zimmer; 4 children. BA in Econ., Washington U., St. Louis, 1970. Founder The Men's Wearhouse Inc., Houston, 1973, chmn., pres., 1974—91, chmn., pres., CEO, 1991—97, chmn., CEO, 1997—. Bd. dir. Apollo Group Inc., 2006—. Bd. dirs. Inst. Noetic Sciences. Office: The Mens Wearhouse 40650 Encyclopedia Cir Fremont CA 94538-2453 also: 5803 Glenmont Dr Houston TX 77081 *

ZIMMER, HANS FLORIAN, composer; b. Frankfurt, Germany, Sept. 12, 1957; m. Suzanne Zimmer; 4 children. Former mem. The Buggles; co-founder Media Ventures LLC. Composer: (films) (with Stanley Myers) Moonlighting, 1982, Success is the Best Revenge, 1984, The Wind, 1987, The Zero Boys, 1987, Taffin, 1988, Terminal Exposure, 1987, Wonderland, 1988, (with Myers) The Nature of the Beast, 1988, (with Luis Bonfa) Prisoner of Rio, 1988, Burning Secret, 1988, (with Myers) Paperhouse, 1988, Rain Man, 1988 (Acad. award nomineee best original score, 1988), A World Apart, 1988, Arcadia, 1988, Black Rain, 1989, Diamond Skulls, 1989, Driving Miss Daisy, 1989, Twister, 1989, Bird on a Wire, 1990, (with Shirley Walker) Chicago Joe and the Showgirl, 1990, Days of Thunder, 1990, Fools of Fortune, 1990, Green Card, 1990, The Neverending Story II: The Next Chapter, 1990, Pacific Heights, 1990, Backdraft, 1991, Regarding Henry, 1991, Thelma and Louise, 1991, Radio Flyer, 1991, The Power of One, 1992, A League of Their Own, 1992, (with Mark Mancina) Where Sleeping Dogs Lie, 1992, Sniper, 1993, (with Bob Telson) Younger and Younger, 1993, Point of No Return, 1993, True Romance, 1993, Calendar Girl, 1993, Cool Runnings, 1993, The House of the Spirits, 1993, I'll Do Anything, 1994, Renaissance Man, 1994, The Lion King, 1994 (Acad. award best original score, 1994, Golden Globe award, 1995), Crimson Tide, 1995 (Grammy award, 1996), Nine Months, 1995, Broken Arrow, 1996, Muppet Treasure Island, 1996, The Preacher's Wife, 1996, The Peacemaker, 1997, As Good As It Gets, 1997, The Prince of Egypt, 1998, The Thin Red Line, 1998, Chill Factor, 1999, The Road to El Dorado, 2000, Gladiator, 2000 (ASCAP award, 2001, Golden Globe award, 2001), Mission: Impossible II, 2000 (ASCAP award, 2001), An Everlasting Piece, 2000, Hannibal, 2001 (ASCAP award, 2002), Pearl Harbor, 2001 (ASCAP award, 2002), Invincible, 2001, Riding in Cars with Boys, 2001, Black Hawk Down, 2001, Spirit: Stallion of the Cimarron, 2002 (ASCAP award, 2003), The Ring, 2002 (ASCAP award, 2003), Tears of the Sun, 2003, Matchstick Men, 2003, The Last Samurai, 2003 (ASCAP award, 2004), Something's Gotta Give, 2003, King Arthur, 2004, Thunderbirds, 2004, Shark Tale, 2004 (ASCAP award, 2005), Lauras Stern, 2004, Spanglish, 2004, Madagascar, 2005 (ASCAP award, 2006), Batman Begins, 2005 (ASCAP award, 2006), The Little Polar Bear 2, 2005, The Weather Man, 2005, The Da Vinci Code, 2006 (ASCAP award, 2007), Pirates of the Caribbean: Dead Man's Chest, 2006 (ASCAP award, 2007), The Holiday, 2006, Pirates of the Caribbean: At World's End, 2007, The Simpsons Movie, 2007, (TV films) Wild Horses, 1985, Millennium: Tribal Wisdom and the Modern World, 1992, The 3rd Reich, in Color, 1998, (TV miniseries) First Born, 1989, (TV series) El Candidato, 1999; music prodr. (films) The Last Emperor, 1987. Recipient Joseph Plateau award of Honor, 2000, Hollywood Film award for Outstanding Achievement in Music in Film, Hollywood Film Festival, 2001, Harry Mancini award, ASCAP, 2003, Career Achievement award, US Nat. Bd. of Rev., 2003. Office: Gorfaine Schwartz Agency 4111 W Alameda Ave Ste 509 Burbank CA 91505-4171 *

ZIMMER, JOHN HERMAN, lawyer; b. Sioux Falls, SD, Dec. 30, 1922; s. John Francis and Veronica (Berke) Zimmer; m. Deanna Langner, 1976; children from previous marriage: Mary Zimmer Quinin, Robert Joseph, Judith Maureen Zimmer Rose. Student, Augustana Coll., Sioux Falls, 1941—42, Mont. State Coll., 1943; LLB, U. S.D., 1948. Bar: S.D. 1948. Pvt. practice, Turner County, SD, 1948—; of counsel Zimmer, Duncan & Cole, Parker, SD, 1992—. States atty., Turner County, 1955—58, Turner County, 1962—64; asst. prof. med. jurisprudence U. S.D.; minority counsel U.S. Senate Armed Svcs. Com. on Strategic and Clin. Materials Investigation, 1962—63; chmn. Southeastern Coun. Govts., 1973—75; mem. adv. coun. U. S.D. Law Sch., 1973—74. Pres. S.D. Easter Seal Soc., 1986—87; Chmn. Turner County Rep. Com., 1955—56; mem. adv. com. S.D. Rep., 1959—60; alt. del. Rep. Nat. Conv., 1958. With AUS, 1943—46, PTO. Decorated Bronze Star, Philippine Liberation Ribbon. Mem.: ATLA, ABA, VFW, S.D. Bar Assn., Fed. Bar Assn., Am. Legion, Shriners, Elks, Phi Delta Phi. Home: PO Box 640 Parker SD 57053-0640 Office: Zimmer Duncan & Cole LLP Law Bldg PO Box 550 Parker SD 57053-0550 Home Phone: 605-297-3265; Office Phone: 605-297-4446. Personal E-mail: jhzim@aol.com.

ZIMMER, LARRY WILLIAM, JR., sports announcer; b. New Orleans, Nov. 13, 1935; s. Lawrence W. Sr. and Theodora (Ahrens) Z.; m. Dawn M. Cailouet, June 4, 1955 (div. June 1972); children: Larry III, Tracey; m. Brigitte Bastian, Nov. 17, 1972. Student, La. State U., 1953-55; BJ, U. Mo., 1957. Sports dir. KFRU Radio, Columbia, Mo., 1960-66; asst. mgr. programming WAAM Radio, Ann Arbor, Mich., 1966-71; broadcaster football, basketball Mich., 1966-70; sportscaster, sports dir. KOA Radio, Denver, 1971—; broadcaster Denver Broncos Football, 1971-96; broadcaster football, basketball U. Colo. Buffaloes, 1971—; broadcaster Denver Rockets, 1972-74. Adj. prof. journalism U. Colo., 2001—. Author: Stadium Stories--The Denver Broncoes, 2004. Bd. mem. Colo. Ski Mus. and Hall of Fame, Vail, 1981-2000, Opera Colo., Denver, 1985—, Colo. chap. Nat. Football Found; former mem. adv. bd. Jefferson Co. Youth Advocacy Ctr. 1st lt. US Army, 1958-60. Named Colo. Sportscaster of the Yr., Nat. Sportscasters and Sportswriters Assn., Salisbury, NC, 1988, 90, 91, 2001, 02, Broadcaster of the Yr., Colo. Broadcaster's Assn., Denver, 1995; recipient Powerade award for best radio/TV sports story of yr. Nat. Sportscasters and Sportswriters Assn., 2000. Avocations: skiing, jogging, opera. Office: KOA Radio 72 Paradise Rd Golden CO 80401 Business E-Mail: larryzimmer@clearchannel.com.

ZIMMER, MARKUS BERNHARD, legal association administrator; b. Basel, Switzerland, Oct. 10, 1946; came to U.S., 1948; s. Max Bernhard and Elisabeth (Sulzmann) Z.; m. Shelley Elaine Melcomian, Jan. 5, 1976; children: Jessica, Christopher. BA in Philosophy, U. Utah, 1971, MA in Philosophy, 1975; MEd, Harvard U., 1977; EdD in Philosophy of Edn., 1980. Rsch. asst. Harvard Law Sch., Cambridge, Mass., 1977-78; teaching fellow law and ethics Harvard U., Cambridge, Mass.; asst. divsn. dir. Div. Continuing Edn. and Tng., Fed. Jud. Ctr., Washington, 1981—83, chief legal svcs. tng. br., 1983—84, chief mgmt. tng. br., 1984-87; adj. assoc. prof. mgmt. U. Md., College Park, 1985-87; clk. of ct., dist. ct. adminstr. US Dist. Ct. Utah, Salt Lake City, 1987—2006; chief ct. mgmt. Internat. Criminal Tribunal, The Hague, Netherlands, 2006—07; project mgr. Ukrainian Adminstrv. Ctr. Restructuring, Kiev, 2007—. Fed. dist. ct. clks. adv. com. Adminstrv. Office US Cts., 1990-96, fed. dist. ct. case mgmt. and stats. umbrella group, 1992-98, dist. ct. efficiencies task force, 1992-93, ct. adminstrn. adv. com., 1995-96, chmn. tech. panel on automation, 1999-2002; interagy. adv. group on tng. and devel. Office of Pers. Mgmt., Washington, 1984-87; ABA Cen. and East European Law Initiative ct. adminstrn. cons. Bulgarian Ministry Justice, Sofia, 1992, legal specialist, Skopje, Macedonia, 1997, faculty, Jud. Tng. Inst., Prague, Czech Republic, 2000-01; chief arch. jud. reform strategy, Serbia, 2005; leader World Bank Regional Justice Sector Capacity Bldg. Program, Prague, Czech Republic, 2003-05; mem. faculty ABA Ceeli Prague Inst. Iraqi Judges, 2004; faculty Internat. Seminar on Jud. Transparency, Chengdu, China, 2005; founding ptnr. and pres. Internat. Assn. Ct. Admin., 2004—; chair US Dist. Cts. Civil/Criminal User Group, 1995-98; ad hoc task force on budget allotment simplification US Cts., 1996-98; dist. clk. liaison US Jud. Conf. IT Com., 1999-2001, internat. jud. rels. com., 2002-04; adv. roundtable on law on cts. Coun. Europe, Rep. of Montenegro, 2001; cons. Abu Dhabi Govt. Jud. Restructuring Program, 2007—, others in field; spkr. in field. Exec. editor Internat. Jour. Court Adminstrn., 2007—; contbr. articles to profl. jours. Exec. bd. Utah Combined Fed. Campaign, 1989-2006, bd. chmn. and statewide campaign dir., 1992, 2002. Fulbright fellow, 1972-73; recipient U.S. Cts. Dir.'s award for outstanding leadership, 1994, Roy B. Gibson Freedom of Info. Act award Utah chpt. Soc. Profl. Journalists, 2000. Mem. ABA (CEELI ct. adminstrn. working group 1991-94, Russian jury trial working group 1993-94, African human rights subcom., 2004—); ASTD (dir. justice sys. trainers 1984-86), Fed. Ct. Clks. Assn. (exec. bd. 1991-92), Internat. Assn. for Ct. Adminstrn., 2004—.

ZIMMER, PAUL GERALD, II, retired community care licensing professional; b. Detroit, Oct. 2, 1946; s. Paul Gerald and Beatrice Mae (Mitchell) Z.; m. Shelly Mardell Hallier, May 23, 1980; children: Paul Gerald III, Carrie Lea. BA in Religion/Social Work, Azusa Pacific U., Calif., 1973. Ordained to ministry So. Bapt. Conf., 1985. Vocat. rehab. counselor dept. vocat. rehab. State of Calif., Riverside, 1986-88, intake specialist social svc. cmty. care licensing, 1988-91, licensing program supr. dept. social svc. cmty. care licensing, 1991-2001; ret., 2001. Instr., adv. bd. mem. Riverside County Office Edn.-Family-to-Family, 1993—; mem. Riverside County Dept. Pub. Social Svcs. Child Advocacy Coun., 1994—; co-chair RICKI com. Riverside County Dept. Health-Immunizations, 1996-98; monthly music evangelist LA Union Rescue Mission, 1984-2005, Christian Concert Assn., 2005-; mem. Fontana chpt. Am. Red Cross, 1983-87. Author (booklet): The Age of Becoming, 1977, Spiritually Broke, 2003; author (books): Prodigal Daze, 2004, Thorn Daze, 2006; author (music album) Day-A-Comin', 1989, (lyrics) Flashback Music, 1996. Dist. exec. Boy Scouts Am., Redlands/Victorville, Calif., 1981-83, mem. Order of Arrow, 1963—; mem./instr. Riverside County Office Edn. Child Care Initiative Project for Spanish Speaking Care Providers Indio, 1994—; appointed mem. State of Calif. Equal Employment Opportunity Adv. Com.-Disability Adv. Com., Sacramento, 1997-2000; min. Ch. in the Park, Hemet, Calif., 1996-2001; bd. dirs. Christian Concert Assn., 2005—. With US Army, 1967-68. Recipient Youth Adv. of Yr. award Riverside County Office Edn., 1993. Mem. Inland Empire Parents Anonymous (group facilitator, crisis counselor 1990-93). Avocations: writing/performing christian music, fitness walking, coin collecting/numismatics. Home: 1188 Wilson Ave Perris CA 92571-4926 Personal E-mail: airskypony@aol.com.

ZIMMER, PAUL JOSEPH, manufacturing executive; m. Lisa Zimmer; 3 children. BBA, Northwood U. Account mgr. Lear Corp., 1985, bus. unit mgr. GM divsn., mgr. Truck Group, Ford divsn., dir. ops. Ford divsn., dir. spl. vehicle platform Ford divsn., truck platform dir. GM divsn., v.p. J.I.T. ops. Truck Group, GM divsn., 1997, pres. seating systems divsn., 2000—03, pres. interior products divsn. Europe, 2003—05, sr. v.p., pres. Global Seating Systems Product Group, 2005—06, sr. v.p., pres. interior systems, 2006—. Office: Lear Corp 21557 Telegraph Rd PO Box 5008 Southfield MI 48086 Office Phone: 248-447-1500. Office Fax: 248-447-1722. *

ZIMMER, RICHARD ALAN, lawyer, retired congressman; b. Newark, Aug. 16, 1944; s. William and Evelyn (Schlank Rader) Zimmer; m. Marfy Goodspeed Zimmer, Dec. 27, 1965; children: Carl William, Benjamin Goodspeed. BA, Yale U., 1966, LLB, 1969. Bar: N.Y. 1971, U.S. Dist. Cts. (so. and ea. dists.) N.Y. 1974, N.J. 1975, U.S. Dist. Ct. N.J. 1975, U.S. Supreme Ct. 1980, D.C. 2005. Assoc. Cravath, Swaine and Moore, NYC, 1969—75; gen. atty. Johnson & Johnson, New Brunswick, NJ, 1976—91; mem. N.J. Gen. Assembly, 1982—87, chmn. state govt. com., 1986—87; mem. N.J. Senate, 1987—91, 102nd-104th Congresses from 12th N.J. dist., Washington, 1991—97; with Dechert, Princeton, NJ, 1997—2001; of counsel Gibson, Dunn & Crutcher, Washington, 2001—. Lectr. pub. and internat. affairs Woodrow Wilson Sch., Princeton U., 1997—2000. Chmn. Citizens for a Better N.J., 1997—2000, Study Commn. on the Implementation of the Death Penalty, 1997—98; trustee Freedom House Found., 1997—2001. Republican. Office: Gibson Dunn & Crutcher 1050 Connecticut Ave NW Washington DC 20036-5306 E-mail: rzimmer@gibsondunn.com.

ZIMMER, ROBERT JEFFREY, academic administrator, mathematician, educator; b. NYC, Nov. 5, 1947; s. Max S. and Harriet (Brokaw) Z.; m. Terese Schwartzman, Oct. 27, 1974; children— David, Benjamin, Alexander. AB summa cum laude, Brandeis U., 1968; PhD, Harvard U., 1975. Asst. prof. US Naval Acad., Annapolis, Md., 1975-77; instr. U. Chgo., 1977-79, assoc. prof., 1979-80, prof. math, 1980—, chmn. math dept., 1991-95, assoc. provost for rsch. & edn., 1995—98, dep. provost for rsch., 1998—2000, dep. provost, 2000—01; pres. U. Chgo, 2006—; prof. math. U. Calif.-Berkeley, 1981-83; provost, Ford Found. prof. math. Brown U., Providence, 2002—06. V.p. rsch. Argonne Nat. Lab., 2000—02. Author: Ergodic Theory and Semisimple Groups, 1984, Essential Results of Functional Analysis; contbr. articles to profl. jours. Sloan Found. fellow, 1979-83 Fellow Am. Acad. Arts & Scis. Office: U Chgo Office of Pres 5801 S Ellis Ave Chicago IL 60637 *

ZIMMER, WILLIAM, art critic; Undergrad., Columbia U.; degree in Art History, U. Tex. With The Soho News, 1977; art critic NY Times, 1981—. Lectr. in field; juried art exhbns. Office: NY Times 229 West 43rd St New York NY 10036

ZIMMERER, KATHY LOUISE, museum director; b. Whittier, Calif., Dec. 9, 1951; BA cum laude, U. Calif., Berkeley, 1974; MA, Williams Coll., 1976. From tour guide to curatorial asst. Sterling and Francine Clark Inst., Williamstown, Mass., 1975-76; spl. asst. dept. modern art L.A. County Mus. Art, 1976-77; mus. edn. fellow Fine Arts Mus. San Francisco, 1977-78; dir. coll. art gallery SUNY, New Paltz, 1978-80; cons. in field, 1980-81; dir. univ. art gallery Calif. State U., Dominguez Hills, 1982—. Project dir. Painted Light: California Impressionist Paintings from the Gardena H.S./L.A. Unified Sch. Dist., 1996—. Mem. Internat. Assn. Art Critics, Art Table. Office: Univ Art Gallery Calif State U 1000 E Victoria St Carson CA 90747-0001 Home Phone: 562-421-1743; Office Phone: 310-243-3334. E-mail: kzimmerer@csudh.edu.

ZIMMERMAN, AARON MARK, lawyer; b. Syracuse, NY, Jan. 28, 1953; s. Julius and Sara (Lavine) Zimmerman. BS, Syracuse U., 1974, JD, 1976. Bar: N.Y. 1977, Pa. 1977, DC 1978, S.C. 1978, Fla. 1978, U.S. Dist. Ct. S.C. 1978, U.S. Dist. Ct. (no. dist.) N.Y. Corp. atty., asst. sec. Daniel Internat. Corp., Greenville, SC, 1977—79; ptnr. Abend, Driscoli & Zimmerman, 1979—81; pvt. practice Syracuse, 1981—. Bd. dirs. Syracuse Friends Amateur Boxing, 1982—92. Mem.: ABA, Fla. State Bar, DC State Bar, S.C. State Bar, Workers Compensation Assn. Ctrl. N.Y. (dir., treas. 1980—95, charter mem.), N.Y. State Bar (mem. exec. com. workers compensation com. 1984—98), Am. Arbitration Assn. (arbitrator). Home: 602 Standish Dr Syracuse NY 13224-2018 Office: 117 S State St Syracuse NY 13202-1103 Office Phone: 315-475-7777. Personal E-mail: az.zimlaw@gmail.com.

ZIMMERMAN, BERNARD, investment banker; b. Bklyn., Dec. 7, 1932; s. Jacob and Pearl (Schechner) Z.; m. Joyce M. Singer, Dec. 24, 1960; children: Wayne Jay, Ellen Holly. BBA, CCNY, 1954; MBA, NYU, 1957. CPA NY. Fin. exec. consumer products Spartans Industries, Inc., NYC, 1961-65; sr. v.p. Scheinman, Hochstin, and Trotta, Inc., NYC, 1965-72; pres. Bernard Zimmerman and Co., Inc., Weston, Conn., 1972—; pres., CEO FCCC, Inc. (formerly First Conn. Capital Corp.), Norwalk, Conn., 2003—. Pres. Beacon Hill Mgmt., Inc., Boston, 1994-97; sr. v.p. corp. fin. Gruntal & Co., Inc., N.Y.C., 1983-84; pres., chmn. bd., pres. St. Lawrence Seaway Corp., Indpls., 1985-93, fin. cons.; sr. v.p. The Zimmerman Group, Inc., 1991-96; chmn. bd. dirs., pres. Beacon Hill Mut. Fund, Inc., Boston, 1994-97; Liquidating trustee Unity Buying Svc. Co. Liquidating Trust, Hicksville, NY; bd. dirs. Sbarro, Inc., Melville, NY; fin. cons. Beautiful Visions-U.S.A., Ltd., Bethpage, NY, Task Mgmt. Co., Ridgefield, Conn., 1998-99; pres. and CEO FCCC, Inc., Norwalk, Conn., 2003—; chmn. bd., pres. GVC Venture Corp., N.Y.C., 2004—. Bd. dirs. Inst. Cancer Rsch. and Molecular Medicine, Temple U., Phila., 1995-; trustee Sharro Family Found., Melville, 1993—; mem. Nat. Assn. Corp. Dir. Blue Ribbon Commn. on Corp. Governance-Best Practice Coun., 1997. With AUS, 1955-57. Mem.: NY State Soc. CPAs. Home and Office: 18 High Meadow Rd Weston CT 06883-2946 Office Phone: 203-226-5165.

ZIMMERMAN, BERNARD, judge; b. Munich, Bavaria, Fed. Republic Germany, May 31, 1946; came to U.S., 1949; s. Sam and Roza Z.; m. Grace L. Suarez, Oct. 23, 1976; children: Elizabeth, Adam, David, Dara Bylah. AB, U. Rochester, 1967; JD, U. Chgo., 1970. Bar: Calif. 1971, La. 1971, U.S. Supreme Ct. 1975, U.S. Dist. Ct. (no., ea., cen. and so. dists.) Calif., U.S. Dist. Ct. (ea. dist.) La., U.S. Ct. Appeals (9th cir.). Law. clk. chief judge U.S. Dist. Ct. (ea. dist.) La., New Orleans, 1970-71; asst. prof. law La. State U., Baton Rouge, 1971-72; ptnr. Pillsbury, Madison & Sutro, San Francisco, 1972-95; legal cons. 3d Constnl. Conv. Commonwealth of the No. Mariana Islands, Northern Mariana Islands, 1995; U.S. magistrate judge U.S. Dist. Ct. (no. dist.) Calif., 1995—. Dep. pub. defender City of San Francisco, 1975; arbitrator U.S. Dist. Ct., San Francisco, AAA; judge pro tem San Francisco Superior and Mcpl. Cts. Bd. dirs., mem. exec. com. San Francisco Lawyers' Com. on Urban Affairs, 1984-95, treas., 1987; mem. regional bd. Anti-Defamation League, 1989-95. Mem. Phi Beta Kappa. Clubs: Olympic (San Francisco). Office: 450 Golden Gate Ave San Francisco CA 94102-3661 Office Phone: 415-522-4093.

ZIMMERMAN, D. PATRICK, psychotherapist, health facility administrator; b. Chgo., Jan. 7, 1942; s. Delores Morley Zimmerman and Steven Joseph Patrick Maloney. BA, Wofford Coll., Spartanburg, SC, 1963; MA, Antioch Coll., Yellow Springs, Ohio, 1976; PhD, Ill. Sch. Profl. Psychology, Chgo., 1986. Cert. Clin. Psychologist Ill. Dept. Profl. Regulation, 1988, Psychoanalyst Chgo. Ctr. Psychoanalysis, 1998. Tchr. Chgo. Pub. Schs., 1967—69; founder, dir. The So. Sch. (Therapeutic Day Sch.), Chgo., 1969—94; post-doctoral fellow Sonia Shankman Orthogenic Sch., U. Chgo., Chgo., 1985—86, coord. rsch., 1987—2002, asst. dir., admissions and psychotherapy svcs., 2002—. Lectr. Com. on Human Devel. U. Chgo., 1998—2004, lectr. Dept. Psychiatry, 1998—. Editor: (jour.) Residential Treatment for Children and Youth; author: (books) The Forsaken Child: Essays on Group Care and Individual Therapy; co-editor: On Transitions from Group Care: Homeward Bound, Psychotherapy in Group Care, Residential Treatment. Mem., sec. Chgo. Ctr. for Psychoanalysis, 2001—04, bd. dirs., 2002—05. Grantee, Found. for Emotionally Disturbed Children, 1998. Fellow: Am. Assn. Children's Residential Centers; mem.: APA, Quadrangle Club, U. Chgo. Office: The Sonia Shankman Orthogenic Sch 1365 East 60th St Chicago IL 60637 Office Phone: 773-834-2728. Office Fax: 773-702-1304. E-mail: pzimmerm@midway.uchicago.edu.

ZIMMERMAN, DIANE LEENHEER, law educator; b. Newton, N.J., Apr. 16, 1941; d. Adrian and Mildred Eleanor (Booth) Leenheer; m. Earl A. Zimmerman, Sept. 24, 1960 (div. Aug. 1982); m. Cavin P. Leeman, Feb. 18, 1984. BA, Beaver Coll., Glenside, Pa., 1963; JD, Columbia U., 1976. Bar: N.Y. 1977, US Supreme Ct. 1983. Reporter, Newsweek mag., N.Y.C., 1963-71; spl. features writer N.Y. Daily News, NYC, 1971-73; law clk. to Hon. Jack B. Weinstein US Dist. Ct. Ea. Dist. N.Y., 1976-77; asst. prof. law N.Y.U. Sch. Law, 1977-80, assoc. prof., 1980-82, prof., 1982—, now Samuel Tilden prof. law; mem. faculty Practicing Law Inst., N.Y.C., 1979, 84, 90, 92, 94, 96-02; Disting. Lee Vis. Prof. Constl. Law Coll. William and Mary, 1994; moderator justice and soc. program Aspen Inst., 1992, 99; Disting. Vis. Hosier Chair Intellectual Property, DePaul Coll. Law, Chgo., 2001; lectr. 17th Ann. Manges Lectr. Intellectual Property, 2004. Recipient citation of merit Columbia U. Sch. Journalism, 1972; Kent scholar and Stone scholar, 1973-76; Mem. ABA (vice chmn. tort liability study com. tort and ins. sect. 1986-87, chair 1st amendment rights com. 1989-94), Am. Law Inst., Assn. of Bar City of N.Y. (chairperson com. civil rights 1981-83), Copyright Soc. USA (trustee 1988-91, 2004—). Office: NYU Sch Law Vanderbilt Hall Rm 332 40 Washington Sq S New York NY 10012-1099 Office Phone: 212-998-6250. Business E-Mail: zimmermd@juris.law.nyu.edu.

ZIMMERMAN, DONALD PATRICK, lawyer; b. Albany, NY, Mar. 20, 1942; s. Bernard M. and Helen M. (Eshelman) Z. Student, McDonogh Sch., 1953—57, Lawrenceville Sch., 1960; BA, Rollins Coll., 1964; JD, Dickinson Sch. Law, 1967. Bar: Pa. 1968, US Dist. Ct. (ea. dist.) Pa., US Ct. Appeals (3rd cir.), US Supreme Ct. 1971. Atty. Legal Aid, 1968-69; pub. defender Lancaster County, Pa., 1969-72; pvt. practice Lancaster, 1974—. Instr. Ct. Common Pleas for Constables, 1976-; solicitor Lancaster County Dep. Sheriff Assn., 1977-, Lancaster County Constable Assn., 1975-; sheriff solicitor Lancaster County Sheriff Office 2004-; instr. sheriff's dept. Lancaster County for Dep. Sheriffs, 1978-85; of counsel to Dep. Sheriff Assn. Pa., 1979-81; spl. counsel Pa. State Constables Assn., 1981; chmn. Bd. Arbitrators Lancaster County, 1975-81; spl. counsel Legislative Com. to Constable Assn. Pa., 1982; v.p. Sheriff's Solicitors Assn., 2006; legal instr. NRA. Author: The Pennsylvania Landlord and Tenant Handbook, 1982, revised edit., 1993; editor (with J. Hatfield and A. Taylor) Pennsylvania Constable Handbook, 1998, Landlord Training Program, Nat. Program Manual; contbr. articles to profl. jours. Legal instr. NRA, 2007; mem. pastoral coun. St. Anthony's Cath. Ch., 1995-98, mandated extraordinary min. of Communion, 2002. Recipient Ofcl. Commendation of Merit, Lancaster County Sheriff's Dept., 1979, Ofcl. Commendation of Merit, F.O.P. State Police Lodge 66, 1985, Disting. Svc. award, 1987, Cert. of Appreciation, Lancaster Crime Commn., 2003, Recognition award City of Lancaster, 2004, Recognition award Borough of Manheim, 2006. Mem. ABA, ATLA, Pa. Bar Assn., Acad. Family Mediators, Lancaster County Bar Assn., W. Hensel Brown Inn of Ct., Lancaster County Constables Assn. (Outstanding Leadership award 1988, Disting. Svc. award as solicitor 1998, 25 Yrs. Dedicated Svc. award 2000, Dedicated Svc. award 2004, 30 Yr. Dedicated Svc. award 2005). Avocation: fencing. Office: 214 E King St Lancaster PA 17602-2977 Office Phone: 717-394-6859. Business E-Mail: patrickzimm@dpzlaw.us.

ZIMMERMAN, EARL ABRAM, neurologist, educator; b. Harrisburg, Pa., May 5, 1937; s. Earl Beckley and Hazel Marie (Myers) Z. BS in Chemistry, Franklin and Marshall Coll., 1959; MD, U. Pa., 1963. Diplomate Am. Bd. Psychiatry and Neurology, Am. Bd. Internal Medicine. Intern Presbyn. Hosp., NYC, 1963-64, resident, 1964-65, Neurol. Inst. CPMC, NYC, 1965-68, research fellow endocrinology, 1970-72; asst. prof. to prof. neurology Columbia U., NYC, 1972-85; prof., chmn. dept. neurology Oreg. Health Sci. U., Portland, 1985-2000; chmn. dept. neurology Albany (N.Y.) Med. Coll., 2000—04; clin. dir. neuroscis. Advanced Imaging Rsch. Ctr., dir. Alzheimer's Ctr., Albany Med. Ctr./GE Global Rsch., 2002—. Dir. neurology Helen Hayes Hosp., Haverstraw, N.Y., 1982-83 Mem. editl. bd. Jour. Histochem. Cytochemistry, 1980-85, 87, Neuroendocrinology, 1985-88, Annals of Neurology, 1985-91, Western Jour. Medicine, 1993-98, Jour. Clin. Endocrinal Metabolism, 1995-99; contbr. numerous articles to profl. jours. Maj. USAF, 1968-70 Rsch. grantee NIH, 1977—. Mem. Am. Neurol. Assn. (program chmn. 1980-82), Am. Acad. Neurology (Wartenber lectr. 1985), Endocrine Soc. Democrat. Mem. United Ch. of Christ Avocations: woodworking, gardening, theater, music, art, skiing, tennis. Office: Albany Med Coll Dept Neurology 47 New Scotland Ave MC-65 Albany NY 12208 Home Phone: 518-785-3638; Office Phone: 518-262-0801. Business E-Mail: zimmere@mail.amc.edu.

ZIMMERMAN, EDWIN MORTON, lawyer; b. NYC, June 11, 1924; s. Benjamin and Tobie (Fuchs) Z.; m. Caroline Abbot, July 3, 1956; children: Sarah Abbot, Lyle Benjamin, Miriam Appleton. AB, Columbia U., 1944, LLB, 1949. Bar: NY 1949, DC 1969, US Supreme Ct 1969. With Hoover Commn. Reorgn. Exec. Br., 1948; law clk. to Hon. Stanley F. Reed U.S. Supreme Ct., 1950-51; law clk. to Judge Simon H. Rifkind U.S. Dist. Ct., 1949-50; pvt. practice law NYC, 1951-59; prof. law Stanford U., 1959-69; with Justice Dept., 1965-69, asst. atty. gen. charge antitrust div., 1968-69; mem. Covington & Burling, Washington, 1969-94, sr. counsel, 1994—. Mem. coun. Adminstrv. Conf. U.S., 1975—78; mem. mfg. studies bd. Nat. Acad. Sci., 1983—87; adj. prof. George Washington Sch. Law, 1996—2001. Trustee Textile Mus., 1983—, pres. bd. trustees, 1987-96; mem. Folger Poetry Bd., 1990—; mem. adv. bd. Partisan Rev., 1996-2003. 1st lt. signal corps US Army, 1944—46. Mem. ABA, Assn. of Bar of City of NY, Am. Law Inst., Coun. Fgn. Rels., Phi Beta Kappa. Home: 1820 Kalorama Sq NW Washington DC 20008-4022 Office: Covington & Burling PO Box 7566 1201 Pennsylvania Ave NW Washington DC 20004-2401 Office Phone: 202-662-5190. Business E-Mail: ezimmerman@cov.com.

ZIMMERMAN, ELYN, artist; b. Phila., Dec. 16, 1945; d. Louis B. and Sylvia (Snyder) Z.; m. Kirk Varnedoe, Oct. 8, 1983. BA in Psychology, UCLA, 1968, MFA in Painting, 1972. Apptd. mem. Commn. Fine Arts, 2003. One-man shows include Univ. Art Mus., Berkeley, Calif., 1974, P.S. 1, Long Island City, N.Y., 1977, Mus. Contemporary Art, Chgo., 1979, Hudson River Mus., Yonkers, N.Y., 1982, Joslyn Art Mus., Omaha, 1984, Wave Hill, Riverside, N.Y., Contemporary Art Mus. U. South Fla., Tampa, 1991, Gagosian Gallery, N.Y.C., 1993, 96, 98, 2001, 03, 04; exhibited in group shows at Whitney Mus. Am. Art, N.Y.C., 1975, Biennale of Sydney, Australia, 1976, Walker Art Ctr., Mpls., 1979, San Diego Mus. Art, 1980, Venice Biennale, USA Pavillion, Italy, 1980, Mus. Contemporary Art, Chgo., 1981, Newport Harbor Art Mus., Calif., 1982, Hirshhorn Mus., Washington, 1983, San Francisco Mus. Modern Art, 1984, Socrates Sculpture Park, N.Y.C., 1996, L.A. County Mus. Art, 1996, Addison Gallery, Andover, Mass., 1998, Marlborough Gallery, N.Y.C., 1998, Chesterwood, Stockbridge, Mass., Montclair Mus., N.J., 1999, Ctr. for Photography, Woodstock, N.Y., Witherspoon Gallery Durham, N.C., 2002; sculpture commns. include Nat. Geographic Soc., Washington, O'Hare Internat. Ctr., Rosemont, Ill., Dade County Justice Ctr., Miami, Fla., Moffit Rsch. Ctr./U. South Fla., Tampa, Market Plz., San Francisco, Birmingham Mus. Art, AT&T Hdqrs., N.J., World Trade Ctr. Meml., N.Y.C. Nat. Endowment for Arts grantee, 1976, 80, 83, Creative Artist Pub. Svc. grantee, 1980; NEA and Japan-U.S. Friendship Commn. fellow, 1982. Mem. Creative Time, Inc. (bd. dirs. 1984-90). Home: 140 Greene St New York NY 10012-3241 Office Phone: 212-219-3224. Business E-Mail: elynzimmerman@nyc.rr.com.

ZIMMERMAN, GIDEON K., retired minister; b. Lehr, ND, Aug. 18, 1920; m. Eleanor Pekrul; children: Paul, Mark (dec.), Thomas. Diploma, N.Am. Baptist Sem., Rochester, NY, 1943; BA, U. ND, 1951; postgrad., Bethany Bibl. Sem., 1958—59, Chgo. Lutheran Sem., 1959—61; BD, N.Am. Bapt. Sem., Sioux Falls, SD, 1960, DD, 1971. Pastor First Bapt. Ch., Auburn, Mich., 1943-47, Grace Bapt. Ch., Grand Forks, N.D., 1947-51, Temple Bapt. Ch., Milw., 1951-55; gen. sec. dept. Christian edn. N. Am. Bapt. Conf., 1955-68, exec. sec., 1968-79, estate planning counselor, 1979-85; ret. Home: 3721 Bardstown Rd Apt 601 Louisville KY 40218-2261

ZIMMERMAN, HAROLD SAMUEL, retired state legislator, publishing executive, state agency administrator; b. Valley City, ND, June 1, 1923; s. Samuel Alwin and Lulu (Wylie) Z.; m. Julianne Williams, Sept. 12, 1946; children: Karen, Steven, Judi Jean (dec.). BA, U. Wash., 1947. News editor Sedro-Woolley (Wash.) Courier-Times, 1947-50; editor, pub. Advocate, Castle Rock, Wash., 1950-57; pub. Post-Record, Camas, Wash., 1957-80; assoc. pub., columnist, dir. Eagle Publs., Camas, 1980-88; ret. Mem. Wash. Ho. of Reps., 1967-80; mem. Wash. Senate, 1981-88, Wash. State Environ. Hearings Bd., Lacey, 1988-93. Mem. Grange, Lions, Kiwanis, Sigma Delta Chi, Sigma Chi. Republican. United Methodist. Personal E-mail: hszim@aol.com.

ZIMMERMAN, HELENE LORETTA, retired business educator; b. Rochester, NY, Feb. 26, 1933; d. Henry Charles and Loretta Catherine (Hobert) Z. BS, SUNY, Albany, 1953, MS, 1959; PhD, U. N.D., 1969. Cert. records mgr. Bus. tchr., chmn. bus. dept. Williamson (N.Y.) Cen. Sch., 1953-69; asst. prof. U. Ky., Lexington, 1969-70; assoc. prof. bus. Cen. Mich. U., Mt. Pleasant, 1970-74, prof., 1974-98. Author General Business, 1977; contbg. author to records mgmt. text book, 1987. Sec. Isabella County Christmas Outreach, Mt. Pleasant, 1983-2004, mem. steering com., 1983—; mem. Internat. Rels. Coun., Mt. Pleasant, 2003—; active Goodrow Fund, 2006—. Mem.: AAUW (pres. 1984—86), Mich. Bus. Edn. Assn. (bd. dirs. 1985—90, pres. 1988—89, bd. dirs. 1995—97), Nat. Bus. Edn. Assn., Internat. Soc. Bus. Edn. (internat. v.p. English speaking nations 1986—88, editor Internat. Rev. 1997—2006), Inst. Cert. Records Mgrs. (sec. 1985—89, exam. devel. com. 1993—2002), Assn. Records Mgmt. and Adminstrn., Gen. Fedn. Women's Clubs (pres. Mt. Pleasant chpt. 2004—05), Delta Kappa Gamma (state pres. 1987—89, internat. fin. com. 1990—94, internat. ad hoc com. on tech. 1996—2000). Avocations: travel, crafts.

ZIMMERMAN, HOWARD ELLIOT, chemist, educator; b. NYC, July 5, 1926; s. Charles and May (Cohen) Zimmerman; m. Jane Kirschenheiter, June 3, 1950 (dec. Jan. 1975); children: Robert, Steven, James; m. Martha L. Bailey Kaufman, Nov. 7, 1975 (div. Oct. 1990); stepchildren: Peter B. Kaufman, Tanya Kaufman; m. Peggy J. Vick, Oct. 1991. BS, Yale U., 1950, PhD, 1953. NRC fellow Harvard U., 1953-54; faculty Northwestern U., 1954-60, asst. prof., 1955-60; assoc. prof. U. Wis., Madison, 1960-61, prof. chemistry, 1961—, Arthur C. Cope and Hilldale prof. chemistry, 1975—. Chmn. 4th Internat. Union Pure and Applied Chemistry Symposium on Photochemistry, 1972; organizer, chmn. Organic Photochemistry Symposium at Pacifchem, Honolulu, 1972, Honolulu, 95, Honolulu, 2000, Honolulu, 05. Author: (book) Quantum Mechanics for Organic Chemists, 1975; mem. editl. bd.: Jour. Organic Chemistry, 1967—71, Molecular Photochemistry, 1969—75, Jour. Am. Chem. Soc., 1982—85, Revs. Reactive Intermediates, 1984—89; contbr. articles to profl. jours. and chpts. to profl. texts. Recipient Halpern award for photochemistry, N.Y. Acad. Scis., 1979, Chem. Pioneer award, Am. Inst. Chemists, 1986, Sr. Alexander vonHumboldt award, 1988, Hilldale award, U. Wis., 1988—89, 1990, Porter medal, IUPAC, 2006. Mem.: NAS, Inter-Am. Photochemistry Assn. (co-chmn. orgnic divsn. 1977—79, exec. com. 1979—86), German Chem. Soc., Chem. Soc. London, Am. Chem. Soc. (James Flack Norris award 1976, Arthur C. Cope Scholar award 1991, XXI IUPAC Porter medal 2006), Phi Beta Kappa, Sigma Xi. Home: 7813 Westchester Dr Middleton WI 53562-3671 Office: U Wis Chemistry Dept 1101 University Ave Madison WI 53706-1322 Business E-Mail: Zimmerman@chem.wisc.edu.

ZIMMERMAN, JAMES M., retail company executive; b. 1944; Chmn. Rich's Dept. Store div. Federated Dept. Stores, 1984-88; pres., COO Federated and Allied Dept. Stores, Cin., 1988-97; CEO Federated Dept. Stores, Cin., 1997—2003, chmn., 1997—. Office: Federated Department Stores Inc 7 W 7th St Cincinnati OH 45202-2424

ZIMMERMAN, JAMES M., lawyer; b. Cin., Apr. 7, 1974; BA, Vanderbilt U., 1996, JD, 1999. Bar: Ohio 1999. Assoc. Taft, Stettinius & Hollister LLP, Cin., 1999—. Mem., oper. bd. Main St. Ventures, Cin. Mem., Adv. Bd. Give Back Cin. Named one of Ohio's Rising Stars, Super Lawyers, 2005, 2006. Mem.: Ohio State Bar Assn., Cin. Bar Assn., Order of Coif. Office: Taft Stettinius & Hollister LLP 425 Walnut St Ste 1800 Cincinnati OH 45202-3957 Office Phone: 513-381-2838. Office Fax: 513-381-0205. E-mail: zimmerman@taftlaw.com.

ZIMMERMAN, JEAN, lawyer; b. Berkeley, Calif., Dec. 3, 1947; d. Donald Scheel Zimmerman and Phebe Jean (Reed) Doan; m. Gilson Berryman Gray III, Nov. 25, 1982; children: Charles Donald Buffum and Catherine Elisabeth Phebe (twins); stepchildren: Alison Travis, Laura Rebecca, Gilson Berryman. BSBA, U. Md., College Park, 1970, JD, Emory U., Atlanta, Ga., 1975. Bar: Ga. 1975, D.C. 1976, N.Y. 1980. Asst. mgr. investments FNMA, Washington, 1970-73; assoc. counsel Fuqua Industries Inc., Atlanta, 1976-79; assoc. Sage Gray Todd & Sims, NYC, 1979-84; from assoc. counsel to sr. v.p., gen. counsel, sec. IBJ Whitehall Bank & Trust Co., NYC, 1984—99; sr. v.p., gen. counsel, sec., bd. dirs. IBJ Schroder Bus. Credit Corp., NYC, 1996-98, Innovest Capital Mgmt., Inc., NYC, 1997-99; sr. v.p., gen. counsel, sec. Innovest Corp., NYC, 1997-99; from gen. counsel, sec. to exec. v.p. ops. and legal ArrowSight, Inc. (formerly ParentWatch.com), Mt. Kisco, NY, 2001—. From asst. sec. to sr. v.p., gen. counsel, sec., bd. dirs. IBJ Whitehall Bus. Credit Corp., IBJ Whitehall Capital Corp., IBJ Whitehall Securities, Inc., Delphi Asset Mgmt., Inc., Innovest Asset Mgmt., Inc., N.Y.C., 1997-99; from asst. sec. to v.p., gen. counsel, sec. IBJ Schroder Internat. Bank, Miami, Fla., 1989-98; sr. v.p., gen. counsel, sec. Execution Svcs., N.Y.C., 1991-93. Founder, officer ERA Ga., Atlanta, 1977-79; bd. dirs. Ct. Apptd. Spl. Advs., 1988-94. Named one of Outstanding Atlantans, 1978-79; recipient Disting. Alumni award Emory U. Sch. Law, 1999. Mem.: ABA, LWV, Am. Soc. Corp. Secs., Inc., Ga. Assn. Women Lawyers (bd. dirs. 1977—79), Assn. Bar City N.Y., Assn. Emory Alumni (N.Y. pres. 1999—2003, bd. govs. 2001—05), DAR. Personal E-mail: jzimmer642@aol.com. Business E-Mail: jean.zimmerman@arrowsight.com.

ZIMMERMAN, JO ANN, retired health science association administrator, educator, retired lieutenant governor; b. Van Buren County, Iowa, Dec. 24, 1936; d. Russell and Hazel (Ward) McIntosh; m. A. Tom Zimmerman, Aug. 26, 1956; children: Andrew, Lisa, Don and Ron (twins), Beth. Diploma, Broadlawns Sch. of Nursing, Des Moines, 1958; BA with honors, Drake U., 1973; postgrad., Iowa State U., 1973—75. RN, Iowa. Asst. head nurse maternity dept. Broadlawns Med. Ctr., Des Moines, 1958—59, weekend supr. nursing svcs., 1960—61, supr. maternity dept., 1966—68; instr. maternity nursing Broadlawns Sch. Nursing, 1968—71; health planner, community rels. assoc. Iowa Health Systems Agy., Des Moines, 1978—82; mem. Iowa Ho. Reps., 1982—86; lt. gov., pres. of Senate, State of Iowa, 1987—91; cons. health svcs., grant writing and continuing edn. Zimmerman & Assocs., Des Moines, 1991—2000; dir. patient care svcs. Nursing Svcs. Iowa, 1996—98; nurse case mgr. Olsten Health Svcs. (now Gentiva Health Svcs.), 1998—2004; founder JAZ Tours, 2002—04, ret., 2004, 2004. Ops. dir. Medlink Svcs., Inc., Des Moines, 1992-96. Contbr. articles to profl. jours. Mem. advanced registered nurse practioner task force on cert. nurse mid-wives Iowa Bd. Nursing, 1980-81, Waukee, Polk County, Iowa Health Edn. Coord. Coun., Iowa Women's Polit. Caucus, Dallas County Women's Polit. Caucus; chmn. Des Moines Area Maternity Nursing Conf. Group. 1969-70, task force on sch. health svcs. Iowa Dept. Health, 1982, task force health edn. Iowa Dept. Pub. Instruction, 1979, adv. com. health edn. assessment tool, 1980-81, Nat. Lt. Govs., chair com. on Agrl. and Rural Devel., 1989; Dallas County Dem. Ctrl. Com., 1972-84, 98—; bd. dirs. Waukee Cmty. Sch. Bd., 1976-79, pres. 1978-79; bd. dirs. Iowa PTA, 1979-83, chair Health Com., 1980-84; mem. steering com. ERA, Iowa, 1991-92; founder Dem. Activist Women's Network (DAWN), 1992; mem. Disciples of Christ Mission Group to El Salvadore, 2003, 04; founder health ministry First Christian Ch., Des Moines, Iowa, 2004. Named to Iowa Women's Hall of Fame, 2005; recipient Woman Achievement award, YWCA Greater Des Moines, 2005, Search Your Heart award, Am. Heart Assn., 2007. Mem. ANA, LWV (health chmn. met. Des Moines chpt.), Iowa Nurses Assn., Iowa League for Nursing (bd. dirs. 1979-83), Family Centered Childbirth Edn. Assn. (childbirth instr., advisor), Iowa Cattleman's Assn., Am. Lung Assn. (bd. dirs. Iowa 1988-92), Dem. Activist Women's Network (founder 1992). Mem. Christian Ch. Avocations: gardening, sewing, reading, bridge.

ZIMMERMAN, JORDAN, advertising and marketing executive; b. NJ; MBA, U. South Fla. Chmn, CEO Zimmerman & Ptnrs. (Omnicom group since 1999), Ft. Lauderdale, Fla., 1984—; ptnr., pres., alt. gov. Fla. Panthers hockey, 2001—. Achievements include led Just Say No marketing initiative during the Carter administration which is one of the most recognizable anit-drug campaigns to date. Office: 2200 West Commerical Blvd Fort Lauderdale FL 33309

ZIMMERMAN, JOSEPH FRANCIS, political scientist, educator; b. Keene, NH, June 29, 1928; s. John Joseph and May Veronica (Gallagher) Z.; m. Margaret Bernardette Brennan, Aug. 2, 1958; 1 child, Deirdre Ann. BA, U. N.H., 1950; MA, Syracuse U., 1951, PhD, 1954. Instr. govt. Worcester Poly. Inst., 1954—55, asst. prof., 1955-57, assoc. prof., 1957-62, prof., 1962-65; lectr. Clark U., Worcester, Mass., 1957-65; prof. polit. sci. SUNY, Albany, 1965—. Staff dir. N.Y. State Joint Legis. Com. Transp., 1967-68, rsch. dir., 1968-73; rsch. dir. N.Y. State Select Legis. Com. Transp., 1977-82, Legis. Commn. on Critical Transp. Problems, 1982-95. Author: State and Local Government, 1962, The Massachusetts Town Meeting: A Tenacious Institution, 1967, The Federated City: Community Control in Large Cities, 1972, Pragmatic Federalism, The Reassingment of Functional Responsibility, 1976, (with Frank W. Prescott) The Politics of the Veto of Legislation in New York, 1980, The Government and Politics of the Empire State, 1981, Local Discretionary Authority, 1981, (with Deirdre A. Zimmerman) The Politics of Subnational Governance, 1983, State-Local Relations: A Partnership Approach, 1983, 2d edit., 1995 (CHOICE award as outstandin acad. book, 1984), Participatory Democracy: Populism Revived, 1986, Federal Preemption: The Silent Revolution, 1990, Contemporary American Federalism, 1992; (with Wilma Rule) United States Electoral System: Their Impact Upon Women and Minorities, 1992, Electoral Systems in Comparative Perspective: Their Impact on Women Minorities, 1994, Curbing Unethical Behavior of Government, 1994, Interstate Relations: The Neglected Dimension of Federalism, 1996, The Recall: Tribunal of the People, 1997, The New England Town Meeting: Democracy in Action, 1999; The Initiative: Citizen Law-Making, 1999, (with Wilma Rule) The U.S. House of Representatives: Reform or Rebuild?, 2000, The Referendum: The People Decide Public Policy, 2001 Interstate Cooperation: Compacts and Administrative Agreements, 2002, Interstate Economic Relations, 2004, Congressional Preemption: Regulatory Federalism, 2005, Interstate Disputes: The U.S. Supreme Court's Original Jurisdiction, 2006, The Silence of Congress: State Taxation of Interstate Commerce, 2007; contbr. articles to profl. jours. Pres. Citizens' Plan E Assn., Worcester, 1960-62, Citizens for Neighborhood Improvement Worcester, 1957-59. Served to capt. USAF, 1951—53. Named 1 of 3 Outstanding Young Men Worcester Jr. C. of C., 1959, 61, 1 of 3 Outstanding Young Men Mass, Jr. C. of C., 1961, disting. citizen award Nat. Conf. on Govt., 1986. Mem. Am. Polit. Sci. Assn. (Outstanding Academician sect. intergovtl. adminstrn. 1997), Am. Soc. Pub. Adminstrn. (Outstanding Federalism Academician 1997), Nat. Mcpl. League. Clubs: German-Am. Social. Roman Catholic. Home: 82 Greenock Rd Delmar NY 12054-4414 Office: SUNY Rockefeller College 135 Western Ave Albany NY 12222 Office Phone: 518-439-9440, 518-442-5378. E-mail: zimmer@albany.edu.

ZIMMERMAN, LAWRENCE A., printing company executive; b. NY, Dec. 2, 1942; BS in Fin., NYU, 1965; MBA, Adelphi U., Garden City, NY, 1967. Dir. budgets to corp. contr. IBM Corp., 1988—94, v.p. fin. Europe, Mid. East and Africa ops. Paris, 1994—96, v.p. fin. and planning server and tech. divsn., 1996—98; exec. v.p., CFO Sys. Software Assoc., Inc., Chgo., 1999; corp. sr. v.p. Xerox Corp., Stamford, Conn., 2002, CFO, 2002—, exec. v.p., 2007—. Bd. dirs. Brunswick Corp., 2005—. Office: Xerox Corp 800 Long Ridge Rd Stamford CT 06904 Office Phone: 203-968-3000. *

ZIMMERMAN, MARLIN U., JR., chemical engineer; b. Akron, Ohio, Aug. 2, 1923; s. Marlin Ulrich and Helen (Nelson) Z. BChemE, Johns Hopkins U., 1944; MBA, Harvard U., 1966. Registered profl. engr., Ohio. Jr. engr. Standard Oil Co. (Ohio), Cleve., 1944-46, engr., 1946-48, sr. engr., 1948-49, process engr. Lima (Ohio) refinery, 1949-50, group engr. Cleve., 1951-55, group supr., 1956-60, supr. process sys. sect., 1961-63, head acrylonitrile task force, 1961, tech. specialist, 1964-66; mgr. long term planning Norton Co., Worcester, Mass., 1966-69; cons. John Van Der Valk & Assocs., NYC, 1970-73; pvt. practice cons. chem. engr. ammonia-urea Hackensack, NJ, 1974—. Head task force to help commercialize Sohio acrylonitrile process. Contbr. articles to profl. jours. Baker scholar, 1966. Mem. AIChE, Johns Hopkins Club, Tudor and Stuart Club, Tau Beta Pi, Omicron Delta Kappa, Beta Theta Pi. Methodist. Achievements include patent for process improvement of Tosco shale process for oil recovery; patent for pig handling for gasoline blender meter testing loop, others. Avocations: travel, photography, reading, investing, computer programming.

ZIMMERMAN, MARTIN B., automotive executive; b. New York City, June 19, 1946; B (hon.), Dartsmouth Coll.; D in Econ., Mass. Inst. of Tech. Faculty mem. Sloan Sch. of Mgmt., Mass. Inst. of Tech.; prof. bus. econ. dept. Univ. Mich. Grad. Sch. Bus. Admin., 1983—85, prof. and chmn. bus. econ. dept., 1985; co. chief economist Ford Motor Co., Dearborn, Mich., 1987—94, exec. dir. govtl. rels. and corp. econ., 1994—99, v.p. govtl. affairs, 1999—2001, group v.p., corp. affairs, 2001—. Sr. economist President's Coun. of Econ. Advisors, Washington, 1985—86; adv. coun. Nat. Aeronautic and Space Admin., 1988—92. Serves on bd. of the Citizens Rsch Coun. of Mich., Cmty. Found. of S.E. Mich. and Detroit Met. Visitors and Conv. Bur. Recipient Blue Chip Econ. Forecasting Award. Mem.: Citizens Rsch. Coun. of Mich., Bus. for Soc. Responsibility (bd. dir.), The Panel of Econ. Advisors to the Congl. Budget Office, Com. for Econ. Devel. (bd. of trustees), Nat. Assn. Bus. Economists, Phi Betta Kappa. Office: Ford Motor Co One American Rd Dearborn MI 48123-1899

ZIMMERMAN, MARY ALICE, performing arts educator; BA, MA, PhD, Northwestern U. Asst. prof. performance studies Northwestern U., Evanston, Ill.; artistic assoc. Goodman and Seattle Repertory Theater; mem. Lookingglass Theater Company, Chicago. Dir.: (plays) The Notebooks of Leonardo da Vinci, The Odyssey, Arabian Nights, Journey to the West, Metamorphoses (Tony award best dir., 2002), Secret in the Wings, Eleven Rooms of Proust, Measure for Measure, Henry VIII, A Midsummer Night's Dream, All's Well That Ends Well, Argonautika, 2006. Active Lookingglass Theatre Co. Recipient MacArthur Fellowship, 1998, 20 Joseph Jefferson Awards for best direction. Fellow: Am. Acad. Arts & Sci. Office: Dept Performance Studies Northwestern U 1920 Campus D Evanston IL 60208

ZIMMERMAN, MICHAEL DAVID, lawyer; b. Chgo., Oct. 21, 1943; s. Elizabeth Porter; m. Lynne Mariani (dec. 1994); children: Evangeline Albright, Alessandra Mariani, Morgan Elisabeth; m. Diane Hamilton, 1998. BS, U. Utah, 1966, JD, 1969, LLD (hon.), 2001. Bar: Calif. 1971, Utah 1978. Law clk. to Chief Justice Warren Earl Burger U.S. Supreme Ct., Washington, 1969-70; assoc. O'Melveny & Myers, LA, 1970-76; assoc. prof. law U. Utah, 1976-78, adj. prof. law, 1978-84, 89-93; of counsel Kruse, Landa, Zimmerman & Maycock, Salt Lake City, 1978-80; spl. counsel Gov. of Utah, Salt Lake City, 1978-80; ptnr. Watkiss & Campbell, Salt Lake City, 1980-84; assoc. justice Supreme Ct. Utah, Salt Lake City, 1984-93, 98-00, chief justice, 1994-98; atty., mediator, arbitrator, ptnr. Snell & Wilmer, Salt Lake City, 2000—. Co-moderator Justice Soc. Program of Snowbird Inst. for Arts and Humanities, 1991, 92, 93, 94, 95, 97, 98; moderator, Tanner lecture panel dept. philosophy U. Utah, 1994; faculty Judging Sci. Program Duke U., 1992, 93; bd. dirs. Conf. of Chief Justices, 1995-98. Note editor: Utah Law Rev., 1968-69; contbr. numerous articles to legal publs. Mem. Project 2000, Coalition for Utah's Future, 1985—96; trustee Hubert and Eliza B. Michael Found., 1994—98; bd. dirs. Rowland-Hall St. Mark's Sch., 1995—2002; bd. assoc. Utah Mus. Natural History Found., 1997—; bd. dirs. Summit Inst. for Arts and Humanities,

1989—2002, chair, 2002—; bd. dirs. Hansen Planetarium, 1997—2001, Snowbird Inst. for Arts and Humanities, 1989—98, Deer Valley Inst. for Arts and Humanities, 1996—98, Kanzeon Zen Ctr., 1999—, chair, 2000—; bd. dirs. Utah Coun. on Conflict Resolution, 1999—2005, chair, 1999—2005; bd. dirs. Pvt. Adjudication Ctr.; mem. Duke U., 2000—02; co-dir. Registry of Ind. Sci. and Tech. Advisors, Duke U., 2000—02; chair Utah Jud. Coun. Task Force on Racial and Ethnic Fairness in the Jud. Sys., 1996—2000. Named Utah State Bar Appellate Ct. Judge of Yr., 1998; recipient Excellence in Ethics Award, Ctr. for Study of Ethics, 1994, Disting. Svc. Award Utah State Bar, 1998, Individual Achievement Award Downtown Alliance, 1997, The Peter W. Billings, Sr. American Arbitration Assoc. Outstanding Dispute Resolution Svc. Award, 1997, Humanitarian award, Nat. Conf. for Cmty. and Justice, 2005. Fellow: Am. Bar Found.; mem.: Am. Acad. Appellate Lawyers, Gov. Radiation Exposure Study Mgmt. Com., Ririe-Woodbury Dance Co. (exec. bd. 1982—84), U.S. Dept. of Energy Dose Assessment Adv. Group of the Off-Site Radiation Exposure Reconstruction Project (Utah citizen rep. 1980—84), Utah Legal Svc. Corp. (Bd. of Trustees 1985—87, 2002—), U. Utah Master of Pub. Adminstrn. Program Practitioners' Adv. Com. (mem 1985—89), U.S. Vet. Adminstrn. Adv. Com. on Environ. Hazards (e.g., agent orange, nuclear radiation 1985—89), Nat. Endowment for the Humanities Scholar in Residence at Utah Valley Cmty. Coll. (Orem, Utah 1990), Order of Coif, Am. Judicature Soc. (bd. dirs. 1995—2001), Am. Inns of Ct. VII, Utah Jud. Coun. (supreme ct. rep. 1986—91, chair 1994—98), Jud. Conf. U.S. (adv. com. civil rules 1985—91), Salt Lake County Bar Assn., Utah Bar Assn., Am. Law Inst., ABA (faculty mem. appellate judges' seminar 1993), Phi Kappa Phi. Office: Snell & Wilmer 15 West South Temple Ste 1200 Salt Lake City UT 84101 Office Phone: 801-257-1964. E-mail: mzimmerman@swlaw.com.

ZIMMERMAN, NANCY PICCIANO, library and information scientist, educator; b. Jeannette, Pa., July 29, 1951; d. Daniel Joseph and Helen Elizabeth (Lipinski) Picciano; m. Lee W. Zimmerman, Aug. 10, 1974; children: Matthew, Renée. BA in English, Carlow Coll., Pitts., 1973; MLS in Libr. Sci., U. Pitts., 1974; MS in Computer Edn. and Cognitive Sys., U. North Tex., 1992; PhD in Libr. and Info. Studies, Tex. Woman's U., 1992. Lic. libr. media specialist, K-12, lang. arts/English 7-12. Libr. media specialist Fairfield (Calif.)-Suisun Sch. Dist., 1976-78; reference libr. Pikes Peak Libr. Dist., Colorado Springs, Colo., 1983; libr. media specialist North Pole (Alaska) H.S., 1984-85, Prince William County Schs., Woodbridge, Va., 1985-89; dir. info. retrieval lab. Tex. Woman's U., Denton, 1989-91; adj. prof., rsch. assoc. U. North Tex., Denton, 1991-92; from asst. to assoc. prof. Sch. Info. and Libr. Studies SUNY, Buffalo, 1993-99; assoc. prof. Sch. Libr. and Info. Scis. U. S.C., Columbia, 1999—. ALISE/OCLC rsch. grantee, 1994, 2004. Mem. ALA (coun. 2000—, chair Libr. Rsch. Round Table 1995-96, chair com. profl. ethics 2006-), Am. Assn. Sch. Librs. (treas. 1996-99, pres. 2002-03, exec. bd. 1996-99, 2001-04), Internat. Assn. Sch. Librs., N.Y. Libr. Assn. (pres. 1999), Nat. Bd. for Profl. Tchg. Stds. (sch. libr. media com. 1997-2000), Phi Delta Kappa, Beta Phi Mu (nat. exec. coun. 1994-99, 2005—, pres. 2007-). Office: U SC Sch Libr and Info Scis 217 Davis Coll Columbia SC 29208-0001 Office Phone: 803-777-1215. Business E-Mail: npz@sc.edu.

ZIMMERMAN, PAUL ALBERT, retired academic administrator, minister; b. Danville, Ill., June 25, 1918; s. Albert Carl and Hanna Marie (Haffner) Z.; m. Genevieve Emmaline Bahls, June 11, 1944; children—Karmin (Mrs. Raymond Philp), Thomas. Student, Concordia Coll., Ft. Wayne, Ind., 1936-39; BA, Concordia Sem., St. Louis, 1941, M.Div., 1944; MA, U. Ill., 1947, PhD, 1951; D.D., Concordia Sem., Springfield, Ill., 1975; LLD (hon.), Concordia Coll., Ann Arbor, Mich., 1994. Prof. theology and sci. Bethany Coll., Mankato, Minn., 1944-53; prof. Concordia Tchrs. Coll., Seward, Nebr., 1953-54, pres., 1954-61, Concordia Luth. Jr. Coll., Ann Arbor, Mich., 1961-73, Concordia Coll., River Forest, Ill., 1973-83, ret., 1983; pastor St. Luke's Luth. Ch., Harrison, Mich., 1983-88. Author and editor: Darwin, Evolution and Creation, 1959, Rock Strata and the Bible Record, 1971, Creation, Evolution and God's Word, 1972; author A Seminary in Crisis: The Inside Story of the Preus Fact Finding Committee, 2007. Chmn. Washtenaw County Red Cross, 1968-70; pres. Ann Arbor Found., 1970-71; mem. Citizens Com. Study Taxation, Ann Arbor, 1972; mem. adv. bd. St. Joseph Mercy Community, 1969-72; chmn. Luth. Ch. Mo. Synod's Bd. for Mission Services, 1982-92, Mission Task Force, 1990-91, adminstrv. asst. pres. Mo. Synod, 1972-73, 93-94, mem. curriculum comm. bd. higher edn., 1963-73, mem. task force constl. revision Mo. Synod, chmn. com. adjudication procedures Mo. Synod, Mo. Synod com. on structure, 1995-98. Fellow Creation Rsch. Assn. Lutheran. Home: 2798 Princeton Dr Traverse City MI 49684-9131

ZIMMERMAN, PHYLLIS ELAINE, music educator, composer, director; b. Pitts., Feb. 22, 1934; d. William H. and Isabelle Anderson Zimmerman. BA in Sociology, Thiel Coll., 1956; BA in Vocal Performance, Concordia Coll., 1959; student in Voice, U. Colo., 1966; student in Choral Techniques and Voice, Meadowbrook Sch. Music, 1967; student in Music, Choral Conducting, Choral Technique & Voice, Occidental Coll., 1968—69. Dir. choral Wellsville (Ohio) H.S., 1959—63, Churchill Area H.S., Pitts., 1963—68; thr. music, dir. choral Santa Barbara (Calif.) H.S., 1969—95; founder, artistic dir. Canticle A Cappella Choir, Santa Barbara, 1995—. Dir. madrigal singers Santa Barbara H.S. Choir, 1969—95, dir. concert tours, 1972—92. Dir.(prodr.): (compact disc) Earth Chants, 1994, Canticle, 1996, My Song in the Night, 2000, O Wondrous Mystery, 2003, Phoenix (27 original compostions and arrangements), 2004, Every Time I Feel the Spirit, 2006; composer: (songs) Seasons of his Mercies, 2003, Four Songs of Concord, 2005, Four Lyrics of Sara Teasdale, 2006, The Gift of God's Grace, 2006. Named Local Hero, Santa Barbara (Calif.) Ind., 1995; recipient Outstanding Contbn. to Cmty. award, Santa Barbara (Calif.) City Coun., 2004, Disting. Alumni award, Concordia Coll., 2006. Mem.: Am. Choral Dirs. Assn. (performer). Home Phone: 805-964-8629.

ZIMMERMAN, ROBERT ALLEN See DYLAN, BOB

ZIMMERMAN, ROGER JOSEPH, fishery biologist; b. Alice, Tex., Dec. 2, 1941; s. Walter George and Laura Virgie (Heine) Z.; m. Domenica Marie DeCaro, Dec. 28, 1976; children: Kathryn, Robert. BS in Biology, Tex. A&I Coll., 1966, MA in Biology and Geology, 1969; PhD in Marine Scis., U.P.R., Mayaguez, 1979. Tchg. asst. biology dept. U. South Fla., Tampa, 1971, rsch. assoc. marine sci. dept. St. Petersburg, 1971-73; rsch. assoc. P.R. Nuclear Ctr. U. P.R., 1974-75, grad. fellow, 1975-78, marine benthic ecologist Ctr. for Energy & Environ. Rsch., 1978-81; fishery ecologist fishery mgmt. divsn. NOAA/NMFS Galveston (Tex.) Lab., 1981-91, divsn. chief fishery ecology divsn., 1991-93, lab. dir., 1993—. Rsch. fellow U.S. Nat. Mus. Natural History, Smithsonian Instn., Washington and Harbor Beach, Fla., summer 1975, 76; vis. instr. marine biology dept. Tex. A&M U., Galveston, summer 1988, 89; vis. instr. biology dept. Corpus Christi (Tex.) State U., 1986; tchg. asst. biology U. South Fla., 1970; lectr.-counselor Tex. A&I U., 1969, lab. coord., tchg. asst., 1968-69; OAS and U.S. AID advisor to Instuto de Pesca de Ecuador, 1985-88; mem. com. coastal ocean estuarine habitat rsch. planning com. NOAA 1987, sci. adv. com., 1989; chair predator-prey com. S.E. Fisheries Sci. Ctr., 1990-91; coord. climate and global change ecol. sys. and dynamics work group NMFS, 1990, spl. asst. to office of sr. scientist, 1990; mem. sci. adv. com. Galveston Bay project Nat. Estuary Program, 1993-96, mgmt. com. Coastal Bend project, 1994-98; bd. dirs. Gulf of Mex. regional marine rsch. program NMFS-SEFSC, 1992-93; rep. programs on coastal fisheries and estuarine ecology SERSC, 1992-95; grad. student advisor, adj. wildlife and fisheries dept. and biology dept. Tex. A&M U., dept. biology Corpus Christi State U., dept. marine scis. La. State U., 1985-89, dept. biology U. Houston, 1983-85; presenter workshops in field. Reviewer for jours. in field, including Fishery Bull., Contbns. to Marine Sci., Marine Ecology Progress Series, Jour. Exptl. Marine Biology and Ecology, Marine Biology, Bull. Marine Sci., Jour. Wetlands Ecology and Mgmt., Estuaries, Coastal and Shelf Sci., also various proposals; editl. reviewer SEFSC Galveston Lab., 1984—; contbr. numerous articles to profl. publs.; author abstracts, revs. in field. Mem. Estuarine Rsch. Fedn., Gulf Estuarine Rsch. Soc., Crustacean Soc., Am. Fisheries Soc., Assn. Marine Labs. of the Caribbean. Office: Nat Marine Fisheries Svc SE Fisheries Sci Ctr 4700 Avenue U Galveston TX 77551-6901

ZIMMERMAN, RYAN WALLACE, professional baseball player; b. Washington, NC, Sept. 28, 1984; s. Keith and Cheryl Zimmerman. Attended, U. Va. Third baseman Washington Nationals, 2005—. Active Nat. Multiple Sclerosis Soc.; founder ziMS Found. Recipient All-Am., Baseball Am., 2005, Nat. Collegiate Baseball Writer's Assn., 2005. Achievements include being the first rookie third baseman to play in 157 games since Dick Allen played 162 in 1964; establishing a franchise rookie record with a 17 game hitting streak. Office: RFK Stadium 2400 E Capitol St SE Washington DC 20003 Office Phone: 202-349-0400. *

ZIMMERMAN, SOL SHEA, pediatrician; b. NYC, June 25, 1948; s. Isaac and Estera (Berkowicz) Z.; m. Diana F. Zimmerman, Aug. 8, 1971; children: Jeffrey, Steven, Andrew. AB, Columbia U., 1968; MD, NYU, 1972. Diplomate Am. Bd. Pediats.; pediat. critical care medicine. Intern dept. pediats. NYU-Bellevue Hosp. Ctr., NYC, 1972-73, resident dept. pediats., 1973-75, chief resident dept. pediats., 1977-78, asst. prof. clin. pediats., 1978-83, assoc. prof. clin. pediats., 1983—, dir. pediat. critical care medicine, 1978-98, assoc. dir. dept. pediats., 1985—; assoc. chair dept. pediats. NYU Sch. of Medicine, NYC, 1997—, assoc. prof. pediat., 2002—. Pres. Pediat. Assocs. N.Y.C., P.C., 1978—; v.p. Univ. Physicians Network, 1996—; chmn. bd. mgrs. Univ. MSO, 1998—; assoc. prof. pediat. NYU-Bellevue Hosp. Ctr., 2002. Editor, author: (textbook) Critical Care Pediatrics, 1985. Chmn. com. on heart, health in the young N.Y.C. affiliate Am. Heart Assn., 1987-93. Maj. USAF MC, 1975-77. Fellow Am. Acad. Pediats., Am. Coll. Chest Physicians, Critical Care Medicine; mem. N.Y. Soc. Pediat. Critical Care Medicine (v.p. 1989-91, pres. 1991-93), Alpha Omega Alpha. Office: Pediat Assocs NYC PC 317 E 34th St New York NY 10016-4974 also: 20 Plaza St E Brooklyn NY 11238-4955

ZIMMERMAN, STEVEN CHARLES, chemistry professor; b. Chgo., Oct. 8, 1957; s. Howard Elliot and Jane (Kirschenheiter) Z.; m. Sharon Shavitt, Aug. 5, 1990; 2 children, Arielle Reneé, Elena Michelle. BS, U. Wis., 1979; MA, MPhil, Columbia U., PhD, 1983. Asst. prof. chemistry U. Ill., Urbana, 1985-91, assoc. prof. chemistry, 1991-94, prof. chemistry, 1994—, Roger Adams prof. chem., interim chem. dept. head; affiliate faculty mem. Beckman Inst. Mem. bioorganic natural products study sect. NIH, 1994—98. Contbr. articles to profl. publs. Presdl. Young Investigator award, NSF, 1988-93; Alfred P. Sloan fellow, 1992-93; recipient Buck-Whitney award, Am. Chem. Soc., 1995, Arthur C. Cope Scholar award, 1997. Home: 55 Chestnut Ct Champaign IL 61822-7121 Office: U Ill 345 Roger Adams Lab 600 S Mathews Ave Urbana IL 61801 E-mail: sczimmer@uiuc.edu.

ZIMMERMAN, WILLIAM EDWIN, editor, writer; b. Bklyn., Feb. 2, 1941; s. George and Ruth (Edelbaum) Z.; m. Teodorina Bello, Dec. 13, 1969; 1 child, Carlota Pastora. BA, Queens Coll., Flushing, 1962. Pres. Guarionex Press, Ltd., NYC, 1979—; with Am. Banker, NYC, 1962-82, editor, sr. v.p., 1982-89; editor in chief Banking Week, 1986-89; dep. editor Sunday Bus. sect. The NY Times, 1989; spl. projects editor, editor Student Briefing Page Newsday, LI, NY, 1989—2004. Author: How to Tape Instant Oral Biographies, 1979, A Book of Questions to Keep Thoughts and Feelings, 1984, Make Beliefs, 1987, Life Lines: A Book of Hope, 1990, The Little Book of Joy, 1995, Dogmas: Simple Truths from a Wise Pet, 1995, Make Beliefs for Kids of All Ages, 1996, A Book of Sunshine, 1997, Cat-e-chisms: Feline Answers to Life's Big Questions, 1997, My Life: An Open Book, 2000, Lunch Box Letters, 2000, Idea Catcher for Kids, 2000, Butterfly Wishes, 2002, My Paper Memory Quilt, 2004, 100 Things Guys Need to Know, 2005, Doodles & Daydreams: Your Passport for Becoming An Escape Artist, 2007. Mem. Am. Oral History Assn., Am. Soc. Bus. Writers, Am. Soc. Bus. Press Editors, NY Fin. Writers Assn., Overseas Press Club, Deadline Club, Dowtown Athletic Club, NY Athletic Club, Sigma Delta Chi. Democrat. Jewish. Personal E-mail: wmz@aol.com.

ZIMMERMANN, FRANK MARTIN, physicist, educator, research scientist; b. Karlsruhe, Germany, May 6, 1964; arrived in US, 1987, naturalized, 2004; s. Manfred Eugen and Herta Zimmermann; m. Yeong-Ah Soh, Oct. 29, 1995 (div. Sept. 2, 2003); 1 child, Ingrid Hana; m. Sophia Tsai, July 2, 2006. MS in Physics, Cornell U., 1993, PhD in Physics, 1995. Rsch. asst. solid state physics Ariz. State U., 1988-89; rsch. asst. surface sci. Cornell U., 1990-95; asst. prof. physics dept. physics and astronomy and lab. surface modification Rutgers U., Piscataway, NJ, 1995-2001, assoc. prof., 2001—. Lectr., presenter in field. Contbr. numerous articles to profl. jours. including Surface Sci. Reports and Phys. Rev. Lett. Fulbright fellow, 1987-88, Internat. Rsch. fellow Sci. and Tech. Agy., Japan, 1996, 98; Rutgers bd. trustees rsch. fellow for scholarly excellence, 2001. Mem. Am. Phys. Soc., Am. Vacuum Soc. (Grad. Rsch. award 1994, Morton M. Traum award 1995), Am. Chem. Soc. (Victor K. LaMer award 1996), Phi Kappa Phi. Achievements include elucidation of mechanisms and dynamics of thermal and photochemical desorption and adsorption using laser spectroscopy. Avocations: whitewater kayaking, downhill skiing, bicycling. Office: Rutgers U Dept Physics 136 Frelinghuysen Rd Piscataway NJ 08854-8019

ZIMMERMANN, JOERG, biophysicist; b. Berlin, July 1, 1971; PhD, Humboldt U., 1990—96. Postdoctoral fellow UC Berkeley, Dept. of Chemistry, Berkeley, Calif., 2001—03; rsch. assoc. The Scripps Rsch. Inst., La Jolla, Calif., 2003—. Recipient Humboldt award, 2001. Mem.: Am. Chem. Soc., The Biophys. Soc., European Soc. for Photobiology. Office: Scripps Rsch Inst CVN-22 10550 N Torrey Pines Rd La Jolla CA 92037

ZIMMERMANN, JOHN JOSEPH, lawyer; b. Chgo., Apr. 30, 1939; s. John Joseph and Ernestine Elizabeth (Leuver) Z.; m. Alice Rose Farrell, July 4, 1964; children: John, Michael, Thomas, Margaret, Kathleen. AB, DePaul U., Chgo., 1962, JD, 1967. Bar: Ill. 1967, US Dist. Ct. (no. dist.) Ill. 1967, US Ct. Appeals (7th cir.) 1967. Ptnr. Raysa & Zimmermann, LLC, Park Ridge, Ill.; village atty. Village of Mt. Prospect, 1968-79, acting village mgr., 1969, 70-71; city atty. City of Wood Dale, Ill., 1975-2002; corp. counsel City of Highland Park, Ill., 1979-99, corp. counsel, 1990-99; atty. Mt. Prospect Pub. Libr., 1982-95; village atty. Village of Mettawa, Ill., 1981—; corp. coun. Village of Schiller Park, Ill., 1993—; dir. Joe Mitchell Buick/GMC Truck, Inc., Mt. Prospect, 1979-; lectr. Ill. Inst. for Continuing Legal Edn., 1979-, Ill. State Bar Assn., 1988—. Mem. St. Paul of the Cross Sch. Bd. of Edn., Park Ridge, 1972-75, pres., 1974-75; mem. sponsoring com. Ann. Men's Prayer Breakfast, Park Ridge, 1979-; charter mem. Ill. Inst. Local Govt. Law, dir., pres., 2000-02. Recipient Ofcl. Commendation Village of Mt. Prospect, 1971, named hon. citizen, 1974; recipient certs. of appreciation Ill. Inst. Continuing Legal Edn., 1980, Chgo. Bar Assn., 1984, Ill. State Bar Assn., 1988. Mem. Internat. Mcpl. Lawyers Assn. (del., lectr., dir., trustee, pres. 2001-02), Ill. State Bar Assn. (sec. 1983, mem. local govt. sect. coun. 1981-91), Ill. Home Rule Attys. Com. (charter mem., chmn. 1978-79), Chgo. Bar Assn. (chmn. local govt. com. 1983-84), Ill. Inst. Local Govt. Law (charter; dir., pres. 2000-02). Roman Catholic. Home: 524 Vine Ave Park Ridge IL 60068-4148 Office: Raysa & Zimmermann LLC 22 South Washington Avenue Park Ridge IL 60068

ZIMMERMANN, PHILIP R., software engineer, consultant; B in Computer Sci., Fla. Atlantic U., 1978. Founder PGP, Inc. (acquired by Network Associates, Inc., then acquired by PGP Corp. in 2002), 1996—97; sr. fellow Network Associates, Inc., 1997—2000; spl. advisor, cons. PGP Corp., 2002—. Cons. on matters of cryptographic for several companies; spkr. in field; fellow Stanford Law Sch., Ctr. for Internet and Soc.; chmn. OpenPGP Alliance; adv. bd. mem. Anonymizer.com, Hush Comm., Encentuate, Qualys. Creator (email encryption software package) Pretty Good Privacy (PGP), 1991— (One of the Top 10 Most Important Products of 1994, Information Week, Network Computing Well-Connected award for Best Security Product, 1996). Adv. bd., Computer Engring. Dept. Santa Clara U. Named one of Net 50-Most Influential on the Internet, Newsweek, 1995, Top 10 Innovators in E-business, InfoWorld, 2000; named to CRN Industry Hall of Fame, 2001, Heinz Nixdorf Mus. Forum Wall of Fame, 2003; recipient Pioneer award, Electronic Frontier Found., 1995, Chrysler award for Innovation in Design, 1995, PC Week IT Excellence award, 1996, Lifetime Achievement award, Secure Computing Mag., 1998, Louis Brandeis award for Privacy Internat., 1999. Mem.: Computer Professionals for Social Responsibility (bd. dir., Norbert Wiener award 1996), League for Programming Freedom, Assn. Computing Machinery, Internat. Assn. Cryptologic Rsch., Roundtable of Scientific Comm. and Nat. Security. Business E-Mail: prz@mit.edu.

ZIMMERMANN, ROBERT LAURENCE, marketing professional; b. Mpls., Jan. 1, 1932; s. Lawrence and Bertha Mabel (Foss) Z. BA, U. Minn., 1954, MA, 1965, PhD, 1970. Asst. prof. psychology U. Winnepeg, Man., Can., 1968-69; research assoc. psychiatry research unit U. Minn., Mpls., 1969-75; sr. scientist biometrics lab. George Washington U., Washington, 1975-76; pvt. cons. research design and data analysis Mpls., 1976-84; sr. research mgr. Maritz Market Rsch., Mpls., 1984—. Clin. asst. prof. psychiatry dept. U. Minn., Mpls., 1976-90; external rev. officer FDA, Washington, 1974-77. Contbr. numerous articles to profl. jours. Fellow NIMH, 1958, 61, 69-71; merit fellow State of Minn. Mem. AAAS, Com. on Space Rsch., Nat. Space Soc., Nat. Space Found., The Planetary Soc., ACLU, Amnesty Internat., Ctr. Pub. Integrity, Oxfam. Democrat. Avocation: writing. Home: 1920 S 1st St Apt 1104 Minneapolis MN 55454-1048 Office: Maritz Market Rsch Inc 7701 France Ave S Minneapolis MN 55435-5288 Personal E-mail: zimmermannbobl@comcast.net.

ZIMMERMANN, THOMAS CALLANDER PRICE, retired historian, educator; b. Bryn Mawr, Pa., Aug. 22, 1934; s. R.Z. and Susan (Goodman) Z.; m. Margaret Upham Ferris. BA, Williams Coll., 1956, Oxford U., 1958, MA, 1964; AM, Harvard U., 1960, PhD, 1964. Asst. prof. Reed Coll., Portland, Oreg., 1964-67, assoc. prof., 1967-73, prof. history, 1973-77, chmn. dept. history, 1973-75; v.p. acad. affairs Davidson (N.C.) Coll., 1977-86, Charles A. Dana prof. History, 1986-99, Charles A. Dana prof. history emeritus, 1999-2000, ret., 2000. Mem. Oreg. Com. for Humanities NEH, 1971—77; mem. Region 14 selection com. Woodrow Wilson Nat. Fellowship Found., Princeton, NJ, 1967—70. Author: Paolo Giovio: The Historian and the Crisis of Sixteenth-Century Italy, 1995 (Helen and Howard R. Marraro Book prize Am. Hist. Assn. 1996, Presdl. Book award Am. Assn. for Italian Studies 1997); co-editor of collected works of Paolo Giovio, 1985; contbr. articles to profl. jours. Pres. Am. Alpine Club, NYC, 1979-82, bd. dirs., 1975-83; bd. dirs. Charlotte Opera Assn., NC, 1980-82, NC Outward Bound Sch., Morganton, 1978-81; bd. advisors Lowell Obs., 1988-93; mem. Rome Prize Jury (Post-Classical Humanistic Studies) Am. Acad. in Rome, 1993; bd. adv. bot. gardens U. NC, Charlotte, 2007—. Danforth fellow, 1956-62, Fulbright fellow, Italy, 1962-64, Villa "I Tatti" fellow Harvard U. Ctr., 1970-71; Am. Council of Learned Socs. fellow, N.Y.C., 1975-76. Mem. Renaissance Soc. Am., Sixteenth Century Studies Conf., Soc. Italian Hist. Studies, Am. Assn. Italian Studies, Phi Beta Kappa.

ZIMMERN-REED, ANNETTE WACKS, psychologist; b. Exeter, Va., Feb. 7, 1933; d. Samuel Cleve and Zella Edith (Nelson) Wacks; m. James Robert Reed; children: Kenneth Zimmern, Ronald Zimmern stepchildren: Susan, Kathleen. RN, Sinai Hosp. Sch. Nursing, 1954; BA, U. Md., 1969, MA, 1971, PhD, 1975. RN Md.; lic. Family-Marriage Therapist Tex. Capt., dir. substance abuse, dir. mental health divsn. USPHS, Rockville, Md., 1976—96. Asst. prof. dept. psychiatry divsn. psychology U. Tex., Dallas, 1985. Author: Violence in America, 1986. Fellow: Am. Assn. Marriage and Family Therapists; mem.: Am. Counselors Assn. Avocations: swimming, reading, writing.

ZIMMETT, MARK PAUL, lawyer, educator; b. Waukegan, Ill., July 4, 1950; s. Nelson H. Zimmett and Roslyn (Yastrow) Zimmett Grodzin; m. Joan Robin Urken, June 11, 1972; children: Nora Helene, Lili Eleanor. BA, Johns Hopkins U., 1972; JD, NYU, 1975. Bar: N.Y. 1976, U.S. Dist. Ct. (so. and ea. dists.) N.Y. 1976, U.S. Dist. Ct. (no. dist.) Calif. 1980, U.S. Ct. Appeals (2d cir.) 1980, U.S. Supreme Ct. 1981, U.S. Ct. Appeals (5th cir.) 1986, U.S. Ct. Appeals (9th cir.) 1988. Assoc. Shearman & Sterling, NYC, 1975-83, ptnr., 1984-90; adj. assoc. prof. internat. law NYU, 1986-88; lectr. internat. comml. litig. and arbitration Practicing Law Inst., 2000—02. Author: Letters of Credit, New York Practice Guide Business and Commercial Law, 1990; contbr. articles to profl. jours. Mem. ABA (subcom. on letters of credit, com. on uniform comml. code sect. bus. law), NY State Bar Assn., Assn. of the Bar of the City of NY (task force on corp. governance, com. on fed. cts., coun. on profl. and jud. ethics), NY County Lawyers Assn. (com. on bus. bankruptcy law, task force corp. governance, com. fed. cts., com. profl. and jud. ethics), Citizens Union. Democrat. Jewish. Office: 126 E 56th St New York NY 10022-3613 Office Phone: 212-755-0808.

ZIMMIE, THOMAS FRANK, civil engineer, educator; b. Scranton, Pa., Jan. 24, 1939; s. Thomas and Stella Josephine (Price) Z.; m. Patricia Joyce Kelly, June 8, 1962 (div. 1979); 1 child, David Thomas; m. Judith Anne Braden, July 13, 1989. BSCE, Worcester Poly. Inst., 1960; MSCE, U. Conn., 1962, PhD in Geotech. Engring., 1972. Registered profl. engr., N.Y., Conn. Staff engr. Union Carbide Corp. (Linde div.), Buffalo, 1964-68; profl. engr. Town of Mansfield, Conn., 1968-72; ptnr. Wang and Zimmie Cons., Troy, NY, 1973-80; v.p. Arch Engring. Cons., Troy, 1984-88; program dir. NSF, Washington, 1988-90; pres., CEO Civrotech Engrs., Inc., Troy, 1993—; prof., chair dept. civil engring Rensselaer Poly. Inst., Troy, 1973—, acting chair dept. civil and environ. engring., 2005—. Postdoctoral researcher Norwegian Geotech. Inst., Oslo, 1972-73; geotech. engr. N.Y. Dept. Environ. Conservation, Albany, 1983-85; town engr. Town of North Greenbush, N.Y., 1985-88. Editor: Permeability and Groundwater Contamination, 1981, Environmental Geotechnology, 2000; contbr. articles to profl. jours. 1st lt. US Army, 1962—64. Fellow Am. Coll. of Forensic Examiner, fellow ASCE (cert., Outstanding Svc. award 1986, 87); mem. ASTM (Spl. Svc. award 1980, Charles Dudley award 1984), Transp. Rsch. Bd., Am. Rd. and Transp. Builders Assn. Achievements include research in environmental protection. Avocation: flying. Home: 39 Zelenke Dr Wynantskill NY 12198-8627 Office: Rensselaer Poly Inst Civil & Environ Engring Dept Soil Mechanics Lab Troy NY 12180 Home Phone: 518-283-6208; Office Phone: 518-276-6939. Business E-Mail: zimmit@rpi.edu.

ZIMNY, MAX, labor union administrator, lawyer, arbitrator; b. Bklyn., Mar. 9, 1925; s. Joseph and Rebecca (Nadelman) Z.; m. Bernice Nelson, June 26, 1948; children: Stuart, Andrew. Student, Bklyn. Coll., 1942—47, LLB cum laude, 1950; postgrad., NYU Grad. Sch. Labor Law, 1950—52. Bar: N.Y. 1950, U.S. Dist. Ct. (so. and ea. dists.) N.Y. 1951, U.S. Ct. Appeals (2nd cir.) 1955, U.S. Supreme Ct. 1962, U.S. Ct. Appeals (D.C. cir.) 1968, U.S. Ct. Appeals (4th cir.) 1969, U.S. Ct. Appeals (9th cir.) 1975, U.S. Ct. Appeals (8th cir.) 1980, U.S. Dist. Ct. (no. dist.) N.Y. 1983, U.S. Ct. Appeals (6th cir.) 1987, U.S. Ct. Appeals (7th cir.) 1988, U.S. Ct. Appeals (3rd and 5th cirs.) 1991. Mem. Zimny & Goldberg, NYC,

1950—52; asst. gen. counsel Textiles Workers Union Am., NYC, 1952—58, Internat. Ladies' Garment Workers' Union, NYC, 1958—63, assoc. gen. counsel, 1963—72, gen. counsel, 1972—95, Union of Needletrades, Indsl. and Textile Employees, 1995—2001. Mem. Vladeck, Elias, Vladeck, Zimny and Englehard, N.Y.C., 1976-78; lectr. NYU Sch. Law, Stetson U. Sch. Law, Indsl. Rels. Rsch. Inst., Nat. Acad. Arbitrators. Editor: Labor Arbitrator Development, 1983, Arbitration: A Guide for Advocates, 1990, Arbitration Casebook, 1997. Mediator, fact finder N.Y. Pub. Employment Rels. Bd., 1968—; chmn. Consumer Adv. Coun. City of N.Y.; mem. Levittown (N.Y.) Bd. Edn.; chmn. Profls. for Histadrut, NYC; arbitrator NYS disciplinary panel; Bd. dirs. Nat. Resources Ctr. for Consumers Legal Svcs., Lawyers Coord. Com. AFL-CIO; bd. dirs. Corsi Labor Mgmt. Inst.; mediator, arbitrator Am. Arbitration Assn.; labor, employment and comml. panels, arbitrator labor and mgmt. panel Fed. Mediation and Concilation Svc.; arbitrator N.Y.C. Office of Collective Bargaining, Electric Boat, Groton, Conn.; mem. nat. adv. coun., chair com. on rules and procedures, chair nat. task force on ADR in employment and due process protocol; mem. steering com. ctr. for Law and Econ. Policy Columbia U. Sch. Law; adv. com. NYU and Fordham Conf. on Labor, 1985—. With US Army, 1943—46. Fellow: Coll. Labor and Employment Lawyers (chair, com. on ethics and civility); mem.: ABA (chmn. com. on arbitration 1977—81, coun. labor sect. 1989—, chair labor and employment sect., pub. rels. com.), Commn. Healthcare Dispute Resolution, Labor Employee Rels. Assn., Bar Assn. City of N.Y. (labor com.), B'nai B'rith Club (pres. lodge), Order of Coif. Home Phone: 516-731-4358; Office Phone: 516-731-4358. E-mail: maxzimny@optonline.net.

ZIMOV, BRUCE STEVEN, software engineer; b. Cin., Oct. 16, 1953; s. Sherman and Sylvia Zimov; m. Cathy Lynn Zimov, July 24, 1999. BS in Physics, U. Cin., 1975, MA in Philosophy, 1979. Physicist Kornylak Corp., Hamilton, Ohio, 1982-83; software engr. Entek Sci. Corp., Cin., 1983-89, project mgr., 1989-95, systems mgr., 1995-2000, AOL sr. tech. mgr., 2000—07, K12 sr dir., 2007—. Inventor chess variants, table tennis variant. Mem. IEEE, Internat. Neural Network Soc., Tri-State Online Philosophy SIG (founder). Avocations: philosophy, chess, Web surfing, computers, economics. E-mail: mindnova@aol.com.

ZIMPHER, NANCY LUSK, academic administrator; b. Gallipolis, Ohio, Oct. 29, 1946; d. Aven Denzle and Elsie Gordon (Hammond) L.; 1 child from a previous marriage, William Fletcher Zimpher; m. Kenneth R. Howey, May 8, 1987. BS, Ohio State U., 1968, MA, 1971, PhD, 1976. Cert. K-12 Tchr., Ohio. English tchr. Montgomery County Schs., Md., 1968, Reynoldsburg (Ohio) Schs., 1970; substitute tchr. Rolla (Mo.) City Schs., 1970-71; tchr. Phelps County Schs., Mo., 1971-72; grad. teaching assoc. Coll. Edn. Ohio State U., Columbus, 1972-73; dir. Coll. of Edn. Ohio State U., Columbus, 1973-74, grad. adminstrn. asst. to dean, 1974-76, dir. field experiences alumni rels., 1976-80, coord. undergraduate programs, 1980-84; asst. prof. Ednl. Policy and Leadership Ohio State U., 1984-86, assoc. prof., 1986-91, full prof., 1991-98, assoc. dean, 1992, dean, 1993, exec. dean, 1994; chancellor, prof. curriculum and instrn. U. Wis., Milw., 1998—2003; pres. U. Cin., 2003—. Prin. investigator U.S. Office Edn. Field Devel. Grant, 1981-83, 85-88; co-principal investigator Metro. Life Found. Grant. 1989—, 1992—; cons. The Holmes Group, Lansing, Mich., 1991—. Book rev., editor: Journal of Teacher Education, 1986-89; co-author: Book Profiles of Preservice Teacher Education, 1989, RATE Profiles, 1987-92, A Time for Boldness: A Case Story of Institutional Change, 2002; co-editor: University Leadership in Urban School Renewal: The President's Role, 2004, Boundary Spanners: A Key to Success in Urban Partnerships, 2006, Recruiting, Preparing and Retaining Teachers for Urban Schools, 2006, Creating a New Kind of University, 2006. Chair Faculty Compensation and Benefits Commn., 1989-90, Fiscal Com., 1991-92, Spousal Equivalency Com., 1990-91, Search Com., v.p. for Fin., 1992, Ohio State U; pres., chair bd. dirs. Holmes Partnership, 1997, chair edn. vision coun. United Way Franklin County, 1997; chair bd. dirs. United Way Franklin County, 1998; chair bd. dirs. Nat. Assn. State Univs. and Land-Grant Colls., 2007; chair Urban Serving Univs., 2005—. Fellow Com. for Instnl. Coop., Acad. Leadership Program. 1989-90; recipient Disting. Rsch. award, Disting. Teacher Educator award Assn. Tchr. Educators, 1990, Adams Professorshi Coll. Edn. Ind. State U., 1990—, Alumni Disting. Tchg. award, The Ohio State U., 1992, Chief Exec. Leadership award Coun. for the Advancement and Support Edn., 2003, Career Woman of Achievement award YWCA, 2004, Profl. Achievement award Ohio State U., 2004; named YWCA Woman of Achievement, 1997. Mem. Am. Edn. Rsch. Assn., Am. Assn. Coll. Teacher Edn. Rsch. Comm., Assn. Tchr. Educators, ASCD, Phi Delta Kappa. Episcopalian. Avocations: watercolorist, golf, sewing. Office: Univ Cin 625 Univ Pavilion PO Box 210063 Cincinnati OH 45221-0063

ZIMPLEMAN, LARRY DONALD, actuary; b. Williamsburg, Iowa, Sept. 7, 1951; s. J. Henry and Clara (Hansemann) Z.; m. Kathleen Margaret Berry, Dec. 29, 1973; children: Jeffrey, Christopher, Thomas. BSBA, Drake U., 1973, MBA, 1979. Enrolled actuary. Actuary student Principal Fin. Group, Des Moines, 1973-77, asst. actuary, 1977-82, dir., 1982-88, 2d v.p., 1989—97, v.p., 1997—99, sr. v.p., 1999—2001, exec. v.p., 2001—03, pres. retirement & investor services, 2003—06, pres., COO, 2006—. Chmn. Princor Fin. Services Corp.; past chmn. Employee Benefit Rsch. Inst.; trustee Actuarial Found.; chmn. Harris Trust com. Am. Council Life Insurers; delegate Nat. Summit on Retirement Savings, 2002—06. Contbr. articles to Drake Law Rev., 1984, Matthew Bender Rev., 1984, Taxes, 1987, Pension Section Newsletter, 1990. Bd. dirs. Prin. Fed. Polit. Action Com. Fellow Soc. of Actuaries; mem. Am. Acad of Actuaries (bd. dirs. Washington 1989—), Des Moines Actuaries Club (pres. 1989-90), Greater Des Moines C. of C. (bd. drs., bus. econ. devel. com. 1990). Avocations: sports, running. Office: Principal Fin Group 711 High St Des Moines IA 50392 *

ZIMRING, FRANKLIN E., lawyer, educator; b. 1942; BA, Wayne State U., 1963; JD, U. Chgo., 1967. Bar: Calif. 1968. Asst. prof. U. Chgo., 1967-69, assoc. prof., 1969-72, prof., 1972-85; co-dir. Ctr. for Studies in Criminal Justice, 1973-75, dir., 1975-86; prof. law dir. Earl Warren Legal Inst., U. Calif., Berkeley, 1985—2002. Author: (with Newton) Firearms and Violence in American Life, 1969; The Changing Legal World of Adolescence, 1982; (with Hawkins): Deterrence, 1973, Capital Punishment and the American Agenda, 1986, The Scale of Imprisonment, 1991, The Search for Rational Drug Control, 1992, Crime is Not the Problem, 1997, American Youth Violence, 1998, Punishment and Democracy, 2001, The Contradictions of American Capital Punishment, 2003, An American Travesty, 2004, American Juvenile Justice, 2005, The Great American Crime Decline, 2007. Mem. Am. Acad. Arts and Scis. Office: U Calif Earl Warren Legal Inst Boalt Hall Berkeley CA 94720 Business E-Mail: zimring@law.berkeley.edu.

ZIMRING, STUART DAVID, lawyer; b. LA, Dec. 12, 1946; s. Martin and Sylvia (Robinson) Z.; m. Eve Axelrad, Aug. 24, 1969 (div. 1981); m. Carol Grenert, May 24, 1981; children: Wendy Lynn Martin, Joseph Noah, Mathew Kevin Grenert, Dov Shimon. BA in U.S. History, UCLA, 1968, JD, 1971. Bar: Calif. 1972, U.S. Dist. Ct. (cen. dist.) Calif. 1972, U.S. Dist. Ct. (no. dist.) Calif. 1984; U.S. Supreme Ct., 1994; cert. specialist in estate planning, probate and trust law. Assoc. Law Offices Leonard Smith, Beverly Hills, Calif., 1971-73; ptnr. Law Offices Smith & Zimring, Beverly Hills, Calif., 1973-76; assoc. Levin & Ballin, North Hollywood, Calif., 1976-77; prin. Levin, Ballin, Plotkin, Zimring & Goffin, A.P.C., North Hollywood, 1978-91, Law Offices Stuart D. Zimring, North Hollywood, 1991—. Lectr. Los Angeles Valley Coll., Van Nuys, Calif., 1974-82. Author: Inter Vivos Trust Trustees Operating Manual, 1994, Durable Powers of Attorney for Health Care--A Practical Approach to an Intimate Document, 1995, Reverse Mortgages--An Update, 1996, Cultural and Religious Concerns in Drafting Advance Directives, 1996, Drafting for Multi-Cultural Diversity in Advance Directives, 2000; co-author: California Guide to Tax, Estate and Financial Planning for the Elderly, 2001-06. Bd. dirs. Bet Tzedek, Jewish Legal Svcs., L.A., 1975-88, chmn. legal svcs. com., 1978-82; bd. dirs. Brandeis-Bardin Inst., Simi Valley, Calif., 1976-80; bd. dirs. Bur. Jewish Edn., L.A., 1973-88, chmn. com. on parent and family edn., 1985-87; trustee Adat Ari El Synagogue, L.A., 1982-2000; bd. dirs. ONEgeneration, 1994, 1st v.p. 1995-97, pres., 1997-2001. Recipient Circle award Juvenile Justice Connection Project, L.A., 1989, Wiley W. Manuel award for pro bono legal svcs., 1994, 95, 96, 97, 98, 2003; named Vol. Atty. of Yr., Bet Tzedek Legal Svcs., 2002. Fellow: Am. Coll. Trusts and Estates Counsel, Nat. Acad. Elder Law Attys. (pres. So. Calif. chpt. 1997, nat. bd. dirs. 1997—2001, sec. 2001—03, pres. 2004—05); mem.: San Fernando Valley Bar Assn. (trustee 1979—86), State Bar Calif. Democrat. Avocations: music, collecting wine, travel, photography. Office: 12650 Riverside Dr Ste 100 North Hollywood CA 91607-3421 Office Phone: 818-755-4848. Business E-Mail: ZIMZIM@ElderLawLA.com.

ZINBERG, DAVID J., lawyer; b. NYC, Apr. 12, 1954; ScB magna cum laude, Brown U., 1974; JD, Harvard U., 1978. Bar: N.Y. 1979, U.S. Dist. Ct. (so. and ea. dists.) N.Y. 1981. Assoc. DeForest & Duer, 1978—81; mem. Rosenman & Colin LLP, NYC, 1981—87, ptnr., 1987—97; v.p. Morgan Guaranty Trust Co., 1997—2000; ptnr. Ingram Yuzek Gainen Carroll & Bertolotti, LLP, NYC, 2000—. Mem.: Assn. Bar City NY (real property sect.), NY State Bar Assn. (real property sect., exec. com. 1999—). Office: Ingram Yuzek Gainen Carroll & Bertolotti LLP 250 Park Ave New York NY 10177 Office Phone: 212-907-9601. Office Fax: 212-907-9681. E-mail: dzinberg@ingramllp.com.

ZINBERG, DOROTHY SHORE, sociologist, educator; b. Boston; m. Norman E Zinberg (dec.); children: Sarah Zinberg Mandel, Anne. BA, MA, Boston U.; PhD, Harvard U., 1966. Research chemist Lever Bros., Cambridge; sr. research assoc. Daniel Yankelovich, Inc., NYC, and; Cambridge Center for Research in Behavioral Scis., 1966-68; NSF research sociologist dept. chemistry U. Coll. London, 1968-69; lectr. Harvard U., 1960—. Mem. adv. com. Office Sci. Pers. NRC, Washington, 1971—74, bd. on engring. edn., 1991; spl. adviser Aspen Inst.; cons. MacArthur Found., 1989—93; vis. scholar NAS, China, 1987, Nat. Inst. Sci. and Tech., Tokyo, 1991; vis. lectr. Inst. for Human Scis., Vienna, 1995; mem. adv. bd. Erik Erikson Inst. for Edn. and Rsch., 1996—; vis. prof. Imperial Coll., London, 2001—04; assoc. Whitehead Inst. Biomed. Rsch., MIT, 2004—; vis. sr. fellow U. Coll. London, 2006—. Columnist: London Times Higher Educ Supplement, 1993—2001, NY Times Syndication, 1994—96. Mem. internat. sci. exchs. NAS, 1994—96, mem comt int relations, 1977—80, mem comt int human resources; chmn adv coun int div NSF, 1978—81; mem coun Int Exchange Scholars, 1978—81; mem comt int exchange engrs NAE, 1987—88; mem adv panel Office Technology Assessment Educ and Employment Scientists and Engrs, 1986—88; trustee Simon's Rock Col, 1971—75; mem panel sci and tech policy NATO, 1995—99; bd. dirs. Fine Arts Workshop, Provincetown, Mass., 1970—86, Bill T. Jones Found for Dance Promotion, 1997—99; bd dirs Gen Scanning, Inc, 1998—99; bd dirs eng educ NRC, 1990—95. Fellow: AAAS (mem comt sci freedom and responsibility 1972—74, comt opportunities in sci 1973—76, comt sci, eng, and pub policy 1982—88, com. exch. scientists with Fed. Republic Germany 1987—91, 1991); mem.: NAS (com. to evaluate Internat. Sci. and Tech. Ctr. Moscow 1995—97), Int Sci Policy Found (adv. bd. 1988—2004), Coun Foreign Relations, Fedn. Am. Scientists (mem. coun. 1980—85, bd. talking sci.). Home: 3 Acacia St Cambridge MA 02138-4818 Office: Harvard U 79 JF Kennedy St Cambridge MA 02138 E-mail: dorothy_zinberg@harvard.edu.

ZINCZENKO, DAVID, editor; s. Bohdan Zinczenko and Janice Sobieski. B, Moravian Coll. Assoc. editor Men's Journal, 1991—93; editl. dir. Men's Health Internat.; editor-in-chief Men's Health Mag., 2000—. Guest expert in field. Author: The Abs Diet, 2004 (named N.Y. Times Best Seller, 2004). Nominee Nat. Mag. award, ASME, 2005; named Folio's 1999 Thirty Under 30, one of People Mag. 50 Most Eligible Bachelors, 2002; named one of Ten Best-Dressed in Media, Ad Age, 2005; recipient 6 gold medals in Folio Mag. CDMA competition, Nat. Mag. award, ASME, 2000. Office: Men's Health 733 Third Ave New York NY 10017 also: Men's Health Rodale 33 E Minor St Emmaus PA 18098 *

ZINDER, NEWTON DONALD, investment advisor, consultant; b. NYC, Aug. 12, 1927; s. Paul and Jennie (Feld) Z.; m. Clarice Katz, Dec. 26, 1954; children— Marla, Andrea, Pamela. BA, NYU, 1948, MBA, 1957; MA, Columbia U., 1949. Securities analyst Ira Haupt & Co., NYC, 1953-60; securities analyst E.F. Hutton & Co., NYC, 1960-63, stock market analyst, 1963-88, Shearson Lehman Bros., NYC, 1988-92; investment cons., 1993—. Served with USN, 1945-46 Mem. Market Technicians Assn. Home: 66 Oak Creek Trail Madison WI 53717-1510 E-mail: newtwiz@webtv.net.

ZINE, LARRY JOSEPH, film rental company executive; b. Williston, ND, Dec. 12, 1954; s. Joseph and Olga (Hapip) Z.; m. Nancy Jane Brude, Aug. 14, 1976. BBA in Mktg., U. N.D., 1977, MS in Acctg., 1979. CPA, N.D. Grad. teaching asst. U. N.D., Grand Forks, 1978-79, instr., 1979-81; acct. Circle K Corp., Phoenix, 1981-82, tax and audit supr., 1982-84, fin. reporting mgr., 1984-87, v.p. fin. reporting, 1987, exec. v.p., CFO, 1988—96, Petro Shopping Ctr., LP, 1996—99, pres., 1999, dir.; exec. v.p., CFO Blockbuster Inc., Dallas, 1999—, chief adminstr. officer, 2001—. Mem. AICPA, Beta Alpha Psi. Avocation: running. Office: Blockbuster Inc 1201 Elm St Dallas TX 75270 Office Phone: 214-854-3000. Office Fax: 214-254-3677. *

ZINGALE, DONALD PAUL, academic administrator, educator; b. Bklyn., Aug. 3, 1946; s. Charles and Helen (Puglisi) Z. BS in Health, Phys. Edn., Bklyn. Coll., 1967; MS in Phys. Edn., U. Mass., 1969; PhD in Phys. Edn., Ohio State U., 1973; MSW, Calif. State U., Sacramento, 1984. Lic. clin. social worker, Calif.; lic. marriage and family counselor, Calif.; cert. health and phys. edn. instr. secondary schs., N.Y.C., N.Y.; cert. Alpine ski instr. Prof., assoc. dean health, human svcs. Calif. State U., Sacramento, 1973-93, assoc. v.p. rsch. and grad. studies, 1993-95, dean LA, 1995—96; dean Coll. Health and Human Svcs. San Francisco State U., 1996—2004; v.p. acad. affairs Calif. Maritime Acad., 2004—. Contbr. articles to profl. jours. and publs. Mem.: APHA, Nat. Coun. U. Rsch. Adminstrs., Am. Assn. Higher Edn., Am. Assn. Health Phys. Edn., Recreation and Dance, Profl. Ski Instrs. Am. Roman Catholic. Avocations: alpine skiing, sailing, travel, cooking, home renovation. Office: Calif Maritime Acad 200 Maritime Academy Dr Vallejo CA 94590-8181

ZINGALE, ROBERT G., surgeon; b. Bklyn., Feb. 9, 1957; s. Joseph and Theresa Zingale; m. Christine A. Smith, Oct. 4, 1986; children:Jillian, Kara, Alec. BS cum laude, Pace U., 1979; MD, SUNY, Bklyn., 1983. Diplomate Am. Bd. Surgery, Surg. Crit. Care, Nat. Bd. Med. Examiners. Resident Maimonides Med. Ctr., Bklyn., 1983-88; trauma fellow Coney Island Hosp, Bklyn., 1988-89; attending physician, dir. trauma, pres. med. staff Huntington (N.Y.) Hosp., 1989—; attending physician Nassau County Med. Ctr., East Meadow, NY, 1991—; clin. instr. SUNY, Stony Brook, 1991—; assoc. clin. prof. surgery N.Y. Med. Coll./North Shore U. Hosp., Valhalla, 1993—; pres. med. staff Huntington Hosp. Dir. surg. svcs. Dolan Health Ctr. Contbr. articles to profl. jours. Fellow ACS, Suffolk Acad. Medicine; mem. AMA, Soc. Laparoendoscopic Surgeons, Am. Soc. Gen. Surgeons, N.Y. Met. Breast Cancer Grop, Med. Soc. N.Y., Suffolk County Med. Soc. Office: 158 E Main St Huntington NY 11743 Office Phone: 631-271-1822.

ZINGER, MICHAEL, reproductive endocrinologist; BA, Brandeis U., Waltham, Mass., 1991; MD, Albert Einstein Coll. of Medicine, NYC, 1995. Diplomate Am. Bd. of Obstetrics and Gynecology, Am. Bd. Reproductive Endocrinology and Infertility. Resident dept. obstetics gynecology North Shore U. Hosp., NYU Coll. of Medicine, Manhasset, 1995—99, chief resident dept. obstetics gynecology, 1998—99; clin. instr. in reproductive endocrinology and infertiilty U. Cin. Coll. Medicine, 1999—2002, fellow in reproductive endocrinology and infertility, 1999—2002; dir. in vitro fertilization Fertility Inst. at Edward, Naperville, Ill., 2002—. Profl. adv. bd. RESOLVE, Chgo., 2003—. Spkr. at ann. symposium RESOLVE, Chgo., 2003. Recipient Merck Sr. Fellow's award, The Endocrine Soc., 2002. Fellow: Am. Coll. of Obstetrics and Gynecology; mem.: Am. Soc. of Reproductive Medicine, Soc. for Reproductive Endocrinology. Achievements include research in reproductive endocrinology. Office: Fertility Inst at Edward 120 Osler Dr #100 Naperville IL 60540 Home Phone: 847-593-1040; Office Phone: 630-428-2229. Office Fax: 630-428-0336. E-mail: mzinger@usa.net.

ZINGG, PAUL JOSEPH, academic administrator; b. Newark, July 22, 1947; s. Carl William Zingg and Dolores Lucking Dulebohn. BA in History, Belmont Abbey Coll., Belmont, NC, 1968; MA in History, U. Richmond, Va., 1969; PhD in History, U. Ga., 1974. Chair and asst. prof., dept. of history and polit. sci. St. Bernard's Coll., Cullman, Ala., 1975-77; dean, academic affairs Daniel Hale Williams U., Chgo., 1977-78; adj asst./assoc. prof., dept. of Am. civilization U. Pa., Phila., 1978—86, asst. dean, academic affairs, Coll. of Arts and Sciences, 1978—79, vice dean, undergraduate studies and admissions, Coll. of Arts and Sciences, 1979—83, Am. Coun. on Edn. Fellow in Academic Adminstrn. and spl. asst. to the pres., 1983—84, exec. asst. to pres., 1984—86; cons. U. Calif., Berkeley, 1986; dean liberal arts and prof., dept. of history St. Mary's Coll., Moraga, Calif., 1986-93; prof., dept. of history Calif. Poly. State U., San Luis Obispo, Calif., 1993—2003, dean liberal arts, 1993-95, provost and acad. v.p., 1995—2003; pres. Calif. State U., Chico, 2004—. Vis. instr. history Ga. Coll., Milledgeville, 1971; cons., contbr. on exhibits Oakland Mus., 1992-94, Calif. Hist. Soc., 2004, PBS-TV documentary film Baseball, 1991-93; editorial cons. U. Nebr. Press, 1994—, U. Ill. Press, 1995-, others. Author: Pride of the Palestra, 1987, Harry Hooper, 1887-1974: An American Baseball Life, 1993, Runs, Hits and Era: The Pacific Coast League, 1903-1958, 1994, 2nd edit., 1996, A Good Round: A Journey Through the Landscapes and Memory of Golf, 1999, The Moraine Country Club 1930-2005, 2005; co-author: Through Foreign Eyes, 1982; editor, co-author: The Academic Penn, 1986; editor, contbr.: The Sporting Image: Readings in American Sport History; editor: In Search of the American National Character, 1984; contbr. numerous articles to profl. jours. Mem. Calif. Hist. Soc., 2000—; charter mem., Calif. Coun., Oakland Mus., 1995—. NEH summer fellow, 1975, summer rsch. grant, 1989, Ctr. for Internat. Study and Rsch. fellow, 1980-82, Am. Coun. on Edn. fellow, 1983-84; U. Pa. Rsch. Found. awards, 1983-85, faculty mem. of the yr., 1984, grantee St. Mary's Coll., 1987, 90, 91, 93, alumni faculty scholarship award, 1992. Mem. Orgn. Am. Historians, Soc. for History Edn., N.Am. Soc. for Study of Sport, Am. Studies Assn., Soc. for Am. Baseball Rsch., Am. Coun. on Edn., Assn. Am. Colls. and Univs., Am. Assn. Higher Edn., Nat. Assn. State Univs. and Land-Grant Colls., Rotary Club, Merion Golf Club, Butte Creek Country Club, Canyon Oaks Country Club, Phi Alpha Theta, Phi Beta Delta. Avocations: golf, labrador retrievers, baseball. Office: Calif State U 400 W First St Chico CA 95928-0155 Office Phone: 530-898-5201. E-mail: pzingg@csuchico.edu.

ZINK, HARRY A., ophthalmologist; MD, Univ. Pa., 1971. Resident, rsch. fellow, glaucoma Barnes Hosp.-Washington Univ. Sch. Med., St. Louis, 1976; asst. clin. prof. Case Western Res. Univ.; pvt. practice Wooster, Ohio. Mem.: Ohio Ophthalmological Soc., Am. Acad. Ophthalmology (chmn. membership adv. com., ad hoc com. on primary eye care, mem. coun. from Ohio Ophthalmological Soc. 1993—95, trustee-at-large 1995—97, sec. mem. svcs. 1998—2004, pres. 2005—). Office: Wooster Eye Ctr 3519 Friendsville Rd Wooster OH 44691 Office Phone: 330-345-7200.

ZINK, JOHN H., III, lawyer; b. Balt., Feb. 14, 1945; BA, Washington & Lee U., 1967, JD, 1970. Bar: Md. 1970, US Dist. Ct. (md.), US Ct. Appeals (DC, 4th cir.), US Supreme Ct. Ptnr., Comml. Litigation practice Venable LLP, Towson, Md. Atty. Grievance Commn. Rev. Bd., 1982; mem. Gov.'s Jud. Nominating Commn., 1982-90. Fellow Md. Bar Found.; mem. ABA, Md. State Bar Assn. (chair ins. trust com.), Md. Def. Counsel, Def. Rsch. Inst., Baltimore County Bar Assn., Phi Delta Phi. Office: Venable LLP PO Box 5517 210 Allegheny Ave Towson MD 21204 Office Phone: 410-494-6254. Office Fax: 410-821-0147. Business E-Mail: jhzink@venable.com.

ZINK, LEE BERKEY, retired academic administrator, economist, educator; b. Salem, Ind., June 7, 1930; s. Otto C. and Lera (Berkey) Z.; m. Patricia Louise Patton, Aug. 16, 1964; children: Kevin Patrick, Barry Lee. BA in Econs. magna cum laude, Ind. U., 1959; PhD in Econs., Okla. State U., 1967. Field rep. GM Acceptance Corp., Louisville, Ky., 1953-54; asst. mgr. Dougherty Motor Sales, Salem, 1954-56; asst. prof. econs. Southeastern State Coll., Durant, Okla., 1964-67, spl. asst. to dir. Tech. Use Studies Ctr., 1964-65, dir., 1965-68, assoc. prof. of Econs., 1967-68; dir., prin. rsch. economist, bur. bus. and econ. rsch. U. N.Mex., Albuquerque, 1968-77; prof. bus. adminstrn. N.Mex. Highlands U., Kirtland, 1974-81; dir. Inst. Applied Rsch. Svcs. U. N.Mex., Albuquerque, 1975-2000, dir. Nat. Energy Info. Ctr. affiliate/U.S. Dept. Energy, 1978-87, assoc. v.p. rsch., bus. and govt. rels., 1988-2000; ret. Mem. Gov.'s adv. com. statis. standards for Okla., 1964-66, sci. and industry Okla., 1965-66, statewide planning com. implemenation of Tech. Svcs. Act, Okla., 1965-66; cons. majority leader U.S. Ho. Reps., 1964-68, So. Okla. Devel. Assn., 1965-68, Gov. Okla., 1965-68, Kiamichi Econ. Devel. Dist., Okla., 1967-68, N.Mex. Corp. Commn., 1969-74, N.Mex. State Planning Office, 1971, Ohio State U. Evaluation Ctr., 1972, others; mem. Gov.'s adv. com. N.Mex. Dept. Devel., 1971; adv. panel spl. tech. assistance program Office Econ. Opportunity, 1972-74; mem. Albuquerque adv. coun. U.S. Small Bus. Adminstrn., 1974-81, chmn. 1977-79; chmn. Gov.'s Coun. Econ. Advisors, 1975-78; sec. econ. devel. Gov.'s Cabinet, 1975-76, policy advisor, 1976-78; econ. devel. task force We. Interstate Commn. Higher Edn., 1979. Mem. edit. review bd. Review of Regional Economics and Business, 1976-85; bd. edit. contbrs. The Albuquerque Tribune, 1979-82; mem. edit. adv. bd. The Southwest Review of Management and Economics, 1981-85; contbr. articles to profl. jours. Organizing pres. Kiamichi Econ. Devel. Dist., Okla., 1966-67; active Monte Vista Christian Ch., 1968—; exec. dir. N.Mex. Coun. Econ. Edn., 1969-75, chmn. operating com., 1976-86; pres. East Holiday Park Neighborhood Assn., 1978-94; adv. coun. city growth and devel. Greater Albuquerque Leadership Devel. Program, 1980-82; adv. bd. U.S. Armed Svcs., 1980-87; adv. bd. econ. devel. City of Albuquerque, 1980-84; community advisor NCAA Vols. for Youth, 1981-85; mem. Bernalillo county Human Svcs. Coalition, 1982-85; apptd. by Gov.-elect Anaya N.Mex. Jobs Task Force, 1982-83; apptd. chmn. by mayor Better Albuquerque Bond Coms., 1983-87, 93-95; trustee U. Albuquerque, 1983-86; bd. dirs. Nat. Tng. Inst. Cmty. Econ. Devel., 1979-82, Inst. Study Cmty. Econ. Devel., 1980-82, Albuquerque Conv. and Vis. Bur., 1984-87, Consumer Credit Counseling Svc. N.Mex., 1985-94, pres. 1989-90, Better Bus. Bur. N.Mex., 1992—; pres. adv. coun. UNICEF, Albuquerque, 1985-95; mem. employment and tng. needs task force City of Albuquerque, 1987-88; evaluation team Congressman Lujan's South Valley task force, 1987; apptd. chmn. by Mayor Saavedra and city coun. pub. forum com. recycling, 1991. 2d lt. U.S. Army, 1951-53, Germany; lt. col. USAR, 1953-71. Fellow Nat. Defense Edn. Act, 1959-62; grantee Nat. Aeronautics and Space Adminstrn., 1964-68, N.Mex. Dept. Devel., 1968-80, HEW, 1968-76, 1971-72, Bank N. Mex., 1969-77, The Albuquerque Model Cities Agy., 1969-70, Four Corners Regional Commn., 1969-80, U.S. Forest Svc.,

1974-77, U.S. Dept. Commerce, 1975-79, 1976-2000, N.Mex. Energy Resources Bd., 1976-77, The Navajo Nation, 1976-78, U.S. Army Corps. Engrs., 1976-78, U.S. Dept. Energy, 1978-87. Mem. Am. Assembly Collegiate Schs. Bus. (rsch., statis., publs. com. 1976-77, small bus. adminstrn. liasion com. 1976-78), Am. Soc. Info. Sci. (frontier chpt. exec. com. 1972-73, chmn.-elect 1972, chmn. 1973), Assn. Univ. Bus. and Econ. Rsch. (exec. com. 1971-78, v.p. 1975-76, pres. 1976-77), Mid continent Rsch. and Devel. Coun. (bd. dirs. 1965-69), Fedn. Rocky Mountain States (chmn. bus. rsch. com. 1969-75), Rocky Mountain Coun. Burs. Bus. and Econ. Rsch. (chmn. 1969-77), N.Mex. Coun. Econ. Edn. (bd. dirs. 1969-90), Am. Guild Organists (dean Albuquerque chpt. 1996-98), Greater Albuquerque C. of C. (edn. com. 1968-73, bd. dirs. 1970-76, 78-82, chmn. growth com. 1972, v.p. 1973-74, pres. 1981), U. N.Mex. Retiree Assn. (pres. 2003-05), Phi Kappa Phi, Phi Beta Kappa (alpha chpt. exec. com., sec. 1973-75), Golden Key (hon.). Democrat. Avocation: pipe organs. Home: 3741 Mount Rainier Dr NE Albuquerque NM 87111-4399 Personal E-mail: drLBZ@aol.com.

ZINKERNAGEL, ROLF MARTIN, immunology educator; b. Basle, Switzerland, Jan. 6, 1944; s. Robert W. and Suzanne (Staehlin) Zinkernagel; m. Kathrin G. Ludin, Mar. 11, 1968; children: Christine, Annelies, Martin. MD, U. Basel, 1968. Intern in surgery Claraspital, Basel, 1968—69; postdoctoral Inst. Biochemistry, Lausanne, 1970—72, Dept. Microbiology, ANU, Canberra, Australia, 1973—75; asst. prof. Dept. Immunopathology, Scripps U., La Jolla, Calif., 1975—80, mem., 1978—79; assoc. prof. Dept. Pathology, Div. Exptl. Pathology, U. Zurich, 1979—92; full prof. Dept. Pathology, Inst. Exptl. Immunology, U. Zurich, 1992—. Editl. bd. Exptl. Cell Biology, 1976—88, Immunogenetics, 1977—, Parasite Immunology, 1978—84, Jour. of Immunology, 1978—80, Thymus, 1979—89, Antiviral Rsch., 1980—88, Jour. of Exptl. Medicine, 1981—84, European Jour. of Immunology, 1981—, Jour. of Environ. Pathology Toxicology and Oncology, 1981—, Cellular Immunology, 1983—, Internat. Jour. of Microbiology, 1983—, and others. Co-recipient Nobel Prize for medicine, 1996; recipient Albert Lasker award for Basic Med. Rsch., 1995. Mem.: others, Deutsche Gesellschaft fur Virologie, Deutsche Gesellschaft fur Immunologie, ENI European Network of Immunol. Instns., Internat. Soc. for Antiviral Rsch., Acadmia Euopea, Swiss Soc. of Cell and Molecular Biology, Swiss Soc. of Microbiology, Swiss Soc. of Pathology, Am. Assn. of Pathologists, Am. Assn of Immunologists, Australian Soc. for Immunology, Swiss Soc. of Allergy and Immunology, Soc. Francaise d'Immunolgie (hon.), Scandinavian Soc. of Immunology (hon.). Achievements include discovery of of MHC-restricted T cell recognition; of the thymus role in determining MHC-restricted T-cell specficity; NK-cell activity in virus infections, T-cell epitope escape virus mutants, tolerances to viruses; research in on role of virus-specific T-cells in causing immunopathology. Office: Univ Hosp Inst Exptl Immunology Schmelzbergstr 12 CH-8091 Zurich Switzerland Office Phone: 0041 44 255 2989. Office Fax: 41 44 255 44 20. Business E-Mail: Rolf.Zinkernagel@usz.ch.

ZINKHAM, W. ROBERT, lawyer; b. Balt., May 30, 1955; s. William H. and Claire A. Z.; m. Theresa McGeehan, July 7, 1985; children: Natalie Anne, Elizabeth Claire. BA, Johns Hopkins U., 1977; JD, U. Md., Balt., 1980. Law clerk to chief judge Md. Ct. Appeals, Balt., 1980-81; assoc. Venable, Baetjer and Howard, Balt., 1981-88, ptnr., 1989—. Bd. dirs. Greater Balt. Med. Ctr. Found., 1992—. Editor Md. Law Rev., 1979. Chmn. Johns Hopkins Hosp. Psychiat. Day Hosp., Balt., 1982-92; pres. Mt. Washington Hills Assn., Balt., 1984-87. Mem. ABA, Am. Acad. Hosp. Attys., Nat. Health Lawyers Assn., Md. Bar Assn., Balt. Bar Assn. Republican. Office: Venable 2 Hopkins Plz Ste 1800 Baltimore MD 21201-2982 E-mail: wrzinkham@venable.com.

ZINKHAN, GEORGE MARTIN, III, marketing educator; b. Balt., Feb. 17, 1952; s. George Martin Jr. and Mary Elizabeth (Stoner) Z.; m. Marie Bruce; children: George M. IV, Lydia F., Sam S., M. Elizabeth S., L. James G. BA in English Lit., Swarthmore Coll., 1974; MBA in Ops. Rsch., U. Mich., 1979, PhD in Bus. Adminstrn., 1981. Stats. lab. counselor U. Mich., Ann Arbor, 1978-79, teaching fellow, 1979-81; asst. prof. U. Houston, 1981-86, Conn prof. mktg., 1989-93; Coca-Cola prof. mktg., dept. head U. Ga., Athens, 1994—. Vis. assoc. prof. U. Pitts., 1987-88; mem. exec. com. Faculty Senate, U. Houston, 1991-92; cons. FTC, Washington, 1992-93, San Francisco, 1994-96. Co-author: Electronic Commerce: The Strategic Perspective, 2000, Consumers, 2002, 2004; editor: Enhancing Knowledge Developments in Marketing, 1995, Advertising Research: The Internet, Consumer Behavior, and Strategy, 2002; editor Jour. Acad. of Mktg. Science, 2003-; editor Jour. Advt., Richmond, Va., 1991-95, (spl. issue) Jour. Bus. Rsch., 1996, 2d edit. 1999, book rev. editor, mem. rev. bd. Jour. of Mktg., College Station, Tex., 1991—; mem. rev. bd. Jour. Current Issues, 1991—, Jour. Bus. Rsch., 1994—, Jour. MacroMarketing, 1998—. Mem. Am. Mktg. Assn. (track chair 1991-96, v.p. for rsch. 1996-98, pres. advt. spl. interest group 1996-2003, acad. coun. 2005), Am. Acad. Advt. (named one of Top 12 Contbrs. to Advt. 1990, one of Top 10 Contbrs. to Svcs. Advt. 1997, one of top 5 Contbrs. to Advt. Lit., Jour. of Advt., 1998, co-chair Nat. Conf., 2001), Acad. Mktg. Sci. (track chair promotion mgmt. 1994, track chair electronic commerce 1998), Assn. Consumer Rsch. (session chair 1990, program com. 1996, 2000, Judge Peabody awards 1996—). Democrat. United Ch. of Christ. Avocations: soccer, basketball, swimming, tennis, chess. Home: 372 Chesterfield Rd Bogart GA 30622-1761 Office: Univ Ga Dept Mktg 138 Brooks Hall Athens GA 30602-6258 Business E-Mail: gzinkhan@terry.uga.edu.

ZINKLE, STEVEN JOHN, engineer, researcher; b. Prairie du Chien, Wis., Nov. 5, 1958; s. Aloysius Peter and Katherine Edith (Brownlee) Z.; m. Teresa Allen Medford, May 26, 1990; children: Austin Chase, Allen Peter. BS, U. Wis., 1980, PhD, 1985. Wigner fellow, 1985—87; rsch. staff Oak Ridge Nat. Lab., Tenn., 1985—2006, corp. fellow, 2004—, dir. materials sci. and tech. divsn., 2006—. Vis. scientist Forschungszentrum Jülich, Germany, 1991-92, Risø Nat. Lab., Roskilde, 1991-92. Assoc. editor: Jour. ASTM Internat., 2003—06. Recipient Rsch. Publ. award Martin Marietta Energy Systems, Oak Ridge, 1991, David Rose Excellence in Fusion Engring. award Fusion Power Assocs., Gaithersburg, Md., 1992, Oak Ridge Nat. Lab. Tech. Achievement award, 1997, 99, 2002, Ernest Orlando Lawrence award in Nuc. Tech. Dept. Energy, 2007. Fellow Am. Ceramic Soc. (Nuc. and Environ. Techs. Best Paper award 1994-95), Am. Soc. Metals Internat. (chair nuc. material com. 2003-05); mem. Materials Rsch. Soc., Am. Nuc. Soc., Materials Sci. and Tech. (exec. com. 2003—), The Minerals, Metals and Materials Soc., Sigma Xi, Phi Kappa Phi. Office: Oak Ridge Nat Lab PO Box 2008 Oak Ridge TN 37831-6132 Home Phone: 865-966-1239; Office Phone: 865-574-4065. E-mail: zinklesj@ornl.gov.

ZINMAN, DAVID JOEL, conductor; b. NYC, July 9, 1936; s. Samuel and Rachel Ilo (Samuels) Z.; m. Leslie Heyman (dec.); children: Paul Pierre, Rachel Linda; m. Mary Ingham, May 19, 1974; 1 child, Raphael. MusB, Oberlin Conservatory, Ohio, 1958; MA, U. Minn., 1961. Asst. to Pierre Monteux, 1961-64; guest condr. U.S. and Europe; music dir. Netherlands Chamber Orch., 1964-77, Rochester (N.Y.) Philharm. Orch., 1974-85; prin. guest condr. Rotterdam (Netherlands) Philharm. Orch., 1977-79; chief condr. Rotterdam Philharm. Orch., 1979-82; prin. guest condr., music dir. designate Balt. Symphony Orch., 1983-85, music dir., 1985—98, Tonhalle Orch., Zurich, Switzerland, 1995; music dir. designate Aspen (Colo.) Music Festival and Sch., 1997, music dir., 1998—; program dir. Am. Acad. Conducting, Aspen, 1998—. Adj. prof. Eastman Sch. Music, Rochester. Rec. artist Phillips, Nonesuch, Decca/London, Decca/Argo, Angel/EMI, Telarc, Sony Classical. Recipient Grand Prix du Disque, 1967, 82, Edison award, 1967, 3 Grammy awards, 1990, Grammophone best selling record award, 1993, Grammophone award, 1994, Deutschen Schallplatten prize, George Peabody medal for outstanding contbn. to music in Am., 1996. Office: PO Box 161 Millville DE 19970 Office Phone: 302-541-8087.

ZINMAN, RICHARD SCOTT, financial planner; s. Norman J. and Florence T. Zinman; m. Audrey Angela Zambetti, Sept. 10, 1988. BA, Duke U., Durham, NC, 1982. Cert. investment mgmt. analyst. V.p. Smith Barney, Harris Upham & Co., NYC; mng. dir. Bank of Am., NYC, 1996—2001; mng. dir. wealth mgmt., sr. advisor Citigroup Family office Smith Barney, NYC, 2001—. Named one of Best 100 Brokers, Barron's, 2006—07. Office: The Atlas Group Smith Barney 31 W 52d St 23rd Fl New York NY 10019 Office Phone: 212-603-6278. Office Fax: 212-765-1057. E-mail: richard.zinman@smithbarney.com. *

ZINMEISTER, KARL, federal official; BA, Yale U., 1981. Legis. asst. to Sen. Daniel Patrick Moynihan, 1981—82; rsch. assoc. Am. Enterprise Inst. for Pub. Policy Rsch., 1982—86, Dewitt Wallace Reader's Digest fellow, 1994—95, J.B. Fuqua fellow, 1997—; self-employed writer, rschr., 1986—94; editor-in-chief The Am. Enterprise mag., 1994—2006; asst. to Pres. for domestic policy The White House, 2006—. Weekly commentator Trend Watch Radio Am., 1985—89; rsch. dir. Working Seminar on Family and Am. Welfare Policy, 1986—87; mem. bd. advisors Nat. Fund for Improvement and Reform of Schools and Tchg., U.S. Dept. Edn., 1988—89, Found. Cmty. and Faith-Centered Enterprise, 2002—04. Author: (book) Boots on the Ground: A Month with the 82nd Airborne in the Battle for Iraq, 2003, Dawn Over Baghdad: How the U.S. Military is Using Bullets and Ballots to Remake Iraq, 2004, Combat Zone: True Tales of G.I.s in Iraq, 2005; editor: Are World Population Trends a Problem?, 1985, In Real Life: Powerful Lessons from Everyday Living, 2005; prodr.: (films) Warriors, 2007. Named Am. at a Crossroads Winne, Corp. Pub. Broadcasting; recipient Media award, 1998, Best in Media award, Nat. Coun. Children's Rights, 1990, Disting. Svc. award for reporting in Operation Iraqi Freedom, 2003. Office: The White House Eisenhower Exec Office Bldg Rm 469 Washington DC 20502

ZINN, HOWARD, historian, educator, playwright; b. NYC, Aug. 24, 1922; s. Edward and Jennie (Rabinowitz) Z.; m. Roslyn Shechter, Oct. 30, 1944; children: Myla, Jeff. BA, NYU, 1951; MA, Columbia U., 1952, PhD, 1958. Instr. history, polit. sci. Upsala Coll., 1953-56; lectr. history Bklyn. Coll., 1955-56; chmn. dept. history, social sci., prof. Spelman Coll., Atlanta, 1956-63; fellow Harvard U. Center for East Asian Studies, 1960-61; dir. Non-Western Studies Program Atlanta U. Center, 1961-62; assoc. prof. govt. Boston U., 1964-66, prof. govt., 1966-88, prof. emeritus, 1988—. Vis. prof. U. Paris, 1974, 78, 84. Author: LaGuardia in Congress, 1959, SNCC: The New Abolitionists, 1964, The Southern Mystique, 1964, New Deal Thought, 1966, Vietnam: The Logic of Withdrawal, 1967, Disobedience and Democracy, 1968, The Politics of History, 1970, Post-War America, 1973, Justice in Everyday Life, 1974, A People's History of the United States, 1980, Declarations of Independence, 1990, Failure to Quit, 1993, You Can't Be Neutral on a Moving Train: A Personal History of Our Times, 1994, The Zinn Reader, 1997, Marx in Soho, 1999, On War, 2001, On History, 2001, Terrorism and War, 2002; co-author (with Anthony Arnove) Voices of A People's History of the United States, 2004; playwright Emma, produced TOMI Theatre, N.Y.C., 1986, London, 1987, Edinburgh Festival, 1987, Tokyo, 1990, Daughter of Venus, produced Theatre for New City, 1985; contbr. articles to profl. jours. Served to 2d lt. USAAF, 1943-45. Decorated Air medal; recipient Albert J. Beveridge prize Am. Hist. Assn., 1958, Thomas Merton award Thomas Merton Ctr., 1991, Olive Br. award Pitts. Writers and Pubs. Alliance for Nuclear Disarmament, 1991. Mem. Dramatists Guild, AAUP.

ZINN, KEITH MARSHALL, ophthalmologist, educator; b. Bklyn., Oct. 15, 1940; s. Victor Zinn and Eve (Lane) Z.; m. Elaine H. Kirban, Apr. 8, 1979. Student, NYU, Bronx, 1961; MD, SUNY, Bklyn., 1965. Diplomate Am. Bd. Ophthalmology; lic. physician, NY, Calif. Intern St. Lukes Hosp., NYC, 1965-66; research assoc. NIH, Bethesda, Md., 1966-68; post-doctoral fellow Retina Found., Boston, 1968-69; post-doctoral fellow dept. ophthalmology Harvard U. Med. Sch., Boston, 1968; asst. resident chief resident dept. ophthalmology Mount Sinai Hosp., NYC, 1969-71, ednl. fellow dept. ophthalmology, 1971-72; chief clin. fellow retina service Mass. Eye & Ear Infirmary, Harvard U. Med. Sch., Boston, 1972-73, Heed fellow dept. ophthalmology, 1972-73; research assoc. dept. retina research Retina Found., Boston, 1972-73; mem. faculty Lancaster Post-Grad. Course Ophthalmology, Harvard U. Med. Sch., Boston, 1970-90; consulting mng. dir. HT Capital Advisors, LLC, 2000—. Guest faculty dept. ophthalmology Harvard U. Med. Sch., Boston, 1969-84; asst. prof. dept. ophthalmology Mt. Sinai Sch. medicine, NYC, assoc. clin. prof., 1976-80, clin. prof., 1980—; attending ophthalmic surgeon NYC, 1980—; attending ophthalmic surgeon Manhattan Eye Ear & Throat Hosp., NYC, 1981—; surgeon cons. Hosp. Joint Diseases, NYC, 1975-83, Patrolmen's Benevolent Assn., NYC, 1977—; lectr. field. Author: The Pupil, 1972, Ocular Fine Structure for the Clinician, 1973, The Developing Visual System, 1975, The Retinal Pigment Epithelium, 1975; author-editor: The Retinal Epithelium, 1979, Clinical Atlas of Peripheral Retinal Disorders, 1988; numerous audio-visual teaching progs. in ophthalmology; contbg. editor Mt. Sinai Jour. Medicine, 1975—; assoc. mem. editorial bd. Ophthalmic Surgery, 1980-89; mem. faculty editorial bd. Clin. Ophthalmology Update, 1982—; inventor field. Served lt. comdr. USPHS, 1966-68. Recipient numerous awards excellence medicine, including: Joseph Globus award Mount Sinai Jour. Medicine, 1979, Abraham Kornzweig Teaching award Mount Sinai Sch. Medicine, 1982. Fellow Am. Acad. Ophthalmology, Otolaryngology, ACS, Internat. Coll. Surgeons, Internat. Eye Found., Soc. Eye Surgeons, NY Acad. Medicine, NY Diabetes Assn., NY Heart Assn., NY Soc. Clin. Ophthalmology, Soc. Heed Fellows, Retina Soc., Ophthalmic Soc. UK, Oxford Ophthal. Congress, Brit. Am. Retinal Group; mem. AMA (Physicians Recognition award 1971, 76, 81, 82, 85), Ophthalmic Laser Surg. Soc. (v.p. 1986-88, pres. 1988-90), Am. Intraocular Lens Implant Soc., NY Acad. Medicine (trustee 1989-90, sec. 1985-86, chmn. ophthalmology sect. 1987-88, David Warfield fellowship com. 1990-92), Am. Bd. Laser Surgery (bd. dir. 1987—). Home: 125 E 87th St Apt 14C New York NY 10128 Office Phone: 212-535-5030.

ZINN, MICHAEL WALLACE, aerospace engineer; b. Washington, Dec. 30, 1962; s. Wallace Bernard and Frances E. AA, Charles County C.C., La Plata, Md., 1983; BS, Tri-State U., Angola, Ind., 1986. Coop student Naval Ordnance Sta., Indian Head, Md., 1980-86, mine decoy engr., 1986-87, airbreathing propulsion engr., 1987-92; airbreathing propulsion engr. Air/Cruise Missile Br. Naval Surface Warfare Ctr., Indian Head, 1992—2005, quality evaluation engr., 2005—. Mem. Joint Army-Navy-NASA-Air Force (JANNAF) airbreathing com., expendable engine subcom., Laurel, Md., 1987—; mem. Internat. Tech. Coop. Program involved in pyrotechnic aging and degradation Key Tech. Area 421, 1994-98. Author several tech. papers for AIAA and JANNAF. Pres. Port Tobacco Players, Inc., La Plata, Md., 1992-93; bd. dirs. Charles County Fair, Inc. Mem. AIAA (life, sr.), Am. Def. Preparedness Assn. (life), Cruise Missile Assn., Internat. Pyrotechnics Soc., Charles County Darts Assn. (webmaster) Achievements include work on aging surveillance programs for expendable gas turbine engines, on aging properties of expendable engines and solid propellant gas generators; assisted in new predictive techniques for ordnance surveillance; assisted in design of mine clearing line charge solid propellant rocket motor. Home: 11922 Charles St La Plata MD 20646-6414 Home Phone: 301-934-6961; Office Phone: 301-744-1434. Business E-Mail: michael.zinn@navy.mil.

ZINN, WILLIAM, musician, composer; b. NYC, Nov. 19, 1924; s. Philip and Anna (Miller) Zinn; m. Sophia Kalish, July 11, 0948; children: Karen Louise Heau, David Benjamin. Student, SUNY, 1952-54. Violinist Balt. Symphony, 1944-45, Indpls. Symphony, 1945-46, Ft. Wayne Philharm., 1946-47, Pitts. Symphony, 1947-49, Mpls. Symphony, 1950-51; concertmaster New Britain Symphony, Conn., 1968-90, Queens Symphony, 1969-71, Ridgefield Symphony, Conn., 1973-76, Chappaqua Symphony, NY, 1976, Yonkers Philharm., 1993—. Tchr. mech. drafting Mondell Inst., 1956; soloist with orchs. on records, radio, TV and recitals, 1993—2003; founder Masterwork Piano Trio, Masterwork Piano Quartet, Classical String Quartet, Zinn's Ragtime String Quartet, Excelsior String Quartet, Queens Festival Orch., Bayside, NY, 1965, Assn. Musical William Zinn, Caracas, Venezuela, 1968, Vitametrics Am., 1976, Internat. Symphony World Peace, 1978, Big Apple chamber Pops, 1983, Excelsior Composer's Festival Competition, 1984; coach ensembles Chamber Music Assocs., 1973—78; engr. NYC Bd. Edn., 1951—57, Bodin-Zinn Corp., 1957—58, Chem. Constrn. Corp., 1958—59; pres. Zinn Originals, Inc., 1959—68, Sparx, Inc., Trademark Hall of Fame, Inc., Nice Realty Corp., MFW Restaurant Corp., Zinn Labs., Inc., 1994, Caramoor Press Internat. Corp., 1996, Dunhill Pub. Co., 1996, ZinnPrint Internat., Inc., 1996, Barclay Holdings Group, Inc., 1998; co-founder Excelsior Music Pub. Co., Visionary Music Pub. Co., Nat. Music Promotion Agy., Telecom. Svcs., 1982, Assoc. Sci. Publs., 1985, Barclay House Pubs., 1985, Excelsior Typographers and Engravers Unltd., 1985, Empco Recs. Internat., 1985, Imperial Editions, 1986, Missing Link Publs., 1986, Krazy Klassics Kompany, 1986, New Age Pubs., 1987, Krazy Klassics Komix, 1988, Zinn Pub. Group, 1989, Zinn Comm., 1989, Decca Books, 1993, Arlington House, 1993, Zinn Labs., Inc.; sec. treas. Spark Industries, Inc., Music Clearing House, 1989, Innovation Records, 1991, Krazy Klassics Records, 1991, Hanover House, 1991; adj. prof. NYU, 1987—; cons. Worldwide Leisure Corp., 1997. Author (with Edward Gordon): Thermography, 1947; author: (with George S. Grosser) Vitametrics I, The Human Formula for Self-Evaluation, 1976, Vitametrics II, The Human Formula for Self-Improvement, 1978; author: The Lost Chord, 1981, To Whom It May Concern, 1995, 1,001 Original Wise Sayings of William Zinn, 1996, 2,600 Wise Sayings, 1997, 3,500 Wise Sayings, 1998, 4,100 Wise Sayings, 1999, 6,000 Wise Sayings, 2000, 6,700 Wise Sayings, 2001, 10,000 Wise Sayings, 2002, 11,000 Wise Sayings, 2003, 12,500 Wise Sayings, 2004, 13,500 Wise Sayings, 2005, 15,000 Wise Sayings, 2006; composer: Chromatique, 1946, Piccolo Concerto, 1948, Violin Concerto, 1950, String Quartet, 1963, Chopinesque, 1965, (ballets) Night Creatures, Andante for Strings, 1967, Concerto for Octahorn, 1976, The International Anthem for World Peace, 1977, String Symphony, 1977, Romance for French Horn or Viola and Piano, 1981; co-author: Concerto for Violin/Viola/Cello/Double Bass and Orchestra, 1985; composer: Kol Nidrei Memorial for String Quartet or String Orchestra, 1985, six concert duos for violin and viola, 1988, 15 Leroy Anderson favorites for string quartet or string orch., 1988, Mia, 1989, Aloha Hawaii, 1989, The Willows, 1990, Our Song of Love, 1990, Symphony in Ragtime, 1990, In Old Hawaii, 1991, Christmas in Hawaii, 1991, A Tribute to the Masters for String Quartet or String Orchestra, 1991, A Stroll in a Japanese Garden for Violin, Cello, Harp trio in 24 movements, 1996; arranger: numerous operatic arias for string quartet or string orch., originator: Musiphonics, 1981, 24 Paganini Caprices for String Quartet, 1992, 10 Sousa marches for string quartet, 1992, The Merry Widow Waltz for string quartet or string orch., 1992, Mozart Symphony # 40, 1992, arranger: 21 Henry Mancini songs for string quartet/string orch., 1992, 16 Duke Ellington songs for string quartet/string orch., 1993, Gold and Silver Waltz, Skater's Waltz for string quartet and string orch., 8 arias from Porgy & Bess for string quartet/string orch., 1992, A Tribute to Fritz Kreisler for violin and piano, 1994, 16 arrangements of Fritz Kreisler works for string quartet/string orch., 1994, 12 Jewish Songs for String Quartet/String Orch., 1995, 6 duets for violin and viola, vol. II, 1996, An Elegy for Mother Teresa, 1997, concerto Hebraic for piano and string orch., Let Freedom Ring, A Tribute to Martin Luther King, Jr. for orch., chorus and narrator, 24 Etudes for solo cello, 1998, Hebraic Lament of Atonement for solo cello and string quartet or string orch., 1999, A Symphonic Portrait of Yonkers, 1999, The Seven Seasons for Orchestera: seven symphonic works commemorating the Jewish holidays of Rosh Hashanah, Yom Kippur, Sukkot, Hanukkah, Purim, Passover, Shavuot, 2000, Siegfried Idyll Rhapsody solo violin and orch., 2001, A Requiem for Jerome G. Sala for soloists, chorus and orch., 2001, 6 Bach cello and solo suites converted to duets with original violin part added, 2002, Dance of the Hours Fantasy for solo violin and orch. or piano, 2002, Meditation for solo violin or flute, harp and string orch., 2002, 28 Beethoven Bagatelles arranged for string quartet or string orch., 2002, Beethoven: Pathetique Sonata, slow movement arranged for string quartet or string orch., 2002, violin and piano The Carnival of the Animals, Nutcracker Suite, 2003, In Hallowed Ground, 9/11/2001 for solo voice chorus, string orch., bass clarinet, 2003, Peter & The Wolf for violin and piano, 2004, String Trio, 2004, A Klezmer Symphony, 2004, 6 Dvorak waltz for quartet or string orch., 2004, String Quartet No. 2, 4 Clarinet Quartet, 2004, concertino for 2 violins and strings, 2004, Elegy for solo trumpet and strings, 2005, concertino for 2 French horns and strings, 2005, Octet Netherworld for low brass and woodwinds, 2005, solo for flute and strings, 2005, solo for clarinet and strings, 2005, solo for trombone and strings, 2005, solo for bassoon and strings, 2006, America for viola and piano, 2007, others. Chmn., bd. dirs. Let Us Remember to Remember, 1984. Recipient 41st Hawaiian Nat. Song Contest award, 1990, Mayor and City Coun. citations for Yonkers, 2000, Symphonic Portrait. Mem.: ASCAP, Am. Fedn. Musicians, NY Humanist Assn., Nat. Coun. Women US, Internat. Platform Assn. Home: 35-19 215th Pl Bayside NY 11361-1725

ZINNEN, ROBERT OLIVER, management consultant, consultant; b. Racine, Wis., June 28, 1929; s. Aloys Henry and Mabel Helen (Holy) Z.; m. Darlene Mary Weyers, Aug. 25, 1956; children: Claudia Jane, Robert O. BBA, U. Wis., 1951, JD, 1956. Bar: Wis. 1956, Ill. 1959, Mass. 1982; CPA, Ill. Tax accountant Price Waterhouse, Chgo., 1956-59; mem. firm Tenney & Bentley, Chgo., 1959-64; assoc. dir. taxes Allstate Cos., Skokie, Ill., 1964-65; v.p. fin. Do-All Co., Des Plaines, Ill., 1965-67; dir. taxes Quaker Oats Co., Chgo., 1967-71; internat. atty. Am. Hosp. Supply Corp., 1971-75; fin. cons. Alexander Proudfoot Co., Chgo., 1975-76; v.p. fin. Milton Bradley Co., Springfield, Mass., 1976-82; co-owner, exec. v.p. Roadmaster Corp., Olney, Ill., 1982-88, cons., 1988—. Mem. Housing and Traffic Commns., Highland Park, Ill., 1963-66; chmn. Congl. Action Com., Springfield; bd. dirs. Assoc. Industries, Mass. Served with U.S. Army, 1951-53. Mem. Toy Mfrs. Am. (bd. dirs. 1984-88), Quail Creek Country Club, Moorings Country Club, Longmeadow Country Club. Republican. Roman Catholic. Personal E-mail: cyberzinn@comcast.net.

ZINNER, ERNST K., physics educator, earth and planetary science educator, researcher; b. Steyr, Austria, Jan. 30, 1937; MS, Tech. U., Vienna, Austria, 1960; PhD in Physics, Wash. U., Mo., 1972. Instr. physics Coll. Vet. Medicine, Vienna, 1963-64; program and calculation magnetic field distbr. Brown-Boveri Co., Switzerland, 1964-65, rsch. assoc., 1972-74, sr. rsch. scientist, 1974-89; rsch. prof. physics Wash. U., St. Louis, 1989—. Vis. scientist Max-Planck Inst. Physics, Germany, 1980, Max-Planck Inst. Chemistry, Germany, 1980, U. Pavia, Italy, 1989. Recipient J. Lawrence Smith medal NAS, 1997. Fellow Am. Physics Soc., Meteoritical Soc.; mem. AAAS, Am. Geophysics Union, Sigma Xi. Office: Wash U Campus Box 1169 1 Brookings Dr Saint Louis MO 63130-4862

ZINNES, ALICE FICH, artist, educator; b. Norman, Okla., June 24, 1956; d. Irving I. and Harriet F. (Fich) Z BA Art History, Swarthmore Coll., 1977; cert. merit in painting, N.Y. Studio Sch., NYC, 1977—80; postgrad., Skowhegan Sch. Art, Maine, 1980; MFA Painting, Queens Coll., CUNY, 1982. Tchr. Pratt Inst., Bklyn., 1999—. Tchr. N.Y.C. Tech. Coll., CUNY,

Bklyn., 1983—88, Bklyn., 1997—, Baruch Coll., CUNY, NYC, 1986, NYC, 1988—97, Coll. S.I., CUNY, 1987—2001, Bklyn. Coll., 1998; guest lectr., vis. critic Millersville U., Pa., 1992, 93, 97, Dartmouth Coll., Hanover, NH, 1997; curator Frankel Pariser & Rudder, NYC, 1994—97; vis. critic N.Y. Studio Sch., NYC, 1997. One-woman shows include Queens Coll. Gallery, 1982, 2002, Swarthmore Coll., 1987, Frankel Pariser & Rudder, 1993, Dartmouth Coll., 1997, Tribes Gallery, N.Y.C., 1998, 2002, Hopper House, Nyack, N.Y., 2002, Delaware Arts Ctr., Narrowsburg, NY, 2006, Galleria Janet Kurnatowski, Bklyn., 2007, exhibited in group shows at Millersville U., 1992, Greenwich House, N.Y.C., 1992, Nat. Acad. Design, 1992, 1994, 1996, Tribeca 148 Gallery, 1992, 1996, 2000, N.Y. Studio Sch., 1993, 1995—2001, Bowery Gallery, N.Y.C., 1993, 1995, Salena Gallery-L.I. U., Bklyn., 1994, 1997, Art Showcase, The Bond Market, N.Y.C., 1998, Elsa Mott Ives Gallery, 1997, 1999, 2001, Grace Gallery, N.Y.C. Tech. Coll., Bklyn., 1999, Artist Space, N.Y.C., 1999, Simon Gallery, Morristown, N.J., 2000, 55 Mercer Gallery, N.Y.C., 2000, William Paterson U., N.J., 2000, Contemporary Mus., Balt., 2000, Key Span Corp. Galleries, Bklyn., 2000, Piergo, 2000—, Seton Hall U., Newark, 2000, NYU, 2000, Drawing Ctr. Registry, N.Y.C., 2001—, John Elder Gallery, 2001, Chelsea Pier 60, 2001, Exit Art, 2002, Sperone Westwater Gallery, 2002, Ayce de Roulet Williamson Gallery, Pasadena, Calif., 2002, Artisi Space, N.Y.C., 2004, Brent Sikkeme Gallery, 2004, Del. Arts Coun., Narrowsburg, N.Y., 2005, Times Square Lobby Gallery, N.Y.C., 2005, Pratt Inst., 2005, Painting Ctr., 2005, Lori Bookstein Fine Art, 2005, Chh'i Contemporary Fine Art, Bklyn., 2006, Michael Ingbar GAllery, NYC, 2007, Windham Fine Art, NY, 2007. Named Barklie McKee Henry Meml. scholar, Skowhegan Sch. Art, 1980, Residency fellow, Va. Ctr. for the Creative Arts, Sweet Briar, 1992, 1997, 1999, 2001, Cummington (Mass.) Cmty. Arts, 1993; recipient Julius Hallgarten prize, Nat. Acad. Design, N.Y.C., 1988, 1990. Avocations: swimming, hiking. Home: 457 15th St Apt 5D Brooklyn NY 11215-5734 Office: NYC Tech Coll 300 Jay St Brooklyn NY 11201-1909 Office Phone: 718-768-3655.

ZINNES, HARRIET FICH, poet, fiction writer, retired English educator, literary and art critic; b. Boston; d. Assir and Sarah (Goldberg) Fich; m. Irving I. Zinnes, Sept. 24, 1943 (dec. 1979); children: Clifford, Alice. BA cum laude, CUNY, 1939, MA, 1944; PhD, NYU, 1953. Editor publs. divsn. Raritan (N.J.) Arsenal, 1942-43; assoc. editor Harper's Bazaar, NYC, 1944-46; tutor Hunter Coll. CUNY, NYC, 1946-49; asst. prof. Queens Coll. CUNY, Flushing, 1949-53, assoc. prof., 1962-78, full prof., 1978-89, prof. emerita, 1989—; lectr. in English Rutgers U., New Brunswick, N.J., 1961-62. Vis. prof. Am. lit. U. Geneva, 1968. Author: Waiting and Other Poems, 1964, An Eye for an I, 1966, I Wanted to See Something Flying, 1976, Entropisms, 1978, Book of Ten, 1981, Lover: Short Stories, 1988, Book of Twenty, 1992, My, Haven't the Flowers Been?, 1995, The Radiant Absurdity of Desire, 1998, Plunge, 2001, Drawing on the Wall: Poems, 2002 (named Notable Book of Yr.), Whither Nonstopping, 2005; editor: Ezra Pound and the Visual Arts, 1980; translator Blood and Feathers: Selected Poems of Jacques Prevert, 1988, rev. edit., 1993; contr. editor, Hollin's Critic, Denver Quarterly; contr. writer, N.Y. Arts Mag.; author numerous poems; contbr. articles to popular mags. MacDowell Art Colony fellow, 1972-74, 77, 2004, Yaddo fellow, 1978, 81, Va. Ctr. for Creative Arts fellow, 1975-76, 81-82, 84, 86, 88-93, resident fellow, Djerassi Found., 1990, La Napoul, 2002; Am. Coun. Learned Socs. grantee, 1978, CUNY summer grantee, 1979, 81, 86. Fellow Poets Editors & Novelists, Nat. Book Critics Circle, Acad. Am. Poets, Internat. Assn. Art Critics, Poetry Soc. Am.; mem. Phi Beta Kappa. Home: 25 W 54th St New York NY 10019-5404 Office: Dept English Queens Coll Flushing NY 11367 Home Phone: 212-582-8315; Office Phone: 212-582-8315. Personal E-mail: hzinnes@rcn.com.

ZINNI, ANTHONY CHARLES, retired military officer; b. Conshohocken, Pa., Sept. 17, 1943; s. Antonio and Lilla (Disabatino) Z.; m. Dale Elaine Bathke, Nov. 19, 1966; children: Lisa, Maria, Anthony. BS in Econs., Villanova U., 1965; MA in Bus., Cen. Mich. U., 1984; MA in Internat. Rels., Salve Regina Coll., Newport, RI, 1986; postgrad., Nat. War Coll., Washington, 1983-84. Commd. 2d lt. USMC, 1965, advanced through grades to gen., 1997, ret., 2000; comdg. officer 2d bn. 8th Marines, Camp Lejeune, N.C., 1980-81, 9th Marines, Okinawa, Japan, 1987-89; instr. Comdt. Staff Coll., Quantico, Va., 1981-83; staff ops. officer Hdqrs. USMC, Washington, 1984-86; chief naval ops. fellow Strategic Studies Group, Newport, 1986-87; chief staff Tng. and Edn. Ctr., Combat Devel. Command, Quantico, 1989-90; dep. ops. officer European Command, Stuttgart, Germany, 1990-91; chief of staff, dep. commdg. gen. Task Force Provide Comfort, 1991-92; dir. ops. Unified Task Force, Stuttgart, Somalia, 1992-93; commdg. gen. I Marine Expeditionary Force, 1994-96; dep. comdr. U.S. Ctrl. Command, 1996-97, comdr., 1997-2000; spl. envoy to the Middle East US Dept. State, 2002—03; disting. sr. advisor Ctr. for Strategic & Internat. Studies, Washington, 2000—; disting. mil. fellow Ctr. for Def. Info., Washington. Co-author (with Tom Clancy & Tony Koltz): Battle Ready, 2004; co-author: (with Michael DeLong & Noah Lukeman) Inside CentCom: The Unvarnished Truth About the Wars in Afghanistan and Iraq, 2004; co-author: (with Tony Koltz) The Battle for Peace: A Frontline Vision of America's Power and Purpose, 2006. Roman Catholic. Office: Ctr for Def Info 1779 Massachusetts Ave NW Washington DC 20036

ZINOBER, PETER WOLFSON, lawyer; b. Bklyn., July 4, 1943; s. Herman Robert and Olga Pauline (Wolfson) Z.; m. Joan Felice Wagner, June 13, 1971; children: Brett, Scott, Bryan, Beth. BA in English Lit., U. Fla., 1965, JD, 1969; LLM in Labor Law, George Wash. U., 1971. Bar: Fla. 1969, D.C. 1970, U.S. Dist. Ct. (no., so. and mid. dists.) Fla. 1976, U.S. Supreme Ct. 1976, U.S. Ct. Appeals (D.C. cir.) 1970, (5th cir.) 1976, (11th cir.) 1981. Atty. U.S. Dept. Labor, Washington, 1969-71, NLRB, Washington, 1971-72; trial atty. NLRB Region 12, Tampa, Fla., 1972-73; ptnr. Carlton, Fields, Ward, et al, Tampa, Fla., 1973-80, dept. head labor employment, 1980-88; ptnr. Zinober & McCrea, Tampa, Fla., 1988—. Asst. editor: BNA - The Developing Labor Law - Treatise, 1979-89, assoc. editor, 1989—. Mem. Fla. Arts Coun., 1977-81, vice chmn., 1980-81; bd. dirs. Tampa Players, 1988-90; bd. govs. The Fla. Orch., 1976-86, 81-83, chmn., 1990-98; bd. govs. Tampa Bay Bus. Commn. Arts, pres. 1996-98; bd. dirs. Urban League, Tampa Hillsborough, 1989-; dirs. Anti-Defamation League, 1988-92, NCCJ, 1989-92; mem. Spl. City/County Task Force of Future of Arts, 1991-93. Mem. ABA (coun. labor and employment law sect. 2004—), Indsl. Rels. Rsch. Assn., Fla. Bar (chmn. labor sect. 1977-78, designation coord. com. 1980-82, chmn. bd. certification, designation and advt. 1982-83, exec. coun. local govt. law sect. 1986-89), U. Club, Tampa Yacht Club. Democrat. Jewish. Home: 1501 Bayshore Blvd Tampa FL 33606-3002 Office: Zinober & McCrea PA 201 E Kennedy Blvd Ste 800 Tampa FL 33602-5863

ZINOMAN, JASON, theater critic; Chief Broadway and Off-Broadway critic Time Out NY Mag.; theater critic, reporter NY Times, NYC. Contbr. New Republic, Esquire, Salon, Slate. Office: NY Times Culture Desk 229 W 43rd St New York NY 10036 Office Phone: 212-556-7329. Office Fax: 212-556-1516.

ZINSER, ELISABETH ANN, former academic administrator; b. Meadville, Pa., Feb. 20, 1940; d. Merle and Fae Zinser. BS, Stanford U., 1964; MS, U. Calif., San Francisco, 1966, MIT, 1982; PhD, U. Calif., Berkeley, 1972. Nurse VA Hosp., Palo Alto, Calif., 1964-65, San Francisco, 1969-70; instr. Sch. Nursing U. Calif., San Francisco, 1966-69; pre-doctoral fellow Nat. Inst. Health, Edn. and Welfare, 1971-72; adminstr. Sch. Medicine U. Wash., Seattle, 1972-75, Coun. Higher Edn., State of Ky., 1975-77; prof., dean. Coll. Nursing U. N.D., Grand Forks, 1977-83; vice chancellor acad. affairs U. N.C., Greensboro, 1983-89; pres. Gallaudet U., Washington, 1988, U. Idaho, Moscow, 1989-95; chancellor U. Ky., Lexington, 1995—2001; pres. So. Oreg. Univ., Ashland, 2001—06. Bd. dir. Assoc. Am. Coll. & Univ., 1999—, Am. Council Edn., Nat Assoc. State Univ. & Land Grant Coll.; bd. mem. Ctr. on Academic Integrity; past chmn. Commn. Outreach & Tech. Transfer. Primary author: (with others) Contemporary Issues in Higher Education, 1985, Higher Education Research, 1988; spkr. in field. Mem. Oreg. Women's Forum; bd. mem. Ashland C. of C., Oreg. Shakespeare Festival, Crater Lake Nat. Park Trust. Leadership fellow Bush Found., 1981-82.

ZINTER, STEVEN L., state supreme court justice; m. Sandra Zinter; 2 children. Doctorate, Univ. So. Dakota, 1975, BS, 1972. Pvt. practice, 1978—86; state atty. Hughes County; cir. judge State of So. Dakota, 1987—97; presiding judge Sixth Judicial Cir., 1997—2002; judge SD Supreme Court, 2002—. Mem. Harry S Truman Found.; trustee So. Dakota Retirement Sys.; elect. pres. So. Dakota Corrections Commn. Mem.: ABA, S.D. Judges Assn. (past pres.), S.D. Bar Assn. Office: SD Supreme Ct 500 E Capital Ave Pierre SD 57501-5070 *

ZIOLKOWSKA-BOEHM, ALEKSANDRA, writer; b. Lodz, Poland, Apr. 15, 1949; arrived in US, 1990; d. Henryk and Antonina Zofia (Laskiewicz) Z.; m. C. Norman Boehm Jr., June 8, 1990; 1 child, Thomas Tomczyk. M in Lit., U. Lodz, 1973; PhD, U. Warsaw, Poland, 1978. Pvt. asst. Melchior Wankowicz, Warsaw, 1972-74; repertoire rsch. staff Warsaw TV Theater, 1977-81. Author: Blisko Wankowicza, 1975, 1978, 1988, Z Miejsca Na Miejsce, 1983, 1986, 1997, Senator Haidasz, 1983, Dreams and Reality, 1984, Kanada, Kanada, 1986, Diecezja Lodzka I Jej Biskupi, 1987, Moje I Zaslyszane, 1988, Kanadyjski Senator, 1989, Na Tropach Wankowicza, 1989, 1999, Proces M. Wankowicza, 1964, 1990, Nie Tyllko Ameryka, 1992, Korzenie Sa Polskie, 1992, Ulica Zolwiego Strumienia, 1995, 2004, Amerykanie Z Wyboru, 1998, The Roots are Polish, 2000, 2d edit., 2004, Korespondencja J. Giedroyc-Wankowicz, 2000, Podroze Z Moja Kotka, 2002, 2004; author: (with Szymon Kobylinski) Nie minelo nic, procz. lat., 2003; author: Kaja od Radoslawa, 2006. Recipient Kontrasty award, 1980, Zloty Exlibris award Ksiaznica Pomorska, 2001; named to Del. Divsn. of Arts, 2006; scholar Oxford (Eng.) Lang. Ctr., 1975, Ont. Ministry of Culture, Toronto, 1981-83, Can. Polish Rsch. Inst., Toronto, 1981-83, A. Mickiewicz Found., Toronto, 1981-83, Inst. Internat. Edn., Washington, 1985, Creative Nonfiction Discipline award Del. Divsn. Arts in Literature, 2006; Fulbright scholar, Warsaw U., 2006-07. Mem. Am. PEN Club, Polish Writers Union, Polish Writers Union Abroad, Polish Inst. Arts and Sci., Zaiks, Kosciuszko Found. (scholar 1990). Avocations: travel, birdwatching, domestic pets. Home: 11 Ridgewood Cir Wilmington DE 19809-2860 Office Phone: 302-764-8345. Personal E-mail: aleksboehm@aol.com.

ZIOLKOWSKI, JAN MICHAEL, medievalist educator; b. New Haven, Nov. 17, 1956; s. Theodore J. and Yetta (Goldstein) Z.; m. Elizabeth Ann Hillenius; children: Saskia Elizabeth, Ada Margaret, Yetta Joy. AB summa cum laude, Princeton U., 1977; PhD, U. Cambridge, Eng., 1982; MA (hon.), Harvard U., 1987. Asst. prof. Harvard U., Cambridge, Mass., 1981-84, John L. Loeb assoc. prof. of the humanities, 1984-87, prof. medieval Latin and comparative lit., 1987—2002, Arthur Kingsley Porter prof. medieval Latin, 2002—. Author: Alan of Lille's Grammar of Sex, 1985, Nigel of Canterbury, Miracles of the Virgin Mary, 1986, Jezebel: A Norman Latin Poem, 1989, On Philology, 1990, Talking Animals: Medieval Latin Beast Poetry, 1993, Nigel of Canterbury, The Passion of St. Lawrence, 1994, The Cambridge Songs, 1994, 98, Obscenity: Social Control and Artistic Creation in the European Middle Ages, 1998, The Medieval Craft of Memory, 2002, Fairy Tales from Before Fairy Tales, 2006; editor Comparative Literature Studies. Pres. Internationales Mittellateiner Komitee, 2000—. Fellow Guggenheim Found., 1987-88, ACLS, 1986, Netherlands Inst. for Advanced Study, 2005—; Rome Prize fellow Am. Acad. in Rome, 1980-81; Marshall scholar, 1977-80. Mem. Medieval Acad. Am. (councillor 1991-94), Dante Soc. Am. (councillor 2004—), Am. Philol. Assn., Phi Beta Kappa. Home: 930 Centre St Newton MA 02459-1266 Office: Harvard Univ Classics 221 Boylston Hall Cambridge MA 02138 Office Phone: 617-496-6062. Business E-Mail: jmziolk@fas.harvard.edu.

ZIOLKOWSKI, THEODORE JOSEPH, literature educator, writer; b. Birmingham, Ala., Sept. 30, 1932; s. Mieczislaw and Cecilia (Jankowski) Z.; m. Yetta Bart Goldstein, Mar. 26, 1951; children: Margaret Cecilia, Jan Michael, Eric Josef. AB, Duke U., 1951, AM, 1952; student, U. Innsbruck, Austria, 1952-53; PhD, Yale U., 1957; DrPhil honoris causa (hon.), U. Greifswald, 2001. Instr., then asst. prof. Yale U., New Haven, 1956-62; assoc. prof. Columbia U., NYC, 1962-64; prof. Germanic langs. and lit. Princeton (N.J.) U., 1964-69, chmn., 1973-79, Class of 1900 prof. modern langs., 1969-2001, prof. comparative lit., 1975-2001, dean Grad. Sch., 1979-92, prof. emeritus, 2001. Vis. prof. Rutgers U., 1966, Yale U., 1967, 75, CUNY, 1971, Bristol U., 1987, U. Munich, 1992; vis. scholar U. Ctr. in Va., 1971, Piedmont U. Ctr., N.C., 1971; Dancy Meml. lectr. U. Montevallo, 1973; Christopher Longest lectr. U. Miss., 1979; Patten Found. lectr. Ind. U., 1980; vis. lectr. Österreichische Akademie der Wissenschaften, 1992; vis. lectr. Korean Ministry of Edn., 1996; chmn. N.Y. State Doctoral Evaluation Program in German, 1975-80; nat. rev. panel for U.S. Nat. Grad. Fellows Program, 1985-87, 91—; chmn. overseers vis. com. on German Harvard U., 1982-88; mem. selection com. for Bennett award, 1988; with German-Am. Acad. Coun., 1993-99; chmn. N.Y. State Humanities Screening Com., 1996; chmn. bd. German-Am. Ctr. for Vis. Scholars, 1997-99; forum assembly spkr. Brigham Young U; mem. evaluation team Rosenzweig Zentrum of Hebrew U., Jerusalem, 1999; mem. search com. for chair in German, Bristol U., 1999; mem. search com. for dean Internat. U. Bremen, 1999-00. Author: Hermann Broch, 1964, The Novels of Hermann Hesse, 1965, Hermann Hesse, 1966, Dimensions of the Modern Novel, 1969, Fictional Transfigurations of Jesus, 1972 (James Russell Lowell prize MLA), Disenchanted Images, 1977, Der Schriftsteller Hermann Hesse, 1979, The Classical German Elegy, 1980, Varieties of Literary Thematics, 1983, German Romanticism and Its Institutions, 1990, Virgil and the Moderns, 1993, The Mirror of Justice, 1997 (Christian Gauss prize Phi Beta Kappa), Das Wunderjahr in Jena, 1998, The View from the Tower, 1998, The Sin of Knowledge, 2000, Berlin: Aufstieg einer Kulturmetropole um 1810, 2002, Hesitant Heroes, 2004, Clio the Romantic Muse, 2004 (Barricelli prize), Ovid and the Moderns, 2005 (Robert Motherwell award Dedalus Found.), Vorboten der Moderne: Eine Kulturgeschichte der Fruehromantik, 2006, Modes of Faith: Secular Surrogates for Lost Religious Belief, 2007; editor: Hermann Hesse, Autobiographical Writings, 1972, Hermann Hesse, Stories of Five Decades, 1972, Hesse: A Collection of Critical Essays, 1972, Hermann Hesse, My Belief: Selected Essays, 1974, Hermann Hesse, Tales of Student Life, 1976, Hermann Hesse, Pictor's Metamorphoses and Other Fantasies, 1982, Hermann Hesse, Soul of the Age: Selected Letters, 1891-1962, 1991, Friedrich Dürrenmatt, Selected Writings 2: Fictions, 2006; mem. editl. bd. Germanic Rev., 1962-95, Publs. MLA, 1971-75, Arbitrium, 1983-, 17th Century Studies, 1985-2005, Germanistik, 1987-, Jahrbuch für Internat. Germanistik, 1997-, World Literature Today, 1998-, Etudes Germaniques, 1998-, Publications of the English Goethe Society, 2003-, Spectrum Lit./Comparative Studies, 2004-; mem. editl. bd. Princeton U. Press, 1972-75, trustee, 1982-95; translator (with Yetta Ziolkowski): The Poetics of Quotation (Herman Meyer) 1968, Hermann Hesse: A Pictorial Biography, 1975; contbr. over 160 articles and 400 revs. Decorated comdr.'s cross Order of Merit (Germany), 2000; recipient Howard T. Behrman award for disting. achievement in humanities, 1978, Wilbur Lucius Cross medal Yale U., 1982, Goethe Inst. gold medal, 1987, Henry Allen Moe prize in humanities, 1988, Festschrift Themes and Structures (ed. Alexander Stephan), 1997, Jakob-und-Wilhelm Grimm prize for German Studies, 1998, Humboldt Sr. Rsch. prize, 1998; Mellon Emeritus Faculty fellow, 2003; Fulbright rsch. grantee, 1958-59, grantee Am. Philos. Soc., 1959, NEH grantee, 1978, Guggenheim fellow, 1964-65, Am. Coun. Learned Socs. fellow, 1972, 76; resident fellow Bellagio Study Ctr., 1993. Mem. MLA (hon. life; exec. coun. 1976-77, pres. 1985), Acad. Lit. Studies, Am. Comparative Lit. Assn., Am. Acad. Arts and Scis., Assn. Lit. Scholars and Critics, Authors Guild, Am. Assn. Tchrs. German (hon. life), Yale Grad. Sch. Assn. (pres. 1974-76), Assn. Grad. Schs. (v.p. 1989-90, pres. 1990-91), Heinrich von Kleist Gesellschaft, Goethe-Gesellschaft, Novalis-Gesellschaft, Internat. Vereinigung für Germanistik (exec. coun. 1985-95, treas. 1990-95), Am. Philos. Soc. (councillor 1991-97), Göttingen Akademie der Wissenschaften, Austrian Akademie der Wissenschaften, Deutsche Akademie für Sprache und Dichtung, Inst. Germanic and Romance Studies London, Phi Beta Kappa. Home: 36 Bainbridge St Princeton NJ 08540-3902 Personal E-mail: tjziol@aol.com.

ZIOMEK, CAROL ANN, medical products executive; BS in Chemistry, Wilkes Coll., Wilkes-Barre, 1972; PhD in Biology, Johns Hopkins U., Balt., 1978. Rsch. assoc. Cambridge U., England, 1978—82; staff scientist Worcester Found. for Exptl. Biology, Shrewsbury, Mass., 1982—90; prin. scientist Genzyme Corp., Framingham, Mass., 1990—93; v.p., devel. GTC Biotherapeutics, Inc, Framingham, 1993—. Fellow, Am. Cancer Soc., 1978—80. Office: GTC Biotherapeutics Inc 175 Crossing Blvd Ste 410 Framingham MA 01702 Office Phone: 508-370-5421. Office Fax: 508-370-5266. Business E-Mail: carol.ziomek@gtc-bio.com.

ZIOMEK, JONATHAN S., journalist, educator; b. Newport News, Va., July 28, 1947; s. Stanley Walter and Joy Carmen (Schmidt) Z.; m. Rosalie Ziomek, Aug. 14, 1977; children: Joseph, Jennifer; 1 stepchild, Daniel. BA in Sociology, U. Ill., 1970, MS in Journalism, 1982. Reporter, labor writer, feature writer, Sun. fin. editor Chgo. Sun-Times, 1970-78; press sec. for U.S. Senate campaign, Chgo., 1979-80; asst. prof. Medill Sch. Journalism, Northwestern U., Evanston, Ill., 1983-88; dir. grad. editl. programs Medill Sch. Journalism/Northwestern U., Evanston, Ill., 1988—2004, asst. dean, 1994—2004, assoc. prof., 1994—. Rapporteur Aspen Inst., Journalism and Soc. Seminar, 2004, McCormick Found. Mil. and Media Conf., 2005-06; presenter, cons. in field. Contbr. articles to popular mags.; editor: Chgo. Journalist Newsletter, 1991-93. Participant Internat. Visitors Ctr., Chgo., 1988—; fact-finder USIA, Bulgaria and Yugoslavia, 1990. Mem. Assn. for Edn. in Journalism and Mass Communications, Soc. Profl. Journalists, Nat. Assn. Sci. Writers, Chgo. Headline Club. Home: 2149 Hartrey Ave Evanston IL 60201-2571 Office: Northwestern Univ Medill Sch Journalism Evanston IL 60208-0001

ZION, ROGER HERSCHEL, retired management consultant, retired congressman; b. Escanba, Mich., Sept. 17, 1921; s. Herschel G. and Helen (Hutchinson) Z.; m. Marjorie Knauss, Feb. 20, 1945; children: Gayle, Scott, Randy. BA, U. Wis., 1943, postgrad., 1944-45. With Mead Johnson & Co., 1946-66, dir. tng. and profl. rels., 1965-66; internat. mktg. mgmt. cons., 1966; mem. 90th-93d congresses from 8th Dist. Ind.; chmn. Rep. Task Force on Energy and Resources; pres. Resources Devel., Inc., Washington, 1975—. Hon. chmn. GoPlus Assn. Author: Keys to Human Relations in Selling, 1963, The Hallowed Howls of Congress, 1994, The Republican Challenge, 1995, The Amazing Adventures of Congressman Zion, 2004 V.p. Buffalo Trace council Boy Scouts Am., 1961; Bd. dirs., chmn. Evansville (Ind.) chpt. ARC, 1960-65. Lt. USNR, 1943-46, PTO. Named Toastmaster, Evansville Press Gridiron dinner, 1963; recipient Citizen of Month award New Image Com. of Evansville's Future, 1962 Mem. Nat. Sales and Mktg. Execs. Assn. (pres. Evansville 1962), Wabash Valley Assn., AMVETS (life), Rotary (dir. Evansville club 1964), Evansville Country Club (dir. 1960-65), Alpha Delta Phi (pres. Wis. chpt. 1941-43) Congregationalist. Home: 7938 E Oak St Evansville IN 47715-7214

ZIPES, DOUGLAS PETER, cardiologist, researcher; b. White Plains, NY, Feb. 27, 1939; s. Robert Samuel and Josephine Helen (Weber) Z.; m. Marilyn Joan Jacobus, Feb. 18, 1961; children: Debra, Jeffrey, David. BA cum laude, Dartmouth Coll., 1961, B of Med. Sci., 1962; MD cum laude, Harvard Med. Sch., 1964. Diplomate Am. Bd. Internal Medicine, mem. subsplty. bd. cardiovasc. disease 1989-99, chmn., 1995-99, chmn. com. cert. in clin. cardiac electrophysiology 1989-96, bd. dirs. 1995-2003, exec. com. 1999-2003, chmn. bd. 2002-03. Intern, resident, fellow in cardiology Duke U. Med. Ctr., Durham, NC, 1964-68; vis. scientist Masonic Med. Rsch. Lab., Utica, NY, 1970-71; from asst. prof. medicine to disting. prof. emeritus Ind. U., Indpls., 1970—2004, disting. prof. emeritus, 2004—, Medtronic Zipes chair cardiology Sch. Medicine, 2004—, Zipes vis. prof., 2005. Bd. dirs. Inst. for Clin. Evaluation; cardiology adv. com NIH, 1991—94; mem. med. adv. bd. ABCNews.com, 2000—; mem. dean's coun. Dartmouth Med. Sch., Ind. Med. Sch.; cons. in field. Author: Comprehensive Cardiac Care, 7th edit., 1991; editor: Slow Inward Current, 1980, Cardiac Electrophysiology and Arrhythmias, 1985, Nonpharmacological Therapy of Tachyarrhythmias, 1987, Cardiac Electrophysiology From Cell to Bedside, 1990, 4th edit., 2004; co-editor: Treatment of Heart Diseases, 1992, Ablation of Cardiac Arrhythmias, 1994, 2d edit., 2002, Antiarrhythmic Therapy: A Pathophysiologic Approach, 1994, Arrhythia and Sudden Death in Athletes, 2000, Heart Disease, A Textbook of Cardiovascular Medicine, 8th edit., 2007, Thoracic Vein Arrhythmias, 2004, Sudden Cardiac Death, A Handbook for Clinical Practice, 2006; mem. editl. bd. Circulation, 1974-78, 83-, Am. Jour. Cardiology, 1979-82, 88-, Am. Jour. Medicine, 1979-90, Jour. Am. Coll. Cardiology, 1983, 2002-, Am. Heart Jour., 1977-97, PACE, 1977-, Circulation Rsch., 1983-90, Am. Jour. Noninvasive Cardiology, 1985-89, Jour. Electrophysiology, 1987-89, Cardiovasc. Drugs and Therapy, 1986-93, Japanese Heart Jour., 1989-, Jour. Cardiovasc. Pharmacology and Therapeutics, 1994-, Jour. Cardiovasc. Pharmacology, 1995—, Cardiovasc. Therapeutics, 1995, Current Clin. Trials, 1995-98, Jour. Interventional Cardiac Electrophysiology, 1996-, Am. Heart Hosp. Jour., Jour. Am. Coll. Cardiology; editor-in-chief: Progress in Cardiology, 1988-92, Cardiology in Rev., 1992-2002, Contemporary Treatments of Cardiovasc. Disease, 1996-98, Am. Coll. Cardiology Extended Learning, 1997-, Ind. Jour. Pacing and Electrophysiology Online, 2001-; founding editor Heart Rhythm, 2004—, Jour. Cardiovasc. Electrophysiology, 1990-2004; contbr. articles to profl. jours.; patentee cardioverter, elec. prevention of arrhythmia, discrimination of atrial fibrillation, fixation of implantable devices, and pericardial delivery of therapeutic and diagnostic agents. Pres., bd. dir. Indpls. Opera Co., 1983-85; mem. study sect. NIH, Washington, 1977-81; mem. nat. merit rev. bd. VA, 1982-85, Cardiology Adv. Com. NHLBL, 1991-98, chmn. steering com. AVID; chmn. Data and Safety Monitoring Bd. AFFIRM, 1996-2002; bd. dir. Am. Bd. Internal Medicine Found., 2002-04; chmn. Am. Bd. Internal Medicine, 2002-03. Named Sagamore of Wabash, Gov. of Ind., 2001; recipient Disting. Achievement award, Am. Heart Assn., 1989, Disting. Alumnus award, Duke U. Med. Ctr., 2007. Master Am. Coll. Cardiology (chmn. ACC/AHA subcom. to assess EP studies, chmn. young investigators award com. 1988-94, trustee 1992-97, 2002-05, chair nominating com. 2003, chmn. devel. com. 1996-2001, sci. sessions program com. 1996-98, v.p. 1999-2000, pres. 2001-02, co-chair ventricular arrhythmias guidelines 2003—, Bethesda (Md.) conf. guidelines athletes with heart disease, chair campaign the future, endowed lectr. 2005, Disting. Scientist award 1996, endowed Douglas P. Zipes Disting. Young Scientist award 2005); fellow ACP, Am. Heart Assn. (exec. com. 1980-88, sci. sessions program 1983-86, chmn. various coms., chmn. 1995, bd. dir. Internat. Cardiology Found. 1993-98, bd. dir. 1994-96, chmn. emergency cardiac care com. 1995-96, Herrick award 1997, Cor Vitae award 2004); mem. Am. Soc. Clin. Investigation, Assn. Univ. Cardiologists (v.p. 1994, pres. 1995), Assn. Am. Physicians, Am. Physiol. Soc., Cardiac Electrophysiology Soc. (pres. 1985-86), Heart Rhythm Soc. (pres. 1988-90, trustee 1990-2000, lectr.

2005, Disting. Scientist award 1995), InterAm. Soc. Cardiology (1st v.p. 1995-98), Ind. Cardiac Electrophysiology Soc. (founder), Argentine Soc. Cardiology (hon. fgn. mem.). Home: 10614 Winterwood Carmel IN 46032-9688 Office: Ind U Sch Medicine 1100 W Michigan St Indianapolis IN 46202-5208 Home Phone: 317-962-0556; Office Phone: 317-697-2406. Business E-Mail: dzipes@iupui.edu.

ZIPF, JENNIFER E., marketing professional; b. Edison, NJ, Nov. 7, 1973; d. James and Patricia Zipf; m. Omar Dablan, Oct. 1, 2005. BA in Journalism, Rider U., Lawrenceville, NJ, 1995. Asst. editor Quadrant Healthcom, Inc., Belle Mead, NJ, 1996, Philip Lief Group, Princeton, NJ, 1996—98; publs. specialist Rec. for Blind & Dyslexic, Princeton, 1998—99; assoc. editor, mktg. comm. Merrill Lynch Investment Mgrs., Plainsboro, NJ, 1999—2001, asst. v.p., e-business, 2001—04; mktg. comm. mgr. MarketingNPV, Princeton, 2004—. Participant, fundraiser Susan G. Komen Race for Cure, Princeton, 2000—06; vol. Friends of Homeless Animals, Princeton, 2002—05, SAVE, Princeton, 2007—; instr. NE Acad. Martial Arts, Mercerville, 2006—; trustee Lawrence Square Village II Bd., Lawrenceville, 2007—; vol. Kerry/Edwards presdl. campaign, Princeton, 2004. Recipient Best Redesign award, APEX, 1999, Hon. Mention, NJ Pub. Rels. Soc. Am., 1999, Gold B-to-B Best E-mail Opt-in Campaign award, MarketingSherpa, 2006. Mem.: Mensa, Phi Sigma Tau, Pi Delta Phi, Omicron Delta Kappa. Democrat. Avocations: travel, kickboxing, music, writing, photography. Home Phone: 609-631-8163; Office Phone: 609-375-2096. Personal E-mail: jz117@comcast.net.

ZIPF, ROBERT EUGENE, JR., legal medicine consultant, pathologist; b. Sept. 18, 1940; s. Robert Eugene and Meriam (Murr) Z.; m. Nancy J. Gaskell, Sept. 11, 1965; children: Karin Lorene, Marjorie Kristine. BA, DePauw U., 1962; MD, Ohio State U., 1966. Diplomate Am. Bd. Pathology. Intern Miami Valley Hosp., Dayton, Ohio, 1966-67; dir. forensic pathology Duke U. Med. Ctr., Durham, NC, 1967-72; dir. radioisotope pathology Riverside Meth. Hosp., Columbus, 1974-78; dep. coroner, forensic pathologist Franklin County, Columbus, 1974-78; regional forensic pathologist State of N.C., Rocky Mount, 1978—; pres. R.E. Zipf, PA, Pathology Assocs., Rocky Mount, NC, 1978—2005. Clin. asst. prof. East Caroline U. Med. Sch., Greenville, N.C., 1979—; adj. prof. Atlantic Christian Coll., Wilson, N.C., 1980-89, dir. Sch. Med. Tech., 1983-89; dir. clin. and diagnostic labs., chief patholgy Nash Gen. Hosp., Rocky Mount, 1978-2006; dir. forensic toxicology lab. Nash Health Care Sys., Rocky Mount, 1990-2000; cons. in field. Contbr. articles to profl. jours. Trustee United Fund, 1979-84; active Mayor's Com. on Drug and Substance Abuse, 1987—; bd. dirs. NC Wesleyan Coll. Found., 2005—, Nash C.C., 2005—; advisor Zipf Charitable Trust and Fund, 1999—; mentor Nash-Rocky Mount Pub. Schs., 1980—. Maj. USAF, 1972-74. Fellow Am. Soc. Clin. Pathologist, Am. Acad. Forensic Scientists; mem. SMS (clin. adv. bd. 1988-91, lab. advisors bd. 1989-91, pres. advisor bd. 1990), Assn. Clin. Scientists, Am. Coll. Nuc. Medicine, N.C. Med. Soc., N.Y. Acad. Scis. (pres. Lab. Users Group 1988-90, 92), Nash County Med. Soc. (pres. 1995). Home: 120 Newby Ct Rocky Mount NC 27804-3322 Office: Nash Gen Hosp Pathology Lab Rocky Mount NC 27804 E-mail: rezpath@email.com.

ZIPKIN, SHELDON LEE, lawyer, educator; b. Washington, June 10, 1951; s. Sol and Selma (Rumerman) Z.; m. Ellen Linda Reitman, July 1, 1973; children: Saul Moshe, Shana Chaya, Joel Mordechai, Abigail Deborah. Student, Hebrew U., Jerusalem, 1970-71; BA, U. Fla., 1973, MA, Cert. in Urban Studies, 1977; JD, Emory U., 1980. Bar: Ga. 1980, Fla. 1980, U.S. Dist. Ct. (so. dist.) Fla. 1983. Assoc. Gladstone Assocs., Miami, Fla., 1973-75; ptnr. Emory Assocs., Atlanta, 1979-80; dep. consumer adv. Metro Dade County, Miami, 1980-81; asst. pub. defender 11th Jud. Cir., Miami, 1981-83; ptnr. Roth & Zipkin, Miami, 1984-86; pvt. practice, Miami, 1986-87, 88-91; chief consumer litigation sect. Fla. Dept. Legal Affairs, Miami and Tallahassee, 1987-88; ptnr. Roth, Zipkin, Cove & Roth, Miami, 1991-95; pvt. practice law, 1995—. Adj. prof. law U. Miami, St. Thomas U., 1998—; pres., chmn. bd. Analytic Prognostication, Inc., Miami, 1988—. Pres., chmn. bd. dirs. Sta. WDNA-FM Pub. Radio, Miami, 1981-82; mem. consumer adv. coun. Fla. Hosp. Cost Containment Bd., Tallahassee, 1988-89. Fellow Soc. for Applied Anthropology; mem. ABA, ATLA, North Dade Bar Assn. (dir. 1997—), Dade County Bar Assn. (dir. 2000), Fla. Bar Assn. (consumer protection com. 1988—), Omicron Delta Kappa. Democrat. Jewish. Avocations: chess, reading. Office: 3rd Fl 2020 NE 163rd St North Miami Beach FL 33162-4927 Office Phone: 305-944-9100. E-mail: zipkin@aol.com.

ZIPP, JOEL FREDERICK, lawyer; b. Shaker Heights, Ohio, Feb. 12, 1948; s. Jack David and Eleanor Adele Zipp; m. Elizabeth Ann Frieden, Dec. 4, 1976; 1 child, Carlyn Leigh. BS, U. Wis., 1970, MS, 1972; JD, Case Western Res. U., 1975. Bar: Ohio 1975, D.C. 1976, U.S. Claims Ct., U.S. Ct. Appeals (D.C. cir.) 1976, U.S. Ct. Appeals (5th cir.) 1979, U.S. Ct. Appeals (11th cir.) 1983, U.S. Supreme Ct. 1983. Trial atty. Fed. Energy Regulation Com., Washington, 1975-79, asst. dir. office of enforcement, 1979; assoc. Morley & Caskin, Washington, 1979-80; ptnr. Morley, Caskin & Generelly, Washington, 1981-98; mng. ptnr. Cameron McKenna LLP, Washington, 1998—2003; gen. counsel, sec. Portland Natural Gas Transmission Sys., 1993-99; ptnr. Bracewell & Giuliani, Washington, 2003—. Notes editor: Energy Law Jour., 1990—98; contbr. articles to profl. jours. Bd. dirs. Westmoreland Children's Ctr., Washington, 1987—88, Found. Energy Law Jour., 1999—2001. Fellow Smithsonian, 1969. Mem.: ABA, Energy Bar Assn. (v.p. 1989—99, past com. chair ann. meeting 1992, 1993, bd. dirs. 1993—96, pres. 2000—01, bd. dirs. 2001—02, mem. nominations com. 2002—05). Jewish. Avocations: skiing, running, bicycling. Home: 9216 Burning Tree Rd Bethesda MD 20817-2251

ZIPP, RONALD DUANE, judge, real estate broker, clergyman; b. New Braunfels, Tex., Dec. 7, 1946; s. Nolan William and Irene Alyce (Stiba) Z.; children: Robert Andrew, Kristi Nicole; m. Saundra Zipp, Mar. 5, 1989. BBA, Tex. A&M U., 1968; JD, St. Mary U., San Antonio, 1971; MA, Oxford U., Eng., 1997. Bar: Tex., US Dist. Ct. (so. dist.) Tex., US Ct. Appeals (5th cir.) 1973, US Supreme Ct. 1974; ordained to ministry Anglican Ch., 1998. Assoc. Kelley, Looney, Alexander & Hiester, Edinburg, Tex., 1971-73; ptnr. Pena, McDonald, Prestia & Zipp, Edinburg, Tex., 1973-81; pvt. practice New Braunfels, Tex., 1981-82, 89—; real estate broker. Judge Comal County Ct.-at-Law, New Braunfels, Tex., 1983—; adj. prof. San Antonio Coll.; real estate broker. Author: local newspaper column; contbr. articles to profl. jours. Bd. dirs. New Braunfels Cmty. Svcs., 1992—, pres., 1981-83, 97-98, sec., 1994; bd. dirs. Child Welfare, vice chmn., 1981-82, chmn., 1982-83; dir. Drover-Comal County Fair Assn.; vol. H.O.S.T.S.; vice chmn. Folkfest, 1994, chmn., 1995—; pres. Cmty. Svc. Ctr., 1997, 2005; bd. dirs., trustee Sr. Citizens Ctr. and Found.; dir. Comal County Fair Assn.; mentor New Braunfels Ind. Sch. Dist.; clergyman, chancellor Anglican Diocese of S.W. Fellow Coll. of State Bar; mem. ABA, Greater New Braunfels C. of C. (legis. com., resources com., heritage com.), Tex. State Jr. Bar (criminal law com. 1975-76), Tex. Criminal Def. Lawyers' Assn. (bd. dirs. 1976-77, various coms.), Tex. Aggie Bar Assn. (charter), Comal County Bar Assn. (past pres.), Comal County A&M Club (pres., treas.), Hidalgo County Bar Assn. (treas. 1972-75), Opa and Kleine Opa of Wurstfest Assn. (chmn. Folkfest), Hidalgo County A&M Club (pres.), Elks, Kiwanis, Lions (sec. 1996, pres. 1997), 100 Club (dir. 2001—), Phi Delta Phi. Lutheran/Anglican. Office: Ste A 831 Landa St New Braunfels TX 78130-5401 Office Phone: 830-629-5600. Office Fax: 830-629-5754. Business E-Mail: rzipp@sbcglobal.net.

ZIPPIN, CALVIN, epidemiologist, educator; b. Albany, NY, July 17, 1926; s. Samuel and Jennie (Perkel) Z.; m. Patricia Jayne Schubert, Feb. 9, 1964; children: David Benjamin, Jennifer Dorothy. AB magna cum laude, SUNY, Albany, 1947; ScD, Johns Hopkins U., Balt., 1953. Rsch. asst. Sterling-Winthrop Rsch. Inst., Rensselaer, NY, 1947-50, Johns Hopkins U., Balt., 1950—53; instr. biostats. Sch. Pub. Health, U. Calif., Berkeley, 1953-55; asst. to full rsch. biostatistician Sch. Medicine U. Calif., San Francisco, 1955-67, asst. prof. preventive medicine, 1958-60; post doctoral fellow London Sch. Hygiene and Tropical Medicine, 1964-65; prof. epidemiology U. Calif., San Francisco, 1967-91, prof. emeritus, 1991—. Vis. assoc. prof. stats. Stanford U., 1962; adv. WHO, 1969—; vis rsch. worker Middlesex Hosp. Med. Sch., London, 1975; com. mem. Am. Cancer Soc. and Nat. Cancer Inst., 1956—; faculty adviser Regional Cancer Centre, Trivandrum, India, 1983—; cons., lectr., vis. prof. in field. Co-author book, book chpts.; author or co-author papers primarily on biometry and epidemiology of cancer; editl. advisor Jour. Stats. in Medicine, 1981-86. Mem., alt. mem. Dem. Ctrl. Com., Marin County, Calif., 1987-96. Recipient Disting. Alumnus award SUNY, Albany, 1969, Lifetime Achievement and Leadership award Nat. Cancer Inst., 2003, also awards, fellowships and grants for work in cancer biometry and epidemiology. Fellow Am. Statis. Assn., Am. Coll. Epidemiology, Royal Statis. Soc. Gt. Britain; mem. Biometric Soc. (mem. internat. coun. 1978-81, pres. Western N.Am. region 1979-80), Calif. Cancer Registrars Assn. (hon.), Internat. Assn. Cancer Registries (hon.), B'nai B'rith (pres. Golden Gate lodge 1970-71, pres. Greater San Francisco unit 21 2003-06, internat. bd. govs. 2005—), Phi Beta Kappa, Sigma Xi, Delta Omega. Office: Univ Calif Dept Epidemiology and Biostats San Francisco CA 94107 Office Phone: 415-514-8000. Business E-Mail: calvin.zippin@ucsf.edu.

ZIPPIN, DAVID BENJAMIN, ecologist, consultant; b. San Francisco, Aug. 20, 1967; s. Calvin and Patricia Jayne Zippin; life ptnr. Thomas Matthew Engels. BA, U. Calif., San Diego, 1989; PhD, U. Tex., Austin, 1997. Biologist Regional Environ. Consultants, San Diego, 1990—91; sr. environ. scientist MHA Environ. Consulting, San Mateo, Calif., 1997—99; prin. Jones & Stokes, San Jose, Calif., 1999—. Author: Habitat Conservation Planning in California (Outstanding Resource Document, Assn. Environ. Profls., 2005). Member-at-large, treas. No. Calif. Rainbow Divers, San Francisco, 2006—07. Mem.: Soc. for Conservation Biology (steering com. 2006 ann. meeting 2004—06). Office: Jones & Stokes 2841 Junction Ave Ste 114 San Jose CA 95112 Office Phone: 408-434-2244. Business E-Mail: dzippin@jsanet.com.

ZIPSER, EDWARD J., meteorologist, educator; BS in Aero. Engring., Princeton U., NJ, 1958; MS in Meteorology, Fla. State U., 1960, PhD in Meteorology, 1965. PhD scientist Nat. Ctr. Atmospheric Rsch., Boulder, Colo., 1966—76, sr. scientist, 1976—90; prof. dept. meteorology Tex. A&M U., Coll. Sta., 1990—99; prof., chair dept. meteorology U. Utah, Salt Lake City, 1999—. Chief scientist Global Atmospheric Rsch. Prog. Nat. Ctr. Atmospheric Rsch., 1971—73, project head Global Atmospheric Rsch. Prog. Atlantic Tropical Expt., 1973—77, head mesoscale interactions sect. Convective Storms Divsn., 1981—84, dir. Convective Storms Divsn. and Cloud Systems Divsn., 1984—87, sci. visitor Mesoscale and Microscale Divsn., 1990—98; rsch. fellow of Natural Environment Rsch. Coun. Imperial Coll., London, 1974—75; Nat. Ctr. Atmospheric Rsch. affiliate vis. prof. dept. atmospheric sci. U. Wash., 1989; head dept. meteorology Tex. A&M U., 1990—95. Contbr. articles to sci. jours.; chair editl. bd.: Bull. of Am. Meteorol. Soc., 2001—. Recipient NOAA award, Outstanding Contbns., 1975; grantee Univ. Space Rsch. Assn. Vis. fellowship, NASA Goddard Space Flight Ctr., 1996—97. Fellow: Am. Meteorol. Soc. (Editor's award 1999, Spl. award, Outstanding Contbns. and Leadership 1977); mem.: Am. Geophys. Union, Sigma Xi. Office: Dept Meteorology U Utah 135 S 1460 E Rm 819 Salt Lake City UT 84112-0110 E-mail: ezipser@met.utah.edu.

ZIRINSKY, BRUCE R., lawyer; b. NYC, Sept. 6, 1947; BS, Cornell U., 1969; JD, NYU, 1972. Bar: N.Y. 1973, U.S. Dist. Ct. (so. and ea. dists.) N.Y. 1973, U.S. Ct. Appeals (2d cir.) 1974, U.S. Ct. Appeals (1st cir.) 1980, U.S. Ct. Appeals (11th cir.) 1981, U.S. Ct. Appeals (5th cir.) 1986, U.S. Supreme Ct. 1991, U.S. Ct. Appeals (6th cir.), 1995. Mem. Weil, Gotshal & Manges, NYC, 1999; ptnr. & chmn. Fin. Restructuring dept. Cadwalader Wickersham & Taft, NYC. Mem. ABA (sect. corp., banking and bus. law), N.Y. State Bar Assn. (mem. com. bankruptcy laws banking and bus. law sects. 1979—). Office: Cadwalader Wickersham & Taft LLP 1 World Fin Ctr New York NY 10281 Office Phone: 212-504-6404. Office Fax: 212-504-6666. Business E-Mail: bruce.zirinsky@cwt.com.

ZIRINSKY, SUSAN, television producer; m. Joe Peyronnin; 1 child, Zoe. Grad., Am. U. Sr. prodr. CBS Evening News, 1986-91, sr. broadcast prodr., 1991-93; sr. prodr. Eye to Eye, 1993-94, exec. prodr., 1994-95, CBS News, 48 Hours, NYC, 1996—. Sr. prodr. CBS News coverage of 1992 Olympic Winter Games, Campaign '96. Co-recipient Edward R. Murrow award, Overseas Press Club, 2006. Office: CBS News 48 Hours 524 W 57th St Fl 5 New York NY 10019-2924

ZIRKLE, WARREN E., lawyer; b. Harrisonburg, Va., 1943; BS, Va. Poly. Inst. and State U., Blacksburg, 1965; JD, U. Va., Charlottesville, 1975. Bar: Va. 1975, US Dist. Ct. Ea. & We. Districts Va. 1976, US Supreme Ct. 1980, US Ct. Appeals 11th Cir. 1987, US Ct. Appeals 4th Cir. 1989, US Ct. Appeals Fed. Cir. 1998, US Ct. Appeals 3rd Cir. 2004. Ptnr. McGuire-Woods LLP, Richmond, Va., McLean, Va., 2000—, now chair firm. comml. litig. dept., mem. bd. partners, 1995—2001. Adj. prof. law U. Richmond, 1993—94. Office: McGuireWoods LLP Ste 1800 1750 Tysons Blvd Mc Lean VA 22102-4215 Office Phone: 703-712-5371. Office Fax: 703-712-5262. Business E-Mail: wzirkle@mcguirewoods.com.

ZIRNHELD, JENNIFER L., engineering educator, researcher; b. Buffalo, May 12, 1969; d. Mark D. McMahon and Carolyn V. Pfeil; m. Mark J. Zirnheld, May 22, 1993. BSEE, SUNY, Buffalo, 1993, MS, 1997, PhD, 2004. Lectr. SUNY, Buffalo, 1997—2004; co-prin., investigator, dep. dir. Energy Systems Inst., 2005—. Contbr. articles to profl. jours. Recipient Milton Plesur award, U. Buffalo Student Assn., 2000—01; Bergquist Doctoral fellow, SUNY, Buffalo, 1998—2002, James Clerk Maxwell Primex doctoral fellow, 2000—01. Mem.: IEEE (treas. 2000, newsletter editor 2000—, chair 2001—02), Am. Phys. Soc., Am. Soc. Engring. Edn., Eta Kappa Nu. Office: University of Buffalo 312 Bonner Hall Buffalo NY 14260 Business E-Mail: zirnheld@eng.buffalo.edu.

ZIROLI, DENNIS F., state agency administrator; married; 1 child. BS in Mgmt. and Acctg., Bryant Coll., 1972. With Columbus Nat. Bank, RI Divsn. Taxation; prin. bank examiner divsn. banking RI Dept. Bus. Regulation, 1983, assoc. dir., supt. banking regulation divsn., 1998—. Office: Banking Regulation Divsn RI Dept Bus Regulation 233 Richmond St Providence RI 02903 Office Phone: 401-222-2405. Office Fax: 401-222-5628. E-mail: dziroli@dbr.state.ri.us.

ZISCHKE, DOUGLAS ARTHUR, foreign service officer; b. Sioux Falls, SD, May 24, 1929; s. Arthur Gustav and Alice Minetta (Wedeking) Z.; m. Janice Mae Kuehnemann, June 8, 1957; children: Mark Douglas, Deborah Jan, Todd Lincoln. BS in Journalism cum laude, U. Wis., 1951, MS, 1952. Joined U.S. Fgn. Svc., 1957; tech. editor Forest Svc., Madison, 1955-57; asst. info. officer USIS, Montevideo, Uruguay, 1957-58, La Paz, Bolivia, 1958-59; asst. cultural affairs officer, br. pub. affairs officer Mexico, 1960-65; info. specialist Washington, 1965-67; pub. affairs officer Tegucigalpa, Honduras, 1967-69; dep. pub. affairs officer Buenos Aires, 1969-71; pub. affairs officer Guatemala City, Guatemala, 1971—74; assigned to U.S. Army War Coll., 1974-75; dep. pub. affairs officer Am. embassy Tehran, Iran, 1975-78; cultural coord. USICA, Washington, 1979-80; internat. cons., 1980-86; fgn. affairs advisor State Dept., 1986-98. Author monograph. Bd. dirs. Boy Scouts Am; dir. Lutheran Ch. 1973-74. Served with Signal Corps, AUS, 1953-55. Mem. Diplomatic and Consular Officers Ret.

ZISCHKE, MICHAEL HERMAN, lawyer; b. Yokahama, Japan, Dec. 30, 1954; s. Peter H. and Alice Marian (Oliver) Z.; children: Julia Carol, Jessica Marian; m. Nadin Sponamore, Sept. 30, 2006. BA magna cum laude, Dartmouth Coll., 1977; JD, U. Calif., Berkeley, 1982. Bar: Calif. 1982. Legis. asst. Congressman Bob Carr, Washington, 1977-79; assoc. Miller, Starr & Regalia, Oakland, Calif., 1982-87, McCutchen, Doyle, Brown & Enersen, Walnut Creek, Calif., 1987-91, counsel, 1991-93; ptnr. Landels Ripley & Diamond LLP, San Francisco, 1993—2000, Morrison & Foerster LLP, San Francisco, 2000—06, co-chmn. land use and environ. law practice group, 2003—06; ptnr. Cox Castle & Nicholson, LLP, 2007—. Lectr. land use issues U. Calif. Extension, 1988—, U. Calif. Davis Sch. Law, 1993-2001, U. Southern Calif. Law Sch., 1995-. Co-author: Land Use Initiatives and Referenda in California, 1990, Practice Pursuant to the California Environmental Quality Act, 1993, 2d edit., 2006; contbr. articles to profl. jours. Dir. Boys & Girls Clubs Oakland, 1988-2000. Mem. ABA, Calif. State Bar Assn. (exec. com. environ. law sect., 1995-2004), Calif. Bldg. Industry Assn. (select com. on industry litigation), Bar Assn. San Francisco. Democrat. Episcopalian. Office Phone: 415-262-5109.

ZISKIN, LAURA, television producer, film producer; b. Mar. 3, 1950; Grad., USC, 1973. Asst. to Jon Peters; co-founder Frogwood Films, 1984; founder, pres. Fox 2000, Beverly Hills, Calif., 1994—99; founder Laura Ziskin Productions, 1999—. Films include: (assoc. prodr.) Eyes of Laura Mars, 1978; (prodr.) Murphy's Romance, 1985, No Way Out, 1987, D.O.A., 1988, Everybody's An American, 1988, The Rescue, 1988, What About Bob?, 1991, The Doctor, 1991, Hero, 1992, To Die For, 1995, Spider-Man, 2002, Spider-Man 2, 2004, Stealth, 2005, Spider-Man 3, 2007; (exec. prodr.) Pretty Woman, 1990, As Good As it Gets, 1997; (TV) Fail Safe, 2000, Dinner with Friends, 2001, 74th Ann. Acad. awards, 2002, Tarzan, 2003, The Spaces, 2003., prodr.(TV) How I Learned to Drive, 2001. Named one of 100 Most Powerful Women in Entertainment, Hollywood Reporter, 2004, 2005, 2006. Office: Laura Ziskin Prodns 10201 W Washington Blvd Astaire Bldg Culver City CA 90232 Office Phone: 310-244-7373. Office Fax: 310-244-0073. *

ZISKIND, ANDREW A., cardiologist, medical educator, health facility administrator; b. Boston, Aug. 31, 1958; s. Alan and Barbara (Schiff) Z.; m. Geraldynn Landry, May 16, 1990; children: Katherine, Rebecca. AB, Bowdoin Coll., 1980; MD, U. Pa., 1984; MBA, Loyola Coll. Md., 1999. Diplomate Am. Bd. Cardiology, Am. Bd. Internal Medicine. Intern, resident Mass. Gen. Hosp., Boston, 1984-87, fellow in cardiology, 1987-90; asst. prof. medicine U. Md., Balt., 1990-96, assoc. prof., 1996-99, U. Washington, 1999—2005, assoc. dean clin. affairs/assoc. v.p. clin specialty program, 1999—2005; pres. Barnes-Jewish Hosp., St. Louis, 2005—; prof. Washington U. Sch. Medicine, St. Louis. Dir. cardiac catheterization lab. U. Md., 1990-95, dir. cardiac network, 1995-99, v.p. clin. svcs. Univ. Care, 1997-99. Fellow Am. Coll. Cardiology, Am. Coll. Physicians, Soc. Cardiac Angiography & Interventions; mem. Am. Coll. Physicians Execs., Am. Fedn. Clin. Rsch. Avocation: woodworking. Office: Barnes-Jewish Hosp 1 Barnes-Jewish Hosp Plaza Saint Louis MO 63110 Home Phone: 314-821-0477; Office Phone: 314-362-5400.

ZISMAN, BARRY STUART, retired lawyer; b. NYC, Sept. 18, 1937; s. Harry and Florence Rita (Tucker) Z.; m. Maureen Frances Brumond, Dec. 30, 1979; children: Michael Glenn, Marlene Ann. AB, Columbia U., 1958, JD, 1961. Bar: D.C. 1962, N.Y. 1965, Tex. 1986, U.S. Dist. Ct. (ea. and so. dists.) N.Y. 1967, U.S. Ct. Appeals (D.C. cir.) 1967, U.S. Dist. Ct. (no. and so. dists.) Tex. 1986, U.S. Ct. Appeals (5th cir.) 1988, U.S. Supreme Ct. 1967. With U.S. Govt., 1962-66; pvt. practice Syosset, N.Y., 1966-71; sr. counsel CBS Inc., NYC, 1972-75; asst. gen. counsel, asst. sec. M. Lowenstein & Sons, NYC, 1975-79; gen. counsel Grumman Allied Indsl. Inc., Bethpage, N.Y., 1979-83; asst. gen. counsel Grumman Corp., Bethpage, 1982-83; sr. atty. FDIC, Dallas, 1984-87; of counsel Arter & Hadden, Dallas, 1987-88, ptnr., 1988, Winstead, McGuire, Sechrest & Minick, Dallas, 1988-90, Arter & Hadden, Dallas and Washington, 1990-91, Rubinstein & Perry, Dallas, 1991-93, The Zisman Law Firm, P.C., Dallas, 1993—2005; ret., 2006. Advisor in field; vice-chmn. Assn. of Bank and Thrift Receivership Coun. Editor and author: Banks and Thrifts: Government Enforcement and Receivership Law, 1991. With U.S. Army, 1961-62. Home and Office: 905 Murl Dr Irving TX 75062-4441 Office: Ste 1100 800 W Airport Freeway Irving TX 75062 Home Phone: 972-659-0703; Office Phone: 972-659-1110. Personal E-mail: zislaw@aol.com.

ZISMAN, DAVID ABRAM, medical educator, health facility administrator; b. Washington, Mar. 1, 1966; s. Elias Zisman and Adela Del Vecchio; m. Raquel Kizer, May 2, 1992; children: Nicole Alexandra, Iliana, Karen Michelle. MD, Ctrl. U. Venezuela, 1991. Diplomate in internal medicine, pulmonary medicine and critical care medicine Am. Bd. Internal Medicine. Med. dir., interstitial lung disease program, pulmonary and critical care divsn. UCLA, 2003—, co-dir., pulmonary function labs., 2003—; asst. prof. medicine David Geffen Sch. Medicine, UCLA, 2003—. Instr. medicine Mayo Clinic, Mayo Grad. Sch. of Medicine, Jacksonville, Fla., 1998—2000; founder, dir. interstitial lung disease program U. Pa. Sch. of Medicine, Phila., 2000—03, asst. prof. medicine, 2000—03. Named Seminal Investigation of Yr., Critical Care Medicine, Am. Coll. Chest Physicians, 1997; recipient Chest Found. Clin. Rsch. award, 2001; NIH grantee. Fellow: Am. Coll. Chest Physicians; mem.: World Assn. Sarcoidosis and Other Granulomatous Diseases, Internat. Soc. for Heart and Lung Transplantation, Am. Thoracic Soc. Achievements include research in association between pulmonary fibrosis and coronary artery disease. Office: UCLA Hosp 10833 Le Conte Ave 37-131 CHS Los Angeles CA 90095 Home Phone: 818-879-9913; Office Phone: 310-825-8689. Office Fax: 310-206-8622. E-mail: dzisman@mednet.ucla.edu.

ZISSER, MARTIN SHEPHERD, fur apparel manufacturer, investor, securities trader; b. Bklyn., Jan. 30, 1942; s. Irving and Jean (Shepherd) Z. Student, NYU, 1960-63. Wall St. investor and trader. Sec. treas. Fur Dressers Union Local 2A, N.Y.C., 1989-92; v.p. UFCW Local 174, N.Y.C., 1992—. Recipient Ofcl. Brit. Coat of Arms, Queen Elizabeth II. Mem. Internat. Soc. Philosophical Enquiry, Mensa. Republican. Jewish. Avocations: study of history, politics, world current events, economics. Home: 2801 Emmons Ave Apt 3F Brooklyn NY 11235-2218 Office Phone: 718-444-3749. Personal E-mail: stargate18000@aol.com.

ZITO, BARRY, professional baseball player; b. Las Vegas, Nev., May 13, 1978; Student, U. Calif., Santa Barbara, Pierce Jr. Coll., U. So. Calif. Pitcher Oakland Athletics, 2000—06, San Francisco Giants, 2006—. Named to, Am. League All-Star team, 2002, 2003; recipient Am. League Cy Young award, 2002. Achievements include has appeared on TV shows including JAG, Arli$$, and the Chris Isaak Show; led American League in Wins, 2002. Office: Pac bell Park 24 Willie Mays Plz San Francisco CA 94107 *

ZITO, FRANK R., lawyer, accountant; b. Haverhill, Mass., Mar. 14, 1946; s. Dan and Anne (Grieco) Z.; m. Carol S. Tandy, Sept. 19, 1976. BS, U. Mass., 1969; JD, Suffolk Law Sch., 1972; LLM, NYU, 1973. Bar: Mass. 1972, U.S. Supreme Ct. 1982, U.S. Tax Ct. 1984. Gen. mgr. Sun Ray Baking Co., 1973-79; atty., mem. Tofias P.C., Cambridge, Mass., 1979—.

Contbr. articles to law jour. Mem. ABA (mem. forum com. 1982-84), Mass. Bar Assn., Am. Inst. CPA's, Mass Soc. CPA's. Home: 8 Livermore Rd Belmont MA 02478-4516 Office Phone: 617-761-0510. Business E-Mail: fzito@tofias.com.

ZITO, NICK, horse trainer, breeder; b. NY, Feb. 6, 1948; m. Kim Zito; 2 children from previous marriage. Former asst. trainer John Campo, LeRoy Jolley; horse trainer. Recipient C.V. Whitney Award, the New York Turf Writers Assoc., 1994, 2000. Achievements include trained winning horse Strike Gold, Kentucky Debry, 1991, Go for Gin, 1994, Louis Quatorze, Preakness Stakes, 1996, Birdstone, Belmont Stakes, 2004; training for George Steinbrenner, Rick Pitino, Marylou Whitney; being elected to horse racing Hall of Fame, 2005. Office: NTRA 2525 Harrodsburg Rd Lexington KY 40504

ZITO, ROBERT JOHN AMADEUS, lawyer; b. NYC, Sept. 11, 1956; s. Joseph J. and Phyllis A. (Esposito) Z.; m. Dana Sabin Cole, July 4, 1992. BA, Tulane U., 1978; JD, N.Y. Law Sch., 1981. Bar: N.Y. 1985, U.S. Dist. Ct. (so. and ea. dists.) N.Y. 1983, (no. dist.) 1993, U.S. Ct. Appeals (2nd Cir.) 1988, U.S. Ct. Appeals (9th Cir.) 2000, U.S. Tax Ct. 1984, U.S. Supreme Ct. 1988; ordained deacon Epis. Ch. of U.S., 2001; parish deacon, Ch. of the Incarnation, N.Y.C. Assoc. LaRossa Cooper, NYC, 1981-85, Spengler Carlson, NYC, 1985-90; ptnr. Zito & Assocs., NYC, 1990-91, Sullivan Donovan, NYC, 1991-93, Tanner Propp & Farber, NYC, 1993—98, Fischbein Badillo Wagner Harding, NYC, 1998—2003, Schiff Hardin, LLP, NYC, 2003—07, Carter Ledyard & Milburn LLP, NYC, 2007—. Lt. col. (ret.) N.Y. Guard, 1991-2001; editl. adv. bd., Episcopal New Yorker. Recipient Bklyn. Achievement award Bklyn. Dems., 1994; N.Y.S. Long and Faithful Svc. award, N.Y.G. Achievement Medal. Mem. ABA, N.Y. Bar Assn., Fed. Bar Coun., Columbian Coun., Ancient Chpt. RAM, Holland Lodge F & AM (past master), Knights Templar, the Most Venerable Order of the Hosp. of St. John of Jerusalem (officer brother), Royal Order Merit Ho. of Savoy (knight). Republican. Episcopalian. Avocations: musical instruments, sailing. Office: Carter Ledyard & Milburn LLP 2 Wall St New York NY 10005 E-mail: zito@clm.com.

ZITO, ROBERT THOMAS, pharmaceutical executive; b. Bayonne, NJ, Nov. 20, 1953; s. Thomas W. and Rose (Scarito) Z. BA in English, Fairfield U., Conn., 1975. Asst. sports editor Bridgeport Telegram, Conn., 1975-79; account exec. Hill and Knowlton, Inc., NYC, 1979-83; v.p. CN Comm., Rahway, NJ, 1983-87; mng. dir. advt. and comm. svcs. NY Stock Exch., 1987-90, exec. v.p. comm.; v.p. corp. comm. Sony USA Inc. and Sony Software Corp., NYC, 1990; with Bristol-Myers Squibb, 2004—, sr. v.p. corp. and bus. comm., chief comm. officer. Pres. Lotsa' Pasta, Inc., Iselin, NJ, 1982-87; cons. Arctic Sports Shops, Inc., Bridgeport, 1976-82; bd. dirs. HDC, Inc., Bayonne. Dir. youth basketball progs. YMCA, Trumbull, Conn., 1977; basketball coach Barlow HS, Redding, Conn., 1977; bd. mem. Bristol-Myers Squibb Found., St. Peter's Prep., FDNY Found., Cento Amici. Recipient Ellis Island Medal of Honor, 1998. Mem. Nat. Sportscasters and Sportswriters Assn., Trenta Amici Club (pres.), Wisemen, PR Seminar. Office: Bristol Myers Squibb 345 Park Ave New York NY 10154-0037 *

ZITRIN, ARTHUR, physician; b. Bklyn., Apr. 10, 1918; s. William and Lillian (Elbaum) Z.; m. Charlotte Marker, Oct. 4, 1942; children— Richard Alan, Elizabeth Ann. BS, City Coll. N.Y., 1938; MS, N.Y. U., 1941, MD, 1945; certificate psychoanalytic medicine, Columbia, 1955. Diplomate: Am. Bd. Psychiatry and Neurology. Research fellow animal behavior Am. Museum Natural History, 1939-42; intern King County Hosp., 1945-46; resident psychiatry Bellevue Hosp., 1948-51; instr. physiology Hunter Coll., NYC, 1948-49; mem. faculty N.Y.U. Sch. Medicine, 1949-97, prof. psychiatry, 1967-97, prof. emeritus, 1997—; mem. staff Bellevue Hosp., NYC, 1951—, dir. psychiatry, 1955-68, N.Y.C. Dept. Hosps., 1962- 64; pvt. practice, 1949—; attending psychiatrist Univ. Hosp., NYC. Cons. psychiatrist Manhattan Va Hosp. Author papers in field. Served to capt., M.C. AUS, 1946- 48. Fellow Am. Psychiat. Assn. (life), N.Y. Acad. Medicine; mem. AMA, N.Y. Soc. Clin. Psychiatry (pres. 1966- 67), Am. Psychoanalytic Assn. (life), Sigma Xi, Alpha Omega Alpha. Home: 56 Ruxton Rd Great Neck NY 11023-1529 Office: 550 1st Ave New York NY 10016-6402

ZITTEL, ANDREA, painter, sculptor; b. Escondido, Calif., 1965; BFA in Painting & Sculpture, San Diego State U., 1988; MFA in Sculpture, RI Sch. Design, 1990. Founder A-Z Adminstrv. Svcs., 1992—; co-organizer High Desert Test Sites. One-man shows include A-Z Living Units, Jack Hanley Gallery, San Francisco, 1993, A-Z Carpet Furniture, Christopher Grimes Gallery, Santa Monica, Calif., 1993, one-woman shows include Purity, Andrea Rosen Gallery, NY, 1993, Comfort, Anthony d'Offay Gallery, London, 1994, Three Living Systems, Carnegie Mus. Art, Pitts., 1994, A series of rotating installations, Andrea Rosen Gallery, NY, 1994, 1995, New Work, San Francisco Mus. Modern Art, 1995, Social Fictions, Barbara & Steven Grossman Gallery, Sch. Mus. Fine Arts, Boston, 1996, New Art 6, Cin. Art Mus., 1996, A-Z Travel Trailer Units, La. Mus. Modern Art, Humlebaek, Denmark, 1996, A-Z Escape Vehicles, Andrea Rosen Gallery, NY, 1996, RAUGH, 1998, A-Z Personal Panels, Sadie Coles HQ, London, 1999, Point of Interest, Public Art Fund, Central Park, NY, 1999, A-Z Time Trials: Free Running Rhythms, Regen Projects, LA, 2000, A-Z Sorting Trays, Susan Inglett, NY, 2001, Andrea Rosen Gallery, NY, 2002, Regen Projects, LA, 2002, Philomene Magers Projekte, Munich, Germany, 2003, Sammlung Goetz, Munich, Germany, 2003, Small Liberties, Whitney Mus. Am. Art, NYC, 2006, exhibited in group shows at Ornament: Ho Hum All Ye Faithfull, John Post Lee Gallery, NY, 1991, One Leading to Another, 303 Gallery, NY, 1992, Writing on the Wall, 1992, Radio Show, Artist's Space, NY, 1992, Add Hot Water, Sandra Gering Gallery, NY, 1993, Don't Look Now, Thread Waxing Space, NY, 1994, Sense & Sensibility, Mus. Modern Art, NY, 1994, Light for the Dark Days of Winter, A/D Gallery, NY, 1995, About Place: Recent Art of Am., Art Inst. Chgo., 1995, Whitney Biennial, Whitney Mus. Am. Art, NY, 1995, 2004, Just Past, Mus. Contemporary Art, LA, 1996, Staging Surrealism, Wexner Ctr. Arts, Ohio, 1997, Patrick Painter Editions, Lehmann-Maupin Gallery, NY, 1997, Travel & Leisure, Paula Cooper Gallery, NY, 1998, Inglenook, Feigen Contemporary, NY, 1998, Art in Pub. Places at Miami Design District, Dacra Companies, Miami Beach, 1999, Elysian Fields, Centre Georges Pompidou, Paris, 2000, Threshold: Invoking Domestic in Contemporary Art, Contemporary Art Ctr. Va., 2000, Drawings, Regen Projects, LA, 2001, Against Design, Mus. Contemporary Art, San Diego, Calif., 2001, Everything Can Be Different, Calif. Ctr. Arts, 2002, Tempo, Mus. Modern Art, NY, 2002, Just Love Me, Bergen Art Mus., 2003, Living Units, Triple Candie, Harlem, NY, 2003, and others. Recipient Distinction Art, San Diego State U., 1988, Award Excellence, RI Sch. Design, 1989, 1990, catalogue support prize, Alfried Krupp Von Bohlen und Halbach Found., 1999, Lucelia Artist Award, Smithsonian Am. Art Mus., 2005; Deutschen Akademischen Austauschdienst Grant, Berlin, Germany, 1995, Coutts Contemporary Arts Found., Zurich, Switzerland, 1996. Mailing: c/o Andrea Rosen Gallery 525 West 24th St New York NY 10011

ZITTRAIN, JONATHAN L., law educator; b. Pitts., Dec. 24, 1969; s. Lester and Ruth Zittrain. BS, Yale U., 1991; JD, Harvard U., 1995, MPA, 1995. Bar: Pa. 1995, D.C. 1996, U. S. Ct. Appeals (D.C. cir.) 1996. Chief forum adminstr. Compuserve Info. Svc., 1984—86; editl. columnist Computer Shopper, 1986-90; program mgr. Microsoft Corp., Redmond, Wash., 1990; with U.S. Dept. State, Washington, 1991; staff U.S. Senate Select Com. on Intelligence, Washington, 1992, 94; law clk. U.S. Ct. Appeals, Washington, 1995; exec. dir. Berkman Ctr. for Internet & Society, Harvard Law Sch., Cambridge, Mass., 1997—2000, faculty co-dir., 2000—; lectr. law Harvard Law Sch., Cambridge, Mass., 1997—99, asst. prof., 2000—, Jack N. and Lillian R. Berkman asst. prof. for entrepreneurial legal studies, 2001—; chair internet governance & regulation Oxford U., 2005—. Office: Berkman Ctr for Internet & Society Harvard Law Sch Baker House 1587 Massachusetts Ave Cambridge MA 02138 Business E-Mail: zittrain@law.harvard.edu.

ZITZEWITZ, ERIC, economics professor; s. Paul and Barbara Zitzewitz; m. Christine Foley; children: Zachary, Zoe, Alexander. BA in Econs., Harvard Coll., Cambridge, Mass., 1993; PhD, MIT, Cambridge, 2001. Econ./bus. analyst McKinsey & Co., Washington, 1993—97; asst. prof. econs. Stanford Grad. Sch. Bus., Calif., 2001—. Grad. Rsch. fellowship, NSF, 1998—2001. Office: Stanford Graduate School of Business 518 Memorial Way Stanford CA 94305 Office Phone: 650-724-1860.

ZIV, JACOB, communications engineer; b. Tiberias, Israel, Nov. 27, 1931; BSc, Israel Inst. Tech., 1954, MSc, 1957; DSc, MIT, 1962. Sr. rsch. engr. Israel Ministry Defense, 1955—59, head comm. divsn., 1962—68; sr. rsch. engr. Melpar, Inc., 1961—62; mem. tech. staff Bell Labs., 1968—70; Herman Gross prof. elec. engring. Technion, Israel Inst. Tech., 1970—. Dean, faculty elec. engring. Technion, 1974—76, v.p. academic affairs, 1978—82. Recipient Israel prize in Exact Scis., 1993, Internat. Marconi award, 1995, Richard W. Hamming medal, IEEE, 1995, Claude E. Shannon award, Info. Theory Soc., 1997, Basic Rsch. award, Eduard Rhein Stiftung, 1998. Fellow: IEEE; mem.: Israel Acad. Sci., Israel Acad. Scis. and Humanities (pres.), NAS (fgn. assoc. 2004), Am. Acad. Engring. (assoc.). Office: Faculty Elec Engring 668 Meyer Technion City Haifa 3200 Israel

ZIVELONGHI, KURT DANIEL, painter, computer graphics artist, designer; b. Barstow, Calif., Oct. 3, 1960; s. Vincent Otto and Beverly Dean (Schwind) Z. Student, Pasadena City Coll., Calif., 1984-85, Art Students League, NYC, 1988-89; BFA, Art Ctr. Coll. of Design, 1993. Self employed fine artist, Pomona, Calif., 1990—. Art dir. movies Seagull's Journey, Gizmo LLC, The Innocent Bystander, Mad Dogs Prodns., 1998. One-man show at Coll. of Design Art Ctr., Pasadena, Calif., 1993; group shows include Flux Gallery, Eagle Rock, Calif., 1993, Art Students League, NYC, 1989, Artexpo, NY, 2000, Marbella, Spain, 2000, AR+21, Las Vegas, 2000, 10th Internat. Biennial Portraiture-Drawings-Graphics, Tuzla, 2002, Aaron Gallery, Washington, 2003, Scottsdale Art Festival, 2003, Orlando Gallery, 2004, Omma Ctr. for Arts, Santa Barbara, Calif., 2005. Mem.: Am. Acad. Poets. Avocations: piano, weightlifting, theater, chess, films.

ZIVIN, NORMAN H., lawyer; b. Chgo., Aug. 10, 1944; s. Alfred E. and Irene (Scher) Z.; m. Lynn F., Dec. 27, 1967; children: Allison, Stephen, Michael. E.M. in Mining Engring., Colo. Sch. Mines, 1965; JD cum laude, Columbia U., 1968. Bar: N.Y. 1968, Ill. 1970, U.S. Supreme Ct. 1975. Assoc. Cooper & Dunham LLP (and predecessor firms), NYC, 1968-70, 71-75, ptnr., 1976—. Mem. Bd. Ethics New Castle (N.Y.), 1974-79. Mem. ABA, Assn. of Bar of City of N.Y., Am. Intellectual Property Law Assn., N.Y. Intellectual Property Law Assn., Soc. Mining Engrs., U.S. Trademark Assn., Fed. Bar Coun., Town Club of Newcastle (pres. 1982-84). Office: Cooper & Dunham LLP Ste 2200 1185 Avenue Of The Americas New York NY 10036-2615 Office Phone: 212-278-0400. E-mail: nzivin@cooperdunham.com.

ZLATOFF-MIRSKY, EVERETT IGOR, violinist; b. Evanston, Ill., Dec. 29, 1937; s. Alexander Igor and Evelyn Ola (Hill) Z.-M.; m. Janet Dalbey, Jan. 28, 1976; children from previous marriage— Tania, Laura. B.Mus., Chgo. Mus. Coll., Roosevelt U., 1960, M.Mus., 1961. Mem. faculty dept. music Roosevelt U., Chgo., 1961-66. Founding mem., violinist, violist Music of the Baroque, 1971-2003. Violinist orch. Lyric Opera of Chgo., 1974-2003; concert master, pers. mgr., 1974-2003, violinst, violist, Contemporary Chamber Players U. Chog., 1964-82, solo violinist, Bach Soc., 1966-83; violist, violinist, Lexington String Quartet, 1966-81; rec. artist numerous recs., radio-TV and films; solo violinist appearing throughout U.S. Recipient Olive Ditson award Franklin Honor Soc., 1961 Mem. Nat. Acad. Rec. Arts and Scis. Republican. Roman Catholic. Home: 1600 Old Pecos Trail Santa Fe NM 87505 E-mail: jdzm@aol.com.

ZLOCH, WILLIAM J., federal judge; b. Ft. Lauderdale, Fla., 1944; BA, U. Notre Dame, 1966; JD, Notre Dame Law Sch., 1974. Pvt. practice, Ft. Lauderdale, 1974—85; judge US Dist. Ct. (So. Dist.) Fla., Ft. Lauderdale, 1985—, chief judge. Lt. USN, 1967—69. Office: US Dist Ct 299 E Broward Blvd Fort Lauderdale FL 33301-1944

ZLOTNICK, NORMAN LEE, lawyer; b. Bklyn., Nov. 2, 1947; s. Harry S. and Frances Zlotnick; m. JoAnn L. Zlotnick, Nov. 26, 1976; m. Sharon Harris, Mar. 12, 2000. BA in History, CCNY, 1969; JD, Rutgers U., 1972. Bar: N.J. 1972, U.S. Dist. Ct. N.J. 1972, U.S. Ct. Appeals (3d cir.) 1974, U.S. Supreme Ct. 1976, N.Y. 1990. Assoc. Perskie & Callinan, 1972-77; ptnr. Perskie, Bloom & Zlotnick, P.A., 1977-79, Bloom & Zlotnick, 1979-82, Marione, Biel, Zlotnick & Feinberg, P.A., Atlantic City, 1982—. Contbr. Rutgers-Camden Law Jour. Mem. ABA, ATLA, N.J. Bar Assn., N.Y. Bar Assn., Cape May County Bar Assn., Atlantic County Bar Assn. (N.J. Supreme Ct. spl. ethics master, Atlantic County civil case arbitrator, cert. civil trial atty.). Office: 3201 Atlantic Ave Atlantic City NJ 08401-6216 Address: 20 Devon Dr Egg Harbor Township NJ 08234-7569 Office Phone: 609-344-1173. Business E-Mail: normanzlotnick@mbzflaw.com.

ZLOTOWSKI, MARTIN, psychologist; b. Lodz, Poland, Aug. 10, 1934; s. Pawel and Helen Zlotowski; m. Judith Ann Lifschitz, May 17, 1974; children: David, Steven, Laura. BA, NYU, 1955; MA, Mich. State U., 1958, PhD, 1960. Rsch. assoc. Grad. Sch. Pub. Health U. Pitts., 1960-61; rsch. assoc., lectr. Boston U., 1961-62; staff psychologist VA Hosp., Coatesville, Pa., 1962-65, unit chief, 1965-73; clin. dir. St. Mary Providence, 1966-70; assoc. prof. spl. edn. West Chester (Pa.) U., 1973—2003. Grad. coord., 1987-2000; dir. Counseling Assocs., Paoli, Pa., 1973-85, exec. dir., 1985—. Pres. Chester County Family Acad., 1999-2002, bd. trustees 2002-04; v.p. Victim Witness Svcs. Chester County, 1976-77. Fellow: Phila. Psychol. Assn., Phila. Soc. Clin. Psychologists (pres. 1978—79, sec. human svcs. ctr. 1982), Am. Orthopsychiat. Assn. (life); mem.: APA, Pa. Fedn. Coun. Exceptional Children (pres. Pa. divsn. behavior disorders 2000—04). Democrat. Jewish. Home: 241 Torrey Pine Ct West Chester PA 19380 Office Phone: 610-647-8270.

ZNAMIEROWSKI, DAVID M, insurance company executive; BA, Colby Coll.; MBA, Amos Tuck Sch. of Bus., Dartmouth Coll. V.p. corp. fin. Salomon Bros., 1986—91; portfolio mgr., v.p, investment strategy and policy Aetna Life & Casulty Co., 1991—96; dir., risk mgmt. strategy Hartford Life, Conn., 1996—97, sr. v.p., dir., life investment strategy Conn., 1997—99, sr. v.p., chief investment officer Conn., 1999—2001; pres. Hartford Investment Mgmt. Co. (HIMCO), Conn., 2001—; chief investment officer The Hartford Fin. Svcs. Group, Inc., Conn., 2001—. Mem. bd. govs. Investment Co. Inst., Am. Coun. of Life Ins.; dir., pres. Hartford sponsored mutual funds. Office: Hartford Fin Svc Group Inc Hartford Plaza 690 Asylum Ave Hartford CT 06115 *

ZOBEL, RYA WEICKERT, federal judge; b. Germany, Dec. 18, 1931; AB, Radcliffe Coll., 1953; LLB, Harvard U., 1956. Bar: Mass. 1956, U.S. Dist. Ct. Mass., 1956, U.S. Ct. Appeals (1st cir.) 1967. Assoc. Hill & Barlow, Boston, 1967-73, Goodwin, Procter & Hoar, Boston, 1973-76, ptnr., 1976-79; judge U.S. Dist. Ct. Mass., Boston, 1979—; dir. Fed. Jud. Ctr., Washington, 1995-99. Mem. Boston Bar Assn., Am. Bar Found., Mass. Bar Assn., Am. Law Inst. Office: US District Ct 1 Courthouse Way Boston MA 02210-3002

ZOBRAS, HELEN, gynecologist, director; b. Sydney, NSW, Australia, Jan. 27, 1954; d. Michael Levas and Despina Mavrogiannis; m. David Gillett, Apr. 17, 2004; m. Stephen Zorbas, Mar. 8, 1975 (div. 1996); children: Danielle Zorbas, Peter Zorbas, Alexano Zorbas. MBBS, U. Sydney, 1978, B of Surgey, 1977. Gen. practitioner, Sydney, NSW, 1981—93; breast physician Sydney Sq. Diagnostic Breast Clinic, Sydney, 1989—96; coord. breast cancer NBCC, RACCD, Sydney, 1996—2000; staff specialist, breast physician Royal Prince Alfred Hosp., Sydney, 1998—; clin. dir. Sydney Breast Clinic, 2003, NBCC, Sydney, 2000—04, dir., 2004—. Conf. presenter in field; mem. numerous coms. on breast cancer including: Breast Screen Australia, Australian Cancer Network, Commonwealth Govts. Cancer Strategy Group, Nat. Breast Cancer Audit, Nat. Health Com., Cancer Inst. NSW, numerous others. Contbr. numerous articles to profl. jours. Fellow: Australiasian Soc. Breast Physicians; mem.: European Soc. Mastology, COSA. Office: Nat Breast Cancer Ctr 92 Parranatta Rd Camperdown 2050 Australia

ZOBRIST, GEORGE WINSTON, computer scientist, educator; b. Highland, Ill., Feb. 13, 1934; s. George H. and Lillie C. (Augustin) Z.; m. Freida Groverlyn Rich, Mar. 29, 1955; children: Barbara Jayne, George William, Jean Anne. BS, U. Mo., 1958, PhD, 1965; MS, Wichita State U., 1961. Registered profl. engr., Mo., Fla. Electronic scientist U.S. Naval Ordnance Test Sta., China Lake, Calif., 1958-59; rsch. engr. Boeing Co., Wichita, 1959-60; instr. Wichita State U., 1960-61; assoc. prof. U. Mo., Columbia, 1961-69, U. So. Fla., Tampa, 1969-70; chmn. elec. engring. dept. U. Miami, Coral Gables, Fla., 1970-71; prof. U. South Fla., Tampa, 1971-72, 73-76; prof., chmn. dept. elec. engring. U. Toledo, 1976-79; dir. computer sci. and engring. Samborn, Steketee, Otis, Evans, Inc., Toledo, 1979-82; prof. computer sci. Grad. Engring. Ctr. U. Mo., St. Louis, 1982-85, prof. computer sci. Rolla, 1985-99, chmn. dept., 1994-99, prof. emeritus, 1999—. Rsch. prof. U. Edinburgh, Scotland, 1972-73; lectr. U. Western Cape, South Africa, 1995 summer; cons. Wilcox Electric Co., Bendix Corp., both Kansas City, Mo., 1966-68, ICC, Miami, 1970-71, Def. Comm. Agy., Washington, 1971, 72, U.S. Naval Rsch. Labs., Washington, 1971, Med. Svc. Bur., Miami, 1970-71, NASA, Kennedy Space Ctr., Fla., 1973-76, 88, 89, 93, 94, Prestolite Corp., Toledo, 1977-79, IBM, Lexington, Ky., 1983-86, Wright-Patterson AFB, Ohio, 1986, PAFB, Fla., 1987, McDonnell Douglas, Mo., 1989, Digital Systems Cons., Mo., 1989, Oak Ridge Nat. Labs., 1992. Author: Network Computer Analysis, 1969, Progress in Computer Aided VLSI Design, 1988-90; editor Internat. Jour. Computer Aided VLSI Design, 1989-91, Object Oriented Simulation IEEE Press, 1996, Computer Sci. and Computer Engring. Monograph series, 1989-91, Internat. Jour. Computer Simulation, 1990-96, VLSI Design, 1992-2002; editor IEEE Potentials Mag., 1996-99, 2003; assoc. editor, 1984-96, 99—; contbr. articles to profl. jours. Served with USAF, 1951-55. Named Young Engr. of Yr. ctrl. chpt. Mo. Soc. Profl. Engrs., 1967; NSF summer fellow, 1962, 64; NASA, IBM, DOE, UES/AFOSR, McDonnell Douglas rsch. grantee, 1967-88. Fellow IEEE (life, mem. IEEE Press editl. bd. 1998—); mem. Am. Legion, Rotary, Sigma Xi, Tau Beta Pi, Phi Eta Sigma, Eta Kappa Nu, Pi Mu Epsilon, Upsilon Pi Epsilon. Home: 12030 Country Club Dr Rolla MO 65401-7469 Office: U Mo Rolla Dept Compuer Sci 1870 Miner Cir Rolla MO 65409-0001 Business E-Mail: zobrist@umr.edu.

ZOCCHI, LOUIS JOSEPH, product designer, game company executive; b. Chgo., Feb. 16, 1935; s. Louis Alexander and Martha (Adams) Z.; m. Elissa Lorelei Scott, June 8, 1959 (Sept. 1976); children: David, Suzanne, LaRee, Lisa; m. Sharon Annette Olson, May 25, 1985; 1 child, Heidi Olson. Cert. air traffic controller, 1955, air traffic control instr., 1964. Commd. USAF, 1954, advanced through grades to tech. sgt., air traffic contr. Offut AFB, Nebr., 1954, Lincoln AFB, Nebr., 1955-59, Misawa AFB, Japan, 1959-63, Holloman AFB, N.Mex., 1963-64, air traffic control instr. Keesler AFB, Miss., 1964-70, air traffic contr. Mather AFB, Calif., 1970-71, Kimpo AFB, Korea, 1971-72, George AFB, Calif., 1972-73, Biloxi, Miss., 1973-75, ret., 1975; commd. 1st lt. Miss. State Guard, 1991, advanced through grades to capt., 1993; owner Zocchi Distbrs., Victorville, Calif., 1972—; pres. Gamescience, Inc., Cedarhurst, N.Y., 1974—. Cruise dir. Europa Star cruise ship, 1988; cons. Dupuy Inst., 1995. Designer (games) Battle of Britain, 1968, Star Fleet Battle Manual, 1977 (Gamesday award 1981), Basic and Advanced Fighter Combat, 1980 (H.G. Wells award 1981); inventor Zocchihedron 100-sided dice, 1985, inventor 16 sided die, 5-sided die, 3-sided die, 14 Sided Die Major Ala. State Guard, 1997—, col., 2003. Recipient Hobbyist award Metro Detroit Gamers, 1979, Spl. Svc. award Strategists Club, 1982, Charles Roberts Adventure Gaming Hall of Fame award, 1987, Gama Honor of Svc. award 1991, George award Coastcon, 2005 Mem. Game Mfrs. Assn. (chmn. membership com. 1978-84, v.p. 1978-84, bd. dirs. 1985), Internat. Brotherhood Magicians (Order of Merlin 2000), Hobby Industry Assn. (pres. gaming div. 1981), Gulf Coast Jazz Soc. (pres.), Soc. Am. Magicians (pres.). Avocations: playing jazz music, ventriloquism, magic. Home and Office: Gamescience Inc 7604 Newton Dr Biloxi MS 39532-2830 Home Phone: 228-392-4177; Office Phone: 228-392-4177.

ZOCHOWSKI, T. ROBERT, JR., lawyer; b. New Brunswick, NJ, 1964; BS in Fgn. Svc., Georgetown U., 1986; JD, NYU, 1989. Bar: NJ 1989, NY 1990. Assoc., project fin. group law firm, NYC, 1989—93; assoc. Shearman & Sterling LLP, NYC, 1993—99, ptnr., structured fin., hiring ptnr., 1999—2006; ptnr. Paul, Weiss, Rifkind, Wharton & Garrison LLP, NYC, 2006—. Articles editor NYU Law Rev. Office: Paul Weiss Rifkind Wharton & Garrison LLP 1285 Ave Americas New York NY 10019 Office Phone: 212-373-3762. Office Fax: 212-492-0762. E-mail: rzochowski@paulweiss.com. *

ZOE, RACHEL (RACHEL ZOE ROSENZWEIG), fashion stylist; b. NYC, Sept. 1, 1971; m. Rodger Berman. Grad., George Washington U., 1993. With YM Mag.; fashion stylist for various celebrities including Cameron Diaz, Kate Beckinsale, Jennifer Garner, Paris Hilton, Keira Knightley; fashion stylist to Nicole Richie, 2004—06. TV appearances The Simple Life, 2006, Project Runway, 2006. *

ZOELLER, DAVID LOUIS, lawyer, bank executive; b. Indpls., Nov. 26, 1949; s. John Louis and M. Maxine (Snoderly) Z.; m. Wesley Anne Carlton, Aug. 14, 1971; children: Laura Anne, David Carlton. BA, So. Meth. U., Dallas, 1971; JD, Ind. U., 1974. Bar: Ind. 1974, US Dist. Ct. (so. dist. Ind.) 1974. Asst. sec., legal counsel Stokely-Van Camp Inc., 1974-83; legal mgmt. positions through exec. v.p., sec., gen. counsel Nat. City Corp., Cleve., 1983—. Mem. ABA, Ind. Bar Assn., Indpls. Bar Assn., Ohio Bar Assn., Cleve. Bar Assn., Am. Soc. Corp. Secs., Lawyers Coun. Fin. Svcs. Roundtable. Republican. Presbyterian. Office: Nat City Corp Nat City Ctr 1900 E 9th St Cleveland OH 44114-3484 Office Phone: 216-222-2000. *

ZOELLER, DONALD J., lawyer; b. Queens Village, NY, Mar. 18, 1930; s. Henry Adolph and Marion Elizabeth (Brodie) Z.; m. Susan Josephine Campisi, Sept. 3, 1955; children— Paul Joseph, Jean Marie, Diane Marie AB, Fordham Coll., 1951; LL.B., Fordham Sch. Law, NYC, 1958. Bar: N.Y. 1959, D.C. 1967. Law clk. to judge U.S. Dist. Ct. (so. dist.) N.Y., NYC, 1958-59; assoc. Mudge Rose Guthrie Alexander & Ferdon, NYC, 1959-68, ptnr., 1968-95, exec. ptnr., 1991-95, chmn. exec. com., 1995; counsel Carter, Ledyard & Milburn, NYC, 1995-96, ptnr., 1997-98, of counsel, 1999—2003, ret., 2003. Adj. prof. law Fordham U. Law Sch., 1989—; lectr. in field. Contbr. articles to legal pubis. Trustee Oyster Bay-East Norwich Bd. Edn., 2007—. 1st lt. US Army, 1951—53, Korea. Mem.: Bar Assn. City of NY. Republican. Roman Catholic. Avocations:

skiing, swimming, tennis, reading. Office Phone: 516-922-7205. Business E-Mail: dzoeller@optonline.net. *Notable cases include: Matsushita Electric Indsl. Co. Ltd. et al vs. Zenith Radio Corp. et al, 475 U.S. 574, 89 L. edit. 2d 538, 106, s.ct. 1438.*

ZOELLER, JACK CARL, diversified financial services company executive; b. Buffalo, Feb. 26, 1949; s. Ronald Carl and Margaret Lillian (Wademan) Z.; m. Kathryn Louise Helmke, Apr. 25, 1981; children: Andrew, Alexander, Charles (dec.). BS, U.S. Mil. Acad., 1970; M of Pub. Policy, Harvard U., 1972; M of Letters, Oxford U., Eng., 1974. Program budget officer Army Chief of Staff's Office, Pentagon, Washington, 1978-80; v.p. E.F. Hutton & Co., Inc., NYC, 1982; pres. E.F. Hutton Indemnity Group, NYC, 1983-85, Capital Risk Mgmt., Iselin, NJ, 1985-87; exec. v.p., bd. dirs. Comfed Mortgage Co., Lowell, Mass., 1987-88, pres., 1988-91, ComFed Savs. Bank, Lowell, 1990-91; chmn. chief exec. officer ComFed Bancorp., Cambridge, Mass., 1990-95; pres. The Zoeller Group, Washington, 1993-95. Bd. dirs. N.Am. Health Plans, Inc., Amherst, NY, 1995—99; pres. AtlantiCare Risk Mgmt. Corp., 1995—2004; chmn., CEO AtlantiCare, Inc., 1995—2004; pres. N.Am. Health & Life Ins., Barbados, 1996—2006; vis. rsch. prof. George Washington U., 2005—. Mem. exec. com. Lowell Devel. and Fin. Corp., 1989-91, class gift com. U.S. Mil. Acad., 1990-95; youth sports coach, 1990-96; Am. chmn. 750th Ann. Campaign Univ. Coll., Oxford, Eng., 1998-2002; parent group leader Maret Sch., Washington, 1998-2003; bd. dirs. Transcommunity FinCorp., Va., 2006-. Served to capt. US Army, 1970—80. Decorated Meritorious Svc. medals; Rhodes scholar, Oxford U., 1972. Mem. West Point Soc. N.Y. (bd. govs. 1985-87), West Point Soc. D.C., Am. Friends Univ Coll. Oxford, Inc. (v.p. 1999—), Fed. Nat. Mortgage Assn. (N.E. regional adv. bd. 1990-91), Assn. Am. Rhodes Scholars (bd. dirs. 2004—, treas. 2006—), New Eng. Hist. Geneal. Soc., Soc. Mayflower Descs. Home and Office: 2810 31st St NW Washington DC 20008-3523 Home Phone: 202-342-5553. Personal E-mail: jackzoeller@yahoo.com.

ZOELLICK, ROBERT BRUCE, President of the World Bank, former federal agency administrator; b. Evergreen Park, Ill., July 25, 1953; s. William T. and Gladys Zoellick; m. Sherry Lynn Ferguson, June 28, 1980. BA with honors, Swarthmore Coll., 1975; M in Pub. Policy, Harvard U., 1981, JD magna cum laude, 1981; LittD (hon.), St. Joseph's Coll., 2002. Bar: DC 1981. Spl. asst. to dep. atty. gen. criminal divsn. US Dept. Justice, Washington, 1978-79; pvt. law practice, 1981-82; law clk. to Hon. Patricia M. Wald, US Ct. Appeals (DC Cir.), Washington, 1982-83; v.p., asst. to chmn. & CEO Fannie Mae, Washington, 1983-85; from sec., dep. asst. sec. for fin. instns. policy, to counselor to sec. & exec. sec. US Dept. Treasury, Washington, 1985-88; counselor with rank under sec. US Dept. State, Washington, 1989-92, under sec. for econ. & agrl. affairs, 1991-92; dep. chief of staff, asst. to Pres. The White House, Washington, 1992-93; exec. v.p. housing & law Fannie Mae, Washington, 1993-97; Olin prof. nat. security US Naval Acad., Annapolis, Md., 1997-98; pres., CEO Ctr. Strategic & Internat. Studies, Washington, 1998-99; resident fellow German Marshall Fund US, Washington, 1999—2001; rsch. scholar Belfer Ctr. Sci. and Internat. Affairs Harvard U., Cambridge, Mass.; U.S. Trade Rep. Exec. Office of the Pres., Washington, 2001—05; dep. sec. US Dept. State, Washington, 2005—06; vice chmn. internat. The Goldman Sachs Group, Inc., NYC, 2006—07; pres. The World Bank Group, Washington, 2007—. Decorated Knight Comdr.'s Cross (for work on German unification, Germany); recipient Alexander Hamilton award US Treasury Dept., 1988, Disting. Svc. award US State Dept, 1992, Disting. Pub. Svc. medal Dept. Def., 2006-07; fellow Luce Found., Hong Kong, 1980. Mem. DC Bar Assn., Phi Beta Kappa. Office: The World Bank Group 1818 H St NW Washington DC 20433 Office Phone: 202-458-2500.

ZOFFER, H. JEROME, business educator, dean; b. Pitts., July 23, 1930; s. William and Sarah Leah (Fisher) Z.; m. Maye Rattner, July 19, 1959; children: Gayle Risa, William Michael. BBA, U. Pitts., 1952, MA, 1953, PhD, 1956; CPCU, Am. Inst., Phila., 1954. Sales and mgmt. cons., 1952—60; instr. Sch. Bus. Adminstrn., U. Pitts., 1953—56; asst. prof. Sch. Bus. Adminstrn. U. Pitts., 1956—59, assoc. prof. Joseph M. Katz Grad. Sch. Bus., 1959—66, prof. Sch. Bus. Adminstrn., Grad. Sch. Bus., 1966—, chmn. dept. real estate and ins., 1958—60, dir. spl. studies, 1960—62, asst. dean acad. affairs, 1962—65, assoc. dean for adminstrn., 1965—68, dean Grad. Sch. Bus., 1968—96, dean emeritus, 1996—. Ford Found. fellow in applied math. U. Pa., Phila., 1961—62; mem. visitation com. Am. Assembly Collegiate Schs. of Bus., 1972—2000, mem. stds. com., 1974—78, mem. exec. com., 1975—87, chmn. accreditation rsch. com., 1974—84, v.p. bd. dirs., 1984—85, pres., 1985—86, chmn. Mid. State Evaluation Accrediting Teams, 1967—85. Author: The History of Automobile Liability Insurance Rating: 1900-1958, 1959; also monographs.; contbr. articles to profl. jours. Bd. dirs., v.p. Leadership Inst. for Community Devel., 1968-73, Allegheny chpt. Epilepsy Found. Am., 1971-77; bd. dirs. Pitts. Dist. Export Coun., 1974-77, Sch. Advanced Jewish Studies, 1976-79, Czech Mgmt. Ctr., 1989—2005, Travelers Aid Soc., Pitts., 2006—; bd. govs. Internat. Ins. Seminars, Inc., 1968-77; pres. Temple Sinai Congregation, 1979-81; mem. festival bd. Three Rivers Art Festival, 1988-93; mem. steering com. Leadership Pitts., 1986-91; sec. Am. Jewish Com., 1993-95; bd. dirs. Student Cons. Project, U. Pitts., 1970-96, Consortium for Coop. and Competitiveness, 1986-96, Moral Force in the Workplace, 1986-96; investment com. United Jewish Fedn., 1992-95; sec.-treas., bd. dirs. David Berg Found., 1995—. Named Man of Yr. in Edn., Vectors Pitts., 1986, Disting. Alumnus, 1989, U. Pitts. Alumni Assn. Mem. Soc. Psychol. Study Social Issues, Mid. Atlantic Assn. Colls. Bus. Adminstrn. (pres. 1972-73), Am. Assn. Univ. Adminstrs. (exec. com. 1971-79, pres. 1975-77, dir. 1980-83, pres. found. 1983-95), Univ. Club (bd. dirs. 1988-94, sec. 1990-91, v.p. 1991-92, pres. 1992-93), Omicron Delta Gamma, Beta Gamma Sigma (pres. Beta chpt. 1964-68). Home: 220 N Bellefield Ave Ph 1201 Pittsburgh PA 15213-1468 Office: U Pitts Pitts Campus Katz Grad Sch Bus Pittsburgh PA 15260 Office Phone: 412-624-7678. Business E-Mail: zoffer@katz.pitt.edu.

ZOFFER, RACHELLE, telecommunications industry executive; b. Pitts., 1967; BS, U. Mich.; MBA, U. NC Chapel Hill. Variuos mgmt. positions Oracle, The Walt Disney Co.; v.p. bus. devel. ShadowTV, Softel-USA; dir. interactive TV Verizon Comm. Inc., NYC, 2006—. Office: Verizon Comm Inc 140 West St New York NY 10036 *

ZOGHBI, HUDA Y., neurologist, geneticist, educator; b. Beirut, June 29, 1955; BSc, Am. U. Beirut; MD, Meharry Med. Coll., 1979. Prof. pediat. neurology and geriatrics Baylor Coll. Medicine, Houston, 1994—; investigator Howard Hughes Med. Inst., 1996—; pediatrician Tex. Children's Hosp. and Ben Taub Gen. Hosp. Elected mem. Inst. of Medicine, 2000; sci. adv. bd. Internat. Rett Syndrome Assn.; med. rsch. adv. bd. Nat. Ataxia Found.; sci. issues com. Am. Acad. Neurology. Recipient Sidney Carter award, Acad. Neurobiology, Javits award, NIH, E. Mead Johnson award for pediat. rsch., Derek Denny-Brown Neurological Scholar award, Am. Neurol. Assn. Mem.: Am. Acad. Neurology (sci. issues com.), Inst. Medicine, NAS. Achievements include discovery (with others) of gene that causes spinocerebellar ataxia type 1; discovery of MECP2 gene that causes Rett syndrome; identifying Math1 gene that governs development of inner-ear hair cells. Office: Baylor College of Medicine T 807 1 Baylor Plz Houston TX 77030-3411 Office Phone: 713-798-6558. Office Fax: 713-798-8728. Business E-Mail: hzoghbi@bcm.tmc.edu.

ZOHN, MARTIN STEVEN, lawyer; b. Denver, Oct. 22, 1947; s. William and Alice Zohn; m. Carol Falender, June 6, 1980; children: David Joseph, Daniel Robert. BA, Ind U., 1969; JD, Harvard U., 1972. Bar: Calif. 1972, Ind. 1973, US Ct. Claims 1980, US Supreme Ct. 1980, US Ct. Appeals (9th cir.) 1981. Assoc. Cadick, Burns, Duck & Neighbors, Indpls., 1972-77, ptnr., 1977-80, Pacht, Ross, Warne, Bernhard & Sears, Inc., LA, 1980-86, Shea & Gould, LA, 1986-89, Proskauer Rose LLP, LA, 1989—. Pres. Indpls. Settlements, Inc., 1977-79. Bd. dirs. Pub. Counsel, 2001—, treas., 05, sec., 06. Mem. Fin. Lawyers Conf. (mem. bd. govenors), LA County Bar Assn. (exec. com. prejudgment remedies sect. 1985-92, exec. com. bankruptcy sect. 2001—), Beverly Hills Bar Assn. (exec. com. bus. law sect. 1985-92, exec. com. bankruptcy sect. 2003—), Phi Beta Kappa. Office Phone: 310-284-5648. Business E-Mail: mzohn@proskauer.com.

ZOIS, CONSTANTINE NICHOLAS ATHANASIOS, meteorologist, educator; b. Newark, Feb. 21, 1938; s. Athanasios Konstantinos and Asimina (Speros-Biekas) Zois; m. Elyse Stein, Dec. 26, 1971; children: Jennifer, Jonathan. BA, Rutgers U., 1961; MS, Fla. State U., 1965; PhD, Rutgers U., 1980. Draftsman Babcock and Wilcox Corp., Newark, 1956; designer Foster Wheeler Corp., Carteret, NJ, 1956; instr. Rutgers U., New Brunswick, NJ, 1961-62; grad. asst. Fla. State U., Tallahassee, 1962-65; rsch. meteorologist Nat. Weather Svc., Garden City, LI, NY, 1965-67; prof. Kean Coll. N.J., Union, 1967—. Founder meteorology program Kean Coll. N.J., Union, 1967—, chmn. all coll. promotion com., 1991—93; cons. Connell, Foley, Geiser, Roseland, NJ, 1986—88. Author, editor: Papers in Marine Science, 1971; author: Observation of the Newark NJ Nocturnal Heat Island and Its Consideration in Terms of a Physical Model, 1980, Dynamical and Physical Oceanography, 1988, Atmosphere Dynamics: Exercises and Problems, 1988, Climatology Workbook, 1988, Weather Map Folio, 1989; co-author: Outcomes Assessment at Kean College at NJ, 1992, Synoptic Meterology-Exercises and Readings, Vols. 1-3, 1995, Weather Folio, Vol. 2, NWS Map Anthology, 2003. Mem.: AAAS, N.J. Marine Scis. Consortium, N.Y. Acad. Scis. (vice chmn. atmospheric scis. sect. 1986—87, chmn. 1987—88, mem. adv. com. atmospheric sci. sect. 1988—), Am. Meteorol. Soc. (pres. N.J. chpt. 1980—81), Nat. Weather Assn., Phi Beta Kappa. Republican. Greek Orthodox. Avocations: guitar, banjo, fishing, baseball, snorkeling. Home: 2798 Carol Rd Union NJ 07083-4831 Office: Kean Coll of NJ Dept Meteorology Morris Ave Union NJ 07083-7117 Office Phone: 908-737-3693. *It is water that consecrates the atmosphere as a cathedral of wonderment, as it is water that incarnates the sea as an oasis of life.*

ZOLA, GARY PHILLIP, rabbi, historian; b. Chgo., Feb. 17, 1952; m. Stefani Paula Rothberg; children: Amanda Roi, Jorin Benjamin, Jeremy Micah, Samantha Leigh. BA in Am. History with distinction, U. Mich., 1973; MA in Counseling Psychology, Northwestern U., 1976; PhD in Am. Jewish History, Hebrew Union Coll., Cin., 1991. Ordained rabbi, 1982. Dir. informal edn. and youth activities Temple Israel, Mpls., 1973-74; regional youth dir., asst. camp dir. Olin-Sang-Ruby Union Inst., UAHC, Chgo., 1974-77; student pulpit B'nai Israel Congregation, Williamson, W.Va., 1978-79; mem. student pulpit Anshe Sholom Congregation, Olympia Fields, Ill., 1979-80, Columbus Hebrew Congregation, Columbus, Ind., 1981-82; rabbi for high holy days Chgo. Jewish Experience, Chgo., 1982-94; nat. dir. admissions Hebrew Union Coll.-Jewish Inst. Religion, Cin., 1982-89, nat. dean admissions and student affairs, 1989-91, nat. dean admissions, student affairs and alumni rels., 1991-98; exec. dir. Jacob Rader Marcus Ctr. Am. Jewish Archives at Hebrew Union Coll., Cin., 1998—; assoc. prof. Am. Jewish Experience Hebrew Union Coll. Jewish Inst. of Religion. Del. Emerging Leaders Conf., Am. Coun. for Internat. Leadership, 1989, 91; bd. dirs. Am. Jewish Com., Cin., 1982—, mem. exec. com., 1984—; bd. dirs. Hillel U. Cin., 1991-94, Jewish Fedn., Cin., 1993-95; pres. Greater Cin. Bd. Rabbis, 1993-95, Jewish Cmty. Rels. Coun., (bd. dir.,1994—); founding mem. Kehillah of Cin., Jewish Think Tank; pres. Martin Luther King Jr. Coalition Cin., 2003-05; chair Commn. for Commemorating 350 Years of Am. Jewish History. Author: Isaac Harby of Charleston, 1994; editor: Hebrew Union College--Jewish Institute of Religion--A Centennial History, 1875-1975, (Michael A. Meyer), 1992, Women Rabbis: Exploration and Celebration, 1996, The Dynamics of American Jewish History, 2003, A Place of Our Own: The Rise of Reform Jewish Camping, 2006; editor: The American Jewish Archives Jour., 1998—; contbr. numerous scholarly articles to profl. jours.; mem. editl. bd. Reform Judaism. Bd. dirs. ethics com. Jewish Hosp., Cin.; life mem. N.Am. Fedn. Temple Youth; active NCCJ. Mem. Ctrl. Conf. Am. Rabbis, Orgn. Am. Historians, Assn. Jewish Studies, So. Jewish Hist. Soc., Am. Jewish Hist. Soc., N.Am. Fedn. Temple Youth (life). Office: Hebrew Union Coll Jewish Inst Religion 3101 Clifton Ave Cincinnati OH 45220-2404

ZOLA, MICHAEL S., lawyer; b. Madison, Wis., Dec. 15, 1942; s. Emanuel and Harriet (Sher) Zola; 1 child, Emanuel David. BS cum laude, U. Wis., 1964; LLB, Columbia U., 1967. Bar: D.C. 1968, Wis. 1968, U.S. Dist. Ct. (we. dist.) Wis. 1968, Calif. 1969, U.S. Dist. Ct. (no. dist.) Calif. 1969, U. S. Ct. Appeals (9th cir.) 1969, Hawaii 1981, U.S. Dist. Ct. Hawaii 1981. Law clk. to judge U.S. Dist. Ct. (we. dist.) Wis., 1967—68; mng. atty. San Francisco Neighborhood Legal Assistance Found., 1968—70; sole practice Calistoga, Calif., 1970—73; directing atty. Mendocino Legal Svcs., Ukiah, Calif., 1973—76; state chief of legal svcs. State of Calif., Sacramento, 1976—78, dep. state pub. defender, 1978—79; sole practice Kailua-Kona, Hawaii, 1981—. Mem. adv. bd. Kona Salvation Army, 1983—93; chmn. Mendocino County Dem. Ctrl. Com., Ukiah, 1975—76; pres. Kona Beth Shalom Congregation, 1991—94. Reginald Heber Smith Poverty Law fellow, 1968—70. Mem.: Legal Aid Soc. Hawaii (bd. dirs. 1985—86), Nat. Assn. Criminal Def. Lawyers, Hawaii Assn. Criminal Def. Lawyers (bd. dirs. 1989—), Rotary Club Kona (pres. 1998—99). Office: 75-5744 Alii Dr Ste 223 Kailua Kona HI 96740-1740 Business E-Mail: zolalaw@verizon.net.

ZOLANDZ, MICHAEL E., JR., lawyer; BA cum laude, George Washington U., 1998, JD with high honors, 2001. Bar: DC, Md. Assoc. Arent Fox Kintner Plotkin & Kahn, Washington, 2001—02; assoc., pub. law & policy strategies group Sonnenschein Nath & Rosenthal LLP, Washington, 2002—. Office: Sonnenschein Nath & Rosenthal LLP Ste 600, E Tower 1301 K St NW Washington DC 20015 Office Phone: 202-408-9204. Office Fax: 202-408-6399. Business E-Mail: mzolandz@sonnenschein.com.

ZOLER, MITCHEL L., journalist; b. NYC; PhD, SUNY, Buffalo, 1979. Journalist Phila. bur. Internat. Med. News Group, Wynnewood, Pa., 1992—. Office: Internat Med News Group 262 Trent Rd Wynnewood PA 19096

ZOLLA-PAZNER, SUSAN, hospital administrator, biologist, biomedical researcher; MD, U. Calif., San Francisco, PhD in Med. Microbiology, 1967. NIH postdoctoral fellow NYU Med. Ctr., 1967—69; dir., immunology rsch. lab. Veterans Affairs Med. Ctr., NYC, dir. rsch. AIDS ctr. U.S. chair U.S.-Japan Commn. on AIDS Rsch.; editorial bd. mem. AIDS Rsch. and Human Retroviruses, Cellular Immunity, Journ. Immunologic Methods. Author: more than 240 scientific papers on cancer, AIDS and various human pathogens. Office: VET 18 18147N 423 E 23 St New York NY 10010 *

ZOLLAR, ALFRED, computer company executive; M in Applied Math., U. Calif., San Diego. Sys. engr. trainee IBM, San Francisco, 1977, gen. mgr. e-network software, sr. v.p. develop. tivoli software, lab dir. software group Raleigh, NC, DB2 product mgr. Santa Teresa, Calif., gen. mgr., network software, 1996—98, gen. mgr. network computing software divsn., 1998—2000, gen. mgr. lotus software Cambridge, Mass., 2000—03, gen. mgr., eServer iSeries, 2003—. Bd. dirs. Chubb Corp.; mem. Leadership Coun. of Ctr. Bus. and Govt., John F. Kennedy Sch. Govt., Harvard U. Mem.: Greater Boston C. of C. (exec. com.). Office: IBM 1 Rodgers St Cambridge MA 02142 also: IBM 1133 Westchester Ave White Plains NY 10604

ZOLLARS, WILLIAM D., freight company executive; b. 1948; BA, Univ. Minn., 1969. Various exec. positions with Eastman Kodak, 1970—94; sr. v.p. Ryder Integrated Logistics Ryder Sys., Inc., 1994—96; pres. Yellow Freight Sys., 1996-99; chmn., pres., CEO Yellow Roadway Corp., Overland Park, Kans., 1999—. Bd. dir. Cigna Corp., Cerner Corp., Butler Mfg. Co. Trustee ProLogis Trust, Midwest Rsch. Inst.; bd. mem. Heart of Am. United Way, Civic Council of Greater Kans. City, Carlson Sch. Mgmt., Univ. Minn., NAM. Mem.: Am. Trucking Assn. (bd. mem.), Phi Beta Kappa. Office: Yellow Corp 10990 Roe Ave Overland Park KS 66211-1213 *

ZOLLER, MICHAEL, otolaryngologist, head and neck surgeon, educator; b. New Orleans, July 21, 1947; s. Harry and Mildred (Daitch) Z.; m. Linda Kramer, Dec. 21, 1974; children: Rebecca, Jonathan. BS, U. New Orleans, 1971; MD, Tulane U., 1972. Resident in gen. surgery Jewish Hosp., St. Louis, Washington U. Sch. Medicine, 1972—74; resident in otolaryngology Mass. Eye and Ear Infirmary, Harvard U. Med. Sch., Boston, 1974—77; pres. Ear, Nose and Throat Assocs., Savannah, Ga., 1977—; chmn. eye, ear, nose and throat dept. Candler Hosp., 1996—98. Asst. clin. prof. surgery Med. Coll. Ga., Augusta, 1982—96, assoc. clin. prof. surgery, 1996—2003; assoc. prof. surgery Mercer Med. Sch., 2000—; dir. otology otoneurology dept. St. Joseph's Hosp., Savannah, 1994—; bd. dirs. Darby Bank and Trust, 2007. Chmn. med. divsn. United Way, Savannah, 1990, chmn. profl. divsn., 1991, 94-2001, vice chmn. campaign, 2002, chmn. campaign, 2003, bd. dirs., 2002-07, vice chmn. bd. dirs., 2004-05, chmn. bd. dirs., 2005-2006; mem. allocation panel, 1997-2002; bd. dirs. Am. Cancer Soc., Savannah, 1993-2000, pres. Chatham County unit, 1996-97, chmn. bd., 1997-98; bd. dirs. Savannah Country Day Sch., 1993-97, chmn. ann. campaign, 1995-96; bd. dirs. St. Joseph's Candler Found., 2001-07; pres. Savannah Jewish Fedn., 1991-93; active Savannah Jewish Fedn. Endowment Bd., 1995-99; mem. med. adv. bd. South Coll., 1996-2000; mem. parents coun. Washington U., St. Louis, 1997-2001, Tulane U., 2002-05, Tulane Med. Sch., 2005-06, Tulane Med. Alumni Assn, 2007; bd. dirs. Leadership Savannah, 1996-98, Darby Bank & Trust, 2007. Recipient Young Leadership award Savannah Jewish Fedn., 1985, Boss of Yr. award Savannah Jaycees, 1993, Celebrate Savannah award for outstanding contbns. to Savannah, Ga. Guardian, 1996; Harvard U. Med. Sch. fellow, 1976-77. Fellow: ACS; mem.: AMA, So. Med. Assn. (otolaryngology sec. 2006—07), Ga. Soc. Otolaryngology (pres. bd. trustees 1997—98, editor newsletter 1998—2001, Lester Brown Lifetime Achievement award 2005), Med. Assn. Ga. (mem. ho. of dels. 1990—2005, bd. dirs. 1995—2004, editl. bd. 2001—07, Ga. Cup award 1993, Ayest-Wyeth Cmty. Svc. award 1996, Cmty. Svc. award 2001), 1st Dist. Med. Assn. (pres. 1987—88), Ga. Med. Soc. (pres. 1992, chmn. bd. trustees 1997, chmn. endowment fund 2004—, John B. Rabun Cmty. Svc. award 1995, Hero's award 2001), Am. Neurotology Soc., Am. Soc. Head and Neck Surgery, Am. Acad. Otolaryngology and Head and Neck Surgery (tonsils and adenoids com. 1996—99, sleep disorders com. 1996—2002, pediat. otolaryngology com. 2003—, equilibrium com. 2005—). Office: Ear Nose and Throat Assocs Savannah 5201 Frederick St Savannah GA 31405-4501 Personal E-mail: MZ47ent@aol.com.

ZOLLINGER, CYNTHIA, financial consultant; BA, Wellesley Coll.; MBA, U. Chgo. Co-founder Cornerstone Rsch., mng. dir. Menlo Park, Calif., 1989—2007, pres., CEO, 2007—. Taught, grad. sch. bus. U. Chgo.; taught, grad. sch. bus. and law sch. Stanford U. Office: Cornerstone Research 1000 El Camino Real Menlo Park CA 94025 Office Phone: 650-853-1660. Business E-Mail: czolling@cornerstone.com. *

ZOLNO, MARK S., lawyer; BA Polit. Sci., No. Ill. Univ., 1965; JD, John Marshall Law Sch., 1978; MA cum laude Internat. Rels., Universidad de las Américas, Mexico, 1974. Bar: Ill. 1978, U.S. Dist. Ct. (no. dist.) Ill. 1979, U.S. Ct. Internat. Trade 1979, U.S. Ct. Appeals (fed. cir.) 1979. With U.S. Customs Svc., Dept. Commerce, U.S. Trade Rep's. Office, Internat. Trade Commn., Fed. Trade Commn., FDA; ptnr. Katten, Muchin, Rosenman, Chgo., 1988—. Past chmn. Chgo. Bar Assn. Customs and U.S. Trade Law Com.; lectr. in field. Contbr. articles to profl. jours. Office: Katten Muchin Rosenman 525 W Monroe St Ste 1900 Chicago IL 60661-3693 Office Phone: 312-902-5436. Business E-Mail: mark.zolno@kattelaw.com.

ZOLOT, MARVIN MITCHELL, internist; b. Chgo., May 10, 1931; s. Eli Zolot and Gussie Gagerman; m. Diane Rachel Calo, June 25, 1955; children: Madeline Eve Baron(dec.), Eric Adam, Amy Louise. BS, U. Ill., Urbana, 1952; MD, U. Ill., Chgo., 1956. Diplomate Am. Bd. Internal Medicine. Intern Phila. Gen. Hosp., 1956—57; resident internal medicine U. Ill. Rsch., Chgo., 1957—58; resident internal medicine, chief resident U. Wis. Gen. Hosp., Madison, 1960—62; pvt. practice Madison, 1960—85; med. dir. Trustmark Ins. Co., Lake Forest, Ill., 1985—95; cons. to ins. industry Chgo., 1995—2000; ret. Assoc. clin. prof. medicine U. Ill. Med. Sch., Chgo., 1960—85; dir. edn. U. Wis. at Madison Gen. Hosp., 1978—82; chmn. dept. internal medicine Madison Gen. Hosp., 1980—84; pres. Madison Gen. Rsch. Found., 1980—85. Author: B.S. Medicine, 1998. Chmn. social action com. Temple Beth El, Madison, 1980—82. Capt. USAR, 1958—60. Fellow: ACP (50 Yr. award 1996); mem.: AMA. Jewish. Avocation: antiques. Home: 5440 Caddis Bend #416 Fitchburg WI 53711

ZOLOTH, LAURIE SUSAN, bioethicist; b. LA, June 15, 1950; d. Arthur and Helen (Cohen) Zoloth; m. Henry Levy (div. June 1980); m. Daniel Zoloth Dorfman, Aug. 17, 1986; children: Matthew, Noah, Benjamin, Joshua, Sarah. BA cum laude, U. Calif., Berkeley, 1974; BSN, SUNY, 1982; MA in English, San Francisco State U., 1991; MA, PhD in Theology and Jewish Studies, Grad. Theol. Union, 1993. Instr. adult edn. Jewish studies Lehrahaus Judaica, 1988-93; cons. ethicist Nat. Kaiser Permanente HMO, Berkeley, Calif., 1987; prof. ethics, dir. Jewish Studies prog. San Francisco State U., 1995—2003; dir. Ctr. Bioethics, Sci. and Soc. Northwestern U., Chgo., dir. bioethics Ctr. Genetic Medicine, Ctr. Regenerative Medicine and Inst. Nanotechnology; prof. med. ethics and humanities Northwestern U. Feinberg Sch. Medicine; prof. religion, mem Jewish Studies faculty Northwestern U. Weinberg Coll. Arts and Scis. Instr. ethics Chapman Coll., 1989; lectr. clin. bioethics prog. Stanford U. Grad. Theol. Union, 1991—92, instr. bioethics prog., 1994; asst. prof. Calif. State U., Sonoma, 1994; mem. Nat. Adv. Coun. NASA, mem. Planetary Protection Adv. Com., mem. Interagency Nat. Animal Care and Use Com.; chair bioethics adv. bd. Howard Hughes Med. Inst.; mem. data safety monitoring bd. NIH Asia AIDS Vaccine Trials. Mem. editl. bd.: Am. Jour. Law, Medicine and Ethics, Jour. Clin. Ethics, Am. Jour. Bioethics; author: Health Care and The Ethics of Encounter, 1999; co-editor: Notes From a Nattow Ridge: Religion and Bioethics, Riding on Faith: Religion, Popular Culture and the World of Disney, Margin of Error: The Ethics of Mistakes in Medicine, The Human Embryonic Stem Cell Debate: Ethics, Religion and Policy. Recipient NASA Nat. Pub. Svc. award, 2005. Mem.: Am. Acad. Religion (chair sect. on women), Soc. Women's Health Rsch. (bd. mem.), Soc. Neuroethics (bd. mem.), Soc. Scriptural Reasoning (bd. mem.), Internat. Soc. Stem Cell Rsch. (bd. mem.), Am. Soc. Bioethics and Humanities (pres. 2001). Jewish. Office: Ctr Bioethics Sci and Soc Northwestern U 676 N St Clair Rm 1260 Chicago IL 60611 Office Phone: 312-926-2924. Business E-Mail: lzoloth@northwestern.edu.

ZOLVINSKI, SUSAN KAYE, medical director; b. Berrien Springs, Mich., Sept. 17, 1962; Degree in practical nursing, Lake Mich. Coll., 1982; AAS, Commonwealth Bus. Coll., 1997; BS in Healthcare Adminstrn., Kennedy-We. U., 2001; MBA, Argosy U., 2007. Office nurse Office of John H. Phillips, M.D., 1988-91; staff nurse St. Anthony Hosp., Michigan City, Ind., 1989-91; DON Med Watch, P.C., Michigan City, Ind., 1991-96; med. dir. Commonwealth bus. coll. Brown Mackie Coll., Michigan City, 1995—. Vol. instr. ARC, Michigan City, 1990—; guild vol. St. Anthony

Hosp., Michigan City, 1998. Mem. Am. Assn. Office Nurses, Nat. Assn. Physician's Nurses, Am. Med. Technologists, Am. Assn. Med. Assts., Nat. Network Health Career Programs, Nat. Assn. Physician Office Laboratorians, Alpha Beta Gamma. Office: Brown Mackie Coll 325 E Us Highway 20 Michigan City IN 46360-7362

ZOMBIE, ROB (ROBERT CUMMINGS), musician, filmmaker; b. Haverhill, Mass., Jan. 12, 1966; m. Sheri Moon, Oct. 31, 2002. Founding mem. White Zombie, 1985—96. Musician: (albums) (with White Zombie) Psycho-Head Blowout, 1986, Soul Crusher, 1987, Make Them Die Slowly, 1989, La Sexorcisto, 1992, Astro-Creep 2000, 1995, Supersexy Swingin' Sounds, 1996, (solo albums) Hellbilly Deluxe, 1998, American Made Music to Strip By, 1999, The Sinister Urge, 2001, Educated Horses, 2006; prodn. asst. (TV series) Pee-wee's Playhouse, 1986, writer, dir. (films) House of 1000 Corpses, 2003, writer, dir., prodr. The Devil's Rejects, 2005 (Chainsaw award, 2006), actor Slither, 2006, writer The Haunted World of El Superbeasto, 2006. Office: c/o The Firm Ste 1026 60 Madison Ave New York NY 10010

ZON, LEONARD I., pediatrics educator, researcher; b. Hartford, Conn. BS in Chemistry and Natural Sciences, Muhlenberg Coll., Allentown, Pa., 1979; MD, Jefferson Med. Coll., 1983. Diplomate Am. Bd. Internal Medicine; lic. physician, Mass. Rsch. asst. Jefferson Med. Coll., Phila., 1980-82; intern New Eng. Deaconess Hosp., Boston, 1983-84, from jr. to sr. resident in internal medicine, 1984-86; rsch. fellow Children's Hosp., Boston, 1987-90, founder, dir. Stem Cell Rsch. Program, Grousbeck prof. hematology/oncology; instr. Harvard Med. Sch., Boston, 1989-91, asst. prof. pediatrics, 1991—, mem. faculty grad. program biol. and biomed. scis., 1994—, prof. pediat. medicine, Children's Hosp. Boston; investigator Howard Hughes Med. Inst., 1993—. Guest faculty Okla. Health Scis. Ctr., 1993; lectr. in field. Contbr. articles to Am. Jour. Physiology, Jour. Clin. Microbiology, Lancet, Am. Jour. Medicine, Br. Jour. Haematology, Nature, Biotechniques, Molecular Cell Biology, Biology of Hematopoiesis, Jour. Biol. Chemistry. Recipient Hyman Menduke Rsch. awrd, 1983; Friends of the Farber fellow, 1987, Dana-Farber Cancer Inst. fellow, med. oncology, 1986-89; grantee NSF, 1978, NIH, 1980, 89—, Chalres H. Hood Found., 1990-92, Hoffmann-La Roche, 1991-94. Mem. AMA, AAAS, ACP, Am. Soc. Clin. Oncology, Am. Soc. Hematology, Am. Fisheries Soc., Mass. Med. Soc., Inst. Medicine., Internat. Soc. for Stem Cell Rsch. (founder, past pres.) Achievements include research in hematopoiesis, development, genetics. Office: Childrens Hosp Boston 300 Longwood Ave Karp-7 Boston MA 02115 also: Howard Hughes Med Inst New Rsch Bldg Rm 7211 1 Blackfan Cir Boston MA 02115 Office Phone: 617-919-2069. Office Fax: 617-730-0222. E-mail: zpn@enders.tch.harvard.edu.

ZONANA, VICTOR, lawyer, educator; b. Zagazig, Eqypt, Aug. 28, 1940; s. Isaac A. and Fortunee (Cohen Beyda) Z.; m. Mary Linda Haynie, Aug. 22, 1964; children: David A., Nancy B. Zonana Dickinson. BS in Econs., Hofstra U., 1961; LLB, NYU, 1964, LLM, 1966. Bar: N.Y. 1965. Assoc. Kaye, Scholer, Fierman, Hays & Handler, NYC, 1966-69; prof. NYU, 1969-80, adj. prof., 1981—, Charles S. Lyon vis. prof., 1994; dep. tax legis. counsel U.S. Dept. Treasury, 1975-76; cons. to asst. commr. IRS, 1975, office of chief counsel, 1994; counsel, ptnr. Kaye, Scholer, Fierman, Hays & Handler, NYC, 1980-87, Arnold & Porter, NYC, 1988—2001; prof. Bklyn. Law Sch., 1996—2002; prin. KPMG LLP, London, 2002—. Mem., chmn. adv. bd. NYU Tax Inst. Fellow Am. Coll. Tax Counsel; mem. ABA, N.Y. State Bar Assn. (co-chmn. com. on fgn. activities of U.S. taxpayers, chmn. com. on depreciation and investment credit, co-chmn. com. tax acctg. matters, com. tax policy). Office: KPMG LLP 8 Salisbury Sq London EC4Y 8BB England Home Phone: +44 (0)207 976 6964; Office Phone: +44 (0)207 694 1737.

ZONAY, THOMAS A., lawyer; b. 1963; BS; JD, Vt. Law Sch. Bar: Vt. 1988. Criminal def. lawyer Carrol, George & Pratt, Rutland, Vt.; ptnr. Ford & Zonay, P.C., Woodstock, Utah, 2000—. Mem.: Vt. Bar Assn. (pres. 2004—, mem. bd. mgrs.). Office: Ford & Zonay PC PO Box 388 Woodstock VT 05091-0388 Office Phone: 802-457-1000. Office Fax: 802-457-1874. E-mail: tazonay@sover.net. *

ZONIA, DHIMITRI, artist; b. St. Louis, June 12, 1921; s. Ligori and Polixenna Zonia; m. Margaret C. Wieland, July 11, 1927; children: Margaret E., Susan C., Carolynn L., Laura E. Ind. study, Italy and Eng., 1972. Editl. cartoonist Postmark Prague, 1984—86; editl. cartoonist illustrator Cry Justice Now, St. Louis, 1998—2000; staff mem. The Scene Newspaper, 2002—05. Vis. artist Albanian Nat. Gallery, Tirane, 2005. *Served in the intelligence unit with the 8th Air Corps in Europe during WWII. After receiving an honorable discharge worked for the Veterans Administration as an illustrator. Newspaper work starting with St. Louis Post Dispatch as a quality supervisor, and as an editorial cartoonist for Postmark Prague, Czech Republic, Cry Justice Now, an advocacy newspaper for prison inmates worldwide, and Zoa, a locally published charitable publication and The Scene, a campus newspaper of Forest Park Community College, St. Louis.* One-man shows include Tattershall Castle, London, 1982, Nat. Gallery Art, Tirana, Albania, 2001—05, Forest Pk. CC, St. Louis, 2004—05, exhibitions include Oak Grove Mauselium, 1972, Palais de Congress, Paris, 1976, Yamaha Corp., Madison Sq. Garden, NYC, 1977, Jewish Cmty. Ctr., 1978, Macdonnel Planetarium, St. Louis, 1978, Mo. Botanical Garden, 1988, Polish Bi-ennial, Warsaw, 1992, Anheuser-Busch Breweries Employees, 1992, St. Louis C.C., 2007, Represented in permanent collections St. Bernadette Mus. Sacred Art, Albuquerque, Okla. Art Ctr., Oklahoma City Ark. Art Ctr., Little Rock, Albrecht Art Ctr., St. Joseph, Mo., Rapid City Art Ctr., SD, Butler Inst. Am. Art, Youngstown, Ohio, pvt. collections, Am., Europe, Japan, Australia, cover photo, Savvy Family mag., 2006; author: Art and Poetry, 2006. Bd. govs. St. Louis Artists Guild, St. Louis, 1967. Recipient 1st prize for editl. art, Mo. Coll. Media Assn., 2002—05, 3d pl. award, 2006, Journalism award, ACLEU, 2006. Mem.: Soc. Ind. Artists (life; hon.). Mailing: 4680 Karamar Dr Saint Louis MO 63128 Personal E-mail: weizon@aol.com.

ZONIS, MARVIN, political scientist, educator; b. Boston, Sept. 18, 1936; s. Leonard and Clara (Barenberg) Z.; m. Lucy Salenger, Jan. 3, 1976; children by previous marriage-Nadia E. Leah; 1 stepdaugher, Brix E. Smith. AB, Yale U., 1958; postgrad., Harvard Grad. Sch. Bus., 1958-59; PhD, M.I.T., 1968; candidate, Inst. for Psychoanalysis, Chgo., 1977-85. Mem. faculty U. Chgo., 1966—, assoc. prof. and prof. behavioral scis., 1973-89—, prof. Grad. Sch. Bus., 1989—; dir. U. Chgo. (Center for Middle Eastern Studies), 1976-79; pres. Marvin Zonis and Assocs., Internat. Cons., 1991—. Cons. in field; chmn. com. on Middle East Am. Coun. Learned Socs.-Social Sci. Rsch. Coun., 1970-76; pres. Am. Inst. Iranian Studies, 1969-71; bd. dirs. CNA Fin. Corp. Author: The Political Elite of Iran, 1971, Khomeini, The Islamic Republic of Iran, and the Arab World, 1987, Majestic Failure: The Fall of the Shah, 1991, The East European Opportunity: The Complete Business Guide and Source Book, 1992; co-author The Kimchi Matters: Global Business and Local Politics in a Crisis Driven World, 2002; contbr. articles to profl. jours. Served with USAF, 1959-60. Recipient Quantrell award for excellence in teaching U. Chgo., 1979 Home: 4950 Chicago Beach Dr Chicago IL 60615 Office: U Chgo 5807 S Woodlawn Ave Chicago IL 60637-1515 Office Phone: 773-702-8753. Business E-mail: marvin.zonis@chicagogsb.edu. *Psychoanalytic approaches to the study of political phenomena open new vistas to understanding as well as facilitating the design of U.S. policy.*

ZOOG, ERIC JAMES, emergency physician; b. Hamilton Square, NJ, Aug. 9, 1969; s. James Edgar and Lorraine Zoog; m. Kimberly Lynne Simpson, Sept. 6, 1998; 1 child, Samantha Elise. MD, Med. Coll. Pa., Phila., 1995. Diplomate Am. Bd. Emergency Medicine, 2000, hyperbaric medicine team tng. Internat. ATMO, Inc., 2001, cert. EMT - Tactical Fed. Protective Svc., Dept. Homeland Security, 2005. Intern internal Medicine Ea. Va. Med. Sch., 1996, resident emergency medicine, 1999; mng. ptnr. Emergency Medicine Assocs. Jackson, Flowood, Miss., 2001—; med. dir. emergency dept. Miss. Bapt. Med. Ctr., Jackson, 2000—; ptnr. ER Innovations, PLLC, Flowood, 2006—. Med. team mgr. Va. Task Force 2, Fed. Emergency Mgmt. Agy., Virginia Beach, Va., 1998—99; dir. med. support Miss. Bur. Narcotics, Jackson, 2005—; ptnr. Tactical Med. Support, Brandon, Miss., 2006—. Contbr. chapters to books. Fellow: Am. Coll. Emergency Physicians. Home: 76 Grandview Cir Brandon MS 39047 Office: Emergency Medicine Associates of Jackson 2506 Lakeland Dr Ste 203 Flowood MS 39232 Home Phone: 601-829-0154; Office Phone: 601-936-6001. Office Fax: 601-936-8616. Personal E-mail: ericzoog@bellsouth.net.

ZOOGMAN, NICHOLAS JAY, lawyer; b. NYC, Apr. 2, 1947; s. Morris William and Hannah (Stern) Z.; m. Carla Ganz, June 7, 1970; children: Sarah Elizabeth, Peter William. BA, NYU, 1967; MA, Harvard U., 1969, JD, 1973. Bar: N.Y. 1974, U.S. Dist. Ct. (so. and ea. dists.) N.Y. 1974, U.S. Ct. Appeals (2d cir.) 1975, U.S. Supreme Ct. 1979, U.S. Dist. Ct. (ea. dist.) Mich. 1988, U.S. Ct. Appeals (D.C. cir.) 1990, U.S. Ct. Appeals (6th cir.) 1993, U.S. Ct. Appeals (5th cir.) 1997. Assoc. Donovan Leisure Newton & Irvine, NYC, 1973-75; ptnr. Anderson Kill & Olick, NYC, 1976-2000; counsel Dickstein Shapiro LLP, NYC, 2000—05, ptnr., 2006—. Mem. ABA, N.Y. State Bar Assn., Assn. Bar City of N.Y., Phi Beta Kappa, Pi Sigma Alpha. Office: Dickstein Shapiro LLP 1177 Avenue of Americas New York NY 10036-2714 Home Phone: 212-222-2720.

ZOOK, JOHN EDWIN, physician, surgeon, missionary; b. Tabor, Iowa, Oct. 3, 1924; s. Abram Eyster Zook and Eunice (Francis) Brenneman; m. Jeanne Pierson, Sept. 7, 1952; children: Rebecca Clair, Daniel John, Paul Michael. BA, Lewis and Clark Coll., 1950; MD, U. Oreg., 1954; cert. tropical medicine Antwerp Sch. Tropical Medicine, Belgium, 1956. Diplomate Am. Bd. Surgery. Intern Emanuel Hosp., Portland, Oreg., 1954-55; resident in surgery Good Samaritan Hosp., Portland, 1965-69; ednl. missionary Unevangelized Tribes Mission, Congo, 1943-46; med. missionary Congo Inland Mission, 1955-65; dir. med. activities Africa Intermennonite Mission, Republic of Congo, 1961-65, surgeon, 1969-77; practice medicine specializing in gen. surgery, Portland, 1977—2005; chief staff Mt. Hood Med. Ctr., 1982, Woodland Park Hosp., 1989; mem. bd. dirs., 1988-91; exchange physician China Ednl. Exchange Program, Chungquin Med. Coll., 1984-90. V.p. Mennonite Men of Mennonite Ch. USA, 1982—. Fellow ACS, Internat. Coll. Surgeons (Oreg. regent 1980-84, v.p. 1985), Portland Surg. Soc. Republican. Office: E Portland Surg Clinic 25500 SE Stark St Gresham OR 97030 Home Phone: 503-257-5190. Personal E-mail: jeannezook123@msn.com.

ZOON, KATHRYN CHRISTINE, biochemist; b. Yonkers, NY, Nov. 6, 1948; d. August R. and Violet T. (Pollock) Egloff; m. Robert A. Zoon, Aug. 22, 1970; children: Christine K., Jennifer R. BS, Rensselaer Poly. Inst., 1970; PhD, Johns Hopkins U., 1976. Rsch. chemist divsn. biochem. biophys. Bur. Biologics FDA, Bethesda, Md., 1980-84, rsch. chemist divsn. virology, 1984-88, rsch. chemist divsn. cytokine biology Ctr. Biologics, 1988—92, divsn. dir., 1989-92; dir. Ctr. Biologics Evaluation and Rsch., 1992—2003; dep. dir. Ctr. for Cancer Rsch. Nat. Cancer Inst., NIH, 2003—04; dep. dir. planning and devel. divsn. intramural rsch. NIAID, NIH, 2004—06, dir. divsn. intramural rsch., 2006—. Chmn. expert com. on biol. standardization WHO, 1997-98, 99, 2000, 01; mem. adv. com. of CMR, 2000-03; mem. adhoc expert on biology standardization WHO, 2004—; dir. NIH, NIAID, DIR; lectr. in field. Contbr. articles to rsch. in biol. chemistry to sci. jours.; sect. editor Jour. Interferon and Cytokine Rsch., 1980—. Bd. dirs. Found. Advanced Edn. Scis. 1996-2004, 1st v.p., 1999-03; mem. adv. bd. Def. Advance Rsch. Projects Agy., 1998-00, Inst. Medicine Nat. Acad. Sci., 2002-. Recipient Person of the Yr. award Biopharm, 1992, Pub. Svc. and Genetic Engring. News award, 1995, Presdl. Meritorious Exec. Rank award, 1994, Grateful Patient award Nat. Assn. Cancer Patients, 1997, Rensselaer Alumni Assn. award, 1997, Sec.'s award for disting. svc. Dept. Health and Human Svcs., 2001, 03, Disting. Alumnus award Johns Hopkins U., 2003; NY State Regents fellow, 1970, Interferon rsch. fellow NIH, Bethesda, 1975-77, staff fellow, 1979-80. Mem. Am. Soc. Biochem. and Molecular Biology, Intenat. Soc. Interferon and Cytokine Rsch. (pres. elect 1998-99, pres. 2000-01), Internat. Assn. Biol. Standardization (mem. adv. coun. 2000—), Inst. of Medicine. Roman Catholic. Office: NIAID/NIH Bldg 10 Rm 4A30A 10 Center Dr Bethesda MD 20892 Office Phone: 301-496-3006. Business E-Mail: kzoon@niaid.nih.gov.

ZOPF, EVELYN LANOEL MONTGOMERY, retired guidance counselor; b. Laurel, Miss., July 10, 1932; d. Arthur LaNoel and Ruby Lee (Lewis) Montgomery; m. Paul Edward Zopf, Aug. 5, 1956; 1 child, Eric Paul. MusB in Edn., U. So. Miss., 1953, MA, 1954. Guidance counselor U. So. Miss., 1953—54, U. Fla., 1954—56; tchr. New Orleans City Schs., 1956—57; pub. sch. music tchr., band dir., choral dir. Putnam County Schs., Fla., 1957—59; pvt. music tchr. voice, piano, clarinet and trumpet, 1953—61; substitute tchr. Guilford County Schs., 1959—93. Mem. arts series com. Guilford Coll., 1973—77; interim choir dir. New Garden Friends Meeting, 1961, chmn. music com., 1974—76; adviser to fgn. students, 1954—56, 1959—62; mem. First Internat. Congress on Quaker Edn. Com., 1987—88, Guilford Coll.'s Sesquicentennial Com., 1985—87; spkr. various religious and art groups. Vol. ARC, Boy Scouts Am.; active U. Fla. Union Bd., 1955—56; vol. com. worker NC dist. auditions Met. Opera, 1999—2001; precinct del. County Dem. Conv., 1977, 1979, precinct worker, 1980, campaign worker, 1980; bd. dirs. Greensboro Friends of Music, 1970—71; bd. dirs. Greensboro chpt. NC Symphony Bd., 1979—83; feeder bd. Guilford Coll. Friends of the Lib. Bd., 1993—94, exec. bd., 1994—95. Mem.: United Soc. of Friends Women (pres. 1979—81), Internat. Fellowship Quaker Women, Guilford Coll. Cmty. Chorus, Women's Soc. (dir. 1978—82), Guilford Coll. Arts Appreciation (v.p. 1980—81, pres. 1981—82), Guilford Gourmet Club, Phi Mu. Home: 815 George White Rd Greensboro NC 27410-3317

ZOPFI, EMMA G., elementary school educator; arrived in U.S., 1961; d. Gilberto L. and Maria B. Garcia; m. Charles W. Zopfi, Dec. 2, 1975; children: Charles W. Jr., Catherine Marie. BS in Bilingual Elem. Edn., U. Tex., El Paso, 1989. 2d grade tchr. North Loop Elem., El Paso, 1989—2000, 3d grade tchr., 2001—02, 4th grade tchr., 2002—. Gifted & talented tchr. North Loop Elem., El Paso, 2003—06; grade level rep. CEIC-North Loop Elem., 2005—; tchr. rep. Bel Air area Sci. Scope & Seq. Revision Com., El Paso, 2005—06. Vol. Bel Air HS Theater, El Paso, 2001—02, Christo Rey Ch., El Paso, 2001—02. Named Tchr. of the Yr., YISD, 1998—99, 2002—03; grantee. Mem.: ATPE, State Tchr. Sci. Assn., Soc. for the Advancement of Chicanos in Sci. Assn. Avocations: sewing, crafts. Office: North Loop Elem 412 Emerson El Paso TX 79915 Business E-Mail: ezopfi@yisd.net.

ZOPP, ANDREA LYNNE, lawyer, retail executive; b. Rochester, NY, Jan. 25, 1957; d. Reuben K. and P. Greta (Hurst) Davis; m. William E. Zopp, Jr., Oct. 7, 1989; children: Alyssa, Kelsey, William. BA cum laude, Harvard Coll., 1978; JD, Harvard U., 1981. Bar: Ill. 1981, U.S. Dist. Ct. (no. dist.) Ill. 1981, U.S. Ct. Appeals (7th cir.) 1982. Law clk. Hon. George N. Leighton, U.S. Dist. Ct., Chgo., 1981-83; asst. U.S. atty. U.S. Atty.'s Office, Chgo., 1983-86, dept. chief OCDETF, 1986-88, dep. chief criminal lit., 1988-90; ptnr. McDermott, Will & Emery, Chgo., 1990-91; chief narcotics prosecutions bur. Cook County State's Attys. Office, Chgo., 1991-92, first asst. state's atty., 1992—96; ptnr. Sonnenschein Nath & Rosenthal, 1997—2000; v.p., dep. gen. counsel Sara Lee Corp., 2000—03; sr. v.p., gen. counsel Sears, Roebuck & Co., Hoffman Estates, Ill., 2003—. Mem. Gov.'s Commn. on Capital Punishment, State of Illinois, 2000—. Bd. dirs. Aux. Bd., Art Inst. Chgo., 1987-2000; bd. dirs. Chgo. Regional Bd. of Jr. Achievement, 1991-95, Chgo. Area Project, 1992—. Fellow Leadership Greater Chgo., 1989-90; Kizzy Scholarship Fund award, 1991-92. Fellow Am. Bar Found., Am. Coll. Trial Lawyers; Mem. ABA, Chgo. Bar Assn., Chgo. Inn of Ct., Cook County Bar Assn., Black Women Lawyers Assn., Leadership Greater Chgo. (bd. dirs.). Avocations: running, music, theater. Office: Sears Roebuck & Co 3333 Beverly Rd Hoffman Estates IL 60179 *

ZORC, RENEE, school librarian; m. Bill Zorc; children: Katie, Danny. Libr. Daniel Wright Jr. HS, Lincolnshire, Ill. Recipient Collaborative Sch. Libr. Media award, AASL, 2007. Mem.: Ill. Sch. Libr. Media Assn., Nat. Bd. Profl. Teaching Standards, N. Suburban Libr. Sys. Office: Daniel Wright Jr HS 1370 Riverwoods Rd Lincolnshire IL 60069 Office Phone: 847-259-1560.

ZORE, EDWARD JOHN, financial services executive; b. Milw., July 5, 1945; s. Joseph F. and Marie A. Z.; m. Diane Widemshek, Aug. 19, 1967; children: Annemarie, Kathryn. BS in Econs., U. Wis., Milw., 1968, MS in Econs., 1970. With investment dept. Northwestern Mut. Fin. Network, Milw., 1969—, chief investment officer, 1990—98, CFO, 1995—98, exec. v.p. life and disability income ins., 1998—2000, pres., 2000—, CEO, 2001—. Bd. trustees Northwestern Mut. Fin. Network, 2000—; bd. dirs. Manpower, Inc., 2000—. Republican. Roman Catholic. Office: Northwestern Mutual 720 E Wisconsin Ave Milwaukee WI 53202-4797 *

ZORIE, STEPHANIE MARIE, lawyer; b. Walla Walla, Wash., Mar. 18, 1951; d. Albert Robert and L. Ruth (Land) Z.; m. Francis Benedict Buda, Apr. 18, 1981 (div. 1985). BA, U. Fla., 1974, JD, 1978. Bar: N.Mex. 1991, Fla. 1978, U.S. Dist. Ct. (so. and mid. dists.) Fla. 1979, U.S. Ct. Appeals (5th cir.) 1979, U.S. Tax Ct. 1980, U.S. Ct. Customs and Patent Appeals 1980, U.S. Customs Ct. 1980, U.S. Ct. Mil. Appeals 1980, U.S. Ct. Claims 1981, U.S. Ct. Internat. Trade 1981, U.S. Ct. Appeals (11th cir.) 1981, U.S. Ct. Appeals (fed. cir.) 1982, U.S. Supreme Ct. 1988; cert. civil ct. mediator Fla. Supreme Ct.; cert. family mediator, N.Mex. Assoc. Richard Hardwich, Coral Gables, Fla., 1978-79, Brown, Terrell & Hogan P.A., Jacksonville, Fla., 1979-80, Dorsey, Arnold & Nichols, Jacksonville, Fla., 1980-81; sole practice Jacksonville, Fla., 1981-84; ptnr. Blakeley & Zorie P.A., Orlando, Fla., 1985-86; sole practice Orlando, Fla., 1986—, Santa Fe. Owner Coyote Cody Co., 1991. Recipient Rep. Claude Pepper award, 1978. Mem. John Marshall Bar Assn., Spanish-Am. Law Students Assn., Phi Alpha Delta (local sec.-treas. 1978-79). Avocations: water sports, needlecrafts, cooking. Office: PO Box 2898 Santa Fe NM 87504-2898 also: PO Box 372118 Satellite Beach FL 32937-0118 Home Phone: 505-986-6121, 321-777-0593; Office Phone: 505-660-8412, 321-777-0593. Personal E-mail: zorieblue@yahoo.com.

ZORN, ERIC STUART, retail executive; b. Newark, Oct. 2, 1948; s. Arthur and Evelyn (Bernstein) Z.; m. Lois Karen Green, Nov. 29, 1979. Student, Fairleigh Dickinson Coll., Wayne, NJ, Upsala Coll., East Orange, NJ. Cash ops. supr. Vornado Inc., Garfield, N.J., 1966-69; corp. auditor Mangel Stores Corp., NYC, 1969-70; sr. v.p. Jamesway Corp., Secaucus, NJ, 1970; pres. Omnia Protective Services Inc., Ft. Lee, NJ, 1979, 1530 Owners Corp. (coop. bldg.), Ft. Lee; regional v.p. Wal-Mart Stores Inc., 1993—97, v.p. realty, 1997—99, sr. v.p. realty, 1999, pres. realty, 2003—05, exec. v.p. Wal-Mart Realty, 2005—. Mem. Internat. Mass Retailing Inst. (chmn. loss prevention group 1979-82), NJ Retail Mchts. Assn. (chmn.), Internat. Soc. Stress Analysts, Soc. Strategic Planning, Internat. Coun. Shopping Centers (trustee). Republican. Jewish. Office: Wal-Mart Realty 2001 SE 10th St Bentonville AR 72712-6489

ZORN, JOHN, composer, musician; b. NYC, Sept. 2, 1953; Band mem. Naked City, NYC, 1989—94; founder, mem. Masada, 1994—; founder & exec. prodr. Tzadik record label, NYC, 1995—. Numerous commissions including NY Philharm., Kronos Quartet, Am. Composers Orch., Bklyn. Philharm., Stephen Drury, Bayerische Staatsoper, WDR Orch. Köln. Major compositions include: Christabel, 1972, Conquest of Mexico, 1973, Mikhail Zoetrope, 1974, Lacrosse, 1977, Hockey, 1978, Fencing, 1978, The Book of Heads, 1978, Pool, 1979, Archery, 1979, Track & Field, 1980, Locus Solus, 1982, Sebastopol, 1983, Rugby, 1983, Cobra, 1984, Xu Feng, 1985, Godard, 1985, Spillane, 1986, Hu Die, 1986, Ruan Lingyu, 1987, Hwang Chin-ee, 1988, Cat O'Nine Tails, 1988, Quê Trân, 1988, For Your Eyes Only, 1989, Bézique, 1989, Torture Garden, 1990, Grand Guignol, 1990, Dead Man, 1990, Elegy, 1991, Leng Tch'e, 1991, Carny, 1992, Memento Mori, 1992, Kristallnacht, 1992, Absinthe, 1992, Angelus Novus, 1993, Masada, 1993-97, The Sand's Share, 1994, Redbird, 1995, Dark River, 1995, Aporias, 1995, Music for Children, 1996, Duras, 1996, Kol Nidre, 1996, Orchestra Variations, 1996, Etant Donnés, 1997, Shibboleth, 1997, Cycles du Nord, 1998, Rituals, 1998, The String Quartets, 1999, Cartoon S&M, 2000, Love, Madness & Mysticism, 2001, Hockey, 2002, Hemophiliac, 2002, Magick, 2004, Rituals, 2005, Mysterium, 2005, Moonchild, 2006; composer for films: White & Lazy, 1986, She Must Be Seeing Things, 1987, Distribution of Lead, 1988, The Golden Boat, 1990, Maohgai, 1993, Hollywood Hotel, 1994, Zigrail, 1995, The Black Glove, 1997, Trembling Before G-d, 2001, Secret Lives: Hidden Children & Their Rescuers During WWII, 2002, Shaolin Ulysses, 2003, Invitation to a Suicide, 2004, Protocols of Zion, 2005, The Treatment, 2006; appears in films: Rising Tones Cross, 1985, Put More Blood Into the Music, 1987, The Revenge of the Dead Indians, 1993, Sabbath in Paradise, 1998, A Bookshelf on Top of the Sky: 12 Stories About John Zorn, 2002, Jack Smith & the Destruction of Atlantis, 2006. MacArthur fellow, John D. & Catherine T. MacArthur Found., 2006. Office: Tzadik PMB 126 200 E 10th St New York NY 10003 E-mail: info@tzadik.com.

ZORN, ROBERT LYNN, education educator; b. Youngstown, Ohio, Mar. 22, 1938; s. Robert S. and Frances L. Zorn; m. Joan M. Wilkos, Apr. 26, 1957; children: Deborah Lynn, Patricia Lynn. BS in Edn., Kent State U., 1959; MEd, Westminster Coll., 1964; PhD, U. Pitts., 1970. Tchr. West Branch (Ohio) Pub. Schs., 1961—62; H.S. unit prin. Boardman Schs., 1967—70; dir. adminstrv. svcs. Mahoning County Schs., 1970—73, asst. supt., 1973—76; elem. prin. Poland Schs., 1962—67, supt. schs., 1976—. Adj. prof. edn. Westminster Coll., 1985—; chmn. Ohio Adv. Com. State Dept. Edn., McGuffey Hist. Soc. Nat. Educator's Hall of Fame. Author: Speed Reading, 1989, rev. edit., 1997; contbr. articles to profl. jours. Chmn. Mahoning County chpt. Am. Cancer Soc.; pres. bd. trustees Poland Meth. Ch.; trustee Mahoning County chpt. Am. Heart Assn. To lt. USAF, 1959—61. Mem.: Am. Assn. Sch. Adminstrs., Doctoral Assn. Educators (life), Ohio PTA (life), Rotary, Fonderlac County Club, Protestant Men's Club, Phi Delta Kappa. Republican. Office: 30 Riverside Dr Youngstown OH 44514-2049 Office Phone: 330-757-7000. Business E-Mail: polarz@access-k12.org.

ZORNES, MILFORD, artist; b. Camargo, Okla., Jan. 25, 1908; s. James Francis and Clara Delphine (Lindsay) Z.; m. Gloria Codd, 1935; 1 son, Franz Milford; m. Patricia Mary Palmer, Nov. 8, 1942; 1 dau., Maria Patricia. Student, Otis Art Inst., Los Angeles, 1929, Pomona Coll., 1930-34. Instr. art Pomona Coll., 1946-50; art dir. Vortox and Padua Hills Theatre, Claremont, 1954-66. Exhibited at Calif. Watercolor Soc., Met. Mus., Am. Watercolor Soc., Corcoran Gallery, Bklyn. Mus., Denver Mus., Cleve. Mus., L.A. Mus., Brooks Gallery, London, Bombay Art Assn., Chgo. Art Inst., Butler Mus., Gallery Modern Masters, Washington, Santa Barbara (Calif.) Mus., Cin. Mus., Laguna (Calif.) Art Gallery, Oklahoma City Mus., Springville (Utah) Mus., Claremont (Calif.) Fine Arts, Anderson Art Gallery, Sunset Beach, Calif., Aartists Trail GAllery, Claremont;

represented in permanent collections at L.A. Mus., White House Collection, Met. Mus., Pentagon Bldg., Butler Mus., UCLA, Nat. Acad., San Diego Mus., L.A. County Fair, Home Savs. and Loan Assn., L.A., Corcoran Gallery, Washington; mem. art com., Nat. Orange Show, San Bernardino, Calif., 1963-65; author: A Journey to Nicaragua, 1977, The California Style: California Watercolor Artists, 1925-1955, 1985; subject of book by Gordon McClelland: Milford Zornes, Hillcrest Press, 1991. Served with U.S. Army, 1943-45, CBI. Recipient Paul Prescott Barrow award Pomona Coll., 1987, David Prescott Burrows award, 1991, A Most Disting. Citizen award So. Utah State Coll., 1988, Am. Artist Achievement award Am. Artist Mag., 1994; named Nat. Academician. Mem. NAD, Am. Watercolor Soc., Southwestern Watercolor Soc., Watercolor West, Nat. Watercolor Soc., Utah Watercolor Soc. Address: 2136 Brescia Ave Claremont CA 91711-1804 *It has been my effort in life to have awareness: not to have all knowledge because no one can encompass all knowledge; not to have only wealth or only success, because there is no dimension of completeness of wealth or success; not to achieve complete goodness, because goodness and right are relative; not to enjoy the epitomy in taste because taste is a gratification of self alone; but rather to seek and achieve understanding of relative values and a concept of the completeness of life. With this as my effort and my inner goal, I find success within the areas of my limited abilities, my meager knowledge, and my frail grasp of the infinite.*

ZORNOW, DAVID MERRILL, lawyer; b. NYC, Mar. 31, 1955; s. Jack and Marion (Gilden) Z.; m. Martha Malkin, July 21, 1985; children: Samuel Morris, Hannah Jane, Ethan Lewis. AB summa cum laude, Harvard U., 1976; JD, Yale U., 1980. Bar: NY 1981, DC 1988, US Ct. Appeals (3d cir.) 1982, US Dist. Ct. (so. dist.) NY 1983, US Ct. Appeals (2d cir.) 1984, US Dist. Ct. DC 1989, US Ct. Appeals (DC cir.) 1989, US Dist. Ct. (ea. dist.) NY 1993. Law clerk to Hon. Herbert J. Stern US Dist. Ct. NJ, Newark, 1980-82; assoc. Kramer Levin Kamin Nessen & Frankel, NYC, 1982-83; asst. US atty. So. Dist. NY US Atty.'s Office, NYC, 1983-87; assoc. ind. counsel Office Ind. Counsel-Iran/Contra Investigation, Washington, 1987-89; ptnr., head NY white collar criminal def. practice Skadden, Arps, Slate, Meagher & Flom LLP, NYC, 1989—. Chmn. NYC Civilian Complaint Rev. Bd., 1994-96; vis. faculty Trial Advocacy Workshop Harvard Law Sch., Cambridge, Mass., 1988, Benjamin N. Cardozo Sch. Law; spkr. and writer on white collar crime issues. Contbr. articles to profl. publ. Mem. Fed. Bar Coun., Assn. Bar City NY, NY Coun. Def. Lawyers., Phi Beta Kappa. Office: Skadden Arps Slate Meagher & Flom LLP 4 Times Sq Fl 39 New York NY 10036-6595 Office Phone: 212-735-2890. Office Fax: 917-777-2890. E-mail: dzornow@skadden.com.

ZOROWSKI, CARL FRANK, engineering educator, academic administrator; b. Pitts., July 14, 1930; s. Stanley and Mary Josephine (Kozuch) Z.; m. Sarah Jane Crossley, Aug. 7, 1954 (dec. 1983); children: Kathleen Ann, Karl Alan, Kristine Alaine; m. Louise Parrish Lockwood, Apr. 13, 1985. BSME, Carnegie Inst. Tech., 1952, MSME, 1953, PhD, 1956. Instr. Carnegie Inst. Tech., Pitts., 1952-56, asst. prof., 1956-61, assoc. prof., 1961-62; prof. dept. mech. and aero. engring. N.C. State U., Raleigh, 1964-66; R.J. Reynolds Industries prof., 1966-97; assoc. dept. head, 1964-72; dept. head, 1972-79; assoc. dean acad. affairs Sch. Engring., 1979-85; dir. Integrated Mfg. Sys. Inst., 1986-92; dept. head, 1992-93; dir. Succeed/NSF Coalition, 1993-97; assoc. dean acad. affairs, 1993-94; R.J. Reynolds Industries emeritus prof., 1997—. Contbr. articles to profl. jours.; patentee in field. 2d lt. USAR, 1952-58. Recipient Rsch. award Sigma Xi, 1967. Fellow ASME (Richards Meml. award 1975), Fellow Am. Soc. Engring. Edn. (We. Electric award 1968); mem. Fiber Soc. (Achievement award 1970). Home: 103 Windyrush Ln Cary NC 27511-9758 Office: NC State U PO Box 7901 Raleigh NC 27695-0001 Home Phone: 919-851-3145. Personal E-mail: zorowski@mindspring.com. Business E-Mail: zorowski@eos.ncsu.edu.

ZORTHIAN, BARRY, communications executive; b. Kutahia, Turkey, Oct. 8, 1920; naturalized, US, 1930; s. Herbert Peter and Annaly (Markarian) Zorthian; m. Margaret Aylaian, June 6, 1948; children: Gregory Jannig, Stephen Arnak. BA, Yale U., 1941; LLB, N.Y. U., 1953; LLD (hon.), Ind. Inst. Tech., 1970. Bar: NY 1953. Newspaper reporter, 1936-42; newspaper and radio reporter, 1947-48; news and policy editor USIA, 1948-56, program mgr. Voice of Am., 1956-61; dep. pub. affairs. officer USIS, India, 1961-64; min.-counselor for info. Am. Embassy, Vietnam, 1964-68; v.p. Time, Inc., 1969-79, v.p. govt. affairs, 1974-79; pres. Time-Life Broadcast, 1969-73, Washington/Balt. Regional Assn., 1979-81; sr. v.p. Gray and Co., Washington, 1981-84; ptnr. Alcalde & Fay, Arlington, Va., 1984—. Bd dirs Am. Univ. Armenia, Armenian Gen Benvolent Union, Internat. Rsch. and Exchs. With USMC, 1942—46, col USMCR, 1946—73. Mem.: Marine Corps Res. Officers Assn., Washington Inst. Fgn. Affairs, Am. Fgn. Svc. Assn., Coun. Fgn. Rels., Congl. Country Club (Washington), Met. Club (Washington), Burning Tree Club (Washington), Century Assn. Club (N.Y.C.). Home: 4201 Cathedral Ave NW Apt 405E Washington DC 20016-4914 Office: Alcalde & Fay 2111 Wilson Blvd Ste 850 Arlington VA 22201-3051 Office Phone: 703-841-0626. Personal E-mail: barzor2@aol.com.

ZOSIKE, JOANIE FRITZ, theater director, actress; b. Bklyn., July 6, 1949; d. Nathan and Gloria S. (Greenberg) Hieger; m. Godson Zosike. BA in Theatre, NYU, 1980. Actor The Living Theatre, NYC, 1990—. Co-dir. DADAnewyork; co-founder and co-dir. Action Racket Theatre, N.Y.C., 1998—; artist-in-residence Living Theatre Workshops (USA) Author: (stage prodns.) You Told Me That the Carousel Was Crystal, Frames, Inside, 12 Steps to Murder; author: (with Hanon Reznikov) And Then The Heavens Closed; actress (stage prodns.) Chisciotte, Not in My Name, Mysteries and Smaller Pieces, Utopia, Anarchia, Humanity, Body of God, I and I, Midsummer Night's Dream, Mother Courage, Resistance, (solo performances) All Right So I AM the Earth, Harpies Complex, Ereshkigal's Peg, Fritzgabriel Cabaret, Alen Mak Festival (Bulgaria), Festival des Politisches Liedes (Germany), (films) Mass and Masses, Human Flesh; vocalist (radio show) Women on the Edge of Time; contbr. Between Ourselves: Letters Between Mothers and Daughters (edited by Karen Payne), Women in American Theatre (edited by Helen Krich Chinoy and Linda Walsh Jenkins); contbr. poetry and articles to artistic jours. Bd. dirs. N.Y.C. Peoples Life Fund; participating artist Theatres Against War. Mem. War Resisters League, New Yorkers Against the Death Penalty. Office: The Living Theatre 21 Clinton St New York NY 10009

ZOTTER, BRUCE C., lawyer; b. New Britain, Conn., Sept. 18, 1942; BSME, MIT, 1965, MSME, 1966; JD with honors, George Washington U., 1975. Bar: Va. 1975, DC 1976, registered: US Patent & Trademark Office. Ptnr. Finnegan, Henderson, Farabow, Garrett & Dunner LLP, Washington, leader, Mech. Practice Group. Mem.: Am. Intellectual Property Law Assn., ABA, Va. Bar Assn., Bar Assn. DC, DC Bar, Sigma Xi, Pi Tau Sigma. Office: Finnegan Henderson Farabow Garrett & Dunner LLP 901 New York Ave NW Washington DC 20001-315 Office Phone: 202-408-4000. Office Fax: 202-408-4400. Business E-Mail: zotterb@finnegan.com.

ZOU, CHANGPING, research scientist, educator; arrived in U.S., 1986; d. Daming Zou and Yidi Zhao; m. Sui Zhang; children: Aaron Tan Zou-Zhang, Philip Tigar Zou-Zhang. MD, Beijing Med. Coll., 1983; MPH, U Tex., Houston, 1990; PhD, U. Tex., Houston, 1994. Postdoctoral fellow U. Tex. MD Anderson Cancer Ctr., Houston, 1994—97, instr., 1997—98, asst. prof., 1998—2003; faculty mem. Grad. Sch. Biomed, Sci. U. Tex., Houston, 1998—2003; assoc. prof. U. Ariz., Tucson, 2003—. Grantee, Ovarian Cancer Rsch. Fund, 2004—05, Cervical Cancer Rsch., 2000—01, 2002—03; Cancer Prevention Grad. fellow, NCI, 1994—95. Mem.: Internat. Soc. Cancer Chemoprevention, Am. Soc. Preventive Oncology, Am. Assn. Cancer Rsch., Peking U. Alumni Assn. (bd. dirs. 2000—03). Achievements include patents pending for nutral products in cancer chemoprevention; research in Vitamin A derivatives in head and neck cancer chemoprevention; Vitamin A derivatives in bladder cancer chemoprevention. Office: U Ariz 1501 N Campbell Ave Tucson AZ 05078 Home Phone: 713-592-9838; Office Phone: 520-626-8883. Office Fax: 520-626-9287. Personal E-mail: zou@email.arizona.edu.

ZOU, DEKUN, research scientist; PhD, NJ Inst. Tech., Newark, 2005. Rsch. asst. NJ Inst. Tech., 2001—05; rschr. Thomson Corp. Rsch., Princeton, NJ, 2005—. Recipient Best Paper award, Internat. Workshop on Digital Watermarking, 2006. Mem.: IEEE. Achievements include patents pending for nethod and apparatus for lossless image data hiding that does not generate salt-pepper noise and is robust against compression; system and method for data hiding using inter-word space modulation; film grain technology based video watermarking.

ZOU, LINDA, bank executive; BS in Bus. Adminstrn., Baruch Coll. Various positions in banking; with Country Bank, The Bank of East Asia, Ltd., Independence Cmty. Bank; asst. v.p., underwriter Valley Nat. Bank, NYC; v.p. NY Bus. Devel. Corp., Albany, 2006—. Office: NY Bus Devel Corp 50 Beaver St Albany NY 12207 Office Phone: 212-803-3670. E-mail: lzou@nybdc.com.

ZOUBAREFF, KATHY OLGA, administrative assistant; b. Hassalt, Belgium; d. Vladimir F. and Kataryna (Sarcov) Z. Grad. in TV acting, J.R. Powers Sch.-Model Agy.; BA in Polit. Sci., Wayne State U.; postgrad., Ann Parsley Sch. Dance, Clinton Twp., Mich., 1990-95, Mary Skiba Sch. Dance, 1995—; A in Gen. Studies, Drama, Macomb Community Coll.; fitness and nutrition cert., Internat. Corr. Schs. Ctr., Scranton, Pa.; voice studies, Ctr. for Creative Studies, Detroit, 1994—; drama studies, Wayne State U., 1994—; broadcasting studies, Macomb C.C., Warren, Mich., 2001. Acct./adminstrv. asst. Univ. Orthopaedic Assocs. Detroit, P.C., 1990-96, office mgr., 1996-98; with The Zoubareff Co., 1998—. Actress, dancer, fashion, TV comml. and photog. model/film screen extra, Hawaiian Tropic Pageants; fragrance model Coty Fragrances, Celion Dion; swimsuit model Ujena; nat. spokesperson Dryell, Physique, Pantene, Oil of O'Lay, Vidal Sassoon, Cover Girl, Coca Cola, Marlboro, Nascar, Indy 400, others; voice over talent, Mae West look-alike; beauty cons. Olay, Cover Girl, Rimmell, London, Lee Jeans. Mem. Renaissance Ctr. Fashion Panel, Detroit, 1989-91; rsch. bd. advisors Am. Biog. Inst.; mem. Internat. Biog. Centre Adv. Coun., 1992, St. Clair Shores Players; contbg. Am. Film Inst., L.A., 2006 Avocations: art, drawing, exercise. Home: 38579 Delta Dr Clinton Township MI 48036-1711 Office Phone: 373-577-3447. Personal E-mail: madonna48036@yahoo.com.

ZOUHARY, JACK, federal judge; b. Toledo, Dec. 18, 1951; BA cum laude, Dartmouth Coll., 1973; Rufus Choate scholar; JD, U. Toledo Coll. Law, 1976. Atty. Robison, Curphey & O'Connell, Toledo, 1976—99, Fulley & Henry, Ltd., Toledo, 2004—05; sr. v.p. & gen. counsel S.E. Johnson Companies, Maumee, Ohio, 2000—03; judge Lucas County Common Pleas Ct., 2005—06, US Dist. Ct. (No. dist.) Ohio, 2006—. Mem.: ABA, Inns of Ct. - Morrison Waite ch., Am. Assn. Trial Lawyers, Toledo Bar Assn., Ohio Bar Assn. Office: 203 US Ct House 1716 Spielbusch Ave Toledo OH 43604-1363 Office Phone: 419-213-5675. Office Fax: 419-213-5680. *

ZOURARAKIS, DEMETRIO PERIFERACHIS, natural resource scientist; b. Buenos Aires, Argentina, Mar. 2, 1952; s. Jorge Demetrio Zourarakis and Elena Periferachis, Jorge Periferachis and Palmira Angela Comerci; m. Joyce Carol Zourakis, July 13, 1945; 1 child, Zachary Alexander. BS, Universidad Nacional de Buenos Aires, 1977; MSc, Iowa State U., Ames, 1987; PhD, U. Ky., Lexington, 1992. Geog. info. sys. processing specialist divsn. conservation Ky. Dept. Natural Resources, Frankfort, 2000—04; remote sensing and geog. info. sys. analyst divsn. geog. info. Commonwealth Office Tech., Frankfort, 2004—. Adj. prof. dept. geography and geosciences U. Louisville, 1998—. J. Fielding Reed fellow, Potash and Phosphate Inst., 1988. Fellow: Soil and Water Conservation Soc. (mem. Ky. Bluegrass chpt.); mem.: Mensa, Gamma Sigma Delta, Sigma Xi (hon.). Home: 5011 Venetian Way Versailles KY 40383 Office: Commonwealth Office Tech Divsn Geog Info 403 Wapping St Ste 340 Frankfort KY 40601 Home Phone: 859-873-2177. Personal E-mail: demetrio.zourarakis@gmail.com. Business E-Mail: demetrio.zourarakis@ky.gov.

ZRNIC, DUSAN S., research scientist, educator; b. Belgrade, Serbia, Serbia-Monteneg (Yugoslavia), June 3, 1942; s. Slobodan J. and Vera D. Zrnic. PhD, U. Ill., 1969. Rsch. asst. U. Ill., Urbana, 1965—69; prof. dept. elec. engring. Calif. State U., Northridge, 1969—78. Leader Doppler Radar Project, sr. scientist Nat. Severe Storms Lab., Norman. Author: (R&D, edn.) Doppler Radar and Weather Observations, 1993 (IEEE Harry Diamond award, 1988). Recipient Presdl. Rank Award, 2005. Mem.: NAE. Office: NOAA/NSSL 1313 Halley Cr Norman OK 73069 Office Phone: 405-366-0403.

ZSCHAU, JULIUS JAMES, lawyer; b. Peoria, Ill., Apr. 1, 1940; s. Raymond Johann Ernst and Rosamond Lillian (Malicoat) Z.; m. Leila Joan Krueger, Aug. 7, 1971; children: Kristen Elisabeth, Kimberly Erna, Kira Jamie White, Karla Johanna. BS, U. Ill., Champaign, 1964, JD, 1966; LLM, John Marshall Law Sch., 1978. Bar: Ill. 1966, Fla. 1975. Atty. Ill. Central Gulf R.R. Co., Chgo., 1966-68; assoc. Coin & Sheerin, Chgo., 1968-70, Snyder, Clarke et al, Waukegan, Ill., 1970-72; counsel Ill. Ctr. Corp., Chgo., 1972-74; v.p., gen. counsel, sec. Am. Agronomics Corp., Tampa, Fla., 1974-76; pres. Sorota & Zschau, Clearwater, Fla., 1976-90; shareholder Baynard, Harrell, Ostow & Ulrich PA, 1990-94, Johnson, Blakely, Pope, Bokor, Ruppel and Burns, Clearwater, 1994—2002, Pennington Moore Wilkinson Bell & Dunbar PA, 2002—. Bd. dirs. Attys. Title Ins. Fund, Inc., chmn. bd. dirs., 1994—95; chmn. com. on land trusts Fla. Bar, past chmn. Real Property, Probate and Trust Law sect., vice chair grievance com., 1985—87, chair leadership conf., 1987; chmn. Jud. Nominating Commn. of 6th Jud. Dist., 1991—94; chmn. jud. nominating com. Ct. Appeals (2d dist.). Mem. Pinellas County Exec. Com., Tampa Regional Planning Coun., 1988-92. Served to capt. USNR, 1962-92. Fellow: Am. Bar Found. (life); mem.: ABA (chmn. standing com. lawyers title guaranty funds 1991, chmn. land trust com., chmn. standing com. lawyers title guaranty funds 2004—07), Fla. Bar Found. (chmn. jud. nominations procedures com. 1992—93, legal aid to poor com.), Fla. Con. Bar Assn. (past pres., past chmn. vol. bar liaison com.), Clearwater Bar Assn. (past pres.), Chgo. Bar Assn., Ill. Bar Assn., Am. Coll. Real Estate Lawyers (past chmn. condominium com.), Clearwater C. of C. (bd. govs., exec. com., past v.p.), Countryside Country Club. Republican. Home: 1910 Saddlehill Rd N Dunedin FL 34698-2437 Office: Julius J Zschau 1247 S Myrtle Ave Clearwater FL 33756-3469 Home Phone: 727-784-8490.

ZSCHAU, MARILYN, singer; b. Chgo., Feb. 9, 1944; d. Edwin Arthur Eugene and Helen Elizabeth (Kelly) Z.; m. Franz Baars, Sept. 2006. BA in Radio, TV and Motion Pictures, U. N.C., 1959; grad., Juilliard Sch. Music, 1965; studied opera theatre with Christopher West, studied voice with Florence Page Kimball, studied with John Lester. Toured with Met. Nat. Co., 1965-66; debut, Vienna Volksoper, in Die Tote Stadt, 1967, Vienna Staatsoper, in Ariadne auf Naxos, 1971; with N.Y.C. Opera in La Fanciulla del West, 1978; debut Royal Opera, covent Garden in La Boheme, 1982, Met. Opera, in La Boheme, 1985, La Scala, in Die Frau ohne Schatten, 1986; has toured and sung in many countries including S.Am., Japan, and Australia. Office: 4245 Wilshire Blvd Oakland CA 94602-3549 Home Phone: 510-336-9269; Office Phone: 510-484-7742. E-mail: marilynzschau@yahoo.com.

ZSIGMOND, VILMOS, cinematographer, film director; b. Szeged, Hungary, June 16, 1930; came to U.S., 1957, naturalized, 1962; s. Vilmos and Bozena (Illichmann) Z.; children: Julia, Susi. MA, U. Film and Theater Arts, Budapest, Hungary, 1955. Free-lance cinematographer for numerous commls., also ednl., documentary and low-budget feature films, 1965-71; now dir., cinematographer on commls. (winner several nat. and internat. awards); feature films, 1971-; films include McCabe and Mrs. Miller, 1971; Images, 1972, Deliverance, 1972, The Long Goodbye, 1973, Scarecrow, 1973, Cinderella Liberty, 1973, The Sugarland Express, 1974, Obsession, 1976, Close Encounters of the Third Kind, 1977 (Acad. award 1977), The Last Waltz, 1978, The Rose, 1978, The Deerhunter, 1978 (Acad. award nomination and Brit. Acad. award), Heavens Gate, 1979, The Border, 1980, Blow Out, 1980, Jinxed, 1981, Table for Five, 1982, The River, 1983 (Acad. award nomination), No Small Affair, 1984, Real Genius, 1985, Witches of Eastwick, 1986, Journey to Spirit Island, 1988, Fatman and Little Boy, 1989, Two Jakes, 1989, Bonfire of the Vanities, 1990, Stalin, 1991 (CableAce award, Direction of Photography and/or Lighting Direction in a Dramatic/Theatrical Special/Movie or Miniseries, ASC award, Emmy award), Sliver, 1992; dir. The Long Shadow, 1992, Intersection, 1993, Maverick, 1993, The Crossing Guard, 1994, Assassins, 1995, The Ghost and the Darkness, 1996 (ASC Award nomination), Fantasy for a New Age, 1997, Playing By Heart, 1998, The Body, 1999, The Mists of Avalon, 2000, Life as a House, 2001, (opera film) Bánk Bán, 2002, Jersey Girl, 2003, Melinda and Melinda, 2004, The Black Dahlia, 2005. Recipient lifetime achievement award Worldfest, Flagstaff, 1998. Mem. Acad. Motion Picture Arts and Scis., Dirs. Guild, Am. Soc. Cinematographers (lifetime achievement award 1998). Home Phone: 310-305-8258; Office Phone: 818-753-6300. Personal E-mail: vilmoszsigmond@hotmail.com. Business E-Mail: patty@themackagency.net.

ZUBER, CATHERINE, costume designer; MFA, Yale Sch. Drama. Costume designer (plays) Brand, Frankenstein, Two Gentlemen of Verona, The Merchant of Venice, Silence, Cunning, Exile, Jack's Holiday, Troilus and Cressida, The Grey Zone, King Lear, Cowgirls, Nightmare Alley, Violet, Misalliance, The Primary English Class, Captains Courageous, The Musical, An Experiment with an Air Pump, Saturday Night, Time and Again, Servicemen, Othello, Andorra, Boys and Girls, Play Yourself, Far Away, The Mercy Seat, Julius Caesar, The Harlequin Studies, Beckett/Albee, The Beard of Avon (Lucille Lortel award, outstanding costume design, 2004), The Regard Evening, Frozen, Intimate Apparel (Lucille Lortel award, outstanding costume design, 2005), Engaged (Obie award, Village Voice, design, 2005), Last Easter, Five by Tenn, The Paris Letter, The House in Town, 2006, Love's Labor's Lost, 2007 (Helen Hayes award outstanding costume design, 2007), (Broadway plays) The Red Shoes, 1993, Philadelphia, Here I Come!, 1994, The Rose Tattoo, 1995, London Assurance, 1997, Triumph of Love, 1997, Ivanov, 1997, The Sound of Music, 1998, Twelfth Night, 1998, Dinner at Eight, 2002, Frozen, 2004, Dracula, the Musical, 2004, Little Women, 2005, Doubt, 2005, The Light in the Piazza, 2005 (Tony award, best costume design of a musical, 2005), Awake and Sing!, 2006 (Tony award, best costume design of play, 2006), Defiance, 2006, The Coast of Utopia, 2006 (Outer Critics Cir. award outstanding costume design, 2007, Drama Desk award outstanding costume design, 2007, Tony award best costume design of play, 2007). Recipient Obie award, sustained achievement in costume design, 1997, Henry Hewes award, outstanding costume design, 2003. *

ZUBER, MARIA T., geophysicist, educator; married; 2 children. BA in Astrophysics & Geology, U. Penn., 1980; SsM in Geophysics, Brown U., 1983, PhD in Geophysics, 1986. Rsch. asst. geological sciences Brown U., 1980—86; NRC rsch. assoc., Geodynamics Branch NASA/Goddard Space Flight Ctr., 1985—86, geophysicist, Geodynamics Branch, 1986—92, sr. rsch. scientist, Lab. for Terrestrial Physics, 1994—; assoc. rsch. prof. geophysics Johns Hopkins U., 1991—92, assoc. prof. geophysics, 1991—95, prof. geophysics, 1995; cons. aerospace div. MIT Lincoln Lab., 2002—; prof. geophysics & planetary sci. MIT, 1995—98, E.A. Griswold prof. geophysics, dept. earth, atmospheric & planetary scis., 1998—, head dept. earth, atmospheric & planetary sciences, 2003—. Visiting asst. prof. geophysics Johns Hopkins U., 1990; guest investigator Woods Hole Oceanographic Institution, 1996—2004; sr. sci. fellow Radcliffe Inst. for Advanced Study, 2002—03; visiting scholar Harvard U., 2002—03; bd. dirs. Planetary Soc., 2000—; mem. advisory council Jet Propulsion Lab., 2000—; mem. Independent Status Review Bd., NASA Mars Exploration Rover, 2003—. President's Commn. on Implementation of US Space Exploration Policy, 2004. Mem. bd. reviewing editors Science, 2000—. Recipient NASA Peer award, 1988, NASA Outstanding Performance award, 1988, 1989, 1990, 1991, 1992, NASA Exceptional Scientific Achievement medal, 1995, Scientific Achievement award, Am. Inst. of Aeronautics & Astronautics, 2002, NASA Disting. Public Service medal, 2004. Fellow: Am. Acad. Arts & Sciences, Am. Geophysical Union; mem.: NAS, Am. Astronomical Soc., AAAS. Office: MIT Dept Earth Atmospheric & Planetary Scis 54-518 77 Mass Ave Cambridge MA 02139 Business E-Mail: zuber@mit.edu.

ZUBERBIER, JO ANN, elementary school educator; b. Perryville, Mo., Mar. 8, 1936; d. Henry Herman and Marcella Mae (Koeneman) Schaefer; m. Orlan Gene Zuberbier, June 11, 1960; children: Todd Alan, Gregg Milo, Dawn Cheryl Zuberbier Flatt. BA magna cum laude, U. Wis., Green Bay, 1971. Cert. life tchr., Wis. Tchr. St. John's Luth. Sch., Red Bud, Ill., 1954-55, St. Paul's Luth. Sch., Mt. Prospect, Ill., 1956-61, Kennedy Elem. Sch., Green Bay, Wis., 1971-92, Christa McAuliffe Elem. Sch., Green Bay, 1992—97; ret., 1997. Vol. gen. ednl. devel./HS equivalency diploma tchr. St. Croix County Jail, Hudson, Wis. Mem. ASCD, NEA, Green Bay Edn. Assn., WEAC. Home: 1146 County Rd H New Richmond WI 54017-6125 Personal E-mail: jazubie@frontiernet.net.

ZUBERNIS, LYNN SMITH, psychologist, counselor; d. Kevlin Walter and Carol Luckins Smith; m. James J. Zubernis, June 25, 1983 (div. Mar. 1994); children: Emily Kevlin, Jeffrey James. BA in Psychology, Rosemont Coll., 1994; MA in Sch. Psychology, Bryn Mawr Coll., 1997, PhD in Clin., Devel. and Sch. Psychology, 2002. Cert. Sch. Psychologist Pa., 1997, lic. Psychologist Pa., 2005. Intern psychologist Marple Newtown Sch. Dist., Newtown Square, Pa., 1996—97, Child Study Inst., Bryn Mawr, Pa., 1996—98, St. Gabriel's Hall, Audubon, Pa., 1997—98; sch. psychologist Tower Hill Sch., Wilmington, Del., 1999—; intern psychologist Friends Hosp., Phila., 2000—01; therapist Penn Friends Behl Health, Phila., 2001—02; counselor St. Josephs U., Phila., 2002—, asst. dir., Counseling Ctr. Instr. West Chester State U., 1999, adj. prof., 2006; adj. Haverford Coll., 2000. Contbr. articles to profl. jours. Mem.: APA, Pa. Psychol. Assn., Delta Epsilon Sigma, Alpha Sigma Lambda. Avocations: writing, films. Office: St Josephs Univ Counseling Ctr 5600 City Ave Philadelphia PA 19131 Business E-Mail: lzuberni@sju.edu.

ZUBIETA, ALBERTO ALEMAN, construction executive; b. Panama City, Panama; Degree in indsl. engring., civil engring., Tex. A & M U. Adminstr. Panama Canal Commn., 1998—2000, Panama Canal Authority, 1998—. Recipient Fed. Engr. of Yr. award, ASCE, 1998, Personality 2001 award, Seatrade Orgn. Mem.: Young Profls. Assn. (Panama Chpt.), Panama Architects and Engrs. Assn., Panamanian Chamber of Constrn. (William Ross Medal 1992). Office: Panama Canal Authority PO Box 526725 Miami FL 33152-6725

ZUBKOFF, DANIEL J., lawyer; b. Buffalo, May 28, 1957; AB magna cum laude, Cornell U., 1979; JD cum laude, Harvard Law Sch., 1982. Bar: NY 1983. Co-adminstr. ptnr. Cahill Gordon & Reindel LLP, NYC, ptnr., Fin. Securities & Banking Practice Group. Mem.: Phi Beta Kappa. Office: Cahill Gordon & Reindel LLP 80 Pine St New York NY 10005-1702 Office Phone: 212-701-3466. Office Fax: 212-378-2383. Business E-Mail: dzubkoff@cahill.com.

ZUBKOFF, MICHAEL, medical educator; b. NYC, June 2, 1944; s. Harry and Catherine (O'Brien) Z.; children: Steven, Joel, Lisa; m. Leslee Ann Michaels, 1991. BA, Am. Internat. Coll., 1965, LLD (hon.), 1981; MA, Columbia U., 1966, cert. Internat. Fellow program, 1966, PhD, 1968; MA (hon.), Dartmouth Coll., 1980. Research assoc. conservation human resources Columbia U., NYC, 1966-67; assoc. prof. econs. Fisk U., Nashville, 1967-70; assoc. prof. health econs., assoc. chmn. dept. family and community health Meharry Med. Coll., Nashville, 1967-75; assoc. prof. econs. Vanderbilt U., Nashville, 1970-75; prof. econs. and mgmt. Amos Tuck Sch. Bus., prof. chmn. dept. cmty. and family medicine Med. Sch. Dartmouth Coll., Hanover, NH, 1975—. Mem. inst. medicine Nat. Acad. Scis., 1982—, mem. assembly engrs. inst. med. com. on tech. and health care, 1977-79, grad. med. ednl. nat. adv. com., 1977-81., com. on grad.-med. edn. programs for mil. services Nat. Acad. Scis., 1980-82., nat. research council commn. on human resources Nat. Acad. Scis., 1980-84, com. on aging soc. Nat. Acad. Scis., 1984-89; corr. com. human rights Nat. Acad. Scis., 1983—, nat. rsch. coun. com. computer tech. and svc. sector productivity Nat. Acad. Scis., 1991-94; instr. econs. Harvard U., Yale U., and Columbia U., 1967-68. Co-author: Urban Health Services: The Case of New York, 1971, Consumer Incentives for Health Care, 1974, Health: A Victim of Cause of Inflation, 1976, Framework for Government Intervention in the Health Sector, 1978, Hospital Cost Containment: Selected Notes for Public Policy, 1980, Problem Based Learning of Social Science & Humanities by Fourth Year Medical Students, 1986, The Medical Outcomes Study: An Application of Methods for Monitoring the Results of Medical Care, 1989, Measuring Functional Status & Well Being: The Medical Outcomes Study Approach, 1992, Health Society & The Physician: Problem Based Learning of Social Sciences & Humanities, 1993; contbr. numerous articles to profl. jours. Del., health spokesman White House Summit on Inflation, 1974. Fellow Woodrow Wilson Found., 1964-66, Fulbright Found., 1967-68, USPHS, 1966-67. Mem. Am. Econ. Assn., Am. Pub. Health Assn. Home: RR 1 Fairlee VT 05045-9801 Office: Dartmouth Med Sch Dept Comty & Family Med HB7250 Hanover NH 03755

ZUBOV, SERGEI, professional hockey player; b. Moscow, July 22, 1970; m. Irina Zubov; children: Pavel, Anastasia. Defenseman NY Rangers, 1992-95, Pitts. Penguins, 1995-96, Dallas Stars, 1996—. Player NHL All-Star Game, 1998—2000. Recipient Second All-Star Team, 2006. Achievements include being a member of Stanley Cup Champion NY Rangers, 1994, Dallas Stars, 1999. Avocations: fishing, basketball. *

ZUBRETSKY, JOSEPH M., insurance company executive; BSBA, Univ. Hartford. Ptnr. Coopers & Lybrand, 1990—96; exec. v.p., CFO Healthsource Inc., 1996—97; exec. v.p. bus. develop., CFO MassMutual Fin. Group, 1997—99; pres., CEO GAB Robins Group, 1999—2005; sr. v.p. fin., investments & corp. develop. UnumProvident Corp., 2005—07; exec. v.p., CFO, chief risk officer Aetna Inc., Hartford, Conn., 2007—. Office: Aetna Inc 151 Farmington Ave Hartford CT 06156 *

ZUBRITSKY, ALEXANDER NICKOLAEVICH, pathologist; b. Severo-Kurilsk, Sakhalin, Russia, Mar. 14, 1949; s. Nickolay Alexandrovich and Kaleriya Andreevna (Chechulina) Z.; children: Vladimir, Sergey Yashin. MD in Med. Scis., Med. Inst., 1974. Hosp. attendant dept. pathology City Hosp. N21, Sverdlovsk, Russia, 1965—67; hosp. attendant Medico-Legal Morgue N1, Sverdlovsk, 1967—68; nurse Sta. of Emergencies Care N1, Sverdlovsk, 1971—72; head pathology dept. Ctrl. Regional Hosp., Neviyansk, Russia, 1975—76; chief pathology dept., head pathologist Sverdlovsk Rd. Hosp., 1976—83; lectr. pathol. anatomy Med. Sch. Sverdlovsk Rd., 1976—77; chief dept. pathology mcpl. instn. Taldom Ctrl. Regional Hosp., 1983—; pathologist City Clin. Hosp., Moscow, 2004—. Contbr. articles to profl. jours. Recipient award Am. Coll. Chest Physicians, 1990, Pathology Rsch. Practice award, Taldom-Innsbruck, 1993, Internat. Peace prize UCC, 2003, Internat. Scientist Yr. Gold Medal, 2004, Man of Achievement award for Outstanding Contbns. to Pathol. Anatomy of Cor Pulmonale, 2005, Best People of Russia medal, 2006; named Internat. Man Yr., 1994-95, 03. Mem.: AASS, Atlantic-Euro-Mediterranean Acad. Med. Scis., N.Y. Acad. Sci., Internat. Soc. Diagnostic Quantitative Pathology, Internat. Soc. Heart Rsch. (European sect.), Internat. Union Against Tb and Lung Disease, European Soc. Pathology. Avocations: music, walking. Home: Prospekt Mira 101B/79 129085 Moscow Russia Office Phone: (7-496)-20-6-02-57. Personal E-mail: alex_79zubr@yahoo.com. Business E-Mail: zubr5taldom@mail.ru.

ZUBROFF, LEONARD SAUL, surgeon; b. Minersville, Pa., Mar. 27, 1925; s. Abe and Fannie (Freedline) Z. BA, Wayne State U., 1945, MD, 1949. Diplomate Am. Bd. Surgery. Intern Garfield Hosp., Washington, 1949-50, resident in surgery, 1951-55, chief resident surgery, 1954-55; pvt. practice medicine specializing in surgery, 1958-76; med. dir. Chevrolet Gear and Axle Plant, Forge Plant, GM, Detroit, 1977-78; divsnl. med. dir. Detroit Diesel Allison divsn., Detroit, 1978-87; regional med. dir. GM, 1987-89; ret., 1989. Chief of surgery, chief profl. svcs. N.E. Air Command, Pepperell AFB, Newfoundland. With USAF, 1956—58. Mem.: Le Vine Found. (trustee). Home and Office: 22511 S Bellwood Dr Southfield MI 48034-2116

ZUCARO, ALDO CHARLES, insurance company executive; b. Grenoble, France, Apr. 2, 1939; s. Louis and Lucy Zucaro; m. Gloria J. Ward, Oct. 12, 1963; children: Lucy, Louis, Faye. BS in Acctg, Queens Coll., NYC, 1962. C.P.A., N.Y., Ill. Ptnr. Coopers & Lybrand (and predecessor), Chgo. and NYC, 1962-76; exec. v.p., chief fin. officer Old Republic Internat. Corp., Chgo., 1976-81, pres., 1981—, CEO, 1990—93, chmn., CEO, 1993—. Pres., bd. dirs. Old Republic Life Ins. Co., Old Republic Life of N.Y., Old Republic Ins. Co., Internat. Bus. and Merc. Reassurance Co., Republic Mortgage Ins. Co., Old Republic Nat. Title Ins. Co., Home Owners Life Ins. Co. Editor: Financial Accounting Practices of the Insurance Industry, 1975, 76. Mem. AICPAs. Roman Catholic. Office: Old Republic Internat Corp 307 N Michigan Ave Chicago IL 60601-5311

ZUCH, LEAH D.T., language educator; b. Lehighton, Pa., June 12, 1961; s. Robert Thompson and Muriel Gwendolyn (Brent) Zuch; m. Richard G. Lewis, June 4, 1994. BA in English, Clarion U., Pa., 1986; MA in English, U. Soc. Maine, Gorham, 1996. Tchr. English as 2d lang. Scarborough H.S. and Mid. Sch., Maine, 1992—. Mem.: TESOL. Green Party. Lutheran. Avocations: bicycling, gardening. Home: 47 Inverness St Portland ME 04103 Office: Scarborough High Sch 20 Gorham Rd Scarborough ME 04074

ZUCK, ALFRED MILLER, public administration educator; b. East Petersburg, Pa., Aug. 27, 1934; s. Walter Newton and Mary (Miller) Z.; m. Geraldine Connelly, July 21, 1957; children: Susan, David. BA, Franklin and Marshall Coll., 1957; MPA, Syracuse U., 1958. Dir. fed. program Presdl. Commn. on Youth Opportunities, Washington, 1967-68; dir evaluation Employment and Tng. Adminstrn., Dept. Labor, Washington, 1968-70, dir adminstrn. and mgmt., 1970-75; comptroller U.S. Dept. Labor, Washington, 1975-77; exec. dir. Commn. on Exec., Legis. and Jud. Salaries, Washington, 1980; asst. sec. Dept. Labor, Washington, 1977-83, acting sec., 1981; asst. adminstr. EPA, Washington, 1983; exec. dir. Nat. Assn. Schs. of Pub. Affairs and Adminstrn., Washington, 1983-97; disting. prof. Am. U., Washington, 1996—2005, emeritus prof., 2005—. Pres. Internat. Inst. Adminstrv. Scis., Brussels, 1989-92, Am. Consortium for Internat. Pub. Adminstrn., Washington, 1984-89; bd. dirs. Pub./Pvt. Venture, Inc., Phila., 1984-90. Recipient Presdl. Disting. Exec. award Pres. of U.S., 1980; Disting. Alumni award Franklin and Marshall Coll., 1980. Fellow Nat. Acad. Pub. Admisntrn. (trustee 1989-95, chmn. bd. trustees 1993-95); mem. Phi Beta Kappa. Personal E-mail: alzuck@aol.com.

ZUCKER, ALEXANDER, physicist, researcher; b. Zagreb, Croatia, Aug. 1, 1924; came to U.S., 1939; s. William and Bertha (Klopfer) Z.; m. Joan-Ellen Jamieson, Nov. 28, 1953; children: Rebecca, Claire, Susannah. BA, U. Vt., Burlington, 1947; MS, Yale U., New Haven, 1948, PhD, 1950. Physicist Oak Ridge Nat. Lab., 1950-60, assoc. dir. electro-nuclear div., 1972-75, dir. heavy ion project, 1988, assoc. dir. phys. scis., 1973-88, acting lab. dir., 1988, assoc. dir. for nuclear techs., 1989-93; exec. dir., environ. studies bd. NAS-NAE, Washington, 1970-72; prof. physics U. Tenn., 1996—. Mem. U.S. del. to USSR on Peaceful Uses of Atomic Energy, 1963; Ford prof. physics U. Tenn., Knoxville, 1968-73; U.S. del. to Pugwash Conf., 1971; research coordination council Gas Research Inst., Chgo., 1978-85; com. Army manpower Nat. Research Council, Washington, 1982-83; adv. panel on technologies to reduce U.S. materials import vulnerability Office of Technology Assessment, Washington, 1982-85; council on energy engring. research Dept. of Energy, Washington, 1983—; industry, nat. lab. steel initiative White House, Washington, 1984 Editor Internat. Jour. Nuclear Sci. Applications, 1980—; cons. editor Ency. and Yearbook of Sci. and Tech. McGraw-Hill Pub. Co., 1989; mem. editorial bd. Science, 1981-82; contbr. articles to profl. jours. Pres. Oak Ridge Civic Music Assn., Oak Ridge Arts Coun.; bd. chair Ridgeview Psychiatric Hosp. Guggenheim fellow, 1966-67; Fulbright-Hays Research scholar, 1966-67 Fellow Am. Phys. Soc., AAAS, Sigma Xi; mem. ASME, Nat. Acad. Scis. (nuclear physics del. to People's Republic of China 1979), Internat. Union Pure and Applied Physics (mem.-at-large U.S. nat. com. 1976-78) Achievements include research in nuclear physics with heavy ions and protons; accelerators, especially cyclotrons; materials research programs, especially high-temperature materials and surfaces; nuclear power reactors, especially gas-cooled reactors; research reactor with ultra high neutron flux.

ZUCKER, ALFRED JOHN, English and history educator, academic administrator, historian; b. Hartford, Sept. 25, 1940; s. Samuel and Rose (Zucker) Z.; m. Sallie Lea Friedheim, Dec. 25, 1966; children: Mary Anne, John James Jr., James Patrick, Patrick Jonathan, Anne-Marie Kathleen, Kathleen Mary. AA, LA Valley Coll., 1960; AB in English, UCLA, 1962, AB in Speech, MA in English, 1962, MA in Speech, 1963, PhD, 1966; postgrad., U. So. Calif., Harvard U.; MA in history, Calif. State U., Long Beach, 2000, MA in Polit. Sci., 2004. Prof. English and history, chmn. div. humanities LA SW Coll., 1968-72; prof. English El Camino Coll., 1985—, LA Valley Coll., 1989—, chmn. dept. English, honors sponsor, 1997—. Contbr. articles to profl. jours. Mem. LA Coll. Dist. Senate, 1969—. Mem. AAUP, LA Coll. Tchrs. Assn. (dir.), Calif. Jr. Coll. Assn., Calif. Tchrs. Assn., World Affairs Coun., Calif. Scholarship Fedn., Mensa, KC, Gold Key, Phi Beta Kappa, Phi Delta Kappa (pres. UCLA chpt. 1966-67, v.p. 1967-68), Tau Alpha Epsilon, Phi Theta Kappa, Phi Alpha Theta, Phi Kappa Phi, Phi Delta Gamma. Office: 5800 Fulton Ave Van Nuys CA 91401-4062 Home: 1701 Simplicity Irvine CA 92620 Office Phone: 818-947-2343. Business E-Mail: zuckeraj@lavc.edu.

ZUCKER, DAVID F., information technology executive; b. Wichita Falls, Tex., Aug. 8, 1962; s. Paul Zucker and Margaret Anne (Keating) Chisholm. BA in Econ., Princeton U., 1984; MBA, Harvard, 1988. Fin. analyst Goldman, Sachs & Co., NYC, 1984-86; exec. pub. ABC, Inc., Travel Agent Mag., NYC, 1988-90; mgr. current series programming ABC Entertainment, LA, 1991; dir. programming Eurosport, London, Paris, 1992-93; v.p. programming to exec. v.p. ESPN, Inc., Bristol, Conn., 1993-94; sr. v.p., managing dir. ESPN Internat., NYC, 1995—99; pres., CEO Diva Systems Corp., 1999—2000, Skillgames LLC, 2000—02; mng. dir. Walker Digital LLC, 2000—02; pres., COO Playboy Enterprises, Inc., 2002—03; pres., CEO Midway Games, Inc., 2003—. Office: Midway Games Inc 2704 W Roscoe St Chicago IL 60618

ZUCKER, JEFFREY, broadcast executive; b. Homestead, Fla., Apr. 9, 1965; m. Caryn Stephanie Nathanson, 1996; children: Andrew, Elizabeth, Peter. BA in Am. History, Harvard Coll., 1986. Rschr., 1988 Olympic Games, Seoul, Korea NBC Sports, 1986—88; field prodr. NBC News, 1989; exec. prodr. Today, 1992—93, Now with Tom Brokaw and Katie Couric, NBC Nightly News with Tom Brokaw, 1993, Today, 1994—2000; pres. NBC Entertainment, 2000—03, NBC Entertainment, News and Cable Group, 2003—05; CEO NBC Universal TV, 2005—07; pres., CEO NBC Universal, 2007—. Exec. prodr.: (news segments) Russian coup, 1991, Persian Gulf War, 1991, 1993 and 1997 presdl. inaugurations, the bombing of Centennial Olympic Pk., 1996, 1996 and 2000 polit. conventions, Decision 2000; writer: The Games of the XXIV Olympiad (Emmy award, outstanding writing, 1988); supervising prodr.: "Senator Edward Kennedy" Today (Emmy award, outstanding interview, 1991); exec. prodr.: "California Fire" Now with Tom Brokaw and Katie Couric (Emmy award, outstanding coverage of a single breaking news story, 1993), "Tragedy in Rwanda" Now with Tom Brokaw and Katie Couric (Emmy award, outstanding background/analysis of a single current story, 1994), "The Brain" Now with Tom Brokaw and Katie Couric (Emmy award, outstanding informational or cultural program, 1994). Jewish. Office: NBC 3000 W Alameda Ave Burbank CA 91523-0002 also: NBC Universal 52nd Fl 30 Rockefeller Plz New York NY 10112 *

ZUCKER, JERRY, chemical manufacturing executive; b. Tel-Aviv, Israel, Aug. 24, 1949; s. Leon and Zipora (Shlifkovitz) Z.; m. Anita Goldberg, June 21, 1970; cildren: Jonathan Michael, Andrea Michelle, Jeffrey Mark. BS, U. Fla., 1968, MEE, 1972. Electronics design engr. Vital Industries, Inc., Gainesville, Fla., 1968-71; devel. engring. group dir. Cons. Engrs., Inc., Gainesville, 1971-73; supr. process engring. and tech. svcs. Hudson Pulp & Paper Corp. (now Ga. Pacific), Palatka, Fla., 1973-78; dir. mfg. and tech. svcs. Raybestos Manhattan, Inc., North Charleston, SC, 1978-82; chmn. bd., pres., CEO InterTech Group, Inc., 1983—; chmn., CEO Polymer Group, Inc., 1996—2003; gov., CEO Hudson's Bay Co., Canada, 2006—. Bd. dirs. High Tech. Coatings Corp., Advanced Chem. Techs., Inc., Tighitco, Inc., Ecosys, Inc., ConX Inc., Tycon Inc., Worthington Products Inc., Aerospace Def. Inc., Technetics Group, Inc., Thantex, Inc., Global Golf, Inc., Daramic, Inc., RemGrit Corp., Polyionix, Inc.; cons. phosphate mining, pulp and paper and sugar industries. Contbr. articles to tech. hours.; patentee in electrochem., mech. and chem. fields. Bd. dirs. Trident United Way, Charleston Jewish Fedn.; former pres. Hotline Inc., Hebrew Benevolent Soc., Hebrew Orphan Soc., Orgn. Rehab. Tng.; chair S.C. Aquarium; former pres. Synagogue Emanuel, 1996-98; mem. exec com., incoming pres. Coastal Coun., Boy Scouts Am.; co-chair Charleston Regional Devel. Alliance; chmn. Jewish studies adv. bd. Coll. Charleston; mem. electronics engring. tech. bd. Trident Tech. Coll.; mem. electronics tech. adv. bd. Garrett Acad. Tech. Named one of Forbes' Richest Americans, 2006. Mem. IEEE, TAPPI (nat. elec. engring. com. 1977-95), Am. Chem. Soc., Charleston Metro C. of C. (bd. dirs.), Am. Israeli C. of C. Jewish. Office: The InterTech Group Inc PO Box 5205 4838 Jenkins Ave North Charleston SC 29405-4816

ZUCKER, ROBERT A(LPERT), psychologist; b. NYC, Dec. 9, 1935; s. Morris and Sophie (Alpert) Z.; m. Martine Latil; children: Lisa, Alex, Eleanor; m. Kristine Ellen Freeark, Mar. 10, 1979; 1 child, Katherine. B.C.E., CCNY, 1956; postgrad., UCLA, 1956-58; PhD, Harvard U., 1966. Diplomate Am. Bd. Profl. Psychology (clin.); lic. psychologist, Mich. From instr. to asst. prof. psychology Rutgers U., 1963-68; from asst. prof. to assoc. prof. to prof. Mich. State U., 1968-94; prof. psychology in psychiatry and psychology U. Mich., 1994—, dir. Addiction Rsch. Ctr., 1994—, dir. substance abuse sect. Dept. Psychiatry, 1994—, faculty assoc. RCGD Inst. for Social Rsch., 1996—. Vis. prof. U. Tex., Austin, 1975; vis. rsch. prof. psychology in psychiatry U. Mich., 1990-91; vis. scholar Nat. Inst. Alcohol Abuse and Alcoholism, 1980; dir. clin. tng. Mich. State U., 1982-94; lectr. Nebr. Symposium on Motivation, 1986; cons. in field. Co-author, editor: Further Explorations in Personality, 1981, Personality and the Prediction of Behavior, 1984, The Emergence of Personality, 1987, Studying Persons and Lives, 1990, Personality Structure in the Life Course, 1992, The Development of Alcohol Problems: Exploring the Biopsychosocial Matrix of Risk, 1994, Alcohol Problems Among Adolescents: Current Directions in Prevention Research, 1995, Alcohol Problems and Aging, 1998, Multiproblem Youth: Intervention and Treatment, 2004; contbr. chpts. and articles to profl. publs. Bd. dirs. Nat. Coun. on Alcoholism-Mich., 1978-82; mem. Psychosocial Initial Rev. Group, Nat. Inst. Alcohol Abuse and Alcoholism, 1989-92; mem. HPRB study sect. Ctr. for Sci. Rev., NIH, 1998-2000. Recipient Fellow's award, Inst. Children Youth and Families, Mich. State U., 1993, Excellence in Clin. Rsch. award, Blue Cross-Blue Shield Mich. Found., 1997; Method for External Rsch. in Time grantee, NIH, 2003—. Fellow AAAS, APA (pres. addictions divsn. 50 1997-98), APS, Am. Orthopsychiat. Assn.; mem. Midwestern Psychol. Assn., Rsch. Soc. on Alcoholism (sec., bd. dirs. 2000-03, bd. dirs. 2007—), Polish Soc. Rsch. Addictions, Polish Soc. Psychiatrists (hon., named to Hall Fame 2007). Office: Univ Mich Addiction Rsch Ctr 4250 Plymouth Rd Ann Arbor MI 48109-5740 Office Phone: 734-232-0280. Business E-Mail: zuckerra@umich.edu.

ZUCKER, STEFAN, tenor, writer, editor, commentator; b. NYC; BS, Columbia U., 1967; postgrad., NYU, 1967-72. Freelance tenor concerts and operas in U.S. and Europe, 1965—; philosophy lectr. Coll. Ins. NYC, 1972; tenor RCA Records, NYC, 1972-77; guest singer radio and TV programs U.S. and Europe, 1975—; radio producer, host WKCR-FM, NYC, 1980-94; opera critic N.Y. Tribune, 1983-84; host web radio program Opera Fanatic www.belcantosociety.org, 2002—. Lectr. The Mannes Coll. Music, 2000—. Author: The Origins of Modern Tenor Singing, 1997; appeared in film Opera Fanatic: Stefan and the Divas, 1998; record producer including Rossini's Rivals: Music By Then-Famous, Now-Obscure, Italian Composers, 1984; restorer films of opera singers, 1987—; singer, producer, stage dir., adminstr. various operas, 1967—; editor Opera Fanatic mag., 1986—; commentator and singer (TV series) Bel canto: Tenors of the 78 Era, 1996-97; contbr. articles to Internat. Dictionary of Opera, Opera News, The Opera Quar., Am. Record Guide, Opera Fanatic, Globe & Mail, News World, Professione Musica, others. Pres. Bel Canto Soc., Inc., 1985—. Named Worlds Highest Tenor by Guinness Book of World Records, 1979—; subject of record Stefan Zucker: The World's Highest Tenor, 1981. Mem. NYU Philosophy Assn. (pres. 1969-72, v.p. 1968), Music Critics Assn., Assn. Furtherment Bel Canto (pres. 1967-80). Office: Bel Canto Soc Inc 11 Riverside Dr New York NY 10023-2504

ZUCKERBERG, MARK ELLIOT, Internet company executive, entrepreneur, programmer; b. Dobbs Ferry, NY, May 14, 1984; Attended, Harvard U. Co-founder Facebook.com, Palo Alto, Calif., 2004—. Named one of 50 Who Matter Now, Business 2.0, 2007. Achievements include development of one of the most widely used networking websites among college and high school students with over 11 million users throughout the U.S., Canada and Europe; the ninth most highly trafficked website in U.S. *

ZUCKERMAN, BRIAN DAVID, lawyer; m. Jennifer Zuckerman; children: Jake, Mason. BA, SUNY, Binghampton, NY, 1991; JD, Temple U., 1994. Bar: Pa., NJ. Assoc. Klehr, Harrison, Harvey, Branzburg & Ellers, Phila., 1994—97; atty. Pepper Hamilton, Phila., 1997—99; gen. counsel, sec. Pep Boys, Phila., 1999—. Office: The Pep Boys 3111 W Allegheny Ave Philadelphia PA 19132 Office Phone: 215-430-9169.

ZUCKERMAN, GREGG J., mathematics professor; PhD, Princeton Univ., 1975. Prof. math. Yale Univ., and dir. undergraduate studies in math. Fellow, Alfred P. Sloan Found., 1979—83. Achievements include being one of 18 top mathematicians and computer scientists (Atlas of Lie Groups Project) from the US to successfully map E8, one of the largest and most complicated structures in mathematics. Office: Dept Math Yale Univ PO Box 208241 New Haven CT 06520-8241 Office Phone: 203-432-4198. Office Fax: 203-432-7316. Business E-Mail: gregg@math.yale.edu. *

ZUCKERMAN, HARRIET, sociologist, educator; b. NYC, July 19, 1937; d. Harry and Anne D. (Wiener) Z; m. Robert K. Merton, 1993. AB, Vassar Coll., Poughkeepsie, NY, 1958; PhD, Columbia U., NYC, 1965. Asst. prof. sociology Columbia U., 1965-72, assoc. prof., 1972-78, prof., 1978-92, prof. emerita, 1993—; sr. rsch. scholar, 1993—; chmn. dept. Columbia U., 1978-81; v.p. Andrew W. Mellon Found., 1991-98, sr. v.p., 1998—. Vis. scholar Russell Sage Found., 1971—72, 1985—87; mem. adv. bd. Social Sci. Citation Index Inst. Sci. Info., 1972—98; dir. Ann. Revs., Inc.; trustee Am. Savs. Bank, 1978—83. Author: Scientific Elite: Nobel Laureates in the United States, 1977, rev. edit., 1996; co-editor: Toward A Metric of Science: The Advent of Science Indictors, 1978, The Outer Circle: Women in the Scientific Community, 1991; mem. editorial bd. Scientometrics, 1977-, Am. Jour. Sociology, 1972-74, 77-79, Am. Sociol. Rev, 1972-74, 87-91, Sci., 1985-86; contbr. articles to profl. jours. Bd. dir. Social Sci. Rsch. Coun., 1974-76, AAAS, 1980-84, Women's Forum, 1989-91; trustee Ctr. for Advanced Study in Behavioral Scis., 1976-88, 89-2001, 03—; mem. ednl. adv. bd. John Simon Guggenheim Meml. Found., 1986-93, mem. com. on selection, 1989-91. Woodrow Wilson fellow, 1958-59; Ctr. for Advanced Study in Behavioral Scis. fellow, 1973-74; Guggenheim fellow, 1980-81; Phi Beta Kappa vis. scholar, 1982-83; recipient Dean's award for Disting. Achievement Columbia U. Grad. Sch., 1998. Mem. Am. Philos. Soc. (councillor 1997-03, 2005—, v.p. 2006-,chmn. Class III membership com. 2002-05), Am. Acad. Arts and Scis. (chmn. class III membership com. 1991-94), Soc. Social Studies Sci. (pres. 1989-91), The Century Assn., Coun. on Fgn. Rels.

ZUCKERMAN, HERBERT LAWRENCE, lawyer; b. Newark, June 11, 1928; s. David and Adele Zuckerman; m. Janet Albert, Sept. 10, 1950; children: Julia, Elizabeth, William. BSBA, Lehigh U., 1949; JD, Rutgers U., 1953. Acct. Zuckerman & Black, Newark, 1949-56; pvt. practice law Newark, 1956-71; ptnr. Zuckerman, Aronson & Horn, Newark, 1971-81; ptnr., v.p. Sills Cummis, Newark, 1981-98, sr.counsel, 1998—. Bd. dirs. Am. Jewish Com., 1990—; vol. The Hospice, Glen Ridge, N.J., 1985-93. Fellow Coll. of Tax Counsel; mem. ABA, N.J. Bar Assn., Fed. Bar Assn., Essex County Bar Assn., Mental Health Assn. (bd. dirs. 1997-99), Mensa. Avocations: tennis, music, theater, opera, reading. Office: Sills Cummis 1 Riverfront Plz 13th Fl Newark NJ 07102-5400 Home Phone: 973-763-7386; Office Phone: 973-643-7000. Business E-Mail: hzuckerman@sillscummis.com.

ZUCKERMAN, MARC ABRAHAM, finance educator; b. NYC, May 30, 1951; s. Henry and Rela (Ast) Z.; m. Sue Carol Kezurer, Dec. 6, 1981; 1 child, Sam David. BA cum laude, CUNY, Bronx, 1973; MA, Columbia U., 1974; MBA, Manhattan Coll., 1984. Cert. mgmt. acct., treasury profl., credit executive. Dir. corp. credit Clinton Swan Clothes, NYC, 1978-80; dir. fin. Lord Jeff, Norwood, N.J., 1980-88; dir. corp. credit Bernard Chaus, Inc., Secaucus, N.J., 1988-89; asst. treas. Warnaco, Bridgeport, Conn., 1989; treas. Bernard Chaus, Inc., Secaucus, 1989-95; corp. contr. Precision Custom Coatings, Totowa, N.J., 1996-99; v.p. ops., CFO Triboro Quilt

Mfg. Corp., 1999—. Pres. Meadowlands Fin. Group, 1991-95; adj. prof. fin. Contbr. articles to profl. jours. Pack com. mem. Ridgewood Boy Scouts Am., 1997-2000, treas. 1997-2000. Mem. Inst. Mgmt. Accts., Treas. Mgmt. Assn., Treas. Mgmt. Assn. N.J., Nat. Assn. Credit Mgmt., N.J. Corp. Treas. Mgmt. Assn. (treas. 1996-99), Nat. Apparel Mfrs. Credit Assn. (bd. dirs. 1993-95), Bergen Rockland Inst. Mgmt. Accts. (bd. dirs. 1996-97). Avocations: jogging, golf. Home: 153 Lincoln Ave Ridgewood NJ 07450-4105 Office: Triboro Quilt Mfg Corp 172 South Broadway White Plains NY 10605

ZUCKERMAN, MARVIN, retired psychologist; b. Chgo., Mar. 21, 1928; s. Eli and Sophia (Pilder) Z.; children: April B. Zuckerman Schanoes, Steven H. BA, NYU, 1949, PhD, 1954. Rsch. assoc. Inst. Psychiat. Rsch., Ind. U. Med. Ctr., 1956-59; asst. prof. psychology Bklyn. Coll., 1959-62; rsch. assoc. Albert Einstein Med. Ctr., Phila., 1963-69; prof. psychology U. Del., Newark, 1969—2002, prof. emeritus, 2002—, ret., 2002. Author: (with C.D. Spielberger) Emotions and Anxiety, 1976, Sensation Seeking: Beyond the Optimal Level of Arousal, 1979, Biological Bases of Sensation Seeking, Impulsivity and Anxiety, 1983, Psychobiology of Personality, 1991, 2d edit. 2005, Behavioral Expressions and Biosocial Bases of Sensation Seeking, 1994, Vulnerability to Psychopathology, 1999, Sensation Seeking and Risky Behavior, 2007. Fellow APA, Am. Psychol. Soc.; mem. Internat. Soc. Study Individual Differences (past pres.). Home: 1500 Locust St Apt 4013 Philadelphia PA 19102-4326 Office Phone: 215-732-2408. Business E-Mail: zuckerma@udel.edu.

ZUCKERMAN, MEL (MELVIN ZUCKERMAN), hotel executive; b. May 1928; m. Enid Zuckerman. Co-founder, chmn. Canyon Ranch Health Resort, Inc., Tucson, 1979—. Founder Wellness Coun. of Ariz. (formerly Wellness Coun. of Tucson), 1984, pres. emeritus, bd. advisors; bd. dirs. Crescent Real Estate Equities. Bd. dirs. U. Ariz. Found.; adv. bd. U. Ariz. Arthritis Ctr., Ariz. Prevention Ctr. Named to Condé Nast Traveler Mag. Hall of Fame, 1997. Office: Canyon Ranch 8600 E Rockcliff Rd Tucson AZ 85750 Office Phone: 520-749-9000. *

ZUCKERMAN, MORTIMER BENJAMIN, publishing executive, real estate developer; b. Montreal, Ont., Can., June 4, 1937; arrived in US, 1961, naturalized, 1977; s. Abraham and Esther Zuckerman. BA in Econs. and Polit. Theory with 1st class honors, McGill U., Montreal, 1957, LLB with honors, 1961; MBA with distinction, U. Pa., 1962; LLM, Harvard U., 1962. Sr. v.p. Cabot, Cabot & Forbes, Boston, 1965—69; co-founder, chmn. bd. Boston Properties Co., 1970—, also dir., 1997—; pres., chmn. bd. Atlantic Monthly Co., Boston, 1980—99; chmn., editor-in-chief US News & World Report, 1984—; chmn., co-pub. NY Daily News, 1993—2004, chmn., pub., 2004—. Lectr., then assoc. prof. Harvard U. Grad. Sch. Design, 1966—74; vis. lectr. city and regional planning Yale U., 1967—69; dir., mem. exec. com. Stride Rite Corp., 1970—83; dir. Property Capital Trust Co., 1979—80, RET Income Found., 1976—79; pub. interest dir. Fed. Home Loan Bank of Boston, 1972—73; mem. JP Morgan Nat. Adv. Bd., Internat. Inst. Strategic Studies, Washington Inst. Near East Policy. Founder Zuckerman Fellowships Harvard U., 2004—; pres. bd. trustees Sidney Farber Cancer Inst., Boston, 1980; trustee Meml. Sloan-Kettering, Aspen Inst., NYU, Hole in the Wall Gang Fund, Inc., Center for Comm. Named one of Forbes' Richest Americans, 2006; recipient Commandeur De L'Ordre des Arts et des Lettres, France, Lifetime Achievement Award, Guild Hall, Gold Medal, Am. Inst. Architecture. Mem.: Coun. Fgn. Rels., Harmonie (NYC), Harvard Club (Boston and NYC). Office: New York Daily News 450 W 33rd St Fl 3 New York NY 10001-2681 also: US News & World Report 1050 Thomas Jefferson St NW Washington DC 20007-3817 also: Boston Properties 599 Lexington Ave Rm 1800 New York NY 10022-6030 Office Phone: 212-326-4013, 202-955-2000. *

ZUCKERMAN, PAUL HERBERT, lawyer; s. Max B. and Minnie (Mendelson) Z.; m. Sara Shiffman, Aug. 25, 1963; children: David Isaac, Daniel Mark. BS in Econs., Wharton Sch., U. Pa., 1957; MBA in Corp. Fin., NYU, 1964; JD, Bklyn. Law Sch., 1967. Bar: N.Y. 1968, U.S. Dist. Ct. (so. and ea. dists.) N.Y. 1975, U.S. Tax Ct. 1977, U.S. Ct. Appeals (2d cir.) 1972, U.S. Supreme Ct. 1973. Security analyst U.S. Trust Co., NYC, 1962-66; sr. security analyst CNA Mgmt. Rsch. Corp., NYC, 1966-71, mgr. dept. investment rsch., 1971-73; sole practice NYC, 1973—. Speaker and writer in field; radio, TV appearances. Served to lt. (j.g.) USN, 1957—60. Mem.: Wharton Bus. Sch., NYC Bar Assn. Office: 8th Fl 226 W 26th St New York NY 10001-6785 Office Phone: 212-367-1900. Office Fax: 212-255-6562. Business E-Mail: EstatesWillsTrusts@gmail.com.

ZUCKERMAN, RICHARD ENGLE, lawyer, educator; b. Yonkers, NY, Aug. 2, 1945; s. Julius and Roslyn (Ehrlich) Z.; m. Denise Ellen Spoon, July 14, 1968; children: Julie Ann, Lindsay Beth. BA, U. Mich., 1967; JD cum laude, Southwestern U., 1974. Bar: Calif. 1974, Mich. 1976, Nev. 1986, U.S. Dist. Ct. (ea. and we. dists.) Mich. 1977, U.S. Ct. Appeals (6th cir.) 1977, U.S. Ct. Appeals (9th cir.) 1982, U.S. Ct. Appeals (2d and 7th cirs.) 1994, U.S. Tax Ct. 1980, U. S. Supreme Ct. 1985, U.S. Ct. Appeals (4th cir.) 2001. Spl. atty. organized crime and racketeering sect. U.S. Dept. Justice, Detroit, 1974-77; sr. ptnr. Raymond, Rupp, Wienberg, Stone & Zuckerman, P.C., Troy, Mich., 1977-87, Honigman, Miller, Schwartz & Cohn, Detroit, 1987—, chair litigation dept., 1996—2002, also bd. dirs., 1999—2003. Adj. prof. Detroit Coll. Law, 1978—98, 2004—06; mem. Mich. Atty. Grievance Commn., 1995—2001, vice-chmn., 1999—2000, chmn., 2000—01; judicial qualification com. State Bar Mich., 2005—. Served to lt. USN, 1967-71, Vietnam. Mem. ABA (grand jury com. criminal justice sect., state bar com. on judicial qualifications, 2006), Fed. Bar Assn. (chmn. criminal law sect. Detroit chpt. 1985-90, bd. dirs. 1985-94, co-chair criminal def. com. 1990-95), Knollwood Country Club (West Bloomfield, Mich.), Std. Club (Detroit), Am. Inns Ct. (master of bench 1995-97), Tam O'Shanter Country Club. Republican. Jewish. Office: Honigman Miller Schwartz & Cohn 2290 First National Bldg Detroit MI 48226 Office Phone: 313-465-7618. Business E-Mail: rez@honigman.com.

ZUCKERT, CATHERINE HELDT, political science educator, writer, editor; b. Miami, Fla., Oct. 20, 1942; d. Henning and Agneta Dom (Christensen) Heldt; m. Michael Paul Zuckert, Sept. 11, 1965; children: Rachel, Larissa, Emily. BA, Cornell U., 1964; MA, U. Chgo., 1967, PhD, 1970. From asst. to full prof. Carleton Coll., Northfield, 1971-98; instr. St. Olaf Coll., Northfield, Minn., 1972; assoc. prof. Claremont (Calif.) McKenna Coll., 1976-77; prof. polit. sci. U. Notre Dame, Ind., 1998—, Nancy Reeves Drew prof. polit. sci., 1999. Wm. R. Kenan Jr. prof. Carleton Coll., 1997-98; vis. prof. honors edn. U. Del., Newark, 1989-90; vis. disting. prof. Fordham U., Bronx, N.Y., 1994-95; vis. prof. U. Mich., Ann Arbor, 1996; cons., panelist NEH, Washington, 1976-97; cons. Ford Found., N.Y.C., 1988-97. Author: Natural Rights and the American Imagination, 1990 (Most Outstanding Book Published in Philosophy of Religion 1990), Postmodern Platos, 1996; co-author: The Truth About Leo Strauss, 2006; editor: Understanding the Political Spirit, 1988 (Choice award 1989); editor-in-chief The Review of Politics, 2004— Named to honor roll Templeton Found., Pa., 1997. Mem. Am. Polit. Sci. Assn., N.Am. Soc. for Study of Greek Thought, Midwest Polit. Sci. Assn. Office: U Notre Dame 547 Flanner Hall 350 Decio Notre Dame IN 46556 Office Phone: 574-631-6620.

ZUE, VICTOR W., engineering educator; ScD in Elec. Engring., MIT, Cambridge, Mass., 1976. Prof. elec. engring. and computer sci. MIT, Cambridge, dir., Computer Sci. and Artificial Intelligence Lab, Delta Electronics chair. Chair Info. Sci. and Tech. study group Defense Advanced Rsch. Projects Agency, US Dept. Defense, 1996—98. Contbr. articles to profl. jours. Fellow: Acoustical Soc. Am.; mem.: NAE, IEEE. Independent. Office: MIT Computer Sci and Artificial Intelligence Lab Stata Ctr, Bldg 32 32 Vassar St Cambridge MA 02139 Office Phone: 617-253-8513. Business E-Mail: zue@csail.mit.edu.

ZUERLEIN, DAMIAN JOSEPH, priest; b. Norfolk, Nebr., May 28, 1955; s. Victor Damian and Elizabeth P. (Wegener) Z. BA, U. St. Thomas, St. Paul, 1977; MDiv, St. Paul Sem., 1981. Ordained priest Roman Cath. Ch., 1981. Tchr. Norfolk Cath. HS, 1981—85; asst. pastor Sacred Heart/St. Mary's Parish, Norfolk, 1981—85; assoc. pastor St. Pius X Cath. Ch., Omaha, 1985-88, Mary Our Queen Cath. Ch., Omaha, 1988-90; pastor Our Lady of Guadalupe Parish, Omaha, 1990—2004, St. Agnes Parish, Omaha, 1997—2004, St. Francis of Assisi Parish, Omaha, 2002—03, St. Columbkille Parish, Papillion, Nebr., 2004—. Cons. Archdiocesan Vocations Office, Omaha, 1985-95; chmn., co-founder Omaha Together One Cmty., 1991-95; co-founder Weaving, Women's Advocacy Group, Omaha, 1988—, co-founder IXIM Spirit of Solidarity, 2004—. Presenter (video) Loving Your Marriage, 1990, El Matrimonio: Una Jornada Para Todo Una Vida, 1995; co-author: (manual) Hispanic Pastoral Plan, 1991. Advisor Mayor P.J. Morgan, Omaha, 1991—95; active Gov. Nelson's Urban Adv. Task Force, 1994, Domestic Violence Coordinating Coun. Greater Omaha, 1996—, Nat. Campaign for Human Devel. Adv. Bd., 1997—2000, Nebr. Gov.'s Task Force on Immigration, 1999—2000; founder, dir. Guadalupe-Ines Mission Sch., 1998—2004; del. Omaha City Charter Rev. Conv., 2003; pres. Omaha Presbyn. Coun., 2003—06, Greater Omaha Clergy Assn., 1987—88; bd. dirs. United Cath. Social Svcs., Omaha, 1990—96, Chicano Awareness Ctr., Omaha, 1991—98, Omaha Food Bank, 2000—, Vis. Nurse Assn., 1996—2000, Omaha 100 Inc., 1991—96, chair, 1991—93; bd. dirs. South Omaha Neighborhood Assn., 1992, pres., 1994—98. Mem. Pax Cristi, Amnesty Internat., Fontenelle Forest Assn. Avocations: canoeing the bwca, skiing, travel, hiking. Home and Office: 200 E 6 St Papillion NE 68046 Home Phone: 402-933-5815; Office Phone: 402-339-3285. Personal E-mail: damzuer@aol.com.

ZUETEL, KENNETH ROY, JR., lawyer; b. LA, Apr. 5, 1954; s. Kenneth Roy Sr. and Adelle Francis Z.; m. Cheryl Kay Morse, May 29, 1976; children: Bryan, Jarid, Christopher, Lauren. BA, San Diego State U., 1974; JD, U. San Diego, 1978. Bar: Calif. 1978, Nev. 2006, US Ct. Appeals (9th cir.) 1979, US Dist. Ct. (ctrl. dist.) Calif. 1979, US Dist. Ct. (so. and no. dists.) Calif. 1980, US Dist. Ct. (ea. dist.) 1981. Clk. to fed. Judge Martin Pence US Dist. Ct. Hawaii, Honolulu, 1978-79; assoc. litigation Buchalter, Nemer, LA, 1979-83, Thelen, Marrin, LA, 1983-88; ptnr. Zuetel & Torigian, Pasadena, Calif., 1988—. Superior ct. arbitrator LA Superior Ct., 1982-90, superior ct. settlement officer, 1988-93; judge pro tem LA Mcpl. Ct., 1983-94, LA Superior Ct., 1989-94; guest lectr. Loyola U. Sch. Law, 1986-95; CEB lectr. Author: Civil Procedure Before Trial, 1992—; cons. editor: Cal. Civ. Proc., 1992; contbr. articles to profl. jours. Recipient Recognition award LA Bd. Suprs., 1988. Mem. State Bar Nev., State Bar Calif. (mem. adv. com. continuing edn. 1985-88, trial practice subcom. 1985-88, disciplinary examiner 1986), Los Angeles County Bar Assn. (chair trial atty. project 1982-83, mem. LA del. conf. of dels. 1986-96, chair LA de. conf. of dels. 1995, exec. com. barristers 1984-88, superior ct. com. 1985-88, civil practice com. 1992-94, exec. com. litigation sect. 1989-90), Pasadena Bar Assn., Inns of Ct. (barrister LA chpt. 1991-92), Mensa, Phi Beta Kappa, Phi Kappa Phi, Phi Alpha Theta, Pi Sigma Alpha. Republican. Presbyterian. Office: Zuetel & Torigian 2 N Lake Ave Ste 550 Pasadena CA 91101 Office Phone: 626-449-5144. Business E-Mail: krzuetel@ztlaw.net.

ZUFRA, MINDY MARIE, mathematics educator; d. Thomas W. Holl and Kathleen Mae Tikva; m. Todd Michael Zufra, Apr. 4, 1997; children: Kyle Jacob, Lauren. BS, Mount Union Coll., Alliance, Ohio, 1996; MA, Akron U., Ohio, 1998. Tchr. Springfield H.S., Akron, 1996—2000, Barberton H.S., Ohio, 2000—. Student coun. advisor Barberton H.S., 2000—, 11th grade advisor, 2000—. Grantee, Martha Holden Jennings Found., 2005, Barberton Cmty. Found., 2005. Mem.: Beta Xi. Office: Barberton HS 555 Barber Rd Barberton OH 44203

ZUFRYDEN, FRED S., academic administrator, finance educator, researcher; b. Grenoble, France, June 13, 1943; came to U.S., 1956; s. Henri and Cecile (Frymer) Z.; m. Toby Marlene Levin, Dec. 24, 1967; 1 child, Ryan BA in Math., UCLA, 1965, MBA, 1966, PhD in Bus. Adminstrn., 1971. Rsch. engr. mil. ops. and systems analysis group N.Am. Aviation, Inc., LA, 1966-67; rsch. assoc. resources rsch. dept. Planning Rsch. Corp., LA, 1967-68; ops. rsch. specialist data systems div. Litton Systems, Inc., LA, 1968-70; asst. prof. dept. mgmt. scis. Sch. Bus. and Econs., U. Calif., Northridge, 1970-71; asst. prof. dept. mktg. Grad. Sch. Bus. U. So. Calif., LA, 1971-75, assoc. prof., 1975-82, prof., 1982—, Ernst Hahn prof. mktg., 1991—, chmn. mktg. dept., 1987-90, rsch. dir. internat. bus. econs. and rsch. Grad. Sch. Bus., 1983—. Mem. editorial bd. Jour. Advt. Rsch., 1981—, Mktg. Sci., 1979—, Jour. Mktg., 1978—; mem. cons. and planning com. Mktg. Sci. Jour., 1979; referee Jour. Mktg. Rsch., Mgmt. Sci., Decision Sci., Jour. Internat. Rsch. in Mktg.; mem. abstract writing staff International Abstracts in Operations Rsch./Mgmt. Sci., 1973; contbr. articles to profl. jours. including Jour. Mktg. Rsch., Mktg. Sci., Jour. Operational Rsch. Soc., Mgmt. Sci., Decision Scis., Jour. Mktg., Jour. Advt. Rsch., Jour. Internat. Rsch. in Mktg., Jour. Royal Statis. Soc., Interfaces, Rsch. in Mktg., Jour. of Mktg. Rsch. Soc., Jour. of Bus., others Rsch. grantee U. So. Calif., 1973, 75, 76, 77, 78, A.C. Nielsen Co., 1988-90. Mem. Am. Mktg. Assn. (cert. recognition 1974), Ops. Rsch. Soc. Am., Inst. Mgmt. Sci., Omega Rho, Beta Gamma Sigma

ZUG, ELIZABETH E., concert pianist, educator; b. Phila., Oct. 8, 1907; d. Nathan Walter and Amelia Elizabeth (Nelson) Zug. BA in Music, Irving Coll., 1928. Mem. faculty Nat. Guild Piano Tchrs., 1949. Judge piano auditions Yr. in Music, Nat. Guild Piano Tchrs., 1949. Debut N.Y. Town Hall, 1938; concert pianist, S.Am. tour, 1941. Named Outstanding N.Y. Debut as Pianist, 1938, Judge of the Yr. Nat. Guild Piano Tchrs., 1949. Mem. Music Tchrs. Nat. Assn., Pa. Music Tchrs. Assn. United Ch. Christ. Avocations: writing, designing, landscaping. Studio: 12 N 4th St Reading PA 19601-3910

ZUGIBE, FREDERICK THOMAS, retired pathologist, forensic specialist; b. Garnerville, NY, May 28, 1928; s. Benjamin and Anna (Zarick) Z.; m. Catherine Frances O'Leary, Apr. 7, 1951; children: Frederick T., Thomas P., Cathryn T. Blaber, Theresa A. Mandracchia, Mary E. Raleigh, Matthew M., Kevin J. BS, St. Francis Coll., 1951; MS, U. Chgo., 1959, PhD, 1960; MD, W.Va. U., 1968. Diplomate Am. Bd. Pathology-Anatomic, Am. Bd. Pathology-Forensic, Am. Bd. Family Practice. Rsch. histologist Lederle Labs., Pearl River, NY, 1950-52, rsch. chemist, 1953-55; rsch. assoc. ophthalmic rsch. Columbia U., NYC, 1955-56; dir. cardiovascular rsch. U.S. VA, Pitts., 1960—65; chief med. examiner County of Rockland, Pomona, NY, 1969—2003. Adj. assoc. prof. pathology Columbia U., 1972—; bd. dirs. Hudson Techs. Inc., Hillburn, N.Y., Rockland Westchester Found. for Sudden Infant Death, White Plains, N.Y.; med. dir. Rockland County Emergency Med. Svcs. N.Y.S. Dept. Health, Pomona, 1990-2003; supervising med. officer disaster med. assistance team Nat. Disaster Med. Assistance, Pomona, 1992-2003; expert on crucifixion and Shroud of Turin. Author: Eat, Drink and Lower Your Cholesterol, 1964, Diagnostic Histochemistry, 1970, 14 Days and a Healthy Heart, 1986, The Cross and Shroud: A Medical Inquiry into Crucifixion, 1988, Dissecting Death, 2005, The Crucifixion of Jesus: A Forensic Inquiry, 2005; contbr. numerous articles to profl. jours. and chpts. to books; appeared in TV documentaries on Discovery Channel, History Channel, Learning Channel, In Search Of, Nat. Geographic, CNN, CBC, others. Named Knight by His Royal Highness Dom Duarte Pio, Duke of Braganca, Head of Royal House Portugal, 2002, Dr, Frederick T. Zugibe Forensic Unit (formerly Rockland County Med. Examiner's Office), legis. action, 2003; named one of 25 people in Rockland County, N.Y. who most influenced this region in the 20th century; recipient Disting. Citizens award, Assn. Visually Impaired, 1998, Physician Recognition awards, more than 75 law enforcement, govtl. and med. awards, 1971—, numerous others, Presdl. Tribute, 1998, Spl. Congressional Recognition award, 1998; Dr. Frederick T. Zugibe Forensic Unit named in his honor, Rockland County Med. Examiners Office, 2003. Fellow Coll. Am. Pathologists (emeritus), Am. Coll. Cardiology (emeritus), Am. Acad. Forensic Scis. (emeritus), NY Cardiology Soc., Coun. Arteriosclerosis of Am. Heart Assn., Assn. Scientists and Scholars Internat. for the Shroud of Turin (pres., founder), Sigma Xi. Roman Catholic. Achievements include first to describe glycoprotein storage disease (Zugibe-Gilbert Syndrome), the defect in the syndrome of the sea blue histocyte and arthrodentoosteodysplasia. an acroosteolysis syndrome, a mask to eliminate odors of putrefaction, and a demummifaction technique for finger-printing; invented ac/dc cardiopulmonary resuscitator, many others. Home and Office: 1 Angelus Dr Garnerville NY 10923-2022 Office Phone: 845-354-1333. Personal E-mail: ftzugibe@msn.com.

ZUHDI, NAZIH, retired surgeon; b. Beirut, May 19, 1925; arrived in US, 1950, naturalized, 1960; s. Omar and Lutfiye (Atef) Z.; children by previous marriage: Omar, Nabil; m. Annette McMichael; children: Adam, Leyla, Zachariah BA, Am. U., Beirut, 1946, MD, 1950. Diplomate Am. Bd. Surgery, Am. Bd. Thoracic Surgery. Intern St. Vincent's Hosp., SI, NY, 1950-51, Presbyn.-Columbia Med. Ctr., NYC, 1951-52; resident Kings County SUNY Med. Ctr., NYC, 1952-56; fellow SUNY Downstate Med. Ctr., Bklyn., 1953-54; resident Univ. Hosp., Mpls., 1956, Okla. City, 1957-58, practice surgery specializing in cardiovasc. and thoracic, 1958-87, Nazih Zuhdi Transplant Inst. adminstr., 1985-99, ret., 1999. Founder, chmn., dir., surgeon-in-chief Oklahoma Transplantation Inst. (renamed Nazih Zuhdi Transplant Inst., Aug., 1999) Bapt. Med. Ctr., 1984-99, chmn. dept. transplantation, Baptist Hosp., Okla. City, 1994-99; co-founder, chmn. Okla. Cardiovasc. Inst., Okla. City, 1983-84, Okla. Heart Ctr., Okla. City, 1984-85 Contbg. author Cardiac Surgery, 1967, 2d edit., 1972; contbr. articles to profl. jour.; developer numerous med. devices, techniques, rsch. and publs. on cardiopulmonary bypass, internal hypothermia, assisted circulation, heart surgery and transplantation of thoracic organs; developer heart-lung machines; designer, use of exptl. plastic bypass hearts; originator of clin. non-hemic primes of heart-lung machines producing total intentional hemodilution, at present, the universally accepted principle of cardiopulmonary bypass for partial and total body perfusion, use of banked citrated blood for surgical field blood loss replacement if needed beyond the cell-saver during open heart surgery, heart transplantation, and lung transplantation; researcher in cardiovasc. studies. Founder Islamic Ctr., Inc., Oklahoma City, 1985-1986; Internat. Bd. Vis., U. Okla., 1996-. Named to Okla. Hall of Fame, 1994. Fellow ACS; mem. AMA, NCCJ (Humanitarian award 1996), Am. Thoracic Soc., Okla. Thoracic Soc., So. Med. Assn., Okla. Med. Assn., Internat. Coll. Angiology, Am. Coll. Chest Physicians, Oklahoma City C. of C., Oklahoma County Med. Soc., Oklahoma City Clin. Soc., Okla. Surg. Assn., Oklahoma City Surg. Soc., Southwestern Surg. Congress, Am. Coll. Cardiology, Am. Soc. Artificial Internal Organs, Soc. Thoracic Surgeons (founding mem.), Am. Assn. for Thoracic Surgery, Internat. Cardiovasc. Soc., Okla. State Heart Assn., Osler Soc., So. Thoracic Surg. Assn., Lillehei Surg. Soc., Internat. Soc. Heart Transplantation, Dwight Harken's Founder's Group Cardiac Surgery, Westaby's Pioneers in Cardiac Surgery, Internat. Soc. Cardiothoracic Surgery (Japan, founding mem.), Am. Soc. Transplant Surgeons, Milestones of Cardiology of Am. Coll. Cardiology, Okla. City Golf and Country Club, Okla. Hall of Fame. Moslem. Achievements include first to use banked citrated blood for cardiopulmonary bypass for open heart surgery; invention of experimental and clinical non-hemic primes of heart-lung machines producing total intentional hemodilution. Home: 7305 Lancet Ct Oklahoma City OK 73120-1430 Personal E-mail: anz70@aol.com.

ZUICHES, JAMES JOSEPH, sociologist, educator; b. Eau Claire, Wis., Mar. 24, 1943; s. William Homer and Bronnie Monica (Stich) Z.; m. Carol Ann Kurilo, Aug. 19, 1967; children:; James Daniel, Joseph Kurilo. BA in Philosophy, U. Portland, 1967; MS in Sociology, U. Wis., 1969, PhD in Sociology, 1973. Instr., asst. prof., assoc. prof. sociology Mich. State U., East Lansing, 1971-82, prof., 1982; assoc. program dir. in sociology NSF, Washington, 1979-80, program dir. in sociology, 1980-82; assoc. dir. rsch. Cornell U., Ithaca, N.Y., 1982-86; assoc. dean Coll. Agr. and Home Econs., Wash. State U., Pullman, 1986-94, dir. Agrl. Rsch. Ctr., 1986-94; program dir. food sys. and rural devel. W.K. Kellogg Found., Battle Creek, Mich., 1994-95; dean Coll. Agr. and Home Econs. Wash. State U., Pullman, 1995—2003, prof. Dept. Cmty. and Rural Sociology, 1986—. Mem. adv. subcom. NSF, 1977-79; sci. adv. com. USDA Nat. Rsch. Initiative, Washington, 1992-93; com. on future land grant univ. bd. on agr., NRC, Washington, 1994-96; pub. Wash. Land and People Mag., 1987-92; mem. Bd. Natural Resources, Wash. State, 1995-2003. Co-editor: The Demography of Rural Life, 1993; contbr. articles to profl. jours. Pres., bd. dirs. Edgewood Village Children's Ctr., East Lansing, 1978-79. Recipient sustained superior performance award NSF, 1981; rsch. grantee NIMH, 1973, ERDA, 1978. Fellow AAAS; mem. Rural Sociol. Soc. (pres. 1992-93, editor 50th Anniversary Rsch. Series, 5 vols. 1988-93), Am. Sociol. Assn., Population Assn. Am. Roman Catholic. Avocations: skiing, swimming, hiking, reading. Office Phone: 509-335-8540.

ZUICK, ERNEST RONALD, JR., career officer, advertising executive; b. San Bernardino, Calif., Nov. 2, 1935; s. Ernest Ronald Sr. and Catherine Louise (Leach) Z.; m. Johnnie Fern Lemons, Aug. 19, 1966. BA, Fresno State U., 1964, MA, 1968; MPA, Auburn U., 1974; postgrad., Air Command and Staff Coll., 1974, Air War Coll., 1982. Cert. tchr., Calif. Joined Calif. Air N.G., 1958, advanced through grades to col., 1984; advt. acct. exec., sports and polit. cartoonist Turlock (Calif.) Jour., 1956-62; advt. acct. exec. Fresno (Calif.) Bee, 1965-76; various assignments Calif. Mil. Dept., Sacramento, 1976-85, dir. legis., 1985-95, spl. projects dir., 1999—2001; dir. Media Svcs., 2001—04. Mem. ancillary staff Res. Forces Policy Bd., Office of Sec. of Def., 1982-95. Co-editor: Grizzly Mag., 2005—; contbr. articles to profl. jours. Mem. N.G. Assn. Calif. (pres. 1983-84). Avocations: writing, cartooning, video production.

ZUIDEMA, GEORGE DALE, surgeon, educator; b. Holland, Mich., Mar. 8, 1928; s. Jacob and Reka (Dalman) Z.; m. Joan K. Houtman, June 2, 1953; children: Karen Sue, David Jay, Nancy Ruth, Sarah Kay. AB, Hope Coll., 1949, D.Sc. (hon.), 1969; MD, Johns Hopkins U., 1953. Diplomate: Am. Bd. Surgery. Intern Mass. Gen. Hosp., 1953-54, asst. resident surgeon, then chief resident surgeon, 1954, 57, 58, 59; asst. prof. surgery, then assoc. prof. U. Mich. Sch. Medicine, 1960-64; prof. surgery, dir. dept. Johns Hopkins Sch. Medicine; also surgeon in chief Johns Hopkins Hosp., 1964-84; prof. surgery, vice provost med. affairs U. Mich., 1984-94. Cons. Walter Reed Army Med. Center, Sinai Hosp., Balt., Balt. City Hosp., Clin. Center of NIH; chmn. Study on Surg. Svcs. for U.S., 1970-75 Editor: (with O.H. Gauer) Gravitational Stress in Aerospace Medicine, 1961; (with G.L. Nardi) Surgery-A Concise Guide to Clinical Practice, 1961, 4th edit., 1982; (with R.D. Judge and F. Fitzgerald) Physical Diagnosis, 1963, 6th edit., 1997; (with W.F. Ballinger and R.B. Rutherford) Management of Trauma, 1968, 4th edit., 1985; (with L. Schlossberg) Atlas of Human Functional Anatomy, 1977, 4th edit., 1997, Shackelford's Surgery of the Alimentary Tract, 5th edit., 2001; editor Jour. Surg. Rsch., 1966-72, assoc. editor, mem. editl. bd., 1972—; mem. editl. bd. Surgery Ann., 1968-75, Surgery, 1970-97, co-editor in chief, 1975-97. Bd. dirs. Md. divsn. Am. Cancer Soc., 1964-68; trustee William Beaumont Hosp., Royal Oak, Mich., 1984-94, Hope Coll., Holland, Mich, 1987—. Capt. M.C., USAF, 1954-56. John and Mary R. Markle scholar academic medicine, 1961-66; recipient Henry Russell award U. Mich., 1963 Fellow ACS,

Royal Coll. Surgeons Ireland (hon.); mem. Assn. Am. Med. Colls., Ctrl. Soc. Clin. Rsch., Soc. Univ. Surgeons, Am. Surg. Assn., So. Surg. Assn., Soc. Clin. Surgery, Soc. Vascular Surgery, Internat. Cardiovascular Surgery, Halsted Soc., Nat. Inst. Medicine, Assn. Acad. Surgeons (pres. 1967-69), Allen O. Whipple Soc., Coun. on Grad. Med. Edn., Ft. Del. Soc. (dir., 2006—), Del. Acad. Soc. (pres., 1994-1996, 2004—, dir., 1990—), Phi Beta Kappa, Tri Beta, Alpha Omega Alpha. Home and Office: 983 Willow View Ct Holland MI 49424-6615

ZUK, CARMEN VEIGA, psychiatrist; b. Buenos Aires, Mar. 5, 1939; arrived in U.S., 1971; d. Carlos and Carmen Villella Veiga; m. Gerald Harvey, May 7, 1974; children: Cary Elizabeth and Gabrielle Ann (twins). MD, U. Buenos Aires, 1964, cert. psychiatry, 1969. Diplomate Am. Bd. Psychiatry and Neurology. Intern Med. Coll. Pa., Phila., 1974—75; resident in psychiatry Norristown State Hosp., Norristown, Pa., 1977—79; child psychiatry fellowship Med. Coll. Pa. and Ea. Pa. Psychiat. Inst., Phila., 1979—81; dir. child and adolescent unit Hosp. of Med. Coll. Ga., Augusta, 1981—83; dir. treatment team New Orleans Adolescent Hosp., 1983—85; assoc. Psychiatry Med. Group, Calif., 1985—86; mental health psychiatrist L.A. County Dept. Mental Health San Fernando Mental Health Svcs., 1986—88; psychiatrist-ptnr. So. Calif. Permanente Med. Group, Van Nuys, 1988—98, ptnr., 1988—98; staff psychiatrist Santa Clarita Child and Family Ctr., 1999—2002; ret., 2005. Asst. prof. dept. psychiatry Med. Coll. Ga., 1981-83; clin. asst. prof. dept. psychiatry and neurology Tulane U., 1983-85. Co-author: Psychology of Delusion, 2005; contbr. articles to profl. jours. Mem. AMA, Internat. Soc. for Adolescent Psychiatry. Avocations: reading, cooking, gardening, swimming, music. Home: 7620 Hollister Ave 219 Goleta CA 93117 Personal E-mail: carmenzuk@msn.com.

ZUKER, CHARLES S., neuroscientist, biology professor; PhD, MIT. Investigator Howard Hughes Medical Inst.; prof. biology & neurosciences U. Calif., San Diego, 1986—. Scientific advisor Avalon Ventures; scientific co-founder Aurora Biosciences, 1995, Senomyx, Inc., 1999; mem. scientific adv. bd. Ambit Biosciences, CMEA Ventures. Recipient Alcon award, AAAS, 1999, Gogan award, 2000; fellow, Jane Coffin, U. Calif. Berkeley, Whitaker Health Scis. Found., MIT. Mem.: Am. Acad. Arts and Scis., Nat. Acad. Scis.

ZUKERMAN, MICHAEL, lawyer; b. Bklyn., Oct. 3, 1940; s. Charles Morris and Gertrude Ethel Zukerman; m. Claire J. Goldsmith, June 25, 1961 (div. 1986); children: Steven, Amy; m. Elaine DeMasi, Nov. 21, 1986 (div. 1999); children: Jaclyn, Laura; m. Janey Alexander, Feb. 2, 2001. BS, U. Fla., 1961; LLB, St. John's U., 1964; LLM, NYU, 1966. Bar: NY 1965, Pa. 1983, U.S. Tax Ct. 1984. Credit analyst, loan officer Franklin Nat. Bank, 1964-66; assoc. Jaffin, Schneider, Kimmel & Galpeer, NYC, 1966-67; ptnr. Zukerman, Licht & Friedman and predecessors, NYC, 1967-79, Baskin & Sears, P.C., NYC, 1979-85, Graubard, Moskowitz, Dannett, Horowitz & Mollen, NYC, 1985-86, Gersten, Savage, Kaplowitz & Zukerman, NYC, 1986-89; of counsel Olshan, Grundman, Frome & Rosenzweig, NYC, 1990-95, Graham & James, NYC, 1995-2000, Bryan Cave LLP, 2000—03; exec. v.p. Brookhill Group, 1986-89; of counsel Sonnenschein Nath and Rosenthal, NYC, 2003—04, Warshaw Burstein Cohen Schlessinger & Kuh LLP, NYC, 2004—. Pres. First Ptnrs. Credit Corp., NYC, 1988—93; bd. dirs. Interjurist Ltd., Whitestone Realty Capital, LLC; mng. dir. Nat. Aspbergers Rsch. Found., 1993—, trustee, 2001—; lectr. in field. Contbr. articles to profl. jours. Trustee Temple Beth Torah, Melville, N.Y., 1972-80, YMHA Suffolk County, Hauppague, N.Y., 1980-85; bd. dirs. Dayton Mgmt. Corp., 1974-2001, Suffolk Jewish Cmty. Planning Bd., Hauppague, 1982-85, Congregation Bnai Elohim, 1994, 2nd v.p., 1995; co-chmn. bus. adv. coun. Town of Greenburgh, 1992. Mem.: ABA. Home: 915 Cherry Ln Valley Stream NY 11581-2722 Office: Warshaw Burstein Cohen Schlessinger & Kuh LLP 11th Fl 555 Fifth Ave New York NY 10016 Home Phone: 516-792-0220; Office Phone: 212-984-7836. E-mail: mzukerman@whitestonerealty.com.

ZUKERMAN, PINCHAS, concert violinist, violist, conductor; b. Tel Aviv, July 16, 1948; came to U.S., 1962; s. Yehuda and Miriam (Lieberman) Z.; m. Eugenia Rich, May 26, 1968 (div.); children: Natalia, Arianna; m. Tuesday Weld, 1985 (div.); m. Amanda Forsyth, Mar. 2004. Student, Juilliard Sch. Music, 1965-68; MusD (hon.), Brown U., 1989. Ind. concert violinist, 1968—. With impresario, Sol Hurok, 1967-76; condr., soloist English Chamber Orch., 1974, Mostly Mozart Festival, N.Y.C., 1975; guest condr., soloist Los Angeles Philharm., Boston Symphony, Chgo. Symphony, Pitts. Symphony, Phila. Orch., N.Y. Philharm.; music dir. South Bank Festival, London, 1978-80, St. Paul Chamber Orch., 1980-87, Nat. Arts Ctr. Orch., 1998—; prin. festival condr. Dallas Internat. Summer Music Festival, 1990-94; prin. guest condr. Dallas Symphony, 1993-95; toured with Isaac Stern; mem. trio with Daniel Barenboim and Jacqueline du Pre; (rec. artist) CBS, EMI, Philips Classics labels, RCA Victor Red Seal, BMG Classics. Winner Internat. Levintritt Competition, 1967, Medal of Arts, 1983, Isaac Stern award Nat. Arts Awards, 2002. Office: care Kirshbaum Demler & Assoc 711 W End Ave Apt 5KN New York NY 10025-6821

ZUKOSKI, CHARLES FREDERICK, IV, chemical engineering educator, academic administrator; b. Birmingham, Ala., Aug. 17, 1955; BA in Physics, Reed Coll., 1977; PhD in Chem. Engring., Princeton U., 1984. Asst. prof. dept. chem. engring U. Ill., Urbana, 1985-90, assoc. prof., 1990-93, prof., 1994—, alumni prof. chem. engring., 1994—, head chem. engring., 1995—, vice chancellor rsch., William H. and Janet G. Lycan prof. Contbr. articles to profl. jours. Fulbright scholar, Dept. Applied Math., U. Melbourne, 1992; recipient NSF Presdl. Young Investigator award, 1986, Everitt Tchg. award, 1992, Ralph K. Iler award, Am. Chem. Soc., 1997, Alpha Chi Sigma award, AIChE, 2002. Mem.: NAE. Office: U Ill Dept Chem Engring 109 Roger Adams Lab MC-712 Box C-3 600 S Mathews Ave Urbana IL 61801 Office Phone: 217-333-0034. Office Fax: 217-333-5052. E-mail: czukoski@uiuc.edu. *

ZULAUF, SANDER (SANDER WILLIAM ZULAUF), poet, educator, editor; b. Paterson, NJ, Nov. 5, 1946; s. S. William Z. and Marion Ann Zulauf; m. Christianne Beresford, June 15, 1968 (div. 1976); 1 child, Scott; m. Madeline Ruth Slocum, May 26, 1979; stepchildren: Michael, Mary Beth. BA, Gettysburg Coll., 1968; MA, Ind. U., 1973. Tchr. Martin Luther King Sch., Paterson, NJ, 1968—69, Hanover Park Regional H.S., East Hanover, NJ, 1969-71; prof. County Coll. Morris, Randolph, NJ, 1973—. Editor, pub. Ars Poetica, Lake Hopatcong, N.J., 1996-99. Author: (poetry) Succasunna New Jersey, 1987, Living Waters, 2005; editor: The Poets of New Jersey: From Colonial to Contemporary, 2005, Jour. N.J. Poets, 1989—; founding editor Index Am. Periodical Verse, 1971—82. Sec.-treas. Forest South Homeowners Assn., Byram Twp., 1989—94, pres., 2004—; lay eucharistic min. St. Dunstan's Episcopal Ch., Succasunna, 1974—. Named 1st Poet Laureate, Diocese of Newark, 1999—; recipient Allen Ginsberg award, Poetry Ctr., Passaic, N.J., 1993, 2001, 2002, Excellence in Print award, Jour. N.J. Poets Pub. Radio's Poet and the Poem, 2002; fellow NEH, Princeton, 1987; grantee N.J. Arts Coun., 1992—93. Mem. Acad. Am. Poets, Poetry Soc. Am., Poets House, Kenneth Burke Soc., Thoreau Soc., Assn. Writers and Writing Programs, Skylands Writers and Artists Assn. (sec. treas. 1994-98, v.p. 1999-2000). Democrat. Episcopalian. Avocations: camping, boating, environmental preservation, gardening, travel. Home Phone: 973-347-1068; Office Phone: 973-328-5471. Personal E-mail: sanderzpoet@msn.com. Business E-Mail: szulauf@ccm.edu.

ZULCH, JOAN CAROLYN, retired medical publishing company executive; b. Great Neck, NY, Apr. 10, 1931; d. Walter Howard and Edna Ruth (Howard) Z. BS in Biology, Allegheny Coll., 1952; postgrad., Hunter Coll., 1954. Med. sec. E.R. Squibb & Sons, NYC, 1952; with Macmillan Pub. Co., NYC, 1952-88, editorial asst. med. dept., 1952-56, asst. editor med. dept., 1956-58, editor med. dept., 1958-61, med. editor coll. and profl. div., 1961-75, sr. editor medicine, coll. and profl. div., 1975-78, exec. editor med. books, profl. books div., 1978-79, editor-in-chief, 1979-80, asst. v.p., editor-in-chief profl. books div., 1980-82, v.p., pub. med., nursing, health sci. dept., 1982-85, v.p., pub. med. books, sci., tech., med. dept., 1985-88. Recipient Best Illustrated Med. Book award Assn. Med. Illustrators, 1977, Outstanding Book in Health Sci. award Assn. Am. Pubs., 1982, Woman of Distinction award, 15th Dist. NYS Assembly, 2006. Mem. AAAS, Post Libr. Assn., L.I.U. (rec. sec. 1990-93, exec. coun. 1990—96), Friends of Locust Valley Libr. (pres. 1991-93, 94-96, 98-2000, 2004—06, treas. 1993-94, 96-98, 2000-02, 1st v.p. 2002-04, 2006-), Locust Valley C. of C. (bd. dirs. 1997—), Alpha Gamma Delta, Delta Sigma Rho. Republican. Home: 36 Wood Ln Lattingtown PO Box 547 Locust Valley NY 11560-0547

ZULKER, CHARLES BATES, broadcasting company executive; b. Pleasantville, NJ, Dec. 20, 1926; s. William John and Virginia (Carr) Z.; m. Virginia Wright, June 24, 1949; children: Connie Lee, Timothy Scott Charles. Adminstrv. officer Princeton (N.J.) U., 1950-60; asst. mgr. Sta. WPEL, Montrose, Pa., 1960-65; gen. mgr. Sta. WCHR, Trenton, NJ, 1965—. Trustee Princeton Evang. Fellowship, 1973-83; bd. council Word of Life Internat., Schroon Lake, N.Y., 1974-82; mem. exec. bd. Upper Makefield Community Assn., 1972-79; deacon Westerly Rd. Ch., Princeton, 1999-2002. With U.S. Army, 1945-46. Mem. Wooden Canoe Heritage Assn. Am., Nat. Religious Broadcasters, Nat. Assn. Broadcasters, Squam Lakes Assn. (Holderness, N.H.). Office: 119 Locktown Rd Flemington NJ 08822-4715 Office Phone: 215-493-4252. E-mail: czulker@nassaubroadcasting.com.

ZUMBRUN, ALVIN JOHN THOMAS, law and criminology educator; s. Orrell Sylvester Tilton and Mary Kathryn (Sprinkle) Zumbrun; m. Marianne Jane Nolan; children: Mary Susan, Alvin J. T. Jr., Steven M., Diane, MaryAnn, Mary Kathleen. BA, U. Md., 1952, MA, 1956; MEd in Spl. Edn., Coppin State U., 1972, MEd in Adminstrn., 1974; JD, U. Balt., 1970. Probation officer Supreme Bench of Balt., 1950-52; budget and program dir. Cmty. Chest, Balt., 1953-55; mng. dir. Criminal Justice Commn., Balt., 1956-59; exec. dir., criminologist Md. Crime Investigating Com., Balt., 1960—93; dept. chmn., prof. criminal justice Catonsville CC, Md., 1968-94; dept. chmn., dir. grad. program, prof. criminal justice U. Balt., 1974-76. Adj. prof. criminal justice U. Md., Hood Coll., Coppin State U., Md. State Police Acad., Balt. County Polic Acad., 1969—; mem. adv. bd. Balt. Criminal Justice Program, 1976—94; cons. Am. Edn. Assn., Washington, 1980—85; mem. senate Catonsville CC, 1970—83; mem. Nat. Disaster Med. Sys., 1993—; mem. acad. stds. senate com. U. Md., College Park, 1997—99; rschr. in field. Author: Maryland Crime Report, 5 vols., 1959—94, Directory of Criminal Justice Agencies, 22 vols., 1962—94, Civil Disturbance Riots of 1968, 1969. Mem. scholarship com. Md. Troopers Assn., Pikesville, 1990—93; pres. Maplewoods Home Owners Assn., 1996—97; lay pres., mem. coun. Salem Luth. Ch., Catonsville, 1956—59, 1965—68; mem. adv. bd. articulation com. U. Md., College Park, 1977—94. Lt. (j.g.) USN. Recipient Superior Pub. Svc. award, Afro Am. Newspaper, 1962, Excellence in Tchg. award, Md. State Bd. CCs, 1987, Superior Ednl. Svcs. award, Balt. County Police Chief, 1994, citation for ednl. achievements, Gov. of Md., 1994, Hon. Trooper 25 Yrs. Acad. Tchg., Md. State Police, 1995. Mem.: VFW (life), Internat. Assn. Chiefs Police, Nat. Dist. Attys. Assn., Intenrat. Soc. Criminology, Md. Acad. Criminal Justice Profs. (pres. 1971—94), Am. Legion (life). Avocations: walking, bicycling, travel. Home and Office: 438 Maple Forest Rd Catonsville MD 21228-1783 Office Phone: 301-405-0172. Personal E-mail: azumbrun@comcast.net.

ZUMBRUNNEN, DAVID ARNOLD, engineering educator; b. Salt Lake City, Sept. 3, 1955; m. Elizabeth Buck. B in Mech. Engring., U. Minn., 1977; MS in Mech. Engring., Purdue U., 1984, PhD in Mech. Engring., 1988. Registered profl. engr., Ind., SC. Co-founder NSF Ctr. Advanced Engring. Fibers and Films; asst. prof. mech. engring. Clemson U., SC, 1988—93, assoc. prof. mech. engring., 1993—97, prof. mech. engring., 1997—2003, Warren H. Owen-Duke Energy prof. mech. engring., 2003—. Lt. USN, 1977—82. Presdl. Faculty Fellow The White House/NSF, 1992-97. Fellow: ASME; mem.: AAAS, Polymer Processing Soc., Material Rsch. Soc., SPE, Am. Chem. Soc., AIChemE. Achievements include invention of structured materials formed by chaotic advection and smart blending technology. Office: Dept Mech Engring Clemson Univ Clemson SC 29634-0921 Business E-Mail: zdavid@clemson.edu.

ZUMERCHIK, JOHN, urologist; b. Chgo., Ill., Nov. 29, 1932; s. John and Anna (Marchuk) Z.; m. Eileen Heraty, June 14, 1958; children: Cheryl Ann, John Francis, David Lee, Steven Jay, Patricia Eileen, James Jacob, Janine Marie. AA, Wilson Jr. Coll., Chgo., 1953; student, U. Ill., Chgo., 1953-54; MD, Loyola U., 1958. Diplomate Am. Bd. Urology. Rotating intern Cook County Hosp., Chgo., 1958-59, urology resident, 1960-63; gen. surg. resident MacNeal Meml. Hosp., Berwyn, Ill., 1959-60; pvt. practice Drs. Ross-Zumerchik Partnership, Evergreen Park, Ill., 1964-67, Drs. Ross, Zumerchik, Boctor, Evergreen Park, 1970-83, Southwest Urology Assocs., Evergreen Park, 1983—. Staff urologist Little Co. of Mary Hosp., chmn. divsn. urology, dept. surgery, 1977-80, 82-84; staff urologist Ingalls Meml. Hsop.; mem. resident edn. attending staff dept. urology Cook County Hosp., 1961-85, grad. edn. asst. prof., 1963-85; clin. instr. urology med. student edn. Loyola U. Chgo., 19562-72. Pres. 98th and Kedzie Corp., Evergreen Park, 1988, 96-97. Lt. col. M.C. U.S. Army, 1968-70. Fellow ACS (mem. examining com. 1978-84, 92-96); mem. AMA, Am. Urol. Assn. (north ctrl. sect.), Am. Assn. Clin. Urologists, Chgo. Urol. Soc. (exec. com. 1987), Ill. Urol. Soc., Ill. Med. Soc., Chgo. Med. Soc., Pan-Pacific Surg. Assn., Royal Soc. Medicine, Am. Soc. Andrology, Am. Fertility Soc., Am. Inst. Ultrasound in Medicine, Endourology Soc. Avocations: tennis, skiing, biking, photography, carpentry. Office: Southwest Urology Assocs 9760 S Kedzie Ave Evergreen Park IL 60805-3123 Business E-Mail: swuroloty9760@sbcglobal.net.

ZUMWALT, RICHARD DOWLING, flour mill executive; b. Amarillo, Tex., Dec. 1, 1912; s. Richard Dowling and Cora Bell (Pate) Z.; m. Florine Anita Nelson, Oct. 23, 1938; 1 dau., Alexandra Anita (Mrs. Klaus Schwabe). Student, Met. Bus. Coll., 1930; ext. student, Tex. Tech. Coll., 1931, Dallas Coll., 1949. With Pearlstone Mill & Elevator Co., summers 1929/30, J. C. Crouch Grain Co., 1931-44, Burrus Mills, Inc., Dallas, 1944-83, exec. v.p. Regla, Cuba plant, 1952, pres., 1964-83; sec.-treas. Zumwalt Inc., 1973—; ret. gen. mgr. Burrus milling dept. Cargill, Inc. Past pres. Bulgur Assos., Washington, Dallas Grain Exch. Mem. Millers Nat. Fedn., Tex. Mfrs. Assn. (past dir.). Home: 7353 Blairview Dr Dallas TX 75230-5416 Personal E-mail: ddzumwalt@aol.com.

ZUMWALT, ROGER CARL, hospital administrator, consultant; b. Eugene, Oreg., Oct. 26, 1943; s. Robert Walter and Jean Elaine (Adams) Z.; children: Kathryn Nicole Zumwalt DeWeber, Timothy Robert. Student, Boise State U., 1963—65; BA, We. Oreg. U., 1969; postgrad., U. Iowa, 1969—71; MA cum laude, Oreg. State U., 1973. Adminstr. Coulee Cmty. Hosp., Grand Coulee, Wash., 1973-75, Eastmoreland Hosp., Portland, Oreg., 1975-81; exec. dir. Cmty. Hosp., Grand Junction, Colo., 1981-97; pres., healthcare cons. accreditation Zumwalt Consulting, Salem, Oreg., 1997—; dir. adminstrv. svcs. divsn. SAIF Corp., Salem, 1998—. Chmn., bd. dirs. Alphabet House Pediat. Rehab. and Edn., 1998—2000, Castle Rock Med. Group, Inc., Denver, 1998—2003; part owner, chmn. bd. dirs. Castle Rock Med. Ctr., Colo., 1998—, N.W. Okla. Regional Med. Ctr. Cherokee, 2000; spkr. numerous local and nat. presentations, subjects including healthcare, hosp. mktg./success/costs, 1981—97; guest lectr. Mesa State Coll., 1992—98, Colo. Christian Coll., 1996—98. Newspaper columnist, 1973-75; contbr. articles, presentations to profl. publs. Commr. Multnomah County Health Care Commn., Portland, 1978-81; health cons. Grant County Housing Auth., Grand Coulee, 1974-75; mem. pk. bd. City of Tigard, Oreg., 1976-78; caucus rep. Mesa County Rep. Party, Grand Junction, 1988; mem. adv. com., pres.'s office Mesa State Coll., Grand Junction, 1989; bd. dirs. Hospice of Grand Valley, Grand Junction, 1992-97, mem. devel. com., 1993-97, vice chmn. bd. dirs., 1994-97; bd. dirs. Grand Valley Hospice, 1992-96; com. mem. Salem Coalition on Youth Literacy, 2000—. Fellow Coll. Osteo. Healthcare Execs. (bd. dirs. 1985-88, pres. 1987, examiner 1989—, Disting. Svc. award 1989); mem. Am. Osteo. Healthcare Assn. (bd. dirs. 1987-98, treas. 1992-93, 1st v.p. 1994-95, 2d v.p. 1993-94, vice chairperson 1994-95, chmn. 1996-97, chairperson 1997-98, past chmn. 1998), Am. Osteo. Assn. (ex-officio mem. bd. dirs. 1996), Bur. Healthcare Facilities Accreditation (v.p. 1994, advisor 1995-98, accreditation cons. 1995—, accreditation surveyer 1978—, accreditation survey instr. 1994—), Joint Commn. on Am. Healthcare Orgn. (task force on small and rural hosps. 1994-98), Colo. Hosp. Assn. (bd. dirs. 1987-92), Mountain States Vol. Hosp. Assn. (bd. dirs. 1984-98, exec. com. 1991-98, v.p. 1993, vice chmn. bd. dirs. 1992-98), We. Coll. Ind. Practice Assn. (Medicine Mauls Measles com., fin. com. 1991-92), We. Colo. Health Care Alliance (bd. dirs. 1989-94, v.p. 1992, chmn. bd. dirs. 1993), Mesa County Mental Health Assn. (bd. dirs. 1988-89, 91-92), Grand Junction C. of C. (bd. dirs. 1991-93), Rotary (Grand Coolee, Wash. 1973-75, Portland 1975-81, Grand Junction 1981-98, Salem 1998—, chmn. fund raising com. 2000-01, bd. dirs. 2001-02), Western Oreg. U. Alumni Assn. (bd. dirs. 2006—, v.p. bd. dirs. 2006-07, pres.-elect 2007—), Masons, Shriners (pres. Grand Junction club 1989, bd. dirs. El Jebel 1986-90, 1st v.p. Western Colo. club 1989), KC. Republican. Roman Catholic. Avocations: golf, camping, fishing, hunting. Home: 592 Meadowbrook Ln Stayton OR 97383 Office: SAIF Corp 440 Church St SE PWB 2 Salem OR 97312-2000 Fax: 503-315-3086. E-mail: rogzum@netzero.com, rogzum@netzero.net.

ZUMWALT, ROSS EUGENE, forensic pathologist, educator; b. Goodrich, Mich., July 18, 1943; s. Paul Lawrence and Lila Ann (Birky) Z.; m. Theresa Ann Schar, Sept. 12, 1970 (div. Apr. 1988); children: Christopher Todd, Tenley Ann; m. Cheryl Lynn Willman, Sept. 4, 1988; 1 child, David Willman Zumwalt. BA, Wabash Coll., 1967; MD, U. Ill., 1971. Diplomate in anat. and forensic pathology Am. Bd. Pathology. Intern, resident in pathology Mary Bassett Hosp., Cooperstown, NY, 1971-73; resident in anat. and forensic pathology Southwestern Med. Sch., Dallas, 1973-76; asst. med. examiner Dallas County, Dallas, 1974-76; staff pathologist, dir. labs. Naval Regional Med. Ctr., Camp Lejeune, NC, 1976-78; dep. coroner Cuyahoga County, Cleve., 1978-80, Hamilton County, Cin., 1980-86; assoc. prof. pathology U. Cin. Sch. Medicine, 1980-86; prof. pathology U. N.Mex. Sch. Medicine, Albuquerque, 1987—; chief med. investigator Office of Med. Investigator, Albuquerque, 1991—; pres. Am. Bd. of Pathology, Tampa, 2000—01. Trustee Am. Bd. Pathology, Tampa, Fla., 1993—. Lt. comdr. USN, 1976-78. Fellow Am. Acad. Forensic Scis., Coll. Am. Pathologists; mem. AMA, Nat. Assn. Med. Examiners (bd. dirs. 1984-96, pres. 1995-96), Am. Soc. Clin. Pathologists, Am. and Can. Acad. Pathologists. Avocation: golf. Home Phone: 505-344-7480; Office Phone: 505-272-0710. Business E-Mail: rzumwalt@salud.unm.edu.

ZUNG, THOMAS TSE-KWAI, architect; b. Shanghai, Feb. 8, 1933; came to the U.S., 1937, naturalized, 1954; 1 child, Thomas Bates. Student, Drew U., 1950-51, Va. Poly. Inst., 1951-53, Columbia U., 1955-57; BArch, U. Mich., 1960; MS in Design Sci., Internat. Coll., 1982. Project arch. Edward Durell Stone, Arch., NYC, 1958, 60-65; arch. Cleve., 1967—. Pres. Buckminster Fuller, Sadao and Zung, Archs., 1979—; disting. sr. fellow Stanford U. Librs.; John Denver Windstar Found. Symposium spkr., Aspen, Colo., 2004. Author editor: Buckminster Fuller, Anthology for the New Millennium; prin. works include City Cleve. Pub. Utilities Bldg., Cleve. State U. Geodesic Elongated Dome, Mayfran, Inc., Sawmill Creek Lodge, U. Akron Guzzetta Hall, Music, Speech and Theater Arts Ctr., Alumni Ctr. Bowling Green State U., U. Akron Master Plan-West, City of East Cleveland, Superior Euclid beautification plan, student recreation ctr. Bowling Green State U., Glenville Pub. Libr., campus bldg. Tex. Wesleyan Coll., recreation, health and phys. edn. bldg. Wittenberg U., Medina Res. Park Office, arena, health, phys. edn. complex U. Akron, Dyke Coll., Lima State Prison, Cleve. Children's Christian Home, State of Ohio Pre-Release Ctr. Cleve., Lorain-Grafton State Prison, Mayfield H.S., Asian Village Project, Cleve. Metroparks Tropical Rainforest Bldg., Student Union Wittenberg U., YWCA, Salem, Ohio, China Internat. Trade Ctr., People's Rep. China, additions to Cleve. Hopkins Internat. Airport, Ohio State U. Coll. of Dentistry-Postle Hall and Hist. Costume and Textile Mus., Master Plan Schreiner Coll. and Cailloux Student Ctr., Griffin Welcome Ctr., Master Plan Walsh Univ., Walsh Student Union, Columbus, Western Res. Psychiat. Hosp., Ohio, Trumbull State Prison, Ohio Dept. Transp. Prototypical Rest Stop Design; patentee in field. Trustee Pace Assn., 1970-73, Karamu House, 1974-80, Cleve. Inst. Music, 1979-86, Chinese Cultural Assn., 1980-84, Ohio Arts Coun., 1982-84; task force chmn. Greater Cleve. Growth Assn., 1970; mem. Coun. Human Rels., 1972, Leadership Cleve. Class '77; cubmaster local Boy Scouts Am., 1977-79; vestryman St. Christopher-by-River, 1980-83; bd. dirs. Buckminster Fuller Inst., 1983—, Pearl S. Buck Found., 1989-98, cons. arch. hist. house com.; mem. Adv. Coun. Aging, State of Ohio, 1997—; founder, pres. Bratenahl 100, 2006-. With Signal Corps, U.S. Army, 1953-55. Decorated 5 medals; recipient Pub. Works award, State of Ohio, 1971, Design award, Korean Inst. Constrn. Tech., 1984, Ohio Valley ABC Design Excellence award, Wittenberg U. Student Union, 1989, Synergeticists N.E. Corridor award, 2005, Buckminster Fuller SNEC award, 2005, others; Disting. sr. fellow, Stanford U. Librs. Mem. AIA (dir. Cleve. chpt. 1980, Design award Cleve. chpt. 1972, Design award 1989), Am. Soc. Planning Ofcls., English Speaking Union (trustee 1972-75), Ohio Soc. Archs., Ohio Assn. Minority Archs. and Engrs. (trustee 1982-90), Hermit Club, City Club (dir. 1972-74, v.p. 1974), Rotary. Office: Buckminster Fuller Sadao & Zung 1 Bratenahl Pl Cleveland OH 44108-1181

ZUNGOLO, EILEEN H., dean; BS, MEd, EdD, Columbia U. Prof., dean Sch. Nursing Northeastern U., Boston, assoc. dean Bouve Coll. Health Scis. Office: Northeastern Univ Sch Nursing 360 Huntington Ave Boston MA 02115-5000 E-mail: ezungolo@lynx.dac.neu.edu.

ZUNZ, OLIVIER JEAN, history professor; b. Paris, July 19, 1946; s. Jean R. and Monique M. (Blin) Z.; m. Christine M. Crommen, July 3, 1970; children: Emmanuel, Sophie. Licence in history and geography, U. Paris X, 1968, M in History, 1969; Doctorat-ès-Lettres, U. Paris I, Panthéon-Sorbonne, 1982. Scientist Ctr. Nat. de la Recherche Scientifique, Paris, 1976-78; asst. prof. dept. history U. Va., Charlottesville, 1978-83, assoc. prof., 1983-88, prof., 1988-99, Commonwealth prof., 1999—. Vis. prof. Ecole des Hautes Etudes en Scis., Sociales, Paris, 1985—, Coll. France, 1997; dir. seminar for Coll. Tchrs. NEH, 1989, 92. Author: The Changing Face of Inequality: Urbanization, Industrial Development, and Immigrants in Detroit, 1980-1920, 1982, Making America Corporate, 1870-1920, 1990, Why the American Century?, 1998; editor, co-author: Reliving the Past: The Worlds of Social History, 1985; editor: Alexis de Tocqueville, Democracy in America (transl. A. Goldhammer), 2004; co-editor: (with David Ward) The Landscape of Modernity: Essays on New York City, 1900-1940, 1992, (with Leonard Schoppa and Nobuhiro Hiwatari): Social Contracts under Stress: The Middle Classes of America, Europe, and Japan at the Turn of the Century, 2002, (with Alan S. Kahan): The Tocqueville Reader: A Life in Letters and Politics, 2002; mem. editl. bd. Revs. in Am. History, 1990-98; contbr. articles, book revs. to profl. jours. Jr. fellow Mich. Soc. Fellows, 1973-76, John Simon Guggenheim Meml. Found. fellow, 1986-87; grantee U. Mich.-Ford Found. Population

Devel. Fund, 1974-76, NSF, 1976-78, NEH, 1979-81, 84-87, Ford Found., 2004-07; also recipient numerous rsch. grants. Mem. Am. Hist. Assn., Orgn. Am. Historians, The Tocqueville Soc. (pres. 2001—06). Home: 1368 Hilltop Rd Charlottesville VA 22903-1225 Office: U Va Corcoran Dept of History PO Box 400180 Randall Hall Charlottesville VA 22904-4180 Business E-Mail: oz@virginia.edu.

ZUPAN, MARK A., dean, business professor; b. Rochester, NY, July 28, 1959; s. Janez and Maria (Močnik) Zupak; m. Carol Shuherk; children: Will, Walker. BA in economics, Harvard U., 1981; PhD in economics, MIT, 1987. Teaching fellow dept. economics Harvard U., Cambridge, 1983-86; asst. prof. to prof. economics Marshall Sch. Bus., U. So. Calif., 1987—97, assoc. dean masters programs; dean, prof. economics Eller Coll. Bus. and Pub. Adminstrn., U. Ariz., 1997—2004; dean Simon Grad. Sch. Bus., U. Rochester, NY, 2004—, prof. economics and pub. policy. Vis. prof. Amos Tuck Sch. Bus. Adminstrn., Dartmouth Coll.; mem. editl. bd. Pub. Choice, Jour. Bus. Economics, Rsch. in Law and Economics. Co-author: (with E.K. Browning) Microeconomic Theory and Applications, (with T. W. Gilligan, A. M. Marino) Microeconomic Cases and Applications; Contbr. articles to profl. journals. Mem. Phi Beta Kappa. Lodges: Rotary. Office: William E Simon Grad Sch Bus Adminstrn U Rochester CS-2202H Carol Simon Hall Rochester NY 14627-0107 Office Phone: 585-275-3316. Business E-Mail: mark.zupan@simon.rochester.edu. *

ZUPANSKI, DUSANKA, research scientist; b. Yugoslavia; BS, U. Belgrade, Serbia, 1981, MS, 1989, PhD, 1994; postgrad., U. Corp. Atmospheric Rsch., Camp Springs, Md., 1994—96. Postdoctoral fellow U. Corp. for Atmospheric Rsch., Camp Springs, Md., 1994—96, rsch. scientist, 1996—2001, Colo. State U./Coop. Inst. for Rsch. in the Atmosphere, Ft. Colins, 2001—. Mem.: European Geophys. Soc., Am. Geophys. Union, Am. Meteorol. Soc. Achievements include first to data assimilation; model error estimation. Office: Colo State U 1375 Campus Delivery Fort Collins CO 80523-1375 Office Phone: 970-491-8642. Business E-Mail: zupanski@cira.colostate.edu.

ZUPKO, MISCHA SARCHÉ, composer, church music director; b. Chgo., June 29, 1971; s. Ramon Eugene and Vonette Sarché Zupko; m. Minkyoo Shin, May 17, 2003. BA in Piano Performance, Northwestern U., Evanston, Ill., 1994; MA in Composition, Ind. U., Bloomington, 1998, DM in Composition, 2003. Invited participant masterclass in composition Aspen Summer Music Festival, 1998. Composer: (concert music) Visions of a Forgotten Soul for Baritone and String Quintet, 1996, Evolutions for Woodwind Quartet, 1996, Etude for Flute and Piano, 1997, Lumens for Orchestra, 1997 (Jacob Druckman prize Aspen Music Festival, 1998), Sonata for Bassoon and Piano, 1998, Mourning Song for Cello, 1998, Facing the Wind for Violin and Piano, 1998, Jasmine's Looking Glass for Flute, Clarinet, Violin, Cello, Percussion and Piano, 1998 (Commd. Aspen Music Festival, 1998), Shunt for Piano and Tape, 1999, Fahrenheit for Piano and Chamber Orchestra, 1999, Canter Into Black for Orchestra, 2000, In Transit for Alto Saxophone and Piano, 2000, Despedida for Harp, 2000 (USA Internat. Harp Competition Composition Contest winner, 2003), Five Etudes for Piano, 2001 (Ruth and Emil Beyer award Nat. Fedn. of Music Clubs, 2000), Femme Fatale, 2002, The Seventh Seal for Alto Saxophone and Organ, 2002, Towards You for Mezzo Soprano, Clarinet, Violin, Viola and Cello, 2002, Seven Deadly Sins, 2002 (Lee Ettelson prize, 2004), Harpsichord Concerto for Harpsichord and String Quartet, 2002, Processional for Alto Saxophone and Organ, 2003, Ghost Variation for Piano, 2003 (Commd. Gilmore Internat. Keyboard Festival, 2003), Still for Orchestra, 2004 (Commd. Pacific Symphony, 2003), Addendum for Soprano and Piano, 2004, Ichabod for Orchestra, 2004 (Commd. Minn. Orch., 2004), Shades of Grey for Violin and Piano, 2005 (Commd. Barlow Endowment, 2005), Nuevo Dia, 2006 (Commd. Music Inst. of Chgo., 2006), Dawning for Organ, 2006. Finalist Rome Prize Competition (Prix de Rome), Am. Acad. in Rome, 2004; named a participant in Soc. of Electro-accoustic Music in the U.S. Y2K Conf., 2000, participant Minn. Orch. Reading Sessions and Composers Inst., Minn. Orch., 2002; recipient Am. Composer's Competition winner, Pacific Symphony Orch., 2003, Margaret Buehler-White Meml. award, Nat. Soc. of Arts and Letters/Bloomington Chpt.'s 2001 Music Competition, 2001, First Music 17 competition winner, NY Youth Symphony, 2000, Cola Heiden Meml. award, Nat. Soc. of Arts and Letters/Bloomington Chpt.'s 2000 Music Competition, 2000, Tom Brown Meml. award, 1998; grantee, St. Olaf Symphonic Band, 2006, Fromm Found. (Harvard U.), 2002. Mem.: ASCAP (1st Pl. Kaplan award Morton Gould Young Composer Awards 2001, Morton Gould Young Composer award 1999, 2000), Am. Music Ctr., Soc. of Composers Inc. Home: 5801 N Sheridan Rd #6B Chicago IL 60660 Office: Lutheran Ch of the Ascension 460 Sunset Ridge Rd Northfield IL 60093 Home Phone: 773-784-0937; Office Phone: 847-446-8335. Office Fax: 847-446-8308. Personal E-mail: mzupko@sbcglobal.net. Business E-Mail: mischa@ascension-church.org.

ZUPSIC, MATTHEW MICHAEL, insurance company executive; b. Pitts., Aug. 30, 1950; s. Joseph Matthew and Antoinette (Birsic) Z.; children: Tina Elizabeth, Matthew Quay. BA, Marietta Coll., 1972. Mktg. rep. Hartford Ins., Pitts., 1972-76; ins. agt. Githens Ins. Ctr., Belle Vernon, Pa., 1976-77; v.p., ptnr. Burchill Ins. Agy., Inc., Pitts., 1977-88; pres. Harte, Hawke & Zupsic Ins. Agy., Pitts., 1989—. Mem. Pa. Assn. Ind. Ins. Agts. (bd. dirs. 1980-88), Ind. Ins. Agts. Pitts. (treas. 1983, 1st v.p. 1984-86, pres. 1986-88), B&S Investment Club (pres 1985-87). Democrat. Roman Catholic. Avocations: sailing, skiing, boating, gardening. Office Phone: 724-940-7540. Business E-Mail: mzupsic3@connecttime.net.

ZURBENKO, IGOR GEORG, science educator; s. George and Leokadia Zurbenko; m. Laura M. Close, June 1, 1991. MSC, Moscow State U., 1978, PhD, 1981. Chair nat. statis. lab. Moscow U., 1980—90; prof. biostatistics U. Albany, 1991—. Author: Spectral Analysis of Time Series. Mem.: Am. Statis. Assn. Liberal. Roman Catholic. Achievements include research in New Computer Algorithms In Spectral Analysis. Avocations: travel, hiking, swimming. Home: One Univ Pl 141 Rensselaer NY 12144 Office: RPI 110 Eigteen St Troy NY 12180 Office Phone: 518-276-6452. Home Fax: 518-402-0381. Business E-Mail: izurbenko@uamail.albany.edu.

ZURCHER, ZEAN WILLIAM, retired music educator, musician; s. Harvey George Sheldon and Audrey Phyllis (Jones) Zurcher; m. Kay Alice Kneip, Sept. 1, 1955; children: Robert William, Linda Kay Pedersen. MusB Edn., Morningside Coll. Conservatory of Music, Sioux City, Iowa, 1956; MA, Columbia U., NYC, 1959, profl. diploma, 1960, EdD, 1973. Cert. tchr. of music NY State, 1960, sch. adminstrn. and supervision NY State, 1973. Vocal and instrumental music tchr. (part time) Homer Pub. Schools, Homer, Nebr., 1955—58, Winnebago Pub. Schools, Winnebago, 1956—58; asst. in music edn. Teachers Coll., Columbia U., NYC, 1959—60; instrumental music tchr. Middletown Pub. Schools, 1960—63, Baldwin Pub. Schools, NY, 1960—96; ret. Music rschr. Nat. Symposium on Rsch. in Music Behavior, 1975—87; rsch. lectr., panelist NY State Sch. Music Assn., 1975—88; mem. Columbia U. Consortium on Competency-Based Tchr. Edn., NYC, 1977—78; presenter in field. Co-author: Applications of Research in Music Behavior: The Alabama Project (Music, Society and Education in America) (named Nationally-Recognized Rschr., 1987), Design for Music Learning, Research in Music Behavior: Modifying Music Behavior in the Classroom; performer: Newport Jazz Festival Nat. Tour, Tommy Vig Trio, The Roland Wiggins Quintet, Don Glasser Band, Ernie Rudy Band, Am. Opera Soc. Orch., Little Orch. Soc., Russian State Symphony. With 21st Army Band, 1954—55, Ft. Lewis, Wash. Named to All-American Bandmasters Band, Am. Bandmasters Assn., Chgo., 1957; recipient Hon. Life Membership, NY State Congress of Parents and Tchrs., 1966, Plaque for Outstanding Contbns., Badwin Band and Orch. Mothers' Club, 1969, PTA Plaque in appreciation for 20 yrs. of dedication to the students of Baldwin Harbor Jr. HS, Parent Tchrs. Assn., 1983. Mem.: NY State Sch. Music Assn. (recognized for 30 yrs. of dedicated svc. 1993), Baldwin Teachers Assn. (v.p. 1986—2000), NY State United Tchrs. (del. 1986—2000), Am. Fedn. Tchrs. (del. 1986—2000, recognized for 30 yrs. of dedicated svc.), Music Educators Nat. Conf., Phi Mu Alpha Sinfonia Music Frat. (life; pres. of Beta Gamma chpt. 1959—60). Christian Science. Achievements include music rsch. cited in numerous publ. including Achieving Ednl. Excellence by Sulzer-Azaroff and Mayer. Avocations: concerts, opera, theater, travel. Home: 81 Lester Ave Freeport NY 11520-5912 Home Phone: 516-868-4084. Personal E-mail: wzurcher@aol.com.

ZURHEIDE, CHARLES HENRY, consulting electrical engineer; b. St. Louis, May 9, 1923; s. Charles Henry and Ollie C. Z.; m. Ruth M. Plueck, June 25, 1949; children— Barbara Anne, Pamela S BS in Elec. Engring, U. Mo., Columbia, 1944. Registered profl. engr., Mo. Distbn. engr. Laclede Power & Light Co., St. Louis, 1944-45; sub-sta. engr., then indsl. engr. Union Electric Co., St. Louis, 1945-51; chief elec. engr. Fruin-Colnon Contracting Co., St. Louis, 1951-54; a founder, treas., v.p. Smith-Zurheide, Inc., St. Louis, 1954-65; pres. Zurheide-Herrmann, Inc., St. Louis, 1965—, chmn. bd., 1988—2002; ret. Chmn. Elec. Code Rev. Commn., St. Louis, 1965-, Mo. Bd. Profl. Engrs., 1977-82, St. Louis Indsl. Devel. Commn., 1965-67; mem. adv. panel region 6 GSA, 1977—; plan commn., City of Ferguson, Mo., 1968-73; tech. adv. com. St. Louis C. of C., 1977; mem. Mo. Pub. Svc. Commn. Task Force on Retail Wheeling of Electricity, 1998 Recipient Dist. Svc. in Engring. award, U. Mo., 1976. Fellow Am. Cons. Engrs. Council; mem. Mo. Soc. Profl. Engrs. (Engr. of Year award 1970), Cons. Engrs. Council Mo., IEEE, Illuminating Engring. Soc., Engrs. Club St. Louis (Achievement award 2003), Tau Alpha Pi. Clubs: Norwood Hills Country. Mo. Athletic Home: 14336 Spyglass Rdg Chesterfield MO 63017-2140 Office: Zurheide-Herrmann Inc 4333 Clayton Ave Saint Louis MO 63110-1684 Business E-Mail: czurheide@zhideas.com.

ZURICK, JACK, electrical engineer, consultant; b. Bklyn., May 28, 1952; s. Joseph and Edelgard (Wendland) Zurick; m. Nenita Cardinal, Apr. 28, 1990. AAS, Queensborough CC, 1973. Cert. assoc. engring. technician. Elec. designer Ebasco Svcs., Inc., NYC, 1973-76; design engr. Gibbs & Cox, Inc., NYC, 1976-78; elec. designer Sci. Design Co., Inc., NYC, 1978-85; design engr. Vikonics, Inc., Secaucus, NJ, 1985-87; sr. elec. designer H-R Internat., Inc., Edison, NJ, 1988-93; sr. elec. engr. Kleinknecht Elec. Co. NJ, Maplewood, 1993-94; cons. Rotator Svcs., Inc., East Brunswick, NJ, 1994-95; elec. design engr. ICF Kaiser Engrs., Inc., Iselin, NJ, 1995-97; sr. elec. designer Fluor Daniel, Inc., Marlton, NJ, 1997, Orbital Engring. Inc., Bensalem, Pa., 1997; design mgr. Automated Control Concepts, Inc., Neptune, NJ, 1998—2006; sr. elec. designer Altran Solutions Inc., Cranbury, NJ, 2006—. Cons. Sherman Svcs., Inc., Somerset, 1988, Gen. Indsl. Techs., Inc., Valleystream, NY, 1987—88, Allied Resources Tech. Cons., Inc., 1997. Mem.: Nat. Inst. Cert. Engring. Technols. (assoc. engring. technician), Tau Alpha Pi (v.p. 1972—73). Avocations: golf, guitar, electronics, scuba diving. Home: 59 Pheasant Run Freehold NJ 07728-7767 Office: Altran Solutions Inc 2525 Rte 130 Cranbury NJ 08512 Office Phone: 609-409-9790 ext. 1333. Personal E-mail: jzurick@optonline.net. Business E-Mail: jzurick@altransolutions.com.

ZURIER, ROBERT BURTON, rheumatology educator; b. Passaic, NJ, Feb. 19, 1934; s. Milton and Lillian (Matzner) Z.; m. Catherine Elizabeth Miers, June 3, 1962; 1 child, Adam Wheaton. BS, Rutgers U., 1955; MD, U. Tex. Southwestern Med. Sch., Dallas, 1962; MA (hon.), U. Pa., 1981. Intern, then resident in medicine Boston City Hosp., 1962-64; fellow in medicine St. Lukes Hosp., NYC, 1964-66; fellow in rheumatology NYU, 1970-73; pvt. practice internal medicine Holden, Mass., 1967-70; asst. prof. medicine U. Conn., Farmington, 1973-76, assoc. prof., 1976-80; prof., chief. rheumatology U. Pa., Phila., 1980-91; prof. medicine, dir. rheumatology div. U. Mass. Med. Ctr., Worcester, 1991—2006, prof. medicine, 2006—. Served to capt. USAR, 1956-68. Guggenheim Found. fellow, 1986. Mem. AAAS, Am. Coll. Rheumatology (master), Am. Soc. Clin. Investigation, Interurban Clin. Club (pres. 1989-90). Office: U Mass Med Ctr 55 Lake Ave N Worcester MA 01655-0002 Office Phone: 508-856-6246. Business E-Mail: robert.zurier@umassmed.edu.

ZUSCHLAG, NANCY HANSEN, environmental and nature resources educator; d. Irving Djalmar and Carmen Mary Zuschlag. BA in Biology cum laude, Coe Coll., 1977; MA in Biology, U. Kans., 1982. Regional conservation educator and coord. Mo. Conservation Dept., Jefferson City, 1982-84; coord. sch. programs Denver Mus. Natural History, 1986-87; program dir. dept. natural resources and environ. edn. Coop. Ext. Colo. State U., 1988-98; dir. ops. and edn. Mad Sci. of Denver, 1998-99; pres. Green Triangle Internat., 1997—; instr. and sci. specialist Colo. Acad., 2000—; internat. coord. Cultural Programs Can., Europe and S.Am., 2001, 2004. Instr. environ. educator Mus. Natural History, U. Kans., Lawrence, 1976-82, assoc. pub. edn. dept., 1986-89; lectr. William Woods Coll., 1982-84; study, rsch. rev. group Canary Islands, 1985; cons. Kongskilde Field Study Edn. Ctr., Soro, Denmark, 1985; assoc. zool. Denver Mus. Natural History, 1988; cons. and educator Mus. Zool., U. Copenhagen, 1984-85, 95-96; co-dir., sci. coord., instr. Colo. Acad., 2000-04; environ. edn. coord., instr. Cherry Creek Sch. Sci., 2004; natural and phys. adj. prof., instr. U. N. Colo., 2006, lectr. urban edn., 2006. Author, editor: Back to Ancient Egypt, 1987; (with others) Science - Natur/Teknik, Assessment and Learning Studies and Educational Theory Curriculum, Vol. 22, 1995; editor: (with others) Contributions to Vertebrate Ecology and Systematic; a Tribute to Henry S. Fitch, 1983; contbr. articles to profl. jours. State edn. coord. Colo. Earth Day is Every Day campaign, Boulder, 1990; bd. dirs. Foothills Nature Ctr., Boulder, Colo., 1987-89, Colo. Found. Agr., Denver, 1992-95, edn. bd., 1993, World Coun. Elders, 2003—; facilitator and presenter UN Program Youth in the Environment, U. Colo., Boulder, 1993; chair environ. and natural resources future's task force com., Colo. State U. Coop. Ext., 1993; nat. natural resources and environ. mgmt. support team coop. states, rsch. ext. edn. sys., USDA, 1993-96; synthesis team and original document writing team, Colo. Environ. Edn. Master Plan, 1994; state steering com. Denver Urban Resources Partnership, 1996—, Denver Youth Naturally Project, 1995. Recipient N.J. award AUW, County Achievement award Nat. Assn. Counties, 1989, Environ. Scholar award USEPA, 1990, region 8 Outstanding Women's Contbns. in Environ. Edn. award, 1992, Nat. Environ. Coun. award, 1992, 94, Celebrate Colo. Environ. Leadership award Colo. State Gov., 1993; scholar Coe Coll., 1973-74; Virginia Harkness-Sawtelle Found. scholar Coe Coll. and U. Kans., 1976-78; Fulbright scholar U. Copenhagen Zool. Mus., 1984-85, Fulbright scholar assoc. Royal Danish Sch. Edn., 1995-96. Mem. Am. Assn. Biol. Scis., Nat. Wildlife Fedn. (mem. steering com. Naturlink 1993), North Am. Assn. Environ. Edn., Alliance Environ. Edn., Nat. Assn. Interpreters, Am. Arachnological Assn., Colo. Alliance Environ. Edn. (bd. dirs. 1988-92, pres. 1990-91, adv. bd. 1997), Colo. Assn. Tchrs., Fulbright Alumni Soc., Phi Sigma, Epsilon Sigma Phi (State Early Career Excellence award 1990). Avocations: hiking, writing on nordic and celtic myth, nature and culture, jewelry-making, travel. Office: Green Triangle Internat PMB 223 4255 S Buckley Rd Aurora CO 80013 Office Fax: 303-699-1358. Personal E-mail: nhzgreentri@hotmail.com.

ZUSSY, NANCY LOUISE, librarian; b. Tampa, Fla., Mar. 4, 1947; d. John David and Patsy Ruth (Stone) Roche; m. R. Mark Allen, Dec. 20, 1986. BA in Edn., U. Fla., 1969; MLS, U. So. Fla., 1977, MS in Pub. Mgmt., 1980. Cert. librarian, Wash. Ednl. evaluator State of Ga., Atlanta, 1969-70; media specialist DeKalb County Schs., Decatur, Ga., 1970-71; researcher Ga. State Libr., Atlanta, 1971; asst. to dir. reference Clearwater (Fla.) Pub. Libr., 1972-78, dir. librs., 1978-81; dep. state libr. Wash. State Libr., Olympia, 1981-86, state libr., 1986—2002; owner Nancy Zussy Allen Massage Therapy, 2003—. Chmn. Consortium Automated Librs., Olympia, 1982-97; cons. various pub. librs., Wash. and other U.S. states, Uzbekistan, Russia, 1981—; exec. officer Wash. Libr. Network, 1986-90; v.p. WLN (non-profit orgn.), 1990-93. Contbr. articles to profl. jours. Treas. Thurston-Mason Community Mental Health Bd., Olympia, 1983-85, bd. dirs., 1982-85; mem. race com. Seafair Hydroplane Race, Seattle, 1986—, mem. milk carton derby team, 1994—, announcer, prodr. air show; co-chair Pub. Info. Access Policy Task Force, 1995-96; mem. Gov.'s Work Group on Comml. Access to Govt. Electronic Records, 1996-97; mem. K-20 Telecomms. Oversight and Policy Com., 1996-2002. Mem. ALA, Assn. Specialized and Coop. Libr. Agys. (legis. com. 1983-86, chmn. 1985-87, vice chmn. state libr. agys. sect. 1985-86, chmn. 1986-87, chmn. govt. affairs com. Libr. Adminstrn. and Mgmt. Assn., 1986-87), Freedom To Read Found. (bd. dirs. 1987-91), Chief Officers of State Libr. Agys. (bd. dirs.-at-large 1987-90, v.p., pres.-elect 1990-92, pres. 1992-94), Wash. Libr. Assn. (co-founder legis. planning com. 1982-2002, fed. rels. coord. 1984-2002), Fla. Libr. Assn. (legis. and planning com. 1978-81), Pacific N.W. Libr. Assn., Rotary (bd. dirs. 1995-96), Phi Kappa Phi, Phi Beta Mu. Avocations: hiking, barbershop quartets, boating, cross country skiing. Office: 1722 Harrison Ave NW Olympia WA 98502

ZUTAUT, STEVEN ERIC, systems analyst, application developer; s. James and Magdaline Zutaut. BS in Computer Sci./Chemistry, U. Ala., Huntsville, 1984, PhD in Materials Sci., 1993. Journeyman knowledge-based applications developer Minn., cert. internet application developer Oracle Corp., solution developer.net Microsoft Corp., developer for JavaTM 2 Platform Sun Microsystems, Inc. Assoc. systems analyst Unisys, Montgomery, Ala., 1984—87; knowledge engr. PEAKSolutions Corp., Bloomington, Minn., 1987—89; rsch. assoc. U. Ala., Huntsville, 1993—96; rsch. scientist Nichols Rsch. Corp., Huntsville, 1996—99; sr. cons. Computer Scis. Corp., Huntsville, 1999—2001; software developer (cons.) AEROTEK, Huntsville, 2001—02; sr. systems analyst III Teledyne Solutions, Inc., Huntsville, 2002—04; software developer (cons.) TEKSystems, Huntsville, 2005—06; software engr. Westar Aerospace and Def. Group, 2006—. Contbr. articles to profl. jours. Mem.: IEEE, Assn. Computing Machinery. Home: 7801 Regent Pl SW Apt 6 Huntsville AL 35802-1471 Personal E-mail: sezutaut@msn.com.

ZVETINA, JAMES RAYMOND, pulmonologist; b. Chgo., Oct. 14, 1913; s. John and Jennie (Albrecht) Z.; m. Florence Courtney, Feb. 4, 1944. BS, Loyola U., 1940; MD, U. Ill., 1943. Intern West Suburban Hosp., Oak Park, Ill., 1944, resident physician, 1944-45; asst. ward med. officer USNH, NOB, Norfolk, Va., 1945; staff physician Pulmonary TB Svc. VA Med. Hosp., Hines, Ill., 1946-54; asst. chief Pulmonary Svc. VA Med. Hosp., Hines, Ill., 1954-68, sect. chief, 1968-88, attending physician, 1988-91, cons., 1992—; clin. prof. medicine Coll. Medicine, U. Ill., Chgo., 1978—. Mem. adv. bd. Coll. Medicine, U. Ill., 1985—; rep. Rsch. Conf. in Pulmonary Disease, VA Armed Forces, 1946-74. Contbr. articles to profl. jours. V.p. Chgo. Cath. Physicians, 1979, pres., 1978. Comdr. USNR, 1945-46, med. officer USNR, ret. Recipient Svc. award 40 Yrs. VA Adminstrn., 1985, Svc. award 30 Yrs. U. Ill. Med. Sch., 1978. Fellow Am. Coll. Chest Physicians; mem. AMA, Ill. State Med. Soc. (Fifty Yr. club), Chgo. Med. Soc., Third Order of St. Dominic. Roman Catholic. Achievements include research in area of pulmonary infections. Home: 96 Forest Ave Riverside IL 60546-1977 Office: VA Hines Hines IL 60141

ZVIJAC, JOHN E., orthopedist, surgeon; b. Buffalo, Ny, Mar. 22, 1960; s. John and Ann Zvijac; m. Gail Zvijac. MD, SUNY Buffalo Sch. of Medicine, 1986. Cert. Am. Bd. of Orthop. Surgeons, 1994. Orthop. surgeon UHZ Sports Medicine Inst., Coral Gables, Fla., 1992—; prof. U. of Miami Sch. of Edn., Dept. of Exercise Sci. & Sports Medicine, Fla., 1992—2006; mem., athletic tng. educatin adv. bd. Fla. Internat. U., Miami, 1992—, courtesy prof. in exercise and sports sci., 2005—. Chief of staff Doctors Hosp., Coral Gables, 2004—; team physician Tampa Bay Buccaneers, Fla., 1998—, Fla. Internat. U., Miami, 1992—, Chaminade-Madonna Coll. Prep. Sch., Hollywood, 2002—. Contbr. chapters to books. Bd. mem. Doctors Hosp., Coral Gables, Fla., 2004—. Fellow: Arthroscopy Assn. of N.Am., Am. Orthop. Soc. for Sports Medicine, Am. Acad. of Orthop. Surgeons; mem.: Fla. Orthop. Soc., NFL Physicians Soc., Internat. Soc. of Arthroscopy, Knee Surgery & Orthop. Sports Medicine. Office: UHZ Sports Medicine Inst 1150 Campo Sano Ave Ste 200 Coral Gables FL 33146 Office Phone: 305-669-3320. Office Fax: 305-669-3353. E-mail: jzvijac@uhzsmi.com.

ZWANGER, JEROME, physician; b. NYC, Apr. 4, 1923; m. Bernice E. Lomazov, May 22, 1955; children: Susan, Roberta (dec.), Melissa, Betsy. AB, U. Pa., 1943; MD, Chgo. Med. Sch., 1947. Diplomate Am. Bd. Radiology. Intern Wyckoff Heights Hosp., Bklyn., 1947-49; resident L.I. Coll. Hosp., Bklyn., 1949-52; practice medicine specializing in radiology; asst. dir. dept. radiology L.I. Coll. Hosp., NYC, 1953-54; radiologist L.I. Jewish Hosp., 1955-60; dir. radiology North Shore U. Hosp., Plainview, NY, 1961—, also bd. dirs. Asst. prof. clin. radiology SUNY, Stony Brook, 1974-80; governing bd. Nassau-Suffolk Health Systems Agy.; mem. N.Y. State Bd. Medicine, Bd. Profl. Med. Conduct N.Y. State Dept. Health. Mem. vis. com. Met. Mus. Art, Phila. Art Mus.; bd. overseers Sch. Arts and Scis., U. Pa. Fellow: Nassau Acad. Medicine (founding fellow, past pres.), Am. Coll. Radiology (councilor 1975—); mem.: AMA, Soc. for Breast Imaging, Am. Inst. Ultrasound in Medicine, L.I. Radiol. Soc. (past pres.), N.Y. State Radiol. Soc. (pres. 1986—87), Radiol. Soc. N.Am., Nassau County Med. Soc. (past pres.), Med. Soc. N.Y., U. Pa. Alumni Assn. (bd. overseers 1997). Office: 126 Hicksville Rd Massapequa NY 11758-5822

ZWANZIG, ROBERT WALTER, chemist, physical science educator; b. Bklyn., Apr. 9, 1928; s. Walter and Bertha (Weil) Z.; m. H. Frances Ryder, June 6, 1953; children: Elizabeth Ann, Carl Philip. BS, Poly. Inst. Bklyn., 1948; MS, U. So. Calif., 1950; PhD, Calif. Inst. Tech., 1952. Rsch. assoc. Yale, 1951-54; asst. prof. Johns Hopkins, 1954-58; phys. chemist Nat. Bur. Standards, 1958-66; rsch. prof. U. Md., College Park, 1966—, disting. prof. phys. sci., 1980-88, disting. prof. emeritus, 1988—; rsch. chemist NIH, Bethesda, Md., 1988—. Assoc. editor: Jour. of Chem. Physics, 1965-67, Jour. of Math. Physics, 1968-70, Transport Theory and Statistical Physics, 1970, Chem. Physics, 1973—; Contbr. articles profl. jours. Dept. Commerce Silver medal, 1965 Fellow Am. Phys. Soc., Am. Acad. Arts and Scis., AAAS; mem. Nat. Acad. Scis., Am. Chem. Soc. (Peter Debye award in phys. chemistry 1976, Irving Langmuir award 1984, Joel H. Hildebrand award 1994). Home: 5314 Sangamore Rd Bethesda MD 20816-2355 Office: NIH Nat Inst Digestive and Diabetes and Kidney Diseases Bethesda MD 20892-0001

ZWASS, VLADIMIR, computer science and information systems educator; b. Lvov, USSR, Feb. 3, 1946; came to U.S., 1970, naturalized, 1979; s. Adam and Friderike (Getzler) Z.; m. Alicia Kogut, Apr. 24, 1977; 1 child, Joshua Jonathan MS, Moscow Inst. Energetics, 1969; MPhil, Columbia U., 1974, PhD, 1975. Mem. profl. staff IAEA, Vienna, 1970; asst. prof. computer sci. Fairleigh Dickinson U., Teaneck, NJ, 1975-79, assoc. prof., 1979-84, prof., 1984—, prof. computer sci. and mgmt. info. sys., 1990—, disting. prof. computer sci. and mgmt. info. sys., 1999—, chmn. com. computer sci., 1976—. Cons. U.S. Govt., Met. Life Ins. Co., Citibank, Diebold Group; seminar assoc. Columbia U., 1986—; speaker nat. and internat. meetings. Author: Introduction to Computer Science, 1981, Programming in Fortran, 1981, Programming in Pascal, 1985, Programming in Basic, 1986, Management Information Systems, 1992, Foundations of Information Systems, 1998; editor-in-chief: Jour. Mgmt. Info. Sys., 1983—, Internat. Jour. Electronic Commerce, 1996—, Advances in Mgmt.

Info. Systems, —; contbr. articles to profl. jours. and publs., Ency. Britannica, N.Y. Times, chpts. to books. Columbia U. fellow, 1970-71; Helena Rubinstein Found. scholar, 1971-75; grantee USN, other agys. Mem. IEEE, Assn. Computer Machinery, Assn. for Info. Sys., Sigma Xi, Eta Kappa Nu. Home: 19 Warewoods Rd Saddle River NJ 07458-2712 Office: Sch Computer Sci and Info Sys Fairleigh Dickinson U Teaneck NJ 07666 Office Phone: 201-327-9239. Personal E-mail: zwass@fdu.edu.

ZWEBACK, STANLEY, psychologist, educator; s. Harry and Belle Zweback; m. Dianne Barbara Fain, Dec. 24, 1964; children: Franklin Edward, Jessica Ellen. PhD, U. Md., 1972; BA, Coll. N.J., 1964. Diplomate Am. Bd. Profl. Disability Consultants. Assoc. prof. psychology Towson U., Md., 1970—; dir. svcs. Pers. Screening Sys., Severna Park, Md., 1985—. Cons. Balt. City Pub. Sch. Sys., 1999—2003; dir. svcs. Drs. Zweback, Driscoll and Assocs., Severna Park, 1989—98; psychol. cons. Arthur Slade Regional Sch., Glen Burnie, Md., 1973—. Contbr. articles to profl. jours. Pres. Bello Machre, Inc., Pasadena, Md., 1987—96. Experienced Tchr. fellow in sch. psychology, U.S. Office Edn., 1967—68. Mem.: APA (continuing edn. com. 1989—90). Office: Towson U 8000 York Rd Towson MD 21252 Office Phone: 410-704-3210. Personal E-mail: stanzwe@yahoo.com. E-mail: zweback@towson.edu.

ZWEBEN, STUART HARVEY, information scientist, educator, dean; b. Bronx, NY, Apr. 21, 1948; s. Max D. and Ruth (Schwartz) Z.; m. Rochelle T. Small, June 13, 1971; 1 child, Naomi. BS, CUNY, 1968; MS, Purdue U., 1971, PhD, 1974. Sys. analyst IBM Corp., Kingston, NY, 1969-70; asst. prof. Ohio State U., Columbus, 1974-80, from vice chmn. to acting chmn. computer sci. dept., 1982-84, assoc. prof., 1980-92, prof., 1992—, chmn., 1994—2005, assoc. dean academic affairs and adminstrn. Coll. Engring., 2006—. Pres. Computing Scis. Accreditation Bd., Stamford, Conn., 1989-91, v.p. 1987-89, sec., treas. 1986-87; sec.-treas. Fedn. on Computing in the U.S., Washington, 1992. Contbr. articles to profl. jours. Rsch. grantee NSF, 1981-83, 88-97, 2005-06, Army Rsch. Office, 1980-83, Dept. Edn., 1983-85, Applied Info. Tech. Rsch. Ctr., 1990-91, Honda R&D, 1998-2006, Dayton, Ohio, 2003-; Equipment grant AT&T Bell Labs, 1984, 86-88. Fellow Accreditation Bd. Engring. and Tech., Inc. (computing accreditation commn. exec. com. 2001—, vice chmn. ops., 2005-06, chair elect, 2006-), Assn. for Computing Machinery (pres. 1994-96, v.p. 1992-94, coun. mem. 1982-88, chpt. bd. chmn. 1982-85, publications bd. 1988-92, fin. com. 1990-92, nominating com. chmn. 1999-2000, fellows com. chmn. 2003, constn. and bylaws chmn. 1988-92, Recognition of Svc. award 1980, 85, 87-88, Outstanding Contbn. award 1997); mem. AAUP, IEEE Computer Soc. (assoc. editor 1990-98), Computing Rsch. Assn. (bd. dirs. 1997-2004, Spl. Svc. award 2006), Coun. Sci. Soc. Presidents (sec. 1998), Columbus Tech. Coun. (Tech. Person of Yr. award 2000). Avocations: sports, stamp collecting/philately. Office: Ohio State U Computer Scis 2015 Neil Ave Columbus OH 43210-1210 Office Phone: 614-292-9526. Business E-Mail: zweben@cse.ohio-state.edu.

ZWEIBEL, ALAN, writer; b. Brooklyn, NY, 1950; Grad., Univ. Buffalo, 1972. Former script writer Saturday Night Live, NYC, 1975—80; prodr. HBO's Curb Your Enthusiasm, 2004—. Publ. spkr. Speakers Network. Screen writer: TV Specials The Beach Boys Special, 1976, The Paul Simon Special, 1977, Dragnet, 1987, North, 1994, The Story of Us, 1999, TV series Good Sports, 1991, Saturday Night Live (five Emmy awards, six Ace awards, two Writer's Guild awards), TV films I am Your Child, 1997; author: (novels) The Other Shulman, 2006 (The Thurber Prize for American Humor, 2006), North, (memoir) Bunny-Bunny: Gilda Radner-A Sort of Love Story; playwright: Between Cars, Comic Dialogue. Office: Speakers Network Ste 190 4719 Reed Rd Columbus OH 43220 *

ZWEIBEL, JOEL BURTON, retired lawyer; b. NYC, Feb. 7, 1935; s. Jacob and Ruth (Fleischner) Z.; m. Lynn Herzog (dec. Nov. 1984); children: Jane, Emily; m. Chrystine Marie Trichter. BBA magna cum laude, CCNY, Baruch Coll., 1955; LLB, Yale Law, 1958. Bar: NY 1959. Ptnr. Kaye, Scholer, Fierman, Hays & Handler, NYC, 1969-79, Gelberg & Kronovet, NYC, 1979-81, Kramer, Levin, Nessen, Kamin & Frankel, NYC, 1981-90, O'Melveny & Myers, NYC, 1990—2001, ptnr. in-charge N.Y. office, 1998—2000. Lectr. 2d Ann. Uniform Comml. Code Law Inst., 1968, Practicing Law Inst. Sr. Workout Officers Roundtable. Author: Creditors' Rights Handbook, 1980; co-author: Herzog's Bankruptcy, Forms and Practice, 6th edit., 1980; contbr. articles to profl. jours. Recipient award Bankruptcy and Reorgn. Divsn. Fedn. United Jewish Appeal, 1989. Mem. ABA, Assn. Bar City NY (chmn. com. on bankruptcy and corp. reorgn. 1981-84), Nat. Bankruptcy Conf. (chmn. com. on avoiding powers 1983-2000, mem. exec. com., treas. 1991-2000), Yale Law Sch. Alumni Assn. (bd. dirs. 2004-), Am. Coll. Bankruptcy (dir., regent 2d cir.), (co-founder, mem. steering com. execs. on campus program, Baruch Coll., CUNY, advisor prelaw soc. 2002-). Avocations: art, theater, music, photography, tin whistle. Office: 570 Park Ave New York NY 10021 Home Phone: 212-751-5718. Personal E-mail: jbzweibel@aol.com.

ZWEIFACH, LAWRENCE J., lawyer; b. NYC, July 5, 1947; BA magna cum laude, Lehigh U., 1969; JD cum laude, George Washington U., 1973. Bar: NY 1974, US Dist. Ct., NY (So., No., We. & Ea. Dist.), US Ct. of Appeals, Second & Tenth Circuits, US Tax Ct. Law clerk to Judge Harold A. Stevens NY State Ct. of Appeals, 1974; law clerk to Judge Henry Bramwell US Dist. Ct., NY, Ea. Dist., 1975—76; asst. US atty. US Attys. Office, NY Ea. Dist., 1977—86, dep. chief, criminal div., 1983, chief, criminal div., 1984—86; various positions including co-chair, litigation dept. Gordon Altman Weitzen Shalov & Wein LLP, 1986—2000; ptnr. Heller Ehrman LLP, 2000—, chair litigation, NY Office. Mem.: ABA (mem. fed. regulation of securities com., mem. bus. law section), Fed. Bar Council, NY Council of Defense Lawyers, NYC Bar Assn. (mem. securities regulation & judicial conduct com.), NY State Bar Assn. Office: Heller Ehrman LLP Times Square Tower 7 Times Square New York NY 10036 Office Phone: 212-847-8762. Office Fax: 212-763-7600. Business E-Mail: lawrence.zweifach@hellerehrman.com.

ZWEIFEL, DAVID ALAN, newspaper editor; b. Monroe, Wis., May 19, 1940; s. Cloyence John and Uva Lorraine (Skinner) Z.; m. Sandra Louise Holz, Sept. 7, 1968; children: Daniel Mark, Kristin Lynn. BJ, U. Wis., 1962. Reporter The Capital Times, Madison, Wis., 1962-71, city editor, 1971-78, mng. editor, 1978-83, editor, 1983—. V.p. Simpson St. Free Press, 2001—; bd. dirs. Swiss Am. Ctr., Friends of Monona Terrace, Capital Times Co., Madison Newspapers Inc., William T. Evjue Charitable Trust. V.p. Alliance for Children and Youth, Madison, 1983—; bd. dirs. United Cerebral Palsy Dane County, Madison, 1984-91. Lt. U.S. Army, 1963-65; col. USNG, ret. Named Investigative Reporter of Yr. Madison Press Club, 1972; Disting. Journalism grad., U. Wis., 2003 Mem.: Soc. Profl. Journalists (Spl. Achievement award 1992, 1996), Wis. Freedom of Info. Coun. (pres. 1986—2000), Wis. AP (pres. 1987—88), Am. Soc. Newspaper Editors (com. freedom of info., Pulitzer Prize juror 2000, 2001), U. Wis. Alumni Assn., Wis. N.G. Assn. (trustee 1975—81), Elks. Avocations: running, bowling, book collecting. Home: 5714 Tecumseh Ave Monona WI 53716-2964 Office: The Capital Times PO Box 8060 Madison WI 53708-8060

ZWEIFEL, DONALD EDWIN, editor, lobbyist, consultant; b. LA, Nov. 30, 1940; s. Robert Fredrick and Eugenia Bedford (White) Z.; m. Donna Jean Croslin; 1 son, Phillip Matthew. Student, Orange Coast Coll., 1963-67, 90-92, U. Calif., Irvine, 1968-70, Western State U. Coll. Law, 1973, Irvine U. Coll. Law, 1974-75, Rancho Santiago Jr. Coll., 1988, Chapman U., 1993—97; grad., Aviation Ground Sch., 1990; student, USAF Air U., 1994—95, USAF Air. U., 2000—01. Cert. student pilot, registered lobbyist Calif. State Legislature. Devel. tech. Hughes Aircraft, Newport Beach, Calif., 1963-64; co-founder, station mgr. Sta. KUCI-FM, Irvine, Calif., 1970; owner, mgr. Zweifel Jaguar Car Sales and Svc., Santa Ana, Calif., 1975-76; pres. Zweifel & Assocs. Inc., Santa Ana, 1977-86, Zweifel South Coast Exotic Cars, Orange, Calif., 1987-96, ret., 1996; assoc. editor, cons. Compliance News Pub. Co., Long Beach, Calif., 1998—. Mem. small bus. coun. CalTrans, 2000—; legis. com., small bus. adv. coun. Calif. Dept. Gen. Svcs., 2005—; environ. air and water quality com. Associated Gen. Contractors, 2007—. Co-author: Challenge 2000, Regaining the America's Cup, 1996; editor: (coll. textbook) The Dream Is Alive, Space Flight and Operations In Earth Orbit. Vol. emergency coord. emergency mgmt. divsn. Orange County Fire Authority, 1985-87, Navy Relief Soc., 1993, 1st. lt. CAP Squadron 88 Group VII, 1993-95, sr. programs officer, 1993-94, asst. transp. officer Calif. Wing Hdqrs., 1994-95, Group VII Facilities officer, 1994-95, 2000-02, squadron pers. officer, 1993-95, 2000-02, Calif. wing rep. to Orange County Vol. Orgns. Active in Disaster, ARC, 1994-95, Calif. wing vol. Office Emergency Svcs., Calif., 1994-96, 2000-21, grad. Squadron Leadership Sch., 1993, Wing Supply Officers Sch., 1995, squadron safety officer, pub. affairs officer, asst. aerospace edn. officer, 1998-2001; program coord. Young Astronaut Coun., 1989-90; cadet CAP, USAF aux., Long Beach, Calif., 1953-59; mem. Orange County Homeless Issues Taskforce, 1994-95, 1997-2000, Orange County Homeless Svc. Providers for the Reuse of Marine Corps Air Sta., Tustin, Calif., 1994-95; legis. com. Orange County Vets. Adv. Coun., 1998-2006; chmn. tech. rev. subcom. Marine Corps Air Sta., El Toro, Calif., 1998-2001; apptd. to CalEPA DTSC Adv. Group Mil. Base Closure, 1995-99, CalEPA Dept. Toxic Substances Control Adv. Group pro-bono cons., Orange County Citizen's Adv. Commn. and El Toro Local Redevel. Authority, 1996-2001; vol. mediator Victim-Offender Reconciliation program, 1995-96; restoration adv. bd. MCAS Tustin, 1994—, co-chair, 2003—; restoration adv. bd. MCAS, El Toro, Calif., 1994—; active Freedom Com. of Orange County; cmty. emergency response team City of Placentia, 2003—; homeless vets. com. United Vets. Orgn. Orange County; fed. advocate for Disabled Veteran Bus. Enterprise, 2004; dir. Orange County Walk of Honor, 1998 With U.S. Army Nat. Guard, 1958—59. Recipient 6 certs. achievement Fed. Emergency Mgmt. Agy., 1989-96, 2 certs. appreciation CAP, 2 certs commendation, 1994, cert. appreciation Southwest Divsn. Naval Facilities Engring. Commd., 2000, Meritorious Svc. award, Calif. State Assembly Restoration Adv. Bd. Assemblyman John Campbell, 2001. Mem. Air Force Assn. (vice-chmn. civilian recruitment Calif. state membership com. 1988-91, v.p. govt. rels. Calif. 2006—, v.p. membership, Gen. Doolittle chpt. bd. dirs. 1987-89, 90-92, dir. Gen. Jimmy Doolittle chpt. 2005—, Exceptional Svc. award Gen. Jimmy Doolittle chpt. 1988, 91, Calif. Meritorious Svc. award 1988, v.p. membership Gen. Curtis E. LeMay Orange County chpt. 2000-02, 2004), Calif. Assn. for Aerospace Edn. (fellow), Marine Corps Hist. Found. (life), Aerospace Edn. Found. (Gen. Jimmy Doolittle fellow 1988, Gen. Ira Eaker fellow 1989, Pres.'s award 1988), US Naval Inst., AIAA (Cert. of Appreciation 1989, LA chpt. hist. com. 1989), Gulf & Vietnam Vets. Strategic Studies Archives (cons., co-founder 1983—, dir.), Marine Corps League (assoc., capt. Heinsey detachment 2000-02), Confederate Air Force (col.1989), AmVets (nat. jr. coord. com. 2003-05, Calif. jr. coord. 2003-04, 2d vice comdr. dist. II, Dept. Calif 2003-04, 1st vice comdr. dist. 2004-05, 2d vice-comdr. post 18 2006—, So. Calif. JROTC awards coord. 2007—), Masons, Saddleback Master Chorale of Orange County. Avocations: sailing, travel, flying. Home: 386 Hawaii Way Placentia CA 92870-6036 Personal E-mail: dzweifel@sbcglobal.net.

ZWEIFEL, PAUL FREDERICK, retired physics professor; b. NYC, June 21, 1929; s. Fritz and Dorothy Mary Zweifel; m. Kathleen Anne McKay, Nov. 13, 1967; children: Christen Anne Whitten, Frederick Feza, Evan Rudolph, Kathryn Clements. BS, Carnegie Inst. of Tech., Pitts., Pa., 1948; PhD, Duke Univ., Durham, NC, 1949. Rsch. assoc., mgr. theoretical physics, consulting physicist GE Knolls Atomic Power Lab., Schenectady, NY, 1953—58; from assoc. prof. to prof. of nuc. engring. U. Mich., Ann Arbor, 1958—68; from prof. to univ. disting. prof. Va. Poly. Inst. and State U., Blacksburg, 1968—96; univ. disting. prof. emeritus Va. Poly. Inst. and State Univ., Blacksburg, 1996—. Cons. numerous orgns. including U.S. AEC, Oak Ridge, Argonne and Los Alamos Nat. Labs., 1958—88; vis. prof. numerous univs. including both U.S. and fgn. in Italy, Germany, Slovenia, Turkey; mem. numerous editl. bds. Translator opera supertitles; contbr. music articles, including opera program notes. Recipient E.O. Lawrence medal, US Govt. (Atomic Energy Commn.), 1972; Guggenheim fellowship, John Simon Guggenheim Found., 1974-75. Fellow: Am. Phys. Soc.; mem.: Fed. Am. Scientists (sec. 1956—59), Am. Math. Soc. Liberal. Episcopalian. Avocations: music, travel, bridge, flight instructor, sportswriter. Home and Office: 6820 Sahalee Cir Radford VA 24141 Home Phone: 540-639-1295; Office Phone: 540-639-1295. Personal E-mail: zweifel@alumni.duke.edu.

ZWEIFEL, RICHARD GEORGE, curator; b. LA, Nov. 5, 1926; s. Harold Charles and Kathleen Marguerite (Garland) Z.; m. Frances Ann Wimsatt, July 30, 1956; children: Matthew Karl, Kenneth Paul, Ellen Katrina. BA, UCLA, 1950; PhD, U. Calif., Berkeley, 1954. Mem. staff Am. Mus. Natural History, NYC, 1954-89, chmn. curator dept. herpetology, 1968-80, curator emeritus; 1989—; sci. attaché Gondwana, 1974-75. Served with AUS, 1945-46. Mem. Soc. Study Amphibious and Reptiles, Am. Soc. Ichthyologists and Herpetologists. Home: PO Box 16354 Portal AZ 85632-1354

ZWEIG, STEVEN FREDERICK, statistician; s. Sammuel and Shirley Zweig. BS in Animal Sci., U. of Ga., 1979; MA in Econ., Va. Commonwealth U., 1985; MS in Biostatistics, Med. Coll. of Va., 1993. Retail mgr. Pk. Drug Store, Petersburg, Va., 1980—91; cons. InfoStat Cons., Columbus, 1994—96; statis. Covance, Inc., Princeton, NJ, 1996—2000; sr. statistician Target Rsch. Associates, New Providence, NJ, 2000—01; mgr. of biostatistics MDS Pharma Services, King of Prussia, Pa., 2001—03, SFBCI/New Drug Svcs. MNGR Biostats., Kennett Sq, Pa., 2003—04; cons. biostatistician Premier Rsch., Phila., 2004—05; cons. biostatistician Bristol-Myers Squibb, NJ, 2005—06; cons. sr. biostatistician Glaxo Smith Kline, NJ, 2006—. Sec. Columbus Jaycees, Columbus, Ohio, 1994—96. Recipient Dan O'Kane award, Columbus Jaycees, 1996. Mem.: Drug Info. Assn., Am. Statis. Assn. Home: 10 Sunflower Lane Yardville NJ 08620-3002 Personal E-mail: stevenfzweig@netscape.net. Business E-Mail: steven.f.zweig@gsk.com.

ZWEIMAN, BURTON, allergist, immunologist, educator; b. NYC, June 7, 1931; s. Charles and Gertrude (Levine) Z.; m. Claire Traig, Dec. 30, 1962; children: Amy Beth, Diane Susan. AB, U. Pa., 1952, MD, 1956. Diplomate Am. Bd. Internal Medicine, Am. Bd. Allergy & Immunology. Intern Mt. Sinai Hosp., NYC; Hosp. U. Pa., Bellevue Hosp. Ctr. Hosp. U. Pa., Bellevue Hosp. Center, 1957-60; fellow NYU Sch. Medicine, 1960-61; mem. faculty dept. medicine U. Pa. Sch. Medicine, Phila., 1963—, prof. medicine, chief allergy and immunology divsn., 1975-98. Cons. U.S. Army, NIH; co-chmn. Am. Bd. Allergy and Immunology, 1979-81. Editor Jour. Allergy Clin. Immunology, 1988-93; editor Allergy and Asthma: Disease Management Center, 1998—, now med. editor; contbr. articles to med. jours. Served with M.C., USNR, 1961-63. Allergy Found. Am. fellow, 1959-61 Fellow ACP, Am. Acad. Allergy, Asthma and Immunology (past pres.); mem. Am. Assn. Immunologists, Am. Fedn. Clin. Rsch., Phi Beta Kappa, Alpha Omega Alpha. Office: Hosp U Pa 527 Maloney Bldg 34th & Spruce St Philadelphia PA 19104 Business E-Mail: bzweiman@mail.med.upenn.edu.

ZWERDLING, ALEX, language educator; b. Breslau, Germany, June 21, 1932; came to U.S., 1941, naturalized, 1946; s. Norbert and Fanni (Alt) Z.; m. Florence Goldberg, Mar. 23, 1969; 1 son, Antony Daniel. BA, Cornell U., 1953; postgrad. (Fulbright scholar), U. Munich, Germany, 1953-54; MA, Princeton U., 1956, PhD, 1960. Instr. English Swarthmore Coll., 1957-61; asst. prof. English U. Calif., Berkeley, 1961-67, asso. prof., 1967-73, prof., 1973-86, prof. English Berkeley, 1988—, chmn. grad. studies, 1985-86; univ. prof. George Washington U., 1986-88. Vis. prof. Northwestern U., 1977; dir. edn. abroad program U. Calif., London, 1996-98; mem. advanced placement exam. com. Ednl. Testing Svc., 1975-79; mem. fellowship panel Nat. Endowment for Humanities, 1977-82, 84-87, Nat. Humanities Ctr., 1989-90; fellow Ctr. for Advanced Study in Behavioral Scis., 1964-65. Author: Yeats and the Heroic Ideal, 1965, Orwell and the Left, 1974, Virginia Woolf and the Real World, 1986, Improvised Europeans: American Literary Expatriates and the Siege of London, 1998; mem. adv. com. PMLA, 1978-82. Recipient Berkeley citation U. Calif., Berkeley, 2003; Am. Coun. Learned Socs. fellow, 1964-65; NEH fellow, 1973-74; Guggenheim fellow, 1977-78; Woodrow Wilson Ctr. fellow, 1991-92, fellow Nat. Humanities Ctr., 1992-93. Mem. MLA (chmn. 20th Century Brit. lit. div. 1969-70, 85-86). Office: U Calif Dept English Berkeley CA 94720-1030

ZWERDLING, DANIEL, news correspondent; Staff writer New Republic; with Nat. Pub. Radio, 1980—, investigative corr., 1980—94, Nairobi, Kenya, 1989—93, sr. host All Things Considered (Weekend), 1993—99, TV corr. on NOW with Bill Moyers, 2002—04, nat. desk corr., 2004—. Adj. prof. media ethics Am. U. Comm. dept., Washington; assoc. Bard Coll. Inst. for Lang. & Thinking, NY. Author: Workplace Democracy, 1980. Recipient Journalism award, AAAS, 1986, Lowell Thomas award, Overseas Press Club Found., 1995, Edward R. Murrow award, Radio-TV News Dirs. Assn., 2005, Investigative Reporters & Editors award, 2005, Robert F. Kennedy Journalism award, 2005, 2007, Nat. Press Club award for Internat. Reporting, Champion-Tuck award for Econ. Reporting. Office: Nat Pub Radio 635 Massachusetts Ave NW Washington DC 20001 *

ZWERLING, GARY LESLIE, retired investment company executive; b. NYC, Aug. 6, 1949; s. Seymour Joseph and Evelyn Rhoda (Posner) Z.; m. Marierose Miraglia, Aug. 25, 1974; children: Cara Marisa, Craig Harris. BEngring., SUNY, Stony Brook, 1970; MBA, SUNY, Albany, 1972. V.p. Chase Manhattan Bank, NYC, 1972-78; ptnr. Goldman, Sachs & Co., NYC, 1978-96; ret., 1996. Trustee Babson Coll., United Jewish Appeal Fed. No. NJ; bd. overseers Mus. Jewish Heritage-A Living Meml. to the Holocaust; sec., bd. govs. NY chpt. Arthritis Found.; bd. dirs. Am. Fedn. Aging Rsch. Mem. Thoroughbred Owners and Breeders Assn., Nat. Thoroughbred Racing Assn. Jewish.

ZWERN, ARTHUR LOUIS, computer company executive; b. NYC, Mar. 29, 1960; s. Simon and Blanche (Rubin) Z. BS in Applied Physics, Ga. Inst. Tech., Atlanta, 1981; MBA, Harvard U., 1985. Sys. engr. Hughes Aircraft Co., El Segundo, Calif., 1981-83; group leader mfg. engring. KLA Instruments, Santa Clara, Calif., 1985-88, mfg. mgr., 1988-89, product mktg. mgr., 1990-91, mktg. mgr., 1991-92; pres. Voice Innovation, San Jose, Calif., 1992-94, Gen. Reality Co., San Jose, 1994—. Cons. Chryschem, Riverside, Calif., 1987-88. Patentee in field. Bd. dirs. Big Bros., Big Sisters, Santa Clara, 1990-96, pres. bd. dirs. 1993-95. Avocations: skiing, scuba, travel, music. Home: 2226 Coastland Ave San Jose CA 95125-2611

ZWICK, EDWARD M., director, producer, scriptwriter; b. Winnetka, Il., Oct. 8, 1952; s. Allen and Ruth Ellen (Reich) Z.; m. Lynn Liberty Godshall, Oct. 24, 1982. BA, Harvard U., 1974; MFA, Am. Film Inst., 1976. Editor, feature writer The New Republic, Rolling Stone, 1972-74; co-founder The Bedford Falls Co., 1985. Writer, prodr., dir.: (TV series) Family, 1976-80 (Humanitas prize 1980), (TV spl.) Spl. Bull., 1983 (Emmy award for outstanding drama spl. 1983, Dir. Guild award 1983, Writers Guild award 1983, Humanitas prize 1983), (films) The Seige, 1998, The Last Samurai, 2003; dir.: (TV movies) Paper Dolls, 1982, Having It All, 1982, Extreme Close-Up, 1990, (films) About Last Night, 1986, Glory, 1989, Leaving Normal, 1992, Legends of the Fall (also prodr.), 1994, Courage Under Fire, 1996, Blood Diamond (also prodr.), 2006; prodr. Shakespeare in Love, 1998 (Oscar award for best picture, 1998, BAFTA award for best picture, 1999, Golden Satellite award for best picture, 1998), Traffic, 2000 (NY Film Critics Circle award for best picture, 2000, Golden Satellite award for best picture, 2000), I Am Sam, 2001, Women Vs. Men (TV movie), 2002, Abandon, 2002, Lone Star State of Mind (exec. prodr.), 2002; co-creator, exec. prodr.: (with Marshall Herskovitz) Thirtysomething, 1987-91 (Emmy award for outstanding drama series 1988), Dream Street, 1989, My So-Called Life, 1994-95, Relativity, 1996-97, co-creator, prodr. Once and Again, 2000; author: Literature and Liberalism, 1975. *

ZWICK, GARY ALAN, lawyer; b. Cleve., July 7, 1954; s. Coleman David and Eleanor Elaine (Brodsky) Z.; m. Linda Hollander, June 29, 1980; children: Melissa Ann, Daniel Benjamin. BBA in Acctg. and Fin., Kent State U., 1976; JD, Cleve.-Marshall Coll. Law, 1980; LLM in Taxation, Georgetown U., 1982. CPA Ohio, 1981; bar: Ohio 1980, US Tax Ct. Staff acct. Coleman D. Zwick, Cleve., 1976-80; shareholder, dir. tax Cohen & Co., Cleve., 1982-97; tax atty., dir. Walter & Haverfield, LLP, Cleve., 1997—, head tax & wealth mgmt. sect., chair fed. tax grp. Adj. prof. tax law Cleve. State U. Coll. Law. Named an Ohio Super Lawyer, Law & Politics Mag., 2004—07; named one of Top 100 Attys., Worth mag., 2005—06. Office: Walter & Haverfield LLP The Tower at Erieview 1301 E 9th St Ste 3500 Cleveland OH 44114-1821 Office Phone: 216-928-2902. Office Fax: 216-916-2340. E-mail: gzwick@walterhav.com. *

ZWICK, KENNETH LOWELL, lawyer, director; b. Cleve., Oct. 30, 1945; s. Alvin Albert Zwick and Selma (Mack) Durbin; m. Ruth Winifred Epstein, June 21, 1969; children: Tara, Monica. BSME,BS in Mgmt., MIT, 1969; JD, Temple U., 1976. Bar: Pa. 1976. Engr. Raytheon Corp., Norwood, Mass., 1969-71; tech. mgr. On-Line Systems, Inc., Phila., 1971-76; staff atty. Mead Data Cen., Washington, 1976-83; dir. litigation support office U.S. Dept. Justice, Washington, 1983-88, dir. mgmt. programs office, 1988—. Recipient Presdl. rank award, 1994. Mem. ASME (assoc.). Democrat. Jewish. Home: 9316 Wescott Pl Rockville MD 20850-3452 Office: US Dept Justice 3140 Main Justice Bldg Washington DC 20530-0001 Home Phone: 301-251-0684; Office Phone: 202-514-4552. Business E-Mail: ken.zwick@usdoj.gov.

ZWICKLER, ALLEN, investment advisor, educator; b. NYC, Mar. 18, 1958; s. Seymour Zwickler and Sandra Lewin; m. Ellen Karen Pikitch; children: Scott Emlen, Adam, Randi. BS Mgmt., SUNY, Binghamton, 1979; MBA, NYU, 1986. Registered rep. N.Y. Stock Exch., 1979. Rsch. analyst Ladenburg Thalmann, NYC, 1981—89; investment advisor First Manhattan, NYC, 1989—. Lectr. NYU Sch. Continuing Edn., NYC, 2000—05. Trustee Phil Zwickler Charitable and Meml. Found., NYC, 1992—; bd. dirs. Metro Club Sch. Mgmt. SUNY, Binghamton. Avocations: scuba diving, basketball. Home: 420 E 72 St Apt 12-L New York NY 10021 Office: First Manhattan Co 437 Madison Ave New York NY 10022-7001

ZWIENER, DAVID K., financial consultant, former insurance company executive; Bachelor's Degree, Duke U.; MBA in Fin. and Mktg., Northwestern U. Asst. treas. internat. ops. Kimberly Clark, 1984—87; sr. v.p., treas. Heller Internat. Corp., exec. v.p. capital markets; CFO, exec. v.p. ITT Fin., 1993—95; exec. v.p., CFO Hartford Fin. Svcs. Group, 1995—2000, pres., COO property & casualty ops., 2000—07; mng. dir. fin. inst. group The Carlyle Group, Washington, 2007—. Office: The Carlyle Group 1001 Pennsylvania Ave NW Washington DC 20004-2505 *

ZWIER, TIMOTHY S., chemistry professor; BS in Chemistry, Calvin Coll., 1977; PhD Chem. Physics, U. Colo., Boulder, 1981. Postdoctoral rsch. assoc. U. Chgo. James Franck Inst., 1981—83; asst. to assoc. prof. chemistry Calvin Coll., 1983—88; asst. prof. chemistry Purdue U., West Lafayette, Ind., 1988—93, assoc. prof., 1993—97, prof., 1997—. JILA vis. fellow, 1994—95; assoc. head dept. chemistry Purdue U., 2001—03, head dept. chemistry, 2004—. Contbr. articles to profl. jours.; co-editor: Internat. Revs. in Phys. Chemistry, 1998—2003; mem. editl. bd. Molecular Physics, 2001—; sr. editor: Jour. Phys. Chemistry, Am. Chem. Soc., 2003—. Alfred P. Sloan Rsch. fellow, 1989—91. Fellow: Am. Phys. Soc. (mem. exec. com. divn. chem. physics, Earle K. Plyler prize for Molecular Spectroscopy 2007); mem.: AAAS, Am. Astron. Soc., Am. Chem. Soc. Office: Purdue U Rm B155 Dept Chemistry 560 Oval Dr West Lafayette IN 47907-2084 E-mail: zwier@purdue.edu. *

ZWILICH, ELLEN TAAFFE, composer; b. Miami, Fla., Apr. 30, 1939; d. Edward Porter and Ruth (Howard) Taaffe; m. Joseph Zwilich, June 22, 1969 (dec. June 1979). MusB, Fla. State U., 1960, MusM, 1962; D Mus. Arts, Juilliard Sch., 1975; studies with Roger Sessions and Elliott Carter; MusD (hon.), Oberlin Coll., 1987, Converse Coll., 1994; LHD (hon.), Manhattanville Coll., 1991, Marymount Manhattan Coll., 1994, N.Y. New Sch., Mannes, 1995, Mich. State U., 2006. Francis Eppes disting. prof. Fla. State U., Tallahassee, 1999—. Composer in residence Santa Fe Chamber Music Festival, 1990, Am. Acad. Rome, 1990; first Composer's Chair, Carnegie Hall, 1995-99, Saratoga Chamber Music Festival, 2004. Premiere, Symposium for Orch., Pierre Boulez, N.Y.C., 1975, Chamber Symphony and Passages, Boston Musica Viva, Richard Pittman, 1979, 82, Symphony 1, Gunther Schuller, Am. Composers Orch., 1982; violinist Am. Symphony, N.Y.C., 1965-73; composer: Sonata in Three Movements, 1973-74; String Quartet, 1974; Clarino Quartet, 1977; Chamber Symphony, 1979; Passages (for Soprano and Chamber Ensemble), 1981; String Trio, 1982; Symphony 1:3 Movements for Orch., 1982 (Grammy nomination New World Records, 1987); Divertimento, 1983; Einsame Nacht, 1971; Emlekezet, 1978; Im Nebel, 1972; Passages for Soprano and Orch., 1982; Trompeten, 1974; Fantasy for Harpsichord, 1983; Intrada, 1983; Prologue and Variations, 1983; Double Quartet for Strings, Chamber Music Soc. of Lincoln Ctr., 1984; Celebration for Orch., Indpls. Symphony, John Nelson, 1984; Symphony #2 (Cello Symphony) San Francisco Symphony, Edo De Waart, 1985, Symphony #2 Louisville Orch. recording, L.L. Smith (Grammy nomination 1991); Concerto Grosso 1985, Handel Festival Orch., Steven Simon, 1986; Concerto for Piano and Orch., Detroit Symphony, Gunther Herbig, Marc-André Hamelin, 1986; Images for 2 Pianos and Orch., Nat. Symphony Orch., F. Machetti, 1987; Tanzspiel, Peter Martins N.Y.C. Ballet, 1987; Praeludium Boston chpt. AGO, 1987; Trio for piano, violin and cello; Kalichstein, Laredo, Robinson trio, 1987; Symbolon, Zubin Mehta and the N.Y. Philharm., Leningrad and Moscow (USSR), N.Y.C. (Koussevitsky Internat. Rec. award nominee 1990), 1988; concerto for trombone and orch. J. Friedman, Sir Georg Solti, Chgo. Symphony, 1989, concerto for trombone and orch. Christian Lindberg, James De Priest, Malmö Symphony, concerto for flute and orch. D.A. Dwyer, Seija Ozawa, Boston Symphony, 1990, quintet for clarinet and string quartet David Schiffrin, Chamber Music N.W., Lincoln Ctr. Chamber Mus. Soc., 1990; concerto for oboe and orch. John Mack, Christoph von Dohnanyi, Cleve. Orch., 1991; concerto for bass trombone strings, timpani and cymbals Chgo. Symphony Orch. Ch. Vernon, Daniel Barenboim, 1991; concerto for violin, violoncello and orch. Jaime Laredo, Sharon Robinson, Louisville Orch., L. Smith, 1991; Immigrant Voices Peter Leonard, St. Lukes Orch., N.Y. Internat. Festival of the Arts Chorus, Ellis Island, 1991, concerto for flute and orch, D.A. Dwyer, J. Sedares, London Symphony Orch., 1992, Symphony # 3 (Grammy nominee 1993), J. Ling, N.Y. Philharmonic, 1993, concerto for bassoon and orch., Nancy Goeres, Lorin Maazel, Pitts. Symphony, 1993, concerto for horn and string Orch., David Jolley, Rochester Philharm., L.L. Smith., 1993, Fantasy for Orch., JoAnn Falletta, Long Beach Symphony Orch., 1994, American Concerto Doc Severinsen, J. Falletta San Diego Symphony, 1994, A Simple Magnificat, 1994, Triple Concerto Kalichstein, Laredo, Robinson Trio Zdenek Macal, Minn. Orch., 1995, for piano and orch., Peanuts Gallery, 1996, violin concerto, Pamela Frank, H. Wolff, 1997; String Quartet # 2, 1998, Emerson Quartet; Upbeat! 1998, Nat. Symphony Orch., conducted by Anthony Aibel, Symphony # 4 (orch., chorus, children's chorus) Mich. State U., L. Gregorian 2000, Lament for solo piano Carnegie Hall, 2000, Millenium Fantasy for Piano & Orch., J. Biegel, J. Cobos-Lopez, Cin. Symphony, 2000, Lament for Cello & Piano, Met. Mus., N.Y.C., 2000, Partita for Violin & String Orch., Carnegie Hall, 2001, One Nation, 2002, Openings for Orch., 2002 JoAnn Falletta Va. Symphony, Clarinet Concerto, D. Shifrin, Chamber Music Soc. of Lincoln Ctr., Buffalo Philharm, 2002, Episodes for Violin & Piano, Itzhak Perlman, 2003, Quartet for Oboe & Strings, Saratoga Festival, 2004, Rituals for 5 Percussionists and Orchestra, Iris Orchestra, Nexus, 2004, LUVN BLM, Calif. Ear Unit, 2005, Naxos Am. Classics, Violin Concerto and Rituals, M.Stern, Frank, 2005; New World Records: Music By Ellen Taaffe Zwilich; N.Y. Philharm. conducted by Zubin Mehta. Bd. dir. Copland Fund. Named Martha Baird Rockefeller Fund rec. grantee, 1977, 1979, 1982, Guggenheim fellow, 1981; named to, Fla. Artists Hall of Fame, 1994; recipient Elizabeth Sprague Coolidge Chamber Music prize, 1974, Gold medal, G.B. Viotti, Vercelli, Italy, 1975, citation, Ernst von Dohnanyi, 1981, Pulitzer prize for music, 1983, Composers award, Lancaster Symphony Orch., Arturo Toscanini Music Critics award, 1987, Alfred I. DuPont award, 1991, Performing Arts award, Miami Ctr. Performing Arts, 2000, named, Musical Am. Composer of Yr., 1999, Key to the City Cinn., 2001. Fellow: Am. Acad. Arts & Sci.; mem.: AAAL (Acad. award 1984), Guggenheim Found. (bd. dirs.), MacDowell Colony (bd. dirs.), Am. Fedn. Musicians (hon.; life), BMI Found. (bd. dirs.), Am. Music Ctr. (v.p. 1982—84, bd. dirs.). Office: Coll Music Fla State Univ Tallahassee FL 32306-1180 Office Phone: 850-644-4744. Office Fax: 850-644-2033.

ZWILLINGER, MARC J., lawyer; b. NYC; BA in Polit. Sci., magna cum laude, Tufts U., 1991; JD magna cum laude, Harvard U., 1994. Bar: Ill. 1994, DC 1996; Cert. Info. Systems Security Profl. Law clk. to Judge Mark L. Wolf US Dist. Ct. Dist. Mass., 1994—95; assoc. Kirkland & Ellis, Chgo., 1995—97; trial atty. computer crime & intellectual property sect., criminal divsn. US Dept. Justice, 1997—2000; ptnr. Kirkland & Ellis, Washington, 2000—03, head cyberlaw & info. security group, 2001—03; ptnr. Sonnenschein Nath & Rosenthal LLP, Washington, 2003—, chair firm info. security & internet enforcement practice group, 2003—. Office: Sonnenschein Nath & Rosenthal LLP Ste 600, E Tower 1301 K St NW Washington DC 20015 Office Phone: 202-408-9171. Office Fax: 202-408-9171. Business E-Mail: mzwillinger@sonnenschein.com.

ZWINGE, RANDALL JAMES HAMILTON See RANDI, JAMES

ZWISLOCKI, JOZEF JOHN, neuroscience educator, researcher; b. Lwow, Poland, Mar. 19, 1922; arrived in U.S., 1951; s. Tadeusz and Helena (Moscicki) Z.; m. Ruth Gerber, Oct. 29, 1945 (div. May 1954); m. Sylvia Claire Goldman, July 11, 1954 (dec. July 17, 1992); m. Jadwiga M. Morrison, Dec. 2, 1993. Diploma, Fed. Tech. Inst., Zurich, Switzerland, 1944, ScD, 1948; D honoris causa, U. Adam Mickiewicz, Poznán, Poland, 1991, Syracuse U., NY, 2004. Head electroacoustic lab. dept. otolaryngology U. Basel, Basel, Switzerland, 1945-51; rsch. fellow psychoacoustic lab. Harvard U., Cambridge, Mass., 1951-57; dir. Bioacoustic Lab. Syracuse U., 1958-63, founder, dir. Lab. of Sensory Communication, 1963-73, founder dir. Inst. for Sensory Rsch., 1973—84, prof. neurosci., 1984—88, disting. prof. neurosci., 1988—92, disting. prof. emeritus, 1992—; prof. communicative disorders dept. spl. edn. Syracuse U. Sch. Edn., 1982—92; rsch. prof. SUNY Health Sci. Ctr., Syracuse, 1967—. Affiliate prof. bioengring. L.C. Smith Coll. Engring., Syracuse U., 1986-92; Carhart Meml. lectr. Am. Auditory Soc., 1992; Richard C. Heyser Meml. lectr. Audio Engring. Soc., 2005; mem. exec. coun. Com. Hearing, Bioacoustics and Biomechanics, NRC, Washington, 1965-68, chmn., 1967-68; mem. rev. panel on communicative scis. NIH, Bethesda, Md., 1966-70, chmn., 1969-70; mem. Communicative Disorders Program Project rev. com. NIH, Bethesda, 1971-75; chmn. Bd. Sci. Advs. Ctr. Health Scis., U. Wis., Madison, 1975-78. Inventor acoustic ear simulator, acoustic bridge, several types of ear defenders; contbr. articles to profl. jours.; author: Auditory Sound Transmission: An Autobiographical Perspective, 2002. Recipient Faculty Rsch. award Syracuse chpt. Sigma Xi, 1973, Internat. Ctr. Ricerche e Studi Amplifon prize, 1976, Chancellor's citation for exceptional acad. achievement Syracuse U., 1980, Javits Neurosci. Investigator award NIH, 1984, Kwiek medal Acoustics Inst., A. Mickiewicz U., Poland, 1991, medal Acoustical Soc. Poland, 1991, Hugh Knowles prize Northwestern U., 1992, Life Achievement award, Am. Auditory Soc., 2007; named Carhar Meml. lectr. Am. Auditory Soc., 1992, Legend of Auditory Sci., Am. Acad. Audiology, 2006. Fellow Acoustical Soc. Am. (chmn. tech. com. on psychol. and physiol. acoustics 1962, 63, exec. coun. 1982-85, recipient 1st Bekesy medal 1985, chmn. long-range planning com. 1983-86, nominating com. 1986-87, mem. com. on tutorials 1988-91, com. on meetings 1988-91, chmn. spring meeting, 1989), Am. Speech and Hearing Assn., The Polish Inst. Arts and Scis. Am.; mem. NAS, Polish Acad. Scis., Internat. Soc. Audiology (v.p. 1967-72), Internat. Union of Physiol. Scis. (commn. on auditory physiology 1982-89), Internat. Union Pure and Applied Physics (Commn. on Acoustics 1982-89), Collegium Oto Rhino Laryngologicum Amicitiae Sacrum, Assn. for Rsch. in Otolaryngology (award of merit 1988), Am. Otol. Soc. (assoc.), Hearing Rsch. (editl. bd.). Avocations: skiing, tennis, trout fishing, inventions. Home Phone: 315-251-2270; Office Phone: 315-443-9718. Business E-Mail: joe_zwislocki@isr.syr.edu.

ZWOYER, EUGENE MILTON, retired consulting engineering executive; b. Plainfield, NJ, Sept. 8, 1926; s. Paul Ellsworth and Marie Susan (Britt) Z.; m. Dorothy Lucille Seward, Feb. 23, 1946; children: Gregory, Jeffrey, Douglas. Student, U. Notre Dame, 1944, Mo. Valley Coll., 1944-45; BS, U. N.Mex., 1947; MS, Ill. Inst. Tech., 1949; PhD, U. Ill., 1953. Mem. faculty U. N.Mex., Albuquerque, 1948-71, prof. civil engring., dir. Eric Wang Civil Engring. Rsch. Facility, 1961-70; rsch. assoc. U. Ill., Urbana, 1951-53; owner, cons. engr. Eugene Zwoyer & Assocs., Albuquerque, 1954-72; exec. dir., sec. ASCE, NYC, 1972-82; pres. Am. Assn. Engring. Socs., NYC, 1982-84; exec. v.p. T.Y. Lin Internat., San Francisco, 1984-86, pres., 1986-89; owner Eugene Zwoyer Cons. Engr., 1989—2002; COO, treas. Polar Molecular Corp., Saginaw, Mich., 1990, exec. v.p., 1991-92; ret., 2002. Trustee Small Bus. Research Corp., 1976-80; trustee Engring. Info., Inc., 1981-84; internat. trustee People-to-People Internat. 1974-86; v.p. World Fedn. Engring. Orgns., 1982-85. Served to lt. (j.g.) USN, 1944-46. Named Outstanding Engr. of Yr. Albuquerque chpt. N.Mex Soc. Profl. Engrs., 1969, One Who Served the Best Interests of the Constrn. Industry, Engring. News Record, 1980; recipient Disting. Alumnus award the Civil Engring. Alumni Assn. at U. Ill., 1979, Disting. Alumnus award Engring. Coll. Alumni Assn., U. N.Mex., 1982, Can.-Am. Civil Engring. Amity award Am. Soc. Civil Engrs., 1988, Award for Outstanding Profl. Contbns. and Leadership Coll. Engring. U. N.Mex., 1989 Mem. AAAS, ASCE (dist. bd. dirs. 1968-71), NSPE, AFTRA, Am. Soc. Engring. Edn., Nat. Acad. Code Adminstrn. (trustee, mem. exec. com. 1973-79), Engrs. Joint Coun. (bd. dirs. 1978-79), Engring. Soc. Commn. on Energy (bd. dirs. 1977-82), Sigma Xi, Sigma Tau, Chi Epsilon. Home: 6363 Christie Ave Apt 1326 Emeryville CA 94608-1940 E-mail: eugenezwoyer@comcast.net.

ZYCHICK, JOEL DAVID, lawyer; b. Cleve., June 23, 1954; s. Eugene K. and Myra (Rotblatt) Z. BBA, George Washington U., 1976; JD, Case We. Res. U., 1979; LLM in Taxation, NYU, 1979. Bar: Ohio 1979, N.Y. 1985, D.C. 1985, U.S. Tax Ct. 1980, U.S. Ct. Claims 1980, U.S. Ct. Appeals (fed. cir.) 1982. Assoc. Jones, Day, Reavis & Pogue, Cleve., 1980-83, Milbank, Tweed, Hadley & McCloy, NYC, 1983-85; ptnr. Hertzog, Calamari & Gleason, NYC, 1986-98; pres. Zcounsel LLC; pres., CEO, GETKO Group, Inc., Westbury, NY, 1998—2001. Former gen. counsel, dir. The Egg Factory, LLC, Va. Contbr. articles to profl. jours. Dir., treas. Northside Ctr. for Child Devel., N.Y.C. Mem. ABA (past sec., dir. coun. tax sect., nominating com., former chmn. sales and fin. trans. com., past vice chmn. regulations com. govt. submissions), Am. Coll. Tax Counsel, N.Y. State Bar Assn. Avocations: hiking, music, travel. Home: PO Box 1097 Amagansett NY 11930-1097 Office Phone: 516-680-2715. E-mail: JZ@Zcounsel.com.

ZYGOCKI, RHONDA I., oil industry executive; b. St. John's, Newfoundland, Can., July 1957; B.Civil Engring., Meml. U. of Nfld., 1980. Petroleum engr. Chevron Can. Resources, Calgary, Canada, gen. mgr. strategic bus. svcs., 1993—94; profit ctr. mgr. Chevron U.S.A. Prodn. Co., Houston, 1994—97; CFO Chevron Can. Resources, Calgary, 1997—99; mgr. strategic planning Chevron Corp., San Ramon, Calif., 1999—2000, advisor to chmn. bd., 2000—01; mng. dir. ChevronTexaco Australia Pty. Ltd., Perth, Australia, 2001—03; v.p. health, environment and safety Chevron Corp., San Ramon, Calif., 2003—07, corp. v.p. policy, govt. & pub. affairs, 2007—. Mem.: Engrs. Without Borders (bd. dirs.), Internat. Petroleum Industry Environ. Conservation Assn. (bd. dirs.), Internat. Assn. Oil and Gas Prodrs. (bd. dirs.). Office: Chevron Corp 6001 Bollinger Canyon Rd San Ramon CA 94583-2324 *

ZYROFF, ELLEN SLOTOROFF, information scientist, classicist, educator; b. Atlantic City, Aug. 1, 1946; d. Joseph George and Sylvia Beverly (Roth) Slotoroff; m. Jack Zyroff, June 21, 1970; children: Dena Rachel, David Aaron. AB, Barnard Coll., 1968; MA, The Johns Hopkins U., 1969, PhD, 1971; MS, Columbia U., 1973. Instr. The Johns Hopkins U., Balt., 1970-71, Yeshiva U., NYC, 1971-72, Bklyn Coll., 1971-72; libr., instr. U. Calif., 1979, 81, 91, San Diego State U., 1981-85, 94; prof. San Diego Mesa Coll., 1981-95; dir. The Reference Desk Rsch. Svcs., La Jolla, Calif., 1983—; prin. libr. San Diego County Libr., 1985—. V.p. Archaeol. Soc. Am., Balt., 1970-71. Author: The Author's Apostrophe in Epic from Homer Through Lucan, 1971, Cooperative Library Instruction for Maximum Benefit, 1989; contbr. articles to profl. jours. Pres. Women's Am. ORT, San Diego, 1979-81, Zionist Orgn. of Am., San Diego dist., 1997-2000; mem. adv. bd. With Israel Now. Mem.: ALA (chair divsn. and roundtable coms. 1982—, dir. grant programs, coun. 2003—), Libr. Congress Cataloging in Publs. Adv. Group, Assn. Jewish Librs., Am. Classical League, Calif. Libr. Assn. (assembly 1993—99, editor Calif. Librs. 1997—99, pres. mgmt. sect. 2000—01), Am. Philol. Assn., Toastmasters, Beta Phi Mu. E-mail: eszyroff@hotmail.com.

ZYWICKI, ROBERT ALBERT, retired electric power industry executive; b. Chgo., Sept. 23, 1930; s. Martin Albert and Margaret Irene (Mackowski) Z.; m. Barbara Joan Hagerty; children: Robert, Cheryl, Cindy, Carrie. B in Commerce, Northwestern U., 1966. Teller Chgo. Title and Trust Bank, Chgo., 1949-50; painter Getz Molding Co., Chgo., 1950-51; purchasing agt. Woodworker's Tool Works, Chgo., 1953-54; serviceman Addressograph Multigraph, Chgo., 1954-55; mem. Chgo. Fire Dept., 1955-62; v.p. Anixter Bros. Inc., Skokie, Ill., 1955-87; co-owner A-Z Industries, Northbrook, Ill., 1987—2003; ret., 2003. Served as cpl. U.S. Army, 1951-53. Mem. Am. Legion (comdr.). Republican. Roman Catholic. Avocations: thoroughbred horse racing, classical music, baseball card collecting, tennis. Home: 1330 Sprucewood Ln Deerfield IL 60015-4771 Personal E-mail: peter1330@comcast.net. *Love your family, respect your friends and co-workers, value your customers and suppliers. Always keep each in its proper perspective. Most of all, remember - love, value and respect are all two-way streets.*

Geographic Index

UNITED STATES

ALABAMA

Alabaster
Counce, Diane Ryder *neurologist, researcher*
Harvey, James Mathews, Jr. *public relations administrator*
McChesney, Robert Michael, Sr. *retired academic administrator*

Albertville
Chandler, Terry Winford *insurance company executive, real estate developer, small business owner*
Rice, Fuhrman D. (Runt Rice) *retired paper company executive*

Alexander City
Towery, Sarah Carlisle *artist, retired educator*

Andalusia
Fuller, William Sidney *lawyer*
Patterson, Edwin *minister*

Anniston
Ayers, Harry Brandt *editor, publisher, columnist*
Howell, Laura Clark *biologist, educator, small business owner*
Klinefelter, James Louis *lawyer*
Woodrow, Randall Mark *lawyer*

Arab
Black, Daniel Hugh *retired social studies educator*

Ashland
Ingram, Kenneth Frank *retired state supreme court justice*

Athens
Baird, Debra *dean, education educator*
Busick, Sean R. *history professor, writer*
Kemp, Ann *retired librarian*
Lafevor, Kimberly Ann *human resources specialist, educator*
Smith, Patricia Crawford *elementary school educator*

Attalla
Saffels, Anna Wayne Brothers *retired mathematician, educator*

Auburn
Agrawal, Prathima *engineering educator*
Amacher, Richard Earl *retired literature educator*
Ball, Donald Maury *agronomist, consultant*
Clark, Janet Eileen *retired political science professor*
Cochran, John Euell, Jr. *aerospace engineer, educator, lawyer*
Galbraith, Ruth Legg *retired dean, home economist*
Govil, Narendra Kumar *mathematics professor*
Hanley, Thomas Richard *engineering educator*
Hatfield, Donald Gene *retired art educator*
Housel, David *retired athletic director*
Irwin, John David *electrical engineering educator*
Jaeger, Richard Charles *electrical engineer, educator, science association director*
Jones, Allen *history educator, archivist*
Klesius, Phillip Harry *microbiologist, researcher*
Kouzmitcheva, Galina A. *molecular biologist, researcher*
Lewis, Walter David *historian, educator*
Littleton, Taylor Dowe *humanities educator*
Miller, Wilbur Randolph *academic administrator*
Millman, Richard George *architect, educator*
Neely, William Charles *chemistry professor, consultant, research scientist*
Parsons, Daniel Lankester *pharmaceutics educator*
Philpott, Harry Melvin *former university president*
Seroka, James Henry *social studies educator, academic administrator*
Sforzini, Richard Henry *aerospace engineer, educator*
Shippen, Margaret Ellen *special education educator*
Srivastava, Puneet *engineering educator, researcher*
Tian, Hanqin *ecologist, educator*
Tolbert, Clinton Jame *army officer, machinist*
Tuberville, Tommy *college football coach*
Turner, Louise (Lee) Kreher *retired dance educator*
Vasquez, Ramon Francisco *music educator*
Voitle, Robert Allen *dean, physiologist*
Zallen, Harold *academic administrator, chemist*

Auburn University
Dodge, Timothy de K. *school librarian*
Eden, Mario Richard *engineering educator*
Gibson, Keith E. *education educator*
Gogue, Jay (G. Jay Gogue) *academic administrator*
Jackson, Robert Lee *mechanical engineer, educator*
MacEwan, Bonnie *librarian, dean*
Mosjidis, Jorge *agricultural studies educator, researcher*
Strom, Paris Scott *education educator*
Wu, Chwan-Hwa John *adult education educator*

Bay Minette
Simon, Janice Crowder *language educator, consultant*

Bessemer
Collins, Patricia Ann *pastor, pastoral counselor*
Garlikov, Patricia Moodie *education educator*
Stevens, Elizabeth McCartha *secondary school educator*

Birmingham
Adkison, David Paul *orthopedic surgeon*
Albritton, William Harold, IV, *lawyer*
Alexander, James Patrick *lawyer, educator*
Alford, Margie Searcy *lawyer, writer*
Allen, Christopher C. *publishing executive*
Allen, Lee Norcross *historian, educator*
Allen, Maryon Pittman *former senator, clothing designer, journalist*
Andrews, James R. *orthopedic surgeon*
Ayasoufi, Anahita *engineer, researcher*
Baker, David Remember *lawyer*
Balch, Samuel Eason *lawyer*
Banton, Julian Watts *banker*
Barrow, Richard Edward *architect*
Beard, Craig Wyeth *librarian*
Beasley, James Barnie, Jr. *utilities executive*
Bennett, Joe Claude *pharmaceutical executive*
Bennett, Thomas B. *federal judge*
Berte, Neal Richard *academic administrator*
Bittner, Vera *cardiologist*
Blackledge, Brett J. *reporter*
Blan, Ollie Lionel, Jr. *retired lawyer*
Bloomer, Joseph Robert *physician, educator*
Boardman, Mark Seymour *lawyer*
Bonatz, Ekkehard *hand surgeon*
Bono, Alexander Dominic (Lex Bono) *lawyer*
Boomershine, Donald Eugene *bureau executive, development official*
Bozzelli, Richard *publishing executive*
Bradley, Laurence Alan *psychologist*
Briggs, Dick Dowling, Jr. *physician, educator*
Bueschen, Anton Joslyn *physician, educator*
Burden, Cedric Jerome, Sr. *language professor*
Campbell, Charles Alton *transportation executive*
Carmody, Richard Patrick *lawyer*
Carruthers, Thomas Neely *lawyer*
Carter, Frances Tunnell (Fran) *fraternal organization administrator*
Cates, Marshall E. *pharmacist, medical educator*
Caulfield, James Benjamin *pathologist, educator*
Chapman, Lavonya Kelley *lawyer, director*
Childs, Alex Joseph *gynecologist*
Clark, William Northington *lawyer, retired military officer*
Clayton, Orville Woolford *surgeon*
Cockerham, William Carl *sociologist, educator*
Cohen-DeMarco, Gale Maureen *pharmaceutical executive*
Cole, Charles DuBose, II, *law educator*
Coleman, Brittin Turner *lawyer*
Coleman, John James III *lawyer, educator*
Coleman, Stephen Beasley, Jr. *real estate broker, writer*
Comer, Donald III *investment company executive*
Cooper, Karen René *health facility administrator, nursing administrator*
Cooper, Max Dale *pediatrician, researcher*
Cooper, N. Lee *lawyer*
Copeland, Hunter Armstrong *retired real estate company executive*
Corliss, Deane Kenworthy *lawyer*
Coyne, Edward James, Sr. *international business educator*
Culpepper, Mary Kay *editor*
Curtis, John J. *medical educator*
Davis, Stacey Ann *lawyer*
Deal, William Brown *medical school dean, physician, educator*
Denson, William Frank III *lawyer*
Dhall, Rohit *neurologist*
Diasio, Ilse Wolfartsberger *volunteer*
Dick, John R. *bank executive*
Diethelm, Arnold Gillespie *surgeon*
Duke, J. Richard *lawyer*
Elewski, Boni Elizabeth *dermatologist, educator*
Etterer, Sepp *industrial relations specialist, consultant, application developer*
Farley, Joseph McConnell *lawyer*
Finley, Sara Crews *medical geneticist, educator*
Finley, Wayne House *medical educator*
Fisher, Winfield Stitt III *medical educator*
Fleming, William Cary *retired physician, consultant*
Floyd, John Alex, Jr. *editor*
Francavilla, Donna T. *journalist*
Freeman, Arthur Merrimon III *psychology professor, dean*
Friend, Edward Malcolm III *lawyer, educator*
Gale, Fournier Joseph III *lawyer*
Garner, Robert Edward Lee *lawyer*
Garrison, Carol Z. *academic administrator*
George, Frank Wade *small business owner, antiquarian book dealer*
Gilchrist, William Aaron *architect*
Givhan, Robert Marcus *lawyer*
Goldman, Jay *industrial engineer, educator, dean emeritus*
Goodrich, Thomas Michael *engineering and construction executive, lawyer*
Gorrie, M. Miller *construction executive*
Griffin, Eleanor *publishing executive, editor*
Grinney, Jay *health facility company executive*
Hall, Robert Alan *construction company executive*
Hanson, Victor Henry, II, *newspaper publisher*
Harris, Aaron *management consultant*
Haskell, Wyatt Rushton *lawyer*
Haworth, Michael Elliott, Jr. *aerospace company executive*
Hedden, William James *plastic surgeon*
Hendley, Dan Lunsford *retired finance company executive*
Hilliard, Earl Frederick *congressman, lawyer*
Hinton, James Forrest, Jr. *lawyer*
Hirschowitz, Basil Isaac *physician*
Hoidal, David *health facility administrator*
Horsley, Richard David *banker*
Houston, James Gorman, Jr. *retired state supreme court justice*
Howell, William Ashley III *lawyer*
Hudson, C. B., Jr. *insurance company executive*
Hughey, James Fletcher, Jr. *lawyer*
Hull, William Edward *theology studies educator*
Huntley, Horace *history professor*
Hutchison, Larry M. *lawyer*
James, Donald M. *construction materials executive*
Janjua, Naveed Zafar *research scientist*
Jo, Young Gyun *nuclear engineer*
Johns, John D. *insurance company executive, lawyer*
Johnson, Wylie Pierson *electric utility executive*
Johnston, Carden *emergency physician, pediatrician, educator*
Jones, D. Paul, Jr. *bank executive, lawyer*
Jones, William O. *not-for-profit fundraiser*
Keller, Armor *artist, arts advocate*
Kennedy, Joe David, Jr., (Joey Kennedy) *editor*
Kimberly, Robert Parker *medical educator*
Kirby, Russell Stephen *epidemiologist, researcher, geographer*
Kirchner, John Shirk *orthopedic surgeon*
Klein, Michael J. *pathologist, surgeon*
Koomullil, Roy Paulose *mechanics and engineering educator*
Koopman, William James *medical educator, internist, immunologist*
Korf, Bruce Richard *clinical geneticist, neurologist*
Kracke, Robert Russell *lawyer*
Kreisberg, Robert A. *dean, medical educator*
Lacy, Alexander Shelton *retired lawyer*
Laeger, Therese Roach *performing arts educator*
Langum, David John *law educator, historian*
Lisovicz, Nedra Ford *director*
Long, Deborah Joyce *lawyer*
Long, Thad Gladden *lawyer*
Lowman, John D., Jr. *physical therapist, researcher*
Marchase, Richard Banfield *cell biologist, educator, research administrator*
Marks, Charles Caldwell *retired banker, manufacturing executive*
Markstein, Daniel H. III *lawyer*
Mc Callum, Charles Alexander *academic administrator*
McKinley, Cameron Sharbel *elementary school educator*
Mc Millan, George Duncan Hastie, Jr. *lawyer, former state official*
McWhorter, Hobart Amory, Jr. *lawyer*
Meezan, Elias *pharmacologist, educator*
Mendler, Joel A. *lawyer*
Mills, William Hayes *lawyer*
Miyagawa, Ichiro *physicist*
Mohon, Earlene Mann *counselor*
Molen, John Klauminzer *lawyer*
Moore, Jackson Watts *bank executive*
Morgan, Hugh Jackson, Jr. *retired bank and energy executive*
Morgan, Kathryn Diane *criminology educator*
Morgan, Michael Darold *academic administrator*
Morrisey, Michael A. *health economics educator*
Moturi, Sricharan *psychiatrist*
Nash, David J. *engineering and construction company executive, retired military officer*
Neal, Phil Hudson, Jr. *retired manufacturing executive*
Nettles, Bert Sheffield *lawyer*
Newton, Alexander Worthy *lawyer*
Newton, Don Allen *economic development consultant*
Nielsen, Vance Girard *anesthesiologist, researcher*
Noah, James William *biochemist, researcher*
Northen, Charles Swift III *retired bank executive*
Nunn, Grady Harrison *retired political science professor*
Oakes, Walter Jerry *pediatric neurosurgeon*
Omura, George Adolf *medical oncologist*
Oparil, Suzanne *cardiologist, educator, researcher*
Owens, Sandra Nell *nurse*
Palmer, Robert Leslie *lawyer*
Peeples, William Dewey, Jr. *mathematics professor*
Perry, Helen *medical/surgical nurse, secondary school educator*
Persaud, Tarek O. *ophthalmologist*
Piassick, Joel Bernard *lawyer*
Pickett, Stephen Alan *hospital administrator*
Pittman, Constance Shen *endocrinologist, educator*
Pittman, James Allen, Jr. *endocrinologist, educator*
Pizitz, Richard Alan *retail executive, real estate company officer*
Pointer, Sam Clyde, Jr. *retired federal judge, lawyer*
Pollick, G. David *academic administrator, philosopher*
Potter, John Leith *retired mechanical and aerospace engineer, retired educator, consultant*
Powell, Jerry W. *lawyer*
Powell, Larry *communications educator*
Powell, William Arnold, Jr. *retired bank executive*
Pryor, William Holcombe, Jr. *federal judge, former state attorney general, educator*
Quick, Frances King *lawyer*
Reynolds, Jeffrey Warren *music educator*
Rich, Robert Regier *physician, medical educator, immunologist*
Ritter, C. Dowd *diversified financial services company executive*
Robinson, Edward Lee *retired physics professor, consultant*
Rogers, Betsy *elementary school educator*
Rogers, Ernest Mabry *lawyer*
Rotch, James E. *lawyer*
Roth, William Stanley *hospital foundation executive*
Rountree, Asa *lawyer*
Russell, Richard Olney, Jr. *retired cardiologist*
Sabbaj, Steffanie *research scientist*
Scarritt, Thomas Varnon *newspaper editor*
Schafer, James Arthur *physiologist*
Seitz, Karl Raymond *editor*
Selfe, Edward Milton *lawyer*
Sibley, David Hurley *cardiologist*
Siegel, Herrick Jove *orthopedic surgeon*
Sirmans, Barbara C. *library director*
Sisiopiku, Virginia P. *civil engineer*
Sklenar, Herbert Anthony *industrial products manufacturing company executive*
Small, Clarence Merilton, Jr. *lawyer*
Smyth, Rich *publishing executive*
Spence, Paul Herbert *librarian*
Spransy, Joseph William *corporate lawyer*
Stabler, Lewis Vastine, Jr. *lawyer*
Stelzenmuller, Cyril Vaughn *lawyer*
Stephens, Deborah Lynn *health company executive*
Stephens, James T. (J.T. Stephens) *publishing executive*
Stephens, Jerry Wayne *librarian, director*
Stevenson, Edward Ward *retired otolaryngologist, surgeon*
Stewart, Joseph Grier *lawyer*
Stitt, Frank *food service executive*
Styslinger, Lee Joseph, Jr. *manufacturing executive*
Taub, Edward *psychology researcher*
Thomas, Huw Francis *dean, dental educator*
Trigg, Jack Walden, Jr. *retired physician*
Trimmier, Charles Stephen, Jr. *lawyer*
Tucker, Thomas James *retired investment company executive*
Vasconez, Luis Oswaldo *plastic surgeon, educator*
Vila-Carriles, Wanda Helena *research scientist*
Vinson, Laurence Duncan, Jr. *lawyer*
Volanakis, John Emmanuel *immunologist, rheumatologist*
Vyazovkin, Sergey *chemistry professor*
Ward, Liesl Hope *language educator*
Ward, Perry W. *college president*
Watkins, Donald V. *lawyer, entrepreneur*
Weatherly, Robert Stone, Jr. *banker*
Weeks, Arthur Andrew *lawyer, educator*
Wells, Huey Thomas, Jr. *lawyer*
Westmoreland, Andrew *academic administrator*
Whatley, Joe Ramon, Jr. *lawyer*
Wheeler, Cathy Jo *federal agency administrator*
Wheeler, Ruric E. *mathematics professor*
Wheeler, Susie Weems *retired school system administrator*
Whigham, Mark Anthony *computer scientist*
Whittington, John P. *lawyer*
Wilson, James Charles, Jr. *lawyer*
Winstead, Nathaniel Scott *gastroenterologist*
Woodbury, Max Atkin *mathematics professor*
Wrinkle, John Newton *lawyer*
Yoder, Stephen Alan *lawyer*

Brilliant
Franks, Gracie G. *elementary school educator*

Camp Hill
Melzer, John T.S. *translator, editor*

Citronelle
Surry, Melinda Owen *reading coach*

Clanton
Baughman, Bruce Prentiss *state agency administrator*
Jackson, John Hollis, Jr. *lawyer*

Coosada
Reynolds, Linda Ann *elementary school educator*

Crossville
Blessing, Maxine Lindsey *secondary school educator*

Cullman
Morris, Sylvia June Burbank *retired physician*

Daphne
Crosby, Samuel Neil *lawyer*
Curreri, Peter William *health facility administrator, consultant*
Jeffreys, Elystan Geoffrey *petroleum consultant*
Kauffman, Carl Herbert *retired music educator*

Decatur
Julich, Nancy C. *secondary school educator*
Mays, John E. *lawyer*
Michelini, Sylvia Hamilton *auditor*
Powell, Valerie Jean *elementary school educator*
Smith, Trina *academic administrator*
Smith, Troy Alvin *aerospace research engineer*
Talley, Richard Woodrow *accountant*

Demopolis
Dinning, Woodford Wyndham, Jr. *lawyer*
Lloyd, Hugh Adams *lawyer*

Dothan
Baxley, Wade H. *lawyer*
Fleming, Jennie M *retired education educator*
Flowers, V. Anne *retired academic administrator*
Huskey, Dow Thobern *lawyer*
Lord, Jacqueline Ward *retired accountant, photographer, artist*
Malugen, J.T. (Joe Thomas) *retail executive*
Peterson, Roger *community bank executive, retired international investment banker, manufacturing executive, air force officer*
Wright, Burton *sociologist*

Elberta
Wilkinson, Edward Anderson, Jr. *retired military officer, manufacturing executive*

Enterprise
Parker, Ellis D. *retired military officer*

Eufaula
Conniff, Alexandra Acosta *secondary school educator*

Fairfield
McCaslin, LaTanya *art educator*

Fairhope
Gwin, John Michael *retired economics professor, management consultant*
Mozley, Paul David *retired obstetrics and gynecology educator*

Falkville
Dunn, Donna R. *public health service officer*
Templeton, Richard Raymond *special education educator, consultant*

Florala
Duplechin, D. James *lawyer*

Florence
Badger, Phillip Charles *agricultural engineer*
Eich, Wilbur Foster III *retired pediatrician*
Foote, Avon Edward *web developer/producer, communications educator*
Foote, Dorothy Gargis *nursing educator*
Hansen, Vagn Keith *political science educator, college administrator*
Johnson, Johnny Ray *retired mathematics professor*
Knight, Karen Anne McGee *artist, educator, educational research administrator*
Lee, Soojeong *music educator, soprano*

Foley
St. John, Henry Sewell, Jr. *utility company executive*

Gadsden
Farr, Dwayne Louis *automotive executive*
Grimm, James R. (Ronald) *management consultant*

Gardendale
McKay, Marie Conyers *librarian, writer*

Grand Bay
Taylor, Anne Wilkerson *elementary school educator*

Greensboro
Massey, James Earl *retired clergyman, retired educator*

Gulf Shores
Virden, Frank Stanley *retired military officer*
Wallace, John Loys *retired aviation services executive*

Hanceville
Holmes, Kristen Jones *academic administrator*

Hartselle
Slate, Joe Hutson *psychologist, educator*

Hayden
King, Vickie Ruth *minister*

Helena
Coulter, Fern Goshen *retired secondary school educator*

Homewood
Nance, Marione E. *biology educator*

Hueytown
Nelson, Susan Rhodes *media specialist, educator*

Huntsville
Abram, Stephen *librarian, writer*
Allan, Barry David *research chemist, government official*
Baird, James Kern *educator, consultant, academic administrator*
Baldaia, Peter *curator*
Bearden, Thomas Eugene *research scientist*
Bendickson, Marcus J. *engineering company executive*
Brandon, Walter Wiley, Jr. *retired physicist, retired aerospace engineer*
Burko, Lior M. *physicist, educator*
Burrows, Shania Kay *civilian military employee*
Contreras, Frank R. *musician*
Costes, Nicholas Constantine *aerospace scientist, educator, retired government agency administrator*
Daussman, Grover Frederick *electrical engineer, consultant*
Franz, Frank Andrew *academic administrator, physicist, educator*
Freas, George Wilson, II, *computer scientist, consultant*
Gillani, Noor Velshi *atmospheric scientist, researcher, educator*
Graves, Benjamin Barnes *business administration educator*
Hawley, Harold Patrick *educational consultant*
Hoover, Richard Brice *astrobiologist*
Huber, Donald Simon *physician*
Hunter, Herbert Erwin *aerospace engineer*
Jaenisch, Holger Marcel *physicist*
King, David A. *aerospace engineer*
Laughlin, Edward Humes *surgeon, educator*
Lundquist, Charles Arthur *academic administrator*
McIntyre-Ivy, Joan Carol *data processing executive*
Moore, Ann Roy *school system administrator*
Morgan, Beverly Hammersley *secondary school educator, artist*
Morgan, John Derald, Sr. *electrical engineer, educator, writer, researcher*
Norman, Ralph Louis *retired physicist, consultant*
Nuessle, William Raymond *surgeon*
Ooi, Teng Keong *aerospace and mechanical engineer, educator*
Parnell, Thomas Alfred *physicist*
Pittman, William Claude *electrical engineer*
Pruitt, Alice Fay *mathematician, engineer*
Ratchford Merchant, Betty Jo *retired elementary school educator*
Richardson-Weninegar, Loretta Lynne *biologist, educator*
Ryan, L. Thomas, Jr. *lawyer*
Sackheim, Robert Lewis *aerospace engineer, educator*
Schumann, J. Paul *retired federal agency administrator*
Schwinghamer, Mary Denise *veterinarian*
Smith, Robert Earl *space scientist*
Smothers, Deloris Rice *computer career educator*
Stewart, Verlindsey Laquetta *accounting educator*
Stuhlinger, Ernst *physicist*
Sturges, Keith *information technology executive*
Su, Ching-Hua *materials scientist*
Turner, Mary Alice *curriculum specialist*
Vaughan, William Walton *atmospheric scientist*
Watson, Raymond Coke, Jr. *engineering executive, consultant, academic administrator*
Watson, S.A. *lawyer, retired judge*
Wieland, Paul Otto *environmental control systems engineer*
Williamson, Donald Ray *retired career Army officer*
Wright, John Collins *retired chemistry professor*
Wu, Shi Tsan *science research administrator, educator*
Zutaut, Steven Eric *systems analyst, application developer*

Hurtsboro
Bouilliant-Linet, Francis Jacques *global management consultant*

Jacksonville
Bundrum, Kenneth Owen *lawyer, writer*
Chargois, Deborah Majeau *psychology professor, researcher*
Dunaway, Carolyn Bennett *retired sociology professor*
Dunaway, William Preston *retired school system administrator*
Hubbard, William James *library director*
McAbee, Sonja Louise *library administrator*
Spector, Daniel Earl *historian, educator*
Wight, Nathan *music educator*

Jasper
Rowland, David Jack *retired academic administrator*
Sparkman, Brandon Buster *secondary school educator, consultant, writer*
Stallsmith, Becki Laughlin *music educator*
Thomas, Steven Allen *lawyer*

Lafayette
Woody, Mary Florence *nursing educator, academic administrator*

Leeds
Wilson, Maggie Isabelle Lovell *secondary school educator*

Lexington
Freeman, Sandra Dianne *insurance agent, educator*

Lillian
Burnette, Ollen Lawrence, Jr. *historian*
Ray, Betty Jean G. *retired lawyer*

Livingston
Day, Richard M. *computer educator*
Green, Asa Norman *academic administrator*
Holland, Richard D. *academic administrator*

Loachapoka
Schafer, Elizabeth Diane *historian, writer*
Schafer, Robert Louis *agricultural engineer, researcher*

Madison
Brannan, Eulie Ross *educational consultant*
Dannenberg, Konrad K. *aeronautical engineer*
Emerson, William Kary *engineering company executive*
Gibson, John Thomas *academic administrator, consultant*
Jones, Christine Regina *secondary school educator*
Parlier, Greg H. *military officer, analyst, engineer, researcher*
Petty, Margaret *elementary school educator*

Marion
Cleveland, Willie Mae *elementary school educator*
Gosselin, Karen Chowning *music educator*

Maylene
Copes, Marvin Lee *academic administrator*

Mc Calla
Kes, Vicki *museum director*

Midfield
Daniels-Rogers, LaTausha *social sciences educator, entrepreneur*

Millbrook
Boartfield, Ernest William *music educator*

Mobile
Barik, Sailen *biomedical scientist, educator*
Bostwick, Robert Otis *government agency administrator*
Braswell, Louis Erskine *lawyer*
Brogdon, Byron Gilliam *radiologist, educator*
Butler, Charles Randolph, Jr. *federal judge*
Clark, Jack *retired health facility administrator*
Clarke, Charles Kendall *metallurgical engineer, consultant*
Clausell, Deborah Deloris *artist*
Collins, Harold R. *director*
Conlon, James Edward *retired art educator, sculptor*
Cox, Emmett Ripley *federal judge*
Edwards, Jack *congressman, lawyer*
Ellzey, Wayne Ewell *retired accountant*
French, Elizabeth Irene *biology professor, musician*
Goff, William M., Jr. *art director, graphics designer, animator, artist*
Graddick, Charles Allen *judge*
Granade, Callie Virginia Smith *federal judge*
Guarino, Anthony Michael *pharmacologist, educator, consultant, counselor*
Hamid, Michael *electrical engineering educator, consultant*
Hariadi, John Wesley *otolaryngologist, surgeon*
Harris, Benjamin Harte, Jr. *lawyer*
Hart, Eric Mullins *consumer products company executive*
Helmsing, Frederick George *lawyer*
Holland, Lyman Faith, Jr. *lawyer*
Holmes, Broox Garrett *lawyer*
Howard, Alex T., Jr. *federal judge*
Islam, Samantha *civil engineer, researcher*
Johnston, Neil Chunn *lawyer*
Jones, Joseph Seymour *small business owner, poet*
Kargleder, Charles Leonard *language educator*
Lipscomb, Oscar Hugh *archbishop*
Littleton, Jesse Talbot III *radiology educator*
McCleery, Winston Theodore *information technology executive*
Meigs, Walter Ralph *lawyer, dry dock and shipbuilding company executive*
Milling, Bert William, Jr. *judge*
Murchison, David Roderick *lawyer*
Parman, Tracy Le *application developer*
Peebles, E(mory) B(ush) III *lawyer*
Pierce, Donald Fay *lawyer*
Pitcock, James Kent *otolaryngologist*
Pittman, Virgil *federal judge*
Quina, Marion Albert, Jr. *lawyer*
Rewak, William John *retired academic administrator, clergyman*
Rhodes, Deborah Jean Johnson *prosecutor*
Richelson, Paul William *curator*
Rodning, Charles Bernard *surgeon*
Roedder, William Chapman, Jr. *lawyer*
Rummel, Harold Edwin *travel company, retail executive*
Scantlebury, Velma Patricia *surgeon*
Shuayto, Marwan Ibrahim *neurologist*
Smith, Jesse Graham, Jr. *dermatologist, educator*
Suess, James Francis *retired clinical psychologist*
Sumlin, Margaret (Margie) Brown *special education educator*
Taylor, Aubrey Elmo *physiologist, educator*
Wisner, Pamela L. *social worker*

Montevallo
Stephens, Scott *art educator*

Montgomery
Baker, Jimmy H. *former state finance administrator*
Black, Robert Coleman *judge, lawyer*
Blount, Winton Malcolm III *investment executive*
Bolin, Michael F. *state supreme court justice*
Boncek, John James *mathematics professor*
Brown, Jean Williams *former state supreme court justice*
Byars, Walter Ryland, Jr. *lawyer*
Campbell, Maria Bouchelle *lawyer, consultant*
Canary, Leura Garrett *prosecutor*
Carnes, Edward E. *federal judge*
Cassels, Martha Beasley *realtor, investor*
Chapman, Beth Killough *state official*
Cobb, Sue Bell *state supreme court justice*
Copeland, Jacqueline Turner *music educator*
Cornett, Lloyd Harvey, Jr. *retired historian*
Das, Sunil R. *computer scientist, educator*
Dees, Morris Seligman, Jr. *lawyer*
Dixon, Larry Dean *state legislator*
Dubina, Joel Fredrick *federal judge*
Ely, Robert Eugene *lawyer, author, educator*
Folsom, Jim (James Elisha Folsom Jr.) *lieutenant governor, former governor*
Glassroth, Stephen R. *lawyer*
Godbold, John Cooper *federal judge*
Greenhaw, (Harold) Wayne *writer*
Gregory, William Stanley *lawyer*
Hamner, Reginald Turner *lawyer*
Harrison, John D. *state agency administrator*
Hester, Douglas Benjamin *lawyer*
Hobbs, Truman McGill *federal judge*
Hoffman, Richard William *retired banker*
Ivey, Kay Ellen *state official*
Jewell, Jason Eric *adult education educator*
Johnson, Mark Matthew *museum administrator*
Kennedy, Kamela Denise *director*
Kim, Ki Hang *mathematician*
King, Troy *state attorney general*
Kloess, Lawrence Herman, Jr. *retired lawyer*
Laurie, Robin Garrett *lawyer*
Lawson, Thomas Seay, Jr. *lawyer, actor*
Leslie, Henry Arthur *lawyer, retired bank executive*
Leventhal, William E. (Willy) Siegel *writer*
Lowder, Robert E. *bank executive*
Luna, Patricia Adele *marketing executive*
Maddox, Alva Hugh *retired state supreme court justice*
May, Cecil Richard, Jr. *academic administrator*
McElvy, James Douglas *lawyer*
McFadden, Frank Hampton *lawyer, former judge*
McPherson, Vanzetta Penn *magistrate judge*
Mitchell, Rebecca *library director*
Morton, Joseph *school system administrator*
Munson, Edward Harry, Jr. *medical investigator*
Murdock, Glenn *state supreme court justice*
Murkett, Philip Tillotson *human resource executive*
Myers, Ira Lee *physician*
Napier, Cameron Mayson Freeman *historic preservationist*
Owes, Jaunita *library director*
Parker, Tom *state supreme court justice, lawyer*
Patterson, John Malcolm *judge*
Petty, Willie Clifford *musician, composer, educator*
Proctor, David Ray *lawyer*
Riley, Bob (Robert Renfroe Riley) *governor*
Rose, Shirley Kelly *retired language educator*
Salmon, Joseph Thaddeus *lawyer*
Sass, Neil Leslie *toxicologist*
See, Harold Frend *state supreme court justice*
Segall, Robert D. *lawyer*
Shepard, Judith Bethea *librarian*
Smith, Larry Steven *financial analyst, accountant, farmer*
Smith, Patricia M. (Patti) *state supreme court justice*
Steele, Rodney Redfearn *judge*
Stevenson, Bryan Allen *lawyer*
Stuart, Jacquelyn L. *state supreme court justice*
Taylor, Watson Robbins *construction company executive*
Tennimon, Dannie Earl *academic administrator, educator*
Turley, Susan Lynn Welker *military officer*
Uzzell-Baggett, Karon Lynette *career officer*
Volz, Charles Harvie, Jr. *lawyer*
Wall, William Herbert *state coordinator student loan programs*
Watkins, W(illiam) Keith *federal judge*
Wendzel, Robert Leroy *political science professor*
Westhauser, Karl E. *historian*
Williamson, Donald Ellis *public health service officer, state agency administrator*
Witkosky, David V. *language educator*
Wood, James Jerry *lawyer*
Woodall, Thomas A. *state supreme court justice*

Moody
Brasher, Terrie Walker *secondary school educator*

Moulton
Dutton, Mark Anthony *lawyer*

Mountain Brook
Southerland, Henry DeLeon, Jr. *retired lawyer, civil engineer*

Normal
Journey, G. Edward *art educator*

Opelika
Jenkins, Richard Lee *manufacturing executive*
Samford, Yetta Glenn, Jr. *lawyer, director*

Orange Beach
Conrad, Marcel Edward *hematologist, oncologist, educator*

Pelham
Lee, James A. *health facility finance executive*

Pell City
Passey, George Edward *psychologist, educator*

Phenix City
Romey, Barbara Sassmann *gifted and talented educator*

Point Clear
Englund, Gage Bush *dancer, educator*
Holt, Thaddeus *lawyer*

Prattville
Hickman, Walter Dixon, II, *information technology manager*

Ramer
Napier, John Hawkins III *historian*

Salem
Gibbons, Dona Alden Coe *electrical engineer, director*

Seale
Harris-Stokes, Joyce A. *secondary school educator*

Selma
Calhoun-Bates, Carolyn E. *social services administrator*
Fitts, Alston III *writer*
Inge, DeAndres Gates *mathematics educator*

Semmes
Phelps, James Franklin *retired county official*

Sheffield
Hamby, Gene Malcolm, Jr. *lawyer*

Somerville
Johnson, Loyd *agricultural engineer, researcher*

Spanish Fort
Economos, Cora Matheny *librarian*
van Aken, John Henry *retired marine engineer*

Sumiton
Rizzo, Stephen Wayne Burton *secondary school educator, music minister*

Talladega
Jeffers, Trellie Lee James *language educator, dean*
Lanier, Anita Suzanne *musician, educator*
McKinney, John Paul *performing company executive*
Swain, Mary Madgalene Dickerson *pediatrics nurse*

Theodore
Carbo, Tammera Melissa *counselor, counseling administrator*
Hollis, Julia Ann Roshto *critical care, medical, and surgical nurse*

Thomasville
Davis, Gene *retired civil engineer*

Troy
Allard, Catherine *music educator, musician*
Blum, Elizabeth Dian *history professor*
Davidson, Barry Sheldon *academic administrator, comparative and adult education educator*
Manners, Pamela Ann *psychology professor*
Rinehart, James Forrest *political science professor, department chairman*

Trussville
Jacobson, James Edmund *retired newspaper editor*

Tuscaloosa
Axel, Bernard *finance executive*
Baklanoff, Eric Nicholas *economist, educator*
Barfield, Robert F. *mechanical engineer, educator, retired dean*
Bassett, Debra Lyn *lawyer, educator*
Blackburn, John Leslie *small business owner*
Cook, Camille Wright *retired law educator*
Cramer, Dale Lewis *retired economics professor*
Crowley, John William *literature and language professor*
Darden, William Howard, Jr. *biology professor*
Dixon, David Adams *chemistry professor, researcher*
Farahat, Medhat S. *researcher*
Fish, Mary Martha *economics professor*
Freyer, Tony Allan *historian, educator*
Grogg, Jill Elaine *library and information scientist*
Gup, Benton Eugene *banking educator*
Hendrix, Mary Elizabeth *language educator, researcher*
Hocutt, Max Oliver *retired philosophy educator*
Janiga-Perkins, Constance Gabrielle *language educator*
Jemison, Sandra J. *educational association administrator, educator*
Keeton, J. E. *retired psychiatrist*
LaMoreaux, Philip Elmer *geologist, hydrologist, consultant*
Leonard, James *law librarian, educator*
Lopez-Bautista, Juan Manuel *biology professor, research scientist*
Mancini, Ernest Anthony *geologist, educator, researcher*
Mayer, Morris Lehman *marketing educator*
McFarland, James William *real estate company executive, consultant*
McFarland, James William, Jr. *real estate manager*
McNealey, Ernest *college president*
Moynihan, Gary Peter *industrial engineering educator*
Orcutt, Ben Avis *retired social work educator*
Osburn, Charles Benjamin *retired librarian, dean*
Pass, Charlotte Louise *literature educator, consultant*
Periaswamy, Padmini *materials scientist, researcher*
Pieroni, Robert Edward *internist, educator, military officer*
Pitschmann, Louis A. *librarian, dean, educator*
Randall, Kenneth C. *dean, law educator*
Rankin, Margaret McIsaac *elementary school educator*
Ray, Nelda Howton *financial consultant*
Ray, Paul Sukhamay *engineering educator, researcher*
Reinhart, Kellee Connely *journalist*
Ross, Daniel J.J. *publishing executive*
Saban, Nick Lou *college football coach, former professional football coach*
Sinclair, Robert Ewald *retired physician*
Smalley, Donna Wesson *lawyer, educator*
Smith, Ralph Harrison *lawyer*
Thomas, Joab Langston *retired academic administrator, biologist, educator*
Vincent, John Bertram *chemist, educator*
Williams, Roger Courtland *lawyer, arbitrator, mediator*
Witt, Robert E. *academic administrator*

Tuskegee
Abu-elenin, Sherif Mohamed *electrical engineer, educator*
Clark, Shawn L. *psychologist, educator*
Egiebor, Nosa O. *engineering educator, consultant*
Gray, Fred David *lawyer*
Green, Elbert P. *retired academic administrator*
Powell, Nichole Larai *chemistry professor, researcher*
Rangari, Vijaya Kumar *chemistry professor, researcher*

Tuskegee Institute
Casimire-Etzioni, Athema Louise *veterinary pathologist*
Datiri, Benjamin Chumang *soil and environmental scientist*
Paris, Deidre Eileen *artificial intelligence researcher, educator*

Valley
Ogle, D. Clark *textiles executive*

Vernon
Maddox, Frederick Lynn *mathematics educator*

Vestavia
Nuckols, Frank Joseph *psychiatrist*

Webb
Knowles, Julie Nall *secondary school educator*

ALASKA

Anchorage
Bond, Marc Douglas *lawyer*
Braund-Allen, Julianna Elise *librarian*
Brigham, Lawson Walter *oceanographer, researcher*
Brown, Keith E. *lawyer*
Bryner, Alexander O. *state supreme court justice*
Burgess, Timothy M. *federal judge, former prosecutor*
Burke, Marianne King *state agency administrator, finance company executive, consultant*
Butler, Rex Lamont *lawyer*
Byrd, Milton Bruce *academic administrator*
Cantor, James Elliot *lawyer*
Christensen, Ronald E. *physician*
Claman, Matthew W. *lawyer*
Cohen, Nelson P. *prosecutor*
Comeau, Carol Smith *school system administrator*
Cuddy, Daniel Hon *bank executive*
Davis, Bettye Jean *school system administrator, state legislator*
De Lisio, Stephen Scott *lawyer, director, pastor*
Ealy, Jonathan Bruce *lawyer*
Eastaugh, Robert L. *state supreme court justice*
Etzel, Ruth Ann *pediatrician, epidemiologist, educator*
Fabe, Dana Anderson *state supreme court justice*
Fleischer, Hugh William *lawyer*
Grahame, Heather H. *lawyer*
Hickel, Walter Joseph *investment company executive, government agency administrator*
Holl, Roger Elmo *lawyer*
Hughes, Mary Katherine *lawyer*
Jay, Christopher Edward *stockbroker*
Jones, Jewel *social services administrator*
Jones, Mark Logan *educational association executive, educator*
Katcher, Jonathon A. *lawyer*
Keller, Karen A. *library director*
Kincaid, Karen Owers *nursing educator*
Knowles, Tony *former governor*
Langworthy, Robert H. *law educator*
Lindeman, Janet Claire *psychologist, educator*
Linxwiler, James David *lawyer*
Matthews, Warren Wayne *state supreme court justice*
Maynard, Kenneth Douglas *architect*
McClintock, Donald William III *lawyer*
Mills, William James, Jr. *orthopedist, surgeon, researcher*
Nielsen, Jennifer Lee *molecular ecologist, researcher*
Norris, Frank B. *historian*
North, Douglas McKay *academic administrator*
Nosek, Francis John *lawyer, diplomat*
Obermeyer, Theresa Nangle *sociology educator*
Oesting, David W. *lawyer*
Ostrovsky, Lawrence Zelig *lawyer*
Owens, Robert Patrick *lawyer*
Parker, Walter Bruce *arctic research specialist, consultant*
Parnell, Sean *lieutenant governor, former state legislator, lawyer*
Porcaro, Michael Francis *advertising executive*
Rasmuson, Edward Bernard *banker*
Reed, Frank Metcalf *bank executive, director*
Reeves, James N. *lawyer*
Riendl, Robin Wendy *wealth advisory specialist, financial advisor*
Roberts, John Derham *lawyer*
Ross, Wayne Anthony *lawyer*
Ruedrich, Randy *political party official*
Rylander, Robert Allan *financial service executive*
Sandberg, Arlene *elementary school educator*
Schnell, Roger Thomas *small business owner, retired state official*
Schwietz, Roger L. *archbishop*
Serdahely, Douglas J. *lawyer, former state judge*
Shively, John Terry *cruise line executive*
Strohmeyer, John *writer, retired editor*
Sturgulewski, Arliss *state legislator, director*
Sullivan, George Murray *transportation executive, consultant, retired mayor*
Thomas, Lowell, Jr. *writer, retired military officer, state senator*
Thurber, Sharon Lee *elementary resource educator*
Tobin, William Joseph *newspaper editor*
Trevithick, Ronald James *underwriter*
Ulmer, Frances Ann *academic administrator, retired state official*
von der Heydt, James Arnold *federal judge*
Weinig, Richard Arthur *lawyer*
Williams, Deborah Lee *foundation administrator*
Williams, Eleanor Joyce *retired government air traffic control specialist*
Wohlforth, Eric Evans *lawyer*

Auke Bay
d'Armand, John Berger *music educator*
Waldrip, Karen Marie *career planning administrator*

Barrow
Blankenship, Trent *school system administrator, educator*

Bethel
Owen, Lauri J. *lawyer*
Turner, Kathy Ann *special education services professional, director*

Big Lake
Gillette, Muriel Delphine *nurse*

Chiniak
Griffin, Elaine B. *educator*

Chugiak
Mandell, Gordon Keith *aerospace engineer*

Cordova
Bugbee-Jackson, Joan *sculptor, educator*

Dillingham
Bouker, Ina B. *elementary school educator*

Eagle River
Cotten, Samuel Richard *fisheries consultant, former state legislator, consultant*
Sparks, Jack Norman *dean*

Elmendorf Afb
Fassler, Kerin Irene *accountant*

Fairbanks
Beistline, Earl Hoover *mining consultant*
Cahill, Catherine Frances *environmental scientist, educator*
Celaire, Jaunelle Roberta *music educator*
Chapin, F. Stuart III *ecologist*
Doran, Timothy Patrick *academic administrator*
Duffy, Lawrence Kevin *biochemist, educator*
Fathauer, Theodore Frederick *meteorologist*
Freer, Fred-Christian *artist*
Hamilton, Mark R. *academic administrator*
Helfferich, Merritt Randolph *industry and education consultant*
Irish, Joel David *anthropologist*
Jones, Stephen B. *academic administrator*
Kessel, Brina *ornithologist, educator, researcher*
Kleinfeld, Andrew J. *federal judge*
Kramm, Gerhard *meteorologist, researcher*
Lin, Chuen-Sen *mechanical engineer, educator*
Lingle, Craig Stanley *glaciologist, educator*
Margraf, Francis Joseph, Jr. *marine biologist, educator*
Mayer, Sister Patricia E. *elementary school educator*
Murkowski, Frank Hughes *former governor, former senator*
Nakoneczny, Michael Martin *artist*
Roederer, Juan Gualterio *retired physics professor*
Romanovsky, Vladimir Evgeni *physics professor*
Shier, Juliet Marie *social studies educator*
Thompson, Daniel Emerson *vending machine service company executive*
Tiemessen, John J. *lawyer*

Girdwood
Trautner, John James *real estate executive*

Haines
Kaufman, David Graham *construction executive*

Homer
Graber, Elizabeth *communications educator, literature educator*

Juneau
Carpeneti, Walter L. *state supreme court justice*
Colberg, Talis J. *state attorney general*
Cole, Charles Edward *lawyer, state attorney general*
Galvin, Patrick *state official*
Kohring, Victor H. *state legislator*
Palin, Sarah Heath *governor*
Pugh, John Robert *academic administrator, educator, retired state official*
Rozell, William Barclay *lawyer*
Sampson, Roger *school system administrator*
Schorr, Alan Edward *librarian, publishing executive*
Shelton, Kathryn H. *librarian*
Shepard, Beatrice L. *retired microbiologist, historian*
Siddeek, M. S.M. *marine biologist, educator*
Smith, Charles Anthony *foundation administrator, director*
Stevens, Gary Lee *state senator*
Usera, Vincent L. *state agency administrator*
Wessen, Douglas John *psychologist*
Weyhrauch, Bruce Butler *lawyer, former state legislator*

Kodiak
Jamin, Matthew Daniel *lawyer, judge*
Ott, Andrew Eduard *lawyer*
Selby, Jerome M. *mayor*

Nondalton
Gay, Sarah Elizabeth *lawyer*

North Pole
James, Jeannette Adeline *state legislator, accountant, small business owner*
McGee, Michael Vanhook *writer, playwright*

Palmer
Young-Campbell, Laura L. *speech pathology/audiology services professional*

Saint Marys
Alstrom-Beans, Gail *Native American tribal leader*

Saint Paul Island
Lestenkof, Aquilina Debbie *environmental advocate*

Salcha
Rice, Julian Casavant *lawyer*

Sitka
Graham, David Antony *lawyer*

Skagway
Sanders, Debra Kay *curator*

Soldotna
Moore, Hubert, Jr. *retired addictions counselor, consultant*
Stuart, Jodi Marie *language educator*

Thorne Bay
Sylvia, Dennis Ashton *geologist*

Wrangell
Miller, Jennifer L. *elementary school educator, small business owner*
Smith, Kimmie Christine *small business owner*

ARIZONA

Amado
Criswell, Stephen *astronomer*

Anthem
Bennett, Sister Elsa Mary *retired secondary school educator*

Apache Junction
Bracken, Harry McFarland *philosophy educator*
Maher, John *literature educator, writer*

Avondale
Chan, Kathleen Ann *writer, social worker*

Benson
Erden, Sybil Isolde *artist*

Bisbee
Holland, Robert Dale *retired judge*
Moreno, Patricia Frazier *lawyer*

Carefree
Mangouni, Norman *publishing executive*
Putney, Mark William *lawyer, utilities executive*
Smoot, David Paul *finance company executive*
Wearly, William Levi *retired manufacturing executive*
Whittington, Thomas Lee *lawyer*

Casa Grande
Landers, Patricia Glover *language educator*
McGillicuddy, Joan Marie *psychotherapist, consultant*

Cave Creek
Collins, Jack Adam *mechanical engineer*

Chandler
Bailey, Gregory Emmett *systems engineer*
Basha, Edward N., Jr. *grocery chain owner*
Braunisch, Henning *electronics engineer, researcher*
Brown, Brenda *library director*
Brunello-McCay, Rosanne *sales executive*
Casteel, Camille *school system administrator*
Chang, Je-Young *electronics engineer*
D'Angelo, Frank Joseph *literature and language professor*
Fons, Margaret E. *elementary school educator*
Fordemwalt, James Newton *microelectronics engineering educator, consultant*
Goyer, Robert Stanton *retired communications educator and administrator*
Janakiram, Mani *manufacturing engineer*
Kim, James Joo-Jin *electronics company executive*
Meieran, Eugene Stuart *materials scientist*
Newman, Phyllis *retired counselor, therapist, hypnotist*
Simon, Diane Rose *music educator, writer, poet*
Wang, Jinlin *chemical engineer*
Williams, James Eugene *management consultant*

Chinle
Coor, Caren Barbara *art educator*
Hodson, William David *elementary school educator, consultant*

Chino Valley
Norton, Douglas Ray *former auditor general*

Coolidge
Laursen, Lin L. *women's college basketball coach, educator*

Cottonwood
Masters, Arlene Elizabeth *singer*

Davis Monthan Afb
Miller, Charles Wallace *historian, environmental geologist, educator*

Desert Hills
Evans, Carol Ann *reading specialist*

Duncan
Ouzts, Eugene Thomas *minister, secondary education educator*

Eloy
O'Leary, Thomas Michael *lawyer*

Flagstaff
Baron, Patricia Burrell *university director*
Bolin, Richard Luddington *industrial development specialist, consultant*
Cortner, Hanna Joan *retired political scientist, researcher*
Everett, Judith *merchandising educator*
Haeger, John Denis *academic administrator*
Hammond, Howard David *retired botanist, editor*
Herkenhoff, Kenneth Edward *geologist, researcher*
Lapsley, James Norvell, Jr. *minister, educator*
McDonald, Craydon Dean *psychologist*
Millis, Robert Lowell *astronomer, science observatory director*
Pavlik, William Bruce *psychologist, educator*
Pickett, A. Dean *lawyer*
Price, Peter Wilfrid *ecology educator, researcher*
Shoemaker, Carolyn Spellman *planetary astronomer*
Stewart, Roger Charles *consumer products executive*
Stoops, Daniel J. *lawyer*

Florence
Mosby, Nora Jane *music educator*

Fort Huachuca
Sleeper, Nancy JoAnn *mental health services professional*

Fountain Hills
Israel, Robert Allan *statistician*
Jan, George Pokung *political science professor*
Mousseux, Renate *language educator*
Sorenson, Gretchen Hartley *elementary school educator*
Tyl, Noel Jan *retired vocalist, astrologer, writer*
Wright, C. T. Enus *former academic administrator*

Gilbert
Eitner, James William *physician, medical consultant, administrator*
Metcalf, Virgil Alonzo *economics professor*

Glendale
Almstead, Sheila Louise *art gallery owner*
Bai, Haowei *aerospace engineer, aerospace scientist*
Cacciatore, Joanne *social worker*
Cota, Lisa Foley *secondary school educator*
Cotton, Sally Jean *retired music educator*
Doan, Shane *professional hockey player*
Gretzky, Wayne Douglas *retired professional hockey player, professional hockey coach*
Honsa, Vlasta *retired librarian*
Maloney, Don *professional sports team executive, retired professional hockey player*
Nolan, Owen *professional hockey player*
Pang, Darren *hockey analyst, retired professional hockey player*
Patton, Lynn Radonic *pharmacist, educator*
Sweat, Ken Gunter *educator, consultant*
Wise, John Macgregor *speech educator*
Yazzie, Aaron Franklin *events laborer*

Goodyear
Borton, George Robert *retired airline captain*
Carlson, Norman A. *retired federal agency administrator*
Eppen, Gary Dean *business educator*
Molina, Tanya E. *school librarian*

Grand Canyon
Bryant, Leland Marshal *business and nonprofit executive*

Green Valley
Bachman, David Christian *orthopedic surgeon*
Brewington, Arthur William *retired English language educator*
Foley, Teresa A. *psychologist*
Forsyth, Garyfallia Lillian *nurse educator*
Fuer-Davis, Beverly Jean *retired elementary school educator*
Johnson, Charles Foreman *architectural firm executive*
Lusk, Harlan Gilbert *national park superintendent, business executive*
Moser, Robert Harlan *internist, educator, writer*
Pike, George Harold, Jr. *religious organization administrator, clergyman*
Ragan, James Thomas *communications executive*
Ramette, Richard Wales *chemistry professor*
Reichlin, Seymour *endocrinologist, educator*
Smith, Raymond Lloyd *former university president, consultant*

Hereford
Hirth, John Price *metallurgical engineering educator*
Seeland, Arthur David *bishop*

Higley
Chris, Haidet Todd *minister, event producer*

Kingman
Basinger, Richard Lee *lawyer*

Lake Havasu City
Hurt, Nathan Hampton, Jr. *mechanical engineer*
Livingstone, E. Franklin *rehabilitation physician, director*

Lake Montezuma
Loveland, John Bigelow *editor, writer*

Lakeside
Mack, Ina Leah *secondary school educator, pre-school administrator*
McBride, Janet Marie *small business owner*
Seely, Dennis M. *secondary school educator*

Litchfield Park
McKeighen, Ronald Eugene *physicist*

Marana
Davidson, Gilbert *city manager*
Steckler, Larry *publishing executive, writer*

Maricopa
Kimball, Bruce Arnold *soil scientist*

Mesa
Ahearn, Geraldine *medical/surgical nurse, writer, poet*
Cooley, Jack Crain *cadriovascular surgeon*
Cox, Heidi Pinkerton *pediatric surgeon*
David, Susan Holcombe *child and family therapist*
de Masi, Kenneth Forrest *secondary school educator*
DeRosa, Francis Dominic *chemical company executive*
Dillenberg, Jack *dean*
Doyle, Matthew Brian *computer graphics designer*
Duvall, Debra *school system administrator*
Gordon, Marvin F. *retired social sciences educator*
Gunderson, Brent Merrill *lawyer*
Hagen, Nicholas Stewart *medical educator, consultant*
Hawker, Keno *mayor, trucking company executive*
Hudkins, John W. *lawyer*
Hundley, Shelli *mathematics educator*
Johnson, Doug *advertising and public relations executive*
Linxwiler, Louis Major, Jr. *retired finance company executive*
Luth, William Clair *geochemist, retired research manager*
Molina-Walters, Debi Ann *education educator*
Murphy, Edward Francis *sales executive*
Rummel, Robert Wiland *aeronautical engineer, writer*
St. Cyr, Margaret Ann (Peggy St. Cyr) *writer*
Schvaneveldt, Roger Wayne *science educator, consultant*
Singhal, Avinash Chandra *engineering administrator, educator*
Skoldberg, Phyllis Linnea *musician, educator*
Weber, Yvonne Roebuck *research administrator, educator*
Wolf, Heather *library director*

Oracle
Rush, Andrew Wilson *artist*

Oro Valley
Abbassian, Assad *urologist*
Haller, Archibald Orben *sociologist, educator*
Swalin, Richard Arthur *scientist, company executive*

Paradise Valley
Burkholder, Peter Miller *retired physician, educator*
Cohen, Robert *plastic surgeon*
Day, Richard Putnam *marketing professional, arbitrator, employee benefits consultant*
Howard, Lucia Fakonas *retired lawyer*
Lorenzen, Robert Frederick *ophthalmologist*
Quinn, Brian Grant *sculptor, art educator*
Russell, Paul Edgar *electrical engineering educator*
Targovnik, Selma E. Kaplan *dermatologist*
Tubman, William Charles *lawyer*
Tyner, Neal Edward *retired insurance company executive*
Unruh, James Arlen *bank executive*

Parker
Cravath, Jay Lewis *cultural educator*

Patagonia
La Noue, Terence David *artist, educator*

Payson
Hershberger, Robert Glen *architect, educator*
Lasys, Joan *medical/surgical nurse, educator*
Stephenson, Larry Kirk *geography educator, financial planner*

Peoria
Bailey, Claudia Jean *artist, retired librarian*
Cook, Mary Margaret *steamfitter, educator*
Gould, Dorothy Mae *executive secretary, soprano*
Jenkins, Carol Anne *educator*
Murgatroyd, Eric Neal *data processing executive*
Nelson, Mary Kathryn *bilingual counselor, small business owner, real estate agent, artist, insurance agent*
Schindler, William Stanley *retired public relations executive*
Willard, Garcia Lou *artist*
Willis, Edward Oliver *management consultant, state agency administrator*

Phoenix
Adkerson, Richard C. *mining executive*
Aksoy, Hakan *mechanical engineer*
Allen, Robert Eugene Barton *lawyer*
Alsentzer, William James, Jr. *lawyer*
Altiere, Lauren M. *music educator, consultant*
Ammon, John Richard *anesthesiologist*
Andersen, Ib *performing company executive*
Anderson, Lawrence Ohaco *United States magistrate judge, lawyer*
Anderson, Vicki *retired librarian*
Armstrong, Nelson William, Jr. *gaming company executive*
Atkinson, Joseph Matthew *lawyer*
Bain, C. Randall *lawyer*
Baker, William Dunlap *lawyer*
Bakker, Thomas Gordon *lawyer*
Bales, W. Scott *state supreme court justice*
Barbosa, Leandro Mateus *professional basketball player*
Begam, Robert George *lawyer*
Beggs, Harry Mark *lawyer*
Bell, Raja *professional basketball player*
Bellamy, Fredric *lawyer*
Berch, Rebecca White *state supreme court justice, lawyer*
Bidwill, William V. *professional sports team executive*
Binns, James Hazlett, Jr. *entrepreneur*
Birk, David R. *lawyer, electronics executive*
Blanchard, Charles Alan *lawyer, retired state senator*
Boldin, Anquan *professional football player*
Bolin, Vladimir Dustin *chemist*
Breland, Sandy Ann *broadcast executive, director*
Brewer, Janice Kay *state official*
Broomfield, Robert Cameron *federal judge*
Brown, Jack A. *state representative, rancher, real estate broker*
Burke, Timothy John *lawyer*
Burnham, Rebecca Lynne *lawyer*
Bushee, Ward III *newspaper editor*
Canby, William Cameron, Jr. *federal judge*
Carroll, Earl Hamblin *federal judge*
Carter, Ronald Martin, Sr. *pharmaceutical executive*
Case, David Leon *lawyer*
Chadwick, Simon *management consultant*
Charlton, John Kipp *pediatrician*
Chavez, Nelba R. *state and former federal agency administrator*
Church, Steve *electronics executive*
Clements, John Robert *real estate company executive*
Cocking, Jill Hager *protective services official*
Coghill, William Thomas, Jr. *retired lawyer*
Cohen, Jon Stephan *lawyer*
Cole, George Thomas *lawyer*
Colton, Sterling David (David Colton) *lawyer*
Comer, James V. *academic administrator*
Comus, Louis Francis, Jr. *lawyer*
Condo, James Robert *lawyer*
Cooledge, Richard Calvin *lawyer*
Cooper, Alice (Vincent Damon Furnier) *popular musician*
Coor, Lattie Finch *university president*
Cowley, Samuel C. *lawyer, transportation services executive*
Coyle, Linda Marie *elementary school educator*
Crozier, Scott A. *lawyer*
Culnon, Sharon Darlene *special education educator, reading specialist*
Curcio, Christopher Frank *deputy director*
D'Antoni, Mike (Michael Andrew D'Antoni) *Professional basketball coach and sports team executive, former player*
Davies, David George *lawyer, educator*
Dawson, John Joseph *lawyer*
De Michele, O. Mark *real estate company executive*
Derdenger, Patrick *lawyer*
Derouin, James Gilbert *lawyer*
Dewane, John Richard *retired manufacturing executive, small business owner*
Dib, Nabil *cardiologist, researcher*
Dickey, Robert J. *publishing executive*
Diethrich, Edward Bronson *heart institute executive, cardiovascular surgeon*
Donovan, Timothy R. *lawyer*
Doss, Sylvia M. *psychologist, educator*
Doto, Irene Louise *statistician*
Drain, Albert Sterling *business management consultant*
Dunipace, Ian Douglas *lawyer*
Duyck, Kathleen Marie *poet, musician, retired social worker*
Edens, Gary Denton *broadcast executive*
Ehmann, Anthony Valentine *lawyer*
Elmore, James Walter *architect, educator, retired dean*
Everett, James Joseph *lawyer*
Everett, Paul Marvin *physicist*
Everroad, John David *lawyer*
Eyring, Michael Borth *forensic specialist*
Farmer, Kenneth Lloyd, Jr. *health facility administrator, retired military officer*
Farney, Charlotte Eugenia *musician, educator*
Feinstein, Allen Lewis *lawyer*
Fellows, Gerald Lee *lawyer*
Fenzl, Terry Earle *lawyer*
Finch, Carol *librarian*
Flickinger, Don Jacob *lawyer*
Francis, Philip L. *retail executive*
Franke, William Augustus *investor*
Freeman, Stacey Vicario *director, model*
Frehner, Patricia Ann *education educator, consultant*
Freyermuth, Clifford L. *structural engineering consultant*
Friedman, Shelly Arnold *cosmetic surgeon*
Fullmer, Steven Mark *engineering executive*
Gaffney, Donald Lee *lawyer*
Gaines, Francis Pendleton III *judge*
Galbut, Martin Richard *lawyer*
Gallagher, Michael L. *lawyer*
Garagiola, Joe, Jr. *baseball team executive*
Garcia, Ernest G. *audiologist, technologist*
Garvey, Toni *library director*
Genrich, Mark L. *corporate communications director*
Giedt, Bruce Alan *paper company executive*
Gilbert, Donald Roy *lawyer*
Gillette, Robert J. *aerospace transportation executive*
Giltner, Phil (F. Phillips Giltner III) *food distributing executive*
Goddard, Terry *state attorney general*
Goldstein, Stuart Wolf *lawyer*
Gomez, David Frederick *lawyer*
Gordon, Phillip Bruce *mayor*
Grant, Merwin Darwin *lawyer*
Griller, Gordon Moore *legal association administrator, consultant*
Grimwood, Helen Perry *lawyer*
Guerra, Aldo Benjamin *plastic and cosmetic surgeon*
Gwozdz, Kim Elizabeth *interior designer, furniture designer*
Halpern, Barry David *lawyer*
Hamada, Rick *electronics executive*
Hammond, Larry Austin *lawyer*
Hanley, Fred William *librarian, educator*
Hanneman, LeRoy C., Jr. *real estate executive*
Hantel, Philip Edward *lawyer*
Hardwick, Catherine R. *lawyer*
Harris, Jack F. *police chief*
Harrison, Mark Isaac *lawyer*
Hathaway, Peter S. *corporate financial executive*
Hawkins, Jasper Stillwell, Jr. *architect*
Hawkins, Michael Daly *federal judge*
Hay, John Leonard *lawyer*
Hayden, William Robert *lawyer*
Heppell, Jacques Philippe *surgeon, educator*
Hernandez, Heather Marie *organist, music director*
Hicks, William Albert III *lawyer*
Hill, Grant *professional basketball player*
Hochuli, Edward G. *lawyer*
Hoecker, Thomas Ralph *lawyer*
Hooper, Daniel Lee *music educator, composer*
Howard, William Matthew *arbitrator, lawyer, writer*
Hoxie, Joel P. *lawyer*
Hudson, Orlando Thill *professional baseball player*
Huelster, Jeffery James *social studies educator*
Huffman, Edgar Joseph *oil industry executive*
Hunt, Linda *hospital administrator*
Huntwork, James Roden *lawyer*
Hurwitz, Andrew D. *state supreme court justice*
Jacobsen, William M. *plastic surgeon*
Jakubczyk, John Joseph *lawyer*
James, Charles E., Jr. *lawyer*
James, Edgerrin Tyree *professional football player*
Jirauch, Charles W. *lawyer*
Johnson, Christopher D. *lawyer*
Johnson, Elizabeth Misner *health services executive*
Johnson, Mystie L. *obstetrician, gynecologist, department chairman*
Johnson, Randy (Randall David Johnson) *professional baseball player*
Johnston, Logan Truax III *lawyer*
Jones, Charles E. *retired state supreme court chief justice*
Jones, Eddie *architect*
Kamins, Edward *electronics executive*
Kant, Robert S. *lawyer*
Kenney, Thomas Frederick *broadcast executive*
Kerr, Steve (Stephen Douglas Kerr) *professional sports team executive, retired professional basketball player*
Khan, Mohammed Yousuf *physician, consultant*
King, Robert L. *foundation and former academic administrator*
Kirkland, Joseph *voice educator*
Klahr, Gary Peter *retired lawyer*
Klausner, Jack Daniel *lawyer*
Klepinger, John William *trailer manufacturing company executive*
Knoller, Guy David *lawyer*
Kunkel, Joe Carroll *finance company executive*
Kurn, Neal *lawyer*
Kuzma, George Martin *retired bishop*
Kyl, Jon Llewellyn *senator*
Laufer, Nathan *cardiologist*
Leach, John F. *editor, director, journalist, educator*
Lee, Barbara S. *special education educator*
Lee, Richard H(arlo) *lawyer*
Leinart, Matt *professional football player*
Lemon, Leslie Gene *retired diversified financial services company executive, lawyer*
Leshner, Stephen I. *lawyer*
Levetown, Robert Alexander *lawyer*
Lewis, Orme, Jr. *real estate company executive, land use adviser*
Lindeman, Richard Russell *electronics engineer*
Loftin, Nancy Carol *lawyer, utilities executive*
Long, Michael Alan *musician, writer*
Loscher, Tricia Diane *curator, director*
Lovett, William Lee *surgeon*
Lubin, Stanley *lawyer*
Manhold, John Henry *dental educator, consultant*
Marion, Shawn *professional basketball player*
Martone, Frederick J. *judge*
Martori, Joseph Peter *lawyer*
Mason, Michael Lamott *librarian, researcher, writer*
Mast, Gregory Lewis *lawyer*
Masters, Jonathan Edward *clinical psychologist*
May, Bruce Barnett *lawyer*
McAuliffe, Daniel Joseph *lawyer*
McConnell, Albert Lynn *director*
McGregor, Ruth Van Roekel *state supreme court justice*
McKellips, Gordon Wayne, Jr. *lawyer, land developer*
McNamee, Stephen M. *federal judge*
McRae, Hamilton Eugene III *lawyer*
Meeks, Jacquelynn *city health department administrator*
Meschkow, Jordan M. *lawyer*
Meyer, Hermann Belton Perrin *retired neonatologist, health facility administrator, bioethicist*
Miller, Michael Jon *survey engineer*
Miller, Robert J. *lawyer*
Mitchell, Wayne Lee *retired health facility administrator*
Mofford, Rose *former governor of Arizona*

Mondry, Lawrence N. *automotive executive*
Moyer, Alan Dean *retired newspaper editor*
Moyes, Jerry C. *transportation executive*
Mullen, Daniel Robert *finance company executive*
Napolitano, Janet Ann *governor*
Nash, Steve *professional basketball player*
Newman, Donald Lynn *psychologist, consultant*
Nijinsky, Tamara *actress, puppeteer, author, librarian, educator*
Noone, Laura Palmer *academic administrator, lawyer*
Norris, John Steven *healthcare company executive*
Olsen, Alfred Jon *lawyer*
O'Steen, Van *lawyer*
Pasholk, Paul Douglas *retail executive, government official*
Patel, Naresh Pratap *medical educator, physician, consultant*
Pepicello, William J. *academic administrator*
Peralta, Everett Figueroa *education educator, department chairman*
Perry, Lee Rowan *retired lawyer*
Pershad, Ashish *cardiologist*
Phillips, Steve *electronics executive*
Pietzsch, Michael Edward *lawyer*
Pitman, Jim *professional sports team executive*
Placenti, Frank Michael *lawyer*
Platt, Warren E. *lawyer*
Plattner, Richard Serber *lawyer*
Post, William Joseph *utility executive*
Price, Charles Steven *lawyer*
Ralston, Barbara Jo *bank executive*
Reed, Wallace Allison *anesthesiologist*
Refo, Patricia Lee *lawyer*
Rethore, Bernard M. *lawyer*
Reyes, Anna Maria *broadcast executive*
Richardson, Judy McEwen *investment banker, consultant, cartoonist*
Rister, Gene Arnold *humanities educator*
Rivera, Jose de Jesus *lawyer*
Roberts, Christopher Wayne *psychologist, educational consultant*
Roof, Sally Jean-Marie *library and information scientist, educator*
Rose, David L. *lawyer*
Rose, Jalen *professional basketball player*
Rose, Scott A. *lawyer*
Rosenfeld, Lawrence J. (Larry) *lawyer*
Ross, Richard Frederick *lawyer*
Rotellini, Felecia A. *state agency administrator*
Rudolph, Gilbert Lawrence *lawyer*
Ryan, Michael D. *state supreme court justice*
Sadowski, Raymond *electronics executive*
Sage, Webster LeGene, Jr. *ophthalmologist*
Salmon, Matt *former congressman, communications company executive*
Sanchez, Steven M. *financial executive*
Sanders, Barry R. *lawyer*
Sarver, Robert G. *professional sports team owner*
Schenkel, Barbara Ann *minister, nurse, social worker*
Schiffner, Adrienne Anita *art historian, educator*
Schiffner, Charles Robert *architect*
Schneider, Elizabeth Kelley *law librarian, educator*
Schrader, Susan Rae *elementary school educator*
Schroeder, Mary Murphy *federal judge*
Sertich, Kelli Ann *land use planner*
Sherk, Kenneth John *lawyer*
Short, Dean Chilton, II, *lawyer*
Shortliffe, Edward Hance *internist, medical educator, computer scientist*
Silver, Roslyn Olson *federal judge*
Silverman, Alan Henry *lawyer*
Silverman, Barry G. *federal judge*
Singer, Jeffrey Alan *surgeon*
Smith, George *marketing professional*
Smock, Timothy Robert *lawyer*
Snider, Timothy R. *mining executive*
Sochacki, Andrzej *mechanical engineer, researcher, tourism educator*
Sperling, John Glen *education company executive, educator*
Steckler, Phyllis Betty *business and publishing consultant*
Steffey, Lela *state legislator, banker*
Stegmayer, Joseph Henry *housing industry executive*
Stern, Richard David *investment company executive*
Stone, Hazel Anne Decker *artist*
Storey, Norman C. *lawyer*
Stoudemire, Amare Carsares *professional basketball player*
Strand, Roger Gordon *federal judge*
Sutton, Samuel J. *lawyer, educator, engineer*
Swartz, Melvin Jay *lawyer, writer*
Tarbell, Mark *chef*
Taurasi, Diana Lurena *professional basketball player*
Taylor, Elizabeth Jane *investment advisor, real estate company executive, marketing executive*
Teague, Robert Cole *physician*
Tennen, Leslie Irwin *lawyer, consultant*
Thompson, Joel Erik *lawyer*
Thompson, Terence William *lawyer*
Tyus, Gordon *graphics designer, educator*
Udall, Vesta Hammond *special education educator*
Ulrich, Paul Graham *lawyer, writer, editor*
Upson, Donald V. *retired corporate financial executive*
Vallee, Roy A. *electronics executive*
Valverde, Jose Rafael *professional baseball player*
Van Fleet, David Dominic *management educator*
Verbin, Jeffrey Harold *lawyer*
Vryhof, John C. *lawyer*
Walker, Richard K. *lawyer*
Walker, Thomas Carlton *music educator*
Warner, Teddy Fleming *lawyer*
Webb, Brandon Tyler *professional baseball player*
Weisenburger, Theodore Maurice *retired judge, poet, educator*
Welker, Kristina Diane *psychologist*
Wells, GladysAnn *library director*
Welts, Rick *professional sports team executive*
Westhead, Paul *professional basketball coach*
Wheaton, Marilyn *musician*
White, Edward Allen *electronics executive*
Williams, Quinn Patrick *lawyer*
Willocks, Robert Max *retired librarian*
Wilson, Stephen Rip *public policy consultant*
Winthrop, Lawrence Fredrick *judge*
Wirken, Charles William *lawyer*
Wolf, G. Van Velsor, Jr. *lawyer*
Wolf, Irna Lynn *psychologist*
Wright, Margaret Taylor *marketing consultant, publisher*
Yamamoto, Alice M. *secondary school educator*
Yarnell, Michael Allan *mediator, arbitrator, law educator*
Zerella, Joseph T. *retired pediatric surgeon*
Zidich, John M. *publishing executive*

Pinetop
Gilbert-Tiegs, Marion Ann *gifted and talented educator, consultant*

Portal
Zweifel, Richard George *curator*

Prescott
Anderson, Parker Lynn *columnist, playwright*
Beatty, Jametha Ann *communications educator*
Bieniawski, Zdzislaw Tadeusz Richard *engineering educator, writer, consultant*
Chesson, Eugene *retired civil engineering educator, consultant, volunteer*
Forth, Kevin Bernard *beverage distributing industry consultant*
Garcia-Buñuel, Luis *neurologist*
Garvey, Daniel Edward *foundation administrator, educator*
Goodman, Mark N. *lawyer*
Kahne, Stephen James *systems engineering educator, engineering company executive, academic administrator*
Madden, Paul Robert *lawyer, director*
Masotti, Louis Henry *real estate educator, consultant*
Parkhurst, Charles Lloyd *electronics executive*
Rinde, Andrea J. *mathematics educator*
Semon, Warren Lloyd *information scientist, educator*
Waldock, William David *aerospace transportation executive, educator*
Waterer, Bonnie Clausing *retired secondary school educator*

Prescott Valley
Shelley, Bonnie J. *retired voice educator*

Quartzsite
Michel, Verlyn Lyle *mayor, consultant*

Rio Rico
Lowell, J(ames) David *geological consultant, cattle rancher*

Rio Verde
Culligan, John Austin *thoracic surgeon*
Harding, John Hibbard *retired insurance company executive*
Ramsey, David Selmer *retired health facility administrator*
Scott, Louis Edward *advertising executive*
Vanselow, Neal Arthur *retired academic administrator, internist*

Saddlebrooke
Taviss, Patricia Ann *management consultant, library association executive*

Safford
Kaliher, Michael Dennis *historian, librarian*

San Luis
Kryger, Jerri Renee *elementary school educator*

Scottsdale
Afsary, Cyrus *artist*
Allen, A. William, III, (Bill) *food service executive*
Andermann, Mary Annette *application developer, consultant*
Baker, Edward Martin *engineering and industrial psychologist*
Ballinger, Charles William *sanitary engineer, consultant*
Birkelbach, Albert Ottmar *retired oil industry executive*
Blinder, Martin S. *management consultant, art dealer*
Bradway, John Kent *orthopedist*
Brown, Frederick Lee *health facility administrator*
Brown, Shirley Margaret Kern (Peggy Brown) *interior designer*
Bullerdick, Kim H. *lawyer, petroleum executive*
Buri, Charles Edward *lawyer*
Calise, Nicholas James *lawyer*
Coutts, Lawrence Robert *publisher*
Crawford, Robert F. *lawyer*
Dahl, Mark Victor *dermatologist, educator*
Dean, Bruce Linton *radiologist*
Doede, John Henry *investment company executive*
Doglione, Arthur George *data processing executive*
Dorrance, Bennett *real estate company executive*
Drake, Albert Estern *retired statistics educator, farming administrator*
Duran, Roberto *retired boxer*
Evans, Tommy Nicholas *obstetrician, gynecologist, educator*
Farley, James Newton *retired manufacturing executive, electrical engineer*
Ferree, John Newton, Jr. *fundraising specialist, consultant*
Freedman, Stanley Marvin *manufacturing executive*
Friesen, Oris Dewayne *software engineer, historian*
Fukuda, Nobuo *chef*
Gans, Eugene Howard *cosmetic and pharmaceutical company executive, consultant*
Garfield, Ernest *bank executive, consultant*
Gentry, Warren Miller *investment company executive*
Getz, Bert Atwater *investment company executive*
Gookin, Thomas Allen Jaudon *civil engineer*
Gregory, Robert Erb *surgeon*
Grenell, James Henry *retired manufacturing company executive*
Grier, James Edward *hotel executive, lawyer*
Gwinn, Mary Dolores *organization administrator, writer, lecturer*
Hamilton, Rita *library director*
Harrison, Nedra Joyce *surgeon*
Hill, Louis Allen, Jr. *retired dean, civil engineer, consultant*
Howard, William Gates, Jr. *electronics company executive*
Hutchison, Stanley Philip *retired lawyer*
Inman, William Peter *lawyer*
Jacobson, Frank Joel *cultural organization administrator*
Jarman, Beth S. *former state agency administrator, consultant*
Jayaraman, Ganapathi Subramaniam *healthcare industry executive*
Jesky, T. J. *pharmaceutical products executive*
Johnson, Micah William *television newscaster, director*
Jorden, Douglas Allen *lawyer, municipal official*
Joseph, Gregory Nelson *media critic, writer, actor, advocate*
Kathuria, Rajeev S. *cardiovascular surgeon, thoracic surgeon*
Kilburn, Penelope White *retired data processing executive*
Kinney, Carolyn *physician*
Kinsinger, Jack Burl *chemist, educator*
Kolander, David J. *retired chemicals executive*
Krane, Susan *museum director, curator*
Krupp, Clarence William *lawyer, health facility administrator*
Kumar, Kv *management consultant*
Land, George Ainsworth *philosopher, consultant, writer*
Lavenson, Susan Barker *hotel corporate executive, consultant*
Leonard, George Edmund *bank executive, credit manager, marketing professional*
Leonard, Jeffrey S. *lawyer*
Levine, Stanley Walter *chemical company executive*
Lewis, John Christopher *allergist*
Lindgren, D(erbin) Kenneth, Jr. *retired lawyer*
Lloyd, Eugene Walter *retired construction company executive*
Lloyd-Lee, Beverly *interior designer*
Lowry, Edward Francis, Jr. *lawyer*
Lundeen, Bradley Curtis *lawyer*
Marks, Merton Eleazer *lawyer, international arbitrator, mediator, consultant*
McCollum, Alvin August *consultant, real estate company executive, real estate developer*
Meyers, Marlene O. *retired hospital administrator*
Mohraz, Judy Jolley *foundation administrator*
Newman, Ursula Irene *music educator*
Nielsen, Greg Ross *lawyer*
Northey, William Thomas *microbiologist, educator*
Ogilvy, Geoff *professional golfer*
Orford, Robert Raymond *physician, consultant*
Overgaard, Cordell Jersild *lawyer, rancher, director*
Parish, James Michael *medical educator*
Parson, Shaun D. *plastic surgeon*
Parsons, Bob (Robert R. Parsons) *entrepreneur, domain register and web host company executive*
Pelham, Judith *health system administrator*
Phillips, Wanda Charity *secondary school educator, writer*
Quayle, Dan (James Danforth Quayle) *former Vice President of the United States*
Quayle, Marilyn Tucker *wife of former United States Vice President, lawyer*
Rethore, Bernard Gabriel *manufacturing and mining company executive, consultant*
Reznick, Richard Howard *pediatrician*
Richardson, Mary L. *psychotherapist*
Roarke, Michael Charles *medical educator, nuclear medicine physician*
Rodriguez, Douglas *chef*
Sanderson, David R. *physician*
Schleifer, Thomas C. *management consultant, author, lecturer*
Schmitz, Shirley Gertrude *marketing professional, sales executive*
Sheridan, Donald Charles *orthopedist, hand surgeon*
Shors, Clayton Marion *retired cardiologist*
Shower, Robert Wesley *corporate financial executive*
Slager, Donald W. *waste management executive*
Smith, David Burnell *lawyer, state legislator*
Stone, Alan Jay *retired academic administrator*
Stott, Brian *software company executive, consultant*
Strock, James Martin *communications executive, writer, entrepreneur*
Summerhill, Ronald Raymond *psychotherapist, psychologist*
Tazelaar, Henry Dale *physician, educator*
Thompson, Bradford *chef*
Timmons, Evelyn Deering *pharmacist*
Trimble, Thomas James *retired utilities executive, lawyer*
Underwood, Paul Lester *cardiologist*
Vairo, Robert John *insurance company executive*
Van Brunt, Gary T. *tire dealer company executive*
Walsh, Edward Joseph *food products and cosmetics executive*
Washburn, Jerry Martin *accountant, corporate executive*
Watkins, Eugene Leonard *surgeon, educator*
Weaver, Linda Marie *pharmacist, education educator*
Weil, Louis Arthur III *retired newspaper publishing executive*
White, Jo Lynn *lawyer*
Williams-De Silva, Lisa Annette *small business owner, adult nurse practitioner*
Wilson, Robert E. *academic administrator*
Winkler, Sheldon *dentist, educator*
Wojcik, Martin Henry *not-for-profit executive*
Wong, Joe Bing *retired architect*
Woods, Duane C. *waste management executive*
Wu, Eric *entrepreneur*
Zillmer, John J. *waste management administrator*

Sedona
Briney, Allan King *retired radiologist*
Coleman, M.L. (Michael Lee) *artist*
Copeland, Suzanne Johnson *real estate company executive*
Dansby, John Walter *retired oil industry executive*
Hawkins, David Ramon *psychiatrist, writer, researcher, spiritual teacher*
Sasmor, James Cecil *publishing representative, educator*

Sells
Ostrum, Robert F. *orthopaedic surgeon*

Show Low
Pershing, Robert George *retired telecommunications industry executive*

Sierra Vista
Boughan, Zanetta Louise *music educator*
Ponder, Herman *geologist*
Sizemore, Nicky Lee *computer scientist*
Smith, Barbara Jane *computer scientist, educator*

Sonoita
Coates, Wayne Evan *agricultural engineer*
Cook, William Howard *architect*

Sun City
Blanchet, Jeanne Ellene Maxant *artist, educator, performer*
Crisman, Mary Frances Borden *librarian*
Davies, Percy (Pete) Charles *mechanical engineer*
Hamilton, Ronald Ray *minister*
Hauer, James Albert *lawyer*
Joyce, Jeffrey *research scientist, consultant*
Keesling, Karen Ruth *lawyer*
Nicchi, Vincent, Jr. *cardiologist*
Oppenheimer, Max, Jr. *foreign language educator, consultant*
Randall, Claire *retired religious organization administrator*
Reynolds, John Francis *insurance company executive*
Thompson, Betty Jane *retired small business owner*
Treece, James Lyle *retired lawyer*
Williams, William Harrison *retired librarian*

Sun City West
Berkenkamp, Fred Julius *management consultant*
Brown, Ruth Geisler *retired electronics engineer*
Forti, Lenore Steimle *business consultant*
Schrag, Adele Frisbie *business education educator*
Stevens, George Richard *business consultant, public information officer*

Sun Lakes
Sharpless, Joseph Benjamin *retired county official*
Thompson, Loring Moore *retired academic administrator, writer*

Surprise
Bradford, Mariah *elementary school educator, consultant*
Burns, Clare Marie *retired elementary school educator*
Clark, Lloyd *historian, writer, educator*
Eastman, Donna Kelly *composer*
Fennelly, Jane Corey *lawyer*
Koessel, Donald Ray *retired bank executive*
Lazar, Max Seymour *retired pharmaceutical company executive*
Miller, James Rumrill III *finance educator*
Neuman, Isabel *mathematics educator*
Sawyers, Norma Ann *elementary school educator, real estate agent, property manager*
Telban, Ethel *retired librarian*

Tempe
Adrian, Ronald John *science educator*
Anand, Suresh Chandra *physician*
Arkfeld, Louraine C. *judge*
Askland, Andrew *law educator, director*
Balanis, Constantine Apostle *electrical engineering educator*
Bauer, Ernst Georg *physicist, researcher*
Berman, Neil Sheldon *retired chemical engineering professor*
Boudreau, Diane *writer*
Brack, O. M., Jr. *language educator*
Bradford, Steven Paul *film educator, department chairman*
Bush, Jeffrey E. *music educator, art association administrator*
Carpenter, Ray Warren *engineering educator, materials engineer*
Chiriac, Victor Adrian *aerospace engineer, researcher*

Colgate, Catharine Pamella *secondary school educator*
Cortright, Barbara Jean *public relations executive, writer*
Crellin, Alan W. *air transportation executive*
Crouch, Peter E. *engineering educator*
Crow, Michael M. *academic administrator*
Crown, Eric J. *information systems executive*
Crown, Timothy A. *computer technology company executive*
Curtiss, Roy III *life sciences professor*
Dhillon, Janet L. *lawyer, air transportation executive*
Dustman, Patricia (Jo) Allen *elementary school educator, consultant*
Duvernay, Jennifer *librarian*
Emerson, Charles LeRoy *religious studies educator*
Erickson, Dennis *college football coach, former professional football coach*
Fanning, Francis Gerard *lawyer*
Farmer, Richard G. *engineering educator*
Fennessy, Richard A. *information technology executive*
Ferry, David Keane *electrical engineering educator*
Fulton, Ira *construction executive*
Gordon, Leonard *retired social sciences educator*
Goronkin, Herbert *physicist*
Green, Monica H. *history professor*
Haggerson, Nelson Lionel, Jr. *education educator*
Harris, Warren Lynn *computer engineer*
Hechter, Michael Norman *sociologist*
Hickson, Robin Julian *mining company executive*
Hölldobler, Berthold Karl *zoologist*
Iverson, Peter James *historian, educator*
Jacobs, Mark *biology professor, dean*
Jang, Jin-Wook *electronics engineer*
Johanson, Donald Carl *physical anthropologist*
Jungbluth, Kirk E. *real estate appraiser*
Juvet, Richard Spalding, Jr. *chemistry professor*
Kambhampati, Subbarao *computer scientist, educator*
Karády, George György *electrical engineering educator, consultant*
Kaufman, Herbert Mark *finance educator*
Kerr, Derek J. *transportation executive*
Kim, Joochul *urban planner, educator*
Kirby, J. Scott *air transportation executive*
Laybourne, Stanley *computer technology company executive*
Lewis, William Raymond *art educator, artist*
Lombardi, Eugene Patsy *retired conductor, musician, educator*
MacKinnon, Stephen R. *Asian studies administrator, educator*
Mahajan, Subhash *electronic materials educator*
Marchant, Gary Elvin *lawyer*
Matheson, Alan Adams *law educator*
Maynard, Michael *librarian*
McKelvy, Michael John *chemist, research scientist*
Meehan, Robert Henry *human resources, business educator, electronics executive*
Milke, Linda Jean *elementary school educator*
Mittelstaedt, Robert E., Jr. *dean*
Moore, Carleton Bryant *geochemistry educator*
Myint, Soe Win *geographer, educator*
Nagrin, Daniel *dancer, educator, choreographer, writer*
O'Clair, Katherine Clemens *library and information scientist*
Page, Robert Eugene, Jr. *biology professor*
Pany, Kurt Joseph *finance educator, consultant*
Parker, Doug (William Douglas Parker, W. Douglas Parker) *air transportation executive*
Patel, Vimla L. *research scientist*
Pettit, George Robert *chemist, educator, cancer researcher*
Pohlman, Craig Steven *application developer*
Poste, George Henry *biology professor, former pharmaceutical company executive*
Prescott, Edward C. *economist, educator*
Raby, William Louis *writer, consultant*
Rankin, William Parkman *communications educator, academic administrator*
Reckers, Philip Merle *accountant, educator*
Richards, Gale Lee *communications educator*
Rogers, Mark Nicholl *lawyer*
Rowley, Beverley Davies *sociologist*
Sackton, Frank Joseph *public affairs educator*
Schmidt, Sherrie *library director, dean*
Schneller, Eugene Stewart *health administration and policy educator*
Si, Jennie *engineering educator*
Simes, Michael Louis *lawyer*
Simon, Sheldon Weiss *political science professor*
Smith, David John *physicist, researcher*
Smith, Harvey Alvin *mathematics professor, consultant*
Smith, V. Kerry *economics professor*
Spritzer, Ralph Simon *lawyer, educator*
Theodore, David *research scientist*
Thor, Linda M. *college president*
Thums, Charles William *designer, consultant*
Tsakalis, Konstantinos *electrical engineer, educator*
Turner Thorne, Charli *women's college basketball coach*
Uttal, William R(eichenstein) *psychology and engineering educator, research scientist*
Vittal, Vijay *electrical engineer, educator*
Wang, Ning *education educator*
Warner, Kurt(is) *professional football player*
Weigend, Guido Gustav *geographer, educator*
Wetsel, William David *literature educator*
Whisenhunt, Ken *professional football coach*
White, Patricia Denise *dean, law educator*
Wong, Timothy C. *language and literature educator*
Yau, Stephen Sik-sang *computer and information scientist, educator*
Zeitlin, Marilyn Audrey *museum director*

Tubac
Chilcote, Samuel Day, Jr. *trade association administrator*
Pardue, A. Michael *retired plastic and reconstructive surgeon*

Tucson
Abelt, Ralph William *bank executive*
Ablin, Richard Joel *immunologist, educator*
Acker, Loren Calvin *medical products executive*
Addis, Ilana Beth *obstetrician*
Adjarian, Maude Madeleine *literature educator, researcher*
Aguilar, Darla J. *adult education educator*
Ahern, Geoffrey Lawrence *behavioral neurologist*
Alberts, David Samuel *physician, pharmacologist, educator*
Allvin, Paul G. *communications educator*
Alo, Adeniyi *pharmacist, federal agency administrator*
Alpert, Joseph Stephen *cardiologist, educator*
Amhowitz, Harris J. *lawyer, educator*
Anderson, Dayna *medical researcher*
Angel, James Roger Prior *astronomer*
Arnell, Walter James William *engineering educator, consultant*
Aurand, Charles Henry, Jr. *music educator*
Axinn, George Harold *rural sociology educator*
Barrett, Bruce Richard *physics professor*
Barrette-Mozes, Susan Jean *counselor, psychotherapist*
Bartlett, David Carson *state legislator*
Barton, Stanley Faulkner *retired management consultant*
Beezley, William H. *history professor*
Bernstein, Carol *molecular biologist*
Betteridge, Frances Carpenter *small business owner, retired lawyer, mediator*
Birkinbine, John, II, *philatelist*
Blackman, Jeffrey William *lawyer*
Block, Michael Kent *economics and law professor, former government official*
Bloembergen, Nicolaas *physicist, researcher*
Bluemer, Bevan *acrobatics company executive*
Bootman, J. Lyle *pharmacy educator*
Boyle, Christopher George *language educator, counseling administrator*
Brammer, J. William, Jr. *judge, lawyer*
Breiger, Ronald Louis *social sciences educator*
Brennan, Carrie *principal*
Brunton, Daniel William *mechanical engineer*
Brusca, Richard Charles *biologist, researcher, educator, science administrator*
Butcher, Russell Devereux *writer, photographer*
Cain, Vernon *retired diversified financial services company executive*
Capp, Michael Paul *pediatrician, educator*
Carleton, Willard Tracy *retired finance educator*
Carney, Kevin *principal*
Carroll, Dennis Jerome *aerospace transportation executive*
Chiorazzi, Michael Gerard *law librarian, educator*
Christie, Nancy Gail *psychology professor, department chairman*
Clarke, James Weston *political science professor, writer*
Click, Carrie *public relations executive*
Coan, Richard Welton *psychologist, educator*
Cohen, Gary J. *lawyer*
Coker, Mich *lawyer*
Coleman, Anita S. *professor of library science*
Conant, Howard Somers *artist, educator*
Cook, Paul Christopher *intelligence officer*
Cooper, Corinne *communications consultant, lawyer*
Cooper, Jean Saralee *retired judge*
Cope, Thom K. *account executive, lawyer*
Corrigan, James John, Jr. *pediatrician, educator, dean*
Crawford, David L. *astronomer*
Crooks, Roselyn June *artist, writer*
Dale, Deborah *foundation executive*
Dalen, James Eugene *cardiologist, educator*
D'Antonio, James Joseph *lawyer*
Davenport, Sandra *cultural organization administrator*
Davis, Rendell Ashton *retired minister, social worker*
Davis, Stanley Nelson *hydrologist, educator*
De Concini, Dennis *lawyer, retired senator, consultant*
DeLuca, Dominick *medical educator, researcher*
Demeure, Michael J. *surgeon, researcher*
De Young, David Spencer *astrophysicist, educator*
Diáz, Elena R. *community health nurse*
Dinnerstein, Leonard *historian, educator*
Dobbs, Dan Byron *lawyer, educator*
Donoghue, John Charles *application developer, consultant*
Druke, William Erwin *judge, lawyer*
Dunn, Floyd *biophysics and biomedical engineering professor*
Dyer-Raffler, Joy Ann *retired special education diagnostician, educator*
Enquist, Brian Joseph *ecologist, educator*
Erickson, Robert Porter *genetics researcher, educator, clinician*
Esposito, Joseph Louis *lawyer*
Ewy, Gordon Allen *cardiologist, researcher, educator*
Falco, Charles Maurice *physicist, researcher*
Fan, Xiaohui *astrophysicist, educator*
Farhang, Ali J. *lawyer*
Favre, Kelly Ann *surgeon*
Fay, Mary Anne *retail executive*
Feldman, Stanley George *lawyer*
Fishkind, William J. *ophthalmologist*
Flint, Willis Wolfschmidt (Willi Wolfschmidt) *artist, sculptor*
Foley, Louise *medical educator, retired military officer*
Francesconi, Louise L. *defense equipment manufacturing company executive*
Frank, Michael J. *neuroscientist, educator*
Fredericksen, Dick Hartman *retired computer programmer*
Fritts, Harold Clark *botanist, educator*
Froman, Sandra Sue *lawyer*
Gaither, William Samuel *civil engineering executive, consultant*
Galloway, James Malcolm *cardiologist*
Gantz, David Alfred *lawyer, academic administrator*
Gelfand, Howard Michael *history professor*
Gerba, Charles Peter *microbiologist, educator*
Girardeau, Marvin Denham *physics professor*
Goldfarb, Robert Paul *neurological surgeon*
Goldman, Gloria A. *lawyer*
Goltz, Pat *artist, web site designer*
Gonzales, Sarah *women's organization director*
Graham, Anna Regina *pathologist, educator*
Grana, William A. *orthopedist, surgeon*
Grand, Marcia *civic worker*
Grand, Richard D. *lawyer*
Green, Richard Frederick *astronomer*
Gruhl, James *energy scientist, artist*
Gutsche, Carl David *chemistry professor*
Hale, William Bryan, Jr. *newspaper editor*
Hall, Henry Kingston, Jr. *chemistry professor*
Hamner, Rome *social services administrator*
Haney, Robert Locke *retired insurance company executive*
Hanson, Thor *retired health agency executive, retired naval officer*
Harcleroad, Fred Farley *education administrator, consultant*
Harrington, Roger Fuller *electrical engineering educator, consultant*
Harris, David Thomas *immunology educator*
Hattery, Robert Ralph *radiologist, educator*
Hawke, Robert Francis *dentist*
Haynes, Caleb Vance, Jr. *geology and archaeology educator*
Hays, James Fred *geologist, educator*
Healy, Stephanie Lemme *hospital organization administrator*
Heller, Frederick *retired mining executive*
Hellon, Michael Thomas *tax specialist, political organization worker*
Herrnstadt, Richard Lawrence *American literature educator*
Hildebrand, John G(rant) *neuroscientist, educator*
Hill, Henry Allen *physicist, researcher*
Horne, William McHenry *finance educator*
Houser, Harold Byron *epidemiologist*
Hubbard, William Bogel *planetary sciences educator*
Hughes, Malcolm Kenneth *dendrochronologist, educator, administrator*
Hull, Herbert Mitchell *botanist, researcher*
Hunten, Donald Mount *planetary scientist, educator*
Ingram, Charles Owen *priest, educator*
Jamison, Harrison Clyde *retired oil company executive*
Janes, Raena *private school educator*
Jannuzi, Buell T. *astronomer*
Jaramillo, Alba *community educator*
Jefferies, John Trevor *astrophysicist, director*
Jeter, Wayburn Stewart *retired microbiologist, educator*
Johnson, John Gray *retired university chancellor*
Johnson, Paula D. *veterinarian*
Jones, Frank Wyman *management consultant, director, mechanical engineer*
Kaltenbach, C(arl) Colin *dean, educator*
Karkoschka, Erich *planetary science researcher, writer*
Katakkar, Suresh Balaji *hematologist, oncologist*
Kearney, Joseph Laurence *retired athletic conference administrator*
Kececioglu, Dimitri Basil *reliability engineering educator, consultant*
Kennedy, Lydia *human resources specialist*
Kennicutt, Robert Charles, Jr. *astronomer*
Kerwin, William James *electrical engineering educator, consultant*
Kessler, John Otto *physicist, researcher*
King, James Edward *retired museum director, consultant*
King, Joseph Willet *child psychiatrist*
Kischer, Clayton Ward *human embryologist, educator*
Koerber, Erica *photographer*
Kohloss, Frederick Henry *retired engineer*
Kozolchyk, Boris *law educator, consultant*
Kuklin, Susan Beverly *lawyer, librarian, educator*
Kuykendall, Gregory John *lawyer*
Lamb, Willis Eugene, Jr. *physicist, researcher*
Larson, Jon M. *physiatrist*
Larwood, Laurie *psychologist*
Ledeboer, Nancy *library director*
Leonard, Michael A. *retired automotive executive*
Levenson, Alan Ira *psychiatrist, physician, educator*
Levine, Norman *physician*
Lewis, Wilbur H. *educational management consultant*
Lomicka, William Henry *investor*
Longan, George Baker III *real estate company executive*
Lunine, Jonathan Irving *astronomer, educator*
Macleod, Hugh Angus McIntosh *optical science educator, physicist, consultant*
Macys, Sonja *science association director*
Maker, Carol June *gifted and talented education educator*
Marcialis, Robert Louis *planetary astronomer*
Marcus, Frank Isadore *cardiologist, educator*
Marquez, Alfredo C. *federal judge*
Márquez-Peterson, Lea *business broker*
Martin, June Johnson Caldwell *journalist*
Martin, Loren Winston *allergist*
Martin, Marci *writer, former advertising specialist*
Massaro, Toni Marie *dean, law educator*
Matthew, Neil Edward *artist, educator*
Maxon, Don Carlton *mining and construction executive, consultant*
Mc Donald, John Richard *lawyer*
McNulty, Terence Patrick *metallurgist, consultant*
Meehan, Michael Joseph *lawyer*
Meislin, Harvey Warren *emergency healthcare physician, professional society administrator*
Mense, Allan Tate *research and development engineering executive*
Mercker, Mary Alice *aviation school administrator*
Miller, Michael Douglas *lawyer*
Moeckel, Steven *concertmaster*
Moon, Bongki *computer scientist, educator*
Moran, Nancy A. *ecologist, educator*
Morrow, James Franklin *lawyer*
Moten, Darlene *elementary school educator*
Mould, Jeremy Richard *astronomer*
Mullen, Rod *nonprofit organization executive*
Neal, Alaine (Diann Neal) *nursing administrator*
Neff, Terry Ann R. *art director, consultant*
Nelson, Edward Humphrey *architect*
Neugebauer, Marcia *physicist, researcher*
Neuman, Shlomo P. *hydrologist, educator*
Noonan, James C. *lawyer, mediator, arbitrator*
Nord, Myrtle Selma *writer, researcher*
Ogilvie, T(homas) Francis *marine engineering educator*
Orr, Ethan *non-profit organization executive*
Osborne, John Edwards *lawyer*
Pace, Thomas M. *lawyer*
Paravano, Dino *artist*
Pedersen, Arlene *web design company executive*
Peeler, Stuart Thorne *gas industry executive, consultant*
Perry, Lewis Charles *emergency medicine physician, osteopath*
Peters, Charles William *nuclear energy industry executive*
Petersen, Frederick J. *lawyer*
Peterson, Thomas W. *engineering educator*
Pierce, Roger Arnold, II, *pharmacist, director*
Popson, Lucy (Maria D. Popson) *elementary school educator*
Portney, Paul Rogers *dean*
Powell, Winona *music educator*
Powers, Linda Sue *biophysicist, educator, biomedical engineer*
Prewitt, Charles Thompson *geochemist*
Protas, Josh *non-profit organization director*
Quan, Stuart Fun *internist, educator*
Raab, Diane *special education educator*
Reinius, Michele Reed *executive recruiter*
Reitan, Ralph Meldahl *clinical neuropsychologist, former educator*
Repp, Page W., Jr. *construction executive*
Rieke, Marcia J. *astronomer, educator*
Rietschel, Robert Louis *dermatologist*
Riggs, Lew *foundation executive*
Riley, Mark Richard *biochemical engineer, educator*
Roberts, J. Berry *elementary school educator, sports official*
Robles, Maricela *architect*
Roemer, Elizabeth *retired astronomer, educator*
Rogers, Lee Frank *radiologist*
Roll, John McCarthy *judge*
Rollins, Tony James *organizational consultant*
Rose, Carol Marguerite *law educator*
Rose, Hugh *management consultant*
Russell, Findlay Ewing *physician*
Ryan, Kenneth J. *immunologist, educator*
Samet, Dee-Dee *lawyer*
Sampsel, Hunter *mortgage company executive*
Schannep, John Dwight *brokerage house executive*
Scholly, Edwin *chef*
Schorr, S. L. *lawyer*
Schulz, Renate Adele *German studies and second language acquisition educator*
Schwebel, Milton *psychologist, educator*
Seaman, Arlene Anna *retired musician*
Seehausen, Richard Ferdinand *architect*
Serido, Joyce *psychologist, researcher*
Shahidullah, Mohammad *medical researcher, medical educator*
Shaul, David Leedom *linguist, archivist*
Shelton, Robert Neal *academic administrator, physics professor, researcher*
Shropshire, Donald Gray *hospital executive*
Simmons, Sarah R. *lawyer*
Slack, Donald Carl *agricultural engineer, educator*
Smerdon, Ernest Thomas *engineering educator*
Smith, David Wayne *psychologist, educator*
Smith, Kenneth Rodger *finance educator*
Snyder, Richard Gerald *research scientist, administrator, educator, consultant*
Soren, David *archaeologist, educator, writer, filmmaker*
Spaeth, Jan Mills *jury consultant*
Sprague, Ann Louise *aerospace scientist*
Staubitz, Arthur Frederick *retired lawyer, health products executive*
Stitt, Mari Leipper *poet*
Stoffle, Carla Joy *university library dean*
Strittmatter, Peter Albert *astronomer, educator*
Strong, John William *lawyer, educator*
Tang, Esther Don *real estate developer, consultant, social worker*
Tersigni, Jennifer M. *not-for-profit fundraiser*
Thompson, Raymond Harris *retired anthropologist, educator*
Thorpe, Jason M. *non-profit organization director*
Thurman, Robert Kenneth *retired military officer*
Tifft, William Grant *retired physics professor, scientist*
Tindall, Robert Emmett *lawyer, educator*
Tirrell, John Albert *organization executive, consultant*
Titley, Spencer Rowe *geology educator*
Tollin, Gordon *retired chemistry professor*
Tompkins, Emil *chiropractor*
Treadwell-Rubin, Pamela A. *lawyer*
Underwood, Jane Hainline Hammons *anthropologist, educator*

Venkata, Subrahmanyam Saraswati *engineering educator, researcher*
Villica-a, Taunya *corporate financial executive*
Walker, Franklin Curtis *federal agency administrator*
Walker, Ronald Hugh *retired management consultant*
Walkup, Robert E. *mayor*
Wallach, Leslie Rothaus *architect*
Weil, Andrew Thomas *physician, educator*
White, Herbert Spencer *library and information scientist, educator, dean*
Wickham, John Adams, Jr. *retired army officer*
Wilder, Janos *chef*
Williams, Alan Keiser *management consultant*
Willoughby, Stephen Schuyler *mathematics professor*
Wolff, Sidney Carne *astronomer, science administrator*
Woolfenden, James Manning *nuclear medicine physician, educator*
Wrae, Natasha *lawyer*
Wyant, James Clair *engineering company executive, educator*
Yoon, Jeong-Yeol *biological engineer, educator*
Yuan, Nicole Patricia *healthcare educator*
Yurkanin, J. Paul *surgeon, educator*
Zegura, Stephen Luke *biologist, anthropologist, educator*
Zhang, Donna D. *toxicologist, educator*
Zheng, Wenxin *gynecologist, pathologist*
Ziehler, Tony Joseph *insurance agent*
Zou, Changping *research scientist, educator*
Zuckerman, Mel (Melvin Zuckerman) *hotel executive*

Waddell
Turner, Warren Austin *state legislator*

West Sedona
Lane, Margaret Anna Smith *property manager, real estate developer*

Wickenburg
Brooks, Donna Jean *counselor, educator*
Daniel, James Richard *accountant, corporate financial executive*

Wikieup
Brattstrom, Bayard Holmes *biology professor*

Youngtown
Black, Robert Frederick *retired gas industry executive*

Yuma
Anderson, John Albert *physician*
Hodson, Roy Goode, Jr. *retired logistician*
Hossler, David Joseph *lawyer, educator*
Houggard, Santa Carol Hall *family nurse practitioner, consultant*
Hudson, John Irvin *retired career officer*
Kiley, Thomas *rehabilitation counselor*
McCarthy, Sherri Nevada *psychologist, educator, educational consultant*
Norton, Dunbar Sutton *economic developer*
Rush, Dorie Mae *nursing educator*
Smith, Jimmie Dee *lawyer*

ARKANSAS

Arkadelphia
Dunn, Charles DeWitt *academic administrator*
Elrod, Ben Moody *academic administrator*
Futrell, Alvin *director*
Grant, Daniel Ross *retired academic administrator*
Graves, John William *historian*
Nelson, Leon *retired data processing professional*
Pemberton, Barbara Butler *religious studies educator*
Taylor, Michael Ray *media specialist, educator*
Webster, Robert Lee *accounting educator, researcher*

Ashdown
Edmonson, Phyllis Denty *artist*
Finley, John Cyrus III *lawyer, judge*

Bald Knob
Barber, Leah Adrianne *elementary school educator, literacy educator*

Batesville
Bordeau, Catherine *French Professor*
Carius, Robert Wilhelm *mathematics professor, retired military officer*
Harkey, John Norman *judge*
Meinzer, Beverly Anne *chemist, educator*

Bella Vista
Johnson, A(lyn) William *chemistry professor, writer, researcher, consultant*
Medin, Alice Louise *librarian*
Medin, Myron James, Jr. *city manager*
Pogue, William Reid *retired astronaut, foundation administrator, aerospace scientist, consultant*

Benton
Krueger, Marlo Bush *retired lawyer*

Bentonville
Castro-Wright, Eduardo *retail executive*
Chambers, Susan (M. Susan Chambers) *retail executive*
Curran, Patricia A. *retail executive*
Dillman, Linda M. *retail executive*
Dobbs, Johnnie *retail executive*
Duke, Michael T. *retail executive*
Fleming, John E. *retail executive*
Ford, Rollin *retail executive*
Gean, Thomas C. *lawyer, former prosecutor*
Glass, David D. *retail and professional sports team executive*
Hefner, Linda P. *retail executive*
Herkert, Craig R. *retail executive*
Holley, Charles Murphy, Jr. *retail company executive*
Hyde, Thomas D. *lawyer*
McMillon, Doug *retail executive*
Menzer, John Bruce *retail executive*
Mora, Alberto J. *retail executive, lawyer*
Schoewe, Thomas M. *retail executive*
Scott, H(arold) Lee, Jr., (Lee Scott) *retail executive*
Simon, William *retail executive*
Walton, Jim Carr *bank executive*
Walton, (Samuel) Rob(son) *discount department store chain executive*
Zorn, Eric Stuart *retail executive*

Berryville
Brown, Frances Louise (Grandma Fran) *artist, art gallery director*

Cherokee Village
Hollingsworth, John Alexander *retired science and mathematics educator, writer*

Conway
Cloyd, J. Timothy *academic administrator*
Duan, Qiang *computer scientist, educator*
Hatcher, Joe Branch *management consultant*
Horton, Joseph Julian, Jr. *economics and finance educator*
Johnson, David Randall *radio director*
Johnson, James Douglas (Jim Johnson) *lawyer*
Leffler, Jean Riise *religious organization administrator*
McNew, Bennie Banks *retired finance educator*
Stiritz, Marette McCauley *English language educator, consultant*
Wu, Hui *language educator*
Ziegler, John Alan *historian, political scientist, educator*

Crossett
Hubbell, Billy James *lawyer*

Earle
Swift, Peggy Lynette *elementary school educator*

El Dorado
Barnes, Harry Francis *federal judge*
Cossé, Steven A. *lawyer, oil industry executive*
Deming, Claiborne Payne *oil industry executive*
Doerr, Harvey *oil industry executive*
Fitzgerald, Kevin Gerard *oil industry executive*
Lee, Vernon Roy *minister*
Nolan, William C., Jr. *oil industry executive*
Tommey, Charles Eldon *retired surgeon*
Watkins, Jerry West *retired oil company executive, lawyer*
Wood, David M. *oil industry executive*

Eureka Springs
McCullough, V. Beth *pharmacist, educator*

Farmington
Schoppmeyer, Martin William, Jr. *school system administrator*

Fayetteville
Bajwa, Sreekala G. *agricultural engineer, educator*
Banks, David Russell *former health care executive*
Bassett, Woodson William, Jr. *lawyer*
Bell, Debbie McCulley *science educator*
Brown, Avert Hayden *animal scientist, educator*
Brown, Connell Jean *retired animal science educator*
Broyles, Frank (John Franklin Broyles) *athletic director, retired college football coach*
Collen, Tom *women's college basketball coach*
Costrell, Robert Michael *economist*
Epley, Lewis Everett, Jr. *retired lawyer*
Ferritor, Daniel E. *retired chancellor*
Fink, William James *retired surgeon*
Gaddy, James Leoma *chemical engineer, educator*
Hightower, Randall Dee *oncologist*
Jones, Phillip John *librarian*
Karim, Khursheed *engineering educator, researcher*
Kellogg, David Wayne *agricultural studies educator, researcher*
Kester, Charles Melvin *lawyer*
King, Jerry Wayne *chemist, researcher, engineer*
Levine, Daniel Blank *classical studies educator*
Malone, David Roy *retired educational association administrator, director*
Morris, Justin Roy *food scientist, consultant*
Musacchia, X(avier) J(oseph) *physiology and biophysics educator*
Musick, Gerald Joe *retired entomology educator*
Nowlin, William B. *surgeon*
Nutt, Houston *university football coach*
O'Brien, Douglas J. *lawyer, educator*
Parker, Lee Bryan *retired physician*
Pearson, Charles Thomas, Jr. *lawyer, director*
Pelphrey, John *men's college basketball coach*
Pittman, Harrison M. *lawyer, educator*
Rosenberg, Leon Joseph *marketing educator*
Schaper, Louise Levy *library director*
Schoppmeyer, Martin William *education educator*
Smith, Lavenski R. (Vence) *federal judge*
Smith, Robert Victor *academic administrator, educator*
Steele, Kenneth Franklin, Jr. *hydrologist*
Thorup, Shawna Saavedra *librarian*
Venkatesh, Viswanath *information systems professional, educator, consultant*
White, Donald D. *finance educator, consultant*
White, John Austin, Jr. *academic administrator, engineering educator*
Wilkins, Charles L. *chemist, educator*
Williams, Miller *retired poet, writer, translator*
Wilson, Charles Banks *artist*
Woods, Randall Bennett *history professor*

Fort Smith
Bailey, Donald Keith *music educator, composer, musician*
Balfe, Robert Cramer III *prosecutor*
Churchey, Randy L. *health facility administrator*
Colbert, Alice Taylor *history professor*
Cooper, Richard F. *lawyer*
Davidson, Robert A. *trucking executive*
Flanders, Donald Hargis *manufacturing executive*
Gooden, Benny L. *school system administrator*
Howell, James Tennyson *allergist, immunologist, pediatrician*
Karr, Charles *lawyer*
Meadors, C. Brian *lawyer*
Snider, James Rhodes *radiologist*
Warner, Carol M. *mathematics professor*
Young, Robert A. III *freight systems executive*

Gravette
Duncan, Jean Marie *language educator*
Legler, Kristin M. *music educator*

Greenwood
Walters, Bill *retired state senator*

Greers Ferry
Martindale, Carla Joy *retired librarian*
Robbins, Etta Jo *music educator*

Harrison
Sprott, James D. *lawyer*

Heber Springs
Rawlings, Paul C. *retired government official*

Helena
Roscopf, Charles Buford *lawyer*

Hindsville
Peirce, Carole *elementary school educator*

Holiday Island
Pischke, Frank John *retired otolaryngologist*

Hot Springs
Farris, Jefferson Davis *university administrator*
Hugo, Janet *director*
Kamel, Hosam Kamal *medical educator, researcher, geriatrician*

Hot Springs National Park
Haupt, Robert J. *hotel and real estate developer*

Hot Springs Village
Philpott, Larry La Fayette *retired horn player*

Huntsville
Roach, Lonnie Calvin *social studies educator*

Jefferson
Schwetz, Bernard Anthony *toxicologist*

Jonesboro
Bartee, Neale *music educator, musician, conductor*
Deacon, John C. *lawyer*
Elkins, Francis Clark *historian, educator, director*
Groves, Mark *music director*
Hanners, G(ary) Dale *retired psychological mental health professional*
Jones, Kenneth Bruce *surgeon*
Malinsky, Marci Ann *education educator*
Smith, Eugene Wilson *retired academic administrator, education educator*
Tims, Robert Austin *data processing official, pilot*

Lake Village
Schwartz, Robert P. *lawyer*

Little Rock
Adcock, Robert H., Jr., (Bunny) *state agency administrator*
Allen, H(enry) William *lawyer*
Alsobrook, David Ernest *library director, archivist, historian*
Anderson, Philip Sidney *lawyer*
Arnold, Morris Sheppard *federal judge*
Ashcraft, Carolyn *state librarian*
Banks, Alicia *elementary school educator*
Bass, Evelyn Elizabeth *elementary school educator*
Beebe, Mike (Michael Dale Beebe) *governor, former state attorney general, lawyer*
Bell, Richard Eugene *agricultural products executive, state official*
Bemis, Michael B. *utility company executive*
Bird, Samuel N. *judge*
Bissada, Nabil Kaddis *urologist, educator, researcher, author*
Bohannon, Charles Tad *lawyer*
Bradford, Jay Turner *insurance company executive, state legislator*
Braithwaite, Wilfred John *physics professor*
Britt, Billy Jean *retired elementary school educator, economic education specialist*
Brosnahan, Godela *nephrologist, medical educator*
Brown, Larry Douglass *research consultant, writer*
Bruce, Thomas Allen *physician, educator*
Campbell, Gilbert Sadler *surgeon, educator*
Casciano, Daniel Anthony *biologist, educator*
Cawood, Gary Kenneth *photography educator*
Chahoud, Georges *medical educator, preventive medicine physician*
Chappelle, Richard Allen, Sr. *bishop*
Cheek, James Richard *ambassador*
Chiang, Chia-Chu *computer scientist, educator*
Chilcote, Lugean Lester *retired architect, researcher*
Coleman, Marshia Adams *social sciences educator*
Corbin, Donald L. *state supreme court justice*
Cross, J. Bruce *lawyer*
Daniels, Charlie L. *state official*
Danielson, Paul E. *state supreme court justice*
Darsey, Jerome Anthony (Jerry Darsey) *chemistry professor, consultant*
Davis, Suanna Jeanette *mezzo-soprano, retired music educator*
Dillard, William, II, *department store chain executive*
Elders, Joycelyn (Minnie Jocelyn Elders, Minnie Joycelyn Lee) *public health service officer, endocrinologist, former Surgeon General of the United States*
Fitzhugh, Kathryn Corrothers *law librarian*
Ford, Joe Thomas *telephone company executive, former state senator*
Ford, Scott T. *telecommunications industry executive*
Frazier, Elizabeth Ann *pediatric cardiologist*
Fribourgh, James Henry *retired university administrator*
Gasaway, Sharilyn *telecommunications industry executive*
Gealt, Michael A. *environmental microbiologist, educator*
Givens, John Kenneth *automotive executive*
Glaze, Thomas A. *state supreme court justice*
Good, Mary Lowe *investment company executive, educator*
Goodner, Norman Wesley *governmental relations specialist*
Green, Johnnie D. *loan officer*
Greenberg, Paul *editor*
Griffin, William Mell III *lawyer*
Gulley, Wilbur Paul, Jr. *retired savings and loan association executive*
Gunter, James Houston, Jr. *state supreme court justice*
Gunter, Russell Allen *lawyer*
Hagen, Jody Lynn *neuropsychologist, educator*
Hall, John Wesley, Jr. *lawyer*
Halter, Bill (William A. Halter) *lieutenant governor*
Hannah, James *state supreme court justice*
Hart, Ronald Wilson *radiobiologist, educator, toxicologist, business adviser*
Haught, William Dixon *lawyer, writer*
Hinson, Jack Allsbrook *research toxicologist, educator*
Hoover, Paul Williams, Jr. *lawyer*
Hope, Ronald Arthur *lawyer*
Hough, Aubrey Johnston, Jr. *pathologist, physician, educator*
Hussman, Walter E., Jr. *publishing executive*
Hutchins, Laura Fulper *physician, medical educator*
Imamura, Michiaki *cardiac surgeon, pediatric and congenital cardiothoracic surgery*
Imber, Annabelle Clinton *state supreme court justice*
James, T. Kenneth *school system administrator*
Jansen, G. Thomas *dermatologist*
Jaquiss, Robert Douglas Benjamin *pediatric cardiac surgeon*
Jones, Stephen Witsell *lawyer*
Julian, Jim Lee *lawyer*
Kaza, Greg John *economist, educator*
Lang, Nicholas Paul *surgeon*
Ledbetter, Calvin Reville, Jr., (Cal Ledbetter) *political science professor, legislator*
Lemke, Judith A. *lawyer*
Levy, Eugene Pfeifer *architectural firm executive, architect*
Lewis, Johanna Miller *historian, educator*
Light, Jo Knight *stockbroker*
Lucy, Dennis Durwood, Jr. *neurologist, educator*
Marshall, William Taylor *lawyer*
Martin, Floyd W. *art educator*
Massey, Richard N. *lawyer, telecommunications industry executive*
May, Ronald Alan *lawyer*
McCaleb, Annette Watts *executive secretary*
McDaniel, Dustin *state attorney general*
McIntyre, Nina M. *counseling administrator*
Mehta, Jawahar Lal *cardiologist*
Metzer, Walter Steven *neurologist, educator*
Mulkey, Jack Clarendon *retired library director*
Murphey, Arthur Gage, Jr. *law educator*
Nelson, Edward Sheffield *lawyer, retired utilities executive*
Nunn, Patarica Dian *poet*
O'Brien, Mark Stephen *pediatric neurosurgeon*
Olden, Kevin William *medical researcher*
Pennington, Jodie A. *education outreach educator*
Portis, Charles McColl *reporter, writer*
Priest, Sharon Devlin *retired state official, not-for-profit developer*
Prince, David Cannon *lawyer*
Pryor, David Hampton *former senator*
Ramsay, Richard L. *lawyer*
Raney, Miriam Day *actress*
Raza, Asim *psychiatrist*
Roaf, Andree Layton *judge*
Schroeder, Paul J., Jr. *lawyer*
Shell, Robert J. *construction executive*
Sherman, William Farrar *lawyer, former state legislator*
Shoffner, Martha Ann *state official*
Smith, Griffin, Jr. *executive editor*
Sotomora-von Ahn, Ricardo Federico *pediatrician, educator*
Stewart, Amy Lee *lawyer*
Stockburger, Jean Dawson *lawyer*
Stodola, Mark Allen *mayor, former prosecutor*
Terry, William Leake *lawyer*
Trice, William Henry III *lawyer*
Truemper, John James, Jr. *retired architect*
Truex, Dorothy Adine *retired university administrator*
Ursery, Frederick Stanley *lawyer*
Vinikas, Vincent *historian, educator*
Ward, Harry Pfeffer *hematologist, retired academic administrator*
Waters, Zenobia Pettus *retired finance educator*
Weiss, Richard A. *state official*
Whiteside, Charles B. III *investment company executive*

Whitlow, Mary Ann *retired elementary school educator*
Wight, Patricia Anne *neuroscience educator*
Wilson, I. Dodd *dean*
Wilson, William R., Jr. *federal judge*
Witherspoon, Carolyn Brack *lawyer*
Wright, Susan Webber *federal judge*
Young, Hays Wilson Jorden *research scientist*

Lonoke
Ross, Philip Rowland *retired library director*

Lowell
Garrison, Wayne *transportation executive*
Thompson, Kirk *transportation executive*

Magnolia
Harrison, Betty Carolyn Cook *retired education educator, administrator*

Malvern
Dodd, Jerry Lee *lawyer*
Selix, Karen Elizabeth *writer, artist, vocalist*

Marion
Hughes, Michael Randolph *evangelist*

Mena
Eddleman, Floyd Eugene *retired language educator*
Thrailkill, Daniel B. *lawyer*
Wiles, Betty Jane *accountant*

Monticello
Babin, Claude Hunter *history professor*
Ball, William Kenneth *lawyer*

Mountain Home
Baker, Robert Leon *military officer*

Nashville
Martin, Marie Ann *art association administrator*

Newport
Thaxton, Marvin Dell *lawyer*

North Little Rock
Jackson, Willie *writer, researcher*
Patty, Claibourne Watkins, Jr. *lawyer*
Turner, (Clyde) Tab (Clyde Tab Turner) *lawyer*
Welch, Morgan E. *lawyer*

Palestine
Taylor, Barbara Mae Helm *artist, educator*

Pearcy
Burch, Bobby Joe *secondary school educator*

Pine Bluff
Engle, Carole Ruth *aquaculture economics professor*
Jones, John Harris *retired lawyer*
Jones-Woolfolk, Jerald Maxine *dean, educator*
Long, Edward Arlo *management consultant, retired manufacturing executive*
Sims, David Lloyd *lawyer*
Strode, Joseph Arlin *lawyer*
Walker, Richard Brian *chemistry professor*

Pocahontas
Moss, Linda Elaine *science educator*

Prairie Grove
Dunn, Anne Ewald Nefflen *retired elementary school educator*

Prescott
Vasser, Albert Glenn *lawyer*

Rogers
Cooper, John Alfred, Jr. *community development company executive*
Myers, Dane Jacob *lawyer, podiatrist*

Russellville
Barker, Stephanie Anne *middle school mathematics educator*
Morris, Lois Lawson *retired education educator*
Vance, Sue Ann *musician, educator*

Scranton
Uzman, Betty Ben Geren *retired pathologist*

Searcy
Burks, David Basil *academic administrator, educator*
Hughes, Thomas Morgan III *lawyer*

Sherwood
Cantu, Jennifer St. John *gifted and talented educator*
George, James Edward *accountant*

Siloam Springs
Wubbena, Jan Helmut *music professor*

Springdale
Bond, Richard L. *food products executive*
Gonzalez-Pita, J. Alberto *lawyer, food products executive*
Hogensen, Margaret Hiner *retired librarian*
Holman, L. Charlene *elementary school educator*
Hudson, R. Read *lawyer, food products executive*
Leatherby, Dennis *food products executive*
Minkel, Justin *elementary school educator*
Miquelon, Wade D. *food products executive*
Schaffer, Archie III *food products executive*
Tyson, John H. *food products executive*

State University
Barredo, Ronald De Vera *physical therapist, educator*
Hannigan, Robyn E. *science educator, researcher*
Milner, Clyde A., II, *historian*

Texarkana
Petty, Marsha *chemistry educator*
Stroud, John Fred, Jr. *judge*

Tontitown
McMennamy, Roger Neal *automotive executive*

Walnut Ridge
Wheeless, Charlotte Ann *science educator*

Ward
Rudy, Janet Faye Walker *science educator*

West Fork
Higgins, Sarah Jean *literature and language professor*

West Memphis
Fogleman, Julian Barton *lawyer*
Howell, Kathy Aileen *advertising executive*
Peoples, Johnny Ray *music educator*

White Hall
Scott, Vicki Sue *school system administrator*

Wickes
Riley, Faith Lynch *retired historian, writer*

Winslow
Burggraf, Frank Bernard, Jr. *landscape architect, retired educator*

CALIFORNIA

Agoura Hills
Canatsey, Ken *nurse*
Currie, Malcolm Roderick *aerospace and automotive executive, research scientist*
deCiutiis, Alfred Charles Maria *oncologist, television producer*
Gressak, Anthony Raymond, Jr. *sales executive*
Kuzmanovic, Jane Violet *academic administrator*
Merchant, Roland Samuel, Sr. *health facility administrator, educator*
Schmidt, Frank Broaker *executive recruiter*
Teresi, Joseph *publishing executive*

Alameda
Bartalini, C. Richard *judge*
Billings, Thomas Neal *computer and publishing executive, management consultant, entrepreneur, journalist, writer*
Boltwood, Russell Lewis *lawyer, telecommunications industry executive*
Brooks, Aaron Lafette *professional football player*
Caldwell, William Mackay, IV, *cloning and stem cell research company executive*
Davis, Allen *professional football team executive*
Earle, Sylvia Alice *research biologist, oceanographer*
Janowitz, Jeffrey Mark *management consultant*
Jordan, LaMont *professional football player*
Kiffin, Lane *professional football coach*
LaRose, Katherine Stencel *music educator*
Lu, Hong Liang *telecommunications industry executive*
Potash, Jeremy Warner *public relations executive*
Robinson, Joanne Adele *retired secondary school educator, volunteer*
Rubin, Charles Alexis *writer*
Russell, JaMarcus *professional football player*
Sapp, Warren Carlos *professional football player*
Troll, Lillian Ellman *psychologist, educator*
Verrill, Kathleen Wills *special education educator*
Whorton, M. Donald *physician, epidemiologist*
Willson, Clyde D. *biologist, educator*

Alamo
Liggett, Lawrence Melvin *vacuum equipment manufacturing company executive*
Madden, Palmer Brown *lawyer*
Schreiber, John T. *lawyer*
Shiffer, James David *retired utilities executive*
Whalen, John Sydney *management consultant*

Albany
Meidav, Joshua Sinclair Ethan *ecologist, researcher*
Schwimmer, Sigmund *food enzymologist*

Alhambra
Determan, John David *lawyer*
Duke, Donald Norman *publishing executive*
Huang, Jia-Sheng Jack *optics scientist, researcher*
Im, Jaemo *research scientist*
Suzuki, Bob H. *retired academic administrator*

Aliso Viejo
Blum, Scott Allen *Internet company executive*
Cohen, Sasha (Alexandra Pauline Cohen) *ice skater*
Dunn, Dana-Lori *counselor*
Dutile, Robert Arthur *executive management consultant*
Fisher, Lawrence N. *lawyer, engineering and construction management company executive*
Grover, Neel *Internet company executive*
Harder, Wendy Wetzel *communications executive*
Kizer, Kenneth Wayne *emergency physician, executive, educator*
La Marca, Jeffry Peter *language educator, consultant*
Steuert, Douglas Michael *engineering and construction management company executive*

Alpine
Greenberg, Byron Stanley *newspaper and business executive, consultant*
Oliverio, Ponzio *protective services official, educator*
Roberts, Dwight Loren *engineering consultant, writer*

Alta Loma
Campbell, Ellen Feyk *elementary school educator*
Haskvitz, Alan Paul *elementary school educator, consultant*
Klein, Henry *lawyer*
Maloof, Sam *woodworker*
Straka, Laszlo Richard *retired publishing consultant*

Altadena
Burden, Jean Prussing *retired poet, editor*
Coles, Donald Earl *retired engineering educator*
Dutton, Pauline Mae *fine arts and reference librarian*
Eisen, Glenn Philip *management consultant, educator*
Klages, Karen Louise *musician, educator*
Mkryan, Sonya *geophysicist, educator, research scientist*
Willans, Jean Stone *bishop, religious organization administrator*
Wilson, Nancy *singer*

Alviso
Ramsay, Michael *communications company executive*
Rogers, Thomas Sydney *communications company executive*
Sordello, Steve *communications executive*

Anaheim
Barry, Sandra *school system administrator*
Bennett, Genevieve *artist*
Bertuzzi, Todd *professional hockey player*
Browne, Autumn Lee *theater educator, actress, theater director*
Burke, Brian *professional sports team executive*
Carlyle, Randy *professional hockey coach, retired professional hockey player*
Getzlaf, Ryan *professional hockey player*
Giguere, Jean-Sebastien *professional hockey player*
Glazer, Sidney *physician, director*
Gobar, Alfred Julian *retired economic consultant, educator, investor*
Goodspeed, Kathryn Ann *pre-school educator*
Green, Travis *professional hockey player*
Guajardo, Elisa *counselor, educator*
Guerrero, Vladimir Alvino *professional baseball player*
Lackey, John Derran *professional baseball player*
Lano, Charles Jack *retired financial executive*
Lee, Donna Jean *retired nurse*
Litvak, David A. *surgeon*
McNulty, James Francis *engineering executive*
Miller, Mark A. *information technology training executive*
Moreno, Arturo (Arte Moreno) *major league baseball team owner, former advertising executive*
Nelipovich, Sandra Grassi *artist*
Niedermayer, Scott *professional hockey player*
Pronger, Chris *professional hockey player*
Rodriguez, Francisco Jose *professional baseball player*
Schneider, Mathieu *professional hockey player*
Selanne, Teemu *professional hockey player*
Unan, George Vincent *adult education educator*
Warring, Jerome Thomas *management consultant*
Watson, Oliver Lee III *aerospace engineer, manufacturing executive*
Weaver, Jered *professional baseball player*
Yocum, Lewis Albert *orthopedist, surgeon*

Antelope
Nenov, Ivo P. *mathematical and software researcher*

Antioch
Adams, Liliana Osses *music performer, harpist*
Archuleta, Keith Anthony *entrepreneur, business and management consultant*
Stamm, Barbara Marie Anderson *elementary school educator, interior designer*

Apple Valley
Yule, Caroll Jane *real estate broker*

Aptos
Boesewetter, William Lawrence *elementary school educator, artist*
Bohn, Ralph Carl *educational consultant*
Heron, David Winston *librarian*
Hirsch, Bette G(ross) *academic administrator, language educator*
Miura, Masako Kusayanagi *retired dermatologist*
Nicholson, Joseph Bruce *real estate developer*
Trounstine, Philip John *communications consultant, academic administrator*

Arcadia
Baerg, Richard Henry *podiatrist, surgeon*
Baltz, Patricia Ann (Pann) *retired elementary school educator*
Belnap, David F. *journalist*
Chih, Luke *music educator, conductor*
Gelber, Louise C(arp) *lawyer*
Matsuura, Kenneth Ray *counseling administrator*
Ulrich, Peter Henry *banker*
Yen, Wen-Hsiung *language and music professional, educator*

Arcata
Bailey, Stephen Fairchild *retired museum director, ornithologist, birding tour guide*
Emenhiser, JeDon Allen *political science professor, dean*
Land-Weber, Ellen *photography professor*
McCrone, Alistair William *retired academic administrator*

Arleta
Kelley, Frances A. *occupational therapist, consultant*

Aromas
Fleischman, Paul *children's author*

Arroyo Grande
Benedict, Lawrence Neal *foreign service officer*
Grisez, James Louis *physician, plastic surgeon*
Oseguera, Palma Marie *retired career officer*
Saari, David John *retired law educator*
Willis, Ralph Walker *retired firefighter*
Wobrock, Jesse Lucas *biomechanical engineer*

Atascadero
Locke, Virginia Otis *writer*
Ogier, Walter Thomas *retired physics educator*
Rios, Evelyn Deerwester *columnist, musician, artist, writer*

Atherton
Anderson, Harry W. (Hunk) *retired food service executive*
Baran, Paul *computer executive*
Coleman, Robert Griffin *geology educator*
Ferris, Robert Albert *lawyer, venture capitalist*
Fried, John H. *chemist*
Gill, Stephen Paschall *retired physicist, mathematician*
Goodman, Sam Richard *electronics executive*
Hogan, Clarence Lester *retired electronics executive*
Lane, Joan Fletcher *academic administrator*
Lowry, Larry *engineering company executive*
Sollman, George Henry *venture capitalist*

Auburn
Ferber, Robert Rudolf *retired physics researcher, educator, science administrator*
Henrikson, Donald Merle *forensic pathologist*
Hess, Patrick Henry *chemist, researcher*
Jeske, Howard Leigh *retired insurance company executive, lawyer*
Olesen, Erik L. *psychotherapist, writer*
Rothwell, Elaine B. *artist*
Sanborn, Dorothy Chappell *retired librarian*

Azusa
Liegler, Rosemary Menke *dean*
Miyake, Stephanie Ann *psychology professor, director, marriage and family therapist*
Pacino, Maria Antonieta *education educator, department chairman*

Bakersfield
Ashburn, Roy *state senator*
Bacon, Leonard Anthony *accounting educator*
Barmann, Bernard Charles, Sr. *lawyer*
Bernard, Alexander *protective services official*
Chidgey, Guy Clement *marketing executive*
Duquette, Diane Rhea *library director*
Enriquez, Carola Rupert *museum director*
Fiedler, Joseph Robert *mathematician, educator*
Flachmann, Michael Charles *English language educator*
Frazier, Jo Frances *religious organization administrator, writer*
Gong, Gloria Margaret *lawyer, pharmacist*
Hawkins, Brandon James *podiatrist, surgeon*
Hersberger, Rodney M. *library association executive, school librarian*
Huerta, Dolores Fernandez *labor union administrator*
Kegley, Jacquelyn Ann *philosophy educator*
McAlister, Michael H. *architect*
Meyers, Christopher *humanities educator, consultant*
Osterkamp, Dalene May *psychology educator, artist*
Peterson, Pamela Carmelle *language educator*
Provencio, Roberto Enrique *music educator, music minister*
Prunes, Fernando *plastic surgeon, educator*
Reep, Edward Arnold *artist*
Sawyer, Nelson Baldwin, Jr. *credit union executive*
Sharma, Sanjiv *cardiologist*
Sio, Jimmy Ong *embryologist*
Spinello, Irene M. *internist*
Stone, Shelley Clyde III *art educator, archaeologist*
Tornstrom, Robert Ernest *lawyer, oil industry executive*
Zarra, Ernest Joseph III *secondary school educator, researcher*

Baldwin Park
Driskill, James Lawrence *minister*
Feng, Mark I. *urologist, surgeon*

Banning
Gladden, Garnett Lee *psychologist, educator*

Barstow
Gibbon, Mary-Lynn *special education educator*

Bass Lake
Park, Penny Sheran *retired elementary school educator*

Bayside
Cocks, George Gosson *retired chemical microscopy professor*

Beaumont
Youngren, Delvana Hope *secondary school educator*

Bell Canyon
Labbett, John Edgar *financial analyst*

Belmont
Ellis, Eldon Eugene *retired surgeon*
Endriz, John Guiry *retired electronics executive*
Musmann, Klaus *librarian*
Musmann, Lois S. *conductor, music educator*
Vieux, Alex Serge *computer company executive, educator, journalist, entrepreneur*

Belvedere
Hugenberg, Patricia Ellen Petrie *product designer*
Wallerstein, Robert Solomon *retired psychiatrist*

Belvedere Tiburon
Allan, Walter Robert *lawyer*
Collins, Dennis Arthur *retired foundation administrator*
Fishman, Robert Allen *retired neurologist, educator, department chair*
Hoffman, Julien Ivor Ellis *pediatrician, cardiologist, educator*
Kramer, Lawrence Stephen *journalist*
McFarland, Ronald G. (Ron McFarland) *composer, music educator, musician*
Rayner, Arno Alfred *investment company executive, consultant*
Rosenthal, Robert Jon *newspaper editor, journalist*
Stotter, Lawrence Henry *lawyer*

Benicia
Nelson, Elmer Kingsholm, Jr., (Kim Nelson) *political scientist, educator, writer, mediator, consultant*
von Studnitz, Gilbert Alfred *state official*

Berkeley
Abel, Carlos Alberto *immunologist*
Aggarwal, Vinod K. *political science professor*
Agogino, Alice Merner *computer scientist, mechanical engineer, educator*
Akerlof, George Arthur *economics professor*
Alhadeff, David Albert *economics professor*
Alivisatos, Armand Paul *chemist, educator*
Alter, Robert Bernard *literature educator, critic*
Anderson, William Scovil *classics educator*
Arguedas, Cristina Claypoole *lawyer*
Arveson, William Barnes *mathematics professor*
Attwood, David Thomas *physicist, researcher*
Auerbach, Alan Jeffrey *economist, educator*
Baack, Lawrence James *energy executive, history professor*
Bagdikian, Ben Haig *journalist, educator*
Baldwin, Bruce Gregg *botany educator, researcher*
Banfield, Jillian *mineralogist, geomicrobiologist, educator*
Barnes, Thomas G. *law educator*
Barr, Robert *lawyer, educator*
Barrett, Reginald Haughton *wildlife management educator*
Bartlett, Neil *chemist, emeritus educator*
Basri, Gibor *astronomy educator, academic administrator*
Baumrind, Diana *research psychologist*
Bea, Robert G. *civil engineering educator*
Bell, Alexis T. *chemical engineer, educator*
Bellah, Robert Neelly *sociologist, educator*
Benedict, Burton *retired museum director, anthropologist*
Berger, Stanley Allan *mechanical and biomechanical engineering educator*
Bergman, George Mark *mathematician, educator*
Bergman, Robert George *chemist, educator*
Berk, Jonathan Bryan *finance educator*
Berlekamp, Elwyn Ralph *mathematics professor*
Berring, Robert Charles, Jr. *law educator, librarian, association administrator*
Bertozzi, Carolyn R. *chemistry professor*
Bickel, Peter John *statistician, educator*
Birdsall, Charles Kennedy *electrical engineer*
Birgeneau, Robert Joseph *academic administrator, physicist, researcher*
Bissell, Mina J. *lab administrator, biochemist*
Blackburn, Robert Parker *lawyer*
Blanch, Harvey Warren *chemical engineering educator*
Blume, James Beryl *investment advisor*
Bogy, David B(eauregard) *mechanical engineering educator*
Botchan, Michael R. *molecular biologist, biochemist*
Bousso, Raphael *physicist, educator*
Bragg, Robert Henry *physicist, researcher*
Brandes, Stanley Howard *anthropology educator, writer*
Brenner, Sydney *molecular biologist, researcher*
Brewer, Eric A. *computer science educator*
Brocchini, Ronald Gene *architect*
Brooke, Tal (Robert Taliaferro) *writer*
Browne, G.M. Walter Shawn *journalist, publisher*
Buckland, Michael Keeble *librarian, educator*
Bucklin, Louis Pierre *business educator, consultant*
Buell, Evangeline Canonizado *advocate*
Buffler, Patricia Ann *epidemiologist, educator, dean*
Bustamante, Carlos J. *biophysicist, educator*
Buxbaum, Richard M. *lawyer, educator*
Cairns, Elton James *chemical engineering professor*
Calendar, Richard Lane *biochemistry educator*
Callenbach, Ernest *writer, editor*
Campbell, John *philosopher, educator*
Campion, Edmund Joseph *composer, educator*
Cardwell, Kenneth Harvey *architect, educator*
Casey, James *engineering educator*
Casida, John Edward *toxicology and entomology professor*
Cerny, Joseph III *chemistry professor, retired dean, director*
Chamberlin, Michael John *retired biochemistry professor*
Chapela, Ignacio H. *biologist, researcher*
Cheit, Earl Frank *economist, educator*
Chen, Lu *neurobiologist, biology professor*
Chetin, Helen Campbell *writer*
Chew, Geoffrey Foucar *physicist*
Chihara, Charles Seiyo *philosophy educator*
Chirurg, James Thomas *holding company executive*
Choper, Jesse Herbert *law educator, dean*
Chorin, Alexandre Joel *mathematician, educator*
Christ, F. Michael *mathematics professor*
Chu, Steven *physics professor, director*
Clarke, John *physics professor*
Cline, Thomas Warren *geneticist, educator*
Coats, Robert Noyce *hydrologist*
Coffin, Grange Simons *pediatrician*
Coffman, Robert Lee *pharmaceutical executive*
Colella, Philip *mathematician*
Collier, David *political science professor*
Consey, Kevin Edward *museum administrator*
Cooper, William Secord *information science educator*
Costa, Gustavo *Italian studies scholar*
Cranz, Galen *architecture educator, sociologist*
Crews, Frederick Campbell *humanities educator, writer*
Cuffey, Kurt M. *geophysicist, geochemist, educator*
Culler, David Ethan *computer science educator*
Day, Lucille Lang *museum administrator, educator, writer*
Deck, Richard Allen *political scientist, consultant, writer, volunteer*
De Goff, Victoria Joan *lawyer*
Delory, Gregory Townsend *aerospace scientist, consultant*
Derenzo, Stephen E. *electrical engineering and computer science educator, researcher*
Dharan, Hari *mechanical engineer, educator*
Diamond, Marian Cleeves *neuroscientist, educator*
Diamond, Richard Martin *nuclear chemist*
diSessa, Andrea A. *education educator*
Donghi, Tulio Halperin *history professor*
Dornfeld, David Alan *engineering educator*
Doyle, Fiona Mary *dean, metallurgical engineer, educator*
Dudley, Anna Carol *singer, voice educator*
Dunlop, Neil *computer scientist, department chairman*
Duster, Troy *sociology educator*
Edelman, Lauren B. *sociologist, law educator*
Eisenberg, Melvin A. *law educator*
Eisenbud, David *mathematics professor*
Enoch, Jay Martin *optometrist, research scientist, educator*
Fenves, Gregory L. *engineering educator*
Filippenko, Alexei Vladimir *astrophysicist, educator*
Fleiszig, Suzanne Mariane Janete *optometry educator*
Fleming, Graham Richard *chemistry educator*
Fowler, Thomas Kenneth *physicist*
Fréchet, Jean *chemistry professor*
Freedman, David Amiel *statistics educator, consultant*
Freedman, Sarah Warshauer *education educator*
Freedman, Stuart Jay *nuclear science educator*
Frisch, Joseph *mechanical engineer, educator, consultant*
Fuerstenau, Douglas Winston *mineral engineering educator*
Gaillard, Mary Katharine *physicist, educator*
Gallagher, M. Catherine *English literature educator*
Garrison, William Louis *civil engineering educator*
Genn, Nancy *artist*
Gilbert, Neil Robin *social work educator, writer, consultant*
Ginger, Ann Fagan *lawyer*
Glaser, Donald Arthur *physicist*
Gluss, Brian *mathematician, statistician, engineer, systems expert*
Goldberg, Evgueni *computer scientist*
Goldberg, Kenneth Yigael *computer engineering educator, artist*
Goldhaber, Gerson *astrophysicist, researcher*
Govindjee, Sanjay *engineering educator*
Graham, Susan Lois *computer scientist, consultant*
Green, David *nonprofit organization administrator*
Grossman, Bonnie *art gallery director*
Grossman, Elmer Roy *pediatrician*
Grubb, Erica B. *lawyer*
Gumbs, Pam *pharmacist*
Hagar, Sammy *musician, vocalist, composer*
Hahn, Erwin Louis *physicist, researcher*
Hakansson, Nils Hemming *economist, educator*
Halbach, Edward Christian, Jr. *law educator*
Haley, George Patrick *lawyer*
Haller, Eugene Ernest *materials scientist, educator*
Halpern, Martin Brent *physics professor*
Harlan, Robert Dale *library and information scientist, educator, academic administrator*
Harris, Michael Gene *optometrist, lawyer, educator*
Hartman, Robert Leroy *artist, educator*
Hearst, John Eugene *retired chemistry professor, consultant, researcher*
Heathcock, Clayton Howell *chemistry educator, researcher*
Helson, Henry Berge *publisher, educator, retired mathematician*
Herr, Richard *history professor*
Hertelendy, Paul *critic, writer, poet*
Hill, Lorie Elizabeth *psychotherapist*
Hobbs, Christopher Rollin *botanist, writer*
Hoffman, Darleane Christian *chemistry professor*
Hsu, Chieh Su *applied mechanics engineering educator, researcher*
Hu, Chenming *engineering educator*
Imbrie, Andrew Welsh *composer, educator*
Jackson, J(ohn) David *physicist, researcher*
Janney, Daniel S. *health products executive*
Jeanloz, Raymond *geophysics educator*
Jones, Vaughan Frederick Randal *mathematician, educator*
Jorde, Thomas *law educator*
Joyce, Rosemary Alexandria *anthropology educator, department chairman*
Kadish, Sanford Harold *law educator*
Kagan, Robert Allen *law educator*
Karabel, Jerome Bernard *sociologist, educator*
Karp, Richard Manning *computer science educator*
Kastenberg, William Edward *engineering professor, former academic administrator*
Katzen, Mollie *writer*
Kay, Herma Hill *law educator*
Kay, Paul de Young *linguist*
Keasling, Jay D. *chemistry professor, research scientist*
Keeler, Theodore Edwin *retired economics professor*
Kerth, Leroy T. *physics professor*
King, Cary Judson III *chemical engineer, educator, academic administrator*
King, Nicole *molecular biologist, educator*
Kirz, Janos *physicist*
Klinman, Judith Pollock *biochemist, educator*
Kluger, Richard *writer, editor*
Knox, Helene Margrethe *poet, editor*
Kuh, Ernest Shiu-Jen *electrical engineering educator*
Kurtzman, Ralph Harold, Jr. *biochemist, researcher, consultant*
Langridge, Robert *biophysicist, educator, computational biologist*
Lashof, Joyce Cohen *public health service officer, educator*
Lee, Ronald Demos *demographer, economist, educator*
Leemans, Wim Pieter *physicist*
Leitmann, George *mechanical engineer, educator*
Leonard, Thomas C. *librarian, dean*
Lerner, Michael *rabbi*
Lesser, Wendy *editor, writer, consultant*
Lester, William Alexander, Jr. *chemist, educator*
Letiche, John Marion *economist, educator*
Levine, Mark David *science administrator, director*
Lewis, Edwin Reynolds *biomedical engineering educator, academic administrator*
Lidicker, William Zander, Jr. *zoologist, educator*
Liepmann, Dorian *engineering educator*
Lin, Robert Peichung *physicist, educator, researcher*
Linn, Marcia Cyrog *education educator*
Linn, Stuart Michael *biochemist, educator*
Lipps, Jere Henry *biology and geology professor*
Litwack, Leon Frank *historian, educator*
Lloyd, Elisabeth Anne *philosophy educator*
Long, Anthony Arthur *classics educator*
Ma, Chung-Pei Michelle *astronomer, educator*
Ma, Fai *mechanical engineering educator*
Majumdar, Arunava *mechanical engineer, educator*
Mandelstam, Stanley *physicist*
Manga, Michael *earth science educator, geophysicist*
Marcy, Geoffrey W. *astronomer, physicist, educator*
Markowitz, Samuel Solomon *chemistry professor*
Marletta, Michael A. *biochemistry educator, researcher*
Maslach, Christina *psychology professor*
Maurer, Stephen Mark *academic program director*
Mavroudi, Maria *philologist, educator*
McFadden, Daniel Little *economist, educator*
McKee, Christopher Fulton *physicist, astronomer, educator*
McLaughlin, Sylvia Cranmer *volunteer, environmentalist*
McNulty, John Kent *lawyer, educator*
Meador, Ross DeShong *lawyer*
Medak, Susan Lee *performing company executive*
Menell, Peter Seth *law educator*
Merges, Robert Patrick *law educator, writer*
Mettinger, Karl Lennart *pharmaceutical executive*
Middlekauff, Robert Lawrence *historian, educator, academic administrator*
Miles, Raymond Edward *retired dean, organizational behavior and industrial relations educator*
Miller, William Hughes *theoretical chemist, educator*
Minudri, Regina Ursula *librarian, consultant*
Mishkin, Paul J. *lawyer, educator*
Miyasaki, George Joji *artist*
Monismith, Carl Leroy *civil engineering educator*
Moran, Rachel *law educator*
Morris, John William, Jr. *metallurgy educator*
Muir, William Ker, Jr. *political science professor*
Muller, Richard Stephen *electrical engineer, educator*
Muscatine, Charles *language educator, writer*
Myers, Miles Alvin *educational association administrator, researcher*
Myrick, Alissa B. *parasitologist, science educator*
Nader, Laura *anthropologist, educator*
Norgaard, Richard Bruce *economist, educator, consultant*
Ofteness, Ove (O.V. Michaelsen) *writer, musician*
Osserman, Robert *mathematician, educator, writer*
Oster, George F. *molecular biologist, environmental scientist*
Ott, David Michael *engineering company executive*
Pagni, Patrick John *mechanical engineering science educator, safety engineer, researcher*
Partridge, Loren Wayne *art historian, educator*
Patek, Sheila N. *biologist, educator*
Patterson, David Andrew *computer scientist, educator, consultant*
Pavlath, Attila Endre *chemist, researcher*
Pearson, P. David *dean*
Penzien, Joseph *structural engineering educator*
Perlmutter, Saul *astrophysicist, educator*
Perry, Dale Lynn *chemist*
Petiet, Carole Anne *psychologist*
Pigford, Thomas Harrington *nuclear engineering educator*
Pines, Alexander *chemistry educator, researcher, consultant*
Pister, Karl Stark *engineering educator*
Polak, Elijah *engineering educator, computer scientist*
Pope, Alexander H. *retired lawyer*
Power, Mary Eleanor *biology professor*
Prausnitz, John Michael *chemical engineer, educator*
Preston, Paul Michael *anthropologist, writer*
Price, Paul Buford *physicist, researcher*
Purcell, Alexander Holmes *entomologist, educator*
Quail, Peter Hugh *biologist, educator*
Quigley, John Michael *economist, educator*
Quinn, Nigel William Trevelyan *research scientist*
Rasmussen, John Oscar *nuclear research scientist*
Rauch, Irmengard *linguist, educator*
Rausser, Gordon C(lyde) *agricultural and resource economics educator*
Raymond, Kenneth Norman *chemistry professor, researcher*
Reich, Michael *economics professor*
Reich, Robert Bernard *political economics educator, former secretary of labor*
Reid, Frances Evelyn Kroll *freelance/self-employed cinematographer, film director, communications executive*
Reingold, Arthur Lawrence *epidemiologist, educator*
Ritchie, Robert Oliver *materials science educator, department chairman*
Romanowicz, Barbara *geology and geophysics professor*
Romer, David *economics professor*
Rosenzweig, Mark Richard *psychologist, neuroscientist, educator*
Roy, Prabir Kumar *physicist*
Ruppenthal, Karl M. *author, educator*
Saraph, Prasad Vaman *research scientist, industrial engineer*
Sastry, Sosale Shankara *electrical engineer, computer scientist, educator*
Scheffler, Samuel *philosophy educator*
Scheiber, Harry N. *law educator*
Schekman, Randy W. *molecular biology administrator, biochemist*
Schoenfeld, Alan Henry *mathematics education professor, researcher*
Schultz, E. Eugene, Jr. *computer engineer, director*
Scotchmer, Suzanne Andersen *economics professor*
Scott, Eugenie Carol *science foundation director, anthropologist*
Seil, Fredrick John *retired neuroscientist*
Seligman, Brad *lawyer*
Selz, Peter Howard *art historian, educator*
Séquin, Carlo H. *computer science educator*
Sessler, Andrew Marienhoff *physicist*
Shannon, Thomas Frederic *German language educator*
Shapiro, Martin *law educator*
Shortell, Stephen Michael *dean, health services researcher*
Shugart, Howard Alan *physicist, researcher*
Simon, Horst D. *computer scientist*
Simpson, David William *artist, educator*
Slaman, Theodore A. *mathematics professor*
Slezkine, Yuri *history professor*
Smith, Alan Jay *computer science educator, consultant*
Smith, Charles Lee *writer*
Smolensky, Eugene *economics professor*
Smoot, George Fitzgerald III *astrophysicist*
Sobel, Noam *science educator*
Somorjai, Gabor Arpad *chemist, educator*
Staff, Virgil Clinton *retired history educator*
Staubus, George Joseph *finance educator*
Steiner, Herbert Max *physics professor*
Stoller, Claude *architect*
Strauss, Herbert Leopold *chemistry professor*
Streitwieser, Andrew, Jr. *retired chemistry professor*
Sulloway, Frank Jones *social sciences educator, historian*
Susskind, Teresa Gabriel *publishing executive*
Taruskin, Richard Filler *musicologist, educator*
Taylor, John Lockhart *retired municipal official*
Tedford, Jeff *college football coach*
Teeguarden, Dennis Earl *forest economist, educator*
Tempelis, Constantine Harry *immunologist, educator*
Thompson, Anthony Wayne *metallurgist, educator, consultant*
Thorner, Jeremy W. *biology professor*
Townes, Charles Hard *physics professor*
Tutashinda, Kweli (Brian P. Altheimer) *chiropractic physician, educator*
Tyson, Laura D'Andrea *economics professor, former dean, federal official*
Valentine, James William *paleontologist, educator, writer*
Vanden Heuvel, Kathleen *law librarian*
Varaiya, Pravin P. *electrical engineer*
Varian, Hal Ronald *economics professor*
Vega, Reinaldo *research scientist*
Veklerov, Eugene *mathematician, computer scientist*
Voiculescu, Dan Virgil *mathematics professor*
Vojta, Paul Alan *mathematics professor*
Wagner, David *computer scientist, educator*
Wake, Marvalee Hendricks *biology professor*
Walker, Peter *landscape architect*
Waters, Alice *executive chef, restaurant owner, writer*
Weir, Margaret *sociologist, political science professor*
Welch, Claude (Raymond) *theology studies educator*
Westheimer, Gerald *optometrist, educator*
White, Timothy Douglas *biology professor, educator*
Wieczorek, John Richard *application developer, systems analyst*
Wiegel, Robert Louis *consulting engineering executive*
Wilensky, Harold L. *political science professor, sociologist, researcher*
Williamson, Oliver Eaton *economics and law professor*

Winkelstein, Warren, Jr. *physician, educator*
Wolf, Joseph Albert *mathematician, educator*
Wolfinger, Raymond Edwin *retired political science professor*
Wolfram, Charles William *law educator*
Woodhouse, Thomas Edwin *lawyer, trust company administrator*
Wright, Paul Kenneth *mechanical engineer, educator*
Yang, Peidong *material science researcher*
Yeung, Ronald Wai-Chun *engineering educator, researcher*
Yoo, John Choon *law educator, former federal agency administrator*
Yu, Bin *statistician, educator*
Zaentz, Saul *film producer, former record company executive*
Zelmanowitz, Julius Martin *mathematics professor, academic administrator*
Zimring, Franklin E. *lawyer, educator*
Zwerdling, Alex *language educator*

Berry Creek
Miller, Joseph Arthur *manufacturing engineer, consultant, educator*

Beverly Hills
Abdul, Paula (Paula Julie Abdul) *singer, dancer, choreographer*
Aboolian, Andre *plastic surgeon*
Abrams, J.J. (Jeffrey Jacob Abrams) *television producer, scriptwriter*
Affleck, Ben *actor*
Ahmanson, Howard, Jr. *Philanthropist*
Ahmanson, Roberta *Philanthropist*
Alessi, David Michael *surgeon*
Alfonso, Frank A. *lawyer*
Allen, Howard Norman *cardiologist, educator*
Allen, Joan *actress*
Allen, Ted *television personality*
Allen, Tim (Timothy Allen Dick) *actor, comedian*
Alter, Gary *plastic and reconstructive surgeon, urologist*
Amado, Honey Kessler *lawyer*
Ambrose, Lauren (Lauren Anne D'Ambruoso) *actress*
Anderson, Kenneth Allen *lawyer, hotel executive*
Anderson, Pamela Denise *actress*
Anderson, Wes (Wesley Wales Anderson) *film director*
Aniston, Jennifer *actress*
Ann-Margret, (Ann-Margret Olsson) *actress, performer*
Apatow, Judd *scriptwriter, television and film producer*
Arieff, Allen Ives *physician*
Arnold, Tom *actor, comedian, television producer*
Arquette, Patricia *actress*
Avary, Roger Roberts (Frank Brauner) *film director, producer, writer*
Aykroyd, Daniel Edward *actor, writer*
Azaria, Hank *actor*
Bacon, Kevin *actor*
Bader, Diedrich *actor*
Balash, Jeffrey Linke *investment banker*
Baldwin, Alec (Alexander Rae Baldwin III) *actor*
Ball, Alan *screenwriter*
Banderas, Antonio *actor*
Bao, Katherine Sung *pediatric cardiologist*
Barkin, Ellen *actress*
Barrymore, Drew *actress*
Basichis, Gordon Allen *writer, scriptwriter, novelist, marketing consultant, media consultant*
Bass, Ronald *screenwriter*
Bateman, Jason *actor*
Bay, Michael Benjamin *film director*
Beatty, Warren *actor, film director, film producer*
Bell, Zoë *stunt-woman, actress*
Bello, Maria Elana *actress*
Belushi, James A. *actor*
Bening, Annette *actress*
Benjamin, Andre Lauren (Dre, André 3000) *vocalist, actor*
Berenger, Tom (Thomas Michael Moore) *actor*
Berg, Jeffrey Spencer *talent agency executive*
Berger, Andre *plastic surgeon*
Bergman, Andrew *scriptwriter, film director*
Bergman, Nancy Palm *real estate investment company executive*
Berkus, James *talent agent*
Biel, Jessica *actress, model*
Bisset, Jacqueline *actress*
Black, Jack (Thomas Black) *actor*
Blaine, David *magician*
Blanchett, Cate (Catherine Elise Blanchett) *actress*
Bogdanovich, Peter *film director, writer, producer, actor*
Bollenbach, Stephen Frasier *hotel executive*
Bonham-Carter, Helena *actress*
Bortman, David *lawyer*
Bosworth, Kate *actress*
Bradshaw, Terry (Terry Paxton Bradshaw) *sports announcer, former professional football player*
Bridges, Beau (Lloyd Vernet Bridges III) *actor*
Bridges, Jeff *actor*
Brillstein, Bernie J. *producer, talent manager*
Brockovich-Ellis, Erin *legal researcher*
Broderick, Matthew *actor*
Brokaw, Norman Robert *talent agency executive*
Brown, Clancy *actor, publishing executive*
Buckland, Marc *television director*
Burnett, Carol *actress, comedienne, singer*
Burnham, John Ludwig *agent*
Burns, Marvin Gerald *lawyer*
Burstyn, Ellen (Edna Rae Gillooly) *actress*
Bush, Sophia *actress*
Bymel, Suzan Yvette *talent manager, film producer*
Byrne, Gabriel *actor*
Campbell, Neve *actress*
Cantor, Alan Bruce *management consultant, application developer*
Capshaw, Kate (Kathy Sue Nail) *actress*
Carpenter, John Howard *director, screenwriter*
Carrey, Jim *actor*
Caruso, David *actor*
Casey, Sue (Suzanne Marguerite Philips) *actress, real estate broker*
Castellaneta, Dan (Daniel Louis) *actor*
Caster, Andrew Ian *ophthalmologist*
Castle-Hughes, Keisha *actress*
Caton-Jones, Michael *film director, film producer*
Cattrall, Kim *actress*
Catz, Boris *endocrinologist, educator*
Caviezel, James Patrick *actor*
Channing, Carol *actress*
Chappelle, Dave (David Chappelle) *actor, comedian*
Chase, David (David DeCaesare) *scriptwriter, television director and producer*
Christensen, Hayden *actor*
Chritton, George A. *theater producer*
Clarkson, Kelly Brianne *singer*
Clemens, Bruce Archer *lawyer*
Clooney, George *actor*
Close, Glenn *actress*
Coates, Anne V. *film editor*
Collette, Toni *actress, singer*
Columbus, Chris J. *film director, screenwriter*
Condon, Tom *sports agent*
Condon, William (Bill) *director, writer, producer*
Congdon, Amanda *actress, web video blogger, writer*
Connelly, Jennifer *actress*
Connery, Sir Sean (Thomas Sean Connery) *actor*
Cook, Dane (Dane Jeffrey Cook) *comedian, actor*
Corbett, John *actor*
Corbin, Barry *actor, writer*
Corbin, Frederic H. *plastic surgeon*
Corwin, Stanley Joel *book publisher*
Covitz, Carl D. *investment company executive, federal and state official*
Cox Arquette, Courteney *actress*
Cristofer, Michael *actor, writer, playwright, scriptwriter*
Croll, Tony *cinematographer, television director*
Cronenberg, David *film director*
Crowe, Cameron *screenwriter, film director*
Cruz, Penelope *actress*
Curry, Tim *actor*
Curtis, Jamie Lee *actress*
Cusack, Joan *actress*
Cusack, John *actor*
Daly, Tyne *actress*
Daniels, Jeff *actor, playwright*
Danson, Ted (Edward Bridge Danson III) *actor*
Davis, Geena (Virginia Davis) *actress*
Davis, Jonathan, Jr. *broadcast executive*
DeGeneres, Ellen *actress, comedienne, talk show host*
Delaney, Kim *actress*
De Niro, Robert *actor, film producer and director, restaurant owner*
Depp, Johnny *actor*
Dern, Bruce MacLeish *actor*
DeVito, Danny Michael *actor, film director*
Diesel, Vin (Mark Vincent) *actor*
Donner, Richard *film director, producer*
Dorff, Stephen *actor*
Dourdan, Gary *actor*
Drescher, Fran *actress*
Driver, Minnie *actress*
Duchovny, David *actor*
Duhamel, Josh David *actor*
Duke, Patty (Anna Marie Duke) *actress*
Duncan, Michael Clarke *actor*
Eastwood, Clint (Clinton Eastwood Jr.) *actor, film director and producer*
Eisner, Michael Dammann *investment and former entertainment company executive*
Elfman, Jenna (Jennifer Mary Butala) *actress*
Elliott, Sam *actor*
Emanuel, Ari (Ariel Z. Emanuel) *talent agent*
Epps, Omar *actor*
Estevez, Emilio *actor, writer, director*
Evans, Louise *investor, retired psychologist*
Eyre, Chris *film director*
Fagel, Bruce G. *lawyer, former emergency physician*
Falco, Edie *actress*
Fallon, Jimmy *actor*
Farrelly, Bobby (Robert Leo Rarrelly Jr.) *scriptwriter, film director and producer*
Favreau, Jon *actor, film director, film producer*
Fein, William *ophthalmologist*
Ferguson, Craig *actor*
Ferrell, Conchata Galen *actress, performing arts educator*
Ferrell, Will (John William Ferrell) *actor*
Fey, Tina *actress*
Filosa, Gary Fairmont Randolph, II, *columnist, film producer*
Fincher, David *film director and producer*
Fine, Richard Isaac *lawyer*
Fisher, (Donald) Garth *plastic surgeon*
Flaum, Marshall Allen *television producer, writer, director*
Fleder, Gary *film director, producer*
Fleming, Peggy Gale *professional ice skater*
Flockhart, Calista *actress*
Foch, Nina *actress, creative consultant, film director, educator*
Foley, James *film director*
Fonda, Jane *actress*
Ford, Tom *apparel designer and executive*
Forsythe, William *actor*
Fox, Michael J. (Michael Andrew Fox) *actor*
Fox, Vivica *actress*
Foxx, Jamie (Eric Bishop) *actor, comedian*
Franken, Al (Alan Stuart Franken) *comedian, writer, actor*
Fraser, Brendan *actor*
Friedman, Robert Lee *film company executive*
Friendly, David T. *film executive, producer*
Futterman, Dan *actor, scriptwriter*
Gabler, Elizabeth Brand *film company executive*
Gaghan, Stephen *scriptwriter, film director*
Gandolfini, James *actor*
Ganis, Sidney *film company executive, producer*
Garofalo, Janeane *actress, comedienne*
Garr, Teri (Ann) *actress*
Gelbart, Larry *scriptwriter, television and theater producer*
Gilpin, Peri *actress*
Glass, David J. *lawyer*
Glazer, Guilford *real estate developer*
Glenn, (Theodore) Scott *actor*
Glotzer, Liz *film company executive*
Glover, John *actor*
Glover, Savion *actor, dancer*
Goldsmith, Bram *banker*
Golshani, S. Daniel *plastic surgeon*
Gooding, Cuba, Jr. *actor*
Goodman, John *actor*
Gordy, Berry *entrepreneur, film producer, recording industry executive*
Gores, Tom T. *investment company executive*
Gossett, Louis, Jr. *actor*
Graham, Heather *actress*
Graham, Lauren *actress*
Grant, Hugh *actor*
Grant, Michael Ernest *educational administrator, management educator*
Gray, Thomas Knox *film producer*
Grazer, Brian *film company executive*
Grenier, Adrian *actor*
Griffin, Anthony *plastic surgeon*
Griffin, Kathy *comedienne, actress*
Griffith, Andy (Andrew Samuel Griffith) *actor*
Griffith, Clark Dexter *corporate financial executive*
Grimwade, Richard Llewellyn *lawyer*
Groening, Matthew (Abram) *writer, cartoonist*
Guest, Christopher *actor, director, screenwriter*
Guggenheim, Barbara Sue *art consultant*
Gugino, Carla *actress*
Gyllenhaal, Jake *actor*
Gyllenhaal, Maggie *actress*
Hackford, Taylor *film director*
Hackman, Gene (Eugene Alden Hackman) *actor*
Hallstrom, Lasse *film director*
Hamilton, Linda *actress*
Hamlin, Harry Robinson *actor*
Hanks, Tom *actor, film producer, film director*
Hannah, Daryl *actress*
Hanson, Curtis *film director, scriptwriter*
Harden, Marcia Gay *actress*
Hardy, Sean *chef*
Harrelson, Woody *actor*
Harris, Mel (Mary Ellen Harris) *actress*
Harris, Neil Patrick *actor*
Hart, Matthew J. *hotel and recreation executive*
Hart, Melissa Joan Catherine *actress*
Hartnett, Josh *actor*
Hawke, Ethan Green *actor*
Hawn, Goldie *actress*
Haworth, Randal Digby *plastic surgeon*
Hayek, Salma *actress*
Haysbert, Dennis *actor*
Heasley, Thomas Allen *composer, musician*
Heaton, Patricia *actress*
Heder, Jon *actor*
Hefter, Lee *chef*
Heller, Paul Michael *film company executive, producer*
Herrmann, Edward Kirk *actor*
Hersh, Neal Raymond *lawyer*
Heston, Charlton (John Charlton Carter) *actor*
Hewitt, Jennifer Love *actress, singer*
Hill, David *broadcast executive*
Hilton, (William) Barron *hotel executive*
Hoffman, Dustin Lee *actor*
Hogan, Steven L. *lawyer*
Holmes, Katie (Katherine Noelle Holmes) *actress*
Hopkins, Sir Anthony (Philip) *actor*
Hopkins, Stephen *film director, producer*
Hopper, Dennis *actor, writer, photographer, film director*
Howard, Ron *film director*
Hughes, John W. *film producer, director, screenwriter*
Hunt, Bonnie *actress*
Hunt, Helen (Helen Elizabeth Hunt) *actress*
Hurd, Gale Anne *film producer*
Hurley, Elizabeth (Liz Hurley) *actress, model*
Hurt, William *actor*
Huston, Anjelica *actress*
Hutton, Timothy *actor*
Idle, Eric *actor, scriptwriter, film producer, lyricist*
Imperioli, Michael *actor*
Isaacman, Alan L. *lawyer*
Israel, Richard Stanley *investment banker*
Jackson, Janet (Damita Jo) *vocalist, dancer*
Jaffe, F. Filmore *lawyer, retired judge*
Janseen, Famke *actress*
Johansson, Scarlett *actress*
Johnson, Douglas L. *lawyer*
Johnson, Magic (Earvin Johnson Jr.) *professional sports team and development company executive, former professional basketball coach and player*
Jolie, Angelina *actress*
Jones, Cherry *actress*
Jordan, Glenn *film, television and theater director*
Jordan, Neil Patrick *film director, writer*
Josephson, Nancy *talent agency executive*
Joyner, Jeffrey K. *lawyer*
Judd, Ashley *actress*
Kadz, Bruce B. *plastic surgeon*
Kalawski, Eva *lawyer*
Karlin, Michael Jonathan Abraham *lawyer*
Karpman, Harold Lew *cardiologist, educator, writer*
Kaufman, Robert *lawyer*
Kavner, Julie *actress*
Keach, Stacy, Jr. *actor, theater director and producer, musician, composer*
Keener, Catherine *actress*
Keitel, Harvey *actor*
Kelly, Moira *actress*
Kerkorian, Kirk *investor, former motion picture company executive, consultant*
Kerns, Joanna de Varona *actress, writer, director*
Khan, Chaka (Yvette Marie Stevens) *singer*
Kidman, Nicole *actress*
Kim, David Edwin *plastic surgeon*
Kingston, Alex (Alexandra Kingston) *actress*
Klein, Arnold William *dermatologist*
Kleiner, Madeleine A. *lawyer, hotel executive*
Klum, Heidi *model, actress*
Knight, Theodore Raymond (T.R. Knight) *actor*
Knoxville, Johnny (Philip John Clapp) *actor*
Komisar, Ken *recording industry executive*
Kotler, Robert *cosmetic surgeon*
Krause, Peter *actor*
Kressley, Carson *television personality*
La Forgia, Robert M. *hotel executive*
Lahti, Christine *actress*
Lake, Ricki (Ricki Pamela Lake) *talk show host, actress*
Lane, Diane *actress*
Lane, Nathan (Joseph Lane) *actor*
Langella, Frank *actor*
Lansbury, Angela Brigid *actress*
Laurie, Hugh *actor*
Law, Jude (David Jude Law) *actor*
Lawrence, Martin *actor, comedian*
Lear, Norman Milton *producer, writer, director*
Leder, Mimi *television and film director, producer*
Lee, Ang *film director*
Lee, Jason *actor*
Lee, Jason Scott *actor*
Leguizamö, John *actor, comedian*
Lehmann, Michael Stephen *film director*
Leigh, Jennifer Jason (Jennifer Leigh Morrow) *actress*
Lesowitz, Jessica R. *lawyer*
Levant, Brian *film director*
Levinson, Barry L. *film director*
Levy, Eugene *actor, film director, screenwriter*
Lewis, Juliette *actress*
Li, Linda (Linda Jian-Yuh Li) *plastic surgeon*
Limato, Edward Frank *talent agent*
Lindo, Delroy *actor*
Linney, Laura *actress*
Liotta, Ray *actor*
Liu, Lucy *actress*
Lloyd, Christopher *actor*
Lloyd, Christopher *television writer and producer*
Lohan, Lindsay Dee *actress*
Lond, Harley Weldon *editor, publishing executive*
Lord, Marjorie *actress*
Lovett, Richard *talent agency executive*
Lowe, Rob *actor*
Lynch, David K. *film director, writer*
Mac, Bernie *actor, comedian*
MacLaine, Shirley *actress*
Macy, William H. *actor*
Madsen, Michael *actor*
Maher, Bill *television personality and producer, comedian*
Maisel, David *entertainment company executive*
Malick, Terrence (David Whitney II) *film director*
Mandel, Babaloo *scriptwriter*
Mandel, Howie *actor, comedian*
Manheim, Camryn *television and film actress*
Mann, Michael Kenneth *film director, producer*
Mantello, Joseph *theater director*
Margulies, Julianna *actress*
Marsden, James (James Paul Marsden) *actor*
Marshak, Harry *plastic surgeon*
Martin, Steve *actor, comedian*
Martinson, Constance Frye *television personality and producer*
Masterson, Mary Stuart *actress*
Mastrantonio, Mary Elizabeth *actress*
Matheson, Tim *actor*
Matise, John J. *investment company executive*
McAdams, Rachel *actress*
McCarthy, Jenny *actress*
McDermott, Dylan *actor*
McKean, Michael *actor*
McKenzie-Swarts, Molly *human resources specialist, hotel executive*
Meirelles, Fernando *film director*
Mendelsohn, Daniel *writer, humanities professor*
Mendes, Eva *actress*
Menkes, John Hans *pediatric neurologist*
Messing, Debra *actress*
Metcalf, Laurie (Lauren Ophelia Metcalfe) *actress*
Meyer, Breckin *actor*
Meyers, Nancy Jane *screenwriter, producer, director*
Miller, Bennett *film director*
Miller, Sienna *actress*
Miller, Wentworth *actor*
Moelleken, Brent Roderick Wilfred *surgeon*
Mol, Gretchen *actress*
Molina, Alfred *actor*
Moore, Demi (Demi Guynes, Demetria Gene Guynes) *actress*
Moore, Julianne (Julie Anne Smith) *actress*
Moore, Mandy (Amanda Leigh Moore) *actress, singer*
Moore, Mary Tyler *actress*
Moore, Michael *film director, writer*
Mortensen, Viggo *actor, writer*
Morton, Samantha *actress*
Moynahan, Bridget (Kathryn Bridget Moynahan) *actress*
Mullally, Megan *actress*
Mulroney, Dermot *actor*
Muniz, Frankie (Francisco James Muniz IV) *actor*
Murphy, Brittany *actress*
Murphy, Cillian *actor*
Murray, Bill *actor, writer*
Najimy, Kathy *actress*
Nassif, Paul S. *facial plastic and reconstructive surgeon*
Neville, Aaron *musician*
Nicita, Rick *agent*
Nixon, Cynthia *actress*
O'Donnell, Chris *actor*

Olmos, Edward James *actor*
Owen, Clive *actor*
Pacino, Al (Alfredo James Pacino) *actor, film director, film producer*
Palmer, Francis Roger III *plastic surgeon*
Paltrow, Gwyneth *actress*
Pantoliano, Joe *actor*
Parker, Mary-Louise *actress*
Parker, Sarah Jessica *actress*
Patinkin, Mandy *actor, singer*
Patton, Antwan Andre (Big Boi) *vocalist*
Paxton, Bill *actor, film director*
Peet, Amanda *actress*
Pepper, Barry *actor*
Perlman, Jon Arthur *plastic surgeon*
Pezzullo, Ralph Michael *writer, playwright*
Phillippe, Ryan *actor*
Pitt, Brad *actor*
Platt, Oliver *actor*
Plummer, Christopher (Orme) (Arthur Plummer) *actor*
Pohost, Gerald Michael *cardiologist, medical educator*
Polanski, Roman *film director, writer, actor*
Pollack, Sydney *film director*
Pompeo, Ellen *actress*
Portman, Natalie *actress*
Posey, Parker *actress*
Pressman, Edward R. *motion picture producer*
Prinze, Freddie, Jr. *actor*
Pullman, Bill *actor*
Quaid, Dennis *actor*
Quinn, Patricia K. *literary agent*
Rai, Aishwarya *actress*
Ramer, Bruce M. *lawyer*
Rapino, Michael *music company executive*
Reese, Della (Deloreese Patricia Early) *singer, actress*
Reeves, Keanu *actor*
Reiner, Carl *director, actor, writer*
Reiner, Rob *film director, actor*
Rey, Robert M. *plastic surgeon*
Rhames, Ving (Irving) *actor*
Rhys-Meyers, Jonathan *actor*
Ricci, Christina *actress*
Richardson, Patricia *actress*
Richie, Nicole *television personality*
Richman, Keith *communications executive*
Riess, Gordon Sanderson *management consultant*
Ringwald, Molly *actress*
Rinsch, Maryann Elizabeth *occupational therapist*
Rivers, Joan *entertainer*
Roberts, Julia Fiona *actress*
Robinson Peete, Holly *actress, writer*
Rogers, Mimi *actress*
Rose, Jessica Lee *actress*
Rosenthal, Mark David *screenwriter*
Rosenthal, Richard Jay *psychiatrist*
Ross, Tracee Ellis (Tracee Joy Silberstein) *actress, model, fashion editor*
Rossellini, Isabella *actress, model*
Roth, Eric *screenwriter*
Rowles, Michael G. *lawyer*
Rudd, Paul *actor*
Rudkin, George Henry *plastic surgeon*
Ruffalo, Mark *actor*
Rush, Geoffrey *actor*
Russell, Keri *actress*
Russell, Kurt *actor*
Russo, Anthony *film director*
Russo, Joe *film director*
Ryan, Frank Harry *plastic surgeon*
Ryan, Meg (Margaret Mary Emily Ann Hyra) *actress, film producer*
Saget, Bob *actor, comedian, writer, television director*
Samberg, Andy *actor*
Sambery, Andy *actor*
Sandrich, Jay H. *television director*
Sarsgaard, Peter *actor*
Schaff, Manya *foundation administrator*
Schaffer, Akiva *writer, director*
Schiff, Gunther Hans *lawyer*
Schneider, Charles Ivan *newspaper executive*
Schneider, Rob *actor*
Schulian, John (Nielsen Schulian) *screenwriter, author*
Scott, Ridley *film director*
Scott-Thomas, Kristin *actress*
Seacrest, Ryan (Ryan John Seacrest) *television and radio personality, entrepreneur*
Sedgwick, Kyra *actress*
Seidel, Joan Broude *securities dealer, investment advisor*
Semel, George Herbert *plastic surgeon*
Sevigny, Chloë *actress*
Sewell, Rufus *actor*
Seymour, Jane *actress*
Shadyac, Thomas *film director, producer*
Shalhoub, Tony *actor, television producer*
Shanley, John Patrick *playwright, screenwriter*
Shapiro-Mathes, Angela *broadcast executive*
Shatner, William *actor*
Sherwood, Kehela (Karen Kehela Sherwood) *broadcast executive*
Shlosberg, Stuart R. *prosthodontist*
Short, Martin *actor, comedian, film critic*
Shue, Elisabeth *actress*
Shuler Donner, Lauren *film producer*
Shyamalan, M. Night (Manoj Nelliyattu Shyamalan) *film director*
Siciliano, Rocco Carmine *cultural institute executive*
Sigler, Mary Ann *investment company executive, accountant*
Silverman, David *film director, television producer, television director, animator*
Silverman, Sarah *comedienne, actress*
Simmons, Gene (Chaim Witz, Gene Klein) *musician*
Simpson, Jessica Ann *singer, actress*
Simpson, Mike *talent agent*
Singer, Bryan *film producer, director, writer, actor*
Sinise, Gary *actor*
Skerritt, Tom *actor*
Slater, Christian *actor*
Smith, Jaclyn *actress*
Smith, Marilyn Noeltner *retired science educator*
Smith, Yeardley *actress*
Snowden, David L. *protective services official*
Sobelle, Richard E. *lawyer*
Sommers, Stephen *film director, producer, scriptwriter*
Sonnenfeld, Barry *director, cinematographer*
Sorkin, Aaron *scriptwriter, television producer, playwright*
Spacek, Sissy (Mary Elizabeth Spacek) *actress*
Spader, James *actor*
Spelling, Tori (Victoria Davey Spelling) *actress*
Spielberg, Steven (Allan) *film director, producer*
Stamos, John *actor*
Statham, Jason *actor*
Steinem, Gloria *writer, editor, advocate*
Stern, Sandor *film director, writer*
Stiles, Julia *actress*
Streep, Meryl (Mary Louise Streep) *actress*
Sutherland, Donald *actor*
Sutherland, Kiefer *actor*
Suvari, Mena *actress*
Swayze, Patrick *actor, dancer*
Sykes, Wanda *comedienne, actress*
Symone, Raven (Raven-Symoné Christina Pearman) *actress, singer*
Tabak, Steven William *cardiologist*
Taccone, Jorma *writer, director*
Tamblyn, Amber Rose *actress*
Tambor, Jeffrey *actor, theater director, educator*
Tamkin, Curtis Sloane *real estate development company executive*
Taylor, Christine *actress*
Taylor, Lili *actress*
Theron, Charlize *actress*
Thompson, Emma *actress*
Thompson, Larry Angelo *film and television producer, lawyer, motivational speaker, writer*
Thompson, Richard Dickson *lawyer*
Thurman, Uma Karuna *actress*
Tilly, Jennifer *actress*
Tomei, Marisa *actress*
Traugott, Peter *television producer*
Travolta, John *actor*
Tripplehorn, Jeanne *actress*
Tucci, Stanley *actor*
Tucker, Chris *comedian, actor*
Turner, Kathleen *actress*
Turturro, Nicholas *actor*
Tyler, Liv *actress*
Underwood, Blair *actor, television producer*
Utley, Nancy *film company executive*
Van Dyke, Dick *actor, comedian*
Van Zandt, Steven *actor, musician, radio personality*
Vardalos, Nia *actress, screenwriter*
Vaughn, Vince *actor*
Victor, Robert Eugene *real estate company executive, lawyer*
Visnjic, Goran *actor*
Wachowski, Andy *film director*
Wachowski, Larry *film director*
Walker, William Tidd, Jr. *investment banker*
Ward, David Schad *scriptwriter, film director*
Ward, Sela *actress*
Watts, Naomi *actress*
Wayans, Marlon *actor, film producer, writer*
Wayans, Shawn *actor, film producer, writer*
Weaver, Sigourney (Susan Alexandra Weaver) *actress*
Weir, Peter Lindsay *film director*
Weisz, Rachel *actress*
Whaley, Frank *actor*
White, Betty *actress, comedienne*
White, Meg(an) (Martha) *musician, vocalist*
Whitford, Bradley *actor*
Wiatt, James Anthony *theatrical agency executive*
Williams, Michelle *actress*
Williams-Paisley, Kimberly *actress*
Willis, Walter Bruce (Bruce Willis) *actor, vocalist*
Wilson, Luke *actor*
Wilson, Owen *actor*
Winkler, Henry Franklin *actor, film producer, director*
Winkler, Irwin *motion picture producer*
Winthrop, John *wines and spirits company executive*
Wirtschafter, David *talent agency executive*
Wolper, David Lloyd *motion picture and television executive*
Wood, Elijah *actor*
Woods, James *actor*
Wright, Jeffrey *actor*
Wright Penn, Robin *actress*
Wu, Yusen (John Woo) *film director*
Yorn, Rick *talent agent*
Yuan, Robin Tsu-Wang *plastic surgeon*
Zane, Billy *actor*
Zanuck, Richard Darryl *motion picture company executive*
Zarem, Abe Mordecai *management consulting executive*
Zellweger, Renee *actress*

Big Pine
Reynaud-Roepke, Suzanne *psychologist*

Bloomington
Lawrence, William, Jr. *retired elementary school educator*

Blythe
Wells, James Wayne *retired secondary school educator*

Bodega Bay
Clegg, James Standish *physiologist, biochemist, educator*
Sorensen, Linda *lawyer*

Bolinas
Harris, Paul *sculptor*
Okamura, Arthur Shinji *artist, educator*

Bonita
Deane, Debbe *psychologist, journalist, editor, consultant*
Ling, Jahja Wang-Chieh *conductor*
Pesavento, Gary D. *psychologist*

Boonville
Hanes, John Ward *civil engineer, sculptor, rancher, director*

Boron
Fisher, Richard Paul *chemist*

Borrego Springs
Strong, John Oliver *plastic surgeon, educator*

Bradbury
Campbell, Robert Charles *minister, theology studies educator*

Brawley
Kinder, Joseph Donald *principal*

Brea
Brown, Ronald Malcolm *engineering corporation executive*
Oh, Tai Keun *business educator, consultant*
Painchaud, Phillip Andre *metrologist*
Tamura, Cary Kaoru *consultant*
Xiu, Faxian *research scientist*

Brentwood
Albers, Lucia Berta *land developer*
Groseclose, Wanda Westman *retired elementary school educator*
Hansen, B. J. (Bobby J. Hansen) *management consultant, real estate investor and developer*

Brisbane
Baadh, Valerie *choreographer, movement educator, theater producer, production designer*
Daniels, Caroline *publishing executive*
Mashouf, Manny *apparel executive*

Buellton
Hashimoto, Tadao *engineering company executive*
Porter, Bruce Jackman *computer engineer, application developer, portfolio manager, civil engineer*

Burbank
Aviv, Oren R. *film company executive*
Baker, Rick *make-up artist*
Bender, Jack *television producer, television director, actor*
Berman, Bruce *entertainment company executive, television producer*
Berwick, Frances *broadcast executive*
Big Boy, (Kurt Alexander) *radio personality, actor*
Bird, Andy *film company executive*
Bower, Richard James *minister*
Branch, Michelle (Michelle Jaquet DeSevren Branch) *musician*
Brandis, Bernardine *lawyer*
Braverman, Alan N. *lawyer*
Bublé, Michael *singer*
Buck, Peter *musician, guitarist*
Burk, Bryan *television producer*
Bush, Billy *television personality*
Caouette, David Paul *public relations executive*
Cheng, Albert *communications executive*
Chiarelli, Robert Charles *audio engineer*
Clapton, Eric *musician, singer*
Clark, Dick *performer, producer*
Cohen, Polly *film company executive*
Connelly, Mary *television producer*
Cook, Richard W. (Dick Cook) *film company executive*
Crane, David *producer*
de Ravin, Emilie *actress*
Downey, Susan *film company executive*
Fishburne, Laurence III *actor*
Fogerty, John Cameron *musician, composer*
Franco, James *actor*
Garner, Scott *communications executive*
Glavin, Edward P. *television producer*
Handel, William Wolf *radio personality*
Hansen, Libby *broadcast executive*
Henley, Don *singer, drummer, songwriter*
Higgins, Jean *television producer*
Horn, Alan F. *film company executive*
Howard, James Newton *composer*
Iger, Bob (Robert Allen Iger) *entertainment company executive*
Janollari, David *television broadcasting executive, cable and television producer*
Joseff, Joan Castle *manufacturing executive*
Jovovich, Milla (Natasha Militza Jovovich) *model, actress*
Kadin, Heather *broadcast executive*
Kaye, Jhani *radio station executive, television producer and director*
Kilgariff, Karen *television producer*
Kingsley, Bob *radio personality*
Kroll, Sue *broadcast executive*
Kwan-Rubinek, Veronika *broadcast executive*
Lakshmi, Padma *actress, television host, model*
Lang, K. D. (Katherine Dawn Lang) *country music singer, composer*
Lassner, Andy *television producer*
Lindelof, Damon *television producer, scriptwriter*
Marinelli, Janice *broadcast executive*
McGraw, Tim *country music singer*
McPherson, Stephen *broadcast executive*
Meyer, Barry Michael *motion picture executive*
Michel, Donald Charles *editor*
Miller, Clifford Albert *merchant banker*
Mitchell, Joni (Roberta Joan Anderson) *singer, songwriter, artist*
Moore, Ryan Natalie *creative director*
Navarro, Dave (David Michael Navarro) *musician, recording artist*
Nelson, Diane W. *broadcast executive*
O'Quinn, Terry (Terrance Quinn) *actor*
Ostroff, Dawn T. *broadcast executive*
Pedowitz, Mark *broadcast executive*
Petty, Tom (Thomas Earl Petty) *musician, composer*
Piddock, James Anthony *actor*
Pope, Katherine Collins *television executive*
Raulinaitis, Pranas Algis *electronics executive, consultant*
Rawlinson, Joseph Eli *foundation administrator, lawyer*
Remini, Leah *actress*
Renner, Andrew Ihor *surgeon*
Rhimes, Shonda *producer, director, writer*
Rivera, Miluka *actress, journalist, poet*
Robinov, Jeff *film company executive*
Robinson, James G. *film production executive*
Ross, Rich *broadcast executive*
Rzeznik, Johnny *singer, musician*
Schlaerth, John Burr *oncologist, gynecologist*
Shore, Howard Leslie *composer*
Silver, Joel *film producer*
Sklar, Marty (Martin A. Sklar) *entertainment company executive*
Staggs, Thomas O. *entertainment company executive*
Stewart, Rod (Roderick David Stewart) *singer*
Sweeney, Anne M. *cable television company executive*
Taubin, Dawn *film company executive*
Thornton, Cameron Mitchell *financial planner*
Wandell, Morgan *broadcast executive*
Weiskopf, Wanda *mezzo soprano, writer, poet*
Wells, John Marcum *producer, writer*
Wiseman, Jane *broadcast executive*
Wonder, Stevie (Steveland Hardaway Judkins, Stevland Morris) *musician*
Younger, Laurie *broadcast executive*
Zhao, Chonghao *neurologist, educator*
Zimmer, Hans Florian *composer*
Zucker, Jeffrey *broadcast executive*

Burlingame
Azarnoff, Daniel Lester *pharmaceutical executive, consultant*
Corcoran, Elizabeth Anne *journalist*
Cotchett, Joseph Winters *lawyer, writer*
Denten, Christopher Peter *lawyer*
Mendelson, Lee M. *film company executive, producer, director, writer*
Schwantes, Robert Sidney *international relations executive*
Slabach, Stephen Hall *lawyer*

Calabasas
Dreier, R. Chad *construction and mortgage company executive*
Geckle, Timothy J. *lawyer*
Goldfield, Emily Dawson *finance company executive, artist*
Hawkins, John N. *education educator, writer*
Jones, Richard K. *information technology executive*
Mozilo, Angelo R. *diversified financial services company executive*
Rubin, Rick (Frederick Jay Rubin) *record producer*
Sambol, David E. *diversified financial services company executive*
Samuels, Sandor Eli *lawyer, diversified financial services company executive*
Sieracki, Eric P. *diversified financial services company executive*
Stark, Martin J. *management consultant*
Walling, Donovan Robert *editor, writer*

California City
Paiva, Clifford Anthony *physicist, consultant*

Camarillo
Arthington, Carol Ann *elementary school educator*
Baehr, Theodore *religious organization administrator, writer, communications executive*
Bowman, Bruce *art educator*
Bryan, Bob Charles *professional tennis player*
Bryan, Mike Carl *professional tennis player*
Cleary, Thomas Charles *technology company executive*
Cobb, Shirley Ann Dodson *public relations consultant, journalist*
Epperson, Stuart W. *religious raido broadcaster*
Gigas, Gunter George *retired physicist, physician*
Kaiman, Sarah *retired physician*
MacAlister, Robert Stuart *retired oil industry executive*
Rush, Richard R. *academic administrator*
Smith, David Michael *financial planner*
Sullivan, Michael Evan *investment company executive*
Van House, Robert Arthur *small business owner, contractor*
Wakelee, Daniel William *academic administrator*
Weiss, Carl *aerospace company executive*

Cambria
Harden, Marvin *artist, educator*
Morse, Richard Jay *human resources specialist, consultant*

Cameron Park
Vorce-Tish, Helene R. *writer*

Camino
McCarthy, Brian Nelson *real estate developer*

Campbell
Battista, Richard *chef, educator*
Levy, Salomon *mechanical engineer*
Ross, Hugh Courtney *electrical engineer*
Vincent, David Ridgely *financial consultant*

Canoga Park
Lederer, Marion Irvine *cultural administrator*

Canyon Country
Catalani, Richard William *forensic specialist, writer*
Rivero, Luis Raul *aerospace physician, military officer*

Canyon Lake
Schilling, Frederick Augustus, Jr. *geologist, consultant*
Sparks, Dale Boyd *allergist, health facility administrator*

Capistrano Beach
Dithridge, Elizabeth *civic worker*

Capitola
Jackson, Kingsbury Temple *educational and financial consultant*

Carlsbad
Baker, Donna M. *research and development company executive, lawyer*
Benjamin, Theresa Mary *retired psychotherapist*
Chopra, Deepak *preventive medicine physician, writer*
Craig, Jenny *human services manager*
Crooke, Stanley Thomas *pharmaceutical executive*
Farrell, Warren Thomas *author*
Fikes, Jay Courtney *anthropology educator, art dealer*
Gibson, Terry Grant *security firm executive*
Golding, Brage *university president*
Halberg, Charles John August, Jr. *mathematics professor*
Howard, Robert Staples *newspaper publisher*
Kauderer, Bernard Marvin *retired naval officer, consultant*
McCracken, Steven Carl *lawyer*
Mezzullo, Louis Albert *lawyer*
Misiorowski, Elise Besson *museum director*
Missett, Judi Sheppard *dancer, jazzercise company executive*
Nosanow, Barbara Shissler *museum director, curator*
Okamoto, Allen M. *real estate company executive*
Ritchie, Doris Lee *executive secretary*
Smarsh, James David *retired military officer*
Smith, Warren James *optical scientist, consultant, lecturer, author*
Wilson, Donald Grey *engineering management consultant*
Wollam, Jean Farr *retired diplomat*
Workman, Jerome James, Jr. *chemist*

Carmel
Aurner, Robert Ray, II, *retail development executive*
Barton, Hugh Perry *bank executive*
Bengert, W. Raymond *lawyer, chemical engineer*
Bohannon-Kaplan, Margaret Anne *non-profit organization executive, lawyer*
Chung, Kyung Cho *Korean history specialist, writer, educator*
Creighton, John Wallis, Jr. *writer, former management educator, consultant, small business owner*
de Vos, Paula Francesca *finance company executive, investment advisor, consultant*
Dobey, James Kenneth *banker*
Faul, June Patricia *education specialist*
Felch, William Campbell *internist, editor*
Freed, Sharon Lou *retired principal*
Gordon, David Jamieson *tenor*
Hamilton, Beverly Lannquist *investment executive*
Hamilton, Lyman Critchfield, Jr. *telecommunications industry executive*
Hobbs, C. Fredric *artist, filmmaker, writer*
Jacobs, Ralph, Jr. *artist*
Koeppel, Gary Merle *publishing executive, art gallery owner, writer*
Mollman, John Peter *publishing executive*
Pippi, Mike *entertainment management*
Skidmore, Howard Franklyn *public relations counsel*
Smith, Gordon Paul *management consultant*
Vardamis, Alex A. *foundation administrator, retired military officer*
Winfield, Rodney M. *artist, retired art educator*
Wright, Constance Storey *retired humanities educator*
Youngdahl, Paul Frederick *mechanical engineer*

Carmel Valley
Chapman, Robert Galbraith *retired hematologist, administrator*
Kasson, James Matthews *electronics executive*
Meckel, Peter Timothy *arts administrator, educator*
Wolfe, Maurice Raymond *retired museum director, educator*

Carmichael
Friedman, Mary Kathleen *secondary school educator*
Hellmuth, William Frederick *economics professor*
O'Leary, Marion Hugh *retired dean, chemist*
Oprsal, Nancy Upshaw *retired elementary school educator*
Ryan, Gretchen Margarete Frieda *art educator*
Throner, Guy Charles, Jr. *aerospace engineering executive, scientist, inventor, consultant*

Carpinteria
Adizes, Ichak *management consultant, writer*
Morgan, Alfred Vance *management consulting company executive*
Puzder, Andrew F. *food service executive, lawyer*
Schmidhauser, John Richard *retired political science professor*
Williams, Benjamin V., IV, *headmaster, history educator*

Carson
Anuakan, Robyn Iset *archivist, educator, film producer*
Beckham, David (David Robert Joseph Beckham) *professional soccer player*
Bensussen, Gale K. *health products company executive*
Berenato, Joseph C. *manufacturing executive*
Heiser, James S. *manufacturing executive*
Hirsch, Gilah Yelin *artist, writer*
Ivers, Louise H. *art history professor*
Lalas, Alexi (Panayotis Alexander Lalas) *professional sports team executive, retired professional soccer player*
Mende, Howard Shigeharu *mechanical engineer*
Mori, Allen Anthony *academic administrator, consultant*
Oropeza, Jenny *state official*
Paige, Dorothy Billiard *retired secondary school educator, educational consultant*
Palmer, Beverly Blazey *psychologist, educator*
Ruiz Gutierrez, Carlos Humberto *professional soccer player*
Schmid, Sigi *professional soccer coach*
Siegel, Neil Gilbert *computer engineer, consultant*
Stuart, Nancy Giovinazzo *secondary school educator*
Zimmerer, Kathy Louise *museum director*

Castro Valley
Evans, Robert William *psychologist, theologian*
Morrison, Glenn Leslie *minister*
West, Doyle Thomas *retired music educator*
Wycoff, Charles Coleman *writer, retired anesthesiologist*

Castroville
Guglielmo, Eugene Joseph *computer scientist*

Cathedral City
Berry, Ester Lorée *vocational nurse*
Jackman, Robert Alan *retail executive*

Century City
Clark, Shaun C. *lawyer*

Cerritos
Lee, Jhemon Hom *physician*
Woodson-Glenn, Yolanda *social worker*

Chatsworth
Bhartia, Prakash *defense research management executive, educator*
Cassar, Jon Francis *television director, film director*
Klein, Jeffrey S. *lawyer, media executive*
Strieby, B. Lorraine *artist*
Weisbrod, Ken (Joseph Louis Weisbrod) *marketing professional*

Chico
Akimoto, Martin Wayne *mental health services professional*
Allen, Charles William *mechanical engineer, educator*
Curry, William Sims *management consultant*
Golightly, Douglas Raymond *artist*
Hornaday, Richard H. *artist, retired educator*
Hyde, Geraldine Veola *retired secondary school educator*
Kistner, David Harold *biology professor*
Livingston, Myran Jay *author, film writer, director and producer*
McNall, Scott Grant *sociologist, educator, academic administrator*
Mejia, Barbara Oviedo *retired chemistry professor*
Reinhardt, Deborah Ann *music educator*
Ritter, Dale William *obstetrician, gynecologist*
Roth, Ronald Lee *engineering educator*
Smith, Valene Lucy *anthropologist, educator*
Zingg, Paul Joseph *academic administrator*

Chino
Goodman, Lindsey Alan *furniture manufacturing executive, architect*
Lee, Sung Ho *psychiatrist*
Wiegand, Penelope Tarleton *elementary school educator*

Chino Hills
Fisher, Teresa Marie *psychologist, forensic specialist*
Ofner, William Bernard *investor, lawyer*
Pearson, April Virginia *lawyer*

Chula Vista
Albala, A. Ari *medical educator, director, psychiatrist*
Allen, Henry Wesley *biomedical researcher, consultant*
Blankfort, Lowell Arnold *newspaper publisher*
Briggs, Franklin Henry *retired naval officer*
Capehart, Bonnie *language educator*
Cohen, Elaine Helena *pediatrician, cardiologist, educator*
McKenzie, Scott Arthur *public health service officer, consultant*
Nelson, Carl Alfred *writer, international business educator*
Palmer, David J. *library director, municipal official*
Ryan, Candace I. *writer, director, editor*
Weiss-Cornwell, Amy *interior designer*
Worthington, George Rhodes *retired naval officer*
Wyatt, Edith Elizabeth *elementary school educator*

Citrus Heights
Daves, Sandra Lynn *poet, lyricist*
Leisey, Donald Eugene *learning materials executive*
Osaki, Mark Stephen *foundation administrator, writer*

City Of Commerce
Martin, Richard J. *food wholesale executive*
Plamann, Alfred A. *wholesale distribution executive*

City Of Industry
Cavanaugh, Janis Lynn *protective services official, educator*
Contreras-Sweet, Maria *bank executive*
Roski, Edward P., Jr. *real estate developer, professional sports team executive*

Claremont
Ackerman, Gerald Martin *art historian, consultant*
Alexander, John David, Jr. *college administrator*
Ansell, Edward Orin *lawyer*
Atlas, Jay David *philosopher, consultant, linguist, educator*
Barron, Hal S. *historian, history professor*
Bekendam, Carol Helen *psychologist*
Benjamin, Karl Stanley *artist, educator*
Bennett, William John (Bill Bennett) *radio personality, former secretary of education*
Blizzard, Alan *artist*
Borcherding, Thomas Earl *economist*
Burdekin, Richard Charles Keighley *economics professor*
Burns, Richard Dean *historian, educator, writer*
Christian, Suzanne Hall *financial planner*
Coleman, Courtney Stafford *mathematician, educator*
Cramer, Alfred William *musician, educator*
Csikszentmihalyi, Mihaly *psychology professor*
Davis, Nathaniel *humanities educator*
Deese, E(thel) Helen *retired literature and language professor*
Detwiler, Daniel Paul *retired physics professor*
Dunye, Cheryl *artist, filmmaker*
Dym, Clive Lionel *engineering educator*
Ferguson, Cleve Robert *lawyer, educator*
Forti, William Bell *manufacturing executive*
Furman, David Stephen *artist, educator*
Gann, Pamela Brooks *academic administrator*
Halpern, Diane F. *psychology educator, professional association executive*
Hansch, Corwin Herman *chemistry professor*
Hawkins, Gregory J. *consumer products company executive*
Helliwell, Thomas McCaffree *physicist, researcher*
Henriksen, Melvin *mathematician, educator*
Huang, Hao H. *music educator, department chairman*
Hwang, Wei-Chin *psychology professor*
Jaffa, Harry Victor *political philosophy educator emeritus*
Johnson, Jerome Linné *cardiologist, educator*
Jones, Nancy Langdon *financial planner, writer*
Klawe, Maria Margaret *academic administrator, engineering and computer science educator*
Kucheman, Clark Arthur *philosophy and religious studies educator*
Lasswell, Marcia Lee *psychologist, educator*
Liggett, Thomas Jackson *retired seminary president*
Likens, James Dean *economics professor*
Lipman-Blumen, Jean *public policy and organizational behavior educator*
Lofgren, Charles Augustin *historian, educator*
Los, Cornelis Albertus *economist, finance educator, risk analyst*
Maguire, John David *academic administrator, educator, writer*
Martin, Jay Herbert *psychoanalyst, language professor, political science professor*
McKirahan, Richard Duncan *classics and philosophy educator*
Molinder, John Irving *engineering educator, consultant*
Monson, James Edward *electrical engineer, educator*
Moss, Myra Ellen (Myra Moss Rolle) *philosophy educator*
Myhre, Janet *mathematician, educator*
Nelson, Mark D. *music educator, arts education administrator*
Oxtoby, David William *academic administrator, chemistry professor*
Pedersen, Richard Foote *diplomat, academic administrator*
Phillips, M. Ian *physiologist, educator*
Pinney, Thomas Clive *retired English language educator*
Pippenger, Nicholas John *mathematician, researcher, computer scientist, educator*
Platt, Joseph Beaven *former college president*
Rankaitis, Susan *artist*
Rossum, Ralph Arthur *political science professor*
Sanders, James Alvin *retired minister, retired religious studies educator*
Segal, Daniel Alan *anthropologist, educator*
Silverman, Victor *history professor, writer, filmmaker*
Skandera Trombley, Laura Elise *academic administrator, literature educator*
Sontag, Frederick Earl *philosophy educator*
Stanley, Peter William *former academic administrator*
Stokes, Anne Dorothy *retired educational association administrator*
Strauss, Jon Calvert *retired academic administrator*
Tanenbaum, Basil Samuel *engineering educator*
Tang, Yao Liang *medical educator, researcher, surgeon*
Tilden, Wesley Roderick *writer, retired application developer*
Tollenaere, Lawrence Robert *retired industrial products company executive*
Wachtel, Albert *writer, educator*
Wakefield, Andre *history professor*
Wallace, David Foster *writer*
Weis, Frederick M. *academic administrator*
Wheeler, Geraldine Hartshorn *historian, writer*
Woodress, James Leslie, Jr. *language educator*
Zehr, Connie *sculptor, art educator*
Zornes, Milford *artist*

Clayton
Bower, Fay Louise *academic administrator, nursing educator*

Clovis
Badgley, Clifford W. *music educator*
Brahma, Chandra Sekhar *civil engineering educator*
Kawashima, Hope Nozomi *musician*
Shields, Allan Edwin *writer, photographer*
van der Paardt, Tamara Ann *music educator*
Von Prince, Kilulu Magdalene *retired occupational therapist, sculptor*

Coachella
Trover, Ellen Lloyd *lawyer, rancher, art dealer*

Coalinga
Frame, Ted Ronald *lawyer*

Colton
Allen, Blair Hamilton *writer, poet, artist, editor, photographer*
Brown, Jack H. *supermarket company executive*

Colusa
Carter, Jane Foster *agricultural industry executive*

Compton
Drew, Sharon Lee *sociologist*
Dymally, Mervyn Malcolm *retired congressman*
McKnight, Carl Phillip *psychologist*
Shiloh, Allen *writer*

Concord
Accatino, Steven C. *instrumental music educator, orchestra conductor*
Blair, Virginia Devoto *music educator*
Borson, Daniel Benjamin *lawyer, educator, physiologist, researcher*
Braunesreither, Lori Jean *environmental services administrator*
Broadbent, Amalia Sayo Castillo *graphic arts designer*
Crandall, Ira Carlton *electrical engineer, consultant*
Hooper, Mark Scheller *electrical engineer, educator*
Randle, Ellen Eugenia Foster *opera and classical singer, educator*
Seshadri, Srivatsan *optics scientist*
Turnbull, Thomas Leigh *social studies educator, secondary school educator*
Uremovich, Michael Elliot *transportation company executive*

Copperopolis
Whisnand, Rex James *association housing executive*

Corona
Chao, Allen Y. *pharmaceutical executive*
Holt, Chifra *dancer, educator, choreographer, artist*
White, Joy Mieko *retired communications executive*
Wood, Brenda Jean *pastor, evangelist*

Corona Del Mar
Allen, Russell G. *lawyer*
Britten, Roy John *biophysicist*
Delap, Tony *artist*
Freeman, Richard Dean *new business start-up service company executive*
Jacobs, Donald Paul *architect*
Khurgel, Tatiana *music educator, director*
O'Brien, John William, Jr. *management consultant*
Tobis, Jerome Sanford *physician*
Yeo, Ron *architect*

Coronado
Axelson, Joseph Allen *professional sports team and publishing executive*
Baumer, Edward Ferdinand *finance company executive*
Butcher, Bobby Gene *retired military officer*
Herring, Charles David *lawyer, educator*
Hostler, Charles Warren *retired ambassador, international affairs consultant*
Kasbeer, Stephen Frederick *retired university official, investor*
Mariya, Deborah Luethje *minister*
Mock, David Clinton, Jr. *internist*
Raushenbush, Walter Brandeis *retired law educator*
Sack, Edgar Albert *electronics company executive*
Smith, Albert Cromwell, Jr. *investment company executive, writer*

Corte Madera
Dalpino, Ida Jane *retired secondary school educator*
Tate, John William *consumer products company executive, former food products executive*

Costa Mesa
Afrasiabi, Peter R. *lawyer*
Aguilera, A. Eric *lawyer*
Allen, Merrill James *marine biologist*
Andrassy, Kyra E. *lawyer*
Barbarosh, Craig A. *lawyer*
Brady, John Patrick, Jr. *electronics educator, consultant*
Caldwell, Courtney Lynn *lawyer, real estate consultant*
Cohen, Stanley *commercial real estate developer*
Daniels, James Walter *lawyer*
Daucher, Donald Alfred *lawyer*
Elliott, Kelli Jeanette *biology professor*
Frieden, Clifford E. *lawyer*
Giannini, Valerio Louis *investment banker*
Grogan, Virginia S. *lawyer*
Hara, Tadao *educational administrator*
Harley, Halvor Larson *bank executive, lawyer*

Hay, Howard Clinton *lawyer*
Hopkins, Denise S. *marketing executive*
Hurst, Charles Wilson *lawyer*
Jones, H(arold) Gilbert, Jr. *lawyer*
Kiang, Assumpta (Amy Kiang) *brokerage house executive*
Lattanzio, Stephen Paul *astronomy educator*
Marshall, Ellen Ruth *lawyer*
Matsen, Jeffrey Robert *lawyer*
Metzger, Vernon Arthur *management educator, consultant*
Mohajer, Dineh *cosmetics company executive*
Mooradian, George T. *lawyer*
Morrow, Donald L. *lawyer*
Muller, Jerome Kenneth *photographer, art director, editor*
Mumford, Lawrence R. *composer, educator*
Ortlund, Anne (Elizabeth Anne Ortlund) *writer, musician*
Rose, I. Nelson *lawyer, educator*
Ruben, Richard S. *lawyer*
Schaaf, Douglas Allan *lawyer*
Schaller, Gordon A. *lawyer*
Scheuneman, Christine A. *lawyer*
Shallenberger, Garvin F. *retired lawyer*
Sharpe, Constantine *engineer, consultant, mathematics professor*
Tennyson, Peter Joseph *lawyer*
Williams, William Corey *theology educator, consultant*

Cotati
Hill, Debora Elizabeth *writer, journalist, screenwriter*

Coto De Caza
Sheehy, Jerome Joseph *electrical engineer*

Cottonwood
Stewart, John Norman *scenic artist*

Covina
Baker, Elenora Frances *retired elementary school educator*
Paulson, Raymond Arnold *science engineering executive*

Cowan Heights
Ruttencutter, Brian Boyle *manufacturing company executive*

Crescent City
Carter, Neville Louis *geophysicist, educator*

Crestline
Douglas, Cindy Holloway *financial consultant*
Merrill, Steven William *research and development company executive*
Noble, Lawrence Alan *artist*

Crockett
Sexton, Randall C. *art educator*

Cromberg
Kolb, Ken Lloyd *writer*

Culver City
Baer, Amy Bosley *film company executive*
Blake, Jeff *film company executive, lawyer*
Boonshaft, Hope Judith *public relations executive*
Brooks, James L. *film producer, director*
Brooks, Mel *film producer and director, actor, scriptwriter*
Chaffin, Ceán *producer*
Davidson, Gordon *theater producer and director*
Eckel, James Robert, Jr. *financial planner*
Ehrlich, Steven David *architect*
Evans, Linda (Linda Evanstad) *actress*
Finkelman Cox, Penney *film producer*
Fischer, Bradley J. *film company executive*
Fisher, Lucy *film producer*
Gordon, Florence Irene *graphics designer, illustrator*
Grant, Joan Julien *artist*
Jacobs, Betty Jane Lazaroff *communications educator*
Kaufman, Richard Stuart *conductor*
Landau, Yair *film company executive*
Leve, Alan Donald *electronics executive*
Lynton, Michael *film company executive*
Maltzman, Irving Myron *psychology professor*
Mann, Michael Martin *engineering executive*
Mark, Laurence Maurice *film producer*
Marshall, Garry K. (Garry Kent Marsciarelli) *film producer, director, writer*
Milano, Adam *film company executive*
Moss, Eric Owen *architect*
Muller, Jenny Helen *physician, psychiatrist*
Netzel, Paul Arthur *fundraising management executive, consultant*
Nicholas, Frederick M. *lawyer*
Pascal, Amy Beth *film company executive*
Sebastian, Joan (José Manuel Figueroa) *musician*
Simmons, Kimora Lee *apparel designer, television personality, model*
Sussman, Deborah Evelyn *interior designer, small business owner*
Thomas, Marlo (Margaret Julia Thomas) *actress*
Trebek, Alex *television game show host*
Van Galder, Valerie *marketing executive*
Vollack, Lia *broadcast executive*
Wick, Douglas *producer*
Wigan, Gareth *film company executive*
Ziskin, Laura *television producer, film producer*

Cupertino
Bregman, Mark *information technology executive*
Carnie, Kay C. *artist, educator*
Clyde, Robert Allan *computer software engineer*
Cook, Timothy D. *computer company executive*
Courville, Arthur F. *lawyer*
Draper, Paul *winemaker*
Fadell, Anthony M. (Tony) *computer company executive*
Fletcher, Homer Lee *librarian*
Gallegos, Vernon David *theater educator*
Haskell, Barry Geoffry *computer engineer, researcher*
Ive, Jonathan *information technology executive, product designer*
Jobs, Steve(n) (Paul) *computer company executive*
Johnson, Ron *information technology executive*
Knapp, George Griff Prather *retired insurance executive*
Lyon, Mary Lou *retired secondary school educator*
Mathias, Leslie Michael *electronic manufacturing company executive*
Nielsen, Tod *information technology executive*
Oppenheimer, Peter *computer company executive*
Rosenberg, Donald Jay *lawyer, computer company executive*
Schiller, Philip W. *information technology executive*
Serlet, Bertrand *information technology executive*
Sobrato, John A. *construction executive*
Svalya, Phillip Gordon *lawyer*
Tamaddon, Sina *information technology executive*
Thompson, John W. *information technology executive*

Cypress
Cully, Joseph Andrew *hazard substance scientist*
Edmonds, Ivy Gordon *retired writer*
Olschwang, Alan Paul *lawyer, crossword and variety puzzle author*
Romero, Tony *information technology executive*
Scott, Gregory W. *health care company executive*

Daly City
Batlin, Robert Alfred *retired newspaper editor*
Hargrave, Sarah Quesenberry *consulting company and public relations executive*

Dana Point
Fisher, Delbert Arthur *pediatric endocrinologist, educator, retired health facility administrator*
Mallory, Frank Linus *lawyer*
Wolf, Karl Everett *aerospace transportation executive, communications executive*

Danville
Bergsten, James Robert *computer technology architect*
Candland, D. Stuart *lawyer*
Cross, Christopher T. *educational association administrator, consultant*
Frerk-Demaria, Deborah *language educator*
Harks, Helene Louise *elementary school educator*
Jones, Orlo Dow *retired lawyer, retired pharmaceutical executive*
Wisniewski, Stephen Adam *professional football player*

Darwin
Palazzo, Robert Paul *lawyer, accountant*

Davis
Al-Asaad, Hussain *electrical engineer, educator*
Altisent, Marta *humanities educator*
Ardans, Alexander Andrew *veterinarian, educator, lab administrator*
Ball, Barry Allen *veterinarian, researcher*
Barbour, Michael G(eorge) *botanist, educator, ecologist, consultant*
Bartosic, Florian *lawyer, educator*
Baskin, Ronald Joseph *biophysicist educator, dean*
Bauer, Ross *composer, music educator*
Biggart, Nicole Woolsey *dean*
Bombardelli, Fabián Alejandro *hydraulic engineer, researcher*
Bower, John Richard Fenn *archaeologist, educator*
Bruch, Carol Sophie *law educator*
Bryant, Brenda K. *psychologist, educator*
Bunch, Richard Alan *writer, educator, poet, philosopher*
Burri, Betty Jane *research chemist*
Cahill, Thomas Andrew *physicist, researcher*
Cardiff, Robert Darrell *pathology educator*
Chancellor, William Joseph *agricultural engineering educator*
Cheney, James Addison *civil engineering educator*
Cohen, Lawrence Edward *sociologist, educator, criminologist*
Colvin, Harry Walter, Jr. *physiology educator*
Conn, Eric Edward *plant biochemist*
Day, Howard Wilman *geology educator*
DePaoli, Geri M. (Joan DePaoli) *artist, historian*
Doi, Roy Hiroshi *biochemist, educator*
Druzhnikov, Yuri Ilya *literature educator, writer*
Eastin, Delaine Andree *education educator*
Enders, Allen Coffin *anatomy educator*
Epstein, Emanuel *plant physiologist*
Fannjiang, Albert *mathematician, educator*
Fuhs, G. Wolfgang (Georg Wolfgang Fuhs) *environmental research manager*
Gardner, Murray Briggs *pathologist, educator*
Gates, Bruce Clark *chemical engineer, educator*
Greenwood, M. R. C. *biologist, nutrition educator, former academic administrator*
Groth, Alexander Jacob *political science professor*
Hayden, John Olin *English literature educator, writer*
Hess, Charles Edward *environmental horticulture educator*
Hinshaw, Virginia *academic administrator*
Hoffman, Michael Jerome *humanities educator*
Holyoak, Marcel *ecologist, educator*
Imwinkelried, Edward John *law educator*
Jensen, Hanne Margrete *pathologist, educator*
Johnson, Kevin Raymond *law educator*
Jones, Edward George *neuroscientist, educator*
Jungerman, John Albert *physics professor*
Kass, Philip Howard *epidemiology educator*
Knittel, Christopher Roland *economics professor, consultant*
Kowalczykowski, Stephen Charles *microbiologist, cellular and molecular biologist, educator*
Kurlaender, Michal *education educator*
Langley, Charles Hunt *geneticist, educator*
Lavernia, Enrique Jose *materials science and engineering educator*
Liu, Kai *physics professor*
Major, Clarence Lee *writer, painter, poet, educator*
Marino, Miguel Angel *engineering educator*
Mason, William A(lvin) *psychologist, educator, researcher*
Maurer, Frank W, Jr. *land trust administrator*
McHenry, Henry Malcolm *anthropologist, educator*
Meyer, Margaret Eleanor *retired microbiologist*
Moyle, Peter Briggs *marine biologist, educator*
Mukherjee, Amiya K. *metallurgy and materials science educator*
Murphy, Terence Martin *biology professor*
Musolf, Lloyd Daryl *political science professor, educational association administrator*
Oakley, John Bilyeu *law educator*
Owings, Donald Henry *psychologist, educator*
Palmer, Philip Edward Stephen *radiologist*
Perschbacher, Rex Robert *dean, law educator*
Pritchard, William Roy *former university systems administrator*
Prokosch, Mark David *research scientist*
Qualset, Calvin O. *agronomist, educator*
Rappaport, Lawrence *plant physiology and horticulture educator*
Rhode, Edward Albert *veterinary medicine educator, veterinary cardiologist*
Richman, David Paul *neurologist, educator, researcher*
Rooks, George Malcolm *writer, educator, small business owner*
Rost, Thomas Lowell *retired botany educator*
Roth, John Roger *geneticist, biology educator*
Schaefer, Saul *cardiologist*
Schneeman, Barbara Olds *nutritionist, educator*
Schoener, Thomas William *zoology educator, researcher*
Shackelford, James Floyd *materials science educator, researcher*
Sharrow, Marilyn Jane *library administrator*
Sillman, Arnold Joel *physiologist, educator*
Simonton, Dean Keith *psychology professor*
Smith, Michael Peter *social sciences educator, researcher*
Spindler, George Dearborn *anthropologist, educator, writer*
Springer, Sally Pearl *university administrator*
Stern, Judith Schneider *nutritionist, researcher, educator*
Stroeve, Pieter *chemical engineering researcher, educator*
Sumner, Daniel Alan *economist, educator*
Sun, Qiang *botanist*
Tanno, John W. *university librarian*
Tchobanoglous, George *civil engineering educator*
Tracy, Craig Arnold *mathematics educator*
Troy, Frederic Arthur, II, *medical biochemistry professor*
Turcotte, Donald Lawson *geophysical sciences educator*
Van Alfen, Neal K. *plant pathologist*
Vanderhoef, Larry Neil *academic administrator*
Waddington, Raymond Bruce, Jr. *language educator*
Wang, Shih-Ho *electrical engineer, educator*
Watt, Kenneth Edmund Ferguson *zoology educator*
Wegge, Leon Louis François *retired economics educator*
Williamson, Alan Bacher *literature educator, poet, writer*
Willis, Frank Roy *historian, educator*
Wolk, Bruce Alan *law educator*
Wydick, Richard Crews *lawyer, educator*
Yilma, Tilahun Daniel *virologist, veterinarian, educator, researcher*

Del Mar
Farquhar, Marilyn Gist *cell biologist, pathologist, educator*
Fricke, Martin Paul *science company executive*
Kaye, Peter Frederic *columnist*
Marcus, Larry David *broadcast executive*
Morton, Frederic *author*
Quinn, Katherine Sarah *psychologist*
Seitman, John Michael *arbitrator, mediator, lawyer*
Smith, Geoffrey Arthur *museum staff member, surgeon*
Wilkinson, Eugene Parks *nuclear engineer, director*

Delano
Salmassi, Sadegh *physician*

Denair
Hale, Lois J. *retired mathematics educator*

Desert Hot Springs
Laws, Maurice Wesley *set decorator, museum exhibit designer*
Zarres, Sharon L. *marriage and family therapist, health facility administrator*

Diablo
Burnison, Boyd Edward *lawyer*

Diamond Bar
Domeño, Eugene Timothy *elementary education educator, principal*
Snoop Dogg, (Calvin Broadus) *vocalist, actor*

Dinuba
Surabian, Carol Anne *language educator, consultant*

Downey
Achon, Raquel Andrea *music educator, consultant*
Brooks, Lillian Drilling Ashton (Lillian Hazel Church) *adult education educator*
Hackney, Jack Dean *physician*
Perry, Jacquelin *orthopedist, surgeon*
Robles, Darline P. *school system administrator*
Shapiro, Richard Stanley *physician*
Todd, Margaret Donnellan *library director*

Duarte
Margolin, Kim Allyson *internist, hematologist, oncologist*
Riggs, Arthur D. *health facility administrator, research scientist*
Smith, Steven Sidney *molecular biologist*

Dublin
Chen, John S. *computer company executive*
Whetten, John D. *food products executive*

East Palo Alto
Bates, William III *lawyer*
Frankle, Diane Holt *lawyer*
Hantash, Basil M. *dermatologist, educator*
Lesser, Henry *lawyer*
Rinsky, Arthur C. *lawyer*
Schelling, Donald Lawrence *lawyer*

Edwards
Brand, Vance Devoe *astronaut, director*

El Cajon
Thomas, Esther Merlene *elementary and adult education educator*
Yoshizu, Jeri *public relations executive*

El Centro
Gaede, Robert Matthew *music educator*

El Cerrito
Alldredge, Noreen S. *librarian*
Burger, Edmund Ganes *architect*
Herzberg, Dorothy Crews *retired secondary school educator*
Kao, Yasuko Watanabe *retired library director*
Koths, Kirston Edward *biochemist*
Ma, L. Eve Armentrout *television producer, television director, educator*

El Dorado Hills
Bartlett, Robert Watkins *metallurgist, educator, consultant*
Blasier, Robert Dalton, Jr. *lawyer*
Briggs, Rex *marketing executive, writer*
Sparks, Robert Dean *medical administrator, gastroenterologist*
Tierney, Kevin Allen *elementary school educator*

El Granada
Heere, Karen R. *astrophysicist*

El Macero
Stowell, Robert Eugene *pathologist, retired educator*

El Monte
Hwang, Tzu-Yang *minister*
White-Whitfield, Lisa Denise *social worker*

El Segundo
Abdul-Jabbar, Kareem (Lew Alcindor, Lewis Ferdinand Alcindor) *professional basketball coach, retired professional basketball player*
Bryant, Kobe *professional basketball player*
Buss, Jerry (Gerald Hatten Buss) *professional sports team owner*
Carey, Chase (Charles G.) *broadcast executive*
Churchill, Bruce B. *broadcast executive*
Doyle, Patrick T. *broadcast executive*
Eckert, Robert A. *consumer products company executive*
Fisk, Hayward Dan *lawyer, computer services company executive*
Freeland, Pete *aerospace transportation executive, consultant*
Hamel, Michael A. *career officer*
Harwick, Wayne Thomas *economist*
Hsia, Irene Yee *electrical engineer*
Hunter, Larry Dean *lawyer, broadcast executive*
Jones, Wes *architect*
Keane, Michael E. *computer services company executive*
Kilpatrick, Frank Stanton *marketing executive*
Kupchak, Mitchell *professional sports team executive, retired professional basketball player*
Laphen, Michael W. *computer services company executive*
McCarty, Shirley Carolyn *retired aerospace executive*
Muhlbach, Robert Arthur *lawyer*
Musk, Elon *aerospace transportation executive*
Normile, Robert J. *lawyer*
Odom, Lamar Joseph *professional basketball player*
Palkovic, Michael W. *broadcast executive*
Pontual, Romulo *broadcast executive*
Schohl, Joseph *lawyer*
Shanks, Eric *communications executive*
Suranyi, John B. *broadcast executive*
Thiry, Kent J. *health products executive*
Toler, Penny *former professional basketball player, sports team executive*
Vollrath, Frederick E. *human resources specialist, career officer*
Webb, Darryl Willard *systems engineer*
Willis, Judy Ann *lawyer*

Elk Grove
Forbes, Kenneth Albert Faucher *retired urological surgeon*
McDavid, Douglas Warren *executive research consultant*
Moe, Janet Anne *elementary school educator, church organist*

Elmira
Montoya, Malaquias *art educator, artist*

Emeryville
Anderson, Darla K. *animated film producer*
Catmull, Edwin E. *film company executive, computer graphics engineer*
Chang, Ying-Lan *technologist*
Chiasson, William B. *electronic games executive*
Chung, Caleb *inventor, toymaker, toy company executive*
Fields, Howard Lincoln *neurologist, physiologist, educator*
Goldstein, Jack *biopharmaceutical executive, microbiologist*
Gombocz, Erich Alfred *biochemist*
Houghton, Michael *geneticist*
Howe, Drayton Ford, Jr. *lawyer*
Kalinske, Thomas J. *education, video game and toy company executive*
Katz, Jeffrey G. *electronic games executive*
Lasseter, John A. *film company executive, computer animator*
Masri, Merle Sid *biochemist, consultant*
Pao, Bing Shih *emergency physician*
Pien, Howard *pharmaceutical executive*
Renton, Hollings C. *health products executive*
Roth, Joe *motion picture company executive*
White, Raymond Leslie *geneticist*
Zwoyer, Eugene Milton *retired consulting engineering executive*

Encinitas
Deets, Dwain Aaron *retired aerospace technology executive*
Ford, William Francis *retired bank holding company executive*
Hale, David Fredrick *biotechnology executive*
Kim, Kyehee *environmental engineer, consultant*
Lougeay, Denruth Colleen *clinical psychologist, educator*
Mazak, Arlene Patricia *marriage and family therapist*
Williams, Michael Edward *lawyer*

Encino
Altschul, David Edwin *record company executive, lawyer*
Bright, Kevin S. *producer*
Church, Kathy Lynn *education educator, consultant*
Darvish, Daniel K. *research and development company executive, director*
Ehrlich, Kenneth James *television producer*
Elkins, Brad S. *ophthalmologist*
Friedman, George Jerry *aerospace engineering executive*
Genga, John Michael *lawyer*
Glickman, Daniel Robert *motion picture association executive, former congressman*
Greenberg, Allan *advertising and marketing research consultant*
Ingels, Marty *agent, broadcast executive*
Irmas, Audrey Menein *not-for-profit developer*
Kempisty, Michael *artist, writer, actor*
Knuth, Eldon Luverne *engineering educator*
Lesavoy, Malcolm Alan *plastic surgeon*
Luna, Barbara Carole *financial analyst, accountant*
Parrott, Dennis Beecher *retired insurance industry executive*
Pisano, A. Robert *former actors guild executive, former film company executive*
Rawitch, Robert Joe *journalist, educator*
Rosner, Louis Joseph *medical educator*
Schulweis, Harold Maurice *rabbi*
Shire, David Lee *composer*
Smith, Selma Moidel *lawyer, composer*
Sungaila, Mary-Christine (M.C. Sungaila) *lawyer*
Taylor, Renee *actress, writer*
Teplinsky, Joel Jack *plastic surgeon*
Westmore, Michael George *make-up artist, writer*

Escalon
Barton, Gerald Lee *food products executive*

Escondido
Briggs, Edward Samuel *naval officer*
Brown, Brian Ellis *protective services official*
Carlson, Mary Lou *elementary school educator, sister*
Damsbo, Ann Marie *psychologist*
Ehrhart, Joseph Edward *retired broadcast technician*
Gerhardt, Emery William *food products executive*
Guinn, Stanley Willis *retired lawyer*
Linzey, Verna May *minister, writer*
McCarberg, Bill Harold *physician*
Moore, Marc Anthony *retired academic administrator, writer, retired military officer*
Newman, Barry Ingalls *retired bank executive*
Rockwell, Elizabeth Goode *dance company director, consultant, educator*
Sanders, Adrian Lionel *retired educational consultant*
Sloan, Anne Elizabeth *food scientist, writer*
Tomomatsu, Hideo *chemist*
Walker, Patricia Ann *special education educator*

Eureka
Bowker, Lee Harrington *sociologist, educator, writer*
Hannaford, Peter Dor *public relations executive, writer*
Hise, Mark Allen *dentist*

Fair Oaks
Chernev, Melvin *retired beverage company executive*
Hutton, Essex Clark, Sr. *adult education educator*
Lemke, Herman Ernest Frederick, Jr. *retired elementary school educator, consultant*
Potter, George Kenneth *artist*

Fairfax
Kadoyama, Margaret *museum educator, management consultant*

Fairfield
Edson, William Alden *retired electrical engineer, researcher*
Gelpke, Peter Hall *science educator*
Mary, Diane Bradley *elementary school educator, secondary school educator*
Ornellas, Maile Louise *filmmaker, educator*
Schunke, Hildegard Heidel *accountant*
Spake, Reuben Michael *mathematics professor, researcher*

Fallbrook
Cordes, Kathleen Ann *retired physical education educator, director*
Freeman, Harry Lynwood *retired accountant*
Harsha, Philip Thomas *retired aerospace engineer*
Ragland, Jack Whitney *artist*

Felicity
Istel, Jacques Andre *mayor*

Folsom
Anderson, Jeffrey Lee *physician, anesthesiologist, consultant*
Chowdhury, Ali Asraf *electrical engineer, researcher, director*
Ettlich, William F. *electrical engineer*
Ewing, Russell Charles, II, *physician*
Haga, Enoch John *computer educator, writer, editor*
Jefferds, William John *military officer*
Krishnaswamy, Dilip *computer architect*
Regan, William Joseph, Jr. *energy company executive*
Terranova, Elizabeth (Elisa) Jo *artist*

Fontana
Ferreri, Michael Victor *optometrist*
Rainsberry, Patrick Ryan *engineer*

Fort Bragg
Gjerde, Rosalie Carolyn *music educator, conductor*
Lehan, Jonathan Michael *judge*

Foster City
Alton, Gregg H. *lawyer*
Burke, Kevin *finance company executive*
Coghlan, John Philip *corporate financial executive*
Denny, James M. *pharmaceutical and former retail executive*
Fry, Derek A. *finance company executive*
Hotz, Henry Palmer *retired physicist*
Karnazes, Elizabeth Marie Barnson *lawyer, photojournalist*
Liu, Leonard *software services company executive*
Lutvak, Mark Allen *computer company executive*
Martin, John C. *pharmaceutical company executive*
Milholland, Terence V. *finance company executive*
Miller, Jon Philip *marketing professional, pharmaceutical executive*
Pollitt, Byron H., Jr. *retail executive*
Rabbat, Guy *electronics executive, consultant*
Rosen, Howard B. *biopharmaceutical company executive*
Saunders, Joseph W. *finance company executive*
Sommer, Kenneth *finance company executive*
Yan, Martin *celebrity chef*
Zaidi, Iqbal Mehdi *biochemist, research scientist*

Fountain Valley
Armstrong, Jeffrey Lee *representative, oceanographer*
Berman, Steven Richard *computer company executive*
Crecelius, Daniel Neil *history professor*
Davis, Jeremy Matthew *chemist*
Einstein, Stephen Jan *rabbi*
Hoffman, Richard W. *automotive executive*
Kieu, Quynh Dinh *pediatrician, not-for-profit developer*
Nguyen, Thanh-Van *otolaryngologist*
Otto, Marie (Bertha Otto) *educational administrator, educational consulting company executive*
Smith, Marie Edmonds *real estate agent, property manager*
Treadway-Dillmon, Linda Lee *actress, stuntwoman, dancer, dispatcher, athletic trainer*
Wilhite, Steve *automotive executive*

Fowler
Bowman, Joseph Paul *protective services official, writer, retired military officer*

Frazier Park
Edwards, Sarah Anne *social worker, psychologist*

Fremont
Alsborg, Thomas C. *electronics executive*
Bagley, James W. *semiconductor equipment company executive*
Bray, Richard Daniel *librarian*
Chao, Kwang-Chu *chemical engineer, educator*
Chen, Wai-Kai *electrical engineering and computer science educator, consultant*
Chien-Hale, Elizabeth *lawyer*
Cummings, John Patrick *lawyer*
Grant, Alan J. *business executive, educator*
Gupta, Anu *lawyer*
Hinson, Duane Keith *minister, counselor*
Hofacket, Jean *library director*
Huang, Robert *electronics executive*
Khalsa, Prabhjot Singh *neurologist*
Kitta, John Noah *lawyer*
Korn, Laurence *health products executive*
Le, Thuy Trong *nuclear engineer, educator*
Leung, Simon *lawyer, electronics executive*
Monajemi, Pezhman *electrical engineer*
Newberry, Stephen G. *semiconductor equipment company executive*
Pelton, Alan Roy *engineer, researcher, engineering educator*
Polk, Dennis *electronics executive*
Rusch, Thomas William *manufacturing executive*
Sanchez, Marla Rena *communications executive*
Smith, Bernald Stephen *retired pilot*
Stinnett, Terrance LLoyd *lawyer*
Tang, John *network technician, information scientist, educator*
Venturini, Judith Anne *education educator*
Wood, Linda May *librarian*
Wu, James Chen-Yuan *aerospace engineering educator*
Yamamoto, Masako *music educator, director*
Yaoi, Takuro *biochemist*
Zandi, Iraj *plastic surgeon*
Zimmer, George A. *men's apparel executive*

Fresno
Autry, Alan *film company executive, mayor, actor, former professional football player*
Berman, Richard P. *lawyer*
Bosch Cobb, Karen *library director*
Bundy-DeSoto, Teresa Mari *language educator, vocalist*
Burnett, Lynn Barkley *health science educator*
Corless, Dorothy Alice *nursing educator*
Cornish, Bonita Clark *retired secondary school educator*
Coyle, Robert Everett *federal judge*
Cunningham, Mark Alan *surgeon*
Dackawich, S. John *sociology educator, academic administrator*
Darden, Edwin Speight, Sr. *architect*
Dauer, Donald Dean *investment company executive*
De La Cruz-Reyes, Pilar L. *nursing administrator*
Epperson, Robert Dale *farmer*
Ewell, A. Ben, Jr. *lawyer, small business owner*
Fortune, Larry M. *real estate broker*
Ganulin, Judy *public relations professional*
Garrison-Finderup, Ivadelle Dalton *writer, educator*
Genini, Ronald Walter *retired history educator, historian*
Harris, Breck Anthony *business educator, writer, researcher*
Ishii, Anthony W. *judge*
Jenkins, David Ray *lawyer*
Joishy, Suresh K. *oncologist*
Joseph, James William *political scientist, consultant, educator*
Kauffman, George Bernard *chemistry professor*
Kouymjian, Dickran *art historian, educator*
Lagle, John Franklin *lawyer*
Lambe, James Patrick *lawyer*
Lanter, Lanore *writer, educator*
Leigh, Hoyle *psychiatrist, educator, writer*
Little, Kevin Gerard *lawyer*
McConnell, Charles Prescott *retired science educator*
Misakian, Jo Ellen Priest *school librarian, dean*
O'Connor, Kevin John *psychologist, educator*
O'Neill, Lawrence Joseph *federal judge*
Ortiz, John Michael *provost*
Palmer, Samuel Copeland III *lawyer*
Patnaude, William Eugene *architect*
Patton, Jack Thomas *family practice physician*
Pings, Anthony Claude *architect*
Riggs, Krista Dyonis *music educator, librarian*
Rubingh, Jonathan Patrick *environmental health specialist*
Runyon, Brett L. *lawyer*
Shmavonian, Gerald S. *political organization administrator*
Smith, Richard Howard *banker*
Stewart, Deborah Claire *dean*
Tellier, Richard Davis *management educator*
Tudman, Cathi Graves *elementary school educator*
Tyckoson, Dave *library director, library association executive*
Waters, Rosemary R. *biology professor*
Welty, John Donald *academic administrator*
Wilson, James Ross *communications educator, broadcast executive*
Winslow, Norman Eldon *small business owner*
Xiong, Tousu Saydangnmvang *minister, theology studies educator*

Fullerton
Ackerman, Richard Charles *lawyer, state legislator*
Ayala, John L. *retired librarian, dean*
Bjorklund, Nancy Basler *history professor*
Bush, William Merritt *lawyer*
Carrithers, Joseph Edward *English composition and literature educator*
Choi, John U. *periodontist, educator*
Donoghue, Mildred Ransdorf *education educator*
Fischer, Robert Blanchard *academic administrator, researcher*
Foote, Paul Sheldon *business educator, administrator, consultant*
Frizell, Samuel *law educator*
Garrett, Scott T. *medical products executive*
Goldstein, Edward David *lawyer, former glass company executive*
Johnson, Carolyn Elizabeth *librarian*
Kaisch, Kenneth Burton *psychologist, priest*
Levesque, Paul Joseph *religious studies educator*
Lewandoski, Robert Henry *editor, publisher*
Miller, Arnold *electronics executive*
Moerbeek, Stanley Leonard *lawyer*
Montgomery, Thom Mathew *health program administrator, counselor*
Roberts, Mark Scott *lawyer*
Rubin, Arthur Leonard *systems engineer, mathematician*
Sadrudin, Moe *humanitarian organization executive*
Shapiro, Mark Howard *physicist, educator, dean*
Smith, Ephraim Philip *academic administrator*
Steinmeyer, Robert Jay *retired lawyer*
Sugarman, Michael *physician, rheumatologist*
Woyski, Margaret Skillman *retired geology educator*
Zettel, Laura A. *psychology professor, researcher*

Garberville
Nyokka, Suzette *artist, natural health educator*

Garden Grove
Cochrum, Ellen Joan *language educator*
Schuler, Robert Harold *minister, writer*
Williams, J(ohn) Tilman *insurance company executive, real estate agent, municipal official*

Garden Valley
Price, Lew Paxton *writer, engineer*

Gardena
Hite, Janet Sue *elementary school educator*
Kelly, Sean *entrepreneur*
Martin, Melissa Carol *radiological physicist*

Gilroy
McCarty, Robert Clarke *mathematician*

Glen Ellen
Berkland, James Omer *geologist*
Haslag, Karen Christine *art educator, musician*
Hurlbert, Roger William *information technology executive*

Glendale
Calabro, Alfred A. *lawyer*
Coleman, Lewis Waldo *film company executive, former bank executive*
Cross, Richard John *bank executive*
Dallas, Saterios (Sam Dallas) *aerospace engineer, researcher, consultant*
Daly, Ann Michelle *broadcast executive*
de Grassi, Leonard *art historian, educator*
Early, Alexander Rieman III *judge*
Enrico, Roger A. *film and retired soft drink company executive*
Fox, John *film company executive*
Gedjeyan, Gaiane Diana (Astvatsatrian) *pianist, physical therapist*
Geffen, David Lawrence *film company and former recording company executive*
Gibbons, Leeza *television and radio talk show host, entertainment reporter*
Grillo, Leo *actor, photographer*
Halaby, Noelle M. *lawyer*
Hoffman, Donald M. *lawyer*
Hughes, Bradley Wayne *storage company executive*
Hunt-Coffey, Nancy *library director*
Jacobson, Nina R. *film producer and former company executive*
Katzenberg, Jeffrey *film company executive*
Kay, Alan C. *computer scientist, nonprofit organization executive*
Kazanjian, Phillip Carl *lawyer, educator*
Kazarian, Poghos F. *physicist, researcher, educator*
Kelley, Jan *publishing executive, musician*
Kendrick, Katherine *lawyer*
Levy, Murray *business educator*
Lund, John Richard *entertainment company executive*
MacDonald, Kirk Stewart *lawyer*
MacDonald, Laurie *film company executive*
Martinetti, Ronald Anthony *lawyer*
Michelson, Lillian *librarian, researcher*
Misa, Kenneth Franklin *management consultant*
Parkes, Walter F. *film company executive*
Phipps, Robert Lee *information technology manager*
Robinson, Smokey (William Robinson) *singer, composer*
Scott, A. Timothy *lawyer*
Shou, Sharon Louise Wikoff *vocational rehabilitation counselor*
Snider, Stacey *film company executive*
Sotelo, Eduardo (El Piolín) *radio personality*
Spring, Carl Chaffee, Jr. *writer*
Stack, Kevin J. *lawyer*
Stewart, Julia A. *food service executive*
Whalen, Lucille *retired academic administrator*
White, Jennifer Elizabeth Belk *corporate training specialist*
Woolls, Esther Blanche *library science educator*

Glendora
Lasko, Allen Howard *pharmacist*

Gold River
Andrew, John Henry *lawyer, writer*
Shaw, Eleanor Jane *newspaper editor*

Goleta
Everhart, Thomas Eugene *retired academic administrator, engineering educator*
Gilbert, Richard Keith *biology professor, researcher*
Jerphagnon, Olivier L. *telecommunications industry executive*
Nahra, Lynda J. *bank executive*
Sensiper, Samuel *electrical engineer*
Zuk, Carmen Veiga *psychiatrist*

Granada Hills
Aller, Wayne Kendall *psychologist, educator, computer company executive, property manager*
Lehtihalme, Larry K. (Lauri Lehtihalme) *financial planner*
Shoemaker, Harold Lloyd *information scientist*

Granite Bay
Hartmann, Frederick Howard *retired political science professor*
Holtz, Sara *marketing consultant*
Kemper, Dorla Dean Eaton (Dorla Dean Eaton) *real estate broker*

Grass Valley
Cassella, Dennis Gene *retired county official*
Cheney, Margaret *writer, retired editor*
Ely, Parry Haines *dermatologist, educator*
Engles, Eric William *editor, writer*

Hawkins, Richard Michael *lawyer*
Lynn, David Lawrence *music educator*
Washington, Allyn Jarvis *writer*

Greenbrae
Blatt, Morton Bernard *medical illustrator*
Bonapart, Alan David *lawyer*
Cohn, Bruce *film and television company executive*
Freedman, Albert Z. *publishing executive*
Parnell, Francis William, Jr. *otolaryngologist*
Tyng, Anne Griswold *architect*

Gridley
Stiles, Owen Rodger *social studies educator*

Gualala
Ring, Alice Ruth Bishop *retired preventive medicine physician*

Guerneville
Mannino, J. Davis *psychologist, educator, author*

Gustine
Ramirez, Nola Marie *librarian*

Hacienda Heights
Dodson, Arleen Cecilia *language educator*
Love, Daniel Joseph *consulting engineer*

Half Moon Bay
Fennell, Diane Marie *marketing professional, process engineer*
Lambert, Frederick William *lawyer, educator*
Robertson, Abel L., Jr. *pathologist*

Happy Camp
Black, Barbara Ann *publisher*

Hat Creek
Shepard, David Haspel *film restoration specialist*

Hawthorne
Brann, Donald Lewis, Jr. *school superintendent*
Fila, John Charles *psychoanalyst*

Hayward
Bachicha, Joseph Alfred *physician, educator*
Beck, Edward William *lawyer*
Duncan, Doris Gottschalk *information systems educator*
Garcia, Melva Ybarra *counseling administrator, educator*
Hammond, Marian Corleene *retired literature educator*
Kohl, John Preston *finance educator, consultant*
McKenzie, Brian Bruce *finance educator*
Rees, Norma S. *academic administrator*
Reevy-Manning, Gretchen Maria *psychologist, educator*
Sabharwal, Ranjit Singh *mathematician*
Smith, John Kerwin *lawyer*
Staudohar, Paul David *economics professor, labor arbitrator*

Healdsburg
Eade, George James *retired military officer, researcher*
Keane, Douglas *chef*
Kemp, Alson Remington, Jr. *lawyer, retired educator*
Myers, Robert Eugene *writer, educator*
Vedros, Neylan Anthony *microbiologist, educator*
Wunderlich, Alfred Leon *artist, educator*

Hemet
Berger, Lev Isaac *physicist, researcher*
Clark, Harold L. *technology company executive, consultant*
Culverwell, Albert Henry *historian*
Mata, David Joseph *physician*

Hercules
Richards, Gerald Thomas *lawyer, educator, writer*
Tandy, Carla M. *dancer, educator*
Tyson, Kathleen Hayhurst *educational association administrator*

Hermosa Beach
Battles, Roxy Edith *novelist, consultant, educator*
Kokalj, James Edward *retired aerospace administrator*
Wickwire, Patricia Joanne Nellor *psychologist, educator*
Winthrop, Kenneth Ray *insurance executive*
Zartman, Patrick Joseph *secondary school educator*

Highland
Miller, R. Warburton *psychologist, farmer*
Tacal, Jose Vega, Jr. *retired public health official, veterinarian*

Hillsborough
Keller, John Francis *retired food products executive, mayor*
Kraft, Robert Arnold *retired medical educator, physician*
Packard, Peter *retired internal medical educator*
Westerfield, Putney *management consulting executive*

Hollister
Monaco, Reb Leon *county official*
Schallhorn, Charles Dean *social sciences educator, labor union administrator*

Hollywood
Adams, William James, Jr., (Will.i.am) *rap artist*
Berryman, Guy *musician*
Brooks, Lila *animal rights activist, retired hotel executive*
Buckland, Jon *musician*
Champion, Will *musician*
Diamond, Mike (Mike D) *recording artist*
Fisher, Joel Marshall *political scientist, educator, wine consultant*
Greenwood, Jonathan Richard Guy (Jonny Greenwood) *musician*
Hoesli, Hanna *dentist*
Lewis, Huey (Hugh Anthony Cregg III) *singer, composer, bandleader*
Lynne, Shelby (Shelby Lynn Moorer) *country singer*
Martin, Chris *vocalist*
McAdams, Frank Joseph III *communications educator*
Melchior, Ib Jorgen *scriptwriter, author, film director*
Michaels, Mia *choreographer, dancer*
Miles, Joanna *actress, playwright, director*
Minnelli, Liza *singer, actress*
Parks, Robert Myers *appliance manufacturing company executive*
Perth, Rod *network entertainment executive*
Roberts, Mel (Melvin Richard Kells) *retired film editor*
Schuster, Peggy Lindner (Pravrajika Brahmaprana) *sister, nun*
Warren, Diane *lyricist*
Yauch, Adam Nathaniel (MCA) *recording artist*
Yorke, Thomas Edward *musician, vocalist*

Hopland
Jones, Milton Bennion *retired agronomist*

Huntington Beach
Baroni, Michael L. *lawyer*
Burson, Thomas Daniel *retired aerospace executive*
Carter, Henrietta McKee *music educator, department chairman*
Davidson-Shepard, Gay *secondary school educator*
De Massa, Jessie G. *media specialist*
Dostourian, Dick *computer systems executive*
Flakes, Susan *playwright, theater director*
Foose, Chip *automotive designer, television personality*
Garrels, Sherry Ann *lawyer*
Houck, Aleda Jean *dean*
Jensen, Dennis Lowell *lawyer*
Leveton, Ian Sinclair *civil engineer*
Martin, Wilfred Wesley Finny *psychologist, property owner and manager*
McKay, David E. *mathematics professor*
McKnight, Robert B., Jr. *sporting goods manufacturing executive*
Nguyen, Han Van *mechanical engineer*
Pineda, Anselmo *neurosurgery educator*
Ramphal, Julie Frances *retired secondary school educator*
Slater, Kelly (Robert Kelly Slater) *professional surfer*
Sward, Andrea Jeanne *information and computer scientist, musician*
Welsh, William Daniel *geriatric medicine family practice physician*
Winterowd, Walter Ross *language educator*
Yglesias, Kenneth Dale *college president*

Huntington Park
Gaines-Page, Rena L. *science educator*

Idyllwild
Jones, William Lee, Jr. *psychologist, educator*
Schneider, Paul *writer*

Imperial Beach
Merkin, William Leslie *retired lawyer*

Indian Wells
Gassman, Andrea C. *paralegal, artist*
Hrabal, Antonin *physician, educator*
Jennings, Richard Milburn *resort developer*
Jorgensen, Gordon David *retired engineering company executive*
Kelley, John Paul *communications consultant*
McDermott, Thomas John, Jr. *lawyer*

Indio
De Salva, Christopher Joseph *lawyer, consultant*
Garra, Raymond Hamilton, II, *marketing executive*
Hamilton, Allen Philip *financial advisor*
Houghton, Robert Charles *secondary school educator*
Olson, Phillip David LeRoy *agriculturist, chemist*

Inglewood
Dorr, Lawrence D. *orthopedic surgeon*
Epstein, Marsha Ann *public health service officer, physician*
Zarif, Farid *internist, nutritionist*

Irvine
Aigner, Dennis John *economics professor, consultant*
Aitken, Ashleigh E. *lawyer*
Alch, Mark Lee *finance educator, researcher, real estate investor*
Alexopoulos, Nicolaos George *electrical engineering educator, dean*
Alspach, Philip Halliday *manufacturing executive*
Andersen, Erik M. *lawyer*
Ang, Alfredo Hua-Sing *civil engineering educator*
Avzaradel, Bob *music educator*
Ayala, Francisco José *geneticist, educator*
Bander, Myron *physics professor, dean*
Barsamian, Harut *computer scientist, consultant*
Bartkus, Richard Anthony *magazine publisher*
Basombrio, Juan C. *lawyer*
Bastiaanse, Gerard C. *lawyer*
Beard, Ronald Stratton *lawyer*
Benford, Gregory Albert *physicist, writer*
Boyd, Carolyn Patricia *history professor*
Bruce-Novoa, Juan David *literature and language professor, writer*
Bryant, Susan V. *academic administrator*
Burton, Michael Ladd *anthropology educator*
Callé, Craig R.L. *finance company executive*
Catrakis, Haris John *science educator*
Chelapati, Chunduri Venkata *civil engineering educator*
Chernock, Michelle Leigh *medical researcher*
Christensen, Becky Vanderhoof *lawyer*
Chronley, James Andrew *real estate executive*
Clark, Bruce Robert *geologist, consultant*
Clegg, Michael Tran *genetics educator, researcher*
Cole, Robert K. *diversified financial services company executive*
Coleman, J. Edward *computer company executive*
Crawford, Denise F. *lawyer*
Crowley, Daniel Francis, Jr. *transportation and logistics executive*
Danziger, James Norris *political science professor*
Demetrescu, Mihai Constantin *research scientist, educator, computer company executive*
Drake, Michael V. *academic administrator, ophthalmologist, educator*
DuBose, Guy Steven *lawyer*
Dull, David A. *lawyer*
Dzyaloshinskii, Igor Ekhielievich *physicist*
Farrar, Donald Keith *retired finance company executive*
Feldman, Martha Sue *political scientist, educator*
Feldstein, Paul Joseph *management educator*
Finkelstein, Mark *mathematician, educator*
Finlayson-Pitts, Barbara Jean *chemistry professor*
Fleischer, Everly Borah *academic administrator, department chairman*
Freeman, Douglas K. *lawyer*
Friedenberg, Richard Myron *radiologist, physician, educator*
Gallardo, Miguel E. *psychologist*
Galuppo, Lynn T. *lawyer*
Gardiner, David M. *biologist, educator*
Ge, Nien-Hui *chemist, educator*
Gibson, Patrick Daniel *accountant, historian*
Gilbert, Margaret P. *philosophy professor, researcher*
Grabowski, Richard Joseph *lawyer*
Gylseth, Doris Hanson (Doris Lillian Gylseth) *retired librarian*
Halvorsen, Clay A. *lawyer, construction executive*
Hancock, S. Lee *lawyer, business executive*
Harpen, Shawn M. *lawyer*
Hensley, William Michael *lawyer*
Hinderaker, Ivan *retired political science professor*
Hine, Robert Van Norden, Jr. *historian, educator*
Hoffman, Donald David *cognitive and computer science educator*
Horne, Terry *publishing executive*
Huang, Wendy Wan-Juoh *lawyer*
Huff, C(larence) Ronald *sociologist, criminologist, educator*
Ingram, Douglas Stephen *lawyer*
James, Anthony Amadé *molecular biologist, educator*
Jamshidipour, Yousef *bank executive, economist, financial advisor*
Jitomirskaya, Svetlana *mathematics professor*
Jones, Joie Pierce *entrepreneur, acoustician, writer, educator*
Jorion, Philippe *education educator*
Keller, Jennifer L. *lawyer*
Knobbe, Louis Joseph *lawyer, educator*
Kohli, Gurmander Singh *plastic surgeon*
Kraemer, Kenneth Leo *architect, urban planner, educator*
Lave, Charles Arthur *economics professor*
Le Bon, Douglas Kent *investment manager*
Lenhoff, Howard Maer *biological sciences educator, academic administrator*
Lesonsky, Rieva *editor-in-chief*
Li, Peter Wai-Kwong *mathematics professor*
Lillyman, William John *language educator, academic administrator*
Lin, Kwei-Jay *education educator, researcher*
Lowe, Kathlene Winn *lawyer*
Luce, R. Duncan (Robert Duncan Luce) *psychology professor*
Madden, Thomas A. *finance educator*
Manasson, Vladimir Alexandrovich *physicist*
Maradudin, Alexei A. *physics professor*
Margolis, Julius *economics professor*
Matros, Richard K. *insurance company executive*
Mattson, Robert Marvin, Jr. *lawyer*
McCubbin, Sharon A. *elementary school educator*
McGregor, Scott A. *electronics company executive*
McLaughlin, Calvin Sturgis *biochemistry professor*
Merken, Leo *lawyer*
Micic, Miodrag *chemist, researcher*
Miledi, Ricardo *neurobiologist*
Mohraz, Ali *engineering educator*
Morhaime, Mike *video game company executive*
Morton, Roger Larkin *finance educator*
Munoff, Gerald J. *university librarian*
Nalcioglu, Orhan *radiologist, educator*
Nowick, Arthur Stanley *metallurgy and materials science educator*
Ozonian, Steve *real estate company executive*
Pal, Sukumar *immunologist, researcher*
Pardo, Robert *game designer, video game software company executive*
Parnes, Andrew H. *financial executive*
Penny, Simon *art educator*
Petrasich, John Moris *lawyer*
Phalen, Robert Franklynn *environmental scientist*
Pocock, J. Michael *communications executive*
Policano, Andrew J. *dean, finance educator*
Pomeranz, Kenneth L. *history professor*
Power, Francis William *newspaper publisher*
Premchand, Arigapudi *retired financial consultant*
Pyott, David Edmund Ian *pharmaceutical executive*
Qin, Yufen *immunologist, researcher*
Quilligan, Edward James *retired obstetrician, gynecologist, educator*
Randerson, James T. *geophysicist, educator*
Rankin, James *finance company executive*
Re, Joseph R. *lawyer*
Riley, Sally Jean *science educator*
Ritz, Thorsten *biophysics professor*
Rogan, James Edward *former federal agency administrator, former congressman*
Rooklidge, William Charles *lawyer*
Rose, Irwin A. (Ernie Rose) *biochemist, educator*
Rowland, Frank Sherwood *chemistry professor*
Ruyter, Nancy Lee Chalfa *dance educator*
Rynn, Nathan *physics professor, consultant*
Saari, Donald Gene *mathematician, department chairman, economist*
Samueli, Henry *electrical engineer, educator, entrepreneur*
Scarborough, Stephen J. *construction executive*
Schaefer, Ronald Dean *secondary school educator*
Scheithauer, Christopher C. *lawyer*
Schoendorfer, Donald W. *engineer*
Schonfeld, William Rost *political science professor*
Seals, David W. *lawyer*
Seller, Gregory Erol *marketing executive, consultant, writer*
Shadpour, Hamed *research assistant*
Shea, Kenneth J. *chemistry professor*
Sherwood, Rod(erick) III *computer company executive*
Shirilau, Mark Steven *utilities executive*
Siegel, Barry *journalist, writer, literature educator*
Sirignano, William Alfonso *aerospace and mechanical engineer, educator*
Sklansky, Jack *electrical and computer engineering educator, researcher*
Smith, Andrew Donald *plastic surgeon*
Smoot, Skipi Lundquist *psychologist*
Snyder, Rick (Richard D. Snyder) *computer company executive*
Specter, Richard Bruce *lawyer*
Sperling, George *psychologist, educator*
Stack, Geoffrey Lawrence *real estate developer*
Stanbridge, Eric John *biology professor*
Starostina, Natasha *research scientist*
Stern, Jean *museum director*
Stone, Samuel Beckner *lawyer*
Stubberud, Allen Roger *electrical engineering educator*
Sunshine, Steven H. *lawyer*
Tachner, Leonard *lawyer*
Theologides, Stergios *lawyer, real estate company executive*
Thigpen, Stephen P. *horticulture products company executive*
Ting, Albert Chia *biomedical engineer, researcher*
Tyler, Michael Robert *lawyer*
Umberg, Thomas John *lawyer*
Vandell, Kerry Dean *real estate consultant, educator, director, finance educator*
Vines, Henry Ellsworth III *lawyer, accountant, financial planner*
Wallis, Richard Fisher *physicist, researcher*
Wan, Frederic Yui-Ming *mathematician, educator*
Weller, Stephen G. *botanist, educator*
Welsh, John Joseph (Jay) *lawyer*
Werlin, Lawrence B. *obstetrician, gynecologist, endocrinologist*
Wetterau, Mark S. *food products/distributor executive*
White, Douglas Richie *anthropology educator*
White, Stephen Halley *biophysicist, educator*
Wickramasinghe, Hemantha Kumar *electrical engineer, physicist*
Windsor, Adrian Sharon *real estate broker, literature and language professor*
Wintrode, Ralph Charles *lawyer*
Wong, Nathan Donald *medicine and epidemiology researcher, educator*
Yazdi, Ahmad *computer scientist, researcher*

Jackson
Tyler, Clifford Ernest *director*

Joshua Tree
Hope, Harry Joe (Joeseph) *retired corporate communications specialist, writer*

Kensington
Appelman, Evan Hugh *retired chemist*
Connick, Robert Elwell *retired chemistry professor*
Littlejohn, David *writer*
Oppenheim, Antoni Kazimierz *mechanical engineer*
Stent, Gunther Siegmund *molecular biologist, educator*

Kentfield
Blum, Joan Kurley *not-for-profit fundraiser, marketing executive, consultant*
Dargel, Jan Kay *college administrator, institute president, lawyer*
Edgar, James Macmillan, Jr. *management consultant*
German, Donald Frederick *physician*
Halprin, Anna Schuman (Mrs. Lawrence Halprin) *dancer*
Schmid, Rudi (Rudolf Schmid) *retired internist, educator, academic administrator*

La Canada Flintridge
Baines, Kevin Hays *astronomer, planetary scientist*
Byrne, George Melvin *physician*
Costello, Francis William *lawyer*
Lamson, Robert Woodrow *retired school system administrator*
Macmillan, Robert Smith *electronics engineer*

La Crescenta
Purcell, Lee (Lee Jeune Williams) *actress, film producer*
Riccardi, Vincent Michael *pediatrician, educator, entrepreneur*

La Habra
Chase, Cochrane *advertising agency executive*
Estrada, Isabel Victoria *obstetrician, gynecologist*

La Habra Heights
Agajanian, Gilda *pianist*

La Jolla
Adams, Marc Anthony *medical statistician, researcher*
Akiskal, Hagop Souren *psychiatric researcher, educator*
Andre, Michael Paul *physicist, educator*
Anthony, Harry Antoniades *retired city planner, architect, educator*
Antin, David *poet, critic*
Arnold, James Richard *chemist, educator*
Asbeck, Peter Michael *engineering educator*
Ashley, Christopher *performing company executive*
Asmus, John Fredrich *physicist*
Atai, Manucher *retired surgeon*
Atkinson, Richard Chatham *academic administrator, cognitive scientist*
Backus, George Edward *theoretical geophysicist*
Bailey, David Nelson *pathology educator, dean, academic administrator*
Baran, Phil S. *chemistry professor*
Bardwick, Judith Marcia *management consultant*
Bavasi, Peter Joseph *sports management executive*
Beebe, Mary Livingstone *curator*
Bellugi, Ursula *neuropsychologist, educator*
Berger, Wolfgang H. *oceanographer, educator, geologist*
Blanchard, Daniel G. *cardiologist*
Blantz, Roland C. *nephrologist, educator*
Boger, Dale L. *chemistry professor*
Branscomb, Lewis McAdory *physicist, researcher*
Brooks, Charles Lee III *computational biophysicist, educator*
Buchholz, Debby *lawyer*
Burbidge, E. Margaret *astronomer, educator*
Burbidge, Geoffrey *astrophysicist, educator*
Cain, William Stanley *experimental psychologist, educator, researcher*
Carmichael, David Burton *physician*
Cavenee, Webster K. *director*
Chandler, Marsha *academic administrator, educator*
Chang, William Shen Chie *electrical engineering educator*
Chao, Edward C. *internist*
Chien, Shu *physiology and bioengineering educator*
Chisari, Francis V. *pathologist*
Chrispeels, Maarten Jan *biology professor*
Cleveland, Don W. *biomedical researcher*
Coburn, Marjorie Foster *psychologist, educator*
Coden, Daniel Jay *ophthalmologist*
Colbert, James, Jr. *academic administrator*
Continetti, Robert E. *chemistry professor*
Copley, David C. *newspaper publishing company executive*
Counts, Stanley Thomas *retired military officer, retired electronics executive*
Covell, Ruth Marie *medical educator, academic administrator*
Cox, Charles Shipley *oceanography researcher, educator*
Dalessio, Donald John *internist, neurologist, educator*
Davies, Hugh Marlais *museum director*
Davis, Brian Keith *biophysicist, researcher*
Dillin, Andrew *medical researcher, educator*
Dimsdale, Joel Edward *psychiatry educator*
Dixon, Frank James *pathologist, educator*
Dixon, Jack Edward *biological chemistry professor, consultant*
Drake, Hudson Billings *aerospace and electronics executive*
Driscoll, Charles Frederick *physicist, educator*
Edelman, Gerald Maurice *biochemist, neuroscientist, educator*
Edgington, Thomas S. *pathologist, molecular and vascular biologist, educator*
Edwards, Charles Cornell *surgeon, medical association administrator*
Elander, Richard Paul *microbiologist, consultant*
Elman, Jeffrey Locke *cognitive sciences educator*
Evans, Ronald M. *microbiologist, educator*
Farson, Richard Evans *psychologist*
Feher, George *biophysicist, educator*
Foley, L(ewis) Michael *real estate company officer*
Fowler, Raymond Dalton *psychologist, educator*
Foxe, Marye Anne *academic administrator*
Freedman, David Noel *religious studies educator*
Freedman, Jonathan Borwick *journalist, writer, educator*
Fung, Yuan-Cheng Bertram *bioengineering educator, writer*
Gabay, Janis T. *literature and language educator*
Gandhi, Tarak *computer engineer*
Garland, Cedric Frank *epidemiologist, educator*
Geckler, Richard Delph *retired metal products executive*
Gilbert, James Freeman *geophysics educator*
Gill, Gordon N. *medical educator*
Goldman, Mitchel Paul *dermatologist*
Granger, Clive William John (Sir Clive Granger) *retired economist*
Guillemin, Roger C.L. *physiologist*
Halkin, Hubert *mathematics professor, researcher*
Hallin, Daniel Clark *communications educator*
Hamburger, Robert N. *pediatrician, educator, consultant*
Han, Jiahuai *medical researcher*
Harris, Philip Robert *management and space psychologist*
Harris, T. George *editor*
Hawkinson, Tim *sculptor*
Haxo, Francis Theodore *marine biologist*
Haymet, Anthony Douglas-John *research scientist, chemistry educator*
Heeb, Mary Jo *biochemist, researcher*
Helinski, Donald Raymond *biologist, educator*
Hemingway, George Thomson *marine biologist, educator, priest*
Hendrickson, David Norman *chemistry professor*
Hermann, Thomas C. *chemistry professor*
Hofmann, Alan Frederick *biomedical researcher, educator*
Holmes, Edward Warren *dean, medical educator*
Horner, Anthony Adam *pediatrician, educator*
Hunter, Tony (Anthony Rex) *molecular biologist, educator*
Ideker, Trey *computational and molecular biologist*
Imana, Jorge Garron *artist*
Itano, Harvey Akio *biochemistry educator*
Jacobson, Gary Charles *political science professor*
Jensen, Henrik Wann *computer graphics designer, educator*
Johnson, Gayle Ann *cardiology nurse*
Kaback, Michael *medical educator*
Kadonaga, James Takuro *biochemist*
Karbhari, Vistasp M. *engineering educator, researcher*
Karin, Michael *educator, molecular biologist, consultant*
Karlen, Peter Hurd *lawyer, writer*
Katinsky, Steven B. *communications company executive*
Katzman, Robert *neurologist, educator*
Kearns, David Richard *chemistry professor*
Kehler, Andrew S. *computer scientist, educator*
Kelly, Jeffrey W. *chemist, educator*
Kennel, Charles Frederick *atmospheric physics professor, academic administrator, government official*
Khan, Imran *research scientist, educator*
Kirchheimer, Arthur E(dward) *lawyer, business executive*
Kitada, Shinichi *biochemist*
Klonoff-Cohen, Hillary Sandra *epidemiologist*
Kolodner, Richard David *biochemist, educator, director*
Kooyman, Gerald Lee *physiologist, researcher*
Kuperman, William A. *oceanographer, educator*
Lal, Devendra *nuclear geophysics educator*
Langacker, Ronald Wayne *linguistics educator*
Lauer, James Lothar *physicist, researcher*
Levy, Ralph *engineering executive, consultant*
Lewin, Ralph Arnold *biologist*
Linden, Paul Fredrick *environmental engineer, educator*
Linshaw, Andrew Ross *mathematician*
Liu, Shumo *molecular biologist*
Low, Mary Louise (Molly) *documentary photographer*
Low, Philip Steven *research scientist, entrepreneur*
Lydon, Nicholas B. (Nick Lydon) *biochemist, pharmaceutical executive, researcher*
Ma, Wenxue *medical scientist*
Macagno, Eduardo R. *biology professor, dean*
Machina, Mark Joseph *economist*
Mah, Silvia Armitano *director, educator*
Mandler, George *psychologist, educator*
Mandler, Jean Matter *psychologist, educator*
Maple, M. Brian *physics professor*
Marti, Kurt *chemistry professor*
Martin, James John, Jr. *systems analyst, retired research and development company executive*
Mayer, James Hock *lawyer, mediator*
McCammon, James Andrew *chemistry professor*
McDonald, Marianne *classicist*
McKay, Dianne Brenda *nephrologist*
Mendoza, Stanley Atran *pediatric nephrologist, educator*
Miller, Carol *elementary school educator, counselor*
Miller, David R. *academic administrator*
Miller, Scott R. *plastic surgeon*
Milstein, Laurence Bennett *electrical engineering educator, researcher*
Molina, Mario Jose *physical chemist, educator*
Moossa, A. R. *surgeon, educator*
Morello, Candis Marguerite *pharmacist, educator*
Morgens, Warren Kendall *retired lawyer*
Nahavandi, Amir Nezameddin *retired engineering firm executive*
Nakamura, Robert Motoharu *pathologist*
Nemat-Nasser, Sia *engineering educator, researcher*
Nicolaou, K. C. *chemistry professor*
Nyhan, William Leo *pediatrician, educator*
Olafson, Frederick Arlan *philosophy educator*
Onuchic, José Nelson *biophysics educator, electrical engineer*
Oreskes, Naomi *science historian*
Palsson, Bernhard O. *engineering educator*
Patton, Stuart *biochemist, educator*
Penner, Stanford Sol *engineering educator*
Peterson, Paul Ames *lawyer, educator*
Poole, Keith T. *political science professor*
Rahman, Yueh-Erh *biologist*
Rajasekar, Arcot *computer scientist*
Rauch, James E. *economics professor*
Rearden, Carole Ann *clinical pathologist, educator*
Reed, John C. *physician, researcher*
Reynolds, Roger Lee *composer, educator*
Richman, Douglas Daniel *medical virologist, educator, internist*
Ride, Sally Kristen *physics professor, research scientist, retired astronaut*
Rinaker, Samuel Mayo, Jr. *retired utilities executive*
Rotenberg, Manuel *physics professor*
Rubenstein, Howard S. *physician, writer*
Rubin, Lewis J. *physician, researcher*
Rudee, Mervyn Lea *engineering educator, researcher*
Schimmel, Paul Reinhard *biochemist, biophysicist, educator*
Schmid-Schoenbein, Geert Wilfried *biomedical engineer, educator*
Schneider, Benjamin *psychology professor, consultant*
Schneider, Gerald L. *plastic surgeon*
Schottlaender, Brian E.C. *university librarian*
Schroeder, Julian Ivan *biology professor*
Scull, Andrew T. *sociologist, educator*
Seagren, Stephen Linner *oncologist*
Shakespeare, Frank *ambassador*
Sham, Lu Jeu *physics professor, physicist*
Shannahan, William Paul *lawyer*
Sharpless, K. Barry *chemist, educator*
Sherman, Irwin William *biological sciences educator, academic administrator*
Shor, George G., Jr. *geophysicist, oceanographic administrator, engineer*
Shuler, Kurt Egon *chemist, educator*
Siegel, Jay Steven *chemistry educator*
Silver, Dee Edward *physician, neurologist*
Singer, Robert *plastic surgeon*
Snyder, Evan *cloning and stem cell company administrator, neuroscientist, educator*
Somerville, Richard Chapin James *atmospheric scientist, educator*
Stark, Harold Mead *mathematics educator*
Starr, Ross Marc *economist, educator*
Steinberg, Daniel *preventive medicine physician, educator*
Stone, Donald Diamond *investment and sales executive*
Sullivan, Robert S. *college dean*
Swain, Judith Lea *cardiologist, educator*
Tan, Eng Meng *immunologist, biomedical researcher*
Taupenot, Laurent *medical educator, researcher*
Taur, Yuan *physicist, researcher*
Taylor, Palmer W. *pharmacology educator*
Telengator, Alexander M. *engineer*
Terras, Audrey Anne *mathematics professor*
Thomas, Charles Allen, Jr. *molecular biologist, educator*
Thompson, Charlotte Ellis *pediatrician, educator, writer*
Tsien, Roger Yonchien *chemist, cell biologist*
Tsuang, Ming Tso *psychiatrist, educator*
Tsuji, Frederick Ichiro *biochemist, molecular biologist*
Tsybakov, Boris Solomon *information theory and communication networks researcher, educator*
Van Lint, Victor Anton Jacobus *physicist*
Vogt, Peter K. *oncologist*
Vucinic, Dejan *neuroscientist*
Waddy, Lawrence Heber *writer*
Wahl, Geoffrey Myles *biology professor*
Walker, Richard Hugh *orthopaedic surgeon*
Wallach, Nolan R. *mathematician, consultant*
Wang, Lei *biochemist*
Watson, Kenneth Marshall *physics professor*
Wesling, Donald Truman *English literature educator*
West, John Burnard *physiologist, educator*
Whaley, Storm Hammond *retired federal agency administrator*
Wilkie, Donald Walter *retired biologist, aquarium administrator*
Wilkins, Floyd, Jr. *retired lawyer*
Wilson, Bonnie Jean *lawyer, educator, investor*
Wolynes, Peter Guy *chemistry researcher, educator*
Wong, Wade Hwu *radiologist, educator*
Wright, Andrew *English literature educator*
Wulbert, Daniel Eliot *mathematician, educator*
Zimmermann, Joerg *biophysicist*

La Mesa
Canzoneri, Lois H. *retired church musician*
Hansen, Grant Lewis *retired air transportation executive*
Schmidt, James Craig *retired bank, savings and loan association executive*

La Palma
Knowles, Marie L. *transportation executive*
Levy, Elaine Ann *music educator*
McNamee, Lawrence Ross, Jr. *manufacturing executive*

La Puente
Chico, Darlene Ehrich *elementary school educator*
Hitchcock, Frederick E., Jr., (Fritz) *automotive company executive*
Pleitez, Concepcion Maria *elementary school educator*
Ver Kuilen, Marion Jane *retired instructional aide*
Vetter, Lawrence Anthony *art educator, consultant*

La Quinta
Calvin, James Willard *thoracic and vascular surgeon*
Eversole, Barbara Louise *administrative assistant*
Pitkin, Roy Macbeth *retired obstetrician, educator*
Rothrock, Roger Lee *corporate financial executive, retired military officer*

La Verne
Fleck, Raymond Anthony, Jr. *retired academic administrator*
Izaguirre, George *microbiologist*
Jalbert, Janelle Jennifer *executive recruiter, secondary school educator*
Lou, Yiming *chemical engineer*
McDonough-Treichler, Judith Dianne *medical educator, consultant*
Morgan, Stephen Charles *academic administrator*
O'Brien, James D. *language educator, communications executive*

Ladera Ranch
Skidmore, Michelle Marie *elementary school educator, principal*

Lafayette
Davies, Paul Lewis, Jr. *retired lawyer*
Dethero, J. Hambright *banker*
Edwards, Aura C. *political organization worker, volunteer*
Freeman, Tom M. *lawyer*
Kang, Isamu Yong *retired nuclear medicine physician*
Krueger, Robert Edward *mechanical engineer, manufacturing executive*
Lewis, Sheldon Noah *technology consultant*
Lichterman, Martin *history professor*
Morehouse, Valerie Jeanne *librarian*
Shurtleff, Akiko Aoyagi *artist, consultant*

Laguna Beach
Arnold, John David *management counselor*
Bent, Alan Edward *political science professor*
Challis, Diane Leslie *theater director*
Chevli, Lyn *writer*
Hanauer, Joe Franklin *real estate company officer*
Pelton, Virginia Lue *small business owner*
Simons, Barry Thomas *lawyer*

Laguna Hills
DeGrave, Douglas Michael *lawyer*
Hammond, R. Philip *chemical engineer*
Lagrew, David Crutcher *obstetrician, gynecologist, medical association administrator, director*
Mathews, Stanton Terry *lawyer*
Reinglass, Michelle Annette *lawyer, mediator, arbitrator*
Rossiter, Bryant William *chemistry consultant*
Widyolar, Sheila Gayle *dermatologist*

Laguna Niguel
Axon, Donald Carlton *architect*
Carr, Bernard Francis *hospital administrator*
Greenberg, Lenore *public relations professional*
McEvers, Duff Steven *lawyer*
York, James Orison *real estate executive*

Laguna Woods
Badgley, John Roy *architect*
Berk, Jack Edward *gastroenterologist, educator*
Hussey, William Bertrand *retired diplomat*
McClure, Hal H. *film producer*
Ross, Mathew *medical educator*
Walker, Donald Ezzell *retired academic administrator*
Wheatley, Melvin Ernest, Jr. *retired bishop*

Lagunitas
Holman, Arthur Stearns *artist*

Lake Arrowhead
Fitzgerald, John Charles, Jr. *investment banker*

Lake Elsinore
Druskoff, Barbara Therese *elementary school educator*
Young, Patricia Janean *speech pathology/audiology services professional*

Lake Forest
Bukaty, Raymond M. *lawyer*
Coyne, John F. *computer company executive*
Cranmer, Scotty *professional trick bike rider*
Fahim, Amr *electrical engineer*
Higby, Lawrence M. *medical products executive*
Massengill, Matthew H. *computer company executive*
Schroeder, John A. *systems engineering consultant, educator*
Shakeel, Arif *computer company executive*

Lake View Terrace
McCraven, Eva Stewart Mapes *health service administrator*

Lakewood
Bogdan, Carolyn Louetta *financial specialist, retired small business owner*
Carr, Firpo Wycoff *bible scholar, educator, writer*

Lancaster
Campano, Ruwanthi *surgeon*
Hodges, Vernon Wray *mechanical engineer*
Holley, Susan L. *psychologist*
Strom, Susan G. *special education educator*
Wooster, Larry D. *music educator*

Larkspur
Greenberg, Myron Silver *lawyer*
Hanna, Nessim *marketing educator*
Ratner, David Louis *retired law educator*

Lemoore
Gerhard, H. John *orthopaedic surgeon, military officer*

Lincoln
Chong, Vernon *retired surgeon, military officer*
Dorn, Mary Ann *retired auditor*
Helzer, James Dennis *retired health facility administrator*
Johnson, Ursula Anne *artist*
Maupin, Michael Dennis *quality assurance professional*
Patten, Thomas Henry, Jr. *retired finance educator, personnel director*

Live Oak
Spilman, Janet Lynne *special education educator*

Livermore
Alder, Berni Julian *physicist, researcher*
Anastasio, Michael R. *science foundation director*

Bollinger, William Anthony *security specialist, educator*
Cook, Robert Crossland *chemist, researcher*
Cowgill, Donald Franklin *physicist*
Darter, Thomas Eugene, Jr. *composer, musician, writer*
Goodwin, Bruce T. *engineer*
Hah, Sang Soo *biomedical researcher*
Hallquist, John O. *engineering company executive*
Hiskes, Dolores G. *language educator*
Hooper, Edwin Bickford *physicist*
Johnson, Roy Ragnar *electrical engineer, researcher*
Kidder, Ray Edward *physicist, consultant*
King, Ray John *electrical engineering educator, engineering company executive*
Kirkwood, Robert Keith *applied physicist*
Leith, Cecil Eldon, Jr. *retired physicist*
Nuckolls, John Hopkins *physicist, researcher*
Radousky, Harry Brian *physicist*
Sack, Seymour *nuclear scientist*
Santer, Benjamin David *atmospheric scientist*
Shotts, Wayne J. *nuclear scientist, federal agency administrator*
Spiller, Eberhard Adolf *physicist, researcher*
Tarter, Curtis Bruce *physicist, science administrator*
Tripodes, James G. *nuclear safety and environmental regulatory affairs professional*
Weber, Stephen Vance *physics researcher*
Wilson, James Ricker *physicist, consultant*
Zalk, David Mark *industrial hygienist, occupational health researcher*

Livingston
Foster, Ron *agricultural products supplier and executive*

Lodi
Bernhoft, Franklin Otto *psychotherapist, psychologist*
Reinold, Christy Diane *school counselor, consultant*
Tan, Robert C. *music educator*

Loma Linda
Bailey, Leonard Lee *surgeon*
Behrens, Berel Lyn *physician, academic and health facility administrator*
Bull, Brian Stanley *pathologist, educator*
Chan, Philip J. *medical educator*
Cimpoeru, Petre *archivist, educator*
Coggin, Charlotte Joan *cardiologist, educator*
Condon, Stanley Charles *gastroenterologist*
Goodacre, Charles J. *dean, educator*
Herrmann, Paul C. *physician, chemist*
Kyle, James Lewis *dean, physician*
Lee, Sean S. *dentist, researcher*
Llaurado, Josep G. *nuclear medicine physician, researcher*
Llerandi Phipps, Carmen Guillermina *nutritionist and dietitian*
Longo, Lawrence Daniel *physiologist, obstetrician, gynecologist, educator*
Molnar, Violet *mental health nurse*
Pendergraft, Janice Gayle *volunteer*
Schwab, Ernest Roe III *physiology educator, researcher, academic administrator*
Slater, James Munro *radiation oncologist*
Slattery, Charles Wilbur *biochemistry educator*
Sorajjakool, Siroj *religious studies educator, psychology professor*
Strother, Allen *biochemical pharmacologist, researcher*
Taylor, Barry Llewellyn *microbiologist, educator*
Wareham, Ellsworth Edwin *cardiothoracic surgeon, educator*
Wood, Virchel Edgar *orthopedist, surgeon, educator*

Lomita
Balcom, Orville *engineer*
Welch, Lynne G. *language and music educator*

Lompoc
Bongiorno, James William *electronics executive*
Jack, Morgann Tayllor *writer, artist*
Lyra, Jon Robert *music educator, artist*
Means, James Andrew *retired engineer*
Wagner, Geraldine Marie *nursing educator, consultant*

Long Beach
Adkinson, Theodore H. *lawyer*
Adler, Jeffrey D. *media consultant, management consultant*
Alexander, F. King *academic administrator*
Alkana, Linda Kelly *history professor*
Baber, Walter Franklin *political science professor*
Barron, (Mary Lou) Slater *artist, retired educator*
Bauer, Roger Duane *chemistry professor, consultant*
Brown, Lester B. *social worker, educator*
Brown, Roxanne (Jerene Roxanne Brown) *sales executive*
Burnett, Ella M. Glenn *education educator*
Bursley, Kathleen A. *lawyer*
Calhoun, John R. *lawyer*
Chiou, Shiun-Kwei *medical researcher*
Cook, Karla Joan *elementary school educator*
Davies, Grace Lucille *real estate educator*
DelGaudio, Julian Joseph *history professor*
Deukmejian, George *lawyer, retired governor*
Dillon, Michael Earl *mechanical engineering executive, educator*
Duran, Matias Martin *retired adult education educator*
Elston, Joan Wilma *adult education educator, real estate agent*
Engle, Robert Irwin *music educator, translator*
Fiebert, Martin Stephen *psychology professor*
Fischler, Sandy Lynn *charitable and informational organization executive*
Fleming, Jane Williams *retired elementary school educator, writer*
Foster, Robert G. (Bob Foster) *mayor*
Halili, Antonio Marquez *facilities maintenance mechanic*
Hancock, John Walker III *banker*
Helwick, Christine *lawyer*
Higginson, John *retired career officer*
Hu, Chi Yu *retired physicist, educator*
Janssen, Maridith Annette *recreational therapist, educator*
Jeynes, William Hettich *education educator, religious organization administrator, minister*
Karentte, Betty *state legislator*
Kumar, Rajendra *electrical engineering educator*
Kwaan, Jack Hau Ming *retired physician*
Lathrop, Irvin Tunis *retired dean*
Lauda, Donald Paul *retired dean*
Levine, Arthur M. *law educator*
Macer, George Armen, Jr. *orthopedic hand surgeon*
Mathieu, Susan Leifer *recreational therapist, educator*
McGaughey, Charles Gilbert *retired biochemist*
Mills, Don Harper *pathology and psychiatry educator, lawyer*
Molina, Joseph Mario (Mario Molina) *medical administrator*
Monson, Dan *men's college basketball coach*
Moon, Hojin *mathematical statistician, educator*
Mullins Berg, Ruth Gladys *nurse*
Myers, John Wescott *air transportation executive*
Nguyen, Huong Tran *former elementary and secondary language educator, former district office administrator*
Papazian, George Ara *dentist*
Prince Crystal, Christina *minister, media specialist*
Proust, Joycelyn Ann *retired librarian*
Reed, Charles Bass *chief academic administrator*
Rutherford, Vicky Lynn *special education educator*
Sato, Eunice Noda *former mayor, consultant*
Schmidt, Eleanore *library director*
Schubel, Jerry Robert *marine scientist educator, dean*
Sidhwa, Frank N. *engineering executive*
Sinclitico, Dennis J. *lawyer*
Sosoka, John Richard *consulting firm executive, engineer*
Springer, Wilma Marie *retired elementary school educator*
Stanton, Julia A. *lawyer*
Viola, Bill *artist, writer*
Wagdy, Mahmoud F. *engineering educator*
Wise, George Edward *lawyer*
Wollmer, Richard Dietrich *statistics and operations research educator*
Worcester, Howard Lester *internist*
Wu, Sing-Yung *physician, researcher*
Yousef, Fathi Salaama *communications educator, management consultant*

Los Alamitos
Aberman, Harold Mark *veterinarian*
Eckelman, Richard Joel *engineering specialist*
Kirkpatrick, James Joseph *psychologist*
Weinberger, Frank *information management consultant*
Wu, Henry H. *urologist, surgeon*

Los Alamos
Daly, John T *research scientist*

Los Altos
Beer, Clara Louise Johnson *retired electronics executive*
Bergrun, Norman Riley *aerospace executive*
Carsten, Jack Craig *venture capitalist*
Collins, Gordon Dent *recording industry executive*
Fraknoi, Andrew *astronomer, educator*
King, Chi-Yu *research scientist*
Larson, Carol S. *foundation administrator, lawyer*
Marder, Janet *rabbi*
Michael, Harold Kaye (Bud Michael) *sales, marketing and operations executive*
Nivison, David Shepherd *language educator, philosopher*
Orman, Nanette Hector *psychiatrist*
Peterson, Victor Lowell *aerospace engineer, consultant*
Scifres, Donald Ray *finance company executive*
Sharpe, Roland Leonard *structural engineer, consultant*
Welsh, Doris McNeil *early childhood education specialist*
Wilbur, Colburn Sloan *foundation consultant, trustee, former executive*
Yang, Roxana Hwu *lawyer, investor*

Los Altos Hills
Archibeque, Charlene Paullin *retired music educator*
Fondahl, John Walker *civil engineering educator*

Los Angeles
Abbe, Alexander *lawyer*
Abdy, Pamela *film producer*
Abell, Nancy L. *lawyer*
Aberbach, Joel David *political science professor, writer*
Abich, Yvette M. *lawyer*
Abidi, Asad Ali *electrical engineer, educator*
Abrams, Norman *retired law educator, former academic administrator*
Abramson, Leslie Hope *lawyer*
Acain, Michael P. *lawyer*
Acosta, Maritoni A. *lawyer*
Adamek, Charles Andrew *lawyer*
Adams, Thomas Merritt *lawyer*
Adell, Hirsch *lawyer*
Adleman, Leonard M. *computer scientist, educator*
Adler, Erwin Ellery *lawyer*
Adler, Fred Peter *retired electronics company executive*
Adler, Michael I. *lawyer*
Adler, Robert L. *lawyer*
Adler, Sara *arbitrator, mediator*
Agnew, John A. *science educator*
Aguilar, Valentin G., II, *lawyer*
Ahrens, Mary Elizabeth *lawyer*
Alarcón, Arthur Lawrence *federal judge*
Alden, John W. *lawyer*
Alexander, Erika *actress*
Alkalay, Arie L. *pediatrician*
Alkon, Ellen Skillen *physician*
Allen, Michael John Bridgman *language educator*
Allen, Sharon *accounting firm executive*
Allen, Suzanne *financial planning executive, insurance agent, writer, educator*
Allen, Walter Recharde *sociology educator*
Allen, William Richard *retired economist*
Allred, Gloria Rachel *lawyer*
Alpers, Edward Alter *history professor*
Altman, Scott *law educator, dean*
Alvarado, Pablo *day laborer organizer, immigrant rights activist*
Álvarez, Rodolfo *sociology educator, consultant*
Aman, Kalley R. *lawyer*
Aminian Baghai, Arash *lawyer*
Amir, Michael M. *lawyer*
Anawalt, Patricia Rieff *anthropologist, researcher*
Andersen, Ronald Max *health services researcher, educator*
Anderson, John Edward *diversified holding company executive, lawyer*
Anderson, Joshua E. *lawyer*
Anderson, W. French (William French Anderson) *biochemist, physician, educator*
Angel, Arthur Ronald *lawyer, consultant*
Angeloff, Dann Valentino *brokerage house executive*
Anka, Paul *singer, composer*
Annaud, Jean-Jacques *film director, producer, scriptwriter*
Ansley, Julia E. *retired elementary school educator, poet, writer*
Antin, Michael *lawyer*
Aoki, Masanao *economics professor*
Apfel, Gary *lawyer*
Apple, Jacki (Jacqueline B.) *artist, educator, writer*
Apt, Charles *artist*
Apt, Leonard *physician*
Apuzzo, Michael Lawrence John *neurological surgeon*
Aranas, Pauline *law librarian, educator*
Arbisser, Aton *lawyer*
Arbit, Beryl Ellen *legal assistant*
Archerd, Army (Armand A. Archerd) *columnist, retired commentator*
Arenella, Peter Lee *law educator*
Armstrong, Lloyd, Jr. *academic administrator, physics professor*
Arnett, Will *actor*
Arney, Randall *artistic director*
Arnkra, Joe *legal administrator, writer*
Arnold, Dennis B. *lawyer*
Aronoff, Vera *law librarian*
Aronowitz, Joel Alan *plastic and reconstructive surgeon*
Aronson, Seth *lawyer*
Aronzon, Paul S. *lawyer*
Asperger, James *lawyer*
Atchley, Raymond Deval *technology company executive*
Austen, Karl Ramsdell *lawyer*
Avidan, Alon Y. *physician*
Azad, Susan Stott *lawyer*
Bacharach, Burt *composer, conductor*
Baer, Walter S. *think-tank executive*
Bahr, Ehrhard *Germanic languages and literature educator*
Bain, Conrad Stafford *actor*
Bakaly, Charles George, Jr. *lawyer, mediator*
Baker, Donald *literature educator*
Baker, Robert Frank *molecular biologist, educator*
Baker, Valerie L. *federal judge*
Banerjee, Utpal *biology professor, research scientist*
Banks, Tyra (Tyra Lynne Banks) *retired model, television personality*
Barberie, Jillian *newscaster, meteorologist*
Barker, Bob (Robert William Barker) *television personality*
Baron, Melvin Farrell *pharmacy educator*
Barrack, Thomas J., Jr. *real estate investor, lawyer*
Barren De Serres, Bruce Willard (H.R.H. The Duke Bruce Willard Barren de Serres) *merchant banker*
Barrett, Jane Hayes *lawyer*
Barron, Stephanie *curator*
Bart, Peter Benton *editor, film producer, writer*
Barth Menzies, Karen *lawyer*
Barton, Alan Joel *lawyer*
Barza, Harold A. *lawyer*
Basile, Paul Louis, Jr. *lawyer*
Bates, Marcia Jeanne *information scientist educator*
Battista, Richard *entertainment company executive*
Baum, Michael Lin *lawyer*
Baumann, Richard Gordon *lawyer*
Baumbach, Noah *screenwriter*
Baumgarten, Ronald Neal *lawyer*
Baylor, Elgin Gay *professional sports team executive and retired basketball player*
Beart, Robert W., Jr. *colon and rectal surgeon, educator*
Beatty, Ned *actor*
Beaver, James Norman, Jr., (Jim Beaver) *actor, writer*
Beck, (Beck Hansen) *musician, songwriter*
Begley, Ed, Jr. *actor*
Bekey, George Albert *computer scientist, educator*
Belkind, Elizabeth *chef*
Bell, Lee Phillip *television personality, producer*
Bell, William J., Jr. *television producer*
Beltramo, Michael Norman *management consultant*
Bender, Charles William *lawyer*
Bendiksen, Oddvar Olav *aerospace engineer, educator*
Bendix, Helen Irene *lawyer*
Bennett, Charles Franklin, Jr. *biogeographer, educator*
Bennis, Warren Gameliel *business administration educator*
Benson, Sidney William *chemistry researcher*
Berg, Yehuda *rabbi, author, television personality*
Berger, Albert *film producer*
Bergman, Emily Anne *librarian*
Bergman, Marilyn Keith *lyricist, writer*
Berk, Blair *lawyer*
Berman, Geoffrey Louis *diversified financial services company executive*
Berman, Myles Lee *lawyer*
Bernacchi, Richard Lloyd *lawyer*
Bernstein, Arthur Harold *venture capital executive*
Bernstein, Leslie *academic administrator, biostatistician, epidemiologist*
Bernstein, Sol *cardiologist, educator*
Bessman, Samuel Paul *pediatrician, educator, biochemist*
Beyer, Robert D. *corporate financial executive*
Bhaumik, Mani Lal *physicist*
Bibicoff, Hillary Sue *lawyer*
Bice, Scott Haas *dean, law educator*
Biele, Hugh Irving *retired lawyer*
Biggs, Jason *actor*
Binder, Gordon M. *venture capitalist*
Bing, Steve *film producer*
Bird, Terry W. *lawyer*
Birren, James Emmett *research and development company executive*
Bishop, Leah Margaret *lawyer*
Bitting, William M. *lawyer*
Black, Keith Lanier *neurosurgeon, educator*
Black, Lewis *comedian, actor*
Blahd, William Henry *nuclear medicine physician, director*
Blake, Rob *professional hockey player*
Blencowe, Paul Sherwood *lawyer, private investor*
Bloch, Paul *public relations executive*
Bloom, Claire *actress*
Bloomberg, Coe Arthur *lawyer*
Blue, Violet (Ada Mae Johnson) *blogger*
Blumberg, Grace Ganz *lawyer, educator*
Bobbitt, Leroy *lawyer*
Bodey, Bela *immunologist, pathologist, oncologist*
Bodkin, Henry Grattan, Jr. *lawyer*
Boehm, Barry William *computer science educator*
Bogen, Andrew E. *lawyer*
Bohle, Sue *public relations executive*
Boime, Albert Isaac *art historian, educator*
Boles, Richard Gregory *clinical geneticist, researcher*
Bondareff, William *psychiatrist, educator*
Bonesteel, Michael John *lawyer*
Bonner, Robert Cleve *lawyer*
Bordy, Michael Jeffrey *lawyer*
Borenstein, Daniel Bernard *psychiatrist, educator*
Borsting, Jack Raymond *business administration educator*
Bosley, Tom *actor*
Boswell, James Douglas *medical research executive*
Bottjer, David John *earth science and biology educator*
Bowers, Terree A. *lawyer*
Boxer, Lester *lawyer*
Boyce, David S. *lawyer*
Boyd, Malcolm *minister, writer*
Boyer, Paul D. *biochemist, educator*
Boyle, Barbara Dorman *film company executive*
Boyle, Kevin Richard *lawyer*
Boyter, Cale *film company executive*
Brackmann, Derald E. *otolaryngologist*
Bradley, Lawrence D., Jr. *lawyer*
Bradshaw, Murray Charles *musicologist, educator*
Branca, John Gregory *lawyer, consultant*
Brand, Michael *museum director*
Brandler, Jonathan M. *lawyer*
Brandt, William Arthur, Jr. *consulting executive*
Bratton, William J. *police chief, former commissioner*
Braun, Harland W. *lawyer*
Braunstein, Glenn David *physician, educator*
Brendel, Bettina *abstract artist*
Breslow, Lester *public health physician, educator*
Bressan, Paul Louis *lawyer*
Breuer, Stephen Ernest *religious organization administrator, consultant*
Brewer, David L. III *school system administrator, retired military officer*
Brian, Brad D. *lawyer*
Brill, Laura W. *lawyer*
Bringardner, John Michael *lawyer, clergyman*
Broad, Eli *foundation administrator, art collector*
Brolin, James (James Brunderlin) *actor*
Brown, Jason Robert *composer, arranger*
Brown, Jim *investment company executive*
Brown, Kathleen *diversified financial services company executive*
Brown, Kwame *professional basketball player*
Brown, Michael K. *lawyer*
Brown, Pat Crawford *actress*
Bruce, William A. *airport executive*
Brusa, Amilcar *boxing trainer*
Bryan, Greyson *lawyer*
Bryan, Karen Smith *lawyer*
Bryant, Taimie L. *law educator*
Buffington, Gary Lee Roy *safety engineer, construction executive*
Bufford, Samuel Lawrence *federal judge*
Bugliosi, Vincent T. *lawyer*

Buonemani, James Paul *church musician, director, composer*
Burch, Robert Dale *lawyer*
Burcham, David W. *law educator*
Burke, Robert Bertram *lawyer, political scientist, lobbyist*
Burke, Yvonne Watson Brathwaite (Mrs. William A. Burke) *lawyer*
Burnett, T-Bone (Henry John Burnett) *music producer, musician*
Burten, Barry Lee *lawyer*
Burton, Brian Joseph (Danger Mouse) *sound recording engineer, musician*
Burton, Tim (Timothy William Burton) *film director, film producer*
Bush, Wesley G. *aerospace transportation executive*
Bustamante, Cruz M. *former lieutenant governor*
Butcher, Larry L. *neuroscientist, educator*
Buter, Irwin *lawyer*
Byrd, Christine Waterman Swent *lawyer*
Byrnes, James Bernard *museum director, consultant*
Caine, Michael *actor*
Calabrese, Joseph A. *lawyer*
Campbell, Christian Bethune *actor*
Campion, Robert Thomas *manufacturing executive*
Capron, Alexander Morgan *lawyer, educator, bioethicist*
Caram, Eve La Salle *language educator, writer*
Carey, Stevens Anthony *lawyer*
Carleson, Lennart A.E. (Lennart Axel Edvard Carleson) *mathematics professor*
Carlson, Robert Edwin *lawyer*
Carlton, John L. *lawyer*
Caroompas, Carole Jean *artist, educator*
Carr, Willard Zeller, Jr. *retired lawyer*
Carrey, Neil *lawyer, educator*
Carrillo, Elpidia *actress*
Carroll, Pete *college football coach*
Casamassima, Christopher T. *lawyer*
Cassavetes, Nick *film director, actor*
Cassell, Samuel James *professional basketball player*
Castro, Leonard Edward *lawyer*
Cate, Jan Harris *lawyer*
Cates, Gilbert *television and film producer, theater director*
Catlin, Don H. *molecular pharmacologist, educator*
Cecere, Domenico *homebuilding company executive*
Cee-Lo, (Thomas DeCarlo Callaway) *singer*
Cermak, John Frank, Jr. *lawyer*
Chambers, Justin *actor*
Champagne, Duane Willard *sociology educator*
Champlin, Charles Davenport *television personality, critic, writer*
Chan, David Ronald *tax specialist, lawyer*
Chan, Thomas Tak-Wah *lawyer*
Chandor, Stebbins Bryant *pathologist*
Chang, Henry C. *library administrator*
Chang, Jane P. *chemical engineering educator*
Chapman Collins, Janice *school system administrator*
Charen, Mona *columnist*
Charisse, Cyd (Tula Ellice Finklea) *actress, dancer*
Charney, Dov *apparel executive*
Chavez, Victor Edwin *judge*
Chazen, Stephen I. *oil industry executive*
Cheeseboro, Margrit *retired economics educator*
Chen, Tony F. *mathematics professor, dean*
Cheng, Hong *library and information scientist*
Cheng, Tsen-Chung *electrical engineering educator*
Chernin, Peter F. *multimedia company executive*
Cherry, James Donald *pediatrician*
Cheung, Sheri T. *lawyer*
Chiate, Kenneth Reed *lawyer*
Cho, Eung-Rae (Brian) *bank executive*
Chobotov, Vladimir Alexander *aerospace engineer, educator*
Choi, Myong Yong *chemist, researcher*
Chopra, Inder Jit *endocrinologist*
Choudhury, Bikram *yoga instructor, writer, entrepreneur*
Christol, Carl Quimby *lawyer, political science professor*
Christopher, Warren Minor *lawyer, former secretary of state*
Chu, Chi-Cheng *research scientist*
Chu, Morgan *lawyer*
Chu, Robert Lance *physician*
Chui, Chi On *electrical engineer, educator*
Chung, Tong Soo *lawyer*
Chuong, Cheng-Ming *pathologist, educator*
Churgin, Amy *publishing executive*
Clair, John J., Jr. *lawyer*
Clark, Burton Robert *sociologist, educator*
Clark, Irene L. *literature and language professor*
Clark, R(ufus) Bradbury *lawyer, director*
Clarke, Peter *communications and health educator*
Clarke, Steven Gerard *chemistry professor*
Cleary, William Joseph, Jr. *lawyer*
Clemente, Carmine Domenic *anatomist, educator*
Clow, Lee *advertising agency executive*
Coates, Thomas J. *medical association administrator*
Cochran, Steve *lawyer*
Cohee, Kevin *bank executive*
Cohen, Cynthia Marylyn *lawyer*
Cohen, S(tephen) Marshall *philosophy educator*
Colacurcio, Michael J. *English professor*
Cole, Carolyn *photojournalist*
Cole, K.C. *journalist, writer*
Cole, William Louis *lawyer*
Coleman, Paul Jerome, Jr. *physicist, researcher*
Coleman Smith, Salaam *communications executive*
Colletti, Ned *professional sports team executive*
Collier, Anna *photographer*
Collier, Charles Arthur, Jr. *lawyer*
Collins, Audrey B. *judge*
Concoff, Gary O. *lawyer*
Cong, Jason Jingsheng *computer scientist, educator, consultant, researcher*
Conley, Mark A. *lawyer*
Connor-Dominguez, Billie Marie *science information professional*
Cook, Ian Ainsworth *psychiatrist, researcher, educator*
Cook, Melanie K. *lawyer*
Cooley, Steve *prosecutor*
Cooper, Chris *actor*
Cooper, Michael Jerome *professional basketball coach and former player*
Cooper, Robert E. *lawyer*
Cora, Cat *chef*
Cordova, Richard D. *hospital administrator*
Corman, Julie Ann *producer, director*
Corman, Roger William *film director*
Cornwall, John Michael *physics professor, consultant*
Coroniti, Ferdinand Vincent *physics and astronomy professor*
Corwin, Norman *scriptwriter, film producer, film director*
Cote, Richard James *pathologist, researcher*
Coupe, James Warnick *lawyer*
Couturier, Darrel J. *art dealer, director*
Cowan, Marie Jeanette *dean, nurse, educator*
Cox, Brian *actor*
Crabtree-Ireland, Duncan *lawyer*
Craft, Cheryl Mae *neurobiologist, anatomist, researcher*
Crampon, Jean Elaine *librarian*
Crawford, Marc *professional hockey coach*
Crockett, Donald Harold *composer, music educator*
Crombie, Douglass Darnill *aerospace communications system engineer*
Crosby, Peter Alan *management consultant*
Crumm, Max (Aaron Maximillian Crumm) *actor*
Cuadra, Carlos Albert *library and information scientist, consultant*
Curran, Darryl Joseph *photographer, educator*
Curtiss, Thomas, Jr. *lawyer*
Cushman, John C. III *real estate company executive*
Cyrus, Billy Ray *country music performer, actor*
Dabrowska, Dorota Maria *statistician, educator*
D'Accone, Frank Anthony *music educator*
Daly, Heather Eileen *toxicologist*
Daly, Robert Anthony *international relief organization, former professional sports team and film company executive*
Dane, Eric *actor*
D'Angelo Melby, Donna Marie *lawyer*
Daniels, Gregory Martin *screenwriter*
Daniels, John Peter *lawyer*
Daniels, William David (Bill Daniels) *actor*
Danoff, Dudley Seth *surgeon, urologist*
Danziger, Bruce Edward *structural engineer*
Dapkus, Paul D. *engineering educator*
Darby, G(eorge) Harrison *lawyer*
Darby, Michael Rucker *economist, educator*
Darden, Christopher Allen *lawyer, actor, writer*
Dastin, Barry L. *lawyer*
Daum, John F. *lawyer*
Davidson, Ezra C., Jr. *obstetrician, gynecologist, academic administrator, educator*
Davis, Gray (Joseph Graham Davis) *lawyer, former governor*
Davis, John A. *film producer*
Davis-Fernandes, Tina Denise *secondary school educator, coach*
Day, Robert Addison, Jr. *investment management company executive*
Dayton, Sky *telecommunications company executive*
De Brier, Donald Paul *lawyer, oil industry executive*
DeCarlo, John T. *lawyer*
de Castro, Hugo Daniel *lawyer*
Decker, Richard Jeffrey *lawyer*
Dee, Ruby (Ruby Dee Davis) *actress, writer, film director*
Dekmejian, Richard Hrair *political science professor*
De La Hoya, Oscar *boxer*
Delaney, Matthew Sylvester *mathematics professor, academic administrator*
De Larios, Dora *artist*
de la Rocha, Castulo *health services executive*
Delgadillo, Rockard J. (Rocky Delgadillo) *lawyer*
Del Toro, Benicio *actor*
Delugach, Albert Lawrence *journalist*
DeMann, Freddy *film, play and television producer*
Demick, Barbara *journalist*
Demoff, Marvin Alan *lawyer*
Dempsey, Patrick *actor*
Denham, Robert Edwin *lawyer, investment company executive*
Denson, Nikkole *film producer, company executive*
dePaolis, Potito Umberto *food company executive*
De Robertis, Edward M. F. *research scientist, educator*
Detels, Roger *epidemiologist, retired dean*
Devereux, Mara *sculptor, artist*
Dewey, Donald Odell *dean, academic administrator*
Dhir, Vijay K. *mechanical engineering educator*
Diamond, Jared Mason *biologist, writer*
Diamond, Jason Brett *facial plastic surgeon, otolaryngologist*
Diamond, Stanley Jay *lawyer*
Diaz, Maria G. *lawyer*
Didkovsky, Leonid V. *engineer*
Diehl, Dolores *performing company executive*
Dienes, Louis Robert *lawyer*
DiMeglio, David J. *lawyer*
Dinel, Richard Henry *lawyer*
Dixon, Patrick Richard *prosecutor*
Dodd, Jan Eve *lawyer*
Dolan, Mary Anne *journalist, columnist*
Doll, Lynne Marie *public relations agency executive*
Don, Manuel *medical researcher*
Donaldson, Michael Cleaves *lawyer*
Donovan, John Arthur *lawyer*
Dorff, Elliot *rabbi*
Dorfman, William M. *dentist*
Dorman, Albert A. *engineering executive, consultant, architect*
Dorrell, Karl *college football coach*
Dows, David Alan *chemistry professor*
Dr. Dre, (Andre Young) *rapper, record producer*
Drooyan, Richard E. *lawyer*
Dr. Phil, (Phillip Calvin McGraw) *psychologist, television personality*
Dudziak, Mary Louise *law educator*
Duke, Margaret Joyce *sound recordist, broadcast engineer*
Dumitrescu, Domnita *Spanish language educator, researcher*
Dummett, Clifton Orrin *dentist, educator*
DuMont, James Kelton, Jr. *actor, theater producer*
Dunham, Scott H. *lawyer*
Dunleavy, Michael Joseph, Sr. *professional basketball coach*
Dunn, Bruce Sidney *materials scientist, educator*
Duritz, Adam *musician*
Dworsky, Daniel Leonard *architect, educator*
Dwyre, William Patrick *journalist*
Eatman, Louis Perkins *lawyer*
Eckhart, Aaron *actor*
Edelman, Scott Alan *lawyer*
Edgerton, Bradford Wheatly *plastic surgeon*
Edmonds, Tracey E. *film company executive*
Edwards, Blake *film director*
Edween, Julie *plastic surgeon*
Efron, Zac *actor, singer*
Eisenstein, Edward Milton *psychologist, physiologist, radiologist, educator*
Eley, Hunter R. *lawyer*
Ellenbogen, Richard *plastic surgeon*
Ellickson, Bryan Carl *economics professor*
Ellingsen, Richard D. *lawyer*
Ellis, James G. *dean, finance educator*
Elrod, Lu *music educator, actress*
Elswit, Robert *cinematographer*
Emigh, Rebecca Jean *social sciences educator*
Engel, Jerome, Jr. *neurologist, neuroscientist, psychiatry professor*
Engel, William King *neurologist, educator*
Engvall, Bill *comedian, actor*
Enstrom, James Eugene *epidemiologist*
Eo, SuRak *plastic surgeon, educator*
Erdos, Joanna E. *school counselor, secondary school educator*
Erichsen, Peter Christian *foundation administrator*
Estrich, Susan Rachel *law educator*
Estrin, Deborah Lynn *computer engineer, educator*
Etessami, Hirbod (Hiri Etessami) *endodontist, educator*
Ettenger, Robert Bruce *physician, pediatric nephrologist*
Evans, Gregory Hinojosa *lawyer*
Ezer, Mitchel J. *lawyer*
Faber, George Donald *retired communications executive*
Fairbank, Robert Harold *lawyer*
Fairchild, Morgan (Patsy McClenny) *actress*
Fanselow, Michael Scott *psychology professor*
Farias-Eisner, Robin P. *gynecologic oncologist, educator*
Farmer, Robert Lindsay *lawyer*
Farrell, Joseph *film producer and company executive, financial analyst, writer, sculptor*
Fathpour, Sasan *optical engineer, researcher*
Feig, Stephen Arthur *pediatrician, preventive medicine physician, hematologist, oncologist, educator*
Feigen, Brenda S. *lawyer, film producer, writer*
Fein, Irving Ashley *television and motion picture executive*
Fein, Ronald Lawrence *lawyer*
Feinstein, Michael Jay *singer, pianist, musicologist, actor*
Feldman, Larry Robert *lawyer*
Feldman, Lewis G. *lawyer*
Feldman, Robert C. (Bob) *public relations executive*
Feng, Lei *medical researcher*
Fenning, Lisa Hill *lawyer, mediator, retired judge*
Ferrera, America Georgine *actress*
Fickett, Edward Hale *architect, educator, arbitrator*
Field, Ted (Frederick) *film company and recording industry executive*
Fielding, Jonathan Evan *city health department administrator, pediatrician*
Fields, Bertram Harris *lawyer*
Fields, Henry Michael *lawyer*
Figlin, Robert Alan *hematologist, oncologist*
Fincher, Edgar Franklin *dermatologic surgeon*
Findley, John Allen, Jr. *publishing executive*
Finegold, Sydney Martin *microbiology educator*
Finkel, Evan *lawyer*
Finnegan, Michael J. *lawyer*
Firstenberg, Jean Picker *film institute executive*
Fischer, Alfred George *geology educator*
Fisher, Barry Alan *lawyer*
Fitz-Carter, Aleane *retired elementary school educator, composer*
Flagel, Mark Alan *lawyer*
Flanagan, Fionnula Manon *actress, writer, theater director*
Flanigan, James J(oseph) *journalist*
Fleer, Keith George *lawyer, film company executive*
Fleischmann, Ernest Martin *performing arts executive, consultant*
Fleming, Macklin *retired judge*
Floyd, Tim *men's college basketball coach, former professional basketball coach*
Fodor, Peter Bela *plastic surgeon, educator*
Foley, Martin James *lawyer*
Follick, Edwin Duane *law educator, dean, chiropractor*
Fongwa, Marie Ngetiko *nurse midwife*
Fonkalsrud, Eric Walter *pediatric surgeon, educator*
Forness, Steven Robert *educational psychologist*
Forrester, James Stuart *cardiologist, medical educator*
Foster, Sutton *actress*
Frackman, Russell Jay *lawyer*
Fragner, Matthew Charles *lawyer*
Franceschi, Ernest Joseph, Jr. *lawyer*
Francis, Charles K. *medical educator*
Frank, Peter Solomon *art historian, curator, critic*
Franz, Dennis *actor*
Fredericks, Beverly Magnuson *artist*
Fredman, Howard S. *lawyer*
Freehling, Allen Isaac *rabbi*
Freier, Elliot G. *lawyer*
Frimmer, Paul Norman *lawyer*
Fulco, Armand John *biochemist*
Furcal, Rafael *professional baseball player*
Futami, Norman *lawyer*
Gabriel, Ronald Samuel *child neurologist*
Gabriel, Stuart A. *real estate professor, director*
Gallo, Jon Joseph *lawyer*
Galton, Stephen Harold *lawyer*
Ganas, Perry Spiros *physicist*
Ganz, Patricia Anne *medical educator, physician*
Garbacz, Gregory A. *lawyer*
Garcia, Andrew Bernard *chemical engineer*
Garciaparra, Nomar (Anthony Nomar Garciaparra) *professional baseball player*
Garrett, Elizabeth *law educator, academic administrator*
Garrett, Spencer *actor, writer, director*
Gasich, Welko Elton *retired aerospace defense executive, management consultant*
Gasparetti, Lorenzo E. *lawyer*
Gasson, Judith C. *research scientist*
Gatti, Richard A. *medical educator, medical geneticist*
Gaviola, Karen Z. *television director*
Gehry, Frank Owen *architect*
Geller, Kenneth Allen *otolaryngologist*
Geller, Stephen Arthur *pathologist, educator*
Gengaro, Christine Lee *music educator*
Geoffrion, Arthur Minot *management scientist*
Geragos, Mark John *lawyer*
Gest, Howard David *lawyer*
Gewertz, Bruce Labe *surgeon, educator*
Ghez, Andrea Mia *astronomy and physics educator*
Gianopulos, Jim *film company executive*
Giffin, Margaret Ethel (Peggy Giffin) *management consultant*
Gifford, Kathie Lee *television personality, vocalist*
Gilbertson, John T. *lawyer*
Gilligan, Thomas W. *dean, finance educator*
Gilman, John Joseph *research scientist*
Girard, Robert David *lawyer*
Girardi, Thomas Vincent *lawyer*
Glazer, Michael *lawyer*
Glazier, Kenneth M. *lawyer*
Goedde, Alan George *financial company executive*
Goin, Marcia Kraft *physician*
Gold, Jonathan *restaurant critic, columnist*
Goldberg, Herb *psychologist, educator*
Goldberg, Robert B. *molecular biologist, educator*
Golden, Arthur *writer*
Goldman, Allan Bailey *lawyer*
Goldman, Benjamin Edward *lawyer*
Goldman, Donald Aaron *lawyer*
Goldman, Joel A. *lawyer*
Goldsman, Melvin Saul *lawyer*
Goldstein, Robert David *law educator*
Golomb, Solomon Wolf *mathematician, electrical engineer, director, educator*
Gondry, Michel *film director*
Gonick, Harvey Craig *nephrologist, educator*
Goo, Valerie M. *lawyer*
Good, Edith Elissa (Pearl Williams) *writer*
Goodman, Max A. *lawyer, educator*
Goodwin, Scott Craig *interventional radiologist*
Gordon, Allen Barry *musician, composer*
Gordon, Basil *retired mathematics professor*
Gordon, David *writer, educator*
Gordon, Malcolm Stephen *biology professor*
Gordon, Mark, II, *film producer*
Gores, Alec E. *venture capitalist*
Gorman, Joseph Gregory, Jr. *lawyer*
Gorney, Roderic *psychiatrist, educator*
Gosling, Ryan (Ryan Thomas Gosling) *actor*
Goss, Kent *lawyer*
Gothold, Stuart Eugene *school system administrator, education educator*
Gottfried, Ira Sidney *management consulting executive*
Gould, David *lawyer*
Gould, Elliott *actor*
Govan, Michael *museum director*
Grammer, Kelsey *actor*
Graves, Anna Marie *lawyer*
Gray, Jan Charles *lawyer, business owner*
Gray, Jeremy J.F. *lawyer*
Greaves, John Allen *lawyer*
Green, William Porter *lawyer*
Greenberg, Barry Michael *talent executive*
Greenberg, Gordon Alan *lawyer*
Greenberger, Martin *biotechnologist, information scientist, educator*
Grinnan, Katie *artist*
Grinnell, Alan Dale *neuroscientist, educator*
Grobe, Charles Stephen *lawyer, accountant*
Grode, Susan A. *lawyer*
Grody, Wayne William *physician, educator*
Gronnier, Henry Maurice *violinist, educator*
Gross, Allen Jeffrey *lawyer*
Gross, Larry Paul *communications educator*
Gross, Lee *chef*
Grossman, Steven L. *lawyer*
Grotjahn, Mark *painter*

McLurkin, Thomas Cornelius, Jr. *lawyer*
McNevin, Christopher J. *lawyer*
McQueen, Justice Ellis (L. Q. Jones) *actor, television director*
McRee, Lisa *television host, producer*
Meaders, Donald W. *lawyer*
Meer, Jon Douglas *lawyer*
Meisinger, Louis M. *lawyer*
Melby, Donna D. *lawyer*
Mellinkoff, Sherman Mussoff *medical educator*
Mellor, Ronald John *history professor*
Melnick, Michael *geneticist, educator*
Mendel, Jerry Marc *electrical engineering educator*
Mendoza, Ron *chef*
Mentzer, Roslyn *academic administrator*
Merwine, David Karl *neurophysiologist, educator*
Mesereau, Thomas Arthur, Jr. *lawyer*
Meshki, Hamed *lawyer*
Metzger, Robert Streicher *lawyer*
Meyer, Bruce D. *lawyer*
Meyer, Catherine Dieffenbach *lawyer*
Meyer, Michael Edwin *lawyer*
Mezger, Jeffrey T. *construction executive*
Michaelson, Jon *lawyer*
Michel, Gregg L. *cruise line executive*
Midler, Laurence H. (Larry) *lawyer*
Mihan, Richard *retired dermatologist*
Milchan, Arnon *film producer*
Miles, Jack (John Russiano) *journalist, educator*
Millard, Neal Steven *lawyer, educator*
Miller, Milton Allen *lawyer*
Miller, Timothy Alden *plastic and reconstructive surgeon*
Min, Soo Bong *bank executive*
Minkova, Donka *language educator*
Minor, Rickey *composer, television producer, music director*
Mintz, Marshall Gary *lawyer*
Miranda, M. Jeanne *psychiatrist*
Miscavige, David *head of religious order*
Mobley, Cuttino Rashawn *professional basketball player*
Mock, Theodore Jaye *finance educator*
Modabber, Zia F. *lawyer*
Moe, Stanley Allen *architect, consultant*
Mohr, Anthony James *judge*
Mohr, John Luther *biologist, environmental consultant*
Molina, Gloria *municipal official*
Mondino, Bartly J. *ophthalmologist*
Montoya, Velma *economist, consultant*
Moor, Carl H. *lawyer*
Moore, Shemar *actor*
More, Philip Harvey Birnbaum *business administration educator*
Moreno, Rita (Rosita Dolores Alverio) *actress*
Morgan, Elizabeth *plastic surgeon*
Morgan, Marshall T. *emergency physician*
Morgenthaler-Lever, Alisa *lawyer*
Morgner, Aurelius *economist, educator*
Moriuchi, K. Derek *secondary school educator*
Morrell, Ernest Davis *literature and language professor*
Morrissey, J. Richard *lawyer*
Morrow, Margaret M. *lawyer, judge*
Morrow, Winston Vaughan *financial executive*
Morton, Joe *actor*
Mosich, Anelis Nick *accountant, writer, educator, consultant*
Mosk, Richard Mitchell *judge*
Moskowitz, Joel Steven *lawyer*
Moss, Jerome (Jerry) S. *recording industry executive*
Motykie, Gary *plastic surgeon*
Moxley, John Howard III *internist*
MoY, Ronald Leonard *dermasurgeon*
Mueller, Carl Richard *theater arts educator, author*
Muldaur, Diana Charlton *actress*
Muntz, Eric Phillip *aerospace and mechanical engineering educator, consultant*
Murdock, David H. *food products executive*
Murphree, A. Linn *ophthalmologist*
Murphy, Elaine (Frances Elaine Murphy) *musician, harpist, flutist*
Murray, Alice Pearl *data processing company executive*
Murray, Anthony *lawyer*
Myers, Albert F. *aerospace executive*
Myrth, Judy G. *editor*
Nachshin, Robert Jay *lawyer*
Nadler, Gerald *management consultant, educator*
Nakanishi, Don Toshiaki *Asian American studies educator, writer*
Nakra, Tanuj *plastic surgeon*
Natale, Ronald Bruno *oncologist*
Nazarian, Sam *film producer*
Needleman, Jack *education educator, researcher*
Neelin, J. David *meteorologist, educator*
Neely, Sally Schultz *lawyer*
Neiter, Gerald Irving *lawyer*
Nelson, Howard Joseph *geographer, educator*
Nelson, James Augustus, II, *real estate company executive, architect*
Nelson, Larry Dean *telecommunications and computer systems company executive, consultant*
Nelson, Marvin Dale, Jr. *radiologist, educator*
Neufeld, Elizabeth Fondal *biochemist, educator*
Neutra, Dion *architect*
Newhart, Bob (George Robert Newhart) *entertainer*
Newman, David Wheeler *lawyer*
Newman, Gary *broadcast executive*
Newman, Michael Rodney *lawyer*
Newman, Richard G. *engineering company executive*
Newton, Jim *editor*
Ng, Kim (Kimberly J. Ng) *professional sports team executive*
Nicholas, William Richard *lawyer*
Nicholson, Jack *actor*
Nikias, Chrysostomos L. (Max Nikias) *engineering educator*
Niles, John Gilbert *lawyer*
Nilles, John Mathias (Jack Nilles) *futurist*
Nilles, Laila Padorr *musician, music company executive*
Nimni, Marcel Ephraim *biochemistry educator*
Nissenson, Allen Richard *physician, educator*
Nobe, Ken *chemical engineering professor*
Noble, Douglas *architecture educator*
Noble, Ernest Pascal *pharmacologist, biochemist, educator, psychiatrist*
Noble, James Wilkes *actor*
Nobumoto, Karen S. *prosecutor*
Noce, Walter William, Jr. *hospital administrator*
Nochimson, David *lawyer*
Nogales, Luis Guerrero *investment company executive*
Noguchi, Thomas Tsunetomi *writer, pathologist*
Norris, Edwin L. *lawyer*
Norris, William Albert *lawyer, mediator, retired judge*
North, Oliver Laurence (Ollie North) *syndicated columnist, retired military officer*
Nottage, James H. *museum administrator, curator, historian*
Nuechterlein, Keith H. *psychology professor*
Nugent, Gary W. *lawyer*
Oakes, Jeannine *education educator*
Oberstein, Norman S. *lawyer*
O'Brien, Robert Charles *lawyer*
Ochoa, Arthur J. *lawyer, hospital administrator*
O'Connell, Kevin *lawyer*
O'Donnell, Pierce Henry *lawyer*
Ogilvie, Lloyd John *clergyman*
Oh, Angela E. *lawyer*
Ohlmeyer, Donald Winfred, Jr. *film and television producer*
Okrent, David *engineering educator*
Olah, George Andrew *chemist, educator*
Oldman, Gary *actor*
O'Leary, Prentice Lee *retired lawyer*
Olian, Judy D. *dean*
Olivas, Daniel Anthony *lawyer*
Oliver, Dale Hugh *lawyer*
Olivier, Kathy Ricks *college basketball coach*
Olsen, Frances Elisabeth *law educator, theorist*
Olson, Ronald Leroy *lawyer*
O'Neil, Harold Francis *psychologist, educator*
O'Neill, Russell Richard *engineering educator*
Oppenheim, Charles B. *lawyer*
Oppenheimer, Randy (Mark Randall Oppenheimer) *lawyer*
Ordin, Andrea Sheridan *lawyer*
Orme, Antony Ronald *geography educator*
O'Shea, James E. *editor-in-chief*
Osher, Stanley Joel *mathematician, researcher*
Ostroff, Peter I. *lawyer*
Owen, Michael Lee *lawyer*
Oyeyipo, Bolanle T. *geriatrician*
Ozcan, Aydogan *electrical engineer, educator*
Pachino, Barton P. *lawyer*
Palevsky, Max *industrialist, director*
Palmer, Charles Francis *lawyer*
Palmer, James F. *aerospace transportation executive*
Palmer, Keke (Lauren Keyana Palmer) *actress*
Palmieri, Victor Henry *lawyer, director, investment advisor*
Panish, Brian Joseph *lawyer*
Papadopoulos, John K. *archaeology educator*
Parente, Robert Bruce *electrical engineer, consultant*
Park, Lee (Lee Parklee) *artist*
Park, No-Hee *dean, academic administrator*
Parks, Michael Christopher *journalist, educator*
Parmelee, Arthur Hawley, Jr. *pediatric medical educator*
Parsky, Gerald Lawrence *lawyer*
Parsons, Terence Dwight *linguist, educator*
Pascotto, Alvaro *lawyer*
Pasich, Kirk Alan *lawyer*
Patrick, Robert *playwright*
Patron, Susan Hall *librarian, writer*
Paulson, Donald Robert *chemistry professor*
Pearl, Judea *computer scientist, educator*
Peel, Mark *chef, restaurant owner*
Peng, Weimin *biochemist, molecular biologist*
Penn, Sean *actor*
Penny, Brad (Bradley Wayne Penny) *professional baseball player*
Perkins, William Clinton *manufacturing executive*
Perlis, Michael Fredrick *lawyer*
Perrine, Richard Leroy *environmental engineer, educator*
Perron, Edward Adrian *lawyer*
Perry, Ralph Barton III *lawyer*
Pesta, Ben W., II, *lawyer, writer*
Petak, William John *systems management educator*
Peterson, Kurt C. *lawyer*
Peterson, Linda S. *lawyer*
Petrocelli, Daniel M. *lawyer*
Petroff, Laura R. *lawyer*
Phelps, Barton Chase *architect, educator*
Philbin, Ann *art facility director*
Phillips, Geneva Ficker *academic editor*
Phillips, Keith Wendall *minister*
Phillips, Stacy D. *lawyer*
Phoenix, Joaquin Raphael *actor*
Pi, Edmond Hsin-Tung *psychiatry educator*
Pickens, James T., Jr. *actor*
Pierskalla, William Peter *dean, finance, engineering educator*
Piller, Charles Leon *journalist*
Pircher, Leo Joseph *lawyer, director*
Pittman, Amanda Nelson *music educator*
Piuze, Michael Joseph *lawyer*
Plate, Thomas Gordon *columnist, educator*
Plath, Kathrin *biology professor, biomedical researcher*
Poa, Li *cardiac surgeon*
Poindexter, William Mersereau *lawyer*
Poledna, Mathias *video artist*
Pollock, John Phleger *lawyer*
Port, Sidney Charles *mathematician, educator*
Porter, John E. *lawyer*
Porter, Verna Louise *lawyer*
Powell, James Lawrence *educational association administrator, museum director, geologist*
Power, John Bruce *lawyer*
Prager, Susan Westerberg *academic administrator, law educator*
Preonas, George Elias *lawyer*
Presant, Sanford Calvin *lawyer, educator, writer, tax specialist*
Prewitt, Jean *not-for-profit organization executive*
Price, William Charlie *lawyer*
Priselac, Thomas M. *health facility executive, educator*
Pritzker, Jean *film producer*
Pugsley, Robert Adrian *law educator*
Qiao, Jian-Hua *pathologist, researcher*
Quicksilver, William Todd *lawyer*
Quinlan, Catherine *university librarian*
Quinn, John B. *lawyer*
Quinn, John J. *lawyer*
Rabinovitz, Joel *lawyer, educator*
Racine, Scott H. *lawyer*
Racklin, Barbara Cohen *fundraising consultant*
Raeder, Myrna Sharon *lawyer, educator*
Rafeedie, Edward *federal judge*
Rakow, Jay *lawyer, film company executive*
Raksin, Alex *reporter, writer*
Ramanathan, Rangasamy *pediatrician*
Ramer, Lawrence Jerome *corporation executive*
Ramo, Simon *retired engineering executive*
Ramos, Jorge *newscaster*
Rando, John *theater director*
Rao, Narsing A. *ophthalmologist, pathologist, educator*
Rappeport, Ira J. *lawyer*
Rasmussen, Robert Kenneth *dean, law educator*
Rath, Howard Grant, Jr. *lawyer*
Ratzenberger, John Deszo *actor, writer, film director*
Raven, Bertram H(erbert) *psychology professor*
Ray, Gilbert T. *lawyer*
Reddick, C.N. (Frank)lin III *lawyer*
Reed, Irving Stoy *electrical engineer*
Reeves, Barbara Ann *lawyer*
Reilly, Kevin *broadcast executive*
Reinisch, John Ferdinand *plastic surgeon, educator*
Reinman, Glenn D. *computer scientist, educator*
Reisman, Ellen Kelly *lawyer*
Reiss, Howard *chemistry professor*
Renwick, Edward S. *lawyer*
Resnick, Lynda *corporate financial executive*
Resnick, Stewart Allen *diversified company executive*
Reuben, Don Harold *lawyer*
Reyes Robbins, Ann Marie *lawyer, researcher, educator, former magistrate judge*
Reynolds, Burt *actor, film director*
Reynolds, Charles Patrick *pediatric oncologist, researcher*
Rice, Regina Kelly *marketing executive*
Rice, Thomas Howard *healthcare educator*
Rich, Alan *music critic, writer*
Rich, Andrea Louise *museum administrator*
Richards, Eric Albert Stephan *lawyer*
Richards, Keith *musician*
Richardson, James *chef*
Richardson, John Vinson, Jr. *library and information science professor*
Richland, Kent Lewis *lawyer*
Richter, Stuart M. *lawyer*
Rickles, Donald Jay *comedian, actor*
Riegler, Alan Martin *bank technology consultant*
Riff, Lawrence P. *lawyer*
Rimoin, David Lawrence *medical geneticist*
Riordan, George Nickerson *investment banker*
Rishwain, James Michael, Jr. *lawyer*
Rising, Kevin D. *lawyer*
Roberts, Emma Rose *actress*
Roberts, Eric *actor*
Roberts, Paul Harry *mathematics professor*
Roberts, Robert Winston *social worker, educator, dean*
Roberts, Sidney *biological chemist*
Roberts, Virgil Patrick *lawyer, judge*
Robertson, Hugh Duff *lawyer*
Robison, William Robert *lawyer*
Robitaille, Luc *sports team executive, retired professional hockey player*
Robson, Glenn R. *engineering and design company executive*
Rodriguez, Daniel *tenor, former protective services official*
Rodriguez, Ensor *physician, scientist, writer*
Roeder, Richard Kenneth *business owner, lawyer*
Roeser, Andy *professional sports team executive*
Rogers, David Booth *lawyer*
Rogers, Wayne M. *actor, investor, investment strategist, consultant*
Rohrer, Susan Earley *film producer, film director, scriptwriter*
Rosenberg, Alan *actors guild executive*
Rosenfeld, John Lang *geology educator*
Rosenstock, Linda *dean, medical educator*
Rosenthal, J. Thomas *hospital administrator, medical educator*
Rosenthal, Sol *lawyer*
Rosenzweig, Richard Stuart *publishing company executive*
Rosett, Arthur Irwin *lawyer, educator*
Ross, Ami L. *insurance company executive, finance company executive*
Ross, Bruce Shields *lawyer*
Ross, Marion *actress*
Roth, Tim *actor*
Rothenberg, Alan I. *lawyer, professional sports association executive*
Rouse, Richard Hunter *historian, educator*
Rouze, Jeffrey Alan *real estate executive*
Roven, Alfred Nathan *surgeon*
Rowell, Victoria *actress*
Rowen, Howard *financial consultant*
Rozanski, Stanley Howard *lawyer*
Rubin, Robert Terry *psychiatrist, researcher, educator*
Rubin, Stanley Creamer *television producer, film producer*
Rubinstein, Moshe Fajwel *engineering educator*
Rush, Herman E. *television executive*
Ruskin, Joseph Richard *actor, director*
Russo, Rene *actress*
Rust, Neil W. *lawyer*
Rustand, Kay *lawyer*
Ruthberg, Miles N. *lawyer*
Rutter, Marshall Anthony *lawyer*
Ryan, Stephen Joseph, Jr. *ophthalmologist, educator*
Saban, Haim *investment company executive, television producer*
Sachs, George *biology professor, physician*
Sacks, Robert A. *lawyer*
Sadraie, Hamid Reza *civil engineer, researcher*
Safadi, M. Oussama *engineering educator*
Safonov, Michael George *electrical engineering educator, consultant*
Sager, Kelli L. *lawyer*
Sahimi, Muhammad *engineering educator*
Saito, Takashi *professional baseball player*
Saltzman, Joseph *journalist, educator, television producer*
Salvaty, Benjamin Benedict *lawyer*
Salzman, David Elliot *entertainment industry executive*
Samet, Jack I. *lawyer*
Sample, Steven Browning *academic administrator*
Samuels, Mark A. *lawyer*
Sands, Rick (Richard Sands) *film company executive*
Santaolalla, Gustavo *musician, composer, record producer*
Sarnat, Bernard George *plastic surgeon, educator, researcher*
Sarnoff, Thomas Warren *television executive*
Saxe, Deborah Crandall *lawyer*
Sayed, M. Gary *healthcare administrator, educator, scientist*
Scates, Allen Edward *coach*
Schaefer, William David *language educator*
Scheibel, Arnold Bernard *psychiatrist, educator, research director*
Schelbert, Heinrich Ruediger *nuclear medicine physician*
Schill, Michael H. *dean, law educator*
Schindler, David J. *lawyer*
Schlesinger, Adam *musician*
Schmidt, Jason *professional baseball player*
Schnebelen, Pierre *resort planner and developer, consultant*
Scholtz, Robert Arno *electrical engineering educator*
Schopf, James William *paleobiologist, researcher, educator*
Schreiber, Liev (Isaac Liev Schreiber) *actor*
Schuetze-Coburn, Marje *university librarian*
Schulberg, Budd *author*
Schulman, Cathy *film producer*
Schwartz, Robert M. *lawyer*
Schwarz, Ernst Ruediger *cardiologist, researcher*
Schwimmer, George *writer, film producer*
Scott, Robert Lane *chemist, educator*
Scott, Tony *film director*
Scoular, Robert Frank *lawyer*
Sears, David O'Keefe *psychology professor*
Sedaris, Amy *writer, actress*
See, Carolyn *English language educator, writer, book critic*
Selleck, Tom *actor*
Seto, Theodore Paul *lawyer, educator*
Settles, F. Stan, Jr. *engineering educator, manufacturing executive*
Sewell, William George III *electronics engineer, writer*
Shacter, David Mervyn *lawyer*
Shaiman, Marc *composer, arranger, orchestrator*
Shakely, John Bower (Jack Shakely) *foundation executive*
Shank, Russell *librarian, educator*
Shanks, Patricia L. *lawyer*
Shapiro, Jerald Steven *chemist, bank executive*
Shapiro, Mel *playwright, educator, theater director*
Shapiro, Robert *lawyer*
Shay, Anthony Victor *choreographer, dance historian*
Shearer, Derek Nocross *political science professor, diplomat, academic administrator*
Sheehan, Lawrence James *lawyer*
Sheller, John Willard *lawyer*
Shen, Wei-Chiang *medical educator*
Sherman, Randolph *plastic and reconstructive surgeon, educator*
Sherrell, John Bradford *lawyer*
Sherwood, Allen Joseph *retired lawyer*
Shideler, Ross Patrick *literature and language educator, writer, translator, poet*
Shields, William Donald *physician, educator*
Shneidman, Edwin S. *psychologist, thanatologist*
Shoaf, R. Wayne *librarian*
Shortz, Richard Alan *lawyer*
Shostak, S. Richard *lawyer*
Shuger, Debora Kuller *humanities educator*
Shultz, John David *lawyer*
Shuster, Alvin *journalist, reporter*
Shuster, Beth *editor*
Siegel, Michael Elliot *nuclear medicine physician, educator*
Siegel, Robert (Bob) A. *lawyer*
Siegel, Sheldon C. *pediatrician, immunologist, allergist*
Siegel, Stuart Elliott *pediatric oncologist, educator*
Silbergeld, Arthur F. *lawyer*
Silva, Clarice F. (Clarice F. Chavira-Sliva) *lawyer*
Silverstein, Suzanne *art therapist*
Simmons, Donna Marie *neuroscientist, histotechnologist, neuroendocrine anatomist, researcher*
Simmons, Richard J. *lawyer*
Sinay, Joseph *retail executive*
Singer, Joel *real estate company executive*
Singer, Martin Dori *lawyer*

Singleton, Joan Vietor *publishing executive, writer, film producer*
Sinner, Steve *sculptor*
Sitrick, Michael Steven *communications executive*
Skaggs, David L. *orthopedist, educator*
Sklar, Richard Lawrence *political science professor*
Slavkin, Harold Charles *dean, biologist*
Sloan, Harry Evans *film company executive*
Sloan, Sheldon Harold *lawyer*
Smiley, Tavis *radio talk show host, writer*
Smith, Chadwick Fitzhugh *orthopaedic surgeon, educator*
Smith, Emil L. *biochemist, educator*
Smith, Jean Webb (Mrs. William French Smith) *civic worker*
Smits, Jimmy *actor*
Smooke, Michael G. *lawyer*
Snider, Darryl *lawyer*
Sohn, Sung Won *bank executive*
Solish, Jonathan Craig *lawyer*
Solomon, David Harris *geriatrician, educator*
Song, Yongyi *librarian*
Sonnenschein, Ralph Robert *physiologist*
Soohoo, Elena *strategic planning administrator*
Soria, Samuel Salvador *musician*
Speyer, Jason Lee *aeronautical engineer, educator*
Spindler, Paul *communications executive, consultant*
Spitzer, Matthew Laurence *law educator*
Spivak, Kenin Mathew *personal care industry executive*
Springsteen, Bruce (Bruce Frederick Joseph Springsteen) *musician, singer*
Stall, Richard J., Jr. *lawyer*
Stamm, Alan *lawyer*
Stancill, James McNeill *finance educator, consultant*
Stanish, Charles *anthropologist, educator*
Stanton, Harry Dean *actor*
Stanton, Robert James, Jr. *geologist, educator*
Stapleton, Jean (Jeanne Murray) *actress*
Starostin, Aleksandr B. *nuclear scientist, researcher*
Starr, Kevin *librarian, educator*
Starrett, Lucinda *lawyer*
Steh, Bill Drago *neuropsychologist*
Stein, James Eric *pediatric surgeon*
Stein, Laurence Jay *lawyer*
Stein, Sheryl E. *lawyer*
Stellwagen, Robert Harwood *biochemistry professor*
Stephens, Loren M. *publishing executive, writer*
Sterling, Donald T. *real estate mogul, professional sports team owner*
Stern, Mariana Carla *epidemiologist, educator*
Stern, Susan Toy *human resources specialist*
Stevenson, Robert Murrell *music educator*
Stiehm, E. Richard *pediatrician, educator*
Stinehart, William, Jr. *retired lawyer*
Stockwell, Robert Paul *linguist, educator*
Stoddart, J(ames) Fraser *chemistry professor*
Stone, Gregory Paul *lawyer*
Stone, Lawrence Maurice *lawyer, educator*
Stoughton, W. Vickery *healthcare executive*
Stout, Lynn Andrea *law educator*
Straatsma, Bradley Ralph *ophthalmologist, educator*
Strack, Stephen Naylor *psychologist*
Streeter, Oscar Edward, Jr. *radiation oncologist*
Streisand, Barbra Joan *singer, actress, film director*
Strick, Jeremy *curator*
Strickland, Julia B. *lawyer*
Strong, Gary Eugene *university librarian*
Strong, George Gordon, Jr. *lawyer, management consultant*
Sugar, Ronald D. *aerospace transportation company executive*
Sullivan, Stuart Francis *anesthesiologist, educator*
Sutterby, Larry Quentin *internist*
Swamikannu, Xavier *environmental engineer, state official*
Swanson, Daniel G. *lawyer, economist*
Sweeney, Paul W., Jr. *lawyer*
Swofford, Beth *agent*
Synolakis, Costas E. *engineering educator*
Szego, Clara Marian *cell biologist, educator*
Tabachnick, Norman Donald *psychiatrist, educator*
Taggart, Jennifer T. *lawyer*
Takahashi, Masato *pediatric cardiologist, educator*
Takei, George Hosato *actor*
Takesh, Fahi *lawyer*
Talley, Vernon Andrew *museum administrator*
Tamkin, S. Jerome *manufacturing executive, consultant*
Tang, Christopher S. *finance educator*
Tao, Terence Chi-Shen *mathematics professor*
Tardio, Thomas A. *public relations executive*
Tarr, Ralph William *lawyer, former federal government official*
Tassler, Nina *broadcast executive*
Tatro, René P. *lawyer*
Taylor, Charles Ellett *biologist, educator*
Taylor, Leigh Herbert *dean*
Taylor, Minna *lawyer*
Taylor, Peter J. *diversified financial services company executive*
Taylor, Shelley E. *psychology researcher, educator*
Taymor, Julie *theater, film and opera director, designer*
Tellem, Nancy Reiss *broadcast executive*
Telles, Cynthia Ann *psychologist*
Tepper, R(obert) Bruce, Jr. *lawyer*
Tepstein, Daniel C. *lawyer*
Territo, Mary C. *health facility administrator, hematologist, educator*
Terry, Timothy P. *lawyer*
Terry, W. Burks *lawyer*
Tevrizian, Dickran M., Jr. *judge*
Thomas, Geoffrey L. *lawyer*
Thomas, John David *composer, musician, compact disc artist, photographer, music and arts business owner*
Thompson, Anne Kathleen *entertainment journalist*
Thompson, Earl Albert *economics professor*
Thompson, Judith Kastrup *nursing researcher*
Thompson, Paul Matthew *neuroscientist*
Thompson, Richard Frederick *psychologist, neuroscientist, educator*
Thoren-Peden, Deborah Suzanne *lawyer*
Thorne, Richard Mansergh *physicist*
Thorpe, Geogory B. *lawyer*
Timlin, Robert J. *judge*
Tirador, Gabriel *insurance company executive*
Tobisman, Stuart Paul *lawyer*
Tolo, Vernon Thorpe *orthopedist, educator*
Toman, Mary Ann *federal official*
Tomlin, Lily *actress*
Torres, Cynthia Ann *marketing professional*
Torres-Gil, Fernando M. *academic administrator*
Totten, George Oakley III *political science professor*
Treister, George Marvin *lawyer*
Trembly, Cristy *television executive*
Trembly, Dennis Michael *musician*
Trenton, Patricia Jean *art historian*
Trimble, Stanley Wayne *hydrologist*
Tritle, Lawrence Alan *history professor*
Trope, Sorrell *lawyer*
Troy, Nancy J. *art history educator*
Trumbull, Stephen Michael *entrepreneur, musician*
Trygstad, Lawrence Benson *lawyer*
Tsao, Jennie Ching-I *research scientist, educator*
Turner, Ralph Herbert *sociologist, educator*
Udvar-Hazy, Steven F. *leasing company financial executive*
Udwadia, Firdaus Erach *engineering educator, consultant*
Ukropina, James R. *lawyer*
Ullman, Tracey *actress, singer*
Underwood, Carrie Marie *singer*
Utz, Sarah Winifred *nursing educator*
Uva, Joe *broadcast executive*
Valdez, Jeff *broadcast executive, television producer*
Valentine, Dean *film producer*
Valenzuela, Manuel Anthony, Jr. *lawyer*
Valladares-Barbush, Lisette Marie *mathematics educator*
Van Buren, Abigail (Jeanne Phillips) *columnist, educator*
van Dam, Heiman *psychoanalyst*
Van de Kamp, John Kalar *lawyer*
Vanyo, Bruce Gordon *lawyer*
Varat, Jonathan D. *law educator, dean*
Vari, Sandor George *physician, research scientist*
Varner, Carlton A. *lawyer*
Vaughn, William Weaver *retired lawyer*
Verdi, Robert *jewelry designer, fashion expert, television personality*
Verreos, Nick *apparel designer*
Ver Steeg, Donna Lorraine Frank *nurse, sociologist, educator*
Vescio, Robert Allen *oncologist, educator*
Vidale, John Emilio *geologist*
Villablanca, Jaime Rolando *neuroscientist, medical educator*
Villaraigosa, Antonio Ramon *mayor*
Vincent, Dirk L. *lawyer*
Volpert, Richard Sidney *lawyer*
von Kalinowski, Julian Onesime *lawyer*
Vredevoe, Donna Lou *academic administrator, microbiologist, educator, biomedical researcher*
Wagar, Elizabeth Ann *microbiologist, director*
Wagner, Christian Nikolaus Johann *materials engineering educator*
Wagner, Paula *film company executive, film producer*
Wagner, William Gerard *dean, information scientist, consultant, physicist, investment manager*
Waits, Thomas Alan *composer, actor, singer*
Walden, Dana *broadcast executive*
Walendowski, George Jerry *accounting and business educator*
Walken, Christopher *actor*
Walker, Paul R. *lawyer*
Walker, Raymond John *physicist*
Wallach, Howard Frederic *psychiatrist*
Walsh, Kate *actress*
Walter, Jessica *actress*
Ward, Leslie Allyson *journalist, editor*
Warren, Robert Stephen *lawyer*
Washington, Isaiah *actor*
Wasser, Dennis Matthew *lawyer*
Wasser, Laura Allison *lawyer*
Wasserman, Casey *management consultant*
Wasserman, Marcia Watson *legal administration consultant*
Wasserman, William Phillip *lawyer*
Wasterlain, Claude Guy *neurologist*
Waterman, Christopher *dean*
Waterman, Michael Spencer *mathematics and biology professor*
Waterston, Samuel Atkinson *actor*
Watson, Glenn Robert *lawyer*
Watson, Sharon Gitin *psychologist*
Wayne, June Claire *artist*
Wayte, Alan (Paul) *lawyer*
Weatherup, Roy Garfield *lawyer*
Weiner, Leslie Philip *neurology educator, researcher*
Weiner, Perrie M. *lawyer*
Weisberg, Ruth *artist*
Weiss, Kenneth R. *newswriter*
Weiss, Martin Harvey *neurosurgeon, educator*
Weiss, Walter Stanley *lawyer*
Weissman, Barry Leigh *lawyer*
Weitz, Brett *broadcast executive*
Welch, Lloyd Richard *electrical and communications engineer, educator, consultant*
Wells, Annie *photographer*
Wells, Bradley W. *foundation administrator*
Wells, David Lee *professional baseball player*
Wells, Kenneth Brooks *medical educator, researcher*
Westerfield, Randolph W. *finance educator, former dean*
Weston, John Frederick *business educator, consultant*
Westreich, Benzion Joseph *lawyer*
Wexler, Robert *academic administrator*
Whitaker, Forest *actor*
White, Brett *real estate company executive*
White, Robert Joel *lawyer*
Whiteman, David Bruce *librarian, poet*
Whitten, Charles Alexander, Jr. *physics professor*
Whybrow, Peter Charles *psychiatrist, educator, director, author*
Wilkerson, LuAnn *dean, medical educator*
Wilkinson, Alan Herbert *nephrologist, educator*
Willett, Robert E. *lawyer*
Williams, Bart H. *lawyer*
Williams, Harold Marvin *lawyer, retired foundation, academic and federal agency administrator*
Williams, James M. *foundation administrator*
Williams, Kenneth Scott *entertainment company executive*
Williams, Norma Jean *lawyer*
Williams, Richard Thomas *lawyer*
Williams, Robert E. *lawyer*
Williams, Ronald Dean *minister, religious organization administrator*
Willner, Alan Eli *electrical engineer, educator*
Wilson, Chandra Danette *actress*
Wilson, Ed *broadcast executive*
Wilson, Gary Thomas *engineering executive*
Wilson, Miriam Geisendorfer *retired physician, educator*
Wincor, Michael Z. *psychopharmacology educator, clinician, researcher, director*
Wine, Mark Philip *lawyer*
Winterman, Craig L. *lawyer*
Winters, Barbara Jo *musician*
Withers, Hubert Rodney *radiotherapist, radiobiologist, educator*
Witherspoon, Reese (Laura Jean Reese Witherspoon) *actress*
Wittrock, Merlin Carl *educational psychologist*
Wittry, David Beryle *physicist, researcher*
Wlaschin, Ken *cultural organization administrator, writer*
Wolfen, Werner F. *lawyer*
Wolpe, David *rabbi*
Wong, James Bok *economist, chemical engineer, technologist, consultant*
Wong, Wing-Yen *hematologist, educator*
Wood, James Nowell *foundation administrator, former museum director*
Wood, Nancy Elizabeth *psychologist, educator*
Wood, Willard Mark *lawyer*
Woodley, David Timothy *dermatology educator*
Woodruff, Fay *paleoceanographer, geological researcher*
Woods, Daniel James *lawyer*
Woodsome, Edwin Valentine, Jr. *lawyer*
Wooler, John William *multi-media specialist*
Wortham, Thomas Richard *literature and language professor*
Wright, Edward Leonard *astronomy educator*
Wright, Ernest Marshall *physiologist, consultant*
Wright, Kenneth Brooks *lawyer*
Wright, Otis Dalino, II, *judge*
Wu, George H. *federal judge*
Wu, Shi-Qi (Samuel Wu) *medical geneticist*
Wyle, Noah *actor*
Xue, Yongkang *science educator*
Yablonovitch, Eli *electrical engineering educator*
Yager, Thomas C. *retired judge*
Yamaguchi, Dean Takao *medical educator, researcher*
Yang, Bingen *mechanical engineering educator*
Yang, Debra Wong *lawyer, former prosecutor*
Yang, Henry S. (Hong Yang) *metallurgist, materials engineer*
Yari, Bob *film company executive, producer*
Yen, Teh Fu *civil and environmental engineering educator*
Yersiz, Hasan *medical educator*
Yerxa, Ron *film producer*
Yoakam, Dwight *country western musician*
York, Gary Alan *lawyer*
York, Michael (Michael York-Johnson) *actor*
Young, Christopher *composer*
Zacchino, Narda *newspaper editor*
Zalavras, Charalampos *orthopedic surgeon*
Zame, William R. *economist, mathematician, educator*
Zamos, Jerome *lawyer, real estate consultant*
Zeithammer, Robert *adult education educator*
Zeitlin, Maurice *sociology educator*
Zelon, Laurie Dee *judge*
Zemeckis, Robert L. *film director*
Ziffren, Kenneth *lawyer*
Zisman, David Abram *medical educator, health facility administrator*

Los Gatos
Allan, Lionel M. *director for-profit and non-profit companies, educator*
Carson, Sol Kent *artist, educator*
Hastings, Reed *film rental company executive, former education association administrator*
Janvier, Pascal Paul *chef, educator*
Mintz, Marilyn D. *artist, writer*
Ohanjanian, Ruzanna *clinical psychologist*
Rosenheim, Donald Edwin *electrical engineer*
Saha, Samar Kanti *electronics engineer, educator*

Los Osos
Kreitzer, David Martin *artist*
Kreitzer, Jacalyn Bower *vocalist, voice educator*

Lower Lake
Garcia, Beatrice Maude *social worker, director*

Lynwood
Nelson, Maurice Sandy, Jr. *metal products company executive*
Sitomer, Alan Lawrence *literature and language educator*
Sterling, Arthur James *retired legal assistant*

Madera
Glynn, James A. *sociology educator, writer*
Pollack, Henry Clinton III *pediatric emergency physician*

Malibu
Almond, Paul *film director, film producer, scriptwriter, writer*
Baskin, Otis Wayne *business educator*
Bedrosian, Edward *retired electrical engineer*
Benton, Andrew Keith *academic administrator, lawyer*
Bush, Kristian *musician*
Dankanyin, Robert John *management consultant*
Davenport, David *lawyer, educator, academic administrator*
DeMieri, Joseph L. *retired bank executive*
Dominguez, Sylvia Margarita *electrical engineer, researcher*
Dowd, Ned *film producer*
Ensign, Richard Papworth *transportation executive*
Factor, Max III *arbitrator, mediator*
Hanson, Gary A. *lawyer, educator, academic administrator*
Harris, Ed (Edward Allen Harris) *actor*
Holmes, Henry W. *lawyer*
Hunt, Valerie Virginia *electrophysiologist, educator*
LaChanze, (R. LaChanze Sapp, Rhonda Sapp) *actress*
Larson, Edward John *history and law professor*
Liu, David Shiao-Kung *research scientist, consultant*
Marshall, Donald Glenn *English language and literature educator*
Morgenstern, Leon *surgeon*
Naegele, Timothy Duncan *lawyer*
Nelson, Grant Steel *law educator*
Nettles, Jennifer *singer*
Pepper, David M. *scientist, educator, writer, inventor, consultant*
Phillips, Ronald Frank *academic administrator*
Roosa, Mark S. *dean, librarian*
Smith, Yvonne Smart *advertising executive*
Starr, Kenneth Winston *dean, lawyer*
Tyler, Ronald Lee *religious studies educator*
Vereen, Ben *actor, singer, dancer*
Warder, Michael Young *academic administrator*

Manhattan Beach
Allmon, Michael Bryan *accountant, financial consultant*
Blanton, John Arthur *architect, writer*
Grollman, Julius Harry, Jr. *cardiovascular and interventional radiologist*
Mandel, Martin Louis *lawyer*
McQuillin, Richard Ross *management consultant*
Pettersen, Thomas Morgan *accountant, corporate financial executive*
Pruetz, Adrian Mary *lawyer*
Rae, Matthew Sanderson, Jr. *lawyer*

Manteca
Talmage, Kenneth Kellogg *consumer products company executive*
Tonn, Elverne Meryl *pediatric dentist, dental benefits consultant, forensic odontologist*

Marina
Mettee-McCutchon, Ila *municipal official, retired military officer*
Paget, Ruth Pennington *librarian, educator, writer*
Shane, William Whitney *astronomer*

Marina Del Rey
Bennett, Joel Herbert *construction executive*
Dexheimer, Henry Phillip, II, *insurance agency executive*
Donzis, Paul Bennett *lawyer, finance educator, ophthalmologist*
Gold, Carol Sapin *international management consultant, speaker, writer*
Gregg, Lucius Perry, Jr. *aerospace executive*
Heath, Berthann Jones *educational association administrator*
Jeffrey, John Orval *Internet company executive, lawyer*
Khurana, Sanjay Kumar *spine surgeon, director*
Lindheim, Richard David *broadcast executive, director*
Neuman, Clifford *computer scientist, educator*
Rimer, John Thomas *language educator, academic administrator, writer*
Schulman, Robert S. *lawyer*
Stevens, William Grant (Grant Stevens) *plastic surgeon*
Stoker, David Allen *plastic surgeon*
Swartout, William R. *mathematician, educator, director*

Mariposa
Bruce, John Anthony *artist*
Rogers, Earl Leslie *artist, educator*

Martinez
Meyer, Jarold Alan *oil company research executive*
Thomas, Walter Dill, Jr. *retired forest pathologist, consultant*
Tong, Siu Wing *computer programmer*
Williams, Charles Judson *lawyer, writer*

Marysville
Myers, Elmer *psychiatric social worker*

Mckinleyville
Peithman, Roscoe Edward *physicist, educator*
Stuart, Henry Lee *retired rail transportation executive*
Thueson, David Orel *pharmaceutical executive, researcher, writer, educator*

Mendocino
Masterson, William A. *retired judge*

Menifee
Aguilar, Shelley Kezer *biology professor, research scientist*
Balow, Irving Henry *retired education educator*

Menlo Park
Allen, Matthew Arnold *physicist*
Altman, Drew E. *foundation executive*
Baez, Joan Chandos *vocalist*
Bales, Royal Eugene *retired philosophy educator*
Bernstein, Lawrence R. *inorganic chemist, pharmaceutical chemist*
Bourne, Charles Percy *information scientist, educator*
Brest, Paul A. *law educator, foundation administrator*
Brinegar, Claude Stout *retired oil industry executive*
Brodsky, Stanley Jerome *physics educator, consultant*
Bukry, John David *geologist*
Bynum, Gretchen Luepke *geologist*
Carlson, Curtis R. *electronics research industry executive*
Cassidy, Mike *online game company executive*
Chao, Howard H. *lawyer*
Cohen, Danny *computer engineer*
Collins, Nancy Whisnant *foundation administrator*
Crosley, David Risdon *chemical physicist*
Currie, Francis Sparre *lawyer*
Davies, Paul Lewis III *venture capitalist*
Doerr, (L.) John *venture capitalist*
Dorfan, Jonathan Mannie *physicist, researcher*
Drell, Persis Sydney *physicist*
Drell, Sidney David *physicist, arms control and national security specialist*
Dubinsky, Donna L. *information technology executive*
Dyer, Charles Arnold *lawyer*
Edwards, John Wesley, II, *lawyer*
Fenton, Noel John *venture capitalist*
Fisher, Ora T. *lawyer*
George, Dileep *electrical engineer*
Goldstein, Jon *investment advisor*
Gunderson, Robert Vernon, Jr. *lawyer*
Halperin, Robert Milton *retired electrical machinery company executive*
Harris, Edward Day, Jr. *physician*
Haslam, Robert Thomas III *lawyer*
Hazen, Paul Mandeville *banker*
Hearst, William Randolph III *lawyer, former newspaper publisher*
Heller, Esther A. *writer, educator*
Heuman, Donna *lawyer*
Hewlett, Walter B. *application developer*
Hoffman, Thomas Edward *dermatologist*
Holmquest, Donald Lee *health organization director, nuclear medicine physician, lawyer, retired aerospace engineer*
Honey, Richard Churchill *retired electrical engineer*
Jackson, Jeanne Pellegren *apparel executive*
Jaros, John A. *physics professor*
Joy, Bill (William Nelson Joy) *venture capitalist, former computer software company executive*
Kamin, William Stephen *food products executive, photographer*
Karel, Steven *lawyer*
Kaufman, Christopher Lee *lawyer*
Kelly, Daniel Grady, Jr. *lawyer*
Kennelly, Dennis L. *lawyer*
Kerman, Peter F. *lawyer*
Khosla, Vinod *investment company executive*
Kirk, Cassius Lamb, Jr. *retired lawyer, investor*
Kovachy, Edward Miklos, Jr. *psychiatrist, consultant*
Kramlich, C(harles) Richard (Dick) *venture capitalist*
Kuwabara, James Shigeru *research hydrologist*
Kvamme, Mark D. *marketing professional*
Labiosa, William Bruce *civil engineer, researcher*
Lane, Laurence William, Jr. *retired ambassador, publisher*
Levenson, Milton *chemical engineer, consultant*
Lipman, Peter W. *research scientist*
Lucas, Donald Leo *investor*
Lynch, Charles Allen *investment company executive, director*
Madison, James Raymond *lawyer*
Marks, Michael E. *electronics executive*
Marquardt, David F. *venture capitalist*
McCarthy, Roger Lee *mechanical engineer*
McDonald, Warren George *accountant, mortage company, savings and loan association executive, consultant*
Medearis, Mark A. *lawyer*
Mendelson, Alan Charles *lawyer*
Messmer, Harold Maximilian, Jr., (Max Messmer) *financial services executive*
Mill, Theodore *chemist, researcher*
Moos, Walter Hamilton *pharmaceutical company executive*
Moritz, Michael J. *venture capitalist*
Mozley, Anita Ventura *retired curator, retired art historian*
Mummery, Daniel R. *lawyer*
Neumann, Peter Gabriel *computer scientist*
Pallotti, Marianne Marguerite *foundation administrator*
Penzias, Arno Allan *astrophysicist, information scientist, researcher*
Perkins, Tom (Thomas James Perkins) *venture capital company executive*
Quinn, Kevin Anthomy *investment banker*
Richter, Burton *physicist, educator*
Roberts, George R. *investment banker*
Ruspini, Enrique Hector *research scientist*
Saifer, Mark Gary Pierce *pharmaceutical executive*
Schmidt, Chauncey Everett *banker, director*
Scholes, Myron S. *financier, former law and finance educator*
Scoble, Robert *podcast network company executive, blog writer*
Smith, Marshall Savidge *foundation executive*
Stern, Julian Nathaniel *lawyer, pharmaceutical executive*
Sutherland, Ivan E. *computer scientist*
Taft, David Dakin *chemicals executive*
Taylor, Richard Edward *physicist, researcher*
Vane, Sylvia Brakke *anthropologist, writer*
VanHook, Tracie Lynnette *small business owner*
Vaughan, Gregory V. *financial planner*
Waddell, M. Keith *human resources specialist*
Westcott, Brian John *manufacturing executive*
White, Cecil Ray *librarian, consultant*
Wolfson, Mark Alan *investor, educator, dean*
Yang, Joseph *lawyer*
Zollinger, Cynthia *financial consultant*

Merced
Hallman, Max O. *humanities professor, philosophy professor, director*
Lashley, Lenore Clarisse *lawyer*
Tomlinson-Keasey, Carol Ann *academic administrator*

Midway City
Allen, Frances Michael *publisher*

Mill Valley
Castleman, Breaux Ballard *health management company executive*
Cole, Richard Charles *lawyer*
D'Amico, Michael *architect, urban planner*
Harner, Michael James *anthropologist, educator*
Harris, Jeffrey Saul *physician, consultant, health facility administrator*
Kolb, Felix Oscar *physician*
Leslie, Jacques Robert, Jr. *journalist*
McNamara, Stephen *newspaper executive*
Mumford, Christopher Greene *corporate financial executive*
Nemir, Donald Philip *lawyer*
Padula, Fred David *filmmaker*
Premo, Paul Mark *oil industry executive*
Schreyer, Chara *foundation administrator, art collector*
Schwartzbach, M. Gerald *lawyer*
Selvig, Jettie Pierce *lawyer*

Millbrae
Thomlinson, Ralph *demographer, educator*

Milpitas
Allen, Irma M. *adult education educator*
Chiu, Peter Yee-Chew *physician*
Corrigan, Wilfred J. *computer company executive*
DuChene, Todd Michael *lawyer*
Hasler, William Albert *electronics executive*
Levy, Kenneth *computer company executive*
Ligan, Warren J. *corporate financial executive*
Lin Chien, Chester *electronics executive*
London, Craig *electronics executive*
O'Connor, Kevin *electronics executive*
Ogawa, Joichi Raphael *director, consultant*
Patel, Kiran *manufacturing executive*
Simson, Claudine *computer company executive*
Talwalkar, Abhi Y. (Abhijit Y. Talwalkar) *computer company executive*
Tufano, Paul J. *computer company executive*
Wang, Susan S. *manufacturing executive*

Mission Hills
Niku, Soheil Daniel *urologist*

Mission Viejo
Faley, Robert Lawrence *retired instruments company executive*
Glasky, Alvin Jerald *retired medical research scientist*
Lake, Jane Burford *special education educator, hypnotherapist, small business owner*
Ruben, Robert Joseph *lawyer*
Tuohey, Conrad Gravier *lawyer*

Modesto
Barnes, William David *non-profit charities consultant, publisher*
Czopek, Vanessa *library director*
Gallo, Joseph E. *vintner*
Jones, Mary Cunningham *music educator*
Khanna, Kanwal *rheumatologist*
Kushar, Kent *information technology executive*
Moe, Andrew Irving *veterinarian*
Morrison, Robert Lee *physical scientist*
Murphy, John Thomas *lawyer*
Mussman, William Edward III *lawyer*
Nicholson, Coy Lee *English educator, writer*
Piccinini, Robert M. (Bob Piccinini) *grocery store chain executive*
Price, Robert William *school superintendent, consultant*
Smith, Heather Lynn *psychotherapist, recreational therapist*
Suntra, Charles Ratapol *surgeon, educator*
Tidball, Lee Falk *elementary school educator, writer*
Whiteside, Carol Gordon *foundation executive*

Moffett Field
Berenji, Hamid Reza *research scientist, educator*
Chen, Bin *materials scientist*
Cohen, Malcolm Martin *psychologist, researcher*
Friedmann, E(merich) Imre *biologist, educator*
Glass, Brian Jay *aerospace scientist*
Harper, Lynn D. *biologist*
Kittel, Peter *research scientist*
Lissauer, Jack Jonathan *astronomy educator*
Makeev, Maxim A. *physicist*
Mattioda, Andrew Lige *chemist, researcher, space scientist*
Sharma, Surendra Prasad *aerospace engineer, scientist*
Statler, Irving Carl *aerospace engineer*

Mojave
Binnie, Brian *pilot, transportation executive*
Melvill, Michael W. *aircraft company executive, experimental test pilot*
Rutan, Burt (Elbert Leander Rutan) *aircraft designer, aircraft company executive*

Monarch Beach
Dougherty, Elmer Lloyd, Jr. *retired chemical engineering professor, consultant*

Monrovia
Edwards, Kenneth Neil *chemical engineering executive*
Fannin, Daniel Paul Clark *information systems executive*
Jemelian, John Nazar *management consultant*
Kimnach, Myron William *botanist, horticulturist*
Lim, SallyJane *financial planner, diversified insurance and financial advisor, realtor*
Pray, Ralph Emerson *metallurgical engineer*
Stevens, Gary *retired jockey*

Montara
Calman, Sandra Gogins *physician, researcher*

Montebello
Calderon, Ronald *state official*
Lopez, Donald Robert *parochial school educator, writer*

Montecito
Braun, David A(dlai) *lawyer*
Hanley, Kevin Lance *maintenance company executive*
Meghreblian, Robert Vartan *manufacturing executive, physicist*
Purl, O. Thomas *retired electronics company executive*
Wheelon, Albert Dewell *physicist*

Monterey
Black, Robert Lincoln *pediatrician, educator*
Boger, Dan Calvin *science professor, consultant*
Bomberger, Russell Branson *lawyer, writer*
Brook, Douglas Alan *former civilian military employee*
Browder, John Glen *former congressman, educator*
Butler, Jon Terry *computer engineering educator, researcher*
Denning, Peter James *computer scientist, engineer*
Franke, Jack Emil *foreign language educator*
Gaver, Frances Rouse *lawyer*
Goldstein, Kenneth F. *entertainment and publishing company executive*
Hanlon, James Allison *confectionery company executive*
Hoivik, Thomas Harry *military educator, international consultant*
Lehr, Jeffrey Marvin *immunologist, allergist*
Matthews, David Fort *career officer*
Nesheim, Robert Olaf *retired food products executive*
Neta, Beny *mathematics educator, researcher*
Oder, Broeck Newton *history educator, director*
Oliver, Daniel T. *military education administrator, career officer, retired*
Packard, Julie *aquarium administrator*
Peet, Phyllis Irene *women's studies educator*
Pinkham, Frederick Oliver *foundation executive, consultant*
Reneker, Maxine Hohman *librarian*
Robinson, Marla Holbrook *community care nurse*
Schrady, David Alan *civilian military employee, educator*
Soskin, William H. *lawyer, accountant*
Yao, Lihua *research scientist, statistician*

Monterey Park
Goei, Bernard Thwan-Poo (Bert Goei) *retired architectural and engineering firm executive*
Grasse, Wanda Gene *lawyer, writer*
Maronde, Robert Francis *internist, pharmacologist*
Smith, Betty Denny *county official, administrator, fashion executive*
Stankevitz, Diane Lynn *athletic trainer*
Stapleton, Jean *journalism educator*
Wilson, Linda *librarian*

Moorpark
Young, Victoria E. *occupational health nurse, lawyer*

Moraga
Allen, Richard Garrett *healthcare educator*
Kilbourne, George William *lawyer*
O'Brien, Bea Jae *artist*
Silcox, Frances Eleanor *museum and exhibits planning consultant*
Tom, Randolph L. *corporate financial executive, lawyer*

Moreno Valley
Bajor, Renee Allyson *special education educator*
Calley, Tranquil Hudson *retired travel consultant, educator*
Guerrero, Donna Marie *sales executive*
Marshall, Debra Lynn *secondary school educator*
White, Charles R. *former mayor*

Morgan Hill
Freimark, Robert (Bob) *artist*
Horning, Barbara Hortense Scheer *retired elementary school educator*
Nchekwube, Emeka J. *neurologist, surgeon*
Singh, Loren Chan *writer, educator*

Moss Beach
Glauthier, T. J. *management consultant*

Moss Landing
Brewer, Peter George *ocean geochemist*
Clague, David A. *geologist*
Lange, Lester Henry *mathematics professor*
McNutt, Marcia Kemper *geophysicist*
Robison, Bruce H. *marine biologist*

Mount Hamilton
Guggenheim, Alan Andre Albert Paul Edouard *international consultant*

Mountain View
Abel, Elizabeth Ann *dermatologist*
Armstrong, Tim *information technology executive*
Baker, Mitchell *computer software developer, foundation administrator*
Balogh, Aristotle N. *information technology executive*
Bennett, Stephen M. *computer software company executive*
Bills, Robert Howard *political party executive*
Bishop, Robert R. *computer company executive*
Bloch, Joshua J. *software designer*
Brilliant, Larry (Lawrence Brilliant) *preventive medicine physician, epidemiologist, technology pioneer, writer, educator, entrepreneur, social venture capitalist*
Brin, Sergey Mihailovich *information technology executive*
Brown, Shona L. *information technology executive*
Bunnell, Ben *information technology manager*
Cabrol, Nathalie Agnes *research scientist*
Campbell, William V. *computer company executive*
Cerf, Vinton Gray *information technology executive*
Chu, Wai C. *engineer, researcher*
Cook, Scott David *computer software company executive*
Coughran, William M., Jr. *information technology executive, researcher*
Davidson, Gordon Kirby *lawyer*
de Geus, Aart J. *computer software company executive*
Di Muccio, Mary-Jo *retired librarian*
Drummond, David C. *information technology executive, lawyer*
East, John *computer company executive*
Eschelbeck, Gerhard *information technology executive*
Eustace, Alan *information technology executive*
Fennell, Laura A. *lawyer*
Garg, Ashutosh *computer scientist, researcher*
Gillis, Edwin *information technology executive*
Gitlin, Richard D. *telecommunications technology executive*
Graham, Paul *Internet company executive, writer*
Halvorsen, Per-Kristian *software company executive, former educator, researcher*
Healy, Jodi *library services manager*
Hoagland, Albert Smiley *electrical engineer, researcher*
Hoffman, Donald Clinton *physicist, researcher*
Hoffman, Reid *Internet company executive*
Hughes, Gregory *information technology executive*
Hwang, Dennis (Dennis Hwang-Jung-moak) *graphic computer artist*
Isaacs, Nicholas Stephen *music educator, director*
Johnson, Conor Deane *mechanical engineer*
Kobza, Dennis Jerome *architect*
Koo, George Ping Shan *business consultant*
Kordestani, Omid *information technology executive*
Mayer, Marissa Ann *information technology executive*
Nash, Horace Lyons *lawyer*
Nucci, Antonio *information technology executive*
Nye, Dan *Internet company executive*
Page, Larry (Lawrence E. Page) *information technology executive*
Pasahow, Lynn Harold *lawyer*
Qureishi, A. Salam *computer company executive*
Reyes, George *information technology executive*
Roper, William Alford, Jr. *Internet company executive*
Rosenberg, Jonathan *information technology executive*
Sarukkai, Sekhar *information technology executive*
Schickli, Jeanne Hlavka *virologist, researcher*
Schmidt, Eric Emerson *information technology executive*
Showalter, Mark Robert *astronomer*
Singh, Sangita *information technology and marketing executive*
Stapleton, James John *marketing executive, writer*
Summers, David Patrick *chemist, astrobiologist*
Walker, John Kent, Jr. *lawyer*
Wang, Sheldon *information technology executive, insurance company executive*
Warren, Richard Wayne *obstetrician, gynecologist*
Weiss, Rhett Louis *lawyer*
Wildman, Iris J. *retired law librarian*

Murrieta
deVries-White, Donna Lynn *education educator, consultant*
Geffe, Philip Reinhold *electrical engineer, consultant*
Lake, Bruce Meno *physicist*
Rose, Norma Louise *retired human services manager*

Napa
Battisti, Paul Oreste *retired municipal official*
Cahill, Richard Frederick *lawyer*
Chiarella, Peter Ralph *vintner*
Chiarello, Michael *chef*
Crosthwaite, Rachel Anspach *editor*
Eissmann, Walter James *consulting company executive*
Hess, Donald Marc *diversified financial services company executive*
Kuntz, Charles Powers *lawyer*
Pickett, Justus Cunningham *medical association administrator*
Schmidt, Hollie *secondary school educator*
Shin, Ernest Eun-Ho *physicist, educator, researcher*

National City
Beauchamp, Miles Philip *editor, columnist, consultant*

Nevada City
Chalpin-Fleitas, Susan Gail *environmental health specialist, forester*
Clausen, Jeanne Lorraine *musician*

Newark
Gupta, Anju *risk management consultant*
Shah, Haresh Chandulal *civil engineering educator*

Newbury Park
Bleiberg, Leon William *surgeon, podiatrist*
Fisk, Charles John *meteorologist, researcher, consultant*
Lindsey, Joanne M. *flight attendant, poet*

Newhall
Stein, Karl N. *plastic and reconstructive surgeon*

Newport Beach
Allen, Terrence R. *lawyer*
Artusi, Daniel A. *Internet company executive*
Baskin, Scott David *lawyer*
Batniji, Rami K. *facial plastic surgeon*
Belić Weiss, Zoran *artist, design educator, director*
Bennett, Bruce W. *retired construction executive, civil engineer*
Bissell, George Arthur *architect*
Blankenship, Edward G. *architect*
Boras, Scott D. *professional sports agent*
Bren, Donald L. *real estate company executive*
Bron, Guillermo (Bill Bron) *lending company executive*
Brown, Giles Tyler *history professor, lecturer*
Bruggeman, Terrance John *corporate financial executive*
Bryant, Thomas Lee *magazine editor*
Carmichael, David Richard *lawyer, insurance company executive*
Casey, Thomas Clark *retired trust company executive, investment advisor*
Chiu, John Tang *physician*
Clark, Thomas P., Jr. *lawyer*
Connolly, John Earle *surgeon, educator*
Currie, Robert Emil *retired lawyer*
Dean, Paul John *magazine editor*
Domanskis, Edward *plastic surgeon*
Fawcett, John Scott *real estate developer*
Fehner, Michael Richard *lawyer*
Fielding, Roy Thomas *software scientist*
Goldstein, Michael Gerald *lawyer, director*
Gross, William H. (Bill Gross) *financial analyst, investment company executive*
Grover, Sanjay *plastic surgeon*
Hancock, Ellen Marie *communications executive*
Herron, J. Jay *lawyer*
Hueston, John Charles *lawyer*
Ip, T. Y. Steven *plastic surgeon*
Johnson, William Stanley *metal distribution company executive*
Kaye, Michael S. *corporate executive*
Kenney, William John, Jr. *real estate developer*
Klink, Fredric J. *lawyer*
Kolyer, John McNaughton *materials scientist, retired chemist*
Koontz, Dean Ray *writer*
Krischer, Gordon Eugene *lawyer*
Landau, Martin *actor*
Leets, Peter J. *consulting firm executive*
Livingston, Lori Winder *lawyer*
Lyon, William, Sr. *construction executive*
Marcoux, Carl Henry *insurance company executive, writer, historian*
Matzdorff, James Arthur *investment banker, internet marketing professional*
McCue, Dennis Michael *management consultant*
Mc Culloch, Samuel Clyde *history professor*
Millar, Richard William, Jr. *lawyer*
Morris, James T. *insurance company executive*
Mullin, Stan *real estate company executive*
O'Donnell, Bernard Joseph, Jr. *lawyer*
Olenicoff, Igor *real estate company executive*
Prince, Thomas E. *bank executive*
Richardson, Walter John *architect*
Schiff, Laurie *lawyer*
Schnapp, Roger Herbert *lawyer, consultant*
Shackleton, Robert James *finance company executive*
Shamoun, John Milam *plastic surgeon*
Shonk, Albert Davenport, Jr. *advertising executive*
Singer, Gary James *lawyer*
Smeal, Kemp Leslie *psychotherapist, musician*
Solmer, Richard *surgeon*
Spitz, Barbara Salomon *artist*
Steelberg, Chad *broadcast advertising company executive*
Steelberg, Ryan *broadcasting advertising company executive*
Steinberg, Leigh William *sports agent*
Thorp, Edward Oakley *investment management company executive*
Tracy, James Jared, Jr. *retired legal association administrator*
Tran, Khanh T. *insurance company executive*
Turner, Jana L. *real estate company executive*
Ueberroth, Lindsey *hotel executive*
Viehe, Richard B. *podiatrist*
Wade, Michael Robert Alexander *marketing specialist*
Weissbard, Samuel Held *lawyer*
Wentworth, Diana von Welanetz *author*
Wentworth, Theodore Sumner *lawyer*
Whittemore, Paul Baxter *psychologist*
Wozniak, Steve (Stephen Gary Wozniak) *computer scientist, philanthropist*

Newport Coast
Evanoff, George C. *retired consumer products company executive*
Pavony, William H. *financial consultant, management consultant*
Rollans, James O. *service company executive*
Swan, Peer Alden *public utility executive*

Nicasio
Richardson, Jerome Lynn (Jerry Richardson) *secondary school educator*

Norco
Lu, Guiyang *electrical engineer, executive*
McNeal, Phyllis Paulette *parole agent*
Morrison, James V. *biology professor*

North Fork
Flanagan, James Henry, Jr. *lawyer, finance educator*

North Hills
Deets, Richard M. *secondary school educator, consultant*
Iacocca, Lee (Lido Anthony) *venture capitalist, retired automotive executive*

North Hollywood
Ajalat, Sol Peter *lawyer*
Calva, Robert Baraquiel *music educator*
Campos, Luis *puzzle writer*
Chang, Wung *academic administrator, investment advisor, educator*
Davis, Edmond Ray *lawyer*
de la Houssaye, Brette Angelo-Pepe *electrical engineer, researcher, educator*
Elliott, John Foster *psychotherapist, writer*
Fanning, Dakota *actress*
Holmes, Michael *performing arts company executive, educator*
Krayzie Bone, (Anthony Henderson) *rap artist*
Kreger, Melvin Joseph *lawyer*
Newton-John, Olivia *singer, actress*
Roth, David Lee *singer*
Sacco, Tony *cinematographer, television director, film director*
Smothers, Tom *actor, singer*
Stone, Sharon *actress*
Thomson, John Ansel Armstrong *biochemist*
Toplitt, Gloria H. *music educator, actress, vocalist*
Totton, Carl Allen, II, *psychologist*
Zimring, Stuart David *lawyer*

Northridge
Bassler, Robert Covey *artist, educator*
Boberg, Dorothy Kurth *author*
Bradshaw, Richard Rotherwood *engineering executive*
Cartwright, Nancy *actress, television producer*
Curzon, Susan Carol *academic administrator*
Dart, John Seward *journalist, editor*
Duran, Karin Jeanine *librarian*
Haskell, Peter Abraham *actor, director*
Jumonville, Felix Joseph, Jr. *physical education educator, real estate company officer*
Karels, Tim J. *ecology professor*
Kiddoo, Robert James *engineering service company executive*
Koester, Jolene *academic administrator*
Lampert, Lynn Denise *librarian, educator*
Logan, Lee Robert *orthodontist, department chairman*
Loudon, Craig Michael *video specialist*
Luedders, Jerry Duane *music educator, academic administrator*
Mitchell, James Andrew *education educator*
Mitchell, Rie Rogers *psychologist, counselor, educator*
Omatsu, Glenn *Asian American studies professor*
Orenstein, Michael (Ian Orenstein) *philatelic dealer, columnist*
Ro, Won Woo *engineering educator, researcher*
Rowlands, Kathleen Dudden *education educator*
Runquist, Lisa A. *lawyer*
Smathers, James Burton *medical physicist, educator*
Torgow, Eugene N. *electrical engineer*
Walcher, Alan Ernest *lawyer*

Norwalk
Ernest, Roger Craig *language educator*

Novato
Bibeault, Donald Bertrand *corporate executive, investor*
Criswell, Eleanor Camp *psychologist*
Jaeger, Patsy Elaine *retired secondary school educator, artist*
Kassel, Arthur David *retired orthopaedic surgeon*
Lane, Michele Jeanne *special education educator*
McNamara, John Stephen *artist, educator*
Patterson, W. Morgan *college president*
Peters, Thomas *foundation administrator*
Thompson, Peter Layard Hailey, Sr. *landscape and golf course architect, architectural firm executive*

Oak Park
Vinson, William Theodore *lawyer*

Oak View
Tennant, John Randall *management consultant*

Oakdale
Saletta, Mary Elizabeth (Betty Saletta) *sculptor*

Oakhurst
Cantwell, Christopher William *artist*

Oakland
Allen, Jeffrey Michael *lawyer*
Al Malik, Amir Isa *entrepreneur, consultant, musician*
Ames, Bruce Nathan *biochemisty and molecular biology professor, department chairman*
Andrasick, James Stephen *transportation executive*
Banke, Kathy M. *lawyer*
Beane, Billy (William Lamar) *professional sports team executive*
Beasley, Bruce Miller *sculptor*
Berry, Kathleen A. *English language educator*
Berry, Phillip Samuel *lawyer*
Brust, David *physicist*
Bryant, Arthur H. *lawyer*
Butterworth, Paul *information technology executive*
Carwell, Hattie Virginia *health physicist*
Chavez, Eric *professional baseball player*
Cohan, Christopher J. *professional sports team owner*
Crane, Robert Meredith *health facility administrator*
Dailey, Garrett Clark *publisher, lawyer*
Davies, Colleen T. *lawyer*
Davis, Baron *professional basketball player*
DeFazio, Lynette Stevens *dancer, choreographer, violinist, actress, educator*
Dellums, Ronald Vernie *mayor, retired congressman*
Deming, Willis Riley *retired lawyer*
Der, David F. *family practice physician, retired general surgeon*
De Vos, George Alphonse *psychologist, anthropologist*
Diaz, Sharon *education administrator*
Dibble, David Van Vlack *visually impaired educator, lawyer*
DiMaggio, Debbi *realtor*
Drexel, Baron Jerome *lawyer*
Dynes, Robert C. *academic administrator, physicist*
Ellis, Monta *professional basketball player*
Epstein, Ervin Harold, Jr. *dermatologist, educator, researcher*
Fleming, Jayne Elizabeth *lawyer*
Foley, Jack (John Wayne Harold Foley) *poet, writer, editor-in-chief*
Foust, Lawrence L. *lawyer*
Frye, L. Thomas *curator*
George, Donald Warner *online columnist and editor, freelance writer*
Geren, Bob (Robert Peter Geren) *professional baseball manager*
Gleick, Peter H. *conservationist*
Glover, Danny *actor*
Gomes, Wayne Reginald *academic administrator*
Gonzalez, Arthur Padilla *artist, educator*
Green, David Edward *retired librarian, priest, translator*
Hafey, Joseph Michael *health association executive*
Haiman, Franklyn Saul *writer, communications educator*
Halvorson, George Charles *healthcare insurance company executive*
Haren, Dan (Daniel John Haren) *professional baseball player*
Haskell, Arthur Jacob *retired water transportation executive*
Hawkins, Robert B. *think-tank executive*
Heinrich, Daniel J. *chemicals executive*
Henel, Carolyn E. *lawyer*
Hoffinger, Scott A. *pediatric orthopaedic surgeon*
Holmgren, Janet L. *academic administrator*
Jakubowsky, Frank Raymond *religious writer*
Jaramillo, Carlos Alberto *civil engineer*
Jensen, D. Lowell *federal judge*
Johnson, Kenneth F. *lawyer*
Joseph, Marc Alter *philosopher, educator*
Kane, Jacqueline *human resources specialist*
Kazan, Steven *lawyer*
Kendall, Jason Daniel *professional baseball player*
Kepner, William Raymond, Jr. *retired secondary school educator*
Killebrew, Ellen Jane (Mrs. Edward S. Graves) *cardiologist, educator*
Kimpton, Laura *artist*
Klatsky, Arthur Louis *cardiologist, epidemiologist*
Knauss, Donald R. *consumer products company executive*
Kohn, Steven M. *lawyer*
Kotsay, Mark Steven *professional baseball player*
Krauss, Ronald Maxwell *research scientist, endocrinologist, educator*
Lake, Suzanne *singer, music educator*
Lanzone, Jim *Internet company executive*
Lazar, John Edward *social services administrator, not-for-profit developer*
Lebda, Douglas R. *Internet company executive*
Lee, Ella Louise *librarian, educator*
Lee, Jong Hyuk *accountant*
Lee, Low Kee *electronics engineer, consultant*
Leslie, Robert Lorne *lawyer*
Linford, Rulon Kesler *physicist, electrical engineer*
Macmeeken, John Peebles *foundation executive, educator*
Martinez, Carmen Lorena *library director*
Masover, Gerald Kenneth *microbiologist*
McKinney, Judson Thad *broadcast executive*
Miller, Barry *researcher, psychologist*
Mullin, Christopher Paul *professional sports team executive, retired professional basketball player*
Neeley, Beverly Evon *sociologist, consultant*
Nelson, Donald Arvid (Nellie Nelson) *professional basketball coach*
Newsome, Randall Jackson *judge*
Ng, Lawrence Ming-Loy *pediatrician*
Pang, Dachling *neurosurgeon, educator*
Parker, Melissa Bernice *advertising executive*
Piazza, Mike (Michael Joseph Piazza) *professional baseball player*
Preston, Elizabeth A. *psychologist*
Price, Gary *librarian*
Quinby, William Albert *lawyer, arbitrator, mediator*
Rath, Alan T. *sculptor*
Reese, Charles Woodrow, Jr. *lawyer*
Richardson, Jason Anthoney *professional basketball player*
Robinson, Charles Furlonge *lawyer*
Robinson, Ellen M. *vocalist, educator*
Rosen, Frederick Semenov *otolaryngologist*
Rowell, Robert *professional sports team executive*
Rubin, Rhea Joyce *library consultant*
Saunders, Raymond Jennings *artist, educator*
Schacht, Henry Mevis *writer, consultant*
Schell, Farrel Loy *transportation engineer*
Schrag, Peter *editor, writer*
Shapiro, David W. *prosecutor*
Sharpton, Thomas *physician*
Silverberg, Robert *writer*
Smith, Christopher Allen *information technology executive, financial executive*
Stein, Laura *lawyer, consumer products company executive*
Stetler, Russell Dearnley, Jr. *investigator*
Stewart, John Lincoln *former academic administrator*
Street, Huston *professional baseball player*
Tchaikovsky, Leslie J. *federal judge*
Theroux, David Jon *economist, educator, research and development company executive*
Trautman, William Ellsworth *lawyer*
Wallis, Eric G. *lawyer*
Wang, Michael Lee *ophthalmologist*
Weaver, Pauline Anne *lawyer*
Westergren, Tim *music company executive*
Widener, Mary Lee *non-profit financial executive*
Wood, James Michael *lawyer*
Wood, Larry (Mary Laird) *journalist, writer, public relations executive, educator, environmental consultant*
Woodbury, Marda Liggett *librarian, writer*
Zschau, Marilyn *singer*

Oakley
Hirning, Fredric Carl *pharmacist*

Oakville
Mondavi, Robert Gerald *winery executive*

Occidental
Archer, Richard Joseph *lawyer*
Rumsey, Victor Henry *electrical engineering educator emeritus*

Oceano
Scott, Donald Michael *writer, educator*

Oceanside
Beck, Marilyn Mohr *columnist*
Curtin, Thomas Lee *ophthalmologist*
Daniel, Susan Qualls *secondary school educator*
Garfin, Louis *retired actuary*
Hertweck, E. Romayne *psychology professor*
Klaas, Nicholas Paul *management consultant*
Lange, Clifford Elmer *retired librarian*
Lyon, Richard *retired mayor, military officer*
McLean, Arthur Frederick *mechanical engineer*
Miller, Donald Eugene *retired air traffic controller*
Miyagawa, Hiroaki *materials scientist, researcher*
Montgomery, Michael Davis *research and development company executive, real estate investor*
Peckham, Donald *computer company executive*
Sullivan, Patrick James *lawyer*
Wright, Darcy Laureen *leadership educator, writer*
Yurist, Svetlan Joseph *mechanical engineer*

Ojai
Allen, David Ratcliff *management consultant, writer*
Mulligan, Michael K. *headmaster*
Parsons, Richard Walter *construction executive*
Paxton, Glenn Gilbert *composer*
Shagam, Marvin Hückel-Berri *private school educator*

Olivehurst
Green, Tim M. *mathematics educator*

Ontario
Chavez, Virginia *counselor*
Dastrup-Hamill, Faye Myers *city official*
Dunn, Donald Jack *law librarian, educator, dean*
Fangerow, Kay Elizabeth *nurse*
Kloepfer, Marguerite Fonnesbeck *writer*
Myers, Christopher D. *bank executive*
Previtti, James P. *real estate executive*

Orange
Abolhoda, Amir *surgeon*
Ahlquist, John B. *application developer*
Alkire, Michael T. *anesthesiologist, researcher*
Amin, Alpesh N. *internist*
Armstrong, David Ligon *psychiatrist*
Banning, Donna Rose *art educator*
Barr, Ronald Jeffrey *dermatologist, pathologist*
Batchelor, James Kent *lawyer*
Borghei, Peyman *medical researcher*
Brown, Tod David *bishop*
Busby, Nita June *small business owner*
Carriere, Brother William Joseph *school system administrator*
Chang, Jae Chan *hematologist, oncologist, educator*
Christian-Brougham, Ruby Rosalie *education educator*
Cramer, Steven Craig *neurologist, educator*
Crumley, Roger Lee *surgeon, educator, otolaryngologist*
Curt, Alan Sandman *neuroscientist, educator*
DiSaia, Philip John *obstetrician, gynecologist, radiology educator*
Dorne, Howard Leslie *radiologist*
Duncan, John Alexander *lawyer*
Duzey, Robert Lindsey *lawyer*
Fisher, Mark Jay *neurologist, neuroscientist, educator*
Hamilton, Harry Lemuel, Jr. *academic administrator, science educator*
Haydon, Michael *obstetrician, gynecologist*
Hubbell, Floyd Allan *internist, educator*

Kaempen, Charles Edward *manufacturing executive*
Kraft, Arthur *dean*
Lott, Ira Totz *pediatric neurologist*
Matallana, Lynne *medical association administrator*
Mc Farland, Norman Francis *bishop*
Meier, Steven W. *orthopedist, surgeon, consultant*
Morgan, Beverly Carver *pediatrician, educator*
Palafox, Brian A. *surgeon*
Rowen, Marshall *radiologist*
Simjee, Aisha *ophthalmologist, educator*
Smith, John LeRoy *mathematician, educator*
Smith, Ronald Edward *ophthalmologist*
Stevens, Cherita Wyman *social sciences educator, writer*
Tuggle, Francis Douglas *entrepreneur, consultant, management educator, scientist*
Uslay, Can *finance educator*
Vaziri, Nosratola Dabir *internist, nephrologist, educator*
Williams, Benjamin R. *health facility administrator*
Williams, Danna Beth *reading specialist, educator*
Wong, Brian Jet-Fei *surgeon*
Yu, Jen *medical educator*

Orangevale
Gibson, Gordon Ronald *chemist*

Orinda
Counelis, James Steve *education educator*
Hartog, John A. *lawyer*
Hetland, John Robert *law educator*
Migdale, Lawrence D. *photographer*
Schneider, Peter A. *urologist, surgeon*
Strong, Susan Clancey *writer, communications executive, editor*
Trowbridge, Thomas, Jr. *mortgage company executive*
Walsh, Joseph Richard *lawyer*

Oroville
Barnes, William Wayne *geographer, writer*

Oxnard
Hill, Alice Lorraine *historian, researcher, genealogist*
Kirschbaum, Alan Ira *air force officer, systems integration specialist*
Leedy, Wallace Curtis *former educator*
O'Connell, Hugh Mellen, Jr. *retired architect*
O'Hearn, Michael John *lawyer*
Sands, Velma Ahda *lawyer*
Tolmach, Jane Louise *community activist, municipal official*
Woolsey, Robert Paul *church musician*

Pacific Grove
Davis, Robert Edward *retired communications educator*
Lim, Byung-Joon Lucas *language educator, department chairman*
Longman, Anne Strickland *special education educator, consultant*
Yep, Laurence Michael *author*

Pacific Palisades
Beck, John Christian *physician, educator*
Cale, Charles Griffin *lawyer, real estate and corporate financial company executive*
Caster, Jacqueline Jacobs *not-for-profit executive*
Chesney, Lee Roy, Jr. *artist*
Claes, Daniel John *physician*
Copeland, John Howard *communications executive, television producer*
Daniels, John R. *oncologist, educator*
Diehl, Richard Kurth *retail executive, consultant*
Flattery, Thomas Long *lawyer, administrator*
Griver, Jeanette A. *psychologist, consultant*
Hadges, Thomas Richard *media consultant*
Hagenbuch, Rodney Dale *financial consultant*
Hoffenberg, Marvin *retired political science professor*
Hubbs, Donald Harvey *foundation executive*
Jennings, Marcella Grady *rancher, investor*
Katz, George Gershon *psychologist, lawyer*
Kelley, Thomas Joseph *lawyer*
Kirkgaard, Valerie Anne *media group executive, radio host, writer, radio producer, consultant*
Lewis, Carl (Frederick Carlton Lewis) *Olympic track and field athlete*
Longaker, Richard Pancoast *retired political science professor, academic administrator*
Love, Susan Margaret *surgeon, educator, writer*
Mulryan, Henry Trist *mining executive, consultant*
Outcalt, David Lewis *academic administrator, mathematics professor, consultant, musician*
Perloff, Marjorie Gabrielle *literature educator*
Rachelefsky, Gary Stuart *medical educator*
Ritter, Jason *actor*
Sevilla, Stanley *lawyer*
Share, Richard Hudson *lawyer*
Verrone, Patric Miller *lawyer, writer*
Wales, Ken *film producer*

Pacifica
Cole, David Macaulay *journalist, consultant*
Kelly, Kevin *editor*
Latham, Benjamin Erwin *music educator*

Palm Desert
Anderson, R. Christian *photographer, media consultant, art director*
Ayling, Henry Faithful *editor, consultant, journalist, poet*
Bantz, Jody Lenore *psychologist*
Baxter, Betty Carpenter *academic administrator*
Benn, Theodore Alexander (Alec Benn) *writer*
Bernhard, Herbert Ashley *lawyer*
Epstein, Marvin Morris *retired construction company executive*
Karson, Lillian P. *risk management consultant*
Miller, Donald Ross *management consultant*
Osborne, Bartley Porter, Jr. *aeronautical engineer*
Owings, Thalia Kelley *elementary school educator*
Ponder, Catherine *clergywoman*
Reinhardt, Benjamin Max *lawyer, arbitrator, mediator*
Sausman, Karen *zoological park administrator*
Stenhouse, Everett Ray *clergy administrator*
Unterman, Eugene Rex *aviation sales and consulting company executive*
Wallace, Franklin Sherwood *lawyer, director*
Widran, Jerrold Joseph *urologist*

Palm Springs
Arnold, Stanley Norman *management consultant, educator*
Coffey, Nancy *real estate broker*
Diodosio, Charles Joseph *lawyer*
Ellsworth, Frank L. *not-for-profit executive*
Gaede, James Ernest *physician, educator*
Gerard, James Wilson *publishing consultant*
Jones, Milton Wakefield *publisher*
Kimberling, John Farrell *retired lawyer*
Krans, Michelle M. *publishing executive*
Nelson, K. Bonita *literary agent*
Petermann, Hans Jürgen *research scientist*
Scott, Walter, Jr. *business consultant*
Wiesner, John Joseph *retail chain store executive*
Wouk, Herman *writer*

Palmdale
Bevilaqua, Paul M. *aeronautical engineer*
Farr, Donald Eugene *engineering scientist*
Kilanowski, Dana Marcotte *historian, writer, filmmaker, archaeologist*
Phillips, Ruthanne *special education administrator*
Yore, Joseph N. *communications executive*

Palo Alto
Abrams, William F. *lawyer*
Adamson, Geoffrey David *endocrinologist, surgeon*
Andersen, Torben Brender *optical researcher, astronomer, software engineer*
Anderson, Charles Arthur *retired science administrator*
Ashford, John Wesson, Jr. *psychiatrist, researcher*
Balzhiser, Richard Earl *research and development company executive*
Banerjee, Prith *computer company executive, computer engineering professor*
Baron, Frederick David *lawyer*
Baum, Brandon *lawyer, educator*
Beatus, Brian J. *lawyer*
Bennett, Alan Jerome *electronics executive, physicist*
Bensch, Klaus George *pathology educator*
Benton, Lee F. *lawyer*
Beutler, Larry Edward *psychologist, educator*
Bianchini, Gina *Internet company executive*
Blessing-Moore, Joann Catherine *allergist, pulmonologist*
Bouchard, Gilles *computer company executive*
Bradley, Donald Edward *lawyer*
Bradley, (R.) Todd *communications and computer company executive*
Breyer, James William *venture capitalist*
Britton, M(elvin) C(reed), Jr. *rheumatologist*
Brown, David Randolph *electrical engineer*
Card, Stuart Kent *psychologist, researcher*
Chace, William Murdough *former university administrator, literature educator*
Chang, Carmen *lawyer*
Charnas, Charles N. *lawyer, computer company executive*
Chen, Stephen Shi-hua *pathologist, biochemist*
Cherno, Melvin *humanities educator*
Chinnis, C. Cabell, Jr. *lawyer*
Climan, Richard Elliot *lawyer*
Cohen, Karl Paley *nuclear energy consultant*
Craparo, John S. *information technology executive*
Curtis, Mark T. *financial planner*
Daniels, Russell *information technology executive*
del Calvo, Jorge A. *lawyer*
Dement, William Charles *medical researcher, educator*
Denzel, Nora *information technology executive*
Diffie, Whitfield (Whit) *computer and communications engineer*
Dillon, Adrian T. *financial executive*
Druker, David *medical association administrator*
Dubin, Anne *medical educator*
Dugger, Marguerite J. *retired special education educator*
Dunn, Debra L. *computer company executive*
Dwyer, John Charles *lawyer*
Ernst, Wallace Gary *geology educator, dean*
Estrin, Judith *computer company executive*
Feldman, Boris *lawyer*
Flanagan, Robert Joseph *economics professor*
Flaum, Keith Avery *lawyer*
Flaxman, Jon E. *computer company executive*
Flory, Curt Alan *research physicist*
Forbes, Alfred Dean *religious studies researcher*
Fordis, Jean Burke *lawyer*
Fries, James Franklin *internal medicine educator*
Fromm, Jeffery Bernard *lawyer*
Fruchterman, James Robert, Jr. *computer company executive, not-for-profit executive*
Furbush, David Malcolm *lawyer*
Gaither, James C. *lawyer*
Galel, Susan Alpert *transfusion medicine physician*
Gallo, Penny Howe *lawyer*
Gibson, Virginia Lee *lawyer*
Giza, David Alan *lawyer*
Gorman, Maureen J. *lawyer*
Greco, Joseph A. *lawyer*
Greene, Diane *information technology executive*
Guertin, Timothy E. *medical products executive*
Haddad, Francois *cardiologist, researcher*
Halloran, Jean M. *human resources specialist*
Halluin, Albert Price *lawyer*
Hamilton, David Mike *publishing executive*
Hays, Marguerite Thompson *nuclear medicine physician, educator*
Heneveld-Story, Christy Jean *educational researcher*
Herrick, Tracy Grant *fiduciary*
Herring, (William) Conyers *retired physicist, educator*
Hiscox, Frank S. *lawyer*
Hoak, Jonathan S., Sr. *lawyer*
Hodge, Philip Gibson, Jr. *mechanical and aerospace engineering educator*
Holman, Halsted Reid *physician, educator*
Holston, Michael Joseph *lawyer, computer company executive*
Horngren, Charles Thomas *finance educator*
Huberman, Bernardo A. *physicist*
Hurd, Mark V. *computer company executive*
Ivey, Thomas J. *lawyer*
Jackson, Cynthia L. *lawyer*
Jacobson, Van *computer scientist, researcher*
Johnson, Noble Marshall *research scientist*
Joshi, Vyomesh I. *computer company executive*
Kapoor, Ashok Kumar *engineer*
Katz, Ronald Stanley *lawyer*
Kawasaki, Guy *venture capitalist, investment banker, evangelist, entrepreneur, blog writer, writer*
Keeffe, Emmet Britton *medical educator*
Keshavarzian, Abtin *electrical engineer, researcher*
Kim, Wan Hee *engineering educator*
King, Kenton J. *lawyer*
Klein, Robert Nicholas, II, *real estate developer*
Knoles, George Harmon *history educator*
Korman, Martin *lawyer*
Lal, Dhananjay *information technology executive, researcher*
Lesjak, Catherine A. *computer company executive*
Lo, Yee On *composer*
Loewenstein, Walter Bernard *nuclear energy industry executive*
Lucente, Sam *industrial designer*
Lynch, Timothy Jeremiah-Mahoney *lawyer, educator, theologian, realtor, writer*
Lyons, Cathy *computer company executive*
Martin, Robert Bruce *chemistry professor*
Masur, Joshua Michael *lawyer*
McCall, Jennifer Jordan *lawyer*
McIntyre, Robert Wheeler *retired conservation organization executive*
Michels, Dirk *lawyer*
Michie, Sara H. *pathologist, educator*
Miller, Michael Patiky *lawyer*
Miller, Scott D. *lawyer*
Moll, John Lewis *retired electronics engineer*
Mommsen, Katharina *retired literature and language professor, foundation administrator*
Monroy, Gladys H. *lawyer*
Moore, Cassandra Chrones *real estate broker*
Moos, Rudolf H. *psychologist, researcher*
Morrison, William Fosdick *business educator, retired electrical company executive*
Moss, Richard B. *pediatrician*
Mott, Randy (Randall D. Mott) *computer company executive*
Neal, Stephen Cassidy *lawyer*
Neale-May, Donovan *marketing executive*
Needleman, Philip *cardiologist, pharmacologist*
Nichols, William Ford, Jr. *foundation, health science association administrator, educator*
Ning, Shoucheng *cancer biologist, head and neck surgeon*
Nopar, Alan Scott *lawyer*
Nuchi, Lior O. *lawyer*
Park, Marina H. *lawyer*
Patten, Valerie Lynn *lawyer*
Patterson, Robert Edward *lawyer*
Peng, Stanford Lee-Yu *physician*
Perez de Alonso, Marcela *human resources specialist, information technology executive*
Perl, Martin Lewis *physicist, educator, chemical engineer*
Perlroth, Mark Guido *medical educator*
Petkanics, Donna M. *lawyer*
Pizzo, Philip A. *pediatrician, educator, dean*
Pooley, James Henry *lawyer*
Quate, Calvin Forrest *engineering educator*
Radcliffe, Mark Flohn *lawyer*
Raffin, Thomas A. *physician*
Randall, Jeffrey G. *lawyer*
Ranganathan, Parthasarathy *computer scientist*
Reback, Gary *lawyer*
Renfro, John M. *human resources specialist*
Richardson, Tom (Edward Thompson Richardson) *artist*
Robinson, Walter J. III *lawyer*
Robison, Shane V. *computer company executive*
Roos, John Victor *lawyer*
Sack, John R. *library and information scientist*
Salmon, Denis R. *lawyer*
Salvatierra, Oscar, Jr. *transplant surgeon, urologist, educator*
Sanders, William John *research scientist*
Saxena, Arjun Nath *physicist*
Schafer, Ronald William *electrical engineering educator*
Schendel, Stephen Alfred *surgeon, educator*
Schnabel, Rockwell Anthony *former ambassador*
Schurman, David Jay *orthopedic surgeon, educator*
Scitovsky, Anne Aickelin *economist, researcher*
Seethaler, William Charles *manufacturing executive*
Sherlock, Phyllis Krafft *psychologist*
Shi, Qin *lawyer, technologist*
Shuer, Lawrence Mendel *neurosurgery educator*
Shulman, Ron E. *lawyer*
Silverman, Norman Henry *cardiologist, educator*
Skoll, Jeffrey S. *philanthropist, former internet company executive*
Skoog, Douglas Arvid *retired chemistry educator, writer*
Smith, Gregory C. *lawyer*
Smith, Julie Ann *pharmaceutical executive*
Solomon, Darlene J.S. *electronics executive*
Sonsini, Larry W. *lawyer*
Spohn, Nor Rae *computer company executive*
Staprans, Armand *electronics executive*
Strober, Samuel *immunologist, educator*
Sullivan, Dennis C. *lawyer*
Sullivan, William P. *electronics executive*
Taylor, John Joseph *nuclear engineer, researcher*
Ticknor, Carolyn M. *computer company executive*
Tiffany, Joseph Raymond, II, *lawyer*
Title, Alan M. *astrophysicist*
Tsien, Richard Winyu *biology professor*
Tune, Bruce Malcolm *pediatrics educator, renal toxicologist*
Unkovic, Nicholas C. *lawyer*
Urquhart, John *medical researcher, educator*
Varney, Robert Nathan *retired physicist, researcher*
Vaughn, Issac J. *lawyer*
Voight, Jerry D. *lawyer*
Walker, Ann Yvonne *lawyer*
Waller, Peter William *public relations executive*
Waltzer, Garrett J. *lawyer*
Webb, Maynard G., Jr. *Internet company executive*
Wheeler, Raymond Louis *lawyer*
White, Rick *lawyer, former congressman*
Winkler, Michael *computer company executive*
Wong, Y(ing) Wood *real estate investment company executive, real estate development company executive, venture capital investment company executive*
Yuan, Nanci *pediatrician, pulmonologist, educator*

Palo Cedro
Haggard, Merle Ronald *songwriter, recording artist*

Palos Verdes Estates
Abbott, A. Dwight *retired astronautical engineer*
Blackman, Lee L. *lawyer*
Brigden, Ann Schwartz *mediator, educator*
DeLuce, Richard David *lawyer*
DiPaul, Christopher *psychologist*
Lazzaro, Anthony Derek *academic administrator*
Mennis, Edmund Addi *investment management consultant*
Myhre, Byron Arnold *pathologist, educator*
Paulikas, George Algis *retired physicist*
Raue, Jorg Emil *electrical engineer*
Seide, Paul *civil engineering educator*
Yarbrough, Allyson Debra *electrical engineer*

Palos Verdes Peninsula
Ahmady, Ali *lab administrator, director*
Alkon, Paul Kent *language educator*
Christie, Hans Frederick *retired utilities executive*
Denke, Paul Herman *retired aircraft engineer*
Grant, Robert Ulysses *retired manufacturing executive*
Leone, William Charles *retired manufacturing executive*
Manning, Christopher Ashley *finance educator, consultant*
Mirels, Harold *aerospace engineer*
Narasimhan, Padma Mandyam *physician*
Slayden, James Bragdon *retired retail executive*
Slusser, Robert Wyman *aerospace transportation executive*
Thomas, Claudewell Sidney *psychiatrist, educator*
Thomas, Hayward *retired manufacturing executive*
Van Der Meulen, Joseph Pierre *neurologist*
Wilson, Theodore Henry *retired electronics executive, aerospace engineer*

Panorama City
Bass, Harold Neal *pediatrician, medical geneticist*
Janis, Elinor Raiden *artist, educator*
Lugg, Marlene Martha *immunization coordinator, health information systems specialist, health planner*
Sue, Michael Alvin *allergist*

Paradise
Barr, Donald Roy *statistics and operations research educator, statistician*
Bernstein, Elizabeth Ann *retired executive secretary*

Paramount
Hall, Howard Harry *lawyer*

Pasadena
Albee, Arden Leroy *geologist, educator*
Allen, Clarence Roderic *geologist, educator*
Andersen, Richard Alan *physiologist*
Anderson, David J. *biology professor*
Anderson, Don Lynn *geophysicist*
Arnold, Frances Hamilton *chemistry educator*
Arnott, Robert Douglas *investment company executive*
Asimow, Paul D. *geophysicist, educator*
Axelson, Charles Frederic *retired accounting educator, food products executive*
Baltimore, David *former academic administrator, microbiologist, educator*
Barish, Barry C. *physics professor, researcher*
Barnes, Charles Andrew *physicist, researcher*
Beauchamp, Jesse Lee (Jack Beauchamp) *chemistry professor*
Becker, Christopher *educator, chef*
Beer, Reinhard *atmospheric scientist*
Bischoff, Rick *admissions director*
Bishop, Robert Calvin *pharmaceutical company executive*
Boehm, Felix Hans *physicist, researcher*
Bogaard, William Joseph *mayor, lawyer, educator*
Boochever, Robert *judge*
Bosley, Edward Richmond *historical site administrator*

Bradley, James Edwin *religious studies educator*
Breckinridge, James Bernard *optical engineer*
Bridges, William Bruce *electrical engineer, educator, researcher*
Brogden-Stirbl, Shona Marie *writer, researcher*
Brotman, Richard Dennis *counselor*
Brown, Michael E. *astronomer, astronomy educator*
Buchwald, Jed Zachary *environmental health researcher, science history educator*
Bunt Smith, Helen Marguerite *lawyer*
Byun, Sung Hun *research scientist*
Caine, Stephen Howard *data processing executive*
Call, Merlin Wendell *lawyer*
Calleton, Theodore Edward *lawyer, educator*
Candes, Emmanuel Jean *mathematics professor*
Chahine, Moustafa Toufic *atmospheric scientist*
Chameau, Jean-Lou *academic administrator*
Chan, Sunney Ignatius *retired chemistry educator*
Chen, Sandra Yi-Ting *political organization worker*
Chu, Benjamin K. *hospital administrator*
Crowley, John Crane *real estate developer*
Culick, Fred Ellsworth Clow *engineering and physics professor*
Cutri, Roc Michael *research scientist*
D'Angelo, Robert William *lawyer*
Davidson, Eric Harris *molecular and developmental biologist, educator*
Davis, Mark E. *chemical engineering educator*
Dervan, Peter Brendan *chemistry professor*
Dimitrius, Jo-Ellan *trial consultant*
Douglas, Kimberly *university librarian*
Dressler, Alan Michael *astronomer*
Duxbury, Thomas Carl *planetary scientist*
Eisenstein, James P. *physicist, educator*
Elachi, Charles *aerospace engineer*
Fernandez, Ferdinand Francis *federal judge*
Fisher, Raymond Corley *federal judge*
Flagan, Richard Charles *chemical engineering educator*
Frautschi, Steven Clark *physicist, researcher*
Fredericks, Ward Arthur *venture capitalist*
Freedman, Wendy Laurel *astronomer, educator, director*
Freeman, Ralph Carter *investment banker, management consultant*
Fu, Lee-Lueng *oceanographer*
Gillis, Christine Diest-Lorgion *financial planner, stockbroker*
Gilman, Richard Carleton *retired academic administrator*
Glovsky, Myron Michael *medical educator*
Goldreich, Peter Martin *astrophysics and planetary physics educator*
Goldschmidt, Walter Rochs *anthropologist*
Goldweber, Robert *emergency physician*
Golombek, Matthew Philip *research scientist, planetary geologist*
Goodstein, David Louis *physics professor*
Goodwin, Alfred Theodore *federal judge*
Gould, Roy Walter *engineering educator*
Gray, Harry Barkus *chemistry professor*
Gregory, Timothy Peter *historian, consultant*
Gross, Bill *energy executive*
Grotzinger, John Peter *paleontologist, educator*
Grubbs, Robert Howard *chemistry professor*
Gurnis, Michael Christopher *geological sciences educator*
Haight, James Theron *lawyer*
Hall, Cynthia Holcomb *federal judge*
Halsted, Margo *music educator, carillonneur*
Harvey, Joseph Paul, Jr. *orthopedist, educator*
Heath, James R. *chemistry educator*
Heindl, Clifford Joseph *physicist, researcher*
Helmberger, Donald Vincent *geophysical educator, researcher*
Helou, George *science administrator, educator*
Hernandez, Enrique, Jr., (Rick Hernandez) *security firm executive*
Hilbert, Robert S(aul) *optical engineer*
Hirschmann, James William III *diversified financial services company executive*
Hitlin, David George *physicist, researcher*
Holmes, Louis Ira *physician assistant, educator, photojournalist*
Holzmann, Gerard Johan *computer science researcher*
Horak, Jan-Christopher *filmmaker, educator, curator*
Hornung, Hans Georg *aeronautical engineering educator, science administrator*
Hou, Thomas Yizhao *mathematician*
Huang, Alice Shih-hou *biologist, educator, virologist*
Hunt, Gordon *lawyer*
Hunt, Hazel Analue Stanfield *retired accountant*
Hunter, Milton *construction company executive, retired career military officer*
Jennings, Paul Christian *civil engineering educator, academic administrator*
Johnson, Barbara Jean *retired judge, lawyer*
Johnson, William Lewis *materials scientist, educator*
Jun, Insoo *nuclear scientist, researcher*
Kamionkowski, Marc Paul *astrophysicist, educator*
Kanamori, Hiroo *geophysicist, professor emeritus*
Kaplan, Gary *executive recruiter*
Kavanagh, Ralph William *physics professor*
Keller, Herbert Bishop *mathematics professor*
Keys, Scott *bank executive*
Kleinpeter, Amy E. Clark *lawyer*
Knowles, James Kenyon *applied mathematician, educator*
Koch, Christof *biologist, educator*
Konishi, Masakazu *neuroscientist, educator*
Koshalek, Richard *academic administrator, former museum director, consultant*
Kousser, J(oseph) Morgan *historian, educator*
Kozinski, Alex *federal judge*
Lake, Kevin Bruce *medical association administrator*
Lange, Andrew E. *astrophysicist*
Ledyard, John Odell *economics professor, consultant*
Leeson, Peter J., IV, *lawyer*
Lester, Henry Allen *biology professor*
Liashkov, Peter *artist, educator*
Lingenfelter, Sherwood Galen *academic administrator, retired anthropologist*
List, Ericson John *environmental engineering science educator, consultant*
Logan, Francis Dummer *retired lawyer*
Lopes, Rosaly Mutel Crocce *astronomer, planetary geologist*
Marcus, Rudolph Arthur *chemist, educator*
Markley, William C. *lawyer*
Marlen, James S. *chemical, plastics and building materials manufacturing company executive*
Martin, Craig Lee *engineering company executive*
Matthews, Mildred Shapley *retired editor*
Mayo, Stephen L. *biochemist*
McAfee, R. Preston *economics professor*
Mc Carthy, Frank Martin *oral surgeon, educator*
McGill, Thomas Conley *physics educator*
Mc Koy, Basil Vincent Charles *theoretical chemist, educator*
McNulty, James F. *construction company executive*
Menefee, John William III *cinematographer, film producer*
Meyerowitz, Elliot Martin *biologist, educator*
Miller, Susan Calabrese *lawyer, consumer products company executive*
Mosher, Sally Ekenberg *lawyer, musician*
Mueth, Joseph Edward *lawyer*
Munger, Edwin Stanton *political geography educator*
Muñoz Fernández, Michela *electrical engineer, researcher*
Murray, Richard M. *engineering educator*
Myers, R(alph) Chandler *lawyer*
Nackel, John George *health facility administrator*
Nelson, Dorothy Wright *federal judge*
Ng, Dominic *bank executive*
O'Bryant, Daniel R. *consumer products company executive*
Oemler, Augustus, Jr. *astronomer, educator*
O'Linger, JoAnn C. *astronomer*
Opel, William *medical research administrator*
Ortiz, Michael *engineering educator*
Paez, Richard A. *federal judge*
Palfrey, Thomas Rossman *economics professor, political science professor*
Parker, Robert Allan Ridley *federal agency administrator, astronaut*
Pashgian, Margaret Helen *artist*
Patton, Richard Weston *retired mortgage company executive*
Perry, Michael W. *bank executive*
Phillips, Robert *engineering educator, researcher*
Plott, Charles Raymond *economics educator*
Politzer, Hugh David *physicist, educator*
Poon, Peter Tin-Yau *engineer, physicist*
Preskill, John Phillip *physics professor*
Revel, Jean-Paul *biology professor*
Rinaldi, James J. *federal agency administrator*
Roberts, John D. *chemist, educator*
Roshko, Anatol *aeronautical engineer*
Rymer, Pamela Ann *federal judge*
Sabersky, Rolf Heinrich *mechanical engineer*
Sandage, Allan Rex *astronomer*
Sanders, Jan W. *librarian, Library Association Executive*
Sargent, Anneila Isabel *astrophysicist*
Sargent, Wallace Leslie William *astronomer, educator*
Schwarz, John Henry *theoretical physicist, educator*
Scott, David Clinton *research scientist*
Scudder, Thayer *anthropologist, educator*
Seinfeld, John Hersh *chemical engineering professor*
Sekanina, Zdenek *astronomer*
Sharif, Masoud *electrical engineer, researcher*
Shaw, Anthony *pediatric surgeon, retired educator*
Shimada, Katsunori *retired electrical engineer*
Short, Elizabeth M. *internist, educator, retired federal agency administrator*
Shuster, Marguerite *minister, educator*
Sidick, Erkin *optical engineer*
Siemon-Burgeson, Marilyn M. *education administrator*
Silverstein, Robert P. *lawyer*
Smith, Howard Russell *manufacturing executive, director*
Smith, Michael Robert *electro-optical engineer, physicist*
Smith, Milan Dale, Jr. *federal judge*
Smith, Ora Everett *corporate executive, lawyer*
Solis, Carlos *lawyer*
Spector, Phil (Harvey Phillip Spector) *record company executive*
Spilker, Linda Joyce *aerospace scientist*
Staehle, Robert L. *foundation executive*
Steidel, Charles C. *astronomy educator*
Stevens, Roy W. *sales and marketing executive*
Stevenson, David John *planetary scientist, educator*
Stone, Edward C. *physicist, researcher*
Stroupe, Ashley W. *engineer*
Sullivan, William Francis *lawyer*
Tanner, Dee Boshard *retired lawyer*
Tashima, Atsushi Wallace *federal judge*
Telleria, Anthony F. *lawyer*
Thomas, Joseph Fleshman *retired architect*
Thorne, Kip Stephen *physicist, researcher*
Tirrell, David A. *research scientist, educator*
Tombrello, Thomas Anthony, Jr. *physics professor*
Valone, Keith Emerson *psychologist, psychoanalyst*
Vance, Rodney *film producer, writer*
van Schoonenberg, Robert G. *lawyer, consumer products company executive*
Varshavsky, Alexander Jacob *molecular biologist*
Vogt, Rochus Eugen *physicist, researcher*
Wadden, Christopher David *food products executive*
Wang, Jia *research scientist*
Wardlaw, Kim A. McLane *federal judge*
Wasserburg, Gerald Joseph *geology and geophysics educator*
Watkins, John Francis *management consultant*
Watson, Noel G. *construction executive*
White-Thomson, Ian leonard *retired mining executive*
Wilcox, Jaroslava Zitkova *physicist*
Williams, Bradley Bennett *historian*
Winbush, Olga Joyce *education educator, consultant*
Winter, Ralph D. *Christian world missionary, professor*
Wise, Mark B. *physics professor*
Wong, Raymond Shiu-Loong *radiologist*
Wood, Lincoln Jackson *aerospace engineer*
Wyatt, Joseph Lucian, Jr. *lawyer, writer*
Yariv, Amnon *electrical engineering educator, research scientist*
Yeager, Caroline Hale *writer, retired radiologist, consultant*
Yeomans, Donald Keith *astronomer*
Yohalem, Harry Morton *lawyer*
Zewail, Ahmed Hassan *chemistry and physics educator, consultant, editor*
Zuetel, Kenneth Roy, Jr. *lawyer*

Paso Robles
Boxer, Jerome Harvey *data processing executive, accountant, management consultant, vintager*
Brown, Benjamin Andrew *retired journalist*
Gerstung, Estella Rose *literature and language professor*
Pasky, Gary Jerome *consumer products company executive*
Webster, David Arthur *retired life insurance company executive*

Patterson
Keller, David Patrick *real estate broker*

Pauma Valley
Fitzgerald, Shane Michael *engineer*
Lewis, Gerald Jorgensen *judge*

Pearblossom
Goldman, Gary Steven *computer scientist, consultant*

Pebble Beach
Dallmann, William Charles *speech educator, writer*
Mortensen, Gordon Louis *artist, printmaker*
Neville, Roy Gerald *research scientist, chemical executive, consultant*

Penn Valley
Ingram, Jeffrey Charles *lawyer, educator*
Sands, Sharon Louise *graphics designer, artist*
Whitsel, Richard Harry *retired biologist, entomologist*

Penngrove
Haslam, Gerald William *writer, educator*

Perris
Cohen, Joseph I. *forensic pathologist*
Zimmer, Paul Gerald, II, *retired community care licensing professional*

Petaluma
Bailey, Preston Edward *music educator*
Castagnola, George Joseph, Jr. *arbitrator, secondary school educator*
Frederickson, Arman Frederick *mining executive, petroleum engineer*
Gervais, Cherie Nadine *small business owner*
Hass, Robert L. *writer, literature educator*
Laporte, Leo *writer, blogger, radio personality*
McChesney, Robert Pearson *artist*
Meyer, Julie Cathleen *marketing executive, director*
O'Hare, Sandra Fernandez *education educator*
Pronzini, Bill John (William Pronzini) *writer*
Purcell, Steven Richard *international management consultant, engineer, economist*
Sebold, Alice *writer*
Skalagard, Hans Martin *artist*
Spiegelman, Art *writer, cartoonist*
Thomas, Nancy Hinckley *special education educator*

Phillips Ranch
Chambers-Belida, Candace R. *radio personality, writer, television producer, educator*

Piedmont
Montgomery, Theodore Ashton *physician*
Putter, Irving *retired French language educator*
Reich, Stanley Benjamin *radiologist, medical educator*
Seavey, William Arthur *lawyer, vintner*

Pinedale
Falcone, Patricia Jeanne Lalim *investor, foundation administrator*

Pinole
Emmanuel, Jorge Agustin *chemical engineer, environmental consultant*
Naughton, James Lee *internist*

Pittsburg
Gustafson, Sally Ann *counselor, cosmetologist, educator*
Williams-Thomas, Elizabeth A. *financial planner, consultant*
Williscroft-Barcus, Beverly Ruth *retired lawyer*

Placentia
Cash, Jeanie Maritta *educational association administrator*
Zweifel, Donald Edwin *editor, lobbyist, consultant*

Placerville
Nesbitt, Paul Edward *historian, author, educator*
Sundgren, Donald E. *construction executive*
Vandenberg, Byron F. *cardiologist*
Wessels-McCoy, Denise Wendy *pre-school administrator, consultant*
Wilkinson, Rosemary Regina Challoner *poet, writer*

Playa Del Rey
Baker, Robert M.L., Jr. *academic administrator, research scientist*
Cairns, Diane Patricia *motion picture executive*
McNeill, Daniel Richard *writer*
Mishelevich, David Jacob *medical products executive*
Raymer, Daniel P. *aeronautical engineering company executive, aeronautical engineer*
Weir, Alexander, Jr. *chemical engineer, consultant*

Pleasant Hill
Bastrenta, Brigitte Elisabeth *school administrator*
Fischer, Laurence Eliot *literature educator, consultant*
Hollister, Arthur Clair, Jr. *epidemiologist, consultant, retired public health service officer*
Otis, Roy James *lawyer*
Schrank, Shirley Ann *artist*

Pleasanton
Askanas, Mark S. *lawyer*
Balmuth, Michael A. *retail executive*
Burd, Steven A. *food service executive*
Ching, David T. *food products executive*
Edwards, Robert L. *corporate financial executive*
Everette, Bruce L. *retail executive*
Ferber, Norman Alan *retail executive*
Fine, Marjorie Lynn *lawyer*
Gordon, Robert A. *food products executive, lawyer*
Novak, Randi Ruth *systems engineer, computer scientist*
Opperwall, Stephen Gabriel *lawyer*
Renda, Larree M. *retail executive*
Roshong, Dee Ann Daniels *dean, educator, counselor*
Scott, G. Judson, Jr. *lawyer*
Shaw, Charles Alden *engineering executive*
Stallings, Charles Henry *retired physicist*
Van Dreser, Merton Lawrence *ceramics engineer*

Point Richmond
Edginton, John Arthur *lawyer*

Pollock Pines
Rickard, Margaret Lynn *library director, consultant*

Pomona
Agvanian, Youri *mathematician, educator, physicist*
Ambrose, William Wright, Jr. *dean, educator, academic administrator*
Bidlack, Wayne Ross *nutritional biochemist, toxicologist, food scientist*
Cranston, John Welch *historian, educator*
Dishman, Rose Marie Rice *academic administrator, researcher*
Fetterly, Barbara Louise *artist*
Gambone, Joseph Charles *medical educator, consultant*
Gupta, Eric K. *pharmacist, educator*
Jackson, Mary Ellen *librarian, consultant*
Lin, Lianlian *management educator*
Mezey, Robert *poet*
Rao, Yallapragada S. *oncologist*
Teague, Lavette Cox, Jr. *systems educator, consultant*
Tomiyasu, Kiyo *retired consulting engineer*
Trotter, F(rederick) Thomas *retired academic administrator*
Vo, Huu Dinh *pediatrician, educator*
Wagner, Edward John *physiologist, educator*
Wilson, Stanley Charles *artist, educator, curator, art gallery director, consultant*

Port Hueneme
Schneider, Arthur Paul *retired videotape and film editor, author*

Porterville
Kusserow, James *music educator*
Syrdahl, Rickelle Lyn *biology professor*

Portola Valley
Carnochan, Walter Bliss *retired humanities educator*
Fogarty, Thomas James *surgery educator*
Garsh, Thomas Burton *publisher*
Graham, William James *packaging company executive*
Hafkenschiel, Joseph Henry, Jr. *cardiologist, educator*
Kuo, Franklin F. *computer scientist, electrical engineer*
March, James Gardner *social sciences educator*
Nycum, Susan Hubbell *lawyer*
Olson, Walter Gilbert *lawyer*
Ward, Robert Edward *retired political science professor, academic administrator*

Poway
Conant, Kim Untiedt *retired elementary school educator*
Hunt, George Wayne *real estate appraiser*
Mueller, Gerhard Gottlob *retired financial accounting executive, educator*

Quartz Hill
McAllister, Bruce Richard *art educator*
Nettelhorst, Robin Paul *academic administrator, writer*

Quincy
Hall, Anthony Elmitt *agriculturist, physiologist*

Ramona
Hoffman, Wayne Melvin *retired airline official*

Rancho Cordova
Gosfield, Margaret *secondary school educator, school system administrator, consultant, editor*
Hall-Barron, Deborah *lawyer*
Harrell, Gary Paul *lawyer*
Ling, Robert Malcolm *banker, publishing executive*
Mesa, Reinaldo Humberto *information scientist, educator*

Rancho Cucamonga
Alvarez, Tirso Reyes, Jr. *engineer*
Gavin, Mary Ellen *marketing professional, consultant*
Kennedy, Mark Alan *secondary school educator*
Quinn, D. Michael *history professor*
Shields, Andrea Lyn *psychologist, coach, educator*
Squires, Kelley Elizabeth *music educator*

Rancho Dominguez
Janura, Jan Arol *apparel manufacturing executive*

Rancho Mirage
Abel, Michael L. *marketing executive*
Atiba, Joshua Olajide Oluwabunmi *internist, philanthropist, oncologist, educator, pharmacologist*
Blixseth, Timothy *real estate developer*
Chuang, Tsu-Yi *dermatologist, epidemiologist, educator*
Cohn, M. James *radiologist*
Cone, Lawrence Arthur *medical educator*
Fromm, Erwin Frederick *retired insurance company executive*
Kramer, Gordon *mechanical engineer*
Leydorf, Frederick Leroy *lawyer*
Leydorf, Mary Malcolm *physician, writer*
Nelson-Walker, Roberta *management software company executive*
Novak, Joe *artist*
Pierno, Anthony Robert *lawyer*
Shen, Alfred C. *neurosurgeon*
Steele, Charles Glen *retired accountant*
Stone, Richard Alan *medical educator*
Weil, Max Harry *internist, cardiologist, educator, researcher*

Rancho Murieta
Irelan, Robert Withers *retired metal products executive*

Rancho Palos Verdes
Curtis, Carole Ortale *executive recruiter, consultant*
Douglass, Craig Bruce *computer technology executive*
Frassinelli, Guido Joseph *retired aerospace engineer*
Gordon, Stewart Lynell *musician, educator*
Hillinger, Charles *journalist, writer*
Kwan, Benjamin Ching Kee *ophthalmologist*
Mac Innes, David Harold *artist, small business owner*
Neilan, Aidan Joseph *radiologist*
Schimmenti, John Joseph *lawyer*
Silver, Arnold Herbert *retired physicist*
Vanderlip, Elin Brekke *professional society administrator, volunteer*
Works, Margaret Elizabeth *retired art educator*
Yassin, Robert Alan *museum director, curator*

Rancho Santa Fe
Affeldt, John Ellsworth *retired physician*
Best, Jacob Hilmer, Jr. *retired hotel chain executive*
Byrd, Betty Rantze *writer*
Carr, David Turner *physician*
Creutz, Edward Chester *physicist, museum director*
Derbes, Daniel William *manufacturing executive*
Dieffenbach, Otto Weaver III *real estate company executive*
Jordan, Charles Morrell *retired automotive designer*
Kessler, A. D. *business and financial consultant, investment advisor, real estate consultant, educator, writer*
Matthews, Leonard Sarver *advertising and marketing executive*
Nadler, Henry Louis *pediatrician, educator, geneticist*
O'Driscoll, Margaret Millar (Peggy O'Driscoll) *real estate broker*
Peterson, Nad A. *retired lawyer*
Rockoff, S. David *radiologist, physician, educator*
Root, Alan Charles *diversified manufacturing company executive*
Ruiz, Ramón Eduardo *history professor*
Step, Eugene Lee *retired pharmaceutical executive*
Woolley, Roger Swire *lawyer*

Rancho Santa Margarita
Berta, Melissa Rose *mathematics professor*
Bunkis, Juris *plastic surgeon*
Curtis, John Joseph *lawyer, writer*
Lawson, Thomas Cheney *fraud examiner*
Parth, Frank R. *consulting company executive, educator*
Shusterman, Neal Douglas *writer, scriptwriter*

Redding
Emmerson, Archie Aldis (Red Emmerson, A.A. Emmerson) *sawmill owner*
Matenaer, Tegwin A. *artist, retired educator, consultant*
Nwangburuka, Okechukwu Nkem *psychiatrist*
Renard, Ronald Lee *allergist*

Redlands
Burgess, Larry Eugene *library director, historian, educator*
Clopine, Gordon Alan *consulting geologist, educator*
Coleman, Arlene Florence *retired pediatrics nurse*
Goto, Toshiko *retired art educator*
Hanks, Richard Alan *archivist*
Hanson, Gerald Warner *retired county official*
Heiss, David James *editor*
Huntley, William Barney *religious studies professor*
Nassar, William Michael *lawyer*
Pick, James Block *business professor, writer*
Rankin, Alex C. *management executive*
Ristau, Jacob Robert *art educator, graphics designer*
Simnjanovski, Riste *counseling administrator*
Skomal, Edward Nelson *retired aerospace transportation executive, electromagnetic environments consultant*
Skoog, William Arthur *retired oncologist*
Wilson, Lois Fair *school system administrator, educator*

Redondo Beach
Abernethy, Robert John *real estate developer*
Brodsky, Robert Fox *aerospace engineer, educator, author*
Crean, Maureen Rose *educational consultant*
Foster, John Stuart, Jr. *physicist, former defense industry executive*
Kagiwada, Reynold Shigeru *electronics executive*
McWilliams, Margaret Ann *home economist, educator, writer*
Mulvey, Gerald John *meteorologist*
Neely, Alexis *lawyer*
Richards, Denise *actress*
Sloan, Michael Dana *information systems specialist, management consultant*

Redwood City
Bell, Frank Ouray, Jr. *lawyer*
Bene, Steven G. *lawyer, game systems company executive*
Block, Keith *computer software company executive*
Bremser, George, Jr. *electronics executive*
Burkhardt, Roger *information technology executive*
Catz, Safra A. *computer software company executive*
Coddington, Clinton Hays *lawyer*
Cooperman, Daniel *lawyer, computer software company executive*
Ellison, Larry (Lawrence Joseph) *computer software company executive*
Fitzpatrick, Will *lawyer*
Grandsaert, John Leo *judge*
Henley, Jeffrey O. *computer software company executive*
Johnson, James Harding *advertising executive*
Kurian, Thomas *computer software company executive*
Lee, V. Paul *entertainment software company executive*
LeVoir, Lurese Cherene *dietetic technician*
Linzner, Joel *lawyer*
Millard, Richard Steven *lawyer*
Minton, Jennifer *computer software company executive*
Mockapetris, Paul V. *computer scientist, information technology executive*
Moore, Peter *interactive entertainment software company executive*
Mullooly, Michael Sean *pilot*
Nosler, Peter Cole *construction company executive*
Pape, Glenn Michael *lawyer, financial planner*
Penner, Susanne Mary *communications executive*
Phillips, Charles E., Jr. *computer software company executive*
Powers, Matthew Douglas *lawyer*
Probst, Lawrence F. III *interactive software/gaming executive*
Riccitiello, John S. *interactive software/gaming executive, venture capitalist*
Rohde, James Vincent *software systems company executive*
Rottler, Juergen *computer software company executive*
Rozwat, Charles *computer software company executive*
Spangler, Nita Reifschneider *volunteer*
Sullivan, Kathleen Marie *lawyer, educator, former dean*
Sweet, Victoria *medical educator, physician*
Trobough, John *communications executive*
Verhoeven, Charles K. *lawyer*
Vrabeck, Kathy Patterson *video game company executive*
Wang, Chen Chi *electronics executive, real estate company executive, diversified financial services company executive*
Wilhelm, Robert Oscar *lawyer, civil engineer*
Wookey, John *computer software company executive*

Redwood Valley
Speed, Cynthia Agnes *retired mathematics professor*

Reedley
Dick, Henry Henry *minister*
Walter, Burl Leroy, Jr. *retired music educator*

Rescue
Ackerly, Wendy Saunders *construction company executive*

Reseda
Hoover, Pearl Rollings *nurse*

Rialto
Alav, Faramarz *cardiologist, internist*
Hunley, John Dillard *retired historian, ombudsman*

Richmond
Arnon, Stephen Soulé *physician, research scientist*
Biddle, Michael *plastics company executive*
Corbin, Rosemary MacGowan *former mayor*
Dolberg, David Spencer *lawyer*
Janda, John Michael *microbiologist*
Jenkins, Everett Wilbur, Jr. *lawyer, writer, historian*
O'Rear, Dennis John *chemical engineer, consultant*
Shaw, Angelynn Renee *protective services official*
Shladover, Steven Elliot *transportation research professional*
Sibitz, Michael William *school system administrator*
Wessel, Henry *photographer*
Ziesenhenne, John William *insurance agent*

Ridgecrest
Bennett, Harold Earl *physicist, optics researcher*
Bennett, Jean Louise McPherson *physicist, research scientist*
Ferguson, Earl Wilson *cardiologist, medical executive, telemedicine consultant*
Miears-Cutsinger, Mary Ellen *artist, art gallery owner*
Sellers, Claudia Lee *biology professor*
St-Amand, Pierre *geophysicist*

Ripon
Freeman, Janice Kalina *elementary school educator*

Riverside
Akintimoye, Akindele D. *lawyer, consultant*
Balandin, Alexander A. *electrical engineer, educator*
Ballantyne, Ryan Johns *pipe organ builder, small business owner*
Barkin, Kenneth David *history professor*
Bartnicki-Garcia, Salomon *microbiologist, educator*
Bell, Helen Lavin *artist*
Beni, Gerardo *electrical engineer, educator*
Boldt, William Gregory *academic administrator, consultant*
Bosse, Mark Thomas *social services administrator*
Bricker, Neal S. *physician, educator*
Calfee, Robert Chilton *psychologist, educator*
Carpenter, Mark Warren *social sciences educator*
Case, Janice Chang *trust officer, property manager, naturopathic physician, psychologist, lawyer*
Chamberlain, Willard Thomas *retired metal products executive*
Chang, Sylvia Tan *health facility administrator, educator*
Custen, Barbara S. *library director*
Darling, Scott Edward *lawyer*
Day, Renee Noelle *secondary school, special education educator, special education educator*
Deal, Kevin Paul *furniture designer*
Elliott, Emory Bernard *language educator, school system administrator*
Evangelista, Allan *surgeon, medical researcher*
Fontana, Sandra Ellen Frankel *special education educator*
Geraty, Lawrence Thomas *academic administrator, archaeologist, educator*
Green, Dolores L. *medical association administrator*
Green, Harry Western, II, *geology and geophysics educator*
Grey, Robert Dean *academic administrator, biology educator*
Griffin, Keith Broadwell *retired economics professor*
Heiting, James Otto *lawyer*
Holmes, Dallas Scott *judge, educator*
Hyman, Bradley Clark *biology professor, geneticist*
Jackson, Ruth Moore *university librarian*
James, Etta (Jamesetta Hawkins) *recording artist*
Jung, Timothy Tae Kun *otolaryngologist*
Larson, Stephen G. *federal judge*
Lee, Raejin *music educator, soprano*
Linaweaver, Walter Ellsworth, Jr. *physician*
Mancilla, Faustina Ramirez *retired psychologist*
Marlatt, Michael James *lawyer*
McGill, Leonard John *lawyer*
McHughen, Alan *geneticist, educator*
Millar, Jocelyn G. *entomologist, educator*
Page, Albert Lee *soil science educator, researcher*
Peterson, Arthur Laverne *foundation administrator*
Petrinovich, Lewis Franklin *psychologist, educator*
Rabenstein, Dallas Leroy *chemistry professor*
Rainey, Susan J. *school system administrator*
Ratliff, Louis Jackson, Jr. *mathematics professor*
Rosenthal, Robert *psychology professor*
Russo, Marisa Natalina *educational consultant*
Salzman, Michele Renee *historian, educator*
Schwartz, Bernard Julian *lawyer*
Schwitzgebel, Eric *philosopher, educator*
Shapiro, Victor Lenard *mathematics professor*
Sklar, Wilford Nathaniel *lawyer, real estate broker*
Smith, Dorothy Ottinger *apparel designer, volunteer*
Smith, Elden Leroy *recreational vehicle and manufactured housing company executive*
Smith, Richard Charles *not-for-profit administrator, educator, consultant, advocate*
Snyder, Henry Leonard *historian, educator, writer*
Sokolsky, Robert Lawrence *journalist*
Stewart, David Wayne *marketing educator, psychologist, consultant, dean*
Suyenaga, Elsie Sakae *retired elementary school educator*
Turk, Austin Theodore *social studies educator*
Van Gundy, Seymour Dean *plant pathologist, educator*
Warren, Katherine Virginia *art gallery director*
White, Clara Jo *small business owner, consultant*
Yacoub, Ignatius I. *dean*
Yount, Gwendolyn Audrey *humanities educator*

Rocklin
Blank, Lenore Kim *literature and language professor, consultant*
Bowen, Brenda Denise *literature and language professor*
Dwyer, Darrell James *finance company executive*
Tal, Jacob *electronics executive*
Wiens, Beverly Jo *psychology professor*
Yates, Coleen Denise *special education educator*

Rohnert Park
Arminana, Ruben *academic administrator, educator*
Babula, William *dean, writer*
Byrne, Noel Thomas *sociologist, educator*
Steiner, John Michael *sociologist, educator*

Rolling Hills
Ehrlich, Michelle *dermatologist*
Rumbaugh, Charles Earl *arbitrator, mediator, educator, lawyer*

Rolling Hills Estates
Bellis, Carroll Joseph *surgeon, educator*
Conrad, Paul Francis *cartoonist*
Diaz-Zubieta, Agustin *nuclear physicist, engineering executive*
Wong, Sun Yet *engineer, consultant*
Zerunyan, Frank Vram *lawyer, councilman*

Romoland
Nail, Phil *information technology executive*

Rosemead
Bouknight, Lon (J.A. Bouknight Jr.) *lawyer, utilities executive*
Bryson, John E. *utilities executive*
Featherstone, Diane L. *utilities executive*
Fohrer, Alan J. *utilities company executive*
Gault, Polly L. *utilities executive*
House, Cecil R. *utilities executive*
Jin, Jing Yi *photographer, film director*
McDaniel, Thomas R. *utilities executive*
Parsky, Barbara J. *utilities executive*
Rosenblum, Richard Mark *utilities executive*
Yazdi, Mahvash *utilities executive*

Roseville
Grant, Barbara *venture capitalist*
Netto, Paul V. *critical care nurse*
Reichmann, Péter Iván *mathematics professor*
Riepenhoff-Talty, Marie *retired virologist*

Ross
Godwin, Sara *writer*
Nicholson, William Joseph *energy and environmental consultant*
Pierce, Carole Jean *artist*

Running Springs
Liddle, Sidney George *retired mechanical engineer, researcher*
Marcus, John Richard *lawyer*

Rutherford
Staglin, Garen Kent *computer company executive, venture capitalist*

Sacramento
Abdur-Rahim, Shareef (Julius Shareef Abdul-Rahim) *professional basketball player*
Acree, G. Hardy *airport executive*
Ailman, Christopher J. *investment company executive*
Aldrich, Thomas Albert *former brewing executive, consultant*
Allan, William George *artist, educator*
Amezcua, Esther Hernandez *elementary school educator*
Artest, Ron (Ronald William Artest Jr.) *professional basketball player*
Baccigaluppi, Roger John *agricultural products executive*
Barankin, Joseph Paul *director, consultant*
Barasch, Eugene Franklin *radiologist, physicist, researcher*
Bass de Martinez, Bernice *academic administrator, consultant*
Behrman, Bruce Ward *social sciences educator*
Bell, Wayne S. *lawyer, state agency official*
Bersin, Alan Douglas *state agency administrator, lawyer*
Betts, Bert A. *retired treasurer, accountant*
Bibby, Mike *professional basketball player*
Blake, D. Steven *lawyer*
Bleckley, Jeanette A. *lawyer*
Block, Alvin Gilbert *academic director*
Bogren, Hugo Gunnar *radiology educator*
Bond, Linda Grace *educational consultant*
Boucek, Jenny *professional basketball coach*
Bowen, Debra Lynn *state official, former state legislator*
Brown, Jerry, Jr., (Edmund Gerald Brown Jr.) *state attorney general, former mayor, governor*
Bruce, Thomas Edward *thanatologist, psychology professor*
Burks, Rocky Alan *disability access manager and consultant*
Burton, Randall James *lawyer*
Byer, Renee C. *photographer*
Callahan, Consuelo Maria *federal judge*
Campbell, Tom *state agency administrator, dean, former congressman*
Carr, Gerald Francis *language educator*
Caso, Anthony T. *lawyer*
Chapman, Michael William *orthopedist, educator*
Chu, Judy May *assemblywoman*

Clover, Haworth Alfred *elementary school educator, historian*
Cole, Glen David *minister*
Costigan, Richard III *lawyer*
Covin, David L. *retired political science professor*
Crawford, Robert Lawrence *mathematics professor*
Crimmins, Philip Patrick *retired metallurgical engineer, lawyer*
Cunningham, Mary Elizabeth (Mary Cunningham-Lusby) *physician*
Davies, Angela *oncologist, educator*
Day, James McAdam, Jr. *lawyer*
Dong, Michael Hon *toxicologist*
Drachnik, Catherine Meldyn *recreational therapist, artist, counselor*
Drummond, Marshall Edward (Mark) *academic administrator*
Duan, Lian *civil engineer*
Dunnett, Dennis George *retired state official*
Fait, Glenn A. *lawyer, educator*
Fargo, Heather *mayor*
Felderstein, Steven Howard *lawyer*
Fitzgerald, Faith Thayer *internist*
Flamm, Melvin Daniel, Jr. *cardiologist*
Forsyth, Nicole Young *animal scientist*
Forsyth, Raymond Arthur *civil engineer, consultant*
Franz, Jennifer Danton *public opinion and marketing researcher*
Friedman, Morton Lee *retired lawyer*
Fung, Maxwell Alexander *medical educator*
Gandara, David Raymond *internist, oncologist, educator*
Garamendi, John R. *lieutenant governor, former state legislator*
Gardner, Jerry Lee *financial consultant*
Gerringer, Elizabeth (The Marchioness de Roe Devon, Poet Julie de Vontine) *writer, lawyer*
Gerth, Donald Rogers *retired university president, educator*
Ghuzlan, Khalid A. *civil engineer*
Giles, Scott Marcus Anthony *composer, artist*
Gold, Anne Marie *library director*
Gray, Walter P. III *historian, archivist, consultant*
Gray-Fuson, Joan Lorraine *lawyer*
Griffith, Yolanda Evette *professional basketball player*
Guisepi, Robert Anthony *historian, writer*
Hales, Robert Ernest *psychiatrist, educator*
Hayward, Fredric Mark *social reformer*
Heaphy, Janis Besler *newspaper executive*
Henson, Glenda Maria *newswriter*
Hildreth, Susan *state librarian*
Houpt, James Edward *lawyer*
Howell, Lydia Pleotis *pathologist, educator*
Huh, Joan *lawyer*
Hull, Frederick Albert *artist, writer*
Hummel, John *information technology executive*
Hunter, Patricia Rae (Tricia Hunter) *state official*
Jackson, Richard Joseph *epidemiologist, educator, pediatrician, preventive medicine physician*
Janigian, Bruce Jasper *lawyer, educator*
Karlton, Lawrence K. *federal judge*
Kasch, Mary Courteol *occupational therapist*
Keiner, Christian Mark *lawyer*
Kelley, Michael A. *state agency administrator*
Kennedy, Harold Lee *physician*
Killian, Richard M. *library director*
Kuehl, Sheila James *state legislator*
Lamb, Philina May Ann *dermatologist, educator*
Laslett, Lawrence J. *physician, educator*
Lathi, Bhagawandas Pannalal *retired electrical engineering educator*
Lee, Edmond *internist, cardiologist*
Leong, Albin B. *pediatric pulmonologist, allergist, educator*
Levi, David F. *federal judge*
Lim, Alan Young *plastic surgeon*
Lionakis, George *architect*
Lippold, Roland Will *retired surgeon*
Lockyer, Bill (William Lockyer) *state official, former state attorney general*
Lundstrom, Marjie *editor*
Lynch, Peter John *retired dermatologist*
Majesty, Melvin Sidney *psychologist, consultant*
Makker, Sudesh Paul *physician*
Malloy, Michael Patrick *law educator, consultant*
Maloof, Gavin Patrick *professional sports team executive*
Maloof, Joseph *professional sports team owner*
Marin, Rosario *state agency administrator, former federal agency administrator*
Mazzaferro, James Joseph *music educator*
McCann, Kim Lou M. *theater educator, director*
McGrath, William Arthur *arbitrator, mediator, lawyer, real estate broker*
Meindl, Robert James *language educator, poet*
Morgan-Prager, Karole *lawyer, publishing executive*
Moulds, John F. *judge*
Nagy, Stephen Mears, Jr. *physician, allergist*
Newland, Chester Albert *public administration educator*
Nice, Carter *conductor*
O'Connell, Jack *school system administrator*
Opperman, Rosanna Resendez *vice principal*
Orey, Daniel Clark *mathematics professor*
Parker, Elizabeth Rindskopf *dean, law educator*
Parsapour, Kourosh *medical educator*
Patino, Douglas Xavier *government agency administrator, academic administrator*
Pavley, Fran J. *state representative*
Petrie, Geoffrey Michael *professional sports team executive, retired professional basketball player*
Piper, Jami Kathleen *music educator, composer, musician*
Pomeroy, Claire *dean*
Post, August Alan *retired economist, artist*
Pruitt, Gary B. *publishing company executive*
Purdy, James Aaron *medical physics professor*
Quinn, Francis A. *bishop*
Rab, George T. *pediatric orthopedic surgeon*
Rainwater, Eric *composer, music educator*
Reynolds, Jerry Owen *professional sports team executive*
Roberts, Paul Dale *state agency administrator, writer*
Robinson, Muriel Cox *psychiatrist*
Rodriguez, Rick *executive editor*
Root, Gerald Edward *legal administrator*
Rosenberg, Dan Yale *retired plant pathologist*
Rosenfeld, Arthur H. *physics professor, researcher*
Rossiter, Stephen J. *surgeon*
Schott, Robert James *internist, cardiologist*
Schwarzenegger, Arnold Alois *governor*
Scott, McGregor W. *prosecutor, lawyer*
Sharma, Arjun Dutta *cardiologist*
Sherwood, Robert Petersen *retired social sciences educator*
Shriver, Maria Owings *news correspondent*
Silva, Joseph, Jr. *dean, medical educator*
Stevenson, Thomas Ray *plastic surgeon*
Strickland, Anthony *state representative*
Styne, Dennis Michael *physician, educator*
Swatt, Stephen Benton *communications executive, consultant*
Theus, Reggie Wayne *professional basketball coach, retired professional basketball player*
Thomas, John *professional sports team executive*
Tong, John *plastic surgeon, educator, ophthalmic surgeon*
Tran, Van Thai *state legislator*
Tung, Prabhas *plastic surgeon*
Unde, Madhavji Anant (Mark Unde) *engineering executive*
Van Camp, Brian Ralph *judge*
Walsh, Denny Jay *reporter*
Walters, Daniel Raymond *political columnist*
Wasserman, Barry L(ee) *architect*
Wiens, Robert Niessen *retired financial analyst*
Williams, Arthur Cozad *retired broadcasting executive*
Willis, Dawn Louise *legal assistant, small business owner*
Wilson, Donald Eugene *management consultant*
Wishek, Michael Bradley *lawyer*
Wolfman, Earl Frank, Jr. *surgeon, educator*
Wolkov, Harvey Brian *oncologist, researcher*
Wyatt, Kyle K. *curator, historian*
Wyland, Mark *state official*
Yee, Leland Y. *state senator*
Yen, Andrew W. *internal medicine physician*
Zaidi, Emily Louise *retired elementary school educator*

Saint Helena

Backen, Howard J. *architect*
Darter, Robert Wells *surgeon, physician*

Salinas

Bernhard, Nancy Lynn *secondary school educator*
Bolles, Donald Scott *lawyer*
Borgman, Sylvia *artist, activist*
Helmer, James John, Jr. *physician, educator*
Huston, Velvali deAyxa *elementary school and voice educator*
Jeffries, Russell Morden *communications company official*
Mathews, Valinda Gail *elementary school educator, theater educator, gifted and talented educator*
Newberry, Conrad Floyde *aerospace engineering educator*
Puckett, Richard Edward *artist, consultant, former recreation executive*
Rosen, Jacqueline I. *musician, educator*
Stevens, Wilbur Hunt *accountant*

San Andreas

Breed, Allen Forbes *social services administrator*
Cretan, Donna *neonatal nurse, lactation consultant*

San Anselmo

Chiaverini, John Edward *construction company executive*
Murphy, Barry Ames *lawyer*
Symington, Toby *foundation administrator*
Truett, Harold Joseph, III, (Tim) *lawyer*

San Bernardino

Baek, Eun-Ok *instructional technology educator*
Burgess, Michael (Robert Reginald Burgess) *librarian, writer*
De Haas, David Dana *emergency physician*
Del Riego, Rutilio J. *bishop*
Fortune, Lowell *judge*
Fullerton, Robert Victor *lawyer*
Hansen, Anne Katherine *poet*
Martinez, Benjamin Ray *security officer, retired military non-commissioned officer*
Mian, Lal Shah *entomologist, educator*
Roberts, Katharine Adair *retired bookkeeper*
Roop, Ophelia Georgiev *library director*
Wilkin, Linda D. *sports medicine physician, educator*
Willis, Harold Wendt, Sr. *real estate developer*

San Bruno

Bradley, Charles William *podiatrist, educator*
Leung, Prudence Marguerite *pharmacist*
Reider, Suzie *Internet company executive, marketing professional*

San Carlos

Eberhard, Martin *automotive executive, electronics engineer*
Eby, Michael John *marketing research and technology consultant*
Foster, Mark Edward *lawyer, consultant, international lobbyist*
Hoffman, Paul Jerome *psychologist, statistician*
Lee, John Jin *lawyer*
Oliver, Nancy Lebkicher *artist, retired elementary school educator*
Rathmann, George Blatz *genetic engineering company executive*
Schumacher, Henry Jerold *museum director, retired military officer*
Symons, Robert Spencer *electronics engineer*
Vanderryn, Jack *environmental services administrator*
Wolff, Ronald Keith *toxicologist, researcher*

San Clemente

Clark, Earnest Hubert, Jr. *tool company executive*
Konney, Paul Edward *health products executive, lawyer*
Petruzzi, Christopher Robert *business educator, consultant*
Steinberg, Howard *chemical company executive, consultant*
Taylor, James Walter *business and management educator*
Wolfram, Thomas *physicist, educator*

San Diego

Adams, Loretta *marketing executive*
Adler, Christopher Alan *composer, educator*
Adriaan, Saint Claire Marlin *elementary school educator*
Aguirre, Michael Jules *lawyer*
Allen, P. Blake *lawyer*
Altman, Steven *financial consulting company executive, academic administrator*
Altman, Steven R. *telecommunications executive*
Anderson, Karl Richard *aerospace engineer, consultant*
Anderson, Paul Maurice *electrical engineering educator, researcher, consultant*
Armstong, Robert G. *lawyer*
Astroth, Margo Foltz *mental health nurse, nurse psychotherapist*
Auld, Robert Henry, Jr. *biomedical engineer, educator, consultant, writer*
Austad, Eric David *plastic and reconstructive surgeon*
Ball, Edward David *hematologist, oncologist*
Ballinger, Charles Edwin *educational association administrator*
Barr, Edward Sheldon *military officer, writer*
Bartus, Raymond Thomas *neuroscientist, writer, pharmaceutical executive*
Batchelder, David H. *investment advisory firm executive*
Bates-Romeo, Delores Alvenia *music educator, consultant*
Baxter, Robert Hampton *insurance company executive*
Beeson, Stephen Charles *physician*
Behrens, Henry William *international business educator, investment company executive*
Bell, Robert Jeffrey *lawyer*
Benirschke, Kurt *retired pathologist, educator*
Bernstein, Sanford Irwin *biology professor*
Blas, Marlene Jambaro *academic administrator, educator*
Bleiler, Charles Arthur *lawyer*
Bliesner, James Douglas *municipal/county official, consultant*
Bloom, Floyd Elliott *internist, neuroscientist*
Boggs, William S. *lawyer*
Bosco, Fernando Javier *geographer, educator*
Bowie, Peter Wentworth *judge, educator*
Brandes, Charles H. *investment company executive*
Brandes, Raymond Stewart *historian, educator, dean*
Breen, Stephen P. *editorial cartoonist*
Brewster, Rudi Milton *judge*
Brierton, Cheryl Lynn *lawyer*
Brom, Robert H. *bishop*
Brooks, John White *lawyer*
Brown, LaMar Bevan *lawyer*
Brownlie, Robert William *lawyer*
Bryan, John Rodney *management consultant*
Burgin, George Hans *computer scientist, educator*
Buska, Sheila Mary *chief financial officer, columnist, writer*
Butterfield, Alexander Porter *air transportation executive, former federal official*
Callahan, LeeAnn Lucille *psychologist*
Campbell, Ian David *opera company director*
Cantor, Charles Robert *biochemistry professor*
Celentino, Christopher *lawyer*
Chambers, Henry George *orthopedic surgeon*
Chatroo, Arthur Jay *lawyer*
Chaudhri, Javade *lawyer, utilities executive*
Clark, Grant Lawrence *corporate lawyer*
Cohn, Marjorie F. *law educator, legal association administrator*
Conly, John Franklin *retired engineering educator*
Copeland, Robert Glenn *lawyer*
Corbett, Luke Robinson *lawyer*
Covey, Dana Curtis *military officer, orthopaedic surgeon*
Crutchfield, Susan Ramsey *neurophysiologist*
Dahlberg, Kenneth C. *engineering executive*
Darmstandler, Harry Max *retired military officer*
Dawe, James Robert *lawyer*
Dean, Richard Anthony *mechanical engineering executive*
De Angelis, Flavio *electrical engineer, researcher*
Delawie, Homer Torrence *retired architect*
DeMaria, Anthony Nicholas *cardiologist, educator*
Devine, Brian Kiernan *pet food and supplies company executive*
DiRuscio, Lawrence William *advertising executive*
Dollarhide, Mary C. *lawyer*
Dorne, David J. *lawyer*
Dulbecco, Renato *biologist, educator*
Dunlop, Marianne *retired language educator*
Dunn, David Joseph *investment company executive*
Dyer, Charles Richard *law library director, educator*
Early, Teri Wilson (Denise Wilson) *elementary school educator, educator*
Ecker, Joseph R. *plant molecular and cellular biologist*
Eckhart, Walter *molecular biologist, educator*
Edwards, Darrel *psychologist, researcher*
Eigner, William Whitling *lawyer*
Estep, Arthur Lee *lawyer*
Felsinger, Donald E. *utilities corporation executive*
Fernandez, Alfredo Tumbaga, Jr. *military officer*
Fike, Edward Lake *newspaper editor*
Fisch, Sanford Michael *lawyer*
Flettner, Marianne *opera administrator*
Forbes, Brian L. *lawyer*
Forster, Geoffrey Peter *engineering executive*
Friedlander, Sheila Fallon *dermatologist, educator*
Friedman, Arthur Daniel *electrical engineer, computer scientist, investment company executive, educator*
Friedman, Paul Jay *retired radiologist*
Gage, Fred H. *neuroscientist, educator*
Gates, Antonio *professional football player*
Gengor, Virginia Anderson *financial planning executive, educator*
Gerber, Robert Scott *lawyer*
Getis, Arthur *geography educator*
Giles, Brian Stephen *professional baseball player*
Golding, Susan G. *former mayor*
Goldstein, Mark Kingston Levin *information technology executive, researcher*
Goltz, Robert William *dermatologist, educator*
Gonzalez, Irma Elsa *federal judge*
Graham, Ginger L. *pharmaceutical executive*
Greenberg, Barry *physician*
Gregoire, Mathieu *artist, consultant*
Grosser, T.J. *not-for-profit fundraiser*
Gupta, Madhu Sudan *electrical engineering educator*
Hagarty, Mark *lawyer*
Hager, Michael W. *museum director*
Haile, Lisa A. *lawyer*
Hales, Alfred Washington *mathematics professor, consultant*
Harris, James Michael *sales executive*
Harutunian, Albert T(heodore) III *judge*
Hasl, Rudolph Carl *dean, law educator*
Hayes, Claude Quinten Christopher *research scientist, inventor*
Heaton, Roger Laurence *lawyer*
Heidrich, Robert Wesley *lawyer*
Herriman, Darleen Ann *music educator*
Hewitt, Karen Peckham *prosecutor*
Hofflund, Paul *lawyer*
Hoffman, Trevor William *professional baseball player*
Hollis, Richard B. *pharmaceutical executive*
Hoston, Germaine Annette *political science professor*
Humes, Edward *journalist, writer*
Hunt, Barnabas John *priest, religious organization administrator*
Idos, Margarita de Leon *elementary school educator*
Inoue, Michael Shigeru *industrial and electrical engineer*
Insogna, Anthony M. *lawyer*
Isaac, Charles Edward *environmental scientist, director*
Jacobs, Irwin Mark *communications executive*
Jacobs, Paul E. *communications company executive*
Jacoby, Irving *physician*
Jagoda, Barry Lionel *communications executive, writer*
Jamieson, Stuart William *surgeon, educator*
Jellison, Beverly Irene *literature and language educator*
Jenkins, Adrienne *women's health nurse*
Jeub, Michael Leonard *financial consultant*
Jing, Zhigang *electrical engineer*
Kameir, Christian *marketing executive*
Kaplan, George Willard *urologist*
Kaufman, Julian Mortimer *broadcasting company executive, consultant*
Kaushansky, Kenneth *medical educator*
Kaysen, Gavin N. *chef*
Kellogg, Huston Glenn *pediatrician, medical educator*
Kim, Lee Ann *reporter, newscaster*
Kinsbruner Bush, Jennifer *lawyer*
Klein, Herbert George *newspaper editor*
Klicperova-Baker, Martina *psychologist, researcher*
Klinedinst, John David *lawyer*
Knuth, Dean Leslie *research and development company executive, golf consultant, writer*
Koenig, Harold Martin *former United States Navy surgeon general*
Koka, Prasad S. *biomedical researcher*
Krejci, Robert Harry *not-for-profit developer, consultant*
Krous, Henry Franklin *pathologist, educator*
Krulak, Victor Harold *newspaper executive*
Kuki, Atsuo *pharmaceutical executive*
Kuniyuki, Ken Toshio *mathematics professor*
Kyle, Robert Campbell, II, *publishing executive*
Lam, Carol Chien-Hua *communications executive, former prosecutor, lawyer*
Lane, Gloria Julian *foundation administrator*
Lane, Sylvia *economist, educator*
Lang, Linda A. *food service executive*
Langenberg, Bret James *surgeon*
L'Annunziata, Michael Frank *chemist, nuclear scientist, consultant*
Lansdowne, William M. *police chief*
Lao, Lang Li *nuclear scientist, physicist*
Larson, Arvid Gunnar *electrical engineer*
Larson, Mark Devin *communications executive*
Latherow, Robert L. *retired music educator*
Lathrop, Mitchell Lee *lawyer*
Lechner, Roger A. *priest*
Lederer, Richard Henry *writer, educator, columnist*
Lerach, William S. *lawyer*
Levine, Harvey Robert *lawyer*

Levy, Jerome *dermatologist, retired military officer*
Lewis, Alan James *pharmaceutical executive, pharmacologist*
Lewis, Shirley Jeane *retired psychologist*
Lieber, Richard Louis *biomedical engineering scientist, educator*
Longenecker, Martha W. *museum director*
Lyons, Mary E. *academic administrator*
Maloney, Ellen Claire *elementary school educator*
Markowitz, Harry Max *finance and economics educator*
Mathes, James R. *bishop*
Mayer, George Roy *education educator*
McBrayer, Sandra L. *educational director, homeless outreach educator*
McClellan, Craig Rene *lawyer*
McCoy, Lilys D. *lawyer*
McCurine, William, Jr. *lawyer*
McGinnis, Robert Earl *lawyer*
McKeown, Mary Margaret *federal judge*
Mc Kinnon, Clinton Dan *aerospace transportation executive*
McMahon, Gerald Lawrence *lawyer*
Mebane, Julie S. *lawyer*
Meirowitz, Randy Emil *research scientist, consultant*
Meno, Lionel R. *academic administrator*
Meskell, Kristin Marie *psychologist*
Mittermiller, James Joseph *lawyer*
Moore, Linda A. *art dealer, curator*
Morris, Grant Harold *law educator*
Mullen, James Joseph III *lawyer*
Mulvaney, James Francis *lawyer*
Murphy, Mary *choreographer, dancer*
Myers, Douglas George *zoological society administrator*
Myers, James M. *pet products executive*
Nahm, Walter K. *dermatologist, researcher*
Nelson, Craig Alan *management consultant*
Neumann, Linda Kay *marketing professional*
Nicholas, Blair *lawyer*
Nickell, Robert E. *electric power industry executive*
North, Robert L. *computer software executive*
Nugent, Robert J., Jr. *fast food company executive*
O'Brien, Jack George *artistic director*
Obright, Neil Allen *data processing executive*
Oldham, Maxine Jernigan *real estate broker*
Olshevsky, George *editor*
O'Malley, James Terence (Terry) *lawyer*
Overton, Marcus Lee *performing arts association administrator, actor, writer*
Padovani, Roberto *communications executive*
Pagan, Keith Areatus *music educator, academic administrator*
Panetta, Joseph Daniel *biotechnologist, director*
Parthemore, Jacqueline Gail *internist, educator, hospital administrator*
Payack, Paul J.J. *marketing professional, writer*
Payne, Margaret Anne *lawyer*
Peavy, Jake (Jacob Edward Peavy) *professional baseball player*
Petersen, Martin Eugene *curator*
Pfiffner, Patrick Meehan *musician, educator*
Pincus, Howard J. *geologist, engineer, educator*
Pincus, Robert Lawrence *art critic, historian*
Pitt, William Alexander *cardiologist*
Plotkin, Allen *aerospace engineer, educator*
Plourd, Christopher John *lawyer, consultant*
Pordon, William Philip *music educator*
Poss, William Bradley *physician*
Pray, Ralph Marble III *lawyer*
Pugh, Richard Crawford *lawyer, educator*
Quigley, Rob Wellington *architect*
Raczka, Tony Michael *artist*
Rady, Ernest S. *thrift and loan association executive*
Rahmani, Reza Mossaver *writer, retired Iranian Air Force officer, banker, tour operator*
Rains, Cameron Jay *lawyer*
Rasochova, Lada *research scientist*
Rastetter, William H. *biotechnology company executive*
Rautenstrauch, Gary M. *marketing executive*
Ray, Albert *physician, educator*
Ray, Gene Wells *industrial executive*
Reading, James Edward *transportation executive*
Rehmus, Charles Martin *arbitrator*
Reinhard, Christopher John *merchant banker, venture capitalist, biotechnologist, director*
Resnik, Robert *medical educator*
Rice, Clare I. *electronics company executive*
Rice, Thomas Hilary (Speedy Rice) *lawyer*
Riedy, Mark Joseph *finance educator*
Robbins, Darren J. *lawyer*
Robbins, Tony (Anthony Robbins) *writer*
Roberts, James McGregor *retired trade association administrator*
Roberts, William S. *lawyer*
Robertson, Michael *Internet company executive*
Rodenberg, Johanna Kristine *education educator, consultant*
Rodriguez, Daniel B. *dean, law educator*
Rohn, William R. *biotechnology company executive*
Roizen, Michael F. *anesthesiologist, medical educator, writer*
Root, George Lincoln, Jr. *lawyer*
Roseman, Charles Sanford *lawyer*
Ross, John, Jr. *cardiologist, educator*
Ross, Terry D. *lawyer*
Rotter, Paul Talbott *retired insurance executive*
Rowe, Peter A. *columnist*
Rowson, Sebastian *engineering executive*
Ruane, James Edward, Jr. *engineering executive*
Saito, Frank Kiyoji *import and export firm executive*
Sanders, Jerry *mayor, former social services executive*
Santee, Dale William *lawyer, air force officer*
Sarkar, Sandip *telecommunications industry executive, researcher*
Sauer, David Andrew *librarian, writer*
Sceper, Duane Harold *lawyer*
Schmale, Neal E. *utilities company executive*
Schmidt, Joseph David *urologist*
Schmidt, Terry L. *healthcare executive*
Schmidt, Thomas Charles *biomedical engineer, researcher*
Schoville, Dennis A(rnold) *lawyer*
Schwartz, Alfred *former dean*
Scott, Douglas Edward *lawyer*
Scott, Richard Malachi *psychologist*
Sejnowski, Terrence Joseph *science educator*
Sell, Robert Emerson *electrical engineer*
Shapiro, Philip Alan *lawyer*
Shedroff, Sharon D. *psychologist, researcher, anthropologist, consultant*
Sheldon-Morris, Tiffini Anne *clinical psychologist, consultative examiner*
Shelton, Dorothy Diehl Rees *lawyer*
Shepard, Jean M. *city health department administrator*
Shepherd, Bruce P. *lawyer*
Shields, Patricia Allene *retail executive*
Shippey, Sandra Lee *lawyer*
Shneour, Elie Alexis *biophysicist, researcher, historian*
Short, Jay Milton *biotechnology company executive*
Simpson, William *information technology manager, consultant*
Skwara, Erich Wolfgang *writer, poet, critic, literature educator*
Slate, John Butler *biomedical engineer*
Smith, A.J. *professional sports team executive*
Smith, Steven Ray *law educator*
Snaid, Leon Jeffrey *lawyer*
Snell, Mark A. *utilities executive*
Snyder, David Richard *lawyer*
Sopp, Mark W. *corporate financial executive*
Spanos, Alexander Gus *construction and professional sports team executive*
Spira, Patricia Goodsitt *retired association executive*
Squire, Larry Ryan *neuroscientist, psychologist, educator*
Stambaugh, Larry G. *financial consultant*
Steen, Paul Joseph *retired broadcasting executive*
Stein, Franklin Joseph *language educator*
Stepner, Michael Jay *architect*
Stoessinger, John George *political science professor*
Sullivan, Michelle Cornejo *lawyer*
Suycott, Mark Leland *program manager, retired military officer*
Swinton, Stephen P. *lawyer*
Tatár, Anna *library director*
Taylor, Marcus Keene *physiologist, researcher*
Thomas, Robert McGuffey *automotive executive, educator*
Thompson, David Renwick *federal judge*
Thompson, Gordon, Jr. *federal judge*
Thorud, Jeffrey Scott *lawyer, legal studies director*
Timoshchuk, Victor Arkadyevich *research scientist*
Tom, Lawrence *technology executive*
Tomlinson, LaDainian *professional football player*
Tozer, William Evans *entomologist, educator*
Tricoles, Gus Peter *electrical engineer, physicist, consultant*
Turner, Norv(al) (Eugene) *professional football coach*
Turrentine, Howard Boyd *federal judge*
Unger, Richard Jonathan *medical educator, anesthesiologist*
Valliant, James Stevens *lawyer*
Vanderbilt, Kermit *language educator*
Van Tassel, Lowell Thomas *mathematics professor*
Vasudevan, Sriram *risk management consultant, energy executive*
Vause, Edwin Hamilton *research foundation administrator*
Vega, Carolyn Jane *elementary educator, consultant, writer*
Verma, Inder M. *biochemist*
Vitek, Reg(inald) A. *lawyer*
Wadlington, W. M. *retired commodity futures trader, financial engineer*
Wagner, Sandra M. *lawyer*
Wallace, Candy *Culinary Association Administrator*
Wallace, J. Clifford *federal judge*
Ward, Charles Raymond *systems engineer*
Warner, John Hilliard, Jr. *technical services company executive*
Wasserman, Stephen Ira *allergist, immunologist, educator*
Wawrytko, Sandra Ann *humanities educator*
Weaver, Michael James *lawyer*
Weber, Stephen Lewis *academic administrator*
Weeks, John Robert *geographer, social studies educator*
Wertheim, Robert Halley *national security consultant*
West, James Harold *finance company executive*
Whittington, Anne Elizabeth *diabetes educator*
Widder, Kenneth Jon *pathologist, educator*
Wiesler, James Ballard *retired banker*
Willis, Norman Hunt *author, writer, director, producer*
Winfield, Dave (David Mark Winfield) *professional sports team executive, retired professional baseball player*
Wing, Thomas M. *military officer, systems engineer*
Winner, Karin E. *editor-in-chief*
Withee, Diana Keeran *art historian, art dealer, educator*
Wolfe, Deborah Ann *lawyer*
Yacovone, Ellen Elaine *banker*
Yie, Junming *research scientist*

San Fernando

Shannon, George Raymond *gerontologist, educator*

San Francisco

Abbott, Barry Alexander *lawyer*
Abbott, Richard Lee *academic administrator*
Abramson, Norman *retired engineering educator, electronics executive*
Adelson, Jay *Internet company executive*
Agard, David A. *biochemistry and biophysics educator*
Alberts, Bruce Michael *cell biologist, former foundation administrator*
Alderman, William Fields *lawyer*
Aldrich, Michael Ray *library curator, health educator*
Alexis, Geraldine M. *lawyer*
Alioto, Angela Mia *lawyer*
Allecta, Julie *lawyer*
Allen, Jose R. *lawyer*
Alvarado, Jorge A. *ophthalmologist, researcher*
Alvarez-Buylla, Arturo *neurobiologist, researcher*
Amend, William John Conrad, Jr. *physician, educator*
Anastacia, (Anastacia Lyn Newkirk) *singer*
Anderson, Chris W. *editor-in-chief*
Anderson, Edward Virgil *lawyer*
Anderson, R. John *apparel executive*
Anooshian, Robert Vahan *plastic surgeon*
Appleman, Nate *chef*
Arbuthnot, Robert Murray *lawyer*
Arnold, Lauren *art historian, writer*
Atkins, Howard Ian *bank executive*
Atkinson, Gordon C. *lawyer*
August-deWilde, Katherine *banker*
Auwers, Linda S. *lawyer*
Babcock, Jo *artist, educator*
Bailey-Wells, Deborah *lawyer*
Bainton, Dorothy Ford *pathologist, educator*
Bajwa, Hashem *advertising executive*
Baker, Cameron *lawyer*
Baker, Joy Doreen *art educator, artist*
Bancel, Marilyn *fund raising management consultant*
Barbagelata, Robert Dominic *lawyer*
Bardsley, Kay *historian, archivist, dance professional*
Barlow, William Pusey, Jr. *accountant*
Barondes, Samuel Herbert *psychiatrist, educator*
Barzelatto, Jose S. *social welfare organization executive*
Basbaum, Allan I. *medical educator, researcher*
Batterman, Boris William *physicist, educator, academic administrator*
Bauch, Thomas Jay *financial consultant, retired lawyer, apparel executive*
Bauer, Steven M. *lawyer*
Baxter, Marvin Ray *state supreme court justice*
Baxter, Ralph H., Jr. *lawyer*
Baxter-Lowe, Lee Ann *science educator*
Baysinger, Kara *lawyer*
Bea, Carlos Tiburcio *federal judge*
Beall, Dennis Ray *artist, educator*
Bechtel, Riley Peart *engineering company executive*
Bechtel, Stephen Davison, Jr. *retired engineering company executive*
Bechtle, Robert Alan *artist, educator*
Bee, Robert Norman *banker*
Béhar, Yves *industrial designer*
Behrens, M. Kathleen *medical researcher*
Bell, C. Gordon *computer architect and engineer, entrepreneur, researcher*
Benet, Leslie Zachary *pharmacologist, educator*
Benezra, Neal *museum director, curator*
Benioff, Marc *Internet company executive*
Bensinger, David August *dentist, dean*
Benvenutti, Peter J. *lawyer*
Bereuter, Douglas Kent *foundation administrator, former congressman*
Berning, Paul Wilson *lawyer*
Bernstein, Gerald William *management consultant, researcher*
Berzon, Marsha S. *federal judge*
Bettinger, Walter W., II, *investment company executive*
Beyer, Molly M. *museum program director*
Bierly, Shirley Adelaide *communications executive*
Biesty, Jennifer *chef*
Bikle, Daniel David *research physician*
Bitterman, Mary Gayle Foley *foundation executive*
Blaise, Clark Lee *writer, educator*
Blanc, Maureen *public relations executive*
Bleich, Jeffrey Laurence *lawyer, educator*
Blohm, Kenneth E. *lawyer*
Blum, Robert M. *lawyer*
Bochy, Bruce *professional baseball team manager and retired player*
Bocobo-Balunsat, Dalisay *librarian, journalist*
Boles, Roger *otolaryngologist*
Bomse, Stephen V. *lawyer*
Bondoc, Rommel *lawyer*
Bonds, Barry Lamar *professional baseball player*
Borowsky, Philip *lawyer*
Bostwick, James Stephen *lawyer*
Bothwell, Anthony Peirson Xavier, Sr. *lawyer, educator*
Botvinick, Elias H. *nuclear medicine physician, researcher, medical educator*
Bourne, Henry R. *pharmacology professor, department chairman, researcher*
Boutros, George F. *investment banker*
Boven, Douglas George *lawyer*
Bracken, Thomas Robert James *real estate investment executive*
Bradford, David S. *surgeon*
Brand, Jeffrey S. *dean, law educator*
Brandel, Roland Eric *lawyer*
Bratton, Christopher Alan *academic administrator, videographer, art educator*
Brechka, Frank Tilson *retired librarian, historian*
Brice, Charles Steven *airline executive*
Briscoe, John *lawyer*
Bronstein, Phil *publishing executive*
Brosnahan, James Jerome *lawyer*
Brothers, Lynda Lee *lawyer*
Brotman, Martin *gastroenterologist*
Brown, Donald Wesley *lawyer*
Brown, Eric Joel *biomedical researcher*
Brown, Walter Francis, Jr. *lawyer*
Browning, James Robert *federal judge*
Broyles, Deborah J. *lawyer*
Bruen, James A. *lawyer*
Buchanan, John Edward, Jr. *museum director*
Buckmaster, Jim *online community bulletin board company executive*
Buckner, John Knowles *investor*
Bull, Henrik Helkand *architect*
Burden, James Ewers *lawyer*
Burgard, Timothy Anglin *curator*
Burlingame, Alma Lyman *chemist, educator*
Burns, Brian Patrick *lawyer*
Buse, Elizabeth L. *finance company executive*
Bushnell, Roderick Paul *lawyer*
Butenhoff, Susan Grace *public relations executive*
Butter, Karen Ann *school librarian*
Byrne, Robert William *lawyer*
Cabraser, Elizabeth Joan *lawyer*
Calhoun, John Joseph (Jack) *retail executive*
Callahan, Patricia R. *bank executive*
Callison, Russell James *lawyer*
Cameron, Heather Anne *publishing executive*
Campbell, Jeffrey C. *health products executive*
Campbell, Scott Robert *lawyer, former food products executive*
Canady, Richard Warren *lawyer*
Canales, James Earl, Jr. *foundation president*
Caniparoli, Val William *choreographer, dancer*
Capaldini, Lisa Claire *physician, educator*
Cartmell, Nathaniel Madison III *lawyer*
Casnocha, Benedict T. *entrepreneur*
Cepeda, Orlando *retired professional baseball player*
Chambers, Guy Wayne *lawyer*
Chao, Cedric C. *lawyer*
Chapman, William B. *lawyer*
Chase, Alexandra Nin *psychologist, writer*
Cherny, Robert Wallace *historian, educator*
Chin, Ming W. *state supreme court justice*
Chin, Sue Soone Marian (Suchin Chin) *artist, photojournalist*
Ciccarone, Daniel *medical educator, researcher, physician*
Cirese, Robert Charles *economist, real estate consultant*
Clements, John Allen *physiologist*
Clever, Linda Hawes *physician*
Clifford, Geraldine Joncich *retired education educator*
Clowes, John Howard *lawyer*
Cluff, Lloyd Sterling *earthquake geologist*
Cobbs, Price Mashaw *social psychiatrist*
Cohen, Bram *web programmer*
Cohen, Fred Ehrenkranz *biophysics professor*
Cohn, Cindy A. *lawyer*
Cohn, Kathleen Mandry *writer*
Coleman, Thomas Young *lawyer*
Collins, Mary Ann *lawyer*
Colton, Roy Charles *management consultant*
Cominos, Dion Nicholas *lawyer*
Conway, Craig A. *retired computer company executive*
Coombe, George William, Jr. *lawyer, retired bank executive*
Cooper, Allen David *medical researcher, educator*
Corash, Michèle B. *lawyer*
Cornett, Patricia Anne *oncologist, educator*
Corrigan, Carol A. *state supreme court justice*
Corrigan, Robert Anthony *academic administrator*
Costa-Zalessow, Natalia *foreign language educator*
Cranston, Mary Bailey *lawyer*
Crawford, J. Brooks *ophthalmologist, educator*
Crawford, Michael Howard *cardiologist, educator, researcher*
Crawford, Roy Edgington III *lawyer*
Croughan, Mary *medical educator*
Cuggino, Michael Joseph *financial executive*
Curran, Mary *lawyer*
Czachor, Bruce *lawyer, consultant*
Dachs, Alan Mark *investment company executive*
Danko, Gary J. *chef*
Danoff, Eric Michael *lawyer*
Dans, Michael Jay *dermatologist, educator*
Darbee, Peter A. *utilities executive*
Darney, Philip Dempsey *gynecologist, educator*
David, George *psychiatrist, economic theory lecturer*
Davidson, Keay *newswriter*
Davis, Patricia Margaret Alice *psychology and religion educator*
Davis, Roger Lewis *lawyer*
Dawson, Chandler Robert *ophthalmologist, educator*
Dawson, Peter A. *corporate financial executive*
Deamer, Bartley C. *lawyer*
Deicken, Raymond Friedrich *neuropsychiatrist, neuroscientist*
Del Campo, Martin Bernardelli *architect*
Dell, Robert Michael *lawyer*
Dellas, Robert Dennis *investment banker*
Demarest, David Franklin, Jr. *banker, retired government official*
DeMuro, Paul Robert *lawyer*
Dennehy, Raymond Leo *philosopher, educator*
DeRisi, Joseph L. *biochemist, educator*
Des Jardins, Traci *chef, restaurant owner*
DeSoto, Lewis Damien *artist, educator*
de Vries, Brian *gerontologist, researcher*
Dickey, Glenn Ernest, Jr. *sportswriter*
Dickinson, Eleanor Creekmore *artist, educator*
Dickinson, Wade *oil industry executive, educator*
Diekmann, Gilmore Frederick, Jr. *lawyer*
Dill, Kenneth Austin *pharmaceutical chemistry educator*
Dolby, Ray Milton *electrical engineer, company executive*
Dolinko, Robert A. *lawyer*
Dommen, Mark *chef*
Donnelly, Thomas M. *lawyer*
Donnelly, Trisha *artist*
Donovan, Charles Stephen *lawyer*
Doumani, Lissa *chef*

Dracup, Kathleen Anne *dean, nursing educator*
Draper, William Henry III *venture capitalist*
Dryden, Robert Eugene *lawyer*
Dubreuil, Francis W. *lawyer*
Dugoni, Arthur A. *retired dean, orthodontics educator*
Dunne, Kevin Joseph *lawyer*
Durdik, Paul A. *lawyer*
Durie, Daralyn J. *lawyer*
Duscha, Julius Carl *journalist*
Dworkin, Michael Leonard *lawyer*
Dwyer, Carrie Elizabeth *lawyer, investment company executive*
Eastham, Thomas *retired foundation administrator*
Edwards, Robin Morse *lawyer*
Effel, Laura *lawyer*
Egan, Kristin *otolaryngologist*
Egan, Patricia Jane *foundation administrator, retired director*
Eggers, Dave *fiction writer, magazine editor*
Eigner, Richard Martin *lawyer*
Elliott, Scott D. *lawyer*
Ellis, John *urban designer*
El-Sayed, Ivan Homer *otolaryngologist, researcher*
Emery, Vince *writer, educator*
Enfield, Donald Michael *insurance company executive*
Engleman, Ephraim Philip *rheumatologist*
Enscoe, Jon *lawyer*
Epsen, Robert A. *lawyer*
Epstein, Charles Joseph *pediatrician, geneticist, biochemist, educator*
Epstein, John Howard *dermatologist*
Ericson, Bruce Alan *lawyer*
Estes, Carroll Lynn *sociologist, educator*
Eth, Jordan David *lawyer*
Etheridge, Melissa Lou *singer, lyricist*
Eurich, Judith *art appraiser, printmaker*
Fainaru-Wada, Mark *journalist*
Fairman, Marc P. *lawyer*
Falk, Jerome B., Jr. *lawyer*
Falk, Steven B. *newspaper publishing executive*
Falkner, Elizabeth *chef*
Fanning, Shawn *information technology executive*
Featherstone, John Douglas Bernard *dean, biochemistry educator*
Felstiner, Mary Lowenthal *retired history professor*
Feng, Wendy Lai *lawyer*
Fergus, Gary Scott *lawyer*
Ferlinghetti, Lawrence *poet*
Ferriero, Donna M. *pediatric neurologist*
Ferris, Russell James, II, *writer*
Fessel, Walford Jeffrey *rheumatologist*
Field, Carol Hart *writer, news correspondent, journalist*
Field, John Louis *architect*
Fifer, Sally Jo *broadcast executive, editor*
Finberg, James Michael *lawyer*
Finberg, Laurence *pediatrician, educator, dean*
Finck, Kevin William *lawyer*
Fink, Scott Alan *lawyer*
Fisher, Donald G. *retail executive*
Fisher, Doris *retail executive*
Fisher, Kathleen V. *lawyer*
Fisher, Robert J. *retail executive*
Fisher, Robert Morton *foundation and academic administrator*
Fleishhacker, David *school administrator*
Fletcher, William A. *federal judge, educator*
Flittie, Clifford Gilliland *retired petroleum company executive*
Floum, Joshua R. *finance company executive, lawyer*
Fogel, Paul David *lawyer*
Folberg, Harold Jay *lawyer, educator, dean*
Folkman, David H. *retail, wholesale and consumer products consultant*
Folkman, Susan *research psychologist*
Fong, Kevin Murray *lawyer*
Fontana, Gary Lynn *lawyer*
Foret, Mickey Phillip *retired air transportation executive*
Foster, David Scott *lawyer*
Foulke, Laura Taylor *not-for-profit fundraiser*
Fox, Patrick John *sociology educator*
Fox, Steve *editor-in-chief*
Frank, Karen Susanna *lawyer*
Freund, Fredric S. *real estate broker and manager*
Frick, Oscar Lionel *pediatrician, educator*
Friedman, Gary *plastic surgeon*
Friedman, K. Bruce *lawyer*
Friese, Robert Charles *lawyer*
Fuller, James William *financial planner*
Fullerton, Dorothy Mallan *artist*
Furth, Frederick Paul *lawyer*
Fury, Michael Andrew *materials scientist, research and development company executive*
Gamson, Joshua Paul *sociology educator, writer*
Ganem, Donald E. *immunologist*
Ganong, William F(rancis) *physiologist, educator*
Garchik, Leah Lieberman *journalist*
Garcia, Michael *Sommelier*
Gardner, Annette Lenore *health policy researcher, political scientist*
Garvey, Joanne Marie *lawyer*
Gekelman, Diana *dentist, dental educator, researcher*
Gellin, Gerald Alan *dermatologist*
Gensler, M. Arthur, Jr. *architect*
George, Ronald M. *state supreme court chief justice*
German, William *newspaper editor*
Gibbs, Michael G. *not-for-profit fundraiser*
Gibbs, Patricia Hellman *physician*
Gibney, Robert L., Jr. *lawyer*
Gillette, Frankie Jacobs *retired savings and loan association executive, federal agency administrator, social worker*
Gillette, Patricia K. *lawyer*
Giovinco, Joseph *non profit agency administrator, writer*
Glantz, Stanton A. *medical researcher*
Glazer, Jack Henry *lawyer*
Glogau, Richard G. *dermatologist*
Glueckman, Alan Jay *writer, producer, director*
Gockley, (Richard) David *opera company director*
Goldberg, Adele J. *computer scientist*
Goldman, Richard N. *foundation administrator*
Goldstein, David Baird *energy executive, physicist*
Goldstein, Sydney Rachel *photographer, writer, radio producer*
Goldstine, Stephen Joseph *art educator*
Golub, Howard Victor *lawyer*
Goode, Erica Tucker *internist*
Gooding, Charles Arthur *radiologist, physician, educator*
Gooding, Gretchen Ann Wagner *physician, educator*
Goodwin, David B. *lawyer*
Gore, Al (Albert Arnold Gore Jr.) *former Vice President of the United States*
Graff, Joan Messing *lawyer*
Granik, Vladimir *mechanic engineering educator, researcher*
Graysmith, Robert *political cartoonist, author*
Greenspan, Deborah *dental educator*
Greenspan, Francis S. *physician*
Greenspan, John S. *dental and medical educator, researcher, academic administrator*
Gresham, Zane Oliver *lawyer*
Griggs, Lewis Brown *executive producer, speaker, trainer*
Grodsky, Gerold Morton *biochemistry professor*
Gross, David F. *lawyer*
Grossman, William *medical researcher, educator*
Gruel, Steven Francis *lawyer*
Grumbach, Melvin Malcolm *pediatrician, educator*
Guggenheim, Davis *film and TV director, producer*
Guggenhime, Richard Johnson *lawyer*
Guttentag, Lucas *advocate, lawyer*
Gwire, William *lawyer*
Haas, Raymond P. *lawyer*
Haas, Robert Douglas *apparel executive*
Haber, Scott R. *lawyer*
Haerle, Paul Raymond *judge*
Hafner, Katie *reporter*
Hagenbuch, John Jacob *investor*
Hale, Victoria G. *chemist, pharmaceutical executive*
Halliday, John Meech *investment company executive*
Hamilton, Joan Nice *editor-in-chief*
Hammergren, John H. *health products executive*
Hanahan, Douglas *biochemist, educator*
Hansen, Carol Louise *literature and language professor*
Hansen, Marka *retail executive*
Harlan, Neil Eugene *retired health facility administrator*
Harris, Kamala D. *prosecutor*
Harriss, Cynthia Therese (Cynthia Therese Clarke) *retail executive*
Harvey, D. Peter *lawyer, educator*
Harvey, Kent M. *utilities executive*
Hasson, Kirke Michael *lawyer*
Hastings, Edward Walton *theater director*
Hatt, David *application developer, composer*
Havel, Richard Joseph *physician, educator*
Hawkins, Trip *electronics executive*
Hecker, Peter S. *lawyer*
Heilbron, David Michael *lawyer, arbitrator, mediator*
Hellman, F(rederick) Warren *investor*
Henderson, Isaac Craig *oncologist, researcher*
Henderson, Thelton Eugene *federal judge*
Hendrick, James T. *lawyer*
Henson, Ray David *law educator, consultant*
Hernandez, Gary A. *lawyer*
Herrera, Dennis J. *lawyer*
Herrera, Luis *library director*
Herringer, Frank Casper *diversified financial services company executive*
Hewitt, Conrad W. *former commissioner, accountant*
Heyman, Melvin Bernard *pediatric gastroenterologist*
Heyneman, Donald *parasitology and tropical medicine educator*
Higashida, Randall Takeo *radiologist, neurosurgeon, medical educator*
Higgins, Daniel B. *lawyer*
Highman, Bruce James *lawyer*
Hills, Austin Edward *vineyard executive*
Hilton, Stanley Goumas *lawyer, educator, writer*
Hinman, Harvey DeForest *lawyer*
Hirsch, (William) Reece *lawyer*
Hirschmann, Peter *video game company executive*
Hisert, George Arthur *lawyer*
Hoffman, William Yanes *plastic surgeon*
Hofmann, John Richard, Jr. *retired lawyer*
Holden, Frederick Douglass, Jr. *lawyer*
Holzemer, William L. *nursing educator*
Honig, Al *artist*
Hosie, Spencer *lawyer*
Hoskins, H. Dunbar *ophthalmologist, medical association administrator*
Howard, Carl *retired lawyer*
Hoyt, Craig Simmons *ophthalmologist, educator*
Hoyt, David A. *bank executive*
Hsu, Chi-yuan *nephrologist, researcher*
Hubbell, Robert B. *lawyer*
Hudner, Philip *lawyer, rancher*
Hudson, Darril *political scientist, educator*
Huhs, John I. *lawyer*
Hunt, James L. *lawyer*
Hunter, William Dennis *lawyer*
Huntting, Cynthia Cox *artist*
Ikeda, Clyde Junichi *plastic and reconstructive surgeon*
Ikuta, Sandra Segal *federal judge*
Illston, Susan Y. *federal judge*
Im, Subin *marketing educator*
Innes, Kenneth Frederick III *lawyer*
Ireland, David *artist*
Jacobs, Michael Allen *lawyer*
Jaffe, Seth Roth *lawyer, retail executive*
James, David Lee *lawyer, writer, international advisor*
James, George Barker, II, *financial executive*
James, Thomas Larry *chemistry professor*
Jamison, Dean Tecumseh *economist*
Jan, Lily Yeh *physiology, biochemist*
Jarvis, Donald Bertram *judge*
Jennings, Jim *architect*
Jewett, George Frederick, Jr. *forest products company executive*
Ji, Tingting *mortgage company executive, consultant*
Johns, Christopher P. *utilities executive*
Johnson, Alexander D. *biochemist, molecular biologist, educator*
Johnson, Daniel, Jr. *lawyer*
Johnson, Michelle L. *lawyer*
Johnson, Stephen Patrick Howard *lawyer*
Jones, Frances Mary *law librarian*
Jones, J. Gilbert *private investigator*
Jones, Stanton William *management consultant*
Jonsen, Albert R(upert) *retired medical ethics educator*
Joseph, Allan Jay *lawyer*
Jossel, Laurence *chef*
Judd, Bruce Diven *architect*
Julian, Paul C. *health products executive*
Julius, David *biochemist*
Juster, Kenneth Ian *lawyer*
Kamm, John *non-profit organization administrator, human rights activist*
Kan, Yuet Wai *hematologist, educator*
Kane, Mary Kay *academic administrator, law educator*
Kantor, Gail *Internet company executive, concert producer*
Kao, John Sterling *mathematician, educator*
Kapor, Mitchell David *application developer, foundation administrator*
Katz, Mitchell H. *city health department administrator*
Katzung, Bertram George *pharmacologist*
Kee, Terry Michael *lawyer*
Keenan, Richard *lawyer*
Keeshan, Lawrence W. *lawyer*
Kegeles, Susan M. *medical educator, researcher*
Keker, John Watkins *lawyer*
Kelley, Michael Garhart Roosevelt *historian, educator, writer*
Kelly, J. Michael *lawyer*
Kelly, James Anthony *priest*
Kennard, Joyce L. *state supreme court justice*
Kennedy, Raoul Dion *lawyer*
Kenyon, Cynthia J. *medical researcher*
Kerlikowske, Karla *research scientist*
Kern, Brad D. *lawyer*
Kern, John McDougall *lawyer*
Kertzman, Mitchell E. *former software company executive, venture capitalist*
Kessler, David Aaron *dean, medical educator*
Kielarowski, Henry Edward *marketing executive*
King, Talmadge E. *physician*
Kirincic, Paul E. *health products executive*
Klammer, Joseph Francis *retired management consultant*
Klein, Marc S. *editor, publishing executive*
Kline, Howard Jay *cardiologist, educator*
Knapp, Charles Lincoln *law educator*
Knutzen, Martha Lorraine *lawyer*
Koeppel, John A. *lawyer*
Koffel, Martin M. *engineering company executive*
Kolkey, Daniel Miles *former judge, lawyer*
Koo, John Ying Ming *psychiatrist, dermatologist*
Koutsoftas, Demetrious Charles *geotechnical engineering consultant*
Kovacevich, Richard M. *bank executive*
Kozloff, Lloyd M. *dean, microbiologist, educator*
Kozloff, Theodore J. *lawyer*
Krane, Hilary K. *lawyer, apparel executive*
Krasinski, Nicole *chef*
Krevans, Rachel *lawyer*
Kriken, John Lund *architect*
Krippner, Stanley Curtis *psychologist*
Kuhl, Paul Beach *lawyer*
Kunz, Heidi *healthcare company executive*
Kushner, Lawrence *rabbi*
LaBelle, Thomas Jeffrey *research executive, academic administrator*
La Farge, Timothy *retired plant geneticist*
Lahlou, Mourad *chef*
Lamberson, John Roger *insurance company executive*
Lane, Fielding H. *lawyer*
Lane, Nathan III *lawyer*
Laret, Mark R. *health facility executive*
Larrabee, Matthew L. *lawyer*
Larson, John William *lawyer*
Lau, Jenny Kwok Wah *theater educator, consultant, film educator, consultant*
Lauterbach, Michael Alan *artist*
Lazarus, David *journalist*
LeBlanc, Tina *dancer*
Lee, Pamela Anne *bank executive, accountant, financial analyst*
Lee, Richard Diebold *lawyer, educator*
Lee, Samuel Sangwon *civil engineer, environmental engineer, agricultural engineer*
LeFurgy, Rich *advertising executive*
Lenk, Edward C. (Toby) *retail executive*
Leonard, Geoffrey Porter *lawyer*
Leong, Belinda *chef*
Leshy, John David *lawyer, solicitor, educator*
Lester, W. Howard *retail executive*
Levie, Mark Robert *lawyer*
Levin, Barry Steven *lawyer*
Levine, Alison *entrepreneur, leadership development consultant, adventurer*
Leviton, Alan Edward *curator*
Lieff, Robert Lawrence *lawyer*
Likova Mineva, Lora T. *research scientist*
Lindstrom, Gregory P. *lawyer*
Little, Jan Nielsen *lawyer*
Liu, Peter *bank executive*
Livermore, Samuel Morgan *lawyer*
Livsey, Robert Callister *lawyer*
Lo, Bernard *medical educator*
Londen, Jack W. *lawyer*
Lopes, James Louis *lawyer*
Loughlin, Michael J. *bank executive*
Low, Arnold Kinman *systems executive*
Low, Randall *internist, cardiologist*
Lowell, Frederick K. *lawyer*
Lowenthal, Steven R. *lawyer*
Lucia, Marilyn Reed *physician*
Lyon, David William *research executive*
Lyons, James Elliott *lawyer*
Maas, Corey *plastic surgeon*
Macahilig, Suzanne *pianist, educator*
MacNaughton, Angus Athole *finance company executive*
Magowan, Peter Alden *professional sports team and retail executive*
Mahley, Robert W. *health facility administrator*
Mahoney, David L. *former pharmaceutical wholesale and healthcare management company executive*
Mahoney, Michael James *investment company executive*
Malkin, Joseph M. *lawyer*
Maly, Michael Kip *lawyer*
Mann, Bruce Alan *lawyer, investment banking executive*
Manning, Jerome Alan *retired lawyer*
Marduel, Alix *venture capitalist*
Markoff, John *reporter*
Márquez-Magaña, Leticia Maria *biology professor*
Marshall, Grayson William, Jr. *materials scientist, biomedical engineer, health sciences educator, dentist*
Marshall, Patrick C. *lawyer*
Marshall, Raymond Charles *lawyer*
Marston, Michael *economist, consultant*
Martel, John Sheldon *lawyer, writer*
Martin, Fred *artist, academic administrator*
Martinetto, Joseph R. *investment company executive*
Martinez, Belinda *health insurance company executive*
Masaoka, Jan *not-for-profit executive*
Mason, Dean Towle *cardiologist*
Masters, Joseph *lawyer, construction executive*
Mathes, Stephen John *plastic and reconstructive surgeon, educator*
Mattern, Douglas James *think-tank executive*
Mattes, Martin Anthony *lawyer*
Matthews, Gilbert Elliott *investment banker*
McAninch, Jack Weldon *urological surgeon, educator*
McCauley, Matthew K. *apparel executive*
McClintock, Jessica *fashion designer*
McCormick, Frank *research scientist*
McCracken, Harry *journalist*
McCulley, Timothy J. *ophthalmologist, surgeon, educator*
McDiarmid, Bruce W. *lawyer*
McDonald, Mary Ann Melody *investment management executive*
McElhinney, Bruce *finance company executive*
McElhinny, Harold John *lawyer*
McFadden, Nancy Elizabeth *utilities executive*
McGettigan, Charles Carroll, Jr. *investment banker*
McGinnis, James Landon *lawyer*
McGrath, Don John *bank executive*
McGuckin, John Hugh, Jr. *lawyer*
McGuire, Kathleen Alison *conductor*
McGuire, William Albert *humanities educator*
McKenzie, John F. *lawyer*
Meadows, John Frederick *lawyer*
Mellor, Robert E. *building materials company executive, lawyer*
Mendlin, Ronald C. *employment specialist, writer*
Merrick, Fred Harold *retired marine engineer*
Michelman, Douglas *finance company executive*
Miller, Ann G. *lawyer*
Miller, Ronald D. *medical educator, researcher*
Miller, Walter Luther *pediatrician, educator*
Miller, William Napier Cripps *lawyer*
Minar, Paul G. *interior designer, consultant*
Minnick, Malcolm David *lawyer*
Minor, Halsey *multimedia company executive*
Mitchell, Bruce Tyson *lawyer*
Mitchell, Theodore Reed *educational association administrator, former academic administrator*
Modjtabai, Avid *bank executive*
Monach, Andrew E. *lawyer*
Moore, Megan M. *mathematics educator, department chairman*
Moreno, Carlos R. *state supreme court justice*
Moris, Lamberto Giuliano *architect*
Morrissey, John Carroll, Sr. *lawyer*
Moyle, Michael R. *lawyer*
Murdoch, Colin *academic administrator*
Muren, Dennis E. *special effects expert*
Murphy, Glenn T. *retail executive*
Murphy, Kathleen Anne Foley *marketing communications executive*
Murphy, Richard A. *health science association administrator*
Murray, Kathleen Anne *lawyer*
Musfelt, Duane Clark *lawyer*
Mustacchi, Piero *preventive medicine physician, educator*
Myers, Peter Scott *lawyer*
Needleman, Jacob *philosophy educator, writer*
Newmark, Craig Alexander *communications executive*
Newsom, Gavin *mayor*
Newton, Nell Jessup *dean, law educator*
Nguyen, Ann Cac Khue *pharmaceutical and medicinal chemist*
Noonan, John T., Jr. *federal judge, educator*
Norris, Philip John *medical educator, researcher*
Oberman, Ida *research and evaluation director, consultant*
O'Brien, Sean *chef*
O'Connor, G(eorge) Richard *ophthalmologist*
Odgers, Richard William *lawyer*

Offer, Stuart Jay *lawyer*
Okeke, Christian Nwachukwu *law educator*
Olsen, Steven Kent *dentist*
Olson, Karl *lawyer*
Olson, Robert Howard *lawyer*
O'Neal, Stephen V. *lawyer*
O'Neill, Brian *national recreation area administrator*
Osborne, Donald Eugene *performing company executive*
Osher, Bernard *philanthropist, former investment company executive*
Ostler, Clyde W. *banker*
Ousterhout, Douglas Kenneth *plastic surgeon*
Owen, Marc *health products executive*
Owens, Ronald Stephen (Ronn Owens) *radio talk show host*
Palmer, Venrice Romito *lawyer, educator*
Palmer, William Joseph *accountant*
Park, Hyun *lawyer, utilities executive*
Park, Roger Cook *law educator*
Parker, Diana Lynne *restaurant manager, special events director*
Parker, Harold Allen *lawyer, real estate company officer*
Parrish, Jenni *law librarian, educator*
Patel, Marilyn Hall *judge*
Paterson, Eva *legal association director, educator*
Paterson, Richard Denis *corporate financial executive*
Paxton, Jay L. *lawyer*
Payne, Eugene C. III *lawyer*
Pazour, Don *publishing executive*
Peck, Art *retail executive*
Penhoet, Edward *foundation administrator, former biochemicals company executive, former dean*
Penskar, Mark Howard *lawyer*
Pera, Renee Reijo *biology professor*
Pereira, P.J. *media consultant*
Perlman, David *journalist*
Perry, E. Lynn *lawyer*
Petersen, Roland *artist, printmaker*
Peterson, Linda Lou *special education educator*
Petrakis, Nicholas Louis *epidemiologist, medical researcher, educator*
Petty, George Oliver *lawyer*
Pfaff, Laura King *auction house executive*
Pfau, George Harold, Jr. *investment advisor*
Phan, Charles *chef*
Philipp, Peter Eric *investment company executive, educator*
Philipsborn, John Timothy *lawyer, writer*
Phillips, Theodore Locke *radiologist, educator*
Pickett, Donn Philip *lawyer*
Pipes, Sally C. *think-tank executive*
Plishner, Michael Jon *lawyer*
Pollack, Jeffrey Lee *restaurateur*
Pope, Carl *environmental organization administrator*
Pope, Marcia L. *lawyer*
Popofsky, Melvin Laurence *lawyer*
Potter, James G. *lawyer, food products executive*
Pottruck, David Steven *venture capitalist*
Preovolos, Penelope Athene *lawyer*
Presniakov, Alexander *artist, sculptor, inventor, writer*
Preuss, Charles Frederick *lawyer*
Pringle, Paul C. *lawyer*
Pritzker, John A. *leisure services executive*
Privett, Stephen A. *academic administrator, priest*
Pure, Pamela J. *health products executive*
Quittner, Josh *editor*
Radlo, Edward John *lawyer, mathematician*
Raeber, John Arthur *architect, construction consultant*
Ragan, Charles Ransom *lawyer*
Raglin, Jonny *Bar Chef*
Rajagopal, Usha *plastic surgeon*
Ratum, Cecilia Bangloy *retired psychologist*
Reding, John Anthony, Jr. *lawyer*
Redo, David Lucien *investment company executive*
Reese, John Robert *lawyer*
Reilly, William Kane *former government official, educator, lawyer, conservationist*
Renfrew, Charles Byron *lawyer*
Renne, Paul A. *lawyer*
Rice, Denis Timlin *lawyer*
Rice, Dorothy Pechman *medical economist*
Richards, Norman Blanchard *lawyer*
Richtel, Matt (Theron Heir) *reporter, cartoonist*
Rieger, Julie *marketing executive*
Rivlin, Gary *writer, reporter*
Robertson, Armand James, II, *judge*
Robertson, Dawn H. *retail executive*
Robertson, Merle Greene *art historian, academic administrator*
Robinson, Patrick *apparel designer*
Robinson, Ralph W. *lawyer*
Rock, Arthur *venture capitalist*
Rodgers, Judy *chef*
Roe, Benson Bertheau *surgeon, educator*
Roethe, James Norton *lawyer*
Rogan, Richard A. *lawyer*
Roger, Kent M. *lawyer*
Rosales, Suzanne Marie *hospital coordinator*
Rosedale, Philip E. *computer software company executive*
Rosen, Evan Mark *executive communication advisor, journalist*
Rosen, Joshua Nathan *lawyer*
Rosen, Sanford Jay *lawyer*
Rosenberg, Pamela *opera director, conductor*
Rosenberg, Rand L. *utilities executive*
Rosenfeld, Robert A. *lawyer*
Rosenheim, Daniel Edward *journalist, television news director*
Rosenstein, Barry *investment company executive*
Rosinski, Edwin Francis *medical educator*
Ross, Elizabeth *marketing executive*
Ross, Jeffrey S. *lawyer*
Rowen, Harvey Allen *investment company executive*
Rowland, John Arthur *lawyer*
Royer, Kathleen Rose *pilot*
Rubenstein, Donald P. *lawyer*
Rubenstein, Steven Paul *newspaper columnist*
Rubin, Michael *lawyer*
Rubin, Seth Isaiah *psychologist*
Rudolph, Abraham Morris *pediatrician, educator*
Rudolph, Peter *chef*
Rugoff, Ralph *curator*
Runnicles, Donald *conductor*
Rusher, William Allen *writer, commentator, columnist*
Russell, Sabin *newswriter*
Russoniello, Joseph Pascal *lawyer*
Rutherford, George Williams III *preventive medicine physician*
Ryan, Joan *columnist*
Ryan, Kevin Vincent *lawyer, former prosecutor*
Sabean, Brian R. *professional baseball team executive*
Sachs, Marilyn Stickle *writer, educator, editor*
Saeger, Rebecca *advertising executive*
Safreno, Casey *investment banker*
Sage-Gavin, Eva Marie *retail executive*
Sakamoto, Katsuyuki *retired academic administrator, psychologist, educator*
Sali, Andrej *chemistry professor*
Sanders, Joel Steven *lawyer*
Sano, Emily Joy *museum director*
Sansweet, Stephen Jay *journalist, writer, marketing executive*
Sarkar, Rajabrata *surgeon*
Sasaki, Robert J. *financial services executive*
Satin, Joseph *language educator, retired dean*
Satre, Derek Davies *psychologist, researcher*
Saul-Gershenz, Leslie *entomologist, consultant, ecologist, director*
Saunders, Sally Love *poet, educator*
Savage, Mark Randall *lawyer*
Savage, Michael Alan (Michael Weiner) *radio personality, commentator*
Sax, Paul J. *lawyer*
Schechter, Naomi R. *oncologist*
Schenkkan, Dirk McKenzie *lawyer*
Schioldager, Amy Lee *investment company executive*
Schmidt, Robert Milton *preventive medicine physician, educator, medical association administrator*
Schools, Scott N. *prosecutor*
Schrock, Theodore R. *surgeon*
Schroeder, Steven Alfred *medical educator*
Schwab, Charles R. *investment company executive*
Schwarz, Glenn Vernon *newspaper editor*
Schwarzer, William W. *federal judge*
Seabolt, Richard L. *lawyer*
Sedway, Lynn Massel *real estate economist*
Seebach, Lydia Marie *physician*
Seegal, John Franklin *lawyer*
Seeger, Laureen E. *lawyer, health products executive*
Seelenfreund, Alan *retired pharmaceutical company executive*
Seff, James M. *lawyer*
Seneker, Carl James, II, (Kim) *lawyer*
Shackley, Douglas John *fire alarm company executive*
Shanahan, Lauri M. *lawyer, retail executive*
Shank, J. William *art conservator*
Shansby, John Gary *investor*
Shaw, Richard Eugene *cardiovascular researcher*
Sheedy, William M. *finance company executive*
Shenk, George H. *lawyer*
Sheppard, Dean *medical educator*
Sherr, Elliott Harold *neurologist, researcher*
Sherratt, Holly *art appraiser*
Shiffman, Michael A. *lawyer*
Shinefield, Henry Robert *pediatrician*
Shinohara, Katsuto *medical educator*
Shorenstein, Douglas W. *corporate executive*
Shorenstein, Walter Herbert *commercial real estate development company executive*
Shostak, Linda E. *lawyer*
Shushkewich, Kenneth Wayne *structural engineer*
Silk, Thomas *lawyer*
Simini, Joseph Peter *accountant, financial consultant, writer, former educator*
Simmons, Russel *Internet company executive, entrepreneur*
Simon, John R. *utilities executive*
Singer, Allen Morris *lawyer*
Siniscalco, Gary Richard *lawyer*
Slipsager, Henrik C. *building services company executive*
Smegal, Thomas Frank, Jr. *lawyer*
Smith, Brian D. *lawyer*
Smith, David Elvin *physician*
Smith, Jennie *artist*
Smith, Kerry Clark *lawyer*
Smith, Lloyd Hollingsworth *physician*
Smith, Quincy *Internet company executive*
Sneed, Joseph Tyree III *federal judge*
Snyder, Darin W. *lawyer*
Soberon, Presentacion Zablan *state bar administrator*
Soh, Chunghee Sarah *anthropology educator*
Sparks, Thomas E., Jr. *lawyer*
Speidel, John Joseph *public health professional, educator*
Speier, Jackie (Karen Jacqeline) *lawyer, former state senator*
Spivey, Bruce E. *ophthalmologist, educator, health facility administrator*
Spratt, Randall N. *health products executive*
Sproul, John Allan *retired utilities executive*
Stahr, Celia Suzanne *art historian, educator*
Stamper, Robert Lewis *ophthalmologist, educator*
Staring, Graydon Shaw *lawyer*
Stauffer, Thomas Michael *university president*
Steel, Michael J. *lawyer*
Steer, Reginald David *lawyer*
Steinsmith, William *internist, research scientist*
Stephens, Elisa *college president*
Steskal, Christopher James *lawyer, former prosecutor*
Stewart, Richard Edwin *insurance consulting company executive*
Steyer, Thomas Fahr *investment company executive*
Stoppelman, Jeremy *Internet company executive, entrepreneur*
Story, Joan H. *lawyer*
Street, Paul Shipley *lawyer*
Stromberg, Ross Ernest *lawyer*
Strother, James M. *lawyer*
Stump, David James *philosopher, educator*
Stumpf, John G. *bank executive*
Su, Hua *medical educator*
Subbiondo, Joseph L. *academic administrator*
Suess, Fred *plastic surgeon*
Sueyoshi, Amy Haruko *social sciences educator*
Sugarman, Myron George *lawyer*
Sugarman, Paul William *lawyer*
Sullivan, Robert Edward *lawyer*
Sutton, John Paul *lawyer*
Syhabout, James *chef*
Talbot, David Lyle *online magazine publisher, former editor*
Tang, Man-Chung *civil engineer, company executive*
Tarnoff, Peter *federal agency administrator, consultant*
Tarun, Robert Walter *lawyer*
Tasooji, Michael B. *retail executive*
Taylor, William James (Zak Taylor) *lawyer*
Ternar, Mine Y. *artist, art educator*
Thacker-Estrada, Elizabeth Lorelei *librarian, historian*
Thiebaud, Wayne Morton *artist*
Thiel, Peter A. *investment company executive*
Thomas, William Scott *lawyer*
Thompson, Patrick S. *lawyer*
Thompson, Robert Charles *lawyer*
Thornton, Charles Victor *lawyer*
Titelbaum, Daniel E. *lawyer*
Tlsty, Thea Dorothy *research scientist, educator*
Tobin, James Michael *lawyer*
Tolstedt, Carrie L. *bank executive*
Tomasson, Helgi *dancer, choreographer, company executive*
Toney, Anita Karen *printmaker*
Torme, Margaret Anne *public relations executive, management consultant*
Traynor, J. Michael *lawyer*
Tricaro, Robert Collet *biologist, educator, editor, poet*
Tripp, Alan H. *educational association administrator, consultant*
Trott, Mena *application developer*
Tully, Herbert Bullard *chemical manufacturing executive*
Turek, Paul John III *construction executive*
Uilkema, John K. *lawyer*
Ullman, Myron Edward, III, (Mike Ullman) *retail executive*
Uri, George Wolfsohn *accountant*
Uyehara, Otto Arthur *mechanical engineering educator emeritus, consultant*
Vail, Thomas Parker *orthopaedic surgeon*
Van Buskirk, Ronald E. *lawyer*
Van Dyck, Wendy *dancer*
Van Dyke, Craig *psychiatrist, director*
Van Hoesen, Beth Marie *artist, printmaker*
Vazquez-Azpiri, A. James *lawyer*
Veaco, Kristina *lawyer*
Vega, Frank J. *newspaper publishing executive*
Venning, Robert Stanley *lawyer*
Vesely, Jeffrey M. *lawyer*
Vidwans, Smruti Jayant *microbiologist*
Vizquel, Omar Enrique *professional baseball player*
Volpe, Peter Anthony *surgeon*
Wakabayashi, Seiji *chef*
Wald, Peter Allen *lawyer*
Walker, Vaughn R. *federal judge*
Walker, Walter Herbert III *lawyer, educator, writer*
Walsh, Joan *editor-in-chief*
Walter, Peter *biochemist*
Wang, Wayne *film director*
Wang, William Kai-Sheng *law educator*
Warnecke, John Carl *architect*
Warner, Harold Clay, Jr. *banker, investment company executive*
Warner, Paul L. *lawyer*
Warner, Rollin Miles, Jr. *economics educator, real estate broker*
Way, E(dward) Leong *pharmacologist, toxicologist, educator*
Weber, Arnold I. *lawyer*
Weber, Paula M. *lawyer*
Weihrich, Heinz *management educator*
Weiner, Michael W. *neuroscientist, researcher, educator*
Weisel, Thomas W. *investment company executive*
Weitzel, Mark P. *lawyer*
Welborn, Caryl Bartelman *lawyer*
Werdegar, Kathryn Mickle *state supreme court justice*
Wernick, Sandra Margot *advertising and public relations executive*
Wescott, William Burnham *oral maxillofacial pathologist, educator*
Whitehead, David Barry *lawyer*
Wild, Nelson Hopkins *lawyer*
Wilkinson, Jeffery Alan *animal scientist*
Williams, Evan *Internet company executive*
Williams, Lance *journalist*
Williams, Linda C. *lawyer*
Williams, R. Neil *finance company executive*
Winblad, Ann *investment company executive*
Wingate, C. Keith *law educator*
Winn, Steven Jay *critic*
Wintroub, Bruce Urich *dermatologist, educator, researcher*
Wirum, Andrea A. *lawyer*
Wolfe, Cameron Withgot, Jr. *lawyer*
Wolff, Sheldon *radiobiology educator*
Wolford, Richard G. *food products executive*
Wong, Stanton D. *lawyer*
Wonner, Paul John *painter*
Wood, Robert Warren *lawyer*
Woo Ho, Doreen *investment banker*
Worthington, Bruce R. *lawyer, energy executive*
Wyle, Frederick S. *lawyer*
Wyse, Roger Earl *physiologist, department chairman*
Yamamoto, Keith Robert *molecular biologist, educator*
Yao, John Sen *physician*
Yellen, Janet Louise *bank executive*
Ying, Weihai *biomedical researcher, educator*
Yost, Nicholas Churchill *lawyer*
Young, Bryant Llewellyn *lawyer*
Young, Douglas Rea *lawyer*
Young, Lowell Sung-yi *health facility administrator, medical educator*
Zaccaria, Adrian *utilities executive*
Zeldin, Kim S. *lawyer*
Zellerbach, William Joseph *retired paper company executive*
Zieff, Susan Gail *healthcare educator*
Ziegler, R. W., Jr. *lawyer, consultant*
Ziering, William Mark *lawyer*
Zimmerman, Bernard *judge*
Zippin, Calvin *epidemiologist, educator*
Zito, Barry *professional baseball player*

San Gabriel

Chen, John Calvin *retired psychiatrist, educator*
Shao, Zhenhua *electrical engineer, consultant*

San Jacinto

Hert, Theresa M. *mathematics educator*
Stange, Sharon (Sherri) *science educator*

San Jose

Alexander, Katharine Violet *lawyer*
Arvizu, Charlene Sutter *elementary school educator*
Avakoff, Joseph Carnegie *medical and law consultant*
Bannick, Matthew *Internet company executive*
Beizer, Lance Kurt *priest, lawyer*
Bell, W. Donald *electronics executive*
Belluzzo, Rick E. (Richard) *information technology and former computer software company executive*
Bennion, David Jacobsen *lawyer*
Bewley, Jeffrey Michael *lawyer*
Boac, Thelma Blantucas *principal*
Bohn, Robert Herbert *lawyer*
Bostrom, Susan L. *marketing executive*
Capellas, Michael D. *telecommunications industry executive*
Carey, Peter Kevin *reporter*
Carle, Matt *professional hockey player*
Cedolini, Anthony John *psychologist*
Ceppos, Jerome Merle (Jerry Ceppos) *newspaper editor*
Ceran, Jennifer Ellen *treasurer*
Chambers, John Thomas *computer systems network executive*
Chandler, Mark D. *computer systems network executive, lawyer*
Cheechoo, Jonathan *professional hockey player*
Chizen, Bruce R. *computer company executive*
Chuang, Alfred S. *information technology executive*
Clark, Michael Steven *accountant*
Cobb, William C. *Internet company executive*
Coleman, William T. *information technology executive*
Collins, Alison *opera singer, music educator*
Compton, Charles (Kip) *communications executive*
Connors, Mary Jean *communications executive*
Craford, M. George *physicist, research administrator*
Dalis, Irene *mezzo soprano, performing arts association administrator*
D'Arrigo, Stephen, Jr. *agricultural company executive*
Davido, Scott *retail executive*
DCamp, Kathryn Acker *human resources executive*
Dennison, Ronald Walton *engineer*
Denver, Thomas HR *lawyer*
Derr, Kenneth T. *energy executive*
Diamond, Diana Louise *editor, journalist*
Doan, Gerald Xuyen Van *lawyer*
Doody, Gregory L. *lawyer, energy executive*
Dorsa, Gene J. *secondary school educator*
Dutta, Rajiv *Internet company executive*
Effren, Gary Ross *financial executive*
Ellner, Michael William *art educator*
Emmett, Brian *software developer*
Estabrook, Reed *artist, educator*
Fawcett, Matthew Knowlton *lawyer*
Fishback, Dennis *information technology executive*
Fister, Michael J. *computer company executive*
Fitzgerald, Timothy K. *writer, political organizer, non-profit administrator*
Fry, John C. *electronics executive*
Gallo, Joan Rosenberg *lawyer*
Gill, Hardayal Singh *electrical engineer*
Gonzales, Daniel S. *lawyer*
Grandison, Tyrone Wilberforce André *systems administrator*
Gross, Lawrence Alan *lawyer*
Ha, Kiet Tuan *hospital administrator*
Hall, Robert Emmett, Jr. *investment banker, realtor*
Hannon, Timothy Patrick *lawyer, judge, educator*
Harris, Jay Terrence *communications educator*
Haycock, Kenneth Roy *academic administrator, educator, consultant*
Helleboid, Olivier *information technology executive*
Hernández, Fernando Vargas *lawyer*
Hernandez, Jo Farb *museum director, consultant*
Hill, Richard S. *manufacturing executive*
Holland, David K. *treasurer*
Hughes, Daniel David *performing company executive*
Hung, Donald Lu-Cheng *electrical engineer, computer engineer, educator*

San Juan Bautista

San Juan Capistrano

San Leandro

San Luis Obispo

San Luis Rey

San Marcos

San Marino

San Mateo

San Pablo

San Pedro

San Rafael

San Ramon

San Ysidro

Sand City

Santa Ana

Santa Barbara

Comanor, William S. *economist, educator*
Conley, Philip James, Jr. *retired air force officer*
Crawford, Donald Wesley *philosophy educator, university official*
Crispin, James Hewes *engineering and construction company executive*
Crowell, John C(hambers) *geology educator, researcher*
Cung, Thiep H. *architectural firm executive*
Curland, David Joseph *retired language educator*
Davidson, Roger H(arry) *political science professor*
Del Chiaro, Mario Aldo *art historian, archaeologist, etruscologist, educator*
Dubroff, Henry Allen *editor, journalist, entrepreneur*
Dunne, Thomas *geology educator*
Egan, Susan Chan *securities analyst, writer*
Egenolf, Robert F. *lawyer*
Eguchi, Yasu *artist*
Ellis, Eugene Joseph *cardiologist*
Emmeluth, Bruce Palmer *investment company executive, venture capitalist*
Emmons, Robert John *corporate executive, poet*
Erasmus, Charles John *anthropologist, educator*
Evans, Anthony Glyn *materials scientist, educator*
Falstrom, Kenneth Edward *lawyer*
Feigin, Joel *composer, educator*
Fingarette, Herbert *philosopher, educator*
Fisher, Steven Kay *neurobiology educator*
Ford, Peter C. *chemistry professor*
Fredrickson, Glenn Harold *chemical engineering and materials educator*
Gartrell, David Christian *archivist*
Giddings, Steven B. *physics professor*
Göllner, Marie Louise *musicologist, retired educator*
Goodchild, Michael Frank *geographer, educator*
Gossard, Arthur Charles *physicist, researcher*
Gross, David Jonathan *physicist*
Gunn, Giles Buckingham *language, religios studies and global and international studies educator*
Gunner, Michael Richard *real estate manager, hotel executive*
Gutierrez-Jones, Carl Scott *English educator*
Handel, Neal *plastic surgeon, researcher*
Hayward, Jean *artist, musician, interior designer*
Heeger, Alan Jay *physicist, educator*
Helgerson, Richard *English literature educator*
Homsy, George *mechanical and chemical engineer, educator*
Hong, Dongwoo *electrical engineer*
Horne, Marilyn Berneice *mezzo-soprano*
Howorth, David *producer, director*
Hubbard, Arthur Thornton *chemist, educator*
Humphreys, Richard Stephen *history professor, researcher*
Jackson, Beverley Joy Jacobson *columnist, educator*
Jochim, Michael Allan *archaeologist*
Johnsen, Eugene Carlyle *mathematician, educator*
Jovanovic, Lois *medical researcher*
Kalman, Laura *history professor*
Karpeles, David *museum director*
Kendler, Howard H(arvard) *psychologist, educator*
Kennedy, John Harvey *chemistry professor*
Kohn, Roger Alan *surgeon*
Kohn, Walter *physicist, retired educator*
Kokotovic, Petar V. *electrical and computer engineering educator*
Kramer, Edward John *materials engineering educator*
Kroemer, Herbert *electrical engineering educator*
Kruger, Kenneth Charles *architect*
Kryter, Karl David *retired research scientist*
Larsgaard, Mary Lynette *librarian, writer*
Lawrance, Charles Holway *retired civil and sanitary engineer*
Levine, Joshua H. *medical products executive*
Lick, Wilbert James *mechanical engineering educator*
Liebhaber, Myron I. *allergist*
Lovelace, Jon (Jonathan Bell Lovelace) *investment management company executive*
Lucas, Gene *academic administrator*
Luyendyk, Bruce Peter *geophysicist, educator, academic administrator*
Macdonald, Ken Craig *geophysicist*
Mack, Judith Cole Schrim *retired political scientist*
Mahlendorf, Ursula Renate *literature educator*
Mathews, Barbara Edith *gynecologist*
Mayer, Richard Edwin *psychology professor*
McCaw, Wendy Petrak *publishing executive*
McCoy, Lois Clark *retired social services administrator, retired county official, editor*
Mc Duffie, Malcolm *oil industry executive*
McGee, James Sears *historian, educator*
McKee, Kathryn Dian Grant *human resources consultant*
McMeeking, Robert Maxwell *mechanical engineer, educator*
Metzinger, Timothy Edward *lawyer*
Minc, Henryk *mathematics professor*
Mitchell, Shawne Maureen *author*
Mitra, Sanjit Kumar *electrical and computer engineering educator*
Murdoch, William Wilson *ecologist, educator*
Nabi, Robin *communications educator*
Nakamura, Shuji *engineering educator*
Obern, Vivian Marie *volunteer*
O'Dowd, Donald Davy *retired university president*
Peale, Stanton Jerrold *physics educator*
Perloff, Jean Marcosson *property manager, retired lawyer*
Pilgeram, Laurence Oscar *biochemist*
Pochini, Judy Hay *interior designer, writer, editor*
Polchinski, Joseph G. *physicist, science educator*
Prindle, William Roscoe *retired glass company executive*
Ramsay, William Charles *writer, composer*
Ray, Charles Dean *neurosurgeon, spine surgeon, bioengineer, inventor*
Rehm, Susan J. *social services professional*
Rose, Mark Allen *humanities educator*
Rosenthal, Earl Edgar *art history educator*
Russell, Jeffrey Burton *historian, educator*
Salotti, Kathryn E. *marriage and family therapist*
Sanger, Robert Marshall *lawyer*
Scheinfeld, James David *retired travel company executive*
Schneider, Edward Lee *botanist, researcher*
Schultz, Arthur Warren *retired communications executive*
Sherman, Alan Robert *retired psychologist, educator*
Simons, Stephen *mathematics professor, researcher*
Sinsheimer, Robert Louis *retired academic administrator, educator*
Sneddon, Thomas William, Jr. *prosecutor*
Tilton, David Lloyd *savings and loan association executive*
Tirrell, Matthew V. *engineering educator*
Tucker, Shirley Lois Cotter *botanist, educator*
Vos, Hubert Daniel *investor*
Wade, Glen *electrical engineer, educator*
Weidemann, Celia Jean *social sciences educator, management consultant, financial consultant*
White, Robert Stephen *retired physics professor*
Wilkins, Burleigh Taylor *philosophy educator*
Witherell, Michael S. *physicist, educator*
Yang, Henry T.Y. *chancellor, educator*
Young, Michael Kent *physics professor*

Santa Clara

Barrett, Craig R. *electronics company executive*
Barrett, Ronald W. *biopharmaceutical executive*
Bechtolsheim, Andy (Andreas) *information technology executive*
Bell, Genevieve *anthropologist*
Benson, Jon H. *information technology executive*
Berg, Carl E. *real estate developer*
Beveridge, Crawford W. *information technology executive*
Bray, Tim (Timothy William Bray) *computer company executive, software developer*
Bryant, Andy D. *computer company executive*
Burke, Conrad *energy executive*
Castellino, Ronald Augustus Dietrich *radiologist, educator*
Chan, Shu-Park *electrical engineering educator*
Chastain, Brandi Denise *professional soccer player*
Chin, Albert Kae *research physician*
Clark, John M. III *lawyer*
Congistre, John Huber *electronics engineer, retired military officer*
Culbertson, Leslie S. *computer company executive*
Cundy, Kenneth Charles *pharmaceutical executive*
Dafforn, Geoffrey Alan *biochemist*
Dai, Guang-ming George *optics scientist*
Dai, Weili *information technology executive*
Dave, Tushar A. *Indo-US venture capital company executive*
Davis, George S. *manufacturing executive*
Denholm, Robyn *information technology executive*
Dessau, Nigel *information technology executive*
Dham, Vinod K. *Indo-US venture capitalist company executive*
Dillon, Michael A. (Mike) *lawyer, information technology executive*
Dobberphul, Daniel *engineering company executive*
Elkus, Richard J., Jr. *electronics company executive*
Faggin, Federico *electronics executive*
Field, Alexander James *economics professor, dean*
Foldvary, Fred Emanuel *economist, educator*
Fowler, John *information technology executive*
Fuller, Dale L. *software security company executive*
Gadre, Anil *information technology executive*
Gelsinger, Patrick P. *computer company executive*
Gilbert, Lucia Albino *psychology professor*
Glancy, Dorothy Jean *lawyer, educator*
Goodchild, Lester Francis *higher education educator*
Grantham, Don *information technology executive*
Green, Rich *information technology executive*
Grossman, Jeremiah *information technology executive*
Grove, Andrew Steven *electronics executive*
Halla, Brian L. *electronics executive*
Harris, David M. *information technology executive*
Heel, Joe *information technology executive*
Hofstetter, Jane Robinson *artist, educator*
Hopkinson, Shirley Lois *library and information scientist, educator*
Howe, Bill *information technology executive*
Hsieh, Marina Cing *lawyer, educator*
Huang, Jen-Hsun *electronics executive*
Hutcheson, Jerry Dee *manufacturing company executive*
Kamal, Abu Hena M. *electrical engineer, researcher*
Kirk, David B. *computer scientist*
Lane, Holly Diana *artist*
Lee, Chan-Yun *physicist, process engineer, educator*
Lehman, Michael Evans *information technology executive*
Lempert, Dennis Alan *lawyer*
Lieto, Tim *information technology executive*
Locatelli, Paul Leo *academic administrator*
MacGowan, Bill *information technology executive*
Maloney, Sean M. *computer company executive*
McCabe, Eugene *information technology executive*
McGowan, Stephen T. *corporate financial executive*
McNealy, Scott Glenn *information technology executive*
Medepalli, Kamesh *engineer, researcher, educator*
Miller, Dan *information technology executive*
Moore, Gordon E. *electronics executive, researcher*
Morgan, James C. *manufacturing executive*
Morris, Sandra K. *computer company executive*
Mukherjee, Sayandev *electrical engineer, researcher*
Murdock, Ian *information technology executive*
Murray, Patricia *electronics company executive*
Nolan, Mike *professional football coach*
Nordlund, Donald Craig *lawyer, electronics executive*
Ostwald, Venice Eloise Varner *librarian, educator, minister, writer*
Otellini, Paul S. *electronics company executive*
Papadopoulos, Gregory Michael *information technology executive*
Parden, Robert James *engineering educator, management consultant*
Pinto, Mark R. *manufacturing executive*
Polden, Donald *dean, law educator*
Pollace, Pamela L. *public relations executive*
Poyadue, Florene Stewart *nurse, foundation administrator*
Roknaldin, Farzam *mechanical engineer, educator*
Roy, Abhra *plasma engineer, researcher*
Rudolph, Ronald Alvin *human resources specialist*
Schwartz, Jonathan Ian *information technology executive*
Sewell, D. Bruce (Bruce Sewell, Durward Bruce Sewell) *lawyer*
Shannon, David M. *lawyer*
Shavers, Cheryl L. *technology and business consultant*
Simmons, Janet Bryant *writer, publishing executive*
Simon, James Lowell *lawyer*
Smith, Alex *professional football player*
Smith, Stephen Allen *mathematician, educator*
Sodhani, Arvind *computer company executive*
Somani, Seema *optics scientist*
Splinter, Michael R. *manufacturing executive*
Stern, Hal *information technology executive*
Sutardja, Sehat *information technology executive*
Sutphin, Brian *information technology executive*
Sweeney, Joseph J. *lawyer, manufacturing executive*
Tremblay, Marc *information technology executive*
Urdan, Timothy Cameron *psychology professor, consultant*
Van Den Hoogen, Ingrid *information technology executive*
Wang, Min *electronics engineer*
White, Ian *information technology executive*
Yen, David Wei-Luen *information technology executive*

Santa Clarita

Boyer, Carl III *not-for-profit developer, retired mayor, municipal official, secondary school educator*
Feldman Nebenzahl, Bernardo *composer, educator*
Kotler, Richard Lee *lawyer*
Lavine, Steven David *academic administrator*
Plew, Paul Timothy *music educator, dean*
Sturges, Sherry Lynn *recording industry executive*
Walker, Robert F. *social studies educator*

Santa Cruz

Bian, Zhixi *research scientist*
Blumenthal, George *academic administrator, astronomy and astrophysics professor*
Brown, George Stephen *physics professor*
Bunnett, Joseph Frederick *chemist, educator*
Carson, Benjamin Leeds *composer, educator*
Chemers, Martin M. *psychologist, educator*
Cheung, Yin-Wong *economics professor*
Davis, Angela Yvonne *political activist, educator, writer*
Dilbeck, Charles Stevens, Jr. *real estate company executive*
Epps, Harland Warren *astronomy educator, optical design consultant*
Faber, Sandra Moore *astronomer, educator*
Flatté, Stanley Martin *physicist, researcher*
Garcia-Luna-Aceves, J.J. *education educator*
Goldenkranz, Andrew *principal, educator*
Griggs, Gary Bruce *oceanographer, geologist, educator, director*
Haussler, David H. *molecular biologist, educator*
Hersley, Dennis Charles *environmentalist, software systems consultant*
Hill, Terrell Leslie *chemist, researcher, biophysicist*
Huskey, Harry Douglas *information and computer science educator*
Kahn, Philippe *telecommunications industry executive, entrepreneur*
Kang, Sung-Mo (Steve Kang) *electrical engineering educator*
Kraft, Robert Paul *astronomer, educator*
Langenheim, Jean Harmon *biologist, educator*
Langhout, Regina D. *psychology professor*
Lay, Thorne *geosciences educator*
Machotka, Pavel *psychology and art educator*
Margon, Bruce Henry *astrophysicist, educator*
Pettigrew, Thomas Fraser *social psychologist, educator*
Pletsch, Marie Eleanor *plastic surgeon*
Pratkanis, Anthony Richard *social psychologist, educator*
Rabus, Dominik Gerhard *electrical engineer, researcher*
Resneck-Sannes, Helen *psychologist*
Ripma, Mary *librarian*
Roby, Pamela Ann *sociologist, educator*
Rothwell, Wendy *biology educator*
Sadjadpour, Hamid Reza *engineering educator*
Sands, Matthew Linzee *physicist, researcher*
Seligmann, William Robert *lawyer, author*
Shorenstein, Rosalind Greenberg *internist*
Smith, M(ahlon) Brewster *retired psychologist, educator*
Steel, Virginia (Ginny) *university librarian*
Stevens, Stanley David *historian, researcher, retired librarian, archivist*
Stormes, John Max *systems analyst*
Varma, Anujan *computer engineer, educator*
Wiberg, Donald Martin *electrical engineering educator, consultant*
Widom, Harold *mathematician, educator*
Williams, Terrie M. *biology professor*
Winston, George *solo pianist, guitarist, harmonica player*
Wipke, W. Todd *chemistry professor*
Woosley, Stanford Earl *astrophysicist*

Santa Maria

Lewis, Mark Kevin *history professor, minister*
Roadarmel, Stanley Bruce *civilian military employee*

Santa Monica

Aaron, David L. *diplomat, author*
Alexander, Peter Houston *artist*
Almqvist, Pelle *singer*
Alpert, Herb *composer, recording artist, producer, painter*
Amos, Reed C. *lawyer*
Appleton, Marc *architect*
Archambault, Nicole Marie *speech pathology/audiology services professional, consultant*
Bachrach, Charles Lewis *advertising agency executive*
Bosman, Richard *artist, printmaker*
Brook, Robert Henry *public health service officer, internist, educator*
Bruckheimer, Jerry Leon *producer*
Buxton, William Glenton *neurologist, director*
Calacanis, Jason McCabe *internet entrepreneur, blogger*
Calcanis, Jason McCabe *Internet company executive*
Cameron, James *film director, screenwriter, producer*
Carr, Ruth Margaret *plastic surgeon*
Carrabba, Christopher Ender *singer*
Chapman Holley, Shawn Snider *lawyer*
Cooper, Jay Leslie *lawyer*
Cornell, Chris (Christopher John Cornell) *singer, musician*
Crichton, Michael (John Michael Crichton) *writer, film director*
Curran, Leigh *actress, playwright*
Davie, Jill *chef*
Davis, Stephen Edward Folwell *banker*
Doran, Lindsay *film producer, executive*
Ellickson, Phyllis Lynn *political scientist*
Eminem, (Marshall Mathers III) *rap artist*
Eve, (Eve Jihan Jeffers) *rap artist, actress*
Feltheimer, Jon *entertainment company executive*
Feniger, Susan *chef, television personality, writer*
Fisher, Frances *actress*
Foley, Jane Deborah *foundation executive*
Friedman, Monroe *psychologist, educator, consultant, editor, writer*
Friedman, Robert Glenn *film company executive*
Geiser, Thomas Christopher *lawyer, insurance company executive*
Genego, William Joseph *lawyer*
Giannulli, Mossimo *designer, apparel business executive*
Goldman, Charles A. *science administrator*
Grace, Maggie *actress*
Gray, Laura B. *psychology professor, counselor*
Greenberg, Sarah *film company executive*
Griffith, Arnold Koons *computer consultant*
Griffith, Huw *advertising executive*
Gritton, Eugene Charles *nuclear engineer, director*
Grossman, Marshall Bruce *lawyer*
Gupta, Rishab Kumar *medical association administrator, educator, researcher*
Hannigan, Alyson *actress*
Heimbuch, Babette E. *bank executive*
Hinerfeld, Robert Elliot *lawyer*
Hirsch, Richard Gary *lawyer*
Hoefflin, Steven M. *plastic surgeon*
Hornstein, James E. *lawyer*
Horowitz, Zachary I. *entertainment company executive*
Hu, Kelly *actress*
Huffington, Arianna (Arianna Stassinopoulos) *writer*
Intriligator, Devrie Shapiro *physicist*
Jain, John Kumar *medical educator, health facility administrator*
Jones, William Allen *lawyer*
Kanin, Josh David *film studies educator*
Katina, Elena Sergejevna *singer*
Katz, Roger *pediatrician, allergist, immunologist, educator*
Kawamoto, Henry K. *plastic surgeon*
Kayton, Myron *engineering company executive*
Kemper, Tom A. *secondary school educator*
Kennedy, Kathleen *film producer*
Kinney, James Howard *lawyer, real estate company executive*
Kirkland, John C. *lawyer*
Klowden, Michael Louis *think-tank executive*
Kurtzman, Joel Allan *economist*
Lederman, Bruce Randolph *investment company executive, retired lawyer*
Lempert, Philip *advertising executive, writer, news correspondent*
Levin, Gerald M. (Jerry Levin) *former media and entertainment company executive*
Levin, Marvin Eugene *lawyer*
Lincoln, Thomas L. *pathologist, educator*
Littlefield, Warren *television executive*
Lohner, Henning *composer, filmmaker*
Louis-Dreyfus, Julia *actress*

Manson, Marilyn (Brian Hugh Warner) *singer, musician*
Markoff, Steven C. *finance company executive*
Masucci, Michael James *artist*
Mayne, Thom *architect*
McCreary, Lori L. *entertainment business executive*
McGlynn, Elizabeth A. *health policy analyst*
McGuire, Michael Francis *plastic surgeon*
McMillan, M. Sean *lawyer*
Milken, Michael R. *think-tank executive, philanthropist*
Milliken, Mary Sue *chef, television personality, writer*
Modisett, Jeffrey A. *lawyer, former state attorney general*
Mora, Philippe *screenwriter, producer, director, painter*
Morgan, Kermit Johnson *lawyer*
Morgenstern, Joe *film critic*
Moses, Samuel B. *accountant, consultant*
Moskos, Charles C. *social studies educator*
O'Connor, Edward Joseph *neurologist*
Ovitz, Michael S. *communications executive*
Palmatier, Malcolm Arthur *editor, consultant*
Patel, Chandra Kumar Naranbhai *communications executive, educator, entrepreneur, researcher*
Peña, Michael Anthony *actor*
Postaer, Larry *advertising executive*
Preble, Laurence George *lawyer*
Rand, Robert Wheeler *neurosurgeon, educator*
Redford, Robert (Charles Robert Redford) *actor, film director*
Resnick, Jeffrey I. *plastic surgeon*
Reville, Robert T. *economist*
Rice, Donald Blessing *corporate executive, former federal official*
Rice, Pamela Ann *marriage and family therapist*
Rich, Michael David *think-tank executive, lawyer*
Rifkin, Arnold *film company executive*
Risman, Michael *lawyer, real estate developer, broker*
Roney, Robert Kenneth *retired aerospace transportation executive*
Rubenstein, Paul D. *lawyer*
Rubin, Gerrold Robert *advertising executive*
Ruble, John *architect*
Ryan, Jane Frances *corporate communications executive*
Sacchi, John *film company executive*
Salveson, Melvin Erwin *management sciences company executive, educator*
Schaeffer, Leonard David *health insurance company executive*
Schultz, Victor M. *physician*
Scott, Jill *poet, musician*
Sekularac, Nadezda *software architect, researcher*
Shahani, Sudhin *entrepreneur, Internet company executive*
Sherman, Victor *lawyer*
Sherman, Zachary *civil engineer, aerospace engineer, consultant*
Shiffrin, Nancy *writer, educator*
Shim, Elisabeth K. *dermatologist*
Shults, Roy L. *lawyer*
Siart, William Eric Baxter *non-profit education organization administrator*
Singer, Frederick Raphael *medical researcher*
Smith, James Patrick *economist*
Snedaker, Catherine Raupagh (Kit Snedaker) *editor*
Soloff, Laura J. *academic administrator*
Soodik, Lynn *lawyer*
Stern, Walter Eugene *neurosurgeon, educator*
Stewart, Patrick *actor*
Stiehm, Judith Hicks *political scientist*
Summer, Donna (La Donna Adrian Gaines) *singer, songwriter, actress*
Sun, Li *statistician*
Suschitzky, Peter *cinematographer*
Teitelbaum, Steven *plastic surgeon*
Tennenbaum, Michael Ernest *investor*
The Edge, (David Howell Evans) *musician*
Thompson, Dennis Peters *plastic surgeon*
Thomson, James Alan *think-tank executive*
Timbaland, (Timothy Z. Mosley) *recording industry executive, rap artist*
Timmer, Barbara *state agency administrator*
Tito, Dennis Anthony *former aerospace engineer, financial advisor*
Tompkins, Ronald K. *retired surgeon, educator*
Tunney, John Varick *lawyer, former senator*
Unterman, Thomas *venture capitalist, lawyer*
Wachs, Martin *urban planning educator, author, consultant*
Wangard, Gregg *chef*
Watros, Cynthia *actress*
Watson, Doc (Arthel Lane Watson) *vocalist, guitarist, banjoist, recording artist*
Weitzman, Howard L. *lawyer, former film company executive*
Welker, Kara *agent*
Wilson, Hugh Steven *lawyer*
Wolf, Charles, Jr. *economist, educator*
Yudell, Buzz (Robert Yudell) *architect*
Zarem, Harvey Alan *plastic surgeon*

Santa Paula
Broughton, Margaret Martha *mental health nurse*
Edwards, Samuel Roger *retired internist*
Lattimore, Steven *classicist, educator*

Santa Rosa
Aman, Reinhold Albert *philologist, writer*
Andriano-Moore, Richard Count *retired military officer, secondary school educator, elementary school educator*
Ash, John *chef*
Banks, Peter Morgan *physics professor*
Biderman, Charles Israel *diversified financial services company executive*
Bozdech, Marek Jiri *physician, educator*
Callum, Myles *magazine editor, writer*
Clement, Clayton Emerson *lawyer*
Cohn, Joseph David *surgeon*
Courteau, Girard Robert *retired prosecutor*
Goldberg, Steven Murray *lawyer*
Grundy, Richard David *engineer*
Handelman, Albert G. *lawyer*
Hoskins, Anthony Glenn *librarian*
Jackson, Jess S. *vintner*
Jandrey, Becky Lee *psychologist*
Jann, Gregg *counselor, sales executive, consultant*
Kim, Seung-bum (Sab) *research scientist*
Kopes-Kerr, Colin P. *physician, publishing executive*
McAvoy, John Martin *plastic surgeon*
Meekins, Deborah *bank executive*
Mir-Sepasi, M. Hossein *cardiac thoracic surgeon*
Monk, Diana Charla *small business owner*
Pearson, Roger Lee *library director*
Person, Evert Bertil *retired newspaper and radio executive*
Rosaschi, Jim *librarian*
Smith, Thomas Kent *retired radiologist*
Swofford, Robert Lee *editor, journalist*
Wagner, Harold A. *retired gas industry executive*
Webb, Charles Richard *retired university president*

Santee
Hardy, Ben(son B.) *orchid nursery executive*
Morris, Henry Madison III *minister, writer, speech professional, consultant*
Peters, Raymond Eugene *historian, writer*
Schenk, Susan Kirkpatrick *nursing educator, consultant, small business owner*

Saratoga
Barna, Lillian Carattini *school system administrator*
Greenleaf, John Edward *human research consultant*
Houston, Elizabeth Reece Manasco *correctional education consultant*
Houston, Joseph Brantley, Jr. *optical instrument company executive*
Reagan, Joseph Bernard *retired aerospace executive, management consultant*
Rollo, F. David *healthcare company executive, cardiologist*
Syvertson, Clarence Alfred *management consultant, engineer*

Sausalito
Apatoff, Michael John *entrepreneur*
Battelle, John *journalist, educator, writer, entrepreneur*
Berkman, William Roger *lawyer, army reserve officer*
Gordon, Robert Eugene *lawyer*
Hansen, Charles Morton *editor, retired military officer*
O'Connor, Paul Daniel *lawyer*
Ornish, Dean *medical association administrator, medical educator*
Sinclair, Cameron *architect*

Scotts Valley
Crandell, Kenneth James *management consultant, entrepreneur*
Hudson, William L. *lawyer, electronics executive*
Janssen, James Robert *consulting software engineer*
Luczo, Stephen J. *computer equipment company executive*
Park, Chong S. *computer company executive*
Pope, Charles C. *computer hardware company executive*
Watkins, William D. *computer hardware company executive*
Wingert, Michael J. *computer company executive*

Seal Beach
Burge, Willard, Jr. *software company executive*
Matz, Sean Cormick *electrical engineer*
Pipes, Doris Perry *secondary school educator, consultant*
Weitzman, Marc Herschel *lawyer*
Whelan, David A. *engineering executive*

Seaside
Anderson, David Louis *academic administrator, history professor*
Gales, Samuel Joel *retired civilian military employee, counselor*
May, James Harvey *communications educator*
Mendoza, Ruben G. *anthropologist, educator, archaeologist*
Panetta, Leon Edward *former White House chief of staff, former congressman*

Sebastopol
Marler, Joan *writer, educator*
McCarthy, Thomas Edward *retired telecommunications executive*
Norman, Arnold McCallum, Jr. *engineer*
O'Reilly, Tim *computer book publishing company executive, open sourcer advocate*
Rappaport, Stuart Ramon *lawyer*
Sabsay, David *library director, consultant*

Sepulveda
Yano, Elizabeth Martin *epidemiologist, researcher*

Shadow Hills
Bangs, Cate (Cathryn Margaret Bangs) *film production designer, interior designer*

Sherman Oaks
Ardalan, Pezhman Christopher *lawyer*
Beck, Glenn *radio personality*
Caren, Robert Poston *aerospace scientist*
Clark, Susan (Nora Goulding) *actress*
Cook, Paul Maxwell *technology company executive*
Crump, Gerald Franklin *retired lawyer*
Drudge, Matt *journalist, celebrity blogger*
Elfman, Danny *composer*
Ferguson, Lisa Beryl *accountant*
Gibbs, Antony (Tony Gibbs) *film editor*
Grossman, Peter H. *plastic surgeon*
Heffner, Daniel Jason *film producer*
Hein, Todd Jonathan *accountant*
Howe, Daniel Walker *historian, educator*
Jordan, Bonnie *television producer*
Karras, Alex *actor, retired professional football player*
Krueger, Kenneth John *nutritionist, educator*
Levin, Evanne Lynn *lawyer, educator*
Lorber, Jeffrey H. *jazz musician, composer*
Medearis, Miller *lawyer*
Merritt, Jean *consulting firm executive, psychotherapist*
Mersel, Marjorie Kathryn Pedersen *lawyer*
Michelson, Louis Eli *lawyer*
Mikesell, Richard Lyon *lawyer, financial counselor*
Milgrim, Darrow A. *insurance company executive*
Norwood, Brandy Rayana (Brandy) *singer, actress*
Platus, Libby *journalist, art educator, sculptor, artist*
Powell, John *composer*
Reiner, Thomas Karl *manufacturing executive, engineering scientist*
Schlessinger, Laura *radio talk show host*
Stein, Kira D. *psychiatrist*
Taylor, Elizabeth (Dame Elizabeth Rosemond Taylor) *actress*
Yasnyi, Allan David *communications company executive*

Sierra Madre
Nation, Earl F. *retired urologist, educator*

Signal Hill
Vandament, William Eugene *retired academic administrator*

Silverado
Mamer, James Michael *secondary school educator*

Simi Valley
Blackwood, (R.) Duke *library director*
Eberhard-Neveaux, Christine *aviation executive, dispute resolution executive*
Erzinger, Kathy McClam *nursing educator*
Lewis, Richard B. *manufacturing and logistics executive*
Ritacco, Patsy Richard *sales executive*
Sproles, Kevin *entrepreneur, Internet company executive*

Solana Beach
Agnew, Harold Melvin *physicist*
Ellsworth, Robert Fred *investment executive, former government official*

Solvang
Roberts, Monty *horse trainer, writer*

Somerset
Carr, Les *psychologist, educator*

Somis
Kehoe, Vincent Jeffré-Roux *photographer, cosmetics executive*
Premack, Ann J. *writer*

Sonoma
Beckmann, Jon Michael *publishing company executive*
Emery, John Edward *plastic surgeon, vintner*
Fellows, Alice Combs *artist*
Hobart, Billie *education educator, consultant*
Kizer, Carolyn Ashley *poet, educator*
Markey, William Alan *health facility administrator, consultant*
Muchmore, Robert Boyer *engineering executive, consultant*
Obninsky, Victor Peter *lawyer*
Sasaki, Y(asunaga) Tito *engineering executive*

Sonora
Chandler, Edwin Russell *clergyman, writer*
Clarke, Paula Katherine *anthropologist, researcher, social studies educator*

Soquel
Cureton, Glen *pharmaceutical executive*
Tomash, Erwin *retired computer company executive*

South Lake Tahoe
Nason, Rochelle *conservation organization administrator*

South Pasadena
Askin, Walter Miller *artist, educator*
Finnell, Michael Hartman *mining executive*
Fuller, Kathy J. *special education educator, consultant, researcher*
Girvigian, Raymond *architect*
Hsieh, Ming *information technology executive*
Kopp, Eugene Howard *communications and electrical engineer, consultant*
Whang, Sukoo Jack *pathologist, microbiologist*

South San Francisco
Brewer, Richard B. *biotechnology company executive*
Caro, Ivor *dermatologist*
Desmond-Hellmann, Susan *medical products manufacturing executive*
Ferrara, Napoleone M.A. *molecular oncologist*
Goodman, Corey Scott *neuroscientist, biotechnologist, educator*
Hull, Cordell William *engineering, construction, and project management executive, investor*
Humphrey, Patrick Paul *pharmacologist*
Hurst, Deborah *pediatric hematologist*
Khawli, Leslie Albert *research scientist, educator*
Lacey, David *biotechnology company executive*
Lee, Ann L. *biotechnology company executive*
Lee, Leonard S. *health facility administrator*
Lewis, Jason Alvert, Jr. *communications executive*
Lipsky, Ian David *biochemical manufacturing executive, director*
Potter, Myrtle S. *research and development company executive*
Ryan, Tom *reporting applications platform company executive*
Scheller, Richard H. *physiologist, science educator*
Tananbaum, James *medical engineering company executive*
Tessier-Lavigne, Marc Trevor *neurobiologist, researcher*
Walsh, J. Michael *wholesale distribution executive*

Spring Valley
Siddiqui, Razia Sultana *retired psychotherapisst, educator*

Stanford
Abraham, (Edward) Spencer *former Secretary of Energy*
Abrams, Herbert LeRoy *radiologist, educator*
Alexander, Janet Cooper *law educator*
Anderson, Theodore Wilbur *statistics educator*
Andreopoulos, Spyros George *writer*
Arber, Daniel Alan *hematologist, pathologist*
Archer, Cristina Lozej *meteorologist*
Arrow, Kenneth Joseph *economist, educator*
Arvin, Ann Margaret *microbiology and immunology educator, researcher*
Aziz, Khalid *petroleum engineering educator*
Baker, Keith Michael *history professor*
Baldwin, Robert Lesh *biochemist, educator*
Bandura, Albert *psychologist, educator*
Barron, Brigid *education educator*
Bauer, Eugene Andrew *dermatologist, educator*
Baylor, Denis Aristide *neuroscientist, educator*
Beaver, William Henry *accounting educator*
Bell, Susan Groag *historian, researcher*
Berg, Paul *biochemist, educator*
Bienenstock, Arthur Irwin *physicist, educator, federal official*
Blandford, Roger David *science educator*
Blau, Helen Margaret *pharmacology educator*
Block, Steven Michael *biophysicist, educator*
Boahen, Kwabena *bioengineering educator*
Boaler, Jo *education educator*
Bobo, Lawrence D. *sociologist*
Boudart, Michel *chemical engineer, consultant, chemist, educator*
Bower, Gordon Howard *psychologist, educator*
Bowlsby, Bob *athletic director*
Brauman, John I. *chemist, educator*
Briggs, Winslow Russell *plant biologist, educator*
Brody, Richard Alan *political science educator, researcher*
Brooks, Helen Bousky *literature and language professor, performing arts educator*
Brown, J. Martin *oncologist, educator*
Brown, Patrick O. *molecular biologist, educator*
Brunger, Axel Thomas *biophysicist, researcher, educator*
Bube, Richard Howard *retired materials scientist, educator*
Bulow, Jeremy Israel *economist*
Bunzel, John Harvey *political science professor*
Campbell, Allan McCulloch *bacteriology educator*
Cannon, Robert Hamilton, Jr. *aerospace engineering educator*
Cantwell, Brian *aeronautical engineer, educator*
Cavalli-Sforza, Luigi Luca *geneticist, educator*
Chase, Robert Arthur *surgeon, educator*
Cohen, Albert *musician, educator*
Cohen, Harvey Joel *pediatric hematology and oncology educator*
Cohen, Stanley Norman *geneticist, educator*
Cohen, William *law educator*
Collman, James Paddock *chemistry professor*
Conquest, Robert (George Robert Acworth Conquest) *writer, historian, poet*
Cook, Karen S. *sociologist, professor*
Cork, Linda Katherine *veterinary pathologist, educator*
Corn, Wanda Marie *art educator*
Cottle, Richard Warren *retired operations research educator*
Cox, Donald Clyde *electrical engineering educator*
Craswell, Richard *law educator*
Curet, Myriam Jeanette *surgeon, educator*
Daily, Gretchen Cara *ecologist, environmental services administrator*
Dally, William J. *computer science educator*
Damon, William Van Buren *developmental psychologist, educator, writer*
Danielson, Elena Schafer *retired archivist*
David, Paul Allan *economist, economic historian*
Davis, Mark M. *microbiologist, educator*
Davis, Ronald Wayne *genetics researcher, biochemistry educator*
Deisseroth, Karl A. *neuroscientist, educator*
Dekker, George Gilbert *literature professor, writer, former academic administrator*
Derksen, Charlotte Ruth Meynink *librarian*
Diamond, Larry *political scientist*
Dickson, Lance E. *former law librarian, educator*
Dirzo, Rodolfo *biologist, educator, researcher*
Djerassi, Carl *writer, retired chemistry professor*
Donaldson, Sarah Susan *radiologist*
Duffie, Darrell *finance educator*
Duus, Peter *retired historian*
Efron, Bradley *statistician, educator*
Egbert, Peter Roy *ophthalmologist, educator*
Ehrlich, Paul Ralph *biology professor*
Ehrlich, Thomas *law educator*
Eisner, Elliot W. *education educator*
Eitner, Lorenz Edwin Alfred *art historian, educator*

Eliashberg, Yakov *mathematician, educator*
Elliott, David Duncan III *science company executive*
Enge, Per Kristian *engineering educator*
Enthoven, Alain Charles *economist, educator*
Eshleman, Von Russel *electrical engineering educator, aerospace scientist*
Etchemendy, John *academic administrator, educator*
Eustis, Robert Henry *design company executive, mechanical engineer*
Falkow, Stanley *microbiologist, educator*
Fan, Shanhui *engineering educator*
Farquhar, John William *physician, educator*
Fayer, Michael David *chemist, educator*
Fee, Willard Edward, Jr. *otolaryngologist*
Feigenbaum, Edward Albert *retired computer science educator*
Felstiner, John *literature educator, translator*
Fetter, Alexander Lees *theoretical physicist, educator*
Fetterman, David Mark *anthropologist, educator*
Findlen, Paula Elizabeth *history educator*
Fire, Andrew Z. *pathologist, educator, geneticist*
Francke, Uta *geneticist, educator*
Franklin, Gene Farthing *engineering educator, consultant*
Franklin, Marc Adam *law educator*
Fredrickson, George Marsh *history professor*
Friedman, Gary David *epidemiologist*
Friedman, Lawrence M. *law educator*
Fuchs, Victor Robert *economist, educator*
Fuller, Gerald G. *engineering educator*
Fuller, Margaret Tatnall *biomedical researcher*
Gage, Nathaniel Lees *retired psychologist, educator*
Garber, Alan Michael *internist, educator, economist*
Gelpi, Albert Joseph *language educator, department chairman, critic*
Glover, Gary H. *radiologist, educator*
Goldstein, Paul *lawyer, educator*
Goodman, Joseph Wilfred *electrical engineering educator*
Gould, William Benjamin, IV, *lawyer, federal agency administrator, educator*
Gray, Robert Molten *electrical engineering educator*
Greely, Henry T. (Hank) *law educator*
Grousbeck, Harold Irving *professional sports team owner, management educator*
Grundfest, Joseph Alexander *law and business educator*
Gumbrecht, Hans Ulrich *literary criticism philosophy educator*
Hall, Robert Ernest *economics professor*
Hanawalt, Philip Courtland *biology professor, researcher*
Hanrahan, Patrick M. *computer scientist*
Hansen, Peter Reinhard *economics professor*
Harbaugh, Jim (James Joseph Harbaugh) *college football coach, retired professional football player*
Harbaugh, John Warvelle *geologist, educator*
Harbury, Pehr A.B. *biochemist, educator*
Harrison, Robert Pogue *literature educator*
Harrison, Walter Ashley *physicist, researcher*
Henderson, Victor Warren *behavioral and geriatric neurologist, epidemiologist, researcher, educator*
Hennessy, John L. *academic administrator*
Henriksen, Thomas Hollinger *researcher*
Hesselink, Lambertus *electrical engineering and physics educator*
Hickman, Bert George, Jr. *economist, educator*
Hlatky, Mark Andrew *cardiologist, researcher*
Holloway, Charles Arthur *public and private management educator*
Horowitz, Mark A. *electrical engineering and computer science educator*
Horwitz, Ralph Irving *internist, epidemiologist, educator, dean*
Howard, Ronald A. *systems engineer, educator*
Hoxby, Caroline Minter *economics professor*
Hunt, Sharon Ann *cardiologist*
Huntington, Hillard Griswold *economist*
Inkeles, Alex *sociology educator*
Jacobs, Charlotte De Croes *oncologist, educator*
Jardetzky, Oleg *retired medical educator, researcher*
Jollimore, Troy *philosophy professor, poet*
Joss, Robert L. *dean*
Jurafsky, Daniel *linguist*
Kailath, Thomas *electrical engineer, educator*
Kamil, Michael *education educator*
Karlan, Pamela Susan *law educator*
Karlin, Samuel *mathematics professor, researcher*
Kays, William Morrow *academic administrator, mechanical engineer*
Keller, Joseph Bishop *mathematician, educator*
Keller, Michael Alan *librarian, musicologist*
Kennedy, David Michael *historian, educator*
Kennedy, Donald *environmental scientist, educator, editor*
Keren, Kinneret *biophysicist*
Khosla, Chaitan S. *chemical engineer*
Kino, Gordon Stanley *electrical engineering educator*
Klausner, Michael David *law educator*
Klima, Roger Radim *physiatrist*
Knuth, Donald Ervin *computer sciences educator*
Koller, Daphne *computer scientist*
Kool, Eric T. *chemist, educator*
Kornberg, Arthur *biochemist, educator*
Kornberg, Roger David *biochemist, structural biologist*
Kovach, Robert Louis *geophysics educator*
Koza, John R. *medical educator, writer*
Kraemer, Helena Antoinette Chmura *psychiatry educator*
Kramer, Larry *dean, lawyer, educator*
Krasner, Stephen David *federal agency administrator, political science educator*
Krawinkler, Helmut *engineering educator, consultant*
Kroo, Ilan M. *aeronautical engineer, educator*
Krumboltz, John Dwight *psychologist, educator*
Kurz, Mordecai *economics professor*
Kwon, Young-Nam *environmental engineer*
Lai, Tze Leung *mathematician, educator*
Laitin, David Dennis *political science professor*
Lambers, James Vincent *mathematician, researcher, petroleum engineer*
Laughlin, Robert B. *academic administrator, physics professor*
Leckie, James Oliver *engineering educator*
Lehman, I(srael) Robert *biochemist, educator*
Leibel, Steven Arnold *radiologist*
Lemley, Mark Alan *law educator*
Lepper, Mark Roger *psychologist, educator*
Lessig, L. Lawrence III *lawyer, educator, writer*
Levy, Ronald *medical educator, researcher*
Lewis, John Wilson *political science professor*
Linehan, John H. *engineering educator, biomedical engineer*
Linvill, John Grimes *engineering educator*
Little, William Arthur *physicist, researcher*
Loeb, Susanna *education educator*
Loftis, John (Clyde), Jr. *language educator*
Lomio, J. Paul *law librarian, researcher*
Long, Sharon Rugel *dean, molecular biologist, educator*
Lotan, Rachel *education educator*
Lyman, Richard Wall *foundation administrator, academic administrator, historian*
Maccoby, Eleanor Emmons *psychology professor*
Macovski, Albert *electrical engineer, educator*
Malenka, Robert C. *psychiatrist, educator*
Mansour, Tag Eldin *pharmacologist, educator*
Mark, James B. D. *surgeon, educator*
Marmor, Michael Franklin *ophthalmologist, educator*
Marrinan, Michael Joseph *art historian, educator*
Marsh, Martha H. *hospital administrator*
Marshall, Lawrence C. *law educator*
Martin, Joanne *social sciences educator*
Martin, Richard Peter *classics educator, consultant*
Martinez, Jenny S. *lawyer*
Matson, Pamela Anne *environmental scientist, science educator*
McCarthy, John *computer scientist, educator*
McCarty, Perry Lee *civil and environmental engineering educator*
McClelland, James Lloyd *psychologist, educator, cognitive neuroscientist*
McConnell, Susan K. *neuroscientist*
McDevitt, Hugh O'Neill *immunologist, educator*
McDonald, John Gregory *financial investment educator*
McDougall, Iain Ross *nuclear medicine educator*
Mc Lure, Charles E., Jr. *economist, consultant*
Mc Namara, Joseph Donald *researcher, retired protective services official*
McQuillen, Michael Paul *neurologist, educator*
Meng, Teresa H. *electrical engineer, educator*
Mignot, Emmanuel *medical researcher*
Milgrom, Paul Robert *economics educator*
Miller, William Frederick *research and development company executive, educator, financial consultant*
Mitchell, Beverly Shriver *hematologist, oncologist, educator*
Mitchell, Reginald Eugene *mechanical engineering educator*
Mobley, William C. *neuroscientist*
Moerner, William Esco *physical chemist, educator*
Montgomery, David Bruce *marketing educator*
Montgomery, Mike *professional basketball coach*
Mooney, Harold Alfred *plant ecologist*
Moore, Thomas Gale *economist, educator*
Moretti, Franco *professor of comparative literature*
Moskalenko, Igor Vladimirovich *physicist, astrophysicist*
Mueller, Holger *physicist*
Noll, Roger Gordon *economist, educator*
Oberhelman, Harry Alvin, Jr. *surgeon, educator*
Olcott, Cornelius, IV, *surgeon*
Orr, Franklin Mattes, Jr. *petroleum engineering educator*
Osheroff, Douglas Dean *physics professor, researcher*
Ott, Wayne Robert *environmental engineer*
Owens, Douglas K. *physician, researcher*
Oyer, Paul *economist*
Palm, Charles Gilman *academic administrator*
Parkinson, Bradford Wells *astronautical engineer, educator*
Paté-Cornell, Marie-Elisabeth Lucienne *finance, engineering educator*
Paulraj, Arogyaswami Joseph *engineering educator, consultant*
Pea, Roy *education educator*
Pearson, Scott Roberts *retired economics professor*
Penn, Lee *information scientist, consultant, journalist*
Pentcheva, Bissera V. *art history educator*
Perry, William James *engineering educator, former secretary of defense*
Pfeffer, Jeffrey *business educator*
Plummer, James D. *electrical engineering educator*
Polan, Mary Lake *obstetrics and gynecology educator*
Quake, Stephen R. *physics professor, researcher*
Rabin, Robert L. *law educator*
Rai, Varun *physical chemist*
Raisian, John *academic administrator, economist*
Reddy, Vadiyala Mohan *cardiothoracic surgeon*
Reitz, Bruce Arnold *cardiac surgeon, educator*
Rhode, Deborah Lynn *law educator*
Ricardo-Campbell, Rita *economist, educator*
Riggs, Henry Earle *academic administrator, engineering educator*
Robbins, Robert Clayton *surgeon*
Roberts, Donald John *economics, business professor, consultant*
Robinson, Paul Arnold *historian, educator, writer*
Rosenberg, Saul Allen *oncologist, educator*
Ross, John *physical chemist, educator*
Roughgarden, Joan E. *biology professor*
Rubenstein, Edward *physician, educator*
Rubin, Karl Cooper *mathematics educator*
Sag, Ivan A. *linguist, educator*
Saller, Richard Paul *classics educator*
Schatzberg, Alan Frederic *psychiatrist, researcher*
Schoen, Richard Melvin *mathematics professor, researcher*
Scott, Kenneth Eugene *lawyer, educator*
Scott, W(illiam) Richard *sociology educator*
Segall, Paul *geologist, educator*
Shapiro, Lucy *molecular biology educator*
Shatz, Carla J. *biology professor, researcher*
Shaw, Richard H. *dean*
Sheehan, James John *historian, educator*
Shenker, Stephen *physics professor*
Shooter, Eric Manvers *retired neurobiology professor, consultant*
Shulman, Lee S. *educational association administrator*
Shultz, George Pratt *economics professor, former secretary of state*
Siekierski, Maciej M. *curator*
Smith, Anna Deavere *actress, playwright, educator*
So, Yuen T. *neurologist, educator*
Sofaer, Abraham David *lawyer, judge, educator, consultant*
Solomon, Edward Ira *chemistry professor, researcher*
Somerville, Christopher Roland *botanist, educator*
Sowell, Thomas *economist, syndicated columnist*
Spence, Andrew Michael *former dean, finance educator*
Springer, George Stephen *mechanical engineering educator*
Spudich, James A. *biology professor*
Stamey, Thomas Alexander *urologist, educator*
Stansky, Peter David Lyman *historian, writer, retired professor*
Stearns, Timothy P. *biology professor, geneticist*
Steele, Claude Mason *psychology professor*
Steele, Shelby *writer, educator*
Stefanick, Marcia Lynn *medical educator, researcher*
Stone, William Edward *academic administrator, consultant*
Street, Robert Lynnwood *civil, mechanical and environmental engineer*
Strober, Myra Hoffenberg *education educator, consultant*
Stryer, Lubert *biochemist, educator*
Sturrock, Peter Andrew *space science and astrophysics educator*
Suppes, Christine Johnson *publishing executive*
Susskind, Leonard *physicist, educator*
Swartz, James R. *chemical engineer, educator*
Sweeney, James Lee *engineering educator*
Theriot, Julie *microbiologist, medical educator*
Thompson, Buzz (Barton H. Jr.) *law educator*
Thompson, George Albert *geophysicist, educator*
Thrun, Sebastian Burkhard *computer science educator, researcher*
Tomlin, Claire J. *aeronautical engineer, educator*
Traugott, Elizabeth Closs *linguist, educator, researcher*
Trost, Barry Martin *chemist, educator*
Ullman, Jeffrey David *computer scientist, educator*
VanDerveer, Tara *women's college basketball coach*
Van Dyke, Milton Denman *aeronautical engineering educator*
Van Horne, James Carter *economist, educator*
Veinott, Arthur Fales, Jr. *university educator*
Vincenti, Walter Guido *aeronautical engineer, emeritus educator*
Wagoner, Robert Vernon *astrophysicist, educator*
Walt, Martin *physicist, educator*
Wandell, Brian A. *neuroscientist, educator*
Weiner, Allen Sydney *law educator*
Weissman, Irving L. *medical researcher*
Wender, Paul Anthony *chemistry professor*
White, Robert Lee *electrical engineer, educator*
Whitney, Rodger Franklin *academic administrator*
Whittemore, Alice *biostatistician*
Widom, Jennifer *computer science and electrical engineering educator*
Williams, Howard Russell *law educator*
Wojcicki, Stanley George *physicist, researcher*
Wolff, Tobias (Jonathan Ansell Wolff) *writer*
Wotipka, Christine Min *education educator*
Yanofsky, Charles *retired biology professor*
Zare, Richard Neil *chemistry professor*
Zarins, Christopher Kristaps *surgeon, educator*
Zimbardo, Philip George *psychologist, educator, writer*
Zitzewitz, Eric *economics professor*

Stevenson Ranch

Krainin, Julian Arthur *film director, producer, cinematographer, writer*

Stinson Beach

Metz, Mary Seawell *retired foundation administrator, retired academic administrator*
Schwarm, Harold Chambers *artist*

Stockton

Biddle, Donald Ray *aerospace transportation executive*
Blodgett, Elsie Grace *small business owner, property manager*
Cobb, Judy Lynn *elementary school educator*
DeRicco, Lawrence Albert *retired college president*
DeRosa, Donald V. *academic administrator*
Fish, Tom *special education and vocational school educator*
Ford, Shirley Griffin *science educator, pharmacist*
Fung, Rosaline Lee *language educator*
Gertler, Fred *librarian, dean*
Gilbertson, Philip *academic administrator*
Hackley, Carol Ann *public relations educator, consultant*
Jacobs, Marian *advertising executive*
Knapp, Christian Jakob *lawyer*
Limbaugh, Ronald Hadley *retired historian, cultural organization administrator*
Magness, Rhonda Ann *retired microbiologist*
McCarty, Lois Leone *retired sociologist*
Meissner, Katherine Gong *municipal official*
Michailoff, Ian Robert *real estate broker, land use planner*
Murphy, Jeremiah T. *professional sports team, construction executive*
Nakanishi, Alan *ophthalmologist, state representative*
Null, Paul Bryan *minister*
Oak, Claire Morisset *artist, educator*
Parish, William Henry *lawyer*
Plovnick, Mark Stephen *business educator*
Ren, Jianhua *education educator*
Rencher, Natalie R. *library director*
Roll, Renée F. *retired psychologist, publishing executive*
Samoshin, Vyacheslav Vladimirovich *chemistry professor, science educator, researcher*
Singleton, Marvin Ayers *state legislator, otolaryngologist*
Sorby, Donald Lloyd *retired dean*
Sumida, Gregory Zio *artist, photographer, musician, astronomer*
Taylor, Francis Michael *auditor, municipal official*
Weick, Cynthia Wagner *business educator*
Whiteker, Roy Archie *retired chemistry professor*
Wilcox, Helena Marguerita (Helena Rita Wilcox) *music educator*
Wong, Patricia M.Y. *library director*
Yamashita, Kenneth Akira *library administrator, librarian*

Studio City

Boyett, Joan Reynolds *performing company executive*
Carradine, David *actor, director*
Childs, Erin Therese *psychotherapist*
Delnik, Alexander *engineering executive, consultant*
Easterson, Sam *artist*
Frumkin, Simon *political organization worker, writer*
Gold, Arnold Henry *judge*
Hamill, Dorothy Stuart *professional ice skater*
Kenney, H. Wesley, Jr., (Harry Wesley Kenney Jr.) *television producer, television director*
King, Carole (Carole Klein) *lyricist, singer*
Laba, Marvin *management consultant*
La Cava, Donald Leon *communications executive*
Lewis, Dawnn *actress*
Mc Donald, Meg *public relations executive*
Meenan, Alan John *clergyman, theology studies educator*
Moseley, Chris Rosser *marketing executive*
Najee, (Jerome Najee Rasheed) *musician*
Parish, James Robert *writer, cinema historian*
Setlin, Alan John *entrepreneur*
Silver, Jeffrey *film producer*
Silverman, Bruce Gary *advertising executive, consultant*
Steinberg, Roy Bennett *television producer, director, educator*
Weiner, Sandra Samuel *critical care nurse, consultant*
Werner, Tom *television producer, professional baseball team executive*
Williscroft, Robert G. *retired military officer, writer*

Summerland

Bauer, Marvin Agather *retired lawyer*
Cannon, Louis Simeon *journalist, writer*

Sun City

Schmoll, Edith Margaret *music educator*

Sun Valley

Casey, Paul Arnold *writer, producer, photographer, composer, director*
Mayhue, Richard Lee *dean, minister, writer*
Miller, Flemon Marshall *public works manager*
Sweet, Harvey *set and lighting designer*

Sunland

Nepales, Ruben Viado *journalist*

Sunnyvale

Andreessen, Marc *software company executive, internet innovator*
Bazzi, Samer *software developer, consultant*
Bowman, Eugene William *retired mathematics professor*
Brachman, Ron *research and development company executive*
Brigden, John *lawyer*
Burkett, Marvin D. *electronics executive*
Butterfield, Stewart *Internet company executive*
Calderoni, Robert M. *software company executive*
Callahan, Michael John *lawyer*
Cambou, Bertrand *information technology executive*
Chang, William Zhi-Ming *research scientist*
Chen, Xiao *process engineer*
Choi, Hoon *electrical engineer*
Coleman, Gregory G. *former magazine publisher, Internet company executive*
Colligan, Edward T. *computer company and communications executive*
Decker, Sue (Susan Lynne Decker) *Internet company executive*
Doluca, Tunc *electronics executive*
Doyle, Mary E. *lawyer*
Dunaway, Cammie *marketing executive*
Ensminger, Dale *retired mechanical and electrical engineer*

Ewald, Robert Hansen (Bo Ewald) *computer software company executive*
Filo, David *Internet company executive*
Gifford, John F. *retired electronics executive*
Goo, Jung-Suk *semiconductor company research engineer*
Gozani, Tsahi *nuclear physicist*
Guan, Xiang *electrical engineer*
Hawkins, Jeff *information technology company executive*
Jayanarayanan, Sankaran Kartik *electrical engineer*
Jorgensen, Blake J. *Internet company executive*
Karnstedt, David *marketing executive*
Koogle, Timothy K. *communications executive*
Kriens, Scott G. *information technology executive*
Lanaro, Clara Marrama *music educator, writer*
Leong, Chia Ken *mechanical engineer*
Lin, Frank C. *computer company executive*
Lundberg, Carl-Erik Wilhelm *telecommunications executive, researcher*
McCollam, Craig A. *manufacturing executive*
McCoy, Thomas M. *information technology executive*
McReynolds, Stephen Paul *lawyer*
Nash, Jill *communications executive*
Oei, Lok S. *digital communications systems and DSP engineer, researcher*
Olson, James (Jim Olson) *telecommunications industry executive*
Parnafes, Itzik *Internet company executive*
Payton, Paul Max *application developer*
Ratchev, Boris A *management consultant*
Rosensweig, Daniel L. *Internet company executive*
Rubin, Gary Andrew *entrepreneur, computer engineer*
Ruiz, Hector de Jesus *information technology executive*
Sartain, Libby *human resources specialist*
Schneider, Hilary A. *Internet company executive*
Schwartz, Eleanore Anita *retired elementary school educator, small business owner*
Semel, Terry S. *Internet company executive*
Uchibori, Chihiro J. *materials scientist, researcher*
Wehde, Albert Edward *lawyer*
Weinberg, William Henry *chemical engineer, physicist, educator*
Xie, Ken *software company executive*
Yang, Jerry *Internet company executive*

Sunol
Rebello, Marlene Munson *speech pathologist, consultant*

Sunset Beach
Pridham, Thomas Grenville *retired microbiologist*

Susanville
Gartner, Harold Henry III *lawyer*
Rogers, Winton (Larry) Lawrence *public information officer*

Sylmar
Corry, Dalila Boudjellal *internist, educator*
Foster, Dudley Edwards, Jr. *musician, educator*
Froelich, Beverly Lorraine *foundation administrator*
Kamangar, Nader *physician, director, researcher, pulmonologist, educator*
Scheib, Gerald Paul *art educator*
Tutor, Ronald N. *construction executive*

Tarzana
Goldberg, Harvey *corporate financial executive*
Hansen, Robert Clinton *electrical engineer, consultant*
Lauter, James Donald *retired stockbroker*
Lindley, Charles Alexander *aerospace engineer, consultant*
Neece, Olivia Helene Ernst *investment company executive, consultant*
Richman, Peter Mark *actor, painter, film producer*
Smith, Mark Lee *architect*
Teitell, Michael Alan *immunologist*
Weil, Leonard *banker*
Zeitlin, Herbert Zakary *college administrator, real estate consultant, writer*

Tehachapi
Mitchell, Betty Jo *publishing executive, writer*
Smith-Thompson, Patricia Ann *public relations consultant, educator*
Sprinkle, Martha Clare *elementary school educator*

Temecula
Cherrington, Pamela Jo *special education educator*
Minogue, Robert Brophy *retired nuclear engineer*
Ojeda, Nelson A., II, *musician*

Temple City
Lau, Bobby Wai-Man *marketing professional, investment advisor*

Templeton
Abernathy, Shields B. *allergist, immunologist, internist*
Foster-Wells, Karen Margaret *artist*
Gandsey, Louis John *petroleum and environmental consultant*
Girolo, Nella Sue *retired voice educator*

The Sea Ranch
Baas, Jacquelynn *museum director, art historian*
Carter, Richard Duane *management educator*
Hayflick, Leonard *cell biologist, biogerontologist, microbiologist, educator, writer*
Robertson, David Govan *lawyer*

Thousand Oaks
Albertson, Marty P. *music company executive*
Allan, Brent Russotto *public health service officer*
Baek, Kwang-Hyun *research scientist*
Bobzin, Steve *chemist, researcher*
Bonanni, Fabrizio *medical products executive*
Bradway, Robert *medical products executive*
Brogden, Stephen Richard *library director*
Bustillos, Timothy D. *management consultant*
Daly, Jim *medical products executive*
Dere, Willard Honglen *medical products executive*
Eisenberg, Paul Richard *cardiologist, consultant, educator*
El Fattah, Yousri M. *computer scientist*
Farshidi, Ardeshir B. *cardiologist, educator*
Fenton, Dennis Michael *medical products executive*
Flanagan, Thomas James *medical products executive*
Fulton, Michael L. *optical company executive, researcher*
Gregory, Calvin *real estate investor*
Harper, Sean *medical products executive*
Herman, Joan Elizabeth *health insurance company executive*
Hudson, Barbara *writer, actor*
Klein, Joseph Mark *retired mining executive*
Kroeger, Chad *musician*
Lieberman, Judith L. *retired special education educator*
Loren, Sophia *actress*
Marshall, David B. *structural ceramics professional*
McCarter, Nancy R. *graphics designer, educator, artist, small business owner*
McNamee, Brian *medical products executive*
Miletich, Joseph P. *medical products executive*
Miller, Elizabeth Joan *artist, guidance counselor*
Morrow, George J. *medical products executive*
Pakula, Anita Susan *dermatologist*
Peake, Ryan *musician*
Perlmutter, Roger *medical products executive*
Pipes, Gary Dale *biochemist*
Remmele, Richard L., Jr. *research scientist, director*
Rooney, Mickey (Joe Yule Jr.) *actor*
Scott, David J. *lawyer, medical products executive*
Sharer, Kevin W. *medical products executive*
Sladek, John R., Jr. *academic administrator, neurobiology and anatomy educator*
Sladek, Lyle Virgil *mathematician, educator*
Sloane, J.P. *television producer, theologian, entertainer, writer*
Valdez, Josh *health insurance company executive*
Venable, Diane Dailey *retired elementary school educator*
Wolff, Stuart *online real estate executive*
Zhang, Zhongqi *chemist*
Zhou, Sophia Huai *biomedical engineering scientist*

Tiburon
Widman, Gary Lee *lawyer*

Toluca Lake
Nunez, Oscar *actor*
Ragan, Ann Talmadge *media and production consultant, actor*

Torrance
Adelsman, Jean (Harriette Adelsman) *newspaper editor*
Amemiya, Koichi *motor vehicle company executive*
Bhargave, Ashish A. *research scientist*
Black, James Jens *plastic surgeon*
Brasel, Jo Anne *pediatrician, educator*
Brass, Eric Paul *internal medicine and pharmacology educator, academic administrator*
Brown, Adriane M. *aerospace transportation executive*
Bryan, Sharon Ann *lawyer*
Budoff, Matthew Jay *cardiologist*
Carlson, Terrance L. *lawyer, aerospace transportation executive*
Daar, Eric Steven *medical educator*
Ebeling, Vicki *marriage and family therapist, writer*
Emmanouilides, George Christos *physician, educator*
Enright, Stephanie Veselich *investment company executive, financial consultant*
Esmond, Donald V. *transportation executive*
Hammer, Terence Michael *physician*
Hansen, James Edward *medical educator, researcher*
Ibe, Basil Obijiaku *biochemist, educator*
Imbarus, Aura *language educator, consultant*
Katz, Ronald Lewis *physician, educator*
Kerstiens, Gene J. *mathemagenician, consultant*
Kim, Keehoon *cybernetic scientist*
Kopple, Joel D. *medical educator*
Kuc, Joseph A. *research scientist*
Mehringer, Charles Mark *medical educator*
Moore, Christopher M. *lawyer*
Muley, Arun *aerospace engineer*
Omari, Bassam O. *cardiothoracic surgeon*
Oudiz, Ronald *cardiologist*
Paulson, Robert Lawrence *aerospace engineer, consultant*
Petillon, Lee Ritchey *lawyer*
Rogers, Howard H. *retired chemist*
Sorstokke, Susan Eileen *systems engineer*
Stabile, Bruce Edward *surgeon*
Sun, Nora Chi-Jun *pathologist*
Swerdloff, Ronald S. *physician, educator, researcher*
Tanaka, Kouichi Robert *hematologist, educator*
Van Emburgh, Joanne *lawyer*

Trabuco Canyon
Addy, Jo Alison Phears *economist*

Tracy
Hay, Dennis Lee *lawyer*
Kiggins, Mildred L. *marketing professional*
Waziri, Ghaus Ghulam *diplomat*

Truckee
Todd, Linda Marie *nutrition researcher, circulation manager, financial consultant, pilot*

Tujunga
Ancu, Edward Florin *veterinarian*
Loehwing, Lord Rudi Charles *publicist, radio broadcasting executive, journalist*

Tulare
Gorelick, Ellen Catherine *museum executive director, chief curator, artist, educator, civic volunteer*
Pinto, Marie Malania *academic administrator, consultant*
Regan, Timothy James *grain company executive*

Turlock
Ahlem, Lloyd Harold *psychologist*
Burns, James Wesley *academic administrator, researcher, consultant*
Parker, John Carlyle *retired librarian and archivist, editor*
Shirvani, Sir Hamid *architect, educator, philosopher, writer, university president*

Tustin
Herdeg, Howard Brian *retired physician*
Hester, Norman Eric *chemical company technical executive, chemist*
Kim, Han Pyong *researcher*
Madory, Richard Eugene *lawyer*

Twain Harte
Kinsinger, Robert Earl *property company executive, educational consultant*
Schneider, James Richard *orthopedist*

Twentynine Palms
Clemente, Patrocinio Ablola *secondary school educator*
Fultz, Philip Nathaniel *management analyst*

Ukiah
McClintock, Richard Polson *dermatologist*
Newell, Barbara Ann *coatings company executive*
Sager, Madeline Dean *lawyer*
Scheffey, David Harold *civil engineer, musician*

Union City
Feinberg, Richard Alan *psychologist*
Lindsey, Tommie *secondary school educator*
Muñoz, Eduardo Rafael *elementary school educator*

Universal City
Bismuth, Pierre *artist*
Bowen, Andrea *actress*
Bromstad, Angela *broadcast executive*
Chavira, Ricardo Antonio *actor*
Cross, Marcia *actress*
Denton, James *actor*
Finkelstein, Rick *film company executive*
Gaspin, Jeff *broadcast executive*
Graboff, Marc *broadcast executive*
Hammer, Bonnie *broadcast executive*
Hatcher, Teri *actress*
Huffman, Felicity (Flicka Huffman) *actress*
Husband, Bertram Paul *lawyer*
Langley, Donna *film company executive*
Linde, David *film company executive*
Longoria, Eva (Eva Jacqueline Longoria, Eva Longoria Christopher) *actress*
Lowe, Kristin *film company executive*
McCormack, Eric *actor*
Merkerson, S. Epatha *actress*
Meyer, Ron *film company executive*
Parent, Mary *film company executive*
Press, Terry *marketing executive*
Reitman, Ivan *film director, producer*
Rocco, Nikki *film company executive*
Savant, Doug *actor*
Sheridan, Nicollette *actress*
Shmuger, Marc *film company executive*
Silverman, Ben *broadcast executive, television producer*
Strong, Brenda *actress*
Stuber, Scott *film company executive*
Weinberg, Teri Ellen *television executive, television producer*
Wolf, Dick (Richard A. Wolf) *television producer*
Woodard, Alfre *actress*

Upland
Goodman, John M. *construction executive*
Jordan, Charles Wesley *retired bishop*
Sheridan, Christopher Frederick *financial consultant, human resources executive*

Vacaville
Che, Maggie *endocrinologist, researcher*

Valencia
Anguiano, Lupe *advocate*
Buchanan, Nancy Page *artist, educator*
Joy, Alexa *small business owner, artist, educator*
Lambirth, Timothy A. *mediator*
Levy, Ezra Cesar *aerospace scientist, real estate agent*
Mann, Alfred *pharmaceutical executive*
Millar, Michael William *musician*
Pocrass, Richard Dale *management consultant*
Samadi, Albert A. *urologist*
Windsor, William Earl *consulting engineer, sales representative*

Vallejo
Brown, Earl Kent *historian, minister*
Davis, William Albert *parks director*

McGowan, Thomas Randolph *retired religious organization administrator*
Toms, Kathleen Moore *nurse*
Towne, Sarah Patton *physician*
Wilson, Carrie Lee Stroud *principal*
Womack, Thomas Houston *manufacturing executive*
Zingale, Donald Paul *academic administrator, educator*

Valley Center
Arciniega, Tomas Abel *university president*
Camp, Joseph Shelton, Jr. *film producer, director, writer*

Valley Ford
Mulkern-Kolosey, Sandy Kathleen *college counselor, educator, realtor*

Valley Springs
Vitrac, Jean-Jacques Charles *international business consultant*

Valley Village
Barkin, Elaine Radoff *composer*
Bench, Johnny Lee *retired professional baseball player*
Diller, Phyllis (Phyllis Ada Driver Diller) *actress, writer*
Finley, Mordecai *rabbi*
Oka, Masi (Masayori Oka) *actor*

Van Nuys
Arabian, Armand *arbitrator, mediator, lawyer*
Becker, Frawley *writer, dialogue director, location manager*
Boone, Deborah Ann (Debby Boone) *singer*
Cook, Jenik Esterm (Jenik Esterm Cook Simonian) *artist, educator*
Dea, Fay Suey *counselor, educator*
Ewing, Guin Porter *historian, art collector*
Graham, Roger John *photography and journalism professor*
Greene, Albert Lawrence *healthcare executive*
Harutyunyan, Armine *billing company executive*
Vasilyeva, Anna *artist, writer*
Walsh, Thomas Francis, Jr. *producer, writer, director*
Wright, Judith Ann *elementary school educator*
Zucker, Alfred John *English and history educator, academic administrator, historian*

Venice
Alf, Martha Joanne *artist*
Beery-Polglase, Penelope (Pixie) *education educator*
Bill, Tony *producer, director*
Binns, Tom *jewelry designer*
Chartoff, Robert Irwin *film producer*
Choo, Kristy *chef*
Eliot, Alexander *writer*
Eversley, Frederick John *sculptor, engineer*
Padilla, Mario René *literature educator, writer*

Ventura
Abul-Haj, Suleiman Kahil *pathologist*
Armstrong, Dianne Owens *language educator*
Barber, Jerry Randel *retired medical device company executive*
Bircher, Andrea Ursula *retired psychiatric mental health clinical nurse specialist*
Bradley, Jerry Alan *psychologist, consultant*
Chouinard, Yvon *sportswear outfitter executive*
Downs, Floella McIntyre *retired ferry pilot, instructor, flight examiner*
Gaynor, Joseph *chemical engineer, management consultant*
Howry, Joe R. *newspaper editor*
Naurath, David Allison *engineering psychologist, researcher*
Turturro, John *actor*
Villaveces, James Walter *allergist, immunologist, consultant*

Vernon
Kim, Ho Gill *poet*

Victorville
Hauk, Beth MacKenzie *elementary school educator, writer*
Quadri, Fazle Rab *lawyer, government official*
Scott, Deborah Elizabeth *school system administrator, poet*
Sedeño, Eugene Raymond *electronics engineer, consultant*

Villa Park
Britton, Thomas Warren, Jr. *retired management consultant*
Hawe, David Lee *manufacturing consultant, venture capitalist*

Visalia
Crowe, John T. *lawyer*
Gray, Kris Diane *nursing consultant, forensic specialist*
Levine, Suzin Nancy Leah *religious organization administrator*
O'Leary, Deanna Kay *benefits compensation analyst, consultant*
Porterfield-Pyatt, Chaumonde R. *music educator, advocate*
Riegel, Byron William *ophthalmologist*

Vista
Cavanaugh, Kenneth Clinton *retired real estate consultant*
Ferguson, Margaret Ann *tax specialist, consultant*
Hawk, Tony *professional skateboarder*
Hennenhoefer, James A. *lawyer*
Mitchell, Thomas Edward, Jr. *communications cabling executive*
Way, Danny *professional skateboarder*

Walnut
Budzak, Stephen Howard *tax specialist, consultant*

Johnson, Keith Liddell *retired chemicals executive*
Karr, Joanne Fern *theater educator*
McKee, Catherine Lynch *lawyer, educator*
Tran, Nam Van *secondary school educator*

Walnut Creek
Bakshi, Nandini *neurologist*
Bryant, Warren F. *retail executive*
Cannon, Grace Bert *retired immunologist*
Carlin, Herbert J. *electrical engineering educator, researcher*
Carson, Jay Wilmer *pathologist, educator*
Chu, Valentin Yuan-ling *author*
Collen, Morris Frank *retired medical association administrator, physician, consultant, researcher*
Costa, Walter Henry *architect*
Gill, Margaret Gaskins *lawyer*
Ginsburg, Gerald J. *lawyer, management consultant*
Grandi, Lois A. *theater director, choreographer, actor*
Hanschen, Peter Walter *lawyer*
Hanson, Robert Duane *engineering educator*
Hassid, Sami *architect, educator*
Henshaw, Guy Runals *management consultant*
Lilly, Luella Jean *retired academic administrator*
Man, Pang Ling *retired psychiatrist*
McCauley, Bruce Gordon *financial consultant*
Nolan, Janiece Simmons *health facility administrator*
Nord, Paul Elliott *lawyer, accountant*
Novotny, Glenn W. *consumer products company executive*
Ostrander, Willis Frederick *retired real estate appraiser*
Pagter, Carl Richard *lawyer*
Parker, Denny S. *engineering company executive*
Rainey, William Joel *lawyer*
Reimann, Arline Lynn *artist*
Rhody, Ronald Edward *bank, communications executive*
Rihn, Richard John *retired physician*
Saavedra, Charles James *banker*
Scott, Phillip W. *financial consultant*
Seaborg, David Michael *evolutionary biologist*
Skaggs, Sanford Merle *lawyer*
Swaney, Thomas Robbins *venture capitalist*
Walston, Roderick Eugene *federal official*
Wu, Tse Cheng *chemist, researcher*

Watsonville
Brown, Alan Charlton *retired aeronautical engineer*
Dorey, William G. *construction executive*
Futch, Michael *lawyer, construction executive*
Watts, David H. *construction company executive*

Weed
Schaefer, M. Elaine *music educator, conductor*

Weimar
Kerschner, Lee R(onald) *academic administrator, political scientist, educator*

West Covina
Ebiner, Robert Maurice *lawyer*
Galen, Albert John *retired lawyer*
McHale, Edward Robertson *retired lawyer*
Musich, Robert Lorin *motivational speaker*
Torres, Esteban Edward *former congressman, trade association administrator*

West Hills
Alexander, Sue *writer*
Christenson, Allen Cecil *retired mathematics educator*
Monosson, Ira Howard *physician*

West Hollywood
Annakin, Kenneth Cooper *film director, writer*
Antin, Jonathan *hairstylist, entrepreneur*
Barker, Clive *artist, film director and producer, scriptwriter*
Berry, Halle Maria *actress*
Burke, Clem *musician*
Cage, Nicolas (Nicolas Coppola) *actor*
Cole, Natalie Maria *singer*
Destri, Jimmy *musician*
DeWolfe, Chris T. *Internet company executive*
Einstein, Clifford Jay *advertising executive*
Estevez, Luis de Galvez *designer, manufacturer*
Franklyn, Audrey Pozen *talent promoter, television personality*
Grey, Brad *film company executive*
Harper, Robert *actor*
Harry, Deborah Ann *singer*
Holloway, Josh *actor*
Huntsberry, Frederick D. *film company executive*
Jackson, Randy *music producer, television personality, musician*
Krabbe, Jeroen Aart *actor*
Lefebvre, Ludovic *chef*
Margolin, Bruce M. *lawyer*
Morris, Brian *advertising executive*
Mulholland, Julie A. *marketing executive*
Presley, Priscilla (Pricilla Ann Wagner, Priscilla Beaulieu Presley) *actress*
Riehl, Joyce K. *veterinarian*
Romijn, Rebecca *actress, model*
Routh, Brandon *actor*
Sackett, Barnard (Barney) *actor, film producer, director, scriptwriter*
Shaye, Robert Kenneth *film company executive*
Shearmur, Alli *broadcast executive*
Slade, Bernard *playwright*
Stein, Ben(jamin) (Jeremy) *television personality, writer, lawyer, economist*
Stein, Chris *musician*
Tarantino, Quentin Jerome *film director, scriptwriter*
Thornton, Billy Bob *actor, film producer*

West Sacramento
Anderson, William Wallace *financial executive*
Coyne, William J. *retail executive, former member house representatives*
Teel, Joyce Raley *retail executive*
Wilson, Eric F.G. *information technology executive*

Westlake Village
Caligiuri, Joseph Frank *retired engineering executive*
Carter, C. Michael *lawyer*
Colburn, Keith W. *electronics executive*
Dalton, Allan D. *real estate company executive*
DeLorenzo, David A. *food products executive*
Detterman, Robert Linwood *financial planner*
Dimitriadis, Andre C. *health care executive*
Doerr, Patricia Marian *elementary and special education educator*
Dotrice, Roy Louis *actor*
Erdelyi, Eileen Edith *financial planner and advisor*
Hoefflin, Richard Michael *lawyer, judicial administrator*
Lereah, David Alan *economist*
Munson, John Backus *computer scientist, retired data processing executive*
Power, J.D., III, (James David Power III) *marketing executive*
Seymour, Jeffrey Alan *governmental relations consultant*
Sindon, Geoffrey Stuart *lawyer*
Strote, Joel Richard *lawyer*
Troxell, Lucy Davis *management consultant*
Weissman, Robert Allen *lawyer, real estate broker*
Yassky, Alan *real estate company executive*

Westminster
Amalsad, Meher Dadabhoy *writer, speaker, seminar leader*
Luong, Khanh Vinh Quoc *nephrologist, researcher*
Nguyen, Khue Vu *molecular biologist, researcher*
Nguyen, Lan Thi Hoang *physician, educator*
Pieper, Michael Joseph *television producer, actor, talk show host*
Zeng, Eddy Yongping *chemist*

Whittier
Arenowitz, Albert Harold *psychiatrist*
Cruz, Denis J. *elementary school educator*
Johnson, Julia Marty *psychologist, educator*
Kirsch, Scott Douglas *family practice physician, director*
Korf, Jean Prinz *retired theater educator*
McKenna, Jeanette Ann *archaeologist*
Paddy, David *literature and language professor*
Pencall, Constance McConnell *retired secondary school educator*
Prickett, David Clinton *physician*
Stahl, James F. *engineer*

Wilmington
Hamai, James Yutaka *manufacturing executive*

Wilton
Harrison, George Harry, III, (Hank Harrison) *publishing executive, author*

Windsor
Fieri, Guy *chef*
Sparks, Bennett Sher *military officer*

Woodland
Bauer, Cynthia Renae *nurse*
Melton, Barry *lawyer, musician*
Squires, Richard Felt *research scientist*

Woodland Hills
Adreani, Michael B. *lawyer*
Babayans, Emil *financial planner*
Berry, Barbara Cochran *education educator, writer*
Brandewie, Richard Anthony *laser and optics consultant*
Clarey, Patricia T. *health insurance company executive, former state official*
Ennis, Thomas Michael *management consultant*
Even, Randolph M. *lawyer*
Feiman, Thomas E. *investment company executive*
Fox, Stuart Ira *physiologist*
Gellert, Jay M. *health and medical products executive*
Glick, Earl A. *lawyer*
Granger, David *editor*
Greaves, Roger F. *health and medical products executive*
Harris, Barbara S. *publishing executive, editor-in-chief*
Helwig, David S. *healthcare insurance company executive*
Jacobson, Sidney *editor*
Jason, Sonya *writer*
Kern, Russell Marc *marketing executive*
Mayhew, Karin D. *health and medical products executive*
McCluggage, Kerry *film and television executive*
Morishita, Akihiko *trading company executive*
Mund, Geraldine *judge*
O'Connor, Brian D.A. *music educator, French horn musician*
Olson, David W. *health and medical products executive*
Pettit, John W. *health facility administrator*
Piersol, Allan Gerald *mechanical engineer*
Pregerson, Harry *federal judge*
Preston, John Elwood *lawyer*
Rich, Marvin P. *health association executive*
Russell, Anne M. *editor-in-chief*
Scheff, Jonathan H. *health and medical products executive*
Sharma, Brahama D. *chemistry professor*
Sivori, John P. *health and medical products executive*
Tiano, Linda V. *lawyer, insurance company executive*
Tuthill, Walter Warren *accountant, management consultant*
Westen, Brodie Curtis, Jr., (Curt) *lawyer*
Woys, James E. *health and medical products executive*
Yates, Gary L. *marriage and family therapist*
Zeitlin, Eugenia Pawlik *librarian, educator, writer*

Woodside
Arthur, Greer Martin *leasing firm executive*
Blum, Richard Hosmer Adams *foundation administrator, educator*
Fisher, Kenneth Lawrence *investment management firm executive*
Freitas, Antoinette Juni *insurance company executive*
Gates, Milo Sedgwick *retired construction company executive*

Yorba Linda
Lunde, Dolores Benitez *retired secondary school educator*
Lynch, Frank Thomas *aeronautical engineer, consultant*
McCune, Brenda L. *lawyer*
Medland, Maurice Blue *writer*
Naftali, Timothy J. *library director, historian, educator, writer*
Porcello, Leonard Joseph *engineering research and development executive*
Stavropoulos, Rose Mary Grant *community activist, volunteer*

Yosemite National Park
Forgang, David M. *curator*

Yountville
Bedell, Jay Dee *small business owner, writer*
Keller, Thomas A. *chef*
Lee, Corey *chef*
Savage, Michael John Kirkness *oil industry executive, performing arts company executive*

Yreka
Smith, Vin *editor, small business owner, writer*

Yuba City
Doughty, Mark Anthony *lawyer*
Kemmerly, Jack Dale *retired state official*
Leverett, Dawn R. *disability education consultant*
Price, Ardythe Bernadeane *nurse*

Yucaipa
Crise, Robert D., Jr. *mathematics professor*

COLORADO

Alamosa
Taylor, Wallace Edmondson, Jr. *otolaryngologist*

Arvada
Bett, Robert Scott *music educator*
Halley, Diane Esther *artist*
Holden, George Fredric *food products executive, consultant, public information officer, writer*
Krohnfeldt, Gretchen Ann *secondary school educator, genealogist*
Mullineaux, Donal Ray *geologist*
Peck, Kenneth E. *lawyer*
Powers, Christopher Sheridan *science educator, web site designer*
Weitzel, Ginger M. *entrepreneur, critical care nurse*
Yamamoto, Kaoru *retired psychology professor*

Aspen
Berkeley, Edward *performing arts association administrator, music educator*
Bucksbaum, Melva *foundation administrator*
Fischl, Eric *artist*
Hayes, Mary Eshbaugh *editor, writer*
Manosevitz, Martin *psychologist*
Mitchell, Karen Frances *artist, jewelry designer*
Newman, Ruth Gallert *psychologist*
Oden, Robert Rudolph *surgeon*
Peirce, Frederick Fairbanks *lawyer*

Aurora
Alvero, Ruben J. *medical educator*
Balle, James Christian *information technology manager*
Battaglia, Frederick Camillo *physician*
Bunn, Paul A., Jr. *oncologist, educator*
Churchill, Mair Elisa Annabelle *medical educator*
D'Amico, Sandra Hathaway *art educator*
Dooley, J. Gordon *food scientist*
Doze, Maureen Adele (Maureen Adele Mee) *social studies educator*
Grace, William Pershing *petroleum geologist, real estate developer*
Haas, Robert Lance *surgeon, consultant*
Katz, Michael Jeffery *lawyer*
Kellogg Fain, Karen *retired history educator*
Morrow, Caroline Donovan *retired social worker*
Nekritz, Edward Steven *lawyer*
Nelson, Marvin Ray *retired life insurance company executive*
Nicholas, Thomas Peter *municipal official*
Nichols, Clyde Richard *minister, consumer products company executive*
Nora, Audrey Hart *physician*
Olson, Allison W. *social studies educator*
Ritchie, Coy Doyle *management consultant*
Roberts-Ramsbotham, Hazel Ruth *piano educator*
Sheffield, Nancy *city agency administrator*
Shore, James H(enry) *psychiatrist*
Stauffer, Scott William *lawyer, accountant*
Stifel, Frederick Benton *minister, biochemist, nutritionist*
Ton, Paul *investor, educator*
Weedin, James Frank *biology professor, researcher*
Zuschlag, Nancy Hansen *environmental and nature resources educator*

Basalt
Shipp, Dan Shackelford *lawyer*

Bayfield
Collins, William Leroy *retired telecommunications engineer*
Horton, Frank Elba *academic administrator, geographer, educator*
Korns, Leota Elsie *writer, mountain land developer, insurance broker*

Black Hawk
Jones, Linda May *tour guide, writer*

Boulder
Anderson, Ronald Delaine *education educator*
Anseth, Kristi S. *tissue engineer, educator*
Armstrong, David Michael *biology professor*
Arslan, Haydar *civil engineer, researcher*
Bangs, F(rank) Kendrick *former business educator*
Barnes, Frank Stephenson *electrical engineer, educator*
Beer, Francis Anthony *political science professor emeritus*
Beylkin, Gregory *mathematician*
Bhat, Rajiv *physicist, researcher*
Bintliff, Barbara Ann *library director, law educator*
Bolomey, Roger Henry *sculptor*
Borko, Hilda *education educator*
Born, George Henry *aerospace engineer, educator*
Bourne, Lyle Eugene, Jr. *psychology professor*
Bruff, Harold Hastings *law educator, former dean*
Burns, Daniel Hobart *management consultant*
Byerly, Radford, Jr. *science administrator*
Canup, Robin M. *astrophysicist, science administrator*
Caruthers, Marvin Harry *biochemistry educator*
Cathey, Wade Thomas *electrical engineering educator*
Chappell, Charles Franklin *meteorologist, consultant*
Charteris, Frances I.A. *art educator, artist*
Churchill, Ward L. *social sciences educator, advocate*
Clark, Gary M. *statistician*
Clark, Melvin Eugene *chemical company executive*
Clark, Noel A. *physics professor*
Clifford, Steven Francis *science administrator, director*
Cordell, Linda S. *anthropologist, educator, museum director*
Cornell, Eric Allin *physics professor*
Corotis, Ross Barry *civil engineer, educator, academic administrator*
Davies, David Huw *electronics executive, engineering company executive*
Davis, Robert Heater *chemical engineering educator*
Deaktor, Darryl Barnett *lawyer*
DePuy, Charles Herbert *chemist, educator*
Dryer, Murray *physicist, educator*
Dubin, Mark William *neuroscientist, educator, academic administrator*
Dudhia, Jimy *atmospheric scientist*
Echohawk, John Ernest *lawyer*
Ellis, Homer Godsey *mathematics professor, physicist, researcher*
El Mallakh, Dorothea Hendry *editor, publishing executive*
Engel, Barbara Alpern *history professor*
Faller, James Elliot *physicist, researcher*
Fenster, Herbert Lawrence *lawyer*
Fiflis, Ted James *lawyer, educator*
Fink, Robert Russell *music educator and theorist, retired dean*
Fleming, Rex James *meteorologist*
Flowers, William Harold, Jr. *lawyer*
Floyd, Ted *ornithologist, writer*
Garstang, Roy Henry *astrophysicist, educator*
Getches, David Harding *lawyer, educator, dean*
Glover, Fred William *information scientist, director, educator*
Gosling, John Thomas *space plasma physicist, researcher*
Gray, William R. *lawyer*
Greenberg, Edward Seymour *political science professor*
Guild, Nancy Ann *biology professor*
Hall, Joan Lord *literature and language educator*
Hall, John Lewis *physicist, researcher*
Hanna, William Johnson *electrical engineering educator*
Hauser, Ray Louis *engineer, researcher, entrepreneur*
Hawkins, Brian Lee *educational association administrator*
Hayes, Richard Johnson *association executive, retired lawyer*
Heath, Josephine Ward *foundation administrator*
Hermann, Allen Max *physics professor*
Hess, John Warren *professional society administrator*
Hibbs, John David *computer company executive, electrical engineer, small business owner*
Hill, David Allan *electrical engineer*
Hill, Janet Swan *library and information scientist, educator*
Hill, Mary C. *hydrologist*
Hill, Melvin James *retired oil industry executive*
Hogg, David Clarence *physicist*
Holdsworth, Janet Nott *women's health nurse*
Horikis, Theodoros *research scientist*
Jessor, Richard *psychologist, educator, director*
Jin, Deborah *physicist, educator*
Jin, Xiaoying *electrical engineer, computer engineer, researcher*
Johnson, Maryanna Morse *business owner*
Johnstone, Sally Mac *educational association administrator, psychology educator*

Joselyn, Jo Ann *space scientist*
Joy, Edward Bennett *electrical engineer, educator, consultant*
Kapteyn, Henry Cornelius *physics professor, engineering educator*
Kellogg, William Welch *meteorologist, researcher*
Kenney, Belinda Jill Forseman *information technology executive*
Killeen, Timothy Laurence *aerospace scientist, science administrator*
King, Edward Louis *retired chemistry professor*
Kintsch, Walter *retired psychology professor*
Knoelker, Michael T.F. *science observatory director*
Koren, Norman Lee *computer company executive*
Kotter, Rita Joan *theatre educator, design consultant*
Kuhn, Timothy R. *communication educator*
Landesman, Howard M. *retired academic administrator*
LeMone, Margaret Anne *atmospheric scientist*
Limerick, Patricia Nelson *history professor*
Linsky, Jeffrey Lawrence *astrophysicist*
Low, Boon Chye *physicist*
Mahlman, Jerry David *retired meteorologist*
Malde, Harold Edwin *retired federal government geologist*
Mancino, John Gregory *software company executive*
Matthews, Eugene Edward *artist*
McFarland, Robert Bruce *physician*
McGuire, Robin K. *engineering company executive*
Mehalchin, John Joseph *entrepreneur, finance company executive*
Meier, Beverly Joyce Loeffler *science educator, educational consultant*
Meier, Mark Frederick *research scientist, educator, artist, small business owner*
Melicher, Ronald William *finance educator*
Menken, Jane Ava *demographer, educator*
Middleton-Downing, Laura *psychiatric social worker, artist, small business owner*
Minger, Terrell John *public administration and natural resource institute executive*
Mitchell, Joan LaVerne *research scientist*
Mooney, William Piatt *actor*
Mulhern, Martin Robert *engineer*
Murnane, Margaret Mary *engineering and physics educator*
Mycielski, Jan *retired mathematics professor*
Nam, Sae Woo *physicist*
Nehls, Richard Charles *lawyer*
Neinas, Charles Merrill *sports association executive, consultant*
Nordgren, Ronald Paul *retired engineering educator, researcher*
O'Brien, Elmer John *librarian, educator*
Oh, Seongshik *physicist, researcher*
Ostrovsky, Lev Aronovich *physicist, oceanographer, educator*
Pankove, Jacques Isaac *retired physicist, researcher*
Peterson, Courtland Harry *law educator*
Peterson, G. P. (Bud Peterson) *academic administrator*
Phelps, Arthur Van Rensselaer *physicist, consultant*
Pierce, Christopher A. *neuropsychologist, consultant*
Pneuman, Linda Jackson *retired physician*
Porzak, Glenn E. *lawyer*
Princeton, Joy Carol *retired nursing educator*
Purvis, John Anderson *lawyer, educator*
Randa, James Paul *physicist, electrical engineer*
Ravishankara, Akkihebal R. *chemist*
Reitsema, Harold James *aerospace engineer*
Roble, Raymond Gerald *science administrator*
Roellig, Leonard Oscar *physics professor*
Rood, David S. *linguistics educator*
Sable, Barbara Kinsey *retired music educator*
Sani, Robert LeRoy *chemical engineering professor*
Sarson, John Christopher *television producer, director, writer*
Schneider, Vivian I. *psychologist, researcher*
Serafin, Robert Joseph *science center administrator, electrical engineer*
Smith, Ernest Ketcham *electrical engineer*
Smith, Paul E. *lawyer*
Smythe, William Rodman *physicist, researcher*
Snow, Theodore Peck *astrophysics educator*
Sodal, Ingvar Edmund *electrical engineer, science administrator*
Southwick, Charles Henry *zoologist, educator*
Staehelin, Lucas Andrew *cell biology professor*
Stanton, William John, Jr. *marketing educator, author*
Stepanek, Joseph Edward *real estate developer, consultant*
Steuben, Norton Leslie *lawyer, educator*
Stevens, Glenn H. *lawyer*
Tans, Pieter P. *research scientist*
Tatarskii, Valerian Il'Ich *physics researcher*
Templeton, Alexis S. *biogeochemist, educator*
Timmerhaus, Klaus Dieter *chemical engineering professor*
Tolbert, Bert Mills *biochemist, educator*
Tolbert, Margaret A. *geochemistry educator*
Trenberth, Kevin Edward *atmospheric scientist*
Tuck, Adrian Francis *meteorologist, physical chemist*
Uberoi, Mahinder Singh *aerospace engineer, researcher*
Walker, Deward Edgar, Jr. *anthropologist, educator*
Washington, Warren Morton *meteorologist*
Wertheimer, Marilyn Lou *librarian, educator*
White, Cindy Hagemeier *adult education educator*
Wieman, Carl E. *physics professor*
Willam, Kaspar J. *civil engineer, educator*
Williams, James Franklin, II, *dean, librarian*
Wilson, M. Roy *academic administrator, medical educator*
Wittemyer, John *lawyer*
Wood, William Barry III *biologist, educator*
Ye, Jun *physicist, researcher*
Yee, Sienho *law educator*
Zable, Jack Louis *mechanical engineer, educator*

Brighton
Rinkenberger, Richard Krug *physical scientist, geologist, consultant*
Wagner, Samuel Albin Mar *state agency administrator*

Broomfield
Baker, Charles E. *lawyer*
Boulos, Paul Fares *civil and environmental engineer*
Crowe, James Quell (Jim) *communications executive*
Flanders, Eleanor Carlson *community volunteer*
Hoover, R. David *packaging company executive*
O'Hara, Kevin J. *information technology executive*
Parker, Bobby Douglas *secondary school educator*
Scott, Gregory Kellam *former state supreme court justice, lawyer*
Seabrook, Raymond J. *corporate financial executive*
Williams, John James, Jr. *architect*

Brush
Gabriel, Donald Eugene *science educator*

Buena Vista
Scott, Gerald Wesley *retired American diplomat*

Calhan
Henderson, Freda LaVerne *elementary school educator*

Canon City
Cochran, Susan Mills *research librarian*
Ward, Larry Thomas *social program administrator*

Carbondale
Cowgill, Ursula Moser *biologist, educator, environmental consultant*

Castle Rock
Barnard, Rollin Dwight *retired financial executive*
Hendrick, Hal Wilmans *human factors educator*
Wolfer, Dale *retired music educator*
Yamnik, Dale Arthur *quality assurance professional, food products executive*

Centennial
Bryan, A(lonzo) J(ay) *retired service club official*
Chandramouli, Srinivasan (Chandra Chandramouli) *management and systems consultant*
Fevurly, Keith Robert *educational administrator*
Frame, Roger Everett *school psychologist*
Goughnour, Roy Robert *civil engineer, educator, director*
Grant, Paul *chemical engineer, real estate broker, lawyer*
Heath, Jayne Marie *music educator*
Lessey, Samuel Kenric, Jr. *foundation administrator*
Milliken, Douglas Gordon *financial consultant, municipal official*
Milliken, John Gordon *research economist*
Owens, Marvin Franklin, Jr. *oil industry executive, director*
Wilks, Dana Lyn *protective services official, writer*

Cherry Hills Village
Conroy, Mary Elizabeth *history professor*
Stapleton, Katharine Hall (Katie Stapleton) *commentator, writer*
Van Loucks, Mark Louis *venture capitalist, financial planner*

Clifton
Konola, Claudette June *finance company executive, consultant*
Menard, Michael Joseph *museum director*

Colorado Springs
Abbott, Gina *municipal government executive*
Adams, Bernard Schroder *retired college president*
Adams, Deborah Rowland *lawyer*
Adams, Janelle R. *mathematics educator, gifted and talented educator*
Adnet, Jacques Jim Pierre *astronautical and electrical engineer, consultant*
Anderson, Paul Nathaniel *oncologist, educator*
Ansorge, Iona Marie *musician, educator, real estate agent*
Baack, Paula D. *music educator, director*
Baldvins, Lynn Ann *medical/surgical nurse, army officer*
Barber, Michael J. *cardiologist, educator*
Beard, Amanda *swimmer, Olympic athlete*
Bobek, Nicole *professional figure skater*
Bowen, Clotilde Marion Dent *retired military officer, psychiatrist*
Brooks, Glenn Ellis *political science professor, educational association administrator*
Budington, William Stone *retired librarian*
Burdo, Amy *elementary school educator*
Bybee, Rodger Wayne *science administrator*
Cameron, Paul Drummond *health facility administrator*
Cash, Swin (Swintayla Marie Cash) *professional basketball player*
Celeste, Richard F. *academic administrator, retired ambassador, governor*
Cheek, Joey *Olympic athlete*
Christensen, C. Lewis *real estate developer*
Colangelo, Jerry John *professional sports team executive*
Coppock, Richard Miles *retired not-for-profit administrator*
Corry, Charles Elmo *geophysicist, not-for-profit developer*
Coughlin, Natalie *Olympic swimmer*
Cramer, Owen Carver *classics educator, department chairman*
Dassanowsky, Robert von *language and film professor, writer, producer*
Deeny, Raymond M. *lawyer*
Dobson, James Clayton *psychologist, author*
Driscoll, Lori *neuroscientist, educator*
Evans, Paul Vernon *lawyer*
Everson, Steven Lee *lawyer, real estate company executive*
Fagin, Barry Steven *computer science educator, writer*
Farrer, Claire Anne Rafferty *anthropologist, educator*
Fielden, C. Franklin III *early childhood education consultant*
Gardner, Rulon E. *Olympic athlete*
Gibson, John Robert *software engineer*
Gifford, Marilyn Joyce *emergency physician, consultant*
Goehring, Kenneth *artist*
Hall, Gary, Jr. *Olympic athlete*
Hamilton, Tyler *professional cyclist, Olympic athlete*
Harvey, William Tarver *biomedical engineer, chronic disease physician*
Hawley, Nanci Elizabeth *professional society administrator*
Hayes, Joanna *Olympic track and field athlete*
Heffron, Michael Edward *software engineer, computer scientist*
Hegarty, Joseph Lee *neurotologist*
Heilman, John Edward *engineering consultant*
Hinkle, Betty Ruth *retired academic administrator*
Howard, Larry Bruce *forensic specialist, consultant*
Kane, Robyn A. *economist*
Kendall, Phillip Alan *retired lawyer*
Killian, George Ernest *retired educational association administrator*
Kleiner, John Philip *cardiologist*
Kubida, William Joseph *lawyer*
Kwan, Michelle Wing *professional figure skater*
Lamborn, Douglas L. *congressman*
LeMieux, Linda Dailey *museum director*
Liebscher, Gregory J. *plastic surgeon*
Loux, Gordon Dale *philanthropic consultant*
Lyddane, Anne Alexandra *retired writer*
MacDougall, Malcolm Edward *lawyer*
May, Misty *Olympic athlete*
Mayweather, Floyd, Jr. *professional boxer*
McCool, Courtney *Olympic athlete*
McDade, Roberta Clark *secondary school educator*
Metz, Brian K. *cardiologist*
Miller, Paula J. *library director*
Miller, Zoya Dickins *civic worker, consultant*
Morris, Steven Lynn *engineering consultant, retired military officer*
Mou, Thomas William *retired physician, medical educator, consultant*
Noyes, Richard Hall *bookseller*
Ogrean, David William *sports association executive*
Partridge, Garold Clyde *marketing executive*
Patterson, Carly *Olympic gymnast*
Payne, Billy (William Porter Payne) *real estate lawyer, sports association executive*
Peirsol, Aaron *Olympic swimmer*
Phelps, Michael *Olympic swimmer*
Purvis, Randall W. B. *lawyer*
Randall, Jessy *curator, writer*
Renuart, Victor Eugene, Jr., (Gene Renuart) *career military officer*
Rhodes, Daisy Chun *writer, researcher, historian*
Rivera, Lionel *mayor*
Roberts, John, II, *television producer, writer*
Sargent, Walter Harriman, II, *lawyer*
Schultz, Richard Dale *national athletic organization executive*
Scott, Carla Anne *musician, educator*
Shockley-Zalabak, Pamela Sue *academic administrator*
Simmons, George Finlay *retired mathematics professor*
Sinclair, William Donald *state legislator, retired church official*
Skora, Wayne Philip *retired air force officer*
Slivka, Michael Andrew *lawyer*
Son, Seung Hwan *mathematician, researcher*
Spicer, Ronald L. *financial services educator*
Stanley, David John *research and development company executive*
Stavig, Mark Luther *language educator*
Strickland, Sylvia Raye *social worker*
Swihart, James W., Jr. *diplomat*
Teter, Hannah *Olympic athlete*
Torres, Dara *Olympic athlete*
Tucker, Frank Hammond *history professor*
Tueting, Sarah *professional hockey player*
Vandeputte, Dixie Dianne *psychologist, educator*
Venugopal, Veerakumar *materials scientist, physicist, researcher*
Walker, Jonathan Lee *lawyer*
Walsh, Kerri Lee *Olympic athlete*
Wariner, Jeremy *Olympic track and field athlete*
Watts, Oliver Edward *engineering company executive*
Weslin, Anna Therese *clinical nurse specialist, dance consultant*
West, R. Leland *veterinarian*
White, Gayle Clay *aerospace company executive*
Willis, Frank Edward *retired air force officer*
Yaney, George *retired history professor*
Yanney, Patrick Steven *human resources specialist*
Zapel, Arthur Lewis *book publishing executive*
Ziemer, Rodger Edmund *electrical engineering educator, consultant*

Columbine Valley
Gagin, Lawrence Vincent *ceramics engineer, consultant*

Commerce City
Hogan, Aden Ellsworth, Jr. *city government administrator*
Trujillo, Lorenzo A. *lawyer, educator, consultant, director*

Conifer
Boese, Michelle Lynne *accountant, consultant*

Cortez
Kristin, Karen *artist*

Denver
Abo, Ronald Kent *freelance/self-employed architect*
Adelman, Jonathan Reuben *political science professor*
Adkins, Jeanne M. *state agency administrator*
Adler, Charles Spencer *psychiatrist*
Albino, Judith Elaine Newsom *university president*
Allen, Nancy H. *dean, library director*
Amore, Shirley C. *library director*
Anderson, Donald H. *energy executive*
Anderson, John David *architect*
Anderson, Norma V. *retired state legislator*
Anthony, Carmelo *professional basketball player*
Aro, Edwin Packard *lawyer*
Ashton, Rick James *retired librarian*
Austin, H(arry) Gregory *lawyer*
Avi, (Avi Wortis) *author*
Axelrod, Evan M. *psychologist, educator*
Babayev, Djangir Ali Ikram *physicist, researcher*
Bader, Gerald L., Jr. *lawyer*
Baer, Richard N. *lawyer, telecommunications industry executive*
Bain, Donald Knight *lawyer*
Balboa, Marcelo *professional soccer player*
Banks, Britt D. *lawyer*
Barber, Patricia Louise *clinical specialist*
Barbour, Alton Bradford *retired human communication studies educator*
Barry, Henry Ford *chemicals executive*
Bartlit, Fred Holcomb, Jr. *lawyer*
Beatty, Michael L. *lawyer*
Belitz, Paul Edward *lawyer*
Bell, Stephen D. *lawyer*
Bender, Michael Lee *state supreme court justice*
Benson, Robert Eugene *lawyer*
Benton, Auburn Edgar *lawyer*
Berry, Robert Worth *lawyer, retired military officer, educator*
Bess, Charles Wayne *lawyer*
Bialasiewicz, Jan Tadeusz *electrical engineering educator*
Black, Gary D. *investment company executive*
Blair, Andrew Lane, Jr. *lawyer, educator*
Blatter, Frank Edward *travel company executive*
Blitz, Stephen M. *lawyer*
Bluher, John H. *lawyer, diversified financial services company executive*
Blum, Gary Bernard *lawyer*
Boggs, Gil *principal ballet dancer*
Boyer, William Joseph *food products executive*
Breeskin, Michael Wayne *lawyer*
Brega, Charles Franklin *lawyer, director*
Brega, Kerry Elizabeth *physician, researcher*
Briggs, Steve Clement *lawyer*
Brown, Hank *academic administrator, former senator*
Brown, Keith Lapham *retired ambassador*
Brownson, Jacques Calmon *architect*
Buckstein, Caryl Sue *writer*
Bufe, Charles Glenn *geophysicist, researcher*
Burrows, Bertha Jean *retired academic administrator*
Butler, Daphne *lawyer*
Butler, David *lawyer*
Byrne, Thomas J. *lawyer*
Byyny, Richard Lee *former academic administrator, physician, educator*
Cain, Douglas Mylchreest *lawyer*
Calvin, Charles D. *lawyer*
Camby, Marcus D. *professional basketball player*
Campbell, Leonard M. *lawyer*
Carlson, Erik B. *lawyer*
Carrigan, Jim R. *arbitrator, mediator, retired judge*
Case, Paul Watson, Jr. *communications executive*
Case, Steve (Stephen M.) *healthcare investment company executive, former media and entertainment company executive*
Cashman, Michael Richard *small business owner*
Chamberlain, Adrian Ramond *transportation engineer*
Chapman, Rex *professional sports team executive and retired basketball player*
Chaput, Charles J. *archbishop*
Charlip, Ralph Blair *military officer, health facility administrator*
Chavez, Jeanette *editor*
Cheroutes, Michael Louis *lawyer*
Cherowitzo, William Edward *mathematics professor*
Childears, Linda *foundation administrator*
Chu, Roderick Gong-Wah *educational association administrator*
Clark, Gary R. *newspaper editor*
Clark, Phillip R. *lawyer*
Clark, Suzanne *accountant*
Clinch, Nicholas Bayard III *small business owner*
Coan, Patricia A. *judge*
Coats, Nathan B. *state supreme court justice*
Cobban, William Aubrey *paleontologist*
Coffman, Mike (Michael H. Coffman) *state official, former state legislator*
Cohen, Andrew *news analyst, lawyer*
Cohen-Vader, Cheryl Denise *municipal official*
Considine, Terry *real estate company executive*
Cook, Albert Thomas Thornton, Jr. *financial advisor*

Coombe, Bob (Robert D.) *academic administrator*
Cooper, Billy J. *lawyer*
Cooper, Paul Douglas *lawyer*
Cope, Thomas Field *lawyer*
Copeland, Eugene Leroy *lawyer, writer*
Cox, William Vaughan *arbitrator, lawyer*
Crawford, Joe Jay *real estate company executive*
Crow, Nancy Rebecca *lawyer*
Cuba, Stanley L. *government official*
Curl, Layton Seth *psychologist, consultant, educator*
Dallas, Sandra *writer*
Dance, Francis Esburn Xavier *communication educator*
Danos, Robert McClure *retired oil company executive*
Dauer, Edward Arnold *law educator*
Davis, R. Steven *lawyer, telecommunications industry executive*
Dean, James Benwell *lawyer*
De Marino, Thomas John *lawyer*
Deutsch, Harvey Elliot *lawyer*
Dobersen, Michael Joseph *pathologist, researcher*
Dolan, Andrew Kevin *lawyer*
Dominick, Peter Hoyt, Jr. *architect*
Dorr, Robert Charles *lawyer*
Dowdle, Patrick Dennis *lawyer*
Drake, Sylvie (Jurras) *theater critic*
Driver, Michael J. *lawyer*
Ducker, Bruce *writer, lawyer*
Duffy, William J. *lawyer*
Dunham, Joan Roberts *administrative assistant*
Dunn, Randy Edwin *lawyer*
DuVivier, Katharine Keyes *lawyer, educator*
Dyer, Edward James *public utilities commissioner*
Eaton, Gareth Richard *chemistry professor, dean*
Ebel, David M. *federal judge*
Edelman, Joel *health facility administrator*
Ehret, Josephine Mary *microbiologist, researcher*
Eickhoff, Theodore Carl *infectious disease physician, epidemiologist*
Eid, Allison *state supreme court justice*
Eid, Troy A. *prosecutor*
Elliff, J(ohn) Eric *lawyer*
Emmet, Thomas Addis, Jr. *college administrator, consultant*
Engdahl, Todd Philip *editor*
Eppler, Jerome Cannon *investment advisor*
Faatz, Jeanne Ryan *councilman*
Fails, Thomas Glenn *geologist*
Fay, Richard James *mechanical engineer, engineering executive, educator*
Felter, Edwin Lester, Jr. *judge*
Fennessey, Paul Vincent *pediatrics and pharmacology educator, researcher*
Finegan, Cole *lawyer*
Fowler, Daniel McKay *lawyer*
Frederick, Robert Allen *history professor*
Fredmann, Martin *ballet company artistic director, educator, choreographer*
Freedman, Robert *psychiatrist*
Freiheit, Clayton Fredric *zoo director*
Fuentes, Brian Christopher *professional baseball player*
Fujioka, Jo Ann Ota *educational association administrator, consultant*
Fulkerson, Richard J. *state agency administrator*
Fulkerson, William Measey, Jr. *college president*
Fuller, Robert Kenneth *architect, urban designer*
Gabow, Patricia Anne *internist, health facility executive*
Gampel, Elaine Susan *investment company executive, consultant*
Garcia, June Marie *librarian*
Gehres, James *retired lawyer*
George, Russell Lloyd *lawyer, former state legislator*
Ghiselli, Gary *spine surgeon*
Giguere, Francois *professional sports team executive*
Golitz, Loren Eugene *dermatologist, pathologist, medical association administrator*
Gorsuch, Neil McGill *federal judge, lawyer*
Graham, Pamela Smith *artist, educator*
Grant, Patrick Alexander *lawyer*
Grant, William West III *banker*
Gravlee, Glenn P(age) *anesthesiologist, educator, director*
Green, Jersey Michael-Lee *lawyer*
Greenberg, David Ethan *communications consultant*
Greyson, Clifford Russell *internist*
Grinspoon, David H. *astrobiologist, writer, museum administrator*
Grissom, Garth Clyde *lawyer, director*
Guber, Myles Stuert *surgeon*
Haddon, Harold Alan *lawyer*
Hainer, Eugene *state librarian*
Hale, Allan L. *lawyer*
Hall, Larry Dean *utilities executive, lawyer*
Hall, Richard Murray, Jr. *finance executive, consultant*
Hanna, Juliet Marie *lawyer*
Harris, Dale Ray *lawyer, arbitrator, mediator*
Harris, James Robert *structural engineer*
Hartley, James Edward *lawyer*
Hayter, Anthony *finance educator, department chairman*
Hecox, Morris B. *academic administrator*
Hegarty, George John *university president, literature and language professor*
Heisler, Todd *photojournalist*
Hejduk, Milan *professional hockey player*
Helton, Todd *professional baseball player*
Hendrix, Lynn Parker *lawyer*
Hickenlooper, John W. *mayor*
Hoagland, Donald Wright *lawyer*
Hobbs, Gregory James, Jr. *state supreme court justice*
Hodges, Joseph Gilluly, Jr. *lawyer*
Hogan, Curtis Jule *labor union administrator, industrial relations specialist, consultant*
Hohner, Kenneth Dwayne *retired fodder company executive*
Holme, Richard Phillips *lawyer*
Hoover, George Schweke *architect*
Hopfenbeck, George Martin, Jr. *lawyer*
Houtsma, Peter C. *lawyer*
Huang, Linda Chen *plastic surgeon*
Hughes, Brad, Jr. *economist*
Hughes, Bradley Richard *finance company executive*
Hughes, J(ohnson) Donald *history professor, editor*
Hurdle, Clint *professional athletics manager*
Ibarra, Irene M. *foundation administrator*
Imhoff, Walter Francis *investment banker*
Imig, William Graff *lawyer, lobbyist*
Irwin, R. Robert *lawyer*
Iseman, Michael Dee *medical educator*
Iverson, Allen Ezail *professional basketball player*
Jacobs, Paul Alan *lawyer*
Jafek, Bruce William *otolaryngologist, educator*
Jarles, Ruth Sewell *education educator*
Johnson, Candice Elaine Brown *pediatrician, educator*
Johnson, Walter Earl *geophysicist*
Johnston, Richard Boles, Jr. *pediatrician, educator, biomedical researcher*
Jones, Irvin R. *engineering educator*
Jones, M. Douglas, Jr. *pediatrician, educator*
Jones, Richard Michael *lawyer*
Jordan, Stephen M. *academic administrator*
Judd, Joel Stanton *lawyer*
Kahane, Jeffrey *conductor, pianist*
Kahn, Edwin Sam *lawyer*
Kane, John Lawrence, Jr. *judge*
Kappy, Michael Steven *pediatrics educator*
Karl, George *professional basketball coach*
Karsh, Philip Howard *retired advertising executive*
Kassan, Stuart S. *rheumatologist*
Keep, Marcus Floyd *neurosurgeon*
Keithley, Roger Lee *judge*
Keller, Glen Elven, Jr. *lawyer*
Kelly, John Fleming *lawyer*
Kelly, Margaret M. *real estate company executive*
Kemper, J. Mariner *bank executive*
Kendig, Lynne E. *physician*
Kennedy, Cary *state official*
King, James M. *lawyer*
Kintzele, John Alfred *lawyer*
Kirshbaum, Howard M. *retired judge*
Knight, Greg *professional sports team executive*
Koul, Hari Krishen *surgery professor, scientist*
Kourlis, Rebecca Love *director, former state supreme court justice*
Kraus, Joseph Roland *reference librarian*
Krendl, Cathy Stricklin *lawyer*
Krieger, Marcia Smith *federal judge*
Krikos, George Alexander *pathologist, educator*
Kruger, Paula *telecommunications industry executive*
Krugman, Richard David *pediatrician, academic administrator, educator*
Kuppireddi, Sireesh *computer scientist*
LaMendola, Walter Franklin *technology business executive, educator*
Landess, Mike (Malcolm Lee Landess III) *newscaster*
Landon, Susan Melinda *petroleum geologist*
Langsley, Pauline Royal *psychiatrist*
Larsen, Gary Loy *physician, researcher*
Larson, Randall J. *energy executive*
Lassonde, Pierre *mining executive*
Lazarus, Steven S. *management and marketing consultant*
Lee, Lela A. *dermatology educator, researcher*
Leone, William J. *lawyer, former prosecutor*
Leprino, James G. *food products executive*
Levinson, Shauna T. *financial services executive*
Levy, Mark Ray *lawyer*
Lewis, Evan Larson *urologist*
Lincoln, Alexander III *financial analyst, lawyer, private investor*
Lindenfeld, JoAnn *physician, educator*
Lipkin, Alan F. *otolaryngologist*
Livingston, Johnston Redmond *manufacturing executive*
Low, Andrew M. *lawyer*
Low, John Wayland *lawyer*
Low, Merry Cook *civic worker*
Lubeck, Marvin Jay *ophthalmologist*
Lucero, Carlos *federal judge*
Lutz, John Shafroth *lawyer*
Lyons, James M. *lawyer*
Macey, William Blackmore *oil industry executive*
MacGregor, George Lescher, Jr. *freelance/self-employed writer, brokerage house executive*
Mackey, Pamela Robillard *lawyer*
Mahoney, Andrea Noel *lawyer*
Maldonado, Kirk Francis *lawyer*
Mandarich, David D. *real estate corporation executive*
Manzanares, Lawrence *city attorney*
Marquess, Lawrence Wade *lawyer*
Marrack, Philippa Charlotte *immunologist, researcher*
Martin, Richard Jay *medical educator*
Martinez, Alex J. *state supreme court justice*
Martz, Clyde Ollen *lawyer, educator*
Mathis, Karen J. *lawyer, legal association administrator*
Matkowski, Bette *academic administrator*
Mayer, Frederick Rickard *oil industry executive*
McCabe, John L. *lawyer*
McCandless, Bruce, II, *aerospace engineer, retired astronaut*
McClinton, David Anthony *performing company executive*
McCollum, Marianne *pharmacist, educator, medical researcher*
McConnell, John *environmental activist, founder of Earth Day*
McConnell, Michael Theodore *lawyer*
McDermott, Sandra *national park administrator*
McDowell, Karen Ann *lawyer*
McFarlane, Willis McKee *buffalo company executive*
McInnis, Scott Steve *lawyer, former congressman*
McIntosh, Carolyn Leigh *lawyer*
McLain, William Allen *lawyer*
McMichael, Donald Earl *lawyer*
McMorris, Jerry *transportation company, sports team executive*
McWilliams, Robert Hugh *federal judge*
Mears, Carolyn Lunsford *education educator*
Meeks, Patricia Lowe *literature and language educator, consultant*
Mehler, Philip S. *internist*
Meiklejohn, Alvin J., Jr. *state legislator, lawyer, accountant*
Mencer, Sue (Constance Suzanne Mencer) *former federal agency administrator*
Menke, Sean E. *air transportation executive*
Merker, Steven Joseph *lawyer*
Meyers, Arlen *physician*
Miller, Andre *professional basketball player*
Miller, Gale Timothy *lawyer*
Miller, Robert Nolen *lawyer*
Miller, Walker David *judge*
Mitchem, Allen P. *lawyer*
Mizel, Larry A. *housing construction company executive*
Mogg, Jimmy W. *gas industry executive*
Moloney, William J. *school system administrator*
Montgomery, C. Michael *lawyer*
Moore, Ernest Eugene, Jr. *surgeon, educator*
Moore, Gregory L. *editor*
Morgan, David Forbes *minister*
Morin, Christopher Joseph *vascular surgeon*
Morrison, Kendra Ann *environmental scientist*
Mueller, Edward A. *telecommunications industry executive*
Mueller, Kathryn Lucile *medical educator*
Mullarkey, Mary J. *state supreme court chief justice*
Murane, William Edward *lawyer*
Murdy, Wayne William *mining company executive, financial officer*
Myhren, Trygve Edward *communications company executive*
Nelson, Sarah Milledge *archaeology educator*
Nemiro, Beverly Mirium Anderson *author, educator*
Neumann, Herschel *retired physics professor*
Newcom, Jennings Jay *lawyer, director*
Newman, Kimberly Eileen *adult education educator*
Nicholson, Will Faust, Jr. *bank executive*
Notebaert, Richard C. *telecommunications industry executive*
Nottingham, Edward Willis, Jr. *federal judge*
Oakes, Terry Louis *apparel executive*
O'Brien, Barbara *lieutenant governor*
O'Brien, Richard T. *mining executive*
Olsen, M. Kent *lawyer, educator*
Ormes, Jonathan Fairfield *astrophysicist, researcher, educator*
Orullian, B. LaRae *retired bank executive*
Osman, Lee R. *lawyer*
O'Toole, James Joseph *business educator*
Otten, Arthur Edward, Jr. *lawyer*
Owen, Elizabeth Marie *art historian, educator*
Palmer, David Gilbert *lawyer*
Payne, Stanley E. *mathematics professor*
Peters, Stephen C. *lawyer*
Petros, Raymond Louis, Jr. *lawyer*
Petty, Thomas Lee *internist, educator*
Phelps, Robert Frederick, Jr. *lawyer*
Phillips, Paul David, Jr. *lawyer*
Plummer, Ora Beatrice *nursing educator, consultant*
Pomerantz, Marvin *thoracic surgeon*
Popham, David Kentner *minister*
Porfilio, John Carbone *federal judge*
Pozner, Larry S. *lawyer, educator*
Prosser, John Martin *architecture educator*
Quenneville, Joel *professional hockey coach*
Quiat, Gerald M. *lawyer*
Rael, Henry Sylvester, Sr. *retired health administrator, financial and management consultant*
Raine, Stanley M. *lawyer*
Rainer, William Gerald *cardiac surgeon*
Raznick, Carol *lawyer*
Repine, John Edward *internist, educator*
Reshotko, Eli *aerospace engineer, educator*
Rice, Nancy E. *state supreme court justice*
Rich, Robert Stephen *lawyer*
Richards, Thomas E. *telecommunications industry executive*
Richardson, John W. *telecommunications industry executive*
Richardson, Thomas A. *lawyer*
Ritter, Bill (August William Ritter Jr.) *governor, former prosecutor*
Robertson, Jerry D. *lawyer*
Rockwood, Linda Lee *lawyer*
Rodriguez, Juan Alfonso *information technology executive*
Roesler, John Bruce *lawyer*
Roth, Robert Charles *lawyer*
Rothman, Paul Alan *publishing executive*
Rovira, Luis Dario *state supreme court justice*
Rubin, Cathy Ann *secondary school educator*
Sakai, Joseph Thomas *psychiatrist, educator*
Sakic, Joe (Joseph Steve Sakic) *professional hockey player*
Saltz, Howard Joel *newspaper editor*
Samuels, Donald L. *lawyer*
Satter, Raymond Nathan *judge*
Sayre, John Marshall *lawyer, former government official*
Scheid, Steven L. *investment company executive*
Schiff, Donald Wilfred *pediatrician, educator*
Schmidt, L(ail) William, Jr. *lawyer*
Schrier, Robert William *physician, educator*
Schwartz, Jeffrey H. *distribution facilities executive*
Search-Winters, Michelle Dawn *corporate financial executive, consultant*
Seawell, Donald Ray *lawyer, performing company executive*
Sharp, Lewis Inman *museum director, curator*
Shea, Kevin Michael *lawyer*
Sheeler, Jim *journalist*
Sheeran, Michael John Leo *priest, academic administrator*
Shepherd, John Frederic *lawyer*
Shively, John D. *lawyer*
Shlay, Judith Carol *physician*
Shwayder, Elizabeth Yanish *sculptor*
Singleton, William Dean *publishing executive*
Sinoff, Harry *religious studies educator, director*
Slotta, Oliveann Davis *mathematics educator, consultant*
Smith, Dwight Morrell *chemistry professor, academic administrator*
Smith, Sallye Wrye *librarian*
Smyth, Ryan *professional hockey player*
Snead, Kathleen Marie *lawyer*
Snyder, Charles Royce *sociologist, educator*
Sokol, Ronald Jay *pediatric gastroenterologist, researcher*
Song, John I. *otolaryngologist, surgeon*
Staelin, Earl Hudson *lawyer*
Stamm, Carol Ann *obstetrician, gynecologist*
Starrs, Elizabeth Anne *lawyer*
Steefel, David Simon *lawyer*
Storey, Brit Allan *historian*
Sujansky, Eva Borska *pediatrician, geneticist, educator*
Sumner, Stephen C. *academic administrator*
Suthers, John William *state attorney general*
Switzer, Teri Reynolds *library association executive*
Szefler, Stanley James *pediatrics and pharmacology educator*
Takis, Stephanie *retired state senator*
Talley, Steven K. *lawyer*
Tatum, Christine *editor*
Taussig, Lynn Max *healthcare administrator, pulmonologist, pediatrician, educator*
Taylor, Edward Stewart *obstetrician, educator*
Taylor, Robert A. *veterinarian*
Taylor, Teresa *telecommunications industry executive*
Theodore, Jose *professional hockey player*
Thomasch, Roger Paul *lawyer*
Thompson, Lohren Matthew *oil company executive*
Thornton, Roland *telecommunications industry executive*
Timmins, Edward Patrick *lawyer*
Tisdale, Douglas Michael, Sr. *lawyer*
Toll, Henry Wolcott, Jr. *pathologist*
Tombaugh, Dorothy Elve *retired secondary school educator, author, lecturer*
Touff, Michael *lawyer*
Tregemba, Robert D. *telecommunications industry executive*
Trueblood, Harry Albert, Jr. *oil industry executive*
Tymkovich, Timothy Michael *federal judge*
Ulrich, Theodore Albert *lawyer*
Vigil, Daniel Agustin *academic administrator*
Villano, Stephen Paul *lawyer*
Waak, Patricia Ann *political organization administrator, environmental association executive*
Wagner, Judith Buck *investment firm executive*
Walker, Samuel David *lawyer*
Warkentien, Mark *professional sports team executive*
Weber, Matthew George *lawyer*
Wedgle, Richard Jay *lawyer*
Weihaupt, John George *geophysics educator, academic administrator*
Welton, Charles Ephraim *lawyer*
Wheeler, Malcolm Edward *lawyer, educator*
White, Joyce Louise *librarian*
Wilke, LeRoy *retired church administrator*
Williams, Michael Anthony *lawyer*
Williams, Suzanne *state senator*
Wilson, Steve *museum director*
Winn, Joan *adult education educator*
Witt, Catherine Lewis *neonatal nurse practitioner, writer*
Wohlgenant, Richard Glen *lawyer, director*
Wolf, Timothy Van de Wint *food products executive*
Wolman, Jonathan Paley *journalist*
Woodward, Lester Ray *lawyer*
Wunnicke, Brooke *lawyer*
Yost, Dan *telecommunications industry executive*
Zimet, Carl Norman *psychologist, educator*

Dillon

Dugan, Michael Joseph *former career officer, health agency executive*
Follett, Robert John Richard *publisher*

Dolores

Harper, Laura Lee *principal*
Kreyche, Gerald Francis *retired philosophy educator*
Rice, Wayne *artist, educator, small business owner*
Winterer-Schulz, Barbara Jean *graphics designer, writer*

Durango

Balas-Whitfield, Susan *artist*
Barter, Mary F. *academic administrator*
Burnham, Bryson Paine *retired lawyer*
Cristol, Stanley Jerome *retired chemistry professor*
Fogleman, Ronald Robert *retired air force officer, consultant*
Foster, James Henry *advertising and public relations executive*
Wigton, Chester Mahlon *physician*
Zeller, Christopher Lee *preservation archaeologist*

Edwards

Chambers, Joan Louise *retired librarian, dean*

Eldorado Springs
Lovins, L. Hunter *public policy institute executive, consultant, educator*

Elizabeth
Brownson, Sue McPherson *music educator*

Englewood
As-Salaam, Jamaal (William Louis Williams Jr.) *poet, film producer, writer*
Bailey, Champ *professional football player*
Bennett, Robert R. *telecommunications company executive*
Bloch, Clifford Alan *pediatric endocrinologist*
DeMuth, Laurence Wheeler, Jr. *lawyer, utilities executive*
Erickson, William Hurt *retired state supreme court justice*
Ervin, Patrick Franklin *nuclear engineer*
Flowers, David J. *corporate financial executive*
Fries, Michael T. *communications executive*
Gertz, David Lee *homebuilding company executive*
Gloss, Lawrence Robert *fundraising executive*
Han, Bernard L. *communications executive*
Hardy, Wayne Russell *insurance and investment broker*
Keesling, Ruth Morris *foundation administrator*
Knize, David Maurice *plastic surgeon*
Kubik, Timothy Robert White *director, history educator*
Lynch, John Terrence *professional football player*
Maffei, Gregory B. *media company executive, former computer software company executive*
Malone, John C. *media company executive*
Manley, Richard Walter *insurance company executive*
Markowski, Elizabeth M. *lawyer*
McCallie, Spencer Wyatt *lawyer*
McGraw, Jack Wilson *federal agency administrator*
Morton, John Douglas *retail executive*
Moskowitz, David K. *lawyer*
Neiser, Brent Allen *foundation executive, public affairs and personal finance speaker, consultant*
Olcer, Nuri Yelman *engineering researcher, educator*
Peterson, Ralph Randall *engineering executive*
Rosser, Edwin Michael *mortgage company executive*
Rowe, Mike *television personality*
Schleyer, William T. *cable company executive*
Shanahan, Mike *professional football coach*
Smith, Rod *professional football player*
Spencer, Margaret Gilliam *lawyer*
Steinhauser, John William *retired lawyer*
Tanabe, Charles Y. *lawyer*
Vogel, Carl E. *communications executive*

Erie
Nichols, Janet Hildreth *elementary school educator, childbirth and parenting educator*

Estes Park
Ojalvo, Morris *civil engineer, educator*
Piper, Mark Harry *retired banker*
Ryder, Susan R. *elementary school educator*
Varilek, Julie *music educator*
Webb, Richard C. *engineering company executive*

Evergreen
Dobbs, Gregory Allan *journalist*
Evans, David Lynn *management consultant*
Haun, John Daniel *petroleum geologist, educator*
Heyl, Allen Van, Jr. *geologist*
Jackson, William Richard *entrepreneur*
Prichard, Vincent Marvin *lawyer*

Fort Collins
Abt, Steven R. *civil engineer, educator*
Ahmann, John Stanley *retired psychologist*
Baldwin, Lionel Vernon *retired university president*
Bamburg, James Robert *biochemistry professor*
Barbezat, Eugene LaVar *computer engineer, retired military officer*
Bennett, Thomas LeRoy, Jr. *clinical neuropsychology educator*
Black, William Cormack, IV, *insect geneticist, statistician*
Bloemen, Crystal Lynn *secondary school educator*
Chorpenning, H. R. III *minister*
Colbert, Debora A. *director*
Eddy, Gladys Louise *retired educational administrator*
Egger, Erick *veterinarian*
Ewing, Jack Robert *accountant*
Fixman, Marshall *chemist, educator*
Follett, Ronald Francis *soil scientist*
Gandy, H. Conway *retired judge, state official*
Grandin, Temple *industrial designer, science educator*
Harper, Judson Morse *retired university administrator, consultant, educator*
Hughes, Harrison G. *horticulture educator*
Jensen, Margaret *real estate broker*
Johnson, Donald Edward, Jr. *lawyer*
Johnson, Robert Britten *geology educator*
Kaufman, Harold Richard *mechanical engineer and physics educator*
Keim, Wayne Franklin *retired agronomist, geneticist*
Kinnison, Robert Wheelock *retired accountant*
Lumb, William Valjean *veterinarian*
Maher, Thomas George *academic administrator, producer, media educator*
Matthies, Frederick John *civil and environmental engineer*
May, Stephen James *communications educator, writer*
Mc Clellan, William Monson *retired library director*
McComb, David Glendinning *history professor*
Meyers, Albert Irving *chemistry professor*
Mielke, Paul William, Jr. *statistician, consultant*
Morgan, George Arthur *psychologist*
Mortvedt, John Jacob *soil scientist, researcher*
Murphy, Dennis Joseph *lawyer*
Neil, Stuart *management consultant, real estate broker*
Notaros, Branislav M. *electrical engineer, educator*
Peng, Junhua *molecular biologist, botanist*
Penley, Larry Edward *academic administrator, finance educator*
Peterson, Gary Andrew *agronomics researcher*
Phemister, Robert David *veterinary medical educator*
Richardson, Everett Vern *hydraulic engineer, educator, administrator, consultant*
Roesner, Larry August *civil engineer*
Rogers, Garth Winfield *lawyer*
Rolston, Holmes III *theology studies educator, philosopher*
Savage, Eldon Paul *retired environmental health educator*
Schaffer, Robert (Bob Schaffer) *former congressman*
Schumm, Stanley Alfred *geologist, educator*
Schwartz, Allen R. *lawyer*
Sedei Rodden, Pamela Jean *psychologist, director*
Seidel, George Elias, Jr. *zoology educator*
Seward, Nathan William *biologist, researcher*
She, Chiao-Yao *physics professor, researcher*
Suinn, Richard Michael *psychologist*
Thompson, David W.J. *atmospheric scientist, educator*
Wang, Tian *immunologist, educator*
Watz, Martin Charles *brewery consultant*
Zupanski, Dusanka *research scientist*

Fort Garland
Boyer, Lester Leroy, Jr. *architecture educator, consultant*
Taylor-Dunn, Corliss Leslie *marriage and family therapist*

Fountain
Hazlett, David Lawrence *social studies educator*

Frederick
Emlen, Warren Metz *retired computer company executive*

Frisco
Helmer, David Alan *lawyer*

Georgetown
Stern, Mort(imer) P(hillip) *communications educator, editor, reporter, consultant*

Glenwood Springs
Jaffrey, Ira *oncologist, educator*
Kelley, Robert Daryl *retired biology professor, mathematics professor*

Golden
Baron, Robert Charles *publishing executive*
Bettinghaus, Erwin Paul *research scientist*
Bickart, Theodore Albert *university president emeritus*
Carney, Deborah Leah Turner *lawyer*
Coors, Peter Hanson *brewery company executive*
DeSanto, John A. *physicist, educator, mathematics professor*
Dickinson, Carol Rittgers *art historian, writer*
Eckley, Wilton Earl, Jr. *humanities educator*
Eiberger, Carl Frederick *lawyer*
Hamilton, Warren Bell *geologist, geophysicist, educator, researcher*
Kazmerski, Lawrence Lee *scientist, research facility executive*
Kiely, W. Leo III *brewery company executive*
Kopel, David Benjamin *lawyer*
Krauss, George *metallurgist*
Metzger, Wyatt K. *physicist*
Mocker, Hans Walter *physicist*
Olson, Marian Katherine *management consultant*
Pegis, Anton George *retired language educator*
Petrick, Alfred, Jr. *economist, educator*
Phillipson, Donald E. *lawyer*
Rodgers, Frederic Barker *judge*
Scoggins, M. W. (Bill Scoggins) *academic administrator*
Shea, Dion Warren Joseph *academic administrator, fundraiser*
Siegrist, Robert L. *engineering educator, consultant*
Sloan, Earle Dendy, Jr. *chemical engineering educator*
Taylor, Philip Craig *physics professor*
Trefny, John Ulric *retired college president*
Truly, Richard H. *academic and federal agency administrator, retired pilot*
von Roedern, Bolko Graf *energy executive, researcher*
Weimer, Robert Jay *geology educator, energy consultant, civic leader*
Zhang, Ruichong *civil and mechanical engineer, educator*
Zimmer, Larry William, Jr. *sports announcer*

Grand Junction
Armstrong, Alden Arthur *retired elementary school educator, photographer, writer*
Bishop, Tilman Malcolm *retired state legislator*
Bragdon, Lynn Lyon *library administrator*
Burdick, Margaret Seale (Marge Burdick) *interior designer*
Hoagland, Christina Gail *occupational therapist, industrial drafter*
Janson, Richard Anthony *plastic surgeon*
Skogen, Haven Sherman *investment company executive*

Greeley
Bond, Richard Randolph *foundation administrator*
Carrico, Stephen J. *construction company executive*
Christiansen, Matthew Lane *mathematics educator*
Cook, Donald Evan *pediatrician, educator*
Cordell, Larry Kenneth (L. Kenny) *agricultural products executive*
Downey, Matthew T. *history professor, writer*
Duff, William Leroy, Jr. *retired dean, finance educator*
Hawthorne, Barbara L. *anthropologist, educator*
Jaouen, Richard Matthie *plastic surgeon*
Linde, Lucille Mae (Lucille Jacobson) *motor-perceptual specialist*
Miller, Diane Wilmarth *retired human resources director*
Miller, Nathaniel Gregory *mathematics professor*
Morgensen, Jerry Lynn *construction company executive*
Murray, Robert Patrick *music educator, musician*
Reardon, James F. *adult education educator*
Rovit, Sam Brian *food products executive*
Schrenk, Gary Dale *foundation executive*
Seager, Daniel Albert *university librarian*
Silcock, Raymond P. *food products executive*
Smith, Jack Lee *bank executive*
Szczyrba, Igor Nicholas *mathematical physicist, consultant*
van Gorp, Gary Wayne *minister*
Willis, Connie (Constance E. Willis) *writer*
Wiseman, Donald F. *lawyer*
Womble, Ken *theater educator, film director, writer, actor*
Worley, Lloyd Douglas *language educator*

Greenwood Village
Appel, Joel *household cleaner manufacturing executive*
Arvizu, Dan Eliab *mechanical engineer*
Aspinwall, David Charles *lawyer, insurance company executive*
Bain, James William *lawyer*
Benson, Robert Craig III *business consultant*
Chico, Beverly Ann *history professor, humanities educator*
Corboy, James McNally *investment banker*
Davidson, John Robert (Jay) *bank executive*
Dewald, Bruce Wayne *lawyer*
Duques, Ric (Henry C. Duques) *information technology company executive*
Dymond, Lewis Wandell *lawyer, educator*
Elway, John Albert *retired professional football player*
Gallegos, Larry Duayne *lawyer*
Gold, Christina A. *data processing company executive*
Grainger, John R. *medical association administrator*
Haliw, Jerome Michael *civil engineer*
Holloman, Kenneth Raymond *pathologist, educator*
Jaegers, Donna Marie *securities analyst*
Karr, David Dean *lawyer*
Lidstone, Herrick Kenley, Jr. *lawyer*
Money, David R. *lawyer, information technology executive*
Nixon, Scott Sherman *lawyer*
Poe, Robert Alan *lawyer*
Rairdon, James Lee *paralegal, educator*
Ramsey, John Arthur *lawyer*
Rothrock, Lindsey Nichole *lawyer*
Schlapbach, David *lawyer*
Sims, Douglas D. *bank executive*
Wittman, Vanessa Ames *communications executive*

Gunnison
Gelwicks, James M. *retired communications educator*
Lavigne, Peter Marshall *conservationist, lawyer, educator*
Wacker, John M. *music educator, director*

Henderson
Reibold, Dorothy Ann *accountant, researcher*

Highlands Ranch
Brierley, James Alan *biohydrometallurgy consultant*
Bublitz, Deborah Keirstead *pediatrician*
Hagen, Glenn W. *lawyer*
Harris, Douglas Clay *retired newspaper executive*
Judson, Philip Livingston *retired lawyer, consultant*
Krinsky, Fredda S. *clinical chemist, consultant*
Mierzwa, Joseph William *lawyer, consultant*
Sapienza, David Victor *social studies educator*
Scalfari, Larry Alan *music educator, director*
Snell, Michael Steven *music educator*
Townsend, James Douglas *controller, accountant*
Wittbrodt, Edwin Stanley *financial planner, consultant, retired military officer*

Hot Sulphur Springs
Edwards, Daniel Walden *prosecutor, lawyer*

Howard
Hopkins, Donald J. *retired lawyer*

Jefferson
Maatsch, Deborah Joan *manufacturing executive*

Joes
Crawford, Dorothy Hill *retired secondary school educator, art educator, artist*

Lafayette
Lee, Robert Anthony *church musician, accompanist*
Mehl, Albert L. *pediatrician, poet, composer*
Thornbury, John Rousseau *radiologist, physician*

Lake George
Norman, John Barstow, Jr. *graphics designer, educator*

Lakewood
Axley, Hartman *retired estate planner, underwriter*
Barrett, Michael Henry *civil engineer*
Colaiannia, Louis Mario *dentist, composer, pianist*
Eikleberry, Lois Schillie *physician*
Guyton, Samuel Percy *retired lawyer*
Hadley, Marlin LeRoy *financial planner, consultant*
Hansen, Richard Olaf *geophysicist, educator, director*
Heath, Gary Brian *manufacturing executive, engineer*
Humphrey, Charles Edward, Jr. *lawyer*
Isely, Henry Philip *association and business executive, integrative engineer, writer, educator*
Knott, William Alan *library director*
Kulkarni, Kishore Ganesh *economics professor, consultant*
Martinen, John A. *travel company executive*
McBride, Guy Thornton, Jr. *college president emeritus*
McElwee, Dennis John *lawyer, former pharmaceutical company executive*
Meyer, Lynn Nix *lawyer*
Nelson, Deborah Jane *family and consumer science educator*
Nichols, Vicki Anne *financial consultant, librarian*
Peters, Julie Anne *writer*
Quinn, John Michael *physicist, geophysicist*
Reed, Joan-Marie *special education educator*
Shenoi, Ranee Melanie *physiatrist*
Stromberg, Patricia Roberts *retired school librarian*
Thome, Dennis Wesley *lawyer*
Winters, Richard Allen *mineral economist*

Lamar
Banker, Carol Anne *elementary school educator*

Laporte
Riba, Shirley *artist*

Leadville
Watson, Jack Crozier *retired state supreme court justice*

Littleton
Aigner-Clark, Julie *consumer products company executive*
Alykova, Valentina *musician, music educator*
Asbjörnson, Kevin Donald *musician, small business owner*
Battilega, John A. *research and development company executive*
Colvis, John Paris *aerospace engineer, mathematician, research scientist*
Dasgupta, Arijit (Bapi) *agricultural products executive*
Day, Susan Marie *music educator, composer*
Ergen, Charles W. *communications professional*
Forstot, Stephan Lance *ophthalmologist*
Fryt, Monte Stanislaus *petroleum company executive, speaker, advisor*
Greenberg, Elinor Miller *director, consultant*
Grounds, Vernon Carl *seminary administrator*
Hopping, William Russell *hospitality industry consultant, appraiser*
Keats, Donald Howard *composer, educator*
Keogh, Heidi Helen Dake *advocate*
Kielmeyer, William Henry *ceramics engineer, researcher*
Kleinknecht, Kenneth Samuel *retired air transportation executive*
Kullas, Albert John *management consultant, systems engineer*
Lode, Trygve Tennyson *entrepreneur, actor*
Marion, John Martin *instructional technology educator*
Meyer, Milton Edward, Jr. *retired lawyer, artist*
Norman, Marcia Macy *writer, realtor*
Paull, Richard Allen *geologist, educator*
Reinker, Mary Stefanich *musician, educator*
Shepherd, Donna Lou *interior designer*
Tucker, James Raymond *primary school educator*
Udevitz, Norman *publishing executive*
Vail, Charles Daniel *veterinarian, consultant*
Volpe, Richard Gerard *insurance accounts executive, consultant*

Livermore
Tkachev, Sergey Nikolayevich *geophysicist*

Lone Tree
Miller, Allan Marquess *hematologist*
Spelts, Richard John *lawyer*
Spisak, John Francis *corporation executive*
Washington, Reginald Louis *pediatric cardiologist*

Longmont
Dierks, Richard Ernest *veterinarian, academic administrator*
Doyle, James Thomas *electronics engineer*
Jones, Beverly Ann Miller *nursing administrator, retired patient services administrator*
Newman, Dean Gordon *business consultant*
Sandler, Thomas R. *accountant, director*
Watkins, John Goodrich *psychologist, educator*
Wohler, Wayne L. *information scientist*
Yost, Byron A. *retired physician*

Louisville
Adams, Eula L. *data storage executive*
Brault, James William *physicist*
Bravo, Adele *elementary school educator*
Maddock, Jerome Torrence *library and information scientist*
Martin, Patrick J. *technology company executive*
Schonbrun, Michael K. *senior housing developer and operator*
Syed, Yasser Fouad Khaderi *electrical engineer*

Loveland
Balsiger, David Wayne *television director, writer, television producer, television director, researcher*
Bierbaum, J. Armin *petroleum company executive, consultant*
Bierbaum, Janith Marie *artist*
Clark, Roger Earl *lawyer*
Fleischer, Gerald Albert *industrial engineer, educator*
Harrison, Craig Donald *water rights broker, real estate and land use planner*
King, Joan Caluda *medical educator, neuroscientist*
Rodman, Alpine C. *arts and crafts company executive, photographer*

Lyons
Spring, Kathleen *writer*

Mancos
Seney, Robert William *retired education educator*
Whitehead, Linda Sue *literature and language educator, history educator, special education educator*

Meeker
Omer, Robert Wendell *hospital administrator*

Monte Vista
Rausch, Paul Matthew *financial executive*

Montrose
Gates, Viola R. *writer*
Kontny, Vincent L. *rancher, retired engineering executive*
Radovich, Donald *painter, illustrator, retired art educator*

Monument
Boggs, Steven Eugene *real estate broker, lawyer*
Breckner, William John, Jr. *retired military officer*
De Francesco, John Blaze, Jr. *public relations consultant, writer*
McIver, Deborah Kay *tax specialist, entrepreneur, small business owner*
Rokke, Ervin Jerome *military officer, academic administrator*

Morrison
Bowen, Peter Geoffrey *arbitrator, business educator*
Myers, Harry J., Jr. *retired publisher*

Nederland
Lutz, Frank Wenzel *education administration educator*
Sutton, Philip D. (Philip Dietrich Sutton) *psychologist, educator*
Thomas, Daniel Foley *retired diversified financial services company executive*

Niwot
Farrington, Helen Agnes *personnel director*

Northglenn
Hemlock, Roberta Leigh *veterinary technician*
Kappler, Karen L. *musician, educator*

Norwood
Brantingham, Andrya J. *special education educator*
Reagan, Harry Edwin III *lawyer*

Ordway
Fosdick, Jacque Janelle *literature and language educator, theater educator*

Pagosa Springs
Kelly, Reid Browne *lawyer*

Palisade
Fay, Abbott Eastman *history professor*

Paonia
Noonan, Robert Harry *art and music educator*
Ring, Ray *editor*

Parachute
Leonard, Betsy Ann *director, writer*

Parker
McCauley, John Michael *real estate appraiser, consultant*
Parker, Juston Scott *travel company executive*

Pine
Jones, David Milton *economist, educator*

Pueblo
Becker, Charles A. *adult education educator*
Deasy, Irene M. *retired protective services official*
Farley, Thomas T. *lawyer*
Lytle, William David *lawyer*
Occhiato, Michael Anthony *municipal official*
Pierce, Jina *curator, artist*
Ramirez, Monica E. *education educator, consultant*
Sisson, Ray L. *retired dean, author*

Ridgway
Lathrop, Kaye Don *nuclear scientist, educator*

Rocky Ford
Mendenhall, Harry Barton *lawyer*

Salida
Strawn, Melvin Nicholas *artist, educator*

Sedalia
Bean, Sharon Louise *music educator*
Cooley, Andrew Lyman *computer company executive*

Silverthorne
Riley, Mary Jane *computer scientist*

Snowmass Village
DiBiaggio, John A. *university president*
Strand, Curt Robert *hotel executive*

Springfield
Wessler, Melvin Dean *farmer, rancher*

Steamboat Springs
Moylan, James Joseph *lawyer*
Potter, William Bartlett *diversified financial services company executive*

Sterling
Mitchell, Stacy Marie *medical transcriptionist*

Superior
Forshee, Gladys Marie *insurance agent, writer*
Middlebrooks, Eddie Joe *environmental engineer*

Thornton
Fritze, Sheila Kay *librarian*
Shih, Franklin *physician*

Trinidad
Marshall, Sandra Lee *historian, writer*

Twin Lakes
Homan, Ralph William *finance company executive*

U S A F Academy
Born, Dana H. *dean, career military officer*
Galema, Joseph M. *music director*
Merchant, P. Glenn, Jr. *military officer, physician*
Musselman, Randall L. *electrical engineer, educator*
Regni, John F. *academic administrator, career military officer*
Reynolds, Jeff *men's college basketball coach*
Veverka, Donald Victor *science educator*
Westermann, Edward Burton *military officer, analyst, educator*

Vail
Bevan, William Arnold, Jr. *emergency physician*
Kelton, Arthur Marvin, Jr. *real estate developer*
McGee, Michael Jay *protective services official, educator*
Philippon, Marc Joseph *orthopaedic surgeon*
Vosbeck, Robert Randall *architect*

Walsh
Lancaster, Robert Carl *secondary school educator*

Wellington
Grant, Lewis O. *agricultural products executive, meteorology educator*

Westminster
Eaves, Stephen Douglas *high school and vocational administrator, educator, consultant*
Kopperud, Marilyn Sue *music educator*
Reynolds-Sakowski, Dana Renee *science educator*
Sherk, George William *lawyer, educator*
White, John David *composer, musician*

Wheat Ridge
Brown, Steven Brien *radiologist*
Fleischaker, Gordon Henry, Jr. *pediatrician*
Hockenberry, E'Rena *music educator*
Morriss, Frank *writer, educator*
Scherich, Erwin Thomas *civil engineer, consultant*
Wilcox, Mary Marks *retired Christian education consultant, educator*

Windsor
Downey, Arthur Harold, Jr. *lawyer, mediator*
Mayer, Victor James *geologist, educator*

Wolcott
Flacke, Joan Wareham *physician, anesthesiologist, educator*

Woodland Park
Cockrille, Stephen *art director, business owner*
Critchlow, Bryan Douglas *music educator*

Woody Creek
Jenkins, Robert Berryman *real estate developer*

CONNECTICUT

Ansonia
Kerpa, Gary J. *computer science consultant*

Avon
Godbout, Arthur Richard, Jr. *lawyer*
Griggs, Julie Hinds *foundation administrator*
Harrison, Thomas Flatley *lawyer, environmental consultant*
Hinz, Carl Frederick, Jr. *immunologist, educator*
Kling, Phradie (Phradie Kling Gold) *small business owner, educator*
Mazur, Edward John, Jr. *financial planner*
Nagel, Miriam Carlson *freelance/self-employed writer*
Shulman, Steven J. *health services company executive*

Beacon Falls
Vignola, Andrew Michael, Sr. *computer company executive*

Bethany
Niederman, James Corson *retired internist, educator*

Bethel
Kurfehs, Harold Charles *real estate executive*
Medvecky, Thomas Edward *lawyer*
Shepard, Jean Heck *retired publishing consultant*
Tomasko, Edward A. *financial planner*

Bloomfield
Baccus, R. Eileen Turner *retired academic administrator, educational consultant*
Coburn, Richard Joseph *electronics executive, electrical engineer*
Cordani, David M. *insurance company executive*
Cornell, Robert Witherspoon *retired mechanical engineer*
Cronin, Daniel Anthony *emeritus archbishop*
De Maria, Anthony John *electrical engineer*
Hermann, Robert Jay *former manufacturing executive, consultant*
Kissa, Karl Martin *electrical engineer*
Mamlok, Walter Joseph *music educator, musician*
Messemer, Glenn Matthew *lawyer*
Nelson-Kauffman, Wendy *history educator*
Rendock, Mary Kay *elementary school educator*
Storrer, Scott A. *insurance company executive*
Stravalle-Schmidt, Ann Roberta *lawyer*
Thorpe, James *retired researcher*

Branford
Chapman, Roger Stevens, Jr. *construction company executive*
Gejdenson, Sam *former congressman*
Johnson, Eva Jo *educational consultant*
Petrie, Stewart Judson *retired obstetrician, gynecologist*
Resnick, Idrian Navarre *foundation administrator*
Rothberg, Jonathan M. *medical products executive, researcher*
Sipprell, George Sidney *aerospace engineer, consultant*
Whitaker, Thomas Russell *English literature educator*

Bridgeport
Aleali, Seyed Hossain *internist*
Bowen, Patrick Harvey *lawyer, consultant*
Eginton, Warren William *federal judge*
King, Sister Eleace *special education services professional*
Kosinski, Edward John *cardiologist, educator*
Lobdell, David Hill *pathologist*
Lori, William E. *bishop*
Macdonald, Karen Crane *occupational therapist, geriatrics services professional*
Maiocco, Kenneth Joseph *dermatologist*
Maloney, Maureen Murphy *social sciences educator*
Mcpherson, Craig A. *cardiologist, educator*
Psarras, Mary Auten *language educator, tax specialist*
Rahrig, Carol Ann *literature and language educator*
Richard, Ellen *theater executive*
Salam, Adil *pulmonary critical care physician*
Semple, Cecil Snowdon *retired manufacturing executive*
Simoneau, Cynthia Lambert *editor, educator*
Trefry, Robert J. *health facility administrator*
Wilchinsky, Mark E. *orthopaedic surgeon*

Bridgewater
Crooke, Robert Andrew *media consultant, writer, educator*

Bristol
Barnes, Carlyle Fuller *manufacturing executive*
Barnes, Wallace *manufacturing executive*
Berman, Chris *sportscaster*
Bodenheimer, George *broadcast executive*
Brantley, Jeffrey Hoke *baseball analyst, retired professional baseball player*
Corso, Lee *former football coach, football analyst*
Gammons, Peter *columnist, commentator*
Greenberg, Mike *sportscaster*
Gwynn, Anthony Keith (Tony Gwynn) *former professional baseball player*
Jaworski, Ron *sports analyst*
Jha, Manish *communications executive*
Johnson, Keyshawn *sportscaster, retired professional football player*
Kolber, Suzy *sportscaster*
Kruk, John Martin *retired professional baseball player, sportscaster*
LaGanga, Donna Brandeis *dean*
Levy, Steve *sports anchor, studio host*
Magnus, Burke *broadcast executive*
Mayne, Kenny *sports anchor*
Mortensen, Chris *sports analyst, reporter*
Olney, Robert Stanbury III *sportswriter and baseball analyst*
Scott, Stuart *sports anchor*
Simmons, Bill *sportswriter*
Skipper, John *publishing executive*
Smith, Emmitt (Emmitt James Smith III) *sportscaster, retired professional football player*
Sutcliffe, Rick (Richard Lee Sutcliffe) *professional baseball player*
Theismann, Joe (Joseph Robert Theismann) *sportscaster, retired professional football player*
Tirico, Mike *sportscaster*
Vitale, Dick *commentator*
Vojtek, RoseAnne OBrien *principal*
Wolff, Russell *broadcast executive*

Broad Brook
Kement, Isabella Viniconis *retired construction company executive*

Brookfield
Cohen, Mark Steven *dentist*
Vladimiroff, Maxim *music educator, composer*

Brooklyn
McIlvane, Edward James *stained glass artist, educator*

Canaan
Lerner, Abram *museum director, artist*
Thorne, Francis *composer*

Canterbury
Yaworski, James John III *elementary school educator*

Canton
Richardson, Dana Roland *technology consultant*

Canton Center
Humphrey, Samuel Stockwell *town official, physicist*

Centerbrook
Grover, William Herbert *architect*

Cheshire
Keiser, David Wharton *pharmaceutical executive*
Rowland, Ralph Thomas *retired architect*
Tufte, Edward Rolf *statistician, educator*
Twomey, Teresa Marie *lawyer*

Chester
Frost-Knappman, (Linda) Elizabeth *publishing executive, editor, writer*
Hilsman, Roger *political scientist, educator*

Clinton
Adler, Peggy Ann *writer, illustrator, consultant, protective services official*

Colchester
Bartkowski, Kathleen Susan *musician*
Nikirk, Susan Silva (Susan Silva) *minister, writer, dancer, consultant*

Colebrook
Burrows, John Edward *communications company executive, writer*
McNeill, William Hardy *retired historian, writer*

Cos Cob
Kane, Jay Brassler *banker*
Murphy, R. Blair *management consulting company executive*

Coventry
Aho, Sandra Christine *textile conservator*
Dimmock, Virginia Ellen *literature and language educator, consultant*

Cromwell
Donohue, Richard William *musician, conductor*
Günther-Stirn, Dagmar Dorothea *retired social sciences educator*

Danbury
Agoora, Lammia Hasson *mathematics educator*
Anderson, Alan Reinold *real estate company and computer security firm executive, consultant*
Angel, Stephen F. *chemicals executive*
Bassett, Robert Andrews *lawyer*
Breedlove, James (Jim Breedlove) *lawyer*
Collar, Emilio, Jr. *information systems consultant*
Good, Jennifer L. *pharmaceutical executive*
Grimes, Margaret Whitehurst *artist, educator*
Hawkes, Carol Ann *academic administrator*
Kavasch, Elizabeth Barrie *writer, educator, illustrator*
Leebens, Patricia Kay *psychiatrist*
Mann, Richard O. *public relations consulting company executive*
Meyers, Abbey S. *foundation administrator*
Moskowitz, Stanley Adam *finance company executive*
Nelson, Willie Hugh *musician, lyricist*
Proctor, Richard Jerome, Jr. *business educator, expert witness, accountant*
Reynolds, Jean Edwards *publishing executive*
Saghir, Adel Jamil *art educator, painter, sculptor*
Sawyer, James S. *manufacturing executive*
Tolor, Alexander *psychologist, educator*
Yamin, Robert Joseph *lawyer*

Darien
Beach, Stephen Holbrook *lawyer*
Becker, Ralph Edward *broadcast executive, consultant*
Brooke, Avery Rogers *publisher, writer*
Cronk, Leonard *management consultant*
Dale, Erwin Randolph *retired lawyer, writer*
Dordelman, William Forsyth *food company executive*
Forman, J(oseph) Charles *chemical engineer, consultant, writer*
Himmelreich, David Baker *lawyer*
Koontz, Carl Lennis, II, *retired investment counselor*
Lim, Ralph Wei Hsiong *finance educator*
McKim, Paul Arthur *management consultant, retired gas industry executive*
Prince, Kenneth Stephen *lawyer*
Schell, James Munson *finance company executive*
Smith, Elwin Earl *mining and oil company executive*
Sprole, Frank Arnott *retired pharmaceutical executive, lawyer*
Workman, Sharon Joy *journalist*

Dayville
Funk, Michael S. *food products executive*

Derby
Katz, David Lawrence *preventive medicine physician, researcher*
McEvoy, Sharlene Ann *law educator*

East Granby
Scanlon, Lawrence Eugene *language educator*

East Haddam
Borton, John Carter, Jr., (Terry Borton) *theatrical producer*
Clarke, Cordelia Kay Knight Mazuy *management consultant, artist*
Clarke, Logan, Jr. *management consultant*

Conant, Jan Royce *artist*
Frost, Susan Beth *theater producer*

East Hampton
Tucceri, Clive Knowles *writer, science educator, consultant*

East Hartford
Barredo, Rita M. *auditor*
Dubin, Joseph William *federal mediator*
Jackson, Joseph Essard *religious organization administrator*
Jacobson, Clas A. *engineering educator, director*
Lautzenheiser, Barbara Jean *insurance company executive*
McLarney, Thomas Joseph *physician*
Staroselsky, Alexander *mechanical engineer, materials scientist*

East Haven
Vermette, Raymond Edward *retired health facility administrator*

Easton
Enos, Randall *cartoonist, illustrator*
Lorenz, Lee Sharp *cartoonist*
Maloney, John Joseph *writer*
Meyer, Alice Virginia *state official*

Ellington
Evarts, Brian *social worker, educator*

Enfield
Doty, Victoria Skower *elementary school educator*
Oliver, Bruce Lawrence *retired information systems educator*
Smith, Spencer Thomas *lawyer*
Squires, William Allen *distribution company executive*

Essex
Galiette, Brad W. *entrepreneur*
Hieatt, Allen Kent *retired language educator*
Hieatt, Constance Bartlett *English language educator*
Lorenze, Mark David *orthopedist, surgeon*
Miller, Elliott Cairns *retired bank executive, lawyer*
Miller, Walter Neal *insurance company consultant*
Pfarr, John S. *lawyer*
Thompson, George Lee *retail executive, consultant*

Fairfield
Backman, Gerald Stephen *retired lawyer*
Beccalli-Falco, Ferdinando *manufacturing executive*
Booth, George Keefer *corporate financial executive*
Brett, Arthur Cushman, Jr. *banker*
Bryan, Barbara Day *retired librarian*
Burd, Robert Meyer *hematologist, oncologist, educator*
Caruso, Daniel F. *lawyer, judge, former state legislator*
Cooper, L.E., Jr. *bank executive, lawyer, writer*
Daley, Pamela *diversified services, technology and manufacturing company executive*
Denniston, Brackett Badger III *lawyer*
Dineen, John C. *manufacturing executive*
Donnelly, Scott C. *manufacturing executive*
Eigel, Edwin George, Jr. *mathematics professor, retired university president*
Fash, Victoria R. *business executive*
Gad, Lance Stewart *investment advisor, lawyer, private investor*
Henson, Daniel S. *marketing executive*
Howell, Karen Jane *private school educator*
Huth, William Edward *lawyer*
Immelt, Jeffrey R. *diversified technology and services company executive*
Janki, Daniel C. *corporate financial executive*
Johnsen, Walter Craig *manufacturing executive*
Kaff, Albert Ernest *reporter, writer*
Kleine, Herman *economist*
Luther, David Byron *management consultant*
Lynch, John F. *human resources specialist*
Miles, Leland Weber *retired academic administrator*
Miller, Frederick Edwin, Jr. *history professor, government agency administrator*
Morehouse, Sarah McCally *retired political science professor*
Morrison, Murray Allan *orthopaedic surgeon*
Neal, Michael A. *corporate financial executive*
Newton, Lisa Haenlein *philosopher, educator*
Osis, Daiga Guntra *lawyer*
Paolini, Claire Jacqueline *dean, educator*
Peters, Susan P. *human resources specialist*
Reif, Deborah *manufacturing executive*
Reiner, Gary M. *diversified technology and services company executive*
Rice, John G. *diversified technology and services executive*
Shelton, Carolyn Johnson *professional society administrator*
Sherin, Keith S. *corporate financial executive*
Stanton, Robert Alan *orthopaedic surgeon*
Trotter, Lloyd G. *manufacturing executive*
Ury, Frederic Stephen *lawyer*
Wales, Gwynne Huntington *retired lawyer*
Wexler, Herbert Ira *retail company executive*
Wright, Bob (Robert Charles Wright) *diversified technology and services company executive, former broadcast executive*

Falls Village
Cronin, Robert Lawrence *painter*
Purcell, Mary Louise Gerlinger *retired adult education educator*
Toomey, Jeanne Elizabeth *animal activist*

Farmington
Bronner, Felix *physiologist, biophysicist, educator, painter*
Centofanti, Joseph *accountant*
Deckers, Peter John *dean*
Donaldson, James Oswell III *neurologist, educator*
Ford, Burch Tracy *headmaster*
Goodson, Richard Carle, Jr. *chemist*
Grafstein, Joel M. *lawyer*
Grunnet, Margaret Louise *retired pathologist, educator*
Hall, Robert Stevens *dentist*
Liebowitz, Neil Robert *psychiatrist*
McCann, John Joseph *lawyer*
McCawley, Austin *psychiatrist, educator*
Osborn, Mary Jane Merten *biochemist, educator*
Owens, Guy *retired neurosurgeon*
Reeves, John Drummond *retired English language professional, writer*
Robinson, Peter J. *dean, periodontal educator, pathologist*
Rothfield, Lawrence I. *microbiology educator*
Rothfield, Naomi Fox *physician*
Runowicz, Carolyn Dilworth *physician*
Schenkman, John Boris *pharmacologist, educator*
Shanley, John David *epidemiologist*
Silverman, David Irving *cardiologist*
Spencer, Richard Paul *biochemist, physician, educator*
Trani, John M. *former consumer products company executive*
Treggor, Josef Philip *music educator, composer, researcher*
Wiechmann, Eric Watt *lawyer*

Gaylordsville
Dunn, Virginia *artist*

Georgetown
Julian, Alexander, II, *menswear designer*

Glastonbury
Bailey, Barbara *library director*
Cassotto, Mary Lou Grace *counselor, educator, lawyer*
Googins, Sonya Forbes *state legislator, retired banker*
Singer, Paul Richard *ophthalmologist*

Greens Farms
Deford, Frank *sportswriter, commentator, writer*

Greenwich
Alonzo, Martin Vincent *mining and aluminum company executive, investor, financial consultant*
Applegarth, Paul Vollmer *investment and development executive*
Asness, Clifford S. *investment company executive*
Atkins, Ronald Raymond *lawyer*
Ball, John Fleming *advertising and film company executive*
Bara, Jean Marc *finance and communications executive, artist*
Bedrosian, Gregory Ronald *investment banker*
Berkley, William Robert *insurance holding company executive*
Bjornson, Edith Cameron *foundation administrator, communications consultant*
Blumberg, Joel Myron *cardiologist*
Bonheim, Nelson Alfred *gastroenterologist, educator*
Brandrup, Douglas Warren *lawyer*
Brant, Peter M. *magazine publishing executive, real estate developer*
Cameron, Dort *electronics executive*
Carmichael, William Daniel *management consultant, educator*
Clements, Robert *insurance executive*
Coleman, Joel Clifford *lawyer*
Davenport, Lee Losee *physicist*
Davidson, Thomas Maxwell *oil industry executive*
DeCrane, Alfred Charles, Jr. *petroleum company executive*
Dettmer, Robert Gerhart *retired beverage company executive*
Donley, James Walton *management consultant*
Duff, Philip *investment company executive*
Ewald, William Bragg, Jr. *writer, consultant*
Farbish, Alfred B. *waterproofing materials executive*
Fleming, Martin *economist, strategist*
Ford, William E. *investment company executive*
Fuller, Theodore *retired insurance executive*
Ganek, David Kent *investor*
Gelfman, Robert William *retired lawyer*
Genachowski, Julius *communications executive*
George, Cynthia Coulter *lawyer*
Gierer, Vincent A., Jr. *tobacco and wine holding company executive*
Goergen, Robert B. *consumer products company executive*
Gonzalez, Mario M. *librarian*
Grant, Ronald Alfred *psychiatrist, pastoral counselor, psychoanalyst*
Grossman, Sanford Jay *former economics professor, financial consultant*
Hanson, Janet Tiebout *investment company executive*
Hewitt, Dennis Edwin *financial executive*
Hoberman, Mary Ann *author*
Horton, Jared Churchill *retired diversified financial services company metal products executive*
Johnson, Herbert Michael *publisher*
Jones, Paul Tudor, II, *investment executive*
Kessler, Murray S. *consumer products company executive*
Kneeland, Michael J. *rental company executive*
Krauser, Robert Stanley *healthcare executive*
Kreiger, Bruce D. *lawyer*
Lampert, Edward S. (Eddie Lampert) *investment company executive*
Landau, Jon *music producer, manager*
Lanning, Christopher Glenn *lawyer*
Lederman, Ira Seth *insurance company executive, lawyer*
Lynch, William Redington *retired lawyer*
Macaulay, William Edward *financial executive*
Mandel, Stephen, Jr. *investment company executive*
Mango, Wilfred Gilbert, Jr. *construction, real estate company executive*
Matthaei, Gay Humphrey *interior designer*
Moffly, John Wesley, IV, *magazine publishing executive*
Moore, John Plunkett Dennis *publisher*
More, Douglas McLochlan *lawyer*
Nemser, Earl Harold *lawyer*
Nevin, Crocker *investment banker*
Nimetz, Matthew *lawyer, investment company executive*
Owens, Bill (William Forrester Owens) *investment company executive, former governor*
Pascarella, Henry William *lawyer*
Paul, Roland Arthur *lawyer*
Paulson, Paul Joseph *advertising executive*
Perless, Ellen *advertising executive*
Rudy, Kathleen Vermeulen *small business owner*
Schneider, John Arnold *investor*
Schoonmaker, Samuel Vail III *lawyer*
Schwed, Roger E. *lawyer, rental company executive*
Scott, Mariette A. *marketing executive*
Selby, Leland Clay *lawyer*
Sexton, David Farrington *lawyer, bank executive*
Shimchick, Marie *music educator*
Smith, Rodger Field *financial executive*
Srere, Benson M(ortimer) *communications executive, consultant*
Stauffer, Valerie Vilas *civic volunteer*
Sternberg, Betty J. *school system administrator*
Stockman, David Alan *investment banker, former congressman*
Storms, Clifford Beekman *lawyer*
Tarantino, Dominic A. *retired professional services firm executive*
Tournillon, Nicholas Brady *investment company executive*
Urstadt, Charles J. *real estate company officer*
von Braun, Peter Carl Moore Stewart *finance company executive*
Wallach, Magdalena Falkenberg (Carla Wallach) *writer*
Welling, Kathryn Marie *editor*
Welt, Philip Stanley *lawyer, consultant*
Wharton, Bernard Mapes *architect*
Wiener, Malcolm Hewitt *historian, writer*
Winkler, Charles Howard *investment company executive*
Wyman, Ralph Mark *multifamily office firm executive*

Groton
English, James Fairfield, Jr. *former college president*
Firebaugh, Millard S. *naval engineer*
Galbraith, Marian *elementary school educator*
Kennedy, Evelyn Siefert *foundation executive, textiles executive*
Leeds, Robin Leigh *transportation executive*
Stoddard, Patrick Clare *retired military systems consultant, computer engineer*
Swindell, Archie Calhoun, Jr. *statistician, consultant*
Wager, Carrie Brockway *chemist, researcher*

Guilford
Britt, David Van Buren *retired educational communications executive*
Chatt-Ellis, Allen Barrett *psychologist, neuroscientist*
Colish, Marcia Lillian *history professor*
Hare, Peter Hewitt *philosophy educator*
Morgan, Leon Alford *retired utilities executive*
Pâquin, Trudy *gerontological nurse*
Pease, David Gordon *artist, educator*
Shelton, Darlene *psychologist, consultant*
Speth, James Gustave *dean, environmental studies educator, lawyer*

Hamden
Adair, Eleanor Reed *environmental biologist*
Brown, Jay Marshall *retired secondary school educator*
Dahl, Robert Alan *political science professor*
Forman, Charles William *religious studies educator*
He, Xiaohong *finance educator*
Ibbotson, Roger G. *financial educator*
Kagan, Donald *historian, educator*
Malherbe, Abraham Johannes *retired religious studies educator, writer*
Margulies, Martin B. *lawyer, educator*
McClellan, Edwin *literature educator*
Nuland, Sherwin *surgeon, writer*
Peterson, George Emanuel, Jr. *retired lawyer*
Reiser, Morton Francis *psychiatrist, educator*
Roche, (Eamonn) Kevin *architect*
Sheikh, Aamer *accounting educator*
Smith, David Martyn *retired forestry educator*
Weinstein, Stanley *Buddhist studies educator*

Hartford
Ahman, Arnold J. *pediatrician*
Alfano, Charles Thomas, Sr. *lawyer*
Amatuli, Robert Alexander *architect*
Anthony, Julian Danford, Jr. *lawyer*
Apruzzese, Philip John *educational association administrator, educator*
Ayer, Ramani *insurance company executive*
Berall, Frank Stewart *lawyer*
Bergenn, James Walter *lawyer*
Bertolini, Mark T. *insurance company executive*
Bieluch, William Charles *judge*
Blumberg, Phillip Irvin *law educator*
Blumenthal, Richard *state attorney general*
Bombara, Beth Ann *insurance company executive*
Bonee, John Leon III *lawyer*
Borden, David M. *state supreme court justice*
Bousbib, Ari *manufacturing executive*
Brennan, Troyen A. *insurance company executive, physician, educator, lawyer*
Bronzino, Joseph Daniel *electrical engineer*
Bryant, Vanessa Lynne *federal judge, lawyer*
Buck, Gurdon Hall *lawyer, urban planner, mediator*
Bucknall, William L., Jr. *human resources professional*
Butler, Gregory B. *lawyer, utilities executive*
Bysiewicz, Susan *state official*
Cain, George Harvey *lawyer, association administrator*
Campbell, Timothy R. *insurance company executive*
Carter, Annette Wheeler *state legislator*
Carter, David George, Sr. *academic administrator*
Carver, Stephen D. *publishing executive, former broadcast executive*
Casazza, William James *insurance company executive, lawyer*
Chedekel, Lisa *journalist*
Chênevert, Louis *manufacturing executive*
Cole, Solon Robert *pathologist, educator*
Coleman, George A. *school system administrator*
Coyle, Michael Lee *lawyer*
Curran, Ward Schenk *economist, educator*
Darnis, Geraud *manufacturing executive*
David, George Alfred Lawrence *manufacturing executive*
Davis, Andrew Neil *lawyer, educator*
Delgado, Joao *emergency physician, toxicologist*
Del Negro, John Thomas *lawyer*
deRaismes, Ann M. *insurance company executive, human resources specialist*
Doucette, John J. *manufacturing executive*
Droney, Christopher F. *judge*
Dupont, Antoinette Loiacono *judge*
Dworkin, Paul Howard *pediatrician*
Eshoo, Barbara Anne Rudolph *non-profit administrator*
Fahrbach, Ruth C. *state legislator*
Fedele, Michael Christian *lieutenant governor, computer company executive*
Finger, Stephen N. *aircraft manufacturing executive*
Fiszel, Geoffrey Lynn *investment banker, investment advisor*
Frost, James Arthur *former university president*
Gale, John Quentin *lawyer*
Geisler, James E. *corporate financial executive*
Geyer, James A *insurance company executive*
Giannaros, Demetrios Spiros *economist, educator, state representative*
Godfrey, Robert Douglas *lawyer*
Gould, Bruce Elliott *physician, medical educator, academic administrator*
Gunderson, Gerald Axel *economics professor*
Hammer, Alfred Emil *artist, educator*
Harden, Jon Bixby *publishing executive*
Hay, Leroy E. *school system administrator*
Hayes, Gregory J. *corporate financial executive*
Herzog, Brigitte *lawyer*
Jahiel, Rene Ino *physician*
Jepsen, George C. *state legislator, lawyer*
Johnson, David M. *insurance company executive*
Jones, James Fleming, Jr. *academic administrator, language educator*
Jung, Betty Chin *epidemiologist, educator, nurse*
Kaimowitz, Jeffrey Hugh *librarian*
Katz, Joette *state supreme court justice*
Kauffman, Matthew *journalist*
Kennedy, Jack Stanners *lawyer*
Killian, Robert Kenneth, Jr. *judge, lawyer*
Kirk, Darcy *law librarian, educator*
Klimek, Joseph John *physician, educator*
Knox, Thomas Isaac *cardiologist*
Kreczko, Alan James *lawyer, insurance company executive*
Leonhardt, Clifton Andrew *lawyer, public information officer*
Lloyd, Alex *lawyer*
Lotstein, James Irving *lawyer*
Louden, Wm. Bruce *lawyer*
Lyon, James Burroughs *lawyer*
Macaluso, Christie A. *bishop*
Mansell, Henry J. *archbishop*
Mardinly, Susan J. *musician, music educator*
Margulies, Beth Zeldes *state attorney general*
Markham, Ian Stephen *theology studies educator, dean*
Marra, Thomas M. *investment company executive*
Mattson, Ingrid *theology studies educator, religious organization administrator*
McHale, David R. *utilities executive*
McQuillan, Mark K. *school system administrator*
Merriam, Dwight Haines *lawyer, land use planner*
Mills, Corinne C. *music educator*
Moore-Beckham, Rosalind Elizabeth *retired social worker*
Mullane, Denis Francis *insurance company executive*
Mushinsky, Mary M. *state legislator*
Nappier, Denise L. *state official*
Newman, Jon O. *federal judge*
Noel, Don Obert, Jr. *retired editor, columnist*
Nolan, John Blanchard *lawyer*
Norcott, Flemming L., Jr. *state supreme court justice*
O'Donnell, Edward Francis, Jr. *lawyer*
Olivier, Leon J. *utilities executive*
Orth, Paul William *retired lawyer*
Pach, Peter Barnard *columnist, editor*
Page, Stephen Franklin *aerospace transportation executive*
Painter, Robert Lowell *surgeon, educator*
Palmer, Richard N. *state supreme court justice*
Peters, Ellen Ash *retired judge*
Pitkin, Howard F. *state agency administrator*
Price, Robert J. *insurance company executive*
Ramanan, Sundaram V. *internist, hematologist, oncologist*
Rell, M. Jodi *governor*
Reynolds, Scott Walton *academic administrator*
Rich, Tracy Leon *lawyer, insurance company executive*
Richter, Donald Paul *lawyer*

Rogers, Chase Theodora *state supreme court justice*
Ryan, David Thomas *lawyer*
Sargent, Joseph Denny *insurance executive*
Schaller, Barry R. *judge*
Scully, John Carroll *life insurance marketing research company executive*
See, Edmund M. *lawyer*
Shivery, Charles W. *utilities executive*
Silk, Mark Reuel *religious studies educator, writer*
Space, Theodore Maxwell *lawyer*
Squatrito, Dominic J. *judge*
Strasser, Kurt Albert *law educator, researcher, author, dean*
Sullivan, William J. *state supreme court justice*
Sussman, Mark Richard *lawyer*
Tancredi, James J. *lawyer*
Taylor, Allan Bert *lawyer*
Teutsch, Clifford L. *editor-in-chief*
Trachsel, William Henry *corporate lawyer*
Valentine, Debra A. *lawyer*
Vertefeuille, Christine Siegrist *state supreme court justice*
Vincensi, Avis A. *sales executive, medical educator*
Voigt, Richard *lawyer*
Wiggin, Kendall French *state librarian*
Wilde, Wilson *insurance company executive*
Williams, Ronald A. *health insurance company executive*
Winter, Miriam Therese (Gloria Frances Winter) *nun, religious studies educator*
Wolin, Neal Steven *lawyer*
Wright, Douglass Brownell *retired judge, lawyer*
Wright, Elease *insurance company executive*
Yardley, Bill *journalist*
Young, Roland Frederic III *lawyer*
Zarella, Peter T. *state supreme court justice*
Znamierowski, David M *insurance company executive*
Zubretsky, Joseph M. *insurance company executive*

Higganum
de Brigard, Emilie *anthropologist, consultant*

Ivoryton
Bendig, William Charles *editor, artist*
Osborne, John Walter *historian, educator, author*

Jewett City
Pucel, Robert Albin *electronics engineer, researcher*

Kensington
Harwin, S. Martin *pediatrician*
Murphy, Thomas John *publishing executive*

Kent
Friedman, Frances *public relations executive*

Lakeville
Estabrook, Robert Harley *journalist*
Jerome, John James *lawyer*
Jones, Ronald David *retired lawyer*
Lipton, Lester *ophthalmologist, entrepreneur*
Mattoon, Robert H., Jr., (Skip) *headmaster*

Lebanon
Brodie, Kevin Stuart *social studies educator*

Ledyard
Chiang, Albert Chinfa *polymer chemist*
Harwood, Harold James, Jr. *biochemist*
McGrattan, Mary K. *state legislator*

Litchfield
Booth, John Thomas *private investor*
Fiederowicz, Walter Michael *lawyer*
Fishman, Mitchell Steven *lawyer*
Kenagy, Robert Coffman *planning consulting company executive*
Kennedy, Susan Orpha *physical education educator, consultant, sports official*
Martin, R. Keith *business and information systems educator, consultant*
Mullins, Patty *artist*
Sherva, Dennis G. *retired investment company executive*

Lyme
Bessie, Simon Michael *publisher*
Bloom, Barry Malcolm *research and development company executive, consultant*

Madison
Clendenen, William Herbert, Jr. *lawyer*
Drought, James Henry *healthcare business owner, exercise physiologist*
Egbert, Emerson Charles *retired publisher*
Golembeski, Jerome John *manufacturing executive*
James, John Whitaker, Sr. *finance company executive*
Kay, Herbert *retired energy executive*
Kilbourne, Edwin Dennis *virologist, educator*
Snell, Richard Saxon *anatomist*
Stevenson, Robert Edwin *microbiologist, consultant*

Manchester
Daube, Jonathan Mahram *academic administrator*
Galasso, Francis Salvatore *materials scientist*
Scholsky, Martin Joseph *retired priest*

Mansfield Center
Petrus, Robert Thomas *internet business owner, investor*

Mashantucket
Yale, John Paul *computer systems developer*

Meriden
Curran, Louis Jerome, Jr. *choral master*
Horton, Paul Chester *psychiatrist*
Lee, Henry C. *forensic scientist*
Losada-Zarate, Gloria *psychologist*
Lowry, Houston Putnam *lawyer*
Shapiro, Philip Edwin *dermatologist, dermatopathologist, educator*
Tamburine, Jean Helen *sculptor, painter, illustrator*

Middlebury
Fickenscher, Gerald H. *chemicals company executive*
Phillips, Walter Mills III *psychologist, educator*

Middletown
Bohan, Lawrence Stewart *retired insurance company executive*
Bonin, John Paul *economics professor*
Buel, Richard Van Wyck, Jr. *retired history professor, editor, writer*
Ebrecht, Ronald *musician*
Ettre, Leslie Stephen *chemist*
Fusco, George Matthew *retired military officer, engineer*
Gillmor, Charles Stewart *historian, researcher, educator*
Janes, Norman K. *lawyer*
Linton, Fred Ernest Julius *mathematics professor, publishing executive*
Lovell, Michael C. *retired economics professor*
Meyer, Priscilla Ann *literature and language professor*
Miller, Richard Alan *retired economist, educator*
Pomper, Philip *historian, educator*
Reed, Joseph Wayne *American studies educator, artist*
Roth, Michael S. *academic administrator, art educator*
Scheibe, Karl Edward *psychology professor*
Schwarcz, Vera *historian, educator, poet*
Shapiro, Norman Richard *literature and language professor*
Slotkin, Richard Sidney *literature educator*
Starr, Francis *physics professor*
Turco, Alfred, Jr. *language educator*
Wasch, William Karl *gerontologist, consultant*
Wensinger, Arthur Stevens *literature and language professor, writer, translator*

Milford
Berchem, Robert Lee, Sr. *lawyer*
Boyer, Carolyn Merwin *school psychologist*
Bubencik, John William, II, *civil engineer, consultant, transportation engineer*
Curt, Denise Morris *painter, photographer*
DeLuca, Fred *food service executive*
Fagan, Alanna *artist, printmaker*
Foster, Patrick R. *historian, writer*
Gallop, Sophronia Langston *elementary school educator*
Henderson, Albert Kossack *publishing and food products executive, consultant*
Hogan, John W., Jr. *lawyer*
Krall, Vita *psychologist*
Muth, Eric Peter *optician, consultant*
Palazzi, Joseph Lazarro *manufacturing executive*
Scaniffe, Joseph Albert *anesthesiologist, consultant*
Schwartz, Richard Edward Derecktor *retired sociologist, educator*

Monroe
Lindskog, David Richard *lawyer*
Oliver, Milton McKinnon *lawyer, translator*

Moodus
Cumming, Robert Emil *editor, writer*

Mystic
Ballard, Robert Duane *marine geologist*
Burrow, Gerard Noel *internist, educator*
Nolf, David M. *financial consultant*
Rooney, Maria Dewing *photographer*
Thompson, Robert Allan *aerospace engineer*

Naugatuck
Flannery, Joseph Patrick *manufacturing executive, director*
Mannweiler, Mary-Elizabeth *painter*
Suscovich, David J. *neuropsychologist, marriage and family therapist*

New Britain
Beatt, Bruce H. *lawyer, metal products executive*
Biskupski, Mieczyslaw Boleslaw *historian, writer*
Chasse, Emily Schuder *librarian, educator*
Emeagwali, Gloria Thomas *humanities educator*
Leeds, Barry Howard *literature and language professor*
Loree, James M. *consumer products company executive*
Lundgren, John F. *consumer products company executive*
Margiotta, Mary-Lou Ann *application developer*
McGowan, Jeffrey *mathematician, educator*
Meskill, Thomas J. *federal judge*
Mooney, Kenneth Frank *design educator*
Murphy, Christopher S. *congressman, former state senator*
O'Connell, Brian Michael *computer scientist, educator*
Petit, William Arthur, Jr. *endocrinologist*
Shen, Xiaoping *geography educator*
Stathos, Lifteria K. *retired educational association administrator*

New Canaan
Ackerman, Sigurd Howard *psychiatrist*
Allen, Joseph Henry *retired publishing company executive*
Bisbee, Gerald Elftman, Jr. *investment company executive*
Burns, Ivan Alfred *grocery products and industrial company executive*
Burns, John Joseph, Jr. *financial and insurance holding company executive*
Cohen, Richard Norman *insurance executive*
Coughlin, Francis Raymond, Jr. *surgeon, educator, lawyer*
Crossman, William Whittard *retired wire cable and communications executive*
Dean, Robert Bruce *architect*
Despres, Louise Fay *secondary school educator*
Ferro, Guy (Gaetano Ferro) *lawyer*
Fredericks, Jeanne Maria Judson *literary agent*
Grace, Julianne Alice *retired investment company executive*
Kamerschen, Robert Jerome *retired business executive, private investor, consultant*
Kovatch, Jak Gene *artist*
MacEwan, Nigel Savage *retired merchant banker*
McKeough, Susan Anne *elementary school educator*
Means, David Hammond *retired advertising executive*
Papp, Laszlo George *retired architect*
Pike, William Edward *retired investment company executive*
Resor, Stanley Rogers *retired lawyer*
Richards, Glenora *artist*
Risom, Jens *furniture designer, consultant, manufacturing executive*
Sachs, John Peter *carbon company executive*
Stadther, Michael Jon *entrepreneur, writer, publisher*
Steinmetz, Richard Bird, Jr. *lawyer*
Ward, Richard Vance, Jr. *management consultant*
Wolff, Sanford Irving *lawyer*
Ylvisaker, James William *insurance executive*

New Fairfield
Price, Richard Galen *sound recording engineer, music producer, conductor*

New Haven
Abdelsayed, Wafeek Hakim *accounting educator*
Abramson, Arthur Seymour *linguistics educator, researcher*
Ackerman, Bruce Arnold *law educator*
Adair, Robert Kemp *physicist, educator*
Alexander, Bruce Donald *real estate executive, educator*
Alpern, Robert J. *dean, medical educator*
Altman, Sidney *biology professor*
Anderson, Carl Albert *fraternal organization administrator, lawyer, dean*
Anderson, John Fredric *science administrator, entomologist, researcher*
Andrews, Donald Wilfrid Kao *economics professor*
Applegate, Debby *biographer*
Ariyan, Stephan *plastic surgeon*
Armbruster, Paula *social worker, director, child mental health educator*
Aronson, Peter Samuel *physiologist, researcher*
Arterton, Janet Bond *federal judge*
Askenase, Philip William *medicine and pathology educator*
Bailey, William Harrison *artist, educator*
Bakhos, Charles Tanos *surgeon*
Balay, Robert Elmore *editor, librarian*
Baltay, Charles *physicist, educator*
Baltimore, Robert Samuel *pediatrician, epidemiologist*
Barash, Paul George *anesthesiologist, educator*
Bartoshuk, Linda M. *otolaryngologist, educator*
Behar, Kevin L. *neuroscientist*
Behling, Paul Lawrence *lawyer, educator*
Behrman, Harold Richard *endocrinologist, physiologist, educator*
Bell, Wendell *sociologist, educator, futurist*
Benfer, David William *hospital administrator*
Benson, Richard *dean, photographer*
Berdon, Robert Irwin *judge*
Berke, Brett Alan *neuroscientist, research scientist*
Berland, Gretchen K. *medical educator, filmmaker*
Berson, Jerome Abraham *chemistry professor*
Birnbaum, Irwin Morton *educational consultant, lawyer*
Blatt, Sidney Jules *psychology professor, psychoanalyst, investigator*
Bloom, Harold *humanities educator, writer*
Bloomer, Kent Cress *architecture educator*
Bloomgarden, Gary Michael *neurosurgeon*
Blum, John Morton *historian, educator*
Borroff, Marie *English language educator*
Boyer, James Lorenzen *internist, educator*
Bracken, Paul *political science professor*
Brand, Myles *sports association and former academic administrator*
Braverman, Irwin Merton *dermatologist, educator*
Brenzel, Jeffrey *dean*
Bresnick, Martin *composer, educator*
Briggs, Derek Ernest Gilmor *science educator*
Brill, Steven *magazine editor*
Brilmayer, R. Lea *lawyer, educator*
Brooks, Peter (Preston) *literature educator, department chairman, writer*
Brown, Thomas Huntington *neuroscientist*
Brownell, Kelly David *psychologist, educator*
Brudvig, Gary W. *chemistry professor*
Bundy, James Abbott *performing company executive*
Burt, Robert Amsterdam *lawyer, educator*
Bynum, Terrell Ward *humanities educator, consultant*
Cabranes, José Alberto *judge*
Calabresi, Guido *federal judge, educator*
Carty, Paul Vernon *lawyer*
Casten, Richard Francis *physicist, educator*
Cha, Charles *surgical oncologist, hepatobiliary surgeon*
Chevalier, Judith A. *economics professor, finance professor*
Chilton, William David *architect*
Chupka, William Andrew *chemical physicist, educator*
Cleary, Paul David *sociomedical educator*
Coe, Michael Douglas *retired anthropologist*
Cohen, Lawrence Sorel *internist, educator*
Coifman, Ronald R. *mathematician, educator*
Collier, David Beebe *lawyer, consultant*
Collins, William F., Jr. *neurosurgery educator*
Comer, James Pierpont *psychiatrist, educator*
Conklin, Harold Colyer *anthropologist, educator*
Crakes, Gary Michael *economics professor*
Cullen, Mark Richard *medical educator*
Curran, Lisa M. *environmental scientist, educator*
Daly, Radley Hutchinson *retired academic administrator*
Danaher, John Anthony III *prosecutor*
Davey, Lycurgus Michael *neurosurgeon*
Days, Drew S. III *lawyer, educator*
De Camilli, Pietro V. *cell biologist*
Degutis, Linda Christine *adult education educator, epidemiologist, researcher*
DeMille, David P. *physics professor*
De Rose, Sandra Michele *psychotherapist, educator, administrator*
Donoghue, Michael John *biologist, educator*
Donohue, John Joseph *law educator*
Dorsey, Peter Collins *federal judge*
DuBois, Arthur Brooks *physiologist, educator*
Duke, Steven Barry *law educator*
Dyson, William R. *state legislator, educator*
Ehrenkranz, Richard Allan *pediatrician*
Elimelech, Menachem *environmental and chemical engineering educator*
Ellickson, Robert Chester *law educator*
Ember, Carol R. *anthropology educator, writer*
Ember, Melvin Lawrence *anthropologist, educator*
Engelman, Donald Max *molecular biophysics and biochemistry educator*
Erikson, Kai *sociologist, educator*
Errington, James Joseph *anthropology educator*
Eskridge, William Nichol, Jr. *law educator*
Esty, Daniel Cushing *lawyer, educator*
Evenson, Robert Eugene *economist, educator*
Falco, Thomas Gilbert *historian, researcher*
Fassler, Margot Elsbeth *music educator, religious studies educator*
Feigenbaum, Joan *computer scientist, mathematician*
Feinstein, Rochelle *artist, educator*
Feldman, Grace A. *music educator*
Ferholt, J. Deborah Lott *pediatrician*
Fikrig, Erol *rheumatologist, medical educator*
Fischer, Michael John *computer science educator*
Fishman, Mark I. *lawyer*
Fiss, Owen M. *law educator*
Forget, Bernard G. *hematologist, educator*
Foster, Roger Sherman, Jr. *surgeon, educator, health facility administrator*
Frank, Roberta *literature educator*
Freed, Daniel Josef *law educator*
Friedlaender, Gary Elliott *orthopedist, educator*
Fuchs, Elinor *film critic, playwright, educator*
Gallant, Brad (Keith Bradoc Gallant) *lawyer*
Galston, Arthur William *biology professor*
Garen, Alan *biophysicist, educator*
Garten, Jeffrey E. *finance educator*
Gastwirth, Donald Edward *lawyer, literary agent*
Genel, Myron *pediatrician, educator*
Gewirtz, Paul D. *lawyer, educator*
Gilbert, Creighton Eddy *art historian*
Gildea, Brian Michael *lawyer*
Girvin, Steven Mark *physicist, researcher*
Goffart, Walter André *history professor*
Goldstein, Daniel Robert *cardiologist*
Gonzalez, Caleb *ophthalmologist, educator*
Goodrich, Isaac *neurosurgeon, educator*
Graetz, Michael J. *law educator*
Grausman, Philip *sculptor*
Green, Donald Philip *political scientist, educator*
Greene, Liliane *literature and language educator, editor*
Greenfield, James Robert *lawyer*
Grey, Margaret *nursing educator*
Gross, Ian *academic pediatrician, neonatologist*
Hallo, William Wolfgang *literature and language professor, writer*
Hansmann, Henry Baethke *law educator*
Harries, Karsten *philosophy educator, researcher*
Harrison, Henry Starin *real estate appraiser, educator, entrepreneur*
Hayden, Dolores *author, architecture educator*
Hebert, Steven C. *medical educator*
Heninger, George Robert *psychology professor, researcher*
Hennah, Vivian Lisa *school system administrator*
Hersey, George Leonard *retired art historian*
Hickey, Leo Joseph *museum curator, educator*
Hollander, John *humanities educator, poet*
Horwich, Arthur L. *medical educator*
Hostetter, Margaret K. *pediatrician, medical educator*
Howe, Roger Evans *mathematician, educator*
Huwiler, Joan P. *public relations executive, consultant*
Hyman, Paula E(llen) *history professor*
Insler, Stanley *philologist, educator*
Jacob, Deirdre Ann Bradbury *manufacturing executive, finance educator, consultant*
Jaisi, Deb P. *geologist, researcher*
Jatlow, Peter I. *pathologist, medical educator, researcher*
Johnson, Lester Fredrick *artist*
Johnstone, Quintin *law educator*
Jolls, Christine Margaret *law educator*
Jorgensen, William L. *chemistry educator*
Kalyanpur, Arjun *radiologist*
Kaplan, Edward H. *operations research specialist*
Kashgarian, Michael *pathologist, educator*
Kauffman, Stephen Blair *law librarian, educator*
Kevles, Daniel Jerome *historian, educator, writer*
Khoshnood, Kaveh *epidemiologist, educator*
Kim, Tae Hoon *biology professor*
King, Robert Alan *psychiatrist, educator*
Kirshbaum, Daniel Joseph *researcher*
Koh, Harold Hongju *dean, law educator*
Korchagin, Vladimir *astrophysicist*
Korenaga, Jun *geophysicist, educator*
Krauss, Judith Belliveau *nursing educator*

Kronman, Anthony Townsend *dean, law educator*
Krumholz, Harlen Marc *cardiologist, internist, educator*
Kushlan, Samuel Daniel *internist, educator, hospital administrator*
Lamar, Howard Roberts *academic administrator, historian*
Langbein, John Harriss *lawyer, educator*
LaPalombara, Joseph *political science educator, industrial management educator*
Leckman, James Frederick *psychiatry and pediatrics educator*
Leeney, Robert Joseph *newspaper editor*
Leffell, David Joel *dermatologist, surgeon, writer, photographer, medical school administrator, educator*
Lehman, Robert Wylie *music educator*
Lentz, Thomas Lawrence *biomedical educator, dean, researcher*
Leo, Martha E. *advocate, counselor*
Lesser, Robert Lewis *ophthalmologist*
Levin, Rick (Richard Charles Levin) *academic administrator, economist*
Levine, Robert John *internist, medical educator, ethicist*
Lifton, Richard P. *medical educator, researcher*
Lindroth, Linda (Linda Hammer) *artist, writer, curator*
Longo, Walter E. *colon and rectal surgeon, educator, director*
Lopez, Javier *psychiatrist*
Lord, Ruth *retired researcher, philanthropist, writer*
Lorimer, Linda Koch *university educator*
Lytton, Bernard *urology educator*
Macey, Jonathan R. *law educator*
Manley, Lawrence G. *literature educator*
Marchesi, Vincent Thomas *biochemist, educator*
Marcus, Edward Leonard *lawyer, political organization worker*
Marcus, Ruth Barcan *philosopher, educator, writer, lecturer*
Margulis, Gregory A. *mathematics and science professor, researcher*
Marks, Lawrence Edward *psychologist, educator*
Marmor, Theodore Richard *political science professor, writer*
Massey, William S. *mathematician, educator*
Mayhew, David Raymond *political science professor*
Mazzotta, Giuseppe Francesco *literature and language professor*
McClain, Brenda C. *pain management physician*
McCorkle, Ruth *oncological nurse, educator, researcher*
McGuire, William James *psychologist, educator*
McNamara, Julia Mary *academic administrator, foreign language educator*
Meyers, Amy *museum director*
Miller, I. George *physician, educator, researcher*
Mineur, Yann Sébastien *neuroscientist*
Mostaghimi, Mehdi *economist, educator*
Mostow, George Daniel *mathematics professor*
Mukherjee, Sandip Kumar *cardiologist*
Musto, David Franklin *medical researcher, educator, historian, consultant*
Narendra, Kumpati Subrahmanya *electrical engineer, educator*
Newick, Craig David *architect*
Nolan, Victoria *theater director*
Norbeck, Timothy Burns *medical association executive*
Novick, Peter J. *cell biologist, educator*
O'Connor, Kevin James *prosecutor, lawyer*
Okerson, Ann Shumelda Lillian *librarian*
Pagani, Mark *education educator, researcher*
Parker, Peter D.M. *physicist, educator, researcher*
Patterson, Peyton R. *bank executive*
Pelli, Cesar *architect*
Persing, John Arthur *surgeon*
Peterson, Linda H. *English language educator*
Phillips, Caryl *writer*
Phillips, Peter Charles Bonest *economist, educator, researcher*
Podolny, Joel M. *dean, management educator*
Pollard, Thomas Dean *cell biologist, educator*
Pollitt, Jerome Jordan *art historian, educator*
Pospisil, Leopold Jaroslav *anthropologist, law educator*
Post, Robert Charles *law educator*
Powsner, Seth M. *psychiatrist, educator*
Priest, George L. *law educator*
Prochaska, Alice *historian, librarian*
Prout, William H., Jr. *lawyer*
Prown, Jules David *art historian, educator*
Quinn, Ian *music educator*
Ramirez, Ainissa *materials scientist*
Randell, Linda L. *utilities executive, lawyer*
Ranis, Gustav *economist, educator*
Rawson, Claude Julien *literature and language professor*
Redmond, Donald Eugene, Jr. *neuroscientist, educator*
Reed, Mark Arthur *research scientist, educator*
Reisman, William Michael *lawyer, educator*
Robinson, Dorothy K. *lawyer*
Robinson, Fred Colson *language educator*
Roemer, John E. *economics educator*
Romano, Roberta *law educator*
Rose, Aron D. *ophthalmologist, educator*
Rose-Ackerman, Susan *law and political economy educator*
Rosenbluth, Frances McCall *political scientist, educator*
Roth, Harold *architect*
Russett, Bruce Martin *political science professor*
Sandweiss, Jack *physicist, researcher*
Sartorelli, Alan Clayton *pharmacologist, educator*
Sasaki, Clarence Takashi *surgeon, educator*
Saunders, Martin *chemistry educator, researcher*
Schlessinger, Joseph *pharmacology educator*
Schloss, Irving Steven *lawyer*
Schneider, David Walter *lawyer*
Schottenfeld, Richard Steven *psychiatrist*
Schowalter, John Erwin *child and adolescent psychiatry educator*
Schuck, Peter Horner *lawyer, educator*
Schultz, T. Paul *economics professor*
Scully, Vincent Joseph, Jr. *architectural historian, educator, writer*
Seashore, Margretta Reed *physician, educator*
Shapiro, Eugene David *pediatrician, epidemiologist, educator*
Shaywitz, Bennett Arthur *medical educator*
Shepherd, Gordon Murray *neuroscientist, educator*
Shiller, Robert James *economist, educator*
Shore, Marci *historian*
Shubik, Martin *economics professor*
Shulman, Gerald I. *physician, scientist, endocrinologist, educator*
Shulman, Robert Gerson *biophysics professor*
Silberschatz, Abraham (Avi Silberschatz) *computer scientist, educator, researcher*
Singer, Jon Douglas *foundation administrator, writer*
Skowronek, Stephen Lee *political scientist, educator*
Smith, Brian Richard *hematologist, oncologist, pathologist*
Smith, John Edwin *philosophy educator*
Snowden, III, Frank Martin *history professor*
Sommer, Miriam Goldstein (Mimi G. Sommer) *writer, photographer*
Sonnenfeld, Jeffrey Alan *management educator*
Sorkin, Jenni *curator, critic*
Spence, Barbara E. *former publishing company executive*
Spence, Jonathan Dermot *historian, educator*
Spencer, Dennis Dee *medical educator, director*
Stahl, Nanette *librarian, biblicist*
Stahl, Richard Sheldon *surgeon*
Stapleton, James Francis *lawyer*
Stern, Robert *psychiatrist*
Stevens, Joseph Charles *psychology professor*
Stiber, Julie Anne *social worker*
Stith-Cabranes, Kate *law educator*
Stuehrenberg, Paul Frederick *librarian*
Sullivan, Shaun Stuart *lawyer*
Summers, William Cofield *science educator*
Sykes, Gwendolyn *academic administrator, former federal agency administrator*
Tirro, Frank Pascale *music educator, composer, writer*
Trumble, Angus A. G. *curator, writer*
Tsai, James C. *ophthalmologist, researcher*
Tully, John Charles *research chemical physicist*
Turner, Frank Miller *historian, educator*
Underdown, David Edward *historian, educator*
Van Cleve, Libby (Elizabeth W. Van Cleve) *music educator, writer*
Venclova, Tomas A. *literature and language professor, writer*
Volkmar, Fred Robert *psychiatrist, educator, director*
Waggoner, Paul Edward *agricultural scientist*
Wagner, Allan Ray *psychology professor*
Wagoner, Walter Dray, Jr. *lawyer*
Walker, John Mercer, Jr. *federal judge*
Wandycz, Piotr Stefan *historian, educator*
Warshaw, Marvin D. *conductor, educator, musician*
Waxman, Stephen George *neurologist, neuroscientist*
Weidhaas, Joanne Barnes *medical educator*
Weiss, Robert M. *urologist, educator*
Winroth, Anders *historian, educator*
Winter, Ralph Karl, Jr. *federal judge*
Wolf, Werner Paul *physicist, researcher*
Wolterstorff, Nicholas Paul *philosophical theology educator*
Wynn, Karen *psychologist, educator, researcher*
Yeargan, Michael *scenic designer*
Yeazell, Ruth Bernard *English language educator*
Zaret, Barry Lewis *cardiologist, medical educator*
Zedillo Ponce de León, Ernesto *former president of Mexico*
Zelitch, Israel *retired scientist*
Zeller, Michael Edward *physicist, researcher*
Zhang, Yawei *epidemiologist*
Zigler, Edward Frank *psychologist, educator*
Zuckerman, Gregg J. *mathematics professor*

New London
Asselin-Connolly, John Thomas *lawyer*
Bald, Ronald James *military officer*
Carpenter, Bruce William *information technology manager, director*
Clarke, Florence Dorothy *minister, educator*
Fainstein, Norman *sociology professor, former academic administrator*
Higdon, Leo Ignatius, Jr., (Lee) *academic administrator*
Johnstone, Philip MacLaren *lawyer*
Morgan, John Richard *writer, publishing executive*
Partnoy, Ronald Allen *lawyer*
Reardon, Robert Ignatius, Jr. *lawyer*
Ringel, Faye Joyce *literature educator*
Schoenberger, Steven Harris *physician, research consultant*
Tassinari, Melissa Sherman *teratologist, developmental toxicologist*
Urbanetti, John Sutherland *internist, consultant*
Van Sice, James *career military officer, academic administrator*

New Milford
Fabricand, Burton Paul *physicist, researcher*
Mullen, John E. *orthopedist, surgeon*

New Preston
Grizzard, George *actor*

Newington
Anderson, Kathryn Parks *music educator*
Chiarenza, Frank John *language educator*
Cohen, Fern K. *music educator*
Peterson, Mary Elizabeth Dreisbach *mechanical engineer*
Sumner, David George *trade association administrator*

Newtown
Babbitt, Martha E. *science educator*
Cole, Richard John *marketing executive*
Cottingham, Robert *artist*
Forger, Robert Durkin *retired professional association administrator*
Goodwick, David Lee *retired advertising executive*
Johnstone, Gregg Martin *communications executive*

Niantic
Butler, Jonathan Putnam *architect*
Danos, Harry John *architect, educator, artist*
Deakyne, William John *library director, musician*
Douglas, Robert Gordon, Jr. *physician*
Hunt, Francis Howard *retired navy laboratory official*
Roman, José Luis *nursing administrator*

Norfolk
Jessup, Philip Caryl, Jr. *retired lawyer*
Mermann, Alan Cameron *retired pediatric educator, chaplain*

North Branford
Gasparine, Barbara Ellen *elementary school educator*
Houghton, Alan Nourse *educational association administrator, consultant*
Ingram, George *manufacturing executive*
Logan, John Arthur, Jr. *retired foundation executive*
Mead, Lawrence Myers, Jr. *retired engineering executive*

North Canton
Swibold, Gretchen Ann *librarian, writer*

North Haven
Fuggi, Gretchen Miller *education educator*
Glaser, Gilbert Herbert *retired neuroscientist, educator*
Herzenberg, Arvid *physicist, researcher*
Hudson, Richard L. *retired adult education educator, minister*
Morrissey, Charles Richard, Sr. *retired elementary school educator*
Westerfield, Carolyn Elizabeth Hess *urban planner*

North Stonington
Keane, John Patrick *retired secondary school educator*
Svengalis, Kendall Frayne *law librarian, educator, publishing executive, writer*

Northford
Gregan, Edmund Robert *landscape architect*
James, William Hall *former state official, educator*

Norwalk
Alvey, Brian *blogger*
Baylis, Robert Montague *investment banker*
Bays, John Theophanis *consulting engineer*
Boyd, Jeffery Hawthorne *travel company executive, lawyer*
Brown, William Terrel *psychology professor, educational consultant*
Burton, David K. *lawyer*
Cammaker, Sheldon Ira *lawyer*
Carius, Michael Lee *emergency medicine physician*
Carlucci, David R. *information technology executive*
DeCesare, Donald E. *broadcast executive*
Eagan, Sherman G. *producer, communications executive*
Falsone, Jack Joseph *physician*
Gold, Richard N. *management consultant*
Greene, Karen Sandra *actress, educator, singer*
Guzzi, Anthony J. *construction executive*
Harris, Holton Edwin *plastics machinery manufacturing executive*
Hathaway, Carl Emil *investment company executive*
Jacobs, Mark Randolph *lawyer*
Johnson, Robert James *psychology educator*
Knopp, Alex *lawyer, mayor*
MacInnis, Frank T. *construction and holding company executive, securities trader*
Nightingale, William Joslyn *management consultant*
Perry, Charles Owen *sculptor*
Piper, Thomas Laurence III *banker*
Raikes, Charles FitzGerald *retired lawyer*
Rosado, Rodolfo Jose *psychologist, educator*
Smith, Gordon Eugene *pilot*
Soper, Jeannine *real estate agent*
Walker, Kellye L. *lawyer*
White, Tony L. *health and medical products executive*
Yeosock, Michael Michael *funeral director, civil engineer*

Norwich
Cote, Michael Richard *bishop*
Hart, Daniel Anthony *bishop*
Pudlo, Steven Edward *computer technician*

Oakville
Carroll, Constance Marie *pianist, music educator*

Old Greenwich
Allen, Jefferson F. *oil industry executive*
DeOrchis, Frankie Juanita *forester, writer*
Dixon, John Morris *magazine editor*
Gayda, Michael D. *lawyer*
Lorefice, Laurence Santo *psychiatrist*
McClelland, Kate *librarian*

Old Lyme
Comfort, William Wistar *mathematics professor*
Doersam, Charles Henry, Jr. *engineer, educator, entrepreneur, writer*
Fairfield-Sonn, James Willed *management educator, consultant*
Johnson, James Myron *psychologist, educator*
Mangin, Charles-Henri *electronics company executive*
Osborne, Judith Barbour *artist*
Willauer, George Jacob *English literature educator*

Old Saybrook
Neal, Irene Collins *artist, educator*
Norcia, Stephen William *advertising executive*
Phillips, William E. *advertising agency executive*
Purcell, Bradford Moore *publishing company executive*
Smith, David Clark *research scientist*

Orange
Davies, Richard Warren *lawyer*
Davis, David Brion *historian, educator*
Lobay, Ivan *mechanical engineering educator*
Powers, Timothy H. *electric power industry executive*

Oxford
Marano, Richard Michael *judge*

Pawcatuck
Gnanaraj, Joseph Sathiya *scientist*

Plainville
Chase, Peter *library director*
Glassman, Gerald Seymour *metal products executive*
Perkins-Banas, Melissa Veronica *neuropsychologist*

Pleasant Valley
Decker, Robert Owen *history professor, clergyman*

Pomfret
Chase, Thomas Stanhope *language educator, department chairman*

Portland
Nocek, Janet *library director*

Prospect
Powell, Raymond William *financial planner, school administrator*

Putnam
Ames, Sandra Cutler *secondary school educator*
Day, John Anthony, Jr. *pulmonologist*
Desaulniers, Rene Gerard Lesieur *retired optometrist*

Quaker Hill
Hasse, Wilma Hahn *retired English professor*

Redding
Addison, Jason Lawrence *multifamily community development executive*
Begell, William *publisher*
Benyei, Candace Reed *psychotherapist*
Gooch, Anthony Cushing *retired lawyer*
Kobak, James Benedict *management consultant*
Poulos, Christopher *literature and language educator*
Quinn, Andrew Peter, Jr. *lawyer, retired insurance company executive*
Welsh, John Francis *retired advertising executive*

Ridgefield
Brewster, Carroll Worcester *former academic administrator*
Burridge, Robert *former mathematics educator, scientific advisor*
Dussan V., Elizabeth B. *scientific adviser*
Egan, Kenneth J. *dermatologist*
Grinberg, Nelu *chemist*
Levine, Paul Michael *paper company executive, consultant*
Lindsay, Dianna Marie *educational administrator*
Lodewick, Philip Hughes *equipment leasing company executive*
McConnell, John Edward *retired electrical engineering company executive*
Mesznik, Joel R. *investment banker*
Taylor, Edwin R. *music director*
Wiegley, Roger Douglas *lawyer*

Riverside
Coulson, Robert *retired professional society administrator, arbitrator, writer*
Deering, Allan Brooks *retired soft drink company executive*
Geismar, Richard Lee *communications executive*
McSpadden, Peter Ford *retired advertising agency executive*
Powers, Claudia McKenna *state legislator*
Schur, Jeffrey *advertising executive*

Rocky Hill
Chu, Hsien-Kun *chemist, researcher*
Mandell, Joel *lawyer*
Wilson, Karen Lynn *esthetician*

Roxbury
Friedman, John Maxwell, Jr. *lawyer*
Gurney, Albert Ramsdell *playwright, educator*
Styron, Rose *human rights activist, poet, journalist*

Salisbury
Block, Zenas *retired management consultant, educator*
Dresser, James van Benschoten *retired management consultant*
Kilner, Ursula Blanche *genealogist, educator, writer*

Sandy Hook
Rosenblatt, Stephen Paul *marketing and sales promotion company executive*

Sharon
Gordon, Nicholas *broadcast and performing arts executive*
Johns, Jasper *artist*
Learsy, Raymond J. *private investor*
Lisle, Laurie *author*
Mesniaeff, Gregory *economist, securities analyst*

Shelton
Kantrowitz, Jonathan Daniel *publishing executive, educator, lawyer*

Sherman
Cowley, Robert William *editor, writer, consultant, lecturer*

Simsbury
Berberich, Patricia Louise *librarian*
Borges, Francisco Lopes *venture capitalist*
Long, Michael Thomas *lawyer, manufacturing executive*
Roberts, Celia Ann *librarian*
Yagudin, Alexei *Olympic athlete, ice skater*

Somers
Blake, Stewart Prestley *retired ice cream company executive*

South Glastonbury
Schroth, Peter William *lawyer, management, educator*

South Kent
Baker, John Milnes *architect*
Keehner, Michael Arthur Miller *investment banking executive*
Samartini, James Rogers *retired appliance company executive*

South Windsor
Baretta, Marsha Motyl *elementary school physical education educator*
Carman, Gary Olen *child welfare consultant*
Famiglietti, Nancy Zima *computer company executive*
Hobbs, David Ellis *mechanical engineer*
Plummer, Daria Marie *elementary school educator*
van Dokkum, Jan *electric power industry executive*

Southbury
Atwood, Edward Charles *economist, educator*
Bergen, Polly *actress*
Bowen, Christopher Edward *researcher, director*
Caravatt, Paul Joseph, Jr. *communications executive*
Foxworth, Johnnie Hunter *retired state agency administrator*
Hopf, Frank Rudolph *retired dentist*
Rorick, William Calvin *retired librarian, portrait artist*
Russell, Allan David *lawyer*
Welton, Sharon Marie *food service executive*

Southington
Byeff, Peter David *hematologist, oncologist*

Southport
Ambrosino, Ralph Thomas, Jr. *retired telecommunications executive*
Damson, Barrie Morton *oil and gas exploration company executive*
Sanetti, Stephen Louis *lawyer*
Twiname, John Dean *minister, human services administrator*
Wheeler, Wilmot Fitch, Jr. *diversified manufacturing company executive*
Wilbur, E. Packer *investment company executive*

Stafford
Klatell, Robert Edward *retired electronics executive, lawyer*

Stamford
Allott, Anthony J. *packaging industry executive*
Babson, Jane Frances *artist, writer*
Bainton, J(ohn) Joseph *lawyer*
Barker, James Rex *water transportation executive, director*
Barreca, Christopher Anthony *lawyer*
Bennett, Carl *retired discount department store executive*
Bostin, Marvin Jay *hospital and health services consultant*
Britt, Glenn Alan *media company executive*
Burns, Ursula M. *printing company executive*
Burston, Richard Mervin *marketing executive*
Burton, Robert Gene *printing company executive*
Buzzard, James A. *paper, packaging and chemical company executive*
Cacace, Michael Joseph *lawyer*
Caldwell, Philip *retired automobile manufacturing and finance company executive*
Carter, Jerome N. *human resources specialist, paper company executive*
Cassidy, Denis Andrew *artist, architect*
Chang, Ted T. *chemist*
Chickering, Howard Allen *insurance company executive, lawyer*
Cohen, Steven A. *investment company executive*
Colthup, Norman Bertram *retired spectroscopist*
Cook, Colin Burford *psychiatrist*
Critelli, Michael J. *manufacturing executive, lawyer*
Cutler, Kenneth B., Jr. *dermatologist, educator*
Dammerman, Dennis Dean *diversified technology and services company executive*
Daniels, Daniel Lloyd *lawyer*
Dell, Warren Frank, II, *management consultant*
Della Rocco, Kenneth Anthony *lawyer*
Dennies, Sandra Lee *city official*
Dodd, Meghan P. *mathematics educator*
Dolan, Thomas J. *printing company executive*
duPont, Augustus Irénée *lawyer*
Engel, Gerald L. *engineering educator*
Erichson, Robert B. *hematologist, oncologist*
Evans, Robert Sheldon *manufacturing executive, director*
Faraci, John Vincent, Jr. *paper company executive*
Fast, Eric Carson *manufacturing executive*
Fein, Ronnie *journalist, writer*
Firestone, James A. *printing company executive*
Frank, Laura Jean *computer scientist*
Friedman, Michael *pharmaceutical executive*
Gladstone, Herbert Jack *manufacturing executive*
Glassman, Hilary E. *lawyer, communications executive*
Gold, Steven Michael *lawyer*
Goldsmith, Donna *sports association executive*
Gonnelli, Patrick M. *finance company executive*
Goodhue, Peter Ames *obstetrician, gynecologist, educator*
Griffith, Forrest Lee III *lawyer*
Gross, Ronald Martin *forest products executive, consultant*
Handler, Evelyn *former academic administrator*
Hawkins, John Donald, Jr. *lawyer*
Hawley, Frank Jordan, Jr. *venture capital executive*
Herlands, E. Ward *poet, printmaker*
Hicks, Wayland R. *rental company executive*
Hogan, Frank W. III *lawyer, manufacturing executive*
Hollinger, Morton *small business owner, artist*
Horowitz, Steven F. *cardiologist*
Horrigan, D. Gregory *packaging products executive*
Hubschman, Henry A. *lawyer*
Hudson, Harold Jordon, Jr. *retired insurance executive*
Jason, J. Julie *portfolio manager, writer, lawyer*
Johnson, Dwayne Douglas (The Rock) *actor, professional wrestler*
Karp, Steve *agent*
Klein, Neil Charles *physician*
Koproski, Alexander Robert *real estate company executive*
Kucic, Joseph *management consultant, industrial engineer, network engineer, information security specialist*
Lalli, Michael Anthony *lawyer*
Lane, Hana Umlauf *editor*
La Penta, Robert Vincent *venture capitalist*
Leader, Leonard *lawyer*
Lesko, Newland A. *paper company executive*
Levitan, Gutman *research and development company executive, communications engineer*
Liu, Don H. *lawyer, printing company executive*
Loh, Arthur Tsung Yuan *finance company executive*
Luke, John Anderson, Jr. *paper, packaging and chemical company executive*
Mac Donald, Michael C. *printing company executive*
Mactas, Mark V. *diversified financial services company executive*
Macurdy, John Edward *bass*
Malloy, Dannel Patrick *mayor*
Martin, John K. *communications executive*
Martin, Murray D. *manufacturing executive*
Mayes, Michele Coleman *lawyer*
McGeeney, John Stephen *lawyer*
McGrath, Richard *lawyer*
Mc Kinley, John Key *retired oil company executive*
McMahon, Linda E. *sports association executive*
McMahon, Vince (Vincent Kennedy McMahon) *sports entertainment company executive*
Merritt, William Alfred, Jr. *retired lawyer, real estate company executive*
Miller, Gregory James *lawyer*
Miller, Wilbur Hobart *retired management consultant*
Morse, Jonathan Kent *religious organization administrator*
Motroni, Hector John *printing company executive*
Mulcahy, Anne Marie *printing company executive*
Munera, Gerard Emmanuel *manufacturing executive*
Nagaraj, Devaraysamudram R. *engineer, researcher*
Nazemetz, Patricia *human resources specialist*
Neal, A. Michael *utilities executive*
Nevans, Roy Norman *food products executive, producer*
Nichols, Ralph Arthur *lawyer*
Nissen, David R. *corporate financial executive*
Olschan, Jacqueline Nicola *lawyer*
Pansini, Michael Samuel *financial analyst, tax specialist*
Pappas, Alceste Thetis *consulting company executive, educator*
Parrs, Marianne M. *paper and lumber company executive*
Perle, Eugene Gabriel *lawyer*
Peterson, Elizabeth Holly *art association administrator*
Pickel, Alan Scott *lawyer*
Reardon, Michael J. *finance company executive*
Ressel, Teresa Mullett *diversified financial services company executive, former federal agency administrator*
Robins, Robert Sidwar *political science professor, department chairman*
Rose, Richard Loomis *lawyer*
Rosenstock, Arthur Richard *plastic surgeon, educator*
Sarner, Richard Alan *lawyer*
Schiff, Jayne Nemerow *underwriter*
Shanman, James Alan *lawyer*
Shassian, Donald R. *telecommunications company executive*
Sherman, Mickey (Michael Sherman) *lawyer*
Silver, Charles Morton *communications company executive*
Silver, R. Philip *packaging products executive*
Skidd, Thomas Patrick, Jr. *lawyer*
Snediker, David E. *lawyer*
Staab, Diane D. *lawyer*
Stern, Brian E. *printing company executive*
Stillings, Irene Ella Grace Cordiner *retired foundation executive*
Teeters, Nancy Hays *economist, director*
Teitell, Conrad Laurence *lawyer, writer*
Thomas, Dennis *retired paper company executive, federal official*
Valentine, Bobby (Robert John Valentine) *professional baseball manager*
Vandebroek, Sophie Verdonckt *printing company executive*
Walsh, Kevin P. *energy executive, financial services executive*
Walsh, Thomas Joseph *ophthalmologist*
Weitzel, William Conrad, Jr. *lawyer*
Wilderotter, Maggie (Mary Agnes Wilderotter) *software company executive, former cable television executive*
Wilens, Michael Engber *information technology executive, biologist, microscopist*
Williams, Reba White *corporate financial executive, writer, researcher*
Willkie, Wendell Lewis, II, *lawyer*
Wilson, Mark *corporate financial executive*
Zimmerman, Lawrence A. *printing company executive*

Stonington
Brown, Meredith M. *lawyer*
Cole, Richard A. *retired lawyer*
Elliott, Inger McCabe *apparel designer, consultant, textiles executive*
Elliott, Osborn *journalist, educator, retired dean*
Simmons, Robert Ruhl *former congressman*
Stoddard, Alexandra *interior designer, educator, writer*

Storrs Mansfield
Auriemma, Geno *women's college basketball coach*
Baldwin, Carlita Rose *minister*
Bartram, Ralph Herbert *physicist*
Baxter, Donald Leon Murray *education educator*
Beall, J. C. *philosopher, educator*
Bzymek, Zbigniew Marian *engineering educator*
Calhoun, Jim *men's college basketball coach*
Cazel, Fred A., Jr. *history professor*
Charters, Ann *literature educator*
Coons, Ronald Edward *historian, educator*
Dennis, Kelly *art history professor*
Devereux, Owen Francis *retired metallurgy educator*
Franklin, Brinley *library director*
Gross, Robert Alan *history professor*
Hogan, Michael J. *academic administrator*
Holsinger, Kent Eugene *biology professor, educator*
Jones, Clyde Adam *artist, educator*
Katz, Leonard *psychology professor, researcher*
Kerr, Kirklyn M. *academic administrator, veterinarian, pathologist*
Klemens, Paul Gustav *physicist, researcher*
Kline, Nancy Mattoon *librarian*
Laufer, Hans *developmental biologist, educator*
MacDonald, John Thomas *school system administrator*
Marcus, Harris Leon *materials science educator*
Marcus, Philip Irving *virology educator, researcher*
McNeal, Ralph B. *social studies educator*
Nicholls, Peter J. *academic administrator*
Petrovic, Kimberly Ann *nursing researcher, nursing educator*
Pitkin, Edward Thaddeus *aerospace engineer, consultant*
Price, Glenda Delores *dean, college president*
Rajasekaran, Sanguthevar *computer science educator*
Rasmussen, Theodore Peter *biology professor*
Reifsnider, Kenneth Leonard *metallurgist, educator*
Rimland, Lisa Phillip *writer, composer, lyricist*
Rose, Dale A.J. *performing arts educator*
Shaw, Montgomery Throop *chemical engineering professor*
Smirnova, Alevtina Leonidovia *physical chemistry educator, researcher*
Sriram, S. *educator*
Stephens, Jack Edward *civil engineer, consultant*
Stwalley, William Calvin *physics and chemistry professor*
Tucker, Edwin Wallace *law educator*
Wang, Fei *pharmacist, educator*
Wilsted, Thomas P. *archivist, director*
Woods, David G. *dean*

Stratford
Blair, Sylvia H. *aerospace engineer*
Feinberg, Dennis Lowell *dermatologist*
LaDonna, Frank *psychologist*
Mahoney, Maurice Jeremiah *medical educator*

Suffield
Bianchi, Maria *critical care specialist, acute care nurse practitioner*
Hanzalek, Astrid Teicher *public information officer, consultant*
Montalto, Paul *academic administrator*

Taconic
Medvecky, Patricia *retired elementary school educator*

Terryville
Doughty-Jenkins, Bonnie-Marie *middle school educator*

Thomaston
Mühlanger, Erich *ski manufacturing company executive*

Torrington
Drobena, Thomas John *minister, educator*
Leard, David Carl *lawyer*
Lippincott, Walter Edward *law educator*
Rolfe, Ellen Mary *retired music educator*
Wall, Robert Anthony, Jr. *lawyer*

Trumbull
Allen, Richard Stanley (Dick Allen) *literature and language professor, writer*
Berg, Charles G. *insurance company executive*
Ewing, Anna M. *stock exchange executive*
Lang, James Richard *software designer, magician*
Nevins, Lyn (Carolyn A. Nevins) *school disciplinarian*
Norcel, Jacqueline Joyce Casale *educational association administrator*
Ouyang, Hao *research scientist*
Watson, Donald Ralph *architect, dean, writer, artist*
Williams, Ronald Doherty *lawyer*

Uncasville
Douglas, Katie (Kathryn Elizabeth Douglas) *professional basketball player*
Lobo, Rebecca *professional basketball player*
Thibault, Mike *professional basketball coach*

Vernon Rockville
Courtney, Joe (Joseph D. Courtney) *congressman*
Marmer, Ellen Lucille *pediatrician, cardiologist*
Purnell, Oliver James III *judge*
Wolff, Gregory Steven *insurance company executive*

Voluntown
Caddell, Foster *artist*
Thevenet, Patricia Confrey *social studies educator*

Wallingford
Cline, John Carroll *psychologist*
Cohen, Gordon S. *health products executive*
Dionne, Karen Marie *veterinary technician, educator*
Hartz, Richard Allen *research scientist*
Karotkin, Rose A. *marketing professional*
Lauttenbach, Carol *artist*
Lelas, Snjezana *pharmacologist, researcher*
Loeffler, Martin H. *electronics executive*
Shanahan, Edward J. *headmaster*
Velentine, Ralph Burnet *music educator, department chairman*

Washington
Leab, Daniel Joseph *history professor*

Washington Depot
Tracy, Michael Cameron *choreographer, educator*

Waterbury
Chabria, Shiven B. *physician, educator*
Dost, Mark W. *lawyer*
Dudrick, Stanley John *surgeon, research scientist, educator*
Fischbein, Charles Alan *pediatrician*
Garsten, Joel Jay *gastroenterologist*
Harper, Barbara Clara *educational program administrator, counselor*
Johnson, Lorelei Marie *artist*
Lang, Christine JoAnn *elementary school educator*
Luedke, Frederick Lee *manufacturing executive*
Martone, Eric Anthony Domenic *history educator*
McDonald, Francis Michael *judge trial referee, retired state supreme court justice*
Pape, William James, II, *newspaper publisher*
Ramirez, Sandra Ivelisse *case manager*
Sanders, Richard L. *academic administrator*
Schefsky, Lynn A. *lawyer, chemicals executive*
Smith, James Copenhaver *bank executive*
Upson, Thomas Fisher *judge, retired state senator, lawyer*
Wolfe, Harriet Munrett *lawyer*
Wood, Robert L. *chemicals executive*
Zasada, Mary Eileen *nursing administrator*

Waterford
Commire, Anne *playwright, writer, editor*
Hinkle, Janet *financial analyst*
Hinkle, Muriel Ruth Nelson *naval warfare analysis company executive*
Johnson, Gary William *environmental scientist, consultant*
Walsh, Peter Joseph *marketing professional*
Weidenbaum, Rhoda Sussman *history educator, researcher*

West Cornwall
Engel, Jeffrey Mark *musician, music educator*
Estern, Neil Carl *sculptor*
Simont, Marc *artist*

West Hartford
Alexandrin, Julie Richmond *special education educator, consultant*
Braus, Ira L. *music educator, researcher*
Calip, Roger *writer, educator*
Chase, Carol Johnson *mathematics educator*
Collins, Alma Jones *language educator, writer*
Detmar-Pines, Gina Louise *business strategy and policy educator*
Faude, Wilson Hinsdale *museum director, consultant*
Gerjuoy, Herbert George *information scientist, educator, psychologist, consultant, poet*
Gitterman, Alex *social work educator*
Glasser, Joseph *management consultant, educator*
Gould, Laurence Ira *physicist*
Harrison, Walter Lee *university president*
Mackey, William Arthur Godfrey *analytical testing company executive*
Malone, Thomas Francis *academic administrator, meteorologist*
Markham, Claire Agnes (M. Clare Markham) *retired chemistry educator, consultant*
Raffay, Stephen Joseph *manufacturing executive, director*
Silver, Herbert *physician*
Swerdloff, Ileen Pollock *lawyer*

Swerdloff, Mark Harris lawyer
Tonkin, Humphrey Richard academic administrator, educator
Wilder, Michael Stephen former insurance company executive
Wolman, Martin lawyer
Zhou, Hong engineering educator

West Haven
Boronico, Jess Stephen management science educator, dean
Haley, George Thomas marketing educator
Kyriakides, Tassos Constantino biostatistician
Onton, Ann Louise Reuther chemist
Sacco, Kari Lynn psychologist

Westbrook
Gilmore, Clarence Percy editor-in-chief, writer

Weston
Aibel, Howard James arbitrator, mediator
Bleifeld, Stanley sculptor
Diforio, Robert George literary agent
Falber, Harold Julius marketing professional
Fredrik, Burry theater producer, director
Kilty, Jerome Timothy playwright, theater director, actor
Murray, Stephen James lawyer
Murray, Thomas J. advertising executive
Oliver, Sandra art dealer, painter
Thompson, N(orman) David insurance company executive
Wiseman, Carter Sterling writer, educator
Zimmerman, Bernard investment banker

Westport
Baker, Leonard Morton manufacturing executive
Barberi, Robert Obed lawyer
Birinyi, Laszlo financial analyst, investment advisor
Blau, Barry marketing professional, financial consultant
Breitbarth, S. Robert manufacturing executive
Carr, Cynthia lawyer
Chernow, Ann Levy artist, educator
Clausman, Gilbert Joseph retired medical librarian
Cohen, Eric I. lawyer
Cramer, Allan P. lawyer
Dalio, Raymond T. investment company executive
Daw, Harold John lawyer, director
DeFeo, Philip D. private equity firm executive
Defeo, Ronald M. machinery manufacturing executive
Donaldson, James Neill banker
Dunham, Christopher Cooper lawyer
Feliciano, José entertainer
Feskoe, Gaffney Jon management consultant
Fisher, Leonard Everett artist, educator, writer
Freedman, Judith Greenberg retired elementary school educator, state legislator
Frese, Edward Scheer, Jr., (Ted Frese) information technology executive, consultant
Fried, Burton Theodore lawyer
Griggs, Nina M. retired realtor
Hedge, Arthur Joseph, Jr. manufacturing executive
Heyman, Ronnie Feuerstein lawyer
Hotchner, Aaron Edward author
Kelly, Paul Knox investment banker
Kramer, Sidney B. publishing executive, literary agent, lawyer
Kuroghlian, Gerald E. English educator
Kurz, Mitchell Howard marketing communications executive
Lewis, Margaret Mary marketing professional
Lust, Herbert Cohnfeldt III securities trader
MacCormack, Charles Frederick international relief organization executive
Manley, John Frederick political scientist, educator
Margolis, Emanuel lawyer, educator
McCormack, Donald Paul newspaper consultant
McKane, David Bennett business executive
Newman, Paul actor, food products executive, race car driver
O'Keefe, John David brokerage house executive
Razzano, Pasquale Angelo lawyer
Ready, Robert James finance company executive
Reilly, Nancy (Anne Caulfield Reilly) painter
Riordan, Thomas J. manufacturing executive
Rudd, Nicholas investor, consultant
Sacks, Herbert Simeon psychiatrist, educator, consultant
Samberg, Arthur J. (Art Samberg) investment company executive
Saxl, Richard Hildreth lawyer
Scheinman, Stanley Bruce corporate financial executive
Schriever, Fred Martin management consultant, financial investor
Sheiman, Ronald Lee lawyer
Siff, Marlene Ida artist, designer
Smith, Andrew James Thomas music educator
Solum, John Henry flutist, educator, author
Stern, Robert D. publishing executive
Stewart, Martha Kostyra entrepreneur, lecturer, author
Stolz, Alan Jay youth camp executive
Walton, Alan George venture capitalist
Warner, Kerstin Julianna gifted and talented educator

Wethersfield
Osborne, Louise publishing executive
Terk, Glenn Thomas lawyer

Willimantic
Barbuto, Leah M. early childhood and technology educator, consultant
Escoto, Carlos Aurelio psychology professor, researcher
Pocock, Emil history professor
Wilson, Margaret Sullivan retired executive dean, consultant

Willington
Zhang, Heng research scientist, educator

Wilton
Adams, Thomas Tilley lawyer
Bair, Thomas J. publishing executive
Bishop, William Wade advertising executive
Brown, James Thompson, Jr. operations research specialist, information scientist
Burki, Arde A. retired military officer
Davis, Joel publisher
Duke, Robert Dominick lawyer
Frank, Robert Allen media consultant
Fricke, Richard John lawyer
Healy, James Casey lawyer
Hersh, Ira Paul tax specialist, financial consultant
Kaskell, Peter Howard professional society administrator, lawyer
Mitchell, Richard Boyle security firm executive
Nickel, Albert George advertising agency executive
Poundstone, Sally Hill library director
Reilly, Kathleen C. director, retired secondary school educator
Seitz, Nicholas Joseph editor, journalist
Slater, Ralph Evan lawyer
Tarde, Jerry (Gerard Tarde) editor-in-chief

Windsor
Christian, George library organization administrator
Ferraro, John Francis corporate financial executive
Weigel, Russell H. headmaster

Windsor Locks
Coelho, Sandra Signorelli secondary school educator, consultant, elementary school educator

Winsted
Stawicki, Joseph John, Jr. marketing executive

Woodbridge
Alvine, Robert industrialist, entrepreneur, world business leader, philanthropist, business owner
Dupré, Louis retired philosopher, educator
Haering, Margaret Elaine lawyer
Kleiner, Diana Elizabeth Edelman art historian, educator, academic administrator
Malloy, Ina Arlene secondary school educator, photographer
Mason, John Wayne psychoneuroendocrinologist, retired medical educator

Woodbury
Giuliano, Rosemary E. lawyer
Skinner, Brian John geologist, educator

Woodstock Valley
Allaby, Stanley Reynolds clergyman

DELAWARE

Bear
Hudson, Kelly Marie music educator
Yannul, Edward chemical engineer, writer

Bethany Beach
Gale, Robert L. retired educational association administrator, consultant
Klein, Gershon A. pediatrician

Camden Wyoming
Bailey, Kay Wood management consultant
Pfeuffer, Robert John musician

Dagsboro
Davis, Marica Nanci Ella Riggin retired artist
Hanna, Anne Marie artist
Mortenson, Thomas Theodore health products executive, management consultant

Dover
Amick, Steven Hammond state legislator, lawyer
Braverman, Ray Howard secondary school educator
Carney, John C., Jr. lieutenant governor
Danberg, Carl Christian state agency administrator, former state attorney general
Denn, Matthew P. lawyer
Ennis, Bruce Clifford retired lawyer
Glen, Robert Alexander state agency administrator
Gregory, Frank R. history professor
Jones, Geraldine Ann Johnson secondary school educator
Kim, Dae Ryong management information systems educator
Markell, Jack A. state official
Minner, Ruth Ann governor
Norman, Anne E. C. state librarian
Ridgely, Henry duPont state supreme court justice
Sessoms, Allen Lee academic administrator, physicist, educator, retired diplomat
Smyth, Joel Douglas newspaper executive
Sorenson, Liane Beth McDowell director, state legislator
Taylor, Suzonne Berry Stewart real estate broker
Wetherall, Robert Shaw librarian
Wilson, Samuel Mayhew surgeon
Windsor, Harriet Smith state official
Woodruff, Valerie school system administrator

Felton
Vansant, Franklin Steven mathematician, educator

Georgetown
Holland, Randy James state supreme court justice
Lane, William H. education educator

Greenville
DeWees, Donald Charles security firm executive
Miller, Duane King health and beauty care company executive
Parets, Paul L. music educator
Reeder, Charles Benton retired economic consultant
Reynolds Cooch, Nancy D. sculptor
Rocek, Jan retired chemist
Schroeder, Herman Elbert scientific consultant

Hockessin
Croyle, Barbara Ann health facility administrative executive
Mertz, Anne Morris writer, researcher, journalist, educator
Stone, F. L. Peter lawyer
Ulmer, William H., Sr. dentist
Valbuena-Briones, Angel Julian retired language educator, author

Laurel
Lydic, Garrett Walton elementary school educator
Selby, Cora Norwood retired elementary school educator

Lewes
Beaufait, Frederick W(illiam) retired engineering educator
Costigan, Constance Frances artist, educator
Fried, Jeffrey Michael health care administrator
Saliba, Anis Khalil surgeon
Spence, Sandra retired trade association administrator
Warden, Richard Dana government labor union official

Middletown
Cataldi-May, Lauren Michelle head of religious order, music director
Hall, Peter Michael physics professor, electronics engineer
Roach, Daniel T., Jr., (Tad Roach) headmaster

Millsboro
Bethke, Frederick Randall microbiologist, researcher
Lasher, Hiram Nelson entrepreneur, consultant

Millville
Zinman, David Joel conductor

Milton
Carrow, Milton Michael law educator
Provost, Thomas Taylor dermatology educator, researcher

New Castle
Almquist, Don illustrator, artist
Brownson, Kenneth C. dean
Cansler, Leslie Ervin retired newspaper editor
Rolland, Kathy Ann elementary school educator
Sanderson, Devon Lee elementary school educator
von Hoelle, John Jacob Lewis publisher, commercial developer

Newark
Allen, Herbert Ellis environmental chemistry educator
Attoh-Okine, Nii Otokunor Nii civil and environmental engineering educator
Bailey, Daniel Carl higher education administrator
Barteau, Mark Alan chemical engineering and chemistry educator
Beris, Antony Nicolas chemical engineer, educator
Bilinsky, Yaroslav political scientist
Brown, Hilton artist, educator, writer
Brynteson, Susan library director
Burmeister, John Luther chemistry professor, consultant
Butkiewicz, James Leon economics professor, researcher, consultant
Byrne, John Michael energy and environmental educator
Campbell, Linzy Leon molecular biology researcher, educator
Colton, David Lem mathematician, educator
Day, Robert Androus literature and language professor, retired library director, editor, publisher
DeLorme, Michael toxicologist, researcher
DeVivo, Sal J. newspaper executive
DiRenzo, Gordon James sociologist, psychologist, educator
Di Toro, Dominic M. engineering educator
Dybowski, Cecil chemistry educator
Elson, Charles Myer law educator
Farstrup, Alan E. educational association administrator
Fox, Alan philosophy educator
Gantzer, Mary Lou medical products executive
Gardner, Timothy Joseph surgeon, educator
Gehrlein, William Vincent business professor
Gibson, Ann Eden art historian, educator
Harker, Patrick Timothy academic administrator, systems engineer, educator
Homer, William Innes art history educator, expert, writer
Jackson, Marvin Dennis journalism educator, writer
Klevinsky, Thomas Jason information technology executive
Korber, Louise Ann artist
Lathrop, Thomas Albert language educator, publisher
Le Min, Thomas Francis law enforcement official, educator
Lemole, Gerald Michael surgeon
Luke, David Russell mathematician, educator
Mangone, Gerard J. international maritime law educator
Mitchell, Peter Kenneth educational consultant
Murray, Richard Bennett retired physics professor
Neal, James Preston state senator, project engineer
Prasad, Ajay Krishna mechanical engineering educator
Rayle, Heather Lynnette chemist
Roselle, David Paul retired academic administrator, mathematician, educator
Rowe, Charles Alfred artist, graphics designer, educator
Russell, Thomas William Fraser chemical engineer, educator
Sandler, Stanley Irving chemical engineering educator
Semmel, Stuart history professor
Smith, Carrie Veronica psychology professor
Sparks, Donald Lewis soil chemistry educator
Steiner, Roger Jacob linguistics educator, writer, researcher
Stick, Thomas Howard Fitchett architect, construction litigation consultant
Swany, Douglas Martin education educator
Velury, Uma finance educator, researcher
Wagner, Norman Joseph III chemical engineering educator, researcher
Wei, Bingqing engineering educator
Weintraub, Stanley arts and humanities educator, writer
Wolters, Raymond historian, educator
Woo, S. B. (Shien-Biau Woo) retired state official, physicist, educator

Ocean View
Taylor, Stan retired state agency administrator

Odessa
Butler, Janet C. shop owner

Rehoboth Beach
Little, R. Donald real estate entrepreneur
Penrose, Cynthia C. retired health care consultant
Stokes, Richard Francis lawyer

Rockland
Cosgrove, Howard Edward, Jr. utilities executive
Levinson, John Milton obstetrician, gynecologist
Rubin, Alan A. pharmaceutical and biotechnology consultant

Wilmington
Abdel-Misih, Raafat Z. surgeon, educator
Alexander, Michael Allen pediatrician, educator
Alonso, Caridad elementary school educator
Ambro, Thomas L. federal judge
Anton, David L. research and development company executive, biotechnologist, researcher
Axente, Liviu Mircea management consultant
Bader, John Merwin retired lawyer
Baker, John David health facility administrator, not-for-profit fundraiser, real estate agent
Barthold, Julia Spencer urologist, researcher
Baumann, Julian Henry, Jr. lawyer
Baxter, Beverley Veloris economic association administrator, educator
Benes, Solomon retired biomedical scientist, physician
Berger, Carolyn state supreme court justice
Biden, Beau (Joseph Robinette Biden III) state attorney general, lawyer
Blankenship, Roy conservator, artist, writer
Bloom, David Andrew communications operations director
Borel, James Calvin chemical company executive
Bounds-Seemans, Pamella J. artist
Bruni, Stephen Thomas museum director
Carpenter, Edmund Nelson, II, retired lawyer
Cecala, Ted Thomas, Jr. banker, accountant
Cohen, Betsy Z. bank executive
Connelly, Thomas M., Jr. chemicals executive
Connolly, Colm F. prosecutor
Copeland, Tatiana Brandt accountant
Darko, Denis F. research scientist, educator, physician
Davis, John Ripoll manufacturing executive
DiLiberto, Richard Anthony, Jr. lawyer
Emmert, Richard Eugene retired industrial and professional association executive
Esrey, Elizabeth Gove Goodier chemist, biologist
Fidance, Christina Marie human services administrator
Finkelstein, Jesse Adam lawyer
Floyd, Israel J. lawyer, chemicals executive
Fredrick, Susan Walker tax company manager
Frelick, Robert Westcott physician, consultant
Fullerton, Ann Elizabeth retired biology educator
Genetta, Ann H. psychologist, neuropsychologist
Goldberg, Morton Edward pharmacologist
Gonzalez, Ricardo surgeon, educator
Goodmanson, Richard R. chemicals executive
Granite, Edwin L oral surgeon
Green, James Samuel lawyer
Griffin, Jo Ann Thomas retired financial planner, tax specialist
Grossman, Jerome Kent lawyer, accountant
Gulyas, Diane H. manufacturing executive
Gurley, Elisabeth Anne art historian, educator, writer
Hartzell, Charles R. science foundation director, cell biologist, biochemist
Herdeg, John Andrew lawyer
Higgins, Roxanne Snelling educational consultant
Holliday, Chad (Charles O. Holliday Jr.) chemicals executive
Holtzman, Arnold Harold chemical company executive
Holzman, James L(ouis) lawyer
Jacobs, Jack Bernard state supreme court justice
Jaycox, Gary Delmar research scientist
Johnston, William David lawyer
Jolles, Janet K. Pilling lawyer
Kalil, James, Sr. investment executive
Keefer, Jeffrey L. chemicals executive
Kirk, Richard Dillon lawyer
Kirkpatrick, Andrew Booth, Jr. lawyer

Kissa, Erik *retired chemist, consultant*
Klayman, Barry Martin *lawyer*
Kneavel, Ann Callanan *humanities educator, communications consultant*
Kneavel, Thomas Charles, Jr. *psychologist, educator*
Kristol, Daniel Marvin *retired lawyer*
Krulak, Charles Chandler *bank executive*
Kullman, Ellen Jamison *chemicals executive*
Kwolek, Stephanie Louise *chemist, researcher*
Lassen, John Kai *development company executive*
Lee, James Harold *investment company executive*
Linderman, Jeanne Herron *priest*
Magee, Thomas Hugh *lawyer*
Malik, John Stephen *lawyer*
Mand, Martin Gary *financial executive*
Marcali, Jean Gregory *retired chemist*
McDonough, Kenneth Lee *pharmaceutical company medical administrator*
McGeever, Elizabeth M. *lawyer*
McLeer Free, Laureen Dorothy *drug development and pharmaceutical professional*
Meitner, Pamela *lawyer, educator*
Mekler, L. Arlen *lawyer, chemist*
Messina, Charles *artist*
Mobley, Stacey J. *lawyer, chemicals executive*
Mukherjee, Partha S. *research scientist*
Nichols, George Leon, Jr. *minister*
Nolen, Samuel Augustus *lawyer*
Nottingham, Robinson Kendall *insurance company executive*
Parshall, George William *chemist, researcher*
Parsons, Donald Francis *judge*
Paschetto, John J. *lawyer*
Pell, Sidney *epidemiologist*
Peterson, Russell Wilbur *environmental services administrator, retired governor*
Porter, John Francis III *banker*
Reed, Thomas James *law educator*
Reeves, Grafton Dulany *pediatric endocrinologist*
Robinson, Sue L(ewis) *federal judge*
Rodgers, Stephen John *lawyer, physician, consultant*
Rogerson, Craig Allan *manufacturing executive*
Rogoski, Patricia Diana *corporate financial executive*
Rose, Selwyn H. *chemicals executive*
Roth, Jane Richards *federal judge*
Sager, Philip Travis *pharmaceutical executive, cardiologist, researcher*
Salinger, Frank Max *lawyer*
Saltarelli, Michael A. *priest*
Schmerling, Erwin Robert *counselor, retired physicist*
Semple, James William *lawyer*
Shah, Udayan Kanaiyalal *surgeon*
Shipley, Samuel Lynn *advertising and public relations executive*
Sippel-Wetmore, Frances Marie *microbiologist, retired business owner*
Smith, Craig Bennett *lawyer*
Smith, S(tewart) Gregory *ophthalmologist, inventor, product developer, consultant, author*
Sparks, W. Donald, II, *lawyer*
Stapleton, Walter King *federal judge*
Stargatt, Bruce M. *lawyer*
Steele, Myron Thomas *state supreme court chief justice*
Sullivan, Lawrence Matthew *lawyer*
Tolles, Bryant Franklin, Jr. *retired history and art professor*
Tumas, Michael B. *lawyer*
Turover, Benjamin Philip *account executive*
Uffner, Michael S. *automotive executive*
Vaddi, Krishna *pharmaceutical executive*
Vecchione, Kenneth A. *corporate financial executive*
Vinocur, Charles David *pediatric surgeon*
Waisanen, Christine M. *lawyer, writer*
Wallace, Jesse Wyatt *pharmaceutical scientist*
Ward, Rodman, Jr. *lawyer, director*
Waritz, Richard Stefan *toxicologist, researcher*
Wasson, Robert E. *state agency administrator*
Wesler, Ken *performing arts company executive*
Whetzel, Robert William *lawyer*
Wier, Richard Royal, Jr. *lawyer*
Williams, Richmond Dean *library consultant and appraiser*
Winslow, Helen Littell *lawyer*
Ziolkowska-Boehm, Aleksandra *writer*

DISTRICT OF COLUMBIA

Bolling Afb

Dendinger, William J. *career officer, chaplain*

Fort McNair

Raines, Edgar Frank, Jr. *historian*

Pentagon

Gourley, Robert *information technology executive*

Washington

Aaron, Henry Jacob J. *economics professor*
Aaronson, David Ernest *lawyer, educator*
Abbott, Alden Francis *lawyer, federal official*
Abdenur, Roberto Mameri Pinto *ambassador*
Abell, Charles S. *federal official*
Abell, Richard Bender *federal judicial officer, lawyer*
Abercrombie, Neil *congressman*
Able, Edward H. *association executive*
Abrams, Elliott *federal official*
Abshire, David Manker *former ambassador, research executive*
Acheson, David Campion *retired lawyer, policy analyst, writer*
Ackerman, Gary Leonard *congressman*
Acta, Manny (Manuel Elias Acta) *professional baseball manager*
Adams, A. John Bertrand *public affairs consultant, director*
Adams, David G. *lawyer*
Adams, Frances Grant, II, *lawyer*
Adams, Robert Edward *journalist*
Adams, Roger C. *federal official, lawyer*
Adamson, Jeremy E. *library director*
Adamson, Richard Henry *pharmacologist*
Adamson, Terrence Burdett *lawyer*
Addington, David S. *federal official, lawyer*
Adducci, Steven A. *lawyer*
Adelman, Kenneth Lee *journalist, former ambassador*
Adelstein, Jonathan Steven *commissioner*
Aderholt, Robert B. *congressman, lawyer*
Adler, Howard Bruce *lawyer*
Adler, Robert Martin *lawyer*
Affronti, Lewis Francis, Sr. *microbiologist, educator*
Ágoston, Gábor *history professor*
Agrast, Mark David *lawyer*
Aguirre, Eduardo, Jr. *ambassador, former federal agency administrator*
Ahlgren, James David *oncologist*
Ahmed, Akbar S. *religious studies educator*
Ahmed, Atif Ali *pathologist*
Aikens, Martha Brunette *park service administrator*
Ain, Sanford King *lawyer*
Aisen, Paul S. *neurologist, researcher, educator*
Aitken, Andrew C. *lawyer*
Ajami, Fouad *professor of middle eastern studies*
Akaka, Daniel Kahikina *senator*
Akin, Todd (William Todd Akin) *congressman, former state legislator*
Akukwe, Chinua *public health physician, health service executive*
Alatis, James Efstathios *university dean emeritus*
Alberg, James L. *lawyer*
Albrecht, Kathe Hicks *art historian, visual resources manager*
Albrecht, Ralph P. *lawyer*
Albright, Madeleine Korbel *former secretary of state*
Aldock, John Douglas *lawyer*
Aldonas, Grant D. *lawyer, former federal agency administrator*
Aleinikoff, Thomas Alexander *dean, law educator*
Alexander, Clifford Joseph *lawyer*
Alexander, Donald Crichton *lawyer*
Alexander, Joseph Kunkle, Jr. *physicist*
Alexander, (Andrew) Lamar *senator, former secretary of education, governor*
Alexander, Rodney M. *congressman*
Alito, Samuel Anthony, Jr. *United States supreme court justice*
Allam, Hannah *journalist*
Allan, Richmond Frederick *lawyer*
Allan, Ronald Gage *academic research coordinator*
Allard, Nicholas W. *lawyer*
Allard, (Alan) Wayne *senator, veterinarian*
Allegra, Francis M. *federal judge, retired federal official*
Allen, Beverly E. *medical librarian*
Allen, Dwayne LeRoy *information systems specialist*
Allen, Henry Southworth *journalist, critic*
Allen, Thad William *career military officer*
Allen, Thomas H. *congressman, lawyer*
Allen, William Jere *minister*
Alleyne, Sir George A.O. *public health administrator, educator*
Allgeier, Peter Frederick *ambassador*
Allred, C. Stephen *federal agency administrator*
Almaguer, Frank *ambassador*
Almquist, Katherine J. *federal agency administrator*
Alperovitz, Gar *author, educator*
Altenburg, John D., Jr. *lawyer, retired military officer*
Altmire, Jason *congressman*
Altschul, Alfred Samuel *airline executive*
Alvarez, Scott G. *lawyer*
Alward, Ruth Rosendall *nursing consultant*
Amarelo, Monica A. *public relations executive, writer*
Ambrose, Myles Joseph *lawyer*
Ames, Frank Anthony *musician, film producer*
Ames, Robert G. *lawyer*
Amos, Deborah Susan *foreign correspondent*
Ampy, Franklin Roosevelt *zoologist, educator*
Amron, Cory M. *lawyer*
Anand, Rajen S. *physiologist, educator*
Andersen, Margo K. *federal agency administrator*
Andersen, Robert Allen *retired federal official*
Anderson, Frederick Randolph, Jr. *lawyer, educator*
Anderson, James E. *lawyer*
Anderson, Stanton Dean *lawyer*
Anderson, Vinton Randolph *bishop*
Anderson, William Carl *civilian military employee, lawyer*
Andres, Jose *chef*
Andrew, Giaccia A. *lawyer*
Andrew, James M. *federal agency administrator*
Andrew, Joseph Jerald *lawyer*
Andrews, Bruce *automotive executive, lawyer*
Andrews, John Frank *editor, author, educator*
Andrews, Mark Joseph *lawyer*
Andrews, Peter Michael *biology professor*
Andrews, Robert Ernest *congressman, lawyer*
Andrews, Terrence Michael *senior policy advisor*
Andril, David T. *lawyer*
Angell, Lois Louise *writer, actor, comedienne, poet*
Angel-Urdinola, Diego Fernando *economist*
Angier, Natalie Marie *science journalist*
Ansary, Cyrus A. *investment company executive, lawyer*
Anthony, Donald Barrett *engineering executive*
Anthony, Stephen Pierce *lawyer*
Anthony, Virginia Quinn Bausch *medical association executive*
Anton, Frank A. *publishing executive*
Antony, Paul T. *military officer, physician executive*
Aoki, Steven *federal agency administrator*
Apatoff, David B. *lawyer*
Apple, Daina Dravnieks *federal agency administrator*
Apple, James Glenn *lawyer, educator*
Apple, Martin Allen *science executive and educator*
Applebaum, Anne *journalist, writer*
Aranoff, Shara L. *federal official*
Archer, Glenn LeRoy, Jr. *federal judge*
Arenas, Gilbert *professional basketball player*
Arend, Anthony Clark *social studies educator, academic administrator*
Arietti, Michael Ray *ambassador*
Arkilic, Galip Mehmet *mechanical engineer, educator*
Arling, Bryan Jeremy *internist*
Arling, Donna Dickson *social worker*
Arlook, Ira Arthur *advocate, communications executive*
Armen, Robert K. (Kelly) III *federal judge*
Armey, Dick (Richard Keith Armey) *state representative*
Armstrong, Alexandra *financial planner*
Arnall, Roland E. *ambassador*
Arndt, Richard Tallmadge *writer, consultant, cultural administrator*
Arnez, Nancy Levi *educational leadership educator*
Arnold, William Edwin *health advocate, consultant*
Arnovitz, Benton Mayer *editor*
Aron, Nan *lawyer, association executive*
Arrott, Elizabeth *journalist*
Artman, Carl Joseph *federal agency administrator*
Asfaw, Abay *economist, consultant, research scientist*
Asker, James Robert *magazine editor*
Åslund, Anders *economist*
Atherton, Charles Henry *federal commission administrator*
Atkins, Paul S. *commissioner*
Atlas, Liane Wiener *writer*
Atlas, Terry *journalist*
Attinger, Christopher Ernst *medical educator*
Attridge, Daniel F. *lawyer*
Auberger, Marcia A. *lawyer*
Augustine, Hilton H., Jr. *computer company executive*
Ausbrook, J. Keith *lawyer*
Avery, Gordon Bennett *medical educator, neonatologist*
Avil, Richard Daniel, Jr. *lawyer*
Aviles, Dionel Michael *civilian military employee, former federal agency administrator*
Aviv, Diana L. *public policy analyst, psychotherapist*
Axelrod, Jonathan Gans *lawyer*
Ayer, Donald Belton *lawyer*
Ayres, Mary Ellen *federal official*
Azcuenaga, Mary Laurie *government official*
Babayi, Robert S. *lawyer*
Babby, Ellen Reisman *educational association executive*
Babby, Lon S. *lawyer*
Baca, Joe *congressman*
Bachman, Kenneth Leroy, Jr. *lawyer*
Bachmann, Michele *congresswoman, former state legislator*
Bachula, Gary R. *federal official*
Bachus, Spencer T. III *congressman, lawyer*
Backlin, Jim *legislative staff member*
Bacon, Sylvia *judge, educator*
Bader, W(illiam) Reece *lawyer*
Badillo, Alejandro *lawyer*
Baer, Michael Alan *political scientist, educator*
Baer, William J. *lawyer*
Bagnoli, David Christopher *architect*
Baicker, Katherine (Kate) *federal official, economics professor*
Baigis, Judith Ann *nursing educator, academic administrator*
Bailar, John Christian III *retired public health educator, physician, statistician*
Baim, Eric M. *lawyer*
Bain, Scott E. *lawyer*
Bainum, Peter Montgomery *aerospace engineer, consultant*
Bair, Sheila Colleen *federal agency administrator*
Baird, Brian N. *congressman*
Baird, Donna Selma *counselor, educator*
Baker, David Harris *lawyer*
Baker, Douglas B. *federal official*
Baker, Howard Henry, Jr. *lawyer, former ambassador, senator*
Baker, James Edgar *federal judge, educator*
Baker, P. Jean *lawyer, mediator*
Baker, Richard Hugh *congressman*
Baker, Stewart Abercrombie *federal agency administrator, lawyer*
Baldridge, J. Douglas *lawyer*
Baldwin, Sheryl Denise *chemist, editor, writer*
Baldwin, Tammy *congresswoman, lawyer*
Ball, Markham (Robert Ball) *lawyer, arbitrator, educator*
Ball, William Lockhart III *lobbyist, former civilian military employee*
Ballard, Frederic Lyman, Jr. *lawyer*
Ballen, Robert Gerald *lawyer*
Bandler, Donald Keith *international consultant, former ambassador*
Bank, Rita M. *lawyer*
Banks, Richard Charles *ornithologist*
Banoun, Raymond *lawyer*
Banta, James Elmer *epidemiologist, educator, dean*
Banzhaf, John F. III *legal association administrator, educator*
Baquet, Dean Paul *editor*
Baran, Jan Witold *lawyer, educator*
Barbash, Barry P. *lawyer*
Barber, Ben Bernard Andrew *journalist*
Barbosa, Rubens Antonio *former ambassador*
Barcella, Ernest Lawrence, Jr. *lawyer*
Barclay, George N. *lawyer*
Bardin, David Jonas *lawyer*
Barnes, Donald Michael *lawyer*
Barnes, Frederic Wood, Jr. *journalist, political analyst*
Barnes, Julian E. *editor*
Barnes, Mark James *lawyer*
Barnet, Robert Joseph *cardiologist, philosopher*
Barnett, Helaine M. *lawyer*
Barnett, Robert Bruce *lawyer*
Barnett, Thomas O. *federal agency administrator*
Barnette, James D. *lawyer*
Barno, David W. *retired military officer*
Barrasso, John Anthony *senator, orthopedic surgeon*
Barreto, Hector V., Jr. *not-for-profit organization executive, former federal agency administrator*
Barrett, Jane Frances *lawyer*
Barrett, Richard David *university director, consultant, retired bank executive*
Barrett, Thomas J. *federal agency administrator, retired military officer*
Barrie, John Paul *lawyer, educator*
Barron, Myra Hymovich *lawyer*
Barrow, John Jenkins *congressman, lawyer*
Barry, Dennis M. *lawyer*
Barry, Paul H. *utilities executive*
Barshefsky, Charlene *lawyer, former federal official*
Bartlett, Bruce Reeves *economist, columnist*
Bartlett, Charles Leffingwell *foundation executive*
Bartlett, Roscoe G. *congressman*
Bartnoff, Judith *judge*
Barton, Joe Linus *congressman*
Barton, Robert Leroy, Jr. *judge, educator*
Bartuska, Ann *government official, biologist*
Baruah, Sandy K. (Santanu Kumar Baruah) *federal agency administrator*
Barusch, Ronald Charles *lawyer*
Baskerville, Lezli *educational association administrator*
Baskin, Maurice *lawyer*
Baskir, Lawrence M. *federal judge*
Bass, Gary D. *advocate, director*
Basseches, Robert Treinis *lawyer*
Bateman, Paul William *federal agency administrator*
Bates, James T. *chief of staff*
Bates, John D. *federal judge*
Batshaw, Mark Levitt *pediatrician*
Battista, Robert James *federal agency administrator, lawyer*
Battle, Michael A. *lawyer, former federal agency administrator, prosecutor*
Baucus, Max Sieben *senator*
Bauer, Richard P. *lawyer*
Bauer, Robert F. *lawyer*
Baum, Ingeborg Ruth *librarian*
Baumann, Linda Adriene *lawyer*
Baum-Villavicencio, Lynne Miriam *lawyer*
Baxter, Nathan Dwight *dean*
Baxter, Sandra L. *government agency administrator*
Bayh, Birch Evans, Jr. *lawyer, former senator*
Bayh, Evan (Birch Evan Bayh III) *senator, former governor*
Bayly, John Henry, Jr. *judge*
Beale, Susan Yates *social worker*
Beall, Julianne *librarian*
Bean, Melissa *congresswoman*
Bea Roberts, Barbara Ann *legal secretary*
Beato, Cristina V. *government agency administrator*
Becerra, Xavier *congressman, lawyer*
Becker, Brandon *lawyer*
Becker, Brenda L. *medical products executive, former federal official*
Becker, Mary Louise *political scientist*
Becker, Stephan E. *lawyer*
Beckwith, Edward Jay *lawyer*
Bednash, Geraldine *educational association administrator*
Beehler, Bruce McPherson *research zoologist, ornithologist, conservationist*
Beers, Nathaniel Brittingham Savio *pediatrician*
Begala, Paul Edward *television personality, political scientist, consultant*
Beghe, Renato *federal judge*
Behan, Kathleen A. (Kitty Behan) *lawyer*
Behney, Clyde Joseph *health policy researcher*
Beier, David *medical products executive*
Beinart, Peter Alexander *editor, columnist*
Beisner, John Herbert *lawyer*
Belak, Michael James *information technology executive*
Bell, Ford Watson *museum association administrator*
Bell, Jerry Alan *science education association administrator*
Bell, Joseph Charles *lawyer*
Bell, Sheila Trice *lawyer*
Bell, Stephen Robert *lawyer*
Beller, Herbert N. *lawyer*
Bellinger, John B. III *lawyer, federal official*
Bellows, Keith Adams *editor-in-chief, writer*
Belson, James Anthony *judge*
Belt, Bradley Deck *financial services executive*
Bender, David Ray *retired library association executive*
Benjamin, Ernst *educational association administrator*
Benjamin, Georges Curtis *emergency physician, consultant*
Benner, C. Jonathan *lawyer*
Bennett, Alan R. *lawyer*
Bennett, Alexander Elliot *lawyer*
Bennett, Philip *editor*
Bennett, Robert F. *senator*
Bennett, Robert Stephen *lawyer*
Benoit, Marilyn B. *psychiatrist, consultant*
Ben-Veniste, Richard *lawyer*
Berdahl, Robert Max *history professor, association and former academic administrator*
Berendzen, Richard *astronomer, educator, author*
Berenson, Bradford A. *lawyer*
Beresford, Douglas Lincoln *lawyer*
Berg, Patricia Elene *molecular biologist*

Berger, Sandy (Samuel R. Berger) *former national security advisor*
Bergmann, Barbara Rose *economics professor*
Bergner, Jane Cohen *lawyer*
Bergner, Jeffrey Thomas *federal agency administrator*
Berkley, Shelley (Rochelle Levine Berkley) *congresswoman, lawyer*
Berl, Joseph M. *lawyer*
Berlack, Evan Raden *lawyer*
Berlin, Kenneth *lawyer*
Berman, Ellen Sue *energy and telecommunications executive, theatre producer*
Berman, Howard Lawrence *congressman, lawyer*
Berman, Joshua G. *lawyer*
Berman, Paul Justin *lawyer*
Bernabei, Lynne Ann *lawyer*
Bernanke, Ben Shalom *chairman board of governors of the Federal Reserve System*
Bernard, Lawrence B. *lawyer*
Bernardi, Roy A. (Romolo Albert Bernardi) *federal agency administrator*
Berner, Frederic George, Jr. *lawyer*
Bernhard, Berl *lawyer*
Bernhardt, David Longly *federal agency administrator*
Bernstein, Mitchell Harris *lawyer*
Bernthal, Eric L. *lawyer*
Bernthal, Frederick Michael *research association executive*
Berrington, Craig Anthony *lawyer*
Berry, Marion *congressman*
Berthelsen, Richard A. *lawyer*
Bertin, Margaret A.H *museum administrator*
Berz, David Richard *lawyer*
Besen, Stanley Martin *economist*
Besozzi, Paul Charles *lawyer*
Best, Judah *lawyer*
Betancourt Lopez, Antonio L. *association executive*
Beyrle, John R. *ambassador*
Bhatia, Karan K. *ambassador*
Biden, Joseph Robinette, Jr. *senator*
Bieber, Sander M. *lawyer*
Bierly, Eugene Wendell *meteorologist, science foundation director*
Bierman, James Norman *lawyer*
Biesenbach-Lucas, Sigrun *language educator, consultant*
Biggert, Judith Borg *congresswoman, lawyer*
Biggs, Jeffrey Robert *political scientist*
Bilbray, Brian Patrick *congressman*
Bilirakis, Gus Michael *congressman, former state representative*
Billauer, Barbara Pfeffer *lawyer, educator*
Billington, James Hadley *librarian, historian*
Bingaman, Jeff, Jr., (Jesse Francis Bingaman) *senator*
Bintz, Edward E. *lawyer*
Bird, Kai *journalist, historian*
Birnbaum, Charles A. *landscape architect*
Birnbaum, Norman *writer, humanities educator*
Birnkrant, Henry Joseph *lawyer*
Bishop, James Dodson *lawyer, mediator*
Bishop, Rob *congressman*
Bishop, Sanford Dixon, Jr. *congressman, lawyer*
Bishop, Timothy H. *congressman*
Black, Scott C. *career military officer, lawyer*
Black, Stephen Franklin *lawyer, writer*
Blackburn, Marsha *congresswoman*
Blackburne-Rigsby, Anna *state supreme court justice*
Blackwelder, Brent Francis *environmentalist*
Blackwill, Robert D. *former federal agency administrator*
Blahous, Charles P. *federal official*
Blair, Bruce G. *think-tank executive*
Blair, James Pease *freelance photographer*
Blair, Robert Allen *lawyer*
Blake, Jonathan Dewey *lawyer*
Blakely, Robert T. *financial executive*
Blakey, Marion Clifton *federal agency administrator*
Blalack, K. Lee *lawyer*
Blanchard, Bruce *civil engineer, consultant*
Blanchard, James Johnston *ambassador, retired governor*
Blankley, Tony *editor*
Blazek-White, Doris *lawyer*
Blazy, Louis Joseph III *federal agency administrator*
Bleakley, Peter Kimberley *lawyer*
Bliley, Thomas Jerome, Jr. *former congressman*
Blitzer, Wolf *news correspondent*
Bloch, Scott J. *lawyer*
Bloch, Susan Low *law educator*
Block, Joseph G. *lawyer*
Block, Lawrence J. *federal judge*
Bloom, David I. *lawyer*
Bloomfield, Sara J. *museum director*
Bloomquist, Michael *lawyer*
Blumenfeld, Jeffrey *lawyer, educator*
Blumenthal, Susan Jane *physician, psychiatrist, educator*
Blumenthal, William *lawyer*
Blunt, Roy D. *congressman*
Boardman, Joseph H. *federal agency administrator*
Boaz, David Douglas *foundation executive*
Bodansky, Robert Lee *lawyer*
Bodine, Susan P. *federal agency administrator*
Bodman, Samuel Wright III *secretary of energy, former specialty chemicals and materials company executive*
Bodner, John, Jr. *lawyer*
Boehm, Steven Bruce *lawyer*
Boehner, John Andrew *congressman*
Bogard, Lawrence Joseph *lawyer*
Boggs, George Robert *educational association administrator*
Boggs, George Trenholm *lawyer*
Boggs, Judith Susan *lawyer, health policy analyst*
Boggs, Thomas Hale, Jr. *lawyer, director*
Bohigian, David Steele *federal agency administrator*

Boisture, Robert A. *lawyer*
Boland, Christopher Thomas, II, *lawyer*
Bolger, Robert J., Jr. *lawyer*
Bolten, Joshua Brewster *White House chief of staff*
Bolton, Claude M., Jr. *civilian military employee, retired military officer*
Bomar, Mary Amelia *federal agency administrator*
Bond, Christopher Samuel (Kit Bond) *senator, lawyer*
Bondareff, Joan M. *lawyer, retired government agency administrator*
Bonicelli, Paul J. *federal agency administrator*
Bonner, Josiah Robins, Jr., (Jo Bonner) *congressman*
Bono, Mary Whitaker *congresswoman*
Bonosaro, Carol Alessandra *professional society and retired federal agency administrator*
Bonvillian, William Boone *lawyer*
Booker, Salih *human rights organization executive*
Bookoff, Leslie *lawyer*
Boozman, John *congressman*
Bopp, Michael D. *lawyer*
Bordallo, Madeleine Zeien (Mrs. Ricardo Jerome Bordallo) *congresswoman*
Boren, Daniel David *congressman*
Borenstein, David Gilbert *internist, writer, rheumatologist*
Borg, Joseph Philip *securities association administrator, lawyer*
Born, Brooksley Elizabeth *retired lawyer*
Borsari, George Robert, Jr. *lawyer, commentator*
Bosch, Michele C. *lawyer*
Bosco, Mary Beth *lawyer*
Boskey, Bennett *lawyer*
Boss, Alan Paul *astrophysicist*
Boss, Lenard Barrett *lawyer*
Bost, Eric M. *ambassador, former federal agency administrator*
Boswell, Eric J. *federal official*
Boswell, Leonard L. *congressman*
Boucher, Richard A. *federal agency administrator*
Boucher, Rick (Frederick C. Boucher) *congressman, lawyer*
Bourne, Peter Geoffrey *physician, educator, writer*
Boustany, Charles W., Jr. *congressman, surgeon*
Bowden, Aisha L. *elementary school educator*
Bowman, Dorothy Louise *artist*
Bowman, Frank Lee (Skip Bowman) *retired military officer*
Boxer, Barbara *senator*
Boyce, Ralph L. (Skip Boyce) *ambassador*
Boyd, Benjamin S. *lawyer*
Boyd, F. Allen, Jr. *congressman, farmer*
Boyd, Thomas Marshall *lawyer*
Boyda, Nancy *congresswoman*
Boyer, Jan E. *federal agency administrator*
Boykin, William G. (Jerry Boykin) *federal agency administrator, career military officer*
Braden, Gregory C. *lawyer*
Bradford, Monica M. *editor*
Bradlee, Benjamin Crowninshield *former editor*
Bradley, John A. *career military officer*
Bradley Gardner, Janice *federal agency administrator*
Bradshaw, Richard Eugene *science and technology government relations consultant*
Bradtke, Robert A. *ambassador*
Brady, Kevin Patrick *congressman*
Brady, Robert A. *congressman*
Braga, Stephen Louis *lawyer*
Brailer, David J. *federal agency administrator*
Braker, Gregory S. *lawyer*
Braley, Bruce *congressman*
Brame, Joseph Robert III *lawyer*
Bramson, Leon *social scientist, educator*
Brand, Rachel L. *federal agency administrator, lawyer*
Branegan, James Augustus III *journalist*
Braswell, Mark K. *lawyer*
Braverman, Jordan *columnist*
Brazeal, Aurelia Erskine *former ambassador*
Breathitt, Linda K. *energy advisor, former federal energy commissioner*
Breaux, John Berlinger *lawyer, communications professor, former senator*
Bregman, Arthur Randolph *lawyer, educator*
Brenner, Janet Maybin Walker *lawyer*
Brenner, Joel F. *federal agency administrator*
Bresnahan, Pamela Anne *lawyer, mediator, arbitrator*
Bretzfelder, Deborah May *retired museum staff member*
Brewster, Robert Charles *diplomat, consultant*
Breyer, Stephen Gerald *United States supreme court justice*
Briggs, Alan Leonard *lawyer*
Briggs, Ethel DeLoria *federal agency administrator*
Briggs, Kerri Layne *federal agency administrator*
Briggum, Sue Marie *corporate executive*
Brimmer, Andrew Felton *economist, consultant*
Brinkmann, Robert Joseph *lawyer*
Brobeck, Stephen James *consumer advocate*
Brock, Gregory E. *editor*
Broder, David Salzer *reporter, writer*
Brody, Peter Martin *lawyer*
Brogan, Stephen (Steve) J. *lawyer*
Bromwich, Michael Ray *lawyer*
Bronstein, Alvin J. *lawyer*
Brooks, Jane K. *real estate agent, educator*
Brooks, Renana Esther *clinical psychologist, business and political consultant, researcher*
Broome, David *federal official*
Brosnan, Carol Raphael Sarah *retired art association administrator*
Brouillette, Dan R. *former federal agency administrator*
Broun, Elizabeth *art historian, curator*
Broun, Paul C., Jr. *congressman, physician*
Brower, Charles Nelson *lawyer, judge*
Brower, Gregory A. *lawyer*

Brown, Barbara Berish *lawyer*
Brown, Campbell *newscaster*
Brown, Corrine *congresswoman*
Brown, Dana A. *federal agency administrator*
Brown, David Nelson *lawyer*
Brown, Harold *former secretary of defense*
Brown, Henry E., Jr. *congressman*
Brown, Janice Rogers *federal judge, former state supreme court justice*
Brown, John Patrick *publishing executive, financial consultant*
Brown, Lawrence George *medical director*
Brown, Lester Russell *research and development company executive*
Brown, Michael D. *shadow senator*
Brown, Morgan *federal agency administrator*
Brown, Nadine *sommelier*
Brown, Pamela Wedd *artist*
Brown, Preston *lawyer*
Brown, Sherrod Campbell *senator, former congressman, former state official*
Brown, Thomas Philip III *lawyer*
Brown, Warren *chef*
Brownback, Sam Dale *senator, lawyer*
Browne, Richard Cullen *lawyer*
Brownell, F. William *lawyer*
Browner, Carol M. *management consultant, former federal agency administrator*
Brown-Hruska, Sharon *economist, former commissioner*
Browning, Steven Alan *ambassador*
Bruce, Carol Elder *lawyer*
Bruce, Derek Andrew *neurosurgeon, educator*
Bruce, Estel Edward *lawyer*
Bruemmer, Russell John *lawyer*
Bruggink, Eric G. *federal judge*
Brunner, Thomas William *lawyer*
Bruno, Philippe M. *lawyer*
Brunsvold, Brian Garrett *lawyer, educator*
Bruzelius, Nils Johan Axel *journalist*
Bryson, William Curtis *federal judge*
Brzezinski, Zbigniew *political science professor, former national security advisor*
Buben, Jeffrey Alan *restaurant owner, chef*
Buc, Nancy Lillian *lawyer*
Buchan, Douglas Charles *gas industry executive, government agency administrator*
Buchanan, Gale Arlon *federal agency administrator, former dean*
Buchanan, Vern (Vernon G. Buchanan) *congressman*
Buckenmaier, Chester III *military officer, anesthesiologist*
Buckley, Jeremiah Stephen *lawyer*
Bucklin, Donald Thomas *lawyer*
Buechner, Jack W(illiam) *lawyer, consultant, educational association administrator*
Buffon, Charles Edward *lawyer*
Buffone, Samuel J. *lawyer*
Buhler, Leslie Lynn *museum director*
Bullard-Bates, Patricia Carol *psychologist, neuropsychologist*
Bulleit, Thomas Nelson, Jr. *lawyer*
Bumpus, Jeanne *lawyer*
Bunch, Lonnie III *museum director*
Bunning, Jim (James Paul David Bunning) *senator, former professional baseball player*
Burchfield, Bobby Roy *lawyer*
Burdett, James R. *lawyer*
Burgess, Michael C. *congressman*
Burgess, Ronald L., Jr. *federal agency administrator, career military officer*
Burgin, Walter Hotchkiss, Jr. *retired academic administrator*
Burk, Martha Gertrude *political psychologist*
Burka, Robert Alan *lawyer*
Burke, Edmund W. *lawyer*
Burke, John *priest*
Burke-Ables, Kim S. *biology educator*
Burnett, Arthur Louis, Sr. *judge*
Burnham, David Bright *writer, educator*
Burnley, James Horace, IV, *lawyer*
Burns, Conrad Ray *former senator*
Burns, David Mitchell *writer, retired diplomat*
Burns, R(obert) Nicholas *federal agency administrator, former ambassador*
Burns, Stephen Gilbert *lawyer*
Burns, William Joseph *ambassador, former federal agency administrator*
Burr, Richard M. *senator, former congressman*
Burris, Boyd Lee *psychiatrist, psychoanalyst, physician, educator*
Burris, Howard L. *investment company executive*
Burris, James Frederick *federal healthcare administrator, educator*
Burrus, William Henry *labor union administrator*
Burt, Jeffrey Amsterdam *lawyer*
Burtless, Gary Thomas *economist, consultant*
Burton, Dan L. *congressman*
Burton, William Joseph *engineering executive*
Busby, David *lawyer*
Buscemi, Peter *lawyer*
Buser, Carolyn Elizabeth *adult education educator*
Bush, George Walker *43rd President of the United States*
Bush, Karen Lee *lawyer*
Bush, Laura Welch *First Lady of United States*
Bush, Lynn Jeanne *federal judge*
Butchart, Mark Steven *diplomat*
Butcher, Karen A. *lawyer*
Butler, (James) Caron *professional basketball player*
Butler, Mary K. *prosecutor*
Butler, Michael Francis *lawyer*
Butterfield, George Kenneth, Jr. *congressman, former state supreme court justice*
Buyer, Steven Earle *congressman, lawyer*
Byrd, Robert Carlyle *senator*
Cabral, Anna Escobedo *federal official*
Cabrera, Orlando J. *federal agency administrator*
Cafritz, Peggy Cooper *communications executive*
Cain, James P. *ambassador, lawyer*
Calamaro, Raymond Stuart *lawyer*
Calder, Kent Eyring *political science professor, federal agency administrator*

Calhoun, Noah Robert *oral maxillofacial surgeon, educator*
Calingaert, Michael *non-profit organization executive*
Callahan, Debra Jean *political organization worker*
Callaway, Clifford Wayne *physician*
Callender, Clive Orville *surgeon*
Callery, Grant *financial industry regulatory authority general cousel*
Callery, T. Grant *lawyer*
Calvani, Terry *lawyer*
Calvert, Ken *congressman*
Cameron, Carl (Karl Lamberg-Karlovsky) *political correspondent*
Cameron, Donald B., Jr. *lawyer*
Camp, David Lee *congressman, lawyer*
Campanelli, Richard M. *federal agency administrator*
Campbell, Benton J. *federal agency administrator*
Campbell, Bradford P. *government agency administrator*
Campbell, John B. T. III *congressman, former state senator*
Campbell, Laura Elizabeth *library administrator*
Campbell, Nancy Duff *lawyer*
Campbell, William Henry, Jr. *rail transportation executive, former federal agency administrator*
Campbell-Smith, Patricia *federal official*
Campos, Roel C. *lawyer, former commissioner*
Cannon, Carl M. *reporter*
Cannon, Christopher Black *congressman, lawyer*
Cantor, Eric I. *congressman, lawyer*
Cantor, Herbert I. *lawyer*
Cantwell, Maria E. *senator*
Capito, Shelley Moore *congresswoman*
Capka, J. Richard (Joseph Richard Capka) *federal agency administrator, retired military officer*
Caplin, Mortimer Maxwell *lawyer, educator*
Capps, Lois Ragnhild Grimsrud *congresswoman, former school nurse*
Caproni, Valerie E. *lawyer, federal agency administrator*
Capuano, Michael Everett *congressman, lawyer*
Carbonell, Josefina G. *federal agency administrator*
Cardin, Benjamin Louis *senator, former congressman*
Cardoza, Dennis *congressman*
Carey, Sarah Collins *lawyer*
Carfine, Kenneth E. *government agency administrator*
Carhart, Homer Walter *retired research scientist*
Carliner, David *lawyer*
Carlisle, Linda Elizabeth *lawyer*
Carluzzo, Lewis R. *federal judge*
Carmody, Carol Jones *transportation executive, former federal agency administrator*
Carnahan, Russ (John Russell Carnahan) *congressman, lawyer*
Carneal, George Upshur *lawyer*
Carney, Christopher Paul *congressman, political science educator*
Carney, Robert Thomas *lawyer*
Carpenter, Russell H., Jr. *lawyer*
Carpenter, Sheila Jane *lawyer*
Carpenter, Ted Galen *political scientist*
Carper, Thomas Richard *senator, former governor*
Carr, Bob *congressman, lawyer*
Carr, Carolyn Kinder *art gallery director*
Carr, Lawrence Edward, Jr. *lawyer*
Carranza, Jovita *federal agency administrator, retired delivery service executive*
Carrier, Warren Pendleton *retired university chancellor, writer*
Carroll, Andrew Patrick Keating *writer*
Carroll, M(argaret) Lizbeth Carr *art educator, graphics designer, photographer*
Carson, Johnnie *former ambassador, academic administrator*
Carson, Julia M. *congresswoman*
Carson, Thomas Bode *bank executive, consultant*
Carter, Barry Edward *law educator*
Carter, John Rice *congressman, lawyer*
Carter, William Joseph *lawyer*
Cartwright, Brian Grant *federal agency administrator, lawyer*
Cartwright, James E. *career military officer*
Cary, George S. *lawyer*
Case, Larry D. *agricultural education specialist*
Casellas, Gilbert F. F. *lawyer*
Casey, George William, Jr. *career military officer*
Casey, Kathleen L. *commissioner*
Casey, Robert Patrick, Jr., (Bob Casey) *senator*
Casscells, Samuel Ward III *federal agency administrator, cardiologist, educator*
Casserly, James Lund *lawyer*
Casserly, Michael David *educational association administrator*
Cassidy, Robert Charles, Jr. *lawyer*
Castagnetti, David A. *political strategist*
Castle, Michael N. *congressman, lawyer*
Caswell, James L. *government agency administrator*
Catoe, Bette Lorrina *pediatrician, educator*
Cavalier, Gina M. *lawyer*
Cavanagh, John Henry *political economist*
Cavanaugh, James Michael *lawyer*
Cavaney, Red *trade association administrator*
Cavett, Deborah J. *federal agency administrator*
Centanni, Steve *national news correspondent*
Chabot, Elliot Charles *lawyer*
Chabot, Herbert L. *federal judge*
Chabot, Steven Joseph *congressman, lawyer*
Chalk, Rosemary Anne *health science association administrator*
Chalkley, Jacqueline Ann *retail company executive*
Challinor, David *retired biologist*
Chamberlain, John Loomis III *retired pediatrician, educator*
Chambers, Letitia Pearl Caroline *consulting firm executive*
Chambliss, Saxby (C. Saxby Chambliss) *senator*

Chamot, Dennis *science policy executive*
Chan, Wing-Chi *cultural consultant and organization administrator, musicologist*
Chandler, Ben (Albert Benjamin Chandler III) *congressman, former state attorney general*
Chandler, James Phillip III *law educator*
Chandrasekaran, Rajiv *editor, writer*
Chang, Sam Hsien-Cheng *lawyer*
Chanin, Michael Henry *lawyer*
Chao, Elaine Lan (Hsiao) *secretary of labor*
Chapman, Paulette Elaine *lawyer*
Chapman, Thomas B. *air transportation executive*
Charytan, Lynn R. *lawyer*
Chase, Thomas Newell *neurologist, researcher, educator*
Chatilovicz, Peter *lawyer*
Chavarria, Adam *federal agency administrator*
Chavous, Kevin P. *lawyer*
Chealander, Steven Russell *federal agency administrator*
Chellaraj, Rajkumar *federal agency administrator*
Cheney, Dick (Richard Bruce Cheney) *Vice President of the United States*
Cheney, Lynne Vincent *humanities educator, writer*
Cheng, Tsung O. *cardiologist, educator*
Cherry, Schroeder *federal agency administrator*
Chertoff, Michael *secretary of homeland security, former federal judge*
Chesanow, Charles *psychiatrist*
Chester, Alexander Campbell III *physician*
Chiarelli, Peter W. *career military officer*
Chiechi, Carolyn Phyllis *federal judge*
Chien, Nguyen Tam *ambassador*
Chilton, Bart (Bartholomew Hamilton Chilton) *commissioner*
Chorba, Timothy A. *lawyer, former ambassador*
Choudhury, Raj Deo *automotive executive*
Choukas-Bradley, James Richard *lawyer*
Christian, Betty Jo *lawyer*
Christian-Christensen, Donna Marie *congresswoman*
Christopherson, Charles Richard, Jr., (Chuck Christopherson) *federal agency administrator*
Chu, David S.C. *federal agency administrator, economist*
Chun, Shinae *federal agency administrator*
Churchill, John Hugh *college academic administrator*
Chused, Richard Harris *law educator*
Chute, Mary L. *library director*
Ciatto, Frank A. *lawyer*
Ciccoella, Charles S. (Chick) *federal agency administrator*
Cicerone, Ralph John *foundation administrator, research scientist*
Ciesla, Fred John *astrophysicist, meteoriticist, researcher*
Cino, Maria *political organization administrator, former federal agency administrator*
Cirulnick, Arthur E. *lawyer*
Citronelle, Michel Richard *chef*
Clagett, Brice McAdoo *lawyer, writer, genealogist*
Clapper, James R., Jr. *federal agency administrator, retired military officer*
Clark, Jeffrey Raphiel *research and development company executive*
Clark, Jim *labor union president*
Clark, LeRoy D. *law educator*
Clark, Michael *artist*
Clark, Michell C. *federal agency administrator*
Clark-Bourne, Kathryn Orpha *retired consul*
Clarke, Yvette Diane *congresswoman*
Clay, William Lacy, Jr. *congressman*
Clayman, Paul F. *lawyer*
Clayton, Carol A. *lawyer*
CLayton, Michael F. *lawyer*
Cleaver, Emanuel, II, *congressman, former mayor, minister*
Cleland, Joseph Maxwell (Max Cleland) *federal official, former senator*
Clement, Paul Drew *federal agency administrator, lawyer*
Clerihue, Randolph James *federal agency administrator*
Clevenger, Raymond Charles III *federal judge*
Clewell, Beatriz Chu *director, researcher*
Clift, Eleanor *news correspondent, writer*
Clifton, James K. *market research company executive*
Cline, Eric H. *archaeologist, anthropologist, classicist, educator*
Cline, William Richard *economist, educator*
Clinton, Hillary (Hillary Diane Rodham Clinton) *senator, lawyer, former First Lady of United States*
Cloud, John Albert, Jr. *ambassador*
Clyburn, James Enos (Jim Clyburn) *congressman*
Coan, Carl A.S., Jr. *lawyer*
Coats, Daniel Ray *lawyer, former ambassador, senator*
Cobb, Calvin Hayes, Jr. *lawyer*
Cobb, Ty *lawyer*
Cobbs, Nicholas Hamner *lawyer, judge*
Coble, (John) Howard *congressman, lawyer*
Coburn, Tom (Thomas Allen Coburn) *senator*
Cochran, Thad (William Thad Cochran) *senator*
Cofer, Jonathan H. *career officer*
Coffey, Matthew B. *senior advisor to industry*
Coffield, Shirley Ann *lawyer, educator*
Coffin, Beatriz de Winthuysen *landscape architect*
Coffina, Scott A. *lawyer*
Cogman, Don V. *public relations executive*
Cohen, Benedict S. *lawyer*
Cohen, David Blair *lawyer*
Cohen, Herman Nathan *private investigator*
Cohen, Larry *labor union administrator*
Cohen, Louis Richard *lawyer*
Cohen, Marc R. *lawyer*
Cohen, Mary Ann *federal judge*
Cohen, Michael *educational association administrator*
Cohen, Sheldon Stanley *lawyer*
Cohen, Steve (Stephen Ira Cohen) *congressman, former state legislator*
Cohen, Wayne R. *lawyer*
Cohen, William Sebastian *consultant, former Secretary of Defense*
Cohn, Sherman Louis *lawyer, educator*
Colaizzi, Roger A. *lawyer*
Cole, Bruce Milan *federal agency administrator, art historian*
Cole, John Pope, Jr. *lawyer*
Cole, Kenneth W. *automotive executive*
Cole, Lorraine *women's association executive*
Cole, Robert Theodore *lawyer*
Cole, Tom *congressman*
Coleman, Bernell *physiologist, educator*
Coleman, Milton *editor*
Coleman, Norman, Jr. *senator, former mayor*
Coleman, William Thaddeus, Jr. *lawyer, former secretary of transportation*
Coll, Stephen Wilson *journalist*
Collamore, Thomas Jones *corporate financial executive*
Colley, Mark Douglas *lawyer*
Collingsworth, Connie Renee *lawyer*
Collins, Daniel Francis *lawyer*
Collins, James Franklin *retired ambassador*
Collins, Robert Ellwood *surgeon*
Collins, Susan Margaret *senator*
Collins, Wayne Dale *lawyer*
Collinson, Dale Stanley *lawyer*
Colon, Jose Ernesto *pathologist*
Colson, Earl Morton *lawyer, educator*
Coltman, Edward Jeremiah *communication executive*
Colton Skolnick, Judith A. *artist*
Colvin, John O. *federal judge*
Comas, Daniel L. *manufacturing executive*
Combs, Linda Morrison *federal official*
Combs, Roberta *religious organization administrator*
Comerford, Cristeta *chef*
Compton, Ann Woodruff *news correspondent*
Comstock, Amy L. *social services administrator*
Comstock, Robert Francis *lawyer*
Conaway, Mike *congressman*
Condrell, William Kenneth *lawyer*
Coneway, Peter Richard *ambassador, retired diversified financial services company executive*
Conlin, Linda Mysliwy *bank executive, former federal agency administrator*
Connaughton, James L. *federal official*
Connaughton, Sean Thomas *federal agency administrator*
Connelly, Warren E. *lawyer*
Conner, Charles F. *federal agency administrator*
Conner, Frank M. (Rusty) III *lawyer*
Conrad, Kent (Gaylord Kent Conrad) *senator*
Conron, Michael William *lawyer*
Conte, Tony *chef*
Convey, John J. *academic administrator*
Conway, James Terry *career military officer*
Conway, John Thomas *federal agency administrator, lawyer, engineer*
Conwill, Kinshasha Holman *museum director*
Conyers, John, Jr. *congressman*
Cook, Charles Edward, Jr. *editor, political analyst*
Cook, David *editor*
Cook, Frances D. *management consultant*
Cook, Harry Clayton, Jr. *lawyer*
Cook, Michael Blanchard *government executive*
Cook, Michael Harry *lawyer*
Cook, William E., Jr. *lawyer*
Cooke, Edmund *lawyer*
Cooney, John Fontana *lawyer*
Cooper, Alan Samuel *lawyer, educator*
Cooper, Byron Stanley *internist, educator*
Cooper, Charles Justin *lawyer, former federal agency administrator*
Cooper, Daniel L. *federal agency administrator*
Cooper, Ginnie *library director*
Cooper, J. Michael *lawyer*
Cooper, James Hayes Shofner (Jim Cooper) *congressman, lawyer*
Cooper, Matthew *journalist*
Cooper, Richard Melvyn *lawyer*
Cooper, Ronald Stephen *lawyer*
Cooper, Thomas J. *lawyer*
Cope, John R(obert) *lawyer*
Copps, Michael Joseph *commissioner*
Corbin, Michael *diplomat*
Corell, Robert Walden *science administrator, educator*
Coreth, Joseph Herman *investment advisor*
Corker, Bob (Robert Phillips Corker Jr.) *senator*
Corn-Revere, Robert *lawyer*
Cornyn, John *senator*
Corrigan, Janet M. *health science association administrator*
Corso, John Anthony *management consultant, educator*
Cortese, Alfred William, Jr. *lawyer, consultant*
Corts, Paul Richard *educational association and former federal agency administrator*
Corwin, Carolyn F. *lawyer*
Cosgrove, John Patrick *editor*
Costa, Jim *congressman*
Costello, Jerry F., Jr. *congressman, former county official*
Coston, William Dean *lawyer*
Cothron, Tony L. *career military officer*
Couch, Robert M. *lawyer, federal agency administrator*
Coulter, Ann *writer, political columnist, lawyer*
Couvillion, David Irvin *federal judge*
Covault, Craig *editor*
Covington, Eileen Queen *secondary school educator*
Covucci, George E. *lawyer*
Cowan, Edward *journalist, editor*
Cowan, Eric Ward *lawyer*
Cowan, Joyce A. *lawyer*
Cox, Ana Marie *writer, former political blogger*
Cox, (Charles) Christopher *federal agency administrator, former congressman*
Cox, John W. *federal agency administrator*
Cox, M. Carolyn *lawyer*
Cox, Rebecca Gernhardt *air transportation executive*
Cox, Warren Jacob *architect*
Coyne, Patrick Joseph *lawyer*
Craft, Robert Homan, Jr. *lawyer*
Craig, Gregory Bestor *lawyer*
Craig, John Tucker *economist, consultant*
Cramer, Robert E., Jr., (Bud Cramer) *congressman, lawyer*
Crane, Edward Harrison III *academic administrator, financial analyst*
Craner, Lorne Whitney *not-for-profit institute executive, former federal agency administrator*
Crapo, Michael Dean *senator, former congressman, lawyer*
Crawford, Brett A. *lawyer*
Crawford, Hunt Dorn, Jr. *retired military officer, educator, diplomat*
Crawford, Lester Mills, Jr. *former federal agency administrator*
Crawford, Susan Jean *federal judge*
Crawford-Mason, Clare Wootten *television producer, journalist*
Crea, Vivien S. *career military officer*
Creel, Harold Jennings, Jr. *federal commission administrator, lawyer*
Crenshaw, Albert Burford *journalist*
Crenshaw, Ander *congressman, lawyer*
Cresanti, Robert Charles *federal agency administrator*
Crocker, Chester Arthur *diplomat, federal agency administrator*
Crocker, Thomas Edward *lawyer*
Crocker, William Henry *ethnologist, researcher*
Crockett, Kristen Michelle *director*
Crosby, William Duncan, Jr. *lawyer*
Cross, Meredith B. *lawyer*
Cross, Terry M. *career military officer*
Crowder, Richard Thomas *ambassador*
Crowe, William James, Jr. *former Chairman of the Joint Chiefs of Staff, international consultant*
Crowley, Joseph *congressman*
Crowley, Juanita A. *lawyer*
Crown, Michele Fleurette *lawyer*
Cruden, John Charles *lawyer*
Crump, John *lawyer*
Cubin, Barbara Lynn *congresswoman*
Cuellar, Henry *congressman, lawyer*
Culberson, John Abney *congressman, lawyer*
Cullman, Lewis B. *philanthropist*
Culp, H. Lawrence *manufacturing executive*
Cummings, Elijah E. *congressman*
Cummings, Frank *lawyer*
Currie, Charles Leonard *educational association administrator*
Curris, Constantine William *educational association administrator*
Curry, Thomas J. *federal and former state agency administrator*
Curtin, Peter J. *lawyer*
Curtis, Charles B. *former federal agency administrator*
Curtiss, Richard Holden *magazine editor, writer*
Cushing, Michael *federal agency administrator*
Cusick, Robert Irwin *federal official, lawyer*
Cutler, Bernard Joseph *editor-in-chief, writer*
Cutler, Walter Leon *diplomat, foundation executive*
Cylke, Frank Kurt *librarian*
Cymrot, Mark Alan *lawyer*
Cynamon, David J. *lawyer*
Cys, Richard L. *lawyer*
Dacey, Robert Frank *accountant*
Dach, Leslie Alan *public relations company executive*
D'Agostino, Thomas Paul *federal agency administrator*
Dailey, Dell Lee *federal agency administrator, military officer*
Dale, Adrianne Marie *information technology executive, consultant*
Dale, Shana L. *federal agency administrator*
Daley, Henry J. *lawyer*
Dalley, George Albert *lawyer, consultant*
Daly, George Garman *dean*
Daly, Kenneth *business association executive*
Damelin, Harold D. *lawyer, former federal agency administrator*
Damich, Edward John *federal judge*
Damjanovich, Chaslav M. (Casey Diamond) *filmmaker, television producer, writer*
Danas, Andrew Michael *lawyer*
Dane, Stephen Mark *lawyer*
D'Aniello, Daniel A. *investment company executive*
Daniels, Stephen M. *government official*
Danilovich, John J. *federal official, former ambassador*
Danziger, Raphael *political scientist, researcher*
Darman, Richard *investor, former federal official*
Davidow, Charles E. *lawyer*
Davidson, Dan Eugene *educational association administrator, director, language educator*
Davidson, Daniel Ira *lawyer*
Davidson, Daniel Morton *lawyer*
Davidson, Donetta Lea *federal official, former state official*
Davidson, Eugene Abraham *biochemist, educator, academic administrator*
Davidson, Jo Ann *political organization executive, retired state legislator*
Davidson, Tom William *lawyer*
Davies, Charles R. *retired lawyer*
Davies, J. Clarence (Terry Davies) *public information officer, consultant*
Davila, Robert R. *academic administrator*
Davis, Artur *congressman, lawyer*
Davis, Danny K. *congressman*
Davis, David Lee *congressman*
Davis, David Oliver *radiologist, educator*
Davis, Donald Ray *entomologist*
Davis, Geoff *congressman*
Davis, Jo Ann S. *congresswoman*
Davis, Lincoln *congressman*
Davis, Michele A. *federal agency administrator, former mortgage company executive*
Davis, Morris D. *military officer, lawyer*
Davis, Nathaniel (Nate) A. *broadcast executive*
Davis, Randy Lee *soil scientist*
Davis, Rex Darwin *business consultant*
Davis, Robert Nolan *federal judge, educator*
Davis, Smith Wormley *lawyer*
Davis, Susan A. *congresswoman*
Davis, Thomas M. III *congressman*
Davis, William E. *lawyer*
Davison, Calvin *retired lawyer*
Dawson, Howard Athalone, Jr. *federal judge*
Dawson, Mimi Weyforth *public policy consultant*
Day, Charles Williamson *commentator*
Day, Doris (Doris von Kappelhoff) *singer, actress*
Day, Lincoln Hubert *demographer, educator*
Day, Melvin Sherman *information and telecommunications company executive*
Deal, Jill B. *lawyer*
Deal, Nathan J. *congressman, lawyer*
Deal, Timothy *association executive, former diplomat*
Dean, Howard Brush III *political organization administrator, former governor*
Dean, John F. *federal judge*
Dean, Paul Regis *retired law educator*
Deason, Jonathan Pierce *environmental engineer, federal agency administrator*
Debevoise, Eli Whitney, II, *federal official, lawyer*
Debolt, Paul A. *lawyer*
de Borchgrave, Arnaud *editor, writer, lecturer*
Decker, Brett M. *bank executive*
Deeb, Mary-Jane *editor, educator*
Dees, C. Stanley *lawyer*
Deese, Pamela McCarthy *lawyer*
DeFazio, Peter Anthony *congressman*
DeFrank, Thomas Michael *journalist*
DeGioia, John J. *academic administrator*
DeGraffenreidt, James H., Jr. *gas company executive*
deKieffer, Donald Eulette *lawyer*
Delahay, John N. *orthopedist, surgeon*
Delahunt, William D. *congressman*
DeLauro, Rosa L. *congresswoman*
de Leon, Sylvia A. *lawyer*
Delgado, Jane *health policy executive, writer, psychologist*
Della Torre, Edward *electrical engineer, educator*
De Martino, Ralph Victor *lawyer*
Dembling, Paul Gerald *lawyer, former government official*
Dempsey, Joan *federal agency administrator*
DeMuth, Christopher Clay *think-tank executive*
Denett, Paul Alfred *federal official*
Denger, Michael Louis *lawyer*
Denison, Mary Boney *lawyer*
Dennis, Gary C. *neurosurgeon, educator*
Denysyk, Bohdan *marketing professional, consultant*
DeParle, Nancy-Ann Min *former federal agency administrator, lawyer*
DePaul, Christina *dean, artist*
de Puget, Albert Borg Olivier *magistrate judge*
de Quadros, Ciro A. *epidemiologist, educator*
de Rato y Figaredo, Rodrigo *international banking official*
Derby, Susan Eileen *not-for-profit fundraiser*
DeSchryver, David Alan *lawyer*
DeSutter, Paula A. *federal agency administrator*
DeTrani, Joseph *federal agency administrator*
Deutsch, Peter R. *former congressman*
Deutsch, Stanley *retired anesthesiologist, educator*
Devaney, Earl E. *federal agency administrator*
DeWaal, Caroline Smith *education and advocacy organization executive, lawyer*
Dewey, Elizabeth R. *lawyer*
Dey, Radheshyam Chandra *cytologist*
Dezenhall, Eric B. *management consultant, writer*
Dhillon, Uttam *federal agency administrator*
Dhue, Stephanie *television producer, reporter*
Diaz, Alphonso Vincent *federal agency administrator*
Diaz, Nils Juan *federal agency administrator*
Diaz-Balart, Lincoln *congressman, lawyer*
Diaz-Balart, Mario *congressman*
Dicello, Francis P. *lawyer*
Dickens, William Theodore *economic researcher*
Dicks, Norman De Valois *congressman*
DiConti, Michael Andrew *not-for-profit executive*
Diehl, Jackson Kemper *journalist*
Dienelt, John F. *lawyer*
Diercks, Walter Elmer *lawyer*
DiGanci, Todd T. *financial regulatory service executive*
diGenova, Joseph E. *lawyer*
Di Lella, Alexander Anthony *biblical studies educator*
DiLenge, Thomas *lawyer*
Dillin, John Woodward, Jr. *retired editor, reporter*
Dillon, Veronica *publishing executive, lawyer*
Dillon, Wilton Sterling *anthropologist, foundation administrator*
Dimberg, Lennart Axel *medical researcher, physician*
Dinan, Donald Robert *lawyer*
Diner, Bryan C. *lawyer*
Dingell, John David *congressman*
Dinh, Viet D. *law educator*
Dionne, E. J., Jr. *columnist*
DiPerna, Frank Paul *photographer, educator*
Disheroon, Fred Russell *lawyer*
Doan, Lurita Alexis *federal agency administrator*
Doan, Michael Frederick *editor*
Dobriansky, Paula Jon *federal agency administrator, ambassador*
Dodd, Christopher John *senator*
Dodgen, Daniel W. *health policy advisor, psychologist*
Doebbler, Curtis F.J. *lawyer*

Doggett, Lloyd Alton, II, *congressman, retired judge*
Dolan, Michael William *lawyer*
Dole, Bob (Robert Joseph Dole) *lawyer, retired senator*
Dole, Elizabeth Hanford (Liddy) *senator, former federal agency administrator*
Dolin, Mitchell F. *lawyer*
Domenech, Edgar A. *federal agency administrator*
Domenici, (Pete) Vichi *senator*
Domingo, Placido *tenor, opera company director*
Donahue, Thomas Reilly *trade union official*
Donaldson, Samuel Andrew *journalist*
Donegan, Charles Edward *lawyer, educator*
Donilon, Thomas E. *lawyer, former federal agency administrator*
Donlon, Claudette *performing company executive*
Donnelly, Joseph *congressman, lawyer*
Donnelly, Shaun Edward *government agency administrator*
Donohoe, Cathryn Murray *journalist*
Donohue, Thomas Joseph *business association administrator*
Donovan, George Joseph *transportation executive, consultant*
Dooley, Calvin Millard *former congressman*
Doolittle, Jesse William, Jr. *lawyer*
Doolittle, John Taylor *congressman*
Doran, Charles Francis *political scientist, consultant*
Dorfman, Cynthia Hearn *government agency administrator*
Dorfman, Marc *lawyer*
Dorgan, Byron Leslie *senator*
Doria, Marilyn L. *lawyer*
Dorn, Georgette Magassy *library official*
Dorn, James Andrew *editor*
Dorn, Jennifer Lynn *professional association executive, former federal agency administrator*
Dorr, Thomas C. *federal agency administrator*
Doty, James Robert *lawyer*
Dougherty, Jude Patrick *philosopher, educator, dean*
Douglas, Leslie *investment banker*
Doumato, Lamia *librarian, historian*
Dowd, John Maguire *lawyer*
Dowd, Maureen *columnist*
Downie, Leonard, Jr. *editor, writer*
Downie, Richard Duncan *government agency administrator, retired military officer*
Downs, Anthony *economist, real estate consultant*
Downs, Clark Evans *lawyer*
Downs, Thomas Michael (Tom Downs) *transportation executive*
Doyle, A. Patrick *lawyer*
Doyle, Michael F. (Mike) *congressman*
Drake, Thelma Day *congresswoman*
Drapeau, Mark David *defense contractor*
Dreeben, Michael R. *federal agency administrator*
Dreier, David Timothy *congressman*
Droms, William George *finance educator, investment advisor*
Duberstein, Kenneth Marc *management consultant, former White House chief of staff*
DuBois, Raymond Francis, Jr. *civilian military employee, former marketing professional*
Duemling, Robert Werner *diplomat, museum director*
Duff, James C. *lawyer*
Duffey, Joseph Daniel *academic administrator*
Duffy, John Fitzgerald *lawyer, educator*
Duffy, Michael F. *commissioner*
Dugan, John Cunningham *federal agency administrator, lawyer*
Duggan, Juanita Donaghey *trade association administrator*
Dujack, Stephen Raymond *editor*
Dunbar, Leslie Wallace *writer, consultant*
Duncan, John J., Jr. *congressman*
Duncan, Mike (Robert Michael) *political organization administrator, lawyer*
Dungy, Gwendolyn Jordan *educational association administrator*
Dunlap, Charles J., Jr. *judge advocate, military officer*
Dunn, David *federal agency administrator*
Dunn, David B. *ambassador*
Dunn, H. Stewart, Jr. *lawyer*
Dunn, James Milton *retired religious organization administrator*
Dunn, Michael V. *commissioner*
Dunne, Patrick W. *federal agency administrator, retired military officer*
Dunner, Donald Robert *lawyer*
Dunton, James Raynor *publisher*
Durbin, Dick (Richard Joseph Durbin) *senator*
Durney, Michael Cavalier *lawyer*
Dutro, John Thomas, Jr. *geologist, paleontologist*
Duvall, Tyler Davis *federal agency administrator*
Dwyer, Maureen Ellen *lawyer*
Dwyer Southern, Kathy *museum administrator*
Dybul, Mark Richard *ambassador*
Dye, Stuart Selley *lawyer*
Dyk, Timothy Belcher *federal judge*
Dyke, Charles William *retired army officer*
Dyson, Michael Eric *religious studies educator, writer*
Eads, George Curtis *economic consultant*
Eagleburger, Lawrence Sidney *former secretary of state*
Earll, Jerry Miller *internist, educator, endocrinologist*
Earp, Naomi Churchill *federal official, lawyer*
Easterbrook, Gregg Edmund *writer*
Eastin, Keith E. *civilian military employee, lawyer*
Eastment, Thomas James *lawyer*
Easton, John Jay, Jr. *lawyer*
Eaton, Judith Sheila *educational association administrator*
Eaton, Sabrina Catherine Elizabeth *journalist*
Eaton, William A. *ambassador, former federal agency administrator*
Eckenhoff, Edward Alvin *health facility administrator, educator*
Eckland, William S *lawyer*
Edelman, Alan Irwin *lawyer*
Edelman, Eric Steven *federal agency administrator, former ambassador*
Edelman, Marian Wright *not-for-profit developer, lawyer*
Edelman, Peter Benjamin *lawyer, educator*
Edge, Joe D. *lawyer*
Edlavitch, Susan T. *lawyer*
Edson, Charles Louis *lawyer*
Edwards, Bob (Robert Alan Edwards) *radio news anchor*
Edwards, Chet (Thomas Chester Edwards) *congressman*
Edwards, Harry Thomas *federal judge*
Edwards, John Frederick *federal official*
Effron, Andrew S. *federal judge*
Efros, Ellen Ann *lawyer*
Eggenberger, Andrew Jon *federal agency administrator*
Eggleston, W. Neil *lawyer*
Ehlers, Vernon James *congressman*
Ehrenhaft, Peter David *lawyer*
Ehrlich, Alan Marshall *lawyer, educator*
Eichen, Jeffrey L. *lawyer*
Eidleman, John C. *lawyer*
Ein, Daniel *allergist*
Eisenberg, Meyer *lawyer*
Eisenberg, Pablo Samuel *non-profit organization executive*
Eisenhower, Susan *business and political consultant*
Eisner, Howard *engineering executive, educator*
Eissenstat, Everett H. *lawyer*
Eizenstat, Stuart Elliot *lawyer, former federal agency administrator*
Ekman, Richard H. *educational association administrator*
Elcano, Mary S. *lawyer*
Elfin, Mel *magazine editor*
El-Fishawy, Saad Samuel *lawyer*
Elias, Thomas Sam *botanist, author*
El Khadem, Hassan Saad *chemistry professor, researcher*
Ellett, Ted (E. Tazewell Ellett) *lawyer*
Ellicott, John LeMoyne *lawyer*
Elliott, Edwin Donald, Jr. *lawyer, educator, federal agency administrator*
Elliott, Emerson John *education consultant, policy analyst*
Elliott, Graham John *music educator, director*
Elliott, Thomas Michael *retired association executive, educator, consultant*
Ellis, Courtenay *lawyer*
Ellis, Joe W. *federal agency administrator*
Ellis, Katheryn *finance company executive*
Ellsworth, Brad (Bradley Ellsworth) *congressman, former police officer*
Elmendorf, Steven A. *political strategist*
Elmer, Brian Christian *lawyer*
Elrod, Eugene Richard *lawyer*
Elsasser, Glen Robert *journalist*
Elwood, Patricia Cowan *city official, political scientist, consultant*
Ely-Raphel, Nancy *diplomat*
Emanuel, Rahm *congressman*
Emden, Craig A. *lawyer*
Emely, Mary Ann *association executive*
Emerson, Jo Ann H. *congresswoman*
Engel, Eliot Lanze *congressman*
Engel, John *lawyer*
England, Gordon Richard *federal agency administrator*
Engler, Renata Johanna Martha *allergist, immunologist, internist, educator*
English, Richard Allyn *sociologist, educator*
Ensenat, Donald Burnham *ambassador, lawyer*
Ensign, John Eric *senator, former congressman*
Entman, Robert Mathew *communications educator, consultant*
Enzi, Michael Bradley *senator, accountant*
Epps, Roselyn Elizabeth Payne *pediatrician, educator*
Epstein, Anthony Charles *lawyer*
Epstein, Gary Marvin *lawyer*
Epstein, Gerald Lewis *technology and security policy analyst*
Epstien, Jay Alan *lawyer*
Erdmann, Charles Edgar (Chip Erdmann) *federal judge, former state supreme court justice*
Erdtmann, Frederick J. *physician, retired military officer*
Ericsson, Sally Claire *not-for-profit consultant*
Ershler, William Baldwin *biogerontologist, educator*
Ervin, Clark Kent *former federal agency administrator*
Escolar, Diana M. *neurologist, researcher*
Esfandiary, Mary S. *physical scientist, operations consultant*
Eshoo, Anna Georges *congresswoman*
Esposo, Arnel *chef*
Etheridge, Bob (Bobby Ray Etheridge) *congressman*
Etter, Delores M. *civilian military employee*
Etzioni, Amitai *sociologist, educator*
Evans, David C. *lawyer*
Evans, Donald Louis *think-tank executive, former secretary of commerce*
Evans, Joy *foundation administrator*
Everett, Ralph Bernard *think-tank executive*
Everett, Terry *congressman*
Evers, Williamson Moore *education policy analyst, political scientist*
Everson, Mark Whitty *international relief organization executive, former federal agency administrator*
Ewing, Ky Pepper, Jr. *lawyer*
Facciola, John Michael *judge*
Faherty, Robert Louis *publishing executive*
Fahey, John M., Jr. *book publishing executive*
Fahmy, Nabil *ambassador*
Fairbanks, Richard Monroe III *lawyer, educator, retired ambassador*
Faleomavaega, Eni Fa'auaa Hunkin *congressman*
Fales, Lisa Jose *lawyer*
Faley, R(ichard) Scott *lawyer*
Falk, Diane M. *research information specialist, librarian, writer, editor, director*
Fanning, Fred Eldridge *public administrator*
Fanone, Joseph Anthony *lawyer*
Farabow, Ford Franklin, Jr. *lawyer*
Farr, George Frank, Jr. *retired federal official*
Farr, Judith Banzer *retired literature educator, writer, lecturer*
Farr, Sam *congressman*
Farrell, Michael W. *judge*
Fattah, Chaka *congressman, former state legislator*
Faust, Emanuel, Jr. *lawyer*
Fedders, John Michael *lawyer*
Feder, Judith *dean*
Feder, Samuel L. *lawyer*
Feeney, Tom *congressman*
Feffer, Gerald Alan *lawyer*
Feil, Michael Bruce *statistician*
Feinberg, Kenneth Roy *lawyer, educator*
Feingold, Russell Dana *senator, lawyer*
Feinstein, Deborah *lawyer*
Feinstein, Dianne *senator*
Feith, Douglas Jay *former federal agency administrator*
Feld, Karen Irma *columnist, journalist, commentator, speech professional*
Feldman, Clarice Rochelle *lawyer*
Felix, Larry R. *federal agency administrator*
Fels, Nicholas Wolff *lawyer*
Fennell, Stephen A. *lawyer*
Fenty, Adrian M. *mayor*
Ferguson, Lewis Hamilton III *lawyer*
Ferguson, Michael A. (Mike) *congressman*
Fernandez, (I)dalia P. *educational association administrator*
Ferrand, Louis George *lawyer*
Ferrara, Ralph C. *lawyer*
Ferrell, Elizabeth Ann *lawyer*
Ferrell, Michael J. *lawyer*
Ferren, John Maxwell *judge*
Ferris, Charles Daniel *lawyer, former government official*
Feshbach, Murray *demographer, educator*
Feulner, Edwin J., Jr. *research foundation executive*
Fiedler, Marc *lawyer, advocate*
Field, Andrea Bear *lawyer*
Fielding, Fred Fisher *federal official, lawyer*
Fields, Stuart Howard *labor relations specialist*
Fields, Suzanne Bregman *syndicated columnist*
Figueroa, Orlando *federal agency executive*
Filner, Bob *congressman*
Fine, Glenn A. *federal agency administrator*
Fineberg, Harvey Vernon *medical institute administrator*
Fineman, Howard David *columnist, news correspondent*
Fingar, Thomas *federal official*
Finkel, David *journalist*
Finkel, Eugene Jay *lawyer*
Finkelstein, James David *physician, educator*
Finkle, Jeffrey Alan *professional association executive*
Finley, James I. *federal agency administrator*
Finn, Timothy John *lawyer*
Finneran, John Patrick, Jr. *finance company executive, educator*
Firestone, Charles Morton *lawyer, educator*
Firestone, Nancy B. *federal judge*
Fischer, Elizabeth (Betsy) *television producer*
Fishbein, Thomas Marlon *general surgeon, transplant surgeon*
Fishburne, Benjamin Postell III *lawyer*
Fishel, Andrew S. *managing director*
Fisher, Alice S. *federal agency administrator, lawyer*
Fisher, Bart Steven *lawyer, educator, investment banker*
Fisher, John R. *district supreme court justice*
Fisher, Miles Mark, IV, *education and religious studies educator, minister*
Fisher, Robert Dale *stockbroker, retired naval officer*
Fishman, Ira *lawyer*
Fitton, Tom (Thomas J. Fitton) *legal foundation administrator*
Fitzgerald, Kevin C. *lawyer*
Fitzmyer, Joseph Augustine *theology studies educator, priest*
Fitzpatrick, James Franklin *lawyer*
Fitzsimmons, Beth Duston (Carolyn Beth Fitzsimmons) *library and information scientist*
Flagg, Ronald Simon *lawyer*
Flaherty, Sister Mary Jean *dean*
Flake, Jeff *congressman*
Flannery, Ellen Joanne *lawyer*
Fleischaker, Marc L. *lawyer*
Fleischman, Aaron I. *lawyer*
Fleisher, Eric Wilfrid *retired foreign service officer*
Flores, Antonio R. *educational association administrator*
Florida, Richard Louis *finance educator, writer*
Flowe, Benjamin Hugh, Jr. *lawyer*
Flowe, Carol Connor *lawyer*
Flügelman, Máximo Enrique *financier, composer*
Flyer, Michael R. *lawyer*
Foer, Franklin *editor*
Foley, April H. *ambassador*
Foley, Maurice B. *federal judge*
Foley, Tom (Thomas Stephen Foley) *former ambassador, former congressman*
Fong, Phyllis Kamoi *federal agency administrator, lawyer*
Forbes, James Randy *congressman*
Ford, Ann K. *lawyer*
Ford, Carl W., Jr. *consulting firm executive, former federal agency administrator*
Ford, Cecilia Sparks *federal agency administrator*
Ford, Charles A. *ambassador*
Ford, Harold Eugene, Jr. *law educator, former congressman*
Ford, Nelson M. *civilian military employee*
Fore, Henrietta Holsman *federal agency administrator*
Foreman, Carol Lee Tucker *consumer advocate*
Foresman, George W. *federal agency administrator*
Forester, John Gordon, Jr. *lawyer*
Forgey, Benjamin Franklin *architecture and art critic*
Forkan, Patricia Ann *foundation executive*
Forrest, Herbert Emerson *lawyer*
Fort, Randall Martin *federal agency administrator*
Fortenberry, Jeffrey Lane *congressman*
Fortuño, Luis *congressman*
Fortuno, Victor M. *lawyer*
Foscarinis, Maria *lawyer*
Foss, Clive Frank Wilson *history professor*
Foster, C(harles) Allen *lawyer*
Foster, Hope S. *lawyer*
Foulke, Edwin Gerhart, Jr. *federal agency administrator, lawyer*
Fowler, Paul Raymond *physician, lawyer*
Fox, Hamilton Phillips, III, (Phil Fox) *lawyer*
Fox, Thomas C. *lawyer*
Fox, William F. *dean, law educator*
Francke, Rend Rahim *former ambassador*
Franco, Omar *government agency administrator*
Francois, Francis Bernard *retired professional society administrator, lawyer, transportation consultant*
Frandsen, Richard A. *lawyer*
Frank, Barney *congressman*
Frank, Richard Asher *lawyer, health products executive*
Frank, Robert J. *lawyer*
Frank, Theodore David *lawyer*
Franklin, Barbara Hackman *former government official*
Franklin, Jonathan S. *lawyer*
Franks, Trent *congressman*
Franzen, Byron T. (John Franzen) *media specialist*
Fraser, William M. III *career military officer*
Fratto, Tony (Salvatore Antonio) *federal official*
Fraulino, Philip Samuel *telecommunications industry executive*
Frazer, Jendayi Elizabeth *federal agency administrator, former ambassador*
Freed, Joel M. *lawyer*
Freedman, Jay Weil *lawyer*
Freeman, Chas W., Jr. *federal agency administrator, writer, ambassador*
Freeman, Peter A. *dean*
Freeman, Sharee M. *federal agency administrator*
Frelinghuysen, Rodney P. *congressman*
French, Valerie *history professor*
Fried, Bruce Merlin *lawyer*
Fried, Daniel *federal agency administrator, former ambassador*
Frieder, Gideon *computer scientist, educator*
Friedman, Alan Jacob *educational association administrator, former museum director*
Friedman, Daniel Mortimer *federal judge*
Friedman, Gregory H. *energy administrator*
Friedman, Robert Sidney *political science professor*
Friedman, Thomas Loren *foreign correspondent, writer*
Friedrich, Dabney Langhorne *lawyer, commissioner*
Fritsche, Claudia *diplomat, ambassador*
Fritts, Edward O. *broadcasting association executive*
Fromer, Kevin *federal agency administrator*
Frost, Edmund Bowen *lawyer*
Frost, Martin, III, (Jonas Martin Frost III) *lawyer, former congressman*
Fujimara, Makota *painter*
Fukushima, Katsuya *chef*
Fuller, Edwin Daniel *hotel executive*
Fulton, Kenneth Ray *professional association administrator*
Furash, Edward Elliott *investment company executive, banker, educator, writer, theater producer*
Furchtgott-Roth, Harold Wilkes *economist, consultant*
Furey, Roger P. *lawyer*
Furgurson, Ernest Baker, Jr., (Pat Furgurson) *writer*
Fusco, Aurilla Marie *director*
Futey, Bohdan A. *federal judge*
Gaa, Willy C. *ambassador*
Gage, John *labor union administrator*
Gage, Larry S. *lawyer*
Gainsborough, Jenni *advocate*
Gajarsa, Arthur J. *judge*
Galbraith, Peter Woodard *former ambassador*
Gale, Joseph H. *federal judge*
Gallagher, Michael David *lawyer, former federal agency administrator*
Gallas, Philip S. *lawyer*
Gallegly, Elton William *congressman*
Gallo, Anthony Ernest *playwright, economist*
Gallo, Kenneth A. *lawyer*
Galloway, Hoyt Wilson *library director*
Galston, William Arthur *political scientist, educator*
Gambatesa, Donald Anthony *federal agency administrator*
Gandhi, Natwar M. *city manager*
Ganter, Susan Lynn *foundation administrator, retired mathematics professor*
Gardiner, Kent A. *lawyer*
Gardner, George Victor *lawyer*
Gardner, James Bailey *historical association administrator*
Gardner, William Albert, Jr. *pathologist, medical products executive*
Garland, Gloria Jean *lawyer*
Garland, Merrick Brian *federal judge*
Garnette, Cheryl Petty *government agency administrator*
Garr, Sally D. *lawyer*
Garre, Gregory *federal agency administrator*
Garrels, Anne *news correspondent*

Garrett, Scott (E. Scott Garrett) *congressman, lawyer*
Garrett, Theodore Louis *lawyer*
Garris, Charles Alexander *mechanical engineer, educator*
Garrish, Theodore John *lawyer*
Garrison, Gwen E. *educational researcher, consultant*
Garthoff, Raymond Leonard *retired diplomat, diplomatic historian*
Garza, Deborah A. *federal agency administrator, lawyer*
Gaskell, Judith Ann *law librarian*
Gates, Robert Michael *secretary of defense, former academic administrator*
Gati, Toby T. *international advisor*
Gavrilis, James *military officer*
Gaynor, Kevin Allen *lawyer*
Gaynor, Suzanne Marie *healthcare executive, researcher*
Gehrig, Leo Joseph *retired surgeon*
Geimann, Steve *radio producer*
Gelb, Joseph Donald *lawyer*
Geller, Kenneth Steven *lawyer*
Geltman, Edward Alan *lawyer*
Genetski, Christian S. *lawyer*
Geniesse, Robert John *lawyer*
Gentner, Paul LeFoe *architect, consultant*
George, Warren S. *labor union administrator*
Gerber, Joel *federal judge*
Gerber, Melanie K. *lawyer*
Geren, Pete (Preston M. Geren III) *civilian military employee, former congressman*
Gerety, Tom R. *former academic administrator, lawyer, educator, philosopher*
Gerlach, Jim (James William Gerlach) *congressman*
Gershman, Carl Samuel *foundation administrator*
Gerson, Michael John *journalist*
Gerson, Stuart Michael *lawyer*
Gerstenmaier, William H. *federal agency administrator, aerospace engineer*
Gesner, Lawrence H. *lawyer*
Gessaman, Donald Eugene *retired government executive*
Gest, Kathryn Waters *public relations executive*
Geyer, Georgie Anne *columnist, educator, commentator, writer*
Giallorenzi, Thomas Gaetano *optical engineer*
Gibbs, Lawrence Blair *lawyer*
Giblin, Vincent J. *labor union administrator*
Gibson, Emmitt E. *career officer*
Gibson, Florence Anderson *talking book company executive, narrator*
Gibson, Reginald Walker *federal judge*
Gideon, Kenneth Wayne *lawyer*
Giffin, Gordon D. *former ambassador, lawyer*
Giffords, Gabrielle *congresswoman, former state senator*
Gilbert, John Albert, Jr. *lawyer*
Gilburne, Miles R. *venture capitalist*
Gilchrest, Wayne Thomas *congressman, secondary school educator*
Gilfoyle, Nathalie Floyd Preston *lawyer*
Gillan, Kayla J. *lawyer*
Gillespie, Ed (Edward Walter Gillespie) *federal official, former political organization administrator*
Gilliam, Sam *artist*
Gillibrand, Kirsten Rutnick *congresswoman, lawyer*
Gillingham, Robert Fenton *economist, consultant*
Gilliom, Judith Carr *federal official*
Gillis, John W. *federal agency administrator*
Gillmor, Paul Eugene *congressman, lawyer*
Gillon, Peter M. *lawyer*
Gilman, Benjamin Arthur *former congressman, lawyer*
Gilmore, James Stuart III *lawyer, former governor*
Gingrey, Phil (John Phillip Gingrey) *congressman*
Gingrich, Newt (Newton Leroy Gingrich) *former congressman*
Ginsberg, Marc Charles *former diplomat, investment company executive*
Ginsburg, Douglas Howard *federal judge*
Ginsburg, Martin David *lawyer, educator*
Ginsburg, Paul B. *health facility administrator*
Ginsburg, (Joan) Ruth Bader *United States supreme court justice*
Gioia, Dana (Michael Dana Gioia) *poet, critic, cultural organization administrator*
Girard, James Emery *chemistry professor*
Gittleman, Richard M. *lawyer*
Giuliano, Louis J. *former industrial manufacturing company executive*
Givhan, Robin Deneen *journalist*
Glancz, Ronald Robert *lawyer*
Glasbrenner, Karl Christian *federal agency administrator*
Glasgow, Norman Milton *lawyer*
Glassman, Cynthia Aaron *federal agency administrator, former commissioner*
Glassman, James Kenneth *editor, writer, publishing executive*
Glazer, Charles Louis *ambassador*
Gleklen, Jonathan Ian *lawyer*
Glendening, Parris Nelson *former governor, political science educator*
Glick, Leslie Alan *lawyer*
Glickman, Stephen H. *judge*
Glynn, Edward F., Jr. *lawyer*
Gnehm, Edward W., Jr. *ambassador*
Godsey, John Drew *retired minister, theology educator emeritus*
Godwin, Kimberly Ann *federal agency administrator, lawyer*
Goeke, Joseph Robert *federal judge, lawyer*
Goelzer, Daniel Lee *lawyer*
Goewey, David W. *lawyer*
Goff, James Franklin *physicist, consultant*
Gohmert, Louis Buller, Jr., (Louie Gohmert) *congressman, former judge, lawyer*
Gold, Peter Frederick *lawyer*
Goldberg, Fred T., Jr. *lawyer*
Goldberg, Jolande Elisabeth *law librarian*
Goldberg, Jonah Jacob *political columnist*
Goldberg, Seth A. *lawyer*
Goldberg, Stanley Joshua *federal judge*
Goldblatt, Steven Harris *law educator*
Goldman, Steven Mark *lawyer*
Goldscheider, Frances K. *sociologist, educator*
Goldsmith, Barry Richard *lawyer, former federal agency administrator*
Goldstein, Allan Leonard *biochemist, educator*
Goldstein, Frank Robert *lawyer*
Goldstein, Michael B. *lawyer*
Goldstein, Thomas C. *lawyer*
Goldway, Ruth Y. *postal regulatory commissioner*
Golkiewicz, Gary J. *federal official*
Gollin, Michael A. *lawyer*
Golodner, Jack *labor association official*
Gonzalez, Cecilia H. *lawyer*
Gonzalez, Charles A. *congressman*
Gonzalez, Emilio T. *federal agency administrator*
Goode, Virgil H., Jr. *congressman*
Goodlatte, Bob (Robert William) *congressman, lawyer*
Goodman, Alfred Nelson *lawyer*
Gordon, Barton Jennings (Bart Gordon) *congressman, lawyer*
Gordon, James Samuel *psychiatrist*
Gorelick, Jamie Shona *lawyer*
Gorham, William *organization executive*
Gorn, Janet Marie *government official*
Gorrell, J. Warren, Jr. *lawyer*
Goshorn, Richard Henley *lawyer*
Gostin, Lawrence O. *lawyer, educator*
Gottfried, Keith Evan *lawyer*
Gottlieb, Robert Gene *lawyer*
Gottschalk, Thomas A. *automotive executive, lawyer*
Graber, Richard William *ambassador, lawyer*
Gradison, Bill (Willis David Gradison Jr.) *former congressman*
Grady, Gregory *lawyer, banker*
Graham, David E. *librarian*
Graham, Donald Edward *publishing company executive*
Graham, John H., IV, *association executive*
Graham, Jonathan P. *lawyer*
Graham, Lindsey Olin *senator*
Graham, Thomas Richard *lawyer*
Grainger, Amanda R. *lawyer*
Gramlich, Edward Martin *public policy educator, former federal official*
Grandmaison, J. Joseph *federal agency administrator*
Granger, Kay *congresswoman*
Grant, Carl N. *communications executive, sales executive*
Grant, Paula DiMeo *lawyer, mediator, nursing educator*
Grapin, Jacqueline G. *economist*
Grassley, Chuck (Charles Ernest Grassley) *senator*
Graves, Samuel B., Jr. *congressman, retired state legislator*
Gray, George M. *federal agency administrator*
Gray, Lyons *federal agency administrator*
Gray, Mary Wheat *statistician, lawyer*
Gray, Sheila Hafter *psychiatrist, researcher*
Grealy, Mary R. *medical association administrator*
Greaux, Cheryl Prejean *federal agency administrator*
Green, Al *congressman*
Green, Donald Hugh *lawyer*
Green, Douglas G. *lawyer*
Green, Gene (Raymond Eugene Green) *congressman*
Green, James Francis *lawyer, consultant*
Green, Joyce Hens *federal judge*
Green, Madeleine F. *educational association administrator*
Green, Richard K. *real estate company executive*
Green, Thomas Charles *lawyer*
Greenberger, I. Michael *lawyer*
Greenberger, Marcia Devins *lawyer*
Greene, Charles M. *federal agency administrator*
Greene, Thomas Hardy *architect*
Greene, William P., Jr. *federal judge*
Greenhalgh, Paul *academic administrator*
Greenhouse, Linda Joyce *journalist*
Gregg, Judd Alan *senator, former governor*
Grenier, Edward Joseph, Jr. *lawyer*
Gribbin, David James, IV, (D.J. Gribbin) *lawyer*
Gribbin, Robert E. III *diplomat*
Griffenhagen, George Bernard *trade association executive*
Griffin, Christine M. *commissioner*
Griffin, David *photojournalist*
Griffin, Kelly Ann *public relations executive, consultant*
Griffin, Michael D. *federal agency administrator, aerospace scientist*
Griffin, Richard J. *federal agency administrator*
Griffin, Robert Thomas *automotive company executive*
Griffis, Kirby T. *lawyer*
Griffith, Thomas Beall *federal judge*
Grigsby, Sharlyn Ann *human resources specialist*
Grijalva, Raul *congressman*
Grimaldi, James V. *journalist*
Grimes, John Grayson *federal agency administrator*
Griner, G. Christopher *lawyer*
Grob, George Frederick *health science association administrator*
Groen, Jeffrey Allan *economist*
Gross, Kenneth Andrew *lawyer*
Gross, Patrick Walter *information technology executive*
Grossman, Claudio M. *dean, law educator*
Grossman, Marc Issaiah *former federal agency administrator*
Grosvenor, Gilbert Melville *journalist, educator, publishing executive*
Grove, Brandon Hambright, Jr. *diplomat*
Grubisich, Tom *web editor*
Gruenberg, Martin J. *federal agency administrator, lawyer*
Grunberg, Nancy R. *lawyer*
Grundstrom, Brian Wilbur *composer*
Grunfeld, Ernie *professional sports team executive, retired professional basketball player*
Guenther, Jack Donald *banker*
Guhin, Michael Alan *ambassador*
Gulland, Eugene D. *lawyer*
Gulliford, James B. *federal agency administrator*
Gumpert, Gunther *artist*
Gunderson, Steven Craig *association executive, former congressman*
Gutierrez, Carlos Miguel *secretary of commerce, former grocery manufacturing company executive*
Gutierrez, Jay Matthew *lawyer*
Gutierrez, Luis V. *congressman, elementary education educator*
Gutman, Harry Largman *lawyer, educator*
Gutman, Roy William *reporter*
Guttman, Egon *law educator*
Guzy, Carol *photojournalist*
Gwaltney, Corbin *publishing executive, editor*
Haber, Jonathan H. *lawyer*
Hadley, Stephen John *national security advisor*
Hagel, Chuck (Charles Timothy Hagel) *senator*
Hagel, Lawrence B. *federal judge*
Hagen, Wendy W. *public relations executive*
Hager, Susan Kulka *public relations executive*
Hagin, Joseph Whitehouse, II, *federal official*
Hagner, John D. *lawyer*
Hahn, Lorna *political organization executive, author*
Hailey, Gary D. *lawyer*
Haines, Harry Allen *federal judge*
Haines, Martha Mahan *lawyer*
Haines, Terry L. *lawyer, consultant*
Halaska, Terrell L. *federal agency administrator*
Halbert, Gary L. *lawyer*
Hale, David M. *ambassador*
Hale, Janet S. *accounting firm executive, former federal agency administrator*
Hale, Martha Larsen *dean, library and information science educator*
Haley, Roger Kendall *librarian*
Hall, H. Dale *federal agency administrator*
Hall, John J. *congressman, musician*
Hall, Ralph Moody *congressman*
Hallgren, Richard Edwin *meteorologist*
Halloran, Michael James *lawyer*
Halperin, Morton H. *political scientist*
Halperin, Samuel *education and training policy analyst*
Halpern, James S. *federal judge*
Halprin, Albert *lawyer*
Halsey, Ashley III *newspaper editor*
Halvorson, Newman Thorbus, Jr. *lawyer*
Hamburg, Margaret Ann (Peggy Hamburg) *public health administrator*
Hamilton, Lee Herbert *educational association administrator, retired congressman*
Hamlisch, Marvin *composer, conductor, musician, entertainer*
Hammond, Allen Lee *editor, consultant, former broadcaster, non-profit policy research center executive*
Hammond, William Michael *historian, educator*
Hampton, Thomas E. *state agency administrator*
Hamre, John J. *think-tank executive, former federal agency administrator*
Hand, John Oliver *museum curator*
Hand, Lloyd N. *lawyer*
Hanley, Allison Anne *federal agency administrator*
Hanlon, Glen *professional hockey coach*
Hanlon, Stephen F. *lawyer*
Hanlon, William R. *lawyer*
Hannah, John P. *federal official*
Hansen, Charles Martin III *lobbyist*
Hansen, Joseph T. *labor union administrator*
Hansen, Kenneth *lawyer*
Hanzlik, Rayburn DeMara *lawyer*
Harbour, Pamela Jones *commissioner, lawyer*
Harding, Fann *retired science administrator*
Hare, Phil (Philip G. Hare) *congressman*
Harkin, Thomas Richard *senator*
Harlem, Susan Lynn *librarian*
Harling, Barbara Jean *social worker*
Harman, Donna Akers *trade association administrator*
Harman, Jane *congresswoman*
Harman, Sidney *audio and video company executive*
Harman, William Boys, Jr. *lawyer*
Harper, Emery Walter *lawyer*
Harpham, Virginia Ruth *violinist*
Harrington, Anthony Stephen *lawyer, diplomat, business executive*
Harrington, Clifford M. *lawyer*
Harrington, Kathleen M. *public relations company executive, former federal agency administrator*
Harris, Don Victor, Jr. *lawyer*
Harris, Jeffrey *lawyer*
Harris, June Leatrice *education coordinator, administrator*
Harris, Scott Blake *lawyer*
Harrison, Earl David *lawyer, real estate company officer*
Harrison, Marion Edwyn *lawyer*
Harrison, Mark B. *lawyer*
Harrison, Patricia de Stacy *broadcast executive, former federal agency administrator*
Harrison, Todd A. *lawyer*
Harrop, William Caldwell *retired ambassador*
Hart, Christopher Alvin *lawyer*
Harter, Donald Harry *neurologist, medical educator*
Hartman, George Eitel *architect*
Hartmann, Robert Sankey *health facility administrator, not-for-profit fundraiser*
Hartwell, Stephen *investment company executive*
Harvey, Eleanor Jones *museum curator*
Harvey, Jane Hull *church administrator*
Harvey, John Collins, Jr. *military officer*
Harvey, Sheila McCafferty *lawyer*
Harvey, Thomas Edward *federal agency administrator*
Harwood, John H., II, *lawyer*
Hassan, Aftab Syed *education specialist, writer, editor*
Hasselmo, Ann Hayes Die *executive recruiter, consultant, psychologist, educator, retired academic administrator*
Hassett, Joseph Mark *lawyer*
Hastert, Dennis (John Dennis Hastert) *congressman*
Hastings, Alcee Lamar *congressman, retired judge*
Hastings, Doc (Richard Norman Hastings) *congressman*
Hastings, Douglas Alfred *lawyer*
Hastings, George L. *federal official*
Hatch, Orrin Grant *senator*
Hatfield, Fred (Frederick William Hattfield) *former commissioner*
Hauptman, Gregory B. *lawyer*
Hauser, Richard Alan *lawyer, foundation administrator*
Hausfeld, Michael D. *lawyer*
Havlicek, Franklin J. *communications executive*
Hawkins, David G. *lawyer*
Hawkins, Philip Linton *real estate executive*
Hayden, Michael Vincent *CIA Director, career military officer*
Hayes, David John *lawyer*
Hayes, John C., Jr. *lawyer*
Hayes, Robin (Robert Cannon Hayes) *congressman*
Haynes, R. Michael *lawyer*
Haynes, William James, II, *lawyer*
Hays, Sharon Lynn *federal official*
Haythe, Winston McDonald *lawyer, real estate investor, educator*
Hazen, Robert Miller *research scientist, writer*
Headden, Susan M. *editor*
Hebert, Jay Howell *lawyer*
Hecht, Marjorie Mazel *editor*
Heckman, Jerome Harold *lawyer*
Heddell, Gordon S. *federal agency administrator*
Hedges, Harry George *retired computer scientist*
Hedges, Kamla King *library director*
Heelan, Patrick Aidan *philosophy educator*
Heenan, Michael Terence *lawyer*
Heffernan, James Vincent *lawyer*
Hefferon, Thomas Michael *lawyer*
Hefter, Laurence Roy *lawyer*
Heideman, Richard D. *lawyer*
Height, Dorothy I. *former foundation administrator*
Hein, Jay F. *federal official*
Heintz, John Edward *lawyer*
Heinz Kerry, Teresa (Maria Teresa Thierstein Simoes-Ferreira) *foundation administrator*
Heiss, Harry Glen *archivist*
Helgerson, John Leonard *federal agency administrator*
Heller, Jack Isaac *lawyer*
Heller, John Roderick III *lawyer, corporate financial executive*
Heller, Mark A. *lawyer*
Helmly, James R. *career military officer*
Helms, Robert Brake *economist*
Hemingway, Thomas L. *career military officer, lawyer*
Hemley, Russell J. *geophysicist*
Henderson, Douglas Boyd *lawyer*
Henderson, Frances J. *lawyer*
Henderson, Karen LeCraft *federal judge*
Henderson, Wade J. *civil rights advocate, law educator*
Henke, Michael John *lawyer, educator*
Henkin, Robert Irwin *neuroscientist, internist, nuclear medicine physician, medical products executive*
Hennessy, Ellen Anne *lawyer, financial consultant, educator*
Henry, Charles Jay *library and information scientist*
Henry, Ed *news correspondent*
Henry, John Cooper *journalist*
Henry, Ronald Kenneth *lawyer*
Hensarling, Jeb *congressman*
Hensler, David J. *lawyer*
Herbst, John Edward *federal agency administrator, former ambassador*
Herger, Walter William *congressman*
Herlihy, Scott C. *lawyer*
Hernandez, Israel *federal agency administrator*
Hernandez, Livan Eisler *professional baseball player*
Heron, Julian Briscoe, Jr. *lawyer*
Herrett, Richard Allison *agricultural research institute administrator*
Herrling, Christopher J. *lawyer*
Hershey, Robert Lewis *mechanical engineer, management consultant*
Hersman, Deborah A. P. *federal agency administrator*
Hertz, Paul Louis *astrophysicist*
Herzstein, Robert Erwin *lawyer*
Hess, Michael Edward *federal agency administrator*
Hess, Stephen *political scientist, writer*
Hevel, Gary Francis *public information officer, consultant*
Hewitt, Emily Clark *federal judge, minister*
Hewitt, Paul Buck *lawyer*
Heyward, Peter E. *lawyer*
Hezir, Joseph S. *energy and environmental executive*
Hiatt, Fred *journalist*
Hiatt, Jonathan Paul *lawyer, labor union administrator*
Hibbert, Robert George *lawyer, food company executive*
Hicks, Jocelyn Muriel *laboratory medicine specialist*
Hiebert, Ray Eldon *writer, educator*
Higgins, Bradford R. *federal agency administrator*
Higgins, Brian *congressman*

Higgins, James Henry III *marketing executive*
Higgins, John P., Jr., (Jack) *federal agency administrator*
Higgins, Kathryn O'Leary (Kitty) *federal agency administrator, former consulting firm executive*
Higgins, Paul John *medical director, career military officer*
Hightower, Dennis Fowler *retired entertainment company executive, educator*
Hileman, Bette *journalist*
Hill, Baron Paul *congressman*
Hill, Christopher R. *federal agency administrator, former ambassador*
Hill, David R. *federal agency administrator, lawyer*
Hill, John H. *federal agency administrator*
Hill, Kent Richmond *federal agency administrator*
Hill, Stephen S. *lawyer*
Hilleary, Van (William Vanderpool Hilleary) *former congressman, lawyer*
Hillman, Jennifer Anne *federal official*
Hills, Carla Anderson *lawyer, former secretary of housing and urban development*
Hills, Roderick M. *lawyer, former government official*
Hills, Stephen P. *publishing executive*
Hillsman, Sally T. *sociologist*
Hinchey, Maurice D. *congressman*
Hinden, Stanley Jay *newspaper editor*
Hinojosa, Rubén *congressman*
Hirji, Rafik F. *water resources expert*
Hirschhorn, Eric Leonard *lawyer*
Hiscock, Richard Carson *legislative staff member*
Hitchens, Christopher Eric *columnist, writer*
Hite, William P. *labor union administrator*
Hittner, George J. *lawyer*
Hoagland, Jimmie Lee *newspaper editor*
Hobbs, Ann S. *lawyer*
Hodes, Paul William, II, *congressman, lawyer*
Hodges, Robert H., Jr. *federal judge*
Hoekstra, Peter *congressman, manufacturing executive*
Hoffa, James Phillip *labor union administrator*
Hoffinger, Adam Steven *lawyer*
Hoffman, Alfred, Jr. *ambassador, real estate developer*
Hoffman, Ann Fleisher *labor lawyer, educator, consultant*
Hoffman, E. Leslie *lawyer*
Hoffman, Joel Elihu *lawyer*
Hoffman, Kenneth R. *lawyer*
Hoffmann, Martin Richard *lawyer*
Hogan, Felicity *artist*
Holbrooke, Richard Charles Albert *investment banker, former ambassador*
Holden, Tim (Thomas Timothy) *congressman, protective official*
Holder, Eric H. *lawyer, former federal agency administrator*
Holladay, Wilhelmina Cole *interior designer, museum director*
Hollingsworth, Joe Gregory *lawyer*
Hollis, Sheila Slocum *lawyer*
Hollman, K. Hollyn *lawyer*
Holmes, Mark V. *judge*
Holt, Rush D. *congressman, physics educator, researcher, consultant*
Honda, Michael M. *congressman*
Hooks, Aubrey *ambassador*
Hooley, Darlene *congresswoman*
Hope, William Duane *retired zoologist, curator*
Hopkins, Charles L. *government agency administrator*
Horahan, Edward Bernard III *lawyer*
Horn, Charles M. *lawyer*
Horn, Marian Blank *federal judge*
Horn, Sharon K. *government agency administrator*
Horne, Michael Stewart *lawyer*
Horner, Constance Joan *federal agency administrator*
Hornyak, Joseph P. *lawyer*
Horowitz, Herbert Eugene *retired diplomat*
Horowitz, Philip Martin *lawyer*
Horton, Philip W. *lawyer*
Horton, Roberta Lazarus *lawyer*
Horvitz, Steven Jay *lawyer*
Hotez, Peter Jay *research scientist, educator*
Houck, James W. *career military officer, lawyer*
House, W(illiam) Michael *lawyer*
Houseman, Alan William *lawyer*
Howard, Glen Scott *lawyer, consultant*
Howard, Jack *industrial relations specialist, consultant*
Howard, Jeffrey Hjalmar *lawyer*
Howard, John *federal agency administrator*
Howard, Robert T. *federal agency administrator*
Howard, Roscoe Conklin, Jr. *lawyer, former prosecutor*
Howe, Fisher *management consultant, retired foreign service officer*
Howell, Mary L. *multi-industry company executive*
Hoyer, Steny Hamilton *congressman*
Hoyt, Robert F. *lawyer*
Hranitzky, Rachel Robyn *lawyer*
Hsia, Judith Ann *physician*
Huang, Margaret *human rights advocate*
Huband, Frank Louis *educational association administrator, electrical engineer, lawyer*
Hubbard, Allan Brooks *federal official, former chemical company executive*
Hubbard, Richard L. *lawyer*
Huberman, Benjamin *technology consultant*
Huberman, Richard Lee *lawyer*
Hudgins, Willie L., Jr. *lawyer*
Hudnut, William Herbert III *political scientist*
Hudson, Michael Craig *political science professor*
Hufbauer, Gary Clyde *economist, lawyer, educator*
Huge, Harry *lawyer*
Hughes, Elizabeth R. (Beth) *lawyer*
Hughes, Karen Parfitt *federal agency administrator*
Hughes, Kent Higgon *economist*
Hughes, Marija Matich *law librarian*
Hughes, Thomas Lowe *foundation executive*
Hulkower, Mark J. *lawyer*
Hulon, Willie T. *federal agency administrator*
Hulse, Carl *newspaper executive*
Hulshof, Kenny Charles *congressman*
Hume, Brit (Alexander Britton) *journalist*
Hume, Cameron R. *ambassador*
Hungar, Thomas G. *federal agency administrator, lawyer*
Hunnicutt, Charles Alvin *lawyer*
Hunt, Albert R. *editor*
Hunt, Earl Stephen *federal agency administrator*
Hunt, Wayne Robert, Sr. *non-profit organization executive*
Hunter, Duncan Lee *congressman*
Hussain, Syed Taseer *biomedical researcher, educator*
Huston, John Wilson *military officer, historian*
Hutchinson, (W.) Asa *lawyer, former federal agency administrator*
Hutchinson, James S. (Jamie) *lawyer*
Hutchinson, Tim *former senator*
Hutchison, Claude B., Jr. *federal agency administrator*
Hutchison, Kay Bailey *senator*
Hutt, Peter Barton *lawyer*
Hutter, Paul J. *lawyer*
Huttler, Stephen B. *lawyer*
Hwang, Jimmy John *internist, oncologist*
Hyman, Lester Samuel *lawyer*
Ijaz, Mansoor *news correspondent*
Iklé, Fred Charles *former federal agency administrator, policy advisor, defense expert*
Indyk, Martin S. *think-tank executive, former ambassador*
Inglis, Bob (Robert Durden) *congressman*
Inhofe, James M. *senator*
Inouye, Daniel Ken *senator*
Inskeep, Steve *radio personality*
Inslee, Jay Robert *congressman*
Insulza, José Miguel *international organization official, former Chilean government official*
Ireland, Oliver *lawyer*
Irving, Thomas L. *lawyer*
Isaacs, Amy Fay *political organization executive*
Isaacs, Joseph C. *medical association administrator*
Isaacson, Walter Seff *think-tank executive, writer*
Isakowitz, Steven Jeffrey *federal agency administrator, aeronautical engineer*
Isakson, Johnny (John Hardy Isakson) *senator, former congressman*
Isbell, David Bradford *lawyer, educator*
Ishaq, Ashfaq *foundation administrator, economist, educator*
Ishimaru, Stuart Jon *commissioner, lawyer*
Iskandar, Harris *attache*
Israel, Steven Jay *congressman*
Israelite, David M. *music publishing executive, prosecutor*
Issa, Darrell E. *congressman*
Iverson, Kristine Ann *federal agency administrator*
Iwry, J. Mark *lawyer*
Jackson, Alphonso Roy *secretary of housing and urban development*
Jackson, Darryl W. *federal agency administrator*
Jackson, Jeanine E. *ambassador*
Jackson, Jesse Louis, Jr. *congressman*
Jackson, John Howard *lawyer, educator*
Jackson, Margaret Elizabeth *science educator*
Jackson, Michael P. *federal agency administrator, former engineering company executive*
Jackson Lee, Sheila *congresswoman*
Jacobs, Alonzo *federal agency contracting officer*
Jacobs, David Ernest *environmental health scientist*
Jacobs, Julian I. *federal judge*
Jacobs, Madeleine *professional society administrator, writer*
Jacobsen, Hugh Newell *architect*
Jacobsen, Raymond Alfred, Jr. *lawyer*
Jacobson, Allen Howard *economist*
Jacobson, David Edward *lawyer*
Jacobson, Louis Alan *journalist*
Jacobson, Michael Faraday *consumer advocate, writer*
Jacobson, Richard Lee *lawyer, educator*
Jacobson, Tracey Ann *ambassador*
Jakes, J. Michael *lawyer*
Jamar, Steven Dwight *law educator*
James, Ronald J. *civilian military employee, lawyer*
Jamison, Antawn *professional basketball player*
Janes, Jackson *research institute executive*
Janes, William Sargent *real estate company executive*
Janney, Christopher G. *lawyer*
Jarmon, Charles *social sciences educator, dean*
Jarque, Carlos M. *former federal official*
Jarvis, Charlene Drew *academic administrator, former scientist*
Jaspersen, Frederick Zarr *economist*
Jatras, James George *lawyer*
Jawad, Said Tayeb (Said Tayeb Djawad) *ambassador, commentator, writer*
Jecklin, Lois Underwood *art corporation executive, consultant*
Jefferson, William Jennings (Jeff Jefferson) *congressman*
Jeffery, Reuben III *federal agency administrator*
Jeffress, William Horace, Jr. *lawyer*
Jenkins, Loren B. *broadcast executive, publisher, writer*
Jenkins, Thomas H. *lawyer*
Jennings, Deborah E. *lawyer*
Jensen, Mark A. *lawyer*
Jensen, Robert Neal *lawyer*
Jensen, Thomas C. *lawyer*
Jenson, William G. *federal agency administrator*
Jimenez, Frank R. *lawyer, civilian military employee*
Jindal, Bobby Piyush *congressman*
Jochum, James J. *lawyer, former federal agency administrator*
Johanns, Michael Owen *secretary of agriculture, former governor*
John, Christopher Charles *lobbyist, former congressman*
John, Frank Herbert, Jr. *real estate appraiser, investor, marketing executive*
Johns, Christopher George *editor-in-chief, photojournalist*
Johnson, Bruce Chr. *librarian*
Johnson, Charles E. *federal agency administrator*
Johnson, Clay III *federal official*
Johnson, Collister, Jr., (Terry Johnson Jr.) *federal official*
Johnson, David Lee *lawyer*
Johnson, David Raymond *lawyer*
Johnson, David Timothy *diplomat*
Johnson, Donald Crandall
Johnson, Eddie Bernice *congresswoman*
Johnson, Esther R. *federal official*
Johnson, James A. *finance company executive*
Johnson, Jennifer J. *federal official*
Johnson, Kelly A. *lawyer, former federal agency administrator*
Johnson, Marlene M. *educational association administrator*
Johnson, Nancy Lee *former congresswoman*
Johnson, Philip McBride *lawyer*
Johnson, Richard A. *lawyer*
Johnson, Richard Kent *publishing executive*
Johnson, Robert Wayne *federal agency administrator*
Johnson, Samuel (Sam Johnson) *congressman*
Johnson, Sheila Crump *entrepreneur*
Johnson, Stephen L. *federal official*
Johnson, Timothy Peter *senator*
Johnson, Timothy Vincent *congressman, lawyer*
Jolly, Bruce O. *lawyer*
Jonas, John Francis *lawyer*
Jonas, Richard Andrew *medical educator*
Jonas, Tina Westby *federal agency administrator*
Jones, A. Elizabeth *corporate communications specialist, former federal agency administrator*
Jones, Aidan Drexel *lawyer*
Jones, Alice Samuels *elementary education educator, federal agency administrator*
Jones, Boisfeuillet, Jr., (Bo Jones) *publishing executive*
Jones, Coletta L. *senior pastor*
Jones, Diane Auer *government education association administrator*
Jones, George Washington, Jr. *lawyer*
Jones, James Robert *ambassador, retired congressman, lawyer*
Jones, Judith Miller *director*
Jones, Kelsey A. *law educator, law administrator*
Jones, Lauren Patricia *psychologist, not-for-profit developer*
Jones, Michael D. *lawyer*
Jones, Richard Henry *ambassador*
Jones, Stanley Boyd *retired researcher*
Jones, Stephanie Tubbs *congresswoman, lawyer, prosecutor*
Jones, Susan Dorfman *real estate broker, writer*
Joo, Douglas D.M. *newspaper and video production and aviation executive*
Jordan, Eddie *professional basketball coach*
Jordan, Jim (James D. Jordan) *congressman, former state legislator*
Jordan, Mosina H. *federal agency administrator*
Jordan, Robert Elijah III *lawyer*
Jose, Pedro A. *physician*
Joyce, Anne Raine *editor*
Joyce, Frederick Mark (Rick) *lawyer*
Joyner, Christopher Clayton *international relations educator*
Justesen, Troy Ralph *federal agency administrator*
Kabalkin, Barry E. *lawyer*
Kabel, Robert James *lawyer*
Kafka, Gerald Andrew *lawyer*
Kagen, Steven L. *congressman, physician*
Kahan, Jonathan Seth *lawyer*
Kahin, Brian *lawyer, computer industry professional, consultant*
Kahlow, Barbara Fenvessy *statistician*
Kahn, Charles N., III, (Chip Kahn) *medical association administrator*
Kahn, Edwin Leonard *retired lawyer*
Kahn, Michael *stage director*
Kahn, Thomas S. *lawyer*
Kail, Floyd Michael *lawyer*
Kaiser, Michael M. *performing company executive*
Kalfatovic, Martin Robert *librarian, writer*
Kaludis, George *management consultant, publishing executive, educator*
Kamber, Victor Samuel *political consultant*
Kammer, Jerry *reporter*
Kamnik, Joseph P. *lawyer*
Kamras, Jason *mathematics educator*
Kanjorski, Paul Edmund *congressman, lawyer*
Kantor, Mickey (Michael Kantor) *lawyer, former secretary of commerce*
Kapikian, Catherine Andrews *artist*
Kaplan, Gilbert B. *lawyer*
Kaplan, Joel David *federal official*
Kaplan, Paul A. *lawyer*
Kaplan, Steven *lawyer*
Kaplun, Paul T. *lawyer*
Kapp, Robert Harris *lawyer*
Kappes, Stephen R. *federal agency administrator*
Kappler, Ann M. *lawyer, finance company executive*
Karle, Isabella L. *chemist*
Karle, Jerome *physicist, researcher*
Karsner, Andy (Alexander Armand Karsner) *federal agency administrator*
Kasold, Bruce Edward *federal judge, lawyer*
Kass, Benny Lee *lawyer*
Kass, Leon Richard *humanities educator*
Kassinger, Theodore William (Ted R. Kassinger) *lawyer, former federal agency administrator*
Kasten, Robert W., Jr. *former senator*
Kato, Ryozo *ambassador*
Kattouf, Theodore E. *former ambassador*
Katyal, Neal Kumar *law educator*
Katz, Hadrian Ronald *lawyer*
Katz, Irv *not-for-profit executive*
Katz, John W. *lawyer, state official*
Katz, Sherman E. *lawyer*
Katzen, Sally *lawyer, educator*
Kaufman, Billie Jo *law librarian, educator*
Kaufman, Joshua Jacob *lawyer*
Kaufman, Thomas Frederick *lawyer, educator*
Kautter, David John *lawyer*
Kauzlarich, Richard Dale *retired ambassador, political scientist, consultant*
Kavanaugh, Brett Michael *federal judge*
Kazin, Michael *historian, writer*
Keaney, Thomas Addis *academic administrator, management consultant, educator, military officer*
Kearney, Stephen Michael *federal agency administrator*
Kearns, Mary Hoyt *psychologist*
Keating, Francis Anthony, II, *retired governor, lawyer*
Keeley, Robert Vossler *retired academic administrator, ambassador*
Keenan, Nancy *pro-choice association executive*
Keeney, John Christopher *lawyer*
Keeney, John Christopher, Jr. *lawyer*
Keeney, Regina Markey *lawyer*
Keenum, Mark Everett *federal agency administrator, former legislative staff member*
Keeny, Spurgeon Milton, Jr. *professional society administrator*
Keiner, R(obert) Bruce, Jr. *lawyer*
Keisler, Peter Douglas *federal agency administrator, lawyer*
Keller, Ric *congressman, lawyer*
Kelley, Colleen M. *labor union administrator*
Kelley, David Christopher *philosopher*
Kelley, Patrick W. *health science association administrator, preventive medicine physician*
Kelliher, Joseph Timothy *commissioner*
Kellner, Leon B. *lawyer*
Kelly, Brian J. *editor*
Kelly, David M. *lawyer*
Kelly, John Joseph, Jr. *federal official*
Kelly, Suedeen G. *commissioner*
Kelly, Thomas J., Jr. *lawyer*
Kelly, William Charles, Jr. *retired lawyer*
Kemp, Geoffrey Thomas Howard *political scientist, consultant*
Kemp, Jack French *former congressman*
Kempthorne, Dirk Arthur *secretary of the interior, former governor*
Kendall, David E. *lawyer*
Kendall, Peter Landis *television news executive*
Kendrick, John Whitefield *economist, educator, consultant*
Kendrick, Kim *federal agency administrator*
Kennard, Mary Elizabeth *lawyer*
Kennard, William Earl *former lawyer*
Kennedy, Anthony McLeod *United States supreme court justice*
Kennedy, Patrick F. *federal agency administrator, former ambassador*
Kennedy, Patrick Joseph *congressman*
Kennedy, Robert Emmet, Jr. *historian, educator*
Kennedy, Roger George *museum program and parks director*
Kennedy, Ted (Edward Moore Kennedy) *senator*
Kennelly, Barbara B. *retired congressman, federal agency administrator*
Kenney, Kristie Anne *ambassador*
Kenney, Robert James, Jr. *lawyer*
Kent, Jill Elspeth *entrepreneur, art appraiser, lawyer*
Kent, M. Elizabeth *lawyer*
Kern, John Worth III *judge*
Kern, Paul John *retired military officer*
Kerr, Orin Samuel *law educator*
Kerry, John Forbes *senator*
Kerwin, Cornelius Martin *academic administrator, educator*
Kesselman, Marc L. *federal agency administrator*
Kessler, Gladys *federal judge*
Kessler, Judd Lewis *lawyer*
Ketchum, James Roe *curator*
Khozeimeh, Issa *electrical engineer, educator*
Kies, Kenneth J. *lawyer*
Kiko, Colleen Duffy *lawyer*
Kiko, Philip George *lawyer*
Kilberg, William Jeffrey *lawyer, director*
Kilby, Theodore Morgan, Jr. *auditor, educator*
Kildee, Dale Edward *congressman*
Kilgore, Edwin Carroll *retired federal agency administrator*
Killefer, Campbell *lawyer*
Killgore, Andrew Ivy *former ambassador*
Kilpatrick, Carolyn Cheeks *congresswoman*
Kim, Mikyong Minsun *education educator*
Kim, Sukhan *lawyer*
Kimbell, Abigail R. *federal agency administrator*
Kimes, Don Mark *artist, educator*
Kimmitt, Robert Michael *federal agency and former business executive*
Kinberg, Robert *lawyer*
Kincannon, Charles Louis (Louis Kincannon) *federal agency administrator*
Kind, Ronald James *congressman, lawyer*
King, Colbert Isaiah *editor*
King, Gwendolyn S. *retired utility company executive, federal official*
King, James C. *retired military officer*
King, Larry (Larry Zeiger) *broadcaster, radio personality*
King, Patricia Ann *law educator*
King, Steve *congressman*
King, Warren R. *judge*
Kingham, Richard Frank *lawyer*
Kingston, Jack *congressman*
Kiplinger, Knight Austin *journalist, publishing executive*
Kirch, Darrell Gene *medical association and former academic administrator, dean*
Kirk, Artemis G. *university librarian*
Kirk, Dennis Dean *lawyer*
Kirk, Donald *journalist*
Kirk, Mark Steven *congressman*

Kirkpatrick, David D. *news correspondent*
Kirsanow, Peter N. *federal agency administrator*
Kirsch, Laurence Stephen *lawyer*
Kiser, Chérie R. *lawyer*
Kissel, Peter Charles *lawyer*
Kittrell, Steven Dan *lawyer*
Kittrie, Nicholas *international lawyer, writer*
Klain, Ronald Alan *lawyer*
Klarfeld, Peter James *lawyer*
Klawiter, Donald Casimir *lawyer*
Klee, Ann Renee *lawyer*
Klein, Michael Roger *investor, foundation administrator*
Klein, Roger A. *lawyer*
Klein, Ronald Jay *congressman, former state legislator, lawyer*
Klepner, Jerry D. *federal agency administrator*
Kline, John *congressman*
Kline, Thomas R. *lawyer*
Klingelhofer, Stephan E. *lawyer*
Klobuchar, Amy Jean *senator, lawyer*
Klose, Kevin *broadcast executive*
Knapp, Richard Maitland *association executive*
Knapp, Rosalind Ann *lawyer*
Kneedler, Edwin S. *federal agency administrator*
Kneuer, John M.R. *federal agency administrator*
Knight, Athelia Wilhelmenia *journalist*
Knight, Bruce Irving *federal agency administrator*
Knollenberg, Joseph Castl (Joe Knollenberg) *congressman*
Knopman, Debra Sara *environmental scientist, director, hydrologist, policy analyst*
Knowles, Jeffrey D. *lawyer*
Kochhar, Kalpana *economist*
Koester, Frederick. H. *aviation systems engineer*
Kohl, Herbert H. *senator, professional sports team owner*
Kohn, Donald L. *federal official, economist*
Kohn, Stephen Martin *lawyer*
Kohr, Howard A. *lobbyist*
Kolasky, William Joseph, Jr. *lawyer*
Kolb, Charles Chester *foundation administrator*
Kolb, Charles Edward Mealey *federal government official, lawyer*
Kolevar, Kevin M. *federal agency administrator*
Kollar-Kotelly, Colleen *federal judge*
Koller, Shirley Leavitt *sculptor*
Kolodner, Robert M. *federal agency administrator, health information technology executive*
Kolzig, Olaf *professional hockey player*
Komarov, Andrei M. *biophysicist, educator, research scientist*
Kondracke, Morton Matt *journalist*
Korb, Donald L. *federal agency administrator, lawyer*
Korman, Can E *engineering educator, department chairman*
Korn, David *pathologist, educator*
Kornicker, Louis Sampson *museum curator*
Korth, Fritz-Alan *lawyer*
Koskinen, John Andrew *foundation executive*
Kostelnik, Michael Charles *commissioner, retired military officer*
Kotler, Milton *marketing company executive*
Kotz, Samuel *statistician, educator, translator, editor*
Kovacic, William Evan *commissioner, law educator*
Kovacs, William Lawrence *lawyer*
Kozusko, Donald D. *lawyer*
Kracov, Daniel A. *lawyer*
Kramer, Andrew Michael *lawyer*
Kramer, Franklin David *lawyer*
Kramer, Noël Anketell *judge*
Kramer, Simon Paul *writer*
Kramer, William David *lawyer*
Krasnow, Erwin Gilbert *lawyer*
Kraus, Margery *management consultant, communications company executive*
Kravis, Marie-Josee Drouin *economist*
Kreidler, Charles W(illiam) *linguist, educator*
Kreig, Andrew Thomas *trade association executive*
Kreinheder, Hazel Fuller *retired genealogist, historian*
Kriesberg, Simeon M. *lawyer*
Kringen, John A. *federal agency administrator*
Kristol, William (Bill Krisol) *editor, political analyst*
Kroener, William Frederick III *lawyer*
Krongard, Howard J. *federal agency administrator, lawyer*
Kroszner, Randall Scott *federal official, economics professor*
Kroupa, Diane Lynn *federal judge*
Krueger, Anne *economist*
Krueger, Keith Roger *educational association administrator*
Krulfeld, Ruth Marilyn *anthropologist, educator*
Krump, Gary Joseph *marketing executive, lawyer, judge*
Kuh, Charlotte Virginia *economist*
Kuhl, Randy (John R. Kuhl Jr.) *congressman, lawyer*
Kulski, Julian Eugeniusz *architect, writer*
Kummant, Alexander K. *rail transportation executive*
Kunder, James R. *federal agency administrator*
Kurin, Richard *museum program director*
Kursh, Gail *lawyer*
Kurtz, Howard *journalist, author*
Kurzweil, Jeffrey *lawyer*
Kushner, Gary Jay *lawyer*
Kushnir, Andrei *artist, consultant*
Kussman, Michael James *federal agency administrator*
Kutler, Alison L. *lawyer*
Kyhos, Thomas Flynn *lawyer*
Labaton, Stephen *journalist, lawyer*
Lackey, Michael E., Jr. *lawyer, educator*
LaFleur, Christopher J. *ambassador*
La Force, Hudson III *federal agency administrator*
Lagon, Mark P. *federal agency administrator*
LaHaye, Beverly *cultural organization administrator*
LaHood, Ray H. *congressman*
Lahreche, Hichem *chef*
Lake, (W.) Anthony *former national security advisor*
Lake, William Truman *lawyer*
Lakner, George Stephen *military officer*
Lamb, Brian Patrick *broadcast executive*
Lambert, Jeremiah Daniel *lawyer, educator*
Lambert, Steven Charles *lawyer*
Lambright, James H. *bank executive*
Lambro, Donald Joseph *columnist*
Lamken, Jeffrey A. *lawyer*
Lamm, Carolyn Beth *lawyer*
Lamont, Bridget Later *librarian, consultant*
Lampl, Peggy Ann *public information officer*
Lampson, Nick (Nicholas Valentino Lampson) *congressman*
Lance, Alan George *federal judge, former state attorney general*
Landrieu, Mary Lorretta *senator*
Landry, Brock R. *lawyer*
Lane, Bruce Stuart *lawyer*
Lane, Charlotte R. *federal official, lawyer*
Lane, John Dennis *lawyer*
Langdale, Mark *ambassador, former hotel executive*
Langdon, James Calhoun, Jr. *lawyer*
Langevin, James R. (Jim Langevin) *congressman, former state official*
Langfeld, Patricia Ann *trade association administrator*
Langfeld, Stanley Chaitt *government executive*
Lanier, Cathy L. *police chief*
Lantos, Thomas Peter *congressman*
Laporte, Gerald Joseph Sylvestre *lawyer*
Lappin, Harley G. *federal agency administrator*
Lardent, Esther Ferster *lawyer, consultant*
Lardner, George, Jr. *journalist, writer*
Lardy, Nicholas Richard *economist, educator*
Laro, David *federal judge*
Larroca, Raymond G. *lawyer*
Larsen, Richard Gary *finance company executive*
Larsen, Richard Ray (Rick Larsen) *congressman*
Larson, Alan Philip *former federal agency administrator*
Larson, John Barry *congressman, insurance executive*
Larson, Judy L. *museum director, curator*
Larson, Philip C. *lawyer*
Lasko, Joel *marketing executive*
LaSpada, Carmella *government agency administrator*
Lasseter, Tom *journalist*
Lastowka, James Anthony *former federal agency administrator, lawyer*
Latham, Patricia Horan *lawyer*
Latham, Patricia S. *physician*
Latham, Peter Samuel *lawyer*
Latham, Tom *congressman*
Latham, Weldon Hurd *lawyer*
Latimer, Allie B. *retired lawyer*
Latimer, Katharine Ruth *lawyer*
Lauerman, William *medical educator*
Laughlin, Felix B. *lawyer*
Laughlin, Gregory H. (Greg Laughlin) *lawyer, former congressman*
Laughlin, James Harold, Jr. *lawyer*
Lautenbacher, Conrad Charles, Jr. *federal agency administrator, retired naval officer*
Lavelle, Joseph P. *lawyer*
Lavin, Franklin Leo *federal agency administrator, former ambassador*
Lavine, Henry Wolfe *lawyer*
Law, Steven J. *business association and former federal agency administrator*
Lawler, William E. III *lawyer*
Lawson, Jennifer *broadcast executive*
Lawson, Kelli *communications executive*
Lazarin, Melissa Y. *director*
Lazarus, Arthur, Jr. *lawyer*
Lazarus, Kenneth Anthony *lawyer*
Lazear, Edward Paul *federal official, economics professor*
Leaf, Howard Westley *retired military officer*
Leahy, Patrick Joseph *senator*
Leamer, Laurence Allen *writer*
Leavitt, Michael Okerlund *secretary of health and human services*
Leavitt, Paul David *director music arts, pianist, composer*
Lebryk, David A. *federal agency administrator*
Leckey, Dolores R. *religious organization administrator, writer*
Ledbetter, Kenneth W. *federal agency administrator*
Lederer, Max Donald, Jr. *lawyer*
Ledley, Robert Steven *biophysicist*
Lee, Barbara *congresswoman*
Lee, Debra Louise *cable television company executive*
Lee, Edward *lawyer*
Lee, Hwa-Wei *librarian, educator, consultant*
Lee, Ronald Derek *lawyer*
Leeds, Charles Alan *publishing executive*
Lefemine, Armand Angelo *thoracic surgeon, educator*
Leff, Deborah *foundation administrator*
Legro, Patrice *museum director*
Lehman, Donald Richard *physicist, educator, academic administrator*
Lehmberg, Robert Henry *retired research physicist*
Lehrman, Margaret McBride *broadcast executive, television producer*
Leibold, Arthur William, Jr. *lawyer*
Leibowitz, Jon *commissioner*
Leipold, James G. *lawyer*
Lelyveld, Gail Annick *actress*
Lemov, Michael R. *lawyer*
Lendsey, Jacquelyn L. *foundation administrator*
Lent, Norman Frederick, Jr. *former congressman*
Leo, Leonard A. *legal association administrator, lawyer*
LeoGrande, William Mark *political science professor, writer*
Leon, Richard J. *federal judge*
Leonard, Bill (J. William Leonard) *federal agency administrator*
Leos, Kathleen *federal agency administrator*
Leshner, Alan Irvin *science administrator*
Lessin, Lawrence Stephen *hematologist, oncologist, educator*
Lettow, Charles Frederick *federal judge*
Leubsdorf, Carl Philipp *publishing executive*
Lever, Jack Q., Jr. *lawyer*
Leveridge, Richard J. *lawyer*
Levett, Todd A. *government agency administrator*
Levey, Stuart A. *federal agency administrator*
Levin, Carl Milton *senator*
Levin, Edward M. *lawyer*
Levin, George Martin *association and organization administrator, aeronautical engineer*
Levin, Robert J. *finance company executive*
Levin, Sander Martin *congressman, lawyer*
Levine, Felice J. *educational association administrator*
Levine, Henry David *lawyer*
Levinger, Matthew B. *historian*
Levinson, Daniel Ronald *federal agency administrator, lawyer*
Levinson, Lawrence Edward *lawyer*
Levinstein, Mark Steven *lawyer, educator*
Levit, Lawrence A. *lawyer*
Levitte, Jean-David *ambassador*
Levy, Gregg H. *lawyer*
Levy, Jill Sondra *educational association administrator*
Levy, Mark Irving *lawyer*
Levy, Michael B. *business educator*
Lewin, John Calvert *medical association administrator*
Lewis, Ann Frank *former government official*
Lewis, Anne McCutcheon *architect*
Lewis, Benjamin Pershing, Jr. *pharmacist, retired public health service officer*
Lewis, Charles Jeremy (Jerry Lewis) *congressman*
Lewis, Charles Joseph *journalist*
Lewis, Daniel Martin *lawyer*
Lewis, David John *lawyer*
Lewis, Dennis M. *federal agency administrator, former hospital administrator*
Lewis, Eleanor Roberts *lawyer*
Lewis, Glenn C. *lawyer*
Lewis, Guy A. *prosecutor*
Lewis, John Robert *congressman*
Lewis, Lorraine *former federal agency administrator*
Lewis, Mark K. *lawyer*
Lewis, Prudence Fox *Christian science practitioner*
Lewis, Robert David Gilmore *retired editor*
Lewis, Roger Kutnow *architect, educator, author*
Lewis, Ron *congressman*
Lewis, William Henry, Jr. *lawyer*
Lewris, Basil J. *lawyer*
Li, Li *research scientist*
Liasson, Mara *news correspondent*
Liberty, Arthur Andrew *judge*
Lichtblau, Eric *journalist*
Lichte, Arthur J. *career military officer*
Lichtenstein, Elissa Charlene *legal association executive*
Lichtman, Allan Jay *historian, educator, consultant*
Liebenson, Gloria Krasnow *interior design executive, freelance writer*
Lieber, Robert James *political science professor*
Lieberman, Joe (Joseph Isadore Lieberman) *senator*
Liebeskind, Richard *lawyer*
Liebman, Ronald Stanley *lawyer*
Liebman, Wilma B. *federal agency administrator*
Lifschitz, Judah *lawyer*
Lightfoot, James Ellison *researcher, director*
Lightfoot, William P., Jr. *lawyer*
Lighthizer, Robert E. *lawyer*
Ligler, Frances Smith *biochemist*
Lincoln, Blanche Lambert *senator*
Lindemann, Adam *communications executive*
Linder, John E. *congressman, dentist*
Lindsey, Seth Mark *lawyer*
Lipinski, Daniel *congressman*
Lippincott, Joan K. *library director*
Lippincott, John *educational association administrator*
Lipsky, John Phillip *international banking official*
Lisboa-Farrow, Elizabeth Oliver *public and government relations consultant*
Litt, Robert S. *lawyer*
Little, John William *plastic surgeon, educator*
Liu, Minetta Chung-sui *oncologist, educator*
Livingood, Wilson S. *protective services official*
Livingston, Bob (Robert Linlithgow Livingston Jr.) *lawyer, retired congressman*
Livingston, Donald Ray *lawyer*
Livingston, Robert Gerald *historian, journalist*
Lloyd, James D. *federal agency administrator*
Lobel, Martin *lawyer*
Locker, Raymond Duncan *editor*
Lockhart, James Bicknell III *federal agency administrator*
Locklear, Arlinda Faye *lawyer*
Loeb, G. Hamilton *lawyer*
Loebsack, Dave *congressman, former political science professor*
Loepere, Carol Colborn *lawyer*
Lofgren, Zoe *congresswoman*
Lofthus, Lee J. *federal agency administrator*
Loftus, Carroll Michael (Michael Loftus) *lawyer*
Lombardo, Fredric Alan *pharmacist, educator*
Longnecker, David Eugene *anesthesiologist, educator*
Loo, Beverly Jane *publishing executive*
Loots, James Mason *lawyer*
Lopatin, Alan G. *lawyer*
Lott, (Chester) Trent *senator*
Lourie, Alan David *federal judge*
Lovejoy, Thomas Eugene *tropical and conservation biologist, association executive*
Lovelace, Gail T. *human resources specialist*
Lowe, Mary Frances *federal official*
Lowe, Randall B. *lawyer*
Lowell, Abbe David *lawyer*
Lowenkron, Barry Frederick *federal agency administrator*
Lowenstein, James Gordon *former diplomat, international consultant*
Lowery, Clay *federal agency administrator*
Lowther, Frederick M. *lawyer*
Loy, James Milton *former federal agency administrator, retired coast guard officer*
Lozansky, Edward Dmitry *physicist, consultant, writer*
Lubar, Jeffrey Stuart *journalist, trade association executive*
Lubic, Benita Joan Alk *travel company executive*
Lucas, C. Payne *development organization executive*
Lucas, James Walter *federal official*
Luchok, Joseph Alan *communications executive, consultant*
Ludwig, Eugene Allan *financial consultant, lawyer, former US Comptroller of the Currency*
Lugar, Dick (Richard Green Lugar) *senator*
Lujan, Manuel, Jr. *think-tank executive, former secretary of the interior, retired congressman*
Lukken, Walter L. *commissioner*
Lundsager, Margrethe (Meg Lundsager) *federal official*
Lungren, Daniel Edward *congressman, former state attorney general*
Lupo, Raphael V. *lawyer*
Luque, Nancy *lawyer*
Lurensky, Marcia Adele *lawyer*
Luskin, Robert David *lawyer*
Lustig, M. Bruce *rabbi*
Lute, Douglas E. *federal official, career military officer*
Luthi, Randall B. *federal agency administrator, former state legislator*
Lutterodt, Clement H. *mathematician, educator*
Luttwak, Edward Nicolae *academic administrator, policy and business consultant, senior advisor*
Luxton, Jane Charlotte *lawyer*
Lybecker, Martin Earl *lawyer*
Lydon, Thomas J. *federal judge*
Lynch, Clifford A. *library and information scientist*
Lynch, Stephen F. *congressman*
Lynn, Karyl Charna (Karyl Lynn Kopelman Zietz) *writer, filmmaker, critic, television producer*
Lyon, Andrew Bennet *economist*
Lyons, Dennis Gerald *lawyer*
Lyons, Francis Xavier *lawyer*
Lyons, Mona *lawyer*
Lytle, Gary R. *telecommunications industry executive*
MacAlister, Rodney J. *President African Development Foundation*
MacBeth, Angus *lawyer*
MacDonald, Bruce E. *military officer, lawyer*
Macdonald, David Robert *lawyer, pension fund administrator*
MacDougall, Gordon Pier *lawyer*
Machen, Ronald C. *lawyer*
Macht, Steven *plastic surgeon, consultant*
Mack, Connie *congressman*
Mack, Connie, III, (Cornelius McGillicuddy III) *former senator*
Mack, Julia Cooper *retired judge*
Macleod, John Amend *lawyer*
Maddaloni, Martin J. *retired labor union administrator*
Madden, Jerome Anthony *lawyer*
Madden, Murdaugh Stuart *lawyer*
Madden, Thomas James *lawyer, educator*
Maddox, Lauren M. *federal agency administrator*
Madras, Bertha Kalifon *federal official, neuroscientist, researcher*
Magee, Charles Thomas *international consultant, retired diplomat*
Magielnicki, Robert L. *lawyer*
Magner, Timothy J. *federal agency administrator, educator*
Magrath, C. Peter *educational association executive*
Magraw, Daniel Barstow, Jr. *lawyer, educator*
Mahar, Ellen Patricia *law librarian*
Mahinka, Stephen Paul *lawyer*
Mahoney, Maureen E. *lawyer*
Mahoney, Tim (Timothy Edward Mahoney) *congressman*
Majoras, Deborah Platt *commissioner*
Malek, Frederic Vincent *finance company executive*
Malinowski, Matthew J. *lawyer*
Mallon, Thomas *writer*
Mallory, Charles King III *lawyer*
Maloney, Carolyn Bosher *congresswoman*
Malveaux, Floyd Joseph *dean*
Manatt, Charles Taylor *lawyer*
Manchester, Paul Brunson *economist*
Mancuso, Mario *federal agency administrator*
Mandel, Harold George *pharmacologist, educator*
Manderson, Easton L. *orthopedist, surgeon*
Manfreda, John J. *federal agency administrator*
Mangano, Philip F. *federal agency administrator*
Maniscalco-Theberge, Mary Elizabeth *surgeon, medical educator*
Mann, Marion *pathologist, educator*
Mann, Oscar *retired physician, internist, educator*
Mann, Thomas *reference librarian*
Mann, Thomas Edward *political scientist*
Manning, David Geoffrey *ambassador*
Manning, Michael J. *lawyer*
Mansfield, Edward Patrick, Jr. *advertising executive*

Mansfield, Gordon Hall *federal agency administrator*
Manson, Joseph Lloyd III *lawyer*
Mantyla, Karen *distance learning consultant*
Manzanares, J. Robert *ambassador*
Manzullo, Donald A. *congressman, lawyer*
Mao, Ho-kwang (Dave Mao) *geophysicist, educator*
Mapes, William Rodgers, Jr. *lawyer*
Maples, Michael D. *federal agency administrator, military officer*
Maran, Stephen Paul *astronomer*
Marburger, John Harmen III *federal official*
Marburg-Goodman, Jeffrey Emil *lawyer*
Marchand, Michael J. *judge, career military officer*
Marchant, Kenny *congressman*
Marcoullis, Erato Kozakou *ambassador*
Marcum, Deanna Bowling *library administrator*
Marcus, Kenneth L. *federal official*
Marcuss, Rosemary Daly *economist*
Marcuss, Stanley Joseph *lawyer*
Margeton, Stephen George *law librarian*
Margolis, Doris May Rosenberg *editor, writer*
Margolis, Lawrence Stanley *federal judge*
Marincola, Elizabeth Mark *nonprofit executive*
Marine, Michael W. *ambassador*
Markey, Edward John *congressman*
Markoski, Joseph Peter *lawyer*
Marks, Herbert Edward *lawyer*
Marks, Richard Daniel *lawyer*
Marlette, Cynthia *lawyer*
Marr, Phebe Ann *retired historian, educator*
Marrett, Michael McFarlene *chaplain*
Marriott, John W. III *hotel executive*
Marriott, John Willard, Jr. *lodging and senior living executive*
Marshall, Alison Buell *lawyer*
Marshall, Jim (James Creel Marshall) *congressman*
Marshall, Joshua Micah *publisher, blog writer, columnist, editor, political journalist*
Martella, Roger Romulus, Jr. *federal agency administrator, lawyer*
Martin, Billy (William R. Martin) *lawyer*
Martin, David Briton Hadden, Jr. *lawyer*
Martin, Guy *lawyer*
Martin, Jerry Lee *organization executive, educator*
Martin, John Charles *lawyer*
Martin, Julie A. *retired insurance company executive*
Martin, Keith *lawyer*
Martin, Kevin J. *federal agency administrator*
Martin, Linda Gaye *demographer, economist*
Martin, Thomas Stephen *lawyer*
Martinez, Carmen Maria *ambassador*
Martinez, Herminia S. *economist, banker*
Martinez, Mel(quiades) (Rafael) *senator, political organization administrator, former secretary of housing and urban development*
Martinez, Rose Marie *health science association administrator*
Martinez Myers, Frances *real estate company executive*
Martinez Tucker, Sara (Sara Alicia Tucker) *federal agency and former educational association administrator*
Marvel, L. Paige *federal judge*
Marventano, David *engineering and construction management company executive*
Marvin, Charles Rodney, Jr. *lawyer*
Masekela, Barbara Joyce Mosima *ambassador*
Mashagbeh, Wassel Khalaf *economist*
Massey, Jeanne Kelly *performing company executive*
Masters, Edward Eugene *association executive, former foreign service officer*
Mateczun, John Matthew *career military officer*
Matheson, James David (Jim) *congressman*
Mathews, Jessica Tuchman *research executive, federal official, newswriter*
Mathias, Edward Joseph *merchant banker*
Matsui, Doris Okada *congresswoman*
Mattsson, Ake *psychiatrist, physician*
Maxwell, David Ogden *federal agency administrator, mortgage company executive*
May, Stephen *writer, federal official, historian*
May, Timothy James *lawyer*
Mayer, Haldane Robert *federal judge*
Mayer, Neal Michael *lawyer*
Mayers, Daniel Kriegsman *lawyer*
Mayo, George Washington, Jr. *lawyer*
Mayo, John W. *finance educator*
Mays, Janice Ann *lawyer*
Mazo, Mark Elliott *lawyer*
Mc Afee, William *government official*
McBee, Susanna Barnes *retired journalist*
McBride, Jonathan Evans *management consultant, director*
McBride, Michael Flynn *lawyer*
McCaffrey, Judith Elizabeth *lawyer*
McCain, John (John Sidney McCain III) *senator*
McCallum, Robert Davis, Jr. *ambassador, former federal agency administrator*
McCann, Clifton Everett *lawyer*
McCarron, Douglas J. *labor union administrator*
McCarthy, Carolyn *congresswoman*
McCarthy, Kevin *congressman, former state legislator*
McCarthy, Peter B. *federal agency administrator*
McCaskill, Claire C. *senator, former auditor*
McCaul, Elizabeth *investment advisor, former state agency administrator*
McCaul, Michael T. *congressman*
McCaw, Susan Rasinski *ambassador*
McClain, Tim S. *lawyer*
McClellan, Mark B. *former federal agency administrator*
McClung, Gwendolyn *soil microbiologist*
McClure, Frederick Donald *lawyer*
McClure, William Pendleton *lawyer*
McCollam, William, Jr. *utilities executive*
McCollum, Betty *congresswoman*
McConnell, Mike (John Michael McConnell) *Director of National Intelligence, retired military officer*
McConnell, (Addison) Mitchell, Jr. *senator, lawyer*
McConnell, Nicholas Stillwell *lawyer*
McConnell, Ted (Theodore) F. *not-for-profit fundraiser, director*
McCormack, Sean Ian *federal agency administrator*
McCormally, Kevin Jay *editor*
McCormick, David Harold *federal agency administrator*
McCormick, Walter Bernard, Jr. *trade association administrator*
McCormick, William Paul *ambassador*
McCoy, Jerry Jack *lawyer*
McCrabb, Donald Raymond *pastoral field educator*
McCrary Anthony, Crystal *writer, producer, lawyer*
McCrery, James (Jim McCrery) *congressman*
McCurdy, David Keith *trade association administrator, former congressman*
McCutchen, Tammy Dee *lawyer, former federal agency administrator*
McDaniels, William E. *lawyer*
McDavid, Janet Louise *lawyer*
McDermott, James A. *congressman, psychiatrist*
McDevitt, Thomas P. *publishing executive*
McDiarmid, Robert Campbell *lawyer*
McDonald, Frances D. *government official, editor, lawyer*
McDowell, Carter K. *lawyer*
McDowell, Heather L. *lawyer*
McDowell, Robert M. *commissioner*
McDowell-Craig, Vanessa Dennise *supervisor, consultant*
McEldowney, Nancy *diplomat*
McElroy, Edward J. *labor union administrator*
McElveen, Junius Carlisle, Jr. *lawyer*
McElveen-Hunter, Bonnie *international relief organization executive*
McEntee, Christine W. *architecture and former medical association administrator*
McEntee, Gerald W. *labor union administrator*
McGee, James M. *federal agency administrator*
McGee, Robert Merrill *oil industry executive*
McGinnis, James Michael *physician*
McGinnis, Patricia Gwaltney *non-profit organization executive*
McGovern, James P. *congressman*
McGovern, Michael *lawyer*
McGrath, Kathryn Bradley *lawyer*
McGrath, Kevin Michael *military analyst, civilian military employee, researcher*
McGuan, Kathleen H. *lawyer*
McGuire, Jack (John F. McGuire) *international relief organization executive*
McGuirl, Marlene Dana Callis *law librarian, educator*
McGurn, William Joseph *speechwriter, editor*
McHenry, Patrick Timothy *congressman*
McHugh, James Lenahan, Jr. *lawyer*
McIntosh, David M. *former congressman*
McIntyre, Marvin H., II, *financial consultant*
McIntyre, Mike (Douglas Carmichael McIntyre II) *congressman*
Mc Kay, Emily Gantz *civil rights and nonprofit professional*
McKay, Margo Marquita *federal agency administrator, lawyer*
McKee, Margaret Jean *federal agency administrator*
McKeever, Joseph Francis III *lawyer*
McKenna, Juliet JoAnn *federal judge*
McKeon, Howard Phillip (Buck McKeon) *congressman, former mayor*
McKinney, David Duane *museum director, architectural historian*
McKinney, James DeVaine, Jr. *lawyer*
McLarty, Thomas F., III, (Mack McLarty) *former White House Chief of Staff*
McLaughlin, David *foundation administrator*
McLaughlin, John J. *broadcast executive, television producer, journalist, political commentator*
McLean, Kathleen *exhibition consultant, museum director*
McLean, R. Bruce *lawyer*
McLucas, William Robert *lawyer, former federal agency administrator*
McMillin, Stephen S. *federal official*
McMorris Rodgers, Cathy *congresswoman*
McMurray, Claudia Anne *federal agency administrator, lawyer*
McNabb, Duncan J. *career military officer*
McNamara, Michael T. *lawyer*
McNamara, Robert Strange *former world bank president, secretary of defense*
McNerney, Jerry (Gerald M. McNerney) *congressman, engineer*
McNulty, Michael Robert *congressman*
McNulty, Paul J. *lawyer, former federal agency administrator*
McNulty, Robert Holmes *non-profit executive*
McPhee, George *professional sports team executive*
Mc Phee, Henry Roemer *lawyer*
Mc Pherson, Harry Cummings, Jr. *lawyer*
McPherson, Peter (M. Peter McPherson) *publishing executive, educational association administrator*
McPhie, Neil Anthony Gordon *federal official*
McQueary, Charles E. (Chuck McQueary) *federal agency administrator*
McQuillan, Laurence Joseph *communications consultant, educator*
McReynolds, Mary Armilda *lawyer*
McSlarrow, Kyle E. *telecommunications association executive, former federal agency administrator*
McSweeny, Dorothy Pierce *art association administrator*
McWilliams, Kenneth L. *lawyer*
Mead, Christopher *lawyer*
Mead, Kenneth Minor *lawyer, former federal agency administrator*
Means, Thomas Cornell *lawyer*
Mederos, Carolina Luisa *public policy consultant*
Medina, Rubens *law librarian*
Medish, Mark *federal government official*
Meece, Roger A. *ambassador*
Meek, Kendrick B. *congressman*
Meese, Ed (Edwin Meese III) *law and public policy educator, former United States attorney general*
Meggers, Betty Jane *anthropologist, researcher*
Megginson, Elizabeth R. *legislative staff member, director, lawyer*
Mehlman, Bruce P. *trade association and formal federal agency administrator*
Mehlman, Ken(neth) (Brian) *lawyer, former political organization administrator*
Meijer, Paul Herman Ernst *physicist, educator*
Meisburg, Ronald Edward *federal agency administrator, lawyer*
Mekkawi, Mohamed *library director*
Melamed, Arthur Douglas *lawyer*
Melancon, Charles *congressman*
Melendy, David Russell *newscaster, reporter*
Mellor, John Williams *economist, consultant*
Meloy, Sybil Piskur *retired lawyer*
Melton, Carol A. *communications executive*
Memmott, Scott A. *lawyer*
Menaker, Frank H., Jr. *lawyer*
Menarchik, Douglas (Edward Douglas Menarchik) *federal agency administrator*
Mencher, Bruce Stephan *judge*
Mendelsohn, Martin *lawyer*
Mendoza, Julie C. *lawyer*
Menendez, Robert (Bob Menendez) *senator, former congressman*
Menkel-Meadow, Carrie Joan *law educator*
Meridor, Sallai *ambassador*
Merow, James F. *federal judge*
Merrifield, Dudley Bruce *finance educator, federal official*
Merrill, Susan L. *financial regulatory service executive, lawyer*
Merritt, Carolyn *government agency administrator*
Mesecar, Doug *federal agency administrator*
Meshulam, Deborah R. *lawyer*
Messiah-Jiles, Sonceria *publishing executive*
Metz, Craig Huseman *lawyer*
Meyer, Dennis Irwin *lawyer*
Meyer, Katherine Anne *lawyer*
Meyer, Lindsay Beardsworth *lawyer*
Meyer, Margaret Vaughan *librarian, educator*
Meyer, Paul *information technology executive*
Meyerrose, Dale William *federal official, retired military officer*
Meyers, Linda Dee *non-profit administrator, researcher*
Meyers, Wayne Marvin *microbiologist, physician*
Meyerson, Adam *foundation administrator*
Meyerson, Harold *journalist*
Mica, John L. *congressman*
Michaels, Gary David *lawyer*
Michaelson, Martin *lawyer*
Michaud, Michael Herman *congressman*
Michel, Paul Redmond *federal judge*
Michelman, Kate *advocate*
Michnich, Marie E. *health policy analyst, consultant, educator*
Mickey, Paul F(ogle), Jr. *lawyer*
Migliore, Marcus Charles *lawyer*
Mikulski, Barbara Ann *senator*
Milam, William Bryant *former ambassador, senior policy scholar*
Milch, Thomas H. *lawyer*
Miles, David Michael *lawyer*
Miles, John Jeffries *lawyer*
Millar, James Robert *economist, educator, university official*
Miller, Andrew Pickens *lawyer*
Miller, Brad (Ralph Bradley Miller) *congressman*
Miller, Candice S. *congresswoman*
Miller, Christine Odell Cook *federal judge*
Miller, Evan *lawyer*
Miller, Ewing Harry *retired architect*
Miller, Gary G. *congressman*
Miller, George *congressman*
Miller, George W. *federal judge, lawyer*
Miller, H. Todd *lawyer*
Miller, Harris N. *educational association administrator*
Miller, James Clifford III *economist*
Miller, James Forrest *lawyer*
Miller, Jeanne-Marie Anderson (Mrs. Nathan J. Miller) *language educator, academic administrator*
Miller, Jeff *congressman*
Miller, John *federal agency administrator, former news correspondent*
Miller, John Ripin *former federal agency administrator, former congressman*
Miller, John T., Jr. *lawyer, educator*
Miller, Laura Ariane *lawyer*
Miller, Margery *psychologist, educator, speech pathology/audiology services professional, mental health services professional*
Miller, Marshall Lee *lawyer*
Miller, Nicole *art columnist*
Miller, Richard N. *former medical association administrator*
Miller, William Green *former ambassador*
Millian, John C. *lawyer*
Millman, Laura Diane *federal official*
Mills, Kevin Paul *lawyer*
Milman, Natalie Bordelon *education educator*
Milstein, Elliott Steven *lawyer, educator, academic administrator*
Minardi, Ann Segura *lawyer, musician*
Mineta, Norman Yoshio *management consultant, former secretary of transportation*
Mirengoff, Paul E. *lawyer, political blogger*
Mirkow, Frank J. *lawyer*
Mirvahabi, Farin *lawyer*
Mishkin, Barbara Friedman *lawyer*
Mishkin, Frederic Stanley *federal official, economics educator*
Missar, Charles Donald *retired librarian*
Mistral, Jacques *economist*
Mitchell, Andrea *journalist*
Mitchell, Harry E. *congressman, former state legislator*
Mitchell, Ross Edward *research scientist, educator*
Mitchell, Ruthie Yvette *human services administrator, director*
Mixter, Christian John *lawyer*
Moates, (G.) Paul *lawyer*
Moe, Richard Palmer *lawyer*
Moe, Ronald Chesney *public administration researcher*
Moeller, Philip D. *commissioner*
Moffitt, William Benjamin *lawyer*
Mogel, William Allen *lawyer*
Mohrman, Kathryn j. *academic administrator*
Mok, Samuel Tinsing *federal agency administrator*
Moler, Elizabeth Anne *utilities executive*
Molinari, Susan *former congresswoman*
Mollohan, Alan Bowlby *congressman*
Mombouli, Serge *ambassador*
Mondello, Lisette McSoud *federal agency administrator*
Monis, Johnny *chef*
Monk, Carl Colburn *legal association and academic administrator, lawyer*
Monroe, Carl Dean III *lawyer*
Monroe, Jane D. *federal agency administrator*
Monroe, Stephanie Johnson *federal agency administrator*
Montanez-Johner, Nancy *federal agency administrator*
Montedonico, Joseph *lawyer*
Monteiro, Maristela Goldnadel *physician, researcher*
Montgomery, John A. *physicist*
Mooney, Marilyn *lawyer*
Moore, Amy Norwood *lawyer*
Moore, Bob Stahly *communications executive*
Moore, Dennis *congressman*
Moore, Donald Emerson III *zoological park administrator, curator, wildlife biologist*
Moore, Gwendolynne S. (Gwen Moore) *congresswoman*
Moore, Jacquelyn Cornelia *retired labor union administrator, editor*
Moore, Jerry A. III *lawyer*
Moore, Kimberly Ann *federal judge*
Moore, Powell Allen *former federal agency administrator*
Moore, Robert Madison *food products executive, lawyer*
Moorehead, Donald V. *lawyer*
Moorman, William A. *federal judge, retired career military officer*
Moot, John S. *lawyer*
Morales, Hector E., Jr. *bank executive, lawyer*
Moran, Anne E. *lawyer*
Moran, Christian J. *federal official*
Moran, Jerry *congressman*
Moran, Jim (James Patrick Moran Jr.) *congressman, stock broker*
Moran, Terry *news correspondent*
Moreno, Jaime *professional soccer player*
Moreno, Luis Alberto *bank executive*
Morford, Craig S. *federal agency administrator, prosecutor*
Morgan, Bruce Ray *management consultant*
Morgan, Daniel Louis *lawyer, educator*
Morgan, Linda Joan *former federal agency administrator, lawyer*
Mori, Yoshiko *language educator*
Morillo, Juan P. *lawyer*
Moring, John Frederick *lawyer*
Moritsugu, Kenneth Paul *federal official, career military officer*
Morrissey, Patricia A. *federal agency administrator*
Morse, Larry Eugene *botanist, conservationist*
Morse, M. Howard *lawyer*
Mosbacher, Robert A. *investment company executive*
Moschella, William Emil *federal agency administrator*
Moseley, T. Michael (Teed Michael Moseley) *military officer*
Moses, Alfred Henry *lawyer, writer, diplomat*
Moshier, David Irwin *church administrator*
Moss, Madison Scott *editor*
Mosso, Lyle David *finance company executive*
Mostoff, Allan Samuel *lawyer, consultant*
Moten, Sarah Elizabeth *federal agency administrator*
Moy, Edmund C. *federal agency administrator*
Muckenfuss, Cantwell Faulkner III *lawyer*
Mudd, Daniel H. *finance company executive*
Mueller, Robert Swan III *FBI director*
Mueller, Sharon Lee (Sherry Mueller) *educational organization executive*
Muir, J. Dapray *lawyer*
Mujica, Barbara Louise *language educator, writer*
Muleta, John B. *lawyer*
Mulford, David Campbell *ambassador, former finance company executive*
Mulhollan, Daniel Patrick *research director*
Mull, Stephen D. *federal agency administrator, former ambassador*
Mullen, Michael G. *career military officer*
Muller, Steven *international studies educator, academic administrator*
Mullick, Florabel Garcia *pathologist, director*
Mulloy, Patrick Aloysius *lawyer*
Munson, Richard Jay *government agency administrator*
Muris, Timothy Joseph *former federal agency administrator, lawyer, educator*
Murkowski, Lisa Ann *senator*
Murphy, Betty Southard *lawyer*
Murphy, Caryle Marie *foreign correspondent*
Murphy, Edward Joseph *government agency administrator*
Murphy, Frances M. *federal agency administrator*
Murphy, Gerard Norris *trade association executive*
Murphy, Joanne Becker *writer*

Murphy, Joseph Albert, Jr. *lawyer*
Murphy, Timothy F. *congressman*
Murray, Christopher Charles III *architect*
Murray, James Joseph III *association executive*
Murray, Patty (Patricia J. Murray) *senator*
Murray, Robert Fulton, Jr. *physician*
Murry, Harold David, Jr. *lawyer*
Murtha, John Patrick, Jr. *congressman*
Musgrave, Marilyn N. *congresswoman*
Mussa, Michael L. *economist, educator*
Mwenda, Kenneth Kaoma *legal association administrator, consultant*
Myers, Ernest M. *otolaryngologist, head and neck surgeon*
Myers, James R. *lawyer*
Myers, Lisa M. *broadcast journalist*
Myrick, Sue Wilkins *congresswoman, former mayor*
Mysen, Bjorn Olav *scientist*
Nabholz, Joseph Vincent *biologist, ecologist*
Nace, Barry John *lawyer*
Nader, Ralph *advocate, lawyer, writer*
Nadler, Jerrold Lewis *congressman, lawyer*
Naeve, Clifford Mike *lawyer*
Nagel, Trevor W. *lawyer*
Nagorski, Zygmunt *political scientist, writer*
Naím, Moises *editor*
Nakayama, Granta Y. *federal agency administrator, lawyer*
Namrow, Eric S. *lawyer*
Nannes, Michael Edward *lawyer*
Napolitano, Grace F. *congresswoman*
Narasaki, Karen Keiko *advocate, lawyer*
Nardi Riddle, Clarine *lawyer, federal official*
Nash, James Lee *poet, security official*
Nash, John Davidson, Jr. *economist*
Nason, David George *federal agency administrator*
Nason, Nicole R. *federal agency administrator*
Natarajan, Aruna *physician, educator, researcher*
Natarajan, Githa *elementary school educator*
Natividad, Irene *women's rights advocate*
Natsios, Andrew Stephen *diplomat, former federal agency administrator*
Nauheim, Stephen Alan *lawyer*
Navarro, Bruce Charles *lawyer*
Navas, William Antonio, Jr. *civilian military employee and retired officer*
Nazareth, Annette LaPorte *commissioner, lawyer*
Neal, Darwina Lee *federal agency administrator*
Neal, Richard Edmund *congressman, former mayor*
Nebeker, Frank Quill *judge*
Negroponte, John Dimitri *federal agency administrator, former national intelligence director, ambassador*
Nelsen, Hart Michael *sociologist, educator*
Nelson, (Earl) Ben(jamin) *senator, former governor, lawyer*
Nelson, Bill (Clarence William Nelson) *senator, former state treasurer*
Nelson, Keith A. *federal agency administrator*
Nemeroff, Michael Alan *lawyer*
Ness, Andrew David *lawyer*
Nethercutt, George Rector, Jr. *lawyer, consultant, former congressman*
Nethery, John Jay *government official, military officer*
Neufeld, Michael John *curator, historian*
Neugebauer, Randy (Robert R. Neugebauer) *congressman*
Neureiter, Norman P. *science association director*
Neviaser, Robert Jon *orthopaedic surgeon, educator*
Newberry, Edward J. *lawyer*
Newell, Mark E. *lawyer*
Newkirk, Thomas Charles *lawyer*
Newman, Pauline *federal judge*
Newman, Sherryl Hobbs *former district secretary*
Nichols, Rob (Robert Stanley Nichols) *think-tank executive, former federal agency administrator*
Nicholson, Jim (Robert James Nicholson) *secretary of veterans affairs, former ambassador*
Nicholson, Richard Selindh *educational association administrator*
Nickel, Henry V. *lawyer*
Nicolson, Dan Henry *retired plant taxonomist*
Niehuss, John Marvin *lawyer*
Niemeier, Charles D. *accountant*
Nightingale, Elena Ottolenghi *pediatric geneticist, academic administrator, educator*
Nightingale, Stuart Lester *public health service officer*
Nims, Arthur Lee III *federal judge*
Nirenberg, Darryl D. *lawyer*
Niskanen, William Arthur, Jr. *economist, think-tank executive*
Nitze, William Albert *government official, lawyer, not-for-profit developer, energy executive*
Nolan, John Edward *lawyer*
Nordhaus, Robert Riggs *lawyer*
Nordlinger, Gerson *investor*
Norland, Donald Richard *retired foreign service officer*
Norquist, David L. *federal agency administrator*
Norquist, Grover Glenn *economist*
Norton, Eleanor Holmes *congresswoman, lawyer, educator*
Norton, Floyd Ligon, IV, *lawyer*
Norwalk, Leslie V. *federal agency administrator*
Norwood, Deborah Anne *law librarian*
Novak, Robert David Sanders *columnist, commentator*
Novelli, William Dominic *retirement association executive*
Novick, Robert T. *lawyer*
Novitch, Mark *physician, retired pharmaceutical executive*
Nuland, Anthony C. J. *lawyer*
Nunes, Devin *congressman*
Nunn, Sam (Samuel Augustus Nunn) *former senator, lawyer*
Nwagbaracha, Joel Onukwugha *academic administrator, educator*
Oakley, Robert Louis *law librarian, educator*
Obama, Barack Hussein, Jr. *senator, former state legislator*
Oberdorfer, John L. *lawyer*
Obering, Trey (Henry A. Obering II) *federal agency administrator, career military officer*
Oberstar, James L. *congressman*
Obey, David Ross *congressman*
Obiozor, George Achulike *ambassador*
O'Brien, Greg *real estate company executive*
O'Brien, Patrick Michael *federal agency administrator*
O'Connell, David M. *academic administrator, priest*
O'Connor, Eileen J. *lawyer, former federal agency administrator*
O'Connor, Karen *political science professor, researcher, writer*
O'Connor, Tom *corporate executive, management consultant*
Odle, Robert Charles, Jr. *lawyer*
Odom, William Eldridge *retired military officer*
O'Donnell, Patrick Emmett *lawyer*
O'Donovan, Leo Jeremiah *former academic administrator, priest, theologian*
O'Dor, Ronald Keith *dean, biology professor, research scientist*
Oehme, Wolfgang Walter *landscape architect*
Oertel, Yolanda Castillo *pathologist, educator*
Ohanian, Bernard Jay *writer, editor*
Ohl, Joan Eschenbach *federal agency administrator*
Oka, Takashi *journalist, consultant, educator*
Okun, Deanna Tanner *federal official*
Olbeter, Erik R. *financial analyst, investment advisor*
Olchyk, Samuel *lawyer*
Oldham, Cheryl *federal agency administrator*
Olding, Michael *plastic and reconstructive surgeon*
Olender, Jack Harvey *lawyer*
Oliphant, Charles Frederick III *lawyer*
Oliphant, Martha Carmichael *civic worker*
Oliver, LeAnn Michelle *government official*
Olmstead, Cecil Jay *lawyer*
Olsen, Jody (Josephine K. Olsen) *federal agency administrator*
Olson, Mark Walter *non-profit corporation administrator, former federal official*
Olson, Pamela Faith *lawyer, former federal agency administrator*
Olson, Theodore Bevry *lawyer, former federal agency administrator*
Olver, John Walter *congressman*
Oman, Ralph *lawyer*
Omass, George A. *federal agency administrator*
O'Neil, Thomas Francis III *lawyer*
O'Neill, Brian Dennis *lawyer*
O'Neill, John H., Jr. *lawyer*
O'Neill, William Patrick *lawyer*
Onel, Suzan *lawyer*
Oosterhuis, Paul William *lawyer*
Opfer, George J. *federal agency administrator*
Oppenheimer, Franz Martin *lawyer*
Oran, Elaine Surick *physicist*
Orbach, Raymond Lee *federal agency administrator, physicist, researcher*
O'Reilly, Kenneth William *retired military officer*
Orr, Bobette Kay *diplomat*
Orszag, Jonathan Marc *economist, consultant*
Orszag, Peter Richard *economist*
Ortiz, Solomon Porfirio *congressman*
Ortner, Donald J. *biological anthropologist, educator*
Oshinsky, Jerold *lawyer*
Osicka, Teresa D. *health economist, consultant*
Osnos, David Marvin *lawyer, director*
Ostendorff, William Charles *federal agency administrator, career military officer*
O'Sullivan, Stephanie L. *federal agency administrator*
O'Sullivan, Terence M. *labor union administrator*
O'Toole, Francis J. *lawyer*
Otremba, Geraldine Marie *congressional and international relations executive*
Otto, Robert L. *information technology executive*
Outlaw, Wanda Cecelia *priest*
Outman, William Dell, II, *lawyer*
Ovechkin, Alexander *professional hockey player*
Overman, Dean Lee *lawyer, investor, writer*
Owen, Henry *former ambassador, consultant*
Owen, Roberts Bishop *lawyer, arbitrator*
Owen, Stephen Lee *lawyer*
Owsley, Douglas W. *forensic osteologist, researcher, anthropologist*
Oxford, Vayl *federal agency administrator*
Oxley, Michael Garver *lawyer, former congressman*
Oyler, Gregory Kenneth *lawyer*
Pace, Peter *Chairman of the Joint Chiefs of Staff*
Pachter, Marc *museum director*
Padden, Preston *broadcast executive*
Padilla, Christopher Alan *federal agency administrator*
Page, Tim *music critic, writer, producer*
Pagel, Scott B. *law librarian, educator, dean*
Paige, Kathleen K. *naval officer*
Paliwal, Dinesh C. *electronics executive*
Pallone, Frank, Jr. *congressman, lawyer*
Palmer, Christopher E. *lawyer*
Palmer, Stacy Ella *periodical editor*
Palumbo, Benjamin Lewis *public relations executive, consultant*
Panero, Hugh Edward *former broadcast executive*
Panetta, Michael *shadow representative*
Pantaleo, Peter S. *lawyer*
Panuthos, Peter J. *federal judge*
Paoletta, Mark R. A. *lawyer*
Pape, Stuart M. *lawyer*
Paper, Lewis J. *lawyer, educator*
Parish, Norman *artist, gallery director*
Parker, Rich *lawyer*
Parr, Carolyn Miller *federal judge*
Parris, Mark Robert *former ambassador, policy advisor*
Parsons, Donald Oscar *economics professor*
Parsons, Gary M. *broadcast executive*
Pascrell, William J., Jr. *congressman*
Pascual, Carlos E. *think-tank executive, former ambassador*
Pasi, Geeta *diplomat*
Passaic, Joseph G. *lawyer*
Pastor, Edward *congressman*
Pasurka, Carl A., Jr. *economist*
Pate, Michael Lynn *lawyer*
Pate, R(obert) Hewitt (III) *lawyer, former federal agency administrator*
Patenaude, Pamela Hughes *federal agency administrator*
Patrick, Richard M. *professional hockey team executive*
Patron, June Eileen *retired government agency administrator*
Patterson, Anne Woods *ambassador, former federal agency administrator*
Patterson, Donna E. *lawyer*
Patton, Sharon F. *museum director*
Patton, Thomas Earl *lawyer*
Paul, John Charles *lawyer*
Paul, William McCann *lawyer*
Paulison, R(obert) David *federal agency administrator*
Paulson, Hank (Henry Merritt Paulson Jr.) *secretary of the treasury, former diversified financial services company executive*
Paulson, Jerome Avrom *pediatrician*
Pavlick, John J., Jr. *lawyer*
Paxon, L. William *former congressman*
Payne, Donald Milford *congressman*
Payne, Fred J. *epidemiologist, educator*
Payton, Sue C. *civilian military employee*
Peacock, Marcus C. *federal agency administrator*
Pearce, Drue *federal official, former state legislator*
Pearce, Steve (Stevan E. Pearce) *congressman*
Pearlman, Ronald Alan *lawyer, educator*
Pearson, Daniel R. *federal official*
Pearson, Rebecca E. *lawyer*
Pearson, Roger *organization executive*
Peck, Louis Moses *editor*
Peck, Robert Stephen *lawyer, educator*
Peck, Suzanne J. *transit authority administrator*
Pedersen, William Francis *lawyer*
Peirce, Neal R. *journalist*
Pelavin, Sol Herbert *research company executive*
Pelham, Ann *publishing executive, department chairman*
Pellegrino, Edmund Daniel *internist, educator, retired academic administrator*
Pelosi, Nancy Patricia *congresswoman*
Pelton, Jeffrey J. *surgeon*
Pemberton, Alan A. *lawyer*
Pence, Michael Richard *congressman*
Pendleton, Miles Stevens, Jr. *diplomat*
Penn, Buddie J. (B.J. Penn) *civilian military employee*
Pensabene, Judith K. *lawyer*
Peretz, Martin *publishing executive, educator*
Perino, Dana Marie *White House press secretary*
Perkins, Nancy Leeds *lawyer*
Perkins, Samuel Thomas *lawyer*
Perl, Peter *editor*
Perle, Richard Norman *former federal agency administrator*
Perlman, Matthew Saul *lawyer*
Perlmutter, Ed (Edwin George Perlmutter) *congressman, former state legislator*
Perlstein, William James *lawyer*
Perry, George Lewis *research economist, consultant*
Perry, Philip J. *lawyer, former federal agency administrator*
Perry, Steven Wayne *statistician*
Persinger, Del Louis *pharmaceutical company executive*
Peters, Frederick Whitten *lawyer*
Peters, Mary Elizabeth *secretary of transportation*
Peters, Marybeth *copyrights register*
Peterson, Charles Hayes *lawyer*
Peterson, Collin C. *congressman*
Peterson, John E. *congressman*
Petito, Margaret L. *foundation president*
Petrash, Jeffrey Michael *lawyer*
Petri, Thomas Evert *congressman*
Petruzzelli, Julie A. *lawyer*
Pfeiffer, Leonard, IV, *executive recruiter, consultant*
Pfeiffer, Margaret Kolodny *lawyer*
Pfeiffer, Steven Bernard *lawyer*
Philbin, Patrick Francis *lawyer, former federal agency administrator*
Phillips, Carter Glasgow *lawyer*
Phillips, James D. *retired diplomat*
Phillips, John R. *lawyer*
Phillips, Karen Borlaug *economist, rail transportation executive*
Phillips, Stanley Davis *ambassador*
Phillips, Susan Meredith *academic administrator, economist*
Phommahaxay, Phanthong *ambassador*
Picarello, Anthony, Jr. *lawyer*
Pickenpaugh, Thomas Edward *archaeologist, anthropologist*
Pickens, Scott E. *lawyer*
Pickering, Chip (Charles Willis Pickering Jr.) *congressman*
Pickholtz, Raymond Lee *electrical engineering educator, consultant*
Pierce, John Randall *medical inspector, pediatrician*
Pierce, Rudolph F. *lawyer*
Pierson, Stuart F. *lawyer*
Pilcher, Carl B. *astrobiologist*
Pincus, Walter Haskell *news editor*
Pines, Wayne Lloyd *public relations executive*
Pionk, Jerome Lee *federal official*
Piorkowski, Joseph D., Jr. *lawyer, physician, educator, military officer*
Pistole, John S. *federal agency administrator*
Pitt, Harvey Lloyd *risk management consultant, former federal agency administrator*
Pittman, R. Allen *federal agency administrator*
Pitts, James T. *lawyer*
Placke, James Anthony *retired diplomat*
Plager, S. Jay *federal judge*
Plaine, Daniel J. *lawyer*
Plaine, Lloyd Leva *lawyer*
Platt, Leslie A. *lawyer*
Plattner, Marc Florea *foundation administrator, editor*
Platts, Howard Gregory *cultural organization administrator, not-for-profit fundraiser, director*
Platts, Todd Russell *congressman, state legislator*
Player, Thelma B. *librarian*
Podberesky, Samuel *lawyer*
Podesta, John David *law educator, former White House chief of staff*
Poe, David Russell *lawyer*
Poe, Ted *congressman, former judge*
Pojeta, John, Jr. *geologist, researcher*
Policy, Vincent Mark *lawyer*
Pollack, Ronald Frank *healthcare organization executive, lawyer*
Pollard, Daniel L. *financial analyst*
Pollock, Alexander John *banker*
Polt, Michael C. *ambassador*
Pomeroy, Earl Ralph *congressman, retired commissioner*
Poneman, Daniel Bruce *lawyer*
Poos, Lawrence Raymond *history educator*
Pope, Andrew *health science association administrator*
Popkin, Joel *economist, consultant*
Popofsky, Mark S. *lawyer*
Porges, Amelia *lawyer*
Porter, John Edward *former congressman*
Porter, John Weston *counselor, consultant, administrator*
Porter, Jon Christopher, Sr. *congressman*
Ports, James Franklin *federal agency administrator, former state legislator*
Posner, Ethan M. *lawyer*
Postol, Lawrence Philip *lawyer*
Potenza, Joseph Michael *lawyer*
Potter, Caryl A. III *lawyer*
Potter, Jack (John E. Potter) *federal agency administrator*
Potter, John Francis *oncologist, surgeon*
Potts, Stephen Deaderick *lawyer*
Povich, David *lawyer*
Powell, Benjamin Albond *federal agency administrator, lawyer*
Powell, Dina Habib *federal agency administrator*
Powell, Donald E. *federal agency administrator*
Powell, Michael Kevin *investment company executive, former federal official*
Powell, Nancy Jo *federal official, former ambassador*
Powers, Mary Ellen *lawyer*
Powers, Richard Edward, Jr. *lawyer*
Pozen, Sharis Arnold *lawyer*
Prater, Mark A. *lawyer, accountant*
Pratt, Dana Joseph *publishing consultant*
Press, Frank *geophysicist*
Preston, Richard McKim *lawyer*
Preston, Stephen W. *lawyer*
Preston, Steven C. *federal agency administrator, former service company executive*
Prestowitz, Clyde Vincent, Jr. *economist, researcher*
Prettyman, Elijah Barrett, Jr. *lawyer*
Prezioso, Giovanni P. *lawyer*
Price, Daniel Martin *lawyer*
Price, David Eugene *congressman, education educator*
Price, Deborah A. *federal agency administrator*
Price, Griffith Baley, Jr. *lawyer*
Price, Joseph Hubbard *lawyer*
Price, Thomas E. *congressman*
Priest, Dana *journalist*
Prina, L(ouis) Edgar *journalist*
Principi, Anthony Joseph *pharmaceutical company executive, former secretary of veterans affairs*
Pritchard, Therese D. *lawyer*
Proger, Phillip A. *lawyer*
Prost, Sharon *federal judge*
Pryor, Mark Lunsford *senator*
Pryor, William C. *judge*
Przypyszny, John R. *lawyer*
Puchalski, Christina M. *physician, medical educator*
Pulley, Lewis C. *lawyer*
Pupkin, Barry A. *lawyer*
Purohit, Rajeev *advocate, writer*
Pusey, William Anderson *lawyer*
Putnam, Adam Hughes *congressman, farmer, rancher*
Putzel, Michael *journalist, editor*
Pyke, Thomas Nicholas, Jr. *science administrator*
Pyle, Robert Noble *public relations executive*
Quainton, Anthony Cecil Eden *diplomat*
Quale, John Carter *lawyer*
Quarles, Steven Princeton *lawyer*
Quello, James Henry *government official*
Quigley, Michael *lawyer*
Quinn, Jack (John Francis Quinn) *former congressman, English language educator*
Quinn, Thomas H. *lawyer*
Quint, Arnold Harris *lawyer*
Rabecs, Robert Nicholas *lawyer*
Rabekoff, Elise Jane *lawyer*
Rabinovitz, Bruce H. *lawyer*
Raby, Julian *art gallery director*
Racine, Karl A. *lawyer*
Racine, Richard B. *lawyer*
Radanovich, George P. *congressman*
Raddatz, Martha *news correspondent*
Rademaker, Stephen Geoffrey *legislative staff member, former federal agency administrator*

Rader, Randall Ray *federal judge*
Radice, Anne-Imelda Marino *museum director, former federal agency administrator*
Radin, Alex *former association executive, consultant*
Radner, Roy *economist, educator, researcher*
Radzely, Howard M. *federal agency administrator, lawyer*
Rahaim, Stephen *lawyer*
Rahall, Nick Joe, II, (Nick Rahall) *congressman*
Raher, Patrick Michael *lawyer*
Railton, W(illiam) Scott *retired commissioner*
Raim, David Matthew *lawyer*
Raimo, Bernard (Bernie) *lawyer*
Rainey, Jean Osgood *public relations executive*
Rales, Mitchell P. *automotive parts company executive*
Rales, Steven M. *automotive parts company executive*
Ralston, Joseph W. *retired military officer*
Ramberg, Walter Dodd *architect*
Ramey, Carl Robert *lawyer*
Ramirez, Ted L. *lawyer*
Ramstad, James *congressman, lawyer*
Ranck, Edna Runnels *academic administrator, researcher*
Randall, Robert L(ee) *ecological economist*
Randolph, A(rthur) Raymond *federal judge*
Randt, Clark Thorp, Jr. *ambassador, lawyer*
Rangel, Charlie (Charles Bernard Rangel) *congressman*
Rankin, Edward Anthony *orthopedist, surgeon*
Rankin, Robert Arthur *journalist*
Ranneberger, Michael E. *ambassador*
Raphael, Louise Arakelian *mathematician, educator*
Rasmus, John Charles *trade association administrator, lawyer*
Raspberry, William James *journalist*
Ratner, Ellen Faith *news analyst and correspondent, writer*
Rauh, Carl Stephen *lawyer*
Raul, Alan Charles *lawyer*
Ravenal, Earl Cedric *international relations educator, writer*
Ray, Charles Aaron *ambassador*
Ray, Joyce Marie *archivist, historian*
Raymond, Lee R. *retired oil company executive*
Rayner, Victoria Leigh *medical educator, consultant*
Razzano, Frank Charles *lawyer*
Reade, Claire Elizabeth *lawyer*
Reaman, Gregory Harold *pediatric hematologist, oncologist*
Reback, Joyce Ellen *lawyer*
Redd, Kenneth Eric *statistician, researcher*
Reddel, Carl Walter *academic administrator*
Redman, Robert Shelton *pathologist, dentist*
Reed, John Francis (Jack) *senator*
Reed, John Hathaway *former ambassador*
Reed, Travis Dean *public relations executive*
Reeder, Joe Robert *lawyer, former federal official*
Rees, Grover Joseph III *lawyer, government official, diplomat*
Reger, Lawrence Lee *trade association administrator*
Regula, Ralph Straus *congressman, lawyer*
Rehberg, Dennis R. *congressman*
Rehnquist, Janet *lawyer, former federal agency administrator*
Rehr, David K. *broadcast association executive*
Reich, Bernard *political science professor*
Reich, John M. *federal agency administrator*
Reich, Walter *psychiatrist, medical educator, political science professor, writer, museum director*
Reichert, David G. (Dave Reichert) *congressman*
Reichertz, Peter Stuart *lawyer*
Reid, Harry Mason *senator*
Reid, Inez Smith *lawyer, educator, judge*
Rein, Bert Walter *lawyer*
Reinsch, William Alan *association executive, educator*
Reischauer, Robert D. *research organization executive*
Relyea, Harold Clarence *political scientist, writer*
Renick, James Carmichael *educational association administrator, former academic administrator*
Renkiewicz, Martin *federal agency administrator*
Renzi, Rick (Richard George Renzi) *congressman*
Repper, George Robert *lawyer*
Retz, William Andrew *naval consultant, retired naval officer*
Retzer, Michael L. *political association executive*
Reyes, Silvestre *congressman*
Reynolds, Jerry (Gerald A.) *federal agency administrator*
Reynolds, Robert Joel *economist, consultant*
Reynolds, Thomas M. *congressman*
Ricciardone, Francis Joseph, Jr. *ambassador*
Rice, Condoleezza *secretary of state, former national security advisor*
Rice, Lois Dickson *retired computer company executive*
Rice, Paul Jackson *lawyer, educator*
Rice, Susan Elizabeth *foreign policy analyst, former federal agency administrator*
Rich, Dorothy Kovitz *educational association administrator, writer*
Rich, John Townsend *lawyer*
Richards, Femi Soyinka *lawyer*
Richards, Suzanne V. *lawyer*
Richardson, Ann Bishop *foundation executive, lawyer*
Richardson, Laura A. *congresswoman*
Richardson, Paul Joseph *economist*
Richardson, Scott *federal official, researcher, writer*
Riche, Robert S. *research and development company executive*
Richeson, James Grady, Jr. *dentist*
Richlen, Scott Lane *federal government program administrator*
Richmond, Marilyn Susan *lawyer*
Rickard, Lisa Ann *lawyer*
Rickert, Anthony H. *lawyer*
Ricks, Thomas Edwin *journalist, writer*
Ridenour, Amy Moritz *research center administrator*
Ridgeway, James Fowler *journalist*
Riehle, B. Hudson *trade association executive*
Rieser, Joseph A., Jr. *tax specialist*
Rifkin, Ned *museum director*
Rigby, Joseph M. *utilities executive*
Riggs, Barbara *federal agency administrator*
Rios, Elena *health association administrator*
Risen, James E. *journalist*
Rissetto, Harry A. *lawyer*
Rives, Jack L. *judge, career military officer*
Rivlin, Alice Mitchell *economics professor, former federal official*
Rizzo, John Anthony *lawyer*
Robb, James Willis *romance languages educator*
Robb, Lynda Johnson *writer*
Robert, Davila R. *academic administrator*
Roberts, Charles Patrick (Pat Roberts) *senator*
Roberts, Cokie (Corinne Boggs Roberts) *newscaster*
Roberts, Gregory *educational association administrator*
Roberts, James Harold III *lawyer*
Roberts, Jeanne Addison *retired literature educator*
Roberts, John *news anchor*
Roberts, John Glover, Jr. *United States Supreme Court Chief Justice*
Roberts, Markley *economist, educator*
Roberts, Michael G. *lawyer*
Roberts, Michael T. *lawyer, educator*
Roberts, Michele A. *lawyer*
Roberts, Walter Ronald *retired diplomat*
Robertson, James *federal judge*
Robinowitz, Carolyn Bauer *psychiatrist, educator, director*
Robinson, Crystal LaTresa *professional basketball coach, retired professional basketball player*
Robinson, Sharon Porter *educational association administrator*
Robison, Victor James, Jr. *retired military officer*
Rochon, Mark *lawyer*
Rockefeller, Edwin Shaffer *lawyer*
Rockefeller, John Davison, IV, (Jay Rockefeller) *senator, retired governor*
Rocque, Vincent Joseph *lawyer*
Rodemeyer, Michael Leonard, Jr. *lawyer*
Rodgers, Clifton Eugene, Jr. *trade association administrator, lobbyist*
Rodley, Carol A. *federal agency administrator*
Rodman, Peter Warren *foreign policy specialist*
Rodriguez, Ciro Davis *congressman*
Roemer, Timothy John *think-tank executive, former congressman*
Rogan, Michael P. *lawyer*
Rogers, Harold Dallas (Hal) *congressman*
Rogers, Judith Ann Wilson *federal judge*
Rogers, Mike (Michael J. Rogers) *congressman*
Rogers, Mike *congressman*
Rogers, Thomasina Venese *commissioner*
Rogers, William Dill *lawyer*
Rogovin, John A. *lawyer*
Rogowsky, Robert Arthur *federal official, educator*
Rohner, Ralph John *lawyer, educator, dean*
Rohrabacher, Dana *congressman*
Rollins, Tree (Wayne Monte Rollins) *professional basketball coach, former professional basketball player*
Romeo, Peter John *lawyer*
Rood, John C. *federal agency administrator*
Rooney, Francis *ambassador*
Rosch, John Thomas (Tom) *commissioner, lawyer*
Rose, George Andrew *application developer, information systems specialist*
Rose, Jonathan Chapman *lawyer*
Rose, Mary McNally *federal official*
Rosebush, James Scott *growth strategy executive, former government official*
Rosen, Gerald Robert *editor*
Rosen, Jeffrey Adam *lawyer*
Rosen, Jeffrey Matthew *law educator, journalist*
Rosenau, James Nathan *political scientist, educator, writer*
Rosenberg, Jerome David *physicist*
Rosenberg, Joel Barry *economist*
Rosenblatt, Jason Philip *literature and language professor*
Rosenblatt, Peter Ronald *lawyer, former ambassador*
Rosenbloom, David Harry *political science and law educator*
Rosenbloom, H(arry) David *lawyer*
Rosenfeld, Arthur F. *federal official, lawyer*
Rosenfeld, Ronald Allen *federal agency administrator*
Rosenhauer, James Joseph (Jim Rosenhauer) *lawyer*
Rosenker, Mark Victor *federal agency administrator*
Rosenkrantz, Steven Jay *lawyer*
Rosenthal, Douglas Eurico *lawyer*
Rosenthal, Seth A. *lawyer*
Rosenthal, Steven Siegmund *lawyer*
Roshwald, Aviel Isaiah *history professor*
Ros-Lehtinen, Ileana Carmen *congresswoman*
Rosman, Michael E. *lawyer*
Ross, Dennis B. *former diplomat*
Ross, Donald K. *lobbyist, environmental organization administrator, lawyer*
Ross, Douglas *lawyer*
Ross, Malcolm *minerals consultant*
Ross, Mike *congressman*
Ross, Robinette Davis *publisher*
Ross, Stanford G. *lawyer, government official*
Ross, Terence P. *lawyer*
Rossides, Eugene Telemachus *lawyer, writer*
Rotberg, Eugene Harvey *investment banker, lawyer*
Rothenberg, Pamela V. *lawyer*
Rother, John *association executive, lawyer*
Rothkopf, Arthur J. *association executive*
Rothman, Steven R. *congressman*
Rothstein, Barbara Jacobs *federal judge*
Rothstein, Paul Frederick *lawyer, educator*
Rotunda, Donald Theodore *public relations consultant*
Rouse, Leo E. *dean, dental educator*
Rouvelas, Emanuel Larry *lawyer*
Rovelstad, Mathilde V(erner) *retired library and information scientist, educator*
Rowden, Marcus Aubrey *lawyer, retired government agency administrator*
Rowe, Richard Holmes *lawyer*
Rowland, Diane *health facility administrator, researcher*
Roybal-Allard, Lucille *congresswoman*
Royce, Ed (Edward Randall Royce) *congressman*
Roycroft, Howard Francis *lawyer*
Royle, David Brian Layton *television producer, journalist*
Rubel, Eric A. *lawyer*
Rubenstein, David M. *investment company executive*
Rubenstein, Laurie R. *lawyer*
Rubin, Kenneth Allen *lawyer*
Ruckman, Roger Norris *pediatric cardiologist*
Ruddy, Frank *lawyer, retired ambassador*
Rudman, Mara E. *government official*
Ruehle, Charles Joseph *pathologist, military officer*
Ruemmler, Kathryn H. *lawyer, former prosecutor*
Ruetter, Gunter H. *surgeon*
Ruiz, Vanessa *judge*
Rule, Charles Frederick (Rick) *lawyer*
Rupp, Kalman *economist*
Ruppersberger, Charles Albert, III, (Dutch) *congressman*
Rusch, Jonathan Jay *lawyer*
Rush, Bobby L. *congressman*
Ruskin, Robert Sterling *educational association administrator*
Russell, Mark *comedian*
Russell, Richard Leavitt *political science professor*
Russell, Richard Mather *federal official*
Russell, William Joseph *educational association administrator*
Russert, Timothy John *broadcast journalist and executive*
Russin, Jonathan *lawyer, consultant*
Russo, Roy R. *lawyer*
Rust, William David, Jr. *retired structural engineer*
Ruta, Frank A. *chef*
Ruthenberg, Kirk R. *lawyer*
Rutherford, Boyd Kevin *federal agency administrator*
Rutstein, David W. *lawyer, food products executive*
Ruttenberg, Charles Byron *lawyer*
Ruttinger, George David *lawyer*
Rutzen, Douglas *lawyer, educator*
Rutzick, Mark Charles *lawyer*
Ruwe, Robert Paul *federal judge*
Ryan, Anthony William *federal agency administrator*
Ryan, David Alan *systems analyst*
Ryan, Edward A. *lawyer, hotel executive*
Ryan, Margaret A. *federal judge*
Ryan, Paul *congressman*
Ryerson, Paul Sommer *lawyer*
Ryn, Claes Gösta *political science professor*
Sachar, Howard Morley *history educator*
Sacher, Steven Jay *lawyer*
Safir, Peter Oliver *lawyer*
Safire, William *journalist, foundation administrator*
St. John, Julie *mortgage company executive*
St. Martin, Jo-Marie *lawyer*
Saladini, Robert *educational association administrator*
Salaman, Alban *lawyer*
Salamon, Linda Bradley *English literature educator*
Salant, Jonathan D. *reporter*
Salazar, John T. *congressman*
Salazar, Ken(neth) Lee *senator, former state attorney general*
Salem, George Richard *lawyer*
Sali, Bill (William Thomas Sali) *congressman, former state legislator*
Salisbury, Dallas L. *researcher, director*
Salsbury, Michael H. *lawyer*
Saltzburg, Stephen Allan *law educator, consultant*
Salyer, Stephen Lee *educational program administrator*
Sams, Ronald F. *career military officer*
Samsot, Robert Louis *editor, consultant*
Samuelson, Kenneth Lee *lawyer*
Sanchez, Linda T. *congresswoman*
Sanchez, Loretta *congresswoman*
Sanchez-Way, Ruth Dolores *public health administrator*
Sanders, Bernard (Bernie Sanders) *senator, former congressman*
Sanders, Robin Renee *former ambassador*
Sanderson, Janet A. *former ambassador*
Sandler, Bernice Resnick *women's rights specialist*
Sandlin, Max Allen, Jr. *former congressman*
Sandlin, Stephanie Herseth *congresswoman, lawyer*
Sandman, James Joseph *lawyer*
Sanger, David E. *news correspondent*
Sant, Roger W. *retired energy executive*
Sant, Victoria P. *museum administrator*
Santora, Kathleen Curry *lobbyist, lawyer*
Santorum, Rick (Richard John) *lawyer, former senator*
Santos, Leonard Ernest *lawyer*
Sarbanes, John Peter Spyros *congressman, lawyer*
Sartori, Michael A. *lawyer*
Sarukhan, Arturo *ambassador*
Satcher, David *public health service officer, former Surgeon General of the United States*
Satloff, Robert B. *think-tank executive*
Satterthwaite, Janet F. *lawyer*
Sauerbrey, Ellen Elaine Richmond *federal agency administrator, former ambassador*
Saunders, Harold Henry *foundation administrator*
Saunders, Mary Jane *lawyer*
Savage, Charles *news correspondent*
Sawhill, Isabel Van Devanter *economist*
Saworotnow, Parfeny Pavlovich *mathematician, educator*
Saxton, Jim (Hugh James Saxton) *congressman*
Sayler, Robert Nelson *lawyer, educator*
Saylor, David J. *lawyer*
Saylor, Maurice Michael *composer, director, music librarian*
Sayre, Edward Vale *chemist*
Sayre, Robert Marion *ambassador*
Scalia, Antonin Gregory *United States supreme court justice*
Scalia, Eugene *lawyer*
Scanlon, Kerry Alan *lawyer*
Scanlon, Terrence Maurice *foundation administrator*
Scarlett, (Patricia) Lynn *federal agency administrator*
Schafer, Jacqueline Ellen *federal agency administrator*
Schafrick, Frederick Craig *lawyer*
Schaitberger, Harold *protective services official, labor union administrator*
Schakowsky, Janice *congresswoman*
Schall, Alvin Anthony *federal judge*
Schapiro, Mary L. *financial regulatory service executive*
Schaumber, Peter Carey *federal agency administrator*
Scheffman, David Theodore *economist, management educator, consultant*
Scheibel, Kenneth Maynard *journalist*
Schellie, Peter D. *lawyer*
Schieffer, Bob *newscaster*
Schieffer, J. Thomas (John Thomas Schieffer, Tom Schieffer) *ambassador, former professional baseball team executive*
Schiff, Adam Bennett *congressman, lawyer*
Schiffer, Lois Jane *lawyer*
Schill, Charles F. *lawyer*
Schiller, Jonathan David *lawyer*
Schimel, David S. *ecologist, science administrator*
Schlesinger, B. Frank *architect, educator*
Schley, Wayne Arthur *political scientist, consultant*
Schlicher, Ronald Lewis *ambassador*
Schlick, Austin C. *lawyer*
Schlickeisen, Rodger Oscar *non-profit environmental organization executive*
Schloss, Howard Monroe *financial regulatory service executive*
Schmidt, Jean *congresswoman*
Schmidt, Susan *journalist*
Schmidt, William Arthur, Jr. *lawyer*
Schmitt, Glenn Ralph *federal agency administrator*
Schmitt, John K. *army officer*
Schmoke, Kurt Lidell *dean, former mayor*
Schneider, Ann Imlah *federal agency administrator, education consultant*
Schneider, Carol Geary *educational association administrator*
Schneider, Cynthia Perrin *former ambassador, political science professor*
Schneider, Lawrence Alan *lawyer*
Schneider, Mark *political science professor*
Schneider, Mark Lewis *foreign policy executive, retired government agency administrator*
Schneider, Matthew Roger *lawyer*
Schneider, Paul Allan *federal agency administrator*
Schneider, Pauline A. *lawyer*
Schneller, Marina Velentgas *lawyer*
Schnitzer, Steven C. *lawyer*
Schoelen, Mary Jeanette *federal judge*
Schoettle, Enid C.B. *federal agency administrator*
Schofield, Regina Brown *federal agency administrator*
Schoomaker, Eric B. *career military officer*
Schor, Laurence *lawyer*
Schornagel, Karl William *government agency administrator*
Schorr, Lisbeth Bamberger *sociologist, researcher*
Schorsch, Louis L. *metal products executive*
Schram, Martin Jay *journalist*
Schroeder, Patricia Scott *trade association administrator, former congresswoman*
Schropp, James Howard *lawyer*
Schulte, Gregory L. *ambassador*
Schultz, William B. *lawyer*
Schumer, Chuck (Charles Ellis) *senator*
Schwaab, Richard Lewis *lawyer*
Schwab, Susan Carroll *ambassador, former academic administrator*
Schwalb, Brian L. *lawyer*
Schwartz, Allyson Y. *congresswoman*
Schwartz, Daniel C. *lawyer*
Schwartz, Norton A. *career military officer*
Schwartz, Victor Elliot *lawyer, educator*
Schwartzman, Andrew Jay *lawyer*
Schwarz, Gerard *conductor, musician, music director*
Schwebel, Stephen Myron *arbitrator, mediator, legal advisor*
Schwelb, Frank Ernest *judge*
Schwinger, David *lawyer*
Scoblic, J. Peter *magazine editor*
Scolese, Christopher *federal agency administrator*
Scott, Charneta Claudetta *psychologist, educator*
Scott, David Albert *congressman*
Scott, Gary Thomas *historian*
Scott, Robert Cortez *congressman, lawyer*
Scott, Stephanie D. *city official*

Scott, Thomas Jefferson, Jr. *lawyer, electrical engineer*
Scovel, Calvin L. III *federal agency administrator*
Scowcroft, Brent *former national security advisor, retired military officer*
Scriven, Wayne Marcus *lawyer*
Scrivner, Ellen M. *psychologist*
Scully, Thomas A. *lawyer, former federal agency administrator*
Seats, Peggy Chisolm *public affairs executive*
Seaver, Barton *chef*
Seck, Mamadou Mansour *ambassador, military officer*
Sedgwick, Jeffrey Leigh *federal agency administrator, political science professor*
Sega, A. Christopher *lawyer*
Sega, Ronald Michael *civilian military employee, former dean*
Segal, Theodore D. *lawyer*
Segall, Wynn H. *lawyer*
Seidman, L(ewis) William *television commentator, publisher*
Seifert, Jeffrey W. *political scientist, researcher*
Selig, William Paul *advocate, cultural organization administrator*
Selin, Ivan *entrepreneur*
Sell, Clay (Jeffrey Clay Sell) *federal agency administrator*
Sellin, Theodore *diplomat, consultant*
Semas, Philip Wayne *editor*
Sensenbrenner, F(rank) James, Jr. *congressman*
Sentelle, David Bryan *federal judge*
Sequeira, Leon R. *federal agency administrator*
Serrano, José Enrique *congressman*
Sessions, Jeff (Jefferson Beauregard Sessions III) *senator, former state attorney general*
Sessions, Pete *congressman*
Sessions, William Steele *lawyer, former FBI director*
Severino, Roberto *language educator, academic administration executive*
Shadegg, John Barden *congressman*
Shaffer, David James *lawyer*
Shah, Rahul K. *surgeon, researcher*
Shakir, Faiz *writer, political blogger*
Shambaugh, David Leigh *political scientist, educator, writer*
Shamim, Mah Talat *chemist*
Shanahan, Sheila Ann *pediatrician, educator*
Shane, Jeffrey Neil *federal agency administrator, lawyer*
Shanks, Hershel *editor, writer*
Shannon, Donald Hawkins *retired editor*
Shannon, Thomas A., Jr. *federal agency administrator*
Shapero, Donald Campbell *physicist, government official*
Shapiro, Howard M. *lawyer, former prosecutor*
Shapiro, Walter Elliot *columnist*
Sharma, Tina *lawyer*
Sharp, Walter L. (Gary Sharp) *career military officer*
Shaw, Russell Burnham *writer, journalist*
Shaw, William Frederick *statistician*
Shaw, William J. *hotel facility executive*
Shay, Albert W. *lawyer*
Shays, Christopher *congressman*
Shea-Porter, Carol *congresswoman, social worker*
Shear, Natalie Pickus *conference and event management executive*
Shearer, Paul Scott *federal agency and trade association administrator*
Sheehan, Neil *reporter, writer*
Shelby, Richard Craig *senator, former congressman*
Shelley, Herbert Carl *lawyer*
Shelton, Hilary O. *civil rights organization administration*
Shenon, Philip *journalist*
Shepard, Julian Leigh *lawyer, humanitarian*
Shepherd, Alan J. *construction executive, management consultant*
Shepherd, Leslie L. *architect*
Sheppard, Scott S. *astronomer*
Sherer, Samuel Ayers *lawyer, urban planner, consultant*
Sherman, Bradley James *congressman*
Sherman, Cary Howard *lawyer*
Sherman, Gerald Howard *lawyer, educator*
Sherman, Jonathan Henry *lawyer*
Sherman, Lawrence Jay *lawyer*
Sherzer, Harvey Gerald *lawyer*
Shields, Christopher Andrew *website director*
Shimkus, John Mondy *congressman*
Shinn, David Hamilton *former diplomat, educator, writer*
Shirzad, Faryar *federal official*
Shore, Bill *nonprofit organization executive*
Shrier, Adam Louis *investment company executive, consultant*
Shrinsky, Jason Lee *lawyer*
Shriver, Timothy Perry *sports association executive*
Shulenburger, David Edwin *educational association administrator, economics educator, former academic administrator*
Shuler, James Mannie *health physicist*
Shull, Joe A. *lawyer*
Shulman, Stephen Neal *lawyer*
Sibolski, John Alfred, Jr. *educational association executive*
Siegel, David B. *lawyer*
Siegel, Frederic Richard *geology educator*
Siegel, Lloyd Harvey *architect, real estate developer, consultant*
Siegel, Ned Lawrence *real estate developer*
Siegel, Robert Charles *broadcast journalist*
Siegel, Robert Steven *internist, oncologist, educator*
Siggins, Jack Arthur *university librarian*
Sikora, Clifford S. *lawyer*
Sikorski, Gerry *congressman*
Silberg, Jay Eliot *lawyer*
Silbert, Earl J. *lawyer*
Silver, Harry R. *lawyer*
Silver, Paul G. *geophysicist*
Silverman, Leslie E. *commissioner*
Silverman, William A. *lawyer*
Silverstein, Martin J. *lawyer, former ambassador*
Simko, Jan *English, foreign language and literature educator*
Simmons, Anne L. *federal official*
Simon, Barry S. *lawyer*
Simon, Gary Leonard *internist, educator*
Simon, Gregory *lawyer*
Simon, John A. *investment company executive*
Simon, Kenneth Mark *lawyer*
Simon, Raymond Joseph *federal agency and former school system administrator*
Simons, Barbara M. *lawyer*
Simons, Lawrence Brook *lawyer*
Simonson, Stewart Gerard *retired federal agency administrator*
Simowitz, Lee H. *lawyer*
Simpson, Cam *reporter*
Simpson, James S. *federal agency administrator*
Simpson, John M. *lawyer*
Simpson, Louis A. *insurance company executive*
Simpson, Michael K. *congressman*
Sims, Joe *lawyer*
Sinel, Norman Mark *lawyer*
Singer, Daniel Morris *lawyer*
Singer, Linda J. *attorney general*
Singer, Maxine Frank *retired biochemist, science association director*
Singer, Richard M. *lawyer*
Singleton, Harry Michael *lawyer*
Sinick, Marshall S. *lawyer*
Sinn, Jerry L. *army officer*
Sires, Albio *congressman, former state legislator*
Sirri, Erik R. *federal agency administrator, economist*
Skall, Gregg P. *lawyer*
Skancke, Nancy J. *lawyer*
Skelton, Ike (Isaac Newton Skelton IV) *congressman*
Skinner, Richard L. *federal agency administrator*
Skinner, Robert Earle, Jr. *civil engineer, engineering executive*
Skinner, Thomas V. *federal agency administrator*
Skol, Michael *counter-money laundering consultant*
Skolnik, Merrill I. *electrical engineer*
Slafka, Kristi Lynne *journalist*
Slater, Jim *sportswriter, journalist*
Slater, Rodney E. *lawyer, emergency management executive, former secretary of transportation*
Slater, Valerie A. *lawyer*
Slatkin, Leonard Edward *musician, conductor, director*
Slaughter, Kenneth S. *lawyer*
Slaughter, Louise McIntosh *congresswoman*
Sloan, Melanie Togman *lawyer, former prosecutor*
Slocombe, Walter Becker *lawyer, former federal official*
Sly, Ridge Michael *pediatrician, allergist, immunologist, educator*
Smalley, Robert Manning *diplomat*
Smith, Adam *congressman*
Smith, Adrian M. *congressman, real estate agent*
Smith, Brian William *lawyer, former government official*
Smith, Christopher (Kit Smith) *lawyer*
Smith, Christopher Henry *congressman*
Smith, Daniel Clifford *lawyer*
Smith, Dean *communications advisor, arbitrator*
Smith, Demaurice F. *lawyer*
Smith, (J.) Dorrance *federal agency administrator*
Smith, Dwight Chichester III *lawyer*
Smith, Elaine Diana *foreign service officer*
Smith, George Vinal *librarian*
Smith, Gordon Harold *senator*
Smith, Herbert G., II, *lawyer*
Smith, Jack Carl *import/export company executive*
Smith, Jeffrey Hartman *lawyer*
Smith, Jessie P. Dowling *retired social services administrator*
Smith, John B. *publishing executive*
Smith, Kingston Earl *lawyer*
Smith, Lamar Seeligson *congressman*
Smith, Lee Elton *surgery educator, retired military officer*
Smith, Loren Allan *federal judge*
Smith, Molly D. *theater director*
Smith, Patricia Grace *federal official*
Smith, R. Jeffrey *reporter*
Smith, Roy Philip *judge*
Smith, Russell Louis *lawyer*
Smith, Stephen Grant *journalist*
Smith, Stuart Seaborne *writer, government and union official*
Smith, Susan A. *photojournalist*
Smith, Tefft Weldon *lawyer*
Smith, Turner Taliaferro, Jr. *lawyer*
Smith, William S., Jr. *education association administrator*
Smutny, Abby Cohen *lawyer*
Smyth, Paul Burton *lawyer*
Snowbarger, Vince *former congressman*
Snowe, Olympia J. *senator*
Snyder, Allen Roger *lawyer*
Snyder, Jed C. *foreign affairs specialist*
Snyder, John Michael *lobbyist, public relations executive*
Snyder, Vic *congressman, physician*
Sobel, Clifford M. *ambassador*
Sohn, Michael N *lawyer*
Sokal, Allen Marcel *lawyer*
Sokler, Bruce Douglas *lawyer*
Solberg, Mary Ann *federal official*
Solinger, Janet W. *museum executive*
Solis, Hilda Lucia *congresswoman, educational administrator*
Sollers, Joseph Sedwick III *lawyer*
Solodky, Howard N. *lawyer*
Solomon, Elinor Harris *economics professor*
Solomon, Eric *federal agency administrator*
Solomon, Richard Harvey *think-tank executive*
Solomon, Sean Carl *geophysicist, lab administrator*
Solomons, Mark Elliott *lawyer, art dealer, entrepreneur*
Sommers, Jill E. *commissioner*
Sommers, Mark *lawyer*
Sonde, Theodore Irwin *lawyer*
Sonnenfeldt, Helmut *former government official, educator, consultant, writer*
Sontag, Ed *former federal agency administrator*
Sorenson, Arne M. *hotel executive*
Sorokowski, Andrew Dennis *lawyer, historian*
Sottile, James *lawyer*
Souder, Mark Edward *congressman*
Souter, David Hackett *United States supreme court justice*
Space, Zack (Zachary T. Space) *congressman*
Spaeder, Roger Campbell *lawyer*
Spagnoletti, Robert James *lawyer, former attorney general*
Spagnolo, Samuel Vincent *internist, pulmonary specialist, educator*
Spear, Scott Lawrence *plastic surgeon*
Spears, James M(it) *lawyer*
Specter, Arlen *senator*
Spector, Melbourne Louis *retired foreign service officer*
Spellings, Margaret LaMontagne *secretary of education*
Spencer, Harrison Clark, Jr. *public health administrator, educator*
Spiegel, Daniel Leonard *lawyer*
Spies, James B. *radiologist, educator*
Spiliotes, Nicholas James *lawyer*
Spitzer, Marc Lee *commissioner, former state legislator*
Spivak, Mark R. *lawyer*
Splete, Allen Peterjohn *educational association administrator, educator*
Splitt, David Alan *lawyer, writer*
Sprague, Mary Gabrielle *lawyer*
Spratt, John McKee, Jr. *congressman, lawyer*
Springer, Linda M. *federal official*
Sproat, Edward F., III, (Ward Sproat) *federal agency administrator*
Spurgeon, Dennis Ray *federal agency administrator, former manufacturing executive*
Squire, Daniel Harris *lawyer*
Stabenow, Deborah Ann *senator, former congresswoman*
Stack, Robert B. *lawyer*
Stadtler, Walter Edward *diplomat*
Stamberg, Susan Levitt *radio personality*
Stanley, Daniel Raymond, Sr. *federal agency administrator*
Stanley, Jean-Daniel *geological oceanographer*
Staples, George McDade *federal agency administrator, former ambassador*
Stapleton, Craig Roberts *ambassador*
Stark, Fortney Hillman (Pete Stark) *congressman*
Starr, Judson Wilmarth *lawyer*
Stayin, Randolph John *lawyer*
Steadman, John Montague *judge*
Stearns, Clifford Bundy *congressman, diversified financial services company executive*
Steel, Robert K. *federal agency administrator, former diversified financial services company executive*
Steele, Ana Mercedes *retired federal agency administrator*
Steer, John Richard *lawyer*
Stein, Daniel Alan *lawyer*
Steinberg, Andrew B. *federal agency administrator, lawyer*
Steinberg, David Isaac *social sciences educator, consultant*
Steiner, David Miller *lawyer*
Steiner, Ruth *musicologist, educator*
Steinhardt, Ralph Gustav III *law educator*
Steinwurtzel, Richard A. *lawyer*
Stelzer, Irwin Mark *economist*
Stent, Angela E. *political scientist, educator, director*
Stephanopoulos, George Robert *political reporter, former federal official*
Stephens, Joe Alan *investigative reporter*
Stephenson, Sherry Madeline *trade economist*
Stern, (Sol) Alan *science administrator, astrophysicist, researcher*
Stern, Andrew L. (Andy Stern) *labor union administrator*
Stern, Carl Leonard *retired news correspondent, federal official, educator*
Stern, Elizabeth Espin *lawyer*
Stern, Gerald Mann *lawyer*
Stern, Kenneth P. *broadcast executive*
Stern, Marcus A. *journalist*
Stern, Paula *international trade consultant*
Stern, Samuel Alan *lawyer*
Stern, Todd D. *government official, lawyer*
Stetson, Catherine E. *lawyer*
Stevens, Herbert Francis *lawyer, educator*
Stevens, John Paul *United States supreme court justice*
Stevens, Paul Schott *lawyer*
Stevens, Roberta A. *librarian*
Stevens, Ted (Theodore Fulton) *senator*
Stevenson, Frances Kellogg *retired museum program director*
Stevenson, Nancy Nelson *museum director*
Stewart, David Pentland *lawyer, educator*
Stewart, Debra Wehrle *educational association administrator, political science professor*
Stich, Roberta Lynn *not-for-profit fundraiser, social worker*
Stine, Jeffrey Kim *environmental historian, curator*
Stock, Ann *federal official*
Stock, Stuart Chase *lawyer*
Stockman, Jennifer Blei *political organization administrator*
Stoiber, Susanne A. *health science organization administrator*
Stolberg, Sheryl Gay *journalist*
Stoll, Richard Giles *lawyer*
Stone, Florence Smith *film presenter and film festival producer, consultant*
Stone, Roger David *environmentalist*
Stoner, John Richard *federal agency administrator*
Stossel, Scott Hanford *editor, writer*
Stottlemyer, Todd A. *business association executive*
Stouck, Jerry *lawyer*
Stovall, Lou *printmaker*
Strand, Margaret N. *lawyer*
Strasser, Richard Joseph, Jr. *federal agency administrator*
Strauss, Paul *shadow senator*
Strauss, Stanley Robert *lawyer*
Strenio, Andrew John, Jr. *lawyer*
Stromberg, Clifford Douglas *lawyer*
Stroup, Richard L. *lawyer*
Struelens, Michel Maurice Joseph Georges *political science professor, consultant*
Stuart, Pamela Bruce *lawyer*
Stucky, Scott Wallace *federal judge, lawyer*
Stupak, Bart T. *congressman, lawyer*
Subbarao, Kalanidhi *economist*
Subiaul, Francys *anthropologist, psychologist, educator*
Suboleski, Stanley C. *federal agency administrator, mining engineer*
Sugarbaker, Paul H. *oncologist, surgeon*
Sullivan, Andrew M. *online journalist, editor, news blogger*
Sullivan, Brendan V., Jr. *lawyer*
Sullivan, Daniel S. *federal agency administrator*
Sullivan, Dwight H. *military lawyer*
Sullivan, Emmet G. *judge*
Sullivan, Jerome H. *educational association administrator*
Sullivan, John A. *congressman*
Sullivan, John David *business association executive*
Sullivan, John J. *lawyer*
Sullivan, Kevin F. *federal official*
Sullivan, Mark J. *federal agency administrator*
Sullivan, Mary Anne *lawyer, government agency administrator*
Sullivan, Michael J. *labor union administrator*
Sullivan, Timothy *lawyer*
Sultan, Terrie Frances *curator*
Summers, Edwin C. *lawyer, electronics executive*
Sumwalt, Robert Llewellyn III *federal agency administrator, pilot*
Sundermeyer, Michael S. *lawyer*
Suneja, Vince H. *lawyer*
Sunshine, Steven C. *lawyer*
Sununu, John Edward *senator*
Suro-Bredie, Carmen Cecilia *federal official*
Sussman, Monica Hilton *lawyer*
Sutherland, J.J. *journalist*
Sutter, Eleanor Bly *retired diplomat*
Sutton, Betty *congresswoman, lawyer*
Svoboda, Patricia Helen *art historian*
Swad, Stephen M. *mortgage company executive*
Swagel, Phillip L. *federal agency administrator*
Swain, Susan Marie *communications executive*
Swankin, David Arnold *lawyer, consumer products company executive*
Sweeney, Dawn M. *trade association administrator*
Sweeney, John Joseph *labor union administrator*
Sweeney, Margaret Mary *federal judge*
Sweeney, Richard James *finance professor*
Swendiman, Alan Robert *lawyer*
Swift, Stephen Jensen *federal judge*
Swimmer, Ross Owen *federal official*
Swygert, Haywood Patrick *academic administrator*
Szamosfalvi, Jozsef *corporate financial executive, consultant*
Szymanski, Patrick Joseph *lawyer*
Tabb, Vandoster Langford, Sr. *retired military officer*
Tacha, Athena *sculptor, artist, educator*
Taft, William Howard, IV, *lawyer*
Talbert, Kent Dean *federal agency administrator, lawyer*
Talbott, Strobe *think-tank executive*
Tallent, Stephen Edison *lawyer*
Tamargo, Mauricio J. *federal agency administrator*
Tancredo, Thomas G. *congressman*
Tannen, Deborah Frances *writer*
Tannenwald, Peter *lawyer*
Tanner, John S. *congressman, lawyer*
Tannon, Jay Middleton *lawyer*
Tanous, Peter Joseph *investment advisor*
Taronji, Jaime, Jr. *lawyer*
Tars, Eric *lawyer, consultant*
Tate, Deborah Taylor *commissioner*
Tate, Sheila Burke *public relations executive*
Tatel, David Stephen *federal judge*
Taubman, Nicholas F. *ambassador*
Taubman, Philip M. *editor*
Taurman, John David *lawyer*
Tauzin, Billy, II, (Wilbert Joseph Tauzin II) *trade association executive, former congressman*
Taylor, David Kerr *international business educator, consultant*
Taylor, Estelle Wormley *language educator, dean*
Taylor, Gene (Gary Eugene Taylor) *congressman*
Taylor, Jeffrey A. *prosecutor*
Taylor, John E. *foundation administrator, lawyer*
Taylor, Nancy Elizabeth *lawyer*
Taylor, Ralph Arthur, Jr. *lawyer*
Taylor, William B., Jr. *ambassador*
Teague, Randal Cornell, Sr. *lawyer*
Teare, Richard Wallace *retired foreign service officer*
Tedeschi, George *labor union administrator*
Teegarden, Lisa A. *psychologist, military officer*
Teich, Albert Harris *professional society administrator*
Temko, Stanley Leonard *lawyer*
Tendler, Paul Marc *lawyer*
Tenenbaum, Jeffrey S. *lawyer*
Tenet, George John *diplomacy professor, former CIA director*
Tenorio, Pedro A. *resident representative*

Wine, L. Mark *lawyer*
Winfrey, Carey Wells *journalist, editor*
Winland, Thomas W. *lawyer*
Winnick, Steven Yale *lawyer*
Winston, Judith Ann *lawyer*
Winter, Donald C. *civilian military employee, former science administrator*
Winter, Douglas E. *lawyer, writer*
Winter, Thomas Swanson *publishing executive*
Wintrol, John Patrick *lawyer*
Wirth, Timothy Endicott *foundation administrator, retired senator*
Wise, Bob (Robert Ellsworth Wise Jr.) *former governor, former congressman*
Wise, Joan S. *lawyer*
Wise, Lorraine E. *educational consultant*
Wiseman, Alan M(itchell) *lawyer*
Wiseman, Laurence Donald *foundation executive*
Wiseman, Thomas G. *lawyer*
Wiss, Marcia A. *lawyer*
Witek, John W. *history professor*
Witorsch, Philip *internist, educator*
Witt, James Lee *management consultant, former federal agency administrator*
Wixon, Henry N. *lawyer*
Wofford, Harris *senator, lawyer*
Wolanin, Barbara Ann Boese *curator, art historian*
Wolanin, Thomas Richard *federal agency administrator, educator*
Wolf, Craig (M. Craig Wolf) *trade association administrator*
Wolf, Frank Rudolph *congressman, lawyer*
Wolf, John S. *ambassador, federal agency administrator*
Wolf, William B., Jr. *lawyer*
Wolfe, Leslie R. *think-tank executive*
Wolfe, Sidney Manuel *physician*
Wolff, Candida (Candi) *federal official*
Wolff, Elroy Harris *lawyer*
Wolff, Otto J. *federal agency administrator*
Wolff, Paul Martin *lawyer, sculptor*
Wolfowitz, Paul Dundes *former President of the World Bank, former federal agency administrator*
Wolski, Victor J. *federal judge, lawyer*
Wolters, Curt Cornelis Frederik *foreign service officer*
Wongswan, Jon *economist*
Wood, James *magazine editor, literary critic*
Wood, Michael M. *ambassador*
Woodall, Samuel Roy, Jr. *lawyer*
Woodley, John Paul, Jr. *civilian military employee, lawyer*
Woodson, Ruby Garrard *educational administrator, chemistry educator*
Woodward, Bob (Robert Upshur Woodward) *newspaper reporter, writer*
Woodworth, Ramsey Lloyd *lawyer*
Woofter, Vivien Perrine *interior designer, consultant*
Woolsey, Lynn C. *congresswoman*
Worden, Robert L. *government agency administrator, researcher*
Work, Charles Robert *lawyer*
Worsley, James Randolph, Jr. *lawyer*
Worthy, K(enneth) Martin *retired lawyer*
Worthy, Patricia Morris *lawyer, educator*
Wortley, George Cornelius *congressman, consultant*
Wraase, Dennis Richard *utilities executive, accountant*
Wrathall, James R. *lawyer*
Wray, Christopher Asher *lawyer, former federal agency administrator*
Wray, Robert *lawyer*
Wright, Daniel V. *career military officer, judge*
Wuzor, Geoffrey Onyema *psychotherapist*
Wyden, Ron(ald) (Lee) *senator*
Wynn, Albert Russell *congressman*
Wynne, Michael Walter *civilian military employee*
Wysocki, Susan *women's health nurse practitioner*
Wyss, John Benedict *lawyer*
Yablon, Jeffery Lee *lawyer*
Yamamoto, Donald Yukio *ambassador*
Yambrusic, Edward Slavko *lawyer, consultant*
Yanikoski, Richard Alan *educational association and academic administrator*
Yannucci, Thomas David *lawyer*
Yarmuth, John Allan *congressman*
Yarwood, Bruce *health science association administrator*
Yasutake, Noriaki *chef*
Yerkes, David Norton *architect*
Yeutter, Clayton Keith *lawyer, former secretary of agriculture*
Yochelson, Ellis L(eon) *paleontologist*
Yoches, Edward Robert *lawyer*
Yock, Robert John *federal judge*
Yoder, Ronnie A. *judge*
Yost, Paul Alexander, Jr. *foundation executive, retired military officer*
Young, Bill (Charles William Young) *congressman*
Young, Donald Alan *federal agency administrator*
Young, Donald E. *congressman*
Young, Howard J. *lawyer*
Young, John Jacob, Jr. *federal agency administrator*
Young, William H. *labor union administrator*
Youtcheff, John Sheldon *physicist*
Yulish, Charles Barry *retired public relations executive*
Zacarías, Karen *playwright*
Zacharias, Norbert *astronomer*
Zagaris, Bruce *lawyer*
Zane, Phillip Craig *lawyer*
Zarate, Juan Carlos *federal official*
Zarychta, William Alex *medical officer, physician assistant*
Zaucha, Jerome J. *lawyer*
Zax, Leonard A. *lawyer*
Zeidman, Philip Fisher *lawyer*
Zentay, John H. *lawyer*
Zhang, Zhiwei *research scientist*
Ziebold, Eric *chef*
Ziegler, Janice H. *lawyer*
Zikmund, Barbara Brown *minister, religious organization administrator, educator*
Ziman, Barry Russell *government relations executive*
Zimmer, Richard Alan *lawyer, retired congressman*
Zimmerman, Edwin Morton *lawyer*
Zimmerman, Ryan Wallace *professional baseball player*
Zinmeister, Karl *federal official*
Zinni, Anthony Charles *retired military officer*
Zoeller, Jack Carl *diversified financial services company executive*
Zoellick, Robert Bruce *President of the World Bank, former federal agency administrator*
Zolandz, Michael E., Jr. *lawyer*
Zotter, Bruce C. *lawyer*
Zwerdling, Daniel *news correspondent*
Zwick, Kenneth Lowell *lawyer, director*
Zwiener, David K. *financial consultant, former insurance company executive*
Zwillinger, Marc J. *lawyer*

FLORIDA

Alachua
Gaines, Weaver Henderson *lawyer*
Schneider, Richard T(heodore) *optics scientist, researcher, engineer*

Altamonte Springs
Chong, Stephen Chu Ling *lawyer*
Diefenbach, Dale Alan *retired law librarian*
Hoogland, Robert Frederics *lawyer*
LeBlanc, Janet M. *addictions and relationship counselor*
Nazari, Kourosh *ophthalmologist*

Altoona
Westbrook, Clinton Howard *retired military petty officer, retired protective services official*

Alva
Darlow, George Anthony Gratton *investor*

Amelia Island
Adelman, Robert Paul *retired construction executive, lawyer*
Lilly, Wesley Cooper *marine engineer*
Schiebler, Gerold Ludwig *pediatrician, educator*

Anna Maria
Hoffmann, Carl Konrad *lawyer*

Apopka
Leslie, John William *public relations and advertising executive*

Arcadia
Spangler, Colleen Ann *marketing professional*
White, Will Walter III *public relations consultant, writer*

Atlantic Beach
Gartland, Alice Johnson *artist*
Preble, Robert Curtis, Jr. *insurance executive*
Walker, Richard Harold *pathologist, educator*

Atlantis
Daniel, George K. *cardiologist*

Aventura
Fishel, Peter Livingston *finance company executive*
Flood, Henry *non-profit organization executive*
Garcia, Marc Anthony *diplomat*
Kliger, Milton Richard *diversified financial services company executive*
McKenna, Peter Dennis *lawyer*
Meltzer, Brad *writer*
Perkel, Robert Simon *photojournalist, educator*
Schwartz, Gerald *public relations and fundraising agency executive*
Wolfenson, Azi U. *electrical, mechanical and industrial engineer, consultant*

Avon Park
Cranfill, Virginia May *retired nursing administrator*

Babson Park
Morrison, Kenneth Douglas *writer, columnist*

Bal Harbour
Horton, Jeanette *municipal government official*
Spiegel, Siegmund *architect*

Bartow
Cury, Bruce Paul *lawyer, judge, educator*
Kincart, Robert Owen *technological executive*
Meuser, Fredrick William *retired church administrator, historian*

Bascom
Brooten, Kenneth Edward, Jr. *lawyer, writer, rancher*
Hart, James Whitfield, Jr. *retired public relations executive, lawyer*

Bay Harbor Islands
Rosenbluth, Morton *periodontist, educator*

Bay Pines
Jewell, Vanessa yoder *surgical physician's assistant*
Law, David Hillis *physician*
Okano, Takeshi *thoracic surgeon*

Belle Glade
Grear, Effie Carter *principal*
Liang, Lee Z. *biology professor*
Roberts, Thomas Andrew, II, *development executive*

Belleair Beach
Ayers, Richard Wayne *electric power industry executive, writer, journalist*
Fuentes, Martha Ayers *playwright*

Belleair Bluffs
Alexander, Christina Anamaria *translator, performing company executive*
Sexton, Donald Lee *retired business administration educator*

Big Pine Key
Fleischer, Roland Edward *art history professor*

Boca Grande
de Saint Phalle, Thibaut *investment banker, financial consultant*

Boca Raton
Agler, Richard Dean *rabbi*
Anise, Nader *lawyer*
Arden, Eugene *retired university provost*
Barbarosh, Milton Harvey *merchant banking executive*
Beber, Robert H. *lawyer, diversified financial services company executive*
Boykin, Anne Jane *dean*
Braisted, Mary Jo *elementary school educator*
Breakstone, Robert Albert *information technology executive, consumer products company executive, consultant*
Brogan, Frank T. *academic administrator, former lieutenant governor*
Buchbinder, Ligaya H. *dermatologist*
Buckstein, Mark Aaron *lawyer, educator, mediator*
Comment, Anna Mae *retired principal*
Cowen, Edward S. *lawyer, consultant*
Dickenson, Katharine Horn *historic preservationist*
Dorfman, Allen Bernard *international management consultant*
Dunhill, Robert *advertising executive*
Feld, Joseph *construction executive*
Fishman, Barry Stuart *lawyer*
Foreman, Barbara Blatt *healthcare facility administrator*
Friedland, Michael Lawrence *dean, medical educator*
Friend, Harold Charles *neurologist*
Furman, Mark Evan *neuroscientist*
Garelick, Martin *retired transportation executive*
Garlick, Michael *lawyer*
Godofsky, Stanley *lawyer*
Goldberger, Melvin Tobias *bank executive*
Golis, Paul Robert *lawyer*
Goo, Jahyun *humanities educator*
Gracin, Hank *lawyer*
Gralla, Eugene *natural gas company executive*
Hampton, Benjamin Bertram *brokerage house executive*
Handel, Morton Emanuel *film company executive, management consultant*
Harris, S. Buddy *architect, interior designer*
Haugen, Christine *plastic surgeon*
Hayman, Harry *professional society administrator, electrical engineer*
Iacobucci, Edward E. *air transportation and former software company executive*
Jessup, Jan Amis *arts volunteer, writer*
Joskow, Jules *economic research company executive*
Kartagener, Carol A. *lawyer*
Kassner, Herbert Seymore *lawyer*
Kaye, Barry *insurance company executive*
Keyes, Daniel *author*
Kitzes, William Fredric *lawyer, advocate, researcher*
Koch, Robert Charles *lawyer, community activist*
Kramer, Cecile Edith *retired medical librarian*
Laine, Iris Ruth *minister, advertising executive, public relations executive*
Lampasona, Eydi M. *art educator*
Langbort, Polly *retired advertising executive*
Langfield, Raymond Lee *real estate developer*
Lazar, Charna L. *education educator, retired CIA officer, security consultant*
Leary, William James *educational association administrator*
Lee, Xiaoyang *scientist*
Lemanski, Larry Fredrick *medical educator, academic administrator*
Levine, Irving R. *commentator, dean, writer, educator*
Lin, Yukweng M. *engineer, educator*
Louda, J. William *chemist, biochemist, educator*
Man, Daniel *plastic surgeon*
Marcus, Andrea Candace Sills *lawyer*
Martin, James Russell *lawyer*
McFarland, Thomas *English literature educator*
McQueen, Scott Robert *broadcast executive*
Miles, Jesse Mc Lane *retired accounting company executive*
Miller, Eugene *business educator, consultant*
Morris, Stuart R. *lawyer*
Mussenden, Georg Antonio *electronics engineer*
Oussani, James John *manufacturing executive*
Parra-Davila, Eduardo *surgeon, educator*
Pasternack, Stefan Alan *psychiatrist, psychoanalyst*
Perel, David *editor*
Pratt, David *lawyer*
Reinstein, Joel *lawyer*
Rhein, Arthur *computer company executive*
Ricciardi, Salvatore *wholesale distribution executive*
Richardson, R(oss) Fred(erick) *insurance company executive, consultant*
Richman, Joseph Herbert *retired public health service officer*
Roselli, Richard Joseph *lawyer*
Rosenberg, Lee Evan *financial planner*
Ross, Kevin McAndrew *academic administrator*
Rothberg-Blackman, June Simmonds *retired nursing educator, psychotherapist*
Samuels, William Mason *physiology association executive*
Shalom, Galit *psychologist*
Sigel, Marshall Elliot *financial consultant*
Silver, Barry Morris *lawyer*
Sperry, Len Thomas *psychiatrist and preventive medicine educator*
Tennies, Robert Hunter *headmaster*
Tescher, Donald R. *lawyer*
Tracy, James Frederick *media educator*
Trunzo, Candace *editor-in-chief*
Vissicchio, Andrew John, Jr. *linen service company executive*
Wallach, Steven Ernst *lawyer, pilot*
Weiner, Howard Marc *physician*
Weissbach, Herbert *biochemist, researcher*
Wertheimer, Esther *sculptor*
Willis, John Alexander *lawyer*
Wilson, James Laurence *real estate development executive, financial services consultant, educator*
Wolf, Jerome L. *lawyer*
Wyatt, James Luther *drapery hardware company executive*
Yoder, Patricia Doherty *public relations executive*
Young, David L. *entrepreneur, retail executive*

Bonita Springs
Becker, Richard Charles *retired college president*
Boothby, Richard Alfred *gynecologist, educator*
Borchers, Janet Marise *elementary school educator, counselor*
Brown, Theodore Lawrence *chemistry professor*
Costley, Gary Edward *food company executive*
Dignan, Thomas Gregory, Jr. *lawyer*
Dougherty, James *retired orthopedist*
Dunning, Herbert Neal *government agency administrator, chemist*
Elliott, Donna Louise *artist*
Gillis, James R. *consumer products company executive*
Hastings, Vivien N. *lawyer*
Hauserman, Jacquita Knight *management consultant*
Hustrulid, William A. *mining engineer, consultant*
Johnson, Franklyn Arthur *academic administrator*
Katzen, Raphael *consulting chemical engineer*
Knight-McDowell, Victoria *former elementary school educator, health products executive*
Kopf, George Michael *retired ophthalmologist*
Rainey, Barbara White *insurance company executive*
Sargent, Charles Lee *manufacturing executive*
Starkey, Jerry L. *real estate developer*
Tuchman, Alan *consumer products company executive*

Boynton Beach
Allison, Dwight Leonard, Jr. *investor*
Bartholomew, Arthur Peck, Jr. *accountant*
Bernstein, Edwin S. *judge*
Bryant, Donald Loyd *insurance company executive*
Charles, Joel *forensic audio and video recording analyst, voice identification consultant*
DeVries, Janet Mary *archivist, curator*
Glickman, Franklin Sheldon *dermatologist, educator*
Honeycutt, Kevin *construction executive, consultant*
Jacobs, Wendy *editor, realtor*
Jensen, Reuben Rolland *former automotive company executive*
Klein, Bernard *publishing executive*
McNair, Russell Arthur, Jr. *lawyer*
Meridy, Howard William *rabbi, anesthesiologist*
Mittel, John J. *diversified financial services company executive, economist*
Pataky, Paul Eric *ophthalmologist*
Polinsky, Janet Naboicheck *retired state official, retired state legislator*
Shang, Charles Yulin *medical physicist*
Sondak, Arthur *retired management consultant*
Turner, Lisa Phillips *human resources executive*
Warga, Jack *mathematician, educator*
Warshaw, Stanley Irving *federal official, consultant*
Waterman, Daniel *mathematician, educator*
Wick, Mitchell A. *physician*

Bradenton
Bailey, Higgins D. *health products executive*
Beall, Robert Matthews, II, *retail executive*
Blanchard, Leonard Albert *writer, consultant, educator*
Brenner, Frank *lawyer*
Brunk, William Edward *astronomer*
Carnes, James Edward *retired electronics executive*
Castro, Valentino *psychologist, counseling administrator*
Crouthamel, Thomas Grover, Sr. *editor, consultant*
Diana, John Nicholas *physiologist*
Driscoll, Constance Fitzgerald *education educator, writer, consultant*
Dryden, Stephen David *artist, product designer*
Dudley, Perry, Jr. *retired electronics executive*
Engelman, Melvin Alkon *retired dentist, dental products executive*
Garvick, Kenneth Ryan *broadcast engineer, announcer, educator*
Grace, David *physician*
Green, Raymond Ferguson St. John *marketing and advertising executive*
Groseclose, Lynn Hunter *lawyer*
Haas, Tommy (Thomas Mario Haas) *professional tennis player*
Hashmi, Sajjad Ahmad *finance educator, dean*
Houston, Stanley Dunsmore *retired public relations executive*
Howe, Carroll Victor *construction equipment company executive*
Lopacki, Edward Joseph, Jr. *lawyer*
McFarland, Richard Macklin *retired journalist*
McRae, Leslie *minister*

Moore, John Hampton *academic administrator*
Padgett, Gail Blanchard *lawyer*
Peterson, Richard J. *surgeon*
Pillot, Gene Merrill *retired school system administrator*
Price, Edgar Hilleary, Jr. *manufacturing executive, consultant*
Rutstein, Stanley Harold *apparel retailing company executive*
Shapiro, Richard Michael *lawyer*
Vereb, Teresa B. *psychiatrist*
Voorhees, Stephanie Robin Faught *retired art educator*
Watkins, William, Jr. *electric power industry executive*
White, Dale Andrew *journalist*
Wilburn, Donald Lee *military officer, retail executive*
Wolf, John Michael *adult education seminar consultant*
Woodson-Howard, Marlene Erdley *former state legislator*

Brandon
England, Lynne Lipton *lawyer, pathologist*
Pantano, Daniele *poet, educator*
Stephens, Robert David *environmental engineering executive*

Brooksville
Anderson, Richard Edmund *city manager, management consultant*
Cario, Jeffrey Peter *lawyer*
Chamberlain, Daniel Robert *retired college president*
Flannery, Michael Sidney *environmental scientist*
McBride, Tamera Shawn Dew *geologist*

Bushnell
Hagin, T. Richard *lawyer*

Cape Canaveral
Hess, Terry Lee *writer, educator, logistician*

Cape Coral
Bradley, Jean Irene *elementary school educator*
Graham, Dorothy E. *elementary school educator*
(Pickett) Harrison Flint, Nancy Elizabeth *retired medical administrator*
Hopkins, Lee Bennett *writer, educator*
Martin, Benjamin Gaufman *ophthalmologist*
Milaski, John Joseph *management consultant*
Nightingale, Suzanne M. *management consultant*
Parrett, Sherman O. *lawyer*
Shuman, Carolyn Rae (Thorburn) *psychologist, columnist, writer, nurse*
Stuart, Robert *container manufacturing executive*
Vamos, Florence M. *lawyer*
Wendel, Joan Audrey *music educator*

Casselberry
Pantuso, Vincent Joseph *food service consultant*
Renee, Lisabeth Mary *small business owner, glass artist*

Cedar Key
Starnes, Earl Maxwell *retired urban and regional planner, architect, educator*

Celebration
Johnson, Derrick M. *information technology executive*
Renard, Meredith Anne *marketing and advertising professional*
Schroeder, James White *retired lawyer*
Whelden, Craig B. *retired army officer*

Chattahoochee
Carrasco, José Aníbal *recreational therapist*

Clearwater
Aragones, Tesa *advertising executive*
Bailey, Robin Keith *medical educator*
Barry, Joyce Alice *dietician, consultant*
Blumencranz, Peter William *surgeon*
Campolettano, Thomas Alfred *international contract manager*
Chisholm, William DeWayne *retired contractor*
Christ, Karyn Lynn *apparel designer, poet*
Coleman, Jeffrey Peters *lawyer*
Crites, Richard Ray *financial planner, finance company executive, investment advisor*
Cross, Beverly Jean *music educator*
Dougall-Sides, Leslie K. *lawyer*
Dutkowsky, Robert M. *computer company executive*
Falkner, William Carroll *lawyer*
Feldman, Marvin Herschel *financial consultant*
Fine, A(rthur) Kenneth *lawyer*
Glymph, Dianne Tyler *librarian*
Halsey, Jean Michele *nursing educator*
Howells, Jeffrey P. *computer company executive*
Johnson, Timothy Augustin, Jr. *lawyer*
Kiehl, E. Robert *manufacturing executive, consultant*
Maxwell, Richard Anthony *retail executive*
McCormack, John Robert *lawyer*
Mitchell, Scott Patrick *advertising executive, Internet company executive*
Peters, Robert Timothy *judge*
Peterson, James Robert *engineering psychologist*
Platau, Gerard Oscar *chemist, consultant*
Raymund, Steven A. *computer company executive*
Sandefer, G(eorge) Larry *lawyer*
Slade, Roy *artist, college president, museum director*
Smith, Marion Pafford *retired avionics company executive*
Tragos, George Euripedes *lawyer*
Turley, Stewart *retired retail company executive*
VanMeer, Mary Ann *publishing executive, writer, webmaster*
Vetter, David R. *lawyer*
Weidemeyer, Carleton Lloyd *lawyer*
Zschau, Julius James *lawyer*

Clermont
Richardson, Dot (Dorothy Gay) *former Olympic softball player, physician*

Clewiston
Burroughs, Jeannette *elementary school educator*
Griffith, Lonzo, Jr. *technology specialist, educator, farmer*

Cocoa Beach
Adkisson, Hubert Keith *military officer*
Antolik, Michael *geophysicist*
Tewksbury, Russell Baird *media consultant, internet strategist, educator*

Coconut Creek
Brenner, Egon *academic administrator, consultant*
Diffine, Suzanne Michele *language educator*
Kaufmann, Vicki Marie *social services administrator*

Coconut Grove
Arboleya, Carlos Joaquin *lawyer, broker*
Softness, John *public relations executive*

Cooper City
Maugere, Dennis Paul *historian, educator*

Coral Gables
Anthony, Andrew John *lawyer*
Balzebre, Anthony Francis, Sr. *real estate developer, investor*
Banks, Russell *financial planner, consultant*
Brandt, Frederic Sheldon *dermatologist*
Brownell, Edwin Rowland *banker, civil engineer, land surveyor*
Buchsbaum, Karen Fuson *public relations executive, consultant*
Burini, Sonia Montes de Oca *apparel manufacturing executive, public relations executive*
Cano, Mario Stephen *lawyer*
Coe, Jack Martin *lawyer, consultant*
Cole, Todd Godwin *management consultant transportation*
Dady, Robert Edward *lawyer*
De Sena, Ferdinando *composer, educator*
Einspruch, Norman Gerald *physicist, engineering educator*
Fitzgerald, John Thomas, Jr. *religious studies educator*
Friedman, Marvin Ross *lawyer*
Frohock, Fred Manuel *political science professor*
Giuffrida, Theodore John *dermatologist*
Glaser, Luis *biochemistry educator*
Gould, Taffy *Internet company executive, real estate executive*
Graham, H. Dillon III *lawyer*
Green, Stephanie *lawyer*
Haggard, William Andrew *lawyer*
Harriell, Kysha *athletic trainer, educator*
Heisenbottle, Richard John *architect*
Hertz, Arthur Herman *communications executive*
Hirschberg, Joseph Gustav *physicist, educator*
Hirschhorn, Joel *lawyer*
Hoffman, Carl H. *lawyer*
Humphries, Joan Ropes *psychologist, educator*
Jackson, Yvonne Ruth *former pharmaceutical executive*
Kohen, Elli *science educator*
Landon, Robert Kirkwood *volunteer*
Leblanc, Roger Maurice *chemistry professor*
Lomonosoff, James Marc *marketing professional*
Lucà-Moretti, Maurizio *research scientist, nutritionist*
Mangravite, Ronald *education educator, writer*
Milton, Jose *real estate development company executive*
Moss, Ambler Holmes, Jr. *lawyer, educator, former ambassador*
Murai, Rene Vicente *lawyer*
Nijman, Jan *geographer, educator*
Nunez-Portuondo, Ricardo *investment company executive*
Perez, Josephine *psychiatrist, educator*
Prilleltensky, Isaac *dean*
Quillian, Warren Wilson, II, *pediatrician, educator*
Roberts, Samuel Smith *television news executive*
Sabat-Rivers, Georgina *Latin American literature educator*
Sacasas, Rene *lawyer*
Saffir, Herbert Seymour *structural engineer, consultant*
Shalala, Donna Edna *academic administrator, former secretary of health and human services*
Shyu, Mei-Ling *information scientist, educator*
Spivey, Donald *history professor*
Steinberg, Alan Wolfe *investment company executive*
Stone, Bruce *lawyer*
Sumanth, David Jonnakoty *industrial engineer, educator*
Swan, Alan Charles *law educator*
Temares, M. Lewis *academic administrator*
Tien, James M. *dean, engineering educator, consultant*
Touby, Kathleen Anita *lawyer*
Van Vliet, Carolyn Marina *physicist, researcher*
Walker, William D. *library director*
Wolf, Aizik Loft *neurosurgeon*
Zvijac, John E. *orthopedist, surgeon*

Coral Springs
Autry, Herman Allen, Sr. *lobbyist, writer, music executive*
Becker, Benjamin *professional tennis player*
Burg, Ralph *art association executive*
Hershenson, Miriam Hannah Ratner *librarian*
Kristofferson, Kris *singer, lyricist, actor*
Polin, Alan Jay *lawyer*
Sommerer, John *accountant, former mayor*

Cortez
Levine, Harvey Davis *retired dentist*

Crawfordville
Brumby, James Remley, III, (Knox Brumby) *retired priest*

Crestview
Scott, George Gallmann *accountant*

Dade City
Brennan, Thomas Emmett *lawyer*
Brown-Waite, Virginia (Ginny Brown-Waite) *congresswoman*
Burdick, Glenn Arthur *physicist, engineering educator*

Dania Beach
Messer, Allen Person *mechanical engineer, construction executive*
Satin, Claire Jeanine *sculptor, artist*
Spieler, Richard Earl *oceanographer, educator*

Davie
Capers, Dom (Dominic Capers) *professional football coach*
Collins, Mary Lynn *education educator*
Green, Trent Jason *professional football player*
Penhollow, Tina Marie *health science researcher, educator*
Snyder, William Albert *lawyer*
Taylor, Jason Paul *professional football player*
Thomas, Zach Michael *professional football player*
Upadhiaya, Umesh Chandra *engineer, consultant*
Walkinshaw, Nicole M. *performing arts educator*
Wang, Xiao *language educator*

Daytona Beach
Ahn, Shi Hyun *professional golfer*
Alvarez, Marianne *artist, photographer, educator*
Amick, William Walker *golf course architect*
Andrews, Donna L. *professional golfer*
Barker, Robert Osborne (Bob Barker) *mediator, educator*
Bivens, Carolyn Vesper *sports association administrator, former advertising executive*
Bodine, Geoff *race car driver*
Bower, Roger Harrison *endocrinologist, director*
Cardwell, Harold Douglas, Sr. *retired rehabilitation services professional*
Castrale, Nicole *professional golfer*
Cavalleri, Silvia *professional golfer*
Creamer, Paula *professional golfer*
David, Valentina S. *physics professor*
Davidson, Herbert M., Jr., (Tippen) *newspaper owner*
Davies, Laura *professional golfer*
DeLuca, Annette *professional golfer*
Duma, Richard Joseph *epidemiologist, microbiologist, educator, pathologist, researcher, physician*
Duval, Cynthia *art historian, museum administrator, consultant, curator*
France, Brian Z. *sports association executive*
France, James C. *professional sports executive*
Green, Betty Nielsen *education educator, consultant*
Han, Hee-Won *professional golfer*
Harris, Christy Franklin *lawyer*
Helfrick, Albert Darlington *electronics engineering educator, consultant, department chairman*
Inkster, Juli *professional golfer*
Jang, Jeong *professional golfer*
Kerr, Cristie *professional golfer*
Kim, Mi Hyun *professional golfer*
Kruse, Marylin Lynn *retired language educator*
Kung, Candie *professional golfer*
Lawson, Scott D. *oral surgeon*
Lee, Seon-Hwa *professional golfer*
Libby, Gary Russell *museum director emeritus, writer*
Lincicome, Brittany *professional golfer*
Mc Collister, John Charles *writer, minister, educator*
Mears, Casey *race car driver*
Neitzke, Eric Karl *lawyer*
Ochoa, Lorena *professional golfer*
Pak, Se Ri *professional golfer*
Pang, Shuo *engineering educator*
Park, Hee-Jung (Hee Jong Park) *professional golfer*
Poitier, Constance Rena *music specialist, educator*
Prammanasudh, Stacy *professional golfer*
Pressel, Morgan *professional golfer*
Rosales, Jennifer *professional golfer*
Scott, John Brooks *retired research and development company executive*
Seenith, Sivasundaram *mathematician, educator*
Sheehan, Patty *professional golfer*
Sigerson, Marjorie Lorraine *librarian*
Smith, Marilynn *retired professional golfer*
Solomon, George *physician, military officer*
Sorenstam, Annika *professional golfer*
Steinhauer, Sherri *professional golfer*
Votaw, Ty M. *golf association commissioner*
Webb, Karrie *professional golfer*
Whitworth, Kathrynne Ann *professional golfer*
Wie, Michelle Sung *professional golfer*
Zenkovsky, Betty Jean *modern languages educator*

Debary
Coble, Alicia Sharon *retired elementary and secondary school educator*

Deerfield Beach
Allaire, Gaston George *music educator, researcher*
Brown, Colin *automotive executive*
Gambino, S(alvatore) Raymond *lab administrator, educator*
King, Don *boxing promoter*
Laser, Charles, Jr. *oil company executive*
Panitz, Daniel R. *psychologist, consultant*
Siegel, Steven L. *finance company executive, consultant*
Solomon, Barry Jason *human services administrator, consultant*
Ward, L. Taylor III *lawyer*
Yerves, Ken *information technology executive*

Deland
Bailey, T. Wayne *political science professor*
Benet, Helen Curry *retired toxicologist, artist*
Bradford, Jane Turner *librarian*
Caccamise, Genevra Louise Ball (Mrs. Alfred E. Caccamise) *retired librarian*
Dascher, Paul Edward *dean, accounting educator*
Freeman, Ronald Eugene *environmental engineer*
Goldberg, Paul Bernard *gastroenterologist, clinical researcher*
James, Craig T. *former congressman*
Langston, Paul T. *dean, composer, music educator*
Musco, Lynn Ann *music educator*
Niemann, Chester S., Jr. *retired band director, customer service administrator*
Plane, Donald Ray *retired management science educator*
Rattman, William John *electronics and electro-optic engineer*
Rouse, Robert Kelly, Jr. *judge*

Delray Beach
Autelitano, Philip M. *marketing professional, consultant, writer*
Brewer, Robert H. *consumer products company executive*
Brown, Charles E. *consumer products company executive*
Campbell, Cynthia *consumer products company executive*
Charyk, Joseph Vincent *retired satellite telecommunications executive*
Chavin, Walter *biological sciences educator, researcher*
Dye, Thomas Roy *political science professor*
Ehrlich, Geraldine Elizabeth *management consultant*
Ellsweig, Phyllis Leah *retired psychotherapist*
Fannin, David Cecil *lawyer, consumer products company executive*
Goldenberg, George *retired pharmaceutical executive*
Hardiman, Joseph Raymond *security firm executive*
Hegstrom, William Jean *retired mathematics professor*
Hofman, Elizabeth Elveretta *retired mathematics educator, guidance counselor, dean*
Holifield, Mark *retail executive*
Larry, R. Heath *lawyer, director*
Levinson, Harry *psychologist, educator*
Luechtefeld, Monica *consumer products company executive*
Make, Isabel Rose *multicultural studies educator, adult education educator, small business owner*
McKay, Patricia A. *consumer products company executive*
Moline, Jennifer M. *consumer products company executive*
Odland, Steve *consumer products company executive*
Rippeteau, Darrel Downing *retired architect*
Rosenfeld, Steven Ira *ophthalmologist*
Ross, Donald Edward *former academic administrator*
Rubin, Chuck (Carl Rubin) *consumer products company executive*
St. George, Elaine *art educator*
Salsberg, Arthur Philip *publishing executive*
Schechterman, Lawrence *lawyer, chef, business consultant*
Schenkel, Suzanne Chance *retired natural resource specialist*
Schwartz, Diane N. *secondary school educator, researcher*
Simon, Albert *retired physicist, engineer, educator*
Sparrow, Kathleen Gail *retired secondary school educator*
Stewart, Patricia Carry *foundation administrator*
Vanderlinde, Daisy *consumer products company executive*
Zarwyn, Berthold *physicist, consultant*

Deltona
Bondinell, Stephanie *counselor, academic administrator*
Marrett, Caroline Denise *special education educator*

Destin
Burns, Jurate *library director*
Davis, Christopher Kevin, Sr. *sales executive*
Deel, Frances Quinn *retired librarian*
Robinson, Wilkes Coleman *retired federal judge*

Doral
Brioso-Mesa, Maureen Diane *mental health services professional*

Dover
Pearson, Walter Donald *editor, columnist*

Duck Key
Prout, George Russell, Jr. *medical educator, urologist*

Dunedin
Jacobs, Marilyn Arlene Potoker *gifted education educator, consultant, author*
Klingbiel, Paul Herman *retired information scientist*
Metcalf, Robert John Elmer *industrial consultant*
Rosa, Raymond Ulric *retired banker*
Ruff, Kenneth *management consultant, information technology manager*

Dunnellon
Dixon, W(illiam) Robert *retired psychologist*

Eglin Afb
Vail, Thomas Leighton *military officer*

Elfers
Milana-Panopoulos, Maria *artist, inventor, model*

Ellenton
Edson, Herbert Robbins *retired foundation and hospital executive, military officer*

Englewood
McCall, Gene William *conservator, sculptor, artist, furniture designer*
Sanders, W(illiam) Eugene, Jr. *retired internist*
Simis, Theodore Luckey *investment banker, information technology executive*
Van Leuven, Robert Joseph *lawyer*

Estero
Brown, William Robert *trade association administrator, consultant*
Morgan, Dennis Richard *lawyer*
Routh, Donald K(ent) *psychologist, educator*

Eustis
Chorosinski, Eugene Conrad *writer, poet, author*
King, Robert Howard *marketing professional*
Metz, Larry Edward *lawyer*

Fernandina Beach
Ash, Frederick Melvin *retired manufacturing executive*
Barlow, Anne Louise *pediatrician, medical researcher*
Kurtz, Myers Richard *retired hospital administrator*
Smeeton, Thomas Rooney *government affairs consultant*

Fort Lauderdale
Adams, Nancy R. *nurse, retired military officer*
Adams, S.C. (Chase) *lawyer, writer, radio and television commentator, financial consultant*
Albatineh, Ahmed Najeeb *statistician, researcher*
Alpert, Martin Jeffrey *chiropractic physician*
Ambrose, Judith Ann *retired wedding and floral designer*
Arneson, Margaret Susan *lawyer*
Austin, John Norman *classics educator*
Bamberg, Louis Mark *wealth planning and business insurance specialist*
Barclay, David A. *lawyer*
Baskies, Jeffrey Alan *lawyer*
Beach, Cecil Prentice *librarian*
Beach, Marcia Ellen *judge*
Benjamin, James Scott *lawyer*
Berrard, Steven R. *investment company and former automotive retail company executive*
Bogenschutz, J. David *lawyer*
Bunnell, George Eli *lawyer, director*
Burleigh, A. Peter *ambassador*
Bustamante, Nestor *lawyer*
Cameron, Cam (Malcolm Cameron) *professional football coach*
Cane, Marilyn Blumberg *law educator*
Cannon, Robert Eugene *library director*
Cantwell, John Walsh *advertising executive*
Carter, James Thomas *contractor, pilot*
Carter Pereira, Claudine Renee *forensic specialist*
Cavendish, Kim L. Maher *museum administrator*
Chernow, Bart *critical care physician*
Chung, Chia Mou (Charles Chung) *former Oriental art business owner*
Cobb, David Keith *accountant*
Cole, Jonathan Edward *lawyer*
Coleman, Phyllis *law educator*
Cox, Linda Susan *allergist, immunologist*
Crawford, Claire Cressman *volunteer, educator*
Dressler, Robert A. *lawyer*
Droege, Marcus *medical educator, researcher*
Dutko, Michael Edward *lawyer*
Dwors, Robert F. *retail executive*
Edmund, Norman Wilson *educational researcher*
Ferrando, Jonathan P. *lawyer, automotive executive*
Fine, Howard Alan *management consultant*
Fischler, Abraham Saul *retired academic administrator, educator*
Fleetwood, Clifford Gene ("The Father of Philosophical Art") *lawyer, publishing and recording industry executive, author*
Franz, William Mathew *lawyer*
Gagnon Blodgett, Michelle Dawn *psychologist*
Gardner, Russell Menese *lawyer*
Glick, Richard Stephen *internist, rheumatologist*
Goldberg, Alan Joel *lawyer*
Golden, E(dward) Scott *lawyer*
Gonzalez, Jose Alejandro, Jr. *federal judge*
Gray, Phillip Lee *religious studies educator, pastor*
Greenberg, Howard *publishing executive*
Gunzburger, Suzanne Nathan *municipal official, social worker*
Haliczer, James Solomon *lawyer*
Hall, David *principal*
Hanbury, George Lafayette, II, *academic administrator*
Hargrove, John Russell *lawyer*
Hess, George Franklin, II, *lawyer*
Hills, John Merrill *educational association administrator, consultant, public relations executive, researcher*
Hirsch, Jeffrey Allan *lawyer*
Hoines, David Alan *lawyer*
Huizenga, H. Wayne *entrepreneur, professional sports team executive*
Itkin, Ivan *nuclear scientist, mathematician*
Jackson, Michael J. *automotive retail company executive*
Jarvis, Robert Mark *law educator*
Johnson, Mary Margaret Dickens *governmental and commercial researcher, consultant*
Jotcham, Thomas Denis *marketing communications consultant*
Katz, Thomas Owen *lawyer*
Kelly, John Patrick *lawyer*
Kjellmark, Eric William, Jr. *management consultant, performing company executive*
Kornblau, Barbara L. *physical therapist, educator*
Krause, Roy G. *office staffing firm executive*
Kubler, Frank Lawrence *lawyer*
Leach, Ralph F. *banker*
LeRoy, Miss Joy *model, apparel designer*
Levy, Michael *electronic manufacturing company executive*
Li, Min-Tang *systems engineer*
Lichtinger, Moises *obstetrician, gynecologist*
Lilley, Mili Della *insurance company executive, entertainment management consultant*
Littman, Marlyn Kemper *information scientist, educator*
Lodwick, Gwilym Savage *radiologist, educator*
Loos, John Thompson *business owner*
Lyons, Bruce Martin *lawyer*
Mahan, Mary Hoyle *retired physical educator*
Maniscalco-Feichtl, Maria *pharmacist, educator*
Markos, Chris *retired real estate company executive*
Markus, Robert Michael *retired journalist*
Maroone, Michael E. *automotive executive*
Maucker, Earl Robert *editor, publishing executive*
McCan, James Lawton *education educator*
McCluskey, Neil Gerard *gerontologist, educator, literary agent*
McCormick, Queen Esther Williams *clergyman*
Meeks, William Herman III *lawyer*
Mintz, Joel Alan *law educator*
Moorhead, Rolande Annette Reverdy *artist, educator*
Morris, Gerald Michael *lawyer, educator*
Morris, Sharon *librarian*
Moss, Stephen Bruce *lawyer*
Nyce, John Daniel *lawyer*
O'Brien, Patrick T. *lawyer*
O'Connor, James E. *waste management executive*
Olson, John Karl *judge*
Oltman, John Harold *patent lawyer*
Packer, Billy *sports announcer (broadcast)*
Padula, Stephen Joseph *lawyer*
Parker, Sasha Smilka *medical educator, nurse, consultant*
Parrish, Lori Nance *property appraiser*
Peltzer, Douglas Lea *manufacturing executive*
Polish, Sheldon S. *lawyer*
Potparic, Zoran *plastic surgeon*
Randi, James (Randall James Hamilton Zwinge) *magician, educator*
Ray, Raymond B. *federal judge*
Rentoumis, Ann Mastroianni *psychotherapist*
Revis, Don Ray, Jr. *plastic surgeon*
Richmond, Gail Levin *law educator*
Riggs, Donald Eugene *librarian, academic administrator*
Rojas, Jesus Jon *health products executive, researcher*
Rubinson, Howard Alan *physician*
Ruffner, Frederick G., Jr. *book publisher*
Russell, Terrence Joseph *lawyer*
Sanders, Dale R. *lawyer*
Santis, Jorge Hilker *curator*
Schneider, Laz Levkoff *lawyer*
Schneider, Ursula Wilfriede *author*
Schreiber, Alan Hickman *lawyer*
Scotti, Diego *marketing executive*
Seltzer, Barry S. *federal judge*
Shen, Michael Yue-Hua *cardiologist*
Sherman, Richard Allen, Sr. *lawyer*
Sherr, Brian J. *lawyer*
Shoemaker, William Edward *corporate financial executive*
Short, Michael J. *automotive executive*
Siegel, Michael Alan *dental educator*
Smith, Frank M. *lawyer*
Smith, Mark W. *management consultant*
Snow, Lurana S. *judge*
Spector, Israel *oncologist*
Stayton, James Michael *music educator*
Sullivan, Edward Delano *lawyer, investor*
Sun, Junping *computer science professor*
Thayer, Charles James *investment banker*
Tristano, Antonio Gino *medical researcher*
Trubey, Lillian Priscilla *retired secondary school educator*
Turner, Hugh Joseph, Jr. *lawyer*
Uchin, Robert Allen *dean, endodontist*
Udolf, Bruce Lee *lawyer*
Vasquez, William Leroy *business educator, consultant*
Velez, Ines *oral pathologist, educator*
Vladem, Paul Jay *investment advisor*
Webster, Ernest Wesley *musician, educator*
Weiss, David I. *real estate company executive, lawyer, writer*
Whitmore, Douglas Michael *physician*
Wich, Donald Anthony, Jr. *lawyer*
Williamson, William Paul, Jr. *journalist*
Wojcik, Cass *decorative supply company executive, retired municipal official*
Wood, James McKean *application developer*
Zimmerman, Jordan *advertising and marketing executive*
Zloch, William J. *federal judge*

Fort Myers
Antonic, James Paul *international marketing consultant*
Barbour, William Rinehart, Jr. *retired book publisher*
Beever, James William III *biologist*
Blanchard, Richard Emile, Sr. *retired management services executive, consultant*
Blanchard, Susan Manning *academic administrator, director, engineering educator*
Canham, Pruella Cromartie Niver *music educator*
Carothers, Douglas Edward *special education educator*
Colasurd, Richard Michael *lawyer*
Colgate, Doris Eleanor *sailing school owner, administrator*
Curtin, Constance O'Hara *language educator, writer*
Curtin, David Yarrow *chemist, educator*
Dalton, Anne *lawyer*
Drushal, Mary Ellen *retired education educator*
Edmonds, Scott A. *apparel executive*
Fulker, Edmund Norman *management consultant*
Goyak, Elizabeth Fairbairn *retired public relations executive*
Harris, Connie *gifted and talented educator*
Haug, Warren R. *research and development consultant*
Horecker, Bernard Leonard *retired biochemistry professor*
Laboda, Gerald *oral and maxillofacial surgeon*
Lamach, Bernard D. *professional engineer, county commissioner*
Lounsbury, David Arthur *protective services official, educator*
Mandelkorn, Robert Marc *ophthalmologist*
Mc Queen, Robert Charles *retired insurance executive*
Medvecky, Robert Stephen *lawyer*
Meng, Gunter Richard *surgeon*
Missimer, Thomas Michael *geologist*
Pouliot, Assunta Gallucci *retired business school owner, director, consultant*
Robertson, Mary Amos *mathematics educator*
Sappenfield, Charles Madison *architect, educator*
Schoonover, Jack Ronald *senior judge*
Schwartz, Carl Edward *artist, printmaker*
Scott, Kenneth Elsner *mechanical engineering educator*
Shafer, Robert Tinsley, Jr. *judge*
Sprinkel, Beryl Wayne *economist, consultant*
Thurman, Cynthia Denise *human services administrator*
Trudnak, Stephen Joseph *landscape architect*
Wendeborn, Richard Donald *retired manufacturing executive*
Zeldes, Ilya M. *forensic scientist, lawyer*

Fort Pierce
Belcher, Dorothy S. *state correctional department administrator*
Calvert, David Victor *soil science educator*
Channon, Christopher T. *ophthalmologist*
Conklin, Howard Lawrence *lawyer*
Hurley, William Joseph *retired information technology executive*
Jefferson, Zanobia Bracy *artist, educator*
Rice, Mary Esther *biologist*
Schwenger, Wilbur John *mathematics educator, mathematics professor*
Sneed, Richard Durwood, Jr. *lawyer*
Starner, Don Edward *radiologist, educator*
Steel, Philip S. *manufacturing executive*
Swenson, Ada Perez *artist*
Thoma, Richard William *chemical safety and waste management consultant*
Weingart, S. Len *foundation administrator*
Widder, Edith Anne *biologist*

Fort Walton Beach
Hicks, Patricia J. *secondary school educator*
Moran, Kimberly Dianne *secondary school educator, artist*
Register, Annette Rowan *literature educator*
Williams, Bethtina Qubré *minister*

Gainesville
Acholonu, Wilfred W., Jr. *clinical pharmacy specialist, educator*
Agresti, Alan *statistics educator*
Anderson, Timothy J. *chemical engineering professor*
Arbogast, Richard Terrence *entomologist, researcher*
Balaban, Murat Omer *food science educator*
Balabanian, Norman *electrical engineering educator*
Barber, Charles Edward *publishing executive, journalist*
Bartlett, Rodney J. *chemistry and physics educator*
Baz, Maher Afif *internist, educator, medical director lung transplant program*
Behnke, Marylou *pediatrician, educator*
Berns, Kenneth Ira *physician*
Besch, Emerson Louis *physiologist, educator, retired dean*
Blanch, Paul Bradford *biomedical engineer, researcher*
Boothroyd, Herbert J. *insurance company executive*
Borkhataria, Rena Rebecca *ecologist, researcher*
Boyes, Patrice Flinchbaugh *lawyer*
Brewer, Corey Wayne *college basketball player*
Brodeur, Michael Stephen *dean*
Brown, Myra Suzanne *university librarian*
Brown, William Samuel, Jr. *communication sciences and disorders educator*
Bryan, Robert Armistead *academic administrator, educator*
Burns, Theodore Weber *gastroenterologist*
Burridge, Michael John *veterinarian, educator, research director*
Bzoch, Kenneth Rudolph *speech and language educator, department chairman*
Cantliffe, Daniel James *horticulture educator*
Capehart, Barney Lee *industrial and systems engineer, educator*
Carlson, David Edward *journalism educator, journalist, consultant*
Carter, Christopher Scott *health facility administrator*
Catalanotto, Frank A. *dentist*
Challoner, David Reynolds *academic administrator, endocrinologist*
Chambers, Robert Hunter III *academic administrator, consultant, historian, educator*
Cheek, Jimmy Geary *academic administrator, agricultural studies educator*
Conti, Charles Richard *medicine and cardiology educator*
Copeland, Edward Meadors III *surgeon, educator*
Cousins, Robert John *nutritional biochemist, educator*
Criser, Marshall M. *lawyer, retired academic administrator*
Cristescu, Nicolaie Dan *engineering educator*
Davis, Richard Hunt, Jr. *historian*
Delfino, Joseph John *environmental engineering sciences educator*
DesForges, Deborah Waln *music educator*
Dewsbury, Donald Allen *psychologist*
Dickinson, Joshua Clifton, Jr. *museum director, educator*
Dilcher, David Leonard *paleobotany educator, researcher*
Dinculeanu, Nicolae *mathematician, educator*
Dolan, Teresa A. *dean, educator, researcher*
Donovan, Billy (William John) *men's college basketball coach*
Drago, Valeria *neurologist, researcher*
Drummond, Willa Hendricks *neonatologist, educator, information technology executive*
Drury, Kenneth Clayton *biologist*
Dunford, James Christopher *entomologist, educator*
Favini, Paul Furey *costume designer, educator*
Flotte, Terence Robin *pediatrician, pulmonologist*
Foley, Jeremy N. *athletic director*
Fossum, Jerry George *electrical engineering educator*
Fouke, Janie M. *academic administrator, educator*
Fregly, B. J. *engineering educator*
Freifeld, Alice *history professor*
Gets, Lispbeth Ella *retired educational administrator*
Graham-Hutchinson, Joanna *counselor, minister*
Green, Alex Edward Samuel *physicist, mechanical engineering educator*
Green, Eleanor Myers *veterinarian, educator*
Greer, Melvin *medical educator*
Gridley, Kelly Elizabeth *biotechnologist, researcher*
Grobman, Arnold Brams *retired biology educator, academic administrator*
Grove, David D. *anthropology professor*
Gutekunst, Richard Ralph *retired microbiology professor*
Hanrahan, Robert Joseph *chemist, educator*
Hardt, Nancy Sisson *pathology and laboratory medicine educator*
Harrison, Faye Venetia *anthropologist, educator, writer*
Hartigan, Karelisa Voelker *classics educator*
Heflin, Martin Ganier *diplomat, political scientist*
Herzog, Roland W. *medical educator*
Hiers, Richard Hyde *lawyer, educator, writer*
Himes, James Albert *retired veterinary medicine educator*
Hochmuth, George J. *horticultural educator*
Holland, Norman Norwood *critic*
Hollien, Harry Francis *communications engineer*
Hoy, Marjorie Ann *entomology educator*
Isaacs, Gerald William *retired agricultural engineering educator, consultant*
Israel, Jerold Harvey *law educator*
Jacobs, Alan Martin *physicist, researcher*
Javid, Nikzad Sabet *dentist, prosthodontist educator*
Jerry, Robert Howard, II, *dean, law educator*
Jones, Gregory R. *theater educator*
Jones, Richard Lamar *entomology educator*
Kaimowitz, Gabe Hillel *lawyer*
Kaplan, John *photojournalist, educator, consultant*
Katritzky, Alan Roy *chemistry professor*
Keebaugh, Aaron Christopher *music educator, historian*
Kersey, Talana S. *mental health counselor*
Khargonekar, Pramod Prabhakar *engineering educator*
Kohen, Martha *architecture educator*
Kraft, John *dean*
Kumar, Pradeep *physics professor, researcher*
Kurrus, Thomas William *lawyer*
Kurzweg, Ulrich Hermann *engineering science educator*
Law, Mark Edward *electrical engineer, educator*
Lee, Won Suk *engineering educator*
LeVeen, Robert Frederick *radiologist*
Link, William Allen *history educator*
Logan, William *poetry critic, literature and language professor, poet*
Lowe, John Thomas, Jr. *church and concert musician*
Lowenstein, Ralph Lynn *university dean emeritus*
Machen, James Bernard *academic administrator*
Maple, Marilyn Jean *educational media coordinator*
Marshall, Kevin A. *director*
Maurer, Virginia Gallaher *law educator*
Mazzaferri, Ernest Louis *endocrinologist, educator*
McClellan, Richard Augustus *retired small business owner*
Mead, Frank Waldreth *taxonomic entomologist*
Meyer, Urban *college football coach*
Micha, David Allan *chemistry and physics professor*
Milanich, Jerald Thomas *archaeologist, writer, curator*
Milbrath, Robert Henry *retired petroleum industry executive*
Mills, Jon *dean emeritus, law educator*
Modell, Jerome Herbert *anesthesiologist, educator*
Moore, John Hartwell *anthropology educator, consultant*
Mosier, Arvin Ray *chemist, researcher*
Mubarak, Kamal K. *pulmonologist, intensivist*
Nair, Ramachandran P.K. *agroforestry educator, researcher*
Neiberger, Richard Eugene *pediatrician, nephrologist, educator*

Neims, Allen Howard *pediatrician, educator, dean, researcher*
Nguyen, Ru *entomologist*
Nicoletti, Paul Lee *retired veterinarian, educator*
O, Kenneth Kyongyop *engineering educator*
Ohrn, Nils Yngve *chemistry and physics educator*
Oliver, Robert Bruce *retired investment company executive*
Opdyke, Neil Donald *geology educator*
Oppenheimer, David Gray *botanist, educator*
Paul, Ouida Fay *music educator*
Peck, Merton Joseph *economist, educator*
Pepine, Carl John *physician, educator*
Pfaff, William Wallace *medical educator*
Phillips, Winfred Marshall *academic administrator, mechanical engineer, educator, biomedical researcher*
Pleasants, Julian McIver *history educator, summer school director*
Price, Donald Dennis *neuroscientist, psychologist*
Price, Mary Kathleen *law librarian, educator*
Puckett, Ruby Parker *nutritionist, food service executive, writer*
Purcifull, Dan Elwood *retired plant virologist, retired educator*
Quesenberry, Kenneth Hays *agronomy educator*
Raghavan, Sivakumar *food scientist*
Ramos-Caro, Francisco A. *dermatologist, educator*
Rhoton, Albert Loren, Jr. *neurosurgeon, educator*
Rosenberger, Margaret Adaline *retired elementary school educator, writer*
Rubin, Melvin Lynne *ophthalmologist, educator*
Russell, Judith *librarian, dean*
Sah, Chih-Tang *electrical and computer engineering educator*
Saucerman, Alvera Adeline *elementary school educator*
Schmertmann, John Henry *civil engineer, educator, consultant*
Schmidt-Nielsen, Bodil Mimi (Mrs. Roger G. Chagnon) *retired physiologist, educator*
Schultz, Gregory S. *biochemist*
Seale, James Lawrence, Jr. *agricultural studies educator, trade association administrator, researcher*
Sherif, S. A. *engineering educator*
Shugan, Steven Mark *finance educator*
Singley, John Edward, Jr. *retired environmental scientist, consultant*
Skoblar, Barry *neuroscientist*
Slavickas, Rimas Anthony *electrical engineer, educator, researcher*
Small, Natalie Settimelli *retired pediatric mental health counselor*
Small, Parker Adams, Jr. *pediatrician, educator*
Smith, David Thornton *lawyer, educator*
Smith, Jo Anne *writer, retired communications educator*
Soltis, Pamela S. *botanist, educator*
Suzuki, Howard Kazuro *retired anatomist, educator*
Teitelbaum, Philip *psychologist*
Teixeira, Arthur Alves *food engineer, educator, consultant*
Terza, Joseph Vincent *economics professor*
Tisher, Charles Craig *nephrologist, educator, dean*
Toskes, Phillip Paul *gastroenterologist, educator, researcher*
Tuleko, James Stanley *engineering educator, nuclear engineer*
Uthman, Basim Mohammad *neurologist, epileptologist, consultant*
Vaidyanathan, Balachandran *operations research specialist, industrial engineer*
Van Alstyne, W. Scott, Jr. *lawyer, educator*
Verink, Ellis Daniel, Jr. *metallurgical engineering educator, consultant*
Vierck, Charles John, Jr. *retired neuroscience educator*
Viessman, Warren, Jr. *dean, civil engineering educator*
von Mering, Otto Oswald *anthropology educator*
Wass, Hannelore Lina *educational psychology educator*
Weinrich, Brian Erwin *mathematician, computer scientist*
Weinstein, David A. *endocrinologist, director*
Weyrauch, Walter Otto *law educator*
Wing, Elizabeth Schwarz *museum curator, educator*
Wingard, John Reid *medical educator*
Xie, Huikai *engineering educator*
Yamamoto, Janet Kazuko *science educator*
York, E. Travis *retired academic administrator*
York, Vermelle Cardwell *retired real estate broker and developer*
Yu, Simon Shyi-Jian *entomologist, educator*
Yuan, Zhen *biomedical researcher*

Gonzalez
Plischke, Le Moyne Wilfred *chemist, researcher*

Graceville
Kinchen, Thomas Alexander *college president*
Moon, Kimberle Irene *voice educator*

Grand Island
Johnson, Tesla Francis *data processing executive, educator*

Green Cove Springs
Davidson, Joy Elaine *retired mezzo soprano*
Slade, Tom *manufacturing executive, political organization worker*

Gulf Breeze
Bothfeld, Robert *retired industrial engineer, director, retired mechanical engineer, director*
Menzer, Robert Everett *retired toxicologist, educator*

Gulf Stream
Nalen, Craig Anthony *federal agency administrator*

Gulfport
Miller, Rosiland *retired art history educator, writer*
Podgor, Ellen Sue *law educator*

Haines City
Clement, Robert William *retired air force officer*
Kirk, Sherwood *retired librarian*
Mc Dougall, Dugald Stewart *retired lawyer*

Hallandale
Braverman, Stanley Deems *ophthalmologist*
Lublinski, Michael *lawyer*

Hallandale Beach
Duffy, Earl Gavin *hotel executive*
Engel, Tala *lawyer*
Geller, Bunny Zelda *poet, writer, publisher, sculptor, artist*

Havana
Beare, Muriel Anita Nikki *public relations executive, author*

Heathrow
Argirion, Michael *editor*
Darbelnet, Robert Louis *automobile association executive*

Hernando
Rodgers, John Joseph III *educational administration consultant, educator*

Hialeah
Agrawal, Piyush C. *school system administrator*
Arrarás, Maria Celeste *newscaster, journalist*
Browne, Donald Victor *broadcast executive*
Diaz, Diane Linda *library director*
Engler, Eva Kay *dental and veterinary products company executive*
Jenkins, Dawn Paula *special education educator, dancer*
Medvinsky, Nathalia *library director*
Roman, Eloy *oncologist*
Sosa, Jorge Luis *surgeon*

Highland Beach
Frager, Albert S. *retired food products executive*
Lane, James McConkey *retired investment banker*
Tolf, Robert Walter *writer*
Upbin, Hal J. *consumer products company executive*

Hillsboro Beach
Donoho, Tim Mark *not-for-profit executive*
Marshall, Jo Taylor *social worker*
O'Connell, Richard (James) *English literature educator, poet*

Hobe Sound
Blumengarten, Jerry *educational consultant*
Casey, Edward Paul *manufacturing executive*
Caspersen, Finn Michael Westby *diversified financial services company executive*
Houser, Constance (Connie) W. *writer, artist*
Houser, Jim (James Cowing Houser Jr.) *artist*
Markoe, Frank, Jr. *lawyer, health facility administrator*
Parker, H. Lawrence *retired investor, rancher, investment banker*
Snook, Stover Hoffman *social sciences educator, researcher*

Holiday
Peterson, George Folke *retired insurance company executive, writer*

Hollywood
Angstrom, Wayne Raymond *communications executive*
Barish, Randall David *application developer*
Duffner, Lee R. *ophthalmologist*
Giulianti, Mara Selena *mayor*
Isenberg, Abraham Charles *shoe manufacturing company executive*
Korthals, Candace Durbin *lawyer*
Lopez, Filemon *broadcast executive*
Phillips, Gary Stephen *lawyer*
Rogovin, Lawrence H. *lawyer*
Sadowski, Carol Johnson *artist*
Sandberg, Joel S. *ophthalmologist*
Sofman, Michael S. *dermatologist*
Spencer, Richard Thomas III *health products executive*
Sundel, Martin *management consultant, psychologist, educator*

Holmes Beach
Dunne, Nancy Anne *retired social services administrator*
Kaiser, Albert Farr *manufacturing executive*

Homestead
Armenteros, Eduardo Carlos *psychologist, educator*
Ireland, Patricia *lawyer*
Roberts, Larry Spurgeon *biological science educator, zoologist*
Whitehorton, Thelma *educational administrator*

Homosassa
Carmichael, Roberta Kay *writer*

Hutchinson Island
Welch, Martha Lynn *environmentalist, educator*

Indialantic
Pavlakos, Ellen Tsatiri *sculptor*
Scrivener, Lois Doing *principal, educator*

Indian Harbor Beach
Scanlon, Charles Francis *retired military officer, writer, publisher*
Traylor, Angelika *stained glass artist*

Indian River Shores
Wiegner, Edward Alex *financial and energy executive*

Indian Rocks Beach
DeLucia, Gene Anthony *government administrator, computer company executive*

Inverness
Esquibel, Edward V. *psychiatrist, health facility administrator*

Islamorada
Gates, Richard Daniel *retired manufacturing executive*

Jacksonville
Aldana, Philipp Roque *neurosurgeon*
Aleschus, Justine Lawrence *retired real estate broker*
Ansbacher, Barry Barnett *lawyer*
Appel, Laurence Bruce *lawyer, retail executive*
Arbogast, Gordon Wade *systems engineer, educator, consultant, retired military officer*
Barrow, Sally Settle *retired media specialist, retired librarian*
Bartley, George B. *ophthalmologist, surgeon*
Beattie, Donald A. *aerospace scientist, consultant*
Bedell, Elizabeth Snyder (Betty Bedell) *editor-in-chief, marketing professional*
Beytagh, Francis X. *law educator*
Bickett, Brent B. *insurance company executive*
Blount, Yolanda Denise *social services administrator, psychologist*
Bodkin, Lawrence Edward *inventor, essayist, research and development company executive, consultant*
Bodkin, Ruby Pate *retired real estate broker, educator*
Bosworth, William Posey *physician, physical education educator*
Boyer, Tyrie Alvis *lawyer*
Boyer, Tyrie William *judge, law educator*
Boylan, Kevin Bernard *neurologist*
Braddock, Donald Layton *retired lawyer, accountant, real estate broker, investor*
Bradford, Dana Gibson, II, *lawyer*
Buckner, Jan Craig *oncologist, educator*
Callender, John Francis *lawyer*
Camacho, George *internist*
Campo, Dave *professional football coach*
Cannon, Carl N. *publishing executive*
Cannon, L. Kinder III *lawyer*
Carpenter, JoAnn Deakin *history professor*
Cavendish, Michael Robert *lawyer*
Chambers, Jack Allen *application developer, educator*
Cherry, Barbara Waterman *speech and language pathologist, physical therapist*
Christian, Gary Irvin *lawyer*
Clarkson, Charles Andrew *real estate investment executive*
Cobb, James E. *lawyer*
Coker, Howard Coleman *lawyer*
Commander, Charles Edward *lawyer, real estate consultant*
Coxe, Henry M. III *lawyer*
Davis, Craig Anderson *school system administrator, educator*
Davis, Fred *journalist, educator*
Davis, Linda Lennon McConnell *critical care nurse*
Delaney, John Adrian *academic administrator*
Delaney, Kevin Francis *retired military officer, consultant*
Del Rio, Jack *professional football coach, former professional football player*
Dundon, Margo Elaine *museum director*
Eden, F. Brown *artist*
Edwards, Marvin Raymond *investment counselor, economical consultant*
Fahner, Harold Thomas *marketing executive*
Farmer, Guy Otto, II, *lawyer*
Fawbush, Andrew Jackson *lawyer*
Fisher, Michael D. *retail executive*
Fitzsimmons, Ellen Marie *lawyer*
Foley, William Patrick, II, *insurance company executive*
Folk, David Wilbur *occupational health and safety administrator*
Francis, James Delbert *oil industry executive*
Gabel, George DeSaussure, Jr. *lawyer*
Gerkens, Henry H. *trucking executive*
Godfrey, John Munro *economic consultant*
Goldhagen, Jeffrey Lee *city health department administrator*
Gooding, David Michael *judge*
Goodwin, Jane Ayers *pediatric anesthesiologist*
Grabowski, Rodney Michael *academic administrator, consultant*
Halil, Susan Terrell *dental hygienist*
Hartman, Frederick Cooper *retired biochemist*
Hartmann, Frederick William *newspaper editor*
Hill, Debra S. *lawyer*
Hill, James Clinkscales *federal judge*
Holliday, Patricia Ruth McKenzie *evangelist*
Homsley, Denise Louise *music educator*
Howard, Marcia Morales *federal judge*
Hughes, Carolyn Wright *elementary school educator, director*
Ibold, Catherine Buhaly *lawyer, director*
Israel, Kimberly Held *lawyer*
Jamrich, John Xavier *retired university administrator*
Johnson, Douglas William *radiologist*
Kalas, Frank Joseph, Jr. *financial, information systems consultant*
Kelso, Linda Yayoi *lawyer*
Kent, John Bradford *lawyer*
Killea, Michael F. *lawyer*
Kinne, Frances Bartlett *academic administrator*
Kneller, Michael K. *transportation services executive*
Koetter, Dirk J. *professional and former college football coach*
Laucks, Richard Conrad *otolaryngologist*
Lee, Lewis Swift *retired lawyer*
Leftwich, Byron Antron *professional football player*
Lehmbeck, John Pierce *journalist, writer*
Link, Robert James *lawyer, educator*
Lovett, Radford Dow *marine terminal real estate and investment company executive*
Lynch, Peter L. *retail executive*
Lyon, Wilford Charles, Jr. *insurance executive*
Mack, Jeannette Ana *medical technician*
Main, Edna Dewey (June Main) *education educator*
Main, James L. *lawyer*
Mantle, Raymond Allan *lawyer*
Marks, Dennis *music educator, musician, composer*
Mass, M. F. *allergist, immunologist*
Matta, Mark W. *human resources specialist, manufacturing executive*
Maxwell, W(ilbur) Richard *retired management consultant*
McBurney, Charles Walker, Jr. *lawyer*
McCook, Richard Paul *grocery chain financial executive*
Melton, Howell Webster, Sr. *federal judge*
Mercer, Erica Schalow *urologist, educator*
Mills, David Michael *ophthalmologist, plastic surgeon*
Milton, Joseph Payne *lawyer*
Mizrahi, Edward Alan *allergist*
Monsky, John Bertrand *investment company executive*
Mooradian, Arshag Dertad *internist, educator*
Moreno-Aspitia, Alvaro *physician, researcher*
Morgan, William Newton *architect, educator*
Moseley, James Francis *lawyer*
Motsett, Charles Bourke *retired sales, marketing and leadership executive*
Mueller, Cherone *religious organization administrator, writer, minister*
Mueller, Edward Albert *retired transportation engineer*
Munoz, Oscar *corporate financial executive*
Nussbaum, Bennett *food products executive*
O'Connor, R. D. *retired healthcare executive*
Olin, Marilyn *secondary school educator*
O'Neal, Michael Scott, Sr. *lawyer*
Osborn, Marvin Griffing, Jr. *educational consultant*
Otto, Elizabeth Hall *education educator*
Page, Willis *conductor*
Payne, Timothy D. *information technology executive*
Perdikis, Galen *plastic surgeon*
Phillips, John Michael *lawyer*
Pillans, Charles Palmer III *lawyer*
Portell, Keith S *application developer, consultant*
Prussin, Jeffrey A. *management consultant*
Quirk, Raymond R. (Randy Quirk) *insurance company executive*
Raynor, Eileen Margolies *otolaryngologist, educator*
Rinaman, James Curtis, Jr. *lawyer*
Roberts, Ricky Elias *linguist, educator*
Sadowski, Peter T. *lawyer*
Sanders, Marion Yvonne *retired geriatrics nurse*
ScarborougH, Marion Nichols *nutritionist, recreational facility executive*
Schlesinger, Harvey Erwin *judge*
Schultz, Frederick Henry *investor, former government official*
Scott, Kamela Koon *psychologist, educator*
Sederbaum, William *marketing professional*
Sheppard, William J. *lawyer*
Shula, Mike (Michael John Shula) *professional football coach, former college football coach*
Siegel, Edward *lawyer*
Skinner, Halcyon E. *lawyer*
Smith, David A. *medical services executive*
Smith, Stephen Mark *music educator*
Stanley, Helen Camille *composer, musician*
Stein, Keith Lance *health system administrator*
Stinson, Alan Lynn *insurance company executive*
Taylor, Fred *professional football player*
Taylor, Robert M. *minister*
Thomas, Archibald Johns III *lawyer*
Thomas, Lee Muller *forest products company executive, former government official*
Thorsteinsson, Gudni *physiatrist*
Tjoflat, Gerald Bard *federal judge*
Tomlinson, William Holmes *management educator, retired military officer*
Van Cleve, Robert Baldwin *cardiologist*
Vane, Terence G., Jr. *finance company executive, lawyer*
Vasana, Susan (Chun-Ye) *engineering educator*
Videla, Fabian *investment company executive, consultant*
Vincent, Norman Fuller *broadcast executive*
Ward, Michael J. *rail transportation executive*
Weaver, Dianne Jay *lawyer*
Welch, Philip Burland *electronics and office products company executive*
White, Edward Alfred *lawyer*

Jacksonville Beach
Mahorner, James G. *lawyer*
McWilliams, John Lawrence III *lawyer*
Saltmarsh, Sara Elizabeth *lawyer*
Saltzman, Irene Cameron *consumer products company executive*

Jasper
McCormick, John Hoyle *lawyer*

Jensen Beach
Dahn, Conney Colley *special education educator*
Gamble, Raymond Wesley *retired marriage and family therapist, clergyman*
Kraynak, Helen *special education consultant*
McHale, Michael John *lawyer*
Peterson, David Frederick *retired government agency administrator*
Skrupky, Elaine Charlotte *art educator*

Juno Beach
Dewhurst, Moray P. *utilities executive*

Frevert, James Wilmot *retired financial planner, investment advisor*
Hay, Lewis III *utilities executive*
Knapp, George M. *lawyer*
Robo, James L. *utilities executive*
Tancer, Edward F. *lawyer, utilities executive*
Woltz, Kenneth Allen *retired management consultant*

Jupiter
Baum, Herbert Merrill *consumer products company executive*
Click, David Forrest *lawyer, investment advisor*
De George, Lawrence Joseph *diversified financial services company executive*
Ernst, Calvin Bradley *retired vascular surgery educator*
Farner, Gordon Noble *retired orthopedist, surgeon*
Feinberg, Herbert *apparel executive, real estate company executive*
Garfinkel, Harmon Mark *retired specialty chemicals company executive*
Gerson, Irwin Conrad *advertising executive*
Jacobson, Jerry Irving *biophysicist, theoretical physicist, medical researcher*
Migliaro, Marco William *electrical engineer*
Moore, Jon Alistair *biology professor, researcher*
Nessmith, H(erbert) Alva *dentist*
Pumphrey, Gerald Robert *lawyer*
Secrest, Glenn James *artist*
Vanatta, Bob *athletic administrator*
Weissmann, Charles *molecular biologist, educator*
Wolff, Edward Alvin *electronics engineer*
Zelnick, Ronald Stuart *surgeon*

Kennedy Space Center
Amador, José Jorge *computer engineer, researcher*
Darwood, John Joseph *physician*
Feldman, Stephen *academic administrator*

Key Biscayne
Cardozo, Arlene Rossen *writer*
Cardozo, Richard Nunez *marketing professional, educator, entrepreneur*
Clay, Cynthia Joyce *writer, editor-in-chief*
de la Cruz, Carlos *wholesale distribution executive*
de la Cruz, Rosa *art collector*
Evans, Peter Kenneth *advertising executive*
Pope, John Edwin *editor, columnist*
Ross, Marilyn J. *language and communications educator*
Stephens, William Theodore *lawyer*
Wilson, Robert Gordon *investment banker*

Key Largo
Daenzer, Bernard John *insurance company executive, consultant*
Davidson, Thomas Noel *metal products executive*
Mattson, James Stewart *lawyer, environmental scientist, educator*
Schmetterer, Robert Allen *advertising executive*

Key West
Buffett, Jimmy (James William Buffett) *vocalist, songwriter, writer*
Kalb, Chester H. *mathematics professor*
MacDougall, Peter *retired lawyer*
Mathews, Harry Burchell *poet, writer, educator*
McIntosh, Jon Charles *illustrator, graphics designer, painter*
Taylor, Victoria *real estate rehabilitator, sculptor*
Trammell, Herbert Eugene *retired physicist*
Wisniewski, P. Michelle *retired obstetrician, gynecologist*

Keystone Heights
Ohanian, Mihran Jacob *nuclear engineer, educator, dean, researcher*

Kissimmee
Goode, Betty Ruth *retired social worker*
Haynes, Ulric St. Clair, Jr. *retired dean*
McCann, Jean Friedrichs *artist, educator*
Toothe, Karen Lee *elementary and secondary school educator*

Lady Lake
Akins, Zane Vernon *agricultural products executive*
Di Benedetto, Ann Louise *retired accounting administrator*
Granger, Robert Alan *mechanical and aerospace engineering educator*
Langevin, Thomas Harvey *retired educational association administrator, consultant*
McCully, Joanna Patricia *small business owner*
Pflum, William John *physician*

Lake Alfred
Kender, Walter John *horticulturist, educator*

Lake Buena Vista
Rasulo, James A. *theme park executive*
Schmudde, Lee Gene *resort executive, corporate lawyer*

Lake City
Gay, John Marion *retired federal agency administrator, financial analyst*

Lake Forest
Ross, Jimmy Douglas *retired military officer*

Lake Helen
Finn, Stephen Martin *media producer, venture capitalist*

Lake Mary
Bachmann, Bill *photographer*
Bindley, William Edward *pharmaceutical executive*
Cosler, Steven Douglas *diversified financial services company executive*
Silver, Elaine Terry *lawyer*
Swonger, Thomas K. H., Jr. *insurance company executive*

Lake Placid
Adams, Herbert Ryan *management consultant, retired minister, mediator*
Roberts, William B. *lawyer*
Viater, John Ronald *investment company executive*
Walter, William Paul *retired bioengineer*

Lake Suzy
Ogan, Russell Griffith *real estate broker*

Lake Wales
Connor, John Thomas, Jr. *portfolio manager*
Echols, Verna K. *volunteer*
Luing, Gary Alan *financial management educator*

Lake Worth
Bachrach, Howard L. *biochemist*
Carlisle, Ervin Frederick *university provost, educator*
Goldstein, Jerome Charles *retired professional society administrator, otolaryngologist, surgeon*
Jacobs, Roxanne *development director*
Rose, Norman *retired lawyer, accountant*
Saffir, Leonard *public relations executive*
Sheehy, Betty Jo *real estate company executive, investment advisor*
Wilson, William J. *language educator*

Lakeland
Attaway, John A., Jr. *lawyer*
Ayaz, Sandra M. *educational association administrator*
Barnett, Hoyt R. (Barney) *supermarket company executive*
Chapman, Angela Marie *science educator*
Cooper, James Russell *retired law educator*
Hatten, William Seward *manufacturing executive, consultant*
Hrabusa, John T. *human resources specialist, food products executive*
Jacobson, Barbara Dinger *music educator*
Jenkins, Howard M. *supermarket executive*
Jurbala, Brian Michael *orthopedic surgeon*
Knowlton, Kevin Charles *lawyer*
MacDonald, Susan Priest *media specialist, writer*
McFarlin, Richard Francis *retired industrial chemist, researcher*
Meads, Walter Frederick *communications executive, consultant, writer*
Mutz, Oscar Ulysses *manufacturing and distribution executive*
Pepine, Mary *dermatologist*
Phillips, David P. *grocery company executive*
Pospichal, Marcie W. *neuroscientist, psychologist, educator*
Reich, David Lee *library director*
Rogers, James Gordon, Jr. *art educator*
Schultz, David Franklin *psychologist*
Siedle, Robert Douglas *management consultant*
Stark, Bruce Gunsten *artist*
Washington, Gloria Dunn *secondary school educator*

Land O Lakes
Mallon, Kellie Jane *special education educator*
O'Connell, Carmela Digristina *appraisal executive, consultant*
Quackenbush, Roger E. *retired secondary school educator*
Wilkinson, Denise V. *psychologist*

Lantana
Balis, Moses Earl *biochemist, educator*
Barrett, Robert James III *investment banker*
Caughman, Patricia Ann *mathematics educator*

Largo
Benoit, Christopher Louis *music educator*
Bush, Debra W. *occupational health nurse*
Dolan, John E. *retired utilities executive, consultant*
Grove, Jeffrey Scott *family practice physician*
Hamlin, Robert Henry *public health service officer, educator, management consultant*
Krolick, Merrill A. *cardiologist*
Moscato, Joseph Louis, Jr. *health facility administrator, military officer*
Shillinglaw, Gordon *retired finance educator*
Trevena, John Harry *lawyer*
Wheat, Myron William, Jr. *cardiothoracic surgeon*

Lauderdale By The Sea
Wynne, Brian James *retired professional society administrator*

Lauderhill
Swisher, Charles Francis *electrical engineer, consultant*

Lecanto
Max, Buddy (Boris Max Pastuch) *musician*
Wheatley, Deborah A. *music educator*

Leesburg
Austin, Robert Eugene, Jr. *lawyer*
Duffy, John Lewis *retired Latin, English and reading educator*
Fechtel, Vincent John *legal administrator*
Genzen, Gary Carl *minister*
Moore, Wistar *cardiovascular surgeon*
Smith, Kathy L. *elementary school educator, cosmetics executive, consultant*

Lighthouse Point
Gauthier, Doreen Ann *librarian*

Lithia
Kulkarni, Kavita-Vibha Arun *chemist*
Richmond, Nancy Mason *retired state agency administrator*

Live Oak
Peters, Lee Ira, Jr. *public defender*

Longboat Key
Bryan, Thomas Lynn *lawyer, educator*
Dalgleish, Stuart McNaught *retired manufacturing executive*
Gollobin, Leonard Paul *chemical engineer*
Hazan, Marcella Maddalena *writer, educator, consultant*
McCollough, Newton Clark III *orthopaedic surgeon*
Morse, Marvin Henry *retired judge*
Stapleton, Harvey James *physics professor*
Workman, George Henry *structural engineering consultant*

Longwood
Bernabei, Raymond *management consultant*
Cirello, John *utility and engineering company executive*
Faller, Donald E. *marketing and operations executive*
Gasperoni, Emil, Sr. *realtor, real estate developer*
Hernandez, H(ermes) Manuel *lawyer*
Hunter, Joel Carl *clergyman, educator*
Johnson, Nancy Plattner *retired secondary school educator*
Smyth, Joseph Patrick *retired military officer, physician*
Tomasulo, Virginia Merrills *retired lawyer*

Loxahatchee
Russell-Tyson, Pearl Leonie *elementary school educator*
Wisnicki, Jeffrey Leonard *plastic surgeon*

Lutz
Anderson, Karl Franklin *systems engineer, researcher*
Corbitt, Doris Orene *retired real estate agent, dietician*
Cualing, Hernani Del Mundo *physician, researcher*
Currey, Cecil Barr *retired history professor*
Ellis, Leslie Elaine *psychotherapist*
Hayes, Timothy George *lawyer, consultant*
Koff, Fred William *retired research chemist*
Kolb, Richard Maurice *sports writer, sportscaster*
Miller, Bonnie Sewell *marketing professional, writer*

Lynn Haven
Birdwell, Jamie *music educator, department chairman*

Macclenny
Edwards, Gregory Lawrence *lawyer*

Madison
Hiss, Sheila Mary *librarian*

Maitland
Bailey, Michael Keith *lawyer*
Cicilioni, Orlando Joseph *plastic surgeon*
Nelson, Stephen D. *music educator*
Rijken, Pieter *medical association administrator*
Vallee, Judith Delaney *environmentalist, writer, not-for-profit fundraiser*
Von Hilsheimer, George Edwin III *neuropsychologist*
Wilder, Charles David *lawyer*

Malabar
de Vos, Peter Jon *ambassador*

Marathon
Giffen, Lois Key *artist, psychotherapist*
Wiecha, Joseph Augustine *language educator*

Marco Island
Cooper, Thomas Astley *bank executive*
Guerrant, David Edward *retired food company executive*
Kelly, Robert Donald *management consultant*
Kerstetter, Wayne Arthur *law educator*
Krause, Charles Joseph *otolaryngologist*
Moore, Faye Halfacre *jewelry manufacturer*
Pettersen, Kjell Will *securities trader, consultant*
Truesdell, Timothy L. *private investor*

Mary Esther
McTyeire, Robert Adams *sound engineer, music company executive, consultant*
Scherf, John George, IV, *lawyer*

Medley
O'Meara, Vicki A. *lawyer*

Melbourne
Arrasmith, William W. *engineering educator*
Ballantyne, Richard Lee *lawyer*
Bostater, Charles R., Jr. *marine engineer, educator*
Brown, Seymour R. *retired lawyer*
Buchanan, Richard Kent *electronics company executive*
Burton, Dale Edward *aerospace engineering exectuve*
Cacciatore, S. Sammy *lawyer*
Catanese, Anthony James *academic administrator*
Cavallucci, Eugene S. (Gene Cavallucci) *lawyer*
Dixon, Richard Dean *lawyer, educator*
Fox, Thomas George *academic administrator*
Greenblatt, Hellen Chaya *immunologist, microbiologist*
Grenevicki, Lance Francis *surgeon*
Hament, Andrew Stanton *lawyer*
Hughes, A. N. *psychotherapist*
Jones, Elaine Hancock *humanities educator*
King, Virginia Shattuck *painter, retired school nurse, educator*
Koenig, Harold Paul *management consultant, ecologist, evangelist, writer*
Lakshmikantham, Vangipuram *mathematics professor*
Lance, Howard L. *communications executive, industrial engineer*
Laposata, Joseph Samuel *army officer*
Magee, Thomas Henry *radiologist, educator*
Maloratsky, Leo G. *electrical engineer*
Mikolajczyk, Mark S. *publishing executive*
Nelson, Gordon Leigh *chemist, educator*
Pocoski, David John *cardiologist*
Simokaitis, Frank Joseph *military officer, lawyer*
Storrs, Eleanor Emerett *science administrator, consultant*
Trachtman, Jerry H. *lawyer*
Trefry, John H. III *chemical oceanographer, educator*
Ward, William Francis, Jr. *real estate investment broker*
Weaver, Lynn Edward *academic administrator, consultant, editor*
Wiseman, Floyd Landis *chemist*
Zabel, Dianne Donnelly *retired elementary school educator*

Melbourne Beach
Carter, Mikele Stander *lawyer*
Glaubinger, Lawrence David *retired manufacturing company executive*

Melrose
Burt, Alvin Victor, Jr. *journalist*

Merritt Island
McClanahan, Leland *university director*
Roub, Bryan R(oger) *electronics executive*
Smith, David Edward *small business owner, aerospace engineer, aerospace scientist*
Yoh, William Harry, Jr. *music educator*

Mexico Beach
Mullen, John P. *retired government executive*

Miami
Acosta, Alex (Rene Alexander Acosta) *prosecutor, former federal agency administrator*
Addy, Dawn Emerson *adult education educator, consultant*
Aguirre-Sacasa, Francisco Xavier *international banker, diplomat*
Ajamil, Luis *civil engineer*
Allen, Charles Norman *television, film and video producer*
Alperin, Stanley I. *writer, editor, consultant*
Alschuler, Al *freelance/self-employed writer*
Alvarez, Cesar L. *lawyer*
Amber, Laurie Kaufman *lawyer*
Amos, Betty Giles *food service executive, accountant*
Anderson, Douglas Richard *ophthalmologist, educator, researcher*
Anderson, Terence James *law educator*
Angones, Frank R. (Francisco Angones) *lawyer*
Arango, Jorge Sanin *architect*
Arango, Penelope Corey *psychologist, consultant*
Arison, Micky *cruise line company executive, professional sports team owner*
Arison, Shari *investment company executive*
Arsht, Adrienne *lawyer, broadcast executive, bank executive*
Baker, Thomas Eugene *law educator*
Bandstra, Emmalee S. *physician, pediatrician, researcher, educator*
Bannard, Walter Darby *artist, art critic*
Barkett, Rosemary *federal judge*
Batcheller, Joe Ann *entrepreneur*
Baumberger, Charles Henry *lawyer*
Becerra, Robert John *lawyer*
Becker, Steven Richard *beverage corporation executive, consultant*
Beckwitt, Richard *construction executive*
Benestante, Vincenzo *writer*
Benjamin, Latanya T. *dermatologist*
Berley, David Richard *lawyer*
Berman, Bruce Judson *lawyer*
Bird, Vincent G. *urologist, researcher, educator*
Birns, Ira Michael *corporate financial executive*
Black, Creed Carter *newspaper executive*
Black, Roy *lawyer*
Blechman, Wilbur Jordan *medical educator*
Block, Norman Louis *oncologist, educator*
Bloom, Mark David *lawyer*
Blumberg, Edward Robert *lawyer*
Bogusky, Alex *advertising executive*
Bolooki, Hooshang *cardiac surgeon*
Borkan, William Noah *electronics executive, biomedical engineer, entrepreneur, venture capitalist, real estate developer*
Bowden, Helen Frances *psychologist*
Braman, Norman *automotive and former sports team executive*
Bravo, Irene Maria *psychologist, educator*
Brochin, Robert M. *lawyer*
Brodsky, Richard Eugene *lawyer*
Bronis, Stephen Jay *lawyer*
Brooten, Dorothy *retired dean, nursing educator*
Brown, Robert Donald *lawyer*
Buchwald, Peter Sandor *science association director*
Burke, Redmond Paul *pediatric cardiologist, surgeon*
Burnett, Henry *lawyer*
Burr, Scott Allen *lawyer*
Camner, Howard *writing educator, writer, poet*
Cano, Margarita *artist, consultant, retired librarian*
Capraro, Franz *accountant*
Cardenas, Diana Delia *academic administrator, retired physician, educator*
Casey, Daniel Arthur *lawyer*
Cento, Juan N. *delivery service executive*
Cenziper, Debbie *journalist*
Chabrow, Penn Benjamin *lawyer*

Chaplin, Harvey R. *wine and liquor wholesale executive*
Chapman, Alvah Herman, Jr. *retired newspaper executive*
Chasen, Jerry Simon *lawyer*
Chen, JiuHua *physicist, geophysicist, educator, materials scientist*
Chidsey, John W. *food service executive*
Chiron, Harlan S. *orthopedic surgeon, educator*
Chisholm, Robert E. *architect*
Clarke, Peter John *computer scientist, educator, educational consultant*
Clarkson, John G. *academic administrator, ophthalmologist*
Clemence, Cheryl Lynn *systems administrator*
Codina, Armando M. *real estate developer*
Cohen, Jeffrey Michael *lawyer*
Comras, Rema *retired library director*
Connor, Terence Gregory *lawyer*
Cooper, Johnnie Edward, Jr. *advocate*
Cosgrove, John Francis *lawyer, mayor*
Cotayo, Charles *journalist, film producer, writer, critic*
Cristol, A. Jay *federal judge*
Critchlow, Richard H. *lawyer*
Curtis, Karen Haynes *lawyer*
Dann, Oliver Townsend *psychoanalyst, psychiatrist, educator*
Dasburg, John Harold *restaurant executive*
David, Christopher Mark *lawyer*
Davis, Edward Bertrand *retired federal judge, lawyer*
de Cespedes, Jorge L. *pharmaceutical executive*
Dede, Mehmet Ismet Can *robotics researcher, educator*
Delehanty, Suzanne *museum director*
de Leon, Lidia Maria *magazine editor*
Diaz, Manuel A. *mayor*
Dimitrijevic, Marko *finance company executive*
Dimitriou, Dolores Ennis *computer consultant*
DJ Craze, (Aristh Delgado) *disc jockey*
Dominguez-Bendala, Juan *medical educator*
Donelan, Mark Anthony *physicist*
Dorion, Robert Charles *entrepreneur, investor*
Duchesne, Carlos A. *epidemiologist, military officer*
Dunn, Richard M. *lawyer*
Eaton, Joel Douglas *lawyer*
Eftekhari, Nasser *physiatrist*
Ehrlich, Morton *marketing executive, management consultant*
Eisdorfer, Carl *psychiatrist, health facility administrator*
Ellek, Antonio *management consultant*
Elsas, Louis Jacob, II, *medical educator*
England, Arthur Jay, Jr. *lawyer, former state justice*
Enriquez, Cristino Catud *radiologist, internist, cardiologist*
Epstein, Gary M. *lawyer*
Eshraghi, Adrien A. *head and neck surgeon, medical educator, researcher*
España, Lourdes Maria *mathematics professor*
Essen, Richard Joel *lawyer*
Fain, Richard David *cruise line executive*
Falco-Leshin, JoAnna M. *literature and language professor*
Fatovic, Robert Dean *lawyer*
Feinberg, Wendie *television producer*
Feito, Jose *architect*
Fernandez, Alberto De Dios *physician*
Fernandez, Jorge Luis *lawyer*
Ferrell, Milton Morgan, Jr. *lawyer*
Fichtner, Margaria *journalist*
Fine, Rana Arnold *chemical and physical oceanographer*
Fish, Stanley Eugene *dean, language educator*
Fishman, Lewis Warren *lawyer, educator*
Fleming, Joseph Z. *lawyer*
Floyd, Suzanne Elvira Izzo *music educator*
Foote, Edward Thaddeus, II, *academic administrator, lawyer*
Freeman, Gill Sherryl *judge*
Freeman, Lewis Bernard *forensic accountant, lawyer*
Freire, Jose A. *physicist, writer*
Freshwater, Michael Felix *hand surgeon, educator*
Frigo, James Peter Paul *industrial hardware company executive*
Frost, Phillip *pharmaceutical executive, dermatologist*
Furst, Alex Julian *thoracic and cardiovascular surgeon*
Galatas, Ruth Ann *musician, publishing executive, educator*
Gang, Robert C. *lawyer*
Garrett, Richard G. *lawyer*
Gilbert, John Ray *geneticist, researcher*
Ginsberg, Myron David *neurologist*
Glaser, Thomas William *educational administrator*
Goel, Steve *treasurer*
Golden, John Dennis *lawyer*
Goldstein, Adam M. *cruise line executive*
Gómez Martinez, Juan Carlos *advertising executive*
Gong, Edmond Joseph *lawyer*
Gonzalez, Eddie *advertising executive*
Goodwin, Kelly Dee *microbiologist, researcher*
Gragg, Karl Lawrence *lawyer*
Green, Barth *neurosurgeon*
Green, Jonathan H. *lawyer*
Greer, Alan Graham *lawyer*
Gross, Bruce E. *construction executive*
Gross, Leslie Jay *lawyer, real estate broker, mortgage company executive*
Grossman, Robert Louis *lawyer*
Gutiérrez, Nicolás, Jr. *lawyer*
Gyllenhaal, Anders *editor*
Hall, Adam Stuart *lawyer*
Hall, Andrew Clifford *lawyer*
Halsey, Douglas Martin *lawyer*
Hampton, John Lewis *retired newspaper editor*
Hampton, Mark Garrison *architect*
Harezi, Ilonka Jo *medical technology research executive*
Harmon, Monica Renee *music educator*
Harrison, Stanley L. *editor, educator, writer*
Hartz, Steven Edward Marshall *lawyer, educator*
Heggen, Arthur William *insurance company executive*
Helfand, Leonard T. *lawyer*
Henderson, Gene M. *marketing professional*
Heros, Roberto Cosme C. *neurosurgeon*
Herz, Marvin Ira *psychiatrist, researcher*
Heuer, Robert Maynard, II, *opera company executive*
Hickey, John Heyward (Jack) *lawyer*
Hicks, Jeff J. *advertising executive*
Highsmith, Shelby *federal judge*
Higley, Bruce Wadsworth *orthodontist*
Himburg, Susan Phillips *dietician, educator*
Hochstein, Leonard Mark *plastic surgeon*
Hoffman, Kenneth Cary *lawyer*
Hoffman, Larry J. *lawyer*
Houlihan, Gerald John *lawyer*
Howell, Ralph Rodney *pediatrician, geneticist, educator*
Huang, Xiao-Lan *chemist*
Hudson, Robert Franklin, Jr. *lawyer*
Humphrey, Christine M. *lawyer*
Ibarguen, Alberto *foundation administrator, former newspaper executive*
Imperato, Joseph John *lawyer, composer*
Irwin, Robert W. *medical educator*
Iver, Robert Drew *dentist*
Jacobson, Bernard *lawyer*
Jaffe, Jonathan M. *construction executive*
Jamieson, Mark T. *corporate financial executive*
Jhabvala, Farrokh *lawyer*
Johnston, Philip Connelly *lawyer*
Jones, William Kinzy *materials engineering educator*
Kahn, Barbara E. *dean, marketing educator*
Kahn, Jack Merrill *television producer*
Kanet, Roger Edward *political science professor*
Kaplan, Betsy Hess *retired school board member*
Karp, Carol *ophthalmologist, educator*
Kasbar, Michael J. *energy executive*
Katz, Sandra *educational consultant, psychologist, education educator*
Kavoukjian, Michael Edward *lawyer*
Kent, Amy Elizabeth *criminologist*
King, Booker Terry, Jr. *surgeon*
King, James Lawrence *federal judge*
Kislak, Jean Hart *art director*
Kitsos, Constantine Nicholas *plastic surgeon*
Klass, Roni *literature and language professor*
Klock, Joseph Peter, Jr. *lawyer*
Korchin, Judith Miriam *lawyer*
Kravitz, Steven J. *lawyer*
Kreitzer, Michael N. *lawyer*
Krieger, Albert J. *lawyer*
Kurzban, Ira Jay *lawyer*
Lampen, Richard Jay *lawyer, investment banker*
Lancaster, Kenneth G. *lawyer*
Landsberg, David *publishing executive*
Landy, Burton Aaron *lawyer*
Lasseter, Kenneth Carlyle *pharmacologist*
Lawrence, David, Jr. *journalist, early childhood advocate*
Leatherman, Stephen Parker *geologist, educator, writer*
Leeder, Ellen Lismore *literature and language professor, literary critic*
Leibowitz, Mark Alan *lawyer*
Lemberg, Louis *cardiologist, educator*
Levine, Robert Jeffrey *lawyer*
Levy, Cesar *mechanical engineer, educator*
Lew, Salvador *radio station executive*
Lewis, John Milton *cable television company executive*
Lipcon, Charles Roy *lawyer*
Lippman, Marc Estes *oncologist, educator, medical researcher*
Llorente, Maria Dorta *psychiatrist, geriatrician, educator*
Long, Maxine Master *lawyer*
Loria, Jeffrey H. *sports team executive*
Louis, Paul Adolph *lawyer*
Lubarsky, David Alan *anesthesiologist, educator*
Lynch, Catherine Gores *social services administrator*
Magrath, Kathleen Barry *retired municipal official*
Maidique, Modesto Alex *academic administrator*
Makki, Shamila *project manager engineer, researcher*
Marcus, Stanley *federal judge*
Martin, Jacques *professional hockey coach and sports team executive*
Martinez-Canas, Maria *photography educator*
Martinez-Fraga, Pedro J. *lawyer*
Mathee, Kalai *research scientist, educator*
Maulion, Richard Peter *psychiatrist, physician, neurolinguist*
Mayfield, (Britt) Max *meteorologist*
McCabe, Robert Howard *college president*
McLaughlin, Margaret Brown *adult education educator, writer*
Medina Milgrom, Genie *pharmaceutical company executive*
Mehta, Eileen Rose *lawyer*
Melesse, Assefa Mekonnen *engineering educator, researcher*
Mena, Daniel *lawyer, arbitrator*
Menendez Cambo, Patricia *lawyer*
Michaels, Todd Jordan *lawyer*
Miller, Raymond Vincent, Jr. *lawyer*
Miller, Stuart A. *construction executive*
Miller Udell, Bronwyn *judge*
Milstein, Richard Craig *lawyer*
Moody, Jacqueline Elaine *music educator*
Mooers, Christopher Northrup Kennard *physical oceanographer, educator*
Morgan, Marabel *writer*
Muench, Karl Hugo *clinical geneticist*
Murphy, Timothy James *lawyer*
Nadeau, Joseph Eugene *health care management, information systems consultant*
Nahmad, Albert H. *manufacturing executive*
Natoli, Joseph T. *financial administrator, former publishing executive*
Navlakha, Jainendra *computer scientist, educator, dean*
Nestor Castellano, Brenda Diana *real estate company executive*
Neu, Charles Eric *historian, educator*
Newton, Terry Fernando *health facility specialist, writer*
Nostro, Louis *lawyer*
Nuernberg, William Richard *lawyer*
Nunez-Lawton, Miguel G. *financial analyst*
O'Bryon, Linda Elizabeth *broadcast executive*
O'Connor, Kathleen Mary *lawyer*
Olvey, Stephen Earl *internist*
O'Neal, Shaquille Rashaun *professional basketball player*
Orlin, Karen J. *lawyer*
Osinski, Martin Henry *healthcare consultant*
Osman, Edith Gabriella *lawyer*
Ovelmen, Richard J. *lawyer*
Page, Larry Keith *neurosurgeon, educator*
Panthaki, Zubin Jal *medical educator, plastic surgeon*
Papy, Charles C. III *lawyer*
Parks, Arva Moore *historian*
Pastoriza, Julio *lawyer*
Patrie, Cheryl Christine *elementary school educator*
Payton, Gary Dwayne *professional basketball player*
Pelton, Margaret Marie Miller *retired art educator, academic administrator, artist*
Perez, Jorge M. *real estate developer*
Pericak-Vance, Margaret A. *medical geneticist, educator, health facility administrator*
Persoff, Myron Mayer *plastic surgeon*
Pfeiffer, Mary Louise *artist, educator*
Pfund, Randy (Randell Pfund) *professional sports team executive*
Pham, Si Mai *cardiothoracic surgeon*
Pilafian, Audrey Kalenian *music educator*
Pitts, Leonard Garvey, Jr. *columnist, writer*
Podhurst, Aaron Samuel *lawyer*
Pomeranz, Felix *accounting educator*
Ponzi Kay, Marylou *human resources specialist*
Porter, Wayne Randolph *dermatologist*
Poston, Rebekah Jane *lawyer*
Pratt, John Patrick *lawyer*
Puliafito, Carmen Anthony *ophthalmologist, healthcare executive*
Quentel, Albert Drew *lawyer*
Quirantes, Albert M. *lawyer*
Raffel, Leroy B. *real estate developer*
Ramirez, Hanley *professional baseball player*
Rawl, Arthur Julian (Lord of Cursons) *corporate director, retail executive, consultant, accountant, writer*
Reilly, Kenneth James *lawyer*
Reiter, Luis *lawyer*
Richards-Vital, Claudia *small business owner, recreational facility executive*
Ricordi, Camillo *surgeon, researcher*
Riley, Patrick James *professional basketball coach, professional sports team executive*
Risi, Louis James, Jr. *manufacturing executive*
Robins, Craig *construction executive*
Robles, Carlos *hematologist, oncologist*
Rodriguez, Irmina Bestard *science educator*
Rodriguez, Josefa Nieves *special education educator, language educator*
Rodriguez, René F. *orthopedic surgeon*
Rodriguez-Walling, Matilde Barcelo *special education educator*
Roman, Ediberto *law educator*
Rosenbaum, Allan *public administration educator, academic administrator, international governance advisor*
Rosinek, Jeffrey *judge*
Rossi, William Matthew *lawyer*
Rothman, David Bill *lawyer*
Rothstein, Ronald *professional basketball coach*
Rourke, Diane McLaughlin *librarian*
Rubell, Donald *gynecologist, hotel executive, art collector*
Rubin, Steven D. *lawyer*
Rubino, Frank A. *lawyer*
Rusconi, Paolo *pediatric cardiologist*
Russell, Elbert Winslow *neuropsychologist*
Russell, James Webster, Jr. *editor, columnist*
Saland, Deborah *psychotherapist, educator*
Saldana, Alfonso Manuel *lawyer*
Salinas, María Elena *newscaster, columnist*
Salvaneschi, Luigi *real estate developer, management consultant, educator*
Samole, Myron Michael *lawyer, management consultant*
Sanchez, Danmary *research scientist*
Santiago, Raymond *library director, educator*
Savage, James Francis *editor*
Schafer, Marie *nurse, educator*
Schally, Andrew Victor *endocrine oncologist, researcher*
Scheer, Mark Jeffrey *lawyer*
Schor, Olga Seemann *mental health counselor, real estate broker*
Schuette, Charles A. *lawyer*
Schulman, Clifford A. *lawyer*
Schwartz, Kessel *modern language educator*
Scully, Sean Patrick *orthopaedic surgeon, educator*
Sears, John Patrick *lawyer*
Seitz, Patricia Ann *judge*
Shannon, Randy Lannard *college football coach*
Sherman, Andrew Lawrence *physiatrist, educator*
Sherman, Beatrice Ettinger *hotel executive*
Shore, H. Allan *lawyer*
Shulman, Allan T. *architect*
Shusterman, Nathan *underwriter, financial consultant*
Siegel, Paul *judge*
Silber, Norman Jules *lawyer*
Simmons, Sherwin Palmer *lawyer*
Simpson, Joe Leigh *obstetrics and gynecology educator*
Sirvén, José E. *lawyer*
Skolnick, S. Harold *lawyer*
Skyler, Jay S. *medical educator, consultant*
Small, Daniel I. *lawyer*
Smalling, William E. *pediatrician, neonatologist*
Smith, Richard C. (Dick) *lawyer*
Solomon, Michael Bruce *lawyer*
Spear, Laurinda Hope *architect*
Stanley, Sherry A. *lawyer*
Stansell, Leland Edwin, Jr. *lawyer, mediator, educator*
Stavridis, Jim (James George Stavridis) *career military officer*
Stebbins, Paul H. *energy executive*
Stein, Allan Mark *lawyer*
Steinbaum, Bernice *art dealer*
Steinberg, Marty *lawyer*
Stewart, Adam Mark *hotel executive*
Stokes, Paul Mason *lawyer*
Strafer, G. Richard *lawyer*
Sustana, Mark *lawyer, construction executive*
Swienton, Gregory T. *transportation company executive*
Tejada, Francisco *physician, educator*
Thaller, Seth Ray *plastic surgeon*
Thornburg, Frederick Fletcher *lawyer, educator*
Traurig, Robert Henry *lawyer*
Treyz, Joseph Henry *librarian*
Tsai, John Jengshyong *publishing executive*
Underwood, Joseph Warren *athletic trainer, educator*
Ungaro-Benages, Ursula Mancusi *federal judge*
Upshaw, Anthony N. *lawyer*
Van Wyck, George Richard *insurance company executive*
Vento, M. Thérèse *lawyer*
Veziroglu, Turhan Nejat *mechanical engineering educator, researcher*
Wade, Dwyane (Dwayne Tyrone Wade Jr.) *professional basketball player*
Walton, Rodney Earl *lawyer*
Walz, Leo R. *conductor*
Warren, Mark Edward *cruise line executive, lawyer*
Wated, Guillermo *psychology educator*
Watson, Doug *information technology executive*
Wax, William Edward *photojournalist*
Weiner, Lawrence *lawyer*
Weinger, Steven Murray *lawyer*
Weinstein, Alan Edward *lawyer*
Weinstein, Andrew H. *lawyer*
Weiser, Ralph Raphael *oil industry executive*
Weiser, Sherwood Manuel *hotel and corporation executive, lawyer*
West, Macdonald *real estate executive*
Wheeler, Steve Dereal *neurologist*
Williams, Jason Chandler *professional basketball player*
Willis, Dontrelle *professional baseball player*
Wilson, Thomas Strong, Jr., (Tam) *judge*
Wing, James David *lawyer*
Wiseheart, Malcolm Boyd, Jr. *lawyer*
Wolff, Grace Susan *pediatric cardiologist*
Wolfson, Aaron Howard *radiation oncologist, educator*
Woolworth, Eric S. *professional sports team executive*
Zack, Stephen Neal *lawyer*
Zaleski-Vegazo, Ilene *librarian*
Zayas-Bazan, Eduardo *foreign language educator*
Zaydon, Thomas John, Jr. *plastic surgeon*
Zubieta, Alberto Aleman *construction executive*

Miami Beach
Arbuz, Joseph Robert *lawyer*
Camber, Diane Woolfe *museum director*
Carnase, Thomas Paul *graphics designer, consultant*
Cohen, Philip Herman *accountant*
Foote, Gwendolyn Sue *middle school educator, artist*
Freshwater, Shawna Marie *neuropsychologist, clinical psychologist, cognitive neuroscientist*
Gardiner, Pamela Nan *performing company executive*
Gitlow, Abraham Leo *retired dean*
Howard, Melvin *financial executive*
Justiniani, Federico Roberto *internist, educator*
Kalsner-Silver, Lydia *psychologist*
Katz, Brian Jeffrey *dermatologist*
Lanzkron, Rolf Wolfgang *manufacturing executive*
Lawson, Eve Kennedy *dancer*
Mandy, Stephen Howard *dermatologist, educator*
McMahon, Joseph Einar *lawyer, consultant*
Palamara, Sherry A. *psychologist*
Popper, Joanna *marketing executive, filmmaker*
Rosenhaus, Drew *professional sports agent*
Rut, Wanda E. *artist, educator, writer*
Sharlach, Jeffrey *public relations executive*
Shula, Don Francis *retired professional football coach, professional sports team executive*
Taylor, Leslie George *mining and finance company executive*
Todd, Christopher Michael *marketing executive, consultant*

Miami Gardens
Bell, Taunjah Patrease *research scientist*
Cabrera, Miguel (Jose Miguel Cabrera) *professional baseball player*
Conley, James W. *English language educator, language arts educator*
Ersek, Gregory Joseph Mark *lawyer*
Light, Alfred Robert *law educator*
Robinson, Beatriz Gonzalez *academic administrator*
Vangates, Dess *retired military officer*

Miami Lakes
Cohen, Ronald J. *lawyer*

Miami Shores
Diener, Betty Jane *business educator*
Favalora, John Clement *archbishop*
Gonzalez, Pedro Blas *philosopher, educator*

Miami Springs
Neasman, Annie Ruth *health facility administrator*

Milton
Collins, Joda Lee *minister*
McKinney, George Harris, Jr. *training systems analyst*

Miramar
Abbott, Paul Scott *writer, public relations executive, consultant*
Asika-Enahoro, Chidi Maureen *rehabilitation services professional, consultant, writer*
Catalano, Carl Philip *small business owner*
Huang, Guiyou *dean, English studies educator, writer*
Navarro, Richard *banker*
Stewart Simpson, Donnamay Angela *interior designer*

Monticello
Johnson, Artis *educational administrator, clergyman*

Montverde
Revis-Pyke, Robin Lynn *director*

Mount Dora
Crone, Eugene N. *addictions specialist, retired educator*
Kirton, Jennifer Myers *artist*
Scharfenberg, Margaret Ellan *retired elementary school educator*
Trundle, W(infield) Scott *publishing executive newspaper, lawyer*

Mulberry
Bowman, Hazel Lois *retired English language educator*

Naples
Adams, John Marshall *lawyer*
Alpert, Hollis *writer*
Anderson, John Thomas *lawyer*
Askins, Wallace Boyd *manufacturing executive*
Badash, Sandi B. *artist, art educator*
Berman, Robert S. *marketing consultant*
Bileydi, Sumer *advertising agency executive*
Blevins, Charles Russell *publishing executive*
Blumenthal, Ronnie *lawyer*
Bradley, Charles MacArthur *retired architect*
Bruce, Jackson Martin, Jr. *lawyer*
Budd, David Glenn *lawyer*
Burdick, Robert W. *newspaper editor*
Butler, Frederick George *retired drug company executive*
Capelle-Frank, Jacqueline Aimee *writer*
Cimino, Richard Dennis *lawyer*
Clapp, Roger Howland *retired publishing executive*
Clarke, John Patrick *retired newspaper publisher*
Cobb, Brian Eric *broadcast executive*
Cotrone, Janice Lynne *nursing consultant*
Cox, Joe Bruce *lawyer*
Crandall, Blane Mitchell *obstetrician, gynecologist*
Crehan, Joseph Edward *lawyer*
Delano, Victor *retired naval officer*
Dorio, Martin Matthew, Jr. *real estate company executive, investor*
Doub, William Offutt *lawyer*
Dykstra, David Allen *real estate broker*
Eldridge, David Carlton *art and antique appraiser*
Ericson, Roger Delwin *lawyer, forest resource company executive*
Faison, William Franklin, II, *lawyer, retired manufacturing corporation executive*
Frantzen, Henry Arthur *retired investment company executive*
Frazer, John Howard *tennis association and retired manufacturing executive*
Gade, Marvin Francis *retired paper company executive*
Gehring, David Austin *cardiologist, physician, health facility administrator*
Gelfand, Neal *oil industry executive*
Goldman, Joel J. *retired lawyer*
Gopman, Jonathan E. *lawyer*
Greene, David *surgeon, researcher*
Hall, Beverly Barton *librarian*
Hansen, Claire V. *financial executive*
Jones, Philip Howard *broadcast journalist*
Keller, Theodore G., Jr. *investment property owner and manager*
Kirby, Charles William, Jr. *dancer, choreographer*
Kley, John Arthur *banker*
Kozitka, Richard Eugene *retired consumer products company executive*
Kvetko, Colleen M. *bank executive*
LaRusso, Anthony Carl *company executive, lecturer, consultant*
Leitner, Alfred *retired mathematical physicist, educator, educational film producer*
Lewis, Gordon Gilmer *golf course architect*
Lickhalter, Merlin *architect*
Llewellyn, Leonard Frank *real estate broker, investment company executive*
Lowery, William Herbert *lawyer*
Ludwig, Richard Joseph *small business owner*
Lynn, Larry (Verne Lauriston Lynn) *engineering executive*
Madigan, Joseph Edward *financial executive, director, consultant*
Mahalawich, Anne Mary *retired mathematics educator*
Marienthal, George *telecommunications industry executive*
Marino, William Francis *telecommunications industry executive, consultant*
Marshall, Charles *communications company executive*
Martinuzzi, Leo Sergio, Jr. *banker*
Mavrides, Elaine *retired mental health services professional, retired social worker*
McSwiney, Charles Ronald *lawyer*
Mehaffey, John Allen *marketing executive, publishing executive*
Mills, Dorothy Jane (Dorothy Z. Seymour) *writer, editor, consultant*
Monaghan, Thomas Stephen *philanthropist*
Moore, Mechlin Dongan *communications executive, management consultant*
Myers, Robert Jay *retired aerospace transportation executive*
Norton, Elizabeth Wychgel *retired lawyer*
Ordway, John Danton *retired pension fund administrator, lawyer, accountant*
Parry, Timothy R. *lawyer*
Peck, Bernard Sidney *lawyer*
Penniman, Nicholas Griffith, IV, *retired newspaper publisher*
Petersen, David L. *lawyer*
Pfister, Raymond Lawrence *otolaryngologist*
Randall, Neil Warren *gastroenterologist*
Riggs, Fletcher Eugene *economist, consultant*
Rigor, Bradley Glenn *lawyer*
Rosen, Michel *retired prosthodontist*
Rowe, Herbert Joseph *retired trade association executive*
Salentine, Thomas James *pharmaceutical executive*
Sampson, John Eugene *food products executive, consultant*
Schwartz, Stephen Gregory *ophthalmologist*
Seavey, Christopher Gordon *psychotherapist, alcohol/drug abuse services professional*
Sekowski, Cynthia Jean *health products executive, medical consultant, contact lens specialist*
Silvestri, Vito Nicholas *communications educator*
Slaff, Allan Paul *military officer, academic administrator, educator, entrepreneur*
Smith, Numa Lamar, Jr. *lawyer*
Sowman, Harold Gene *ceramics engineer, researcher*
Stastny, John Anton *real estate executive*
Stevens, William Kenneth *lawyer*
Suziedelis, Vytautas A. *retired engineering corporation executive*
Swanson, Donald Frederick *retired food company executive*
Temple, Donald *retired allergist, dermatologist*
Thampi, Mohan Varghese *environmental health and civil engineer*
Thomas, Gary Lynn *information technology executive*
Thomas, John Melvin *retired surgeon*
Vanderslice, Thomas Aquinas *electronics executive*
Vickrey, Robert Remsen *artist*
von Arx, Dolph William *food products executive*
Vumbacco, Joseph V. *health services executive*
Wedel-Cowgill, Millie Redmond *secondary school, performing arts, communication and education educator*
Weiss, Daniel Edwin *minister, educator*
Westman, Carl Edward *lawyer*
White, Roy Bernard *performing arts association administrator*
Whitman, Burke William *health services executive*
York, Tina *painter*

Navarre
Bare Grounds, Patricia Kelly *athletic trainer, small business owner*

Neptune Beach
Palmer, Jane G. *music educator*

New Port Richey
Adams, Jean Marie *biology professor*
Assini, Vincent Paul *financial executive*
Charters, Karen Ann Elliott *critical care nurse, health facility administrator*
Day, Peter Rodney *geneticist, educator*
Focht, Theodore Harold *lawyer, educator*
Hanahan, James Lake *retired insurance executive*
Lake, Victor Hugo *former manufacturing company executive*
Maysilles, Daniel Bruce *pharmaceutical services executive*
Miller, Harvey William *retired military officer*
Mills, Edward Warren *corporation executive*
O'Farrell, Mark Theodore *religious organization administrator*
Rhodes, Eric Foster *employee relations consultant, writer*
Sebring, Marjorie Marie Allison *former home furnishings company executive*
Vajk, Hugo *manufacturing executive*

New Smyrna Beach
Faherty, Sandra Lee *social worker, psychotherapist*

Newberry
Thornton, J. Ronald *technology consultant*

Niceville
Crawford, Jackie R. *retired federal agency administrator*
DeLucca, Michael C. *business executive*
Havens, Jason Edward *lawyer*
Litke, Donald Paul *acquisition executive, retired military officer*
Rasmussen, Robert Dee *retired real estate appraiser*
Warren, J. Richard *editor, retired humanities educator*

Nokomis
Beck, George William *retired industrial engineer*
Hawley, Phillip Eugene *investment banker*
Lockledge, Jack E. *retired principal*
Novak, Robert Louis *civil engineer, pavement management consultant*

North Fort Myers
Bayuk, Thomas M., Sr. *restaurant owner, writer*
Gray, Carlos Gibson *restaurant manager, agricultural products supplier, entertainer, television producer*
Miller, William Charles *lawyer*

North Miami
Plotkin-Spotts, Sharon Lee *protective services official, educator*
Stills, Stephen *musician, vocalist, composer*

North Miami Beach
Clanton, Wendy McCarley *elementary school educator, assistant principal*
Kropp, James Herbert, Sr. *investment manager*
Sorosky, Jeri P. *academic administrator*
Zipkin, Sheldon Lee *lawyer, educator*

North Palm Beach
Brophy, Gilbert Thomas *lawyer*
Dreyfoos, Alexander W., Jr. *investor, research scientist*
Hayman, Richard Warren Joseph *conductor*
Higgins, Jay F. *diversified financial services company executive*
Kaplan, Muriel Sheerr *sculptor*
Lavine, Alan *columnist, writer*
Lynch, William Walker *banker*
Nicklaus, Jack William *professional golfer*
Stein, Mark Rodger *allergist*

Oakland Park
Atkinson, Christopher Lee *county official*
Kilpatrick, Clifton Wayne *book dealer*

Ocala
Altenburger, Karl Marion *allergist*
Booth, Jane Schuele *real estate company officer, real estate broker*
Hammes, C. Leslie Greene *musician, educator*
Harris, Charles Edison *banker, lawyer*
Hodges, William Terrell *federal judge*
Hudson, Ann Elizabeth *music educator*
Kilmark, Robert Martin *retired lab administrator*
Massa, Conrad Harry *retired religious studies educator*
Mishkin, Michael Lawrence *psychologist, educator*
Ray, Ruth Alice Yancey *retired rancher, real estate developer*
Schwenk, Gordon Cameron *ophthalmologist*
Sostilio, Robert Francis *office equipment marketing consultant*
Strait, William Robert *computer technician*
Tesmer, Nancy Ann Stutler *retired librarian*

Ocean Ridge
Mueller, Gerard *realtor, investor, former Internet executive*

Ocoee
Godsell, Richard Vernon *elementary school educator, researcher*

Okeechobee
Bishop, Sid Glenwood *union official*

Oldsmar
Brunner, George Matthew *management consultant, retired manufacturing executive*
Caronis, George John *insurance executive*
Craft Davis, Audrey Ellen *writer, educator*
Gambone, Victor, Jr. *internist, geriatrician*
Thompson, Mack Eugene *historian, educator*

Opa Locka
Sample, Althea Merritt *retired secondary education educator, conductor*
Wright, Jeanne Elizabeth Jason *advertising executive*

Orange City
Brakeman, Louis Freeman *retired university official*
Orgega, Gregory Luis *hematologist, oncologist*
Ortega, Gregory Luis *hematologist, oncologist*

Orange Park
Fetchero, John Anthony, Jr. *otolaryngologist*
Hunt, J(ulian) Courtenay *artist*
Rice, Ronald James *hospital administrator*

Orlando
Abbott, Charles Warren *retired lawyer*
Ahlers, Glen-Peter, Sr. *law library director, educator, consultant*
Allison, Anne Marie *retired librarian*
Arkin, J. Gordon *lawyer*
Ashe, Diane Davis *psychology professor, sport psychology consultant*
Atwell, George Michael *composer, conductor, musician*
Baker, Peter Mitchell *science association director, laser scientist*
Beckner, Cynthia Byrd *music and elementary school educator*
Bersia, John Cesar *political science educator, editorial writer*
Bhutta, Adeel Aslam *computer engineer, educator*
Bigum, Randall K. *retired military officer*
Blackwell, Bruce Beuford *lawyer*
Blaher, Neal Jonathan *lawyer*
Bodager, Dean W. *epidemiologist*
Boyles, William Archer *lawyer*
Brouillard, Robert Paul *maintenance planning manager*
Brownlee, Thomas Marshall *manufacturing executive*
Brumby, Andrew M. *lawyer*
Caracciolo, Joseph M. *film producer*
Cawthon, Frank H. *retired construction company executive*
Christiansen, Patrick T. *lawyer*
Clem, Alexander Murphree *lawyer*
Clinton, Stephen Michael *academic administrator*
Comfort, Iris Tracy *writer*
Connolly, Joseph Francis, II, *academic administrator, government consultant*
Conti, Louis Thomas Moore *lawyer*
Delfyett, Peter *engineering educator*
DeMara, Ronald Francis *computer engineer, educator*
Deo, Narsingh *computer scientist, educator*
DeVos, Richard Marvin, Sr. *professional sports team owner, former network marketing company executive*
Doppelt, Ava K. *lawyer*
Dunn, William Bruna III *journalist*
Eagan, William Leon *lawyer*
Eastmond-Robinson, June Patricia *nursing educator*
Edwards, James Alfred *lawyer*
Efthimiou, Costas John *physicist, educator, researcher*
Fawsett, Patricia Combs *federal judge*
Fildes, Richard James *lawyer*
Fleming-Brown, Julie A. *attorney, legal consultant*
Flinchbaugh, David Edward *physicist*
Flitsiyan, Elena S. *physicist, physics educator*
Forbes, Daniel Merrill *minister*
Frey, Louis, Jr. *lawyer, federal official*
Fritz, Jim *professional sports team executive*
Gerber, Daniel J. *lawyer*
Gidel, Robert Hugh *real estate investor*
Gilbert, Suzanne E. *lawyer*
Gill, Michele Gregoire *education educator*
Goings, Everett Vernon (Rick) *consumer products company executive*
Gold, I. Randall *lawyer*
Graham, Eleanore Davis *elementary school educator*
Gray, J. Charles *lawyer, cattle rancher*
Haas, Brian D. *surgeon*
Hall, Charlotte Hauch *editor*
Handley, Leon Hunter *lawyer*
Hitt, John Charles *academic administrator*
Hoctor, James Joseph *lawyer*
Hodel, Mary Anne *library director*
Hoepner, Theodore John *banker*
Hornick, Richard Bernard *physician*
Howard, Dwight David, II, *professional basketball player*
Hsu, C.T. *architect*
Hughes, David Henry *manufacturing executive*
Jordan, Grace Carol *music educator*
Kelaher, James Peirce *lawyer*
Kellison, Stephen George *actuarial consultant*
Kennedy, James W. *aerospace transportation executive*
Kincaid, John Peter *science educator*
Klemenz, Christine F. *science educator, researcher*
Knowles, Patricia Marie *science educator*
Kolattukudy, Pappachan Ettoop *medical center executive, biochemist, educator*
Kollas, Chad D. *medical educator*
Krise, Thomas Warren *academic administrator, literature and language professor, retired military officer*
Lefkowitz, Ivan Martin *lawyer*
Leonard, Joseph B. *airline company executive*
Leonhardt, Frederick Wayne *lawyer*
Lewis, Rashard Quovon *professional basketball player*
Liboff, Richard Lawrence *physicist, researcher*
Llewellyn, Ralph Alvin *physics professor*
Lorenz, Mathias *art director*
Madsen, Andrew H. *food service executive*
Marinescu, Dan Cristian *computer sciences educator, consultant*
Martins, Alex *professional sports team executive*
Mason, J. Cheney *lawyer*
Maupin, Elizabeth Thatcher *theater critic*
McMahon, Ed *television and radio personality*
Mock, Frank Mackenzie *lawyer*
Morgan, Thomas I. *manufacturing executive*
Morrisey, Marena Grant *art museum administrator*
Murphrey, Elizabeth Hobgood *history professor, librarian*
Murrah, Ann Ralls Freeman *historical association executive*
Murrell, Robert George *lawyer*
Nadeau, Robert Bertrand, Jr. *lawyer*
Nants, Bruce Arlington *lawyer*
Naser, Saleh A. *medical researcher, educator*
Nashed, M. Zuhair *mathematics professor, editor*
Okun, Neil Jeffrey *vitreoretinal surgeon*
Oneal-Coble, Leslie *lawyer*
Otis, Clarence, Jr. *restaurant executive*
Pierce, Jerry Earl *publishing executive*
Pierce, John Gerald (Jerry) *lawyer*
Pollack, Robert William *psychiatrist, corporate financial executive*
Pyle, Artimus (Thomas Delmar Pyle) *musician*
Qahwash, Murad *engineer, educator*
Ragland, Robert Allen *lawyer*
Rayle, Stephen Lane *criminal justice educator*
Redick, J.J. (Jonathan Clay Redick) *college basketball player*
Reed, John Alton *lawyer*
Reese, Charles Edgar *columnist*
Rosene, Paul Earl *music educator*
Rounsaville, Keith Eugene *lawyer*
Russ, James Matthias *lawyer*
Salzman, Gary Scott *lawyer*
Schultz, Victoria L. *harpist, entertainer, music educator*
Shanahan, Rebecca M. *lawyer*
Sharp, Christina Krieger *retired nursing educator*
Shirek, John Richard *retired savings and loan executive*
Shives, Paula J. *lawyer*
Shub, Harvey Allen *surgeon*
Sims, Roger W. *lawyer*
Skambis, Christopher Charles, Jr. *lawyer*
Smetanka, Sally S. *small business owner*
Smetheram, Herbert Edwin *management consultant*
Smith, Otis Fitzgerald *professional sports team executive, former professional basketball player*
Smyth, Joseph Vincent *manufacturing executive*
Spoonhour, James Michael *lawyer*
Stepter, Charles Raymond, Jr. *law librarian*
Stockton, Richard Lee *lawyer*

Taitt, Earl Paul *psychiatrist, military officer*
Thorpe, Janet Claire *judge*
Vander Weide, Bob *professional sports team executive*
Van Gundy, Stan *professional basketball coach*
Varvak, Mark *mathematician, researcher*
Vaughn, Rosalyn Mae *academic administrator*
Wade, David Allen *graphics designer*
Walker, Roger Craig *mathematics professor*
Wallace, Mark Raymond *physician*
Waltz, Kathleen M. *publishing executive*
Warren, Dean Stuart *artist*
Weaver, Earl D. *theater educator*
Weiss, Christopher John *lawyer*
Wenski, Thomas Gerard *bishop*
Williams, Pat *professional sports team executive*
Wilson, Brenda Marie *secondary school educator*
Yates, Leighton Delevan, Jr. *lawyer*
Yesawich, Peter Charles *advertising executive*
Young, George Cressler *federal judge*
Yu, Chuanzhao *electrical engineer, researcher*

Ormond Beach
Burke, Marguerite Jodi Larcombe *application developer, consultant*
Burt, Wallace Joseph, Jr. *insurance company executive*
Connors, Michele Perrott *wholesale beverage company executive*
Hayes, Larry B. *retired lawyer*
Hodkinson, Sydney Phillip *composer, educator, musician, conductor*
Kanfer, Julian Norman *biochemist, educator*
Keller, Steven Ray *security consultant*
Logan, Sharon Brooks *lawyer*
Lynn, Evelyn Joan *state senator, consultant*
Sugiyama, Akiko *artist*

Osprey
Caradonna, Stephanie Ann *dermatologist*
Dyche, David Bennett, Jr. *management consultant*
Goffard, Lucien H. *language educator*
Jones, George Yovicic *civil engineer*
Partoyan, Garo Arakel *lawyer*
Weathermon, Sidney Earl *retired elementary school educator*

Oviedo
Drummer, Donald Raymond *diversified financial services company executive, educator*
Duda, Richard Frank *architect, engineering executive*
Gendron, Mary W. *retired educator*
MacKenzie, Charles Sherrard *academic administrator*

Ozona
Bennett, John Joseph *electronics executive*

Palatka
~~Baldwin, Allen Adail *retired lawyer, writer*~~
Embree, Mary Evelyn *retired secondary school educator*
Ginn, John Arthur, Jr. *financial consultant*

Palm Bay
Colman, Charles Kingsbury *academic administrator, criminologist*
Elliott, Scott *minister, retired lawyer*
Pattyn, Sue *publishing executive*
Sheets, Fredrick Sidney *retired military officer, auditor*
Whitten, Shannon Nicole *education educator*

Palm Beach
Adler, Frederick Richard *lawyer, corporate financial executive*
Alton, Howard Robert, Jr. *lawyer, food company executive, real estate executive*
Bagby, Joseph Rigsby *financial investor*
Bagby, Martha L. Green *real estate holding company executive, writer, publishing executive*
Callahan, Edward William *chemical engineer, retired manufacturing executive*
Canary, Nancy Halliday *lawyer*
Coleman, Denis Patrick, Jr. *investment banker*
Coudert, Dale Hokin *real estate executive, marketing consultant*
Crawford, Sandra Kay *lawyer*
Devins, Robert Sylvester *retired lawyer*
Dillard, Rodney Jefferson *real estate executive*
Elson, Suzanne Goodman *social services administrator*
Fisher, Fenimore *business development consultant*
Flanagan, Joseph Patrick *advertising executive*
Floeckher, Louise Byrne Weldon *volunteer*
Frankel, Charles James III *banker*
Gaudieri, Alexander V.J. *art historian, educator, museum director*
Harper, Mary Sadler *wealth advisor and relationship manager*
Hope, Margaret Lauten *retired civic worker*
Javits, Joan (Zeeman) *writer, inventor*
Johnson, Theodore Mebane *brokerage house executive*
Karman, James Anthony *manufacturing executive*
Karp, Richard M. *advertising and communications executive*
Kay, Marcia Chellis *writer*
Klotsche, Charles Martin *real estate company executive, photographer, writer, financial columnist*
Levine, Audrey Pearlstein *foundation administrator*
McCarter, Thomas Nesbitt III *investment company executive, consultant*
Moloney, Thomas Walter *management consultant*
Monath, Norman *publishing company executive*
Parker, Ellis Jackson III *lawyer, broadcaster*
Pryor, Hubert *editor, writer, consultant*
Rumbough, Stanley Maddox, Jr. *industrialist*
Simon, Harold *radiologist*
Smith, Jeffery W. *architect*
Tiefel, William Reginald *hotel company executive*

Palm Beach Gardens
Andrews, Holdt *investment banker*
Auerbach, Paul Ira *lawyer*
Baynham, G. Clay *surgeon*
Choi, K.J. (Kyung-ju Choi) *professional golfer*
Couples, Frederick Steven *professional golfer*
Daly, John Patrick *professional golfer*
Duval, David Robert *professional golfer*
Falk, Bernard Henry *trade association executive*
Farina, John *lawyer*
Fleisher, Seymour *manufacturing executive*
Freedman, Warren *lawyer, educator, judge*
Furyk, Jim (James Michael Furyk) *professional golfer*
Gillette, Frank C., Jr. *retired mechanical engineer*
Giordano, Andrew Anthony *retired naval officer*
Granat, Richard Stuart *lawyer, educator*
Harnett, Joseph Durham *oil industry executive*
Holloway, Edward Olin *human services manager*
Jaffe, Jeff Hugh *retired food products executive*
Kahn, David Miller *lawyer, educator*
Kapnick, Samuel Jason *oncologist*
Kleinberg, Lawrence H. *investor, consultant*
Levitt, George *retired chemist*
Mendelson, Richard Donald *former communications company executive*
Mergler, H. Kent *investment counselor*
Mickelson, Phil (Philip Alfred Mickelson Jr.) *professional golfer*
Mills, Christopher James *neurophysiologist, electroneurodiagnostic technologist*
Nelson, Larry Gene *professional golfer*
Newman, Stephen Michael *lawyer*
O'Brien, Thomas George III *lawyer*
Peck, Maryly VanLeer *retired academic administrator, chemical engineer*
Runge, Donald Edward *food wholesale company executive*
Samuels, Fern Jacqueline *artist, educator*
Sonnier, Joseph A. *lab administrator, physician*
Squier, Jack Leslie *sculptor, retired art educator*
Staub, W. Arthur *health care products executive*
Tauber, Mark J. *retired lawyer*
Van Allen, Veronica Elaine *marketing and public relations professional*
VanButsel, Michael R. *real estate broker, construction executive*
Verplank, Scott Rachal *professional golfer*
Wadkins, Lanny Lanston *professional golfer*
Woods, Tiger (Eldrick Woods) *professional golfer*
Zane, Jeffrey P. *lawyer*
Ziglar, James W. *biometrics industry executive, lawyer, educator*

Palm City
Conklin, George Melville *retired food products executive*
Mc Hale, John Joseph *baseball club executive*
Wishart, Ronald Sinclair *retired chemical company executive*

Palm Coast
Afflick, Gilbert Leslie *editor, journalist*
Barnes, Judith Ann *real estate company executive*
Boyer, Kaye Kittle *association management executive*
Cook, Gloria Houston *civic leader*
Duncan, Donald William *lawyer*
Lewis, William Headley, Jr. *manufacturing executive*
Slatner, Thomas Allen *bookseller*

Palm Harbor
Barker, Larry Lee *communications educator*
Calhoun, John Vincent *research scientist*
Grace, John Eugene *business company executive*
Harrell, Carl Randall *plastic surgeon*
Hewitt, Sarah Nichole *educational consultant, researcher*
Jones, Winona Nigels *retired media specialist*
Jordan, Patricia Colgan *physical education educator*
Katzen-Guthrie, Joy *performance artist, engineering executive*
Perkins, Robert Edward *retired secondary school educator*
Rezanka, Thomas W. *lawyer*
Richeson, Hugh Anthony, Jr. *lawyer*
Schultz, Barbara Marie *investment advisor*
Summers-Powell, Alan *lawyer*
Williams, Thomas Arthur *biomedical computing consultant, psychiatrist*

Palm Springs
Abou-Sayed, Hatem *plastic surgeon*

Palmetto Bay
Nakashima, Tadayoshi *retired biochemist, researcher*
Weeks, Marta Joan *retired priest*

Panama City
Barloga, Scott B. *lawyer*
Cortes, Enric *marine biologist*
D'Arcy, Gerald Paul *engineering executive, consultant*
Fejer, T. William *musician, composer, architect, furniture designer*
Hough, Douglas Ralph *museum director*
Lucas, Truett LaVan *retired communications technician*
Patterson, Christopher Nida *lawyer*
Roberts, Paul Craig III *economics professor, writer, columnist*
Rockhill, Marsha *special education educator*
Schafer, John Stephen *poet*

Panama City Beach
Birdwell, Michelle Marie *music educator*
Nelson, Edith Ellen *dietician*
Reading, Anthony John *retired psychiatrist, educator*

Parkland
Froehlich, Fritz Edgar *communications educator, telecommunications scientist*
Harris, Jacqueline Myers *speech/language pathology services professional*

Patrick Afb
Kohn, Paul Franklin *mathematician*
McAlwee, Martin Frederick *lawyer*

Pembroke Pines
Alber, Oro Linda *healthcare educator, consultant*
Embergher, Mary Louise *elementary school educator*
Feldman, Jacqueline *retired small business owner*
Maynard, Shirley *educational association administrator*
Poore, Paul Michael *school system administrator*
Schaefer, Bonnie (E. Bonnie Schaefer) *retail executive*
Schaefer, Marla L. *retail executive*

Pensacola
Apap, Antonio *finance educator, portfolio manager*
Appleyard, Diane Paige *human service administrator*
Arnold, Barry Raynor *philosophy educator, medical ethicist*
Blankenship, Lawrence L. *retired minister*
Bookman, Alan B. *lawyer*
Bowden, Jesse Earle *editor, writer, cartoonist, journalist, educator*
Bozeman, Frank Carmack *lawyer*
Brown, Ernest L. *education educator*
Brown, Susan Louise *philosopher, educator*
Bullock, Ellis Way, Jr. *architect*
Canady, Alexa Irene *pediatric neurosurgeon, educator*
Di, Xu *education educator*
Ewing, Charles William, Jr. *healthcare educator*
Ford, Kenneth M. *computer scientist, educator*
Geeker, Nicholas Peter *lawyer, judge*
Gill, Becky Lorette *retired psychiatrist*
Jones, Harry Gordon *electronics executive*
Kichler, Jack *dermatologist*
Killian, Lewis Martin *sociology educator*
Larson, Barbara Jean *art history professor*
Levin, Fredric Gerson *lawyer*
Maddock, Lawrence Hill *retired language educator, writer*
Maki, Hope Marie (Countess Hope Marie Maki) *artist, educator*
Maygarden, Jerry Louis *healthcare foundation executive*
Mazzeo, Daniel Patrick *aerospace engineer, consultant*
McKenzie, James Franklin *lawyer*
~~Mountcastle, William Wallace, Jr. *retired*~~ *philosophy and religion educator*
Ricard, John H. *bishop, educator*
Robinson, Harold Gilbert *retired military officer, civilian military employee*
Rubardt, Peter Craig *conductor, educator*
Shimmin, Margaret Ann *retired women's health nurse*
Soloway, Daniel Mark *lawyer*
Story, Susan N. *utilities executive*
Stuart, Walter Bynum III *retired banker*
Vinson, C. Roger *federal judge*
Vuksta, Michael Joseph *surgeon*
Windham, John Franklin *lawyer, educator*
Woolf, Kenneth Howard *architect*

Placida
McClister, Michael *writer*
Prabhudesai, Mukund M. *pathology educator, health facility administrator, researcher, academic administrator*

Plant City
Buchman, Kenneth William *lawyer*
Henry, J. Myrle *pharmacist*
Sparkman, Steven Leonard *lawyer*

Plantation
Alisetti, Edwin Luis *engineer, corporate financial executive*
Costa, Paul Joseph *psychologist*
Fellows, John *delivery service executive*
Gewirtzman, Garry Bruce *dermatologist*
Gonshak, Isabelle Lee *nurse, volunteer*
Harris, Eleanor Lynne K. *theology studies educator*
Hsu, Jiun-Jia *engineering educator, transportation engineer*
Nair, Krishnakumar R. *application developer, researcher*
Schink, Robert Kelly *sales executive*
Young, William Benjamin *retired special education educator*

Poinciana
Spero, Barry Melvin *retired health facility administrator*
Williams, Donald John *physicist, researcher*

Polk City
Carr, Richard William *federal program manager*

Pompano Beach
Baslaw-Finger, Annette *education educator, consultant*
Cherla, Gautam V. *physician, nephrologist, researcher*
Endahl, Ethelwyn Mae *elementary education educator, consultant*
Grossman, Daniel V *investor*
Gude, Nancy Carlson *lawyer*
Hinson, Robert William *advertising executive, consultant*
Johnson, Dorothy Curfman *elementary school educator*
Kester, Stewart Randolph *banker*
Phillips, Floyd Leigh *plastic surgeon*
Rifenburgh, Richard Philip *investment company executive*
Roen, Sheldon R. *psychologist, publishing executive*
Shulmister, M(orris) Ross *lawyer*
Williams, Cloretta Mae *retired elementary school educator*

Ponte Vedra
Singh, Vijay *professional golfer*

Ponte Vedra Beach
Agassi, Andre Kirk *retired professional tennis player*
Azinger, Paul *professional golfer*
Blake, James Riley *professional tennis player*
Calcavecchia, Mark *professional golfer*
Campbell, Chad *professional golfer*
Cink, Stewart *professional golfer*
Coria, Guillermo *professional tennis player*
Curtis, Ben Clifford *professional golfer*
Davis, Wendell, Jr. *lawyer*
de Selding, Edward Bertrand *retired bank executive*
Els, Ernie (Theodore Ernest Els) *professional golfer*
Finchem, Tim *sports association executive*
Garcia, Sergio *professional golfer*
Gaudio, Gaston *professional tennis player*
Ginepri, Robby (Robert Louis Ginepri) *professional tennis player*
Green, Hubert *professional golfer*
Grosjean, Sebastien Rene *professional tennis player*
Hamilton, William Berry, Jr. *retired transportation executive*
Harris, John Borgeson *plastic surgeon*
Howell, Charles III *professional golfer*
Johnson, Zach (Zachary Harris Johnson) *professional golfer*
Langer, Bernhard *professional golfer*
Leek, Jay Wilbur *management consultant*
MacKowski, John Joseph *retired insurance company executive*
Montgomerie, Colin Stuart *professional golfer*
Moya, Carlos *professional tennis player*
Nalbandian, David *professional tennis player*
Novak, Jiri *professional tennis player*
O'Brien, Raymond Vincent, Jr. *banker*
Patterson, Oscar III *academic administrator*
Pavin, Corey Allen *professional golfer*
ReMine, William Hervey, Jr. *retired surgeon*
Rodriguez, Chi Chi (Juan Rodriguez) *professional golfer*
Scott, Adam *professional golfer*
Scott, Marie Claudine *ceramic artist, writer*
Slayton, Gus *foundation administrator*
Soderberg, Nancy *former government official, writer*
Strange, Curtis Northrop *professional golfer*
~~Stricker, Steve *professional golfer*~~
Watson, John Lawrence III *former trade association executive*
Wood, Quentin Eugene *oil industry executive*
Wu, Hsiu Kwang *economist, educator*
Young, Mark V. *sports association executive*

Port Charlotte
Donovan, William Alan *retired librarian*
Hegleh, Joseph A. *ophthalmologist*
Hill, Richard Earl *academic administrator*
Kidd, A. Paul *health facility and government agency administrator*
Kok, Hans Gebhard *consulting engineer*
Levin, Allen Jay *lawyer*
Norris, Dolores June *elementary school educator*
Reynolds, Helen Elizabeth *management consultant*
Von Holden, Martin Harvey *psychologist*
Winters, Stanley B. *history professor, consultant, writer*

Port Orange
Chesnut, Nondis Lorine (Angel Love) *education educator, writer, learning specialist, scriptwriter*
Collyer, Robert B. *retired trade association administrator*
DeMarsico, Jonnette M. *theater educator, consultant*
Johnson, Susan F. *elementary school educator*
Millar, Gordon Halstead *mechanical engineer, agricultural products executive*

Port Richey
Long, Michael Eldon *government and history educator*

Port Saint Lucie
Augelli, John Pat *geographer, educator, writer, consultant, rancher*
Austin, Philip *research scientist*
Beatrice, Ruth Hadfield *hypnotherapist, retired elementary school educator, financial administrator*
Earley, Deborah Loraine *education educator, researcher*
Guglielmino, Lucy Margaret Madsen *education educator, researcher, consultant*
Guglielmino, Paul Joseph *educator*
Harris, Eric *accountant, auditor*
Lambert, George Robert *lawyer, realtor*
Malcolm, Edith *elementary school educator*
Olson, Edward Charles *entrepreneur, conservationist, foundation administrator, consultant, ecologist, writer*
Priore, Louis Vincent *pharmacist*
Rothschild, Mary Ann *music educator*
Staub, Carol Anne *artist*
Whitesell, William Mayberry III *legal association administrator*

Punta Gorda
Bailey, F. Lee (Francis Lee Bailey) *lawyer*
Fullman, Robert Louis *metallurgy consultant*

Haswell, Carleton Radley *banker*
Klarik, Bela William James Clark *retired school system administrator*
Lynch, Constance *reading specialist*
O'Neal, Lyman Henry *biology educator*
Ott, Walter Richard *information technology executive, writer*
Pollard, Herschel Newton *artist, psychologist*
Presley, Brian *investment company executive*
Sehring, Adolf *artist, sculptor*
Spaulding, Mar *retired special education educator*
Stratas, Teresa (Anastasia Strataki) *soprano*

Redington Beach
Alpert, Barry Mark *insurance company and banking executive*

Riviera Beach
Berliner, Hans Jack *retired computer scientist*

Rockledge
Means, Michael David *hospital administrator*

Ruskin
Briscoe, Anne M. *retired science educator*

Safety Harbor
Banks, Allan Richard *artist, art historian, researcher*
Dail, Joseph Garner, Jr. *retired judge*

Saint Augustine
Bishop, Claire DeArment *small business owner, retired librarian*
Brady, James Joseph *labor arbitrator*
Couture, Sister Diane Rhea *sister, artist, educator*
Gilmore, H. James *film producer, educator*
Harper, Robert Walter III *museum director*
Henderson, Hazel *economist, writer*
Jurgens, Julie Graham *mathematics professor*
Lund, Frederick Henry *aerospace and electrical engineer*
McCarty, Doran Chester *religious organization administrator*
Nolan, Joseph Thomas *journalism educator, communications consultant*
Preysz, Louis Robert Fonss III *management consultant, educator*
Proctor, William Lee *college chancellor*
Puma, Vincent Douglas *literature and language professor*
Sappington, Sharon Anne *retired school librarian*
Storey, Robert Davis *retired lawyer*
Wilkes, Delano Angus *architect*
Yonkman, Fredrick Albers *lawyer, management consultant*

Saint Cloud
Everett, Woodrow Wilson *electrical engineer, educator*

Saint Leo
Hammond, Bruce Ray *academic administrator, consultant*
Neuhofer, Mary Dorothy *archivist, librarian*

Saint Petersburg
Allaster, Stacey *sports association executive*
Allshouse, Merle Frederick *educational organization administrator*
Andruk, Marjorie Dean *artist, educator*
Armacost, Peter Hayden *academic administrator*
Bairstow, Frances Kanevsky *arbitrator, mediator, educator*
Barnes, Andrew Earl *former newspaper executive*
Battaglia, Anthony Sylvester *lawyer*
Belich, John Patrick, Sr. *journalist, private investigator*
Betzer, Susan Elizabeth Beers *physician, geriatrician*
Biasotti, Robert E. *lawyer*
Bolhofner, Brett Robinson *orthopedist*
Bryant, Timothy Clark *investment brokerage executive*
Buckspan, Randy Jay *plastic surgeon*
Byrd, Isaac Burlin *retired biologist*
Cardenas-Valencia, Andres Manuel *chemical engineer, researcher*
Carroll, Charles Michael *music educator*
Chapin, Lloyd Walter *academic administrator*
Clijsters, Kim *retired professional tennis player*
Collins, Carl Russell, Jr. *industrial engineer*
Collins, Paul Steven *vascular surgeon*
Connelly, David O'Brien *museum administrator, journalist*
Coraggio, James Thomas *educational researcher, measurement consultant*
Corty, Andrew P. *publishing executive*
Craybas, Jill *professional tennis player*
D'Elia, Christopher Francis *marine biologist, educator, academic administrator*
Dementieva, Elena *professional tennis player*
Dinsdale, Carol Ellen *special education educator*
Emerson, William Allen *retired investment company executive*
Erman, Aila *small business owner*
Escarraz, Enrique III *lawyer*
Felice, William F. *political science professor*
Fleming, William Sloan *energy and computer company executive*
Fraser, John Wayne *insurance executive, consultant, underwriter*
Frazier, A. D., Jr. *information technology executive, lawyer*
Freeman, Corinne *financial analyst, retired mayor*
Gaines, Mary S. *library director*
Georges, Richard Martin *lawyer, educator, poet*
Gilbert, Gordon Joel *neurologist, electroencelographer*
Glass, Roy Leonard *lawyer*
Godbold, Francis Stanley *investment banker, security firm executive*
Grube, Karl Bertram *judge*
Haiman, Robert James *editor, journalist, educator, media consultant, expert witness, critic*
Hamilton, John McFarland *plastic surgeon, real estate developer*
Hooker, Robert Wright *journalist*
Huber, Liezel *professional tennis player*
Hurley, John Kenneth *real estate company and merchant banking executive*
Jacob, Bruce Robert *law educator*
James, Thomas A. *investment company executive*
Janney, Oliver James *lawyer*
Jenkins, Robert Norman *reporter, editor*
Johnson, Edna Ruth *editor*
Jordan, William Reynier, Sr. *retired therapist, poet*
Kanstoroom, David Arnold *real estate developer, entrepreneur*
Kazmir, Scott *professional baseball player*
Kent, Allen *library and information sciences professor*
Kubiet, Leo Lawrence *media consultant*
Kuznetsova, Svetlana *professional tennis player*
Lang, Joseph Hagedorn *lawyer*
Lanza, Donald Charles *otolaryngologist, rhinologist*
Lemoi, Brian André *religious organization administrator, religious studies educator, writer*
Lewis, Chris A. *manufacturing executive*
Linhart, Joseph Wayland *retired cardiologist, educational administrator*
Maddon, Joe *professional baseball coach*
Main, Timothy L. *electronics company executive*
Mann, Sam Henry, Jr. *retired lawyer*
Matecki, Paul L. *lawyer*
McCluskey, Charles James, Jr. *physician assistant*
McNeill, Felita Gale *nurse, military officer*
Meyer, Robert Allen *finance educator*
Miller, G(erson) H(arry) *science administrator, mathematician, computer scientist, chemist*
Mills, William Harold, Jr. *construction executive*
Morean, William D. *manufacturing executive*
Mueller, O. Thomas *molecular geneticist, pediatrics educator*
Myskina, Anastasia *professional tennis player*
Naimoli, Vincent Joseph *diversified financial services company executive*
Naughton, James Martin *journalist*
Nichols, Katie *investment company executive*
Patterson, Eugene Corbett *retired editor, publishing executive*
Paver, Robert L. *lawyer*
Petty, M. S. Marty *publisher*
Petty, Marty *publishing executive*
Pittman, Robert Turner *retired newspaper editor*
Root, Allen William *pediatrician, educator*
Rosenblum, Martin Jerome *ophthalmologist*
Rosenblum, Zina Michelle Zarin *psychology professor, marketing professional, researcher*
Ross, Howard Philip *lawyer*
Scott, Kathryn Fenderson *lawyer*
Sharapova, Maria *professional tennis player*
Shaughnessy, Meghann *professional tennis player*
Short, James F. *investment company executive*
Shuck, Robert F. *financial executive*
Southworth, William Dixon *retired education educator*
Steele, Alison *lawyer*
Tash, Paul Clifford *editor, publishing executive*
Upton, B.J. (Melvin Emanuel Upton) *professional baseball player*
Wales, Jimmy Donal (Jimbo Wales) *Internet company executive*
Wasserman, Susan Valesky *accountant, artist, small business owner*
Wedding, Charles Randolph *architect*
White, June Miller *mathematics professor, educational consultant*
Young, Delmon Damarcus *professional baseball player*
Young, June Hurley *elementary school educator, writer*
Zimmer, Donald William *former professional baseball coach, professional baseball manager, retired professional baseball player*

Saint Petersburg Beach
Garnett, Stanley Iredale, II, *utilities executive, lawyer*
Hurley, Frank Thomas, Jr. *realtor*

San Antonio
Beverland, Jack Edwin *retired retail executive, folk artist*

Sanford
Belanger, Devon Taylor *small business owner*
Capps, James Leigh, II, *lawyer, military officer*
Dettman, Mary *biology professor*
Drewry, Marcia Ann *physician*
Heindl, Phares Matthews *lawyer*
Mena, Michele M. *counselor, educator*
Oostwouder, Peter Henry *physician*
Scott, Mellouise Jacqueline *retired media specialist*
Terrell, Maurice L., Sr. *music educator*

Sanibel
Ball, Armand Baer *former association executive, consultant*
Crown, David Allan *criminologist, educator*
Hasselman, Richard B. *retired rail transportation executive*
Rothschild, Donald Phillip *retired lawyer, arbitrator*
Trevor, Alexander Bruen *information technology consultant*

Santa Rosa Beach
Rees, Lane Charles *industrial relations consultant*

Sarasota
Allen, Charles Franklin *music educator*
Apfelbach, George Leonard, Jr. *urologist*
Atwell, Robert Herron *academic administrator*
Aull, Susan *physician*
Bailey, Robert Elliott *financial executive*
Balliett, John William *entrepreneur, real estate company executive*
Beck, Robert Alfred *hotel executive, educator*
Benowitz, June Melby *historian, educator*
Berkoff, Charles Edward *pharmaceutical and biotech consultant*
Boersma, June Elaine (Jalma Barrett) *retired writer, photographer*
Boersma, Lawrence Allan (Larry Allan) *animal welfare administrator, photographer*
Bowers, Charles Richard *surgeon*
Brandhorst, Wesley Theodore *retired library and information scientist*
Brown, Stephen Ira *philosophy professor*
Burkett, Helen *artist*
Bushey, Alan Scott *retired insurance holding company executive*
Carr, Patricia Ann *community health nurse*
Cavanagh, Denis *gynecologist, obstetrician, educator, gynecological oncologist*
Clark, Eugenie *zoologist, educator*
Cleland, Sherrill *college president*
Clough, William Robert *minister, educator*
Conetta, Tami Foley *lawyer*
Cooper, William Ewing, Jr. *retired army officer*
Corrigan, William Thomas *retired broadcast news executive*
Culkin, Charles Walker, Jr. *retired trade association administrator*
Cummings, Martin Marc *physician, educator, academic administrator*
Daoust, Donald Roger *pharmaceutical executive, microbiologist, cosmetics executive*
De Gennaro, Richard *retired library director*
Derr, Frederick Mueller *civil engineer*
Deutsch, Sid *biomedical engineer, educator*
Doores, Stephen Curtis *manufacturing executive*
Drake, Diana Ashley *retired financial planner*
Dryce, H. David *accountant, consultant*
Dungy, Kathryn R. *humanities educator*
Edwards, Michael Donald *artistic director, drama educator*
Ehrlich, Bernard Herbert *lawyer, trade association administrator*
El Shahawy, Mahfouz *internist, educator, cardiologist*
Faron, Sally Rogers *performing arts association administrator, consultant*
Fendrick, Alan Burton *retired advertising executive*
Fetterman, James Charles *lawyer*
Field, Suellen R. *not-for-profit developer*
Freeman, Richard Merrell *retired lawyer*
Garland, Richard Roger *lawyer*
Gauch, Eugene William, Jr. *retired air force officer*
Gordon, Sanford Daniel *economics professor*
Greenfield, Robert Kauffman *retired lawyer*
Harris, Judith Ann White *occupational health nurse, educator*
Heiser, Rolland Valentine *former army officer, foundation administrator*
Heitler, George *lawyer*
Herb, Frank Steven *lawyer*
Hilt, Thomas Harry *minister*
Hueter, Robert Edward *marine biologist, researcher*
Hughes, Allen *music critic*
Hull, J(ames) Richard *retired lawyer*
Hummel, Dana D. Mallett *librarian*
Iverson, Robert Louis, Jr. *retired internist, physician*
Jackel, Lawrence *publishing executive*
Jacobson, Melvin Joseph *mathematician, educator*
Jelks, Mary Larson *retired pediatrician*
Jellison, Brian D. *manufacturing executive*
Jones, Sally Daviess Pickrell *writer*
Jones, Tracey Kirk, Jr. *retired minister, educator*
Kerr, Donald Craig *retired minister*
Kessler, Leonard *writer, illustrator*
Kimbrough, Robert Averyt *lawyer*
Knickerbocker, Robert Platt, Jr. *lawyer, consultant*
Landis, Edgar David *business consultant*
Lautner, Jane E. *development associate*
Lee, Nancy Ranck *management consultant*
Lengyel, Alfonz *art history, archeology and museology educator*
Levy, Gerhard *pharmacologist*
Lieberman, Carol *healthcare marketing communications consultant*
Long, Robert Radcliffe *fluid mechanics engineer, educator*
Magenheim, Mark Joseph *physician, epidemiologist, educator*
Mahadevan, Kumar *marine life administrator, researcher*
Marino, Eugene Louis *publishing executive, director*
Marks, Charles *surgeon, educator*
Masters, John Christopher *psychologist, educator*
Mattran, Donald Albert *management consultant, educator*
McCollum, John Morris *tenor*
McFarlin, Diane Hooten *publisher*
McMaster, Gloria (Gloria Bugni Juhn) *mezzo-soprano, educator*
Metzger, Sidney *retired communications engineer*
Meyer, B. Fred *small business executive, builder, home and product designer*
Michalson, Gordon E., Jr. *academic administrator*
Middleton, Norman Graham *social worker, psychotherapist*
Milam, Cathy P. *dermatologist*
Miller, Peggy Gordon Elliott *retired academic administrator*
Miranda, Carlos Sa *food products company executive*
Mitchell, John Noyes, Jr. *retired electrical engineer*
Morris, Gordon James *financial company executive, consultant*
Morrow, William Earl *retired government official, retired law educator*
Mullane, John Francis *pharmaceutical executive*
North, Marjorie Mary *columnist*
O'Malley, Thomas Anthony *gastroenterologist, internist*
Phillips, Elvin Willis *lawyer*
Phillips, Howard William *investment banker*
Pierce, Richard Harry *oceanographer*
Platt, Franklin Dewitt *retired history professor*
Poppel, Harvey Lee *management consultant, investment banker*
Proffitt, Waldo, Jr. *newspaper editor*
Raimi, Burton Louis *lawyer*
Retzer, Mary Elizabeth Helm *retired librarian*
Runge, Paul E. *ophthalmologist, educator*
St. John, Terri *secondary school educator*
Sarakatsannis, Leonidas Nicholas *musician, concert pianist, music educator, composer, conductor*
Scalera, Michelle *conservator*
Scanlon, Janice Lynn *retired gifted and talented educator*
Schlegel, John Frederick *management consultant, personal trainer*
Schmalzried, Marvin Eugene *financial consultant*
Shulman, Arthur *communications executive*
Stevens, Elisabeth Goss (Mrs. Robert Schleussner Jr.) *journalist, writer, graphic artist*
Stewart, Donald George *musician, composer, music industry executive*
Stolley, Alexander *advertising executive*
Straight, Elsie Hosking *retired librarian, sculptor*
Tachna, Ruth C. *retired lawyer*
Taplin, Winn Lowell *historian, retired federal agency administrator*
Thompson, Annie Figueroa *retired academic administrator*
Torrey, Richard Frank *utilities executive*
Wadsworth, Dyer Seymour *minerals executive*
Watson, Joyce Morrissa *forensic and clinical psychologist*
Weber, Joanna *curator*
Weeks, Albert Loren *writer, educator, journalist*
Wendlandt, Dorothea Schnepf *artist, writer*
West, Bob *pharmaceutical executive*
Wetenhall, John *museum director*
Wilson, Kenneth Jay *writer*
Zahn, Carl Frederick *museum program director, photographer, graphics designer*
Zavon, Mitchell Ralph *occupational medicine physician*

Satellite Beach
Clark, John F. *space systems engineering educator*
Loney, Mary Rose *former airport administrator, aviation industry consultant*
Newbold-Coco, Rain L. *social services administrator*
Rains, Baxter Smith *sculptor, consultant*
Van Arsdall, Robert Armes *engineer, retired military officer*

Sea Ranch Lakes
Gore, George Henry *lawyer*

Sebastian
Burns, Robert Edward *dean, retired history professor*
Lagin, Neil *landscape designer, consultant*
Mauke, Otto Russell *retired college president*
Pieper, Patricia Rita *artist*

Sebring
McCollum, James Fountain *lawyer*
Parrett, Janelle Swilley *secondary school educator*
Sherrick, Daniel Noah *real estate broker*
Trombley, Michael Jerome *lawyer*
Westberry, Paula I. *nursing administrator*
Wright, Leonard Douglas *protective services official, retired military officer*

Seffner
Seaman, Jeffrey *consumer products company executive*

Seminole
Carrere, Charles Scott *judge, educator*
Evans, Thomas Passmore *management consultant*
McKeown, H. Mary *lawyer, educator*

Singer Island
Dixson, J. B. *communications executive*

South Daytona
Fernández, Lianne *elementary school educator, consultant*

South Miami
Keedy, Christian David *lawyer*
Leinoff, Andrew Morris *lawyer*
Villacian, Vanessa Luisa *psychologist*

Sparr
Tovi, Murray *futurist, research scientist*

Spring Hill
Del Toro-Politowicz, Lillian *medical association administrator, geriatrics services professional, consultant*
Rothenberg, Linda Ann *science educator*
Vanderburg, Paul Stacey *insurance executive, consultant*
Wood, Shelton Eugene *education educator, minister, consultant*

Stuart
Ankrom, Charles Franklin *golf course architect, consultant*
Bowdish, James L.S. *lawyer*

Cocoves, Anita Petzold *psychotherapist*
Derrickson, William Borden *manufacturing executive*
Gary, Willie E. *lawyer*
Gilbert, Glenn Gordon *retired linguistics educator*
Grieve, William Roy *psychologist, educator, educational administrator, researcher*
Kirkpatrick, Harold (Kirk) Wayne *telecommunications industry executive*
Patterson, Robert Arthur *physician, health care consultant, retired health care company executive, retired air force officer*
Robinson, Michael Hill *retired zoological park director, biologist*
Sabol, Stuart J. *otolaryngologist*
Slaihem, Ameer Abdullah *career officer*
Stark, Richard Boies *surgeon, artist*
Viener, John D. *lawyer*

Sugarloaf

Greenberg, Linda Garrett *education educator, volunteer, singer*

Summerfield

Lynne-O'Brien, Vincent *theater director, actor*
McNulty, Carrell Stewart, Jr. *retired manufacturing executive, architect*

Sun City Center

Chapman, Lenora Rosamond *day care provider, social service organization director*
Crow, Harold Eugene *physician, educator*
Edwards, Paul Beverly *retired science and engineering educator*
Jeffries, Robert Joseph *retired engineer, information technology executive, educator*
Malkin, Moses Montefiore *retired employee benefits administration company, diversified financial services company executive*
Petersen, Carolyn Ashcraft *retired psychologist*

Sunny Isles Beach

Edelcup, Norman Scott *management and financial consultant*

Sunrise

Garramone, Charles *plastic surgeon*
Goldenberg, Felix *retired electrical engineer, researcher*
Kitchen, Mike *professional hockey coach, retired professional hockey player*
Maken, Sonny *real estate company executive, real estate developer*
Nieuwendyk, Joe *retired professional hockey player, consultant*
Sorensen, Allan Chresten *service company executive*

Tallahassee

Anderson, Theresa Ann *science educator*
Anstead, Harry Lee *state supreme court justice*
Aurell, John Karl *lawyer*
Baggett, Fred W. *lawyer*
Barnett, Martha Walters *lawyer*
Bartlett, Richard Adams *historian, writer, retired history professor*
Bell, Kenneth B. *state supreme court justice*
Blair, Maudine *psychotherapist, communications executive, management consultant*
Blanton, Faye Wester *legislative official*
Bowden, Bobby (Robert Cleckler Bowden) *college football coach*
Bowen, Paul L. *information systems and accounting educator*
Braswell, Jackie Boyd *state agency administrator*
Browning, Kurt S. *state official*
Buck, Thomas Randolph *retired lawyer, diversified financial services company executive*
Burkman, Ernest, Jr. *education educator*
Butler, Robert Olen *writer, educator*
Bye, Raymond Erwin, Jr. *academic administrator*
Calhoun, Joseph Patrick *economics professor, researcher*
Cantero, Raoul G. III *state supreme court justice*
Carson, Leonard Allen *lawyer*
Choppin, Gregory Robert *chemistry professor*
Clifford, Dorothy Ring *journalist*
Coleman, Robert Hemphill III *theater educator*
Coloney, Wayne Herndon *civil engineer*
Corzine, Jennifer Jean *music educator*
Crist, Charlie (Charles Joseph Crist Jr.) *governor, former state attorney general*
Cronin, Jerome Joseph, Jr. *marketing educator, consultant*
Curtin, Lawrence N. *lawyer*
Dadisman, Joseph Carrol *retired newspaper executive*
Dariotis, Terrence Theodore *lawyer*
Davis, William Howard *lawyer*
Dea, David Young Fong *electrical engineer, consultant*
Deeb, Larry Charles *pediatric endocrinologist, epidemiologist*
DeFoor, J. Allison, II, *lawyer, priest*
De Forest, Sherwood Searle *agricultural engineer, agricultural products executive*
Delp, Roy Edward *music educator, singer*
Dennis, Lawrence C. (Larry) *dean, physics professor*
Dresang, Eliza T. *library and information scientist*
Elsner, James Brian *meteorologist, educator*
Ervin, Charles Phifer, Jr. *education educator, retired military officer*
Ervin, Robert Marvin *lawyer*
Fiore, Carole Diane *library consultant*
Fonvielle, Charles David *lawyer*
France, Belinda Takach *lawyer, business owner*
Gilmer, Penny Jane *biochemist, educator*
Gilmer, Robert *mathematics professor*
Gleeson, Thomas Alexander *retired meteorologist*
Golden, Leon *classicist, educator*
Goldstein, Julia Sonia *librarian*
Gor'kov, Peter (Lev Petrovich) *biomedical engineer*
Grant, Sydney R. *education educator, consultant*
Grimes, Stephen Henry *retired state supreme court justice*
Guy, Mary Ellen Johnston *political science professor*
Hall, Houghton Alexander *electrical engineer, municipal official*
Halpern, Paul G. *retired history professor*
Harper, Robert Augustus *lawyer*
Harrison, Luvada A. *voice educator, singer*
Harsanyi, Janice *retired soprano, educator*
Hatchett, Joseph Woodrow *lawyer, former federal judge*
Hernandez, Jose Yolando Balagtas *surgeon*
Hernandez, Minerva Cuadrante *physician, consultant*
Herndon, Roy Clifford *physicist*
Holcomb, Lyle Donald, Jr. *retired lawyer*
Holcombe, Randall Gregory *economics professor*
Humphrey, Louise Ireland *civic worker, equestrienne*
Hunt, John Edwin *insurance company executive, consultant*
Hunt, Mary Alice *retired humanities educator*
Ilich, Jasminka Z. *dietician, educator*
Johnson, Kelly Overstreet *lawyer*
Johnson, Margaret Anderson *writer, publishing and agricultural products executive*
Kaelin, Eugene Francis *retired philosophy educator*
Keating, Kevin *academic administrator, chef*
Kercheval, Alec Norton *mathematician*
Kerns, David Vincent *lawyer*
Khalil, Mohammed K. *research scientist, medical educator*
Kitchen, E.C. Deeno *lawyer*
Klick, Jonathan *law educator*
Laird, Doris Anne Marley *retired humanities educator, musician*
Laird, William Everette, Jr. *economics professor*
Laughlin, William Eugene *retired electric power industry executive*
Lee, Peter John *research engineer*
Levine, A. Kenneth *lawyer*
Lewis, R. Fred *state supreme court justice*
Lewis, Tom E., Jr. *architect*
Lick, Dale Wesley *educational leadership educator, mathematician*
Lisenby, Dorrece Edenfield *realtor*
Maguire, Charlotte Edwards *retired pediatrician*
Marshall, Alan George *chemistry and biochemistry educator*
Mayhall, Clifford Wesley *lawyer*
McClure, Charles Robert *library and information science educator, consultant*
McCollum, Bill (Ira William McCollum Jr.) *state attorney general, former congressman*
McCord, Guyte Pierce, Jr. *retired judge*
Mele, Alfred R. *philosophy educator*
Miller, Gregory R. *prosecutor*
Miller, Morris Henry *lawyer*
Mills, Belen Collantes *early childhood education educator*
Minnick, Bruce Alexander *lawyer*
Mooney, Krista Michele *academic administrator*
Morgan, Lucy Ware *news correspondent, journalist*
Morgan, Robert Marion *educational research educator*
Morgante, John-Paul *human resources specialist*
Mortham, Sandra Barringer *former state official, medical association administrator*
Nam, Charles Benjamin *demographer, sociologist, educator, writer*
Nasser, Joseph Yousef *public safety administrator, consultant*
Navon, Ionel Michael *mathematics professor*
Nichols, Eugene Douglas *mathematics professor*
Norton, William Alan *lawyer*
Palladino-Craig, Allys *museum director, educator*
Pariente, Barbara J. *state supreme court justice*
Pettijohn, Fred Phillips *retired publishing executive*
Phipps, Benjamin Kimball, II, *lawyer*
Quince, Peggy A. *state supreme court justice*
Rahman, Saleh Mahmudur *medical educator*
Reid, Sue Titus *law educator*
Richard, Barry *lawyer*
Ring, Judith A. *state librarian*
Robson, Donald *physics professor*
Rogers, William Warren *historian, educator, publishing executive, writer*
Rosenberg, Mark B. *academic administrator*
Ross, Levi Andre *public health educator*
Saxon, Don B. *state agency administrator*
Schrieffer, John Robert *physics professor, science administrator*
Scott, Fran *adult education educator*
Shaftel, Matthew Robert *music educator, tenor, conductor*
Sink, Adelaide Alexander *state official*
Sliger, Bernard Francis *academic administrator, economist, educator*
Srivastava, Sanjeev Kumar *electrical engineer, researcher*
Steele, Richard J. *management consultant*
Streem, James Kenneth *musician, educator*
Strickland, Delphene Coverston *judge*
Terry, Anne Curtis *lawyer, writer*
Thiele, Herbert William Albert *lawyer*
Thomas, James Bert, Jr. *retired federal agency administrator*
Thompson, Gregory Lee *social sciences educator*
Thompson, Jean Tanner *retired librarian*
Tourtet, Christiane Andrée *writer, photojournalist, reporter, advocate*
Waas, George Lee *lawyer*
Waas, Harriet Issner *elementary school educator*
Walker, Karen D. *lawyer*
Webster, Peter David *judge*
Weems, Lori K. *lawyer*
Weidner, Donald J. *dean, law educator*
Weissman-Berman, Deborah *biostatistics and composites engineer, researcher*
Wells, Charles Talley *state supreme court justice*
Wetherell, Thomas Kent *academic administrator*
Wiegand, Wayne August *library and information science educator*
Winn, John L. *school system administrator*
Yecke, Cheri Pierson *educational researcher, administrator, policymaker, writer*
Yerg, Beverly Johnson *retired physical education educator, researcher*
Yu, Ming *engineering educator, researcher*
Zachert, Martha Jane *retired librarian*
Zaiser, Kent Ames *lawyer*
Zwilich, Ellen Taaffe *composer*

Tamarac

Auletta, Joan Miglorisi *construction company executive, mortgage and insurance broker*
Krause, John L. *retired optometrist*

Tampa

Afield, Walter Edward *psychiatrist, educator, health facility administrator*
Agazzi, Siviero *neurosurgeon*
Albritton, Arthur Dallas *lawyer*
Alexander, William Olin *retired finance company executive*
Alstott, Michael Joseph (Mike Alstott) *professional football player*
Anton, John Peter *philosopher, educator*
Armstrong, Peter F. *surgeon, pediatrician, orthopedist*
Bachman, Gregg Paul *communications educator*
Barbas, Stephen Michael *lawyer*
Barkin, Marvin E. *lawyer*
Barness, Lewis Abraham *physician*
Barrow, Lionel Ceon, Jr. *communications and marketing consultant*
Barton, Bernard Alan, Jr. *lawyer*
Bedgood, Alvin J. *information technology manager, director*
Bedke, Michael A. *lawyer*
Bereday, Thaddeus Matthew Sigmund *lawyer*
Berne, Patricia Higgins *psychologist, writer, educator*
Bishopric, Karl *insurance company executive, retired investment banker, real estate company executive, retired advertising executive*
Black, Caroline Kapusta *lawyer*
Boutros, Linda Nelene Wiley *medical/surgical nurse*
Branch, Mary Fletcher Cox *secondary school educator*
Branch, William Terrell *urologist, educator*
Brooks, Derrick Dewan *professional football player*
Brown, Troy Anderson, Jr. *retired electric power industry executive*
Buesing, Karen Meyer *lawyer*
Bunker-Soler, Antonio Luis *physician*
Campbell, Richard Bruce *lawyer*
Carnahan, Robert Paul *civil engineer, educator, researcher, consultant*
Castellano, Josephine Massaro *medical records specialist*
Castor, Kathy *congresswoman*
Christian, Terry Clifton *lawyer*
Coats, Janet S. (Janet Weaver) *executive editor*
Coleman, Rodney Albert *political scientist, consultant*
Collins, Jessica Ann *military officer*
Corcoran, Clement Timothy III *lawyer, mediator, retired judge*
Cunningham, Anthony Willard *lawyer*
Dalton, William Steven *oncologist, educator*
Davidson, Charles Thomas *lawyer*
Davis, Blondell Gilliam *business manager, evangelist, artist, author, poet*
Davis, Helen Gordon *retired state senator*
Davis, Jim *lawyer, former congressman*
Davis, Richard Earl *lawyer*
de Lama, Alberto *artist*
Dempsey, Martin E. *career military officer*
de Quesada, Alejandro Manuel *film and museum consultant, writer*
Dessureault, Sophie *oncologist, surgeon, educator*
Diehr, Beverly Hunt *lawyer*
Doliner, Nathaniel Lee *lawyer*
Edwards, Charles M. *medical educator*
Eichberg, Rodolfo David *physiatrist, educator*
El-Hadidy, Bahaa *information scientist, educator, consultant*
Ellwanger, Thomas John *lawyer*
Fallon, William Joseph *career military officer*
Feaster, Jay *professional sports team executive*
Flom, Edward Leonard *retired metal products executive*
Forsythe, Robert Elliott *economics professor*
Freedman, Sandra Warshaw *former mayor*
Friedlander, Edward Jay *journalist, educator*
Gabrilovich, Dmitry I. *immunologist, educator*
Gallagher, Scott Farrell *surgeon, researcher*
Galwankar, Sagar Chandramohan *public health service officer*
Garcia, Jeff (Jeffrey Jason Garcia) *professional football player*
Garrett, Howard Leon *lawyer*
Genshaft, Judy Lynn *academic administrator, psychologist, educator*
Genter, John Robert *grocery industry executive*
Ghiu, Silvana Melania Stefania *process and development engineer*
Gilbert, Leonard Harold *lawyer*
Gilbert-Barness, Enid F. *pathologist, educator*
Gironda, Ronald James *psychologist*
Glazer, Malcolm *professional sports team executive*
Goldman, Mark S. *alcohol/drug abuse services professional, educator, reseracher*
Gomes, Neil Domnic *director*
Gonzalez, Joe Manuel *lawyer*
Grammig, Robert James (Bob Grammig) *lawyer*
Greenfield, George B. *radiologist*
Gruden, Jon *professional football coach*
Guida, Wayne Charles *medical educator, research scientist*
Haggis, Arthur George, Jr. *retired military officer, educator, publisher*
Hamilton, William F. *lawyer*
Hanford, Agnes Rutledge *retired investment advisor*
Hankenson, E(dward) Craig, Jr. *performing arts executive*
Harkness, Mary Lou *librarian*
Hegarty, Thomas Joseph *retired history professor*
Henard, Elizabeth Ann *controller*
Hernandez, Gilberto Juan *accountant, auditor, management consultant*
Hlavay, Jay Alan *financial analyst*
Holliday, Ronald Sturgis *lawyer*
Howey, John Richard *architect, writer*
Hudson, Sherrill W. *energy executive*
Huey, Peggy J. *communications educator, performing company executive*
Hulls, James Robert *emergency physician*
Humphrey, Deborah A. *medical educator, internist*
Huneycutt, Alice Ruth *lawyer*
Hunter, Larry Lee *retired electrical engineer*
Jacobs, Timothy Andrew *epidemiologist, consultant*
Jacobson, Howard Newman *obstetrics and gynecology educator, researcher*
Jacobus, Mary *publishing executive*
Jenkins, Elizabeth Ann *federal judge*
Jennewein, James Joseph *architect*
Johnson, Anthony O'Leary (Andy Johnson) *meteorologist, consultant*
Johnson, Thomas S. *electronics executive*
Jones, Franklin Ross *education educator*
Jones, John Arthur *lawyer*
Kadow, Joseph J. *lawyer*
Keach, Michael Andrew *library and information scientist*
Keller, Shari Ann *small business owner*
Kelly, Thomas Paine, Jr. *retired lawyer*
Kimmel, Ellen Bishop *psychologist, educator*
Knox, Michael Dennis *medical educator, research center administrator*
Koch, Karl R. *policy advisor*
Koren, Edward Franz, Jr. *lawyer*
Kriz, Frank Kenneth, Jr. *surgeon*
Krone, Norman Bernard *real estate developer, lawyer*
Lane, Robin R. *lawyer*
Lau, Mary Applegate *lawyer, arbitrator, mediator*
Lebouitz, Martin Frederick *diversified financial services company executive, consultant*
Lecavalier, Vincent *professional hockey player*
Leopold, Blake *music educator*
Leto, Sharon Ann *secondary school educator, consultant*
Levine, Jack Anton *lawyer*
Lockey, Richard Funk *allergist, immunologist, educator*
Loiselle, Joan Brenda *elementary school educator, art educator*
Luddington, Betty Walles *retired multi-media specialist*
Macferran, Ernest Leslie *mechanical engineer*
MacManus, Susan Ann *political science professor, researcher*
Malone, John I. *pediatrics educator, biomedical researcher*
Mangiapane, Joseph Arthur *retired consulting company executive, physicist*
Martin, Gary Wayne *lawyer*
Martinez, Bob *former federal official, governor*
Matheny, Charles Woodburn, Jr. *former army officer, civil engineer, city official*
McAdams, John Pope *lawyer*
McCook, Kathleen de la Peña *librarian, educator*
McDevitt, Sheila Marie *retired lawyer, energy executive, business consultant*
McIlwain, Harris H. *physician, researcher*
Meisels, Gerhard George *academic administrator, chemist, educator*
Michaels, John Patrick, Jr. *investment banker, media broker*
Mitchell, Mozella Gordon *language educator, minister*
Moffett, Susan L. *information technology manager*
Moszkowski, Neal *health products executive*
Muroff, Lawrence Ross *nuclear medicine physician, educator*
Murphy, Robin Roberson *computer scientist, robotics engineer*
Nord, Walter Robert *business administration educator, researcher, consultant*
Odierno, Raymond T. *career military officer*
Older, Jay Justin *ophthalmic plastic surgeon*
Olson, Eric Thor *career military officer*
Olson, Robert Eugene *physician, biochemist, educator*
O'Neill, Albert Clarence, Jr. *lawyer*
Palmer, Denise E. *publishing executive*
Pankau, Barbara Ropes *lawyer*
Pasetti, Louis Oscar *retired dentist*
Pedowitz, Robert Alan *orthopaedic surgeon, researcher*
Pellett, Jon Michael *lawyer*
Perret, Gerard Anthony, Jr. *orthodontist*
Perry, James Frederic *philosophy educator, writer*
Petraeus, David Howell *career military officer*
Pfeiffer, Eric Armin *psychiatrist, gerontologist, writer*
Piper, John Richard *political science professor*
Platt, Jan Kaminis *former county official*
Plumeri, Joseph James, II, *financial executive*
Powers, Pauline Smith *psychiatrist, educator, researcher*
Preston, Brett Joseph *lawyer*
Purcell, Henry III *real estate developer*
Reed, Donna Marie *editor*
Reiske, Steven Robert Warren *human services manager*
Richards, Brad *professional hockey player*
Roberson, Bruce Heerdt *lawyer*
Robinson, John William, IV, *lawyer*

Rowlands, David Thomas *pathology educator*
Russell, Diane Elizabeth Henrikson *career counselor*
Rydberg, Marsha Griffin *lawyer*
St. Louis, Martin *professional hockey player*
Sanberg, Paul Ronald *medical educator*
Sanchez, Mary Anne *retired secondary school educator*
Sanchez-Ramos, Juan Ramon *physician, medical educator*
Sasso, Gary L. *lawyer*
Schild, Nancy Lois *realtor, music educator*
Schueler, John R. *newspaper executive*
Schumacher, Margaret Lynn *not-for-profit fundraiser, director*
Schwenke, Roger Dean *lawyer*
Seiler, Christine Kay *history professor*
Shenefelt, Philip David *dermatologist*
Shephard, Bruce Dennis *obstetrician, educator, medical writer*
Sigety, Charles Birge *investment company executive*
Silbiger, Martin L. *radiologist, educator, dean*
Smith, David John, Jr. *plastic surgeon*
Smith, William Reece, Jr. *lawyer*
Somers, Clifford Louis *lawyer*
Sopher, Vicki Elaine *appraiser*
Spellacy, William Nelson *obstetrician, gynecologist, educator*
Spielberger, Charles Donald *psychologist, educator*
Spofford, George Edson, IV, *lawyer*
Stagg, Clyde Lawrence *lawyer*
Stair, Wilson Alfred, Jr. *urban designer, landscape architect*
Stallings, (Charles) Norman *lawyer*
Stefanov, Ivanka *music educator*
Stines, Joe *library director, educator*
Studer, William Allen *security consultant, retired military officer*
Sullebarger, John Thompson *internist, educator, cardiologist*
Sullivan, Joseph Peter *risk and insurance management consultant*
Taub, Theodore Calvin *lawyer*
Thomas, Gregg Darrow *lawyer*
Thomas, Wayne Lee *lawyer*
Tillson, Albert Holmes, Jr. *history educator*
Tortorella, John *professional hockey coach*
Tully, Darrow *newspaper publisher*
Tunstall, Graydon Allen *history professor, professional society administrator*
Turner, Stephen Park *philosopher, sociologist, educator*
Vila, Hector *anesthesiologist, department chairman*
Wagner, Frederick William (Bill) *lawyer*
Waller, Edward Martin, Jr. *lawyer*
Watkins, Joan Marie *retired osteopath, retired physician*
Watson, Roberta Casper *lawyer*
Weiner, Irving Bernard *psychologist*
Whatley, Jacqueline Beltram *lawyer*
Willett, Nikki *computer company executive*
Williams, Kimberly Elizabeth *history professor*
Wilson, Charles Reginald *federal judge*
Wolfson, Jay *public health and medical educator, researcher, consultant, lawyer*
Wujcik, Theo Frank *artist*
Yang, Grace H. *lawyer*
Yerrid, C. Steven *lawyer*
Yeshion, Theodore Elliot *crime laboratory director*
Young, Gwynne A. *lawyer*
Zinober, Peter Wolfson *lawyer*

Tarpon Springs
Crismond, Linda Fry *public relations executive*
Jones, Marshall David *musician, minister*
Leisner, Anthony Baker *publishing company executive*

Tavares
Gross, Paul Allan *health products executive*
Kaiser, Robert Lee *retired engineering executive*

Temple Terrace
Crispell, Brian Lewis *history professor*
Reynolds, Jerald M. *music educator*
Rink, Wesley Winfred *retired bank executive*

Tequesta
Swets, John Arthur *psychologist, researcher*
Turrell, Richard Horton, Sr. *banker*

The Villages
Dupies, Donald Albert *retired civil engineer*
Oetjen, David L. (Jon David Douglas) *writer, film producer*
Phillips, Patricia Jeanne *retired school system administrator*

Tierra Verde
Gaffney, Thomas Francis *private investor*
Stewart, John Murray *bank executive*

Titusville
Duffy, John Charles *psychiatrist, educator, consultant*
Morton, Craig Richard *real estate investor*
O'Sullivan, Patricia Ann *principal, writer*
Robinson, Christina Anne *secondary school educator*
Samuelson, Fred Binder *artist, educator*
Stewart, David Witherington *business consultant*

Treasure Island
Dunn, Craig Andrew *entertainer, conductor, writer, composer, educator*

Trenton
Ivey, James Frederick, Jr. *physician*

University Park
Compain, Rita *librarian*
Walker, Jane Stewart *small business owner, publishing executive, educator*

Valparaiso
Merritt, Phyllis June *music educator, director*

Venice
Abernathy, George Thomas *cardiologist, consultant*
Asp, William George *librarian*
Barritt, Evelyn Ruth Berryman *nurse, educator, dean*
Bluhm, Barbara Jean *communications agency executive*
Clarke, Edward Owen, Jr. *lawyer*
Delaney, Robert Finley *retired columnist, political sociologist, lecturer*
Feldmann, Edward George *pharmaceutical chemist, pharmacologist*
Felker, Ouida Jeanette Weissinger *special education educator*
Girman, Dee-Marie *retired artist, singer*
Gooding, Charles Thomas *psychologist, educator, retired academic administrator*
Hrachovina, Frederick Vincent *retired osteopathic physician*
Lanford, Luke Dean *retired electronics company executive*
Meyerhoff, Jack Fulton *corporate financial executive*
Miller, Allan John *retired lawyer, oil industry executive*
Nevins, John J. *bishop*
Przemieniecki, Janusz Stanislaw *engineering executive, former government senior executive and college dean*
Shamsham, Fadi Michel *cardiologist*
Slate, Floyd Owen *retired engineering educator*
Tausan, Carol A. *music educator*

Vero Beach
Ahrens, William Henry *architect*
Ahrensfeld, Thomas Frederick *retired lawyer*
Bennett, Jack Franklin *oil industry executive*
Beran, Denis Carl *publisher*
Bewkes, Eugene Garrett, Jr. *investment company executive, consultant*
Bigler, Harold Edwin, Jr. *retired investment company executive*
Binney, Jan Jarrell *publishing executive, marketing professional*
Bright, Willard Mead *retired manufacturing executive, director*
Case, Douglas Manning *lawyer*
Christopher, Robert Paul *retired physical medicine physician*
Conway, Earl Cranston *business educator, retired manufacturing company executive, educator*
Crosby, John Griffith *investment banker*
Ferrell, Catherine K. *sculptor, painter*
Fish, Mardy *professional tennis player*
Fisher, Andrew *management consultant*
Freeman, Donald Wilford *real estate developer, horse breeder*
Gedeon, Lucinda Heyel *museum director*
Gibson, James Elliott *architect*
Grimes, Howard Ray *management consultant*
Hardie, James Carl *academic administrator, consultant*
Havens, Charles William III *retired lawyer*
Higgs, John H. *lawyer*
Ingwersen, Martin Lewis *water transportation executive*
Janicki, Robert Stephen *retired pharmaceutical executive*
Kamman, Alan Bertram *communications consulting company executive*
Koontz, Alfred Joseph, Jr. *financial analyst, consultant*
Leonsis, Ted *media and professional sports team executive*
Massey, Howard Clayland *writer*
McNamara, Francis Joseph, Jr. *retired foundation executive, lawyer*
McNamara, John J(oseph) *advertising executive, writer*
Nichols, Carl Wheeler *retired advertising agency executive*
Proctor, William Gilbert, Jr. *writer*
Reed, Sherman Kennedy *chemicals executive, consultant*
Riefler, Donald Brown *financial consultant*
Ryce, Donald Theodore, Jr. *lawyer*
Satuloff, Barth *accountant, dispute resolution professional, investment strategist, publishing executive, rancher*
Schwarz, Berthold Eric *psychiatrist*
Sheehan, Charles Vincent *investment banker*
Spivak, Alvin A. *retired public relations executive*
Standish, John Spencer *textile manufacturing company executive*
Wilcox, Harry Wilbur, Jr. *retired manufacturing executive*

Viera
Nessel, Edward Harry *swimming coach*

Village Of Golf
Birle, James Robb *investor*
Boer, F. Peter *chemical company executive*
Sutter, William Paul *lawyer*

Weeki Wachee
Finney, Roy Pelham, Jr. *urologist, surgeon, inventor*
Luffsey, Walter Stith *air transportation executive, consultant*

Wellington
Behren, Robert Alan *lawyer, accountant*

Wesley Chapel
Mendelsohn, Louis Benjamin *financial analyst*
Revelle, Donald Gene *manufacturing and health care company executive, consultant*

West Palm Beach
Aaron, M. Robert *electrical engineer*
Ackerman, David P. *lawyer*
Addison, Ferguson Lofton Lightbourne *retired bank executive*
Barre, Steven Craig *lawyer*
Beall, Kenneth Sutter, Jr. *lawyer*
Beasley, James W., Jr. *lawyer*
Bergmann, Arthur M. *writer, retired journalist, retired county official*
Berner, Thomas Franklyn *lawyer*
Bernhardt, Marcia Brenda *mental health counselor*
Brown, Paul A. *medical services executive*
Brumback, Clarence Landen *physician*
Burgess, R(oy) Brandon *communications executive*
Chapman, Roger Eugene *historian, educator*
Chen, Ming *quality assurance professional*
Chimney, Michael John *aquatic biologist/limnologist, consultant*
Chopin, L. Frank *lawyer*
Chopin, Susan Gardiner *lawyer*
Clark, David William *lawyer, councilman*
Damsel, Charles H., Jr. *lawyer*
Davis, Paul B. *retired mechanical and civil engineer*
Djokic, Walter Henry *lawyer*
Fanjul, Alfie, Jr., (Alfonso Fanjul) *food products executive*
Fanjul, Pepe (Josè Fanjul) *food products executive*
Floyd, Raymond Loran *professional golfer*
Furlaud, Richard Mortimer *pharmaceutical executive*
Gildan, Phillip Clarke *lawyer*
Giuffrida, Tom A. *publisher*
Gold, Bela *economist, educator*
Grant, Joi Odom *mathematics educator*
Gu, Binhe *environmental scientist*
Hale, Marie Stoner *performing company executive*
Henry, Thornton Montagu *lawyer*
Herrick, John Dennis *financial planner, consultant, retired food products executive*
Hill, Thomas William, Jr. *lawyer, educator*
Jacobson, Robert Julian *oncologist, director*
Jenkins, Ruben Lee *chemicals executive*
Johnson, Martin Allen *publishing executive, artist*
Kiely, Dan Ray *fund manager, consultant, real estate company executive*
Koch, William I. *energy company executive*
Koffler, Warren William *lawyer*
Koslow, Stephen Hugh *health science association administrator, pharmacologist, neuroscientist*
Kramer, Eleanor *retired real estate broker, tax specialist, financial consultant*
Kulok, William Allan *entrepreneur, venture capitalist*
Lamb, Kevin Thomas *lawyer*
Lampert, Michael Allen *lawyer*
Lane, Matthew Jay *lawyer*
Levin, Ronald Mitchell *geriatrician*
Link, Scott J. *lawyer*
Livingstone, John Leslie *accountant, economist, management consultant, educator*
Loring, Arthur *lawyer, diversified financial services company executive*
Marini, Alex P. *manufacturing executive*
Marshall-Beasley, Elizabeth *landscape architect*
McAfee, William James *lawyer*
Merey, John Howard *ophthalmologist*
Miller, Richard Jackson (Rick Miller) *lawyer*
Montgomery, Robert Morel, Jr. *lawyer*
Moore, George Crawford Jackson *lawyer*
Mrachek, Lorin Louis *lawyer*
Newmark, Emanuel *ophthalmologist*
Nolan, Richard Thomas *clergyman, educator*
Ogden, John Clifton III *environmental scientist, director*
Orlovsky, Donald Albert *lawyer*
Paine, James Carriger *federal judge*
Pantone, David *academic administrator*
Passy, Charles *writer*
Pingpank, Robert Charles *retired mathematics educator*
Pottash, A. Carter *psychiatrist, hospital executive*
Raab, Ira Jerry *lawyer, judge*
Robinson, Raymond Edwin *conductor, music educator, writer*
Ronan, William John *management consultant*
Ross, Edward Joseph *architect*
Rukeyser, M.S., Jr. *television consultant, writer*
Schneider, Lisa A. *lawyer*
Sims, Ashley Jane *accountant*
Spillias, Kenneth George *lawyer*
Stauderman, Bruce Ford *advertising executive, writer*
Strolla, Cory C. *lawyer*
Terwillegar, Jane Cusack *librarian, educator*
Thomashow, Steven Roy *military officer, intelligence officer*
Vecellio, Leo Arthur, Jr. *construction company executive*
Vilchez, Victoria Anne *lawyer*
Westman, Steven Ronald *rabbi*
Whitfield, Graham Frank *orthopedic surgeon*
Zeller, Ronald John *lawyer*

Weston
Alexander, Cynthia Louise *psychologist, educator*
Barnes, William Douglas *advertising executive*
Berry, Becky *music educator*
Gordon, Lori Heyman *psychotherapist, author, educator*
Holtzman, Gary Yale *retired diversified financial services company executive*
Kortlander, Susan Elizabeth *psychologist*
Lazar, Marioara *psychiatrist*
Marino, Dan (Daniel Constantino Marino Jr.) *sportscaster, retired professional football player*
Messa, Charles Angelo III *plastic surgeon*
Napp, Gudrun F. *artist*
Nogueras, Juan Jose *surgeon*

Wewahitchka
de Abreu, Sue *elementary school educator*

Wimauma
Shober, Amy *education educator*

Windermere
Cerri, Robert Noel *photographer*
Hahn, Dowon *pharmaceutical researcher, educator*
McGuire, Edward David, Jr. *lawyer*
Powell, Thomas Ervin *financial consultant, small business owner*

Winter Garden
Ellis, Missie Lynne *music educator*
Gillet, Pamela Kipping *special education educator*
Reeher, James Irwin *minister*
Stoddart, Mervin *religious studies educator, pastor*

Winter Haven
Bennett, Samuel *elementary school educator*
Boully, LaJuan Bonnie *minister, religious studies educator*
Burns, Arthur Lee *architect*
Goodman, Karen Lacerte *financial services executive*
Grierson, William *retired agriculturist*
Johnson, Gordon Selby *consulting electrical engineer*
Schepis, Anthony Joseph *artist, educator*
Susac, John Obren *neurologist, consultant*

Winter Park
Ackert, T(errence) W(illiam) *lawyer*
Alfond, Theodore B. *retired shoe company executive*
Bagley, Priscilla Annette *music educator, performing arts association administrator*
Benedict, Dorothy Jones *genealogist, researcher*
Bloodworth, Velda Jean *librarian, educator*
Blossey, Erich Carl *chemistry professor*
Carpan, Ann Carolyn *school librarian, educator*
Dempsey, Bernard Hayden, Jr. *lawyer*
Desmarais, Paul Leo *critical care nurse*
Douglas, Kathleen Mary Harrigan *retired psychotherapist, educator*
Granberry, Edwin Phillips, Jr. *safety engineer, consultant*
Gray, Anthony Rollin *retired finance company executive*
Hadley, Ralph Vincent III *lawyer*
Haendiges, Anne R. *marriage and family therapist*
Halladay, Laurie Ann *public relations consultant, food products executive*
Heinle, Richard Alan *lawyer*
Helms, Roger D. *lawyer*
Johnson, Constance Ann Trillich *web site designer*
Johnson, Kraig Nelson *lawyer, arbitrator, mediator*
Jontz, Jeffry Robert *lawyer*
Kincaid, Rodney Lyle *construction company executive*
Kindlund, Newton Carlton *retail executive*
Kittleson, Henry Marshall *lawyer*
Kraft, Kenneth Houston, Jr. *insurance agency executive*
Mason, Aimee Hunnicutt Romberger *retired philosophy and humanities educator*
McKean, Thomas Wayne *retired dentist, retired military officer*
Merrill, Harvie Martin *manufacturing executive, director*
Morgan, Mary Ann *lawyer*
Pineless, Hal Steven *neurologist*
Powers, Ronald George *management consultant*
Rogers, Rutherford David *librarian*
Rooks, Linda *writer*
Seymour, Thaddeus *language educator*
Short, Edmund Coen *retired education educator*
Starr, Martin Kenneth *management educator*
Steward, Sherry Ann *information technology executive, educator*
Swann, Richard Rockwell *lawyer, banker*
Therrien, Francois Xavier, Jr. *business and tax consultant*
Troutman, Holmes Russell *lawyer*
Wallace, Curtis Wilbern, Jr. *music director, organist*
Whitworth, Hall Baker *forest products company executive*
Wilson, Cecil Bruce *internist*
Wilson, Robley Conant, Jr. *language educator, editor, writer*
Wrancher, Elizabeth Ann *music educator, opera singer*
Zhang, Wenxian *librarian*

Winter Springs
McNeal, Mary Kay *secondary school educator*
San Miguel, Sandra Bonilla *social worker*

Zephyrhills
Barron, Ilona Eleanor *elementary school educator, consultant*
Walton, Shirley Dawn *retired medical technician*

GEORGIA

Acworth
Oloni, Anthony Olushegun *medical association administrator, director*
Pope, Robert Daniel *lawyer*

Adairsville
Dobson, Suzanne *science educator*

Albany
Erhardt, Walter L., Jr. *medical association administrator*
Forsyth, Rosalyn Moye *middle school educator*
Johnson, Debra Pope *education educator*
Marbury, Ritchey McGuire III *engineering executive, surveyor*

Peach, Paul E. *physician, health facility administrator*
Ratz, John Louis *dermatologist*
Rodriguez, Sergio Raul *music educator, conductor*
Wernick, Joel *health facility administrator*

Alpharetta

Adams, Kenneth Francis *automotive executive*
Bolton, Robin Jean *artist, painter*
Brands, James Edwin *medical products executive*
Bridges, Alan Lynn *physicist, researcher, application developer, computer scientist*
Bunker, Kimberly LeAnn *critical care nurse, emergency nurse practitioner*
Corby, Francis Michael, Jr. *business executive*
DiBattiste, Carol A. *military officer*
Filliat, Elizabeth Hartley *retired secondary school educator*
Fowler, Vivian Delores *insurance company executive*
Frankel, Andrew Joel *management consultant, information scientist*
Goetz, Richard J. *communications executive*
Hatcher, Barbara A. *lawyer*
Herbig, Joan E. *information technology executive*
Kurtz, Robert Arthur *finance company executive*
Myers, Michael Todd *accountant, telecommunications industry executive, director*
Reed, Wendy *management consultant company executive, information technology executive*
Sierra Mejia, Mauricio Andres *communications engineer*
Thomas, Robert L. *retired manufacturing company executive*
Walker, Thomas H. *real estate developer*
Weitz, John Jerome, Jr. *city planner*
Whitley, Lena Frances *French educator*
Winegar, Albert Lee *computer company executive*
Yeatman, Henry Clay *mechanical engineer*

Americus

Capitan, William Harry *university president emeritus*
Hooks, George Bardin *state legislator, insurance and real estate company executive*
Isaacs, Harold *history professor*
Reckford, Jonathan Thomas More *nonprofit organization administrator*
Stanford, Henry King *college president*
Tu, Chanh M. *ophthalmologist*

Andersonville

Boyles, Frederick Holdren *historian*

Athens

Adams, Michael Fred *academic administrator, political scientist, educator*
Algeo, John Thomas *association executive, retired educator*
Allsbrook, Ogden Olmstead, Jr. *retired economics professor*
Ames, Kathryn S. *library director*
Andrews, Grover Jene *retired adult education educator, administrator*
Baile, Clifton A. *biologist, researcher*
Baumann, Nancy *school librarian*
Beaird, James Ralph *lawyer, educator, dean*
Bennetzen, Jeffrey L. *molecular biologist*
Bertsch, Gary Kenneth *political science professor*
Black, Clanton Candler, Jr. *biochemistry professor, researcher*
Bullock, Charles Spencer III *political science educator, author, consultant*
Carlson, Ronald Lee *law educator*
Castenell, Louis Anthony *academic administrator*
Chu, Chung Kwang *medicinal chemistry professor*
Clute, Robert Eugene *political science professor*
Cook, J. Vincent *lawyer*
Cook, Joel *radiologist*
Crowley, John Francis III *university dean*
Darvill, Alan G. *biochemist, botanist, educator*
Davis, Claude-Leonard *lawyer, academic administrator*
Donovan, James M. *librarian, anthropologist*
Dunham, Richard E. III *lighting designer, consultant, set designer, educator*
Dunn, Delmer Delano *political science professor*
Ellington, Charles Ronald *lawyer, educator*
Evans, Damon *university athletics director*
Feldman, Edmund Burke *art critic*
Fincher, Cameron Lane *psychology professor*
Fink, Conrad Charles *journalist, educator, communications executive, consultant*
Garbin, Albeno Patrick *sociology educator*
Hellerstein, Walter *lawyer*
Herbert, James Arthur *retired art educator, artist, filmmaker*
Houser, Ronald Edward *lawyer, arbitrator, mediator*
Hoyt, Robert E. *dean, management educator*
Huszagh, Fredrick Wickett *lawyer, information technology executive, educator*
Johnson, Michael Kenneth *chemistry professor*
Kaufman, Glen Frank *art educator*
Kibler, James Everett *English language educator, writer*
Kretzschmar, William Addison, Jr. *language educator*
Kurtz, Paul Michael *law educator*
Law, John Harold *biochemistry educator*
Leebens-Mack, James H. *biologist*
McBee, Mary Louise *retired state legislator, academic administrator*
McCutcheon, Steven Clifton *civil and environmental engineer, hydrologist*
Melton, Wayne Charles *real estate executive*
Miller, Herbert Elmer *accountant*
Miller, Ronald Baxter *language educator, writer*
Mills, Mike *popular musician*
Mohamoud, Yusuf Mohamed *agricultural engineer*
Moran, Mary (Molly) Hurley *English language educator*
Nelson, Stuart Owen *agricultural engineer, researcher, educator*
Nichols, William Curtis *psychologist, educator, marriage and family therapist, consultant*
Olsen, Richard James *artist, educator*
Paul, William Dewitt, Jr. *retired art educator, photographer, videographer, museum director*
Pollack, Robert Harvey *psychology professor*
Potter, William Gray, Jr. *university librarian*
Puckett, Elizabeth Ann *law librarian, educator*
Rashleigh, Brenda *ecologist*
Richt, Mark *college football coach*
Schaefer, Henry Frederick III *chemistry professor*
Schleyer, Paul von Ragué *chemistry educator*
Shipley, David Elliott *lawyer, educator*
Smagorinsky, Peter *education educator*
Smith, Susan Carlton (Susan Carlton Smith Cavanagh) *artist, illustrator, sculptor*
Soloski, John *journalism and communications educator*
Staub, August William *theater producer, educator*
Stipe, Michael *musician, film producer*
Tolley, Edward Donald *lawyer*
Tyler, David Earl *retired veterinary medical educator*
Wessler, Susan R. *biologist, educator*
White, Rebecca Hanner *dean, law educator*
Winfield, Richard Dien *humanities educator*
Wraga, William Gerard *education educator*
Yang, Charles Qi-Xiang *chemistry educator, researcher, consultant*
Zinkhan, George Martin III *marketing educator*

Atlanta

Aaberg, Thomas Marshall, Sr. *academic administrator*
Aaron, Hank (Henry L. Aaron) *professional baseball team executive*
Abbott, Gay O. *bank executive*
Abdel-Khalik, Said Ibrahim *nuclear and mechanical engineering educator*
Abney, David P. *delivery service executive*
Abrams, Harold Eugene *lawyer*
Addison, James W. *lawyer*
Affonso, Dyanne D. *dean*
Aiken, Vernoy Fred *government agency administrator*
Albert, Marv *sportscaster, program director*
Albert, Ross Alan *lawyer*
Aldridge, John *lawyer*
Alexander, Alonzo III *music educator, composer*
Alexander, Cecil Abraham *academic administrator, consultant, retired architect*
Alexander, Kent B. *lawyer*
Alexander, Miles Jordan *lawyer*
Allan, Alexander R.C. (Sandy Allan) *food products executive*
Allen, Pinney L. *lawyer*
Allen, Randall L. *lawyer*
Allison, Stuart Anthony *chemistry professor, researcher*
Allitt, Patrick Nicholas *history professor, writer*
Altman, Robert *lawyer*
Amanpour, Christiane *news correspondent*
Ames, Matthew B. *lawyer*
Ames, William Francis *mathematician, educator*
An, Dorothy *lawyer*
Andersen, Morten *professional football player*
Anderson, Al H., Jr. *communications executive*
Anderson, Peter Joseph *lawyer*
Anderson, Ray C. *carpet company executive*
Anderson, Richard H. *air transportation executive*
Anthony, Barbara Cox *foundation administrator*
Arani, Ardy A. *marketing professional, sports association administrator*
Arias, Ileana *psychiatrist, educator*
Arroyo, F. Thaddeus *telecommunications industry executive*
Arthur, Thomas Carlton *former dean, law educator*
Asbill, Richard M. *lawyer*
Ashby, Eugene Christopher *chemistry professor*
Attridge, Richard Byron *lawyer*
Austin, Jesse Hinnant III *lawyer*
Bahl, Roy Winford *economist, educator, consultant*
Bainbridge, Frederick Freeman III *architect*
Baird, Marianne Saunorus *critical care clinical nurse specialist, administrator*
Baker, Thomas William *lawyer*
Baker, Thurbert E. *state attorney general*
Bales, Virginia Shankle *health science association administrator*
Bankoff, Joseph R. *art association administrator*
Bao, Gang *biomedical engineer, educator*
Barker, William Daniel *hospital administrator*
Barkley, Charles Wade *sportscaster, retired professional basketball player*
Barkoff, Rupert Mitchell *lawyer*
Barnes, David A. *delivery service executive*
Barnett, Preston B. *lawyer, communications executive*
Barr, Robert Laurence, Jr. *lawyer*
Barron, Patrick Kenneth *bank executive*
Barros, Paulino R., Jr. *communications executive*
Barry, R. Michael *lawyer*
Bastian, Edward H. *air transportation executive*
Batson, Richard Neal *lawyer*
Baum, Stanley M. *lawyer*
Bayne, Katie J. (Katherine) *marketing executive*
Beazer, Brian C. *construction executive*
Beckham, Walter Hull III *lawyer*
Beerman, Joel I. *lawyer, chemical manufacturing company executive*
Belkin, Steven *professional sports team owner*
Bell, Griffin Boyette *lawyer, former United States attorney general*
Bell, Thomas Devereaux, Jr. *real estate company executive*
Bellamy, Ivory *elementary school educator, consultant*
Bellamy, Walter *professional basketball player*
Bellanca, Joseph Paul *engineering construction executive*
Benario, Herbert William *classicist, educator*
Benham, Robert *state supreme court justice*
Bennett, Jay D. *lawyer*
Benston, George James *accountant, economist*
Benveniste, Lawrence M. *dean*
Berga, Sarah L. *obstetrician, gynecologist, educator*
Berger, Mitchell Zachary *oncologist*
Bergeson, Donna Pottis *lawyer*
Berkelhamer, Jay Ellis *pediatrician*
Berkelman, Ruth *medical educator*
Bernardino, Carlo Roberto *ophthalmologist, educator*
Berry, Dennis (G. Dennis Berry) *publishing executive*
Berryman, Robert Mogabgab *systems engineer*
Beystehner, John J. *transportation executive*
Bibb, Daniel Roland *art restorer*
Biggins, J. Veronica *bank executive*
Bijol, Vanesa *nephrologist, educator, pathologist, researcher*
Billington, Barry E. *lawyer*
Birch, Stanley Francis, Jr. *federal judge*
Bird, Wendell Raleigh *lawyer*
Bisher, James Furman *journalist, writer*
Black, Kenneth, Jr. *retired insurance company executive*
Blackburn, William Stanley *lawyer*
Blackford, Barbara L. *lawyer, manufacturing executive*
Blackstock, Jerry B. *lawyer*
Blake, Frank (Francis Stanton) *consumer products company executive, lawyer*
Blalock, Rebecca A. *information technology specialist*
Blank, A(ndrew) Russell *lawyer*
Bleicher, Michael Nathaniel *mathematics professor*
Block, Andrew *lawyer*
Bloodworth, Albert William Franklin *lawyer*
Blum, Terry Christine *dean*
Boden, Scott David *orthopedic surgeon, spine surgeon, educator*
Boisseau, Richard Robert *lawyer*
Bolch, Carl Edward, Jr. *oil industry executive, lawyer*
Bonds, John Wilfred, Jr. *lawyer*
Bondurant, Emmet Jopling, II, *lawyer*
Boone, J. William *lawyer*
Booth, Gordon Dean, Jr. *lawyer*
Bostic, James E., Jr. *paper company executive*
Bowden, Henry Lumpkin, Jr. *lawyer*
Bowen, Harold J. (Jay) III *investment company executive*
Bowers, W. Paul *utilities executive*
Bowling, Daniel S. III *lawyer*
Boynton, Frederick George *lawyer*
Bradshaw, Rod Eric *personnel consultant*
Branch, Thomas Broughton III *lawyer*
Brandenburg, David Saul *gastroenterologist, educator*
Braswell, Robert M. *state agency administrator*
Bratton, James Henry, Jr. *lawyer*
Braun, Robert David *aerospace engineer, educator*
Brecher, Armin George *lawyer*
Breeden, Mimi *bank executive*
Brelsford, Theodore William, Jr. *theology studies educator*
Bremer, Karen Ingrid *food service executive*
Bremner, James Douglas *psychiatrist, researcher, education educator*
Brewster, William Howard *lawyer*
Bridges, Shirley Walton *air transportation executive*
Bright, David Forbes *academic administrator, classicist, educator*
Broadnax, Walter D. *university president, educator*
Brock, John F. *beverage company executive*
Brooks, Martha Finn *consumer products company executive*
Brown, Janine *lawyer*
Brown, Lorene B(yron) *retired library educator*
Brown-Olmstead, Amanda *public relations executive*
Bryant, Gregory Alexander *bishop*
Buffenstein, Daryl R. *lawyer*
Bull, Frank James *retired architect*
Burge, William Lee *retired credit manager*
Burns, Thomas Samuel *history professor*
Butler, Gloria Singleton *state legislator*
Butterworth, S. Kendall *lawyer*
Byrne, Granville Bland III *lawyer*
Cadenhead, Alfred Paul *lawyer*
Cagle, Casey *lieutenant governor*
Calhoun, Scott Douglas *lawyer*
Campbell, Michael H. *air transportation executive*
Carbonell, Joaquin R. III *telecommunications industry executive, lawyer*
Carley, George H. *state supreme court justice*
Carnes, Julie Elizabeth *judge*
Carpenter, David Allan *lawyer*
Carter, Dudley Rochelle *lawyer*
Carter, Jimmy (James Earl Carter Jr.) *39th President of the United States*
Carter, Stephen M. *telecommunications manufacturing industry executive*
Cates, Christopher Upton *cardiologist*
Cathy, S. Truett *food products executive*
Chafee, Ingrid Roberta Hoover Coleman *retired language educator*
Chambers, Anne Cox *publishing executive, former diplomat*
Chancy, Mark A. *bank executive*
Chandler, Elizabeth B. *lawyer*
Chandler, Robert Charles *healthcare consultant*
Chapman, Hugh McMaster *banker*
Chasen, Sylvan Herbert *data processing executive, financial planner*
Chau, Pin Pin *bank executive*
Cheatham, Sharif *lawyer*
Chiang, Tze I. *economist, researcher, consultant*
Chilivis, Nickolas Peter *retired lawyer*
Cilella, Mary Winifred *director*
Circeo, Louis Joseph, Jr. *research scientist, civil engineer*
Clarke, Thomas Hal *lawyer*
Cleage, Pearl Michelle *writer, playwright, journalist*
Clearo, Kellie Anne *internist, pharmacist, psychiatrist*
Clough, (Gerald) Wayne *academic administrator*
Cobb, Charles Kenche, Jr. *lawyer, real estate broker*
Cohen, Ezra Harry *lawyer*
Cohen, George Leon *lawyer*
Cohen, Lori G. *lawyer*
Cohen, N. Jerold *lawyer*
Coleman, Terry Lewis *state legislator*
Collins, Steven M. *lawyer*
Compans, Richard W. *microbiology educator*
Comstock, Robert Donald, Jr. *real estate executive*
Conboy, Kevin Patrick *lawyer*
Connelly, Terrence John, Sr. *broadcast executive*
Cook, Philip Carter *lawyer*
Cooper, Gerald Rice *clinical pathologist*
Cooper, Jerome Maurice *architect*
Cooper, Marc-Antonie *finance educator*
Cooper, Simon F. *hotel executive*
Cooper-Ruspoli, Annie Nataf *psychiatrist, director*
Copenhaver, John Barns *not-for-profit executive, lawyer*
Corr, James Vanis *furniture manufacturing executive, accountant*
Correa, Adolfo *epidemiologist, educator*
Costello, John H. III *business and marketing executive*
Cox, Bobby (Robert Joe Cox) *professional baseball manager*
Cox, Kathy *school system administrator*
Cox, Nancy Jane *microbiologist*
Cramer, Howard Ross *geologist, environmental consultant*
Crawford, Kyle A. *industrial engineer*
Cressler, John David *electrical engineering educator*
Croft, Terrence Lee *lawyer, mediator, arbitrator*
Crow, Tim *consumer products company executive*
Crump-Caine, Lynn *food service executive*
Culhane, John Joseph *lawyer, food products executive*
Cummings, Alexander B., Jr. *food products executive*
Curran, James W. *epidemiologist, educator, dean*
Curtis, J. Vaughan *lawyer*
Curtis, Philip Kerry *executive recruiter, lawyer*
Cutshaw, Kenneth Andrew *lawyer*
Dalton, John Joseph *lawyer*
Danielson, Gilbert Lawrence *consumer products company executive*
Darden, Claibourne Henry, Jr. *marketing research professional*
Darden, George Washington, III, (Buddy Darden) *former congressman, lawyer*
David, Todd R. *lawyer*
Davis, Benjamin Alando *lawyer*
Davis, D. Scott *delivery service executive*
Davis, Erroll Brown, Jr. *academic administrator, former utilities executive*
Davis, Frank Tradewell, Jr. *lawyer*
Davis, Lawrence William *radiation oncologist*
Davis, Marvin Arnold *manufacturing executive*
Davis, Michael *medical educator*
Dawson, Robert G. *telecommunications industry executive*
Dayhoff, Diane *retail executive*
Dean, James Edward *retired state official*
Deane, Richard Hunter, Jr. *former federal judge, lawyer*
DeAngelo, Joseph J. *consumer products company executive*
Dearman, Andrew J. III *utilities executive*
Deason, Stephen Earl *computer company executive*
Declercq, Nico Felicien *research scientist*
DeCosta, Benjamin R. *airport executive*
de Heer, Walter A. *physics professor*
DeLong, Mahlon R. *neurologist, educator*
Deming, N. Karen *lawyer*
Denny, Richard Alden, Jr. *retired lawyer*
DePaoli, Lou *professional sports team executive*
DeRodes, Robert P. *consumer products company executive*
De Rosa, Christopher Thomas *biomedical researcher*
de Waal, Frans B.M. *biologist, psychology professor*
Dickinson, Robert Earl *atmospheric scientist, educator, retired science administrator*
Diedrich, Richard Joseph *architect*
Dierker, David F. *bank executive*
Dietz, William Harry *pediatrician*
Dobbins, Benjamin Knox *lawyer*
Dobson, Rick *metals company executive*
Domby, Arthur H. *lawyer*
Donald, James Edward *retired career officer, government agency executive*
Dorfman, Richard *bank executive*
Dorris, William E. *lawyer*
D'Orsi, Carl Joseph *medical educator, radiologist, researcher*
Dotson, Albert *not-for-profit fundraiser*
Douglas, J. Alexander M. (Sandy) *beverage company executive*
Douglas, John Lewis *lawyer*
Douglas, William W. *food products executive*
Dowling, Roderick Anthony *investment banker*
Doyle, Michael A. *lawyer*
Dramis, Francis (Fran) A., Jr. *communications executive*
Driver, Walter W., Jr. *lawyer*
Duffey, William Simon, Jr. *federal judge, former prosecutor*
Duffie, L. Traywick *lawyer*
Duffy, Bill *professional sports team executive*
Dunlevie, Steven S. *lawyer*
Durrett, James Frazer, Jr. *retired lawyer*

Dutt, Kamla *medical educator*
Dykes, Ronald Mitchell *retired telecommunications industry executive*
Dyson, James David *lawyer*
Ebersole, W. Daniel *state official*
Eckert, Charles Alan *chemical engineering educator*
Eckl, William Wray *lawyer*
Edmondson, J.L. (James Larry Edmondson) *federal judge*
Edwards, Stephen Allen *lawyer*
Egan, Michael Joseph *retired lawyer, state legislator*
Eiselstein, William P. (Billy Eiselstein) *lawyer*
Elgison, Martin J. *lawyer*
Ellingwood, Bruce Russell *structural engineer, educator*
Elliott, Mark Lee *lawyer*
Eskew, Michael L. *package distribution company executive*
Esser, Patrick J. *communications executive*
Etheridge, Jack Paul *arbitrator, mediator, retired judge*
Evans, Dwight H. *utilities executive*
Evans, Orinda D. *federal judge*
Faber, Olaf Ulrich *structural engineer*
Fajardo, Geroncio Cagigas *epidemiologist*
Falk, Henry *pediatrician, epidemiologist, researcher*
Fancher, Kristen L. *lawyer*
Fanning, Thomas Andrew *utilities executive*
Farnham, Clayton Henson *lawyer*
Faulkner, Kristine *communications executive*
Fayard, Gary P. *beverage company executive*
Felton, Jule Wimberly, Jr. *lawyer*
Fenton, Jeffrey J. *management consultant, wholesale distribution executive*
Ferris, James Leonard *academic administrator*
Finan, Irial *beverage company executive*
Finkelstein, David Ritz *physicist, educator, consultant*
Finley, Michael Valton *foundation executive*
Fischbach, Peter *pediatrician*
Flagg Davis, Vivian Annette *librarian, researcher, public information officer*
Fleming, Julian Denver, Jr. *lawyer*
Fleury, Marc *application developer*
Foege, William Herbert *public health administrator, educator*
Forbes, Theodore McCoy, Jr. *arbitrator, mediator, retired lawyer*
Forney, Larry J. *chemical engineer, educator*
Forry, Robert H. *lawyer*
Fortin, Raymond D. *lawyer, bank executive*
Fortuna, Julian Anthony *lawyer, accountant*
Foster, John Witherspoon *lawyer*
Fowler, Bruce Andrew *toxicologist, researcher, public health service official*
Fox, Ronald Forrest *physicist, educator*
Francis, Julie *beverage company executive*
Franklin, Robert Michael, Jr. *academic administrator, theology studies educator*
Franklin, Shirley Clarke *mayor*
Frederick, Paula J. *lawyer*
Freedman, Louis Martin *dentist*
Freeman, Thomas E. *bank executive*
Frias, Jaime Luis *retired pediatrician, educator*
Gailey, Chan, Jr., (Thomas Chandler Gailey) *college football coach*
Galambos, John Thomas *internist, medical educator*
Gallagher, Thomas C. *diversified manufacturing executive*
Gambrell, David Henry *lawyer*
Ganaway, George Kenneth *psychiatrist, psychoanalyst, educator, researcher*
Gangwal, Rakesh *air transportation executive*
Garland, LaRetta Matthews *psychologist, nursing educator*
Garrett, E. Reid *lawyer*
Garrett, Michael D. *utilities executive*
Gary, Kenneth J. *lawyer*
Gay, Robert Derril *behavioral health consultant*
Gayle, Helene D. *pediatrician, public health service officer*
Gearon, John Michael, Sr., (Michael Gearon) *professional sports team owner*
Gearon, John Michael, Jr., (Michael Gearon) *professional sports team owner, communications executive*
Genberg, Ira *lawyer*
Gephardt, Dick (Richard Andrew Gephardt) *consulting compay executive, lawyer, former congressman*
Gerakitis, Richard *lawyer*
Gerberding, Julie Louise *federal agency administrator*
Gershenhorn, Alan *delivery service executive*
Giddens, Don Peyton *engineering educator, researcher*
Girth, Marjorie Louisa *lawyer, educator*
Glaser, Arthur Henry *lawyer, mediator*
Glass, Roger I. *virologist*
Goldfarb, Eric Daniel *information technology executive*
Goldman, John Abner *rheumatologist, immunologist, educator*
Goldstein, Elliott *lawyer, director*
Goldstein, Eric L. *historian, educator*
Gonzalez, Ruben Rene *biochemist, researcher, educator*
Goodman, Seymour Evan *computer science and international studies educator, researcher, consultant*
Goodwin, George Evans *public relations executive*
Gordon, Frank Jeffrey *medical educator*
Gorman, Steve M. *communications executive*
Grady, Kevin E. *lawyer*
Gramlich, Larry E. *lawyer*
Grant, Susan *television executive*
Graves, Judson *lawyer*
Gray, Charnelda L. *pharmacist*
Green, Holcombe Tucker, Jr. *investment company executive*
Greene, Kevin C. *lawyer*
Greene, Mary Katherine *lawyer*
Gregory, Mel Hyatt, Jr. *retired insurance company executive*
Gregory, Wilton D. *archbishop*
Grice, Richard W. *lawyer*
Groton, James Purnell *lawyer, arbitrator*
Grout, Robert W. *lawyer*
Guberman, Sidney *painter, writer*
Guerra, Larry Cacao *engineer, researcher*
Guest, Rita Carson *interior designer*
Gupta, Sanjay *neurosurgeon, educator, medical correspondent, journalist*
Hackett, Stanley Hailey *lawyer*
Hakes, Jay Edward *library director, former federal agency administrator*
Hall, Beverly L. *school system administrator*
Hall, Wilbur Dallas, Jr. *medical educator*
Hallen, Barry *philosopher, educator*
Handel, Karen *state official*
Hanna, Frank Joseph, Jr. *credit company executive*
Hao, Chunhai *pathologist, researcher*
Harkey, Robert Shelton *retired lawyer*
Harris, Clifford Joseph, Jr., (T.I., Tip Harris) *rap artist*
Harris, Harold Stephen, Jr. *lawyer*
Harrison, George Brooks *engineer, researcher, retired military officer*
Hartle, Robert Wyman *retired literature and language professor*
Hartley, Bob *professional hockey coach*
Harvey, Adia M. *sociology professor*
Harvey, James A. *lawyer*
Hasson, James Keith, Jr. *lawyer, educator*
Hatch, Helen Davis *architect*
Hatcher, Charles Ross, Jr. *surgeon, health facility administrator*
Hatcher, James A. *lawyer*
Hauenstein, Glen W. *air transportation executive*
Hawks, Barrett Kingsbury *lawyer*
Hay, Peter Heinrich *law educator*
Hayes, Jimmy W. *media company executive*
Hays, Richard R. *lawyer*
Hays, William Grady, Jr. *corporate financial and banking consultant*
Heady, Eugene Joseph *lawyer*
Healy, Bridget M. *lawyer*
Heberton, George H. *lawyer*
Heit, Marny *lawyer*
Heller, Dan L. *lawyer*
Henry, Ronald James Whyte *academic administrator, physicist, educator*
Henry, Thomas Reid *education educator, researcher*
Herman, John C. *lawyer*
Hess, Dennis William *chemical engineering educator*
Hester, Francis Bartow, III, (Frank Hester) *lawyer*
Hester, Thomas Roderick, Jr. *plastic surgeon, educator*
Higginbotham, Eve Juliet *ophthalmologist, educator, dean*
Hill, Allen Edward *delivery service executive*
Hilliard, Robert Glenn *insurance company executive, lawyer*
Hinchey, John William *lawyer*
Hines, Preston Harris *state supreme court justice*
Hinkel, Daniel Farris *lawyer, writer, investment company executive*
Hinson, H. Douglas *lawyer*
Hobby, Scott M. *lawyer*
Hodges, Dewey Harper *aerospace engineer, educator*
Hoff, Gerhardt Michael *lawyer, insurance company executive*
Hoffman, Fred L. *human resources specialist*
Hoffman, Michael William *lawyer, accountant*
Hogan, John Donald *retired college dean, finance educator*
Holland, George Edison, Jr., (Ed) *lawyer, utilities executive*
Hollis, Timothy Martin *bank executive*
Holly, Timothy Arnold *security firm executive*
Honaman, J. Craig *health facility administrator*
Hopkins, Donald Roswell *public health physician*
Hopkins, John David *lawyer*
Hopping, Janet Melinda *educational association administrator*
Horsley, Alex *director*
Hough, Leslie Seldon *educational association administrator*
Howard, Harry Clay *lawyer*
Howard, Ralph O'Sullivan, Jr. *geologist, researcher*
Howell, Arthur *lawyer*
Hubbell, Fred Shelton *insurance company executive*
Hudgins, Roger J. *pediatric neurosurgeon*
Huff, Rolla P. *Internet company executive*
Hug, Carl Casimir, Jr. *pharmacology and anesthesiology educator, medical ethics educator*
Hughes, James Mitchell *epidemiologist, educator*
Hull, Frank Mays *federal judge*
Humann, L. Phillip *bank executive*
Hunstein, Carol *state supreme court justice*
Hunter, Forrest Walker *lawyer*
Huo, Xiaoming *mathematician, educator*
Hussey, Kent J. *consumer products company executive*
Hyland, Gregory E. *home building products executive*
Ide, Roy William III *lawyer*
Igietseme, Joseph Ugbodaga *biomedical researcher, educator*
Isaf, Fred Thomas *lawyer*
Isdell, (Edward) Neville *beverage company executive*
Israili, Zafar Hasan *pharmacologist, educator*
Izard, John *lawyer*
Jackson, Geraldine *entrepreneur*
Jaffe, Harold W. *federal agency administrator*
James, Anthony R. *utilities executive*
Janney, Donald Wayne *lawyer*
Jefferson, Jonathan Kenneth *dean*
Jeffery, Geoffrey Marron *medical parasitologist*
Jenkins, Albert Felton, Jr. *lawyer*
Jett-Parmer, Jonathan Jackson *mechanical engineer*
Johns, Michael Marieb Edward *otolaryngologist, academic administrator*
Johnson, Carl Frederick *marriage and family therapist*
Johnson, Carrie Clements *executive*
Johnson, Ernie, Jr. *sportscaster*
Johnson, Joe Marcus *professional basketball player*
Johnson, John H. *lawyer*
Johnson, (Frederick) Ross *international management advisory company executive*
Johnson, Weyman Thompson, Jr. *lawyer*
Jolley, Samuel Delanor, Jr. *academic administrator*
Jones, Andruw Rudolf *professional baseball player*
Jones, Chipper (Larry Wayne Jones Jr.) *professional baseball player*
Jones, Glower Whitehead *lawyer*
Jordak, John A., Jr. *lawyer*
Juang, Fred (Biing-Hwang Juang) *engineering educator*
Judd, George R. *wholesale distribution executive*
Jurkiewicz, Maurice John *surgeon, educator*
Kaelin, Darryl Louis *medical educator*
Kahn, Bernd *radiochemist, educator*
Kalafut, George Wendell *retired distribution company executive, retired naval officer*
Kaminshine, Steven J. *dean, law educator*
Karp, Herbert Rubin *neurologist, educator*
Katz, Joel Abraham *lawyer*
Kaufman, Mark David *lawyer*
Kaufman, Mark Stuart *lawyer*
Kaywood, Sam K., Jr. *lawyer*
Keiller, James Bruce *clergyman, dean*
Kelley, Brian P. *beverage and former relocation services company executive*
Kelley, Linda Elaine Spadafora *school psychologist, educator*
Kelly, Craig James *bank executive*
Kelly, Geoffrey J. *lawyer, beverage company executive*
Kelly, James Patrick *lawyer*
Kennedy, James Cox *publishing and media executive*
Kennedy, Robert *political science professor*
Kent, Muhtar *beverage company executive*
Keough, Donald Raymond *investment and former beverage company executive*
Kessler, Richard Paul, Jr. *lawyer*
Ketchum, Mark D. *consumer products company executive*
Khoury, Kenneth F. *lawyer, air transportation executive*
Kilgore, Cada T. III *lawyer*
Killorin, Robert Ware *lawyer*
King, K(imberly) N(elson) *computer science educator*
King, Linda Orr *museum director, consultant*
King, Spencer Bidwell III *cardiologist, educator, medical educator*
Kingsbury, Michael Bryant *organist, retired elementary school educator, retired secondary school educator*
Kirby, C. Eugene, Jr. *bank executive*
Kitchens, William H. *lawyer*
Klein, Jonathan *broadcast executive*
Klibanoff, Hank *journalist*
Kline, Lowry F. *beverage company executive, lawyer*
Klippel, John H. *physician, medical association administrator*
Kloer, Philip Baldwin *critic*
Knapp, Charles Boynton *economist, former university president, educator*
Kneisel, Edmund M. *lawyer*
Knight, Billy (William R. Knight) *professional sports team executive*
Knowles, Marjorie Fine *law educator, dean*
Kolshak, Joseph C. *air transportation executive*
Kontio, Peter *lawyer*
Kovalchuk, Ilya *professional hockey player*
Krishnamurthy, Ramesh Saligrama *environmental scientist, researcher*
Kuehn, Kurt P. *delivery service executive*
Kuklenyik, Zsuzsanna *chemist, researcher*
Kung, Lisa *lawyer*
Kuntz, Marion Lucile Leathers *classicist, historian, educator*
Lackland, Theodore Howard *lawyer*
Lamberth, James A. *lawyer*
Lamon, Harry Vincent, Jr. *lawyer*
Landau, Michael B. *law educator*
Landen, Ashley Renee *mechanical engineer*
Landon, James Henry *lawyer*
Laney, James Thomas *former ambassador, educator*
Latham, John L. *lawyer*
Lawley, Thomas Joseph *dean, medical educator*
Lazarus, Mark *broadcast executive*
Leach, James Glover *lawyer*
Leonard, David Morse *lawyer*
Lester, Charles Turner, Jr. *lawyer*
Lewcock, Ronald Bentley *architect, educator*
Lewis, Earl *academic administrator*
Lewis, Stephen E. *lawyer*
Lieberman, Laura Crowell *arts administrator, artist, critic*
Liebman, Gregg *communications executive*
Liebmann, Seymour W. *construction executive, consultant*
Lim, Sung Kyu *computer scientist, educator*
Lin, Ming-Chang *physical chemistry professor, researcher*
Linder, Harvey Ronald *lawyer, arbitrator, mediator*
Linkous, William Joseph, Jr. *lawyer*
Lipshutz, Robert Jerome *lawyer, former government official*
Liu, Zheng *economist, educator*
Lobb, William Atkinson *financial services executive*
Lockhart, Dennis P. *bank executive*
Loewy, Robert Gustav *aerospace executive, engineering educator*
Long, Leland Timothy *retired geophysics educator, seismologist*
Long, Robert Richard *banker*
Looby, Brian William *lawyer, lobbyist*
Loomis, Kenan Gregg *lawyer*
Love, Gay McLawhorn *manufacturing executive*
Loveland, L. Joseph, Jr. *lawyer*
Loven, Andrew Witherspoon *environmental engineering company executive*
Lowe, Jonathan Wayne *lawyer*
Lower, Robert Cassel *lawyer, educator*
Lu, Hanchao *humanities educator, writer*
Lubin, Michael Frederick *physician, educator*
Luce, Richard *university librarian*
Luce, Willard Ray *historian, director*
Luckovich, Mike *cartoonist*
Luger, Richard *economics professor*
Lund, Victor L. *healthcare company executive*
Lunsford, Mike (Michael Cameron Lunsford) *Internet company executive*
Ly, Hinh *science educator*
Lynch-Stieglitz, Jean *geophysicist, educator*
Lynn, David G. *biology and chemistry professor*
Macadam, Stephen E. *wholesale distribution executive*
Macenczak, Lee Andrew *air transportation executive*
Mackay, Gregory James *plastic surgeon*
MacLeish, Peter R. *neuroscientist*
Malhotra, Naresh Kumar *marketing educator*
Malone, Adam *lawyer*
Malone, James Hiram *graphics designer, journalist, writer*
Manley, David Bott III *lawyer*
Manning, George Taylor *lawyer*
Mansour, Kamal A. *cardiothoracic surgeon*
Marohn, William D. *consumer products company executive*
Marr, Daniel G. *food products executive*
Marshall, John Treutlen *lawyer, educator*
Martin, David Edward *health sciences educator*
Marvin, Charles Arthur *law educator*
Mason, Karol V. *lawyer*
Massey, Walter Eugene *retired academic administrator, physicist*
Mast, Kent E. *lawyer*
Mathews, Brian Scott *librarian*
Matschullat, Dale Lewis *lawyer*
McAlister, Harold Alister *astronomer*
McAlpin, Kirk Martin *lawyer*
McCann, Brian Michael *professional baseball player*
McCarthy, Ian J. *construction executive*
McChesney, Michael C. *computer company executive*
McClure, Teri Plummer *lawyer, delivery service executive*
McCrary, Charles D. *utilities executive*
McDavid, Sara June *librarian*
McDevitt, John *delivery service executive*
McDonald, Kristen *lawyer*
McDowell, David Lynn *mechanical engineering educator*
McFall, John *performing company executive*
McGibbon, James R. *lawyer*
McGowan, Angela Kay *government agency administrator, researcher*
McGuinn, Michael Edward III *retired army officer*
McIntire, Larry Vern *biomedical engineering educator*
McLean, James Albert *artist, educator*
McMahon, Donald Aylward *investor, corporate director*
McNabb, Dianne Leigh *investment banker, accountant*
McNeill, Thomas Ray *lawyer*
McTier, Charles Harvey *foundation administrator*
Mecke, William Moyn *public information officer*
Meindl, James Donald *electrical engineering educator, academic administrator*
Mellott, John C. *publishing executive*
Melton, Harold D. *state supreme court justice*
Menear, Craig *retail executive*
Mercer, John T.W. *lawyer*
Merdek, Andrew Austin *publishing and media executive, lawyer*
Merkel-Moran, Christa Ilse *investor, linguist, educator*
Merrill, Allan P. *construction executive*
Meyer, James Sampson *art historian, educator*
Meyer, Richard W. *university librarian*
Mialon, Hugo *economics professor*
Mildenhall, Jonathan *beverage company executive*
Miller, Douglas Linn *lawyer*
Miller, Sue *information technology executive*
Miller, Zell Bryan *former senator, governor*
Minneman, Kenneth Paul *pharmacology educator*
Mitchell, Stephen Milton *investment company executive*
Mize, Gerald L., Jr. *lawyer*
Mobley, John Homer, II, *lawyer*
Moeling, Walter Goos, IV, *lawyer*
Moeller, Joseph W. *forest products company executive*
Mogabgab, Rose-Warren Berryman *academic administrator, writer*
Moore, Philip Nicholas *author*
Morant, Brenda White *publishing executive, small business owner, investor*
Morgan, Elizabeth Ann *lawyer*
Mowrey, Robert D. *lawyer*
Mull, Gale W. *lawyer*
Muller, Edward Robert *energy executive, lawyer*
Mullin, Bernard James *professional sports team executive*
Murphy, James Jeffrey *electronics executive*
Murphy, Kenyon W. *lawyer*
Muth, Richard Ferris *economics professor*
Nagel, Vernon J. *chemicals and eletronics executive*
Nahai, Foad *plastic surgeon, educator*

Nahmias, David E. *prosecutor*
Neil, Robert F. *broadcast executive*
Nelson, Allen W. *lawyer, insurance claims management company executive*
Nemeroff, Charles Barnet *neurobiology and psychiatry educator*
Nerem, Robert Michael *engineering educator, consultant*
Newman, Stuart *lawyer*
Newton, Floyd Childs III *lawyer*
Nix, Jerry W. *automotive executive*
Noe, Elizabeth Hardy *lawyer*
Norman, Albert George, Jr. *lawyer*
Norman, Elaine Mitchell *information technology executive*
Nosakhere, Akilah Shukura Montsho *librarian, consultant, editor, writer*
Nunn, Donald Ray *plastic surgeon*
Nurkin, Sidney J. *lawyer*
Oakley, Godfrey Porter, Jr. *medical educator*
Oakley, Mary Ann Bryant *lawyer*
O'Day, Stephen Edward *lawyer*
O'Kelley, William Clark *federal judge*
Olansky, Sidney *retired dermatologist*
O'Leary, Robert C. *publishing and media executive*
Oliker, Vladimir *mathematician, educator*
Oliver-Warren, Mary Elizabeth *retired library science educator, library and information scientist*
Orr, A. Summey III *lawyer*
Osburne, Robert Carl *endocrinologist, educator*
Osgood, Christopher Mykel *radio sales manager*
Osorio, Claudio E. *computer company executive*
Ossewaarde, Anne Winkler *real estate company executive*
Ouweleen, Michael *communications executive*
Owens, Christine M. *delivery service executive*
Owens, Laura Lewis *lawyer*
Palmer, Charles F. *lawyer*
Palmer, Vicki R. *food products executive*
Pan, Yi *computer science educator*
Parsons, Leonard Jon *marketing educator, consultant*
Partlett, David F. *dean, law educator*
Patterson, Dennis M. *bank executive*
Patton, Carl Vernon *academic administrator, educator*
Patton, Laurie Louise *religious studies educator, writer*
Peacock, Lamar Batts *retired physician*
Pelypenko, Elizabeth *lawyer*
Penn, Darren W. *lawyer*
Pennington, Richard J. *police chief*
Peponis, John *architect, educator*
Perdue, George (Sonny Perdue) *governor, former state legislator*
Perera, Unil A.G. *physics educator, researcher*
Perez, Beatriz R. *marketing executive*
Perry, Timothy Sewell *lawyer*
Persons, (W.) Ray (W. Ray Persons) *lawyer, legal association administrator*
Petrik, Michael Thomas *lawyer*
Pike, Larry Samuel *lawyer*
Pilcher, James Brownie *lawyer*
Pindle, Arthur Jackson, Jr. *philosopher, researcher*
Pless, Laurance Davidson *lawyer*
Polhamus, Barbara *nutritionist, educator*
Polk, James Ray *journalist*
Polk, Malcolm *chemistry professor*
Portman, John C., Jr. *architect, developer*
Pottle, Steven L. *lawyer*
Powers, Susan J. *information technology executive*
Price, Elizabeth Anne *lawyer*
Prince, M. David (Morris David Prince) *retired electronics executive, computer graphics designer, educator*
Pritchett, Amy R. *aerospace engineer, educator*
Prucino, Diane L. *lawyer*
Pu, Calton *computer scientist*
Pulgram, William Leopold *architect, space designer*
Quillian, J. Kirk *lawyer*
Quittmeyer, Peter Charles *lawyer*
Raby, Kenneth Alan *lawyer, retired military officer*
Rachel, David P. *lawyer*
Rafuse, Nancy E. *lawyer, director*
Ragland, William McKenzie, Jr. *lawyer, real estate developer*
Rahnema, Farzad *engineering educator, department chairman*
Ramsey, Ira Clayton *retired petroleum industry executive*
Raper, Charles Albert *retired management consultant*
Ratcliffe, David M. *utilities executive*
Rawls, James C. *lawyer*
Raymond, Usher, IV, (Usher) *vocalist, actor*
Reece, Richard Kent *finance executive*
Reed, Glen Alfred *lawyer*
Reed, James Whitfield *internist, educator, endocrinologist*
Reed, William R., Jr. *bank executive*
Reinhardt, Daniel Sargent *lawyer*
Remar, Robert Boyle *lawyer*
Renteria, Edgar *professional baseball player*
Rhodes, Thomas Willard *lawyer*
Riccio, Felix *professional sports team owner*
Riddell, Stephen W. *lawyer*
Ridley, Clarence Haverty *retail executive*
Riggs, Gregory Lynn *lawyer*
Riordan, Robert P. *lawyer*
Robelot, Jane *anchor*
Roberts, Edward Graham *librarian*
Robinson, J. Patrick *consumer products company executive*
Robison, Carolyn Love *retired librarian*
Rodríguez, Rocío *artist*
Rogers, Brenda Gayle *educational administrator, educator, consultant*
Rogers, DeWitt Ralph *lawyer*
Rogers, William H., Jr. *bank executive*
Rohr-Kirchgraber, Theresa M.B. *adolescent medicine*
Rojas, Carlos *literature and language educator*
Rouhani, Shahrokh *civil engineering environmental educator, consultant*
Rucchin, Steve *professional hockey player*
Rusche, Mark C. *lawyer*
Rushdie, Salman (Ahmed Salman Rushdie) *writer, educator*
Ryan, J. Brennan *lawyer*
Ryan, J. Bruce *healthcare management consulting executive*
Salant, Richard Frank *mechanical engineer, educator*
Salmon, Marla E. *nursing educator, dean*
Sams, Louise S. *broadcast executive, lawyer*
Sanders, Carl E. *lawyer, former governor*
Sands, Jeff Michael *medical educator*
Saslow, Debbie L. *cancer control specialist, director*
Savera, Adnan Tabrez *surgical pathologist, director*
Sawyer, John C. *lawyer*
Schmitt, Edward A. *manufacturing executive*
Schneider, Ryan A. *lawyer*
Schroder, Jack Spalding, Jr. *lawyer*
Schroeder, Eric Peter *lawyer*
Schuchat, Anne *health facility administrator*
Schuerholz, John Boland, Jr. *professional baseball executive*
Schulte, Jeffrey Lewis *lawyer*
Scott, Donald Lavern *city manager, librarian, former army officer*
Scott, Marian Alexis *journalist*
Sears, Leah Ward *state supreme court justice*
Seeger, Guenter Otto *chef*
Seegers, Harvey *retail executive*
Seffrin, John Reese *health science association administrator, educator*
Sexson, William Robert *pediatrician, educator*
Seydel, Rutherford (John), (II) *professional sports team owner, lawyer*
Shapiro, George Howard *retired lawyer*
Shapiro, Michael Edward *museum director*
Shaw, Brad *communications executive*
Shepherd, Craig Allen *environmental services administrator*
Sherbinski, Linda Anne *nurse anesthetist, nursing educator*
Shlanta, Paul R. *lawyer*
Shrestha, Ram K. *economist, researcher*
Shufeldt, Robert Charles *bank executive*
Sibley, James Malcolm *retired lawyer*
Sigman, Stanley T. *telecommunications industry executive*
Silverstein, Leonard A. *lawyer*
Simao, Paul *news agency executive*
Simpson, Allan Boyd *real estate company executive*
Singer, Ross *library and information scientist*
Singh, Narendra *cardiologist, researcher, medical educator*
Sizemore, Michael Maynard *architectural firm executive*
Slade, Scott *radio personality*
Sloan, Mary Jean *retired media specialist*
Small, Gus H. *lawyer*
Smith, Alexander Wyly, Jr. *lawyer*
Smith, Edward Kendrick *lawyer*
Smith, Frank G. III *lawyer*
Smith, Jeffrey Michael *lawyer*
Smith, Joanne *marketing executive*
Smith, John Francis, Jr., (Jack Smith) *retired automotive executive*
Smith, Richard F. *financial services company executive*
Smith, Robert Boulware III *vascular surgeon, educator*
Smith, Scott C. *lawyer, legal association administrator*
Smith, Sidney Oslin, Jr. *lawyer*
Smoltz, John Andrew *professional baseball player*
Snarey, John Robert *psychologist, educator*
Snyder, James C., Jr. *lawyer, consumer products company executive*
Snyder, Robert Lyman *materials scientist, educator*
Somerhalder, John W., II, *energy executive*
Sophianopoulos, Judy Ann *environmental scientist*
Soupata, Lea N. *human resources specialist*
Spangler, Dennis Lee *physician*
Spangler, John I. III *lawyer*
Spano, Robert *conductor, music director*
Speckhart, Dawn Seidner *bone marrow transplant/leukemia psychologist*
Spikes, Jesse J. *lawyer*
Spillett, Roxanne *social services administrator*
Spitznagel, John Keith *retired microbiologist, immunologist, physician*
Sprecher, Jeffrey C. *commodities exchange executive*
Sprinkle, Shannon M. *lawyer*
Stacey, Weston Monroe, Jr. *nuclear engineer, physicist, educator*
Stallings, Ronald Denis *lawyer*
Steele, Charles, Jr. *civil rights association executive, former state legislator*
Stein, Grant T. *lawyer*
Steinhaus, John Edward *retired anesthesiologist, educator*
Stent, Terry *pilot, art collector*
Stephenson, Mason Williams *lawyer*
Stewart, Michael McFadden *speech professional*
Stillwagon, Gary Bouldin *radiation oncologist*
Stockton, David A. *lawyer*
Stoffel, Robert E. *delivery service executive*
Stokes, James Sewell *environmental services administrator, not-for-profit developer*
Stormont, Richard Mansfield *hotel executive*
Strekowski, Lucjan *chemistry professor*
Strickland, Frank B. *lawyer*
Sullivan, Timothy E. *bank executive*
Sweeney, Neal James *lawyer*
Swift, Charles D. *career military officer, lawyer, educator*
Swift, Frank Meador *lawyer*
Szabo, John F. *library director*
Tait, C. Downing, Jr., (Columbus Downing Tait Jr.) *physician, medical educator*
Tanenbaum, Allan Jay *lawyer*
Tatum, Beverly Daniel *academic administrator, writer, psychology and education educator*
Taylor, Andrew T., Jr. *radiologist, educator*
Taylor, David Randy *museum staff member, consultant*
Taylor, George Kimbrough, Jr. *lawyer*
Taylor, Mark *former lieutenant governor*
Taylor, Tom *marketing executive*
Teepen, Thomas Henry *editor, journalist*
Teixeira, Mark Charles *professional baseball player*
Tennant, Thomas Michael *lawyer*
Tentzeris, Emmanouil Manos *engineering educator, researcher*
Terwilliger, J. Ronald *real estate company executive*
Thacker, Stephen Brady *medical association administrator, epidemiologist*
Thattassery, Emil George *cardiologist*
Thomas, Lizanne *lawyer*
Thompson, Hugh P. *state supreme court justice*
Thompson, Shirley Williams *mathematics professor*
Thoms, Jannet *rapid transit executive*
Thorpe, Jane Fugate *lawyer*
Thrower, Randolph William *lawyer*
Thuesen, Gerald Jorgen *industrial engineer, educator*
Thursby, Jerry Gilbert *economics professor, consultant, department chairman*
Tighiouart, Mourad *statistician, researcher*
Tillman, Mary Norman *urban affairs consultant*
Tinsley, Barbara V. *lawyer*
Tomaszewski, Richard Paul *market representation executive*
Tome, Carol B. *consumer home products company executive*
Toner, Michael F. *journalist*
Travis, Robert M. *lawyer*
Trethewey, Natasha *poet, literature educator*
Trevathan, James E. *waste management executive*
Tripodi, Joseph V. *beverage company executive, former insurance company executive*
Tucker, Cynthia Anne *journalist*
Turner, Beau (Reed Beauregard Turner) *professional sports team owner, philanthropist*
Udoff, Eric Joel *diagnostic radiologist*
Vachon, Reginald Irenee *mechanical engineer*
VanWoerkom, Jack A. *lawyer, consumer products company executive*
Varner, Chilton Davis *lawyer*
Veal, Rex R. *lawyer*
Veatch, Julian Lamar, Jr. *library director*
Vega, J. David *thoracic surgeon*
Verrill, F. Glenn *advertising executive*
Vigtel, Gudmund *retired museum director*
Vito, Raymond P. *engineering educator, researcher*
Volentine, Richard J., Jr. *lawyer*
Vulgamore, Allison *performing arts association administrator*
Waddell, Don *professional sports team executive*
Wade, Nicole Jennings *lawyer*
Wagner, James Warren *academic administrator, engineering educator*
Wald, Michael Leonard *public relations executive*
Wallace, Gladys Baldwin *librarian*
Wallace, Julia Diane *newspaper editor*
Wallace, Peter Marsden *radio personality and producer, commentator, writer*
Walsh, W. Terence *lawyer*
Walton, Carole Lorraine *clinical social worker*
Walton, Jim *news network executive*
Wang, Yuhang *science educator*
Ward, Horace Taliaferro *federal judge*
Warren, Stephen Theodore *human geneticist, educator*
Waterhouse, Richard *museum administrator, artist*
Waters, John W. *minister, educator*
Weatherly, Alvis Morrison, Jr. *retired association developer*
Webb, Robert W., Jr. *lawyer*
Weed, Roger Oren *rehabilitation services professional, educator*
Weidman, Sheila *marketing professional*
Wellon, Robert G. *lawyer*
Wells, James M. III *bank executive*
Wenger, Nanette Kass *cardiologist, researcher, educator*
Wentworth, Lynn A. *housing products company executive, former telecommunications industry executive*
Weyand, Cornelia Maritta *medical educator*
Wheeler, Chris D. *investment company executive*
White, Benjamin Taylor *lawyer*
Whitt, Richard Ernest *reporter*
Wieland, John *real estate executive*
Wiesenfeld, Kurt Arn *physicist, researcher*
Wigmore, Steven P. *lawyer*
Wilding, Diane *computer scientist, consultant*
Wilkins, Dominique (Jacques Dominique Wilkins) *professional sports team executive, retired professional basketball player*
Williams, David Howard *lawyer*
Williams, Gary Randall *lawyer*
Williams, James Bryan *banker*
Williams, Neil, Jr. *retired lawyer*
Williams, Ralph Watson, Jr. *retired security firm executive*
Williams, Robert P., II, *lawyer*
Williams, S. Linn *lawyer*
Williamson, R. Mark *lawyer*
Wilmer, Mary Charles *artist*
Wilson, Brent Lawrence *lawyer, mediator*
Wilson, James Hargrove, Jr. *lawyer*
Winchester, Jesse Gregory *finance company executive*
Winckler, Alicia Jean *human resources director*
Winer, Ward Otis *mechanical engineer, educator*
Wineski, Lawrence E. *medical educator, biomedical researcher*
Winestock, James F. *delivery service executive*
Winkler, Allen Warren *lawyer, educator*
Winograd, Audrey Lesser *retired advertising executive*
Winsberg, Harris Bryan *lawyer*
Withrow, William N., Jr. *lawyer*
Wong, Ching-Ping *chemist, materials engineer*
Wood, L. Lin, Jr. *lawyer*
Wood, William C. *surgeon, medical educator, academic chairman*
Woodard, Diane E. *music educator*
Woodson, Mike *professional basketball coach*
Wright, Frederick Lewis, II, *lawyer*
Wright, Peter Meldrim *lawyer*
Wu, De Ting *mathematics professor, researcher, writer*
Wu, Jeff (Chien-Fu Wu) *engineering educator*
Wussler, Robert Joseph *broadcast executive, media consultant*
Wylly, Barbara Bentley *volunteer*
Yaccarino, Linda *marketing executive*
Yancey, Asa Greenwood, Sr. *physician, educator*
Yancey, Carolyn Dunbar *retired education policymaker*
Yates, Ella Gaines *librarian, consultant*
Yates, Jerome William *scientific administrator, researcher*
Yavari, Arash *engineering educator*
Yoganathan, Ajit Prithiviraj *biomedical engineer, educator*
Young, Michael Anthony *lawyer*
Zacks, David M. *lawyer*
Zadeh, Javad Hamadani *mathematics professor*
Zealey, Sharon Janine *lawyer*
Zeliazkova, Mariona Georgieva V. *music educator*
Zhitnik, Alexei *professional hockey player*

Auburn
Hutchinson, Leslie Julian *preventive medicine physician*

Augusta
Atteberry, Linda Rose *surgeon, retired military officer*
Baker, Carleton Harold *physiology educator*
Baker, Philip Steven *dentist, educator*
Bollag, Wendy Bollinger *medical educator, scientist*
Carroll, James Edwin *child neurologist, researcher*
Champion, Susan Michele *music educator*
Cooney, William J. *lawyer*
Davis, Catherine Lucy *psychologist, diabetes researcher*
Davis, Minnie P. *minister*
Denton, Frank M. *publishing executive*
Dolen, William Kennedy *allergist, immunologist, pediatrician, educator*
Drisko, Connie Lee Hastings *dean, dental educator*
Dyer, James Harold, Jr. *language educator*
Ellison, Lois Taylor *internist, educator, medical association administrator*
Fincher, Ruth Marie Edla *medical educator, dean*
Gillespie, Edward Malcolm *hospital administrator*
Given, Kenna Sidney *surgeon, educator*
Hooks, Vendie Hudson III *surgeon*
Horuzsko, Anatolij *medical researcher*
Hsu, Stephen De *medical educator*
Inscho, Edward William *physiology educator*
Johnson, William Michael *physician*
Knox, Wyckliffe Austin, Jr. *lawyer*
Kutlar, Ferdane *genetics educator, researcher*
Lanier, Troy *lawyer*
Lapp, Carol Anne *oral biology educator*
Lee, Gregory Price *neuropsychology educator*
Luxenberg, Malcolm Neuwahl *ophthalmologist, educator*
MacLeod, James L. *minister, finance company executive, art gallery owner*
Mansberger, Arlie Roland, Jr. *surgeon*
Mixon, Kenneth Wayne *history professor, department chairman*
Ownby, Dennis Randall *pediatrician, allergist, educator, researcher*
Phillips, Marjorie Shaw *pharmacist, educator*
Pryor, Carol Graham *obstetrician, gynecologist*
Puryear, Joan Copeland *academic administrator*
Rogers, Michael Bruce *orthodontist*
Ryan, James Walter *physician, researcher*
Schultz, Nancy Jansson *artist*
Tedesco, Francis Joseph *retired academic administrator, medical educator*
Wood, Lisa Godbey *federal judge, former prosecutor*
Woodhurst, Robert Stanford, Jr. *architect*
Wray, Betty Beasley *allergist, immunologist, pediatrician*

Austell
Cohn, Charles Erwin *retired physicist*
Halwig, J. Michael *allergist*
Orr, Zellie *entrepreneur, educator, writer, researcher*
Pope, Jacqueline Privette *music educator*
Scott, Yvonnie Michelle *special education educator, diagnostician, paralegal*

Avondale Estates
Bastin, Clinton *retired chemical engineer, nuclear scientist*

Bainbridge
Dixon, Lugenia *psychology educator*
Kirkland, William Michael *history professor*
Miley, Jenna Yvonne *education educator, consultant*
Vanstone, Catherine *library and information scientist*

Ball Ground
Tucker, Robert Dennard *health care products executive*

Barnesville
Adams, Cynthia Ann *librarian, media specialist, language educator*
Anderson, Nancy Dixon *librarian*
Brown, Angelia *poet*

Baxley
Williams, David Alfred *elementary school educator*
Williams, Sonia Kay *retired secondary school educator*

Big Canoe
Bendelius, Arthur George *engineering firm executive*

Bishop
Bower, Douglas William *counseling administrator, psychotherapist, clergyman*

Blairsville
Barrett, David Eugene *judge*
Jones, Mary Emma B. *psychologist*
Kerr, Walter Belnap *retired electrical engineer, language researcher, consultant*
Stainback, Susan Bray *retired education educator*

Braselton
Copper, James Robert *manufacturing executive*

Brooklet
McCormick, Paula Shurling *elementary school educator*

Brunswick
Herndon, Alice Patterson Latham *public health nurse*
Iannicelli, Joseph *chemical company executive, consultant*
Mihal, Sandra Powell *research scientist*
Moran, John Bernard *retired government official*
Patrick, Connie L. *federal official*
Perniciaro, Charles Vincent *dermatologist, educator, entrepreneur*
Pittman, Catherine Sylvia *secondary school educator*

Buford
Byrd, Larry Donald *behavioral pharmacologist*
Coakley, Deirdre *columnist, writer*

Byron
Morton, Eric *liberal arts educator*

Calhoun
Lorberbaum, Jeffrey S. *textiles executive*
Perillo, Salvatore J. *lawyer*

Canton
Angulo, Charles Bonin *foreign service officer, lawyer*
Wilson, Brian Andrew *computing performance consultant, educator, writer, editor*

Carrollton
Cochran, J. Guyton, Jr. *corporate financial executive*
Hunter, Thomas Rogers *political science professor*
Hynes, Thomas John *academic administrator*
Morton, Elizabeth Gron *art historian, educator*
Pope, W. Alan *psychology professor, psychotherapist*
Sethna, Beheruz Nariman *academic administrator, educator, management consultant*
Thorn, Stuart Wallace *marketing and financial executive*
Wanager, Charles Raymond, Jr. *reporter, editor*

Cartersville
Kordecki, Don Harry *theater director*
Morgan, Derek *chef*
Swanson, William Fredin III *manufacturing executive*

Cataula
Averill, Ellen Corbett *retired secondary education science educator, administrator*

Cedartown
Garner, Robby Glen *software research executive, roboticist*

Clarkesville
Dowden, Thomas Clark *telecommunication executive*

Clarkston
Charania, Barkat *real estate consultant*

Cleveland
Edwards, John Carver *retired archivist*

Cochran
Agnew, Charlie Martin *art educator, artist*
Ricks, John Addison III *history professor*

College Park
Hogan, Ernestine Dearing *retired mathematics educator, retired school system administrator*
Patterson, P(ickens) Andrew *lawyer*
Stokes, Arch *lawyer, writer*

Columbus
Amos, Daniel Paul *insurance company executive*
Amos, Paul Shelby, II, *insurance company executive*
Anthony, Richard E. *bank executive*
Baker, Janet *insurance company executive*
Beall, Charles Donald *former special education educator*
Blanchard, James Hubert *finance company executive*
Blanck, Susan *insurance company executive*
Branch, Jason *lawyer*
Brinkley, Jack Thomas *lawyer, retired congressman*
Bryant, Mollie Annette *rehabilitation services professional, director*
Carr, Leila S. *bank executive*
Chan, Philip *retired dermatologist, retired military officer*
Cloninger, Kriss III *insurance company executive*
Cox, Kermitt L. *insurance company executive*
Davis, Rebecca C. *insurance company executive*
Duncan, Frances Murphy *retired special education educator*
Friou, Phillip J. (Jack Friou) *insurance company executive*
Golden, Joseph David *music educator*
Green, Fred L. III *bank executive*
Griffith, G. Sanders III *lawyer, finance company executive*
Grimsley, Reagan Louis *archivist, educator*
Haneman, Vincent Siering, Jr. *consulting engineer, educator, dean*
Harbison, Ed *state legislator, broadcast journalist, motivational speaker*
Harp, John Anderson *lawyer*
Hart, Angela *insurance company executive*
Herbert, Jeff *insurance company executive*
Hiatt, Florence Ellen *musician*
James, Elizabeth R. (Lee Lee James) *bank executive*
Janke, Kenneth S., Jr. *insurance company executive*
Jeffery, William Jeremy *insurance company executive*
Jinright, Noah Franklin *security firm executive, retired vocational school educator*
Johnson, Walter Frank, Jr. *lawyer*
Kirkland, Ronald E. *insurance company executive*
Laney, John Thomas III *federal judge*
Lester, James D. III *insurance company executive*
Loudermilk, Joey M. *lawyer, insurance company executive*
McFarland, Samuel P., Jr. *psychologist*
McGlamry, Max Reginald *retired lawyer*
Montgomery, Anna Frances *elementary school educator*
Norah, Patricia Ann *retired music educator*
Ottman, Bob *insurance company executive*
Page, William Marion *lawyer*
Patrick, James Duvall, Jr. *lawyer*
Poydasheff, Robert Stephen *lawyer*
Pringle, David L. *insurance company executive*
Purol, R.M. Scott *psychiatric nurse*
Riggsby, Dutchie Sellers *education educator*
Rogers, Ralph A., Jr. *insurance company executive*
Shields, Gerald W. *insurance company executive*
Simmons, Lynda Teel *nurse, healthcare executive*
Sweeney, Robert David *retired communications engineer*
Tillman, Audrey Boone *insurance company executive*
Tipton, James D. *retired military officer, education educator*
White, Teresa Lynne *insurance company executive*
Wooten, Joel Orba, Jr. *lawyer*

Conley
Marcus, James Elbert *manufacturing executive*

Conyers
Grider, Rhonda Patriece *elementary school educator, writer*
Kelly, John Hubert *diplomat*
Skipper, James Hulett, Jr. *music educator*
Spearman, Maxie Ann *financial analyst, administrator*

Cordele
Bell, Andrew C. *music educator*

Covington
Norwood, Brandi Aisha *middle school educator*

Crawford
Spears, Louise Elizabeth *minister, secondary school educator*

Cumming
Drew, Paul S. *entrepreneur*
Johnston, Melissa *school librarian*

Dahlonega
Newman, Thomas Daniel *archaeologist, school system administrator, minister*
Williams, Linda Stallworth *literature and language professor*

Dalton
Bouckaert, Carl M. *manufacturing executive*
Ford, Katherine Michelle *special education educator*
Nielsen, Mary Tanzy *literature and language professor, department chairman*
Turner, Jackson Parks *financial company executive*

Dawsonville
Jorgensen, Alfred H. *retired information technology educator*

Decatur
Brown, William Virgil *internal medicine educator*
Cavallaro, Joseph John *retired microbiologist*
Clarke, Erskine *religious history professor, writer*
Cox, Thomas A. *lawyer*
Dillingham, William Byron *literature educator, author*
Duffy, Thomas M. *transportation services executive, lawyer*
Farley, Monica M. *medical educator*
Gebhart, Ronald John *infectious disease specialist, administrator*
Grace, George H. *not-for-profit fundraiser*
Hamilton, Frank Strawn *musician, composer, educator*
Henderson, Ralph Hale *physician*
Hinman, Alan Richard *public health physician, epidemiologist*
Jones, Debbie Jo *finance educator*
Kiss, Elizabeth *academic administrator, philosophy educator*
Knight, Walker Leigh *publishing executive, minister*
Majette, Denise *former congresswoman*
Manley, Frank *language educator, writer*
Mc Intosh, James Eugene, Jr. *interior designer*
McKinney, Cynthia Ann *former congresswoman*
Moore, Wayland D. *artist*
Peacock, Scott *chef*
Posey, Douglas Harris *pathologist*
Ray, Amy *vocalist, guitarist*
Rosenberg, Mark L. *health facility administrator*
Saliers, Emily *singer, musician*
Shaw, Jeanne Osborne *editor, poet*
Showers Johnson, Violet Mary-Ann Iyabo *history professor*
Wheelan, Belle S. *educational association administrator*
Williams, Rita Tucker *lawyer*

Demorest
Rogers, Elizabeth (Betty) Carlisle *education educator, consultant*

Donalsonville
Ponder, Dan E., Jr. *former state legislator, food service executive*

Doraville
Wempner, Gerald Arthur *engineering educator*

Douglas
Hayes, Dewey *lawyer*
McCrea, Derek Duane *military officer, artist*
Sims, Rebecca Littleton *lawyer*
Vickers, Dana Tate *school psychologist, researcher*

Douglasville
Smith, Stephanie Renae *middle school educator*
Walker, Pam *biology educator*

Dublin
Giannini, A. James *psychiatrist, educator, researcher, author*
Shuman-Riley, Brenda *literature and language educator*
Yauck, F. Alan *biology educator*

Duluth
Brody, Aaron Leo *food and packaging consultant*
Colwell, Gene Thomas *engineering educator*
Cothrun, Thomas Keith *secondary school educator*
Cunningham, Richard Anthony *science administrator*
Evans, Paul *osteopath*
Guillory, Barbara Ann *elementary school educator*
Johnston, William David *biotechnologist, director*
Laubscher, Robert James *consumer products company executive*
Lupton, Stephen D. *lawyer*
McCracken, William Henry *retired mining executive*
Moss, Shad Gregory (Bow Wow, Lil' Bow Wow) *rap artist*
Polstra, Larry John *lawyer*
Reed, Ralph Eugene, Jr. *political consultant, former political organization administrator*
Richenhagen, Martin H. *manufacturing executive*
Sloan, Donnie Robert, Jr. *lawyer*
Tewes, R. Scott *lawyer*

Dunwoody
Callison, James W. *retired lawyer, air transportation executive*
Hendrix, Jane Galloway *art educator*
Maddox, Jerry Aven *retired catalog executive, writer*

East Point
Bridgewater, Herbert Jeremiah, Jr. *radio personality*
Johnson, Hardwick Smith, Jr. *school psychologist*

Eatonton
Digby, Pamela Annette *elementary school educator*

Evans
Feldman, Elaine Bossak *medical nutritionist, educator*
Zachert, Virginia *retired psychologist*

Fairburn
Holyfield, Evander *professional boxer*
Milam, Lynne Morgan *special education educator*

Fayetteville
Cokuslu, Lynda Elizabeth McCord *medical assistant*
De Revere, David Wilsen *retired professional society administrator*
Neal, Joan Burkes *librarian*
Turnipseed, Barnwell Rhett III *journalist, public relations consultant*

Fitzgerald
Newsome, John David, Jr. *music educator*

Flintstone
Ragon, Robert Ronald *clergyman*

Flowery Branch
Abraham, John *professional football player*
Blank, Arthur M. *professional sports team and retired lumber company executive*
Coll, Edward Girard, Jr. *university president*
Crumpler, Alge *professional football player*
Hall, DeAngelo *professional football player*
Harrington, Joey (John Joseph Harrington) *professional football player*
Horn, Joe *professional football player*
McKay, Richard James *professional sports team executive*
Petrino, Bobby *professional football coach*
Reynolds, George Anthony, Jr. *engineering executive*

Folkston
Crumbley, Esther Helen Kendrick *retired real estate agent, retired secondary school educator, councilman*

Forest Park
Honoré, Russel L. *career military officer*
Lambert, Ethel Gibson Clark *secondary school educator*

Forsyth
Coleman, Steven Andrew *surveyor*

Fort Benning
Gittins, Timothy *military officer*
Kotwal, Russ Steven *military officer, physician*

Fort Mcpherson
Stultz, Jack C. *career military officer*

Fort Stewart
McCarthy, Dorothy A. (Landers) *educator*
Stone, Joshua James *military officer*
Thompson, Frankie Mazie *school psychologist*
Warner, Christopher Hugh *psychiatrist*

Gainesville
Burd, John Stephen *retired academic administrator, music educator*
Floyd, Hazel McConnell *special education educator*
Frank, Mary Lou Bryant *psychologist, educator*
Jones, William Benjamin, Jr. *retired electrical engineering educator*
Leet, Richard Hale *oil industry executive*
Lowrey, Alex Andre *biology professor*
Nichols, Dana *language educator*
Schuder, Raymond Francis *lawyer*
Stewart, Jon Douglas *lawyer*

Glennville
Craft, Mary Faye *public relations executive, consultant, television producer, poet*

Greensboro
Copelan, Ann Hanson *artist, psychologist*

Griffin
Doyle, Michael Patrick *microbiologist, educator, director*

Grovetown
Jones, Jerry W. *protective services official, investor*

Hamilton
Byrd, Gary Ellis *lawyer*
McEachern, Beverley C. *priest*

Hartwell
Rushing, Tonnie Austin Page *musician, educator*

Hawkinsville
Whipple, Woodrow Thomas *artist, educator*

Hephzibah
Smith, Charles Joe, Sr. *music educator*

Hiawassee
Davis, Nighta J. *photographer, artist*

Hinesville
Etheridge, James Ralph *history professor*
Smith, Barbara *bank executive*
Thomas, James, Jr. *retired engineering executive, retired military officer*

Hiram
Stevens, Charles Thomas, Sr. *drafting technology educator*

Hoschton
Campbell, Leslie Caine (Caine Campbell) *writer, historian*
Sneed, Larry Allan *history professor*

Ila
Greene, Sheree' Jeane *elementary school educator, consultant*

Jasper
Ledford, Shirley Louise *practical nurse*
Marger, Edwin *lawyer*
Wiltse, James Cornelius *retired electrical engineer*

Jeffersonville
Capece, Michelle René *elementary school educator*
Hawthorne, Sarah Beck *reading educator*

Jekyll Island
Bentley, James Luther *former journalist*

Jonesboro
Galvin, John Rogers *retired army officer, law educator*
Harris, Queen Wiggs *mathematician, educator*
Perez, Maritza E. *elementary school educator*

Kennesaw
Adams, Dean (Lewis Adams) *theater director*
Bonaparte, Rudolph *engineering company executive*
Kidonakis, Nikolaos *physicist*
Martinez, Ricardo *emergency medicine company executive*
McCoy, R. Wesley *biology educator*
Paterson, Paul Charles *retired private investigator, security consultant*
Robinson, Kenneth Charles *management educator*
Roebuck, Deborah Mae Britt *management consultant, educator*
Siegel, Betty Lentz *university president*
Smith, Carol L. *human services administrator, consultant*
Whittingham, Harry Edward, Jr. *retired banker*

Kingsland
Barlow, Paula C. *nurse*
Huygens, Remmert William *architect*

Lagrange
Callaway, Mark Clayton *investment company executive*
Copeland, Robert Bodine *internist, cardiologist*
Gittinger, Laurie Ellen *music educator, elementary school educator*
Hudson, Charles Daugherty *insurance executive*
West, John Thomas *retired surgeon*

Lake Park
Blanton, Vallye J. *elementary school educator*

Lawrenceville
Ahn, Steven *finance company executive, educator*
Bannick, Janice Carol *automotive dealerships executive*
Brannon, Ronald Roy *retired minister*
Crain, Mary Ann *elementary school educator*
Davidson, Brook A. *lawyer*
Davies, David B. *communications executive*
Fetner, Robert Henry *radiobiologist*
Folds, Frank Elliott *music educator*
Gericke, Paul William *minister, educator*
McDonald, James Francis *electronics company executive*
Schoen, Marc Alan *pension and employee benefits executive*
Swanson, Lynnette Sue *special olympics coordinator, special education educator*
Wall, Clarence Vinson *state legislator*

Leesburg
Hilley, Mary Kay *music educator*

Lilburn
Bendelius, Bonnie Sue *elementary school educator*
Magnan, Sarah E. *court reporter*
Neumann, Thomas William *archaeologist*

Lithonia
Baxter, Gene Francis *chemical researcher, consultant*
Johnson, Henry C. (Hank Johnson) *congressman, lawyer*
Sigh, Robert Virgil *public health physician*

Loganville
Smelser, Thelma Ann *writer, tax specialist*

Lovejoy
Onukwuli, Francis Osita *computer scientist, secondary school educator, mathematician*

Lyons
Eernisse, Susan Freeman *music educator*

Mableton
Reeves, Denise Moseley *dancer, educator*
Rowe, Bonnie Gordon *music company executive*

Macon
Aldridge, Melvin Dayne *engineering educator*
Anderson, Robert Lanier III *federal judge*
Brown, Stephen Phillip *judge*
Cole, John Prince *lawyer, academic administrator*
Cranford, James Michael *lawyer*
Davis, David Scott *academic administrator, chemistry professor*
Dunwody, Eugene Cox *architect*
Ennis, Edgar William, Jr. *lawyer*
Faircloth, Laurie Ricketson *critical care nurse*
Floyd, Daisy Hurst *dean, law educator*
Franklin, Roosevelt *minister*
Good, Estelle M. *minister*
Hails, Robert Emmet *retired aerospace engineer, manufacturing executive, retired military officer*
Hershner, Robert Franklin, Jr. *judge*
Huffman, Joan Brewer *history professor*
Jones, Frank Cater *retired lawyer*
Kitchens, William Charlie *accountant*
Leonard, Michael Steven *industrial engineering educator*
Lewis, Sandra Combs *research psychologist, writer*
Papagan, Harry Gregory *literature and language professor*
Patterson, Kenneth *nurse*
Pilcher, Christie W. *retired special education educator*
Robinson, Joe Sam *neurosurgeon, educator*
Robinson, W. Lee *lawyer*
Steeples, Douglas Wayne *retired university dean, consultant, researcher*
Weaver, Jacquelyn Kunkel Ivey *artist, educator*
Wood, Frank Maxwell *prosecutor, lawyer*
Young, Henry E. *tissue engineering medical educator*

Madison
DuBose, Charles Wilson *lawyer*

Marietta
Ahlstrom, Michael Joseph *lawyer*
Aronoff, Craig Ellis *business educator, consultant*
Barksdale, Daryl *historic preservationist*
Bentley, Fred Douglas, Sr. *lawyer*
Berryhill, Henry Lee, Jr. *retired geologist*
Bivens, Mitchel Lee *school system administrator, minister*
Blount, Daniel J. *lumber company executive*
Bollinger, Frances L. *elementary school educator*
Carnes, James Donald *real estate manager*
Choi, Sukhwan *engineer*
Clarkson, Lawrence William *air transportation executive*
Devigne, Karen Cooke *retired amateur athletics executive*
Dudley, Gary Edward *psychologist*
Edwards, Charles Mundy III *financial consultant*
Fuller, Frank Robert *political scientist, director*
Garrett, Joseph Edward *aerospace engineer*
Hammond, Elea Anne *special education educator*
Hays, Robert William *communications educator, consultant, writer*
Hellrung, Stephen Andrew *lawyer*
Houston, Dorothy Middleton *elementary school educator*
Howard, Bruce Allen *social studies educator*
Huddleston, Connie Marie *archaeologist, consultant*
Humphrey, Stephen M. *paperboard company executive*
Ingram, Robert D. *lawyer*
Kelly, William Watkins *educational association executive*
Kendall, Susan Gardes *librarian*
Laframboise, Joan Carol *middle school educator*
Lahtinen, Silja Liisa *artist*
McEntire, Betty *health facility administrator*
Miles, Thomas Caswell *aerospace engineer*
Nowland, James Ferrell *lawyer*
O'Neil, Kelly Lynn *pharmacist*
Opre, Thomas Edward *retired editor, film company executive*
Overstreet, Regina Nix *mathematics educator*
Paquin, Jeffrey Dean *lawyer*
Ranu, Harcharan Singh *biomedical scientist, administrator, orthopaedic biomechanics educator*
Roach, Carole Hyde *music educator*
Rossbacher, Lisa Ann *academic administrator*
Scheible, David W. *paper company executive*
Short-Mayfield, Patricia Ahlene *business owner*
Sigler, Paulette Terry *music educator*
Smith, Baker Armstrong *management executive, lawyer*
Smith, George Thornewell *retired state supreme court justice*
Smith, Irene Helen-Nordine *music educator*
Spann, George William *management consultant*
Wenk, Michael Scott *environmental services administrator*
Williamsen, Dannye Sue *personal development educator, publisher*

Martinez
Colborn, Gene Louis *anatomy educator, researcher*
Meyers, Nicholaus *music educator*

Mc Rae
Allen, Annette *minister*

Mcdonough
Mauney, Brandi Savage *special education diagnostician*
Wilson, Russell Edward *music educator*

Metter
Guido, Michael Anthony *evangelist*

Milledgeville
Childre, Amy *education educator*
Davis, Matthew Scott *curator, history professor*
Engerrand, Doris Dieskow *retired business educator*
Williamson, John Thomas, Sr. *minerals company executive*

Morrow
Culver, Dan Louis *federal agency administrator*
Gooden, Randall Scott *historian, archivist*
Totty, Totty Okoro *soccer coach*

Moultrie
Collum, Rick Daniel *lawyer*
Vereen, William Jerome *uniform manufacturing company executive*

Mount Berry
Davis, John Edward *music educator, musician*
Mew, Thomas Joseph, III, (Tommy Mew) *artist, educator*

Nashville
Haywood, Mary Gwendolyn *music educator*

Newnan
Barron, Thomas Willis *real estate broker*
Culbreth, Lucretia Joy *science educator*
Drake, W. Homer, Jr. *federal judge*
Franklin, Bruce Walter *lawyer*
Krach, Dale James *science educator, athletic trainer*

Norcross
Conway, Hobart McKinley, Jr. *futurist*
Cramer, James Perry *management strategist, architectural author, educator*
Emery, William David *consulting company executive*
Galfas, Timothy, II, *wholesale distribution executive*
Granger, Philip Richard *minister*
Herron, Bonnie L. *management consulting company executive*
Jablonski, Zygmunt *lawyer*
Mangum, Mylle Bell *information technology executive*
Metz, Robert C. *media company executive*
Ockwell, Gary *electrical engineer, marketing professional*
Rubright, James Alfred *paperboard and packaging company executive*
Wagner, Robert Earl *retired agronomist*
Xie, Jeff Zhengquan *lawyer*

Oakwood
Jondahl, Terri Elise *importing and distribution company executive*
Phillips, Ernie Howard *music educator*

Oxford
Cody, William Bermond *political science professor*

Peachtree City
Barnes, Marylou Riddleberger *retired academic administrator*
Clark, James Kermit, Jr. *real estate executive*
Day, Annette J. *music educator*
Ebneter, Stewart Dwight *utility industry management consultant*
Nix, Kemie Richards *educational association administrator, editor*
Roobol, Norman Richard *chemistry professor, consultant*

Pearson
Delk, Charlotte Turley *elementary school educator*

Perry
Geiger, James Norman *lawyer*
Jackson, Rutha Mae *pastor, military reserve officer, secondary school educator*

Pine Mountain
Bishop, Michael *writer*
Callaway, Howard Hollis *resort executive*

Powder Springs
Creighton, Peggy Milam *media specialist, writer*

Rincon
Purcell, Ann Rushing *state legislator, human services manager*

Robins Afb
Wolfe, Sarah Catharine *curator*

Rockmart
Vinson, Victoria Dean *middle school educator*

Rome
Davis, Susan Lynn *musician, educator*
Doyle, James Donald, Jr. *librarian*
Johnson, Alberta Clark *psychology professor*
Mosley, Mary Mac *retired librarian*
Murphy, Harold Loyd *federal judge*
Sender, James LeRoy *retired military officer, retired federal agency administrator*

Roopville
Huckeba, Emily Causey *retired elementary school educator*

Roswell
Abernathy, Robert E. *health products executive*
Baker, Anita Diane *lawyer*
Bauer, Joanne B. *health products executive*
Birmingham, Richard Gregory *lawyer*
Bruckner, William J. *lawyer*
Burgess, John Frank *retired utilities executive*
Caughman, Richard Bankston *retired manufacturing executive*
Christopher, Lin *artist*
Dolan, Dennis Joseph *pilot, lawyer*
England, John Melvin *lawyer, clergyman*
Feldman, Joel Martin *retired judge*
Gottung, Lizanne C. *health products executive*
Herron, Harriette A. *retired occupational health nurse*
Hill, Donald Dee *management consultant, educator, writer*
Klein, John Jacob *retired economist*
Ludacris, (Chris Bridges) *musician, actor*
McCloud, Melody T. *obstetrician-gynecologist, surgeon*
Mimms, Thomas Bowman, Jr. *lawyer*
Moseley, Marc Robards *sales executive*
Nilsen, Arthur Christian *lawyer*
Peterson, Donald Robert *editor, vintage automobile consultant*
Polatty, Rose Jackson *civic worker*
Rogers, Richard Hilton *hotel executive*
Roland, Raymond William *lawyer, mediator*
Siepi, Cesare *opera singer*
Spencer, Jan B. *health products executive*
Welch, Robert Bennett *retired music educator, retired conductor*
Yune, Marc E. *surgeon*

Saint Marys
Hall, Lois Bremer *secondary school educator, volunteer*
Smith, Charles Courtland, Jr. *lawyer, state legislator*

Saint Simons Island
Bell, Ronald Mack *university foundation administrator, consultant*
Douglas, William Ernest *retired commissioner*
Edwards, Edith Martha *lawyer*
Keenan, William W. (Kip) III *public relations executive*
Mathis, Luster Doyle *academic administrator, political scientist, educator*
Schneider, Duane Bernard *English literature educator*
Spivey, Ted Ray *language educator*
Taylor, Philip Raymond *lawyer*
Thau, William Albert *lawyer*
Turbidy, John Berry *investor, management consultant*
Walker, Charls Edward *economist, consultant*
Webb, Lamar Thaxter *architect*

Sandy Springs
Owen, Robert Hubert *lawyer, real estate broker*

Savannah
Aja-Herrera, Marie *fashion designer, educator*
Berry, Jack K. *lawyer*
Boland, John Kevin *bishop*
Booth, Edmund A., Jr. *prosecutor*
Bowman, Catherine McKenzie *lawyer*
Cartledge, Raymond Eugene *retired paper company executive*
Cebula, Richard John *economist, educator*
Chong, Bruce Simon *dean, broadcast executive*
Clemmons, John B. *bank executive, director, retired mathematics educator*
Coffey, Thomas Francis, Jr. *retired writer*
Conner, David Michael *lawyer*
Craib, Kenneth Bryden *research and development company executive, physicist, economist*
Dennison, D. Brian *lawyer*
Dickey, David Herschel *lawyer, accountant*
Dodge, William Douglas *risk management consultant*
Eaves, George Newton *health facility administrator, educator*
Edenfield, Berry Avant *federal judge*
Fishburne, John Ingram, Jr. *retired obstetrician/gynecologist, educator*
Foley, Marilyn Lorna *artist*
Forbes, Morton Gerald *lawyer*
Granger, Harvey, Jr. *retired manufacturing executive*
Greco, Richard Jude *plastic and reconstructive surgeon*
Henne, Preston A. *engineering executive*
Holland, Robert D. *music educator*
Houngues, Desire Mensanh *dean*
Hsu, Ming-Yu *engineering educator*
Hung, Chin-Cheng *artist, educator*
Johnson, Eric B. *state legislator*
Krahl, Enzo *retired surgeon*
Leighton, Richard Frederick *retired dean*
Lindley, James Gunn, Jr. *neurosurgeon*
Lindqvist, Gunnar Jan *management consultant, international trade consultant*
Lombardo, Joseph T. *aerospace transportation executive*
Martin, Grace Burkett *psychologist*
McCracken, Eugene Luke *lawyer*
Moore, William Theodore, Jr. *federal judge*
Mukhtar, Mohamed Haji *social sciences educator*
Otter, John Martin III *retired television advertising consultant*
Polite, Evelyn C. *retired elementary school educator, evangelist*
Rowan, Richard G. *former academic administrator*
Rozantine, Gayle Stubbs *psychologist*
Sanders, James Grady *biogeochemist*
Searcy, William Nelson *lawyer, director*
Siuta, Abby Mae *primary school educator*
Skelton, William Douglas *physician*
Smith, David Lee *retired editor*
Smith, Elizabeth Mackey *retired financial consultant*
Spitz, Seymour James, Jr. *retired fragrance company executive*
Stillwell, Walter Brooks III *lawyer*
Swartz, Anne *art historian*
Taggart, Helen M. *adult education educator, nurse*
Thomas, Dwight Rembert *writer*
Thompson, Larry James *retired gifted and social studies education educator*
Thompson, Richard S. *lawyer, former prosecutor*
Wallace, Paula S. *academic administrator*
Walter, Paul Hermann Lawrence *chemistry professor*
Windom, Herbert Lynn *oceanographer, environmental scientist*
Wirth, Fremont Philip, Jr. *neurosurgeon, educator*
Yagami, Kazuo *historian*
Zoller, Michael *otolaryngologist, head and neck surgeon, educator*

Sea Island
Revoile, Charles Patrick *lawyer*

Sky Valley
Geer, Ronald Lamar *mechanical engineer, consultant, retired oil industry executive*
Wilkinson, Albert Mims, Jr. *lawyer*

Smyrna
Atkins, William Austin, Sr., (Bill Atkins) *former state legislator*
Jeffords, Keith (Kelland Keith Jeffords Jr.) *plastic surgeon*
Lnenicka, Wade Sheridan *purchasing agent, councilman*
Seigler, Michael Edward *lawyer, librarian*
Tripp, Victor K. *electrical engineer, researcher*

Snellville
Blankenship, Colleen Marie-Krick *secondary school educator, writer*

Social Circle
Penland, John Thomas *retired import/export and development company executive*

Statesboro
Adhikari, Dharma Nanda *journalist, writer, educator*
Bartels, Jean Ellen *nursing educator*
Brogdon, W.M. *lawyer*
Diamanduros, Terry Davis *psychology professor, director*
Edenfield, Gerald M. *lawyer*

Franklin, James Burke *lawyer*
Henry, Nicholas Llewellyn *public administration educator*
Kersey, Scott N. *mathematician, educator*
Lloyd, Margaret Ann *psychologist, educator*
Mitchell, Wilfrid Bede *librarian, library association executive*
Molina, Gustavo *engineering educator, researcher*
Murkison, Eugene Cox *finance educator*
Nettles, Saundra R. Murray *psychologist, writer, educator*
Wilson, LeVon Edward *lawyer, educator*

Stockbridge
Friedman, Robert Barry *neurosurgeon*
Grimes, Richard Allen *banker, educator*

Stone Mountain
Allen (Irvin M.N.), Georgianne Lydia Christian *writer, poet*
Bacon, Louis Albert *retired consulting civil engineer*
Brown, Rhonda Jean *special education educator*
Dees, Julian Worth *retired academic/research administrator*
Fairweather, Daniel Edward *music educator*
Farngalo, Rosemarie Merritt *school psychologist*
Gotlieb, Jaquelin Smith *pediatrician*
Jones, Ellen *elementary school educator*
Reichert, Leo Edmund, Jr. *biochemist, department chairman, endocrinologist*
Torbush, Deborah Nickels *psychologist*

Suwanee
Brewer, Brenda Neal *assistant principal, educator*
Cox, Albert Harrington, Jr. *retired economist*
Decker, Michael John *neuroscientist*
Stanley, Gwen G. *elementary school educator*
Williams, Terry Neal *secondary school educator*

Swainsboro
Watt, (Arthur) Dwight, Jr. *computer programming and microcomputer specialist*

Thomasville
Avera, Stephen R. *food products company executive, lawyer*
Deese, George E. *food products company executive*
Flowers, Langdon Strong *food company executive*
Tillinghast, Nancy *library director*

Tifton
Dorminey, Henry Clayton, Jr. *allergist*
Reinhardt, George Robert *lawyer*
Roberts, Curtis Creed *minister, writer*
Waldrop, Sherry Hutchinson *elementary school educator*

Toccoa
Cross, Kim L. *engineer, sales executive*
Maypole, John Floyd *real estate company executive*

Toccoa Falls
Council, Thomas Maurice *music educator*
Gardner, Donna Rae (Donna Rae Diehl) *education educator*
Stufft, William David *music educator*

Townsend
Hicks, Harold Eugene *chemical engineer*

Tucker
Jiali, Ye *medical researcher*
Stewart, Connie Ward *retired academic administrator*
Streeb, Gordon Lee *diplomat, economist*

Union City
Drake-Hamilton, Lillie Belle *retired secondary school educator*
Malcolm, Gloria J. *small business owner*

Valdosta
Bailey, Hugh Coleman *academic administrator*
Beal, John M. *surgeon, medical educator*
Burnette, Ada M. Puryear *program coordinator*
Cronin, Kevin Stewart *historian, educator*
Halter, Henry James, Jr., (Diamond Jim Halter) *retail executive*
Morgan, Joe Leland *physician, psychiatrist*
Sinnott, John Patrick *lawyer, educator*

Vidalia
Fountain, Edwin Byrd *minister, librarian, poet*

Villa Rica
Abney, Martha McEachern *music educator*
Blevins, Ernest Everett *genealogist, researcher, historian*
Carroll, Linda Lovell *elementary school educator*

Waleska
Ast, Thesesa Lynn *history professor*
Gustafson, Deborah Ann *mathematics educator*

Warner Robins
DePriest, C(harles) David *engineering executive, retired military officer*
Gayton, Johnny Lee *ophthalmologist, educator, recreational facility executive*
Merk, P. Evelyn *retired librarian*
Nugteren, Cornelius *air force officer*

Watkinsville
Vaughn, Lisa Michelle *assistant principal*
Wight, Robert Joseph *lawyer*

West Point
Albarado, Rebecca Hill *elementary school educator*
Andrews, Gerald Bruce, Sr. *business executive*
Glover, Clifford Clarke *retired construction company executive*

Whitesburg
Nicholson, Diane M. *special education educator*

Wildwood
Dombrowski, Bob *artist, writer*

Woodbine
Konetzni, Albert H., Jr. *career officer*

Woodstock
Austin, John David *retired financial executive*
Barthlow, Michelle Jones *science educator*
Collins, David Browning *religious institution administrator*
Furuta, Soichi *poet, art consultant, educator*

Young Harris
Cox, Cathy *academic administrator, former state official*
March, Boyd Lee *political science professor, researcher*
Richardson, Vernal Edward *retired music educator*
Wolfersteig, Eloise Smith *retired music educator*

HAWAII

Aiea
Manabe, Shari A *physical education educator*

Camp H M Smith
Keating, Timothy J. *career military officer*

Ewa Beach
Lewis, Mary Jane *film producer, film director, scriptwriter*

Haleiwa
Shigemasa, Teresa *mental health services professional, educator*

Hawaii National Park
Swanson, Donald Alan *geologist*

Hickam Afb
Paddock, Lori Ann *military officer*
Tallman, Sean Dale *anthropologist*

Hilo
Binder, Philippe-Michel *physicist, educator*
Dinges, Richard Allen *entrepreneur*
Kojima, Sheri S. *high school business educator*
Pezzuto, John Michael *dean, pharmacology educator*
Tseng, Rose *academic administrator*

Holualoa
Scarr, Sandra Wood *retired psychology educator, researcher*

Honolulu
Abbott, Isabella Aiona *retired biology educator*
Acoba, Simeon Rivera, Jr. *state supreme court justice, educator*
Adams, Jo-Ann Marie *lawyer*
Ahmed, Iqbal *psychiatrist, consultant*
Ahrari, Ehsan M. *political science professor, dean*
Aiona, James R., Jr. *lieutenant governor*
Akiba, Lorraine Hiroko *lawyer*
Akinaka, Asa Masayoshi *lawyer*
Ako, Harry *engineering educator, researcher*
Albano, Andres, Jr. *real estate developer, real estate broker*
Baker, Rosalyn Hester *state senator*
Bender, Byron Wilbur *linguistics educator*
Bennett, Mark J. *state attorney general*
Berg, John Townsend *physiologist, researcher*
Betts, Barbara Stoke *artist, educator*
Betts, James William, Jr. *financial analyst, consultant*
Bitterman, Morton Edward *psychologist, educator*
Bloede, Victor Carl *lawyer, consultant, director*
Boas, Frank *retired lawyer*
Botsai, Elmer Eugene *architect, educator, retired dean*
Brady, Stephen R. P. K. *physician*
Brill, Richard C. *physical science educator*
Bronster, Margery S. *retired state attorney general, lawyer*
Cadman, Edwin Clarence *health facility administrator, retired educator*
Callies, David Lee *lawyer, educator*
Case, Edward E. *former congressman, lawyer*
Case, James Hebard *lawyer*
Castle, Alfred *administrator*
Chapman, Duane Lee (Dog) *bail enforcement agent, television personality*
Char, Vernon Fook Leong *lawyer*
Chen, Wai-Fah *civil engineering educator*
Chesne, Edward Leonard *physician*
Ching, Chauncey Tai Kin *agricultural studies educator, economist*
Cho, Lee-Jay *social scientist, demographer*
Chyba, Monique *mathematics professor*
Clifton, Richard Randall *federal judge*
Cowan, Stuart Marshall *lawyer*
Cox, Richard Horton *civil engineering executive*
Crumpton, Charles Whitmarsh *lawyer*
Curb, Jess David *medical educator, researcher*
Dang, Marvin S.C. *lawyer*
Deaver, Phillip Lester *lawyer*
Devenot, David Charles *human resources specialist, artist*
Devens, Paul *retired lawyer*
Doane, W. Allen *water transportation executive*
Duffy, James Earl, Jr. *state supreme court justice*
Dupont, Ralph Paul *lawyer, educator*
Dyen, Isidore *linguistic scientist, educator*
Englert, Peter *academic administrator, director*
Erickson, Jackie Mahi *lawyer, electric power industry executive*
Finucane, Melissa Lucille *psychologist, researcher*
Fischer, Joel *social work educator*
Fok, Agnes Kwan *retired cell biologist, educator*
Fong, Bernard W.D. *physician, educator*
Fong, Peter C. K. *lawyer, judge*
Franz, Charles Norman *engineer*
Fried, L. Richard, Jr. *lawyer*
Fukumoto, Leslie Satsuki *lawyer*
Fullmer, Daniel Warren *former psychologist, educator*
Gay, E(mil) Laurence *lawyer*
Gee, Chuck Yim *dean*
Gelber, Don Jeffrey *lawyer*
Ghasemi Nejhad, Mehrdad N. *mechanical engineering educator*
Gillmor, Helen *federal judge*
Godbey, Robert Carson *lawyer*
Goldstein, Sir Norman *dermatologist*
Goodhue, William Walter, Jr. *pathologist, military officer, educator*
Greeley, Burnham H. *lawyer*
Griffin, Dominic B. III *state agency administrator*
Gubler, Duane J. *virologist, educator, researcher*
Guerrero, Reuben Castro *oncologist, internist*
Guthrie, Edgar King *artist*
Hac, Anna Barbara *computer scientist, educator*
Hack, Randolph C. *advocate, educator, counselor*
Haight, Warren Gazzam *investor*
Halloran, Richard Colby *writer, reporter, communications executive, editor*
Hamada, Duane Takumi *architect*
Hamamoto, Patricia *school system administrator, educator*
Hannemann, Mufi *mayor*
Hart, Brook *lawyer*
Hawke, Bernard Ray *planetary scientist, researcher*
Hays, Ronald Jackson *career officer*
Hazlett, Mark A. *lawyer*
Heller, Ronald Ian *lawyer*
Hey, Richard Noble *marine geophysicist*
Hirai, Craig Kazuo *accountant*
Hirono, Mazie Keiko *congresswoman, former lieutenant governor*
Ho, Reginald Chi Shing *medical educator*
Hoffmann, Kathryn Ann *humanities educator*
Hook, Ralph Clifford, Jr. *business educator*
Hue, Nguyen Van *soil scientist, chemist, educator*
Hughes, Robert Harrison *former agricultural products executive*
Ihrig, Judson La Moure *chemist*
Imanaka, Mitchell Akio *lawyer*
Ingersoll, Caroline Yee *director*
Ingersoll, Richard King *lawyer*
Ishikawa-Fullmer, Janet Satomi *psychologist, educator*
Issell, Brian F. *oncologist, internist*
Iwai, Wilfred Kiyoshi *lawyer*
Jewitt, David *astronomer*
Johnson, Lawrence M. *retired bank executive*
Jordan, Amos Azariah, Jr. *foreign affairs educator, retired military officer*
Kaholokula, Joseph Keaweaimoku *psychologist, researcher*
Kamemoto, Fred Isamu *retired zoologist*
Kane, Thomas Jay III *surgeon, educator*
Kanehiro, Kenneth Kenji *risk management consultant, educator*
Karl, David Michael *oceanographer, educator*
Katayama, Robert Nobuichi *retired lawyer*
Kawachika, James Akio *lawyer*
Kawamura, Georgina K. *finance company executive, state official*
Keil, Klaus *geology educator, consultant*
Keith, Kent Marsteller *academic administrator, motivational speaker, lawyer, writer*
Kelley, Richard Roy *hotel executive*
Kennedy, Faye *retired social worker, author*
Keogh, Richard John *firearms and explosives consultant*
Kessler, Cristy *education educator*
Keyes, Saundra Elise *newspaper editor*
Khan, Mohammad Asad *geophysics educator, retired minister, former senator of Pakistan*
Kim, S. Peter *psychiatrist, educator, health facility administrator, researcher*
Kim-Rupnow, Weol Soon *education educator*
Kobayashi, Bert Takaaki, Jr. *lawyer*
Koide, Frank Takayuki *electrical engineering educator*
Konan, Denise *academic administrator, economics professor*
Kong, Laura S. L. *geophysicist*
Kudritzki, Rolf-Peter *astronomer, educator*
Kupchak, Kenneth Roy *lawyer*
Lacy, John Robert *lawyer*
Laney, Leroy Olan *economist, banker, educator*
Langhans, Edward Allen *drama and theater educator*
Lau, Constance H. (Connnie Lau) *electric power industry executive*
Lau, Eugene Wing Iu *lawyer*
Lau, H. Lorrin *obstetrician, gynecologist*
Lebedev, Konstantin Vladimirovich *oceanographer, researcher*
Lee, Dale W. *lawyer*
Lee, Lorrin L. *internet marketing entrepreneur, architect, writer*
Lee, Yeu-Tsu Margaret *surgeon, educator*
Levinson, Steven Henry *state supreme court justice*
Lewis, Peter Cushman *electric company executive*
Lilly, Michael Alexander *lawyer, writer*
Lingle, Linda *governor*
Lombardi, Dennis M. *lawyer*
Longstreth, Robert Mayne *lawyer*
Louie, David Mark *lawyer*
Lum, Jean Loui Jin *nursing educator*
Mader, Charles Lavern *chemist*
Magaoay, Michael Y. *state representative*
Mandel, Morton *molecular biologist*
Marks, Michael J. *lawyer*
Mau-Shimizu, Patricia Ann *lawyer*
McClain, David Stanley *academic administrator, business and management professor*
McMurtry, Gary Michael *geochemist, educator*
Merrifield, Donald Paul *ministries coordinator*
Midkiff, Robert Richards *trust company, finance company executive, consultant*
Miller, Clifford Joel *lawyer*
Miller, Richard Sherwin *law educator*
Miyasaki, Shuichi *lawyer*
Mochida, Paula T. *library director*
Moon, Ronald T.Y. *state supreme court chief justice*
Moore, Ernest Carroll III *lawyer*
Moreno-Cabral, Carlos Eduardo *cardiac surgeon*
Morrison, Charles Edward *think-tank executive*
Morse, Jack Craig *lawyer, arbitrator*
Muranaka, Jami *biology educator*
Nakata, Gary Kenji *lawyer*
Nakayama, Paula Aiko *state supreme court justice*
Nasky, H(arold) Gregory (Harold Gregory Nasky) *lawyer*
Ng, Wing Chiu *accountant, educator, application developer, lawyer, advocate*
Nguyen, Thanh Truc Thi *computer animator, educator*
Nishimura, Pete Hideo *oral surgeon*
Niyekawa, Agnes Mitsue *foreign language professor*
Noguchi, Hideo *insurance company executive*
Nordyke, Eleanor Cole *demographer, researcher, public health nurse*
Obana, William G. *neurosurgeon*
O'Brien, Kendra Allen *psychologist, researcher*
Ogburn, Hugh Bell *chemical engineer, consultant*
Okinaga, Lawrence Shoji *lawyer*
Oldenburg, Ronald Troy *lawyer*
O'Neill, Charles Kelly *marketing professional, retired advertising executive*
O'Shaughnessy, Edward Joseph *urologist, retired medical educator*
Owen, Cathy Hesse *science administrator*
Paige, Glenn Durland *political scientist, educator*
Pakvasa, Sandip *physicist*
Palia, Aspy Phiroze *marketing educator, researcher, consultant*
Parsa, Fereydoun Don *plastic surgeon*
Pedersen, Paul Bodholdt *psychologist, educator*
Perkins, Frank Overton *academic administrator, marine biologist*
Pickens, Alexander Legrand *retired education educator*
Pickens, Frances Jenkins *artist, educator*
Pilar, L. Prudencio R. *financial services executive*
Pinckney, Neal T. *psychologist, retired educator*
Portnoy, Jeffrey Steven *lawyer*
Potts, Dennis Walker *lawyer*
Raleigh, Cecil Baring *geophysicist*
Ramler, Siegfried *foundation administrator, researcher*
Reber, David James *lawyer*
Rehg, Kenneth Lee *linguistics educator*
Reinke, Stefan Michael *lawyer*
Rhee, Mooweon *business educator*
Riggs, Fred Warren *retired political science professor*
Robinson, Robert Blacque *foundation administrator*
Sagawa, Yoneo *horticulturist, educator*
Saiki, Patricia *federal agency administrator, congressman*
Sakamoto, Norman Lloyd *state legislator, civil engineer*
Sakamoto, Ronald Rikio *lawyer, construction executive*
Sato, Glenn Kenji *lawyer*
Schatz, Irwin Jacob *cardiologist, educator*
Schindler, Jo Ann *librarian, director*
Seff, Karl *zeolite chemist, chemistry educator*
Sia, Jeffrey H.K. *lawyer*
Silva, Clarence *bishop*
Silva, Mary Barnes *retired elementary school educator*
Simonds, John Edward *retired newspaper editor*
Soifer, Aviam *dean, law educator*
Solidum, James *finance and insurance executive*
Sparks, Robert William *retired publishing executive*
Staats, Arthur W. *psychology professor*
Starshak, James L. *lawyer*
Steinmann, John Colburn *architect*
Stephan, John Jason *historian, educator*
Sterrett, James Melville *accountant, consultant*
Streltzer, Jon *psychiatry professor*
Sugiki, Shigemi *ophthalmologist, educator*
Suh, Dae-Sook *political science professor*
Sumida, Kevin P.H. *lawyer*
Swanson, Richard William *retired statistician*
Takumi, Roy Mitsuo *state legislator*
Tanner, Jerré E. *composer, retired publishing executive*
Tanoue, Donna A. *bank executive, former federal agency administrator*
Tarui, Nori *economics professor*
Taylor, Carroll Stribling *lawyer*
Tiwari, Atul *chemist, researcher*
Turbin, Richard *lawyer*
Uejo, Colleen Misaye *elementary school educator*
Uhl, Philip Edward *artist, photographer, cinematographer*
Umebayashi, Clyde Satoru *lawyer*
Usui, Leslie Raymond *apparel executive*
Varley, Herbert Paul *Japanese language and cultural history educator*
Wang, Jaw-Kai *bioengineering educator*
Watanabe, Corinne Kaoru Amemiya *judge, state official*
Wee, Christine Dijos *elementary school educator*
Weight, Michael Anthony *lawyer, former judge*
Wellein, Marsha Diane Akau *military educator, director*
Wesselkamper, Sue *academic administrator*

White, Emmet, Jr. *retirement community administrator*
White, Gary Richard *electrical engineer*
Wilson, William James *healthcare executive*
Wolff, Herbert Eric *banker, former army officer*
Woo, Vernon Ying-Tsai *lawyer, real estate developer*
Wright, Chatt Grandison *academic administrator*
Yee, Florence *library director*
Yeh, Raymond Wei-Hwa *architect, educator*
Yew, David *physician, director*

Kahului
Domingo, Cora Maria Corazon Encarnacion *minister*
Tolliver, Dorothy *librarian*
Yamamoto, Irwin Toraki *editor, publishing executive*

Kailua
Bone, Robert William *writer*
Buratynski, Theresa Joan *physician*
Shank, Charles Vernon *science administrator, educator, physicist*
Stamper, Ewa Szumotalska *psychologist*
Tavares, Samantha *psychologist, educator*
Wong, Wallace *real estate investor*
Wright, John Cotton *archivist, consultant*

Kailua Kona
Diama, Benjamin *retired secondary school educator, artist, composer, writer*
Iolana, Patricia Elvira *foundation administrator, consultant*
Leonardo, Ann Adamson *marketing and sales consultant*
Pratt, Alan John *business and marketing consultant*
Spitze, Glenys Smith *retired teacher and counselor*
Zola, Michael S. *lawyer*

Kamuela
Chen, Chien-hsing *Chinese traditional health practices educator*
Richards, Phyllis Anderson *psychologist*

Kaneohe
Ashley, Elizabeth *dean, educator*
Lagoria, Georgianna Marie *curator, writer, editor, visual art consultant*
Strang, Nathan Thomas *military officer*
Vincent, Thomas James *retired manufacturing executive*
Young-Pohlman, Colette Lisa *music educator*

Kapaa
Caspillo, Carol A. *secondary school educator*
Klontz, Bradley T. *psychologist, consultant*
Veylanswami, Satguru Bodhinatha *head of religious order*

Kapaau
Jankowski, Theodore Andrew *artist*
McFee, Richard *electrical engineer, physicist*
Ralston, Joanne Smoot *public relations executive*

Kapolei
Stewart, Bobby Gene *laboratory director*
Zabanal, Eduardo Olegario *lawyer*

Keaau
Alton, Lloyde Loren *retired defender*

Kihei
Borchers, Robert Reece *physicist, science administrator*
Burns, Richard Gordon *retired lawyer, writer, consultant*
Galesi, Deborah Lee *artist*
McGuire, Michael William *communications executive*

Koloa
Donohugh, Donald Lee *physician*

Kula
Maloney, Michael Patrick *lawyer, mediator, arbitrator*
Richardson, Robert Allen *retired lawyer, educator*
Rohlfing, Frederick William *lawyer, retired judge, political scientist*

Lahaina
Percy, Helen Sylvia *physician*

Laie
Miller, Ronald Mellado *education educator*
Shumway, Eric Brandon *academic administrator*

Lihue
Culliney, John James *radiologist, educator*
Stevens, Robert David *librarian, educator*

M C B H Kaneohe Bay
Liu, Derek C. *military officer*

Makawao
Huff, Harriet *artist, educator*

Mililani
Camery, John William *computer engineer*
Gardner, Sheryl Paige *gynecologist*
Hunkele, Lester Martin III *retired federal agency administrator*
Magee, Donald Edward *retired national park service administrator*
Okita, George Torao *retired pharmacologist*
Olsen, Harris Leland *diplomat, writer, real estate company executive, educator*

Mountain View
Peterson, Gerald Joseph *aerospace executive, consultant*

Ocean View
Baglow, David Richard *marine facility administrator*

Pahoa
Lewis, Jack (Cecil Paul Lewis) *publishing executive, editor*

Paia
Loomis, James Cook *mathematician, cyberneticist, writer, educator, navigator*
Richman, Joel Eser *lawyer, arbitrator, mediator*

Pearl City
Awakuni, Gene I. *academic administrator, psychologist*
Fujita, James Hiroshi *history educator*
Sue, Alan Kwai Keong *dentist*

Pearl Harbor
Willard, Robert F. *career military officer*

Volcano
Nicholson, Marilyn Lee *arts administrator*

Waianae
Bourke-Faustina, Marlene Frances *music educator*

Waikoloa
Calvert, Delbert William *retired energy executive*
Copman, Louis *radiologist*
Morris, Victor Franklin, Jr. *retired meteorology educator*

Waipahu
Chang, Walter Tuck, Sr. *draftsman, real estate agent, religious studies educator*

IDAHO

Boise
Aitken, Paul Arthur *composer, conductor*
Andrus, Cecil Dale *academic administrator*
Appleton, Steven R. *electronics executive*
Badke, Frederick Robert *cardiologist*
Benham, James H. *state official*
Benson, Kenneth Victor *manufacturing executive, lawyer*
Black, Pete *retired state legislator, educator*
Brownson, Mary Louise *counselor, educator, artist*
Burdick, Roger S. *state supreme court justice*
Burton, Timothy Alan *biologist*
Chenoweth, Tim *information scientist, educator*
Cleary, Edward William *retired diversified forest products company executive*
Clemins, Archie Ray *career officer*
Cory, Wallace Newell *retired civil engineer*
Crane, Ron G. *state official*
DeMotte, John Buck *educational consultant*
Eiriksson, Charles Einar *cardiologist*
Eismann, Daniel T. *state supreme court justice*
Fawcett, Charles Winton *lawyer*
Gee, Gavin M. *state agency administrator*
Geston, Mark Symington *lawyer*
Gowler, Vicki Sue *editor-in-chief*
Griffin, Sylvia Gail *reading specialist*
Hanks, Stephen Grant *construction executive, lawyer*
Harad, George Jay *retired manufacturing executive*
Herbert, Kathy J. *retail executive*
Hlobik, Lawrence S. *agricultural products executive*
Hoagland, Samuel Albert *lawyer, pharmacist*
Hofflund, Mark *theater director*
Holt, Isabel Rae *radio program producer*
Hunsucker, (Carl) Wayne *architectural firm executive, educator*
Ilett, Frank, Jr. *trucking executive, educator*
Jones, James Thomas *state supreme court justice, former state attorney general*
Jones, Warren Eugene *state supreme court justice*
Joslin, Ann *state librarian*
Keough, Shawn *state legislator*
Kustra, Robert W. (Bob Kustra) *former state official, academic administrator*
LaRocco, Larry *former congressman*
Leroy, David Henry *lawyer*
Lewis, Roderic W. *electronics executive, lawyer*
Lodge, Patti Anne *state senator*
Long, William D. *grocery store executive*
Luna, Thomas *school system administrator*
Mahoney, James E. *information technology executive*
Maloof, Giles Wilson *academic administrator, educator, author*
McDevitt, Charles Francis *retired judge, lawyer*
McGown, John, Jr. *lawyer*
McLuskie, Ed *communications educator*
Meier, Joseph M. *lawyer*
Meyer, Christopher Hawkins *lawyer*
Minnich, Diane Kay *legal association administrator*
Moss, Thomas E. *prosecutor*
Myers, William Gerry III *lawyer*
Nelson, Kristin Schad *cosmetic surgeon*
Nelson, Thomas G. *federal judge*
Noack, Harold Quincy, Jr. *lawyer*
Otter, Butch (C. L. Otter, Clement Leroy Otter) *governor, former congressman*
Overgaard, Willard Michele *retired political scientist*
Parent, Mark Gordon *cardiologist*
Park, William Anthony (Tony) *lawyer*
Parry, Richard D. *lawyer, construction executive*
Petersen, Chris *college football coach*
Pfouts, Ralph William *economist, consultant*
Priest, Marshall Franklin III *cardiologist*
Redshaw, James Douglas *neurologist*
Richardson, Betty H. *lawyer, former prosecutor*
Risch, Jim (James E.) *lieutenant governor, former governor, state legislator*
Seale, Walter Louis *cardiologist*
Shurtliff, Marvin Karl *lawyer*
Silak, Cathy R. *lawyer, former state supreme court justice*
Simplot, Jack (John Richard Simplot) *diversified food products company executive*
Simplot, Scott R. *diversified food products company executive*
Slaughter, Richard Arthur *political scientist, economist, educator*
Smith, Marsha H. *state agency administrator, lawyer*
Stephens, William Thomas *forest products manufacturing company executive*
Sullivan, James Kirk *management consultant*
Terteling-Payne, Carolyn Ann *city official*
Trott, Stephen Spangler *federal judge*
Trout, Linda Copple *state supreme court justice*
Van Helden, Pete *food products executive*
Wasden, Lawrence *state attorney general*
Washington, Dennis R. *contracting company executive*
Wilson, Jack Fredrick *retired federal government official*
Winmill, B. Lynn *federal judge*
Ysursa, Ben T. *state official*
Zarges, Thomas H. *engineering executive*

Burley
Little, Glen Gordon *retired circus clown, educator*

Caldwell
Angresano, James *economics professor*
Hendren, Robert Lee, Jr. *academic administrator*
Hoover, Robert Allan *university president*
Kerrick, David Ellsworth *lawyer*

Coeur D' Alene
Clabby, Michael *computer graphics designer, educator*
Dahlgren, Dorothy *museum director*
McCormick, Chad Donald *otolaryngologist*

Donnelly
Ferensowicz, Michael Jay *real estate company executive*

Eagle
Ricks, Thomas Aaron *real estate developer*

Emmett
Bennett, Gary Lee *physicist, consultant*

Fort Hall
Himmler, Bruno Jon *physician, military officer*

Gooding
Larson, Lynn Wood *artist, musician*

Hailey
Hogue, Terry Glynn *lawyer*

Harrison
Carlson, George Arthur *artist*

Hayden
Griffith, William Alexander *former mining company executive*

Idaho Falls
Abbott, Michael Lehman *environmental scientist*
Barbe, Betty Catherine *marketing professional, retired financial analyst*
Harris, Darryl Wayne *publishing executive*
Jue, Jan-Fong *materials scientist*
Lee, Glenn Richard *medical association administrator, educator*
Miller, Gregory Kent *structural engineer*
Paviet-Hartmann, Patricia *chemist, researcher*
Planchon, Harry Peter, Jr. *research development manager*
Riemke, Richard Allan *nuclear engineer*
Rydalch, Ann *federal agency administrator*
Thorsen, Nancy Dain *real estate broker*

Inkom
Ambrose, Tommy W. *chemical engineer, engineering executive*
Jackson, Allen Keith *retired museum administrator*

Jerome
Bell, Maxine Toolson *state legislator, librarian*
Ricketts, Virginia Lee *historian, researcher*

Ketchum
McElhinny, Wilson Dunbar *banker*
Parry, Janet *retired health facility administrator*
Ziebarth, Robert Charles *management consultant*

Kimberly
Strausbaugh, Carl Alan *plant pathologist*

Lewiston
Marshall, Josie *secondary school educator*
Tait, John Reid *lawyer*
Thomas, Dene Kay *academic administrator, educator*

Moscow
Abraham, Terry *school librarian*
Anderson, Clifton Einar *writer, corporate communications specialist*
Bobisud, Larry Eugene *mathematics professor*
DeShazer, James Arthur *biological engineer, educator, research administrator*
Fiske, Janet Murray *volunteer, elementary school educator, researcher*
Force, Ronald Wayne *retired librarian*
Goetschel, Roy Hartzell, Jr. *mathematician, researcher*
Greever, Janet Groff *history professor*
Griffiths, Peter Roughley *chemistry professor, consultant*
Guy, Stephen Otto *agronomist, educator*
Harris, Robert Dalton *retired history professor, researcher, writer*
Jankowska, Maria Anna *school librarian, educator*
Kreutzer, Natalie Ruth Jones *music educator*
Miller, Maynard Malcolm *geologist, educator, science administrator, former state legislator*
Renfrew, Malcolm MacKenzie *chemist, educator*
Roberts, Lorin Watson *botanist, educator*
Shreeve, Jean'ne Marie *chemist, educator*
Vaughan, Karen Lynn *soil scientist*
Vincenti, Sheldon Arnold *lawyer, educator*
White, Timothy Peter *academic administrator, physical education educator*

Nampa
Bowers, Curtis Ray, Jr. *chaplain*
Hagood, Richard A. *academic administrator, educator*

Ola
Farr, Reeta Rae *special education administrator*

Parma
Sharkey, (John) Mick *biology educator*

Pocatello
Bennett, Byron Lee *chemistry professor, researcher*
Eichman, Charles Melvin *counselor*
Jacobsen, Richard T. *mechanical engineering educator*
Lawson, Jonathan Nevin *academic administrator, educator*
Nye, W. Marcus W. *lawyer*
Piland, Neill Finnes *health services economist, researcher, educator*
Risinger, Fred Owen *pharmacologist*
Robinson, Evelyn Etta *principal*
Smith, Norman Randy *federal judge*
Stucki, Margaret Elizabeth *art gallery director, writer, painter*
Vailas, Arthur C. *biomechanics educator*
Valentine, Ralph Schuyler *chemical engineer, director*

Post Falls
Brede, Andrew Douglas *science administrator, botanist*
Hasalone, Annette Leona *radio personality, research and development company executive*
Riggs, Jack Timothy *emergency physician, retired lieutenant governor*

Priest River
Booker, Bruce Robert *rabbi*

Rexburg
Barrus, Charles LaMar, Jr. *music educator*
Clark, Kim Bryce *academic administrator*
Ivers, John Joseph *language educator, dean*

Rogerson
Boss, Marylin Jeanette *elementary school educator*

Sandpoint
Benbrook, Charles Mallard *executive consulting company*
Bowne, Martha Hoke *editor, consultant*
Daarstad, Erik *cinematographer*
Glock, Charles Young *sociologist, writer*
Staff, Jack Robert *economist, author, monk*

Sun Valley
Cassell, William Comyn *retired college president*
Stewart, John Todd *economist, consultant*
Tillinghast, Charles Carpenter III *retired marketing company executive*

Twin Falls
Berry, L. Clyel *lawyer*
Cowger, Shari Ann *music educator*
Eaton, Curtis Howarth *banker, lawyer*
Hohnhorst, John Charles *judge*
Wright, Frances Jane *educational psychologist*

Wayan
Carney Nelson, Ellen B. *elementary school educator*

Yellow Pine
Auth, Robert Ralph *art educator*

ILLINOIS

Abbott Park
Ashley, Richard W. *pharmaceutical executive*
Burke, Sandra E. *information technology executive*
Dempsey, William G. *pharmaceutical executive*
Frazier, Douglas Byron *healthcare manufacturing manager*
Freyman, Thomas C. *pharmaceutical executive*
Gonzalez, Richard A. *pharmaceutical executive*
Jeng, Tzyy-Wen *biochemist, researcher*
Krivoshik, Andrew Peter *engineer, physician*
Krueger, Allan C. *chemist*
Liepmann, Holger A. *pharmaceutical executive*
Nemmers, Joseph M., Jr. *pharmaceutical executive*
Schumacher, Laura J. *lawyer, pharmaceutical executive*
White, Miles D. *pharmaceutical executive*

Addison
McDonald, David Eugene *transportation operator*

Alexander
Eck, Gail Ann *elementary school educator*

Algonquin
Wise, Jack Ronald *music educator*

Alsip
Fournier, Maureen Mary *physical education educator*

Alton

Boyle, Ann M. *dean, dental educator*
Kessler, William Eugene *healthcare executive*
Struif, L. James *lawyer*

Anna

Pleinta, Tod Algiers *philosopher, educator*

Argonne

Abrikosov, Alexei Alexeyevich *physicist*
Ahmed, Shabbir *chemical engineer*
Bader, Samuel David *physicist*
Ban, Stephen Dennis *gas industry executive*
Buth, Christian *physicist, researcher*
Chang, Yoon Il *nuclear engineer*
Derrick, Malcolm *physicist*
Kolesnikov, Alexander Ivanovich *physicist*
Kumar, Romesh *chemical engineer*
Lawson, Robert Davis *theoretical nuclear physicist*
Lindert, Eric Alton *operations research specialist, small business owner*
Myles, Kevin Michael *metallurgical engineer*
Peshkin, Murray *physicist*
Saricks, Christopher Lee *retired transportation analyst*
Schriesheim, Alan *science administrator*
Shpyrko, Oleg G. *physicist*
Steindler, Martin Joseph *chemist*
Sumant, Anirudha *materials scientist, researcher*

Arlington Heights

Ammar, Alia N. *neuropsychologist, educator*
Baptist, Allwyn J. *healthcare consultant*
Baumann, Daniel E. *publishing executive*
Ehrenpreis, Eli Daniel *physician, educator, biomedical researcher*
Ehrmann, Susanna *language educator, photographer, writer*
Fields, Sara A. *travel company executive*
Griffin, Jean Latz *political strategist, writer, publisher*
Hudson, Ronald Morgan *aviation planner*
Jensen, Lynn Edward *retired medical association administrator, economist*
Lampinen, John A. *newspaper editor*
Li, Norman N. *chemicals executive*
Ray, Douglas Kent *newspaper executive*
Rivkin, William B. *physicist*
Ruder, John Regan *physician*
Smith, Norman Obed *retired physical chemist, educator*
Tongue, William Walter *economics and business consultant, educator*
Tucker, Bowen Hayward *lawyer*

Aurora

Cain, Thomas Robert *interventional radiologist*
Camic, David Edward *lawyer*
Daugherty, Patricia Ann *retired elementary school educator*
Elgar, Sharon Kay *science educator*
Koopman, Richard Nelson *engineer, consultant*
Lee, Robert Hugh *management executive*
Lloyd, Johnny Keith *biology professor*
Lowe, Ralph Edward *lawyer*
Mitchinson, Milliam J. *social studies educator*
Noglows, William P. *electronics executive*
Pappas, Margene *retired music educator*
Stephens, Steve Arnold *real estate broker*

Barrington

Burrows, Brian William *retired research and development company executive*
Carter, Jeanie *performing company executive*
Chung, Joseph Sang-hoon *economics professor*
Graham, Berta *humanities educator, researcher*
Hybels, Bill *Pastor*
Kunkel, Nancy Angela *psychologist*
Lee, William Marshall *lawyer*
Murphy, Robert *executive search consultant*
Nadig, Gerald George *retired manufacturing executive*
Perry, I. Chet *petroleum company executive*
Ross, Frank Howard III *management consultant*
Scanlon Hobbs, Laurie Ann *public relations professional*
Stephens, Norval Blair, Jr. *marketing consultant*
Wood, Andrée Robitaille *archaeologist, researcher*
Wyatt, James Frank, Jr. *lawyer*
Wynn, Thomas Joseph *judge, educator*
Young, Michael Phillip *orthopedist, surgeon*

Bartlett

Plaskacz, Edward John *computer scientist, engineer, mathematics professor*

Batavia

Bardeen, William Allan *research physicist*
Brown, Gerald Curtis *retired military officer, engineering executive*
Jonckheere, Alan Mathew *physicist*
Morefield, Michael Thomas *financial executive*
Oddone, Piermaria Jorge *physicist*
Raja, Rajendran *physicist*
Rakhno, Igor *physicist*

Belleville

Bauman, John Duane *lawyer*
Boyle, Richard Edward *lawyer*
Braxton, Edward K. *bishop*
Fietsam, Robert Charles *accountant*
Hedges, Patrick Armand *security firm executive*
Hess, Frederick J. *lawyer*
Hilgenbrink, Robert J. *academic administrator*
Hundsdorfer, Beth *reporter*
Jones, Donald Leigh *retired music educator*
Miller, Jan Paul *lawyer, former prosecutor*
Pawlaczyk, George *reporter*
Pounds, Regina Dorothea *writer*
Ripplinger, George Raymond, Jr. *lawyer*
Shim, Sang Koo *mental health services professional*
Stanford, Edward Joseph *gynecologist*
Studer, Louis *priest, religious organization administrator*
Terveer, Joyce Ann *academic administrator, English language educator*
Thien-Stasko, Vicki Lynn *civil engineer*
Urban, Donald Wayne *lawyer*

Bellwood

Miller, Denyce Karlina *tax specialist*
Nader, Nadine Ann *social studies educator*

Belvidere

Luhman, William Simon *community development administrator*
Mc Nelly, Frederick Wright, Jr. *psychologist*
Wells, April *language educator*

Benton

Gilbert, J. Phil *federal judge*

Berwyn

Forst, Edmund Charles, Jr. *communications educator, administrator, consultant*
Galinsky, Dennis Lee *radiation oncologist, educator*
Hudik, Martin Francis *hospital administrator, educator, consultant, writer*
Misurec, Rudolf *physician, surgeon*
Parker, Alan John *veterinary neurologist, educator, researcher*
Wunderlich, Dorothy Anastasia *superintendent*

Bloomingdale

Flaherty, John Joseph *quality assurance company executive*
Roskam, Peter James *congressman, former state legislator, lawyer*
Wolande, Charles Sanford *former computer company executive*

Bloomington

Beeler, Charlotte Jean *oil and supply company executive, interior design business executive*
Blackburn, John D. *insurance company executive*
Bridges, Roger Dean *historian*
Brown, Jared *theater director, educator, writer*
Brunner, Kim M. *insurance company executive, lawyer*
Curry, Alan Chester *actuary*
Dietz, William Ronald *corporate management professional*
Laurenti, Joseph Luciano *language educator, writer*
Pannell, Thierry Edgard *engineer, information technology manager*
Rust, Edward Barry, Jr. *insurance company executive, lawyer*
Skillrud, Harold Clayton *minister, retired bishop*
Spears, Larry Jonell *lawyer*
Sullivan, Laura Patricia *lawyer, insurance company executive*
Switzer, Jon Rex *architect*
Tipsord, Michael L. *insurance company executive*
Trefzger, Richard Charles *surgeon*
Vayo, David Joseph *composer, music educator*
Ward, Jon David *retired insurance company executive*
Wilson, Richard F. *academic administrator*

Bolingbrook

Alvarado, Serafin *wine connoisseur*
Day, Mary Ann *medical/surgical nurse*
Malicay, Manuel Alaban *physician*
Price, Theodora Hadzisteliou *individual, child and family therapist*
Sabau, Carmen Sybile *retired chemist*
Sheehan, James Patrick *printing company executive, former media company executive*
Tot, Zvonimir *musician, composer, music educator*

Bourbonnais

Dalton, Martha Gomer *music educator*
Gipple, Ellen A. *elementary school educator*
McClure, Thomas Edward *lawyer*
Sayson, Joselito *physical therapist, educator*
Wilkey, Elmira Smith *illustrator, artist, writer, educator*
Woodruff, Neal *music educator*

Bridgeview

Guppy, John *professional sports team executive*

Broadview

Bland, Pamela June *special education educator*
Lazar, Jill Sue *home healthcare company executive*

Brookfield

Rabb, George Bernard *zoologist, conservationist*
Rudnick, Jamie *geneticist, research scientist*

Buffalo Grove

Johnson, Craig Theodore *portfolio manager*
Kuennen, Thomas Gerard *journalist*
Samors, Neal *publishing executive, writer*
Ward, Michael W. *lawyer*

Burr Ridge

Bottom, Dale Coyle *marketing executive, director, management consultant*
Decker, Richard Knore *lawyer*
McCormack, Robert Cornelius *investment banker*
Rosenberg, Robert Brinkmann *information technology executive*
Wyatt, Robert Odell *journalism educator*
Zaccone, Suzanne Maria *sales executive*

Calumet City

Muñoz, Romeo Solano *audio visual curator*
Scullion, Annette Murphy *lawyer, educator*

Carbondale

Asoh, Derek Ajesam *information scientist, educator*
Baker, Clora Mae *business educator*
Bauner, Ruth Elizabeth *library director*
Benford, Robert Dee *social studies educator, editor*
Burr, Brooks Milo *zoology educator*
Carlson, David Harold *library director, dean*
Clemons, John Robert *lawyer*
Cole, Brad *mayor*
Dixon, Billy Gene *academic administrator, educator*
Duggan, James Edgar *law librarian*
Hahn, Robert Alan *philosophy educator*
Headrick, Todd Christopher *mathematical statistician, educator*
Kawewe, Saliwe Moyo *social work educator, researcher*
Lanigan, Richard Leo, Jr. *humanities educator, writer, editor*
LeFebvre, Eugene Allen *zoology educator, ecologist*
Lowery, Christopher M. *men's college basketball coach*
Malkin, Marjorie J. *recreational therapist, educator*
Mathur, Ike *finance educator*
M'Cormack, Fredanna Antoinette Durosimi *dietician, educator*
Neuman, Edward George *mathematician, educator*
Oyana, Tonny J. *geoscientist, educator*
Poshard, Glenn (Glendal W. Poshard) *academic administrator, former congressman*
Scott, Shirley Clay *dean*
Snyder, Carolyn Ann *education educator, librarian, director*
Treviño, Fernando Manuel *academic administrator, medical educator*
Weeks, Theodore R. *history professor*
Whitlock, John Joseph *museum director*
Whittington, Rebecca Ann *lawyer*

Carlyle

Spihlmann, Kris Ann *mathematics educator*

Carol Stream

Armerding, Hudson Taylor *retired college president, consultant*
Bemis, Mary Ferguson *magazine editor*
Franzen, Janice Marguerite Gosnell *magazine editor*
Gale, Neil Jan *Internet company executive, computer scientist, consultant*
Yancey, Philip David *editor, author*

Carrollton

Strickland, Hugh Alfred *lawyer*

Carterville

Krapf, Keith Alan *science educator*

Carthage

Glidden, John Redmond *lawyer*

Cary

Irey, Robin Elizabeth *performing company executive, performing arts educator*

Centralia

Whitten, Mary Lou *nursing educator*

Champaign

Arnould, Richard Julius *economist, educator, consultant, dean*
Baillargeon, Renee *psychology professor*
Baker, Jack Sherman *architect, educator*
Balbach, Harold Edward *environmental scientist*
Batzli, George Oliver *ecology educator*
Boubekri, Mohamed *architecture educator*
Boyle, Francis Anthony *law educator*
Brighton, Gerald David *retired finance educator*
Brustein, William Irving *sociology educator*
Buschbach, Thomas Charles *geologist, consultant*
Cartwright, Keros *hydrogeologist, researcher*
Chang, Kathy Kuhl *computer programmer, analyst*
Cho, In-Koo *economist, educator*
Clark, Nicholas Leland *contractor*
Davis, James Henry *retired psychology educator*
Dmitriev, Dmitry A. *entomologist, researcher*
Douglas, George Halsey *language educator, writer*
Dulany, Elizabeth Gjelsness *editor*
Eriksen, Charles Walter *psychologist, educator*
Fredrickson, L(awrence) Thomas *composer*
Freedman, Philip *internist, educator*
Ghosh, Avijit *dean*
Gold, Paul Ernest *psychology and behavioral neuroscience educator*
Gomez, Terrine *school director*
Greene, James K. *military officer, educator*
Gross, David Lee *geologist*
Guttenberg, Albert Ziskind *planning educator*
Herman, Richard H. *academic administrator*
Hopkins, Lewis Dean *architecture educator*
Hurd, Heidi M. *dean, humanities and law educator*
Ikenberry, Stanley Oliver *education educator, director, former university president*
Johnston, Janis L. *law librarian, educator*
Justice, Patricia *academic administrator, educator*
Katehi, Linda P.B. *engineering educator*
Kindt, John Warren *lawyer, educator*
Korst, Helmut Hans *mechanical engineer, educator*
Kotoske, Roger Allen *artist, educator*
Krause, Harry Dieter *law educator*
Kroner, Fred L. *journalist*
Krug, Edward Charles *environmental scientist*
Levin, Geoffrey Arthur *botanist*
Loeb, Jane Rupley *academic administrator, educator*
Maggs, Peter Blount *lawyer, educator*
Mamer, Stuart Mies *lawyer*
May, Linda Karen Cardiff *occupational health nurse, safety engineer, consultant*
McConkie, George Wilson *education educator*
McCulloh, Judith Marie *editor*
McGlathery, James Melville *retired foreign language educator*
McKay, JoAnn *retired musician, composer*
Meyer, August Christopher, Jr. *broadcast executive, lawyer*
Mies, John Charles *Internet company executive*
Miller, Harold Arthur *lawyer*
Moore, Jerry Jay *sales executive, retired archaeologist*
Nowak, John E. *law educator*
Perry, Kenneth Wilbur *finance educator*
Rawles, Edward Hugh *lawyer*
Rayward, Warden Boyd *librarian, educator*
Rebeiz, Constantin Anis *plant biochemist, educator, lab administrator, foundation administrator*
Richardson, Selma Katherine *retired library and information scientist*
Ridlen, Samuel Franklin *agriculture educator*
Riley, Robert Bartlett *landscape architect*
Roese, Neal J. *psychology professor, consultant*
Rose, Walter Deane *retired engineering educator*
Ruan, Lian Jin *library director*
Schoenfeld, Hanns-Martin Walter *finance educator*
Semonin, Richard Gerard *retired state official*
Smith, Ralph Alexander *cultural and educational policy educator*
Spice, Dennis Dean *financial consultant*
Spodek, Bernard *early childhood educator*
Stone, Victor J. *retired law educator*
Stotler, Edith Ann *retired grain company executive*
Strauser, David Ross *healthcare educator, director*
Summerfield, Gale *director, educator*
Triandis, Harry Charalambos *psychologist, educator*
Turquette, Atwell Rufus *logician*
Turquette, Frances Bond *editor*
Unsworth, John M. *dean, library and information science educator*
Urban, Richard J. *library and information scientist*
Watts, Emily Stipes *retired English language educator*
Watts, Robert Allan *publisher, lawyer*
Wolfram, Stephen *physicist, computer company executive*
Young, Paul *graphic designer, edcator*

Channahon

Blomstedt, Erik Ragnar *library administrator*

Charleston

Coutant, Mary McElwee *retired editor*
Daum, John LaVern *retired band director, educator*
Eberly, Charles *counseling and student development educator*
McBride, Jonica Helene *mathematics professor*
O'Rourke, Kathleen Ann *education educator*
Ramsey, Charles Estel *retired physician, retired surgeon*
Rives, Stanley Gene *retired academic administrator*
Surles, Carol D. *academic administrator*
Thornburgh, Daniel Eston *retired university administrator, journalism educator*

Chatham

Chew, Keith Elvin *health facility administrator*

Chebanse

McLaughlin, Barbara Lyn *elementary school educator*

Chester

Welge, Donald Edward *food manufacturing executive*

Chicago

Abcarian, Herand *surgeon, educator*
Abelson, Herbert Traub *pediatrician, educator*
Abrams, Lee Norman *lawyer*
Abt, Ralph Edwin *lawyer*
Achatz, Grant *chef*
Acker, Ann E. *lawyer*
Acker, Frederick George *lawyer*
Adams, Austin A. *bank executive*
Adams, Edward A. *legal journalist*
Adams, John S. *insurance company executive*
Adelman, Pamela Bernice Kozoll *education educator*
Adelman, Stanley Joseph *lawyer*
Adelman, Steven Herbert *lawyer*
Adelson, Lawrence Seth *electronics executive, lawyer*
Alberts, Barry S. *lawyer*
Albrecht, Ronald Frank *anesthesiologist*
Albright, Chris *professional soccer player*
Alcantara, Anita Luisa *community arts administrator*
al-Chalabi, Suhail Abdul-Jabbar *transport economist, consultant*
Alexander, Karen *museum staff member*
Allen, Belle *management consulting firm and communications executive*
Allen, Henry Sermones, Jr. *lawyer*
Allen, Ronald Jay *law educator*
Allen, Thomas Draper *lawyer*
Almen, Lowell Gordon *church official*
Amberg, Thomas L. *public relations executive*
Amboian, John Peter, Jr. *investment company executive*
Andersen, Burton Robert *immunologist, educator, medical historian*
Anderson, Cathy C. *lawyer*
Anderson, Craig Allen *retired art educator, artist*
Anderson, David Boyd *lawyer, metal products executive*
Anderson, J. Trent *lawyer*
Anderson, John Leonard *academic administrator, chemical engineering educator*
Anderson, Karl Stephen *editor*
Anderson, Kimball Richard *lawyer*
Anderson, Thomas Caryl *dean*

Andolino, Rosemarie S. *airport terminal executive*
Andreoli, Kathleen Gainor *nurse, educator, dean*
Angst, Gerald L. *lawyer*
Anthony, Michael Francis *lawyer*
Antonio, Douglas John *lawyer*
Anvaripour, M. A. *lawyer*
Apelbaum, Phyllis L. *delivery messenger service executive*
Apollo, Brian *psychologist, poet*
Appel, Nina Schick *law educator, dean, academic administrator*
Arnold, Damon Theodore *physician*
Aronson, Virginia L. *lawyer*
Arpino, Gerald Peter *performing company executive*
Arruda, Jose *nephrologist*
Artner, Alan Gustav *art critic, journalist*
Arvanitakis, Zoe *neurologist, researcher*
Ash, J. Marshall *mathematician, educator*
Athas, Gus James *lawyer*
Aubin, Barbara Jean *artist*
Auerbach, Marshall Jay *lawyer*
Avery, Robert Dean *lawyer*
Axley, Frederick William *lawyer*
Babcock, Lyndon Ross, Jr. *environmental engineer, educator*
Babcock, Sandra L. *lawyer, educator*
Bacevicius, John Anthony, V, (John Bace) *research and development company executive*
Badel, Julie *lawyer*
Baer, John Richard Frederick *lawyer*
Bailey, Robert, Jr. *advertising executive*
Bailey, Robert Converse *epidemiologist, anthropologist, educator*
Baines, Harold Douglass *retired professional baseball player, baseball bench coach*
Baird, Douglas Gordon *law educator, dean*
Baird, James *lawyer*
Bajich, Milena Tatic *psychologist*
Bakay, Roy Arpad Earle *neurosurgeon, educator*
Baker, Bruce Jay *lawyer*
Baker, Pamela *lawyer*
Bakris, George L. *nephrologist, educator, clinical researcher*
Balanoff, Clem *county election director*
Balasi, Mark Geoffrey *architect*
Baldwin, DeWitt Clair, Jr. *pediatrician, educator*
Baldwin, Shaun McParland *lawyer*
Baldwin, Shawn D. *investment company executive*
Baley, Joan Marie *elementary school educator*
Balk, Robert A. *medical educator*
Balzekas, Stanley, Jr. *museum director*
Banerjee, Prashant *industrial engineer, computer scientist, educator*
Bannon, John A. *lawyer*
Banoff, Sheldon Irwin *lawyer*
Barazani, Morris *artist, educator*
Barber, Bruce Jackson, II, *musician*
Barbour, Claude Marie *minister, educator*
Barden, Larry A. *lawyer*
Barker, Walter Lee *thoracic surgeon*
Barker, William Thomas *lawyer*
Barnes, Brenda C. *food products executive*
Barnes, James Garland, Jr. *lawyer*
Barney, Carol Ross *architect*
Barnhard, Steve *travel company executive*
Baron, Joseph Mandel *hematologist*
Barr, Emily L. *broadcast executive*
Barr, John Robert *retired lawyer*
Barr, Sanford Lee *dentist*
Barré, Laura *finance company executive*
Barron, Harold Sheldon *lawyer*
Barron, Howard Robert *lawyer*
Barron, John *editor*
Bart, Susan Therese *lawyer*
Bartholomay, William C. *insurance brokerage company and professional sports team executive*
Barton, John Joseph *obstetrician, gynecologist, administrator, educator, researcher*
Bartter, Brit Jeffrey *investment banker*
Basden, Cameron *dancer*
Bashwiner, Steven Lacelle *lawyer*
Bauer, William Joseph *federal judge*
Baugher, Peter V. *lawyer*
Baum, Bernard Helmut *sociologist, educator*
Baumgartner, William Hans, Jr. *lawyer*
Bayless, Rick *chef*
Beasley, DaMarcus Lamont *professional soccer player*
Beck, Philip S. *lawyer*
Beck, Robert N. *nuclear medicine educator*
Becker, Gary Stanley *economist, educator*
Becker, Michael Allen *internist, rheumatologist, educator*
Becker, Scott *lawyer*
Becker, Theodore Michaelson *lawyer*
Beem, Jack Darrel *retired lawyer*
Behnia, Roya *lawyer*
Behnke, Michael Clare *academic administrator*
Beilock, Sian Leah *psychology professor, psychologist*
Bell, Angela Marie *accountant*
Bell, Carl Compton *psychiatrist, researcher*
Bell, James A. *aerospace transportation executive*
Bellows, Laurel Gordon *business lawyer*
Belluschi, Anthony C. *architect*
Benedict, Kennette Mari *foundation executive, researcher*
Bennett, Edward James *lawyer*
Bennett, Robert William *law educator*
Bennington, Thomas Francis *lawyer, county official*
Bensinger, Peter Benjamin *consulting firm executive*
Benson, Al Bowen III *oncologist, educator*
Benson, George W. *lawyer*
Bentley, Carol Ligon *retired library and information scientist*
Ben-Yoseph, Miriam *social sciences educator*
Berens, Mark Harry *lawyer*
Berenzweig, Jack Charles *lawyer*
Berger, Miles Lee *land economist*
Berger, Robert Michael *lawyer*
Bergonia, Raymond David *venture capitalist*
Bergstein, Melvyn *information technology executive*
Berhalter, Gregg *professional soccer player*
Berish, Brad A. *lawyer*
Berkoff, Adam T. *lawyer*
Berkoff, Mark Andrew *lawyer*
Berkowitz, Sean M. *lawyer*
Berman, Arthur Leonard *retired state legislator*
Berman, Debbie L. *lawyer*
Berman, Laura *sex therapist*
Bernardin, Thomas L. *advertising executive*
Bernatowicz, Frank Allen *management consultant*
Bernick, David M. *lawyer*
Bernick, Howard Barry *manufacturing executive*
Bernstein, Charles Bernard *lawyer*
Bernstein, H. Bruce *lawyer*
Berolzheimer, Karl *lawyer*
Bess, Ronald W. *advertising executive*
Bettman, Suzanne (Sue Bettman) *lawyer*
Betz, Hans Dieter *theology studies educator*
Beugen, Joan Beth *communications executive*
Bevington, David Martin *English literature educator*
Bezanilla, Francisco *biomedical researcher*
Bidwell, Charles Edward *sociologist, educator*
Biebel, Paul Philip, Jr. *lawyer*
Biggs, Robert Dale *Near Eastern studies educator*
Bindenagel, James Dale *university executive*
Binion, Celious *retired parochial school educator*
Birnbaum, Barry William *special education educator*
Bitner, John Howard *lawyer*
Bixby, Frank Lyman *retired lawyer*
Blackman, Everett Allan *writer*
Blake, Aileen B. *finance company executive*
Bleiweiss, Shell J. *lawyer*
Block, Neal Jay *lawyer*
Block, Philip Dee III *retired investment company executive*
Blount, Michael Eugene *lawyer*
Bluhm, Neil Gary *real estate company executive*
Blust, Larry D. *lawyer*
Bobins, Norman R. *banker*
Bobrinskoy, Charles Kellogg *investment banker*
Bocanegra, Carlos *professional soccer player*
Bodenstein, Ira *lawyer*
Boehnen, Daniel A. *lawyer*
Bogaard, Jonathan Harvey *lawyer*
Boggs, Joseph Dodridge *pediatric pathologist, educator*
Boho, Dan L. *lawyer*
Boies, Wilber H. *lawyer*
Bolger, David P. *insurance company executive*
Bona, Jerry Lloyd *mathematician, educator*
Bondra, Peter *professional hockey player*
Bonomi, Philip David *physician*
Bonow, Robert Ogden *medical educator*
Borenstine, Alvin Jerome *search company executive*
Bosowski, Edward M. *manufacturing executive*
Bosselman, Fred Paul *law educator*
Bostwick, Jarrett T. *lawyer*
Botica, Matthew J. *lawyer*
Boulanger, Victor *director*
Bouma, Robert Edwin *lawyer*
Bourdon, Cathleen Jane *professional society administrator*
Bowe, William J(ohn) *lawyer*
Bowen, Stephen Stewart *lawyer*
Bower, Glen Landis *judge, lawyer*
Bowman, James Edward *pathologist, educator*
Bowman, Leah *fashion designer, consultant, photographer, educator*
Boyer, John William *history professor, dean*
Boykin, Richard Renarda *lawyer, former legislative staff member*
Boykins, Michael L. *lawyer*
Bradley, Thomas A. *insurance company executive*
Brake, Cecil Clifford *retired diversified manufacturing executive*
Bramnik, Robert Paul *lawyer*
Bramson, James B. *dentist, dental association administrator*
Bratcher, Juanita *journalist*
Brennan, Joseph *lawyer*
Brennan, Noelle C. *lawyer*
Brice, Roger Thomas *lawyer*
Bridgman, Thomas Francis *retired lawyer*
Brininstool, David *architect*
Brinkman, John Anthony *historian, educator*
Briones, Teresita Landicho *medical researcher, educator*
Brizzolara, Charles Anthony *lawyer, director*
Bro, Ruth Hill *lawyer*
Brodsky, William J. *investment company executive*
Bromley, Richard *lawyer*
Brookens, Carl *psychologist*
Brooker, Thomas Kimball *oil industry executive*
Brown, Alan Crawford *lawyer*
Brown, Carole L. *transportation executive*
Brown, Donald James, Jr. *lawyer*
Brown, Elizabeth McCarthy *social services administrator*
Brown, Gregory K. *lawyer*
Brown, Jeremy Earle *advertising executive*
Brown, Joel S. *evolutionary ecologist, educator*
Brown, Matthew S. *lawyer*
Brown, Richard Holbrook *library director, historian, researcher*
Brown, Steven Spencer *lawyer*
Brummel, Mark Joseph *religious organization administrator*
Bryan, John Henry *food and consumer products company executive*
Bryant, David J. *lawyer*
Bryant, Fred Boyd *psychology professor*
Bucklo, Elaine Edwards *United States district court judge*
Bucksbaum, John *real estate company executive*
Bucksbaum, Matthew *real estate investment trust company executive*
Buehrle, Mark *professional baseball player*
Bulger, Brian Wegg *lawyer*
Buniak, Raymond *educational professional*
Burck, Joseph Russell *medical educator, consultant, minister*
Burgdoerfer, Jerry *lawyer*
Burke, Anne M. *state supreme court justice*
Burke, John Michael *lawyer*
Burke, Michelle C. *lawyer*
Burke, Thomas Joseph, Jr. *lawyer*
Burkhardt, Edward Arnold *rail transportation executive*
Burns, Robert Patrick *law educator*
Burroughs, Margaret Taylor Goss *artist*
Burt, Richard K. *physician, educator*
Burton, Cheryl *newscaster*
Busey, Roxane C. *lawyer*
Butler, John William, Jr. *lawyer*
Bynoe, Peter Charles Bernard *real estate developer, lawyer*
Byrne, Rhonda *television producer*
Byther-Smith, Ida W. *social services administrator*
Cafferty, Pastora San Juan *education educator*
Calabresi, Steven G. *law educator*
Callahan, Michael R. *lawyer*
Callahan, Timothy T. *real estate company executive*
Cameron, Kenzie Alynn *medical researcher, educator*
Campbell, Alex *mobile marketing executive*
Campbell, Gavin Elliott *real estate investor and developer*
Campbell, William J., Jr. *lawyer*
Camper, John Jacob *writer, academic administrator*
Canmann, Michael *investment banker*
Canty, Dawn M. *lawyer*
Cappo, Joseph C. *journalist, writer*
Card, Deborah R. *orchestra administrator*
Carey, Charles P. *mercantile exchange executive*
Carlin, Dennis J. *lawyer*
Carlson, LeRoy Theodore, Jr. *telecommunications industry executive*
Carlson, Michael *chef*
Carlson, Walter Carl *lawyer*
Caro, William Allan *physician, educator*
Carpenter, David William *lawyer*
Carr, Jeffrey W. *lawyer, manufacturing executive*
Carr, Walter Stanley *lawyer*
Carren, Jeffrey P. *lawyer*
Carroll, David *writer, illustrator*
Carroll, William Kenneth *lawyer, educator, psychologist, theologian*
Cascino, Anthony Elmo, Jr. *lawyer, insurance company executive*
Case, Donni Marie *investment company executive*
Case, Gregory C. *insurance company executive*
Cassens Weiss, Debra Sue *professional association administrator, publishing executive*
Castillo, Mario Enrique *artist, educator*
Castillo, Ruben *federal judge*
Castorino, Sue *communications executive*
Ceko, Theresa C. *lawyer, educator*
Celesia, Gastone Guglielmo *neurologist*
Cesario, Robert Charles *marketing executive*
Chacko, Samuel *association official*
Chafetz, Barry Richard *lawyer*
Chakrabarty, Ananda Mohan *microbiologist*
Chaleff, Carl Thomas *investment company executive*
Chambers, Donald Arthur *biochemistry and molecular medicine educator*
Chan, Lawrence Siu-Yung *dermatologist, educator*
Chandler, Kent, Jr. *lawyer*
Chang, Peter M.J. *musicologist, educator*
Chanyungco, Delly Yangco *dean*
Chapman, Alger Baldwin *financial services company executive, lawyer*
Chapman, Stephen James *columnist*
Charles, Allan G. *obstetrician, educator*
Charrow, Joel *pediatrician, geneticist, educator, director*
Chatterton, Robert Treat, Jr. *reproductive endocrinology educator*
Cheely, Daniel Joseph *lawyer*
Chemers, Robert Marc *lawyer*
Chen, David *spinal cord injury physician*
Cherdunolo, Steve *professional soccer player*
Cherry, Daniel Ronald *lawyer*
Chiles, Stephen Michael *lawyer*
Chin, Cheng *physicist, educator*
Ching, Brian *professional soccer player*
Chinniah, Nim *academic administrator*
Chizewer, David J. *lawyer*
Chmell, Samuel Jay *orthopedic surgeon*
Choldin, Marianna Tax *librarian, educator*
Chomicz, Thomas E. *lawyer, consultant*
Christianson, Stanley David *finance company executive*
Christoffel, Katherine Kaufer *pediatrician, epidemiologist, educator*
Chromizky, William Rudolph *accountant*
Chung, Paul Myungha *mechanical engineer, educator*
Chunprapaph, Boonmee *physician, educator*
Cicero, Frank, Jr. *lawyer*
Citera, Peter M. *mortgage company executive*
Claeys, Jerome Joseph III *investment company executive*
Clark, Frank M. *utilities executive*
Clark, Gerda Margarete *special education educator*
Clark, James Allen *lawyer, educator*
Clark, James E. *lawyer*
Clark, Michael A. *lawyer*
Clarke, Peter D. *lawyer*
Clemens, Richard Glenn *lawyer*
Clifford, Robert A. *lawyer*
Cline, Philip J. *police superintendent*
Cline, William Chambers *automotive executive*
Clinton, Edward Xavier *lawyer*
Cloonan, James Brian *investment company executive*
Coase, Ronald Harry *economist, educator*
Coe, Fredric L. *internist, educator, researcher*
Coffey, Susanna Jean *artist, educator*
Cohen, Charles Emil *art historian, educator*
Cohen, Frederick H. *lawyer*
Cohen, Melanie Rovner *lawyer*
Cohen, Melvin R. *physician, educator*
Cohen, Ted *philosopher, educator*
Cohler, Bertram Joseph *psychologist, educator*
Cole, Brian Jared *orthopedist*
Cole, Thomas Amor *lawyer*
Collen, John *lawyer, educator*
Colley, Karen J. *medical educator, researcher*
Comiskey, Michael Peter *lawyer*
Congalton, Christopher William *lawyer*
Conklin, Thomas William *lawyer*
Conlon, Suzanne B. *federal judge*
Conlon, William F. *lawyer*
Conrad, Jimmy *professional soccer player*
Convey, Bobby (Robert Francis Convey) *professional soccer player*
Conway, James Joseph *radiologist, educator*
Conway, Michael Maurice *lawyer*
Cook, Bruce Lawrence *editor*
Cooke, Michael *editor-in-chief, publishing executive*
Cooper, Charles Gilbert *cosmetics executive*
Copeland, Edward Jerome *lawyer*
Corboy, Philip Harnett *lawyer*
Cordero, Vincent C. *television network executive*
Cosentino, Barbara *counseling administrator*
Costello, Ellen M. *bank executive*
Costello, John William *lawyer*
Costin, Joseph Laurence, Jr. *information services executive*
Coulson, William Roy *lawyer*
Covalt, Robert Byron *chemicals executive*
Cox, Allan James *management consultant*
Cox, Charles C. *economist*
Coyle, Dorothy *government agency administrator*
Coyne, Jerry Allen *ecologist, educator*
Craig, John Bruce *former ambassador, air transportation executive*
Craine, Thomas Knowlton *not-for-profit developer*
Crane, Barbara Bachmann *photographer, educator*
Crane, Charlotte *law educator*
Crane, Christopher M. *utilities executive*
Crane, Edward M. *lawyer*
Crane, Sir Peter Robert *botanist, geologist, paleontologist, educator*
Craven, George W. *lawyer*
Cressey, Bryan Charles *venture capitalist*
Crisham, Thomas Michael *lawyer*
Crone, Anna Lisa *Russian literature educator*
Cronin, James Watson *physicist, researcher*
Cropsey, Joseph *retired political science professor*
Crosby, John Bartlett *lawyer, health science association administrator*
Cross, Robert Clark *journalist*
Crossan, John Robert *lawyer*
Crow, Steven D. *educational association administrator*
Crown, James Schine *investment company executive*
Crown, Lester *manufacturing executive*
Cruickshank, John Douglas *publishing executive*
Crull, Jan, Jr. *lawyer, investment banker, consultant*
Csar, Michael F. *lawyer*
Cudahy, Richard D. *federal judge*
Cueto, Rochelle E. *elementary school educator*
Cullen, Charles Thomas *historian, librarian*
Culp, Kristine Ann *dean, theology studies educator*
Cummings, Andrea J. *lawyer*
Cunningham, Robert James *lawyer*
Cunningham, Thomas Justin *lawyer*
Cuno, James *museum director*
Currie, David Park *law educator*
Curry, Raymond Howard *physician*
Curwen, Randall William *journalist, editor*
Cusack, John Thomas *lawyer*
Custer, Charles Francis *lawyer*
Czestochowski, Joseph Stephen *administrator, publisher, investor*
Dabrowski, Edward John *television technical director*
Daley, Michael Joseph *lawyer*
Daley, Richard Michael *mayor*
Daley, Susan Jean *lawyer*
Daley, Vincent Raymond, Jr. *real estate company executive, consultant*
Daly, Patrick F. *real estate executive, architect*
Dam, Kenneth W. *law educator, former federal agency administrator*
D'Amato, Anthony *law educator*
Dan, Bernard W. *former commodities exchange executive*
Dancewicz, John Edward *investment banker*
Dandridge, LeNor *paralegal*
Daniel, Elnora D. *academic administrator*
Daniel, T. *mime performer, theater director, choreographer*
Daniels, John Draper *lawyer*
Danzer, Gerald Arlin *history professor*
Darby, Edwin Wheeler *retired columnist*
Darchun, Lino Auksutis *real estate professional*
Dardai, Shahid Moinuddin *computer science educator*
Davidson, Michael H. *cardiologist, researcher*
Davidson, Richard Laurence *geneticist, educator*
Davis, Addie L. *mathematics educator*
Davis, Mary Ellen K. *educational association administrator*
Davis, Michael W. *lawyer*
Davis, Muller *lawyer*
Davis, Scott Jonathan *lawyer*
Davison, Richard *internist, educator*
Dawdy, Shannon Lee *archaeologist, historical anthropologist*
Dawson, Caron *medical and legal consultant*
Dawson, Michael C. *political science professor*
Dayal, Vijay Shanker *physician, educator*
Deamant, Catherine D. *internist*

De Armas, Frederick Alfred *foreign language educator*
Debus, Allen George *historian, educator*
Dechene, James Charles *lawyer*
Dee, Ivan Richard *book publisher*
Dees, Richard Lee *lawyer*
DeHart, Jacob *Internet company executive*
de Hoyos, Debora M. *lawyer*
Deitrick, William Edgar *lawyer*
deKool, L.M. (Theo DeKool) *food products executive*
Deli, Anne Tynion *retail executive*
DeLong, Ray *editor*
Delp, Wilbur Charles, Jr. *lawyer*
Dembowski, Peter Florian *foreign language educator*
D'Emilio, John *humanities educator, writer*
DeMoss, Jon W. *insurance company executive, lawyer*
Dempsey, Clinton (Clint) Drew *professional soccer player*
Dempsey, Mary A. *library commissioner, lawyer*
Dempster, Ryan Scott *professional baseball player*
Deng, Luol *professional basketball player*
Desjardins, Claude *physiologist, dean*
Desmond, Bevin *investment research company executive*
D'Esposito, Julian C., Jr. *lawyer*
Despres, Leon Mathis *lawyer, former city official*
Devine, Richard A. (Dick DeVine) *lawyer*
DeWoskin, Margaret Fogarty *real estate company executive*
DeYoe, David P. *lawyer*
Diamond, Seymour *physician*
Diamond, Shari Seidman *law and psychology professor*
Dickman, Martin J. *federal agency administrator*
Dienst, Daniel W. *metal products executive*
Ditelberg, Joshua L. *lawyer*
Dittmer, Frances R. *curator*
Dix, Rollin C(umming) *mechanical engineering educator, consultant*
Dixon, Stewart Strawn *lawyer, consultant*
Dockterman, Michael *lawyer*
Doetsch, Virginia Lamb *former advertising executive, writer*
Doherty, Brian Gerard *alderman*
Dolan, Thomas Christopher *professional society administrator*
Dold, Robert Bruce *journalist*
Domanskis, Alexander Rimas *lawyer*
Dondanville, Patricia *lawyer*
Donlevy, John Dearden *lawyer*
Donnelley, James Russell *printing company executive*
Donner, Ted A. *lawyer*
Donohue, Craig S. *mercantile exchange executive*
Donovan, Landon *professional soccer player*
Doris, Carole R. *rail transportation executive*
Douglas, Charles W. *lawyer*
Downs, Robert K. *lawyer*
Doyle, John Robert *lawyer*
Draft, Howard Craig *advertising executive*
Dragonette, Rita Hoey *public relations executive*
Drake, Francis LeBaron *law librarian*
Driskell, Claude Evans *college director, educator, dentist*
Drizin, Steven A. *lawyer, educator*
Dube, Monte I. *lawyer*
DuCanto, Joseph Nunzio *lawyer, educator*
Dudley, Rick (Richard C. Dudley) *professional sports team executive*
Duffy, Terrence A. *mercantile exchange executive*
Duhl, Michael Foster *lawyer*
Dunaif, Andrea Elizabeth *endocrinologist*
Duncan, Arne *school system administrator*
Duncan, John Patrick Cavanaugh *lawyer*
Dunea, George *nephrologist, educator*
Dunn, Edwin Rydell *lawyer*
Dunning, Jean *artist*
Dupree, Candice *professional basketball player*
Durburg, Jack E. *real estate company executive*
Durchslag, Stephen P. *lawyer*
Durkin, Kevin P. *lawyer*
Dutta, Mitra *engineer, educator*
Dwivedi, Yogesh *science educator*
Dwyer, Dennis D. *information technology executive*
Dye, Jermaine *professional baseball player*
Dyer, Colin *real estate services executive*
Dykstra, Paul Hopkins *lawyer*
Easterbrook, Frank Hoover *federal judge*
Eastman, Dean Eric *physicist, researcher*
Eaton, Maja Campbell *lawyer*
Ebert, Roger Joseph *film critic*
Edelman, Daniel Joseph *public relations executive*
Edelstein, Teri J. *art educator, director, consultant*
Edlis, Stefan T. *plastics company executive*
Edwards, Charles Lloyd *lawyer*
Edwards, Christine Annette *lawyer*
Egan, Kevin James *lawyer*
Eggert, Russell Raymond *lawyer*
Eimer, Nathan Philip *lawyer*
Eisenberg, Daniel *filmmaker*
Ekdahl, Jon Nels *lawyer*
Elden, Gary Michael *lawyer*
Elias, Sherman *obstetrician, gynecologist, clinical geneticist, educator*
Elshtain, Jean Bethke *social sciences educator*
Elson, Alex *lawyer, educator, arbitrator*
Elson, John S. *law educator*
Emerson, Carter Whitney *lawyer*
Enenbach, Mark Henry *community action agency executive, educator*
English, John Dwight *lawyer*
Epstein, Bennett L. (Buzz Epstein) *lawyer*
Epstein, Lee Joan *political science and law professor*
Epstein, Raymond *engineering and architectural executive*
Epstein, Sidney *architect, civil engineer*
Erber, Thomas *mathematics and physics professor*
Erens, Jay Allan *lawyer*
Erkes, Jason *sports association executive*
Ernest, J. Terry *ocular physiologist, educator*
Esrick, Jerald Paul *lawyer*
Essex, Joseph Michael *visual communication planner*
Etherton, Regina Picone *lawyer*
Eubanks-Pope, Sharon G. *real estate company executive, entrepreneur*
Evanich, Kevin Reese *lawyer*
Evans, Charles L. *bank executive*
Evans, Thelma Jean Mathis *internist*
Even, Francis Alphonse *lawyer*
Eze, Emmanuel Chukwudi *philosophy professor*
Ezgur, Michael H. *real estate company executive*
Fagan, Shawn Francis *investment company executive*
Fahner, Tyrone C. *lawyer, former state attorney general*
Fahnestock, Jean Howe *retired civil engineer*
Falls, Robert Arthur *artistic director*
Fanton, Jonathan Foster *foundation administrator*
Farber, Bernard John *lawyer*
Farhadi, Ashkan *physician, researcher, writer*
Farina, Dennis *actor*
Farman, Gerrie P. *research scientist*
Farrakhan, Louis (Louis Eugene Walcott) *religious organization administrator*
Fawcett, Joy Lynn *retired professional soccer player*
Fazio, Peter Victor, Jr. *lawyer*
Feagley, Michael Rowe *lawyer*
Feder, Robert *columnist*
Feingold, Daniel Leon *anesthesiologist, consultant*
Feinstein, Fred Ira *lawyer*
Feldman, Mark I. *lawyer*
Feldman, Ted *cardiologist*
Fellows, Jerry Kenneth *lawyer*
Felsenthal, Steven Altus *lawyer*
Fenton, Clifton Lucien *investment banker*
Ferber, Leonard *lawyer*
Ferguson, Diana S. *food products executive*
Ferguson, Mark Kendric *surgeon, educator*
Ferguson, Stanley Lewis *lawyer*
Fernandez, Geno *insurance company executive*
Fernandez, James *anthropology educator*
Ferrara, Annette *editor, educator*
Ferrini, James Thomas *lawyer*
Fetridge, Clark Worthington *publishing executive*
Field, Karen Ann (Karen Ann Schaffner) *real estate broker*
Field, Marshall *retail executive*
Field, Robert Edward *lawyer*
Fiels, Keith Michael *executive director American Library Association*
Filpi, Robert Alan *lawyer*
Findlay, Donald Cameron *lawyer, former federal agency administrator, insurance company executive*
Finke, Robert Forge *lawyer*
Finnegan, Sheila *lawyer*
Fischbach, Charles Peter *rail transportation executive, consultant, lawyer, arbitrator, mediator*
Fisher, Eugene *marketing professional, community leader*
Fitzgerald, Patrick J., Jr. *prosecutor*
Fitzgerald, Robert Maurice *financial and retired bank executive*
Fitzgerald, Thomas Robert *state supreme court justice*
Fitzpatrick, Robert John *museum director*
FitzSimons, Dennis Joseph *broadcast and publishing executive*
Flaherty, Timothy Thomas *radiologist*
Flaum, Joel Martin *federal judge*
Fleming, Richard H. *finance executive*
Florine, Jane L. *musicology educator*
Fogel, Robert William *economist, educator, historian*
Foland, Jeffrey T. *air transportation sales executive*
Foley, Father John P. *school system administrator, reverend*
Fontanarosa, Phil Bernard *medical journal executive editor, emergency physician, educator*
Forbes, Dorsey Connors *commentator, journalist*
Forbes, John Edward *retired financial consultant*
Fort, Jeffrey C. *lawyer*
Fossett, Steven (J. Steven Fossett) *retired investor, adventurer*
Foster, Ian Tremere *computer scientist*
Foster, James Reuben *travel company executive*
Fotopoulos, James *artist*
Foudree, Bruce William *lawyer*
Foudy, Julie Maurine *retired professional soccer player, Olympic athlete*
Fowler, Don Wall *lawyer*
Fowler, Martin *software engineer, consultant*
Fox, Paul T. *lawyer*
Fraley, Andrea Lyn *physiatrist*
Franch, Richard Thomas *lawyer*
Franco, Carlo Diaz *surgeon, anatomist, anesthesiologist*
Francuch, Paul Charles *broadcast journalist*
Franklin, Richard Mark *lawyer*
Frano, Andrew Joseph *lawyer, civil engineer*
Frantzen, Allen John *English language educator*
Fraumann, Willard George *lawyer*
Frazen, Mitchell Hale *lawyer*
Frederick, John Eugene *science educator*
Frederick, Thomas James *lawyer*
Freeborn, Michael D. *lawyer*
Freed, Karl Frederick *chemistry professor*
Freehling, Daniel Joseph *lawyer, consultant*
Freeman, Lee Allen, Jr. *lawyer*
Freeman, Leslie Gordon *anthropologist, educator*
Freeman, Louis S. *lawyer*
Freeman, Susan Tax *anthropologist, educator, culinary historian*
Freidheim, Cyrus F., Jr. *publishing and former food products executive*
Freitag, Frederick Gerald *osteopathic physician*
Freund, Kristen P. *bank executive*
Frey, James Harrison *fundraising professional*
Fried, Jason *software development company executive*
Friedman, Lawrence Milton *lawyer, finance company executive*
Friedman, Marla Lee *human resources specialist, marketing professional*
Friedman, Michael *surgeon*
Friedman, Roselyn L. *lawyer, mediator*
Fukui, Yoshio *biology professor*
Funderburk, Raymond *judge*
Funk, Carla Jean *library association director*
Furcon, John Edward *management and organizational consultant*
Furlane, Mark Elliott *lawyer*
Furth, Yvonne *advertising executive*
Futterman, Ronald L. *lawyer*
Gabarra, Carin Leslie *professional soccer player, professional soccer coach*
Gadus, Peg *pastoral associate*
Gaggini, John Edmund *lawyer*
Gal, Susan *anthropologist, educator*
Galainena, M. David *lawyer*
Galante, Jorge Osvaldo *orthopedic surgeon, educator*
Galatzer-Levy, Robert Milton *psychiatrist*
Gallopoulos, Gregory Stratis *lawyer*
Galowich, Ronald Howard *real estate company executive, venture capitalist, pilot*
Gamba, Sandro *chef*
Gand, Gale *chef, restaurateur*
Gang, Jeanne *architect*
Gangemi, Columbus Rudolph, Jr. *lawyer, educator*
Gannon, Sister Ann Ida *retired philosophy educator*
Garanzini, Michael J. *academic administrator, priest*
Garber, Philip Robert *academic administrator, researcher*
Garber, Samuel B. *lawyer, retail executive*
Garcia, Paul R. *lawyer*
Gardner, Chris(topher) *securities trader, entrepreneur*
Gardner, Howard Alan *travel company executive, writer, editor*
Garg, Vijay Kumar *telecommunications engineer*
Garman, Rita B. *state supreme court justice*
Garner, Margaret *construction executive*
Garofalo, Douglas *architectural firm executive, educator*
Gary, Warlene D. *educational association administrator*
Garzolini, Judith A. *information technology manager*
Gavin, John Neal *lawyer*
Gearen, John Joseph *lawyer*
Gecker, James M. *lawyer*
Geiman, J. Robert *lawyer*
Geleerd, James D. (Jake Geleerd) *property manager*
Geller, Laurence S. *hotel executive*
Gelman, Andrew Richard *lawyer*
Genson, Edward Marvin *lawyer*
Geoga, Douglas Gerard *real estate developer, lawyer*
George, Francis Eugene Cardinal *cardinal*
George, John Martin, Jr. *lawyer*
Georges, Mara Stacy *lawyer*
Geraghty, Diane C. *law educator*
Geraldson, Raymond I., Jr. *lawyer*
Gerber, Dean N. *lawyer*
Gerbie, Albert Bernard *obstetrician, gynecologist, educator*
Gerdes, Neil Wayne *library director, educator*
Geren, Gerald S. *lawyer*
Gern, Ronald L. *lawyer, real estate company executive*
Gerstner, Robert William *structural engineering educator, consultant*
Gertz, Theodore Gerson *lawyer*
Gervais, Mark G. *physical education educator*
Gewurz, Anita Tartell *physician, medical educator*
Geyer, Michael *history professor*
Gianos, Diane E. *lawyer*
Gibbons, William John *lawyer*
Giblin, Nan J. *psychologist, educator*
Gibson, McGuire *archaeologist, educator*
Giesen, Richard Allyn *manufacturing executive*
Giger, Maryellen Lissak *medical physicist, educator*
Gilbert, Howard N(orman) *lawyer, director*
Gilford, Steven Ross *lawyer*
Gill, Phupinder *mercantile exchange executive*
Gillis, Ruth Ann M. *utilities executive*
Gilson, Jerome *lawyer, writer*
Ginsburg, Allen J. *lawyer*
Gittler, Michelle S. *physiatrist*
Givone, Donna Marie *pharmacologist*
Gladden, James Walter, Jr. *lawyer*
Glass, Ronald Bernhard Jacob *radiologist*
Glenner, Richard Allen *dentist, dental historian*
Glickman, Robert Jeffrey *bank executive*
Glieberman, Herbert Allen *lawyer*
Godfrey, Richard Cartier *lawyer*
Golan, Stephen Leonard *lawyer*
Gold, Allan Harold *architect, structural engineer, educator*
Goldberg, Arnold Irving *psychoanalyst, educator*
Goldblatt, Stanford Jay *lawyer*
Goldring, Norman Max *marketing professional*
Goldsmith, John Anton *linguist, educator*
Goldstein, William A. *investment counsel*
Golomb, Harvey Morris *hematologist, oncologist, educator*
Goltz, Jay *small business owner*
Gomer, Robert *chemistry professor*
Gómez, Martín *library association executive*
Good, Steven Loren *real estate consultant*
Goodman, Larry J. *health facility administrator*
Goodman, Steven Michael *conservation biologist*
Gorbien, Martin John *medical educator, geriatrician*
Gorchow, Bruce D. *investment company executive*
Gordon, Ben *professional basketball player*
Gordon, Ellen Rubin *candy company executive*
Gordon, Howard Lyon *advertising and marketing executive*
Gordon, James A. *investment company executive*
Gordon, James S. *lawyer, director*
Gordon, Leo I. *hematologist, oncologist, educator*
Gordon, Melvin Jay *food products executive*
Gordon, Phillip *lawyer*
Goroff, David B. *lawyer*
Goss, Howard S(imon) *financial executive*
Gossett, Philip *musicologist*
Gottschall, Joan B. *judge*
Gould, John Philip *economist, educator*
Graber, Doris Appel *political scientist, writer, editor*
Graber, Thomas M. *orthodontist, researcher*
Graham, Bruce S. *dean, educator*
Grant, Burton Fred *lawyer*
Grant, Robert McQueen *humanities educator*
Grant, Robert Nathan *lawyer*
Gratz, Jay M.
Gray, Hanna Holborn *historian, educator*
Greaves, William Webster *chemist*
Green, Judson C. *marketing agency executive*
Green, RuthAnn *marketing and management consultant*
Greenbaum, Lewis *lawyer*
Greenberg, Bernard *retired entomologist*
Greenberg, Richard T. *lawyer*
Greenberger, Paul Allen *allergist, immunologist, educator, medical researcher*
Greenspan, Jeffrey Dov *lawyer*
Gregory, Stephanie Ann *hematologist, educator*
Grevious, Mark Allen *plastic surgeon*
Griem, Katherine Leslie *radiation oncologist*
Griffin, Kenneth C. *investment company executive*
Grimm, Terry M. *lawyer*
Gross, Theodore Lawrence *university administrator, author*
Grossman, Kate Nadia *journalist*
Grossman, Robert Mayer *lawyer*
Grubbe, Frederick H. *real estate appraisal executive*
Guillen, Ozzie (Oswaldo Jose Barrios Guillen) *professionall baseball manager*
Gulati, Martha *health facility administrator, cardiologist*
Gunning, Tom *art educator*
Gupta, Krishna Chandra *mechanical engineering educator*
Guralnick, Sidney Aaron *engineering educator*
Guthman, Jack *lawyer*
Gutstein, Solomon *lawyer*
Haben, Mary Kay *candy company executive*
Hacker, Eileen Danaher *nursing educator, researcher*
Hackl, Donald John *architect*
Haffner, Charles Christian III *retired printing company executive*
Hagan, Kate (Kathryn T. Hagan) *library director, editor*
Hahn, Arthur W. *lawyer*
Hahn, Frederic Louis *lawyer*
Hahnemann, Marcus *professional soccer player*
Haley, George *Romance languages educator*
Hallinan, Joseph Thomas *journalist*
Halperin, Errol R. *lawyer*
Halpern, Jack *chemist, educator*
Halprin, Rick (Richard Allan Halprin) *lawyer*
Hamada, Robert S(eiji) *dean, educator, economist, entrepreneur*
Hambrick, Ernestine *retired colon and rectal surgeon*
Hamburger, Philip Andrew *law educator*
Hamm, Mia (Mariel Margaret Hamm) *retired professional soccer player*
Hammond, Celeste M. *law educator*
Hannah, Wayne Robertson, Jr. *lawyer*
Hannay, William Mouat III *lawyer*
Hanrath, Linda Carol *librarian, archivist*
Hansen, Carl R. *management consultant*
Hanson, Floyd Bliss *mathematician*
Hanson, Mark S. *bishop*
Hanson, Ronald William *lawyer*
Hansson, David Heinemeier *application developer*
Hardaway, Ernest, II, *oral and maxillofacial surgeon, public health service officer*
Hardgrove, James Alan *lawyer*
Hardin, Terrence Armstrong *former radio broadcasting manager*
Harmon, Teresa Wilton *lawyer*
Harrelson, Ken *sports broadcaster*
Harrington, Carol A. *lawyer*
Harrington, James Timothy *lawyer*
Harris, Daniel Mark *lawyer*
Harris, Gerald David *surgeon*
Harris, Gregory Scott *state representative*
Harris, Neil *historian, educator*
Harris, Phillip H. *lawyer*
Harris, Shirley *elementary and secondary and adult education school educator*
Harrison, Holly A. *lawyer*
Harrison, Louis S. *lawyer*
Harrold, Bernard *lawyer*
Harrow, Martin *psychologist, educator*
Hart, William Thomas *federal judge*
Hartnett, James Patrick *engineering educator*
Hartz, Michael O. *lawyer*
Harvey, Allison Charmaine *chemist*
Harvey, Paul *commentator, writer, columnist*
Harvey, Ronald Gilbert *research chemist*
Hast, Adele *historian, editor, writer*
Hast, Malcolm Howard *biomedical scientist, educator*
Hasten, Joseph Erwin *bank executive*
Hastie, Reid *psychology professor*
Hatziavramidis, Katie *lawyer*
Hawkins, Loretta Ann *retired secondary school educator, playwright*
Hayden, Harrold Harrison *communications executive*
Hayes, Alice Bourke *academic administrator, biologist, researcher*

Hayes, David John Arthur, Jr. *legal association executive*
Hayley, Kathryn *consulting company executive*
Hayward, Robert M. *lawyer*
Hayward, Thomas Zander, Jr. *lawyer*
Healy, Sondra Anita *consumer products company executive*
Heatwole, Mark M. *lawyer, director*
Heckman, James Joseph *economist, educator*
Hefner, Christie Ann *publishing executive*
Heidemann, Lyle G. *retail executive*
Heider, Anne Harrington *music educator*
Heineman, Ben Walter *corporation executive*
Heineman, Natalie (Mrs. Ben W. Heineman) *civic worker*
Heinemann, Allen W. *rehabilitation psychologist*
Heinrichs, April *soccer coach*
Heinz, John Peter *lawyer, educator*
Heinz, William Denby *lawyer*
Heisler, Quentin George, Jr. *lawyer*
Heisley, Michael E., Sr. *manufacturing executive, professional sports team owner*
Hellie, Richard *historian, educator*
Hellman, Samuel *radiologist, educator*
Helman, Robert Alan *lawyer*
Helmholz, R(ichard) H(enry) *law educator*
Heltne, Paul Gregory *researcher, museum director*
Henderson, Janet E. E. *lawyer*
Henning, Joel Frank *lawyer, writer*
Henry, Brian Thomas *lawyer*
Herald, J. Patrick *lawyer*
Herbert, William Carlisle *lawyer*
Herbst, Arthur Lee *obstetrician, gynecologist*
Herman, Sidney N. *lawyer*
Herron, David A. *stock exchange executive*
Herzenberg, Caroline Stuart Littlejohn *physicist*
Hess, Sidney J., Jr. *lawyer*
Hibbard, Judith Usher *obstetrician*
Hickey, Jerome Edward *investment company executive*
Hickey, John Thomas, Jr. *lawyer*
Hilbert, David R. *philosopher, educator*
Hildebrand, Roger Henry *astrophysicist, physicist*
Hill, Barbara Benton *healthcare executive*
Hill, Shepard W. *air transportation executive*
Hilliard, David Craig *lawyer, educator*
Hilliker, Donald Beckstett *lawyer*
Hillocks, George, Jr. *language educator, researcher*
Hill Rotman, Carlotta H. *physician*
Himmelfarb, John David *artist*
Hinkelman, Ruth Amidon *insurance company executive*
Hinrichs, Charles A. *paper company executive*
Hirsch, Martin *dentist*
Hirt, Jane *editor*
Hlavacek, Roy George *publishing executive*
Hobson, Mellody *investment company executive*
Hodes, Scott *lawyer*
Hodge, Linda M. *former educational association administrator*
Hodgman, David Renwick *lawyer*
Hofer, Roy Ellis *lawyer*
Hoff, John Scott *lawyer*
Hoffman, David H. *city manager*
Hoffman, Richard Bruce *lawyer*
Hofrichter, David Alan *management consultant*
Holabird, John Augur, Jr. *retired architect*
Holleb, Marshall Maynard *lawyer*
Hollis, Donald Roger *management consultant*
Hollis-Sawyer, Lisa Ann *psychologist, gerontologist, researcher*
Holtschneider, Dennis H. *academic administrator, priest*
Homburger, Thomas Charles *lawyer*
Honig, George Raymond *pediatrician*
Hoogenboom, Carol Annette *clinical neuropsychologist*
Hoplamazian, Mark Samuel *hotel executive*
Horwich, Allan *lawyer*
Horwood, Richard M. *lawyer*
Hoskins, Richard Jerold *lawyer*
Howard, Tim *professional soccer player*
Howe, Henry Franklin *ecology educator*
Howe, Jonathan Thomas *lawyer*
Howell, R(obert) Thomas, Jr. *lawyer, former food company executive*
Hsieh, Patrick C. *neurosurgeon*
Hsueh, Wei *pathologist, educator*
Hubberman, Ron *state official*
Huckman, Michael Saul *neuroradiologist, educator*
Hucles, Angela Khalia *professional soccer player*
Huebner, Jeff *art journalist, freelance writer*
Huggins, Lois M. *human resources specialist, consumer products company executive*
Hughes, John Russell *neurologist, educator*
Hummel, Gregory William *lawyer*
Hung, Wu *art historian, educator*
Hunt, Craig A. *lawyer, paper company executive*
Hunt, Lawrence Halley, Jr. *lawyer*
Hunt, Richard *sculptor*
Hunter, James Galbraith, Jr. *lawyer*
Huntley, Robert Stephen *newspaper editor*
Husting, Peter Marden *advertising consultant*
Huttenlocher, Janellen *psychology educator, psychologist*
Hwang, Yujong *information scientist, educator*
Hynes, Brian *lawyer, lobbyist*
Idol, Anna Catherine *magazine editor*
Inan, Zabrin *psychiatrist*
Inwang, Rosie L. *education educator*
Iqbal, Zafar Mohd *biochemist, molecular biologist, pharmacologist, cancer researcher, toxicologist, consultant*
Isaacson, Samuel B. *lawyer*
Ismail, Tarek *lawyer*
Ivankovich, Anthony D. *anesthesiologist, educator*
Ivanov, Kamen Petkov *engineering educator*
Iyer, Kishore *transplant surgeon*
Jachino, Daneen L. *legal administrator*
Jackson, Jesse Louis *political organization worker, clergyman*
Jacobs, Caryn Leslie *lawyer, former prosecutor*
Jacobson, Marian Slutz *lawyer*
Jacobson, Michael Harold *principal*
Jacobson, Richard Joseph *lawyer*
Jacoby, John Patrick *lawyer*
Jacoby Hurd, Jennifer *foundation administrator*
Jacoby Hurd, Jennifer Beth *not-for-profit executive*
Jaconetty, Thomas Anthony *lawyer*
Jacover, Jerold Alan *lawyer*
Jager, Melvin Francis *lawyer*
Jahns, Jeffrey *lawyer*
Jameson, James Larry *medical educator, endocrinologist, internist*
Jampol, Lee Merrill *ophthalmologist, educator*
Janners, Erik Nikolas *music educator, conductor*
Jao, Chiang *information technology educator*
Jarrett, Valerie Bowman *real estate company executive, former stock exchange executive*
Jeff, Kevin Iega *choreographer, performing company executive*
Jegen, Sister Carol Frances *religious studies educator*
Jelsema, Jerry Richard *music director*
Jenkins, John Balester *academic administrator*
Jenks, Bobby (Robert Scott Jenks) *professional baseball player*
Jensen, Harold Leroy *medical liability insurance administrator, physician*
Jerome, Jerrold V. *retired insurance company executive*
Jezuit, Leslie James *manufacturing executive*
Jilhewar, Ashok *gastroenterologist*
Joern, Charles Edward, Jr. *lawyer*
Johanson, Gregory John *psychotherapist, minister*
John, Peter C. *lawyer*
Johnson, Eddie *professional soccer player*
Johnson, Elmer William *lawyer*
Johnson, Garrett Bruce *lawyer*
Johnson, Gary Thomas *cultural organization administrator*
Johnson, Glenn Thompson *retired judge*
Johnson, Janet Helen *literature educator*
Johnson, Richard Fred *lawyer*
Johnson, Timothy Patrick *health and social researcher*
Jones, Cobi *professional soccer player*
Jones, Emil, Jr. *state legislator*
Jones, Linda *communications educator*
Jones, Mary Laura *not-for-profit developer*
Jones, Sandra Yvonne *lawyer*
Jones, Sharon Elaine *lawyer*
Jones, Tony *academic administrator*
Joseph, Robert Thomas *lawyer*
Joslin, Rodney Dean *lawyer*
Judge, Bernard Martin *editor, publishing executive*
Junewicz, James J. *lawyer*
Kadanoff, Leo Philip *physicist, educator*
Kaegi, Walter Emil *history professor*
Kahnweiler, David R. *real estate company executive*
Kahrilas, Peter James *medical educator, researcher*
Kallick, David A. *lawyer*
Kalt, David *diversified financial services company executive*
Kamerick, Eileen Ann *corporate financial executive, lawyer*
Kaminsky, Richard Alan *lawyer*
Kamyszew, Christopher D. *film executive, educator, curator*
Kapala, Frederick J. *federal judge*
Kaplan, Howard Gordon *lawyer*
Kaplan, Jared *lawyer*
Kaplan, Joel H. *lawyer*
Kaplan, Morton A. *political science professor*
Kaplan, Wayne S. *lawyer*
Karanikas, Alexander *language educator*
Karlin, Edward J. *lawyer*
Katz, Adrian Izhack *medical educator*
Katz, Avrum Sidney *lawyer*
Katz, Friedrich *history educator*
Katz, Stuart Charles *lawyer, musician*
Kaufman, Andrew Michael *lawyer*
Kawitt, Alan *lawyer, arbitrator*
Kearney, John Walter *sculptor, painter*
Keenan, Barbara Byrd *professional society administrator*
Keenan, James George *classics educator*
Keiderling, Timothy Allen *chemistry educator, researcher*
Keller, Kasey *professional soccer player*
Kellman, Sandra Y. *lawyer*
Kelly, Arthur Lloyd *investment company executive*
Kelly, Charles Arthur *lawyer*
Kelly, Curtis Hartt *retired publishing executive*
Kelly, Jerry Bob *social services administrator*
Kelly, Peter McClorey, II, *lawyer*
Kenney, Crane H. *lawyer*
Kenney, Frank Deming *lawyer*
Kerbis, Gertrude Lempp *architect*
Kerr, Michael H. *stock exchange executive, lawyer*
Kerwin, Thomas P. *architect*
Khabibulin, Nikolai *professional hockey player*
Khan, M. Wasiullah *academic administrator*
Khodarev, Nikolai Nikolaevich *biologist, researcher*
Kiani, Reza *endocrinology and internal medicine educator*
Kikoler, Stephen Philip *lawyer*
Kilbride, Thomas L. *state supreme court justice*
Kim, Mi Ja *dean, academic administrator*
Kim, Michael Charles *lawyer*
Kimbarovsky, Ross Edward *lawyer*
Kincaid, Richard D. *real estate company executive*
King, Andre Richardson *architectural graphic designer*
King, Sharon Louise *lawyer*
King, Tim *charter school administrator*
Kirkpatrick, Anne Saunders *systems analyst*
Kirsch, Lloyd *academic administrator*
Kirschner, Barbara Starrels *gastroenterologist*
Kirsner, Joseph Barnett *physician, educator*
Kissel, Richard John *lawyer*
Kistenbroker, David H. *lawyer*
Kitch, Paul R. *lawyer*
Kite, Steven B. *lawyer*
Kittle, Charles Frederick *surgeon*
Klapthor, James *broadcast executive*
Klatt, Wayne Roy *editor, writer*
Klaviter, Helen Lothrop *magazine editor*
Klebba, Raymond Allen *property manager*
Klemens, Thomas Lloyd *editor*
Klenk, James Andrew *lawyer*
Klenk, Timothy Carver *lawyer*
Klinger, Steven J. *paper company executive*
Kloss, Linda L. *medical association administrator*
Knapp, Paul Raymond *think-tank executive*
Knappenberger, Paul Henry, Jr. *science museum director*
Kniffel, Leonard John *editor, librarian*
Knight, Christopher Nichols *lawyer*
Knight, Cranston S. *history professor*
Knox, James Marshall *lawyer*
Knuepfer, Robert Claude, Jr. *lawyer*
Kobs, James Fred *direct marketing consultant*
Koch, Steven *lawyer, investment banker, finance company executive*
Koellner, Laurette *aerospace transportation executive*
Koernig, Stephen K. *marketing professional, educator*
Kohn, Shalom L. *lawyer*
Kojaian, C. Michael *real estate company executive*
Kokonas, Nick J. *restaurant owner*
Kolata, David *advocate*
Kolek, Robert Edward *lawyer*
Kolmin, Kenneth Guy *lawyer*
Komiske, Bruce King *hospital administrator*
Konerko, Paul *professional baseball player*
Kopelman, Ian Stuart *lawyer*
Koppelman, Andrew Martin Mayer *law educator*
Kouvel, James Spyros *physicist, educator*
Kozak, John W. *lawyer*
Krakowski, Richard John *lawyer, public relations executive*
Kramer, Andrea S. *lawyer*
Krashesky, Alan *newscaster*
Kraus, Herbert Myron *public relations executive*
Krause, James R. *mercantile exchange executive*
Kravitt, Jason Harris Paperno *lawyer*
Krawetz, Arthur Altshuler *chemist, science administrator*
Kreis, Jason *professional soccer coach, retired professional soccer player*
Krent, Harold J. *dean, law educator*
Kriss, Robert J. *lawyer*
Krivkovich, Peter George *advertising executive*
Kroll, Barry Lewis *retired lawyer*
Krueger, Bonnie Lee *editor, writer*
Krupnick, Elizabeth Rachel *human resources consulting firm and former insurance company executive*
Kubistal, Patricia Bernice *educational consultant*
Kuczwara, Thomas Paul *federal agency administrator, lawyer*
Kudish, David J. *financial executive*
Kuiken, Todd Alan *medical researcher, rehabilitation services professional, educator*
Kullberg, Duane Reuben *accounting firm executive*
Kunda, Dolores *marketing executive*
Kuner, Charles *retired secondary school educator*
Kurtz, David S. *lawyer*
Lach, Alma Elizabeth *food and cooking writer, consultant*
Ladd, Jeffrey Raymond *lawyer*
Laidlaw, Andrew R. *lawyer*
Lal, Anil *health facility administrator*
Landerholm, Elizabeth Jane *early childhood education educator*
Landes, William M. *law educator*
Landow-Esser, Janine Marise *lawyer*
Landsberg, Lewis *dean, endocrinologist, medical researcher*
Laner, Richard Warren *lawyer*
Lang, Gordon, Jr. *retired lawyer*
Langman, Lauren *sociology educator*
Lanznar, Howard S. *lawyer*
Larson, Allan Louis *political scientist, educator, lay worker*
Larson, Nancy Celeste *information technology manager*
Larson, Roy *journalist, publishing executive*
Latimer, Kenneth Alan *lawyer*
Laumann, Edward Otto *sociology educator*
Lavani, Romeen M. *physician*
Lawler, Gregory Francis *mathematics professor*
Lawler, James Ronald *French language educator*
Lazar, Ludmila *concert pianist, music educator*
Lazarus, Steven *technology company exective*
Leadbetter, Tiffany *hotel executive*
Learner, Howard Alan *lawyer*
Lease, John G. *plastic surgeon*
LeDuc, John Andre *lawyer*
Lee, Bao-Shiang Bob *biochemist, researcher*
Lee, Derrek Leon *professional baseball player*
Lee, Gyungho *engineering educator*
Lee, Raphael Carl *plastic surgeon, biomedical engineer*
Lee, Yoon Mo *state official*
Lefco, Kathy Nan *law librarian*
Leff, Alan Richard *medical educator, researcher*
Lefkow, Joan Humphrey *federal judge*
Legge Kemp, Diane *architect, landscape consultant*
Lehman, Dennis Dale *chemistry professor, department chairman*
Leighton, George Neves *retired judge*
Leinenweber, Harry D. *federal judge*
Leonard, Laura L. *lawyer*
Lerman, Zafra Margolin *science educator, public policy professor*
Lerner, Alexander Robert *insurance company executive*
Lerner, Barbara *writer, researcher*
Lerner, Wayne M. *healthcare executive*
LeRoy, Spencer III *lawyer*
Leszinske, William O. *investment company executive*
Levandowski, Barbara Sue *education educator*
Leventhal, Bennett Lee *psychiatry and pediatrics educator, academic administrator*
Levi, John G. *lawyer*
Levin, Charles Edward *lawyer*
Levin, Jack S. *lawyer*
Levin, Lawrence Daniel *lawyer*
Levine, Jenny *library and information scientist, writer*
Levine, Laurence Harvey *lawyer*
Levinson, Michael R. *lawyer*
Levitt, Steven D. *economics professor*
Levmore, Saul *dean, law educator*
Levy, Deborah *security company executive*
Levy, Donald Harris *chemistry professor*
Levy, Peter A. *lawyer*
Lewis, Eddie *professional soccer player*
Leyhane, Francis John III *lawyer*
Liao, Shutsung *biochemist, molecular oncologist*
Libowsky, Stephen David *lawyer*
Lien, John Donovan *lawyer*
Lies, Valerie Sharp *foundation administrator*
Liggio, Carl Donald *lawyer*
Lin, James Chih-I *biomedical and electrical engineer, educator*
Linden, Henry Robert *chemical engineer, researcher*
Lindquist, Lee A. *geriatrician, educator*
Linklater, William J. *lawyer*
Lipinski, Ann Marie *publishing executive*
Lipton, Lois Jean *lawyer*
Listrom, Linda L. *lawyer*
Litwin, Burton Howard *lawyer*
Liu, Ben-chieh *economist*
Liu, Derong *electrical and computer engineer, educator*
Livingston, Bradford Lee *lawyer*
Lochbihler, Frederick Vincent *lawyer*
Lockwood, Gary Lee *lawyer*
Loesch, Katharine Taylor *communications educator, theater educator*
Logemann, Jerilyn Ann *speech pathologist, educator*
Lombardo, Robert *composer, educator*
Lona, Marie A. *lawyer*
Longworth, Richard Cole *journalist*
Looman, James R. *lawyer*
Lopez, Carolyn Catherine *physician*
Lorch, Kenneth F. *lawyer*
Lorch, Robert K. *corporate financial executive*
Lorenz, Hugo Albert *retired insurance executive, consultant*
Lorenz, Katherine Mary *bank executive*
Lotti, Michael *marketing professional*
Lovejoy, Paul Robert *lawyer, air transportation executive*
Lowe, Sandra Elveta *psychologist*
Lower, Joseph *air transportation executive*
Lowinger, Frederick Charles *lawyer*
Lowry, James Hamilton *management consultant*
Lubin, Donald G. *lawyer*
Lucas, Robert Emerson, Jr. *economist, educator*
Luchins, Daniel Jonathan *psychiatrist*
Lufrano, Michael Richard *lawyer*
Lundquist, Dana Richard *health facility administrator*
Luning, Thomas P. *lawyer*
Lurain, John Robert III *gynecologist*
Lurie, Ann LaSalle *foundation administrator*
Luscombe, George A., II, *lawyer*
Lusk, Peggy June *retired counseling administrator*
Lutter, Paul Allen *lawyer*
Luttig, J(ohn) Michael (John Michael Luttig) *aerospace transportation executive, former federal judge*
Lyerla, Bradford Peter *lawyer*
Lynch, John James *lawyer*
Lynch, John Peter *lawyer*
Lyon, Charles Herbert Randolph *investment banker*
Lythcott, Marcia A. *newspaper editor*
Macaulay, Susan Jane *lawyer, educator*
MacCarthy, Terence Francis *lawyer*
MacDougal, Gary Edward *corporate board member, foundation trustee*
Mack, Alan Wayne *interior designer*
Madara, James Lee *dean, pathologist, educator, epitheliologist*
Madigan, John William *publishing executive*
Madigan, Lisa *state attorney general*
Madsen, Dorothy Louise (Meg) *writer*
Maehr, Kate *social services organization executive*
Mahaffey, John Christopher *medical association executive*
Mahaley-Johnson, Hosanna *school system administrator*
Mahani, Mohammad Shadbakht *engineering educator*
Majer, John M. *psychologist, educator*
Makinen, Marvin William *biophysicist, educator*
Malinowski, Arthur Anthony *lawyer, arbitrator*
Malkin, Cary Jay *lawyer*
Malkinson, Frederick David *dermatologist, educator*
Mallory, Robert Mark *controller, finance company executive*
Malovany, Howard *lawyer*
Mancoff, Neal Alan *lawyer*
Mandell, Floyd A. *lawyer*
Manelli, Donald Dean *scriptwriter, film and television producer*
Manning, Frederick James *insurance company executive*
Manning, Sylvia *language educator*
Mansfield, Karen Lee *lawyer*
Manske, Susan E. *investment advisor*
Mansueto, Joseph Daniel *publisher*
Mantuano, Tony *chef*
Manzo, Edward David *lawyer*
Marcovici, Michael *investment company executive*

Marick, Michael Miron *lawyer*
Mariotti, Jay Anthony *journalist*
Marshall, Cody *bishop*
Marshall, Kerry James *artist*
Martin, Arthur Mead *lawyer*
Martin, Gary Joseph *medical educator*
Martin, Ionis Bracy *artist, educator*
Martin, Laura Keidan *lawyer*
Martin, Lauralee *real estate company executive*
Martinez, Natalie *newscaster*
Marwedel, Warren John *lawyer*
Mascherin, Terri Lynn *lawyer*
Mason, Richard J. *lawyer*
Mason, Terry *city health department administrator, urologist*
Mason, William *opera company director*
Mastroeni, Pablo *professional soccer player*
Matanky, James E. *real estate developer*
Mateles, Richard Isaac *biotechnologist*
Matis, Nina B. *lawyer*
Matsakis, Elias N. *lawyer*
Matthei, Edward Hodge *architect*
Matuano, Tony *chef*
May, Aviva Rabinowitz *music educator, musician, linguist*
Mayer, Raymond Richard *business administration educator*
Mayo, Cora Louise *educator*
McCaleb, Malcolm, Jr. *lawyer*
McCallister, Richard Anthony *business consulting company executive*
McCann, Renetta *advertising executive*
Mc Carter, John Wilbur, Jr. *museum executive*
McCarthy, Patrick M. *surgeon*
McCaskey, Raymond F. *insurance company executive*
McCaul, Joseph Patrick *chemical engineer*
McChesney, Fred S. *law educator*
McClain, Shawn *chef*
McCloskey, Deirdre Nansen *economics and history educator*
McCloskey, Michael *social sciences, psychology, and sociology educator*
McClure, James Julius, Jr. *lawyer, former city official*
McConnell, E. Hoy, II, *advertising and public policy executive*
McCormick, Steven D. *lawyer*
McCracken, Thomas James, Jr. *lawyer*
McCrank, Lawrence J. *dean, school librarian*
McCrohon, Craig *lawyer*
McCue, Judith W. *lawyer*
McCullagh, Grant Gibson *retired architect*
McCullagh, Suzanne *curator*
McCullough, Richard Lawrence *advertising executive*
McCurry, Margaret Irene *architect, furniture, interior designer, educator*
McCutcheon, Jennifer Lynne *horse breeder, lawyer*
McDermott, John H. *lawyer*
McDonagh, Steve *chef*
McDonald, Sally J. *lawyer*
McDonald, Theresa Beatrice Pierce (Mrs. Ollie McDonald) *church official, minister*
McDonald, Thomas Alexander *lawyer*
McDonnell, David Croft *diversified financial services company executive*
McDonough, John Michael *lawyer*
McElheny, Josiah G. *sculptor*
McGaan, Andrew Raymond *lawyer*
McGee, Edwin C., Jr. *surgeon*
McGowan, Michael Jeremy *lawyer*
McGrail, Jeane Kathryn *artist*
McGrath, William Joseph *lawyer*
McIntyre, Sarah Elizabeth *soprano*
McKee, Keith Earl *manufacturing technology executive*
McKenzie, Robert Ernest *lawyer*
McKinley, Anne C. *lawyer*
McKinney, Megan *writer*
McLaren, Richard Wellington, Jr. *lawyer*
McLaughlin, T. Mark *lawyer*
McLean, Ian P. *utilities executive*
McMasters, James *law librarian, educator*
McMath, Lula Wray *retired elementary school educator, realtor*
McMenamin, John Robert *lawyer*
McNally, Andrew, IV, *publishing executive, director*
McNeill, G. David *psychologist, educator*
McNerney, James, Jr., (W. James McNerney) *aerospace transportation executive, former manufacturing executive*
McNulty, Timothy J. *editor*
McPherson, Michael Steven *academic administrator, economist*
McVisk, William Kilburn *lawyer*
Meccia, Francis (Frank) Anthony *physician assistant*
Mehlman, Mark Franklin *lawyer*
Mehrberg, Randall Eric *lawyer, utilities executive*
Melamed, Leo *global consulting firm executive*
Melbinger, Michael S. *lawyer*
Melman, Richard *restauranteur*
Melnick, Jane Fisher *writer, educator, photographer*
Melton, David Reuben *lawyer*
Meltzer, Robert Craig *lawyer, educator*
Menchetti, David Barry *lawyer*
Menchin, Robert Stanley *marketing executive*
Messner, Leonard Vincent *optometrist, educator*
Metcalf, James S. *manufacturing executive*
Metz, Charles Edgar *radiology educator*
Meyers, Kenneth Raymond *telecommunications industry executive*
Michaels, Richard Edward *lawyer*
Michaels, Robert A. *real estate development company executive*
Michaels, Walter Benn *English professor, writer*
Michod, Susan Alexander *artist, painter*
Migala, Lucyna J. *journalist, broadcast executive, artistic director*
Mikesell, Marvin Wray *geography educator*
Mikva, Abner Joseph *lawyer, retired judge*
Milbrett, Tiffeny Carleen *professional soccer player*
Miletich, Ivo *library and information scientist, bibliographer, educator, linguist, literature research specialist*
Miller, Benjamin K. *retired state supreme court justice*
Miller, Irving Franklin *chemical, biomedical engineer, academic administrator, educator*
Miller, Kenneth W. *lawyer*
Miller, Lee I. *lawyer*
Miller, Paul J. *lawyer*
Miller, Peter C. *lawyer*
Miller, Stephen Ralph *lawyer*
Miller, Verne William *computer engineer, consultant*
Millichap, Joseph Gordon *neurologist, educator*
Miner, Thomas Hawley *entrepreneur*
Minichello, Dennis *lawyer*
Minkowycz, W. J. *mechanical engineering educator*
Minogue, John P. *academic administrator, educator, priest*
Minow, Josephine Baskin *civic volunteer*
Minow, Newton Norman *lawyer, educator*
Mirza, Leona Lousin *elementary school educator, director*
Mitchell, J. Barry *corporate financial executive*
Mitchell, Lee Mark *private equity investor, executive*
Mityas, Sherif *management consultant*
Montgomery, Charles Barry *lawyer*
Montgomery, Charles Howard *retired bank executive*
Montgomery, Julie-April *lawyer*
Montgomery, William Adam *lawyer*
Moore, Patrick J. *paper company executive*
Moran, James Byron *federal judge*
More, José *photojournalist*
Morency, Paula J. *lawyer*
Morewitz, Stephen John *behavioral scientist, consultant, sociologist, educator*
Morgan, Betsy Stelle *lawyer*
Morgan, Donna Evensen *lawyer*
Morgan, Elaine R. *hematologist, oncologist, medical educator*
Morrison, Portia Owen *lawyer*
Morris-Rogers, Cheryl-Ann *daycare provider, director, educator*
Morrow, John E. *lawyer*
Morrow, Richard Martin *retired oil company executive*
Morsch, Thomas Harvey *lawyer, educator*
Mosena, David R. *museum administrator*
Moster, Mary Clare *public relations executive*
Motherway, Nicholas J. *lawyer*
Mudd, Anne Chestney *mediator, law educator, real estate broker*
Mugnaini, Enrico *neuroscience educator*
Mukai, Ai *physiatrist*
Mullen, J. Thomas *lawyer*
Mullen, Michael T. *lawyer*
Muller, Kurt Alexander *lawyer*
Muller, Leon *writer*
Murata, Tadao *engineering and computer science educator*
Murdock, Charles William *lawyer, educator*
Murphy, Kevin M. *economics professor*
Murphy, Michael Emmett *retired food company executive*
Murray, Daniel Charles *trial lawyer*
Murray, Daniel Richard *lawyer*
Murrin, Michael J. *literature educator, writer*
Murtaugh, Christopher David *lawyer*
Myers, Lonn William *lawyer*
Myerson, Roger Bruce *economist, educator*
Naclerio, Robert Michael *otolaryngologist, educator*
Nadler, Judith *library director*
Nahrstadt, Bradley Charles *lawyer*
Nahrwold, David Lange *surgeon, educator*
Nair, R. Shankar *structural engineer*
Najita, Tetsuo *history professor*
Nambu, Yoichiro *physics professor*
Napleton, Robert Joseph *lawyer*
Narahashi, Toshio *pharmacology educator*
Nash, Donald Gene *federal investigator, economist*
Nash, Jessie Madeleine *journalist, science writer*
Nashat, Guity *historian, education educator, researcher*
Natarus, Burton F. *land use consultant, lawyer*
Nault, William Henry *publishing executive*
Neff, David M. *lawyer*
Neis, James Michael *lawyer*
Neithercut, David J. *real estate company officer*
Neumeier, Matthew Michael *lawyer, educator*
Newcomb, Martin Eugene, Jr. *chemistry professor*
Newlin, Charles Fremont *lawyer*
Newman, Terry E. *lawyer*
Nicholas, Ralph Wallace W. *anthropologist, educator*
Nichols, John Doane *diversified manufacturing corporation executive*
Nickell, Jake *internet retail executive, apparel designer, web site designer*
Nicklin, Emily *lawyer*
Nicolaides, Mary *retired lawyer*
Niehaus, Mary C. *lawyer*
Niehoff, Philip John *lawyer*
Nijman, Jennifer T. *lawyer, department chairman*
Niro, Cheryl *lawyer*
Nitikman, Franklin W. *lawyer*
Niyogi-Salhi, Ruma *science educator*
Noel, Carol Adele *music educator, opera singer*
Noonan, Jack *analytics software and solutions company executive*
Nord, Henry J. *transportation executive*
Nord, Robert Eamor *lawyer*
Nordland, Gerald *museum administrator, historian, consultant*
Norgle, Charles Ronald, Sr. *federal judge*
Notz, John Kranz, Jr. *arbitrator, mediator, retired lawyer*
Novack, Julie Ruth *internet marketing executive*
Novak, John G. *construction executive*
Novak, Mark *lawyer*
Novak, Theodore J. *lawyer*
Novich, Neil S. *metals distribution company executive*
Novotny, David Joseph *lawyer*
Nowacki, James Nelson *lawyer*
Nugent, Lori S. *lawyer*
Nühn, Adriaan *food products executive*
Nusbaum, Edward E. *accounting company executive*
Nussbaum, Bernard J. *lawyer*
Nyhan, Lawrence J. (Larry) *lawyer*
Nyhus, Lloyd Milton *retired surgeon, educator*
O'Brien, Gregory Michael St. Lawrence *academic administrator*
O'Brien, James Phillip *lawyer*
O'Brien, John *professional soccer player*
Ochoa, Juan A. *not-for-profit business association executive*
O'Connor, Pamela Johnson *relocation company executive*
Oehme, Reinhard *physicist, researcher*
Oesterle, Eric Adam *lawyer*
Offutt, Gerald M. *lawyer*
O'Hagan, James Joseph *lawyer*
O'Hare, John Mitchell *lawyer*
Olian, Robert Martin *lawyer*
Oliver, Harry Maynard, Jr. *retired brokerage house executive*
Olk, Frederick James *county official, legal assistant*
Olopade, Olufunmilayo Falusi (Funmi Olopade) *geneticist, educator, oncologist, hematologist*
Olsen, Ben *professional soccer player*
Olsen, Edward John *geologist, educator, curator*
Olsen, Rex Norman *trade association executive*
Olson, Jack Conrad, Jr. *geriatrician*
Olson, Steven R. *lawyer*
O'Malley, John Daniel *lawyer, educator, banker*
O'Neil, Michael C. *lawyer*
Ong, Michael King *mathematician, educator, bank executive*
Onyewu, Oguchi *professional soccer player*
Opitz, Donald L. *science historian*
O'Reilly, Charles Terrance *university dean*
O'Reilly, Heather Ann *Olympic athlete*
Osborn, William A. *investment company executive*
Osborne, Robert Stephen *automotive executive, lawyer*
Ostfeld, Gregory Edward *lawyer*
O'Toole, William George *lawyer*
Overton, Bo *professional basketball coach*
Padberg, Helen Swan *violinist*
Padron, D. Lorenzo *state agency administrator*
Page, Ernest *retired medical educator*
Paley, Vivian Gussin *writer*
Pallasch, B. Michael *lawyer, director*
Pallasch, Magdalena Helena (Mrs. Bernhard Michael Pallasch) *artist*
Pallmeyer, Rebecca Ruth *judge*
Palmer, John Bernard III *lawyer*
Palmer, Patrick Edward *radio astronomer, educator*
Palmer, Robert Towne *lawyer, bank executive*
Panich, Danuta Bembenista *lawyer*
Panko, Jessie Symington *education educator*
Pappas, David Wayne *guidance counselor, consultant*
Pappas, George Demetrios *anatomist, cell biologist, educator*
Pappas, Philip James *real estate company executive*
Parcells, Frederick R. *underwriter*
Park, Thomas Joseph *biology researcher, educator*
Parker, Bonita M. *civil rights organization executive*
Parkhurst, Beverly Susler *lawyer, judge*
Parkhurst, Todd Sheldon *lawyer*
Parr, Virginia Helen *retired librarian*
Parrish, Overton Burgin, Jr. *pharmaceutical corporation executive*
Partridge, Mark Van Buren *lawyer, educator, mediator, writer*
Pascal, Roger *lawyer*
Pascale, Mark *curator, educator*
Patel, Homi Burjor *apparel executive*
Paterakis, Angela Gregory *art educator, writer*
Paul, Ronald Neale *management consultant*
Pavalon, Eugene Irving *lawyer*
Pavelich, Daniel L. *retired account and tax management consulting executive*
Paxson, John *professional sports team executive, retired professional basketball player*
Pedersen, Peer *lawyer*
Peerman, Dean Gordon *magazine editor*
Pehlke, Richard W. *real estate company executive*
Pelton, Russell Meredith *lawyer*
Peltzman, Sam *economics professor*
Pendleton, Elisha Donshell *molecular biologist, researcher*
Pengra, R. Rene *lawyer*
Pensler, Jay Michael *plastic surgeon, educator*
Peponis, Harold Arthur *insurance agent, portfolio manager*
Pepper, J. David, II, (Dave Pepper) *construction executive*
Peres, Judith May *journalist*
Perez, David *utilities executive*
Perez, William D. (Bill Perez) *candy company executive, former sports apparel company executive*
Perez, Ziomara Darlene *pre-school educator*
Perzek, Philip John *lawyer*
Peter, Bernard George *lawyer*
Peters, Charles H.R. *lawyer*
Petersen, Donald Sondergaard *lawyer*
Peterson, Randall Theodore *law librarian, educator*
Peterson, Ronald Roger *lawyer*
Petitan, Debra Ann Burke *elementary school educator, counselor, design engineer, writer*
Philbin, Jack *communications executive*
Phillip, Cynthia A. *librarian*
Phillips, Frederick Falley *architect*
Picker, Randal C. *law educator*
Piekarski, Victor J. *lawyer*
Pilcher, James Eric *physicist*
Pincus, Theodore Henry *public relations executive*
Piniella, Lou (Louis Victor Piniella) *professional baseball team manager*
Pinna, Graziano *biologist, researcher*
Pinnell-Stephens, June Alicia *information broker, consultant, librarian*
Pippin, Robert B. *philosopher, educator*
Pirok, Edward Warren *lawyer, consultant*
Pitt, George *lawyer, investment banker*
Pizer, Howard Charles *sports and entertainment executive*
Plotkin, Manuel D. *management consultant, educator, former corporate executive, former government official*
Plotnick, Harvey Barry *publishing executive*
Plotnik, Arthur *writer, columnist*
Pollak, Lisa *radio producer*
Pollock, Earl Edward *lawyer*
Pope, Eddie *professional soccer player*
Pope, Kerig Rodgers *retired magazine executive*
Pope, Michael Arthur *lawyer*
Portnoy, Elliott Ivan *lawyer*
Posner, Kathy Robin *retired communications executive*
Posner, Richard Allen *federal judge*
Postiglione, Corey M. *artist, critic, art educator*
Power, Joseph Aloysius, Jr. *lawyer*
Powers, William Bryan *academic administrator*
Poznanski, Andrew Karol *pediatric radiologist*
Prather, Susan Lynn *public relations executive*
Preciado, Pamela *artist*
Preece, Lynn Sylvia *lawyer*
Presser, Stephen Bruce *lawyer, educator*
Preuss, Daphne *geneticist, biology professor*
Price, Paul L. *lawyer*
Primm, Earl Russell III *publishing executive*
Primo, Quintin E. III *real estate company executive*
Prinz, Richard Allen *surgeon*
Prior, Gary L. *lawyer*
Prior, Mark *professional baseball player*
Pritchard, Jonathan K. *geneticist, educator*
Pritikin, David T. *lawyer*
Pritikin, James B. *lawyer*
Pritzker, Nicholas J. *diversified financial services company executive*
Pritzker, Penny *investor*
Pritzker, Thomas Jay *hotel executive*
Prochnow, Douglas Lee *lawyer*
Provus, Barbara Lee *retired executive search consultant*
Ptak, Frank Stanley *manufacturing executive*
Pugh, Carla M. *surgeon, educator*
Pulliam, Yvonne Antoinette *gifted education educator*
Qasim, Imad Isa *lawyer*
Quaini, Duane C. *lawyer*
Quinlan, Thomas J. III *printing company executive*
Quinn, Patrick *lieutenant governor*
Rabin, Joseph Harry *marketing research company executive*
Radomski, Robyn L. *marketing executive*
Rafeyan, Roueen *psychiatrist, educator*
Ralph, Damani *professional soccer player*
Ramsey-Goldman, Rosalind *physician*
Rankin, James Winton *lawyer*
Ranney, George A., Jr. *lawyer*
Raphaelson, Joel *retired advertising agency executive*
Rappaport, Richard J. *lawyer*
Rasin, Rudolph Stephen *corporate financial executive*
Raskin, Richard D. *lawyer*
Ratner, Gerald *lawyer*
Raynal, Lazar Pol *lawyer*
Reardon, John E. *broadcast executive*
Reddick, Catherine Anne (Cat Reddick) *Olympic athlete*
Redish, Martin Harris *law educator*
Redmond, Andrea *executive recruiter*
Reed, M. Scott *accounting company executive*
Reed, Vastina Kathryn (Tina Reed) *child and adolescent psychotherapist*
Reich, Allan J. *lawyer*
Reicin, Ronald Ian *lawyer*
Reidy, Daniel Edward *lawyer*
Reiffel, Leonard *physicist, consultant*
Reilly, Anne Huedepohl *university educator, researcher*
Reilly, Robert Frederick *investment banker*
Reinsdorf, Jerry Michael *professional sports team owner, real estate company executive, accountant, lawyer*
Reis, Leslie Ann *lawyer, educator*
Reisman, Andrew Louis *information technology executive, lawyer*
Reitman, Jerry Irving *advertising agency executive*
Relias, John Alexis *lawyer*
Remini, Robert Vincent *historian*
Renwick, Scott *lawyer*
Replogle, Robert Lee *cardiovascular surgeon, thoracic surgeon*
Resnick, Donald Ira *lawyer*
Reum, James Michael *lawyer*
Reum, W. Robert *manufacturing executive*
Reyes, Victor H. *lawyer*
Reyna, Claudio *professional soccer player*
Reynolds, Ruth Carmen *school administrator, secondary school educator*
Rhind, James Thomas *lawyer*
Rhone, Elvie Sue *educational administrator*
Rice, Linda Johnson *publishing executive*
Rice, William Edward *journalist*
Rich, Nancy Jean *lawyer*
Rich, S. Judith *public relations executive*
Richard, Howard M. *lawyer*
Richards, Brian F. *lawyer*
Richardson, John Thomas *academic administrator, clergyman*
Richman, Harold Alan *social welfare policy educator*
Richman, John Marshall *lawyer, food products executive*

Richman, Lawrence I. *lawyer*
Richmond, James Glidden *lawyer*
Richter, Frank M. *geophysicist, educator*
Rieger, Mitchell Sheridan *lawyer*
Riggs, Kenneth P., Jr. *real estate company executive*
Rikoski, Richard Anthony *electrical engineering executive*
Riley, James B., Jr. *lawyer*
Riley, Robert H. *lawyer*
Rishworth, Susan Knoke *archivist, researcher*
Ritchie, William Paul *lawyer*
Ritz, Stephen Mark *lawyer*
Rizzello, Joseph Samuel *stock exchange executive*
Rizzi, Joseph Vito *banker*
Rizzo, Ronald Stephen *lawyer*
Robbins, Audrey *county employee*
Robbins, Ellen Sue *lawyer*
Roberts, John Charles *law educator*
Roberts, Peter C. *real estate company executive*
Robertson, Donna Virginia *architect, educator, dean*
Robertson, William Wright, Jr. *orthopedist, educator*
Robins, Joel *import/export company executive*
Robinson, June Kerswell *dermatologist, educator*
Robinson, Reginald R. *musician*
Robinson, Robin *newscaster*
Rodgers, James Foster *insurance research executive, economist*
Roeper, Richard *columnist*
Rogers, Desiree Glapion *utilities executive*
Rogers, Eugene Jack *retired medical educator*
Rogers, John L. III *lawyer*
Rogers, John W., Jr. *investment company executive*
Rohrman, Douglass Frederick *lawyer*
Roizen, Nancy J. *physician, educator*
Roizman, Bernard *virologist, educator*
Ronan, John *architect*
Rondeau, James Edward *curator*
Rooney, Matthew A. *lawyer*
Rooney, Phillip Bernard *service company executive*
Roos, Raymond Philip *medical educator*
Roper, Harry Joseph *lawyer*
Ropski, Gary Melchior *lawyer*
Rosales, Veronica *language educator*
Rose, Mark E. *real estate company executive*
Rosen, Barry S. *lawyer*
Rosen, George *economist, educator*
Rosen, Steven Terry *oncologist, hematologist*
Rosenblatt, Brian A. *lawyer*
Rosenbloom, Lewis Stanley *lawyer*
Rosenfeld, Howard H. *lawyer*
Rosenfield, Andrew M. *lawyer, educator*
Rosenthal, Albert Jay *advertising executive*
Rosner, Jonathan Lincoln *physicist, researcher*
Rosner, Robert *astrophysicist, educator*
Ross, Curtis Bennett *lawyer*
Ross, Robin S. *investment company executive*
Rosseau, Gail L. *neurosurgeon, educator*
Rossiter, Peter L. *lawyer*
Roth, Robert A. *newspaper executive*
Rovner, Ilana Kara Diamond *federal judge*
Rowe, John William *utilities executive*
Rowley, Janet Davison *physician*
Roy, David Tod *literature educator*
Roy, Kevin *newscaster*
Royster, Lynn Christine *academic administrator, educator*
Rubin, E(rwin) Leonard *lawyer*
Ruder, David Sturtevant *government official, lawyer, educator*
Rudnick, Lewis G. *lawyer*
Rudnick, Paul David *lawyer*
Rudstein, David Stewart *law educator*
Rundio, Louis Michael, Jr. *lawyer*
Running, Andrew Richard *lawyer*
Ruo, Bernice *physician, researcher*
Rupert, Donald William *lawyer*
Rutkoff, Alan Stuart *lawyer*
Ruxin, Paul Theodore *lawyer*
Ryan, Edward F. *lawyer*
Ryan, J. Brendan *advertising executive*
Ryan, Patrick G. *diversified financial services company executive, director*
Ryan, Thomas F. *lawyer*
Rynkiewicz, Stephen Michael *journalist*
Sabbagha, Rudy Elias *obstetrician, gynecologist, educator*
Sabl, John J. *lawyer*
Sacoff, Robert W. *lawyer*
St. Eve, Amy J. *federal judge*
Salopek, Paul F. *news correspondent*
Salpeter, Alan N. *lawyer*
Samuelson, Peter A. *management consultant*
Sanchez, Vincent A. *lawyer*
Sandberg, Craig M. *lawyer*
Sanders, Jacquelyn Seevak *psychologist, educator*
Sanders, Richard Henry *lawyer*
Sandler, Richard H. *pediatric gastroenterologist*
Sandlow, Leslie Jordan *gastroenterologist, educator*
Santangelo, Mario Vincent *retired dentist*
Sathy, Anup *lawyer*
Saunders, George Lawton, Jr. *lawyer*
Savage, Terry *television personality, journalist, stockbroker*
Savard, Denis Joseph *professional hockey coach, former professional hockey player*
Sawyer, Deborah *environmental engineering company executive*
Sawyier, Michael Tod *lawyer, director*
Saylors, Charles J. *educational association administrator, construction executive*
Scanlan, Thomas Cleary *publishing executive, editor*
Schafer, Michael Frederick *orthopedic surgeon*
Schaffer, Henry M. *lawyer*
Schaffner, Howard Sheldon *lawyer*
Schanwald, Steve *professional sports team executive*
Scharf, Stephanie A. *lawyer*
Schenck, Robert Roy *hand surgeon*
Schiele, Michele M. *not-for-profit fundraiser, medical association administrator*
Schieser, Hans Alois *education educator*
Schiller, Donald Charles *lawyer*
Schilsky, Richard Lewis *oncologist, researcher*
Schindler, Judi(th) (Judith Kay Schindler) *public relations executive, marketing professional, consultant*
Schink, James Harvey *lawyer*
Schmidt, John R. *lawyer*
Schneider, Dan W. *lawyer, consultant*
Schneider, Robert Jerome *lawyer*
Schneider, Wesley Clair *marketing communications company executive*
Schoenfield, Rick Merrill *lawyer*
Schoonhoven, Ray James *retired lawyer*
Schopf, William Grant *lawyer*
Schorer, Joseph U. *lawyer*
Schornack, John James *accountant*
Schoumacher, Bruce Herbert *lawyer*
Schreck, Robert A., Jr. *lawyer*
Schriver, John T. III *lawyer*
Schroeder, Christopher *literature and language professor, writer*
Schroeder, Douglas Fredrick *architect*
Schubert, William Henry *curriculum studies educator*
Schueppert, George Louis *financial executive*
Schulte, David Michael *investment banker*
Schulz, Keith Donald *corporate lawyer, writer*
Schumann, William Henry III *corporate financial executive*
Schupp, Anastasia Luka *retired lawyer*
Schwab, Stephen Wayne *lawyer*
Schwartz, Alan Gifford *sport company executive*
Schwartz, Donald Lee *lawyer*
Schwertfeger, Timothy R. *investment company executive*
Sciarra, John J. *obstetrician, gynecologist, educator*
Scogland, William Lee *lawyer*
Scommegna, Antonio *obstetrician, gynecologist, educator*
Scott, Nancy L. *information technology manager, health facility administrator, consultant*
Scott, Stephen Brinsley *theater producer*
Scully, John Edward, Jr. *banker*
Scurry, Briana Collette *professional soccer player*
Seal, Robert A. *library director*
Seaman, Donna Jean *editor, writer*
Seeler, Ruth Andrea *pediatrician, educator*
Segal, Mindy *chef*
Segerstrale, Ullica Christina *social sciences educator, researcher*
Selman, Russell Bertram *lawyer, department chairman*
Senior, Donald Paul *religious organization administrator*
Senior, Richard John Lane *linen and uniform services executive*
Sennet, Charles Joseph *lawyer*
Sennett, Michael *lawyer*
Sergi, Vincent A.F. *lawyer*
Serrano, Justin Forbes *education executive*
Serrell, Beverly *museum consultant*
Serritella, William David *lawyer*
Serry, Cyrus *medical educator*
Serwer, Alan Michael *lawyer*
Sessions, Joan T. *director, educator*
Sewell, William Hamilton, Jr. *historian*
Sfikas, Peter Michael *lawyer, educator*
Shadur, Milton Irving *judge*
Shafer, Eric Christopher *minister*
Shanahan, Betty *professional society administrator*
Shank, Suzanne Adams *lawyer*
Shannon, Iris Reed *health facility administrator, consultant*
Shapiro, Keith J. *lawyer*
Shapiro, Stephen Michael *lawyer*
Shapiro, Steven A. *lawyer*
Shapo, Helene S. *law educator*
Shapo, Marshall Schambelan *lawyer, educator*
Shaughnessy, Edward Louis *language educator*
Shaver, Joan Louise Fowler *dean, women's health nurse*
Sheffield, Jeffrey T. *lawyer*
Sheppard, Berton Scott *lawyer*
Shepro, Richard W. *lawyer*
Sherman, Ian Matthew *lawyer*
Sherman, Jeremy P. *lawyer*
Shields, Thomas Charles *lawyer*
Shields, Thomas William *surgeon, educator*
Shindler, Donald A. *lawyer*
Short, Marion Priscilla *neurogenetics educator*
Shuftan, Robert L. *lawyer*
Shulruff, Stuart P. *lawyer*
Siegel, Howard Jerome *lawyer*
Siegler, Mark *internist, educator*
Sigmon, Joyce Elizabeth *professional society administrator*
Silberman, Alan Harvey *lawyer*
Silverman, Gary R. *lawyer*
Silverman, Ross O. *lawyer*
Simmons, Adele Smith *foundation executive, former educator*
Simon, Arthur Joseph *lawyer*
Simon, George T. *lawyer*
Simon, John Bern *lawyer*
Simons, Helen *school psychologist, psychotherapist, educator*
Simpson, Dick Weldon *political science educator*
Sivananthan, Sivalingam *science educator*
Sive, Rebecca Anne *public relations executive*
Skiles, Scott Allen *professional basketball coach*
Skilling, Raymond Inwood *lawyer*
Skinner, Mary Jacobs *lawyer*
Sklarsky, Charles B. *lawyer*
Skolds, John L. (Jack Skolds) *utilities executive*
Slansky, Jerry William *investment company executive*
Slawkowski, David John *lawyer*
Sljivic-Simsic, Biljana B. *Slavic and Baltic languages educator*
Smagner, John Patrick *applied behavior analyst, educator*
Smale, Stephen *mathematics professor*
Small, Richard Donald *travel company executive*
Smart, Allen Rich, II, *retired lawyer*
Smedinghoff, Thomas J. *lawyer*
Smith, Adrian Devaun *architect*
Smith, Art *chef*
Smith, Arthur B., Jr. *lawyer*
Smith, Earl Charles *nephrologist, educator*
Smith, Elizabeth Angele Taft *curator*
Smith, Joanne C. *physiatrist*
Smith, Lewis J. *medical educator, researcher*
Smith, Raymond Thomas *anthropology educator*
Smith, Sam *columnist, writer*
Smith, Scott Clybourn *publishing executive*
Smith, Stan Vladimir *economist, finance company executive*
Smith, Todd A. *lawyer*
Smolen, Lee M. *lawyer*
Snodgrass, S. Gary *utilities executive*
Snyder, Edward Adams *dean, economics professor*
Snyder, Graydon F. *religion educator*
Sochen, June *history professor*
Socol, Michael Lee *obstetrician, gynecologist, educator*
Solaro, Ross John *physiologist, biophysicist*
Solovy, Jerold Sherwin *lawyer*
Solow, Michael Barry *lawyer*
Solow, Sheldon L. *lawyer*
Sonderby, Susan Pierson *federal bankruptcy judge*
Song, David *plastic surgeon, medical educator*
Soriano, Alfonso Guilleard *professional baseball player*
Sorrentino, Matthew Joseph *internist, educator*
Southwell, Donald G. *insurance company executive*
Spanjol, Jelena *finance educator*
Sparberg, Marshall Stuart *gastroenterologist, educator*
Spector, David M. *lawyer*
Spellmire, George W. *lawyer*
Spergel, Irving Abraham *social worker, researcher*
Spiegler, Joseph Andrew *lawyer*
Spindler, George S. *lawyer, retired oil industry executive*
Spock, Michael *museum administrator*
Spring, Bonnie Joan *preventive medicine educator*
Springer, Jerry (Gerald Norman Springer) *television talk show host, radio personality*
Sproger, Charles Edmund *retired lawyer*
Stacey, James Henry *writer, columnist*
Stack, Paul Francis *lawyer*
Stack, Stephen S. *manufacturing executive*
Staller, John Edward *archaeologist, anthropologist, educator*
Stallworth, Stanley B. *lawyer*
Stamler, Jeremiah *physician, educator*
Stanhaus, James Steven *lawyer*
Stanos, Steven Peter, Jr. *osteopath*
Starkman, Gary Lee *lawyer*
Stassen, John Henry *lawyer*
Stead, James Joseph, Jr. *security firm executive*
Stearns, Neele Edward, Jr. *investment company executive*
Steinberg, Morton M. *lawyer*
Steinberg, Rubin *retired art educator, artist*
Steinberg, Salme Elizabeth Harju *academic administrator, historian*
Steiner, Donald Frederick *biochemist, physician, educator*
Steinfeld, Manfred *furniture manufacturing executive*
Steinhorn, Robin H. *neonatologist, educator*
Stephens, Richard *aerospace transportation executive*
Stern, Carl William, Jr. *management consultant*
Sternstein, Allan J. *lawyer*
Stetler, David J. *lawyer*
Stevens, Linda K. *lawyer*
Stevens, Stanley M. *lawyer*
Stevenson, Adlai Ewing III *lawyer, retired senator*
Stewart, Donald M. *college president*
Stick, Michael Alan *lawyer*
Stiegel, Michael Allen *lawyer*
Stigler, Stephen Mack *statistician, educator*
Stillman, Nina Gidden *lawyer*
Stirling, James Paulman *investment banker*
Stoklosa, Gregory A. *publishing executive*
Stoll, John Robert *lawyer, educator*
Stone, Alan *container company executive*
Stone, Geoffrey Richard *lawyer, educator*
Stone, Susan A. *lawyer*
Strassner, Howard Taft, Jr. *obstetrician, educator*
Stratman, Deborah *filmmaker, film and video educator*
Strauss, Deborah *foundation administrator*
Strauss, Mark *editor*
Strobel, Pamela B. *energy executive*
Strohm, Bruce C. *lawyer, real estate company executive*
Stroscio, Michael Anthony *physicist, researcher*
Strubel, Ella Doyle *advertising executive, public relations executive*
Strubel, Richard Perry *Internet company executive*
Stulberg, Samuel David *surgeon, physician*
Such, Domingo P. III *lawyer*
Suchomel, Mark *publishing executive*
Sufian, Sandy M. *education educator*
Sulkin, Howard Allen *academic administrator*
Sullivan, Barry *lawyer*
Sullivan, Bernard James *accountant*
Sullivan, Marcia Waite *lawyer*
Sullivan, Peggy *librarian, consultant*
Sullivan, Thomas Patrick *lawyer*
Sviokla, John Julius *technology consultant*
Swanson, Don Richard *university dean*
Swibel, Howard Jay *lawyer*
Swibel, Steven Warren *lawyer*
Swiger, Elinor Porter *lawyer*
Swinand, Andrew *advertising executive*
Szerlag, Chester Theodore *health care executive*
Szydlowski, Joseph Edward *music librarian*
Tabin, Julius *lawyer, physicist*
Talbot, Pamela *public relations executive*
Tallon, Dale *professional sports team executive*
Tangora, Anthony Joseph *director*
Tangora, Martin Charles *mathematician, educator*
Tanna, Angelo Peter *ophthalmologist, educator, researcher*
Tarlov, Alvin Richard *foundation administrator, physician, educator*
Tartakoff, David Stephen *mathematics professor, researcher*
Tatar, Arnold Marshall *internist, educator*
Taub, Richard Paul *social sciences educator*
Teichner, Lester *general management executive*
Telfer, Margaret Clare *internist, hematologist, oncologist*
Terkel, Studs (Louis Terkel) *writer, journalist*
Tescher, Jennifer *bank executive*
Tessing, Louise Scire *graphic designer*
Tetzlaff, Theodore R. *lawyer*
Thaden, Edward Carl *history professor*
Theobald, Edward Robert *lawyer*
Thisted, Ronald Aaron *statistician, educator, consultant*
Thomas, Cherryl T. *former federal agency administrator*
Thomas, Dale E. *lawyer*
Thomas, Eddie *composer, recording industry executive, producer, promoter*
Thomas, Frederick Bradley *lawyer*
Thomas, Leona Marlene *healthcare educator*
Thomas, Rhonda Churchill *lawyer*
Thomas, Robert R. *state supreme court justice*
Thomas, Stephen Paul *lawyer*
Thompson, George Fletcher *editor, publishing executive*
Thompson, James Robert, Jr. *lawyer, former governor*
Thompson, Jayne Carr *public relations and communications executive, lawyer*
Thompson, Michael *lawyer*
Thompson, Richard Ellis *secondary school educator*
Thurston, Stephen John *pastor*
Tigerman, Stanley *architect, educator*
Tilton, Glenn F. *air transportation executive*
Tipton, Margaret Ann *religious organization administrator, writer*
Toback, Paul A. *recreational facility executive*
Tomaino, Joseph Carmine *former retail executive, former postal inspector*
Tomar, Russell Herman *pathologist, educator, researcher*
Toohey, James Kevin *lawyer*
Topinka, Judy Baar *state official, political organization worker*
Torchetti, John *professional hockey coach*
Torgersen, Torwald Harold *architect, consultant*
Toth, Bruce A. *lawyer*
Townsend, Robert Morris *economics professor, researcher*
Trafimow, Jordan Herman *orthopedist*
Trammell, Alan Stuart *professional baseball coach, retired professional baseball player*
Treston, Sherry S. *lawyer*
Tribbett, Charles *executive recruiter*
Trio, Edward Alan *lawyer, accountant*
Trost, Eileen Bannon *lawyer*
Trotter, Charlie *chef*
Trotter, Cortez *city official, former fire commissioner*
Truran, James Wellington, Jr. *astrophysicist, educator*
Tryban, Esther Elizabeth *lawyer*
Turilli, M. Louise *lawyer*
Turner, Michael Stanley *astrophysics professor, researcher*
Turow, Scott F. *writer, lawyer*
Tyler, W(illiam) Ed *finance company executive*
Tyree, James C. *insurance company executive*
Tyson, Kirk W. M. *management consultant*
Umans, Alvin Robert *manufacturing executive*
Umbdenstock, Richard J. *medical association administrator*
Underwood, Robert Leigh *venture capitalist*
Ungaretti, Richard Anthony *lawyer*
Upshaw, Harry Stephan *psychologist, educator*
Usiskin, Zalman Philip *mathematics educator*
Utecht, Andrea E. *lawyer*
Valukas, Anton Ronald *lawyer, former prosecutor*
Valyi-Nagy, Tibor G. *neuropathologist, virologist*
Van Demark, Ruth Elaine *lawyer*
Van Den Hende, Fred J(oseph) *human resources executive*
VanderBeke, Patricia K. *architect*
Van Gorp, Jon D. *lawyer*
Van Pelt, Robert Irving *retired firefighter*
Van Tine, Matthew Eric *lawyer*
Van Zandt, David E. *dean, law educator*
Ventrelli, Anita Marie *lawyer*
Venturini, Tisha Lea *professional soccer player*
Verschoor, Curtis Carl *writer, consultant*
Vezeau, Timothy J. *lawyer*
Vie, Richard Carl *insurance company executive*
Vigneswaran, Wickii Thambiah *cardiothoracic surgeon, educator*
Vincent, Jim *performing company executive*
Vishneski, John Stanley III *lawyer*
Vojcanin, Sava Alexander *lawyer*
Volgman, Annabelle Santos *cardiologist, educator*
Von Mandel, Michael Jacques *lawyer*
von Rhein, John Richard *music critic, journalist, writer*
Vrablik, Edward Robert *import/export company executive*
Vree, Roger Allen *lawyer*
Vroman, Kendal *investment company executive*
Wagner, Annette M. *dermatologist, surgeon*
Wagner, Randy Susan *travel company executive*
Wahlen, Edwin Alfred *lawyer*
Wakschlag, Milton Samuel *lawyer*

Walberg, Herbert John *psychologist, educator, consultant*
Walker, Thomas Ray *city aviation commissioner*
Wall, James McKendree *minister, editor*
Wallace, Ben *professional basketball player*
Walsh, Matthew M. *construction executive*
Walsh, Michael S. *lawyer*
Walton, Robert Lee *plastic surgeon*
Wambach, Abby (Mary Abigail Wambach) *Olympic athlete*
Wander, Herbert Stanton *lawyer*
Wang, Albert James *violinist, educator*
Ward, Jonathan P. *investment banker*
Warner, Carrie *architectural engineer*
Wasan, Darsh Tilakchand *academic administrator, chemical engineer, educator*
Wasendorf, Russell R., Sr. *brokerage house executive*
Wasson, Jeffrey *music educator*
Waters, Ronald V. III *candy company executive*
Watts, Michael H. *real estate company executive*
Weaver, Timothy Allan *lawyer*
Webb, Dan K. *lawyer*
Webb, Robert W. *lawyer*
Weber, Hanno *architect*
Webster, James Randolph, Jr. *physician*
Weese, Benjamin Horace *architect*
Weinberg, David B. *investor*
Weinberg, Lila Shaffer *editor, writer*
Weinberg, Walter S. *lawyer*
Weiner, Gerald Arne *stockbroker*
Weinfurter, Daniel Joseph *business services executive*
Weinkopf, Friedrich J. *lawyer*
Weinsheimer, William Cyrus *lawyer*
Weinstein, David M. *not-for-profit organization executive*
Weinstein, Lisa *marketing executive*
Weinstein, Margo *lawyer*
Weintraub, Joseph Barton *publishing executive*
Weiss, John Robert *lawyer*
Weiss, Steven Allan *lawyer*
Weissman, Michael Lewis *lawyer*
Welch, Lyman W. *lawyer*
Welsh, Kelly Raymond *lawyer, investment company executive*
Werner, Raymond J. *lawyer*
Westbrook, Brian *professional football player*
Westerberg, Gary W. *lawyer*
Weston, Roger Lance *banker*
Whalen, Wayne W. *lawyer*
Wham, David Buffington *secondary school educator*
Wheeler, Daniel Harding *architect, educator*
White, C. Vanessa *director*
White, Henry F., Jr. *legal association administrator, retired military officer*
White, Linda Diane *lawyer*
Whiting, Oran F. *lawyer*
Whitington, Peter Frank *pediatric hepatologist, educator*
Whitney, Kent R.E. *securities trader*
Whitney, Patrick Foster *design educator*
Whyte, Alison Anne *conservator*
Wieczorek, Dennis E. *lawyer*
Wied, George Ludwig *physician*
Wier, Patricia Ann *publishing executive, consultant*
Wildman, Max Edward *lawyer, director*
Wilhelm, David C. *investment company executive*
Wilhelm, John L. *health facility administrator*
Wille, Lois Jean *retired editor*
Williams, Ann Claire *federal judge*
Williams, Frederick Tyrone *entrepreneur, pastor*
Williams, Kim Allan *cardiologist, educator*
Williams, Marsha C. *travel company executive*
Williams, Philip Copelain *obstetrician, gynecologist*
Williams, Richard Lucas III *electronics executive, director, lawyer*
Williamson, Wayne C. *internist, geriatrician*
Willoughby, William Franklin, II, *retired physician, researcher*
Wilmouth, Robert K. *commodities trader*
Wilson, Cleo Francine *foundation administrator*
Wilson, Roger Goodwin *lawyer*
Wimer, Ross *architect*
Wimmer, Markus Anton *biomedical engineer, educator*
Wine-Banks, Jill Susan *lawyer*
Winfrey, Oprah *television talk show host, actress, television producer*
Winslow, Robert A. *real estate company executive*
Winstein, Bruce Darrell *physics professor*
Wirszup, Izaak *mathematician, educator*
Wirtz, William Wadsworth *real estate company executive, professional sports team executive*
Wise, William Jerrard *lawyer*
Witcoff, Sheldon William *lawyer*
Wittbrodt, Elizabeth S. *occupational therapist, educator*
Wolf, Charles Benno *lawyer*
Wolfe, David Louis *lawyer*
Wolff, Josh *professional soccer player*
Wong, Thomas Tang Yum *engineering educator*
Wood, Diane Pamela *federal judge*
Wood, Kerry *professional baseball player*
Wood, Mark D. *lawyer*
Wood, Patrick Henry III *former federal official*
Woodford, Peter C. *lawyer*
Wooldridge, Patrice Marie *marketing professional, personal trainer*
Wright, Judith Margaret *law librarian, educator, dean*
Wrigley, William, Jr., (Bill Wrigley Jr.) *candy company executive*
Yale, Seymour Hershel *dental radiologist, educator, gerontologist, dean*
Yamada, Tohru *biologist, educator, researcher, director*
Yamamoto, Hisashi *chemistry professor*
Yao, Tito Go *pediatrician*
Yeager, Mark Leonard *lawyer*
Young, John F. *utilities executive*
Young, Lauren Sue Jones *education educator*
Youngman, Owen Ralph *newspaper executive*
Yu, Anthony C. *religion and literature educator*
Yu, Clement Tak *educator, researcher, consultant*
Yudkowsky, Rachel *medical educator*
Zabel, Sheldon Alter *lawyer, educator*
Zagar, Robert John *psychologist, researcher*
Zagel, James Block *federal judge*
Zagel, Margaret Maxwell *lawyer*
Zajicek, Jeronym *retired music educator*
Zambrano, Carlos Alberto *professional baseball player*
Zee, Phyllis C. *physician, educator, researcher*
Zeine, Rana Ramsey *neuropathologist, research professor*
Zell, Samuel *real estate company executive*
Zellner, Arnold *economics, econometrics and statistics professor*
Zemm, Sandra Phyllis *lawyer*
Zenner, Sheldon Toby *lawyer*
Zheng, James *architectural firm executive*
Zhu, Mingzhao *immunologist, microbiologist*
Zimmer, Robert Jeffrey *academic administrator, mathematician, educator*
Zimmerman, D. Patrick *psychotherapist, health facility administrator*
Zolno, Mark S. *lawyer*
Zoloth, Laurie Susan *bioethicist*
Zonis, Marvin *political scientist, educator*
Zucaro, Aldo Charles *insurance company executive*
Zucker, David F. *information technology executive*

Chicago Heights
Buishas, Kristin Maureen *elementary school educator*
Cifelli, John Louis *lawyer*
Kavis, George *engineer, photographer*
Nowocin, Debra Terese *gifted and talented secondary education educator*
Reed, Scott C. *musician, educator, writer*
Yalavarthi, Ramaraja *physician*

Chillicothe
Tallon, Edward Joseph *social studies educator*

Cicero
Paprocki, Thomas John *lawyer, priest*

Cissna Park
McCullough, Edward L. *artist, educator*

Clarendon Hills
Choice, Priscilla Kathryn Means (Penny) *retired educational association administrator*
Moritz, Donald Brooks *mechanical engineer, consultant*

Coal City
DiGiusto, Elaine Bessie *science educator*

Country Club Hills
Snyder, Caroline Jean *secondary school educator*

Crete
Langer, Steven *human resources specialist, consultant, psychologist*

Crystal Lake
Anderson, Lyle Arthur *retired manufacturing executive*
Chamberlain, Charles James *railroad labor union executive*
Chechopoulos, Peter *photographer, educator*
Fleming, Marjorie Foster *freelance writer, artist*
Gosalia, Keyoor Chetan *electrical engineer*
Haas, Sheila Jean *secondary school educator*
Halperin, Richard George *information technology executive*
Janes, Brian D. *electronics specialist*
Keller, William Francis *publishing consultant*
Kruper, John Gerald (Jack Kruper) *sales and marketing executive*
Pearson, Nels Kenneth *retired manufacturing executive*
Salvesen, B. Forbes *artist*
Shank, William O. *lawyer*
Siebel, Carl A. *manufacturing executive*
Thoms, Jeannine Aumond *lawyer*
Wade, Edwin Lee *lawyer, writer*

Darien
Gardner, Howard Garry *pediatrician, educator*
Hanson, Martin Philip *mechanical engineer, farmer*
Kulkarni, Bidy *reproductive endocrinologist, biomedical researcher, consultant*

Davis
Fulfer, Matrona Penny *retired school librarian, educator, columnist*

Decatur
Camp, William H. *agricultural products executive*
Coryell, Sandra Kay *music educator*
Dunn, John Francis *lawyer, state representative*
Jones, Penny Lee *elementary school educator*
Koucky, John Richard *metallurgical engineer, manufacturing executive*
Mayfield, Peggy Lee *counselor*
Mulhollem, Paul B. *agricultural products executive*
Munoz, Joseph Mark *education educator, consultant*
Reising, Richard P. *lawyer*
Rice, John D. *agricultural products executive*
Schmalz, Douglas J. *agricultural company executive*
Smith, David James *lawyer*
Staley, Henry Mueller *manufacturing executive*
Vigneri, Joseph William *lawyer*
Woertz, Patricia Ann *agricultural company executive, retired oil company executive*

Deerfield
Bialek, Paul Richard *mathematics professor*
Birmingham, William Joseph *retired lawyer*
Blanchard, Eric Alan *lawyer*
Boyd, Joseph Don *diversified financial services company executive*
Carbonari, Bruce A. *consumer products company executive*
Davis, Robert M. *medical products executive*
Gershteyn, Yefim *application developer, researcher*
Green, Dana I. *lawyer, human resources specialist*
Heiman, Marvin Stewart *finance company executive*
Howell, George Bedell *investment company executive*
Lezak, Carol Spielman *communications executive, editor, writer, design consultant, medical librarian*
Lichtenstein, Susan R. *lawyer, medical products executive*
Meyer, Mara Ellice *special education educator, consultant, academic administrator*
Nitzki-George, Diane M. *pharmacist, medical writer*
Omtvedt, Craig P. *consumer products executive*
Parkinson, Robert L., Jr. *medical products executive, health facility administrator*
Persky, Marla Susan *lawyer*
Prete, Gayle Compton *advertising and marketing executive*
Ramirez, Ralph Henry *nurse, corporate executive*
Reich, Victoria J. *consumer products company executive*
Reid-Anderson, James *diagnostic equipment company executive*
Rein, Jeffrey A. *retail executive*
Riedl, George J. *retail executive*
Roche, Mark A. *lawyer, consumer products company executive*
Rudolphsen, William M. *retail executive*
Saida, Toyoyasu *chemical and biochemical engineer*
Sanner, John Harper *retired pharmacologist*
Schnabel, Eckhard Johannes *theologian, educator*
Scott, John Joseph *lawyer*
Scott, Theodore R. *retired lawyer*
Shakno, Robert Julian *hospital and social services administrator*
Taylor, Trent E. *retail executive*
Vollen, Robert Jay *lawyer*
Wagner, Mark A. *retail executive*
Wasson, Gregory D. *retail executive*
Wilson, Stephen Ray *fertilizer manufacturing company executive*
Wrobbel, Karen *education educator, consultant*
Zywicki, Robert Albert *retired electric power industry executive*

Dekalb
Crosser, Carmen Lynn *marriage and family therapist, social worker, consultant*
Dyshkant, Alexander Sergeevich *physicist, researcher*
Gau, Jenn-Terng *engineering educator*
Gelman, Alexander *theater director, educator*
Goldenberg, William Bruce *musician, educator*
Hamilton, David Arnold *retired librarian*
Kimball, Clyde William *physicist, researcher*
Legg, J. Ivan *academic administrator*
Lotshaw, David Paul *physiologist, educator*
Monat, William Robert *university official*
Piot, Philippe Regis-Guy *educator, researcher*
Richoz, Joan Kathryn *real estate agent, retired school nurse*
Shernoff, David Jordan *psychology professor*
Slotsve, George Aaron *economist, educator, consultant*
Stahl, Norman A. *literature and language professor, department chairman*
Troyer, Alvah Forrest *agricultural products executive, horticulturist*

Des Plaines
D'Anca, John Arthur *psychotherapist, educator*
Drake, Ann M. *consumer products company executive*
Frank, James S. *automotive executive*
Giampietro, Nicholas L. *lawyer*
Gochnauer, Richard Wallis *wholesale distribution executive*
Henrikson, Arthur Allen *political cartoonist, educator*
Johnston, Kurt Malcolm *pharmaceutical company executive*
Kaczor, Diane L. *marketing professional, researcher*
Lee, Margaret Burke *college president, language educator*
Martan, Joseph Rudolf *lawyer*
O'Dwyer, Mary Ann *automotive executive*
Page, Helen (Lyn) Bard Ward *literature educator*
Pestova, Ekaterina *scientist*
Quintanilla, Antonio Paulet *retired physician, educator*
Relwani, Nirmal Murlidhar (Nick Relwani) *mechanical engineer*
Sampson, David Allan *insurance association executive, former federal agency administrator*
Santisteban, Joseph Henry *human resources specialist*
Valdes, Annmarie *history professor, researcher*
Vancastle, Robin *bank executive*

Dixon
Huber, Marianne Jeanne *art dealer and appraiser*

Dow
Schuler, Dorothy R. *education educator, consultant, retired elementary school educator*

Downers Grove
Ames, Sandra Patience *sales executive*
Brekke, Stewart Ernest *retired chemistry and physics educator*
Clement, Paul Platts, Jr. *performance technologist, educator*
Cornell, Susan *medical educator*
Dahdal, Wafa Y. *pharmacologist, educator*
Feeney, Don Joseph, Jr. *psychologist*
Fraleigh, Christopher J. *food products executive*
Green, David William *chemist, educator*
Hornish, Ronald Frederick *music educator*
Hubbard, Lincoln Beals *medical physicist, consultant*
Kaput, Jim L. *lawyer*
McGarr, Frank James *retired federal judge, consultant*
Mrozek, Ernest J. *customer service administrator*
Nolan, James W. *food products executive*
Palmore, Rick (Roderick A.) *lawyer, food products executive*
Porter, Chris *food products executive*
Roselieb, Craig Alan *band director*
Saricks, Joyce Goering *librarian*
Schwemm, John Butler *printing company executive, lawyer*
Siedlecki, Nancy Therese *lawyer, funeral director*
Soenen, Michael J. *consumer products company executive*
Spainhour, J. Patrick (James Patrick Spainhour) *outsourcing company executive, former apparel executive*
Veluchamy, Pethinaidu *marketing executive*
Yeager, David P. *transportation executive*

Du Quoin
Ibendahl, Jean Ayres *retired elementary and secondary educator*

Dundee
Carlini, James *management consultant*
Weck Farrag, Kristin W. *bank executive*

East Alton
Clark, Mark Jeffrey *paralegal, researcher*

East Dubuque
Kussmaul, Donald *academic administrator*

East Peoria
Bell, Lori (Lorelei Junot) *library director, library and information scientist*
Kuehn, Brian Allen *lawyer*
Pope, Kitty *library director*
Twitty, Susan Kay *music educator*
Wadsworth Walker, Cherilee *music educator*

East Saint Louis
Lane-Trent, Patricia Jean *social worker*
Thomas, Mary Lee *property manager*
Wright, Katie Harper *educational administrator, journalist*

Edwardsville
Anderson, Mary Jane *music educator*
Browne, Dallas *anthropologist, educator*
Brugam, Richard Blair *biology educator*
Carlson, Jon Gordon *lawyer*
Crowder, Barbara Lynn *judge*
DeGarmo, Denise Kay *political scientist, educator*
Douglas, Thomas John *finance educator*
Gupchup, Gireesh Vijay *pharmacist, educator*
Hampton, Phillip Jewel *artist, educator*
Madison, Grace Lenore *retired medical/surgical nurse, psychologist, educator*
Malone, Robert Roy *artist, art educator*
Petry, Alice Hall *scholar, educator, writer*
Schultz, Norbert J. *retired music educator*
Stranc, Cathleen L. *music educator*
Wiley, Lakesha M. *pharmacist, educator*

Effingham
Fatheree, Joseph G. *informaation technology educator*

Elburn
Hansen, H. Jack *management consultant*
L'Allier, James Joseph *training services executive, educator*

Elgin
Beyer, Karen Haynes *social worker*
FitzGerald, Timothy J. *corporate financial executive*
Kuforiji, Pamela DeLois *school system administrator*
Mao, Ruixuan (Rick Mao) *dean*
Medal, Carole Ann *library director*
Puotinen, Arthur Edwin *college president, minister*
Reimer, Judy Mills *pastor, religious executive*
Roeser, Ronald O. *lawyer, consultant*
Rogers, Carleton Carson, Jr. *trade show and convention executive*
Turnquist, Jerry L. *communications educator, journalist*
Yarkony, Gary Michael *physician, researcher*

Elk Grove Village
Brace, Frederic F. (Jake Brace) *air transportation executive*
Jan, Chwu-Ching Hwang *environmental chemistry consultant*
Szadokierski, Cindy *air transportation executive*

Elmhurst
Blain, Charlotte Marie *internist, educator*
Choyke, Phyllis May Ford (Mrs. Arthur Davis Choyke Jr.) *management executive, editor, poet*
Duchossois, Craig J. *manufacturing executive*
MacInnes, Sally Ackerman *computer education educator*
Parker, James John *engineer, marketing professional*
Pruter, Margaret Franson *editor*
Scurlock, Jo Ann *history professor, researcher*
Stanger, John Goodman *literature and language professor, archivist*

Elmwood Park
Spina, Anthony Ferdinand *lawyer*

Elwood
Ligon, Demond L., Sr. *sales executive*

Eureka
Henry, Joseph Dean *music educator, director*
Staudenmeier, William John, Jr. *academic administrator, dean, sociology professor*

Evanston
Achenbach, Jan Drewes *engineering scientist*
Allred, Albert Louis *chemistry professor*
Arrington, Michael Browne *foundation administrator*
Backman, Vadim *biomedical engineer, educator*
Bazant, Zdenek Pavel *engineering educator*
Beatty, Virginia Lewis *librarian, archivist, consultant*
Belytschko, Ted *engineering educator*
Bethel, Kathleen Evonne *librarian*
Bienen, Henry Samuel *academic administrator, political scientist, educator*
Bloomer, William David *radiologist, oncologist, educator*
Bobco, William David, Jr. *consulting engineering company executive*
Borcover, Alfred Seymour *journalist*
Boye, Roger Carl *academic administrator, journalism educator*
Braeutigam, Ronald Ray *economics professor, educational association administrator*
Brazelton, William Thomas *chemical engineer, educator, dean*
Brendler, Charles Burgess *urologist, educator*
Brown, Laurie Mark *physicist, researcher*
Calkins, Tim *marketing professor*
Cao, Hui *physics and astronomy professor*
Carr, Stephen Howard *materials engineer, educator*
Cates, Jo Ann *library director*
Chang, R. P. H. *materials science educator*
Christian, Richard Carlton *dean, former advertising agency executive*
Colgate, J. Edward *mechanical engineering educator*
Conger, William Frame *artist, educator*
Corey, Gordon Richard *financial advisor, former utilities executive*
Crawford, James Weldon *psychiatrist, educator, administrator*
Crawford, Susan *library director, educator, editor, writer*
Creamer, Robert Allan *lawyer*
Dallos, Peter John *neurobiologist, educator*
Danilov, Victor Joseph *museum administrator, educator, writer*
Daskin, Mark Stephen *engineering educator*
Davis, Shani *Olympic athlete*
Davis, Stephen Howard *applied mathematics professor*
Deming, Thomas Edward *publishing executive*
Devinatz, Allen *retired mathematician, educator*
Dranove, David Stuart *business educator, consultant, economist*
Dumas, Lawrence B. *academic administrator*
Eberley, Helen-Kay *opera singer, recording industry executive, poet*
Enroth-Cugell, Christina Alma Elisabeth *neurophysiologist, educator*
Felknor, Bruce Lester *publishing executive, consultant, writer*
Fessler, Raymond R. *metallurgical engineering consultant*
Fine, Morris Eugene *materials engineer, educator*
Fisher, Andrew Taylor *computer software developer*
Frey, Donald Nelson *industrial engineer, educator, retired manufacturing executive*
Gaiha, Vishnu Das *cardiologist*
Galati, Frank Joseph *stage and opera director, educator, screen writer, actor*
Galvin, Kathleen Malone *communications educator*
Ghiglione, Loren Frank *journalism professor*
Gibbons, William Reginald, Jr. *poet, writer, translator, editor*
Godwin, Hilary A. *chemistry professor, research scientist*
Goldstick, Thomas Karl *biomedical engineering educator*
Gordon, Julie Peyton *foundation administrator*
Gordon, Robert James *economics professor*
Grunsfeld, Ernest Alton III *architect*
Hall, Bruce A. *music educator*
Hemke, Frederick L. *academic administrator*
Hoffman, Brian M. *chemistry professor*
Hughes, Edward F. X. *healthcare educator, preventive medicine physician*
Hurter, Arthur Patrick *economist, educator*
Ibers, James Arthur *chemist, educator*
Ionescu Tulcea, Cassius *research mathematician, educator*
Irons, William George *anthropology educator*
Jacobs, Donald P. *finance educator*
Jacobs, Norman Joseph *publishing executive*
Jain, Dipak Chand *dean, marketing educator, consultant*
Jennings, Hamlin Manson *materials scientist, educator*
Jerome, Joseph Walter *mathematics professor*
Jones, Robert Russell *retired magazine editor*
Kalai, Ehud *economist, researcher, educator*
Keer, Leon Morris *engineering educator*
Kertész, Imre *writer*
Khandekar, Janardan Dinkar *oncologist, educator*
Kotler, Philip *marketing educator, writer*
Krizek, Raymond John *engineering educator, consultant*
Kuenster, John Joseph *editor*
Kujala, Walfrid Eugene *musician, educator*
Lamb, Robert Andrew *molecular biologist, virologist, educator*
Lambert, Joseph Buckley *chemistry professor*
Larson, Paul William *public relations executive*
Lewis, Charles A. *foundation administrator*
Lewis, Dan Albert *education educator*
Macsai, John *retired architect*
Manin, Yuri Ivanovich *mathematician*
Margoliash, Emanuel *biochemist, educator*
Marks, Tobin Jay *chemistry educator*
Matkowsky, Bernard Judah *mathematician, educator*
McCarron, John Francis *editor*
McDonough, Bridget Ann *music theatre company director*
Medin, Douglas *psychology professor*
Menke, Allen Carl *retired manufacturing executive*
Miller, Stephen Herschel *surgeon, educator*
Mills, Edwin Smith *economics professor*
Mineka, Susan *psychology professor*
Moore, C. Bradley *chemistry professor*
Morrison, John Horton *lawyer, arbitrator*
Murphy, Gordon John *electrical engineer, educator*
Mustoe, Thomas Anthony *physician, plastic surgeon*
Neaman, Mark Robert *hospital administrator*
Nechin, Herbert Benjamin *lawyer*
Novales, Ronald Richards *zoologist, educator*
Oakes, Robert James *physics and astronomy professor*
Oh, John Kie-Chiang *political science professor, academic administrator*
Olmstead, William Edward *mathematics professor*
Olszewski, Wojciech *economist, mathematician*
Ottino, Julio Mario *engineering company executive, educator*
Otwell, Ralph Maurice *retired newspaper editor*
Peck, Abraham *editor, writer, educator, media consultant*
Peters, Gordon Benes *retired musician*
Peterson, Lance Robert *physician*
Peterson, Penelope Loraine *dean, education educator*
Power, Peggy Ann *elementary school educator*
Prince, Thomas Richard *accountant, educator*
Pritchard, Sarah Margaret *library director*
Reiss, Lenore Ann *language educator, retired secondary school educator*
Reiter, Stanley *economist, educator*
Richeson, Jennifer Anne *psychology professor, researcher*
Rielly, John Edward *educational association administrator*
Rittmann, Bruce Edward *environmental engineering educator, researcher*
Robbins, Henry Zane *public relations and marketing executive*
Robertson, David Alan *museum director, educator*
Sachtler, Wolfgang Max Hugo *chemistry professor*
Salem, Richard Allen *mediator*
Satterthwaite, Mark A. *economics professor*
Sawhney, Mohanbir S. *finance educator*
Schatz, George C. *chemist, educator*
Schofer, Joseph Landy *civil engineer, educator*
Scholten, Menno Nico *banking consultant*
Schwartz, Neena Betty *endocrinologist, educator*
Scott, Walter Dill *management educator*
Seidman, David N(athaniel) *materials scientist, engineer, educator*
Sener, Stephen Francis *oncologist, surgeon*
Shah, Surendra Poonamchand *engineering educator*
Sheldon, Mark *assistant dean*
Sheridan, James Edward *history professor*
Silverman, Richard Bruce *chemist, educator, biochemist*
Siniscalchi, Marciano *economist*
Smith, Spencer Bailey *engineering and business educator*
Sprang, Milton LeRoy *obstetrician, gynecologist, educator*
Stern, Louis William *marketing educator, consultant*
Stumpf, David Allen *pediatric neurologist*
Taflove, Allen *electrical engineer, educator, researcher, consultant*
Tanner, Martin Abba *statistician, educator*
Thrash, Patricia Ann *retired educational association administrator*
Tornabene, Russell C. *communications executive*
Traisman, Howard Sevin *retired pediatrician*
Ulmer, Melville Paul *physics and astronomy educator*
Van Duyne, Richard Palmer *analytical chemistry educator, chemical physics educator*
Van Ness, James Edward *electrical engineering educator*
Van Zanten, David Theodore *humanities educator*
Vick, Nicholas A. *neurologist*
Watson, Christopher *dean*
Weber, Arnold Robert *academic administrator*
Weertman, Johannes *materials science educator*
Weertman, Julia Randall *materials engineering educator*
Weil, Irwin *literature and language professor*
Weisbrod, Burton Allen *economist, educator*
Wessels, Bruce W. *materials scientist, educator, department chairman*
Widom, Jonathan *biology professor*
Wills, Garry *historian*
Wright, John *classics educator*
Wu, Tai Te *biological sciences and engineering educator*
Zelinsky, Daniel *mathematics professor*
Zimmerman, Mary Alice *performing arts educator*
Ziomek, Jonathan S. *journalist, educator*

Evergreen Park
Wigsmoen, Susan Catania *elementary school educator*
Zumerchik, John *urologist*

Flora
Shrum, John *equal rights officer*

Flossmoor
Cary, William Sterling *retired church executive*
Garrison, Ray Harlan *lawyer*
Pierce, Shelby Crawford *oil industry executive, consultant*
Sayler, Donna L. *secondary school educator, director*

Forest Park
Creighton, Robert Emmett *retired language educator, retired chaplain*

Forreston
Braker, William Paul *music educator*
Harn, Amy Helen *music educator, director*

Forsyth
Graf, Karl Rockwell *nuclear engineer*

Fox Lake
Smith, Justin Stuart *mathematics educator*

Fox River Grove
Abboud, Alfred Robert *banker, investor, consultant, director*

Frankfort
Burhoe, Brian Walter *automotive executive*
Chin, Davis *lawyer*

Franklin Park
Miller, Bryan Michael *music educator*
Simpson, Michael *retired metals service center executive*

Freeport
Giaimo, Paul Sebastian *English and philosophy educator*
Vogt, Lorna Corrine *retired librarian, small business owner*
Weaver, Michael Glenn *pharmacist*

Galena
Alexander, Barbara Leah Shapiro *clinical social worker*
Bezkorovainy, Anatoly *medical educator, retired biochemist*
Crandall, John Lynn *retired insurance company executive, consultant*
Sipiera, Paul P., Jr. *foundation administrator, retired geology and astronomy professor*

Galesburg
Coatney, Louis Robert *librarian, historian*
Haywood, Bruce *retired academic administrator*
Hellenga, Robert Riner *language educator, writer*
Mustain, Douglas Dee *lawyer*
Polay, Bruce *musician, conductor, educator*
Schwartzman, Peter David *environmental scientist, educator*
Taylor, Roger Lee *academic administrator, lawyer*

Galva
Everett, Reynolds Melville, Jr. *lawyer*
Swatos, William Henry, Jr. *priest, sociologist*

Geneva
Montgomery, Joel Robert *communications executive, consultant*
Tyler, Lloyd John *retired lawyer*
Young, Jack Allison *financial executive*

Genoa
Cromley, Jon Lowell *lawyer*

Gilman
Ireland, Herbert Orin *retired engineering educator*

Glen Carbon
Jarabak, Phyllis A. *music educator*
Lazerson, Earl Edwin *retired academic administrator*

Glen Ellyn
Anderson, Barbara Jean *biology professor*
Baloun, John Charles *retired wholesale distribution executive*
Bollendorf, Robert Fredrick *retired education educator, psychologist*
Conti, Paul Louis *management consulting company executive*
Cook, Joann Catherine *computer professor*
Cummings, Joan E. *health facility administrator, educator*
Cvengros, Joseph Michael *manufacturing company executive*
Dieter, Raymond Andrew, Jr. *physician, thoracic and vascular surgeon*
Emano, Dennis Jose Marmol *psychology professor*
Finley, Claudia D. *secondary school educator, consultant*
Frateschi, Lawrence Jan *economist, statistician, educator*
Holman, James Lewis *financial consultant, management consultant*
Hudson, Dennis Lee *lawyer, retired arbitrator, federal official*
King, Peggy Marsha *special education educator, researcher*
Mooring, F. Paul *physics editor*
Neurauter, Elizabeth Strain *secondary school educator*
Nunamaker, Susan Sun *mathematics professor*
O'Connell, Daniel James *lawyer*
Poromanska, Margarita Kirilova *science educator, environmental scientist*
Rothmaler, Peter Antell *mathematician, educator*
Sandrok, Richard William *lawyer*
Slusar, Linda *library and information scientist*

Glencoe
Dean, H. Clark *retired civil engineer, genealogist*
Isaacs, Roger David *public relations executive*
Milloy, Frank Joseph, Jr. *surgeon*
Nebenzahl, Kenneth *rare book and map dealer, author*
Perlberg, Jules Martin *lawyer*
Silver, Ralph David *financial planner*
Siske, Regina *artist*

Glendale Heights
Cook, Doris Marie *retired accountant, educator*

Glenview
Berkman, Michael G. *lawyer*
Blase, Anthony Idomeneus *retired electronics executive, writer, poet*
Brady, Sharon *engineering executive*
Brunner, Robert E. *engineering executive*
Bruns, Nicolaus, Jr. *retired agricultural products executive, lawyer, educator*
Casas, Laurie Ann *plastic surgeon*
Corley, Jenny Lynd Wertheim *elementary school educator*
Coulson, Elizabeth Anne *physical therapist, educator, state representative*
Dul, John A. *lawyer, electronics executive*
Farber, Isadore E. *psychologist, educator*
Flaum, Russell M. *engineering executive*
Franklin, Lynne *corporate communications specialist, writer*
Geller, William Alan *criminologist, consultant, protective services official*
Gillis, Marvin Bob *retired chemical executive, consultant*
Graff, Jeffrey G. *emergency physician*
Gresh, Philip M. *engineering executive*
Grubbs, Robert W. *computer services company executive*
Haebich, Arthur T. *retired thoracic surgeon*
Hagy, James C. *lawyer*
Hansen, Thomas J. *engineering executive*
Hickey, John Thomas *retired electronics company executive*
Hindman, Craig A. *engineering executive*
Hough, Winston *artist*
King, Billie Jean Moffitt *retired professional tennis player*
Kinigakis, Panagiotis *research scientist, engineer, inventor, writer*
Knox, James Edwin *lawyer*
Kropp, Ronald D. *engineering executive*
Levin, Donald Robert *business and finance executive, motion picture producer, professional sports team owner*
Marmet, Gottlieb John *lawyer*
Martel, Roland M. *engineering executive*
Mukoyama, James Hidefumi, Jr. *security firm executive*
Olson, Roy Arthur *retired government official*
Panarese, William C. *civil engineer*
Parry, David C. *engineering executive*
Rorig, Kurt Joachim *chemist, science association director, educator*
Santi, E. Scott *engineering executive*
Smith, Harold B. *manufacturing executive*
Speer, David Blakeney
Sutherland, Allan C. *engineering executive*
Van Zelst, Theodore William *civil engineer, engineering company executive*
Whipple, Matthew Robert *secondary school educator*
Wooten, James H., Jr. *lawyer, engineering executive*
Zentmyer, Hugh J. *engineering executive*

Godfrey
King, Ordie Herbert, Jr. *oral pathologist*

Granite City
Cowan, Robert Randall *science educator*
Humphrey, Owen Everett *retired education administrator*
Rarick, Philip Joseph *lawyer, retired state supreme court justice*

Grayslake
Cayari, Christopher *music educator*
Fonté, Richard W. *educational consultant, former academic administrator*

Great Lakes
Bienek, Diane Rose *research scientist*

Greenville
Filby, Ivan Leonard *management educator*

Griggsville
Evans, H. Todd *music educator*

Gurnee
Hall, Terry *accountant*
Sommerlad, Robert Edward *environmental research engineer*

Hanover
Bleveans, John *lawyer*

Harrisburg
Rushing, Philip Dale *retired social worker*

Harvey
Heilicser, Bernard Jay *emergency physician*

Harwood Heights
Rudel, Barbara Elizabeth *elementary school educator*

Hazel Crest
Freed, Melvyn Norris *retired educational association administrator, writer*

Hennepin
Bumgarner, James McNabb *judge*

Herrin
Gauto, Nelson Fernando *plastic surgeon, consumer products company executive*

Highland Park
Afterman, Allan B. *accountant, educator, financial consultant, researcher*
Bakalar, John Stephen *printing company and publishing executive*
Cohen, Burton David *food service executive, lawyer*
Dirsmith, Ronald *architect*
Dubin, Arthur Detmers *retired architect*
Gash, Lauren Beth *lawyer, state legislator*
Greenblatt, Miriam *writer, editor, educator*
Harris, Thomas L. *public relations executive*
Hershenson, Martha Bradford *history educator*
Hobson, Stephen Gilbert *conductor, music educator*
Hoseman, Daniel *lawyer*
Johnson, Curtis Lee *publishing executive, editor, writer*
Karol, Nathaniel H. *lawyer, consultant*
Korzenski, Robert M. *manufacturing executive*
Nelson, Richard David *lawyer*
Pattis, S. William *publishing executive*
Reed, Jan Stern *lawyer*
Rudo, Milton *retired manufacturing executive*
Rutenberg-Rosenberg, Sharon Leslie *retired journalist*
Schindel, Donald Marvin *retired lawyer*
Slavick, Ann Lillian *retired art educator*
Stein, Paula Jean Anne Barton *hotel real estate company executive, real estate broker*
Tobin, Calvin Jay *retired architect*
Tribbey, Fern *mathematics educator*
Uhlmann, Frederick Godfrey *securities trader*

Highwood
Brown, Lawrence Haas *retired banker*

Hillsboro
Mulch, Robert F., Jr. *physician*

Hillside
Savic, Jelena *technologist, educator*

Hines
Best, William Robert *internist, educator, dean*
Zvetina, James Raymond *pulmonologist*

Hinsdale
Brueschke, Erich Edward *physician, researcher, educator*
Dederick, Robert Gogan *economist*
Kaminsky, Manfred Stephan *physicist*
Kim, Micaela *speech pathology/audiology services professional*
Lonchyna, Vassyl A. *thoracic surgeon*
Mehuron, William Otto *retired federal official*
Unikel, Eva Taylor *interior designer*
Urbik, Jerome Anthony *financial consultant*
Whitney, William Elliot, Jr. *advertising agency executive*

Hoffman Estates
Block, Janice L. *lawyer*
Crowley, William C. *retail executive*
Dziezak, Judie D. *lawyer*
Good, Mark *retail executive*
Harker, William R. *lawyer*
Kahn, Elizabeth *language educator, department chairman*
Lee, Gregory A. *human resources specialist*
Lewis, Aylwin B. *retail executive, former food service company executive*
McCullough, Gary E. *education company executive*
Nicholas, Arthur Soterios *manufacturing executive*
Rooney, John Edward *communications company executive*
Zopp, Andrea Lynne *lawyer, retail executive*

Homewood
Olofsson, Daniel Joel *lawyer*
Parker, Eugene Newman *retired physicist, retired educator*
Schillings, Denny Lynn *retired history professor, educational and grants consultant*

Hoopeston
Hicks, Carol Ann *small business owner, educator*

Hudson
Mills, Frederick VanFleet *art educator, watercolorist*

Huntley
Balk, Alfred William *journalist*
Saporta, Jack *psychologist, educator*

Indian Head Park
Bamberger, Mary Ann *archivist, consultant*

Ingleside
D'Andrea, Dana M. *medical/surgical nurse, lawyer*

Irvington
Brown, Robert William *elementary school educator*

Itasca
Balasa, Mark Edward *investment consultant*
Civgin, Don *corporate financial executive*
Duncan, Sam K. *retail executive*
Gallagher, J. Patrick, Jr. *insurance company executive*
Porter, Ethel Mae *publishing executive*

Jacksonville
Findley, Paul *former congressman, author, educator*
Gallas, Martin Hans *librarian*
Hardin, Susan Jean *social studies educator, department chairman*
Johns, Beverley Anne Holden *special education administrator*
Kuster, Larry Donald *lawyer*

Jerseyville
Sharp, Elaine Cecile *obstetrician, gynecologist*

Joliet
Easton, Kenneth Glenn *retired utilities executive*
Holmgren, Myron Roger *social sciences educator*
Johnston, James Robert *library director*
Kaffer, Roger Louis *bishop*
Layman, Dale Pierre *retired medical educator, researcher, writer*
Lenard, George Dean *lawyer*
McMiller, Anita Williams *leasing company executive*
Ring, Alvin Manuel *pathologist, educator*
Teas, Richard Harper *lawyer*
Tokatlioglu, Theresa Diaz Lopez *elementary school educator*

Justice
Casselle, Corene *pre-school educator*

Kankakee
Roy, Sudipta D. *education educator*

Kenilworth
Bott, Harold Sheldon *accountant, management consultant*
Bowen, Gilbert Willard *minister*
Cook, Stanton R. *media company executive*
Corrigan, John Edward, Jr. *retired banker, lawyer*
McKittrick, William Wood *lawyer*
Schneider-Criezis, Susan Marie *architect*
Weaver, Clifford Lee *retired lawyer, winery owner*
Weaver, Donna Rae *winery executive*

La Grange
Hoisington, Steven H. *industrial engineer*
Kerr, Alexander Duncan, Jr. *lawyer*
Mehlenbacher, Dohn Harlow *civil engineer, consultant*
Zethmayr-Lolakos, Ellen *music educator, writer*

La Grange Park
Butler, Margaret Kampschaefer *retired computer scientist*
Hixon, Carl Kilmer *retired advertising executive, writer*
Perkins, William H., Jr. *retired finance company executive*

Ladd
Shea, Mary Frances *retired elementary school educator*

Lake Barrington
Worrell, Sharyn Dianne Kelley *volunteer, retired flight attendant*

Lake Bluff
Fletcher, Dorothy Jean *hospital administrator, educator*
Fryburger, Vernon Ray, Jr. *advertising executive, finance educator*
Griem, John Michael *management consultant*
Kyncl, John Jaroslav *pharmacologist*
Marozsan, John Robert *retired publishing company executive*
Schreiber, George Richard *publishing executive, writer*
Snader, Jack Ross *retired publishing company executive*

Lake Forest
Begley, Christopher B. *pharmaceutical executive*
Benson, Cedric *professional football player*
Bramhall, Robert Richard *management consultant*
Brewer, Paul Huie *advertising executive, artist, portrait painter*
Carroll, Barry Joseph *manufacturing and real estate executive*
Carter, Donald Patton *retired advertising executive*
Chieger, Kathryn Jean *consumer products company executive*
Covington, George Morse *lawyer*
Crawford, Robert W., Jr. *furniture rental company executive*
Doyle, Joseph E. *lawyer, manufacturing executive*
Dreimann, Leonhard *manufacturing executive*
Emerson, William Harry *retired lawyer*
Feinberg, Jeffrey Enoch *religious studies educator, writer*
Galatz, Henry Francis *lawyer*
Griese, Brian *professional football player*
Grossman, Rex *professional football player*
Hamilton, Peter Bannerman *manufacturing executive, lawyer*
Hammar, Lester Everett *retired manufacturing executive*
Howard, John Lawrence *lawyer*
Johnson, Richard Darrell *management consultant*
Jones, Gordon Kempton *dentist, retired military officer*
Kelly, Daniel John *physician*
Keyser, Richard Lee *distribution company executive*
Krasnewich, Kathryn *water transportation executive*
Lambert, John Boyd *chemical engineer, consultant*
Larson, Peter N. *manufacturing executive*
Leemputte, Peter G. *manufacturing executive*
Levy, Nelson Louis *immunologist, educator, surgeon*
Loux, P. Ogden *distribution company executive*
McCaskey, Michael B. *professional football team executive*
McCoy, Dustan Elwood *manufacturing executive, lawyer*
Miller, Arthur Hawks, Jr. *librarian, archivist*
Mohr, Roger John *retired advertising agency executive*
Morell, William Nelson, Jr. *retired foreign trade association executive, government agency administrator*
Murphy, Karen *sports association executive*
O'Mara, Thomas Patrick *manufacturing executive*
Orton, Kyle *professional football player*
Palmer, Ann Therese Darin *lawyer*
Pawl, Ronald Phillip *neurosurgery educator*
Rand, Kathy Sue *public relations executive, consultant*
Romans, Donald Bishop *manufacturing executive*
Ross, Robert Evan *bank executive*
Ryan, James T. *wholesale distribution executive*
Sadri, Ahmad *sociologist, educator*
Salter, Edwin Carroll *retired pediatrician*
Schulze, Franz, Jr. *critic, educator*
Seaman, Irving, Jr. *banker*
Sherrill, Gregg M. *automotive executive*
Sikorovsky, Eugene Frank *retired lawyer*
Smith, Brian J. *lawyer*
Smith, Lovie *professional football coach*
Stecko, Paul T. *packaging company executive*
Swanton, Virginia Lee *writer, publisher*
Swift, Edward Foster III *investment banker*
Taylor, Barbara Ann Olin *writer, educational consultant*
Urlacher, Brian Keith *professional football player*
Weinberg, Milton, Jr. *retired cardiovascular and thoracic surgeon*
Weston, Arthur Walter *chemist, consultant, retired chemicals executive*
Weston, Dawn Thompson *artist, researcher*
Wilbur, Richard Sloan *medical association administrator, physician*
Young, Ronald Faris *commodities trader*
Ysasi-Diaz, Gloria *wholesale distribution executive*

Lake In The Hills
Kay, Dennis Matthew *retired publishing company official*
Shirazi, Eman Ali *dentist*

Lake Zurich
Juknelis, Nick *music educator*
Krolopp, Rudolph William *retired industrial designer, consultant*
Schultz, Carl Herbert *real estate developer*

Lanark
Abbott, David Henry *manufacturing executive*

Lebanon
Jewett, Thomas O. *science educator, writer*
Ottinger, David *art educator, artist*

Lemont
Anitescu, Mihai *computer scientist, mathematician*
Doebert, Sandra L. *school system administrator*
Hayes, Randy Alan *family therapist, process improvement specialist*
Williams, Jack Marvin *research chemist*

Libertyville
Baraniewski, Henry M. *surgeon*
Bush, Eugene Nyle *retired pharmacologist, pharmacist*
DeSanto, James John *lawyer*
Grote, Jonathan *chemist, researcher*
Maczulski, Margaret Louise *event marketing professional, meeting manager*
Mahoney, Kathleen Marie *social studies educator*
Pegg, Richard Anderson *curator*
Rallo, Douglas *lawyer*
Ritson, Scott Campbell *management consultant*
Szini, Istvan Janos *electronics engineer*
True, Raymond Stephen *editor, writer*
Trzyna, Chris *physical education educator*
Tullman, Glen *management consultant*

Lincoln
Wilson, Robert Allen *religion educator*

Lincolnshire
Anderson, David J. *manufacturing executive*
Campbell, David D. *consumer products company executive*
Fradin, Russell P. *human resources company executive, former computer company executive*
Michalik, John James *legal association administrator*
Para, Gerard Albert *lawyer, real estate broker, consultant*
Ryan, John *lawyer*
Ryan, John M. *lawyer, human resources company executive*
Schauble, John Eugene *physical education educator*
Simes, Stephen Mark *pharmaceutical executive*
Zorc, Renee *school librarian*

Lincolnwood
Beck, Cynthia Marie *archivist, researcher*
Carroll, Howard William *state legislator*
Earnest, Craig Hopkins *psychologist, consultant*
Kamensky, Marvin *lawyer*
Lebedow, Aaron Louis *consulting company executive*
Zaremski, Miles Jay *lawyer*

Lindenhurst
Eron, Madeline Marcus *psychologist*
Theis, Peter Frank *engineering executive*

Lisle
Colbert, Marvin Jay *retired internist, educator*
Hayes, Richard J., Jr. *engineering company executive*
Hecht, Louis Alan *lawyer*
Krehbiel, Frederick August, II, *electronics executive*
Krehbiel, John H., Jr. *retired electronics company executive*
Ruyle-Hullinger, Elizabeth Smith (Beth Ruyle) *municipal financial advisor, consultant*
Slark, Martin P. *electronics executive*
Smith, Jared Russell William *research executive, research scientist, consultant, poet*
Townsley, Lisa Gail *mathematics professor*
Ware, George Henry *botanist*

Litchfield
Talley, Hayward Leroy *communications executive*

Lombard
Ahlstrom, Ronald Gustin *artist*
Bachop, William Earl, Jr. *retired anatomist, zoologist*
Barnholt, Brandon K. *retail executive*
Benning, Joseph Raymond *principal*
Garrett, Paul James *financial planner*
Hambley, Douglas Frederick *geological and environmental engineer*
Harris, Jeff M. *waste management executive*
Henkin, Robert Elliott *nuclear medicine physician*
McCoy, Jeanie Shearer *analytical chemist, consultant*

Long Grove
Ausman, Robert K. *surgeon, research and development company executive*
Conway, John K. *lawyer*
Davis, Britton Anthony *retired lawyer*
Obert, Paul Richard *lawyer, manufacturing executive*

Loves Park
Dixon, John James *music educator*

Lovington
Duncan, Linda B. *social sciences educator*

Machesney Park
Vaughn, Linda Marie *municipal official*

Macomb
Bauerly, Ronald John *marketing educator*
Chu, Felix T. *school librarian*
Dexter, Donald Harvey *surgeon, educator*
Ellickson, Jean *anthropology educator*
Goldfarb, Alvin *academic administrator*
Hayes, Paul Robert *retired field and clinical experiences coordinator*
Hopper, Stephen Rodger *hospital administrator*
Kim, Chung-Ha *music educator*
Merrett, Christopher Douglas *geographer, educator*
Walker, Tammie Leigh *music educator*
Walzer, Norman Charles *retired economics professor*
Wehrman, Elizabeth Ann *music educator*

Madison
Purdes, Alice Marie *retired adult education educator*

Mahomet
Thompson, Margaret M. *physical education educator*

Maple Park
Carter, Ethel Ilene *secondary school educator*

Marengo
Franks, Herbert Hoover *lawyer*
Mrkvicka, Edward Francis, Jr. *writer, finance company executive*

Marion
Crane, Hugh Wingate *railroad executive*
Munas, Falies A. *psychiatric physician*

Markham
Peacock, Marilyn Claire *retired primary school educator*

Marseilles
Nellett, Gaile H. *adult education educator*

Maryville
Stark, Patricia Ann *psychologist*

Matteson
van der Hoek, Sherry A. *counselor*
Wigell, Raymond George *lawyer*

Mattoon
Black, Todd Ronald *music educator*
Horsley, Jack Everett *retired bank executive, writer, lawyer*
Phipps, John Randolph *retired army officer*

Maywood
Akhavan-Heidari, Mehdi *cardiothoracic surgeon*
Albain, Kathy S. *oncologist*
Aranha, Gerard V. *surgeon*
Barbato, Anthony L. *hospital administrator, medical educator*
Bermes, Edward William, Jr. *biochemist, educator*
Biller, Jose *neurologist, educator*
Dado, Diane Valentina *plastic and reconstructive surgeon*
Flanigan, Robert Charles *urologist, educator*
Gianopoulos, John George *obstetrician*
Hanin, Israel *pharmacologist, educator*
Hummel, Patricia *pediatric nurse practitioner, researcher*
Lid, Glenn David *chemistry educator*
Light, Terry Richard *orthopedic hand surgeon*
Miele, Lucio *physician, medical researcher, pharmacologist*
Moran, John Francis *cardiologist*
Nand, Sucha *medical educator*
Newman, Barry Marc *pediatric surgeon*
Origitano, Thomas Charles *neurological surgeon*
Schultz, Richard Michael *biochemistry educator, researcher*

Stankiewicz, James A. *otolaryngologist*
Warpeha, Raymond Leonard *surgeon, educator*
Wheeler, John S., Jr. *urologist*

Mc Gaw Park
Bernardo, Angelito Alday *nephrologist, medical products executive*

Mchenry
Chisu, Ioan *artist*

Melrose Park
Bernick, Carol Lavin *consumer products company executive*
Cernugel, William John *consumer products company executive, distributor*
Giancola, James J. *bank executive*
Klein, Lloyd William *cardiologist, researcher*
Kloster, Carol Good *wholesale distribution executive*
Lai, Robert *urologist, surgeon*
Marino, V. James *consumer products company executive*
Schmidt, Gary P. *lawyer, personal care industry executive*

Metamora
Harbers, Rebecca Ann *physical education educator*

Mokena
Hunter, Steven L. *medical center administrator*
Sangmeister, George Edward *lawyer, consultant, congressman*

Moline
Arnell, Richard Anthony *radiologist*
Cleaver, William Lehn *lawyer*
Gleich, Carol S. *health professions education executive*
Jenkins, James Robert *lawyer, manufacturing executive*
Johnson, Mary Lou *lay worker, educator*
Jones, Nathan Jerome *farm machinery manufacturing company executive*
Lane, Robert W. *farm equipment manufacturing executive*
Mack, Michael J., Jr. *manufacturing executive*
Maroney, Sharon A *special education educator*
Middleton, Marc Stephen *corporate insurance risk manager*
Penn, J. B. *economist, former federal agency administrator*
Stodt, F. Chloe *piano educator*
Taylor, Byron Keith *industrial engineer*

Monmouth
Godde, James Scott *molecular biologist*

Morris
Rooks, John Newton *lawyer*

Morton Grove
McKenna, Andrew James *wholesale distribution, printing company, sports association executive*
Smolyansky, Julie *consumer products company executive*
Vega, Steve *poet, protective services official*

Mount Prospect
Eliason, Birdell *painter, educator*
Epstein, Stephen Roger *financial executive*
Sayers, Gale *computer company executive, retired professional football player*

Mount Sterling
Tracy, Patrick F. *food products executive*

Mount Vernon
Hall, Sharon Gay *retired language educator, artist*
Harvey, Morris Lane *lawyer*
LeMay, Nicholas K. *broadcast executive*
Withers, W. Russell, Jr. *broadcast executive*

Mundelein
Ackley, Robert O. *lawyer*

Murphysboro
McCann, Maurice Joseph *lawyer*

Naperville
Arzoumanidis, Gregory G. *chemist*
Bell, Bradley J. *water treatment company executive*
Benson, Kevin E. *transportation executive*
Briseno, Kathleen *education educator*
Broad, Matthew *lawyer*
Bufalino, Vincent John *cardiologist, medical administrator*
Calamos, John Peter, Sr. *brokerage house executive*
Corvino, Beth Byster *lawyer*
Cowlishaw, Mary Lou *government educator*
Crawford, Raymond Maxwell, Jr. *management consultant*
Desch, Theodore Edward *retired insurance company executive, lawyer*
Dombeck, Harold Arthur *insurance company executive*
Everett, C(harles) Curtis *retired lawyer*
Finzer, Carolyn Lauing *artist*
Folk, Frank Anton *surgeon, educator*
Fritz, Roger Jay *management consultant*
Gilmore, Brenda René *literature and language educator, theater director*
Gracey, Paul C., Jr. *lawyer, utilities executive*
Grimley, Jeffrey Michael *dentist*
Holba Puacz, Jeanne *librarian, educator*
Joyce, William H. *engineering company executive, chemical engineer*
Katai, Andrew Andras *chemical company executive*
Kotynek, George Roy *mechanical engineer, educator, marketing executive*
Landsman, Stephen N. *lawyer*
Larson, Mark Edward, Jr. *lawyer, educator, financial planner*
McCallum, Gerald Christopher *clinical psychologist*
Miller, Charles E. *gynecologist*
Modery, Richard Gillman *retired marketing and sales executive*
Nortell, Bruce *lawyer*
Penisten, Gary Dean *entrepreneur*
Pollak, Raymond *general and transplant surgeon*
Prabhu, Krish Anant *telecommunications industry executive, educator*
Raccah, Dominique Marcelle *publisher*
Rosenthal, Edward Leonard *secondary school educator*
Sellers, Gregory Jude *physicist*
Shanine, George *sales executive, information technology executive*
Sherren, Anne Terry *chemistry professor*
Smetana, Mark *food products executive*
Snyder, Carl *information technology executive*
Stangl, Peter E. *transportation executive*
Strobel, Russ M. *gas industry executive, lawyer*
Tan, Li-Su Lin *accountant, insurance company executive, consultant*
Tibble, Douglas Clair *lawyer*
Vanagas, Rimantas (Ray) Andrius (Ray Vanagas) *entrepreneur, real estate developer, real estate company executive*
Vora, Manu Kishandas *chemical engineer, consultant*
Wake, Richard W. *food products executive*
Wake, Thomas G. *food products executive*
Wilde, Harold Richard *college president*
Zinger, Michael *reproductive endocrinologist*

Nashville
Barber, Donald Gene, Jr. *purchasing agent*
Karmeier, Lloyd A. *state supreme court justice*

New Baden
Franke, Louise Anna *early childhood educator, farmland manager*

New Lenox
Heffernan, Debra Jane *administrator*

Niles
Beton, John Allen *communications company executive*
Ditkowsky, Kenneth K. *lawyer*
Herb, Marvin J. *food products executive*
Roepenack, Dwight Elmer *public health service officer*
Schyvinck, Christine *electronics executive*

Normal
Alferink, Larry Allen *psychology professor*
Bender, Paul Edward *lawyer*
Brehm, Joan M. *social sciences educator*
Brown, Lauren Evans *zoologist, researcher, educator*
Conant, Brian *secondary school educator*
Cooley, William Emory, Jr. *radiologist*
Devinatz, Victor Gary *industrial relations specialist, educator*
Laudner, Kevin *athletic trainer, educator*
Miller, Wilma Hildruth *education educator*
Olsen, Patrice Elizabeth *history professor, photographer*
Presley, John Woodrow *academic administrator*
Rochelle, Victor Cleanthus *retired lawyer*
Shields, John Charles *literature educator*
Stevenson, Cheryl D. *science educator, researcher*
Trouille, Mary Seidman *foreign language educator*
Ward, Dane Michael *academic administrator*

Norridge
Petrakis, Myron Titos *retired mechanical engineer*

North Barrington
Hogan, Harlan Robert *voice-over actor*

North Chicago
Barsano, Charles Paul *medical educator, dean*
Chedid, Antonio *pathologist, educator, researcher*
Gall, Eric Papineau *internist, educator*
Hawkins, Richard Albert *medical educator, administrator*
Hutchinson, Douglas K. *chemist*
Kim, Yoon Berm *immunologist, educator*
Loga, Sanda *physicist, researcher*
Nair, Velayudhan *pharmacologist, educator, academic administrator*
Sierles, Frederick Stephen *psychiatrist, educator*

Northbrook
Abbey, G(eorge) Marshall *lawyer, retired health facility administrator*
Ben-Arie, Ronit Peleg *elementary school educator*
Boettcher, Robert Walter *civil engineer*
Bohlender, Hugh Darrow *lawyer*
Brune, Catherine S. *insurance company executive*
Byun, Michael *plastic surgeon*
Clarey, John Robert *executive recruiter, consultant*
Colburn, David Dunton *investment advisor*
Cripe, Frederick F. *insurance company executive*
Crockett, Joan M. *insurance company executive*
Cruikshank, John W. III *insurance agent*
Cucco, Ulisse P. *retired obstetrician, gynecologist*
Di Spigno, Guy Joseph *industrial psychologist, international management consultant*
Edelson, Ira J. *venture capitalist*
Feibel, Frederick Arthur *financial consultant*
Gratalo, John, Jr. *banker, small business owner*
Hale, Danny Lyman *insurance company executive*
Hindo, Walid Afram *radiology educator, researcher*
Hohmann, James E. *insurance company executive*
Kahn, Sandra S. *psychotherapist*
Keehn, Silas *retired bank executive*
King, Robert Charles *biologist, educator*
Lapin, Harvey I. *lawyer*
Levenfeld, Milton Arthur *lawyer*
Levy, Arnold S(tuart) *real estate company executive*
Liddy, Edward M. *insurance company executive*
McCabe, Michael J. (Mick) *insurance executive, lawyer*
Metz, Adam S. *real estate company executive*
Perelman, Jeffrey E. *real estate company executive*
Pesmen, Sandra (Mrs. Harold William Pesmen) *editor, educator*
Pike, Robert William *insurance company executive, lawyer*
Pulsifer, Edgar Darling *retired leasing and sales company executive*
Roche, Michael J. *insurance company executive*
Rosemarin, Carey Stephen *lawyer*
Ross, Debra Benita *marketing executive, jewelry designer*
Ruebenson, George E. *insurance company executive*
Ruter, Allan J. *literature and language educator*
Sernett, Richard Patrick *lawyer*
Sewright, Charles William, Jr. *mortgage banking advisory services company executive*
Simonson, Eric A. *insurance company executive*
Sorenson, Steven P. *insurance company executive*
Sprieser, Judith A. *former software company executive*
Sudbrink, Jane Marie *sales and marketing executive*
Sylla, Casey J. *insurance company executive*
Wajer, Ronald Edward *management consultant*
Walker, Joan H. *insurance company executive*
Wallace, Harry Leland *lawyer*
Warchol, Judith Marie *small business owner*
Wilson, Thomas Joseph *insurance company executive*

Northfield
Carlin, Donald Walter *retired food products executive, consultant*
Grimes, Sally *marketing professional*
Hadley, Stanton Thomas *manufacturing executive, director, lawyer*
Irgang, Carole A. *marketing executive*
Knight, James Atwood *manufacturing executive*
Lubawski, James Lawrence *healthcare consultant*
Lynch, Kirsten *food products executive*
Mamet, David Alan *playwright, scriptwriter*
McLevish, Timothy R. *food products executive*
Pratt, Murray Lester *manufacturing executive*
Rosenfeld, Irene B. *food products company executive*
Shabica, Charles Wright *geologist, earth science educator*
Shillestad, John Gardner *diversified financial services company executive*
Smeds, Edward William *retired food company executive*
Sneed, Paula Ann *food products executive*
Stepan, Frank Quinn *chemicals executive*
Stepan, Frank Quinn, Jr., (F. Quinn Stepan Jr.) *chemical company executive*
Vilim, Nancy Catherine *advertising executive*
Zupko, Mischa Sarché *composer, church music director*

Northlake
Haack, Richard Wilson *retired police officer*

O Fallon
Voellger, Gary A. *business consulting executive, retired air force officer*

Oak Brook
Alvarez, Ralph *food products executive*
Barnes, Karen Kay *lawyer*
Bennett, Margaret Airola *lawyer*
Biedron, Theodore John *publishing and advertising executive*
Christian, Joseph Ralph *physician*
Ciccarone, Richard Anthony *financial executive*
Congalton, Susan Tichenor *lawyer*
DeLorey, John Alfred *printing company executive*
Dillon, Mary *food products executive*
Ding, Jianchi *embryologist, researcher*
Duerinck, Louis T. *retired rail transportation executive, lawyer*
Fenton, Tim *food service executive*
Fields, Janice L. *food service executive*
Floersch, Richard *human resources specialist*
Grimes, Steven P. *corporate financial executive*
Hodnik, David F. *retail company executive*
Hoffmann, Joan Carol *retired academic dean*
Iles, Eileen Marie *bank executive, risk management consultant, accountant*
Imran, Ayesha *internist*
John, Richard C. *enterprise development organization executive*
Klinger, Gail Greaves *art educator, illustrator*
Mlsna, Kathryn Kimura *lawyer*
Nelson, Robert Eddinger *retired management consultant*
O'Brien, Walter Joseph, II, *lawyer*
Oldfield, E. Lawrence *lawyer*
Paull, Matthew H. *food service executive*
Peckenpaugh, Robert Earl *investment advisor*
Santona, Gloria *lawyer, food products executive*
Skinner, James A. (James A. Skinner) *food products executive*
Spohr, Earl Clyde *retired investment advisor, military officer*
Thompson, Don *food products executive*

Oak Forest
Kogut, Kenneth Joseph *engineer, consultant*

Oak Lawn
Jachna, Joseph David *photographer, educator*
McSweeney, Sean Thomas *director*
Minarik, Carol T. *elementary school educator*
Sullivan, Michael *writer, retired mathematics professor*

Oak Park
Adelman, William John *retired academic administrator, industrial relations specialist*
Cannon, Patrick Francis *public relations executive*
Clark, John Peter III *engineer, consultant*
Devereux, Timothy Edward *advertising executive*
Fisher, Lawrence Edgar *market research executive, anthropologist*
Greer, Julianna Patterson *not-for-profit administrator*
Hiestand, Edgar Leroy *minister*
Matsuda, Takayoshi *surgeon, educator, biomedical researcher*
Schubert, Blake H. *lawyer*
Sengpiehl, Paul Marvin *lawyer, retired state official*
Varchmin, Thomas Edward *public health service officer*
Venerable, Shirley Marie *retired gifted and talented educator*
Young, Jessica S.E. *secondary school educator*

Oakbrook Terrace
Becker, Robert Jerome *allergist, consultant*
Hegenderfer, Jonita Susan *public relations executive*
Keller, Dennis James *management educator*
Tang, George Chickchee *investment company executive*
Taylor, Ronald Lee *academic administrator*

Oakland
Eriksen, Barbara Ann *writer, researcher*

Oregon
Haynes, Gary Allen *photojournalist, editor*

Orland Park
Antia, Kersey H. *industrial and clinical psychologist, consultant*
Burfeind, Betty Ruth *retired secondary school educator, coach*
Carroll, Michael F. *lawyer*
Drugas, Theodore George *retired surgeon*

Oswego
Johnson, Dawn Sundene *chemistry educator*

Ottawa
Ballowe, James *writer, educator*
Thornton, Edmund B. *philanthropist*

Palatine
Bassi, Suzanne Howard *retired secondary school educator, volunteer*
Bokhari, Naila Qureshi *mathematician, educational consultant*
Cotsakis, Patricia Joan *music educator*
Hershenhorn, Robert Gene *bank executive*
Kieft, Gerald Nelson *mechanical engineer*
Pohl, Frederik *freelance/self-employed writer*
Spinner, Lee Louis *accountant*
Victor, Michael Gary *lawyer, physician*
Zamarin, Ronald George *lawyer*

Palos Heights
Hassert, Derrick Lawrence *psychology professor*

Palos Hills
Crawley, Vernon Obadiah *academic administrator*
Mc Intyre, James R. *history professor, researcher*
Skender, Joseph *construction executive*

Palos Park
Nelson, Lawrence Evan *manufacturing executive, consultant*

Park Forest
Billig, Etel Jewel *theater director, actress*
Dalke, Carl D. *school system administrator, consultant*
Goodrich, John Bernard *lawyer, consultant*
Orr, Marcia *primary school educator, consultant, director*
Williams, Jack Raymond *civil engineer*

Park Ridge
Albert, Elizabeth Franz (Mrs. Henry B. Albert) *investor, artist, conservationist*
Bitran, Jacob David *internist*
Campbell, Bruce Crichton *hospital administrator*
Carr, Gilbert Randle *retired railroad executive*
Delany, Jim (James Edward Delany) *sports association administrator, lawyer*
Ewald, Robert Frederick *insurance company executive, consultant*
Hegarty, Mary Frances *lawyer*
Kenney, John Patrick *dentist*
LaRue, Paul Hubert *retired lawyer*
Matthews, Roy S. *management consultant*
Pannke-Smith, Peggy *regional vice chairperson*
Pippen, Jennifer Lynn *therapist, consultant*
Russell, William Steven *treasurer*
Samuels, Brian Louis *oncologist, researcher*
Taillon, Armand Philip *mechanical engineer*
Wasko, Steven E. *lawyer*
White, John Vincent *surgeon, consultant*
Wilson, George Malcolmson *application developer*
Zimmermann, John Joseph *lawyer*

Pekin
Dancey, Charles Lohman *retired newspaper executive*
Miller, Ronald H. *energy executive*

Peoria
Allen, Lyle Wallace *lawyer*

Banwart, Sidney C. *human resources executive*
Bertschy, Timothy L. *lawyer*
Buda, James B. *lawyer, manufacturing executive*
Budzinski, Ronald J. *architect*
Burritt, David B. *manufacturing executive*
Chamberlain, Joseph Miles *retired astronomer, educator*
Coletta, Ralph John *retired lawyer*
Frederick, Richard C. *emergency physician, educator*
Golan, Kim Marie *facility interior designer*
Grebner, Bernice Prill *author, astrological counselor*
Heiple, James Dee *retired state supreme court justice*
Hindi, Riyadh *engineering educator, researcher*
Inman, Samantha Mae *music educator*
Kelly, Grace Dentino *secondary school educator*
Lanzino, Giuseppe *physician*
Levenick, Stuart L. *manufacturing executive*
Lichtenstein, Steven Jay *ophthalmologist*
McConnell, John Thomas *publishing executive*
Meriden, Terry *physician*
Mihm, Michael Martin *federal judge*
Murphy, Sharon Margaret *retired communications educator*
Nielsen, Harald Christian *retired chemist, researcher*
Oberhelman, Douglas R. *tractor company executive*
O'Brien, Daniel Robert *lawyer*
Owens, James W. *manufacturing executive*
Parsons, Donald James *retired bishop*
Parsons, Richard Hugo *lawyer*
Perrilles, Angela Terese *physical therapist*
Peters, Margaret Myrl *retired music educator*
Prusak, Maximilian Michael *lawyer*
Sanderson, Kenneth Jerome *school system administrator, consultant*
Saxon, Randall Lee *pastor, author, educator*
Shaheen, Gerald L. *manufacturing executive*
Vaughan, David John *corporate financial executive*
Vittecoq, Gerard R. *manufacturing executive*
Vroman, David Cole *music educator*
Walker, Philip Chamberlain, II, *health facility administrator*
Winget, Walter Winfield *retired lawyer*
Woods, Michael Lee *lawyer*
Wunning, Steven H. *manufacturing executive*
Xia, Kaiming *mechanical engineer*

Peotone
Kanosky, Albert Leo *history educator, small business owner*

Peru
Carus, Milton Blouke *children's periodicals publisher*

Petersburg
Wood, Harlington, Jr. *federal judge*

Pinckneyville
Cawvey, Clarence Eugene *retired physician*
Johnson, Don Edwin *lawyer*

Plainfield
Chakrabarti, Subrata Kumar *marine research engineer*
D'Arcy, Margaret Jeanette *volunteer*
Matlock, B. Jane *science educator*
Schinderle, Robert Frank *retired hospital administrator*
Serna, Phillip Woodrow *music educator, musician*
Vargo, Louise Ann *landscape artist, music educator*

Pleasant Plains
Thomas, Evelyn B. *agricultural products supplier*

Pontiac
Ewing, Thomas William *congressman, lawyer*

Princeton
Collins, N. Dana *art gallery owner, consultant, retired art educator*
Webber, Adam Brooks *science educator*

Prospect Heights
Aldinger, William F. III *diversified financial services company executive*
Byrne, Michael Joseph *manufacturing executive*
Cloney, Terence J. *lawyer*
Leopold, Mark F. *lawyer*
Lynch, William Thomas, Jr. *advertising executive*
Mooney, Timothy *playwright, actor, theater director*
Robinson, Martin (Marty Robinson) *television and radio broadcaster, media consultant*

Quincy
Centanni, Ross J. *engineering executive*
Gehrich, Leonora Suppan *artist, musician, German literature educator*
Mallory, Troy L. *accountant*
Reynolds, Judith Amy *nutritionist, consultant, animal scientist, educator*
Tomczak, Patricia Ann *dean, archivist*
Tyer, Travis Earl *librarian, consultant*

Richton Park
Nevins, Patrick Fredrick *librarian*
Pierce, Mary E. *retired elementary school educator, public relations consultant*
Piucci, Virginio Louis *academic administrator*

River Forest
Batlivala, Robert Bomi D. *oil industry executive, economics professor*
Carroll, Donna M. *academic administrator*
Coe, Donald Kirk *retired academic administrator*
Douglas, Kenneth Jay *food products executive*
Jackson, William Vernon *Latin American studies and library science educator*
Moore, Vernon John, Jr. *pediatrician, consultant, lawyer*
O'Meara, Thomas Franklin *priest, educator*
Stephens, Michael *library and information scientist, educator*
Tiesenga, Marvin Francis *surgeon*
Wirsching, Charles Philipp, Jr. *retired brokerage house executive, securities trader*

River Grove
Litzsinger, Richard Mark *retail executive*
Stanton, Kathryn *retail executive*
Stein, Thomas Henry *social sciences educator*

Riverside
Dengler, Robert Anthony *management consultant*
Dunn, Barbara Ann *language educator*
Smith, Ronald Forrest *retired history educator*
Van Cura, Joyce Bennett *librarian*

Riverwoods
Bartlett, Robert William *lawyer*
Douglas, Bruce Lee *oral and maxillofacial surgeon, occupational and geriatric health educator, consultant*
Georgiadis, Margaret H. (Margo) *finance company executive*
Gold, Deidra D. *lawyer*
Guthrie, Roy A. *financial company executive*
Hochschild, Roger C. *finance company executive*
Mandel, Karyl Lynn *accountant*
Nelms, David W. *finance company executive*
Offereins, Diane M. *finance company executive*
Smith, E. Follin *retired energy executive*

Robinson
Mallard, Carrie Charlene *science educator*
Wolfe, Ellen Darlene *school librarian, elementary school educator*
Wolven, Ann Reed *literature and language professor, journalist*

Rochester
Mashbern, William Allen *minister, retired religious organization administrator*
Petterchak, Janice A. *writer*

Rock Island
Anderson, Richard Charles *geology educator*
Bahls, Steven Carl *academic administrator, educator*
Banas, John Stanley *obstetrician, gynecologist*
Horstmann, James Douglas *retired academic administrator*
Kirklin-Darif, Dianna Lynn *small business owner*
Lardner, Henry Petersen (Peter Lardner) *insurance company executive*
Leinicke, Kris Gayman *museum director, educator*
Rafferty, Genevieve Kennedy *social service agency administrator*
Symons, Van Jay *humanities educator*

Rockford
Albert, Janyce Louise *human resources specialist, retired business educator, banker, consultant*
Aniol, Scott Michael *pastor*
Bippus, David Paul *manufacturing executive*
Borling, John Lorin *military officer*
Clodius, Robert LeRoy *retired economist*
Cyrs, Michael Thomas *lawyer*
Doran, Thomas George *bishop*
Egan, Terrence *foundation administrator*
Eliason, Jon Tate *electrical engineer*
Gieras, Jacek Franciszek *engineering educator, research scientist*
Gregory, Dola Bell *bishop, customer service administrator*
Heerens, Robert Edward *physician*
Heflin, Tom Pat *artist*
Homewood, Elizabeth Holmes Nash *elementary school educator*
Hoshaw, Lloyd *retired historian, educator*
Howard, John Addison *former academic administrator*
Jacobi, Fredrick Thomas *newspaper publisher*
Johnson, Elizabeth Ericson *retired educator*
Johnson, Thomas Stuart *lawyer*
King-Sturdivant, Constance Maria *social services administrator*
Mottram, Lisa Marie *pediatric psychologist*
O'Donnell, William David *retired construction firm executive*
Reinhard, Philip Godfrey *federal judge*
Reno, Roger *lawyer*
Roberts, James Brian *engineer*
Schlub, Teresa Rae *minister*
Steele, Carl Lavern *academic administrator*
Tuite, Gerald Francis *lawyer, commercial real estate manager*
Wilson, L. C. *superintendent*

Rockton
Bolger, Jacqueline E. *literature and language educator*
Pennell, Danny Joe *social worker*

Rolling Meadows
Bohlin, Dawn Lenore *electrical engineer*
Roti, Thomas David *judge*

Romeoville
Hoppe, Elizabeth Anne *philosopher, educator*

Rosemont
Doheny, Daniel P. *corporate financial executive*
Good, William Allen *professional society executive*
Leggett, Scott *chef, consultant*
Le Menager, Lois M. *incentive merchandise and travel company executive*
Meinert, John Raymond *apparel executive, investment banker*
Reyes, J. Christopher *food products distribution executive*
Tinaglia, Michael Lee *lawyer*

Round Lake
Bui, Mai Ha *molecular biologist, researcher*

Round Lake Beach
Harold, Kathleen T. *elementary school educator*

Rushville
Dohner, Russel Rowland *physician*

Saint Charles
Clancy, Wendell White *mediator, lawyer*
Ghaderi, Bahram *plastic surgeon*
LaHood, Julie Ann *small business owner*
Larsen, David Allen *educational consultant*
Malinowski, MaryEllen *photographer, artist*
Nellemann, Lynne O'Shea *management consultant*

Sandwich
Kola, Ramesh *oncologist*

Savoy
Bednar, Susan Gail *social worker, mediator, consultant, social sciences educator*
McConnell, William Stewart *application developer*
Sinclair, James Burton *retired plant pathology educator, consultant*

Schaumburg
Adrianopoli, Barbara Catherine *librarian*
Aryanfar, Farshid *electrical and electronics engineer*
Borth, David E. *telecommunications industry executive, researcher*
Brown, Gregory Q. *communications executive*
Colberg, Linda *physical education educator*
Delaney, Eugene A. *electronics executive*
Desai, Samir T. *electronics executive*
Fattori, Ruth A. *human resources specialist, electronics executive*
Fox, Thomas J. *communications executive*
Galvin, Robert W. *electronics executive*
Hill, Raymond Joseph *packaging company executive*
Janssen, Carron Joyce *music educator*
Karp, Jeff *construction executive*
Keller, Casey (Kenneth Charles Keller Jr.) *communications executive*
Kornowski, Robert Richard *engineer, science educator*
Lawson, A. Peter *lawyer*
Little, Bruce Washington *professional society administrator*
Maluchnik, Rosemary Pellicore *elementary school educator*
Mark, Kelly S. *telecommunications industry executive, investment advisor*
Marshall, John David *lawyer*
Meredith, Thomas J. *communications, investment company executive*
Moloney, Daniel M. *electronics executive*
Morrison, Patricia B. *information technology executive*
Nehs, (William) Scott *lawyer*
Nottenburg, Richard N. *electronics executive*
O'Connor, James, Jr., (Jim O'Connor) *telecommunications industry executive*
Otis, James, Jr. *architect*
Reed, Stuart C. *electronics executive*
Richter, Glenn *retail executive*
Riffel, Karen Sheffer *music educator*
Roman, Ray *communications executive*
Soon-Shiong, Patrick *pharmaceutical executive*
Tompson, Marian Leonard *professional society administrator*
Warrior, Padmasree *communications executive*
Zander, Edward J. *communications executive*

Seymour
Carringer, Robert *language educator*

Shorewood
Heaphy, John Merrill *lawyer*

Sigel
Stapleton, Patricia Jean *elementary school educator*

Silvis
Kontos, George John, Jr. *surgeon*

Skokie
Anthony, Carolyn Additon *librarian*
Brennan, William P. (Bill Brennan) *computer company executive*
Bush, Gail *librarian, educator, director, writer*
Corley, William Gene *engineering research executive*
Fein, Roger Gary *judge*
Gleason, John Patrick, Jr. *trade association executive*
Griffiths, Robert Pennell *banker*
Hong, In Chul *research scientist*
Langguth, Margaret Witty *health facility administrator*
McCarthy, Michael Shawn *health care company executive, lawyer*
Mierswa, David P. *lawyer, real estate investor*
Plotnick, Paul William *lawyer*
Polus Gerstner, Lillian *educational association administrator, director*
Sahagian, Arthur H. *artist*
Siegal, Burton Lee *product designer, consultant, inventor*
Sperzel, George E., Jr. *former personal care industry executive*

South Barrington
Kissane, Sharon Florence *writer, consultant, educator*

Spring Valley
Gallagher, Donald *physician*

Springfield
Adcock, Eric *application developer*
Beard, Rick *cultural organization administrator*
Beckwith, Peter Hess *bishop*
Bell, John Perry *minister, religious organization administrator*
Bergschneider, David Philip *legal administrator*
Blagojevich, Rod R. *governor, former congressman*
Brown, Malcolm Charles *conservator*
Cobb-Myers, Janet Lea *music educator*
Collins, Annazette R. *state representative*
Craig, Ann *library director*
Currie, Barbara Flynn *state legislator*
Daniels, Lee Albert *state legislator*
Darby, Karen Sue *law educator*
Dodge, Edward John *retired insurance company executive*
Evans, Charles H. *federal judge*
Evans, William Kendall *nuclear scientist*
Frank, Stuart *cardiologist*
Giannoulias, Alexi *state official*
Godwin, John E. *hematologist*
Hallmark, Donald Parker *museum director, educator*
Hannig, Gary L. *state representative*
Heaton, Rodger A. *prosecutor*
Hicks, David Eric *retired sports association executive*
Holland, John Madison *retired family practice physician*
Hynes, Daniel W. *comptroller*
Immke, Keith Henry *lawyer*
Jackson, Jacqueline Dougan *literature educator, writer*
Jefferson, Charles E. *state representative*
Kerr, Gary Enrico *lawyer, educator*
Kersten, Christian George *university administrator*
Klingler, Gwendolyn Walbolt *state representative*
Koch, Christopher A. *school system administrator*
Kocis, Janet Kay *elementary school educator*
Kosel, Renée *state representative*
LeBlang, Theodore Raymond *law educator, lawyer*
Londrigan, Thomas Foster *lawyer*
Madigan, Michael Joseph *state legislator*
Martinez, Iris *state senator*
Masternak, Michal Mateusz *biotechnologist, educator, molecular biologist, researcher*
Mathewson, Mark Stuart *lawyer, editor*
McCown, Linda Jean *medical technology educator*
Mikell, Frank Leonard *cardiologist*
Mills, Richard Henry *federal judge*
Morris, Donald *tax specialist*
Morse, Saul Julian *lawyer*
Munyer, Edward Arnold *zoologist*
Myers, Phillip Ward *otolaryngologist*
Neginsky, Rosina *literature educator, writer, poet*
Pankau, Carole *state senator*
Parke, Terry Richard *state legislator*
Phelps, David Dwain *state agency administrator, former congressman*
Phillips, John Robert *political scientist, educator*
Poorman, Robert Lewis *retired academic administrator*
Quinlan, William J. *lawyer*
Reddy, Ranga Vallela *anesthesiologist*
Reed, James Walter, Jr. *educational association administrator*
Reed, Robert Phillip *lawyer*
Schroeder, Joyce Katherine *state agency administrator, research analyst*
Schroeder, Raymond Ernest *educational administrator*
Schroeder-Lein, Glenna Ruth *librarian, historian*
Simpson, William Arthur *insurance company executive*
Stremsterfer, John Gary *foundation administrator, consultant*
Stroh, Raymond Eugene *retired personnel executive*
Temple, Wayne Calhoun *historian, writer*
Travis, Lawrence Allan *accountant*
Van Meter, Abram DeBois *lawyer, retired banker*
Wehrle, Leroy Snyder *economist, educator*
White, Jesse *state official*
Woodson, Gayle Ellen *otolaryngologist*
Yaffe, Stuart Allen *physician*

Sterling
Pace, Ole Bly III *lawyer*
Tóth, Peter Paul *physician, researcher*

Stoy
Rhoten, Kenneth Dale *writer*

Sugar Grove
Debartolo, Hansel Marion, Jr. *otolaryngologist, plastic surgeon*
DeLay, Larry Gene *science educator, photographer*
Del Medico, Amy *mathematics professor*

Swansea
Tillery, Stephen M. *lawyer*

Sycamore
Ballee, Shawn Alexander *engineering educator*
Burzynski, James Bradley *state legislator*
Stone, Van Courtright *not-for-profit developer*
Whisenhunt, Donald Wayne *historian, educator, dean*

Table Grove
Thomson, Helen Louise *artist*

Taylorville
Austin, Daniel William *lawyer*
Spears, Ronald Dean *judge*

Tinley Park
Daniels, Kurt R. *speech and language pathologist*
Freitag, Carol Wilma *political scientist*

Kenny, Mary Alice *lawyer*
Lobes, Mark Robert *graphic design educator, coach*

Union
Perlick, Richard Allan *steel company executive*

University Park
Alozie, Emmanuel C. *writer, educator*
Hakala, Reino William *mathematician, educator*
Keys, Paul Ross *academic administrator, educator*
Maimon, Elaine Plaskow *academic administrator*
Patton, June Odessa *writer, consultant, educator, researcher*

Urbana
Adesida, Ilesanmi *engineering educator, researcher, dean*
Althaus, Scott L. *political science professor*
Amenu, Geremew Gurmessa *engineering educator, researcher*
Antonsen, Elmer Harold *Germanic languages and linguistics educator*
Arnstein, Walter Leonard *retired historian*
Baer, Werner *economist, educator*
Baker, David Hiram *nutritionist, educator*
Balbach, Stanley Byron *lawyer*
Barenberg, Ernest John *engineering educator, consultant*
Beak, Peter Andrew *chemistry professor*
Bennett, Scott Boyce *retired librarian, consultant*
Berenbaum, May Roberta *entomology educator*
Bergeron, Clifton George *engineer, educator*
Bernard, Richard Lawson *retired geneticist, educator*
Blahut, Richard Edward *electrical and computer engineering educator*
Braatz, Richard Dean *chemical engineer*
Brichford, Maynard Jay *archivist*
Buckius, Richard O. *mechanical engineer, educator*
Buetow, Dennis Edward *physiologist, educator*
Burkholder, Donald Lyman *mathematician, educator*
Carmen, Ira Harris *political scientist, educator*
Carroll, Robert Wayne *mathematics professor*
Ceperley, David Matthew *physics professor*
Chao, Bei Tse *mechanical engineering educator*
Chato, John Clark *mechanical and bioengineering educator*
Chow, Poo *forester*
Christians, Clifford Glenn *communications educator*
Coleman, Paul Dare *physics and electrical engineering educator*
Conry, Thomas Francis *mechanical engineering educator*
Crang, Richard Francis Earl *botanist, writer, research scientist*
Crofts, Antony Richard *biochemistry and biophysics educator*
Dash, Leon DeCosta, Jr. *journalist*
Dovring, Karin Elsa Ingeborg *writer, poet, playwright, media specialist*
Eddy-Johnson, Deanna M. *home health care advocate*
Eden, James Gary *electrical engineer, physicist, educator, researcher*
Edgar, Jim *former governor*
Ehrlich, Gert *science educator, researcher*
Erdman, John W. *nutritionist, educator*
Ezeji, Thaddeus Chukwuemeka *microbiologist, educator*
Fitz-Gerald, Roger Miller *lawyer*
Frazzetta, Thomas Henry *evolutionary biologist, educator*
Frederick, Robert George *lawyer*
Gabriel, Michael *psychology professor*
Garcia, Marcelo Horacio *engineering educator, consultant*
Giles, Eugene *anthropology educator*
Gove, Samuel Kimball *retired political science professor*
Granato, Andrew Vincent *physics professor, researcher*
Greene, Joseph E. *material science researcher*
Greene, Laura Helen *physicist*
Greenough, William Tallant *psychobiologist, educator*
Grossman, Margaret Rosso *law educator*
Gruebele, Martin *chemistry and biophysicist professor*
Haile, H. G. *German language and literature educator*
Hall, William Joel *retired civil engineer, educator*
Hannon, Bruce Michael *engineering educator*
Hedlund, Ronald *baritone*
Heichel, Gary Harold *agronomist, educator*
Hendrick, George *retired English language educator*
Henson, C. Ward *mathematician, educator*
Hess, Karl *engineering educator, science educator*
Hoeft, Robert Gene *agricultural studies educator*
Holonyak, Nick, Jr. *electrical engineering educator*
Holt, Donald A. *agronomist, consultant, researcher, retired academic administrator*
Hoxie, Frederick Eugene *history professor*
Huang, Thomas Shi-Tao *electrical engineering educator, researcher*
Iben, Icko, Jr. *astrophysicist, educator*
Jacobson, Sheldon Howard *engineering educator*
Jiang, Shengxiang *electrical engineer, researcher*
Jonas, Jiri *chemist, educator*
Jones, Benjamin Angus, Jr. *retired agricultural engineering educator, science administrator*
Kaufman, Jerome Benzion *retired neurosurgeon*
Kaufman, Paula T. *university librarian*
Kaufmann, Urlin Milo *English literature educator*
Kelleher, Neil L. *chemist, educator*
Kieffer, Susan Werner *geologist, educator, media consultant*
Kim, Chin-Woo *linguist, educator*
Klein, Miles Vincent *physics professor*
Koenker, Diane P. *history professor*
Krein, Philip T. *electrical engineer, educator, electronics executive*
Krock, Curtis Josselyn *pulmonologist*
Kuhlenschmidt, Mark Stuart *microbiologist, researcher*
Kumar, Panganamala Ramana *electrical and computer engineering educator*
Larkin, Denis M. *geneticist, researcher*
Leggett, Anthony James *physics professor, researcher*
Leon, Arturo Segundo *civil engineer, researcher*
Leuthold, Raymond Martin *agricultural economics professor*
Lieberman, Laurence *poet, educator*
Liebman, Judith Rae Stenzel *retired operations research specialist*
Loui, Michael Conrad *engineering educator*
Love, Joseph LeRoy *history professor, former cultural studies center administrator*
Lu, Yi *chemistry professor*
Lüschen, Günther Rudolf Friedo *social sciences educator*
Makela, Jonathan James *engineering educator*
Martinez, Todd J. *chemistry professor*
Maxwell, William Hall Christie *civil, environmental engineer, educator*
McColley, Robert McNair *historian, educator*
McFarquhar, Greg M. *meteorologist, educator*
Meng, Ling-Jian *engineering educator*
Meyer, Richard Charles *microbiologist, educator*
Miley, George H. *nuclear and electrical engineering educator, plasma engineer, energy conversion scientist*
Nanney, David Ledbetter *geneticist, educator*
Neal, Larry Dwight *retired economic historian, educator*
Nelson, Cary Robert *language educator*
Nelson, Ralph Alfred *physician*
Nettl, Bruno *anthropologist, musicologist, educator*
O'Brien, Nancy Patricia *librarian, educator*
Oliphant, Uretz John *physician, surgeon*
O'Morchoe, Charles Christopher Creagh *anatomist, surgeon, educator*
Ono, Kent Alan *communications educator*
Powers, Richard S. *writer, educator*
Prussing, Laurel Lunt *mayor, economist*
Ra, Hyungshim Yoo *biologist, researcher*
Rao, Nannapaneni Narayana *electrical engineer*
Resek, Robert William *economist*
Rich, Robert F. *law educator, political science professor*
Ridgway, Marcella Davies *veterinarian*
Robinson, Gene Ezia *biologist, educator*
Rodgers, Daryl Mark *language educator*
Rowland, Theodore Justin *physicist, researcher*
Schmidt, Stephen Christopher *agricultural economist, educator*
Schweizer, Kenneth Steven *physics professor*
Searing, Susan Ellis *librarian*
Seebauer, Edmund Gerard *chemical engineer, educator*
Seigler, David Stanley *botanist, educator, chemist*
Snoeyink, Vernon L. *civil engineer, educator*
Snyder, Lewis Emil *astrophysicist, educator*
Solberg, Winton Udell *historian, educator*
Solomon, Wayne C. *aerospace engineer, educator*
Song, Xiaodong *geophysicist, seismologist*
Spitze, Robert George Frederick *agricultural studies educator*
Splittstoesser, Walter Emil *botanist, educator*
Stewart, D. Scott *engineering educator, consultant*
Stukel, James Joseph *academic administrator, mechanical engineer, educator*
Suslick, Kenneth Sanders *chemistry professor*
Switzer, Robert Lee *biochemistry professor*
Talbot, Emile Joseph *French language educator*
Thompson, Robert Lee *agricultural economist, educator*
Tischkau, Shelley Ann *physiologist, educator*
Tondeur, Philippe Maurice *mathematician, educator*
Visek, Willard James *nutritionist, animal scientist, physician, educator*
Wah, Benjamin Wan-Sang *electrical and computer engineering educator*
Warren, Pamela A. *psychologist*
Watson, Paula D. *retired librarian*
Watson, William Douglas *astrophysicist*
Webber, Carl Maddra *lawyer*
Weir, William Bradley *emergency physician*
Whitt, Gregory Sidney *evolution educator*
Williams, Martha Ethelyn *information science educator*
Williamson, Kent D. *educational association administrator*
Wirt, Frederick Marshall *retired political scientist, educator*
Woese, Carl R. *biophysicist, microbiology educator*
Xu, Dong *biophysicist, researcher*
Youngen, Gregory Keith *medical librarian*
Yu, George Tzuchiao *political science professor*
Zimmerman, Steven Charles *chemistry professor*
Zukoski, Charles Frederick, IV, *chemical engineering educator, academic administrator*

Vandalia
Jett, Charlene M. *biologist, researcher*

Vermont
Datcu, Ioana *artist*

Vernon Hills
Cho, Yong Hyo *education educator, consultant*
Claassen, W(alter) Marshall *employment company executive*
Edwardson, John Albert *information technology executive*
Klein, Barbara A. *information technology executive*
Krasny, Michael P. *investment company executive*
Leahy, Christine A. *lawyer, information technology executive*
Ling, Chung-Mei
Powers, Anthony Richard, Jr. *educational sales professional*
Richards, Alan Edward *lawyer*

Villa Park
Gordon, Rachel Singer *editor*
Pittelko, Roger Dean *clergyman, theology studies educator*

Wadsworth
Ahmad, Moghisuddin *chemist, researcher*

Warrenville
Boardman, Robert A. *retired lawyer*
Covey, Steven K. *lawyer*
Data, Art J. *information technology executive*
Hand, Ann Sparenberg *marketing executive*
Horne, John R. *farm equipment company executive*
Johnson, Douglas Wells *lawyer*
Lannert, Robert Cornelius *manufacturing executive*
Ustian, Daniel C. *trucking executive*
Zhang, Li *neurologist*

Washington
Stine, Robert Howard *retired pediatrician, allergist*

Waterloo
Hoffmann, Mary Jukich *voice educator*

Waterman
Arends, Ann M. *elementary school educator, pianist*

Watseka
Freed, Susan Dianne *health facility administrator*

Wauconda
Gotthardt, Mary Jane *retired religious studies educator*
Meehan, Jean Marie Ross *human resources, occupational health and safety management consultant*

Waukegan
Akouris, Dianne *elementary school educator*
Bairstow, Richard Raymond *retired lawyer*
Drapalik, Betty R. *volunteer, artist, educator*
Henrick, Michael Francis *lawyer*
Houle, Jeanne Larson *retired music educator*
Miller, Helen Elizabeth *art educator, adult education educator, artist*
Stone, Jed *lawyer*

West Chicago
Noonan, Josette Marie *music educator*
Paulissen, James Peter *retired pediatrician, county official*

Westchester
Clarke, Richard Lewis *health science association administrator*
Faison, Ralph E. *communications equipment manufacturing executive*
Faulkner, Robert Lloyd *advertising executive, graphics designer*
Hynes, Mary Ann *lawyer, food products executive*
Lightford, Kimberly A. *state legislator*
Masterson, John Patrick *retired language educator*
Pavelka, Elaine Blanche *mathematics professor*
Scott, Samuel C. *food products executive*
Webb, Emily *retired plant morphologist*

Western Springs
Hanson, Heidi Elizabeth *lawyer*
Virant, Paul *chef*
Zamora, Marjorie Dixon *retired political science professor*

Westmont
Schefdore, Ronald L. *dentist*
Tieken, Robert W. *relocation services company executive, retired tire manufacturing company executive*
Warner, H. Ty *entrepreneur, manufacturing executive*

Wheaton
Back, Robert Wyatt *investment company and pharmaceutical executive, consultant*
Benson, Bruce Ellis *philosophy educator*
Ford, Andrew Thomas *former academic administrator*
Kincaid, John Bruce *lawyer*
LaFrancis, Nicole Marie *secondary school educator*
Lawrence-Water, Bette Ann *community health leader*
Leston, Patrick John *judge*
Litfin, A. Duane *academic administrator*
Long, Charles Franklin *retired corporate communications executive*
Martin, Marcia Gray *retired architecture educator, artist, designer*
Pape, Patricia Ann *social worker, consultant*
Pappas, Barbara Estelle *biblical studies educator, author*
Riley, Betty Anne *psychologist, educator*
Schwanda, Grace Elaine *music educator*
Schwanda, Tom *religious studies educator*
Shuster, Robert Douglas *archivist*
Stein, Lawrence A. *lawyer*
Taylor, Mark Douglas *publishing executive*
Thompson, Bert Allen *retired librarian*
Tucker, Beverly Sowers *library and information scientist*
Warner, William Kent, Jr. *religious organization administrator, consultant*

Wheeling
Beemster, Joseph Robert *risk management consultant*
Keats, Glenn Arthur *manufacturing executive*
Levitin, Yelena *surgeon*
Long, Sarah Ann *librarian*
Meehan, Tamiye Marcia *library director*
Roalkvam, Donald L. *library and information scientist*

Willow Springs
Jashel, Larry Steven (L. Steven Rose) *entrepreneur, media consultant*

Willowbrook
Foley, Joseph Lawrence *sales executive*
Walton, Stanley Anthony III *lawyer*

Wilmette
Albright, Townsend Shaul *brokerage house executive, consultant*
Baisley, James Mahoney *retired lawyer*
Bowman, George Arthur, Jr. *retired judge*
Boyle, Antonia Barnes *writer, editor*
Brink, Marion Francis *trade association administrator*
Bunge, Jonathan Gunn *lawyer*
Coughlan, Gary Patrick *pharmaceutical executive*
Day, Emerson *physician*
Ellis, Helene Rita *social worker*
Hansen, Andrew Marius *retired library director*
Hier, Daniel Barnet *neurologist*
Hurley, Andrew John *musician*
Jampole, Michael *music educator, composer*
Mandel, Judith Lynn *primary school educator*
Miripol, Jerilyn Elise *poet, writer, writing therapist*
Monter, E. William *retired history professor*
Olson, Patricia Hagey *retired elementary school educator*
Pearlman, Jerry Kent *electronics company executive*
Schloss, Nathan *retired economist*
Smutny, Joan Franklin *academic director, educator*
Stump, Patrick Martin *musician*
Trohman, Joseph Mark *musician*
Wadden, Richard Albert *environmental engineer, educator, science administrator, consultant*
Walker, Ronald Edward *psychologist, educator*
Wentz, Peter (Peter Lewis Kingston Wentz III) *musician*
Wishner, Maynard Ira *retired finance company executive, lawyer*

Winnetka
Berner, Robert Lee, Jr. *lawyer*
Bundy, Blakely Fetridge *advocate*
Burke, John Edward *communications editor*
Cole, Kathleen Ann *advertising executive, social worker*
Crowe, Robert William *lawyer, mediator*
Ellwood, Scott *lawyer*
Greenblatt, Ray Harris *lawyer*
Hales, Daniel B. *lawyer*
Hickman, Frederic W. *retired lawyer*
Huggins, Charlotte Susan Harrison *retired secondary school educator, writer, travel company executive*
Klapperich, Frank Lawrence, Jr. *investment banker*
Krueger, Deborah A. Blake *school psychologist, consultant*
Ladd, David Scott *music educator*
Markey, Maurice *food products executive*
McKee, Judith Nelson *elementary school educator, educational consultant*
McWhirter, Bruce J. *retired lawyer*
Piper, Robert Johnston *retired architect, urban planner*
Plowden, David *photographer*
Puth, John Wells *manufacturing executive, consultant*
Quaal, Ward Louis *broadcast executive*
Rossi, Ennio C. *internist, educator*
Rubnitz, Myron Ethan *pathologist, educator*
Schlossman, John Isaac *architect*
Sick, William Norman, Jr. *technology company executive*
Thomas, John Thieme *management consultant*
Webster, David Macpherson *lawyer*
Weldon, Theodore Tefft, Jr. *marketing executive*

Wood Dale
Bullen, Daniel Bernard *mechanical engineering educator*
Goodwin, James E. *retired air transportation executive*
Storch, David *manufacturing executive*

Wood River
Shelton, Michael Patrick *principal*

Woodridge
Farrug, Eugene Joseph, Sr. *retired lawyer*
Jandes, Kenneth Michael *retired superintendent of schools*
O'Connor, William Michael *search company executive*
Puthenpurakal, Joseph Mathew *information technology executive*
Shen, Sin-Yan *physicist, acoustical engineer, musicologist*
Stall, Alan David *packaging company executive*

Woodstock
Dorn, Diane M. *science educator*

Yorkville
Freese, Carolyn Lee *art educator*

Zion
Hilyard, Nann Blaine *librarian*

INDIANA

Albany
Patrick, Alan K. *artist*

Alexandria
Irwin, Gerald Port *physician*

Anderson
Bracken, Linda Darlene *medical/surgical nurse*
Carrell, Terry Eugene *manufacturing executive*
Clanin, Douglas Edward *editor, researcher*
Conrad, Harold August *retired religious pension board executive*
King, Charles Ross *physician*
Lambert, Lloyd Laverne *minister*
Nicholson, Robert Arthur *college president*
Woodruff, Randall Lee *lawyer*

Angola
Cain, Tim J. *lawyer*

Batesville
Classon, Rolf Allan *pharmaceutical company executive*
de Maynadier, Patrick D. *lawyer*
Soderberg, Peter H. *health products executive*

Bedford
Hunter, Harlen Charles *orthopedic surgeon*

Beech Grove
Hughes, Charles E. III *plastic surgeon*

Bicknell
Ford, Andrea Michelle *mathematics educator*
Risley, Gregory Byron *retail executive, interior designer*

Bloomington
Aman, Alfred Charles, Jr. *law educator*
Anderson, Judith Helena *English language educator*
Arnove, Robert Frederick *education educator*
Asai, Rika *musicologist, educator*
Barnes, A. James *dean*
Basu, Abhijit *geologist, educator*
Baude, Patrick Louis *law educator*
Becker, William Edward *economist, consultant*
Belth, Joseph Morton *retired business educator*
Bertenthal, Bennett Ira *dean, psychologist, educator*
Bishop, Michael D. *emergency physician*
Bonser, Charles Franklin *public administration educator*
Bornholdt, Laura Anna *academic administrator*
Brehm, Sharon Stephens *psychology professor, former academic administrator*
Brinkman, Paul Del(bert) *retired foundation administrator, journalist, educator*
Brown, Keith *musician, educator*
Buente, Wayne Gerald *information scientist, researcher*
Calinescu, Adriana Gabriela *curator, art historian*
Cameron, John M. *nuclear scientist, educator, administrator*
Chaifetz, Marshal Lawrence *educational consultant, educator*
Choksy, Jamsheed Kairshasp *historian, religious scholar, humanities educator, language educator*
Clevenger, Sarah *botanist, consultant*
Connally, Sandra Jane Oppy *freelance/self-employed artist, educator*
Conrad, Geoffrey Wentworth *archaeologist, educator*
Cook, William Alfred *medical products executive*
Dalmau, Michelle *library and information scientist*
Dalton, Dan R. *finance educator, former dean*
DeHayes, Daniel Wesley *business educator*
Dilts, Jon Paul *law educator*
Dunn, Jon Michael *logician, dean*
Dunning, Jeremy David *application developer, dean, educator*
Easton, Susan Dawn *biochemist, educator*
Edmondson, Frank Kelley *retired astronomer*
Effron, David Louis *conductor, performing company executive*
Engber, Cheryl Ann *retired language educator, linguist*
Estelle, Mark *biology professor*
Estes, William Kaye *psychologist, educator*
Gordon, Paul John *management educator*
Gros Louis, Kenneth Richard Russell *humanities educator*
Guth, Sherman Leon (S. Lee) *psychologist, educator*
Hanson, Gail G. *physicist, researcher*
Hanson, Karen *philosopher, educator*
Hattin, Donald Edward *geologist, educator*
Henson, Jane Elizabeth *information management professional, adult education educator*
Hites, Ronald Atlee *chemist, educator*
Huffman, John Curtis *chemist*
Hustad, Thomas Pegg *marketing educator, association executive*
Jacobi, Peter Paul *journalism educator, writer*
Johnson, Owen Verne *historian, educator*
Juergens, George Ivar *history professor*
Kauffman, Erle Galen *geologist, paleontologist*
Kibbey, Hal Stephen *science writer*
Kiesgen, Paul *music educator*
Kuratko, Donald F. *entrepreneurial educator, consultant*
Lebano, Edoardo Antonio *foreign language educator*
Lee, Don Yoon *publishing executive, academic administrator, writer*
Letsinger, Robert Lewis *chemistry professor*
Lim, Youn-kyung *design educator*
Macfarlane, Malcolm Harris *physicist, educator*
Mac Watters, Virginia Elizabeth *singer, music educator, actress*
Martins, Heitor Miranda *foreign language educator*
Mehlinger, Howard Dean *education educator*
Meho, Lokman I. *library and information scientist, educator*
Mellencamp, John (John Cougar) *singer, lyricist*
Mickel, Emanuel John *foreign language educator*
Mobley, Tony Allen *foundation administrator, former dean, recreation educator*
Moore, Ward Wilfred *medical educator*
Morrison, Clarence Clapp *retired economics professor*
Nolan, Val, Jr. *retired biologist, lawyer*
Nunn, Ken *lawyer*
O'Hearn, Robert Raymond *stage designer*
O'Loughlin, Valerie Dean *medical educator*
O'Meara, Patrick O. *political science professor*
Ostrom, Elinor *political science professor, researcher*
Ostrom, Vincent A(lfred) *political science professor*
Patrick, John Joseph *social sciences educator*
Pauwels, Colleen Kristl *library director, educator*
Pedersen, Paul Mark *sportswriter, educator, columnist*
Peebles, Christopher Spalding *anthropologist, educator, dean, academic administrator*
Peters, Dennis Gail *chemist*
Peterson, M. Jeanne *historian, educator*
Phillips, Harvey G. *musician, performing arts educator*
Pollock, Robert Elwood *nuclear scientist*
Poplawski, Nikodem J. *physicist, researcher*
Prosser, Franklin Pierce *computer scientist*
Purdom, Paul Walton, Jr. *computer scientist*
Puri, Madan Lal *mathematics professor*
Ransel, David Lorimer *history professor*
Reingold, David Ami *sociologist, educator*
Reinisch, June Machover *psychologist, educator, researcher*
Rieseberg, Loren *botanist, educator*
Robel, Lauren *dean, law educator*
Robinson, Jennifer Meta *academic administrator, consultant*
Rocha, Luis M. *physics professor, director*
Rosenberg, Samuel Nathan *French and Italian language educator*
Rudolph, Lavere Christian *library director*
Ruesink, Albert William *biologist, plant sciences educator*
Rugman, Alan Michael *international business educator*
Ryan, John William *academic administrator*
Sampson, Kelvin Dale *college basketball coach*
Schurz, Scott Clark *journalist*
Shreve, Gene Russell *law educator*
Sinor, Denis *history professor, linguist*
Skosnik, Patrick David *neuroscientist, researcher*
Smith, Carl Bernard *education educator*
Smith, Daniel C. *dean, finance educator*
Smith, David Hunt *systems analyst, educator*
Smith, Janet Sue *systems process specialist*
Smith, Linda B. *psychology professor*
Smith, Ronald Thomas *environmental scientist*
Solomon, Bruce Michael *mathematician, educator*
Spera, Dominic Gregorio *music educator, writer*
Steele, Patricia Ann *librarian, dean*
Stoeltje, Beverly June *liberal studies educator*
Studwell, William Emmett *librarian, writer*
Svetlova, Marina *ballerina, retired choreographer*
Temam, Roger M. *mathematician, educator*
Thorelli, Sarah V. *economist, researcher*
Tsutsumi, Tsuyoshi *musician, educator*
Ward-Steinman, David *composer, music educator, pianist*
Webb, Charles Haizlip, Jr. *retired dean*
Webb, Lisa Michelle *regulatory affairs manager*
Weinberg, Eugene David *microbiologist, educator*
Wentworth, Jack Roberts *business educator, consultant*
Wigley, Diana Gail *respiratory therapist*
Wilson, George Macklin *history educator, cultural studies center administrator*

Bluffton
Brockmann, William Frank *retired health facility administrator*

Boonville
Campbell, Edward Adolph *judge, electrical engineer*

Brownsburg
Conway, Dwight Colbur *retired chemistry professor*
Strahle, Ron E. *elementary school educator, social studies educator*

Brownstown
Robertson, Joseph Edmond *grain processing company executive*

Burlington
Roussakis, Peter Ellwood *minister, publisher*

Carmel
Bostick, Russell M. *information technology executive*
Burkett, Robert E., Jr. *lawyer, insurance company executive*
Cohen, Marlene Lois *pharmacologist*
Eden, Barbara Janiece *commercial and residential interior designer*
Fadely, James Philip *writer, educator*
Fisher, Mark Leighton *software engineer*
Husman, Catherine Bigot *retired insurance company executive, consultant*
Mahoney, Margaret Ellis *advertising executive*
McLaughlin, Harry Roll *architect*
Pickens, Robert Bruce *retired accountant*
Prieur, C. James *insurance company executive*
Rand, Leon *academic administrator*
Rati, Robert Dean *retired data processing executive*
Rund, Rex Benjamin *music director*
Rychlak, Joseph Frank *psychologist, educator*
Shoup, Charles Samuel, Jr. *chemicals and materials executive*
Sukapdjo, Wilma Irene *language educator*
Walseth, David G. *lawyer, insurance company executive*
Walsh, John Charles *investment company executive, director*
Winslow, Catherine P. *plastic surgeon*

Cedar Lake
Bocock, Scott Gregory *historian*

Chesterton
Crewe, Albert Victor *physicist, researcher, artist*
Martino, Robert Salvatore *orthopedic surgeon*
Petrakis, Harry Mark *author*

Clarksville
von Allmen, Dion S. *mathematics educator, department chairman, mathematics professor*

Columbus
Able, Warren Walter *natural resource company executive, physician*
Abts, Henry William *retired banker*
Blackwell, Jean Stuart *manufacturing executive*
Boll, Charles Raymond *engine company executive*
Bowden, David *conductor*
Crump, Francis Jefferson III *lawyer*
Eynon, Richard S. *lawyer*
Garton, Robert Dean *state legislator*
Harrison, Patrick Woods *lawyer*
Lim, Yoon-Mi *muisc director, organist*
Loughrey, F. Joseph *manufacturing executive*
MacAvery, Tristan Alexander (Tristan Black Bear) *small business owner, writer, actor*
Miller, William Irwin *finance company executive*
Osborn, DeVerle Ross *insurance company executive*
Rose, Marya Mernitz *lawyer*
Sharpnack, John Trent *judge*
Solso, Theodore M. *manufacturing executive*
Wall, John *manufacturing executive*
Williams, Robert Joseph *behavioral health services executive, psychologist*

Connersville
Newton, Cindy Lynn *elementary school educator, media specialist*

Corydon
Miller, Judith Elaine *retired middle school educator, musician*

Crawfordsville
Barnes, James John *historian, educator*
White, Patrick E. *academic administrator*

Crown Point
Back, Michael Wayne *lawyer*
Dywan, Jeffery Joseph *judge*
Hendricks, Stanley Marshall, II, *executive recruiter, consultant*
Litko, Kenneth R. *aerospace engineer, researcher*
Shaffer, Peggy S. *music educator*

Danville
Baldwin, Jeffrey Kenton *lawyer, educator*
Baldwin, Patricia Ann *lawyer*

Dyer
Crnkovich, Ruth Anne *art appraiser, museum director*

East Chicago
Chukwulebe, Bernard Obioma *manufacturing executive, consultant*

Elkhart
Bloom, Terry Raymond *chemical engineer*
Carnall, Timothy W. *music educator*
Drexler, Rudy Matthew, Jr. *professional law enforcement dog trainer*
Eddy, Darlene Mathis *poet, educator*
Free, Helen Murray *chemist, consultant*
Gassere, Eugene Arthur *lawyer, investment company executive*
Khilnani, Vinod M. *manufacturing executive*
Mathias, Margaret Grossman *manufacturing company executive, leasing company executive*
Mischke, Frederick Charles *retired manufacturing executive*
Treckelo, Richard M. *lawyer*
Vite, Frank Anthony *realtor*

Ellettsville
Young, Frederic Hisgen *information systems executive, data processing consultant*

Evansville
Baker, Gloria Marie *artist*
Berger, Charles Lee *lawyer*
Brill, Alan Richard *entrepreneur*
Capshaw, Tommie Dean *judge*
Clouse, John Daniel *lawyer*
Culver, Gregory K. *science educator*
Ellerbrook, Niel Cochran *gas industry executive*
Fritz, Edward Lane *dentist*
Gaither, John Francis *accountant, consultant*
Harrison, Joseph Heavrin *lawyer*
Hayes, Philip Harold *lawyer*
Hoy, George Philip *clergyman, county official, state legislator*
Jennings, Stephen Grant *academic administrator*
Kimberling, Clark Hershall *mathematics professor, small business owner*
Koch, Robert Louis, II, *manufacturing company executive, mechanical engineer*
Miller, Daniel Raymond *prosecutor*
Morgan, George Henry *patent agent, consultant*
Muehlbauer, James Herman *manufacturing and distribution executive*
Raibley, Parvin Rudolph *dentist*
Reed, Helen Skuggedal *law librarian, musician*
Reed, R. Douglas *music educator*
Scheer, John C. *librarian*
Shoulders, Patrick Alan *lawyer, educator*
Streetman, John William III *museum director*
Wallace, Keith M. *lawyer*
Zion, Roger Herschel *retired management consultant, retired congressman*

Fishers
Christenson, Le Roy Howard *missions mobilizer*
Shults, Anna *elementary school educator*
Thomas, John Arlen *pharmacologist, educator, science administrator*

Fort Wayne
Bacchus, Harold Mustapha *physician*
Balint, David Lee *communications executive*
Beineke, Lowell Wayne *mathematics professor*
Busse, Keith E. *manufacturing executive*
Carroll, Betty Jean *retired application developer*
Cast, Anita Hursh *retired small business owner*
Colvin, Sherrill William *lawyer*
Cooper, Charles Bradford III *educational association administrator*
Curtis, Douglas Homer *small business owner*
Dunsire, P(eter) Kenneth *insurance company executive*
Egly, Sharon Kay *speech pathology/audiology services professional, director*
Fink, Thomas Michael *lawyer*
Frost, Helen Marie *writer*
Gehring, Ronald Kent *lawyer*
Glick, Anna Margaret *real estate broker, consultant*
Gutreuter, Jill Stallings *financial consultant, planner*
Helmke, Paul (Walter Paul Helmke Jr.) *lawyer, former mayor*
Hippensteele, David Simon *engineer*
Kennedy, Elizabeth *health facility administrator*
Klugman, Stephan Craig *newspaper editor*
Krull, Jeffrey Robert *library director*
Langhinrichs, Ruth Imler *playwright, writer*
Lawson, Jack Wayne *lawyer*
Lee, Shuishih Sage *pathologist*
Lee, Timothy Earl *international agency executive, paralegal*
Lee, William Charles *judge*
Lyons, Jerry Lee *mechanical engineer*
Mann, David William *minister*
Marine, Clyde Lockwood *agricultural products supplier, consultant*
Miller, Dawn L. *composition literature educator*
Murray, Shaun Michael *lobbyist, consultant*
Ogle, James Workman *aerospace engineer*
Philpott, Jonathan M. *surgeon*
Pope, Mark Andrew *lawyer, academic administrator*
Raby, Arend Christopher *sales executive*
Rhoad, Richard E. *manufacturing executive*
Richardson, Joseph Hill *physician, medical educator*
Shoaff, Thomas Mitchell *lawyer*
Skinner, Jauneth *art educator, graphic artist*
Snyder, Arthur E. *academic administrator*
Sperone, Kenneth J. *transportation executive*
Steiner, Paul Andrew *retired insurance executive*
Stoll, Wilhelm *mathematics professor*
Streeter, Robert Davenport *electrical engineer, consultant*
Tourkow, Joshua Isaac *lawyer*
Tucker, Dale Keith *church musical director, organist*
Wartell, Michael Alan *academic administrator*
Wooten, Marc *hospital administrator, medical educator*

Fortville
Horner, Sylvia Ann *minister, real estate broker*
Ramanathan, Chitra *artist, art educator*

Frankfort
Borland, Kathryn Kilby *writer*
Stonehill, Lloyd Herschel *gas industry executive, mechanical engineer*

Franklin
Hamner, Lance Dalton *prosecutor*
Nuwer, Henry Joseph (Hank Nuwer) *journalist, educator*
Stone, Mary Ann *literature and language educator*

Gary
Kilibarda, Zoran *geologist, educator*
Lewis, Robert Lee *lawyer*
Michelstetter, Stanley Hubert *lawyer*
Osan, Ana M. *language educator*
Schoon, Kenneth James *science educator, writer*
Sia, Kimberlee Jean *principal*
Smith, Vernon G. *education educator, state legislator*

Goshen
Meyer, Albert James *educational researcher*
Nolt, Steven M. *historian*

Granger
Craypo, Charles *labor economics professor*
Morgan, Ardys Nord *school improvement consultant*
Thomas, Debi (Debra J. Thomas) *ice skater*

Greencastle
Anderson, John Robert *retired mathematics professor*
Bottoms, Robert Garvin *academic administrator*
Dittmer, John Avery *history professor*
Hall, David *newspaper editor*
Phang, May *music educator*
Spicer, Harold Otis *retired English language educator, communications educator*
Weiss, Robert Orr *speech educator*

Greenwood
Broscoe, Peter A. *mortgage company executive, consultant*

Gaunce, Michael Paul *insurance company executive*
Hagedorn, Alan Patrick *social studies educator*
Knapp, Sylvia Clare *retired language educator*
Van Valer, Joe Ned *lawyer, real estate developer*
Waldkoetter, Raymond Oliver *psychologist, consultant*

Griffith
Luetschwager, Mary Susan *educational consultant*

Hammond
Boggs, William Norman *marketing professional, educator*
Capp, David A. *prosecutor*
DeGuilio, Jon E. *lawyer*
Delph, Donna Jean (Maroc) *education educator, consultant, academic administrator*
Diamond, Eugene Christopher *lawyer, health facility administrator*
Fisher, Jeffrey L. *psychologist*
Hansen, Jack Winsor *musician, educator*
Lozano, Rudolpho *federal judge*
Pierson, Edward Samuel *engineering educator, consultant*
Ruman, Saul I. *lawyer*
Van Bokkelen, Joseph Scott *federal judge, former prosecutor*

Hanover
Batchvarova, Madlen Todorova *music educator, conductor*

Highland
Forsythe, Randall Newman *paralegal, educator*
Gladish, David Stephen *lawyer*
Steen, Lowell Harrison *retired physician*

Hobart
Arand, Frederick Francis *accountant, finance company executive*
Hanley, Roberta Lynn *alternative education coordinator, educator*

Howe
Bowerman, Ann Louise *writer, secondary school educator, genealogist*

Indianapolis
Addai, Joseph *professional football player*
Albright, Terrill D. *lawyer*
Allen, David James *lawyer*
Allen, Stephen D. (Stephen Dean Allen) *pathologist, microbiologist*
Anderson, Maxwell L. *museum director*
Anderson, Walter Ernest *church musician*
Andretti, Michael Mario *racing company executive, retired professional race car driver*
Anwar, Sohel *engineering educator*
Aprison, Morris Herman *retired experimental and theoretical neurobiology educator*
Armitage, Robert Allen *lawyer, pharmaceutical executive*
Avery, Melissa J. *lawyer*
Ayars, Patti *human resources specialist, health products executive*
Babsky, Andriy M. *biologist, researcher*
Badger, David Harry *lawyer*
Baetzhold, Howard George *retired language educator*
Banya, Santonino Ku'Caya *science educator*
Barcus, Robert Gene *retired educational association administrator*
Barker, Sarah Evans *judge*
Barkley, James M. *lawyer, real estate company executive*
Beckwith, Lewis Daniel *lawyer*
Bein, Frederick L. *geography educator*
Bepko, Gerald Lewis *retired academic administrator, law educator*
Bergstein, Jerry Michael *nephrologist*
Bird, Larry Joe *professional sports team executive, retired professional basketball player*
Blythe, James David, II, *lawyer*
Bodenhamer, David Jackson *historian, educator*
Boehm, Theodore Reed *state supreme court justice*
Boldt, Michael Herbert *lawyer*
Boling, Joseph Edward *numismatist, retired military officer*
Born, Samuel Roydon, II, *retired lawyer, mediator*
Bowman, Frank O. *law educator*
Boxer, Mark L. *healthcare insurance company executive*
Braly, Angela Fick *health insurance company executive, lawyer*
Bramble, Laura *library director*
Brandt, Ira Kive *pediatrician, geneticist*
Brash, Susan Kay *principal*
Brater, Donald Craig *dean, educator*
Braun, Robert Clare *retired association and advertising executive*
Brenner, Mark Lee *academic administrator, physiologist, educator*
Brickley, Richard Agar *retired surgeon*
Brooker, Roberta L. *library director*
Brooks, Susan W. *prosecutor*
Broome, Marion *dean*
Brown, Edwin Wilson, Jr. *preventive medicine physician, educator*
Brown, Randy *human resources specialist, health insurance company executive*
Broxmeyer, Hal Edward *medical educator*
Buckley, Pamela Kay *educational association administrator*
Buechlein, Daniel Mark *archbishop*
Buhner, Byron Bevis *health science facility administrator*
Buranello, Raymond Terrence *quality assurance executive, chemist*
Burgomaster, Frederick *music director*
Burnett, Judith Jane *public relations executive*
Burr, David Bentley *anatomy educator*
Butt, P. Lawrence *lawyer*
Caine, Virginia A. *city health department administrator*
Capello, William Naldo *surgeon*
Cardwell, Sue Webb *psychology professor*
Carlisle, Sheila A. *judge*
Carney, Joseph Buckingham *lawyer*
Carter, Steve *state attorney general*
Catchings, Tamika Devonne *professional basketball player*
Chandler, Julie Light *secondary school educator*
Cheng, Liang *pathologist*
Choplin, John M., II, *lawyer*
Christen, Arden Gale *dental educator, researcher, consultant*
Clark, Charles M., Jr. *medical school administrator*
Cliff, Johnnie Marie *mathematics and chemistry professor*
Coffey, Charles Moore *communication research professional, writer*
Cohen, Alan H. *retail executive*
Cohen-Gadol, Aaron *neurosurgeon*
Cole, Roland Jay *lawyer*
Coleman, John Joseph III *surgery educator*
Connelly, Deirdre P. *pharmaceutical executive*
Connor, Ulla M. *linguistics educator*
Conour, William Frederick *lawyer*
Corley, William Edward *hospital administrator*
Cowen, Carl C. *mathematics professor*
Cravens, Gary Dean *information scientist, physician*
Crews, Kenneth Donald *law educator, consultant, dean*
Croffie, Joseph M. *gastroenterologist, educator*
Crow, Paul Abernathy, Jr. *retired minister*
Dai, Yuan-Shun *education educator*
Dalsing, Michael Cletus *surgeon, educator*
Daly, Walter Joseph *medical educator*
Daniels, Deborah Jean *lawyer, former federal agency administrator*
Daniels, Mitchell Elias, Jr. *governor, former federal official*
Davis, Edgar Glenn *healthcare executive, educator*
Davis, Kenneth Wayne *language educator, business communication consultant*
Dawes, Dominique *Olympic athlete*
DeForge, Anna *professional basketball player*
DeVeydt, Wayne S. *health insurance company executive*
Dickinson, Richard Donald Nye *clergyman, theology studies educator*
Dickson, Brent E. *state supreme court justice*
Divita, James J. *retired social studies educator, writer, researcher*
Dorocke, Lawrence Francis *lawyer*
Dorr, Marjorie W. *healthcare insurance company executive*
Downs, Thomas K. *lawyer*
Drentlicher, David *lawyer, educator, physician*
Dungy, Tony *professional football coach*
Dutton, Stephen James *lawyer*
Dyken, Mark Lewis, Jr. *neurologist, educator*
Eigen, Howard *pediatrician, educator*
Einhorn, Lawrence Henry *oncologist, medical educator*
Elberger, Ronald Edward *lawyer*
Elvin, George *architecture educator*
Elzer, Robert W. *lawyer*
Engleman Connors, Ellen Gayle *former federal agency administrator*
Enright, William Gerald *religious institute administrator*
Everly, Jack *conductor*
Ewbank, Thomas Peters *lawyer, retired banker*
Farag, Sherif Shafik *physician scientist, educator*
Faulk, Marshall Williams *retired professional football player*
Fehrenbacher, John W. *surgeon*
Fels, James Alexander *lawyer, mediator*
Fife, Wilmer Krafft *retired chemistry professor*
Fine, Pamela B. *newspaper editor*
Finley, Katherine Mandusic *professional society administrator*
Fisher, Gene Lawrence *controller, accountant*
FitzGibbon, Daniel Harvey *lawyer*
Floyd, James M., Jr. *adult education educator*
Foley, Brian Scott *physiatrist, medical educator*
Foster, Kennard P. *magistrate judge*
Foster, Richard S. *urologist, educator*
Fox, Stephen Lee *language educator*
Freeney, Dwight *professional football player*
French, Tarence Wade, Sr. *minister*
Fridell, Jonathan Aaron *transplant surgeon*
Fruehwald, Kristin Gail *lawyer*
Funk, David Albert *retired law educator*
Furlow, Mack Vernon, Jr. *retired chief financial officer, treasurer, financial analyst*
Garmel, Marion Bess Simon *retired arts journalist*
Gerdes, Ralph Donald *fire safety consultant*
Ghetti, Bernardino Francesco *neuropathologist, educator*
Gilliland, John Campbell, II, *lawyer*
Gilman, Alan B. *restaurant company executive*
Gilroy, Sue Anne *hospital administrator, former state official*
Glasscock, Larry Claborn *health insurance company executive*
Gnat, Raymond Earl *librarian*
Goldblatt, Lawrence I. *dean, educator, researcher*
Goodwin, William Maxwell *financial executive*
Gooldy, Patricia Alice *retired elementary school educator*
Greene, Maurice *Olympic athlete, track and field athlete*
Gregg, Stephen Thompson *political scientist, consultant*
Griffith, Roy Lloyd *design engineer*
Griswold, Tom *radio personality*
Grosfeld, Jay Lazar *surgeon, educator*
Grube, F. William *refining company executive*
Hackman, Marvin Lawrence *lawyer*
Handel, David Jonathan *health facility administrator*
Hansell, Richard Stanley *obstetrician, gynecologist, educator*
Harden, Anita Joyce *nurse*
Harden, Annette C. *recreation director*
Hardin, Boniface *academic administrator*
Harper, Terrance G. *journalism organization administrator*
Harrison, Marvin *professional football player*
Harrold, John Andrew *education educator, consultant*
Hartsfield, James Kennedy, Jr. *orthodontist, geneticist*
Hastings, Hill *surgeon*
Hegel, Carolyn Marie *farm owner and organization executive*
Helper, Debra J. *gastroenterologist*
Henry, Barbara Ann *publishing executive*
Hiner, Leslie Davis *lawyer, consultant*
Hitchens, William Randolph (Randy) *healthcare executive*
Holden, James R. *state agency administrator*
Holden, Robert Watson *radiologist, educator, dean*
Horn, Brenda Sue *lawyer*
Horwitz, Javan Lee *neuropsychologist*
Hovde, F. Boyd *lawyer*
Huler, Robert Jay *surgeon*
Hunt, Robert G. *construction company executive*
Ilgen, Dorothy L. *arts foundation executive*
Inui, Thomas Spencer *physician, educator*
Irsay, James Steven *professional football team owner*
Irwin, Glenn Ward, Jr. *medical educator, physician, academic administrator*
Irwin, Marilyn M. *librarian, educator*
Jackson, Valerie Pascuzzi *radiologist, educator*
Jegen, Lawrence A. III *law educator*
Johnston, Cyrus Conrad, Jr. *medical educator*
Johnstone, Robert Philip *retired lawyer*
Jones, Marion *track and field athlete*
Kalwara, Joseph John *engineer*
Kappes, Philip Spangler *lawyer*
Kaufman, Barton Lowell *financial services company executive*
Kautzman, John Fredrick *lawyer*
Keaton, Margaret-Ann Coleman *education educator*
Kemper, James Dee *lawyer*
Kenley, Howard *state legislator*
Kennedy, Russell Edward *academic administrator*
Kenney, Philip G. *construction executive*
Kerr, William Andrew *lawyer, educator*
Kessler, Marcia Lynn *school psychologist*
Kevoian, Bob *radio personality*
Kinney, Eleanor De Arman *law educator*
Kirk, Carol *lawyer*
Kirkham, James Alvin *manufacturing executive*
Kirkpatrick, Robert Hugh *communications executive*
Kitterman, Laura Ann *occupational therapist*
Klaper, Martin Jay *lawyer*
Kleiman, Mary Margaret *lawyer*
Kleinhans, Frederick William *biophysicist, educator*
Knebel, Donald Earl *lawyer*
Knoebel, Suzanne Buckner *cardiologist, educator*
Koch, Edna Mae *lawyer, nurse*
Koeller, Robert Marion *lawyer, director*
Kohart, Mary Beth *real estate company executive*
Krasean, Thomas Karl *historian*
Kunkler, Arnold William *retired surgeon, educator*
Kury, Bernard Edward *lawyer*
Lacy, Andre Balz *industrial executive*
LaGrotto, Louisa *middle school educator*
Lamkin, Martha Dampf *lawyer, foundation administrator*
Lau, Pauline Young *chemist*
Lazaran, Frank *former retail executive*
Lechleiter, John C. *pharmaceutical executive*
Lee, Stephen W. *lawyer*
Lemberger, Louis *pharmacologist*
Lewis, Randall J. *healthcare insurance company executive*
Li, Shuyu *research scientist*
Lindseth, Erik Lars *humanities educator*
Lisher, John Leonard *lawyer*
Lobley, Alan Haigh *retired lawyer*
Lofton, Thomas Milton *lawyer*
Lorell, Beverly H. *medical products executive*
Lowe, Louis Robert, Jr. *lawyer*
Lugar, Thomas R. *manufacturing executive*
Lumeng, Lawrence *physician, educator*
Lytle, L(arry) Ben *insurance company executive, lawyer*
MacDougall, John Duncan *thoracic surgeon*
Madura, James Anthony *surgeon, educator*
Malachowski, Robert Michael *retired pediatrician*
Malloy, William Xavier *pharmacist*
Malone, Jean Hambidge *educational consultant*
Manders, Karl Lee *neurosurgeon*
Manning, Peyton Williams *professional football player*
Martinez-Mier, Esperanza Angeles *dental educator, researcher*
Mason, Thomas Alexander *historian, educator, author*
Mattar, Wissam Elias *physician*
Mays, William G. *chemical company executive*
McCarthy, Kevin Bart *lawyer*
McConnell, William F., Jr. *medical products executive*
McDonald, Brenna Cathleen *psychologist*
Mc Farland, H. Richard *food products executive*
McKeag, Douglas Bruce *physician, educator*
McKeand, Patrick Joseph *newspaper publisher, educator*
McKinney, E. Kirk, Jr. *retired insurance company executive*
McKinney, Larry J. *federal judge*
Merrill, William H., Jr. *lawyer, corporate financial executive*
Mirsky, Arthur *retired geologist, educator*
Miyamoto, Richard Takashi *otolaryngologist*
Moelhman, Amy Jo *social worker*
Moffatt, Michael Alan *lawyer*
Molitoris, Bruce Albert *nephrologist, educator*
Montoya, Juan Pablo *professional race car driver*
Morway, David S. *professional sports team executive*
Mourdock, Richard E. *state official*
Mullen, Thomas Edgar *real estate consultant*
Muncie, Ronald James *environmental services administrator, minister*
Murphy, Anthony J. *pharmaceutical executive*
Murphy, Meissa Bleu *music educator, behaviorist*
Mutz, John Massie *foundation administrator, former state official, former energy executive*
Najjar, Diana *elementary school educator*
Neff, Robert Matthew *lawyer, finance company executive*
Newman, Norman Richard *lawyer*
Nolan, Alan Tucker *lawyer, writer, arbitrator*
Norins, Arthur Leonard *dermatologist, educator*
Nurnberger, John I., Jr. *psychiatrist, educator*
Nussbaum, Samuel R. *healthcare insurance company executive, medical educator*
O'Brien, Jim *professional basketball coach*
Ochs, Sidney *neurophysiology researcher, educator*
Odell, James Calvin *history professor, theology studies educator*
Oldham, Steve Anthony *lawyer*
Olson, Byron Louis *biochemist, educator*
O'Neal, C. Duane *lawyer*
O'Neal, Jermaine *professional basketball player*
Onochie, Florence N. *accountant*
Padgett, Gregory Lee *lawyer*
Page, Curtis Matthewson *minister*
Paul, Stephen Howard *lawyer*
Paul, Steven M. *pharmaceutical executive*
Pence, Linda Lee *lawyer*
Pennamped, Bruce Michael *lawyer*
Peribere, Jerome A. *agricultural products executive*
Perkins, Stephen W. *plastic surgeon*
Petersen, James L. *lawyer*
Peterson, Bart *mayor*
Pishchalnikov, Yuri A. *researcher*
Pitt, Henry Anthony *surgeon, researcher, medical educator*
Pitts, Beverley J. *academic administrator*
Plater, William Marmaduke *literature and language professor, academic administrator*
Pockrass, Joseph Craig *music educator*
Poinsette, Donald Eugene *engineering executive, management consultant*
Polak, Jonathan Garland *lawyer*
Polston, Mark Franklin *minister*
Ralston, Ronald Lee *retired manufacturing tradesman*
Ramakrishnan, Divakar *pharmaceutical executive*
Reed, Suellen Kinder *school system administrator*
Reid, William Hill *mathematics professor*
Reuben, Lawrence Mark *lawyer*
Reynolds, Robert Hugh *lawyer*
Rhoades, Rodney Allen *physiologist, educator*
Rice, Derica W. *pharmaceutical executive*
Richter, Judith Anne *pharmacologist, educator*
Riegsecker, Marvin Dean *pharmacist, state senator*
Ripley, Judith G. *state agency administrator*
Robbins, N. Clay *foundation administrator*
Roberts, William Everett *lawyer*
Roger, Janice Lowenstein *cantor*
Rogers, Robert Ernest *medical educator*
Rokita, Todd *state official*
Roscoe, Michael Shannon *physician assistant, educator*
Rosenblatt, Alice F. *healthcare insurance company executive*
Ross, Edward *cardiologist*
Roth, Lawrence Max *pathologist, educator*
Ruben, Gary A. *marketing and communications consultant*
Rucker, Robert D. *state supreme court justice*
Russell, David Williams *lawyer*
Russell, Frank Eli *retired newspaper publishing executive*
Rusthoven, Peter James *lawyer*
Rutledge, Joanne *artist, consultant*
Ryder, Henry Clay *lawyer*
Ryerson, Dennis *editor*
Santini, Gino *pharmaceutical executive*
Saxena, Romil *pathologist, educator*
Scaletta, Phillip Ralph III *lawyer*
Schenk, William Earl III *senior special agent, criminal investigator*
Schlegel, Fred Eugene *lawyer*
Schmetzer, Alan David *psychiatrist*
Schmid, John A. *musician, voice educator*
Schreckengast, William Owen *retired lawyer*
Schroyer, Michael Kevin *healthcare consultant, hospital executive*
Scism, Daniel Reed *lawyer*
SerVaas, Beurt Richard *manufacturing executive*
SerVaas, Cory *editor-in-chief*
Sheehan, Kevin Edward *venture capitalist*
Shepard, Randall Terry *state supreme court chief justice*
Shula, Robert Joseph *lawyer*
Siderys, Harry *surgeon, educator*
Simon, David *real estate company officer*
Simon, Herbert *real estate developer, professional sports team owner*
Simon, Melvin *real estate developer, professional sports team owner*
Skillman, Becky Sue *lieutenant governor, former state legislator*
Smith, Curt *think tank executive, journalist*
Smith, Donald Archie *religious business executive, consultant*
Smith, James Warren *pathologist, educator, microbiologist, parasitologist*
Smith, K. Clay *machinery transport company executive*

Sokolov, Richard Saul *real estate company executive*
Solomon, Marilyn Kay *primary school educator, consultant, small business owner*
Sommer, James Koch *lawyer*
Sorley, Rebecca Ellen *music educator*
Spanogle, Robert William *marketing and advertising company executive, association administrator*
Speth, Gerald Lennus *educational consultant, management consultant*
Stayton, Thomas George *lawyer*
Stehman, Frederick Bates *obstetrician, gynecologist, educator*
Stevens, Brad K. *men's college basketball coach*
Stewart, Paul Arthur *pharmaceutical company executive*
Stitle, Stephen A. *bank executive*
Strain, James Arthur *lawyer*
Stuhldreher, David Brosnan *urologist*
Sullender, Joy Sharon *retired elementary school educator*
Sullivan, Frank, Jr. *state supreme court justice*
Sundaram, Chandru P. *urologist*
Sutton, Gregory Paul *obstetrician, gynecologist*
Sweezy, John William *political party official*
Swhier, Claudia Versfelt *lawyer*
Swindle, Ralph Wilson, Jr. *research psychologist*
Sykes, Linda Diane *elementary school educator, music educator*
Tabler, Bryan G. *lawyer*
Tabler, Norman Gardner, Jr. *lawyer*
Talesnick, Stanley *lawyer*
Taurel, Sidney *pharmaceutical executive*
Taylor, Angelo *Olympic athlete*
Taylor, Nolan J. *information systems educator*
Tempel, Eugene Raymond (Gene Tempel) *foundation administrator, speaker, researcher*
Terry, Linda Faye *librarian*
Thomas, Jerry Arthur *soil scientist*
Towne, Edgar Arthur *theologian, educator*
Townsend, Earl C., Jr. *lawyer, writer*
Tribble, Hazel R. *elementary school educator*
Turner-Wright, Marie Annetta *retired librarian*
Vandivier, Blair Robert *lawyer*
Van Lieu, Thomas Jerry *school system administrator*
Van Natta, Bruce Wayne *plastic surgeon*
Venzago, Mario *conductor, music director*
Vereen, Robert Charles *retired trade association administrator*
Vinatieri, Adam Matthew *professional football player*
Walsh, Donnie (Joseph Donald Walsh Jr.) *professional sports team executive*
Warkel, Harriet G. *curator*
Watanabe, August Masaru *physician, educator, retired pharmaceutical executive*
Watkins, Harold Robert *minister*
Watts, John S., Jr. *insurance company executive*
Weber, George *oncology and pharmacology educator, researcher*
Welch, Cody M. *transportation and warehousing executive*
Wellnitz, Craig Otto *lawyer, English language educator*
Wensits, David L. *aerospace transportation executive*
Westra, Mitzi Sue *music educator*
Whale, Arthur Richard *retired lawyer*
White, James Patrick *law educator*
Whitfield, Erica Sharon *director, career planning administrator*
Willham, Lorann Ellyn *assistant principal*
Williams, Bernard *Olympic athlete*
Williams, Luida K. *retired elementary school educator*
Wilson, Fred M., II, *ophthalmologist, educator*
Wilson, Richard Harry, Jr. *congressional chief of staff*
Winters, Brian Joseph *professional basketball coach*
Wishard, Gordon Davis *lawyer*
Wong, David T. *biochemist, researcher*
Woodring, DeWayne Stanley *religious organization administrator*
Woody, John Frederick *retired secondary school educator*
Woolling, Kenneth Rau *vascular internist*
Wright, David Burton *retired newspaper publishing company executive*
Yao, Yongxue *immunologist*
Yates, C. Daniel *lawyer*
Yeager, Joseph Heizer, Jr. *lawyer*
Yee, Robert Donald *ophthalmologist*
Young, Philip Howard *library director*
Yovits, Marshall Clinton *information scientist, educator, dean*
Yung, Chi-Wah Rudy *ophthalmologist, educator*
Zipes, Douglas Peter *cardiologist, researcher*

Inglefield
James, Marion Ray *retired publishing executive, editor*

Jasper
Brenner, Raymond Anthony *priest*
Eck, Kenneth James *agronomist*
Newman, Leonard Jay *retail jewel merchant, gemologist*

Jeffersonville
Chilton, Ronald Hanley *broadcasting executive, actor*
Hoehn, Elmer Louis *lawyer, state and federal agency administrator, educator, consultant*
Reisert, Charles Edward, Jr. *realtor, real estate developer*

Knightstown
Richardson, Shirley Maxine *editor*

Knox
Weiss, Randall A. *television and radio producer, supermarket executive, television station owner*

Kokomo
Coppock, Janet Elaine *mental health nurse*
Miller, Robert Frank *retired electronics engineering educator*
Ramos, Jamie *information scientist*
Roales, Robert R. *natural science educator*
Stein, Eleanor Bankoff *retired judge*
Wysong, Earl Edward *sociologist, educator*

La Porte
Bakwin, Edward Morris *banker*
Johnson, Bruce Ross *elementary school educator*
Kaminski, Leon R. *lawyer*
Morris, Leigh Edward *mayor, retired health facility administrator*

Lafayette
Conley, Shawn *agriculturist*
Etzel, James Edward *environmental engineering educator*
Fox, Robert William *mechanical engineering educator*
Gartenhaus, Solomon *physicist, educator*
Geddes, Leslie Alexander *engineering educator, forensic engineer, physiologist*
Hamdi, Hamid S. *neurologist, neurorehabilitation specialist, consultant, researcher*
Hardin, Lowell Stewart *retired economics professor*
Hart, Russell Holiday *retired lawyer*
Jischke, Martin C. *retired academic administrator*
Kanne, Michael Stephen *federal judge*
Langston, Edward Lee *physician, pharmacist*
Layden, Charles Max *lawyer*
Liley, Peter Edward *retired engineering educator*
Loeffler, Frank Joseph *physicist, educator*
McBride, Angela Barron *nursing educator*
McCully, Thomas Richardson *lawyer*
McKowen, Dorothy Keeton *librarian, educator*
Meyer, Brud Richard *retired pharmaceutical executive*
Minor, Ronald Ray *minister*
Mobley, Emily Ruth *library director, educator, dean*
Nicholson, Ralph Lester *botanist, educator*
Novak, Julie Cowan *nursing educator, researcher, clinician*
Osborn, John Robert *retired engineering educator*
Pipes, Robert Byron *mechanical engineer, educator*
Porile, Norbert Thomas *chemistry professor*
Renzetti, Phyllis Jean *retired technical editor*
Roush, Nadine Marie *elementary school educator*
Scaletta, Helen Marguerite *volunteer*
Schönemann, Peter Hans *psychologist, educator*
Schweickert, Richard Justus *psychologist, educator*
Troutner, Joanne Johnson *director, consultant, secondary school educator*

Lagrange
Brown, George E. *judge, educator*

Lawrenceburg
Dautel, Charles Shreve *retired mining company executive*

Liberty
Pringle, Lewis Gordon *marketing professional, educator*
Sowers, Marilyn Rae *librarian*

Lizton
King, Richard Gene *superintendent*

Logansport
Bland, Leonard A. *auditor, consultant*
Brewer, Robert Allen *physician*
Walter, Patricia L. *psychotherapist, consultant*

Madison
Gotts, Edward Earl *psychologist, researcher*
Grahn, Ann Wagoner *retired science administrator*
Jones, Richard Sheffield *veterans service officer*
Snodgrass, Robert Eugene *retired psychiatrist*
Tatera, James Frank *chemist*

Marion
Fisher, Pierre James, Jr. *physician*
Lessly, Chris Ann *music educator, director, conductor*
Miller, Peter Karl *music educator*
Steenbergh, Timothy Allen *psychology professor*
Walker, Corean Jones *evangelist*

Merrillville
Compton, Clyde D. *lawyer*
Han, Dennis Paul *physician*
Miller, Richard Allen *lawyer*
Nguyen, Thach Ngoc *cardiologist*
Skaggs, Robert C., Jr. *utilities executive, lawyer*
Smith, Arthur Edward, Jr. *lawyer*
Tlapa, Richard Joseph *retired priest*
Willadsen, Michael Chris *marketing professional, sales executive*
Yu, Peter Legaspi *rehabilitation physician*

Michigan City
Mothkur, Sridhar Rao *radiologist*
Varro, Barbara Joan *retired editor*
Wiegand, Elizabeth Grieger *musician, educator*
Zolvinski, Susan Kaye *medical director*

Middlebury
Corson, Thomas Harold *retired manufacturing executive*
Guequierre, John Phillip *manufacturing executive*
Mulholland, Janet Lynn Healy *retired language educator, writer*

Mishawaka
Haley, David Alan *healthcare executive*
Ponko, William Reuben *architect*
Rubenstein, Pamela Silver *manufacturing executive*
Sobol, Zbigniew W. *orthopedist, surgeon*
Troyer, LeRoy Seth *architect*
Watts, Mark Edwin *secondary school educator, professional volleyball player*

Muncie
Ali, Mir Masoom *retired statistician, educator*
Amman, E(lizabeth) Jean *academic administrator*
Anderson, Stefan Stolen *retired banker*
Barber, Earl Eugene *management consultant*
Bell, Stephen Scott (Steve Bell) *journalist, educator*
Blume, Peter Frederick *museum director*
Bogg, Richard Allan *sociologist, educator*
Call, David Andrew *meteorologist, educator*
Cheng, Chu Yuan *economics professor*
Dolak, Fritz *librarian, information administrator*
Gora, JoAnn M. *academic administrator*
Harris, Joseph McAllister *retired chemist*
Hendrix, Jon Richard *biology professor*
Henzlik, Raymond Eugene *zoophysiologist, educator*
Hoffman, Mary Catherine *retired nurse, anesthetist*
Kelly, Eric Damian *lawyer, educator*
Kitchens, Frederick Lynton III *education educator, researcher*
Lawhead, Victor Bernard *education educator*
Martínez, Iván David *language educator, translator*
Maurer, Kathleen Marie *music educator, vocalist*
Mertens, Thomas Robert *biology professor*
Nanko, Raymond S. *physician*
Norris, Tracy Hopkins *retired public relations executive*
Roch, Lewis Marshall, II, *ophthalmic surgeon, medical entrepreneur*
Schaefer, Patricia *retired librarian*
Seymour, Richard Deming *technology educator*
Shobe, Franklin Dale *mathematician, educator*
Shoemaker, Helen E. Martin Achor *civic worker*
Stewart, Rita Joan *academic administrator*
Swartz, B. K., Jr., (Benjamin Kinsell Swartz Jr.) *archaeologist, educator*
Thornbro, William Graden *writer*
Van Ness, Ross Howard *education educator*
Wise, Charles Davidson *science educator*
Yeamans, George Thomas *librarian, educator*
Zhuk, Sergei Ivanovich *history professor, researcher*

Munster
Amber, Douglas George *lawyer*
Corsiglia, Robert Joseph *retired electrical construction company executive*
Neff, Bonita Dostal *communication development facilitator*
Potempa, Philip Matthew *journalist, columnist, communications educator*
Taylor, Gloria A. *minister, educator*

New Albany
Chowhan, Naveed Mahfooz *oncologist*
Orth, Susan Lynn *judge*
Rhodes, Betty Fleming *rehabilitation services professional, nurse*
Riehl, Jane Ellen *education educator*

New Harmony
Rice, David Lee *university president emeritus*

New Haven
Powelson, Gale Dawn *elementary school educator*

Newburgh
Slovachek, Donn Richard *obstetrician, gynecologist*
Tierney, Gordon Paul *real estate broker, genealogist*

Noblesville
Church, Douglas D. *lawyer*
Morrison, Joseph Young *transportation executive, consultant*
Wilson, Norman Glenn *church administrator, writer*

North Manchester
Mason, Stephen Olin *not-for-profit developer*
Switzer, Jo Young *college president*

North Vernon
Hicks, Gregory Steven *government agency administrator*

Notre Dame
Appleby, R(obert) Scott *history educator*
Arnold, Peri Ethan *political scientist*
Bartell, Ernest *economist, educator, priest*
Burish, Thomas Gerard *academic administrator, psychology professor*
Burns, Peter C. *science and engineering educator*
Crosson, Frederick James *retired dean, humanities educator*
Davis, Stacy Nicole *religious studies educator*
Despres, Leo Arthur *sociologist, anthropologist, educator, academic administrator*
Edmonds, Edmund P. *law librarian, educator, dean*
Garg, Umesh *physicist, researcher*
Goulet, Denis André *development ethicist*
Gray, William Guerin *engineering educator*
Gunn, Alan *retired law educator*
Hallinan, Maureen Theresa *sociologist, educator*
Hayes, Stephen Matthew *librarian*
Huber, Paul William *biochemistry professor, researcher*
Incropera, Frank Paul *mechanical engineering educator*
Jemielity, Thomas John *language educator*
Jenkins, John I. *academic administrator*
Jensen, Richard Jorg *biologist, educator*
Kogge, Peter Michael *computer scientist, educator*
Kulpa, Charles F. *microbiologist, educator*
Ladewski, Roman Sebastian *priest, educator*
Lanzinger, Klaus *language educator*
Malloy, Edward Aloysius *academic administrator*
Marino, Joseph Paul, Sr. *dean, chemist, researcher*
Marmion, Daniel Keith *school librarian*
Matthias, John Edward *English literature educator*
Maurice, Patricia Ann *geochemist, educator*
McInerny, Ralph Matthew *philosopher, educator, writer*
Meisel, Dan *chemist*
Merz, James Logan *electrical and materials engineering educator, researcher*
Michel, Anthony Nikolaus *electrical engineering educator, researcher*
Mirowski, Philip Edward *economics professor*
Noll, Mark A. *history professor*
O'Hara, Patricia Anne *dean, law educator*
O'Meara, Onorato Timothy *academic administrator, mathematician*
O'Rourke, William Andrew *literature and language professor, writer*
Ovaert, Timothy Christopher *mechanical engineering educator*
Pollard, Morris *microbiologist, educator*
Raymer, John David *literature and language professor*
Reilly, Frank Kelly *business educator*
Robinson, John Hayes *law educator*
Scheidt, W. Robert *chemistry educator, researcher*
Schmitz, Roger Anthony *chemical engineer, educator, academic administrator*
Shannon, William Norman III *finance educator, food service executive*
Shrader-Frechette, Kristin *science educator*
Smith, James Ormal *engineering educator*
Sommese, Andrew John *mathematics professor*
Stadtherr, Mark A. *chemical engineer, educator*
Stamper, John W. *architecture educator, academic administrator*
Trozzolo, Anthony Marion *chemistry professor*
Vakulenko, Sergei Borisovich *medical researcher, educator*
Valenzuela, Julio Samuel *sociologist, educator*
Vecchio, Robert Peter *business management educator*
Weigert, Andrew Joseph *sociology educator*
Weis, Charlie *college football coach*
Welch, Michael R. *sociologist, educator*
Williams, Oliver Franklin *priest, educator*
Woo, Carolyn Yauyan *dean*
Younger, Jennifer A. *university librarian*
Zuckert, Catherine Heldt *political science educator, writer, editor*

Pendleton
Kischuk, Richard Karl *insurance company executive*

Pittsboro
Swango, Colleen Jill *science educator*

Plainfield
Cullin, Rob *librarian*
Fivel, Steven Edward *lawyer, communications executive*
Laikin, Robert J. *electronics executive*

Portage
Popp, Joseph Bruce *manufacturing executive*
Schroeder, Marvis Lynn *accountant, artist*

Richmond
Angell, Stephen W. *religious studies educator*
Farber, Evan Ira *librarian*
Howanitz, E. Paul *thoracic surgeon*
Kirk, Thomas Garrett, Jr. *librarian*

Roanoke
Cutshall-Hayes, Diane Marion *elementary school educator*

Russiaville
Berry, Patricia A. *middle school educator*

San Pierre
Begley, Heidi Marie *nurse, entrepreneur*

Santa Claus
Edwards, James Dallas III *management consultant*

Schererville
Galante, Gustavo E. *plastic surgeon*
Jarrett, Alexis *insurance agent, lawyer*
Opacich, Milan *protective services official, musician*
Platis, Chris Steven *adult education educator*

Scottsburg
Kho, Eusebio *surgeon*

Seymour
Lewis, Judith Susanna *artist*
Pardieck, Roger L. *lawyer*

Shelbyville
Lisher, James Richard *lawyer*
McNeely, James Lee *lawyer*

Shoals
Boyd, Earl E., Jr. *councilman*

South Bend
Agbetsiafa, Douglas Kofi *academic administrator, financial and management consultant*
Anderson, Kenneth Paul *nephrologist, administrator*
Bell, Wishart Bryan *music educator, conductor*

Brueseke, Harold Edward *judge*
Carey, John Leo *lawyer*
Carrington, Michael Davis *criminal justice and security consultant*
Cohen, Ronald S. *accountant*
Cook, Pamela Margaret *French educator*
Davis, Glen Anthony *pediatrician*
Dowty, Alan Kent *political scientist, educator*
Harriman, Gerald Eugene *retired business administrator, economics professor*
Hellyer, Timothy Michael *protective services officer*
Horsbrugh, Patrick *architect, educator, environologist*
Hunt, Mary Reilly *organization executive*
Jones, Wellington Downing III *banker*
Jorgensen, Robert William *aerospace engineer*
Larkin, Eugene David *artist, educator*
Manion, Daniel Anthony *federal judge*
Miller, Robert L., Jr., (Bob Miller) *federal judge*
Muniz, Jorge *composer, music educator*
Norton, Sally Pauline *lawyer*
Reinke, William John *lawyer*
Ripple, Kenneth Francis *federal judge*
Rodgers, Grace Anne *university official*
Seall, Stephen Albert *lawyer*
Shaffer, Thomas Lindsay *lawyer, educator*
Sharp, Allen *federal judge*
Shepherd, Terry Lynn *special education educator*
Smith, E. Berry *television and radio consultant*
Smith, Thomas Gordon *architect*
Storin, Matthew Victor *academic administrator, educator, retired editor*
van Inwagen, Peter Jan *philosophy educator*
Vogel, Nelson J., Jr. *lawyer*

Spencerville
Clark, Donna M. *retired elementary school educator*

Sullivan
Chavez, Mary Ann *osteopathic family physician*

Sweetser
Hueston, Travis Earl *protective services official*

Tell City
Thrasher, Mary Ahlf Marcroft *educator, social worker*

Terre Haute
Aldridge, Sandra *civic volunteer*
Badar, M. Affan *engineering educator*
Bagert, Donald Joseph *computer scientist, educator*
Baker, Ronald Lee *folklore educator*
Benjamin, Lloyd William III *academic administrator*
Bopp, James, Jr. *lawyer*
Britton, Louis Franklin *lawyer*
Chambers, Curtis Allen *clergyman, church administrator*
Dando, William Arthur *academic administrator, geography and geology educator*
Davis, Lant B. *lawyer*
De Marr, Mary Jean *English language educator*
Frey, Susan M. *information specialist*
Gennaro, Rocco Joseph *philosopher, educator*
Gilman, David Alan *education educator*
Guthrie, Frank Albert *chemistry professor*
Hunt, Effie Neva *retired dean, literature educator*
Inlow, Jennifer Kay *chemistry professor, researcher*
Kesler, John A. *lawyer, real estate developer*
Leach, Ronald George *education educator, librarian*
Leigh, Janis *clinician*
Malooley, David Joseph *electronics and computer technology educator*
McCallister, Myrna J. *school librarian, administrator*
McCarter, David Harold *historian, volunteer*
Roshel, John Albert, Jr. *orthodontist*
Steinbaugh, Robert P. *management and finance educator*
Vincent, Richard C. *communications educator, researcher*

Upland
Kesler, Jay Lewis *retired academic administrator*

Valparaiso
Blaschke, Lawrence Raymond *electronic security services professional*
Canganelli, Vincent Guglielmo *retired psychiatrist*
Cook, Addison Gilbert *chemistry professor*
Mundinger, Donald Charles *retired college president*
Mundt, Marvin Glen *retired mathematics professor*
Olson, Lynn *sculptor, painter, writer*
Peters, Howard Nevin *foreign language educator*
Pritchett, Daniel R. *music educator*
Schlender, William Elmer *management sciences educator*
Schnabel, Robert Victor *retired academic administrator*

Vincennes
Emison, Ewing Rabb, Jr. *lawyer*
Smith, Bruce Arthur *lawyer*

Wabash
Ford, Richard Edwin *volunteer*
Scales, Richard Lewis *retired sales executive*

Walton
Chu, Johnson Chin Sheng *retired physician*

Wanatah
Moser, Sandra Kay *secondary school educator*

Warsaw
Binder, Jeffrey R. *medical products executive*
Dvorak, David C. *medical products executive, lawyer*
Elliott, J. Raymond *medical products executive*
Mroczkowski, Matthew *biomedical engineer*

Washington
Graham, David Bolden *food products executive*

Waterloo
Johnson, George Axil III *television producer*
McAlhany, Toni Anne *lawyer*

West Lafayette
Abhyankar, Shreeram Shankar *mathematics professor*
Abu-Omar, Mahdi M. *chemistry professor*
Adams, Robin Sue *engineering educator*
Adelman, Steven Allen *chemist, educator*
Albright, Lyle Frederick *chemical engineering educator*
Amstutz, Harold Emerson *veterinarian, educator*
Andrews, Theodora Anne *retired librarian, educator*
Arabi, Mazdak *hydrologist, researcher*
Barany, James Walter *industrial engineering educator*
Barnes, Virgil Everett, II, *physics professor*
Baumgardt, Billy Ray *professional society administrator, agriculturist*
Beering, Steven Claus *academic administrator, medical educator*
Belcastro, Patrick Frank *pharmacist, researcher*
Bertolet, Rodney Jay *philosophy educator*
Bisi, Arnab *management educator*
Blakesley, David Edward *language educator, small business owner*
Borowitz, Joseph Leo *pharmacologist, educator*
Broden, Thomas Francis III *French language educator*
Buckmaster, Dennis Rene *agricultural engineer, educator*
Chang, Ching-jer *medicinal chemistry educator*
Christian, John Edward *health science association administrator, educator*
Cicirelli, Victor George *psychologist*
Cohen, Raymond *retired mechanical engineer, educator*
Connor, John Murray *economics professor*
Contreni, John Joseph, Jr. *humanities educator*
Cooks, R(obert) Graham *chemist, educator*
Cooper, Arnold Cook *management educator, researcher*
Cooper, James Albert, Jr. *electrical engineering educator*
Córdova, France Anne-Dominic *academic administrator, astrophysicist*
Cosier, Richard A. *dean, finance educator*
Cramer, William Anthony *biochemistry and biophysics researcher, educator*
Cuendet, Muriel *research scientist*
Danielli-Garofalo, Donatella *mathematics professor*
Dasgupta, Anirban *statistician, researcher*
Delleur, Jacques William *retired engineering educator*
Diamond, Sidney *chemist, educator*
Drnevich, Vincent Paul *engineering educator*
Dyrenfurth, Michael John *education educator, academic administrator*
Edwards, Charles Richard *entomology and pest management educator*
Fanwick, Phillip Edward *crystallographer*
Farris, Paul Leonard *agricultural economist*
Fouad, Mohamed Raouf *science educator*
Frankenberger, Jane Rossing *agricultural engineer*
Frey, Harley Harrison, Jr. *retired anesthesiologist*
Gennett, Timothy *academic administrator*
Grace, Richard Edward *engineering educator*
Gruen, Gerald Elmer *psychologist, educator*
Hambrusch, Susanne *computer engineering educator*
Hollich, George J. *psychology professor*
Horwich, George *economist, educator*
Hunt, Michael O'Leary *wood science and engineering educator*
Ichiyama, Dennis Yoshihide *art educator, educational association administrator*
Jackson, Mark James *engineering educator*
Jamieson, Leah H. *engineering educator*
Jang, SooCheong (Shawn) *education educator*
Johannsen, Chris Jakob *agronomist, educator, administrator*
Judd, William Robert *engineering geologist, educator*
Kirksey, Avanelle *nutrition educator*
Ladisch, Michael R. *engineering educator*
Landgrebe, David Allen *electrical engineer*
Lechtenberg, Victor L. *agricultural studies educator*
Le Master, Dennis Clyde *retired forester, economist, educator*
Lewellen, Wilbur Garrett *management educator, consultant*
Lin, Pen-Min *electrical engineer, educator*
Lipschutz, Michael Elazar *chemistry professor, consultant, researcher*
Lord, Victoria Lynn *artist*
Lu, Chang *engineering professor*
Markee, Katherine Madigan *librarian, educator*
Marshall, Francis Joseph *aerospace engineer*
Mc Bride, William Leon *philosopher, educator*
McMillin, David Robert *chemistry professor*
Mork, Gordon Robert *historian, educator*
Morrison, Harry *chemistry professor*
Moskowitz, Herbert *management educator*
Moyars-Johnson, Mary Annis *retired academic administrator*
Mullins, James Lee *librarian, dean*
Naik, Sameer Vijaykumar *mechanical engineer, educator*
Namkung, Young *educator, researcher*
Negishi, Ei-ichi *chemistry professor*
Nelson, Philip Edwin *food scientist, educator*
Nixon, Judith May *librarian*
Ohm, Herbert Willis *agronomy educator, agriculturist*
Ong, Chee-Mun *engineering educator*
Overhauser, Albert Warner *physicist*
Peck, Garnet Edward *pharmacist, educator*
Peroulis, Dimitrios *engineering educator, consultant*
Perrucci, Robert *sociologist, educator*
Poulos, James Thomas *endocrinologist, educator*
Preckel, Paul Veitch *agricultural economics educator, researcher*
Ramkrishna, Doraiswami *chemical engineering educator, researcher*
Rau, Raghavendra *economist, educator*
Reklaitis, Gintaras Victor *chemical engineer, educator*
Ringel, Robert Lewis *academic administrator*
Roberts, Randy W. *history professor*
Rossmann, Michael George *biochemist, educator*
Rud, Anthony Gordon, Jr. *education educator*
Rutledge, Charles Ozwin *pharmacologist, educator*
Salvendy, Gavriel *industrial engineer, educator*
Sanders, David Avram *biochemist, researcher*
Schendel, Dan Eldon *management consultant, finance educator*
Scholer, Sue Wyant *retired state legislator*
Schwartz, Richard John *electrical engineering educator, researcher*
Shaw, Stanley Miner *pharmacist, educator*
Sherman, Louis Allen *biology professor, department chairman*
Shertzer, Bruce Eldon *education educator*
Silva, Tony *education educator, editor*
Sims-Curry, Kristy *women's college basketball coach*
Stob, Martin *retired physiology educator*
Swensen, Clifford Henrik, Jr. *psychologist, educator*
Taber, Margaret Ruth *retired engineering technology educator*
Tacker, Willis Arnold, Jr. *medical educator, researcher*
Thomas, Marlin Uluess *industrial engineer, educator, academic administrator*
Tyner, Wallace Edward *agricultural economics educator*
VanFossen, Phillip J. *academic administrator*
Varma, Arvind *chemical engineering educator, researcher*
Versyp, Sharon *women's college basketball coach*
Viskanta, Raymond *mechanical engineering educator*
Vitter, Jeffrey Scott *academic administrator, computer science educator, researcher*
Vroom, Govert *finance educator*
Wankat, Phillip Charles *chemical engineering educator*
Weidenaar, Dennis Jay *retired economics professor*
Weinstein, Michael Alan *political science professor*
Williams, David Jon *historian, artist*
Williams, Theodore Joseph *engineering educator*
Won, You-Yeon *engineering educator*
Wood, Terry Lee *mathematics educator*
Woodman, Harold David *historian, educator*
Xin, Yan Ping *special education educator*
Yao, Bin *mechanical engineering educator*
Yu, Jiu-Kang *mathematics professor*
Zwier, Timothy S. *chemistry professor*

Westfield
Basil, Douglas Constantine *writer, educator*
Bradbury, Betty Marie *history and music educator*
Hayashi, Tetsumaro *retired literature educator, writer, editor*

Westville
Serwatka, Judy Ann *computer and information systems educator*

Winamac
Ligocki, Gordon Michael *artist, educator*

Winona Lake
Davis, John James *religion educator*
Julien, Thomas Theodore *religious denomination administrator*

Zionsville
Garfunkel, Art *singer, actor*

IOWA

Akron
Hultgren, Dennis Eugene *farmer, management consultant*

Alden
Oliver, Kerryn Hinrichs *music educator, religious studies educator*

Algona
Aboud, John Anthony *music educator*

Altoona
Berkenes, Joyce Marie Poore *social worker, director*

Ames
Abbott, David L. *agricultural products executive*
Ahoy, Christopher Keen *educational association administrator, architect*
Allen, Benjamin J. *academic administrator*
Alumbaugh, JoAnn McCalla *magazine editor*
Anderson, Lloyd Lee *physiologist, educator*
Anderson, Robert Morris, Jr. *electrical engineer*
Angelici, Robert J. *chemistry educator*
Armstrong, Daniel Wayne *chemist, educator*
Avalos, Hector Ignacio *language educator*
Barnes, Richard George *physicist, researcher*
Barton, Thomas Jackson J. *chemistry professor, researcher*
Baumann, Edward Robert *environmental engineering educator*
Beran, George Wesley *veterinary microbiology educator*
Black, James Robert *industrial engineer*
Blaser, Brock Cameron *agronomist*
Bonomi, Ferne Gater *public relations executive*
Bowler, Nicola *engineering educator*
Brown, Robert C. *engineering educator*
Buchele, Wesley Fisher *retired agricultural engineering educator*
Bugeja, Michael Joseph *director, educator, writer*
Bytautas, Laimutis *chemist, educator*
Chimenti, Dale E. *engineering educator*
Clark, Lynn G. *botanist, educator*
Clem, John Richard *physicist, educator*
Courteau, Joanna *foreign language educator*
Crabtree, Beverly June *retired dean*
Dahiya, Rajbir Singh *mathematics professor, researcher*
David, Herbert Aron *retired statistician, educator*
Davis, Wayne Pitman *public relations executive*
Dogandzic, Aleksandar *electrical engineer, educator*
Ebbers, Larry Harold *education educator*
Fox, Karl August *retired economist, educator, eco-behavioral scientist*
Fritz, James Sherwood *chemist, educator*
Fuller, Wayne Arthur *statistics educator*
Geoffroy, Gregory L. *academic administrator, educator*
Greve, John Henry *veterinary parasitologist, educator*
Gschneidner, Karl Albert, Jr. *metallurgist, educator, editor, consultant*
Hallauer, Arnel Roy *geneticist*
Harl, Neil Eugene *economist, educator, lawyer, writer*
Hatfield, Jerry Lee *plant physiologist, agricultural meteorologist*
Hoffman, Elizabeth *academic administrator, economics professor*
Hong, Mei *chemistry professor*
Horowitz, Jack *biochemistry educator*
Jackson, George Arthur *dean, educator*
Jacobson, Robert Andrew *chemistry professor*
Jenks, Cynthia J. *research scientist*
Johnson, Lawrence Alan *cereal technologist, educator, administrator*
Kaufmann, Jeffrey Baer *finance educator*
Koziel, Jacek *agricultural engineer, educator*
Kushner, Mark Jay *engineering and physics educator*
Larsen, William Lawrence *engineering educator*
Lee, Seong-Jae *research scientist*
Lewis, Calvin Fred *architect, educator*
Lo, Chester C.H. *research scientist*
Madison, Olivia *librarian, dean*
Mallapragada, Surya K. *science educator*
Manatt, Richard *retired education educator*
Mattila, Mary Jo Kalsem *elementary school educator, special education educator, art educator*
Maxwell Dial, Eleanore *foreign language educator*
Mengeling, William Lloyd *retired veterinarian, virologist*
Mertins, James Walter *entomologist*
Moore, Kenneth James *agronomist, educator*
Munkvold, Gary P. *plant pathologist, educator*
Nostwich, Theodore Daniel *literature educator, researcher*
O'Berry, Phillip Aaron *retired veterinarian*
Okiishi, Theodore Hisao *mechanical engineering educator*
Opriessnig, Tanja *veterinary pathologist*
Palermo, Gregory Sebastian *architect*
Retallick, Michael S. *agricultural studies educator, director*
Robyt, John F. *chemistry professor*
Ross, Richard Francis *veterinarian, educator, dean, microbiologist*
Ruedenberg, Klaus *theoretical chemist, educator*
Sanders, Wallace Wolfred, Jr. *civil engineer*
Schlagel, Deborah "Devo" Lynn *chemist, materials scientist*
Seaton, Vaughn Allen *retired veterinary pathology educator*
Shonrock, Diana Donner *science and technology librarian, consultant, Library Association Executive*
Smith, John Francis *materials science educator*
Tabatabai, M. Ali *chemist, biochemist*
Thompson, Louis Milton *agronomy educator, researcher*
Topel, David Glen *agricultural studies educator*
Tylka, Gregory L. *plant pathologist, educator*
Wickert, Jonathan Adam *engineering educator*
Wilder, David Randolph *retired materials engineer*
Willham, Richard Lewis *zoology educator*
Willis, Jerry Weldon *computer systems educator, writer*
Yeung, Edward Szeshing *chemist*

Ankeny
Keese, Jan *elementary school educator*
Myers, Robert J. *retail executive*
Stahr, Curtis Brent *photographer, art association administrator, educator*

Bettendorf
Hatch, Lori S. *physical education educator*
Hengst, Herbert Randall *retired adult education educator*
Heyderman, Arthur Jerome *engineer, civilian military employee*
Myatt, William Howard *theater educator, director, actor*
Rathje, James Lee *broker*
Schulz, Sally Ann *pastoral musician, conductor, educator*
Skora, Susan Sundman *lawyer*
Taylor, Paulette Ann *special education educator, educational consultant*

Burlington
Gerdner, Linda Ann *nursing researcher, educator*
Hoth, Steven Sergey *lawyer, educator*

Cambridge
Colvin, Thomas Stuart *agricultural engineer, farmer*

Carlisle
Berning, Robert William *librarian*

Cedar Falls
Blakesley, Kimberly Kay *art educator, consultant*
Broadie, Richard R. *history professor*
Cai, Mingshui *education educator*
Chesnutt, Rod Martin *music educator*
Clohesy, William Warren *philosopher, educator*
Fanelli, Michael Paul *musician, educator, writer*
Haack, Joel K. *mathematics professor, academic administrator*
Huber, Mary Therese *museum director, consultant*
Koob, Robert Duane *chemistry professor, academic administrator*
Lettow, Lucille Jane *school librarian, education educator*
Lindberg, Duane R. *bishop, historian*
Lundy, Sherman Perry *secondary school educator*
Rajendran, Kadiampatti Natarajan *marketing educator*
Schnucker, Robert Victor *historian, educator*
Skaine, James C. *retired communications educator*
Skaine, Rosemarie Keller *writer, consultant, publisher*
Taylor, Darrell Richard *art gallery director, artist*

Cedar Rapids
Baermann, Donna Lee Roth *real estate property executive, retired insurance analyst*
Bahadur, Birendra *displays research specialist*
Baldwin, Cynthia Ann *industrial hygienist*
Baldwin, George Koehler *retired retail executive*
Brighi, Robert J. *principal*
Chadick, Gary Robert *lawyer*
Collins, Kevin Heath *lawyer*
Dangerfield, Joseph Allen *composer, educator*
Fitzpatrick, John Charles *humanities educator, curator*
Hansen, David Rasmussen *federal judge*
Jones, Clayton M. *computer and electronics company executive*
Keller, Eliot Aaron *broadcast executive*
Maikon, Marc Steven *podiatrist*
Mc Manus, Edward Joseph *federal judge*
Melloy, Michael J. *federal judge*
Nazette, Richard Follett *lawyer*
Norris, Albert Stanley *psychiatrist, educator*
Nyquist, John Davis *retired radio manufacturing company executive*
O'Brien, David A. *lawyer*
Pundt, Richard Arthur *lawyer*
Renter, Lois Irene Hutson *retired librarian*
Riley, Tom Joseph *lawyer*
Rohr, Carol Ann *composer, pianist, music educator*
Smith, Bruce Vaughn *electrical engineer*
Snell, Jennifer Sue *school system administrator, psychologist*
Stephens, Ralph Renne *massage therapy educator*
Stolte, Larry Gene *marketing executive, retired computer and publishing company executive*
Urbanowski, Melena Haskovec *elementary school educator*
Wax, Nadine Virginia *retired bank executive*
Whipple, William Perry *foundation administrator*
Wiese, Daniel Edward *marketing and communications researcher*
Wilson, Robert Foster *lawyer*
Ziese, Nancylee Hanson *social worker*

Centerville
Moritz, Dana Dee *language educator*

Chariton
Stuart, William Corwin *judge*

Charles City
Mc Cartney, Ralph Farnham *lawyer*

Cherokee
Gordon, Roma Dianne *music educator*

Clear Lake
Broshar, Robert Clare *retired architect*
Brown, Robert Grover *engineering educator*
Enabnit, Ted *retired lawyer*
Siska, Robert John *software engineer*

Clinton
Kearney, Michael John *banker*
Smith, Lauren Ashley *lawyer, clergyman, physicist, journalist*
Woodman, Grey Musgrave *psychiatrist*

Clive
Miller, Kenneth Edward *sociologist, educator*
Neis, Arthur Veral *healthcare and development company executive*

Coralville
Behlke, Mark Aaron *biotechnologist, research scientist*
Coulter, Charles Roy *lawyer*
McAndrew, Paul Joseph, Jr. *lawyer*

Council Bluffs
Alley, Mary Lou Vande Woude *retired medical/surgical nurse*
Kurt, Johnny Thomas *music educator*
Lippoldt, Vaughn Arthur *retired music educator*
Montgomery Linman, Sina Jo *pediatric nurse practitioner*
Peterson, Richard William *retired judge, lawyer*

Cresco
Fontes, Edward Michael *graphics designer*

Creston
Dillenburg, Carolyn Eva Lauer *retired secondary school educator*
Lockard, Kathleen Ann *educational association administrator*
Nurnberg, Roger C. *county official*

Davenport
Babbitt, Margaret Sargent *museum administrator*
Beckman, Robert W. *pharmacist*
Bush, Michael Kevin *lawyer*
Dcamp, Charles Barton *music educator*
Dettmann, David Allen *lawyer*
Foster, James Franklin *professional sports management executive*
Holleran, Karen Elaine *literature and language professor*
Hudson, Celeste Nutting *education educator, consultant, reading clinic administrator*
Johansen Kastell, Christina Marie *curator*
Juckem, Wilfred Philip *manufacturing executive*
Patterson, Nicholas Noel *language educator, journalism educator*
Robinson, Michelle *curator*
Runge, Kay Kretschmar *library consultant*
Shammas, Nicolas Wahib *internist, cardiologist*
Sheehey, Patricia Ann *secondary school educator*

Decorah
Farwell, Elwin D. *minister, consultant*
Martin, Spencer L. *musician, educator*
Monson, Larry Lee *music educator*

Des Moines
Abel, Gregory E. *utility company executive*
Appel, Brent Robert *state supreme court justice, lawyer*
Barnhart, Dorothy May (Kohrs) *retired small business owner*
Bartschat, Klaus Richard Wilhelm *physics professor*
Begleiter, Martin David *law educator, consultant*
Bergman, Bruce E. *municipal official*
Boettger, Nancy J. *state legislator*
Bremer, Celeste F. *judge*
Brickman, Kenneth Alan *state agency administrator*
Brooks, Roger Kay *insurance company executive*
Burn, Barbara Louise *literature and language educator*
Burns, Bernard John III *public defender*
Butler, Gayle *editor-in-chief*
Cady, Mark S. *state supreme court justice*
Carroll, Frank James *lawyer, educator*
Carter, James Harvey *retired state supreme court justice*
Charron, Joseph L. *bishop*
Cherney, Eugene Joseph *plastic surgeon, director*
Claypool, David L. *lawyer*
Colloton, Steven M. *federal judge*
Conlin, Roxanne Barton *lawyer*
Corning, Joy Cole *retired state official*
Critelli, Nicholas *lawyer, barrister*
Crook, Charles Samuel III *lawyer*
Culver, Chet (Chester John Culver) *governor*
Damos, Craig *construction executive*
Deluhery, Patrick John *retired state official*
Demorest, Allan Frederick *retired psychologist*
Devine, Michael Buxton *attorney, barrister, educator*
DeWulf Nickell, Karol *editor-in-chief*
Doyle, Richard Henry, IV, *lawyer*
Fagg, George Gardner *federal judge*
Fisher, Thomas George *lawyer, retired media company executive*
Fisher, Thomas George, Jr. *lawyer*
Fitzgerald, Michael Lee *state official*
Foxhoven, Jerry Ray *lawyer*
Frederici, C. Carleton *lawyer*
Gaines, Ruth Ann *secondary school educator*
Gartner, Michael Gay *editor, baseball and television executive*
Gersie, Michael H. *insurance company executive*
Godlasky, Thomas C. *insurance company executive*
Graham, Diane E. *newspaper editor*
Graziano, Craig Frank *lawyer*
Griswell, J. Barry *insurance company executive*
Gronstal, Thomas B. *state agency administrator*
Habib, Shahid *medical association administrator*
Hansell, Edgar Frank *lawyer*
Harris, Charles Elmer *retired lawyer*
Harris, K. David *senior state supreme court justice*
Hecht, Daryl L. *state supreme court justice*
Heiden, Cara *mortgage company executive*
Hill, Luther Lyons, Jr. *lawyer*
Hollingsworth, Laura L. *publishing executive*
Jacobs, Libby Swanson *state official*
Jarvey, John Alfred *federal judge*
Jeffrey, Judy *school system administrator*
Jensen, Dick Leroy *lawyer*
Jochum, Pam *state representative*
Judge, Patty Jean *lieutenant governor, nurse*
Kalainov, Sam Charles *insurance company executive*
Kelley, Bruce Gunn *insurance company executive, lawyer*
Kerr, William T. *publishing and broadcast executive*
Koehn, William James *lawyer*
Lacy, Stephen M. *publishing and broadcasting executive*
Larson, Jerry Leroy *state supreme court justice*
Lavorato, Louis A. *retired state supreme court justice*
Longstaff, Ronald Earl *federal judge*
MacKinnon, Douglas Jerome *retired radio and magazine publishing executive*
Martens, Harvey Arthur *retired government worker, academic administrator*
Mauro, Michael Anthony *state official*
Maxwell, David E. *academic executive, educator*
McGiverin, Arthur A. *former state supreme court chief justice*
Miller, Thomas J. *state attorney general*
Mitchell, Stuart *medical entomologist, consulting physician*
Myers, Mary Kathleen *publishing executive*
Nelson, Charlotte Bowers *public administrator*
Nickerson, Don C. *lawyer, retired prosecutor, judge*
O'Keefe, Mary A. *marketing executive*
Olds, John Ward *internist*
Oropeza, Dawn Martinez *art association administrator, artist, curator*
Pappajohn, John G. *venture capitalist*
Paterik, Frances Sue *secondary school educator, actress*
Peddicord, Roland Dale *lawyer*
Poppe, Pamela J. *accountant*
Quirmbach, Herman Charles *economics professor*
Ragan, Amanda *state senator*
Ramsden, Mary Catherine *substance abuse specialist*
Reece, Maynard Fred *artist, writer*
Rosenberg, Steven Joel *urologist*
Scholten, Gary P. *finance company executive*
Shaff, Karen E. *lawyer, insurance company executive*
Shors, John Dennis *lawyer*
Simpson, Lyle Lee *lawyer*
Smith, Diana Marie *business educator*
Sokol, David L. *energy services provider company executive*
Song, Joseph *pathologist, educator*
Stier, Mary P. *publishing executive*
Streit, Michael J. *state supreme court justice*
Ternus, Marsha K. *state supreme court chief justice*
Thompson, Jerome Lafayette *curator*
Vaughan, Therese Michele *insurance educator*
Vietor, Harold Duane *federal judge*
Wallace, Samuel Taylor *health system administrator*
Walters, Clayton William *health facility administrator, rehabilitation services professional, consultant*
Walters, Ross A. *federal judge*
Washburn, Carolyn K. *editor-in-chief*
Wattleworth, Roberta Ann *physician*
Webb, Mary Christine *reading recovery and in-class educator*
Wegner, Mary *state librarian*
Whitaker, Matthew George *prosecutor*
Wiggins, David Stewart *state supreme court justice*
Williams, Carl Chanson *insurance company executive*
Witke, David Rodney *retired newspaper editor, consultant*
Wolle, Charles Robert *judge*
Zimpleman, Larry Donald *actuary*

Dubuque
Burkhart, John Ernest *minister, theology studies educator*
Crahan, Jack Bertsch *retired manufacturing executive*
Hammer, David Lindley *lawyer, writer, investor*
Hanus, Jerome George *archbishop*
Haugen, Jane S. *elementary school educator*
Jorgensen, Gerald Thomas *psychologist, educator, lawyer*
Lickteig, Mary Joan *elementary school educator*
Toale, Thomas Edward *school system administrator, minister*
Tully, Thomas Alois *building materials executive, consultant, educator*

Eldridge
Downing, Paul R. *sports science educator*

Emmetsburg
Farnsworth, Steven Robert *safety engineer*

Epworth
Boice, Daniel Gene *college librarian*

Fairfield
Rogers, Benjamin Franklin *retired history professor*

Forest City
Biggs, Douglas Lee *historian, educator*

Fort Madison
Lorimer, Thomas Harold *minister*
Sodey, Angela Ann *gifted and talented educator*

Glenwood
Campbell, William Edward *mental hospital administrator*

Grinnell
Adelberg, Arnold Melvin *mathematics professor, researcher*
Kintner, Philip L. *history professor*
Michaels, Jennifer Tonks *foreign language educator*
Mitchell, Orlan E. *clergyman, academic administrator*
Osgood, Russell King *academic administrator*
Swartz, James Edward *chemistry professor, educator, dean*
Walker, Waldo Sylvester *biologist, educator, academic administrator*

Grundy Center
Kliebenstein, Don *retired lawyer*

Harlan
Salvo, J. C. *lawyer*

Humboldt
Dodgen, John N. *manufacturing executive*

Ida Grove
Snell, Bruce M., Jr. *judge*

Indianola
Dyer, Cynthia Myers *college librarian, archivist*
Larsen, Robert LeRoy *artistic director*
Mapel, Patricia Jolene *farmer, consultant*
Ouderkirk, Mason James *lawyer*

Iowa City
Abboud, Francois Mitry *physician, educator*
Abdel-Malek, Karim A. *biomedical engineer, educator*
Addis, Laird Clark, Jr. *philosopher, educator, musician*
Albrecht, William Price *economist, educator, government official*
Anderson, Rachel L. *healthcare educator, researcher*
Andreasen, Nancy Coover *psychiatrist, educator, neuroscientist*
Apicella, Michael Allen *microbiologist, educator*
Aspel, Paulene Violette *retired language educator*
Baker, Nancy L. *university librarian, educator*
Baker, Richard Graves *geologist, palynologist, educator*
Baumann, Mark *minister, director*
Beaver, Hilary A. *medical educator, ophthalmologist*
Bedell, George Noble *internist, educator*
Bell, Marvin Hartley *poet, language educator*
Bentz, Dale Monroe *retired librarian*
Bhattacharya, Debashish *environmental scientist, educator*
Bishara, Samir Edward *orthodontist*
Bonfield, Arthur Earl *law educator*
Boyd, Willard Lee *academic administrator, educator, lawyer, museum director*
Bozeman, Theodore D. *religion educator*
Brennan, Robert Lawrence *educational director, psychometrician*
Broffitt, James Drake *statistician, educator*
Buckwalter, Joseph Addison *orthopedic surgeon, educator*
Buckwalter, Kathleen C. *academic administrator, educator*
Burns, C(harles) Patrick *hematologist, oncologist*
Burton, Donald Joseph *chemistry professor*
Campbell, Kevin Peter *physiology and biophysics educator*
Clifton, James Albert *physician, educator*
Collins, Daniel W. *accountant, educator*
Conway, Thomas William *biochemist, educator*
Cooper, Reginald Rudyard *orthopedic surgeon, educator*
Densen, Paul Maximillian *retired health facility administrator*
Donelson, John Everett *biochemistry professor, molecular biologist*
Downer, Robert Nelson *lawyer*
Dreher, Melanie Creagan *dean, nursing educator*
Duff, Kevin *neuropsychologist, psychiatry professor*
Eckstein, John William *internist, educator, retired dean*
Eichenberger Gilmore, Julie Mae *research scientist*
El-Shanti, Hatem Isam *pediatrician, geneticist*
Ertl, Wolfgang *German language and literature educator, artist*
Feldt, Leonard Samuel *academic administrator, educator*
Fellows, Robert Ellis *medical educator, researcher*
Ferentz, Kirk *college football coach*
Ferguson, Richard L. *educational association administrator*
Fethke, Gary C. *economics professor, former dean*
Fiegel, Jennifer *biomedical researcher, educator*
Folsom, Lowell Edwin *language educator*
Fuller, John Williams *economics professor*
Galask, Rudolph Peter *obstetrician, gynecologist*
Gantz, Bruce Jay *otolaryngologist, educator*
Gelfand, Lawrence Emerson *historian, educator*
Geweke, John Frederick *economics professor*
Gibson, David Thomas *microbiology educator*
Gittler, Josephine *law educator*
Green, Peter Morris *classics educator, writer, translator*
Gronbeck, Bruce Elliot *communications educator*
Grose, Charles Frederick *pediatrician, epidemiologist*
Gurnett, Donald Alfred *physics professor*
Hammond, Harold Logan *oral and maxillofacial pathologist, retired educator*
Hausler, William John, Jr. *microbiologist, educator, public health service officer*
Hawley, Ellis Wayne *historian, educator*
Heistad, Donald Dean *cardiologist*
Hines, Norman William *law educator, retired dean*
Hobart, Thomas D. *lawyer*
Hogg, Robert Vincent, Jr. *mathematical statistician, educator*
Holland, Charles Joseph *lawyer*
Hovenkamp, Herbert *law educator*
Hunter, William Curt *dean, finance educator*
Husted, Russell Forest *research scientist*
Huttner, Sidney Frederick *librarian*
Jepsen, David Andrew *retired counselor, educator*
Johnsen, David C. *dean, dental educator*
Johnson, Nicholas *writer, lawyer, educator*
Jones, Carolyn *dean, law educator*
Jones, Catherine Clarissa *retired secondary school educator*
Jorgensen, Palle E.T. *mathematician, educator*
Katen-Bahensky, Donna *health facility administrator*
Kennedy, Colleen M. *medical educator*
Kerber, Linda Kaufman *historian, educator*
Kerber, Richard E. *cardiologist*
Kessel, Richard Glen *zoology educator*
Kim, Chong Lim *political science professor*
Konety, Badrinath R. *surgeon, researcher*
Kottick, Edward Leon *musician, educator*
Kurtz, Sheldon Francis *lawyer, educator*
Lamping, Kathryn G. *medical educator, medical researcher*
Lauer, Ronald Martin *pediatric cardiologist, researcher*
Lee, Inah *psychology professor*

Lickliter, Todd *men's college basketball coach*
Lie, Erik *finance educator*
Lim, Ramon (Khe-Siong Lim) *neuroscience educator, researcher*
Loewenberg, Gerhard *political science professor*
MacGillivray, Leonard R. *chemistry professor*
Magboul, Magboul M. *anesthesiologist, educator*
Mason, Edward Eaton *surgeon*
Mason, Sally Kay Frost *academic administrator, biology professor*
Mather, Roger Frederick *retired music educator, writer*
Maxson, Linda Ellen *biologist, educator*
McCartney, David Farnham *archivist, educator*
McKee, Christopher Fulton *historian, educator*
Medh, Jheem D. *medical educator, biochemist, researcher*
Merrill, Christopher Lyall *writer*
Miller, Dwight Merrick *archivist, historian*
Mills, Margaret H. *linguist*
Montgomery, Rex *biochemist, educator*
Morriss, Frank Howard, Jr. *pediatrics educator*
Muir, Ruth Brooks *alcohol/drug abuse services professional, consultant*
Mullan, Brian *medical educator*
Mullins, Robert F. *cell biologist*
Murray, Jeffrey C. *medical educator, pediatrician*
Myers, Virginia Anne *art educator*
Nathan, Peter E. *psychologist, educator*
Nelson, Herbert Leroy *psychiatrist*
Neumann, Roy Covert *architect*
Newell, Steven Wayne *secondary school educator, consultant*
Niebyl, Jennifer Robinson *obstetrician, gynecologist, educator*
Olin, William Harold *orthodontist, educator*
Park, Joon Bu *biomedical engineer, researcher, educator*
Patel, Virendra Chaturbhai *mechanical engineer, educator*
Perkins, Edward S. *ophthalmologist*
Pessin, Jeffrey E. *physiology educator*
Plapp, Bryce Vernon *biochemistry educator*
Ponseti, Ignacio Vives *orthopaedic surgery educator*
Porter, Nancy Lefgren *reading recovery educator*
Preucil, Doris Bogen *music educator*
Prisinzano, Thomas Edward *chemistry professor, researcher*
Raeburn, John Hay *language educator*
Richerson, Hal Bates *internist, allergist, immunologist, educator*
Riesz, Peter Charles *marketing educator, consultant*
Robertson, Timothy Joel *statistician, educator*
Robillard, Jean Eugene *dean, educator*
Russell, Stephen Richard *medical educator*
Schmeiser, Cynthia Board *educational organization executive*
Schmidt, Julius *sculptor*
Scott, John Beldon *art history educator, writer*
Sheffield, Val C. *medical geneticist*
Siebert, Calvin D. *economist, educator*
Skinstad, Anne Helene *psychologist, researcher*
Snyder, Peter M. *medical educator, medical researcher*
Solbrig, Ingeborg Hildegard *retired literature educator, writer*
Spies, Leon Fred *lawyer*
Spriestersbach, Duane Caryl *academic administrator, speech pathology/audiology services professional, educator*
Stay, Barbara *zoologist, educator*
Stein, Robert A. *writer, educator, military officer*
Strauss, John Steinert *dermatologist, educator*
Titze, Ingo Roland *physics professor*
Tsalikian, Eva *physician, educator*
Van Gilder, John Corley *neurosurgeon, educator*
Wasserman, Edward Arnold *psychology professor*
Weintraub, Neal L. *medical educator, cardiologist*
Welsh, Michael James *medical educator, biophysicist, educator*
Williams, Richard Dwayne *physician, educator, urologist*
Wing, Adrien Katherine *law educator*
Wunder, Charles C(ooper) *physiologist, biophysicist, educator*
Wurster, Dale Erwin *pharmacist, educator, retired dean*
Ziegler, Ekhard Erich *pediatrics educator*

Jefferson
Pauley, James Leroy, Jr. *retired lawyer*

Johnston
Vawter, Toni Valentine *artist*

Kellogg
Anderson, Dale C. *state agency professional, travel consultant*

Keokuk
Hoffman, James Paul *lawyer*

Le Mars
Rebstock, Theodore Lynn *chemist, educator, retired research scientist*

Madrid
Handy, Richard Lincoln *civil engineer, educator*

Manchester
Cook, Sharon Lee Delancey *retired elementary school educator, musician*

Maquoketa
Krum, Dee *secondary school educator*
Tubbs, Edward Lane *banker*

Marion
Pate, Paul Danny *mayor*

Marshalltown
Brennecke, Allen Eugene *lawyer*
Cassidy, Eugene Patrick *pathologist*
Thomas, David Llewellyn *physician*

Mason City
Backlin, William Wayne *music educator, composer*
Collison, Jim *publishing executive*
Davis, Joe Daughtry III *communications educator, writer*
Funkhouser, David Edward *lawyer*
Heiny, James Ray *lawyer*
Leet, Richard Eugene *artist, museum director*
Winston, Harold Ronald *lawyer*

Mount Pleasant
Brereton, Todd Richard *history professor*
Crane, Frederick Baron *retired music educator*
Edwards, Jason Ray *music educator, musician*
Vance, Michael C. *lawyer*

Mount Vernon
Will, Frederic *academic administrator, educator, writer*

Moville
Baker, Kent Alfred *broadcasting and publishing company executive*

Muscatine
Askren, Stan A. *manufacturing executive*
Housh, E. William *manufacturing executive*
Mowl, Linda *special education educator*
Nepple, James Anthony *lawyer*
Stanley, Richard Holt *consulting engineer*
Thomopulos, Gregs G. *consulting engineering company executive*

Nevada
Countryman, Dayton Wendell *lawyer*

Newton
Ward, Doree Maxine *secondary school educator*

North Liberty
Brenneman, Tami K. *not-for-profit fundraiser*

Norwalk
Augspurger, Mark Christian *elementary school educator*

Oelwein
Flaucher-Falck, Velma Ruth *retired special education educator*
McFarlane, Beth Lucetta Troester *retired mayor*

Okoboji
Pearson, Gerald Leon *food products executive*

Orange City
Barker, Jeff *theater and speech educator*

Osage
Christensen, Pamela Karen *pediatric nurse*

Osceola
Reynoldson, Walter Ward *retired judge, lawyer*

Oskaloosa
Anderson, Roxanna Marion *psychology professor*
Burrow, Paul Irving *secondary school educator*
Porter, David Lindsey *history and political science professor, writer*
Robbins, Janet Linda *language educator*

Ottumwa
Krafka, Mary Baird *lawyer*
Lang, Janelle J. *accountant*
Luman, Richard Gordon *retired religious studies educator*
Newquist, Judy Lynne Roos *elementary school educator, education educator*
Tuller, Joey David *manufacturing engineer*

Panora
Hartman, James Austin *retired geologist*

Pella
Den Adel, Raymond Lee *classics educator*
Dout, Anne Jacqueline *manufacturing and sales company executive*
Steele, Mildred Romedahl *educator*

Pocahontas
Jarvis, Sue Kay *science educator*

Rock Valley
Bulthuis, Sidney Aaron *secondary school educator*
Ortman, Don L. *principal*

Sheffield
VanHorn, Bradley Kent *musician*

Sioux City
Andersen, Leonard Christian *former state legislator, real estate investor*
Ayi, Bertha Serwa *infectious disease specialist, internist*
Bennett, Michael L. *agricultural products executive*
Clovis, Samuel Harvey, Jr. *academic administrator*
Doyle, Donald Vincent *retired state legislator, lawyer*
Hassenger, James Michael *writer, retired small business owner*
Madsen, George Frank *lawyer*
Mounts, Nancy *secondary school educator*
Peterson, Delaine Charles *lawyer, bank executive*
Rants, Carolyn Jean *academic administrator, educator*
Waller, Ephraim Everett *retired association executive*
Warnstadt, Jacqueline Rae *elementary school educator*

Spirit Lake
Quaday-Gray, Ailene Diann *retired speech pathology/audiology services professional*

Storm Lake
Bochtler, Stanley Edwin *education educator*
Safley, Holli Ewoldt *music educator*

Tipton
Farwell, Walter Maurice *vocalist, educator*

Toledo
Lyon, Norma Duffield *sculptor, agriculturist*

Urbandale
Hoyt, Kenneth Boyd *education educator, writer*

Walford
Brooks, Debra L. *healthcare executive, neuromuscular therapist*

Waterloo
Alfrey, Marian Antoinette *retired education educator*
Green, Nancy Loughridge *publishing executive*
Kaaki, Bilal *obstetrician, gynecologist*
Kober, Arletta Refshauge (Mrs. Kay L. Kober) *supervisor*
Waters, Ronald W. *theology studies educator, church administrator, pastor*

Waverly
Brunkhorst, Robert John *computer programmer, analyst*
Eick-Gamm, Kimberly Marie *social worker*
Menzel, Ferol Schricker *academic administrator*
O'Konski, Marjorie Katherine *music educator*
Rose, Mary Mabel *retired elementary school educator*

West Bend
Wuebker, Colleen Marie *retired librarian*

West Branch
Forsythe, Patricia Hays *development professional*
Mather, Mildred Eunice *retired archivist*
Walch, Timothy George *library director*

West Des Moines
Alberts, Marion Edward *retired physician*
Bakari, Rosenna *educational psychology professor, consultant*
Conner, William Bruce *facilty engineer*
Dooley, Donald John *retired publishing executive*
Gleason, Robert Lyle *financial analyst, realtor*
Henderson, Jason Craig *financial advisor*
Hockenberg, Harlan David *lawyer*
Houser, Thomas J. *lawyer*
Johnson, John Paul *lawyer, judge*
Lynch, David William *physicist, retired educator*
Marshall, Russell Frank *consulting company executive*
Matthews, Alexander *health facility administrator*
Owens, Fredric Newell *animal nutritionist, educator*
Pearson, Ronald Dale *retail food stores corporation executive*
Pomerantz, Marvin Alvin *manufacturing executive*
Power, Joseph Edward *lawyer*
Rosen, Matthew Stephen *retired botanist*
Stines, Fred, Jr. *publisher*
Tully, Robert Gerard *lawyer*
Weresh, Matthew John *orthopedic surgeon*

Windsor Heights
Beadel, Stephen Jay *author*

Zearing
Britten, William Harry *editor, publisher*

KANSAS

Abilene
Holt, Dan *library director*

Arkansas City
Templar, Ted Mac *lawyer*

Atchison
Lane, Elizabeth Ann *genealogist, researcher*

Baldwin City
Baker, Margaret Moore-Fritz *retired school librarian, humanities educator*
Long, Patricia N. *academic administrator*

Baxter Springs
Whiteley, Henry Howard *religious studies educator, minister*

Bern
Dassel-Stuke, Donna Jane *psychologist, educator*

Caney
Wilmoth, Marsha H. *elementary school educator*

Chanute
Dillard, Dean Innes *English language educator, academic administrator*
Smith, David *music educator*

Chase
Stull, Evalyn Marie *artist*

Chetopa
Reid, William R. *agricultural studies educator*

Claflin
Burmeister, Paul Frederick *farmer*
Lewis, Robert V., Jr. *computer programmer*

Clay Center
Braden, James Dale *former state legislator*

Clifton
Compton, Doris Martha *lay worker*

Coffeyville
Garner, Jim D. *state official, lawyer*
Hawley, Raymond Glen *pathologist*

Colby
Lamm, Freddie Ray *research agricultural engineer*
Morrison, James Frank *optometrist, state legislator*

Coldwater
Adams, Elizabeth Herrington *banker*

Concordia
Fowler, Wayne Lewis, Sr. *internist*

Copeland
Birney, Walter Leroy *religious administrator*

Cottonwood Falls
Dodez, Diane M. *principal*

De Soto
Strubbe, Thomas R. *insurance industry executive*

Derby
Helms, Neville Troy *manufacturing company administrator*

Dighton
Stanley, Ellen May *historian, consultant*

Dodge City
Rebein, David James *lawyer*

El Dorado
Langley, William M. *educator*

Emmett
Byers, Walter *athletic association executive*

Emporia
Alshare, Khaled A. *information systems educator*
Bartruff, Jim *theater educator, director*
Catlett, Robert Bishop *economics professor*
Fowler, Barbara J. *middle school educator*
Lovett, Christopher C. *history professor, consultant*
Phelps, Connie Lea *psychology and special education educator*
Sundberg, Marshall David *biology professor*

Enterprise
Wickman, John Edward *librarian, historian*

Eskridge
Taylor, Russell Benton *mining executive*

Eudora
Miller, David Groff *insurance agent*

Eureka
Pitko, Pamela Ann *physical education educator, coach*

Fort Leavenworth
Anderson, David Allen *military officer, educator*
Barker, Ray Todd *archivist, writer*
Cupp, Orville Shawn *military officer*
King, Curtis Steeble *history professor*
O'Neill, Mark E. *military officer*
Wilhelm, Gary Bretz *physician*

Fort Scott
Hudson, Leigh Carleton *lawyer*

Frontenac
Wilson, Donald Wallin *academic administrator, communications educator*

Garden City
Alam, A.N.M. Mahbub Ul *engineer, educator*
Loyd, Ward Eugene *lawyer*

Garden Plain
Stovall, Carla Jo *former state attorney general*

Geuda Springs
Moore, BettyJane *elementary school educator*

Goddard
Molz, Carol Jean *elementary school educator*

Great Bend
Rittenhouse, Nancy Carol *elementary school educator*

Greeley
Fisher, William Ralph *retired geologist*

Hays
Caprez, Judith V. *social worker, director*
Coyne, Patrick Ivan *physiological ecologist*
Kuksi, Kris M. *artist*

Hiawatha
Searight, Karen S. *language educator*

Humboldt
Finney, Paul *acupuncturist, Chinese herbologist, entrepreneur*

Hutchinson
Baumer, Beverly Belle *journalist*
Brewer, William Thomas *theater educator, theater director*
Buchanan, Bruce *publishing executive*
Buzbee, Richard Edgar *retired newspaper editor*
Crater, Timothy Andrews *internist*
Davis, Mary Elizabeth *speech pathologist, educator, counselor*
Dick, Harold Latham *manufacturing executive*
Hayes, John Francis *lawyer*
Kerr, Dave *state official, marketing professional*

O'Neal, Michael Ralph *state legislator, lawyer*
Swearer, William Brooks *lawyer*
Widener, Charlene *theater director, educator*

Independence
Wright, Tami LaDonna *pre-school educator*

Iola
Lynn, Emerson Elwood, Jr. *retired newspaper editor/publisher*
Strickler, Ivan K. *dairy farmer*
Tebbets, Gary Duane *music educator*

Junction City
Werts, Merrill Harmon *retired management consultant*

Kansas City
Anderson, Harrison Clarke *pathologist, educator, biomedical researcher*
Arakawa, Kasumi *physician, educator*
Atkinson, Barbara F. *dean, medical educator, executive vice chancellor*
Baska, James Louis *wholesale grocery company executive*
Burke, Thomas Richard *community college administrator*
Caruthers, Loyce Ellenor *education educator*
Choi, In-Young *science educator*
Clifton, Thomas E. *academic administrator, minister*
Damjanov, Ivan *pathologist, educator*
Drake, Kenneth David *geologist*
Dunn, Marvin Irvin *physician*
Godwin, Harold Norman *pharmacist, educator*
Grantham, Jared James *nephrologist, educator*
Hudson, Robert Paul *medical educator*
Huet, Raul *psychiatrist*
Jerome, Norge Winifred *nutritionist, anthropologist, educator*
Johnson, Joy Ann *diagnostic radiologist*
Jones, Charles W. *labor union executive*
Keleher, James P. *bishop*
Lawrence, Walter Thomas *plastic surgeon*
Lee, Kyo Rak *radiologist, educator*
Lungstrum, John W. *federal judge*
McCallum, Richard Warwick *medical researcher, clinician, educator*
Meyers, David George *internist, cardiologist, educator*
Miller, Karen L. *dean, nursing educator*
Mohn, Melvin Paul *anatomist, educator*
Naumann, Joseph F. *archbishop*
Olofson, Tom William *technology company executive*
Penick, Elizabeth C. *psychologist*
Perez, Victor Manuel *physician, plastic surgeon*
Rawitch, Allen Barry *medical educator, academic administrator*
Schloerb, Paul Richard *surgeon, educator*
Sciolaro, Charles Michael *cardiothoracic and vascular surgeon*
Suzuki, Tsuneo *molecular immunologist*
Taylor, Sarah Ann *oncologist, educator*
Vacek, James *cardiologist*
Voogt, James Leonard *medical educator*
Vratil, Kathryn Hoefer *federal judge*
Warne, Alan M. *continuing education educator, consultant*
Waxse, David John *judge*
Xiao, Zhousheng *pharmacologist, bone biologist*
Ziegler, Dewey Kiper *neurologist, educator*

Lansing
Huhn, Theresa J. *social studies educator*

Larned
Rehorn, Lois M(arie) (Lois Marie Smith) *nursing administrator*

Lawrence
Alexander, John Thorndike *historian, educator*
Alterman, Michail A. *biochemist, researcher*
Ammar, Raymond George *physicist, researcher*
Angino, Ernest Edward *retired geology and engineering educator*
Armitage, Kenneth Barclay *retired biology professor*
Barnett, William Arnold *economics professor*
Beedles, William LeRoy *finance educator, consultant*
Benjamin, Bezaleel Solomon *structural engineer, educator*
Blaga, Otilia M. *psychologist, researcher*
Briscoe, Mary Beck *federal judge*
Buck, Henry William, Jr. *obstetrician, gynecologist*
Byers, George William *retired entomology educator*
Casad, Robert Clair *legal educator*
Cienciala, Anna Maria *history professor*
Clowes, Edith W. *language educator, consultant, literature educator, consultant*
Conard, John Joseph *finance company executive*
Crowe, William Joseph *librarian*
Darwin, David *engineering educator, consultant*
Dickinson, William Boyd, Jr. *media consultant*
Dooley, Patrick John *graphic designer, educator*
Dreschhoff, Gisela Auguste Marie *physicist, researcher*
Earle, Jonathan Halperin *history professor*
Eldredge, Charles Child III *art history educator*
Enos, Paul *geologist, educator*
Frederickson, Horace George *retired academic administrator, humanities educator*
Gerhard, Lee Clarence *geologist, educator*
Grabow, Stephen Harris *architecture educator*
Green, Don Wesley *chemical and petroleum engineering educator*
Grzymala-Busse, Jerzy Witold *engineering educator*
Gunn, James Edwin *language educator*
Hajdu, Michael A. *cardiologist*
Hale, Richard Lee *magazine editor*
Haricombe, Lorraine *library director, dean*
Haufler, Christopher Hardin *botany educator*
Heller, Francis Howard *retired law and political science educator*
Hemenway, Robert E. *academic administrator, language educator*
Hilding, Jerel Lee *music and dance educator, retired dancer*
Himmelberg, Charles John III *mathematics professor, researcher*
Hirschey, Mark *finance educator, investment advisor*
Johnston, Richard Fourness *biologist, educator*
Kaesler, Roger L. *paleontologist, educator*
Knorr, Patrick *communications executive*
Lan, Chuan-Tau Edward *aerospace engineering educator*
Landgrebe, John Allan *chemistry professor*
Lariviere, Richard Wilfred *academic administrator, educator*
Lerner, David Evan *mathematician*
Li, Chu-Tsing *art historian, educator*
Lichtwardt, Robert William *mycologist*
Locke, Carl Edwin, Jr. *academic administrator, engineer, educator*
Mattila, Edward Charles *music educator*
McAllister, Stephen Robert *dean, law educator*
Mc Coin, John Mack *social worker*
Merriam, Daniel F(rancis) *geologist*
Michener, Charles Duncan *entomologist, researcher, educator*
Miller, Don Robert *surgeon, educator*
Mitscher, Lester Allen *chemist, educator*
Moore, Richard Kerr *electrical engineering educator*
Muirhead, Vincent Uriel *retired aerospace engineer*
Pasik-Duncan, Bozenna Janina *mathematics professor, researcher*
Peterson, Nancy *special education educator*
Pozdro, John Walter *retired music educator, composer*
Rath, Eric Clemence *history professor*
Roskam, Jan *aerospace engineer*
Rowland, James Richard *electrical engineering educator*
Saul, Norman Eugene *historian, educator*
Schoeck, Richard J. *English and humanities scholar, poet*
Schowen, Richard Lyle *retired scientist*
Self, Bill *men's college basketball coach*
Shankel, Delbert Merrill *microbiologist, biologist, educator*
Simons, Dolph Collins, Jr. *publishing executive, editor*
Stella, Valentino John *chemistry professor*
Sterbenz, James Philip Guenther *computer network scientist*
Stull, Donald David *anthropologist, educator*
Tacha, Deanell Reece *federal judge*
Tsubaki, Andrew Takahisa *theater director, educator*
Turnbull, Ann Patterson *special education educator, consultant, research director*
Turnbull, H. Rutherford III *lawyer, educator*
Tuttle, William McCullough, Jr. *history professor*
Wiechert, Allen LeRoy *educational association administrator*
Willhite, G. Paul *chemical engineer, petroleum engineer, educator*
Winter, Winton Allen, Jr. *lawyer, state legislator*
Woelfel, James Warren *philosophy and humanities educator*
Worth, George John *retired English literature educator*

Leavenworth
Crow, Michael P. *lawyer*

Leawood
Barnthouse, Chris David *orthopedic surgeon*
Bortnick, Daniel Philip *plastic surgeon*
Dykes, Archie Reece *finance company executive*
Garwood, Julie *writer*
Gray, Thomas Alva, Jr. *writer, minister, retired protective services official*
Gregory, Lewis Dean *trust company executive*
Gutek, E(dward) Philip *plastic and reconstructive surgeon, educator*
Hartzler, Geoffrey Oliver *retired cardiologist*
Ivey, Donald James *historian, archivist*
Joslin, Janine Elizabeth *preservationist, consultant*
Karmeier, Delbert Fred *engineer, consultant, realtor*
King, Barbara Sackheim *travel company executive*
Mooney, Justin David *motel executive, consultant*
Nouhan, Regina Marie *plastic surgeon*
Talley, Melvin Gary *academic administrator*
Terry, Robert Brooks *food products executive, lawyer*

Lenexa
Ascher, James John *pharmaceutical executive*
Jackson, Charles Wayne *food products and former telecommunications industry executive*
Rawlings, Gregory Owen *science educator, consultant*
Warenskjold, Dorothy *singer, educator*

Liberal
Hicks, Linda Reona *elementary school educator*
Richard, Loren Dru *bank executive*
Smothermon, Reba Maxine *elementary school educator*

Lincoln
Crangle, Robert D. *lawyer, management consultant, entrepreneur*

Lindsborg
Fisk, Irwin Wesley *financial investigator*
Mahraun, Daniel Allen *musician, director*

Logan
Manion, Kay Daureen *financial and office manager*

Louisville
Jabbar, Abdul *physician, educator, gastroenterologist*

Manhattan
Amtoft, Torben *adult education educator, researcher*
Argoti, Andres *chemical engineer, researcher*
Babcock, Michael Ward *economics professor*
Barkley, Andrew Paul *economics professor*
Begum, Khurshida *zoologist, researcher*
Bhadriraju, Subramanyam Venkata *entomologist, consultant*
Coffman, James Richard *academic administrator, veterinarian, educator*
Di Terlizzi, Roberta *pathologist, educator*
Durkee, William Robert *retired internist*
Erickson, Howard Hugh *veterinarian, physiology educator*
Foerster, Bernd *architecture educator*
Gillispie, Harold Leon *minister*
Gorton, Robert L. *retired mechanical engineer*
Hawley, Jana Marie *educator, department head*
Higham, Robin *historian, editor, publisher*
Jin, Hyun Seung *communications educator*
Johnson, William Howard *retired agricultural engineer, educator*
Kaufman, Donald Wayne *research ecologist*
Kirkham, M. B. *plant physiologist, educator*
Klabunde, Kenneth J. *chemistry professor, researcher*
Le, Anh-Thu *physicist, researcher*
Lee, E(ugene) Stanley *engineering educator*
Leslie, John Franklin *pathologist, educator*
Li, Dong *economics professor*
Liu, Kelly H. *geophysicist, educator*
Martin, Frank (Francisco J. Martin) *men's college basketball coach*
McKee, Richard Miles *retired agricultural studies educator*
Mortenson, Kristin Oppenheim *musician*
Muir, William Lloyd III *academic administrator*
Murray, John Patrick *psychologist, educator, researcher*
Myers, Richard Bowman *former joint chiefs of staff chairman, educator*
Oehme, Frederick Wolfgang *medical researcher, educator*
Olds, David Andrew *food scientist, educator*
Patterson, Deb *women's college basketball coach*
Posler, Gerry Lynn *agronomist, educator*
Prins, Harald Edward Lambert *anthropologist, educator*
Seaton, Edward Lee *editor, publishing executive*
Shanklin, Carol W. *dietician, educator*
Simons, Gale Gene *nuclear and electrical engineer, educator*
Singh, Devinder *chemical engineer*
Stevenson, Jeffrey Smith *physiologist, educator*
Thomas, Lloyd Brewster *economics professor*
Wefald, Jon *academic administrator*
Wesch, Michael *anthropology educator, cultural anthropologist, media ecologist*

Mankato
Underwood, Deanna Kay *librarian*

Marysville
Underwood, Earl Frederick, Jr. *clergyman*

Mcpherson
Coppock, Doris Ellen *retired physical education educator, retired music educator*
Tomlison, Rondal Scott *music educator*

Meade
Brannan, Cleo Estella *retired elementary school educator*

Mission
Bresky, Steven J. *agricultural products executive*
Churchill, James Garton *retired finance company executive*
Trevino, Lee Buck *professional golfer*
Walker, H. Reed *lawyer*

Mission Hills
Rose, Stephen F. *columnist*

Neosho Falls
Bader, Robert Smith *biology and zoology educator, researcher*

Newton
Morford, Marie Arlene *insurance company executive*

North Newton
Ediger, Marlow *retired education educator*
Eitzen, David Stanley *sociologist, educator*
Goering, Jacob D. *retired psychoanalyst*
Snider, Marie Anna *syndicated columnist*
Sprunger, Keith L. *historian, educator*

Olathe
Anderson, Joshua M. *speech educator*
Anderson, Peggy C. *retired elementary school educator*
Burrell, Gary *retired manufacturing executive*
Dodd, James B. *Internet executive*
Eichholz, Mark Joseph (Mick) *lawyer*
Epp, Garrett Wayne *music educator*
Goodwin, Becky K. *educational technology resource educator*
Harmon, Roger E. *environmentalist*
Haskin, J. Michael *lawyer*
Kao, Min H. *manufacturing executive*
Kline, Phillip D. *prosecutor*
Monzon, Carlos Manuel *physician*
Morrison, Ray Leon *library director, education educator*
Obenhaus, Steven Lee *secondary school educator*
Roby, Brian L. *bank executive*
Scott, Robert Gene *lawyer*
Stevens, Diana Lynn *elementary school educator*

Onaga
Dillinger, Susan Alice *reading specialist*

Ottawa
Davidson, Medora Lea *dance educator*

Overland Park
Amundson, Beverly Carden *artist*
Baldwin, William Allen *application developer*
Barger, Donald Gordon, Jr. *freight company executive*
Betts, Gene M. *telecommunications industry executive*
Burger, Henry G. *linguist, anthropologist, writer*
Callahan, Michael Thomas *arbitrator, consultant, construction executive, writer*
Carpenter, Nancy E. *mathematics professor*
Christian, Shirley Ann *journalist, author*
Churay, Daniel J. *lawyer*
Cummings, Jan Norman *interior designer, educator*
Ferrell, James Edwin *nuclear energy industry executive*
Fuller, Michael B. *communications executive*
Gaar, Norman Edward *lawyer, former state senator*
Gerke, Thomas A. *telecommunications industry executive, lawyer*
Goetz, Kenneth Lee *cardiovascular physiologist, research consultant, writer*
Green, John Lafayette, Jr. *strategic planning executive, former educational association administrator*
Guckenheimer, Daniel Paul *financial advisor*
Hettinger, Michael Eugene *corneal surgeon*
Hill, Lloyd Lester *food service executive*
Horen, Jeffrey Harry *telecommunications executive*
Johnston, Jocelyn Stanwell *paralegal*
Keplinger, Bruce (Donald Keplinger) *lawyer*
Landry, Mark Edward *podiatrist, researcher*
Lucas, James Raymond *company executive, writer, consultant, speaker*
McCann, Vonya B. *federal agency administrator, telecommunications industry executive*
Murphy, Mark D. *lawyer, real estate developer*
Murray, Thomas Veatch *lawyer*
Ostby, Frederick Paul, Jr. *meteorologist, retired government official, science administrator*
Paulsen, Ruth Ann *French and Spanish language educator*
Rodman, Leonard C. *engineering and construction executive*
Stanton, Roger D. *lawyer*
Stem, Carl Herbert *business educator*
Strandjord, M. Jeannine *telecommunications industry executive*
Velicer, Janet Schafbuch *retired elementary school educator*
Voska, Kathryn Caples *consultant, facilitator*
Vratil, John Logan *state legislator, lawyer*
Woods, Richard Dale *lawyer*
Zollars, William D. *freight company executive*

Ozawkie
Blodig, Allison Marie *environmental services administrator*

Parsons
Lomas, Lyle Wayne *agricultural research administrator, educator*
Walker, Robert R. *music educator*

Pittsburg
Chubb, Richard Marshall *retired physician*
Harris, James Dean *computer scientist, educator*
Lee, Earl Wayne *library science educator*
Morgan, Lyle Warner, II, *medical educator*
Nettels, George Edward, Jr. *retired mining executive*
Sullivan, William John *osteopath*
Trent, Darrell M. *ambassador, academic administrator, transportation executive*

Pleasanton
Earnest, Ola May *curator*

Pomona
Gentry, Alberta Elizabeth *elementary school educator*

Prairie Village
Fairchild, Robert Charles *pediatrician*
Vogel, Arthur Anton *clergyman*

Pratt
Hart, Don Lee *academic administrator, writer*
Hayden, (John) Michael *state official, former governor*
Loomis, Howard Krey *banker, director*
Rehman, Qaiser *rheumatologist, researcher*
Shrack, Christopher George *curator, educator*

Saint John
Robinson, Alexander Jacob *retired psychologist*

Salina
Horst, Deena Louise *state legislator*
Toelle, Jennifer M. *museum staff member*

Sharon Springs
Picknick, Kevin M. *commodities trader*

Shawnee
Poplau, Ronald W. *social studies educator*

Shawnee Mission
Allen, Janet Lee *special education educator*
Badgerow, John Nicholas *lawyer*
Becker, David M. *lawyer*
Bell, Deloris Wiley *physician*
Bond, Richard Lee *lawyer, state senator*
Braude, Michael *commodities trader, researcher*
Breen, Katherine Anne *speech and language pathologist*
Fleming, Michael O. *physician*
Flora, Jairus Dale, Jr. *statistician*

Gamet, Donald Max *appliance company executive*
Helder, Jan Pleasant, Jr. *lawyer*
Henley, Douglas E. *medical association administrator*
Johnson, Bradford McClure *financial consultant, investor*
Mandl, Herbert Jay *rabbi*
Martin, Donna Lee *retired publishing company executive*
McEachen, Richard Edward *banker, lawyer*
Mealman, Glenn *corporate marketing executive*
Moeller, Laura Lee *retired retail executive, library and information consultant*
Nulton, William Clements *retired lawyer*
Pressman, Ronald R. *utilities executive*
Price, James Gordon *physician, educator*
Putman, Dale Cornelius *management consultant, lawyer*
Sader, Carol Hope *former state legislator*
Smith, Edwin Dudley *lawyer*
Snyder, Willard Breidenthal *lawyer*
Sparks, Billy Schley *lawyer*
Starrett, Frederick Kent *lawyer*
Sweeney, Leo Joseph *university administrator*
Thomas, Christopher Yancey III *surgeon, educator*
Vandever, William Dirk *lawyer*

Sublette
Swinney, Carol Joyce *secondary school educator*

Topeka
Allegrucci, Donald Lee *state supreme court justice*
Beier, Carol Ann *state supreme court justice*
Brandau, Christie Pearson *librarian*
Bunten, William Daniel *retired banker*
Cantrell, Duane L. *retail executive*
Carlin, Sydney *state representative*
Concannon, James M. *lawyer, educator, dean*
Crow, Sam Alfred *judge*
Davis, Robert Edward *state supreme court justice*
Dimmitt, Lawrence Andrew *lawyer, educator*
Dunning, John Wilson, II, *music educator, vocalist*
Dye, Gloria A. *education educator*
Elrod, Linda Diane Henry *lawyer, educator*
Farley, Jerry B. *academic administrator*
Frahm, Sheila *association executive, academic administrator, former government official*
Fyler, Carl John *retired dentist*
Goetz, Roger Melvin *minister*
Gordon, Lana G. *state representative*
Griffin, Ronald Charles *law educator*
Hayse, Richard Franklin *lawyer*
Hedrick, Lois Jean *investment company executive, state official*
Hejtmanek, Danton Charles *lawyer*
Irick, Larry D. *lawyer, energy executive*
Jenkins, Lynn M. *state official, former state legislator*
Johnson, Lee Alan *state supreme court justice*
Karst, Gary Gene *retired architect*
Kirk, Nancy A. *state legislator, nursing home administrator*
Luckert, Marla Jo *state supreme court justice*
Marquardt, Christel Elisabeth *judge*
Massey, Michael J. *lawyer, retail executive*
Mc Candless, Barbara J. *financial consultant*
McFarland, Kay Eleanor *state supreme court chief justice*
McFarland, William Joseph (Joe McFarland) *academic administrator*
Menninger, William Walter *psychiatrist*
Millsap, Gina J. *library director*
Moore, William B. *energy executive*
Morrison, Paul J. *state attorney general, former prosecutor*
Nuss, Lawton R. *state supreme court justice*
Parkinson, Mark Vincent *lieutenant governor, former state legislator*
Peters, Barbara Waterman *artist, educator*
Petty, Marge D. *state senator*
Porzig, Ullrich E. *retail executive*
Rogers, Richard Dean *federal judge*
Rosen, Eric S. *state supreme court justice*
Rubel, Matthew Evan *retail executive*
Saville, Pat *state senate official*
Schellman, Elizabeth Turney *vocalist, educator*
Schmidt, Derek *state legislator*
Schroer, Gene Eldon *lawyer*
Schultz, LeAnne *violinist, performer, music educator*
Schultz, Richard Allen *lawyer, farmer*
Sebelius, Kathleen Gilligan *governor*
Sheldon, Roy Albert *literature and language professor*
Sipes, Karen Kay *communications executive*
Slaughter, Jerry *medical association administrator*
Slemmons, Robert Sheldon *architect*
Spencer, William Edwin *retired telecommunications industry executive, engineer*
Spohn, Herbert Emil *psychologist*
Thornburgh, Ron E. *state official*
Thull, Tom (John Thomas Thull) *state agency administrator*
Varner, Charleen LaVerne McClanahan *nutritionist, educator, dietician*

Uniontown
Conard, Norman Dale *secondary school educator*

Wichita
Arnel, Kevin J. *lawyer*
Ayres, Ted D. *lawyer*
Badger, Ronald Kay *lawyer*
Berner-Harris, Cynthia Kay *library director*
Brown, Wesley Ernest *federal judge*
Burket, George Edward, Jr. *retired family physician*
Cadman, Wilson Kennedy *retired utilities executive*
Cobb, Jill *pathologist*
Da'Luz Vieira-Jones, Lorraine Christine C. *acupuncturist, researcher*
Dierks, Melinda Adair *science educator*
Docking, Thomas Robert *lawyer, former state lieutenant governor*
Dorr, Stephanie Tilden *psychotherapist*
Feilmeier, Steve *corporate financial executive*
Guthrie, Diana Fern *nursing educator*
Guthrie, Richard Alan *physician*
Hatteberg, Larry Merle *photojournalist*
Herr, Peter Helmut Friederich *sales executive*
Holden, Mark V. *lawyer*
Holland, Phillip Kent *aerospace engineer*
Johnson, C. Nicholas *dance company executive*
Johnson, Kevin Blaine *lawyer, educator*
Jones, Schuyler *museum director, anthropologist*
Knight, Robert G. *mayor, investment banker*
Koch, Charles de Ganahl *industrial company executive*
Lerman, Kenneth Barry *marketing professional, consultant*
Marshall, Gregg *men's college basketball coach*
McKee, George Moffitt, Jr. *civil engineer, consultant*
Melgren, Eric Franklin *prosecutor, lawyer*
Menefee, Frederick Lewis *advertising executive*
Meyer, Russell William, Jr. *air transportation executive*
Moore, Leon, Jr. *social studies educator*
Moore, Tim J. *lawyer*
Park, Chan Hyung *cell biologist, physician*
Parks, Linda S. *lawyer*
Pottorff, Jo Ann *state legislator*
Powell, Shirley Theressa *elementary school educator*
Racer, William Eugene *retired music educator*
Randels, Ed L. *lawyer*
Rieger, James A. *plastic surgeon*
Rosenberg, Matthew William *plastic surgeon*
Schuster, James Edward *defense equipment manufacturing company executive*
Sevart, Daniel Joseph *lawyer*
Sorensen, Harvey R. *lawyer*
Spurgeon, Kenneth R. *history professor*
Stephenson, Richard Ismert *lawyer*
Thompson, Lee (Morris Thompson) *lawyer*
Vliet, Marni *foundation administrator*
Waters, Mary A. *literature and language professor*
Wilhelm, William Jean *civil engineering educator*
Winkler, Dana John *lawyer*

Winfield
Gray, Ina Turner *fraternal organization administrator*

Yates Center
Stockebrand, Larry Dean *physical education educator, director*

KENTUCKY

Ashland
Hatfield, Bennett K. *mining executive*

Bellevue
Carpenter, Woodrow Wilson *manufacturing executive, ceramics engineer*

Benton
Glass, Mary Jean *management executive*

Berea
Drake, Richard Bryant *retired history professor*
Krug, John Carleton (Tony Krug) *academic administrator, library director, consultant*
Lamb, Irene Hendricks *medical researcher*

Bowling Green
Ahmed, S. Basheer *research and development company executive, educator*
Atwell, Nedra Wheeler *education educator, consultant*
Berry, Mark Sean *music educator*
Burch, Barbara G. *academic administrator*
Cangemi, Joseph Peter *psychologist, consultant, educator*
Collett, Walter Lee *electrical engineer, educator*
Garrison, Geneva *retired administrative assistant*
Haynes, Robert Vaughn *retired academic administrator, historian*
Holland, John Ben *clothing manufacturing company executive*
Huddleston, Joseph Russell *retired judge, mediator, arbitrator*
Jackson, Carlton Luther *history professor, writer*
Minton, John D., Jr. *state supreme court justice*
Slocum, Donald Warren *chemist, researcher*
Wilcher, Larry K. *lawyer*

Brandenburg
Bowen, Patricia Lederer *dental educator*

Brooksville
Dorton, Truda Lou *medical/surgical and geriatrics nurse*

Burlington
Frohlich, Anthony William *lawyer, judge*
Mitchell, Timothy Lynn *music educator*

Campbellsville
Burch, John Russell, Jr. *library director*
Martin, J(ames) Kenneth *music educator*
McArthur, Lisa R. *music educator, musician*

Catlettsburg
Nixon, Ronda Lynn *paralegal*

Corbin
Barton-Collings, Nelda Ann *retired political organization worker, retired bank executive, entrepreneur*
Doby, John Thomas *social psychologist*

Covington
Berg, Lorine McComis *retired guidance counselor*
Froesel, David W., Jr. *medical products executive*
Gemunder, Joel Frank *healthcare company executive*
Hausrath, David L. *lawyer*
Kerr, Thomas Robert *lawyer*
Kobasuk, Mark G. *lawyer, pharmaceutical executive*
Land, Suzanne Prieur *lawyer*
McQueen, Regenia *writer*
O'Brien, James J. *manufacturing executive*
Quin, Joseph Marvin *manufacturing executive*
Robinson, William T. III *lawyer*
Schaeffer, Andrew *lawyer*
Sloan, David B. *lawyer*
Smith, Pete A. *lawyer*
Stepner, Donald Leon *lawyer*
Surber, David Francis *public relations executive, consultant, television producer, journalist*
Tenkotte, Paul Allen *history and international studies educator*
Wolnitzek, Stephen Dale *lawyer*

Crescent Springs
Chellgren, Paul Wilbur *energy industry executive*

Crestwood
Perry, Norah D. *language educator*
Ray, Ronald Dudley *lawyer*
Roy, Elmon Harold *minister*

Cynthiana
Bandurski, Bruce Lord *retired ecologist, environmental scientist*
Florence, Joyce Fritz *mathematics professor*

Danville
Breeze, William Hancock *academic administrator*
Levin, William Robert *art historian*
Morris, Alvin Leonard *retired dentist, academic administrator*
Nickens, Harry Carl *medical association administrator*
Pappas, Marjorie L. *library studies educator*
Roush, John A. *academic administrator*

Elizabethtown
Rahman, Rafiq Ur *oncologist, educator*

Elkton
Manthey, Frank Anthony *physician, director*

Erlanger
Cuneo, Dennis Clifford *automotive company executive*

Eubank
Karriker, Danny Allen *small business owner, protective services official*

Florence
Gorman, Gayla Marlene Osborne *consumer affairs executive*
Hartman, Rome *television producer*

Fort Campbell
Clark, Cecil Lee *military officer*
Griffin, Johnny Lee *military officer*

Fort Knox
Tucker, Brenda Brunette *elementary school educator*

Fort Mitchell
Malayery, Nasrin *educational consultant*
More, Donna *lawyer*
Silvers, Gerald Thomas *retired publishing executive*

Fort Thomas
Whalen, Paul Lewellin *lawyer, educator, mediator*
Yelton, Dianne Burgess *secondary school educator*

Fort Wright
Sullivan, Connie Castleberry *artist*

Frankfort
Bowling, Charles Bryan *legal association administrator*
Carroll, Julian Morton *lawyer, retired governor, state senator*
Chadwick, Robert *lawyer, judge*
Cunningham, Bill *state supreme court justice*
Embry, Michael Dale *writer, editor, educator*
Erwin, Barbara F. *school system administrator*
Fletcher, Ernie (Ernest Lee Fletcher) *governor, former congressman*
Fletcher, Winona Lee *theater educator*
Frye, Wilbur Wayne *retired soil science educator, researcher, administrator*
Gibbons, Judith A. *librarian*
Gomelsky, Boris *geneticist, educator*
Grayson, Trey (C.M. Grayson) *state official*
Hatchett, Edward Bryan, Jr. *lawyer*
Huebner, Ruth A. *science educator, researcher*
Lambert, Joseph Earl *state supreme court chief justice*
Lawrence, Cordell G. *state agency administrator*
Miller, Jonathan S. *state official*
Noland, Kevin M. *school system administrator*
Onkst, Wayne *state librarian*
Palmore, John Stanley, Jr. *retired lawyer*
Palumbo, Ruth Ann *state legislator*
Pence, Stephen Beville *lieutenant governor*
Rainey, Jo Anne *psychologist, educator*
Richards, Jody *state legislator, communications educator, small business owner*
Schroder, Wil *state supreme court justice*
Scott, Will T. *state supreme court justice*
Sisney, Sherleen Sue *secondary school educator*
Sonego, Ian G. *assistant attorney general*
Stine, Katie Kratz *state legislator*
Stumbo, Gregory D. *state attorney general*
Zourarakis, Demetrio Periferachis *natural resource scientist*

Franklin
Law, Jerriann Marcella *artist, poet, writer*

Ft Campbell
Gutheinz, Michael John *military officer, lawyer*

Georgetown
Bates, Clyde Thomas *retired economics professor*
Caroland, William Bourne *structural engineer*
Klotter, James C. *historian, educator*
Lookadoo, Regan *psychology professor*
Wiseman, Frank L., Jr. *chemistry professor*

Glasgow
Baker, Walter Arnold *lawyer*
Coomer, Merle Joan *retired language educator*
Whittaker, Bill Douglas *minister*

Greenville
Walters, Sue Fox *broadcast executive, accountant*

Grethel
Hughes, Cindi Baker *special education educator*

Guston
Yundt, Betty Brandenburg *elementary school educator*

Hardin
Morrow, Bruce William *academic administrator, management consultant*

Harlan
Greene, James S. III *school administrator*

Harrods Creek
Keeney, Steven Harris *lawyer*

Harrodsburg
Worley, Carolyn Ann Hiner *retired secondary school educator*

Hazard
Cory, Cynthia Strong *mathematics professor*
Stewart, Sharon Rose *mathematics professor*

Henderson
Sullivan, William Litsey *lawyer*

Highland Heights
Donnelly, Sharlotte K. B. Neely *anthropology educator, writer*
Kenny, Gregory B. *industrial equipment executive*
Luse, Kimberly Ann *radiologist, educator*
Ramage, James Alfred *history professor*

Hopkinsville
Neville, Thomas Lee *food service company executive*
Redmon-Holliday, Rose Marie *secondary school educator*
Soberal, Isabel M. *minister, music educator, social worker*
Wilkinson, Daniel Melvin *music educator*

Independence
Brewer, Edward Cage III *law educator*
Hopgood, James F. *anthropologist, educator*

La Grange
Morgan, Mary Dan *librarian*

Lexington
Allison, Jonathan Mackinnon *university professor, researcher*
Anderson, James Wingo *physician*
Arrington, Michael Irvin *communications educator*
Baker, Merl *engineering educator*
Bell, Randall Keith *writer*
Bennett, Victoria Elizabeth *rehabilitation nurse, dialysis nurse and technician*
Beshear, Steven Lynn *lawyer*
Boyd, James Robert *energy executive*
Bricker, John Timothy *pediatric cardiologist*
Brock, Carolyn Pratt *chemist, educator*
Brock, Louis Milton, Jr. *engineering educator, researcher*
Calvert, C. Emmett *former state agency administrator*
Cameron-Mickens, Vertrelle Diane *singer, conductor, voice educator*
Canales, Denise Niles *software company executive*
Chance, Kenneth Bernard, Sr. *endodontist educator, academic administrator*
Charnigo, Richard John, Jr. *statistician, educator*
Chi, Keon Soo *editor, educator, researcher*
Clawson, David Kay *orthopedic surgeon*
Coffman, Edward McKenzie *retired history professor*
Coffman, Jennifer Burcham *judge*
Cole, Henry Philip *educational psychology educator*
Cole, Vincent J. *lawyer*
Cross, Alvin Miller (Al Cross) *journalist*
Curlander, Paul Joseph *technology executive*
Davey, Diane Davis *pathologist, educator*
DeLuca, Patrick Phillip *pharmacist, educator, medical association administrator*
Dhir, Anir *surgeon*
Diedrichs, Carol Pitts *library director, dean*
Drake, Vaughn Paris, Jr. *electrical engineer*
Ehmann, William Donald *chemistry professor*
Espinosa, Patricio Sebastian *neurologist, researcher*
Ettensohn, Frank Robert *geologist, educator*
Fryman, Virgil Thomas, Jr. *lawyer*
Gable, Robert Elledy *real estate investment company executive*

Gallagher, Eugene Bennett *sociologist, medical educator*
Garman, Ray Fillmore *occupational physician, director*
Gillispie, Billy Clyde *men's college basketball coach*
Girard, C. Jack *artist, educator*
Goldman, Alvin Lee *lawyer, educator, arbitrator*
Guskey, Thomas Robert *education educator*
Hagen, Michael Dale *family physician educator*
Hamilton-Kemp, Thomas Rogers *organic chemist, educator*
Hickey, John King *lawyer, career officer*
Hinds, Sara Feagan *elementary school educator*
Hochstrasser, Donald Lee *cultural anthropologist, community health and public administrator*
Hojahmat, Marhaba *research scientist*
Holsapple, Clyde Warren *decision and information systems educator*
Holsinger, James Wilson, Jr. *cardiologist, physician*
Huberfeld, Nicole Lauren *healthcare educator*
Huffman, Gerald P. *science administrator, educator*
Humphries, Asa Alan, Jr. *biologist, educator, dean*
Imhoff, Kathleen Ruth Tostrud *library administrator*
Iocono, Joseph Anthony *pediatric and trauma surgeon*
Johnson, Jane Penelope *freelance/self-employed writer*
Kaplan, Martin P. *allergist, immunologist, pediatrician*
Kasperbauer, Michael John *plant physiology educator, researcher*
Keeling, Larry Dale *journalist*
Keller, James *retired state supreme court justice*
Kelly, Timothy Michael *newspaper publisher*
Kern, Bernard Donald *retired physicist*
Kibler, William Benjamin *orthopedist, surgeon*
Kissling, Fred Ralph, Jr. *publishing and insurance agency executive*
Lester, Roy David *lawyer*
Lewis, Robert Kay, Jr. *fundraising executive*
Male, Alan Thomas *engineering educator, foundation administrator*
Mason, Ellsworth Goodwin *retired librarian*
McCoy, R. Burl *lawyer*
McRoberts, J. William *urologist, surgeon, researcher*
Means, Robert Taylor, Jr. *hematologist, educator, researcher*
Michael, Douglas Charles *law educator*
Millard, James Kemper *marketing executive*
Miller, Pamela Gundersen *retired mayor*
Miller, Thomas William *psychologist*
Mitchell, George Ernest, Jr. *zoology educator*
Moliterno, David J. *cardiologist, educator*
Mostert, Paul Stallings *retired mathematician*
Mukherjee, Debabrata *cardiologist, researcher*
Nau, David Paul *pharmacist, educator*
Noble, Mary C. *state supreme court justice*
O'Hurley, John *actor*
Oser, Carrie B. *sociologist, educator*
Pollack, Rhoda-Gale *theater educator, director*
Prado, Edgar *horse racing jockey*
Puffer, James C. *sports medicine physician, educator, medical association administrator*
Rahman, Shafiqur *neuropharmacologist, scientist, educator*
Reed, Michael Robert *agricultural economist*
Reynolds, Eric William *medical educator*
Roach, John C. *state supreme court justice*
Robinson, Thomas Christopher *health science educator*
Romanowitz, Byron Foster *architect, engineer*
Sandoval, Arturo Alonzo *artist, educator*
Sexton, Robert Fenimore *educational organization executive*
Sineath, Timothy Wayne *librarian, educator, dean*
Sogin, David Warren *music educator*
Steensland, Ronald Paul *librarian*
Steinhubl, Steven Rudolf *cardiologist, educator*
Stempel, John Dallas *international studies educator*
Straus, Robert *behavioral sciences educator*
Thapar, Amul R. *prosecutor*
Thelin, John Robert *historian, educator, researcher*
Timoney, Peter Joseph *veterinarian, educator, virologist, consultant*
Todd, James Marion *retired lawyer*
Todd, Lee Trover, Jr. *academic administrator, electrical engineer*
Tollison, Joseph W. *family practice physician*
Turley, Robert Joe *lawyer*
Turner, Sharon P. *dean, dentist, educator*
Varellas, Sandra Motte *judge*
Vestal, Allan W. *dean, law educator*
Walsh-Piper, Kathleen A. *museum director*
Warth, Robert Douglas *history professor*
Weitzel, William David *psychiatrist*
Whayne, Thomas French, Jr. *cardiologist, educator*
Wildasin, David E(arl) *economics professor*
Woodring, John Howell *radiologist*
Worell, Judith P. *psychologist, educator*
Young, Paul Ray *medical association administrator, physician*
Young, Sandra Cooper *retired librarian*
Zito, Nick *horse trainer, breeder*

London

Dyche, Jane Winkler *lawyer*
Keller, John Warren *lawyer*
Siler, Eugene Edward, Jr. *federal judge*

Louisville

Adams, Robert Waugh *state agency administrator, economist, educator*
Amin, Mohammad *urology educator*
Andrews, Billy Franklin *pediatrician, educator*
Ardery, Philip Pendleton *lawyer*
Aronoff, George Rodger *medicine and pharmacology educator*
Atcher, Joseph Ray *director*
Ballantine, John Tilden *lawyer*
Ballew, Laurie K. *psychiatrist*
Barr, James Houston III *lawyer*
Beck, Peter *marketing executive, minister*
Becker, Gail Roselyn *museum director*
Belanger, William Joseph *chemist, consultant*
Bell, Mary Margaret *archivist*
Bhola, Rahul *ophthalmologist*
Blandford, Jim, Jr. *social studies educator*
Bloem, James H. *managed health care executive*
Boggs, Danny Julian *federal judge*
Boykin, Gladys *retired religious organization administrator*
Breidenbach, Warren Conrad *plastic surgeon, hand surgeon*
Brown, Bonnie Maryetta *lawyer*
Buckaway, William Allen, Jr. *lawyer*
Buthod, Craig *library director*
Byerlein, Anne P. *human resources specialist, food products executive*
Cafaro, Debra A. *real estate company executive*
Callen, Jeffrey Phillip *dermatologist, educator*
Campbell, Christian Larsen *lawyer*
Carlisle, Douglas R. *health facility administrator*
Cecil, Bonnie Susan *elementary school educator*
Chagpar, Anees Bahadurali *surgeon*
Chien, Sufan *surgeon, educator*
Choi, Namok *education educator*
Clayton, M. Courtland *management consultant*
Cohen, Burton Jack *otolaryngologist, educator*
Conner, Stewart Edmund *lawyer*
Cook, Terrance *business executive*
Cornelius, Wayne Anderson *electrical and computer engineering consultant*
Cowan, Frederic Joseph *judge*
Dale, Judy Ries *religious organization administrator, consultant*
Danzl, Daniel Frank *emergency physician*
Davidson, Gordon Byron *lawyer*
Deering, Ronald Franklin *librarian, minister*
DeMunbrun-Harmon, Donne O'Donnell *retired family physician*
Diaz, Paul J. *health products executive*
Dudley, George Ellsworth *lawyer*
Duffy, Martin Patrick *lawyer*
Early, Jack Jones *foundation executive*
Elin, Ronald John *pathologist, educator*
Ethridge, Larry Clayton *lawyer*
Evans, Robert L. *sports venue executive*
Ewald, Robert Charles *lawyer*
Farman, Allan George *radiologist, pathologist, educator*
Fenner, Chris *pastor*
Fenton, Thomas Conner *lawyer*
Foster, William R. *zoological park administrator*
French, Michael Bruce *business executive*
Fuchs, Olivia Anne Morris *lawyer*
Galandiuk, Susan *colon and rectal surgeon, educator*
Gall, Stanley Adolph *immunologist, researcher*
Garcia, Rafael Jorge *retired chemical engineer*
Garretson, Henry David *neurosurgeon*
Gilman, Sheldon Glenn *lawyer*
Glogower, Michael Howard *real estate company executive, consultant*
Goldstein, Irvin L. *elementary school educator*
Goodman, Bruce *health products executive*
Greaver, Joanne Hutchins *mathematics educator, writer*
Gregory, James Francis *electrical engineer*
Grevious, Inez Cobble *health facility administrator*
Griffith, Mary H. *bank executive*
Guillaume, Raymond Kendrick *banker*
Hallenberg, Robert Lewis *lawyer*
Hanson, Dennis Michael *retired health facility administrator*
Hathcock, Bonita Catherine (Bonnie Hathcock) *managed health care company executive*
Hayes, William Meredith *pilot, retired military officer*
Hearl, Peter R. *food service executive*
Heiden, Charles Kenneth *metal products executive, consultant, retired military officer*
Herrington, E. Paul III *lawyer*
Heyburn, John Gilpin, II, *federal judge*
Hickey, Bobby Ray *underwriting assistant*
Hiestand, Sheila Patricia *lawyer*
Hipwell, Arthur P. *lawyer, managed health care company executive*
Hopson, Edwin Sharp *lawyer*
Hua, Shiping *political science professor*
Huber, David L. *prosecutor*
Ivey, Denise Hassell *publishing executive*
Ivory, Bennie L. *executive editor*
Jenne, Sue Oak *secondary school educator*
Johnson, Alan Arthur *physicist, educator, consultant*
Jones, David A., Jr. *insurance company executive*
Jones, Veronnie Faye *medical educator, dean*
Kantardzic, Mehmed M. *engineering educator*
Kaplan, Henry Jerrold *ophthalmologist, educator*
Kaplan, Joel A. *academic administrator*
Karwowski, Waldemar *adult education educator*
Kehrt, Bettie F. *medical transcriptionist*
Kelly, Thomas Cajetan *archbishop*
Klotter, John Charles *retired law educator*
Kragthorpe, Steve *college football coach*
Kuntz, Edward Lawrence *healthcare executive*
Landan, Henry Sinclair *financial and business consultant*
Lay, Norvie Lee *law educator*
Lechleiter, Richard A. *medical products executive*
Lin, Stephen Houng Tze *music educator*
Linen, Jonathan S. *diversified financial services company executive*
Luber, Thomas J(ulian) *lawyer*
Lunsford, W. Bruce *health facility administrator and products executive*
Lyndrup, Peggy B. *lawyer*
Mackey, Thomas Clyde *historian*
Maggiolo, Allison Joseph *lawyer*
Manly, Samuel *lawyer*
Margulis, Heidi *health products executive*
Martin, Boyce Ficklen, Jr. *federal judge*
Martin, David Allen *application developer, computer scientist*
Martinez-Maldonado, Manuel *academic administrator, dean, medical and science educator*
Mather, Elizabeth Vivian *healthcare executive*
Mathews, William Gregory *social services administrator*
McAnulty, William E., Jr. *state supreme court justice*
McCall, John Richard *lawyer*
McCallister, Michael B. *insurance company executive*
McCormick, Steven Thomas *insurance company executive*
McKim, Ruth Ann *financial planner*
Mellen, Francis Joseph, Jr. *lawyer*
Mohler, Richard Albert, Jr. *academic administrator, theologian*
Morrin, Peter Patrick *museum director*
Mountz, Wade *retired healthcare executive*
Moya, Steve *health products executive*
Nahata, Babu L. *economics professor, researcher*
Nasraoui, Olfa *computer scientist, educator, electrical engineer*
Newell, Elizabeth Carolyn *retired secondary school educator*
Noah, Christopher Ray *history educator*
Noland, Thomas Turley, Jr. *managed healthcare company executive*
Northern, Richard *lawyer*
Novak, David C. *restaurant company executive*
Osborn, John Simcoe, Jr. *lawyer*
Parker, Joseph Corbin, Jr. *pathologist, educator, department chairman*
Parkins, Frederick Milton *dental educator, dean*
Pelfrey, D. Patton *lawyer*
Pence, Hobert Lee *physician*
Pettyjohn, Shirley Ellis *lawyer, real estate company executive*
Phillips, William Ault *pediatric dentist*
Pitino, Rick *men's college basketball coach*
Portes, Pedro René *psychology professor, department chairman*
Pottinger, Ronald Wayne *food products executive*
Rainer, Thomas Spratling *pastor*
Ramsey, James R. *academic administrator*
Richardson, James David *surgeon*
Riedman, Mary Suzanne *lawyer*
Ronald, Peter *utilities executive*
Rose, Charles Alexander *lawyer*
Rosky, Theodore Samuel *insurance company executive*
Rothstein, Laura *dean, law educator*
Runyon, Keith Leslie *lawyer, editor*
Ruter, Ruth Evelyn *elementary school educator*
Saunders, Robert Samuel *venture capitalist*
Schoo, Bernard John *surgeon*
Schwab, John Joseph *psychiatrist, educator*
Scott, Ralph Mason *retired radiologist, educator*
Shaikun, Michael Gary *lawyer*
Shield, Gene *health products executive*
Shirwan, Haval *immunologist, educator*
Shobe, David Soren *librarian, director*
Silverthorn, Robert Sterner, Jr. *lawyer*
Simpson, Charles R. III *judge*
Skees, William Leonard, Jr. *lawyer*
Smith, Donald Ray *magazine dealer*
Smith, R(obert) Michael *lawyer*
Spalding, Catherine *lawyer*
Staffieri, Victor A. *energy executive*
Stanton, M(orris) Duncan *psychologist, researcher, dean*
Street, William May *retired beverage company executive*
Swain, Donald Christie *retired academic administrator, historian, educator*
Syed, Ibrahim Bijli *medical educator, physicist*
Talbott, Ben Johnson, Jr. *lawyer*
Tanguay, Peter Eugene *child and adolescent psychiatry educator*
Tasman, Allan *psychiatry educator*
Taylor, Robert Lewis *management educator*
Tobin, Gordon Ross *surgery educator*
Towles, Donald Blackburn *retired publishing executive*
Tran, Long Trieu *industrial engineer*
Travis, Nigel *food service executive*
Varga, Paul C. *beverage products executive*
Vincenti, Michael Baxter *lawyer*
Vish, Donald H. *lawyer, writer, photographer*
Vogel, Werner Paul *retired machine company executive*
Waddell, William Joseph *pharmacologist, toxicologist*
Wagner, James Miller *funeral director*
Walz, Jeff (Jeffrey J. Walz) *women's college basketball coach*
Weisskopf, Bernard *pediatrician, child behavior, development and genetics specialist, educator*
Welsh, Sir Alfred John *lawyer, investment advisor*
Westberry, Robert Kent *lawyer*
Wiseman, Dennis R. *science educator*
Wright, Jeffrey A. *biology, physics educator*
Wright, Jesse Hartzell *psychiatrist, educator*
Yazdanpanah, Mehdi Mohammad *research scientist*
Zepeda, Susan Ghozeil *foundation administrator*
Zimmerman, Gideon K. *retired minister*

Madisonville

Kington, Barry Clark *investor, consultant*
Livers, Thomas Henry *not-for-profit fundraiser, consultant*
May, Richard Warren *writer*
Parrent, Jonathan Vince *dean*
Spain, Thomas B. *retired state supreme court justice*
Stulc, Jaroslav Peter *surgeon, educator*

Masonic Home

Coryell, Glynn Heath *financial services executive*

Midway

Critchfield, Alison *education educator*

Monticello

Sexton, Scotty Eugene *music educator, gifted and talented educator*

Morehead

Besant, Larry Xon *retired librarian, administrator, consultant*
Detweiler, Greg Jeffrey *music educator*
Kantrovich, Adam J. *education educator*
Klecker, Beverly McCauley *academic administrator*
Mason, Patrick Samual *manufacturing engineer*
Miller, Green Russell *economist, educator*
Mohammed, Jaby *engineering educator*
Pritchard, Elsie Tomlinson *librarian*

Mount Sterling

Aileen-Donohew, Phyllis Augusta *educational consultant*

Murray

Boston, Betty Lee *investment company executive, financial planner, consultant*
Dunn, Randy J. *academic administrator*
Ferreyra, Rafael Andres *agricultural and biological engineer, consultant, researcher*
Guy, Sallie T. *artist*
Keller, Randal Joseph *toxicology educator*

Newport

Castellini, Robert H. (Bob Castellini) *food products executive, professional sports team executive*
Clinkenbeard, James Howard *principal*
Siverd, Robert Joseph *lawyer*

Nicholasville

Midkiff, Dinah Lee *retired elementary and middle school educator*

Owensboro

Caplan, Geralyn Marie *biology professor*
Matally, M. Garswa *minister*
McRaith, John Jeremiah *bishop*
Miller, James Monroe *lawyer*
Thomas-Löwe, Christine L. *small business owner*
Webb, Otis D. *retired underwriter*

Paducah

Fejes, Robert R. *minister*
Foreman, James Louis *retired judge*
Justice, Phillip Howard *marketing professional*
Kirk, Terri G. *library media specialist*
Mittendorf, Kimberly Ann *secondary school educator, real estate consultant*
Stice, Dwayne Lee *broadcasting company executive*
Talbert, Debra Kaiser *elementary school educator, artist*

Paintsville

Hovee, Mark John *psychologist*

Paris

Gallardo, Sandra Silvana *television producer, actress*
Steffer, Robert Wesley *clergyman*

Pewee Valley

Gill, George Norman *newspaper publishing company executive*

Pikeville

Van Tatenhove, Gregory F. *federal judge, former prosecutor*

Princeton

Earnest, Melissa Webb *education educator*
Faughn, Dale *biology educator*
McNeill, Samuel Gaither *farm management extension agent, educator, engineering educator*
Noffsinger, Nancy Leigh *retired special education educator*

Prospect

Aberson, Leslie Donald *lawyer*
Willenbrink, Rose Ann *retired lawyer*

Radcliff

Cole, Jessie Mae *nursing assistant, freelance/self-employed writer*

Richmond

Ballard, Michael Ray (Mickey Ballard) *minister, music educator*
Branson, Branley Allan *biology professor*
Burch, John Russell *retired military officer*
Chenault, James Stouffer *judge*
Dunston-Coleman, Aingred Ghislayne *history professor*
Hall, Kathy *health facility administrator*
Huch, Ronald Kind *historian, educator*
Inman, Larry Joe *basketball coach*
Machado-Echezuria, Marianella Perpetua *composer, writer, educator*
Wright, John Daniel *minister*

Russellville

Harper, Shirley Fay *nutritionist, educator, consultant, lecturer*

Shelbyville

Miller, Mary Helen *retired state government administrator*

Simpsonville

Burkhardt, Susanne M. *elementary school educator*

Somerset

Pennington, Aubrey El *director*
Prather, John Gideon *lawyer*

Southgate
Glenn, Jerry Hosmer, Jr. *retired language educator*

Stanford
Baughman, James Carson *minister, sports official*

Sturgis
Thornsberry, Willis Lee, Jr. *chemist*

Vanceburg
Aker, Duncan Danforth, Jr. *minister, educator*

Versailles
Farish, William S. *former ambassador, horse breeder*
Stober, William John, II, *economics professor*
Troutt, Kenny *communications executive*

Villa Hills
Giesbrecht, Martin Gerhard *retired economics professor, musician*

Waco
Hackman, Vicki Lou *physician*

Wickliffe
Frueh, Deborah K.A. (Debi Frueh) *artist, poet*
Shadoan, William Lewis *retired judge*

Wilmore
Kinlaw, Dennis Franklin *clergyman, religious organization administrator*
Pohl, Gunther Erich *retired library administrator*

Winchester
Book, John Kenneth (Kenny) *retail store owner*
Cantrell, Georgia Ann *realtor*
Snowden, Ruth O'Dell Gillespie *artist*
Studebaker, John Milton *utilities engineer, consultant, educator*

LOUISIANA

Alexandria
Gist, Howard Battle, Jr. *lawyer*
Gootee, Christy Beck *minister, educator*
Hanley, Henry Gorman *cardiologist*
Maples, Mary Lou *elementary school educator*
Mathews, Peggy Anne *nurse*
Phillips, Virginia *retired federal employee*
Smith, Joe Dorsey, Jr. *retired newspaper executive*
Thevenot, Maude Travis *retired home economist*
Wesse, David Joseph *higher education administrator, consultant*

Amite
Duncan, Johnny Lee *historian*
Wedig, Regina Scotto *lawyer*

Angie
Kennedy, Joan Pace *school librarian, educator*

Baker
Baker, Otis McDowell *small business owner*
Baker, Yvonne Bell *elementary school educator*
Cross, James Edward *electrical engineering educator*

Baton Rouge
Acosta, Lydia M. *library director*
Arceneaux, William *historian, educator, association administrator*
Baron, Stuart *artist, art educator, director*
Bedeian, Arthur George *business educator*
Bensman, Stephen J. *school librarian, researcher*
Bernhard, James M., Jr. *engineering executive*
Besch, Everett Dickman *veterinarian, dean emeritus, educator*
Blackman, John Calhoun, IV, *lawyer*
Blanco, Kathleen Babineaux *governor*
Boren, James Edgar *lawyer*
Boyce, Bert Roy *university dean emeritus, library and information science educator*
Bray, George August *internist, researcher, educator*
Brewer, Ralph Wright, Jr. *lawyer*
Brooks, Burke Jay, Jr. *oncologist*
Broussard, Malcolm Joseph *pharmacist, consultant*
Buchmann, Molly O'Banion *choreographer, educator*
Burns, Paul Yoder *forester, educator*
Caffey, Horace Rouse *academic administrator, agricultural company executive*
Calabrese, Michael Raphael *manufacturing executive, lawyer, consultant*
Camp, John Bliss *journalist, television producer*
Cargill, Jennifer S. *library director, dean, educator*
Casey, Robert Reisch *lawyer*
Chancellor, Van *women's college basketball coach*
Chen, Peter Pin-Shan *engineering, computer science and Internet/web educator, data processing executive*
Cherry, William Ashley *surgeon, state health official, educator*
Cole, Luther Francis *former state supreme court associate justice*
Combe, John Clifford, Jr. *lawyer*
Cooper, William James, Jr. *history professor*
Corripio, Armando Benito *retired chemical engineering professor*
Cramer, Gail Latimer *economist*
Crawford, William Edward *law educator*
Crumbley, Donald Larry *accounting educator, writer*
Culbert, David Holbrook *historian, educator, editor, writer*
Dardenne, Jay (John Leigh Dardenne Jr.) *state official, former state legislator, lawyer*
DeVille, Donald Charles *accountant*
Dhurandhar, Nikhil V. *biomedical researcher, educator*
Doty, Gresdna Ann *theatre historian, educator*
Ducrest, John P. *state agency administrator*
Dugas, David Roy *prosecutor, lawyer*
Fishman, Richard Glenn *lawyer, accountant*
Foti, Charles C., Jr. *state attorney general*
Gammon, Malcolm Ernest, Sr. *surveying and engineering executive*
Gettys, Thomas Wigington *medical researcher*
Graphia, Gary P. *lawyer*
Green, Stuart Paul *law educator*
Guedry, Leo J. *agricultural economics educator*
Hackney, Marcella Wichser *biology professor*
Hamilton, Rebecca L. *state librarian*
Hansel, William *biology professor*
Hardy, John Edward *language educator, writer*
Harper, Sandra Stecher *academic administrator*
Harrelson, Clyde Lee *retired secondary school educator*
Head, Jonathan Frederick *cell biologist*
Hymel, L(ezin) J(oseph) *lawyer, former prosecutor*
Ishler, Harold LeRoy, Jr. *retired physician*
Johnson, Joseph Clayton, Jr. *lawyer*
Kastin, Abba Jeremiah *endocrinologist, researcher*
Kennedy, John Neely *state official*
Khonsari, Michael M. *mechanical engineering educator*
Kidd, James Marion III *allergist, immunologist, educator*
Koehler, Robert Brien *priest*
La Carna, John Edward *writer, social worker*
Landrieu, Mitchell Joseph *lieutenant governor*
Litvinoff, Saul *lawyer, educator*
Livesay, Thomas Andrew *museum director, educator*
Lombardi, John V. *academic administrator, historian*
Lopez, Mandi J. *veterinarian, scientist*
Lusk, Glenna Rae Knight (Mrs. Edwin Bruce Lusk) *librarian*
Lusted, Dona Sanders *music educator, consultant, organist*
Madden, David *author*
Mathews, Sharon Walker *performing company executive, secondary school educator*
Mc Call, Jerry Chalmers *retired federal official*
Mc Cameron, Fritz Allen *retired university administrator*
McCoy, Wesley Lawrence *musician, educator, conductor*
McDonald, Alden J., Jr. *bank executive*
Mc Glynn, Sean Patrick *physical chemist, educator*
McKay, Michael Wendell *lawyer*
Miles, Les *college football coach*
Moody, Gene Byron *engineering executive, small business owner, minister*
Moréteau, Olivier *law educator*
Mueller, Lisel *writer, poet*
Nave, J. L. *performing company executive*
Noland, Christine A. *judge*
Norem, Richard Frederick, Sr. *musician, educator*
O'Connell, Robert Francis *physics professor*
O'Keefe, Sean Charles *academic administrator, former federal agency administrator*
Oxley, James Grieve *mathematics professor*
Parker, John Victor *judge*
Parks, James William, II, *public facilities executive, lawyer*
Pastorek, Paul G. *school system administrator, lawyer*
Patterson, Charles Darold *librarian, educator*
Phillabaum, Leslie Ervin *publisher*
Pike, Ralph Webster *chemical engineer, educator, academic administrator*
Polozola, Frank Joseph *federal judge*
Prestage, James Jordan *university chancellor, consultant*
Pugh, George Willard *law educator*
Puyau, Francis Albert *retired radiology educator, physician*
Quartararo, Philip, Jr. *mathematics professor*
Reich, Robert Sigmund *landscape architect*
Ricapito, Joseph Virgil (Giuseppe Ricapito) *literature educator*
Richards, Marta Alison *lawyer*
Riddick, Winston Wade, Sr. *lawyer*
Riedlinger, Stephen C. *federal judge*
Risinger, Beth N. *elementary school educator*
Robinson, James William *chemistry professor*
Rubin, Michael Harry *lawyer, educator*
Sabliov, Cristina Mirela *humanities educator*
Sandoz, George Ellis, Jr. *political science educator*
Shindo, Charles J. *historian, director*
Sinclair, Glenn Bruce *mechanical engineering educator, researcher*
Smith, Michael *academic administrator*
Smith, Richard James *retired music educator*
Spell, Derrick W. *oncologist, educator*
Stapp, Dan Ernest *retired lawyer, utilities executive*
Starkey, Bob (Robert G. Starkey) *women's college basketball coach*
Superneau, Duane William *geneticist, physician*
Tandberg, Gerilyn Gay *theater educator, costume designer*
Tarver, Dave L. *medical association administrator*
Taylor, John McKowen *lawyer*
Thomas, Jeffrey Cone *financial executive, consultant*
Tipton, Kenneth Warren *retired agricultural administrator, researcher*
Traynham, James Gibson *chemist, educator*
Tumay, Mehmet Taner *geotechnical engineering educator, researcher, consultant*
Unglesby, Lewis O. *lawyer*
Vallas, Paul G. *school system administrator*
Vidal, Martin Andreas *veterinarian*
Warner, Isiah Manuel *chemistry professor*
Wheeler, Otis Bullard *retired language educator, retired director*
Witcher, Robert Campbell, Sr. *bishop*
Wong, Wai Hing *marine biologist, researcher*
Xu, Feng *research scientist, educator*
Yarbrough, Martha Cornelia *music educator*
Young, David P. *physics professor*
Zhou, Liming *environmental scientist*

Belle Chasse
Arimura, Akira *biomedical researcher, educator*

Benton
Rivers, Christine D. *academic administrator*

Bogalusa
Gallaspy, Dixie *interior designer, innkeeper*
Villarrubia, Glenda Boone *reading specialist, reading coordinator, educational consultant, educator*

Bossier City
Paris, Norma Jean *psychologist, educator*

Chauvin
Sammarco, Paul William *ecologist, researcher*

Choudrant
Ford, John Charles *artist*
Lofton, Brenda M. *secondary school educator*

Coushatta
Wiggins, Mary Ann Wise *small business owner, educator*

Covington
Blossman, Alfred Rhody, Jr. *banker*
Doody, Louis Clarence, Jr. *retired accountant*
Gilman-Anderson, Susan Ellen *real estate company executive, consultant*
Maurin, James E. *real estate executive*
Paddison, David Robert *lawyer*
Perez de la Mesa, Manuel Jose *swimming pool company executive*
Rice, Winston Edward *lawyer, priest*
Snyder, Charles Aubrey *lawyer*
Stahr, Beth A. *librarian*
Vercellotti, John Raymond *chemist, researcher*

Crowley
Foreman, Alfred G. *theologian, philosopher*

Cut Off
Mestayer, Mary Frances *science educator*

Denham Springs
Anderson, Alexis *minister*
Grimmer, Cindy C. *social studies educator*
May, Kenneth Nathaniel *retired food industry consultant*

Deridder
Smith, Mabel Hargis *retired secondary school educator, musician*

Destrehan
Ates, J. Robert *lawyer*
Griffith, Steven Franklin, Sr. *lawyer, insurance agent*

Donaldsonville
Watson, Stanley Ellis *clergyman, small business owner*

Dry Prong
McLain, Paul King *systems analyst*

Dubach
Straughan, William Thomas *structural engineering consultant, educator*

Eunice
Attole, Mary Bertha *writer*

Fort Polk
Rolin, Daniel Wayne, Jr. *military officer*

Franklin
Fairchild, Phyllis Elaine *school counselor*
Rouly, Ellie Arceneaux *dancer, educator*

Gilbert
Bell, Wallace Edward *minister, insurance agent*

Glenmora
Burns, Linda D. *elementary school educator*

Gonzales
Kidd, Ruth Price *retired secondary school educator*

Grambling
Judson, Horace Augustus *academic administrator, chemistry educator*
Porter, Wilma Jean *retired educational consultant*

Hammond
Parish, Richard Lee *engineer, consultant*
Parker, Clea Edward *retired university president*
Siegel, Wendy Lowe *special education educator*
Voegel, Phillip Donovan *chemistry professor*

Harahan
O'Neal, Edgar Carl *psychology professor*

Harvey
Simon, Keith R. *safety engineer, petroleum engineer, radio personality*
Weekley, Judy Liddington *special education educator*

Houma
Colasurdo, Irma Louise *secondary school educator, department chairman*
Hukins-Rodrigue, Dana Ann *nurse*

Iowa
Kuykendall, Richard G. *music educator*

Jackson
Kondrup, John Thomas *retired research scientist*

Jefferson
Conino, Joseph Aloysius *lawyer*

Jennings
Marcantel, Bernard Norman *lawyer, judge*

Kenner
Farber, George Allan *dermatologist, educator*
Hallila, Bruce Allan *welding engineer*
Kuebler, David Wayne *insurance company executive, private investigator*
McShan, Clyde Griffin, II, *diversified financial services company executive*

La Place
Blair, Ruth Reba *retired government official, notary public*
Cicet, Donald James *lawyer*
Fiffie Proctor, JoAnn *media and technology specialist*

Lafayette
Angers, Winston Thomas *lawyer, publishing executive*
Appley, Alan J. *neurosurgeon*
Authement, Ray Paul *college president*
Barry, Mildred Castille *artist*
Brasseaux, Carl Anthony *historian, educator, academic administrator, curator*
Breaux, Paul Joseph *lawyer, pharmacist*
Broussard, Richard C. *lawyer*
Cain, Judith Sharp *mathematics professor, consultant*
Carolina, Monteiro *ecologist*
Carstens, Jane Ellen *retired library science educator*
Colbert-Cormier, Patricia A. *secondary school educator*
Cormier, Joseph Bowman *private investigator, consultant*
Damico, Jack Samual *speech educator*
Davidson, James Joseph III *lawyer*
Davis, William Eugene *federal judge*
Domingue, James Neal *neurologist*
Duhe, John Malcolm, Jr. *federal judge*
Gaines, Ernest James *author*
Hail, Karen L. *bank executive*
Harrison, Frank W., Jr. *geologist*
Judice, Marc Wayne *lawyer*
Mansfield, James Norman III *lawyer*
Marceaux, Linda d'Augereau *elementary school educator*
Marinkovic, Serge Peter *urologist, educator, surgeon*
Marshak, Alan Howard *electrical engineer, educator*
Menutis, Ruth Ann *small business owner*
Meza, Luis Alberto *internist, researcher*
Myers, Stephen Hawley *lawyer*
Neuner, Frank X., Jr. *lawyer*
Raffel, Burton Nathan *literature educator, poet, translator*
Rout, Bibhudutta *research scientist*
Roy, James Parkerson *lawyer*
Sides, Larry Eugene *advertising executive*
Skinner, Michael David *lawyer, lobbyist, consultant*
Stravinska, Sarah *dance educator*
Totaro, Michael Wayne *information scientist, educator*

Lake Charles
Batchelor, Karen Sue *music educator*
Beam, James Carroll (Jim Beam) *retired newspaper editor*
Clement, Richard Joseph *retired obstetrician, gynecologist*
Drez, David Jacob, Jr. *orthopedic surgeon, educator*
Fields-Gold, Anita *retired dean*
Gunderson, Clark Alan *orthopedic surgeon*
Lacoste, Alan Daniel *physician, educator, medical company executive*
Lee, Brandi Gremillion *elementary school educator*
Levingston, Ernest Lee *engineering company executive*
Mount, Willie Landry *state legislator*
Sanchez, Walter Marshall *lawyer*
Stacey, Truman *journalist, consultant*
Veron, J. Michael *lawyer, writer*

Leesville
Gutman, Lucy Toni *social worker, educator*
Thompson, Darlene Bennett *realtor, musician*

Luling
Scherer, Donald James, II, *systems administrator, researcher*

Madisonville
Young, Lucy Cleaver *retired physician*

Mandeville
Arrowsmith, Marian Campbell *elementary school educator, supervisor, educator*
Cargille, Charles M. *internist, educator*
Childress, Joel M. *music educator*
Deano, Edward Joseph, Jr. *lawyer, retired state legislator*
Donahue, Maura W. *construction executive*
Ewen, Pamela Binnings *retired lawyer*
Lamid, Sofjan *physician, educator*
Landry, Joseph L., Jr. *retired affirmative action specialist*
Treuting, Edna Gannon *retired nursing administrator, educator*

Many
Dutton, Frank Elroy *data processing executive, writer*

Marksville
Riddle, Charles Addison III *district attorney, former state legislator*

Marrero
Kushner, Frederick Gary *cardiologist, medical educator*

Metairie
Album, Jerald Lewis *lawyer*
Banton, Kathleen Ariatti *artist, educator*
Blunt, Joyce Omega *special education educator*
Brees, Drew (Drew Christopher Brees) *professional football player*
Burns, William Glenn *lawyer*
Bush, Reggie *professional football player*
Casselli, Henry Calvin, Jr. *artist, painter*
Chambers, Thomas Edward *academic administrator, psychologist*
Crosby, Deborah Berry *artist*
Crosby, Marena Lienhard *retired academic administrator*
deLaup, S. Guy *lawyer*
Dickerson, Lon Richard *library administrator*
Edisen, Clayton Byron *physician*
Evans, Carol Rockwell *nursing administrator*
Falco, Maria Josephine *political scientist*
Fantaci, James Michael *lawyer*
Ford, Robert David *lawyer*
Fuhrmann, Emile Frederick *architect*
Gereighty, Andrea Saunders *diversified financial services company executive, poet*
Grau, Shirley Ann (Mrs. James Kern Feibleman) *writer*
Grimm, John Lloyd *marketing professional*
Grotkowski, Edward Michael *music educator, director*
Hardy, Ashton Richard *lawyer*
Jacobs, Benjamin Franklin *cardiologist*
Lake, Wesley Wayne, Jr. *internist, allergist, medical educator*
Loomis, Mickey *professional sports team executive*
Metzner, David Mark *plastic and reconstructive surgeon*
Nehrbass, Seth Martin *lawyer*
Nicoladis, Michael F. *engineering company executive*
O'Neill, James H. *psychotherapist, educator*
Payton, Sean (Patrick Sean Payton) *professional football coach*
Rosen, Charles, II, *retired lawyer*
Roussos, Christopher Wayne *dental association administrator*
Snyder, David Warren *cardiologist*
Villarrubia, Todd M. *lawyer*
Wood, Jonathan Stuart *economist, educator*

Minden
Kemmerly, James Robert *obstetrician, gynecologist*

Monroe
Chardkoff, Joan Corb *language educator*
Cooksey, John Charles *ophthalmologist, retired congressman*
Curry, Robert Lee III *lawyer*
Fouts, James Fremont *mining company executive*
Galle, Jeffrey Wayne *literature and language professor, department chairman*
Hawley, Jeffrey Lance *investments executive, accountant*
Huntington, Lisa Lynee *music educator*
Post, Glen Fleming III *telecommunications industry executive*
Sartor, Daniel Ryan, Jr. *lawyer*
Smith, Donald Raymond *librarian*
Trapp, A. C. *retired music educator*

Napoleonville
Blanchard, Donald Pierre, Jr. *engineer*

Natchitoches
Egan, Shirley Anne *retired nursing educator*
LeBreton, Marietta M. *history professor*
Wells, Carol McConnell *genealogist, retired archivist*
Wolfe, George Cropper *retired private school educator, artist, writer*

New Iberia
Hamilton, Roger Paul, Jr. *lawyer*
Hockless, Mary Fontenot *educational consultant*

New Orleans
Abaunza, Donald Richard *lawyer*
Abbott, Hirschel Theron, Jr. *lawyer*
Acomb, Robert Bailey, Jr. *lawyer, educator*
Agrawal, Krishna Chandra *pharmacology educator*
Allen, Rondall E. *pharmacist, educator*
Alsobrook, Henry Bernis, Jr. *lawyer*
Amoss, Walter James, III, (Jim) *editor*
Andrews, E. Wyllys *archaeologist, educator*
Bacot, Marie *management consultant, researcher*
Balée, William L. *anthropology educator*
Ball, F. Macnaughton, Jr. *architect*
Ball, Millie (Mildred Porteous Ball) *editor, journalist*
Barach, Jeffrey Alvan *management educator*
Barry, Francis Julian, Jr. *lawyer*
Beahm, Franklin D. *lawyer*
Beard, Elizabeth Letitia *physiologist, educator*
Beck, David Edward *surgeon*
Beer, Peter Hill *federal judge*
Benjamin, Adelaide Wisdom *retired lawyer, community volunteer and activist*
Benjamin, Edward Bernard, Jr. *lawyer*
Berenson, Gerald Sanders *physician*
Berrigan, Helen Ginger *federal judge*
Bieck, Robert Barton, Jr. *lawyer*
Blackwell, James E. *retired science educator*
Blakely, Edward James *city manager, economics professor*
Bookhardt, Fred Barringer, Jr. *architect*
Boudreaux, Kenneth Justin *economist, educator*
Bronfin, Fred *lawyer*
Brown, Jerry A. *federal bankruptcy judge*
Brumfield, William Craft *Slavic studies educator, photographer, writer*
Bullard, Edgar John III *museum director*
Calogero, Pascal Frank, Jr. *state supreme court justice*
Carlson, Robert Marshall *health facility administrator*
Carter, James Clarence *pastor, educator*
Casellas, Joachim *art gallery executive*
Cheatwood, Roy Clifton *lawyer*
Christen, Carol A. *principal*
Claverie, Philip deVilliers *lawyer*
Clement, Edith Brown *federal judge*
Cody, Wilmer St. Clair *educational policy researcher*
Cohn, Isidore, Jr. *surgeon, educator*
Coleman, James Julian *lawyer*
Coleman, James Julian, Jr. *lawyer, industrialist, real estate company executive*
Collins, Harry David *forensic, mechanical and nuclear engineer, claims consultant*
Conroy, David Jerome *lawyer*
Cook, Victor Joseph, Jr. *business educator, consultant*
Cospolich, James Donald *electronics executive, consultant*
Cowen, Scott S. *academic administrator*
Crumley, David Oliver *publishing executive, writer, corporate executive*
Crusto, Mitchell Ferdinand *lawyer, educator*
Culbertson, Richard Allen *healthcare educator, health facility administrator*
Culotta, Vincent Anthony, Jr. *obstetrician, gynecologist*
Dahlberg, Carl Fredrick, Jr. *entrepreneur*
David, Robert Jefferson *lawyer*
Denault, Leo P. *energy executive*
Dennis, James Leon *federal judge*
Doley, Harold Emanuel, Jr. *securities company executive*
Dumez, Steve *architect*
Duncan, Margaret Caroline *physician*
Duval, Stanwood Richardson, Jr. *judge*
Easson, William McAlpine *psychiatrist, educator*
Elkins, Gary J. *lawyer*
Espinoza, Luis Rolan *rheumatologist, researcher*
Eustis, Richmond Minor *lawyer*
Ewin, Dabney Minor *surgeon*
Fagaly, William Arthur *curator*
Falgoust, Dean Thomas *lawyer, accountant*
Ferguson, Charles Austin *retired newspaper editor*
Fierke, Thomas Garner *lawyer*
Fisher, James William *pharmacologist, medical educator*
Force, Robert *law educator*
Frantz, Phares Albert *architect*
Friedmann, Patricia Ann *writer*
Frohlich, Edward David *medical educator*
Frost, Dan R. *history professor, department chairman*
Fuselier, Harold Anthony, Jr. *urologist, director, educator*
Gay, Esmond Phelps *lawyer*
Gertler, Meyer H. *lawyer*
Giles, Thomas Davis *cardiologist, internist, educator*
Glancy, David Lucas *internist*
Goins, Richard Anthony *lawyer, educator*
Gordon, Joseph Elwell *university official, educator*
Gould, Harry J. III *neurology educator*
Grant, Arthur Gordon, Jr. *lawyer, educator*
Griffin, Jeffrey Farrow *surgeon*
Hall, Gwendolyn Midlo *historian, educator*
Hardin, Harry S. III *lawyer*
Hasselbach, Karlheinz *retired literature educator*
Healy, George William III *lawyer, mediator*
Herman, Russ Michel *lawyer*
Hoffman, Donald Alfred *lawyer*
Hollier, Larry Harold *vascular surgeon, hospital administrator, dean*
Hovland, Eric Jeffrey *dean, endodontics educator*
Howard, Richard Ralston, II, *medical health advisor, researcher, financial consultant*
Hughes, Alfred Clifton *archbishop*
Hurley, Grady Schell *lawyer*
Hyslop, Newton Everett, Jr. *infectious disease specialist*
Incaprera, Frank Philip *internist*
Irons, Paulette Riley *state legislator, lawyer*
Ivens, Mary Sue *microbiologist, medical mycologist*
Jenkins, James Stephen *internist*
Johnson, Bernette Joshua *state supreme court justice*
Johnson, Peter Forbes *transportation executive, business owner*
Jones, Glenn Earle *property management executive*
Jones, Philip Kirkpatrick, Jr. *lawyer*
Judell, Harold Benn *lawyer*
Kelly, Eamon Michael *economic development professor, retired university president*
Kenney, Brigid *media company executive*
Kewalramani, Laxman Sunderdas *surgeon, consultant*
Kimball, Catherine D. *state supreme court justice*
Kline, David Gellinger *neurosurgery educator*
Klingman, John Philip *architect, educator*
Knoll, Jeannette Theriot *state supreme court justice*
Kolinsky, Michael Allen *emergency physician*
Landry, Sherry S. *lawyer*
Langston, Thomas Samuel *political science professor*
Lannes, William Joseph III *electrical engineer*
Lemann, Thomas Berthelot *lawyer*
Leonard, J. Wayne *energy executive*
Letten, James B. *prosecutor*
Liljeberg, Genevieve Brocato *artist*
Lind, Thomas Otto *barge transportation company executive*
Link, Donald *chef*
Livaudais, Marcel, Jr. *federal judge*
Locke, William *retired endocrinologist*
Looney, Joseph W. *lawyer*
Lopez, Manuel *immunology and allergy educator*
Lowe, Robert Charles *lawyer*
Luza, Radomir Vaclav *historian, educator*
Marcus, Bernard *lawyer, arbitrator, mediator*
Marks, Charles Dennery *insurance consultant*
Martin, David Hubert *internist, epidemiologist, educator*
Martin, Louis Frank *surgery and healthcare outcomes analyst*
Masinter, Paul James *lawyer*
Mathes, Edward Conrad *architect*
McCall, John Patrick *college president, educator*
McGlone, Michael Anthony *lawyer*
McMillan, Lee Richards, II, *lawyer*
McSwain, Norman Ellsworth, Jr. *surgeon, educator*
Meekers, Dominique Armand *public health professor, demographer*
Melcher, Joe A. *audiologist, educator*
Michney, Todd Michael *history professor*
Millikan, Larry Edward *dermatologist*
Milling, R(oswell) King *bank executive, lawyer*
Mintz, Albert *lawyer*
Mitchell, Kenneth David *physiologist, educator*
Moely, Barbara E. *psychologist, educator*
Moffett, James Robert *mining executive*
Nagin, Ray (Clarence Ray Nagin Jr.) *mayor*
Navar, Luis Gabriel *physiology educator, director, researcher*
Nicholl, Jeffrey Scott *neurologist, educator*
Nichols, Ronald Lee *surgeon, educator*
Novakov, George John, Jr. *gifted and talented educator, consultant, administrative assistant*
Nuzum, Robert Weston *lawyer*
Ochsner, John Lockwood *thoracic-cardiovascular surgeon*
Olson, Richard David *psychology professor*
O'Quinn, April Gale *obstetrician, gynecologist, educator*
Osakwe, Christopher *lawyer, educator*
Palmer, Vernon Valentine *law educator*
Pankey, George Atkinson *internist, educator, researcher*
Paolini, Gilberto *literature educator*
Paradise, Louis Vincent *education educator, dean*
Pearce, John Y. *lawyer*
Perdew, John Paul *physics professor*
Perlis, Sharon A. *lawyer*
Phelps, Ashton, Jr. *newspaper publisher*
Poesch, Jessie Jean *art historian*
Pomes, Stephen Vincent *school librarian*
Ponoroff, Lawrence *dean, law educator, consultant*
Pope, John Marvin *journalist*
Porteous, G. Thomas, Jr. *judge*
Porter, George Homer III *physician, medical foundation executive*
Prockop, Darwin Johnson *biochemist, medical educator*
Prudhomme, Paul *chef, restaurant owner*
Query, Lance D. *dean, university librarian*
Reck, Andrew Joseph *philosopher*
Reyes, Raul Gregorio *surgeon*
Reza, Ali Hajmohammad *cardiologist*
Riddick, Frank Adams, Jr. *physician, healthcare administrator*
Roberts, Louise Nisbet *philosopher, educator*
Rosensteel, George Thomas *physics professor, nuclear physicist*
St. Julien, Thais Mary *soprano, musician*
Scelfo, Chris *university football coach*
Schalow, Frank Hickey *philosopher, educator*
Schehr, Kevin John *art gallery owner*
Schexnayder, Randall V. *pharmacist, dean*
Schnabel, Marta-Ann *lawyer*
Schnoebelen, Ian *chef*
Schulte, Francis B. *retired archbishop*
Sherman, Edward Francis *dean, law educator*
Shinn, George *professional sports team owner*
Simon, H(uey) Paul *lawyer*
Skinner, Robert Earle *librarian, writer*
Sloan, Robert D. *energy executive, lawyer*
Smith, Juanita Bérard *lawyer, artist*
Smith, Richard J. *energy executive*
Steeg, Moise S., Jr. *lawyer*
Taylor, Phyllis Miller *energy executive*
Tetlow, Elisabeth Meier *writer, researcher, lawyer*
Thompson, Martyn Philip *political and literary studies educator, translator*
Threefoot, Sam Abraham *physician, educator*
Timmcke, Alan Edward *colon and rectal surgeon*
Tipler, Frank Jennings III *physicist*
Toledo, Bob *college football coach*
Traylor, Chet D. *state supreme court justice*
Ukpolo, Victor *economics educator*
Vance, Robert Patrick *lawyer*
Vaudry, J. William, Jr. *lawyer*
Ventura, Hector Osvaldo *cardiologist*
Victory, Jeffrey Paul *state supreme court justice*
Waggonner, Joseph David III *architect*
Wang, Ting *mechanical engineering educator*
Waring, William Winburn *pediatric pulmonologist, educator*
Weimer, John L. *state supreme court justice*
Wiener, Jacques Loeb, Jr. *federal judge*
Williams, Ronald David *telecommunications industry executive*
Wolfe, Richard Peel *lawyer*
Worley, Robert Bruce, Jr. *lawyer*
Yang, DaGang *mathematician, educator*

New Roads
Hymel, Melissa K. *librarian*

Newllano
Boren, Lynda Sue *gifted education educator*

Opelousas
Lafleur, Kenneth Charles *ophthalmologist*
Pinac, André Louis III *obstetrician, gynecologist*
Underwood, Lorainne Ballard *literature and language educator*

Pearl River
Cantrell, Joseph Sires *chemistry professor*
Thiel, David Brian *physician assistant*

Pineville
Hamlett, Curt *music educator, director*
Lott, Johnnye Jo *elementary school educator, writer*
Nanna, Michael Edward *chemist, researcher*
Thrasher, Fay C. *clinical psychologist*
Webb, Watts Rankin *surgeon*

Ponchatoula
Kuechmann, Christopher Robert *library director*
Kuhn, James Edward *judge*
Warden, Waldia Ann *retreat center administrator, director*

Prairieville
Biri, Toni Roppolo *elementary school educator*

River Ridge
Didriksen, Caleb H. III *lawyer*

Ruston
Bourgeois, Patricia McLin *academic administrator, women's health and pediatrics nurse, educator*
Cochran, James J. *mathematics professor, researcher*
Dodge Robbins, Dorothy Ellin *language educator*
Dua, Sumeet *computer scientist, educator*
Freasier, Aileen W. *special education educator*
Hudnall, Jarrett, Jr. *management consultant, educator, marketing professional*
Maxfield, John Edward *retired university dean*
Mesak, Hani Ibrahim *marketing educator*
Nassar, Raja *statistics educator, researcher, consultant*
Phillips, Thomas J., Jr. *accountant, educator*
Roach, Susan *literature educator*
Sale, Tom S. III *financial economist*
Sterling, Raymond Leslie *civil engineering educator, researcher, consultant*
Taylor, Foster Jay *retired university president*

Saint Martinville
Fournet, Patricia Sibley *retired secondary school educator*

Schriever
Shaffer, Margaret Minor *retired library director*

Shreveport
Brannon, Guy Emilio *psychiatrist*
Brazile, Orella Ramsey *library director*
Bryant, J(ames) Bruce *lawyer*
Burton, George Aubrey, Jr. *accountant*
Carmody, Arthur Roderick, Jr. *lawyer, director*
Casey Wall, Holly *plastic surgeon*
Chu, Quyen Dinh *surgeon, educator, oncologist*
Conrad, Steven Allen *critical care and emergency physician, biomedical engineer, educator*
Cox, John Thomas, Jr. *lawyer*
Foreman, John Patrick *electrical engineer*
Fort, Arthur Tomlinson III *obstetrician, educator*
Goodman, Robert Uhle *lawyer*
Goodman, Sylvia Klumok *film center executive*
Hall, Amy Matthews *science educator*
Heacock, Donald Dee *social worker*
Hetherwick, Gilbert Lewis *lawyer*
Hughes, Mary Sorrows *artist*
Jawahar, Ajay *neurosurgeon, educator*
Jones, Kenneth B., Jr. *surgeon*
Kendrick, Rhonda Lynn *poet, small business owner*
Lazarus, Allan Matthew *retired newspaper editor*
McDonald, John Clifton *surgeon*
McLemore, Laura Lyons *archivist, history educator*
Misra, Raghunath Prasad *physician, educator*
Morelock, Jasmine Crawford *artist*
Nathan, Cherie-Ann Olympia *surgeon, educator*
Nelson, Ralph Stanley *lawyer*
Payne, Roy Steven *lawyer*
Pelton, James Rodger *library director*
Perlman, Jerald Lee *lawyer*
Politz, Nyle Anthony *lawyer*
Raley, Kelli B. *forensic specialist*
Robinson, Garry Lewin *television news executive*
Russell, Robert L. *real estate appraiser*
Shelby, James Stanford *surgeon, researcher*
Shemwell, Robert H. *federal judge*
Staats, Thomas Elwyn *neuropsychologist*
Stewart, Carl E. *federal judge*
Veeramachaneni, Ravindra *pathologist*
Wall, Simeon Heninger, Jr. *plastic surgeon*
Washington, Donald W. *prosecutor*
Webb, Donald Arthur *minister*
Wolf, Robert Edward *physician, educator*
Wood, Julienne Louise *librarian, historian*
Wray, Geraldine Smitherman (Jerry Wray) *artist*

Slidell
Dabdoub, Paul Oscar *academic administrator*
Dearing, Reinhard Josef *curator, retired city official*
Fincher, Margaret Ann *retired secondary school educator*
Ladner, Norma Foley *elementary school educator*
McBurney, Elizabeth Innes *dermatologist, physician, educator*
Muller, Robert Joseph *gynecologist*
Shamis, Edward Anthony, Jr. *lawyer*
Singletary, Alvin D. *lawyer*
Stuart, Charles Edward *electrical engineer, oceanographer*
Tewell, Joseph Robert, Jr. *retired electrical engineer*
Winsor, William John III *engineer, consultant*

Springhill
Morgan, Larry Ronald *minister*
Thomas, Faye Evelyn J. *elementary and secondary school educator*

Sulphur
Fuller, Betty Stamps *music educator*
Toniette, Sallye Jean *physician*

Thibodaux
Harris, Rose M. *academic administrator*
Hulbert, Stephen Thompson *academic administrator*

Tioga
Brandow, Stephen Jon *priest*

Ville Platte
Patsicostas, Susan Joanna *mental health services professional, psychotherapist*

Vivian
Collier, Samuel Melvin *aerospace engineer*

West Monroe
Ford, Mary Ann *secondary school educator*

Westlake
Grantham, Camille Renee Theriot *high school librarian, media specialist*

Westwego
Brehm, Loretta Persohn *retired art educator, librarian, consultant*

Zachary
Price, Carol Leah *mathematics educator*

MAINE

Alna
Beerits, Janet Penrose Robinson *sculptor*

Andover
Kaltsos, Angelo John *electronics executive, educator, photographer*

Auburn
Clifford, Robert William *state supreme court justice*

Augusta
Baldacci, John Elias *governor, former congressman*
Bourque, Bruce Joseph *archaeologist, educator*
Clark, Beth *retired minister*
Cragin, Charles Langmaid *lawyer*
Crosby, Nathaniel Howard *elementary school educator*
Dunlap, Matthew Gordon *state official, former state legislator*
Edmonds, Beth *state legislator*
Gendron, Susan Ann *school system administrator*
Gervais, Paul Nelson *foundation administrator, psychotherapist, writer, public relations executive*
Hussey, John Francis *physician, geriatrician*
Johnson, Phillip Edward *lawyer*
LaFond, Peter B. *lawyer*
LaFountain, Lloyd P. III *state agency administrator*
Lemoine, David G. *state official*
Martin, John Lewis *state legislator*
McCormick, Dale *state official*
Nichols, J. Gary *state librarian*
Nickerson, John Mitchell *political science professor*
Randall, Richard J. *academic administrator*
Rowe, G. Steven *state attorney general*

Bangor
Baber, Brett D. *lawyer*
Ballesteros, Paula Mitchell *nurse*
Bickford, Meris J. *lawyer, bank executive*
Coffman, Michael S. *international organization official, ecologist*
Foster, Walter Herbert, Jr. *real estate company executive*
Kelley, Barbara Bannin *retired physical education educator*
King, Stephen Edwin *novelist, scriptwriter*
MacTaggart, Terrence Joseph *education educator, researcher, former academic administrator*
McKinnon, Carolyn Ann *retired child care center director*
Pattenaude, Richard Louis *academic administrator, educator*
Rea, Ann W. *librarian*
Rudman, Paul Lewis *lawyer, former state supreme court justice*
Silver, Warren M. *state supreme court justice*

Bar Harbor
Carpenter, William Morton *language educator, writer*
Krevans, Julius Richard *academic administrator, internist*
Leiter, Edward Henry *cell biologist, researcher*
Nass, Meryl J. *physician, writer, research scientist*
Swazey, Judith Pound *academic administrator, science educator*

Bass Harbor
Ervin, Spencer *lawyer*

Bath
Galleher, Gay *psychologist*

Belfast
DeSilvey, Dennis Lee *cardiologist, educator, academic administrator*
Griffith, Patricia King *journalist*

Belgrade Lakes
Kany, Judy C(asperson) *retired state senator*

Biddeford
Daly, Frank *anatomist*
Ford, Charles Willard *medical educator*

Bremen
Wilson, Linda Smith *retired academic administrator*

Brewer
Dauphinee, Jo Anne Louise *retired nurse*

Bristol
Sabin, William Albert *writer*

Brooklin
Schmidt, Klaus Dieter *marketing professional, management consultant, educator*
Schmidt, Lynda Wheelwright *psychotherapist*

Brunswick
Aranson, Robert *physician, director*
Fuchs, Alfred Herman *psychologist, educator*
Greason, Arthur LeRoy, Jr. *retired university administrator*
Hodge, James Lee *German language educator*
King, Angus S., Jr. *former governor*
Levine, Daniel *historian, educator*
Mills, Barry *academic administrator, lawyer*
Owen, H. Martyn *retired lawyer*
Pfeiffer, Sophia Douglass *retired state legislator, lawyer*
Schwartz, Elliott Shelling *composer, writer, music educator*
Visser, Richard Edgar *minister*

Bryant Pond
Conary, David Arlan *investment company executive*

Bucksport
Ives, Edward Dawson *folklore educator*

Camden
Daly, Sean G. *bank executive*
Dyer, Barbara F. *retired accountant, writer*

Cape Elizabeth
Cotter, Joseph Francis *retired bank executive, hotel executive*
Rich, John Hubbard, Jr. *news correspondent*

Casco
Brown, Ronald Osborne *telecommunications and computer systems consultant*

Castine
Berleant, Arnold *philosopher*
Bernstein, Lester *editorial consultant*
Davis, Peter Frank *filmmaker, writer*
Wiswall, Frank Lawrence, Jr. *lawyer, educator*

Chebeague Island
Traina, Salvatore Albert *publishing executive*

Corea
Harward, Donald West *retired academic administrator*

Cumberland Foreside
Martin, Joseph Robert *retired corporate financial executive*

Damariscotta
Blake, Bud (Julian Watson) *cartoonist*

Deer Isle
Wheeler, Gerald *church musician, educator*

Dennysville
Hobart, Rebecca Weston *retired elementary school educator*

Dixmont
Cummings, James William *poet*

Dresden
Iserbyt, Charlotte Thomson *researcher, writer, educational consultant*
Turco, Lewis Putnam *language educator*

East Boothbay
Eldred, Kenneth McKechnie *acoustician, consultant*
Ford, Richard *writer*
Gibson, Barry Joseph *editor*

Edgecomb
Carlson, Suzanne Olive *architect*

Ellsworth
Richards, (A)lbert Dewey *retired physician, medical educator, writer*
Whedon, Ralph Gibbs *manufacturing executive*
Young, Lucia Patat *psychotherapist*

Falmouth
Cabot, Lewis Pickering *manufacturing company executive, art consultant*
Pierce, Philip Sargent *clinical psychologist*
Rohsenow, Warren Max *retired mechanical engineer, educator*
Schraft, Susan *radiologist*
Winton, Linda *international trainer, consultant*

Farmington
Barigar, Elizabeth Gayle *painter, art educator*
Kalikow, Theodora June *academic administrator*
Lounsbury, Dave Edmond *medical editor, retired medical educator, military officer*
Mathews, Linnea Koons *science educator, librarian*

Fort Fairfield
Shapiro, Joan Isabelle *lab administrator, medical/surgical nurse*

Freeport
Cushman, Margaret Jane *herbalist, nurse*
Panish, Morton B. *retired physical chemist*

Friendship
Cowan, Diane *research scientist, educator*
MacIlvaine, Chalmers Acheson *retired financial executive, former association executive*

Gardiner
Dunbar, Robert Everett *writer, educator*
Gosline, Norman Abbot *real estate appraiser, consultant*

Georgetown
Chapin, Richard *trustee, director*

Gorham
Chaulet, (Frédérique) Emmanuelle *performing company executive, actress, educator, writer*
Chen, Ray Gow Hwei *artist, educator, department chair*
Sanford, Robert Melvin *environmental scientist, educator*
Wallace, David Eric *craftsman, retired military officer*

Hampden
Scroggins, M. Suzanne Paonessa *budget analyst*

Hancock
Silvestro, Clement Mario *museum director, historian*

Harrington
Ray, Brittany E. *literature and language educator*

Hollis Center
Kaake, Norman Bradford *quality assurance professional*

Islesboro
Rogers, William Raymond *retired academic administrator, psychologist, educator*

Kennebunk
Betts, Edward *artist*
Damon, Edmund Holcombe *retired plastics company executive*

Kennebunkport
Featherman, Bernard *steel company executive*
Featherman, Sandra *retired academic administrator, political science professor*
Mulvihill, James Edward *periodontist, educator*

Kingfield
Wescott, Seth *Olympic athlete*

Kittery
McNally, James Henry *physicist, defense consultant*

Kittery Point
Green, Edward Crocker *research scientist*

Lamoine
Schmidt, Christine Alice *art gallery owner*

Lewiston
Hansen, Elaine Tuttle *academic administrator*
Reich, Jill *dean*
Tardif, Donna Lynn *elementary school educator*

Lincoln
Kneeland, Douglas Eugene *retired newspaper editor*

Lincolnville
Denaco, Parker Alden *state official, lawyer, arbitrator*

Little Deer Isle
Mills, David Harlow *psychologist, professional society administrator*

Lubec
Hayes, Ernest M. *podiatrist*

Milbridge
Enslin, Theodore Vernon *poet*

Mount Desert
Crawford, Richard Bradway *biologist, biochemist, educator*

New Gloucester
Connolly, Paul K., Jr. *lawyer, energy executive*
Jaccaci, August Thayer, Jr. *social architect, educator*
Jasinski, Kenneth M. *energy executive*

New Harbor
Carr, James Revell *writer, curator, retired museum director*
Fradley, Frederick Macdonell *retired architect*
Lyford, Cabot *sculptor*

New Vineyard
Smith, Frederick Orville, II, *agricultural products executive, retired military officer*

Newfield
Patten, Ronald James *university dean*

North Yarmouth
Fecteau, Rosemary Louise *educational administrator, educator, consultant*

Ogunquit
West, Norman Ellsworth *artist*

Old Orchard Beach
Day, Marlene E. *elementary school educator*

Old Town
Alex, Joanne DeFilipp *elementary school educator*
Ritz, George F. *forester, consultant*

Orono
Butterfield, Stephen Alan *education educator*
Causey, Robert Crawford *veterinarian, researcher*
Cohn, Steven Frederick *sociology educator, consultant*
Goldstone, Sanford *psychologist, educator*
He, Zhongqi *chemist, researcher*
Kennedy, Robert Alan *educational administrator*
Landis, Eric N. *civil engineer, educator*
Szymanski, Edna Mora *provost*
Tisher, Sharon S. *lawyer*
Townsend, David W. *oceanographer, educator*
Weiss, Robert Jerome *retired psychiatrist, educator*
Wiersma, G. Bruce *dean, forester, educator*

Orrs Island
Nelson, Robert Louis *lawyer*

Palermo
Anderson, Alfred Oliver *mathematician, consultant*

Peaks Island
Bohan, Thomas Lynch *physicist, lawyer*

Penobscot
dePaolo, Ronald Francis *editor-in-chief, writer*

Portland
Alexander, Donald G. *state supreme court justice*
Blair, Bonnie Kathleen *former professional speedskater, former Olympic athlete*
Bradford, Carl O. *judge*
Buckley, Paul Richard, Sr. *insurance executive*
Calkins, Susan W. *state supreme court justice*
Carter, Gene *judge*
Chimsky-Lustig, Mark Evan *editor, consultant*
Corry, Steve *chef*
Dana, Howard H., Jr. *lawyer, retired state supreme court justice*
Dill, William Rankin *college president*
Duff, John A. *law educator*
Dyro, Frances Mary Agnes *medical educator,*
Glassman, Caroline Duby *state supreme court justice*
Graffam, Ward Irving *lawyer*
Hayward, Sam *chef*
Hornby, David Brock *federal judge*
Hunt, David Evans *lawyer*
Ives, Samuel Clifton *minister*
Jones, Blair Anthony *lawyer*
Kayatta, William J., Jr. *lawyer*
Kessler, Carol Farley *retired English language educator*
Khoury, Colleen A. *law educator, former dean*
Lancaster, Ralph Ivan, Jr. *lawyer*
LeBlanc, Richard Philip *lawyer*
Levy, Jon D. *state supreme court justice*
Lipez, Kermit V. *federal judge, former state supreme court justice*
Masrani, Bharat B. *bank executive*
McKusick, Vincent Lee *retired chief justice, arbitrator, lawyer, mediator*
Mead, Andrew M. *state supreme court justice*
Miller, Buffy *dancer*
O'Brien, Murrough Hall *lawyer*
Opperman, John R. *lawyer*
Pitegoff, Peter Robert *dean, law educator*
Powers, Ross *Olympic athlete*
Reid, Rosemary Anne *insurance agent*
Rundlett, Ellsworth Turner III *lawyer*
Ryan, William J. *bank executive*
Saufley, Leigh Ingalls *state supreme court chief justice*
Schwanauer, Francis *philosopher, educator*
Silsby, Paula D. *prosecutor*
Stanley, Eliot Hungerford *small business owner, writer, lawyer*
Stauffer, Eric P. *lawyer*
Suehrstedt, Wendy P. *bank executive*
Thompson, Peter L. *lawyer*
Thompson, William Irwin *writer, educator*
Vincent, Christine *academic administrator*
von Schack, Wesley W. *utilities executive*
Weir, Anne *writer*
White, Jeffrey Munroe *lawyer*
Whiting, Stephen Clyde *lawyer*
Wipfler, William John *health facility administrator*
Wood, Joseph S. *academic administrator*
Zarr, Melvyn *lawyer, educator*

Raymond
Coughlan, Patrick Campbell *lawyer, mediator*

Rockland
Collins, Samuel W., Jr. *judge*
Crosman, Christopher Byron *museum director*

Rockport
Goodwin, Doris Helen Kearns *historian, writer*

Saco
Ames, Ted *environmental scientist*

Saint Francis
Hafford, Faye O'Leary *writer*

Sanford
Allan, Jonathan David *autograph dealer, pop culture historian*

Sangerville
Harris, Norman Edwin *food scientist, consultant*

Scarborough
Britton, Janet Lynn *lawyer*
Clark, Gordon Hostetter, Jr. *physician*
Raisbeck, Gordon *systems engineer, consultant*
Sadik, Marvin Sherwood *art historian, consultant, retired museum director*
Shire, Donald Thomas *retired chemicals executive, lawyer*
Zuch, Leah D.T. *language educator*

Seal Harbor
Forbes, Peter *architect*

Sedgwick
Donnell, William Ray *small business owner, communications executive*
Schroth, Thomas Nolan *editor*

Skowhegan
Ross, James Owen *education educator, researcher*

South Bristol
Lasher, Esther Lu *minister*
Wells, Arthur Stanton *retired manufacturing executive*

South Paris
Eichorn, Daniel J. *lawyer*

South Portland
Delva, Paul D. *lawyer*
Harris, Penny Smith *fundraising consultant*
Manuel, Peter Jay *poet, singer/songwriter, dramatist, language professor, librettist*
Thompson, Mark S. *electronics executive*
Webster, Peter Bridgman *lawyer*
Wheeler, Hewitt Brownell *surgeon, educator*

Southport
Gibson, Edgar Thomas *retired surgeon, educator*

Standish
Clements, Kathleen Kiley *education educator*

Stockton Springs
Snyder, Arnold Lee, Jr. *retired military officer, research director*

Stonington
Pitts, Edgar Thurlow *writer, retired educator*

Sullivan
Davis-Wexler, Ginia *singer, director*

Sumner
Rudd, David William *management consultant, chemical engineer, consultant*

Surry
Pickett, Betty Horenstein *psychologist*

Tenants Harbor
Bates, John Cecil, Jr. *lawyer*

Topsham
Arnold, Charles Burle, Jr. *retired psychiatrist*

Vinalhaven
Indiana, Robert (Clark) *artist*

Walpole
Dorgan, Kelly M. *marine biologist*

Waterford
Stockwell, William F. *not-for-profit fundraiser, consultant*

Waterville
Adams, William D. *academic administrator*
Bassett, Charles Walker *literature and language professor*
Benissan, Jordan Messan *music educator*
Cook, Susan Farwell *director*
Gemery, Henry Albert *economics professor*
Gilkes, Cheryl Louise Townsend *sociologist, educator, minister*
Laurence, Robert Lionel *chemical engineering professor*
Muehlner, Suanne Wilson *library director*
Simon, David L. *art historian*
Yeterian, Edward Harry *psychologist, educator, administrator*

Wells
Carleton, Joseph George, Jr. *lawyer, state legislator*

West Boothbay Harbor
Marshall, Howard Lowen *musicologist, retired music educator*

Whitefield
Marden, Kenneth Allen *advertising executive*

Wiscasset
Leslie, Seaver *artist*

Yarmouth
Bischoff, David Canby *retired university administrator*
Grover, Mark Donald *application developer, computer scientist*
Hart, Loring Edward *academic administrator*
Haynes, Peter Lancaster *utilities executive*
Northrup, Christiane *obstetrician, gynecologist*

York
Freeman, Neal Blackwell *communications corporation executive*
Hallam, Beverly (Beverly Linney) *artist*
Lyman, William Welles, Jr. *retired architect*
Roché, Robert Richard *artist*
Smart, Mary-Leigh Call (Mrs. J. Scott Smart) *civic worker*

MARYLAND

Aberdeen Proving Ground
Carrieri, Arthur Helmut *physicist, researcher*
Clayton, John Daniel *mechanical engineer, researcher*
Cozby, Richard Scott *electronics engineer, military officer*
Halstead, Rebecca S. *career military officer*
Kuperman, Roman Gregory *toxicologist, ecologist*
Mackay, Raymond Arthur *chemist*
Steger, Ralph James *chemist*
Stuebing, Edward Willis *research scientist*
VanLandingham, Mark Reed *materials engineer*

Abingdon
Wolf, Martin Eugene *lawyer, educator*

Accokeek
Beddow, Richard Harold *retired judge*
Kutchi, Judith Ann *elementary school educator*

Adamstown
Church, Martha Eleanor *retired academic administrator*
Munson, John Christian *acoustician*
Tidball, Charles Stanley *computer scientist, educator*

Adelphi
Agwu, Idika Ume *chemist, educator, reading specialist*
Brandt, Howard Edward *physicist*
Gaunaurd, Guillermo C. *physicist, researcher, engineer*
Kirwan, William English, II, *academic administrator, mathematics professor*
Nguyen, Lam Huy *electronics engineer*
Sutherland, Alan Roy *business educator*
Walker, Mamie Odena *retired secondary school educator*

Annapolis
Ames, Steven Reede *financial planner*
Andrews, Archie Moulton *retired federal official*
Barve, Kumar P. *state legislator*
Battaglia, Lynne Ann *judge*
Bontoyan, Warren Roberts *chemist, lab administrator*
Bowen, Linnell R. *director*
Branand, Claire Diane *advertising executive, writer*
Brann, Eva Toni Helene *philosophy educator*
Busch, Michael *state legislator*
Clagett, Virginia Parker *state official*
Clotworthy, John Harris *oceanographic consultant*
Connolly, Janet Elizabeth *retired sociologist, retired criminal justice educator*
Cooper, Robert Alfred *electrical engineer*
Crawford, Carol Gloria *mathematician, educator*
Criscimagna, Ned Henry *engineer*
Crosby, Ralph Wolf *communications executive*
Doory, Ann Marie *legislator*
Ferris, William Michael *lawyer*
Finerty, Martin Joseph, Jr. *editor, military officer*
Fowler, Jeffrey L. *academic administrator, career military officer*
Fry, Virginia Milne *artist, poet*
Gavian, Peter Wood *securities analyst*
Goldwater, Marilyn R(ubin) *medical/surgical nurse, state legislator*
Greene, Clayton, Jr. *judge*
Grooms, Bruce Estes *career military officer*
Halpern, Joseph Alan *physician*
Hammer, Jacob Myer *physicist, consultant*
Hollinger, Paula Colodny *state legislator*
Jansson, John Phillip *architect, consultant*
Johnson, Bruce *engineering educator*
Kamoie, Laura Croghan *history professor*
Kelley, Delores Goodwin *state legislator*
Klejnot, Getha Jean *school nurse practitioner, music educator*
Kopp, Nancy Kornblith *state official*
Kushner, Jack *retired physician*
Levitan, Laurence *lawyer, retired state senator*
Lillard, John Franklin III *lawyer*
Love, Mary Ann E. *state legislator*
Lucas, George Ramsdell, Jr. *philosophy educator*
Lucas, Steven Mitchell *lawyer*
Madden, Martin Gerard *former state legislator*
Markman, Ronald *artist, educator*
Martino, Peter Dominic *lawyer, financial software company executive, real estate developer, real estate broker, federal agency administrator, consultant, management consultant*
Mason-Chaney, Lisa *curator*
Miller, John Grider *writer*
Miller, Richards Thorn *naval architect, engineer*
Miller, William Charles *academic administrator, retired naval officer*
Nolan, Theresa A. *retired judge, mediator, arbitrator*
O'Malley, Martin Joseph *governor, former mayor, lawyer*
Papenfuse, Edward Carl, Jr. *archivist, state official*
Perkins, Roger Allan *lawyer*
Poe, Luke Harvey, Jr. *lawyer*
Rogers, David Freeman *aerospace engineering educator*
Ruben, Ida Gass *state senator*
Salem, Thomas Eric *electrical engineer, educator*
Schleicher, Nora Elizabeth *bank executive, treasurer, accountant*
Seep, Dorothy M. *music educator*
Seznec, Jean-Francois *international trade and investment manager*
Shapiro, Susan Stobbart *lawyer*
Sheff, Ronald B. *lawyer*
Stern, Margaret Bassett *retired special education educator, author*
Tosé, Maurice B. *communications executive*
Trescott, Sara Lou *water resources engineer*
Trost, Carlisle Albert Herman *retired naval officer*
Weese, John Augustus *retired mechanical engineer*
Welch, Robert Bond *ophthalmologist, educator*
Werking, Richard Hume *librarian, historian, academic administrator*
Wolf, Alfred A. *physicist, educator*

Annapolis Junction
Koplow, Ellen *lawyer, brokerage house executive*

Arnold
Constants, Dorothy Marie *manufacturing executive*
Gagné, Doreen Frances *nurse practitioner, educator*
Harris, Roger Clark *psychiatrist, consultant*
Lee, Yu-Jin *retired military physician*
Marder, Barbara Hermling *theater educator, department chairman*
Smith, Martha A. *academic administrator*
Williams, James Arthur *retired military officer, information technology executive*

Ashton
Smith, Kent Ashton *information scientist, consultant*
Whelan, Roger Michael *lawyer, educator*
Zehner, Lee Randall *entrepreneur, chemist*

Baldwin
Kiper, Mel, Jr. *sports commentator*

Baltimore
Abeloff, Martin David *medical administrator, educator, researcher*
Abrams, Rosalie Silber *retired state agency official*
Achinstein, Peter Jacob *philosopher, educator*
Achuff, Stephen Charles *cardiologist*
Adams, Harold Lynn *architect*
Alarcon, Cesar L *electrical engineer*
Allan, Janet D. *dean*
Allen, Ronald John *astrophysics educator, researcher*
Alsop, Marin *conductor, violinist, music director*
Anderson, Gerard Fenton *economist, academic administrator*
Aneja, Alka *child psychiatrist*
Angelos, Peter G. *professional sports team executive, lawyer*
Apsel, Alyssa *electrical and computer engineer*
Archibald, James Kenway *lawyer*
Aronson, Neal Irwin *neurosurgeon, medical educator*
Arrindell, Nicholas J. *academic administrator, educator*
Arsham, Hossein *operations research analyst*
Askew, Laurin Barker, Jr. *architect*
Astrue, Michael James *lawyer*
Aumann, R. Karl *commissioner, former state official*
Aurelian, Laure *medical sciences educator*
Babb, Barbara A. *lawyer, educator*
Bahrami, Hossein *epidemiologist, physician*
Baines, Henry T., Sr. *supermarkets executive*
Baker, Constance H. *lawyer*
Baker, R. Robinson *surgeon*
Baker, Timothy Danforth *physician, educator*
Baker, William Parr *lawyer*
Baldwin, Henry Furlong *banker*
Baldwin, John Wesley *history professor*
Ball, Gregory Francis *biological psychology educator*
Ball, Marion Jokl *academic administrator*
Bardhan, Tridip K. *engineering educator, researcher*
Barnhart, Jo Anne B. *federal agency administrator*
Barnhill, Gregory Hurd *investment banker*
Barth, John Simmons *writer, educator*
Bartlett, James Wilson III *lawyer*
Baskakov, Ilia V. *biotechnologist, researcher*
Batten, Sonja Victoria *psychologist, educator*
Baumgartner, William Anthony *cardiac surgeon*
Beer, Michael *biophysicist, educator, environmentalist*
Beilenson, Peter Lowell *former public health official*
Bell, Robert M. *judge*
Belzberg, Allan Joel *neurosurgery educator*
Berlage, Jan Ingham *lawyer*
Berns, Peter Vernon *lawyer*
Bigelow, George E. *psychology and pharmacology scientist*
Billig, Donal Michael *surgeon*
Bjerkaas, Allan Wayne *associate dean, physicist*
Blake, Catherine C. *judge*
Blakeslee, Wesley Daniel *lawyer, consultant, director*
Blanton, Edward Lee, Jr. *lawyer*
Blattner, William Albert *physician, epidemiology researcher*
Blau, Robert *editor*
Bluh, Pamela M. *library director, library association executive*
Blumenthal, Roger Scott *cardiologist*
Boardman, John Michael *mathematician, educator*
Bochner, Bruce Scott *immunologist, educator*
Bolger, Doreen *museum director*
Bowman, Donald Eugene *investment advisor*
Bradley, Wanda Louise *librarian*
Brady, Joseph Vincent *behavioral biologist, educator*
Bredar, James Kelleher *judge*
Brem, Henry *neurosurgeon, educator, researcher*
Bridges, John Francis Patrick *healthcare educator, researcher*
Brieger, Gert Henry *medical educator*
Bright, Margaret *sociologist*
Brockmeyer, Michael F. *lawyer*
Broda-Hydorn, Susan *entomologist*
Brodie, Angela M. *biomedical researcher, educator*
Brodie, Menasha Jacob (Jay) *architect, city planner, government executive*
Brody, Eugene Bloor *psychiatrist, educator, editor*
Brody, William Ralph *academic administrator, radiologist, educator*
Broening, Walter Stephens, Jr. *journalist, history educator*
Brooks, Thomas V. *energy executive*
Brotman, Phyllis Block *advertising and public relations executive*
Brown, Anthony Gregory *lieutenant governor, lawyer*
Brown, Donald David *biology professor*
Brown, Eddie C. *investment company executive*
Buccino, Daniel L. *psychotherapist, consultant*
Budimirovic, Dejan B. *academic child psychiatrist*
Burch, Francis Boucher, Jr. *lawyer*
Burns, Scott Patrick *lawyer*
Busuttil, Steven James *surgeon*
Byron, William James *minister, retired academic administrator, finance educator*
Calvert, Walter Randolph *lawyer*
Cameron, Duke Edward *cardiac surgeon, educator*
Campbell, Jacquelyn C. *community health nurse*
Cao, Dengfeng *pathologist*
Caplan, Sharon M. *real estate company executive*
Capute, Courtney G. *lawyer*
Carbine, James Edmond *lawyer*
Carlin, Paul Victor *legal association executive*
Carnell, Teresa Burt *lawyer*
Carney, Stephen Patrick *lawyer, retired insurance company executive*
Carper, Gertrude Esther *small business owner, real estate developer*
Carrier, France *medical educator*
Carson, Benjamin Solomon *neurosurgeon*
Cason, Alan C. *lawyer*
Catania, A(nthony) Charles *psychologist, educator*
Chagnon, Kathleen *lawyer*
Chalk, David *lawyer*
Chapelle, Suzanne Ellery Greene *history professor*
Chaplin, Peggy Louie *lawyer*
Chaudhary, Mohammad Ashraf *biostatistician, researcher*
Chen, Yu *acupuncturist, Chinese herbologist*
Chiu, Hungdah *law educator*
Choudhury, Dipa *mathematician, educator*
Chylinski-Polubinski, Roger *academic administrator*
Ciccolo, Angela *lawyer*
Civiletti, Benjamin Richard *lawyer, former United States attorney general*
Clarizio, Lynda M. *advertising executive, lawyer*
Cohen, Steven Paul *anesthesiologist, researcher*
Cohen, Warren I. *history professor*
Cole, Emried Dargan, Jr. *lawyer*
Collins, John R. *energy executive*
Collins, Marquis Tyrone *investment company executive*
Colwell, Rita Rossi *microbiologist, former federal agency administrator, medical educator*
Connaughton, James Patrick *psychiatrist*
Constantine, Andrew *conductor*
Conway de Macario, Everly *immunologist, molecular biologist*
Cook, Bryson Leitch *lawyer*
Cooper, Jerrold Stephen *historian, educator*
Cooper, Joseph *political scientist, educator*
Coppel, Lawrence David *lawyer*
Corley, Rose Ann McAfee *government official*
Cornwell, Edward E. III *surgeon*
Craig, Nancy L. *molecular biologist, educator, geneticist*
Crowe, Thomas Leonard *lawyer*
Cummings, Charles William *otolaryngologist, educator*
Curley, John Francis, Jr. *mutual fund executive*
Curran, J. Joseph, Jr. *former state attorney general*
Curran, Robert Bruce *lawyer*
D'Alfonzo, Samuel Donald *real estate company executive*
Dalrymple, Robert Anthony III *civil engineering educator*
Dang, Chi Van *hematology and oncology educator*
Dannenberg, Arthur Milton, Jr. *experimental pathologist, immunologist, educator*
Davis, Guy Donald *research scientist*
Dawson, Valina L. *science educator*
DeAngelis, Catherine D. *pediatrics educator*
Deeley, C. Carey, Jr. *lawyer*
DeLateur, Barbara Jane *medical educator*
DePaulo, J. Raymond, Jr. *psychiatrist, researcher*
Derby, Ernest Stephen *retired judge*
Derwart, Gregory M. *state agency administrator*
de Soto, Lisa *lawyer*
Deutsch, Robert William *physicist*
Devan, Deborah Hunt *lawyer*
DeVito, Mathias Joseph *retired real estate company executive*
Devreotes, Peter Nicholas *biochemistry educator*
DeVries, Donald Lawson, Jr. *lawyer*
Dewar, Donald John III *property manager*
DeWeese, Theordore L. *radiation oncologist*
Dewey, Joel Allen *lawyer*
Diaz-Montes, Teresa P. *oncologist, obstetrician, gynecologist*
DiBiagio, Thomas Michael *lawyer, former prosecutor*
Dicello, John Francis, Jr. *physicist, researcher*
Dickey, George Edward *economist, educator, lobbyist, federal official*
Dickfeld, Timm-Michael *electrophysiologist, cardiologist, educator*
Dickinson, Jane W. *retired executive secretary, volunteer*
Dixon, Sheila *mayor*
Dobs, Adrian Sandra *endocrinologist, educator*
Donkervoet, Richard Cornelius *architect*
Donovan, Dianne Francys *journalist*
Dorsey, John Russell *journalist*
Dorsey, Susan G. *neuroscientist, educator*
Dougherty, John C. *lawyer*
Drachman, Daniel Bruce *neurologist, educator*
Dubé, Lawrence Edward, Jr. *lawyer*
Dunn, Jeffrey A. *lawyer*
Duquette, Jim *professional sports team executive*
Durbin, Dean D. *marketing executive*
Egan, Cynthia L. *investment company executive*
Eichhorn, Gunther Louis *chemist, researcher*
Eisenberg, Howard Michael *neurosurgeon*
Eisner, Jonathan David *lawyer*

Elias, Sarah Davis *retired English language educator*
Ellin, Marvin *lawyer*
Ellis, Brother Patrick (H. J.) *academic administrator*
Englar, Nancy Ellen *nurse, consultant, nursing educator*
Epstein, Daniel Mark *poet, dramatist, biographer*
Erdman, Marie Mimmie *small business owner*
Erozan, Yener Sahir *pathologist, educator*
Erwin, H. Robert *lawyer*
Ettinger, David Seymour *oncologist*
Evans, Nolly Seymour *lawyer*
Eveleth, Janet Stidman *law association administrator*
Ferentz, Kevin Scott *physician*
Fergenson, Arthur Friend *lawyer*
Ferro, Elizabeth Krams *lawyer*
Finnerty, Joseph Gregory, Jr. *lawyer*
Finney, Jervis Spencer *lawyer, former prosecutor*
Fisher, Alan Hall *guidebook writer*
Fisher, Morton Poe, Jr. *lawyer*
Foster, Lester Anderson, Jr. *metal products executive*
Fox, Harold Edward *obstetrician, researcher, gynecologist, educator*
Franklin, Paula Anne *artist, writer, psychologist*
Franklin, Timothy A. *editor*
Frerichs, Herbert Donald, Jr. *lawyer*
Friedman, Louis Frank *lawyer*
Fuentealba, Victor William *professional society administrator*
Fulton, Thomas *theoretical physicist, educator*
Gabriel, Donald Albert *real estate company executive*
Gaither, John Francis, Jr. *lawyer, health products executive*
Gall, Joseph Grafton *biologist, researcher, educator*
Gallo, Robert Charles *research scientist*
Gamaldo, Charlene Edie *medical educator*
Gansler, Douglas F. *state attorney general, former prosecutor*
Garbis, Marvin Joseph *judge*
Garten, Morris L. *lawyer*
Gately, Mark Donohue *lawyer*
Gauvey, Susan Kathryn *judge*
Geman, Donald *mathematics professor*
Gendron, Andrew *lawyer*
Giacconi, Riccardo *astrophysicist, educator*
Gifford, Donald George *dean, law educator, consultant*
Gilbert, Blaine Louis *lawyer*
Gillece, James Patrick, Jr. *lawyer*
Gimenez, Luis Fernando *physician, educator*
Glassman, Jon David *aerospace executive*
Godenne, Ghislaine Dudley *physician, psychotherapist, educator*
Goldberg, Alan Marvin *toxicologist, educator*
Goldberg, Morton Falk *ophthalmologist, educator*
Goldman, Brian Arthur *lawyer, accountant*
Goldman, Duff (Jeffrey Adam Goldman) *chef*
Goldman, Lynn Rose *medical educator*
Goldman, Meir *lawyer*
Goldman, Stuart Miles *podiatrist*
Gontrum, Barbara *law librarian, educator*
Gonya, Jeffrey Keenan *lawyer*
Gonzales, Louise Michaux *lawyer*
Goodman, William Richard *insurance adjusting company executive*
Gordis, Leon *physician*
Gordon, Bruce S. *civil rights organization executive, former telecommunications company executive*
Grasmick, Nancy S. *school system administrator*
Gray, Frank Truan *lawyer*
Gray, Oscar Shalom *lawyer*
Green, Bert Franklin, Jr. *retired psychology professor*
Green, Robert Edward, Jr. *physicist, researcher*
Greenough, William Bates III *medical educator*
Greider, Carol Widney *molecular biologist*
Griffin, Diane Edmund *research physician, virologist, educator*
Griffin, John W. *neurologist, medical educator*
Griffith, Lawrence Stacey Cameron *cardiologist, educator*
Guben, Jan K. *lawyer*
Guler, Osman *education educator, researcher*
Haas, Mark *pathologist*
Hackerman, Willard J. *construction executive*
Haeri, Niloofar M. *linguist, educator*
Hafets, Richard Jay *lawyer*
Haig, Frank Rawle *physics professor, priest*
Hanks, James Judge, Jr. *lawyer*
Hansen, Barbara Caleen *physiologist, science educator*
Harris, James Carol Overton, Jr. *psychiatrist, pediatrician*
Harris, Reginald Mervyn, Jr. *librarian, writer*
Harrison, Michael *opera company director*
Harvey, Alexander, II, *retired federal judge*
Hauser, Michael George *astrophysicist*
Hayden, Carla Diane *library director, educator*
Hayes, Dennis Courtland *civil rights association executive, lawyer*
Hecht, Alan Dannenberg *insurance executive*
Hecht, Donald D. *lawyer*
Heldman, Alan Wohl, Jr. *medical educator*
Hellmann, David Bruce *medical educator*
Helm, Donald Cairney *geologist, engineer, educator*
Henderson, Donald Ainslie *public health service officer*
Herpel, Laura Bogan *pulmonologist, researcher*
Hicks, Sherman Gregory *pastor*
Himelfarb, Richard Jay *investment company executive*
Hirsh, Allan Thurman, Jr. *publishing executive*
Hoehn-Saric, R. Christopher *educational organization executive*
Hofkin, Gerald Alan *gastroenterologist*
Hofmann, Irene E. *art museum director*
Honemann, Daniel Henry *lawyer*
Hopkins, Henry Holt *mutual fund attorney*
Hopkins, Samuel *retired investment banker*
Hopps, Raymond, Jr. *lawyer, film producer*
Howard, J. Woodford, Jr. *retired political science professor*
Howard, John Vincent, Jr. *lawyer*
Howell, Harley Thomas *lawyer*
Howes, James Guerdon *communication and transportation executive*
Hrabowski, Freeman Alphonsa III *academic administrator*
Huang, Judy *neurosurgeon*
Hug, Richard Ernest *small business owner*
Huganir, Richard Lewis *neuroscientist, educator, researcher*
Huggins, Amy Branum *music educator*
Hulbert, Jarl O. *music educator*
Hungerford, David Samuel *orthopedic surgeon, educator*
Hussain, Mehboob *medical educator*
Ihrie, Robert *oil, gas and real estate company executive*
Immelt, Stephen J. *lawyer*
Irwin, John Thomas *humanities educator*
Jaar, Bernard Georges *nephrologist, researcher*
Jackson, Stanley Edward *retired special education educator*
Jacobson, Katherine Louise *musician, educator*
Jahren, (A.) Hope *geochemist, educator*
Jelinek, Frederick *electrical engineer, educator*
Johns, Richard James *physician, educator*
Johnson, E. Scott *lawyer*
Johnson, Harry Sterling *lawyer*
Johnson, Kenneth Peter *neurologist, researcher*
Johnson, Michael Paul *historian, educator*
Johnson, Richard Tidball *microbiology and neuroscience educator, virologist, researcher*
Johnston, Edward Allan *lawyer*
Johnston, George W. *lawyer*
Jones, Hendree Evelyn *research scientist, psychologist*
Jones, John Martin, Jr. *lawyer*
Jones, Nicholas Patrick *civil engineering educator*
Judd, Brian Raymond *physicist*
Judson, Horace Freeland *history professor, writer*
Justice, Christopher *communications and language educator*
Kandel, Nelson Robert *lawyer*
Kaplan, Alexander Efimovich *physics educator, engineering educator*
Karni, Edi *economics professor*
Kastor, John Alfred *cardiologist, educator*
Katz, Joseph Louis *chemical engineer, educator*
Kavoussi, Louis Raphael *urologist*
Kelen, Gabor David *emergency physician*
Kennedy, James Aloysius Charles *investment company executive*
Kenney, Brigid E. *lawyer*
Kent, Edgar Robert, Jr. *investment banker*
Kerr, Douglas Anthony *neurologist, researcher*
Kessler, Herbert Leon *art historian, educator, academic administrator*
Kessler, Irving Isar *epidemiologist, consultant*
Kimbrough, Natalie *history professor*
Kirkhart, Matthew Wayde *psychology professor*
Klimantov, Alexius George *engineering executive*
Klitzke, Theodore Elmer *arts consultant, retired college dean*
Knapp, David Allan *pharmaceutical educator, researcher, dean*
Knight, Franklin W. *historian, educator*
Koch, Edgar Frank *protective services official*
Kolkin, Mitchell *lawyer*
Kremen, Richard M. *lawyer*
Krolik, Julian Henry *astrophysicist, educator*
Kumin, Libby Barbara *speech language pathologist, educator*
Kurth, Lieselotte *foreign language educator*
Kuryk, David Neal *lawyer*
Kwon, Chul Soo *psychiatrist*
Langmead, Joseph Michael *accountant, consultant, educator*
Larch, Sara Margaret *healthcare executive*
Lawrence, Robert Swan *physician, educator*
Lawson, Edward Earle *neonatal/perinatal nurse practitioner*
Lazarus, Fred, IV, *academic administrator*
Lazarus, Gerald Sylvan *dermatologist, educator, dean*
Lee, Steven Xavier *museum director, artist and environmentalist*
Lee, Yung-Keun *physicist, researcher*
Legg, Benson Everett *federal judge*
Legum, Jeffrey Alfred *holding company executive*
Lemer, Andrew Charles *engineer, economist*
Lemke, Thomas P. *lawyer, brokerage house executive*
Leonard, Angela Michele *librarian, educator*
Leonard, Joseph Howard *staff specialist*
Leppert, Cynthia L. *lawyer*
Levien, David Harold *surgeon*
Levin, Edward Jesse *lawyer*
Levine, Richard E. *lawyer*
Lewis, Ray *professional football player*
Liberto, Joseph Salvatore *retired bank executive*
Lidtke, Doris Keefe *retired computer science educator*
Lidtke, Vernon LeRoy *history professor*
Liebmann, George W. *lawyer*
Litrenta, Frances Marie *psychiatrist*
Little, Robert *reporter*
Littlefield, John Walley *geneticist, cell biologist, pediatrician*
Liu, Jun O. *pharmacologist, educator*
Long, Donlin Martin *surgeon, educator*
Longo, Dan Louis *internist, researcher, oncologist*
Loucks, Allen Frazier *prosecutor, lawyer*
Lundy, Audie Lee, Jr. *lawyer*
Macario, Alberto Juan Lorenzo *physician*
Maccini, Louis John *economist, educator*
MacPhail, Andrew B. *professional sports team executive*
MacWilliams, Michael Broughton *lawyer*
Magnuson, Nancy *librarian*
Makarov, Danil Victor *urologist*
Marsh, Bruce David *geologist, educator*
Mason, Raymond Adams (Chip) *diversified financial services company executive*
Massof, Robert William *neuroscientist, educator*
Matheson, Nina W. *medical researcher*
Mathias, James D. *lawyer*
Mathias, Robert Joseph *lawyer*
McAdam, Paul Edward *retired library administrator*
McCarthy, Patricia Anne *reading educator*
McClung, A(lexander) Keith, Jr. *retired lawyer*
McGahee, Willis Andrew *professional football player*
McHugh, Paul R. *psychiatrist, neurologist, educator*
McKhann, Guy Mead *neurologist, educator*
McKusick, Victor Almon *geneticist, educator, physician*
McNair, Steve LaTreal *professional football player*
McPartland, James Michael *academic administrator*
McPherson, Donald Paxton III *lawyer*
McWilliams, John Michael *lawyer*
Meagher, Anthony L. *lawyer*
Melick, Clifford Francis *sociologist, researcher*
Meltzer, Arthur Adam *researcher*
Mendell, Joshua T. *molecular biologist, geneticist, educator*
Merchenthaler, Istvan Jozsef *neuroscientist, morphologist*
Mfume, Kweisi *civil rights association executive, former congressman*
Miller, Decatur Howard *lawyer*
Miller, Edward Doring *anesthesiologist, hospital administrator, dean*
Miller, Michael *physician, educator*
Millspaugh, Martin Laurence *real estate developer, consultant*
Miser, Ann *retired government researcher*
Mixson, Archibald James *research scientist, internist, endocrinologist*
Mocko, George Paul *minister*
Moos, H. Warren *physicist, educator, astronomer, director*
Morris, David Michael *insurance executive, lawyer*
Moser, M(artin) Peter *lawyer*
Motz, Diana Gribbon *federal judge*
Motz, John Frederick *federal judge*
Mountcastle, Vernon Benjamin *retired neuroscientist*
Muccie, Mary Rose *publishing executive*
Murphy, Billy (William H. Murphy Jr.) *lawyer*
Murphy, Frances Louise, II, *retired newspaper publisher*
Myers, Eric B. *lawyer*
Myslinski, Norbert Raymond *medical educator*
Nasr, Nadia *library and information scientist*
Nathanson, Harvey Charles *electrical engineer*
Nelkin, Barry David *oncology researcher and educator*
Nelson, Douglas W. *foundation administrator*
Nichols, David Gregory *anesthesiologist, pediatrician, educator*
Nichols, Stephen George *Romance languages educator*
Niemeyer, Paul Victor *federal judge*
Nilson, George Albert *lawyer*
Nonogaki, Hirofumi *research scientist*
Noren, Marc B. *lawyer*
Norman, Colin Arthur *astrophysics educator*
Norman, Philip Sidney *physician*
Nussbaum, Paul M. *lawyer*
O'Brien, Edwin Frederick *archbishop*
Ogden, Jonathan *professional football player*
Ohly, D. Christopher *lawyer*
Oji, Pauline E. *secondary school educator*
Olson, Peter L. *geophysicist, educator*
Orman, Leonard Arnold *lawyer*
Otal, Monica D. *music educator*
O'Toole, Tara Jeanne *medical educator, former federal agency administrator*
Padilla, Irene *library director*
Palmeiro, Rafael Corrales *professional baseball player*
Pappas, George Frank *lawyer*
Park, Mary Woodfill *information consultant, librarian, writer*
Parvis, Peter P. *lawyer*
Passley, Josef Antonio *psychologist, educator, writer*
Patel, Chintan *adult education educator*
Paulson, Ronald Howard *language educator, humanities educator*
Perler, Bruce Alan *vascular surgeon*
Perlman, Beth S. *information technology executive*
Peterson, Ronald R. *health service administrator*
Pickett, Eugenia V. *social worker*
Plank, Kevin A. *apparel executive*
Plant, Albin MacDonough *lawyer*
Pollak, Mark *lawyer*
Posner, Gary Herbert *chemist, educator*
Powe, Neil Richard *physician, educator, epidemiologist, public health service officer*
Provorny, Frederick Alan *lawyer, educator*
Quinn, Thomas Charles *medical researcher, educator*
Rabb, Hamid *nephrologist, educator*
Radding, Andrew *lawyer*
Radhakrishnan, Malathi *biologist, educator*
Radowich, Jeffrey J. *lawyer*
Ranum, Orest Allen *historian, educator*
Rasgon, Jason Laurence *entomologist, microbiologist, educator*
Ravenell, Kenneth W. *lawyer*
Ray, Carol Reneé *researcher*
Rayson, Glendon Ennes *internist, preventive medicine specialist, writer*
Redfield, Robert R. *virologist, medical educator*
Reno, Russell Ronald, Jr. *lawyer*
Reynolds, William Leroy *lawyer, educator*
Riess, Adam Guy *astronomer, educator*
Ripken, Cal (Calvin Edwin Ripken Jr.) *retired professional baseball player*
Roberts, Brian Michael *professional baseball player*
Robinson, Brooks Calbert, Jr. *retired professional baseball player, sports commentator, business consultant*
Robinson, Carrie *pastor*
Robinson, Sally Shoemaker *lay associate*
Robinson, Zelig *lawyer*
Rodowsky, Lawrence Francis *retired state judge*
Rodricks, Daniel John *columnist, television commentator*
Rogers, Brian Charles *portfolio manager, investment company executive*
Rose, Noel Richard *immunologist, microbiologist, educator*
Roseman, Saul *biochemist, educator*
Rosenberg, Edwin Harold *systems analyst*
Rosenberg, Henry A., Jr. *petroleum executive*
Rosenstein, Rod J. *prosecutor*
Rosenthal, William J. *lawyer*
Ross, Richard Starr *retired medical school dean, cardiologist, educator*
Rothenberg, Karen H. *dean, law educator*
Roupe, James Paul *accountant*
Rousuck, J. Wynn *theater critic*
Rubin, Aviel David *computer science educator, writer*
Rumbaugh, Jeffrey Arlin *neurologist, neuroscientist*
Ryan, Timothy *publishing executive*
Rzepkowski, James Edward *state agency administrator*
Sack, George Henry, Jr. *molecular geneticist*
Salamon, Lester Milton *political science professor*
Samet, Jonathan Michael *epidemiologist, educator*
Sanders, Julius Ray *music company executive*
Saudek, Christopher D. *medical educator*
Savonenko, Alena *neuroscientist, educator*
Scales, Robert H., Jr. *former academic administrator, retired army officer*
Schaefer, Robert Wayne *banker*
Schilling, Franklin Charles, Jr. *retail management professional*
Schlaff, Barbara E. *lawyer*
Schochor, Jonathan *lawyer, educator*
Schoenrich, Edyth Hull *internist, preventive medicine physician*
Schultheis, Patricia Ann *writer, editor*
Schumann, Jill *religious organization administrator*
Schwartz, Glenn Martin *archaeologist, educator*
Schwartz, Howard S. *lawyer*
Scriggins, Larry Palmer *lawyer, director*
Seurkamp, Mary Pat *college president*
Shamoo, Adil Elias *biochemist, educator*
Shannon, Joe *art critic, painter*
Shapiro, Harry Dean *lawyer*
Sharfstein, Joshua M. *city health department administrator, pediatrician*
Shattuck, Mayo Adams III *utilities executive*
Shea, James L. *lawyer*
Shelton, Robert Arthur *lawyer*
Shepherd, Kevin L. *lawyer*
Shiffman, Bernard *mathematician, educator*
Short, Alexander Campbell *lawyer*
Sidransky, David *molecular biologist*
Silbergeld, Ellen Kovner *epidemiologist, toxicologist, researcher*
Silver, Michael Joel *lawyer*
Silverstone, Harris J. *chemistry professor*
Singh, Om V. *biotechnologist, researcher*
Sinha, Neeti *biophysicist, researcher*
Sirota, Wilbert H. *lawyer*
Skirpan, Richard Michael *conductor, music educator*
Skolnik, Sandra J. *educational association administrator*
Sleeman, Bill *library and information scientist*
Slezak, Sheri *plastic surgeon*
Smith, Lisa J. *lawyer*
Smith, Robert G. *lawyer*
Smith, Robert W., Jr., (Jay) *lawyer*
Snead, James Arrington *architect*
Snell, Steven Layne *lawyer, consultant*
Snyder, Solomon Halbert *psychiatrist, pharmacologist*
Somer-Greif, Penny Lynn *lawyer*
Sommer, Alfred *ophthalmologist, medical educator, researcher*
Sorkin, Alan Lowell *economist, educator*
Standiford, Harold C. *medical educator*
Starfield, Barbara Helen *pediatrician, educator*
Steensgaard, Anthony Harvey *federal agency administrator*
Steiner, Robert Frank *biochemist*
Sterne, Joseph Robert Livingston *editor, educator*
Stewart, Doris Mae *biology professor*
Stohler, Christian S. *dean, dental educator*
Strickland, Marshall Hayward *bishop*
Strull, Gene *technology consultant, retired manufacturing executive*
Suggs, Kenneth *lawyer*
Sutherland, Donald Sinclair *music educator, musician*
Sykes, Melvin Julius *lawyer*
Tabb, Winston *library director*
Talalay, Paul *pharmacologist, educator*
Talbot, Donald Roy *management consultant*
Tamargo, Rafael J. *neurological surgeon, educator*
Taylor, Carl Ernest *preventive medicine physician, epidemiologist, educator*
Tchantchou, Flaubert *medical researcher*
Tejada, Miguel (Odalis) *professional baseball player*
Temirkanov, Yuri Khatuevich *conductor, music director*
Tenser, Beth Hillary *graphics designer, art director*
Terry, Peter Browne *medical educator*
Thakor, Nitish Vyomesh *biomedical engineering educator*
Thompson, Otho M. *lawyer, former solicitor*
Tiburzi, Paul A. *lawyer*

Tilghman, Richard Carmichael, Jr. *lawyer*
Townsend, Craig Arthur *chemistry educator*
Trembley, Dave *professional baseball manager*
Trombley, Edward Francis III *registrar*
Trpis, Milan *vector biologist, educator*
Trujillo, J. Roberto *virologist*
Ts'o, Paul On-Pong *biophysical chemist, educator*
Tucker, Abigail *journalist*
Tucker, James L., Jr. *artist, educator*
Turnbaugh, Charles W. *state agency administrator*
Tyler, Anne (Mrs. Taghi M. Modarressi) *writer*
Tyler, Ralph Sargent III *lawyer*
Urban, Theodore W. *lawyer, brokerage house executive*
Valentine, April Sue *elementary school educator, department chairman*
Van Riper, Robert Austin *writer, retired public relations executive*
Velculescu, Victor E. *oncologist, educator*
Vogelstein, Bert *oncology educator*
Wahington, Anthony William *volunteer coordinator*
Walker, Irving Edward *lawyer*
Walsh, Patrick Craig *urologist*
Walter, Harold Mark *lawyer*
Warren, Melissa Allison *lawyer*
Wasserman, Richard Leo *lawyer*
Wasta, Vanessa A. *media specialist, web site designer*
Watkins, John B. *lawyer*
Weaver, Kenneth Newcomer *geologist, state agency administrator*
Weisfeldt, Myron Lee *cardiologist, educator*
Weiss, James Lloyd *cardiology educator*
Welker, James Anthony *physician*
West, James Edward (James Edward Maceo West) *acoustical engineer, educator*
Weyandt, Daniel Scott *retired naval officer, engineer, physicist*
White, Pamela Janice *lawyer*
Whitman, Marland Hamilton, Jr. *lawyer*
Wierman, John Charles *mathematician, educator*
Williams, Michael J. *philosopher, educator*
Willis, John T. *former secretary of state*
Wilson, Donald Edward *internist, educator, dean*
Wilson, Thomas Matthew III *lawyer*
Winn, James Julius, Jr. *lawyer*
Wolf, Cyd Beth *lawyer, entrepreneur*
Wolf, Larry M. *lawyer*
Wolfe, Nathan *epidemiologist*
Wolman, M. Gordon *geography educator*
Wright, James Dorsey *lawyer*
Yantis, Steven George *psychology educator*
Yoskowitz, Irving Benjamin *lawyer, energy executive*
Young, Barbara *psychiatrist, psychotherapist, educator, photographer*
Yue, Wusi *mechanical engineer, researcher*
Zaccagnini, Anthony Jackson *lawyer*
Zhao, Xianfeng Frank *pathologist, educator*
Ziff, Larzer *literature and language professor*
Zinkham, W. Robert *lawyer*

Bel Air
Helfrich, Cornelius David *lawyer*
Kramer, Keith Allan *music educator, composer*
Lu, David John *historian, writer*
Miller, Dorothy Eloise *education educator*
Miller, Max Dunham, Jr. *lawyer*
O'Bryon, James Fredrick *defense consultant*
Thursfield, Fred Falconer, II, *foundation administrator*

Belcamp
Tapp, Mamie Pearl *educator*

Beltsville
Bae, Hanhong *molecular biologist, researcher*
Basinger, William Daniel *computer programmer*
Bruckner, Daniel Raymond *history educator*
Davis, Robert Edward *plant pathologist*
Johnson, Phyllis Elaine *chemist, researcher, federal official*
Miller, Ted Robert *management consultant*
Nemes, Attila *soil scientist, researcher*
Palm, Mary Egdahl *mycologist*
Quirk, Frank Joseph *management consulting company executive*
Ritz, David M. *photographic retail company executive*
Schneider, Edwin Kahn *research scientist*
Shukla, Jagadish *science educator*
Tso, Tien Chioh *federal agency administrator, researcher, agronomist*
Young, Peter Robert *library director*

Berlin
Brodsky, Allen *retired biophysicist*
Hammond, Michelle *middle school educator*
Passwater, Barbara Gayhart *real estate broker*
Passwater, Richard Albert *biochemist, author*

Bethesda
Abdoo, Elizabeth A. *lawyer*
Abrams, David B. *federal agency administrator*
Ahn, Sohyun *neuroscientist, researcher*
Aisenberg, Irwin Morton *retired lawyer*
Akhondi, Hossein *internist, researcher*
Aldridge, Edward Cleveland, Jr., (Pete Aldridge) *former federal agency administrator*
Alexander, Duane Frederick *federal agency administrator, pediatrician, researcher*
Allmon, Charles W. *investment advisor*
Allnutt, Robert Frederick *management consultant, lawyer*
Alter, Harvey J. *hematologist, educator*
Alving, Barbara *federal agency administrator, hematologist*
Anderson, George Kenneth *physician, retired military officer, foundation administrator*
Apud, Jose Antonio *psychiatrist, educator*
Arons, Bernard S. *psychiatrist, educator, health services administrator*
Austin, Christopher *neurologist, researcher*
Avila, Nilo Alonso *radiologist*
Baird, Bruce Allen *lawyer*
Banik, Sambhu Nath *psychologist*
Barton, Jean Marie *psychologist, educator*
Basavappa, Ravi *biophysical science educator*
Battey, James F., Jr. *federal agency administrator, neurologist*
Bauersfeld, Carl Frederick *lawyer*
Beall, Robert Joseph *foundation executive*
Bebchick, Leonard Norman *lawyer*
Becker, Bruce Clare *clinical psychologist, neuropsychologist, administrator*
Becker, Edwin Demuth *chemist, director*
Bennink, Jack Richard *microbiologist, researcher*
Benson, Elizabeth Polk *art specialist*
Berg, Jeremy Mark *federal agency administrator, biochemist, researcher*
Berger, Robert Lewis *retired biophysicist*
Berman, Marshall Fox *lawyer*
Berzofsky, Jay A. *medical researcher*
Bowsher, Charles Arthur *retired government official, financial executive*
Brady, Roscoe Owen *neurogeneticist, educator*
Brown, Dudley Earl, Jr. *psychiatrist, educator, health science association administrator, federal agency administrator, retired military officer*
Buetow, Kenneth H. *federal agency administrator*
Bukh, Jens *medical researcher*
Bunger, Rolf *physiology educator*
Burdeshaw, William Brooksbank *engineering executive*
Burkhalter, Susan Shively *music educator, organist*
Burns, Drusilla Lorene *microbiologist*
Cai, Tao *biomedical researcher*
Candotti, Fabio *pediatrician*
Castelli, Alexander Gerard *accountant*
Chanock, Robert Merritt *pediatrician*
Chebaane, Mohamed *water management specialist, consultant*
Chen, Kevin Gang *oncologist, researcher, molecular pharmacologist*
Child-Olmsted, Gisèle Alexandra *retired language educator*
Chronister, Gregory Michael *newspaper editor*
Clark, A. James *real estate company executive*
Cleary, Timothy Finbar *professional society administrator*
Cody, Thomas Gerald *management consultant, writer*
Cohen, Robert Abraham *retired physician*
Cohen, Sheldon Gilbert *physician, historian, immunologist*
Collins, Francis S. *federal agency administrator, geneticist, physician*
Comey, James B., Jr. *lawyer, aerospace company executive, former federal agency administrator*
Conger, Lucinda *retired librarian*
Corn, Milton *dean, physician, consultant*
Cornish, Edward Seymour *magazine editor*
Coutts, Robert B. *aerospace transportation executive*
Cox, Kenneth Allen *retired lawyer, communications executive, consultant*
Crout, J(ohn) Richard *pharmacologist, researcher*
Cruz, Wilhelmina Mangahas *critical care physician, educator*
Damico, Nicholas Peter *lawyer*
Danforth, David Newton, Jr. *surgeon, oncologist*
Daniel, Charles Dwelle, Jr. *retired military officer*
Daniels, Michael Paul *lawyer*
Datiles, Manuel Bernaldes III *ophthalmologist, researcher*
Day, Robert Dwain, Jr. *foundation administrator, lawyer*
De Cherney, Alan Hersh *obstetrics and gynecology educator*
Deckelbaum, Nelson *lawyer*
Dennin, Joseph Francis *former government official, lawyer*
de Vries, Margaret Garritsen *economist*
Dietrich, Robert Anthony *pathologist, consultant, medical association administrator*
Dignac, Geny (Eugenia M. Bermudez) *sculptor*
Di Paolo, Joseph Amedeo *geneticist*
DiPietro, Ralph John *lawyer*
Doroshow, James Halpern *federal agency administrator, oncologist*
Downey, Arthur Thomas III *lawyer*
Dulin, Maurine Stuart *volunteer*
Duncan, Constance Catharine *psychologist, educator, researcher*
Durek, Thomas Andrew *computer company executive*
Eaton, William A. *biomedical researcher*
Ehrenfeld, Ellie (Elvera Ehrenfeld) *biologist, researcher*
Elliott, George Armstrong III *artist, journalist*
Emanuel, Ezekiel J. *oncologist, bioethicist*
English, Michela *entertainment company executive*
English, William deShay *lawyer, director*
Fales, Henry Marshall III *chemist*
Farci, Patrizia *medical educator, researcher*
Fauci, Anthony Stephen *federal agency administrator, allergist, immunologist*
Fee, Elizabeth *medical historian, administrator*
Fefferman, Hilbert *government official, lawyer*
Feuerstein, Donald Martin *lawyer*
Fleisher, Thomas Arthur *physician*
Fleming, Patricia Stubbs (Patsy Fleming) *artist*
Forster, Peter C. *construction executive*
Frank, Martin *physiologist, educator, medical association administrator*
Frank, Richard Sanford *retired magazine editor*
Fraser, Catriona Trafford *art gallery director, photographer*
Frosh, Brian Esten *lawyer, state senator*
Gaarder, Marie *speech pathologist*
Gabelnick, Henry Lewis *medical research administrator*
Gallin, John I. *medical researcher*
Gastwirth, Glenn Barry *medical association administrator*
Gershengorn, Marvin Carl *internist, researcher, educator*
Giedd, Jay Norman *psychiatrist*
Goldstein, Murray *medical epidemiologist and research administrator*
Goodwin, Frederick King *psychiatrist*
Gottesman, Michael Marc *biomedical researcher*
Gottlieb, Jonathan W. *lawyer*
Gould, W. Scott *financial administrator*
Grady, Patricia A. *federal agency administrator*
Graeff, Alan S. *health association executive*
Grau, John Michael *trade association executive*
Greenberg, Judith Horovitz *geneticist*
Greenwald, Peter *health facility administrator, director, epidemiologist, researcher*
Grisham, Joe Wheeler *cell biologist, educator*
Guttmacher, Alan Edward *physician, medical educator*
Guttman, Helene Nathan *biomedical consultant, transpersonal counselor*
Hagberg, Viola Wilgus *lawyer*
Hallett, Mark *neurologist, educator, medical researcher, director*
Harford, Joe B. *federal agency administrator*
Harlan, Linda Carol *epidemiologist*
Harris, Curtis Craig *medical researcher*
Harris, Stanley S. *retired judge, arbitrator, mediator*
Haseltine, Florence Pat *obstetrician, gynecologist, medical association administrator*
Hausman, Steven Jack *health science association administrator*
He, Liusheng *biomedical researcher*
Heath, Ralph D. *aerospace transportation executive*
Hemming, Val G. *retired dean, educator*
Herman, Edith Carol *journalist*
Herman, Mary Margaret *neuropathologist*
Hewes, Laurence Ilsley III *lawyer, management consultant*
Highfill, Philip Henry, Jr. *retired language educator*
Himelfarb, Stephen Roy *lawyer*
Hingson, Ralph W. *medical educator*
Hodes, Richard J. *federal agency administrator, immunologist, researcher*
Hoffman, Ira Eliot *lawyer*
Holloman, Marilyn Leona Davis *lobbyist, non profit administrator, family practice nurse practitioner, new product developer*
Holmberg, Ted *journalist, consultant*
Hrynkow, Sharon Hemond *federal agency administrator, neuroscientist, researcher*
Hsu, S. Dana *technologist*
Huebner, John Stephen *geologist*
Hutchins, Michael *non-profit scientific society administrator, conservation biologist*
Hutton, John Evans, Jr. *surgeon, educator, retired military officer*
Insel, Thomas R. *federal agency administrator, psychiatrist*
Ito, Yoichiro *pathologist, researcher*
Jacobson, Kenneth Alan *chemist, researcher*
Jaffe, Elaine Sarkin *pathologist*
Jamieson, Graham A. *biochemist, researcher, retired organization official*
Johnson, Eugene Clare *data processing company executive*
Johnson, Joyce Marie *psychiatrist, public health service officer, epidemiologist*
Johnson, Robert Louis *professional sports team owner, former broadcast executive*
Johnson, Thomas Dale *publishing executive*
Jonas, Gary Fred *healthcare executive*
Jones, John Franklin, Jr., (Jack F. Jones) *federal agency administrator*
Joy, Robert John Thomas *medical educator*
Joyce, Bernita Anne *retired federal agency administrator*
Kalish, Heather Rachel *chemist, researcher*
Kapikian, Albert Zaven *physician, epidemiologist*
Kaplan, Marjorie *broadcast executive*
Katz, Stephen Ira *federal agency administrator*
Kavanaugh, Everett Edward, Jr. *trade association executive*
Kawazoe, Robin Inada *federal official*
Kem, Richard Samuel *retired army officer*
Kemelhor, Robert E(lias) *mechanical engineer*
Kempster, Norman Roy *journalist*
Kingsley, Mary Lee *writer, researcher, consultant, retired marketing executive*
Kinsey, John Allen *systems engineer, technical director*
Kirby, Harmon Elwood *retired ambassador*
Kirschstein, Ruth Lillian *physician*
Klee, Claude Blenc *medical researcher*
Knachel, Philip Atherton *librarian*
Koonce, Calvin Scott *brokerage firm executive, physicist*
Korn, Edward David *biochemist*
Kramer, Barnett Sheldon *oncologist*
Krause, Richard Michael *medical scientist, government official, educator, researcher*
Kresge, Nicole *editor*
Kruger, Gustav Otto, Jr. *retired oral surgeon, educator, department chairman*
Kubasik, Christopher E. *aerospace transportation executive*
Kunos, George *pharmacologist*
Kutemeyer, Peter Martin *industrial engineering executive*
Laingen, Lowell Bruce *diplomat*
Landis, Story Cleland *federal agency administrator, neurobiologist*
Lane, H. Clifford *internist*
Larrabee, Barbara Princelau *retired intelligence officer*
Larrabee, Donald Richard *publishing executive*
Larsen-Basse, Jorn *mechanical and materials engineering educator, researcher, consultant*
Less, Anthony Albert *retired naval officer*
Levine, Zachary Thomas *neurosurgeon*
Li, Qingdi Quentin *physician, research scientist, medical educator*
Lindberg, Donald Allan Bror *library director, pathologist, educator*
Linehan, William Marston *urologic surgeon, cancer researcher*
Lipman, David J. *medical association administrator, researcher*
Lorber, Mortimer *retired physiology educator*
Lowy, Douglas Ronald *oncologist, researcher*
Lystad, Mary Hanemann (Mrs. Robert Lystad) *sociologist, writer*
Mackall, Crystal L. *medical researcher*
Maguire, Joanne M. *aerospace transportation executive*
Malloy, Edward Michael *diplomat, educator*
Manasse, Henri Richard, Jr. *pharmaceutical executive*
Marini, Ann Marie *medical researcher, educator*
Marriott, Richard Edwin *hotel and contract services executive*
Masur, Henry *internist*
Mattison, Donald Roger *gynecologist, toxicologist, educator, medical association administrator, public health service officer*
McClure, Brooks *management consultant*
McCurdy, Harry Ward *otolaryngologist*
McDonough, Thomas P. *health care company executive*
Mc Gurn, Barrett *communications executive, writer*
McMurphy, Michael Allen *energy company executive, lawyer*
Meakem, Carolyn Soliday *investment executive, financial planner, money manager, consultant*
Melenhorst, Jan Joseph *immunologist*
Mellor, James Robb *retired electronics executive*
Metzger, Henry *federal research institution administrator*
Miller, Judith Wolfe Cohen *management consultant*
Mishkin, Mortimer *neuropsychologist*
Mock, Beverly A. *geneticist, researcher*
Monjan, Andrew Arthur *neuroscientist*
Morgan, John Davis *government agency administrator, consultant*
Morrison, Bruce Andrew *federal official, public information officer*
Moshman, Jack *statistical consultant*
Moss, Bernard *virologist, researcher*
Mullan, Fitzhugh *public health physician*
Murayama, Makio *biochemist*
Murphy, James Paul *lawyer*
Murrett, Robert B. *federal agency administrator, career military officer*
Musil, Robert Kirkland *global environmental politics professor*
Nabel, Elizabeth Guenthner *cardiologist, researcher*
Nassetta, Christopher J. *hotel facility executive*
Neill, Denis Michael *management consultant*
Nejelski, Paul Arthur *retired judge, freelance writer*
Nelson, Ethelyn Barnett *civic worker*
Nelson, John Howard (Jack Howard Nelson) *journalist*
Nelson, William Eugene *lawyer*
Neumann, Ronald Daniel *nuclear medicine physician, educator*
Niederhuber, John Edward *federal agency administrator, oncologist, surgeon, immunologist*
North, A. Frederick *physician*
North, William Haven *foreign service officer*
Nussbaum, Robert L. *senior genetics investigator*
Nyirjesy, Istvan *obstetrician, gynecologist*
Obrams, Gunta Iris *clinical research administrator*
O'Callaghan, Jerry Alexander *federal agency administrator*
Oddis, Joseph Anthony *health associations executive*
Ognibene, Frederick Peter *internist*
Olmsted, Jerauld Lockwood *telephone company executive*
Olson, Lynn *editor*
Ommaya, Ayub Khan *neurosurgeon, educator*
O'Neill, Malcolm R. *aerospace executive*
Ostrander, Elaine A. *federal agency administrator, geneticist*
Pacher, Pál *pharmacologist, educator, researcher*
Padgett, Nancy Weeks *retired law librarian, lawyer, consultant*
Palmer, James Alvin (Jim Palmer) *baseball commentator*
Palumbo, James Fredrick *finance company executive*
Paul, William Erwin *immunologist*
Peck, Edward Lionel *retired foreign service officer, corporate executive*
Pemberton, S. Macpherson *government official, educator*
Perlin, Seymour *psychiatrist, educator*
Peterson, Charles Marquis *medical educator*
Petralia, Ronald Sebastian *entomologist, neurobiologist*
Pettigrew, Roderic I. *federal agency administrator, radiologist, researcher*
Pickerell, James Howard *photojournalist*
Pinn, Vivian W. *federal agency administrator, pathologist*
Pipkin, James Harold, Jr. *lawyer*
Pollard, Harvey B. *medical educator, neuroscientist*
Polsby, Gail K. *psychotherapist*
Pospisil, George Curtis *health science administrator*
Purcell, Robert Harry *virologist, researcher*
Quinnan, Gerald Vincent, Jr. *medical educator*
Quon, Michael James *medical researcher, internist*
Rabson, Alan Saul *federal agency administrator, pathologist, educator*
Rapoport, Judith *psychiatrist*
Raullerson, Calvin Henry *retired political scientist, consultant*
Reed, Berenice Anne *cultural organization administrator, educator, artist*
Reed, Miriam Bell *legislative staff member*

Rennert, Owen Murray *pediatrician, geneticist, educator*
Reynolds, Herbert Young *internist*
Rhim, Johng Sik *physician, medical researcher*
Rice, Charles Lane *surgeon, educator*
Rice, Jerry Mercer *biochemist, consultant, pathologist*
Richardson, John *retired international relations executive*
Robbins, John Bennett *medical researcher*
Robinson, Sharon Beth *health science association administrator*
Rosenbaum, Greg Alan *merchant banker, consultant*
Rosenberg, Mark Louis *lawyer*
Rossouw, Jacques E. *preventive medicine physician, researcher*
Rowell, Edward Morgan *retired foreign service officer, educator*
Ruffin, John *federal agency administrator, researcher*
Ruiz-Bravo, Norka *federal agency administrator*
Saffiotti, Umberto *pathologist*
Salmoiraghi, Gian Carlo *physiologist, educator*
Samelson, Lawrence Elliot *medical researcher*
Sarnoff, Lili-Charlotte (Lolo Sarnoff) *artist*
Saul, B. Francis, II, *bank executive, director*
Saunders, Charles Baskerville, Jr. *retired association executive*
Saville, Thorndike, Jr. *coastal engineer*
Schaeffer, Charles Perry *writer, editor*
Schifter, Richard *lawyer*
Schlom, Jeffrey Bert *research scientist*
Schmidt, Raymond Paul *military officer, historian, government agency administrator*
Schoettler, James Anthony, Jr. *lawyer*
Schrump, David Stuart *medical association administrator, researcher*
Schwarz, Louis Jay *financial advisor*
Shin, Eui-Cheol *medical researcher*
Shulman, Lawrence Edward *biomedical researcher, rheumatologist*
Sieving, Paul A. *federal agency administrator, ophthalmologist, educator*
Silver, David *lawyer*
Singer, Dinah S. *federal agency administrator, immunologist, researcher*
Smoller, Bruce Melvyn *psychiatrist*
Sobel, Mark Esar *pathologist, researcher*
Sokoloff, Louis *retired physiologist, neuroscientist*
Solomon, Henry *university dean*
Solomon, Robert *economist*
Spector, Eleanor Ruth *manufacturing executive*
Springfield, Sanya A. *federal agency administrator*
Sprott, Richard Lawrence *foundation administrator, researcher*
Stadtman, Earl Reece *biochemist, researcher*
Stanfield, Brent B. *federal agency administrator*
Starkey, Russell Bruce, Jr. *energy executive*
Stetler-Stevenson, William George *pathologist*
Stoddard, Philip Hendrick *foreign affairs analyst, consultant, writer*
Stone, Jeremy Judah *professional society administrator*
Stover, Ellen L. *health scientist, psychologist*
Strickler, Scott Michael *lawyer*
Sturtz, Donald Lee *surgeon, educator, military officer*
Tabak, Lawrence A. *federal agency administrator, dentist*
Tanner, Bruce L. *aerospace transportation executive*
Taylor, Lindsay David, Jr. *healthcare executive, bank executive, federal agency administrator*
Taylor, William Jesse, Jr. *international security studies educator, research institute senior advisor*
Teimourian, Bahman *plastic surgeon*
Tilley, Carolyn Bittner *information scientist*
Tourino, Ralph Gene *aerospace transportation executive*
Tracy, Thomas Miles *international health organization official*
Trus, Benes Louis *structural chemist*
Ursano, Robert Joseph *psychiatrist*
Vaitukaitis, Judith Louise *medical researcher*
van der Linden, Frank Morris *historian*
Vaughan, Martha *biochemist, educator*
Vest, George Southall *retired diplomat*
Volkow, Nora Dolores *medical researcher, director*
Wagner, Cynthia Gail *editor, writer*
Waldmann, Thomas Alexander *medical researcher, physician*
Walter, W. Edward *hotel and corporate financial executive*
Webber, Derek *aerospace executive, space tourism entrepreneur*
Webster, Henry de Forest *neuroscientist*
Webster, Thomas Glenn *psychiatrist, educator*
Weinberger, Alan David *lawyer, business executive*
Weinberger, Daniel R. *psychiatrist, neurologist*
Weiss, George Herbert *mathematician, consultant*
Welch, John Kirtland *nuclear energy industry executive*
Wellems, Thomas E. *federal agency administrator*
Western, Karl August *physician, epidemiologist*
White, Jeffrey D. *federal agency administrator*
Wickner, Sue Hengren *biochemist*
Wiese, Wolfgang Lothar *physicist, researcher*
Willenbring, Mark Leon *psychiatrist*
Wise, Allen F. *health care company executive*
Witkop, Bernhard *chemist*
Wolf, Dale B. *health care company executive*
Wolpert-DeFilippes, Mary K. *science administrator*
Woodall, Jerry M. *research scientist, educator*
Wu, Carl *medical researcher*
Yamada, Kenneth Manao *cell biologist*
Yang, Key Paik *librarian, archivist*
Zerhouni, Elias Adam *federal agency administrator*
Zheng, Gang *mathematician, statistician, researcher*
Zielinski, Thomas C. *lawyer, insurance company executive*
Zipp, Joel Frederick *lawyer*
Zoon, Kathryn Christine *biochemist*
Zwanzig, Robert Walter *chemist, physical science educator*

Betterton

Kohl, Benjamin Gibbs *historian, educator*

Bowie

Baker, Marshina *physical education educator*
Buell, Duncan Alan *computer scientist*
Bushnell, David Sherman *social psychologist, consultant*
Cook, Hardy Merrill III *literature and language professor*
Gourdine-Tyson, Natachia *investment company executive, writer*
Hillsman, Joan Rucker *music educator*
Kardiasmenos, Katrina Suzanne *psychology professor*
LeCounte, Lola Houston *literature and language professor, educational consultant*
Littlefield, Roy Everett III *association executive, law educator*
Lowe, Calvin W. *university president*
McCarthy, Kevin John *lawyer*
Speller-Brown, Barbara Jean *pediatric nurse practitioner*
Sterling, Richard Leroy *English and foreign language educator*
Stone, Edward Harris, II, *landscape architect*
Wardrip, Elizabeth Jane *retired librarian*
Yager, Joseph Arthur, Jr. *economist, consultant*

Boyds

Bu, Rulei *artist, educator*

Bozman

Wyatt, Wilson Watkins, Jr. *communications executive, writer*

Brandywine

Jaffe, Morris Edward *insurance company executive, financial analyst*
Johnson, Madge Richards *business owner, fundraiser, consultant, recruiter*

Brentwood

Kaskey, Raymond John *sculptor*

Burtonsville

Hudson, McKinley *retired military officer, retired zoological park administrator*
Penska, Keith Henry *psychiatrist*

Cabin John

Shropshire, Walter, Jr. *biophysicist, pastor*
Townsend, John William, Jr. *physicist, retired federal agency administrator*

California

Galligan, James *retired guidance counselor*
Powell, Melchior Daniel *educational administrator, lawyer*

Cambridge

Digges, Edward S(imms) *business management consultant*
Spahr, Elizabeth *environmental research administrator*

Capitol Heights

Gerstl, Cynthia Koren *foreign and English language educator*
Johnson, Louise Street *medical/surgical nurse*

Catonsville

Hubbard, Herbert Hendrix *lawyer*
Oden, Gloria *language educator, poet*
Toomey, Sister Stephana *liturgical consultant, designer*
Wynn, John Charles *clergyman, retired theology studies educator*
Zumbrun, Alvin John Thomas *law and criminology educator*

Centreville

Griffith, Alan Richard *retired banker*

Chester

Dalrymple, Ronald Gerald *psychologist*

Chestertown

Amos, James Lysle *photographer*
Clarke, Garry Evans *composer, educator, academic administrator, musician*
Docksteader, Karen Kemp *marketing professional*
Mowell, George Mitchell *lawyer*
Rather, Lucia Porcher Johnson *library administrator*
Wendel, Richard Frederick *economist, educator, consultant*

Cheverly

Miller, Mark Karl *journalist, editor*

Chevy Chase

Adler, James Barron *publishing executive*
Albright, Raymond Jacob *federal official*
Alexander, Arthur Jacob *economist*
Alpert, Seymour *anesthesiologist, educator*
Auerbach, Seymour *architect*
Bacon, Donald Conrad *writer, editor*
Baruch, Jordan Jay *retired management consultant*
Basa, Enikö Molnár *retired librarian*
Bisconti, Ann Stouffer *public opinion research company executive*
Bissinger, Frederick Lewis *retired manufacturing executive*
Broide, Mace Irwin *public information officer*
Bruder, George Frederick *retired lawyer*
Bruno, Harold Robinson, Jr. *retired journalist, writer*
Cech, Thomas Robert *medical association administrator, chemistry professor*
Cheng, David Keun *engineering educator*
Choppin, Purnell Whittington *science administrator*
Cline, Ruth Eleanor Harwood *translator*
Coerper, Milo George *lawyer, priest*
Cowen, Eugene Sherman *broadcast executive*
Croft, Joseph David *medical educator*
Curzan, Myron Paul *lawyer*
Dufresne, Craig Roger *plastic surgeon, educator*
Eng, Gloria D. *retired pediatrician*
Ewing, Frank Marion *paper company executive, real estate developer*
Feldman, Bruce Allen *otolaryngologist*
Fern, Alan Maxwell *art historian, retired museum director*
Gildenhorn, Joseph Bernard *lawyer, real estate company executive, retired diplomat*
Glaser, Vera Romans *journalist*
Goldsmith, Stephen *investment company executive, former mayor*
Hani, Antoine George *psychiatrist, psychoanalyst*
Harlan, William Robert, Jr. *internist, educator, researcher*
Hersh, Stephen Peter *psychiatrist, psycho-oncologist, chronic pain expert, educator*
Hickman, R(obert) Harrison *political pollster, strategist*
Hunt, Frederick Talley Drum, Jr. *association executive*
Kandel, Eric Richard *neuroscience educator*
Kay, Stephen R. *surgeon*
Khairalla, Eric William *plastic surgeon*
Kilborn, Peter Thurston *journalist*
Kranking, Margaret Graham *artist, retired educator*
Kriegsman, Alan M. *arts critic*
Krupnick, Janice Lee *psychologist, psychotherapist, educator*
Kurochkina, Natalya Alexandrovna *biophysicist*
Lebow, Irwin Leon *communications engineering consultant*
Lennan, Anne Celeste *trade association and educational software company executive*
Linowes, David Francis *finance educator, corporate financial executive*
Lynn, D. Joanne *physician, researcher*
Meyerson, Christopher Cortlandt *lawyer*
Michaelis, Michael *management and technical consultant*
Mielke, James Edward *geochemist*
Murphy, John Condron, Jr. *lawyer*
Nichols, Henry Eliot *lawyer, realtor, banker, columnist*
Noonan, Patrick Francis *conservation executive*
Norwood, Bernard *economist*
Norwood, Janet Lippe *economist*
Opper, Barbara Negri *financial economist*
Pedersen, Wesley Niels M. *public relations and public affairs counselor*
Pirie, Robert Burns, Jr. *defense analyst*
Pogue, John Marshall *physician*
Pollard, Michael Ross *lawyer, health science association administrator*
Posnick, Jeffrey Craig *plastic surgeon*
Rayburn, Wendell Gilbert, Sr. *educational consultant*
Reilly, Edward Francis, Jr. *federal agency administrator, former state senator*
Resnik, Harvey Lewis Paul *psychiatrist*
Rockwell, Theodore *nuclear engineer*
Rose, John Charles *internist, educator*
Shannon, Stephen Curtis *medical association administrator, occupational health physician*
Shipler, David Karr *journalist, writer*
Shogan, Robert *news correspondent*
Sinclair, Rolf Malcolm *retired physicist*
Smith, Hedrick Laurence *journalist, television producer*
Sperling, Godfrey, Jr. *retired journalist*
Toth, Robert Charles *retired journalist*
Towsner, Cynthia Merle *academic administrator, educator*
Toy, Charles David *lawyer, business manager*
Weiss, Harlan Lee *lawyer*
Wiesel, Sam W. *medical educator, academic administrator*
Williams, Charles Laval, Jr. *retired preventive medicine physician*

Clarksville

Hung, Mei-Jong Chow *social worker*

Clinton

Sander, Clarence Ellis, Jr. *retired protective services official*
Whittington, Ralph Edward *retired curator, librarian*

Cockeysville

Barnes, Peter *federal official*

Cockeysville Hunt Valley

Elkin, Lois Shanman *business systems company executive*
Whitehurst, William Wilfred, Jr. *management consultant*

College Park

Adams, Jeffrey *mathematics professor*
Anderson, John David, Jr. *aerospace engineer*
Antman, Stuart Sheldon *mathematician, educator*
Ayyub, Bilal M. *engineer, company executive, educator, researcher*
Baecher, Gregory B. *civil and environmental engineer, educator*
Barbe, David Franklin *electrical engineer, educator*
Beasley, Maurine Hoffman *journalism educator, historian*
Bedos-Rezak, Brigitte Miriam *historian, educator*
Bellardo, Lewis Joseph, Jr. *archivist*
Benedick, Richard Elliot *diplomat*
Brazile, Donna *advocate*
Brush, Stephen George *historian, educator*
Chopra, Nikhil *systems engineer, researcher*
Coffey, Timothy *physicist*
DeFries, Ruth S. *earth system scientist, researcher*
Deshmukh, Om Dadaji *electrical engineer, researcher*
DeSilva, Alan W. *physics professor, researcher*
Destler, I. M(ac) *political scientist, foreign policy writer*
Diener, Theodor Otto *plant pathologist, researcher*
Dieter, George Elwood, Jr. *academic administrator*
Dorn, Norman Philip *management consulting firm executive*
Dragt, Alexander James *physicist, educator*
Dusold, Laurence Richard *chemist, computer specialist*
Dylla, H. Frederick *science administrator, physicist*
Epstein, Norman B. *psychologist, marriage and family therapist, educator*
Fanning, Delvin Seymour *soil science educator*
Farquhar, James *geochemist, researcher*
Farvardin, Nariman *engineering educator*
Fawcett, Sharon Kay Atchison *archivist*
Fenselau, Catherine Clarke *chemistry professor*
Fisher, Michael Ellis *physicist, educator, chemist*
Frank, Howard *dean, information technology executive*
Frese, Brenda S. *women's college basketball coach*
Fu, Michael C. *management science educator*
Galloway, Gerald Edward, Jr. *civil engineer, educator*
Gansler, Jacques Singleton *public policy educator*
Gates, Sylvester James, Jr. *physics professor, researcher*
Gaylin, Ned L. *psychologist, educator*
Gomery, Douglas *communications educator, writer*
Granatstein, Victor Lawrence *electrical engineer, educator*
Greenberg, Oscar Wallace *physicist, researcher*
Griem, Hans Rudolf *physicist, researcher*
Gupta, Ashwani Kumar *mechanical engineering educator*
Hall, William Sterling *psychology educator*
Hallett, Judith Peller *classical studies educator*
Helz, George Rudolph *chemistry professor*
Hill, Clara Edith *psychologist, educator*
Imig, David Gregg *education educator, retired educational association administrator*
Ingold, Catherine White *academic administrator*
Izaurralde, Roberto César *science educator, researcher*
Jeffery, William Richard *developmental biology educator, researcher*
Johnson, Haynes Bonner *journalist, writer, commentator*
Johnson, Raymond Lewis *mathematician*
Just, Richard Eugene *economist, consultant, agriculturist, educator*
Kang, Kyeongpyo *transportation engineer, researcher*
Katz, Ronald Alan *dermatologist*
Khoury, Bernard V. *educational administrator*
Korhonen, Fawna J. *geologist, researcher*
Kundu, Mukul Ranjan *physics and astronomy professor*
Kurtz, Michael Joseph *archivist, educator*
Langenberg, Donald Newton *retired academic administrator, physicist*
Lathan, Corinna Elisabeth *aerospace engineer*
Lent, Robert William *psychologist*
Levine, William Silver *electrical engineer, educator*
Lowell, Howard Parsons *archivist, federal agency administrator*
Lowry, Charles Bryan *librarian, dean*
Lubkin, Gloria Becker *physicist*
Lucas, Henry Cameron, Jr. *information scientist, educator, writer*
Marcus, Steven Irl *electrical engineering educator*
Meagher, Joseph Patrick *law educator, consultant*
Miller, Raymond Edward *computer science educator*
Miller, Raymond Jarvis *agronomy educator*
Minker, Jack *computer scientist, educator*
Misner, Charles William *physics professor*
Montgomery, William Layton *music educator, educator, musician*
Morphy, Martha A. *archivist*
Mosley, Raymond A. *archivist*
Mote, Clayton Daniel, Jr. *academic administrator, mechanical engineer, educator*
Murdoch, Amelia Clara *educational association administrator*
Neal, Edward Garrison *lawyer*
Nerlove, Marc Leon *economics professor*
Newcomb, Robert Wayne *electrical engineer educator*
Nusinovich, Gregory Semeon *physicist, researcher*
O'Connor, John Dennis *biology professor*
Olson, Charles Eric *economist*
Olson, Keith Waldemar *historian, educator*
Oster, Rose Marie Gunhild *foreign language professional, educator*
Panichas, George Andrew *language educator, critic, editor*
Pasch, Alan *philosopher, educator*
Pease, John Alan *sociology educator*
Petraitis, Karel Colette *lawyer*
Preece, Jennifer J. *dean, information scientist, educator*
Presser, Harriet Betty *social studies educator*
Presser, Stanley *social sciences educator, researcher*
Quester, George Herman *political science professor*

Quick, Edward Raymond *museum director, educator, curator*
Rabin, Herbert *physicist, educator, dean*
Redish, Edward Frederick *physicist, researcher*
Richardson, W. C. *painter*
Rosenberg, Norman Jack *agricultural meteorologist, educator*
Sacks, Charles Bernard *psychiatrist, educator*
Schelling, Thomas Crombie *economist*
Shen, Qing *urban planning educator, researcher, associate dean*
Sigall, Harold Fred *psychology professor*
Silverman, Joseph *chemistry professor*
Sims, Henry P., Jr. *management educator*
Smidts, Carol *mechanical engineer, educator*
Sorenson, Georgia Lynn Jones *political science professor*
Sreenivasan, Katepalli Raju *mechanical engineer, educator*
Stewart, Gilbert Wright *computer science educator*
Stover, Carl Frederick *foundation executive*
Taylor, Leonard Stuart *engineering educator, consultant*
Tilley, David Rogers *engineering educator, researcher*
Toll, John Sampson *retired academic administrator, physics professor*
Walters, William Ben *chemistry professor*
Wasserman, Paul *library and information science professor*
Weart, Spencer Richard *historian*
Weinstein, Allen *archivist*
White, Marilyn Domas *information science educator*
Whittemore, Edward Reed, II, *poet, retired educator*
Williams, Ellen D. *physics professor*
Yoo, Jin-Hyeong *research scientist*
Zen, E-an *research geologist, educator*
Zhang, Da-lin D. *meteorologist, educator*

Columbia
Bennett, P. Tyson *lawyer*
Campbell-Alston, Deirdre Adina *anatomist, physiologist, researcher*
Carter, Karen Zepp *music educator, elementary school educator*
Closson, Walter Franklin *child support prosecutor*
Davis, Benjamin George *theologian, educator*
Deering, Anthony Wayne Marion *real estate developer*
Drexler, Milton *medical association administrator*
Festa, (Al)Fred E. *chemicals executive*
Fishbune, Robert *food products executive*
Fisher, Dale John *retired chemist, medical investigator*
Gillespie, Charles Kevin *priest, educator*
Gregorie, Corazon Arzalem *operations research specialist*
Greyson D'Otazzo, Meaghan Regina *literary critic*
Gruhl, Andrea Morris *librarian*
Hyman, Lawrence Robert *psychiatrist*
Jones-Wilson, Faustine Clarisse *retired education educator*
Kearns, Ronald Edwin *music educator, performance artist*
Khare, Mohan *chemist, researcher*
Klein, Sami Weiner *librarian*
Kurlander, Neale *accountant, law educator*
Marshall, Linda Murphy *linguist, government official*
Maseritz, Guy B. *lawyer*
McCuan, William Patrick *real estate company executive*
McGregor, Douglas A. *real estate company executive*
Nie, Guojun *research scientist*
Norris, Paul J. *chemicals executive*
Pacifico, Joseph Carl *counselor*
Piou-Brewer, Magalie *psychotherapist, educator, small business owner*
Purcell, James Nelson, Jr. *cultural organization administrator*
Rogers, Thomas Francis *foundation administrator*
Rovelstad, Gordon H. *dentist, researcher*
Saini, Simarjeet Singh *electronics engineer*
Scates, Alice Yeomans *retired federal official*
Scornaienchi, Joan Webb *educational association administrator, consultant*
Shaw, Donald Hardy *lawyer*
Strahlman, Richard Scott *pediatrician*
Straja, Sorin Radu *chemical engineer, mathematician, computer programmer*
Terry, Robert Eli *physicist, aerospace scientist, educator*
Tietz, Dietmar Juergen *website engineer, scientist*
Valencia Lavao, Jesus M. *electrical engineer, consultant*
Weems, Helen Rachel *musician, educator*
Whiting, Albert Nathaniel *former university chancellor*
Zeng, Dongsong *computer scientist*

Crofton
Laurenson, Robert Mark *mechanical engineer*
Mahaffey, Redge Allan *movie producer, director, writer, actor, scientist, business executive*
Ross, E(dwin) Clarke *association executive, educator*
Vranish, John Michael *electrical engineer, researcher*
Williams, J. Linda *librarian*

Crownsville
Campbell, Walter Everett *adult education educator*
Irish, Leon Eugene *lawyer, non-profit organization executive, educator*

Cumberland
Heckert, Paul Charles *sociologist, educator*
Riggs, Robert Meldrum *French educator*

Damascus
Styer, Joanne Louise *retired dietician*

Darnestown
Cohen, Sanford Irwin *physician, educator*
Gottlieb, Julius Judah *retired podiatrist*

Davidsonville
Montague, Brian John *consulting company executive*

Dayton
Ferrera, Arthur Rocco *food distribution company executive*
Fischell, Robert Ellentuch *physicist*

Derwood
Crawford, Stephen *national association executive*
Mylonakis, Stamatios Gregory *research scientist, lawyer*
Stadtman, Thressa Campbell *biochemist*

Dickerson
Duncan, Jack G. *lawyer*

District Heights
Parham, Sheila D. *elementary school educator*

Easton
Behm, Mark Edward *academic administrator, consultant*
Brodt, Burton Pardee *retired chemical engineer, writer, researcher*
Chambers, Will Earl *retired freelance writer*
Colton, Elizabeth Wishart *government agency administrator*
Ikenberry, Henry Cephas, Jr. *lawyer*
Kerr, James Wilson *engineer*
Maffitt, James Strawbridge *lawyer*
Peterson, James Kenneth *manufacturing executive*
Rever, George Wright *psychiatrist, health facility administrator*
Shepard, William Seth *diplomat, writer*

Edgewater
Cotter, George R. *retired information scientist*
Dierking, Lynn D. *educational administrator*
Falk, John H. *educational administrator*
McCamy, Calvin Samuel *retired optics scientist*

Elkridge
Morgan, Gary Lorin *systems engineer, director, researcher*

Elkton
Jasinski-Caldwell, Mary L. *insurance company executive*
Mayer, Margaret Ellen *medical coding specialist*
Xu, Ping *chemist*

Ellicott City
Bruley, Duane Frederick *academic administrator, consultant, engineer*
Cooke, Catherine E. *pharmacist, consultant*
Estin-Klein, Libbyada *advertising executive, writer*
Lilly, John Richard, II, *lawyer*
Loerke, William Carl *art historian, educator*
McNaughton, Kenneth John *former publisher*
Pairo, Preston Abercrombie, Jr. *lawyer*
Webster, Sharon B. *economist*

Emmitsburg
Cade, Gregory Brian *federal agency administrator, fireman*

Essex
Bunn, Wm. Jeffrey *secondary school educator, director*

Fort George G Meade
Alexander, Keith B. *federal agency administrator, career military officer*
Black, William B., Jr. *federal agency administrator*
Deitz, Robert L. *lawyer*
Schmitt, Robert Lee *computer scientist*

Fort Meade
Potenza, Vito *lawyer*

Fort Washington
Alexander, Gary R. *lawyer, state legislator, lobbyist*
Cameron, Rita Giovannetti *writer, publishing executive*
Caveny, Leonard Hugh *mechanical engineer, aerospace scientist, consultant*
Satterthwaite, George, II, *security firm executive*
Smoot, Burgess Howard *federal official*
Vaughan, James Joseph Michael *lawyer*

Frederick
Albright, Joseph William *civilian military employee*
Anderson, Arthur Osmund *pathologist, immunologist, bioethicist, military officer*
Baker, Joanne Evelyn *retired government agency administrator*
Borison, Scott Craig *lawyer*
Burkhard, Fred (Bud) *academic administrator*
Byron, Beverly Butcher *retired congresswoman*
Carlson, David Emil *physicist, researcher*
Copeland, Neal G. *medical researcher*
Garver, Robert Vernon *retired research physicist*
Henderson, Madeline Mary (Berry) *chemist, researcher, consultant*
Hogan, Ilona Modly *lawyer*
Hughes, Stephen H. *virologist, researcher*
Iverson, Warren Philip *retired microbiologist, research scientist, consultant*
Keefer, Larry Kay *medical researcher*
Knisely, Ralph Franklin *retired microbiologist*
Lin, George *research and development company executive, biomedical researcher*
Lucas, Joe N. *biophysicist, researcher*
Malin, Howard Gerald *podiatrist*
Marquez, Victor E. *medical researcher*
McDowell, Eugene Charles *systems analyst, bioethicist*
Merrill, Daniel A. *program manager*
Pastoor, Robertus Antonius *academic administrator*
Randall, Frances *technical writer*
Reynolds, Craig W. *research scientist*
Sharifi, Nima *oncologist, researcher*
Whelihan, Alan Stuart *real estate developer, automotive executive*
Wiltrout, Robert H. *federal agency administrator*

Friendship
Clagett, Diana Wharton Sinkler *museum docent*
Levy, David Lawrence *retired lawyer, legal association administrator*

Frostburg
Bauman, Jon Ward *retired music educator*
Gibralter, Jonathan C. *academic administrator*
Horner, Ronald George *musician, educator*
Root, Edward Lakin *education educator, academic administrator*

Fulton
Hamlin, George L. *writer*

Gaithersburg
Aiuto, Russell *science education consultant*
Boettinger, William J. *metallurgist*
Bremenstuhl, David P. *elementary school educator*
Broderick, John Caruthers *retired librarian*
Brodine, Charles Edward *physician*
Burnett, John Huszagh *physicist*
Byers, Christopher Gordon *veterinarian*
Caplin, Jerrold Leon *health physicist*
Carasso, Alfred Sam *mathematician*
Carey, John Edward *communications executive*
Caswell, Randall Smith *physicist*
Celotta, Robert James *physicist*
Clark, Charles Winthrop *physicist*
Cookson, Alan Howard *electrical engineer, researcher*
Dermody, William Christian *biomedical consultant*
DeRose, Paul Christian *chemist, researcher*
Dowd, Carolyn Lay *social worker*
Ferrell, Charles Madison *nuclear engineer, physicist*
Fratantoni, Joseph Charles *medical researcher, biotechnologist, hematologist*
French, Judson Cull *federal official*
Glass, Lawrence *research scientist*
Gloyd, Rita A. *retired social worker*
Hall, Arthur Raymond, Jr. *retired minister*
Harman, George Gibson *physicist, consultant*
Hertz, Harry Steven *government official*
Jacox, Marilyn Esther *chemist*
Jahanmir, Said *materials scientist, mechanical engineer*
Jeffrey, William Alan *federal agency administrator, physicist*
Jestrab, Frank F. *retired lawyer*
Jiang, Zhi-Gang *neuroscientist*
Johnson, George H. *finance company executive*
Landel, Michel *food service and management company executive*
Lenfant, Claude Jean-Marie *physician, director*
Levine, Robert Sidney *chemical engineer, consultant*
Lynn, Jeffrey Whidden *research physicist, educator*
McCann, Joseph Leo *lawyer, former government official*
McDowell, Donna Schultz *lawyer, educator*
Naylor, Phyllis Reynolds *writer*
Phillips, William Daniel *physicist*
Pierce, Daniel Thornton *physicist*
Quraishi, Mohammed Sayeed *retired health facility administrator, research scientist*
Reader, Joseph *physicist*
Rosenblatt, Joan Raup *mathematical statistician*
Rupert, Hoover (Lynn Hoover Rupert) *minister, writer*
Ruth, James Perry *financial planner*
Schwartzberg, Allan Zelig *psychiatrist, educator*
Semerjian, Hratch Gregory *federal agency administrator*
Sengers, Johanna M. H. Levelt *physicist*
Tarrio, Charles *physicist*
Tirumala, Vijaya Raghavan *materials scientist*
Wang, Francis Wei-Yu *biomedical materials scientist, researcher*
Weber, Alfons *physicist*
Werner, Samuel Alfred *physicist, educator*
Wiederhorn, Sheldon Martin *materials scientist engineer*
Wright, Richard Newport III *retired engineering executive, engineering educator*

Galena
Hunsperger, Elizabeth Jane *art and design consultant, educator*

Galesville
Whaley, Garwood *music company executive*

Garrett Park
Baldwin, Calvin Benham, Jr. *retired science administrator*
Kornberg, Warren Stanley *journalist*

Germantown
Byrd, Wyatt *microbiologist, researcher*
Carper, Fern Gayle *small business owner, writer*
Fread, Joan P. *lawyer*
Harris, William Norman *music educator*
Iqbal, Zafar *neuroscientist, biochemist, educator*
Kaul, Pradman *communications executive*
Khan, Tapan Kumar *adult education educator*
Kilani, Ahmed Fathy *lab administrator, director*
Lewis, Robert John Cornelius Koons *retired library director*
Naake, Joan Murray *English professor*
Norcross, Marvin Augustus *veterinarian, researcher, retired federal official*
Patrinos, Aristides *environmental scientist, federal agency administrator*
Ritter, Nadine M. *research scientist*
Sorensen, John Noble *retired mechanical and nuclear engineer*
Warren, Frank *blogger, small business owner*

Gibson Island
Forster, William Hull *management consultant*

Glen Arm
Jackson, Theodore Marshall *retired oil industry executive*

Glen Burnie
Jamaris, Joseph Kastytis *neurosurgeon*
Mc Cabe, Gerard Benedict *retired library administrator*
Sanchez-Barnett, Susan Lynn *historian, educator*
Watts, Virginia Agnes *retired special education educator*

Glenwood
Hansen, Christopher Agnew *lawyer*

Glyndon
Renbaum, Barry Jeffrey *lawyer*

Great Mills
Bufis, Matthew Peter *music educator*

Greenbelt
Acuña, Mario H. *astrophysicist*
Amato, Deborah Douglass *aerospace engineer*
Bernstein, Kenneth J. *secondary school educator*
Bonsib, Robert Charles *lawyer*
Chasanow, Howard Stuart *retired judge, mediator*
Comiso, Josefino Cacas *research scientist*
Danchi, William C. *astrophysicist*
DelloRusso, Neil *astrochemist*
Ericsson, Aprille Joy *aerospace engineer*
Fax, Charles Samuel *lawyer*
Fontaine, Kathleen Sturey *policy analyst*
Gehrels, Neil (Cornelius A. Gehrels) *astrophysicist*
Greenwald, Andrew Eric *lawyer*
Jenkins, Norman *accountant*
Kniffen, Donald Avery *astrophysicist, educator, researcher*
Kuchner, Marc Jason *astrophysicist*
Mather, John Cromwell *astrophysicist*
Matthews, Darryl R., Sr. *not-for-profit fundraiser*
Messitte, Peter Jo *judge*
Miller, Alwin Vermar *educational association administrator, consultant*
Moore, Virginia Bradley *librarian*
Mumma, Michael Jon *research scientist*
Obamogie, Mercy A. *physician*
Parkinson, Claire L. *climatologist*
Simpson, Joanne Malkus *meteorologist*
Titus, Roger Warren *judge*
U-yen, Kongpop *electrical engineer*
Wollack, Edward J. *astrophysicist*
Wood, H(oward) John III *astrophysicist, astronomer*

Gwynn Oak
Hughes, Catherine L. (Cathy Hughes) *radio personality, broadcast executive*

Hagerstown
Baykan, Mary Catherine *library administrator*
Berkson, Jacob Benjamin *lawyer, writer*
Dunlap, John B. *lawyer, educator*
Harrison, Lois Smith *hospital executive, educator*
Higgins, M. Eileen *management consultant, educator*
Ksienski, Aharon Arthur *retired electrical engineer*
Shaper, Christopher Thorne *sales executive*
Stonestreet, Jeannine Lee *edcuator*
Warner, Charles David III *academic administrator*

Hampstead
Dotterweich, Patrick Timothy *social studies educator*

Hanover
Bisciotti, Stephen J. *staffing company executive, professional sports team executive*

Harwood
Dudley, William Sheldon *historian*

Havre De Grace
Wetter, Virginia Forwood Pate *broadcast executive*

Hollywood
Newhouse, Alan Russell *retired federal official*

Hunt Valley
Guthrie, Phillip Patrick *division production manager*
Igusa, Jun-Ichi *mathematician, educator*
Kinstlinger, Jack *engineering executive, consultant*

Hyattsville
Asongu, Januarius Jingwa *business executive*
Golden, Marita *literature educator, writer, foundation administrator*
Gonzalez, Joe Fred, Jr. *mathematical statistician, educator*
Goodwin, Robert Cronin *lawyer*
Lovick, Norman *accountant*
O'Connor, Kevin Thomas *religious organization administrator*
Rodgers, Mary Columbro *literature educator, writer, academic administrator*
Shestack, Alan *museum administrator*
Supanick, Beverly Jane *language educator*

Wuerl, Donald William *archbishop*

Jefferson
Beall, James Robert *toxicologist, consultant*

Jessup
Spievack, Alan R. *research and development company executive, surgeon*

Joppa
Bates, Martha Copenhaver *elementary school educator*

Kensington
Chiazze, Leonard, Jr. *biostatistician, epidemiologist, educator*
Dauster, William Gary *lawyer, economist*
Ellwanger, Albert Thompson III *secondary school educator*
Fasusi, Jimmy Adebayo *small business owner*
Forrest, Sidney *clarinetist, music educator*
Freeman, Ernest Robert *retired engineering executive*
Hum, Vance York *technology consulting executive*
Mathias, Joseph Marshall *lawyer, judge*
Mirkin, Gabe Baron *physician, medical educator, writer, radio personality*
Murray, Thomas James *financial planner, publisher*
Oweiss, Ibrahim Mohamed *economist, educator*
Rosenthal, Alan Sayre *government official, lawyer*
Suraci, Charles Xavier, Jr. *retired federal agency administrator, air transportation executive, consultant*
Szára, Stephen István *pharmacologist, consultant*

Kingsville
Akehurst, Wallace Edward *marketing professional, consultant*
Standiford, Ronald Dawson *minister, educator*

La Plata
Herdman-Fisher, Carolyn A. *music educator*
Stephanic, Barbara Jean *art historian, writer, curator, researcher*
Zinn, Michael Wallace *aerospace engineer*

Landover
Grasselli, Margaret Morgan *curator*
Luchs, Alison *curator, art historian*
Penny, Nicholas Beaver *museum curator*
Powell, Earl Alexander III *art museum director*
Rogers, Joseph Shepperd *art educator*

Lanham
Cheng, Jian-Yu *mechanical engineer, researcher, application developer*
Degnan, John James III *physicist*
Gavin, James Raphael III *biochemist*
Lyons, James Edward (Jed) *publishing executive*
McClain, George Nelson *economist, lawyer*

Lanham Seabrook
Liggins, Alfred C. III *broadcasting company executive*

Largo
Haines, Corrie Gerald *history professor*

Laurel
Babin, Steven Michael *atmospheric scientist, researcher*
Bartley, Shawn *lawyer*
Buffkins, LeRachel Harombe *small business owner*
Cecil, J. Robb *lawyer*
Chrismer, Ronald Michael *federal agency administrator*
Damarla, Thyagaraju *electronics engineer*
Dorsey, John Wesley, Jr. *retired academic administrator, economist*
Eaton, Alvin Ralph, Jr. *aeronautical engineer, applied physics executive, systems engineer*
Harbottle, Heather C. *microbiologist, researcher*
Heaton, Harold Irving, Jr. *research scientist, consultant*
Hoffman, David John *physiologist, ecotoxicologist*
Knecht, Glen Charles *minister*
Krimigis, Stamatios Mike *physicist, researcher, educator, engineering executive, consultant*
Kroshl, William Mark *operations research specialist*
Land, H. Bruce III *electronics engineer, aerospace engineer*
Land, Henry Bruce III *electronics engineer, researcher*
Levitt, Gerald Steven *engineering executive*
Lui, Anthony Tat Yin *physicist*
Maurer, Richard Hornsby *physicist*
McConnaughey, James Walter *economist*
McNutt, Ralph Leroy, Jr. *astrophysicist*
Pikas, Christina Kirk *librarian, researcher*
Rorie, Conrad Jonathan *research scientist, retired military officer*
Stumpff, Robert Thomas *retired academic administrator*
Teeters, Joseph Lee *mathematician, consultant*
Weerackody, Vijitha *electrical engineer, researcher*
Williams, Barbara Ivory *educational researcher*

Lexington Park
Donely, George Anthony Thomas III *retired economist*

Linthicum
Ehrlich, Bob (Robert Leroy Ehrlich Jr.) *lawyer, former governor, congressman*

Linthicum Heights
Skillman, William Alfred *consulting engineering executive*
Stein, David Eric *physicist, defense analyst, futurist, retired military officer*

Lonaconing
Puddy, William (Bill) Curtiss *retired military officer, not-for-profit developer*

Lothian
Flowers, Murhl Lynn *retired pharmacist*
Messenger, Barbara Beall *artist*

Lusby
Eshelman, Ralph Ellsworth *historian, consultant, paleontologist*
Ladd, Culver Sprogle *secondary school educator*
Sprague, Edward Auchincloss *retired professional society administrator, economist*

Lutherville
Aitken, Christopher Charles *investment consultant*
Elma, Bayani Borja *physician*
Freeland, Charles *lawyer, accountant*
Goodman, Valerie Dawson *psychiatric social worker*
Parekh, Dhirajlal Gokaldas *electrical engineer*
Smith, Michelle Sun *psychologist*

Lutherville Timonium
Auwaerter, Paul Gisbert *physician, educator*
Brown, Ellyn L. *lawyer, consultant*
Brustein, Abram Isaac *sales executive, insurance company executive*
Cappiello, Frank Anthony, Jr. *investment advisor*
Cedrone, Louis Robert, Jr. *retired critic*
Meyer, Jon Keith *psychiatrist, psychoanalyst, educator*
Muuss, Rolf Eduard *retired psychologist, author*
Park, Lee Crandall *psychiatrist*
Sternberger, Ludwig Amadeus *neurologist, educator*

Madison
Hoffman, Alicia Coro *retired federal executive*
Hoffman, Kenneth Myron *mathematician, educator*

Marion Station
Handy, Mary Thomas *retired elementary school educator*

Marriottsville
Strange, Donald Ernest *healthcare company executive*

Marydel
LaBarge, Christopher W. *priest*

Millersville
Culver, Catherine Marie *secondary school educator*

Mitchellville
Ball, Robert M. (Robert Myers Ball) *retired social security, welfare and health policy specialist, writer, lecturer*
Blasier, Cole *political scientist*
Brubaker, Lauren Edgar *minister*
Embree, Ainslie Thomas *history professor*
Gordon, Lincoln *political economist*
Griffen, Clyde Chesterman *retired historian*
Hammer, Jane Amelia Ross *advocate*
Heald, Morrell *humanities educator*
Kendall, Katherine Anne *social worker*
Marsh, Caryl Amsterdam *retired curator, psychologist*

Monkton
Parker, Robert M., Jr., (Bob Parker) *wine critic, writer*

Montgomery Village
Durning, Steven James *internist, educator*
Kushner, Lawrence Maurice *physical chemist, consultant*
Murray, Peter *retired metallurgist, manufacturing executive*
Robinson, Henry Ward *meteorologist*

Mount Airy
Spohn, William Gideon, Jr. *mathematician, retired musician*
Swetcharnik, William Norton *visual artist, instructor, consultant*

New Market
Young, Russell Dawson *physicist, consultant*

North Bethesda
Edinger, Stanley Evan *clinical chemist*
Flax, Herman Jacob *physiatrist*
Friedman, Roger Jay *plastic surgeon*
Lerner, Theodore *real estate company executive*
Szabo, Daniel *federal official*

North East
Zatalava, Christine Michelle *science educator*

North Potomac
Kapsch, Robert James *engineering and architectural historian*
Lehman, Leonard *retired lawyer, consultant*
Lide, David Reynolds *editor-in-chief*

Oakland
Harman, Yolanda Michelle *science educator*

Ocean City
Bright, Bruce Frederick *lawyer*
Corun, Ronald Lewis *asphalt refining executive*
Phillips, J. Harrison III *lawyer*

Ocean Pines
Crawford, Norman Crane, Jr. *academic administrator, consultant*

Odenton
Lambert, Vickie Ann *retired dean, nursing consultant*

Olney
Baker, Carl Gwin *retired science administrator, educator*
Delmar, Eugene Anthony *architect*
Taggarse, Jyotsna Sharad *mathematics educator*
Uscinski, Ronald Henry *medical educator*

Owings
O'Neill, Patricia Tydings *performing arts educator, language educator*
Oring, Stuart August *audio-visual specialist, writer, photographer, researcher*

Owings Mills
Billick, Brian *professional football coach*
Chernow, Jeffrey Scott *lawyer, educator, writer*
Colussy, Dan Alfred *aviation executive*
Heck, Albert Frank *retired neurologist*
McNiesh, Celeste Angela *sales executive*
Newsome, Ozzie *professional sports team executive*
Ryan, Judith W. *geriatrics nurse, educator*
Sanner, George Bradley *bank executive*
Smith, Troy *professional football player*
Swartz, Eugene Robert, Jr. *music educator, minister*
Vogel, James Edmond *plastic surgeon*

Oxford
Bellinger, Edgar Thomson *lawyer*

Parkton
Fitzgerald, Edwin Roger *physicist, researcher*

Parkville
Hill, Milton King, Jr. *retired lawyer*
Jensen, Arthur Seigfried *retired engineer, physicist, consultant*

Pasadena
Asti, Alison Louise *lawyer*
De Pauw, Linda Grant *historian, educator, writer*

Patuxent River
Charlot, Joseph Leonce, Jr. *preventive medicine physician*
Stroup, Darryl Ray *systems engineer*

Perry Point
Jones, Scott Nelson *psychologist*

Perryville
Quesenbery, Erika Lynn *media specialist, curator*

Phoenix
Hairston, Walter Albert *school system administrator*

Pikesville
Putzel, Constance Kellner *lawyer*
Stein, Bernard Alvin *retail executive, consultant*

Point Of Rocks
Peppe, Ron *lawyer*

Potomac
Bulger, Roger James *academic administrator*
Christian, John Kenton *publishing executive, marketing professional, consultant*
Cotton, William Robert *retired dentist*
Crowson, Henry Lawrence *mathematician, educator*
Dickerman, Serafina Poerio *real estate broker, consultant*
Druckman, Daniel *social sciences educator, consultant, researcher*
Eaves, Maria Perry *realtor*
Epstein, Mark Robert *electronics executive*
Foley, Joseph Patrick *public relations executive*
Fox, Arthur Joseph, Jr. *editor*
Fthenakis, Emanuel John *aerospace transportation and communications executive*
Gaston, Marilyn Hughes *physician, administrator, public health expert, author*
Hall, William Darlington *lawyer*
Harvey, John Collins *internist, educator*
Hey, Nancy Henson *retired educational administrator*
Ingram, Richard Thomas *retired president, consultant, writer*
Karnow, Stanley *journalist, writer*
Keefe, Arthur Thomas III *non-profit fund raising executive*
Kessler, Ronald *author*
Korengold, George Matthew *physician*
Kuykendall, Crystal Arlene *educational consultant, lawyer*
Lannan, Maura Anne Kelly *reporter*
Medin, A. Louis *computer company executive*
Medin, Julia Adele *mathematics professor, researcher*
Meyer, Lawrence George *lawyer*
Mullenbach, Linda Herman *lawyer*
Navarro, Joseph Anthony *retired statistician, consultant*
Oertel, Goetz Kuno Heinrich *physicist, professional society administrator*
Pastan, Linda Olenik *poet*
Peter, Phillips Smith *lawyer*
Redding, Robert Ellsworth *lawyer*
Reichley, A. James *political scientist*
Rhode, Alfred Shimon *finance educator*
Roesser, Jean Wolberg *state official*
Rosenberg, Sarah Zacher *retired cultural organization administrator*
Rotberg, Iris Comens *social scientist*
Schmeltzer, Edward *lawyer*
Shapiro, Richard Gerald *retail executive, consultant*
Sherwood, Arthur Lawrence *lawyer*
Shirvinski, Adam John *management consultant*
Sundick, Sherry Small *journalist, writer, poet*
Tai, Tsze Cheng *aerodynamicist, researcher*
Tressel, George Walter *TV producer, science educator, consultant*
Troffkin, Howard Julian *lawyer*
Vadus, Gloria A. *scientific document examiner*
Waugaman, Richard Merle *psychiatrist, educator*
Williams, Peter MacLellan *nuclear engineer*
Wolman, Eric *health care consultant*
Wonnacott, Paul *retired economics professor*

Princess Anne
Brockett, Ramona *criminologist, educator*
Chigbu, Paulinus *fisheries biologist, educator, research scientist*
Johnson, Andrea *biologist, researcher*
Sharma, Dinesh Kumar *management science educator*
Thompson, Thelma Barnaby *university president, classical languages educator*

Pylesville
Roth, George Stanley *biochemist, physiologist, researcher*

Queenstown
Corn, Morton *environmental engineer, educator*

Randallstown
Holt, John J. *mediator, arbitrator, retired human resources specialist*

Reisterstown
Broadbent, J. Streett *engineering executive*
Frank, Robert Louis *lawyer*
Stefano, Toni Amanda *voice educator*
Tannenbaum, Harvey *defense technology consultant*
Tirone, Barbara Jean *retired health insurance administrator*

Riverdale
Brown, Yvonne Nardin *secondary school educator*

Rockville
Abron, Lilia A. *chemical engineer*
Adelsperger, Jennifer *forensic scientist*
Ashar, Hansraj G. *structural engineer, nuclear regulator*
Avery, Bruce Edward *lawyer*
Banthin, Jessica S. *economist, researcher*
Bardack, Paul Roitman *cultural organization administrator*
Barkley, Brian Evan *lawyer, political consultant*
Baughman, Robert William *neuroscientist, director*
Berryman, Richard Byron *lawyer*
Birns, Mark Theodore *physician*
Bough, Kristopher *pharmacologist*
Bradshaw, Sheldon *lawyer*
Buchanan, John Donald *retired nuclear scientist*
Burdick, William MacDonald *biomedical engineer*
Burt, Marvin Roger *financial advisor, investment manager*
Cantelon, Philip Louis *historian*
Carlton, Jane M.R. *geneticist*
Chen, Genshe *research scientist*
Cheston, Sheila Carol *lawyer*
Chiogioji, Melvin Hiroaki *retired federal official, entrepreneur*
Clancy, Carolyn M. *internist, federal agency administrator*
Clark, Harry Westley *federal agency administrator*
Clarke, Nina Honemond *historian, writer, retired principal*
Cline, Terry L. *federal agency administrator*
Conroy, J. Michael *lawyer, judge*
Croyle, Robert T. *federal agency administrator, psychologist, educator*
Cyr, Karen D. *lawyer*
Dal Pan, Gerald J. *federal agency administrator*
Davies-Venn, Christian *environmental engineer*
Davis, Beverly Watts *federal agency administrator*
De Jong, David Samuel *lawyer*
Donnally, Robert Andrew *lawyer*
Drum, Bruce Alan *physicist*
Duke, Elizabeth M. *federal agency administrator*
DuPont, Robert Louis *psychiatrist, physician*
Edwards, Bert Tvedt *accountant*
Epstein, Jay Stuart *federal agency administrator*
Fein, Stephanie Lynne *language educator*
Foreman, Todd Matthew *professional sports team owner, communications executive*
Frye, Roland Mushat, Jr. *lawyer*
Geem, Zong Woo *engineer*
Gibson, William M. *technology company executive*
Gluckstein, Fritz Paul *veterinarian, biomedical information specialist*
Gonzalez-Licea, Augustin *pathologist, public health service officer*
Goodman, Jesse *physician, director, public health facility administrator, research scientist*
Gray, Paulette Styles *federal agency administrator, biologist*
Griffith, Jerry Dice *energy executive, management consultant*
Grim, Charles W. *federal agency administrator*
Groban, Mark D. *health care company executive*
Haber, Margaret Wilson *informatics specialist, director*
Haffner, Marlene Elisabeth *internist, public health administrator*
Hamilton, Parker *library director*
Hawk, Ernest T. *federal agency administrator*
He, Junkun *research scientist*
Hepfer, Cheryl Lynn *lawyer*
Hewlett, Richard Greening *historian*
Hoffman, Stephen Lev *physician*
Jacques, Joseph William *investment advisor*
Jaczko, Gregory Bela *commissioner, physicist*
Kadish, Richard L. *lawyer*
Karson, Emile *lawyer*
Katz, Steven Martin *lawyer, accountant*
Kerxton, Alan Smith *lawyer*
Kim, Bong-Jo *molecular biologist, researcher*
Klein, Dale Edward *federal agency administrator, engineering educator*

Kline, Raymond Adam *professional organization executive*
Klosson, Michael *public policy director*
Kohlmeier, Louis Martin, Jr. *newspaper reporter*
Kowarski, Allen Avinoam *endocrinologist, educator*
Kruger, Jerome *materials science educator, consultant*
Landon, John Campbell *research and development company executive*
Lavoie, Daniel Joseph, II, *archivist, historian*
Leach, Berton Joe *medical educator*
LeCompte, Andrew C. *freelance/self-employed interpreter*
Lessenco, Gilbert Barry *retired lawyer*
Levenson, Bruce *professional sports team owner, communications executive*
Leventhal, Carl M. *neurologist, consultant, retired government agency administrator*
Levin, Alexander B. *mathematics professor*
Lloyd, Douglas Seward *physician, public health administrator*
Long, Cedric William *health facility administrator*
Lumpkin, Murray M. *federal agency administrator*
Lushniak, Boris D. *public health service officer*
Lyons, Peter B. *commissioner*
MacArthur, Diana Taylor *advanced technology executive*
Madle, Robert Albert *writer*
Malik, Waheed Ahmad *cardiologist*
Manderscheid, Ronald William *program administrator*
Marcuccio, Phyllis Rose *retired educational association administrator, editor*
Massie, Tammy Jeanne Parliment *statistician*
McDonald, Capers Walter *biomedical engineer, manufacturing executive, entrepreneur, educator*
McMurry, James Finley, Jr. *endocrinologist, researcher*
Merrifield, Jeffrey S. *commissioner*
Miller, Claire Ellen *editor, educator, writer*
Miller, Kenneth Michael *electronics executive, director*
Morgan, William Bruce *naval architect*
Mummaneni, Padmaja *research scientist, educator*
Nelson, Kevin *statistician*
Niewiaroski, Trudi Osmers (Gertrude Niewiaroski) *social studies educator*
O'Donnell, James Francis *retired health scientist administrator*
Parham-Hopson, Deborah *health programs administrator*
Pehrson, Gordon Oscar, Jr. *lawyer, venture capitalist*
Peskowitz, Ed *professional sports team owner, communications executive*
Power, A. Kathryn *federal agency administrator*
Proffitt, John Richard *information technology executive, educator, public official*
Raker, Irma S. *judge*
Ralph, Robert Alan *ophthalmologist, educator*
Rao, Potarazu Krishna *environmental consultant*
Reddy, Thikkavarapu Ramachandra *electrical engineer*
Renninger, Mary Karen *retired librarian*
Robinson, Cheryl Jeffreys *special education educator*
Rosen, Saul Woolf *research scientist, health facility administrator*
Roth, Clifford Joel *lawyer, consultant*
Rothenberg, Alan David *lawyer*
Rutstein, David C. *United States public health service administrator*
Ryan, Kevin William *virologist, clinical research administrator*
Sansalone, William Robert *biochemist, educator, biomedical researcher*
Schindler, Albert Isadore *physicist, researcher*
Schwarz, Sidney Howard *rabbi*
Scully, Martha Seebach *speech and language pathologist*
Seagle, Edgar Franklin *environmental engineer, consultant*
Senger, Jeffrey M. *lawyer*
Shapiro, Maurice Mandel *nuclear astrophysicist*
Shekar, Sam S. *federal agency administrator*
Stansfield, Charles W. *educational administrator*
Steinberg, William Mark *physician*
Strausberg, Robert L. *federal agency administrator*
Sundlof, Stephen Frederick *veterinary administrator*
Tabor, Edward *medical researcher*
Tandon, Narendra Nath *research scientist, director*
Tanenbaum, Richard Hugh *lawyer*
Tang, Kaizhi *research scientist*
Taubenberger, Jeffery Karl *pathologist, molecular biologist*
Telesetsky, Walter *federal agency administrator*
Temple, Robert *physician, federal agency administrator*
Thompson, James Lee *lawyer*
Throckmorton, Douglas Carl *federal agency administrator*
Tomar, Richard Thomas *lawyer*
Toro, Jorge R. *dermatologist, researcher*
Uhl, Kathleen *federal agency administrator*
Um, Ki Sung *research scientist*
Umbreit, Wayne William *bacteriologist, educator*
van Dyck, Peter Cuyler *federal agency administrator*
Van Grack, Steven *lawyer*
Venter, J. Craig (John Craig Venter, Craig Venter) *science foundation director, geneticist*
von Eschenbach, Andrew C. *federal agency administrator, oncologist, urologic surgeon*
Vorosmarti, James *physician*
Wallenmeyer, William Anton *retired physicist*
Watkins, Frederick Harvey *plastic surgeon*
Watkins, H. Thomas *biopharmaceutical company executive*
Weinel, Pamela Jean *nurse administrator*
Whitescarver, Jack Edward *federal agency administrator*
Woodcock, Janet *federal official*
Yoshikawa, Hiromi *pharmaceutical executive*
Zaphiriou, George Aristotle *lawyer, educator*

Rocky Ridge
Rall, Priscilla *artist, educator*

Saint Marys City
Clifton, Lucille Thelma *author*
Froom, David *composer, music educator*
O'Brien, Jane Margaret *academic administrator*
Sullivan, Martin Edward *museum director*

Saint Michaels
Brown, Omer Forrest, II, *lawyer*
Feisel, Lyle Dean *retired dean, electrical engineer, educator*
Peck, Charles Edward *retired construction and mortgage executive*

Salisbury
Booker, Betty Mae *poet*
Bowden, Derek Thomas *orchestra director, educator*
Cathell, Dale Roberts *judge*
Chambers, Dustin Lee *economics professor*
Kleiman, Gary Howard *broadcast, advertising and cellular communications consultant*
Moultrie, Fred *geneticist, researcher*
Nutter, David George *city planner*
Perdue, James A. (Jim Perdue) *food products executive*
Wolter, John Amadeus *librarian, federal official*

Severn
Freeman, Joel Arthur *author, organizational cultural change facilitator*

Severna Park
Allison, John Langsdale *naval architect, marine engineer*
Davis, Clayton *writer, pilot, photographer*
Hall, Marcia Joy *non-profit organization administrator*
Humphreys Troy, Patricia *foundation administrator*
Lesikar, James Daniel, II, *physicist, engineer*
Meima, Ralph Chester, Jr. *retired diplomat, real estate company executive*
Rheinstein, Peter Howard *healthcare company executive, physician, lawyer*
Schick, Edgar Brehob *language educator*
Windsor, Patricia (Katonah Summertree, Perrin Winters, Anna Seeling) *author, educator, lecturer*

Shady Side
Devine, Donald J. *political science professor, consultant*

Silver Spring
Alexander, Herbert E. *political scientist*
Altschul, B. J. *public relations counselor*
Aranya, Gwendalin Qi *painter, priest, educator, yoga educator*
Arvin, Linda Lee *counselor*
Bassett, William, Jr. *geospatial intelligence officer*
Bate, Marilyn Anne *psychologist*
Beach, Bert Beverly *clergyman*
Beard, Lillian B. McLean *pediatrician, consultant*
Bennett, Carol(ine) Elise *retired reporter, actress*
Berger, Allan Sidney *psychiatrist, educator*
Biberman, Lucien Morton *retired physicist*
Blakeney, Barbara A. *public health service officer*
Borkovec, Vera Z. *literature and language professor*
Brandt, Carl David *research virologist*
Brandt, Elsa Lund Erickson *music educator*
Brog, David *former air force officer, consultant*
Brush, Julianna R. *marine biologist*
Burgos-Sasscer, Ruth *chancellor emeritus*
Burke, Margaret Ann *computer company and communications executive*
Calinger, Ronald Steve *historian*
Calvert, Gordon Lee *retired legal association executive*
Carson, Steven Lee *newspaper publisher*
Carter-Johnson, Jean Evelyn *management consultant*
Chery, Reginald *minister*
Ciment, Melvyn *mathematician*
Coates, Robert Jay *retired electronics executive*
Cohen, Sharon Claire *history educator, consultant*
Cole, Wayne Stanley *historian, educator*
Coles, Anna Louise Bailey *retired dean, nurse*
Cooper, Nannie Coles *education educator, consultant*
Corwin, Jeff *biologist, anthropologist, television host*
Craig, Paul Max, Jr. *retired lawyer*
Daniel, J. Christopher *health facility executive, family medicine physician, military officer*
Dentali, Steven J. *chemist*
de Zafra Atwell, Dorothea Elizabeth *retired government agency administrator*
Doherty, William Thomas, Jr. *historian, retired educator*
Dunnigan, John H. *federal agency administrator*
Ehrlich, Charles David *physicist*
Eiserer, Leonard Albert Carl *publishing executive*
Ewing, Blair Gordon *federal official*
Fitzgerald, Joseph Patrick *artist*
Fockler, Herbert Hill *foundation executive*
Freilich, Daniel Adam *epidemiologist*
Ganley, Charles James *federal agency administrator, internist*
Gaydos, Joel Carl *physician*
Gilbert, Charles Richard Alsop *obstetrician, gynecologist, surgeon, educator*
Gunn, Will A. *foundation administrator, retired military officer, lawyer*
Guzman, Martha Patricia *science educator*
Haynes, Leonard L. III *director*
Hendricks, John S. *broadcast executive*
Heppner, Donald Gray, Jr. *immunology research physician, army officer*
Herbers, Tod Arthur *publisher*
Hsueh, Chun-tu *political scientist, educator, foundation administrator, historian*
Hudson, Ralph P. *physicist*
Jacobs, George *broadcast engineering consulting company executive*
Johnson, David L. *federal agency administrator, retired military officer*
Johnson, Richard August *literature and language professor*
Kant, Gloria Jean *retired neuroscientist*
Kline, Jerry Robert *retired administrative judge, ecologist*
Koltnow, Peter Gregory *engineer, consultant*
Koppel, Ted *newscaster*
Kriegel, Robin *medical association administrator*
Kurata, Phillip Cedomir *journalist*
Latson, Richard Charles *retired audio-visual specialist*
Lipstein, Robert A. *lawyer*
Maas, Joe (Melvin Joseph Maas) *retired federal agency administrator*
Mahoney, James R. *federal agency administrator*
Makris, Margaret Lubbe *retired elementary school educator*
Martin, Michiko Jeannette *oceanographer, meteorologist, educational association administrator*
McCray, Lora *real estate developer*
Miller, Karla Patricia *elementary school educator*
Miller, Kendra Danette *art services business owner*
Mlay, Marian *retired government official*
Mohr, Christina *retired economist*
Mok, Carson Kwok-Chi *structural engineer*
Montalvo, Eileen *communications executive*
Moon, Marilyn Lee *economist*
Moreno, Donna Marie *communications executive*
Mosholder, Andrew Donald *psychiatrist*
Niebuhr, David William *epidemiologist, educator*
Null, Elisabeth Higgins *librarian, editor*
Oliver, Kimberly *primary school educator*
Oswald, Rudolph A. *economist*
Papas, Irene Kalandros *English language educator, poet, writer*
Peiperl, Adam *sculptor, photographer*
Rachanow, Gerald Marvin *lawyer, pharmacist*
Rayburn, Carole Ann (Mary Aida) *psychologist, researcher, writer, consultant*
Rice, Michelle *communications executive*
Rice, Rick Blackburn *application developer, systems analyst*
Rodgers, Johnathan *broadcast executive*
Rothberg, Morey David *historian, editor*
Sammet, Jean E. *computer scientist*
Saperstein, David Nathan *rabbi, lawyer, educator*
Scipio, L. Albert, II, (Louis Albert Scipio II) *retired aerospace science engineering educator, historian*
Secular, Sidney *actor, writer, fundraiser, business consultant*
Shalowitz, Erwin Emmanuel *civil engineer*
Shih-Carducci, Joan Chia-mo *food service executive, educator, medical technologist, writer, biochemist*
Sirken, Monroe Gilbert *statistician*
Smedley, Lawrence Thomas *retired organization executive*
Spinrad, Richard William *federal agency administrator, oceanographer*
Striner, Herbert Edward *economics professor*
Supanich, Barbara Ann *physician*
Tobe, Barbara Gaines *information technology executive*
Vernon, Weston, III, (Wes Vernon) *broadcaster, writer, actor*
Waldrop, Francis Neil *physician*
Ware, Thaddeus Van *retired government official*
Weiss, Leonard *mathematician, consultant*
Whalen, John Philip *retired academic administrator, priest, lawyer*
Whitaker, Joel *publishing executive, public official*
White, Edmund William *chemical engineer*
Whitmore, Frank Clifford, Jr. *retired geologist*
Whitten, Leslie Hunter, Jr. *writer, poet, reporter*
Williams, Paul *retired federal agency administrator*
Winston, Michael Russell *foundation executive, historian*
Yasher, Michael *retired accountant*
Young, Jay Alfred *chemical safety and health consultant, editor, writer*
Zaslav, David M. *broadcast executive*

Simpsonville
Altschuler, Bruce Robert *research dentist*
Bluher, Gregory *computer scientist, mathematician*

Solomons
Dorsey, James Francis, Jr. *naval officer*
Harrington, John Vincent *retired communications executive, engineer, educator*
Wright, David Alan *environmental toxicology professor, consultant*

Sparks
Lawless, Robert J. *food products executive*
Rallo, James Gilbert *management company executive*
Skelton, Robert W. *lawyer, food products executive*

Springdale
Keith, Patricia *multi-media specialist*

Stevenson
Hendler, Nelson Howard *physician, health facility administrator, director*
Hilgenberg, John Christian *corporate financial executive, consultant*

Stevensville
Barrett, John Anthony *publishing and printing company financial executive*
Engel, Bradford Charles *educational association administrator, secondary school educator*
Lain, David Cornelius *health scientist, researcher*

Street
Spangler, Ronald Leroy *retired television and aircraft executive, automobile consultant*

Suitland
Brooks, Richard C. *electrical engineer, federal official*
Johnson, Jessica Susan *conservator*
McClain, Edward Fifer, Jr. *retired physicist*
Reupke, William Albert *engineer*

Sunderland
Franklin, Jon Daniel *writer, journalist, educator*

Swanton
Cummins, Delmer Duane *academic administrator, historian*

Takoma Park
DeVaris, Panayotis Eric *architect*
Fatiadi, Alexander John *retired chemist*
Stephenson, Patricia Ann *public health researcher, educator*
Urciolo, John Raphael, II, *finance and real estate educator, developer*

Taneytown
Anderson, Mary Ann Grasso *business executive*

Temple Hills
Ourisman, Mandell Jack *automotive executive*
Smith, Irving *gerontologist*
Strauss, Simon Wolf *chemist, materials scientist*

Thurmont
Schuettinger, Bruce Michael *conservator*

Timonium
Forrester, Alfred Whitfield *psychiatrist, educator*
Sagerholm, James Alvin *retired naval officer*
Zeren, Karl Joseph *dentist, educator*

Towson
Adams, Joseph Andrew *internist, health facility administrator, educator*
Ahearn, Elizabeth Lowe *performing arts educator*
Ali, Omar H. *history professor*
Ayres, Jeffrey Peabody *lawyer*
Baker, Jean Harvey *history professor*
Bowen, Lowell Reed *lawyer*
Brennan, Michael J. *lawyer*
Caret, Robert Laurent *academic administrator*
Carney, Bradford George Yost *lawyer, educator*
Chase, Jacquelyn Veronica *marketing professional*
Comeau, Michael Gerard *lawyer*
Coughlin, James Patrick *mathematician, educator*
Crawford, Leneida Marie *singer, educator*
Feng, Jinjuan *information scientist, educator*
Fenton, Charles E. *lawyer*
Fish, James Henry *library director*
Forrest, Juliet *dancer, educator, choreographer*
Gilliss, Edward Johnson *lawyer*
Hoch, David Allen *athletic director*
Huang, Joseph Chen-Huan *civil engineer*
Jothen, Michael Jon *music educator, composer, conductor*
Koetter, Cornelia M. *lawyer*
Kues, Irvin William *financial planner*
Lutz, Randall Matthew *lawyer*
Mangan, Michael D. *corporate financial executive*
Meny, Robert George *former medical research administrator, physician*
Miller, Herbert H. *lawyer*
Nelson, H. Wayne *gerontologist, advocate*
Passano, E. Magruder, Jr. *management consultant*
Proctor, Kenneth Donald *lawyer*
Propst, M. Teresa Carson *historian*
Shah, Shirish Kalyanbhai *computer science, chemistry and environmental science educator*
Spodak, Michael Kenneth *forensic psychiatrist*
Tull, Willis Clayton, Jr. *retired librarian*
Vettori, Paul Marion *lawyer*
Wilkinson, Charles P. *ophthalmologist*
Zink, John H. III *lawyer*
Zweback, Stanley *psychologist, educator*

Trappe
Blades, G(ene) Granville *accountant*
Burns-Bowie, Maureen Elizabeth *sculptor*
Paul, James Caverly Newlin *law educator, retired dean*

Union Bridge
Hannah, Judy Challenger *private education tutor*

University Park
Beckenstein, Myron *journalist*
Holder, Sallie Lou *training and meeting management consultant, coach*

Upper Marlboro
Buffenbarger, (Robert) Thomas *labor union administrator*
Bune, Karen Louise *state agency administrator, legal assistant*
Harrell, Glenn T., Jr. *judge*
Jones-Lukács, Elizabeth Lucille *physician*
Seibel, Charles Burgess *accountant, educator*
Symlar, Jesse Lee *finance executive*
Zane, *writer, publishing executive*

Waldorf
Raiman, Rosemary A. *advocate*
Wiggins, Stephen Edward *physician*

West Bethesda
Jessup, Stuart Dodge *marine engineer*
Scully, Roger Tehan, II, *lawyer*
Sevik, Maurice *acoustical engineer, researcher*
Vogelgesang, Sandra Louise *former ambassador, writer, consultant*

West River
Atkinson, Dorothy Scott *retired accountant*

Westminster
Dulany, William Bevard *lawyer*
Erb, Betty Jane *retired real estate agent*
Lippy, Karen Dorothy Fethe *nurse psychotherapist*
Madsen, Stephanie D. *psychology professor*
Preston, Charles Michael *lawyer*
Saxton, Celeste Dawn *social studies educator, consultant*
Staples, Lyle Newton *lawyer*

Wheaton
White, Martha Vetter *allergist, immunologist*

White Hall
Radigan, Frank Xavier *retired pharmaceutical executive*

Woodbine
Mc Indoe, Darrell Winfred *retired nuclear medicine physician*
Nuss, Barbara Gough *artist*
Uhl, Scott Mark *state agency administrator*

Worton
Rienhoff, William Francis III *retired surgeon, thoracic surgeon*

Wye Mills
Farley, Gregory Scott *biology professor*
Schnaitman, William Kenneth *retired finance company executive*

MASSACHUSETTS

Acton
An, Hong *engineer*
Benz, Edward John, Sr. *clinical pathologist*
Boghani, Ashok Balvantrai *entrepreneur, management consultant*
Conoby, Joseph Francis *chemist*
Evans, Robert, Jr. *economics professor*
Hicks, Walter Joseph *electrical engineer*
Kalavade, Asa *telecommunications industry executive*
Smith, Raoul Normand *computer science educator*

Agawam
Goodwin, Beverly Ann *elementary school educator*
Kantor, Simon William *chemistry professor*
Sylvester, John Andrew *social studies educator*

Allston
Cort, Julia *television director, television producer, scriptwriter*
Liota, Vincent *television producer*
Mills, Daniel Quinn *business educator, consultant, author*
Spencer, Lara *television personality, journalist*

Amesbury
Bartnicki, Karen Jo *social services administrator*
Heyman, Joseph Martin *gynecologist*

Amherst
Adrion, William Richards *academic administrator, computer and information sciences educator, writer*
Anderson, Ronald Trent *artist, educator*
Archer, Ronald Dean *chemist, educator*
Averill, James Reed *psychology professor*
Baker, Lynne Rudder *philosophy educator*
Bentley, Richard Norcross *regional planner, writer, educator*
Berger, Seymour Maurice *social psychologist*
Bridegam, Willis Edward, Jr. *retired librarian*
Brooks, A. Taeko *historian*
Call, Gregory S. *academic administrator, mathematics professor*
Cornish, Geoffrey St. John *golf course architect*
Cox, David Archibald *mathematics professor*
Dabrowski, Thaddeus E. *art educator, consultant, painter*
Daehler, Marvin William *psychology professor*
Donohue, Therese Brady *artistic director, choreographer, costume and set designer*
Fink, Richard David *chemist, educator*
Fleischman, Paul Robert *psychiatrist, writer*
Franks, Lewis E. *electrical and computer engineering educator, researcher*
Gibson, Walker *retired language educator, poet, writer*
Goldstein, Joseph Irwin *materials scientist, educator*
Hallock, Robert Bruce *physics professor*
Hartwell, Alfred Stedman (Ash Hartwell) *international relations educator, consultant*
Hexter, Ralph J. *academic administrator, literature educator*
Howland, Richard Moulton *retired lawyer*
Immerman, Neil *academic administrator, computer science educator*
Kinney, Arthur Frederick *humanities educator, writer*
Klare, Michael Thomas *social sciences educator, director*
Larson, Joseph Stanley *environmentalist, educator*
Lasch, Pat *artist, educator*
Levin, Robert Eugene *food scientist, educator*
Liebling, Jerome *photographer, educator*
MacKnight, Carol Bernier *educational association administrator*
MacKnight, William John *chemist, educator*
Manz, Charles Craig *management educator*
Margulis, Lynn (Lynn Alexander) *evolutionist, educator*
Marx, Anthony W. *academic administrator*
May, Ernest Dewey *academic administrator, musician*
Mullin, William Jesse *physics professor*
Nash, William Arthur *civil engineer, educator*
Oates, Stephen Baery *retired historian*
Palmer, John Derry *physiology educator*
Peterson, Gerald Alvin *physics professor*
Prince, Gregory Smith, Jr. *retired college president*
Pritchard, William H. *literature educator, writer*
Rabin, Monroe Stephen Zane *physicist*
Reed-Penttinen, Daphne Stevenson *artist*
Roberts, Chris *strategy and finance educator, researcher*
Rosbottom, Ronald Carlisle *language and humanities educator*
Sandweiss, Martha Ann *writer, history professor*
Sarat, Austin D. *jurisprudence and political science educator*
Schafer, Gerald Lewis (Jay Schafer) *library director*
Seymour, Charlena *academic administrator*
Spratlan, Lewis *composer, educator*
Strickland, Bonnie Ruth *psychologist, educator*
Swift, Calvin Thomas *electrical and computer engineering educator*
Tate, James Vincent *poet, English educator*
Taubman, Jane Andelman *literature and language professor*
Taubman, William Chase *political science professor, writer*
Tropp, Linda R. *psychology professor*
Vogl, Otto *polymer science and engineering educator*
Wills, David Wood *minister, educator*
Winter, Horst Henning *chemical engineer, educator*
Wolff, Robert Paul *philosophy educator*
Woodbury, Richard Benjamin *anthropologist, educator*
Wyman, David Sword *retired historian, educator*
Yarde, Richard Foster *art educator*

Andover
Agassounon, William B. G. *engineer, researcher, scientist*
Govern, Frank Stanley *health facility and research administrator, healthcare educator, writer*
Jakes, William Chester *electrical engineer*
Keleher, David *electronics executive*
Kurogi, Yasuhisa *chemist*
Warner, Sally Slade *musician*

Arlington
Eastburn, Christopher Amers *composer, choral director*
Junger, Miguel Chapero *retired acoustics researcher*
Keshian, Richard *lawyer*

Ashfield
Gabriel, Peter Paul *business educator*

Ashland
Morrison, Gordon Mackay, Jr. *retired investment company executive*
Pettinella, Nicholas Anthony *corporate financial executive*

Attleboro
Bischoff, Marilyn Brett *clinical social worker, personal life coach, psychotherapist*
Hammerle, Fredric Joseph *metal products executive*
Wroe, Thomas, Jr. *semiconductor company executive*

Auburn
Bachelder, Robert Stephen *minister*
Baker, David Arthur *retired small business owner, manufacturing executive*
Giannini, Antoinette Frances *music educator, researcher*

Auburndale
Aronow, Saul *radiological physicist, consultant*
Drake, Elisabeth Mertz *chemical engineer, consultant*
Fowler, Frederick Victor, Jr. *import company executive*
Kibrick, Anne *retired nursing educator, dean*
Lindgren, Charlotte Holt *language educator*

Ayer
Sizer, Theodore R. *education educator*

Babson Park
Genovese, Francis Charles (Frank) *economist, educator, editor-in-chief, writer*
Rice, Mark P. *dean, management educator*

Barnstable
Mycock, Frederick Charles *lawyer*
Paquin, Thomas Christopher *lawyer*
Temkin, Robert Harvey *accountant*

Barre
Sullivan, James Edward *poet*

Bedford
Cady, Dona M. *humanities educator*
Daltas, Arthur John *management consultant, software services manager*
Jelalian, Albert V. *electrical engineer*
Ludes, Jacob III *educational association administrator*
Payne, Harry Morse, Jr. *architect*
Shepley, Hugh *architect*
Vaughn, Thomas Joseph *earth science educator, administrator*
White, Alan Frederick *academic administrator*
Winter, David Louis *retired systems engineer, human factors scientist*

Belchertown
Burstein, Michael Clifford *enterprise integration consultant*

Belmont
Benes, Francine M. *neuroscientist, psychiatrist*
Bingham, George Walter Chandler *retired sales executive*
Cavarnos, Constantine Peter *philosopher, writer*
Cohen, Bruce Michael *psychiatrist, educator, scientist, health facility administrator*
Colón, Ernie *comic book artist*
Coyle, Joseph Thomas *psychiatrist*
de Marneffe, Francis *psychiatrist, hospital administrator*
Dohanian, Diran Kavork *art historian, educator*
Greer, Gordon Bruce *retired lawyer, writer*
Hauser, George *biochemist, educator*
Kargman, Marie Witkin *marriage and family therapist*
Klein, Martin Samuel *management consultant*
Levendusky, Philip George *psychologist, academic administrator, educator*
Lloyd, Boardman *investment company executive*
Lyon, Richard Harold *physicist, educator*
Magidson, Jay *statistician*
Merrill, Edward Wilson *chemical engineering professor*
Neumeyer, John Leopold *chemistry professor*
Onesti, Silvio Joseph *psychiatrist*
Pope, Harrison Graham, Jr. *psychiatrist, educator*
Raiffa, Howard *economics educator*
Rand, Peter *writer, editor, educator*
Reynolds, William Francis *mathematics professor*
Rich, Sharon Lee *financial planner*
Stoll, Andrew Lawrence *psychopharmacologist*
Zhang, Kehong *pharmacologist, educator*
Zito, Frank R. *lawyer, accountant*

Berlin
Lohr, Harold Russell *retired bishop*

Beverly
Barger, Richard Wilson *hotel executive*
Eastman, W. Dean *secondary school educator*
Grace, Kathleen M *computer scientist, educator, web site designer*
Lister, Graeme George *physicist, journalist*
Manning, William Frederick *retired photographer*
Pierard, Richard Victor *history educator*
Roy, Robert William *artist, educator*
Smith, Derek Armand *information technology executive*

Billerica
DeCrosta, Susan Elyse *graphic designer*
Kinsman, Robert Preston *biomedical plastics engineer*
Kolb, Charles Eugene *research and development company executive*
Srinivasan, Purushothaman *electrical engineer, researcher*

Bolton
Wintle, Suzanne *elementary school educator*

Boston
Abbott, William Saunders *lawyer*
Aber, John William (Jack) *finance educator, consultant*
Ablow, Roz Karol (Roselyn Karol Ablow) *painter, curator*
Aborn, Foster Litchfield *insurance company executive*
Abrahm, Janet Lee *hematologist, oncologist, educator, palliative care specialist*
Abrams, Roger Ian *lawyer, educator*
Abu-moustafa, Adel H. *medical educator, dean*
Adams, Lisa *lawyer*
Adelstein, S(tanley) James *radiologist, educator*
Adler, Dale Steven *internist, cardiologist*
Ainge, Danny Ray *professional sports team executive, retired professional basketball player*
Ainsley, P. Steven (Steve Ainsley) *publishing executive*
Ajemian, Marianne *lawyer*
Akin, Steven Paul *finance company executive*
Akins, Cary Willard *surgeon, educator*
Albert, Martin Lawrence *behavioral neurologist, writer, educator, researcher*
Albright, Eric D. *medical librarian, director*
Alden, Vernon Roger *academic administrator*
Alderman, Marlene H. *law librarian, educator*
Allen, Ray (Walter Ray Allen) *professional basketball player*
Allen, Rosemary M. *lawyer*
Allen, Tony *professional basketball player*
Allinson, Deborah Louise *economist*
Alpert, Joel Jacobs *pediatrician, educator*
Altshuler, David Matthew *geneticist, endocrinologist*
Amaker, Tommy *men's college basketball coach*
Anderson, Kenneth Carl *physician, educator*
Andrews, Nancy Catherine *dean, pediatrician, hematologist, educator*
Angelo, E. Joanne *child, adolescent and adult psychiatrist*
Angelou, Maya (Marguerite Annie Johnson) *writer, actress*
Anissimova, Svetlana Vladimirovna *physicist, researcher*
Annas, George J. *health law educator*
Anselme, Jean-Pierre Louis Marie *chemist*
Antman, Elliott Marshall *cardiologist, educator*
Antman, Karen Hamm *oncologist, educator, dean*
Antonakes, Steven L. *state agency administrator*
Antonellis, Joseph C. *investment company executive*
Aoun, Joseph *academic administrator, linguistics educator, researcher*
Apjohn, Nelson George *lawyer*
Appelbaum, Diana Karter *author*
Appley, Mortimer Herbert *psychologist, retired academic administrator*
Aquilino, Daniel *banker*
Aresty, Jeffrey M. *lawyer*
Armistead, (Ivor) Cary III *lawyer*
Armstrong, Rodney *librarian*
Armstrong, Scott Allen *oncologist*
Arnold, Kirk *information technology executive*
Aronson, Neil H. *lawyer*
Ascenzo, Carl *information technology executive*
Ash, Barbara Lee *education and human services educator*
Auerbach, John M. *city health department administrator*
Auerbach, Joseph *former lawyer, educator*
Auger, Jessie L. *elementary school educator*
Ausiello, Dennis Arthur *nephrologist*
Austen, K(arl) Frank *internist, educator*
Austen, W(illiam) Gerald *surgeon, educator*
Azadzoi, Kazem M. *urologist, educator*
Bachman, Katharine Elizabeth *lawyer*
Bacon, A. Smoki *television host*
Bae, Frank S.H. *law librarian, educator*
Bailin, Michael Traherne *physician*
Baillieul, John Brouard *aerospace engineering and applied mathematics educator*
Baker, Annette L. *pediatric nurse practitioner*
Baker, Charles Duane *business administration educator*
Baker, Hollie L. *lawyer*
Baldwin, John Charles *surgeon, researcher*
Balliro, Joseph James, Sr. *lawyer*
Banks, Henry H. *orthopedist, educator, dean*
Bapooji Ryan, Anita B. *lawyer*
Baram, Michael S. *lawyer, educator*
Bardaglio, Peter Winthrop *humanities educator, former academic administrator*
Barker, Christopher B. *lawyer*
Barker, Edwin Bogue *musician*
Barnard, Deborah E. *lawyer*
Barnett, Guy Octo *physician, educator*
Baron, David Hume *science journalist*
Baron, Martin *editor*
Barouch, Dan Hung *physician, scientist, educator*
Barron, Michael K. *lawyer*
Basagni, Stefano *computer engineer, educator*
Bass, Michael A. *lawyer*
Bates, David Westfall *internist, educator, medical researcher*
Baughman, Kenneth Lee *cardiologist, educator*
Bawa, Kamaljit Singh *biologist, educator*
Beal, Robert Lawrence *real estate executive*
Becker, Fred Ronald *lawyer*
Becker, James Murdoch *surgeon, educator*
Beckett, Joshua Patrick *professional baseball player*
Bekenstein, Joshua *venture capital company executive*
Benacerraf, Baruj *pathologist, educator*
Benjamin, William Chase *lawyer*
Bennett, Clay *cartoonist*
Bennett, George Frederick *retired investment company executive*
Benoist, Christophe O. *immunologist, educator*
Benz, Edward John, Jr. *internist, hematologist, geneticist, educator, health facility administrator*
Berger, Jerome Morris *communications executive*
Berkman, Lisa F. *public health educator*
Bernhard, Alexander Alfred *lawyer*
Bernhard, William Francis *thoracic and cardiovascular surgeon*
Berson, Eliot Lawrence *ophthalmologist, medical educator*
Berstein, Robert L. *investment company executive*
Berube, Brian A. *lawyer, chemicals executive*
Bhatt, Manisha Hemendra *lawyer*
Bieber, Frederick Robert *medical geneticist*
Billings, Rick *chef*
Bills, Jennifer Leah *lawyer*
Bines, Harvey Ernest *lawyer, educator, writer*
Birmingham, Thomas F. *lawyer, former state legislator*
Bistrian, Bruce Ryan *internist, educator*
Black, Edward G. *lawyer*
Black, Paul Henry *medical educator, researcher*
Black, Peter *neurosurgeon, educator*
Black, Scott M. *diversified financial services company executive*
Blacklow, Robert Stanley *internist, educator*
Blakely, Allison *history professor*
Blendon, Robert Jay *health policy educator*
Bloch, Donald Martin *lawyer*
Bloch, Kurt Julius *physician*
Bloom, Barry R. *dean, medical educator*
Blumenthal, David *health policy expert*
Bodner, Randall Wayne *lawyer*
Bodoff, Joseph Samuel Uberman *lawyer*
Bok, John Fairfield *retired lawyer*
Bonauto, Mary *lawyer*
Bonifaz, John Cristopher *lawyer*
Borden, Mark G. *lawyer*
Bornheimer, Allen Millard *lawyer*
Borus, Jonathan Frederick *psychiatrist, educator*
Boudin, Michael *federal judge*
Bourque, Louise *film director, film instructor*
Bower, Joseph Lyon *business administration educator*
Bowler, Marianne Bianca *federal judge*
Boyd, David Preston *business educator*
Braceras, Roberto M. *lawyer*
Bragg, Lawrence D. III *lawyer*
Brain, Joseph David *biomedical researcher, educator*
Braunwald, Eugene *physician, educator*
Brazelton, Thomas Berry *pediatrician, educator*
Breakstone, Marc L. *lawyer*
Brecher, Kenneth *astrophysicist, educator*
Brenner, Barry Morton *physician*
Brenner, Michael Barry *rheumatologist, educator*
Bressler, Richard J. *investment company and former entertainment company executive*

Briscoe, David Michael *physician, scientist, researcher*
Brodley, Joseph F. *lawyer, consultant, dean*
Brody, Richard Eric *lawyer*
Broitman, Selwyn Arthur *microbiologist, educator, assistant dean*
Bromberg, Lee Carl *lawyer*
Brooke, Peter A. *corporate financial executive*
Brown, Michael Robert *lawyer*
Brown, Robert Arthur *academic administrator, chemical engineering professor*
Brown, Roger H. *academic administrator*
Brown, Stephen Lee *retired insurance company executive*
Brown, William L. *retired banker*
Bruns, William John, Jr. *business administration educator*
Buchanan, Robert McLeod *lawyer*
Buchin, Stanley Ira *management consultant, finance educator*
Bunker, Beryl H. *retired insurance company executive, volunteer*
Burgess, John Allen *lawyer*
Burke, Matthew M. *lawyer*
Burleigh, Lewis Albert *lawyer*
Burling, James C. *lawyer*
Burnes, Kennett Farrar *chemicals executive*
Burnett, Elizabeth B. *lawyer*
Burnham, David Henderson *management consultant*
Burns, Thomas David *lawyer*
Burstein, Harold John *oncologist*
Burt, Frank Davies *lawyer, real estate company executive*
Burton, Thomas Russell *lawyer*
Buxbaum, Robert C(ourtney) *internist*
Cabot, Louis Wellington *foundation trustee*
Cahill, Lawrence R. *lawyer*
Cahill, Timothy P. *state official*
Caldeira, Charlene A. *lawyer*
Callow, Allan Dana *surgeon*
Campanelli, Joseph P. *bank executive*
Campbell, David Kelly *theoretical physicist, engineering educator*
Campbell, Levin Hicks *federal judge*
Canavan, Christine Estelle *state legislator*
Canellos, George Peter *hematologist, oncologist, educator*
Canning, David *economist*
Cao, Xinhua *medical researcher*
Caplan, Louis Robert *neurologist, educator*
Caporizzo, A. William *lawyer*
Cardona, Rodolfo *Spanish language and literature educator*
Carey, John Andrew *investment company executive*
Carey, Martin Conrad *gastroenterologist, molecular biophysicist, educator, medical geneticist*
Carmany, George Walter III *finance company executive, consultant*
Carney, J. W., Jr. *lawyer*
Carp, Jeffrey N. *lawyer, investment company executive*
Carroll, James Edward *lawyer*
Carroll, Jill *freelance journalist*
Carter, T(homas) Barton *law educator*
Cash, James Ireland, Jr. *retired business educator*
Casner, Truman Snell *lawyer*
Cavazos, Lauro Fred *medical educator, former secretary of education*
Chabner, Bruce A. *oncologist, researcher*
Chakrabarti, Supriya *space astrophysicist*
Chandler, Harriette Levy *state legislator, management consultant, educator*
Chang, Hemmie *lawyer*
Chang, Shan Nan *education educator, academic administrator*
Chapin, David Chester *lawyer*
Chara, Zdeno *professional hockey player*
Chen, Ching-chih *information science educator, consultant*
Chertavian, Gerald *nonprofit organization executive*
Chiarelli, Peter *professional sports team executive*
Chobanian, Aram *medical educator, cardiologist, former academic administrator*
Choo, Sin H. *neurosurgeon*
Christenson, Charles John *retired business educator*
Christopher, Irene *librarian, consultant*
Church, George McDonald *geneticist, educator, researcher*
Ciraulo, Domenic Anthony *psychiatrist, educator*
Clapham, David E. *pharmacology educator*
Cleary, John Joseph (Jack) *lawyer*
Clinger, William Douglas *computer scientist, educator*
Cloonan, Michele V. *library director*
Coakley, Martha *state attorney general, former prosecutor*
Codinha, J. William *lawyer*
Coffey, James Francis *lawyer*
Coffin, John Miller *medical researcher, biology professor*
Cohen, Alan Barry *researcher, educator*
Cohen, Alan Seymour *internist*
Cohen, Kenneth A. *lawyer*
Cohen, Rachelle Sharon *journalist*
Cohen, Robert Sonné *physicist, philosopher, educator*
Cohen, Saul G. *chemist, educator*
Cohn, Andrew Howard *lawyer*
Cohn, Lawrence H. *cardiothoracic surgeon*
Coleman, Dennis M. *lawyer*
Coleman, Virginia Flood *lawyer*
Collings, Robert Biddlecombe *judge*
Collins, James H., Jr. *architectural firm executive*
Collins, Tucker *pathologist, molecular biologist*
Condrin, J. Paul *insurance company executive*
Connolly, Thomas Edward *judge*
Connors, Jack, Jr. *advertising executive*
Cook, Gareth *reporter*
Cordy, Robert J. *state supreme court justice*
Cornwall, Deborah Joyce *management consultant, consulting firm executive*
Costa, Daniel Lawrence *architect*
Cowin, Judith Arnold *state supreme court judge*
Creedon, Geraldine *state legislator*
Creem, Cynthia Stone *state legislator, lawyer*
Creevy, William R. *orthopedist, surgeon, educator*
Crimlisk, Jane Therese *probation officer*
Crisp, Coco (Covelli Crisp) *professional baseball player*
Cronin, Bonnie Kathryn Lamb *museum director*
Cronin, Philip Mark *lawyer*
Crowley, William Francis, Jr. *endocrinologist, educator*
Crum, Christopher Paul *pathologist, educator*
Cubell, Howard Alan *lawyer*
Curley, Robert Ambrose, Jr. *lawyer*
Curran, Emily Katherine *museum director*
Curran, Michael J. *stock exchange executive*
Curtin, John Joseph, Jr. *lawyer*
Cutrell, Charles C. III *lawyer*
D'Agostino, Ralph Benedict *mathematician, statistician, educator, consultant*
Daley, George Quentin *hematologist, biomedical research scientist*
Daley, Paul Patrick *lawyer*
Daly, Benedict Dudley Thomas, Jr. *cardiothoracic surgeon, educator*
D'Amico, Anthony Victor *radiation oncologist*
Daniels, Norman *philosopher, educator*
Davis, James S. *lawyer*
Daynard, Richard Alan *law educator*
De Amicis, Don S. *lawyer*
DeBevoise, Charles Henry *lawyer*
de Burlo, Comegys Russell, Jr. *investment company executive, educator, retired treasurer*
Deissler, Mary Alice *foundation executive*
DeJuneas, Patricia Ann *lawyer*
Delaney, John White *lawyer*
Del Bono, Irene Lillian (Irene Stone Guild Del Bono) *lawyer*
Del Sesto, Janice Mancini *opera company executive*
De Luca, Carlo John *biomedical engineer, educator*
Demidov, Vadim V. *biotechnologist, writer*
Demling, Robert Hugh *surgeon, researcher*
Dennis, Kevin M. *lawyer*
Dentler, Robert Arnold *sociologist, educator*
DePaola, Dominick Philip *academic administrator*
DePinho, Ronald *research scientist*
de Rham, Casimir, Jr. *lawyer*
Desai, Tejal Ashwin *biomedical engineer, educator*
DeSanctis, Roman William *cardiologist, educator*
Deshpandé, Rohit *business educator*
Devaney, Robert L. *mathematician, educator*
Devlin, Peter J. *lawyer*
Devlin, Phillip M. *radiologist, medical educator*
Diamandopoulos, Peter *philosophy professor*
Dickie, Robert Benjamin *lawyer, educator*
Di Cola, Joan Barbara *lawyer*
Dienstag, Jules Leonard *dean, hepatologist, researcher*
DiGiustini, Antonetta Anna *educational association administrator, educator*
Dillon, James Joseph *lawyer*
Dineen, John K. *lawyer*
Dluhy, Deborah Haigh *dean*
Dluhy, Robert George *physician*
Doherty, Robert Francis, Jr. *aerospace engineer*
Dolin, Raphael *medical educator*
Domini, Amy Lee *portfolio manager*
Dowd, Peter Jerome *public relations executive*
Draper, Thomas B. *lawyer*
Drazen, Jeffrey Mark *medical educator*
Drew, J.D. *professional baseball player*
Duffy, James Francis III *lawyer*
Duquette, Daniel F. *professional baseball team executive*
Dvorak, Harold Fisher *retired pathologist*
Dwyer, Johanna Todd *nutritionist, educator*
Dyleski-Najjar, Debra *lawyer*
Ebb, Peter L. *lawyer*
Eckstein, Jens W. *venture capitalist, biotechnologist*
Eddleston, Kimberly Ann *management educator*
Edmonds, Dean Stockett, Jr. *physicist, educator, director*
Edwards, Richard Lansing *lawyer*
Efstathiou, Jason Alexander *oncologist, radiologist*
Egbert, Richard Michael *lawyer*
Egdahl, Richard Harrison *surgeon, educator, health science association administrator*
Eisenberg, Leon *psychiatrist, educator*
Elasmar, Michael *director, educator*
El-Baz, Farouk *science administrator, educator*
Elefante, Michael Barrett *lawyer*
El-Erian, Mohamed A. *investment manager*
Elfner, Albert Henry III *retired portfolio manager*
Ellis, Franklin Henry, Jr. *surgeon, educator*
Elrifi, Ivor R. *lawyer*
Emerson, Anne Devereux *museum administrator*
Engel, David Lewis *lawyer*
Englander, John C. *lawyer*
Epler, Gary Robert *physician, author, educator*
Epstein, Arnold M. *medical educator*
Epstein, Franklin Harold *internist, educator*
Epstein, Robert *professional sports team owner, real estate company executive*
Epstein, Theo N. *professional sports team executive*
Erban, John Kalil III *medicine educator, cancer specialist, researcher*
Eskandarian, Edward *advertising executive*
Esper, Susan *diversified financial services company executive*
Essex, Myron Elmer *microbiology and virology educator*
Estes, Nathan Anthony Mark III *cardiologist, medical educator*
Estin, Hans Howard *retired investment company executive*
Eurich, Richard Rex *lawyer*
Everett, Jonathan Jubal *lawyer*
Falb, Peter Lawrence *mathematician, educator, investment company executive*
Farmer, Paul Edward *medical anthropologist*
Farrar, Constance Mosher *marketing executive*
Fay, Michael Leo *lawyer*
Federman, Daniel David *academic administrator, endocrinologist, educator*
Feeherry, Anthony M. *lawyer*
Feeney, Joan N. *judge*
Feeney, Mark *journalist*
Fein, Rashi *health sciences educator*
Felix-Getzik, Erika Michele *pharmacist*
Felter, John Kenneth *lawyer*
Fernandez, Manny (Emmanuel Fernandez-Lemaire) *professional hockey player*
Ferzoco, Stephen John *surgeon*
Fesko, Colleene *art appraiser*
Finegold, Maurice Nathan *architect*
Finn, Terrence M. *lawyer*
Finnegan, Neal Francis *retired banker*
Finucane, Anne M. *communications executive, marketing executive*
Firth, Everett Joseph *timpanist*
Fischer, Eric Robert *lawyer, educator*
Fischer, Mark Alan *lawyer*
Fishman, Robert A. *lawyer*
Fitzgerald, Warren Franklin *lawyer*
Flaherty, Lois Talbot *editor, psychiatrist, educator*
Fletcher, Stephen L. *art appraiser*
Flier, Jeffrey S. *dean, endocrinologist*
Flomenbom, Ophir *biophysicist, researcher*
Floor, Richard Earl *lawyer*
Foer, Jonathan Safran *writer*
Folkman, Moses Judah *surgeon, educator*
Fontanes, A. Alexander *insurance company executive*
Foote, Warren Edgar *neuroscientist, psychologist, educator*
Fortier, Albert Mark, Jr. *lawyer*
Foster, James J(ohn) *lawyer*
Fowler, Floyd Jackson, Jr. *researcher*
Fox, Francis Haney *lawyer*
France, Joseph David *financial analyst*
Francona, Terry Jon *professional baseball manager*
Frank, Richard G. *healthcare educator*
Frank-Kamenetskii, Maxim D. *biomedical engineer*
Frankl, Spencer Nelson *dean, dentist*
Fraser, Donald C. *engineering executive, educator*
Fraser, Robert Burchmore *lawyer*
Freedberg, A. Stone *physician*
Freedman, Joel F. *lawyer*
Frei, Emil III *physician, educator, researcher*
Freishtat, Harvey W. *lawyer*
Friedlander, Robert Max *neurosurgeon*
Friedman, Sandra L. *pediatrician*
Fulchino, Stephen A. *State Librarian*
Gaff, Brian Michael *lawyer*
Gagne, Eric *professional baseball player*
Gaither, Edmund Barry *museum director, curator*
Galvin, William Francis *state official*
Gamst, Frederick Charles *social anthropologist*
Garber, Jeffrey Richard *endocrinologist*
Gardner, Geoff *chef*
Garnett, Kevin *professional basketball player*
Garvin, Michele M. *lawyer*
Gates, Jonathan Dean *surgeon, educator*
Gaudreau, Russell A., Jr. *lawyer, educator*
Gault, Robert Mellor *lawyer*
Gauron, Paul R. *lawyer*
Gawande, Atul A. *surgeon, writer*
Gelb, Richard Mark *lawyer*
Gelfand, Jeffrey Alan *physician, educator*
Gelman, Simon *anesthesiologist, educator*
Gifford, Charles K. *banker*
Gifford, Nelson Sage *finance company executive*
Gilbert, David A. *lawyer*
Gill, Robert Tucker *lawyer*
Gilmore, Maurice Eugene *mathematics professor*
Gimbrone, Michael Anthony, Jr. *research scientist, pathologist, educator*
Giner, A. Silvana *lawyer*
Gipson, Ilene Kay *ophthalmologist, educator*
Giso, Frank III *lawyer*
Glass, Renée *educational health foundation executive*
Glassroth, Jeffrey *internist, educator*
Glazer, Martin A. *lawyer*
Gleason, Daniel J. *lawyer*
Gleason, Jean Berko *psychology professor*
Glimcher, Melvin Jacob *orthopedic surgeon*
Glosband, Daniel Martin *lawyer*
Godine, David Richard *publishing executive*
Golan, David Eric *biophysicist, pharmacologist, hematologist, medical educator*
Goldberg, Irving Hyman *molecular pharmacology and biochemistry educator*
Goldberg, Lena G. *lawyer, investment company executive*
Golden, Daniel *journalist*
Golder, Herbert Alan *classics educator*
Goldie, Sue J. *health service researcher*
Goldman, Eric Scot *lawyer*
Goldman, Richard Harris *lawyer, director*
Goldstein, Jane D. *lawyer*
Goldstein, Nathan *artist, writer*
Gomes, Ryan *professional basketball player*
Gonson, S. Donald *lawyer*
Gonzalez, Juan (Alberto Vazquez) *professional baseball player*
Goodman, Louis Allan *lawyer*
Goody, Joan Edelman *architect*
Gorton, Nathaniel M. *federal judge*
Gossels, Claus Peter Rolf *lawyer*
Gotham, Richard Ernest *professional sports team executive*
Gottlieb, Alice B. *dermatologist*
Gozonsky, Edwin O. O. *investment broker*
Greaney, John M. *state supreme court justice*
Greco, Michael S. *lawyer*
Green, Karen F. *lawyer*
Greenblatt, David J. *pharmacologist*
Greenes, Robert A. *medical educator*
Greer, Allen Curtis, II, *lawyer, investment management executive*
Gregory, Shawn Alen *cardiologist, physician, researcher*
Grice, Noreen Alisa-May *astronomer, educator*
Grillo, Hermes Conrad *surgeon*
Groopman, Jerome *medical educator*
Gross, Ira Kenneth *lawyer*
Grossman, Frances Kaplan *psychologist*
Grundfast, Kenneth Martin *otolaryngologist*
Guertin, Robert Powell *physics professor, dean*
Gura, Kathleen Marie *pediatric pharmacist, educator*
Haddad, Ernest Mudarri *lawyer*
Haddad, Mark E. *lawyer*
Halamka, John D. *emergency physician, information technology executive*
Haldeman, Ed (Charles Edgar Haldeman Jr.) *investment company executive*
Haley, Paul Richard *lawyer, state legislator*
Hall, David *law educator, dean, department chairman*
Hall, Henry Lyon, Jr. *lawyer*
Halpert, David H. *lawyer*
Halston, Daniel William *lawyer*
Halström, Frederic Norman *lawyer*
Hammond, Norman David Curle *archaeology educator, researcher*
Hamrah, Pedram *ophthalmologist, scientist*
Handly, Kevin John *lawyer, educator*
Hanlon, Francis X. *lawyer*
Hardy, Victoria Elizabeth *finance educator*
Harkness, John Cheesman *retired architect*
Harmon, William E. *nephrologist*
Harper, Marvin Bruce *pediatrics educator, hospital administrator*
Harrington, John Michael, Jr. *lawyer*
Harris, Barbara Clementine *bishop*
Harris, Gayle Elizabeth *bishop*
Harris, Mitchel Brion *orthopedist, surgeon*
Harris, Roy Jay, Jr. *editor, business journalist*
Harrison, Stephen Coplan *biochemist, educator*
Hart, John William *theology and ecology educator*
Hartigan, Carol *orthopedist*
Harvey, Christopher P. *lawyer*
Harvey, Kenneth L. *lawyer*
Harvey, Mark Sumner *composer, educator, retired minister, musician*
Haseltine, William Alan *virology educator, former biopharmaceutical company executive*
Hawkey, G. Michael *lawyer, real estate developer*
Hawley, Anne *museum director*
Hay, Elizabeth Dexter *embryologist, educator*
Hayes, Andrew Wallace, II, *consumer products company executive*
Hayes, Robert Francis *lawyer*
Hayes, Robert Herrick *technology management educator*
Hayes, Samuel Linton III *business educator*
Healy, Gerald Burke *otolaryngologist*
Healy, Martin Russell *lawyer*
Hebard, Barbara Adams *conservator*
Hedley-Whyte, John *anesthesiologist, educator*
Hedlund, Ronald David *academic administrator, researcher, educator*
Hehir, J. Bryan *priest, educator, social services administrator*
Heidt, Jeffrey L. *lawyer*
Hendren, William Hardy III *surgeon*
Henry, DeWitt Pawling, II, *literature educator, art association administrator, writer*
Henry, John W. *professional sports team executive*
Herndon, James Henry *orthopedic surgeon, educator*
Hershey, Nona *artist, printmaker, educator*
Herzlinger, Regina *economist, educator, writer*
Hiatt, Howard H. *internist, educator*
Hickey, Elizabeth Louise *advertising agency executive*
Hickey, Paul Robert *anesthesiologist, educator*
Hieken, Charles *lawyer*
Hill, Nicholas S. *physician, researcher*
Hill, Richard Devereux *retired banker*
Hillery, Thomas Hungiville *journalist, financial consultant*
Hills, Patricia Gorton Schulze *curator, art historian*
Hintikka, Jaakko *philosopher, educator*
Hobbs, Gerald S. (Jerry) *private equity firm executive*
Hochedlinger, Konrad *biology professor, biomedical researcher*
Hoffman, Stanley Marc *composer, editor*
Holland, James R. *real estate company officer*
Holt, Sidney Clark *journalist*
Hooley, Joseph (Jay) L. *investment company executive*
Hoort, Steven Thomas *lawyer*
Horan, Douglas S. *lawyer, utilities executive*
Horrigan, Brian Richard *economist*
Hoskins, William Keller *pharmaceutical executive, lawyer, mediator, arbitrator*
Hostetter, Amos Barr, Jr. *cable television executive*
Hotchkiss, Andra Ruth *lawyer*
Howard, Gregory Charles *lawyer*
Howard, Sheryl Andrea *lawyer*
Howe, Janice W. *lawyer*
Howley, Peter Maxwell *pathology educator*
Hoyt, Herbert Austin Aikins *television producer*
Hrones, Stephen Baylis *lawyer, educator*
Hu, Chengcheng *biostatician, medical researcher*
Hua, Nian Grace *mathematician, researcher*
Hubel, David Hunter *physiologist, science educator*
Hudd, Timothy R. *pharmacist, educator*
Hudson, Robert E. *library director*
Hunt, William W. *investment company executive*
Hunter, Durant Adams *executive search company executive*

Hurley, Cornelius Keefe, Jr. *law educator*
husbands, andy *chef*
Huston, Julia *lawyer*
Ingwall, Joanne S. *medical educator*
Ireland, Roderick L. *state supreme court justice*
Ives, J. Atwood *financial executive*
Jacoby, Jeff *journalist, commentator*
Jain, Rakesh K. *chemical engineering and tumor biology educator*
James, Bill *baseball writer, statistician*
Janos, Ellen L. *lawyer*
Jehlen, Patricia D. *state legislator*
Jin, Xuefei (Ha Jin) *literature educator, writer*
Jochum, Veronica *pianist*
Johansen, Erling *retired dental educator, dean*
Johnson, Abigail Pierrepont *investment company executive*
Johnson, Edward Crosby, III, (Ned Johnson) *investment company executive*
Johnston, Richard Alan *lawyer*
Johnston, Susan A. *lawyer*
Jones, Daniel Bougere *surgeon*
Jones, Jeffrey Foster *lawyer*
Jones, Sheldon Atwell *retired lawyer*
Jordan, Alexander Joseph, Jr. *lawyer*
Joyce-Brady, Martin Francis *medical educator*
Julien, Claude *professional hockey coach*
Kahn, Barbara B. *endocrinologist*
Kahn, C. Ronald *research laboratory administrator*
Kalkstein, Joshua Adam *lawyer*
Kang, Jing X. *medical researcher, educator*
Kanin, Dennis Roy *lawyer*
Kantoff, Philip W. *oncologist*
Kaplan, Marshall Myles *medical educator, researcher, gastroenterologist*
Kaplan, Robert S. *business educator, former investment banker*
Karelitz, Robert N(elson) *lawyer*
Karnovsky, Morris John *pathologist, biologist*
Kassirer, Jerome Paul *medical educator*
Katsoulomitis, Georgia *foundation administrator, lawyer*
Katz, Peter *lawyer*
Katzman, Lauren I. *special education educator, consultant*
Katzmann, Gary Stephen *judge*
Kaufmann, Patrick J. *business educator*
Kazemi, Homayoun *internist, educator*
Kearns, Ellen Cecelia *lawyer*
Keating, Michael Burns *lawyer, educator*
Kee, Chea-su *optometrist, educator*
Kehoe, William Francis *lawyer*
Keller, Stanley *lawyer*
Kelly, Edmund Francis *insurance company executive*
Kelly, Francis J. III *global marketing company executive*
Kennedy, Joseph Patrick, II, *utilities executive, former congressman*
Kerry, Cameron F. *lawyer*
Kesari, Santosh *neurologist, oncologist, neuroscientist*
Kessel, Phil *professional hockey player*
Kessler, Diane Cooksey *religious organization administrator, minister*
Khalsa, Sat Bir Singh *biomedical researcher*
Khosla, Anil *lawyer*
Kiang, Nelson Yuan-sheng *medical educator*
Kidder, George Howell *lawyer*
Kieff, Elliott Dan *medical educator*
Kim, David Hanwuk *surgeon, orthopedist, researcher*
Kim, Dong H. *neurosurgeon, medical geneticist, educator*
Kim, Ducksoo *radiologist, inventor, educator*
Kindregan, Charles Peter *law educator*
Kircher, Moritz Florian *radiologist, researcher*
Kirchick, William Dean *lawyer*
Kirkpatrick, Edward Thomson *retired academic administrator, mechanical engineer*
Kirsch, Robert L. *lawyer*
Kitz, Richard John *anesthesiologist, educator*
Klarfeld, Jonathan Michael *journalism educator*
Klein, Bennett *lawyer*
Kleiner, Fred Scott *art historian, archaeologist, educator, editor*
Klem, Christopher A. *lawyer*
Klema, Donald David *architect*
Klieman, Rikki Jo *lawyer, legal analyst*
Klotz, Charles Rodger *water transportation and investment company executive*
Knag, Paul Everett *lawyer*
Knight, Norman *volunteer, retired broadcast executive*
Kocher, Mininder Singh *pediatric orthopaedic surgeon, epidemiologist*
Kociubes, Joseph Leib *lawyer*
Koh, Howard Kyongju *academic administrator, educator, former public health commissioner*
Komaroff, Anthony Leader *physician*
Kopelman, Leonard *lawyer*
Kornberg, Sir Hans Leo *biochemist, educator*
Krane, Stephen Martin *rheumatologist, educator*
Kressel, Herbert Yehude *medical educator*
Kumar, Vikram Sheel *information technology executive*
Kuo, Winston Patrick *pediatric and oral medicine dentist, biomedical researcher*
Kuttner, Robert Louis *editor, writer, columnist*
Lahiri, Jhumpa (Nilanjana Sudeshna) *writer*
Lamont, John Thomas *gastroenterologist, educator*
Lampert, James B. *lawyer*
Landsmark, Ted (Theodore C. Landsmark) *academic administrator*
Lane, Kathy S. *information technology executive, consumer products company executive*
Lang, Laura W. *marketing executive*
Lange, Harry W. *investment company executive*
Langer, Robert Martin *retired chemical engineering company executive, consultant*
Langwell, Dennis J. *insurance company executive*
Larkin, Michael John *editor, journalist*
Lasker, Morris E. *judge*
Last, Michael P. *lawyer*
Lataif, Louis Edward *dean*
Laufer, Marc R. *gynecologist*
Lawrence, Merloyd Ludington *editor*
Lawrence, Paul Roger *retired psychology professor*
Lawson, Rodger A. *diversified financial services company executive*
Lazar, Harold Lee *cardiothoracic surgeon*
Leahy, John L. *software development company executive*
Leaman, J. Richard, Jr. *paper company executive*
LeBlanc, Marianne Camille *lawyer*
Lee, Charles *cytologist*
Lee, David Stoddart *retired investment company executive*
Lee, Donald Young (Don Lee) *publishing executive*
Lee, Thomas Henry *internist, cardiologist, healthcare executive*
Lee, William F. *lawyer*
Leland, Timothy *retired newspaper executive*
Lepore, Ralph Thomas III *lawyer*
Le Quesne, Philip William *chemistry educator, researcher*
Lesser, Laurence *musician, educator*
Lettieri, Richard J. (Richard Joseph Lettieri) *lawyer*
Levine, Robert A. *cardiologist*
Levine, William Michael *lawyer*
Levy, Stephen Raymond *retired data processing executive*
Levy, Stuart B. *molecular biologist, educator, science administrator, researcher*
Liangos, Orfeas *nephrologist, researcher*
Licata, Arthur Frank *lawyer*
Lieberman, Michael J. *lawyer*
Lin, Lihui *business educator*
Linde, Edward H. *real estate manager*
Lindsay, Reginald Carl *judge*
Ling, Pei-Ra *medical educator*
Liotta, Jeanne *film director, educator*
Lisbon, Alan *anesthesiologist, critical care physician*
Little, John Bertram *radiologist, educator, researcher*
Litwin, Paul Jeffrey *lawyer*
Liu, Ta-Chiang *research scientist, physician, consultant*
Livingston, David Morse *internist, biomedical researcher*
Livingston, Frederic Holleyman *mechanical engineer*
Lockhart, Keith Alan *conductor, music director*
Loder, John Mark *lawyer*
Lodge, George C(abot) *business administration educator*
Loeser, Hans Ferdinand *lawyer*
Loewenstein, Andrew B. *lawyer*
Logue, Ronald E. *investment company executive*
Looney, William Francis, Jr. *lawyer*
Loretta, Mark *professional baseball player*
Loria, Martin A. *lawyer*
Loscalzo, Joseph *cardiologist, biochemist*
Loth, Renée *editor*
Lovejoy, George Montgomery, Jr. *real estate company executive*
Lowell, Mike *professional baseball player*
Lowell, Richard Lee *music educator, musician*
Lowenstein, Arlene Jane *nursing educator, health facility administrator*
Lowry, Lois (Lois Hammersberg) *writer*
Lucchino, Lawrence *sports team executive, lawyer*
Ludwig, David S. *endocrinologist*
Lundgren, Lena Margareta *social sciences educator, researcher*
Lundgren, Richard John *real estate executive, city planner, preservationist*
Luongo, C. Paul *public relations executive*
Lynch, Barbara *chef, restaurant owner*
Lynch, Sandra Lea *federal judge*
Lyons, David Barry *philosophy and law educator*
Lyons, Paul Vincent *lawyer*
Macauley, William Francis *lawyer*
MacCombie, Bruce Franklin *composer, college administrator*
Macdonald, Peter J. *lawyer*
MacLeish, Roderick, Jr. *lawyer*
Maffeo, Pino *chef*
Magadan, David Joseph *retired professional baseball player*
Maganzini, Brother John Bernard *academic administrator*
Maisel, William Howard *cardiologist, internist*
Maister, David Hilton *consultant*
Malenka, Bertram Julian *physicist, researcher*
Malt, Ronald Bradford *lawyer*
Mandell, James *health facility executive, urologist, educator*
Mannick, John Anthony *surgeon*
Manning, Peter Kirby *criminal justice educator*
Mansfield, Christopher Charles *lawyer*
Manson, JoAnn Elisabeth *endocrinologist*
Marcus, Karen Jean *medical educator*
Marett, Louis J. *lawyer*
Margolis, Bernard Allen *library administrator*
Markey, John K. *lawyer*
Markham, Jesse William *economist, educator*
Marsh, Milton R.W. *composer*
Marshall, Margaret Hilary *state supreme court chief justice*
Marshall, Martin Vivan *business administration educator, consultant*
Martin, Gina Lynn *lawyer*
Martin, Joseph Boyd *neurologist, educator, retired dean*
Martin, Stanley Allen *lawyer*
Masi, Dale A. *project director, social sciences educator, research and development company executive*
Mason, Herbert Warren, Jr. *religion and history educator, author*
Mathisen, Douglas J. *thoracic surgeon*
Matsuzaka, Daisuke *professional baseball player*
Matthews, Roger Hardin *lawyer*
Matuschak, Mark G. *lawyer*
Maxwell, J. B. *financial, marketing professional, consultant*
May, James Warren, Jr. *plastic surgeon, medical association executive*
May, Thomas J. *electric company executive*
Mayer, William P. *lawyer*
Mayers, David *political science professor, department chairman, history professor*
McArthur, John Hector *business educator*
McAuliffe, Rosemary *lawyer*
Mc Carthy, Joseph Michael *historian, educator*
McChesney, S. Elaine *lawyer*
McClelland, Frank *chef, restaurant owner*
McCormick, Marie Clare *pediatrician, educator*
McCraw, Thomas Kincaid *business history educator emeritus, editor, writer*
McDougal, William Scott *urology educator*
McFarlan, Franklin Warren *business administration educator*
McGovern, Lore Harp *communications executive, philanthropist*
McGovern, Patrick J. *communications executive*
McKenzie, Elizabeth McDaniel *law librarian*
McNeil, Barbara Joyce *radiologist, educator*
McPhee, Joan *lawyer*
McPhee, Jonathan *music director, conductor, composer, interim artistic coordinator*
Meal, Douglas H. *lawyer*
Mehra, Pushkar *director, educator*
Meisner, Mary Jo *foundation administrator, former newspaper editor*
Meissner, Walt *dean*
Menino, Thomas M. *mayor*
Menna, Gilbert G. *lawyer*
Menoyo, Eric Felix *lawyer*
Merk, Frederick Bannister *biomedical educator, researcher*
Merrill, John *chef*
Merrill, Stephen *lawyer, consultant, retired governor*
Merton, Robert C. *economist, educator*
Meserve, William George *lawyer*
Meyer, Andrew C., Jr. *lawyer*
Meyer, Jack Edward *radiologist, educator*
Meyerhardt, Jeffrey Abraham *internist, oncologist*
Miaoulis, Ioannis Nikolaos *mechanical engineer, educator*
Mifflin, Jeffrey Allen *archivist, consultant, historian, researcher*
Mihm, Martin Charles, Jr. *pathologist, educator*
Mikels, Richard Eliot *lawyer*
Miller, Bill (William H. Miller III) *diversified financial services company executive*
Miller, Candace Marie *healthcare educator*
Miller, Michelle D. *lawyer*
Miller, Peter M. *lawyer*
Milstein, Richard Sherman *lawyer*
Milunsky, Aubrey *geneticist, pediatrician, educator*
Miner, Tracy A. *lawyer*
Minot, Winthrop Gardner *lawyer*
Mirabito, Anthony Jason *lawyer, educator*
Miron, Alexander *research scientist*
Mitchell, Jon Ceander *music educator, conductor*
Moellering, Robert Charles, Jr. *internist, educator*
Moffitt, Brenda A. *lawyer*
Moncreiff, Robert P. *lawyer*
Mone, Michael Edward *lawyer*
Mongan, James John *healthcare system administrator*
Montgomery, John T. *lawyer*
Montgomery, Susan Barbieri *lawyer*
Mooney, Michael Edward *lawyer*
Moore, Gregory E. *lawyer*
Moore, Richard Lawrence *structural engineer, consultant*
Moorman, Donald Wayne *surgeon, healthcare administrator*
Morgan, James Philip *pharmacology and cardiology educator*
Moriarty, George Marshall *lawyer*
Moriarty, John *opera administrator, artistic director*
Morris, Robert *education educator*
Morton, Edward James *insurance company executive*
Moss, Alan C. *physician, researcher*
Motenko, Neil Philip *lawyer*
Muldoon, Robert Joseph, Jr. *lawyer*
Murley, Susan W. *lawyer*
Myers, Jeff L. *surgeon*
Myers, Richard Hepworth *medical geneticist, educator*
Nadelson, Carol Cooperman *psychiatrist, educator*
Nagle, James W. *lawyer*
Naimi, Shapur *cardiologist, educator*
Nason, Leonard Yoshimoto *lawyer, writer*
Nathan, David Gordon *pediatrician, educator*
Nelson, Patricia L. *lawyer*
Newberg, Joseph H. *lawyer*
Newhouse, Joseph Paul *economist, educator*
Nielsen, Mark D. *former state legislator*
Nissinen, Mikko Pekka *dancer, performing arts company executive, artistic director*
Noel, Alfred *mathematics professor*
Nold, Carl Richard *museum administrator*
Norris, Lonnie Harold *dean*
Notopoulos, Alexander Anastasios, Jr. *lawyer*
Novack, Kenneth Joseph *lawyer*
Nunnally, Allen C. *lawyer*
Nunnelly, Mark Edward *investor*
Nutt, Robert L. *lawyer, educator*
Oates, William Armstrong, Jr. *investment company executive*
O'Brien, J(ohn) Patrick *psychiatrist, educator*
O'Connell, Mary-Kathleen *lawyer*
O'Connor, Francis Patrick *former state supreme court justice*
O'Donnell, Thomas Lawrence Patrick *lawyer*
Odze, Robert D. *pathologist*
O'Hern, Jane Susan *psychologist, educator*
O'Leary, Joseph Evans *lawyer*
Olsen, Hans Peter *lawyer*
Olubodun, Joel Oladapo *medical researcher, physician*
O'Neill, Philip Daniel, Jr. *lawyer, educator*
O'Reilly, William R., Jr. *lawyer*
Oringer, Kenneth *chef, restaurant owner*
O'Rourke, Maureen A. *dean, law educator*
Ortiz, David (David Americo Ortiz Arias) *professional baseball player*
O'Toole, George A., Jr. *judge*
Pagliuca, Stephen *professional sports team owner, investment company officer*
Paine, William H. *lawyer*
Pallotta, Johanna Antonia (Johanna Stephen) *endocrinologist, educator*
Palmer, David Scott *political scientist, educator*
Papelbon, Jon (Jonathan R. Papelbon) *professional baseball player*
Papisov, Mikhail I. *chemist*
Pappalardo, A. John *former prosecutor, lawyer*
Pappone, Michael J. *lawyer*
Parad, Richard Barry *pediatrician, researcher*
Pardee, Arthur Beck *biochemist, educator*
Park, William H(erron) *finance company executive*
Park, William Wynnewood *law educator*
Parker, Olivia *photographer*
Partan, Daniel Gordon *lawyer, educator*
Patrick, Deval Laurdine *governor, lawyer*
Patterson, John de la Roche, Jr. *lawyer*
Paul, Oglesby *cardiologist, educator*
Pearce, Elizabeth Niewoehner *endocrinologist, researcher*
Peckham, John Munroe III *investment executive, author, lecturer*
Peckham, Thomas Elwood *lawyer*
Penney, Sherry Hood *academic administrator, consultant*
Pereira, Julio Cesar *middle school educator*
Perera, Lawrence Thacher *lawyer*
Perkins, John Allen *lawyer*
Phelan, David C. *lawyer*
Picker, Sebastián *artist*
Pierce, Allan Dale *engineering educator, researcher, editor*
Pierce, Paul Anthony *professional basketball player*
Pisani, Anthony Michael *architect*
Pitts, James Atwater *finance company executive*
Pline, Jennifer Alice *trust company executive*
Plotkin, Irving H. (Irving Herman Plotkin) *economist, consultant*
Pochi, Peter Ernest *physician*
Pokross, David R., Jr. *lawyer*
Polebaum, Mark Neal *lawyer*
Pomeroy, Robert Corttis *lawyer*
Ponce de Leon, Monica *architect*
Popeo, R. Robert *lawyer*
Porcelli, Frank Paul *lawyer*
Porter, Jeffrey R. *lawyer*
Porter, Michael E. *competitive strategy educator*
Poss, Stephen Daniel *lawyer*
Poussaint, Alvin Francis *psychiatrist, educator*
Pozen, Robert Charles *investment company executive*
Preston, Jerome, Jr. *retired lawyer*
Price, Michael Witwer *art gallery owner, lawyer*
Price, Robert F. *lawyer*
Price, Steven *venture capitalist, communications executive, lawyer*
Properzio, Paul J. *classicist, educator*
Purcell, Patrick Joseph *newspaper publisher*
Putnam, Thomas J. *library director*
Pytka, Stephen Milton *office equipment executive*
Quayle, Dwight W. *lawyer*
Quick, Jonathan Dickinson *health organization executive*
Quinan, Deborah Pechet *lawyer*
Ra'anan, Uri (Heinz Felix Frischwasser) *international politics educator*
Rabkin, Mitchell Thornton *physician, educator, hospital administrator*
Radloff, Robert Albert *real estate company executive*
Raish, David Langdon *lawyer*
Ramirez, Manny (Manuel Aristides Ramirez) *professional baseball player*
Rao, Anjana *immunologist, educator*
Rapoport, Tom Abraham *cell biology professor*
Rattner, David W. *surgeon*
Rawn, William Leete III *architect*
Reardon, Frank Emond *lawyer*
Redlich, Marc *lawyer*
Reede, Joan Yvonne *academic administrator, medical educator, pediatrician*
Reese, C. Richard *data processing executive*
Reinherz, Helen Zarsky *social worker, researcher*
Reitnauer, Andrew Richard *forensic specialist*
Relman, Arnold Seymour *physician, editor, educator*
Ren, Jian-Guo *cell biologist, researcher*
Renehan, Richard William *lawyer*
Reppert, Sibley Putnam *lawyer*
Reppert, Steven Marion *pediatrician, research scientist, educator*
Resch, Edward J. *investment company executive*
Richie, Jerome Paul *surgeon, educator*
Richmond, Alice Elenor *lawyer*
Ridker, Paul M. *cardiologist, medical educator*
Rimpel, Auguste Eugene, Jr. *management and technical consulting executive*
Rines, Robert Harvey *lawyer, educator, physicist, composer*
Ritt, Roger Merrill *lawyer*
Rivers, Doc (Glenn Anton Rivers) *professional basketball coach*
Robinson, Andrea J. *lawyer*
Robinson, Jeri *museum program director*
Rochinski, Stephen James *musician, educator*
Rockoff, Mark Alan *pediatric anesthesiologist*
Rogeness, Mary Speer *state legislator*
Rogers, Gary Francis *plastic surgeon*
Rogers, Malcolm Austin *museum director, art historian*
Rohrer, Richard Jeffrey *surgeon, educator*
Romney, (Willard) Mitt *former governor*
Ronayne, Michael Richard, Jr. *academic dean*

Rondeau, Patrick John *lawyer*
Ropple, Lisa M. *lawyer*
Rosen, Stanley Howard *humanities educator*
Rosenbaum, Jay D. *lawyer*
Rosenberg, Peter N. *lawyer*
Rosenblatt, Michael *internist, academic administrator, educator, researcher*
Rosenblum, Peter M. *lawyer*
Rosenfeld, Jonathan D. *lawyer*
Rosengren, Eric S. *bank executive*
Ross, Nelson G. *lawyer*
Rossman, Stuart T. *lawyer*
Roth, Sanford Irwin *pathologist, educator*
Rothberg, Robert *lawyer*
Rowe, Larry Jordan *lawyer*
Rubin, Iris Kedar *dermatologist*
Rudavsky, Dahlia C. *lawyer*
Rudman, Jeffrey B. *lawyer*
Rudolph, James Leonard *lawyer*
Russell, Paul Snowden *surgeon, educator*
Rutkove, Seward Brian *neurologist, educator, neuroscientist*
Ryan, Allan Andrew, Jr. *lawyer, director, educator, writer*
Ryan, Sean T. *lawyer*
Ryan, Thomas John *cardiologist*
Sachdeo, Amit *dentist, researcher*
Sachs, David Howard *surgeon, immunologist, educator*
Sadeghi-Nejad, Abdollah *pediatrician, educator*
Sahney, Vinod K. *health care executive*
Salinger, Michael Alvin *economist, educator*
Sallan, Stephen E. *pediatrician*
Saloman, Syd Adam *lawyer*
Sander, Alison Bishop *international consultant*
Saper, Clifford Baird *neurology educator*
Sargeant, Ernest James *lawyer, educator*
Sartory, Thomas J. *lawyer*
Saunders, Donald Leslie *hotel executive, real estate developer*
Sawyer, William C. *lawyer*
Say, Allen *writer, illustrator*
Scadden, David Thomas *hematologist, oncologist, research scientist*
Scanlon, Dorothy Therese *history professor*
Schaller, Jane Green *pediatrician*
Scherkenbach, Frank Everett *lawyer*
Schilling, Curtis Montague *professional baseball player*
Schlosser, Eric *writer*
Schlossman, Stuart Franklin *physician, educator, researcher*
Schlow, Michael *food service executive*
Schneider, Eric C. *medical educator, physician*
Schoenfeld, David Alan *statistician, educator*
Schulz, John Joseph *communications educator*
Schwartz, Eric Lee *neuroscientist, educator*
Schwartz, Lloyd *music critic, poet*
Schwartz, Paul D. *lawyer*
Scott, James Arthur *radiologist, educator*
Scrimshaw, Susan Crosby *academic administrator*
Sears, John Winthrop *lawyer*
Seddon, Johanna Margaret *ophthalmologist, epidemiologist*
Seglin, Jeffrey L. *columnist, educator*
Seidman, Christine E. *medical educator*
Seidman, Jonathan G. *geneticist, educator*
Selkoe, Dennis Jesse *neurologist, researcher, educator*
Sellke, Frank William *cardiothoracic surgeon, researcher*
Seshadri, Sudha *neurologist, educator*
Shabestari, Khosrow Toutounchi (T. Shabestari) *research scientist*
Shapiro, Eli *business consultant, educator, economist*
Shapiro, Robert N. *lawyer*
Shapiro, Sandra *lawyer*
Sharma, Raj *financial consultant*
Shattuck, John *diplomat, civil rights lawyer, educator*
Shearer, Harry Julius *scriptwriter, actor, television director*
Sheehan, Gregory D. *lawyer*
Shemin, Barry L. *actuary*
Sherman, Robert Alan *lawyer*
Shields, Lawrence Thornton *orthopaedic surgeon, educator*
Shilepsky, Nancy Sue *lawyer*
Shin, Sunny Hyucksun *social worker, educator*
Shore, Miles Frederick *psychiatrist, educator*
Shtern, Victor *computer scientist, educator*
Shulkin, Martin B. *lawyer*
Sidman, Richard Leon *neuroscientist, educator*
Sigel, John D. *lawyer*
Silber, John Robert *retired academic administrator, law and philosophy educator*
Simmons, Sylvia Jeanne Quarles (Mrs. Herbert G. Simmons Jr.) *academic administrator, educator*
Simone, Renata *television producer*
Simpson, Bennett *art critic, art museum curator*
Sinden, Harry *professional sports team executive*
Singer, Steven D. *lawyer*
Singh, Reshmi L. *medical educator*
Sinnott, William F. *lawyer*
Sirkin, Joel H. *lawyer*
Slack, Warner Vincent *medical educator, researcher*
Slavin, Peter L. *hospital administrator*
Sloan, Katherine (Kay Sloan) *college president*
Sloan, Steven Richard *medical educator, director*
Sloane, Carl Stuart *corporate executive, educator, management consultant*
Small, Donald MacFarland *biophysics professor, gastroenterologist, department chairman, researcher*
Smith, Craig R. *lawyer*
Smith, Edwin Eric *lawyer*
Smith, Philip Jones *lawyer*
Snydman, David Richard *infectious diseases specialist, educator*
Sodroski, Joseph G. *medical educator*
Solet, Maxwell David *lawyer*
Sonnenschein, David *music educator, composer, conductor*
Soule, Robert Grove *lawyer*
Southard, William G. *lawyer*
Southgate, Richard W. *lawyer, director*
Sparrow, Joshua D. *child psychiatrist*
Speer, Brownlow Main *lawyer*
Speizer, Frank E. *physician, researcher*
Spellman, Mitchell Wright *surgeon, academic administrator, educator*
Sperling, Reisa A. *neurologist, researcher*
Spiegel, Joan Elizabeth *anesthesiologist, educator*
Spieler, Emily A. *dean, law educator*
Spina, Francis X. *state supreme court justice*
Springer, Timothy Alan *health researcher, immunology educator*
Stachel, John Jay *physicist, researcher*
Stahl, Norman H. *judge*
Stair, Thomas Osborne *physician, educator*
Stallman, Richard Matthew *software developer*
Stampfer, Meir Jonathan *epidemiologist, nutritionist, educator*
Stanley, Harry Eugene *physicist, researcher*
Stearns, Richard Gaylore *judge*
Steere, Allen Caruthers, Jr. *physician, educator*
Steinberg, Donald R. *lawyer*
Steinberg, Laura *lawyer*
Stern, Donald Kenneth *lawyer*
Stevenson, Howard Higginbotham *business educator*
Stewart, Craig E. *lawyer*
Stewart, Elizabeth AnNella *gynecologist, researcher*
Stillwell, R. Newcomb *lawyer*
Stobaugh, Robert Blair *oil industry executive*
Stokes, James Christopher *lawyer*
Stollar, Bernard David *biochemist, educator*
Storey, James Moorfield *lawyer*
Stossel, Thomas Peter *medical educator, researcher, director*
Strahler, Alan H. *geography educator, researcher, writer*
Street, Tison *music educator*
Strominger, Jack Leonard *biochemist*
Strothman, Wendy Jo *literary agent*
Stull, Donald LeRoy *architect*
Sugarman, Paul Ronald *lawyer, educator, academic administrator*
Suh, Wonsuk Warren *radiation oncologist*
Suit, Herman Day *radiation oncologist, medical educator*
Sullivan, Michael J. *prosecutor*
Sullivan, Patricia Eileen *physical therapist, educator*
Sullivan Stemberg, Maureen *interior designer*
Sunstein, Bruce David *lawyer*
Surkin, Elliot Mark *lawyer*
Surman, Owen Stanley *psychiatrist*
Swaim, C. Hall *lawyer*
Swain, Scott D. *finance educator, researcher*
Swartz, Morton Norman *medical educator*
Swope, Jeffrey Peyton *lawyer*
Sykes, Megan *immunologist*
Szczerbiak, Wally *professional basketball player*
Szostak, Jack William *molecular biologist, educator*
Tabin, Clifford S. *geneticist, educator*
Talarek, Nicolas *geneticist, researcher*
Tammaro, Kelly Ann *pharmacist, researcher*
Tappé, Albert Anthony *architect*
Tarantino, Louis Gerald *lawyer, management consultant*
Taubman, Martin Arnold *immunologist, educator*
Tauro, Joseph Louis *federal judge*
Tavakkolizadeh, Ali *surgeon*
Taylor, Jeff *Internet company executive*
Taylor, Thomas William *lawyer*
Tehrani, Nader *architect*
Teich, Malvin Carl *electrical engineering educator*
Telegen, Arthur G. *lawyer*
Terrill, Ross Gladwin *writer, educator*
Theoharides, Theoharis Constantin *pharmacologist, physician, educator*
Thibault, George Edwin *medical educator, non-profit healthcare organization administrator*
Tilly, Jonathan L. *obstetrician, gynecologist, reproductive biologist*
Tompkins, Ronald Gary *surgeon, educator, biomedical investigator*
Torruella, Juan R. *federal judge*
Tosteson, Daniel Charles *physiologist, medical school dean emeritus*
Touster, Saul *law educator*
Towers, John R. *manufacturing executive, lawyer*
Trackman, Philip Charles *biochemist, researcher*
Trafidlo, James Francis *marketing communications executive, commercial photographer*
Treves, S. Ted *nuclear medicine physician, educator, hospital administrator*
Trichopoulos, Dimitrios Vassilios *epidemiologist, educator*
Trier, Jerry Steven *gastroenterologist, educator*
Trimmier, Roscoe, Jr. *lawyer*
Trinkaus-Randall, Gregor *librarian, archivist, preservation administrator*
Tromanhauser, Scott Glenn *orthopaedic surgeon*
Troupe, William Harold *lawyer*
Trumbull, David Lewis Kitchen *trade association executive*
Tse, Marian A. *lawyer*
Tuchmann, Robert *lawyer*
Tullis, Gregory Earl *research scientist*
Twombly, Stephen Doane *magazine publisher*
Tyson, Peter *editor-in-chief*
Vacanti, Joseph Philip *pediatric and transplant surgeon*
Valverde, Paloma *biochemist, educator*
Van Allsburg, Chris *writer, artist*
Van Faasen, William C. *health insurance company executive*
Varitek, Jason *professional baseball player*
Vaughan, Herbert Wiley *retired lawyer*
Vermeule, Cornelius Clarkson III *museum curator*
Vermilye, Peter Hoagland *banker*
Vigoda, Robert A. *lawyer*
Vila, Robert Joseph *television personality, real estate developer, space designer*
Vodo, Plarenta *physicist, researcher*
Vollmer, Charles Mahlon, Jr. *surgeon*
von Stackelberg, Katherine Ellen *environmental scientist, consultant*
Voss, Peter S. *investment company executive*
Waite, Charles Prescott *entrepreneur*
Wakefield, Timothy Stephen (Tim Wakefield) *professional baseball player*
Waldinger, Robert Jon *psychiatrist*
Walek, David B. *lawyer*
Walrath, Patricia A. *state legislator*
Walsh, Joseph Hayes *lawyer*
Walz, Thomas *biology professor*
Wang, Zhi *biomedical researcher*
Ward, Aaron *professional hockey player*
Ward, Wayne Conrad *music educator, conductor*
Ware, Donald R. *lawyer*
Ware, Paul F., Jr. *lawyer*
Warro, Edward A. *library director, dean*
Warshaw, Andrew Louis *surgeon, researcher*
Warshaw, Dalit Hadass *composer, educator*
Watanabe, Mark David *pharmacist, educator*
Watkins, Leroy J. III *entrepreneur*
Weinberg, Martin Gary *lawyer*
Weiner, Stephen Mark *lawyer*
Weisner, David *illustrator*
Weiss, Earle Burton *physician*
Weitzel, John Patterson *lawyer*
Wellington, Carol Strong *law librarian*
Wendorf, Richard Harold *library director, educator*
Wermuth, Paul Charles *retired language educator*
Westcott, John McMahon, Jr. *lawyer*
Westra, James R. *lawyer*
Weyman, Jerzy Maria *mathematics professor*
Wheeler, W(illiam) Scott *composer, conductor, music educator*
White, Augustus Aaron III *orthopaedic surgeon*
White, Barry Bennett *lawyer*
White, Dennis J. *lawyer*
White-Lief, David Westcott *lawyer*
Whitlock, John L. *lawyer*
Whittemore, Anthony Dunster *vascular surgeon, chief medical officer*
Whitters, James Payton III *lawyer, educator*
Wiesel, Elie *writer, educator*
Wiesner, David *illustrator, children's writer*
Wigglesworth, Margaret *real estate company executive*
Wilcox, Steven Alan *lawyer*
Williams, Brown F *media specialist, consultant*
Williams, John Taylor *lawyer*
Williams, John Towner *composer, conductor*
Wirth, Dyann Fergus *public health educator, microbiologist*
Wolf, Alice Koerner *state legislator, former mayor*
Woo, Sook-Bin *dentist, educator*
Woodburn, Ralph Robert, Jr. *lawyer*
Wu, Julian K. *neurosurgeon*
Wu, Tung *curator, artist, art historian, educator*
Wyszynski, Diego Federico *epidemiologist, educator*
Yaroslavsky, Anna *biophysicist, educator*
Yeager, Peter Cleary *sociologist, educator*
Yoshida, Hiroyuki *mathematician, computer scientist, educator, medical science educator*
Young, Anne B. *neurologist, educator*
Young, David William *retired management educator*
Young, Laura *choreographer, educator*
Young, Raymond Henry *lawyer*
Young, William Glover *federal judge*
Yuan, Junying *medical educator, researcher*
Zack, Arnold Marshall *lawyer, mediator, arbitrator, judge*
Zaleznik, Abraham *psychoanalyst, management specialist, educator*
Zannieri, Nina *museum director*
Zelnick, Carl Robert *writer, educator*
Zhukovsky, Mikhail Andreyevich *biophysicist*
Zobel, Rya Weickert *federal judge*
Zon, Leonard I. *pediatrics educator, researcher*
Zungolo, Eileen H. *dean*

Bourne
Fantozzi, Peggy Ryone *geologist, environmental planner*

Boxboro
Parmese, Gabriel J. *corporate financial executive*

Boxford
Siegert, Barbara (Barbara Marie Siegert) *health care administrator*

Boylston
Hanshaw, James Barry *pediatrician, educator*
Larson, Roland Elmer *health facility administrator*
Schofield, Edmund Acton, Jr. *botanist, academic administrator, conservationist, writer*

Braintree
Driscoll, Megan *executive recruiter*
Hallenbeck, Rachel Kirsten *music educator, director*
Malloy, Ellen Ann *athletic trainer*
Riccio, Frank Joseph *lawyer, educator*
Watts, Kisha Mann *school system administrator, secondary school educator*

Bridgewater
Heffernan, Peter John *state official*
Kostka, Robert Raymond *social studies educator, department chairman*
Tinsley, Adrian *former college president*

Brighton
Becton, Henry Prentiss, Jr. *broadcast executive*
Garber, Paul William *lawyer*
Holley, Michael *sportswriter, sportscaster*
O'Malley, Sean Patrick Cardinal *Archbishop of Boston, cardinal*
Valianti, Deborah L. *playwright*
Woodall, Bridgette A. *archivist*

Brockton
Carlson, Desiree Anice *pathologist*
Moore, Mary Johnson *retired community health nurse*

Brookfield
Anderson, Theodore Robert *physicist, small business owner*
Couture, Ronald David *art association administrator, web site designer, consultant*

Brookline
Alarcon, Rogelio Alfonso *retired internist, retired researcher*
Barron, Ros *artist*
Bourne, Katherine Day *journalist, educator*
Brenner, Robin E. *librarian*
Buchin, Jacqueline Chase *psychologist*
Cromwell, Adelaide M. *sociology educator*
Frankel, Ernst Gabriel *shipping and aviation business executive, educator*
Goldsmith, Gary Norman *psychiatrist, psychoanalyst*
Hyman, Albert Lewis *cardiologist, educator*
Jakab, Irene *psychiatrist*
Kawada, Janet Hansen *artist, educator*
Michopoulos, Aristotle V. *humanities educator, researcher*
Moon, John Ellis van Courtland *retired historian*
Nash, Leonard Kollender *retired chemistry professor*
Reedy, Harry Lee *financial services executive*
Rubin-Katz, Barbara *sculptor, human services manager*
Schwartz, Bernard *physician*
Swirnoff, Lois *artist, educator*
Tyler, H. Richard *physician*

Burlington
Angle, Colin *electrical engineer, robotic company executive*
Berkoben, John Perri *physician*
Cerveny, David John *lawyer*
Choi, In-Sup *radiologist*
Clerkin, Eugene Patrick *physician, educator*
Cosgrove, Garth Rees *neurosurgeon*
Dyer, Joseph Wendell *retired naval officer*
Freidberg, Stephen Roy *neurosurgeon*
Greiner, Helen *mechanical engineer*
Hurd, Joseph Kindall, Jr. *obstetrician, gynecologist*
Jones, Harvey Royden, Jr. *neurologist*
Maiti, Amitesh *physicist*
Moschella, Samuel L. *dermatology educator*
Oberfield, Richard Alan *oncologist*
Rhee, Sokwoo *mechanical engineer*
Schoetz, David John, Jr. *colon and rectal surgeon, educator*
Seckel, Brooke Rutledge *plastic surgeon*
Sproull, Robert Fletcher *research and development company executive*
Thayer, Stacy E. *research scientist*

Byfield
Doggett, John Martin, Jr., (Marty Doggett) *headmaster*
Kozol, Jonathan *writer*

Cambridge
Abernathy, Frederick Henry *mechanical engineering educator*
Acemoglu, Daron (K. Daron Acemoglu) *economics professor*
Ackerman, James *fine arts educator*
Adams, Charles Gilchrist *theology studies educator, pastor*
Adams, Jody *chef, restaurant owner*
Adelson, Edward H. *vision science educator*
Alberty, Robert Arnold *chemistry professor*
Alcalay, Albert S. *artist, design educator*
Alcock, Charles Roger *science educator*
Alesina, Alberto *economist, educator*
Alexander, Seth *investment company executive*
Alexander, Susan H. *lawyer, pharmaceutical executive*
Allaire, Jeremy *Internet company executive*
Allen, Thomas John *business educator*
Allison, Graham Tillett, Jr. *political science professor, former federal agency administrator*
Alt, James Edward *political science professor*
Anderson, James Gilbert *chemistry professor*
Anderson, Stanford Owen *architect, architectural historian, educator*
Anderson, William Henry *psychobiology educator*
Andrews, William Dorey *law educator*
Angrist, Joshua D. *economics educator*
Anquetil, Patrick Armand *investment company executive, researcher*
Ansolabehere, Stephen Daniel *political science professor*
Antoniadis, Dimitri Alexander *electrical engineering educator*
Apostolakis, George E. *engineering educator, researcher*
Argon, Ali Suphi *mechanical engineering educator*
Arkani-Hamed, Nima *physicist, educator*
Armitage, David Richard *historian*
Aronson, Michael Andrew *editor*
Asani, Ali S. *foreign language and religious studies educator*
Athey, Susan Carleton *economics professor*
Bailyn, Bernard *historian, educator*
Bailyn, Lotte *psychologist, educator*
Bakanowsky, Louis Joseph *artist, architect, educator*
Baker, Tania Ann *biology professor, researcher*
Bane, Mary Jo *dean, political science professor*
Barger, James Edwin *physicist*
Barnhart, Cynthia *engineering educator, researcher*
Barrett, J. Carl *medical researcher, molecular biologist*

Barron, David Jeremiah *law educator*
Bartee, Thomas Creson *computer scientist, educator*
Bartel, David *biology professor, researcher*
Bartholet, Elizabeth *law educator*
Bator, Francis Michel *economist, educator*
Battin, Richard Horace *aeronautical engineer*
Bawendi, Moungi G. *chemist, educator*
Bear, Mark Firman *neuroscientist, educator*
Bebchuk, Lucian Arye *law and finance educator*
Beér, János Miklós *engineering educator*
Belcher, Angela *engineering educator*
Benkler, Yochai *law educator*
Beranek, Leo Leroy *acoustical engineer, consultant*
Berg, Howard C. *biology professor*
Berger, Harvey James *pharmaceutical executive, physician, educator*
Berlowitz, Leslie *cultural organization administrator*
Berndt, Ernst Rudolf *economist, educator*
Berners-Lee, Sir Timothy John *inventor of world wide web, research scientist, writer*
Bertsimas, Dimitris J. *mathematician, researcher, educator*
Berwick, Donald Mark *medical institute administrator*
Bhabha, Homi K. *humanities educator, writer*
Bhatia, Sangeeta N. *biomedical engineer, educator*
Billings, Joshua *literature scholar*
Binzel, Richard P. *astrophysicist, educator*
Bishop, Robert Lyle *retired economist, educator*
Bizzi, Emilio *neurophysiologist, educator*
Blackmer, Donald Laurence Morton *political scientist*
Blair, Ann *historian*
Blanchet, Jose H. *statistics educator, researcher*
Bloom, Kathryn Ruth *public relations executive*
Bloxham, Jeremy *geophysicist, educator*
Bok, Derek Curtis *law educator, former academic administrator*
Bolster, Arthur Stanley, Jr. *history professor*
Borjas, George J(esus) *economics professor*
Botkin, James W. *leadership and executive coach*
Bradt, Hale Van Dorn *physicist, x-ray astronomer, educator*
Bras, Rafael Luis *engineering educator*
Brecher, Aviva *physicist, researcher*
Bremer, Gabriel *chef*
Brennan, Todd *information technology executive*
Brenner, Howard *chemical engineering educator*
Brewer, Scott *law educator*
Brooks, Rodney Allen *information technology executive, educator*
Brusch, John Lynch *physician, educator, hospital administrator*
Brustein, Robert Sanford *literature and language professor, theater director, writer*
Brynjolfsson, Erik *finance educator, researcher*
Bulovic, Vladimir *engineering educator*
Bunn, Matthew G. *political scientist, writer*
Burke, Bernard Flood *physicist, researcher*
Calabrese, Joseph D. *psychologist, educator*
Campbell, Robert *architect, writer*
Canizares, Claude Roger *astrophysicist, educator*
Cansev, Mehmet *physician, researcher*
Caplice, Christopher *engineering educator*
Carr, Daniel Barry *anesthesiologist, endocrinologist, researcher, pharmaceutical executive*
Carter, Ashton Baldwin *former federal agency administrator*
Cestnick, Laurie L. *neuropsychologist, educator, scientist*
Ceyer, Sylvia T. *chemistry professor*
Chakraborty, Arup K. *chemical engineering educator*
Champion, Hale (Charles Hale Champion) *academic administrator, lecturer, government official, consultant*
Chandler, Fay Martin *artist*
Chandra, Satish *psychologist*
Chatterjee, Sharmila *marketing educator*
Chen, Chau-Chyun *chemical engineer*
Chen, Lincoln Chin-ho *medical educator*
Chen, Sow-Hsin *nuclear science and engineering educator, researcher*
Chernoff, Herman *statistics educator*
Chisholm, Sallie Watson *biological oceanography educator, researcher*
Chodorow, Nancy Julia *psychotherapist, educator*
Chomsky, (Avram) Noam *linguistics and philosophy educator*
Chung, Soon-Jo *engineer, researcher*
Ciubotaru, Dan *mathematics professor*
Clark, Robert Charles *law educator, former dean*
Clay, Phillip L. *academic administrator*
Cleary, David Michael *composer, critic, library assistant*
Clifford, Gari David *engineering educator, biomedical engineer*
Cline, Nancy M. *librarian, department chairman*
Cogan, John Francis, Jr. *lawyer*
Cohen, Robert Edward *chemical engineering professor, consultant*
Cohn, Daniel Ross *physicist*
Cole, Heather Ellen *librarian*
Collier, Earl Miller, Jr. *biotechnology company executive*
Colton, Clark Kenneth *chemical engineering professor*
Conley, Tom Clark *literature educator*
Connick, Harry, Jr. *musician, actor, vocalist, composer, lyricist*
Connors, Frank Joseph *lawyer*
Cooper, Richard Newell *economist, educator*
Corey, Elias James *chemistry professor*
Covert, Eugene Edzards *aerospace engineer, aeronautics professor*
Craig, Albert M. *history professor, researcher*
Crandall, Stephen Harry *engineering educator*
Crawley, Edward Francis *aerospace engineering educator*
Cummins, Christopher C. *chemistry professor*
Cushman, Ellen *counselor*
Cutler, David M. *finance educator*
Dalgarno, Alexander *astronomy educator*
Damrosch, Leopold, Jr. *English educator*
d'Arbeloff, Alexander V. *electronics executive*
Darnton, Robert Choate *library director, historian, educator*
Demaine, Erik D. *computer scientist, educator*
de Monteiro, Nadsa *chef*
de Neufville, Richard Lawrence *engineering educator*
Dennis, Jack Bonnell *computer scientist, educator*
Dershowitz, Alan Morton *law educator*
Desan, Christine *law educator*
DesRosier, Thomas J. *lawyer*
Deutch, John Mark *chemistry professor, former CIA director*
de Varon, Lorna Cooke *choral conductor*
de Weck, Oliver *engineering educator, researcher*
Dewey, Clarence Forbes, Jr. *engineering educator*
DiCamillo, Kate *writer*
Dobson, Parrish *photographer, educator*
Dominguez, Jorge Ignacio *political scientist, educator*
Donahue, Charles, Jr. *law educator*
Donahue, John David *federal agency administrator, educator*
Doty, Paul Mead *biochemist, educator, arms control specialist*
Dowling, John Elliott *biology professor*
Drela, Mark *aeronautical engineer, educator*
Dresselhaus, Mildred Spiewak *physics and engineering professor*
Dudley, Richard Mansfield *mathematician, educator*
Duffy, Robert Aloysius *aeronautical engineer*
Dugundji, John *aeronautical engineer*
Dulac, Catherine *biology professor, researcher*
Dunsire, Deborah *pharmaceutical executive*
Dyck, Martin *literary theorist, mathematics historian*
Eagar, Thomas Waddy *metallurgist, educator*
Eagleson, Peter Sturges *civil and environmental engineer, educator*
Eckaus, Richard Samuel *economist, educator*
Edgerly, William Skelton *banker*
Edley, Christopher F., Jr. *dean, law educator*
Eggan, Kevin C. *molecular and cellular biology professor, researcher*
Ehntholt, Daniel James *chemist*
Eisen, Herman Nathaniel *immunology researcher, medical educator*
Elhauge, Einer Richard *law educator*
Elkins, Caroline M. *history professor, writer*
Ellis, David Wertz *retired museum director, consultant, arbitrator*
Ellison, Glenn *finance educator*
Ellison, Peter Thorpe *anthropology professor*
Ellwood, David Tabor *dean, public policy educator*
Emanuel, Kerry Andrew *meteorologist, oceanographer, educator*
Engell, James Theodore *language educator, department chairman*
Erikson, Raymond Leo *biology professor*
Essigmann, John M. *chemistry professor*
Ette, Ene Ikpong *clinical pharmacologist*
Eurich Lazarus, Nell P. *education educator*
Evans, David Albert *chemistry professor*
Ewing, Scott Edwin *physiatrist, educator*
Fallon, Richard H., Jr. *law educator*
Fanger, Donald Lee *Slavic language and literature educator*
Faust, Drew Gilpin (Catharine) *academic administrator, historian*
Fay, James Alan *mechanical engineering educator*
Feininger, Theodore Lux *artist*
Feld, Michael Stephen *physics professor*
Feldman, Gary Jay *physicist, researcher*
Feldstein, Martin Stuart *economist, educator*
Ferguson, Niall Campbell Douglas *history professor, writer*
Ferrari, Raffaele *oceanographer, educator*
Field, Martha Amanda *law educator*
Field, Robert Warren *chemistry professor*
Fink, Yoel *science educator, researcher*
Fiorenza, Francis P. *religion educator*
Fischer, Kurt Walter *education educator*
Fisher, Philip J. *English language and literature educator*
Fisher, Roger Dummer *negotiation expert, law educator*
Fisher, Stephen Carey *musicologist, editor*
Fishman, Mark Charles *biomedical researcher*
Fitzsimmons, William R. *dean*
Flannery, Susan Marie *library administrator*
Flemings, Merton Corson *engineering educator, materials scientist*
Flier, Michael Stephen *Slavic languages educator*
Forbes, Kristin J. *economics professor, former federal official*
Ford, Patrick Kildea *Celtic studies educator*
Forney, G(eorge) David, Jr. *retired electronics executive*
Fox, James Gahan *veterinarian, educator, researcher*
Fox, John Bayley, Jr. *university dean*
Fox, Maurice Sanford *retired molecular biologist, educator*
Fraker, Ford M. *ambassador*
French, Anthony Philip *physicist, educator*
Frey, Daniel D. *engineering educator, researcher*
Frey, Frederick August *geochemist, researcher, educator*
Friedman, Benjamin Morton *economics professor*
Friedman, Jeffrey Robert *psychiatrist, educator*
Friedman, Jerome Isaac *physics professor, researcher*
Frisch, Rose Epstein *population sciences researcher*
Frosch, Robert Alan *retired automobile manufacturing executive, physicist*
Frug, Gerald E. *law educator*
Fu, Gregory Chung-Wei *chemistry educator*
Fujimoto, James G. *electrical engineering educator*
Gabrielse, Gerald *physics professor*
Gagliardi, Ugo Oscar *systems software architect, educator*
Gallager, Robert Gray *electrical engineering educator*
Gardner, Howard Earl *psychologist, educator, writer*
Garland, Carl Wesley *chemist, educator*
Gaskell, Ivan George Alexander De Wend *art museum curator, educator*
Gassend, Blaise Laurent Patrick *technologist, researcher*
Gates, Henry Louis, Jr. *literature and language professor, historian*
Gebbie, Geoffrey *research scientist, oceanographer*
Geller, Margaret Joan *astrophysicist, educator*
Gergen, David Richmond *federal official, magazine editor*
Gibbons, Joe *filmmaker*
Gilbert, Daniel *psychology professor*
Gilbert, Walter *molecular biologist, educator*
Giles, Robert Hartmann *journalist, educator*
Gingerich, Owen Jay *astronomer, educator*
Girguis, Peter Riad *microbiologist, entrepreneur, educator*
Glaeser, Edward Ludwig *research economist, educator*
Glauber, Roy Jay *physics professor*
Glendon, Mary Ann *law educator*
Goldberg, Marc Evan *healthcare venture capitalist*
Goldberg, Ray Allan *agriculturist, educator*
Goldin, Claudia Dale *economics professor*
Goldsmith, Jack Landman III *law educator, former federal agency administrator*
Goldstone, Jeffrey *physicist, educator*
Goldwasser, Shafrira *computer scientist*
Gomes, Peter John *clergyman, educator*
Goodman, Ellen Holtz *journalist*
Graham, Jorie *writer, educator*
Graham, Loren Raymond *historian, educator*
Graham, Patricia Albjerg *education educator*
Graham, William Albert *religious studies and history educator*
Gray, Paul Edward *academic administrator*
Greenberg, Jerry A. *information technology executive*
Greenblatt, Stephen Jay *literature and language professor, writer*
Greene, Frederick Davis, II, *chemistry professor*
Greenspan, Harvey Philip *applied mathematician, educator*
Greenstone, Michael *economics professor, researcher*
Griffith, Linda G. (Linda Griffith-Cima) *biomedical engineer, chemical engineer, educator*
Grindlay, Jonathan Ellis *astrophysics educator*
Gross, Benedict H. *mathematician*
Grossman, Jerome Harvey *medical association administrator, educator*
Grosz, Barbara Jean *computer science educator*
Grove, Timothy Lynn *geology educator*
Gruber, Jonathan H. *economist*
Guarente, Leonard P. *medical geneticist, educator*
Gund, Graham *architectural firm executive*
Guthke, Karl Siegfried *language educator*
Gyftopoulos, Elias Panayiotis *mechanical and nuclear engineering educator*
Halley, Janet E. *law educator*
Halperin, Bertrand Israel *physics professor*
Halperin, Daniel I. *law educator*
Hamner, W. Easley *architect*
Hanan, Patrick Dewes *foreign language professional, educator*
Hansen, Kent Forrest *nuclear engineering educator*
Hanson, Jon D. *law educator*
Harbison, John *composer*
Harris, Wesley L. *aeronautical engineer, educator*
Hart, Oliver D'Arcy *economics professor*
Hastings, Daniel *aeronautical engineer, educator*
Hastings, John Woodland *biologist, educator*
Hauser, John Richard *marketing and management science educator*
Hauser, Marc D. *psychology professor, educator*
Hausmann, Ricardo *economics professor, director*
Havens, Leston Laycock *psychiatrist, educator*
Heineman, Benjamin Walter, Jr. *lawyer*
Helgason, Sigurdur *mathematician, educator*
Heller, Eric Johnson *physicist, educator, digital abstract artist*
Hernquist, Lars Eric *astronomer, educator*
Herr, Hugh Miller *biomechatronics researcher, educator*
Herschbach, Dudley Robert *chemistry professor*
Hewitt, Jacqueline N. *astronomy educator*
Heywood, John Benjamin *mechanical engineering educator*
Hill, Kenneth *demographer, educator*
Hirsch, Martin Stanley *internist, epidemiologist, researcher*
Hockfield, Susan *academic administrator, medical educator*
Hoffman, Paul Felix *geologist, educator*
Hoffmann, Inge Schneier *psychologist, educator*
Holdren, John Paul *physicist, educator, writer*
Holmberg, Arthur Carl *performing arts educator, theater critic*
Holmstrom, Bengt R. *economics professor*
Holton, Gerald *physicist, educator, science historian*
Hopkins, Nancy Haven Doe *biology professor*
Horvitz, Howard Robert *biology professor, researcher*
Hostage, John Brayne Arthur *law librarian*
Howitt, Arnold Martin *academic administrator, educator*
Hubbard, Ruth *retired biology professor*
Huchra, John Peter *astronomer, educator*
Hughes, Libby *writer*
Hunt, Swanee G. *public policy educator, former ambassador*
Hunter, Ian W. *engineering educator, researcher*
Huntington, Samuel Phillips *political science educator*
Huth, John E. *physicist, educator*
Hyman, Steven Edward *academic administrator, physiatrist, educator*
Hynes, Richard Olding *biology researcher, educator*
Ippen, Erich Peter *electrical engineer, educator, physicist*
Iriye, Akira *historian, educator*
Iuliano, Robert W. *lawyer*
Jackiw, Roman *physicist, researcher*
Jackson, Howell E. *law educator*
Jacobsen, Eric N. *chemistry professor*
Jacoby, Henry Donnan *economist, educator*
Jaenisch, Rudolf *biologist, educator*
Jaffe, Arthur Michael *mathematician, physicist, educator*
Jencks, Christopher Sandys *sociologist, educator*
Jo, Sungho *computer scientist, researcher*
John, Richard Rodda *transportation executive*
Johnson, Howard Wesley *retired academic administrator, finance company executive*
Johnson, Jennifer Toby *military officer*
Jonas, Joan (Joan Amerman Edwards) *artist*
Jones, Alex S. *reporter, writer*
Jones, Christopher Prestige *classicist, educator, historian, consultant*
Jorgenson, Dale Weldeau *economist, educator*
Joskow, Paul Lewis *economist, educator*
Joss, Paul Christopher *astrophysicist, atmospheric physicist, educator*
Juma, Calestous *international development educator*
Kaashoek, M. Frans *computer science and engineering educator*
Kac, Victor G. *mathematician, educator*
Kadak, Andrew C. *engineering educator, former company executive*
Kagan, Elena *dean, law educator*
Kagan, Jerome *psychologist, educator*
Kalb, Johannes Andreas *research scientist*
Kamentsky, Louis Aaron *biophysicist*
Kaplan, Benjamin *judge*
Kaplan, Justin *author*
Kaplow, Louis *law educator*
Kaufman, Andrew Lee *law educator*
Kaufman, Gordon Dester *theology studies educator*
Kayden, Jerold S. *lawyer, urban planner*
Kaysen, Carl *economics professor*
Kazimi, Mujid Suliman *nuclear engineer, educator*
Keller, Evelyn Fox *philosophy of science professor*
Kelly, Sean Dorrance *philosophy educator*
Kelman, Steven Jay *education educator*
Kelsey, Robin E. *art history educator*
Keniston, Kenneth *psychologist, educator*
Kennedy, David William *law educator*
Kennedy, Duncan McLean *law educator*
Kennedy, Randall L. *law educator*
Kennedy, Stephen Dandridge *economist, researcher*
Kerman, Arthur Kent *physicist, researcher*
Ketterle, Wolfgang *physics professor*
Keyfitz, Nathan *sociologist, educator, demographer*
Keyser, Samuel Jay *linguist, educator*
Khorana, Har Gobind *chemist, educator*
Khoury, Philip S. *academic administrator*
King, William Bruce *retired lawyer*
Kirby, William C. *history professor, former dean*
Kirtley, James L., Jr. *electrical engineer, educator*
Kleinman, Arthur Michael *medical anthropology and psychiatry educator*
Klemperer, William *chemistry professor*
Kleppner, Daniel *physicist, researcher*
Knickrehm, Glenn Allen *management executive*
Knoll, Andrew Herbert *biology professor*
Knowles, Jeremy Randall *chemist, educator, dean*
Kobus, Richard Lawrence *architect*
Koepp, Donna Pauline Petersen *librarian*
Koester, Helmut Heinrich *history professor*
Kong, Jin Au *electrical engineering educator*
Kraus, Rozann B. *performing company executive*
Krebs, Hermano Igo *research scientist*
Kremer, Michael *economist, educator*
Kruger, Kenneth *architect*
Ladd, Charles Cushing III *civil engineer, educator*
Ladd, Florence Cawthorne *writer*
Lagace, Paul Alfred *aeronautical engineering educator*
Lagemann, Ellen Condliffe *history and education professor, dean*
LaGuardia, Cheryl M. *school librarian, writer*
Laiou, Angeliki Evangelos *history professor*
Lamberg-Karlovsky, Clifford Charles *anthropologist, archaeologist*
Lander, Eric Steven *geneticist, molecular biologist, mathematician*
Langer, Ellen Jane *psychologist, educator, writer, artist*
Langer, Robert Samuel, Jr. *chemical and biomedical engineering educator*
Langmuir, Charles Herbert *geology educator*
Lau, Vincent W. *lawyer*
Lauder, George V. *marine biologist*
Lauga, Eric *physical mathematician, educator*
Lee, Barbara *political activist, foundation administrator*
Lee, Lester P., Jr. *historian*
Lee, Patrick A. *physics educator*
Lee, Se-Hee *electrical engineer, researcher*
Leiden, Jeffrey Marc *venture capitalist, molecular biologist, cardiologist*

Leighton, Frank T. *mathematics professor*
Lenger, John Richard *journalism educator*
Lentz, Thomas W. *museum director, curator*
Leonard, Herman Beukema (Dutch) *public finance, management, and leadership educator*
Leveson, Nancy G. *aeronautical engineer*
Levi, Herbert Walter *biologist, educator*
Lewis, Henry Rafalsky *manufacturing executive*
Lewis, Scott P. *lawyer*
Liau, Gene *medical educator*
Lieber, Charles *chemistry professor, researcher, materials scientist*
Lieberson, Stanley *sociologist, educator*
Light, Richard Jay *statistician, educator*
Lin, Kai *research scientist*
Lindquist, Susan Lee *biology and microbiology professor*
Lindzen, Richard Siegmund *meteorologist, educator*
Linsky, Marty *education educator*
Lipscomb, William Nunn, Jr. *retired chemistry professor*
Little, John Dutton Conant *management scientist, educator*
Liu, David Ruchien *biochemist, educator*
Liu, Xiong *atmospheric physicist*
Livingston, James Duane *physicist, researcher*
Lloyd, Seth *physicist*
Loeb, Abraham (Avi Loeb) *astrophysics educator, researcher*
Lomon, Earle Leonard *physicist, educator, consultant*
London, Irving Myer *physician, educator*
Long, Alan K. *research administrator*
Losick, Richard M. *biology professor*
Lydon, Amanda *chef*
Lynch, Nancy Ann *computer scientist, educator*
MacKinnon, Rebecca *media consultant, researcher*
MacMaster, Robert Ellsworth *historian, educator*
Magee, Christopher L. *systems engineer*
Magnanti, Thomas L. *management and engineering educator*
Maher, Brendan Arnold *retired psychology educator, editor*
Mahoney, Kevin J. *lawyer*
Maier, Charles Steven *history professor*
Maier, Pauline *historian, educator*
Malmstad, John Earl *literature and language professor*
Malone, Thomas W. *business educator, researcher*
Mandl, Robert *application developer*
Mankiw, (Nicholas) Gregory *economics professor, former federal official*
Manning, John F. *law educator*
Mansbridge, Jane Jebb *political scientist, educator*
Marcus, Richard Sargon *research scientist*
Marini, Robert Charles *environmental engineering executive*
Markey, Winston Roscoe *aeronautical engineering educator*
Marks, David Hunter *civil engineering educator*
Marsden, Brian Geoffrey *astronomer*
Martin, Harry Stratton III *law librarian, educator*
Martin, Paul Cecil *physicist, researcher*
Mathews, Joan Helene *pediatrician*
Matsui, Connie L. *pharmaceutical executive*
Maws, Tony *chef*
Mazlish, Bruce *historian, educator*
Mazur, Barry Charles *mathematician, educator*
Mazur, Michael *artist*
McBride, Robert Albert *training services executive*
McCartney, Kathleen *dean, education educator*
McCunney, Robert Joseph *physician*
McDonald, Christie Anne *literature and language professor, writer*
McGarry, Frederick Jerome *civil engineering educator*
McGurk, Michael R. *lawyer*
McMahon, Andrew Paul *embryologist, educator*
McMullen, Curtis T. *mathematics professor*
McNally, Richard James *clinical psychologist, educator*
Mei, Chiang Chung *civil engineer, educator*
Meinert, Edward *computer scientist, management consultant*
Melton, Douglas A. *molecular and cell biology educator*
Meltzer, Daniel J. *law educator*
Menand, Louis *literature educator, writer*
Meng, Sheng *physicist, researcher*
Meselson, Matthew Stanley *biochemist, educator*
Meyer, John Robert *economist, educator*
Micali, Silvio *information scientist, educator*
Mikaelian, Tsoline *aerospace engineer*
Milgram, Jerome H. *marine and ocean engineer, educator*
Miller, Steven E. *professor of international affairs*
Milner, Richard Gerard *physicist*
Mindell, David A. *engineering educator*
Mitten, David Gordon *classical archaeologist*
Moavenzadeh, Fred *engineering educator*
Moniz, Ernest Jeffrey *physics professor*
Moore, Mark Harrison *criminal justice and public policy educator*
Moore, Sally Falk *anthropology educator*
Mootha, Vamsi Krishna *biomedical researcher, educator*
Mora, Elizabeth *comptroller, academic administrator*
Moran, James Michael, Jr. *astronomer, educator*
Morris, Errol M. *filmmaker*
Moses, Joel *computer scientist, educator*
Mrowka, Tomasz *mathematics professor*
Mullen, James C. *biotechnology company executive*
Munguia Tapia, Emmanuel *electrical engineer, researcher, computer scientist*
Murray, Andrew W. *biology professor, researcher*
Narayan, Ramesh *astronomy educator*
Narayanamurti, Venkatesh *engineering educator, physics professor*
Narayanamurti, Venkatesh *health science association administrator*
Nathanson, Larry *medical educator*
Nayeri, Ali *physicist, educator*
Negele, John William *physics professor, consultant*
Negroponte, Nicholas *media specialist, educator*
Neill, Monty *educational association administrator*
Newey, Whitney K. *economist, educator*
Newman, Dava Jean *aerospace engineering educator, director*
Newman, J. Bonnie *political science professor, former federal official*
Nordell, Hans Roderick *journalist, retired editor*
Nye, Joseph Samuel, Jr. *political science professor, former dean*
Nykrog, Per *French literature educator*
O'Connell, Richard John *geophysicist, educator*
Oettinger, Anthony Gervin *mathematician, educator*
Ogletree, Charles J., Jr. *law educator*
Olschwang, Dan *telecommunications industry executive, entrepreneur*
O'Neil, Wayne *linguist, educator*
Oppenheim, Irwin *chemical physicist, educator*
Orchard, Robert John *theater producer, educator*
Orfield, Antonia Marie *optometrist, researcher*
Orr-Weaver, Terry L. *cell biologist, educator*
O'Shea, Erin K. *biomedical researcher*
Owen, Edward Roger John (E. Roger Owen) *Middle Eastern studies professor, writer*
Page, David C. *biologist, educator*
Pardue, Mary-Lou *biology professor*
Parker, Lisa Frederick *music educator, Dalcroze specialist*
Parker, Richard Davies *law educator*
Parlee, Mary Brown *psychology educator*
Patton, Bruce M. *law educator, management consultant*
Paul, William *physicist, researcher*
Penfield, Paul Livingstone, Jr. *electrical engineering educator*
Perdue, Peter C. *history professor*
Perkins, Dwight Heald *economics professor*
Petersen, Ulrich *geology educator*
Pettengill, Gordon H(emenway) *physicist, researcher*
Pierce, Naomi Ellen *biology professor, researcher*
Pilbeam, David Roger *paleoanthropology educator*
Pinker, Steven A. *psychologist, educator*
Poe, Mya *communications executive, director*
Poggio, Tomaso Armando *physicist, educator, computer scientist, researcher*
Porter, Roger Blaine *federal official, educator*
Porter, William Lyman *architect, educator*
Poterba, James Michael *economist, educator*
Pounds, William Frank *management educator*
Power, Samantha J. *public policy educator, writer*
Prinn, Ronald G. *atmospheric science educator*
Pritchard, David Edward *physics professor*
Probstein, Ronald Filmore *mechanical engineering educator*
Putnam, Robert D. *education educator*
Pye, Lucian Wilmot *political science professor*
Rabbat, Nasser O. *architecture educator*
Rabin, Michael Oser *computer scientist, educator*
Ramcharan, Bertrand *former international organization official*
Ramsey, Norman F. *physicist, researcher*
Ramseyer, J. Mark *law educator*
Randall, Lisa *physics professor*
Ratti, Carlo Filippo *architect, researcher, educator*
Redwine, Robert Page *physicist, researcher*
Reichle, Ralph L. *radiologist*
Reif, L. Rafael *academic administrator, engineering educator*
Rensberger, Boyce *science journalism fellowship program administrator*
Reyes-Cubides, William *language educator, researcher, writer, actor*
Rhoda, Janice Tucker *writer, educator, musician*
Rightmire, George Philip *anthropology educator*
Riley, Lynne F. *lawyer*
Ritvo, Harriet *historian*
Rivest, Ronald L. *engineer*
Roberts, Edward Baer *technology management educator*
Roberts, Nancy *computer scientist, educator*
Rodrik, Dani *economics and international affairs educator*
Rogers, Peter Phillips *environmental engineer, educator, urban planner*
Rogoff, Kenneth Saul *economics professor*
Roos, Daniel *engineering educator*
Rose, Robert Michael *materials engineering educator*
Rosenberg, Charles Ernest *historian, educator*
Rosenblum, Nancy Lipton *political science professor*
Rosenkrantz, Barbara Gutmann *science and medicine historian*
Rosovsky, Henry *economist, educator*
Ross, Matthew Alan *real estate company executive*
Rotberg, Robert Irwin *historian, political scientist, educator, academic administrator*
Rowe, Mary P. *organizational ombudsman, management educator*
Rowley, Geoffrey Herbert *management consultant*
Rubin, Donald Bruce *statistician, educator, research and development company executive*
Rubin, Lawrence Gilbert *physicist, science administrator*
Ruina, Jack Philip *electrical engineer, educator*
Russell, Kenneth Calvin *metallurgical engineering educator*
Sabeti, Pardis Christine *researcher*
Sadoway, Donald Robert *materials science educator*
Sahagun, Aaron *entrepreneur, Internet company executive*
Sahagun, Allan *entrepreneur, Internet company executive*
St. Clair, Richard Collins *composer, administrative assistant*
Sampson, Robert J. *sociologist, educator*
Samson, Leona D. *biological engineering educator, research center director*
Samuelson, Paul Anthony *economist, educator*
Sander, Frank Ernest Arnold *law educator*
Sanes, Joshua Richard *neurobiologist, researcher, educator*
Santos, Adèle Naudé *architect, educator*
Sapers, Carl Martin *lawyer, educator*
Sapienza, Tony *public relations executive*
Sapirie, Stephen Alan *public health administrator*
Sapolsky, Harvey Morton *political scientist, educator*
Schaeffer, Robert *educational association administrator*
Schaub, Robert George *pharmaceutical executive*
Schauer, Frederick Franklin *law educator*
Scherer, Frederic Michael *economics professor*
Schiller, Peter Harkai *biomedical engineering and physics educator*
Schmalensee, Richard Lee *dean*
Schmill, Stuart *admissions director*
Schrag, Daniel P. *geochemist, educator*
Schrock, Nancy Carlson *conservator, consultant*
Schrock, Richard Royce *chemistry professor*
Schuessler Fiorenza, Elisabeth *theology studies educator*
Scott, Hal S. *law educator*
Seager, Sara *astronomer, educator*
Sen, Amartya Kumar *economist, educator*
Sevcenko, Ihor *history and literature professor*
Severin, Christina *public health service officer*
Seyferth, Dietmar *chemist, educator*
Shaheen, Jeanne *political scientist, former governor*
Shapiro, David Louis *law educator*
Shapiro, Irwin Ira *physicist, researcher*
Sharp, Phillip Allen *biologist, educator*
Shavell, Steven M. *law educator*
Shaw, Anthony Raymond, Jr. *research executive*
Sheffi, Yossi *engineering educator, researcher*
Sheng, Morgan Hwa-Tze *neuroscientist, educator*
Shinagel, Michael *dean, English literature educator*
Sidanius, James H. *psychology professor*
Siegel, Abraham J. *economics professor, academic administrator*
Sigel, Anthony B. *art conservator*
Silbey, Robert James *chemistry professor, researcher, consultant*
Simon, Eckehard (Peter) *foreign language educator*
Sims, Ezra *composer*
Singer, Isadore Manuel *mathematician, educator*
Sinha, Pawan *research scientist, educator, entrepreneur*
Skocpol, Theda Ruth *sociology and political science educator, former dean*
Skolnikoff, Eugene B. *political science professor*
Slive, Seymour *museum director, art educator*
Slosburg-Ackerman, Jill Rose *artist, educator*
Smith, David Julian *educational consultant*
Smith, Kenneth Alan *chemical engineer, educator*
Smith, Merritt Roe *history professor*
Smith, Michael D. *dean, electrical engineering and computer science professor*
Snyder, James M., Jr. *political science professor, economics professor*
Soljacic, Marin *physicist, educator*
Sollors, Werner *literature and language educator*
Solow, Robert Merton *economist, educator*
Soon, Willie Wei-Hock *environmental scientist*
Spaepen, Frans August *physicist, educator*
Spelke, Elizabeth Shilin *psychology professor*
Staelin, David Hudson *electrical engineering educator, consultant*
Stanley, Richard P. *mathematics professor*
Stauffer, John William *cultural historian*
Steiker, Carol S. *law educator*
Steiner, Henry Jacob *law and human rights educator*
Steinfeld, Jeffrey Irwin *chemistry professor, educator, writer*
Stevens, Kenneth Noble *electrical engineer, educator*
Stock, James H. *economics professor*
Stoddard, Roger Eliot *scholar*
Strandberg, Malcom Woodrow Pershing *physicist*
Strang, Gilbert *mathematics professor*
Strang, William Gilbert *mathematician, educator*
Stroock, Daniel Wyler *mathematician, educator*
Subramanian, Guhan *law educator*
Suresh, Subra *materials engineer, educator*
Susskind, Lawrence Elliott *urban planner, educator, mediator*
Sussman, Joseph *engineering educator, researcher*
Swager, Timothy Manning *chemistry educator*
Szolovits, Peter *computer scientist*
Ta, Tai Van *lawyer, researcher*
Tananbaum, Harvey D. *astrophysicist*
Tannenbaum, Steven Robert *toxicologist, chemist*
Tarokh, Vahid *engineering educator*
Tarrant, Richard J(ohn) *classicist, educator*
Taylor, Richard *mathematics professor*
Termeer, Henricus Adrianus *pharmaceutical executive*
Thaddeus, Patrick *physicist, researcher*
Thernstrom, Stephan *historian, educator*
Thiemann, Ronald Frank *dean, religious studies educator*
Thompson, Dennis Frank *political science professor, consultant*
Thorburn, David *literature educator*
Tinkham, Michael *physicist, researcher*
Todreas, Neil Emmanuel *nuclear engineering educator*
Tomita, Masaru *engineering educator, researcher*
Tonegawa, Susumu *biology professor*
Toomre, Alar *applied mathematician, theoretical astronomer*
Triantafyllou, Michael Stefanos *engineering educator*
Tribe, Laurence Henry *law educator*
Trilling, Leon *aeronautical engineering educator*
Troccoli, Mariano *astrophysicist, researcher*
Trumpbour, John *historian, researcher, director*
Tsai, Li-Huei *pathologist, researcher*
Tsitsiklis, John N. *electrical engineering and computer science educator*
Tsoi, Edward Tze Ming *architect, urban planner, interior designer*
Tucker, Louis Leonard *retired historical society administrator*
Ungar, Eric Edward *mechanical engineer*
Vagts, Detlev Frederick *law educator*
Valiant, Leslie Gabriel *computer scientist, educator*
Vander Velde, Wallace Earl *aeronautical and astronautical engineering educator*
Vanger, Milton Isadore *historian, educator*
Vendler, Helen Hennessy *literature educator, poetry critic*
Verba, Sidney *political science professor, retired library director*
Vessot, Robert Frederick Charles *physicist, researcher*
Vogan, David A., Jr. *mathematics professor*
Vogel, Ezra F. *sociology educator*
von Hippel, Eric Arthur *innovation educator*
Wacker, Warren Ernest Clyde *internist, educator*
Walker, Graham Charles *biology professor*
Ware, Susan W. *historian*
Warren, Alvin Clifford, Jr. *law educator*
Warren, Elizabeth A. *law educator*
Waters, Mary Catherine *sociology educator*
Watson, Rubie S. *museum director*
Watts, Ross Leslie *finance educator*
Waugh, John Stewart *chemist, educator*
Weinberg, Robert Allan *biochemist, educator*
Weinreb, Lloyd Lobell *law educator*
Weitzman, Arthur Joshua *language educator*
Welsch, Roy Elmer *statistician, educator*
Wen, Xiao-Gang *physics professor*
Wheeler, Robert Treide *microbiologist, researcher*
White, David Calvin *electrical engineer, educator, energy executive, consultant*
White, Shelby *art association administrator*
Whiteside, Ann Baird *library director*
Whitesides, George McClelland *chemistry professor*
Whitlock, Charles Preston *former university dean*
Whitman, Robert Van Duyne *civil engineer, educator*
Widnall, Sheila Evans *aeronautical educator, former secretary of air force, university official*
Wilcox, Maud *editor*
Wilczek, Frank Anthony *physics professor*
Wilkins, David Brian *law educator, director*
Williams, James Henry, Jr. *mechanical engineer, educator, consultant*
Willie, Charles Vert *social sciences educator*
Wilson, David Gordon *mechanical engineering educator*
Wilson, Edward Osborne *biologist, educator, writer*
Wilson, William Julius *sociology educator*
Wirasinha, Hemamali Anushka *computer scientist, researcher*
Wirth, Peter *lawyer*
Wodiczko, Krzysztof *artist, architect, educator*
Wolff, Christoph Johannes *music historian, educator*
Wolfman, Bernard *lawyer, educator*
Wolpert, Ann J. *library director*
Wood, John Armstead *planetary scientist, geological sciences educator, artist*
Wood, Pamela Sharon *music educator, soprano*
Wood, Richard Robinson *real estate company executive*
Wren, Christopher R. *computer scientist, researcher*
Wu, Tai Tsun *physicist, researcher*
Wuensch, Bernhardt John *ceramic engineering educator*
Wurtman, Richard Jay *neuroscientist, educator*
Xie, Xiaoliang Sunney *chemist, educator*
Yannas, Ioannis Vassilios *polymer science educator*
Yau, Shing-Tung *mathematics professor*
Yergin, Daniel Howard *writer, consultant*
Yi, Wei *physicist*
Yip, Winnie *health economics educator*
Young, Laurence Retman *biomedical engineer, educator*
Young, Rick (Richard Allen) *molecular biologist, educator*
Zaldarriaga, Matias *cosmologist, physics professor*
Zeckhauser, Richard Jay *economist, educator*
Zeidenstein, George *population educator*
Zhang, Shuguang *biomedical engineer*
Zhuang, Xiaowei *biophysicist, educator*
Zhukovsky, Alexander *mechanical engineer*
Zinberg, Dorothy Shore *sociologist, educator*
Ziolkowski, Jan Michael *medievalist educator*
Zittrain, Jonathan L. *law educator*
Zollar, Alfred *computer company executive*
Zuber, Maria T. *geophysicist, educator*
Zue, Victor W. *engineering educator*

Canton

Allen, Frances L. (Britchford) *marketing executive*
Bentas, Lily Haseotes *retail executive*
Bihldorff, John Pearson *hospital director*
Fireman, Paul Barry *footwear and apparel company executive*
Fuchs, Lawrence Howard *federal official, educator*
Harrington, Paul *apparel executive*
Judson, Arnold Sidney *management consultant*

Kaigler, Denise *communications executive*
Kelley, Irene W. *retired librarian, musician, artist*
Luther, Jon L. *food service executive*
Masiello, Thomas Philip, Jr. *lawyer, risk management consultant*
Parker, Virginia Marie *language educator*
Sawtelle, Carl S. *psychiatric social worker*

Carlisle
Drew, Philip Garfield *retired engineering company executive, consultant*
Fohl, Timothy *investment company executive*

Carver
Neubauer, Richard A. *library science educator, consultant*
Simeone, Wendy Frances *secondary school educator, department chairman*

Centerville
Anderson, Gerald Edwin *retired utilities executive*
Condon, Ann Blunt *psychotherapist*
Scherer, Harold Nicholas, Jr. *electric power industry executive*

Charlestown
Ackerman, Jerome Leonard *biomedical researcher*
Bhide, Pradeep G. *neuroscientist, researcher*
Buckner, Randy L. *psychology professor, neuroscientist*
Cutrer, Fred Michael *neurologist*
English, Todd *food company executive, chef*
Isselbacher, Kurt Julius *internist, educator*
Kazantsev, Aleksey Gregory *medical educator*
Kovacs, Dora Marta *neuroscientist, researcher, educator*
Leaf, Alexander *preventive medicine physician, epidemiologist*
Moskowitz, Michael Arthur *neuroscientist*
Ntziachristos, Vasilis *radiology, bioengineering educator*
Pittet, Mikael J. *research scientist, director*
Potts, John Thomas, Jr. *physician, educator*
Tanzi, Rudolph Emile *neuroscientist, researcher, educator*
Zamecnik, Paul Charles *oncologist, medical researcher*

Chatham
Escalante, Judson Robert *business consultant*
O'Connell, Brian *community organizer, educator, writer*
Popkin, Alice Brandeis *lawyer*
Rhinesmith, Stephen Headley *management consultant*
Stout, Sharon Sparkes *elementary school educator, counselor*

Chelmsford
Cleven, Carol Chapman *retired state legislator*
DiPillo, Patricia Anne *language educator, researcher*
Dulchinos, Peter *retired lawyer*
Edelstein, Robert A. *urologist*
Fulks, Robert Grady *computer company executive*
Lerer, Neal M. *lawyer*
Menitoff, Paul Alan *psychiatrist*

Chelsea
Jenkins, Alexander III *consumer products company executive, consultant*
Kaneb, John A. *oil industry executive*

Chestnut Hill
Altbach, Philip *director, educator*
Batchelder, Samuel Lawrence, Jr. *retired corporate lawyer*
Beaton, Albert Eugene *education educator*
Blanchette, Oliva *philosophy educator*
Boynton, Andrew C. *dean*
Burgess, Ann Wolbert *nursing educator*
Cohen, David Joel *medical educator*
Dahlben, Salin Abraham *neuropsychiatrist*
Flax, Martin Howard *pathologist, retired educator*
Goizueta, Roberto Segundo *theology studies educator*
Gottlieb, Marise Suss *epidemiologist*
Hachey, Thomas Eugene *British and Irish history educator*
Helmick, Raymond Glen *priest, educator*
Kelley, Shana O. *biochemist*
Kosasky, Harold Jack *fertility researcher*
Leahy, William Patrick *academic administrator, historian, educator*
Mahoney, Kevin J. *social worker, educator*
Mc Innes, William Charles *priest, academic administrator*
Moses, Judy *real estate company executive*
Munro, Barbara Hazard *nursing educator, dean, researcher*
Nemerowicz, Gloria *academic administrator*
Netzer, Nancy *museum director, art historian, educator*
O'Block, Robert Paul *management consultant*
O'Toole, James Michael *history educator*
Pendas, Devin Owen *history professor*
Qingwen, Xu *law educator, social worker, educator*
Reed, James Eldin *historian, consultant, educator*
Safizadeh, M. Hossein *finance educator*
Thier, Samuel Osiah *physician, educator*
Valette, Jean Paul *writer*
Valette, Rebecca Marianne *Romance languages educator*
Vance, Verne Widney, Jr. *retired lawyer*
Yavarkovsky, Jerome Harold *library director*

Chicopee
Dame, Catherine Elaine *acupuncturist*

Chilmark
Lazarus, David *physicist, researcher*

Clinton
Lanza, Robert Paul *medical scientist*

Cohasset
Dickstein, Harvey Leonard *pharmaceutical executive, researcher*
Morse, Elizabeth *conservator*
Rabstejnek, George John *healthcare executive*
Replogle, David Robert *publishing executive*
Whipple, Jacqueline Conant *writer, media specialist*

Concord
Bander, Edward Julius *lawyer, librarian emeritus*
Boger, William Pierce III *ophthalmologist*
Brooker, Richard I. *architect*
Coles, Robert *child psychiatrist, educator, writer*
Davidson, Frank Paul *retired macroengineer, lawyer*
Dresden, Jacob A. *headmaster*
Eberle, William Denman *international management consultant*
Fowler, Charles Albert *electronics engineer*
Giles, Kathleen C. *headmaster*
Glovsky, Susan G.L. *lawyer*
Gorny, Marina Dubinsky *music educator*
Heinle, Beverly Diane *publishing executive*
Horwitz, Paul *physicist*
Ihara, Michio *sculptor*
MacNeill, Frederick Douglas *artist*
Parrish, Thomas Kirkpatrick III *marketing consultant*
Plummer, William Torsch *optical physicist*
Schiller, Pieter Jon *retired venture capital executive*
Villers, Philippe *mechanical engineer*
Weiss, James Michael *financial analyst, portfolio manager*
Wickfield, Eric Nelson *investment company executive*

Cotuit
Ballou, Kenneth Walter *retired business executive, dean*
Miller, Robert Charles *retired physicist*

Cummington
Smith, William Jay *author*
Wilbur, Richard Purdy *writer, educator*

Dalton
Crane, Lansing E. *paper company executive*

Danvers
Beauregard, John *college librarian, consultant*
Butz, Stefan Peter *science association director*
Clark, Sharon Jackson *private school administrator*
Dolan, John Ralph *retired electronics executive*
Haber, Frederic *lawyer*
Kocur, Sean Edward *lab administrator*
Waite, Charles Morrison *food products executive*

Dartmouth
Connors, Robert Leo *city official*
Michel, Howard E. *electrical engineer, director*
Sweeney, Shawna Elizabeth *political science professor, researcher*
Washburn, Stewart Putnam *management consultant*
Wisneski, Kurt *art educator*

Dedham
Bolio, Jason S. *lawyer*
Magner, Jerome Allen *performing company executive*

Dennis Port
Singer, Myer R(ichard) *lawyer*

Devens
Currie, Michael J. *military officer*

Dighton
Buote, Rosemarie Boschen *retired special education educator*
Foley, Gerard F. *history educator*

Dorchester
Jackson, Jimmie L. *retired music educator, organist*
Loh, Shaun *radiologist*
Medeiros, Jennifer Lynn *school psychologist, consultant*
Smith, Survilla Marie *social services administrator, artist, poet*

Douglas
Bachelder, Beverly Brandt *secondary school educator, assistant principal, director*

Dover
Aldrich, Frank Nathan *banker*
Bonis, Laszlo Joseph *marketing executive, healthcare professional, chemist*
Buyse, Marylou *pediatrician, geneticist, medical administrator*
Craver, James Bernard *lawyer*
Edwards, Carl Norman *lawyer*
Mehta, Narinder Kumar *marketing executive*
Peirce, Bonnie *librarian*

Dudley
Van de Workeen, Priscilla Townsend *small business owner and executive*

Duxbury
Erickson, Phyllis Traver *marketing executive*
Schwartz, Edward Arthur *lawyer*
Thrasher, Dianne Elizabeth *mathematics educator, computer scientist, consultant*
Wangler, William Clarence *retired insurance company executive*
Zachmann, William Francis *computer and communications industry market research company executive*

East Boston
Coy, Craig P. *airport terminal executive*
Crawford, Linda Sibery *lawyer, educator*
Patinkin, Terry Allan *physician*

East Falmouth
Forte, Wesley Elbert *former insurance company executive, lawyer*

East Longmeadow
Skutnik, Bolesh J. *optics scientist, lay worker, lawyer*

East Orleans
Burkert, Robert Randall *artist*
Natale, Barbara Gustafson *retired librarian*
Romey, William Dowden *geologist, educator*

East Walpole
Paul, Carol Ann *retired academic administrator, biology educator*

Eastham
Tipton, Noel Martin, Jr. *musician, writer, composer*

Easthampton
Perkins, Homer Guy *manufacturing executive*
Prattis, Susan Marie *veterinarian, educator*

Edgartown
Gatting, Carlene J. *lawyer*
Rosenfeld, Walter David, Jr. *architect, writer*

Everett
Blake, Margaret Mary *director*

Fairhaven
Hotchkiss, Henry Washington *real estate broker, financial consultant*

Fall River
Andrade, Manuela Pestana *art educator*
Cabral, Gloria Maria *food service executive, educator*
Wilner, Marion Leonard *art educator*

Falmouth
Adelman, William J., Jr. *biophysicist*
Brock, Nancy Jeanne *music educator, writer*
Goody, Richard Mead *geophysicist*
Litschgi, Richard John *computer manufacturing company executive*
Maness, George Andrew *music educator*
McInnes, Donald Gordon *rail transportation executive*
Milkman, Roger Dawson *genetics educator, molecular biologist, researcher*
Sato, Kazuyoshi *pathologist*
Saunders, John Warren, Jr. *biology professor, consultant*

Fiskdale
Costello, Christine Ann *fine arts director, church organist*

Fitchburg
Jareckie, Stephen Barlow *museum curator*
Niemi, Beatrice Neal *social services professional*
Shemmeri, Thafur *pediatric dentist*
Wellman, Robert Jonathan *psychologist, educator*

Foxboro
Belichick, Bill (William Stephen Belichick) *professional football coach*
Brady, Tom (Thomas Edward Patrick Brady Jr.) *professional football player*
Bruschi, Tedy *professional football player*
Bush, Raymond T. *accountant, architectural firm executive*
Dillon, Corey *professional football player*
Ferron, Jennifer *marketing executive*
Karelitz, Richard Alan *treasurer, lawyer*
Kraft, Robert K. *professional sports team executive*
Martin, Peter Gerard *computer technician, consultant, secondary school educator*
Moss, Randy Gene *professional football player*
Testaverde, Vincent Frank (Vinny Testaverde) *professional football player*
Thompson, Michael David *physician*

Framingham
Aronson, Benjamin *artist*
Austin, Sandra Ikenberry *nursing educator, consultant*
Barron, Arnold S. *retail executive*
Bogard, Carole Christine *soprano*
Bose, Amar Gopal *electronics executive, electrical engineering educator*
Butka, Paul C. *retail executive*
Cammarata, Bernard *retail executive*
Campbell, Donald G. *retail executive*
Campbell, Kristin A. *lawyer, retail executive*
Casper, Leonard Ralph *American literature educator*
Casselman, Frederick Lee *computer artist, printmaker*
Coiner, Maryrose C. *psychologist*
Crossley, Frank Alphonso *retired metallurgical engineer*
DeWerth, Gordon Henry *management consultant*
Doody, Joseph G. *retail executive*
Feldberg, Sumner Lee *retired retail executive*
Flanagan, Timothy James *academic administrator, criminal justice educator*
Flores, Greg *retail executive*
Flutie, Doug (Douglas Richard Flutie) *retired professional football player*
Gilbert, John F. *retail executive*
Harrington, Joseph Francis *educational company executive, history educator*
Heng, Gerald C.W. *lawyer*
Herrman, Ernie *retail executive*
Klapholz, Henry *obstetrician, gynecologist, educator*
Komola, Christine T. *corporate financial executive*
Lesser, Richard G. *retired apparel executive*
Lindenmeyer, Peter W. *retail executive*
Mahoney, John J. *office supply company executive*
Margolis, Bruce Lewis *human resources executive*
McCauley, Ann *lawyer, retail executive*
Meador, Charles Lawrence *management and systems consultant, educator*
Meyrowitz, Carol M. *retail executive*
Miles, Michael A., Jr. *retail executive*
Naylor, Jeffrey Gordon *retail executive*
Parneros, Demos *retail executive*
Ramachandran, Vasan Srini *medical educator*
Rossi, Jerome R. *retail executive*
Ryan, Dennis M. *lawyer, construction executive*
Sargent, Ronald L. *retail office and business products executive*
Sherr, Richard *retail executive*
Sweetenham, Paul *retail executive*
Tripathy, Nirmal K. *retail executive*
Vassalluzzo, Joseph S. *retail company executive*
Welte, A. Theodore *chamber of commerce executive*
Zamvil, Linda Susan *psychiatrist, educator*
Ziomek, Carol Ann *medical products executive*

Franklin
Benjamin, Bernard Edward *school system administrator, director*
LaRowe, Richard Philip *systems engineer*
Maril, David C. *editor*

Gardner
Du Buske, Lawrence Michael *immunologist, rheumatologist*

Georgetown
deNapoli, Dyan *small business owner, educational consultant*

Gloucester
Birchfield, John Kermit, Jr. *lawyer*
Hausman, William Ray *fund raising and management consultant*
Littlefield, Paul Damon *retired management consultant*
McCarl, Henry Newton *economist, geologist, consultant, venture capitalist*
Sallah, Majeed (Jim Sallah) *retired real estate developer*
Steele-Goetemann, Judith Ann *artist, educator, art gallery owner*
White, Harold Jack *pathologist*
White, Horace Council *business manager*
White, Lucette Darby *painter, sculptor*

Granby
Ingham, Norman William *literature educator, genealogist*

Granville
Brown, Stephen Pat *artist*

Great Barrington
Curtin, Phyllis *music educator, dean, vocalist*
Frye-Moquin, Marsha Marie *social worker*
Rodgers, Bernard Francis, Jr. *literature and language professor*

Greenfield
Hutcheson, Thomas Worthington *trade association administrator*

Groton
Commons, Richard B. *headmaster*
Wiggins, D. Scott *headmaster*

Hampden
Joubert, Raymond Ernest *retired electrical engineer*

Hanover
Lonborg, James Reynold *dentist, former professional baseball player*

Hanscom Afb
Altshuler, Edward Elihu *physicist, researcher*
Carney, David John *computer scientist, music theorist*
Harper, David Taylor *civilian military employee*
Johnson, Charles L., II, *military officer*
Mailloux, Robert Joseph *physicist*

Hanson
Norris, John Anthony *health products executive, lawyer, educator*

Harvard
Monath, Thomas Patrick *physician*

Harwich
Caretti, Ann M. *school system administrator*

Harwich Port
Smith, Ralph Wesley, Jr. *retired federal judge*

Hatfield
Yolen, Jane *writer*

Haverhill
Bigelow, Peter *electronics executive*
DeSchuytner, Edward Alphonse *biochemist, educator*

Haydenville
Rupp, Sheron Adeline *photographer, educator*
Shallcross, Doris Jane *education educator*

Heath
Howland, Margaret E.C. *retired librarian*

Hingham
Llewellyn, John Schofield, Jr. *former food company executive*

Menzies, Ian Stuart *newspaper editor*
Noel, Barbara Hughes McMurtry *retired music educator*
Sullivan, Trudy F. *apparel executive*
Zetcher, Arnold B. *apparel executive*

Holbrook
Crandlemere, Robert Wayne *engineering executive*

Holden
O'Neil, William Francis *academic administrator*
Price, Robert DeMille *lawyer*

Holland
McGrory, Mary Kathleen *humanities educator, retired academic administrator*

Holyoke
Damon, Steven William *music educator*
Dearborn, Maureen Markt *speech and language clinician*
Dower Gold, Catherine Anne *music history educator*
Radner, Sidney Hollis *retired retail executive*
Resnic, Burton S. *lawyer*

Hopkinton
Dacier, Paul T. *lawyer, information technology executive*
Goulden, David *information technology executive*
Moran, Wendy Jacqueline *music educator, musician*
Newbrander, William Carl *health economist, management consultant*
Teuber, William J., Jr. *corporate financial executive*
Tucci, Joseph M. *information technology executive*

Hudson
Osoff, Jeffrey Arlin *media company executive*

Hull
Anderson, Timothy Christopher *educational association administrator*
Medalie, Richard James *lawyer*
Medalie, Susan Diane *lawyer, management consultant*

Hyannis
Cochrane, Paul Hollis *general practice physician*
Nicholson, Ellen Ellis *clinical social worker*
O'Brien, Kathleen L. *special education educator*
Segersten, Robert Hagy *lawyer, investment banker*

Hyde Park
Harris, Emily Louise *special education educator*

Ipswich
Dion Faust, Debra *secondary school educator*
Getchell, Charles Willard, Jr. *lawyer, publisher, foundation executive*
Herrmann, Robert Lawrence *biochemist, educator*
Jennings, Frederic Beach, Jr. *economist, saltwater flyfishing guide*
Lombardo, Ann Marie *special education educator, writer, artist*
Roberts, Richard John *molecular biologist, consultant, scientific officer*
Wilson, Doris H. *volunteer*

Jamaica Plain
Pierce, Chester Middlebrook *retired psychiatrist, educator*
White-Hammond, Gloria E. *pastor, pediatrician, human rights advocate*

Lancaster
Dugan, Maureen *biology educator, consultant*

Lawrence
Wasserman, Stephen Alan *lawyer*
Weaver, Peter David *bishop, religious organization administrator*

Leeds
Deane, James Garner *editor, conservationist*

Lenox
Berofsky, Bernard *philosopher, educator*

Leominster
Ford, John Stephen *treasurer*
Kerns, Christian Randolph *chemist*
Lambert, Lyn Dee *law librarian*

Leverett
Margolis, Nadia *language educator, translator, medievalist*

Lexington
Bailey, Fred Coolidge *retired engineering consulting company executive*
Balu, Sanjeev *pharacoeconomist*
Baron, Sheldon *research and development company executive*
Bazzaz, Fakhri A. *plant biology educator, administrator*
Beusch, John Ulrich *engineer, researcher*
Blackwell, William J. *geophysicist*
Brick, Donald Bernard *software company executive*
Brookner, Eli *electrical engineer*
Bussgang, Julian Jakub *electronics engineer, consultant*
Chamberlain, David M. *retail executive*
Coleman, Loring W. *artist*
Collins, Allan Meakin *education educator*
Davis, Robert J. *internet company executive*
Dinneen, Gerald Paul *electrical engineer, retired federal official*
Dionne, Gerald Francis *research physicist, educator, consultant*
Dougherty, Richard Hamlen *management and healthcare consultant*
Drouilhet, Paul Raymond, Jr. *retired science administrator, electrical engineer*
Farb, Thomas Forest *financial executive*
Fillios, Louis Charles *retired science educator*
Freed, Charles *engineering consultant, researcher*
Freitag, Wolfgang Martin *retired librarian*
Fullerton, Derek Paul *public health service officer*
Garing, Ione Davis *civic worker*
Garrelick, Joel Marc *acoustical scientist, consultant*
Gelb, Arthur *electrical and systems engineering executive*
Gibbs, Martin *biologist, educator*
Goell, James Emanuel *electronics executive*
Grousbeck, Wycliffe *professional sports team owner, venture capitalist*
Horowitz, Morris A. *retired economics professor*
Huang, Robin K. *research scientist*
Jordan, Judith Victoria *clinical psychologist, educator*
Keicher, William Eugene *electrical engineer*
Kennedy, X.J. (Joseph Kennedy) *writer*
Kent, Robert Brydon *law educator*
Klein, Lawrence Allen *finance educator*
Letts, Lindsay Gordon *pharmacologist, educator*
Levine, Janice R. *clinical psychologist*
McFarland, Philip James *secondary school educator, writer*
McGirr, David William John *pharmaceutical executive*
Morrow, Walter Edwin, Jr. *electrical engineer, lab administrator*
Nichols, Albert L. *economic consultant*
Ott, John Harlow *museum administrator*
Papanek, Gustav Fritz *economist, educator*
Schafer, Alice Turner *retired mathematics professor*
Silverman, Sam Mendel *physicist, lawyer*
Smith, Robert Louis *construction company executive*
Stonebraker, Michael R. *electrical engineering, computer science educator*
Thernstrom, Abigail *federal agency administrator, writer*
Ting, David *information technology executive*
Waksman, Byron Halsted *immunologist, educator, medical association administrator*
Wilson, Wendy Scott *history educator*
Zayhowski, John J. *electrical engineer, researcher*

Lincoln
Bracken, (Myra) Jeanne Munn *librarian, writer*
Brandt, John Henry *physician*
Donald, David Herbert *writer, history professor*
Giles, Allen *pianist, composer, music educator*
Gnichtel, William Van Orden *lawyer*
Holberton, Philip Vaughan *entrepreneur, educator*
LeGates, John Crews Boulton *information scientist*
Nenneman, Richard Arthur *retired publishing executive*
Payne, Roger Searle *zoologist, researcher, science administrator, conservationist*
Stathos, Margaret Moreland *musician*

Longmeadow
Ezrin, Myer *retired director*
Gallup, John Gardiner *retired paper company executive*
Katz, Barbara Stein *special education educator*
Keady, George Cregan, Jr. *judge*
Leary, Carol Ann *academic administrator*
Lemnios, Andrew Zachery *aerospace engineer, educator, researcher*
Lo Bello, Joseph David *bank executive*

Lowell
Carlsmith, Christopher *history professor*
Curtis, James Theodore *lawyer*
Dubner, Daniel William *pediatrician*
Kannenberg, Lloyd Chambers *physicist, researcher*
Karr, Ronald Dale *librarian, historian*
Lustick, David Scott *science educator, mathematics professor*
Martin, William Francis, Jr. *lawyer*
McAfee, Noelle Claire *philosopher, educator*
Meehan, Martin Thomas (Marty Meehan) *academic administrator, former congressman, lawyer*
O'Donnell, Kathleen Marie *lawyer*
Pullen, David John *physicist, researcher*
Teague, Bernice Rita *accountant*
Ting, John M. *dean, engineering educator*

Ludlow
Budnick, Thomas Peter *social worker*

Lynn
Astuccio, Sheila Margaret *educational administrator*
Chow, Humphrey Wai *mechanical engineer*
Copeland, Paul Michael *endocrinologist*
D'Entremont, Edward Joseph *application developer, educator*
Ryder, Edward Francis *secondary school educator*

Lynnfield
Kerrigan, Nancy *professional figure skater, retired Olympic athlete*
McGivney, John Joseph *lawyer*
Meyer, Piotr Jan *electronics engineer*

Malden
Brooks, Kevin M. *multimedia researcher, technology storyteller*
Driscoll, David P. *school system administrator*
Guild, Richard Samuel *trade association management company executive*

Manchester
Porter, Henry Homes, Jr. *investor*
Prout, Curtis *internist, educator*

Marblehead
Green, Richard John *architect*
Kennedy, Elizabeth Mae *musician*
Page, George Alfred, Jr. *lawyer*
Quigley, Stephen Howard *executive editor*
Speller, Kerstin G. Rinta *psychologist*
Tamaren, Michele Carol *spiritual director, writer, presenter, personal coach, retired special education educator*

Marion
McPartland, Patricia Ann *adult education educator*

Marlborough
Bennett, C. Leonard *electrical engineer*
Chong, James I. *information technology executive*
Johannes, Richard Scott *medical association administrator*
Knight, Douglas A. *mechanical engineer*
Murray, R. Scott *computer software company executive*
Willebeek-LeMair, Marc *information technology executive*

Marstons Mills
Martin, David Standish *education educator*
Martin, Susan Katherine *librarian*

Mashpee
Jamison, John L. *musician, educator*
Kilmartin, Joseph Francis, Jr. *information technology executive*
Tarlin, Sara-Fay *school psychologist, consultant*

Mattapoisett
Mazer, Mike *cardiologist, retired nephrologist, artist*

Medfield
McQuillen, Jeremiah Joseph *distribution executive*

Medford
Abriola, Linda Marie *civil and environmental engineer*
Ambady, Nalini *social psychologist, educator, researcher*
Astill, Kenneth Norman *mechanical engineering educator*
Bacow, Lawrence Seldon *academic administrator, environmental scientist, educator*
Bedau, Hugo Adam *philosophy educator*
Berman, David *lawyer, poet*
Bharucha, Jamshed *academic administrator*
Bosworth, Stephen Warren *dean, former ambassador*
Catley, Andrew Paul *veterinarian, researcher*
Cavallaro, Mary Caroline *retired physics professor*
Caviness, Madeline Harrison *art history educator, researcher*
Conklin, John Evan *sociology educator*
DeBold, Joseph Francis *psychologist, educator*
Dennett, Daniel Clement *philosopher, writer, educator*
Elkind, David *psychology professor*
Fyler, John Morgan *language educator*
Goldberg, Pamela Winer *entrepreneur, educator*
Greif, Robert *mechanical engineering educator*
Jackendoff, Ray Saul *linguistics educator*
Kumar, Krishna *chemistry professor*
Michalak, Jo-Ann *library director*
Miczek, Klaus Alexander *psychology professor*
Penick, Ann Clarisse *minister, counselor*
Salacuse, Jeswald William *lawyer, educator*
Sarno, Christopher Ed *writer*
Schneps, Jack *physics professor, department chairman*
Sherwin, Martin J. *history professor*
Sternberg, Robert Jeffrey *dean, psychology professor, researcher*
Ueda, Reed Takashi *historian, educator*
Uhlir, Arthur, Jr. *electrical engineer, academic administrator*
Wilson, Jonathan Michael *literature educator, writer*

Medway
Hoag, David Garratt *retired aerospace engineer*

Melrose
Desforges, Jane Fay *retired internist, hematologist, educator*
Henken, Bernard Samuel *clinical psychologist, speech pathologist*

Methuen
McNaughton, William John *retired bishop*

Middleton
Stanley, (Malchan) Craig *school system administrator, consultant, psychologist, researcher*

Mill River
Dunsay, Charles William *elementary school educator*
Jaffe, Katharine Weisman *retired librarian*

Millbury
Yonda, Alfred William *mathematician*

Milton
Frazier, Marie Dunn *speech professional, public relations executive, personnel director*
Randall, Lilian Maria Charlotte *museum curator*
Robertson, Robin Alayne *headmaster, anthropologist*
Wengler, Marguerite Marie *counseling administrator*

Zervas, Nicholas Themistocles *neurosurgeon*

Monson
Webster, Ronie Ruth *secondary school educator*

Monterey
Swan, William *actor*

Nantucket
Byrne, Laura G. *music educator, theater educator, vocal coach*
Kales, Paul Albert *engineering educator, cartoonist*
Rorem, Ned *composer, writer*
Saperstein, Lee Waldo *mining engineering educator*

Natick
Abele, John E. *medical products executive*
Berglund, Larry Glenn *mechanical engineer, educator*
Blaha, Michael Douglas *research biologist*
Darehshori, Nader Farhang *publishing sales executive*
Geller, Esther (Bailey Geller) *artist*
Gottlieb, Michael Norman *internist, educator, health facility administrator*
Grassia, Thomas Charles *lawyer, educator, writer*
Kushner, Harold Samuel *rabbi*
Latanision, Ronald Michael *materials science and engineering consultant*
LaViolette, Paul A. *medical products executive*
Law, Jan *artist*
Leno, Sam R. *corporate financial executive*
Marr, David E. *lawyer*
Miller, George David *retired military officer, not-for-profit executive*
Nicholas, Peter M. *medical products executive*
Nirmel, Krishna *neurosurgeon*
Pokorny, Joseph Wenceslaus III *engineer*
Rendell, Kenneth William *rare and historical documents dealer, consultant*
Sandman, Paul William *lawyer*
Sedo, Manuel Arturo *psychologist, researcher*
Strauss, Harlee Sue *environmentalist, consultant*
Tobin, James Robert *biomedical device manufacturing company executive*
Wallace-Taylor, Elizabeth *medical/surgical nurse*
Zarkin, Herbert J. *wholesale distribution executive*

Needham
Bohnen, Michael J. *lawyer, foundation administrator*
Boulding, Elise Marie *sociologist, educator*
Cogswell, John Heyland *retired telecommunications industry executive, financial consultant*
Di Domenica, Robert Anthony *musician, composer*
Grasso, James Anthony *public relations executive, educator*
Greenway, Hugh Davids Scott *journalist*
Holt, Stephen S. *astrophysicist*
Kanojia, Chet *communications executive*
Kenslea, Timothy Joseph *historian, educator*
Miller, Richard Keith *academic administrator, engineering educator*
Osser, David Neal *psychiatrist, educator*
Powell, Adam Clayton *engineering educator, consultant*
Rafferty, James Paul *telecommunications executive*
Rodman, Sumner *insurance company executive*
Ryan, Una Scully *health science association administrator, medical educator*
Safran, Edward Myron *financial consultant, bank executive*
Spelfogel, Scott David *lawyer*
Zambone, Alana Maria *special education educator, consultant*

Needham Heights
Salhany, Lucille S. (Lucy Salhany) *broadcast executive*

New Bedford
Benoit, Richard Armand *lawyer, retired police chief*
Bullard, John Kilburn *educational association administrator*
Matsumoto, Carolee Setsuko *researcher, education developer and administrator*
Murray, Robert Fox *lawyer*

Newburyport
Robinson, Enders Anthony *geophysicist, educator, writer*
Robinson, Joyce McPeake *academic administrator*

Newton
Bagalay, John Earl *information technology executive, venture capitalist, consultant*
Baron, Charles Hillel *lawyer, educator*
Bassuk, Ellen Linda *psychiatrist*
Benner, Mary Wright *freelance/self-employed conference director*
Bernier, George Matthew, Jr. *oncologist, educator, dean*
Burlage, Dorothy Dawson *clinical psychologist*
Chubb, Stephen Darrow *health products executive*
Coquillette, Daniel Robert *lawyer, educator*
Davidson, Barry A. *plastic surgeon*
Dunlap, William Crawford *physicist*
Frankenheim, Samuel *retired lawyer*
Garcia, Eduardo *neurologist, consultant*
Glazer, Donald Wayne *lawyer, corporate financial executive, educator*
Glick-Weil, Kathy *library director*
Holbik, Karel *economics professor*
Huber, Richard Gregory *lawyer, educator*
Hume, Ellen Hunsberger *media analyst, educator, journalist*
Jeanloz, Roger William *biochemist, educator*

Jellinek, Michael Steven *psychiatrist, pediatrician*
Karp, Stephen R. *real estate developer*
Klyosov, Anatole Alex *biochemist, researcher*
Lichtin, Norman Nahum *chemistry professor*
Marrone, Philip A. *chemical engineer*
Marshall, Robert Lewis *musicologist, educator*
Matteson, Carol J. *academic administrator*
May, Harold Louis *retired surgeon, not-for-profit developer*
Metzer, Patricia Ann *lawyer*
Mullen, Maureen Ann *social worker*
Nahigian, Robert John *real estate company executive, consultant*
O'Connell, Sister Virginia M. *school librarian*
Osborne, Charles David *singer, composer, conductor*
Peterson, Lloyd, Jr. *academic administrator, consultant*
Peterson, Osler Leopold *lawyer*
Petrowski, Joseph H. *oil industry executive*
Saffran, Kalman *entrepreneur, venture capitalist*
Sasahara, Arthur Asao *cardiologist, educator, researcher*
Sheridan, Thomas Brown *mechanical engineering and applied psychology educator, researcher, consultant*
Teig, Marlowe Gilman *investment banker*
Wahlberg, Mark *actor*
White, Burton Leonard *retired educational psychologist, writer, consultant*
Winder, Alvin Eliot *public health educator, clinical psychologist*

Newton Center
Adams, F. Gerard *economist, educator*
Copithorne, David A. *public relations executive*
Eichler, Marc *neurosurgeon*
Garvey, John Hugh *dean, law educator*
Schuller, Gunther Alexander *composer*
Snyder, John Gorvers *lawyer*
Williamson, Susan *retired mathematician, educator*

Newton Centre
Anzalone, Filippa Marullo *law librarian, educator*
Peck, Sheldon *orthodontist, educator, dental anthropologist, historian*

Newton Highlands
Bricklin, Daniel *software designer, consultant*
Hummel, Margaret P. *state representative*

Newtonville
Polonsky, Arthur *artist, educator*

North Adams
McConnell, Matthew Stephen *composer, educator*
Thurston, Donald Allen *broadcast executive*

North Andover
Becker, Lawrence Wilfred *headmaster*
Gelb, Harold Seymour *retired manufacturing executive, entrepreneur, consultant*
Goldstein, Charles Henry *architect, consultant*
Herstein, Gary L. *philosophy professor, researcher*
Jannini, Ralph Humbert III *electronics executive*
Kurzweil, Raymond C. *computer scientist, entrepreneur*
Norris, Rebecca Sachs *religious studies educator*
Swallow, Kathleen Clinedinst *chemistry professor*

North Attleboro
Koussa, Harold Alan *insurance account executive*

North Chatham
O'Brien, Robert Emmet *insurance company executive*
Wilson, E. B. *manufacturing executive, consultant, writer*

North Chelmsford
Erkkila-Ricker, Barbara Howell *writer, photographer*
Kotelly, George Vincent *editor, writer, electrical engineer*

North Dartmouth
Barrow, Clyde Wayne *social sciences educator*
Hsu, Jong-Ping *physicist, educator*
Sauro, Joseph Pio *physics professor*
Xu, Haiping *application developer, educator*
Yoken, Mel B(arton) *language educator, writer, radio personality*

North Dighton
Cserr, Robert *psychiatrist, physician, hospital administrator*
Silvia, David Alan *insurance broker*

North Easton
Bundy, Annalee Marshall *library director*
Varella, Hazel L. *historian, educator*

North Grafton
Costa, Lais Rosa Rodrigues *veterinarian, educator, medical researcher*
Schwartz, Anthony *veterinary surgeon, educator*

North Oxford
Carney, Roger Francis Xavier *retired military officer*

North Quincy
Rutherford, Scott *marketing professional, consultant*

Northampton
Christ, Carol Tecla *academic administrator*
Derr, Thomas Sieger *religion educator*
Donfried, Karl Paul *theologian, clergyman*
Elkins, Stanley Maurice *historian, educator*
Fabing, Suzannah *museum director*
Hastings, Wilmot Reed *lawyer, writer*
Holbert, Kelly McKay *exhibition coordinator, art historian*
Mahoney, Maureen A. *academic administrator*
Naegele, Philipp Otto *musician, educator*
Newman, Leslea *writer*
Palser, Barbara F. *retired botanist*
Piccinino, Rocco Michael *librarian*
Robinson, John Alan *information scientist, educator*
Rose, Peter Isaac *sociologist, writer, editor*
Schuleit, Anna *artist*
Smith, Malcolm Barry Estes *philosopher, educator, lawyer*
von Klemperer, Klemens *historian, educator*

Northborough
Cradler, Judith A. *science educator*
Fulmer, Hugh Scott *physician, educator*
Wang, Jun *process engineer, materials scientist*

Norton
Crutcher, Ronald Andrew *academic administrator, music educator*
Worthley, Harold Field *retired minister, educator*

Norwell
Brett, Jan Churchill *illustrator, author*
Case, David Knowlton *management consultant*

Norwood
Berliner, Allen Irwin *dermatologist*
Fishman, Jerald G. *semiconductor executive*
Li, Chiang J. *pharmaceutical executive, physician scientist*
Memishian, Jack *electronics engineer*
Pence, Robert Dudley *biomedical researcher, consultant, hospital administrator*
Seif, Margaret K. *lawyer, electronics executive*
Sheingold, Daniel H. *electrical engineer*
Singer, Paula Noyes *lawyer, computer company executive*

Orange
Rivers, Robert Alfred *microwave company executive*
Strunjo, Jacob Anthony *elementary school educator*

Orleans
Baird, Julian Thompson, Jr. *entrepreneur*
Patterson, Elizabeth C. *choir director*
Rappaport, Margaret Mary Williams Ewing *psychologist, physician, writer, pilot, consultant*

Osterville
Schwarztrauber, Sayre Archie *former naval officer, maritime consultant*
Sommers, William Paul *management consultant, research and development company executive*

Oxford
Holbrook, Howard George *pharmacist*
Schur, Walter Robert *physician*

Palmer
Dupuis, Robert Simeon *sales executive*

Paxton
Clarke, Edward Nielsen *engineering science educator*

Peabody
Bierman, George William *retired food scientist*
Birdsall, Melinda R. *gynecologist*
Dobbs, John McGregor *physicist, mechanical engineer*
Generazzo, Arlene Diamond *retired elementary school educator*
Gordon, Bernard M. *computer company executive*
Lipman, Richard Paul *pediatrician*
Perryman, Jonathan Richard *orthopedist, surgeon*
Peters, Leo Francis *environmental engineer*
Southwick, Paul *retired public relations executive*

Pelham
Fetler, Andrew *author, educator*

Pepperell
Holmes, Jean Louise *real estate investor, humanities educator*

Petersham
Chivian, Eric Seth *psychiatrist, environmental scientist, educator*

Pittsfield
Begley, Charlene *manufacturing executive*
Doyle, Anthony Peter *lawyer*
Feigenbaum, Armand Vallin *systems engineer, information technology executive*
Guzzo, Jessica Ann *music educator*
Hochfelder, Scott Z. *toy company executive, lawyer*
Norris, Jeannie *headmaster*
Rich, Philip Dewey *publishing executive*
Shammas, Nazih Kheirallah *environmental engineer, consultant, engineering educator*
Staley, Greg *retail executive*
Wenner, Gene Charles *arts management executive*
Wood, Elizabeth Ann *special education educator*

Plainville
Zani, Frederick Caesar *retired financial consultant*

Plymouth
Della-Giustina, Jo-Ann *lawyer*
Flood, H. Gay (Hulda Gay Flood) *editor, consultant*
Goldman, Ralph Frederick *research physiologist, educator*
Gregory, Dick *comedian, volunteer*
Joseph, Rodney Randy *art association administrator*
Phillips, Warren G. *secondary school educator*
Staszesky, Francis Myron *electric power industry executive, consultant*
Woodburn, Norma Denman *biology educator, researcher*

Prides Crossing
Garcia, Adolfo Ramon *lawyer, director*
Schlichtmann, Jan Richard *lawyer*

Provincetown
Collins, Larry Richard *artist, educator, art gallery director*
Hutchinson, Peter Arthur *artist*
McCarthy, Christine M. *museum director*
Oliver, Mary *poet*

Quincy
Adams, Ronald G. *elementary school educator*
Hall, John Raymond, Jr. *fire protection executive*
Hayes, Mary Dianne Wixted *lawyer*
Holway, David J. *labor union administrator*
Levin, Robert Joseph *food products executive*
Lippincott, Joseph P. *photojournalist, educator*
Moran, James Joseph, Jr. *insurance company executive*
Motejunas, Gerald William *lawyer*
Young, Richard William *chemicals executive*

Randolph
Cammarata, Richard John *financial advisor*
Huntington, Robert Howard *business management executive*
Johnson, Laurence Michael *lawyer*
Morrissey, Edmond Joseph *philologist*

Reading
Burbank, Nelson Stone *investment banker*
Frey, Joanne Alice Tupper *art educator*
Nordstrand, Nathalie Elizabeth Johnson *artist*

Revere
Anthony, Sylvia *social welfare organization executive*
Paananen, Victor Niles *language educator*
Recupero-Faiella, Anna Antonietta *poet*

Rockland
Blethen, Sandra Lee *pediatric endocrinologist*
Dunne, Myra Schley *nurse, consultant*

Rockport
Bissell, Phil (Charles P. Bissell) *cartoonist*
Harries, James Theodore *psychologist*
Martin, Roger Hemenway *artist, educator*
Nicholas, Thomas Andrew *artist*
Wiberg, Lars-Erik *occupational compatibility consultant*

Roslindale
Girard, Jonathan Richard *conductor*
Sullivan, Dorothy Rona *state official*

Roxbury
Cruthird, Brandy K. *gym owner and fitness instructor*
Peters, Alan *anatomy educator*
Simons, Elizabeth R(eiman) *biochemist, educator*

Salem
Corrigan, Karina Helen Hiltje *museum administrator*
Doran, Kathleen Brewer *dean, consultant*
Goss, Laurence Edward, Jr. *geographer, educator*
Higgins, Gina O'Connell *psychologist, writer*
McKenzie, Walter L. *information technology executive, consultant*
Melby, John B. *composer, educator*
Moran, Philip David *lawyer*
Rabchenuk, Paul Thomas *lawyer*

Sandwich
Parsons, Stuart W. *librarian*
Troy, Robert Sweeney, Sr. *lawyer*

Scituate
Spangler, Stanley Eugene *international relations educator*

Sharon
Berzon, Faye Clark *retired nursing educator*
Edmonds, Nick *sculptor*

Shelburne Falls
Evelyn, Phyllis *minister*
Torras, Joseph Hill *pulp and paper company executive*

Sherborn
Borgeson, Earl Charles *law librarian, educator*
Cushing, Steven *linguist, educator, writer, researcher, consultant*
Goglia, Charles A., Jr. *lawyer*
Hancock, William Frank, Jr. *management consultant*
Kennedy, Chester Ralph, Jr. *retired state official, art director*

Shirley
Hoffmann, Micheal Joseph *theater director*

Shirley Center
Holden, Harley Peirce *retired archivist*

Shrewsbury
Falter, Robert Gary *real estate broker, educator*
Kranich, Margaret Mansley *artist*
Mastroianni, Anthony Robert *real estate company officer*
Nixon, Eugene Ray *chemist, educator*
Onorato, Nicholas Louis *retired program director, economist*

Shutesbury
Abbott, Douglas Eugene *engineering educator*
Creed, Robert Payson, Sr. *retired literature educator*

Siasconset
Albani, Thomas J. *investor*
Rauch, George Washington *lawyer, director*
Smith, Harrison Harvey *journalism consultant*

Somerset
Joseph, George Foster, Jr. *elementary school educator, historian*

Somerville
Austill, Allen *dean emeritus*
Ballman, Chris *public radio reporter*
Brams, Marvin Robert *economist, mental health counselor, interfaith minister, educator*
Curwood, Steve *television producer, host*
Fitzpatrick, Terry *public radio reporter, producer*
Gellerman, Bruce Edward *reporter*
Imende-Cooney, Elizabeth F. *literature educator, consultant*
Klass, Perri Elizabeth *pediatrician, writer*
Suhrstedt, Barbara Lynn *concert pianist, voice educator*

South Dartmouth
Mellberg, Leonard Evert *physicist*
Ward, Richard Joseph *university dean, educator, author*

South Easton
Keith, Michael Curtis *communication educator, writer*

South Hadley
Berek, Peter *literature and language professor*
Bowie, Lee *academic administrator, philosopher, educator*
Brownlow, Frank Walsh *literature and language professor*
Burbine, Thomas Hewey *science educator, researcher*
Creighton, Joanne Vanish *academic administrator*
Elleman, Barbara *editor*
Ewing Browne, Sheila *chemistry professor, physical organic chemist*
Farnham, Anthony Edward *language educator, department chairman*
Fisher, William Thomas *business administration educator*
Hall, Lee *artist, educator, writer*
Horsnell, Margaret Eileen *retired historian*
Townsend, Jane Kaltenbach *biologist, educator*
Williamson, Kenneth Lee *chemistry professor*

South Hamilton
Ryan, Heather Vickers *marketing professional*

South Orleans
Hale, Margaret Smith *insurance company executive, educator*

South Wellfleet
Blau, Monte *retired radiology educator*

South Weymouth
Coombs, Alice A. Tolbert *anesthesiologist, internist*
Young, Michael Chung-En *allergist, immunologist, pediatrician*

South Yarmouth
Nichols, Robert Lyman *retired foreign service officer, lecturer*

Southborough
Chryssis, George Christopher *entrepreneur*
Kriegsman, Edward Michael *lawyer*
Lavin, Philip Todd *medical executive*
Mylotte, John Arnold *writer, educator*
Stubbart, David James *elementary school educator*
Warren, John Coolidge *educational administrator*

Southbridge
Anderson, Ross Barrett *healthcare environmental services manager*
Mangion, Richard Michael *health facility administrator*
Vasey, Ann L. *pre-school administrator, counselor*

Spencer
Robinson, Evelyn Edna *secondary school educator*

Springfield
Burke, Michael Henry *lawyer*
Caprio, Anthony S. *academic administrator*
Castellani, Frederick C. *insurance company executive*
Cook, Kathryn Anne *secondary school educator*
Crandall, Roger W. *insurance company executive*
Dibble, Francis Daniel, Jr. *lawyer*
Engebretson, Douglas Kenneth *architect, interior designer*
Ervin, Billy Maxwell *retired military officer*
Farkas, Paul Stephen *gastroenterologist*
Friedmann, Paul *surgeon, educator, research and development company executive*
Ganai, Sabha *surgeon, researcher*
Glavin, William Francis, Jr. *insurance company executive*
Gunton, Howard E. *insurance company executive*
Habermehl, Lawrence LeRoy *philosophy educator*
Harnois, Veronica *psychologist, educator*
Johnson, Robert Allison *life insurance company executive*
Kirkwood, John Robert *neuroradiologist*

Kottamasu, Mohan Rao (K.V.R. Mohan Rao) *physician, health facility administrator*
Liptzin, Benjamin *psychiatrist*
Mason, Mark D. *lawyer*
McCarthy, Charles Francis, Jr. *lawyer*
McGee, William Tobin *internist*
Melconian, Linda Jean *state senator, lawyer, educator*
Miller, Leroy Paul, Jr. *language educator*
Muhlberger, Richard Charles *museum director, writer, educator*
Murphy, Eileen Bridget *retired mathematics and computer science professor*
Neiman, Kenneth Paul *judge*
Oldershaw, Louis Frederick *retired lawyer*
Parke, David Alan *lawyer*
Reese, Stuart Harry *insurance company executive*
Roellig, Mark D. *lawyer*
Rollings, Michael Thomas *insurance company executive*
Romero, Ricardo Vicente *gastroenterologist*
Santopietro, Albert Robert *lawyer*
Sarsynski, Elaine A. *insurance company executive*
Scibelli, Andrew M. *academic administrator*
Stack, May Elizabeth *retired library director*
Starr, David *editor, publisher*
Susse, Sandra Slone *lawyer*
Utley, F. Knowlton *library director, educator*
Weiss, Ronald Phillip *lawyer*

Squantum
Robertson, Michael Swing *minister*

Stockbridge
Fitzpatrick, Jane *entrepreneur*
Shapiro, Edward Robert *psychiatrist, educator, health facility administrator, psychotherapist*

Stoughton
Gabovitch, Steven Alan *lawyer, accountant*
George, Arthur Charles *lawyer*
Hall, Roger Lee *musicologist, educator, composer*
Joseph, Anthony Barnett *psychiatrist*
Pitkin, Mark *research scientist*

Sudbury
Ames, Lois Winslow Sisson *social worker, educator, writer*
Aronson, David *artist, retired educator*
Deutsch, Marshall E(manuel) *medical products company executive, inventor*
Diette, Kelly A. *psychologist*
Henderson, Ernest III *healthcare executive*
Lamont-Havers, Ronald William *retired physician, medical association administrator*
McCree, Paul William, Jr. *systems design and engineering company executive*
Meltzer, Donald Richard *retired treasurer*

Sunderland
Baritz, Loren *history professor*

Swampscott
Kaufman, William Morris *electrical engineer, consultant*

Taunton
Ricciardi, Louis Michael *brokerage house executive*

Tewksbury
Black, Richard Bruce *corporate executive, consultant*
Faccini, Ernest Carlo *mechanical engineer*
Herlihy-Chevalier, Barbara Doyle *retired mental health nurse*
Shea, William J. *former insurance company executive*
Tabea, Emile Victor *health facility administrator*

Truro
Chaplin, Ansel Burt *lawyer*

Uxbridge
Zeis, Joanne A. *medical writer*

Vineyard Haven
Breuer, Joann Green *theater director*
Kimball, Julie Ellis *small press publisher, humorist, writer*
Ortlip, Paul Daniel *artist*

Waban
Hewlett-Kierstead, Nancy Carrick *psychologist, educator*
Mark, Melvin *mechanical engineering educator, consultant*
Rogoff, Jerome Howard *psychiatrist, psychoanalyst, forensic expert*
Rossolimo, Alexander Nicholas *management consultant, corporate director*
Shklar, Gerald *pathologist, periodontist, educator*

Wakefield
Coletta, Gerard Charles *management consultant*
Lucas, Robert Frank *lawyer*
Trogolo, Jeffrey A. *research scientist*

Waltham
Abbott, Laurence Frederick *physics educator*
Ackerman, Robert Wallace *private equity manager*
Adamian, Gregory Harry *academic administrator*
Altman, Stuart Harold *economist, educator*
Arena, Albert A. *museum director*
Barnes-Brown, Peter Newton *lawyer*
Bernstein, Stanley Joseph *manufacturing executive*
Bleicher, Paul Alan *information technology executive, physician*
Boykan, Martin *composer, music educator*
Bronfman, Charles Rosner *philanthropist, former distillery executive*
Brown, Edgar Henry, Jr. *mathematician, educator*
Buchholz, William James *communications executive, educator*
Caine, Franklyn A. *aerospace transportation executive*
Cantarella, Paolo *former automotive executive*
Chory, John H. *lawyer*
Cox, Howard Ellis, Jr. *venture capitalist*
Dekkers, Marijn E. *electronics executive*
Edmiston, Scott *academic administrator, educator*
Epstein, Irving Robert *chemistry professor*
Erbil, Can *economist, educator*
Faneuil, Edward J. *lawyer*
Fischer, David Hackett *historian, educator*
Floyd, John Taylor *electronics executive*
Foxman, Bruce Mayer *chemist, educator*
Franklin, Charles E. *manufacturing executive*
Galinat, Walton Clarence *research scientist*
Gaskin, Steven Paul *marketing executive, consultant*
Goodheart, Eugene *literary critic*
Gumpertz, Werner Herbert *structural engineering company executive*
Hall, Jeffrey Connor *biology educator, behavioral genetics researcher*
Hanson, Perry *library and information scientist*
Heystee, Susan *information technology executive*
Hill, Anita Faye *law educator*
Hoogasian, Seth H. *lawyer*
Hooper, Marcia Jacobs *venture capitalist, former communications executive*
Hovsepian, Ronald W. *network management software company executive*
Kasputys, Joseph Edward *corporate executive, economist*
Klerman, Lorraine Vogel *public health educator*
Lackner, James Robert *aerospace medicine educator*
Landaw, Stephen Arthur *physician, educator*
Larson, Gloria Ann Cordes *academic administrator, lawyer*
Leach, Robert Ellis *orthopedist, surgeon, educator*
Lian, Bong H. *mathematics professor, department chairman*
Malis, Andrew Gary *telecommunications industry executive*
Marder, Eve Esther *neuroscientist, educator*
McCulloch, Rachel *economist, educator*
Meister, Paul M. *medical products executive*
Messman, Jack L. *network management software company executive*
Metcalfe, Robert M. *venture capitalist, former science engineer, publishing executive, writer*
Miller, Christopher *science educator*
Nelson, Arthur Hunt *real estate company executive*
Notkin, Leonard Sheldon *architect*
Novick, David Kandel *science educator, department chairman*
O'Connell, Jeanne *financial planner, insurance broker*
Quinn, Michael *economics professor*
Reinharz, Jehuda *academic administrator, history educator*
Roosevelt, James, Jr. *insurance company executive, lawyer*
Sachs, Murray *French language and literature educator, researcher*
Saxe, Leonard *social psychologist, educator*
Scheffler, Israel *philosopher, educator*
Schneider, Craig David *health policy analyst*
Schrecker, John *historian, educator*
Sekuler, Robert William *psychologist, educator*
Shepard, Donald Sloane *public policy research educator*
Shyu, Heidi *defense equipment manufacturing company executive, electrical engineer*
Simeonov, Simeon *computer scientist*
Slifka, Eric *oil industry executive*
Snider, Barry B. *organic chemist*
Staves, Susan *humanities educator*
Stephens, Jay B. *lawyer, defense equipment manufacturing company executive*
Stuntz, Linda Gillespie *government official, lawyer*
Sullivan, Mary E. *retired secondary educator, past state legislator*
Swanson, William Henry *defense equipment manufacturing company executive*
Wajsgras, David C. *manufacturing executive*
Wawrzaszek, Susan V. *university librarian*
Wyner, Yehudi *composer, pianist, conductor, educator*

Watertown
Emerson, Charles P. *research scientist*
Gerritson, A. J. *advertising executive*
Kaloosdian, Robert Aram *lawyer*
Pellegrom, Daniel Earl *health and development executive*
Reilly, Thomas F. *former state attorney general*
Rivers, Wilga Marie *language educator*
Tompkins, Curtis Johnston *government agency administrator*

Wayland
Brynjolfsson, Ari *nuclear physicist*
Clark, Melville, Jr. *physicist, consultant, electrical engineer*
Dergalis, George *artist, educator*
Edelman, Stuart Edward *psychiatrist*
Huff, William Braid *retired publishing company executive*
Humphrey, Diana Young *fundraiser*
Moncure, Ashby Carter *surgeon, educator*
Wolff, Peter Adalbert *retired physics professor, researcher*

Webster
Fels, Gerald *insurance company executive*

Wellesley
Auerbach, Jerold S. *academic administrator, educator*
Baker, Charles D. *health insurance company executive*
Bidart, Frank *English educator, poet*
Birkerts, Gunnar *architect*
Bottomly, (H.) Kim *academic administrator, biology professor, researcher*
Burstein, Harvey *lawyer, educator*
Charpie, Robert Alan *physicist, researcher*
Craven, Donald Edward *epidemiologist, researcher*
DiCamillo, Gary Thomas *manufacturing executive*
Falchuk, Kenneth R. *gastroenterologist*
Fineberg, Gerald *real estate company executive*
Gailius, Gilbert Keistutis *manufacturing executive*
Gerety, Robert John *microbiologist, researcher, pediatrician, pharmaceutical executive*
Giddon, Donald B(ernard) *psychologist, educator*
Heisler, Elwood Douglas *hotel executive*
Jacobs, Ruth Harriet *poet, playwright, sociologist, gerontologist*
Kato, Walter Yoneo *physicist*
Lloyd-Jones, Sir (Peter) Hugh (Jefferd) *writer*
Marcus, Richard Greenwald *manufacturing executive*
Martin, Tony *humanities educator*
Marx, Peter A. *lawyer*
McGibbon, Phyllis Isabel *artist, educator*
Mickenberg, David *museum director, art director, historian*
Mistacco, Vicki E. *foreign language educator*
Morant, Ricardo Bernardino *psychology professor*
Murray, Joseph Edward *retired plastic surgeon*
Pike, Judith Robyn *lawyer*
Sangree, Walter Hinchman *social anthropologist, educator*
Sexton, John Joseph *oral and maxillofacial surgeon, educator*
Silberman, Robert A. S. *lawyer*
Snitzer, Elias *physicist*
Stettner, Edward A. *political science professor*
Summe, Gregory Louis *health products executive*
Thayer, Gaylord Bertram, Jr. *retired electronics executive, private investor*
Tierney, Thomas J. *social entrepreneur*
Tofias, Allan *retired accountant*
Tsai, Ming *chef*
Weil, Thomas Alexander *retired electronics engineer*
Wilchins, Stephen N. *lawyer*
Young, Delano Victor *cell biologist, pharmaceutical scientist, biochemist, educator*

Wellesley Hills
Carroll, Deirdre Holden *psychiatric nurse practitioner, educator, medical researcher*
Carroll, Megan *lawyer, educator*
Clarkson, Cheryl Lee *healthcare executive*
Doorley, Thomas Lawrence III *management consultant*
Imbrescia, Marcia *landscape company executive*
Marcus, William Michael *rubber and vinyl products manufacturing company executive*
Spierings, Egilius Leonardus Hendricus *pharmacologist, neurologist, headache specialist, clinical trialist*

Wellfleet
Limpitlaw, John Donald *publishing executive, priest*
Mc Feely, William Shield *historian, writer*
Piercy, Marge *poet, writer*

Wenham
Wang, Dong *history professor, director*

West Brookfield
Higgins, Brian Alton *art gallery owner, artist*

West Chatham
Rowley, Glenn Harry *lawyer*

West Falmouth
Bass, Norman Herbert *neurologist, educator, research scientist, hospital administrator, academic administrator*
Carlson, David Bret *retired lawyer*
King, Richard Hood *retired newspaper executive*

West Hyannisport
Gingold, George Norman *insurance company executive, lawyer*

West Newbury
Dooley, Ann Elizabeth *freelance writers cooperative executive, editor*

West Newton
Spitzer, Toba *rabbi*

West Roxbury
Ellenbogen, George *poet, educator*
Lovell, Francis Joseph *retired investment company executive*
Roach, Maureen S. *primary school educator*

West Springfield
Desai, Veena Balvantrai *obstetrician, gynecologist, educator*

West Tisbury
Méras, Phyllis Leslie *journalist*

West Wareham
Worrell, Cynthia Lee *bank executive*

Westborough
Antalek, Eileen Elizabeth *educational psychologist, consultant*
Bok, Joan Toland *utilities executive*
Gionfriddo, Maurice Paul *aeronautical engineer, research and development company executive*
Horwitz, Eleanor Catherine *public information officer*
Nichols, Guy Warren *retired institute and utilities executive*
Schrager, Mindy Rae *operations research specialist*
Staffier, Pamela Moorman *psychologist*

Westfield
Buckmore, Alvah Clarence, Jr. *computer scientist, ballistician*
Zayac, Linda Mary *sociologist, educator*

Westford
Geary, Marie Josephine *art association administrator*
Paine, Robert J. *environmental scientist, consultant*

Weston
Alcock, George Lewis, Jr., (Peter) *investor, business strategist*
Barry, William Anthony *priest, writer*
Bateman, Thomas Robert *lawyer*
Daly, Charles Ulick *foundation executive*
Goldstein, Arthur Louis *retired utilities executive*
Higgins, Sister Therese *literature educator, former college president*
Jayasankar, Subramanyan *orthopaedic surgeon*
Katz, William Emanuel *retired chemical engineer*
Kraft, Gerald *economist*
Lashman, L. Edward *arbitrator, mediator, consultant*
Lin, Alice Lee Lan *physicist, researcher, educator*
Oates, Mary Josephine *historian, educator*
Saad, Theodore Shafick *retired microwave company executive*
Sanzone, Donna S. *publishing executive*
Stambaugh, Armstrong A., Jr. *restaurant and hotel executive*
Tenney, Sarah G. *music educator*
Thomas, Roger Meriwether *lawyer*
Valente, Louis Patrick (Dan Valente) *financial planner, director*
Wood, Jeremy Scott *architect, urban designer*

Westport
Gormley, Robert John *retired publishing executive*
Nichols, C. Walter III *retired trust company executive*

Westport Point
Fanning, William Henry, Jr. *computer specialist*

Westwood
Bier, Louis Henry Gustav *minister*
Bloomingdale, Lewis Morgan *retired psychiatrist*
Borgman, George Allan *journalist*
Kushner, Jeffrey L. *manufacturing executive*
Phillips, Marion Grumman *civic volunteer, writer*
Riley, Henry Charles *banker*

Weymouth
Fitzsimmons, B. Joseph, Jr. *lawyer*

Whitinsville
Plaud, Joseph Julian *psychology educator*

Williamstown
Bell, Robert *literature educator*
Blair, Phyllis E. *artist*
Bolton, Roger Edwin *economist, educator*
Chandler, John Wesley *educational consultant*
Conforti, Michael Peter *museum director, art historian*
Cramer, Phebe *psychologist*
Crampton, Stuart Jessup Bigelow *physicist, researcher*
Dalzell, Robert Fenton, Jr. *historian, educator*
Dew, Charles Burgess *historian, educator*
Eusden, John Dykstra *theology studies educator, minister*
Fuller, Renee Nuni *psychologist, educational publisher*
Fuqua, Charles John *retired classicist*
Graver, Lawrence Stanley *language educator*
Graver, Suzanne Levy *English literature educator*
Hill, Victor Ernst, IV, *retired mathematics professor, musician*
Kassin, Saul *psychology professor*
Markgraf, J(ohn) Hodge *chemist, educator*
Morgan, Frank *mathematics professor*
Niemeyer, Peter Eduard *history educator*
Norton, Glyn Peter *literature educator*
Oakley, Francis Christopher *historian, educator*
Park, David Allen *physicist, researcher*
Pasachoff, Jay Myron *astronomer, educator*
Pistorius, George *language educator, educator*
Robinson, Hobart Krum *management consulting company executive*
Rudolph, Frederick *history professor*
Schapiro, Morton Owen *academic administrator*
Sheahan, John Bernard *economist, educator*
Sprague, John Louis *management consultant*
Stuebner, Erwin August, Jr. *internist*
Wilkins, Earle Wayne, Jr. *retired surgery educator*
Wobus, Reinhard Arthur *geologist, educator*
Wootters, William K. *physics professor*

Wilmington
Lee, Joohan *materials scientist*
Vakhshoori, Daryoosh *chemicals executive*

Winchester
Blackham, Ann Rosemary *realtor*
Brennan, Francis Patrick *banker*
Ferrara, Lee *graphics designer, artist, educator*
Hansen, Robert Joseph *civil engineer*
Irving, Gitte Nielsen *secondary school educator*
Jackson, Francis Joseph *research and development company executive*
Milburn, Richard Henry *physics professor*
Neuman, Robert Sterling *art educator, artist*
Ockerbloom, Richard C. *newspaper executive*

Taggart, Ganson Powers *management consultant*
Winston, Arthur William *physicist*

Winthrop
Brown, Patricia Irene *retired law librarian, lawyer*
Flockhart, Barbara Townsley *publishing executive*

Woburn
Mehra, Raman Kumar *aerospace and defense technology executive, automotion and control engineering researcher*
Preve, Roberta Jean *librarian, researcher*
Serfaty, Daniel *human systems engineer*
Sharp, William Thomas *information technology executive*
Winson, Ellen-Marie (Macone) *school system administrator, reading specialist*

Woods Hole
Behn, Mark Dietrich *marine geophysicist, educator*
Berggren, William Alfred *geologist, research micropaleontologist, educator*
Burger, Max Marcel *biochemist*
Cohen, Seymour Stanley *biochemist, educator*
Farrington, John William *academic administrator, dean, research scientist*
Felzer, Benjamin Seth *ecologist, researcher*
Gagosian, Robert B. *chemist, educator*
Gifford, Prosser *retired library administrator*
Hart, Stanley Robert *geochemist, educator*
Laster, Leonard *internist, gastroenterologist, academic administrator, educator, writer, researcher*
Ledwell, James R. *oceanographer*
Luyten, James Reindert *research institute director, oceanographer*
Melillo, Jerry M. *ecologist*
Newman, John Nicholas *naval architect educator*
Prendergast, Robert Anthony *pathologist educator*
Sogin, Mitchell L. *biologist, educator*
Speck, William T. *former physician, health facility administrator*
Steele, John Hyslop *marine scientist, oceanographic institute administrator*
Suchy, Albert Francis *marine architect*
Uchupi, Elazar *geologist, researcher*
Verslycke, Tim *research scientist*
Woodwell, George Masters *ecologist, conservationist*

Worcester
Alkassab, Firas *rheumatologist*
Angelini, Michael P. *insurance company executive*
Arthur, Gwendolynne Lee *university librarian*
Bagshaw, Joseph Charles *molecular biologist, educator*
Balaji, Kethandapatti C. *urologist, oncologist, researcher*
Balko, George Anthony III *lawyer, educator*
Banks, McRae Cave, II, *management educator, consultant*
Bassett, John E. *academic administrator, language educator*
Berkey, Dennis Dale *academic administrator*
Bernhard, Jeffrey David *dermatologist, educator, editor*
Billias, George Athan *historian, educator*
Boroff, Henry Jack *federal judge, educator*
Brooks, John Edward *college president*
Byatt, Nancy *psychiatrist*
Camougis, George *health, safety and environmental consultant*
Candib, Murray A. *retail executive, consultant*
Cesareo, Francesco *academic administrator, historian, educator*
Chern, Shyh-Shi Richard *radiologist*
Cosar, Ediz Fergün *pathologist, researcher*
Cowan, Fairman Chaffee *lawyer*
Delorey, John Francis *music educator*
Dolgon, Corey *sociology educator, political activist*
Donnelly, James Corcoran, Jr. *lawyer*
Drachman, David Alexander *neurologist*
Dunlap, Ellen S. *library administrator*
Dwork, Debórah *history professor*
Eppinger, Frederick H., Jr. *insurance company executive*
Fitzgerald, Katherine *molecular biologist, educator*
Greenberg, Nathan *accountant*
Haas, Richard Allen *physician*
Hagar, Richard Joseph *music educator, musician*
Harding, Beth Ann *middle school educator*
Harper, Doreen C. *nursing educator*
Hatfield, Renee S.J. *music educator*
Huber, J. Kendall *lawyer, insurance company executive*
Hunter, Richard Edward *retired physician*
Illanes, Diego Sebastian *obstetrician, gynecologist*
Indic, Premananda *education educator, researcher*
Katz, Robert Nathan *ceramics engineer, educator*
Kennedy, Linda Mann *neuroscience educator, researcher*
Lazare, Aaron *dean, psychiatrist*
Lougee, David Louis *lawyer*
Madison, John Mark *pulmonologist, educator*
Malone, Joseph James *mathematics professor, researcher*
Mardilovich, Ivan P. *education educator, researcher*
Mathisen, Howard *psychologist, educator, minister*
McCorison, Marcus Allen *librarian, cultural organization administrator*
McFarland, Michael C. *academic administrator*
Mello, Craig C. *molecular medicine educator, researcher*
Mirick, John O. *lawyer*
Morse, Leonard J. *epidemiologist, public health service officer*
Moschos, Demitrios Mina *lawyer*
Nelson, Donald Frederick *retired physics educator, researcher*
Ott, Attiat Farag *economist, educator*
Parsons, Edwin Spencer *clergyman, educator*
Reilly, Daniel Patrick *retired bishop*
Selin, Lisa K. *physician*
Shuster, Helen M. *library director*
Stutz, Cathleen Kinsella *education educator*
Tonkonogy, Joseph Moses *physician, neuropsychiatrist, researcher*
Townes, Philip Leonard *pediatrician, educator*
Uhl, Christopher Martin *lawyer*
Uschuplich, Vedran *pathologist*
Van Nostrand, Richard Charles *lawyer*
Varpahovsky, Andrey *computer scientist, educator*
Vaughan, Alden True *history professor*
Venugopal, Thayanithy *biologist, geneticist, researcher*
Vick, Susan *playwright, educator, director, actress*
Welu, James A. *art museum director*
West, Michael D. *cloning and stem cell research company executive*
Woolhouse, Maureen Ann *mathematics professor*
Young, Stephen Bernard *urogynecologist, surgeon*
Zeugner, John Finn *historian, educator, writer*
Zurier, Robert Burton *rheumatology educator*

Wrentham
Bittenbender, Brad James *safety engineer*

Yarmouth Port
Gordon, Benjamin Dichter *pediatrician, educator, health facility administrator*
Hall, James Frederick *retired college president*
Phelps, Judson Hewett *health facility administrator, marketing professional*
Stott, Thomas Edward, Jr. *retired engineering executive*
Weiner, Charles *historian, educator*

MICHIGAN

Ada
Lyall, Lynn *consumer products company executive*
Mason, James Hamilton *surgeon*
Mohr, Michael Arthur *lawyer*
Van Andel, Steve Alan *consumer products company executive*
Weiss, Joseph Joel *consulting company executive*

Adrian
Dodson, John Thomas *orchestra conductor*
Geyer, Richard Douglas *librarian, editor, poet*
Lamprecht, Elizabeth Ann *mathematics professor*
Weathers, Milledge Wright *retired economics professor*

Albion
Cocks, Geoffrey Campbell *history professor*

Allen Park
Johnson, Calvin *professional football player*
Kirby, Dorothy Manville *social worker*
Kitna, Jon *professional football player*
Marinelli, Rod *professional football coach*
Millen, Matt *professional sports team executive*
Pollard, Marcus *professional football player*
Williams, Roy *professional football player*

Allendale
Haas, Thomas Joseph *academic administrator, chemistry educator*
Murray, Diane Elizabeth *librarian*
Parker, Kelly Andrew *philosopher, educator*

Alma
Merwin, Gregory Alan *insurance agent, retired special education educator*
Tracy, Saundra J. *academic administrator*

Alpena
Hunter, Mark John *lawyer, photographer*

Ann Arbor
Abrams, Gerald David *pathologist, educator*
Adriaens, Peter *environmental engineer, consultant*
Agno, John G. *management consultant*
Agranoff, Bernard William *biochemist, educator*
Akerlof, Carl William *physics professor*
Akil, Huda *neuroscientist, educator, researcher*
Akin, Cem *internist, allergist, medical researcher*
Alexander, Buzz (William) *literature and language professor*
Allen, Layman Edward *law educator, research scientist*
Allen-Meares, Paula G. *social work educator, dean*
Anderson, Austin Gothard *lawyer, consultant, academic administrator*
Annchild, Cynthia *educational consultant*
Ansbacher, Rudi *physician*
Anupindi, Ravi *operations research specialist, educator*
Arlinghaus, Sandra Judith Lach *mathematical geographer, educator*
Ashe, Arthur James III *chemistry professor*
Atreya, Sushil Kumar *planetary-space science educator, astrophysicist*
Awtar, Shorya *engineering educator, consultant*
Bacon, George Edgar *pediatrician*
Bagian, James Philip *former astronaut, public health service officer, medical educator*
Bailey, Reeve Maclaren *museum curator*
Baler, Blanche Kimoto *retired child psychiatrist*
Ball, Deborah Loewenberg *dean, education educator*
Barsan, William George *emergency physician*
Bartell, Lawrence Sims *chemist, educator*
Bartlett, Robert Hawes *surgeon*
Bashshur, Rashid L. *health facility administrator, educator*
Bass, Hyman *mathematician, educator*
Beaubien, Anne Kathleen *librarian*
Beaver, Frank Eugene *critic, historian*
Becher, William Don *retired electrical engineer, educator, writer*
Beckley, Robert Mark *architect, educator*
Bedard, Patrick Joseph *editor, writer, consultant*
Beeton, Alfred Merle *lab administrator, director, biologist, educator, environmentalist*
Behling, Charles Frederick *psychologist, educator*
Beilein, John Patrick *men's college basketball coach*
Belcher, Louis David *marketing professional, retired mayor*
Berenson, Red (Gordon A. Berenson) *hockey coach, retired professional hockey player*
Beutler, Frederick Joseph *information scientist*
Beutler, Suzanne A. *retired secondary school educator, artist*
Bierbaum, Rosina M. *federal agency administrator*
Bilello, John Charles *engineering educator, director*
Bishop, Elizabeth Shreve *psychologist*
Blinder, Seymour Michael *chemistry and physics professor, researcher*
Bloom, Jane Maginnis *emergency physician*
Blouin, Francis Xavier, Jr. *history professor*
Blumenthal, Jane Leonardi *library director*
Boehnke, Michael *biostatistics educator*
Bolcom, William Elden *composer, educator, musician*
Bolling, Steven Fredric *cardiac surgeon, educator*
Bornstein, George Jay *literary educator*
Bornstein, Morris *economist, educator*
Bowdler, Anthony John *internist, educator*
Boxer, Laurence Alan *physician, research educator*
Brandon, David A. *food service executive*
Brinkman, Michael *neuropsychologist, researcher*
Brophy, Patrick David *pediatrician, researcher*
Brown, Donald Robert *psychology professor*
Brown, William Ernest *dentist*
Bryant, Barbara Everitt *academic administrator, researcher, retired marketing professional, federal agency administrator*
Buckley, Francis J., Jr. *librarian*
Buesser, Anthony Carpenter *lawyer*
Burdi, Alphonse Rocco *anatomist*
Burke, Robert Harry *surgeon, educator*
Cain, Albert Clifford *psychologist, educator*
Caminker, Evan H. *dean, law educator*
Carlson, Bruce Martin *anatomist*
Carney, Thomas Daly *lawyer*
Carr, Lloyd H. *college football coach*
Casey, Kenneth Lyman *neurologist*
Cerny, Joseph Charles *urologist, educator*
Chaffers, James A. *architect, educator*
Chaffin, Don Brian *industrial engineering educator, research director*
Chang, Chun-Shu *historian, educator, writer*
Chang, Hsueh-lun Shelley *historian, researcher, writer*
Chey, William D *physician, researcher*
Chiodo, Anthony *medical educator*
Chupp, Timothy Edward *physicist, educator, academic administrator*
Clark, Noreen Morrison *behavioral science educator, researcher*
Clark, Thomas B., Sr. *real estate broker*
Clarke, Roy *physicist, researcher*
Clewell, Don B. *microbial geneticist, educator*
Cochran, Kenneth William *toxicologist*
Cohen, Malcolm Stuart *economist*
Cole, David Edward *automotive executive, educator*
Converse, Philip Ernest *retired social sciences educator*
Conway, Lynn *computer scientist, electrical engineer, educator*
Cooper, Edward Hayes *lawyer, educator*
Coran, Arnold Gerald *pediatrician, surgeon*
Courant, Paul Noah *university librarian, economist, educator*
Cowen, Roy Chadwell, Jr. *language educator*
Csere, Csaba *editor-in-chief*
Curley, Edwin Munson *philosophy educator*
Curtin, Joseph *violinmaker*
Darlow, Julia Donovan *lawyer*
Daub, Peggy Ellen *library administrator*
Davis, Robert Leach *retired federal official*
Dawson, William Ryan *zoology educator*
Decker, Raymond Frank *chemicals and metal products executive*
Dekker, Eugene Earl *biochemistry educator*
De Laat, Gilbert *automotive executive*
Delbanco, Nicholas Franklin *language educator, writer*
Del Monte, Monte Anthony *medical educator*
DeVine, Edmond Francis *retired lawyer*
Dew, Thomas Edward *lawyer*
Diana, Joseph A. *retired foundation executive*
Didier, Elaine K. *library director, educator*
Dobranski, Bernard *dean, law educator*
Dolan, Robert J. *dean*
Dominguez, Kathryn Mary *economist, educator*
Donabedian, Avedis *physician, educator*
Dougherty, Richard Martin *library and information science professor*
Doyle, Constance Talcott Johnston *physician, educator, medical association administrator*
Drach, John Charles *research scientist, educator*
Drake, John Warren *aviation consultant*
Driscoll, John *publishing executive*
Dunlap, Connie *librarian*
Dunnigan, Brian Leigh *historian, curator*
Duquette, Donald Norman *law educator*
Easter, Stephen Sherman, Jr. *biology professor*
Eberbach, Steven John *retired electronics company executive*
Eisenberg, Marvin Julius *retired art history educator*
Eisendrath, Charles Rice *journalism educator, farmer, consultant*
Eisenstein, Elizabeth Lewisohn *historian, educator*
Elger, William Robert, Jr. *accountant*
Ellmann, Douglas Stanley *lawyer*
Ellsworth, Phoebe Clemencia *psychology professor*
England, Anthony Wayne *engineering and science educator, dean*
Fajans, Stefan Stanislaus *retired internist*
Farmer, Cheryl Christine *internist, industrial hygienist*
Farrand, William Richard *retired geology educator*
Ferrell, Robert Hugh *historian, educator*
Feuerwerker, Albert *historian, educator*
Filisko, Frank Edward *physicist, researcher*
Fleming, Suzanne Marie *academic administrator, freelance/self-employed writer*
Foley, Daniel Ronald *personnel director, lawyer*
Ford, Betty Ann (Elizabeth Ann Ford) *former First Lady of the United States, health facility executive*
Forsyth, Ilene Haering *art historian*
Fox, David Alan *rheumatologist, immunologist*
Frey, William H. *demographer, educator*
Friedmann, Peretz Peter *aerospace engineer, educator*
Frohna, John G. *pediatrician*
Galea, Sandro *epidemiologist*
Garneau-Tsodikova, Sylvie *chemistry professor*
Garris, Michael Jack *lawyer*
Gelehrter, Thomas David *medical educator, geneticist*
Gibala, Ronald *metallurgical engineering educator*
Gikas, Paul William *medical educator*
Gilbert, Elmer Grant *engineering educator, control theorist*
Gilman, Sid *neurologist*
Ginsburg, David *genetics educator, researcher*
Goldstein, Steven Alan *medical and engineering educator*
Gomez, Luis Oscar *Asian and religious studies educator, clinical psychology educator*
Gordon, Anitra *librarian*
Gray, Whitmore *lawyer, educator*
Greden, John Francis *psychiatrist, educator*
Green, Thomas Andrew *lawyer, educator*
Greenfield, Lazar John *surgeon, educator*
Gregerson, Linda Karen *poet, language educator, critic*
Griess, Robert L., Jr. *mathematics professor*
Griffin, Henry Claude *retired chemistry professor*
Griffith, John Randall *health facility administrator, educator*
Grossman, Esta S. *biology professor*
Gurm, Hitinder S. *cardiologist, educator*
Guy, Ralph B., Jr. *federal judge*
Hackett, Roger Fleming *historian, educator*
Haddock, Fred(erick) T(heodore), Jr. *retired astronomer*
Haefner, Don Paul *retired psychology educator*
Hagel, William Carl *metallurgical consultant*
Hagen, John William *psychology professor*
Hannoosh, Michele Ann *language educator*
Hathaway, James C. *law educator*
Hawkins, Joseph Elmer, Jr. *physiologist, educator*
Hayes, John Patrick *electrical engineering and computer science educator, consultant*
Herzig, David Jacob *retired pharmaceutical company executive, consultant*
Hessler, David William *information and multimedia systems educator*
Heydon, Peter Northrup *farmer, educator, philanthropist*
Hill, Bruce Marvin *statistician, educator*
Hilton, James L. *university librarian*
Hinshaw, Ada Sue *nursing educator, former dean*
Hoff, Julian Theodore *neurosurgeon, educator*
Hollenberg, Paul Frederick *pharmacology educator*
Horowitz, Samuel Boris *biomedical researcher, educational consultant*
Houghtlin, Robert *publishing executive*
House, James Stephen *social psychologist, educator*
Humes, Harvey David *nephrologist, educator, director*
Irvine, Judith Temkin *anthropologist, educator*
Israel, Barbara A. *healthcare educator*
Izzo, Herbert John *language and linguistics educator, researcher*
Jackson, James Sidney *psychologist, educator*
Janko, Richard Charles Murray *humanities educator*
Johnson, Brenda L. *university librarian*
Johnson, Timothy R. B. *obstetrician, gynecologist, educator*
Johnston, Lloyd Douglas *social sciences educator*
Jones, George L. *retail executive*
Jones, Lawrence William *retired physicist*
Joscelyn, Kent Buckley *lawyer*
Kahn, Douglas Allen *law educator*
Kalbfleisch, John David *statistics educator*
Kamisar, Yale *lawyer, educator*
Kaufman, Peter Bishop *biological sciences educator*
Kelch, Robert Paul *former dean, pediatric endocrinologist*
Kelly, Raymond Case *anthropology educator*
Kennedy, David Boyd *foundation executive, lawyer*
Keppelman, Nancy *lawyer*
Kesler, Stephen Edward *geology educator*
Ketefian, Shaké *nursing educator*
Kim, E. Han *financial economist, educator*
Kingdon, John Wells *political science professor*
Klinkman, Michael Scott *medical educator*
Knott, John Ray, Jr. *language educator*
Koren, Yoram *mechanical engineering educator*
Kostyo, Jack Lawrence *physiology educator*
Kothary, Piyush C. *research scientist*

Kozma, Adam *electrical engineer*
Krier, James Edward *law educator, writer*
Krimm, Samuel *physicist, researcher*
Krisch, Alan David *physics professor*
Kuehn, George E. *lawyer*
Kuhl, David Edmund *nuclear medicine physician, educator*
Kunzel, Erich, Jr. *conductor, arranger, educator*
Laycock, Harold Douglas *law educator, writer*
Lazarsfeld, Robert Kendall *mathematician, educator*
Lee, John Chaeseung *nuclear engineering educator*
Levitsky, Melvyn *former ambassador*
Lewis, Robert Enzer *editor, educator*
Lewis, William Arthur *artist, educator*
Lichter, Allen S. *oncologist, educator, dean*
Lichter, Paul Richard *ophthalmology educator*
Lightfoot, Albert J. *clergyman*
Lin, Hai *physicist*
Lozoff, Betsy *pediatrician, educator*
Lupia, Arthur W. *political science educator*
Lyon, Thomas Peyton *finance educator, consultant*
MacCormack, Sabine Gabriele *history educator*
MacKinnon, Catharine Alice *lawyer, educator, writer*
Mancuso, Peter *medical educator*
Manis, Melvin *psychologist, educator*
Margolis, Philip Marcus *psychiatrist, educator*
Markel, Howard *physician, educator*
Markovits, Andrei Steven *political science professor*
Martin, Claude Raymond, Jr. *marketing consultant, educator*
Martin, William Russell *nuclear engineering educator*
Masten, Scott Edward *economics and public policy educator, consultant*
Matthews, Rowena Green *biological chemistry educator*
McCarus, Ernest Nasseph *retired language educator*
McCormack, Terry R. *automotive executive*
Mendez, David *information systems and operations research educator*
Merlin, Roberto Daniel *physicist, educator*
Merte, Herman, Jr. *mechanical engineering educator*
Metcalf, Robert Clarence *architect, educator*
Meyer, John Frederick *engineering educator*
Meyers, Philip Alan *geochemistry educator, researcher*
Miller, Josef M. *otolaryngologist, educator*
Miller, William Ian *law educator*
Mitchell, Edward John *economist, retired educator*
Mizruchi, Mark Sheldon *sociology professor, business administration professor*
Modell, Stephen Mark *medical researcher, educator*
Monto, Arnold Simon *epidemiology educator*
Moore, Thomas Edwin *biologist, educator, museum director*
Morris, Michael David *chemistry professor*
Motawi, Karim *textiles executive*
Mounts, L. David *food products executive*
Mulholland, Michael William *surgeon, researcher*
Munro, Donald Jacques *philosopher, educator*
Muraski, Anthony Augustus *lawyer*
Neal, Homer Alfred *physics professor, researcher, academic administrator*
Neidhardt, Frederick Carl *microbiologist, educator*
Nelson, Roy Jay *retired French educator*
Niehoff, Leonard Marvin *lawyer*
Nikoui, Hossein Reza *quality assurance professional*
Nordman, Christer Eric *chemistry professor*
Nriagu, Jerome Okon *environmental geochemist*
Oakley, Deborah Jane *public health service officer, nursing educator*
Oh, So-Ryeok *research scientist*
Oliver, William John *pediatrician, educator*
O'Meara, John Corbett *federal judge*
Omenn, Gilbert Stanley *academic administrator, internist*
Orringer, Jeffrey S. *dermatologist, educator*
Paige, Jeffery Mayland *sociologist, educator*
Pappas, Janice Louise *paleontologist, researcher*
Parkinson, William Charles *physics professor, researcher*
Parsons, Jeffrey Robinson *anthropologist, educator*
Paul, Ara Garo *university dean*
Payton, Sallyanne *law educator*
Pearlman, Mark *medical educator, researcher*
Pedley, John Griffiths *archaeologist, educator*
Peng Chen, Hsiu-Hui *music educator*
Perkins, Bradford *historian, educator*
Perkins, George *writer, educator*
Pernick, Martin Steven *history professor*
Petrick, Ernest Nicholas *mechanical engineer, researcher*
Petty, Elizabeth Marie *geneticist*
Pierce, John Charles *singer*
Pitt, Bertram *cardiologist, educator, consultant*
Pollack, Martha E. *dean, computer science and engineering educator*
Pollock, Lawrence I. *retail executive, investment company executive*
Pollock, Tresa M. *engineering educator*
Polverini, Peter J. *dean, dental educator*
Potempa, Kathleen M. *dean, nursing educator*
Potter, David Stone *Greek and Latin educator*
Powell, Kenneth Grant *aerospace engineering educator*
Powsner, Edward Raphael *physician*
Prahalad, C.K. *finance educator, corporate strategist*
Railton, Peter Albert *philosophy educator*
Rao, Panduranga S. *nephrologist, educator*
Reddy, Venkat Narsimha *ophthalmologist, researcher*
Reed, John Wesley *lawyer, educator*
Robbins, Jerry Hal *educational administration educator*
Robertson, Richard Earl *physical chemist, educator*
Roe, Byron Paul *physics professor*
Rogers, Bryan L. *dean*
Rogers, Bryan Leigh *dean, artist, art educator*
Romani, John Henry *health science association administrator, educator*
Rosenthal, Amnon *pediatric cardiologist*
Rupp, Ralph Russell *retired audiologist, educator, author*
Ryan, Marianne Elizabeth *lawyer*
Ryland, Jane N. *educational association administrator*
St. Antoine, Theodore Joseph *retired law educator, arbitrator*
St. John, Edward P. *social sciences educator*
Saitou, Kazuhiro *engineering educator*
Saltiel, Alan Robert *biochemist*
Sandalow, Terrance *law educator*
Sanford, Melanie S. *chemist, educator*
Saper, Joel R. *neurologist, educator*
Sarkar, Subrata *medical educator*
Savari, Serap Ayse *engineering educator, researcher*
Scavarda, Donald Robert *composer, artist*
Schacht, Jochen Heinrich *biochemistry educator*
Schottenfeld, David *retired epidemiologist, educator*
Schteingart, David Eduardo *internist*
Schwank, Johannes Walter *chemical engineering educator*
Schwarz, Norbert *psychology professor*
Scott, Norman Ross *electrical engineering educator*
Scott, Rebecca J. *law and history educator*
Seibold, James Richard *physician, educator*
Senior, Thomas Bryan A. *electrical engineering educator, researcher, consultant*
Seyhun, Hasan Nejat *finance educator, department chairman*
Shapiro, Matthew David *economist, educator*
Shaw, Sonia *retired lawyer*
Sheldon, Ingrid Kristina *retired mayor, controller*
Simpson, A.W. Brian *law educator*
Sloan, Herbert Elias *physician, surgeon*
Sloat, Barbara Furin *cell biologist, educator*
Smith, Donald Cameron *retired preventive medicine physician*
Smith, Karen E. *mathematician, educator*
Sobel, Alan *electrical engineer, physicist*
Spence, David Wendel *application developer*
Srinivasan, Ashok *radiologist*
Stafford, Frank P. *economist, educator*
Stafford, Frank Peter, Jr. *economics professor, consultant*
Steel, Duncan Gregory *engineering educator*
Stein, Eric *retired law educator*
Stembridge, John Reese *mathematics professor*
Steward, James *museum director, art history educator*
Stolz, Benjamin Armond *foreign language educator*
Strang, Ruth Hancock *pediatrician, educator, cardiologist, priest*
Stross, Jeoffrey Knight *internist, educator*
Sullivan, Teresa Ann *law and sociology educator, academic administrator*
Sullivan, Thomas Patrick *academic administrator*
Sung, Kyu-Taik *social worker, educator, gerontologist, researcher*
Surovell, Edward David *real estate company executive*
Swaroop, Anand *medical educator*
Sylvester, Dennis Michael *electrical engineer, educator*
Teener, James W. *neurologist, medical educator*
Theut, C. Peter *lawyer*
Thompson, Norman Winslow *surgeon, educator*
Tice, Carol Hoff *intergenerational specialist, consultant*
Todd, Robert Franklin III *oncologist, educator*
Trautmann, Thomas Roger *history professor, anthropology educator*
Turits, Richard Lee *history professor*
Ulaby, Fawwaz Tayssir *engineering educator, director, science administrator*
Ulsoy, Ali Galip *engineering educator*
Vandermeer, John H. *ecologist, educator*
Vanderploeg, Henry A. *ecologist, researcher*
Van der Voo, Rob *geophysicist*
Veltman, Martinus J.G. *retired physics educator*
Vielmetti, Edward Marshall *webmaster*
Vining, (George) Joseph *law educator*
Waggoner, Lawrence William *law educator*
Walsh, James Joseph *lawyer*
Waltz, Susan *political scientist, educator*
Wang, Lumin *nuclear engineer*
Ward, Peter Allan *pathologist, educator*
Ware, Richard Anderson *foundation executive*
Warner, Kenneth E(dgar) *dean, public health educator, consultant*
Warren, Jane Carol *psychologist*
Weder, Alan B(rian) *internist, medical educator*
Weg, John Gerard *physician*
Weiser, Marc *venture capitalist*
White, James Boyd *law educator*
Whitman, Marina von Neumann *economist, educator*
Wilhelm, Edward W. *corporate financial executive*
Wilkins, John P. *university librarian*
Williams, David R. *sociologist, educator, senior research scientist*
Williams, John Andrew *physiology researcher, educator*
Williams, Melvin Donald *anthropologist, educator*
Wilson, Richard Christian *engineering firm executive*
Woronoff, Israel *former psychology educator*
Xie, Yu *adult education educator*
Yamashina, Tadashi (George) *transportation executive*
Yang, Ralph Tzu-Bow *chemical engineer, educator*
Young, Edwin Harold *chemical and metallurgical engineering educator*
Zhang, Youxue *geology educator*
Zucker, Robert A(lpert) *psychologist*

Armada
Kummerow, Arnold A. *superintendent of schools*

Au Gres
Dhawan, Vikas *plastic surgeon*

Auburn Hills
Billups, Chauncey *professional basketball player*
Boyle, Olabisi Ariyo *manufacturing engineer*
Davidson, William M. *manufacturing executive, professional sports team owner*
Dumars, Joe III *professional sports team executive, retired professional basketball player*
Ebeid, Russell Joseph *glass manufacturing executive*
Etefia, Florence Victoria *retired school psychologist*
Farrar, Stephen Prescott *glass products manufacturing executive*
Ford, Cheryl *professional basketball player*
Gasparovic, John J. *lawyer*
Gerson, Ralph Joseph *manufacturing executive*
Hamilton, Richard Clay *professional basketball player*
Hammond, John *professional sports team executive*
Horiszny, Laurene Helen *lawyer*
Johnson, Shannon *professional basketball player*
Kalina, John *auto parts company executive*
Knight, Jeffrey Alan *corporate financial executive*
Laimbeer, Bill *professional basketball coach, retired professional basketball player*
LaSorda, Thomas W. *automotive company executive*
Liu, C. Q. *engineer*
Mandiberg, David Michael *sculptor*
Manganello, Timothy M. *auto parts company executive*
Meyer, Deborah Wahl *automotive executive*
Nardelli, Robert Louis *automotive executive, former consumer home products company executive*
Nolan, Deanna Nicole *professional basketball player*
Ostfield, Alan *professional sports team executive*
Rae, Nancy A. *human resources specialist, automotive executive*
Saunders, Flip (Philip D. Saunders) *professional basketball coach*
Suravajjala, Mamatha *information technology manager*
Unger, Susan J. *automotive executive*
Wallace, Rasheed *professional basketball player, marketing professional*
Webber, Chris (Mayce Edward Christopher Webber) *professional basketball player*
Wilson, Thomas S. *professional sports team executive*
Young, Stacy A. *information technology manager*

Bad Axe
Sullivan, James Gerald *small business owner*

Baroda
Reckline, Sigmund Joseph *publishing executive, editor*

Battle Creek
Baldwin, Susan Olin *commissioner, management consultant*
Banks, Donna Jo *food products executive*
Bryant, John A. *food products executive*
Davis, Laura Arlene *retired foundation administrator*
Fisher, David Russel *business educator*
Jenness, James M. *food products executive*
Lincoln, Margaret *library media specialist*
Mackay, David (A.D. David Mackay) *food products executive*
Matthews, Wyhomme S. *retired music educator, academic administrator*
Montie, Jeffrey W. *food products executive*
Pilnick, Gary H. *food products executive, lawyer*
Risukhin, Vladimir Nikolayevich *aeronautical engineer, educator*
Speirn, Sterling K. *foundation administrator*
Steffel, Vern John, Jr. *lawyer*

Bay City
Greve, Guy Robert *lawyer*
Hiner, John Patrick *newspaper editor*
Lore, John S. *health facility administrator*
Ludington, Thomas Lamson *federal judge*
Powers, David Louis *lawyer*

Belleville
Schaefer, James Theodore *writer, editor, educator*
Stebbins, Donald J. *car parts manufacturing company executive*
Van Tassel, Michael L. *music educator*
Wilson, David James *chemistry researcher, educator*

Belmont
Wooster, Stephanie Lynne *art historian, artist*

Benton Harbor
Binkley, David A. *human resources specialist*
Brown, Mark E. *manufacturing executive*
Fettig, Jeff M. *manufacturing executive*
Hopp, Daniel Frederick *lawyer, manufacturing company executive*
Schults-Berndt, Elfie *music educator*
Swift, David L. *manufacturing executive*
Templin, Roy W. *manufacturing executive*
Thieneman, Michael D. *manufacturing executive*
Todman, Michael A. *manufacturing executive*
Yaggi, W. Timothy *manufacturing executive*
Yoder, Dale Roy *history educator*

Berrien Springs
Hamel, Lorie Ann *psychologist*
Lesher, William Richard *retired academic administrator*
Lundgren, Dennis David *elementary school educator, secondary school educator*
Maguad, Ben Abrico *management educator*

Beulah
Auch, Walter Edward *security firm executive*
Edwards, Wallace Winfield *retired automotive executive*
Tanner, Helen Hornbeck *historian, consultant*

Beverly Hills
Castle, Maurice Emmett *orthopedist, surgeon*
Hertzberg, David Gordon *retired lawyer*
Pardington, Mary Elizabeth *elementary school educator*

Big Rapids
Ryan, Ray Darl, Jr. *academic administrator*
Westman, Craig Ellery *academic administrator*

Bingham Farms
Baumkel, Mark S. *lawyer*
Berman, Leonard Keith *lawyer*
Giles, Conrad Leslie *ophthalmic surgeon*
Goren, Steven Eliot *lawyer*
Gratch, Serge *retired mechanical engineering educator*
Robinson, Steve *real estate company executive*
Silverman, Gilbert B. *retired real estate developer, art collector*

Birch Run
Warnick, Howard James *retired church musician, educator*

Birmingham
Auld, Frank *psychologist, educator*
Demorest, Mark Stuart *lawyer*
Elsman, James Leonard, Jr. *lawyer*
Foxen, Richard William *manufacturing executive*
Kienbaum, Thomas Gerd *lawyer*
Kothari, Rajesh Ujamlal *investment company executive*
Kozlow, Richard *artist*
Maxwell, Jack Erwin *manufacturing executive*
McCuen, John *columnist, educator, consultant on counterinsurgency operations*
Schaefer, John Frederick *lawyer*
Sharf, Stephan *automotive executive*
Smith, George Wolfram *physicist, researcher*
Smith, Todd P. *marketing executive*
Thorpe, Norman Ralph *lawyer, automotive executive, retired military officer*
Zacharski, Dennis Edward *lawyer*

Bloomfield
Kanter, Alan Michael *lawyer*
Reiter, Jesse Matthew *lawyer*

Bloomfield Hills
Adams, Charles Francis *advertising and real estate company executive*
Adams, James Charles *lawyer*
Ball, Patricia Ann *physician*
Banas, C(hristine) Leslie *lawyer*
Berline, James H. *advertising and public relations executive*
Bokhari, Raza Ali Babar *former marketing strategist*
Brent, Robert Lewis *urologist*
Burnett, Patricia Hill *artist, educator*
Burstein, Richard Joel *lawyer*
Charla, Leonard Francis *lawyer, publishing executive*
Clippert, Charles Frederick *lawyer*
Coburn, Ronald Murray *ophthalmologist, surgeon*
Cook, Steven M. *lawyer, construction executive*
Cregg, Roger A. *construction executive*
Cummings, Roger Holt *lawyer*
Dawson, Stephen Everette *lawyer*
Deron, Edward Michael *lawyer*
Devaney, Dennis Martin *lawyer, educator*
Dugas, Richard J., Jr. *construction executive*
Ellinghausen, James R. *construction executive*
Frankel, Richard William *retired vending company executive*
Gagliardi, Raymond Alfred *physician*
Gold, Edward David *lawyer*
Googasian, George Ara *lawyer*
Greenwood, Frank *information scientist, educator*
Haidostian, Alice Berberian *concert pianist, volunteer, not-for-profit fundraiser*
Kasischke, Louis Walter *lawyer*
Keane, Peter J. *construction executive*
Kirk, John MacGregor *lawyer*
Ledwidge, Patrick Joseph *lawyer*
LoPrete, James Hugh *lawyer*
Martin, J(oseph) Patrick *lawyer, judge*
Mathog, Robert Henry *otolaryngologist, educator*
McCuen, John Francis, Jr. *lawyer*
McDonald, Patrick Allen *lawyer, educator, arbitrator*
Mc Gehee, H. Coleman, Jr., (Harry Coleman McGhhe) *retired bishop*
Meyer, George Herbert *lawyer*
Nern, Christopher Carl *lawyer*
Norris, John Hart *lawyer, director*
O'Hara, John Paul III *orthopedic surgeon*
O'Shaughnessy, Robert T. *automotive executive*
Papai, Beverly Daffern *retired library director*
Petruska, Steven C. *construction executive*
Poth, Stefan Michael *retired diversified financial services company executive*
Pulte, William J. *construction executive*
Rader, Ralph Terrance *lawyer*
Robinson, Jack Albert *retail executive*

Sandy, William Haskell *training and communication systems executive*
Simon, Evelyn *lawyer*
Smith, H(arold) Lawrence *lawyer*
Snyder, George Edward *lawyer*
Solomon, Mark Raymond *lawyer, educator*
Sommerfeld, David William *lawyer, educator*
Stewart, Michael B. *lawyer, mechanical and aerospace engineer*
Stunz, John Henry, Jr. *retired physician, consultant*
Swift, Jonathan *television personality, educator*
Syme, Daniel Bailey *rabbi, institution executive*
Taubman, Robert S. *real estate developer*
Victor, Richard Steven *lawyer*
Weil, John William *technology management consultant*
Williams, J. Bryan *lawyer*
Williams, Walter Joseph *lawyer*
Wise, John Augustus *lawyer, director*

Bloomfield Township
Brown, Lynette Ralya *journalist, publicist*

Bloomingdale
Schultheis, Ann Lucia *curriculum specialist*

Brighton
Clark, Robert Thomas *ophthalmologist*
Crabtree, John David *manufacturing company executive*

Burton
Farmer, Philip José *writer*
Johnson, Jolene Carole *music educator*

Cadillac
Walker, Dale Maxwell *city official*

Camden
Falls, Kathleene Joyce *photographer*

Canton
Broniak, Lynn Marguerite *gifted and talented educator, technology educator*
Finnerty, Bryan *sports association executive*

Capac
Wagner, Dorothy Marie *retired senior creative designer, artist*

Carleton
Ely, Deborah D. *elementary school educator*

Caro
Hile, Michele Vera *middle school educator*

Cass City
Althaver, Lambert Ewing *manufacturing executive*

Center Line
Cahill, Kimberly M. *lawyer*

Charlevoix
Miles, David Loren *museum director*

Charlotte
Burpee, Lyle Frederick *retired industrial engineer*
Coirolo, Christina *writer, author representative*
Young, Everett J. *management consultant, agricultural economist*

Chassell
Spain, James Dorris, Jr. *biochemist, educator*

Cheboygan
Ostrowski, Stacey *athletic trainer, educator*

Chelsea
Fry, Richard E. *architectural firm executive*
Kendall, Kay Lynn *interior designer, consultant*
Weinreich, Gabriel *physicist, minister, educator*

Chesterfield
Danielson, Gary R. *lawyer*

Clarkston
Kruzan, James Brendan *financial planner*
Wydra, Frank Thomas *healthcare executive*

Clinton Township
Ho, Robert En Ming *neurosurgeon, educator*
Neal, Larry P. *library director*
Zoubareff, Kathy Olga *administrative assistant*

Commerce Township
Thibideau, Carolyn C. *musician, educator*

Davison
West, Stacy Kathlena *athletic trainer*

Dearborn
Adkins, Elizabeth W. *archivist*
Ahmed, Saleem *management consultant, educator*
Bannister, Michael E. *automotive executive*
Beyer, Roberta Bonnie *dean, education professor, writer, researcher*
Bowersox, Patricia Anne *social worker*
Brown, James Ward *mathematician, educator, author*
Cairns, James Robert *mechanical engineering educator*
Cape, James Odies E. *fashion designer*
Cischke, Susan Mary *automotive executive*
Codina, Francisco *automotive executive*
Fields, Mark *automotive executive*
Ford, Bill (William Clay Ford Jr.) *automotive company executive*
Ford, William Clay *automotive and professional sports team executive*
Fordyce, James George *physician*
Gandhi, Haren S. *chemical engineer*
Henderson, Stanley Elwood *academic administrator, consultant*
Hogan, Brian Joseph *editor*
Hrovat, Davorin D. *engineer*
Johnston, Michael Francis *auto parts company executive*
Kahn, Mark Leo *arbitrator, educator*
Kang, Hong Tae *engineering educator*
Kiska, Timothy Olin *communications educator, radio producer*
Kuzak, Derrick M. *automotive executive*
Laymon, Joe W. *human resources specialist, automotive executive*
Leclair, Don (Donat R. Leclair Jr.) *automotive executive*
Leet, Kenneth H.M. *automotive executive*
Leitch, David G. *automotive executive, lawyer*
Little, Daniel Eastman *philosopher, educator, director*
Little, Robert Eugene *engineering educator*
Lundy, J(oseph) Edward *retired automobile company executive*
Marcin, Robert H. *automotive executive*
Mays, J. C. *automotive executive*
Mi, Chunting Chris *engineering educator*
Mulally, Alan R. *automotive company executive, former aerospace company executive*
Nelson, Alison R. *lawyer*
Ojakli, Ziad S. *automotive executive*
Papazian, Dennis Richard *retired historian, educator, commentator*
Parry-Jones, Richard *automotive executive*
Pestillo, Peter John *auto parts company executive, lawyer*
Popovich, George Lee *theater educator*
Powell, Ronald Rowe *library science educator*
Prasad, Priya *engineer, researcher*
Smither, Nick *automotive executive*
Yang, Guangbin *engineer*
Zhu, Qiang *education educator*
Zimmerman, Martin B. *automotive executive*

Dearborn Heights
Ghrist, Catherine Ann *religious organization administrator*
Johns, Diana *secondary school educator*

Decatur
Kinney, Gregory Hoppes *lawyer*

Detroit
Abramson, Hanley Norman *pharmacy educator*
Abt, Jeffrey *art educator, art historian, artist, writer*
Albom, Mitch David *sports columnist*
Alexander, Sheldon *psychology educator*
Alpert, Daniel *broadcast executive*
Anderson, Gerard M. *energy executive*
Andrews, Caesar *editor*
Anger, Paul *newspaper editor*
Archer, Dennis Wayne *lawyer, former mayor*
Babb, Ralph W., Jr. *bank executive*
Babcock, Mike *professional hockey coach*
Bahl, Gautam *radiologist*
Balon, Richard *psychiatrist, educator*
Barclay, Kathleen S. *automotive executive*
Barrett, Nancy Smith *academic administrator*
Bassett, Tina *communications executive*
Battah, Hammam Jamil *civil engineer, utilities executive*
Baytarian, P. Jeffrey *not-for-profit fundraiser*
Beal, Graham William John *museum director*
Beierwaltes, William Howard *physiologist, educator*
Bell Wilson, Carlotta A. *social services specialist, state official, consultant*
Bennett, Grace *publishing executive*
Beran, John R. *banker*
Bhandari, Akshay *urologist*
Bilstrom, Jon Wayne *lawyer*
Blaszkiewicz, David *investment company executive*
Blomquist, David Wels *journalist*
Bock, Brooks Frederick *emergency physician*
Bonderman, Jeremy *professional baseball player*
Boocock, Stephen William *lawyer*
Bowen, David R. *science and technology educator, consultant*
Bowman, William Scott (Scotty Bowman) *professional hockey coach*
Braid, Ralph M. *economics professor*
Brake, Willie Edward *computer company executive, educator*
Brand, George Edward, Jr. *retired lawyer*
Brill, Lesley *literature and film studies educator*
Brown, Gloria Diane *elementary school educator*
Brunk, Thomas Walter *art historian*
Brustad, Orin Daniel *lawyer*
Bully-Cummings, Ella M. *police chief*
Burns, Lawrence D. *automotive executive*
Burnside, Wanda Jacqueline *elementary school educator*
Burzynski, Susan Marie *newspaper editor*
Butler, David J. *newspaper editor*
Buttigieg, Joseph J. *bank executive*
Calkins, Stephen *lawyer, educator*
Callahan, J(ohn) William (Bill Callahan) *judge*
Candler, James Nall, Jr. *lawyer*
Charfoos, Lawrence Selig *lawyer*
Chauderlot, Fabienne-Sophie *foreign language educator*
Chelios, Chris (Christos K. Chelios) *professional hockey player*
Chou, Clifford Chi Fong *research engineering executive*
Clarke, Troy A. *automotive executive*
Cohan, Leon Sumner *lawyer, retired electric company executive*
Cohen, Norton Jacob *lawyer*
Cohen, Sanford Ned *pediatrician, educator, academic administrator*
Corbitt, Eumiller Mattie *special education educator*
Corrigan, Maura Denise *state supreme court justice*
Cothorn, John Arthur *lawyer*
Covensky, Edith *language educator, poet*
Cox, Sean F. *federal judge*
Cranmer, Thomas William *lawyer*
Curtis, Robert O. *mechanical engineer*
Cyprus, Nicholas Stanley *automotive executive, accountant*
Darr, Alan Phipps *curator, historian*
Datsyuk, Pavel *professional hockey player*
Datta, Sudip *finance educator*
Dauch, Richard E. *automotive executive*
Day, Burnis C. *artist, educator*
Deason, Herold McClure *lawyer*
DeRoo, Sally Ann *biology, geology and environmental science educator*
Devellano, James Charles *professional hockey manager, baseball executive*
DiChiera, David *opera company director*
Diehl, Nancy J. *lawyer*
Dombrowski, David *baseball team executive*
Dombrowski, Mitchell Paul *obstetrician, researcher*
Drescher, Dennis George *biochemist, researcher*
Drutchas, Gregory G. *lawyer*
Dudley, Arthur, II, *lawyer*
Dudley, John Henry, Jr. *lawyer*
Duensing, Dorothy Jean *music educator, vocalist*
DuMouchelle, Ernest J. *art appraiser*
DuMouchelle, Lawrence F. *art appraiser*
Dunn, William Bradley *lawyer*
Dworkin, Aaron P. *violinist, educator*
Dwyer, John M. *mathematician, statistician, computer scientist*
Earley, Anthony Francis, Jr. *utilities company executive, lawyer*
Early, S. Allen III *lawyer*
Edelstein, Tilden Gerald *academic administrator, historian, educator*
Edmunds, Nancy Garlock *federal judge*
Elder, Jack S. *urologist, educator*
Ellyn, Lynne *energy executive*
Enam, Syed Ather *neurosurgeon, researcher*
Faison, W. Mack *lawyer*
Fay, Sister Maureen A. *university president*
Feikens, John *federal judge*
Field, Judith Judy *librarian*
Fleming, George Robert *psychologist*
Forster, Carl-Peter *automotive executive*
Frade, Peter Daniel *chemist, educator, administrator*
Francis, Edward D. *architect*
Frank, Richard Calhoun *architect*
Friedman, Bernard Alvin *federal judge*
Fussell, Karen Marie *social worker, protective services official*
Gardin, Julius Markus *cardiologist, educator*
Gerosa, Peter R. *automotive executive*
Gershel, Alan M. *prosecutor*
Gettelfinger, Ron *labor union administrator*
Gillum, Roderick D. *automotive executive*
Gilmer-Hill, Holly *medical educator*
Glotta, Ronald Delon *lawyer*
Godzak, Roman Paul *archivist*
Goodman, Allen Charles *economist, educator*
Grabowski, Jon *real estate company executive*
Groves, Odessa Marie *science educator*
Guo, Zhongwu *science educator*
Gupta, Suraj Narayan *physicist, researcher*
Haddad, Ramsi *medical geneticist, educator*
Hampton, Verne Churchill, II, *lawyer*
Hanks, Robin *rehabilitation nurse*
Hasek, Dominik *professional hockey player*
Hashimoto, Ken *dermatologist, educator*
Hawley, Robert C., Jr. *pathologist*
Henderson, Frederick A. (Fritz) *automotive executive*
Holland, Ken *professional sports team executive*
Holmstrom, Tomas *professional hockey player*
Hughes, Thomas A. *lawyer, utilities executive*
Hunke, David L. *publishing executive*
Ilitch, Marian *professional hockey team and food service executive*
Ilitch, Michael *professional hockey team and food products executive*
Jackson, Linda Shorter *nutritionist, educator*
Jeffs, Thomas Hamilton, II, *retired bank executive*
Jendrzejewski, Roxanne Marie *social studies educator, language educator*
Johnson, Lester Larue, Jr. *artist, educator*
Jones, James Allen *secondary school educator*
Kalman, Andrew *manufacturing executive, director*
Kaltenbach, James Albert *neurobiologist, educator*
Kamins, John Mark *lawyer*
Keith, Damon Jerome *federal judge*
Kelley, Mark Albert *physician, educator, health products executive*
Kelly, Marilyn *state supreme court justice*
Kennedy, Cornelia Groefsema *federal judge*
Kessler, Philip Joel *lawyer*
Kilpatrick, Kwame Malik *mayor*
Kim, Do Gyoon *biomedical researcher*
Krsul, John Aloysius, Jr. *lawyer*
Kruse, Ronia *information technology executive*
Kummler, Ralph H. *chemical engineer, educator, dean*
Kyff, Kimberly *elementary school educator*
LaNeve, Mark R. *automotive executive*
Lawrence, John Kidder *lawyer*
Lerner, Stephen Alexander *microbiologist, physician, educator*
Levin, Charles Leonard *state supreme court justice*
Lewis, David Baker *lawyer*
Leyland, Jim (James Richard Leyland) *professional baseball manager*
Lidstrom, Nicklas *professional hockey player*
Lim, Henry Wan-Peng *dermatologist*
Lisak, Robert Philip *neurologist, researcher, educator*
Little, Laura Ann *elementary school educator, art educator*
Lockman, Stuart M. *lawyer*
Locniskar, Dana Michael *financial consultant*
Losanoff, Julian Emil *surgeon, educator*
Lowell, Scott *restaurant manager, real estate developer*
Lupulescu, Aurel Peter *medical educator, researcher, physician*
Lutz, Robert Anthony *automotive company executive*
MacDonald, Douglas Andrew *psychologist, educator*
Madgett, Naomi Long *poet, editor, publisher, educator*
Maida, Adam Joseph Cardinal *cardinal*
Maiese, Kenneth *neurologist, neuroscientist*
Mamat, Frank Trustick *lawyer*
Mani, Nandita S. *medical librarian*
Martin, John E *psychologist, educator*
Martz, Mike *former professional football coach*
Maseru, Noble A.W. *city health department administrator*
Maurer, David Leo *lawyer*
McArthur, Steven Francis *psychologist, educator*
McCrae, Jocelyn Diane *psychologist*
McIntyre, Michael John *lawyer, educator*
McKim, Samuel John III *lawyer*
Mclendon, Lloyd *professional baseball coach, retired baseball player*
McWhorter, Sharon Louise *engineering executive, inventor, consultant*
Mika, Joseph John *library director, educator*
Miller, Bruce Abraham *lawyer*
Miller, Orlando Jack *obstetrician, gynecologist, educator, geneticist*
Mitchell, Connie *director*
Mitseff, Carl *lawyer*
Monroe, Craig *professional baseball player*
Morgan, Virginia Mattison *judge*
Moses, Gregory H., Jr. *health services administrator*
Moss, Leslie Otha *homeland security specialist*
Murphy, Stephen Joseph III *prosecutor*
Myers, Rodman Nathaniel *lawyer*
Nabozny, Heather *professional sports team groundskeeper*
Nathanson, Saul David *oncologist, surgeon, educator*
Neithercut, Mark Edward *foundation consultant*
Nemeth, Patricia Marie *lawyer*
Newman, Andrea Fischer *air transportation executive*
Nicholson, James M. *chemicals executive*
Noland, Mariam Charl *foundation executive*
Novak, Raymond Francis *environmental services administrator, pharmacology educator*
Ordonez, Maggilo Jose *professional baseball player*
Ortiz, Francis Robert *lawyer*
Osgood, Chris *professional hockey player*
Ostrea, Enrique Mapua, Jr. *pediatrician, medical educator*
Ouellette, Daniel Ronald *pulmonary and critical care medicine specialist*
Parrish, Maurice Drue *museum executive*
Parry, Dale D. *publisher, editor*
Peck, William Henry *curator, archaeologist, educator, art historian, writer*
Peters, John Douglas *lawyer, artist*
Phillis, John Whitfield *physiologist, educator*
Pietrofesa, John Joseph *psychologist, educator*
Piper, William Howard *bank executive*
Polanco, Placido Enrique *professional baseball player*
Porcher, Robert *restaurant manager, retired professional football player*
Prasad, Ananda Shiva *medical educator*
Rafalski, Brian *professional hockey player*
Rajpurkar, Atul Dattatraya *urologist*
Rassel, Richard Edward *lawyer*
Rathod, Mulchand *mechanical engineering educator*
Raymond, Richard Gerard, Jr. *lawyer*
Reddy, Daniel Joseph *vascular surgeon*
Redman, Barbara Klug *nursing educator*
Reece, Terry Allen *travel company executive, Internet company executive*
Rivers, Emanuel P. *emergency physician, medical educator*
Rivin, Eugeny (Eugene) I. *engineering educator, researcher, consultant*
Rodriguez, Ivan Torres *professional baseball player*
Roehling, Carl David *architect*
Rogers, Kenny (Kenneth Scott Rogers) *professional baseball player*
Rogers, Paulleto *researcher, writer*
Rohr, Richard David *lawyer*
Rosen, Gerald Ellis *federal judge*
Rosman, Howard S. *cardiologist, educator*
Rozof, Phyllis Claire *lawyer*
Ruckdeschel, John Charles *health facility administrator*
Rupley, Jerry T. *lawyer*
Ryan, James Leo *federal judge*
Saxton, William Marvin *lawyer*
Schiffer, Charles Alan *oncologist, educator*
Schlichting, Nancy Margaret *hospital administrator*
Schreiber, Bertram Manuel *mathematics professor*
Schwartz, Alan Earl *lawyer, director*
Schwartz, Matthew Barahal *historian*
Schweitzer, Peter *advertising agency executive*
Schweitzer, Vanessa Gayl *otorhinolaryngologist*
Scott, John Edward Smith *lawyer*
Sedler, Robert Allen *law educator*
Selyuzhenkov, Ilya *research scientist*
Shade, George Henry, Jr. *obstetrician, gynecologist, educator*
Shah, Aashit K. *neurologist*
Shannon, Margaret Anne *lawyer*
Sheffield, Gary Antonian *professional baseball player*
Sherrick, Daniel William *lawyer*
Shi, Weisong *computer scientist, educator*
Silverman, Norman Alan *cardiac surgeon*
Sima, Anders Adolph Fredrik *pathologist*
Skowronski, Nancy *library director*
Skundric, Dusanka S. *medical educator, researcher*
Small, Melvin *historian, educator*
Smith, Gary Richard *technology educator*
Smith, James Albert *lawyer*
Smith, S. Kinnie, Jr. *lawyer*

Smith, Wilbur Lazar *radiologist, educator*
Smyntek, John Eugene, Jr. *editor*
Soave, Anthony *manufacturing executive*
Sokol, Robert James *obstetrician, gynecologist, educator*
Sousanis, Nick *art web site designer*
Sparrow, Herbert George III *lawyer, educator*
Speegle, Laura Ann *elementary school educator*
Spyers-Duran, Peter *librarian, educator*
States, J. Christopher *molecular biology educator, researcher*
Steiman, H. Robert *dean, dental educator*
Stern, Todd *restaurant manager*
Stewart, Melbourne George, Jr. *physicist, researcher*
Szygenda, Ralph J. *automotive executive*
Tarnacki, Duane L. *lawyer*
Taylor, Anna Diggs *federal judge*
Terry, Robin *museum director*
Thelen, Bruce Cyril *lawyer*
Thomas, Craig Damon *protective services official*
Timm, Roger K. *lawyer*
Topacio, Angela *marketing executive*
Turner, Reginald Maurice, Jr. *lawyer*
Tyburski, James Gerard *surgeon*
Valade, Alan Michael *lawyer*
Verlander, Justin Brooks *professional baseball player*
Vigneron, Allen Henry *theology studies educator, rector, auxiliary bishop*
Volz, William Harry *lawyer, educator*
Voudoukis, Ignatios John *internist, cardiologist*
Wagoner, Rick (G. Richard Wagoner Jr.) *automotive executive*
Walls, Amos Louis III *music educator*
Warden, Gail Lee *healthcare executive*
Washington, Olivia Grace Mary *psychotherapist, educator, counselor, researcher*
Whitehouse, Fred Waite *endocrinologist, researcher*
Whiteman, Richard Mark *lawyer*
Whitmer, Richard E. *insurance company executive*
Wiener, Joseph *pathologist, educator*
Williams, Denise *academic administrator*
Wittlinger, Timothy David *lawyer*
Wolf, Barry *geneticist, pediatric educator*
Wu, Frank H. *law educator, journalist*
Wyrick, Jermaine Albert *lawyer*
Yang, Kai *engineering educator*
Yee, Sandra Gayle Brown *library director, dean*
Yzerman, Steve (Stephen Gregory Yzerman) *professional sports team executive, retired professional hockey player*
Zuckerman, Richard Engle *lawyer, educator*

Dewitt
Hutting, Lori A. *language educator*

Dexter
Hanamey, Rosemary T. *nursing educator*

Dowagiac
Murphy, Ellis *association management executive*
Ott, C(larence) H(enry) *ambassador, retired accounting professor*

East Lansing
Abeles, Norman *psychologist, educator*
Abolins, Maris Arvids *physicist, educator*
Abramson, Paul Robert *political scientist, educator*
Aggarwal, Vaneet *research scientist*
Andersland, Orlando Baldwin *retired engineering educator*
Anderson, David Daniel *retired humanities educator, writer, editor*
Anderton, James Franklin, IV, *real estate company executive*
Austin, Sam M. *physicist, educator*
Baillie, Richard Thomas *economist, educator*
Ballbach, Philip Thornton *political consultant, investor*
Bandes, Susan Jane *museum director, educator*
Beckmeyer, Henry Ernest *anesthesiologist, pain management specialist, educator*
Blosser, Henry Gabriel *physicist*
Boehlert, Carl Joseph *materials scientist, educator*
Bromley, Stephen C. *zoology educator*
Brophy, Jere Edward *education educator, researcher*
Brown, Boyd Alex *physicist, researcher*
Bukovac, Martin John *horticulturist, educator*
Byerrum, Richard Uglow *college dean*
Cascarilla, Richard A. *lawyer*
Case, Eldon Darrel *materials science educator*
Chapin, Richard Earl *retired librarian*
Chen, Kun-Mu *electrical engineering educator*
Crewe, Nancy Moe *retired psychologist*
Cross, Aureal Theophilus *geology and botany educator*
Cutts, Charles Eugene *retired engineering educator*
Dennis, Frank George, Jr. *retired horticulture educator*
Dewhurst, Charles Kurt *museum director, curator, language educator*
D'Itri, Frank Michael *environmental research chemist*
Dye, James Louis *retired chemistry professor*
Fisher, Alan Washburn *historian, educator*
Foss, John Frank *mechanical engineering educator*
Fraker, Pamela J. *science educator*
Freedman, Eric *journalist, educator, writer*
Gass, Gertrude Zemon *psychologist, researcher*
Gelbke, Claus-Konrad *nuclear physics educator*
Goodman, Erik David *engineering educator*
Gottschalk, Alexander *radiologist, educator*
Greenberg, Bradley Sander *communications educator*
Hackel, Emanuel *science educator*
Haider, Steven John *economics professor*
Haka, Clifford Hughey *library director*
Harrison, James Francis *chemistry professor, researcher*
Harrison, Jeremy Thomas *dean, law educator*
Harrison, Michael Jay *physicist, researcher*
Hine, Darlene Clark *history educator, administrator*
Honhart, Frederick Lewis III *academic director*
Iglesias, Emma Maria *economics professor*
Izzo, Thomas *college basketball coach*
Kang, Jun-Koo *finance educator*
Kaplan, Thomas Abraham *physicist, educator*
King, Lonnie J. *dean*
Kirk, Edgar Lee *retired musician, educator*
Kirkpatrick, R(obert) James *geologist, educator*
Koo, Anthony Ying Chang *economist, educator*
Kreinin, Mordecha Eliahu *economics professor*
Ladenson, Sharon *university librarian*
Lashbrooke, Elvin Carroll, Jr. *law educator, consultant*
Lenski, Richard Eimer *evolutionary biologist, educator*
Lloyd, John Raymond *mechanical engineering educator*
Luccock, Thomas Nelson *auditor, director*
Luecke, Eleanor Virginia Rohrbacher *civic volunteer*
Manderscheid, Lester Vincent *agricultural economics educator*
McMeekin, Dorothy *botanist, plant pathologist, educator*
Menchik, Paul Leonard *economist, educator*
Merchant, Suzy *women's college basketball coach*
Miracle, Gordon Eldon *advertising educator*
Monson, Carol Lynn *osteopath, psychotherapist*
Natoli, Joseph *language educator*
Noel, Mary Margaret *nutritionist, educator*
Perrin, Robert *writer, consultant*
Pervaiz, Mohammad Hassan *cardiologist*
Petrides, George Athan *ecologist, educator*
Petropoulos, Evangelos *former health institute director, educator, researcher*
Pierre, Percy Anthony *engineering educator*
Preiss, Jack *biochemistry professor*
Press, Charles *retired political science professor*
Pysh, Joseph John *neurologist*
Ralph, David Clinton *communications educator*
Rasmusson, Thomas *lawyer*
Ristow, George Edward *neurologist, educator*
Root-Bernstein, Robert Scott *biologist, educator*
Rosenman, Kenneth D. *medical educator*
Ross, Anthony Dewayne *engineering educator*
Rothert, Marilyn L. *dean, nursing educator*
Saul, William Edward *engineering educator*
Schoenl, William James *history professor*
Seaton, James Everett *humanities educator*
Simon, Lou Anna Kimsey *academic administrator*
Sisk, Cheryl *neuroscientist, educator*
Snoddy, James Ernest *education educator*
Spagnuolo, Mark Mario *retired dentist*
Sparks, Harvey Vise, Jr. *physiologist*
Stapleton, James Hall *retired statistician, educator*
Strampel, William Derkey *dean, medical educator*
Tiedje, James Michael *microbiologist, educator, ecologist*
Todd, Ewen Cameron David *food safety director*
Tzitsikas, Helene *retired literature educator*
von Bernuth, Robert Dean *agricultural engineering educator, consultant*
Wakoski, Diane *poet, educator*
Watson, Ralph Edward *internist, educator*
White, James Alfred *lawyer*
Wilkinson, William Sherwood *lawyer*
Wilson, R. Dale *marketing educator*
Winder, Clarence Leland *psychologist, educator*
Yang, Lijian *educator*

Eastport
Tomlinson, James Lawrence *mechanical engineer*

Edwardsburg
Floyd, Alton David *cell biologist, consultant*

Elk Rapids
Thompson, Richard Thomas *academic administrator*

Escanaba
Wood, D. Ann *language and music educator*

Farmington
Aubertin, Madeline Katherine *retired nursing educator, medical/surgical nurse, mental health services professional*
Ellens, J(ay) Harold *philosopher, educator, psychotherapist, minister*
Ginsberg, Myron *computer scientist*
Neyer, Jerome Charles *consulting civil engineer*
Penberthy, Stanley Josiah, Jr. *publisher*
Shaevsky, Mark *lawyer*
Werba, Gabriel *public relations consultant*

Farmington Hills
Aboulafia, Elie David *vascular surgeon*
Antone, Nahil Peter *lawyer, civil engineer*
Barry, Essie Marilyn *elementary school educator, writer*
Bernstein, Richard *lawyer*
Chapman, Gilbert Bryant *physicist*
Damron, Jayne *librarian*
Ellmann, Sheila Frenkel *investment company executive*
Fenton, Robert Leonard *lawyer, writer, film producer*
Fershtman, Julie Ilene *lawyer*
Foley, Thomas John *lawyer*
Friedman, Rozanne Golston *psychotherapist*
Gordon, Arnold Mark *arbitrator, educator*
Gordon, Craig Jeffrey *oncologist, educator*
Goslin, Gerald Hugh *concert pianist, educator*
Hagerty, Robert E. *academic administrator*
Heiss, Richard Walter *retired bank executive, consultant, lawyer*
Hurd, Mary K. *civil engineer, writer*
Kern, Michael L. III *corporate financial executive*
Mall, Sanford J. *lawyer*
Manna, Martin *public relations executive, marketing executive*
Meyer, Philip Gilbert *lawyer*
Plaut, Jonathan Victor *rabbi*
Purdy, Jan Rae *music educator*
Robinson, Amorie Alexia *psychologist, educator*
Smith, Isabel Francis *financial planner*
Taravella, Christopher Anthony *lawyer*
Theodore, Ares Nicholas *chemist, researcher*
Winzenreid, James Ernest *lawyer, entrepreneur*

Fennville
Kamman, Curtis Warren *retired ambassador*

Ferndale
Forkan, Eveleen *counselor, educator, researcher*
Haberman, Jeremy *music venue executive*
Huvaere, Jason *production company executive*

Fife Lake
Knecht, Richard Arden *family practitioner*

Flat Rock
Cerasuolo, Jennifer Lyn *preservationist*

Flint
Acuff, A. Marshall, Jr. *retired investment company executive*
Belcher, Max *social services administrator, dean*
Cooley, Richard Eugene *lawyer*
Czinder, Thomas Bradley *musician, director*
Hart, Clifford Harvey *lawyer*
Palinsky, Constance Genevieve *hypnotherapist, educator*
Simmons, Robert Randolph *principal*
Smith, Catherine Jean *artist, educator*
Tomblinson, James Edmond *architect*
Wheeler, Michael Thomas *pain medicine specialist, director*
White, David C. *archivist, historian*
White, William Samuel *foundation executive*
Wigston, David Lawrence *biologist, dean*
Williams, Veronica Myres *psychotherapist, social worker*

Flushing
Bain, William David *electronics engineer, writer*
Demankowski, Lisa Renee *architect, educator*
Lopez Negrete, Kariann May *psychologist*

Frankenmuth
Shetlar, James Francis *physician*

Frankfort
Foster, Robert Carmichael *banker*
Gerberding, Miles Carston *lawyer*
Storrer, William Allin *theater educator, consultant*

Franklin
Pappas, Edward Harvey *lawyer*
Reinhart, Anne Christine *special education educator, consultant*
Sax, Mary Randolph *speech and language pathologist*

Fraser
Winget, Larry J., Sr. *automotive industry executive*

Freeland
Lutes, Byron B. *retired surgeon*

Gaylord
Cooney, Patrick Ronald *bishop*
Jones, John Paul *probation officer, psychologist*
Smith, Frank Earl *retired trade association administrator*

Glen Arbor
Wagner, Bruce Stanley *marketing professional*

Grand Ledge
Evert, Sandra Florence (Sandra Wheeler) *medical/surgical nurse, consultant*

Grand Rapids
Anyalebechi, Prince N. *engineering educator, consultant*
Auwers, Stanley John *motor carrier executive*
Baker, Hollis MacLure *furniture manufacturing company executive*
Barnes, Thomas John *lawyer*
Beals, Paul Archer *religious studies educator*
Becker, Robert Joseph *database consultant, application developer, educator, computer science specialist*
Beeke, Joel Robert *minister, educator, writer*
Bell, Robert Holmes *federal judge*
Bolinder, Scott W. *publishing company executive*
Bolt, Eunice Mildred DeVries *artist*
Botsford, Jon Douglas *lawyer*
Bradshaw, Conrad Allan *retired lawyer*
Brenneman, Hugh Warren, Jr. *judge*
Brinkmeyer, Scott S. *lawyer*
Bursch, John Joseph *lawyer*
Bytwerk, Randall Lee *communication educator*
Carlotti, Ronald John *food scientist*
Collier, Brian *history professor*
Crowell, Gregory F. *musician, director*
Currie, William G. *forest products executive*
Curtin, Timothy John *lawyer*
Daniels, Joseph *neuropsychiatrist*
Davis, Henry Barnard, Jr. *lawyer*
DeLapa, Judith Anne *business owner*
DeVries, Robert K. *retired publisher, consultant*
DeYonker, Alex J. *lawyer, food products executive*
Diekema, Anthony J. *college president, consultant*
Dykstra, William Dwight *management executive, consultant*
Evans, Oliver H. *college administrator*
Glenn, Michael B. *forest products executive*
Gordon, Dan A. *food service executive*
Greenfield, John Charles *biochemist, professional society administrator*
Hackett, James P. *manufacturing executive*
Harris, Richard W. *lawyer, educator, accountant*
Harrison, Robert Ward *retired surgeon*
Hoekstra, Mark Rains *information technology executive, consultant*
Horn, Joyce Elaine *retired music educator*
Jennette, Noble Stevenson III *lawyer*
Jonker, Robert James *federal judge*
Kaczmarczyk, Jeffrey Allen *journalist, music and dance critic*
Ljungren, Wendy *engineering executive*
Logie, John Hoult *former mayor, lawyer*
Lubbers, Arend Donselaar *retired academic administrator*
Luttikhuizen, Henry Martin *art historian, curator*
MacDonald, David Richard *industrial psychologist*
Maines, Charles John *electronics manager*
Maupin, Karin Louise *secondary school educator*
McCallum, Charles Edward *lawyer*
Mears, Patrick Edward *lawyer*
Meijer, Hank *retail company executive*
Menninga, Clarence *retired geologist*
Messner, James W. *advertising executive*
Metzler, James Robert *musician*
Miles, Wendell A. *federal judge*
Murray, Mark Andrew *food products executive, former academic administrator, economist*
Noakes, William S., Jr. *lawyer*
Oetting, Roger H. *lawyer*
Petkus, Alan Francis *microbiologist*
Purchase-Owens, Francena *marketing professional, consultant, educator*
Quist, Gordon Jay *federal judge*
Rasmussen, Douglas John *lawyer*
Roberts-Brown, Arlene Maria *executive assistant*
Robson, Larry J. *physician*
Sadler, David G(ary) *manufacturing executive*
Schmidt, Gary David *language educator*
Secchia, Peter F. *forest products executive, former United States ambassador to Italy*
Shoemaker, Allen Leslie *psychology professor, consultant*
Spaulding, Dan *public relations executive*
Spies, Frank Stadler *lawyer*
Sturken, Craig C. *retail executive*
Swanson, Alfred Bertil *orthopaedic and hand surgeon, educator*
Sytsma, Fredric A. *lawyer*
Taber, Rodman Eastman *thoracic surgeon*
Tiemstra, John Peter *economics professor*
Vande Kopple, William John *literature and language professor*
Van Haren, W(illiam) Michael *lawyer*
Verdier, David D'Ooge *ophthalmologist, educator*
Vranish, Kenneth *electrical engineer, consultant*
Vredevoogd Combs, Pat *real estate company executive*
Walsh, James *retail supermarket executive*
Watkins, James Kelley *retired urologist*
Webb, Mark Russell *music educator*
Wendt, Vernon Earl *internist, cardiologist*
Williams, Janice H. *business executive*
Wilt, Jeffrey Lynn *pulmonary and critical care physician, educator*
Woodrick, Robert *food products executive*

Greenbush
Paulson, James Marvin *retired engineering educator*

Greenville
Mullendore, James Myers *lawyer*

Grosse Ile
Smith, Veronica Latta *real estate company officer*
Stryker, Joan Copeland *retired obstetrician, retired gynecologist, educator*

Grosse Pointe
Amsden, Ted Thomas *lawyer*
Bryfonski, Dedria Anne *publishing executive*
Caldwell, John Thomas, Jr. *communications executive*
Casey, Genevieve M(ary) *librarian, educator*
Goss, James William *lawyer*
Hendrie, Janice Ellen *language educator*
Hill, Draper *editorial cartoonist*
Manetta, Richard L. *chemicals executive, lawyer*
Marshall, Douglas William *health research administrator, educator*
Mengden, Joseph Michael *retired investment banker*
Whittaker, Jeanne Evans *retired journalist*
Wilkinson, Warren Scripps *manufacturing executive*

Grosse Pointe Farms
Christian, Edward Kieren *broadcasting station executive*
Fromm, Joseph L. *financial consultant*
Obolensky, Marilyn Wall (Mrs. Serge Obolensky) *metals company executive*
Surdam, Robert McClellan *retired banker*
Thurber, Peter Palms *lawyer*

Grosse Pointe Park
Centner, Charles William *lawyer, educator*
Elsila, David August *editor*
Knapp, Mildred Florence *retired social worker*
Krebs, William Hoyt *industrial hygienist, health science association administrator*
Mogk, John Edward *law educator, association executive, consultant*
Orton, Colin George *medical physicist*

Grosse Pointe Shores
Burke, Thomas Joseph *civil engineer*
Holness, Gordon Victor Rix *engineering executive, mechanical engineer*
LaHood, Mary Anne *real estate investor*
Sphire, Raymond Daniel *anesthesiologist, educator*

Grosse Pointe Woods
Barnhart, Mary C. *health facility administrator*
McWhirter, Glenna Suzanne (Nickie McWhirter) *retired columnist*
Prather, Kenneth Earl *lawyer*
Sul, Yi Chul *neurologist*

Gwinn
Lasich, Vivian Esther Layne *secondary school educator*

Hale
Lixey, Elizabeth Voulgarakis *secondary school educator*

Harbor Beach
Falkenberg, Mary Elaine *small business owner*

Harbor Springs
Cappel, Constance *editor, writer*
Smith, Wayne Richard *lawyer*
Turner, Lester Nathan *lawyer, international trade consultant*

Harsens Island
Woodford, Arthur MacKinnon *retired library director, historian*

Haslett
Hotaling, Robert Bachman *urban planner, educator*
Warrington, Willard Glade *retired university official*

Hastings
Adrounie, V. Harry *retired military medical service officer, science educator, environmentalist*
Jones, Kensinger *advertising executive, educator*

Hickory Corners
Bristol, Norman *lawyer, arbitrator, retired food products executive*
Lauff, George Howard *biologist*

Highland
Brown, Ray Kent *biochemist, physician, educator*
Bullard, Willis Clare, Jr. *lawyer*

Hillsdale
Frudakis, Anthony Parker *sculptor, educator*
Miller, Robert Raymond, Jr. *biology professor*

Holland
Claar, Victor *economist, educator*
Cook, James Ivan *clergyman, educator*
DeBruyn, Maxine *performing arts educator*
Garlough, William Glenn *marketing executive*
Haworth, Richard G. (Dick Haworth) *office furniture manufacturer*
Holmes, Jack Edward *political science professor*
Murphy, Max Ray *lawyer*
Nieuwsma, Milton John *writer, journalist*
Nyenhuis, Jacob Eugene *academic administrator*
Stynes, Stanley Kenneth *retired chemical engineer, educator*
Van Noord, Diane C. *artist, educator*
Van Voorst, Robert E. *theology educator, minister*
Van Wylen, Gordon John *former college president*
Zuidema, George Dale *surgeon, educator*

Holly
Evans Snowden, Audra Lynn *counselor*
Stolpin, William Roger *printmaker*

Holt
Smith, Betty W. *librarian*
Wood, Mary Elizabeth *retired secondary school educator, church musician*

Houghton
Abdelkhalik, Ossama *computer science educator, researcher*
Crittenden, John Charles *engineering educator*
Fink, William Orman *retired federal agency administrator, management consultant*
Heckel, Richard Wayne *metallurgical engineering educator*
Huang, Eugene Yuching *civil engineer, educator*
Hungwe, Kedmon Nyasha *education educator, researcher*
Mukherjee, Abhijit *mechanical engineer, educator*
Narain, Amitabh *aerospace and mechanical engineering educator*
Utt, Glenn S., Jr. *retired medical products executive*

Howell
Rohrabacher, Janet Hammond *genealogist, archivist*
Tupper, Leon F. *manufacturing executive*
Watkins, Curtis WinthroP *artist*

Idlewild
Wooley, Geraldine Hamilton *poet, writer*

Inkster
Bullock, Steven Carl *lawyer*

Interlochen
Kimpton, Jeffrey S. *academic administrator*

Ionia
Ulmer, Evonne Gail *health science association administrator*

Ironwood
Rondeau, Clement Robert *petroleum geologist*

Ishpeming
Steward, James Brian *lawyer, pharmacist*

Ithaca
Price, Gregory *environmentalist*

Jackson
Brunner, James Edwin *lawyer*
Feldmann, Judith Gail *language professional, educator*
Goldsen, Bruce I. *radio executive*
Graham, Donald James *food technologist, hygienic design consultant*
Jacobs, Wendell Early, Jr. *lawyer*
Joos, David W. *energy executive*
Kelly, Robert Vincent, Jr. *metal products executive*
Livesay, Jacqueline Ryder *elementary school educator, music educator, director*
Marcoux, William Joseph *lawyer*
Nugent, Ted (Theodore Anthony Nugent) *musician, radio personality*
Popp, Nathaniel *archbishop*
Smith, Stanton Kinnie, Jr. *lawyer*
Walberg, Tim (Timothy Lee Walberg) *congressman, former state legislator*
Webb, Thomas J. *utilities executive*
Whipple, Kenneth *utilities executive*
Wingblade, Loren Charles *education educator*

Jenison
Kruse, Pamela Jean *lawyer*

Jerome
Dillon, Merton Lynn *historian, educator*

Jonesville
Corwin, Danny Willard *rehabilitation services professional, director*

Kalamazoo
Badra, Robert George *theology studies and humanities educator*
Bailey, Judith Irene *academic administrator, educator, consultant*
Bennett, Arlie Joyce *clinical social worker*
Bernknopf, Allison Cori *pharmacist, educator*
Breisach, Ernst A. *historian, educator*
Burns, James W. *education educator*
Campbell, William Bernard *cardiologist*
Carver, Norman Francis, Jr. *architect, photographer*
Coss, Barbara Sue *humanities educator*
Curry, John Patrick *insurance company executive, management consultant*
Dahlinger, Martha Louise *elementary school educator*
Dybek, Stuart *language educator, writer*
Enslen, Pamela Chapman *lawyer*
Enslen, Richard Alan *federal judge*
Fischell, Tim Alexander *cardiologist*
Gordon, Edgar George *retired lawyer*
Grotzinger, Laurel Ann *librarian, educator*
Haenicke, Diether Hans *academic administrator emeritus, educator*
Hall, Curtis E. *lawyer*
Hudson, Roy Davage *retired pharmaceutical executive*
Jayasingh, Preetha *food scientist*
Julien, Catherine *history professor*
Kujawski, Daniel *science educator*
Lander, Joyce Ann *retired nursing educator, retired medical/surgical nurse*
Lavender, Maryann Michelle *history educator*
Light, Christopher Upjohn *freelance/self-employed writer, photographer*
Light, John Richard *sculptor*
Litynski, Daniel Mitchell *optical engineer, educator, physicist, retired military officer*
Lundquist, C. David *lawyer*
MacMillan, Stephen P. *health products executive*
Marquardt, Michele C. *lawyer*
Marshall, Vincent de Paul *industrial microbiologist, researcher*
Miazga, Ronald C. *language educator*
Ortiz-Button, Olga *social worker*
Palchick, Bernard S. *academic administrator, painter, educator*
Paul, Annegret *mathematics professor*
Petersen, Anne C. (Cheryl Petersen) *foundation administrator, educator*
Ratner, Carl Joseph *opera stage director, baritone*
Saber, Alan A. *surgeon*
Showalter, Shirley H. *former academic administrator*
Sridharan, Sugandhi *neurologist*
Stavig, Richard Thorson *retired literature educator*
Vander Weg, Phillip Dale *art educator, academic administrator, sculptor*
Van Slambrouck, John G. *lawyer*

Kentwood
Yovich, Daniel John *chemist, educator*

Lake Angelus
Kresge, Bruce Anderson *retired physician*

Lake Orion
Berger, Laura Ann *dance studio owner*
Leonard, Jacquelyn Ann *retired elementary school educator*
Robinson, Marietta S. *lawyer*

Lanse
Augustine, Henry Joseph *secondary school educator*

Lansing
Arends, Herman Joseph *former insurance company executive*
Baker, Frederick Milton, Jr. *lawyer*
Birn, Stuart R. *lawyer*
Brewer, Mark Courtland *lawyer*
Brown, Nancy Field *editor*
Cavanagh, Michael Francis *state supreme court justice*
Cherry, John D., Jr. *lieutenant governor, former state senator*
Couto, C. Douglass *state agency administrator*
Cox, Mike (Michael A. Cox) *state attorney general*
Cunningham, Paula Diane *bank executive, former academic administrator*
Demlow, Daniel J. *lawyer*
Feight, Theodore J. *financial planner*
Fink, Joseph Allen *lawyer*
Fisher, John W. *insurance company executive*
Flanagan, Michael P. *school system administrator*
Foster, Joe C., Jr. *lawyer*
Gallagher, Byron Patrick, Jr. *lawyer*
Granholm, Jennifer Mulhern *governor*
Harrison, Michael Gregory *judge*
Hess, Steven Charles *lawyer*
Hoffman, Philip Edward *legislative consultant*
Hopgood, Hoon-Yung *state representative*
Kelley, Frank Joseph *lawyer, former state attorney general*
Kleine, Robert J. *state official*
Kluge, Len H. *director, actor, theater educator*
Land, Terri Lynn *state official*
Lobenherz, William Ernest *consumer products company executive, trade association administrator, lawyer*
Looyenga, Roger L. *insurance company executive*
Markman, Stephen J. *state supreme court justice*
Marvin, David Edward Shreve *lawyer*
McKeague, David William *judge*
Nsofor, Leslie Monagolum *food scientist, researcher*
Reid English, Cristen *bank executive*
Roberston, Nancy R. *state librarian*
Rooney, John Philip *law educator*
Shirtum, Earl Edward *retired civil engineer*
Spence, Howard Tee Devon *retired judge, lawyer, consultant, arbitrator, government agency administrator*
Stockmeyer, Norman Otto *law educator, consultant*
Straus, Kathleen Nagler *academic administrator, educator*
Suhrheinrich, Richard Fred *federal judge*
Taylor, Clifford Woodworth *state supreme court justice*
Vincent, Frederick Michael, Sr. *neurologist, educator*
Watters, Linda A. *state agency administrator*
Winder, Richard Earnest *legal foundation administrator, writer, consultant*
Young, Robert P., Jr. *state supreme court justice*

Lawrence
Applewhaite, Carlisle S. *special education educator, consultant*

Leland
Small, Hamish *chemist*
Soutas-Little, Robert William *mechanical engineer, educator*

Lenox
Shaw, Charles Rusanda *retired government investigator*

Livonia
Barfield, Jon E. *employment company executive*
Baskin, Victoria *child and adolescent psychiatrist*
Bialosky, David L. *lawyer, automotive executive*
Cantie, Joseph S. *automotive executive*
Chowdhury, Subir *management consultant*
Drouin, Joe *automotive executive*
Gepford, Barbara Beebe *retired nutrition educator*
Gepford, William George *minister*
Gilbert, Daniel *professional sports team owner, mortgage company executive*
Haggard, Joan Claire *church musician, piano instructor, accompanist, adjudicator*
Hoffman, Barry Paul *lawyer*
Holtzman, Roberta Lee *French and Spanish language educator*
Katzman, David *investment company and professional sports team executive*
Kujawa, Sister Rose Marie *academic administrator*
Lake, Peter J. *automotive executive*
Lunn, Steven *automotive executive*
Maibach, Ben C., Jr. *consumer products company executive*
Marchuk, Neil *automotive executive*
McCotter, Thaddeus George *congressman*
McDowell, Richard William *academic administrator*
McHard, James Lorin *corporate financial executive, freelance/self-employed composer, writer*
Nahra, Khalil Salim *colon and rectal surgeon*
Nelson, Troy Alan *music educator, church musician*
Plant, John Charles *automotive executive*
Uicker, Joseph Bernard *retired engineering company executive*
Valerio, Michael Anthony *diversified financial services company executive*

Ludington
Puffer, Richard Judson *retired college chancellor*

Mackinaw City
Brisson, Steven Charles *curator*
Evans, Lynn Louise Morand *archaeologist*

Macomb
Farmakis, George Leonard *retired education educator*

Madison Heights
Janke, Kenneth *investment consultant*
Kafarski, Mitchell I. *chemical processing company executive*
Peaslee, Robert Leon *metallurgical engineer, consultant*
Pierce, Jean Lois *elementary school educator*
Scott, George Alfred *advertising executive, writer*
Xia, Jiding *chemical engineering educator*

Manistee
Trussell, Charles Tait *columnist*

Manistique
Jeffcott, Janet Bruhn *statistician, consultant*

Maple City
Duff, James George *retired finance company and automotive executive*

Marine City
Brown, Ronald Delano *endocrinologist*

Marquette
Brege, Dorance Charles *biologist*
Camerius, James Walter *marketing educator, corporate researcher*
Carnahan, George Richard *retired finance educator*
Cotter, June Ann *special education educator*
Keefe, Ronald D. *lawyer*
Lincke, Eric Theodore *retired surgeon*
Mahmood, Tallat *oncologist, hematologist*
Manning, Robert Hendrick *retired audio-visual services executive*
Pesola, William Ernest *restaurant management executive*

Mason
Yoakam, Kelly Lynn *harpist, educator*

Mattawan
Greene, Timothy James *industrial engineering educator*

Mears
Loomis, Norma Irene *marriage and family therapist*

Midland
Adams, Thomas Walton *corrections official*
Banholzer, William F. *chemical company executive*
Barker, Nancy Lepard *university official*
Battle, Leonard Carroll *lawyer*
Burns, Stephanie A. *chemicals executive*
Bus, James Stanley *toxicologist*
Carbone, Anthony J. *chemicals executive*
Chao, Marshall *chemist*
Cook, Phillip H. *chemicals executive*
Crummett, Warren Berlin *analytical chemistry consultant*
Davidson, John Hunter *agriculturist*
Dorman, Linneaus Cuthbert *retired chemist*
Gambrell, Michael R. *chemicals executive*
Haller, Heinz *chemicals executive*
Hampton, Leroy *retired chemical company executive*
Holder, Julie Fasone *chemicals executive*
Kalil, Charles James *lawyer, chemicals executive*
Kepler, David E., II, *chemicals executive*
Kreinberg, Romeo *chemicals executive*
Kresge, Charles T. *chemicals executive*
Liveris, Andrew N. *chemical company executive*
Meister, Bernard John *retired chemical engineer*
Merszei, Geoffrey E. *corporate financial executive*
Nowak, Robert Michael *chemist*
Potts, Sandra *library director*
Robbins, Lanny Arnold *chemical engineer*
Schmidt, William C. *retired chemicals executive*
Veurink, Gary R. *chemicals executive*
Walthie, Theo H. *chemicals executive*

Milford
Bennur, Mallikarjuna *automotive executive*
Oliveri, Eugene Alfred *gastroenterologist*

Millersburg
Bergstedt, Roger Allen *biologist, researcher*

Moline
Grassmid, Ronald Jay *elementary school educator*

Monroe
Cohn, Morton Ray *lawyer*
Darrow, Kurt L. *manufacturing executive*
Lipford, Rocque Edward *lawyer*

Mount Clemens
Robinson, Earl, Jr. *marketing, transportation executive, educator, retired air force officer*

Mount Pleasant
Beehr, Terry A. *psychology professor*
Dietrich, Richard Vincent *geologist, educator*
Messick, Frederic Morton *librarian*
Mohanty, Dillip K. *chemistry professor, researcher*
Oh-Lee, Justin DoHoon *psychology professor*
Petrick, Michael Joseph *journalism educator*
Peyrefitte, Ashton George, Jr. *meteorologist, educator*
Scott, Renay Marie *academic administrator, educator*
Smallwood, Carol *writer*
Stancato, Franklin Anthony *psychology professor*
Traines, Rose Wunderbaum *sculptor, educator*

Muskegon
Akker, Arlene F. *social sciences educator*
Briggs, John Mancel III *lawyer*
Crummett, Allan Warren *psychologist*
Fauri, Eric Joseph *lawyer*
Fitzgerald, Rebecca Anne *curator, historian*
McKendry, John H., Jr. *lawyer*
McKitrick, James Thomas *retired retail executive*
Nehra, Gerald Peter *lawyer*
Ross, Annette Lee *educational consultant*
Roy, Paul Emile, Jr. *county official*

Naubinway
Beaudoin, Robert Lawrence *small business owner*

Negaunee
Hultquist, Thomas Robert *meteorologist*

Niles
Gibbs, Denis Laurel *radiologist*
Marshall, Gerald Francis *optical engineer, consultant, physicist*
Tenney, Jane Morris *real estate developer*

North Branch
Stevenson, James Laraway *engineering company executive, electronics engineer, computer engineer, communications engineer, engineering educator*

Northport
Schultz, Richard Carlton *plastic surgeon*
Scripps, Douglas Jerry *musician, educator, conductor*
Thomas, Philip Stanley *economist, educator*

Northville
Cauley, Patrick C. *lawyer*
Clawson, Curtis J. *manufacturing executive*
Dempsey, Donald Chandler *stockbroker, financial planner*
Green, Jody *real estate company executive, real estate broker*
Hariri, V. M. *arbitrator, mediator, educator*
Leavitt, Martin Jack *lawyer*

Norway
Hunt, Gregory C. *music educator*

Novi
Chow, Chi-Ming *retired mathematics professor*
DiRita, David M. *lawyer, manufacturing executive*
Flinchbaugh, Jamie *training services executive*
Jeffe, Sidney David *automotive executive, engineer*
Johnson, S.A. (Tony Johnson) *automotive executive*
Kinsey, Charles John *industrial auctioneer, consultant, farmer, cattle breeder*
Malcolm, Mark *automotive executive*
McElya, James S. *automotive executive*
Serenson, Lynn Ann *mathematics educator*

Oak Park
Coleman, Dorothy Charmayne *nurse*
Gardin, Hershel *academic administrator, dean, management consultant*

Okemos
Burnett, Jean B. *biochemist, educator*
Edwards, Caryn Louise *educational consultant, special education educator*
Klunzinger, Thomas Edward *writer, actor, film director*
Solo, Robert Alexander *economist, educator*

Owosso
Acton, David L(awrence) *automobile company executive*
McKean, Sherry Lynn *medical technician*
Tompkins, Alice Angeline *artist*

Petoskey
Kleppe, Lars W. *retired pathologist*
Kukla, Edward Richard *rare books and special collections librarian*
Meengs, William Lloyd *cardiologist*
Nicholson, William Noel *clinical neuropsychologist*
Switzer, Carolyn Joan *artist, educator*

Pinckney
Britton, Clarold Lawrence *lawyer, consultant*

Pittsford
Shaffer, Richard Stanley *mechanical engineer, researcher*

Plymouth
Berry, Charlene Helen *librarian, musician*
Leuliette, Timothy D. *automotive executive*
Longhofer, Ronald Stephen *financial consultant*
Lou, Zheng (David) *technical specialist*
Martina, Carlo Jack *lawyer*
Moore-Viculin, Charlotte Anne *artist, musician*
Morgan, Donald Crane *lawyer*
Nowakowski, Nicholas J. *lawyer*
Robinson, Logan Gilmore *lawyer*
Vlcek, Donald Joseph, Jr. *food products executive, wholesale distribution executive, writer*

Pontiac
Anderson, Anita A. *secondary school educator*
Bautista, Marieta Pascual *psychiatrist*
Hampton, Philip Michael *consulting engineering company executive*
Pardee, Jeffrey Clark *county government official*
Pierson, William George *lawyer*
Riley, Mary Jane Stewart *secondary school educator*
Wang, Yucong *engineering executive*

Port Huron
Rowark, Maureen *fine arts photographer*
Ruby, Kathryn Grace *education educator*
Wu, Harry Pao-Tung *retired librarian*

Portage
Brown, John Wilford *health products executive*
Cowart, James D. *psychologist*
Seely, Robert Eugene *management consultant*
Underdal, Olav M. *engineering executive*
Zhang, Charles C. *financial planner*

Quinnesec
Opolka, Jayme Lyn *medical writer, researcher*

Ravenna
Herremans, Paul William *mathematics educator*

Redford
Karpinski, Huberta *library trustee*

Reed City
Rautiola, Norman A. *manufacturing executive*

Republic
Wixtrom, Donald Joseph *translator*

Richland
Atkinson, Arthur John, Jr. *pharmacologist, educator, consultant*
Nott, Robin K. *theater educator, theater director*

Rochester
Clark, Jon Brian *psychologist*
Cordes, Mary Kenrick *psychologist, retired*
Estes, Todd A. *historian*
Loh, Robert N. K. *engineering educator*
Packard, Sandra Podolin *education educator, consultant*
Polis, Michael Philip *engineering educator*
Youn, Anthony Sungjin *plastic surgeon*

Rochester Hills
Akeel, Hadi Abu *robotics executive*
Badalament, Robert Anthony *urologist, oncologist*
Denton, Lawrence A. *automotive executive*
DiCosmo, Nino *engineering company executive*
Parker, Catherine L. *theater educator*
Unakar, Nalin Jayantilal *biological sciences educator*

Rockford
Grady, Kenneth Alan *lawyer, corporate secretary*
Loux, Jonathan Dale *business development consultant, director*

Romeo
Stryker, James William *retired automotive executive, former military officer*
Tsukamoto, Daniel *piano instructor, church organist*

Rothbury
Fischer, Dorothy Virginia *retired small business owner*

Royal Oak
Atchison, Steven *real estate company executive*
Britt, Stephen Thomas *medical educator*
Cain, Lawrence Edward *small business owner, language educator, researcher*
Cook, Noel Robert *manufacturing executive*
DeMaria, Mark *construction executive*
Doty, Angela Joy *emergency physician, military officer*
Dworkin, Howard Jerry *retired nuclear medicine physician, educator*
Fragomeni, James Mark *mechanical engineer, educator*
LaBan, Myron Miles *physician, hospital administrator*
Mengel, Christopher Emile *lawyer, educator*
O'Neill, William Walter *physician, educator*
Pricer, Wayne Francis *counseling consultant*
Proctor, Conrad Arnold *physician*
Schaffner, Adam David *plastic surgeon*
Seidman, Joel C. *pulmonary physician*
Stanalajczo, Greg Charles *computer company executive*

Saginaw
Carlson, Robert James *bishop*
Chaffee, Paul Charles *newspaper editor, publisher*
Cline, Thomas William *real estate leasing company executive, management consultant*
Coughlin, Jeannine Marie *music educator*
Evans, Harold Edward *retired banker*
Ferlinz, Jack *cardiologist, educator*
Hammel, Iriana Simona *geriatrician*
McGraw, Patrick John *judge*
Moyer, Genevieve J. *counselor*
Scharffe, William Granville *academic administrator, educator*
Zanot, Craig Allen *lawyer*

Saint Clair Shores
Hausner, John Herman *retired judge*
Howe, Jennifer Lynn *secondary school educator*
Joslyn, Robert Bruce *lawyer*
Skoney, Sophie Essa *educational administrator*
Ugorowski, Philip Brien *nuclear scientist, researcher*

Saint Joseph
King, George Raleigh *retired manufacturing executive*
Wood, Dirk Gregory *surgeon, physician, forensic consultant*

Saline
Cruden, Robert William *botany educator*

Saugatuck
Genetski, Robert James *economist*

Sault Sainte Marie
Johnson, Gary Robert *political scientist*
Money, Robert McGuffey *history professor*
Morello, Steven John *lawyer*
Youngblood, Betty J. *academic administrator*

Shelby Township
Nagy, Louis Leonard *engineering executive, researcher*
Osuch, Debra K. *materials engineer*

Sodus
Handy, Virginia Mae *writer*

South Haven
LaRocque, Linda Lou *interior designer, educator, playwright*
Llorens, Merna Gee *elementary school educator, retired music educator*
Tyrrell, Cole Brooks *music educator*
Waxman, Sheldon Robert *lawyer*

Southfield
Alapont, José Maria *automotive executive*
Andreoff, Christopher Andon *lawyer*
Barnett, Marilyn *advertising executive*
Bassey, Ronald D. *tax attorney*
Boyce, Daniel Hobbs *finance company executive*
Brackenbury, James M. *manufacturing executive*
Brooks, Ernie L. *lawyer*
Caponigro, Jeffrey Ralph *public relations counselor*
Chambers, Charles MacKay *academic administrator, lawyer, consultant*
Darling, Robert Howard *lawyer*
Dawson, Dennis Ray *lawyer, manufacturing executive*
DelGrosso, Douglas G. *manufacturing executive*
DeLong, Donald Alan *lawyer*
Drebus, John Richard *computer consultant*
Fieger, Geoffrey Nels *lawyer*
Fox, Stacy L. *lawyer*
Fried, Martin L. *lawyer*
Gleichman, John Alan *protective services official*
Goodman, Barry Joel *lawyer*
Gordon, Louis *retired lawyer*
Gouldey, Glenn Charles *manufacturing executive*
Graves, Ray Reynolds *retired judge*
Gregory, Karl Dwight *economics professor, consultant*
Herrera-Lasso, Miguel *manufacturing executive*
Hettiarachchi, Chamil Hiroshan *civil engineer, educator*
Hotelling, Harold *economics professor, lawyer*
Jackson, Roger A. *human resources specialist, automotive executive*
Jacobson, Michael F. *lawyer*
Kalter, Alan *advertising agency executive*
Kamsickas, James *automotive executive*
Kaplow, Robert David *lawyer*
Katz, Robert L. *lawyer*
Lee, James Edward, Jr. *educational consultant*
Leuchtman, Stephen Nathan *lawyer*
Low, James William *lawyer*
Lynch, George Michael *auto parts manufacturing executive*
Maibach, Ben C. III *construction company executive*
Makupson, Amyre Porter *broadcast executive*
Margolis, Sherry *newscaster*
Martin, Marcella Edric *retired community health nurse*
McClow, Roger James *labor lawyer*
McKeen, Alexander C. *retired engineering executive, foundation administrator*
Miller, Nancy Ellen *computer scientist, consultant*
Morganroth, Mayer *lawyer*
Ninivaggi, Daniel A. *lawyer, manufacturing executive*
Osborne, Marie-Angela *journalist*
Perez-Cruet, Mick Jorge (Miguelangelo Jorge Perez-Cruet) *neurosurgeon, educator*
Ponitz, John Allan *lawyer*
Porter, Thomas W.B. *lawyer*
Primo, Joan Erwina *retail and real estate consulting business owner*
Prokop, Kevin *investment company executive*
Ritchie, Alexander Buchan *lawyer*
Rochkind, Louis Philipp *lawyer*
Rossiter, Robert E. *manufacturing executive*
Salvatore, Louis R. *manufacturing executive*
Scott, Raymond E. *manufacturing executive*
Sedler, Rozanne Friedlander *social worker, educator*
Shields, Robert Emmet *merchant banker, lawyer*
Simoncini, Matthew J. *manufacturing executive*
Sobel, Robert A. *retired orthopedic surgeon*
Song, Xubin *mechanical engineer, researcher*
Stern, Marvin *history professor*
Thimotheose, Kadakampallil George *psychologist*
Thurswell, Gerald Elliott *lawyer*
Timmons, Robbie *news anchor*
Toll, Sheldon Samuel *lawyer*
Torpey, Scott Raymond *lawyer*
Torraco, Pamela Louise *psychotherapist*
Turner, Lee Irwin *lawyer*
Vandenberghe, James H. *manufacturing executive*
Weiner, Karen Colby (Karen Lynn Colby) *psychologist, lawyer*
Willingham, Edward Bacon, Jr. *ecumenical minister, administrator*
Wood, Terry David *broadcasting executive*
Zimmer, Paul Joseph *manufacturing executive*
Zubroff, Leonard Saul *surgeon*

Spring Arbor
Bates, Gerald Earl *retired bishop*

Sterling Heights
Fleming, Mac Arthur *retired labor union administrator*
Markey, James Kevin *lawyer*
Novak, Joseph Anthony *law librarian*
Rizk, Maged *cardiologist, researcher*
Weed, Melvin L. *retired railroad conductor, small business owner*

Sturgis
Hair, Robert Eugene *editor, writer, historian*

Swartz Creek
Packer, Matthew James *musician, educator, advertising executive*

Sylvan Lake
Derdarian, Christine Anne *lawyer*

Taylor
Barry, Alan H. *consumer products company executive*
Coleman, Fay *literature and language educator, director*
Hirsch, David L. *lawyer*
Leekley, John Robert *lawyer, consumer products company executive*
Manoogian, Richard Alexander *consumer products company executive*
Wadhams, Timothy *consumer products company executive*

Tecumseh
Buker, Edwin L. *manufacturing executive*
Herrick, Todd W. *manufacturing executive*
Johnson, Kelly *chef*

Three Rivers
Boyer, Nicodemus Elijah *chemist, consultant*
Mundy, B. Jo Ann *minister*

Traverse City
Anderson, Carol Lynn *social worker, educator*
Clous, James M. *electrical equipment company executive, engineer*
Faulmann, Roger Ray *retired music educator*
Ginsberg, David Baron *retired management consultant*
Leuenberger, Betty Lou *psychologist, educator*
Quandt, Joseph Edward *lawyer, educator*
Weaver, Elizabeth A. *state supreme court justice*
Zimmerman, Paul Albert *retired academic administrator, minister*

Trenton
Tang, Cyrus *investment company executive*

Troy
Adderley, Terence Edward *human resources executive*
Alber, Phillip George *lawyer*
Alterman, Irwin Michael *lawyer*
Baker, Vernon G., II, *lawyer, automotive executive*
Battenberg, J. T. III *automotive company executive*
Bishop, Michael *lawyer, state senator*
Buschmann, Siegfried *retired manufacturing executive*
Butler, Kevin M. *electronics executive*
Camden, Carl T. *human resources company executive*
Cantor, Bernard Jack *lawyer*
Chalil, Joseph Mathew *sales executive, consultant, liver disease specialist, medical products executive*
Chapman, Conrad Daniel *lawyer*
Cunningham, Gary H. *lawyer*
Dellinger, Robert J. *corporate financial executive*
Dillon, Joseph Francis *lawyer*
Donlon, James D. III *controller, corporate financial executive*
Elder, Irma *retail executive*
Fritzsche, Hellmut *physics professor*
Gelder, John William *lawyer*
Golusin, Millard R. *obstetrician, gynecologist*
Haron, David Lawrence *lawyer*
Hilton, Michael E. *lawyer*
Hodges, Michele *chamber of commerce executive*
Hucal, Michelle *editor*
Kruse, John Alphonse *lawyer*
Lis, Daniel T. *lawyer*
Mahone, Barbara Jean *automotive executive*
May, Alan Alfred *lawyer*
McClure, Charles G. *automotive executive*
Michaels, Glen *artist, sculptor*
Miller, Robert Stevens, Jr., (Steve Miller) *automotive company executive*
Navarro, Monica *lawyer*
Nefske, Donald Joseph *engineer*
O'Neal, Rodney *automotive company executive*
Opie, John D. *retired electric power industry executive*
Paluda, Andrew Joseph *lawyer, consultant*
Pearce, Harry Jonathan *lawyer, manufacturing executive*
Peters, Thomas M. *lawyer*
Rapson, Richard (Rip Rapson) *foundation administrator*
Schafer, Sharon Marie *anesthesiologist*
Sherbin, David M. *lawyer*
Sloan, Hugh Walter, Jr. *automotive executive*
Strome, Stephen *distribution company executive*
Thoms, David Moore *lawyer*
Walker, Bette *automotive executive*
Walker, Bette M. *information technology executive*
Weber, Mark R. *automotive executive*
Webster, Robert Byron *lawyer*
Weingart, Robert Paul *financial consultant*
Williams, Leonard Todd, Jr. *hotel sales and marketing executive*

University Center
Boyse, Peter Dent *academic administrator*
Clarey, Timothy Lee *geologist, educator*
Clark, Basil Alfred *language educator*
Dadlez, Anna Romana *language educator*
Gilbertson, Eric Raymond *academic administrator, lawyer*
Hall, David McKenzie *business and management educator*
Hill, Alan Gordon *sociologist, educator*
Pelzer, Charles Francis *human molecular geneticist, biologist, educator, research scientist*
Tuttle, Robert Bruce *mechanical engineer, educator*

Utica
Egan, Ron *corporate financial executive*

Van Buren Township
Donofrio, John *lawyer*

Walled Lake
Connelly, Thomas Joseph *lawyer*
Gillespie, J. Martin *sales and distribution company executive*
Seglund, Bruce Richard *lawyer*

Warren
Bell, Julie Marie *health facility administrator, consultant*
Bridenstine, Louis Henry, Jr. *lawyer*
Cai, Mei *materials engineer, researcher*
Cutter, Jeffrey S. *music educator*
Herbst, Jan Francis *physicist, researcher*
Hopp, Anthony James *advertising agency executive*
Kolakowski, Diana Jean *county commissioner*

Washington
Barrows, Ronald Thomas *lawyer*

Waterford
Anderson, Francile Mary *secondary school educator*
Gulda, Edward James *diversified financial services company executive*
Houston, E(rnest) James, Jr. *banker, consultant*
James, William Ramsay *broadcast executive*
Laing, James Thomas *retired not-for-profit developer*
Pronovost, Amy Lynne *dancer, educator*
Randall, Karl W. *air transportation executive, lawyer*
Zielinski, Michael Edmund *osteopath*

Watervliet
Watkins, M(artha) Anne *family practice nurse practitioner*

West Bloomfield
Avery, Karin F. *lawyer*
Barr, Martin *science educator, academic administrator*
Cox, Clifford Ernest *information systems consulting executive, former academic administrator*
Harwood, Julius J. *metallurgist, educator*
Jones, Lewis Arnold, Jr. *physician, radiologist, consultant*
Lit, Mark Alan *recreational facility executive*
Mamut, Mary Catherine *retired entrepreneur*
Marx, Thomas George *economist*
Rauwerdink, William Jay *accountant*
Sarwer-Foner, Gerald Jacob *psychiatrist, educator*
Sawyer, Howard Jerome *physician*
Simpson, Robert Lee *academic administrator, department chairman, biologist, educator*
Smith, Nancy Hohendorf *sales executive, marketing professional*
Sullivan, Robert Emmet, Jr. *lawyer*
Tobin, Bruce Howard *lawyer*
Williamson, Marilyn Lammert *literature educator, academic administrator*

Westland
Geiringer, Steve R. *medical educator*

White Lake
Clyburn, Luther Linn *real estate broker, appraiser*

Whitehall
Squier, David Louis *manufacturing executive*

Williamston
Johnson, Tom Milroy *dean, physician, educator*
Schab, Daniel J. *mathematics educator*

Wilson
Harris, Mary Lynn *science educator, consultant*

Wixom
Becker, John Raymond *pharmacist*
Huff, Alvin Edward *retired engineer*
Sugiyama, Toru Tom *automotive executive*
Welch, Cherie Lynn *healthcare educator*

Wyandotte
Pentiuk, Randall Alan *lawyer*

Wyoming
Couch, Katrina Denise *elementary school educator*

Ypsilanti
Barnes, James Milton *retired physics and astronomy professor*
Barr, John Monte *lawyer*
Bengtsson, Erling Blöndal *musician, educator*
Boone, Morell Douglas *information technology educator*
Cere, Ronald Carl *languages educator, consultant, researcher*
Eggertsen, John Hale *lawyer*
Fairfield, Richard Thomas *art educator*
Farah, Badie Naiem *computer information systems educator, consultant*
Fox, Diane Porretta *nursing educator*
Gillard, Montgomery *dermatologist*
Kolopajlo, Lawrence Hugh *chemistry professor*
Lewis-White, Linda Beth *elementary school educator*
Lottie, Adrian Jerome *writer, educator, consultant*
McLain, Dennis O. *lawyer*
Stuppard-Byars, Doris J. *minister*
Wegner, John Mark *historian*
Weinstein, Jay A. *social sciences educator, researcher*
Willis, Craig Dean *academic administrator*

Zeeland
Volkema, Michael A. *office furniture manufacturer*
Walker, Brian C. *manufacturing executive*

MINNESOTA

Ada
Sillerud, Arlen Roger *retired secondary school educator*

Alexandria
Lillestol, Jane Brush *educational consultant*

Anoka
Chamberlain, Sonja Kay *music educator*
Hicken, Jeffrey Price *lawyer*
Lindbergh, Reeve *writer, poet*
Weidner, Jacque Goodin *educational consultant, not-for-profit developer*

Arden Hills
Ciske, Karen Lysbeth *retired medical/surgical nurse*
Lahann, Jon Clifford *retired music educator*

Austin
Alcorn, Wallace Arthur *minister, writer*
Budd, Jim *communications manager*
Cavanaugh, James W. *lawyer*
Ettinger, Jeffrey M. *food products executive, lawyer*
Rioux, Pierre August *psychiatrist*

Bayport
Bernick, Alan E. *lawyer, accountant*
Garofalo, Donald R. *window manufacturing executive*

Bemidji
Bridston, Paul Joseph *strategic management consultant*
Kief, Paul Allan *lawyer*
Martinson, Ida Marie *retired medical/surgical nurse, physiologist*
McKee, Marcy D'Ette *voice educator*
Rogers, Patricia Louise *education educator, consultant, dean*

Bloomington
Bekrenev, Anatoliy *physicist*
Broeker, John Milton *lawyer*
Dordell, Timothy Paul *lawyer*
Grinnell, Joseph Fox *lawyer*
Knotek, Robert Frank *retired management consultant, educator*
Kuntz, Lila Elaine *business educator*
Larson, Michael Len *newspaper editor, hospital administrator, publishing executive*
Mooty, John William *lawyer*
Nelson, Eric John *lawyer*
Nichols, Donna Mardell *nurse anesthetist*
Smith, Henry Charles III *symphony orchestra conductor*

Blue Earth
Siem, Pauline M. *library director*

Brainerd
Peterson, Donn Neal *forensic engineer, engineering company executive*
Samuelson, Donald B. *former state legislator*

Breezy Point
Anderson, Gail Marie *retired librarian*

Brooklyn Park
DeBusk, Charles Richard *engineer, consultant*

Buffalo
Moon, James Russell *retired technology education educator*

Burnsville
Foss, Emma Thoren *retired social worker*
Hatch, Mike *former state attorney general*
Lakin, James Dennis *allergist, immunologist, director*
O'Brien, Gerald James *utilities executive*

Caledonia
Kranz, Kimberly Renee *elementary music educator*

Canby
Larson, Gary Arthur *farmer, financial consultant*

Chanhassen
Prince, (Prince Rogers Nelson) *musician, actor*
Severson, Roger Allan *bank executive*

Chaska
Cohen, Cheryl Diane Durda *communications executive*

Chatfield
Opat, Matthew John *lawyer*

Chisholm
Peterson, Marjorie *former mayor*

Cloquet
Belanger, Sharon Amling *special education educator*

Coleraine
Jones, Gail *elementary school educator*

Collegeville
Reinhart, Dietrich Thomas *academic administrator, social studies educator*

Coon Rapids
Bordner, Patricia Anne *insurance agent, writer*
Enzenauer, Kirk Karl *elementary school educator*
Vogel, Scott Charles *music educator*
Wilson, Sylvia Alyce *musician, educator*

Crookston
Balke, Victor H. *bishop*
Killough, Alvin Lynard *psychology professor, consultant*
Shol, Kim Durand *accountant, computer scientist*

Detroit Lakes
Stowman, David L. *lawyer*

Duluth
Aufderheide, Arthur Carl *pathologist*
Bowman, Roger Manwaring *real estate company officer*
Burns, Richard Ramsey *lawyer*
Einat, Haim *social sciences educator*
Gallian, Joseph Anthony *mathematics professor*
Harlander, Ronald Stanley, Jr. *pharmacist*
Johnson, Arthur Gilbert *microbiology educator*
Latto, Lewis M. *broadcast executive*
McKee, David Charles *neurologist*
Minor, Elizabeth Colquitt *chemistry professor*
Morath, Max Edward *entertainer, composer, writer*
Pearce, Donald Joslin *retired librarian*
Rapp, George Robert (Rip Rapp) *geology and archeology educator*
Salmela, David Daniel *architect*
Salminen, John Theodore *artist, educator*
Schroeder, Fred Erich Harald *humanities educator*
Stauber-Johnson, Elizabeth Jane *retired elementary school educator*
Thibodeau, Thomas Raymond *lawyer*
Wen, Shixing *school librarian*
Whiteman, Richard Frank *architect*
Wirth, Erin Masson *lawyer*
Ziegler, Richard J. *dean, educator*

Eagan
Bauer, Kris *air transportation executive*
Becker, Michael J. *air transportation executive*
Clemens, T. Pat *manufacturing executive*
Cohen, Neal S. *air transportation executive*
Davis, David M. *air transportation executive*
Dulas, DeAnne L. *lawyer*
Friedel, Jim *air transportation executive*
Gouin, Warner Peter *information technology consultant*
Griffin, J. Timothy *air transportation executive*
Haan, Philip C. *air transportation executive*
Knotek, Crystal *air transportation executive*
Linder, Mary Carroll *air transportation executive*
Matthews, Daniel B. *air transportation executive*
Rainey, Timothy J. *air transportation executive*
Roberts, Andrew C. *air transportation executive*
Sievwright, Julia Ann *elementary school educator*
Steenland, Douglas M. *air transportation executive*
Wise, Theresa *air transportation executive*

East Grand Forks
Crow, Judson Lewis *plastic surgeon*

East Gull Lake
Simons, John Nelson *surgeon, consultant*

Eden Prairie
Arthur, Lindsay Grier *retired judge, editor, writer*
Childress, Brad *professional football coach*
Feuss, Linda Anne Upsall *lawyer*
Gernander, Barton Carl *lawyer*
Gilbert, James H. *lawyer, former state supreme court justice*
Hansen, Erik Frederick *lawyer*
Hanson, Dale S. *retired bank executive*
Henningsen, Peter, Jr. *manufacturing executive*
Higgins, Robert Arthur *electrical engineer, educator, consultant*
Jackson, Darren Richard *retail executive*
Jackson, Michael L. *wholesale distribution executive*
Johnson, Brad *professional football player*
Johnson, Howard Arthur, Jr. *corporate executive, operations analyst, financial officer*
Knickerbocker, Vicky Ann *academic administrator*
Knous, Pamela K. *wholesale distribution executive*
Lindbloom, Chad M. *transportation executive*
Luther, William P. *former congressman*
McCombs, Billy Joe (Red McCombs) *professional football team executive*
Nilles, John Michael *lawyer*
Noddle, Jeffrey *retail and food distribution executive*
Switz, Robert E. *telecommunications executive*
Thompson, Sally Ann *editor*
Wiehoff, John P. *trucking executive*
Woods, Gary V. *professional football team executive, former professional basketball team executive, automotive executive*

Edina
Bakken, Eric Allen *lawyer*
Bisping, Bruce Henry *photojournalist*
Brown, Charles Eugene *retired electronics company executive*
Brown, Laurence David *retired bishop*
Campbell, James Robert *retired bank executive*
Covington, Alec C. *retail executive*
Davidson, Ann D. *lawyer, aerospace transportation executive*
Drewes, Matthew A. *lawyer*
Fenwick, Sheridan Mellon *psychologist, director*
Finkelstein, Phil *retail executive*
Froemming, Herbert Dean *retired retail executive*
Gottesman, Irving I. *psychologist, educator*
Jeffrey-Smith, Lilli Ann *biofeedback specialist, educator, administrator*
Kunin, Myron *hair care company executive*
Leach, Bertram George *retired military officer, securities dealer*
Neff, Fred Leonard *lawyer*
Renz, Christopher P. *lawyer*
Schaibley, Ann M. *lawyer*
Schulze, Chad William *lawyer*
Tagatz, George Elmo *retired obstetrician, gynecologist, educator*
Towey, Anne C. *lawyer*
Worthing, Carol Marie *retired minister*

Eitzen
Euller, Steven C. *lawyer*

Elk River
Richardson, Mark P. *protective services official, educator*

Elysian
Thayer, Edna Louise *health facility administrator*

Excelsior
Bilka, Paul Joseph *retired physician*
Fazio, Anthony Lee *investment company executive*
Fenske, Jerald Allan *minister*
Martinson, Elmer James *retired surgeon*
Oliver, Edward Carl *retired state legislator, insurance company executive, small business owner*
Pfeifer, Polly Lee *elementary school educator*

Faribault
Collins, Ruth Ann *principal*

Farmington
Wurdeman, Lew Edward *Internet company executive, consultant*

Forest Lake
Skrip, Cathy Lee *psychologist*

Fridley
Ellison, Cynthia Kuehl *music educator, musician*

Golden Valley
Ainsworth, Louis Lynde *lawyer, manufacturing executive*
Altafullah, Irfan M. *neurologist*
Breimayer, Joseph Frederick *patent lawyer*
Hogan, Randall J. *manufacturing and electronics executive*
Leppik, Margaret White *municipal official*
Savitt, Steven Lee *computer scientist*
Schlichting, William Henry *lawyer, writer*
Spake, Mary Barbara *music educator*

Goodridge
Hanson, Norma Lee *farmer*

Grand Marais
Hattery, Robert Wilber *political science educator*
Hennessy, William Joseph *prosecutor*

Grand Rapids
Merrill, Arthur Lewis *retired theologian*

Granite Falls
Alness, Mae Christine *retired medical/surgical nurse*

Hallock
Malm, Roger Charles *lawyer*

Harmony
Webster, Jeffrey Leon *graphic designer*

Hastings
Avent, Sharon L. Hoffman *manufacturing company executive*
Mahlen, Tatum L. *voice educator*
May, Nicholas G.B. *lawyer*
Orr, Jennie Marie (Jennie Thomas) *family physician*

Hibbing
Calligan, William Dennis *retired life insurance company executive*

Hopkins
Dunlap, William DeWayne, Jr. *advertising agency executive*
Young, Margaret Labash *librarian, information consultant, editor*

Inver Grove Heights
Koenig, Robert August *minister, educator*
Rone, James Stephen *performing arts association administrator*

Kasson
Brown, Patrick Joseph *corporate financial executive, consultant*

Kenyon
Peterson, Franklin Delano *lawyer*

La Crescent
Gelatt, Charles Daniel *manufacturing executive*

Lake Crystal
Pawlitschek, Donald Paul *management consultant*

Lake Elmo
Tomljanovich, Esther M. *retired judge*

Lake Lillian
Marquardt, Steve Robert *advocate*

Lakeville
Pattee, Steven D. *lawyer*
Setterholm, Jeffrey Miles *systems engineer*

Lauderdale
Resch, Joseph Anthony *neurologist*

Lindstrom
Messin, Marlene Ann *plastics company executive*

Lino Lakes
Jezierski, Scott *wireless monitoring, security, and surveillance company executive*

Little Falls
Morgan, Mary Jo *school system administrator*
Perfetti, Robert Nickolas *educational consultant*
Stobb, Mary Jean *retired association administrator*

Long Lake
Lowthian, Petrena *academic administrator*

Madison
Husby, Donald Evans *engineering company executive*

Mahtomedi
Brainerd, Richard Charles *human resources executive, consultant, educator*
Holmén, Reynold Algott Emanuel *chemist*

Mankato
Dumke, Melvin Philip *dentist*
Janc, John J. *language educator*
Kohlmeyer, Jason C. *lawyer*
Nickerson, James Findley *retired education educator*
Orvick, George Myron *religious organization administrator, minister*
Preska, Margaret Louise Robinson *historian, educational association administrator*
Purscell, Keith William *minister*
Rosengren, Christopher Paul *lawyer*
Schreier, Bradley *management executive*

Maple Grove
Kirpes, Anne Irene *elementary school educator*
Ones, Deniz S. *psychologist, educator*

Mapleton
John, Hugo Herman *natural resources educator*

Marine On Saint Croix
Gavin, Robert Michael, Jr. *educational consultant*

Marshall
Burr, Tracy L. *food products executive*
Paskach, David M. *lawyer, food products executive*
Pichaske, David Richard *language educator*
Pippin, M. Lenny *food products executive*
Sattler, Brian R. *lawyer*
Van Overbeke, Debbie Ann *education educator*

Medina
McConnell, Mary Patricia *lawyer*
Tiller, Thomas C. *manufacturing executive*

Mendota Heights
Cohen, Robert *medical device and pharmaceutical manufacturing and marketing executive*
Cotter, Patrick Linnae *lawyer*
Frechette, Peter Loren *dental products executive*
Friedrichs, Terence Paul *special education educator*

Milaca
Wig, Robert Curtis *retired music educator, conductor*

Minneapolis
Aamoth, Gordon M. *medical association administrator*
Abi-Ghanem, Georges Victor *civil engineer, environmental engineer*
Abramson, Norman M. *lawyer*
Ackerman, Eugene *biophysics professor*
Adams, John Stephen *geography educator*
Ahern, Michael James *lawyer*
Ahlers, Linda L. *retail executive*
Ali, Jeffer *lawyer*
Alton, Ann Leslie *judge, lawyer, educator*
Ambrose, Thomas William *retired broadcast executive*
Anderson, Eric Scott *lawyer*
Anderson, John Edward *mechanical engineering educator*
Anderson, Leslie J. *lawyer*
Ariyur, Kartik Balasubramanian *control systems engineer, researcher*
Arnold, Douglas Norman *mathematician*
Atwood, John Brian *dean*
Augustus, Seimone *professional basketball player*
Avella, Joseph Ralph *university professor*
Bache, Robert James *physician, educator*
Bader, Kathleen M. *chemicals executive*
Baer, Timothy R. *lawyer, retail executive*
Bagan, Mark G. *grain exchange executive*
Baillie, James Leonard *lawyer*
Baker, John Stevenson (Michael Dyregrov) *writer*
Bales, Kent Roslyn *language educator*
Ballintine, Daniel John *lawyer*
Bancroft, Ann E. *polar explorer*
Banerjee, Subir Kumar *science educator*
Barden, Robert Christopher *lawyer, psychologist, educator, writer*
Barnard, Tom *radio personality*
Barnes, Nancy *editor-in-chief*
Bashiri, Iraj *Central Asian studies educator*
Beck, Joshua James *information technology executive*
Beekman, Marvin Lee *lawyer*
Berens, William Joseph *lawyer*
Berg, Thomas Kenneth *lawyer*
Bergerson, David Raymond *lawyer*
Berman, Walter S. *treasurer*
Berry, David J. *former financial services company executive*
Berryman, Robert Glen *accounting educator, consultant*
Berscheid, Ellen S. *psychology professor, writer, researcher*
Binger, Erika L. *foundation administrator*
Bingham, Christopher *statistics educator*
Blackwell, Todd V. *human resources specialist*
Bland, J(ohn) Richard *lawyer*
Boelter, Philip Floyd *real estate company officer, construction executive*
Bonavia, Paul J. *energy executive*
Boone, Bret Robert *professional baseball player*
Borger, John Philip *lawyer*
Bouchard, Thomas Joseph, Jr. *psychology professor, researcher*
Boushek, Randy L. *insurance company executive*
Bowie, Norman Ernest *university official, educator*
Brand, Steve Aaron *lawyer*
Branson, Timothy E. *lawyer*
Brasket, Curt Justin *systems analyst*
Bress, Michael E. *retired lawyer*
Breyer, K. Jon *lawyer*
Brink, David Ryrie *lawyer*
Brown, Robert John *social sciences educator, consultant*
Bruininks, Robert H. *academic administrator, psychologist, educator*
Bruner, Philip Lane *lawyer*
Buchwald, Henry *surgeon, educator, researcher*
Buckingham, Elizabeth C. *lawyer*
Buhrmaster, Robert C. *manufacturing executive*
Buratti, Dennis P. *lawyer*
Burchell, Howard Bertram *retired internist*
Burdick, Lou Brum *public relations executive*
Burke, Forrest G. *lawyer*
Burke, Richard T., Sr. *professional sports team executive*
Burns, Matthew Kevin *psychology professor*
Busdicker, Gordon Gene *retired lawyer*
Camarotto, David Earle *lawyer*
Caplan, Allan Hart *lawyer*
Carlson, Arne Helge *former governor*
Carlson, Jennie Peaslack *bank executive*
Carr, Peter William *chemistry professor*
Cattanach, Robert Edward, Jr. *lawyer*
Cecere, Andrew *bank executive*
Chadwick, Eric Hugh *lawyer*
Champlin, Steven Kirk *lawyer*
Chavers, Blanche Marie *pediatrician, educator, researcher*
Chemberlin, Peg *minister, religious organization administrator*
Chipman, John Somerset *retired economist, educator*
Chosy, James Louis *lawyer, brokerage house executive*
Christiansen, Jay David *lawyer*
Church, Timothy Robert *medical educator, researcher*
Cialkowski, David Michael *lawyer*
Ciresi, Michael Vincent *lawyer*
Clary, Bradley G. *lawyer, educator*
Clemence, Roger Davidson *landscape architect, educator*
Collins, Arthur D., Jr. *medical products executive*
Connelly, Michael C. *lawyer, energy executive*
Constantine, Katherine A. *lawyer*
Cook, William M. *manufacturing executive*
Cooper, William Allen *bank executive*
Cope, Lewis *journalist*
Corwin, Gregg Marlowe *lawyer*
Cowles, John, Jr. *publishing executive, women's sports promoter, philanthropist*
Crabtree, Vicki Gail *musician*
Cracchiolo, James M. *diversified financial services company executive*
Craig, James Lynn *physician, health services administrator*
Crippen, John Raymond *museum director*
Crosby, Jacqueline Garton *newspaper editor, journalist*
Crosmer, Janie Lynn *insurance company executive*
Curler, Jeffrey H. *packaging manufacturing executive*
Cussler, Edward Lansing, Jr. *chemical engineer, educator*
Dale, John Sorensen *investment company executive, portfolio manager*
Dallas, H. James *medical products executive*
Danielson, James Walter *retired research microbiologist*
Davis, Aaron W. *lawyer*
Davis, Howard Ted *engineering educator*
Davis, Michael J. *judge*
Davis, Richard K. *bank executive*
Deach, Jana Aune *lawyer*
deBruin Sample, Anne *human resources specialist*
Degnan, John Michael *lawyer*
DeMane, Michael F. *medical products executive*
DeVries Smith, Kate *lawyer*
DiGangi, Frank Edward *academic administrator*
Diviney, Craig David *lawyer*
Dorenkamp, Theodore III *lawyer*
Doty, David Singleton *federal judge*
Drake, Dallas Sumner *researcher*
Dunn, Brian J. *retail executive*
Durkin, G. Michael *food products executive*
Durocher, Vernle C. (Skip), Jr. *lawyer*
Dworkin, Martin *microbiologist, educator*
Dykstra, Dennis Dale *physiatrist*
Eck, George Gregory *lawyer*
Edwardson, Sandra *dean, nursing educator*
Ellis, Gary *medical products executive*
Eng, Holly S.A. *lawyer*
Engdahl, Brian Edward *psychologist*
Engh, N. Rolf (Rolf Engh) *lawyer*
Erdrich, Louise (Karen Erdrich) *writer, poet*
Erickson, Gerald Meyer *classical studies educator*
Erickson, W(alter) Bruce *business and economics educator, entrepreneur*
Fallon, Patrick R. *advertising executive*
Farah, Caesar Elie *language educator, historian*
Fauth, John J. *venture capitalist*
Feldman, Nancy Jane *insurance company executive*
Fergus, Patricia Marguerita *language educator, writer, editor*
Ferrari, Giannantonio *electronics executive*
Fetler, Paul *retired composer*
Finkelstein, Paul D. *personal care industry executive*
Firchow, Evelyn Scherabon *German language and literature educator, writer*
Firchow, Peter Edgerly *language professional, educator, writer*
Fisch, Robert Otto *medical educator*
Fisher, Michele Renee *lawyer*
Flanagan, Barbara *journalist*
Flom, Gerald Trossen *lawyer*
Flynn Peterson, Kathleen A. *lawyer*
Forneris, Jeanne M. *lawyer*
Forsythe, Thomas M. *communications executive*
Foye, Randy *professional basketball player*
Francis, Michael R. *retail executive*
Frase, Richard S. *law educator*
Freese, Andrew *neurosurgeon, educator*
French, John Dwyer *retired lawyer*
Fulop, Laszlo G. *architect*
Gage, Edwin C., III, (Skip Gage) *travel and marketing services executive*
Gagnon, Craig William *lawyer*
Galambos, Theodore Victor *civil engineer, educator*
Gallagher, Gerald Raphael *venture capitalist*
Gallagher, Patrick J. *lawyer*
Gardenhire, Ronald Clyde *professional athletics manager*
Garner, Shirley Nelson *language educator*
Garon, Philip Stephen *lawyer*
Garrard, William L. *aerospace engineer, educator*
Garton, Thomas William *lawyer*
Geiger, Mark Watson *management educator*
Genereux, L. Joseph *lawyer*
George, William Wallace *former manufacturing executive*
Georgopoulos, Apostolos P. *neuroscientist, neurologist, educator*
Gill, Richard Lawrence *lawyer*
Gjertson, Stephen Arthur *artist, writer*
Gockel, John Raymond *construction executive*
Gogel, Raymond E. *energy executive*
Goldberg, Luella Gross *diversified financial services company executive*
Goldberg, Stanley Morton *surgeon, educator*
Goldman, Allen Marshall *physics professor*
Goodman, Christopher Lawrence *lawyer*
Gordon, Corey Lee *lawyer*
Gorham, Eville *retired ecologist*
Gottschalk, Stephen Elmer *retired lawyer*
Greener, Ralph Bertram *lawyer*
Greenfield, Lee *state legislator*
Griffith, Sima Lynn *investment banker, consultant*
Griswold, William M. *museum director, curator*
Gross, David J.F. *lawyer*
Grundhofer, Jerry A. *bank executive*
Grundhofer, John F. *bank executive*
Gulliver, John Stephen *civil engineering educator*
Haase, Ashley Thomson *microbiology professor, researcher*
Hackman, Anna *pharmacist*
Hadley, Katherine G. (Kit) *library director*
Hagedorn, Hildi *psychologist, researcher*
Hagglund, Clarance Edward *lawyer, publishing executive*
Haines, Stephen John *neurosurgeon*
Halbreich, Kathy *museum director*
Hale, James Thomas *retail executive, lawyer*
Hale, Roger Loucks *manufacturing executive, director*
Halley, James Woods *physics professor*
Hallman, Gary L. *photographer, educator*
Hamel, Mark Edwin *lawyer*
Hamel, William John *church administrator, minister*
Hampl, Patricia *writer, educator*
Hansen, Jo-Ida Charlotte *psychology professor, researcher*
Hansen, Robyn L. *lawyer*
Hanson, Arthur Stuart *physician, consultant*
Hanson, Kent Bryan *lawyer*
Harper, Donald Victor *retired transportation and logistics educator, consultant*
Hart, Buster Clarence *lawyer*
Hawkins, William A. III *medical products executive*
Haynsworth, Harry Jay, IV, *law educator*
Hays, Thomas S. *medical educator, researcher*
Hayward, Edward Joseph *lawyer*
Hebrink, Bob *publishing executive*
Heffelfinger, Thomas Backer *lawyer, former prosecutor*
Heiberg, Robert Alan *lawyer*
Hellman, Geoffrey P. *philosopher, educator*
Helsene, Amy L. *lawyer*
Hemsley, Stephen J. *healthcare company executive*
Hendrixson, Peter S. *lawyer*
Hensley, Mary Lynne Floyd *academic medical center administrator*
Herman, John Hughes *lawyer*
Herr, David Fulton *lawyer, educator*
Hillstrom, Thomas Peter *engineering executive*
Hinderaker, John Hadley *lawyer, political blogger*
Hoffman, Michael J. *manufacturing executive*
Hoffmann, Thomas Russell *business management educator*
Holden, Susan M. *lawyer*
Holen, Norman Dean *artist, educator*
Holt, Robert Theodore *political science professor, educator, dean*
Hom, David Brian *surgeon*
Howland, Joan Sidney *law librarian, educator*
Hudson, Troy *professional basketball player*
Hunt, Kay Nord *lawyer*
Hunter, Donald Forrest *lawyer*
Hunter, Torii Kedar *professional baseball player*
Huntzicker, William Edward *journalism educator, writer*
Hurwicz, Leonid *economist, educator*
Hyslop, David Johnson *retired arts administrator*
Ingbar, David H. *physician, researcher*
Jackson, J. David *lawyer*
Jacob, Bernard Michel *architect*
Jacobs, Irwin Lawrence *diversified corporate executive*
Jacobson, Carrie Isabelle *lawyer*
Jameson, Jennifer A. *lawyer*
Jarboe, Mark Alan *lawyer*
Johnson, Alex Moore *dean, law educator*
Johnson, David Wolcott *psychologist, educator*
Johnson, Donald Clay *librarian, curator*
Johnson, Gary M. *lawyer*
Johnson, John Warren *retired professional society administrator*
Johnson, Kenneth Harvey *veterinary pathologist*
Johnson, Larry Walter *lawyer*
Johnson, Lola Norine *retired advertising and public relations executive, educator*
Johnson, Margaret Ann (Peggy) *library administrator*
Johnson, Richard J. *lawyer*
Johnson, Walter Kline *civil engineer*
Jonason, William A. *lawyer*
Jones, Jeffrey A. *lawyer*
Joseph, Daniel Donald *aeronautical engineer, educator*
Joseph, Marilyn Susan *gynecologist*
Joyce, Joseph M. *lawyer, retail executive*
Judson, Patricia Lynn *obstetrician, gynecologist, oncologist*
Junek, John C. *lawyer, finance company executive*
Kalinsky, Robert A. *lawyer*
Kane, Robert Lewis *public health service officer, educator*
Kantor, David *lawyer*
Kaplan, Sheldon *lawyer, director*
Karras, Ruth Mazo *history professor*
Keane, William Francis *nephrology educator, research foundation executive*
Keets, John David, Jr. *insurance company executive*
Kelly, A. David *lawyer*
Kelly, Charles Harold *advertising executive*
Kelly, Richard C. *energy executive*
Kelly, Tom (Jay Thomas Kelly) *retired professional sports team manager*
Keppel, William James *lawyer, educator, writer*
Keyes, Jeffrey J. *lawyer*
Kilbourne, Barbara Jean *health and housing executive*
Kim, Seong Chan *environmental scientist, researcher*
Kim, Suck-Won *psychiatrist, educator*
King, Lyndel Irene Saunders *museum director*
Kinney, Earl Robert *mutual funds company executive*
Kirtley, Jane Elizabeth *law educator*
Klaas, Paul Barry *lawyer*
Knoke, David Harmon *sociology educator*
Knopf, Matthew J. *lawyer*
Kohlstedt, David Lee *geophysicist, educator*
Kohlstedt, Sally Gregory *historian, educator*
Koneck, John Michael *lawyer*
Korotkin, Fred *writer, philatelist*
Koutsky, Dean Roger *advertising executive*
Kreiser, Frank David *real estate executive*
Kressel, Robert J. *federal judge*
Kudrle, Robert Thomas *economist, educator*
Kuhi, Leonard Vello *astronomer, academic administrator*
Kvalseth, Tarald Oddvar *mechanical engineer, educator*
Laing, Karel Ann *publishing executive*
Lambert, Robert Frank *electrical engineer, educator, consultant*
Lancaster, Peter McCreery *lawyer*
Larson, Sheryl Ann *social worker, researcher, writer*
Lavik, Bricker L. *lawyer*
Lavoie, James A. *lawyer*
Lazar, Raymond Michael *lawyer, educator*
Lebedoff, David Miller *lawyer, writer*
Lebedoff, Jonathan Galanter *retired judge, mediator*
Lee, Jong Y. *medical scientist, educator*
Lehman, Tom (Thomas Edward Lehman) *professional golfer*
Lenehan, James T. *former pharmaceutical executive*
Leon, Arthur Sol *research cardiologist, exercise physiologist*
Leppik, Ilo E. *neurologist, educator*
Lerner, Harry Jonas *publishing executive*
Leuchovius, Deborah *advocate, special education services professional, consultant*
Levinson, David Matthew *engineering educator, civil engineer*
Lewis, Stephen Richmond, Jr. *economist, educator*
Lillehaug, David Lee *lawyer*
Lindell, Edward Albert *academic and religious organization administrator*
Lindsay, Michael Anthony *lawyer*
Lipovetsky, Stan(islav) *statistician, mathematician*
Lloyd, Patrick M. *dean, dental educator*
Loh, Horace H. *pharmacology educator*
Loken, James Burton *federal judge*
Loreno, Nina Louise *elementary school educator*
Loucks, Kathleen Margaret *lawyer*
Lougee, Wendy Pradt *university librarian, educator*
Lucke, Stephen P. *lawyer*
Lueck, Martin R. *lawyer*
Luepker, Russell Vincent *epidemiology educator*
Lumpkins, Robert L. *food products executive*
Magid, Creighton (Chip) Reid *lawyer*
Magnuson, Roger James *lawyer*
Mahoney, Kathleen Mary *lawyer*
Malmquist, Carl Phillip *psychiatrist*
Mandel, Sheldon Lloyd *dermatologist, educator*
Mansfield, William L. *manufacturing executive*
Manthey, Thomas Richard *lawyer*
Marinello, Kathryn V. *information technology executive*
Markus, Lawrence *retired mathematics professor*

Marling, Karal Ann art history educator, social sciences educator, curator
Marshak, Marvin Lloyd physicist, researcher
Marshall, Siri Swenson lawyer, consumer products company executive
Martin, Judith Moran lawyer
Martin, Phillip Hammond lawyer
Martin, Roger Bond landscape architect
Martinson, Bradley James lawyer
Matson, Timothy C. lawyer
Matthews, James Shadley lawyer
Mauer, Joe professional baseball player
Maynard, Hugh M. lawyer
McDonald, John J., Jr. lawyer
McGunnigle, George Francis lawyer, judge
McHale, Kevin Edward professional sports team executive, retired professional basketball player
McIntyre, John Lawrence lawyer
McKee, Tim chef
McLaren, Brian pastor, christian activist
McLaughlin, Patrick J. lawyer
McNamara, Michael John lawyer
McRoberts, Sheryl A. art educator
Meador, Ron newspaper editor, writer
Meier, Lisa M. lawyer
Melendez, Brian lawyer
Mellum, Gale Robert lawyer
Melrose, Kendrick Bascom manufacturing executive
Mengler, Thomas M. dean
Meshbesher, Ronald I. lawyer
Mikan, G. Mike healthcare services company executive
Miller, Alan M. writer, educator, television host
Miller, William Alvin clergyman, author, lecturer
Miner, James Ross emergency physician, educator
Mitau, Lee R. lawyer, bank executive
Moller, James Herman pediatrician, educator
Mondale, Joan Adams wife of former Vice President of United States
Mondale, Walter Frederick lawyer, former Vice President of United States
Monga, Manoj medical educator
Montgomery, Ann D. federal judge, educator
Montgomery, Henry Irving financial planner
Montgomery, Lynn Marie educational consultant
Montpetit, Jeffrey M. lawyer
Moor, Rob professional sports team executive
Moore, Randall Charles biology professor
Moreno, Albert F. lawyer, former apparel executive
Morneau, Justin Ernest George professional baseball player
Morrison, Fred LaMont law educator, dean
Mouser, Les (Lyman Mouser) advertising executive
Mulligan, Donal L. consumer products company executive
Munsell, William A. healthcare insurance company executive
Murphy, Daniel J., Jr. aerospace and defense manufacturing company executive, military officer
Murphy, Diana E. federal judge
Murphy, Joseph Edward, Jr. broadcast executive
Muthyala, Ramaiah chemistry professor, researcher
Najarian, John Sarkis surgeon, educator
Nanne, Louis Vincent professional hockey team executive
Nelson, Julie Loftus lawyer
Nelson, Richard Arthur lawyer
Nemo, Anthony James lawyer
Ness, David Michael lawyer
Nevin, Phillip professional baseball player
Nicholson, Bruce J. insurance company executive
Nixdorf, Donald dentist, researcher
Noel, Franklin Linwood judge
Novak, Leslie Howard lawyer
Nyrop, Donald William air transportation executive
O'Connor, Michael B. biology professor, researcher
Oesterle, Stephen N. medical products executive, cardiologist, educator
Oh, Allen James lawyer
O'Keefe, Michael academic administrator, physicist
O'Keefe, Thomas Michael academic administrator
Olson, James Richard retired transportation executive
O'Neill, Brian Boru lawyer
O'Neill Moreland, Tamara lawyer
Oriani, Richard Anthony metallurgical engineer, educator
Ort, Shannon lawyer
Osadchuk, Margo publishing executive
Osterholm, Michael T. epidemiologist, public health service officer
Ostrom, Don political science professor
Overmier, J. Bruce psychology professor
Paar, Christopher R. lawyer
Page, Gregory R. agricultural products and diversified services company executive
Parhi, Keshab Kumar electrical and computer engineering educator
Parsons, Charles Allan, Jr. lawyer
Paulose, Rachel K. prosecutor
Paulu, Frances Brown retired international center administrator
Payne, William Bruce lawyer, director
Pedersen, James F. lawyer
Peltier, Ronald James real estate corporation officer
Perlman, Lawrence retired information technology executive
Persson, Erland Karl electrical engineer, executive
Peterson, David C. lawyer
Peterson, Neal N. lawyer
Petzold, Linda Ruth computer scientist, educator, researcher
Pfau, James Michael lawyer
Pfender, Emil mechanical engineering educator
Phibbs, Clifford Matthew surgeon, educator
Piper, Addison Lewis securities executive
Platt, Nina law librarian
Pletcher, Carol H. chemicals executive
Pohlad, Carl R. bank executive, professional sports team executive
Pohlad, Robert C. consumer products company executive
Porter, Philip Wayland geography educator
Portoghese, Philip Salvatore medicinal chemist, educator
Potter, David B. lawyer
Powell, Deborah Elizabeth pathologist, dean
Powell, Kendall J. consumer products company executive
Pratte, Robert John lawyer
Preuss, Roger Emil artist
Price, Joseph Michael lawyer
Pyles, Lee Allan cardiologist, biomedical researcher
Quam, Lois insurance company executive
Quie, Paul Gerhardt pediatrician, educator
Radmer, Michael John lawyer, educator
Randall, Roger David publishing executive
Raskind, Leo Joseph law educator
Rasmussen, Teresa J. lawyer, insurance company executive
Ratchye, Boyd Havens lawyer
Reha, Rose Krivisky retired finance educator
Reichgott Junge, Ember Darlene retired senator, lawyer, writer, broadcast commentator, radio personality, communications executive
Rein, Stanley Michael lawyer
Reinhart, Robert Rountree, Jr. lawyer
Reiss, Ira Leonard retired sociology educator, writer
Reister, Raymond Alex retired lawyer
Remele, Lewis Albert, Jr. lawyer
Resnick, Phillip Stanley lawyer
Revnew, Thomas Richard lawyer
Reyelts, Paul C. chemical company executive
Ridder, Par publishing executive
Rockenstein, Walter Harrison, II, lawyer
Rockwell, Winthrop Adams lawyer
Roe, John H. manufacturing executive
Roe, Roger Rolland, Jr. lawyer
Rompala, Richard M. chemical company executive
Rose, Thomas Albert artist, educator
Rosenbaum, James Michael federal judge
Rosenbaum, Robert A. lawyer
Rosenblatt, Cynthia Schaffer lawyer
Ross, Donald, Jr. language educator, academic administrator
Rothenberg, Elliot Calvin lawyer, writer
Rowan, Herman T. art educator, artist
Rudelius, William marketing educator
Ryan, Terry professional sports team executive
Rybak, R. T. mayor
Saeks, Allen Irving lawyer
Safley, James Robert lawyer
Saksena, Marian E. lawyer
Sanger, Stephen W. consumer products company executive
Santana, Johan Alexander professional baseball player
Santana, Lymari Jeanette lawyer
Santosa, Fadil mathematics professor
Satorius, John Arthur lawyer
Sawicki, Zbigniew Peter lawyer
Sawyer, Charles F. lawyer
Scallen, Thomas Kaine broadcast executive
Schermer, Judith Kahn lawyer
Schmaltz, David G. lawyer
Schneider, Elaine Carol lawyer, researcher, writer
Schnell, Robert Lee, Jr. lawyer
Schreiner, John Christian economics consultant, software publisher
Schuh, G(eorge) Edward dean, agricultural economist
Schulkers, Joan M. lawyer
Schulze, Richard M. retail executive
Schwartz, Howard Wyn business and marketing educator, consultant
Scouton, David Earl lawyer
Scovanner, Douglas A. retail executive
Scoville, James Griffin industrial relations professor
Scriven, L. E(dward) engineering educator
Seibert, Troy J. lawyer
Seidel, Robert Wayne science historian, educator
Seifert, James J. lawyer
Serrin, James Burton mathematics professor
Severinsen, Doc (Carl H. Severinsen) conductor, musician
Shaheen, Christopher T. lawyer
Shapiro, Burton Leonard dentist, geneticist, educator
Shaughnessy, Thomas William retired librarian
Shively, William Phillips political scientist, educator
Shnider, Bruce Jay lawyer
Short, Marianne Dolores lawyer
Sidebottom, Charles Benton engineering executive
Sieben, Jeffrey Scott lawyer
Silver, Alan Irving lawyer
Simonson, James S. lawyer
Sinha, Akhouri A. cell and development biologist, researcher
Sipkins, Peter W. lawyer
Sippel, William Leroy lawyer
Sisk, Gregory Charles lawyer, educator
Skare, Robert Martin lawyer, director
Slocum, Rosemarie physician services consultant, recruiter
Smetanka, Mary Jane reporter
Smith, Tubby men's college basketball coach
Soland, Norman R. corporate lawyer
Sorenson, Christopher J. lawyer
Sortland, Paul Allan lawyer
Soule, George William lawyer
Sparrow, Ephraim Maurice mechanical engineering scientist, educator
Spear, Allan Henry state legislator, historian, educator
Spoor, William Howard food products executive
Sprenger, Gordon M. hospital administrator
Srirangarajan, Seshan electrical engineer, researcher
Stack, Jim professional sports team executive
Stageberg, Roger V. lawyer
Steen-Hinderlie, Diane Evelyn social worker, musician
Stein, Robert Allen lawyer, educator, former legal association administrator
Steinberg, Michael music critic, educator
Steinhafel, Gregg W. retail executive
Stenwick, Michael William retired internist, geriatrician, consultant
Stephens, Lee-Ann Williams elementary school educator, educator
Stephenson, Vivian M. former retail executive
Stern, Gary Hilton bank executive
Stern, Leo G. lawyer
Stoeri, William R. lawyer
Stone, Harold B. artist, educator
Strickland, Thomas L. lawyer
Struthers, Margo S. lawyer
Sullivan, Alfred Dewitt academic administrator
Sullivan, E. Thomas law educator
Sullivan, John L. political science professor
Suryanarayanan, Raj Gopalan pharmacist, researcher, consultant, educator
Svendsbye, Lloyd August academic administrator, theologian, educator
Swanson, David P. lawyer
Swenson, Mark Gregory architect
Swiontkowski, Marc Francis orthopedist
Takyar, Mir Shahrouz electrical engineer, researcher
Tandon, Rajiv training company executive
Tanick, Marshall Howard lawyer, educator
Tatlock, Ann writer
Tellegen, Auke retired psychology professor
Thompson, Roby Calvin, Jr. orthopedic surgeon, educator, department chairman
Thompson, Theodore Robert pediatric educator
Thormodsgard, Diane L. bank executive
Thorson, Steven Greg lawyer
Tinkham, Thomas W. lawyer
Toscano, James Vincent medical foundation administrator
Tracy, James Donald historian, educator
Trestman, Frank D. distribution company executive, director
Trucano, Michael lawyer
Truhlar, Donald Gene chemist, educator
Tuckson, Reed V. physician, health insurance company executive
Turner, John Gosney insurance company executive, director
Turner, Ronald L. information services executive
Ulrich, Robert J. retail executive
Ulstrom, Robert A. retired pediatrician
Van Brunt, William A. lawyer
Van Dyke, William Grant manufacturing executive
Vanska, Osmo music director
Veblen, Thomas Clayton management consultant
Vedder, James J. lawyer
Veith, G. John lawyer
Viault, Raymond G. food company executive
Voss, Barry Vaughan lawyer
Wahoske, Michael James lawyer
Walden, John retail executive
Walker, Sally M. writer
Wang, Yang cardiologist, educator, medical researcher
Ward, David Allen sociology educator
Warman, Eduardo Norberto research scientist
Warring, Douglas Franklin education educator, psychologist
Watson, Dennis Wallace microbiologist, educator
Watson, Lucia chef
Wegerson, Edward J. lawyer
Weil, Cass Sargent lawyer
Weinberg, Richard Alan psychologist, educator
Weintraut, Steven James lawyer
Weiss, Gerhard Hans German language educator
Welters, Anthony health services executive
Whelpley, Dennis Porter lawyer
White, Robert James retired columnist
Wichmann, David S. health care services executive
Wickesberg, Albert Klumb retired management consultant
Wicks, John R. lawyer
Wieneke, Darin Scott lawyer
Wikman, Michael Raymond advertising executive
Wild, John Julian surgeon, researcher, medical educator
Wilks, David M. energy executive
Windhorst, John William, Jr. lawyer
Winer, Edward L. lawyer
Wittman, Randy Scott professional basketball coach
Wolford, Kathryn Frances foundation administrator
Wollan, Curtis Noel theater producer, theater director
Wollenberg, Bruce Frederick electrical engineering educator, consultant
Woodman, Stewart chef
Woods, Robert Edward lawyer
Wright, Chris professional sports team executive
Wright, Herbert E(dgar), Jr. geologist
Wurtele, Christopher Angus paint and coatings company executive
Yost, Gerald B. lawyer
Young, Christopher Aaron lawyer
Younger, Judith Tess law educator
Yourzak, Robert Joseph management consultant, educator, engineer
Ysseldyke, James Edward psychology professor
Zaleske, David Joseph surgeon, research scientist, health facility administrator
Zierden, Don professional basketball coach
Zimmermann, Robert Laurence marketing professional

Minnetonka
Anderson, David Wayne entrepreneur, former federal agency administrator
Bahl, Tracy L. healthcare executive
Bean, Glen Atherton entrepreneur
Bjerke, Dana librarian
Erlandson, Patrick J. health products executive
Gillies, Donald Richard marketing and advertising consultant, educator
Kostka, Ronald Wayne marketing consultant
Morisato, Susan Cay actuary
Nelson, Marilyn Carlson hotel executive, travel company executive
Penshorn, John S. health facility administrator
Pillsbury, George Sturgis retired investment advisor
Porter, Jim human resources specialist
Rivet, Jeannine M. health insurance company executive
Robbins, Orem Olford insurance company executive
Rogers, James Devitt judge
Sandy, Lewis Gordon physician, healthcare executive
Schmidt, Russel Alan, II, sales executive
Sheehy, Robert J. insurance company executive
Weisman, Eric music company executive
Wigfield, Rita L. elementary school educator

Moorhead
Boggs, David Bruce art educator
Buckley, Joan N. retired literature and language professor
Dille, Roland Paul college president
Heuer, Gerald Arthur mathematician, educator
Noblitt, Harding Coolidge political scientist, educator
Rothlisberger, Rodney John music educator
Shoptaugh, Terry Lee historian, archivist
Strong, Judith Ann chemist, educator
Trainor, John Felix retired economics professor
Treumann, William Borgen university dean

Morris
Ordway, Ellen biologist, educator, entomologist, researcher

Mound
Reske, Steven David lawyer, writer
Whaley, Roger Glenn music educator

Mounds View
Wang, Aixue translator, writer

Nevis
Stibbe, Austin Jule retired accountant

New Brighton
Appel, William Frank pharmacist

New Ulm
Schubkegel, Joyce Catherine music educator, composer
Weinberg, Justin Peter lawyer

North Mankato
Taylor, Glen A. printing, direct mail and technology executive, professional sports team owner

North Oaks
Engle, Donald Edward retired rail transportation executive, lawyer
McDonald, Malcolm Willis retired real estate company executive

North Saint Paul
O'Brien, Daniel William lawyer, lumber company executive

Northfield
Appleyard, David Frank retired mathematics professor
Cederberg, James retired physics professor
Clark, Clifford Edward, Jr. history professor
Clark, William Hartley political science professor
Iseminger, Gary Hudson philosophy educator
Levin, Burton diplomat
Lundergan, Barbara Keough lawyer
Oden, Robert A., Jr. academic administrator
Paas, John Roger language educator
Schuster, Seymour mathematician, educator
Soule, George Alan literature educator
Sovik, Edward Anders architect, consultant
Steen, Lynn Arthur mathematician, educator
Swanson, Stephen Olney minister, retired English educator
Yandell, Cathy Marleen language educator

Oak Park Heights
Jones, Edwin Channing, Jr. retired electrical and computer engineering educator

Oakdale
Russomanno, Frank P. information technology executive
Tran, Nang Tri research scientist, electrical engineer

Olivia
Cosgriff, James Arthur physician

Osseo
Anya, Adamma Chukwudi special education educator
Boyd, Kelly A. lawyer, educator

Ottertail
Blaha, Verle Dennis consumer products company executive, electrical engineer

Owatonna
Annexstad, Albert T. insurance company executive

Park Rapids
Novak, Larry Ray *secondary school educator, music educator, director*
Shilson, Wayne *artist, educator*

Pequot Lakes
Gray, Allen (Ernest Bungaard) *communications executive*

Plymouth
Friswold, Fred Ravndal *manufacturing executive*
Kahler, Herbert Frederick *manufacturing executive*
Kodali, Dharma Rao *engineering educator*
Mack, Richard L. *lawyer, software company executive*
Prokopanko, James T. *agricultural products executive*
Saville, Derric James *lawyer*
Shadley, Robert D. *retired army officer*
Trump, Stephanie *music educator, choral director*
Vieth, William Chapman *secondary school educator*

Richfield
Amdahl, Douglas Kenneth *retired state supreme court justice*
Anderson, Bradbury H. *retail executive*
Ballard, Shari L. *retail executive*
Devlin, Barbara Jo *school district administrator*
Reilly, Jill Marlene *school system administrator*

Robbinsdale
Anderson, Scott Robbins *hospital administrator*
Harrison, Christopher Eugene *graphics designer, artist, consultant*

Rochester
Bakkum-Gamez, Jamie Nadine *obstetrician, gynecologist*
Bartholomew, Lloyd Gibson *physician*
Bowie, E(dward) J(ohn) Walter *hematologist, researcher*
Brown, Arnold Lanehart, Jr. *pathologist, educator, dean*
Cofield, Robert Hahn *orthopedic surgeon, educator*
Coleman, Mary Ellen *quality assurance professional*
Cortese, Denis A. *healthcare executive, medical educator*
Currier, Bradford Leonard *spine and orthopedic surgeon*
Danielson, Gordon Kenneth, Jr. *cardiovascular surgeon, educator*
Dearani, Joseph Albert *medical educator*
DeRemee, Richard Arthur *retired internist, educator, researcher*
Douglass, Bruce E. *physician*
Engel, Andrew George *neurologist*
Fervenza, Fernando C. *nephrologist, educator*
Forstrom, Lee Arthur *physician*
Fye, W. Bruce III *cardiologist*
Garcia Franco, Carlos Enrique *thoracic surgeon*
Gersh, Bernard J. *cardiologist, researcher, educator*
Gervais, Sister Generose *hospital consultant*
Gibbons, Raymond John *cardiologist*
Gorman, Colum Alphonsus *retired endocrinologist*
Gracey, Douglas Robert *internist, educator, physiologist*
Greenleaf, James Fowler *biophysics educator*
Haddy, Francis John *internist, educator*
Hauri, Peter J. *psychology professor, researcher*
Hunder, Gene Gerald *rheumatologist, educator*
Kantarci, Kejal *radiologist, researcher*
Kao, Pai Chih *clinical chemist*
Key, Jack Dayton *librarian*
Knopman, David S. *neurologist*
Kyle, Robert Arthur *medical educator, oncologist*
LaRusso, Nicholas F. *gastroenterologist, educator, scientist*
Lee, Hon-Chi *medical educator*
Lucas, Alexander Ralph *child psychiatrist, educator, writer*
Mackenzie, Ronald Alexander *anesthesiologist*
Maher, L. James III *molecular biologist*
Malkasian, George Durand, Jr. *obstetrician, educator*
McAlpine, Donald Eugene *physician*
Moir, Christopher Robert *surgeon*
Mrazek, David Allen *child and adolescent psychiatrist*
Neel, Harry Bryan III *surgeon, scientist, educator*
Nelson, Audrey May *physician*
Nevling, Harry Reed *human resources consultant*
Ngaage, Dumbor Laateh *cardiothoracic surgeon*
Ordog, Tamas *research scientist, educator*
Orwoll, Gregg S.K. *lawyer*
Pairolero, Peter Charles *surgeon, educator*
Pang, Yuan-Ping *synthetic and computational chemist*
Perry, Harold Otto *dermatologist*
Phillips, Sidney Frederick *gastroenterologist, educator*
Piepgras, David G. *neurosurgeon, educator*
Pittelkow, Mark Robert *physician, dermatologist, educator, medical researcher*
Platt, Jeffrey Louis *surgeon, director, immunologist, educator, pediatric nephrologist*
Podratz, Karl C. *gynecologic surgeon, oncologist, educator*
Pulido, Jose S. *physician*
Rasimas, Joseph James *psychiatrist*
Rinden, David Lee *clergyman*
Robbins, Thomas Landau *researcher, editor*
Rogers, Roy Steele III *dermatologist, educator, dean*
Rosenow, Edward Carl III *medical educator*
Schneider, Mahlon C. *lawyer*
Scott, John Paul *medical educator*
Seferian, Edward G. *medical educator*
Shampo, Marc Anthony *retired editor*
Siekert, Robert George *retired neurologist, retired educator*
Silber, Michael H. *neurologist*
Sim, Franklin H. *orthopedic surgery educator*
Somsen, Henry Northrop *retired lawyer*
Stegall, Mark D. *surgeon, medical educator*
Stevens, Jeremy R. *lawyer*
Stickler, Gunnar Brynolf *pediatrician*
Stockwell, Linda M. *principal*
Tak, Tahir *cardiologist, researcher*
Talley, Nicholas Joseph *medical educator, research scientist, physician*
Van Dyke, Daniel L. *geneticist*
Ward, Louis Emmerson *retired physician*
Whisnant, Jack Page *neurologist*
Wiebers, David Owen *physician*
Wood, Douglas Lynn *medical educator*
Woods, John Elmer *plastic surgeon*
Wylam, Mark Edward *medical educator, researcher*

Rosemount
Aadland, Thomas Vernon *minister*

Roseville
El-Hilali, Oussama *application developer*
Fisher, Rebecca Rhoda *lawyer*
Fullerton, Denise S.S. *lawyer*
Marten, Gordon Cornelius *agronomist, educator, federal agency administrator*
McMillan, Mary Bigelow *retired minister, volunteer*
Miller, Suzanne Marie *library director, educator*
Seagren, Alice *school system administrator, former state legislator*

Saint Cloud
Godzala, Jesse Thomas *history educator*
Hofsommer, Donovan Lowell *history professor*
Huber-Warring, Tonya *education educator*
Hughes, Kevin John *lawyer*
Inkster, Christine Davis *librarian, educator*
Olson, Barbara Ford *physician*
Prout, Robert Stephen *higher education consultant, law enforcement consultant*
Rice, Steven William *ophthalmologist*
Specht-Jarvis, Roland Hubert *fine arts and humanities educator, dean*
Supanvanij, Janikan *finance educator*
Wertz, John Alan *retired secondary school educator*

Saint Joseph
Kirick, Daniel John *agronomist*
Rowland, Howard Ray *mass communications educator*

Saint Louis Park
Beecher, Lee Hewitt *psychiatrist*
Frestedt, Joy Louise *research scientist, science administrator*
Saliterman, Steven S. *internist, educator*

Saint Paul
Abraham, John Patrick *mechanical engineer, educator*
Abrams, Ronald Lawrence *state legislator*
Ahlvers, Steven J. *athletic trainer*
Allison, John Robert *lawyer*
Alsop, Donald Douglas *federal judge*
Amidon, Paul Charles *publishing executive*
Anderson, G. Barry *state supreme court justice*
Anderson, Paul Holden *state supreme court justice*
Anderson, Russell A. *state supreme court chief justice*
Archabal, Nina M(archetti) *historic site director*
Arnold, Valerie Downing *lawyer*
Axelrod, Leonard *management consultant*
Backstrom, Niklas *professional hockey player*
Baker, Douglas M., Jr. *service industry executive*
Barnwell, Franklin Hershel *zoology educator*
Barry, Anne M. *public health officer*
Bauer, Jean Warner *family economics educator*
Bell, Lawrence T. *lawyer*
Benet, Jay S. *insurance company executive*
Bly, Carol McLean *writer, educator*
Bree, Marlin Duane *publisher, author*
Broccard, Alain Fransois *pulmonologist*
Brooks, Phillip *advertising executive*
Brushaber, George Karl *academic administrator, minister*
Buckley, George W. *manufacturing executive*
Burke, Mary Griggs (Mrs. Jackson Burke) *art collector*
Burton, Charles Victor *neurosurgeon*
Busch, Robert Henry *geneticist, researcher*
Bushway, Deborah *psychologist, educator*
Campbell, Patrick D. *manufacturing executive*
Cavert, Henry Mead *retired physician, educator*
Chaudhary, Satveer *state senator*
Cheng, H. H. *soil scientist, agronomic and environmental science educator emeritus*
Clarke, Charles J. *insurance company executive*
Comer, Beth Megan-Simkins *forensic scientist*
Courtney, Eugene Whitmal *computer company executive*
Crabb, Kenneth Wayne *obstetrician, gynecologist*
Cyr, Lisa Watson *lawyer*
Dahlberg, Eric Ross *music educator*
Daly, Joseph Leo *law educator*
Davis, Margaret Bryan *paleoecology researcher, educator*
Debertin, Jay D. *energy and food products executive*
Demitra, Pavol *professional hockey player*
Diesch, Stanley La Verne *veterinarian, educator*
Doermann, Humphrey *writer, consultant*
Dybvig, Mary McIlvaine *educational consultant, psychologist*
Dykstra, Robert *retired education educator*
Edwards, Jesse Efrem *pathologist, educator*
Ek, Alan Ryan *forester, educator*
Ellison, Keith *Congressman-elect, lawyer*
Ettinger, Irwin R. *insurance company executive*
Feinberg, David Erwin *retired publishing executive*
Fishman, Jay Steven *diversified financial services company executive*
Fisk, Martin H. *lawyer*
Fitzgerald, Kelly Patrick *lawyer*
Fladung, Thom *editor-in-chief*
Flynn, Harry Joseph *archbishop*
Fritze, Steven L. *service industry executive*
Fulton, Robert Lester *sociology educator*
Galvin, Michael John, Jr. *lawyer*
Gehan, Mark William *lawyer*
Geis, Jerome Arthur *lawyer, educator*
Gildea, Lorie Skjerven *state supreme court justice*
Gilmore, Guy L. *publishing executive*
Granger, Steven Tandvig *archivist, consultant*
Green, Gary Jule *lawyer*
Greenwood, Stephen John *environmental engineer*
Hanna, Kathryn Lura *university administrator*
Hanson, Samuel Lee *state supreme court justice*
Hanson, Tom *state official*
Heyman, William Herbert *financial services executive*
Hintz, Chad Jason *lawyer*
Holter, Arlen Rolf *cardiothoracic surgeon*
Hopper, David Henry *theologian, educator*
Hornbach, Daniel J. *biologist, educator*
Hubbard, Stanley Stub *broadcast executive*
Huber, Sister Alberta *academic administrator*
Huggins, Melanie *library director*
Huzar, Eleanor Goltz *historian, educator*
Janzen, Peter S. *lawyer, food products executive*
Jessup, Paul Frederick *financial economist, educator*
Johnson, James Erling *insurance executive*
Johnson, John D. *energy and food products executive*
Johnson, Paul Oren *lawyer*
Jones, C. Paul *lawyer, educator*
Kaliyan, Nalladurai *research scientist*
Kastelic, David Allen *lawyer, energy and food products executive*
Keillor, Garrison Edward *writer, radio personality*
Kelly, Patrick J. *lawyer*
Kent, Patricia Anne *music educator, singer*
King, Jack Burge *academic librarian*
Kirwin, Kenneth Francis *law educator*
Kling, William Hugh *broadcast executive*
Kluempke, Patrick M. *energy and food products executive*
Knutson, Dan *food products executive*
Kommedahl, Thor *plant pathology educator*
Krop, Pamela S. *lawyer*
Kurtz, Harold Paul *foundation executive*
Kyle, Richard House *federal judge*
Labuza, Theodore Peter *food science educator*
Lancaster, Joan Ericksen *judge*
Larson, Thomas D. *energy and food products executive*
Lasansky, Leonardo *artist, educator*
Lebedoff, Randy Miller *lawyer*
Lee, Andrea Jane *academic administrator, nun*
Leighton, Robert Joseph *lawyer*
Lemaire, Jacques *professional hockey coach*
Leonard, Kurt John *retired plant pathologist, director*
Lillie, John Canfield III *lawyer*
Lipp, Robert I. *insurance company executive*
Lofquist, Vicki L. *journalist*
MacLean, Brian W. *insurance company executive*
Mather, Richard Burroughs *retired Chinese language and literature educator*
Maxfield, Lori Rochelle *education educator*
McCormick, James Harold *academic administrator*
McGegan, Nicholas *music director*
McKinnell, Robert Gilmore *retired zoologist, biology professor, geneticist*
McNamee, Sister Catherine *educator*
Meyer, Helen M. *state supreme court justice*
Michael, Alfred Frederick, Jr. *physician, medical educator*
Molnau, Carol L. *lieutenant governor, former state legislator*
Monson, Dianne Lynn *literacy educator*
Mooney, Matthew Thomas *engineering executive*
Murphy, Kevin M. *state agency administrator*
Nash, Nicholas David *retail executive*
Newmark, Richard Alan *chemist*
Ouderkirk, Andrew J. *corporate scientist*
Page, Alan C. *state supreme court justice*
Palmquist, Mark L. *energy and food products executive*
Pampusch, Anita Marie *foundation administrator*
Pappas, Sandra Lee *state senator*
Pawlenty, Timothy James *governor*
Perry, James Alfred *environmental scientist, consultant, science educator, academic administrator*
Phillips, Ronald Lewis *plant geneticist, educator*
Policinski, Chris *food products executive*
Prager, Stephen *chemistry professor*
Pratt, Jon *not-for-profit executive*
Prohofsky, Dennis E. *lawyer, insurance company executive*
Risebrough, Doug *professional sports team executive*
Ritchie, Mark *state official*
Rodríguez, Liliana Cristina *mathematics educator*
Rodriguez, Roberto Miguel *investment company executive*
Rosenberg, Brian C *academic administrator*
Rossmann, Jack Eugene *psychologist, educator*
Rothmeier, Steven George *investment company executive*
Roy, Robert Russell *toxicologist*
Rubens, Sidney Michel *physicist, consultant*
Ruttan, Vernon Wesley *agricultural economist, educator*
Sadowsky, Michael J. *microbiologist, educator*
Schiltz, Patrick Joseph *federal judge*
Schmitz, John *energy and food products executive*
Schnitzer, Alan D. *lawyer*
Schram, Lee J. *manufacturing executive*
Schuman, Allan L. *chemicals executive*
Senkler, Robert L. *insurance company executive*
Seymour, McNeil Vernam *lawyer*
Shepherd, Terry L. *health facility administrator*
Shvartsman, Mikhail Meyer *mathematics professor*
Sisson, Bernice Belair *advocate*
Skillingstad, Constance Yvonne *social services administrator, educator*
Skinner, Pamela J. *adult education educator*
Smith, George Floyd *medical educator*
Smith, Marschall Imboden *lawyer*
Speedie, Marilyn Kay *microbiologist, educator, dean*
Spence, Kenneth F. III *lawyer, insurance company executive*
Starks, Daniel J. *medical technology and services executive*
Stelzig, Samuel Frederic *retired secondary school educator*
Stibbe, Craig Jule *engineer*
Swaiman, Kenneth Fred *pediatric neurologist, educator*
Swanson, Lori A. *state attorney general, lawyer*
Tesch, Phiip C. *dean, minister*
Thompson, Mark K. *lawyer*
Todd, John Joseph *lawyer*
Tylevich, Alexander V. *sculptor, architect*
Van Pilsum, John Franklin *biochemist, educator*
Vecoli, Rudolph John *retired history educator, director*
Volpi, Michele *chemicals executive*
Wagner, Mary Margaret *library and information scientist, educator*
Wehrwein, Austin Carl *freelance/self-employed reporter*
Weiner, Carl Dorian *retired historian*
Weisberg, David Steven *environmental scientist*
Weschcke, Carl Llewellyn *publishing executive*
Westbrock, Leon E. *energy and food products executive*
Westermeyer, Joseph John *psychiatrist*
Wiersma, Kevin *lab administrator*
Williams, Lynell R. *educational association administrator*
Willis, Bruce Donald *judge*
Wilson, Leonard Gilchrist *medical educator*
Wiltz, James W. *medical products executive*
You, Yali *music educator*
Zibell, Donald Fredrick *lawyer*
Ziegler, Richard Ferdinand *lawyer*

Saint Peter
Fister, Barbara Ruth *librarian, educator, writer*
Haeuser, Michael John *library administrator*
Jodock, Darrell Harland *minister, educator*
Mc Rostie, Clair Neil *economics professor*

Shakopee
Eliason, Arlene F. *mathematician, educator*
Gertis, Neill Allan *writer*

Shoreview
O'Dea, Thomas Joseph *clinical engineer, medical physicist*

Sleepy Eye
Jirak, Sarah Reed *secondary school educator*

South Saint Paul
Pugh, Thomas Wilfred *lawyer*

Stillwater
Asch, Susan McClellan *pediatrician*
Erwin, Raymond Maurice *secondary school educator*
Horsch, Lawrence Leonard *venture capitalist, corporate financial executive*

Vadnais Heights
Martinez, Kathryn Marie *music educator*
Polakiewicz, Leonard Anthony *foreign language and literature educator*

Virginia
Knabe, George William, Jr. *pathologist, educator*

Waite Park
Pearson, Andrew R. *lawyer*

Walker
Collins, Thomas William *caterer, consultant*

Waseca
Deike, Keith Lawrence *lawyer*
Frederick, Edward Charles *university official*
Strand, Melvin LeRoy *English educator*

Waterville
Pettis, Patricia Amanda *secondary school educator, farmer*

Waubun
Christensen, Marvin Nelson *venture capitalist*

Wayzata
Blodgett, Frank Caleb *retired food company executive*
Brown, Neil W. *bank executive*
Heckt, Melvin Dean *lawyer*
Luthringshauser, Daniel Rene *manufacturing executive*
Muschenheim, Frederick *retired pathologist*
Nagorske, Lynn A. *bank executive*
Palmer, Brian Eugene *retired lawyer*
Reutiman, Robert William, Jr. *lawyer*
Rich, Willis Frank, Jr. *banker*
Schnobrich, Roger William *lawyer*
Schoen, Charles Judd *service executive*
Skrowaczewski, Stanislaw *conductor, composer*
Staley, Warren R. *agricultural products and diversified services company executive*
Sullivan, Austin Padraic, Jr. *retired diversified food company executive*
Waldera, Wayne Eugene *crisis management executive*
Wyard, Vicki Shaw *investment and insurance company executive*

West Saint Paul
Cento, William Francis *retired newspaper editor*
Nightingale, Edmund Joseph *clinical psychologist, educator, consultant*

White Bear Lake
Bruhn, JoAnn Marie *radiologic technologist, writer, speaker*

Winona
Brosnahan, Roger Paul *retired lawyer*
Holm, Joy Alice *goldsmith, psychology professor, artist, educator*
Nasstrom, Roy Richard *educational consultant*
Oberton, Willard D. *industrial supply company executive*

Woodbury
Beck, Warren Randall *retired glass technologist*
McCalip, David Ray *lawyer*
Woodruff, Ellen Louise *chaplain*

Young America
Luecke, Robert Kenneth *social studies educator, department chairman*

MISSISSIPPI

Aberdeen
Davidson, Glen Harris *federal judge*
Forbes, George Neal *minister*

Ackerman
Coleman, Frances McLean *secondary school educator*
James, Lee J. *agriculture educator*

Alcorn State
Wyatt, Helen J. *special education educator*

Batesville
Carlson, George Clarence, Jr. *state supreme court justice*
Neal, Joseph Lee *vocational school educator*
Smith, Daniel Briggs, Jr. *lawyer*

Bay Saint Louis
Bernstein, Joseph *lawyer*
Hurlburt, Harley Ernest *ocean modeling and prediction scientist*

Biloxi
Brinsmade, Akbar Fairchild *chemical engineering consultant*
Brown, Sheba Ann *elementary school educator*
Love, James Sanford III *communications executive*
Manners, Pamela Jeanne *secondary school educator*
Zocchi, Louis Joseph *product designer, game company executive*

Brandon
Hall, Breda Faye Kimbrough Inman *counselor, educator*
Samsel, Maebell Scroggins (Midge Samsel) *paralegal*

Caledonia
Reed, James Tabor *history educator, consultant*

Carthage
Moran, Mitch *lawyer*

Clarksdale
Lucy, William (Bill Lucy) *labor union administrator*

Cleveland
Boschert, Thomas Neville *historian, educator*
Breland, James Andrew *minister*
Wojcik, John Casimir *music educator, director*

Clinton
Bigelow, Martha Mitchell *retired historian*
Gore, Samuel Marshall *art educator, sculptor*
Hutson, Martha Gillon *social studies educator, consultant*
Montgomery, Keith Norris, Sr. *insurance agent, military officer*

Collins
Lamb, Connie *retired elementary school educator*

Columbus
Jones, Carol A. *nutritionist, artist*
Kantack, Catherine Margaret *retired music educator, retired international and bank broker*
Kaye, Samuel Harvey *architect, educator*
Labensky, Sarah Ross *culinary educator*
Rood, Cynthia Hooper *landscape architect, consultant*
Summer, Emily Eugenia *artist, art educator*
Sumners, Sarah Elizabeth *grant manager, history professor*
Tousley, Rebecca Perkins *retired librarian*
Traynham, Lurene Jones *retired secondary school educator*

Crystal Springs
Nixon, Brenda Joyce *elementary school educator, small business owner*

Decatur
Gordon, Marcus *judge*

Diamondhead
Reddien, Charles Henry, II, *lawyer, diversified financial services company executive, consultant*

Ecru
Mounce, Carolyn P. *retired school librarian*

Ellisville
McNair, Emma Louise *minister*

Fayette
La Salle, Arthur Edward *historic foundation executive*

Flowood
Byrd, Joyce Marie *dentist*
Das, Suman Kumar *plastic surgeon, researcher*
Wilson, William Roberts, Jr., (Bob Wilson) *lawyer, apparel executive*
Zoog, Eric James *emergency physician*

Fulton
Mastin, Lynn P. *biology professor*

Greenville
Martin, Andrew Ayers *lawyer, physician, educator*

Greenwood
Horn, Lawrence Charles *retired music educator*
Swayze, Charles J., Jr. *lawyer*

Grenada
Thomas, Ouida Power *music educator*

Gulfport
Biffle, Tony *editor*
Davis, Wynndi P. *elementary school educator*
Egland, Katherine Tatum *educational consultant, director*
Harral, John Menteith *lawyer*
Opel, Pamela Lynn *elementary school educator*
Phillips, Joy Lambert *lawyer, banker*
Senter, Lyonel Thomas, Jr. *federal judge*
Swetman, Glenn Robert *literature and language professor, poet*
Thatcher, George Robert *banker, writer, journalist, columnist*
Topazi, Anthony J. *utilities executive*

Hattiesburg
Adelman, Michael Schwartz *lawyer*
Bedenbaugh, Angela Lea Owen *chemistry educator, researcher*
Chain, Bobby Lee *electrical contractor, former mayor*
Davis, Charles Raymond *political scientist, educator*
Diket, Mary Read M. *academic administrator, educator*
Doty, Duane Harold *business educator*
Gunther, William David *academic administrator, economics professor*
Hickman, Ronald Lee *media broker, broadcast executive*
Lucas, Aubrey Keith *retired university president*
McRaney, Joan Katherine *artist*
Miao, Wujian *chemistry professor*
Noonkester, James Ralph *retired college president*
Saunders, Martha Dunagin *academic administrator*
Scarborough, William Kauffman *historian, educator*
Stockstill, David H. *musician, research historian, lecturer*
Wiest, Andrew Allen *history professor, writer*
Zelner, Kyle Forbes *historian, educator*

Hernando
Brown, William A. *lawyer, mediator, arbitrator*

Holly Springs
Beckley, David Lenard *academic administrator*

Houston
Griffin, T. David *family physician, pharmacist*

Indianola
Matthews, David *clergyman*

Iuka
Segars, Kelly Scott, Sr. *physician, banker*

Jackson
Adams, Charles P., Jr. *lawyer*
Allison, John S. *state agency administrator*
Anglin, Linda McCluney *retired elementary school educator*
Banks, Fred Lee, Jr. *former state supreme court justice, lawyer*
Barbour, Haley Reeves *governor*
Barksdale, Rhesa Hawkins *federal judge*
Bloom, Sherman *retired pathology educator, photographer*
Boronow, Richard Carlton *gynecologist, educator*
Bounds, Hank M. *school system administrator*
Burns, Robert, Jr. *retired architect, painter*
Carden, Alan L. *hospital chaplain*
Carmichael, Sally W. *volunteer*
Caviness, Kimberly Sweat *environmental engineer*
Chinn, Mark Allan *lawyer*
Clark, David Wright *lawyer*
Clark, Eric C. *state official*
Cobb, Kay Beevers *state supreme court justice, retired state senator*
Coleman, Mary H. *state legislator*
Corlew, John Gordon *lawyer*
Cowan, Bryan D. *medical educator, department chairman*
Creel, Sue Cloer *retired secondary school educator*
Cruse, Julius Major, Jr. *pathologist, educator*
Currie, Edward Jones, Jr. *lawyer*
Daniels, Patsy Jean *literature professor*
de-Shazo, Richard Denson *medical educator, academic administrator*
Diaz, Oliver E., Jr. *state supreme court justice*
Dickinson, Jess H. *state supreme court justice*
Drinkwater, William Wayne *lawyer*
Easley, Charles D., Jr. *state supreme court justice*
Ellingburg, C. Michael *lawyer*
England, John F. *lawyer*
Flowers, Kriste K. *financial analyst*
Gordon, Granville Hollis *church official*
Graves, James E. *state supreme court justice, educator*
Grossi, Jason *mechanical engineer, consultant*
Hafter, Jerome Charles *lawyer*
Hall, John E. *medical educator*
Harkins, Patrick Nicholas III *lawyer*
Hendrix, Albert Randel *social services administrator*
Henegan, John C(lark) *lawyer*
Herndon, Robert McCulloch *neurologist, researcher*
Hood, Jim *state attorney general*
Houston, Gerry Ann *oncologist*
Howell, Joel Walter III *lawyer*
Hughes, Byron William *oil industry executive*
Hughson, Michael Donald *pathologist, researcher, medical educator*
Hupp, James R. *dean, dental educator*
Hutchison, Mark Stevenson *lawyer*
Iliescu, Radu *medical educator*
Izevbigie, Ernest B. *biomedical researcher*
Jolly, E. Grady *federal judge*
Julian, Michael *grocery company executive*
Lamar, Ann Hannaford *state supreme court justice*
Lampton, Dunn O. *prosecutor*
Lampton, Leslie B., Sr. *oil industry executive*
Langford, James Jerry *lawyer*
Lee, Tom Stewart *judge*
Lewis, Robert Edwin, Jr. *pathology and immunology educator, researcher*
Lucas, Frances *academic administrator*
Marshall, Gailen Daugherty, Jr. *allergist, educator*
Mayeaux, Anne Russell *education educator*
McGuire, Sarah Lea *biology professor*
McIntyre, James G. *lawyer*
McLin-Bronson, Hattie Rogers *school system administrator*
Mitchell, Jerry *reporter*
Moize, Jerry Dee *lawyer, federal official*
Moll, George William *pediatrician, educator*
Munera, Pedro Antonio *child and adolescent psychiatrist*
Nix, J. Elmer *retired orthopedist, surgeon*
O'Mara, Charles Snow *surgeon*
Ozerden, Halil Suleyman (Sul) *federal judge*
Phillips, Joshua *pediatrician*
Randolph, Michael K. *state supreme court justice*
Rawson, John Elton *neonatologist, medical educator*
Redmon, Cynthia Ann *poet, songwriter*
Reeves, Tate *state official*
Risley, Rod Alan *educational association administrator*
Roberts, Richard Charlton III *lawyer*
Roy, Sitesh Ranen *pediatrician, allergist, immunologist, educator*
Scanlon, Pat H. *lawyer*
Smith, Carnice *music educator, director*
Smith, James W., Jr. *state supreme court justice*
Smith, Sharman Bridges *state librarian*
Stanton, Sylvia Doucet *artist, gallery owner*
Suess, James Francis *retired psychiatry educator*
Sugg, Robert Perkins *retired judge*
Sweet, Dennis C. III *lawyer*
Tchounwou, Paul Bernard *environmental health specialist, toxicologist, educator*
Thigpen, James Tate *oncologist, educator*
Travis, Jay A. III *lawyer*
Tuck, Amy *lieutenant governor*
Uzodinma, Minta LaVerne Smith *retired nursing administrator, nurse midwife*
Waites, Robert Guinn *utilities executive*
Waller, William Lowe, Jr. *state supreme court justice*
Welch, W(alter) Scott III *lawyer*
West, Carol Catherine *law educator*
Winter, William Forrest *retired governor, lawyer*
Wise, Robert Powell *lawyer*
Young, Brianne Lamonica *rehabilitation services professional*

Laurel
Lacey, Peeler Grayson *diagnostic radiologist*
Lindstrom, Eric Everett *ophthalmologist*

Madison
Grant, Russell Porter, Jr. *lawyer, petroleum landsman*
Watts, Thomas Parrish *history educator, consultant*

Mayhew
Marsh, Patricia Guyton *humanities educator*

Mccomb
Chamberlin, Mary Ellen *music educator*

Meridian
Leewer, William George, Jr. *education educator*

Minter City
Mitchell, Patsy Malier *religious school founder, administrator*

Mississippi State
Babski-Reeves, Kari *industrial and systems engineering educator*
Ballard, Michael B. *archivist*
Chrisman, James Joseph *management educator*
Cook, Susan Deborah *language educator, writer*
Eksioglu, Burak *engineering educator*
Foglesong, Robert H. *academic administrator, career military officer*
Hosie, Thomas Walsh *counselor, educator*
Knudson, Kevin Patrick *mathematics professor*
Lowery, Charles Douglas *historian, dean, educator*
Martin, Edward Curtis, Jr. *landscape architect, educator*
Rabideau, Peter Wayne *dean, chemistry professor, educator*
Reddy, Kambham Raja *botanist, educator*
Sabanadzovic, Sead *virologist, educator*
Swafford, Jeanne *education educator*
Thompson, Joe Floyd *aerospace engineer, researcher*
Truax, Dennis Dale *civil engineer, educator, consultant*
Vance, David A. *information systems educator*

Morton
Cox, Marlina R. *social studies educator*

Moss Point
Bolton, Betty J. *medical/surgical nurse, poet*

Mound Bayou
Kamphefner, Pius *minister*
Robinson, Oliver Dale *counselor, pastor*

Natchez
Bramlette, David C. III *retired federal judge*
Foster, Evaline L. *education educator, researcher*
Golden, Rolland Harve *artist*
Kirk, Susanne Smith *editor*
McLemore, Joan Meadows *librarian, consultant*
Wynn, Bobbye Faye *music educator*

Ocean Springs
Austin, Claude Lidell *retired surgeon*
Biber, Patrick D. *oceanographer*
Culberson, Gary Michael *hotel manager*
Furlow, William Lawrence *retired financial consultant*
Lawson-Jowett, Mary Juliet *lawyer*
Lee, Kathleen Mary *health facility administrator, nursing executive*
Luckey, Alwyn Hall *lawyer*
O'Barr, Bobby Gene, Sr. *lawyer*

Olive Branch
Carnall, George Hursey, II, *lawyer*
Leary, Frances Elizabeth Cooper *secondary school educator*

Oxford
Greenlee, Jim Ming *prosecutor*
Howorth, David Bishop *retired lawyer*
Keiser, Edmund Davis, Jr. *biologist, educator*
Landon, Michael de Laval *retired history professor*
Mills, Michael Paul *judge*
Moorhead, Sylvester Andrew *retired education educator*
Rego, Cesar *science educator, researcher*
Scruggs, Richard F. *lawyer*
Walton, Gerald Wayne *retired university official*

Pass Christian
Henrion, Rosemary Provenza *psychotherapist, educator*
McCardell, James Elton *retired naval officer*

Pearl
Latham, Robert Richard, Jr. *retired emergency services administrator*

Philadelphia
Duncan, Mark *prosecutor*
Montgomery, Kathryn Suzainne *elementary school educator*

Raymond
Simpson, William M. *history professor*

Ridgeland
Harmon, George Marion *academic administrator*

Saltillo
Hopkins, Betty Belinda *elementary school educator*

Saucier
Finley, Emma Rosemary *science educator*

Senatobia
Banham, Sandra Rodgers *language educator*
Latham, Amy Moore *academic administrator*

Shaw
Garner, Mable Tecola *health facility administrator*

Southaven
Taylor, Ronald Louis *lawyer*

Starkville
Eksioglu, Sandra Duni *industrial engineering educator*
Ford, Robert MacDonald III *architect, educator*
Gregg, Billy Ray *seed industry executive, consultant*
Jacob, Paul Bernard, Jr. *electrical engineering educator*
Liu, Qingyun *thermal and mechanical research engineer*
Mabry, Donald Joseph *retired academic administrator, history professor*
Martin, Theodore Krinn *former university administrator*
Mosley, Mary Nell H. *retired elementary school educator*
Oppenheimer, Bonnie Lou *mathematics professor*
Riekels, Lynda Marie *materials engineer*
Thomas, Garnett Jett *accountant*
Westerhold, Ruth Elizabeth *psychologist, educator*

Stennis Space Center
Chin-Bing, Stanley Arthur *physicist, educator*

Stoneville
Morales-Ramos, Juan Alfredo *entomologist, researcher*
Ranney, Carleton David *retired plant pathologist*

Tupelo
Clayton, Claude F., Jr. *lawyer*
Cleveland, Mary Heloise *elementary school educator*
Hill, J. Edward *physician, educator*
Nash, Henry Warren *marketing educator*
Ramage, Martis Donald, Jr. *banker*

Tylertown
Mord, Irving Conrad, II, *lawyer*

University
Bartee, RoSusan D. *educational leadership educator*
Breazeale, Mack Alfred *research scientist, educator*
Cheng, Alexander Hung-Darh *engineering educator, consultant*
Davis, Samuel Marion *dean, law educator, researcher*
Doerksen, Robert John *pharmacy educator*
Dor, George W. K *music educator*
Duke, Stephen Oscar *physiologist, research scientist, educator*
Khayat, Robert Conrad *academic administrator*
Ladner, Renee *women's college basketball coach*
McCurdy, Christopher Robert *pharmacist, educator*
Shughart, William Franklin, II, *economics professor, consultant*
Smith, Allie Maitland *engineering educator*

Vicksburg
Bailess, Robert R. *lawyer*
Houston, James R. *government agency administrator*
Keulegan, Emma Pauline *special education educator*
Mazzeo-Merkle, Linda Lou *legal administrator*
Nichols, William Owen *conservationist*
North, Ryan Elliot *geophysicist, researcher*
Pace, Carol Rebecca *elementary school educator*

Washington
Munyer, Cheryl *museum administrator*

Waynesboro
Crager, Ginny Lee *gifted and talented educator*

Whitfield
Montgomery, John Harold *psychiatrist*

Yazoo City
Woodliff, George Franklin III *priest*

MISSOURI

Advance
Lanpher, Ben Evert *psychologist, researcher*
Thomas, Rich L. *secondary school educator*

Alton
Scott, Lori Denise *music educator, musician*

Arcadia
Davis, Jo *nurse, writer, professional speaker, small business owner, photographer*

Arnold
Kasey, Arthur R. III *secondary school educator*

Ash Grove
Johnson, Iver Christian *retired real estate appraiser*

Bakersfield
Barnes, Sandra Lynn *special education educator*

Ballwin
Ackerson, Charles Stanley *minister, educator, social worker*
Cornell, William Daniel *mechanical engineer*
Luberda, George Joseph *lawyer, educator*
Pallozola, Christine *not-for-profit executive*
Robbert, Louise Buenger *retired historian*

Belton
Blim, Richard Don *retired pediatrician, health facility administrator*
Bryant, Tammi D. *history professor*

Bethel
Coonrod, Delberta Hollaway (Debbie) *retired elementary school educator, consultant*

Bloomfield
Ferrell, Paul Cleveland *writer*

Blue Springs
Hochgrebe, Nolan Robards *secondary school educator*
Lundy, Sadie Allen *small business owner*
Page, Leslie Andrew *retired consumer products company executive*
Peters, Thomas Andrew *library and information scientist, writer*
Washburn, Gladys Haase *retired church musician, educator, director*

Bolivar
Brown, Autry *psychology professor, clergyman*
Goss, Curtis Dale *language educator*
Harris, Beverly Howard *retired mathematics professor, genealogist*
Smith, James O. *history professor, writer*

Bourbon
Heitsch, Leona Mason *artist, writer*

Branson
Lanning, James Wilford *sales executive, retired music educator*
Ownby, Jerry Steve *landscape architect, educator*

Bridgeton
Asma, Lawrence Francis *priest*
Brunngraber, Eric Henry *banker*
Hylla, Linda Kay *sister, social worker*
Kenison, Raymond Robert *fraternal organization administrator, director*

Brighton
Copus, Phyllis Lee *retired federal agency administrator*

Butler
Turner, Vicky Jo *music educator*

Canton
Cochell, Gary G. *mathematician, educator*

Cape Girardeau
Blanton, Lewis M. *federal judge*
Langenfeld, Mark E. *healthcare educator*
Lowes, Albert Charles *lawyer*
McManaman, Kenneth Charles *lawyer*
Sacha, Robert Frank *osteopath, educator*
Smallwood, David Andrew *language educator, education educator*
Smallwood, Glenn Walter, Jr. *utility marketing management executive*

Carl Junction
Pulliam, Frederick Cameron *educational administrator*

Carthage
Haffner, David S. *manufacturing executive*
Jett, Ernest Carroll, Jr. *paper company executive, lawyer*
McAfee, Diana Mae *media specialist, music educator*
Weissenberger, Harry George *lawyer*
Wright, Felix E. *manufacturing executive*

Chesterfield
Ashworth, Ronald Broughton *health facility executive, accountant*
Bunch, C. Robert *oil industry executive, lawyer*
Carpenter, Will Dockery *chemicals executive*
Diamandis, Peter H. *foundation administrator, entrepreneur*
Fujiwara, Hideji *chemist, researcher*
Gerard, Jules Bernard *law educator*
Gietschier, Steven Philip *journalist, historian*
Hier, Marshall David *lawyer*
Landram, Christina Louella *librarian*
Morley, Harry Thomas, Jr. *real estate executive*
Omell, Gary H. *radiologist*
Pollihan, Thomas Henry *lawyer*
Salem, Bakr Ibramim *cardiologist*
Selfridge, George Dever *retired dentist, retired military officer*
Stork, Donald Arthur *advertising executive*
Welshans, Merle Talmadge *retired management consultant*
Williams, Luther Steward *research scientist*
Winter, William Earl *retired beverage company executive*

Clayton
Kemper, David Woods, II, *banker*
Mohan, John J. *lawyer*
Mohrman, Henry Joe, Jr. *lawyer, investment manager*
Novelly, Paul Anthony *petrochemical and refining company executive*
Pain, George H. *lawyer*
Rupp, Joseph D. *metal products executive*
Tremayne, Eric Flory *lawyer*
Vecchiotti, Robert Anthony *management and organizational consultant*

Cleveland
Harper, Bill J. *floral designer, consultant, educator*

Columbia
Almony, Robert Allen, Jr. *librarian*
Anderson, Ralph Robert *endocrinologist, educator*
Bank, Barbara J. *sociology educator*
Bauman, John E., Jr. *chemistry professor*
Beem, John Kelly *retired mathematician, educator*
Berry, William A. *artist, educator*
Biddle, Bruce Jesse *social psychologist, educator*
Bien, Joseph Julius *philosophy educator*
Blevins, Dale Glenn *agronomy educator*
Brown, Olen Ray *microbiologist, biomedical researcher, educator*
Bunn, Ronald Freeze *retired lawyer, academic administrator, political scientist*
Burgoyne, Suzanne *theater educator, writer*
Cogswell, James A. *library director*
Cogswell, Jim *library director*
Colwill, Jack Marshall *physician, educator*
Creighton, Donald Louis *mechanical engineer, consultant*
Crist, William Miles *dean, pediatrician, educator*
Cunningham, Billie M. *accounting educator*
Cunningham, Milamari Antoinella *retired anesthesiologist*
Day, Cecil LeRoy *agricultural engineering educator*
Deaton, Brady J. *academic administrator*
Decker, Wayne Leroy *meteorologist, educator*
Dessem, R. Lawrence *dean, law educator*
Drummond, William Kenneth *small business owner, mechanical engineer, consultant*
Easton, Stephen Douglas *lawyer, educator*
Edgington, Bobbie George *communications engineer, consultant*
Eggers, George William Nordholtz, Jr. *anesthesiologist, educator*
Finkelstein, Richard Alan *retired microbiology educator, consultant*
Fisch, William Bales *law educator*
Flinn, Mark van Doren *education educator*
Flournoy, Nancy *statistician, educator*
Frisby, James Curtis *retired agricultural engineering educator*
Fulweiler, Howard Wells *language professional*
Gehrke, Charles William *biochemistry professor*
George, Melvin Douglas *retired university president*
Giblin, Michael F. *medical researcher, educator*
Goodrich, James William *retired historian executive*
Gupta, Bina *philosopher, educator*
Gysbers, Norman Charles *counselor, educator*
Hardin, Christopher Demarest *medical educator*
Harter, Philip J. *lawyer, educator*
Hawthorne, Marion Frederick *chemistry professor*
Helvey, William Charles, Jr. *communications specialist*
Hensley, Elizabeth Catherine *nutritionist, educator*
Hoffsette, Leon Merle *security specialist, retired military officer*
Horner, Winifred Bryan *humanities educator, researcher, consultant, writer*
Hossain, Maruf *research scientist*
James, Elizabeth Joan Plogsted *pediatrician, educator*
Janda, Mark William *history educator*
Kausler, Donald Harvey *retired psychology professor*
Keown, Linda Jane *language educator*
Keyvan, Shahla *nuclear engineer, educator*
Kirawanich, Phumin *electrical engineer*
König, Peter *pediatrician, educator*
Lamb, Gordon Howard *academic administrator*
Lansford, Raymond William *retired finance educator*
LeMaster, Joseph William *physician, epidemiologist*
Lewis, Michael Robert *medical researcher, educator*
Li, Y. Charles *mathematician, educator*
Libby, Wendy B. *academic administrator*
Loory, Stuart Hugh *journalist*
Looser, Devoney Kay *English literature educator*
LoPiccolo, Joseph *psychologist, educator, author*
Lubensky, Earl Henry *diplomat, anthropologist*
Mashhoon, Bahram *physicist, researcher*
Mays, William Gay, II, *lawyer, real estate developer*
McKinley, Lori *education educator*
Men, Hongsheng *biologist, researcher*
Miller, Paul Ausborn *adult education educator*
Mitchell, Roger Lowry *retired agronomy educator*
Moore, Mitchell Jay *lawyer, educator*
Morehouse, Lawrence Glen *veterinarian, educator, academic administrator*
Mullen, Edward John, Jr. *Spanish language educator*
Mustapha, Azlin *food scientist, educator*
Nikolai, Loren Alfred *accounting educator*
O'Connor, John Thomas *civil engineering educator*
Overby, Osmund Rudolf *art historian, educator*
Parrigin, Elizabeth Ellington *lawyer*
Perry, Michael Clinton *internist, educator, academic administrator*
Phillips, Walter Ray *law educator*
Poehlmann, Carl John *agricultural researcher*
Pringle, Oran Allan *mechanical and aerospace engineering educator*
Puckett, Charles Linwood *plastic surgeon, educator*
Puttler, Benjamin *entomologist*
Randall, Douglas D. *biochemist, educator*
Randall, Linda Lea *biochemist, educator*
Roberts, R. Michael *animal scientist, biochemist, educator*
Rowlett, Ralph Morgan *archaeologist, educator*
Sanders, Keith Page *journalism educator*
Schwartz, Richard Brenton *English language educator, dean, writer*
Shang, Yi *computer scientist, educator*
Srinivasan, Hema *mathematics professor, researcher*
Stack, Frank Huntington *painter, retired art educator*
Stephenson, Hugh Edward, Jr. *retired surgeon*
Strickland, Arvarh Eunice *history professor*
Tarnove, Lorraine *medical association executive*
Timberlake, Charles Edward *historian, educator*
Tobias, Joseph Drew *pediatric anesthesiologist*
Turley, J. William *lawyer*
Vale, Patrice J. *musician, consultant*
Van Sambeek, Jerome William *plant physiologist, educator*
Weisman, Gary Andrew *biochemist*
Welliver, Warren Dee *lawyer, retired judge*
Westbrook, James Edwin *law educator*
Whitman, Dale Alan *lawyer, educator*
Witten, David Melvin *retired radiology educator*
Yanders, Armon Frederick *biological sciences educator, science administrator*
Zhang, Yuwen *mechanical engineer, researcher, educator*

Creve Coeur
Bockserman, Robert Julian *chemist*
Burch, Kelly Joan *pharmacist, consultant*
Randle, Bernadette *musician, composer, graphics designer*
Wasserman, Stephen Miles *communications director*

Cuba
Work, Bruce Van Syoc *small business owner, consultant*

Dearborn
McInnis, Robin Lynn *voice educator*

Doniphan
McCann, Lawrence Alton *music educator*

Earth City
Anderhalter, Oliver Frank *educational organization executive*
Holt, Torry *professional football player*
Kroenke, E. Stanley *real estate developer, professional sports team owner*
Wallace, Bob (Robert Eugene Wallace Jr.) *lawyer*

Edwards
Findley, Kathryn E.C. *psychologist*

Eureka
Lindsey, Susan Lyndaker *zoologist*

Excelsior Springs
Mitchell, Earl Wesley *clergyman*

Farmington
Ashkin, Ronald Evan *international executive*
Lees, William Glenwood *retired finance and retail executive*
Pratte, Geoffrey Lynn *lawyer, arbitrator*

Fayette
Inman, Marianne Elizabeth *academic administrator*
Keeling, Joe Keith *religious studies educator, retired dean*

Fenton
Hoffman, Gilbert L. *information technology executive*
Huber, Scott *transportation services executive*
Lipovsky, Robert P. *marketing executive*
Maritz, W. Stephen *marketing professional, service executive*
Meyer, Joyce *television minister, author*
Stadler, Gerald P. *transportation executive*

Ferguson
Chubb, Charles Ray *physicist, researcher*

Festus
Auchly, Christopher M. *music educator*

Florissant
Ackley, Robert Arthur *mathematics educator, retired military officer*
Conrad, Mary Trench *elementary school educator*
Kralemann, William Joseph *retired chemistry educator*
Linn, Dale E. *secondary school educator*
Luebke, Martin Frederick *retired curator, retired private school educator*
Owen, Robert Frederick *internist, rheumatologist*
Stevens, Robert Edward *engineering company executive*
Stormer, John Anthony *retired minister, writer, publisher*
Tanphaichitr, Kongsak *rheumatologist, allergist, immunologist, internist*
Tomazi, George Donald *retired electrical engineer*

Foristell
Fry, Lowell Lawrence, Jr. *minister*

Forsyth
Klinefelter, Sarah Stephens *retired dean, broadcast executive*

Fort Leonard Wood
Collins, Pamela Marie *forensic specialist, educator*
Craig, Constant Peter *retired military officer, military analyst, consultant*
Meyer, Ronald G. *forensic specialist*

Four Seasons
Bivins, Susan Steinbach *systems engineer*

Fredericktown
Sudmeyer, Alice Jean *art gallery owner*

Fulton
Backer, William Earnest *food products executive*
Hinchie, William Jules *nuclear engineer, director*
Lamkin, Fletcher M., Jr. *academic administrator*

Gainesville
Cline, Thomas William *prosecutor*
Sayles, Wayne Gerald *numismatist, writer*

Grain Valley
Olsson, Björn Eskil *railroad supply company executive*

Granby
Sparkman, Lyle Bruce *academic administrator, education educator*

Gray Summit
Desloge, Christopher Davis, Sr. *real estate company, merchant banking and consulting executive*

Greenwood
Zeller, Marilynn Kay *retired librarian*

Hannibal
Corkern, David E. *music educator*
Reinhard, James Richard *judge*
Terrell, James Daniel *lawyer*
Welch, Joseph Daniel *lawyer*

Hazelwood
Burleski, Joseph Anthony, Jr. *information technology executive*

Hermann
Mahoney, Catherine Ann *artist, educator*
Wilson, C. Daniel, Jr. *library director*

High Ridge
Karll, Jo Ann *retired judge, lawyer*

Hillsboro
Hollander, Lisa Elizabeth Elena *geographer, educator, history professor*
Howald, John William *lawyer*
Jackson, Candine Lee *performing arts, English and speech educator*
Stinson, Stanley Thomas *project manager*

Holden
Martin, Laurabelle *property manager*

Hollister
Lowther, Gerald Halbert *lawyer*

Holt
Merrill, Donna *special education educator*

Independence
Albano, Michael Santo John *lawyer*
Barker, Keith Rene *investment banker*
Burke, Kim Donald *science educator*
Burnett, Crystal Blythe *marketing professional*
Cady, Elwyn Loomis, Jr. *medicolegal consultant*
Devine, Michael J. *library director, educator*
Evans, Margaret Ann *human resources administrator, business owner*
Francis, Mary Frances Van Dyke *small business owner, real estate company executive, retired editor*
Franklin, J. Richard *principal*
House, Lianne Kay *elementary school educator*
Lemon, Leslie Roy *radar meteorologist*
Minton, Kent W. *lawyer*
Nordsieck, Karen Ann *custom apparel company executive*
Pinick, Sariah Kay *music educator*
Potts, Barbara Joyce *retired historic site director*
Rees, Elaine *chemistry educator*
Smith, R(onald) Scott *lawyer*
Terry, Jack Chatterson *lawyer*
Tyree, Alan Dean *clergyman*
Wilding, Richard J. *library director*

Ironton
Sebastian, Phylis Sue (Ingram) *real estate broker, antiques, appraiser*

Jefferson City
Bailes, Shawn Michael *criminalist*
Bartlett, Alex *lawyer*
Blunt, Matt (Matthew Roy Blunt) *governor, former state official*
Brooks, Sean Christopher *criminologist*
Bussabarger, Mary Louise *mental health services professional*
Carnahan, Robin *state official*
Conroy, Margaret M. *library director*
Craver, Charles Henry *illustrator*
Deutsch, James Bernard *lawyer*
Hafley, David Allen *military officer*
Kinder, Peter D. *lieutenant governor, former state senator*
King, D. Kent *school system administrator*
Knox, William Arthur *judge*
Limbaugh, Stephen Nathaniel, Jr. *state supreme court judge*
Mahoney, Carolyn Ray *academic administrator*
McClure, D. Eric *state agency administrator*
McDaniel, Sue Powell *writer*
Mitten, L. Russell *lawyer, former telecommunications industry executive*
Nixon, Jeremiah W. (Jay) *state attorney general*
Novotney, Donald Francis *superintendent of schools*
Price, William Ray, Jr. *state supreme court justice*
Russell, Mary Rhodes *state supreme court justice*
Stith, Laura Denvir *state supreme court justice*
Swarens, Cork (C.C. Swarens) *medical association administrator*
Teitelman, Richard B. *state supreme court judge*
Tettlebaum, Harvey M. *lawyer*
White, Ronnie L. *retired state supreme court justice*
Wolff, Michael A. *state supreme court judge*

Joplin
Daus, Arthur Steven *neurological surgeon*
Dodson, Robert Wayne *surgeon*
Fang, Qiang *history professor*
Habermann, James Herbert *retired pathologist*
Hand, Linda Marie *mathematics professor*
Massa, Richard Wayne *retired communications educator*
Miller, Toni M. Andrews *critical care nurse*
Nodler, Charles Edward, Jr. *archivist, history professor*
Scott, Robert Haywood, Jr. *lawyer*
Wostal, Holly Ann *music educator*

Kansas City
Acheson, Allen Morrow *retired engineering executive*
Amend, Bill *cartoonist*
Anderson, Christopher James *lawyer*
Angoff, Gerald Harvey *cardiologist*
Atkinson, David Neal *law educator*
Ayers, Jeffrey David *lawyer*
Baisden, Eleanor Marguerite *retired airline compensation executive, consultant*
Baker, John Russell *utilities executive*
Baker, Ronald Phillip *service company executive*
Balloun, Joseph Eugene *lawyer*
Barnes, Kay *former mayor*
Bartunek, Robert R(ichard), Jr. *lawyer*
Bass, Lee Marshall *food products company executive*
Bates, William Hubert *lawyer*
Batiuk, Thomas Martin *cartoonist*
Beck, William G. *lawyer*
Beckett, Theodore Charles *lawyer*
Beihl, Frederick *retired lawyer*
Belzer, Irvin V. *lawyer*
Benedict, Stephanie Michelle *purchasing agent, sales consultant*
Benner, Richard Edward, Jr. *marketing consultant, volunteer, investor*
Benton, William Duane *federal judge*
Berenbom, Loren David *cardiologist*
Berkley, Eugene Bertram (Bert) *envelope company executive*
Berkowitz, Lawrence M. *lawyer*
Bernhardt, Mark *orthopedic surgeon, educator*
Bevan, Robert Lewis *lawyer*
Bitner, Teddy Dwight *history professor, military officer*
Blanton, W. C. *lawyer*
Bloch, Henry Wollman *diversified financial services company executive*
Boggs, James Dotson *lawyer*
Bowman, Pasco Middleton, II, *judge*
Bradshaw, Jean Paul, II, *lawyer*
Brandmaier, Jeff *diversified financial services company executive*
Brandt, William Perry *lawyer*
Brett, George Howard *baseball executive, former professional baseball player*
Bridges, Constance Rose *communications educator*
Brous, Thomas Richard *lawyer*
Brown, Peter C. *movie theater company executive*
Brown, Peter W. *lawyer*
Bryant, Richard Todd *lawyer*
Bugher, Robert Dean *professional society administrator*
Busby, Marjean (Marjorie Jean Busby) *retired journalist*
Butler, Merlin Gene *physician, medical geneticist, educator*
Byers-Pevitts, Beverley *college administrator, educator*
Caulfield, Joan *director, educator*
Cheng, Kuang Lu *chemist, educator*
Chesser, Michael J. *gas and electric power industry executive*
Churchman, Michael Steele Bright *educational consultant, educator*
Clancy, Patrick *artist, educator*
Clarke, Milton Charles *lawyer*
Clegg, Karen Kohler *lawyer*
Collins, Kathleen *academic administrator, art educator*
Connor, Kevin M. *lawyer*
Courson, Marna B.P. *public relations executive*
Coveney, Raymond Martin, Jr. *geology educator*
Crawford, Randy M. *lawyer*
Cross, William Dennis *lawyer*
Cunningham, Gunther *professional football coach*
Cunningham, Paul George *minister*
Danner, Kathleen Frances Steele *federal official*
Davis, James Robert *cartoonist*
Davis, John Charles *lawyer*
Davis, Richard Francis *city government official*
Deacy, Thomas Edward, Jr. *lawyer*
Dees, Stephen Phillip *agricultural products executive, lawyer*
Delaware, Richard Raymond *mathematician, educator*
Dias, Jerry Ray *chemistry professor, researcher*
Dicus, Stephen Howard *lawyer*
Diehl, James Harvey *church administrator*
Dietrich, William Gale *lawyer, real estate developer, consultant*
Dillingham, John Allen *marketing professional*
Dimond, Edmunds Grey *medical educator*
Doan, Kirk Hugh *lawyer*
Dunn, Terrence P. *manufacturing executive*
Dwyer, William Michael *health care company advisor*
Eddy, Charles Alan *chiropractor*
Edwards, Cynthia G. *archivist*
Edwards, Herman *professional football coach*
Egan, Charles Joseph, Jr. *lawyer, consumer products company executive*
Eldridge, Truman Kermit, Jr. *lawyer*
Ernst, Mark A. *diversified financial services company executive*
Eubanks, Eugene Emerson *education educator, consultant*
Fetsch, Susan Hackler *nursing administrator, educator*
Fey, Laura Clark *lawyer*
Finch, Floyd Raymond, Jr. *lawyer*
Finn, Robert W. *bishop*
Forker, Alan Duane *medical educator*
Foster, Mark Stephen *lawyer*
Frantze, David Wayne *lawyer*
Freeman, Frederick Roe *lawyer*
Friedlander, Edward Robert *pathologist*
Frisbie, Charles *lawyer*
Funkouser, Mark *mayor*
Gansler, Robert *professional soccer coach*
Gardner, Brian E. *lawyer*
Garrelts, Colby *chef*
Geroe, Michael R. *lawyer*
Gibson, John Robert *federal judge*
Gonzalez, Tony *professional football player*
Gordon, Alex Jonathan *professional baseball player*
Gorman, Gerald Warner *lawyer*
Graebner, Carol F. *diversified financial services company executive, lawyer*
Graham, Harold Steven *lawyer*
Graves, Todd Peterson *lawyer, former prosecutor*
Gray, Helen Theresa Gott *editor*
Green, Frank Earl *retired civil engineer*
Green, Richard Calvin, Jr. *electric power and gas industry executive*
Guilliland, Martha W. *academic administrator*
Gusewelle, Charles Wesley *journalist, writer*
Hagan, John Charles III *ophthalmologist*
Hall, Donald Joyce, Sr. *greeting card company executive*
Hall, Robert T. *pediatrician, medical educator, researcher*
Hamilton, Richard Alfred *academic administrator, marketing executive*
Handley, Gerald Matthew *lawyer, educator*
Harris, Charlie J., Jr. *lawyer*
Haverty, Michael R. *rail transportation executive*
Hebenstreit, James Bryant *agricultural products executive, venture capitalist*
Heeter, James A. *lawyer*
Hindman, Larrie C. *lawyer*
Hoenig, Thomas M. *bank executive*
Hoffmann, Donald *architectural historian*
Holmes, Priest *professional football player*
Howes, Brian Thomas *lawyer*
Huston, Kent Allen *rheumatologist*
Johnson, Larry (Larry Alphonso Johnson Jr.) *professional football player*
Johnson, Linda Diane *environmental health specialist, biologist*
Johnson, Mark Eugene *lawyer*
Johnson, Mark P. *lawyer*
Johnson, Richard Dean *pharmaceutical consultant, educator*
Johnston, John Steven *lawyer*
Jonas, Harry S. *medical education consultant*
Jones, Charles Calhoun *estate and business planning consultant*
Joyce, Michael Patrick *lawyer*
Judd, Barbara Anne *history educator, counselor*
Jung, Craig D. *food products executive*
Kafoure, Michael D. *food products executive*
Kaplan, Harvey L. *lawyer*
Kauk, Janet Lea *not-for-profit developer*
Kemper, Rufus Crosby, Jr. *retired bank executive*
Kemper, R(ufus) Crosby III *library director*
Kilroy, John Muir *lawyer*
Kilroy, William Terrence *lawyer*
Kilway, Kathleen Victoria *chemist, educator, researcher*
Kindred, Lynn Herbert *cardiologist*
Kirch, Donald Allen *writer, composer*
Klamann, John Michael *lawyer*
Koelling, Thomas Winsor *lawyer*
Koerner, Wendell Edward, Jr. *lawyer, mediator*
Krieg, Nancy Kay *social worker, poet, musician*
Krumlauf, Robert Eugene *neuroscientist, educator*
Kuenn, Marjorie Asp *music educator*
Langworthy, Robert Burton *lawyer*
Lashley, Curtis Dale *lawyer*
Laughrey, Nanette Kay *federal judge*
Lednicky, John A. *virologist, microbiologist*
Lee, Margaret Norma *artist*
Leone, Lawrence Joseph *real estate broker*
Levings, Theresa Lawrence *lawyer*
Lindsey, David Hosford *lawyer*
Litan, Robert Eli *lawyer, economist*
Lofland, Gary Kenneth *cardiac surgeon*
Londré, Felicia Mae Hardison *theater educator*
Long, Edwin Tutt *surgeon*
Lotven, Howard Lee *lawyer*
Mackenzie, Nanci *gas company executive*
Magariel, Dale L. *law librarian*
Magill, Kent B. *lawyer*
Marquette, I. Edward *lawyer*
Martin-Bowen, Lindsey *freelance writer*
Martucci, William Christopher *lawyer*
Mast, Kande White *artist*
Matheny, Edward Taylor, Jr. *lawyer*
McCallister, Ben D. *internist, cardiologist, educator*
McCollum, Clifford Glenn *college dean emeritus*
McDonnell, Thomas A. *information technology executive*
McGregor, Douglas Hugh *pathologist, educator*
McGruder, Aaron *cartoonist*
McKenna, George LaVerne *art museum curator*
McLarney, Charles Patrick *lawyer*
McManus, James William *lawyer*
Mc Meel, John Paul *newspaper syndicate and publishing executive*
McPhee, Mark Steven *gastroenterologist, educator*
McSweeney, William Lincoln, Jr. *retired publishing executive*
Meche, Gil (Gilbert Allen Meche) *professional baseball player*
Meilink, Jacqueline Rae *music educator*
Milton, Chad Earl *lawyer*
Molteni, Agostino *pathology educator*
Moore, Stephen James *lawyer*
Mordy, James Calvin *retired lawyer*
Morgison, F. Edward *investment broker*
Murphy, John F. *lawyer*
Mustard, Mary Carolyn *financial executive*
Myers, Betty J. *retired music specialist*
Nagle, Jean Susan Karabacz *retired sociologist, psychologist*
Neaves, William Barlow *cell biologist, educator*
Nelson, Freda Nell Hein *librarian*
Newsom, James Thomas *lawyer*
Northrip, Robert Earl *lawyer*
O'Brien, James Edward *surgeon*
O'Dear, Craig Steven *lawyer*
Oliver, Thornal Goodloe *retired health facility administrator*
Palmer, Cruise *newspaper editor*
Palmer, Dennis Dale *lawyer*
Parizek, Eldon Joseph *geologist, educator, dean*
Parker, Dennis Gene *former sheriff, martial arts instructor*
Patterson, Neal L. *information systems company executive*
Pelofsky, Joel *lawyer*
Pemberton, Bradley Powell *lawyer*
Petosa, Jason Joseph *publisher*
Piepho, Robert Walter *pharmacy educator, researcher*
Plax, Karen Ann *lawyer*
Poston, Walker Seward, II, *medical educator, researcher*
Potter, George William, Jr. *mining executive*
Price, Charles H., II, *former ambassador*
Price, James Tucker *lawyer*
Prugh, William Byron *lawyer*
Pruitt, Stephen Wallace *finance educator*
Rada, David Charles *dermatologist*
Redfearn, Paul L. III *lawyer*
Reed, Michael John *dentist, dean, oral biology educator*
Reitz, Christopher M. *lawyer, gas industry executive*
Respeliers, Patrick J. *lawyer*
Riggins, William G. *electric power industry executive*
Robb, Gary Charles *lawyer*
Robertson, Kenneth Carl *music educator*
Robertson, Leon H. *management consultant, educator*
Rogers, Charles Myers *lawyer*
Roosa, Jan Bertorotta *psychologist, writer*
Rost, William Joseph *chemist*
Rowland, Landon Hill *diversified holding company executive*
Rutherford, Barry D. *cardiologist*
Sampson, William Roth *lawyer*
Sands, Darry Gene *lawyer*
Schaffer, Sandra Sue *artist, educator*
Schall, Jan Joan *curator, educator*
Schult, Thomas P. *lawyer*
Seligson, Frederic Lee *physician, cardiothoracic surgeon*
Seligson, Theodore H. *architect, interior designer, urban planner*
Setser, Patricia A. *music educator*
Setzler, Edward Allan *lawyer*
Sexton, J. Stan *lawyer*
Shaw, John W. *lawyer*
Shields, Will Herthie *professional football player*
Shutz, Byron Christopher *real estate company officer*
Simpson, John W. *lawyer*
Sipho, Ella P. *artist*
Slead, Roger W *lawyer*
Smithson, Lowell Lee *lawyer*
Snelling, Troy Wayne *history educator*
Solberg, Elizabeth Transou *public relations executive*
Spaeth, Nicholas John *lawyer, former state attorney general*
Spalty, Edward Robert *lawyer*
Spear, Joseph E. *architect*
Spigarelli, James L. *science administrator*
Stevens, James Hervey, Jr. *retired financial planner*
Stowers, James Evans, Jr. *investment company executive*
Suni, Ellen Y. *dean, law educator*
Swaffar, Glenda Jean *director*
Tanner, Eric Benson *lawyer*
Thomas, Marcia Markowitz *library director, educator*
Thompson, Mary Elizabeth *application developer*
Tio, Celina *chef*
Todd, Stephen Max *retired lawyer*
Toll, Perry Mark *lawyer, educator*
Truog, William Edward III *pediatrician, educator, researcher*
Tully, Mac *publishing executive*
Tyler, John Edward III *lawyer*
Van Dyke, Thomas Wesley *lawyer*
Vering, John Albert *lawyer*
Versfeld, Leon *lawyer*
Viani, James Laurence *retired lawyer*
Voran, Joel Bruce *lawyer*
Warakomski, Alphonse Walter Joseph, Jr. *sales executive, marketing professional*
Ward, R. Lawrence *lawyer*
Warlen, Stephen Clarence *forensic specialist, consultant*
West, Marc *information technology executive*
Whipple, Dean *federal judge*
Whisler, Joe B. *lawyer*
Whitener, William Garnett *dancer, choreographer*
Whittaker, Judith Ann Cameron *lawyer*
Wilkinson, Ralph Russell *retired biochemistry educator, toxicologist*
Willsie, Sandra Kay *internist, educator*
Willy, Thomas Ralph *lawyer*
Wilson, Marc Fraser *art museum director*
Wirken, James Charles *lawyer*
Wood, John F. *prosecutor*
Woods-Taylor, Cleora Lynesia *mathematics educator, consultant*
Woody, Teresa Ann *lawyer*
Woolley, Brian N. *lawyer*
Wright, Scott Olin *federal judge*
Wyrsch, James Robert *lawyer, educator, writer*
Young, Thomas William *medical examiner*
Zieman, Mark *newspaper editor*

Kingsville
Schreiner, Donald Scott *not-for-profit fundraiser*
Stimac, John Anthony *small business owner, poet, cartoonist, inventor*

Kirksville
Dixon, Barbara Bruinekool *academic administrator*
Festa, Roger Reginald *chemist, educator*
French, Michael Francis *medical educator*
Hanley, Mark Young *historian, educator, researcher*
Holman, Charles Raymond *osteopathic physician*
Ling, Huping *history professor*
Maldonado-Class, Joaquin *language educator*
Rose, Lynn (M. Lynn Rose) *history professor*
Weerts, Richard Kenneth *music educator*

Kirkwood
Holsen, James Noble, Jr. *retired chemical engineer*

Lake Saint Louis
Dommermuth, William Peter *marketing consultant, educator*
Lang, Danny Robert *planning consultant*
Royal, William Henry *retired real estate developer, architect*

Lamar
Geddie, Rowland Hill III *lawyer*

Lees Summit
Brown, Doris Jane *medical technician*
Carter, William Gerald *non-profit corporation executive*
Foudree, Charles M. *financial consultant*

Henley, Joseph Oliver *manufacturing executive*
Hubbard, Harold Mead *energy and environmental systems consultant, retired research executive*
Korschot, Benjamin Calvin *retired investment company executive*
Lord, Heaven *consciousness studies educator, minister, translator*

Liberty
Foskett, Cynthia *nurse, analyst*
Harriman, Richard Lee *performing arts association administrator, educator*
Samuel, Robert Thompson *optometrist*
Tanner, Jimmie Eugene *retired dean*

Louisiana
Smith, Philip G. *lawyer*

Manchester
Forsman, Alpheus Edwin *retired lawyer*

Marshall
Berry, Karen Ann *communications educator*
Sayer, Ronald J. *composer, educator*
Zank, Virginia *literature and language professor*

Marshfield
Frame, Susan S. *special education educator*
Knust, Daniel Max *lawyer*

Maryland Heights
Boudreau, Thomas M. *lawyer, health products executive*
Buselmeier, Bernard Joseph *insurance company executive*
Cooper, Richard Alan *lawyer*
Holmes, Michael *health products executive*
Ignaczak, Edward B. *health products executive*
Lowenberg, David A. *pharmaceutical executive*
McNamee, Patrick *health products executive*
Miller, Steven *medical administrator*
Motchan, Dennis Glenn *physician*
Motheral, Brenda R. *health products executive*
Paz, George *health products executive*
Porter, Douglas W. *health products executive*
Rey-Giraud, Agnès *health products executive*
Steward, David L. *technology company executive*
Stiften, Edward J. *corporate financial executive*

Maryville
Edwards, Carla E. *psychology professor*
Hubbard, Dean Leon *academic administrator*
Kling, Carl Andrew *music educator*
Schultz, Patricia Bowers *vocal music educator, conductor*
Tennihill, Sally Kay *writer, music educator*
Wanorie, Tekle O. *finance educator*

Neosho
Allman, Margaret Ann Lowrance *counseling administrator*

Nevada
Schulze, Cheryl Ranea *secondary school educator*

New Bloomfield
Luebbert, Terry Lynne *elementary school educator*

North Kansas City
Hellman, Richard *endocrinologist*

O Fallon
Gross, Stanley Merhl *chiropractor*
McElhatton, Jerry *credit card company executive*
Ractliffe, Robert Edward George *management executive*
Raeuchle, John Steven *application developer*
Reid, Lorene Frances *middle school educator*

Oak Grove
Davis, Jo *naturopathic physician*

Oregon
Lynn, Brenda *physical education educator*

Osage Beach
Peth, Howard Allen *law educator*
Troutwine, Gayle Leone *lawyer*

Osceola
Johnson, Thomas Moore, II, *curator, lawyer*

Pacific
Hogan, Kurt Avery *music educator*

Parkville
Brackett, Mary Virginia *language educator, writer*
Breckon, Donald John *academic administrator*
Schultis, Gail Ann *library director*

Platte City
Jones, Jay Robert *music educator*
Kalin, D. Jean (Dorothy Jean Kalin) *artist, educator*
Shier, Susan Lynne *music educator*

Poplar Bluff
Black, Ronnie Delane *religious organization administrator, mayor*
Carr, Charles Louis *retired religious organization administrator*
Samuell, Tiechera Dawn *language educator*
Young, William Webb *military officer, aire warfare specialist, poet*

Raymore
Dickerson, Jill Louise *elementary school educator*
Spainhower, James Ivan *retired college president*

Raytown
MacLeod, Linda Ann *secondary school educator*

Reeds Spring
Woods, Dale *retired mathematics professor*

Richmond Heights
Chandler, James Barton *international education consultant*
Shaich, Ronald M. *food service executive*

Rogersville
Hover, Tryphena Machael *music educator*

Rolla
Adawi, Ibrahim Hasan *physics professor*
Alexander, Ralph William, Jr. *physics professor*
Bagnall, Lindsay Lomax *not-for-profit executive*
Carney, John F. III *academic administrator*
Cudney, Elizabeth A.F. *industrial engineer*
Datz, Israel Mortimer *information systems specialist*
Day, Delbert Edwin *ceramic engineering educator*
Galati, Nestore *materials engineer, researcher*
Grimm, Louis John *mathematician, educator*
Ingram, William Thomas III *mathematics professor*
Isaac, Kakkattukuzhy M. *engineering educator, researcher*
Rao, Vittal Srirangam *electrical engineering educator*
Sauer, Harry John, Jr. *mechanical engineer, educator, academic administrator*
Venayagamoorthy, Ganesh Kumar *electrical engineer, computer engineer, educator*
Warner, Don Lee *dean emeritus*
Wray, Kent *academic administrator*
Wu, Shuo-sheng *director*
Yu, Wei-Wen *retired engineering educator*
Zobrist, George Winston *computer scientist, educator*

Saint Ann
Johnson, Harold Gene *lawyer*

Saint Charles
Fitzpatrick, Karey Rose *music educator, director*
Gross, Charles Robert *county official, former state senator, former bank executive*
Martin, Edward Brian *electrical engineer*
Parker, Marsha Marie *dean, actress*
Pundmann, Ed John, Jr. *automotive company executive*
Quiggins, Larry Dale *theater educator*
Ritter, Robert Thornton *lawyer*
Rollings, Dale Linn *lawyer*
Segelhorst, Cindy Marie *pre-school educator*
Tabaka, Sandra Lee *retired medical/surgical nurse*
Wagner, Mary Ann *human resources executive*
Winning, J. Patrick *lawyer*

Saint James
Stevens, Helen Jean *music educator*

Saint Joseph
Bacon, Brian James, Jr. *music and liturgy director*
Boor, Myron Vernon *psychologist, educator*
Chilcote, Gary M. *museum director, reporter*
Gupta, Chakshu *pathologist*
Kranitz, Theodore Mitchell *lawyer*
Malani, Ashok K. *physician*
Rachow, Sharon Dianne *realtor*

Saint Louis
Ackers, Gary Keith *biophysical chemistry educator, researcher*
Agarwal, Banke *gastroenterologist, educator*
Agarwal, Ramesh Kumar *aeronautical scientist, researcher, educator*
Albaugh, James F. *aerospace transportation executive*
Alber, John I. *lawyer*
Allen, Garland Edward *biologist, professor, writer*
Alpers, David Hershel *gastroenterologist, educator*
Anagnostopoulos, Constantine Emmanuel *venture capitalist, former company executive*
Antonacci, Anthony Eugene *retired engineer*
Appleton, R. O., Jr. *lawyer*
Armstrong, J. Hord III *pharmaceutical company executive*
Armstrong, Theodore Morelock *corporate financial executive*
Arnold, Fred English *lawyer*
Arnold, John Fox *lawyer*
Atwood, Hollye Stolz *lawyer*
Aylward, Ronald Lee *lawyer*
Bach, Richard Gordon *internist, cardiologist, educator*
Bachmann, John William *security firm executive*
Bacon, Bruce Raymond *physician*
Baernstein, Albert, II, *mathematician, educator*
Bagby, Robert L. *investment company executive*
Baker, Shirley Kistler *academic administrator, university librarian*
Baker, W. Randolph *brewery company executive*
Balci, Cem N *radiologist*
Baldwin, Edwin Steedman *lawyer*
Ball, Dan H. *lawyer*
Ballinger, Walter Francis *surgeon, educator*
Banerjee, Bhaskar *gastroenterologist, medical educator*
Barken, Bernard Allen *lawyer*
Barksdale, Clarence Caulfield *retired banker*
Barmann, Lawrence Francis *historian, educator*
Bascom, C. Perry *retired foundation administrator*
Baum, Gordon Lee *lawyer, non-profit organization administrator*
Baum, M(ary) Carolyn *occupational therapist*
Baumer, Martha Ann *minister*
Baxter, Warner L. *electric power industry executive*
Bealke, Linn Hemingway *banker*
Beck, Lois Grant *anthropologist, educator, author*
Beltcheva (Belcheva), Mariana *research scientist, educator*
Bender, Carl Martin *physics professor, consultant*
Berg, Darrell Matthews *musicologist*
Berland, David I. *psychiatrist, educator*
Berwick, Philip *law librarian, director, dean*
Bextermiller, Theresa Marie *architect, computer engineer*
Bhalla, Sanjeev *radiologist*
Bickel, Floyd Gilbert III *investment counselor*
Biondi, Lawrence *academic administrator, priest*
Bjerregaard, Preben *cardiologist, educator*
Blake, Allen H. *bank executive*
Blanke, Richard Brian *lawyer*
Blankenship, Robert Eugene *biochemistry educator*
Blanton, Elizabeth Anne *secondary school educator*
Bobak, Mark T. *lawyer*
Boddie, Don O'Mar *recording industry executive*
Boggs, Beth Clemens *lawyer*
Bonacorsi, Mary Catherine *lawyer*
Booth, Betty Jean *retired daycare administrator, poet*
Boothby, William Munger *retired mathematics professor*
Boyce, Gregory H. *energy executive*
Bradley, Edward Joseph, Jr. *electrical engineer*
Bradley, Marilynne Gail *advertising executive, educator*
Brandt, Keith E. *plastic surgeon, educator*
Brandt, Kimberly Glanz *recreational facility executive, director*
Branham, Gregory Harris *facial plastic surgeon*
Brauer, Stephen Franklin *diplomat, manufacturing company executive*
Braverman, Alan Charles *cardiologist, educator*
Brickey, Kathleen Fitzgerald *law educator*
Brickler, John Weise *lawyer*
Brickson, Richard Alan *lawyer*
Bridgewater, Bernard Adolphus, Jr. *retired retail executive*
Bridwell, Keith Happ *orthopedic surgeon*
Briggs, William Benajah *retired aerospace engineer*
Brighton, Louis Andrew *religious studies educator*
Brockhaus, Robert Herold, Sr. *business educator, consultant*
Brody, Lawrence *lawyer, educator*
Browde, Anatole *electronics company executive, consultant*
Browman, David L(udvig) *archaeologist*
Brown, Bettye *librarian, educator*
Brown, JoBeth Goode *food products executive, lawyer*
Brownlee, Robert Hammel *lawyer*
Bryan, Henry C(lark), Jr. *retired lawyer*
Bryant, Donald L., Jr. *insurance and benefits company executive*
Bryant, Ruth Alyne *banker*
Buckley, Kevin William *lawyer*
Buggs, Dwayne Andre *fine arts coordinator, music educator*
Bultas, William Fitzgerald *Internet company executive*
Burgess, James Harland *physics professor, researcher*
Burgess, William Patrick *management consultant*
Burgin, Richard Weston *writer, educator, editor*
Burke, Raymond Leo *archbishop*
Burke, Thomas Michael *lawyer*
Burke, William *neurologist*
Burroughs, Harold R. *lawyer*
Busch, August Adolphus, IV, *brewery company executive*
Byrnes, Christopher Ian *engineering educator*
Cain, James Nelson *arts school and concert administrator*
Cao, Nannan *research scientist*
Carp, Larry *lawyer*
Carpenter, Chris *professional baseball player*
Carr, Gary Thomas *lawyer*
Chambliss, Linda R. *obstetrician, consultant*
Chaplin, David Dunbar *medical research specialist, educator*
Chaplin, Hugh, Jr. *preventive medicine physician, educator*
Chayet, Sergio *finance educator*
Chole, Richard Arthur *otolaryngologist, department chairman*
Clark, John Walter *physics professor*
Clark, Robert G. *construction executive*
Clark, Stephen Robert *lawyer*
Clear, John Michael *lawyer*
Cloninger, Claude Robert *psychiatrist, epidemiologist, educator, researcher*
Colangelo, Carmon *artist, printmaker, educator*
Colletti, Ronald F. *chemist, researcher*
Concibido, Vergel C. *research and development company scientist, plant geneticist, writer, inventor*
Connor-Ward, Dannette Vaudrilyn *research biologist*
Conran, Joseph Palmer *lawyer*
Constantino, John Nicholas *medical educator, researcher*
Copeland, Douglas Allen *lawyer*
Corich, Evelyn Frances *mathematics professor*
Cornfeld, Dave Louis *lawyer*
Cornfeld, Richard Steven *lawyer*
Correa-Perez, Juan Ramon *andrologist, embryologist, researcher*
Costigan, Edward John *retired investment banker*
Cotton, W(illiam) Philip, Jr. *architect*
Covington, Ann K. *lawyer, former state supreme court justice*
Cowsik, Ramanath *physics professor*
Crews, Terrell K. *agricultural products executive*
Crider, Robert Agustine *international financier, protective services official*
Cryer, Philip Eugene *endocrinologist*
Cullen, James D. *lawyer*
Cupples, Stephen Elliot *lawyer*
Curran, Michael Walter *management scientist*
Damiano, Ralph James, Jr. *cardiovascular and thoracic surgeon*
Danforth, John Claggett *lawyer, former ambassador, senator*
Danforth, William Henry *retired academic administrator, physician*
Davidson, John *professional sports team executive, former hockey analyst*
Davis, Irvin *advertising, public relations and broadcast executive*
Deng, Ping *finance educator*
Dewald, Paul Adolph *psychiatrist, educator*
DeWoskin, Alan Ellis *lawyer*
Diekman, Connie *nutritionist*
Dierberg, James F. *bank executive*
DiPersio, John F. *oncologist*
Dodge, Paul Cecil *academic administrator*
Dodge, Philip Rogers *neurologist, educator*
Dorwart, Donald Bruce *lawyer*
Dougherty, Charles Hamilton *pediatrician*
Doughty, Nikedra *academic administrator*
Dowd, Edward L., Jr. *lawyer, former prosecutor*
Dowd, Thomas F. *lawyer*
Downey, Michael Patrick *lawyer*
Dreifke, Gerald Edmond *electrical engineering educator*
Drey, Leo *environmentalist*
Drury, Charles Louis, Jr. *hotel executive*
Dudukovic, Milorad P. *chemical engineering educator, consultant*
Duesenberg, Richard William *lawyer*
Duhme, Carol McCarthy *civic worker*
Dykewicz, Mark Steven *physician*
Eberlein, Timothy J. *surgeon*
Ebert, Robert T. *lawyer*
Eckstein, David Mark *professional baseball player*
Edison, Bernard Alan *retired apparel executive*
Edmonds, James Patrick (Jim Edmonds) *professional baseball player*
Ehrlich, Ava *broadcast executive*
Elder, Dee A. *literature and language educator*
Elgin, Sarah Carlisle Roberts *biology professor, researcher*
Elliott, Howard, Jr. *lawyer, gas industry executive*
Elliott, Susan Spoehrer *information technology executive*
Ellis, Dorsey Daniel, Jr. *lawyer, educator*
Engelhardt, Irl F. *coal company executive*
Engelhardt, Thomas Alexander *editorial cartoonist*
Engsberg, Jack Robert *science educator, researcher*
Epner, Steven Arthur *computer consultant*
Epstein, Robert Harry *lawyer*
Evans, Lawrence E. *lawyer, educator*
Evans, R. Gregory *bioterrorism researcher, educator*
Evens, Ronald Gene *radiologist, educator, health facility administrator*
Evers, Alex Steven *anesthesiologist, internist, educator*
Eyerman, Charlotte *curator, art historian*
Ezenwa, Josephine Nwabuoku *social worker*
Falk, William James *lawyer*
Farnam, Thomas Campbell *lawyer, educator*
Farr, David N. *electronics executive*
Farria, Dione Marie *radiologist, educator*
Felthous, Alan Robert *psychiatrist*
Ferguson, Gary Warren *retired public relations executive*
Fessenden, Ann T. *law librarian*
Filippine, Edward Louis *federal judge*
Fingleton, Thomas D. *retail executive*
Fitch, Coy Dean *internist, educator*
Fitch, Rachel Farr *health policy analyst*
Fitzpatrick, Susan *biochemist, neurologist, foundation administrator*
Fleshman, James W. *medical association administrator*
Fletcher, Bill, Jr. *political organization executive, activist*
Floyd, Walter Leo *lawyer*
Flye, M. Wayne *surgeon, immunologist, educator, writer*
Folz, Carol Ann *benefits compensation analyst*
Fondaw, Ronald Edward *artist, educator*
Fournie, Raymond Richard *lawyer*
Fox, G. Richard *lawyer*
Foy, Betsy D. *health facility administrator, educator*
Fraley, Robert T. *biotechnologist*
Frank, Michael M. *lawyer*
Frank, Terrence Dooley *diversified financial services company executive, director*
Fredericks, Henry Jacob *lawyer*
Frey, Sharon Elizabeth *internist, adult infectious disease physician*
Frieden, Carl *biochemist, educator*
Friedlander, Michael Wulf *physicist, researcher*
Fromm, Ronald A. *apparel executive*
Galvin, Walter J. *electrical equipment manufacturing executive*
Garrett, Ted Eugene *surgeon*
Gass, William H. *writer, educator*
Gauen, Patrick Emil *news correspondent*
Gay, William Arthur, Jr. *thoracic surgeon*
Gelberman, Richard H. *orthopedist, surgeon*
George, Thomas Frederick *academic administrator*
Geslani, Gemma P. *science educator, health researcher*
Gianoulakis, John Louis *lawyer*
Gibbons, Patrick Chandler *physicist, researcher*
Gilhousen, Brent *lawyer*
Gilligan, Sandra Kaye *private school director*
Gillis, John Lamb, Jr. *lawyer*
Godiner, Donald Leonard *lawyer*
Goebel, John J. *lawyer*
Gokel, George William *organic chemist, educator*
Goldberg, Anne Carol *physician, educator*
Goldstein, Julius Lester *biomedical engineer, consultant*
Goldstein, Steven *lawyer*
Goran, Mark H. *lawyer*
Gordon, Jeffrey Ivan *gastroenterologist, educator, molecular biologist, researcher*

Gould, Phillip Louis *engineering educator*
Graff, George Stephen *aerospace transportation executive*
Graham, Robert Clare III *lawyer*
Grant, Hugh *agricultural products executive*
Gray, Charles Elmer *lawyer, rancher, investor*
Greaney, Thomas L. *lawyer, educator*
Green, Dennis Joseph *retired lawyer*
Green, Maurice *molecular biologist, educator, virologist*
Greenbaum, Stuart I. *economist, educator*
Greenley, Beverly Jane *lawyer, educator*
Griggs, Leonard LeRoy, Jr. *air transportation executive, consultant*
Gross, Michael Lawrence *chemistry professor*
Grossberg, George Thomas *psychiatrist, educator*
Grubb, Robert L., Jr. *neurosurgeon*
Gruender, Raymond W. *federal judge, former prosecutor*
Guarigila, Dale A. *lawyer*
Guenther, Charles John *librarian, writer*
Guerri, William Grant *lawyer*
Gupta, Mahendra R. *dean*
Gupta, Surendra Kumar *chemicals executive*
Haas, Daniel Louis *structural engineer*
Hakkinen, Raimo Jaakko *aerospace scientist*
Hamilton, Jean Constance *judge*
Hammerman, Marc Randall *nephrologist, educator*
Hanaway, Catherine Lucille *prosecutor*
Handel, Peter H. *physics professor*
Hanley, Thomas Patrick *obstetrician, gynecologist*
Hansen, Charles *lawyer*
Hansman, Robert G. *artist, educator*
Harris, Harvey Alan *lawyer*
Harris, Whitney Robson *lawyer, educator, military officer, volunteer*
Harvey, David R. *chemical company executive*
Haslett, Jim *professional football coach*
Hassell, Stephen C. *information technology executive*
Hayman, Randy E. *lawyer*
Hays, Howard H. (Tim Hays) *editor, publisher*
Heiken, Jay Paul *physician*
Hellmuth, Theodore Henning *lawyer*
Herbert, Kevin Barry John *classics educator*
Hermeling, Caroline L. *lawyer*
Hiles, Bradley Stephen *lawyer*
Hinton, Velecia Ann *academic administrator*
Hirsch, Raymond Robert *chemicals executive, lawyer*
Holliman, W. G. (Mickey), Jr. *furniture manufacturing executive*
Holmes, Nancy Elizabeth *pediatrician*
Holt, Glen Edward *editor*
Holtzman, David Michael *neurologist*
Hoy, Dawn Riske *musician, director*
Hrubetz, Joan *retired dean, nursing educator*
Hsueh, Eddy C. *surgeon, oncologist*
Hughes, Jeffrey A. *art history educator*
Hunt, Kevin J. *food products executive*
Hunter, Earle Leslie III *retired professional association executive*
Hunter, John C. III *chemicals executive*
Husar, Rudolf Bertalan *mechanical engineering educator*
Hyers, Thomas Morgan *internist, biomedical researcher*
Inkley, John James, Jr. *lawyer*
Israel, Martin Henry *astrophysicist, educator, academic administrator*
Izuchukwu, John Ifeanyichukwu *industrial engineer, mechanical engineer*
Jackson, Carol E. *federal judge*
Jacobs, Donald Louis *medical educator*
James, William W. *financial consultant*
Johnson, Donn S. *communications executive*
Johnson, E. Perry *lawyer*
Johnson, Robert Graham *surgeon, educator, researcher*
Johnson, Sandra Hanneken *law educator*
Joley, Lisa Annette *lawyer, brewery company executive*
Jones, Robert Gerard *lawyer*
Jones, Timothy R. *plastic surgeon, director*
Joyner, Dee Ann *bank executive*
Kaminski, Donald Leon *surgeon, gastroenterologist, educator*
Kandel, Alan Harold *lawyer*
Kariya, Paul *professional hockey player*
Keffler, Karl Joseph *investment company executive, lawyer*
Keller, Juan Dane *retired lawyer*
Kelly, Douglas Laird *lawyer, investment company executive*
Kennelly, Sister Karen Margaret *church administrator, nun, retired academic administrator*
Keyes, Marion Alvah, IV, *manufacturing executive*
Khoury, George Gilbert *printing company executive, sports association executive*
Killenberg, George Andrew *publishing executive, consultant, retired editor*
Kimmey, James Richard, Jr. *foundation administrator*
King, Joseph, Jr. *federal agency administrator*
Kipnis, David Morris *physician, educator*
Klein, Rosemary L. *lawyer*
Klein, Ward M. *consumer products company executive*
Kling, Merle *retired political scientist, retired university official*
Kling, S(tephen) Lee *banker*
Klobasa, John Anthony *lawyer*
Knutsen, Alan Paul *pediatrician, immunologist, allergist*
Koff, Robert Hess *academic administrator, adult education educator*
Kohn, Alan Charles *lawyer*
Kolker, Allan Erwin *ophthalmologist*
Koo, Michele *plastic surgeon*
Kornblet, Donald Ross *communications company executive*
Kornfeld, Stuart A. *hematology educator*
Kouchoukos, Nicholas Thomas *surgeon*
Krasney, Rina Susan *school librarian*
Kuhlmann, Fred Mark *lawyer*
LaBruyere, Thomas Edward *health facility administrator*
Lackey, Kayle Diann *elementary school educator*
Lambright, Stephen Kirk *brewing company executive, lawyer*
La Russa, Tony, Jr., (Anthony La Russa Jr.) *professional baseball manager*
Lauenstein, Ann Gail *librarian*
Lause, Michael Francis *lawyer*
Leavitt, Lynda *school system administrator, educator*
Lebowitz, Albert *lawyer, writer*
Leer, Steven F. *mining executive*
Leguey-Feilleux, Jean-Robert *political scientist, educator*
Lenke, Lawrence Gerald *orthopedic surgeon, educator*
Lents, Don Glaude *lawyer*
Lents, Peggy Iglauer *marketing professional*
Lenzen, Dana Diane *social studies educator*
Leonard, Judith Price *educational advisor*
Leven, Charles Louis *economics professor*
Le Vine, Victor Theodore *retired political science professor*
Lewis, Jeffrey E. *dean, law educator*
Lewis, Jodi A. *secondary school educator, theater educator*
Lewis, Lawrence M. *emergency physician, researcher*
Lewis, Robert David *ophthalmologist, educator*
Ley, Timothy James *hematologist, molecular biologist*
Lieberman, Edward Jay *lawyer*
Liggett, Hiram Shaw, Jr. *retired diversified financial services company executive*
Limbaugh, Stephen Nathaniel *federal judge*
Linehan, Scott *professional football coach*
Lipeles, Maxine Ina *lawyer, law educator*
Litow, Mark I. *lawyer*
Lock, Albert Larry, Jr. *finance company executive*
Lombardi, Mark Owen *academic administrator, international relations educator*
Lonsberg, John V. *lawyer*
Lovelace, Eldridge Hirst *retired landscape architect, city planner, civil engineer*
Lowenhaupt, Charles Abraham *lawyer*
Lowther, Thomas Edward *lawyer*
Lubbock, James Edward *retired writer, photographer, media consultant*
Lucchesi, Lionel Louis *lawyer*
Ludmerer, Kenneth Marc *medical educator*
Lutz, John Thomas *author*
Lybarger, Jerry *lawyer*
Lynch, Robert Martin *lawyer, consultant*
Macias, Edward S. *chemistry professor, dean, academic administrator*
MacInnis, Al *professional sports team executive, retired professional hockey player*
Mackinnon, Susan *plastic surgeon*
Madsen, Matthew J. *lawyer*
Mahan, David James *retired academic administrator*
Mahsman, David Lawrence *writer, church administrator*
Majerus, Philip Warren *physician*
Majerus, Rick *men's college basketball coach*
Mandelstamm, Jerome Robert *lawyer*
Manske, Paul Robert *orthopedic hand surgeon, educator*
Mantovani, John F. *pediatric neurologist*
Marks, Murry Aaron *lawyer*
Marti, Paul Edgar, Jr. *architect, educator*
Martin, Kevin John *nephrologist, educator*
Martin, Lisa Demet *lawyer*
Massa, David J. *lawyer*
Massey, Raymond Lee *lawyer*
Maurer, Frederic George III *bank executive*
McCarter, Charles Chase *lawyer*
McDaniel, James Edwin *lawyer*
McDonald, Douglas Joel *orthopedic surgeon, educator*
McDonnell, Sanford Noyes *air transportation executive*
McGinnis, W. Patrick *diversified company executive*
McGuire, Waller F. *library director*
McKelvey, James Morgan *chemical engineering educator, retired dean*
McKinnis, Michael Bayard *lawyer*
McMahon, Robert M. *physician, lawyer*
Meisel, George Vincent *lawyer*
Meissner, Edwin Benjamin, Jr. *retired real estate broker*
Merrell, James Lee *writer, minister*
Merrill, Charles Eugene *lawyer*
Metcalfe, Elizabeth Brokaw *art educator*
Metcalfe, Walter Lee, Jr. *lawyer*
Michaelides, Constantine Evangelos *architect, educator*
Michenfelder, Albert A. *lawyer*
Middelkamp, John Neal *pediatrician, educator*
Miller, Gary J. *political economist*
Miller, James Gegan *research scientist*
Miller, Judith Braffman *writer*
Mitrophanov, Alexander Yuryevich *mathematician, researcher*
Molloff, Florence Jeanine *speech and language therapist*
Monroe, Thomas Edward *business and financial executive*
Monteleone, Patricia L. *dean*
Moon, Marc R. *cardiac surgeon*
Moore, McPherson Dorsett *lawyer*
Moran, Christopher John *radiologist, educator*
Morley, John Edward *physician*
Morris, Matthew Christian *professional baseball player*
Mowbray, Kevin D. *publishing executive*
Mullens, William Reese *retired insurance company executive*
Mulligan, Michael Dennis *lawyer*
Muns, Raleigh Clayton *school librarian*
Murray, Andy *professional hockey coach*
Murray, George E. *lawyer*
Murray, Robert Wallace *chemistry professor*
Myerson, Robert J. *radiologist, educator*
Nagarkatti, Jai Prakash *chemical company executive*
Nayak, Laxmeesh Mike *plastic surgeon*
Neely, John Gail *otolaryngologist*
Neidorff, Michael F. *health care executive*
Neville, James Morton *retired lawyer, consumer products company executive*
Newman, Andrew Edison *restaurant manager*
Newman, Charles Andrew *lawyer*
Noce, David D. *judge*
Noel, Edwin Lawrence *lawyer*
Norberg, Richard Edwin *physicist, researcher*
North, Douglass Cecil *economist, educator*
Oberlander, Michael I. *lawyer, consumer products company executive*
O'Connell, Daniel Craig *retired psychologist, educator*
O'Donnell, Edward Joseph *bishop, retired editor*
O'Gorman, Gerald Joseph *language educator*
O'Keefe, Michael Daniel *lawyer*
Olney, John William *psychiatry professor*
Olson, Robert Grant *lawyer*
O'Malley, Kevin Francis *lawyer, educator, writer*
Owens, William Don *anesthesiology educator*
Ozawa, Martha Naoko *social work educator*
Pace, Charles *library director*
Pace, Orlando Lamar *professional football player*
Palans, Lloyd Alex *lawyer*
Palmer, Fredrick D. *lawyer, energy executive*
Payne, Meredith Jorstad *physician*
Peck, William Arno *internist, educator, dean, academic administrator*
Peper, Christian Baird *lawyer*
Perotti, Rose Norma *lawyer*
Peters, David Allen *mechanical engineering educator, consultant*
Phoenix, G. Keith *lawyer*
Pickle, Robert Douglas *lawyer, apparel executive*
Pillai, Pragash *communications executive*
Piwnica-Worms, Helen M. *cell biologist, educator*
Pleau, Lawrence Winslow *professional sports team executive*
Pollack, Joe *retired columnist, critic, writer*
Pollack, Seymour Victor *computer science educator*
Poole, William *bank executive*
Pope, Robert E(ugene) *fraternal organization administrator*
Prensky, Arthur Lawrence *pediatric neurologist, educator*
Pryor, David Bram *health science association administrator*
Pujols, Albert (Jose Alberto Pujols) *professional baseball player*
Purkerson, Mabel Louise *physician, educator, physiologist*
Quinn, Jeffry N. *chemicals executive, lawyer*
Rabbitt, Daniel Thomas, Jr. *lawyer*
Raclin, Grier C. *lawyer*
Rainwater, Gary L. *electric power industry executive*
Ramming, Michael Alexander *retired school system administrator*
Randolph, Jennings, Jr., (Jay Randolph) *sportscaster*
Rao, Dabeeru C. (D.C. Rao) *epidemiologist, educator*
Rasche, Robert Harold *banker, retired economics educator*
Raven, Peter Hamilton *botanical garden director, botany educator*
Rednam, Krishna Rao Venkata *ophthalmologist*
Reiss, Craig Keith *cardiologist, educator*
Rendlen, Charles Earnest, III, (Sketch Rendlen) *federal judge, lawyer*
Reynolds, Robert A., Jr. *electric distributor executive*
Rice, Patricia Jane *journalist*
Rice, Rose Ann M. *secondary school educator*
Rich, Harry Earl *corporate financial executive*
Rich, Keith M. *neurosurgeon*
Riddle, Veryl Lee *lawyer*
Riew, K. Daniel *cervical spine surgeon*
Ringkamp, Stephen H. *lawyer, educator*
Ritterskamp, Douglas Dolvin *lawyer*
Robbins, Arnie *editor-in-chief*
Roberts, Jeanne Delores *lawyer*
Robins, Lee Nelken *medical educator*
Rolen, Scott Bruce *professional baseball player*
Roodman, David A. *lawyer*
Rose, Albert Schoenburg *lawyer, educator*
Rosenbaum, Herbert Edwin *neurology educator*
Ross, Monte *electrical engineer, researcher*
Rovak, Stephen H. *lawyer*
Rowan, Steven William *history professor*
Royal, Henry Duval *nuclear medicine physician, educator, director*
Rubenstein, Jerome Max *lawyer*
Rudy, Yoram *biomedical engineer, biophysicist, educator*
Ruland, Richard Eugene *literature educator, critic, historian*
Ryall, Jo-Ellyn M. *psychiatrist*
Sachs, Alan Arthur *lawyer*
Sale, Llewellyn III *lawyer*
Sale, Merritt *classicist, educator, comparatist*
Salisbury, Robert Holt *political science professor*
Saltman, Robert Jon *physician, medical educator*
Sarder, Pinaki *research scientist*
Schaal, Barbara Anna *evolutionary biologist, educator*
Schindler, Laura Ann *piano teacher, accompanist*
Schlafly, Phyllis Stewart *writer*
Schneider, Amanda Jean *lawyer*
Schnuck, Craig D. *grocery store company executive*
Schoch, Alexander C. *lawyer, energy executive*
Schoenhard, William Charles, Jr. *health system executive*
Schonfeld, Gustav *medical educator, researcher, administrator*
Schramm, Paul Howard *lawyer*
Schwartz, Alan Leigh *pediatrician, educator*
Schwarz, Egon *language educator, writer, critic*
Schweizer, Gregory Paul *music educator*
Seabaugh, William F. *lawyer*
Seiler, James Elmer *judge*
Sestric, Anthony James *lawyer*
Setser, Christie Elaine *auditor*
Shanahan, Michael Francis *retired manufacturing executive, former hockey team executive*
Shapiro, Larry J. *pediatrician, educator, scientist, dean*
Shaw, Charles Alexander *judge*
Shepperd, Thomas Eugene *accountant*
Sherby, Kathleen Reilly *lawyer*
Shine, Katina Lynniece Wilbon *neuropsychologist, consultant*
Shostak, Burton H. *lawyer*
Shrauner, Barbara Wayne Abraham *electrical engineer, educator*
Shulkina, Tatyana *botanist, researcher*
Sibbald, John Ristow *management consultant*
Siegel, Barry Alan *radiologist*
Siemer, Paul Jennings *public relations executive*
Sigmund, Greg S. *investment company executive*
Sims, Gary Wayne *music educator*
Skarie, David P. *food products executive*
Skrainka, Alan Frederick *securities analyst*
Slatopolsky, Eduardo *nephrologist, educator*
Slavin, Raymond Granam *allergist, immunologist*
Sly, William S. *biochemist, educator*
Smit, Neil *telecommunications industry executive*
Smith, Arthur Lee *lawyer*
Smith, C. Grant *film producer, scriptwriter*
Smith, Karen Jody *education educator*
Smith, Morton Edward *ophthalmology educator, dean*
Snively, David Frederick *agricultural products company executive, lawyer*
Snyder, William W. *corporate financial executive*
Spector, Gershon Jerry *otolaryngologist, educator, researcher*
Sproule, James Michael *communications educator, writer*
Stacy, Zachary Aaron *pharmacist*
Staines, Gail M. *university librarian*
Stearley, Robert Jay *retired packaging company executive*
Stewart, John Harger *music educator*
Stoecker, David Thomas *retired banker*
Stohr, Donald J. *federal judge*
Stokes, Patrick T. *brewery company executive*
Stoneman, Mark L. *lawyer*
Stookesberry, Denise *music educator, musician*
Storandt, Martha *psychologist*
Stratmann, Gayle G. *lawyer, consumer products company executive*
Stretch, John Joseph *social worker, educator, management consultant*
Strevey, Tracy Elmer, Jr. *army officer, surgeon, health facility administrator*
Strunk, Robert Charles *physician*
Sullivan, Edward Lawrence *lawyer*
Sullivan, Steven R. *lawyer*
Sutera, Salvatore Philip *mechanical engineer, educator*
Sutter, Jane Elizabeth *conservationist, science educator*
Swain, David O. *manufacturing executive*
Swinson, Sara Hope *writer, chaplain*
Switzer, Frederick Michael III *lawyer, arbitrator, mediator*
Szabo, Barna Aladar *engineering educator*
Taylor, Andrew C. *rental and leasing company executive*
Taylor, Jack Crawford *rental and leasing company executive*
Teasdale, Kenneth Fulbright *lawyer*
Teitelbaum, Steven Lazarus *pathology educator*
Telowitz, Marilyn Marie *English and social studies educator*
Templeton, Alan Robert *biology professor*
Ternberg, Jessie Lamoin *pediatric surgeon, educator*
Terry, Nicholas P. *law educator*
Thach, William Thomas, Jr. *neurologist, educator*
Thalden, Barry *architect*
Tibi, Rigobert *seismologist, researcher*
Tiefenbrunn, Alan James *medical educator*
Tishler, Richard Norman *lawyer*
Tkachuk, Keith *professional hockey player*
Trinkaus, Erik *paleoanthropologist, educator*
Turcotte, John Arthur, Jr. *lawyer*
Turley, Michael Roy *lawyer*
Turner, Jonathan Shields *computer science educator, researcher*
Turner-Richard, Lana R. *musician, director, composer*
Tyler, William Howard, Jr. *advertising executive, educator*
van den Berg, Sara Jane *language educator*
Vandiver, Thomas K. *lawyer*
Van Fleet, Lisa A. *lawyer*
Virgo, John Michael *economist, researcher, educator*
Virgo, Katherine Sue *medical researcher*
Virtel, James John *lawyer*
Voss, Thomas R. *electric power industry executive*
Wack, Thomas E. *lawyer*
Wagner, Raymond Thomas, Jr. *lawyer, legal association administrator*
Walker, Doretta Anita *director*
Walker Tucker, Dana *lawyer*
Wallace, Kirk D. *research scientist*
Walsh, David Joseph *pediatric neurologist, educator*
Walsh, Joseph Leo III *lawyer*
Walsh, Thomas Charles *lawyer*
Waters, Richard *retired publishing executive*
Watters, Richard Donald *lawyer*
Weese, Cynthia Rogers *architect, educator*
Weidenbaum, Murray Lew *economist, educator*
Weight, Doug *professional hockey player*
Weiss, Charles Andrew *lawyer*

Weiss, Robert Francis *retired academic and religious organization administrator, consultant*
Weixlmann, Joseph Norman, Jr. *language educator, academic administrator*
Welch, David William *lawyer*
Welch, Michael John *chemistry educator, researcher*
Weldon, Virginia V. *retired food products executive, retired pediatrician*
Wellman, Carl Pierce *philosophy educator*
Wells, Samuel Alonzo, Jr. *surgeon, educator*
Whyte, Michael P. *genetics educator, researcher, director*
Wiggins, Dewayne Lee *financial executive*
Wilbanks, Donnie Jo *healthcare educator*
Wiley, Gregory Robert *publisher*
Wilkins, Addi L. *retired lay worker*
Will, Clifford Martin *physicist, researcher, educator*
Williams, Mary Alice Baldwin *retired home economist, volunteer*
Williams, Theodore Joseph, Jr. *lawyer*
Williamson, Keith Harvey *lawyer*
Williamson, Marilyn *retired secondary school educator*
Wilson, Edward Nathan *mathematician, educator*
Wilson, Margaret Bush *lawyer*
Wilson, Margaret Mary Georgiana *geriatrician, researcher, physician*
Wilson, Michael E. *lawyer*
Winter, Mildred M. *educational administrator*
Winter, Richard Lawrence *diversified financial services company executive*
Withers, W. Wayne *lawyer*
Witherspoon, William *investment economist*
Wolff, Frank Pierce, Jr. *lawyer*
Woolf, Steven Michael *artistic director*
Woolsey, Thomas Allen *neuroscientist, biologist*
Wright, Philip B. *lawyer*
Wrighton, Mark Stephen *academic administrator, chemistry professor*
Yaeger, Douglas Harrison *gas industry executive*
Yamaguchi, Ken *surgeon, educator*
Yarasheski, Kevin Edward *medical educator*
Yi, Xiaobin *anesthesiologist, pain management specialist*
Yokoyama, Wayne Makoto *medical educator, researcher, internist*
Young, Marvin Oscar *lawyer*
Young, Paul Andrew *anatomist*
Young, Vernon Leroy *plastic surgeon, researcher*
Zazulia, Allyson Robyn *neurologist, educator*
Zerman, Allan H. *lawyer*
Zinner, Ernst K. *physics educator, earth and planetary science educator, researcher*
Ziskind, Andrew A. *cardiologist, medical educator, health facility administrator*
Zonia, Dhimitri *artist*
Zurheide, Charles Henry *consulting electrical engineer*

Saint Peters
Beckmann, Bill *mortgage company executive*
Caples, Linda Griffin *retired secondary school educator*
Long, Lydia Ann *literature and composition professor*
Ranner, Shanna *music educator*
Thornton, Girard B., Jr., (Jerry) *elementary school educator*
Wang, William Weiqi *physician*

Salem
Wood, Thomas Wesley *humanities educator, editor*

Sarcoxie
Elliott, Diane Reid *history professor*

Sedalia
Chaar, Bassem T. *hematologist, oncologist*
Rice, James Briggs, Jr. *lawyer*

Smithville
Johnson, Darryl Thomas *communications educator*

Springfield
Amtower, Debra Lynn *nursing consultant*
Armstrong, Bill Howard *artist, educator*
Aull, Elizabeth Berryman *real estate development executive*
Baird, C. Ronald *lawyer*
Bartee, Wayne C. *retired history professor*
Baxter-Smith, Gregory John *lawyer*
Blake, Loretta L. *music educator*
Branstetter, Ann Dyche *psychology professor*
Budzinsky, Armin Alexander *investment banker*
Burgess, Ruth Lenora Vassar *speech and language educator*
Busch, Annie *library director*
Buttacy, Anthony *social studies educator*
Carlson, Thomas Joseph *real estate developer, lawyer*
Cassity, Michael David *music therapy educator*
Champion, Norma Jean *communications educator, state legislator*
Christian, John Catlett, Jr. *lawyer*
Clothiaux, Pierre Laurent *orthopedic surgeon*
Criswell, Charles Harrison (Harry) *analytical chemist, environmental and forensic consultant, executive*
Denton, D. Keith *management educator*
Dissmore, Larry David *musician, educator, conductor*
Easley, June Ellen Price *genealogist*
FitzGerald, Kevin Michael *lawyer, mediator*
Fredrick, LaRita Denise *science educator*
Geter, Rodney Keith *plastic surgeon*
Gill, Angela Sue *clinical psychologist*
Given, Mark *religious studies educator*
Glazier, Robert Carl *publishing executive*
Hackett, Earl Randolph *neurologist*
Hancock, Timothy Daniel *architect, musician*
Henslee, Gregory L. *automotive executive*
Horny, Karen Louise *library administrator*
Johnson, Eugene Lee *political scientist, history professor*
Jura, James J. *electric utility executive*
Kienstra, Matthew Allen *plastic surgeon*
McDonald, William Henry *lawyer*
Moran, Jon S. *humanities educator*
Moulder, T. Earline *musician*
O'Block, Robert *association, publishing executive*
O'Reilly, David E. *auto parts company executive*
Reed, Peggy Anne *education educator*
Rogers, Clayton Rush *application developer, small business owner, consultant*
Schnake, Richard Lane *lawyer*
Sherman, Ruth Todd *counseling administrator, educator*
Spicer, Holt Vandercook *retired theater educator*
Sutton, Kim Rochell *education educator*
Thompson, Clifton C. *retired chemistry professor, academic administrator*
Toste, Anthony Paim *chemistry educator, researcher*
Trask, Thomas Edward *religious organization administrator*
Verret, Daniel Joseph *otolaryngologist*
Wooten, Rosalie (Rosalie O'Reilly Wooten) *automotive company executive*

Stockton
Hammons, Brian Kent *lawyer*

Sturgeon
Fashing, Edward Michael *ranch owner, physical science educator*

Town And Country
Fagerberg, Roger Richard *lawyer*
Levin, Marvin Edgar *physician*

Trenton
Gentry, Shirley *music educator, writer*

Troy
Bockhorst, Barbara Alice *retired secondary school educator*
Lawrence, John R. *academic administrator*

Union
Boehmer, Ann *mathematics professor*
Schmelz, Brenda Lea *paralegal*

University City
McVey, Francis Daniel *mechanical engineer, software developer, educator*
Winter, David Ferdinand *electrical engineering educator, consultant*

Villa Ridge
Laskowski, Leonard Francis, Jr. *microbiologist*

Walker
Martin, Phillip Dwight *bank consulting company executive, mayor*

Walnut Shade
McCall, Charles Barnard *health facility administrator, educator*

Warrensburg
Jurkowski, Odin Lech *education educator*
Leonard, Raymond W. *historian, educator*
Yousef, Mahmoud *mathematics professor, computer scientist, educator*

Warrenton
Dapron, Elmer Joseph, Jr. *communications executive*

Washington
Chambers, Jerry Ray *school system administrator, consultant*
Houseman, Marc Alan *museum director*
Stelzner, Paul Burke *textile company executive*

Webb City
James, Kathryn A. *secondary school educator*

Webster Groves
Becker, Rex Louis *architect*
Conerly, Richard Pugh *retired manufacturing executive*

Wentzville
Berry, Chuck (Charles Edward Anderson Berry) *musician, composer*
Cowger, Gary L. *automotive executive*
Park, Young H. *dean*

West Plains
Wilcoxson, Roy Dell *plant pathologist, researcher, educator*

Wildwood
Truitt, William Harvey *private school educator*

Willow Springs
Jordan, Gilbert Fred *geophysicist, physicist*

Windyville
Condron, Barbara O'Guinn *philosopher, educator, academic administrator, writer*
Condron, Daniel Ralph *academic administrator, metaphysics educator*

Winona
Marshall, Lucille Ruth *retired mathematics professor*

MONTANA

Big Sky
Ryan, Raymond D. *retired steel and insurance company executive*
Strickler, Jeffrey Harold *pediatrician*

Bigfork
Wetzel, Betty Preat *writer*

Billings
Aldrich, Richard Kingsley *lawyer*
Barnea, Uri N. *rabbi, conductor, musician*
Cochran, William Michael *librarian*
Cromley, Brent Reed *lawyer, state senator*
DeRosier, Arthur Henry, Jr. *historian*
DeRosier, Linda Scott *psychologist, educator*
Fagg, Russell *judge, lawyer*
Fried, Michael D. *mathematician, educator*
Glenn, Guy Charles *pathologist*
Habein, Harold Clinton *retired surgeon*
Haughey, James McCrea *lawyer, artist*
Knapp, Howard Raymond *internist, clinical pharmacologist*
Larsen, Kimbert E. *journalist*
Larsen, Richard Lee *city manager, consultant, retired mayor, arbitrator*
Mace, Michael R. *academic administrator, real estate development consultant, mortgage executive*
Malee, Thomas *lawyer*
Mercer, William W. *prosecutor*
Nance, Robert Lewis *oil industry executive*
Paul, Bessie Margrette *retired weather forecaster*
Peterson, Robyn Gayle *museum director*
Sample, Joseph Scanlon *foundation executive*
Sexton, Ronald P. *academic administrator*
Sites, James Philip *lawyer*
Stapleton, Corey *financial planner*
Thomas, Sidney R. *federal judge*
Thompson, James William *lawyer*
Towe, Thomas Edward *lawyer*
Tryon, Margaret A. *director, school psychologist*

Bonner
Smith, Annick *writer*

Bozeman
Biegel, Debra Jeanne *music educator*
Buonamici, April Graham *elementary school and music educator*
Cokelet, Giles Roy *biomedical engineering educator*
Conover, Richard Corrill *lawyer*
Davis, Nicholas Homans Clark *finance company executive*
DeHaas, John Neff, Jr. *retired architecture educator*
Duffié, Mary Katharine *anthropologist, educator*
Gamble, Geoffrey *academic administrator*
Gogan, Peter John Patrick *biologist, researcher*
Gray, Philip Howard *former psychologist, writer, educator*
Grieco, Paul Anthony *chemistry professor*
Han, Jiaping *research scientist*
Horner, John Robert *paleontologist, researcher, curator*
Hufstetler, Mark Allan *historian*
Jacobsen, Jeffrey Scott *environmental scientist*
Nehrir, M. Hashem *electrical engineer, educator*
Nelson, Steven Dwayne *lawyer*
Patten, Duncan Theunissen *ecologist educator*
Sanddal, Nels Dodge *foundation executive, consultant*
Sanks, Robert Leland *environmental engineer, retired educator*
Stanislao, Joseph *engineering educator, consultant*
Vick, Jeffrey Harrison *musician, educator*
Warrick, Kimberley Kaye *language and social studies educator*
Weeden, Norman Frank *geneticist, educator*
Weller, Therese Marie *not-for-profit fundraiser*
Wylie, Paul Richter, Jr. *lawyer*

Butte
Clark, Gloria A. *music educator*
Gilmore, W. Franklin (Frank) *academic administrator*
Harrington, Dan William *state senator*
L'heureux, Richard Allen *academic administrator, consultant*
McCarthy, Bernard Francis *lawyer*
Weight, Willis D. *geologist, writer, engineering educator, consultant*

Clancy
Ekanger, Laurie *retired state official, consultant*

Columbia Falls
Spade-Shenker, George Lawrence (George Shenker) *research scientist*

Cut Bank
Roush, Glenn A. *state senator*

Dayton
Catalfomo, Philip *retired university dean*
von Volborth, Alex (Alexis) *geochemist, geological engineering educator*

Dillon
Storey, Richard D. *academic administrator, biology professor*
Tash, Bill *state senator*

Eureka
Atherton, Michael Ward *music educator*
Kessler-Hodgson, Lee Gwendolyn *actress, performing company executive*

Forsyth
Heser, Cheryl J. *library director*

Glendive
McDonough, Russell Charles *retired state supreme court justice*

Great Falls
Davidson, David Scott *retired architect*
Doherty, Steve *lawyer, state legislator*
Hartelius, Channing Julius *lawyer*
Hugg, Harold J. *music educator, director*
Johnson, Gordon James *performing company executive, conductor*
Knudson, Ruthann *environmental consultant, anthropologist, archaeologist*
Manning, John Willard *lawyer*
Walker, Leland Jasper *civil engineer*

Hamilton
Henley, Jack Carson *retired military officer*
Langton, Jeffrey H. *judge*

Harlem
Andrews, Robert Bruce, Jr. *physician, military officer*
Brekke, Alan Lee *industrial engineer*

Havre
Capdeville, Alex *academic administrator*
Freeman, Neil *accounting and computer consulting firm executive, owner*
Maristuen, Keith A. *lawyer*
Moog, Mary Ann Pimley *lawyer*

Helena
Benyus, Janine M. *writer*
Bohlinger, John C. *lieutenant governor, former state legislator*
Cooney, Mike *former secretary of state*
Cotter, Patricia O'Brien *state supreme court justice*
Fitzpatrick, Lois Ann *library administrator*
Goodwin, Annie M. *state agency administrator*
Gray, Karla Marie *state supreme court justice*
Harrison, John Conway *retired state supreme court justice*
Hill, Richard (Rick) Allan *former congressman*
Hunt, William Edward, Sr. *lawyer, retired state supreme court justice*
Johnson, Brad *state official*
Johnson, John Philip *geneticist, researcher*
Jones, Charles Irving *bishop*
Leaphart, W. William *state supreme court justice*
Maes, Paul Joel *dentist*
Mahlum, Dale Duane *state legislator, small business owner*
Manuel, Vivian *public relations executive*
McCulloch, Linda *school system administrator*
McGrath, Mike *state attorney general*
Meadows, Judith Adams *law librarian, educator*
Morris, Brian *state supreme court justice*
Morrison, John Martin *lawyer*
Nelson, James C *state supreme court justice*
Newell, Bruce *library director*
Pettit, Lawrence Kay *university president*
Probasco, Peggy Lee *lawyer*
Rice, Jim *state supreme court justice*
Schweitzer, Brian *governor*
Staffeldt, Darlene Maria Preble *library director*
Stearns, Sheila MacDonald *academic administrator*
Toole, Joan Trimble *financial consultant*
Warner, John Arnan *state supreme court justice*

Kalispell
Bledsoe, Drew *retired professional football player*
Freiberg, Robert Jerry *engineering executive*
Slater, Allen J. *music educator*
Vickers, Lee Louise *minister*

Lodge Grass
Rockabove, Magdalene M. *special education educator*

Medicine Lake
Nelson, Linda J. *state legislator*

Miles City
Coffman, Richard C. *retired protective services official*
Gerber, Robin *history and social sciences educator*

Missoula
Beal, Jon G. *lawyer*
Bowman, Jean Louise *lawyer, civic worker*
Brewer, Carol A. *biology professor*
Brown, Bob (Robert Joseph Brown) *former state official*
Brown, Perry Joe *dean*
Brown, Robert Munro *museum director*
Brumit, Lawrence Edward III *oil industry executive*
Dennison, George Marshel *academic administrator*
Fawcett, Don Wayne *retired anatomist*
George, Alexander Andrew *lawyer*
Haines, John Meade *poet, translator, writer*
Hulme, Janet A. *physical therapist, writer, small business owner*
Jakobson, Mark John *retired physics professor*
Kittredge, William Alfred *humanities educator*
Lopach, James Joseph *political science professor*
Millin, Laura Jeanne *museum director*
Molloy, Donald William *federal judge, lawyer*
Morales, Julio K. *lawyer*
Nygren, Christian Thomas *lawyer*
Schulte, John C. *lawyer*
Sullivan, Robert John *lawyer*
Tonev, Thomas (Toma) V. *mathematics professor*
Vogelsberg, Ross Timm *education educator, researcher*
Willey, Charles Wayne *lawyer*
Wollersheim, Janet Puccinelli *psychology professor*
Yee, Albert Hoy *writer, retired psychologist, educator*

Monarch
Baker, David Warren *earth scientist*

Polson
Marchi, Jon *retired brokerage house executive, rancher, venture capitalist*
Turnage, Jean Allen *retired state supreme court chief justice*

Pony
Anderson, Richard Ernest *agricultural engineer, consultant, rancher*

Rollins
Greer, Willis Roswell, Jr. *finance educator*

Three Forks
Woodriff, Lee *company executive*

Twin Bridges
Ruppel, Edward Thompson *geologist*

Victor
Davenport, Anne Marilyn *dietitian*

Whitefish
Carmichael, Gary Alan Alan *social studies educator*
DeFranco, Boniface Ferdinand Leonard (Buddy DeFranco) *clarinetist, bandleader*
Miller, Ronald Alfred *family physician*

Whitehall
Bernard, Donald Ray *retired law educator*

Wilsall
Adams, Dirk Standley *lawyer*

Winifred
Butcher, Edward Bernie *state senator*

Wolf Point
Morin, JoyAnn Hauge *education educator*

NEBRASKA

Adams
Nieveen, Teresa J. *elementary school educator*

Alliance
Haefele, Edwin Theodore *political theorist, consultant*

Arlington
Moskus, Jerry Ray *retired academic administrator*

Aurora
Lockmon, Nancy *mathematics educator*

Beatrice
Clawson, Rita Louise *curator*
Riedesel, Laureen Falk *library director*

Bellevue
Evans, Cleveland Kent *psychology professor*
Kayne, Jon Barry *academic administrator, psychologist*
Muller, John Bartlett *university president*

Benkelman
Whiteley, Rose Marie *city clerk, treasurer*

Bennington
Burgher, Louis William *physician, educator, academic administrator*

Blair
Hutton, Delvin Dwayne *retired theology studies educator, minister*

Boys Town
DiBacco, Nadine Louise *retired library director, photographer, writer*
DiBacco, T. Jay *financial services executive, retired military officer*
Lynch, Thomas Joseph *museum director*

Broken Bow
Sennett, John O. *lawyer*

Cedar Bluffs
Fleischman, Brian William *mathematics educator*

Chadron
Bump, Bevin B. *lawyer*
Younglove, Georgia A. *agricultural studies educator*

Chappell
Orr, Jim (James D. Orr) *editor, writer, publishing executive*

Clay Center
Hahn, George LeRoy *agricultural engineer, biometeorologist*

Columbus
Schumacher, Paul Maynard *lawyer*

Crete
Runestad, Kurt S. *music educator*

Elkhorn
Walk, Louis Bernard *physician*

Fort Calhoun
Ware, Frederick *internist, educator, nephrologist*

Fremont
Dunklau, Rupert Louis *financial planner, consultant*

Friend
De Bevoise, Lee Raymond *editor, writer*

Grand Island
Hesterman, Phillip Karl *music educator*

Harrison
Coffee, Virginia Claire *civic worker, former mayor*

Hastings
Dungan, John Russell, Jr., (12th Viscount Dungan of Clane, Hereditary Prince of Fermoy and Arra) *anesthesiologist, health facility administrator*

Holdrege
Hendrickson, Bruce Carl *life insurance company executive*

Kearney
Johnston, Gladys Styles *university official*
Voigt, Steven Russell *lawyer*

Kimball
Kinnison, Daniel E. *manufacturing engineer*
Walker, Judy Lou *special education educator, director*

Lincoln
Anderson, Sonya L. *physical therapist, educator*
Auld, James S. *educational psychologist*
Bahar, Ezekiel *electrical engineering educator*
Beam, Clarence Arlen *federal judge*
Beermann, Allen J. *former state official*
Blanke, Henry H., Jr. *retired theater educator*
Bradley, Richard Edwin *retired academic administrator*
Bruning, Jon Cumberland *state attorney general*
Bruskewitz, Fabian W. *bishop*
Callahan, Bill *college football coach*
Christensen, Douglas D. *school system administrator*
Collier, Nathan Morris *musician, educator*
Connolly, William M. *state supreme court justice*
Connor, Carol J. *library director*
Crump, Linda R. *lawyer*
Deegan, Mary Jo *sociologist*
Digman, Lester Aloysius *management educator*
Dixon, Wheeler Winston *film and video studies educator, writer*
Dunlap, Michael S. *student loan company executive*
Dyer, William Earl, Jr. *retired newspaper editor*
Eckhardt, Craig Jon *chemistry professor*
Edison, Allen Ray *electrical engineer, educator*
Edwards, Donald Mervin *systems engineer, educator, dean*
Fawcett-Yeske, Maxine Ann *music educator*
Fisher, Calvin David *food products executive*
Gale, John A. *state official*
Genoways, Hugh Howard *systematic biologist, educator*
Gerrard, John M. *state supreme court justice*
Giesecke, Joan Ruth *librarian, dean*
Grew, Priscilla Croswell *academic administrator, geologist, educator*
Guthery, John M. *lawyer*
Hansen-Daberkow, Michelle Len *elementary school art educator*
Hanway, Donald Grant *retired agronomist, educator*
Hardin, Martha Love Wood *civic leader*
Hastings, William Charles *retired state supreme court chief justice*
Hawley, Kimra *computer company executive*
Heavican, Michael G. *state supreme court justice*
Heineman, David Eugene *governor*
Hendry, John V. *retired state supreme court justice*
Hoffmann, Richard John *biology professor, dean*
Howlett, Ray *sculptor*
Jones, Lee Bennett *chemistry professor, academic administrator*
Kern, Jeanne Rustemeyer Wood *retired secondary school educator*
Koch Johns, Patricia A. *theater educator*
Koger, Michael Pigott *physician, writer*
Kopf, Richard G. *federal judge*
Kren, Josef *physiology professor*
Kristensen, Douglas Allan *former state legislator*
Lee, Sang M. *management educator*
Leinieks, Valdis *classicist, educator*
Leiter, Richard Allen *law librarian, educator*
Lichty, Warren Dewey, Jr. *lawyer*
Lienemann, Delmar Arthur, Sr. *accountant, real estate developer*
Lundstrom, Gilbert Gene *bank executive, lawyer*
Mach, Jan Ellen Walkenhorst *literature educator, editor*
MacPhee, Craig Robert *economist, educator*
Magorian, James *poet, writer*
Massengale, Martin Andrew *agronomist, educator, university president*
McCormack, Michael *state supreme court justice*
McCutcheon, Allan Lee *statistics educator*
Mendola, Joseph Robert *philosophy professor, department chairman*
Michels, Dale E. *physician*
Miller-Lerman, Lindsey *state supreme court justice*
Milligan, Cynthia Hardin *dean, lawyer*
Montag, John Joseph, II, *librarian*
Mulvaney, Mary Jean *retired physical education educator*
Munn, John *state agency administrator*
Nelson, Darrell Wayne *retired academic administrator, research scientist*
Norton, Hugo Wilbert, Jr. *journalism educator, dean*
Obafunwa, John Oladapo *academic administrator, pathologist, educator*
Ogle, Robbin Sue *criminal justice educator*
Osborn, Shane *state official*
Perlman, Harvey Stuart *academic administrator*
Piester, David L(ee) *magistrate judge*
Preister, Donald George *state legislator, greeting card manufacturer*
Reinhardt, John W. *dean, dental educator*
Rembolt, James Earl *lawyer*
Robak, Kim M. *lawyer*
Rosenow, John Edward *foundation executive*
Rowe, David Winfield *lawyer*
Salyards Burton, Shannon Marie *voice educator, singer*
Sawyer, Robert McLaran *historian, educator*
Schimek, DiAnna Ruth Rebman *state legislator*
Sellmyer, David Julian *physicist, researcher*
Seng, Coleen Joy *mayor*
Sheehy, Rick *lieutenant governor, former mayor*
Sicking, Dean L. *civil engineer, educator*
Smith, L. Dennis *former academic administrator*
Splinter, William Eldon *agricultural engineering educator*
Stange, James Henry *architect*
Starace, Anthony Francis *theoretical atomic physicist*
Steffan, Judy Mae *medical/surgical nurse*
Stephan, Kenneth C. *state supreme court justice*
Steward, Weldon Cecil *architecture educator, architect, consultant*
Stoddard, Robert H. *geography educator*
Sullivan, Robert Emmett *pediatric dentist, educator*
Tadesse, Tsegaye *climatologist, researcher*
Tavlin, Michael John *real estate company and manufacturing executive*
Taylor, Stephen Lloyd *toxicologist, educator, food scientist*
Urbom, Warren Keith *federal judge*
Vidaver, Anne Marie *plant pathology educator*
Wagner, Rod *library director*
White, Tyler Goodrich *composer, conductor*
Wiersbe, Warren Wendell *clergyman, writer, lecturer*
Willborn, Steven L. *dean, law educator*
Wilson, Charles Stephen *cardiologist, educator*
Woollam, John Arthur *electrical engineering educator, physics professor*
Wright, John F. *state supreme court justice*
Yoder, Bruce Alan *chemist*

Lindsay
Parker, Gary Dean *manufacturing executive*

Lyons
Rose, Dwight Dean *music educator*

Mc Cook
Regier, Bryan L. *music educator*
Watts, Susan Helene *theater educator*

Neligh
Kinnan, Sharon Jo *elementary school educator*

Omaha
Achelpohl, Steven Edward *lawyer*
Armitage, James O. *medical educator*
Badeer, Henry Sarkis *physiology educator*
Baker, Gail *director, ESL educator*
Baltaro, Richard J. *pathologist, medical educator*
Bang, Michele Alene *protective services official*
Barker, Thomas B. *information technology executive*
Barrett, Frank Joseph *lawyer, insurance company executive*
Batchelder, Anne Stuart *retired publishing executive, political organization worker*
Belck, Nancy Garrison *dean, educator*
Benson, John Alexander, Jr. *internist, educator*
Bergt, Gregory Paul *chemist, consultant*
Boamah-Wiafe, Daniel *geographer, researcher*
Bolles, Al *food products executive*
Brownrigg, John Clinton *lawyer*
Bruckner, Martha *academic administrator*
Buffett, Warren Edward *entrepreneur, investment company executive*
Caggiano, Joseph *advertising executive*
Caporale, D. Nick *lawyer*
Cappellano, Rosemarie Zaccone *small business owner*
Carson, Ron *investment company executive*
Casale, Thomas Bruce *medical educator*
Chow, Joan K. *food products executive*
Creigh, James Carey *lawyer*
Cross, Walter Thomas *investment company executive*
Crouse, Jerry K. *energy company executive*
Curtiss, Elden Francis *archbishop*
Dahlk, Thomas Harlan *lawyer*
Daub, Hal (Harold John Daub Jr.) *lawyer*
Derrick, Deborah Ball *editor, writer*
De Santiago, Dena Kalene *investment company executive, writer*
Dittrick, William G. *lawyer*
Duffy, Dennis J. *rail transportation executive*
Eggers, James Wesley *executive search consultant*
Eisele, Charles R. *rail transportation executive*
Fahey, Mike *mayor*
Fairfield, Bill L. *finance company executive*
Faith, Marshall E. *grain company executive*
Fellman, Richard Mayer *retired lawyer*
Fennell, Madaline *elementary school educator*
Foster, Betty Louise *secondary school educator*
Fusaro, Ramon Michael *dermatologist, preventive medicine physician, researcher*
Gehring, John F. *food products executive*
Gerteis, Christopher *history educator*
Gleason, James Mullaney *lawyer, insurance company executive*
Goslee, Dwight J. *agricultural products executive*
Grewcock, Bruce E. *construction and mining executive*
Hachten, Richard Arthur, II, *healthcare system executive*
Hamann, Deryl Frederick *lawyer, bank executive*
Hamburg, Marc D. *investment company executive*
Haney, J. Terrence *retired insurance consultant*
Hansen, James Allen *state agency administrator*
Hardy, Jim, Jr. *food products executive*
Hawaux, André J. *food products executive*
Hawks, Howard L. *energy executive*
Heckman, Gregory A. *food products executive*
Hemmer, J. Michael *lawyer, rail transportation executive*
Hermsen, Kenneth Paul *dental educator, forensic odontologist*
Hodgson, Paul Edmund *surgeon, department chairman*
Hoie, Eric B. *pharmacist, educator*
Hollis, Dean *food products executive*
Houser, Kevin *engineering educator*
Howard, Thomas Clement *surgeon*
Hupp, Michael M. *lawyer*
Huse, Frank Peter *lawyer*
Huurman, Walter William *pediatric orthopaedic surgeon, educator*
Imray, Thomas John *radiologist, educator*
Jaksich, Daniel J. *controller*
Jansen, James Steven *lawyer*
Jenkins, Melvin Lemuel *lawyer*
Jensen, Sam *lawyer*
Jetter, Arthur Carl, Jr. *insurance company executive*
Johnson, James David *concert pianist, organist, educator*
Johnson, Owen C. *food products executive*
Khoynezhad, Ali *cardiothoracic surgeon, researcher*
Kimmes, Nicole S. *dentist, educator*
Knight, Robert M., Jr. *rail transportation executive*
Knudsen, Doug *food products executive*
Koraleski, John J. *rail transportation executive*
Korbitz, Bernard Carl *hematologist, consultant*
Krutter, Forrest Nathan *lawyer*
Kuhlman, Thomas Ashford *retired American studies educator, writer*
Lee, Dennis Patrick *lawyer, judge*
Lieben, Thomas Geoffrey *lawyer*
Louis, Virgie Lee *retired secondary school educator*
Louisa, Angelo Joseph *social studies educator, researcher*
Lynch, Benjamin Leo *oral surgeon, educator*
Mactier, Ann Dickinson *state agency administrator*
Madariaga, Miguel G. *epidemiologist*
Mardis, Hal Kennedy *urological surgeon, educator, researcher*
Mark, Wayne Joseph *lawyer*
Maurer, Harold Maurice *pediatrician*
Maydwell, Robert Mason, Jr. *social sciences educator*
McCook, Jacqueline K. Heslop *food products executive*
McCusker, Thomas J. *lawyer, insurance company executive*
Mew, Calvin Marshall *advertising executive*
Moglia, Joseph H. *brokerage house executive*
Mohiuddin, Syed Maqdoom *cardiologist, educator*
Munger, Charles T. *diversified company executive*
Neary, Daniel P. *insurance company executive*
Newton, John Milton *academic administrator, psychologist, educator*
O'Brien, Richard L(ee) *physician, educator, academic administrator*
Pamies, Rubens John *dean*
Perez, Peter Michael *food products executive*
Plotkin, Horacio *pediatric endocrinologist, orthopedic surgeon, educator*
Polsky, Donald Perry *architect*
Pouw, King T. *food products executive*
Rainey, Deana Lee Parks *language educator*
Reiser, Richard Scott *lawyer*
Ricketts, John Joe *securities company executive*
Riley, William Jay *federal judge*
Rock, Harold L. *lawyer*
Rodkin, Gary M. *food products executive*
Rogan, Eleanor Groeniger *oncologist, educator*
Roskens, Ronald William *management consultant, retired academic administrator*
Ross, Donald Roe *federal judge*
Ryan, Mark Anthony *architect, lawyer*
Ryan, Sheila A. *retired dean, nursing educator*
Ryan, Shelli Ann *public relations executive*
Sankaranarayanan, Jayashri *medical educator*
Sass, Rivkah K. *library director*
Sasson, Aaron R. *surgeon*
Schaefer, Barbara W. *rail transportation executive*
Schilken, Michael C. *lawyer*
Schlessinger, Joel *dermatologist, researcher, entrepreneur*
Schropp, Tobin *lawyer*
Scott, Walter, Jr. *telecommunications industry executive*
Seitz, Carole Jane *composer, educator*
Shanahan, Thomas M. *judge*
Sharpe, Robert Francis, Jr. *lawyer, food products executive*
Shilling, Kay Marlene *psychiatrist*
Simmons, Lee Guyton, Jr. *zoological park director*
Skoog, Donald Paul *retired pathologist, educator*
Smithey, Donald Leon *airport authority director*
Sooriyaarachchi, Gamini Sarathchandra *oncologist, hematologist, educator*
Stecher, Joe W. *prosecutor*
Stenberg, Donald B. *lawyer*
Stinson, Kenneth E. *construction and mining company executive*
Strawhecker, Paul Joseph *fundraising consultant*
Strom, Lyle Elmer *judge*
Swindells, Susan *HIV specialist*
Tennison, Lynden *rail transportation executive*
Thorson, Alan Glen *surgeon*
Tinker, John Heath *anesthesiologist, educator*
Tomczyk, Fredric J. *brokerage house executive*
Treves, John *neurosurgeon*
Tunnicliff, David George *retired civil engineer*
Turner, Robert W. *rail transportation executive*
Vosburg, Bruce David *lawyer*
Ward, Vernon Graves *retired internist*
Wells, Roger W. *lawyer*
Werner, Clarence L. *transportation executive*
Werner, Gregory L. *transportation executive*
Wilson, Daniel Richard *anthropologist, physician*
Wilson, John Human III *curator, art historian*
Winter, Jimmy *entrepreneur, systems administrator*
Wunsch, James Stevenson *political science professor*
Young, James R. *rail transportation executive*
Zaiman, K(oichi) Robert *dentist*
Zepf, Thomas Herman *retired physics professor*

Oneill
Hedren, Paul Leslie *parks director, historian*

Papillion
Dvorak, Allen Dale *radiologist*
Snelling, James Anthony *biology professor, technologist*
Zuerlein, Damian Joseph *priest*

Scottsbluff
Kabalin, John Nicholas *urologist*
Shoemaker, Troy *hazardous materials response team coordinator, fire captain*
Wylie, Guy Stephen *psychologist, educator*

Seward
Bork, Ronald Dale *academic administrator*
Wolfram, William Ray *artist, educator*

Sidney
Cabela, Richard N. *retail executive*
Highby, Dennis *retail executive*
Zigweid, Richard Neil *music educator*

Sutton
Johnson, Michael Randy *bank executive*

Taylor
Brown, Kevin Paul *secondary school educator*

Waverly
Jensen, Daniel *history educator*

Wayne
Weixelman, Joseph Owen *history professor*

Winnebago
Bauer-Sanders, Katherine Ann *primary school educator*

York
McNeese, Beverly Diane *language educator*

NEVADA

Boulder City
Fisher, Paul Cary *writing supplies company executive*
Johnsen, Ken C. *steel products company executive*
McBride, Dennis Ray *curator, writer*
Schultheis, Adam John *music educator, consultant*
Stephenson, Arthur Emmet, Jr. *investment company executive*
Wyman, Richard Vaughn *engineering educator, company executive*

Carson City
Agosti, Deborah Ann *retired senior justice*
Alexander, Judy Lynne *investor*
Ayres, Janice Ruth *social services administrator*
Brant, James William *educational consultant, mathematician, educator*
Burns, Dan W. *manufacturing executive*
Cherry, Michael A. *state supreme court justice*
Crawford, John Edward *retired geologist, consultant*
Eftimoff, Anita Kendall *retired educational consultant*
Gibbons, Jim (James Arthur Gibbons) *governor, former congressman*
Gibbons, Mark *state supreme court justice*
Hardesty, James *state supreme court justice*
Jones, Sara Sue Fisher *librarian*
Krolicki, Brian Keith *lieutenant governor, former state official*
Marshall, Kate *state official*
Masto, Catherine Marie Cortez *state attorney general, former county official*
Maupin, A. William *state supreme court justice*
McCarthy, Ann Price *lawyer*
Miller, Ross James *state official, prosecutor*
Parraguirre, Ronald David *state supreme court justice*
Rheault, Keith W. *school system administrator*
Rocha, Guy Louis *archivist, consultant, historian*
Saitta, Nancy M. *state supreme court justice*
Theiss, Jane I. *music educator*
Welch, Richard LeRoy *personal improvement company executive*

Cold Springs
Turner VanLydegraf, Claudia Beth *writer, researcher*

Elko
Heller, Dean *congressman, former state official*
Lesbo, Paula Mae *elementary and secondary education educator*
Puccinelli, Andrew James *lawyer*
Vaughan, Robert Oren *lawyer*

Ely
Alderman, Minnis Amelia *psychologist, educator, small business owner*
Daniels, Frank Emmett *mathematician, educator*

Fallon
Jones, Gilbert Leed *retired law enforcement officer, coroner, author, educator*

Gardnerville
Griffiths, Barbara Lorraine *psychologist, writer, marriage and family therapist*

Genoa
Goode, John Martin *manufacturing executive*

Glenbrook
Goldsmith, Harry Sawyer *surgeon, educator*

Hawthorne
Pierce, Mildred Louise *librarian*

Henderson
Anspaugh, Lynn Richard *research biophysicist*
Berns, Philip Allan *lawyer*
Bruno, Cathy Eileen *management consultant, former state official, social sciences educator*
Cambeiro, Arthur Michael *plastic surgeon*
Cohan, George Sheldon *advertising and public relations executive*
Fay, Thomas F. *library director*
Fehr, Gregory Paris *marketing and distribution company executive*
Freyd, William Pattinson *not-for-profit fundraiser, director*
Goldstein, Morris *retired consumer products company executive*
Holloway, Robert Wester *radiochemist*
Johnson, Joan Bray *insurance company consultant*
Keene, Richard Brian *school system administrator, educational consultant*
Kelley, Michael John *newspaper editor*
Lang, Sheldon *pathologist*
Marcovitz, Leonard Edward *retail executive*
Maryanski, Fred J. *academic administrator*
McKinney, Sally Vitkus *state official*
Meinel, Aden Baker *optics scientist*
Oesterman, Paul Joseph *pharmacist, educator*
Schwartz, Richard *retired lawyer*
Teemant, Melanie J. *middle school educator*
Thomas, James Patrick *special education educator*
Tierno, Joel Thomas *philosopher, educator*
Trivelpiece, Alvin William *physicist, educator, consultant*
Van Noy, Terry Willard *health care executive*
Wax, Arnold *physician*
Wennerstrom, Arthur John *aeronautical engineer*
Wieting, Gary Lee *federal agency executive*
Wills, Robert Hamilton *retired publishing executive*

Incline Village
Duffield, David A. *application developer, former computer software company executive*
Johnston, Bernard Fox *foundation executive, writer*
Jones, Robert Alonzo *economist*
Large, Larry Denton *academic administrator*
Merdinger, Charles John *civil engineer, educator, military officer, academic administrator*
Mitton, Michael Anthony *environmental technology company executive*
Strack, Harold Arthur *retired electronics executive, military officer, financial consultant, musician, writer*
Thompson, David Alfred *industrial engineer*
Yount, George Stuart *paper company executive*

Indian Springs
Dvorak, DeLyle Dennis *music and early childhood educator, consultant*

Las Vegas
Adelson, Sheldon Gary *hotel and gaming company executive*
Ahmad, Shamoon *hematologist, oncologist, consultant*
Ananias, José *retired school system administrator*
Arce, Phillip William *hotel and casino executive*
Arell, Bobby Ray, Jr. *pharmaceutical executive, management consultant*
Arum, Robert *lawyer, sports events promoter*
Ashley, David B. *academic administrator, engineering educator*
Atwood, Charles L. *recreational facility executive*
Baker, Anita *singer*
Baloglu, Seyhmus *hospitality and tourism educator*
Barbagallo, Al T. *real estate company executive*
Becker, Nancy Anne *former state supreme court justice*
Bernhard, Peter C. *lawyer, state agency administrator*
Bernstein, Maureen Ann *theater educator, director*
Bersi, Ann *lawyer*
Bishop, Leo Kenneth *clergyman, educator*
Boman, Keith Gregory *cardiologist*
Boyd, William S. *hotel and gaming company executive*
Brammell, Stephen Harrison *lawyer*
Bridges, B. Ried *lawyer*
Broca, Laurent Antoine *aerospace scientist*
Brock, Holly Melinda *marketing professional*
Bryan, Richard H. *lawyer, educator, former senator*
Buckley, Michael Edward *lawyer*
Buzard, Kurt Andre *ophthalmologist*
Bybee, Jay Scott *federal judge, former federal agency administrator*
Chesnoff, David Zeltner *lawyer*
Cole, Ann Harriet *psychologist, consultant*
Collins, Frank Edwin *lawyer*
Consul, Vincent A. *lawyer*
Culp, Gordon Louis *consulting engineer, management consultant*
Curran, William P. *lawyer*
Das, Biswajit *electrical engineer, educator*
DeBusk, Lorraine *elementary school educator*
Derrick, William Dennis *retired physical plant administrator, consultant*
Dill, Ellen Renée *minister, educator, writer*
Donaghy, Henry James *literature educator, academic administrator*
Douglas, Michael Lawrence *state supreme court justice*
Duke, Edward Marion, III, (Mickey Duke) *health facility administrator, consultant*
Duncombe, Patricia Warburton *retired social worker*
Duva-Mikhail, Donna Marie *financial executive*
Ecker, Howard *lawyer*
Edualino, Emilio Quial *school educator*
Egidio, Martha L. *real estate broker and salesman*
Ehrlich, Bruce Jay *media consultant, psychologist, writer*
Ensign, Michael S. *resort company executive*
Ernst, Suzanne *academic administrator, educator*
Eskin, Jeffrey Laurence *lawyer*
Faiss, Robert Dean *lawyer*
Ferrillo, Patrick J., Jr. *dean, endodontist*
Frances, Marie Cecilia *theater producer, television producer*
Francis, Timothy Duane *chiropractor*
Freeman-Clark, J. P. Ladyhawk *vicar, underwater exploration, security and transportation executive, model*
French, Richard Harry *hydrologic and hydraulic engineer, consultant*
Frigard, Monique Denise *journalist*
Gafford, Mary May Grimes *retired humanities educator*
Gardner, Grace Joely *writer, consultant, psychologist*
Garn, Susan Lynn *art educator*
Gaspar, Anna Louise *retired elementary school educator, consultant*
Gentile, Dominic P. *lawyer*
Gilchrist, Ann Roundey *medical/surgical nurse*
Goldblatt, Hal Michael *photographer*
Goodall, Leonard Edwin *public administration educator*
Goodenberger, Daniel Marvin *medical educator*
Goodman, Oscar Baylin *mayor, lawyer*
Goodwin, John Robert *lawyer, educator, writer*
Gostin, Irwin *retired lawyer*
Greene, Addison Kent *lawyer, accountant*
Griesche, Robert Price *hospital purchasing executive*
Gubler, John Gray *lawyer*
Haas, Robert John *aerospace engineer*
Hall, Gene E. *education educator*
Hardie, George Graham *casino executive*
Hartley, Thomas Y. *gas industry executive*
Hellmuth, Phil (Phillip J. Hellmuth Jr.) *professional poker player*
Henderson, Jeff *chef*
Herridge, Elizabeth *museum director*
Herzlich, Harold J. *chemical engineer*
Higgins, Walter M. III *electric power industry executive*
Hilbrecht, Norman Ty *lawyer*
Hill, Judith Deegan *retired lawyer*
Hobbs, Guy Stephen *financial executive*
Hoepfner, Mark Thomas *surgeon*
Hua, Fred Huizhong *materials scientist*
Huff, Dennis Lyle *marketing professional*
Huston, Joyce A. *entertainment and publishing company executive*
Jabara, Michael Dean *real estate developer, former technology entrepreneur*
Jackson, Charles Anthony *music educator, radio personality*
Jackson, Phillip Ellis *marketing executive, writer*
Jacobs, Gary N. *lawyer, hotel executive*
Jakopec, Carl Thomas *pharmaceutical executive*
James, Mark A. *lawyer, former state legislator*
James, Phyllis A. *lawyer*
Jarvis, Renee Marie *language educator*
Jost, Richard Frederic III *lawyer*
Kamer, Gregory Jay *lawyer*
Kardum, Karmen Ana *lawyer*
Kasama, Hideto Peter *international business and investment advisor*
Kendell, Ken *music educator*
Kennedy, Margaret Alexis *law educator, researcher*
Kirsch, Lynn *lawyer*
Knight, Gladys (Gladys Maria Knight) *singer*
Kondrup, Steven W. *state agency administrator*
Kruger, Lon *men's college basketball coach*
Kurlinski, John Parker *physician*
Lally, Norma Ross *retired federal agency administrator*
Lanni, Terry (Joseph Terrence Lanni) *hotel corporation executive*
Larson, Brian A. *lawyer*
Laub, William Murray, Sr. *retired utilities executive*
Lee, Theodore Bo *real estate developer*
Leleu, Jonathan Paul *lawyer*
Levasseur, Mark *dean*
Lewis, Jerry (Joseph Levitch) *comedian*
Loveman, Gary W. *gaming company executive*
Luckett, Byron Edward, Jr. *chaplain, retired military officer*
MacPherson, Grant *chef*
Mahan, James Cameron *judge*
Manley, Edward Harry, Jr. *professional association administrator, food products executive, retired military officer*
Mansfield, Lorraine J. *lawyer*
Marcella, Joseph *information scientist*
Marlon, Anthony M. *healthcare company executive, cardiologist*
Marnell, Anthony Austin, II, *architect*
Martinez, Adriana *photographer*
Massier, Paul Ferdinand *mechanical engineer*
Mataseje, Veronica Julia *sales executive*
Mc Elroy, John Harley *electrical and industrial engineering educator*
McNulty, James Francis, Jr. *lawyer, consultant*
Meiner, Sue Ellen Thompson *adult nurse practitioner, consultant, gerontologist*
Mellor, Eli *diversified financial services company executive, writer*
Merkin, Albert Charles *pediatrician, allergist*
Merrill, Wendy Jane *financial services company executive*
Messenger, George Clement *engineering executive, consultant*
Michel, Mary Ann Kedzuf *retired nursing educator*
Miller, Valerie Carol *journalist*
Morgan, Richard J. *dean, law educator*
Moritz, Timothy Bovie *psychiatrist*
Moss, Gary Curtis *lawyer*
Muhlenbruck-Fleischer, Deborah Lynn *music educator*
Murren, James Joseph *hotel executive*
Neilsen, Craig H. *hotel executive*
Neumann, Edward Schreiber *transportation engineering educator*
Nicholson, R. Stephen *former cultural organization administrator*
Noback, Richardson Kilbourne *medical educator*
Norville, Craig Hubert *lawyer*
Oshins, Steven Jeffrey *lawyer*
Palmer, Lynne *writer, astrologer*
Palmieri, Frederick William *structural engineer*
Parry, Clint *business coaching executive*
Pierce, Thresia Korte (Tish Pierce) *primary school educator*
Pitaro, Thomas F. *lawyer*
Pro, Philip Martin *judge*
Ramos, Albert A. *electrical engineer*
Ramsey, Inez Linn *librarian, educator*
Rapoport, Nancy B. *law educator*
Rawlinson, Johnnie Blakeney *federal judge*
Rodefer, Jeffrey Robert *lawyer*
Rolff, James Robert *retired locomotive engineer, writer*
Rothrock, Carson *music educator*
Sadineni, Suresh Babu *research scientist*
Sakugawa, June Elizabeth *music educator*
Sanders, Charlotta Elisabeth *nuclear engineer, educator*
Satre, Philip Glen *casino entertainment executive, lawyer*
Schaeffer, Glenn William *casino corporate financial executive*
Schaffer, Martin David *cardiologist*
Scherf, Dietmar *publishing executive, artist, minister*
Shaw, Jeffrey William *gas industry executive*
Sheets, Thomas R. *lawyer, gas industry executive*
Shires, George Thomas *surgeon, educator*
Shively, Judith Carolyn (Judy Shively) *administrative assistant*
Shuman, R. Baird *academic administrator, consultant, language educator, writer*
Sillerman, Robert F. X. *communications executive, banker*
Singer, Clifford *mathematics educator, artist*
Singer, Michael Howard *lawyer*
Sklar, Alan Curtis *lawyer*
Smith, Keith E. *hotel and gaming company executive*
Snyder, Arthur Kress *lawyer, restaurant owner*
Snyder, John Henry *computer science educator, consultant*
Solomon, Jack Avrum, Jr. *lawyer, automotive executive, art dealer*
Sorrell, Michael E. *consulting company executive, hospitality executive*
Speck, Eugene Lewis *internist*
Spencer, Carol Brown *retired educational association administrator*
Stanley, Tim *information technology executive*
Stark, S. Daniel, Jr. *casino and gaming resort company executive*
Stein, Stephen *lawyer*
Stoberski, Michael Edward *lawyer*
Sullivan, Christopher David *real estate broker, real estate attorney*
Tash, Martin Elias *publishing company executive*
Terry, William B. (Bill) *lawyer*
Vogelzang, Nicholas John *medical oncologist*
Wakefield, Marie A. *counselor, educational association administrator*
Walker, Randall H. *air transportation executive*
Walters, Daniel L. *library director*
Weeks, Gerald *psychologist, educator*
Welter, William Michael *marketing and advertising executive*
White, Dana *sports association executive*
Wiemer, Robert Ernest *film and television producer, writer, director*
Wiener, Valerie *state senator, writer, communications executive*
Williams, Mary Irene *business education educator*
Wilson, Joseph Morris III *lawyer*
Wright, Rick (Richard A. Wright) *lawyer*
Wynn, Steve Alan (Stephen A. Wynn) *hotel and gaming company executive*
Yackira, Michael William *electric power industry executive*
Zamboni, William Arnold *plastic and reconstructive surgeon, lab director*

Logandale
Smiley, Robert William, Jr. *investment banker*

Nellis Afb
Malachowski, Nicole *pilot*

North Las Vegas
Folden, Norman C. (Skip Folden) *information systems executive, consultant*
Janzen, Donna Lee (Bricker) *music educator, singer*
Kubilus, Norbert John *information technology executive*
Manley, Audrey Forbes *retired academic administrator, pediatrician, retired military officer*
Nisbett, Robert F. *music educator, consultant*

Pahrump
Evans, Charles Wayne, II, *biologist, researcher*
Noble, Alice L. *writer, researcher*

Reno
Akiyama, Toshio *cardiologist, educator, researcher, director*
Aldrich, Gary O. *singer, educator*
Bell, Robert Cecil *lawyer*
Binns, James Edward *retired banker*
Bonaldi-Moore, Lorraine Kay *nursing educator*
Brunetti, Melvin T. *federal judge*
Carr, James Russell *engineering educator*
Cathey-Gibson, Sharon Sue Rinn *principal, academic administrator*
Chapman, Samuel Greeley *political science professor, criminologist*
Chrystal, William George *retired minister*
Clontz, Donna *lawyer, writer, consultant*

Crognale, Michael Anthony *medical educator, neuroscientist, consultant*
Crowley, Joseph Neil *political science professor, former academic administrator*
Cummings, Nancy *library director*
Cummings, Nicholas Andrew *psychologist*
Cunningham, Steve *orthopedic surgeon*
Daniels, Ronald Dale *conductor*
Danko, George *engineering educator*
Dietrich, Dean Forbes *academic administrator*
Feinhandler, Edward Sanford *writer, photographer, art dealer*
Fletcher, Douglas Charles *lawyer*
Ford, Victoria *retired public relations executive, writer, oral historian*
Fox, Mark *men's college basketball coach*
Frank, Lillian Gorman *human resources executive, management consultant*
Fuerstenau, M(aurice) C(lark) *metallurgical engineer*
Gifford, Gerald Frederic *retired science educator*
Glick, Milton Don *academic administrator, chemist*
Glotfelty, Cheryll *literature and language professor*
Goin, Peter Jackson *art educator*
Goodenow, Rew R. *lawyer*
Gundersen, Wayne Campbell *energy executive, consultant*
Guneyi, Umit Ahmet *physician, consultant*
Harsh, Antoinette Mollett *investor*
Hayes, Steven Charles *psychologist, educator*
Hengstler, Gary Ardell *publisher, editor, lawyer*
Heyvaert, Alan *environmental scientist, educator*
Hibbs, Loyal Robert *lawyer*
Hill, Earl McColl *lawyer*
Howard, Christopher Philip *management consultant, investor*
Hug, Procter Ralph, Jr. *federal judge*
Hunterton, C. Stanley *lawyer*
Jacobson, Raymond Earl *electronics executive*
Johnson, David D. *lawyer, game company executive*
Johnson, Jeffrey David *artist*
Kaleta, Paul J. *lawyer, utilities executive*
Kemmelmeier, Markus *sociologist, psychologist, educator*
Kent, Stephen Smiley *lawyer*
Kleinfeld, Erwin *mathematician, educator*
Kleppe, John Arthur *electrical engineer, educator, company executive*
Leland, Joy Hanson *retired anthropologist, researcher*
MacKintosh, Frederick Roy *oncologist*
Mandl, William John *electronics engineer, researcher*
Matthews, Thomas J. *game company executive*
McCarty-Puhl, J-Petrina *chemistry educator*
McKibben, Howard D. *federal judge*
Middlebrooks, Deloris Jeanette *retired nursing educator*
Mitchell, David Lancaster *research educator*
Murray, Alison Elizabeth *microbiologist, educator, researcher*
Pagni, Albert Frank *lawyer*
Perry, Jean Louise *academic administrator*
Pinson, Larry Lee *pharmacist, state agency administrator*
Price, Jonathan G. *geologist*
Ragavan, Anpalaki Jeyabalasinkham *software developer, researcher*
Raggio, William John *state legislator*
Reed, Edward Cornelius, Jr. *federal judge*
Ross, Robert Donald *library director*
Sandoval, Brian Edward *federal judge, former state attorney general*
Santos, Herbert Joseph, Jr. *lawyer*
Savoy, Douglas Eugene *bishop, writer, religious studies educator*
Scrimgeour, Gary James *writer, educator*
Shoen, Edward Joseph *transportation and insurance companies executive*
Sladek, Ronald John *physics professor*
Small, Elisabeth Chan *psychiatrist, educator*
Svahn, John Alfred *federal agency administrator*
Taranik, James Vladimir *geologist, educator*
Tedford, Jack Nowlan III *construction executive, small business owner*
Walrath, Harry Rienzi *retired minister*
Walther, Steven T. *lawyer*
Weinberg, Leonard Burton *political scientist*
Welcome, Richard Mark *radiologist*
White, John, Jr. *lawyer*
Zager, Bernard Solomon *physician, consultant*
Zaliapin, Ilya *statistician*
Zanjani, Esmail D. *medical educator, research scientist*

Sandy Valley
Viscuglia, Jenny Lou *music educator*

Sparks
Bonham, Harold Florian *research geologist, consultant*
Boyer, Patricia W. *publishing executive, editor*
Holder, Harold Douglas, Sr. *investor, hotel executive*
Trabitz, Eugene Leonard *aerospace company executive*

Winnemucca
Hesse, Martha O. *gas industry executive*
Westmoreland, Jessie Allred *literature educator*

Yerington
Price, Judith Holm *educational psychologist*
Price, Thomas Munro *computer consultant*
Scatena, Lorraine Borba *retired rancher, women's rights advocate, researcher*

Zephyr Cove
Hudzinski, Leonard Gerard *social sciences educator, researcher*

NEW HAMPSHIRE

Alstead
Holloway, Robert Charles *musician, composer*

Amherst
Atwater, Verne Stafford *finance educator*
Johnson, Daryl Diane *painter*
Soneira, Raymond Mario *computer company executive, scientist*

Antrim
Scales, John Thomas *state official*

Auburn
Herman, William George *municipal official*

Bedford
Cronin, Timothy Cornelius III *computer manufacturing executive*
Hall, Pamela S. *environmental services administrator*
Steadman, David Rosslyn Ayton *corporate financial executive, director*

Bennington
Verney, Richard Greville *paper company executive*

Berlin
Doherty, Katherine Mann *librarian, writer*

Bow
Emery, Paul Emile *psychiatrist*

Brentwood
Boozer-Blasco, Claudia Ruth *family and consumer resources educator*

Campton
Benton, Geraldine Ann *preschool owner, director*
Scrimshaw, Nevin Stewart *physician, nutritionist, educator*

Center Harbor
Shaw, Robert William, Jr. *management consultant, venture capitalist*

Center Sandwich
Booty, John Everitt *retired theology studies educator*

Colebrook
Bernard, Susan Shattuck *retired secondary school educator*
Bernard, Wilbert Auguster, Jr. *retired school system administrator*

Concord
Ayotte, Kelly A. *state attorney general*
Bagan, Merwyn *neurological surgeon*
Barbadoro, Paul James *federal judge*
Blankenstein, Elizabeth M. *director, educator*
Bradley, Paula E. *former state legislator*
Broderick, John T., Jr. *state supreme court chief justice*
Brown, Tom Christian *newspaper publishing executive*
Clemons, Jane Andrea *state legislator*
Colantuono, Thomas Paul *prosecutor, former state legislator*
Cote, David Edward *state legislator*
Dalianis, Linda Stewart *state supreme court justice*
DiClerico, Joseph Anthony, Jr. *federal judge*
Duggan, James E., Jr. *state supreme court justice*
Eaton, Thomas R. *state legislator*
Ferland, Brenda L. *state representative*
Flora, Kathleen M. *retired state representative*
Foster, Linda Timberlake *state legislator*
Francoeur, Sheila T. *state representative*
Galway, Richard E., Jr. *state supreme court justice*
Gardner, William Michael *state official*
Gatsas, Ted (Theodore L. Gatsas) *state legislator*
Ginsburg, Ruth *state representative*
Hager, Elizabeth Sears *state legislator, social services administrator*
Heard, Charles Wolfe *lawyer, consultant*
Hicks, Gary Ellis *state supreme court justice*
Hildreth, Peter C. *state agency administrator*
Hill, Donald S. *state commissioner*
Howard, Jeffrey R. *federal judge*
Hutson, John D. *dean, retired military officer*
Jillette, Arthur George, Jr. *school system administrator, educator*
Kaen, Naida *state representative*
Kenney, Kimberly *elementary school educator*
Larsen, Sylvia B. *state legislator*
Lynch, John H. *governor*
Matthews, William R., Jr., (Bill Matthews) *headmaster*
McAuliffe, Steven James *federal judge*
Mevers, Frank Clement *state agency administrator, archivist*
Norelli, Terie Thompson *state legislator*
Nowe, Ronald John *state legislator, small business owner*
Pilliod, James P. *state legislator, physician*
Potter, Fred Leon *lawyer, retired insurance company executive*
Pride, Mike *editor*
Provencher, Catherine A. *state official*
Rath, Thomas David *lawyer, retired prosecutor*
Resnick, Kenneth *photography director*
Roberts, George Bernard, Jr. *management and government relations consultant, former state legislator*
Robinson, V. Gene (The Right Reverend V. Gene Robinson) *bishop*
Stadelmann, Wayne Karl *plastic surgeon*
Stickney, Nancy Carver *state legislator*
Tracy, Lyonel B. *school system administrator*
Uchida, Richard Y. *lawyer*
Vidaver, Robert Maxwell *medical educator*
White, Jeffrey George *healthcare consultant*
York, Michael Charest *librarian*

Contoocook
Held, Wayne Edward *retired military officer*

Cornish
Atkinson, James Blakely *writer, editor*

Deering
Spitzer, Morton Edward *management consultant*

Derry
Holmes, Richard Dale *history consultant*
Katsakiores, George Nicholas *state legislator, retired food service executive*
Sapareto, Frank Vincent, II, *investment advisor, state legislator*

Dover
Beaupre, Timothy *lawyer*
Catalfo, Alfred, Jr., (Alfio Catalfo) *lawyer*
McManus, Anthony Aidan *judicial organization executive*
Nelson, Michael Underhill *educational association administrator*
Parks, Joe Benjamin *entrepreneur, retired state legislator*
Pelletier, Arthur Joseph *state legislator, educator*
Pelletier, Marsha Lynn *secondary school educator, poet*

Dublin
Hale, Judson Drake, Sr. *publishing executive, editor, writer*

Durham
Farrell, William Joseph *university chancellor*
Ford, Daniel (Daniel Francis Ford) *writer*
Gold, Janet Nowakowski *Spanish language educator*
Hapgood, Robert Derry *language educator*
Harris, John William *historian, educator*
Huddleston, Mark Wayne *academic administrator, political scientist, educator*
Irish, James David *oceanographer, educator*
McConnell, Michael *art educator*
Palmer, Stuart Hunter *sociology educator*
Pistole, Thomas Gordon *microbiology professor, researcher, department chairman*
Ray, Stephen Alan *academic administrator, lawyer*
Romoser, George Kenneth *political and social science educator*
Simic, Charles *language educator, poet*
Wheeler, Katherine Wells *retired state legislator*

East Andover
Gould, Donald Everett *retired chemical company executive, consultant*

Enfield
Gamache, R. Donald *retired business development executive*

Etna
Picoult, Jodi *writer*

Exeter
Harmon, Richard Wingate *management consultant*
Kelley, Carolyn *biotechnology educator*
Rimkunas, Barbara *historian, educator*
Schubart, Caren Nelson *psychologist*
Thomas, Jacquelyn May *librarian*
Tingley, Tyler C. *headmaster*
Wicklein, John Frederick *journalist, educator*

Farmington
Panek, William Dominick *systems engineer executive*

Fitzwilliam
Schott, John Robert *international consultant, educator*

Francestown
Milton, Peter Winslow *artist*

Franconia
Leich, Jeffrey R. *museum director*
Schaffer, David Edwin *retired systems administrator*

Gilford
Wool, Alan D. *mathematics educator*

Glen
Zager, Ronald *chemist, consultant*

Goffstown
Day, Russell Clover *state agency administrator*
Holden, Carol Helen *county official*
Martel, Eva Leona *accountant*
Wajenberg, Arnold Sherman *retired librarian, educator*

Grantham
Figley, Melvin Morgan *radiologist, physician, educator*
Grimley, Robert Thomas *chemistry professor*
Hansen, Herbert W. *management consultant*

Greenville
Talbot, Franis *writer*

Hampstead
Hargreaves, David William *retired communications company executive*

Hancock
Pollaro, Paul Philip *artist*

Hanover
Ambros, Victor R. *geneticist, educator*
Bel Bruno, Joseph James *chemistry professor*
Bien, Peter Adolph *language educator, writer*
Boghosian, Varujan Yegan *sculptor, educator*
Bower, Richard Stuart *retired economist*
Brooks, H. Allen *architectural educator, author, lecturer*
Burnham, Patricia White *consultant, advocate, writer, business executive*
Chapman, Robert James *psychiatrist, educator*
Christesen, Paul C. *classical studies educator*
Copenhaver, Marion Lamson *retired state legislator*
Crory, Elizabeth Lupien *retired state legislator*
Curphey, Thomas John *chemist, researcher*
Daniell, Jere Rogers, II, *retired historian*
Danos, Paul *dean, accounting educator*
Demko, George Joseph *geographer*
Dmitrovsky, Ethan *oncologist, medical educator, researcher*
Dong, Kui *music educator, composer*
Doyle, William Thomas *physicist, retired educator*
Ehrlich, David Gordon *film director, educator*
Fesen, Robert A. *astronomer, educator*
Fischel, William Alan *economics professor*
French, Kenneth Ronald *finance educator*
Gardner, Peter Jaglom *lawyer, publishing executive*
Garthwaite, Gene Ralph *historian, educator*
Gazzaniga, Michael S. *neuroscientist, psychologist*
Gert, Bernard *philosopher, educator*
Gilbert, John Jouett *aquatic ecologist, educator*
Goodman, William Beehler *editor, literary agent*
Govindarajan, Vijay *finance educator*
Green, Ronald Michael *bioethics educator*
Horrell, Jeffrey Lanier *library director*
Kantrowitz, Arthur *physicist, researcher, educator*
Kemp, Karl Thomas *insurance company executive*
Kleck, Robert Eldon *psychology professor*
Koop, C. Everett (Charles Everett Koop) *former Surgeon General of the United States, educator*
Kurtz, Thomas Eugene *retired mathematics professor*
Lamperti, John Williams *mathematician, educator*
Langford, George Malcolm *cell biology educator*
Laskaris, Maria *dean*
Logue, Dennis Emhardt *finance educator, writer, banker, consultant*
Lotko, William *engineering educator*
Lundquist, Weyman Ivan *lawyer*
Luxon, Thomas Hyatt *language educator, director*
Lynd, Lee Rybeck *biology educator*
Lyons, Gene Martin *political scientist, educator*
Mannix, Charles Raymond *law educator*
Mansell, Darrel Lee, Jr. *language educator*
Masters, Roger Davis *political scientist, educator, toxicologist*
McIlroy, M. Douglas *computer scientist, educator*
Montgomery, David Campbell *retired physics professor*
Oxenhandler, Neal *literature educator, writer*
Petitto, Laura-Ann *cognitive neuroscience educator*
Queneau, Paul Etienne *retired metallurgical engineering educator*
Riggs, Lorrin Andrews *psychologist, educator*
Rockmore, Daniel Nahum *mathematician*
Rolett, Ellis Lawrence *cardiologist, educator*
Russell, Robert Hilton *Romance languages and literature educator*
Rutter, Jeremy Bentham *archaeologist, educator*
Scherr, Barry Paul *foreign language educator*
Shewmaker, Kenneth Earl *history professor*
Slaughter, Matthew J. *economics professor, former federal official*
Spielberg, Stephen Paul *dean, educator*
Starzinger, Vincent Evans *political scientist, educator*
Wegner, Gary Alan *astronomer*
Wright, James Edward *academic administrator, historian, educator*
Zubkoff, Michael *medical educator*

Henniker
Braiterman, Thea Gilda *economics professor, state legislator*
Nitschke-Shaw, Debra Ann *education educator, dean*

Hillsboro
Nelson, Matthew *graphics designer*

Jackson
Synnott, William Raymond *retired management consultant*

Jaffrey
Press, Fred *artist*
Walling, Cheves Thomson *chemistry professor*

Keene
Baldwin, Peter Arthur *psychologist, educator, author, minister*
Bell, Ernest Lorne III *retired lawyer*
Bleam, Nancy Kay *physical education educator*
Cohen, Richard B. *grocery company executive*
Gardner, Eric Raymond *lawyer*
Hackett, John Thomas *retired economist and financial executive*
Harris, Reuben *wholesale distribution executive*
Higgins, Roland Louis *history professor*
Hoffman, Nancy M. *painter*
Lichtenstein, Sally (Ali) Tucker *small business owner, writer, English and women's studies educator*
Miller, Rita *die-casting company executive, personnel consultant*
Pelletier, John B., Jr. *mathematics professor, consultant*
Salcetti, Marianne *newswriter, educator*

Kingston
Walen, Harry Leonard *historian, lecturer, author*

Laconia
Parthasarathy, Vinod *manufacturing engineer, consultant*

Lancaster
Mekeel, Robert K. *lawyer*

Lebanon
Bernat, James Lawrence *neurologist, educator*
Carr, Charles F. *orthopedist*
Cole, Bernard F. *community and family medicine professor*
Collins, E. Dale *surgeon, educator*
Cronenwett, Jack LeMoyne *vascular surgeon educator*
DeMars, Leslie R. *oncologist, obstetrician, gynecologist, educator*
Emery, Virginia Olga Beattie *psychologist, researcher*
Ferrell, Richard Bradley *neuropsychiatrist*
Fillinger, Mark F. *vascular surgeon, researcher*
Glass, Donald David *anesthesiologist*
Kelley, Maurice Leslie, Jr. *gastroenterologist, educator*
Koval, Kenneth Joseph *orthopedist, surgeon*
McCollum, Robert Wayne *epidemiologist, educator*
Munck, Allan Ulf *physiologist, educator*
Oxman, Thomas Elliot *psychiatrist*
Phillips, Joseph Michael *neurosurgeon*
Rao, Sreeramoju Gautami *oncologist*
Rosenberg, Stanley David *psychologist, educator*
Sedlacek, Martin *nephrologist*
Silberfarb, Peter Michael *psychiatrist, educator*
Torkelson, Andrew Thomas *cardiologist*
van Leeuwen, Dirk Jacob *hepatology educator*
Waugh, Theodore Rogers *orthopedic surgeon*
Whitley, Rob *medical educator, sociologist, researcher*

Lee
Young, James Morningstar *internist, military officer*

Litchfield
Darlington, David William *management consultant*
Miller, Dawn Marie *retired meteorologist*

Littleton
Kelly, Dorothy Helen *pediatrician, educator*
Lucas, Kurt John *health facility director*
Merritt, Thomas Butler *lawyer*

Loudon
Moore, Beatrice *religious organization administrator*

Lyme
Carmichael, Donald Scott *retired lawyer, corporate financial executive*
Cornwell, Gibbons Gray III *retired internist, educator*
Dwight, Donald Rathbun *publishing executive, corporate communications specialist*
McIntyre, Oswald Ross *physician*

Lyndeborough
Roper, Stephanie Abbot *history professor, writer*

Manchester
Arnold, Barbara Eileen *state legislator*
Carrier, Celine A. *psychologist*
Dahar, Eleanor William *lawyer*
Dugan, Kevin F. *lawyer*
Durham, Ian Thomas *physicist, educator*
Ehrlich, Charles Gordon *insurance company executive, lawyer*
Haffer, Edward Anthony *lawyer*
Hood, James Calton *lawyer*
Hower, Philip Leland *semiconductor device engineer*
Ingraham, Alec *mathematics professor*
Lavery, Robert Michael *internist, cardiologist*
McNamara, Richard Bedle *lawyer*
Merideth, Susan Carol *business administration educator*
Middleton, Jack Baer *lawyer*
Monson, John Rudolph *lawyer*
Perkins, Charles III *newspaper and website editor*
Roche, John Edward *college administrator, human resources specialist, educator*
Shaheen, Bill (William Henry) *lawyer*
Stebbins, Henry Blanchard *lawyer*
Vogelman, Lawrence Allen *lawyer, educator*
Wells, Robert Alfred *lawyer*
Wright, Mark A. *lawyer*

Meredith
Hatch, Frederick Tasker *research scientist*
Heald, Bruce Day *English and music educator, historian*

Meriden
Brent, Patricia Lee *health facility administrator, writer*

Merrimack
Gallup, Patricia *computer company executive*

Middleton
Feyler, Carrie A. *elementary school educator*

Milford
Queeney, Deborah Ann *special education educator*

Milton
Edelman, Hendrik *library and information science professor*
Shean, Timothy Joseph *manufacturing executive*

Mirror Lake
Culleton, James Frederick *neurologist*

Mont Vernon
Buckley, Charles E. *retired museum director, curator*

Moultonborough
Patten, Betsey Leland *state legislator*

Nashua
Arthur, Rose Ann Horman *dean*
Bergeron, Paul Robert *city clerk*
Egan, John Frederick *retired electronics executive*
Hahto, Sami K. *physicist*
Hemming, Walter William *retired financial consultant*
Hermansen, Marcus C. *pediatrics professor, director*
Jette, Ernest Arthur *lawyer*
Knights, Edwin Munroe *pathologist*
Lumbard, Eliot Howland *lawyer, educator*
Matarazzo, Maria C. *finance educator, department chairman*
Mitsakos, Charles Leonidas *education educator, consultant*
Pignatelli, Debora Becker *state official*
Siroty, William Charles *physician*
Smith, Thomas Raymond III *software engineer*
Walz, Deborah Sue *application developer, musician*
Woodruff, Thomas Ellis *electronics consulting executive*
Yannone, Ronald Matthew *systems engineer, researcher*

New Castle
Baker, Robert I. *manufacturing executive*
Friese, George Ralph *retail executive*
Klotz, Louis Herman *structural engineer, educator, engineering executive, consultant*
Levin, Harvey Jay *financial institution design and construction specialist, developer, auctioneer*
Mapel, William Marlen Raines *retired bank executive*

New London
Crane, Robert Kendall *engineering educator, researcher, consultant*

Newmarket
Getchell, Sylvia Fitts *librarian*
Jernigan, David Bruce *men's college basketball coach*

Newport
Gayvoronsky, Ludmila *artist, educator*
Stamatakis, Carol Marie *lawyer, former state legislator*

North Hampton
Taylor, Donald *retired manufacturing executive*

Orford
Karol, John J., Jr. *producer, filmmaker*
Martin, Allen *retired lawyer*

Peterborough
Bass, Perkins *retired lawyer, congressman*
Day, John Sidney *management sciences educator*
Eppes, William David *arts and humanities advocate*
Thomas, Elizabeth Marshall *writer*

Pike
Teschner, Douglass Paul *project administrator*

Plainfield
Brown, Judith Olans *retired lawyer, educator*

Plaistow
Goddu, Kevin Albert *secondary school educator*
Libby-Barth, Jennifer *social studies educator*

Plymouth
Berona, David A. *library director, educator*
Bisson, Casey *library and information scientist*
Dutille, Jessica Annie Orf *social services administrator, educator*
Gorin, Stephen H. *social worker, educator*
Hopkins, William Hayes *lawyer, writer*
Hunnewell, Richard *art historian, educator*
Vinogradova, Natalya *mathematician, educator*

Portsmouth
Baumann, Hans D. *engineering executive*
Bourgeault, Ronald *art appraiser*
Boutin II, Bernie L. *information technology executive*
Breen, Edward Deveaux *manufacturing executive*
Cunningham, Valerie S. *historic preservationist, researcher*
Doleac, Charles Bartholomew *lawyer*
Dumont, Mary *chef*
Harter, Hugh Anthony *foreign language educator*
Hopkins, Jeannette Ethel *book publisher, editor*
Lytton, William Bryan *lawyer*
McArdle, Barry Francis *dentist*
Nylander, Jane Louise *museum director, educator, writer*
Powers, Henry Martin, Jr. *oil industry executive*
Tober, Stephen Lloyd *lawyer*
Volk, Kenneth Hohne *lawyer*
Watson, Thomas Roger *lawyer*
Wener, Brian D. *psychologist*

Rindge
Martin, Frederick Nichols *school system administrator*

Rochester
Coviello, Robert Frank *retail executive*
Dworkin, Gary Steven *insurance company executive*
Jones, Franklin Charles *judge*

Rye
Wilson, Ralph Sloan *retinal surgeon*

Salem
Courtois, Michael G. *biology educator*
Simmons, Marvin Gene *retired geophysics educator*
Smith, Laurence Roger *journal editor*
Stone, Patricia A. *special education services professional, consultant*

Sanbornton
Weiant, Elizabeth Abbott *retired biology professor*

Sanbornville
Berg, Warren Stanley *retired bank executive*
Szugda, Sharon A. *elementary school educator*

Seabrook
Ganz, Mary Keohan *lawyer*

Silver Lake
Tregenza, Norman Hughson *investment banker*

Somersworth
Dahms, Bruce John *secondary school educator*
Gow, Linda Yvonne Carignan Cherwin *travel executive*

Stoddard
Cahill, George Francis, Jr. *physician, educator*

Stratham
Green, Catherine Cooper *artist*
Swartz, Jeffrey B. *apparel executive*
Terry, Elizabeth Hays *artist, small business owner*

Walpole
Burns, Ken *documentary filmmaker*

Warner
Coolidge, Daniel Scott *lawyer*
Hunt, Everett Clair *engineering educator, researcher, consultant*

Waterville Valley
Saenger, Bruce Walter *consulting firm executive*

Weare
White, Karen Ruth Jones *information systems executive*

West Chesterfield
Garinger, Louis Daniel *retired religion educator*

West Lebanon
Halperin, George Bennett *education educator, retired military officer*
Lawton, Jacqueline Agnes *retired communications executive, management consultant*

Winchester
MacKay, Neil Duncan *plastics company executive, consultant*

Windham
Arndt, Janet S. *former state legislator, educator*

Wolfeboro
Bonin, Suzanne Jean *artist*

NEW JERSEY

Absecon
Byrne, Shaun Patrick *lawyer*
Cartlidge, Edward Sutterley *mechanical engineer*

Adelphia
Carter, Harry Robert *fire protection consultant*

Allendale
Bisanzo, Mark Thomas *retired sales executive*
DeFeo, Neil P. *consumer products company executive*
Morris, Edward William, Jr. *lawyer*
Rosenblum, Edward G. *lawyer*
Ruth, Rodney *musician, music consultant, contractor, educator*

Allenhurst
Tognoli, Era M. *performing company executive, artistic director*

Allentown
Sulyok, Paul David *music educator, composer*

Annandale
Wu, Margaret *research scientist*

Atco
Goldstein, Benjamin *lawyer, educator*

Atlantic City
Felder, Wilson Norfleet, II, *engineering executive*
Irvine, Robert *chef*
Jamieson, John Edward, Jr. *social services administrator, minister*
Juliano, Mark J. *hotel and gaming company executive*
Knight, Edward R. *judge, psychologist, law educator*
Maddox, Odinga Lawrence, II, *head of religious order*
Zlotnick, Norman Lee *lawyer*

Atlantic Highlands
Hawley, Joseph. B. *property management executive, educator*
Levine, George Lewis *literature and language professor, critic*
Tice, George A(ndrew) *photographer*

Augusta
Martin, Richard L. *retired insurance executive*

Avenel
Berg, Louis Leslie *investment executive*

Avon By The Sea
Bruno, Grace Angelia *accountant, retired educator*
Mataranglo, Robert Patrick *artist, educator*
Potter, Emma Josephine Hill *language educator*

Basking Ridge
Buist, Richardson *retired corporate executive, retired banker*
Collis, Sidney Robert *retired telephone company executive*
Conklin, Donald Ransford *retired pharmaceutical executive*
Craven, Pamela F. *lawyer*
D'Ambrosio, Louis J. *telecommunications industry executive*
Dorsa, Caroline *software company executive*
Drewry, Don Neal *fire protection engineer*
Matthews, Craig Gerard *retired energy executive*
McAdam, Lowell C. *telecommunications industry executive*
Moden, Joleen *communications executive*
Morgan, Samuel P(ope) *physicist, applied mathematician*
Perez, Glad M. *marketing professional*
Riesenberger, John Richard *science administrator*
Schenker, Leo *retired utilities executive*
Schmidt, William Max *management consultant, marketing and business development executive*
Tamarelli, Alan Wayne *venture capitalist*

Bay Head
O'Brien, Robert Brownell, Jr. *banker, consultant, yacht broker, opera company executive*

Bayonne
Fitzpatrick, Harold Francis *lawyer*
Lo Re, Vincent, Jr. *retired academic administrator, municipal official*
Pelosi, Marco Antonio *obstetrician and gynecologist, plastic surgeon*

Bedminster
David, Edward Emil, Jr. *electrical engineer, executive, management consultant*
DeCostanzo, Marybeth *language educator*
Eslambolchi, Hossein *communications executive*
Flaherty, Kathleen Ruth *telecommunications industry executive*
Gardner, David John *communications executive, sound recording engineer*
Hart, Terry Jonathan *communications executive*
Laroia, Rajiv *communications executive*
Ripp, Joseph Allen *information technology executive*
Strigl, Dennis F. *telecommunications industry executive*

Belle Mead
Dyer, Hugh Nelson III *management company owner*
Goodnick, Paul Joel *psychiatrist*
Sarle, Charles Richard *health facility executive*

Belleville
Salvini, Emil Robert *publishing executive, writer, historian*
Shuhan, Janice-Lynn Nazziola *secondary school educator*

Bellmawr
Wilke, Constance Regina *elementary school educator*

Belmar
Downes, Laurence M. *gas industry executive*
Swett, Stephen Frederick, Jr. *artist, educator*

Belvidere
Walsh, John Alfred *retired social worker*

Bergenfield
Clark, Fred *writer, editor*
Davidson, Marilyn Copeland *writer, musician, educator*
Glazer, Gilda F. *musician, educator*

Berkeley Heights
Geusic, Joseph Edward *physicist*
Mac Rae, Alfred Urquhart *physicist, electrical engineer*
Momeni, Reza *plastic surgeon*

Bernardsville
Cooperman, Saul *retired educational administrator*
Dixon, Richard Wayne *retired communications company executive*
Dixon, Rosina Berry *physician, pharmaceutical executive, consultant*
Flynn, Marie Cosgrove *retired portfolio manager, corporate financial executive*
Robinson, Maureen Loretta *retired secondary school educator*
Spofford, Sally (Sally Hyslop) *artist*
Teiger, David *management consultant*

Blackwood
Perkins, Rita Wade *historian, educator*

Blairstown
Bean, Bennett *artist*

Bloomfield
Conta, Richard Vincent *actuary*
Glasser, Lynn Schreiber *publisher*
Glasser, Stephen Andrew *publishing executive, lawyer*
Lordi, Katherine Mary *lawyer*
Weisert, Kent Albert Frederick *lawyer*

Bogota
Condon, Francis Edward *retired chemistry professor*

Boonton
Bona, Frederick Emil *public relations executive*
Walzer, James Harvey *lawyer, author*
Ward, Solveig Maria *marketing professional*

Bordentown
Spitzer, Lois Nancy *language educator*

Bound Brook
Shive, Richard Byron *architect*

Bradley Beach
Unger, Irwin *historian, educator*

Branchville
MacMurren, Harold Henry, Jr. *psychologist, lawyer*
Murphy, Gregory E. *insurance company executive*
Pasvolsky, Richard Lloyd *retired parks, recreation, and environment educator*

Brick
Roache, Patrick Michael, Jr. *management consultant*
Shortess, Edwin Steevin *marketing consultant*

Bridgeton
Howell, James Burt III *retired agricultural products company sales consultant*

Bridgewater
Albrethsen, Adrian Edysel *metallurgist, consultant*
Bernson, Marcella S. *psychiatrist*
DeMaio, Donnalee A. *bank executive*
Fung, Shun Chong *retired chemical engineer*
Glesmann, Sylvia-Maria *artist*
Hart, Karen Jean *special education educator*
Hirsch, Paul J. *orthopedist, surgeon, health facility administrator, medical educator*
Maynard, Kenneth Irwin *pharmaceutical executive, medical educator, researcher*
Patton, Diana Lee Wilkoc *artist, educator, illustrator*
Scully, John Thomas *obstetrician, gynecologist, educator*
Sethi, Shyam Sunder *management consultant*
Skidmore, James Albert, Jr. *management, computer technology and engineering services company executive*
Steinhart, Jessica *lawyer*
Taylor, Duncan Paul *pharmacologist, researcher*
Wood, J(oshua) Warren III *lawyer*

Brookside
Fairchild, Samuel Wilson *investor, retired federal agency administrator, financial services executive*

Browns Mills
Cha, Se Do *internist*
DeWitt, Edward Francis *artist*
Henderson, Kathleen Denise Ross *medical/surgical nurse, educator*
McGrath, Lynn Bernard *surgeon*
Moore, Roger Addison *pediatrician, anesthesiologist*

Budd Lake
Ocello, Claudia Barbara *museum program director*
Webb, John Gibbon III *lawyer*

Burlington
Cobb, Vanessa Wyvette *elementary school educator*
Haws, Elizabeth Anne *psychologist, director*
Rowlette, Henry Allen, Jr. *social worker, counseling psychologist*
Tang, Paul C. *lawyer*

Butler
Ward, Robert Allen, Jr. *advertising executive*

Caldwell
Savage, Joseph George *academic administrator*
Werner, Patrice (Patricia Ann Werner) *academic administrator*

Califon
Rosen, Carol Mendes *artist*

Camden
Ances, I. G(eorge) *obstetrician, gynecologist*
Baveja, Alok *finance educator*
Beck, Susan J. *academic librarian*
Brooks, Gail Denise *school system administrator, consultant*
Brotman, Stanley Seymour *federal judge*
Conant, Douglas R. *food products executive*
Fricks, Ernest Eugene *management consultant*
Galante, Joseph A. *bishop*
Golub, Harvey *food products and former financial services company executive*
Gordon, Walter Kelly *retired academic administrator, retired language educator*
Hillman, Noel L. *federal judge, former prosecutor*
Hollenberg, Steven Michael *physician, researcher*
Irenas, Joseph Eron *judge*
Kaden, Ellen Oran *lawyer, consumer products company executive*
Laskin, Lee B. *judge, state senator*
Parra, Raul O. *urologist, educator*
Parrillo, Joseph Edison, Jr. *allergist, immunologist, cardiologist*
Pomorski, Stanislaw *lawyer, educator*
Pratter, Melvin Richard *medical educator*
Rajaram, Sri-Sujanthy *internist, medical educator*
Reardon, Nancy Anne *food products executive*
Ross, Steven Elliot *surgeon*
Schiffner, Robert A. *food products executive*
Simandle, Jerome B. *federal judge*
Solomon, Rayman Louis *dean, law educator*
Tan, LiQin *artist, educator*
Venegas, Arturo, Jr. *protective services official*
Worrall, John Dennis *economics professor, consultant, writer*
Yamada, Tetsuji *health economist, educator*

Cape May
Fox, Matthew Ignatius *publishing executive*
Savage, Maureen Walls *retired history professor*
Turner, Almon Richard *retired art historian, educator*

Cape May Court House
Altman, Brian David *pediatric ophthalmologist*
Cohen, Daniel Edward *writer*
Cohen, Susan Lois *writer*
Fineberg, Robert Alan *lawyer*

Cape May Point
Chandler, Marguerite Nella *real estate company executive*
Fraser, Malcolm Cavanagh *mayor*
Jordan, Joe J. *architect*

Carteret
Standley, John T. *food market executive*
Strassler, Marc A. *lawyer*
Vitrano, Frank G. *supermarket executive*

Cedar Grove
Carlozzi, Catherine L. *corporate communications consultant, writer*
Mandel, Irwin Daniel *dentist*

Cedar Knolls
Hariri, Robert Joseph *neurosurgeon, research scientist*
Schectman, Stephen Barry *pharmaceutical executive*

Chatham
Brodkin, Adele Ruth Meyer *psychologist*
Earle, Jean Buist *finance executive*
Hurley, Allyson Kingsley *dentist*
Leonett, Anthony Arthur *banker*
Meagher, James Proctor *editor*
Murphy, Joseph James *chiropractic physician*
Tepper, David Alan *hedge fund manager*
Zegas, Alan Lee *lawyer*

Cherry Hill
Batterman, Steven Charles *engineering mechanics and bioengineering professor, consultant*
Blakney, Juanita Mosley *psychotherapist*
Clauser, Donald Roberdeau *retired musician*
Copsetta, Norman George *real estate executive*
D'Alfonso, Mario Joseph *lawyer*
Del Rossi, Christopher *elementary school educator*
Erving, Julius (Winfield), (II) *retired professional basketball player, business executive*
Falese, Robert D., Jr. *bank executive*
Gardner, Joel Robert *writer, historian*
Garrigle, William Aloysius *lawyer*
Goldberg, Jack *hematologist*
Gooden, Linda R. *aerospace transportation executive*
Gorenberg, Charles Lloyd *finance company executive*
Kahn, Marc Leslie *orthopedic surgeon*
Kole, Janet Stephanie *lawyer, writer*
Levin, Joshua Zev *computer scientist, consultant, transportation engineer*
Makous, Bruce B. *fundraiser, writer*
Margolis, Gerald Joseph *psychiatrist, psychoanalyst*
Myers, Daniel William, II, *lawyer*
Olearchyk, Andrew *cardiothoracic surgeon, educator*
Resor, Randolph Richardson *transportation consultant*
Rose, Joel Alan *legal consultant*
Rudman, Solomon Kal *magazine publisher*
Schelm, Roger Leonard *information systems specialist*
Swibinski, Edward Thomas *internist, endocrinologist, educator*
Toogood, James Stephen *artist, educator*
Weinstein, Steven D. *lawyer*
Werbitt, Warren *gastroenterologist, educator*

Chester
Lynch, Beverly Love *language educator*

Cinnaminson
Edwin, Robert *voice educator*

Clark
Barr, Jon-Henry *lawyer*
D'Onofrio, Justin Michael *information technology manager, consultant*

Clayton
Bertenshaw, William Howard III *radio and television producer*

Cliffside Park
Chelariu, Ana Radu *library director*
Diktas, Christos James *lawyer*
Goldstein, Howard Bernard *investment banker*
Perhacs, Marylouise Helen *musician, educator*

Clifton
Bronkesh, Annette Cylia *public relations executive*
DiNicola, Robert J. *consumer products company executive*
Feinstein, Miles Roger *lawyer*
Goldberger, Alan Steven *lawyer*
Lieb, L. Robert *lawyer*
Yau, Edward Tintai *toxicologist, pharmacologist*

Clinton
Isaacman, Jared *entrepreneur*

Colts Neck
Candelora, Deborah Michael *engineer, sculptor*
Crowder-Pagano, Linda Louise *special education educator*
Schmalz, Elizabeth Moody *cosmetics company executive*

Columbia
Timcenko, Lydia Teodora *secondary school educator, biochemist*

Cranbury
Hawver, Dennis A. *psychologist, consultant*
Kemmerer, Peter Ream *financial executive*
Yoseloff, Julien David *publishing company executive*
Zurick, Jack *electrical engineer, consultant*

Cranford
De Luca, Thomas George *lawyer*
Hrycak, Peter *retired engineering educator*
Jenssen, Warren Donald *microbiologist, consultant*
Mack, William L. *real estate investment company executive*
Mazur, Leonard L. *pharmaceutical company executive*
McCreedy, Edwin James *lawyer*
Mendelson, Joel Stuart *allergist, immunologist*
Petryshyn, Wolodymyr V. *retired mathematician*
Russell, John Joseph *English educator*

Cresskill
Benton, Donald Stewart *publishing company executive, lawyer*
Jurasek, John Paul *mathematics professor, counselor*
Uehling, Gordon Alexander, Jr. *investment company executive*

Deal
Becker, Richard Stanley *music publisher*

Delanco
Lane, Carrie Belle (Hairston) *retired music educator*

Demarest
Dornfest, Burton Saul *anatomy educator*

Denville
Doane, Eileen Maloney *learning disabilities teacher consultant*
Minter, Jerry Burnett *electronics executive*
Veech, Lynda Anne *musician, educator*

Deptford
Johns, Michael Douglas *healthcare executive, medical device executive, former federal government official*

Dover
Kassell, Paula Sally *editor, publisher*

Dumont
Sadock, Geoffrey Johnston *English professor*

East Brunswick
Applebaum, Charles *lawyer*
Braun, Anna M. *music educator*
Daniel, Charles Timothy *transportation engineer, consultant*
Dombrowski, Anne Wesseling *retired microbiologist*
Hurst, Gregory Squire *investment company executive, theater director and producer*
Johnson, Edward Elemuel *psychologist, educator*
Kaufman, Matthew *otolaryngologist, plastic surgeon*
Liebowitz, Larry Arnold *electroceramics materials engineer*
McDowell, Wilbur Benedict *retired chemist consultant*
Meningall, Evelyn L. *retired educational media specialist*
Wildnauer, Richard Harry *pharmaceutical executive*

East Hanover
Dodsworth, Roy W. *pharmaceutical company executive*
Nelson, Barbara Kasztan *marketing professional*
Nemecek, Georgina Marie *molecular pharmacologist*
Verma, Anila *epidemiologist*
Zhang, Cynthia Hongbing *lawyer*

East Orange
Agarwal, Shashi Kant *cardiologist*
Chiang, Tom *medical educator, researcher*
Fielo, Muriel Bryant *interior designer*
Hudson-Zonn, Eliza *nurse, psychologist*
Ilogienboh, Caroline O. *protective services official, publishing executive*
Jones-Gregory, Patricia *art educator*
Khanna, Yash Kumar *family practice physician, pediatrician*
McCampbell, Edwin Lee *physician*
Wolff, Derish Michael *economist*

East Rutherford
Carter, Vince *professional basketball player*
Cathey, Gertrude Brown *retired medical/surgical nurse*
Coughlin, Tom *professional football coach*
Frank, Lawrence *professional basketball coach*
Gilbride, Kevin *professional football coach*
Guevara, Amado *professional soccer player*
Jefferson, Richard *professional basketball player*
Kempner, Michael W. *public relations executive*
Kidd, Jason *professional basketball player*
Kluge, John Werner *broadcast and advertising executive*
Manning, Eli (Elisha Nelson Manning) *professional football player*
Mara, John Kevin *professional sports team executive*
Mashburn, Jamal *professional basketball player*
Reese, Jerry *professional sports team executive*
Shockey, Jeremy Charles *professional football player*
Stefanski, Edward *professional sports team executive*
Strahan, Michael Anthony *professional football player*
Thorn, Rodney King *professional sports team executive, retired professional basketball player*
Toomer, Amani *professional football player*
Umenyiora, Osi *professional football player*
Yormark, Brett D. *professional sports team executive*

East Windsor
Shoemaker, Frank Crawford *retired physicist*

Eatontown
Danikas, Dimitrios *plastic surgeon*
Nissov, Morten *telecommunications industry executive*

Edgewater
Berliner, Barbara *retired librarian, consultant*
Pohan, Armand *transportation executive, professional hockey club executive, lawyer*
Siegel, Max Laurence *recording industry executive*

Edgewater Park
Mednick, Sheldon Ira *pharmacist*

Edison
Alexander, John Charles *pharmaceutical executive, preventive medicine physician*
Behr, Omri M. *lawyer*
Blumengold, Jeffrey Gene *health facility administrator*
Chen-Maxham, Li-Chan *soprano*
Currie, Robert *communications executive*
Fan, Shirley Tsui-Yu *music educator*
Giacino, Joseph T. *psychologist, educator*
Gizzi, Martin Sherman *neurologist, neurophysiologist*
Hunter, Michael *publishing executive*
Kijowski, Rosemary Joan *small business owner, retired music educator*
O'Brien, John Graham *lawyer*
Pedescleaux-Muckle, Gail *retired business analyst, writer, artist, consultant*
Riley, Barbara Polk *retired librarian*
Roskoski, John *religious studies educator, coach*
Samek, Edward Lasker *medical transcription executive*
Sinma, Binod K. *urologist, consultant*
Traub, Richard Kenneth *lawyer*
Vercammen, Kenneth Albert *lawyer, prosecutor*
Walters, Arthur Scott *neurologist, educator, clinical research scientist*
Winter, Robin Okner *health facility administrator*

Egg Harbor City
Farris, Vera King *former college president*

Egg Harbor Township
Carney, Michelle Catherine *assistant principal*
Lashman, Shelley Bortin *retired judge*
Polillo, Ronald R. *federal official*
Schreiber, Eileen Sher *artist*

Elizabeth
Barnes, Marjorie *poet, educator*
Berger, Harold Richard *physician*
de la Viña-Sierra, Diana Maria *music educator*
Gellert, George Geza *food importing company executive*
Horan, Gary S. *healthcare executive*
Lucco, James Perry *writer*
Rauh, Linda Ann *rehabilitation services professional, counselor*
Rosenstein, Neil *surgeon, genealogist, researcher*
Sananman, Michael Lawrence *neurologist*

Elmwood Park
Mangano, Louis *lawyer*
Weisberger, James David *hematopathologist*
White, H. Katherine *lawyer*

Englewood
Abramson, David Lawrence *plastic surgeon, educator*
Anuszkiewicz, Richard Joseph *artist*
Boteach, Shmuley *rabbi, television personality, author*
Dardik, Herbert *vascular surgeon, general surgeon*
DeJarnett, Rodney *headmaster*
Deresiewicz, Herbert *retired mechanical engineering educator, consultant*
Elias, Steven *surgeon*
Fay, Toni Georgette *communications executive*
Frieden, Faith Joy *obstetrician*
Goldweit, Richard Scott *cardiologist*
Gulko, Edward *healthcare executive, consultant*
Harish, Ziv *allergist, immunologist*
Kim, Dongsoo *clinical neuropsychologist, researcher*
Kramer, Orin Stuart *investment services company executive*
Minkoff, John *mathematician, educator*
Rotondi, Nicholas John *automotive executive*
Schmidt, Ronald Hans *architect*
Tobias, Geoffrey *otolaryngologist, plastic surgeon*
Wuhl, Charles Michael *psychiatrist*

Englewood Cliffs
Bartiromo, Maria Sara *financial news correspondent*
Books, Roberta Paula *real estate finance executive*
Burnett, Erin *finance newscaster*
Dobrzynski, Judith Helen *journalist, commentator*

Farrell, Patricia Ann *psychologist, educator, writer*
Fisher, Andrew, IV, *newswriter, television producer*
Haltiwanger, Robert Sidney, Jr. *book publishing executive*
Hoffman, Mark *broadcast executive*
Insana, Ronald Gerard *newscaster*
Klauberg, Laura *marketing executive*
Lagnado, Silvia *marketing executive*
Lawrence, James A. *food products executive*
Neis, Arnold Hayward *pharmaceutical company executive*
Saible, Stephanie Irene *editor-in-chief*
Vazacopoulos, Alkis *application developer, educator*
Wernick, Edward Raymond *information technology executive*
Yu, Fei *internist*

Ewing
Brown, Richard Alexander *chemist*
Brunda, Daniel Donald *retired aerospace engineer, consultant, inventor, writer*
Gitenstein, Donna M. *academic administrator*
McCarty, John Albert *management educator*

Fair Haven
McKissock, David Lee *retired manufacturing company executive*
Wyndrum, Ralph William, Jr. *communications consultant*

Fair Lawn
Melen, Alex *entrepreneur, Internet company executive*
Namerow, David Mark *pediatrician*

Fairfield
Connell, William Terrence *lawyer, judge*

Far Hills
Alexandre, Kristin Kuhns *public relations executive, writer*
Burns, Amy Margaret *music educator*
Corash, Richard *lawyer*

Farmingdale
Schluter, Peter Mueller *electronics executive*

Flanders
Hilbert, Rita L. *librarian*
Kuzma, Deborah J. *vice principal, music educator*

Flemington
Buchsbaum, Peter A. *judge*
Huguenel, Jean M. *pharmaceutical executive, director, legal assistant*
Kettler, Carl Frederick *airline executive*
Kiovsky, Douglas George *land use planner*
Lance, Leonard *state legislator*
Lenagh, Thomas Hugh *lawyer, financial advisor*
Miller, Louis H. *lawyer*
Nielsen, Lynn Carol *lawyer, educational consultant*
Rubin, Arkady *biostatistics and data management researcher, executive*
Rushton, Alan R. *physician, medical researcher, historian*
Salamon, Renay *real estate broker*
Thomas, Anne Moreau *former newspaper owner*
Zulker, Charles Bates *broadcasting company executive*

Florham Park
Altieri, James M. *lawyer*
Bossen, Wendell John *retired financial planner*
Cangemi, Michael Paul *accountant, author, consultant*
Chase, Eric Lewis *lawyer*
Hardin, William Downer *retired lawyer*
Hull, Gerald W., Jr. *lawyer*
Javaid, Hassan Bilal *management consultant*
Kahn, Richard *lawyer*
Kandravy, John *lawyer*
Kouroupas, Paul *telecommunications industry executive, lawyer*
Laulicht, Murray Jack *lawyer*
Lavey, Stewart Evan *lawyer*
Long, Stephen R. *lawyer*
Malone, Robert K. *lawyer*
Naimark, George Modell *marketing and management consultant*
Negi, Devendra S. *communications services company administrator*
Nittoly, Paul Gerard *lawyer*
O'Connell, Daniel Francis *lawyer*
Pantel, Glenn Steven *lawyer*
Reid, Charles Adams III *lawyer*
Ridley, John A. *lawyer*
Rosenberg, Paul I. *lawyer*
Rosenthal, Jeffrey M. *lawyer*
Smith, Theodore S. *lawyer*
Stryker, David Michael *lawyer*

Fords
Ayers, Christopher James *special education educator*
Blond, Stuart Richard *magazine editor*

Forked River
Novak, Dennis E. *physician*

Fort Dix
Adams, Keith Robert *military officer*

Fort Lee
Altomara, Rita Ecke *library director, writer*
Armellino, Michael Ralph *retired portfolio manager*
Chessler, Richard Kenneth *gastroenterologist, endocrinologist*
Goldberg, Harry Finck *lawyer, consultant*
Goldfarb, Joel Peter *internist, gastroenterologist*
Huang, Jianzhong *biomedical researcher*
Li, Tien-Shun *obstetrician, gynecologist, educator*
Lippman, William Jennings *investment company executive*
Mack, Earle Irving *former ambassador, real estate company executive*
Orman, Suze *news correspondent, writer*
Seitel, Fraser Paul *public relations executive*
Soejima, Daisuke *diversified financial services company executive, economist*
Stuart, Carole *publishing executive*
Sugarman, Alan William *educational consultant*
Thomopoulos, Michael *music educator*
Umansky, Edith Simon *retired school librarian, retired elementary school educator*
Underwood, Steven Clark *finance company executive*
Weinstock, George David *financial services company executive*
Weiss, Simona *retired paralegal*
Young, Vera Lee Hall *academic administrator, director*

Fort Monmouth
Fritch, John Kenneth *civilian military employee*
Perlman, Barry Stuart *electrical engineer, researcher, director*
Poulos, Andrew, Jr. *protective services official, director*
Schwering, Felix Karl *electronics executive, researcher*
Thornton, Clarence Gould *electronics executive, civilian military employee*

Franklin Lakes
Baker, Cornelia Draves *artist*
Considine, John R. *pharmaceutical company executive*
Klepper, Kenneth O. *healthcare executive*
Ludwig, Edward J. *medical technology executive*
Machlowitz, David Steven *lawyer*
Reed, JoAnn A. *corporate financial executive*
Sherman, Jeffrey Scott *lawyer*
Snow, David B. *pharmaceutical executive*
Williams, Edward David *information technology management consultant*

Freehold
Christ, Duane Marland *retired computer systems engineer*
D'Andrea, Patricia Carlisle *marketing professional, communications executive*
Dinrstein, Charles Robert *vascular surgeon*
Ehling, Elizabeth Sullivan *psychotherapist, marriage and family therapist*
Foster, Eric Harold, Jr. *retail executive*
Greenstein, Gary *periodontist, dental educator*
Jawidzik, Edward Mark *priest*
Newman, James Michael *judge, lawyer*

Galloway
Newell, Eric James *financial planner, retired insurance company executive*

Garfield
Herpst, Robert Dix *lawyer, optical materials company executive*
Nickles, I. MacArthur *librarian*

Garwood
Jannotti, Gene Patrick *business consultant, telecommunications professional*
Smith, Joan Lowell *syndicated columnist, feature writer*

Gibbstown
Krebs, Meiken *chemicals executive*

Gillette
Nathanson, Linda Sue *publishing executive, writer*

Gladstone
Close, Donald Pembroke *management consultant*

Glassboro
D'Augustine, Robert *academic administrator, lawyer*
Donahue, Mary Lee *literature and language professor, editor*
Gephardt, Donald Louis *music educator*
Korieh, Chima J. *history professor*
Mukhoti, Bela Banerjee *economics professor*
Slater, C. Stewart *chemical engineering educator*
Wright, William Cook *archivist, director*

Glen Ridge
Addison, Herbert John *consulting editor, writer*
Agnew, Peter Tomlin *employee benefit consultant*
Connolly, Joseph Thomas *retired lawyer, judge*
Pendley, Donald Lee *association executive*
Rubin, Roberta Gail *retired pathologist*
Vaccaro, John J. *neurologist*
Zbar, Lloyd Irwin Stanley *otolaryngologist, educator*

Glen Rock
Goldstone, Robert Allen *orthopaedic surgeon*
Markey, Brian Michael *lawyer*
Mc Elrath, Richard Elsworth *retired insurance company executive*
Savoie, Brietta Dolores Giger *retired librarian*

Green Brook
Bohanan, David John *management consultant*
Hertzberg, Henry *retired radiologist*
Spoeri, Randall Keith *healthcare company executive*

Green Village
Swift, John Francis *retired health care advertising company executive*

Guttenberg
Wright, Jane Cooke *oncologist, educator, consultant*

Hackensack
Abut, Charles C. *lawyer*
Agress, Harry, Jr. *radiologist, nuclear medicine physician*
Ahearn, James *columnist*
Alvarez, Manuel *hospital executive, medical educator, medical news correspondent*
Borg, Malcolm Austin *publishing executive*
Bronson, Meridith J. *lawyer*
Burt, Gwynne Elayne *minister, theology studies educator*
Caminiti, Donald Angelo *lawyer*
Croland, Barry I. *lawyer*
D'Alessandro, Dianne Marie *public defender*
Duus, Gordon Cochran *lawyer*
Feldman, Vitaly *entrepreneur*
Ferguson, John Patrick *health facility administrator*
Forman, Michael H. *lawyer*
Greenberg, Steven Morey *lawyer*
Haines, Kathleen Ann *pediatrician, educator*
Heilborn, George Heinz *investor*
Horowitz, Donald *lawyer*
Imus, Deirdre (Coleman) *health facility administrator, writer*
Jaye, Daniel *principal*
Koretsky, Alexander *entrepreneur*
Latimer, Stephen Mark *lawyer*
Margulies, James Howard *editorial cartoonist*
Masullo, Alfredo Salvatore *dermatologist*
Mavrovic, Paul J. *information technology executive*
Mullin, Patrick Allen *lawyer*
Navatta, Anna Paula *lawyer*
Pecora, Andrew Louis *hematologist, oncologist*
Peterson, Linda Ellen *lawyer*
Pollinger, William Joshua *lawyer*
Rauscher, Gregory Edwin *plastic surgeon*
Smith, Daniel *oncologist, gynecologist*
Spiegel, Linda F. *lawyer*
Stein, Gary S. *retired judge, lawyer*
Steinbach, Harold I. *lawyer*
Vort, Robert A. *lawyer*
Weiner, Samuel *lawyer*
Williamson, (Eulah) Elaine *elementary school educator*

Hackettstown
Lamour, Kenol *artist, educator*
Mulligan, Elinor Patterson *lawyer*
Singh, Harjit *medical educator, artist*
Van Campen, Stephen Bernard *executive recruiter, consultant*
Walker, Carole A. *advertising executive*
Wiedemann, Charles Louis *dentist*

Haddonfield
Andres, Kenneth G., Jr. *lawyer*
Baltake, Susan *marketing and communications professional*
Bauer, Raymond Gale *sales professional*
Capelli, John Placido *nephrologist, educator*
Ewan, David E. *lawyer*
Fisher, George Ross III *physician, educator*
Fuoco, Philip Stephen *lawyer*
Gatti, Eugene Anthony *immunologist, pediatrician*
Heuisler, Charles William *lawyer*
Iavicoli, Mario Anthony *lawyer*
Jensh, Ronald Paul *retired anatomist*
Spevak, Eric Scott *lawyer*

Hainesport
Sylk, Leonard Allen *manufacturing executive, real estate developer*

Haledon
Dougherty, June Eileen *librarian*

Hamilton
Allen, Stacey R. *forensic specialist*
Ebert, Lawrence Burton *lawyer*
Sporn, Aaron Adolph *physician, educator*

Hampton
Nevins, Arthur Gerard, Jr. *lawyer*

Harrison
Winkleblech, Eileen *computer technology educator, career planning administrator*

Hasbrouck Heights
Perham, Roy Gates III *industrial psychologist*

Haworth
Strum, Brian J. *real estate company officer*

Hazlet
Uriarte, Chris J. *information technology executive*

Helmetta
Gabay, Eleonora V. *mechanical engineer, educator*

Hewitt
Mollenkott, Virginia Ramey *English literature and language educator, writer, guest lecturer*
Selwyn, Donald *engineering administrator, researcher, inventor, educator*

Highland Park
Blum, Lisa Carrie *social worker, researcher*
Brudner, Harvey Jerome *physicist*
Feuerwerker, Elie *biologist, educator*
Fogiel, Max *publishing executive*
Grady, Joyce (Marian Joyce Grady) *psychotherapist, consultant*
Kolodzei, Natalia A. *art association administrator, art historian, curator*
Spencer, Herbert Harry *structural engineer, researcher, computer analyst*

Highlands
Dann, Emily *mathematics educator*
Hansen, Christian Andreas, Jr. *plastics and chemical company executive*
Psuty, Norbert Phillip *marine sciences educator*

Hightstown
Darr, Walter Robert *financial analyst*
Elliott, Frank Nelson *retired college president*
Green, John F. *headmaster*
Hunter, John Stuart *statistician, consultant*
Schorske, Carl Emil *historian, educator*

Hillsborough
Herman, David J. *infectious diseases physician*
Kenyhercz, Thomas Michael *pharmaceutical company executive*
Sun, Wei *electrical engineer*

Hillsdale
Cageao, Carolynn Finnen *language educator*
Copeland, Lois Jacqueline *physician*
Kohan, Lois Rae *community health nurse*

Hillside
Dickerson, Martin Lee *principal*
Wilson, Bertina Iolia *retired music educator*

Ho Ho Kus
Deupree, Marvin Mattox *financial consultant*
Van Slooten, Ronald Henry Joseph *dentist*

Hoboken
Abel, Robert Berger *science administrator*
Boesch, Francis Theodore *electrical engineer, educator*
Bostwick, Randell Armour *retired food service executive*
Fassoulis, Satiris Galahad *communications executive, director*
Griskey, Richard George *chemical engineering professor*
Hakki, Ayesha *editor-in-chief*
Korfiatis, George *academic administrator, engineering educator*
Lawrence, Victor B. *computer and systems engineer*
Malek, Manu *information scientist, educator*
Moon, Deok Hyun *research scientist, educator*
Raveché, Harold Joseph *academic administrator*
Savitsky, Daniel *retired structural engineer, educator*
Schmidt, George *physicist, educator*
Sisto, Fernando *mechanical engineering educator*
Sommers, George R. *lawyer*
Spring, Michael *editor, writer*
Tardiff, Jill Alexandria *publishing executive, photographer*
Ubell, Robert Neil *editor, educator, publishing executive, consultant*
Widdicombe, Richard Palmer *librarian*
Xing, Yiping *electrical engineer, researcher*
Zabarankin, Michael *operations research specialist, educator*

Holmdel
Colmant, Andrew Robert *lawyer*
Kane, Michael Joel *physician*
Kogelnik, Herwig Werner *electronics company executive*
Lang, Howard Lawrence *electrical engineer*
Smith, Sibley Judson, Jr. *historic site administrator, educator*
Smith, Timothy G. *telecommunications industry executive*

Hopatcong
Oken, Robert *retired neuroscientist, consultant*

Hope
McDonald, John Joseph *electronics executive*

Hopewell
Lester, Pamela Robin *lawyer, consultant*
Woodward, Daniel Holt *librarian, researcher*

Howell
Culver, Vicky *art gallery director, artist*

Irvington
Paden, Harry *municipal official*

Iselin
Accardi, Joseph Ronald *accountant*
Dornbusch, Arthur A., II, *lawyer*
Goodman, Barry S. *lawyer*
Ilinich, Oleg *chemist, researcher*
Liu, Xinsheng *chemist*
Perry, Barry W. *manufacturing executive*
Smith, Orin Robert *chemical company executive*

Jackson
Arminas, Scott Arnold *chemist, poet, writer*
Cohen, Walter Stanley *financial consultant*
Hagberg, Carl Thomas *financial executive*
Heck, Roberta M. *poet, writer*
Leveson, Irving Frederick *economist*
Ranone, John Louis *school board executive*
Tague, Charles Francis *retired engineering company executive, real estate company executive, construction executive*
Wagner, Edward Kurt *publishing company executive*
Woodman, G. Roger *management consultant*

Jersey City
Adlershteyn, Leon *retired marine architect, retired engineering educator and researcher*
Amoruso, Leonard J. *lawyer*
Bolcar, Katherine Elizabeth *music educator*
Bulaong, Grace F. *library director*
Collins, John W., Jr. *retired military officer, technologist, educator*
Cornacchia, Eugene John *academic administrator, political science professor*
D'Alessandro, Daniel *lawyer, educator, coach*
Demos, Nicholas John *physician, surgeon, researcher*
Farrior, Evan Bell *special education educator, writer*

Goldberg, Arthur *merchant banker, financial consultant, educator*
Gordon, Robert Dana *transplant surgeon*
Gurevich, Grigory *visual artist, educator, mime*
Hayes, Isaac *rhythm and blues singer, composer*
Healy, Jerramiah *mayor*
Hitchcock, John C. *communications media executive*
Ingrassia, Paul Joseph *publishing executive*
Jeng, Judy Horng *librarian*
Jennings, Sister Vivien *literature and language professor*
Katz, Colleen *publisher*
Klyatis, Lev Matusovich *test and reliability scientist*
Koster, Emlyn Howard *geologist, educator*
Laski, John N. *finance educator*
Lipschutz, Neal S. *editor*
Mahood, Marie I. *counselor, educator*
Merritt, Thomas M. *lawyer*
Ohiwerei, Godwin Oiseozoje *sociologist, educator*
Ott, Gilbert Russell, Jr. *lawyer*
Perhach, James Lawrence *pharmaceutical executive*
Pietrini, Andrew Gabriel *automotive aftermarket executive*
Queen Latifah, (Dana Elaine Owens) *actress, musician*
Riley, Cheryl *artist, educator*
Rodeiro, José M. *art historian, educator*
Signorile, Vincent A. *lawyer*
Singer, Howard Jack *biology professor, researcher*
Soo Hoo, Tsung (Bill) Yao *security studies educator, consultant*
Stine, Rick D. *editor*
Thor, Ira P. *sports director*
Twersky, Laura Harriet *biologist, educator*
Urso, Ida *psychologist*
Warren, Maredia Delois *music educator*
Weaver-Gardner, Priscilla *library director*
Yaworsky, Bohdan *criminal justice educator*

Kearny
Brady, Lawrence Peter *lawyer*
Dunne, Frederick R., Jr. *lawyer*
John, Ricky *state official*

Keasbey
Hari, Kenneth Stephen *painter, sculptor, writer*

Kendall Park
Gupta, Rajat Kumar *lawyer, accountant*
Hershenov, Bernard Zion *research and development company executive*
Kesarwala, Hemant *pediatrician, educator*

Kenilworth
Bertolini, Robert J. *pharmaceutical executive*
Cox, Carrie *pharmaceutical executive*
Gen, Martin *protective services executive*
Hassan, Fred *pharmaceutical executive*
Korfmacher, Walter Averill *chemist, researcher*

Kinnelon
Haller, Charles Edward *engineer, consultant*
Preston, Andrew Joseph *pharmacist, drug company executive*

Lakewood
Appello, Patrick Paul *guitarist, lutenist, educator*
Conklin, Jack L. *education educator*
Doak, Nancy Ann *mathematics educator*
Fanuele, Michael Anthony *retired electronics engineer, research engineer*
Forbes, Gordon Maxwell *sportswriter, commentator*
Houle, Joseph E. *mathematics professor*
Karol, Frederick John *retired industrial chemist*
Levovitz, Pesach Zechariah *rabbi*
Pilgram, Suzanne *artist, art educator*
Williams, Barbara Anne *retired academic administrator*

Lambertville
Cusworth, Christyl J. *conservator, artist*

Lanoka Harbor
Lake, William Robert *school district administrator*

Laurel Springs
Cleveland, Susan Elizabeth *library administrator, researcher*
Roma, Aida Clara *artist*

Lawrenceville
Antonacci, Mark Darryl *orthopedist, surgeon*
Ben-Asher, Daniel Lawrence *photojournalist, retired legislative staff member*
Bishop, James Francis *personnel director, consultant*
Brill, Michael Henry *physicist, editor*
Coleman, Wade Hampton III *management consultant, mechanical engineer, retired banker*
Evans, Frederick John *psychologist*
Jordan, Mildred Rice Loretta *education educator*
Karp, Jonathan D. *biology professor*
Kulak, Chester B. *dentist*
Maxwell, Max Anthony *retired language educator*
Nygren, Lan Ma *finance educator*
Oram, Fern Amy *editor-in-chief, director*
Pouleur, Hubert Gustave *cardiologist, consultant*
Rosenthal, Albert Lester *dermatologist, educator*
Rozanski, Mordechai *academic administrator*
Stark, Albert Maxwell *lawyer*
Stehle, Edward Raymond *secondary education educator, school system administrator*
Stein, Sandra Lou *educational psychology professor*
Tharney, Leonard John *education educator, consultant*
Weaver, Charles Lyndell, Jr. *marketing executive, educational consultant*

Witte, Arnold Stewart *neurologist*

Layton
Seely, Maribeth Walsh *elementary school educator*

Leonardo
Bianchi, Hollis Dolce *writer, poet, artist*

Leonia
Deutsch, Nina *pianist, vocalist*
Greenwald, Martin *publishing company executive*
Kitman, Marvin *journalist*
Kurtz, Anthony David *physicist*

Liberty Corner
Apruzzese, Vincent John *lawyer*
Feeks, J. Michael *bank executive*

Lincoln Park
Sichuk, George *entrepreneur, writer, biochemist, physiologist*

Lincroft
Benham, Helen *music educator*
Ruiz Madas, Yesenia *educational counselor*
Zigo, Paul Edward *historian, educator*

Linden
Bukosky, Richard J. *allergist*
Purves, Dennis Patrick *library director*

Linwood
Sutman, Francis Xavier *retired academic administrator, chemist, writer*

Little Falls
Berra, Yogi (Lawrence Peter Berra) *former professional baseball player, coach, manager*
Casey, Karen Anne *banker*
Shern, Stephanie Marie *investment company executive, accountant*
Varis, Agnes *pharmaceutical executive*

Little Ferry
Briggs, Alice *clinical child psychologist*

Little Silver
Brennan, William Joseph *manufacturing executive*
Marcus, Abir A. *psychiatrist*
Schmidt, Daniel Edward, IV, *lawyer, arbitrator*

Livingston
Adelsberg, Harvey *hospital administrator*
Brody, Martin *hotel executive*
Daman, Ernest Ludwig *mechanical engineer*
Fodero, Joseph Peter *plastic surgeon*
Friedman, Merton Hirsch *retired psychologist, educator*
Gordon, Frederick James *orthopedist, surgeon*
Ingato, Robert Joseph *lawyer*
Jaffe, Leonard *orthopedist, surgeon, educator*
Leone, Joseph M. *finance company executive*
Peek, Jeffrey M. *finance company executive*
Rinsky, Joel Charles *lawyer*
Samojlik, Eugeniusz *medical educator, health facility administrator*
Santoro, Elissa Jeanne *breast oncology surgeon*
Segal, Jeffrey L. *gynecologist, obstetrician, researcher*
Stevens, William Dollard *mechanical engineer, consultant*
Sukoneck, Ira David *lawyer*

Lodi
Karetzky, Joanne Louise *librarian*
Karetzky, Stephen *library director, educator, researcher*
McParland, Robert Patrick *literature educator, writer*
Pitocco, Barbara Mary *psychotherapist, social worker*

Long Branch
Lagowski, Barbara Jean *writer, editor*
Luria, Martin Jay *endocrinologist*
Pachman, Frederic Charles *library director*

Lumberton
Campagnolo, Mary Frances *physician*

Lyndhurst
Bunda, Stephen Myron *political advisor, counselor, lawyer, classical philosopher*
Herndon, John Laird *accounting firm executive*
McNamara, Patrick James *lawyer*
Prevoznik, Michael E. *lawyer*
Scagnelli, John Mark *lawyer*

Madison
Armstrong, Richard William *bank executive, management consultant*
Bull, Vivian Ann *retired academic administrator, educator*
Byrd, Stephen Fred *human resource consultant*
Demain, Arnold Lester *microbiologist, educator*
Ellenbogen, Leon *nutritionist, biochemist, retired pharmaceutical executive*
Essner, Robert Alan *pharmaceutical executive*
Jennings, George Harold *psychology professor*
Kaboub, Fadhel *economics professor, consultant*
Mahady, Joseph M. *former pharmacy products company executive*
Monte, Bonnie J. *performing arts company executive, director, educator*
O'Brien, Mary Devon *communications executive, consultant*
O'Connor, Charles P. *lawyer*
Parker, Henry Griffith III *insurance executive*
Poussot, Bernard Jean *pharmaceutical executive*
Rosales Herrera, Raúl Joaquin *language educator*
Rubinstein, Ernest *librarian, educator*
Skaggs, Merrill Maguire *humanities educator*
Stein, Lawrence V. *lawyer*
Weisbuch, Robert Alan *academic administrator*

Mahwah
Bear, Larry Alan *retired lawyer, educator*
Birnberg, Jack *financial executive*
Gerstein, David Brown *manufacturing and professional sports team executive*
Gibbons, Robert Philip *management consultant, director*
Hailparn, Diana Finnegan *psychotherapist, writer*
Harth, Marshall Stephen *psychology professor, psychotherapist*
Padovano, Anthony Thomas *theologian, literature educator*

Manalapan
Barratt, Donna Lee *elementary school educator*
Stone, Fred Michael *lawyer*

Manasquan
Abate, John E. *electrical engineer, consultant*
Jones, Elizabeth Harding *real estate agent, retired elementary school educator*
Kelman, Marybeth *retired health care consultant, health policy analyst*

Manchester
Madan, Deepak S. *engineering executive*

Mantoloking
Shane, Kevin *apparel executive, entrepreneur*

Maple Shade
Mahon, Katherine A. (Kit Mahon) *public relations executive, writer*

Maplewood
Fiorito, Frank Anthony *secondary educator*
Haggerty, Mary Ann *medical educator*
Joel, Amos Edward, Jr. *telecommunications consultant*
Johnson, Dewey, Jr. *retired biochemist*
Lally, Michael David *writer, actor*
Levine, Benjamin *lawyer*
Safian, Gail Robyn *public relations executive*
Shuttleworth, Anne Margaret *psychiatrist*
Tatyrek, Alfred Frank *retired chemist, environmental engineer*
Woods, Krystyna Janina *artist, pharmacist*

Margate City
Trocki-Videll, Cyla *psychiatrist, medical association administrator*
Videll, Jared Steven *cardiologist*

Marlboro
Bass, David Steven *law educator, arbitrator, mediator*
Kayafas, Stephanie Ann *special education educator, consultant, supervisor, actress*

Marlton
Cheney, Eleanora Louise *retired secondary school educator*
Clemens, David Allen *minister*
Farwell, Nancy Larraine *public relations executive*
Kahn, Sigmund Benham *retired internist, dean*
Klein, Gerhart Leopold *public relations executive*
Sidelsky, Patricia Loney *science educator*

Matawan
Amato, Vincent Vito *marketing and business consultant*
Cohen, Robert L. *film producer*
Liggett, Twila C. *broadcast executive, educator*
Mayo, Douglas Blake *computer scientist, application developer*
Nolan, Sharon Theresa *nurse, educator*
Rivera-Dominguez, Alberto *mathematician, educator, mechanical engineer*
Thompson, Samuel Donald *assemblyman*

Mays Landing
LoBiondo, Frank A. *congressman*
Mooney, Lori *county official*

Mc Afee
Fogel, Richard *lawyer, educator*

Medford
Henderson, Rita Elizabeth *literary agent, journalist*
Lawson-Ndu, Ovunda A. *emergency physician, surgeon*
Mayer, Joyce Harris *artist*
Micko, Alexander S. *corporate financial executive, educator, treasurer*
Nicholas, Leonard G. *music educator*
Sheffer, James Thomas *music educator*
Springer, Douglas Hyde *retired food products executive, lawyer*

Mendham
Hambleton, George Blow Elliott *retired management consultant*
Kirby, Allan Price, Jr. *investment company executive*
Pierson, Robert David *investor*
Posunko, Barbara *retired elementary school educator*

Metuchen
Arbeiter, Joan *artist, educator*
Demkovitz, Russell Bernard *deacon, ceremetary director*
Macarin-Mara, Lynn *psychotherapist, consultant*
Massey, Eleanor Nelson *retired school librarian, media specialist*
Smyth, David *writer, editor*

Middlesex
Baker, James Clifford *school system administrator*

Middletown
Lundgren, Carl William, Jr. *physicist*
Meyler, William Anthony *financial analyst*

Sullivan, Timothy Patrick *telecommunications company executive*
Tomicki, Stephen G. *engineer*

Midland Park
Baum, Richard David *urologist*

Millburn
Bablin, Mark Edward *security administrator, mortgage consultant*
Diamond, Richard S. *lawyer*
Kuttner, Bernard A. *retired judge, lawyer*

Milltown
Haws, Robert John *lawyer*

Millville
Caldwell, Linda E. *critical care nurse*

Monmouth Beach
Ginty, Karen *elementary school educator*
Herbert, LeRoy James *retired accounting firm executive*

Monmouth Junction
Brolin, Robert Edward *physician, surgeon*
Chau, Wai Yip *surgeon*
Kaminker, Marcia Kahn *physical therapist*
Lancaster, Barbara Mae *management consulting company executive*
Lien, Ting-Ting *music educator*
Prestbo, John Andrew *editor, writer, journalist*

Monroe Township
Allen, Katherine Spicer *writer, former chemist*
Cushman, Helen Merle Baker *retired management consultant*
Meshowski, Frank Robert *business consultant*
Reichek, Morton Arthur *retired magazine editor, writer*
Spierer, Robert *family practice physician*
Stein, Florence Taub *retired social worker*
Treatman, Paul *retired school system administrator*
Zelin, Jerome *retired retail executive*

Montclair
Adarkar, Aditya *humanities educator*
Campbell, Stewart Fred *foundation administrator, consultant*
Chemidlin, Michele Lynn *athletic trainer, consultant*
Chinard, Francis Pierre *physiologist, consultant physician, educator*
Cole, Susan A. *academic administrator, language educator*
Cooke, Nicole *school librarian*
Delbourgo, Joëlle Lily *publishing executive*
Delgado, Ramon Louis *theater educator, author, director, playwright, lyricist*
Du, Chunguang Charles *biologist, educator*
Dubrow, Marsha Ann *management consultant, musicologist*
Eager, George Sidney, Jr. *electrical engineer, engineering executive*
Gollob, Herman Cohen *retired publishing executive*
Greenwald, Robert *public relations executive*
Holmes, Nathaniel J. *surgeon*
Jones, Michael A. *mathematics professor*
Jones, Sylvia Calpurnia *investment company executive*
Luftglass, Murray Arnold *corporate financial executive*
McConnell, Lorelei Catherine *retired library director*
Mukherjee, Avinandan *business educator*
Rosen, Allen David *plastic surgeon*
Sims, Patterson *curator*
Walker, George Theophilus, Jr. *composer, music educator, pianist*
Williamson, Philemona *artist*

Montvale
Avedon, Marcia J. *diversified industrial products company and former pharmaceutical executive*
Falcon, Raymond Jesus, Jr. *lawyer*
Henkel, Herbert Ludwig *diversified industrial products company executive*
Nachtigal, Patricia *lawyer*
Politi, Beth Kukkonen *publishing services company executive*

Montville
Birkett, Norman Myles *private school educator, writer*
Buzak, Edward Joseph *lawyer*
Riotto, Scott M. *secondary school educator*

Moonachie
Ueltschi, Albert Lee *air transportation executive*

Moorestown
Bennington, William Jay *management consultant*
Buckman, William H. *lawyer*
Burnham, Lem *psychologist, think-tank executive*
Carson, William Charles *sales and marketing executive*
Clark, Maryliz M. *retired minister*
Felcyn, Diane Annette *art association administrator*
Hyland, William Francis *retired lawyer*
McDaniel, Joanava B. *nurse*
Schwerin, Horace S. *marketing research consultant*
Slemmer, Carl Weber, Jr. *retired lawyer*

Morris Plains
Bennett, John Charles *former engineering and construction executive*
Capellos, Chris Spiridon *chemist*
Ferris, Carlisle Keith *artist*
Goldenberg, David Milton *experimental pathologist, oncologist*
Spong, John Shelby *retired bishop, writer, columnist*

Morristown
Adler, Kenneth R. *oncologist*
Anderson, David J. *corporate financial executive*
Aspero, Benedict Vincent *lawyer*
Bartkus, Robert Edward *lawyer*
Boodey, Cecil Webster, Jr. *retired political science professor*
Bromberg, Myron James *lawyer*
Cameron, Nicholas Allen *manufacturing executive*
Coleman, James H., Jr. *lawyer, former state supreme court justice*
Cote, David M. *diversified technology and manufacturing company executive*
Cregan, Frank Robert *financial executive, consultant*
Deming, Frederick Wilson *retired economist, banker*
Fiel, Stanley Bruce *internist, pulmonologist, educator, researcher*
Finkel, Marion Judith *internist, pharmaceutical administrator*
Fontaine Newsome, Lynn *lawyer*
Fradin, Roger Brent *manufacturing executive*
Fredericks, Robert Joseph *language company executive*
Giacchi, Renato *physician*
Gillen, James Robert *lawyer, insurance company executive*
Gordon, Erin Kathleen *elementary school educator*
Hansbury, Stephan Charles *judge*
Haselmann, John Philip *management consultant*
Hastings, Mary Jane *minister*
Healey, Thomas J. *former government official, brokerage house executive*
Herzberg, Peter Jay *lawyer*
Humick, Thomas Charles Campbell *lawyer*
Jacobs, Andrew Robert *lawyer*
Johnson, David Blackwell *safety engineer*
Kearns, William Michael, Jr. *investment banker*
Kirby, Fred Morgan, II, *finance company executive*
Kirby, Jefferson W. *investment company executive*
Kittelberger, Larry E. *engineering executive*
Korf, Gene Robert *lawyer*
Kreindler, Peter Michael *lawyer*
Lazar, Eric Loren *pediatric surgeon, director*
Lieberman, Lester Zane *engineering company executive*
Martelet, Francois R. *pharmaceutical executive*
McConnell, John Howard *personnel management consultant, writer*
Mertz, Francis James *university president*
Miller, Steven H. *museum director*
Moore, Milo Anderson *banker*
Moritz, Mark William *vascular surgeon*
Musa, John Davis *information technology executive, writer*
Nadaskay, Raymond *architect*
Nolan, J. Michael, Jr. *retired lawyer*
O'Grady, Dennis Joseph *lawyer*
Olcott, John Whiting *air transportation executive*
Parker, Mary Lou *lawyer*
Parr, Grant Van Siclen *surgeon*
Pollock, Stewart Glasson *lawyer, state supreme court justice*
Prince, Leah Fanchon *lab administrator, executive secretary*
Prystauk, Elissa *artist*
Rainal, Attilio Joseph *retired electronics engineer*
Raziq, Yaqub *telecommunications engineer*
Rogachefsky, Arlene Sandra *dermatologist*
Rose, Robert Gordon *lawyer*
Rosenthal, Meyer Louis *lawyer*
Ross, Thomas J., Jr. *personal financial adviser*
Sachs, Richard Gregory *cardiologist*
Scott, Richard Thomas, Jr. *reproductive endocrinologist*
Sherman, Sandra Brown *lawyer*
Smart, Frank Wilson *physician*
Stanton, Patrick Michael *lawyer*
Venezia, William Thomas *school system administrator, counseling consultant*
Waks, Robert Gilman *librarian*
Weidenkopf, Thomas W. *human resources specialist*
Williams, Joseph Dalton *pharmaceutical executive*
Zaubler, Thomas Scot *psychiatrist, educator*

Mount Holly
Mintz, Jeffry Alan *lawyer, mediator*

Mount Laurel
Batory, Ronald Louis *rail transportation executive*
Giampetro, Kathleen A. *school psychologist*
Jones, Marian C. *music educator*
Koplin, Bernice J. *lawyer*
Mann, Louis Eugene *financial planner*
Rabbe, David Ellsworth *oil industry executive*

Mountain Lakes
Daniel, Royal Thomas III *lawyer, mechanical engineer, accountant*
Loomis, Rebecca C. *psychologist*
Wallace, MaryJean Elizabeth *science educator*

Mountainside
Bertsch, Patricia Ann *nature center director*
Helander, Robert Charles *lawyer, arbitrator*
Horner, Shirley Jaye *columnist, writing and publishing consultant*
Lipton, Bronna Jane *marketing communications executive*
Vice, Susan F. *medicinal chemist*

Mullica Hill
Rose, Carol Ann *retired air transportation executive*

Neptune
Aguiar, Adam Martin *chemist, educator*
Laraya-Cuasay, Lourdes Redublo *pediatrician, pulmonologist, educator*
Montgomery, John Harold *environmentalist*
Rice, Stephen Gary *pediatrician, sports medicine physician, educator*
Riordan, John A. *retired food products executive*

Neptune City
Axelrod, Glen Scott *publishing and pet product company executive*

Neshanic Station
Muckenhoupt, Benjamin *retired mathematics professor*

New Brunswick
Aisner, Joseph *oncologist, medical educator*
Alexander, Robert Jackson *economist, educator*
August, David Allen *surgeon*
Bennett, Joan Wennstrom *biology educator*
Bertino, Joseph Rocco *oncologist, educator*
Biribauer, Richard Frank *lawyer*
Borah, Gregory *surgeon, educator*
Bowden, Henry Warner *religion educator*
Boyarsky, Andrew Harold *surgeon, educator*
Bradley, Dondeena G. *consumer products company executive*
Brilliant, Eleanor Luria *retired social work educator*
Bunch, Charlotte *advocate*
Caldwell, Dale Gilbert *management consultant*
Carson, Jeffrey L. *internist*
Chambers, John Whiteclay, II, *history professor*
Chandler, James John *surgeon, educator*
Clauss-Ehlers, Caroline S. *psychologist, educator, journalist*
Corbett, Siobhan Aiden *surgeon*
Coscia, Anthony R. *state agency administrator, lawyer*
Darretta, Robert J. *pharmaceutical executive*
Day-Salvatore, Debra Lynn *medical geneticist*
Denda, Kayo *librarian*
Deyo, Russell C. *health products executive, lawyer*
Dhib-Jalbut, Suhayl S. *physician*
DiPaola, Robert *internist*
Dougherty, Neil Joseph *physical education educator, consultant*
Drachtman, Richard Allan *pediatrician, educator*
Ehrenfeld, David William *biology professor, writer*
Elias, Maurice Jesse *psychology educator*
Ettinger, Lawrence Jay *pediatric hematologist, oncologist, educator*
Feigenson, Mark Daniel *geologist, educator*
Foley, Eugene Arthur *accountant, consultant*
Foster-Cheek, Kaye I. *health products executive*
Friedrich, Gustav William *dean, communications educator*
Funk, Cyril Reed, Jr. *agronomist, educator*
Gaunt, Marianne I. *university librarian*
Gillette, William *historian, educator*
Glasser, Paul Harold *sociologist, educator, social worker, university administrator*
Glickman, Norman Jay *economist, urban policy analyst*
Goggins, Colleen A. *health products executive*
Goldberg, Michael Ira *obstetrician, gynecologist*
Goldrich, Michael Seth *otolaryngologist*
Graham, Alan Morrison *surgeon*
Greenberg, Michael Richard *urban studies and community health educator*
Greenwald, Alfred Emanuel *retired cosmetic surgeon*
Griffin, Gary Arthur *technological products executive*
Grob, Gerald N. *historian, educator*
Haines, William Joseph *retired pharmaceutical executive*
Hartman, Mary Susan *historian, educator*
Horowitz, Irving Louis *publisher, educator*
Huhmann, Maureen Brigitte *dietitian, researcher*
Jaluria, Yogesh *mechanical engineering educator, department chairman*
Jenkins, Alyce Mitchem *writer, educator*
Jenkins, Reese V. *historian, educator*
Kadlec, Kim *media executive*
Kahn, Jeffry *mathematics professor*
Kaufman, Kenneth Roland *psychiatrist, educator*
Khachadurian, Avedis *physician*
Kostis, John Basil *cardiologist*
Kulikowski, Casimir Alexander *computer scientist, engineer, educator*
Lachance, Paul Albert *food science educator, clergyman*
Larsen, Ralph S(tanley) *retired pharmaceutical executive*
Lepore, Frederick Everett *neurologist, educator*
Lesk, Michael E. *library and information science educator*
Leventhal, Elaine A. *internist*
Leventhal, Howard *health psychology educator, researcher*
Libutti, Patricia O'Brien *university librarian*
Makhija, Mohan *nuclear medicine physician*
Mann, Richard Alan *physician, educator*
Maramorosch, Karl *virologist, educator*
Martínez, Tomás Eloy *writer, journalist*
Mazzeo, Anthony R. *chemist*
McCormick, Richard Levis *academic administrator*
Mechanic, David *social sciences educator*
Miller, Arthur Harold *lawyer*
Miller, Lynn Fieldman *lawyer*
Mills, Dorothy Allen *investor*
Mills, George Marshall *financial consultant*
Moreyra, Abel E. *medical educator*
Mullinix, Kathleen Patricia *food products executive, biochemist*
Nelson, Jack Lee *education educator*
Nosko, Michael Gerrik *neurosurgeon, educator*
Notterman, Daniel A. *pediatrician, educator*
Olson, Robert Martin *plastic surgeon*
O'Neill, William Lawrence *retired history professor*
Pandey, Ramesh Chandra *chemist, chemicals executive*
Peterson, Per A. *health products executive*
Pitchumoni, Capecomorin Sankar *gastroenterologist, educator*
Poon, Christine A. *pharmaceutical company executive*
Qualls, Barry V. *literature professor*
Radford, Marie Louise *library science educator*
Raska, Karel Frantisek Julian, Jr. *pathologist, virologist, educator*
Reed, James Wesley *social historian, educator*
Reock, Ernest C., Jr. *retired social studies educator, director*
Robock, Alan *meteorology professor*
Rockoff, Hugh Touff *economist, educator*
Rosenberg, Seymour *psychologist, educator*
Rubin, Eric Howard *oncologist, researcher*
Russell, Louise Bennett *economist, educator*
Saidi, Parvin *hematologist, medical educator*
Salas, Max *pediatrician, educator*
Saracevic, Tefko *information science educator*
Scanlon, Jane Cronin *mathematics professor*
Schneider, Stephen Harley *medical educator*
Scholz, Peter M. *surgeon, director*
Scodari, Joseph C. *health products executive*
Shindler, Daniel *cardiologist*
Smouse, Peter E. *ecologist, educator*
Snyder, Barbara K. *pediatrician, educator*
Sosa, Joseph F. *pharmaceutical executive*
Spotnitz, Alan Jeffrey *cardiothoracic surgeon*
Stanley, Jason *education educator*
Stauffer, George B. *dean, musician, historian, consultant*
Stich, Stephen Peter *philosophy educator*
Strauss, Ulrich Paul *chemist, educator*
Strawderman, William E. *statistics educator*
Strickland, Dorothy *education educator*
Tanner, Daniel *education educator*
Tedrow, John Charles Fremont *soils educator*
Tiger, Lionel *social scientist, anthropology consultant*
Toby, Jackson *sociologist, educator*
Todd, Mary Beth *oncologist, researcher*
Trivers, Robert L. *bioscience and anthropology educator, evolutionary biologist, sociobiologist*
Trooskin, Stanley Z. *surgeon*
Turock, Betty Jane *library and information science professor*
Upton, Arthur Canfield *experimental pathologist, educator*
Valeriani, Nicholas J. *health products executive*
Weinstein, Melvin Phillip *physician educator*
Weiss, Lynne S. *pediatrician, educator*
Weiss, Robert Edward *urologist, educator*
Weldon, William C. *pharmaceutical executive*
Weng, George Jueng-Cious *engineering educator*
Yorke, Marianne *lawyer, real estate executive*

New Milford
Walsh, Joseph Michael *magazine distribution executive*

New Monmouth
Santos, Sharon Lee *parochial school educator*

New Providence
Barnes, Sandra Henley *retired publishing company executive*
Blessing, Leonard C. *secondary school educator*
Bruch, Ruth E. *information technology executive*
Carapezzi, William R., Jr. *telecommunications industry executive, lawyer*
Chandross, Edwin Arthur *chemist, consultant*
Chatterji, Debajyoti *retired manufacturing executive*
Chen, Young-Kai *electronics engineer, researcher*
Del Tiempo, Sandra Kay *sales executive*
Hackenson, Elizabeth *information technology and telecommunications industry executive*
Helfand, Eugene *chemist*
Hirsch, Maxine K. *special education educator, councilman*
Kim, Jeong H. *telecommunications industry executive, communications engineer*
Kritzmacher, John A. *telecommunications industry executive*
McCaffrey, Robert Henry, Jr. *retired manufacturing company executive*
McCarthy, G. Daniel *lawyer*
Mejia, Jose A. *telecommunications industry executive*
Reinsdorf, Judith A. *lawyer*
Ring, Timothy Michael *human services administrator, pharmaceutical executive*
Russo, Patricia F. *telecommunications company executive*
Sivco, Deborah Lee *materials scientist, researcher*
Slusher, Richart Elliott *physicist, researcher*

New Vernon
Dugan, John Leslie, Jr. *foundation executive*
Kushen, Allan Stanford *retired lawyer, corporate executive*
McCormack, John Joseph, Jr. *insurance company executive*

Newark
Adler, Freda Schaffer (Mrs. G. O. W. Mueller) *criminologist, educator*
Akin, Wanda M. *lawyer, literary and sports agent*
Alexander, Mark C. *law educator, policy advisor*
Altenkirch, Robert A. *academic administrator*
Arabie, Phipps *marketing educator, researcher*
Arbuckle, Peggy Trawick *special education educator, consultant*
Aregood, Richard Lloyd *editor*
Aron, Lester *lawyer*
Arwady, George E. *publishing executive*
Asatryan, Rubik *chemistry professor, researcher*
Askin, Frank *law educator*
Baer, Susan M. *airport executive*
Baker, Herman *medical educator, writer*
Bar-Ness, Yeheskel *electrical engineer, educator*
Barry, Maryanne Trump *federal judge*
Bergen, Stanley Silvers, Jr. *retired academic administrator*
Berry, Andrew T. *lawyer*
Bielory, Leonard *allergist, immunologist, medical school administrator*
Bizub, Johanna Catherine *law librarian*
Bloom, Joel S. *academic administrator*
Blount, Susan L. *insurance company executive, lawyer*
Blumrosen, Alfred William *law educator*
Bolden, Marion A. *superintendent*
Booker, Cory Anthony *mayor, lawyer*
Brescher, John B., Jr. *lawyer*
Brodeur, Martin *professional hockey player*
Buck, Rebecca A. *museum administrator, registrar*
Bumb, Renee Marie *federal judge*
Byrd, Stephen C. *utilities executive*
Cahn, Jeffrey Barton *lawyer*
Carbone, Richard J. *insurance company executive*
Caron, Jacques *professional hockey coach*
Carroll, John Douglas *mathematical and statistical psychologist, educator*
Cave, Damien *journalist*
Chaplin, C. Edward (Chuck) *diversified financial services company executive*
Cherniack, Neil Stanley *pulmonologist, educator*
Christie, Christopher James *prosecutor, lawyer*
Christie, Scott S. *lawyer*
Clymer, Brian William *diversified financial services company executive, retired state official*
Cohen, Stanley *pathologist, educator*
Colangelo-Bryan, Jeremy Paul *urban planner, transportation executive*
Collins, Jason L. *psychologist*
Connor, Holly Pyne *curator, art historian*
Contractor, Farok *business and management educator*
Cook, Stuart Donald *neurologist, educator*
Courter, James A. (Jim) *communications executive, retired congressman*
Cummis, Clive Sanford *lawyer*
Cunningham, LeeAnn *assistant prosecutor*
Darmento, Ralph Joseph *religious organization administrator, educator, school system administrator*
Dauth, Frances Kutcher *journalist, editor*
Day, Edward Francis, Jr. *lawyer*
Debevoise, Dickinson Richards *federal judge*
Dee, Francis X. *lawyer*
Defeis, Elizabeth Frances *lawyer, educator*
Depre, Christophe *medical educator*
Dhawan, Atam Prakash *engineering educator, dean*
Dickson, Jim *writer, theater producer*
Edwards, Samuel Lawrence, II, *information technology executive, writer*
Eittreim, Richard MacNutt *lawyer*
Elias, Patrik *professional hockey player*
Ellner, Jerrold Jay *infectious diseases specialist*
Emery, Charles Christian, Jr. *health care and information systems executive*
English, Nicholas Conover *lawyer*
Evans, Hugh E. *pediatrician, educator*
Falck, David Phillip *lawyer, utilities executive*
Feldman, Cecile Arlene *dean, dental educator*
Fenster, Saul K. *retired academic administrator*
Ferguson, Yale Hicks *political scientist, educator*
Friedland, Bernard *electrical engineer, educator*
Fuentes, Julio M. *federal judge*
Gadepalli, Vijaya L. *mathematics educator*
Garde, John Charles *lawyer*
Garth, Leonard I. *judge*
Gauster, Stephen Wilhelm *lawyer, corporate financial executive*
Gettleman, Jeffrey *journalist*
Gibbons, John Joseph *lawyer, retired federal judge*
Gibson, Kathleen M. *computer and electronics executive*
Gionta, Brian *professional hockey player*
Goldman, Glenn *architect, educator*
Goldstein, Bruce I. *lawyer*
Goldstein, Ira Morris *neurosurgeon*
Goldstein, Marvin Mark *lawyer*
Granick, Mark S. *medical educator*
Graycar, Adam *dean, former Australian government official*
Greenaway, Joseph Anthony, Jr. *judge*
Grey, Wilma J. *library director*
Grier, Mark B. *diversified financial services company executive*
Hanesian, Deran *chemical engineer, educator, environmental scientist, consultant*
Haring, Eugene Miller *lawyer*
Haycock, Christine Elizabeth *retired medical educator*
Hiltz, Starr Roxanne *sociologist, educator, writer, consultant, computer scientist*
Hobbs, Patrick Esmond *dean, law educator*
Hochberg, Faith S. *US district court judge*
Holzer, Marc *public administrator educator*
Howard, M(oses) William, Jr. *minister*
Hummel, Donald Keith *priest*
Iffy, Leslie *medical educator*
Izenberg, Jerry *sportswriter, columnist, author*
Izzo, Ralph *utilities executive*
Joffe, Russell T. *former dean*
Jonas, Howard S. *communications executive*
Karp, Donald Mathew *lawyer, banker*
Kelley, Tina *journalist*
Kennedy, Leslie W. *criminal justice educator, former dean*
Koster, Barbara *insurance company executive*
Kott, David Russell *lawyer*
Kou, Victoria *medical educator*
Krovatin, Gerald *lawyer*
Lamoriello, Lou (Louis Anthony Lamoriello) *professional sports team executive*
Langenbrunner, Jamie *professional hockey player*
Lanzerotti, Louis John *physicist*
Laperriere, Jacques (Joseph Hughes Laperriere) *professional hockey coach, retired professional hockey player*
La Rocco, Anthony P. *lawyer*
LaRossa, Ralph *utilities executive*
Lautenberg, Frank Raleigh *senator*
Ledeen, Robert Wagner *neuroscientist, educator*
Levin, Simon *lawyer*
Levis, William *utilities executive*

Little, Alan Brian *gynecologist, educator*
Lopriore, Richard P. *utilities executive*
Lorell, Jeffrey W. *lawyer*
Louria, Donald Bruce *medical educator*
Macal, Zdenek *conductor, music director*
MacLean, John *professional hockey coach, former professional hockey player*
Maqsood, Ahsan *cardiologist, researcher*
Marino, William J. *insurance executive*
McGuire, William B(enedict) *lawyer*
McLean, David J. *lawyer*
Meegoda, Jay Namunu *engineering educator, professional engineer*
Ming, Xue *pediatrician, pediatric neurologist, neuroscientist, pharmacologist*
Mitchell, Jason Wayne *radiologist*
Miura, Robert Mitsuru *mathematician, researcher, educator*
Morales, Grisel *language educator*
Moran, Eileen A. *utilities executive*
Myers, John Joseph *archbishop*
Myers, Priscilla A. *insurance company executive*
Nash, Alicia Lardé *application developer, physicist*
Neuer, Philip David *lawyer, real estate consultant*
Newhouse, Mark William *publishing executive*
Odenath, David R., Jr. *diversified financial services company executive*
O'Flynn, Thomas M. *utilities executive*
Owen, William Franklin, Jr. *academic administrator, former research and development company executive*
Pagán, Gilberto, Jr. *psychologist*
Parveen, Nikhat *microbiologist, educator*
Passantino, Benjamin Arthur *marketing executive*
Patrick, Robert Herbert, Jr. *economist, educator*
Pego, Margaret M. *utilities executive*
Petillo, John J. *former academic administrator, priest*
Pfeffer, Robert *chemical engineer, academic administrator, educator*
Phillips, John C. *lawyer*
Pinkett, Randal D. *entrepreneur*
Price, Mary Sue Sweeney *museum director*
Pryor, Stefan I. *city manager, real estate developer*
Quinn, Kevin J. *utilities executive*
Rak, Lorraine Karen *lawyer*
Reichman, Lee Brodersohn *physician*
Reilly, William Thomas *lawyer*
Risinger, D. Michael *lawyer, educator*
Robertson, William Withers *lawyer*
Robinson, Larry Clark *professional hockey coach*
Rosato, Anthony Dominick *mechanical engineer, educator*
Rothschild, Gita F. *lawyer*
Ryan, Arthur Frederick *diversified financial services company executive*
Ryan, Lisa Kathleen *environmental and medical science educator*
Sarles, Richard R. *rail transportation executive*
Schleifer, Steven J. *psychiatrist, educator*
Schweizer, Karl Wolfgang *historian, educator, author*
Selover, R. Edwin *lawyer, utilities executive*
Siegal, Joel Davis *lawyer*
Simmons, Peter *law and urban planning educator*
Simpson, Elbert C. *utilities executive*
Smothers, Ronald *journalist*
Spillers, William Russell *civil engineering educator*
Steinbaum, Robert S. *publishing executive, lawyer*
Stevens, Scott *retired professional hockey player*
Strangfeld, John R., Jr. *diversified financial services company executive*
Sutter, Brent Colin *professional hockey coach, retired professional hockey player*
Timoni, Stephen Anthony *lawyer, accountant*
Tischman, Michael Bernard *lawyer*
Vajtay, Stephen Michael, Jr. *lawyer*
Vanderbeek, Jeffrey *professional sports team executive*
Varzegar, Minoo *literature educator, reading specialist*
Vatner, Stephen F. *physiologist, researcher, research scientist*
Verkhovsky, Boris *computer scientist, educator*
Vincenti, Gene A. *director, consultant*
Ward, Roger Coursen *lawyer*
Weis, Judith Shulman *biology professor*
Weiss, Gerson *endocrinologist, educator*
Wigenton, Susan Davis *federal judge*
Willse, James Patrick *newspaper editor*
Winters, Robert Cushing *insurance company executive*
Zaborszky, Laszlo *neuroscientist*
Zuckerman, Herbert Lawrence *lawyer*

Newfield
Dreher, Frank H., Jr. *retired optician*

Newfoundland
Van Winkle, Edgar Walling *retired electrical engineer*

Newton
Boulware, Bobbie L. *music educator*
Colizza, Wayne Anthony *orthopaedic surgeon*
Cox, William Martin *lawyer, educator*
MacMurren, Margaret Patricia *secondary school educator, consultant*
Morgenstern, Robert Terence *lawyer*

North Bergen
Archbold, Michael G. *consumer products company executive, former retail executive*

North Branch
Sittler, Ryan Lee *librarian*

North Brunswick
Bern, Ronald Lawrence *management consultant, writer*
Burge, Micah Benjamin *school psychologist*
Frenkiel, Richard Henry *retired systems engineer, consultant*
Jones, Frank A., Jr. *psychiatrist, educator*
Moon, Kathleen K. *language arts educator*

North Caldwell
Meserlian, Donald C. *mechanical engineer, consultant*

Northfield
Margolis, Thomas Ira *vitreoretinal ophthalmologist*
McNeal, Jane Erskine *music educator, musician*

Northvale
Di Mino, André Anthony *manufacturing executive, consultant*
Urgas, Sandra S. *emergency physician*

Norwood
Murburg, Thelma D. *retired elementary school educator*

Nutley
Bridge, Thomas Peter *psychiatrist, researcher*
English, Robert Joseph *electronics executive*
Liu, Chao-Min *biochemist, biotechnologist, researcher*
Mallard, Stephen Anthony *retired utilities executive*
Marée, Kathleen Nancy *retired language educator*
Mostillo, Ralph *medical association administrator*
To, Stephen Edward *editor, writer*

Oak Ridge
Kieren, Thomas Henry *management consultant*

Oakland
Dressel, Margaret Jane *artist, educator*
Keough, Daniel Emmet *retired magazine editor*
Manheimer, Heidi *cosmetics company executive*
Reutty, Michele Marie *library director*
Sosland, Karl Z. *lawyer*

Ocean
Brown, Sanford Donald *lawyer*
Reich, Bernard *communications engineer*

Ocean City
Culbertson, Jane Young *statistician*
Hughes, William John *former congressman, diplomat*
Kyriazis, Arthur John (Athanasios Ioannis Kyriazis) *lawyer, biotechnologist*

Old Bridge
Downs, Thomas Edward, IV, *lawyer*

Old Tappan
Lovitch, Joan *science educator, coach*

Oldwick
Sinfelt, John Henry *chemist*
Snyder, Arthur *publishing executive*

Oradell
Blakeslee, Edward Eaton *lawyer, insurance company executive*
Huntington, Raymond J. *education center executive*
Mavroudis, John M. *lawyer*
Merliss, Harry *orthopedist, surgeon*
Parish, J. Michael *lawyer, mutual fund executive, writer*
Struck, Norma Johansen *artist*

Paramus
Atkins, Yvette *special education educator*
Crow, Lynne Campbell Smith *insurance company representative*
Gartner, Michael Constantin *plastic surgeon*
Gilbert, Stephen Alan *lawyer, organization executive*
Gordon, Scott (Harry Scott Buehlmeier) *entertainer, actor*
Grinberg, Efraim *watch manufacturing company executive*
Grinberg, Gedalio *watch manufacturing company executive*
Hermance, Ronald E., Jr. *bank executive*
Hochberg, Lois J. *school psychologist*
Jacobs, Helen Nichols *artist*
Jenkins, Elaine *middle school educator*
Levy, Joseph *lawyer*
Lieberman, Charles *economist*
Liva, Edward Louis *eye surgeon*
Marcel-Calderon, Linda *music educator*
Michalek, Romuald *environmental engineer, engineering company executive*
Noguere, Suzanne *trade association executive, poet*
Saltzman, Jared *performing arts educator, lighting designer*
Tamburro, Peter James, Jr. *secondary school educator*

Park Ridge
Ciannella, Joeen Moore *small business owner*
Frissora, Mark P. *automobile rental and leasing company executive*
Giovannoli, Joseph Louis *entrepreneur, lawyer*
Kennedy, Brian James *marketing executive*
Koch, Craig R. *automobile rental company executive, automobile leasing company executive*
Rolfe, Harold E. *lawyer*
Siracusa, Paul J. *automotive executive*

Parlin
Mogensen, Charles Ray, Jr. *retired food service executive*

Parsippany
Belmonte, Steven Joseph *hotel chain executive*
Buckman, James Edward *lawyer*
Cox, Melvin Monroe *lawyer*
Ferguson, Thomas George *retired healthcare advertising agency executive*
Garbarini, William Nicholas *pharmaceutical executive*
Holmes, Stephen P. *hotel executive*
Hull, Anthony E. *real estate company executive*
Kallmann, Stanley Walter *lawyer*
Kunz, Thomas R. *real estate company executive*
Langrana, Anita *financial analyst, personal trainer*
McLester, Scott G. *lawyer, hospitality executive*
Nelson, Ronald L. *travel services company executive, former film company executive*
Newman, Mark S. *electronics company executive*
Salerno, F. Robert *travel company executive*
Sclafani, Karen C. *lawyer*
Silverman, Henry Richard *real estate company executive*
Smay, Connie R. *educational media specialist, educator*
Smith, Richard A. *real estate company executive*
Theiss, Richard Edward *electrical engineer, applications engineer*
Wasser, Marilyn J. *lawyer, real estate company executive*
Wechter, Ira Martin *tax specialist, financial planner*
Weller, Robert N(orman) *hotel executive*

Passaic
Lindholm, Clifford Falstrom, II, *engineering executive, mayor*
Sebek, Miklós László *sculptor, educator*

Paterson
Daniels, Cheryl Lynn *pediatrics nurse*
Fields, Marvin Leon *secondary school educator*
Fink, David Leonard *surgeon*
Mussano, Theodore Anthony *retired court services supervisor*
Pou, Nellie *assemblywoman*
Thomas, Alyce M. *nutritionist, consultant*

Peapack
Eddey, Gary Erwin *physician, administrator, educator*
Rost, Peter *pharmaceutical company executive*
Walsh, Philip Cornelius *retired mining executive*

Pennington
Calvo, Roque John *professional society administrator*
Czach, Gabriela Bozena *personal care industry executive*
Donnelly, Gerard Kevin *marketing and retail executive*
Fong, Donald P. *psychiatrist*
Kelly, Quentin Thorn *water and power company executive, writer*
Madison, T. Jerome *business executive*
Townsend, Peggy (Stephanie G.) *headmaster*
Zhang, Hong (Rick) *design engineer, researcher*

Penns Grove
Reilley, James Clark *artist, cartoonist, small business owner*

Pennsauken
Alday, Paul Stackhouse, Jr. *retired mechanical engineer*
Honickman, Harold *food manufacturing company executive*

Perth Amboy
Cruz, Nelson Xavier *healthcare executive*
Richardson-Melech, Joyce Suzanne *music educator, singer*

Phillipsburg
Drago, Joseph Rosario *urologist, educator*
Richards, Jay Claude *photographer, publishing executive, historian*

Pilesgrove
Mohrfeld, Richard Gentel *marketing professional*

Pine Brook
Kim, Dongwook *research and development company executive*

Pine Hill
Albee, Gloria *playwright*

Piscataway
Amaral, Andre Renato Sales *education educator, researcher*
Arnold, Edward (Eddy Arnold) *research scientist, educator*
Balaguru, Perumalsamy *civil engineering educator*
Breslauer, Kenneth J. *science educator, researcher*
Chynoweth, Alan Gerald *retired telecommunications industry executive*
Cohen, Morrel Herman *physicist, biologist, educator*
Colaizzi, John Louis *medical educator*
Colcord, Herbert Nathaniel, III, (Skip) *corporate communications executive*
Conney, Allan Howard *pharmacologist, researcher*
D'Aloia, G(iambattista) Peter *manufacturing executive*
Denhardt, David Tilton *molecular and cell biology educator*
Dill, Ellis Harold *university dean*
Dooner, Hugo K. *plant pathologist, educator*
Ebright, Richard High *molecular biologist*
Escobar, Javier Ignacio *psychiatrist*
Essien, Francine B. *biologist, educator*
Etter, Zana Claire *library director*
Ferstandig Arnold, Gail *research scientist, educator*
Flick, Ferdinand Herman *surgeon, preventive medicine physician*
Gelman, Rochel *psychology professor*
Glashausser, Charles Michael *physicist, researcher*
Goss, Mary E. Weber *sociology educator*
Gustafsson, Mary E. *lawyer*
Idol, James Daniel, Jr. *chemist, educator, inventor, consultant*
Iwaniec, Henryk *mathematics professor*
Kear, Bernard Henry *materials scientist, consultant*
Leath, Paul Larry *physicist, educator, former university official*
Lebowitz, Joel Louis *mathematical physicist, educator*
Lee, Barbara Anne *law educator*
Li, Yanyan *mathematician, educator*
Lindenfeld, Peter *physics professor*
Linke, Richard A. *optical engineer*
Lioy, Paul James *environmental health scientist*
Lu, Yen-Wen *adult education educator*
Manowitz, Paul *biochemist, researcher, educator*
Menza, Matthew A. *psychiatrist*
Mizrahi, Isaac *fashion designer*
Peterson, Donald Robert *psychologist, educator, academic administrator*
Poses, Frederic M. *engineering company executive*
Ranzan, David Aldrich *archivist*
Riss, Richard Michael *research economist, church history educator*
Robbins, Allen Bishop *physics professor*
Rokhlenko, Alexander *research scientist, educator*
Rosalsky, Barbara Ellen *artist, community health nurse*
Sahota, Amrik *medical researcher, educator, lab administrator*
Salkind, Alvin J. *engineering educator, dean, consultant*
Schiano, Greg *college football coach*
Smith, Bob *lawyer, educator, state senator*
Sumner, Floyd G. *retired music educator*
Swee, David Ethan *physician*
Tischfield, Jay Arnold *genetics educator*
Trontell, Marie Celestine *dean*
Vanderbilt, David *physics professor*
Vieth, Wolf Randolph *chemical engineering educator*
Volfson-Doubova, Elena *psychiatrist, researcher*
Wang, Tsuey Tang *science educator, venture capitalist*
Welkowitz, Walter *biomedical engineer, educator*
White, Eileen *science educator, researcher*
Wu, Jian *operations research specialist*
Yacowitz, Harold *biochemist, nutritionist*
Young, Wise *neurosurgeon, educator, medical researcher*
Zerubavel, Eviatar *sociologist, educator*
Zhang, Dajun *biomedical engineering educator*
Zhen, Li *systems analyst, researcher*
Zimmermann, Frank Martin *physicist, educator, research scientist*

Pitman
Cloues, Edward Blanchard, II, *lawyer*
Reinfeld, George *retired communications educator*

Plainfield
Allen (Sup), Stuart *film and television company executive*
Ellington II, Michael L. *lawyer*
Frost, David *retired biology professor, medical editor, consultant*
Green, Gerald B. *state legislator*
Limpert, John H., Jr. *fund raising executive*
Ruiz, Pedro Javier *education educator*
Schram, Henry B. *insurance company executive*

Plainsboro
Baeckler, Virginia Van Wynen *librarian, writer*
Devine, Hugh James, Jr. *marketing executive*
Khan, Sajid A. *management consultant, entrepreneur*
Schreyer, William Allen *retired finance company executive*
Spiegel, Phyllis *public relations consultant, journalist*

Pleasantville
London, Charlotte Isabella *secondary school educator*

Point Pleasant
Greene, Ellin *library service educator*

Point Pleasant Beach
Massey, Dorothy Williams *ophthalmologist, writer*

Pomona
Constantelos, Demetrios John *priest, educator*
Latourette, Audrey Wolfson *law educator*
Sharon, Yitzhak Yaakov *physicist, educator*

Pompton Plains
Gummel, Hermann Karl *retired physicist, lab administrator*
Pischl, Adolph John *school administrator*
Shrem, Charles Joseph *metals corporation executive*

Port Norris
Canzonier, Walter Jude *shellfish aquaculturist*

Princeton
Aarsleff, Hans *linguistics educator*
Ackourey, Peter Paul *lawyer*
Adler, Stephen Louis *physicist*
Agrawal, Shruti *researcher*
Ait-Sahalia, Yacine *finance educator*
Aizenman, Michael *mathematics and physics professor, researcher*
Allen, Stanley T. *architect, dean, educator*
Altmann, Stuart Allen *biologist, educator*
Anderson, Ellis Bernard *retired lawyer, pharmaceutical executive*

Anderson, Philip W. *physicist*
Armstrong, Richard Stoll *minister, educator, poet*
Balch, Stephen Howard *professional society administrator*
Ballou, Janice Donelon *research director*
Bartolini, Robert Alfred *electrical engineer, researcher*
Basáñez, Miguel Ebergenyi *political scientist, educator*
Bassler, Bonnie L. *molecular biologist*
Beidler, Marsha Wolf *lawyer*
Belshaw, George Phelps Mellick *bishop*
Benabou, Roland Jean-Marc *economist, educator*
Bergman, Edward Jonathan *lawyer, educator*
Bergman, Richard Isaac *health information executive*
Bergman, Victoria Besterman *small business owner, consultant*
Bhargava, Manjul *mathematics professor, researcher*
Billington, David Perkins *civil engineering educator*
Blackman, Sue Anne Batey *economics research specialist*
Bland, Calvin *foundation administrator*
Blinder, Alan Stuart *economist, educator*
Bogan, Elizabeth Chapin *economist, educator*
Bombieri, Enrico *mathematician, educator*
Boretz, Naomi Messinger *artist, educator*
Bowersock, Glen Warren *retired historian, educator*
Branker, Anthony Daniel John *music educator, researcher, composer*
Brinkman, William Frank *physicist, research and development company executive*
Brombert, Victor Henri *literature educator, author*
Brown, Leon Carl *historian, educator*
Bryan, Kirk, Jr. *meteorologist, oceanographer, researcher*
Bunnell, Peter Curtis *retired art educator, curator*
Burger, Leslie B. *library director, library association executive*
Burgess, Robert Kyle *lawyer*
Bynum, Caroline Walker *history professor, writer*
Calderbank, Robert *engineering educator, researcher*
Campbell, Mildred Corum *business owner, nurse*
Campbell, Robert Emmett *retired health products executive*
Carr, Marcus Eugene, Jr. *internist*
Carter, Emily Ann *physical chemist, researcher, educator*
Carver, David Harold *retired pediatrician*
Cava, Robert J. *chemistry professor*
Cavanaugh, James Henry *health products executive, retired federal official*
Chaikin, Paul M. *physicist*
Chamberlin, John Stephen *investor, consumer products company executive*
Chang, Sun-Yung Alice *mathematics professor*
Cheiten, Marvin Harold *playwright, manufacturing executive*
Chen, Thomas *mathematical physicist, researcher, educator*
Chou, Stephen Y. *electrical engineer, educator*
Christian, Carole Ann *psychologist, academic administrator*
Christman, Edward Arthur *physicist*
Coffey, Joseph Irving *political scientist, educator*
Connor, Geoffrey Michael *lawyer*
Cook, Michael Allan *social sciences educator*
Cooper, Joel *psychologist, educator*
Cooper, John Madison *philosophy educator*
Cooper, Michael R. *dean*
Corngold, Stanley Alan *language educator, writer*
Cox, Douglas Lynn *management consultant, researcher*
Craigie, James R. *consumer products and former sports equipment apparel company executive*
Crane, David W. *energy executive*
Crawford, Franklin David *publishing executive*
Curtiss, Howard Crosby, Jr. *mechanical engineer, educator*
Das, Jagabandhu *chemist, researcher*
Davidson, Ronald Crosby *physicist, researcher*
Davies, Robert Abel III *consumer products company executive*
Dawes, Trevor A. *school librarian*
Debenedetti, Pablo Gaston *chemical engineering professor*
Deligne, Pierre René *mathematician*
De Lung, Jane Solberger *independent sector executive*
Diller, Elizabeth E. *architect, educator, artist*
Dixon, Keith W. *meteorologist*
Doll, Robert C. *investment company executive*
Donohue, Andrew John *lawyer, securities executive*
Dougherty, Peter Joseph *publisher*
Draine, Bruce Thomas *astrophysicist, educator*
Drakeman, Lisa N. *biotechnologist*
Duncan, Dianne Walker *elementary school educator*
Durst, Robert Joseph, II, *lawyer*
Dyson, Freeman John *retired physics professor*
Engard, Nicole C. *library and information scientist*
Enquist, Lynn William *molecular biologist*
Ermolaev, Herman Sergei *Slavic languages educator*
Fefferman, Charles Louis *mathematics professor*
Felton, Edward William *computer scientist, educator*
Fernholz, Erhard Robert *investment executive*
Fisch, Nathaniel Joseph *physicist*
Fitch, Val Logsdon *physics professor*
Florey, Klaus Georg *chemist, pharmaceutical consultant*
Ford, Jeremiah III *architect*
Fox, Mary Ann Williams *librarian*
Frankfurt, Harry Gordon *philosophy professor*
Frantz, Robert Wesley *lawyer*
Fraser, Alexander G. *research scientist*
Freeman, Bruce George *fundraising consultant*
Frenier, Diane M. *lawyer*
Frey, Julia Bloch *language and art educator, historian*
Friedberg, Aaron Louis *political science professor*
Ganoe, Charles Stratford *banker, consultant*
Garner, Stephen Trent *meteorologist*
George, Thomas *artist*
Ghasemi, Seifi *chemicals executive*
Gillham, John Kinsey *chemical engineering professor*
Giordmaine, Joseph Anthony *physicist*
Girgus, Joan Stern *psychologist, educator, director*
Gmachl, Claire *electrical engineer, educator*
Goddard, Peter *academic administrator, mathematical physicist*
Goheen, Robert Francis *classicist, educator, former ambassador*
Goldblatt, Barry Lance *manufacturing executive*
Goldfarb, Irene Dale *retired financial planner*
Goldston, Robert J. *research scientist*
Gordenker, Leon *political science professor*
Gould, Elizabeth *neuroscientist, educator*
Gould, James L. *biology professor*
Grabar, Oleg *retired art educator*
Grafton, Anthony Thomas *history professor*
Grant, Barbara Rosemary *science educator, researcher*
Grant, Peter Raymond *biologist, researcher, educator*
Graves, Michael *architect, educator*
Green, Claude *information company executive*
Greenman, Jane Friedlieb *lawyer, human resources executive*
Grigger, Jane Elizabeth *earth science educator, photographer*
Grisham, Larry Richard *physicist*
Gross, Charles Gordon *psychology professor*
Groves, John Taylor III *chemist, educator*
Gund, Gordon *venture capitalist, investment company executive*
Gunning, Robert Clifford *mathematician, educator*
Haberman, Shelby Joel *statistician, educator*
Habicht, Christian Herbert *history professor*
Hait, William Neil *oncologist, educator*
Haldane, F(rederick) Duncan M(ichael) *physics educator*
Hall, Robert Turnbull III *lawyer*
Hanks, Richard *information company executive*
Harford, James *writer*
Harman, Gilbert Helms *philosophy educator*
Harvey, Norman Ronald *retired finance company executive*
Hermann, Janie *librarian*
Hill, James Scott *lawyer*
Hillier, J(ames) Robert *architect*
Hochschwender, Karl Albert *international trade and government relations consultant*
Hoebel, Bartley Gore *psychologist, educator*
Hollander, Robert B., Jr. *retired romance languages educator*
Hollander, Toby Edward *education educator*
Howarth, William (Louis) *literature and language professor, writer*
Howell, David Luke *history professor*
Hughes, Robert G. *foundation administrator*
Hynes, Samuel *language educator, writer*
Jeffers, Beverly Maynard *volunteer*
Jenkins, Edward Beynon *research astronomer*
Johnson, Sydney *men's college basketball coach, former professional basketball player*
Johnson-Laird, Philip Nicholas *psychologist*
Johnston, Robert Fowler *venture capitalist*
Jordan, William Chester *historian, educator*
Kahneman, Daniel *psychology professor*
Kaplowitz, Karen (Jill) *lawyer, consultant*
Kassof, Allen H. *foundation administrator*
Kateb, George Anthony *political science professor*
Katz, Nicholas M. *mathematician*
Katz, Stanley Nider *law educator*
Kauzmann, Walter Joseph *chemistry professor*
Keeley, Edmund LeRoy *literature educator, writer, translator*
Keephart, Lydia Fabbro *lawyer, mediator*
Keevey, Richard Francis *federal official, state official, educator*
Kelleher, Kathleen *marketing professional*
Keller, Suzanne *sociologist, psychotherapist*
Kelly, Paul J. *lab administrator, physician, researcher*
Kenen, Peter Bain *economist, educator*
Kenny, Jane M. *government relations consulting executive*
Kenyon, Regan Clair *educational association administrator*
Keohane, Robert Owen *political scientist, educator*
Klainerman, Sergiu *mathematics professor*
Knoepflmacher, Ulrich Camillus *literature educator*
Kobayashi, Hisashi *computer scientist, dean*
Kollár, János *mathematics professor*
Krueger, Alan B. *economics professor*
Krugman, Paul Robin *economics professor*
Kurtzer, Daniel Charles *former ambassador*
Lam, Sau-Hai (Harvey) *aeronautical engineering educator*
Landgraf, Kurt M. *educational association administrator*
Langlands, Robert Phelan *mathematician, educator*
Lavizzo-Mourey, Risa Juanita *medical foundation and academic administrator*
Law, Stuart A., Jr. *lawyer*
Lazarus, Arnold Allan *psychologist, educator*
Lechner, Bernard Joseph *consulting electrical engineer*
Lee, Ruby Bei-Loh *multimedia and computer systems architect*
Leetmaa, Ants *environmental services administrator, educator*
Leonard, Naomi Ehrich *aerospace engineer, educator*
Levin, Simon Asher *mathematician, ecologist, educator*
Levine, Richard James *publishing executive*
Levy, Kenneth *music educator*
Lewis, Bernard *retired social studies educator*
Lewis, John Prior *economist, educator*
Lieb, Elliott Hershel *physicist, mathematician, educator*
Lincoln, Anna *publishing executive, language educator*
Lippincott, Walter Heulings, Jr. *retired publishing executive*
Liu, Bede *electrical engineering educator*
Logue, Judith Felton *psychoanalyst, educator*
Long, Frank Wesley, Jr. *chemist*
Luchak, Frank Alexander *lawyer*
Lumpkin, John Robert *public health physician, state official*
Lustig, Graham *performing company executive*
MacMillan, David W.C. *chemistry professor*
MacPherson, Robert Duncan *mathematician, educator*
Mahmoud, Adel A. *physician, molecular biologist, educator*
Maldacena, Juan Martin *physicist, researcher*
Malkiel, Burton Gordon *economist, educator*
Malkiel, Nancy Weiss *dean, historian, educator*
Manabe, Syukuro *meteorologist*
Manyak, Michael John *urologist, educator, researcher*
Marks, James S. *public health service administrator*
Maskin, Eric Stark *economics professor*
Matlock, Jack Foust, Jr. *diplomat*
McClure, Donald Stuart *physical chemist, educator*
Mc Pherson, James Munro *history professor*
Mc Vicker, Charles Taggart *artist, educator*
Meade, Dale Michael *experimental physicist*
Mehlman, Myron A. *medical educator, toxicologist*
Miles, Richard Bryant *mechanical and aerospace engineering educator*
Miller, George Armitage *psychologist, educator*
Miller, Patrick Dwight, Jr. *religious studies educator, minister*
Mills, Bradford *merchant banker*
Mirzakhani, Maryam *mathematician*
Mollica, Joseph A. *pharmaceutical executive*
Moote, A. Lloyd *history professor*
Morgan, William Jason *geophysics educator*
Morris, Mac Glenn *advertising executive*
Moynahan, Julian Lane *retired literature educator, writer*
Mueller, Peter Sterling *psychiatrist, educator*
Muldoon, Paul *poet, educator*
Murphy, Coleen T. *biomedical researcher, educator*
Murphy, J. Andrew (Drew) *lawyer*
Nash, John Forbes, Jr. *mathematician, researcher*
Nehamas, Alexander *philosophy educator*
Nied, Thomas Herman *retired media specialist*
Nolet, Guust *geophysicist*
O'Brien, Tim *lawyer*
O'Donnell, Laurence Gerard *retired managing editor*
Okounkov, Andrei *mathematics professor*
Olsen, Gregory H. *fiber optic manufacturing executive, researcher*
Onat, Bora M. *research and development company executive, electrical engineer*
Ong, Nai-Phuan *physicist, educator*
Onstott, Tullis *microgeologist, geology professor*
Oppenheimer, Michael *physicist*
Orphanides, Nora Charlotte *ballet educator*
Ostriker, Jeremiah Paul *astrophysicist, educator*
Oxman, Stephen A. *federal official*
Pacala, Stephen W. *ecology educator*
Page, Lyman Alexander, Jr. *physicist*
Painter, Nell Irvin *historian, educator, writer*
Paret, Peter *historian*
Parry, Scott Brink *psychologist*
Pechura, Constance Mary *foundation administrator*
Pfister, Marc *consumer products company executive, physician, researcher*
Picco, Steven Joseph *lawyer*
Pimley, Kim Jensen *financial training consultant*
Polyakov, Alexander M. *physics professor*
Poor, Harold Vincent *electrical engineering educator*
Quandt, Richard Emeric *economics professor*
Rabb, Theodore K. *historian*
Ramaprasad, Kackadasam Raghavachar *physical chemist*
Rapelye, Janet Lavin *dean*
Reinhardt, Uwe Ernst *economist, educator*
Riehl, Christina Pauline *ecologist*
Riordan, Thomas J. *lawyer, chemicals executive*
Rodgers, Daniel Tracy *historian, educator*
Roetteler, Martin Henri *computer scientist, researcher*
Rohrer, Katherine Tinley *academic administrator*
Rosen, Harvey Sheldon *economics professor, former federal official*
Royce, Barrie Saunders Hart *physicist, researcher*
Rozman, Gilbert Friedell *sociologist, educator*
Russel, William Bailey *engineering educator*
Rutherford, Paul Harding *physicist*
Sandman, Peter M. *risk management consultant*
Sarnek, Peter Clive *mathematics professor*
Schroeder, Glenn Carl *lawyer, educator*
Schupbach, Trudi M. (Gertrud Schupbach) *biologist, researcher*
Seawright, James L., Jr. *sculptor, educator*
Seiberg, Nathan *physics professor*
Shapiro, Harold Tafler *economics professor, former academic administrator*
Shear, Theodore Leslie, Jr. *archaeologist, educator*
Shenk, Thomas Eugene *molecular biology educator, academic administrator*
Shimizu, Yoshiaki *art historian, department chairman*
Siegel, Laurie *human resources specialist*
Sierocki, John Stanley *oncologist*
Sigal, Leonard H. *physician*
Sigman, Daniel M. *geochemist, educator*
Silhavy, Thomas Joseph *molecular biology educator*
Sinai, Yakov G. *theoretical mathematician, educator*
Singer, Burton Herbert *statistics educator*
Singer, Peter Albert David *philosophy educator, writer*
Slaughter, Anne-Marie *dean*
Smith, Arthur John Stewart *physicist, researcher*
Song, Zhen *electrical engineer, researcher*
Spence, Donald Pond *psychologist, psychoanalyst*
Spergel, David Nathaniel *astrophysicist, educator*
Starr, Paul Elliot *sociologist, educator, editor, writer*
Stein, Elias M. *mathematician, educator*
Stengel, Robert Frank *engineering and applied science educator*
Sterzer, Fred *research physicist*
Suckewer, Szymon *physics professor*
Sugerman, Abraham Arthur *psychiatrist, educator*
Sullivan, Diane P. *lawyer*
Sutphin, William Taylor *lawyer*
Tarjan, Robert Endre *computer scientist, educator*
Taylor, Edward Curtis *chemistry professor*
Taylor, Joseph Hooton, Jr. *radio astronomer, physicist*
Testa, James A. *lawyer*
Tilghman, Shirley Marie *academic administrator, biology professor*
Torquato, Salvatore *materials scientist, chemistry professor*
Trainer, Karin A. *librarian*
Tremaine, Scott Duncan *astrophysicist*
Treu, Jesse Isaiah *venture capitalist*
Trussell, James *economist, educator, dean*
Tsui, Daniel C. *electrical engineer, physicist*
Tumposky, Daniel L. *education assessment specialist*
Tymoczko, Dmitri *music educator, composer*
Ufford, Charles Wilbur, Jr. *lawyer*
Unruh, Howard K., Jr. *military officer, university administrator*
Van Houten, Franklyn Bosworth *geologist, educator*
VanMarcke, Erik Hector *civil engineer, educator*
Vapnik, Vladimir N. *mathematician, researcher, educator*
Verdu, Sergio *engineering educator*
Vinicombe, Charles James *lawyer*
Voevodsky, Vladimir *mathematician*
von der Schmidt, Edward III *neurosurgeon, veterinarian*
Von Hippel, Frank Niels *public and international affairs educator*
Walter, Hugo Günther *humanities educator, poet*
Walzer, Michael *retired political science professor*
Warren, William L. *lawyer*
Waters, Robyn *writer, marketing consultant*
Wei, James *chemical engineering professor, academic dean*
Weiss, Renée Karol *editor, musician*
West, Charles Converse *retired theologian*
West, Cornel Ronald *humanities educator, writer*
Western, Bruce *sociologist, educator*
Westoff, Charles Francis *demographer, educator*
Wheeler, John Archibald *physicist, educator*
Whipple, William, Jr. *government policy consultant, writer*
White, Morton Gabriel *philosopher, writer, historian, retired educator*
Wieschaus, Eric F. *molecular biologist, educator*
Wightman, Arthur Strong *physicist, researcher*
Wilentz, Sean *historian, educator, writer*
Wiles, Andrew J. *mathematician, educator*
Willig, Robert Daniel *economics professor*
Willingham, Warren Willcox *psychologist*
Wilmerding, John *art historian, educator, curator*
Winder, Bayly Philip *bank executive*
Witkin, Evelyn Maisel *retired geneticist*
Witten, Edward *mathematical physicist*
Woolfolk, Robert Lee *psychologist, educator*
Yu, Ying-Shih *retired history professor, writer*
Zelizer, Viviana *sociologist, educator*
Ziolkowski, Theodore Joseph *literature educator, writer*

Princeton Junction

Amenta, Peter Sebastian *pathologist*
Bair, William Alois *engineer*
Butorac, Frank George *librarian, educator*
Cohen, Florence Emery *retired financial services executive*
Denlinger, Edgar Jacob *retired electronics engineering executive, researcher*
Haddad, James Henry *chemical engineer, consultant*
Hirschman, Barry H. *human resources specialist*
Lull, William Paul *engineering consultant*
Norback, Craig Thomas *writer*
Vahaviolos, Sotirios John *electrical engineer, researcher, engineering executive*

Rahway

Freedman, Stanley Lewis *assistant principal*
Garcia, Maria Luisa *biochemist, researcher*
Kaczorowski, Gregory John *biochemist, researcher, science administrator*
MacCoss, Malcolm *pharmaceutical executive, chemist*

Ramsey

Balter, Leslie Marvin *business communications educator*
Libin, Laurence Elliot *retired curator*

Randolph

Chen, Kevin S. *management executive, consultant, educator*
Ghosh, Ajit Kumar *daycare administrator*

Goldman, Phyllis E. *psychology educator*
Zelante, Thomas Andrew *lawyer*

Raritan
Polak, Lori Lyn *medical products executive*
Yong, Guo *chemist, educator*

Red Bank
Braddom, Randall Lee *physiatrist, educator*
Brown, Valerie Anne *psychotherapist, social worker, educator*
Carmody, Margaret Jean *retired social worker*
Clever, Marcia Sue *psychiatrist*
Daidone, Lewis Eugene *finance company executive*
Fred, Rogers Murray III *veterinary oncologist*
Gutentag, Patricia Richmond *social worker, family counselor, occupational therapist*
Hertz, Daniel Leroy, Jr. *entrepreneur*
Hovnanian, Ara K. *real estate developer*
Hovnanian, Kevork S. *real estate developer*
Kenney-Baden, Linda *lawyer*
McWhinney, Madeline H. (Mrs. John Denny Dale) *economist, director*
Oberst, Robert John *financial analyst*
Pezzutti, Santo Costante *advertising executive, art director*
Reinhart, Peter Sargent *lawyer*
Scaccia, Frank John *plastic surgeon, otolaryngologist*
Sorsby, James Larry *home building company executive*
Walker, Ira Allen *financial consultant*
Watson, Charles M. *financial consultant*

Ridgefield
Riggs, Rory B. *pharmaceutical executive*
Tracey, Matthew Sean *music educator, musician*

Ridgefield Park
D'Avella, Bernard Johnson, Jr. *publishing executive, lawyer*
Denning, Karen Craft *finance educator*
Heidel, Theresa Elizabeth *artist, educator*

Ridgewood
Baddoura, Rashid Joseph *emergency physician*
Bronstein, Eric H. *surgeon*
Carbone, Tracy *pediatrician, educator*
Clements, Lynne Fleming *marriage and family therapist, application developer*
Farrell, Gregory Alan *biomedical engineer*
Fox, Ingrid *curator*
Harris, Micalyn Shafer *lawyer, arbitrator, mediator, educator, consultant*
Healey, Frank Henry *retired chemicals executive*
Kiernan, Richard Francis *publisher*
Kopeloff, Iris Hope *dermatologist*
Le May, Moira Kathleen *retired psychology educator*
Mitgang, Lee David *journalist, writer, educator, foundation administrator*
O'Leary, Paul Gerard *retired insurance company executive*
Ostling, Richard Neil *journalist*
Seigel, Jan Kearney *lawyer*
Sumers, Anne Ricks *ophthalmologist, museum director*
Trocano, Russell Peter *lawyer*
Warner, John Edward *advertising executive*

Ringwood
Barbour, Arthur J. *artist*

River Edge
Gass, Manus M. *accountant, construction executive*

River Vale
Verebey, Karl Geza *toxicologist, pharmacologist, educator*

Riverton
O'Brien, James Jerome *construction management consultant*

Rivervale
Becker, Murray Leonard *corporate financial consultant, actuary*
Moderacki, Edmund Anthony *music educator, conductor*
Posamentier, Alfred Steven *mathematics professor, dean*

Rochelle Park
Gaer, Michael Ira *financial planner*

Rockaway
Allen, Dorothea *secondary school educator*
Husar, Walter Gene *neurologist, neuroscientist, educator*
Kelsey, Ann Lee *library administrator*
Kurtz, Ellen R. *journalist*
Steier, Audrey Keller *music educator*

Roseland
Benson, James Bracken *lawyer*
Brody, Jane L. *lawyer*
Butler, Gary C. *computer company executive*
Byer, Theodore Scott *accountant*
Clemente, Celestino *physician, surgeon*
Eakeley, Douglas Scott *lawyer*
Eichler, Burton Lawrence *lawyer*
Farber, Zulima V. *lawyer, former state attorney general*
Fuller, S(heri) Marce *energy executive*
Golden, Robert Charles *finance company executive*
Hayden, Joseph A., Jr. *lawyer*
Kohl, Benedict M. *lawyer*
Leit, David Edward *lawyer*
Malafronte, Donald *health facility administrator, consultant*
McMahon, Edward Richard *lawyer*
Miceli, Marc Dominick *lawyer*
Panagides, John *pharmacologist*
Positan, Wayne John *lawyer*

Post, John N. *lawyer*
Rosen, Charles Arthur *lawyer*
Slutsky, Kenneth Joel *lawyer*
Smith, Wendy Hope *lawyer*
Stern, Herbert Jay *lawyer*
Sugahara, Byron Masahiko *transportation executive*
Tarino, Gary Edward *lawyer*
Vanderbilt, Arthur T., II, *lawyer*
Vitiello, Anthony F. *lawyer*
Weinbach, Arthur Frederic *computer company executive*
Wovsaniker, Alan *lawyer, educator*

Roselle
Di Marco, Barbaranne Yanus *principal*
Wilson, Arthur Theodore *education consultant*

Rumson
Brenner, Theodore Engelbert *retired trade association administrator*
Rowe, Harrison Edward *electrical engineer*
Strong, George Hotham *private investor, consultant*

Rutherford
Baker, Don L. *band director*
Gerety, Peter Leo *archbishop*
Petrie, Ferdinand Ralph *illustrator, artist*
Suarez, Sally Ann Tevis *health facility administrator, nurse, consultant*

Saddle Brook
Cohn, Albert Linn *lawyer*
Herrmann, Jeffrey W. *lawyer*
Hickey, William V. *manufacturing executive*
Kelsey, David *manufacturing executive*
Knopf, Barry Abraham *lawyer, educator*
Pearlman, Peter Steven *lawyer*
Salerno, William Douglas *cardiologist*

Saddle River
Goodman, Jerome David *psychiatrist*
Lasser, Gail Maria *psychologist, educator*
Noyes, Robert Edwin *publisher, writer*
Roes, Nicholas A. *writer, artist*
Weissmann, Heidi Seitelblum *radiologist, educator*

Salem
Carpenter, Margaret S. (Molly Carpenter) *artist*
Petrin, Helen Fite *lawyer, consultant, mediator*

Scotch Plains
Hallard, Wayne Bruce *retired economist*
Johnsen, Karen Kennedy *marketing professional*
Klock, John Henry *lawyer*
Kraemer, Ira B. *symphony conductor*
Quackenbush, Schuyler *engineer, consultant*
Shaw, Alan *lawyer*

Sea Bright
Plummer, Dirk Arnold *chemical, electrical, and electronics engineer*

Sea Isle City
Tull, Theresa Anne *retired diplomat*

Secaucus
Abrams, Dan *broadcast executive, news correspondent*
Arena, Bruce *professional soccer coach*
Austin, Ski *sports association executive*
Bradley, Bob *professional soccer coach*
Carlson, Tucker *political analyst, writer, television host*
Cosby, Rita Karen *newscaster*
Criqui, Robert J. *sports association executive*
Dabah, Ezra *apparel executive*
Denenberg, David Scott *sports association executive, lawyer*
Diggs, Taye (Scott Diggs) *actor*
Hellmuth, Stephen M. *sports association executive*
Koenig, William S. *sports association executive*
Liao, Paul Foo-Hung *electronics executive*
Marcus, Alan C. *public relations consultant*
Meola, Tony *professional soccer player, actor*
Olbermann, Keith *news analyst, former sportcaster*
Puente, Audrey *meteorologist*
Sakiewicz, Nick *professional sports team executive*
Sanders, Summer *Olympic athlete, news correspondent, newscaster*

Sewell
Crouse, Farrell R. *lawyer*

Shiloh
Garrison, John Raymond *organization executive*

Short Hills
Alesio, Steven W. *financial services company executive*
Austin, Danforth Whitley *media executive*
Bartels, Stanley Leonard *investment banker*
Chaiken, Bernard Henry *internist, gastroenterologist*
Duberstein, Joel Lawrence *internist, pulmonologist, educator*
Fast, Kenneth H. *lawyer*
Gibson, William Lee *financial consultant*
Harwood, Jerry *market research executive*
Hazlehurst, Robert Purviance, Jr. *lawyer*
Howe, James Everett *investment company executive*
Kaye, Marc Mendell *lawyer*
MacKinnon, Malcolm D(avid) *retired insurance company executive*
Mebane, William Black *controller, financial consultant*
Novack, Robert *lawyer*
Ogden, Maureen Black *retired state legislator*
Price, Michael F. *money management executive*
Robbins-Wilf, Marcia *educational consultant*

Schaefer, Charles James III *advertising executive, consultant*
Schaefer, Eleanor Montville *retired publishing executive*
Schirmeister, Charles F. *retired lawyer*
Siegfried, David Charles *retired lawyer*
Soderlind, Sterling Eugene *newspaper industry consultant*
Wharton, Lennard *engineering company executive*
Winter, Ruth Grosman (Mrs. Arthur Winter) *journalist*

Shrewsbury
Baker, Gerald David *marketing executive, consultant*
Elkwood, Andrew Ira *plastic surgeon*
Feeney, John Robert *banker*
Michaelson, Peter Lee *lawyer*
Norwitz, Steven Barry *plastic and reconstructive surgeon, health facility administrator*
Rose, Michael Ian *plastic surgeon*
Rosenblum, Bruce Robert *neurosurgeon*
Westerman, Liane Marie *research scientist executive*

Sicklerville
Browna, Jo McIntyre *nurse*
Miller, Audrey Thornton *retired vice principal*
Simpson, Eugene Thamon *music educator, singer*

Skillman
Brill, Yvonne Claeys *engineer, consultant*
Diaz, Teresita Perez *chemist*
Eiger, Richard William *retired publisher*
Liro, Joseph R. *diversified financial services company executive*
Rhett, Haskell Emery Smith *educational association administrator*
Tenenbaum, Bernard Hirsh *entrepreneur, educator*

Somerdale
Botka, Betsy Jean *industrial arts and career awareness instructor*

Somerset
Aronson, Louis Vincent, II, *manufacturing executive*
Becker, Phyllis *information technology manager*
Brophy, Joseph Thomas *computer company executive*
De Salva, Salvatore Joseph *retired pharmacologist, toxicologist*
Fink, Edward Murray *lawyer, educator*
Green, Jeffrey C. *lawyer*
Karas, James *public relations executive, engineering executive*
Lichtig, Leo Kenneth *health economist*
Pappert, Amy S. *dermatologist, educator*
Soaries, DeForest B., Jr. *former state official*
Tsou, Yu-Min *science administrator, chemistry researcher*
Wallfesh, Henry Maurice *communications executive, writer*

Somerville
Albin, Barry Todd *state supreme court justice*
Fleischman, Joseph Jacob *lawyer*
Hulse, Robert Douglas *biotechnologist*
Hutcheon, Peter David *lawyer*
Lieberman, Marvin Samuel *lawyer*
Ligorano, Michael Kenneth *lawyer*
Norris, Richard A. *lawyer, mediator*
Sivanesan, Sivaruban *mechanical engineer*
Sponzilli, Edward George *lawyer*

South Amboy
Moskal, Anthony John *retired dean, management consultant, educator*

South Bound Brook
Weir, Sonja Ann *artist*

South Hackensack
Cohen, Brett I. *health products executive*

South Orange
Bao, Xue-Ming *librarian, educator*
Budin, Wendy C. *nursing educator, researcher*
Hansell, Phyllis Shanley *nursing educator, administrator, researcher, consultant*
Hecht, Marion B. *counselor*
Hoffert, Eric Michael *application developer, information technology executive*
Nowik, John David *music educator, musician*
Riordan, Rick *writer*
Sahiner, Mehmet Alper *physics professor, researcher*
Sheeran, Robert T. (Monsignor) *academic administrator*

South Plainfield
Brakken, William *construction executive*
Hylbert, Paul W. *construction executive*
Kennedy, John William *engineering company executive*
Kwon, Ik Hyun *internist*
Lewandowski, Andrew Anthony *utilities executive, consultant*
Santoro, Frank Anthony *lawyer*

South River
Kirshner, Jacob *physician*

Southampton
Callaway, Ben Anderson *journalist*
O'Connor, Sheryl Broderick *literature and language educator*
Saltus, Phyllis Borzelliere *music educator*

Sparta
Bhattacharyya, Dev *information technology executive, consultant*
Jacobs-Quam, Vivien Marie *retired music educator*

McMeen, Elmer Ellsworth III *lay minister, musician, retired lawyer*
McMeen, Sheila Taenzler *retired lawyer*
Rosser, Alvin Raymon *artist*
Spence, Robert Leroy *publishing executive*

Spring Lake
Bonhag, Thomas Edward *insurance company executive, financial planner, consultant*
D'Luhy, John James *investment banker*
Harrigan, John Thomas, Jr. *physician, obstetrician, gynecologist*
Krein, Catherine Cecilia *broadcast and journalism educator*
O'Connor, Francis X. *financial executive*
Pandolfe, John Thomas, Jr. *lawyer*

Springfield
Devitt, H. William III *treasurer, corporate financial executive*
Javerbaum, Kenneth S. *lawyer*
Kwartler, Jed Aryeh *otolaryngologist*
Mytelka, Arnold Krieger *lawyer*
O'Desky, Ilyse Hope *psychologist, educator*
Shilling, A. Gary *economist, consultant*
Wurgaft, Jack *lawyer*

Stanton
Kille, John William, Jr. *toxicology and biomedical product consultant*

Stewartsville
Busch, Beverly Gail *English language educator, literature educator, instructional resource center administrator*

Stirling
Walsh, Peter Joseph *physics professor*

Stockton
Mahon, Robert *photographer*
Schoenherr, John (Carl) *artist, illustrator*

Stratford
Levitas, Andrew Stephen *child psychiatrist, educator*

Succasunna
Romance, Mary C. *library director*

Summit
Barer, Sol Joseph *biotechnology company executive*
Carniol, Paul J. *plastic and reconstructive surgeon, otolaryngologist*
Falletta, Jo Ann *conductor*
Fuess, Billings Sibley, Jr. *advertising executive*
Fukui, Hatsuaki *retired electrical engineer, art historian*
Gaudino, Mario *physician, pharmaceutical company executive, scientist*
Gerathy, E. Carroll *retired insurance company executive, real estate developer*
Greenberg, Rosalie *child psychiatrist*
Halperin, John Jacob *neurology educator, researcher*
Hodosh, Richard M. *neurosurgeon*
Katz, Michael Albert *lawyer*
Kenyon, Edward Tipton *lawyer*
Lewis, Donald Emerson *banker*
Lijoi, Peter Bruno *lawyer*
Lindars, Laurence Edward *retired health care products executive*
Lovett, Juanita Pelletier *clinical psychologist*
Macioce, Frank Michael *lawyer, financial services company executive*
Mueller, Paul Henry *retired bank executive*
Pfaltz, Hugo Menzel, Jr. *lawyer*
Phillips, James Charles *physicist, researcher*
Rosensweig, Ronald Ellis *chemical engineer, consultant*
Rousseau, Irene Victoria *artist*
Weinstein, Stephen Brant *communications executive, researcher, writer*
Woller, James Alan *lawyer*
Zachary, Louis George *chemical company consultant*

Sussex
Hoyt, Earl Edward, Jr. *industrial designer*

Swedesboro
Lovell, Theodore *electrical engineer, consultant*

Tabernacle
DiBella, Russell Thomas *federal investigator*

Teaneck
Alperin, Richard Martin *social worker, psychoanalyst*
Brudner, Helen Gross *social sciences educator*
Bullough, John Frank *musician, educator*
Carter, Regina *jazz violinist*
Cassimatis, Peter John *economics professor*
Chen, Zong *computer scientist, educator*
Connola, Donald Pascal, Jr. *management consultant*
Cowan, Wallace Edgar *retired lawyer*
Cowen, John Edwin *education educator*
Dewey, Ralph Jay *school system administrator*
Ehrlich, Ira Robert *mechanical engineering consultant*
Feinberg, Robert S. *plastics company executive, marketing professional*
Fjordbotten, Alf Lee *language educator*
Gordon, Lois G. *language educator*
Graham, Janet Lorraine *music educator*
Haas, Gerhard Julius *microbiologist, educator*
Holmes, Miriam H. *publisher*
Ladenheim, Jules Calvin *neurosurgeon*
Lafer, Fred Seymour *data processing executive*
Lichtenstein, Robert *Education executive*
Meno, John Peter *chorepiscopus*
Reinish, Gloria Brooks *electrical engineer, educator*
Smith, Susan Elizabeth *guidance director*
Solá, Victoria M. *announcer, writer*

Wallmann, Jeffrey Miner *author*
Weinberg, Loretta *state legislator*
Weiss, Mitchell Joseph *librarian*
Wiener, Joel Howard *historian, educator*
Zwass, Vladimir *computer science and information systems educator*

Tenafly
Bernstein, William Robert *banker*
Blank, Marion Sue *psychologist, educator*
Gerst, Paul Howard *physician*
Gold, Marc J. *secondary school educator, supervisor*
Golomb, Frederick Martin *surgeon, educator*
Koons, Irvin Louis *graphics designer, consultant, marketing professional*
Tall, Susan Porter *music educator*

Teterboro
Hagemann, Robert A. *health care company executive*
Mohapatra, Surya N. *laboratory executive*

Three Bridges
Lawrence, Gerald Graham *management consultant*

Tinton Falls
Arminio, Josephine Meconi *elementary school educator*
Hoelzler, Michael Gebhard *veterinarian, surgeon*
Macdonald, Donald Arthur, Jr. *physician, surgeon*
Ostar, Allan William *educational consultant*
Priesand, Sally J. *rabbi*

Titusville
Cooper, Paul *retired mechanical engineer, director, researcher*
Pandina, Gahan J. *psychologist, researcher*
Reema, Jain *pharmacist, pharmaceutical executive*

Toms River
Bosley, Karen Lee Foley *language educator, communications educator*
Donaldson, Marcia Jean *lay worker*
Fox, Daniel Emery *orthopedic surgeon*
Kanarkowski, Edward Joseph *data processing company executive*
Marchese, Michael James, Jr. *radiation oncologist*
Matteo, Christine E. *librarian*
Moran, Jeffrey W., Jr. *county surrogate*

Totowa
Giliberti, Orazio Lucia *ophthalmologist*
Tuthill, Jay Dean, II, *investment executive*

Township Of Washington
Valenti, Thomas Peter *painter*

Trenton
Abelow, Bradley *state official*
Baron, Lisa Ann *environmental scientist*
Baroni, Bill (William E. Baroni Jr.) *state legislator*
Bigham, William J. *lawyer*
Binder, Elaine Kotell *associations consultant*
Biskin, Bruce Howard *psychometrician*
Blackburn, Audrey Peyton *lawyer*
Blake, Norma E. *library director*
Brown, Peggy Lee *academic administrator, consultant, singer*
Caldwell, Wesley Stuart III *lawyer, lobbyist*
Caspersen, Sidney J. *state agency administrator*
Chen, David *reporter*
Christopherson, Elizabeth Good *broadcast executive*
Codey, Richard James (Dick Codey) *state senator, former acting governor*
Cole, Richie Thomas *musician, composer, educator*
Cooper, Mary Little *judge*
Corzine, Jon Stevens *governor, former senator*
Cowen, Robert E. *federal judge*
Davy, Lucille E. *school system administrator*
Deltuvia, John Joseph, Jr. *systems analyst*
Demitry, Elpis Hope *music educator*
Depuglio, Joseph *physics educator*
Doherty, Robert Christopher *lawyer*
Donohue, Patricia Carol *academic administrator*
Fischer, Pamela Shadel *public relations executive*
George, Emery Edward *foreign language and studies educator, writer*
Goldman, Steven M. *state agency administrator*
Gomez, William *orthopedist*
Greenberg, Morton Ira *federal judge*
Gupta, Rajendra Prasad *physician*
Hoens, Helen E. *state supreme court justice*
Holt, Jonathan Turner *public relations executive*
Jones, Dale Edwin *public defender*
Jones, Sophia LaShawn *architect*
Kocieniewski, David *journalist*
Lattanzi, Gregory Denis *archaeologist*
LaVecchia, Jaynee *state supreme court justice*
Leipzig, Melvin *art educator*
Long, Virginia *state supreme court justice*
Mansnerus, Laura *news correspondent*
Martin, James Hanley *state attorney general*
Metzger, John Mackay *lawyer*
Milgram, Anne M. *state attorney general*
Miller, Ruane *artist, educator*
Mojer-Torres, Lisa Nan *lawyer*
Obed, Leonora Rita Villegas *writer*
Old, Hughes Oliphant *theologian, minister*
Palmer, Douglas Harold *mayor*
Powell, Joyce *educational association administrator, secondary school educator*
Pruitt, George Albert *college president*
Rabner, Stuart Jeff *state supreme court justice, former state attorney general*
Riccards, Michael Patrick *academic administrator*
Ritchey, Kenneth William *social services administrator*
Rivera-Soto, Roberto A. *state supreme court justice*
Russell, Joyce Anne Rogers *retired librarian*
Scheiring, Michael James *college official*
Sheridan, Peter Gerard *federal judge, lawyer*
Smallwood, Robert Albian, Jr. *retired secondary education educator*
Socolow, David Jacob *state agency administrator*
Sterns, Joel Henry *lawyer*
Sullivan, John *news correspondent*
Szaky, Tom *agricultural products executive*
Viscomi, Frank Joseph *pharmaceutical executive*
Wallace, John E. *state supreme court justice*
Wells, Nina Mitchell *state official*

Turnersville
DePace, Nicholas Louis *physician*
Rabil, Mitchell Joseph *lawyer*

Union
Bottitta, Joseph Anthony *lawyer*
Callahan, Michael J. *lawyer, retail executive*
Chrusciel, Susan Marie *research scientist, molecular biologist*
Eisenberg, Warren *retail executive*
Feinstein, Leonard *retail executive*
Gorrin, Eugene *lawyer*
Greenstein, Richard Henry *lawyer*
Kim, Youn-Suk Ernest *economist, educator*
Lederman, Susan Sturc *public administration professor*
Marjanczyk, Joseph Anicetus *priest*
Mark, Michael David *lawyer*
Norward, Josephine Norma *social work educator, consultant*
Rauch, Allan N. *lawyer*
Rogge, Rena Wolcott *librarian*
Temares, Steven H. *retail executive*
White, Robert Leslie Gordon, Jr. *aerospace transportation executive*
Zois, Constantine Nicholas Athanasios *meteorologist, educator*

Union City
Bozoyan, Sylvia *elementary school educator*
Englese, Damon Joseph *director*
Portes, Fernando A. *project manager*
Rondon, Edania Cecilia *lawyer*

Upper Montclair
Guha, Dilip K. *retired urban planner*
Ophori, Duke Urhobo *environmental scientist, educator, research scientist, consultant*
Tintle, Carmel Joseph *public relations executive*

Upper Saddle River
Oolie, Sam *manufacturing and investment company executive*
Wallace, William III *engineering executive*

Vauxhall
Jacobs-Smith, Ruby Eudora *retired medical/surgical nurse, public health service officer*
Ross, Mark Samuel *lawyer, educator, funeral director, writer*

Ventnor City
Bolton, Kenneth Albert *management consultant*
Robbins, Hulda Dornblatt *artist, printmaker*

Verona
Ayaso, Manuel *artist*
Cirello, Richard *physician, director*
Malanga, Gerard Anthony *sports medicine physician, director*

Vineland
Clinton, Lawrence Paul *psychiatrist*
Heck, Todd William *lawyer*
Schmid, Patti A. *library director*
Sinakin, Herbert Morris *dermatologist*

Voorhees
Brahms, William Bernard *librarian, publisher, writer*
Correll, Donald L. *water services company executive*
Glasofer, Eric David *allergist, immunologist, pediatrician, educator*
Lampert, S. Henry *retired dentist*
Litman, Bernard *electrical engineer, consultant*
Piermatti, Jack *dentist*
Schwartz, Bennett K. *dermatologist*
Siskin, Edward Joseph *engineering and construction company executive*
Suflas, Steven William *lawyer*

Waldwick
Lynch, Carol *special services director, psychologist, minister*
Sorabella, Philip A. *radiologist*

Wall
Applegate, Donald Edward *history professor*
Dugan, Mariellen *lawyer*
Monaco, Robert Anthony *radiologist*
Motley, John Paul *retired psychiatrist*
Mudd, Mary *historian*
Nucciarone, A. Patrick *lawyer*
O'Neill, James Paul *psychiatrist*
Petrovich, Dorothy *elementary school educator*

Wallington
Safira, Barabara *science educator*

Warren
Baxter, Nancy *medical writer*
Bernstein, Eric Martin *lawyer*
Blass, Walter Paul *management consultant, educator*
Brundage, Maureen A. *lawyer, insurance company executive*
Cox, Robert C. *insurance company executive*
Degnan, John J. *insurance company executive, lawyer*
DiPietro, Ralph Anthony *management and marketing consultant, educator*
Finnegan, John D. *insurance company executive*
Hennings, Dorothy Grant *education educator*
Jacobson, Gary Steven *lawyer*
Kozberg, Donna Walters *rehabilitation services professional*
Kozberg, Ronald Paul *health and human services administrator*
Kraus, Steven Gary *lawyer*
Krump, Paul J. *insurance company executive*
Maull, George Marriner *conductor, educator*
McElwee, Andrew Allison, Jr. *insurance company executive*
Motamed, Thomas Firouz *insurance company executive*
O'Reilly, Michael *insurance company executive*
Rana, Harminderpal Singh *lawyer*
Robusto, Dino E. *insurance company executive*
Ventantonio, James Bartholomew *lawyer*
Yang, Tsong-Toh (T.T.) *pharmacist, researcher*

Watchung
Cohen, Melvin Irwin *retired communications systems and technology executive*
Cox, Archibald, Jr. *investor*
Eisenberg, Richard R. *dermatologist*
Michaelis, Paul Charles *engineering physicist executive*
Miller, John Ronald *minister*
Rubin, Robert Jay *colon and rectal surgeon*
Tornqvist, Erik Gustav Markus *chemical engineer, research scientist, consultant*

Wayne
Arthur, Ray *retail executive*
Arthur, Raymond L. *retail toy and game company executive*
Babrowski, Claire Harbeck *retail executive*
Barbour, John *retail executive*
Brockett, Francesca L. *retail executive*
Cetrulo, Jerry *artist, sculptor*
Creasey, F. Clay *retail executive*
Derby, Deborah *retail executive*
DeRosa, Richard Jerome *composer, musician, educator*
Friedman, Martin Burton *retired chemicals executive*
Garcia, Ofelia *art educator, administrator*
Geiger, David E. *engineer*
Gollance, Robert Barnett *ophthalmologist*
Harrington, Kevin Paul *lawyer*
Heyman, Samuel J. *chemical manufacturing company executive*
Jeffrey, Robert George, Jr. *manufacturing executive*
Kay, Christopher K. *retail executive, lawyer*
Markee, Richard L. *retail executive*
Patnaik, Pradeep Kumar *science educator*
Rogoff, Paula Drimmer *English and foreign language educator*
Rosenthal, Herbert Seymour *orthopedist, surgeon*
Schmidt, Barnet Michael *communications and electronic engineer*
Schwartz, David Jay *lawyer*
Storch, Gerald L. (Jerry Storch) *retail executive*
Sullivan, Glenn D. *music educator*

Weehawken
Hobson, Burton Harold *publishing executive*

West Caldwell
Brundage, Gertrude Barnes *pediatrician*
Dixon, Jo-Ann Conte *management consultant*
Page, Frederick West *business consultant*
Schiff, Robert *healthcare consulting company executive*

West Long Branch
DeRosa, Christopher Samuel *history professor*
Gaffney, Paul Golden, II, *academic administrator, retired military officer*
Lutz, Francis Charles *dean, civil engineering educator*
Martin, Sylvia S. *special education educator, psychology educator*
Pearson, Thomas Spencer *academic administrator*

West Milford
Hannon, Patricia Ann *library director*
Stelpstra, William John *minister*

West New York
Gruenberg, Elliot Lewis *electronics engineer and company executive*
Knopf, Claire *editor, writer*
Koo, Yonghoi *investment banker*
Schmidt, Nancy Anne *psychotherapist*

West Orange
Asaadi, Mokhtar *plastic surgeon*
Atkins, Richard Bart *film and television producer*
Bennett, Alan Hugh *retired medical educator*
Bojsza, Joan E. *elementary school educator*
Bornstein, Lester Milton *retired health facility administrator*
Brodkin, Roger Harrison *dermatologist, educator*
Casella, Anthony John *cardiologist*
Decter, Edward M. *orthopedist, surgeon*
De Lisa, Joel Alan *rehabilitation physician, research executive*
Eisenberg, R. Neal *restoration company executive*
Gans, Bruce Merrill *physiatrist, educator, health facility administrator*
Ghali, Anwar Youssef *psychiatrist, educator*
Hill, George James *physician, educator*
Hwang, Karen *research scientist*
Jordan, Leo John *lawyer*
Kyle, Corinne Silverman *management consultant*
Langsner, Alan Michael *pediatric cardiologist*
Linsenmeyer, Todd Alan *urologist, physician, educator*
Martin, Boston Faust *neurosurgeon*
Mazur, Thomas A. *music educator*
McKinney, John Adams, Jr. *lawyer*
Petrokubi, Marilyn *film company executive, producer, writer, researcher*
Richmond, Harold Nicholas *lawyer*
Rinsky, Judith Sue Lynn *foundation administrator, consultant, educator*
Rogal, Gary Jeffrey *cardiologist*
Rosa, Richard Angelo *orthopedist, surgeon, educator*
Samson, David *lawyer*
Sweeney, Gerald Bingham *lawyer*
Thomas, Gary L. *retired academic administrator*
Tutela, Rocco *plastic surgeon*
Whang, Matthew Ihn Seong *urologist*

West Paterson
Lilley, David *chemicals executive*
Pataki, Andrew *bishop*
Schady, Kathleen *pharmaceutical executive*
Smith, Roy (R. Smith) *lawyer*

West Windsor
Yoseloff, Thomas *publisher*

Westfield
Bhagat, Phiroz Maneck *mechanical engineer*
Bobis, Daniel Harold *lawyer*
Davoren, Steven Michael *marketing professional, psychologist*
Kean, Tom, Jr., (Thomas Howard Kean Jr.) *state senator*
Krivoshik, David Peter *lawyer*
Lechner, Alfred James, Jr., (Jim Lechner) *lawyer, former federal judge*
McLean, Vincent Ronald *former manufacturing company financial executive*
Simon, Martin Stanley *economist, consultant*
Vijayakumar, Asha *ophthalmologist*

Westwood
Fabrikant, Craig Steven *psychologist*
Landzberg, Joel Serge *cardiologist*
Possick, Paul Aaron *dermatologist*
Radakovich, Daniel I. *communications executive, consultant*

Wharton
Krosser, Howard S. *aerospace transportation executive*

Whippany
Alexander, Mark A. *energy executive*
Vallee, Michelle Linda *pre-school educator*
Willans, Joanne Joy *music educator*

Whitehouse
Shelton, Craig *food service executive*

Whitehouse Station
Anstice, David W. *pharmaceutical executive*
Bossidy, Larry (Lawrence Arthur) *pharmaceutical company and former industrial manufacturing executive*
Clark, Richard T. *pharmaceutical company executive*
Deese, Willie A. *pharmaceutical executive*
Fiscus, Philip Wayne *underwriter*
Frazier, Kenneth C. *pharmaceutical executive, lawyer*
Gilmartin, Raymond V. *pharmaceutical company executive*
Graddick-Weir, Mirian *human resources specialist*
Kellogg, Peter Newman *pharmaceutical executive*
Kuhlik, Bruce Neil *lawyer*
McGlynn, Margaret G. *pharmaceutical executive*
McGuire, John Lawrence *pharmaceutical executive*
Scalet, J. Chris (James Christopher Scalet) *pharmaceutical executive*
Weber, Ann *pharmaceutical executive, researcher*
Yarno, Wendy *pharmaceutical executive*

Whiting
Randall, Lynn Ellen *librarian*
Willis, Ben *writer, artist*

Williamstown
Heidemark, George John *elementary school educator*

Willingboro
Bevels, Esther Marie *medical technician, director*
Denslow, Deborah Pierson *primary school educator*
Green, Riva Lee *social worker, minister*
Ingerman, Peter Zilahy *systems analyst, consultant*

Woodbridge
Barcan, Stephen Emanuel *lawyer*
Brown, Morris *lawyer*
Galkin, Samuel Bernard *orthodontist*
Hoberman, Stuart A. *lawyer*
Lepelstat, Martin L. *lawyer*
Santulli, Richard T. *air transportation executive*
Vitale, Joseph F. *state legislator*
Warren, Arthur Lee *secondary school educator, school system administrator*

Woodbury
Adler, Lewis Gerard *lawyer*
Doughty, A. Glenn *minister*
Stambaugh, John Edgar *oncologist, hematologist, educator, pharmacologist*

Woodcliff Lake
Jacobs, Charles Nathan *editor, writer*
Tarlowe, Jeffrey L. *health products executive*

Wyckoff
Gartner, Joseph John, II, *obstetrician, gynecologist*

Ginsberg, Barry Howard endocrinologist, educator
Lavery, Daniel P. management consultant
Marcus, Linda Susan dermatologist
Munson, William Leslie insurance company executive

Yardville

Zweig, Steven Frederick statistician

NEW MEXICO

Abiquiu

Botts, Gregory artist
Howlett, Phyllis Lou retired athletics administrator

Alamogordo

Ashdown, Franklin Donald physician, composer
Ernst, James Allan safety engineer, consultant
Hobson, Suellen Ann Weber retired elementary school educator
Patch, Lisa E. health services director, nurse

Albuquerque

Alexis, Tracy L. project manager, project specialist, information technology manager, small business owner
Alford, Steve (Steven Todd Alford) men's college basketball coach
Allen, Richard Cutler surgeon, researcher
Anaya, Rudolfo writer, educator
Anderson, Kristina Elizabeth writer
Anderson, Lawrence Keith electrical engineer, consultant
Ardelean, Emil Valentin mechanical engineer, researcher
Baca, Vera Jennie Schulte art educator
Bachand, George D. research scientist
Baker, Laura Kay art gallery owner, writer
Bardacke, Paul lawyer
Barker, Lynn M. management consultant
Barry, Steve sculptor, educator
Baum, Carl Edward electrical engineer, researcher
Beach, Arthur O'Neal lawyer
Beiler, Holly Anne education educator
Bell, Stoughton computer scientist, mathematician, educator
Bergman, Barbara E. law educator
Berman, Stanley Zissman allergist, immunologist, educator, internist
Biderman, Paul Leonard lawyer, educator
Bova, Vincent Arthur, Jr. lawyer, consultant, photographer
Brinker, Charles Jeffrey chemistry and chemical engineering educator
Brown, James Hemphill biology professor
Brown, Lee Kelvin pulmonary, critical care and sleep medicine physician, researcher
Byers, Steven N. anthropologist, educator, computer professional
Calkins, Ralph Nelson retired economics professor
Caplan, Edwin Harvey retired dean, finance educator
Cargo, David Francis lawyer, former governor
Carlow, Kathleen M. lawyer
Caruso, Mark John lawyer
Chang, Barbara Karen medical educator, director
Chavez, Martin Joseph mayor, lawyer
Chilton, Lance Alix pediatrician
Clarke, Gray B. psychiatrist
Clarke, Julia L. library director
Cobb, John Candler medical educator
Coleman, Barbara McReynolds artist
Compton, J. Douglas lawyer
Condie, Carol Joy anthropologist, science administrator
Conway, John E. federal judge
Davies, Thomas Mockett, Jr. history professor
Davis, Betty Bourbonia real estate company executive
Davis, Jon L. logistics consultant
DelCampo, Robert Gregory education educator
Deloria, Philip S. (Sam) lawyer
Dorato, Peter electrical and computer engineering educator
Draper, Dorothy E. middle school mathematics educator
Duke, Wanda K. artist
Duryea, Elias J. education educator
Eichenberg, Peter Thompson retired criminal investigator
Eldredge, Jonathan DeForest medical librarian, educator, social informaticist
Emin, David physicist
Enke, Christie George chemistry professor, consultant
Erickson, Sue Alice health educator, consultant, nurse
Everitt, Elizabeth M. school system administrator
Farmer, Terry D(wayne) lawyer
Figueroa, Francisco Armando aerospace transportation executive, accountant
Finch, Robert Jonathan communications engineer, consultant
Florez, Viola E. academic administrator, dean
Flournoy, John Charles, Sr. retired civilian military employee, officer
Foster, Judi interior designer, artist
Franse, R. Nelson lawyer
Freeman, Patricia Elizabeth multi-media specialist, educational consultant
Frias, Shirlee N. elementary school educator
Friberg, George Joseph electronics company executive, entrepreneur
Fuller, Anne Elizabeth Havens English language and literature educator, consultant
Gahala, Estella Marie writer, consultant
Gander, John Edward biochemistry educator
Garcia, F. Chris academic administrator, political scientist, educator
Giller, Edward Bonfoy retired government official, military officer
Goldberg, Catherine T. lawyer
Gomez, Larry prosecutor
Gordon, Larry Jean sanitarian, environmental health consultant
Grady, Dennis Edward physicist, researcher
Graff, Pat Stuever secondary school educator
Green, Francis William investment consultant, former missile scientist
Gutierrez, Sidney M. federal agency administrator
Hadas, Elizabeth Chamberlayne editor
Hager, Gordon Douglas scientist, engineering educator
Hall, Jerome William research engineering educator
Haltom, B(illy) Reid lawyer
Hansen, Curtis LeRoy federal judge
Hansen, Harold B., Jr. assistant principal
Harden, Neva Ninette writer, consultant
Harris, David W. academic administrator
Harris, Fred R. political scientist, educator, retired senator
Hart, Frederick Michael law educator
Hartz, Harris L federal judge
Hayo, George Edward management consultant
Heffron, Warren A. physician, educator
Henderson, Rogene Faulkner toxicologist, researcher
Hersee, Stephen Derek science educator
Hollander, Nancy lawyer
Hopfinger, Anton Joseph education educator, consultant
Horner, Harry Charles, Jr. sales executive
Hsi, David Ching Heng plant pathologist, geneticist, educator
Hunt, Bonnie Jo art association administrator, writer, soprano
Hutton, Paul Andrew historian, educator, writer
Iman, Ronald L. statistician, consultant
Jaramillo, Mari-Luci retired federal agency administrator
Jontz, Dennis Eugene lawyer
Jung, Rex Eugene psychologist, researcher
Kaehele, Bettie Louise accountant
Keleher, Michael Lawrence lawyer
Kierst, Debra B. theater educator, director, actor
King, Lowell Restell pediatric urologist
Knospe, William Herbert medical educator
Korman, Nathaniel Irving research and development company executive
Lambert, Jeffrey Scott secondary school educator
Lang, Thompson Hughes publishing executive
Lange, Dale Lowell language educator, researcher
Lasater, W(illiam) Robert, Jr. lawyer
Lattman, Laurence Harold retired academic administrator
Lawit, John Walter lawyer
Leach, Richard Maxwell, Jr., (Max Leach Jr.) corporate professional, consultant
Leeper, Ramon Joe physicist
Lewis, Linda Kathryn librarian
Liotta, William A. theater educator
Loftfield, Robert Berner biochemistry professor
Long, Robert Leroy retired utilities executive, consultant
Lopez, Martin III lawyer
Madrid, Patricia A. former state attorney general
Mansell, Justin Dennis optical engineer, consultant
Mapel, Douglas Wayne epidemiologist, educator, pulmonologist, critical care specialist
Mauderly, Joe Lloyd pulmonary toxicologist
May, Philip Alan sociologist, educator
McBride, Gerald Francis lawyer
McCrady, Barbara Sachs psychologist, educator
Mock, Joan Bodet music educator
Moore, Charles Loyd lawyer
Moskos, Harry columnist, editor
Mueller, Diane Mayne lawyer
Multhaup, Merrel Keyes artist
Nathanson, Paul S. lawyer, educator
Nelson, Mary Carroll artist, writer
Neville, Bruce David librarian
O'Brien, Daniel J. lawyer
Ofte, Donald retired nuclear energy industry executive
Omer, George Elbert, Jr. orthopaedic surgeon, educator
Orona, Joseph Ryan information technology executive
Orraj, Craig Allen lawyer
Ortiz, Patrick T. lawyer
Paine, Robert Treat chemistry educator
Palmer, Sharon-Joy agricultural research company executive
Parker, James Aubrey federal judge
Payne, Lucy Ann Salsbury law librarian, educator, lawyer
Peck, Ralph Brazelton civil engineering educator, consultant
Peña, Juan José retired interpreter
Pirkl, James Joseph industrial designer, educator, writer
Polley, Richard Donald microbiologist, chemist
Predock, Antoine Samuel architect, educator
Priem, Richard Gregory writer, executive
Prince, Bart architect
Qi, Huaqing special education educator
Qualley, Charles Albert art educator
Quinn, Iain musician
Raburn, Vern L. air transportation executive, former internet company executive
Rasmussen, Kerrie L. theater educator
Reichard, Robert Ross pathologist
Ricco, Edward Robert lawyer
Richter, Harvena retired literature educator, poet
Rivero, Dennis P. orthopedist
Roberts, Dennis William construction executive
Robinson, Charles Paul nuclear energy industry executive, diplomat
Roehl, Jerrald J. lawyer
Rosenberg, Robert D. radiologist, researcher
Royce, Stanton motivational speaker, consultant, marketing professional, sales executive
Ruiz, Carlos Leon nuclear scientist, physicist
Rutherford, Thomas Truxtun, II, state legislator, municipal official
Salazar, John Paul lawyer
Sanchez, Raymond G. former state legislator
Scarnecchia, Suellyn dean, law educator
Schmidt, Charles Otto military officer, engineer
Schmitt, Harrison Hagan former senator, geologist, astronaut, consultant
Schuler, Alison Kay lawyer
Schwerin, Karl Henry anthropology educator, researcher
Sheehan, Michael Jarboe archbishop
Sisk, Daniel Arthur lawyer
Sisson, Laurence P. artist
Slade, Lynn lawyer
Snell, Patricia Poldervaart librarian, consultant
Stahl, Jack Leland real estate company executive
Sterba, Jeffry E. energy executive
Stevenson, Bradford Allen management consultant
Strasburger, Victor C. pediatrician
Stuart, Cynthia Morgan retired academic administrator
Summers, William Koopmans psychiatrist, internist, researcher
Sussman, Arthur H. artist, painter
Tchoumak, Adelina corporate financial executive
Thévenot, Maxine Rachael musician, educator
Thomson, Iain Donald philosopher, educator
Thornton, J. Duke lawyer
Throckmorton, Rex Denton lawyer
Tolendino, Lawrence Francis electrical engineer
Truby, Betsy Kirby artist, illustrator, photographer
Tryon, Patti Ann school psychologist
Uhlenhuth, Eberhard Henry psychiatrist, educator
Van Devender, J. Pace research scientist, science administrator
Varela, Alan Mark state agency administrator, lawyer
Vigil, Charles J. lawyer
Wade, Gaylia Suzanne secondary school educator
Wainio, Mark Ernest insurance company consultant
Weh, Allen Edward aviation executive
Wellborn, Charles Ivey strategic planning consultant
Westwood, Albert Ronald Clifton management consultant, researcher
Wild, Richard music educator, musician
Wilkinson, Frances Catherine librarian, educator
Williams, Juanita Rosalie artist
Wilson, Heather Ann congresswoman
Witkin, Joel-Peter photographer, poet
Woodward, Joan B. science association director
Worrell, Audrey Martiny geriatric psychiatrist
Zink, Lee Berkey retired academic administrator, economist, educator

Artesia

Jensen, Eric Reinhard music educator

Bayard

Foy, Thomas Paul lawyer, retired state legislator, bank executive

Belen

Jolly, Jeffrey Russell musician, educator
Toliver, Lee mechanical engineer

Carlsbad

Christopherson, Ron mathematics educator
Piper, Lloyd Llewellyn, II, engineer, government and service industry executive
Regan Gossage, Muriel librarian

Cerrillos

Lutz, Nancy Cole educational consultant
Lutz, Raymond Price retired industrial engineer, educator

Clovis

Bradley, Walter D. lieutenant governor, real estate broker
Paladugu, Ramesh surgeon

Corrales

Adams, James Frederick psychologist, academic administrator, educator
Arkin, Michael Barry lawyer, arbitrator, writer
Campion, Kathleen Francis lawyer, gifted and talented educator
Eisenstadt, Pauline Doreen Bauman state legislator
Hooker, Van Dorn architect, educator, artist

Deming

Sherman, Frederick Hood lawyer

Dulce

Polczynski, Eric James pharmacist

Edgewood

Hamilton, Jerald musician

El Prado

Young, Jon Nathan archaeologist

Elephant Butte

Lederer, John Martin retired aeronautical engineer

Embudo

Rogers, Benjamin Talbot mechanical engineer, consultant

Farmington

Anderson, Evelyn Louise elementary school educator
Brown, Kimleigh Clayton special education educator, biologist
Espinosa, Nancy Sweet artist, anthropologist, curator
Graham, Warren Kirkland dentist
Moeller, Floyd Douglas lawyer
Neidhart, James Allen oncologist, educator
Perry, Mark Bradley lawyer, minister
Peterson Gerstner, Janet English professor
Thompson, Joseph T., Jr. health facility administrator
Titus, Victor Allen lawyer

Gallup

Cattaneo, Jacquelyn Annette Kammerer artist, educator

High Rolls Mountain Park

Ellison, Luther Frederick oil industry executive

Hobbs

Dill, Gary A. academic administrator
Garey, Donald Lee oil industry executive
Garey, Patricia Martin artist
Reagan, Gary Don state legislator, lawyer

Hondo

Pawley, Ray L. retired zoological park administrator, curator

Kirtland Afb

Tritten, James John federal agency administrator, educator

Las Cruces

Arthur, Paul Keith retired military officer
Bell, M. Joy Miller financial planner, real estate agent
Constantini, Louis O. financial consultant, stockbroker
Egginton, Everett educational administrator
Fitzgearld, Gayl musician, educator
Ford, Clarence Quentin mechanical engineer, educator
Hansuk, Sohn industrial engineer, educator
Heger, Herbert Krueger education educator
Kilmer, Neal Harold application developer
Little, Karen J. counselor
Lopez, Carol Sue artist
Martin, Michael V. academic administrator, economics professor
Muller, David Eugene retired mathematics professor, computer scientist, educator
Neumann, Rita Nunez lawyer
Parsley, Steven Dwayne title company executive
Peterson, Robin Tucker marketing educator
Rayson, Gary Donn chemistry educator
Reynolds, Terry Ray curator, anthropologist, educator
Richardson, Albert Edward chemistry professor, researcher
Roscoe, Stanley Nelson psychologist, aeronautical engineer
Salamanca-Riba, Susana Alicia mathematics professor
Sohn, Hansuk research scientist, educator
Tonn, Robert James retired entomologist

Las Vegas

Fries, James A. academic administrator
Howard, Leland William writer
Immerman, Michael director
Mendez, Celestino Galo mathematics professor, dean
Riley, Carroll Lavern anthropology educator
Simpson, Dorothy Audrey retired speech educator

Lordsburg

Clem, Sarah Lynn special education educator
Moralez, Joselyn Hope special education educator

Los Alamos

Andrews, Malcolm John engineering educator
Atcher, Robert Whitehill chemist, educator
Becker, Stephen A. physicist
Benjamin, Susan Selton elementary school educator
Bergen, Benjamin Karl research scientist
Blagoev, Krastan Blagoev physicist, biophysicist
Brown, Lowell Severt physicist, researcher
Burakovsky, Leonid physicist, researcher
Copenhaver, Carl physicist
Dudziak, Donald John nuclear engineer, educator
Engelhardt, Albert George physicist
Flippo, Kirk research scientist
Gibson, Benjamin Franklin physicist
Gregg, Charles Thornton research and development company executive, molecular biologist, researcher
Grilly, Edward Rogers physicist
Harlow, Francis Harvey physicist, anthropologist, research scientist, artist
Herr, Bruce lawyer
Huynh, My Hang Vo chemist, researcher
Judd, O'Dean P. physicist
Kang, Qinjun mathematician
Keepin, George Robert, Jr. physicist
Kloepper, David Alan retired management consultant
Korber, Bette Tina Marie chemist
Kubas, Gregory Joseph research chemist
Lipnikov, Konstantin mathematician
Masse, William Bruce archaeologist
Mead, William Charles physicist
Mendius, Patricia Dodd Winter retired editor, educator, writer
Michaudon, André Francisque physicist
Mihalas, Dimitri Manuel astrophysicist, educator
Nix, James Rayford nuclear physicist, consultant
Pack, Russell T. theoretical chemist
Picraux, Samuel Thomas physicist, researcher
Press, William Henry physicist, computer scientist
Ramirez, Juan mechanical engineer, researcher
Ramsey, Margie librarian
Rosen, Louis physicist
Sanbonmatsu, Kevin Y. molecular biologist, researcher
Schwarz, Ricardo B. research scientist
Selden, Robert Wentworth physicist, consultant

Sharp, David Howland *physicist*
Sickafus, Kurt Edward *materials scientist, researcher*
Smith, Fredrica Emrich *rheumatologist, internist*
Smith, James Lawrence *research physicist*
Stoddard, Stephen Davidson *ceramics engineer, retired state senator*
Swadener, John Gregory *research scientist*
Swift, Gregory *physicist*
Terrell, (Nelson) James *physicist*
Thompson, Joe D. *physicist*
Vitev, Ivan Mateev *physicist, researcher*
Wang, Yuejian *research scientist*
Weronski, Pawel *physicist, researcher*
Wohlberg, Brendt *electrical engineer, researcher*
Wooten, H. Omar *systems engineer, researcher*

Los Lunas
Seiler, Fritz Arnold *physicist*

Mayhill
Pastor, Stephen Daniel *chemistry professor, researcher, consultant*

Mora
Hanks, Eugene Ralph *real estate developer, rancher, forester, retired military officer, investor*

Moriarty
Cox, Darlene Beth *secondary school educator*
Haver, Jurgen F. *marketing consultant*
Moonwalker, Tu *minister, counselor, artist*

Penasco
Marx, Nicki Diane *sculptor, painter, jeweler*

Placitas
Hidy, George Martel *chemical engineer, engineering executive*
Long, Timothy Scott *chemist, consultant*
Reade, Lewis P. *diplomat, engineer, consultant*
Schoen, Stevan Jay *lawyer*
Smith, Richard Bowen *retired national park superintendent*
Watson-Boone, Rebecca A. *dean, researcher, library and information scientist, educator*

Portales
Carr, Tracy A. *musician, educator*
Dal Porto, Mark Daniel *music educator*
Frost, Everett Lloyd *academic administrator, anthropologist*
Goodwin, Martin Brune *retired radiologist*
Howard, Carolyn F. *elementary school educator*
Musonera, Etienne *finance educator, consultant*
Overton, Edwin Dean *retired campus minister, educator*
Paschke, Donald Vernon *music educator*
YSikes, Juanita Lou *art educator*

Prewitt
Reinhardt, Elizabeth A. *mathematics educator*

Ranchos De Taos
Dickey, Robert Preston *writer, educator, poet*

Raton
Carroll, William *publishing company executive*

Reserve
Wiley, James Dee *retired history and biology educator, national park service ranger*

Rio Rancho
Harmon, Joanna Kimball (Ethel Jo Harmon) *retired archivist, writer*
Nellessen, James Edward *environmental scientist, consultant*
Norman, Phyllis B. *volunteer*
Stevens, Roger Templeton *writer*

Roswell
Anderson, Donald Bernard *oil industry executive*
Baldock, Bobby Ray *federal judge*
Bassett, John Walden, Jr. *lawyer*
Choudhary, Adil Mushtaq *gastroenterologist*
Haines, Thomas David, Jr. *lawyer*
Kitchen, Richard *history professor, researcher*
Kraft, Richard Lee *lawyer*
Peterson, Dorothy Hawkins *artist, educator*
Robinson, Mark Leighton *gas industry executive, petroleum engineer, farmer*
Sun, Hui *industrial engineer, operations research analyst*
Wiggins, Kim Douglas *artist, appraiser, dealer*

Sandia Park
Beffort, Sue Wilson *state legislator*
Greenwell, Ronald Everett *communications executive*
Rager, Rudolph Russell *retired lawyer*
Wilczynski, Janusz S. *manufacturing executive, retired physicist*

Santa Fe
Aarons, Stephen D. *lawyer*
Adams, Mark Kildee *lawyer*
Akeroyd, Richard G., Jr. *library director*
Alfidi, Ralph Joseph *retired radiologist, educator, researcher*
Anderson, Darrell Edward *psychologist, educator*
Ballard, Louis Wayne *composer*
Bienvenu, John Charles *lawyer*
Black, Bruce D. *judge*
Brandt, Richard Paul *communications and entertainment company executive*
Brannen, Jeffrey Richard *lawyer*
Burton, John Paul (Jack Burton) *lawyer*
Carpenter, Richard Norris *retired lawyer, energy consultant*
Casey, Patrick Anthony *lawyer*
Cerny, Charlene Ann *director*
Chavez, Edward L. *state supreme court justice*
Cheetham, Alan Herbert *paleontologist*
Clyde, Larry Forbes *banker*
Connolly, Kevin Jude *lawyer*
Coss, David *mayor*
Cowan, George Arthur *chemist, bank executive, director*
Dasenbrock, Reed Way *state official, former academic administrator, literature educator*
Davis, Tom *biology professor*
Denish, Diane D. *lieutenant governor*
Dirks, Lee Edward *newspaper executive*
Dodds, Robert James III *lawyer*
Dreisbach, John Gustave *investment banker*
Duhaime, Nina Lee *energy and research and development company executive*
Evans, Dick *artist*
Farber, Steven Glenn *lawyer*
Ferguson, Glenn Walker *writer, educator, retired ambassador*
Fisher, Robert Alan *laser physicist*
Franzen, Ulrich J. *architect*
Gaddes, Richard *opera company director*
Gallegos, Mary Ellen *education educator, department chairman*
Garcia, Veronica *school system administrator*
Gell-Mann, Murray *theoretical physicist, educator*
Gilbert, Alan T. *conductor*
Giovanielli, Damon Vincent *physicist, consultant*
Goorley, John Timothy *nuclear engineer*
Groseclose, Everett Harrison *retired editor*
Hammer, Charles F. *retired chemistry professor*
Harding, Marie *ecological executive, artist*
Harroun, Dorothy Sumner *artist*
Herrera, Mary E. *state official*
Hickey, John Miller *lawyer*
Hoffmann, Louis Gerhard *immunologist, educator*
Johnson, Eric B. *police chief*
Johnson, Reverdy *lawyer*
Justice, Jack Burton *retired lawyer, writer*
Kaman, Helen S. *retired aerospace engineer, artist*
Karp, Diane R. *art educator*
Kellner, Richard George *mathematician, computer scientist*
Kelly, Paul Joseph, Jr. *federal judge*
Kiefer, Helen Chilton *emergency and trauma physician, neurologist*
King, Gary K. *state attorney general*
Kingsley, Judith *artist*
Kingsmore, Stephen Francis *physician, research scientist*
Knight, Kenneth Hugh *conductor*
Kronberg, Philipp Paul *physicist, educator*
Lee, David Mallin *physicist*
Lehmberg, Stanford Eugene *historian, educator*
Leibowitz, Jack Richard *physicist, educator*
Leon, Bruno *architect, educator*
Lewis, James Beliven *state official*
Lichtenberg, Maggie Klee *publishing executive*
Long, Timothy Edward *philosopher, research scientist*
Lynn, John Eric *nuclear physicist, researcher, consultant*
Maehl, William Henry *historian, academic administrator, consultant*
Maes, Petra Jimenez *state supreme court justice*
Mauldin, Barbara Barieau *curator*
Mazria, Edward *architectural firm executive*
McClaugherty, Joe L. *lawyer, educator*
Mercer, James Lee *management consultant*
Merrin, Seymour *computer company executive*
Micunis, Gordon Jules *set designer*
Miller, Dwight Richard *professional hair care industry executive, cosmetologist, consultant*
Miller-Engel, Marjorie *foundation administrator, commissioner, small business owner*
Moll, Deborah Adelaide *lawyer*
Morrison, Malcolm Cameron *engineering management professional*
Morrissey, Michael Joseph *investment banker*
Ovitsky, Steven Alan *musician, classical music executive*
Peat, Randall Dean *military analyst, retired military officer*
Peña, Amado Maurilio, Jr. *artist, curator, educator*
Peters, Margaret Annette *English language educator*
Pound, John Bennett *lawyer*
Pulitzer, Roslyn Kitty *social worker, psychotherapist*
Richardson, Bill (William Blaine Richardson III) *governor*
Roybal, James R. *artist*
Rubenstein, Bernard *orchestra conductor*
Scheuer, Ralph H. *lawyer*
Schiller, William Richard *surgeon*
Schwarz, Michael *lawyer*
Serna, Patricio *state supreme court justice*
Sloan, Jeanette Pasin *artist*
Smith, Philip Meek *science administrator, consultant*
Stieber, Tamar *journalist*
Stolley, Richard Brockway *journalist*
Sumner, Gordon, Jr. *retired military officer*
Thornburg, Garrett, Jr. *finance company executive*
Vázquez, Martha Alicia *federal judge*
Verant, William J. *state agency administrator*
Watkins, Stephen Edward *accountant, publishing executive*
Welch, Jasper Arthur, Jr. *security company executive, consultant*
West, Geoffrey B. *theoretical physicist, physics professor*
White, David Hywel *physics professor, researcher*
Williams, Ralph Chester, Jr. *physician, educator*
Williams, Stephen *anthropologist, educator*
Wolkoff, Eugene Arnold *lawyer*
Wotherspoon, Mary Ruth *artist, writer*
Yalman, Ann *judge, lawyer*
Zlatoff-Mirsky, Everett Igor *violinist*
Zorie, Stephanie Marie *lawyer*

Seneca
Monroe, Kendyl Kurth *retired lawyer*

Silver City
Bettison, Cynthia Ann *museum director, archaeologist*
Buhner, Stephen Harrod *research scientist*
Cunningham, John Edward *retired geologist, educator*
Fryxell, David Allen *publishing executive*
Lopez, Linda Carol *social sciences educator*
Parent, Annette Richards *free lance writer, artist*
Remillard, Jean D. *medical association administrator*
Snedeker, John Haggner *university president*

Socorro
Schery, Stephen Dale *physicist*
Wang, Bixiang *mathematician*

Sunspot
Keil, Stephen Lesley *astrophysicist*

Taos
Boles, David LaVelle *lawyer*
Bolls, Imogene Lamb *English language educator, poet*
Brown, David Warfield *management educator, lawyer, academic administrator*
Harmon, Barbara Sayre *artist*
Vickers, Robert Edwin *retired military officer, historian, writer*
Witt, David L. *curator, writer*

Tesuque
MacGraw, Ali *actress*

Tijeras
Knutson, Mark Thomas *sculptor, architectural firm executive*

Truth Or Consequences
Rush, Domenica Marie *health facilities administrator*

NEW YORK

Adams Center
Hood, Thomas Gregory *minister*

Addison
Vona, John David *music educator*

Albany
Aceto, Vincent John *librarian, educator*
Alessi, Robert Joseph *lawyer, real estate developer, pharmacist*
Arseneau, James Charles *physician*
Barsamian, John Albert *lawyer, arbitrator, criminologist, judge, educator*
Baum, Joseph Thomas *lawyer*
Blount, Stanley Freeman *marketing educator*
Bonventre, Vincent Martin *lawyer, educator*
Bowen, Mary Lu *ecumencial administrator*
Brademas, John *retired academic administrator, former congressman*
Bradley, Edward James *state official, computer programmer and analyst*
Brewer, Aida M. *state official*
Bruno, Joseph L. *state legislator*
Capaldi, Elizabeth Ann Deutsch *psychological sciences professor*
Carl, Allen Laurence *surgery educator*
Carson, JoAnne *artist, educator*
Catalano, Robert Anthony *ophthalmologist, hospital administrator, writer*
Clark, John B. *academic administrator*
Cogen, Richard M. *lawyer*
Cole, John Adam *insurance executive*
Colombí-Monguió, Alicia de *language and humanities educator*
Corelli, John Charles *physicist, researcher*
Cortés-Vázquez, Lorraine *state official*
Cromie, William J. *urologist*
Cuomo, Andrew Mark *state attorney general, former secretary of housing and urban development*
Daines, Richard F. *state health commissioner, former health services executive*
Davis, Paul Joseph *endocrinologist*
DeNuzzo, Rinaldo Vincent *pharmacy educator*
Devine, Eugene Peter *supreme court justice*
DiNapoli, Thomas Peter *state official, former state legislator*
Donohue, Mary O. *judge, former lieutenant governor*
Donovan, Robert Alan *language educator*
Dulin, Thomas N. *lawyer*
Dushensky, Jacqueline Amelia *banker, educator*
Ebert, Loretta Caren *librarian*
Eppink, Joseph A. *music educator*
Ericson, David Frank *political scientist, educator*
Eristoff, Andrew S. *state agency administrator*
Evans, Jennifer G. *pharmacist*
Everett, James W., Jr. *lawyer*
Fanuele, Frank John *engineering executive, electrical engineer*
FitzAlan-Howard, Bennett-Thomas Henry Robert *news analyst, consultant, political scientist, theologian*
Flint, Robert Wallace *neuroscientist, educator*
Frank, Joachim *structural biologist, educator, biophysicist*
Frisch, Harry Lloyd *chemist, educator*
Gaddy, Sheila Mae *application developer, geriatrics nurse, writer, volunteer*
Gellis, Zvi Dan *healthcare educator*
Graffeo, Victoria A. *state appeals court judge*
Grannis, Pete (Alexander Banks Grannis) *state official, former state legislator*
Greenberg, Martin Alan *criminologist, educator*
Hancox, David R(obert) *audit administrator, educator*
Happ, Harvey Heinz *electrical engineer, educator*
Heshmat, Hooshang *manufacturing executive*
Howard, Lyn Jennifer *medical educator*
Hubbard, Howard James *bishop*
Jacobs, Rhoda S. *state legislator*
Jennings, Gerald D. (Jerry Jennings) *mayor*
Jones, Theodore T., Jr. *judge*
Joyce, William George, Jr. *transportation executive*
Kaye, Judith Smith *state appeals court judge*
Kelly, Raymond Aloysius, Jr. *lawyer, educator*
Kennedy, William Joseph *novelist, educator*
Kholodenko, Yuri V. *scientist, educator*
Kim, Jai Soo *retired physicist*
Knee, Michael J. *science librarian, consultant*
Koff, Howard Michael *lawyer*
Kruegler, Catherine A. *sister, parochial school educator*
Kuhla, Donald E. *chemicals executive*
Laird, Edward DeHart, Jr. *lawyer*
Langer, Judith Ann *psychologist*
Lefkowitz, Jerome *lawyer*
Lepow, Martha Lipson *pediatric educator, consultant*
Levine, Howard Arnold *judge*
Ley, Ronald *psychologist, educator*
Maloney, Sean Patrick *state official, lawyer*
Mannella, Carmen A. *research scientist*
Marciniak, Macary Weck *pharmacist, educator*
Meader, John Daniel *judge*
Mekonnen, Ademe *meteorologist*
Menges, Susan Debra Favreau *management consultant, retired protective services official*
Merbler, Candace Anne *librarian*
Mills, Richard Paul *school system administrator*
Miner, Roger Jeffrey *federal judge*
Mondello, Joseph N. *political organization administrator*
Mueller, I. Lynn *strategic planning and communications consultant*
Mumpower, Jeryl L. *academic administrator*
Nathan, Richard P(erle) *political science professor*
Noonan, John Daniel *plastic surgeon*
O'Donnell, Denise Ellen *state official, former prosecutor*
Ortloff, George Christian, Sr., (Chris Ortloff) *commissioner, journalist*
Paterson, David Alexander *lieutenant governor, former state legislator*
Picotte, Susan Carroll *lawyer*
Pigott, Eugene F., Jr. *state appeals court judge*
Polimeni, John Matthew *economics professor*
Read, Susan Phillips *state appeals court judge*
Reese, William Lewis *philosophy educator*
Robbins, Cornelius (Cornelius Van Vorse) *educational administration educator*
Rosenfeld, Harry Morris *editor*
Rosenkrantz, Daniel J. *computer science educator*
Rostow, Charles Nicholas *lawyer, educator*
Roy, Rob J. *biomedical engineer, anesthesiologist, educator*
Ruggeri, Robert Edward *lawyer*
Saifi, Javid *surgeon*
Sandhaas, Jill T. *lawyer*
Schalit, Robert Edward *advertising executive*
Schalk, Gerwin *research scientist, software engineer*
Schneider, Allan Stanford *biophysics, neuroscience and pharmacology educator, biomedical research scientist*
Schulman, Ruth Meryl Aronson *research and development company executive*
Scott, William Proctor III *lawyer*
Shtutman, Michael *biologist*
Shubert, Joseph Francis *librarian*
Smith, Ada LaVerne *state legislator*
Smith, Rex William *journalist*
Smith, Robert Sherlock *state appeals court judge*
Snitkoff, Gail Goodman *immunologist, educator*
Spitzer, Eliot Laurence *governor, former state attorney general*
Stavisky, Toby Ann *state legislator*
Swartz, Donald Percy *physician*
Tepper, Clifford *allergist, immunologist, educator*
Thompson, Frank Joseph *political science professor*
Tully, Mathew B. *lawyer*
Veille, Jean-Claude *obstetrician, educator*
Verdile, Vincent Paul *dean, emergency physician*
Volker, Dale Martin *state legislator, lawyer*
Welch, Janet Martin *librarian*
Wilber, Roger Alan *library supervisor, writer*
Wittner, Lawrence Stephen *history professor*
Yanas, John Joseph *lawyer, director*
Zambri, Melissa Marie *lawyer, educator*
Zimmerman, Earl Abram *neurologist, educator*
Zimmerman, Joseph Francis *political scientist, educator*
Zou, Linda *bank executive*

Albertson
Berlin, Mark A. *lawyer*

Albion
Allamon, Karen Henn *minister*
Minier, Lee N. *funeral director*

Alden
Pajak, David Joseph *lawyer, consultant*

Alexandria Bay
Fisher, Lester Emil *retired zoo administrator*

Alfred
Fei, Jun *art educator, graphics designer*
Higby, Wayne (Donald) *artist, educator*
Johnson, Carla Conrad *library dean*
Pye, Lenwood David *materials science educator, researcher, consultant*
Scheer, Joseph H. *artist, education educator*
Smith, Mark Arthur *information scientist, educator*

Alfred Station
Condrate, Robert Adam, Sr. *spectroscopy educator*

Amagansett
Zychick, Joel David *lawyer*

Amenia
Hale, Nathan Cabot *sculptor, artist, poet*

Amherst
Bradford, Michelle M. *social studies educator*
Brogan, Michael Spencer *physical therapist, educator*
Clark, Donald Malin *professional association executive*
Ismail, Abu Zafar Mohamed *physics professor, researcher*
Jen, Frank Chifeng *finance and management educator*
Jones, E. Thomas *lawyer*
Kurtz, Paul *philosopher, educator, writer, publisher*
Nickell, Joe *paranormal expert*
Shook, John Robert *philosopher*

Amityville
Citrano-Cummiskey, Debra Moira *chemist, network technician*
Imbert, Richard Conrad *insurance company executive, real estate developer*
Soloway, Richard Lewis *electronics executive*
Upadhyay, Yogendra Nath *physician, educator*

Ancram
Blechman, R. O. *artist, filmmaker*

Ancramdale
Weinstein, Joyce *artist*

Angola
Green, Gerard Leo *priest, educator*
Ross, Sue Hoisington *music educator*

Annandale On Hudson
Achebe, Chinua *writer, humanities educator*
Ashbery, John Lawrence *language educator, poet, playwright, art critic*
Botstein, Leon *academic administrator, conductor, historian*
Darrow, Emily M. *public relations executive, writer*
Keesing, Felicia *biology professor*
LÊ, An-My *photographer, educator*
Manea, Norman *writer, educator*
Miyagawa, Chiori *theater educator, playwright*
Papadimitriou, Dimitri Basil *economist, educator, academic administrator*
Pfaff, Judy *artist*
Sourian, Peter *writer, language educator, educator*
Tower, Joan Peabody *composer, educator*

Apalachin
Linder, Fannie Ruth *psychotherapist, concert soprano*

Ardsley
Silman, Roberta Karpel *writer, critic*
Swift, Michael Ronald *internist, educator*

Ardsley On Hudson
Guise, David Earl *architect, educator*
Seaman, Alfred Barrett *journalist, writer*
Stein, Milton Michael *retired lawyer*

Armonk
Boies, David *lawyer*
Bolduc, Ernest Joseph *management consultant, not-for-profit developer*
Brown, Joseph W., Jr., (Jay Brown) *insurance company executive*
Daniels, Michael E. *information technology executive*
Donofrio, Nicholas M. *information technology executive*
Dunton, Gary C. *insurance company executive*
Ferguson, Roger Walter, Jr. *reinsurance company executive, former federal official*
Gerstner, Louis Vincent, Jr. *investment company and retired information technology executive*
Harreld, James Bruce *information technology executive*
Horn, Paul M. *information technology executive, crystallographer*
Iwata, Jon C. *computer company executive*
Kelly, John E. III *information technology executive*
Kohnstamm, Abby E. *marketing executive*
Loughridge, Mark *computer company executive*
Mellors, Robert Charles *physician, scientist, educator*
Rosenberg, Michael *lawyer*
Sanchez, Adalio T. *data processing executive*
Wago, Mildred Hogan *retired municipal official*
Walsh, David James *lawyer*
Weber, Robert Carl *lawyer*
Wertheim, Ram D. *lawyer*
Zeitler, William M. *information technology executive*

Astoria
Francesca, Mike *radio personality*
Kaufman, George S. *real estate company executive*
Matheson, Linda *retired social worker*
Salzberg, Russ *sportscaster*
Schwartz, David Peter *curator*
Sirignano, Monica Ann *performing company executive, playwright*
Unsal-Tunay, Nuran *geological engineer, researcher*

Attica
Allen, Susan Diane *educator*
Rogers, Donald L. *music educator, department chairman, animal breeder*

Auburn
Arcuri, Michael A. *congressman*
Dello Stritto, Ellen M. *retired social studies educator*
Pelkey, Lawrence Michael *school psychologist*

Aurora
Ryerson, Lisa M. *academic administrator*

Averill Park
Haines, Walter Wells *retired economics professor*

Babylon
Brackett, Ronald E. *investment company executive, lawyer*
DaSilva, Lynn Judith *special education educator*
Herbst, Jane Elizabeth *school librarian*
Schwartz, Benjamin Michael *gynecologist, oncologist*
Schwarz, Barbara Ruth Ballou *elementary school educator*

Baldwin
Aliano, Joy Caryl *retired elementary school educator*
Chopra, Parveen Chander *management consultant, educator, researcher, community activist*

Baldwin Place
Kurian, George Thomas *publisher*

Baldwinsville
Wilson, Harold Batting *treasurer*

Ballston Spa
Barba, Harry *writer, publisher, educator*
Brown, Ifigenia Theodore *retired lawyer*
Westbrook, Jack Hall *metallurgist, consultant*

Batavia
Schirm, David *art educator, artist*
Steiner, Stuart *college president*

Bath
BetzJitomir, Susan Marie *lawyer, educator, policy analysis researcher*

Bay Shore
Williams, Tonda *entrepreneur, consultant*

Bayside
Chugh, Om Parkash *mathematics professor, researcher, forensics specialist*
Clingan, Edmund *history professor*
Gerus, John Patrick *portfolio manager, retired educator*
Kennedy, Mary Theresa *mental health services professional*
Li, Rowena Liu-ping *media specialist*
Madden, Joseph Daniel *trade association executive*
Mullany, Kevin Fergus *music educator, director*
Ohrenstein, Roman Abraham *economist, educator, rabbi*
Zinn, William *musician, composer*

Beacon
Kanzer, Lynn Karen *medical record technician*
Mc Keown, William Taylor *magazine editor, author*
Metz, Ferdinand *chef, educator, academic administrator*
Rousseau, Christina Jeannie *elementary school educator*
Siejka, George John *artist*

Bedford
Bowman, James Kinsey *publishing executive, rare book dealer*
Chase, Chevy (Cornelius Crane Chase) *comedian, actor, writer*
Husted, William Armstrong *sales executive*
Philip, Peter Van Ness *former trust company executive*
Tischler, Gary Lowell *psychiatrist, educator*

Bedford Corners
Greene, Jesse J., Jr. *former computer company executive*
Singer, Craig *entrepreneur, inventor, executive, investor, consultant*

Beechhurst
Wingate, Constance Blandy *retired librarian*

Bellerose
Miller, Paul J. *orthopedist, surgeon*
Paramekanthi, Srinivasan Mandayam *software services executive*
Roberts, Kathleen Joy Doty *secondary school educator*
Stecher, Pauline *painter, educator*

Bellmore
Andrews, Charles Rolland *library administrator*
Feldman, Harriet Ruth *dean*
Lederman, Gary *dentist*

Bellport
Coonerty, Mary Elizabeth *special education educator*
Regalmuto, Nancy Marie *small business owner, consultant*
Schultheis, Edwin Milford *dean, business educator*
Townsend, Terry *publishing executive*

Belmont
Rush, Deborah L. *art educator, artist*

Bemus Point
Ross, Roderic Henry *retired insurance company executive*

Bethpage
Baglio, Vincent Paul *aerospace transportation executive*
Conti, James Joseph *retired chemical engineer, educator*
Dolan, Charles Francis (Charles "Chuck" Dolan) *media and entertainment company executive*
Dolan, James L. *communications executive, professional sports team owner*
Gottesman, Patricia Ann *marketing executive*
Janczak, Andrew Anthony *marketing professional*
Mahony, Sheila Anne *retired communications executive*
Marcus, Craig Harlan *ophthalmologist*
McCormack, Dermot *communications executive*
Schwartz, Jonathan D. *lawyer*

Big Flats
Keck, Donald Bruce *physicist*
Orsillo, James Edward *computer engineer, information technology executive*

Binghamton
Arcones, Miguel A. *mathematics professor*
Bearsch, Lee Palmer *architect, urban planner*
Beck, Stephanie G. *lawyer*
Best, Robert Mulvane *insurance company executive*
Bix, Herbert Philip *historian, educator*
Bronstein, Laura *social worker, educator*
Cho, Sungdai *linguist, educator*
Coates, Donald Robert *geologist, educator*
DeFleur, Lois B. *academic administrator*
Dimitrov, Nikolay *chemistry professor*
Gaddis Rose, Marilyn *literature educator, translator*
Gates, Gregory Ansel *lawyer*
Gerhart, Eugene Clifton *lawyer*
Gouldin, David Millen *lawyer*
Guay, Robert E. *philosopher, educator*
Hilton, Peter John *mathematician, educator*
Isaacson, Robert Lee *neurobehavioral scientist, educator*
James, Gary Douglas *biological anthropologist, educator, researcher*
Jones, Wayne Elfed, Jr. *chemist, researcher*
Khasawneh, Mohammad Turki *industrial engineer, educator*
Klir, George Jiri *systems science educator*
Kramer, Philip Joseph *lawyer*
Lee, Wendy Wan-Ki *music educator*
Levis, Donald James *psychologist, educator*
Madigan, Kathryn Grant *lawyer*
Mazrui, Ali Al'Amin *political science professor, researcher*
Meador, John Milward, Jr. *dean, librarian*
Naslund, Howard Richard *geological science educator*
Peckham, Eugene Eliot *judge, lawyer*
Regenbogen, Adam *judge*
Sklar, Kathryn Kish *historian, educator*
Stein, George Henry *historian, educator, administrator*
Swain, Mary Ann Price *university official*
Taylor, Kenneth Douglas *stockbroker, finance and computer consultant, educator*
Whittingham, M(ichael) Stanley *chemist*
Wildoner, Nancy Schamu *music educator, fine arts department chairman*
Zhou, Nan *finance educator*

Blue Mountain Lake
Bond, Hallie E. *curator, historian*
Welsh, Caroline Mastin *museum director, curator, art historian*

Blue Point
Owen, Thomas Llewellyn *investment company executive*

Bohemia
Breslin, Eileen Mary *lawyer*
Grandmaster Flash, (Joseph Saddler) *disc jockey*
Rudolph, Scott *pharmaceutical executive*

Boiceville
Thomas, David Clifton *music educator*

Brainard
Isaksen, Robert L. *retired bishop*

Brentwood
Burgess, John Thomas *physical education educator, consultant*
Liebert, Lynn Langenbach *psychologist, educator*
McKeever, Edna *archivist, educator*

Brewster
Mahoney, Joëlle Katherine *astrological consultant, communications educator*
Nadel, Norman Allen *civil engineer*
Perez, Louis Anthony *radiologist*
Shepard, Lance Hastings *marketing professional, consultant, newscaster*

Briarcliff Manor
Bernstein, Nadia Jacqueline *lawyer*
Bhargava, Rameshwar Nath *physicist*
Bingham, J. Peter *electronics research executive*
Bower, Thomas Michael *lawyer*
Cavalcanti, Dave Alberto Tavares *electrical engineer*
Cooper, Gloria *editor, press critic*
Erkamp, Ramon Quido *medical researcher, consultant*
Goldschmidt, Robert Alphonse *financial executive*
Kennell, Richard Wayne *recording industry executive, consultant, small business owner, treasurer, finance company executive*
Kepcher, Carolyn *real estate company executive*
Oakley, Richard Putney *investment banker*
Pousada, Lidia *physician*
Read, John Conyers *non-profit company executive*
Wheeler, Margaret Jane *actress, soprano, voice educator*
Windham, Revish *poet*

Bridgehampton
Cook, Peter Halsey *architect*
Phillips, Warren Henry *publishing executive*
Stuart, Greg *marketing professional, writer*

Brightwaters
Kavanagh, Eileen J. *librarian*
North, E(dward) Lee *retired writer, former aerospace company professional*

Brockport
Blake, Robert William *retired literature and language professor, writer*
Dabbagh, Mahmoud *language educator, linguist, researcher*
Gemmett, Robert J. *dean, English language educator*
Leslie, William Bruce *history professor*
McGhee, Diane Baumann *dance instructor, consultant*
White, Christopher Todd *language educator, anthropologist*

Brocton
Berman, Alexis Danielle *elementary school educator*

Bronx
Abbott, Rick *pediatric neurosurgeon, educator*
Abreu, Bobby *professional baseball player*
Adams, Alice *sculptor*
Afterman, Jean *professional sports team executive*
Ahmose, Nefertari A. *journalism educator*
Alderman, Elizabeth *pediatrician, educator*
Antwi, Ebenezer Yaw *education educator*
Ask-Nanko, Lorraine Charlotte *music educator*
Bacarella, Flavia *artist, educator*
Baker, Blanche *actress*
Balka, Sigmund Ronell *lawyer*
Bark, Nigel Martyn *psychiatrist*
Behnken, William Joseph *artist, educator*
Bella, Jonathan N. *cardiologist*
Bennett, Michael Vander Laan *neuroscience educator*
Bingham, June *playwright*
Blaufox, Morton Donald *hypertension specialist, nuclear medicine physician, educator*
Block, Holly *museum director*
Bowers, Francis Robert *educational consultant, literature educator*
Brandt, Lawrence Jay *internist, gastroenterologist, educator*
Bullaro, Grace Russo *literature, film and foreign language educator, critic*
Burgio, Michael *medical researcher*
Cano, Robinson Jose *professional baseball player*
Carter, Majora J. *urban planner*
Cashman, Brian M. *professional sports team executive*
Chase, Martin Leslie *literature and language educator, priest*
Clemens, Roger (William Roger Clemens) *professional baseball player*
Cohen, Herbert Jesse *pediatrician, educator*
Cohen, Selma *retired librarian*
Cornfield, Melvin *lawyer, director*
Coupey, Susan McGuire *pediatrician, educator*
Damon, Johnny *professional baseball player*
Das, Ashoke Kumar *internist, consultant*
Dean, Nancy *literature educator, retired playwright*
Diaz-Fuentes, Gilda *pulmonologist*
Dolich, Barry H. *plastic surgeon, educator*
Drepaul, Loris Omesh *internist, infectious diseases physician*
DuLaux, Russell Frederick *lawyer*
Dulles, Avery *cardinal, theologian*
Durglishvili, Nana Z. *psychologist, language educator*
Dutcher, Janice Jean Phillips *oncologist*
Elkins, Alfred David *insurance company executive*
Engelke, Charles Edward *physics professor*
Fleischer, Norman Samuel *endocrinology administrator, medical educator*
Fletcher, Judith Ellen *music educator*
Frater, Robert William Mayo *surgeon, educator*
Freeman, Leonard Murray *radiologist, nuclear medicine physician, educator*
Gaveras, Harry *architect*
Giambi, Jason Gilbert *professional baseball player*
Golden, Gail (Gail Golden Icahn) *travel company executive*
Goodrich, James Tait *neuroscientist, neurosurgeon*
Grassano, Thomas David *minister*
Greenstein, Stuart Mark *surgical educator*
Hait, Gershon *pediatric cardiologist*
Hallett, Charles Arthur, Jr. *language educator, humanities educator*
Hartil, Kirsten *research scientist*
Hauser, Bernice Worman *director*
Heagarty, Margaret Caroline *retired pediatrician*
Hennessy, Thomas Christopher *priest, educator, retired dean*
Hilliard, Carol *nurse, educator, consultant, researcher*
Hirano, Asao *neuropathologist, educator*
Hodgson, W(alter) John (Barry Hodgson) *surgeon*
Horwitz, Susan Band *pharmacologist*
Hudson, Frederick Bernard *management consultant*
Hughes, Phil (Philip J. Hughes) *professional baseball player*
Hunt, George William *priest, magazine editor*
Jackson, Reggie (Reginald Martinez Jackson, Mr. October) *retired professional baseball player*
James, Gesille *librarian*
Jeter, Derek Sanderson *professional baseball player*
Juszczyk, James Joseph *artist*
Kahn, Thomas *medical educator*
Kalnicki, Shalom *radiologist, educator*
Kalpana, Ganjam V. *biomedical researcher*
Karesh, William B. *science administrator, director, veterinarian*
Kassoy, Hortense (Honey Kassoy) *artist, sculptor, painter*

Keating, Tedd Michael *adult education educator*
Kelley, Aloysius Paul *academic administrator, priest*
Kelly, Thomas M. *headmaster*
Kitt, Olga *artist*
Koranyi, Adam *mathematics professor*
Korman, Barbara *sculptor*
Kornfeld, Robert Jonathan *playwright, photographer*
Koss, Leopold G. *pathologist, educator*
Kostelny, Albert Joseph, Jr. *lawyer*
Lagares, Portia Octavia *music educator*
Lee, Dong Hwan *business administration educator*
Lieber, Charles Saul *internist, educator*
Lienert, Christoph *physical education educator*
Long, Gregory R. *botanic garden administrator*
Lyons, Maxine Evadney *small business owner, poet*
Macklin, Ruth *bioethics educator*
Martinez, Tino *professional baseball player*
Matsui, Hideki *professional baseball player*
Mazabel, Hector Antonio *psychotherapist, guidance counselor, researcher, journalist, announcer*
McCabe, James Patrick *university librarian*
McShane, Joseph Michael *academic administrator, priest*
Megalli, Maguid Ramzi *health facility administrator*
Menthena, Anuradha *research scientist*
Michler, Robert E. *heart surgeon*
Min, Sang Hee *internist, researcher*
Mittler, Diana (Diana Mittler-Battipaglia) *music educator, pianist*
Mukherjee, Asit Baran *geneticist, educator*
Mullangi, Sivaprasad *surgeon*
Muller, Katherine Lynn *clinical psychologist*
Mussina, Michael Cole *professional baseball player*
Nathanson, Melvyn Bernard *academic administrator, mathematician, educator*
Nierva, Magdelena Lavesores *mathematics educator*
Nitowsky, Harold Martin *physician, educator*
O'Connor, William Riordan *lawyer, educator*
Oertel, Michael *researcher, medical educator*
Oktay, Maja Hrzenjak *medical educator*
Olerud, John Garrett *professional baseball player*
Parker, Everett Carlton *clergyman*
Pena, Antonio Francisco (Tony Pena) *professional athletics coach*
Pettitte, Andrew Eugene (Andy Pettitte) *professional baseball player*
Pomrenze, Colonel *archivist, consultant*
Posada, Jorge Rafael *professional baseball player*
Prabhu, Vrunda P. *mathematics professor*
Purpura, Dominick P. *dean emeritus, neuroscientist*
Radel, Eva *pediatrician, hematologist*
Rego, Simon Alexander *psychologist*
Reichgott, Michael Joel *medical educator, dean, physician*
Reidy, Valerie J. *principal, educator*
Reinus, John F. *hepatologist, medical educator*
Richards, Shana Natalie *physical therapist*
Richman, Murray *lawyer*
Rivera, Mariano *professional baseball player*
Robinson, Gwendolyn Niema *elementary school educator*
Rodriguez, Alex (Alexander Emmanuel Rodriguez) *professional baseball player*
Rose, Israel Harold *mathematics professor*
Rosenstreich, David Leon *medical educator, immunologist, allergist*
Ruben, Robert Joel *pediatric otorhinolaryngologist, educator*
Rubensky, Mitchell *band director*
Sable, Robert Allen *gastroenterologist*
Safyer, Steven Michael *medical association administrator, educator*
Sanchez-Silkman, Jennifer Christine *elementary school educator*
Sanderson, Steven E. *science administrator*
Satir, Birgit H. *medical educator, researcher*
Scanlan, Thomas Joseph *college president, educator*
Schaller, George Beals *zoologist*
Scharff, Matthew Daniel *immunologist, cell biologist, educator*
Schaumburg, Herbert Howard *neurology educator*
Schlussel, Seymour *obstetrician, gynecologist*
Schramm, Vern L. *biochemist, educator*
Seltzer, William *statistician, social science administrator*
Shafritz, David Andrew *physician, research scientist*
Shapiro, Nella Irene *surgeon, educator*
Sherman, Judith Dorothy *theater producer, engineer, recording industry executive*
Sisson, Elisabeth Joanne *elementary school educator*
Sonnenblick, Edmund Hiram *medical educator, cardiologist*
Spatt, Hartley Steven *humanities educator*
Spiegel, Allen Michael *dean, internist*
Spinka, William J. *art educator*
Spitzer, Adrian *pediatrician, educator*
Stanley, E. Richard *biomedical researcher*
Stein, Bernard L. *journalist*
Stein, Ruth Elizabeth Klein *physician*
Steinbrenner, George Michael III *professional baseball team and shipbuilding company executive*
Stertz, Stephen Allen *historian, educator*
Strauch, Berish *plastic surgeon, hand and cosmetic surgeon*
Tellis, Vivian Anthony *transplant surgeon, administrator*
Torre, Joe (Joseph Paul Torre) *professional baseball team manager*
Ultan, Lloyd *historian, educator*
Valgemae, Mardi *language educator*
Veith, Frank J. *vascular surgeon, researcher, educator*
Waelsch, Salome Gluecksohn *geneticist, educator*
Walsh, Christine Ann *cardiologist*
Weil, Gary Ronald *lawyer*
Weiss, Avi *rabbi*
Wertheim, Mary Danielle *educational coordinator*
Wiernik, Peter Harris *oncologist, educator*
Williams, Bernie (Bernabe Figueroa Williams) *professional baseball player*
Wilson, Sarada Amelia Princess *elementary school educator*
Yale (Yeleyenide-Yale), Serina *philanthropist, apparel designer*
Yalow, Rosalyn Sussman *biophysicist*
Zalaznick, Sheldon *retired editor, journalist*

Bronxville

Bertles, John Francis *physician, educator*
Biscardi, Chester *composer, educator*
Brunale, Vito John *aerospace engineer*
Cutler, Kenneth Burnett *lawyer, investment company executive*
Ellinghaus, William Maurice *communications executive*
Frost, A. Corwin *architect, consultant*
Fuller, David Otis, Jr. *lawyer*
Garber, Robert Edward *lawyer, insurance company executive*
Hagendorn, William Hull *lawyer*
Lawrence, Karen R. *academic administrator, literature and language professor*
Lee, Clement William Khan *trade association administrator*
Lombardo, Philip Joseph *broadcasting company executive*
Parsons, Andrew John *management consultant, corporate administrator*
Peters, Sarah Whitaker *art historian, writer*
Pollin, Burton Ralph *language educator*
Rosenthal, Lucy Gabrielle *writer, editor, educator*

Brookhaven

Kouts, Herbert John Cecil *retired physicist*

Brooklyn

Abott, Michael Larry *physician*
Ackerman, Jacob Lewis *ophthalmologist*
Aizman, Alexander *ophthalmologist*
Alfonso, Antonio Escolar *surgeon*
Al-Hafeez, Humza *minister, editor*
Allison, Mary Ann *consulting company executive, writer, speaker*
Altura, Bella T. *physiologist, educator*
Altura, Burton Myron *physiologist, educator*
Amendola, Sal John *artist, educator, writer*
Amon, Carol Bagley *federal judge*
Amrhein, Joe *artist*
Anderson, Lennart *artist*
Armenakas, Anthony Emmanuel *aerospace engineering educator*
Armstrong, John Wallace *film producer*
Armstrong, L. C. *artist*
Bakakos, Diana *middle school educator*
Bandler, Martin *physician*
Barran, Thomas Paul *language educator*
Behm, Dutsi *physician*
Benz, Susan *library and information scientist*
Bernstein, Larry Howard *clinical pathologist*
Berry, Richard S. *physician*
Bianco, Anthony Joseph III *newswriter*
Birenbaum, Leo *retired engineering educator*
Birenbaum, William M. *former university president*
Biro, Laszlo *dermatologist*
Bishar, John Joseph, Jr. *utilities executive, lawyer*
Blasi, Alberto *Romance languages educator, writer*
Bloomfield, David Charles *lawyer, educator, not-for-profit public executive*
Borgen, Patrick Ivan *surgeon*
Bottiglia, Frank Robert *bank executive*
Bramwell, Henry *federal judge*
Bugliarello, George *academic administrator, educator*
Bui, Phong *painter*
Buttaro, Lucia *language educator, consultant*
Campbell, Naomi *artist*
Carswell, Lois Malakoff *botanical garden executive, consultant*
Catell, Robert Barry *gas industry executive*
Chambers, William Edmond *writer*
Chao, Tsai Chung *physician, medical association administrator*
Charton, Marvin *chemist, educator*
Chung, Ping Tsai *education educator*
Clark, Luther Theopolis *physician, educator, researcher*
Cogan, Brian M. *federal judge*
Cohen, Alan *investment banker*
Coleman, Maurice L. *bank executive*
Collins, Ronald Leslie Leopold *neurosurgeon*
Costello, Jeffrey *apparel designer*
Cottrell, James E. *anesthesiologist, medical educator*
Crawford, Clinton *art historian, educator*
Cummings, Josephine Anna *writer, consultant, advertising executive*
Curtis-Tweed, Phyllis Marie *humanities educator*
D'Elia, Nicholas *secondary school educator*
Desmarais, Charles Joseph *museum director, writer*
DiMarzio, Nicholas Anthony *bishop*
Dinnerstein, Harvey *artist*
Dinnerstein, Simon Abraham *artist, educator*
Donaldson, Stephen Reeder *author*
Doucette, David Robert *information technology executive*
Douglass, Melvin Isadore *school system administrator, humanities educator, composer*
Ebesu, Duane Ken *human services administrator*
Eliasi, Jennifer Rebecca *dietician, consultant*
Epstein, Alvin *actor, performance artist, theater director, make-up artist*
Erber, William Franklin *gastroenterologist*
Evans, Beth *library and information scientist*
Faison, Seth Shepard *retired insurance broker*
Fani, Robert J. *gas industry executive*
Felder, Mira B. *dean, academic administrator*
Fischer, R.M. *sculptor*
Fischman, Myrna Leah *accountant, educator*
Flam, Jack Donald *art historian, educator*
Fleischer, Marian *surgeon*
Fletcher, Donna Angella *secondary school educator*
Forsberg, Suzanne *humanities educator*
Fox, Cynthia F. *journalist, writer*
Franco, Victor *theoretical physics educator*
Frank, Hosea (Ze Frank) *web video blogger*
Friedman, Eli A. *nephrologist, educator*
Frisch, Ivan Thomas *academic administrator, educator, computer and communications company executive*
Furchgott, Robert Francis *pharmacologist, educator*
Galatianos, Gus A. *computer company executive, consultant, real estate developer, educator*
Gamble, Cahtina Robyne *elementary school educator*
Garaufis, Nicholas G. *federal judge*
Garrett, Nancy Fales *playwright, educator*
Garrow, Eugene *pediatric surgeon*
Gatten, David *filmmaker*
Gentile, Robert A. *assistant principal*
Germano, Thomas *art educator*
Gershon, Nina *federal judge*
Gianlorenzi, Nona Elena *art dealer, painter*
Gilmartin, MaryAnne *real estate company executive*
Gilmore, Jennifer A.W. *computer specialist, educator*
Gioseffi, Daniela (Dorothy Daniela Gioseffi) *poet, writer, playwright, critic*
Gisolfi, Diana (Pechukas) *art history educator*
Glasser, Israel Leo *federal judge*
Glassman, Paul *library administrator, architecture educator*
Golanski, Alani *lawyer*
Gonsalves, Patricia E. *surgical nurse*
Goodman, David Joel *electrical engineering educator, science facility director*
Gotta, Alexander Walter *anesthesiologist, educator*
Grado, Angelo John *artist*
Gross, Richard A. *chemist, educator*
Gross, Stephen Mark *pharmacist, dean*
Gustin, Mark Douglas *healthcare executive*
Haber, Ira Joel *artist, educator*
Haralick, Robert Martin *electrical engineering educator*
Hawkins, Vivian Agatha *mental health nurse, educator*
Hechtman, Howard *financial analyst*
Hendra, Barbara Jane *public relations executive*
Heron, Earl D. *communications executive*
Herzog, Lester Barry *lawyer*
Hill, Elizabeth Anne *academic administrator, lawyer*
Hill, Victoria Ruth *librarian*
Hollander, Gerald Martin *physician*
Hopkins, Karen Brooks *performing arts executive*
Horowitz, Sara *labor organizer*
Hultin, Jerry MacArthur *academic administrator, former dean*
Ierardi, Eric Joseph *school system administrator*
Irizarry, Dora L. *federal judge*
Isquith, Aaron David *real estate broker, consultant*
Jacobowitz, Israel Jacob *cardiothoracic surgeon*
Jacobson, Barry Stephen *lawyer, judge*
Jones, Rudolph *minister*
Jones, Susan Emily *fashion educator, administrator, educator emeritus*
Josephson, William Howard *retired lawyer*
Kamins, Barry Michael *lawyer*
Kaprov, Susan L. *artist, photographer*
Karmel, Roberta Segal *lawyer, educator*
Kerwick, Colleen *lawyer, artist*
Kilanko, Oyenike Eunice *obstetrician, gynecologist*
Kimmich, Christoph Martin *academic administrator, educator*
King, Margaret Leah *history professor*
Kirshenbaum, Richard Irving *retired public health physician*
Korman, Edward R. *federal judge*
Kramer, Allan Franklin, II, *researcher, botanical garden official*
Kriftcher, Noel N. *humanities educator, director*
Krinsky, Yehuda *rabbi*
Landau, Joel *health services administrator*
Latif-Zade, Alisher *composer*
Laverty, Marilyn T. *public relations executive, media consultant*
Lazansky, Edward *artist, art educator*
Leamer, Robert Eldon *lawyer, hospital administrator*
Lee, Spike (Shelton Jackson Lee) *film director and producer*
Lehman, Arnold Lester *museum official, art historian*
Li, John K.H. *pathologist, department chairman*
Lichstein, Edgar *cardiologist*
Lichter, Stephen Marc *oncologist*
Lieber, Lola *artist*
Lindall, Terrance *artist*
Lipson, Steven Mark *virologist, microbiologist, environmental scientist, educator*
Litto, Judith Cheryl *art educator*
Liu, Yong *engineering educator*
Lobron, Barbara L. *speech educator, editor, photographer, writer*
Lockey, James Peter *public health service officer*
Lopate, Phillip *language educator, writer*
Loum, Anthony Webster *librarian*
Lowery, Robert Chesley *thoracic surgeon, educator*
Luka, Bishoy *pharmacologist, educator*
Luterman, Gerald *electronics company executive*
Mack-Harvin, Dionne L. *library director*
Mann, Roanne L. *federal judge*
Marcus, Donald *lawyer*
Markowitz, Marty (Martin Markowitz) *city manager*
Mauskopf, Roslynn R. *prosecutor*
Mayer, Ira Edward *gastroenterologist*
Mc Clenney, Byron Nelson *community college administrator*
McLean, William Ronald *retired electrical engineer, consultant*
McQuiggan, John A. *theater producer, writer*
Medbury, Scot Daniel *botanical garden executive*
Menezes, Nelson *surgeon*
Merlin, Lisa Ruth *neurologist, researcher*
Middleton, John Edison *management consultant*
Mirra, Suzanne Samuels *pathologist*
Mirski, Sara *real estate developer*
Moehring, Fred Adolf *wholesale distribution executive*
Mook, Sarah *retired chemist*
Morgan, Mary Louise Fitzsimmons *fund raising executive, lobbyist*
Morris, Mark William *choreographer*
Munk, Loren James *painter, writer, critic*
Murillo-Rohde, Ildaura Maria *marriage and family therapist, consultant, educator, retired dean*
Murphy, Kathleen Mary *former law firm executive, alternative healing professional*
Najib, Jadwiga S. *pharmacist, educator*
Nemazie, Siamack *nephrologist, consultant*
Niesen, James Louis *theater director*
Nii, Yuko *artist*
Nye, William Roger *psychologist*
O'Connor, Sister George Aquin (Margaret M. O'Connor) *academic administrator, educator*
O'Doherty, Susan Ann *psychologist, writer*
Ogunkoya, Andrea *marketing executive*
Ortner, Everett Howard *magazine editor, writer*
Orugunta, Raveendra Babu *pediatrician*
Padovano, Anthony John *fine arts educator, artist*
Palmer, Marc *engineer, lawyer*
Panwar, Shivendra Singh *education educator, researcher*
Parlamis, Michael Frank *civil engineer, construction executive*
Pearlstein, Seymour *artist*
Pearsall, Otis Pratt *retired lawyer*
Peker, Elya Abel *artist*
Pennisten, John William *computer scientist, actuary, linguist*
Peters, Mercedes *psychotherapist*
Piene, Chloe *artist, filmmaker*
Pitynski, Andrzej Piotr *sculptor*
Plotz, Charles Mindell *physician, educator*
Poser, Norman Stanley *law educator*
Price, Ely *dermatologist*
Purvin, Jack Mitchell *physician*
Rafiq, Muhammad Amir *nephrologist*
Raggi, Reena *federal judge*
Rathbun, Andrew J. *music educator*
Ratner, Bruce C. *professional sports team owner, real estate developer*
Rauschenbusch, Stephanie *artist, educator, poet*
Reichel, Walter Emil *advertising executive*
Reisler, Helen Barbara *public relations executive*
Remsen, James F., Jr. *biology educator*
Reynolds, Nancy Remick *writer, researcher, editor*
Rezkalla, Laurence *internist*
Reznikov, Lev *process engineer, researcher*
Rice, John Thomas *architecture educator*
Richardson, Alfonso Austin *accountant, financial services executive*
Richmond, Eero *composer, music librarian*
Rogers, Michael Alan *writer*
Roker, Christopher A. *microbiologist, photographer*
Rosenkranz, Richard Irwin *lawyer*
Ross, Randolph Ernest *investor*
Roth, Robert *lawyer, journalist*
Russell, Wayne Delano *activist, educator, poet*
Ryan, Leonard Eames *judge*
Sacchi, Terrence J. *cardiologist*
Sadr, Ali *neurosurgeon*
Sahlene, *singer*
Sakhnovich, Lev Aronovich *mathematics educator, researcher*
Samuel, Carren C. *hospital administrator*
Sanford, David Boyer *journalist, editor*
Savits, Barry Sorrel *surgeon*
Schaefer, Marilyn Louise *artist, writer, educator*
Schiffman, Gerald *microbiologist, educator*
Schneider, Adele Goldberg *librarian, educator*
Schwarz, Richard Howard *obstetrician, gynecologist, educator*
Schweikert, Edgar Oskar *dentist*
Schweikert, Mary Lou *elementary school educator*
Shalita, Alan Remi *dermatologist*
Sharify, Nasser *librarian, educator, writer*
Shaw, Kendall (George) *artist, educator*
Shaw, Leonard Glazer *retired electrical engineering educator, consultant*
Shcherbakova, Estella *chemist, mathematician, educator*
Shedrinsky, Alexander Mikhail *chemistry professor, conservator, consultant*
Shelov, Steven Patrick *pediatrician, educator*
Shivcharan, Jaigobin *secondary school educator, consultant*
Shulman, Abraham *otolaryngology educator, hospital administrator*
Sifton, Charles Proctor *federal judge*
Simons, Barbara *retired elementary school educator*
Singer, Eric T. *investment banker*
Skrobela, Katherine Creelman *music producer, data processing executive*
Slack, Ryan *entrepreneur*
Solan, Lawrence Michael *lawyer*
Song, Mark *surgeon, educator*
Spector, Robert Donald *language educator*
Stevens, Aleksei Reuben *music educator, composer*
Tagliapietra, Robert *apparel designer*

Tamir, Theodor *electrophysics researcher, educator*
Taylor, Ian Logan *dean*
Taylor, Shannon *lawyer, not-for-profit developer*
Teitelbaum, Zalman *rabbi*
Tessler, Sidney *pulmonologist*
Thomas, Lucille Cole *librarian*
Toranzo, Nilsa Caridad *special education services professional*
Townes, Sandra L. *federal judge*
Velázquez, Nydia Margarita *congresswoman*
Vidal, Maureen Eris *theater educator, actress*
Vitaliano, Eric Nicholas *federal judge*
Weber, Michael A. *physician, researcher*
Wei, Xinzhou *engineering educator*
Weill, Georges Gustave *mathematics professor*
Weinstein, Jack Bertrand *federal judge*
Wexler, Joan G. *dean, law educator*
Wiener, Hesh (Harold Frederic Wiener) *publishing executive, consultant*
Wilkow, Brian Richard *hospital administrator and clinician*
Wilson, Robert Warne *philanthropist*
Witherspoon, Maria Bernarda Pena *principal*
Wolf, Edward Lincoln *physicist, educator*
Wolfe, Ethyle Renee *academic administrator*
Wolintz, Arthur Harry *neurologist, ophthalmologist*
Wrotten, Marylean *medical coordinator, counselor*
Zakanitch, Robert Rahway *artist*
Zinnes, Alice Fich *artist, educator*
Zisser, Martin Shepherd *fur apparel manufacturer, investor, securities trader*

Brookville
Swaner, Lynn E *education educator*

Buffalo
Alexandridis, Paschalis *chemical engineer, educator*
Amborski, Leonard Edward *retired chemist*
Ambrus, Clara Maria *physician*
Ambrus, Julian L. *physician, educator*
Baier, Robert Edward *chemist, educator*
Bailey, Thomas Charles *lawyer*
Ballow, Mark *immunologist, educator*
Batt, Ronald Elmer *gynecologist, historian, biomedical research scientist*
Bayles, Jennifer Lucene *museum program director, educator*
Bean, Edwin Temple, Jr. *lawyer*
Bender, James Y. *not-for-profit fundraiser*
Beutner, Ernst Herman *microbiology educator*
Blane, Howard Thomas *alcohol/drug abuse services professional, researcher*
Bobinski, George Sylvan *librarian, educator*
Boden, William Edward *cardiologist, educator*
Brathwaite, Frank B. *education educator*
Brody, Harold *neuroanatomist, gerontologist, educator*
Brown, Byron W., Jr. *mayor, former state legislator*
Brown, Lawrence Charles *lawyer*
Brydges, Thomas Eugene *lawyer*
Buchanan, Richard N. *dean, dental educator*
Bucki, Carl Leo *judge*
Cao, Shousong *medical researcher, educator*
Carlson, Bruce William *diversified holding company executive*
Chang, Ching Ming (Carl) *engineering executive, mechanical engineer, educator, writer*
Chu, Tsann Ming *immunochemist, educator*
Churchill, Melvyn Rowen *chemistry professor*
Clarkson, Elisabeth Ann Hudnut *volunteer*
Coburn, Lewis Alan *mathematics professor*
Coles, Robert Traynham *architect*
Connors, Terrence M. *lawyer*
Creaven, Patrick Joseph *pharmacologist*
Cullen, Paul *medical educator*
Czyrny, James Joseph *physiatrist*
Daley, Ruth Margaret *advertising agency administrator*
Day, Donald Sheldon *lawyer*
Demant, Peter *geneticist, researcher*
DiFranco, Ani *music executive, musician*
Doren, Robert Alan *lawyer*
Dosluoglu, Hasan Haldun *surgeon*
Dreishpoon, Douglas Scott *curator, art historian*
Duax, William Leo *biologist, researcher*
Dubber, Markus Dirk *law educator*
Duchan, Judith Felson *retired speech pathology/audiology services professional*
Ezzo, David Albert *not-for-profit executive, anthropologist, educator*
Feldman, Irving *poet*
Feroleto, John *lawyer*
Feuerstein, Alan Ricky *lawyer*
Finnegan, Marchand Marie (Shonnie Finnegan) *archivist, consultant*
Fisher, Cheryl Smith *lawyer*
Flynn, Terrance Patrick *prosecutor, lawyer*
Frone, Michael R. *psychologist, researcher*
Fryer, Appleton *sales executive, diplomat*
Gardner, Arnold Burton *lawyer*
Genco, Robert Joseph *immunologist, periodontist, educator, scientist*
Germain, Pamela *health facility administrator, educator*
Ghadersohi, Ali *veterinarian, researcher*
Giambra, Joel Anthony *municipal official*
Gielow, Kathleen Louise *career planning administrator, consultant, special education educator*
Glanville, Robert Edward *lawyer*
Goldberg, Neil Alan *lawyer*
Goldblatt, Samuel *lawyer*
Goralski, Donald John *public relations executive, counselor*
Gort, Michael *economics professor*
Grant, S. G. *education educator*
Grasser, George Robert *lawyer, real estate developer, consultant*
Greene, Robert Michael *lawyer*
Gruen, David Henry *financial analyst*
Halbreich, Uriel Morav *psychiatrist, educator*
Halpern, Ralph Lawrence *lawyer*
Harvey, Steven John *not-for-profit developer*
Hauptman, Herbert Aaron *mathematician, educator, researcher*
Headrick, Thomas Edward *lawyer, educator*
Heilman, Pamela Davis *lawyer*
Hoffman, Faith Louise *social worker*
Hohn, David *physician*
Iggers, Georg Gerson *history professor*
Ignatowski, Tracey A. *research scientist, educator*
Irwin, Robert James Armstrong *investment company executive*
Jacobs, Jeremy Maurice, Sr. *diversified financial services company and professional sports team executive*
Jain, Piyare Lal *physics professor*
Jasen, Matthew Joseph *lawyer, retired judge*
Joseph, Ella *artist*
Joseph, Todd M. *lawyer*
Karwan, Mark Henry *engineering educator*
Kelly, Jim (James Edward Kelly) *former professional football player*
Kmiec, Edward Urban *bishop*
Kristoff, Karl W. *lawyer*
Kurlan, Marvin Zeft *retired surgeon*
Lamb, Charles Moody *political scientist, educator*
Lee, Jaekyung *education educator, researcher*
Lele, Amol Shashikant *obstetrician, gynecologist*
Levy, Kenneth Jay *psychology professor, academic administrator*
Lippes, Gerald Sanford *lawyer*
Lipsey, Stanford *newspaper publisher*
Littlewood, Douglas Burden *brokerage house executive*
Lombardo Appleby, Linda Rose *music educator*
Ma, Yingyu *research scientist*
Mahaney, Michael C. *library director*
Manes, Stephen Gabriel *concert pianist, educator*
Manning, Kenneth Alan *lawyer*
Martin, Margaret M. *artist, educator*
Mather, Lynn *law educator, political science professor*
Mattar, Lawrence Joseph *lawyer*
McCormack, Patricia Lynn *retired psychologist*
McElvein, Thomas Irving, Jr. *lawyer*
McKenzie, Denise *religious organization administrator, academic administrator*
McKibbin, William Alex *artist*
Meredith, Dale Dean *civil engineering educator*
Merini, Rafika *humanities educator, writer, language educator*
Merriman, Kevin Thomas *lawyer*
Meshlovitz, Mary E. *educational consultant, special education educator*
Mihich, Enrico *medical researcher*
Milazzo, David Anthony *mathematics educator*
Milgrom, Felix *immunologist, educator*
Miller, Ryan *professional hockey player*
Milligan, John Drane *historian, educator*
Mindell, Eugene Robert *surgeon, educator*
Monahan, John Michael *lawyer*
Mucci, Gary Louis *lawyer*
Murphy, Dennis Patrick *hotel business entrepreneur*
Murray, Glenn Edward *lawyer*
Mutton, Holly Beth *psychiatrist*
Naughton, John Patrick *cardiologist, educator*
Nielsen, Nancy H. *health organization executive*
Nolan, James Paul *internist, educator, researcher*
Odza, Randall M. *lawyer*
O'Loughlin, Sandra S. *lawyer*
Olsen, R. Nills *dean, law educator*
Oppenheimer, Randolph Carl *lawyer*
Pados, Dimitris A. *electrical engineer, educator*
Paige, Susan Mary *adult education educator*
Patel, Mulchand Shambhubhai *biochemist, researcher*
Pearson, Paul David *lawyer, arbitrator, mediator*
Pegels, C. Carl *management consultant, educator*
Peradotto, John Joseph *retired classics educator, editor*
Piver, M. Steven *gynecologic oncologist*
Popat, Saurin Rajnikant *oncologist, surgeon*
Rachlin, Lauren David *lawyer*
Regier, Darcy John *professional sports team executive*
Reich, William Zeev *lawyer*
Reismann, Herbert *engineer, educator*
Reitan, Paul Hartman *retired geologist, educator*
Rich, Robert E., Jr. *frozen foods company executive*
Roberts, Stephen M. *library director*
Ross, Gary Earl *writing educator*
Ruckenstein, Eli *chemical engineering professor*
Ruff, Lindy *professional hockey coach*
Sadler, Robert E., Jr. *bank executive*
Sahlem, James Robert *law librarian*
Salisbury, Eugene W. *lawyer, mediator*
Sarjeant, Walter James *electrical and computer engineering educator*
Segalla, Thomas Francis *lawyer*
Seitz, Mary Lee *mathematics professor*
Seller, Robert Herman *cardiologist, physician*
Shapiro, Stuart Charles *computer scientist, educator*
Shaw, David Tai-Ko *electrical and computer engineering educator, academic administrator*
Shedd, Donald Pomroy *surgeon*
Shick, Richard Arlon *finance educator*
Siedlecki, Peter Anthony *English language and literature educator*
Simpson, John Barclay *academic administrator*
Skretny, William Marion *federal judge*
Spengler, Paul Albert *grants and foundation administrator*
Starks, Fred William *chemicals executive*
Stoll, Howard Lester, Jr. *dermatologist*
Stoss, Frederick Warren *librarian, educator*
Sullivan, Margaret M. *editor-in-chief*
Swenson, William W. *retired dean, aerospace engineer, consultant*
Treanor, Charles Edward *physicist, researcher*
Trevisan, Maurizio *epidemiologist*
Triggle, David John *dean, pharmacist, consultant*
Trotter, Herman Eager, Jr., (Herman Trotter) *retired music critic*
Tucker, Melvin Jay *education educator, researcher*
Twagilimana, Aimable *language educator, writer*
Urban, Henry Zeller *publishing executive*
Veronica, Debra Clarisse *principal*
Vishwanath, Arun *information scientist, educator*
Vladutiu, Adrian O. *physician, educator*
Wang, Jui Hsin *biochemistry educator*
Wiesenberg, Russel John *statistician*
Williams, Lillian Serece *historian, social studies educator*
Wilmers, Robert George *bank executive*
Wisbaum, Wayne David *lawyer*
Woolverton, Diane Marie *literature and language professor*
Wright, John Robert *retired pathologist, educator*
Xu, Jinhui *engineering educator*
Yonkman, Mark William *lawyer*
Zawadzki-Janusz, Stacy Lynn *music educator, performing arts educator*
Zawicki, Joseph Leo *science educator*
Zhong, Sheng *computer scientist*
Zirnheld, Jennifer L. *engineering educator, researcher*

Burnt Hills
DeVries, Robert Charles *research scientist*

Buskirk
Johanson, Patricia Maureen *artist, architect*

Cairo
Ludwig, Laura Lonshein *poet*

Cambria Heights
Welfare, Frederick George *secondary school educator*

Cambridge
Kriss, Gary W(ayne) *priest*

Camillus
Armani, Frank Henry *retired lawyer*
Thompson, Mary Cecilia *nurse midwife*

Campbell Hall
Greenly, Colin *artist*

Canaan
Belknap, Michael H. P. *real estate developer*
Hooper, Ian (John Derek Glass) *retired marketing communications executive*
Lewis, Marjorie *librarian*
Pennell, William Brooke *lawyer*
Walker, William Bond *painter, retired librarian*

Canandaigua
Barden, George V. *county official, watershed specialist*
Beal, Myron Clarence *osteopath*
Ditmars, James Everett *social worker, actor*
Lowther, Frank Eugene *research physicist*
Wormer, Thomas Andrew *surgeon*

Canastota
Mirante, Thomas Anthony *retired secondary education educator*

Canton
Auster, Nancy Eileen Ross *economics professor*
Goldberg, Rita Maria *foreign language educator*
Sullivan, Daniel F. *academic administrator, sociologist, educator*

Carle Place
Mulhern, Edwin Joseph *lawyer*
Seiden, Steven Jay *lawyer*

Carmel
Foster, Lawrence G. *orthopedist, surgeon*
Laporte, Cloyd, Jr. *retired lawyer, manufacturing executive*
Lowe, Edwin Nobles *retired lawyer*

Castle Point
Mehta, Rakesh Kumar *physician, educator*

Castleton On Hudson
Kienzle, John Fred *retired history educator*

Catskill
Johnson, Deborah Jean *director*
Philp, Richard Nilson *writer, editor, journalist, historian*

Cazenovia
Carlson, William Clifford *retired defense industry executive, military officer*
Shattuck, George Clement *retired lawyer*
Wyckoff, Sylvia Spencer *art educator, artist*

Cedarhurst
Cohen, Harris L. *diagnostic radiologist, consultant*
Klein, Irwin Grant *lawyer*
Lagnado, Jennifer M. *assistant principal*
Taubenfeld, Harry S. *lawyer*

Centereach
Alabi, Kehinde *research scientist, mechanical engineer*
Chassman, Karen Moss *educational association administrator*
Feinberg, Sandra Lee *library director*

Centerport
McQueeney, Henry Martin, Sr. *publisher*
Stevens, Martin Brian *publisher*
Trotta, Ric Charles *aerospace transportation executive, consultant*

Central Islip
Bernstein, Stan *federal bankruptcy judge*
Boyle, E. Thomas *federal magistrate judge*
Brown, Alton C. *television personality, chef*
Cyganowski, Melanie L. *bankruptcy judge*
Eisenberg, Dorothy *federal judge*
Feuerstein, Sandra Jeanne *judge*
Hurley, Denis R. *federal judge*
James, Sharon Ann *elementary school educator*
Morris, Jeffrey Brandon *law educator*
Platt, Thomas Collier, Jr. *federal judge*
Seybert, Joanna *federal judge*
Spatt, Arthur Donald *federal judge*
Taylor, Carol Fay *education educator*
Viera, Robert, Sr. *protective services official*
Voigt, Philip Kenneth *music educator*

Chappaqua
Boal, Lyndall Elizabeth *social worker*
Castrataro, Barbara Ann *lawyer*
de Janosi, Peter Engel *research manager*
George, Jean Craighead *author, illustrator*
Graham, Lawrence Otis *lawyer, writer, television commentator*
Laun, Louis Frederick *government official*
O'Neill, Robert Charles *inventor, consultant*
Pollet, Susan L. *lawyer*
Pomerene, James Herbert *retired computer engineer*
Romney, Richard Bruce *lawyer*
Schwarz, Wolfgang *psychologist*

Charlton
Kekes, John *philosopher, educator*

Chatham
Kherdian, David *writer*
Weiner, Jack H. *lawyer*

Chautauqua
Schmidt, Edward Craig *lawyer*

Chazy
Ratner, Gayle *special education educator*

Cheektowaga
Kipler, James Michael *musician, educator*
Mruk, Eugene Robert *retired marketing professional, urban planner*
Staehr, Jonathan Edward *lawyer*
Wagle, A. Tina *education educator, researcher*

Cherry Valley
Humes, Graham *investment banker*

Chester
Amelar, Richard Daniel *urologist*
Holzer-Gargiulo, Alexandra *graphics designer, writer*
Mackerodt, Fred *public relations specialist*

Chestnut Ridge
Burns, Richard Owen *lawyer*
Day, Stacey Biswas *physician, educator*

Chittenango
Baum, Peter Alan *lawyer*
Cassell, William Walter *retired accounting operations consultant*

Churchville
Balch, Glenn McClain, Jr. *academic administrator, minister, writer*
Clarke, Stephan Paul *retired language educator, writer*

Cicero
Pink, (Alecia B. Moore) *singer*

Clarence
Greatbatch, Wilson *biomedical engineer*
Stringer, Gretchen Engstrom *consulting volunteer administrator*
Takeuchi, Esther Sans *chemist*

Claverack
Barrett, William Gary *advertising and marketing executive*

Clifton Park
Hilts, Earl T. *lawyer, government official, educator*
Nair, Laura *retired music educator*
Scher, Robert Sander *instrument design company executive*
Van Slyke, Rosemary *tax specialist*

Clifton Springs
Spoto, Carl Alexander, Jr. *history educator*

Clinton
Kodat, Catherine Gunther *literature and language professor*
Pagani, Albert Louis *aerospace system engineer*
Paris, David C. *political science professor*
Redfield, Robert Horace *mathematician, educator*
Ring, James Walter *physics professor*
Stewart, Joan Hinde *academic administrator*

Cobleskill
Ingels, Jack Edward *horticulture educator*
Rivera, Salvador, Jr. *history and sociology educator, researcher*
Westervelt, Gayle Gaetano *physical education educator*
Wilson, Lewis Lansing *insurance executive*

Cohocton
Sarfaty, Wayne Allen *insurance agent, financial planner*

Cold Spring
Pugh, Emerson William *electrical engineer*

Cold Spring Harbor
Hannon, Gregory J. *biology professor, researcher*

Stillman, Bruce *molecular biologist*
Watson, James Dewey *molecular biologist, educator*

Commack
Kurtz, Joel Barry *finance executive*
Price, Amelia Ruth *not-for-profit foundation president, artist, small business owner*
Somer, Stanley Jerome *lawyer*
Steindler, Walter G. *retired lawyer*

Conesus
Dadrian, Vahakn Norair *retired sociology educator*

Cooperstown
Bordley, James, IV, *surgeon*
Butts, William Lester *entomologist, researcher*
Franck, Walter Alfred *rheumatologist, medical educator, health facility administrator*
Harman, Willard Nelson *malacologist, educator*
Leonardo, James M. *hematologist, educator, oncologist, director*
Mays, Willie Howard, Jr., (Say Hey Kid) *retired professional baseball player*
Petroskey, Dale Alan *cultural organization administrator, former professional society administrator*
Rich, Walter George *railroad transportation executive*
Sutter, Bruce (Howard Sutter) *retired professional baseball player*
Veenema, Ralph James *retired urologist*

Copake
Johnson, Paul Edward *poet, writer*

Coram
Saunders, Audrey J. *tax specialist, writer*

Corning
Asonevich, Walter Jozef *English educator*
Buechner, Thomas Scharman *artist, museum director, retired glass manufacturing company executive*
Cicerchi, Eleanor Ann Tomb *not-for-profit fundraiser*
Flaws, James B. *technology executive*
Hatton, Vincent Paul *lawyer*
Hauselt, Denise Ann *lawyer*
Spillman, Jane Shadel *curator, writer, researcher*
Ughetta, William Casper *lawyer, manufacturing executive, director*
Volanakis, Peter F. *manufacturing executive*
Whitehouse, David Bryn *museum director*

Cornwall On Hudson
Peirce, Karen Patricia *education educator*
Pendley, Stephen *social studies educator, department chairman*

Corona
Beltran, Carlos *professional baseball player*

Cortland
Anderson, Donna Kay *musicologist, educator*
Brush, Florence Clapham *kinesiologist, exercise physiologist, physical education educator*
Lyman, Kristin M. *music educator*
Rohr, Richard Edward *physician, administrator*
Taylor, Leland Baridon *lawyer*

Cortlandt Manor
Lupiani, Jennifer Lynne *school psychologist*
Rosenberg, Marilyn Rosenthal *artist, poet*
Traille, Joy Myra *microbiologist, eldercare service provider*

Coxsackie
Moyna, John Lawrence *priest*

Cranberry Lake
Glavin, James Edward *landscape architect*

Cross River
Lang, Robert Mays, Jr. *manufacturing and not-for-profit executive*
Thorn, Susan Howe *interior designer*

Croton Falls
Curtis, Frank R. *lawyer*
Jakes, John *author*

Croton On Hudson
Hoffman, Paul Shafer *lawyer*
Johann, Anne Dorothy *visual and graphic artist, painter*
Norman, Jessye *soprano*
Plotch, Walter *management consultant, fund raising counselor*
Sayre, Susan Kathryn Greenwald *musician, educator*
Wandel, Sharon Lee *sculptor*

Cutchogue
Dank, Leonard Dewey *medical illustrator, audio-visual consultant*
Schulze, Paul *industrial designer, educator*

Dansville
Dearing, Teresa Allison *librarian*
Vogel, John Walter *lawyer*

Deer Park
Chapman, Ronald Thomas *musician, educator*
Kanders, Warren Beatty *manufacturing executive, investment banker*

Delmar
Button, Rena Pritsker *public relations executive*
Houghton, Raymond Carl, Jr. *education educator*
Matuszek, John Michael, Jr. *environmental scientist, educator, consultant*

Depew
Saleh, David John *lawyer*

Derby
Cuomo, Rivers *singer, songwriter*
Goodell, Joseph Edward *manufacturing executive*
Pordum, Francis J. *former state legislator, educator, marketing professional*

Dix Hills
Braun, Ludwig *retired engineering educator*
Fouladvand, Hengameh *artist*

Dobbs Ferry
Anbinder, Paul *publishing executive, consultant*
Andreadis, Constantine *art educator, therapist*
Fritz, Jean Guttery *writer*
Guggenheimer, Tobias Immanuel Simon *architect*
Kraetzer, Mary C. *sociologist, educator, consultant*
Maiocchi, Christine *lawyer*
Poian, Edward Licio *historian*
Postman, Robert Derek *dean, mathematics professor, writer*
Scudder, Charles Seelye Kellgren *lawyer*
Simon, Lothar *publishing executive*
Sutton, Francis Xavier *social services administrator, consultant*

Douglaston
Balbi, Kenneth Emilio *environmental specialist, researcher*
Levine, Jeffrey E. *real estate developer*
Palatnick, Frank Sidney *educational consultant*
Valero, René Arnold *clergyman*
Walsh, Sean M. *lawyer, computer scientist, criminologist*

Dryden
Baxter, Robert Banning *insurance company executive*
Powell, Marsha *director, educator*
Slocum, Robert Bigney *retired librarian*

Dundee
Miller, Ronald K. *real estate broker, educator*

Dunkirk
Flaherty, Cynthia Mead *music educator*

East Amherst
Ennis, Carol Robbins *retired music educator*
Watson, Stewart Charles *construction executive*

East Aurora
Dohn, Julianne *child protective services specialist*
Woodard, Carol Jane *educational consultant*

East Greenbush
McConville, Edward Patrick *lawyer*
Mucci, Patrick John *financial consultant, realtor, commercial loan broker*
Quenelle, Susannah Sherman *music educator*

East Hampton
Brady, James Winston *commentator, writer, editor*
Bromley, Bruce Ditmas *language educator, writer*
Damaz, Paul F. *architect*
Dello Joio, Norman *composer*
Delson, Sidney Leon *architect*
Ehren, Charles Alexander, Jr. *lawyer, educator*
Garrett, Charles Geoffrey Blythe *physicist, consultant*
Garten, Ina *chef*
Good, Allen Hovey *investment banker, real estate broker*
Jaroff, Leon Morton *retired magazine editor*
Jaudon, Valerie *artist*
Karp, Harvey Lawrence *metal products executive*
Mencher, Stuart Alan *sales and marketing executive*
Metz, Robert Roy *publishing executive, media consultant*
Salzman, Robert Jay *accountant*
Scott, Rosa Mae *art educator, artist*
Strassfield, Christina Mossaides *curator*
Twomey, Thomas A., Jr. *lawyer, educator*
Wainwright, Carroll Livingston, Jr. *retired lawyer*

East Islip
Donohue, Claire P. *retired school librarian*

East Meadow
Adler, Ira Jay *lawyer*
Albert, Gerald *clinical psychologist*
Cymbler, Murray Joel *corporate financial executive*
Fuchs, Jerome Herbert *management consultant*
Hyman, Montague Allan *lawyer, educator*
Jeziorski, Michael A. *social studies educator*

East Northport
Juliano, John Louis *lawyer*
Kehoe, Thomas J. *food products executive*

East Norwich
Busner, Philip H. *retired lawyer, judge*
Rosen, Meyer Robert *chemical engineer*

East Rochester
Murray, James Doyle *accountant, educator*

East Rockaway
Nodiff, Jack *artist, retired pharmacist*

East Setauket
Badalamenti, Fred Leopoldo *artist, educator*
Coccaro, Stephen F. *plastic surgeon*
Dervan, John Patrick *cardiologist*
Malbon, Craig Curtis *pharmacology educator, dean*
Simons, James Harris *technology company executive*

East Syracuse
Duffy, Nancy Keogh *newscaster, broadcast executive*
McGlynn, Sean Edward *secondary school educator*
Nivarthi, Raju Naga *anesthesiology educator*
Williamson, Carolyn *research scientist*

Eastchester
Giuliano, Robert Paul *pharmacist*
Gottschall, Edward Maurice *editor, writer*
Katz, Kenneth Arthur *lawyer, accountant*
Kravath, Alan Wolfe *retired education evaluator*

Eden
Thomas, Jimmy Lynn *retired treasurer*

Edmeston
Blackman, Dorothy J. *library director*

Elba
Kauffman, William Joseph *editor, writer*

Elma
Hawk, George Wayne *retired electronics company executive*
Wirth, Sandra Lee *real estate company owner*

Elmhurst
Brown, Ronald Joseph *religious studies educator*
Cush, John Patrick *priest, theology studies educator*
Lin, Dahang *medical physicist*
Masci, Joseph Richard *medical educator*
Prypchan, Lida D. *psychiatrist*

Elmira
Gordon, June Sacavage *art educator*
Graham, David Richard *orthopedic surgeon*
Leveen, Pauline *retired history professor, government professor*
Meier, Thomas Keith *academic administrator, language educator*
Miran, Patricia Marie *art educator*
Nast, Edward Paul *cardiothoracic surgeon, vascular surgeon*
Reddick, Bryan DeWitt *academic administrator*
Winner, George Henry *lawyer*

Elmont
Butera, Ann Michele *consulting company executive*
Cusack, Thomas Joseph *retired banker*

Elmsford
Demopoulos, Harry Byron *retired pathologist, pharmaceutical researcher*
Miranda, Robert Nicholas *publishing executive, director*
Panitz, Lawrence *physician*
Raymond, George Marc *city planner, educator*

Endicott
Goodwin, Charles Hugh *technology education educator*
Markovich, Voya R. *information technology executive*
Schreiber, Robert Walter *computer scientist*

Endwell
Maliwacki, John M. *secondary school educator*

Fairport
Bartlett, Cody Blake *retired lawyer*
DeMay, Michael F. *secondary school educator, small business owner*
Mullin, Thomas J. *lawyer, food products executive*
Sands, Richard E. *food products executive*
Sands, Robert *food products executive*

Falconer
Halm, Nancye Studd *retired academic administrator*

Far Rockaway
Epstein, Samuel Abraham *sales executive*
Helfgott, Samson *lawyer*
Sussman, Laureen Glicklin *retired elementary school educator*

Farmingdale
Bandyopadhyay, Amitabha *engineering educator*
Goodstone, Michael S. *psychology professor, consultant*
Nolan, Peter John *physics professor*
O'Brien, Joan Susan *lawyer, educator*
Winn, John Arthur, Jr. *mathematics educator*

Fayetteville
Chevli, Renate Naren *gynecologist, obstetrician*
Hadyk-Wepf, Sonia Margaret *artist, real estate manager*
Krathwohl, David Reading *retired education educator*
Meigs, Montgomery Cunningham, Jr. *retired military officer, educator*
Pachter, Irwin Jacob *pharmaceutical consultant*

Fishers Island
Baue, Arthur Edward *retired surgeon, educator, health facility administrator*

Fishkill
Brocks, Eric *ophthalmologist, surgeon*

Floral Park
Chatoff, Michael Alan *lawyer*
Corbett, William John *lawyer, public relations executive, minister, consultant*
Curci, Paula *counseling educator, poet, radio personality*
Daloia, Rachel Rosemary *music educator*
Dudek, Henry Thomas *management consultant*
Giuffré, John Joseph *lawyer*
Goldstein, George A. *school system administrator*

Isenberg, Henry David *microbiology educator*
Kolb, Lisa Marie *music educator*

Flushing
Alou, Moises *professional baseball player*
Anderson, Michelle J. *dean, law educator*
Beveridge, Andrew Alan *sociologist, educator, consultant*
Bird, Thomas Edward *foreign language and literature educator*
Birnstiel, Charles *consulting engineer*
Brody, Roberta *information science educator*
Carlson, Cynthia Joanne *artist, educator*
Castillo, Luis Antonio Donato *professional baseball player*
Chang, Jason *artist, educator*
Cohen, David *lawyer*
Commoner, Barry *biologist, educator*
Delgado, Carlos Juan *professional baseball player*
DellaPina, Mario John *academic administrator*
Evens, Lucie Ann *music educator*
Farago, John Michael *law educator, consultant*
Feng, Ying *painter, art educator*
Fichtel, Rudolph Robert *retired association executive*
Galdamez, Ricardo *internist*
Glavine, Tom (Thomas Michael Glavine) *professional baseball player*
Goldman, Norman Lewis *chemistry professor*
Goldsmith, Howard *writer, consultant*
Hart, Antonio Maurice *musician, educator*
Henderson, Rickey Henley *professional baseball coach, retired professional baseball player*
Hon, John Wingsun *physician*
Hu, Huping *biophysicist, lawyer*
Kim, Hakyong *lawyer, accountant*
Kim, Sun-Hae *retired medical/surgical nurse, writer, retired nurse midwife, retired physical therapist*
Kroeppel, Warren *airport terminal executive*
Martinez, Pedro Jaime *professional baseball player*
Mendelson, Elliott *mathematician, educator*
Minaya, Omar *professional sports team executive*
Mirkin, Michael V. *chemistry professor*
Nussbaum, Michel Ernest *physician*
Park, Chan Ho *professional baseball player*
Pellitteri, John Steven *psychologist, psychotherapist, educator*
Rabassa, Gregory *language educator, translator, poet*
Randolph, Willie (Willie Larry Randolph Jr.) *professional baseball team manager, retired professional baseball player*
Reyes, Jose Bernabe *professional baseball player*
Rosenberg, Deborah A. *special education educator*
Sanborn, Anna Lucille *pension fund administrator, consultant*
Schwartz, Estar Alma *lawyer*
Shen, Ronger *artist, educator*
Smaldone, Edward Michael *composer*
Smith, Charles William *social sciences educator*
Stahl, Frank Ludwig *civil engineer*
Torrence-Thompson, Juanita Lee *editor, public relations executive*
Totakura, Satyanarayana Raju *secondary school educator*
Tytell, John *literature educator, writer*
Wagner, Billy (William Edward Wagner) *professional baseball player*
Wang, Zeng-Yu *neurologist, immunologist*
Wright, David Allen *professional baseball player*
Yeo, Kim Eng *artist*
Zinnes, Harriet Fich *poet, fiction writer, retired English educator, literary and art critic*

Fly Creek
Dusenbery, Walter Condit *sculptor*

Forest Hills
Alves, Flavio P. *researcher, director*
Barger, David J. *air transportation executive*
Battaglia, Alex *air transportation executive*
Brooks, Martin *electronic media company executive*
Buhks, Ephraim *college administrator, technology educator*
Cerveris, Michael *actor*
Chew, Russell G. (Russ) *air transportation executive*
D'Addario, Alice Marie *retired school system administrator*
Eden, Alvin Noam *pediatrician, writer*
Henley, Arthur *writer, editor*
Kilgannon, Corey *journalist*
Kourides, Peter Theologos *lawyer*
Kra, Pauline Skornicki *French language educator*
Mathieu Byers, Deborah Anne *performing company executive*
Morgan, Jacqui *illustrator, painter, art educator, writer*
Neeleman, David G. *air transportation executive*
Nero, Shondel J. *language educator*
Polakoff, Abe *baritone*
Reis, Don *publishing executive*
Seldes, Richard M. *orthopedist, consultant*
Spiegel, Andrea *marketing executive*
Tvildiani, Dimitry *cardiologist*

Forestville
Adams, Lee Towne *lawyer*

Fort Drum
Youngs, Michael Theron, Jr. *non-commissioned officer*

Franklin Square
Cantilli, Edmund Joseph *safety engineer, educator, translator, writer, consultant*
Indiviglia, Salvatore Joseph *artist, retired military officer*
Vanora, Jerome Patrick *lawyer*

Fredonia
Aghazadeh, Seyed-Mahmoud *finance educator*
Arnavut, Ziya *educator*
Benton, Allen Haydon *biology professor*
Croxton, Jack Sanders *director, consultant*

Freeport
Berg, Alan *lawyer, arbitrator*
Ferentino, Sheila Connolly *psychologist, consultant*
Golici, Nicolae *sculptor*
Martorana, Barbara Joan *secondary school educator*
Mitchell, Alice Joyce *retired secondary school educator, retired dietician*
Pullman, Maynard Edward *biochemist*
Zurcher, Zean William *retired music educator, musician*

Fresh Meadows
Godfrey, Philip M. *plastic surgeon*
Greenberg, Robert Jay *law educator*
Male, Ayn Rochelle *psychologist, researcher*
Vigoda, Paul Evan *secondary school educator*

Fulton
Jennings, Meghan Young *music educator*
Long, Robert Emmet *author*

Garden City
Austin, Stuart *lawyer*
Balkan, Kenneth J. *lawyer*
Bouchard, Wendy Ann Borstel *language educator*
Brewer, Bruce William *plastic surgeon*
Calamari, Joseph August *law librarian*
Caputo, Kathryn Mary *paralegal*
Conlon, Brian Thomas *promotion executive*
Conlon, Thomas James *marketing executive*
Cook, George Valentine *lawyer, consultant*
Deane, Leland Marc *plastic surgeon, director*
DiMascio, John Philip *lawyer*
Doucette, Mary-Alyce *computer company executive*
Douglas, Barry K. *plastic surgeon*
Einenkel, Robert Herbert *theater educator, actor, director*
Fishberg, Gerard *lawyer*
Freedman, Monroe Henry *law educator*
Good, Larry Irwin *gastroenterologist, educator*
Gray, Phil R. *band director, musician*
Harwood, Stanley *retired judge, lawyer, arbitrator, mediator*
Hecht, Jennifer Michael *poet, historian*
Ingber, Larry H. *lawyer*
Jenkins, Kenneth Vincent *literature educator, writer*
Kaplan, Joel Stuart *lawyer*
Klein, Arnold Spencer *lawyer*
Kroll, Martin N. *lawyer*
Laureano, Mari *government agency administrator, writer*
Mastaglio, Peter James *lawyer*
McNair, Marcia L. *language educator, writer, editor*
Meng, M. Kathryn *lawyer*
Minicucci, Richard Francis *lawyer, former hospital administrator*
Nogee, Jeffrey Laurence *lawyer*
Okoampa-Ahoofe, Kwame *language educator, historian*
Ostrow, Michael Jay *lawyer*
Paterson, Basil Alexander *lawyer*
Pereira, John William Miller *theater educator*
Persons, John Wade *lawyer*
Podwall, Kathryn Stanley *biology professor*
Posch, Robert John, Jr. *lawyer*
Prabhakar, Kumkum *biology professor*
Rhein, John Hancock Willing III *publishing executive*
Rosenberg, Lee *lawyer*
Russell, Stella Pandell *artist, author, educator*
Schwarz, Carl A., Jr. *lawyer*
Scollard, Patrick John *hospital executive*
Scott, Robert Allyn *academic administrator*
Shuart, James Martin *retired academic administrator*
Spinowitz, Alan Lee *dermatologist*
Storandt, Peter *educational consultant*
Toy, Vivian *journalist*
Walsh Mitchell, Diana *school psychologist, consultant*
Wetherill-Smith, Linda Marie *musician, educator, performing arts association administrator*

Garden City Park
Radu, Bogdan *aerospace engineer*

Gardiner
Mabee, Carleton *historian, educator*

Garnerville
Chapman, Margaret Elizabeth *elementary school educator*
Evers, Gene *writer*
Zugibe, Frederick Thomas *retired pathologist, forensic specialist*

Garrison
Callahan, Daniel John *biomedical researcher*
Murray, Thomas Henry *bioethics educator, writer*

Geneseo
Bauer, Norman James *retired education educator*
Lim, Seong Bae *business educator*
Olczak, Paul Vincent *psychologist, educator*

Geneva
Brind, David Hutchison *lawyer, judge*
Crumlish, Jane C. *pediatrician*
Lieberg, Olaf U. *orthopaedic surgeon*
Roelofs, Wendell Lee *biochemistry professor, consultant*
Siebert, Karl Joseph *food science educator, consultant*
Vecchiotti, Tony V. *insurance agent*

Germantown
Farberman, Harold *conductor, composer*

Ghent
Rao, Natti Sreerama *small business owner, consultant*

Glen Cove
Burnham, Harold Arthur *pharmaceutical executive, physician*
Lewis, Felice Flanery *retired lawyer, educator*
Olsen, Robert C., Jr. *academic administrator, military officer*
Rathkopf, Daren Anthony *lawyer*
Rothberg, Judith *elementary school educator, researcher*

Glen Head
Conway, David Antony *marketing professional*
Huber, Don Lawrence *publisher*
Martin, David S. *retired secondary school educator, administrator*

Glenford
Matalon, Vivian *theatrical director*
Rieder, Naomi *artist*

Glenmont
Bellizzi, John J. *law enforcement association administrator, pharmacist, educator*
Coye, Mary P. *counselor*
Haizlip, Viola *medical/surgical nurse*

Glens Falls
Bartlett, Richard James *lawyer*
McMillen, Robert Stewart *lawyer*
Pearsall, Glenn Lincoln *brokerage house executive*
Vitvitsky, Jack *physician assistant*

Glenwood
Chambers, Denning Jessyca *middle school educator*

Goshen
Watson, Georgianna *retired librarian*

Gouverneur
Kuehl, Alexander Edward *physician, health facility administrator, educator, writer*
Leader, Robert John *lawyer*

Great Neck
Appel, Gerald *investment advisor*
Arams, Frank Robert *electronics executive*
Brill, Steven Charles *financial planner, lawyer*
Christie, George Nicholas *economist, consultant*
Dines, David Michael *surgeon, educator*
Druks, Herbert Michael *history educator*
Feldman, Gary Marc *nutritionist, consultant*
Fisher, Barry G. *orthopedist, surgeon*
Gabriel, Mordecai Lionel *biologist, educator*
Gold, Alan H. *plastic surgeon*
Goldberg, Melvin Arthur *communications executive*
Goldman, Ira Steven *gastroenterologist*
Helstein, Ivy Rae *communications executive, psychotherapist, writer*
Hurwitz, Johanna (Johanna Frank) *writer*
Jacono, Andrew A. *Plastic Surgeon*
Kahn, David *editor, author*
Katz, Edward Morris *banker*
Kechijian, Paul *dermatologist, educator*
Kimm, Michael S. *lawyer*
Lipsky, Jack Bender *insurance company executive*
Lupkin, Stanley Neil *lawyer*
Marcus, Philip *dean*
Minkoff, Jack *retired economics professor*
Panes, Jack Samuel *publishing executive*
Puttlitz, Donald Herbert *microbiologist*
Rosenberg, Richard F. *physician, radiologist*
Samuel, Paul *retired cardiologist*
Scherr, Lawrence *internist, healthcare educator, historian*
Schlesinger, Irwin D. *neurologist*
Seckler, Bernard David *retired mathematics professor, translator*
Seidler, Doris *artist*
Shons, Alan Rance *plastic surgeon, surgical oncologist, educator*
Wolff, Edward *physician*

Great River
Hayman, Martin Arthur *psychiatrist, educator*

Greenfield Center
Bruchac, Joseph *writer, storyteller*
Templin, John Leon, Jr. *healthcare consulting executive*

Greenlawn
Bachman, Henry Lee *electrical engineer, company executive*
Robinson, Kenneth Patrick *lawyer, electronics executive*

Greenport
Jackson, Richard Montgomery *air transportation executive*
Monsell, Thomas Oliver *secondary school educator, writer*
Watts, Harold Wesley *economist, educator*

Greenvale
Araoz, Daniel Leon *psychologist, educator*
Cordaro, Matthew Charles *energy and utility executive, educator*
Halper, Emanuel B(arry) *lawyer, real estate developer, consultant, writer*
Krasnoff, Eric *health products executive*
Kusukawa, Akira *demographer, educator*
Lennox, Pamela Chatterton *academic administrator*
Manzari, Laura Lynn *law educator*
Regazzi, John James III *dean, publishing executive*
Senft, Mason George *musician*
Steinberg, David Joel *academic administrator, historian, educator*
Sugar, Joseph Robert *music educator, conductor, musician*

Greenwich
Edsforth, Maureen McGill *instructional technology specialist*
Smethurst, E(dward) William, Jr. *investment banker*

Groveland
Battersby, Harold Ronald *retired anthropologist, archaeologist, linguist*

Hamburg
Calkins, Evan *physician, educator*
Gaughan, Dennis Charles *lawyer*
Hargesheimer, Elbert III *lawyer*
Markulis, Henryk John *career military officer*

Hamilton
Ammerman, Albert Jay *archaeologist, humanities educator*
Berlind, Bruce Peter *poet, educator*
Chopp, Rebecca S. *academic administrator*
Edmonston, William Edward, Jr. *retired publishing executive, writer, psychology professor*
Frey, Frank Michael *biology professor*
Johnston, Michael (William) *political science educator, university administrator*
Moynihan, William J. *museum executive*
Pagano, Jo Anne *education educator*
Rotter, Andrew Jon *history educator*
Soderberg, Dale LeRoy *language educator, drama director, producer*
Staley, Lynn *literature educator*
Tucker, Thomas William *mathematics professor*

Hampton Bays
Bucicchia, Carolanne Stephanie *elementary school educator*
Jacobs, George Braun *neurosurgeon*
Wille, Rosanne Louise *educational consultant*

Hancock
DeLuca, Ronald *former advertising agency executive, consultant*
Senia, Grace Melanie *language and music educator*

Hannacroix
Schwebler, Stephen *retired chemist*

Harrison
Crawford, R. George *investment company executive, educator, filmmaker*
Kramer, Alan Sharfsin *lawyer*
Northcutt, Marie Rose *elementary school educator, special education educator*
Strone, Michael Jonathan *real estate consultant, lawyer, art consultant*
Wadsworth, Frank Whittemore *foundation administrator, literature educator*

Hartsdale
Aker, Susan K. *elementary school educator, assistant principal*
Bomback, Fred M. *pediatrician*
Chait, Maxwell Mani *physician*
Greenawalt, Peggy Freed Tomarkin *advertising executive*
Katz, John *investment banker*
Lightburn, Anita Louise *dean, social work educator*
Martin, Daniel Richard *pharmaceutical executive*
McMann, Edith Brozak (Edith Brozak) *performing and visual artist*
Pell, Arthur Robert *human resources specialist, consultant, writer*
Schweitzer, Caren S. *social worker*

Hastings On Hudson
Cassella, William Nathan, Jr. *retired not-for-profit organization executive*
Considine, Russel A. *executive recruiter, photographer*
D'Antoni, Philip *television producer*
Edelman, Paul Sterling *lawyer*
Green, Nancy Sue *pediatrician, health science association administrator*
Landau, Peter Edward *editor*
Reich, Herb *editor*
Rosch, Paul John *internist, educator*
Sharpe, Robert Kent *writer, director, producer, photographer*
Stillman, Jeanne Betsock *public health administrator, consultant*
Thornlow, Carolyn *law firm administrator, consultant*
Weinstein, Edward Michael *architect, consultant*

Hauppauge
Bender, Bruce F. *book publishing executive*
Buckley, Robert Matthew *electrical engineer*
Hausman, Howard *electronics executive*
Levy, Steve A. *county official, former state legislator*
Reid, Margaret Elizabeth *elementary school educator, secondary school educator*
Scheine, Edward Robert *lawyer*

Haverstraw
Alpert, Revell Judith *retired data processing executive*
Eidelman, Sharon (Sherry) R. *marriage and family therapist*

Hawthorne
Batstone, Joanna Louise *physicist*
Hodge, Timothy *performing company executive, actor*
Mihaila, George Andrei *computer scientist, researcher*
Nandedkar, Sanjeev Dattatraya *medical researcher, educator*
Pianka, George *orthopedic surgeon*
Ward, Christopher *computer scientist, researcher*
Wen, Sheree *computer company executive*
Yoffa, Ellen J. *information technology executive*

Hempstead
Aaron, Merik Roy *financial executive, lawyer, judge, educator*
Adams, Velma M. *assistant principal, consultant*
Berliner, Herman Albert *academic administrator, economist, educator, dean*
Bose, Meena *political science professor*
Coleman, Benjamin Joseph *music educator*
Coles, Laveranues *professional football player*
Connolly, Melissa Kane *public relations executive*
Dyson, Andre *professional football player*
Ferguson, D'Brickashaw *professional football player*
Freese, Melanie Louise *librarian, educator*
Garuthara, Rohana K. *physics professor*
Goldstein, Stanley Philip *engineering educator*
Graffeo, Mary Thérèse *music educator, performer*
Heuermann-Nowik, Patricia Calhoun *theater director*
Lazarus, Harold *management educator*
Mahon, Malachy Thomas, Sr. *lawyer, educator*
Mangini, Eric *professional football coach*
Masheck, Joseph Daniel *art critic, educator*
Pennington, Chad (James Chadwick Pennington) *professional football player*
Schechtman, Saul *conductor*
Shafritz, Keith Michael *psychology professor*
Sharifov, Rovshan Chingiz *lawyer*
Sodano, Salvatore F. *former stock exchange executive*
Tannenbaum, Mike (Michael B. Tannenbaum) *professional sports team executive*
Watford, Dolores *elementary school educator*
Wattel, Harold Louis *economics professor*
Zagano, Phyllis *religious studies educator*

Henrietta
Byfield, Bert A. *conservative humanitarian novelist*

Herkimer
Durham, Jeanette Randall *artist, educator*
Kirk, Patrick Laine *lawyer*
Lowery, Kathleen Ann *elementary school educator*

Hewlett
Cohen, David Leon *physician*
Colfin, Bruce Elliott *lawyer, video producer*
Steinfeld, Philip Sheldon *pediatrician*
Williams, Tyler James *actor*

Hicksville
Garner, Beth L. *music educator*
Horowitz, Barry Allan *music company executive*
Lieberman, Douglas Mark *lawyer*
Noll, Amy *secondary educator*
Polatsch, Bernard *obstetrician, gynecologist*
Stein, Melvin A. *accountant*
Tucci, Gerald Frank *manufacturing executive*
Yen, Henry Chin-Yuan *computer systems programmer, software engineer, consulting company executive*

Hillsdale
Lunde, Asbjorn Rudolph *lawyer*
Parmet, Herbert Samuel *historian, writer*

Holland
Loockerman, William Delmer *retired educational administrator*

Holley
Lepkowski, Suzanne Joy *language educator*
Ruck, Rosemarie Ulissa *retired social worker, freelance/self-employed writer*

Hollis
Singh, Harbachan *solicitor, barrister*

Holmes
Conyers, Claude Brunson *publishing consultant, editor, dance historian*

Homer
Gustafson, John Alfred *biology professor*

Honeoye Falls
Hillabrandt, Larry Lee *service industry executive*
Masterson-Smith, Julie *librarian*

Hoosick Falls
Dodge, Cleveland Earl, Jr. *retired manufacturing executive, director*

Hopewell Junction
Donovan, Andrew Joseph *financial consultant*
Sellingsloh, Hulda Knipling *retired artist*

Hornell
Hunter, John Orr *retired college president*
Pulos, William Whitaker *lawyer*

Horseheads
Shabanowitz, Harry *electronics engineer, educator*

Houghton
Luckey, Robert Reuel Raphael *retired academic administrator*

Howard Beach
Leiter, Samuel L. *theater educator*

Hudson
Agata, Burton C. *lawyer, educator*

Chambers, William McWillie *artist, art dealer*
Davis, Deborah Lynn *lawyer, art dealer*
Geistfeld, James Gordon *veterinarian*
Howard, Andrew Baker *lawyer*
Miner, Jacqueline *political consultant*

Hudson Falls
Leary, Daniel *artist*

Hunter
Khanzadian, Vahan *tenor*

Huntington
Brettschneider, Rita Roberta Fischman *retired lawyer*
Christiansen, Donald David *electrical engineer, editor, publishing executive, consultant*
Connor, Joseph Robert *editor*
Engstrand, Beatrice C. *neurologist, educator*
German, June Resnick *lawyer*
Hochberg, Ronald Mark *lawyer*
Kirwin, Barbara Rosa *forensic specialist*
LaTourrette, James Thomas *retired electrophysics, electrical engineering and computer science educator*
Munson, Nancy K. *lawyer*
Reiner, John *cartoonist*
Selkirk, Alexander MacDonald, Jr. *lawyer*
Slutsky, Leonard Alan *finance executive, consultant*
Tucker, William P. *lawyer, writer*
Winick, Martin *pediatric surgeon*
Zingale, Robert G. *surgeon*

Huntington Station
Agosta, Vito *mechanical and aerospace engineering educator*
Stevens, Susan Seltenreich Cirillo *special education educator*
Williams, Una Joyce *psychiatric social worker*

Hurley
Culver, Michael Patrick *music educator, composer*
Opdahl, Viola Elizabeth *secondary school educator*
Petruski, Jennifer Andrea *speech and language pathologist*
Smith, Lewis Motter, Jr. *retired advertising and direct marketing executive*

Hyde Park
Hunt, Mark Alan *museum director*
Koch, Cynthia M. *library director*
Rider, Kathleen Mary *dietician*
Ryan, L. Timothy *chef, educator, academic administrator*

Interlaken
Bleiler, Everett Franklin *writer, publishing company executive*

Inwood
Chernov, Yuriy D. *engineering executive*
Kofman, Leonid *consumer products company executive*

Irvington
Carey, Edward John *utilities executive*
Jackson, Thomas Gene *lawyer*
Sherman, Norman Mark *advertising agency executive*
Yablon, Leonard Harold *publishing executive*

Islandia
Artzt, Russell M. *electronics executive*
Buckley, Terrence Patrick *lawyer*
Cooper, Nancy E. *computer software company executive*
Cron, Kenneth D. *information technology executive*
Fliegelman Olli, Amy *lawyer, computer company executive*
Gupta, Yogesh *software company executive*
Handal, Kenneth V. *computer software company executive, lawyer*
Pruzansky, Joshua Murdock *lawyer*
Robinson, Douglas *computer company executive*
Swainson, John A. *software company executive*

Islip
Libert, Nancy Porta *retired elementary school educator*

Ithaca
Abrams, Meyer Howard *language educator*
Alexander, Gregory Stewart *law educator*
Alexander, Martin *microbiologist, educator*
Arquit, Nora Harris *retired music educator, writer*
Ascher, Robert *anthropologist, archaeologist, film producer, educator*
Ashcroft, Neil William *physics professor, researcher*
Barbasch, Dan Mihai *mathematics professor*
Barcelo, John James III *law educator*
Bassett, William Akers *retired geologist, educator*
Bathrick, David *foreign language educator, academic administrator*
Bauman, Dale Elton *nutritional biochemistry professor*
Beneria, Lourdes *economist, educator*
Berkelman, Karl *retired physics professor*
Billera, Louis J(oseph) *mathematics professor*
Bourne, Russell *publisher, author*
Bramble, James Henry *mathematician, educator*
Brazell, Karen Woodard *literature educator*
Burns, Joseph Arthur *planetary science educator*
Cahoon, Richard Stuart *biotechnologist, educator*
Chapman, Lewis Duane *economist*
Clermont, Kevin Michael *law educator*
Colby-Hall, Alice Mary *language educator*
Cottrell, G. Walton *manufacturing executive*
Craighead, Harold Gene *physicist, educator*
Cramton, Roger Conant *lawyer, educator*
Crepet, William Louis *botanist, educator*
Csaki, Csaba *physicist*
Danforth, Bryan Nicholas *entomologist, educator*
Daouk, Hazem *finance educator*
Darlington, Richard Benjamin *retired psychologist, educator, researcher*
Davies, Peter John *plant physiology educator, researcher*
De Boer, Pieter Cornelis Tobias *mechanical and aerospace engineering educator*
Dick, Richard Irwin *environmental engineer, educator*
Dietert, Rodney Reynolds *immunology and toxicology educator*
Durrett, Richard T. *mathematics professor*
Dyckman, Thomas Richard *accountant, educator*
Earle, Clifford John, Jr. *mathematician*
Easley, David *economics professor*
Eastman, Lester Fuess *electrical engineer, educator*
Eddy, Donald Davis *language educator*
Ehrenberg, Ronald Gordon *economist, educator*
Eisenberg, Theodore *law educator*
Eisner, Thomas *biologist, educator*
Emlen, Stephen Thompson *zoology educator*
Emr, Scott David *molecular biologist, director*
Fick, Gary Warren *agronomist, educator*
Firebaugh, Francille Maloch *academic administrator*
Fireside, Harvey Francis *political scientist, educator*
Fitchen, Douglas Beach *physicist, researcher*
Fitzpatrick, John Weaver *ornithologist, researcher*
Fonder, Mark Leslie *music educator*
Foote, Robert Hutchinson *medical educator*
Freed, Jack Herschel *chemist, educator*
Fuchs, W. Kent *engineering educator*
Ganem, Bruce *chemistry educator*
Garrison, Elizabeth Jane *artist*
George, Albert Richard *mechanical and aerospace engineer, educator*
Germain, Claire Madeleine *law librarian, educator*
Ginsparg, Paul *physicist*
Gold, Michael Evan *law educator*
Goldsmith, Paul Felix *astronomy and physics professor*
Greene, Harry W. *biology professor*
Grippi, Salvatore William *artist*
Groos, Arthur Bernhard, Jr. *German studies and music educator*
Gross, Leonard *mathematics professor*
Habicht, Jean Pierre *public health educator*
Hairston, Nelson George, Jr. *ecologist, educator*
Haith, Douglas A. *engineering educator, researcher*
Halpern, Bruce Peter *academic administrator, researcher, educator*
Harris, Robert Lee, Jr. *history professor*
Hartmanis, Juris *computer scientist, educator*
Hay, George Alan *law and economics educator*
Henry, Susan Armstrong *biology professor, dean*
Hess, George Paul *biochemist, educator*
Hillman, Robert Andrew *lawyer, educator*
Hoffmann, Roald *chemist, educator*
Hohendahl, Peter Uwe *German language and literature educator*
Hojnowski, Jules Austin *entrepreneur*
Holcomb, Donald Frank *physicist, academic administrator*
Hopcroft, John Edward *computer scientist, educator*
Hoy, Ronald Raymond *neurobiology educator*
Hull, Isabel Virginia *history professor*
Husa, Karel *composer, conductor, educator*
Jagendorf, André Tridon *physiologist*
James, Doug L. *computer scientist, educator*
Jarrow, Robert Alan *economist, educator*
Just, David Ryan *economist*
Kahn, Alfred Edward *economist, educator, government official*
Kallfelz, Francis A. *veterinary medicine educator*
Kassabov, Martin *mathematics professor*
Kennedy, Kenneth Adrian Raine *biological and forensic anthropologist*
Kennedy, Wilbert Keith, Sr. *agronomy educator, retired university official*
Kenney, Anne *university librarian*
Kimes, Sheryl Elaine *business educator*
Kingsbury, John Merriam *botanist, educator*
Kinoshita, Toichiro *physicist*
Kleinberg, Jon M. *computer scientist, educator*
Korf, Richard Paul *mycology educator*
LaCapra, Dominick Charles *historian, educator*
LaFeber, Walter Frederick *historian, educator, writer*
Laquatra, Joseph *humanities educator*
Lee, David Morris *physics professor*
Leibovich, Sidney *engineering educator*
Lengemann, Frederick William *retired physiology educator*
Lesser, William Henri *marketing educator*
Lewenstein, Bruce Voss *science historian*
Loucks, Daniel Peter *environmental systems engineer*
Lovelace, Richard Van Evera *education educator, research scientist*
Lowi, Theodore Jay *political science professor*
Lumley, John Leask *physicist, researcher*
Lyons, Thomas Patrick *economics professor*
Mai, William Frederick *plant nematologist, educator*
Majumdar, Mukul Kumar *economist, educator*
Maldonado-Mendoza, Ignacio Eduardo *molecular biologist, researcher*
Maxwell, William Laughlin *retired industrial engineering educator*
McConkey, James Rodney *literature and language educator, writer*
McCue, Arthur Harry *artist, educator*
McDougal, Stuart Yeatman *comparative literature educator, author*
McGuire, William *civil engineer, educator*
McLafferty, Fred Warren *chemist, educator*
McMurry, John Edward *chemistry professor*
Merle, H. Etienne *broker, director, restaurateur*
Meyburg, Arnim Hans *transportation engineer, educator, consultant*
Mikus, Eleanore Ann *artist*
Morgan, Robert *writer, poet, educator*
Mortlock, Robert Paul *microbiologist, educator*
Mueller, Betty Jeanne *social work educator*
Nerode, Anil *mathematician, educator*
Nikitin, Alexander Yu. *pathologist*
Norton, Mary Beth *history educator, writer*
Novak, Joseph Donald *science educator*
Olbricht, William Lee *engineering educator*
Oliver, Jack Ertle *geophysicist, educator*
O'Rourke, Thomas Denis *civil engineer, educator*
Paau, Alan Shiukee *academic administrator, biotechnologist, educator*
Pantano, Alessandra *mathematics professor*
Park, Roy Hampton, Jr. *advertising executive*
Parlange, Jean-Yves *environmental engineer, educator*
Pelto, Gretel H. *nutritional anthropologist, educator*
Perry, Margaret *librarian, writer*
Pinstrup-Andersen, Per *economist, educator*
Pohl, Robert Otto *physics professor*
Poleskie, Stephen Francis *retired art educator, artist, writer, publisher*
Pope, Stephen Bailey *mechanical engineer, educator*
Poppensiek, George Charles *retired veterinary scientist, retired educator*
Porte, Joel Miles *language educator*
Provine, William B. *biology professor*
Rader, Nancy Louise de Villiers *psychology professor, consultant*
Radzinowicz, Mary Ann *language educator*
Rawlings, Hunter Ripley III *classicist, former academic administrator*
Regenstein, Joe M. *food scientist, educator*
Rhodes, Frank Harold Trevor *academic administrator, geologist*
Richardson, Robert Coleman *physics professor, researcher*
Rinaldo, Peter Merritt *publishing executive*
Roberts, E. F. *law educator*
Rodríguez, Ferdinand *chemical engineer, educator*
Salpeter, Edwin Ernest *physical sciences educator*
Scheraga, Harold Abraham *retired physical chemistry professor*
Schlafer, Donald Hughes *veterinary pathologist*
Schneiderman, Anne Mercedes *lawyer, neurobiologist*
Schuler, Mary Callaghan *artist, educational association administrator*
Schwab, Stewart Jon *dean, law educator*
Schwartz, Donald Franklin *communication scientist*
Scott, Norman Roy *academic administrator, agricultural engineer, educator*
Seadle, Michael Steven *data processing executive, writer*
Shore, Richard Arnold *mathematics professor*
Silbey, Joel Henry *history professor*
Skorton, David Jan *academic administrator*
Smidt, Seymour *economics professor*
Smith, Julian Cleveland, Jr. *chemical engineering professor*
Smith, Robert John *anthropology educator*
Sosna, Morton Philip *historian, academic administrator*
Squyres, Steven Weldon *astronomy educator, planetary geology researcher*
Stephens, John Charles *audiologist, educator*
Strogatz, Steven H. *mathematics professor*
Stycos, Maria Nowakowska *adult education educator*
Summers, Robert Samuel *lawyer, author, educator*
Swieringa, Robert Jay *dean, accounting educator*
Tardos, Eva *computer scientist, educator*
Thomas, Jacob Earl *retired physicist*
Thorbecke, Erik *economics professor*
Tiwari, Sandip *electrical and computer engineering educator*
Tomek, William Goodrich *agricultural economist*
Trotter, Leslie Earl *operations research specialist, educator*
Urazghildiiev, Ildar R. *mathematician*
Vanek, Jaroslav *economist, educator*
Viands, Donald Rex *plant breeder, educator*
Walcott, Charles *neurobiology and behavior educator*
Waldman, Michael *economist, educator*
Wasserman, Robert Harold *biology professor*
Welch, Ross Maynard *plant physiologist, educator*
Whitaker, Susanne Kanis *veterinary medical librarian*
Widom, Benjamin *chemistry professor*
Williams, Peggy Ryan *academic administrator*
Williamson, Charles Harvey Kaye *mechanical and aerospace engineering educator*
Wills, Michael Stephen *nutritionist, quality assurance professional*
Winter, Travis Ford *social worker*
Wootton, John Francis *physiology educator*
Xu, Chris *physicist, educator*
Yavuz, A. Kadir *aerospace engineer, researcher*
Zaslaw, Neal *musicologist*

Jackson Heights
Chang, Lydia Liang-Hwa *social worker, educator*
Dacey, Paul *artist*
Ryan, Judith Ann *dean*
Sohmer, Bernard *mathematics professor, administrator*

Jamaica
Ambizas, Emily Marguerite *pharmacist, educator*
Angione, Howard Francis *lawyer, retired editor*
Bartilucci, Andrew Joseph *university administrator*
Beliavsky, Ninah *linguistics professor*
Brown, Kenneth Lloyd *lawyer*
Bunshaft, Charles Edward *elementary school educator, consultant*
Cade, Walter III *artist, actor, musician, vocalist*
Cantor, Jerome Owen *surgical pathologist, educator, researcher*
Carter, Timothy Howard *biochemist, educator*
Castro-Blanco, James *law educator*
Chirico, Donna M. *psychologist, educator, researcher*
Cline, Janice Claire *education educator*
Coppa, Frank John *historian, educator*
Daly, Mary C. *dean, law educator*
Davis-Jerome, Eileen George *educational consultant, principal*
Ekbatani, Glayol *language educator, director, writer*
Faust, Naomi Flowe *education educator*
Flake, Floyd Harold *former congressman*
Galante, Thomas W. *library director*
Garcia-Febo, Loida *librarian*
Garner, Steven C. *radiologist, emergency physician*
Gati, William Eugene *architect, educator, industrial designer*
Geffner, Donna Sue *speech pathology/audiology services professional, audiologist, educator*
Grayshaw, James Raymond *judge*
Greenberg, Jacob *biochemist, educator, consultant*
Harrington, Donald James *university president*
Jefferson, Wayne *language educator*
Kaplan, Carolyn Sue *elementary school educator*
Kemeny, M. Margaret *oncologist, surgeon, hospital administrator, educator*
Lam, Sum *medical educator*
Lees, Francis *economics professor*
Meeks, Gregory Weldon *congressman*
Parmet, Robert David *historian, educator*
Pratt-Johnson, Yvonne Karen *education professor*
Sciame, Joseph *university administrator*

Jamesport
Curlee, F. Lynn *illustrator*

Jamestown
DJang, Arthur H.K. *pathologist, preventive medicine physician*
Huston, Lana M. *lawyer*
Idzik, Martin Francis *lawyer*
Kestler, Richard Michael *mathematics educator*
Leising, David Michael *industrial engineer*
Thompson, Birgit Dolores *civic worker, writer*
Walker, Timothy Craig *transportation executive*

Jamesville
DeCrow, Karen *lawyer, educator, writer*

Jefferson
Sullivan, Jim *artist*

Jeffersonville
Craft, Douglas Durwood *artist*
Harms, Elizabeth Louise *artist*

Jericho
Astuto, Philip Louis *retired language educator*
Blau, Harvey Ronald *lawyer, manufacturing executive*
Corso, Frank Mitchell *lawyer*
Edson, Andrew Stephen *public relations executive*
Rosen, Robert Arnold *management consultant, real estate owner, manager, developer, investor, farmer*
Shapiro, Marjorie *accountant*
Shinners, Stanley Marvin *electrical engineer*

Johnson City
Coddington, Arthur Michael, Jr. *pediatrician, dermatologist*
Goddard, Bryan Lance *physician, director*
McMillen, Marieta Louise *art educator*

Johnstown
Swanker-Gibson, Jahnn Hansen *mental health nurse*

Katonah
Bandon, William Edward III *lawyer*
Bashkow, Theodore Robert *electrical engineering consultant, former educator*
Bauman, Jonathan Hugh *psychiatrist*
Fry, John *magazine editor*
Giobbi, Edward Giacchino *artist*
McCauley, Gerard Francis *literary agent*
Simpson, William Kelly *curator, Egyptologist, educator*
Stillman, Michael Allen *dermatologist*
Wenglowski, Gary Martin *economist*

Keeseville
Turetsky, Aaron *lawyer*

Kenmore
Elibol, Tarik *gastroenterologist, educator*
Kenny, John Edward *computer analyst*
Kuhn, William Andrew *music educator*

Keuka Park
Armstrong, James Francis III *retired language educator, writer*

Kew Gardens
Adler, David Neil *lawyer*
Aldea, Patricia *architect*
Chipkin, Frederick *textile designer, consultant, artist, writer*
Marshall, Helen M. *county official*

Kinderhook
McCreight, JoAnn Oakley *retired librarian*

Kings Park
Fay, Thomas A. *philosopher, educator*
Greene, Robert William *communications educator, media consultant*

LaFantano, Elizabeth music educator

Kingston
Johnson, Marie-Louise Tully dermatologist, educator
Tsirpanlis, Constantine N. theology, philosophy, classics and history educator

La Fayette
Cady, Duane Maynard surgeon

Lake Luzerne
Goldstein, Manfred retired management consultant

Lake Placid
Grimmette, Mark Olympic athlete
Johns, Sara Kelly school librarian, library association executive
Martin, Brian Olympic athlete
Pappalardo, Rosa Gloria secondary school educator
Reiss, Paul J. academic administrator
Rossi, Ronald Aldo sports association administrator, Olympic athlete

Lakemont
Brothers, Fletcher Arnold minister, religious organization founder, director

Lakewood
Anderson, Raymond Quintus diversified company executive
Deppas, Louis Anthony financial adviser

Lancaster
Neumaier, Gerhard John environmental services administrator, consultant
Schulenberg, Gary Michael social studies educator

Lansing
Emelett, Stephen John electrical engineer, researcher

Larchmont
Berridge, George Bradford retired lawyer
Bloom, Lee Hurley lawyer, consultant, retired consumer products company executive
Burkett, Bradford Charles lawyer
Cavanna, Dino Francesco chemicals executive
Folter, Roland historian, rare book dealer, writer
Greenwald, Carol Schiro professional services marketing research executive
Hinerfeld, Norman Martin manufacturing executive
Hinerfeld, Ruth G. civic organization executive
Kaufmann, Henry Mark mortgage banker
Levi, James Harry real estate executive, investment banker
McSherry, William John, Jr. lawyer, consultant
Plumez, Jean Paul advertising executive, consultant
Rainier, Robert Paul publisher, consultant
Rockland, Lawrence Howard psychiatrist, educator
Siegel, Nathaniel Harold sociology educator
Sklarew, Robert Jay biomedical research educator, consultant
Stahl, William Martin retired surgeon
White, Thomas Edward lawyer
Wit, David Edmund software company executive

Latham
Catalano, Jane Donna lawyer
Condon, Joseph Dennis broadcasting executive
Schwartz, Robert William management consultant
Stallman, Donald Lee environmental executive
Wilkes, Brent Ames management consultant

Lawrence
Berman, Carol retired commissioner
Bursky, Herman Aaron lawyer
Henriquez, Allen artist

Levittown
Lambert, Bruce journalist
Massie, Clifford Michael music company executive
Vitello, Paul journalist

Lewiston
Cooper, David R. neurosurgeon
Dexter, Theodore Henry chemist
LoTempio, Julia Matild retired accountant

Lindenhurst
Hungerford, Gary A. insurance executive, columnist, writer, editor
Kaufman, Susan Shiffman psychologist

Liverpool
De Long, Jacob Edward real estate broker
Federico, Josephine A.M. music educator
Landers, Mary Dean J. music educator
Wightman, Sharon Leilani librarian

Livingston Manor
Root, Stuart Dowling lawyer, retired government agency administrator, banker

Lloyd Harbor
Sheard, Charles III dermatologist

Lockport
Carr, Edward Albert, Jr. pharmacologist, educator, physician
Koelmel, John R. finance company executive
Leader, Bruce Robert secondary school educator
Penney, Charles Rand lawyer, civic worker
Schultz, Gerald Alfred (Jerry Schultz) retired chemicals executive
Steinagle, Martin Gene contractor, paralegal, poet, writer

Locust Valley
Bentel, Frederick Richard architect, educator
Bentel, Paul Louis architect, educator
Comfort, William Twyman, Jr. banker
Fairman, Joel Martin retired broadcast executive
Fletcher, Mary Lee retired marketing professional
Zulch, Joan Carolyn retired medical publishing company executive

Long Beach
Harris, Steven M. urologist
Levine, Samuel Milton lawyer, retired judge, arbitrator, mediator
Robbins, Jeffrey Howard media consultant, research writer, educator
Shahda Geraci, Carole Anne retired elementary school educator
Solomon, Robert H. lawyer

Long Eddy
Hoiby, Lee composer, concert pianist

Long Island City
Ackerman, Jason food products executive
Belkharraz, Abderrazak Idrissi education educator, researcher
DiGiovanni, Eleanor Elma scaffold installation company executive
Dromm, Daniel Patrick elementary school educator
Henrikson, C. Robert insurance company executive
Leggett, Ann Vaughan artist
Lieberman, Janet Elaine academic administrator
Lucca, Louis Anthony academic administrator
Madden, Steven footwear designer
Markus, Maura bank executive
Rein, Catherine Amelia insurance company executive, lawyer
Sadao, Shoji architect
Wanderman, Susan Mae lawyer
Yiannes, (Iordanides) sculptor, ceramist, educator
Young, Aaron conceptual artist

Loudonville
Burstein, Sharon Ann corporate communications specialist, apparel designer
Doyle, Mathias Francis academic administrator, political scientist, educator
Drake, Robert academic administrator, educator
Ribley-Borck, Joan Grace medical/surgical rehabiliation nurse
Toal, James Francis academic administrator

Lynbrook
Cangemi, Lisa Lynne art director, graphics designer
Wong, Edward Vincent investment company executive

Mahopac
Gonzalez-Tornero, Sergio artist
McCluskey, Frank Bryce director

Malone
Stone, Todd M. military officer

Malverne
Benigno, Thomas Daniel lawyer
Pollio, Ralph Thomas editor, consultant
Van Bosse, Harold J.P. orthopedic surgeon

Mamaroneck
Coleman, Marshall Donald psychiatrist, psychoanalyst
Halpern, Abraham Leon psychiatrist
Martin, Roger Harry retired college president
McEnroe, Patrick former professional tennis player, sports commentator
McLarnon, Mary Frances neurologist
Mizrahi, Abraham Mordechay retired health products executive, pediatrician

Manhasset
Arnofsky, Adam Garett cardiothoracic surgeon
Bernstein, David gastroenterologist
Boal, Bernard Harvey cardiologist, educator, author
Bosworth, Jay L. radiation oncologist
Brand, Oscar folk singer, writer, educator
Budman, Cathy Linda psychiatrist, physician
Burke, Alexander James, Jr. publishing executive
Calvin, Donald Lee stock exchange official
Croce, Anne Lally nurse, commissioner
Dabideen, Darrin research scientist
D'Olimpio, James Thomas oncologist
Esposito, Rick Anthony thoracic surgeon
Evans, Bob (Robert Evans) publishing executive
Foerst, John George, Jr. retired fundraising executive
Foley, Cornelia MacIntyre retired artist
Gardner, Robert financial services executive
Hall, Michael Howard thoracic surgeon
Hartman, Alan Roy surgeon, educator
Kalimi, Robert cardiovascular surgeon
Kaminsky, Arthur Charles lawyer
Milhorat, Thomas Herrick neurosurgeon
Pogo, Gustave Javier cardiothoracic surgeon, educator
Preston, Rob editor-in-chief
Rochelson, Burton L. obstetrician
Savage, Clare Leavy school psychologist
Shelat, Amit Mahesh neurologist
Sirooni, Anahid Alice composer, musician
Stevens, Thelma Kaplan artist, educator
Vatsia, Sheel Kumar cardiothoracic surgeon
Wachtler, Sol lawyer, educator
Weitzner, Steve publishing executive

Manlius
Gibson, Judith W. psychotherapist
Harriff, Suzanna Elizabeth Bahner media consultant
Martonosi, Anthony Nicholas retired biochemistry professor

O'Reilly, Mary environmental scientist, educator
Prior, John Thompson pathology educator

Marcellus
Baker, Bruce Roy artist, illustrator
Pirozzi, Mildred Jean retired nursing administrator
Taylor, Robert Wilson military officer, publishing executive

Maspeth
Blitz, Nelson, Jr. entrepreneur
Heppa, Douglas Van computer specialist

Massapequa
Labow, Theodore Allan dermatologist, educator
Pettersen, Kevin Will investment company executive
Turk, Elizabeth Ann music educator
Zwanger, Jerome physician

Massapequa Park
King, Peter Thomas congressman, lawyer

Massena
Pollard, Fred Don finance company executive, director

Mechanicville
Rhodes, Alan Charles minister

Medford
Brower, Robert Charles rehabilitation counselor, small business owner
Snyder, Mark Jeffrey financial planner, actuary

Medusa
Groom, Winston Francis, Jr. writer

Melville
Bergman, Stanley M. health products executive
Bongiorno, Joseph John, Jr. electrical engineering educator
Breslawski, James P. health products executive
Brown, Peter Stewart lawyer, electronics executive
Bultan, Aykut communications systems engineer
Cahn, Richard Caleb lawyer
Campofranco, Salvatore real estate company executive
Copperman, Stuart Morton pediatrician, educator
Cummings, Anthony William lawyer, educator, banker
Damadian, Raymond Vahan biophysicist
Davidson, Justin music critic
Duval, Daniel Webster electronics executive
Ettinger, Michael Saul lawyer
Feller, Benjamin E. actuary
Gellman, Marc rabbi
Gilroy, Kevin electronics executive
Grayson, Gerald Herbert economist, educator, arbitrator, writer
Handelsman, Walt cartoonist
Hildebrand, John Frederick columnist, educator
Kissinger, Walter Bernhard retired automotive executive
Klurfeld, James Michael journalist
Knight, Timothy P. publishing executive
Komaroff, Stanley lawyer
Kornberg, Fred electronics executive
Krenek, Debby newspaper editor
Lane, Arthur Alan lawyer
Long, Michael J. electronics executive
Mancini, John editor, publishing executive
Mathur, Bhawnesh electronics executive
McMahon, John P. electronics executive
Millman, Bruce Russell lawyer
Mitchell, William Edmund electronics executive
Moran, Paul James journalist, columnist
Morris, M. Catherine electronics executive
Olesen, Robert Lind Ole electrical engineer
Reardon, George Martin lawyer
Reilly, Paul J. electronics executive
Schmid, Charles Ernest acoustical engineer, academic administrator
Schoenfeld, Michael P. lawyer
Settle, Mark information technology executive
Sobol, Elise Schwarcz music educator
Starr, Jeffrey lawyer, bank executive
Strauss, Michael mortgage company executive
Taub, Jesse J. electrical engineering researcher
Waddell, John Comer electronics executive

Mendon
Munson, Harold Lewis education educator

Merrick
Cariola, Robert Joseph artist
Cherry, Harold actuary, consultant
Fleischman, Francine D. secondary school educator
Garfinkel, Lawrence Saul academic administrator, educator, television producer
Harrison, Marjorie Freeman secondary education educator, librarian
Howard, Joyce Anne elementary school educator

Mexico
Halse, Frank Adams, Jr. retired minister
Sade, Donald Stone anthropology educator

Middle Island
Andrews, Gaylen public relations executive
Clarke, Hughette Naomi elementary school educator
Linick, Andrew S. direct marketing expert

Middleburgh
Mau, Lisa Anne special education educator

Middletown
Bedell, Barbara Lee journalist
Joerger, Jay Herman psychologist, entrepreneur
Kossar, Ronald Steven lawyer
Ojeda, Joseph A. psychotherapist

Radeboldt-Daly, Karen Elaine retired medical/surgical nurse

Millbrook
Della-Volpe, Ralph Eugene artist
Flexner, Kurt Fisher economist, educator
Hall, Penelope Coker editor, writer
Likens, Gene Elden biology and ecology educator
Turndorf, Jamie psychotherapist

Millerton
Hastings, Donald Francis actor, writer
Welsh, Donald Emory publisher

Mineola
Bartlett, Clifford Adams, Jr. lawyer
Bartol, Ernest Thomas lawyer
Block, Martin lawyer
Brand, Donald Albert medical researcher, educator
Flanzig, Daniel lawyer
Halloran, Daniel James lawyer
Hammer, Deborah Marie librarian, paralegal
Kokotos, William J. cardiothoracic surgeon
Lynn, Robert Patrick, Jr. lawyer
Miller, Loring Erik insurance agent, broker
Monaghan, Peter Gerard lawyer
Newman, Malcolm mechanical and civil engineering consultant
Niederman, Michael Steven physician, educator
O'Connell, Maureen C. county official, former state legislator
Olsen, Dorothy S. music educator
Rubine, Robert Samuel lawyer
Schaffer, David Irving lawyer
Schubach, Scott Leslie cardiac physician
Smolev, Terence Elliot lawyer, educator
Tannenbaum, Bernard lawyer
Vintzileos, Anthony Mark obstetrician, gynecologist
Will, Alfred Joseph lawyer, engineer

Minoa
Sickler, Michael Allan educator, artist

Monroe
Dierna, Joseph Biagio construction company executive, land development consultant
Fontana, John Arthur employee benefits specialist
Furman-Markowitz, Joanna Florence dance educator

Monsey
Erickson, Barbara Martha historian, writer

Montauk
Butler, Thomas William retired health and social services administrator
Kahn, Richard Dreyfus lawyer

Montgomery
Feldman, Arlene Karp special education educator, director
Moore, Virginia Lee Smith elementary school educator
Teutul, Paul, Sr. television personality, mechanic

Monticello
Dutcher, Joana elementary school educator, singer

Montour Falls
Spencer, Dawn Joyce advocate

Montrose
Reber, Raymond Andrew chemical engineer

Mount Kisco
Curran, Maurice Francis lawyer
Hayworth, Scott David physician
Kilbourn, Joseph A. lawyer
Kohlberg, James A. venture capitalist
Kohlberg, Jerome, Jr., (Jerry Kohlberg) venture capitalist, lawyer
Laster, Richard biotechnologist, consultant
Novak, Gregory marketing professional
Powell, Jeffrey Scott endocrinologist
Schneider, Robert Jay oncologist

Mount Sinai
Feinberg, Sheldon Norman pediatrician, educator
Kopp, Richard Edgar electrical engineer

Mount Vernon
Addesso, Angela Joyce school system administrator
Carty, Mary Ellen psychologist
Chagula, Paul Machiya information technology executive, consultant
Madden, M. Stuart lawyer
NelsonWilliams, Cecelia Elaine dietician, nutritionist
Rossini, Joseph contracting and development corporate executive
Sherrill, Milton Lewis sculptor, painter
Weisman, Richard Scott lawyer
Young, Paula Eva animal shelter director

Mumford
Conrad, Jacob B. curator, historian

Munnsville
Carruth, Hayden poet

Narrowsburg
Krause, Gloria Rose music educator

Nassau
Benamati, Dennis Charles librarian, editor, consultant

Nedrow
Lyons, Oren Native American chieftain, conservationist

Neponsit
Nicastri, Ann Gilbert *science educator*

Nesconset
Burns-Riviello, Michaela Aileen *social studies educator*

New City
Borelli, Francis J(oseph) (Frank Borelli) *diversified financial services company executive*
Fenster, Robert David *lawyer*
McCullagh, James Charles *publishing executive*
O'Dowd, Charles Edwyn *physician*
Sayegh, Nabil *urologist*

New Hampton
Sinnard, Elaine Janice *painter, sculptor*

New Hartford
Anthony, Donald Charles *librarian, educator*
Boyle, William Leo, Jr. *educational consultant, retired academic administrator*
Chapin, Mary Q. *arbitrator, director, mediator, writer*
Weiss, Holly Anne *music educator, singer*

New Hyde Park
Bonagura, Vincent R. *pediatrician, educator, researcher*
Esiason, Boomer (Norman Julius Esiason) *professional football player*
Fried, Wendy B. *obstetrician, gynecologist*
Gecelter, Gary Raymond *gastrointestinal surgeon, researcher*
Hainline, Brian *neurologist*
Handelsman, John Ellis *pediatric orthopedist, surgeon*
Hyman, Abraham *electrical engineer*
Jacobson, Marc Stephen *pediatrician, educator*
Jaffe, Richard S. *lawyer*
Kamler, Kenneth Mark *microsurgeon*
Kolitz, Jonathan Elianhu *hematologist, oncologist*
Lee, Brian Edward *lawyer*
Lehrer, Stanley *magazine publisher, editorial director, museum exhibitor*
Low, Frederick Emerson *language educator*
Mealie, Carl A. *emergency physician, educator*
Medarov, Boris I. *pulmonologist, researcher, critical care physician*
Mehrotra, Bhoomi *hematologist, oncologist*
Offner, Eric Delmonte *lawyer*
Palestro, Christopher J. *physician*
Pegalis, Steven E. *lawyer*
Punwaney, Juanita *dermatologist*
Richards, Bernard *investment company executive*
Rini, Josephine Nancy *nuclear medicine physician*
Schneider, Steven Jack *neurosurgeon*
Seltzer, Vicki Lynn *obstetrician, gynecologist*
Smith, Robin Errol *pediatrician, neurologist, educator*
Vultaggio, Don J. (Dominick Vultaggio) *beverage company executive*
Wolf-Klein, Gisele Patricia *geriatrician*

New Paltz
Azank, Roberto *artist*
Brown, Peter David Gilson *German language educator*
Emanuel-Smith, Robin Lesley *special education educator*
Flanagan Kelly, Anne Marie *academic administrator*
Flood, Ralph F. *educational association administrator*
Gee, David E. *academic administrator*
Lavallee, David Kenneth *chemistry professor, academic administrator*
Nyquist, Corinne Elaine *librarian*
Poskanzer, Steven Gary *academic administrator, lawyer*
Robinson, Anthony Christopher *novelist, educator*
Schnell, George Adam *geographer, educator, demographer*

New Rochelle
Berlage, Gai Ingham *sociologist, researcher*
Black, Page Morton *civic worker, vocalist, musician*
Branch, William Blackwell *playwright, producer*
Cohen, Saul Bernard *retired academic administrator, geographer*
Eaton, Richard Gillette *retired surgeon, educator*
Ferencz, Benjamin Berell *lawyer*
Fitch, Nancy Elizabeth *historian, educator*
Gitler, Bernard *cardiologist, critical care specialist*
Gunning, Francis Patrick *lawyer, insurance company executive*
Gunther, Virginia F. *history educator*
Hasson, Adam Isaac *lawyer*
Herman, William Charles *lawyer*
Leaf, Robert Jay *dental insurance consultant*
Margolin, Harold *metallurgical educator*
Menzies, Henry Hardinge *architect*
Metz, Roxie Anne *art educator*
Perry-Böttinger, Lynne Valencia *interventional cardiologist*
Reddington, Mary Jane *retired secondary school educator*
Rovinsky, Joseph Judah *obstetrician, gynecologist*
Rutstein, Eleanor H. *psychologist*
Saperstein, David *writer, film director, television personality*
Sommer, Jay *writer, literature and language educator*
Tassone, Gelsomina (Gessie Tassone) *metal products executive*
Winstead, Melody *science educator*

New Windsor
Mandel, Joel Emanuel *orthopedist*

New York
Aaron, Roger S. *lawyer*
Aaron, Stewart D. *lawyer*
Abate, Catherine M. *retired state legislator*
Abatemarco, Tracy J. *lawyer*
Abbott, Geoffrey Winston *physiologist, researcher*
Abbott, James Edward *lawyer*
Abboud, Joseph M. *fashion designer*
Abdel Dayem, Hussein Mahmoud *nuclear medicine physician, radiology educator*
Abelman, Arthur F. *lawyer*
Abelson, Alan *columnist*
Abelson, Reed *reporter*
Abelson, Robert Paul *cantor, singer*
Abernathy, James Logan *public relations executive*
Abish, Cecile *artist*
Abrahams, Robert M. *lawyer*
Abramowitz, Elkan *lawyer*
Abrams, Floyd *lawyer, educator*
Abrams, Robert *lawyer, state attorney general*
Abramson, Jill *newspaper publishing executive*
Abuhoff, Daniel Mark *lawyer*
Acampora, Ralph Joseph *brokerage firm executive*
Achenbaum, Alvin Allen *marketing and management consultant*
Ackerman, Arlene *education professor, former school system administrator*
Ackerman, Lisa Marilyn *foundation administrator, consultant*
Ackman, William Albert *investment company executive*
Acrivos, Andreas *chemical engineering professor*
Adams, Bryan *vocalist, composer, photographer*
Adams, Cindy *journalist*
Adams, George Bell *lawyer*
Adams, John Brett *investment banker, pharmaceutical executive*
Adams, John Coolidge *composer, conductor*
Adams, John Hamilton *lawyer*
Adams, Robert Brereton *lawyer*
Adams, Scott *cartoonist*
Adcroft, Patti (Patrice Gabriella) *editor*
Addison, Anne Simone Pomex *television director, consultant, commentator*
Adelson, Kenneth I. *sports association executive*
Adler, Edward I. *media and entertainment company executive*
Adler, Jerry *journalist, writer*
Adler, Margot Susanna *journalist, radio producer, correspondent, writer*
Adler, Norman Tenner *psychology educator, dean*
Adler, Richard *composer, lyricist*
Adler, Stephen J. *editor-in-chief*
Adler, Tracy L. *curator*
Adlersberg, Jay Ben *internist*
Adrian, Barbara (Mrs. Franklin C. Tramutola) *artist*
Agisim, Philip *advertising and marketing executive*
Agostinelli, Robert Francesco *investment banker*
Agranoff, Gerald Neal *lawyer*
Aguilar-Alvarez, Guillermo *lawyer*
Ahmad, Jameel *civil engineer, researcher, educator*
Ahn, Jung Hwan *physiatrist, educator*
Ahrens, Lynn *lyricist*
Aidinoff, M(erton) Bernard *retired lawyer*
Ailes, Roger Eugene *broadcast executive*
Ainbinder, Bruce *lawyer*
Aitken, Doug *artist*
Akon, (Aliaune Thiam) *singer*
Akselrad, Hal (Harold Eaton) *broadcast executive, lawyer*
Aksen, Gerald *arbitrator, mediator, lawyer*
Albano, David Warren *financial executive, business analyst*
Albee, Edward Franklin *playwright, writer*
Albert, Garett J. *lawyer*
Alcott, Mark Howard *lawyer*
Alda, Alan *actor, film director, scriptwriter*
Alden, Steven Michael *lawyer*
Alderson, Philip Otis *radiologist, educator*
Alemany, Ellen R. *bank executive*
Alex, Paula Ann *foundation administrator*
Alexander, Jane (Jane Quigley) *actress, theater educator, writer*
Alexander, Roy *public relations executive, writer*
Alexis, Andrew F. *dermatologist*
Alfano, Michael Charles *university administrator*
Alfieri, Vincent *lawyer*
Alford, Katherine *food products executive*
Alikhani, Zoubin *internist, molecular biologist, researcher*
Alizadeh, Kaveh *plastic surgeon, educator*
Allan, Col *editor-in-chief*
Allard, Linda Marie *fashion designer*
Allen, Alice *communications and marketing executive*
Allen, Betty (Mrs. Ritten Edward Lee III) *mezzo-soprano*
Allen, Claxton Edmonds III *investment banker*
Allen, Herbert Anthony, Jr. *investment company executive*
Allen, Leon Arthur, Jr. *lawyer*
Allen, Oliver E. *writer*
Allen, William Thomas *law educator*
Allerhand, Joseph S. *lawyer*
Allis, David C. *biologist, educator*
Allison, Herbert Monroe, Jr. *investment company executive*
Allison, Michael David *space scientist, educator*
Alliton, Vaughn *brokerage executive*
Almon, Lorie *lawyer*
al-Nasser, Nassir Abdulaziz *ambassador*
Aloe, Paul Hubschman *lawyer*
Alperin, Stuart N. *lawyer*
Alpert, Jon *television producer, director, reporter*
Alpert, William Harold (Bill Alpert) *artist, painter*
Alschuler, Steven *public relations executive, writer, consultant*
Alt, Carol A. *actress, model, entrepreneur, writer*
Altchek, David Wilson *orthopedist, surgeon*
Alter, Eleanor Breitel *lawyer*
Alter, Jonathan Hammerman *journalist*
Alter, Paul R. *lawyer*
Alterman, Daniel L. *lawyer*
Altfest, Lewis Jay *financial planner*
Altieri, Peter Louis *lawyer*
Altman, Lawrence Kimball *physician, journalist*
Altman, Roy Peter *pediatric surgeon*
Alvarez, Julia *writer*
Ambrosio, Anthony G. *broadcast executive*
Amdur, Martin Bennett *lawyer*
Amelan, Bjorn G. *sculptor, set designer*
Amen, Robert M. *manufacturing and retired paper company executive*
Amenoff, Gregory *artist, educator*
Ames, Richard Pollard *physician, educator, lecturer*
Ames, Roger *recording industry executive*
Amos, Tori *musician, singer*
Amster, Linda Evelyn *newspaper executive, consultant*
Amsterdam, Anthony Guy *law educator*
Amsterdam, Mark Lemle *lawyer*
Anastasi, William Joseph *artist*
Ancier, Garth Richard *broadcast executive*
Andelbradt, Mark *chef*
Anders, David Brian *prosecutor*
Andersen, K(ent) Tucker *investment executive*
Andersen, Mark *musician*
Andersen, Richard Esten *lawyer*
Anderson, Arthur Allan *management consultant*
Anderson, David Poole *sportswriter*
Anderson, Fred D. *investment company executive, retired computer company executive*
Anderson, Fred Richard *minister, writer*
Anderson, Gloria Brown *publishing executive*
Anderson, Lisa *political science professor, researcher, former dean*
Anderson, Richard Theodore *trade association administrator, urban planner*
Anderson, Theodore Wellington *portfolio strategist*
Anderson, Walter Herman *editor, educator*
Andolina, Janet *lawyer*
Andolsen, Alan Anthony *management consultant*
Andrade, Andres *vocalist, educator*
Andre, Michael (Kenneth Andre) *editor-in-chief*
Andreassi, John Lawrence *psychologist, educator*
Andree, Tim *advertising executive*
Andreotti, Lamberto *pharmaceutical executive*
Andrews, Gordon Clark *lawyer*
Andrias, Richard T. *judge*
Andriola, Rocco F. *lawyer, diversified financial services company executive*
Andrus, Roger Douglas *lawyer*
Anesh, Mark K. *lawyer*
Angell, Roger *writer, magazine editor*
Angland, Joseph *lawyer*
Angus, Patricia Marie *lawyer*
Antell, Darrick Eugene *plastic surgeon, educator*
Anthoine, Robert *lawyer, educator*
Anthony, Michael *chef*
Anthony, William Graham *artist*
Antonakos, Stephen *sculptor*
Antonuccio, Joseph Albert *management consultant*
Apcar, Leonard M. *online editor*
Apostolakis, James John *shipping company and pharmaceutical executive*
Appel, Albert M. *lawyer*
Appel, Marsha Ceil *advertising executive*
Appelbaum, Ann Harriet *lawyer*
Appelbaum, Paul Stuart *psychiatrist, medical educator, department chairman*
Applebaum, Stuart S. *public relations executive*
Applegate, Jeffrey M. *investment company executive*
Aptekar, Ken *painter*
Aquila, Francis Joseph *lawyer*
Aquilino, Thomas Joseph, Jr. *federal judge, educator*
Arabatzis, Constance Elaine *lawyer*
Arad, Michael Sahar *architect*
Aranda, Benjamin *architect*
Arcangel, Cory *artist, computer technician*
Arditi, Ralph *lawyer*
Arenson, Gregory K. *lawyer*
Arenson, Karen Wattel *reporter*
Arffa, Allan J. *lawyer*
Arias, Ricardo Alberto *ambassador, lawyer*
Arkin, Stanley S. *lawyer*
Arlen, Jennifer Hall *law educator*
Armani, Giorgio *fashion designer*
Armbrust, Joseph W., Jr. *lawyer*
Armen, Garo H. *research and development company executive*
Armenakas, Noel Anthony *medical educator*
Armine, Cindy A. *bank executive*
Armstrong, Neil A. *former astronaut*
Arnold, Ann *artist, illustrator*
Arnold, Martin *editor, journalist*
Arnold, Winfred Raymon *trade association administrator*
Aron, Alan Milford *pediatric neurology educator*
Aronson, Clifford Hank *lawyer*
Aronson, Donald Eric *management and tax consultant*
Aronson, Edgar David *venture capitalist*
Arouh, Jeffrey Alan *lawyer*
Arquit, Kevin James *lawyer*
Arrow, Allen H. *lawyer*
Arroyo, Martina *soprano*
Arvystas, Michael Geciauskas *orthodontist, educator*
Asakawa, Takako *dancer, choreographer, educator, director*
Ascherman, Jeffrey Alan *plastic and reconstructive surgeon*
Aschoff, Lawrence Michael (Mick Aschoff) *computer information scientist*
Ash, Karen Artz *lawyer*
Ashanti, (Ashanti Shequoiya Douglas) *vocalist*
Ashbaugh, Dennis *artist*
Ashdown, Marie Matranga *writer, educator, cultural organization administrator*
Asher, Aaron *retired editor, publisher*
Ashinoff, Reid L. *lawyer*
Ashley, Dwayne *not-for-profit fundraiser*
Ashley, Willard Walden C., Sr. *minister*
Ashton, Dore *writer, educator*
Asimov, Eric *wine critic*
Asner, Edward *actor*
Assael, Henry *marketing educator*
Astley, Amy *editor-in-chief*
Aston, Sherrell Jerone *plastic surgeon, educator*
Astor, David Warren *journalist*
Aswady, Adiyatwidi Adiwoso *diplomat*
Ataeva, Aksoltan *diplomat*
Atkins, Peter Allan *lawyer*
Atlas, James Robert *editor, writer*
Attal, Laurent *cosmetics executive*
Attwood, James Albert, Jr. *investment company executive*
Atwood, Margaret Eleanor *writer*
Audet, Paul L. *diversified financial services company executive*
Aufses, Arthur Harold, Jr. *surgeon, educator*
Augustine, Cynthia H. *educational services company executive, lawyer*
Auletta, Ken *columnist*
Auslander, Mitchell J. *lawyer*
Auster, Paul *writer*
Austin, John H.M. *radiologist*
Ausubel, Jesse Huntley *environmental researcher*
Ax, Emanuel *pianist*
Axel, Richard *pathology and biochemistry educator*
Axelrod, Charles Paul *lawyer*
Axelrod, Deborah Mona *surgeon*
Axelrod, Norman N(athan) *technology and product development consultant*
Axinn, Stephen Mark *lawyer*
Axthelm, Nancy *advertising executive*
Ayafor, Martin Chungong *ambassador*
Ayoub, Elsa *lawyer*
Azzoli, Val *music company executive*
Bacall, Lauren (Betty Joan Perske) *actress*
Bach, Thomas Handford *lawyer, investor*
Bachelder, Joseph Elmer III *lawyer*
Bachner, Barbara LaVerdiere *artist*
Bachrach, Nancy *retired advertising executive*
Backstedt, Roseanne Joan *artist*
Baden, Michael M. *pathologist, educator*
Badertscher, David Glen *law librarian, consultant*
Badgley, Mark *fashion designer*
Baechler, Donald *painter*
Bagger, Richard Hartvig *pharmaceutical executive*
Baglivo, Mary L. *advertising executive*
Bagnall, Roger Shaler *history professor, director*
Baha, Christian J. *investment company executive*
Bahash, Robert J. *information technology executive*
Bahler, Gary M. *lawyer*
Bahlke, Conrad George *lawyer*
Bahr, Lauren S. *publishing executive*
Baier, Bret *news correspondent*
Bailey, Colin Barry *curator*
Bailey, Darlyne *social worker, educator*
Bailey, Glenda *editor-in-chief*
Bailey, Jerome H. (Jerry Bailey) *mercantile exchange executive*
Bains, Leslie Elizabeth *banker*
Baio, Joseph T. *lawyer*
Baird, Lisa P. *marketing executive*
Baird, Penny Drue *interior designer*
Baird, Richard *human resources specialist*
Baird, Zoë *lawyer*
Baity, John Cooley *lawyer*
Baitz, Jon Robin *playwright*
Baja, Lauro Liboon, Jr. *diplomat*
Bakal, Ron Sharone *urologist*
Baker, Al *journalist*
Baker, Daniel Clifton III *plastic surgeon, educator*
Baker, Deborah *editor, writer*
Baker, Elizabeth Calhoun *magazine editor*
Baker, Mark M. *lawyer, law educator*
Baker, Paul Raymond *historian, educator*
Baker, Stuart David *lawyer*
Baker, Susan L. *performing company executive, retired investment banker*
Baker, William Harris *lawyer*
Balamaceda, Casilda *neurologist, oncologist*
Balazs, André T. *hotel executive*
Baldacci, David *writer*
Baldessari, John Anthony *artist*
Baldwin, David Shepard *physician*
Baldwin, Deborah *editor*
Balilty, Oded *photographer*
Balinberg, Edmond B. *physician*
Ball, John Paul *publishing company executive*
Ballard, Charles Alan *investment banker*
Balmori, Diana *landscape designer*
Balter, Bernice *religious organization administrator*
Bamberger, Michael Albert *lawyer, educator*
Ban, Ki-Moon (Ban Ki-Moon) *Secretary General of the United Nations, former South Korean government official*
Bancroft, Margaret Armstrong *lawyer*
Bandier, Martin N. *music publisher*
Bandler, James *reporter*
Banerjee, Neela *reporter*
Banerjee, (Bimal) *artist, educator*
Banga, Ajay *diversified financial services company executive*
Bank, Melissa S. *writer*
Banker, Amy Beth Cohen *artist, writer, educator, curator, actress, poet*
Bankston, Archie Moore *lawyer*
Bannigan, Eugene F. *lawyer*
Bantivoglio, Barbara *broadcast executive*
Bantom, Michael Allen *sports association executive*
Barakat, Richard *oncologist, gynecological surgeon*
Barandes, Robert *lawyer*
Barasch, Clarence Sylvan *lawyer*
Barasch, Mal Livingston *lawyer*
Barbeosch, William Peter *bank executive, lawyer*
Barber, Lionel *journalist*

Barber, Tiki (Atiim Kiambu Barber) *sportscaster, retired professional football player*
Barbour, Catherine Jean *actress, set designer, director, mime*
Barbur, Peter T. *lawyer*
Barchas, Jack David *psychiatrist, medical researcher, educator, behavioral molecular neurobiologist*
Bardach, Joan Lucile *clinical psychologist*
Barist, Jeffrey *lawyer*
Barker, Barbara Ann *ophthalmologist*
Barksdale, James Love *communications executive*
Barlow, Anne Julia *curator*
Barlow, Barbara Ann *surgeon*
Barlow, Matthew *real estate company executive*
Barnard, Kevin Francis *lawyer*
Barnes, Clive Alexander *drama and dance critic*
Barnes, Gregg *costume designer*
Barnes, Jhane Elizabeth *fashion design company executive, designer*
Barnet, Will *artist, educator*
Barnett, Vivian Endicott *curator*
Barnett, Will *painter*
Barolini, Teodolinda *literary critic*
Baron, Andrew Michael *blog website producer, educator, composer*
Baron, Mitchell Neal *lawyer*
Baron, Robert Howard *lawyer*
Baron, Sheri *advertising agency executive*
Barondess, Jeremiah Abraham *physician*
Barquero, Pedro B. *mathematician, researcher*
Barr, John W. *investment company executive, foundation administrator*
Barr, William Pelham *telecommunications industry executive, lawyer, former United States attorney general*
Barrett, David A. *lawyer*
Barrett, Elizabeth Ann Manhart *psychotherapist, consultant, nursing educator*
Barron, James Turman *journalist*
Barron, Susan *clinical psychologist*
Barry, Dan *columnist*
Barry, Desmond Thomas, Jr. *lawyer*
Barry, Nancy Marie *bank executive*
Barry, Thomas Corcoran *investment advisor*
Barry, William Garrett III *publishing company executive*
Barshay, Scott A. *lawyer*
Bart, Roger *actor*
Bartfeld, Daniel D. *lawyer*
Bartholomew, Lincoln Edwin *physician*
Bartlett, Elizabeth Easton *interior designer*
Bartlett, Jennifer Losch *artist*
Bartlett, Joseph Warren *lawyer*
Bartlett, Thomas A. *telecommunications industry executive*
Bartley, Matthew B. *insurance company executive*
Barton, Lewis *food products executive, consultant*
Barton, Richard N. *computer company executive*
Bartow, Diane Grace *marketing professional, sales executive*
Baruch, Ralph M. *communications executive*
Bashir, Martin *news correspondent*
Bashkow, Jack Simon *musician*
Bason, George R., Jr. *lawyer*
Basquin, Mary Smyth (Kit Basquin) *museum administrator*
Bass, Franklin F. *lawyer*
Bassen, Ned Henry *lawyer*
Bastianich, Lidia Matticchio (Lidia Motika) *chef, food service executive*
Batali, Mario Francis *chef*
Batavia, Mitchell *physical therapist, educator*
Bateman, Maureen Scannell *lawyer*
Bateman, Paul *diversified financial services company executive*
Batts, Deborah A. *federal judge*
Bauer, Douglas F. *retired lawyer*
Bauer, Joel J. *surgeon, educator*
Bauer, Marion Dane *writer*
Bauer, Peter F. *publishing executive*
Baumgardner, John Ellwood, Jr. *lawyer*
Baumgarten, Barbara *human resources specialist*
Baumgarten, Sidney *lawyer*
Baumrin, Bernard Stefan Herbert *lawyer, educator*
Bawden, Nina (Mary Bawden) *author*
Bazell, Robert Joseph *science correspondent*
Beal, M. Flint *neurologist*
Bear, Stephen E. *pharmaceutical executive*
Bearse, Carol Irene *education educator*
Beattie, Ann *writer, educator*
Beattie, Richard Irwin *lawyer*
Beattie, E. Scott *cosmetics executive*
Beausoleil, Doris Mae *retired federal agency housing specialist*
Beck, Andrew James *lawyer*
Beck, Martha Ann *curator, director*
Beck, Nathaniel L. *political science professor*
Becker, Franklin *chef*
Becker, Jonathan *photographer*
Becker, Steven H. *lawyer*
Becker, Susan Kaplan *management and marketing communication consultant, educator*
Beckman, Michael *lawyer*
Beckman, Richard David *publishing and advertising executive*
Bederson, Benjamin *physicist, researcher*
Bednar, Rudy *television producer, director*
Bee, Samantha *comedian, actress*
Beecher, William Manuel *management consultant*
Beeken, Timothy K. *lawyer*
Beekman, William Bedloe *lawyer*
Beerbower, Cynthia Gibson *lawyer*
Beerbower, John Edwin *lawyer*
Beeson, Ann *lawyer*
Beeson, Jack Hamilton *composer, educator, writer*
Begley, Louis *writer, lawyer*
Behrens, Kathleen *sports association executive*
Beim, David Odell *investment banker, educator*
Beim, Norman *playwright, actor, theater director, writer*
Beinecke, Candace Krugman *lawyer*
Beinecke, Frances G. *environmentalist*
Beinecke, Frederick William *investment company executive*
Beinecke, William Sperry *retired consumer products company executive*
Belfer, Robert Alexander *oil and gas company executive*
Belgorod, Barry Miles *surgeon, educator*
Belknap, Norton *foundation administrator*
Belknap, Robert Lamont *literature educator*
Bell, David Arthur *retired advertising agency executive*
Bell, Hilari *writer, former librarian*
Bell, Jonathan Robert *lawyer*
Bell, Martin Allen *investment company executive*
Bell, Theodore Augustus, III, (Ted Bell) *writer, former advertising executive*
Bellando, John W. *publishing executive, accountant*
Bellanger, Serge René *bank executive*
Bellas, Albert Constantine *investment executive*
Beller, Gary A. *lawyer, former insurance company executive*
Belliveau, Gerard Joseph, Jr. *librarian*
Bellovin, Steven M. *computer science educator*
Bellows, Carl D. *lawyer*
Belson, Ken *reporter*
Belzer, Richard *actor, comedian*
Ben-Ami, Leora *lawyer*
Ben-Avi, Simon Stephen *biomedical researcher, educator*
Bendelac, Roger E. *investment executive, financial consultant*
Bender, John Charles *lawyer*
Bender, Judith *journalist, editor*
Bender, Thomas *historian, educator*
Benenson, Mark Keith *lawyer*
Benhabib, Jess *adult education educator*
Ben-Haim, Zigi *artist*
Benjamin, Harvey E. *lawyer, sports association executive*
Benjamin, Jeff *lawyer, pharmaceutical executive*
Benkard, James W. B. *lawyer*
Bennack, Frank Anthony, Jr. *publishing company executive*
Bennett, Paul B. *stock exchange executive*
Bennett, Scott Lawrence *lawyer*
Benno, Jonathan *chef*
Bensinger, Steven J. *insurance company executive*
Bentley, Eric *writer, playwright, literature educator*
Benton, Daniel C. *investment company executive*
Beraka, George Joseph *plastic surgeon*
Berendt, John Lawrence *writer, editor*
Berenson, Alex *reporter*
Berezovsky, Boris Abramovich (Platon Elenin) *entrepreneur*
Berg, A(ndrew) Scott *writer*
Berg, Madelaine R. *lawyer*
Bergdoll, Barry G. *architectural historian, educator*
Bergen, Jeffrey Bruce *art gallery owner*
Bergen, John Donald *public relations and communications executive*
Berger, Frank Milan *biomedical researcher, retired pharmaceutical executive*
Berger, George *lawyer*
Berger, Marsha J. *computer scientist, educator*
Berger, Marvin *medical educator*
Berger, Max W. *lawyer*
Berger, Pearl *librarian, dean*
Berger, Stephen *finance company executive*
Berger, Thomas Louis *author*
Berghahn, Volker Rolf *history professor*
Bergman, Arlene *lawyer*
Bergman, Charles Cabe *foundation executive*
Bergman, Donald Arthur *endocrinologist, educator*
Bergmann, Peter George *lawyer*
Bergtraum, Howard Michael *lawyer*
Berk, Paul David *internist, research scientist, educator*
Berke, Barry H. *lawyer*
Berkery, Rosemary Theresa *lawyer, investment company executive*
Berkett, Neil *telecommunications industry executive*
Berkow, Ira Harvey *writer, journalist*
Berkowitz, Brad Alan *portfolio manager*
Berkowitz, Lauren M. *music company executive*
Berkowitz, Richard Lee *obstetrician, gynecologist, director*
Berlin, Andrew Mark (Andy Berlin) *advertising agency executive*
Berlin, Heather Ayn *neuroscientist, philosopher, educator*
Berlind, Robert Elliot *artist, educator*
Berman, Ariane R. *artist*
Berman, Carol Wendy *psychiatrist*
Berman, Greg *think-tank executive*
Berman, Keith *solicitor, lawyer*
Berman, Richard Miles *judge*
Bern, Marc Jay *lawyer*
Bernard, David George *retired management consultant*
Bernard, Richard Phillip *lawyer*
Bernardin, Jamie *information technology executive*
Bernbach, John Lincoln *marketing professional*
Berne, Bruce J. *chemistry professor*
Berner, Andrew Jay *library director, writer*
Berney, Bob *film company executive*
Bernheimer, G. Max *art appraiser*
Bernstein, Daniel Lewis *lawyer*
Bernstein, David William *lawyer*
Bernstein, Donald Scott *lawyer*
Bernstein, Jay L. *lawyer*
Bernstein, Richard *financial analyst, investment advisor*
Bernstein, Richard Allen *food products executive*
Bernstein, Robert Jay *lawyer*
Bernstein, Robert M. *dermatologic surgeon*
Bernstein, Warren J. *lawyer*
Berresford, Susan Vail *foundation administrator*
Berrien, Jacqueline A. *lawyer*
Berruga-Filloy, Enrique *ambassador*
Berry, Dean C. *lawyer*
Berry, John Nichols III *publishing executive, editor*
Berthot, Jake *artist, educator*
Bertolami, Charles Nicholas *dean, dental educator, oral surgeon*
Beshar, Christine *lawyer*
Beshar, Peter Justus *lawyer, insurance company executive*
Beshar, Robert Peter *lawyer*
Beshers, Daniel Newson *retired materials scientist*
Beslow, William S. *lawyer*
Bessey, Palmer Quintard *surgeon*
Bessler, Marc *surgeon, educator*
Best, Wanda *career planning consultant*
Besterman, Douglas *composer, orchestrator*
Bethel, Denise *art appraiser*
Bettis, Jerome Abram *sports commentator, retired professional football player*
Bettman, Gary Bruce *national hockey league commissioner*
Betts, Richard Kevin *political science professor*
Beverley, Cordia Luvonne *gastroenterologist*
Bevilacqua, Louis J. *lawyer*
Bewkes, Jeffrey L. *television broadcasting company executive*
Bezanson, Thomas Edward *lawyer*
Bezozo, Kenneth K. *lawyer*
Bhattacharya, Satyajit *research scientist*
Bialkin, Kenneth Jules *lawyer, director*
Bialler, Nancy *art appraiser*
Bialo, Kenneth Marc *lawyer*
Bibliowicz, Jessica M. *financial analyst*
Bickers, David Rinsey *dermatologist, educator, department chairman, health facility administrator*
Bicks, Peter Andrews *lawyer*
Biddle, Flora Miller *art patron, museum administrator*
Biederman, Barron Zachary (Barry) *advertising agency executive*
Biel, Leonard, Jr. *urologist*
Bienenstock, Martin J. *lawyer*
Biggs, John Herron *retired insurance company executive*
Biglari, Hamid *investment banker*
Bikel, Theodore *actor, singer*
Bilsky, Mark Harvey *neurosurgeon*
Binn, Jason *publishing executive*
Birch, Ian *editor-in-chief*
Bird, Hector Ramón *child psychiatrist, psychoanalyst, educator*
Bird, Paul S. *lawyer*
Birkelund, John Peter *investment company executive*
Birkenhead, Thomas Bruce *theater producer, educator*
Birman, Joseph Leon *physics professor*
Birmelin, Robert *artist*
Birnbaum, Edward Lester *lawyer*
Birnbaum, Sheila L. *lawyer, educator*
Birns, Nicholas Boe *literature educator, editor*
Birstein, Ann *writer, educator*
Bischoff, Theresa Ann *not-for-profit association executive*
Bishop, Susan Katharine *executive search company executive*
Björk, (Björk Guðmundsdóttir) *singer, composer*
Bjorklund, Victoria B. *lawyer*
Black, Barbara Aronstein *legal history educator*
Black, Carole *broadcast executive*
Black, Cathleen Prunty *publishing executive*
Black, Henry Richard *physician*
Black, James Isaac (Jib) III *lawyer*
Black, Jerry Bernard *lawyer*
Black, Louis Engleman *lawyer*
Black, Steven D. *bank executive*
Blackman, Kenneth Robert *lawyer*
Blair, Dike *sculptor, painter*
Blair, Michael Walter *lawyer*
Blair, William Granger *retired reporter*
Blair, William McCormick, Jr. *lawyer*
Blalock, Sherrill *investment advisor*
Blanc, Roger David *lawyer*
Blanchard, Kimberly Staggers *lawyer*
Bland, Frederick Aves *architect*
Blank, Matthew C. *broadcast company executive*
Blankfein, Lloyd C. *diversified financial services company executive*
Blasband, David *lawyer*
Blaser, Martin Jack *medical educator, researcher*
Blassberg, Franci J. *lawyer*
Blavatnik, Leonard *investment company executive*
Blechner, Mark Jacob *psychologist, educator*
Bledel, Alexis (Kimberly Alexis Bledel) *actress*
Bleser, Philip F. *diversified financial services company executive*
Blinder, Albert Allan *judge*
Blinken, Donald *ambassador, investment banker*
Blitzer, Andrew *otolaryngologist, educator, research scientist, writer*
Blivaiss, David Harvey *lawyer, accountant*
Bliwise, Lester Martin *lawyer*
Blobel, Günter *cell biologist, educator*
Block, Dennis Jeffrey *lawyer*
Block, Francesca Lia *writer*
Block, Ned *philosopher, educator*
Bloom, Lisa Read *lawyer*
Bloomberg, Mike (Michael Rubens) *mayor*
Bloomfield, April *chef*
Bloomgarden, Karenne Jo *elementary school educator, small business owner*
Bloomgarden, Kathy Finn *public relations executive*
Blum, David J. *former editor-in-chief*
Blum, Paul *retail executive*
Blume, Judy *author*
Blumkin, Linda Ruth *lawyer*
Boachie-Adjei, Oheneba *orthopedic surgeon*
Boardman, D(ennie) Dixon *investment banker*
Boast, Molly Shryer *lawyer*
Bobrow, Richard S. *lawyer, former diversified financial services executive*
Bochner, Bernard H. *urologic surgical oncologist*
Bochner, Mel *artist*
Bock, Walter Joseph *zoology educator*
Bockstein, Herbert *lawyer*
Boddie, Reginald Alonzo *lawyer*
Bodley, Harley Ryan, Jr. *sportswriter, announcer, editor*
Bodovitz, James Philip *lawyer*
Boehner, Leonard Bruce *lawyer*
Boffey, Philip M. *journalist*
Bogdanich, Walt *journalist*
Bogdanos, Matthew F. *lawyer, reserve military officer, writer, boxer*
Bogdonoff, Morton David *internist, educator*
Bogert, Jeremiah *journalist*
Bohm, Richard D. *lawyer*
Boice, Craig Kendall *management consultant*
Boley, Bruno Adrian *engineering educator*
Bollinger, Lee Carroll *academic administrator, law educator*
Bolotowsky, Andrew Ilyitch *flutist, composer*
Bolton, Michael *singer, songwriter*
Bolton, Roger *public relations executive*
Bond, Alma Halbert *psychoanalyst, author*
Bond, James Max, Jr. *architect, academic administrator*
Bonfante, Larissa *classics educator*
Bonfield, Andrew R.J. *pharmaceutical executive*
Bonino, Fernanda *art dealer*
Bonnell, Bruno *information technology executive*
Bontecou, Lee *artist, sculptor*
Boodro, Michael *editor*
Bookspan, Martin *broadcaster, writer*
Boolbol, Susan K. *surgeon*
Boot, Max *journalist*
Booth, Mitchell B. *lawyer*
Booth Corwin, Tami *publishing executive*
Borchard, William Marshall *lawyer*
Borders, William Alexander *journalist*
Borer, Jeffrey Stephen *cardiologist*
Borisoff, Richard Stuart *lawyer*
Borland, Virginia Ann *journalist, fashion specialist, fiber company executive*
Bornmann, William Gerard *organic chemist*
Bornstein, Gary A. *lawyer*
Borowitz, Sidney *retired physics professor*
Borrelli, John Francis *architect*
Bosl, George Joseph *physician, oncologist*
Bossert, Rex Thomas *editor-in-chief*
Boston, Gretha *actress, vocalist*
Boston, Lloyd *television personality*
Boswell, Gina R. *cosmetics executive*
Bothmer, Dietrich Felix von *curator, archaeologist*
Botkin, Daniel Benjamin *biologist, environmental scientist, writer*
Bottari, Paul J. *lawyer*
Bottomley, Michelle J. *advertising executive*
Boufford, Jo Ivey *health facility administrator, educator*
Boulhosa, Michael L. *lawyer*
Boulud, Daniel *chef, restaurant owner*
Bourgeois, Louise *sculptor*
Boutis, Tom *artist, painter, printmaker*
Bove, John Louis *chemistry and environmental engineering educator, researcher*
Bovin, Denis Alan *diversified financial services company executive*
Bowen, Tim *recording industry executive*
Bowen, William Gordon *foundation administrator, economist*
Bowers, Brent *editor*
Bowers, John M. *labor union administrator*
Bowers, Patricia Eleanor Fritz *economist*
Bowers, William Charles *lawyer*
Bowles, Newton Rowell *United Nations executive*
Bowman, Robert A. *Internet company executive*
Boxer, Leonard *lawyer*
Boxer, Sarah *critic, reporter, writer*
Boyd, Michael Alan *investment company executive, lawyer*
Boyer, Aurelia G. *information technology executive*
Boykin, Keith O. *former government official, writer*
Boylan, Elizabeth Shippee *academic administrator, biologist, educator*
Boyle, Edward J. *lawyer*
Boziwick, George E. *music librarian, composer*
Brabeck, Mary Margaret *dean, psychology professor*
Bracco, Lorraine *actress*
Brach, Richard S. *lawyer*
Bradbury, Ray Douglas *writer*
Bradford, Barbara Taylor *writer, journalist*
Bradley, Bill (William Warren Bradley) *former senator*
Bradley, E. Michael *lawyer*
Bradley, John Francis *financial services company executive*
Bradley, Richard (Richard Blow) *writer*
Bradshaw, Dove *artist*
Brady, Adelaide Burks *public relations agency executive, giftware catalog executive*
Brady, Bruce Morgan *lawyer*
Brafman, Benjamin *lawyer*
Braham, Randolph Lewis *political science professor*
Brams, Steven John *political science professor*
Branch, Taylor *writer*
Brand, Jason *diversified financial services company executive*
Branski, Ryan Comfort *research scientist*
Brant, Henry *composer*
Brant, Sandra J. *magazine publisher*
Brantley, Benjamin David *theater critic*
Brashares, Ann *writer*
Brathwaite, Edward Kamau (Kamau Brathwaite, Lawson Edward Brathwaite) *poet, educator*
Bratten, Millie Martini *editor-in-chief*
Brauchli, Marcus Walker *editor*
Braudy, Susan Orr *writer*
Braun, Jeffrey Louis *lawyer*
Brauner, Gary Jules *dermatologist, cosmetic laser surgeon*
Braunstein, Douglas *bank executive*

Braverman, Robert Jay *management consultant, educator*
Bravo, Luis Fernando *investment banker*
Brazinsky, Irv(ing) *chemical engineering educator, department chairman*
Brecher, John *columnist*
Breen, Kenneth Michael *lawyer, former prosecutor*
Breglio, John F. *lawyer*
Breinin, Goodwin M. *physician*
Brennan, Henry Higginson *architect*
Brennan, Murray Frederick *surgeon, oncologist*
Brennan, Patrick J. *lawyer*
Brenner, Beth Fuchs *publishing executive*
Bresani, Federico Fernando *manufacturing executive*
Breslow, Esther May Greenberg *biochemistry professor, researcher*
Breslow, Ronald Charles *chemist, educator*
Breslow, Stephanie R. *lawyer*
Brestle, Daniel J. *cosmetics executive*
Brett, Barry J. *lawyer*
Brett, Harry P. *lawyer*
Brick, Michael *journalist*
Brieger, George *lawyer*
Briley-Saebo, Karen Catherin *physics professor*
Bring, Murray H. *retired lawyer*
Brinkley, Alan David *provost, historian*
Brinkley, Christie *model, spokesperson, designer*
Briskman, Louis Jacob *lawyer, broadcast executive*
Briskman, Robert David *engineering executive*
Bristow, Cynthia Lynn *immunologist*
Britz Lotti, Diane Edward *investment company executive*
Brizel, Michael Alan *retail executive, lawyer*
Brizendine, Ellanor N. (Bodie) *headmaster*
Broad, William J. *science writer*
Broadwater, Douglas Dwight *lawyer*
Broatch, Robert E. *insurance company executive*
Brock, Charles Lawrence *lawyer, diversified financial services company executive, investment banker*
Broder, Douglas Fisher *lawyer*
Brodie-Baldwin, Helen Sylvia *retired college and human services administrator*
Brodman, Michael Lewis *gynecologist, educator*
Brodsky, David Michael *lawyer*
Brodsky, Samuel *lawyer*
Brody, Alan Jeffrey *investment company executive*
Brody, Catherine Tyler *archivist, historian, writer*
Brody, Jane Ellen *journalist, researcher*
Brody, John *sports association executive*
Brody, Kenneth David *investment banker*
Brody-Lederman, Stephanie *artist*
Brohn, William David *conductor, orchestrator, arranger*
Bromberg, Debra *financial analyst, investment advisor*
Bromberger, Allen Richard *lawyer*
Brome, Thomas Reed *lawyer*
Bronfman, Edgar Miles, Jr. *recording industry executive*
Bronstein, Peter E. *lawyer*
Brooke, Linda Hundley *retired human resources specialist*
Brooks, Daniel Townley *lawyer*
Brooks, Deborah W. *foundation administrator*
Brooks, Gary *crisis management and family business consultant*
Brooks, Roger G. *lawyer*
Brooks, Timothy H. *broadcast executive*
Bross, Matthew W. *information technology executive*
Brothers, Joyce Diane *television personality, psychologist*
Broude, Richard Frederick *lawyer, educator*
Broumand, Stafford R. *Plastic Surgeon*
Browar, Lisa Muriel *librarian*
Browdy, Joseph Eugene *lawyer*
Brown, Andreas Le *retail executive, art gallery owner*
Brown, Arthur Edward *physician*
Brown, Bobbi *cosmetics executive*
Brown, Carol Leslie *gynecological oncologist*
Brown, Carroll *retired diplomat, association executive, consultant*
Brown, Chris (Christopher Maurice Brown) *singer*
Brown, Dan *writer*
Brown, Darrell James *publishing executive*
Brown, David *motion picture producer, writer*
Brown, Edward James, Sr. *utilities executive*
Brown, G(lenn) William, Jr. *bank executive*
Brown, Helen Gurley *editor-in-chief*
Brown, Jason Walter *neurologist, educator, researcher*
Brown, Jennifer Kay *lawyer*
Brown, Jonathan *art historian, educator*
Brown, Joyce F. *academic administrator*
Brown, Katie *columnist*
Brown, Loren H. *lawyer*
Brown, Paul M. *lawyer*
Brown, Ralph Sawyer, Jr. *retired lawyer*
Brown, Renee M. *sports association executive*
Brown, Rita Mae *writer*
Brown, Ronald *retired stockbroker*
Brown, Stuart F. *writer*
Brown, Terrence Charles *art association executive, researcher, lecturer*
Brown, Trisha *dancer*
Browne, Arthur *newspaper editor*
Browne, Joy *psychologist, radio personality*
Browne, Malcolm Wilde *journalist*
Browne, Thom *apparel designer*
Browning, Candace *investment company executive*
Brownstein, Alan P. *health foundation executive, consultant*
Brownstein, Andrew Richard *lawyer*
Brownwood, David Owen *lawyer*
Bruce, Duncan Archibald *investor, writer*
Bruder, Harold Jacob *artist, educator*
Brumm, James Earl *lawyer, import/export company executive*
Brun, Henry *publishing executive*
Brundige, Robert William, Jr. *lawyer*
Bruner, Jerome S. *law educator*
Bruni, Frank *restaurant critic*
Brunie, Charles Henry *investment manager*
Bruno, Antoinette *food service executive*
Brunson, Curtis *communications systems company executive*
Brus, Louis Eugene *physical chemist*
Brusca, Robert Andrew *economist*
Brust, John Calvin Morrison *neurologist, educator*
Brustein, Lawrence *finance company executive*
Bryan, Barry Richard *lawyer*
Brychtova, Jaroslava *sculptor*
Brymer, Charles Edward (Chuck Brymer) *advertising executive*
Bryson, Louise Henry *broadcast executive*
Buatta, Mario *interior designer*
Buch, Jan *medical research administrator, director*
Buchanan, Richard W. *sports association executive, lawyer*
Buchbinder, Ellen Maud *allergist*
Buchwald, Don David *lawyer*
Buchwald, Ephraim *rabbi*
Buck, Joe (Joseph Francis Buck) *sportscaster*
Buck, Louise Zierdt *psychologist*
Buckholz, Robert E., Jr. *lawyer*
Buckles, Robert Howard *retired investment company executive*
Buckley, Christopher Taylor *editor, author*
Buckley, Susan *lawyer*
Buckley, William Frank, Jr. *magazine editor, writer*
Buckman, Thomas Richard *foundation executive, educator*
Budd, Thomas Witbeck *lawyer*
Buehler, Thomas *psychotherapist, expressive therapist, artist*
Buissonnière, Marine *international organization administrator; physician*
Buist, Kathy *artist*
Bujold, Lois McMaster *writer*
Bull, David *fine art conservator*
Buller, Steven E. *diversified financial services company executive*
Bulliet, Richard Williams *historian, educator, writer*
Bundchen, Giselle *model*
Bunts, Frank Emory *artist*
Burak, H(oward) Paul *lawyer*
Burch, Tory *apparel designer*
Burckhardt, Tom *artist*
Burden, Amanda M. *urban planner*
Burdette, Brooks R. *lawyer*
Burgess, Clara Skipwith *retired principal*
Burgess, Lynne A. *lawyer*
Burgheim, Richard *magazine editor*
Burgman, Dierdre Ann *lawyer*
Burgweger, Francis Joseph Dewes, Jr. *lawyer*
Burian, Peter *ambassador*
Burke, James Joseph, Jr. *investment banker*
Burke, Kevin *utilities executive*
Burnett, Len *publishing executive*
Burnett, Mark *television producer*
Burns, Arnold Irwin *lawyer*
Burns, John F. *reporter*
Burns, John MacDougal III *lawyer*
Burns, M. Michele *human resources company executive*
Burns, Red *academic administrator*
Burns, Stephen L. *lawyer*
Burrell, Lizabeth Lorie *lawyer*
Burros, Marian Fox *writer*
Burrows, Kenneth David *lawyer*
Burrows, Michael Donald *lawyer*
Burson, Harold *public relations executive, director*
Burstein, Judd *lawyer*
Burton, Eve Bradley *lawyer*
Burton, Peggy *advertising and marketing executive*
Burtson, James E. *multimedia company executive*
Buryk, Alexis *advertising executive*
Buschke, Herman *neurologist*
Bushnell, Candace *columnist, writer*
Bushnell, George Edward III *lawyer*
Bussel, James *pediatrician, obstetrician, gynecologist, educator*
Bustin, George Leo *lawyer*
Butler, David T. III *communications systems company executive*
Butler, Kerry *actress*
Butler, Samuel Coles *lawyer*
Butler, Vincent Paul, Jr. *internist, educator*
Butte, Amy S. *brokerage house executive*
Buttenwieser, Lawrence Benjamin *lawyer*
Butterly, Kathy *sculptor*
Buttner, Jean Bernhard *diversified financial services company executive*
Buttrick, Harold *architect*
Butts, Hugh Florenz *physician, psychiatrist, psychoanalyst*
Buxton, Douglas Francisco *ophthalmologist, educator*
Byer, Diana *performing company executive*
Bylinsky, Gene Michael *magazine editor*
Byowitz, Michael H. *lawyer*
Byrd, Debra Ann *actor, theater producer, performing company executive*
Byrd, Eva Wilson *communications executive*
Byrne, Gerard Anthony (Gerry) *publishing executive, consultant*
Byron, Eric Howard *sculptor, museum researcher and administrator*
Bystryn, Jean-Claude *dermatologist, educator*
Cabalquinto, Luis Carrazcal *freelance writer*
Cabiallavetta, Mathis *insurance company executive*
Caddick, Sarah J. *medical association administrator, biomedical researcher*
Caffrey, Patricia *diversified financial services company executive*
Caginalp, Aydin S. *lawyer*
Cagliuso, Nicholas Vincent, Sr. *public health service officer*
Cagney, Lawrence K. *lawyer*
Cahill, John Donald *emergency medicine physician, educator*
Cahn, Steven Mark *philosopher, educator*
Caiazzo, Nicholas R. *lawyer*
Cai-Lee, Wendy *entrepreneur*
Caine, Paul Jason *publishing executive*
Cajori, Charles Florian *artist, educator*
Calabrese, Rosalie Sue *management consultant, writer*
Calame, Kathryn Lee *microbiologist, educator*
Calder, James J. *lawyer*
Caldwell, Ian *writer*
Caldwell, L. Scott *actress*
Caldwell, Leslie Ragon *lawyer, former prosecutor*
Caldwell, Zoe *actress, film director*
Calello, Paul *diversified financial services company executive*
Calhoun, Craig Jackson *social scientist, educator*
Calhoun, David L. *information and media company executive*
Califano, Joseph Anthony, Jr. *lawyer, former secretary of health education and welfare*
Calio, Nicholas E. *diversified financial services company executive*
Call, Neil Judson *manufacturing executive*
Callagy, John M. *lawyer*
Callahan, Dennis S. *insurance company executive*
Callahan, Robert F., Jr. *media company executive, former broadcast executive*
Callo, Joseph Francis *writer*
Camacho, Philip Bruce *insurance company executive*
Cambria, Christopher C. *lawyer, communications systems company executive*
Camera, Nicholas J. *lawyer*
Cameron, Timothy G. *lawyer*
Cami, Russell *lawyer*
Camilleri, Louis C. *consumer goods company executive*
Cammarata, Angelo *surgical oncologist*
Cammisa, Frank P., Jr. *surgeon, educator*
Camp, Sharon L. *reproductive health organization administrator*
Campbell, George, Jr. *physicist, university administrator*
Campbell, Judith E. *retired insurance company executive*
Campbell, Magda *retired child psychiatrist, researcher, educator*
Campbell, Mary Schmidt *dean*
Campbell, Naomi *model*
Campbell, Robert David *manufacturing and metal products executive*
Campbell, Ronald Neil *retired graphics designer*
Campise, James F. *lawyer*
Campos, Fernando *editor-in-chief*
Canada, Geoffrey *social welfare administrator, writer*
Cancro, Robert *psychiatrist, educator*
Cane, Jeffrey *editor*
Canedy, Dana *editor*
Canellos, Peter C. *lawyer*
Cannell, John Redferne *lawyer*
Canonero, Milena *costume designer*
Canoni, John David *lawyer*
Canseco, Jose *retired professional baseball player*
Cantor, Melvyn Leon *retired lawyer*
Cantor, Richard Ira *physician, corporate health executive*
Cantrell, Lana *actress, lawyer, singer*
Capalbo, Carmen *theater director, producer*
Caperton, (William) Gaston, (III) *educational association administrator, former governor*
Caples, Richard James *performing company executive, lawyer*
Caploe, Roberta *magazine editor*
Caplow, Ted *environmental engineer*
Capolarello, Joe R. *photojournalist*
Caponnetto, Marianne *information technology executive*
Capozzi, Lou *public relations executive*
Cappellazzo, Amy *art appraiser, writer*
Cappuccio, Paul T. *lawyer, communications executive*
Capriati, Jennifer Maria *professional tennis player*
Capus, Steve *broadcast executive*
Caputo, David Armand *academic administrator, political scientist, educator*
Caputo, Lisa M. *finance company executive*
Caputo, Lucio *trade company executive*
Caputo, Philip Joseph *writer, journalist*
Caraley, Demetrios James *political science professor, writer, editor*
Card, Orson Scott (Byron Walley) *writer*
Cardile, Paul Julius *fine arts dealer*
Cardinale, Kathleen Carmel *retired health facility administrator*
Cardozo, Benjamin Mordecai *lawyer*
Cardozo, Michael A. *lawyer*
Cardwell, Diane *journalist*
Carey, David *publishing executive*
Carey, Peter Philip *writer*
Carey, William Polk *investment banker*
Carhart, Mark Monroe *investment company executive*
Carlin, David H. *lawyer*
Carlson, Donna *art association administrator, director*
Carlson, Gretchen *news correspondent*
Carlson, Marvin Albert *theater educator*
Carlson, P(atricia) M(cElroy) *writer*
Carlson, Richard A. *interior designer*
Carlucci, Paul V. *publishing executive*
Carman, Gregory Wright *federal judge*
Carmellini, Andrew *chef*
Carmichael, Jesse Royal *musician*
Carmona, Wayne *television producer*
Carnabuci, Frank J. III *headmaster*
Carneiro, Robert Leonard *curator, anthropologist*
Caro, Robert Allan *historian, writer*
Carpenter, James *glass innovator*
Carpenter, Randle Burt *lawyer*
Carr, Arthur Charles *psychologist, educator*
Carr, Gladys Justin *publishing executive, consultant, editor, writer*
Carr, James T. *publishing executive*
Carroll, David Paul *social welfare administrator*
Carter, Elliott Cook, Jr. *composer*
Carter, Graydon (Edward Graydon Carter) *editor-in-chief*
Carter, James Hal, Jr. *lawyer*
Carter, Lonnie Tyrone *playwright, educator*
Carter, Marshall Nichols *stock exchange executive*
Carter, Peyton Franklin III *accountant*
Carter, Zachary W. *lawyer*
Carvette, Anthony M. *construction executive*
Casden, Andrew Michael *orthopedist*
Case, David Bartlett *internist, educator*
Case, Robert Brown *physician*
Casella, Jim *publishing executive*
Caserta, Jennifer *communications executive*
Casey, Gerard William *retired food products executive, lawyer*
Casey, Thomas Jefferson *clean energy industry executive and entrepreneur, environmental activist*
Cash, Rosanne *singer, songwriter*
Cashin, Richard M., Jr. *diversified financial services company executive*
Cashman, Gideon *lawyer*
Cassullo, Joanne Leonhardt *foundation administrator*
Castel, P. Kevin *federal judge*
Castellano, Michael John *investment company executive*
Castle, John Krob *merchant banker*
Castoro, Rosemarie *sculptor*
Castro, Jan Garden *writer, art educator, consultant*
Catley-Carlson, Margaret *not-for-profit executive*
Catsimatidis, John Andreas *retail executive*
Cattelan, Maurizio *artist*
Caulfield, Jerome Joseph *lawyer*
Cavallo, Jo Ann *language educator*
Cavallo, Rob *recording industry executive*
Cavanagh, Michael J. *bank executive*
Cavanagh, William G. *lawyer*
Cavenaugh, Matt *actor*
Cavuto, Neil *newscaster, business journalist, television host*
Caws, Mary Ann *literature and language professor*
Cayne, James E. (Jimmy) *diversified financial services company executive*
Caytas, Ivo George *lawyer*
Cazeaux, Isabelle Anne Marie *retired music educator*
Cecil, Donald *retired investment company executive*
Cedarbaum, Miriam Goldman *federal judge*
Celentano, John E. *pharmaceutical executive*
Cembalest, Robin *arts editor, critic*
Cendali, Dale Margaret *lawyer*
Centrello, Gina *publishing executive*
Cephas, Derrick D. *bank executive, lawyer*
Cerfolio, Nina Estelle *psychiatrist, educator*
Cesar, Kamala *dancer, educator*
Cesare, Christine B. *lawyer*
Chabon, Michael *writer*
Chaganti, Raju S. *geneticist, educator, researcher*
Chahinian, A(ram) Philippe *oncologist*
Chai, Nelson J. *stock exchange executive*
Chaitman, Helen Davis *lawyer*
Chajet, Clive *brand and corporate image consultant*
Chalfie, Martin *biology professor*
Chalsty, John Steele *investment banker*
Chamberlain, John Angus *sculptor*
Chammah, Walid A. *investment banker*
Chan, Janet *editor-in-chief*
Chan, Lo-Yi Cheung Yuen *architect*
Chan, Siu-Wai *materials science educator*
Chandler, Michael Jonathan *allergist, physician*
Chandrasekhar, Sujana S. *otologist, educator, neurotologist*
Chang, David *chef*
Chang, Laura *editor*
Chang, Marian S. *filmmaker, composer*
Chang, Stanley *ophthalmologist*
Chang-Robbins, Joyce *diversified financial services company executive*
Channing, Stockard (Susan Antonia Williams Stockard) *actress*
Chanos, James S. *investment company executive*
Chao, James Si-Cheng *maritime executive*
Chapin, Julie Kurtz *lawyer*
Chapin, Samuel R. *investment company executive*
Chapin, Schuyler Garrison *retired cultural organization administrator, retired dean*
Chapman, Craig E. *lawyer*
Chapman, Drew Gordon Lee *lawyer*
Chapman, Max C., Jr. *investment company executive*
Chapman, Paul B. *oncologist*
Chapnick, David B. *lawyer*
Chappell, John Charles *lawyer*
Chappell, Richard Lee *biology educator, neuroscientist*
Charash, Bruce D. *cardiologist, educator*
Charney, Marc D. *editor*
Charon, Rita *internist, medical educator, writer*
Chatillon, Devereux *lawyer, publishing executive*
Chatzinoff, Howard *lawyer*
Chaves, Jose Maria *diplomat, lawyer, foundation administrator, educator*
Chavkin, Jeffrey S. *lawyer*
Chazen, Hartley James *lawyer*
Cheeks, George *lawyer, broadcast executive*
Cheema, Faisal Habib *surgeon, researcher*
Cheh, Huk Yuk *electrochemist*
Chell, Beverly C. *retired media company executive, lawyer*
Chelstrom, Marilyn Ann *political science educator, consultant*
Chemtob, Nancy Nadel *lawyer*

Chen, James Tsing-Fang *art association administrator, cultural organization administrator*
Chen, Jonathan *pediatric surgeon*
Chen, Tak-Ming *retired civil engineer, consultant*
Chen, Wesley *lawyer*
Chen, Xi *research scientist*
Chenault, Kenneth Irvine *finance company executive*
Cheney, Richard Eugene *public relations executive, psychoanalyst*
Chenoweth, Kristin *actress*
Chepiga, Michael Joseph *lawyer*
Cherkasky, Michael G. *insurance company executive*
Chermayeff, Ivan *graphics designer*
Chernis, Mark *educational organization executive*
Cherryh, C. J. *writer*
Chesler, Evan Robert *lawyer*
Chesney, Robert Henry *management consultant, director*
Chesnutt, Jane *editor-in-chief*
Chestnut, Colette *broadcast executive*
Chevigny, Paul Graves *law educator*
Chevray, Rene *engineering educator*
Chiang, Yung Frank *law educator*
Chiarchiaro, Frank John *lawyer*
Chicco, Gianfranco *healthcare communications executive*
Chichilnisky, Graciela *mathematician, economist, educator, writer*
Chida, Junaid Hasan *lawyer*
Childs, David M. *architectural firm executive*
Childs, John Farnsworth *retired bank executive*
Chin, Mel *sculptor*
Chin, Sylvia Fung *lawyer*
Chinn, Yuen Yuey *art educator, painter*
Chira, Susan *editor*
Chirico, Anthony (Tony) *publishing executive*
Chirico, Emanuel *apparel executive*
Chirls, Richard *lawyer*
Chiu, David Tak Wai *surgeon*
Cho, Tai Yong *lawyer*
Chodorow, Jeffrey *restaurant owner*
Chong, Ping *performing company executive*
Chopey, Nicholas P. *editor*
Chou, Ting-Chao *inventor, educator*
Chowdhury, Md Shoaib *engineer*
Christ, Lily Esther Shih *mathematics professor*
Christensen, Anne *art director*
Christensen, Dieter *ethnomusicologist*
Christensen, Henry III *lawyer*
Christian, Leslie Kojo *ambassador*
Christiansen, Keith *curator*
Christodoulou, Marilena *investment banker, finance company executive*
Christoffers, Lynn Beryl *curator, artist*
Christopher, Maurine Brooks *foundation administrator, writer, editor*
Christopher, Nicholas *poet, writer*
Christy, Arthur Hill *lawyer*
Christy, John Hill III *journalist*
Chromow, Sheri P. *lawyer*
Chudnovsky, Maria *mathematician, educator*
Chung, Jen *blog editor*
Chung, Jung Git *retired aerospace engineer*
Chunilal, Damian *investment company executive*
Church, Frank Forrester *minister, writer*
Church, Pamela T. *lawyer*
Chusid, Martin *musicologist, educator*
Chutorian, Abe M. *pediatrician, educator*
Chwast, Seymour *graphic artist*
Ciara, (Ciara Princess Harris) *R&B performer*
Cieply, Michael *editor, writer*
Ciparick, Carmen Beauchamp *state appeals court judge*
Cipolla, Mark *lawyer*
Clair, Bernard E. *lawyer*
Claire, Thomas Andrew *financial executive, consultant, educator, writer*
Clamar, Aphrodite J. *psychologist*
Clapp, Stephen Henry *dean, violinist*
Clark, Bruce E. *lawyer*
Clark, Carolyn Cochran *lawyer*
Clark, Gordie *professional sports team executive*
Clark, Howard Longstreth, Jr. *finance company executive, director*
Clark, James Joseph *lawyer*
Clark, Joan Hardy *retired journalist*
Clark, Jonathan Montgomery *lawyer*
Clark, Merrell Edward, Jr. *lawyer*
Clark, Michael K. *diversified financial services company executive*
Clark, Robert Henry, Jr. *finance company executive*
Clark, Victoria *actress*
Clarke, Frank William *communications executive*
Clarke, Kenneth Kingsley *retired electronics executive*
Clary, Richard Wayland *lawyer*
Claster, Jill Nadell *academic administrator, history educator*
Clayman, Greg *communications executive*
Clayton, Jon Kerry *insurance company executive*
Clayton, Joseph Paul *broadcast executive*
Cleary, Beverly Atlee (Mrs. Clarence T. Cleary) *writer*
Clemens, Rosemary A. *health facility administrator, foundation administrator*
Clemente, Francesco *artist*
Cliff, Walter Conway *lawyer*
Clifford, Stewart Burnett *banker, director*
Clines, Francis X. *journalist*
Clinton, Bill (William Jefferson Clinton) *42nd President of the United States*
Clinton, Chelsea Victoria *financial consultant, former first daughter*
Close, Chuck (Charles Thomas Close) *artist*
Close, Lanny Garth *otolaryngologist, educator*
Close, Michael John *property manager, lawyer*
Clower, Donna *music company executive*
Coatsworth, John Henry *history professor, writer, dean*
Cobb, Henry Nichols *architect*
Cobb, James G. *editor*
Coben, Harlan *writer*
Cockrell, Sanford Alonza III *accountant*
Coe, Sue *artist, journalist*
Coen, Jessica *blog writer, editor*
Coffee, John Collins, Jr. *legal educator*
Coffey, John P. (Sean Coffey) *lawyer*
Coffin, Anne Gagnebin *arts administrator, editor*
Cohen, Abby Joseph *investment company executive*
Cohen, Adam *reporter, lawyer*
Cohen, Cora *artist*
Cohen, David Harris *neuroscientist, educator, academic administrator*
Cohen, Edmund Stephen *lawyer*
Cohen, Ezechiel Godert David *physicist, researcher*
Cohen, Harriet Newman *lawyer*
Cohen, Henry Rodgin (H. Rodgin Cohen) *lawyer*
Cohen, Howard A. *cardiologist*
Cohen, Jeffrey E. *lawyer*
Cohen, Joel Ephraim *biologist, educator, demographer*
Cohen, Jonathan Little *investment banker*
Cohen, Joshua Robert *lawyer*
Cohen, Mildred Thaler *art gallery director*
Cohen, Mitchell S. *political science professor*
Cohen, Noel Lee *otolaryngologist, educator*
Cohen, Patricia *editor, critic*
Cohen, Richard Martin *journalist*
Cohen, Robert Stephan *lawyer*
Cohen, Robin L. *lawyer*
Cohen, Seymour Martin *oncologist, hematologist, educator*
Cohen, Sidney Maximilian *neurologist*
Cohen, Stephen Frand *political scientist, writer, historian, educator, commentator*
Cohn, Bertram Josiah *portfolio manager*
Cohn, David Stephen *lawyer*
Cohn, Gary D. *diversified financial services company executive*
Cohn, Ian J. *architect*
Colacino, Michael *real estate company executive*
Colan, Joanne *video blogger, television personality*
Colburn, Martha *animator, filmmaker, artist*
Cole, Carolyn Jo *brokerage house executive*
Cole, Charles Dewey, Jr. *lawyer*
Cole, Kenneth D. *apparel designer*
Cole, Lewis George *lawyer*
Cole, Willie *artist*
Coleman, Charles Payson, Jr., (Payson Coleman) *lawyer*
Coleman, Donald Jackson *ophthalmologist, educator*
Coleman, Jo-Ann S.E. *social worker*
Coleman, Morton *oncologist, hematologist, educator*
Coleman, Ornette *jazz musician*
Coleman, Stuart H. *lawyer*
Colen, Dan *artist*
Colen, Helen Sass *plastic surgeon*
Colen, Stephen R. *plastic and reconstructive surgeon*
Coles, Joanna *magazine editor-in-chief*
Colibazzi, Tiziano *psychiatrist*
Colicchio, Tom *chef, food service executive*
Colihan, James Charles *lawyer*
Coll, John Peter, Jr. *lawyer*
Coller, Barry Spencer *internist, pathologist, hematologist, educator, department chairman*
Collier, Charlie *communications executive*
Collins, Elwood F. *lawyer*
Collins, J. Barclay, II, *lawyer, oil industry executive*
Collins, John F. *lawyer*
Collins, Kevin T. *lawyer*
Collins, Phil (Philip David Charles Collins) *singer, songwriter, drummer, record producer*
Collins, Richard Lawrence *editor*
Collinsworth, Cris *sportscaster, retired professional football player*
Colmes, Alan *political commentator, radio personality*
Colp, Norman Barry *artist, curator*
Comitas, Lambros *anthropologist, educator*
Compagnon, Antoine Marcel *French language educator*
Compte, Maria Emilia *physician, educator, administrator*
Comstock, Beth (Elizabeth J.) *marketing executive*
Cona, Louis *publishing executive*
Conarroe, Joel Osborne *foundation administrator, editor, educator*
Conboy, Kenneth *lawyer, retired federal judge*
Concannon, Christopher R. *stock exchange executive*
Conde, Yvonne M. *freelance journalist, writer*
Condron, Christopher M. (Kip) *investment company executive*
Conelli, Maria Ann *art educator, dean, architect*
Confessore, Nicholas *journalist*
Conigliaro, Laura Claire *securities analyst*
Conley, Terence P. *human resources specialist*
Conlon, Peggy Eileen *publisher*
Connelly, Michael *writer*
Connery, Michael M. *lawyer*
Connolly, John Joseph *publishing executive*
Connor, W(alter) Robert *foundation administrator, classicist, educator*
Connors, Peter J. *lawyer*
Conrad, Winthrop Brown, Jr. *lawyer*
Conroy, Pat (Donald Patrick Conroy) *writer*
Consagra, Sophie Chandler *academic administrator*
Considine, Jill M. *securities trader*
Consolo, Faith Hope *real estate company executive*
Constantine, Jan Friedman *lawyer*
Constantinides, Minas Spiros *otolaryngologist, plastic surgeon*
Conston, Henry Siegismund *lawyer*
Conway, E. Virgil *financial consultant, lawyer*
Conway, Kevin *actor, performing company executive*
Conway, Richard Francis *investment company executive*
Cook, Blanche Wiesen *historian, educator, journalist*
Cook, Ian M. *consumer products company executive*
Cook, Michael Lewis *lawyer*
Cook, Robert S., Jr. *lawyer*
Cooke, Warren F. *lawyer*
Cooley, Thomas F. *dean, economist, educator*
Cooney, Joan Ganz *broadcast executive, director*
Cooper, Anderson Hays *news correspondent, cable news anchor*
Cooper, Deborah Ellen *lawyer*
Cooper, Helene *editor*
Cooper, James D. *lawyer*
Cooper, Michael *journalist*
Cooper, Michael Anthony *lawyer*
Cooper, Stephen F. *management consultant, corporate recovery executive*
Cooper, Stephen Herbert *retired lawyer*
Cooperman, Leon G. *investment company executive*
Copeland, Michelle *plastic surgeon*
Coppotelli, Blake Albert *lawyer*
Corbin, Herbert Leonard *public relations executive, director*
Corbin, Sol Neil *lawyer*
Corcoran, Barbara *real estate company executive*
Corcoran, David *newspaper editor*
Corddry, Rob *comedian, actor*
Cordeiro, Peter Gabriel *surgeon, plastic surgeon*
Corgan, Billy (William Patrick Corgan) *musician*
Corigliano, John Paul *composer*
Cornelius, James Milton *pharmaceutical company executive*
Cornell, Henry *lawyer*
Cornell, John Robert *lawyer*
Corporon, John Robert *broadcast executive*
Correa, Daniel *energy executive, physics engineer*
Corrigan, E(dward) Gerald *diversified financial services company executive*
Corsaro, Frank Andrew *theater director*
Cortese, Edward *marketing and public relations executive*
Cortez, Ricardo Lee *investment management executive*
Cortina, Betty *magazine editor*
Cosgrave, Paul J. *commissioner*
Costa, Francisco *fashion designer*
Costas, Bob (Robert Quinlan Costas) *sportscaster*
Costikyan, Edward N. *lawyer*
Cotter, Holland *art critic, writer*
Coughlin, Christopher J. *financial executive*
Coulter, David A. *investment banker*
Coupland, Douglas Campbell *writer*
Couric, Katie (Katherine Anne Couric) *newscaster, journalist*
Covey, Lirio S. *research scientist*
Cowan, Rachel *rabbi*
Cowin, Stephen Corteen *biomedical engineering educator, consultant*
Cowing, Charles Ogden *talent agency executive*
Cowles, Charles *art dealer*
Cox, L. Kevin *human resources specialist*
Cox, Larry *human rights organization executive*
Cox, Peter *artist*
Coyle, Pat *professional basketball coach*
Craft, Randal Robert, Jr. *lawyer*
Craig, Charles Samuel *marketing educator*
Craig, Edward Vincent *orthopedic surgeon, educator*
Craig, Elizabeth Coyne *marketing executive*
Craig, Pamela J. *management consulting firm executive*
Cramb, Charles W. *cosmetics executive*
Cramer, Douglas Schoolfield *broadcasting executive*
Cramer, Edward Morton *lawyer, music company executive*
Cramer, Jim (James J. Cramer) *financial information executive*
Crames, Michael J. *lawyer*
Cranch, Laurence E. *lawyer, investment company executive*
Crane, Benjamin Field *lawyer*
Crane, Charles Grant *financial analyst*
Crane, Roger Ryan, Jr. *lawyer*
Crane, Stephen Charles *medical association executive*
Crary, Miner Dunham, Jr. *lawyer*
Crean, Peter Thomas *lawyer*
Creel, Thomas Leonard *lawyer*
Creswell, Julie *reporter*
Crichlow, David A. *lawyer*
Crier, Catherine *newscaster*
Crile, Susan *artist*
Crist, Judith *film and drama critic*
Critchlow, Charles Howard *lawyer*
Crittenden, Danielle Ann *writer, journalist*
Crittenden, Gary Lewis *diversified financial services company executive*
Croce, Arlene *critic*
Crockett, Andrew Duncan *bank executive*
Croft, Kathryn Delaine *social worker, consultant*
Cromwell, Oliver Dean *investment banker*
Cronin, Anne *editor*
Cronin, Doreen *writer, former lawyer*
Cronkite, Walter *radio and television news correspondent*
Cross, George Alan Martin *biochemistry professor, researcher*
Cross, Theodore Lamont *publisher, author*
Crouch, Stanley *writer, musician*
Crovitz, Louis Gordon *publishing executive, journalist, lawyer*
Crowdus, Gary Alan *film company executive*
Crown, Roberta *artist, educator*
Cruz, Juan-Carlos *chef*
Cruz, Zoe *diversified financial services company executive*
Crystal, J. Scott *publishing executive*
Crystal, James William *insurance company executive*
Cubitto, Robert John *lawyer*
Cucin, Robert Louis *plastic surgeon, lawyer*
Cucullu, Santiago *artist*
Cuiffo, Frank Wayne *lawyer*
Culhane, Stephen (David Stephen King Culhane) *lawyer*
Cumming, Ian M. *holding company executive*
Cummings, John W. *diversified financial services company executive*
Cummins, Herman Zachary *physicist*
Cundiff, Victoria Anne *lawyer*
Cuneo, Donald Lane *lawyer, educator*
Cunha, Mark Geoffrey *lawyer*
Cunningham, Francis *artist*
Cunningham, Merce *performing company executive, dancer*
Cunningham-Rundles, Charlotte *physician, educator*
Cuomo, Chris(topher) *newscaster, lawyer*
Cuomo, Mario Matthew *lawyer, former governor*
Cuozzo, Steven David *newspaper editor*
Curiel, Carolyn *former ambassador*
Curley, Thomas *newspaper executive*
Curley, Walter Joseph Patrick *diplomat, investment banker*
Curry, Ann *correspondent, anchor*
Curry, Boykin (Ravenel Boykin Curry IV) *investment manager*
Curry, Jane Louise *writer*
Curtin, Jane Therese *actress, writer*
Curtis, Paul James *performance artist, director*
Curtis, Susan M. *lawyer*
Cusack, John T. *lawyer*
Cushing, Charles R. *architectural firm executive*
Cutler, Bruce *lawyer*
Cutler, Laurence Stephan *architect, museum administrator, writer, advertising executive, educator*
Cutler, Stephen M. *lawyer, former federal agency administrator*
Czajka, James Vincent *architect*
Czárán, Lóránt *geographer, consultant*
Czepiel, Lori Anne *lawyer*
Dabney, H. Slayton, Jr. *lawyer*
Dadakis, John D. *lawyer*
Dahan, Andre *telecommunications industry executive*
Dahl, Jonathan *magazine editor-in-chief*
Daitz, Ronald Frederick *lawyer*
Dajani, Virginia *art association administrator*
Dales, Samuel *microbiologist, virologist, educator*
D'Alessio, Frederick D. *telecommunications company executive*
Daley, Suzanne *editor*
Dallas, William Moffit, Jr. *lawyer*
Dallen, Russell Morris, Jr. *investment company and publishing company executive, lawyer*
Dalton, Dennis Gilmore *political science professor*
Daltrey, Roger Harry *singer*
Daly, Cheryl *communications and broadcast executive*
D'Amato, Alfonse M. *lawyer, senator*
d'Amboise, Jacques Joseph *former dancer, choreographer, educator, director*
D'Ambrosio, Ralph G. *communications systems company executive*
D'Amelio, Frank Anthony *pharmaceutical executive, former telecommunications industry executive*
Dana, F(rank) Mitchell *theatrical lighting designer*
Dana, Will *editor*
Dandonoli, Patricia A. *not-for-profit fundraiser*
D'Angelo, Joseph Francis *publishing executive*
Daniel, David Ronald *management consultant*
Daniel, Samuel J. *hospital administrator, medical educator*
Daniels, George Benjamin *federal judge*
Daniels, Jennifer M. *lawyer*
Daniels, Joseph Carl *foundation administrator*
Daniels, Randy A. *investment company executive, former state official*
Daniels, Susanne *broadcast executive*
Danielson, John M. *educational consultant, former federal agency administrator*
Danilow, Greg A. *lawyer*
Danishefsky, Samuel J. *chemistry professor*
Danitz, Marilynn Patricia *choreographer, video specialist*
Dankner, Jay Warren *lawyer*
Dannhauser, Stephen J. *lawyer*
Dano, Linda *actress*
Dansky, Ira M. *lawyer*
Danto, Arthur Coleman *writer, philosopher, critic*
Danza, Tony *actor*
Danziger, Lucy *editor*
Dargis, Manohla *film critic*
Darlington, Henry, Jr. *retired investment broker*
Darnell, James Edwin, Jr. *molecular biologist, educator*
Darrell, Norris, Jr. *lawyer*
Darrow, Jill E(llen) *lawyer*
Darst, David Martin *investment banker, writer, educator*
Das, Kalyan *lawyer*
Daubs, James Daniel *educational assessment specialist*
Dauman, Philippe P. *multi media company executive*
Dauten, Dale Alan *newspaper columnist*
Davenport, Kirk Addison *lawyer*
David, Hal *lyricist*
David, Miles *marketing executive*
David, Reuben *lawyer*
David, Theoharis Lambros *architect, educator*
Davidovsky, Mario *retired composer*
Davidson, Anthony R. *education educator, consultant*
Davidson, Donald William *advertising executive*
Davidson, Douglas E. *lawyer*
Davidson, George Allan *lawyer*
Davidson, Nancy Brachman *artist, educator*
Davidson, Robert Bruce *retired lawyer*
Davidson, Sheila Kearney *lawyer, insurance company executive*
David-Weill, Michel Alexandre *retired investment banker*
Davis, Christopher James *television producer*

Davis, Clive Jay *record company executive*
Davis, D. Lavelda *dean, academic administrator*
Davis, Evan Anderson *lawyer*
Davis, Florence Ann *lawyer*
Davis, George Linn *banker*
Davis, Gordon J. *lawyer*
Davis, J. Morton *investment company executive, venture capitalist, economist*
Davis, Jacqueline Zurat *library director, arts administrator*
Davis, Jessica G. *geneticist*
Davis, Jordan S. *venture capitalist*
Davis, Karen *insurance company executive, educator*
Davis, Kenneth Leon *psychiatrist, pharmacologist, medical educator*
Davis, Kevin E. *law educator*
Davis, Lisa E. *lawyer*
Davis, Michael Steven *lawyer*
Davis, Owen Kidder *physician, endocrinologist*
Davis, Patti *writer*
Davis, Richard Joel *former government official, lawyer*
Davis, Richard Ralph *lawyer*
Davis, Trayton M. *lawyer*
Davison, Bruce *actor*
Davoren, Peter J. *construction executive*
Day, James *television executive*
Dean, Alan *lawyer*
De Angelis, Judy *anchorwoman*
Deans, Patricia Herrmann *investment banker*
Deaver, James T.H. *lawyer*
DeBellevue, Lucky *sculptor*
Debiec, Jacek *psychiatrist, research scientist, educator*
Debo, Vincent Joseph *lawyer, director, manufacturing executive*
DeBow, Jay Howard Camden *public relations executive*
Debs, Richard A. *investment banker*
DeCarava, Roy R. *photographer, educator*
DeChiara, Dominick *lawyer*
Decter, Midge *writer*
Deem, George *artist*
Deen, Paula H. *television personality, restaurant owner, chef*
Deering, Suzy *advertising executive*
Defendi, Vittorio *medical association administrator, pathologist*
Degener, Carol M. *lawyer*
DeGregorio, Carlo *social studies educator*
Dehn, Cathleen Patterson *health facility administrator*
Dehn, James Keith *investment company executive*
de Kenessey, Stefania Maria *composer*
Delaney, Jeffrey J. *lawyer*
Delaney, Robert Vincent *former gas company executive, economic development consultant*
de Lange, Titia *research scientist, educator*
de la Renta, Oscar *fashion designer*
de Lasa, José M. *lawyer*
Del Forno, Anton *classical guitarist, recording artist, composer, educator*
Delikat, Michael *lawyer*
De Lisi, Nancy *corporate financial executive*
Della Rocca, Steven *lawyer*
DelliBovi, Alfred A. *bank executive, former federal agency administrator*
Delmer, Deborah P. *science educator*
Del Tufo, Robert J. *lawyer, former state attorney general*
DeMasi, Karin A. *lawyer*
deMause, Lloyd *psychologist*
de Menil, Lois Pattison *historian, philanthropist*
Demeny, Paul George *demographer, researcher*
Demetrios, (Demetrios Trakatellis) *archbishop*
Demirtas, K. Ozgur *finance educator*
DeMonte, Claudia Ann *artist, educator*
de Montebello, Philippe Lannes *museum director*
De Natale, Andrew Peter *lawyer*
DeNiro, Mary Lyn S. *lawyer*
Denker, Henry *playwright, author, director*
Denmark, Bernhardt *manufacturing executive*
Denmark, Florence Harriet Levin *psychology professor*
Denmark, Stanley Jay *orthodontist*
Dennis, Diane Joy Milam *retired architect*
Dennis, Donna Frances *sculptor, art educator*
Dennis, Everette Eugene, Jr. *foundation executive, educator, writer*
Dennis, Willie E. *lawyer*
Dennison, Lisa *auction house executive*
Denno, Deborah W. *law educator*
de Notaristefani, Carlo *pharmaceutical executive*
Denson, J. Russell *publishing executive*
Denson, Terry *telecommunications industry executive*
Denton, Nick *publishing executive*
DeNunzio, David Ames *investment banker*
DeOrchis, Vincent Moore *lawyer*
DePreist, James Anderson *conductor*
de Ravel d'Esclapon, Pierre F. *lawyer*
Derman, Cyrus *mathematical statistician*
Derow, Peter Alfred *publishing executive*
Derzaw, Richard Lawrence *lawyer*
Desai, Kiran *writer*
Desai, Vishakha N. *professional society administrator*
De Sear, Edward Marshall *lawyer*
Desiato, Michael *editor-in-chief*
Desloge, Rosemary Byrne *otolaryngologist, educator*
Desmarais, John M. *lawyer*
Desmond, Laura *advertising executive*
Desnick, Robert John *human geneticist*
Despins, Luc *lawyer*
Detjen, David Wheeler *lawyer*
Deull, Charles Brian *lawyer, former publishing executive*
Deutsch, Ayala *sports association executive, lawyer, educator*
Deutsch, Claudia *reporter*
Deutsch, David Neil *investment banker*
Deutsch, Donny *advertising executive*
Deutsch, Eric J. *real estate developer, urban planner*
Deutsch, Martin Bernard Joseph *editor, publishing executive*
DeVard, Jerri *marketing professional*
Deveraux, Jude (Jude Gilliam White) *writer*
De Vido, Alfredo Eduardo *architect*
DeVita, M. Christine *foundation administrator*
Devitre, Dinyar S. *consumer products company and corporate financial executive*
De Vivo, Darryl Claude *pediatrician, neurologist*
Devlin, Robert Manning *diversified financial services company executive*
DeVoe, David F., Sr. *publishing executive*
DeWoody, Beth Rudin *film producer*
Dhondt, Steven Thomas *development officer*
Diamond, Bernard Robin *lawyer*
Diamond, Brian *lawyer*
Diamond, David Howard *lawyer*
Diamond, Heidi Janice *marketing professional*
Diamond, Matthew C. *media and marketing company executive*
Diamonstein-Spielvogel, Barbaralee *writer*
Di Angelo, Christopher J. *lawyer*
Dias Griffin, Anne *investment advisor*
Diaz, Angela *pediatrician, educator*
Diaz-Cruz, Mario III *lawyer*
DiBiasio, Adolf R. *entertainment company executive*
DiBlasi, Gandolfo Vincent *lawyer*
Didion, Joan *writer*
Diercksen, John W. *telecommunications industry executive*
Dierdorf, Daniel Lee (Dan Dierdorf) *sports commentator, football analyst, former professional football player*
Dietl, Bo (Richard A. Dietl) *private investigator, former police officer*
Diggins, Peter Sheehan *arts administrator*
Diker, Charles M. *investment advisor*
Dikkers, Scott *editor*
Dillard, Annie *writer*
Diller, Barry *Internet company executive*
DiLorenzo, Louis Patrick *lawyer*
DiMaggio, Frank Louis *civil engineering educator*
Di Meo, Dominick *artist, sculptor, painter*
Di Mitri, Piero *fashion designer*
Dimling, John Arthur *marketing executive*
Dimon, Jamie (James L. Dimon) *diversified financial services company executive*
Dine, Jeffrey Malcolm *lawyer*
Dinerman, Miriam *social work educator*
Dinerstein, Robert Charles *lawyer, former bank executive*
Dinnerstein, Simone *pianist*
Di Palma, Joseph Alphonse *investment company executive, lawyer*
DiPiazza, Samuel A., Jr. *finance company executive*
DiResta, Gene Robert *biomedical researcher, director*
Disa, Joseph James *plastic surgeon*
DiSalvatore, William P. *lawyer*
DiSciullo, Alan Michael *lawyer*
Diskant, Gregory L. *lawyer*
Disney, Anthea *publishing executive*
Divon, Michael Y. *obstetrician and gynecologist*
Dixon, Wendy L. *pharmaceutical executive*
Dlugoff, Marc Alan *lawyer*
Dobbins, David Foster *lawyer*
Dobbs, John Barnes *artist, educator*
Dobell, Byron Maxwell *magazine consultant*
Dobkin, Jake *online publishing executive, blogger*
Dobrin, Tory *performing company executive, dancer*
Dobrof, Rose Wiesman *gerontology educator*
Doctoroff, Daniel L. *municipal official*
Doctorow, E.L. (Edgar Lawrence) *writer, English educator*
Dodge, Geoffrey A. *publishing executive*
Dodson, Howard *research center administrator*
Doerfler, Ronald John *publishing executive*
Doherty, Thomas *publisher*
Dohrenwend, Bruce Philip *epidemiologist, social sciences educator*
Dokos, Daniel S. *lawyer*
Dolan, Raymond Bernard *insurance company executive, director*
Domino, Fats (Antoine Domino) *pianist, singer, songwriter*
Domowitz, Ian *finance company executive*
Donaghy, James K. *construction executive, contractor*
Donahue, Lisa J. *corporate financial executive, consultant*
Donald, Arnold W. *health science association administrator, former food products executive*
Donald, Norman Henderson III *lawyer*
Donaldson, John Cecil, Jr. *consumer products company executive*
Donneson, Seena Sand *artist*
Donoghue, Denis *language professional, educator*
Donovan, Richard Edward *lawyer*
Doody, John *lawyer*
Dooley, Douglas John *bank executive*
Dooley, Thomas E. *multi media company executive*
Doonan, Simon *window dresser, creative director*
Dooner, John Joseph, Jr. *advertising executive*
Dopf, Glenn William *lawyer*
Dorfman, Howard David *pathologist, educator*
Dorkey, Charles E. III *lawyer*
Dormann, Henry O. *magazine publisher*
Dorsen, Norman *lawyer, educator*
Dorsett, Burt *investment company executive*
Dotson, Robert Charles (Bob Dotson) *news correspondent*
Doud, Randall H. *lawyer*
Douglas, James McCrystal *lawyer*
Douglas, Peter Roderick *lawyer*
Dowell, James Thomas *artist, filmmaker*
Dowling, Danielle *writer*
Downes, Lawrence *editor*
Downey, John Alexander *physician, educator*
Downs, Hugh Malcolm *retired radio and television broadcaster*
Doyle, Eugenie Fleri *pediatrician, cardiologist, educator*
Doyle, John *artistic director, designer*
Doyle, Joseph Anthony *retired lawyer*
Doyle, Michael W. *international official, educator*
Doyle, Paul Francis *lawyer*
Dozier, Kimberly *news correspondent*
Dranovsky, Alex *psychiatrist, researcher*
Draper, James David *art museum curator*
Drapkin, Donald G. *venture capitalist*
Dratch, Rachel *comedienne, actress*
Drayer, Burton Paul *hospital administrator, neuroradiologist*
Drebsky, Dennis Jay *lawyer*
Dreier, Marc S. *lawyer*
Dreifus, Claudia *journalist, educator*
Dreiling, Richard W. *retail executive*
Dresner, Byron *lawyer*
Drew, Ina R. *bank executive*
Drewes, Robert W. *communications systems company executive*
Drexler, Mickey (Millard Steven) *retail executive*
Driscoll, Karen *communications executive*
Driver, Martha Westcott *literature educator, researcher, writer*
Driver, Tom Faw *theologian, writer, advocate*
Droga, David *advertising executive*
Dru, Jean-Marie Paul *advertising executive*
Drucker, Jacquelin F. *lawyer, arbitrator, writer*
Drucker, Jonathan *lawyer*
Drucker, Richard Allen *lawyer*
Drum, Sydney Maria *artist*
Drury, Chris *professional hockey player*
Druskin, Robert A. *diversified financial services company executive*
Drzik, John P. *management consulting firm executive*
D'Souza, Rohit *investment company executive*
Dubin, James Michael *lawyer*
Dubin, Morton Donald, II, *lawyer*
Du Boff, Jill Bonnie Candise *sound effects artist*
Dubois, Michel *anesthesiologist*
Dubrow, John *artist*
Dubuc, Nancy *communications executive*
Ducasse, Alain *chef*
Duch, Stephen *corporate financial executive*
Duchin, Peter Oelrichs *musician*
Duda, Michael *advertising executive*
Dudley, William C. *economist*
Duff, Gill *advertising executive*
Duff, Hilary Ann *singer, actress*
Duff, John Ewing *sculptor*
Duff, William Brandon *lawyer*
Duffy, Edmund Charles *lawyer*
Duffy, James Henry *writer, retired lawyer*
Duffy, Kevin Thomas *federal judge*
Duffy, W. Leslie *lawyer*
Dugger, Celia Williams *journalist*
Dukakis, Olympia *actress*
Duke, Anthony Drexel *retired sociologist, educator, philanthropist*
Duke, Ellen (Bebe Duke) *bank executive*
Dukmejian, Michael *publishing executive*
Dulaine, Pierre *ballroom dancer*
Dullea, Keir *actor*
Du Mont, Nicolas *psychiatrist, educator*
Duncan, Patricia *lawyer, broadcast executive*
Duncan, Pearl Rose *writer*
Dunham, Wolcott Balestier, Jr. *lawyer*
Dunkelman, Loretta *artist*
Dunn, James W. *communications systems company executive*
Dunn, Martin *editor-in-chief*
Dunn, M(orris) Douglas *lawyer*
Dunn, Thomas E. *lawyer*
Dunne, Diane C. *marketing professional*
Dunne, Dominick *writer*
Dunning, Jennifer *dance critic, reporter*
Dunst, Laurence David *advertising executive*
Du Prez, John *composer*
Dupri, Jermaine *recording industry executive, music producer*
DuPuy, Bob (Robert A. DuPuy) *major league baseball executive*
Duran, George *chef*
Durang, Christopher *actor, playwright*
Durkin, Dorothy Angela *university official*
Durrant, M. Patricia *diplomat*
Dusick, Ryan Michael *musician*
Dwek, Cyril S. *bank executive*
Dworetzky, Murray *retired physician, educator*
Dworkin, Ronald Myles *law educator*
Dwyer, Jim *reporter, columnist*
Dylan, Bob (Robert Allen Zimmerman) *singer, musician*
Dyyon, Mario (LeRoy Frazier) *artist*
Eaker, Sherry Ellen *editor*
Eakins, William Shannon *lawyer*
Earl, Christopher D. *health products executive*
Earle, Victor Montagne III *lawyer*
Earling, Debra Magpie *writer, educator*
Eaton, Richard Kenyon *federal judge*
Ebersol, Dick (Duncan Dickie Ebersol) *television broadcasting executive*
Eckert, Allan Wesley *writer*
Eckhardt, Laurel Ann *biologist, researcher, educator*
Eckman, Fern Marja *journalist*
Edelman, Judith H. *architect*
Edelman, Scott A. *lawyer*
Edelson, David Bick *diversified holding company executive*
Edelson, Gilbert Seymour *lawyer*
Edelstein, Barbara A. *radiologist*
Edelstein, David Robert *medical educator*
Edgar, Harold Simmons Hull *legal educator*
Edgerley, Susan *editor*
Edidin, Peter *editor*
Edlin, Richard A. *lawyer*
Edlow, Kenneth Lewis *security firm executive*
Edmiston, Mark Morton *publishing company executive*
Edsall, Thomas Byrne *reporter*
Edsparr, Patrik L. *diversified financial services company executive*
Edward, Jeffrey N. *diversified financial services company executive*
Edwards, Franklin Richard *economist, educator, consultant*
Edwards, Harold Mortimer *mathematics professor*
Edwards, Jeffrey N. *investment company executive*
Effron, Blair Wayne *investment advisor*
Egen, Maureen Mahon *publishing executive*
Egielski, Richard *illustrator*
Ehrenbard, Robert *lawyer*
Ehrenkranz, Joel S. *lawyer*
Eichenwald, Kurt *writer*
Einbond, Linda Saxe *biologist, researcher*
Einhorn, David Allen *lawyer*
Einiger, Carol Blum *investment company executive*
Eins, Stefan *artist, curator, science researcher, writer*
Einstein, Steven Henry *lawyer, investment banker*
Eisen, LizabethAnn R. *lawyer*
Eisen, Robert L. *lawyer*
Eisenberg, Barbara Anne K. *lawyer*
Eisenberg, Herbert *lawyer*
Eisenberg, Lee B. *writer*
Eisenberg, Sonja Miriam *artist*
Eisenman, Peter David *architect, educator*
Eisenstadt, G. Michael *diplomat, writer, educator, researcher*
Eisert, Edward Gaver *lawyer*
Eisler, Edith *violinist, educator*
Eisler, Susan Krawetz *advertising executive*
Eitel, Mitchell Scott *lawyer*
Elder, Janet *editor*
Elderfield, John *art historian, museum curator*
Eldredge, Niles *curator, paleontologist*
Elinson, Jack *social sciences educator*
Elkes, Terrence Allen *communications executive*
Elkin, Judith *lawyer*
Elkin, Michael S. *lawyer*
Ellenhorn, David N. *lawyer*
Ellenson, David *college president*
Ellerbee, Linda (Linda Jane Smith) *reporter*
Elliman, Christopher J. (Kim Elliman) *investment company executive*
Ellin, Doug *film producer, television producer, television director, writer*
Ellington, Mercedes *performing company executive, choreographer, director, producer, educator*
Ellingwood, Susan *editor*
Elliot, Cameron Robert *lawyer*
Elliott, Andrea *reporter*
Elliott, David J. *music educator*
Elliott, Missy (Melissa Arnette Elliot) *musician*
Elliott, Steven G. *bank executive*
Ellis, Bret Easton *writer*
Ellis, Lisa *music company executive*
Ellis, Rosemary *editor-in-chief*
Ellis, Ross *non-profit organization executive*
Ellis, Scott *theatrical director*
Ellison, Nicholas Howell *literary agent*
Ellroy, James *writer*
Elmer, Russell S. *diversified financial services company executive, lawyer*
Elmore, Leonard Joseph *lawyer*
Elsen, Jon *editor*
Elsen, Sheldon Howard *lawyer*
Emme, (Emme Aronson) *model, apparel designer*
Emmerich, Adam Oliver *lawyer*
Emmerich, Toby *film company executive*
Emmrich, Stuart J. *editor*
Enders, Elizabeth McGuire *artist*
Engel, Alison Lange *marketing executive*
Engel, Amy J. *corporate financial executive*
Engel, Ralph Manuel *lawyer*
Engelberg, Gail May *fine arts patron*
Englander, Israel A. *financier*
Engle, Robert F. *finance educator*
English, Mark *artist*
English, Thomas Francis *lawyer*
Engstrom, Erik *publishing executive*
Ennis, Ronald Dov *radiation oncologist*
Ensler, Eve *playwright, actress*
Entwistle, Andrew John *lawyer, consultant*
Epling, Richard Louis *lawyer*
Epstein, Cynthia Fuchs *sociology educator, writer*
Epstein, Jeremy G. *lawyer*
Epstein, Matthew *opera company director*
Epstein, Melvin *lawyer*
Epstein, Michael Alan *lawyer*
Epstein, Stuart Joel *investment banker*
Ercklentz, Alexander Tonio *investment company executive*
Ercklentz, Enno Wilhelm, Jr. *lawyer*
Erdoes, Mary Callahan *bank executive*
Erickson, Mitchell Drake *chemist, environmental scientist*
Ericson, Robert Walter *lawyer*
Erikson, Robert S. *political science professor*
Erlanger, Bernard Ferdinand *biochemist, educator*
Erlenmeyer-Kimling, L. *psychiatrist, researcher*
Ernst, John Louis *management consultant*
Errico, R. Christopher *investment advisor*
Eschenbach, Christoph *conductor, musician, music director*
Esnault, Tony *chef*
Esposito, Louis *real estate developer*
Esposito, Richard Joseph *journalist, executive*
Essig, Jack *magazine publishing executive*
Estabrook, Alison *surgeon, educator*
Esterow, Milton *publishing executive*
Estlund, Cynthia *law educator*
Estraikh, Gennady *humanities educator*
Estreicher, Samuel *lawyer, educator*
Ethan, Carol Baehr *psychotherapist, psychoanalyst*
Ettinger, John Riche *lawyer*
Evanovich, Janet *writer*
Evans, Alfred Lee, Jr. *advertising executive*
Evans, Douglas Hayward *lawyer*
Evans, Greg *cartoonist*

Evans, Sir Harold Matthew *editor, publisher, writer*
Evans, Heidi *journalist*
Evans, John Thomas *lawyer*
Evans, Mark Ira *obstetrician, geneticist*
Evans, Martin Frederic *lawyer*
Evans, Mary Johnston *corporate director*
Evarts, William Maxwell, Jr. *lawyer*
Evnin, Anthony Basil *venture capital investor*
Ewing-Mulligan, Mary *food products executive*
Faber, Neil *advertising executive*
Faber, Peter Lewis *lawyer*
Faber, Robert Charles *lawyer*
Fabian, Larry Louis *academic administrator*
Fabrikant, Geraldine *journalist*
Fader, Bruce E. *lawyer*
Fagen, Leslie Gordon *lawyer*
Fager, Jeffrey *broadcast executive*
Fagin, Allen Ian *lawyer*
Fagin, Claire Mintzer *nursing administrator, educator*
Fagin, Dan *science and environmental writer, reporter*
Fahey, James Edward *brokerage house executive*
Fahim, Kareem *journalist*
Fahn, Stanley *neurologist, educator*
Fajors, Nique *interactive entertainment executive*
Fakahany, Ahmass L. *investment company executive*
Falai, Tacopo *chef*
Falk, Edgar Alan *public relations consulting executive, writer*
Falkenrath, Richard A. *protective services official*
Fallek, Andrew Michael *lawyer*
Fallows, James Mackenzie *journalist*
Fantasia, (Fantasia Monique Barrino) *singer*
Farah, Roger N. *retail company executive*
Farber, Donald Clifford *lawyer, educator*
Farber, Jeffrey Mark *diversified financial services company executive*
Farber, John J. *chemical company executive*
Farber, Seth C. *lawyer*
Fargis, Paul McKenna *publisher, publishing executive, consultant, book developer*
Farhi, Jane-Iris *cardiologist, internist*
Farinelli, Jean L. *management consultant*
Farino, Julian *television director, film director, television producer*
Faris, George N. *management consultant*
Farley, Carole *soprano*
Farley, Katherine G. *real estate company executive*
Farley, Terrence Michael *banker*
Farley, Thomas W. *stock exchange executive*
Farrell, Herman D., Jr., (Denny Farrell) *state legislator, former political organization administrator*
Fasman, Zachary Dean *lawyer*
Fasnacht, Heide Ann *artist, educator*
Fass, Peter Michael *lawyer, educator*
Fast, Julius *writer, editor*
Fastow, Jay N. *lawyer*
Fathallah, Hassana *research scientist*
Faulkner, Walter Thomas *lawyer, director*
Fausel, Alan *art appraiser*
Favorule, Denise *publishing executive*
Fawcett, Christopher Babcock *civil engineer, construction and water resources company executive*
Faxon, Roger *music company executive*
Fazio, Vic (Victor Herbert Fazio Jr.) *lawyer, former congressman*
Fears, Linda *editor-in-chief*
Feczko, Joe *cosmetics executive*
Feczko, Joseph M. *pharmaceutical executive*
Feder, Arthur A. *lawyer, association administrator*
Feder, Barnaby *reporter*
Feder, Benjamin *computer game company executive*
Feder, Harry Simon *bank executive*
Feder, Saul E. *lawyer*
Federle, Michael *publishing executive*
Feigen, Richard L. *art dealer, collector, writer*
Feiler, William S. *lawyer*
Feinberg, Wilfred *federal judge*
Feintuch, Henry Philip *public relations executive*
Feit, Barberi Paull *composer, lyricist, psychotherapist, writer*
Feit, Glenn Martin *lawyer*
Feld, Eliot *dancer, choreographer, performing company executive*
Feldberg, Meyer *investment advisor, university dean emeritus*
Feldberg, Michael Svetkey *lawyer*
Felder, Raoul Lionel *lawyer*
Feldman, Allan Roy *corporate development and marketing executive*
Feldman, Daniel Lee *former state official*
Feldman, Franklin *retired lawyer, printmaker*
Feldman, Helaine *editor, public relations associate*
Feldman, Noah *law educator*
Feldman, Ronald Arthur *sociologist, educator, social worker*
Feldman, Samuel Mitchell *neuroscientist, educator*
Felsher, Steven G. *advertising executive, lawyer*
Feltus, Alan Evan *artist*
Feniger, Jerome Roland, Jr. *broadcast executive*
Fenn, Patrick B. *lawyer*
Fenster, Albert M. *lawyer*
Fensterstock, Blair Courtney *lawyer*
Ferber, Linda S. *museum director*
Feretic, Eileen Susan *editor*
Ferguson, Kitty Gail *writer, educator*
Ferguson, Milton Carr, Jr. *lawyer*
Ferguson, Sarah *The Duchess of York*
Fernandes, Jeanne Mary *retired human resources specialist*
Fernandez, James *retail products executive*
Fernandez, Jose Walfredo *lawyer, department chairman*
Fernández, Teresita *sculptor*
Fernandez de Cordova, Sergio Alonso *advertising executive, publishing executive*
Ferrante, Joan Marguerite *language and literature educator, writer*
Ferraro, Geraldine Anne *lobbyist, former congresswoman*
Ferriero, David S. *library director*
Fertig, Howard *publishing executive*
Fertitta, George A. *marketing executive*
Feuerman, Carole A. *sculptor, artist*
Fewell, Charles Kenneth, Jr. *lawyer*
Fey, Albert Eugene *lawyer*
Feyer, Thomas *editor*
Fialkoff, Francine Susan *editor*
Field, Steven Philip *medical educator*
Fielding, Helen *writer*
Fields, Felicia P. *actress*
Fifty Cent, (Curtis James Jackson) *rap artist*
Fili-Krushel, Patricia *media company executive*
Filimonov, Mikhail Anatolyevitch *investment company executive*
Filkins, Dexter Price *newspaper reporter*
Filler, Ronald Howard *lawyer*
Finch, Edward Ridley, Jr. *lawyer, educator, retired diplomat, ambassador*
Finch, Lawrence Nelson, II, *computer scientist, consultant*
Findakly, Hani K. *investment company executive*
Findlay, Michael Alistair *art dealer, poet*
Fine, Drew S. *lawyer*
Fine, Jo Renée *management consultant*
Fine, Kit *philosophy educator*
Fineman, Steven E. *lawyer*
Fink, Laurence D. *diversified financial services company executive*
Fink, Matthew E. *health facility executive, educator*
Fink, Robert Steven *lawyer, writer, educator*
Finkelson, Allen *lawyer*
Finkelstein, Allen Lewis *lawyer*
Finkelstein, Bernard *lawyer*
Finkelstein, David S. *lawyer*
Finkelstein, Ira Allen *lawyer*
Finkelstein, James A. *media executive*
Finkelstein, Stuart M. *lawyer*
Finley, John G. *lawyer*
Finley, Skip *communications executive*
Finn, Brian D. *financial services executive*
Finn, Edwin Anthony, Jr. *publishing executive*
Finn, Peter *public relations executive*
Finn, Peter Michael *broadcast executive*
Finnerty, Joseph Gregory III *lawyer*
Fins, Joseph Jack *internist, medical ethicist*
Finzi, Benjamin *communications executive*
Fiori, Pamela *publishing executive, writer*
Fiorilla di Santa Croce, John Leopoldo *investment company executive, lawyer*
Firestone, David E. *editor*
Firestone, Louise *lawyer*
First, Michael Bruce *psychiatrist, educator*
Firth, Nicholas *recording industry executive*
Fischbach, Gerald D. *dean, neurobiology educator*
Fischer, Carl *photographer, graphic designer, actor*
Fischer, Herbert Steven *social studies educator*
Fischer, Joseph L. *pharmaceutical executive*
Fischer, Mark David *lawyer*
Fishbein, Peter Melvin *lawyer*
Fisher, Ann Bailen *lawyer*
Fisher, Arnold L. *real estate company executive*
Fisher, Arthur *magazine editor*
Fisher, Joely *actress*
Fisher, Kenneth *real estate company executive*
Fisher, Laura Lani *physician, medical educator*
Fisher, Peter R. *investment company executive, former federal agency administrator*
Fisher, Robert I. *lawyer*
Fisher, Steven *real estate company executive*
Fisher, Vernon *artist, educator*
Fisher, Winston Crawford *real estate company executive*
Fishman, Alan H. *mortgage company and former bank executive*
Fishman, Ellen Beth *lawyer*
Fishman, Fred Norman *lawyer*
Fishman, Steven T. *psychologist*
Fiske, Robert Bishop, Jr. *lawyer, former prosecutor*
Fitch, Janet *writer*
Fitts, Nelson Orus *lawyer*
FitzPatrick, Daniel M. *trust company executive, lawyer*
FitzPatrick, James A., Jr. *lawyer*
Fitzpatrick, Joseph Mark *lawyer*
Flack, Roberta *singer*
Flaherty, Clementina Santi *corporate communications specialist, writer*
Flaherty, Pamela Potter *bank executive*
Flaherty, Stephen *composer, orchestrator*
Flamm, Leonard N(athan) *lawyer*
Flanagan, Sean Patrick *publishing executive*
Flanders, Karen *consumer products company executive*
Flannery, Kate *actress*
Flaum, Sander Allen *advertising and marketing executive*
Flax, Herschel *surgeon*
Flay, Bobby *chef, restaurateur*
Fleder, Robert Charles *lawyer*
Fleischer, Arthur, Jr. *lawyer*
Fleischman, Albert Sidney (Sid Fleischman) *writer*
Fleischman, Barbara Greenberg *public relations consultant*
Fleischman, Edward Hirsh *lawyer, consultant*
Fleischman, Keith M. *lawyer*
Fleischmann, Dennis C. *lawyer*
Fleisher, Michael D. *music company executive*
Fleming, Gregory James *investment company executive*
Fleming, Peter Emmet, Jr. *lawyer*
Fleming, Renée L. *opera singer*
Fleming, Ronald A. *lawyer*
Flescher, Sharon *art historian, educator*
Fletcher, Anthony Lee *lawyer*
Fletcher, Harry George III *library director*
Flinn, Michael de Vlaming *investment company executive*
Flint, George Squire *lawyer*
Flom, Jason *music company executive*
Flom, Joseph Harold *lawyer*
Flood, Richard Sidney *curator*
Florence, Tyler *chef*
Florescue, Leonard George *lawyer*
Floret, Evelyn *sculptor*
Florio, Steven T. *magazine executive*
Florio, Thomas A. *publishing executive*
Flory, Marjorie Anne *writer, editor*
Flowers, Brandon Richard *singer*
Flowers, J. Christopher *investment banker*
Fluhr, Howard *consulting firm executive*
Flumenbaum, Martin *lawyer*
Flynn, John J. *museum curator*
Flynn, Timothy P. *finance company executive*
Flynn, William Joseph *insurance company executive*
Fogel, Irving Martin *consulting engineer*
Fogg, Blaine Viles *lawyer*
Fogg, William V. *lawyer*
Fogge, Len *advertising executive*
Fogler, Dan *actor*
Folio, James M. *publishing executive*
Folta, Carl D. *communications executive*
Foner, Eric *historian, educator*
Fontaine, John C. *foundation administrator, lawyer, former newspaper company executive*
Fontana, Thomas Michael *television producer, scriptwriter*
Forbes, Christopher (Kip Forbes) *publisher*
Forbes, Jim (James D. Forbes) *investment banker*
Forbes, Sally *researcher, editor, curator*
Forbes, Steve (Malcolm Stevenson Forbes Jr.) *publishing executive*
Forbes, Timothy Carter *publishing executive*
Force, Pierre Marie *French language and literature educator*
Ford, Eileen Otte (Mrs. Gerard W. Ford) *modeling agency executive*
Ford, Jack *lawyer, news correspondent*
Ford, Mark Patrick *publishing executive*
Ford, Paul B. *lawyer*
Ford, Ralph A. *lawyer, moving and relocation company executive*
Forden, Diane Claire *magazine editor*
Forelle, Charles *reporter*
Foreman, Richard *theater director, playwright*
Forese, Laura Lee *hospital administrator, orthopedist*
Formento, Daniel *radio company executive, writer*
Forrest, David Vickers *psychiatrist, educator*
Forrest, Katherine B. *lawyer*
Forrest, Kenneth B. *lawyer*
Forsberg, Myra *editor*
Forstadt, Joseph Lawrence *lawyer*
Forster, Arnold *lawyer, author*
Fortner, Joseph Gerald *surgeon, educator*
Fosler, Gail D. *economist*
Foster, Carter *curator*
Foster, Craig Allen *plastic surgeon*
Foulkes, Llyn *artist, educator*
Fowle, Bruce S. *architect*
Fowler, Dennis L. *surgeon, director*
Fowler, John M. *finance executive*
Fox, Andrew *entertainment productions executive*
Fox, Arthur Charles *cardiologist, educator*
Fox, Bette-Lee *journal editor*
Fox, David *lawyer*
Fox, Donald Thomas *lawyer*
Fox, Keith *publishing executive*
Fox, Margalit (Eve) *journalist, editor, writer*
Fox, Matthew *actor*
Fox, Merritt B. *lawyer, educator*
Fox, Mitchell B. *publishing executive*
Fox, Paula *writer*
Fox, Richard Gabriel *anthropologist, educator*
Fox, Robert Frederick, Jr. *architect*
Fox, Sylvan *journalist, educator*
Fraenkel, George Kessler *chemistry professor*
Fraidin, Stephen *lawyer*
France, Kim *editor-in-chief*
Frances, Richard Joseph *psychiatrist*
Franciosa, Joseph Anthony *healthcare consultant*
Franck, Thomas Martin *law educator*
Frank, Elizabeth *writer, educator*
Frank, Frederick *investment banker*
Frank, Lloyd *lawyer, director, retired chemicals executive*
Frank, William Fielding *computer company executive, consultant*
Frank, William P. *lawyer*
Frankel, Adam B. *lawyer*
Frankel, Martin Richard *statistician, educator, consultant*
Frankel, Max *retired journalist*
Frankenthaler, Helen *artist*
Frankfort, Lew *consumer products company executive*
Franklin, Blake Timothy *lawyer*
Franklin, Jason Edward *advocate, researcher*
Franklin, Julian Harold *political science professor*
Franks, Lucinda Laura *journalist*
Franks, Martin Davis *broadcast executive*
Frantz, Andrew Gibson *endocrinologist, educator, dean*
Franzen, Jonathan *writer*
Frasch, Ronald L. *retail executive*
Frazier, Charles Robinson *writer*
Frazza, George S. *lawyer*
Fredericks, Ivy Lindstrom *investment banker*
Fredericks, Wesley Charles, Jr. *lawyer*
Fredericks, William Curtis *lawyer*
Freed, Stanley Arthur *retired museum curator*
Freedberg, David Adrian *art historian, educator*
Freedman, Alfred Mordecai *psychiatrist, educator*
Freedman, Gerald M. *lawyer*
Freedman, Helen E. *judge*
Freedman, Jenna *library and information scientist*
Freedman, Michael Leonard *geriatrician, educator*
Freeland, Chrystia *editor*
Freeman, David John *lawyer*
Freeman, Harold Paul *oncologist, educator, medical center director*
Freeman, Scott M. *lawyer*
Freeman, Steven M. *lawyer*
Frehm, Lynne *painter*
Freiberg, Steven J. *diversified financial services company executive*
Freidheim, Scott J. *investment company executive*
Freilicher, Morton *lawyer, educator*
French, John III *lawyer, director*
Frenkel, Jacob Aharon *insurance company executive*
Frere, Fabrice G. *publishing executive*
Freudenheim, Milton B. *journalist*
Freund, Fred A. *retired lawyer*
Frey, Andrew Lewis *lawyer*
Freyer, Dana Hartman *lawyer*
Freyre, Angela Mariana *lawyer*
Freyre, Fabio *publishing executive*
Fribourg, Paul J. *grain company executive*
Fricklas, Michael David *lawyer, broadcast executive*
Fridson, Martin Steven *finance company executive*
Fried, Donald David *lawyer*
Fried, Richard L. *lawyer*
Friedberg, Barry Sewell *investment banker*
Frieden, Thomas R. *city health department administrator, epidemiologist*
Friedenberg, Daniel Meyer *investor, writer*
Friedman, Alan Roy *lawyer*
Friedman, Bart *lawyer*
Friedman, B(ernard) H(arper) *writer*
Friedman, Caitlin *public relations executive*
Friedman, Debbie *singer, songwriter, religious studies educator*
Friedman, Dennis J. *lawyer*
Friedman, Eugene Stuart *lawyer*
Friedman, George *lawyer*
Friedman, Ira Hugh *surgeon*
Friedman, J. Roger *publisher*
Friedman, Jane *publishing executive*
Friedman, Jeffrey J. *lawyer*
Friedman, Jeffrey M. *medical researcher, educator*
Friedman, Max *lawyer*
Friedman, Robert Laurence *investment company executive*
Friedman, Sam *editor*
Friedman, Samuel Selig *lawyer*
Friedman, Stephen *federal official, former diversified financial services executive*
Friedman, Stephen J. *lawyer*
Friedman, Wilbur Harvey *lawyer*
Frisch, Harry David *lawyer, consultant, investment company executive*
Frischling, Carl *lawyer*
Frommer, Arthur *editor-in-chief, travel writer*
Frommer, William S. *lawyer*
Frost, William Lee *foundation executive*
Fruitman, Frederick Howard *investment banker*
Frumkin, Joseph B. *lawyer*
Fry, Elizabeth H. W. *lawyer*
Fry, Morton Harrison, II, *lawyer*
Frye, Clayton Wesley, Jr. *finance company executive*
Fuchs, Elaine V. *molecular biologist, educator*
Fuchs, Nancy E. *lawyer*
Fuentez, Tania Michele *journalist*
Fuerth, Glenn J. *lawyer*
Fugazy, William Denis *transportation company executive*
Fuhrman, Susan H. *academic administrator, education educator, researcher*
Fukata, Masayuki *gastroenterologist, hematologist*
Fuld, Richard Severin, Jr., (Dick Fuld) *investment banking executive*
Fuller, Bonnie *editor-in-chief*
Furman, Anthony Michael *public relations executive*
Furman, Roy Lance *investment banker, theater producer*
Fusaro, Peter C. *environmental scientist, consultant*
Fuster, Valentin *cardiologist, educator*
Futter, Ellen Victoria *museum administrator*
Fuzesi, Stephen, Jr. *lawyer, communications executive*
Gabay, Donald *lawyer*
Gabriel, Trip (Bertram Gabriel III) *editor*
Gabrielson, Charles *publishing executive*
Gabrilove, Jacques Lester *physician*
Gaffney, Elizabeth Mallory *editor, writer, literature educator, translator*
Gaffney, John T. *lawyer*
Gagosian, Larry *art dealer*
Gainsburg, Roy Ellis *publishing executive*
Galan, Leonidez Vindollo *architect*
Galanter, Eugene *psychologist, educator*
Galanter, Marc *psychiatrist, educator*
Gallagher, Brian John *lawyer*
Gallagher, Ellen *artist*
Galland, Leo *internist, researcher*
Gallo, David *scenic designer*
Gallo, Martha J. *diversified financial services company executive*
Gallo, William Victor *cartoonist*
Galluzzo, Jay A. *lawyer*
Gamble, Theodore Robert, Jr. *investment banker*
Gan, Yong Xue *materials engineer, educator*
Gandy, Sam *neurologist, neuroscientist, educator*
Gangwisch, James Edward *social worker, researcher*
Gans, Herbert J. *sociologist, educator*
Gant, Donald Ross *investment banker*
Ganz, David L. *lawyer*
Ganz, Howard Laurence *lawyer*
Ganzi, Victor Frederick *publishing executive*
Gaon, Simon A. *artist, painter*
Garabedian, Paul Roesel *mathematics professor*
Garber, Donald *Major League Soccer commissioner*
Garbus, Martin Solomon *lawyer*

Garcia, Andy *actor*
Garcia, Michael J. *prosecutor, former federal agency administrator*
Garcia, Nina *publishing executive*
Gardino, Vincent Anthony *broadcast executive*
Gardner, Gary A. *lawyer*
Gardner, H. McIntrye (Mac Gardner) *diversified financial services company executive*
Gardner, Janet Paxton *journalist, film producer*
Gardner, Richard Newton *diplomat, lawyer, educator*
Garfield, Leslie Jerome *real estate executive*
Garfield, Martin Richard *lawyer*
Garfinkel, Barry Herbert *lawyer*
Garfinkel, Lee *advertising agency executive*
Garland, David William *law and sociology educator*
Garment, Leonard *lawyer, author*
Garner, Albert Headden *investment banker*
Garner, Mark *communications executive*
Garner, Melvin C. *lawyer*
Garrett, Laurie *journalist, global health scholar*
Garrett, Robert *investment banker, director*
Garrett, Wendell *antiques appraiser, historian, editor*
Garson, Gary Wayne *lawyer, diversified holding company executive*
Gartner, Murray *lawyer*
Gartner, Steven J. *lawyer*
Garvey, Richard Anthony *retired lawyer*
Garvin, Andrew Paul *computer company executive, writer*
Garzarelli, Elaine Marie *economist*
Gasman, Daniel E. *retired history professor, writer*
Gaspar-Martins, Ismael *Angolian diplomat, former government minister, business executive*
Gatfield, Stephen J. *advertising executive*
Gatje, Robert Frederick *architect, writer*
Gatling, Patricia L. *lawyer, commissioner*
Gaughan, Eugene Francis *lawyer, retired accountant*
Gay, Darrell S. *lawyer*
Gay, Peter *historian, educator, writer*
Gazzara, Ben *actor*
Geary, Hilary R. *society editor*
Gebbie, Kristine Moore *medical educator*
Geckle, Robert Alan *manufacturing executive*
Geddes, John M. *editor*
Geelan, John *lawyer*
Gehringer, Richard George *publishing executive*
Geier, Philip Henry, Jr. *advertising executive*
Geiser, Elizabeth Able *publishing company executive*
Geissbuhler, Stephan *graphics designer*
Geithner, Timothy F. *bank executive*
Gelb, Judith Anne *lawyer*
Gelb, Leslie Howard *writer, lecturer, consultant*
Gelb, Peter *performing company executive*
Gelfand, David R. *lawyer*
Geller, Robert James *advertising executive*
Gellert, Michael Erwin *investment banker*
Gellhorn, Alfred *physician, educator*
Gellman, Barton David *correspondent*
Gelmann, Edward Paul *oncologist, educator*
Gelston, Philip A. *lawyer*
Geltzer, Robert Lawrence *lawyer, arbitrator, mediator, retired retail executive*
Genader, Robert J. *investment company executive*
Gendler, Ellen *dermatologist*
Genova, Joseph Steven *lawyer*
Genty, Philip *law educator*
Geoghegan, Patricia *lawyer*
George, Elizabeth (Susan Elizabeth George) *writer*
Geraghty, Patrick D. *lawyer*
Gerard, Whitney Ian *lawyer*
Gerard-Sharp, Monica Fleur *communications executive*
Gerber, Robert Evan *judge*
Gerberg, Judith Levine *career consultant*
Gerdts, William Henry *art history educator*
Germano, William Paul *dean, former publishing executive*
Gerner, Joan *foundation administrator*
Gero, Anthony George *securities and commodities trader*
Gersony, Welton Mark *pediatrician, cardiologist, educator*
Gerspach, Thomas Joseph *lawyer*
Gertler, Menard M. *physician, educator*
Getnick, Neil Victor *lawyer*
Geurts, Tom Geerd *real estate educator, consultant*
Gewirtz, Elliot *lawyer*
Gewirtz-Friedman, Gerry *editor*
Geyer, Thomas Powick *newspaper publisher*
Ghani, Cyrus *lawyer*
Gharib, Susie *newscaster*
Ghossaini, Soha Nadim *medical educator*
Gialanella, Donald George *broadcast executive, sound recording engineer, sculptor*
Giancotti, Filippo Giusto *molecular biologist, educator*
Gianinno, Susan McManama *advertising executive*
Giannetti, Stephen P. *publishing executive*
Giannetti, Thomas Leonard *lawyer*
Giannini, Giancarlo *actor, director, screenwriter*
Giardina, Elsa Grace Vonna *cardiologist, educator*
Gibbons, Robert John *lawyer*
Giblin, James Cross *writer, publishing executive*
Giblin, Jennifer *chef*
Gibney, Alex *producer, director, writer*
Gibney, James S. *editor*
Gibson, Arlene Joy *retired headmaster*
Gibson, Charles DeWolf *newscaster*
Gibson, John *news anchor, correspondent*
Gibson, Ralph H. (Ralph Holmes Gibson) *photographer*
Giddens-Jones, Emily Jane *architectural and interior designer, consultant*
Gifford, William C. *lawyer, educator*
Gigot, Paul Anthony *editor*
Gilbert, Rose Bennett *journalist*
Gill, E. Ann *lawyer*
Gill, Linda A. *advertising executive*
Gillers, Stephen *law educator*
Gillespie, George Joseph III *lawyer*
Gillespie, John Thomas *retired university administrator*
Gillespie, Michael J. *lawyer*
Gilligan, Carol *psychologist, writer*
Gilligan, Edward P. *diversified financial services company executive*
Gillinson, Sir Clive Daniel *music executive, former musician*
Gillispie, Robert J. *lawyer*
Gilmour, Joseph A. *insurance company executive*
Giniger, Kenneth Seeman *publisher*
Ginsberg, David Lawrence *architect*
Ginsberg, Henry *medical educator, researcher*
Ginsberg, Hersh Meier *rabbi, religious organization administrator*
Ginsburg, Sigmund G. *management and executive search consultant*
Ginter, Valerian Alexius *urban historian, educator*
Ginzel, Andrew H. *artist*
Giordano, Bill A. *psychotherapist*
Giordano, Mary Ann *editor*
Giraldi, Robert Nicholas *film director*
Girardi, Joe (Joseph Elliot Girardi) *sports announcer, former professional baseball manager, former professional baseball player*
Gissler, Sigvard Gunnar, Jr. *journalist, educator, retired editor*
Gitter, Max *lawyer*
Gittes, Franklin M. *lawyer*
Giuliani, Rudy (Rudolph William Louis Giuliani III) *consultant, lawyer, former mayor*
Giusti, William Roger *lawyer*
Gladstone, Bernard *columnist*
Gladstone, Rick *editor*
Gladwell, Malcolm *writer*
Glanze, Walter D. *editor, writer, lexicographer, publishing consultant*
Glasberg, H(erbert) Mark *psychiatrist, educator*
Glasberg, Scot Bradley *plastic surgeon*
Glaser, Milton *graphics designer, illustrator*
Glass, David Carter *psychologist, educator*
Glass, Julia *writer*
Glass, Philip *composer, musician*
Glasser, Stephen C. *lawyer*
Glassman, Alexander Howard *psychiatrist, researcher*
Glassman, Debra *dentist*
Glassman, Steven *dentist*
Glassman, Steven J. *lawyer*
Glater, Jonathan D. *reporter*
Glatt, Mitchell Steven *consumer products company executive*
Glauber, Robert R. *former financial regulatory service executive*
Glazier, Penny Port *property and event manager*
Gleason, Barbara Jo *literature and language professor*
Glekel, Jeffrey Ives *lawyer*
Glesby, Marshall Jay *physician, educator*
Gliatta, Stephen *lawyer*
Glickman, Michael Richard *social studies educator*
Glickman, Robert Morris *health facility administrator, dean*
Glickstein, Steven *lawyer*
Gliedman, Michael Seth *sports association executive*
Gliklich, Jerry *physician, educator*
Glimcher, Arnold B. *art gallery executive*
Glowczewska, Klara *editor-in-chief, translator*
Gluck, Carol *history professor*
Gluck, Matthew *lawyer*
Gluck, Peter L. *architect*
Glück, Sebastian M. *pipe organ builder*
Glusband, Steven Joseph *lawyer*
Gochberg, Thomas *real estate investor, investment banker*
Goddard, Donald Letcher *writer, editor*
Godridge, Leslie V. *bank executive*
Godson, Godfrey Nigel *molecular geneticist, educator*
Goelet, Robert G. *investment company executive*
Goetz, Maurice Harold *lawyer*
Goff, Stephen Payne *molecular biologist, educator*
Gold, Arnold P. *neurologist*
Gold, Jeffrey Mark *investment banker*
Gold, Mari S. *public relations executive*
Gold, Martin Elliot *lawyer, educator*
Gold, Neil D. *lawyer*
Gold, Richard L. *lawyer*
Gold, Sharon Cecile *artist, educator*
Gold, Simeon *lawyer*
Gold, Stuart Walter *lawyer*
Gold, William Elliott *health care management consultant, educator*
Goldbard, Laura E. *lawyer*
Goldberg, Danny *recording industry executive*
Goldberg, Jay *lawyer*
Goldberg, Laurence *investment banker*
Goldberg, Nieca *cardiologist, educator*
Goldberg, Richard W. *federal judge*
Goldberg, Victor Paul *law educator*
Goldberger, Paul Jesse *dean, architecture critic, writer*
Golden, Arthur F. *lawyer*
Golden, Daniel H. *lawyer*
Golden, Michael *publishing executive*
Golden, Thelma *curator*
Golden, William Theodore *trustee, corporate director*
Goldenberg, Charles Lawrence *real estate company executive*
Goldfarb, C. Richard *radiologist, educator*
Goldfarb, David *investment banking executive*
Goldfarb, Donald *industrial engineering educator*
Goldfarb, Will *chef*
Goldfein, Shepard *lawyer*
Goldfrank, Lewis Robert *physician*
Goldman, Charles Norton *retired corporate lawyer*
Goldman, George David *psychologist*
Goldman, Lawrence Saul *lawyer*
Goldman, Louis B. *lawyer*
Goldman, Michael S. *lawyer*
Goldman, Neal *entrepreneur, information technology executive*
Goldman, Peter Louis *writer*
Goldmark, Peter Francis *banker*
Goldschmid, Harvey Jerome *law educator, commissioner*
Goldschmidt, Charles *advertising agency executive*
Goldsmith, Clifford Henry *retired consumer products company executive*
Goldsmith, Lee Selig *lawyer, physician*
Goldsmith, Merwin *actor, theater director*
Goldsmith, Michael Allen *oncologist, educator*
Goldsmith, Stanley Joseph *nuclear medicine physician, educator*
Goldstein, Alvin *lawyer*
Goldstein, Charles Arthur *lawyer*
Goldstein, Gary Sanford *executive recruiter*
Goldstein, Howard Sheldon *lawyer*
Goldstein, Howard Warren *lawyer*
Goldstein, Jeffrey Alan *corporate financial executive*
Goldstein, Jonathan *lawyer*
Goldstein, Kenneth B. *lawyer*
Goldstein, Marc *surgeon, urologist, educator, health facility administrator*
Goldstein, Marcia Landweber *lawyer*
Goldstein, Martin S. *obstetrician, gynecologist, educator*
Goldstein, Matthew *academic administrator*
Goldstein, Sandra Cara *lawyer*
Goldston, James *television producer*
Goldstone, Steven F. *former consumer products company executive*
Golick, Toby *law educator, legal services administrator*
Golin, Mark *editor*
Golomb, Susan L. *literary agent*
Golub, Steven J. *investment company executive*
Gomez, Scott *professional hockey player*
Gomory, Ralph Edward *foundation administrator, mathematician*
Gonnerman, Jennifer *writer, journalist*
Gonzalez, Eugene Robert *investment banker*
Gonzalez-Falla, Sondra Gilman *art collector*
Goodale, James Campbell *lawyer, television producer, columnist, educator*
Goodale, Toni Krissel *research and development company executive*
Goodell, Roger *national football league commissioner*
Goodfriend, Herbert Jay *lawyer*
Goodhartz, Gerald *law librarian*
Goodman, Allegra *writer*
Goodman, Gary A. *lawyer*
Goodman, George Jerome Waldo (Adam Smith) *writer, television journalist, consultant*
Goodman, Kim C. *credit card and former computer company executive*
Goodman, Michael B(arry) *communications educator*
Goodman, Roy Matz *corporate financial executive, former state senator*
Goodridge, Allan D. *lawyer*
Goodstein, Laurie Beth *journalist*
Goodstein, Les *newspaper publishing executive*
Goodwin, Beatrice *nursing educator, consultant*
Goodwin, Michael *labor union administrator*
Goott, Alan F(ranklin) *lawyer*
Gordimer, Nadine *writer*
Gordon, Alan Lee *psychiatrist*
Gordon, David *playwright, theater director, choreographer*
Gordon, David A. *lawyer*
Gordon, Jeffrey Neil *law educator*
Gordon, Jennifer Lynn *lawyer, administrator*
Gordon, Leo Maury *federal judge*
Gordon, Linda *history educator*
Gordon, Mark J. *real estate company executive*
Gordon, Marsha L. *dermatologist*
Gordon, Michael Mackin *lawyer*
Gordon, Robert Jay *lawyer, educator*
Gordon, Stephen Louis *lawyer*
Gordon, Stuart A. *lawyer*
Gordon, Susan C. *broadcast executive*
Gordon, Wycliffe *trombonist, jazz musician, music educator, composer*
Gorenstein, Ethan Ezra *psychologist, educator*
Gore Schiff, Karenna *nonprofit organization administrator, lawyer, writer*
Gorlin, Alexander *architect*
Gorman, James P. *finance company executive*
Gormley, Kenneth *lawyer*
Gorton, Mark Howard *information technology executive, entrepreneur*
Gosin, Barry M. *real estate company executive*
Gosper, Brett *advertising agency executive*
Gossett, Robert Francis, Jr. *merchant banker*
Gotbaum, Betsy *municipal official*
Goto, Midori *classical violinist*
Gotschlich, Emil Claus *physician*
Gottesman, David Sanford *investment company executive*
Gotthoffer, Lance *lawyer*
Gotti, Victoria *columnist, writer, actress*
Gottlieb, Geoffrey Jon *dermatologist*
Gottlieb, Jerrold Howard *advertising executive*
Gottlieb, Paul Mitchel *corporate financial executive*
Gottlieb, Robert W. *lawyer*
Gotto, Antonio Marion, Jr. *internist, educator*
Gotts, Ilene Knable *lawyer*
Gottschalk, Alfred *retired academic and museum administrator*
Gould, Andrew *oil industry executive*
Gould, Emily *editor*
Gould, Harry Edward, Jr. *paper company executive*
Goulden, Joseph Chesley *author*
Goulianos, Konstantin *physicist, educator*
Gourevich, Philip *writer, editor*
Gourevitch, Jacqueline *artist*
Gourevitch, Philip *editor*
Gover, Alan Shore *lawyer*
Grace, Nancy A. *news correspondent, former prosecutor*
Grad, Frank Paul *lawyer, educator*
Graf, John A. *finance company executive*
Graf, Peter Gustav *accountant, lawyer*
Graff, George Leonard *lawyer*
Graff, Randy *actress*
Grafstein, Bernice *physiology and neuroscience educator, researcher*
Grafton, Sue *novelist*
Graham, Alma Eleanor *editor, writer, educational consultant*
Graham, Fred Patterson *news correspondent, journalist*
Graham, John L. *lawyer*
Granath, Herbert A. *television industry executive*
Granito, Frank Henry III *lawyer*
Granoff, Gary Charles *lawyer, investment company executive*
Grant, Cynthia D. *writer*
Grant Goldman, Pamela *journalist, writer*
Grassi, Joseph F. *lawyer, mediator, arbitrator*
Grau, Marcy Beinish *real estate broker, former investment banker*
Graustark, Barbara *editor*
Graves, Earl G., Jr., (Butch Graves) *publishing executive*
Graves, Earl Gilbert *publishing executive*
Gray, Farrah *entrepreneur, writer*
Gray, James L. *investment company executive*
Gray, Jerry *editor*
Gray, Jonathan David *real estate company executive*
Gray, Stacey M. *lawyer*
Grayer, Elizabeth L. *lawyer*
Grayer, Jonathan *education company executive*
Greaney, Michael E. *lawyer*
Grebow, Edward *finance company executive*
Greeff, Douglas Haven *cosmetics executive*
Greegard, Leslie F. *mathematics professor*
Greely, Hannah *artist*
Green, Alvin *lawyer, consultant*
Green, Dan *publishing executive*
Green, Eric Howard *lawyer*
Green, George Joseph *publishing executive*
Green, Mark Joseph *lawyer, author*
Green, Maurice Richard *neuropsychiatrist*
Green, Micah S. *trade association administrator*
Green, Stephen L. *real estate developer*
Green, Wayne Hugo *psychiatrist, psychoanalyst*
Green, William D. *management consulting firm executive*
Greenawalt, Robert Kent *lawyer, educator*
Greenberg, Alan Courtney (Ace Lev Petrovich) *diversified financial services company executive*
Greenberg, Benjamin *physician*
Greenberg, Daniel Lawrence *lawyer*
Greenberg, David I. *consumer products company executive*
Greenberg, Ira George *lawyer*
Greenberg, Jack *lawyer, educator*
Greenberg, Joel I. *lawyer*
Greenberg, Mark *television producer*
Greenberg, Peter S. *travel editor, news correspondent, writer*
Greenberg, Philip Alan *lawyer*
Greenberg, Steve *music company executive*
Greenberger, Howard Leroy *lawyer, educator*
Green-Dorsey, Jean Audrey *information technology executive*
Greene, Bernard Harold *lawyer*
Greene, Frank Edward Wade *foundation administrator, writer*
Greene, Ira S. *lawyer*
Greene, Mark I. *lawyer*
Greene, Richard H. *journalist, writer, policy analyst*
Greenfield, (Henry) Jeff *news analyst*
Greenfield, Lucille Jean *music educator, composer*
Greenfield, Sarah *photo editor*
Greengard, Leslie F. *mathematician, educator*
Greengard, Paul *neuroscientist, educator*
Greenhill, Robert Foster *investment banker*
Greenland, Leo *advertising executive*
Greenman, Frederick F., Jr. *lawyer*
Greenman, Josh *editor*
Greenman, Paula S. *lawyer*
Greenspon, Robert Alan *lawyer*
Greenstein, Abraham Jacob *mortgage company executive, accountant*
Greenthal, Jill A. *investment banker*
Greenwald, David *lawyer*
Greenwald, Julie *recording industry executive*
Greenwald, Sheila Ellen *writer, illustrator*
Greenzang, Katherine *lawyer, insurance company executive*
Gregorian, Vartan *foundation administrator*
Gregory, Jim (James Michael Gregory) *sports association executive, former professional sports team executive*
Gregory, Joseph M. *investment company executive*
Gregory, Robin N. *lawyer*
Grehan, Kevin J. *lawyer*
Greifeld, Robert *stock exchange executive*
Greilsheimer, James Gans *lawyer*
Greiner, Stephen W. *lawyer*
Greitzer, Matt *marketing professional*
Grenquist, Peter Carl *publishing executive, consultant*
Gresham, George *labor union administrator*
Grew, Robert Ralph *retired lawyer*
Griefen, John Adams *artist, educator*
Gries, Michael F. *diversified financial services company executive*
Griesa, Thomas Poole *federal judge*
Griffel, L. Michael *music educator, researcher*
Griffin, Anne *political scientist, educator*
Griffin, Michael Daniel *investment counselor*
Griffin, Michael F. *lawyer*
Griffith, William R. *lawyer*
Griffiths, Sylvia Preston *physician, educator*
Griffy, Timothy T. *human resources specialist, finance company executive*

Grimaldi, Nicholas Lawrence *fundraising executive*
Grimes, William *critic*
Grisham, John *writer*
Grody, Deborah *psychologist, director*
Grogan, John *writer*
Groh, Jennifer Calfa *law librarian*
Gromada, Thaddeus V. *historian, academic administrator*
Gromek, Joseph R. *apparel executive*
Gropper, Allan Louis *judge*
Gross, Amy *editor-in-chief*
Gross, John H. *lawyer*
Gross, Jonathan Light *computer scientist, mathematician, educator*
Gross, Karen Charal *lawyer*
Gross, Steven Ross *lawyer*
Grossman, Barbara *artist, educator*
Grossman, Dan Steven *lawyer*
Grossman, Lawrence Kugelmass *former communications and advertising executive*
Grossman, Michael *economics professor*
Grossman, Nancy *artist*
Grossmann, Edward A. *lawyer*
Groves, Ray John *accountant*
Grubin, Sharon Ellen *lawyer, former federal judge*
Grubman, Allen J. *lawyer*
Gruen, Alison Brett *dermatologist*
Gruenberger, Peter *lawyer*
Grueskin, William Steven (Bill Grusekin) *editor*
Grune, Steven Bryan *publishing executive*
Grunes, Robert Lewis *engineering executive, consultant*
Grunewald, Raymond Bernhard *lawyer*
Grunfeld, A. Tom *history professor*
Grunschlag, Toni *pianist, researcher*
Grushkin, Jay D. *lawyer*
Gruss, Martin David *investor*
Gruss, Shoshanna Lonstein *apparel designer*
Gubert, Walter Alexander *investment company executive*
Guedry, James Walter *lawyer, retired manufacturing executive*
Guehenno, Jean Marie *international organization official*
Guggenheim, Martin Franklin *lawyer, educator*
Guiher, James Morford, Jr. *publisher, writer*
Guillot, Cyril Etienne *international organization administrator*
Gulino, Frank *lawyer, educator*
Gumbel, Bryant Charles *broadcaster*
Gumbinner, Paul S. *advertising and executive recruitment agency executive*
Gumpert, Lynn *gallery director*
Gund, Agnes *retired museum administrator*
Gunn, Tim (Timothy M. Gunn) *apparel executive*
Gupta, Paul R. *lawyer*
Gupta, Rajat Kumar *retired management consultant, electronics executive*
Gural, Jeffrey R. *real estate company executive*
Gure, Anna Valerie *retired social worker, consulting psychotherapist*
Gurfein, Richard Alan *lawyer*
Gutfreund, John Halle *investment company executive, consultant*
Guth, Amber Azniv *surgeon, educator*
Guthrie, Randolph Hobson, Jr. *plastic surgeon, consultant*
Gutman, Henry B. *lawyer*
Gutman, Robert William *retired art educator*
Gutzwiller, Martin Charles *theoretical physicist, research scientist*
Guzman, Kathleen McFadden *antiques appraiser, auctioneer*
Gwathmey, Charles *architect*
Gwathmey, Gaines *lawyer*
Gyles, Robert *mathematics professor*
Haacke, Hans Christoph Carl *artist, educator*
Haas, Richard John *artist*
Haas, Steven B. *orthopedist, surgeon, educator*
Haass, Richard Nathan *federal official*
Habachy, Suzan Salwa Saba *economist, not-for-profit developer*
Haberman, Clyde *columnist*
Haberman, Seth *advertising executive*
Habib, Ibrahim Wahby *computer engineer, educator*
Hackbarth, Steven Lyle *writer, educator, audio-visual specialist*
Hackett, George *editor*
Hackett, Kevin R. *real estate company executive, lawyer*
Hackett, Larry *editor*
Hadas, Rachel *poet, educator*
Haddad, Heskel Marshall *ophthalmologist, educator*
Haddad, Jamil Raouf *retired physician*
Hadden, John Winthrop *immunopharmacology educator*
Haddon, James Francis *banker*
Hadjiangelis, Nicos Pavlos *medical educator, consultant*
Haegele, Patricia *publishing executive*
Haessle, Jean-Marie Georges *artist*
Haffner, Alden Norman *academic administrator*
Haffner, F. Kinsey *lawyer*
Haggerty, Luane Ruth Davis *theater director, educator, actress*
Hague, William Edward *writer*
Haig, Robert Leighton *lawyer*
Haigh, Jennifer *writer*
Haight, Charles Sherman, Jr. *federal judge*
Haight, David Hulen *ophthalmologist*
Haiman, Zoltan *astronomer, educator*
Haimes, Burton Kenneth *lawyer*
Haims, Bruce David *lawyer*
Haines, Thomas Henry *biochemist, educator, researcher*
Hajjar, Katherine Amberson *physician, pediatrician*
Hakala, Thomas John *private banker, financial planner, accountant*
Halaby, Samia Asaad *painter, educator, writer*
Halberstam, Malvina *lawyer, educator*
Haley, James F., Jr. *lawyer*
Hall, Bryan H. *lawyer*
Hall, John Herbert *lawyer*
Hall, Lisa Gersh *broadcast executive, lawyer*
Hall, Michael C. *actor*
Hall, Peter W. *federal judge, former prosecutor*
Hall, Richard *lawyer*
Hall, Thomas J. *lawyer*
Hall, Trish *editor*
Hallake, Marcello *lawyer*
Halliday, Joseph William *lawyer*
Halmi, Robert, Sr. *film, television producer*
Halper, Thomas *political science professor*
Halperin, Jonathan L. *medical school administrator*
Halperin, Mark Evan *editor*
Halperin, Richard E. *lawyer, finance company executive*
Halpern, Merril Mark *retired investment banker*
Halsband, Frances *architect*
Hambrick, George Walter, Jr. *dermatologist, educator*
Hamburg, Charles Bruce *lawyer*
Hamburg, David A. *psychiatrist, foundation administrator*
Hamdan, Lawrence Anise *investment banker, lawyer*
Hamilton, Dorothy Cann *academic administrator*
Hamilton, Laurell K. *writer*
Hamilton Jackson, Marilyn J. *dancer, educator, choreographer*
Hamm, David Bernard *lawyer*
Hammer, Scott M. *medical researcher, educator*
Hammett, Kirk Lee *musician*
Hammond, Darrell *actor*
Hammond, Lou Rena Charlotte *public relations executive*
Hamoy, Carol *artist*
Hanau, Kenneth John III *venture capitalist*
Hance, James Henry, Jr. *former bank executive*
Handelsman, Lawrence Marc *lawyer*
Handler, Arthur M. *lawyer*
Handler, Daniel (Lemony Snicket) *writer*
Handler, Janet Bougash *elementary school educator*
Handler, Richard B. *investment company executive*
Handley, Siobhan A. *lawyer*
Hanft, James *lawyer*
Hanisch, Toula *legal assistant*
Hann, Lucy E. *radiologist, educator*
Hannon, Gerard V. *lawyer*
Hansell, Saul Henry *reporter*
Hansen, James E. *physicist, meteorologist, federal agency administrator*
Hansen, Kristopher M. *lawyer*
Hansen, William D. *educational consultant, former federal agency administrator*
Hansmann, Ralph Emil *investment executive, director*
Hanson, Jean Elizabeth *lawyer*
Hanson, Paula *sports association executive*
Hanson, Stephen *food service executive*
Hara, Eric *chef*
Haracz, Stephen M. *lawyer*
Harbeson, John Willis *political science professor*
Hardin, Melora *actress*
Hardwick, Elizabeth *writer*
Hardy, Hugh *architect*
Hardy, John *artist*
Hargitay, Mariska Magdolina *actress*
Harkrider, John David *lawyer*
Harlan, Leonard Morton *merchant banker*
Harlow, Ruth *lawyer*
Harmon, Jane *theater producer*
Harms, David B. *lawyer*
Harper, Gerard Edward *lawyer*
Harrell, Ray Evans *performing company executive, conductor, educator*
Harris, Adam C. *lawyer*
Harris, Arlene *lawyer*
Harris, David Alan *not-for-profit organization executive*
Harris, David Henry *retired life insurance company executive*
Harris, Ethan S. *diversified financial services company executive*
Harris, Frederick John *foreign language and literature educator*
Harris, Henry William *physician*
Harris, Joel B. (Joel Bruce Harris) *lawyer*
Harris, Julie (Ann) *actress*
Harris, Katherine Safford *speech and hearing educator*
Harris, Theresa *lawyer*
Harris, William Vernon *history professor*
Harrison, Rachel *artist*
Harrison, S. David *lawyer*
Harrow, Nancy (Mrs. Jan Krukowski) *editor, composer, singer*
Hart, Clare *information company executive*
Hart, Gurnee Fellows *investment counselor*
Hart, Karen Ann *advertising executive*
Hart, Mary T. *lawyer*
Hart, Robert M. *lawyer*
Harter, Theo C. *music educator, composer*
Hartl, Roger *physician, researcher*
Hartman, Alan *investment banker*
Hartman, Joan Edna *retired literature educator, dean, provost*
Hartmann, Carl Joseph *lawyer, consultant*
Hartnett, William M. *lawyer*
Harty, Thomas H. *publishing executive*
Hartzell, Andrew Cornelius, Jr. *retired lawyer*
Harvey, David W. *humanities educator*
Harvey, Peter C. *lawyer, former state attorney general*
Hasday, Robert Joel *lawyer*
Haskell, Barbara *curator*
Haskell, John Henry Farrell, Jr. *investment company executive*
Hass, Lawrence Joel *lawyer*
Hassell, Gerald L. *bank executive*
Hastings, Deborah *bass guitarist*
Hatcher, Kendra *advertising executive*
Hathaway, Gerald Thomas *lawyer*
Hathaway, Robin *writer*
Hatheway, John Harris *advertising agency executive*
Hatter, Richard Wayne *foundation administrator, artist*
Hauser, Gustave M. *media specialist*
Hauser, Rita Eleanore Abrams *lawyer*
Hawke, Roger Jewett *lawyer*
Hawkins, Katherine Ann *hematologist, educator, lawyer*
Hayes, Eddie (Edward W. Hayes) *lawyer*
Hayes, Gerald Joseph *lawyer*
Hayes, John D. *diversified financial services company executive*
Hazan, Scott L. *lawyer*
Hazzard, Shirley *author*
Headlam, Bruce *editor*
Headley, Mark J. *lawyer*
Healy, J. Kevin *lawyer*
Healy, Julia Schmitt *artist, educator*
Healy, Mark *editor-in-chief*
Healy, Nicholas Joseph *retired lawyer*
Hearn, George *actor*
Hearn, George Henry *lawyer, water transportation executive*
Hearst, George Randolph, Jr. *publishing executive, real estate company executive*
Heaton, Eric *investment banker*
Hebert, Bliss Edmund *opera director*
Hecht, William David *accountant*
Hedden, Andrew S. *lawyer*
Heeger, David J. *psychology professor*
Heekin, Jim (James Robson Heekin III) *advertising executive*
Heekin-Canedy, Scott H. *publishing executive*
Heffernan, Virginia *television critic*
Heffner, Richard Douglas *historian, educator, communications consultant, television producer*
Hefter, Michael C *lawyer*
Heftler, Thomas E. *lawyer*
Hegarty, John F., Jr. *advertising executive*
Heiferman, Scott *Internet company executive*
Heilbrun, James *economist, educator*
Heimann, John Gaines *investment banker*
Heinemann, Larry C. *writer*
Heinemann, Peter *artist, educator*
Heintz, Florent M. *art appraiser*
Heinzelman, Kris F. *lawyer*
Heinzerling, Larry Edward *communications executive*
Heisler, Stanley Dean *lawyer*
Heitner, Kenneth Howard *lawyer*
Held, Huyler Clark *lawyer*
Heleniak, David William *diversified financial services company executive, lawyer*
Hellenbrand, Samuel Henry *lawyer*
Heller, Robert Martin *lawyer*
Hellerer, Mark R. *lawyer*
Helm, Lenora Zenzalai *musician, educator*
Hemmerdinger, H. Dale *real estate executive*
Hemphill, Clara Jacobs *advocate*
Henderson, Donald Bernard, Jr. *lawyer*
Henderson, Edward Drewry, Jr. *finance company executive*
Hendin, Josephine Gattuso *language educator, writer*
Hendrickson, Wayne A(rthur) *biochemist, educator*
Hendry, Andrew Delaney *lawyer, consumer products company executive*
Hennessee, E. Lee *securities trade executive, financial consultant*
Henriques, Diana Blackmon *journalist*
Henry, Daniel T. *diversified financial services company executive*
Henry, Emil William, Jr. *diversified financial services company executive, former federal agency administrator*
Henry, Frederick B. *foundation administrator*
Henry, Lawrence C. (Lonny Henry) *investment banker*
Henry, Sally McDonald *lawyer*
Henry, Sarah M. *museum staff member, historian*
Hensel, Katherine Ruth *portfolio manager, investment advisor*
Henselmann, Caspar Gustav Fidelis *sculptor*
Henze, William F., II, *lawyer*
Herbert, Bob *columnist*
Herbert, Marilynne *public relations executive, freelance photographer*
Herbst, Abbe Ilene *lawyer*
Herbst, Steven *sports association executive*
Herbst, Todd L. *lawyer*
Herlihy, Edward D. *lawyer*
Herman, Darren *entrepreneur, marketing executive*
Herman, Dorothy *real estate broker*
Herman, Kenneth Beaumont *lawyer*
Herman, Peter Windley *lawyer*
Herman, Stan *fashion designer*
Hernandez, Keith *retired professional baseball player*
Hernandez, Lazaro *apparel designer*
Hernandez-Fallous, Jacqueline *marketing executive*
Hernstadt, Judith Filenbaum *city planner, real estate and broadcast executive*
Herold, Karl Guenter *lawyer*
Herr, Harry Wallace *medical researcher, educator, surgeon, urologist*
Herregat, Guy-Georges Jacques *retired banker*
Herrera, Arturo *artist*
Herrera, Carolina *fashion designer*
Herrera, Paloma *dancer*
Herring, Hubert B. *editor*
Herring, Oliver *artist*
Herrmann, Lacy Bunnell *investment company executive, entrepreneur, venture capitalist*
Herron, Cindy *actress, vocalist*
Hersch, Dennis Steven *bank executive, lawyer*
Herschlein, James D. *lawyer*
Hersh, Seymour Myron *journalist, writer*
Hershcopf, Gerald Thea *retired lawyer*
Hershman, Elliott B. *orthopedist, surgeon*
Herszenhorn, David *journalist*
Hertz, Leon *publishing executive*
Hertz, Michael K. *lawyer*
Hertzig, Margaret E. *psychiatrist*
Herz, Andrew Lee *lawyer*
Herzeca, Lois Friedman *lawyer*
Herzog, John E. *numismatist*
Herzog, Thomas *obstetrician, gynecologist, gynecological oncologist and surgeon, educator*
Herzog, Werner (Werner Stipetic) *film director*
Hess, John B. *oil industry executive*
Hess, Michael David *lawyer*
Hesse, Karen (Karen Sue Hesse) *writer, educator*
Hesselbein, Frances Richards *foundation administrator, writer, editor*
Hesser, Amanda Lea *journalist, chef*
Hetfield, James *singer*
Hewitt, John R. *lawyer*
Hewitt, Vivian Ann Davidson (Mrs. John Hamilton Hewitt Jr.) *retired librarian*
Heyde, Martha Bennett *psychologist*
Heymann, C(lemens) David *author*
Hiaasen, Carl *writer, reporter*
Hickey, Catherine Josephine *school system administrator*
Hicks, Jonathan P. *journalist*
Hicks, Tyler Gregory *publishing company executive, writer*
Hidalgo, David Arthur *plastic surgeon*
Hiden, Robert Battaile, Jr. *lawyer*
Hielscher, Andreas Helmut *biomedical engineer*
Highstein, Jene Abel *sculptor*
Hilchey, Tim *editor*
Hildebrand, Phillip J. *insurance company executive*
Hill, Alfred *law educator*
Hill, J(ames) Tomilson *investment banker*
Hill, Janine *think-tank manager*
Hillenbrand, Laura *writer*
Hillman, Peter N. *lawyer*
Hines, Walter James *stock exchange executive*
Hinz, Theodore Vincent *architect*
Hippeau, Eric *book publishing executive*
Hirsch, Charles S. *city health department administrator*
Hirsch, Edward Mark *language educator, poet*
Hirsch, Harvey Stuart *psychiatrist*
Hirsch, Irving B. *lawyer*
Hirsch, Jerome S. *lawyer*
Hirsch, Jules *physician, researcher*
Hirsch, Roseann Conte *publisher*
Hirschfeld, Michael *lawyer*
Hirschfield, Bradley *rabbi*
Hirschhorn, Bernard *educator, historian, researcher, writer*
Hirschhorn, Kurt *pediatrics educator*
Hirschhorn, Rochelle *genetics educator*
Hirschson, Linda Benjamin *lawyer*
Hirshfield, Stuart *lawyer*
Hirshon, Sheldon Ira *lawyer*
Hirshowitz, Melvin Stephen *lawyer*
Hjortsberg, William Reinhold *writer*
Ho, Betty Juenyü Yülin *retired musician, physiologist, educator*
Ho, David D. (Da-i Ho) *research physician, virologist, scientific organization director*
Hoch, Benjamin *lawyer*
Hochhauser, Richard Michael *marketing professional*
Hochlerin, Diane *pediatrician, educator*
Hochman, Judith Sheryl *cardiologist, researcher*
Hochman, Richard H. *investment company executive*
Hodes, Robert Bernard *lawyer*
Hodge, Roger D. *editor*
Hoeflin, Ronald Kent *philosopher, writer*
Hoekstra, Edward John *foundation administrator*
Hoff, Jonathan M(orind) *lawyer*
Hoffert, Barbara *editor*
Hoffert, Martin Irving *aerospace scientist, educator*
Hoffman, Alice *writer*
Hoffman, Linda M. *chemist, educator*
Hoffman, Linda R. *social services administrator*
Hoffman, Lloyd Alan *plastic surgeon*
Hoffman, Mathew *lawyer*
Hoffman, Nancy *art gallery director*
Hoffman, Ronald L. *manufacturing executive*
Hoffmann, Ingrid *chef, television personality*
Hoffner, Marilyn *university administrator*
Hogan, Mary Beth *lawyer*
Hoge, Warren M. *editor*
Hoglund, Robert N. *utilities executive*
Hohn, Harry George *retired insurance company executive, lawyer*
Holcomb, Kevin Michael *obstetrician, gynecologist, gynecologic oncologist*
Holden, Stephen *film critic*
Holl, Steven Myron *architect, educator*
Holland, Bernard Peabody *music critic*
Holland, Jimmie C. *psychiatrist, educator*
Holland, Michael Francis *investment company executive*
Holley, Steven Lyon *lawyer*
Holliday, Guy D. "Doc" *publishing executive*
Holloway, Ralph Leslie *anthropology educator*
Hollyer, A(rthur) Rene *lawyer*
Holman, Bud George *lawyer*
Holmes, Anna-Marie *ballerina*
Holquist, James Michael *literature educator, department chairman*
Holsenbeck, George Penn *lawyer*
Holstad, Christian *artist*
Holt, Peter Rolf *gastroenterologist, educator*
Holtz, Diane *retail executive*
Holtzman, Elizabeth *lawyer*
Holtzmann, Howard Marshall *lawyer, judge*
Holub, Martin *architect*
Holwell, Richard J. *federal judge*
Holzer, Harold *museum and marketing executive, historian, writer*
Hondros, Chris *photojournalist*
Hong, Michael *communications executive*
Honig, Barry Hirsh *biophysicist, educator*
Honigman, Steven *lawyer*
Hood, Donald Charles *academic administrator, psychologist, educator*
Hooker, Wade Stuart *lawyer*
Hooper, Anthony C. *pharmaceutical executive*

Hopson, craig *chef*
Horan, Anthony J. *diversified financial services company executive*
Hormats, Robert David *economist, investment banker*
Horn, Karen Nicholson *investment company executive, former bank executive*
Horn, Roni *artist*
Hornstein, Mark *financial executive*
Horowitz, Eliot *Internet company executive*
Horowitz, Frances Degen *academic administrator, psychology educator*
Horowitz, Gedale Bob *investment banker*
Horowitz, Steven Gary *lawyer*
Hort, Michael *art collector*
Hort, Susan *art collector*
Horvat, Olga *artist*
Horyn, Cathy *newspaper editor*
Hoskins, Donald W. *retired medical association administrator*
Hoskins, William John *obstetrician, educator, gynecologist*
Hosseini, Khaled *writer*
Hotchner, Holly *museum director, curator, conservator*
Hotz, Robert Lee *writer, editor*
Houck, Rudolph S.(Rob) *lawyer*
Houston, Allan Wade *professional basketball player*
Hovde, Carl Frederick *language professional, educator*
Hoving, Thomas *museum director, consultant, writer*
Howard, Bonnie *bank executive*
Howard, David *retired educational association administrator, writer*
Howard, Lisa Ryan *publishing executive*
Howard, Mildred *sculptor*
Howard, Richard (Joseph) *poet, literary translator*
Howat, John Keith *retired museum executive*
Howat, Kevin John *publishing and healthcare services executive*
Howe, Florence *literature educator, writer, publisher*
Howe, Richard Rives *lawyer*
Howitt, John P. *lawyer*
Hoxter, Curtis Joseph *international economic advisor, public relations executive, communications executive*
Hoye, J.D. *foundation administrator*
Hoyt, Clark Freeland *editor, journalist*
Hoyt, Pamela *nurse*
Hricik, Lorraine E. *bank executive*
Hritz, George F. *lawyer*
Hruska, Alan J. *lawyer, filmmaker*
Hu, Danian *history professor*
Hu, Winnie *journalist*
Hubbard, R(obert) Glenn *dean, former federal official*
Huck, L. Francis *lawyer*
Huckshorn, Kristin *journalist*
Hudes, Nana Brenda *marketing professional*
Hudis, Clifford Alan *internist, oncologist*
Hudson, Christopher John *publisher*
Hudspeth, Stephen Mason *lawyer*
Huebner, Marshall Scott *lawyer*
Huey, John Wesley, Jr. *editor*
Hughes, Brigid *former editor*
Hugo, Norman Eliot *retired plastic surgeon, educator*
Hulbert, Richard Woodward *lawyer*
Hull, Cathy *artist, illustrator*
Hull, Philip Glasgow *lawyer*
Hulsebosch, Daniel Joseph *historian, educator*
Hummel, Keith R. *lawyer*
Hundley, James W. III *think-tank executive, consultant, researcher*
Hunt, Franklin Griggs *lawyer*
Hunter, Billy (G. William) *sports association administrator, lawyer*
Hupper, John Roscoe *retired lawyer*
Hurley, Cheryl Joyce *book publishing executive*
Hurley, Dean C. *bank executive, lawyer*
Hurley, Lawrence Joseph *lawyer*
Hurlin, Dan *theater director*
Hurlock, James Bickford *retired lawyer*
Hurst, Robert Jay *security firm executive*
Hutchings, Peter Lounsbery *retired insurance company executive, director*
Hutchins, Traver *publishing executive*
Hutchinson, Lynda Ronette (Billie Holiday Jr., Princess of Jazz, Munchie) *vocalist, musician, comedian, actress*
Huttner, Constance S. *lawyer*
Hutton, G. Thompson *lawyer*
Huxtable, Ada Louise *architecture critic*
Hwang, David Henry *playwright, screenwriter*
Hyde, David Rowley *lawyer*
Hylton, Kevin Nathaniel *musician, composer*
Hyman, Alan Barry *lawyer*
Hyman, Bruce Malcolm *ophthalmologist*
Hyman, Edward *financial analyst, economist*
Hyman, Jerome Elliot *lawyer*
Hyman, Morton Peter *private equity investment company executive*
Hynes, Aedhmar *public relations executive*
Hynes, Patricia M. *lawyer*
Ianniello, Joseph R. *broadcast executive*
Iannuzzi, John Nicholas *lawyer, author, educator*
Iannuzzi, Salvatore *information technology executive*
Ichel, David W. *lawyer*
Iglauer, Edith *writer, reporter*
Ikouebe, Basile *ambassador*
Ilacqua, Rosario Salvatore *securities analyst*
Ilchman, Warren Frederick *academic and foundation administrator, educator*
Iles, Greg *writer*
Ilkin, Baki *diplomat, Turkish government official*
Ilse-Neuman, Ursula *curator*
Ilson, Bernard *public relations executive*
Imber, Gerald *plastic surgeon*
Immergut, Mel M. *lawyer*
Imparato, Anthony Michael *vascular surgeon, educator, researcher*
Imus, Don (John Donald Imus Jr.) *radio personality*
Incandela, Gerald Jean-Marie *artist*
Indursky, Arthur *lawyer*
Ingrassia, Lawrence *editor*
Ingrassia, Timothy J. *investment banker*
Innis, Roy Emile Alfredo *foundation executive*
Insel, Michael S. *lawyer*
Intriligator, Marc Steven *lawyer*
Iqbal, Syma U. *information technology executive*
Ireland, Jay *broadcast executive*
Ireland, Patrick *artist*
Irish, George Butler *media company executive*
Irvin, Patricia Louise *lawyer*
Irwin, Robert Walter *artist*
Isaacson, Allen Ira *lawyer*
Isaacson, Steven Robert *surgeon*
Iselin, John Jay *academic administrator*
Isenberg, Steven Lawrence *retired publishing executive*
Isherwood, Charles *theater critic*
Ishiguro, Kazuo *writer, scriptwriter*
Iskenderian, Mary Ellen *bank executive*
Isogai, Masaharu *international corporate strategist, retired apparel executive*
Isom, O(ttis) Wayne *thoracic surgeon, educator*
Isquith, Fred Taylor *lawyer*
Issacharoff, Samuel *law educator*
Issler, Harry *lawyer*
Istomin, Marta Casals *retired school president, performing company executive*
Iturbide, Graciela *photographer*
Iuzzini, Johnny *chef*
Ivanhoe, Robert J. *lawyer*
Ivanick, Carol W. Trencher *lawyer*
Ivanov, Iliyan *psychiatrist, researcher, artist*
Ivory, James Francis *film director*
Ivy, Robert Adams, Jr. *architect, editor-in-chief*
Jacker, Corinne Litvin *playwright, writer*
Jackson, Anne (Anne Jackson Wallach) *actress*
Jackson, Cheyenne *actor*
Jackson, Henry Nathaniel *clothing designer*
Jackson, Jack P. *lawyer*
Jackson, Keith MacKenzie *retired sports commentator*
Jackson, Kenneth Terry *historian, academic administrator*
Jackson, Mike *finance company executive*
Jackson, Robert R. *lawyer*
Jackson, Stu *sports association executive, former university basketball coach*
Jacob, Edwin J. *lawyer*
Jacob, Marvin Eugene *lawyer*
Jacobs, Albert Lionel, Jr. *lawyer*
Jacobs, Arnold Stephen *writer, commentator*
Jacobs, Arnold Stephen *lawyer*
Jacobs, Dennis G. *federal judge*
Jacobs, Jim *actor, composer, librettist, playwright*
Jacobs, Lawrence A. *media company executive, lawyer*
Jacobs, Marc *fashion designer*
Jacobs, Paul *lawyer*
Jacobs, Paul A. *music educator*
Jacobs, Randall Scott David *lawyer*
Jacobs, Robert Alan *lawyer*
Jacobsen, Theodore H. (Ted H. Jacobsen) *labor union administrator, secondary school educator*
Jacobson, Gilbert H. *lawyer, director*
Jacobson, Jeffrey E. *lawyer, consultant, educator*
Jacobson, Jerold Dennis *lawyer*
Jacobson, Julius H., II, *vascular surgeon, writer*
Jacoby, Jacob *consumer psychology educator*
Jacoby, Robert Harold *management consulting executive*
Jacquette, Yvonne Helene *artist*
Jaffe, Fredrick F. *surgeon*
Jaffe, Helene D. *lawyer*
Jaffe, Susan *ballerina*
Jaglom, Andre Richard *lawyer*
Jagr, Jaromir *professional hockey player*
Jakes, Peter H. *lawyer*
James, Hamilton Evans (Tony James) *private equity executive*
James, Marc Stephen *brokerage house executive*
James, Robert Leo *advertising executive, director*
Jamieson, Wendell *editor*
Jamison, Douglas W. *venture capitalist*
Jamison, Jayne *publishing executive*
Jamison, Judith *performing company executive, dancer*
Jan, Dominique Michel *surgeon, educator*
Janiak, Anthony Richard, Jr. *investment banker*
Janklow, Morton Lloyd *lawyer, literary agent*
Janney, Stuart Symington III *investment company executive*
Janowitz, James Arnold *lawyer*
Jansky, Jeannette Jefferson *learning disabilities specialist*
Janulis, Theodore P. *investment company executive*
Jarecki, Henry George *physician, financial planner*
Jaroslawicz, David *lawyer*
Jarvik, Robert Koffler *biomedical research scientist*
Jarvis, Jeff *journalist, former critic, news blogger*
Jarvis, Rebecca *financial reporter*
Jasso, Guillermina *sociologist, educator*
Jassy, Everett Lewis *lawyer*
Javitt, Norman B. *medical educator, researcher*
Jay-Z, (Shawn Corey Carter) *music company executive, rap artist*
Jean, Wyclef *musician, recording industry executive*
Jebejian, Sarkis *lawyer*
Jefferson, Denise *dance school director*
Jefferson, Margo L. *journalist*
Jeffrey, Robert (Bob Jeffrey) *advertising executive*
Jelinek, Vera *dean*
Jelks, Glenn William *plastic surgeon*
Jellinek, George *broadcast executive, music educator, writer*
Jenkins, Paul *artist*
Jenner, Jesse Jacob *lawyer*
Jenrette, Richard Hampton *investment and insurance company executive*
Jensen, Bill *editor*
Jepson, Hans Godfrey *investment company executive, director*
Jervis, Robert *political science professor*
Jessell, Thomas M. *medical educator*
Jesselli, Steve *journalist*
Jeydel, Richard K. *lawyer*
Jeynes, Mary Kay *college dean*
Jhabvala, Ruth Prawer *writer*
Jian, Chen *international organization official*
Jing, Bing *business educator*
Jock, Paul F., II, *lawyer*
Joel, Richard Marc *academic administrator, law educator, dean*
Joffe, Robert David *lawyer*
Johansson, Jerker Mats *investment banker*
Johnnes, Daniel *chef*
Johnson, A. Paul *composer*
Johnson, Betsey Lee *fashion designer*
Johnson, Brooke Bailey *broadcast executive*
Johnson, Charles Richard *writer, teacher*
Johnson, Clarke Courtney *financial consultant, educator*
Johnson, David Harrover *lawyer, music company executive*
Johnson, David J., Jr. *lawyer*
Johnson, Harmer Frederik *art appraiser*
Johnson, Harold Earl *human resources specialist*
Johnson, Horton Anton *pathologist*
Johnson, J. Chester *corporate financial executive, consultant, writer*
Johnson, James D. *lawyer*
Johnson, Jeh Charles *lawyer*
Johnson, John William, Jr. *executive recruiter*
Johnson, Kristine *newscaster*
Johnson, Peter James, Jr. *lawyer, legal analyst*
Johnson, Richard *editor*
Johnson, Scott Stuart *merchant banker*
Johnson, Thomas Stephen *banker*
Johnson, Verdia E. *marketing professional*
Johnson, Warren Douglas *infectious diseases physician, researcher*
Johnston, David Cay Boyle *journalist*
Jolly, Thomas Alan *journalist*
Jonas, Saran *neurologist, educator*
Jones, Abbott C. *investment company executive*
Jones, Alan Kent *investment company executive*
Jones, Bill T. *dancer, choreographer*
Jones, David *advertising executive*
Jones, David R. *not-for-profit executive*
Jones, Diana Wynne *writer*
Jones, Frank Joseph *securities exchange executive*
Jones, Jacqueline Eleanor *otolaryngologist*
Jones, James A. III *lawyer*
Jones, Judith *editor*
Jones, Laurie Lynn *magazine editor*
Jones, Richard M. *broadcast executive*
Jones, Sarah *actress, playwright, poet*
Jones Reynolds, Star (Starlet Marie Jones) *television host, lawyer, former prosecutor*
Jong, Erica Mann *writer*
Joo, Michael *artist, educator*
Jordan, Vernon Eulion, Jr. *lawyer*
Josell, Jessica (Wechsler) *public relations executive*
Joseph, Gregory Paul *lawyer*
Joseph, Leonard *lawyer*
Joseph, Michael Sarkies *accountant*
Josephson, Jordan Stuart *otolaryngologist*
Josephson, Marvin *literary agent*
Joyner, Alexandra Leigh *cell biologist*
Joynt, Stephen W. *financial services company executive*
Juceam, Robert E. *lawyer*
Juliber, Lois D. *manufacturing executive*
Jung, Andrea *cosmetics company executive*
Jung, Doris *soprano*
Jurka, Edith Mila *psychiatrist, researcher*
Just, Gemma Rivoli *retired advertising executive*
Kadden, Jack *editor*
Kaden, Lewis B. *bank executive, lawyer, educator*
Kafin, Robert Joseph *lawyer*
Kafka, Barbara Poses *writer, chef*
Kagan, Ilse Echt *librarian, researcher, historian*
Kagan, Julia Lee *magazine editor*
Kaggen, Lois Sheila *non-profit organization executive, advocate*
Kahan, Marlene *professional association executive*
Kahn, Alan Edwin *lawyer*
Kahn, Anthony F. *lawyer*
Kahn, Joseph F. *journalist*
Kahn, Norman *dental educator, pharmacologist*
Kahn, Wolf *artist*
Kailas, Leo George *lawyer*
Kaiser, Walter *language educator*
Kaish, Luise Clayborn *sculptor, painter, educator*
Kaish, Morton *artist, educator*
Kaku, Michio *theoretical nuclear physicist, educator*
Kakutani, Michiko *critic*
Kalajian-Lagani, Donna *publishing executive*
Kalik, Mildred *lawyer*
Kalikow, Peter Stephen *real estate developer, former transportation and publishing executive*
Kalish, Arthur *lawyer*
Kalish, Myron *lawyer*
Kalisher, Simpson *photographer*
Kallir, Jane Katherine *art gallery director, author*
Kallman, Craig *music company executive*
Kallstrom, James K. *state official*
Kalsner, Stanley *pharmacologist, physiologist, educator*
Kalter, Albert *lawyer, educator*
Kamali, Norma *fashion designer*
Kambour, Annaliese Spofford *lawyer, media company executive*
Kamerman, Sheila Brody *social work educator*
Kamin, Sherwin *retired lawyer*
Kaminer, Ariel *editor*
Kaminsky, Alan *lawyer*
Kamlot, Robert *performing arts executive*
Kamm, Linda Heller *lawyer*
Kan, Diana Artemis Mann Shu *painter, art educator, writer*
Kanakaredes, Melina *actress*
Kandarian, Steven A. *insurance company executive*
Kandel, Denise Bystryn *sociologist*
Kandel, Myron *newscaster, columnist*
Kandel, William Lloyd *lawyer, arbitrator, mediator, educator, writer*
Kane, Michael Arthur Christopher *plastic surgeon*
Kane, Richard Joseph *lawyer*
Kane, Siegrun Dinklage *lawyer*
Kane, Thomas Patrick *broadcast executive*
Kanick, Virginia *retired radiologist*
Kann, Peter Robert *retired publishing executive, journalist*
Kanner, Frederick W. *lawyer*
Kanof, Norman B. *dermatologist*
Kanter, Carl Irwin *retired lawyer*
Kanter, Stacy J. *lawyer*
Kanzer, Alan *lawyer*
Kapelman, Barbara Ann *internist, hepatologist, gastroenterologist, educator*
Kaplan, Carl Eliot *lawyer*
Kaplan, Cathy M. *lawyer*
Kaplan, James I. *lawyer*
Kaplan, Jill Rebecca *publishing executive*
Kaplan, Joseph Solte *retired lawyer*
Kaplan, Lawrence Jay *retired economist, educator*
Kaplan, Lewis A. *federal judge*
Kaplan, Madeline *legal administrator*
Kaplan, Mark Norman *lawyer*
Kaplan, Paul Michael *lawyer, educator*
Kaplan, Peter W. *editor-in-chief*
Kaplan, Rick (Richard N. Kaplan) *broadcast executive*
Kaplan, Susan *lawyer*
Kaplan, Theodore Norman *insurance company executive*
Kaplan, Todd P. *diversified financial services company executive*
Kaplitt, Michael Gordon *neurosurgeon, medical educator*
Kaplow, Julie B. *psychologist, educator*
Kapoor, Neera *optometrist, research scientist*
Kappas, Attallah *physician*
Karalekas, George Steven *advertising agency executive, political consultant*
Karan, Donna (Donna Faske) *fashion designer*
Karan, Paul Richard *lawyer*
Karasu, T(oksoz) Byram *psychiatrist, educator, writer*
Karatz, William Warren *lawyer*
Karchin, Louis Samuel *composer, educator*
Kardon, Janet *museum director*
Karelis, Kathleen E. *lawyer, communications systems company executive*
Karlgaard, Rich *publishing executive*
Karmali, Rashida Alimahomed *lawyer*
Karmazin, Mel *broadcast executive*
Karp, Brad S. *lawyer*
Karp, David C. *lawyer*
Karp, Martin Everett *management consultant*
Karp, Nolan S. *plastic surgeon*
Karp, Roberta Schuhalter *retail executive, lawyer*
Karpel, Craig S. *journalist, editor*
Karr, Jane *editor*
Karsen, Sonja Petra *retired literature educator*
Kartiganer, Joseph *retired lawyer*
Kase, Nathan Ginden *dean*
Kasirer, Suri *lobbyist*
Kasowitz, Marc Elliot *lawyer*
Kasparaitis, Darius *professional hockey player*
Kassel, Catherine M. *community, maternal, and women's health nurse, consultant*
Kassel, Terry *human resources specialist*
Kassel, Virginia Weltmer *television producer, scriptwriter*
Kastan, David Scott *literature educator, writer*
Katcher, Richard David *lawyer*
Katsh, Salem Michael *lawyer*
Katz, Abraham *retired foreign service officer*
Katz, Avi *lawyer*
Katz, Bruce Elliot *dermatologist*
Katz, David A. *lawyer*
Katz, Esther *historian, educator*
Katz, Jerome Charles *lawyer*
Katz, Jose *cardiologist, theoretical physicist, educator*
Katz, Lois Anne *internist, nephrologist*
Katz, Robert James *lawyer*
Katz, Ronald Scott *lawyer*
Katz, Stuart Z. *lawyer*
Katzberg, Robert F. *lawyer*
Katzman, John S. *educational organization executive*
Katzmann, Robert Allen *federal judge*
Katzowitz Shenfield, Lauren *philanthropy consultant*
Kauffmann, Stanley Jules *author*
Kaufman, Bel *author, educator*
Kaufman, David Marc *pediatric neurologist*
Kaufman, Henry *diversified financial services company executive*
Kaufman, Robert Max *lawyer, director*
Kaufman, Stephen Edward *lawyer*
Kaufman, Victor A. *broadcast and retired film company executive*
Kaufmann, Mark Steiner *banker, director*
Kavaler, Thomas J. *lawyer*
Kavalerchik, Boris Yakovlevich *application developer, researcher*
Kavesh, Robert A. *economist, educator*
Kayle, Bruce E. *lawyer*
Kayser, Leo III *lawyer*
Kazanjian, John Harold *lawyer*
Kazemi, Farhad *political scientist, educator*
Kean, Hamilton Fish *lawyer*
Keane, Bil *cartoonist*
Keane, Jeff *cartoonist*
Keane, Patrick *marketing executive*
Keany, Sutton *lawyer*
Kearse, Amalya Lyle *federal judge*

Keating, Isabel *actress*
Keegan, Peter W. *diversified holding company executive*
Keenan, John Fontaine *federal judge*
Keenan, Michael Edgar *marketing professional*
Keenan, Terry *anchor, correspondent*
Keene, Donald *writer, translator, language educator*
Keene, Lonnie *lawyer*
Keeney, Scott Neal *molecular biologist*
Kehoe, John P. *investor relations executive*
Kehret, Peg *writer*
Kelleher, Colm *diversified financial services company executive*
Kelleher, Kevin *music company executive*
Kelleher, Kimberly Anderson *magazine publishing executive*
Keller, Bill *executive editor*
Keller, Bruce P. *lawyer*
Kellerman, Jonathan Seth *writer, pediatric psychologist, educator*
Kelley, Darcy B. *biology professor*
Kelley, David N. *lawyer, former United States attorney*
Kelley, Kitty *writer*
Kelley, Mike *artist*
Kelly, Alfred F., Jr. *diversified financial services company executive*
Kelly, Anastasia Donovan (Stasia Kelly) *lawyer, insurance company executive*
Kelly, Christopher M. *lawyer*
Kelly, Ellsworth *painter, sculptor*
Kelly, James *editor*
Kelly, Patrick Joseph *neurosurgeon, educator*
Kelly, R. (Robert Sylvester Kelly) *musician, recording industry executive*
Kelly, Raymond Walter *police commissioner*
Kelly, Robert P. *bank executive*
Kelly, Thomas Jesse, Jr. *molecular biologist*
Kelly, Thomas Michael *lawyer*
Kelly, William Michael *investment company executive*
Kelman, Edward Michael *lawyer*
Kelmenson, Leo-Arthur *advertising executive*
Kelson, Richard B. *metal products executive*
Keltner, Thomas Nethery, Jr. *lawyer*
Kemper, Randy *fashion designer*
Kende, Christopher Burgess *lawyer, educator*
Keneally, Kathryn Marie *lawyer*
Kenneally, Michael E. *diversified financial services company executive*
Kennedy, Adrienne Lita *playwright*
Kennedy, David L. *cosmetics company executive*
Kennedy, Kevin W. *finance company executive*
Kennedy, Robert Francis, Jr. *lawyer, environmentalist*
Kennedy, Thomas Patrick *financial executive*
Kenney, Brian *editor-in-chief*
Kenney, John Joseph *lawyer*
Kenny, Tom *actor*
Keno, Leigh R. *antiques dealer, appraiser*
Keno, Leslie B. *antiques dealer, appraiser*
Kent, Julie *dancer, actress, model*
Kent, Linda Gail *dancer*
Kent, Steven *lawyer*
Kent, Susan *library director, consultant*
Keogh, Kevin *lawyer*
Kepets, Hugh Michael *artist*
Kepke, Matthew Aaron *lawyer*
Keppler, Herbert *publishing executive*
Kercheval, Michael P. *real estate company executive*
Kerik, Bernard Bailey *security firm executive, former police commissioner*
Kern, George Calvin, Jr. *lawyer*
Kern, William Bliem, Jr. *minister*
Kerner, Gerald *lawyer*
Kernochan, John Marshall *lawyer, educator*
Kerrest, Jacques Dominique *broadcasting company executive*
Kerrey, Bob (J. Robert Kerrey) *academic administrator, former senator*
Kerschner, Edward *brokerage house executive*
Kerz, Louise (Louise Hirschfeld) *historian*
Kessel, Mark *lawyer*
Kessinger, Kevin M. *diversified financial services company executive*
Kessler, Eric *broadcast executive*
Kessler, Jeffrey L. *lawyer*
Kessler, Stuart *accountant, financial planner*
Ketchum, Richard G. *stock exchange executive, lawyer*
Keteyian, Armen *news correspondent*
Kezsbom, Allen *lawyer*
Khalil, Mounir A. *librarian, educator*
Khalilzad, Zalmay Mamozy *ambassador*
Khatamee, Masood Ahmad *obstetrician, gynecologist*
Kheel, Robert J. *lawyer*
Kheradpir, Shaygan *information technology executive*
Khuri, Nicola Najib *physicist, researcher*
Kidd, Chip *book designer, writer*
Kid Rock, (Robert James Ritchie) *singer*
Kiekhofer, William Henry *lawyer*
Kiernan, John S. *lawyer*
Kies, David M. *lawyer*
Kiessling, B. Robbins *lawyer*
Kilik, Jon *film producer*
Killian, John F. *telecommunications industry executive*
Killip, Thomas *cardiologist*
Kilpatrick, Auston Marm (A. Marm Kilpatrick) *research scientist*
Kilpatrick, Donald G. *lawyer*
Kim, Ana H. *otolaryngologist, educator*
Kim, Atta *photographer*
Kim, Dow *investment company executive*
Kimball, John Devereux *lawyer*
Kimber, Karen Beecher *ESL educator*
Kimmel Cohn, Roberta *art dealer, educator*
Kimmelman, Michael Simon *art critic*
Kinberg, Judy *television producer and director*
Kindler, Jeffrey B. *pharmaceutical company executive, lawyer*
Kindler, Robert Alan *investment banker*
King, B.B. (Riley B. King) *singer, guitarist*
King, Edward Joseph *clinical chemist, laboratory administrator*
King, Gayle *editor, radio personality, television personality*
King, Henry Lawrence *lawyer*
King, Marcia Gygli *artist*
King, Stephen C. *lawyer, commissioner, educator*
Kinne, David Weir *retired surgeon*
Kinnell, Galway *poet, translator*
Kinney, Catherine R. *stock exchange executive*
Kinney, Gilbert Hart *investor*
Kinney, Stephen Hoyt, Jr. *lawyer*
Kinsolving, Charles McIlvaine, Jr. *marketing executive*
Kinstler, Everett Raymond *artist*
Kinzler, Thomas Benjamin *lawyer*
Kirby, John Joseph, Jr. *lawyer*
Kirdar, Nemir Amin *banker*
Kirkham, D. Collier *lawyer*
Kirman, Igor *lawyer*
Kirpalani, Susheel *lawyer*
Kirsch, Donald *financial consultant*
Kirschbaum, Myron *lawyer*
Kirschenbaum, Alexander *medical educator*
Kirschner, Kenneth Harold *lawyer*
Kirsh, Michael Alan *financial estate planner*
Kislik, Richard William *publishing executive*
Kissel, Howard William *drama critic*
Kisselgoff, Anna *dance critic*
Kitcher, Philip Stuart *philosophy educator*
Kizer, Jorge Ruben *cardiologist, epidemiologist*
Klapholz, Marc *cardiologist*
Klapper, Andrew Mark *plastic surgeon*
Klapper, Richard H. *lawyer*
Klause, Annette Curtis *librarian, writer*
Klausen, Raymond *theatre set and television production designer, sculptor*
Kleber, Herbert David *psychiatrist, educator*
Kleckner, Robert George, Jr. *retired lawyer*
Kleeblatt, Norman L. *museum curator*
Klein, Calvin Richard *fashion designer*
Klein, Cynthia *art appraiser*
Klein, Eleazer *lawyer*
Klein, Harvey *medical educator*
Klein, Jason Evan *publishing executive*
Klein, Jeffrey Peter *investor*
Klein, Joel Irwin *school system administrator*
Klein, Laura Colin *publishing executive*
Klein, Martin I. *lawyer*
Klein, Michael S. *diversified financial services company executive*
Klein, Naomi *journalist*
Klein, Richard S. *lawyer*
Klein, Robert *comedian, actor*
Klein, T(heodore) E(ibon) D(onald) *writer*
Kleinbard, Edward D. *lawyer*
Kleinbaum, Sharon *rabbi*
Kleinberg, Norman Charles *lawyer*
Kleinfeld, Klaus *metal products executive, former electronics executive*
Kleinsinger, Stuart *retired lawyer, music producer*
Klemann, Gilbert Lacy, II, *lawyer*
Kliavkoff, George *sports association executive*
Kligerman, Thomas Alexander *architect*
Kliment, Robert Michael *architect*
Kliment, Stephen Alexander *architect, editor, journalist*
Klimstra, David S. *pathologist*
Kline, Eugene Monroe *lawyer*
Kline, Kevin Delaney *actor*
Klingensmith, Michael *publishing executive*
Klinger, Alan Mark *lawyer*
Klingsberg, David *lawyer*
Klipstein, Robert Alan *lawyer*
Klotz, Martin B. *lawyer*
Kluger, Jeffrey *reporter, author*
Knapp, Albert Bruce *gastroenterologist*
Knapp, Robert Charles *retired obstetrics and gynecology educator*
Knerr, Anthony David *financial consultant*
Knobler, Peter Stephen *magazine editor, writer*
Knopf, Alfred, Jr. *retired publisher*
Kobak, James Benedict, Jr. *lawyer, educator*
Kobi, Daniel Casey *lawyer*
Koblenz, Michael Robert *lawyer*
Kobrin, Lawrence Alan *lawyer*
Koch, David Hamilton *chemical company executive*
Koch, Ed (Edward Irving Koch) *lawyer, former mayor*
Koch, Edward Richard *lawyer, accountant*
Koch, Stephen Bayard *writer, language educator*
Koegel, William Fisher *lawyer*
Koeltl, John George *federal judge*
Koen, Robert G. *lawyer*
Koepp, Stephen *editor*
Koeppel, Noel Immanuel *financial planner, securities broker, real estate broker*
Koerner, Brendan I. *columnist*
Kogod, Robert P. *philanthropist, former real estate company executive*
Kohl, Robert L. *lawyer*
Kohlmann, Susan J. *lawyer*
Kohn, A. Eugene *architect*
Kohn, Immanuel *lawyer*
Kohut, John Walter *corporate executive*
Kojevnikov, Boris Oleg *lawyer, consultant*
Koke, Richard Joseph *writer, curator*
Kolata, Gina *journalist*
Kolatch, Myron *magazine editor*
Kolben, Deborah *editor*
Kolker, Adam Ross *plastic surgeon, educator*
Kolodny, Edwin Hillel *neurologist, geneticist, director*
Kolson, Ann J. *editor*
Komisar, Arnold *otolaryngologist, educator*
Koob, Charles Edward *lawyer*
Koons, Jeff *artist*
Koopersmith, Kim *lawyer*
Kopelman, Richard Eric *management educator*
Kopenhaver, Patricia Ellsworth *podiatrist*
Koplewicz, Harold Samuel *child and adolescent psychiatrist*
Koplik, Michael R. *sales representation company executive*
Koplovitz, Kay *television network executive*
Kopp, Wendy *educational association administrator*
Koppelman, Chaim *artist, educator*
Koppelman, Charles A. *record company executive*
Koppelman, Dorothy Myers *artist, consultant*
Koral, Alan Max *lawyer*
Kordish, Heike Christiane *library director*
Kornberg, Alan William *lawyer*
Kornfeld, Neil S. *lawyer*
Kornreich, Edward Scott *lawyer*
Korotkin, Michael Paul *lawyer*
Kors, Michael (Karl Anderson Jr.) *fashion designer*
Korsten, Susan Snyder *science educator*
Kosakow, James Matthew *lawyer*
Koslow, Jonathan L. *lawyer*
Kostelanetz, Richard *writer, artist*
Koster, Elaine *publishing executive*
Kostova, Elizabeth *writer*
Koteff, Ellen *editor*
Koten, John F. *editor-in-chief*
Kotlowitz, Robert *writer, editor*
Kotuk, Andrea Mikotajuk *public relations executive, writer*
Kotzwinkle, William *writer*
Kourides, Ione Anne *endocrinologist, researcher, educator*
Kove, Miriam *psychotherapist*
Kovner, Bruce S. *investment company executive*
Kowalski, Michael J. *retail products executive*
Kozak, Harley Jane *actress, writer*
Kozinn, Allan *music critic, reporter*
Kozlowski, Cheryl M. *fixed income analyst*
Kraemer, Harry M. Jansen, Jr. *investment and former medical products executive*
Kraemer, Lillian Elizabeth *retired lawyer*
Kraines, Merrill M. *lawyer*
Krakoff, Reed D. *apparel designer*
Kram, Shirley Wohl *federal judge*
Kramarsky, Werner H. *art collector*
Kramer, Daniel Jonathan *lawyer*
Kramer, Linda Konheim *curator, art historian*
Kramer, Marc Z. *publishing executive*
Kramon, Glenn *newspaper business editor*
Krane, Steven Charles *lawyer*
Krantz, Judith Tarcher *novelist*
Krasna, Alvin Isaac *biochemist, educator*
Krasner, Daniel Walter *lawyer*
Krasnow, Richard P. *lawyer*
Kraus, Peter Steven *diversified financial services company executive*
Kraushar, Jonathan Pollack *communications and media consultant*
Krauss, Herbert Harris *psychologist*
Kravis, Henry R. *investment banker*
Kravitz, Lee *editor*
Krawcheck, Sallie L. *diversified financial services company executive*
Krebs, Carl F. *architectural firm executive*
Kreek, Mary Jeanne *physician*
Kreidman, Perry L. *lawyer*
Kreisberg, Neil Ivan *advertising executive*
Kreitzman, Ralph J. *lawyer*
Krell, David *stock exchange executive*
Krementz, Jill *photographer, author*
Kressel, Henry *venture capitalist*
Kreuther, Gabriel *chef*
Krieger, Sanford *lawyer*
Krill, Kay (Katherine Lawther Krill) *apparel executive*
Krinsky, Carol Herselle *art historian, educator*
Krinsky, Robert Daniel *consulting firm executive*
Kristof, Nicholas Donabet *journalist*
Kroeber, Karl *language educator*
Kroell, Devi *accessories designer*
Kroft, Steve *news correspondent, editor*
Kroll, Sol *lawyer*
Krouse, George Raymond, Jr. *lawyer*
Krueger, Richard Bohn *psychiatrist*
Krueger, Sam Quan *museum administrator*
Kruger, Barbara *artist*
Kruger, Steven F. *literature educator*
Krukowski, Jan *communications executive*
Krupman, William Allan *lawyer*
Krupp, Fred D. *lawyer, environmental services administrator*
Kubek, Gary W. *lawyer*
Kuby, Ronald Lawrence *lawyer*
Kuchta, Ronald Andrew *museum director, editor, curator*
Kudisch, Marc *actor*
Kuehn, Coleen P. *advertising executive*
Kuh, Richard Henry *lawyer*
Kuhbach, Robert Gerdes *manufacturing executive*
Kuhn, James D. *real estate company executive*
Kujawski, Elizabeth Szancer *art curator, consultant*
Kulish, Nicholas *reporter*
Kumalo, Dumisani Shadrack *ambassador*
Kumra, Vandana *otolaryngologist*
Kunes, Richard W. *cosmetics executive*
Kuntz, Lee Allan *lawyer*
Kuntz, William Francis, II, *lawyer, educator*
Kuo, John Tsungfen *geophysicist, educator, researcher*
Kuperman, Robert Ian *retired advertising agency executive*
Kurman, Juta *music educator*
Kurnow, Ernest *statistician, educator*
Kurtz, Jerome *lawyer, educator*
Kurz, William Charles Frederick *lawyer*
Kurzweil, Edith *social sciences educator, editor*
Kurzweil, Harvey *lawyer*
Kushner, Jared C. *publishing executive, real estate developer*
Kutosh, Sue *artist*
Kuttler, Judith Esther *retired psychotherapist*
Ky, Alex Jenny *surgeon, educator*
Kya-Hill, Robert *actor, educator*
Kyriakou, Linda Grace *communications executive*
La Barbara, Joan *composer, musician, singer*
LaBarre, Dennis W. *lawyer*
LaBelle, Patti (Patricia Louise Holte) *singer, entertainer*
Labunski, Stephen Bronislaw *professional society administrator*
Lachman, Leigh Jay *plastic surgeon, educator*
Lachman, Marguerite Leanne *real estate investment advisor*
Lachmann, Elisabeth Amanda *physician*
Lack, Andrew R. *music company executive*
Lack, Robert Joel *lawyer*
Lackner, Bernard *hotel executive*
Lackritz, Marc E. *securities industry association executive*
Lacovara, Philip Allen *lawyer*
Lacy, Robinson Burrell *lawyer*
Ladjevardi, Hamid *portfolio manager*
Lafavore, Michael J. *editor-in-chief*
Lagani, Daniel *publishing executive*
Lagani, Joseph A. *publishing executive*
Lahey, John H. *lawyer*
Lai, W(ei) Michael *retired engineering educator*
Lalwani, Anil Kumar *otolaryngologist*
Lam, Derek *apparel designer*
Lamagna, Carlo M. *art educator*
LaMattina, John L. *pharmaceutical executive*
Lamb, Robert Boyden *finance and management educator*
Lamb, Wally *writer*
Lamia, Thomas Roger *lawyer*
Lamle, Hugh Roy *investment advisor, consultant*
Lamm, Donald Stephen *literary agent*
Lamm, Norman *academic administrator, rabbi*
Lammie, James Louis *engineering executive, retired military officer*
Lamont, Lansing *journalist, writer, public affairs and trust executive*
Lamport, Anthony Matthew *venture capitalist*
Lamster, Ira Barry *dean, academic administrator*
Lanchner, Bertrand Martin *lawyer, advertising executive*
Landau, David H. *lawyer*
Landau, Sidney Ivan *lexicographer*
Landman, Jonathan *editor*
Landon, Dain Charles *lawyer*
Landrigan, Philip John *epidemiologist*
Landry, Donald William *physician, educator, director, scientist*
Lane, Jeffrey Bruce *diversified financial services company executive*
Lane, Kenneth Jay *jewelry designer*
Lane, Kenneth Robert *producer, distributor*
Lang, Everett Francis, Jr. *brokerage house executive*
Lang, George *restaurateur*
Lang, Pearl *dancer, choreographer*
Lang, Stephen *actor*
Langan, Richard F., Jr. *lawyer*
Lange, Liz *apparel designer, director*
Lange, Marvin Robert *lawyer*
Lange, Phil C. *retired education educator*
Langer, Bruce Alden *lawyer*
Langer, David J. *neurological surgeon*
Langford, Laura Sue *corporate financial executive*
Langhammer, Fred H. *cosmetics company executive*
Langone, Kenneth G. *investment company executive*
Langton, Cleve Swanson *advertising executive*
Lannamann, Richard Stuart *executive search consultant*
Lans, Deborah Eisner *lawyer*
Lansbury, Edgar George *theatrical producer*
Lansner, Gabrielle *choreographer, dancer, performing company executive, actress*
Lansner, Ruth L. *lawyer*
Lanyon, Ellen *artist, educator*
Lao, Joseph R. *humanities educator, researcher*
Lao, Kenny *restaurant manager*
Lapham, Lewis Henry *editor, television personality, writer*
Lapidus, Mitchell *lawyer*
Lapierre, Dominique *writer, historian, philanthropist*
LaQuaglia, Michael Patrick *pediatric surgeon, neuroblastoma researcher*
Laragh, John Henry *cardiologist, surgeon, educator*
Larberg, John Frederick *retired social welfare executive, wine consultant, educator*
LaRocca, Salvatore *sports association executive*
Larose, Lawrence Alfred *lawyer*
Larsen, Jonathan Zerbe *journalist*
Larson, Steven Mark *physician*
Lasch, Christopher *architect*
Lash, Stephen Sycle *auction company executive*
Lasker, Jonathan Lewis *artist*
Lasker, Joseph L. *artist, illustrator*
Laskin, Richard Sheldon *orthopedic surgeon*
Lasser, Joseph Robert *investment company executive*
Lat, David B. *former assistant US attorney, online-journalist, editor, blogger*
Lataille, Ronald H. *telecommunications industry executive*
Latza, William D. *lawyer*
Lauder, Aerin *cosmetics executive*
Lauder, Evelyn H. *cosmetics executive*
Lauder, Jo Carole *art association administrator*
Lauder, Leonard Alan *cosmetic and fragrance company executive*
Lauder, Ronald Stephen *investor*
Lauder, William P. *cosmetics executive*
Laue, Bruce Antonio *financial consultant, writer*
Lauer, Eliot *lawyer*
Lauer, Matt *television personality*
Laufer, Jacob *lawyer*
Laufer, Mark Vladimir *retired engineering educator*
Laufman, Harold *surgeon, consultant*
Laumont, Philippe Emile *communications executive*
Launer, Leland C., Jr. *insurance company executive*
Lauren, Ralph *fashion designer*
Laurence, Jeffrey Conrad *immunologist, educator*
Laurence, Michael Marshall *foundation administrator*
Laurie, Nancy Walton *retail executive*

Lavin, Howard S. *lawyer*
Lawhon, Charla *editor*
Lawrence, Bryan Hunt *investment company executive*
Lawrence, Christopher Rueckert *investment banker*
Lawrence, Lauren *psychotherapist, writer*
Lawrence, Nina *publishing executive*
Lawson, Nigella *cookbook writer, celebrity chef*
Lawson, William *otolaryngologist, educator*
Lawson-Johnston, Peter, II, *investment company executive*
Lawson-Johnston, Peter Orman *foundation executive*
Lax, Peter David *mathematician, educator*
Laybourne, Geraldine B. *broadcast executive*
Layton, Donald Harvey *retired banker*
Lazarcik, Gregor *economist, educator, financial research company executive*
Lazarus, Adrienne *retail executive*
Lazarus, Shelly (Rochelle Braff Lazarus) *advertising executive*
Lazio, Rick Anthony (Enrico Anthony Lazio) *bank executive, former congressman*
Leach, Bryan *music company executive*
Leahey, Lynn *editor-in-chief*
Leahey, Miles Cary *economist*
Leahy, Michael Joseph *retired newspaper editor*
Leahy, Robert Louis *psychologist*
Leavitt, David Livingstone *architect*
Lebenthal, Alexandra *investment firm executive*
LeBlang, Skip Alan *lawyer*
LeBlond, Richard Knight, II, *banker*
Lebow, Mark Denis *lawyer*
LeClerc, Paul *library director*
Lederberg, Joshua *geneticist, educator*
Lederman, Lawrence *lawyer, writer, educator*
Ledger, William Joe *obstetrician, educator*
LeDoux, Joseph E. *neuroscientist, educator*
Lee, Amy *singer*
Lee, Christopher *chef*
Lee, David Hee-Don *trade association administrator, educator*
Lee, Frances Helen *editor*
Lee, Helie *writer*
Lee, In-Young *lawyer*
Lee, James Bainbridge, Jr. *bank executive*
Lee, Jennifer *journalist*
Lee, Jerome G. *lawyer*
Lee, Paul Lawrence *lawyer*
Lee, Sally A. *editor-in-chief*
Lee, Sandra *food service executive, product designer, chef*
Lee, Thomas F. *art association administrator*
Lee, Tsung-Dao *physicist, researcher*
Lee, Vivian S. *radiologist*
Leech, Katharine (Kitty Leech) *costume designer, educator*
Leeds, Norman E. *medical educator, radiologist*
Leeman, Eve *psychiatrist*
Lees, Alfred William *former magazine editor, writer*
Leet, Mildred Robbins *social welfare administrator, consultant*
Lefcourt, Gerald B. *lawyer*
LeFevre, David E. *lawyer, business executive*
Lefferts, Gillet, Jr. *architect*
Leffler, Marvin *foundation administrator, writer*
Lefkowitz, David S. *lawyer*
Lefkowitz, Howard N. *lawyer*
Legrand, Michel Jean *composer*
Legvold, Robert *political science professor*
Lehman, Edward William *social studies educator, researcher*
Lehman, Mark E. *lawyer*
Lehmann, Ruth *geneticist, educator*
Lehmann-Haupt, Christopher Charles Herbert *book reviewer*
Leiber, Gerson August *artist*
Leibert, Burton M. *lawyer*
Leibovitz, Annie *photographer*
Leibowitz, Herbert Akiba *literature and language professor, writer*
Leibowitz, Martin L. *financial services company executive*
Leichtling, Michael Alfred *lawyer*
Leifer, Edgar *physician, retired medical educator*
Leighton, Lawrence Ward *investment banker*
Leisure, Peter Keeton *federal judge*
Leive, Cynthia *editor-in-chief*
Lekberg, Barbara *sculptor*
Leland, Richard G(uy) *lawyer*
L'Engle, Madeleine (Mrs. Hugh Franklin) *writer*
Lennon, Thomas Furneaux *television producer, writer*
Lenobel, Jeffrey A. *lawyer*
Lenox, Adriane *actress*
Lenz, Dolly (Idaliz Dolly Lenz) *real estate broker*
Leon, Martin Bert *cardiologist, educator*
Leonard, Edwin Deane *lawyer*
Leonard, John *film and literature critic*
Leppard, Raymond John *conductor, musician*
Leritz, Lawrence R. *choreographer, singer, dancer*
Lerner, Eric M. *lawyer*
Lerner, Frederic Howard *finance executive, educator*
Lerner, Jonathan J. *lawyer*
Lerner, Martin *museum curator*
Lerner, Max Kasner *lawyer*
Lerner, Richard E. *lawyer*
Lerner, Sandra *artist*
Lesch, Michael Oscar *lawyer*
Lesk, Ann Berger *lawyer*
Leslie, Seymour Marvin *communications executive, director*
Lesman, Michael Steven *lawyer*
Lessing, Brian Reid *actuary*
Lessing, Stephen M. *finance company executive*
Lessnau, Klaus-Dieter Karl *pulmonologist, director, medical educator*
Leubert, Alfred Otto Paul *management consultant*
Leung, Firman *investment bank executive*
Leung, Sandra *pharmaceutical executive, lawyer*
Levai, Pierre Alexandre *art gallery executive*
Leval, Pierre Nelson *federal judge*
Levander, Andrew Joshua *lawyer*
Leven, Ann Ruth *financial consultant*
Levie, Joseph Henry *lawyer, banker*
Levin, Alan M. *television journalist*
Levin, Ezra Gurion *lawyer*
Levin, Frances R. *psychiatrist, educator*
Levin, Gail *writer, educator, photographer*
Levin, Henry Mordechai *economist, educator*
Levin, Herbert *retired diplomat, foundation administrator*
Levin, Ira *writer, playwright*
Levin, Janna J. *physicist, educator*
Levin, Michael Joseph *lawyer*
Levin, Peter S.W. *lawyer*
Levin, Susan Bass *state agency administrator, lawyer*
Levine, Adam Noah *singer*
Levine, David *artist*
Levine, Ellen R. *editor-in-chief*
Levine, Gail Carson *writer*
Levine, James *conductor, music director, pianist*
Levine, Judy Kendall *real estate broker, interior designer, writer*
Levine, Louis D. *museum administrator, archaeologist*
Levine, Michael J. *sports products company executive*
Levine, Naomi Bronheim *academic administrator*
Levine, Robert H. *medical educator, psychiatrist*
Levine, Robert Jay *lawyer*
Levine, Ronald Jay *lawyer*
Levine, Sherrie *conceptual artist*
Levinson, Paul Howard *lawyer*
Levinson, Robert Alan *textiles executive*
Levinson, Stephen *television producer*
Levinson, Warren Mitchell *broadcast journalist*
Levitan, David M(aurice) *lawyer, educator*
Levitan, Max Fishel *anatomist, geneticist, educator*
Levitan, Steve *lawyer*
Levitt, Arthur, Jr. *investment company executive, former federal agency administrator*
Levitt, Harry *speech and hearing scientist*
Levitz, Paul Elliot *publishing executive*
Levkovich, Tobias M. *financial analyst, investment advisor*
Levoy, Myron *author*
Levy, Albert *physician*
Levy, Clifford J. *reporter*
Levy, Dany *publishing executive*
Levy, Herbert Monte *lawyer*
Levy, Jack *investment banker*
Levy, Shawn Anthony *writer*
Levy, Stanley Herbert *lawyer*
Lew, Jacob *public administration educator*
Lewin, Robert *lawyer*
Lewis, Jerry Lee *country-rock singer, musician*
Lewis, Jonathan Joseph *surgical oncologist, molecular biologist, educator, entrepreneur*
Lewis, Michael *writer, journalist*
Lewis, W. Walker *strategic and financial advisory company executive*
Lewis, William M. *diversified financial services company executive*
Lewy, Robert Max *physician*
Lewyn, Ann Salfeld *retired English as a second language educator*
Lewyn, Thomas Mark *lawyer*
Li, Tze-chung *lawyer, educator*
Liao, Martha *geneticist*
Libby, Daniel M. *pulmonologist*
Libchaber, Albert Joseph *physics professor*
Liberman, Megan Rose *editor*
Libeskind, Daniel *architect*
Libin, Paul *theater producer and director*
LiBretto, John Charles *television director*
Lichtenstein, Warren G. *investment company executive*
Lichtman, Adam David *anesthesiologist, educator*
Liddle, Jeffrey L. *lawyer*
Lieb, Richard Jay *investment banker*
Liebenson, Jeffrey M. *lawyer*
Lieber, Robert C. *investment company executive*
Lieberman, Dave *chef*
Lieberman, James Sanford *physiatrist, neurologist*
Lieberman, Nancy Ann *lawyer*
Liebman, Lance Malcolm *law educator*
Liebman, Pamela *real estate company executive*
Liebman, Theodore *architect*
Liebmann, Jeff S. *lawyer*
Liff, Zanvel A. *psychologist*
Liftin, John Matthew *lawyer*
Lifton, Robert Kenneth *manufacturing executive*
Ligh, Jonathan Kennard *ophthalmologist*
Liles, Kevin *music company executive*
Lilly, Evangeline *actress*
Lim, Phillip *apparel designer*
Lima, Adriana Francesca *model*
Liman, Lewis Jeffrey *lawyer*
Limbaugh, Rush Hudson III *radio talk show host*
Lincoln, Edmond Lynch *investment banker*
Lincoln, Stephen *publishing executive*
Lindahl, Sheena *entrepreneur*
Lindauer, Erik D. *lawyer*
Lindblom, Marjorie Press *lawyer*
Lindley, David Morrison *lawyer*
Lindo, Stephen T. *lawyer*
Lindsay, George Peter *lawyer*
Lindsay-Abaire, David *playwright*
Lingeman, Richard Roberts *editor-in-chief, writer*
Link, Robert O., Jr. *lawyer*
Linker, Arthur S. *lawyer*
Lipkin, Martin *medical educator, researcher*
Lipman, Ira Ackerman *security service company executive*
Lipper, Kenneth *investment banker, film producer, writer*
Lippert, Nels T. *lawyer*
Lippman, Jonathan *judge*
Lippman, Laura *writer*
Lippman, Sharon Rochelle *art historian and therapist, filmmaker*
Lipscomb, James Louis *lawyer, insurance company executive*
Lipscomb, Thomas Heber III *media company executive*
Lipsey, Robert Edward *economist, educator*
Lipsky, Pat *artist*
Liptak, Adam *lawyer, reporter*
Lipton, Charles *public relations executive*
Lipton, Joan Elaine *advertising executive*
Lipton, Martin *lawyer*
Lisanti, Mark V. *blogger, writer*
Liss, Norman *lawyer*
Litman, Jack Theodore *lawyer*
Little, Robert David *library science professor*
Littman, Brett *museum director, art critic*
Littman, Dan R. *microbiologist*
Lituchy, Gregg *dentist*
Litvack, Sanford Martin *lawyer*
Litvin, Joel M. *sports association executive, lawyer*
Litwin, Ethan *lawyer*
Litwin, Leonard *real estate company executive*
Liu, Kai-Lih *epidemiologist*
Liu, Lewis-Guodo *information scientist, educator*
Liu, Tony *chef*
Livingston, Debra Ann *federal judge, educator*
Llinás, Rodolfo Riascos *neuroscientist, researcher*
Lloyd, Jean *retired early childhood educator*
Lloyd, Kenneth L. *columnist*
Lloyd, William Frederick *lawyer*
Lo, Anita *chef*
Loacker, Lynn J. *lawyer*
Loar, Peggy Ann *foundation administrator, museum administrator*
Lobenfeld, Eric Jay *lawyer*
Lobl, Herbert Max *lawyer, writer*
Lobo, Rogerio Arnaldo *obstetrician, gynecologist*
Lobrano, John D. *lawyer*
Lockshin, Michael Dan *rheumatologist*
Lodge, Henry Sears *physician*
Loeb, Daniel Seth *investment company executive*
Loeb, John Langeloth, Jr. *investment counselor, consultant*
Loeb, John Nichols *physician, educator*
Loeb, Larry Morris *communications company executive*
Loeb, Lisa *singer, lyricist*
Loeb, Marshall Robert *journalist*
Loeb, Thomas Wolf *plastic surgeon*
Loengard, John Borg *photographer, editor*
Loengard, Richard Otto, Jr. *lawyer*
Loft, Lloyd Mark *otolaryngologist*
Logan, Kenneth Richard *lawyer*
Logan, Lara *news correspondent*
Lohr, Steve *reporter*
Løj, Ellen Margrethe *ambassador*
Lombardi, Joseph J. *retail executive*
London, Herbert Ira *humanities educator, academic administrator*
London, Martin *lawyer*
London, Nora Eleonor *foundation administrator*
Loney, Glenn Meredith *theater educator*
Longley, Marjorie Watters *newspaper executive*
Longobardi, David *editor-in-chief*
Longstreth, Bevis *lawyer*
Loo, Marcus Hsieu-Hong *urologist, physician, educator*
Loomis, Carol J. *journalist*
Lopez, Ralph Ivan *pediatrics educator*
Lorber, Barbara Heyman *communications executive, event producer*
Lorch, Maristella De Panizza *writer, educator*
Lord, Barbara Joanni *lawyer*
Lord, Marvin *apparel executive*
Loring, John Robbins *artist, writer*
LoSchiavo, Linda Bosco *library director*
Losier, Marie *film director*
Loss, Margaret Ruth *lawyer*
Lothian, James Robert *economist, educator*
Lotwin, Stanford Gerald *lawyer*
Lou, Liza *artist*
Louganis, Greg E(fthimios) *retired Olympic athlete, actor*
Loughlin, Walter P. *lawyer*
Loughran, Peter J. *lawyer*
Love-Hassell, Esther Boyer *special education educator, consultant*
Lovell, Whitfield *artist*
Lowe, Nick *vocalist, musician, producer*
Lowenberg, Marc Gregory *dentist*
Lowenfeld, Andreas Frank *law educator*
Lowenfels, Fred M. *lawyer*
Lowenfels, Lewis David *lawyer*
Lowenstein, Louis *law educator*
Lowitt, Ian T. *investment company executive*
Lowman, David *mortgage company executive*
Lowry, Glenn David *art museum director*
Lowry, Nicholas D. *art appraiser*
Lowy, George Theodore *lawyer*
Lubars, David *advertising executive*
Lubell, Michael Stephen *physicist, educator*
Lubetski, Edith Esther *librarian*
Lubovitch, Lar *dancer, choreographer*
Lucas, James E(vans) *operatic director*
Luce, Charles Franklin *retired utilities executive, lawyer*
Lucht, John Charles *management consultant, writer*
Luckman, Sharon Gersten *arts administrator*
Luke, Douglas Sigler *investment company executive*
Luks, Allan Barry *executive director*
Lum, Larry *lawyer*
Lundberg, George David, II, *medical editor-in-chief, pathologist*
Lunding, Christopher Hanna *lawyer*
Lundquist, John Milton *librarian, Egyptologist, author, travel writer, photographer*
Lundqvist, Henrik *professional hockey player*
Lunemann, Jan D. *neurologist, researcher*
Luntz, Maurice Harold *ophthalmologist*
Luo, Michael *journalist*
Lupert, Leslie Allan *lawyer*
Lupica, Mike (Michael Thomas Lupica) *sports columnist*
LuPone, Patti *actress*
Luria, Mary Mercer *lawyer*
Lurie, Alison *writer*
Lurie, Ranan Raymond *political cartoonist, artist, journalist*
Lutnick, Howard William *brokerage house executive*
Lutz, Tina *apparel designer*
Lutzker, Elliot Howard *lawyer*
Lutzker, Joel E. *lawyer*
Luxenberg, Arthur Martin *lawyer*
Lyddane, John Lawrence Ashton *lawyer*
Lyden, David Charles *oncologist, cell biologist*
Lyman, Peggy *artistic director, dancer, choreographer, educator*
Lynch, Dick *telecommunications industry executive*
Lynch, Gary G. *investment company executive, lawyer*
Lynch, Gerard E. *federal judge*
Lynch, Loretta E. *lawyer, former prosecutor*
Lynch, Luke Daniel, Jr. *lawyer*
Lyne, Susan Markham *multi-media company executive, former broadcast executive*
Lynn, Theodore Stanley *lawyer*
Lynne, Michael *film company executive*
Lyon, Carl Francis, Jr. *lawyer*
Lyons, Daniel *editor, website blogger*
Lyons, John Matthew *telecommunications industry, broadcast executive*
Lyons, Nick *publishing executive*
Ma, Yo-Yo *cellist*
Maack, Thomas *physiology professor*
Maas, Jane Brown *advertising executive*
Maas, Werner Karl *microbiology educator*
Maazel, Lorin *conductor, composer, violinist, music director*
MacAllaster, Archie *investment company executive*
Macan, William Alexander, IV, *lawyer*
MacArthur, John Roderick C. G. (Rick MacArthur) *magazine publisher, journalist*
Macchiarola, Frank Joseph *academic administrator, educator*
MacCrate, Robert *lawyer*
MacDonald, Alan S. *diversified financial services company executive*
Macer-Story, Eugenia Ann *writer*
MacGowan, Sandra Firelli *publishing executive, consultant*
Mack, Dennis Wayne *lawyer*
Mack, John J. *diversified financial services company executive*
MacKay, Malcolm *executive search consultant*
Macken, Daniel Loos *cardiologist, educator*
Mackey, Patricia Elaine *university librarian*
MacKinnon, Roderick *neuroscientist, educator*
MacLachlan, Patricia *author*
MacLean, Babcock *lawyer*
MacLellan, Steve *bank executive*
MacLeod, William Bentley *economics, law professor*
Maclin, Samuel Todd *diversified financial services company executive*
Mac Low, Mordecai-Mark *astrophysicist*
MacRae, Cameron Farquhar III *lawyer*
Macri, Theodore William *book publisher*
Macris, Michael *lawyer*
Madden, John *sportscaster, retired professional football coach*
Madden, John J. *lawyer*
Madden, John Patrick *lawyer*
Madden, Michael Daniel *finance company executive*
Madden, Mickey *musician*
Maddow, Rachel *radio personality, political activist*
Madison, George W. *lawyer, corporate financial executive*
Mager, Ezra Pascal *investment company executive*
Maguire, Gregory *writer*
Maher, Jonathan Bannon *finance executive*
Maheras, Thomas G. *diversified financial services company executive*
Mahon, Arthur Joseph *lawyer*
Mahoney, Margaret Ellerbe *foundation executive*
Maidman, Richard Harvey Mortimer *lawyer*
Maione, Donna *fashion designer*
Maitland, Guy Edison Clay *lawyer*
Maitland, Wendy *real estate company executive, psychotherapist*
Makovsky, Kenneth Dale *public relations executive*
Malamud, Deborah C. *law educator*
Malandrino, Catherine *apparel designer*
Maldonado-Bear, Rita Marinita *economist, educator*
Malernee, James Kent, Jr. *financial consultant*
Malfa, Frances *lawyer*
Malgieri, Nick *food service executive, educator, chef, writer*
Malin, Irving *language educator, critic*
Malina, Michael *lawyer*
Malinowska-Sempruch, Kasia *director*
Malitz, Sidney *psychiatrist, educator*
Malkin, Barry *film editor, consultant*
Malkin, Peter Laurence *lawyer, investor*
Malkin, Stanley Lee *neurologist*
Mallin, Joel *lawyer*
Mallow, Matthew J. *lawyer*
Malone, Beverly Louise *nursing administrator, former dean*
Manassah, Jamal Tewfek *electrical engineer, educator, management consultant*
Mandabach, Caryn *television producer*
Mandel, Carol *university librarian*
Mandelbaum, Harold Neil *accountant*
Mandelbaum, Jay *diversified financial services company executive*
Mandelker, Lawrence Arthur *lawyer*
Mandelstam, Charles Lawrence *lawyer*
Maneker, Morton M. *lawyer*
Maney, Michael Mason *lawyer*
Manger, William Muir *internist, educator, writer, research scientist*
Manges, James Horace *investment banker*

Manilow, Barry (Barry Alan Pincus) *singer, composer*
Manley, James L. *molecular biologist, educator*
Mann, Frank Bert *artist, educator*
Mann, James Brooks *lawyer*
Mann, Katinka *artist*
Manning, Dennis J. *insurance company executive*
Manning, Martha Mary *writer, psychologist*
Manoff, Richard Kalman *advertising executive, writer, public health service officer, consultant*
Mansi, Joseph Anneillo *public relations company executive*
Mansouri, Lotfollah (Lotfi Mansouri) *retired performing company executive*
Mantel, Allan David *lawyer*
Manuel, Charles B., Jr. *lawyer*
Mapes, Glynn Dempsey *newspaper editor*
Marable, Manning *social science educator, writer*
Marangoz, Salih *orthopedist*
Marano, Thomas *diversified financial services company executive*
Maraynes, Allan Lawrence *filmmaker, television producer*
Marbury, Stephon *professional basketball player*
Marceau, Yvonne *ballroom dancer, educator*
Marcosson, Thomas I. *management consultant, advertising executive*
Marcus, Eric Peter *lawyer*
Marcus, Eric Robert *psychiatrist*
Marcus, Gwen Ellen *sculptor*
Marcus, Maria Lenhoff *lawyer, educator*
Marcusa, Fred Haye *lawyer*
Marcuse, Adrian Gregory *academic administrator*
Marden, Brice *artist*
Marder, Michael Zachary *dental educator, researcher*
Mardirosian, Tom *actor, playwright*
Maremont, Mark *reporter*
Margalith, Helen Margaret *retired librarian*
Margolis, Mark Neal *actor*
Margulis, Alexander Rafailo *physician, educator*
Mariani, Michael Matthew *lawyer*
Marin, Deborah B. *psychiatrist, educator*
Marinaccio, Jessica *dean*
Mariner, Jonathan D. *major league baseball executive*
Marino, Peter *architect*
Mark, Reuben *consumer products company executive*
Markel, Gregory Arthur *lawyer*
Markowitz, Gerald E. *historian, educator*
Markowitz, John C. *psychiatrist*
Markowitz, Martin H. *biomedical researcher*
Markowski, James Joseph *lawyer*
Marks, Aaron H. *lawyer*
Marks, Andrew Robert *molecular biologist*
Marks, Lillian Shapiro *retired secretarial studies educator, writer, editor*
Marks, Paul Alan *oncologist, cell biologist, educator*
Marks, Ramon Paul *lawyer*
Marks, Theodore Lee *lawyer*
Marlas, James Constantine *diversified financial services company executive*
Marone, Anthony F., Jr. *quality assurance professional*
Marooney, Richard T. *lawyer*
Marrero, Victor *federal judge, lawyer*
Marriott, David R. *lawyer*
Marriott, Michel *reporter*
Marron, Donald Baird *venture capitalist*
Marshall, Alton Garwood *real estate agent, consultant*
Marshall, Kathleen *choreographer, theater director*
Marshall, Robert *film, television and theater director, choreographer*
Marshall, Sheila Hermes *lawyer*
Marshall, Simone Verniere *psychologist, psychoanalyst*
Marshall, Thomas Carlisle *retired applied physics professor*
Marshall, Tom *publishing executive*
Martin, George J., Jr. *lawyer*
Martin, Judith Sylvia *journalist*
Martin, Malcolm Elliot *lawyer*
Martin, Mary-Anne *art gallery owner*
Martin, Michael Townsend *sports association executive, marketing professional, consultant*
Martin, Paul Ross *editor*
Martin, Renwick D. *lawyer*
Martinez, Lucy *lawyer*
Martínez-López, Carmen Leonor *management consultant, educator*
Martini, Richard K. *theatrical producer*
Martins, Peter *ballet master, choreographer, dancer*
Martone, Patricia Ann *lawyer*
Marvel, Jonathan J. *architect*
Marx, Owen Cox *lawyer*
Marzorati, Gerald *editor*
Masey, Jack *exhibition designer*
Masi, Jane Virginia *marketing and sales consultant*
Masin, Michael Terry *lawyer*
Maslin, Janet *critic*
Masnyj, Yuri *painter, sculptor*
Mason, Andrew S. *lawyer*
Mason, Bobbie Ann *writer*
Mason, Christopher May *lawyer*
Mason, Dan *broadcast executive*
Mason, Frank Herbert *artist, educator*
Mason, Marshall W. *theater director, educator, author*
Masri, Safwan Malek *industrial engineer, educator*
Massad, Timothy G. *lawyer*
Massengill, David E. *lawyer*
Masters, Jon Joseph *corporate governance specialist, management consultant*
Masterson, Ellen Hornberger *accountant*
Masterson, James Francis *psychiatrist*
Masyr, Jesse James *lawyer*
Matalon, J. Rolando *rabbi*
Matarasso, Alan *plastic and reconstructive surgeon*
Materna, Joseph Anthony *lawyer*
Mathas, Theodore A. *insurance company executive, lawyer*
Mathers, William Harris *lawyer*
Mathews, Jack Wayne *journalist, film critic*
Mathias, Andrew *real estate company executive*
Mathieson, Garrett Alfred *insurance brokerage executive*
Mathis, Catherine J. *publishing executive*
Matsuhisa, Nobuyuki *chef, restaurant owner*
Mattei, Ivan E. *lawyer*
Matteson, William Bleecker *lawyer*
Matthews, Christopher John *political commentator, writer*
Matthews, Dave *singer, musician*
Matthews, Edwin Spencer, Jr. *lawyer*
Mattson, Joe *sports marketing executive*
Mattson, Marlin Roy Albin *health facility administrator, psychiatry educator*
Matus, Wayne Charles *lawyer*
Maupin, Armistead Jones, Jr. *writer*
Maurer, Gilbert Charles *media specialist*
Maurer, Jeffrey Stuart *trust company executive*
Maury, Richard *painter*
Mawhinney, Thomas Stephen *education educator, educational consultant*
Maxfield, Guy Budd *lawyer, educator*
Maxwell, Anders John *investment banker*
Maxwell, Carla Lena *dancer, choreographer, educator*
May, Gita *literature educator*
May, Peter William *business executive*
May, William Frederick *manufacturing executive*
Mayer, Carl Joseph *prosecutor, lawyer, educator*
Mayer, Christopher *lawyer*
Mayer, Rosemary *artist*
Mayer, Theodore V.H. *lawyer*
Mayer, William Emilio *investor*
Mayerson, Philip *classics educator*
Mayerson, Sandra Elaine *lawyer*
Mayeux, Richard *hospital administrator, neurologist*
Maynard, John Rogers *language educator*
Maynard, Micheline Ann *journalist, writer*
Maynard, Virginia Madden *foundation administrator*
Mayo-Johnston, Julia A. *psychiatry professor, psychotherapist*
Maysilles, Elizabeth *speech communication professional, educator*
Maysles, Albert H. *filmmaker*
Mazzo, Kay *ballet dancer, educator*
Mazzola, Anthony Thomas *editor, graphics designer, consultant*
Mazzola, John William *retired performing company executive, consultant*
Mbanefo, Arthur Christopher Izuegbunan *diplomat*
McAtee, Darin P. *lawyer*
McAveney, Mary Susan *marketing executive*
McCabe, David J. *lawyer*
McCabe, Jim *publishing executive*
McCabe, Mary F. *marketing professional*
McCaffrey, Carlyn Sundberg *lawyer*
McCall, H. Carl *financial services executive, former state comptroller*
McCann, Robert J. *investment company executive*
McCarrick, Edward R. *publishing executive*
McCarthy, Cormac (Charles Joseph McCarthy) *writer*
McCarthy, Pamela Maffei *magazine editor*
McCarthy, Patrick *publishing executive*
McCarthy, Robert Emmett *lawyer*
McCarty, V. K. *publishing executive, chaplain, librarian*
McCaslin, Teresa Eve *human resources specialist*
McCaw, Robert Bruce *lawyer*
McClelland, Shearwood Junior *orthopaedic surgeon*
McClimon, Timothy John *lawyer*
McCollough, Jack *apparel designer*
McComb, William L. *retail and former pharmaceutical executive*
McCooey, Robert H., Jr. *brokerage house executive*
McCormack, Richard Thomas Fox *diversified financial services company executive, former ambassador*
McCormack, Thomas Joseph *retired publishing executive, playwright*
McCormack, William F. *lawyer*
McCourt, Frank (Francis McCourt) *writer*
McCrary, Eugenia Lester (Mrs. Dennis Daughtry McCrary) *civic worker, writer*
McCredie, James Robert *fine arts educator*
McCree, Donald Hanna III *diversified financial services company executive*
McCrie, Robert Delbert *editor, educator*
McCullough, David *writer, educator*
Mc Cullough, J. Lee *industrial psychologist*
McCumber, Chris *communications executive*
McDade, Herbert H. III *investment company executive*
McDaniel, Raymond W., Jr. *financial information company executive*
McDarrah, Fred William *photographer, editor, writer*
McDavid, William Henry *lawyer*
McDermott, Alice *writer*
McDermott, Ann Elizabeth *chemistry professor*
McDonald, Audra Ann *actress, vocalist*
Mcdonald, Gregory Christopher *author*
McDonald, James S. *investment company executive*
McDonald, John F. *publishing executive, restaurateur*
McDonell, Robert Terry *magazine editor, novelist*
McDonell, Terry *publishing executive, writer, editor*
McDonough, Kristin *library director*
McDowell, David Michael *psychiatrist, educator, researcher*
McElhinney, James Lancel *artist, educator*
McElroy, Kathleen O. *dining editor*
McEwen, Adam *artist*
McEwen, Bruce Sherman *neuroscientist, educator*
McFadden, Cynthia Graham *news correspondent, journalist*
McFadden, Mary Josephine *fashion industry executive*
McFadden, Robert Dennis *reporter*
McFarland, Alan Roberts *investment banker*
McFarland, Kathleen Troia (KT McFarland) *government defense consultant*
McFeely, William Drake *publishing company executive*
McGarr, Keith *information technology executive*
McGee, Hugh E. III *investment company executive*
McGill, Jay *magazine publisher*
Mc Gillicuddy, John Francis *retired banker*
McGinn, Timothy J. *lawyer*
McGinnis, Arthur Joseph, Jr. *public relations executive*
McGonagle, Duncan Francis *mental health nurse, substance abuse counselor*
McGowen, Lorraine S. *lawyer*
Mc Gowin, William Edward *artist*
McGrady, Phyllis *television producer*
McGrath, Christopher Thomas *lawyer*
McGrath, Eleanor Burns *editor, writer*
McGrath, Judy (Judith Ann McGrath) *broadcast executive*
McGrath, Michael G. *management consulting firm executive*
McGrath, Thomas John *lawyer, writer, film producer*
McGraw, Harold W., III, (Terry McGraw) *information company executive*
McGraw, Harold Whittlesey, Jr. *publishing executive*
McGuire, Raymond J. *investment banker*
McGunigle, Brian Edward *lawyer*
McHenry, Barnabas *lawyer*
McHugh, Caril Eisenstein Dreyfuss *art dealer, art gallery director, consultant*
McInerney, Jay *writer*
McInerney, Mark A. *county official*
McInerney, Thomas J. *Internet company executive*
McIntire, Mike *journalist*
McIntyre, Brian P. *sports association executive*
McKean, Henry P. *mathematics institute administrator*
McKeever, Kent *library director, law librarian*
McKenna, William Michael *advertising executive*
McKenzie, Kevin Patrick *performing company executive*
McKenzie, Mary Beth *artist*
McKinley-Haas, Mary *artist*
McKinnell, Hank (Henry A. McKinnell Jr.) *pharmaceutical executive*
McKinnon, Floyd Wingfield *textile executive*
McLane, Charles D., Jr. *metal products executive*
McLaughlin, Joseph Michael *federal judge*
McLaughlin, Joseph Thomas *lawyer*
Mc Lean, Don *singer, instrumentalist, composer*
McLennan, Hamish *advertising executive*
McMahon, James Charles *lawyer*
McManus, Paul M. *hotel executive*
McMullan, William Patrick III *investment banker*
McMurtry, Larry Jeff *writer*
McNally, Michele *editor, photographer*
McNally, Terrence *playwright*
McNamara, J. Donald (John Donald McNamara) *retired lawyer, business executive*
McNamara, Mary Ellen *not-for-profit executive*
Mc Namara, Robert A. *construction company executive*
McNeil, Donald G., Jr. *journalist*
McNeil, Wendy Lawson-Johnston *foundation administrator*
McNulty, James J. *former mercantile exchange executive*
McQuown, Judith Hershkowitz *writer, consultant, financial planner*
McTiernan, Charles E., Jr. *lawyer, energy executive*
Meacham, Jon E. *editor*
Meachin, David James Percy *investment banker*
Meadow, Lynne (Carolyn Meadow) *theater producer*
Meads, Mindy *retail executive*
Mechanic, Jonathan L. *lawyer*
Medina, Kate (Kathryn Bach Medina) *publishing executive, editor*
Meehan, Sandra Gotham *corporate financial executive, consultant, writer*
Meeker, Mary G. *brokerage house executive*
Meeropol, Rachel *lawyer*
Mehler, Gordon *lawyer, former federal prosecutor*
Mehretu, Julie *artist*
Mehta, Linn Cary *literature educator*
Mehta, Sonny (Ajay Singh Mehta) *publishing executive*
Meier, Barry *reporter*
Meier, Richard Alan *architect*
Meiklejohn, Donald Stuart *lawyer*
Meilman, Roy K. *lawyer*
Meiseles, Daniel *sports association executive*
Meisner, Jay *plastic surgeon*
Mellins, Robert B. *pediatrician, educator*
Mello, Dawn *retail executive*
Melloan, George Richard *editor*
Melnick, Peter Rodgers *composer*
Melone, Joseph James *retired insurance company executive*
Melton, Howell Webster, Jr. *lawyer*
Meltzer, Milton *author*
Meltzer, Roger *lawyer*
Mencher, Melvin *journalist, educator*
Mendelson, Edward James *English literature educator*
Mendoza, Roberto G., Jr. *banker*
Menicheschi, Edward John *publishing executive*
Menschel, Robert Benjamin *investment banker*
Menza, Claudia Marcella *literary agent*
Mercado, David *lawyer*
Mergenthaler, Frank *corporate financial executive*
Meriam, Thomas C. *lawyer*
Merkin, Ari *advertising executive*
Meron, Theodor *judge, educator, researcher*
Merow, John *lawyer*
Merrill, George Vanderneth *lawyer, investment executive*
Merriss, Philip Ramsay, Jr. *banker*
Mertens, Joan R. *museum curator, art historian*
Mesnikoff, Alvin Murray *psychiatrist, educator*
Messick, Andrew *sports association executive*
Messner, Thomas G. *advertising executive, copywriter*
Mestres, Ricardo Angelo, Jr. *lawyer*
Metz, Emmanuel Michael *investment company executive, lawyer*
Meyer, Fred Josef *finance company executive*
Meyer, Janis M. *lawyer*
Meyer, Karl Ernest *journalist*
Meyer, Pearl *compensation executive consultant*
Meyer, Scott *communications executive*
Meyer, Tobias *auction house executive*
Meyer-Bahlburg, Heino F.L. *psychology professor*
Meyerhoff, Erich *librarian, director*
Meyers, Dale (Mrs. Mario Cooper) *artist*
Meyerson, Lee A. *lawyer*
Miano, Louis Stephen *arts advisor*
Michaels, Al (Alan Richard Michaels) *sportscaster*
Michaels, Lorne *television producer*
Michaelson, Arthur M. *lawyer*
Michalski, Paul Peter *lawyer*
Michel, Nicolas *international organization official*
Michelis, Michael Frank *nephrologist*
Michels, Robert *psychiatrist, educator*
Michelsen, Christopher Bruce Hermann *surgeon*
Michelson, Gertrude Geraldine *retired retail executive*
Middendorf, John Harlan *English literature educator*
Middlebrook, Diane Wood *English language educator, writer*
Middleton, David *physicist, educator*
Midlarsky, Elizabeth Ruth *psychologist, educator, researcher*
Migiro, Asha-Rose *international organization official*
Migro, Asha-Rose *international organization official*
Mikumo, Akiko *lawyer*
Milch, David *screenwriter, producer*
Milder, Jay *artist*
Mildvan, Donna *infectious diseases physician*
Millard, Robert B. *investment company executive*
Millard, Wenda Harris *multi-media company executive*
Miller, Alan *computer company executive, management consultant*
Miller, Arthur Madden *lawyer, investment banker, brokerage house executive*
Miller, Arthur Raphael *law educator*
Miller, Barbara Kenton *retired librarian*
Miller, Charles Hampton *lawyer*
Miller, Corbin Russell *investment company executive*
Miller, Dennis *comedian*
Miller, Ernest Charles *management consultant*
Miller, Garfield Lankard III *investment banker*
Miller, George Keith *lawyer*
Miller, Harvey R. *lawyer, bankruptcy reorganization specialist*
Miller, Harvey S. Shipley *foundation trustee, philanthropist*
Miller, Heidi G. *diversified financial company executive*
Miller, J. Allen *lawyer*
Miller, Merry *educational association administrator*
Miller, Michael Jeffrey *editor, columnist*
Miller, Nancy K. *literature educator*
Miller, Neil Stuart *advertising executive*
Miller, Nicole Jacqueline *fashion designer*
Miller, Paul Samuel *lawyer*
Miller, Peter N. *historian, educator*
Miller, Philip Efrem *librarian*
Miller, Philip Jay *plastic surgeon*
Miller, Richard Kidwell *artist, actor, educator*
Miller, Robert *advertising executive*
Miller, Robert J. *lawyer*
Miller, Ruby Sills *retired gerontologist*
Miller, Sam Scott *lawyer*
Miller, Stephanie *radio personality*
Miller, Stuart A. *lawyer*
Miller, Theodore Norman *lawyer*
Miller, Theodore T. *radiologist*
Miller-Sydney, Audrey Yvonne *music educator*
Millet, T. Kelley *securities trader*
Mills, Stephanie Ellen *writer*
Mills, Stephen G. *lawyer*
Millson, Rory Oliver *lawyer*
Millstein, Ira M. *lawyer, educator*
Millstein, James Eliot *lawyer*
Millstein, Lincoln *media company executive*
Milmed, Paul Kussy *lawyer*
Milmoe, J. Gregory, Jr. *lawyer*
Milonas, E. Leo *lawyer, former state judge*
Milonas, Minos *artist*
Milstein, Howard P. *bank executive*
Milstein, Paul *real estate developer*
Min, Janice Byung *editor-in-chief*
Mina, Richard T. *apparel executive*
Minarik, Else Holmelund (Bigart Minarik) *author*
Mindich, Eric *investment company executive*
Minick, Michael *publishing executive*
Minkel, Herbert Philip, Jr. *lawyer*
Minkowitz, Martin *lawyer, former state government official*
Minskoff, Edward *architectural firm executive*
Mintz, Norman Nelson *investment banker, educator, retired academic administrator*
Mintz, Samuel Isaiah *language educator, writer*
Mir, Aleksandra *artist*

Mirenburg, Barry Leonard *publishing executive, educator*
Mironer, Merril A. *lawyer*
Mirvis, Theodore Neal *lawyer*
Mischel, Walter *psychology professor*
Mischka, James *fashion designer*
Mitchell, Alison N. *newspaper reporter, editor*
Mitchell, Arthur *dancer, choreographer, performing company executive, educator*
Mitchell, Dennis Anthony *dentist, educator*
Mitchell, George John *entertainment company executive, lawyer, former senator*
Mitchell, Mary Jenkins *public health service officer*
Mitchell, Patricia Edenfield *broadcast museum administrator*
Mitterand, Henri C. *literature educator, writer*
Mitwell, Jill *television director*
Miyake, Issey *fashion designer*
Mnuchin, Alan Geoffrey *investment banker*
Mnuchin, Steven T. *investment company executive*
Modlin, Howard S. *lawyer*
Modruson, Frank B. *information technology executive*
Moehringer, J. R. *writer*
Moerdler, Charles Gerard *lawyer*
Moglen, Eben *law educator*
Mohn, Louis *publishing executive*
Mohr, Jay *comedian, actor*
Mohr, Jay Preston *neurologist, educator*
Molho, Emanuel *publisher*
Molinaro, Samuel L., Jr. *diversified financial services company executive*
Moloney, Thomas Joseph *lawyer*
Moltz, James Edward *brokerage house executive*
Mombaerts, Peter *biology professor*
Momin, Shamim *curator*
Monaghan, Dominic *actor*
Monk, Meredith Jane *artistic director, composer, choreographer, filmmaker*
Monson, Robert Joseph *education educator*
Montero, Sylvia *pharmaceutical executive*
Mooney, Richard Emerson *writer*
Mooney, Ted (Edward Comstock Mooney) *editor, art critic, writer*
Moonves, Leslie *broadcast executive*
Moore, Ann S. *publishing executive*
Moore, Anne *physician*
Moore, Charles Hewes, Jr. *manufacturing executive*
Moore, Christopher *writer*
Moore, Michael Watson *musician, educator*
Moore, Rachel Suzanne *performing company executive, dancer*
Moore, Thomas A. *lawyer*
Moore, Thomas Ronald (Lord Bridestowe) *lawyer*
Morales, Carlos M. *lawyer*
Moran, Martin Joseph *fundraising company executive*
Moran, Thomas J. *insurance company executive*
Morawetz, Cathleen Synge *mathematician*
Moreno, Barry *historian, writer*
Morgan, Frank Edward, II, *corporate financial executive*
Morgan, Mary E. *publishing executive*
Morgan, Suann Lee *information technology manager, consultant*
Morgenson, Gretchen C. *reporter*
Morgenthau, Robert Morris *prosecutor*
Morhouse, Sanford W. *lawyer*
Morial, Marc Haydel *association executive, former mayor*
Morosan, Ronald *artist, educator*
Morphy, James Calvin *lawyer*
Morreale, Joseph Constantino *academic administrator, educator, economist, consultant*
Morris, David S. *publishing executive*
Morris, Dick *columnist, political consultant*
Morris, Doug (Douglas Peter Morris) *recording industry executive*
Morris, Robert Lee *gallery administrator, jewelry designer*
Morris, Stephen Burritt *marketing information company executive*
Morris, William Charles *investor*
Morrison, John Henry *neuroscientist, educator, lab administrator*
Morrison, Stacy Lynne *editor*
Morrissey, Thomas A. *publishing executive*
Morse, Edward Lewis *energy economist, director*
Morse, Robert Parker *investment company executive*
Morse, Stephen Scott *virologist, epidemiologist, immunologist, educator*
Morvillo, Robert Guy *lawyer*
Mosbacher, Georgette Paulsin *cosmetics executive*
Moscowitz, Todd *music company executive*
Mosenson, Steven Harris *lawyer*
Moskin, John Robert *editor, writer*
Moskin, Morton *lawyer, director*
Moskowitz, Harold J. *lawyer*
Moskowitz, Randi Zucker *nurse*
Moskowitz, Ross F. *lawyer*
Mosler, Bruce E. *real estate company executive*
Mosley, Daniel Lynn *lawyer*
Mosley, Walter *writer*
Moss, Adam *editor*
Moss, Sara E. *lawyer, cosmetics executive*
Mosse, Peter John Charles *financial services executive*
Moss-Salentijn, Letty (Aleida) *anatomist, educator*
Motoc, Mihnea Ioan *international organization official*
Moulton, Sara *chef, magazine editor*
Mourning, Paul W. *lawyer*
Moy, Richard L. *research scientist*
Moyer, David S. *executive search consultant*
Moyles, Philip Vincent, Jr. *financial services company executive*
Moyne, John Abel *computer scientist, linguist, educator*
Mroz, John Edwin *political scientist*
Muccia, Joseph William *lawyer*
Muchnick, Richard Stuart *ophthalmologist, educator*
Mukasey, Michael B. *lawyer, former federal judge*
Mullaney, Thomas Joseph *lawyer*
Mullaney, William J. *insurance company executive*
Mullany, Gerry *editor*
Mullen, Peter P. *lawyer*
Mullen, Robert W. *construction executive*
Muller, Charlotte Feldman *economist, educator*
Muller, Jennifer *choreographer, dancer*
Mulligan, Jeremiah T. *lawyer*
Mulligan, John J. *corporate financial executive*
Mundell, Robert Alexander *economist, educator*
Mundheim, Robert Harry *law educator*
Mundinger, Mary O'Neil *nursing educator*
Muñoz, Heraldo (Heraldo Muñoz Valenzuela) *diplomat*
Munroe, George Barber *retired mining and manufacturing company executive*
Munzer, Stephen Ira *lawyer*
Muradian, Vazgen *composer*
Murase, Jiro *lawyer*
Murdoch, Rupert (Keith Rupert Murdoch) *multi media company executive*
Murdock, Robert Mead *curator*
Muriel, Amador Cruz *physicist*
Murphy, Arthur William *lawyer, educator*
Murphy, Austin de la Salle *economist, educator, banker*
Murphy, Donna *actress*
Murphy, James Edward *public relations and marketing executive*
Murphy, John B. *portfolio manager*
Murphy, John Vincent *investment company executive*
Murphy, Karen *film producer*
Murphy, Kenneth F. *human resources specialist*
Murphy, Mark Joseph *enterprise sales executive*
Murphy, Ramon Jeremiah Castroviejo *physician, pediatrician*
Murphy, Richard William *retired diplomat*
Murphy, Rosemary *actress*
Murphy, Sean M. *lawyer*
Murphy, Stacia *health service association executive*
Murray, Eileen K. *investment company executive*
Murray, Richard Maximilian *insurance company executive*
Muscari, Joseph Charles *manufacturing executive*
Muscato, Andrew *lawyer*
Musgrave, R. Kenton *federal judge*
Muskin, Victor Philip *lawyer*
Myerberg, Marcia *investment banker*
Myers, Gerald Eugene *humanities educator*
Myers, Roberta *editor-in-chief*
Myerson, Toby Salter *lawyer*
Nabi, Stanley Andrew *brokerage house executive*
Nadler, David A. *insurance company executive*
Nadler, Ellen R. *lawyer*
Nadler-Hurvich, Hedda Carol *public relations executive*
Naftalis, Gary Philip *lawyer, educator*
Naftolin, Frederick *gynecologist, educator*
Nagourney, Herbert *publishing company executive*
Naidich, Thomas Paul *neuroradiologist, educator*
Nair, Mira *film director, film producer*
Naka, Yoshifumi *surgeon, researcher*
Nally, Dennis Mathew *finance company executive*
Nama, George *artist*
Nance, Allan Taylor *retired lawyer*
Nantz, James William (Jim Nantz) *sportscaster*
Napack, Brian *publishing executive*
Napolitano, Andrew P. *lawyer, judge, analyst*
Napolitano, Steven V. *lawyer*
Nash, Edward L. *advertising executive*
Nash, Paul LeNoir *lawyer*
Nash, Thomas *physician*
Nass, Herbert Evan *lawyer*
Nass, Ruth *pediatric neurologist*
Nassau, Michael Jay *lawyer*
Nasser, Jacques *banker, former automotive company executive*
Nasser, Jennifer Ann *nutritionist, researcher, healthcare educator*
Nathan, Andrew James *political science educator*
Nathan, Frederic Solis *lawyer*
Nathan, Paul S. *retired editor, writer*
Natori, Josie Cruz (Josefina Almeda Cruz Natori) *apparel executive*
Nauman, Bruce *artist*
Navarra, Tova *writer, artist*
Nawab, Akhtar *chef*
Nazem, Fereydoun F. *venture capitalist, entrepreneur*
Neal, James G. *university librarian*
Nederlander, James Morton *theater executive*
Nederlander, Robert E. *entertainment and television executive, lawyer*
Needell, Benjamin F. *lawyer*
Needham, George Austin *investment banker*
Neff, Daniel A. *lawyer*
Neff, Michael Alan *lawyer*
Neff, Thomas Joseph *search firm executive*
Neger, Peter C. *lawyer*
Neidell, Martin H. *lawyer*
Neidich, Brooke Garber *foundation administrator, art patron*
Neier, Aryeh *author, human rights organization administrator*
Neiman, LeRoy *artist*
Neiman, Richard H. *state agency administrator*
Neiman, Shirah *prosecutor*
Nelles, Sharon *lawyer*
Nelly, (Cornell Haynes Jr.) *rap artist*
Nelson, Anne *media consultant, educator, writer*
Nelson, Bill *broadcast executive*
Nelson, Carl *journalist*
Nelson, Dean B. *media company executive*
Nelson, Jim *editor*
Nelson, Kathy *broadcast executive*
Nelson, Martha Jane *editor*
Nelson, Merlin Edward *retired management consultant, lawyer*
Nemazee, Hassan *investment banker*
Neshat, Shirin *artist*
Netzer, Dick *economics professor*
Neubauer, Peter Bela *psychoanalyst*
Neuberg, Hans W. *internist, educator*
Neuborne, Burt *law educator*
Neufeld, Peter *lawyer*
Neugebauer, Cynthia A. *lawyer*
Neuhaus, Richard John *priest, research institute president*
Neuman, Maxine Darcy *cellist, educator*
Neuner, Lynn K. *lawyer*
Neuwirth, Alan James *lawyer*
Neuwirth, Michael G. *orthopedist, surgeon, educator*
Neuwirth, Robert Samuel *obstetrician, gynecologist, educator*
Neveloff, Jay A. *lawyer*
Neville, David *apparel designer*
New, Maria Iandolo *pediatrician, educator*
Newberg, Esther *literary agent*
Newbold, John Lowe *retired banker, financial consultant*
Newhouse, Jeffrey H. *radiologist, educator*
Newman, Andy *journalist*
Newman, Charles Michael *mathematician, physicist, educator*
Newman, Diane *publishing executive*
Newman, Fredric Samuel *lawyer, communications executive*
Newman, Kenneth E. *lawyer*
Newman, Lawrence *lawyer, educator*
Newman, Lawrence Walker *lawyer*
Newman, Randy *singer, songwriter, musician*
Newman, Robert Gabriel *physician*
Newman, William Arthur *lawyer*
Newsome, Frederick V. *medical educator*
Newsome, James E. *mercantile exchange executive*
Newstead, Jennifer G. *lawyer*
Ney, Edward N. *ambassador, advertising and public relations executive*
Nezu, Victor A. *lawyer*
Ng, David *electrical engineer*
Nicholas, Robert A. *lawyer*
Nicholas, Stephen J. *orthopedic surgeon, sports medicine physician*
Nichols, Edie Diane *real estate broker*
Nickoloff, Edward Lee *radiology physicist*
Nicol, Dominik *writer, photographer*
Nicolau, Siobhan *cultural organization administrator*
Nides, Thomas Richard *diversified financial services company executive*
Niederauer, Duncan L. *stock exchange executive*
Niemeth, Charles Frederick *lawyer*
Niemiec, David Wallace *investment company executive*
Nieporent, Drew *restaurant group executive*
Nigam, Hemanshu *lawyer, Internet company executive*
Nigo, *fashion designer*
Nimkarn, Saroj *endocrinologist, researcher*
Nirenberg, Louis *mathematician, educator*
Nisenholtz, Martin Abram *telecommunications executive, educator*
Nish, Wayne Paul *chef, restaurant owner*
Nissenbaum, Robert Jay *law librarian, educator*
Niven, James Graham *auctioneer, art appreciator, philanthropist*
Noam, Eli Michael *telecommunications industry executive, educator*
Noble, Ronald Kenneth *secretary general of Interpol*
Noce, Donna *retail executive*
Nocera, Joseph *editor, writer*
Nolan, William Joseph III *banker*
Nonna, John Michael *lawyer*
Noonan, Peggy *writer*
Norell, Mark Allen *paleontologist, curator*
Noris, Peter Dana *investment company executive*
Norman, Christina *broadcast executive*
Norman, Stephen Peckham *finance company executive*
Norris, Floyd Hamilton *financial journalist*
Norsten, Todd *artist*
North, Julie A. *lawyer*
Northup, Nancy Jean *lawyer*
Norton, David K. *publishing executive, human resources specialist*
Norton, Larry *oncologist, researcher*
Noski, Charles H. *telecommunications executive*
Novick, Nelson Lee *dermatologist, internist, consultant, cosmetic dermasurgeon, writer*
Novick, Richard Paul *research scientist, public health institute administrator*
Novitz, Charles Richard *broadcast executive, reporter*
Novogratz, Michael E. *investment company executive*
Novogrod, Nancy Gerstein *editor*
Nozkowski, Thomas *painter*
Nugent, Nelle *theater, film and television producer*
Nurnberg, Charles Gordon *publishing executive*
Nurse, Sir Paul M. *academic administrator*
Nusbacher, Gloria Weinberg *lawyer*
Nusbaum, Jack Henry *lawyer*
Nussbaum, Bernard W. *federal official, lawyer*
Nussbaum, Jeffrey Joseph *musician*
Nussenzweig, Michel Claudio *immunologist, educator*
Nussle, Jim (James Allen Nussle) *former congressman*
Nye, Bill S. *research scientist, engineer, comedian, writer, inventor*
Nyren, Neil Sebastian *publishing executive, editor*
Nyweide, Jeffrey O. *management and business executive*
O, Cao K. *cultural organization administrator*
Oates, Joyce Carol *writer*
Oberfield, Sharon Elefant *pediatric endocrinologist*
Oberly, Kathryn Anne *lawyer, diversified financial services company executive*
Oberman, Michael Stewart *lawyer*
Obernauer, Marne, Jr. *technology industry executive*
Obogeanu, Madalina Maria *reporter*
Obolensky, Ivan *investment banker, foundation administrator, writer*
O'Brien, Clare *lawyer*
O'Brien, Conan *talk show host, writer, performer*
O'Brien, Kevin J. *lawyer*
O'Brien, Michael J. *lawyer, advertising executive*
Ocampo, Jose Antonio *economist, educator, former international organization official, former Colombian government official*
Ocampo, Manuel *artist*
Ocean, Allyson Joy *oncologist, educator*
Ochoa, Manuel, Jr. *oncologist*
Ochs, Carol Rebecca *theologian, writer, theology studies educator, philosopher*
O'Connell, Maureen Elizabeteh *publishing executive*
O'Connor, Anahad S. *journalist*
O'Connor, Chuck (Charles O'Connor) *painter*
O'Connor, John Joseph *oil industry executive*
O'Connor, Kevin *computer programming executive*
Odenweller, Robert Paul *philatelist, trade association administrator, retired pilot*
O'Doherty, Brian *writer*
Odoner, Ellen J. *lawyer*
O'Donnell, John Logan *retired lawyer*
O'Donnell, Michael E. *microbiologist, educator*
Oechler, Henry John, Jr. *lawyer*
Oelsner, Richard S. *lawyer*
Oestreich, James R. *editor*
Oettgen, Herbert Friedrich *physician*
Offit, Morris Wolf *investment company executive*
Offit, Sidney *writer, educator*
Offutt, Brian *broadcast executive*
Ofri, Danielle *internist*
Oglesby, Charles R. *automotive executive*
O'Grady, John Joseph III *lawyer*
O'Hara, Robert Sydney, Jr. *lawyer*
Ohlson, Douglas Dean *artist, educator*
O'Keefe, Vincent Thomas *clergyman, educational association administrator*
O'Kelley, Winnie *editor*
Okuhara, Tetsu *artist, photographer*
Okun, Herbert Stuart *diplomat, educator*
Okura-Marszycki, Mindy Emi *editor*
Okuwa, Makoto *chef*
Olafsson, Olaf *communications executive*
Oldenburg, Richard Erik *auction company executive*
Oldfield, Barney *entertainment executive*
Oldham, Todd *fashion designer*
Olick, Philip Stewart *lawyer*
Olinger, Carla D(ragan) *medical advertising executive*
Olinger, Chauncey Greene, Jr. *investment company executive, editorial consultant*
Olitzky, Kerry Marc *rabbi*
Oliva, Lawrence Jay *retired academic administrator, history professor*
Oliveri, Paul Francis *lawyer*
Olshan, Bernard *artist*
Olson, Peter *publishing executive*
Olsson, Carl Alfred *urologist, department chairman*
O'Meara, Christopher M. *investment company executive*
Omotoso, Edward *diplomat, journalist*
Omura, Yoshiaki *medical educator*
O'Neal, E. Stanley (Stanley O'Neal) *investment company executive*
O'Neal, Hank *entertainment producer, small business owner*
O'Neil, John Joseph *lawyer*
O'Neil, Scott M. *sports association executive*
O'Neill, Charles K. *lawyer*
O'Neill, Joan *editor*
O'Neill, Judith D. *lawyer*
O'Neill, June Ellenoff *economist*
O'Neill, Matthew *film producer*
O'Neill, Thomas J. (Tom O' Neill) *engineering company executive*
Oppenheim, Robert *beauty industry executive*
Oppenheimer, Paul *literature educator, poet*
Oratz, Ruth *physician*
Orce, Kenneth W. *lawyer*
Ordorica, Steven Anthony *obstetrician, gynecologist, educator*
O'Reilly, Bill (William O'Reilly Jr.) *commentator, writer*
O'Reilly, Richard John *pediatrician*
Oremus, Stephen *composer*
Orender, Donna *sports association executive*
Oreskes, Irwin *biochemistry educator*
Oricchio, Michael *editor*
Orkin, Louis Richard *physician, educator*
O'Rorke, James Francis, Jr. *lawyer*
Orozco, Gabriel *artist*
Orr, Dennis Patrick *lawyer*
Orr, James F. III *foundation administrator*
Ortega, Tony *editor-in-chief*
Osberg, Gregory John *publishing company executive*
Osborn, Donald Robert *lawyer*
Osborn, John W. *lawyer*
Osborn, June Elaine *pediatrician, microbiologist, educator, foundation administrator*
Osborne, Joan Elizabeth *singer, songwriter*
Osborne, Richard de Jongh *mining and metals company executive*
Osgood, Charles *news broadcaster, journalist*
Osgood, Richard Magee, Jr. *electrical engineering professor, researcher*
Osgood, Robert Mansfield *lawyer*
O'Shea, Elizabeth Therese *counselor*
Osnos, Gilbert Charles *management consultant*
Osnos, Peter Lionel Winston *publishing executive*
Osorio, Pepon *artist*
Ostermann, Curt *lighting designer, educator*
Ostling, Paul James *corporate financial executive*
Ostner, Steven Mark *lawyer*
Ostrager, Barry Robert *lawyer*
Ostrander, Thomas William *investment banker*
Ostwald, David F. *theater director, educator*

O'Sullivan, Eugene Henry *retired advertising executive, management consultant*
O'Sullivan, Thomas J. *lawyer*
O'Toole, Patricia Ellen *writer, educator*
Otunnu, Olara A. *childrens organization official*
Ouroussoff, Nicolai *architecture critic*
Owen, Richard *federal judge*
Owens, Richard D. *lawyer*
Oxnam, Robert Bromley *trust company advisor*
Oz, Frank (Frank Richard Oznowicz) *entertainer, film director*
Oz, Mehmet Cengiz *cardiac surgeon, writer*
Ozolinsh, Sandis *professional hockey player*
Paaswell, Robert Emil *civil engineer, educator*
Pace, Eric Dwight *retired journalist*
Pace, Wayne H. *communications executive*
Pack, Sandy (Sandra Lee Pack) *former federal agency administrator*
Packer, George *writer*
Packer, Linda S. *psychotherapist*
Packer, Stuart Howard *medical educator*
Paddock, Anthony Conaway *financial consultant*
Padgett, Douglas Edmund *orthopedist, surgeon, educator*
Padmanabhan, Anand *information technology executive*
Padnick, Jennifer C. *lawyer*
Page, Kenneth R. *lawyer*
Pagnani, Keith A. *lawyer*
Paige, Roderick Raynor *educational consultant, former secretary of education*
Paik, Myunghee Cho *statistician, educator*
Paik, Younhee *artist*
Pak, SuChin *newscaster*
Pakter, Jean *maternal and child health consultant*
Paley, Alan H. *lawyer*
Paley, Michael A. *rabbi*
Palion, Peter Thaddeus *financial planner*
Pall, Ellen Jane *writer*
Palm, Gregory K. *lawyer, investment company executive*
Palmer, Catherine E. *lawyer*
Palmer, Charlie *chef, restaurant manager*
Palmer, Deryck A. *lawyer*
Palmer, Michael *poet*
Palmer, Robert Baylis *librarian*
Palsho, Dorothea Coccoli *information services executive*
Panagos, Steven Gregory *food products executive*
Pandit, Vikram S. *investment banker*
Pandolfi, Frances *health facility administrator*
Paneth, Donald Joseph *editor, writer*
Panicek, David *radiologist*
Panken, Peter Michael *lawyer*
Papalia, Diane Ellen *humanities educator*
Papell, Helen Gertrude *poet, retired librarian*
Papernik, Joel Ira *lawyer*
Pappagallo, Marco *neurologist, pain medicine specialist*
Pappas, Milton J. *venture capitalist*
Papps, Bruce William *financial analyst, investment company executive*
Pardes, Herbert *health facility executive, psychiatrist, educator*
Pareles, Jon *music critic*
Parent, Louise Marie *lawyer, corporate financial executive*
Paretsky, Sara N. *writer*
Park, Cynthia *sociology educator, consultant*
Park, Yong Jin *lawyer*
Parker, Alice *composer*
Parker, C. Allen *lawyer*
Parker, David B. *lawyer*
Parker, Trey *animator*
Parkin, Gerard Francis Ralph *chemistry educator, researcher*
Parnes, Alan P. *lawyer*
Parrett, William G. *accounting company executive*
Parrette, Jean-Briac *communications executive*
Parrish, Steven C. *consumer products company executive*
Parsons, Estelle *actress, director, theater producer*
Parsons, Richard Dean *communications executive*
Pascoe, B. Lynn *international organization official, former ambassador*
Pasierb, Stephen John *advertising executive, marketing professional*
Pask, Scott *set designer*
Paskin, Michael A. *lawyer*
Passlof, Pat *artist, educator*
Paster, Howard G. *public relations and public affairs company executive*
Pastores, Gregory McCarthy *pediatrician, medical geneticist, researcher*
Pastores, Stephen M. *internist*
Pataki, George Elmer *lawyer, former governor*
Paterson, Katherine Womeldorf *writer*
Patmos, Marcia *apparel designer*
Patrick, Hugh Talbot *economist, educator*
Patrick, Stephen C. *consumer products company executive*
Patricof, Alan Joel *investment company executive*
Patrikis, Ernest T. *lawyer*
Patterson, James Brendan, Jr. *writer, former advertising executive*
Patterson, Katheryn Clews *lawyer*
Patterson, Robert Porter, Jr. *federal judge*
Paul, Andrew Mitchell *investment advisor*
Paul, George *television director*
Paul, Herbert Morton *lawyer, accountant, educator*
Paul, James William *lawyer*
Paul, Laurence M. *editor*
Paul, Les *entertainer*
Paul, Robert Carey *lawyer*
Paulson, Loretta Nancy *psychoanalyst*
Pavarotti, Luciano *lyric tenor*
Pavia, George M. *lawyer*
Pawliczko, George Ihor *academic administrator*
Paxton, Robert Owen *historian, educator*
Payard, Francois *food service executive*
Payton-Wright, Pamela *actress*
Pearce, Alan S. *lawyer*
Pearl, Mary Corliss *wildlife conservationist*
Pearlman, Steven Jay *otolaryngologist, surgeon, educator*
Pearlstine, Norman *communications consultant, former editor*
Pearson, Clarence Edward *management consultant, educator*
Pearson, Margit Linnea *management consultant*
Peck, Andrew Jay *federal judge*
Peck, Fred Neil *economist, educator*
Peckolick, Alan *painter, graphics designer, photographer*
Pedley, Timothy Asbury, IV, *neurologist, educator, researcher*
Peery, Shelley *psychologist*
Peet, Charles D, Jr. *lawyer*
Peetz, Karen B. *bank executive*
Pegram, John Braxton *lawyer*
Pelaccio, Zakary *chef*
Pellegrini, John B. *lawyer*
Peloso, John Francis Xavier *lawyer*
Pelster, William Charles *lawyer*
Peltz, Nelson A. *investment company executive*
Peluso, John *lawyer, insurance company executive*
Pelz, Robert Leon *lawyer*
Peninger, Michael J. *insurance company executive*
Penn, Stanley William *journalist*
Pennington, William Mark *sportswriter*
Pennisi, Liz *women's health nurse*
Pennoyer, Peter Morgan *architect*
Pennoyer, Robert M. *lawyer*
Penrod, Steven David *law educator*
Penzer, Michèle Olivier *lawyer*
Pepper, Allan Michael *lawyer*
Pepperman, Richard C., II, *lawyer*
Peppers, Jerry P. *lawyer*
Peppet, Russell Frederick *accountant*
Percus, Jerome Kenneth *physicist, researcher*
Perella, Joseph Robert *investment banker*
Perelman, Ronald Owen *consumer products company executive*
Peretsman, Nancy B. *investment banker*
Perez-Firmat, Gustavo Francisco *writer, language educator*
Pérez-Rivera, Francisco (Frank Rivera) *writer*
Perik, Michael J. *educational organization executive*
Perin, Noel I. *neurosurgeon*
Perkins, Lawrence Bradford, Jr. *architect*
Perkins, Roswell Burchard *lawyer*
Perlgut, Mark Ralph *public relations executive*
Perlis, Donald M. *artist*
Perlman, Doug *sports association executive*
Perlmuth, William Alan *lawyer*
Perlmutter, Alvin Howard *television and film producer*
Perlmutter, Isaac *entertainment company executive*
Perlmutter, Louis *investment banker, lawyer*
Perram Frank, Heather *editor-in-chief*
Perry, Brooke Elizabeth *public relations executive*
Perry, Douglas *opera singer*
Perry, Richard C. *financier*
Perschetz, Martin L. *lawyer*
Persell, Caroline Hodges *sociologist, educator, author, researcher, consultant*
Pershan, Richard Henry *lawyer*
Persichilli Keogh, Karen Mary *political organization worker*
Pesner, Carole Manishin *art gallery owner*
Petach, Ann Marie *diversified financial services company executive*
Petchesky, Rosalind Pollack *social and political scientist, educator*
Peters, Bernadette (Bernadette Lazzara) *actress*
Peters, Roberta *soprano*
Peterson, Peter George *investment company executive*
Petno, Douglas B. *investment company executive*
Petrie, Donald Joseph *banker*
Petronella, Michael A. *publishing executive*
Petrow, George J. *lawyer*
Pettibone, Peter John *lawyer*
Petz, Edwin V. *real estate company executive, lawyer*
Petzal, David Elias *editor, writer*
Pfeffer, David H. *lawyer*
Pfeifer, Tracy M. *plastic surgeon*
Pfeiffer, Jane Cahill *former broadcasting company executive, consultant*
Pfeifler, Brian C. *financial planner*
Phair, Liz *vocalist*
Phelan, John C. *lawyer*
Phelps, Edmund Strother *economics professor*
Philbin, Regis (Francis Xavier) *television personality*
Phillips, Barnet, IV, *lawyer*
Phillips, Gerald Baer *internal medicine scientist, educator*
Phillips, Pamela Kim *lawyer*
Phillips, Reneé *writer*
Picasso, Paloma *fashion designer*
Picciano, Anthony Gerade *academic administrator*
Pickering, Laurel *public health service officer*
Picón, Carlos Arturo *curator*
Pidot, Whitney Dean *lawyer*
Pierce, Charles Eliot, Jr. *library director, educator*
Pierce, David *information technology executive*
Pierce, Morton Allen *lawyer*
Pierson, Jack *artist*
Pierson, Richard Norris, Jr. *medical educator*
Pietruski, John Michael, Jr. *pharmaceutical executive*
Pikitch, Ellen Karen *science educator*
Pilati, Stefano *apparel designer*
Pildes, Richard H. *law educator*
Pile-Spellman, John Martin *radiology and neurosurgery educator*
Pincomb, Jessica *information technology executive*
Pincus, Lionel I. *financial executive, entrepreneur*
Pinczower, Kenneth Ephraim *lawyer*
Pinczuk, Aron *physicist*
Pines, Burton Yale *media executive*
Pinkwater, Julie *publishing executive*
Pinover, Eugene Alfred *lawyer*
Piombino, Nicholas *psychotherapist*
Piovezahn, Alessandro R. *public information officer, marketing professional, consultant*
Pippert, Thomas W. *lawyer*
Pitman, Gerald H. *plastic surgeon*
Pittman, Robert Warren *investor*
Pittoni, Luke M. *lawyer*
Pitts, Andrew J. *lawyer*
Piven, Frances Fox *political scientist, educator*
Planitzer, Russell E. *computer company executive*
Plant, Robert Anthony *singer, composer*
Platnick, Norman I. *curator, entomologist*
Platt, Nicholas *retired ambassador*
Platusich, Christian Michael *underwriter*
Plavinskaya, Anna Dmitrievna *artist*
Plepler, Richard L. *broadcast executive*
Plevan, Bettina B. *lawyer*
Plotkin, Loren H. *lawyer*
Plottel, Jeanine Parisier *foreign language educator*
Plum, Fred *neurologist*
Plummer, William B. *publishing executive*
Pnueli, Amir *computer science educator*
Podesta, Roger E. *lawyer*
Podhoretz, John *editor, writer*
Poe, Randall Ellsworth *public relations executive, author*
Poehler, Amy *comedienne, actress*
Pogue, David *journalist*
Pogue, Donald Carl *federal judge*
Pogue, Velvie Anne *nephrologist, educator*
Pokorny, Jan Hird *architect, educator*
Polak, Vivian Louise *lawyer*
Polenz, Joanna Magda *psychiatrist*
Polevoy, Nancy Tally *lawyer, social worker, genealogist*
Polin, Jane L. *foundation official*
Poliner, Jason M. *lawyer*
Polisi, Joseph William *academic administrator*
Politan, Nicholas H. *lawyer*
Poll, Robert Eugene, Jr. *bank executive*
Pollack, Martin D. *lawyer*
Pollack, Robert Elliot *biologist, educator, writer*
Pollack, Stanley P. *lawyer*
Pollack, Stephen J. *investment company executive, stockbroker*
Pollak, William L. *newspaper publishing executive*
Pollan, Stephen Michael *lawyer, writer, life coach, finance expert*
Pollard, Veronica *automotive executive*
Pollock, Ellen Joan *editor*
Pollock, Jefrey Ian *pollster, political consultant*
Pollock, Paul James *lawyer*
Pollock, Robert B. *insurance company executive*
Pollock-O'Brien, Louise Mary *public relations executive*
Polshek, James Stewart *architect*
Polsky, Cynthia Hazen *artist, art collector, philanthropist*
Poltrack, David F. *broadcast executive, marketing educator*
Polydorides, Alexandros Demetrios *pathologist*
Pomerantz, Charlotte *writer*
Pomerantz, Frederick J. *lawyer*
Pomeroy, Lee Harris *architect*
Pomp, Alfons *surgeon*
Pompadur, I. Martin *communications executive*
Pool, Mary Jane *writer, editor*
Poole, William Daniel *writer, editor*
Poons, Larry *artist*
Poor, Peter Varnum *television producer and director*
Popa, Radu D. *law librarian*
Pope, Liston, Jr. *writer, journalist*
Pope, Martin *chemist, educator*
Portale, Alfred *chef, restaurant owner*
Porter, Grant A. *investment banker*
Porter, Liliana Alicia *artist, photographer, painter, printmaker, filmmaker*
Porter, Marc Bennett *auction house executive*
Porterfield, Christopher *magazine editor, writer*
Portnow, Marjorie *painter*
Posen, Richard L. *lawyer*
Posen, Zac *apparel designer*
Posin, Kathryn Olive *choreographer*
Posner, Jerome Beebe *neurologist, educator*
Posner, Louis Joseph *lawyer, accountant*
Posner, Michael Hoffman *lawyer*
Post, David Alan *broadcast executive*
Postelnek, Stephen A. *lawyer*
Potter, Hollis Gromisch *radiologist*
Potter, Nicholas F. *lawyer*
Potter, William James *investment banker*
Poulet, Anne Litle *museum director, art historian*
Poulson, Richard Jasper Metcalfe *lawyer*
Pouschine, John Laurence *private equity investment executive*
Powell, Julie *writer*
Powell, Richard Gordon *retired lawyer*
Powell, Scott C. *bank executive*
Powers, Edward Alton *minister, educator*
Powers, Scott *television producer, actor*
Prager, David Ellis *lawyer*
Prager, Kenneth Michael *pulmonologist, educator*
Pratt, William *lawyer*
Prelutsky, Jack *author*
Prendergast, Sir Kieran *former international organization official*
Presby, J. Thomas *financial advisor, director, arbitrator*
Prescott, Darrell *lawyer*
Preska, Loretta A. *federal judge*
Press, Jim (James E. Press) *automotive executive*
Preston, Frances Williams *music company executive*
Preston, Julia *journalist*
Prettyman, Alfred Emerson *language and behavioral science educator, publishing executive*
Previn, André (Ludwig) *composer, conductor, pianist*
Price, Frank *motion picture and television company executive*
Price, Hilary B. *cartoonist*
Price, (Mary Violet) Leontyne *retired concert and opera singer, soprano*
Price, Michael J. *investment banker*
Price, Reynolds *writer, educator*
Price, Robert *media and communications executive, investment banker, lawyer*
Primi, Don Alexis *advertising, public relations, rail transportation executive*
Primps, William Guthrie *lawyer*
Prince, Charles O., III, (Chuck Prince) *diversified financial services company executive*
Prince, Harold *theatrical director, producer*
Prince-Ramus, Joshua *architect*
Prins, Richard T. *lawyer*
Priore, Christopher Anselmo *artist*
Pritchard, John F. *lawyer*
Prives, Carol *biologist, educator*
Prizzi, Jack Anthony *investment banking executive*
Procope, Ernesta Gertrude *insurance company executive*
Proctor, Georganne C. *investment company executive*
Profusek, Robert Alan *lawyer*
Prounis, Othon A. *lawyer*
Prozes, Andrew *publishing executive*
Psomiades, Harry John *political science professor*
Ptashne, Mark Steven *molecular biology professor*
Puccio, Thomas Phillip *lawyer*
Pujol, Ernesto *artist*
Pulanco, Tonya Beth *special education educator*
Puleo, Frank Charles *lawyer*
Pulos, Virginia Kate *actress, consultant*
Puris, Martin Ford *media company executive*
Purse, Charles Roe *investment banker*
Purtell, Lawrence Robert *lawyer*
Puschel, Philip P. *textiles executive*
Puth, David W. *diversified financial services company executive*
Putnam, Jerry (Gerald D. Putnam) *stock exchange executive*
Putnam, Jonathan *lawyer*
Putnam, Keri *film company executive*
Pye, Gordon Bruce *economist*
Qazi, Ashraf Jehangir *ambassador*
Qian, Jin *law librarian*
Quackenbush, Margery Clouser *psychoanalyst, researcher*
Quackenbush, Robert Mead *artist, writer, psychoanalyst*
Quale, Andrew Christopher, Jr. *lawyer*
Queler, Eve *conductor*
Quennell, Nicholas *landscape architect, educator*
Quick, Peter *stock exchange executive*
Quigley, James B. *diversified financial services company executive*
Quigley, James H. *accounting firm executive*
Quimby, Fred William *pathology educator, veterinarian*
Quindlen, Anna *journalist, writer*
Quin-Harkin, Janet Elizabeth (Rhys Bowen) *writer*
Quinlan, Guy Christian *lawyer*
Quinlan, Mary Lou *former advertising executive, consultant*
Quinlan, Robert Conrad *real estate developer*
Quinn, Christine Callaghan *councilwoman*
Quinn, Francis Flaherty *lawyer*
Quinn, James W. *lawyer*
Quinn, Jane Bryant *journalist, writer*
Quinn, Yvonne Susan *lawyer*
Quiñones Keber, Eloise *art historian, educator*
Quinson, Bruno Andre *painter, retired publishing executive*
Quint, Ira *retail executive*
Quintero, Ronald Gary *management consultant*
Quirk, John James *investment company executive*
Quisgard, Liz Whitney *artist, sculptor*
Quivers, Robin *radio personality*
Raab, Jennifer J. *city commissioner*
Raab, Sheldon *lawyer*
Rabb, Bruce *lawyer*
Rabb, Harriet Schaffer *academic administrator, lawyer*
Rabin, Jack *lawyer*
Rabinowitz, Jack Grant *radiologist, educator*
Rabinowitz, Stephen L. *lawyer*
Rabiu, Badru I.O. *federal official*
Race, Tim *editor*
Rachow, Louis A(ugust) *librarian*
Rackow, Eric C. *hospital administrator*
Radecki, Jeffrey *sports medicine physician*
Radice, Frank J. *communications executive*
Radin, Amy Janine *financial services company executive*
Radin, Sam *lawyer*
Radke, Kirk A. *lawyer*
Rado, Peter Thomas *lawyer*
Radon, Jenik Richard *lawyer*
Radwin, Jerome J. *public health service officer*
Rafferty, Emily Kernan *museum administrator*
Rafferty, Thomas G. *lawyer*
Raghavan, Sudheer *hotel executive*
Rahm, Susan Berkman *lawyer*
Rainer, Yvonne *choreographer, filmmaker*
Rainess, Alan Edward *psychiatrist, neurologist, educator*
Rainis, Eugene Charles *bank executive*
Raisler, Kenneth Mark *lawyer*
Rakoff, Jed Saul *federal judge, author*
Ralli, Constantine Pandia *lawyer*
Ramachandra, Goutham K. *software architect, software developer*
Ramirez, Maria Fiorini *financial consultant*
Ramirez, Sara *actress*
Ramirez, Tina *performing company executive*
Rampe, David *editor*
Rampe, Kevin M. *real estate developer*

Ramsay, David Leslie *physician, dermatologist, educator*
Rand, Lawrence Anthony *investor, finance company executive*
Rand, William *lawyer, retired judge*
Randall, Francis Ballard *retired historian, educator, writer*
Randall, Jessie *apparel executive*
Randel, Don Michael *foundation administrator, former academic administrator, musicologist*
Randich, Steven J. *financial services company executive*
Randolph, David *conductor*
Rankin, Clyde Evan III *lawyer*
Ranz, Jules M. *psychiatrist, director*
Rao, Sethuramiah Lakshminarayana *demographer, United Nations official*
Rapoport, Bernard Robert *lawyer*
Rapoport, Miles S. *former state official*
Rapp, Adam *writer, playwright*
Rappaport, Charles Owen *lawyer*
Rappaport, Linda Ellen *lawyer*
Rashad, Ahmad *sports broadcaster, former professional football player*
Rathbone, Peter B. *art appraiser*
Rathmann, Peggy *writer, illustrator*
Ratliff, Ben *music critic*
Rattner, Steven Lawrence *investment banker*
Rauch, Arthur Irving *management consultant*
Rauschenberg, Robert *artist*
Rausen, Aaron Reuben *pediatric hematologist, oncologist*
Raven, Abbe *broadcast executive*
Ravetch, Jeffrey Victor *molecular biologist, immunologist, educator*
Ravitch, Diane Silvers *historian, educator, writer, government official*
Raviv, Tal *ophthalmologist*
Rawski, Frederick *lawyer*
Ray, Rachael Domenica *chef, television personality*
Rayfield, Elliot James *medical educator*
Raylesberg, Alan Ira *lawyer*
Raymond, Dorothy Sarnoff *communications consultant, former actress, former singer*
Raynor, Bruce S. *labor union administrator*
Raynor, Richard Benjamin *neurosurgeon, educator*
Read, Ian C. *pharmaceutical executive*
Reals Ellig, Janice *marketing professional, human resources specialist*
Reams, Lee Roy *actor*
Rebell, Arthur Leslie *diversified holding company executive*
Reboul, John W. *lawyer*
Record, William John *librarian*
Reda, James Francis *business consultant*
Redburn, Tom *newspaper editor*
Redding, Markus Carl *management consultant, educator*
Reddy, Krishna Narayana *artist, educator*
Redlener, Irwin Elliot *health facility administrator, educator*
Redlich, Norman *lawyer, educator*
Redmond, Elsa M. *anthropologist*
Redo, S(averio) Frank *retired surgeon*
Redpath, John Sloneker, Jr. *lawyer, publishing executive*
Redstone, Sumner Murray *broadcast executive, lawyer*
Reece, Thomas L. *manufacturing executive*
Reed, Marc C. *telecommunications industry executive, human resources specialist*
Reed, W. Allen *automotive executive*
Reese, Tracy *fashion designer*
Reeves, Dianne *singer*
Reeves, Jennifer Todd *filmmaker*
Reger, Robert J., Jr. *lawyer*
Reges, Marianna Alice *marketing executive*
Rehl, Beatrice Claire *editor*
Reich, Larry Sam *lawyer*
Reich, Steve *composer*
Reichel, Aaron Israel *lawyer, editor, writer, rabbi*
Reichl, Ruth Molly *editor-in-chief*
Reid, Antonio (L.A. Reid) *music company executive*
Reid, Edward Snover III *lawyer*
Reid, John Phillip *law educator*
Reidenberg, Marcus Milton *physician, educator*
Reidy, Carolyn Kroll *publisher*
Reidy, Maureen J. *fashion industry executive*
Reif Cohen, Jessica *broadcast executive*
Reifler, Stewart *lawyer*
Reig, June Wilson *scriptwriter, television director and producer*
Reilly, Edward Arthur *lawyer*
Reilly, Edward T., Jr. *advertising executive*
Reilly, Richard R. *lawyer*
Reilly, William Francis *media company executive*
Reinhard, Keith Leon *advertising executive*
Reinhold, Richard Lawrence *lawyer*
Reininghaus, Ruth *retired artist*
Reinking, Ann H. *dancer, actress*
Reinthaler, Richard Walter *lawyer*
Reisberg, Barry *geriatric psychiatrist, neuropsychopharmacologist*
Reisler, Marc S. *lawyer*
Reisman, Sharyl A. *lawyer*
Reisner, Lorin L. *lawyer*
Reiss, Dale Anne *corporate financial executive*
Reiss, Steven Alan *lawyer, educator*
Reitan, Bernt *metal products executive*
Reitzas, Joshua T. *lawyer, venture capitalist*
Reitzfeld, Alan D. *lawyer*
Remington, Deborah Williams *artist*
Remnick, David J. *journalist, editor-in-chief*
Ren, Christine *surgeon*
Renehan, Edward John *writer*
Renick, Kyle *artistic director*
Rennert, Ira Leon *manufacturing executive*
Renney, Tom *professional hockey coach*
Rennie, John *editor-in-chief*
Repko, William Clarke *banker*
Resika, Paul *artist*
Resnick, Rhoda Brodowsky *psychotherapist*
Resnick, Scott N. *real estate company executive*
Resnicow, Norman Jakob *lawyer*
Ressa, Gregory John *lawyer*
Restani, Jane A. *federal judge*
Reuben, Gloria *actress, singer*
Reutter, Eberhard Edmund, Jr. *education and law educator*
Revenkova, Ekaterina *biologist, researcher*
Reverdin, Bernard J. *lawyer*
Revesz, Richard Luis *dean, law educator*
Revkin, Andrew C. *writer, reporter*
Reynard, Muriel Joyce *lawyer*
Reynolds, Clayton S. *lawyer*
Reynolds, David Spencer *humanities educator, writer*
Reynolds, Fredric G. *broadcast executive*
Reynolds, James *management consultant*
Reynolds, John R. *hospital executive*
Rheins, Carl Jeffrey *historian, director*
Rhoads, Geraldine Emeline *editor, consultant*
Rhodes, David *academic administrator*
Rhodes, Randi *radio personality*
Rhodes, Richard (Lee) *writer*
Rhodes, Rosamond *medical educator, philosophy educator*
Rhodes, Samuel *violist, educator*
Rhodes, William Reginald *banker*
Rhone, Sylvia Marie Miller *recording industry executive*
Ricca, Gregory J. *broadcast executive, management consultant*
Rice, Barbara Lynn *stage manager*
Rice, Charles M. *virologist, educator*
Rice, Donald Sands *lawyer*
Rice, Joseph Lee III *lawyer*
Rice, Luanne *writer*
Rice, Thomas Charles *lawyer*
Rich, Adrienne *poet*
Rich, Frank Hart *journalist, writer*
Rich, Frederic Carl *lawyer*
Rich, R(obert) Bruce *lawyer*
Richard, Stephen O. *sports association executive*
Richard, Virginia Rynne *lawyer*
Richards, Cecile *healthcare network executive*
Richards, David A.J. *law educator*
Richards, David Alan *lawyer*
Richardson, Frank Elmer III *investor*
Richardson, Grace Elizabeth *consumer products company executive*
Richert, John Rolin *neuroimmunologist, educator*
Richieri, Kenneth A. *lawyer, publishing executive*
Richman, Martin Franklin *lawyer*
Richman, Michael Paul *lawyer*
Richman, Sophia *psychologist*
Richtman, Jack *French language educator*
Ridgway, Delissa Anne *federal judge*
Rieder, Eric *lawyer*
Rieff, David Sontag *editor, critic*
Rielly, J(ohn) P. *corporate financial executive*
Riesel, Sheila Ginsberg *lawyer*
Rifkind, Arleen B. *pharmacologist, researcher, educator*
Rifkind, Robert S. *lawyer*
Rigg, Dame Diana *actress*
Riggio, Leonard *book store company executive*
Riggio, Stephen *book store company executive*
Rigolosi, Elaine La Monica *lawyer, educator*
Rikon, Michael *lawyer*
Rikoon, Jonathan J. *lawyer*
Riley, Thomas Edward *lawyer*
Ringel, Dean *lawyer*
Ringgold, Faith *artist*
Ripa, Kelly Maria *television personality, actress*
Ripert, Jean-Maurice *ambassador*
Riss, Eric *psychologist*
Ristich, Miodrag *psychiatrist*
Ritch, Kathleen *diversified financial services company executive*
Ritch, Robert Harry *ophthalmologist, educator*
Ritchie, Richard Lee *media company executive*
Ritter, Jodi Gottesfeld *lawyer*
Rivera, Chita (Conchita del Rivero) *actress, singer, dancer*
Rivera, Geraldo *television personality, journalist*
Rivera, Walter *lawyer*
Rivkin, David Wolfe *lawyer*
Rivlin, Benjamin *political science professor*
Rivlin, Richard Saul *internist*
Rizzuto, Katherine *publishing executive*
Roach, Margaret *publishing executive*
Robb, Kathy McCleskey *lawyer*
Robbins, John Clapp *management consultant*
Robbins, Rachel F. *stock exchange executive, lawyer*
Robbins, Tim (Timothy Francis Robbins) *actor, film director*
Roberts, Burton Bennett *lawyer, retired judge*
Roberts, Donald Munier *retired banker, trust company executive*
Roberts, Fletcher *editor*
Roberts, Francis Stone *advertising executive*
Roberts, Gene *newspaper editor*
Roberts, Howard H., Jr. *transportation executive*
Roberts, Jim *editor*
Roberts, Katy *editor*
Roberts, Kevin *advertising executive*
Roberts, Nora *writer*
Roberts, Robin *newscaster*
Roberts, Thomas Alba *lawyer*
Robertson, Andrew J. *advertising executive*
Robertson, Edwin David *lawyer*
Robertson, Hugh (Elihu F.) *lawyer*
Robertson, Jaquelin Taylor *architect, educator*
Robfogel, Susan Salitan *lawyer*
Robinson, Barbara Paul *lawyer*
Robinson, Dennis R. *sports association executive*
Robinson, Irwin Jay *lawyer*
Robinson, James D. III *venture capitalist*
Robinson, Janet L. *publishing executive*
Robinson, Kim Stanley *science fiction author*
Robinson, Marilynne *writer*
Robinson, Paul M. *lawyer*
Robinson, Peter M. *business association executive*
Robinson, Richard *publishing executive*
Robock, Stefan Hyman *retired economics professor*
Roche, Gerard Raymond *management consultant*
Rock, Allan Michael *ambassador, former Canadian government official*
Rockefeller, David *banker*
Rocklen, Kathy Hellenbrand *lawyer*
Rockwell, John Sargent *dance critic, writer, former arts administrator*
Rodgers, Kathy *legal association administrator, lawyer*
Rodin, Judith Seitz *foundation administrator, former academic administrator, psychologist, educator*
Rodin, Rita Angela *lawyer*
Rodriguez, Alcibiades J. *neurologist, educator*
Rodriguez, Freddy *actor*
Rodriguez, Narciso *fashion designer*
Rodriguez, Vincent Angel *lawyer, director*
Roeder, John Louis *physics educator*
Roeder, Robert Gayle *biochemist, molecular biologist, educator*
Roeding, Cyriac R. *broadcast executive*
Roehrs, Christopher Scott *lawyer*
Roer, Ricki E. *lawyer*
Roethenmund, Otto Emil *finance company and bank executive*
Rogers, James Beeland, Jr., (Jim Rogers) *retired investment company executive*
Rogers, Laurence Steven *lawyer*
Rogers, Robert M. *architect*
Rogers, Theodore Courtney *investment company executive*
Rogers, Theodore Otto, Jr. *lawyer*
Rogin, Gilbert Leslie *editor, author*
Rohatyn, Felix George *diversified financial services company executive, former ambassador*
Roker, Al *newscaster*
Roldan, Kenneth Arroyo *executive recruiter, lawyer*
Rolfe, Ronald Stuart *lawyer*
Rollin, Betty *writer, television journalist*
Rollins, James (Jim Czajkowski, James Clemens) *writer, veterinarian*
Rollins, Sonny (Theodore Rollins) *composer, musician*
Romano, Fernanda (Fefa Romano) *advertising executive*
Romano, John Francis *dermatologist*
Romanos, John, Jr., (Jack Romanos) *publisher*
Romans, John Niebrugge *lawyer*
Romero, Anthony D. *legal association administrator*
Romita, Mauro Charles *plastic surgeon*
Romo, Thomas III *plastic surgeon*
Ronde, John Herman *writer, translator*
Roney, Carley *wedding company executive, writer*
Ronstadt, Linda Marie *singer*
Rooney, Paul C., Jr. *retired lawyer*
Roosevelt, Theodore, IV, *investment banker*
Root, Nina J. *librarian, writer*
Roppel, Mark *lawyer*
Rosaldo, Renato Ignacio, Jr. *cultural anthropology educator*
Rosand, David *art historian, educator*
Rose, Charlie (Charles Peete Rose Jr.) *television journalist*
Rose, Daniel *real estate company executive, consultant*
Rose, Elihu *real estate executive*
Rose, Joanna Semel *volunteer*
Rose, Joanne W. *rating service executive*
Rose, Robert Neal *investment banker*
Rose, Victoria Lasdon *publishing executive*
Rosell, Kurt F. *lawyer*
Rosen, Adam B. *lawyer*
Rosen, Jeffrey J. *lawyer*
Rosen, J(oshua) Philip *lawyer*
Rosen, Matthew A. *lawyer*
Rosen, Michael N. *lawyer*
Rosen, Nathaniel Kent *cellist*
Rosen, Richard Lewis *lawyer, real estate developer*
Rosenbaum, Joan Hannah *museum director*
Rosenbaum, Richard A. *lawyer*
Rosenberg, Alan David *accountant*
Rosenberg, Alan Stewart *lawyer*
Rosenberg, Alex Jacob *art appraiser, educator, art dealer*
Rosenberg, Gerald Alan *lawyer*
Rosenberg, Harold Nmi *preventive medicine physician, consultant*
Rosenberg, Jerome Ira *lawyer*
Rosenberg, John David *language educator, critic*
Rosenberg, Lawrence *lawyer*
Rosenberg, Marc Steven *lawyer*
Rosenberg, Robert Charles *housing corporation executive*
Rosenberg, Robert Jay *lawyer*
Rosenberg, Tina *reporter*
Rosenblatt, Lief D. *investment company executive*
Rosenbloom, Daniel *investment advisor, lawyer*
Rosenblum, Constance *newspaper editor*
Rosenblum, Jay Alan *neurologist*
Rosenblum, William F., Jr. *lawyer*
Rosenfeld, Gerald *investment company executive, financial analyst*
Rosenfeld, Isadore *cardiologist, educator*
Rosenfeld, Steven B. *lawyer*
Rosenfield, Allan *medical educator, dean, obstetrician, gynecologist*
Rosengarten, Frank *retired language educator, retired literature educator, writer*
Rosensaft, Menachem Zwi *lawyer, writer, foundation administrator*
Rosenshine, Allen Gilbert *retired advertising agency executive*
Rosenthal, Andrew Mark *newspaper editor*
Rosenthal, Howard Lewis *political science professor*
Rosenthal, Jacob (Jack Rosenthal) *foundation executive*
Rosenthal, Jane *film company executive*
Rosenthal, Larry W. *cosmetic dentist*
Rosenthal, Shirley Lord *cosmetics magazine executive, novelist*
Rosenthal, Tamara *apparel executive*
Rosenwasser, Mike *lawyer*
Rosenzweig, Charles Leonard *lawyer*
Rosevear, Cora *curator*
Roskam, Catherine S. *bishop*
Roskin, William A. *communications executive*
Rosoff, William L. *lawyer*
Rosow, Stuart L. *lawyer*
Ross, Barry C. *lawyer*
Ross, Brian Elliott *chief investigative correspondent*
Ross, Diana (Diana Ernestine Earle Ross) *singer, actress, entertainer, fashion designer*
Ross, Jerrold *music educator*
Ross, Jo Ann *media buyer*
Ross, Mathew P. *lawyer*
Ross, Matthew *lawyer*
Ross, Norman Alan *publisher*
Ross, Stephen M. *real estate company executive*
Ross, Steve J. *publishing executive*
Ross, Wilbur Louis, Jr. *investment banker*
Rossen, Jordan *lawyer*
Rosset, Barnet Lee, Jr. *publishing executive*
Roth, Eric M. *lawyer*
Roth, Kenneth *human rights advocate*
Roth, Michael I. *communications executive, lawyer*
Roth, Sol *rabbi*
Roth, Steven *real estate company executive*
Rothberg, Gerald *editor, publishing executive*
Rothberg, Glenda Fay Morris *lawyer*
Rothenberg, Eleanore *psychotherapist*
Rothenberg, Jerome *writer, literature educator*
Rothenberg, Laraine S. *lawyer*
Rothenberg, Peter Jay *lawyer*
Rothenberg, Randall *advertising executive*
Rothenberg, Robert Philip *public relations counselor*
Rothfeld, Michael B. *theatrical producer, investor*
Rothman, Barbara Katz *sociology educator*
Rothman, Bernard *lawyer*
Rothman, David J. *historian, educator*
Rothman, Esther Pomeranz *social services administrator, psychologist*
Rothman, Henry Isaac *lawyer*
Rothman, James Edward *cell biologist, educator*
Rothschild, Amalie Randolph *filmmaker, film producer, film director, photographer*
Rothschild, Gideon *lawyer*
Rothschild, Nathaniel Philip (Victor James) *investment company executive*
Roubin, Gary Sidney Samuel *interventional cardiologist, educator, researcher*
Roubini, Nouriel *economics professor*
Roumain, Daniel Bernard *composer, violinist*
Roumani-Denn, Vivienne Rachel *library and information scientist, consultant*
Rouse, Christopher Chapman III *composer, educator*
Rover, Edward Frank *foundation administrator, lawyer*
Rovine, Arthur William *international arbitrator*
Rovit, Richard Lee *neurosurgeon*
Rowe, David Lee *financial advisor*
Rowen, Andrew S. *lawyer*
Rowen, Ruth Halle *musicologist, educator*
Rowland, Esther E(delman) *retired dean*
Rowland, Lewis Phillip *neurology educator, editor, clinical investigator*
Rowley, Cynthia *apparel designer*
Roye, Carol *nursing educator*
Rozbruch, S. Robert *orthopedist, researcher*
Rozen, Jerome George, Jr. *entomologist, curator, researcher*
Rozenberg, Lana *cosmetic dentist*
Rozman, Alexander *lawyer, consultant*
Rubell, Jennifer *writer, hotelier*
Ruben, Lawrence *real estate developer and company executive, lawyer*
Rubenstein, Howard Joseph *public relations executive*
Rubenstein, Joshua Seth *lawyer*
Rubenstein, Leonard *engineering company executive*
Rubenstein, Sanford Marvin *English professor, poet*
Rubenstein, William S. *lawyer*
Rubin, Albert Louis *internist, nephrologist, educator*
Rubin, Harry Meyer *software industry executive*
Rubin, Herbert *lawyer*
Rubin, Jeffrey Wayne *lawyer*
Rubin, Joel Edward *manufacturing executive*
Rubin, Robert Edward *diversified financial services company executive, former secretary of the treasury*
Rubin, Robert Samuel *investment banker*
Rubin, Stephen Edward *publishing executive, editor, journalist*
Rubin, Theodore Isaac *psychiatrist, writer*
Rubinfien, Leo H. *photographer, writer*
Rubino, Victor Joseph *academic administrator, lawyer*
Rubinstein, Aaron *lawyer*
Rubinstein, Frederic Armand *lawyer*
Rubinstein, Javier H. *lawyer*
Rubinstein, Peter J. *rabbi*
Rubin-Vega, Daphne *actress*
Ruda, Howard *lawyer, finance company executive*
Rudavsky, Oren *film producer, cinematographer, film director*
Rudel, Julius *conductor*
Rudenstine, David *dean, law educator*
Rudenstine, Neil Leon *former academic administrator, educator*
Ruder, William *public relations executive*
Rudin, Scott *film and theatre producer*
Rudloff, Udo *surgeon, researcher*
Rudoff, Sheldon *lawyer*
Ruegger, Philip T. III *lawyer*
Ruesterholz, Virginia P. *telecommunications industry executive*
Rule, Sheila *editor*
Rumaker, Michael *writer, language educator*
Rupp, George Erik *international relief organization executive*

Rusch, Valerie Williams *thoracic surgeon*
Rusch, William Graham *religious organization administrator*
Ruscha, Edward *artist*
Rusmisel, Stephen Raymond *lawyer*
Russell, David O. *film director, film producer, scriptwriter*
Russo, Anthony Joseph *public relations professional*
Russo, Thomas Anthony *lawyer*
Russotti, Philip Anthony *lawyer*
Russotto, Paul *artist, educator*
Ruta, Thomas V. *professional sports team and accounting executive*
Rutenberg, Jim *journalist*
Rutherfurd, John *financial information company executive*
Ryan, Antony L. *lawyer*
Ryan, J. Richard *lawyer*
Ryan, Regina Claire (Mrs. Paul Deutschman) *editor, literary agent*
Ryan, Robert Leslie *oil company executive*
Ryan, T. Timothy (Thomas Timothy Ryan Jr.) *diversified financial services company executive, former federal agency administrator*
Ryman, Robert Tracy *artist*
Sabat, Robert Hartman *magazine editor*
Sabel, Bradley Kent *lawyer*
Sacco, Amy *restaurant and nightclub owner*
Sachar, David Bernard *gastroenterologist, educator*
Sachar, Louis *writer*
Sachs, Jeffrey David *economist, educator*
Sack, Robert David *federal judge, educator*
Sacks, Ira Stephen *lawyer*
Sacks, Oliver Wolf *neurologist, writer*
Saddler, Donald Edward *choreographer, dancer*
Sadegh, Ali M. *mechanical engineering educator, researcher, consultant*
Sadick, Neil Scott *dermatologist*
Sadik, Nafis *United Nations administrator*
Sadik-Khan, Janette I. *city manager, former federal agency administrator*
Sadiq, Aamir *investment banker, engineer*
Sadock, Benjamin James *psychiatrist, educator*
Sadove, Stephen Irving *retail executive*
Saeed, Faiza J. *lawyer*
Saffar, Jean-Marc *healthcare consultant*
Safian, Robert L. *executive editor*
Safra, Joseph *bank executive*
Saft, Stuart Mark *lawyer*
Sahid, Joseph Robert *lawyer*
Saint-Donat, Bernard Jacques *finance company executive*
St. Germain, Jean Mary *medical physicist*
St. Martin, Charlotte *trade association administrator*
Salans, Lester Barry *physician, research scientist, educator*
Saleh, Mohammed *diplomat*
Salembier, Valerie Birnbaum *publishing executive*
Salerno-Sonnenberg, Nadja *violinist*
Salgo, Peter Lloyd *internist, writer, anesthesiologist, journalist, commentator*
Salinger, J(erome) D(avid) *author*
Salky, Barry A. *surgeon*
Salmans, Charles Gardiner *banker*
Salmi, Mika *information technology executive*
Salomon, Richard E. *investment company executive*
Salonen, Esa-Pekka *conductor, music director*
Salonga, Lea *actress, singer*
Salter, James *writer*
Salter, Kevin Thornton *lawyer*
Salter, Mary Jo *poet*
Salvati, Edwardo A. *surgeon*
Salvesen, Magda Abercromby *art and garden historian*
Salzberg, Barry *accounting firm executive*
Sampras, Pete *retired professional tennis player*
Sampson, Hugh Albert, Jr. *medical educator*
Samuels, Dorothy J. *journalist, writer*
Samuels, Leslie B. *lawyer*
Samuelsson, Marcus (Kasshun Tsegie) *food service executive*
Sanchez, Karla G. *lawyer*
Sanchez, Manuel *retired social services administrator, writer*
Sand, Leonard B. *federal judge*
Sandelman, Jonathan E. (Jon) *investment banker*
Sander, Elliot Gene (Lee Sander) *transportation executive*
Sanders, Gina Susan *publishing executive*
Sandford, John (John Roswell Camp) *writer, journalist*
Sandhu, Harvinder Singh *spinal surgeon, educator*
Sandler, Irving Harry *art critic, art historian*
Sandler, Lucy Freeman *art history educator*
Sandler, Richard Jay *lawyer*
Sandler, Robert Michael *insurance company executive*
Sandler, Ross *law educator*
Sands, Harry *psychologist, health administrator, researcher*
Sandstedt, J. Erik *lawyer*
Sandy, Sandra V. *psychologist*
Sangiuliano, Barbara Ann *tax consultant*
Sanseverino, Raymond Anthony *lawyer*
Santo, Fred M. *lawyer*
Santos, Nadine *music director*
Saperstein, Richard S. *financial consultant*
Saphir, Richard Louis *pediatrician*
Sapir, Tamir *entrepreneur*
Sarachik, Myriam Paula Morgenstein *physics professor, condensed matter physicist*
Saraf, Peter Nataniel *film producer, executive*
Sarandon, Susan Abigail *actress*
Sard, Susannah Ellen *non-profit executive*
Sareyan, Andy *publishing executive*
Sargent, Pamela *writer*
Sarkozy, Olivier (Pierre Olivier Sarkozy) *investment banker*
Sarnelle, Joseph R. *publishing executive*
Sarnoff, Ann M. *publishing executive, former sports association executive*
Sasman, Irene Deak Handberg *publishing executive*
Sather, Glen Cameron *professional hockey team executive, coach*
Satine, Barry Roy *lawyer*
Saufer, Isaac Aaron *lawyer*
Saul, Andrew M. *investment company executive*
Saunders, Paul Christopher *lawyer*
Savas, Emanuel S. *finance educator, public official*
Savell, Polly Carolyn *lawyer*
Savrin, Louis *lawyer*
Sawers, Sir John *ambassador*
Sawyer, (L.) Diane *newscaster, journalist*
Sawyers, Al Baker *lawyer*
Saxena, Brij B. *endocrinologist, biochemist, educator*
Saxton, Catherine Patricia *public relations executive*
Sayre, Phil *editor*
Sayres, Edwin J., Jr. *animal welfare organization administrator*
Scalamandre, Jill E. *marketing executive*
Scanlon, Rosemary *economist*
Scarborough, Chuck (Charles Bishop Scarborough III) *newscaster*
Scarlett, Austin *apparel designer*
Scarola, John Michael *dentist, educator*
Scarpa, A. Michael *apparel and corporate financial executive*
Scarpa, Michael *apparel executive*
Scarpelli, Bob *advertising executive*
Scaturro, Philip David *investment banker, academic administrator*
Scelsa, Joseph Vincent *sociologist, educator, dean*
Sceusa, Nicholas A. *pharmacologist*
Schaab, Arnold J. *lawyer*
Schachter, James Robert *editor*
Schacter, Ira Jason *lawyer*
Schaedelin, Pierre *chef*
Schaefer, John H. *finance company and security firm executive*
Schaeffer, Richard *mercantile exchange executive*
Schafer, Charles J. *communications systems company executive*
Schafer, Milton *composer, pianist, educator*
Schafer, Oscar S. *investment company executive*
Schaffer, Kenneth B. *communications executive, mechanical engineer, consultant*
Schaffer, Scott R. *lawyer*
Schaffer, Seth Andrew *lawyer*
Schaffner, Bertram Henry *psychiatrist*
Schaffzin, Jonathan A. *lawyer*
Schair, Robin A. *lawyer*
Schallert, Edwin Glenn *lawyer*
Schama, Simon *historian, educator, author*
Schamus, James Allan *film producer and company executive, screenwriter*
Schapiro, Donald *lawyer*
Schapiro, Miriam *artist*
Scharf, Charles W. *bank executive*
Schatz, Gary Stewart *marketing professional*
Schechner, Richard *theater director, educator*
Schechter, Daniel Scott *child and adolescent psychiatrist, researcher*
Scheck, Barry C. *legal association administrator, educator*
Scheeder, Louis *theater producer, director, educator*
Scheiman, Eugene R. *lawyer*
Scheindlin, Raymond Paul *literature educator, religious organization administrator*
Scheler, Brad Eric *lawyer*
Schick, Harry Leon *investment company executive*
Schick, Thomas *diversified financial services company executive*
Schiesel, Seth *reporter*
Schiff, David Tevele *investment banker*
Schiff, Frank *investment company executive*
Schiff, Howard Irwin *urologist*
Schiffer, Stephen *philosopher, educator*
Schiffman, Daniel *lawyer, arts advocate*
Schiller, Justin Galland *antiquarian bookseller, researcher, editor*
Schiller, Vivian *Internet company executive*
Schindel, Ronnie M. *lawyer*
Schirokauer, Conrad *history professor*
Schisgal, Murray *playwright*
Schizer, David Michael *dean, law educator*
Schizer, Zevie Baruch *lawyer*
Schlang, David *retired real estate company executive, lawyer*
Schlegel, Peter Niles *urologist, educator*
Schlein, Michael Edward *diversified financial services company executive*
Schler, Michael Lawrence *lawyer*
Schlesinger, Andrea Batista *think-tank executive*
Schlesinger, Sanford Joel *lawyer*
Schlesinger, Stephen Cannon *foreign policy consultant*
Schley, William Shain *otolaryngologist*
Schlosser, Herbert S. *broadcasting company executive*
Schlussel, Joseph Lazar *business executive*
Schmemann, Serge *journalist*
Schmertz, Eric Joseph *lawyer, educator, commissioner*
Schmertz, Mildred Floyd *editor-in-chief, writer*
Schmidt, Benno Charles, Jr. *lawyer*
Schmidt, Charles Edward *lawyer*
Schmidt, Joseph W. *lawyer*
Schmidt, Stanley Albert *editor, writer*
Schmidt, William E. *editor*
Schmidtberger, Michael J. *lawyer*
Schmidt-Holtz, Rolf *music company executive*
Schmolka, Leo Louis *law educator*
Schneck, Jerome M. *psychiatrist, historian, medical educator*
Schneider, Daniel B. *reporter*
Schneider, Howard *lawyer*
Schneider, JoAnne *artist*
Schneider, Martin Aaron *photojournalist, ecologist, engineer, writer, artist, television director, filmmaker, public advocate, medical researcher, educator*
Schneider, Willys Hope *lawyer*
Schneiderman, Irwin *lawyer*
Schneier, Edward Vincent *political science professor*
Schneier, Marc *rabbi*
Schnell, Laura S. *lawyer*
Schoenfeld, Gerald *performing company executive*
Schoenfeld, Jim *professional sports team executive, former professional hockey coach*
Schoenfeld, Robert Louis *biomedical engineer*
Schoenhut, Frederick W. *stock exchange executive*
Schorer, Suki *ballet teacher*
Schori, Katharine Jefferts *bishop*
Schorr, Brian Lewis *lawyer, writer*
Schorsch, Ismar *theology studies educator, rabbi*
Schotter, Andrew Roye *economics professor, consultant*
Schrade, Robert Warren *classical pianist, educator*
Schrager, Ian *hotel executive*
Schreiber, Jay *journalist*
Schreyer, Leslie John *lawyer*
Schueneman, Diane L. *diversified financial services company executive*
Schulhof, Michael Peter *electronics company executive*
Schulhofer, Stephen Joseph *law educator*
Schulhoff, Karen L. *information specialist*
Schulte, Stephen John *lawyer, educator*
Schulz, David Alan *lawyer, educator*
Schulzrinne, Henning G. *computer science educator*
Schumacher, Harry Richard *lawyer*
Schumacher, Robert Denison *banker*
Schuman, Patricia Glass *publishing company executive, educator*
Schumer, Robert B. *lawyer*
Schupak, Leslie Allen *public relations company executive*
Schuster, Carlotta Lief *psychiatrist*
Schuster, Reid S. *advertising executive*
Schwab, Frank, Jr. *management consultant*
Schwab, George David *social sciences educator, writer*
Schwab, Harold Lee *lawyer*
Schwantner, Joseph *composer, educator*
Schwartz, Alan David *diversified financial services company executive*
Schwartz, Alan Victor *advertising executive*
Schwartz, Anna Jacobson *economist*
Schwartz, Barry Fredric *lawyer, diversified holding company executive*
Schwartz, Gil (Stanley Bing) *broadcast executive, writer*
Schwartz, Herbert Frederick *lawyer*
Schwartz, Jordan M. *lawyer*
Schwartz, Marvin *lawyer*
Schwartz, Max J. *lawyer*
Schwartz, Mischa *electrical engineering educator*
Schwartz, Renee Gerstler *lawyer*
Schwartz, Robert *finance educator*
Schwartz, Robert George *retired insurance company executive*
Schwartz, Theodore H. *neurosurgeon*
Schwartz, Wallace L. *lawyer*
Schwartz, William *lawyer, educator*
Schwartzstein, Adam *lawyer*
Schwarz, Frederick A.O., Jr. *lawyer*
Schwarzman, Stephen Allen (Steve Schwarzman) *investment banker*
Sclafani, Anthony Paul *plastic surgeon, educator, biomedical researcher*
Sclafani, Joseph L. *diversified financial services company executive*
Sclafani, Susan K. *educational consultant, former federal agency administrator*
Scofidio, Ricardo *artist, architect, educator*
Scott, Dale Allan *major league umpire*
Scott, Daniel J. *lawyer*
Scott, Margaret Simon *retired mortgage broker*
Scott, Mimi Koblenz *psychotherapist, actress, journalist, playwright*
Scott, Norman (W. Norman Scott) *orthopedist, sports medicine physician, surgeon*
Scott, Stanley DeForest *real estate company executive*
Scott, Susan Craig *plastic surgeon*
Scott, Tom *broadcast executive*
Scott, William Clement III *investor*
Scribner, Charles III *art historian, writer*
Sculco, Thomas Peter *surgeon*
Scully, Robert William (Bob Scully) *diversified financial services company executive*
Seal, *musician*
Seaman, Alfred Jarvis *retired advertising agency executive*
Seaman, Barbara (Ann Rosner) *author*
Sean Paul, (Sean Paul Henriques) *singer*
Seary, Lawrence Anthony *cinematographer, television producer*
Seborovski, Carole *artist*
Secunda, Eugene *marketing professional, educator*
Sedaka, Neil *singer, songwriter*
Seder, Sam *radio personality*
Sederbaum, Arthur David *lawyer*
Sedlin, Elias David *orthopedist, educator*
See, SawTeen *structural engineer*
Seeger, Pete *folk singer, songwriter*
Seelig, Jill *publishing executive*
Seely, Robert Daniel *cardiologist, medical association administrator*
Segal, Lore *writer*
Segal, Martin Eli *retired actuarial and consulting company executive*
Segal, Sheldon Jerome *biologist, educator, foundation administrator*
Seiden, Henry (Hank Seiden) *advertising executive*
Seiden, Steven Arnold *executive search consultant*
Seidenberg, Ivan G. *telecommunications industry executive*
Seidler, Alan Richard *composer, musician, music company executive*
Seidler, B(ernard) Alan *lawyer*
Seife, Howard *lawyer*
Seifert, Thomas Lloyd *lawyer*
Seiff, Eric A. *lawyer*
Seigel, Jerrold Edward *historian, writer*
Seigel, Stuart Evan *lawyer*
Seinuk, Ysrael A. *architectural engineer*
Seitz, Frederick *former university administrator*
Selby, Cecily Cannan *dean, science educator, scientist*
Selby, Ronald M. *orthopedic surgeon*
Seldes, Marian *actress*
Selig, Bud (Alan Huber Selig) *major league baseball commissioner*
Selig, Karl-Ludwig *literature and language professor*
Seliger, Charles *artist*
Seligman, Daniel *editor*
Seligman, Delice *lawyer*
Sellers, Peter Hoadley *mathematician, educator*
Seltzer, Terry F. *endocrinologist, medical educator*
Selver, Paul Darryl *lawyer*
Semlies, Lori R. *lawyer*
Semple, Robert Baylor, Jr. *editor, journalist*
Sención, Felix *publishing executive*
Sendak, Maurice Bernard *writer, illustrator*
Sendax, Victor Irven *dentist, educator, dental implant researcher*
Sender, Adam D. *investment company executive, art collector*
Senior, Enrique Francisco *investment banker*
Senzel, Martin Lee *lawyer*
Serbaroli, Francis J. *lawyer, educator, writer*
Serchuk, Ivan *lawyer*
Serebrier, José *musician, composer, conductor*
Serota, James Ian *lawyer*
Serota, Susan Perlstadt *lawyer, educator*
Serra, Matthew D. *consumer products company executive*
Serra, Richard *sculptor*
Servodidio, Pat Anthony *broadcast executive*
Serwer, Andy (Andrew E. Serwer) *editor, journalist*
Sessions, Roy Brumby *otolaryngologist, educator*
Setrakian, Berge *lawyer*
Severs, William Floyd *actor*
Sevilla-Sacasa, Frances Aldrich *bank executive*
Seward, George Chester *lawyer*
Sexton, Joe *editor*
Sexton, John Edward *academic administrator, law educator*
Seymour, Everett Hedden, Jr. *lawyer*
Seymour, Karen Patton *lawyer, former prosecutor*
Seymour, Samuel Whitney *lawyer*
Shabto, Uri *vitreo-retinal surgeon*
Shachar, Avishai *lawyer*
Shaffer, Peter (Sir Peter Shaffer) *playwright*
Shafir, Robert S. *finance company executive*
Shafrir, Doree *editor, journalist*
Shah, Jatin Premanand *head and neck surgeon, educator*
Shah, Vivek *publishing executive*
Shainwald, Sybil *lawyer*
Shakespeare, Valerie Monroe *curator, director, art gallery owner*
Shakow, David Joseph *lawyer, educator*
Shamamian, Oscar *architect*
Shamask, Ronaldus *fashion designer*
Shambroom, Paul *artist, photographer*
Shanahan, Brendan Frederick *professional hockey player*
Shanahan, William Stephen *consumer products company executive*
Shane, Penny *lawyer*
Shank, Ron *publishing executive*
Shanks, David *publishing executive*
Shanks, Eugene Baylis, Jr. *banker*
Shannon, Careen Brett *lawyer, writer, law educator*
Shanor, Donald Read *journalism educator, writer*
Shao, Wei *writer, educator*
Shapiro, Gary Evan *newspaper journalist*
Shapiro, Isaac *lawyer*
Shapiro, James Stephen *English professor*
Shapiro, Joel Elias *artist*
Shapiro, Judith R. *academic administrator, anthropology educator*
Shapiro, Mark Jeffrey *lawyer*
Shapiro, Marvin Lincoln *communications company executive*
Shapiro, Meryl *lawyer*
Shapiro, Michael *lawyer*
Shapiro, Neal *broadcast executive, television producer*
Shapiro, Robert Frank *investment company executive*
Shapiro, Steven R. *legal association administrator*
Shapiro, Theodore *psychiatrist, educator*
Sharbel, Jean M. *editor*
Sharfstein, Howard F. *lawyer*
Shargel, Gerald L. *lawyer*
Sharkey, Catherine Moira *law educator*
Sharma, Deven *financial information company executive*
Sharma, Ravi Ivan *lawyer*
Sharoff, Leighsa *nursing educator, researcher*
Sharp, J(ames) Franklin *finance educator, portfolio manager*
Sharpe, Shannon *commentator, retired professional football player*
Shatkin, Jess Parker *psychiatrist*
Shatter, Susan Louise *artist*
Shaw, Adam *broadcast executive*
Shaw, David Elliot *financial executive*
Shaw, Steven A. *information technology executive*
Shaw, Theodore Michael *legal association administrator*
Shawn, Wallace *playwright, actor*
Shea, Edward Emmett *lawyer, educator, writer*
Shea, James William *lawyer*

Shea, Martin M. *broadcast executive*
Shecter, Howard L. *lawyer*
Shedlarz, David L. *pharmaceutical executive*
Shedlin, Gary Stephen *investment banker*
Sheehan, Michael Andrew *former protective services official, former federal agency administrator*
Sheehan, Mike *advertising executive*
Sheehan, Robert C. *lawyer*
Sheehan, Susan *writer*
Sheinman, Mort *editor, consultant, writer, photographer*
Shelanski, Michael L. *cell biologist, educator*
Sheldon, Eleanor Harriet Bernert *sociologist, writer*
Shelley, Carole *actress*
Shen, Michael *lawyer*
Shenker, Joseph C. *lawyer*
Shenkman, Mark Ronald *investment and finance executive*
Shepard, Robert M. *lawyer, investment banker, engineer*
Shepard, Stephen Benjamin *journalist, educator, retired editor*
Shepherd, Gillian Mary *physician*
Sheresky, Norman M. *lawyer*
Sherman, Arthur *theater educator, writer, actor, composer, sculptor*
Sherman, Eric *communications executive*
Sherman, Eugene Jay *retired marketing professional, economist*
Sherman, Jeffrey Barry *retail executive*
Sherman, John Eric *plastic surgeon*
Sherman, Sarai *sculptor, painter*
Sherman, Spencer E. *ophthalmologist*
Sherrod, Philip Lawrence *artist, composer, painter, poet*
Sherwood, Andrew *management consultant*
Shields, Craig M. *lawyer*
Shields, James Joseph *academic administrator, educator, writer*
Shientag, Florence Perlow *lawyer*
Shier, Shelley M. *production company executive*
Shimizu, Masato *chef*
Shinder, Marcella Marie *marketing executive*
Shineman, Edward William, Jr. *retired pharmaceutical executive*
Shinkle, John Thomas *lawyer*
Shinnar, Reuel *engineering educator, consultant*
Shionoiri, Hideo *computer technologist*
Shipley, Walter Vincent *retired bank executive*
Shnayerson, Robert Beahan *editor, consultant*
Shneidman, J. Lee *historian, educator*
Shockey, George R., Jr. *lawyer*
Shoket, Ann E. *editor-in-chief*
Shorris, Anthony Ernest *state agency administrator*
Shorter, James Russell, Jr. *lawyer*
Shortz, Will *puzzle editor*
Shoss, Cynthia Renée *lawyer*
Showalter, David Scott *accounting executive*
Shriver, Lionel (Margaret Ann Shriver) *writer*
Shuler, Laura *marketing executive*
Shulevitz, Uri *writer, illustrator*
Shulman, Max Rees *lawyer*
Shuman, Earl Stanley *songwriter, music publisher*
Shutran, Richard *lawyer*
Shvo, Michael *real estate broker*
Shyer, John D. *lawyer*
Sibley, David Allen *illustrator, writer, ornithologist*
Sibony, Gedi *sculptor*
Sicha, Choire *online editor*
Sidamon-Eristoff, Anne Phipps *not-for-profit developer*
Sidamon-Eristoff, Constantine *lawyer*
Siderow, Neil *real estate company executive*
Sidran, Miriam *retired physicist*
Sidwell, David H. *diversified financial services company executive*
Siebert, John Weston *surgeon, plastic surgeon*
Siebert, Muriel (Mickie) *brokerage house executive, retired bank executive*
Siegel, Arthur Herbert *finance company executive*
Siegel, Edward M. *lawyer*
Siegel, Herbert Jay *communications executive, director*
Siegel, Jeffrey Norton *lawyer*
Siegel, Lucy Boswell *public relations executive*
Siegel, Marc Monroe *television producer, scriptwriter, director*
Siegel, Marvin *newspaper editor*
Siegel, Randy *publishing executive*
Siegel, Stanley *lawyer, educator*
Siffert, John Sand *lawyer, educator, writer*
Sifton, Sam *editor*
Sigal, Elliott *pharmaceutical executive*
Sigal-Ibsen, Rose *artist*
Sigety, Cornelius Edward *real estate developer, director*
Sigmond, Carol Ann *lawyer*
Siguler, George William *diversified financial services company executive*
Sikander, Shahzia *artist*
Siklos, Richard *reporter*
Silberberg, Richard Howard *lawyer*
Silberman, John Alan *lawyer*
Silbersack, John Walter *literary agent*
Silkenat, James Robert *lawyer*
Siller, Stephen I. *lawyer*
Silva, Daniel Joseph *writer*
Silver, Adam *sports association executive*
Silver, Joan Micklin *film director, screenwriter*
Silver, Morris *economist, educator*
Silver, Richard Tobias *oncologist, educator*
Silver, Richard V. *lawyer, diversified financial services company executive*
Silver, Sheldon *state legislator, lawyer*
Silverberg, Jay Lloyd *lawyer*
Silverberg, Michael Joel *lawyer*
Silverman, Allison *scriptwriter, television producer, actress*
Silverman, Arthur Charles *lawyer*
Silverman, Eric F. *lawyer*
Silverman, Laurence A. *lawyer*
Silverman, Martin Morris Bernard *secondary school educator*
Silverman, Moses *lawyer*
Silvers, Robert B. *editor*
Silvers, Sally *choreographer, performing company executive*
Silverstein, Larry A. *real estate developer*
Silverstein, Paul N. *lawyer*
Silverstein, Samuel Charles *cellular biology and physiology professor, researcher*
Simkin, Steven *lawyer*
Simmons, John Derek *retired financial consultant*
Simmons, Joseph (Run Simmons, Reverend Run) *musician*
Simmons, Michael *entrepreneur, publishing executive*
Simmons, Peter Lawrence *lawyer*
Simmons, Sue *newscaster*
Simms, Marsha E. *lawyer*
Simms, Phil *sports commentator, retired professional football player*
Simon, Bruce Harvey *lawyer*
Simon, Eric Jacob *neuroscientist, educator*
Simon, Jacqueline Albert *political scientist, writer*
Simon, Joel *music producer, advertising executive*
Simon, Ronald Charles *curator, educator*
Simonds, Charles Frederick *artist*
Simone, Joseph R. *lawyer*
Simons, Albert III *lawyer*
Simpkins, Neil P. *investment and automotive company executive*
Simpson, Mary Michael *priest, psychotherapist*
Sinclair, Daisy *communications executive*
Sinensky, Jeffrey *lawyer*
Singer, Barbara Helen *photographer, radiographer*
Singer, Joy Daniels *journalist, consultant*
Singh, Jyoti Shankar *international organization executive*
Singleton, Donald Edward *journalist*
Sinsheimer, Warren Jack *lawyer*
Sirgado, Jo Anne E. *lawyer*
Sirkin, Michael S. *lawyer*
Sischy, Ingrid Barbara *editor, art critic*
Siskind, Arthur Michael *lawyer*
Siskind, Donald Henry *lawyer*
Sitarz, Anneliese Lotte *pediatrician, educator, physician*
Sitomer, Richard *air transportation executive*
Sitomer, Sheila Marie *television producer and director*
Sjoblom, Thomas V. *lawyer*
Skaistis, Rachel G. *lawyer*
Skinner, Peter Graeme *retired lawyer*
Skinner, Robert C., Jr. *retail executive*
Skirnick, Robert Andrew *lawyer*
Sklyar, Adelina M. *lawyer*
Skolnik, Richard Alan *plastic surgeon*
Slabe, James F. *publishing executive*
Slacik, Claudia *bank executive*
Sladkus, Harvey Ira *lawyer*
Slavin, Arlene *artist*
Sleed, Joel *columnist*
Sleigh, Sylvia *artist, educator*
Slifkin, Daniel *lawyer*
Sliwa, Curtis *radio personality, volunteer*
Sloan, Allan Herbert *journalist*
Sloane, Howard G. *lawyer*
Sloat, Richard Joel *artist*
Slomanson, Lloyd Howard *architect, musician, photographer*
Slone, Sandi *artist*
Slotkin, Todd *diversified financial services company executive*
Slotnick, Barry Ivan *lawyer*
Sloujitel, Jacob Ben *mathematics professor, researcher*
Slusser, William Peter *investment banker*
Slutsky, Lorie A(nn) *foundation executive*
Small, George LeRoy *geographer, educator*
Small, Jeffrey *lawyer*
Small, Jonathan Andrew *lawyer, consultant*
Smart, Thomas A. *lawyer*
Smeall, Christopher *lawyer*
Smiley, Jane Graves *author, educator*
Smith, Barry Hamilton *foundation administrator, physician*
Smith, Betty *writer, not-for-profit developer*
Smith, Brad *journalist*
Smith, Bradley Youle *lawyer*
Smith, Clare *art appraiser*
Smith, Craig Richey *thoracic surgeon*
Smith, Dennis (Edward Smith) *publishing executive, writer*
Smith, Edward Paul, Jr. *lawyer*
Smith, George Bundy *lawyer, retired state appeals court judge*
Smith, Gordon A. *bank executive*
Smith, Gordon H. *civil and forensic engineer, consultant*
Smith, Hilary Cranwell Bowen *investment banker*
Smith, Ian K. *writer, columnist, physician*
Smith, J. Gordon *automotive executive*
Smith, James Walker *lawyer*
Smith, Jason A. B. *lawyer*
Smith, Jeffrey Austen *lawyer*
Smith, Jeffrey G. *lawyer*
Smith, Karen A. *lawyer*
Smith, Kiki *artist*
Smith, Liz (Mary Elizabeth Smith) *columnist, newscaster*
Smith, Malcolm Bernard *investment company executive*
Smith, Malcolm Sommerville *bass*
Smith, Martin Jay *advertising and marketing executive*
Smith, Phillips Guy *banker*
Smith, Raymond W. *investment banking executive*
Smith, Richard Mills *editor-in-chief*
Smith, Robert Blakeman *lawyer*
Smith, Robert Everett *lawyer*
Smith, Roberta *art critic*
Smith, Shirley *artist*
Smith, Stuart Alan *lawyer*
Smith, Thomas A. *lawyer, investment company executive*
Smith, Thomas Ramsaur, Jr. *lawyer*
Smith, Warren Allen *writer, director, columnist*
Smith, Zak *artist*
Smith-Miller, Henry Houck *architect*
Smotrich, David Isadore *architect*
Snell, Audrey *financial analyst, investment advisor*
Snider, Jerome Guy *lawyer*
Snow, Charles *lawyer*
Snow, Dash *photographer*
Snow, Jack (John William Snow) *investment company executive, former secretary of the treasury*
Snyder, Jon David *dean*
Snyderman, Nancy *surgeon, medical journalist*
Soave, Rosemary *internist*
Sobbott, Susan *diversified financial services company executive*
Sobel, Gerald *lawyer*
Sobel, Howard D. *dermatologist*
Sochet, Mary Allen *psychotherapist, educator, writer*
Softness, Donald Gabriel *marketing professional, manufacturing executive*
Solano, Henry L. *lawyer*
Solarz, Alan H. *lawyer*
Solecki, R. Stefan *anthropologist, educator*
Solender, Michael Samuel *lawyer, diversified financial services company executive*
Solís, Marco Antonio *singer, composer*
Solnit, Rebecca *writer, critic*
Solomon, Andrew P. *lawyer*
Solomon, Gail Ellen *physician*
Solomon, Howard *pharmaceutical executive*
Solomon, Libertina *retired pharmacist, educator*
Solomon, Maynard Elliott *musicologist, retired recording industry executive*
Solomon, Stephen L. *lawyer*
Solomon, Terri Marcia *lawyer*
Solomonoff, Galia *architect*
Solomons, Gus, Jr., (Gustave Martinez) *choreographer, dancer, writer*
Solomons, Seth *marketing executive*
Solotar, Joan S. *securities analyst*
Somerhalder, Ian Joseph *actor*
Somers, John Arthur *insurance company executive*
Sommer, Jeff *journalist*
Sonett, Joshua Robert *medical educator, surgeon*
Sonneman, Eve *artist*
Sono, Masayuki *architect, artist*
Sopanen, Jeri Rainer *photography director*
Sorell, Kitty Julia *public relations executive*
Sorell Stehr, Deborah K. *lawyer*
Sorensen, Gillian Martin *United Nations official*
Sorgi, Leonard *lawyer*
Soriano, Nancy Mernit *editor-in-chief*
Sorkin, Andrew Ross *reporter, columnist*
Sorkin, David James *lawyer*
Sorkin, Ira Lee *lawyer*
Sorkin, Laurence Truman *lawyer*
Soros, George *pension fund administrator*
Sorte, John Follett *investment firm executive*
Sorter, George Hans *accounting and law educator, consultant*
Soter, George Nicholas *advertising executive*
Soth, Alec *photographer*
Sotomayor, Sonia *federal judge*
Sott, Janny *journalist*
Souham, Gérard *communications executive*
Soussloff, Andrew D. *lawyer*
Southworth, Robert Alexander, Jr. *education researcher, educator*
Sovern, Michael Ira *law educator*
Soyer, David *cellist, music educator*
Soyster, Margaret Blair *lawyer*
Spade, Kate (Katherine Noel Spade) *apparel designer*
Spanbock, Maurice Samuel *lawyer*
Spatafora, Marcello *ambassador*
Spatt, Robert Edward *lawyer*
Spear, Harvey M. *lawyer*
Spears, Britney *singer*
Spector, Anita Frohmann *retired buyer*
Spector, Johanna Lichtenberg *ethnomusicologist, former educator*
Spector, Jonathan *business research organization executive, former dean*
Spelfogel, Evan J. *lawyer, educator*
Speller, Robert Ernest Blakefield, Jr. *choreographer*
Spelling, Ian *columnist*
Spellman Sweet, Julie T. *lawyer*
Spence, Sique (Mary Stewart Spence) *art dealer*
Spencer, Charles S. *anthropologist*
Spencer, Frank Cole *medical educator*
Spencer, Michael C. *lawyer*
Sperling, Allan George *lawyer*
Spero, Joan Edelman *foundation administrator*
Speros, James Demitrios *advertising executive*
Speyer, James L. *oncologist*
Speyer, Jerry I. *real estate company executive*
Speziale, Richard Salvatore *financial executive*
Spiegel, Elwyn *advertising executive, art director*
Spiegel, Herbert *psychiatrist, educator*
Spiegel, Jerrold Bruce *lawyer*
Spielvogel, Sidney Meyer *investment banker*
Spikol, Eileen *artist*
Spillane, Dennis Kevin *lawyer*
Spindler, James Andrew *not-for-profit executive*
Spinetta, Jean-Cyril *airline executive*
Spinney, Caroll *entertainer, educator*
Spivak, Leonard A. *lawyer*
Sporn, Michael V. *producer, director*
Sprague, Peter Julian *software company executive, lecturer*
Sprayregen, James H.M. *diversified financial services company executive, lawyer*
Spriggs, David Randall *healthcare administrator, educator*
Sprizzo, John Emilio *federal judge*
Sproule, Michael E. *insurance company executive*
Squeri, Stephen *diversified financial services company executive*
Squire, Walter Charles *lawyer*
Squires, John *publishing executive*
Srulowitz, Marvin *lawyer*
Stackhouse, John Ewell Harbour *judge*
Stacom, Tara Irene *real estate company executive*
Stade, George Gustav *humanities educator*
Stadler, Brian M. *lawyer*
Stainrook, Harry Richard *photographer, retired bank executive*
Staley, James E. *bank executive*
Stanceu, Timothy Charles *federal judge*
Standard, Kenneth G. *lawyer*
Stang, Arnold *actor, writer, film director*
Stang, Rolf Kristian *vocalist, educator, actor, advertising executive, writer*
Stanger, Ila *editor-in-chief*
Stanley, Alessandra *critic*
Stanton, Amy *marketing executive*
Stanton, Ronald P. *export company executive*
Starer, Brian Douglas *lawyer*
Starr, Michael *lawyer*
Starr, Steven Dawson *photographer*
Starr Kins, Gloria *public relations executive, writer, photojournalist, writer, editor*
Stasio, Marilyn Louise *columnist*
Stathis, Nicholas John *lawyer*
Stecher, Esta E. *lawyer, investment company executive*
Steel, Danielle Fernande *author*
Steere, William Campbell, Jr. *pharmaceutical executive*
Steffe, Cynthia *fashion designer*
Steiger, Paul Ernest *editor, journalist*
Stein, David Fred *investment company executive*
Stein, Ellen Gail *information technology manager*
Stein, Elliot, Jr. *business executive*
Stein, Howard S. *retired banker*
Stein, Jacob *computer programmer, analyst*
Stein, Jane Wallison *lawyer*
Stein, Judith *history professor*
Stein, Marvin *psychiatrist, historian*
Stein, Ronald J. *lawyer*
Stein, Stephen William *lawyer*
Stein, Zena A. *retired epidemiologist, educator*
Steinberg, Arthur Jay *lawyer*
Steinberg, Howard Eli *lawyer, diversified financial services company executive*
Steinberg, Jonathan S. *cardiologist, educator*
Steinberg, Leo *art historian, educator*
Steinberg, Milton *retired educational association administrator*
Steiner, David M. *dean*
Steiner, Jeffrey Josef *manufacturing executive*
Steinglass, Peter Joseph *psychiatrist, educator*
Steinhardt, Michael H. *diversified financial services company executive*
Steir, Michael S. *real estate company executive*
Stelwagon, Jennifer Cooper *psychiatrist*
Stengel, Richard *editor*
Stephenson, Alan Clements *lawyer*
Sterling, Robert Lee, Jr. *investment company executive*
Stern, David Joel *national basketball association commissioner*
Stern, Donald Allan *lawyer*
Stern, Fritz Richard *historian, educator*
Stern, Howard Allan *radio personality, television show host*
Stern, James Andrew *investment banker*
Stern, Leonard Norman *real estate developer, former pet supply manufacturing company executive*
Stern, Mitchell *broadcast executive*
Stern, Peter *communications executive*
Stern, Robert Arthur Morton *architect, educator, writer*
Stern, Roslyne Paige *magazine publisher*
Stern, Walter Phillips *investment company executive*
Sternberg, Seymour *insurance company executive*
Sterne, Hedda *artist*
Sternman, Joel W. *lawyer*
Sterns, William S. III *lawyer*
Steuer, Richard Marc *lawyer*
Stevens, Mark Whitney *art critic*
Stevens, Michael N. *lawyer*
Stevens, Risë *performing arts association administrator*
Stevens, Rosemary Anne *medicine and public health historian, artist*
Stevenson, William Henri *author*
Stever, Donald Winfred *lawyer*
Steves, Gale C. *marketing professional, writer, editor-in-chief, publishing executive*
Stewart, E(dward) Nicholson *investment management executive*
Stewart, Ellen D. *theater producer*
Stewart, Geoffrey S. *lawyer*
Stewart, James B. *journalist, writer*
Stewart, Jon (Jonathan Stewart Leibowitz) *comedian, actor*
Stewart, Lynne F. *lawyer*
Stewart, Richard Burleson *law educator*
Stewart, Ruth Ann *public policy educator*
Stiefel, Ethan *dancer, performing company executive*
Stiglitz, Joseph Eugene *economics professor, former federal official*
Stillman, Charles Allen *lawyer*
Stimmel, Barry *cardiologist, educator, internist, dean*
Stimpson, Catharine Rosalind *literature educator, writer*
Sting, (Gordon Matthew Sumner) *musician, songwriter, actor*
Stockton, Susan *food products executive*
Stokes, William James *musician*
Stoll, Neal Richard *lawyer*
Stolper, Pinchas Aryeh *religious organization executive, rabbi*

Volpe, Thomas J. *corporate financial executive*
von Baillou, Astrid *executive search consultant*
von der Heyden, Karl Mueller *retired manufacturing executive*
Von Drasek, Lisa *librarian*
von Fraunhofer-Kosinski, Katherina *bank and advertising executive*
Vongerichten, Jean-Georges *food service executive, chef*
von Mehren, Robert Brandt *retired lawyer*
von Mueffling, William *investment company executive*
Voorsanger, Bartholomew *architect*
Vora, Ashok *financial economist*
Vorhees, Mark *writer*
Voss, Linda I. *finance company executive*
Voto-Bernales, Jorge *ambassador*
Vyskocil, Mary Kay *lawyer*
Wachsberger, Chaim *lawyer*
Wachtell, Herbert M. *lawyer*
Wackermann, William *publishing executive*
Waddell, Mark E. *lawyer*
Wade, Estelle B. *psychologist, psychoanalyst*
Wadsworth, John (Jack) Spencer, Jr. *investment banker*
Wagner, Alan Cyril *television and film producer, consultant, performing arts educator*
Wagner, Robin Samuel Anton *stage and set designer*
Wahlgren, Francis J. *art appraiser*
Wailand, George *lawyer*
Wainwright, Marcus *apparel designer*
Wainwright, Rufus *musician, singer*
Waks, Jay Warren *lawyer*
Wald, Bernard Joseph *lawyer*
Wald, Richard Charles *media consultant, educator*
Wald, Sylvia *artist*
Wald, Wayne A. *lawyer*
Walden, Jennifer Lee *plastic surgeon*
Walden, Shelton Harrison *radio personality, educator*
Waldenberg, Alan S. *lawyer*
Waldman, Seymour Morton *lawyer*
Waldman, Steven *editor*
Waldron, Jeremy James *law educator*
Walk, Charlie *music company executive*
Walker, Alice *writer*
Walker, Charles Dodsley *conductor, organist*
Walker, F(rank) Borden *oil industry executive*
Walker, George H. *investment company executive*
Walker, George Herbert, IV, *investment company executive*
Walker, Jennie Louise *not-for-profit fundraiser, consultant*
Walker, John Lockwood *lawyer*
Walker, Kara *artist*
Walker, Kim A. *lawyer*
Walker, Mort *cartoonist*
Walker, Robert Harris *historian, writer, editor*
Walkovik, Donald C. *lawyer*
Wall, Charles R. *lawyer*
Wallace, Alexandra *broadcast executive, television producer*
Wallace, Christopher *broadcast television correspondent*
Wallace, Edward Corbett *lawyer*
Wallace, Nora Ann *lawyer*
Wallace, Thomas C. *editor, publishing executive*
Wallace, Walter C. *lawyer, government official*
Wallach, Eli *actor*
Wallach, Eric Jean *lawyer*
Waller, Robert James *writer*
Wall Spitzer, Silda *not-for-profit developer, First Lady of New York State*
Walters, Barbara Jill *broadcast journalist*
Walters, Milton James *investment banker*
Walton, Anthony John (Tony Walton) *set designer, illustrator, writer*
Waltuck, David *chef, restaurant owner*
Wanek, William Charles *public relations executive*
Wang, Albert Huai-en *lawyer*
Wang, Frederick Mark *pediatrician, ophthalmologist, educator*
Wang, Guangya *ambassador, international organization official*
Wang, Lu-Hai *medical educator, biochemist*
Wang, Vera *fashion designer*
Wang, Xinsheng *lawyer*
Wank, Gerald Sidney *periodontist, educator*
Wanner, Eric *foundation executive*
Wanzenberg, Alan *architect*
Ward, Geoffrey Champion *writer, editor*
Warden, John Lehman *lawyer*
Wardropper, Ian Bruce *museum curator, educator*
Wareham, Raymond Noble *brokerage house executive*
Waren, Stanley Arnold *academic administrator, performing company executive*
Waricha, Joan *publishing executive*
Warner, Miner Hill *investment banker*
Warner, Peter David *publishing executive*
Warnke, Gordon E. *lawyer*
Warren, Andrew C. *apparel executive*
Warren, Arete Bernice *art historian*
Warren, David P. *stock exchange executive*
Warren, Irwin Howard *lawyer*
Warren, James I. *lawyer*
Warren, Michelle Palmieri *internist, endocrinologist*
Warren, Russell Frederick *orthopedist*
Warren, William Bradford *lawyer*
Washburn, David Thacher *lawyer*
Washburn, Joan Thomas *small business owner*
Wasow, Omar *Internet company executive*
Wasser, Henry *retired American literature and sociology educator*
Wasserman, Steve *literary agent*
Wasserstein, Bruce *investment banker*
Waterman, Millicent Adora *education educator, minister*
Waters, Donald Joseph *data processing executive*
Waters, Sylvia *dance company artistic director*
Watkins, Charles Booker, Jr. *mechanical engineering educator*
Watson, Anthony L. *health facility executive*
Watson, Solomon Brown, IV, *lawyer, publishing executive*
Watt, Douglas (Benjamin Watt) *writer, drama critic*
Wattleton, (Alyce) Faye *educational association administrator, advocate*
Watts, Duncan J. *social sciences educator*
Waxenberg, Jay David *lawyer*
Waxman, Allen *pharmaceutical executive*
Waxman, Anita *theater producer*
Waybourn, Kathleen Ann *lawyer, consultant*
Wayne, Leslie *reporter*
Weber, Lisa M. *insurance company executive*
Weber, Mark *apparel executive*
Weber, Robert Maxwell *cartoonist*
Webster, Catherine T. *telecommunications industry executive*
Webster, Susan *lawyer*
Wedlick, Dennis *architect, writer*
Weeks, David Frank *foundation administrator*
Ween, Martin M. *lawyer*
Weiksner, Sandra S. *lawyer*
Weil, Frank A. *investment banker, lawyer*
Weil-Garris Brandt, Kathleen (Kathleen Brandt) *art historian*
Weill, Sandy (Sanford I. Weill) *former diversified financial services company executive*
Weinberg, Adam D. *museum director*
Weinberg, H. Barbara *art historian, educator, curator*
Weinberg, Jeffrey J. *lawyer*
Weinberg, John Sidney *investment banker*
Weinberg, Peter Amory *investment banker*
Weinberger, Harold Paul *lawyer*
Weinberger, Mark Alan *corporate financial executive, former federal agency administrator*
Weiner, Andrew Jay *lawyer*
Weiner, Earl David *lawyer*
Weiner, Lawrence Charles *artist*
Weiner, Stephen Arthur *lawyer*
Weiner, Walter Herman *bank executive, lawyer*
Weingarten, Marc *lawyer*
Weingarten, Randi (Rhonda) *labor union administrator, lawyer*
Weingrow, Howard Louis *finance company executive*
Weinroth, Lois L. *lawyer*
Weinschel, Alan Jay *lawyer*
Weinstein, Bob (Robert Weinstein) *film company executive*
Weinstein, Harvey *film company executive, film producer*
Weinstein, Herbert *chemical engineer, educator*
Weinstein, Herschel S. *lawyer, pharmaceutical executive*
Weinstein, I. Bernard *oncologist, geneticist, director, educator*
Weinstein, Martin *aerospace transportation executive, manufacturing executive, materials scientist*
Weinstein, Raymond *sculptor*
Weinstein, Sidney *retired university program director*
Weinstock, Leonard *lawyer*
Weintraub, Beverly *editor*
Weintz, Jacob Frederick, Jr. *retired investment banker*
Weisberg-Samuels, Janet S. *psychologist*
Weisbrod, Carl *lawyer, public official*
Weisenburger, Randall J. *advertising executive*
Weiser, Martin Jay *lawyer*
Weiss, Carol Juliet *psychiatrist*
Weiss, Donald S. *real estate developer*
Weiss, Jack Meyar *lawyer*
Weiss, Jonathan Arthur *lawyer, writer*
Weiss, Lawrence N. *lawyer*
Weiss, Lisa Ann *lawyer*
Weiss, Melvyn I. *lawyer*
Weiss, Myrna Grace *management consultant*
Weiss, Paul Richard *plastic surgeon*
Weiss, Samuel Abraham *psychologist, psychoanalyst*
Weissman, David L. *lawyer*
Weissmann, Andrew *lawyer, former prosecutor*
Weissmann, Gerald *internist, researcher, educator, editor, writer*
Weithorn, Stanley Stephen *lawyer*
Weitz, Harvey *lawyer, educator*
Weitz, Perry *lawyer*
Weitzner, Harold *mathematics professor*
Wek, Alek *model*
Welch, Martha Grace *physician, researcher*
Weld, Jonathan Minot *lawyer*
Weld, William F. *former governor*
Welder, Rachael Mae *mathematician, educator*
Welikson, Jeffrey Alan *lawyer*
Welker, Jennifer Carol Marie *artist*
Wellin, Keith Sears *investment banker*
Wellington, Harry Hillel *lawyer, educator*
Wells, Christopher M. *lawyer*
Wells, Theodore V., Jr., (Ted) *lawyer*
Welshimer, Mark J. *lawyer*
Weltman, Edward S. *lawyer*
Wemple, Erik C. *editor-in-chief*
Wender, Ira Tensard *lawyer*
Wender, Phyllis Bellows *literary agent*
Wendlandt, Gary E. *insurance company executive*
Wenegrat, Saul S. *art association administrator, educator*
Wenig, Cindy L. *lawyer*
Wenig, Devin Norse *communications executive*
Wenner, Jann Simon *editor, publisher*
Werder, Richard I., Jr. *lawyer*
Werfelman, William Herman, Jr. *public relations executive*
Werman, David Sanford *psychiatrist, psychoanalyst*
Werner, Robert L. *lawyer, consultant*
Werner, Ryan *film company executive*
Werthamer, Nathan Richard *physicist*
Weschler, Lawrence Michael *writer, journalist*
Wesely, Edwin Joseph *lawyer*
Wesely, Marissa Celeste *lawyer*
Wesley, John Mercer *artist*
Wesley, Richard C. *federal judge*
West, Kanye *rap artist*
West, Paul Noden *writer, playwright*
West, Stephen Kingsbury *lawyer, director*
Westin, David Lawrence *broadcast executive, lawyer*
Westlake, Donald Edwin (Tucker Coe, Richard Stark) *writer*
Westreich, Neil P. *lawyer*
Westrich, Geoffrey Howard *orthopaedic surgery*
Wetmore, Keith Chidester *lawyer*
Wexelbaum, Michael *lawyer*
Wexler, Allan *architect, educator*
Wexler, Leonard Howard *pediatric oncologist*
Wexler, Patricia Susan *dermatologist, surgeon*
Wexler, Peter John *artist, photographer, theatre designer, producer, director*
Weyman, Todd D. *art appraiser*
Weymouth, Elizabeth K. *bank executive*
Whaley, Charles Henry, IV, *communications company executive*
Wharton, Ralph Nathaniel *psychiatrist, educator*
Wheeldon, Christopher *dancer, choreographer*
Wheeler, Jane *investment banker*
Wheeler, William J. *insurance company executive*
Whelan, William J. III *lawyer*
Whitaker, G(eorge) Warren *lawyer*
Whitaker, Mark Theis *broadcast executive, editor*
Whitcomb, James Howard, Jr. *investment banker*
White, Benjamin *communications executive*
White, Fred B. III *lawyer*
White, George Cooke *theater director, foundation administrator*
White, Harry Edward, Jr. *lawyer*
White, Jack (John Anthony Gillis) *musician, producer*
White, John Patrick *lawyer*
White, Kate *editor-in-chief*
White, Katherine Patricia *lawyer*
White, Lawrence J. *economics professor*
White, Lillias *actress*
White, Mary Jo *lawyer, former prosecutor*
White, Peter C. *lawyer*
White, W. Christopher *lawyer*
Whited, Mary Elizabeth *marketing professional*
Whiteman, Douglas E. *publisher*
Whiting, Anthony *executive search consultant*
Whiting, Gordon James *investment banker*
Whiting, Susan Dickinson *media research company executive*
Whitman, Martin J. *portfolio manager*
Whitmer, Frederick Lee *lawyer*
Whitney, Craig Richard *journalist*
Whitney, Jonathan B. *lawyer*
Whitson, Jerry E. *lawyer*
Whittemore, Laurence Frederick *bank executive*
Whittingham, Charles Arthur *library director, publishing executive*
Whoriskey, Robert Donald *lawyer*
Whyatt, Robin M. *healthcare educator*
Wick, Tamara *photographer, artist, writer*
Wickes, R(ichard) Paul *lawyer*
Widing, Eric P. *auction specialist*
Widlund, Olof Bertil *computer science educator, mathematician*
Wiener, Marvin S. *rabbi, editor, executive*
Wiesel, Torsten Nils *neurobiologist, educator*
Wieser, Helmut *metal products executive*
Wijnberg, Sandra S. *investment company executive*
Wilcox, John Caven *lawyer, financial executive*
Wildermuth, Bruce R. *lawyer*
Wilds, Bonnie *writer, volunteer*
Wile, Joan *composer, lyricist, singer*
Wiles, Michael E. *lawyer*
Wiley-Hart, Debra *musician, educator*
Wilford, John Noble, Jr. *science news correspondent*
Wilkerson, Edward *apparel designer*
Wilkins, Amy P. *publishing executive*
Wilkinson, John Hart *lawyer*
Wilkinson, Louise Cherry *psychology professor, dean*
Willett, John A. *lawyer*
Willett, Roslyn Leonore *public relations executive, food service consultant, writer, editor*
Williams, Anthony *lawyer*
Williams, Ben *editorial director online magazine*
Williams, Brian *network news anchor*
Williams, Christopher *investment company executive*
Williams, Christopher *photographer*
Williams, Dave Harrell *investment company executive*
Williams, Helena E. *rail transportation executive*
Williams, Lena *sportswriter*
Williams, Marsha E. *broadcast executive*
Williams, Michael G. *publishing executive*
Williams, Montel *television talk show host*
Williams, Patricia J. *law educator*
Williams, Tod Culpan *architect, educator*
Williams, Vanessa (Vanessa Lynn Williams) *recording artist, actress*
Williams, Vaughn Charles *lawyer*
Williams, Wendy *radio personality, writer*
Williams, William John, Jr. *lawyer*
Williamson, Douglas Franklin, Jr. *lawyer*
Willig, Kenneth C. H. *lawyer*
Willis, William Ervin *lawyer*
Willner, Barry A. *lawyer*
Willner, Judith P. *clinical geneticist, pediatrician, educator*
Willumstad, Robert B. *insurance company executive, retired diversified financial services company executive*
Wilson, Edwin *writer, playwright, educator, theater director*
Wilson, Marie C. *foundation administrator*
Wilson, Mike *journalist*
Wilson, Paul Holliday, Jr. *lawyer*
Wilson, Peter Scott *lawyer*
Wilson, Robin *interior designer*
Wilson, Rowan D. *lawyer*
Wimpfheimer, Michael Clark *lawyer*
Winawer, Sidney J. *physician, educator*
Windels, Paul, Jr. *lawyer*
Windhager, Erich Ernst *physiologist, educator*
Winerip, Michael *reporter*
Winfield, Richard Neill *lawyer*
Wing, John Russell *lawyer*
Winick, Myron *nutrition professor, physician*
Winkelried, Jon A. *investment banker*
Winkler, Matthew Adam *editor-in-chief, reporter*
Winn, H. Richard *surgeon*
Winship, Frederick Moery *journalist*
Winterer, Philip Steele *lawyer*
Winters, William Thomas *bank executive*
Wintner, Mark S. *lawyer*
Wintour, Anna *editor-in-chief*
Wintrob, Jay S. *insurance company executive*
Wise, Aaron Noah *lawyer*
Wise, Damon *chef*
Wise, Robert F., Jr. *lawyer*
Wiseman, Michael Martin *lawyer*
Wisner, Frank George *insurance company executive, former ambassador*
Wit, Harold Maurice *retired investment banker, lawyer*
Witkin, Eric Douglas *lawyer*
Witmeyer, John Jacob III *lawyer*
Witten, Roger Michael *lawyer*
Wittes, Robert E. *physician, science foundation director*
Wittstein, Edwin Frank *theater director, set designer*
Wixom, William David *art historian, museum administrator, educator*
Woetzel, Kurt D. *banking executive*
Wohl, Frank Harold *lawyer*
Wohrle, Marta *publishing executive*
Wolden, Suzanne Leesa *pediatric radiation oncologist*
Woletz, Robert G. *editor*
Wolf, Barry M. *lawyer*
Wolf, Naomi *writer*
Wolf, Peter Michael *investment manager, consultant, writer*
Wolfe, George C. *theater director, producer, playwright*
Wolfe, James Ronald *retired lawyer*
Wolfe, Scott W. *orthopedic hand surgeon*
Wolfe, Tom (Thomas Kennerly Wolfe Jr.) *writer, journalist*
Wolff, Alejandro Daniel *ambassador*
Wolff, Edward Nathan *economist, educator*
Wolff, Jesse David *lawyer*
Wolff, Larry *history professor*
Wolff, Richard Joseph *public relations executive, consultant, historian*
Wolff, Virginia Euwer *writer*
Wolff, William F. III *investment banker*
Wolff, William I. *surgeon, educator*
Wolfson, Howard *political analyst*
Wolfson, Jordan *artist*
Wolgemuth, Richard Lee *pharmaceutical executive*
Wolitzer, Steven Barry *investment banker*
Wolkoff, Neal L. *stock exchange executive*
Wollan, Eugene *lawyer*
Wong, Andrea J. *broadcast executive*
Wong, Elizabeth Hung *organist, choirmaster*
Woo, Alex *jewelry designer*
Wood, Kimba M. *federal judge*
Wood, Ronald *musician*
Woodman, Betty *sculptor*
Woodruff, Bob (Robert Warren Woodruff) *newscaster*
Woodruff, Jay Noel *editor, writer*
Woodruff, Mark Reed *magazine editor*
Woods, John Maynard *lawyer*
Woods, Lebbeus *theoretical architect, educator*
Woods, Stuart *writer*
Wood-Smith, Donald *plastic surgeon*
Woodward, Joanne Gignilliat *actress*
Woodward, Kirk *theater director*
Woolard, Edgar S., Jr. *retired chemical company executive*
Woolery, James C. *lawyer*
Worman, Howard Jay *internist, educator*
Wortman, Marlene Stein *historian*
Wortman, Richard S. *historian, educator*
Wragge, Chris *newscaster*
Wray, Cecil, Jr. *lawyer*
Wren, Gayden *playwright, theater director*
Wren, John D. *advertising executive*
Wright, Deborah C. *bank executive*
Wright, Douglas *playwright*
Wright, Faith-dorian *artist*
Wright, Gwendolyn *writer, architecture educator, historian*
Wright, Jason Howard Sebastian *communications executive*
Wright, Joseph Robert, Jr. *corporate executive*
Wright, Margaret Hagen *computer scientist, administrator*
Wright, Sheena *not-for-profit developer*
Wright, Tony *advertising executive*
WuDunn, Sheryl *journalist, correspondent*
Wunderman, Jan Darcourt *artist*
Wunsch, Hannah *anesthesiologist, researcher*
Wuorinen, Charles Peter *composer*
Wurmfeld, Sanford *artist, educator*
Wyeth, James Browning *artist*
Wylde, Kathryn S. *business organization executive*
Wylie, James Malcolm *adult education educator*
Wynne, William Francis *lawyer*
Wyschogrod, Edith *philosophy educator*
Wyss, David Alen *diversified financial services company executive*
Wyzner, Eugeniusz *diplomat*
Yablon, Heather D. *lawyer*
Yaffe, James *writer*
Yalen, Gary N. *retired insurance company executive*
Yamaguchi, Masaya *musician, educator*
Yamin, Michael Geoffrey *lawyer*
Yancey, Richard Charles *investment banker*
Yankwitt, George B(ruce) *lawyer*
Yao, David Da-Wei *engineering educator*

Yapijakis, Constantine *environmental engineer, educator, consultant*
Yardley, Jim *journalist*
Yarett, Jordan Eliot *lawyer*
Yee, Bennie Sene *construction manager, electrical engineer*
Yegulalp, Tuncel M. *mining engineer, educator*
Yelenick, Mary Therese *lawyer*
Yeo, Patricia *chef*
Yerman, Fredric Warren *lawyer*
Yerushalmi, Yosef Hayim *historian, educator*
Yetman, Gary *investment company executive*
Yetman, Leith Eleanor *academic administrator*
Yeung, Bernard Yin *finance educator*
Yglesias, Helen Bassine *author, educator*
Yodowitz, Edward Jay *lawyer*
Yoffie, Erich H. *religious organization administrator*
Yorio, Kimberly *public relations executive*
York, Janet Brewster *nurse, family and sex therapist, artist*
Yoshiuchi, Ellen Haven *healthcare educator, clinical counselor*
Young, Alice *lawyer*
Young, Brian *chef*
Young, Bruce Kenneth *obstetrician, gynecologist, educator*
Young, Estelle Irene *dermatologist, educator*
Young, Genevieve Leman *publishing executive, editor*
Young, John Lloyd *actor*
Young, Jonathan *lawyer*
Young, Michael Warren *geneticist, educator*
Young, Robert Craig *banker*
Youngwood, Alfred Donald *lawyer*
Yu, Andrew *minister*
Yu, Pauline Ruth *former dean, educational association administrator*
Yu, Yi-Hao *endocrinologist, educator, physician, research scientist*
Yuferov, Vadim *research scientist*
Yunis, Amira *real estate company officer*
Yurchenco, Henrietta Weiss *musicologist, writer*
Yurt, Roger William *surgeon, educator*
Zabel, William David *lawyer*
Zack, Robert G. *lawyer, investment company executive*
Zackheos, H.E. Sotirios *ambassador*
Zagat, Nina *publishing executive*
Zagat, Tim *publishing executive*
Zagoren, Joy Carroll *health facility director, researcher*
Zagorin, Janet Susan *legal firm administrator, marketing professional*
Zahnd, Richard H. *sports association executive, lawyer*
Zaitzeff, Roger Michael *lawyer*
Zalaznick, Lauren *broadcast executive*
Zamarra, Galen *chef*
Zambello, Francesca *opera and theater director*
Zammit, Joseph Paul *lawyer*
Zand, Dale Ezra *business management educator*
Zannino, Richard F. *publishing executive*
Zapata, Angel *pastor*
Zarghami, Cyma *broadcast executive*
Zaslowsky, David Paul *lawyer*
Zauderer, Mark Carl *lawyer*
Zawistowski, Stephen Louis *psychologist, educator*
Zbornak, Kent *television producer*
Zedrosser, Joseph John *lawyer*
Zeitlin, Jide James *investor*
Zeldin, Richard Packer *publisher*
Zelnick, Strauss *entertainment company executive*
Zerin, Steven David *lawyer*
Zeuschner, Erwin Arnold *brokerage house executive*
Zevon, Scott J. *plastic surgeon*
Zhen, Juan *medical researcher*
Ziegler, Henry Steinway *retired lawyer*
Zifchak, William C. *lawyer*
Ziltz, Bob *publishing executive*
Zimand, Harvey Folks *lawyer*
Zimbalist, Michael *publishing executive*
Zimmer, William *art critic*
Zimmerman, Diane Leenheer *law educator*
Zimmerman, Elyn *artist*
Zimmerman, Sol Shea *pediatrician*
Zimmett, Mark Paul *lawyer, educator*
Zinberg, David J. *lawyer*
Zinczenko, David *editor*
Zinman, Richard Scott *financial planner*
Zinn, Keith Marshall *ophthalmologist, educator*
Zinoman, Jason *theater critic*
Zirinsky, Bruce R. *lawyer*
Zirinsky, Susan *television producer*
Zito, Robert John Amadeus *lawyer*
Zito, Robert Thomas *pharmaceutical executive*
Zitrin, Arthur *physician*
Zittel, Andrea *painter, sculptor*
Zivin, Norman H. *lawyer*
Zochowski, T. Robert, Jr. *lawyer*
Zoffer, Rachelle *telecommunications industry executive*
Zolla-Pazner, Susan *hospital administrator, biologist, biomedical researcher*
Zombie, Rob (Robert Cummings) *musician, filmmaker*
Zoogman, Nicholas Jay *lawyer*
Zorn, John *composer, musician*
Zornow, David Merrill *lawyer*
Zosike, Joanie Fritz *theater director, actress*
Zubkoff, Daniel J. *lawyer*
Zucker, Stefan *tenor, writer, editor, commentator*
Zuckerman, Mortimer Benjamin *publishing executive, real estate developer*
Zuckerman, Paul Herbert *lawyer*
Zukerman, Michael *lawyer*
Zukerman, Pinchas *concert violinist, violist, conductor*
Zweibel, Joel Burton *retired lawyer*
Zweifach, Lawrence J. *lawyer*
Zwickler, Allen *investment advisor, educator*

Newark
Hemmings, Madeleine Blanchet *not-for-profit administrator, grant writer, media consultant*

Newburgh
Adams, Barbara *language educator, poet, writer*
Blas, Bryan Allyn *postal maintenance worker, artist*
Liberth, Richard Francis *lawyer*
Milligram, Steven Irwin *lawyer*

Newport
Wilson, Eldon Ray *minister*

Niagara Falls
Askins, Arthur James *accountant, auditor*
Bharadwaj, Prem Datta *physics professor*
DeFelice, Eugene Anthony *internist, educator, magician*
Hawkins De Golier, Danielle *political activist*
Knowles, Richard Norris *chemist*
Levine, David Ethan *lawyer*

Niagara University
Brown, Kathleen *education educator*
Foote, Chandra Jeanet *education and elementary school educator, writer*
Osberg, Timothy Michael *psychologist, educator, researcher*

Niskayuna
Edelheit, Lewis S. *research physicist*
Fatić, Vuk Marko *electrical engineer, educator, researcher*
Huening, Walter Carl, Jr. *retired consulting application engineer*
Kambour, Roger Peabody *retired polymer physical chemist, researcher*
Laskaris, E(vangelos) Trifon *technologist, researcher*
Mangan, John Leo *retired electric power industry executive, international trade specialist*
Nichols, Albert Myron *retired minister*
Rasheed, Adam *aerospace engineer, researcher*
Varanasi, Kripa Kiran *research scientist*
Wright, Theodore Paul, Jr. *political science professor*

North Tonawanda
Beach, Sandra Marie Yudichak *secondary school educator*
Majeroni, Ronald L. *pastoral counselor, consultant*
Powers, Bruce Raymond *writer, language educator, consultant*

North White Plains
Erla, Karen *artist, painter, collagist, printmaker*

Northport
Donenfeld, Kenneth Jay *management consultant*
Graber, Mark L. *internist*
Hohenberger, Patricia Julie *fine arts and antique appraiser, consultant*
Miller, Philip John *insurance agent, consultant*
Reinertsen, Norman *retired air transportation executive*
Richards, Carol Ann Rubright *retired editor, journalist*
Russo, Christine Fiorella *language educator*
Weaver, Eric James *educational administrator*
Weber, Ray Everett *engineering executive, consultant*

Norwood
Church, Richard Dwight *electrical engineer, scientist*

Nyack
Brecht, Warren Frederick *retired business executive*
Chien, Jennie *sculptor*
Degenshein, Jan *architect, planner*
Hendin, David Bruce *literary agent, writer, numismatist, educator*
Karp, Peter Simon *marketing executive*
Mann, Kenneth Walker *retired minister, psychologist*
Oursler, Fulton, Jr. *editor, writer*
Sussman, Richard *music educator, composer*
Tirana, Bardyl Rifat *lawyer*

Oakdale
Poppiti, Kimberly D. *performing arts educator*

Oakland Gardens
Fiedler, Hal (Harold) *painter, printmaker*
Polak, Emil Joseph *history professor, researcher*

Oceanside
Kyler, Arlene *advertising executive*

Old Chatham
Severs, Charles A. III *lawyer*

Old Westbury
Casares, Federico M. *science educator*
Christofides, Fotine *parochial school educator*
O'Brien, Adrienne Gratia *communications educator*
Ozelli, Tunch *economics professor*
van Wie, Paul David *secondary school educator, historian*

Olean
Heyer, John Henry, II, *lawyer*
Ross, Anthony Robert *retired drafting engineer*

Olivebridge
Osborne, Seward Russell *writer*

Oneonta
Freckelton, Sondra *artist*
Hickey, Francis Roger *physicist, researcher*
Horner, Carl Matthew *chemistry professor*
Johnson, Richard David *retired librarian*
Malhotra, Ashok Kumar *philosophy educator*
vom Saal, Walter *psychology professor*

Ontario
Blackman, Lani Modica *copy editor*

Orangeburg
Filippelli, James Anthony *literature and language educator*
Greenberg, William Michael *psychiatrist*
Hawkins, Pamela Leigh Huffman *biochemist*
Lajtha, Abel *biochemist*
Levine, Jerome *psychiatrist, educator*
Rivet, Diana Wittmer *lawyer, farmer*
Yaragudri, Vinod K. *neuroscientist, researcher*

Orchard Park
Askew, Gloria Yarbrough *dietician*
Carducci, Donald Joseph *music educator*
Jauron, Dick (Richard M. Jauron) *professional football coach*
Keenan, John Paul *leadership and management educator, consultant, director, psychologist*
Kwiatkowski, Timothy D. *bank executive*
Lee, Richard Vaille *internist, educator*
Levy, Marv (Marvin Daniel) *professional football team executive and retired coach*
Sullivan, Mortimer Allen, Jr. *lawyer*
Urbanski, Jane F. *retired microbiologist*

Orient
Cochran, Judy Anne *psychiatric nurse practitioner*

Ossining
Beard, Janet Marie *health facility administrator*
Dolmatch, Theodore Bieley *management consultant*
Galef, Sandra Risk *state legislator, educator*
Hall, H(erbert) Glen *lawyer*
Maloney, William James *dentist, educator*
Robinson, Karen Vajda *dietician*
Wolfe, Mary Joan *physician*

Oswego
Fox, Michael David *retired art educator*
Garruto, John *counseling administrator*
Greene, Stephen Craig *lawyer*
Hockey, Christopher Lawrence *academic administrator*
Malgieri, Lewis Joshua *psychologist, consultant*
Smiley, Marilynn Jean *musicologist*

Ovid
Dresser, David Leland *municipal official*
Scoles, Marie Y. *elementary school educator*

Owego
Kemp, Eugene Thomas *retired veterinarian*
Zendle, Howard Mark *systems engineer, researcher*

Oxford
Ryan, Kenneth Eugene *engineer*

Oyster Bay
Coates, Winslow Shelby, Jr. *lawyer*
Joel, Billy (William Martin Joel) *musician*
Landrón, Ana *school psychologist*
Mooney, James David, Jr. *aerial photographer*
Prey, Barbara Ernst *artist*
Schwab, Hermann Caspar *banker*
Smith, Pamela Rosevear *air transportation executive*
Wachsman, Harvey Frederick *lawyer, neurosurgeon*
Walsh, Charles Richard *retired banker*

Ozone Park
Bellamy, Renee Adele *secondary school educator*
Joanidhi, Zhani *mathematician, educator*

Palisades
Andrews, Peter James *application developer, writer*
Broecker, Wallace S. *geophysicist, educator*
Burckle, Lloyd Henry *geologist, researcher*
Chiu, Tzu-Chien *geologist, researcher*
Davis, Dorothy Salisbury *writer*
Kellogg, Herbert Humphrey *metallurgist, educator*
Kent, Dennis V. *earth scientist, educator*
Lenton, Roberto Leonardo *environmental services administrator*
Polk, Milbry Catherine *writer*
Porta, Siena Gillann *sculptor, educator*
Previdi, Michael *meteorologist, research scientist*
Purdy, G. Michael *observatory director*
Richards, Paul Granston *seismologist, geophysics educator*
van Geen, Alexander *geochemist, researcher*

Patchogue
Igneri, David Sebastian *elementary school educator*
Marr, Robert Bruce *physicist, researcher*
McPherson, Sherry Lynn *social worker*

Pawling
Caplan, Ronald Mervyn *obstetrician, gynecologist*
Jones, James Earl *actor*
Lester, Helen Doughty *writer*
Peale, Ruth Stafford (Mrs. Norman Vincent Peale) *not-for-profit executive*

Pearl River
Barringer, William Charles *retired chemist*
Bryant, Karen Worstell *financial advisor, investment company executive*
Lokhnauth, John *chemist, researcher*
Meyer, Irwin Stephan *lawyer, accountant*
Riley, James Kevin *lawyer*
Wang, John Xiaowu *computer company executive*

Peekskill
Black, Carolyn Rebecca *music educator*
Harte, Andrew Dennis *transportation company executive, travel agent*

Pelham
Gaffney, Mark William *lawyer*
Hearle, Douglas Geoffrey *public relations consultant*

Penfield
Kraft, Donald Eugene *architecture and engineering company executive*

Penn Yan
Falvey, W(illiam) Patrick *judge*
Stempien, Joseph Jeffrey *music educator*

Peru
Dawson, James Clifford *environmental science educator, geologist*

Phoenix
Ackerman, Roger G. *ceramics engineer*

Piermont
Berkon, Martin *artist*

Pine Bush
Shepard, Ricahrd *film director, producer, writer*

Pine Island
Rogowski, Cheryl *farmer*

Pine Plains
Trapp, Peter Jarl Rudolf *portfolio manager, farmer*

Pittsford
Barker, Julie A. *school system administrator*
Bernstein, Paul *retired academic dean*
Blyth, John E. *lawyer, educator*
Braunsdorf, Paul Raymond *lawyer*
Buzard, A. Vincent *lawyer*
Coleman, Paul David *neurobiology educator, researcher*
Dobbs, Herbert Hotaling *automotive executive, consultant, research scientist, retired military officer*
Faloon, William Wassell *physician, educator*
French, Henry Pierson, Jr. *retired historian, educator*
Goldstein, David Arthur *biophysicist, educator*
Green, Martin Lincoln *retired medical products executive*
Hampson, Thomas Meredith *lawyer*
Herge, Henry Curtis, Jr. *information technology executive, consultant*
Hollingsworth, Jack Waring *mathematics professor*
Huston, Samuel Richard *health facility executive*
Joos, Felipe Miguel *mechanical engineer, researcher*
Maxey, Joseph T. *marriage and family therapist, educator, hospital administrator*
Saini, Vasant Durgadas *computer software company executive*
Snyder, Donald Edward *finance company executive*
Sproull, Robert Lamb *retired academic administrator, physicist, director*
Steamer, Robert Julius *political science professor*
Stonehill, Eric *lawyer*
Thompson, Brian John *academic administrator, optics scientist, educator*
Turri, Joseph A. *lawyer*
Willett, Thomas Edward *lawyer*

Plainview
Layne, Jeffrey Todd *urologist*
Rich, Charles Anthony *hydrogeologist, consultant*
Sangesland, Odd Einar *mechanical engineer, consultant*

Plandome
Sherwood, James Webster III *writer*

Plattsburgh
Bedworth, David Albert *health educator*
Schueller, Gretel Helena *journalist, educator*
Treacy, William Joseph *electrical and environmental engineer*
Withrow, Gregory B. *director, accountant*

Pleasant Valley
Becofsky, Arthur Luke *arts administrator, writer*
Marshall, Natalie Junemann *economics professor*
Odescalchi, Edmond Péry *international financial consultant, author*

Pleasantville
Alston, Alyce C. *publishing executive, former diamond company executive*
Barkley, James *artist*
Benton, Janetta Rebold *art historian, professor, writer*
Berner, Mary G. *publishing executive*
Clifton, Jean B. *publishing executive*
Dillon, Eva A. *publishing executive*
DuPree, Clifford H. R. *lawyer*
Eschweiler, Peter Quintus *planning consultant*
Geltzeiler, Michael S. *publishing executive*
Grimes, Suzanne *publishing executive*
Leo, Jacqueline M. *editor-in-chief*
McEwen, Laura *publishing executive*
Meisel, Martin *retired English and comparative literature educator*
Mirakian-Escobar, Rachel Ann *language educator*
Newborn, Andrea R. *publishing executive, lawyer*
Pike, John Nazarian *optical engineering consultant*
Schrier, Eric Woodside W. *publishing executive*
Shiri-Garakani, Mohsen *physicist, educator*
Urban, Joseph Jaroslav *engineer, consultant*

Pomona
Frelow, Robert Dean *retired school system administrator, writer*
Landau, Lauri Beth *accountant, consultant*

Port Chester
Ailloni-Charas, Dan *marketing executive*
Gregory, Lisa *marriage and family therapist*
Rosenberg, William Mark *chef, restaurant owner*
Sayles, Eva *artist*
Sotelo-Dynega, Marlene *psychologist*

Port Jefferson
Ahmad, Arif *surgeon*
Dranitzke, Richard J. *surgeon*

Port Jefferson Station
Shockley, Alonzo Hilton, Jr. *school system administrator*
Spahr, Clinton S., Jr. *retired elementary school educator*

Port Washington
Candido, Arthur Aldo *publishing and distribution company executive*
Feuss, Judith Farrar *musician, educator*
Hackett, John Byron *advertising executive, lawyer*
Jay, Frank Peter *retired writer, lexicographer, educator*
Johnson, Tod Stuart *market research company executive*
Kwak, Seung-Keon *research scientist*
Leeds, Richard *computer marketing executive*
Mayer, Renee G. *lawyer*
Ragan, David *publishing company executive*
Rogatz, Peter *retired physician*
Rush, Curt Stefan *lawyer*
Starr, Ringo (Richard Starkey) *musician, actor*
Ullman, Leo Solomon *lawyer*
Williams, George Leo *historian, retired secondary school educator, landmark director*

Potsdam
Chin, Der-Tau *chemical engineer, educator*
Collins, Anthony G. (Tony Collins) *academic administrator*
Fendler, Janos Hugo *chemistry professor*
Ha, Andrew Kwangho *education educator*
Islam, Muhammad Azadul *physicist, educator, researcher*
Lunt, Lora G. *language educator, director*
Matijevic, Egon *chemistry professor*
Naik, Sajo P. *physicist, researcher*
Rudiger, Lance Wade *secondary school educator*
Schwaller, John Frederick *academic administrator, historian, educator*
Scott, Jean A. *university president*

Poughkeepsie
Abraham, Manoj Timothy *plastic surgeon, educator*
Bartlett, Lynn Conant *English literature educator*
Brakas, Nora Jachym *education educator*
Carino, Aurora Lao *psychiatrist, health facility administrator*
Chu, Richard Chao-Fan *mechanical engineer*
Conklin, Donald David *academic administrator*
Daniels, Elizabeth Adams *English language educator*
Deiters, Sister Joan Adele *psychoanalyst, nun, chemistry professor*
Dietz, Robert Barron *lawyer*
Dolan, Thomas Joseph *judge*
Glasse, John Howell *retired philosophy and theology educator*
Hansen, Karen Thornley *accountant*
Harmelink, Herman III *minister, writer, religious studies educator*
Hathaway, Richard Dean *retired language educator*
Heller, Mary Bernita *psychotherapist*
Hill, Catharine Bond (Cappy) *academic administrator, economics professor*
Hytier, Adrienne Doris *French language educator*
Johnson, M(aurice) Glen *political science professor*
Kim, David Sang Chul *publishing executive, evangelist, retired academic administrator*
Klingenberg, Beate *management educator, director*
Kranis, Michael David *lawyer, judge*
Lang, William Warner *physicist*
Levine Simon, Sarah Ann *music educator*
Logue, Joseph Carl *electronics engineer, consultant*
Lowden, Christine C. *school system administrator*
Millman, Jode Susan *lawyer, writer*
Opdycke, Leonard Emerson *retired elementary school educator, publishing executive, writer*
Ostertag, Robert Louis *lawyer*
Padegs, Andris *electrical engineer, company executive*
Peck, H. Daniel *literature educator*
Phipps, Peter A. *psychology professor*
Rosenblatt, Albert Martin *retired state appeals court judge*
Schmidt, Roger R. *engineer*
Sharp, Ronald Alan *language educator, writer, dean*
Shatz, Phillip *lawyer*
Sherman, Ethan *contractor, publisher*
Slade, Bernard Newton *electronics executive*
Taphorn, Joseph Bernard *lawyer*
Taylor, Patricia *director*
Teal, Arabella W. *lawyer, former state attorney general*
VanBuren, Denise Doring *corporate communications executive*
Van Zanten, Frank Veldhuyzen *library director*
Willard, Nancy Margaret *writer, educator*
Wilson, Richard Edward *composer, music educator, pianist*
Wolfersteig, Jean Lois *medical association administrator, educator*

Pound Ridge
Darcy, Keith Thomas *finance company executive, educator, not-for-profit developer*
Ingram, Samuel William, Jr. *retired lawyer*
Rubino, John Anthony *management and human resources consultant*
Schwebel, Renata Manasse *sculptor*

Purchase
Amelio, Bill (William J.) *computer company executive*
Black, Leon David *private investment company executive*
Bryant, Daniel James *food and beverage company executive, former federal agency administrator*
Dunbar, W. Roy *finance company executive*
Ehrman, Lee *geneticist, educator*
Finnerty, Louise Hoppe *food products executive*
Flanagan, Lawrence *finance company executive*
Frost, Elizabeth Ann McArthur *physician*
Gioffre, Bruno Joseph *lawyer*
Goodman, Richard *food products executive*
Hanft, Noah Jonathan *lawyer*
Heuer, Alan J. *finance company executive*
Hudson, Dawn Emily *food service company executive*
Johnson-Wolff, Christina Marie *retail executive*
Johnston, Hugh Francis *corporate development manager*
Kelly, Edmund Joseph *lawyer, investment banking executive*
Macnee, Walter M. *finance company executive*
Magaziner, Elliot Albert *musician, conductor, educator*
McElwaine, James William *music educator*
McWilton, Chris A. *finance company executive*
Michl, Michael W. *finance company executive*
Murdock, Wendy Jean *management consultant*
Newell, Lionel L. III *treasurer*
Newton, Esther Mary *anthropologist, educator*
Nooyi, Indra Krishnamurthy *food products executive*
Phillips, Carly *writer*
Reinemund, Steven S. *retired food products executive*
Roach, John Hendee, Jr. *bank and financial services executive, investment banker*
Ryan, Edward W. *economics professor*
Schmitz, Robert Allen *publishing executive, investor*
Schwarz, Thomas J. *academic administrator, lawyer*
Selander, Robert W. *finance company executive*
Thompson, Larry Dean *lawyer, former federal agency administrator*
Tokarz, Michael Theodore *merchant banker*
Trudell, Cynthia M. *food products executive, former automotive executive*
Ughetta, James C. *lawyer*
Wachenheim, Edgar III *investment company executive*
Wallach, Kenneth L. *paper company executive*
Waller, Gary Fredric *language educator, poet*
Ward, Stephen M., Jr. *computer company executive*
West, Kazuko Ito *mathematics educator, department chairman*
White, Michael Dennis *food products executive*

Quogue
Burkhardt, Ronald Robert *advertising executive, writer, artist, filmmaker*
Hines, William Eugene *banker*

Raquette Lake
Bridger, Beverly Maria *historic site director*

Red Hook
Gudenzi-Ruess, Ida Carmen V. *music educator, artist*
Pastrana, Ronald Ray *theology studies educator, science educator, department chairman, psychotherapist, retired school system administrator*

Rego Park
Davidov, Ludmila G. *psychiatrist*
Feldman, Rachel Beth *psychologist*
Lowey, Nita Melnikoff *congresswoman*
Nakanishi, Yuko Julie *engineering educator, consultant*
Solowey, Carl *dermatologist, educator*
Sotomayor, Alexander *management consultant*

Remsenburg
Billman, Irwin Edward *publishing executive*

Rensselaer
Hull, Raymond Whitford *public relations executive*
Willis, John Patrick *chemist*

Rensselaerville
Fletcher, Raymond Russwald, Jr. *lawyer*

Rexford
Nitecki, Joseph Zbigniew *librarian*
Schmitt, Roland Walter *retired academic administrator*

Rhinebeck
Crum, Albert B. *psychiatrist, consultant*
Ewald, Wendy Taylor *photographer, writer, educator*
Melley, Steven Michael *lawyer*
Scherr, Allan Lee *computer scientist, software executive*
Sloane, Beverly LeBov *writer, instructor, consultant*

Rhinecliff
Conklin, John Roger *retired electronics company executive*

Richmond Hill
Gintautas, Jonas *physician, scientist, administrator*
Malhotra, Madhu Bala *psychiatrist*

Richmondville
Bartholomew, Debra Lee *publishing executive*

Ridge
Adams, Peter David *physicist, writer, editor*
Blume, Martin *physicist*
Carter, Sylvia *journalist*

Riverhead
Carpenter, Angie M. *former small business owner, editor, county legislator*
Maggipinto, V. Anthony *lawyer*
Orben, Jack Richard *investment company executive, director*

Rochester
Adair, Donald Robert *lawyer*
Adams, Carol H. *dean*
Alder, Donna Bordelon *biologist, educator*
Anderson, Porter Warren, Jr. *retired pediatrics educator*
Anthamatten, Mitchell Lewis *chemical engineer, educator*
Ashley, Stephen B. *finance company executive*
Aslin, Richard N. *psychology professor, researcher*
Aydelotte, Myrtle Kitchell *retired nursing administrator*
Bannon, Anthony Leo *museum director*
Baum, John *physician*
Begishev, Ildar *electronics engineer*
Berman, Robert L. *imaging company executive*
Bidlack, Jean Marie *pharmacologist, educator, researcher*
Bigelow, Nicholas Pierre *physicist, researcher*
Black, Candace Regan *language educator*
Blackman, Eric Glen *physics and astronomy professor*
Blanda-Holtzberg, Marianne Lourdes *education educator, consultant*
Blanton, Thomas N. *chemist, researcher*
Bluhm, William Theodore *political scientist, educator*
Blumberg, Neil *hematologist, educator*
Boeckman, Robert Kenneth, Jr. *chemistry professor, organic chemistry researcher*
Bonfiglio, Thomas Albert *pathologist, educator*
Bouyoucos, John Vinton *retired research and development company executive*
Bowen, William Henry *dental researcher, educator*
Braley, Oleta Pearl *community health nurse, writer*
Brody, Bernard B. *internist, educator*
Brooks, Walter S. *dermatologist*
Buckley, Michael Francis *lawyer*
Buff, Frank Paul *chemist, educator*
Buff, Iva Moore *librarian, musicologist*
Burton, Richard Irving *orthopedist, educator*
Cain, Burton Edward *retired chemistry professor*
Campbell, Alma Jacqueline Porter *elementary school educator*
Canzano, Daniel A. *information technology executive*
Carstensen, Edwin Lorenz *retired biomedical engineer, biophysicist*
Caton, Scott Brenon *history professor*
Chess, Patricia R. *pediatrician, medical educator, researcher*
Chey, William Yoon *physician*
Chiarenza, Carl *art historian, critic, artist, educator*
Chiverton, Patricia Ann *dean, nursing educator*
Ciccone, J. Richard *psychiatrist, educator*
Clark, Matthew Harvey *bishop*
Clarkson, Thomas William *toxicologist, educator*
Clifford, Eugene Thomas *lawyer*
Cohen, Ann Ellen *librarian*
Cohen, Jules *former dean, internist, educator*
Cohen, Nicholas *immunologist, educator*
Colabufo, Steven James *mathematics educator*
Colby, William Michael *lawyer*
Collins, Christopher Carl *manufacturing executive*
Conwell, Esther Marly *physicist, researcher*
Coumou, David J. *electrical engineer, consultant*
Cunningham, Robert Del *librarian*
D'Angio, Carl T. *pediatrician, educator*
Deci, Edward Lewis *psychologist, educator*
Destler, William W. *academic administrator*
DeWeese, James Arville *surgeon, educator*
Dimopoulos, Vassilios Georgios *physician, researcher*
Doty, Robert William *neuroscientist, physiologist, educator*
Dow, Ronald F. *librarian, dean*
Doyle, Justin P. *lawyer*
Dreyfuss, Eric Martin *allergist*
Drummond, Malcolm McAllister *electronics engineer*
DuBrin, Andrew John *management educator, writer, behavioral sciences educator, writer*
Duke, Charles Bryan *electronics executive, physicist, educator*
Eisenberg, Richard S. *chemistry professor*
Everett, Claudia Kellam *retired special education educator*
Fallesen, Gary David *journalist, lay worker*
Faraci, Philip J. *imaging company executive*
Farmer, Richard Gilbert *academic physician, foundation administrator*
Fausold, Martin Luther *history professor*
Fenno, Richard Francis, Jr. *political scientist, educator*
Ferbel, Thomas *physicist, educator*
Fitzgerald, John T., Jr. *lawyer*
Frisina, Robert Dana *neuroscientist, educator*
Galbraith, Robert Lyell, Jr. *lawyer*
Gauldin, Robert L. *music educator, composer*
Geiger, Alexander *lawyer*
Goldberg-Schaible, Jocelyn Hope Schnier *market research professional*
Golden, Reynold Stephen *geriatrician, educator*
Golisano, B. Thomas *financial services company and professional sports team executive*
Gootnick, Margery Fischbein *lawyer*
Gordon, Dane Rex *philosophy educator, minister*
Goyer, Virginia L. *accountant*
Gripe, Alan Gordon *minister*
Günter-McCoy, Jane Hutton *singer*
Gustin, Carl E., Jr. *manufacturing executive*
Guzick, David S. *dean, educator*
Haag, Joyce P. *lawyer, imaging company executive*
Hanson, Karen Noble *financial holding company executive*
Harris, Diane Carol *merger and acquisition consulting firm executive*
Harter, Ralph Millard Peter *lawyer, minister, educator*
Hauser, William Barry *historian, educator*
Hellyar, Mary Jane *imaging company executive*
Herminghouse, Patricia Anne *foreign language educator*
Hoch, Edward Dentinger *writer*
Hollis, Susan Tower *history professor*
Hopkins, Thomas Duvall *economics professor*
Houde-Walter, Susan *optics scientist, educator*
Hurlbut, Robert Harold *health care services executive*
Huxlin, Krystel Raluka *neuroscientist, educator*
Jackson, Thomas Humphrey *former academic administrator*
Jain, Manish *researcher*
John, Susan V. *state representative*
Johnson, Bruce Marvin *language educator*
Johnston, Frank C. *psychologist*
Joynt, Robert James *academic administrator, physician*
Judge, Jonathan J. *financial services company executive*
Kaidy, Mitchell *retired journalist, legislative staff member*
Kampmeier, Jack August Carlos *chemist, educator*
Kaupa, Mike *musician, educator*
Keeler, William Conrad III *curator, librarian, archivist*
Kelley, Stephen Michael *lawyer*
Kende, Andrew Steven *chemist, educator*
Khorana, Alok Anand *oncologist, medical researcher*
Kieburtz, Karl David *physician, educator, researcher*
Klinke, Louise Hoyt *volunteer*
Knauer, James Philip *physicist*
Knox, Robert Seiple *physicist, researcher*
Kraus, Sherry Stokes *lawyer*
Kurdziel, Michael Thomas *engineering executive*
Kurlan, Roger *neurologist, educator*
Kurland, Harold Arthur *lawyer*
Kwok, Wingchi Edmund *physicist*
Langley, James T. *imaging company executive*
Lank, Edith Handleman *journalist, educator*
Lansky, Lewis *history professor*
Larson, Joanne Caroline *education educator*
Laties, Victor Gregory *psychologist, educator*
Law, Michael R. *lawyer*
Lebman, Robert Richard *social services administrator*
Levy, Harold David *psycholinguist*
Li, James Chen Min *materials science educator*
Lichtman, Marshall Albert *hematologist, educator, researcher*
Lloyd, William J. *imaging company executive*
Long, John Broaddus, Jr. *economist, educator*
Luckey, George William *chemist, researcher*
Lundback, Staffan Bengt Gunnar *lawyer*
Lyman, Gary Herbert *epidemiologist, cancer researcher, educator*
Lyness, Jeffrey Marc *psychiatrist, educator*
Makous, Walter Leon *visual scientist, educator*
Maples, Philip G. *museum director*
Mapstone, Mark *neuropsychologist, educator*
Maquat, Lynne E. *biomedical researcher*
Marriott, Marcia Ann *business, economics professor, health facility administrator*
McAnarney, Elizabeth R. *pediatrician, educator*
McCrory, John Brooks *retired lawyer*
McDonald, Joseph Valentine *neurosurgeon*
Mc Kenzie, Lionel Wilfred *economist, educator*
McMeekin, Thomas Owen *dermatologist*
Meconi, Honey *musicologist, writer*
Melissinos, Adrian Constantin *physicist, researcher*
Merritt, Howard Sutermeister *retired art educator*
Meyerhofer, David D. *physicist, educator*
Middleton, J. Richard *religious studies educator*
Moore, Duncan Thomas *optics scientist, educator*
Moore, James Conklin *lawyer*
Morrison, Patrice Burgert *lawyer*
Moss, Arthur Jay *physician*
Nace, Morton Oliver, Jr. *human services manager*
Nazarian, Lawrence Fred *pediatrician*
Newport, Elissa L. *psychology professor*
Niemi, Richard Gene *political science educator*
O'Brien, Jeanne H. *medical educator*
Pacala, Leon *retired professional society administrator*
Palermo, Anthony Robert *lawyer*
Paley, Gerald Larry *lawyer*
Palvino, Jack Anthony *retired broadcasting executive*
Parker, Kevin James *electrical engineer, educator*
Pettinella, Edward *real estate company executive*
Phelps, Charles Elliott *economics professor, director*
Pilcher, Webster Hotchkiss *neurosurgeon*
Pitoniak, Scott Michael *sportswriter*
Powers, James Matthew *neuropathologist, educator, researcher*
Price, Richard Edward *lawyer*
Primo, David Martin *political science professor*
Ramirez, Stevan G. *consumer products company executive*
Regenstreif, S(amuel) Peter *political scientist, educator*
Ren, Clement L. *immunologist, researcher*

Rizk, Toufic Assaad *vascular surgeon*
Robbins, Nancy Slinker *volunteer*
Rodgers, Suzanne Hooker *physiologist, consultant*
Rosenhouse, Michael Allan *lawyer, editor, consultant, columnist*
Rosner, Leonard Allen *lawyer*
Rothberg, Abraham *writer*
Rothberg, Paul G. *medical geneticist, educator*
Rulison, Joseph Richard *investment banker*
Sammler, Anne Michelle *healthcare educator*
Santhanam, Kalathur S. V. *chemist, researcher*
Saunders, William Hundley, Jr. *retired chemist, educator*
Schaefer, Katherine L. *medical researcher, educator*
Schanfield, Moses Samuel *geneticist, educator*
Schumacher, Jon Lee *lawyer*
Schwert, G(eorge) William III *finance educator*
Sharma, Gaurav *imaging scientist, electrical engineer*
Sheppard, Luvon *art educator*
Sherman, Fred *biochemist, educator*
Shirley, Bonnie J. *retired elementary school educator*
Sieg, Albert Louis *photographic company executive*
Singer, Alan Daniel *artist*
Siragusa, Charles J. *judge*
Sklarsky, Frank S. *imaging company executive*
Smith, Julia Ladd *oncologist, physician*
Smith, Paula V. *library director*
Sparks, Charles Edward *pathologist, educator*
Sparks, Janet Lindsay Dehoff *pathologist, educator*
Stewart, Sue S. *lawyer*
Stratton, John Alfred *electrical engineer, educator*
Swanton, Susan Irene *retired library director*
Szalapski, Robert Francis *theoretical physicist*
Tantillo, Mary Darlene *nurse*
Terefenko, Dariusz *music educator*
Thorndike, Edward Harmon *physicist*
Tobin, Barbara Kay *minister*
Turner, Scott MacNeely *lawyer*
Twietmeyer, Don Henry *lawyer*
VanderLinden, Camilla Denice Dunn *telecommunications industry executive*
VanGelder, Kim E. *information technology executive*
Vernarelli, Michael Joseph *economics professor, consultant, academic administrator*
Vigdor, Justin Leonard *lawyer*
Wagner, Aureen Pinto *psychologist, educator*
Waite, Stephen Holden *lawyer*
Walton, Joseph Paul *neuroscientist, audiologist*
Wayland-Smith, Robert Dean *retired banker*
Webster, Gordon Visscher, Jr. *minister*
Wegman, Colleen *food service executive*
Wegman, Daniel R. *food service executive*
White, Ann Marie *medical educator*
Wild, Robert Warren *lawyer*
Wiley, Jason LaRue, Jr. *neurosurgeon*
Williams, Thomas Franklin *physician, educator*
Witmer, George Robert, Jr. *lawyer*
Wygant, Patricia Bryans *artist*
Yip, Kwok Leung *physicist, researcher*
Young, Mary Elizabeth *history professor*
Zagorin, Perez *historian, educator*
Zarrella, Ronald L. *pharmaceutical executive*
Zax, Melvin *psychologist, educator*
Zupan, Mark A. *dean, business professor*

Rockville Centre
Beyer, Suzanne *advertising agency executive*
Castleman, Louis Samuel *retired metallurgist, educator*
Fitzgerald, Janet Anne *philosophy educator, academic administrator*
Lewittes, Don Jordan *psychologist*
Lynch, Peter K. *education educator*
Mazzucelli, Colette Grace Celia *author, educator*
Pompan, Jack Maurice *management consultant*
Schwartz, Arthur *playwright, poet*
Teyan, Frederick Gene *pediatrician*

Rocky Point
Falcone, David J. *elementary school educator*
Knapp, Craig Brian *musician, educator*
Meschi, Jennifer Margaret *technology educator*
Scalfani, Carl *secondary school educator*

Rome
Ferens, Daniel Vincent *retired civilian military employee*
Min, Balshik *pathologist*
Simonin, Howard A. *biologist*
Simons, Richard Duncan *lawyer, retired judge*
Walther, Peter C. *church musician*

Romulus
Ostrander, Robert Edwin *retired United Nations interregional advisor, petroleum company executive*

Ronkonkoma
Leventhal, Norman B. *entrepreneur*

Roosevelt
Jackson, Andrew Preston *library director*

Roscoe
Torres, Jacques *food service executive, pastry chef*

Roslyn
Aptekar, Doris Mae Weinberg *psychotherapist, school psychologist, hypnotherapist*
Finke, Leonda Froehlich *sculptor, educator*
Greenberg, Steven M. *physician*
Landsman, Richard *investment company executive, finance educator*
Mazlen, Roger Geoffrey *ophthalmologist, pharmacologist*
Rosegarten, Rory *personal manager, television producer, theater producer, film producer*
Shubin, Joanna *science educator*
Stracher, Dorothy Altman *education educator, consultant*
Ulanoff, Stanley M. *communications executive*

Roslyn Heights
Castillo, Nelson A. *lawyer*
Guthart, Leo A. *electronics executive*
Newmark, Marilyn *sculptor*

Rouses Point
Weierstall, Richard Paul *retired pharmaceutical chemist*

Ruby
Cole, Max *artist*

Rye
Barker, Harold Grant *surgeon, educator*
Bostock, Roy Jackson *investment company executive*
Capps, John Edward *lawyer, consumer products company executive*
Curtin, Brian Joseph *retired ophthalmologist*
Feinberg, Norman Maurice *real estate company executive*
Franklin, Martin E. *consumer products company executive*
Gabelli, Mario J. *diversified financial services company executive*
Gambee, Robert Rankin *investment banker*
Goldstein, Peter Dobkin *lawyer*
Harrington, Diane *librarian, writer*
Hurwitz, Sol *writer, consultant*
Kaufman, Shirona *cantor, educator*
Kaulakis, Arnold Francis *management consultant*
Ketchum, William Clarence *author, educator*
Lawi, David Steven *utilities executive, merchant banker*
Lehman, Lawrence Herbert *consulting engineering executive*
Nelson, Vita Joy *editor, publisher*
Newburger, Howard Martin *psychoanalyst*
Pearson, Nathan Williams *communications, investment executive*
Rolland, Peter George *landscape architect*
Sales, Mitzi S. *science educator*
Waltz, Joseph McKendree *neurosurgeon, educator*
Wilmot, Irvin Gorsage *former hospital administrator, educator, consultant*

Rye Brook
Aquino, Joseph Mario *clinical psychologist*
Berk, Alan S. *accountant*
Kuntzman, Ronald *research and development company executive*
Mariam, Thomas Fred *public relations executive, radio producer*
Masson, Robert Henry *paper company executive*

Sag Harbor
Brody, Eugene David *investment company executive*
Brody, Jacqueline *editor*
Epstein, Jason *publishing company executive*
Pashman, Susan Ellen *writer*

Sagaponack
Cedering, Siv *poet, writer*
Graham, Howard Barrett *publishing company executive*

Saint Albans
Norfleet, Leontine Sandra *retired biologist*

Saint Bonaventure
Anderson, John Thomas *librarian, historian*
Mazon, Margaret Fausold *language educator*
Tenglund, Ann M. *librarian*

Saint Huberts
Neilson, Winthrop Cunningham III *retired communications executive, financial consultant, photographer*

Saint James
Batule, Robert John *priest, writer*
Kelly, Michael Joseph *academic administrator, consultant*

Saint Regis Falls
O'Bryan, Margaret Sundberg *music educator*

Sanborn
Michalak, Janet Carol *childhood education educator, coordinator*
Nowak (Jarosz), Linda Therese *special education educator, consultant*

Sands Point
Cullinan, Bernice Ellinger *education educator*
Hoynes, Louis LeNoir, Jr. *lawyer*
Lear, Erwin *anesthesiologist, educator*
Olian, JoAnne Constance *curator, art historian*
Wurzel, Leonard *retired candy manufacturing company executive*

Saranac
Smith, J. Kellum, Jr. *foundation administrator, lawyer*

Saranac Lake
Caguiat, Carlos Jose *health facility administrator, priest*

Saratoga Springs
Boyers, Robert *literature and language professor*
Carovano, John Martin *not-for-profit developer*
Caruso, Adrienne Iorio *retired language educator*
Ford, Dexter *retired insurance company executive*
Glotzbach, Philip A. *academic administrator, philosopher, educator*
Miller, Anita Diane *psychologist*
Porter, David Hugh *musician, classicist, academic administrator, music educator*
Sainer, Arthur *writer, theater educator*
Stake, Peter *artist, educator*
Upton, Richard Thomas *artist*
Wait, Charles Valentine *banker*

Sayville
Grizzaffi, Kimberly Anne *secondary school music educator*

Scarsdale
Abbe, Colman *investment banker*
Angel, Dennis *lawyer*
Belasco, Steven Ronald *lawyer*
Benedict, James Nelson *lawyer*
Beuchert, Edward William *lawyer*
Blitman, Howard Norton *construction executive*
Borg, Robert Frederic *civil engineer*
Bosses, Stevan J. *mediator, arbitrator*
Brilliant, Richard *art historian, educator*
Carrick, Richard David *composer, performing company executive, music educator*
Clark, Merrell Mays *management consultant*
Cohen, Irwin *economist*
Decaminada, Joseph Pio *retired insurance company executive*
Edis, Gloria Toby *pediatrician*
Erbsen, Claude Ernest *retired journalist*
Gerber, Roger Alan *lawyer, consultant*
Gladstone, William Louis *accountant*
Glickenhaus, Sarah Brody *speech therapist*
Gollin, Stuart Allen *accountant*
Goodman, Jordan Elliot *journalist*
Graff, Henry Franklin *historian, educator*
Hoffman, Richard M. *lawyer*
Holmes, Rupert *playwright, singer, writer*
Johnson, Boine Theodore *manufacturing executive, mayor*
Johnson, William Alexander *clergyman, philosophy and theology educator*
Kaufman, Robert Jules *communications consultant, lawyer*
Laufer, Leonard Justin *management consultant*
Lindsay, Sharon Winnett *lawyer, consultant*
Lipman, Marvin Matthew *physician, medical educator, medical editor, writer*
Macchia, Vincent Michael *lawyer*
Mercando, Anthony Dominic *cardiologist*
Moser, Marvin *physician, educator, author*
O'Brien, Edward Ignatius *corporate financial executive, director, investor, lawyer*
O'Neill, Michael James *editor, author*
Perko, Kenneth Albert, Jr. *lawyer, art dealer*
Porosoff, Harold *chemist, science administrator, research and development company executive*
Port, Lilly Bruck Lieb *retired advocate, columnist, commentator*
Schultz, Harley *consulting company executive*
Soley, Robert Lawrence *plastic surgeon*
Stamas, Stephen *not-for-profit administrator*
Topping, Seymour *writer*
Van Gundy, Gregory Frank *retired lawyer*

Schaghticoke
O'Connor, Abigail Elizabeth *mathematician, educator, science educator*

Schenectady
Ainlay, Stephen Charles *academic administrator, educator*
Board, Joseph Breckinridge, Jr. *political scientist, educator*
Cadieux, Ronald Claude *mathematics educator*
Davis, Lewis Berkley *mechanical engineer*
Depan, Harry John *cardiothoracic surgeon*
Fell, Samuel Kennedy (Ken) *infosystems executive*
Finks, Robert Melvin *paleontologist, educator*
Fleischer, Robert Louis *geology professor*
Frost, Robert Edwin *chemistry professor*
Golub, Lewis *supermarket company executive*
Golub, Neil M. *supermarket chain executive*
Hermance, Myron E., Jr. *conductor, educator*
Hull, Roger Harold *foundation and former academic administrator*
Huszar, Andrew Louis *school psychologist*
Huth, Geoffrey Anthony *archivist, artist*
Katz, Samuel *retired geophysics educator*
Levine, Sanford Harold *lawyer*
Mancuso, J(ohn) James *librarian*
Mikata, Yozo *mechanical engineer, application developer*
Morris, John Selwyn *philosopher, educator, retired academic administrator*
Murray, Edward Rock *insurance broker*
Myers, Darlene Marie *dance studio owner, choreographer*
Oliker, David William *healthcare management administrator*
Philip, A. G. Davis *astronomer, educator, editor*
Ringlee, Robert James *retired consulting engineering executive*
Ritterband, Arnold B. *internist*
Schenck, John Frederic *physician*
Sternlicht, Beno *research and development company executive*
Stevens, Roy W. *microbiologist, researcher, photographer*
Szokody, Aniko *pianist, educator*
Weber, Charles S. *mechanical engineer*

Schoharie
Duncombe, Raynor Bailey *lawyer*

Schroon Lake
Johnson, Donald Raymond *lawyer*

Scotia
de la Rocha, Carlos A. *retired physician*

Scottsville
Williams, Henry Ward, Jr. *lawyer, writer*

Sea Cliff
Picone-Zocchia, Joanne *educational consultant, writer*
Popova, Nina *dancer, choreographer, director*

Seaford
Bongiovi, Stephen *literature and language educator*
Furey, Raymond Joseph *lawyer*
Setzler, William Edward *retired chemicals executive*
Spencer, Jean *retired business executive*

Selden
Connors, William Francis, Jr. *academic administrator*
Cook, Lisa Marie *mathematics professor, mathematics learning center coordinator*
Howard, Douglas L. *literature and language professor*

Selkirk
Christoph, Peter Richard *historical editor, archivist*

Seneca Falls
Norman, Mary Marshall *academic administrator, alcohol/drug abuse services professional, educator*

Setauket
Robinson, Richard M. *communications executive*

Shelter Island
Dowd, David Joseph *banker, construction executive*
Mayer, Martin Prager *writer*
Nicklin, George Leslie, Jr. *psychoanalyst, educator, physician, writer*
Shaw, Alan Roger *finance educator, retired company executive*

Shelter Island Heights
Culbertson, Janet Lynn *artist*
Gage, Beau *artist*

Sherburne
Dodd, Jack Gordon, Jr. *physicist, researcher*

Shokan
Seligman, Frederick *lawyer*

Sidney
Werner, David A. *paper company executive*

Silver Creek
Kurzawa, Marilyn Taylor *educational consultant*

Skaneateles
Behrend, Donald Fraser *academic administrator, educator*

Sleepy Hollow
Chia, David Thien-Shing *internist, gastroenterologist*
Daly, William Joseph *lawyer*
Flynn-Connors, Elizabeth Kathryn *reporter, editor*
Marshall, Michael Borden *marketing executive*
Melvin, Russell Johnston (Jay Melvin) *magazine publishing consultant*
Neill, Richard Robert *retired publishing executive*
Resnick, Adrienne Jo *clinical social worker, psychotherapist*
Schmidt, Klaus Franz *advertising executive*

Slingerlands
Beer, Paul Marius *ophthalmologist, educator*
Ipsen, Carol Anne *psychiatrist, educator*
Zacek, Joseph Frederick *historian, educator*

Smallwood
Golden, Elliott *judge*

Smithtown
Dowis, Lenore *lawyer*
Fritzhand, Irvin Dick *psychologist*
Goodman, Richard Shalem *lawyer, orthopedic surgeon*
Haskins, Debra May *academic administrator, educator*
Koss, Tamara *dermatologist, educator*
Rockensies, John William *mechanical engineer*
Spellman, Thomas Joseph, Jr. *lawyer*
Tuzel, Suzanne L. *psychiatrist*

Snyder
Breverman, Harvey *artist*
Levine, George Richard *language educator*

Somers
Azua, Maria *computer company executive, computer engineer*
Bauman, William Allen *pediatrician, educator, health systems consultant*
Bensen, Annette Wolf *graphic art company consultant*
Beracha, Barry Harris *food products executive*
Berisford, John L. *consumer products company executive*
Bronzo, Neal A. *consumer products company executive*
Cohn, Howard *retired magazine editor*
Crawford, Victor L. *consumer products company executive*
Drewes, Alfred H. *consumer products company executive*
Foss, Eric J. *consumer products company executive*
Franks, Brent J. *consumer products company executive*
Keeffe, John Arthur *lawyer, director*
Rapp, Steven M. *lawyer, consumer products company executive*
Reznick, Steven Michael *orthopedic surgeon, educator*
Rubin, Samuel Harold *internist, consultant*
Sanford, Linda S. *information technology executive*
Trzasko, Joseph Anthony *psychologist, educator*

Wladawsky-Berger, Irving *communications executive*

South Richmond Hill
Scheich, John F. *lawyer*

South Salem
Bongiorno, William J. *public relations executive*
Carpentieri, Carol Ellen *artist, educator*
Cowles, Frederick Oliver *lawyer*

South Setauket
Friedlander, Gerhart *nuclear chemist*
Poli, Kenneth Joseph *editor, writer, photographer*

Southampton
Bolster, Jacqueline Neben (Mrs. John A. Bolster) *communications consultant*
Brokaw, Clifford Vail III *investment banker*
Brophy, James David, Jr. *humanities educator*
Bujese, Arlene *artist, art dealer, curator*
Culp, Michael Bronston *investor, writer, publisher*
Kanovitz, Howard *artist, educator*
Lopez, David *lawyer*
Platt, Jonathan James *lawyer*
Thomas, Violeta de los Angeles *real estate broker*

Sparkill
Dahl, Arlene *actress, writer, designer, cosmetics executive*
Solomon, Pearl Gold *education educator, consultant*

Sparrow Bush
Murray, William Bruce *opera singer*

Spencerport
Broussard, Allison M. *secondary school educator, artist*
Wolsky, Jack *retired art educator*

Spring Valley
Johnson, Judith A. *educational administrator*
Mittleberg, Eric Michael *pharmaceutical executive*

Staatsburg
Wentworth, Dennis Ladd *historic sites and parks administrator*

Stamford
Bergleitner, George Charles, Jr. *investment banker*

Staten Island
Auh, Yang John *librarian, educational administrator*
Berci, Margaret Elizabeth *education educator*
Black, Lawrence *librarian*
Brady, Christine Ellen *education coordinator*
Bruckstein, Alex Harry *internist, gastroenterologist, geriatrician*
Carpenito, Frank Anthony *principal, educator*
Caudle, Fairfid Monsalvatge *psychology professor*
Chohan, Muhammad Omar *neuroscientist, neurologist*
Clark, Sylvia Dolores *business educator*
De Luca, Andrea (Helen Siglain) *psychoanalyst*
Dennery, Linda *newspaper publishing executive*
Fafian, Joseph, Jr. *management consultant*
Ferranti, Thomas, Jr. *lawyer*
Ferzli, George Salem *surgeon*
Fossella, Vito John, Jr. *congressman*
Foster, Paul *playwright*
Franzone, Eric Scott *psychologist*
Fusco, Jo Ellen *music educator*
Gaeta, Rosemarie *psychotherapist*
Gavrity, John Decker *retired insurance company executive*
Gelbein, Jay Joel *accountant*
Holder, Calvin Beresford *history professor*
Humphries, Edward Francis *lawyer*
Klingle, Philip Anthony *law librarian*
Lazzara, Margo Valentine *counselor, writer*
Lewis, Carla Susan *psychology educator*
Maiman, Mitchell *oncologist, gynecologist*
Morales, Tomás D. *academic administrator, educator*
Nelson, Carey Boone *sculptor*
Newhouse, Donald E. *newspaper publishing executive*
Newhouse, Samuel Irving, Jr., (Si Newhouse Jr.) *publishing executive*
Pasciuto, Joseph Doria *priest*
Piegari, James A. *psychologist*
Popler, Kenneth *behavioral health services administrator, psychologist*
Porter, Darwin Fred *writer*
Prince, Danforth *publishing executive, journalist*
Shively, Sarah Elizabeth *actress*
Stathopoulos, Peter *internist*
Stearns, Stephen Jerold *history professor, writer*
Stolz, Theodora *psychologist*
Trogan, Roland Bernard *composer, educator*
Wilson, Van Ray *secondary school educator*
Yang, Song-Yu *medical biochemist*
Zaage, Herman *printmaker, educator*

Stony Brook
Alexander, John Macmillan, Jr. *chemistry professor*
Anderson, Michael Thomas *mathematics professor, researcher, director*
Andriola, Mary Repole *neurologist, pediatrician*
Baker, David A. *obstetrician, gynecologist, educator*
Benitez-Silva, Hugo A. *economics professor*
Bogart, Michele Helene *art history educator*
Bonner, Francis Truesdale *chemist, educator, dean*
Brandwein, Ruth Ann *social welfare educator, social services administrator, writer*
Brown, Gerald Edward *physicist, researcher*
Carr, Edward Gary *psychology professor*
Chiang, Fu-Pen *mechanical engineering educator, researcher*
Cochran, James Kirk *dean, oceanographer, educator, geochemist*
Cole, Steven *psychiatrist, educator*
Corman, Marvin Leonard *surgeon, educator*
Dagum, Alexander B. *plastic surgeon*
Ebin, David Gregory *mathematician, researcher, educator*
Filstrup, (E.) Christian *library director, dean*
Fine, Richard Nisan *pediatrician, educator, dean*
Fritts, Harry Washington, Jr. *internist, educator*
Futuyma, Douglas Joel *ecology educator*
Gambino, Richard Joseph *materials engineer, educator*
Geller, Marvin Alan *meteorology educator, researcher*
Glimm, James Gilbert *mathematician, educator*
Goldberg, Homer Beryl *language educator*
Grim, Patrick Neal *philosopher, educator, logician*
Gulino, Lawrence Carl *mediator*
Harris, Alice *linguist, educator*
Harvey, Christine Lynn *publishing executive*
Hurst, Lawrence *orthopedic surgeon*
Ihde, Don *philosopher, educator*
Jaber, Rajaa *physician, educator*
Jonas, Steven *preventive medicine physician, author*
Kenny, Shirley Strum *academic administrator*
Koppelman, Lee Edward *regional planner, educator*
Kuchner, Eugene Frederick *neurosurgeon, educator, neuroscientist*
Kuspit, Donald Burton *art historian, critic, educator*
Lane, Dorothy Spiegel *preventive medicine physician*
Laspina, Peter Joseph *computer resource educator*
Lawson, H(erbert) Blaine, Jr. *mathematician, educator*
Leakey, Richard Erskine *paleoanthropologist, museum director*
Lennarz, William Joseph *research biologist, educator*
Leske, M. Cristina *medical researcher, educator*
Levin, Richard Louis *retired language educator*
Liang, Jerome Zhengrong *radiology educator*
Lydic, Michael Lynn *medical educator, obstetrician*
Martin, Lawrence B. *academic administrator, anthropologist, educator*
Meyers, Morton Allen *radiologist, educator*
Mignone, Mario B. *language educator*
Milnor, John Willard *mathematician*
Monheit, Alan Goodman *obstetrician, gynecologist*
Moskowitz, Anita Fiderer *art historian, educator*
Ohannessian, Harry Haroutune *travel agency executive*
Ojima, Iwao *chemistry professor*
Pekarsky, Melvin Hirsch *artist*
Priebe, Cedric Joseph, Jr. *retired pediatric surgeon*
Rifkin, Barry R. *dean, dental educator, researcher*
Rohlf, F. James *biologist, educator*
Rosengart, Todd Kenneth *cardiothoracic surgeon, researcher, neurosurgeon, consultant*
Seifert, Frank C. *thoracic surgeon*
Semmel, Bernard *historian, educator*
Shamash, Yacov *dean, electrical engineering educator*
Silverman, Hugh J. *philosophy educator*
Simpson, Louis Aston Marantz *language educator, writer*
Squires, Nancy *psychology professor*
Sreebny, Leo M. *oral biology and pathology professor*
Steigbigel, Roy Theodore *epidemiologist, educator, research scientist*
Stolzberg, Mark Elliott *psychologist*
Stone, Elizabeth Cecilia *anthropology educator*
Swanson, Robert Lawrence *oceanographer, academic program administrator*
Tanur, Judith Mark *sociologist, educator*
Tassiopoulos, Apostolos K. *vascular surgeon*
Tewarson, Reginald Prabhakar *retired mathematics educator, consultant*
Tucker, Alan Curtiss *mathematics professor*
Vlay, Stephen Charles *cardiologist, electrophysiologist*
Weisbrot, Deborah Marcia *psychiatrist*
White, Henry J. *engineering educator, consultant*
Wilson, Thomas Allen *pediatrician, endocrinologist*
Zemanian, Armen Humpartsoum *electrical engineer, mathematician*

Stony Creek
La Grasse, Carol Winter *property rights activist, retired civil engineer*

Stuyvesant
Tripp, Susan Gerwe *museum director*

Suffern
Codispoti, Andre John *allergist, immunologist*
Coronel, Victor Felipe *engineering educator*
Raven, Luisa Antonia *psychotherapist, nurse*

Sugar Loaf
Endico, Mary Antoinette *artist*

Sunnyside
Gil Orrios, Angel *theater director, lighting designer, translator*

Syosset
Bermas, Stephen *lawyer*
Kniffin, Paula Sichel *insurance sales executive*
Ruthchild, Geraldine Quietlake *training and development consultant, writer, poet*
Theodosius, *retired leader of the Orthodox Church in America*

Syracuse
Ackerman, Kenneth Edward *retired lawyer, educator*
Allis, Damian Gregory *chemist, technologist, consultant*
Alston, William Payne *philosophy educator*
Arterian, Hannah R. *dean, law educator*
Baker, Bruce Edward *orthopedic surgeon, consultant*
Baldwin, John Edwin *chemistry professor*
Baldwin, Robert Frederick, Jr. *lawyer*
Barclay, H. Douglas (Hugh Douglas Barclay) *lawyer, legislator, diplomat*
Becker, Lorne Arthur *family physician*
Birkhead, Guthrie Sweeney, Jr. *political scientist, dean*
Blakely, Caroline Miller *retired editor*
Boeheim, Jim *college basketball coach*
Braiman, Mark Stephen *biomedical educator, researcher*
Braungart, Richard Gottfried *political scientist, educator*
Brickwedde, Richard James *lawyer*
Bunn, Timothy David *newspaper editor*
Butler, John Edward *lawyer*
Caldicott, Catherine V. *medical educator, researcher*
Cantor, Nancy *academic administrator*
Caravan, Ronald L. *music educator, composer*
Cirando, John Anthony *lawyer*
Colvin, Ruth Johnson *literacy organization founder*
Cooper, John Ambrose *management consultant, marketing professional*
Costello, Thomas Joseph *retired bishop*
Crane, David Michael *prosecutor, former judge advocate, educator*
Crowston, Kevin Ghen *information scientist, educator*
Driscoll, Charles Thurston, Jr. *civil and environmental engineering educator*
Duerr, Dianne Marie *sports medicine consultant, educator*
Elkins, Elizabeth A. *library director*
Elms, Ben *actor, theater director*
Emery, Robert Allan *minister*
Favalo, John Frank *marketing executive*
Fitzgerald, Harold Kenneth *social work educator, consultant*
Fitzpatrick, James David *lawyer*
Forbes, Peter Edwin *sculptor*
Ford, Steven J. *lawyer, manufacturing executive*
Fortune, John B. *medical educator*
Fredrickson, Bruce E. *orthopedist*
Freund, Deborah A. *academic administrator*
Furze, Edward William *fundraising consultant*
Gaal, John *lawyer*
Gartner, Joseph Charles *retired systems administrator*
Gold, Joseph *medical researcher*
Graver, Jack Edward *mathematics professor*
Gray, Charles Augustus *banker*
Han, Jongwoo *political science professor*
Hayes, David Michael *lawyer*
Hildebrandt, George Frederick *lawyer*
Hole, Richard Douglas *lawyer*
Honig, Arnold *physics professor, researcher*
Horton, Jason A. *biologist*
Irwin, Peter C. *not-for-profit fundraiser*
Jerge, Marie Charlotte *minister*
Kaplan, Eugene Alken *psychiatry professor, department chairman*
Kerr, Darlene Dixon *electric power company executive*
Kim, Yong-Woo *engineer, educator, consultant*
Kriesberg, Louis *sociologist, educator*
Lee, David Ames *lawyer, banker, editor, writer*
Luchsinger, John Francis, Jr. *lawyer*
Luft, Eric V.D. *writer, educator, publisher*
Malhotra, Yogesh *information scientist, consultant, information technology executive, computer engineer*
Marcoccia, Louis Gary *accountant, academic administrator*
McCurn, Neal Peters *federal judge*
Meier, Raymond A. *former state legislator, lawyer*
Meinig, Donald William *geography educator*
Monmonier, Mark *geographer, writer*
Moynihan, James M. *bishop*
Munson, Howard G. *federal judge*
Murphy, Cornelius B., Jr., (Neil Murphy) *academic administrator*
Obbie, Mark Joseph *communications educator*
O'Connor, Michael E. *lawyer*
Orentlicher, John *video research educator, artist*
Ortiz, Fernando, Jr. *commissioner*
Pardee, Otway O'Meara *computer scientist, educator*
Phillips, Larry Arthur *artist*
Pinsky, Roy David *lawyer*
Pooler, Rosemary S. *federal judge*
Powell, James Matthew *history professor*
Prettyman, John A. *English language educator*
Prucha, John James *geologist, educator*
Rabuzzi, Daniel D. *medical association administrator*
Ray, Romita *art historian, educator*
Richardson, M. Catherine *lawyer*
Rivette, Francis Robert *lawyer*
Rogers, Sherry Anne *physician*
Sargent, Robert George *engineering educator*
Scheinman, Steven Jay *dean, medical educator*
Schiff, Eric Allan *physics professor*
Scullin, Frederick James, Jr. *federal judge*
Skoler, Louis *architect, educator*
Smardon, Richard Clay *landscape architect, environmental studies professor*
Smith, Corinne Roth *psychologist*
Smith, Kenneth Judson, Jr. *chemistry professor*
Stam, David Harry *librarian*
Staples, Heidi L *poet, writer*
Steigerwald, Louis John III *corporate executive*
Sternlicht, Sanford *literature educator, writer*
Streeten, Barbara Wiard *ophthalmologist, medical educator*
Suddaby, Glenn T. *prosecutor, lawyer*
Swartz, Michael Frederick *physician assistant*
Szasz, Thomas Stephen *psychiatrist, educator, writer*
Tatham, David Frederic *art historian, educator*
Taylor, Robert Saxton *retired dean*
Thomas, Sidney *fine arts educator, researcher*
Thorin, Suzanne E. *dean, university librarian*
Tolkacheva, Elena *physicist, researcher*
Trop, Sandra *museum director*
Verheyen, Peter David *librarian, conservator*
Verrillo, Ronald Thomas *neuroscience educator, researcher*
von Dran, Raymond *dean, library and information science educator*
Vook, Richard Werner *retired physics professor*
Waddy, Patricia A. *historian, retired architecture educator*
Wallerstein, Mitchel Bruce *dean, educator*
Walsh, James Thomas (Jim Walsh) *congressman*
Wells, Peter Nathaniel *judge, lawyer*
Williams, William Joseph *retired hematologist, educator*
Winter, William Thomas *chemistry educator*
Wolff, Catherine Elizabeth *opera company executive*
Wolff, L. Thomas *physician, educator*
Young, Douglas Howard *lawyer*
Zimmerman, Aaron Mark *lawyer*

Tappan
Cardenas, Raul Rodolfo, Jr. *engineering executive, educator, consultant*
Dell, Robert Christopher *environmental engineer, educator, artist*
Fox, Muriel *retired public relations executive*

Tarrytown
Bergson, Henry Paul *professional society administrator*
Cocchiarella, Antonio *physician, educator*
Ferrari, Robert Joseph *finance educator, retired bank executive*
Field, Barry Elliot *internist, gastroenterologist*
Gutheil, Irene A. *social work educator, researcher*
Hyman, Leonard Stephen *financial consultant, economist, writer*
Kenney, Dion Patrick *information technology executive, entrepreneur*
Kirsch, Abigail *culinary productions executive*
Marcus, Sheldon *school policy and administration educator*
Maun, Mary Ellen *computer consultant*
Mc Murtry, James Gilmer III *neurosurgeon*
Osborne, Robin *library and information scientist*
Safian, Keith Franklin *hospital administrator*
Stein, Sol *publishing executive, writer*
Weiner, Max *psychology professor*
Yancopoulos, George D. *pharmaceutical executive*

Thornwood
Bassett, Lawrence C. *management consultant*

Tivoli
Ratcliff, Carter Goodrich *writer, critic, poet*

Tonawanda
Brunger, Eric Geoffrey *social studies educator, coach*
Drozdziel, Marion John *aeronautical engineer*
Haller, Calvin John *banker*
Loos, William H(enry) *librarian, consultant*

Troy
Acar, Evrim *computer scientist*
Ahlers, Rolf Willi *philosopher, theologian*
Baker, Kim Pearson *education educator*
Belfort, Georges *chemical engineering educator, consultant*
Berg, Daniel *science and technology educator*
Bergles, Arthur Edward *mechanical engineering educator*
Block, Robert Charles *nuclear engineering educator*
Brazil, Harold Edmund *political science professor*
Bryant, Kimberly Ziegler *dental hygienist, educator*
Burch, Mary Seelye Quinn *law librarian, consultant*
Ci, Lijie *materials scientist*
Demertzoglou, Pindaro Epaminonda *systems administrator, educator*
Dobry, Ricardo *engineering educator*
Drew, Donald Allen *mathematical sciences educator*
Dvorak, George J. *mechanics and materials engineering educator*
Ehrlich, Henry Lutz *biology professor*
Ferris, James Peter *chemist, educator*
Finkel, Sanford Norman *lawyer*
Freyssinier Nova, Jean Paul *engineering research professor*
Friedman, Gerald Manfred *geologist, educator*
Friedman, Sue Tyler *technical publications executive*
Gerhardt, Lester A. *engineering educator, dean*
Giaever, Ivar *physicist*
Gill, William Nelson *chemical engineering professor*
Glicksman, Martin Eden *materials engineering educator*
Gutmann, Ronald J. *retired electrical engineering educator*
Haddock, Jorge *industrial engineering educator, consultant*
Haviland, David Sands *retired architectural educator, researcher, administrator*
Hendler, James Alexander *computer science educator, consultant*
Hsu, Cheng *decision sciences and engineering systems educator*
Jackson, Shirley Ann *academic administrator, physicist*
Jones, E. Stewart, Jr. *lawyer*
Kahl, William Frederick *retired academic administrator*

Lahey, Richard Thomas, Jr. *nuclear and fluid mechanics engineer*
Levinger, Joseph Solomon *physicist, researcher*
Linhardt, Robert John *chemistry professor*
Littman, Howard *chemical engineer, educator*
Magdon-Ismail, Malik *computer science professor*
Mayo, Robert Raymond (Bob Mayo) *university librarian*
McDermott, Robert J. *commissioner*
McDonald, John Francis Patrick *electrical engineering educator*
Medicus, Heinrich Adolf *physicist, researcher*
Medicus, Hildegard Julie *retired dentist, orthodontist, educator*
Persans, Peter David *physics educator, researcher*
Phan, Phillip Hin Choi *business educator, consultant*
Phelan, Thomas *clergyman, academic administrator, educator*
Potts, Kevin T. *retired chemistry professor*
Sanderson, Arthur Clark *engineering educator*
Shephard, Mark Scott *civil and mechanical engineering educator*
Shur, Michael *electrical engineer, educator, consultant*
Sperber, Daniel *physicist*
Szymanski, Boleslaw Karol *computer scientist, educator, entrepreneur*
Thompson, Barbara Ellen *occupational therapist, educator*
Toren, Mark *state official, statistician*
Wait, Samuel Charles, Jr. *academic administrator, educator*
Watson, E Bruce *science educator*
Woods, John William *electrical, computer and systems engineering educator, consultant*
Zimmie, Thomas Frank *civil engineer, educator*
Zurbenko, Igor Georg *science educator*

Tuckahoe
Brecher, Bernd *management consultant*
Thornton, Elaine Seretha *oncology clinical nurse specialist*

Tupper Lake
Johnson, David Wesley *lawyer*
Welsh, Peter Corbett *museum director, historian*

Turin
Klossner, Windy *food products executive*

Tuxedo Park
Davis, Shelby Moore Cullom *investment company executive, consultant*
Regan, Ellen Frances (Mrs. Walston Shepard Brown) *ophthalmologist, educator*
Sansone, Heidi L. *primary school educator*
Steinetz, Bernard George, Jr. *endocrinologist*

Uniondale
Berzow, Harold Steven *lawyer*
Bossy, Michael *professional sports team executive, retired professional hockey player*
Cassidy, David Michael *lawyer*
DiPietro, Rick *professional hockey player*
Duffy, James Raymond *lawyer*
Eilen, Howard Scott *lawyer, mediator*
Guerin, Bill *professional hockey player*
Guerrera, Lisa E. *financial planner*
Kotula, Michael Anthony *lawyer*
Lemle, Robert Spencer *lawyer*
Levy, Robert S. *lawyer*
Nolan, Ted (Theodore John Nolan) *professional hockey coach*
Pratt, George Cheney *law educator, retired judge*
Reddy, Gerard Anthony *financial consultant*
Sanchez, Laura Ann *music educator*
Snow, Garth *professional sports team executive, former professional hockey player*
Stewart, Cynthia Willis *minister*
Trottier, Bryan John *professional sports team executive, former professional hockey player and coach*
Wang, Charles B. *professional sports team executive, former computer company executive*

Unionville
Kemnitz, Thomas Milton *publisher*

Upton
Baltz, Anthony John *physicist*
Bari, Robert Allan *physicist*
Bond, Peter Danford *physicist*
Chaudhari, Praveen *science administrator, materials physicist*
Fowler, Joanna S. *chemist*
Fthenakis, Vasilis *chemical engineer, consultant, educator*
Goldhaber, Maurice *physicist, researcher*
Hamilton, Leonard Derwent *physician, molecular biologist*
Harbottle, Garman *chemist*
Hendrie, Joseph Mallam *physicist, nuclear engineer*
Lindenbaum, S(eymour) J(oseph) *physicist*
Lowenstein, Derek Irving *physicist*
Meinhold, Charles Boyd *health physicist*
Rau, Ralph Ronald *retired physicist*
Samios, Nicholas Peter *physicist*
Setlow, Jane Kellock *biophysicist*
Setlow, Richard Burton *biophysicist, researcher*
Steinberg, Meyer *chemical engineer*
Sutherland, Betsy Middleton *biologist*
Tannenbaum, Michael J(ay) *physicist*
Wei, Xiangdong *physicist, researcher*

Utica
Antzelevitch, Charles *research and development company executive*
Baber, Bob *dean*
Brennan, John Joseph *lawyer, administrator*
Cardamone, Richard J. *federal judge*
Fiori-Blanchfield, Joan *artist, historian*
Johnson, Mary Elizabeth *lawyer*
Schweizer, Paul Douglas *museum director*

Wagner, Frederick Reese *retired language educator*

Valatie
Dorsey, Richard J. *lawyer*

Valhalla
Adler, Karl Paul *academic administrator, medical educator*
Aronow, Wilbert Solomon *physician, educator*
Christesen, John D. *business educator*
Cohen, Martin Bruce *physician*
Czarnecki, Anthony J. *correction administrator, educator*
Del Guercio, Louis Richard Maurice *surgeon, educator*
De Nicola, Peter Francis *tax executive*
Fachnie, H(ugh) Douglas *film manufacturing company official*
Frishman, William Howard *cardiologist, educator, department chairman, cardiovascular pharmacologist, gerontologist*
Goodman, Alvin Irwin *internist, nephrologist, educator*
Hankin, Joseph Nathan *college president*
Iatropoulos, Michael John *health research executive, pathology educator*
Inchiosa, Mario Anthony, Jr. *pharmacologist*
Jenks, Eileen A. *academic administrator, real estate agent*
Kline, Susan Anderson *medical educator, internist*
Leone, Stephen Joseph *language educator, computer technician, consultant*
Madden, Robert Edward *surgeon, educator*
Marks, Stephen J. *neurologist, educator*
Niguidula, Faustino Nazario *surgeon, educator*
O'Connell, Ralph Anthony *dean, psychiatrist, educator*
Peterson, Stephen Joseph *internist*
Safai, Bijan *physician, investigator*
Sclafani, Charles Carlo *language educator, department chairman*
Traeger, Nadav *pediatrician, pulmonologist*
Urban, Diane *psychologist, educator*
Williams, Gary Murray *pathologist, educator*

Valley Stream
Datta, Rajiv V. *oncologist, surgeon, department chairman*
Eisenberg, Michael James *music educator*
Ellis, Bernice *financial planner, investment advisor*
Rachlin, Harvey Brant *writer*
Wood, Catherine T. *special education educator*

Verbank
Berry, Maryann Paradiso *minister*

Vestal
Adour, Colleen McNulty *artist, educator*
Grinberg, Raul *internist*
McGuire, John Thomas *lawyer, educator, writer*
Quataert, Donald *historian, educator*

Victor
Morris, G. Michael *science educator*

Waccabuc
Tognino, John Nicholas *diversified financial services company executive*

Wainscott
Henderson, William Charles *editor*
Herzog, Arthur III *author*
Russo, Alexander Peter *artist, educator*

Walden
Miranda, Hermes *school counselor*
Murphy, Pamela Ann *music educator, actress, musician*

Wallkill
Koch, Edwin Ernest *artist, interior designer*
Strauser, Susan Parkyn *performing arts educator, singer*

Wantagh
Berk, Adele L. *composer, music educator*
Blum, Melvin *chemical company executive, researcher*
Glaser, David *painter, sculptor*
Luchs, Jodi Ian *ophthalmologist*
Petris, Elli *paralegal*
Smits, Edward John *historian, consultant*

Wappingers Falls
Hogan, Edward Robert *financial services executive*
Johnson, Jeh Vincent *architect*
Maissel, Leon Israel *physicist, engineer*
Stabile, Patrice Christine *mathematics educator*

Warwick
Fletcher, Robert Alexander *artist, writer*
Linnéa, Sharon *writer, playwright*
Simon, Dolores Daly *copy editor*

Washingtonville
Fontana, Adam Vincent *music educator, musician*
Marcialis, Angelo Vincent *musician, educator*

Water Mill
Hagstrom, Jack Walter Carl Kling *retired pathology educator*
Kreimer, Michael Walter *financial planner, investment company executive*

Waterford
Glavin, A. Rita Chandellier (Mrs. James Henry Glavin III) *lawyer*
Gold, James Paul *museum director*
Novotny, F. Douglas *lawyer*

Watertown
Brett, James Clarence *retired journalism educator*

Coe, Benjamin Plaisted *retired state official*
McHugh, John Michael *congressman*

Watervliet
Alber, Richard Lawrence *quality assurance professional*
Elrahman, O. Abd *environmental and transportation engineer, educator*
Troiano, Edward *mechanical engineer, researcher*

Webster
Curtis, Deana A. *electronics executive, small business owner*
Cusick, Patricia A. *information technology executive*
McWilliams, C. Paul, Jr. *engineering executive*
Nicholson, Douglas Robert *accountant*
Powers, Richard Gerard *history educator*

Wellsville
Van Tyne, Arthur Morris *geologist*

West Harrison
Reichelderfer, Brenda L. *manufacturing executive*
Verano, Anthony Frank *retired banker*

West Hempstead
Guggenheimer, Heinrich Walter *mathematician, educator*

West Hurley
Martucci, Vincent James *composer, pianist*

West Islip
Rifkin, Matthew D. *radiologist*
Theiss, Cynthia C. *home economist, educator*

West Nyack
Pringle, Laurence Patrick *writer*
Zansky, Michael *artist, production designer*

West Point
Boettner, Daisie Dawson *military officer, mechanical engineering educator*
Finnegan, Patrick *dean, military officer, lawyer*
Hagenbeck, Franklin Lee *academic administrator, career military officer*
Jensen, Leslie Dwight *curator*
Keith, Bruce Edward *sociologist*
Williams, Craig Stewart *organist, music educator, director*

West Seneca
Bidlack, Jerald Dean *manufacturing executive*

Westbury
Brooks, David H. *manufacturing executive*
Greenberger, Roni Susan *elementary school educator*
Lorber, Howard Mark *investments executive*
Marks, Debra Jane *special education educator*
Mondello, John Paul *financial consultant*
Ross-Lee, Barbara *dean, educator*
Sandler, Gerald Howard *computer scientist, information technology executive, educator*

Westhampton Beach
Flood, Angela *interior designer, artist*

White Plains
Abrams, Leigh Jeffrey *manufacturing executive*
Adams, Robert T. *lawyer*
Adkins, Rodney *computer company executive*
Aron, Adam M. *air transportation executive*
Baran, Xiaolei Yu *physician, psychiatry professor*
Bender, Joel Charles *lawyer*
Berlin, Alan Daniel *lawyer, real estate company officer, consultant*
Bernard, Robert William *plastic surgeon*
Biers, Martin Henry *physician*
Blass, John Paul *physician, biochemist*
Bober, Lawrence Harold *retired banker*
Bodnar, Peter O. *lawyer*
Brieant, Charles La Monte *federal judge*
Brown, Ronald C. *hotel executive*
Bushkin, Merle Jerome *investment banker*
Carey, John *judge*
Carlisle, Jay Charles, II, *lawyer, educator*
Carlucci, Joseph P. *lawyer*
Chase, Jenny Wei-Lang Kao *singer, music educator*
Colwell, Howard Otis *advertising executive*
Conner, William Curtis *federal judge*
Culleton, James J. *lawyer, former prosecutor*
Davenport, Lindsay *professional tennis player*
Doyle, Dennis T. *lawyer*
Duncan, Bruce W. *hotel and retired real estate company executive*
Feder, Robert *lawyer*
Fisher, Jerome *apparel executive*
Flanigen, Edith Marie *materials scientist, consultant*
Foderaro, Lisa *reporter*
Foster, John Horace *consulting environmental engineer*
Fouse, Jacqualyn A. *consumer products company executive*
Fowlkes, Nancy Lanetta Pinkard *social worker*
Frase, Katharine *information technology executive*
Frazier, Amy *professional tennis player*
Gambardella, Thomas M. *lawyer*
Gilbert, Bradley *professional tennis coach, former professional tennis player, former Olympic athlete*
Gillingham, Stephen Thomas *financial planner*
Gjertsen, O. Gerard *lawyer*
Gottlieb, Lester M. *entrepreneur*
Greenawalt, William Sloan *lawyer*
Greenspan, Leon Joseph *lawyer*
Greenspan, Michael Evan *lawyer*
Haines, Daniel Webster *engineering consultant, engineering educator*
Halpern, Philip Morgan *lawyer*

Hardin, Adlai Stevenson, Jr. *judge*
Hattar, Jacqueline *lawyer*
High, Kemba M. *special education educator*
Howse, Jennifer Louise *foundation administrator*
Huang, Han *systems engineer*
Katz, Michael *pediatrician, educator*
Kroner, Arnold Friedrich *financial consultant, economist*
Kurzman, Robert Graham *lawyer, educator*
Kutscher, Martin L. *pediatrician, neurologist*
Landa, Howard Martin *lawyer, management consultant*
Leish, Kenneth William *retired publishing company executive*
Levasseur, Guy J. *lawyer*
Lightstone, John B. *finance company executive*
Longo, Ronald Anthony *lawyer*
Loranger, Steven R. *industrial manufacturing company executive*
Lukaszewski, James Edmund *communications executive*
MacDonald, J. Randall *information technology executive, human resources specialist*
Machover, Carl *computer graphics designer, engineer, consultant*
Maffeo, Vincent Anthony *lawyer, director*
Manville, Stewart Roebling *archivist*
Marano, Anthony Joseph *cardiologist*
Marino, Jane B. *library director*
McNamara, Michael J. *law educator*
Mills, Steven A. *information technology executive*
Milone, Lydia *lawyer*
Mitchell, Robert Dale *engineer, consultant*
Moffat, Robert W., Jr. *information technology executive*
Munneke, Gary Arthur *law educator, consultant*
Nastasi, Aldo A. *judge*
Nelson, Mario *physiatrist*
Nesci, Vincent Peter *lawyer*
Newman, Marie Stefanini *law librarian, educator*
Null, William Seth *lawyer*
O'Brien, H. Michael *lawyer*
O'Brien, James F. *lawyer*
Ottinger, Richard Lawrence *dean emeritus*
Palmisano, Samuel J. *information technology executive*
Parker, Barrington D., Jr. *federal judge, lawyer*
Payson, Martin F. *lawyer*
Pfeffer, Cynthia Roberta *psychiatrist, educator*
Pirro, Jeanine Ferris *prosecutor*
Prabhu, Vasant M. *corporate financial executive*
Quaranta, Philip *lawyer*
Ramos, Denise L. *corporate financial executive*
Robinson, Nicholas Adams *law educator, department chairman*
Rometty, Ginny (Virginia M. Rometty) *information technology executive*
Ryan, Robert Davis *lawyer*
Sacco, John Michael *accountant*
Scott-Williams, Wendy Lee *library and information scientist*
Sedelmaier, J. J. *filmmaker*
Sheehan, Timothy J. *lawyer*
Siegel, Kenneth S. *lawyer*
Silverberg, Steven Mark *lawyer*
Silverman, Amy Jocelyn *psychiatrist*
Sloan, F(rank) Blaine *retired law educator*
Smith, Gerard Peter *neuroscientist*
Steccato, Carl L. *lawyer*
Sternlicht, Barry Stuart *hotel executive*
Straus, Marc Joshua *internist, poet*
Streisand, Robert L. *thoracic surgeon*
Sussberg, Milton Joel *marketing professional*
Szolnoki, John Frank *special education educator, administrator*
Topol, Robin April Levitt *lawyer*
Tumbarello, Phillip A. *lawyer*
Underweiser, Irwin Philip *mining executive, lawyer*
Vignali, Rosario M. *lawyer*
Waterhouse, Lynette *mathematics educator*
Wedge, Chris *animation director, studio executive*
Weisburger, John Hans *medical researcher*
Weiss, Terri Lynn *lawyer*
Williams, Serena *professional tennis player, apparel designer*
Williams, Ted Vaughnell *physical education educator*
Williams, Venus *professional tennis player*
Wittcoff, Harold Aaron *chemist*
Worby, David E. *lawyer*
Young, Steven L. *lawyer*
Zuckerman, Marc Abraham *finance educator*

Whitestone
Bikoff, J. Darius *beverage company executive*
Kahn, Matt *marketing executive*
Lodico, Cheryl Madeline *secondary school educator*
Oza, Rohan *beverage company executive*
Prisco, Frank J. *psychotherapist*
Rahr, Stewart *health medical products executive*

Williamsville
Ackerman, Philip Charles *utilities executive, lawyer*
Berner, Robert Frank *managerial statistics educator, administrator*
Ciprich, Paula Marie *lawyer, gas industry executive*
Cloudsley, Donald Hugh *retired library administrator*
Dobosiewicz, Elizabeth J. *lawyer*
Drew, Fraser Bragg Robert *language educator*
Jones, Robert Alfred *retired clergyman*
Levite, Laurence A. *publishing executive*
Metzger, Ernest Hugh *aerospace engineer, research scientist*
Neiman, Joseph Bruce *dermatologist, educator*
Ogra, Pearay L. *pediatrician, educator*
Perry, J. Warren *health facility administrator, educator*
Reisman, Robert E. *allergist, educator*
Rekate, Albert C. *physician*

Saveth, Edward Norman *historian, educator*
Whitcomb, James Stuart *videographer, photographer, production company executive*

Williston Park
Lilly, Thomas Joseph *lawyer*
Lynch, Kyle Thomas *lawyer*

Willow
Bley, Carla Borg *composer*

Willsboro
Reuther, David Louis *retired children's book publisher, writer*

Wilton
Concemi, Alfred P. *marketing professional*

Windham
Manno, Robert *composer, conductor*

Windsor
Warner, Roberta Arlene *retired accountant, financial services executive*

Wolcott
Searle, Robert Ferguson *minister*

Woodbury
Agresti, Miriam Monell *psychologist*
Fischoff, Gary Charles *lawyer*
Greenberg, Stephen Todd *plastic surgeon*
Guttenplan, Harold Esau *retired food company executive*
Mangia, Angelo James *lawyer*

Woodmere
Schlissel, Fred *management consultant, educator*
Winick, Bernyce Alpert *artist, photographer*

Woodside
Hofmann, Herbert C. *diversified holding company executive*
Sfiroudis, Gloria Tides *library and information scientist, educator*
Swift, Constance Redmond *special education educator*

Woodstock
Banks, Rela *sculptor*
Currie, Bruce *artist*
Godwin, Gail Kathleen *writer*
Lieberman, Josefa Nina *retired psychologist, writer*
Ober, Stuart Alan *investment advisor, writer*
van Hamel, Manette C. *artist, writer*

Wyandanch
Fonseca, Alejandra *language educator*
Newman, Samuel *retired trust company executive*

Yaphank
Narain, Ralph B. *biologist*

Yonkers
Baumel, Herbert *violinist, conductor*
Baumel, Joan Patricia French *writer, educator*
Capodilupo, Elizabeth Jeanne Hatton *public relations executive*
Connors, James Patrick *lawyer*
Gunner, Murray *retired religious organization administrator*
Holtz, Gilbert Joseph *steel company executive*
Johansen, Robert Joseph *consulting actuary*
Kleman, Kimberly C. *editor-in-chief*
Kopelman, Milton *retired secondary school educator, principal*
Lee, Claudia S. *retired elementary school educator*
Liggio, Jean Vincenza *adult education educator, artist*
Lukach, Arthur S., Jr. *manufacturing executive*
Lupiani, Donald Anthony *psychologist*
McKean, Kevin S. *publishing executive, writer*
Mennin, Gerald Stanley *ophthalmologist*
Neal, Leora Louise Haskett *social services administrator*
Novick, Stephen Alan *cardiologist*
Ortega, Maria A. *security firm executive, educator*
Philipps, Edward William *former banker, real estate appraiser*
Senator, Ronald Paul *composer, writer, retired music educator*
Singer, Cecile Doris *bank executive, former state legislator*
Spagnuolo, Mario *physician*
Speirs, Greg *artist*
Torrese, Dante Michael *prosthodontist, educator*
Trentanelli, John Anthony *educational administrator*
Weston, Francine Evans *secondary school educator*
Westphal, Carol Jean *media specialist*

Yorktown Heights
Avouris, Phaedon *chemical physicist*
Berk, George Ellis *cardiologist*
Das, Koushik K. *industrial researcher*
Dennard, Robert Heath *engineering executive, scientist*
d'Heurle, François Max *research scientist, engineering educator*
Hoffman, Alan Jerome *mathematician, educator*
Iyengar, Arun K. *computer scientist*
Keyes, Robert W. *physicist, researcher*
Kim, Keunwoo *electrical engineer, researcher*
Lang, Norton David *physicist*
Lanzerotti, Mary Yvonne *physicist, researcher*
Lei, Hui *computer scientist*
Mayer, Gerard J. *physician*
Ning, Tak Hung *physicist, microelectronic technologist*
Schiller, Barbara *retired special education educator*
Terman, Lewis Madison *retired electrical engineer, researcher, director*
Tersoff, Jerry David *physicist*
Wade, James O'Shea *editor, writer*
Winograd, Shmuel *mathematician*
Winterton, Joseph Henry *computer software executive*
Wynne, James J. *research scientist*

Youngstown
Alpert, Norman *chemical company executive*
Lamb, Charles F. *retired minister, educator*

NORTH CAROLINA

Advance
Cochrane, Betsy Lane *former state senator*
Guth, Caryl Joy *retired anesthesiologist*

Andrews
Fonda, Ronald Alan *epistemologist*

Ararat
Marsh, Joseph Virgil *real estate broker, retired investment advisor*

Arden
Baker, Kerry Allen *management consultant*

Asheboro
Jones, David M. *zoological park administrator*
Sanders, William Eugene *marketing executive*

Asheville
Bissette, Winston Louis, Jr. *lawyer, mayor*
Brown, David G. *academic administrator*
Chidnese, Patrick Nicholas *retired lawyer*
Coli, Guido John *chemical company executive*
Davis, Roy Walton, Jr. *lawyer*
Dickens, Charles Henderson *retired social sciences educator*
Elmore, Bruce Alexander, Jr. *lawyer*
Haggard, William Henry *meteorologist*
Hamilton, Jackson Douglas *lawyer*
Haynes, John Mabin *retired utilities executive*
Horwitz, Bertrand Nathan *finance educator*
King, Joseph Bertram *architect*
Lavelle, Brian Francis David *lawyer*
Letzig, Betty Jean *financial consultant*
McDevitt, Larry S. *lawyer*
Meyerson, Seymour *retired chemist*
Mundt, Barry Maynard *management consultant*
Pfeiffer, William Sanborn *education educator, writer*
Shuler, (Joseph) Heath *congressman, real estate company executive, retired professional football player*
Smith, James Finley *economist, educator*
Thornburg, Lacy Herman *federal judge*
Turcot, Marguerite Hogan *medical researcher*
Tynes, Robert Dick *artist, educator*
Voigt, Ellen *literature educator*
White, Terry Edward *physician*
Wilson, Thomas Douglas, Jr. *lawyer*

Bakersville
Buchanan, Robin Byington *school system administrator*

Banner Elk
Hutcheson, James Sterling *retired physician, allergist*

Beaufort
Bonaventura, Celia Jean *biochemist, researcher*
Cullman, Hugh *retired tobacco company executive*

Biltmore Forest
Sgro, Joseph Anthony *retired psychologist, educator*

Black Mountain
Belue, Janie A. *music educator*
Blackwell, Anna Nelle *medical educator, medical technician*
Dalton, Robert Edgar *retired mathematician, computer scientist*
Ingle, Robert P. *retail executive*

Blowing Rock
Barnebey, Kenneth Alan *food products executive*

Boone
Austin, Roberta Jones *elementary school educator*
Conrad, David Paul *business broker, real estate developer, retired food service executive*
Duke, Charles Richard *dean*
Durham, Harvey Ralph *retired academic administrator*
Jones, Dan Lewis *psychologist*
Kimmel, Chuck *academic administrator, director*
Lugo, Emil J. *retired secondary school educator*
Martin, Vicki Joan *biology professor*
Mills, Susan Wilson *music educator*
Oelberg, Robert Nathan *landscape architect*

Brevard
Dillon (Kenofer), Doris *artist, historian, educator, interior designer*
Flory, Margaret Martha *retired religious organization administrator*
Foster, Edward John *engineer physicist*
Phillips, Euan Hywel *publishing executive*

Bryson City
Miller, Gary H. *lawyer*

Buies Creek
Hammond, Mark L. *biology professor, academic administrator*
Johnson, George Lloyd *education educator, consultant, writer*
Platt, Rorin Morse *history professor, historian*
Wiggins, Norman Adrian *academic administrator, law educator*

Burlington
Ellington, Beth Elder *librarian*
Holt, Bertha Merrill *state legislator*
King, David Paul *health services executive, lawyer*
MacMahon, Thomas P. *healthcare company executive*
Phillips, Ruth Ann *retired secondary school educator*
Powell, James Bobbitt *health facility administrator, pathologist*
Slayton, John Howard *lawyer, corporate financial executive*
Smith, Bradford T. *lawyer*
Wilson, William Preston *psychiatrist, educator*

Burnsville
Bernstein, William Joseph *glass artist, educator*
Cullom, William Otis *retired trade association executive*
Doyle, John Lawrence *artist*

Camden
Hammond, Roy Joseph *reinsurance company executive*

Camp Lejeune
Chadwick, Christopher Michael *military officer*

Canton
Dixon, Shirley Juanita *retired restaurant owner*
Roberts, Bill Glen *retired protective services official*

Cape Carteret
Mullikin, Thomas Wilson *mathematics professor*

Carrboro
Barbarin, Oscar Anthony *psychologist*
Generous, William Thomas, Jr., (Tom) *coach, educator*
Prather, Donna Lynn *psychiatrist*

Carthage
Gebhardt, Robert Charles *lawyer*

Cary
Bryant, Mynora Joyce *not-for-profit fundraiser*
Buckler, Sheldon A. *technology company executive*
Connally, Mark *statistician, psychometrician*
Conrad, Hans *materials science and engineering educator*
Craig, Harold Kent *mechanical contracting executive, systems analyst*
Goodnight, James H. *software company executive*
Hauser, John Reid *electrical engineering educator*
Kimbrell, Odell Culp, Jr. *internist*
Kung, Pang-Jen *materials scientist, electrical engineer*
Martin, William Royall, Jr. *retired professional society administrator*
Mata, Elizabeth Adams *language educator, land investor*
Montgomery, Charles Harvey *lawyer*
O'Meallie, Kitty *artist*
Sall, John *information technology executive*
Slaattè, Howard Alexander *minister, philosophy educator*
Summers, Suzanne Frances Hemenway *elementary school educator*
Swanson, David C. *publishing executive*
Sweeney, Tim *computer game developer, programmer*
Taylor, David Wyatt Aiken *retired clergyman*
Taylor, Marvin Edward, Jr. *lawyer*
Timothy, David Harry *retired biology professor*
Trebing, David Martin *public policy executive*
Vandergriff, Kenneth Lynn *religious studies educator*
Vick, Columbus Edwin, Jr. *retired civil engineering design firm executive*

Cashiers
O'Connell, Edward James, Jr. *psychologist, educator, systems administrator, consultant*

Chapel Hill
Andreoni, Kenneth A. *surgeon*
Andrews, Richard Nigel Lyon *academic administrator, educator*
Atashili, Julius *epidemiologist*
Azar, Henry Amin *retired medical historian, educator*
Bailey, Herbert Smith, Jr. *retired publisher*
Baker, Edward L., Jr. *public health physician*
Ballard, David Eugene *anesthesiologist*
Baroff, George Stanley *psychologist, educator*
Baron, Samuel Haskell *historian*
Bernard, Stephen Alan *oncologist*
Berne, Suzanne *writer, educator*
Boger, John Charles *law educator, dean*
Bolas, Gerald Douglas *museum director, art historian, educator*
Bondurant, Stuart *physician, educational association administrator*
Bowers, Thomas Arnold *journalism educator, dean*
Bowles, Erskine B. *academic administrator, former White House chief of staff*
Boyarsky, Saul *urologist, educator*
Broad, Molly Corbett (Margaret Corbett Broad) *retired academic administrator*
Brookhart, Maurice S. *chemist*
Brooks, Frederick Phillips, Jr. *computer scientist, educator*
Brower, David John *lawyer, urban planner, educator*
Brown, Frank *social sciences educator*
Browning, Christopher R. *historian, educator*
Bursey, Maurice M. *retired chemistry professor*
Callahan, Leigh Fleming *medical educator, researcher*
Campbell, Bobby Jack *academic administrator*
Campbell, Frances Alexander *psychologist*
Carey, Lisa Anne *oncologist, educator*
Carroll, Roy *retired academic administrator*
Carson, Culley Clyde III *urologist, educator*
Chang, Kuk Won *theology educator, researcher, pastor*
Clark, Arthur Watts *insurance company executive*
Coeytaux, Remy Rene *physician, researcher*
Cole, Richard Ray *communications educator, former dean*
Coles, William Henry *ophthalmologist, educator*
Collier, Albert M. *pediatrician, educator, director*
Crohn, Max Henry, Jr. *lawyer*
Cromartie, William James *medical educator, researcher*
Cronenwett, Linda Houk *dean, nursing educator*
Cummings, Sandra Eileen *medical products executive*
Dangl, Jeffery L. *biology professor*
Davis, Butch (Paul Hilton Davis) *college football coach*
Davis, Morris Schuyler *astronomer*
Davis, Sarah Irwin *retired language educator*
Day, Barbara D. *education educator, association administrator*
Debreczeny, Paul *retired language educator, writer*
De Friese, Gordon H. *health services researcher*
De Rosa, Guy Paul *orthopedic surgery educator*
Desimone, Joseph M. *chemist, educator*
Dirschl, Douglas Ray *surgeon, educator*
Dixon, Frederick Dail *architect*
Drossman, Douglas Arnold *medical investigator, educator, gastroenterologist*
Drutz, David Jules *venture capitalist*
Edwards, Richard LeRoy *dean, social sciences educator, management consultant*
Eliel, Ernest Ludwig *chemist, educator*
Erdem, Nurum Filiz *geriatrician*
Farber, Rosann Alexander *geneticist, educator*
Feinberg, Lawrence Edward *language educator, researcher*
Fieleke, Norman Siegfried *economist, educator*
Fine, J(ames) Allen *insurance company executive*
Finkel, Alan Glen *neurologist, educator*
Fletcher, Suzanne Wright *epidemiologist, medical educator, editor*
Flora, Joseph M(artin) *language educator*
Fordham, Christopher Columbus III *dean, academic administrator, medical educator*
Forman, Donald T. *biochemist, educator*
Fowler, Wesley Caswell, Jr. *obstetrician, gynecologist*
Fox, Mike *college baseball coach*
Frampton, Paul Howard *physics researcher, educator*
Ganley, Oswald Harold *retired director*
Gervais-Gruen, Elizabeth *lawyer*
Girdler, Susan Scott *psychologist, educator, researcher*
Godschalk, David Robinson *architect, urban development planner, educator*
Goldsmith, Lowell Alan *medical educator*
Gordon-Larsen, Penny *nutritionist, educator, researcher*
Goyer, Robert Andrew *pathology educator*
Gray, Virginia Hickman *political science professor*
Green, Paul Eliot, Jr. *retired optical engineer*
Greganti, Mac Andrew *physician, educator*
Grendler, Paul Frederick *historian, educator*
Gressman, Eugene *lawyer*
Griffiths, José-Marie *dean, library and information science educator*
Gritter, Elizabeth *historian, researcher*
Gura, Philip Francis *English and American literature educator*
Hartlyn, Jonathan *political scientist, educator*
Hatchell, Sylvia R. *women's college basketball coach*
Hawkins, David Rollo, Sr. *psychiatrist, educator*
Heninger, Simeon Kahn, Jr. *language educator*
Henson, O'Dell Williams, Jr. *retired anatomy educator*
Herman-Giddens, Gregory *lawyer*
Hobgood, W. Sands *systems engineer*
Houpt, Jeffrey Lyle *psychiatrist, educator, former dean*
Huff, Daniel M. *music educator*
Hulka, Jaroslav Fabian *obstetrician, gynecologist*
James, Alton Everette, Jr. *radiologist*
Jones, Houston Gwynne *archivist, history professor*
Jones, Lyle Vincent *psychologist, educator*
Jones, W. S. (Steve Jones) *dean*
Jorgenson, James Wallace *chromatographer, educator*
Kenan, Thomas Stephen III *philanthropist*
Kinnaird, Eleanor Gates *state legislator, lawyer*
Klein, Martin Jesse *physicist, science historian, educator*
Klinefelter, Anne *law librarian, educator*
Kohn, Richard H. *historian, educator*
Krasno, Richard Michael *foundation executive, educator*
Kremer, Michael *surgeon*
Lachiewicz, Paul Francis *orthopedist, surgeon, educator*
Latané, Bibb *social psychologist*
Lauder, Valarie Anne *editor, educator*
Lavelle, John Paul *urologist*
Lawrence, David Michael *lawyer, educator*
Lee, Kuo-Hsiung *medicinal chemistry professor*
Levine, Madeline Geltman *literature and language educator, translator*
Ligett, Waldo Buford *chemist*
Lilley, Albert Frederick *retired lawyer*
Lochridge, Julie Deane *retired communications executive*
Loeb, Ben Fohl, Jr. *retired law educator*
Lohr, Jacob Andrew *pediatrician, educator*
Lowman, Robert Paul *psychology professor, academic administrator*

Lundblad, Roger Lauren *biotechnology consultant*
Macdonald, James Ross *physicist, researcher*
Magill, Samuel Hays *academic administrator, consultant*
Magnuson, Terry R. *geneticist, educator*
Marchionini, Gary Joseph *information science educator*
Martikainen, A(une) Helen *retired health specialist educator*
Mc Kean, John Rosseel Overton *university dean*
McKinney, Ross Erwin, Sr. *civil engineering educator*
McMillan, Campbell White *pediatrician, educator, hematologist*
Mersini - Houghton, Laura *physicist, educator*
Merzbacher, Eugen *retired physics professor*
Meyer, Philip Edward *journalism educator*
Miller, C. Arden *physician, educator*
Mitchell, Earl Nelson *physicist, researcher*
Moellering, John Henry *aviation maintenance company executive*
Moeser, James Charles *academic administrator*
Moore, Albert Cunningham *lawyer, insurance company executive*
Moran, Barbara Burns *librarian, educator*
Mueller, Nancy Schneider *retired biology professor*
Murray, Michael Dennis *pharmacist*
Neff, Severine *music educator*
Nelson, Philip Francis *musicologist, consultant, conductor*
Norton, Edward C. *economist, educator*
Okun, Daniel Alexander *environmental engineering educator*
Pagano, Joseph Stephen *internist, educator, researcher*
Parr, Robert Ghormley *chemistry professor*
Patz, Edward Frank *retired lawyer*
Peacock, Erle Ewart, Jr. *surgeon, lawyer, educator*
Perreault, William Daniel, Jr. *business administration educator*
Pillsbury, Harold Crockett III *otolaryngologist*
Popkin, Barry Michael *nutrition educator*
Powell, Carolyn Wilkerson *retired music educator*
Prange, Arthur Jergen, Jr. *psychology and psychiatry professor, neuroscientist*
Prinz, Jesse J. *philosophy educator*
Proffit, William Robert *orthodontics educator*
Pruett, James Worrell *librarian, educator, musicologist*
Rabil, Albert, Jr. *humanities educator*
Ramsey, John Michael *chemistry professor, researcher*
Ravenel, Shannon *book publishing professional*
Rezk, Naser Labeeb *biochemist, researcher*
Riggs, Timothy Allan *museum curator*
Rimer, Barbara K. *health facility administrator, educator, dean*
Rindfuss, Ronald Richard *social studies educator*
Roper, William Lee *dean, preventive medicine physician, administrator*
Rosen, Benson *business administration educator*
Ross, Coleman DeVane *accountant, insurance company executive*
Salmon, Edward Dickinson *cell biologist, educator*
Sancar, Aziz *research biochemist*
Sanders, John Lassiter *retired academic administrator*
Schier, Donald Stephen *language educator*
Schoonover, Brenda B. *ambassador*
Schoultz, Lars *political scientist, educator*
Shea, Thomas Charles *physician, educator*
Sheldon, George Frank *medical educator*
Smith, Dean Edwards *retired men's college basketball coach*
Smith, Sidney Rufus, Jr. *linguist, educator*
Smithies, Oliver *geneticist, educator*
Southern, Robert Allen *lawyer*
Spencer, Elizabeth *writer*
Spencer, Roger Felix *psychiatrist, educator*
Stamm, John William Randolph *dentist, educator*
Stenberg, Carl W. III *public administration educator, dean*
Steponaitis, Vincas Petras *archaeologist, anthropologist, educator*
Stipe, Robert Edwin *retired design educator*
Stockman, James Anthony III *pediatrician*
Strauss, Albrecht Benno *retired language educator, editor*
Strauss, Diane Carol Wheeler *librarian, educator, writer*
Stumpf, Walter Erich *cell biology and pharmacology professor, researcher*
Taft, Timothy Ned *orthopedist, surgeon, sports medicine physician*
Taylor, Michael E. *mathematics professor*
Tolley, Aubrey Granville *psychiatrist, health facility administrator*
Trejo, JoAnn *medical researcher*
Treml, Vladimir Guy *economist, educator*
Tsui, Frank *physicist, educator, researcher*
Umminger, Bruce Lynn *government agency administrator, research scientist, educator, consultant*
Vargha, Rebecca B. *university librarian, library association executive*
Wasik, Barbara Hanna *psychologist, educator*
Weakley, Alan Stuart *curator*
Wegner, Judith Welch *lawyer, educator, dean*
Weiss, Shirley F. *retired urban and regional planner, economist, educator*
Wescott, Joseph Warren, II, *academic administrator, education educator*
West, Alisha Nicole *otolaryngologist, surgeon*
White, Raymond Petrie, Jr. *dentist, educator, dean*
Whybark, David Clay *business educator, researcher*
Wilcox, Benson Reid *cardiothoracic surgeon, educator*
Wilfert, Catherine M. *medical association administrator, pediatrician, epidemiologist, educator*
Williams, John N. *dean, dental educator*
Williams, Roy *men's college basketball coach*
Williamson, Joel Rudolph *humanities educator, writer*
Wilson, Glenn *economist, educator*
Winfield, John Buckner *rheumatologist, educator*
Winstanly, Derek Miles *medical practitioner, company executive*
Wolfenden, Richard Vance *biochemistry educator*
Wright, Deil Spencer *political science professor*
Yeatts, Karin Beatrice *epidemiologist*
Yow, Valerie Raleigh *historian, writer, counselor*
Zeisel, Steven H. *nutritionist, scientist, educator*

Charlotte

Alphin, J. Steele *bank executive*
Anderson, Gerald Leslie *finance company executive*
Armstrong, James David *editor, educator, minister*
Aycock, Joseph William *music educator, auto racing official*
Ayscue, Edwin Osborne, Jr. *lawyer*
Baird, Douglas James *investment banker*
Barber, Martha Gayle *lawyer*
Barber, Timothy G. *lawyer*
Barnhill, G. Michael *lawyer*
Barron, Henry B., Jr., (Brew) *energy executive*
Barrows, Frank Clemence *journalist*
Bass-Hollis, Cynthia Gibson *environmental services administrator*
Bauroth, Nancy Ann *journalist, former marketing executive*
Behrman, Michael J. *professional sports team executive*
Belk, Thomas Milburn, Jr., (Tim) *apparel executive*
Bell, Kenneth Davis *lawyer*
Bennett, R. Monty *church organist*
Bessant, Cathy (Catherine Pombier) *bank executive, marketing professional*
Bickerstaff, Bernie (Bernard Tyrone Bickerstaff Sr.) *professional sports team executive, former professional basketball coach*
Blanchfield, Francis J., Jr. *lawyer*
Blowers, Helene *library and information scientist*
Bonnefoux, Jean-Pierre *choreographer, dancer*
Brackett, Martin Luther, Jr. *lawyer*
Bragg, Ellis Meredith, Jr. *lawyer*
Brinkley, Amy Woods *bank executive*
Brooks-Gordon, Elizabeth Faye *history educator*
Brown, Charles M. *library director*
Brown, Edward J III *bank executive*
Brown, Harold Ogden Joseph *religious studies educator*
Browning, Peter Crane *manufacturing executive*
Brynn, Edward Paul *former ambassador*
Buchan, Jonathan Edward, Jr. *lawyer*
Buckley, Charles Robinson III *lawyer*
Cameron, Donald John *retired commodities trader*
Campbell, Hugh Brown, Jr. *judge*
Carr, David *professional football player*
Carroll, James P. *lawyer*
Castro, Mary McDermott *language educator*
Caulkins, Ann *publishing executive*
Chambers, Julius LeVonne *lawyer*
Clark, Ranjana B. *bank executive*
Clodfelter, Daniel Gray *state legislator, lawyer*
Cochran, John R. III *bank executive*
Cochrane, Eugene W., Jr. *foundation administrator*
Connor, Michael S. *lawyer*
Conrad, Robert J., Jr. *federal judge*
Cooke, Steven John *chemical engineer, consultant, scientist*
Cooper, Jason P. *lawyer*
Coss, Stephen K. *lawyer*
Cottingham, Tracy Thomas III *lawyer*
Culbreth, James Harold, Jr. *lawyer*
Cummings, Stephen Emery *investment banking executive*
Czarnecki, Kelly *librarian*
Davis, Stephen *professional football player*
Delhomme, Jake Christopher *professional football player*
Desoer, Barbara J. *bank executive*
Dickson, Thomas Walter *textile company executive*
Dienes, Timothy Paul *mathematician, educator*
DiMicco, Daniel R. *manufacturing executive*
Dubois, Philip Leon *academic administrator, political scientist, educator*
Durham, J(oseph) Porter, Jr. *lawyer, educator*
Economou, Greg *professional sports team executive*
Edmondson, Ruby Johnson *psychologist*
Elanayar, Sunil K. *research and development engineer*
Eppes, Thomas Evans *advertising and public relations executive*
Eppley, Frances Fielden *secondary school educator, writer*
Erdman, David Williams *lawyer*
Ethridge, Mark Foster III *writer, publishing executive, consultant*
Fennebresque, John C. *lawyer*
Ferebee, Stephen Scott, Jr. *retired architect*
Ferriola, John J. *manufacturing executive*
Finley, Glenna *writer*
Fitzpatrick, James Ward, Jr. *retired engineering educator*
Fox, John *professional football coach*
Fox, William J. *bank executive, former federal official*
Freeman, Sidney Lee *minister*
Fretwell, Elbert K., Jr. *retired university chancellor, consultant*
Gage, Gaston Hemphill *lawyer*
Gallagher, Arthur J. *academic administrator*
Gambrell, Sarah Belk *retail executive*
Gantt, Harvey B. *architect, former mayor*
Goldstein, Stuart N. *lawyer*
Good, Lynn J. *energy executive*
Goodwin, William H., Jr. *diversified financial services company executive*
Goolkasian, Paula A. *psychologist, educator*
Gordon, Jeff *race car driver*
Gosnell, Guy R. *lawyer*
Gotta, Joseph D. *music company executive*
Graham, Billy (William Franklin Graham) *evangelist*
Graham, Franklin (William Franklin Graham III) *evangelist, missionary*
Grigg, Eddie Garman *minister, educator*
Gunson, Douglas R. *lawyer*
Hahn, Robert J. *lawyer*
Haines, Kenneth H. *sports television broadcasting and marketing executive*
Halas, Paul Anthony, Jr. *business appraisal and valuation specialist, consultant*
Hall, James Bryan *gynecologist, oncologist*
Hammonds, Bruce L. *bank executive*
Handy, John W. *shipping company executive, retired military officer*
Hankins, Irvin W. III *lawyer*
Hanna, George Verner III *lawyer*
Hauser, David L. *energy executive*
Herring, Rebecca Royce *music educator, consultant*
Higgins, Rod (Roderick Dwayne Higgins) *professional sports team executive, retired professional basketball player*
Hinchey, Tim *professional sports team executive*
Hinson, Bobby D. *lawyer*
Hord, Joy M. *lawyer*
Horn, Carl III *federal judge*
Horoschak, Mark J. *lawyer*
Huberman, Jeffrey Allen *architect*
Hufanda, Joseph *dentist*
Ives, H. Bryan III *lawyer*
Jacobs, Gordon Waldemar *surgeon, educator*
Janson, Julia S. *energy executive*
Jenkins, Benjamin P. III *bank executive*
Johnson, Jimmie *race car driver*
Jones, Milton H., Jr. *bank executive*
Jordan, Michael Jeffrey *professional sports team executive, retired professional basketball player, professional baseball player*
Jordan, Robert Sands *electrical engineer*
Kearney, Christopher J. *manufacturing executive, lawyer*
Kelley, Janet Godsey *lawyer*
Kelly, R. James *retail executive*
Kelly, Stanhope A. *bank executive*
Kennelly, Michael J. *neurologist, surgeon*
Kidda, Michael Lamont, Jr. *psychologist, educator*
Krueger, Joanna Katherine *chemistry professor, researcher*
Kuechle, Scott E. *manufacturing executive*
Larsen, Marshall O. *manufacturing executive*
Lea, Scott Carter *retired packaging company executive*
Levine, Howard R. *retail executive*
Lewis, Kenneth D. *bank executive*
Lilly, James Edward *lawyer*
Lilly, Kevin L. *lawyer, manufacturing executive*
Linnert, Terrence Gregory *lawyer*
Lisenby, Terry S. *manufacturing executive*
Locke, Elizabeth Hughes *retired foundation administrator*
Lott, Hamilton, Jr. *manufacturing executive*
Loughridge, John Halsted, Jr. *lawyer*
Lyerly, Elaine Myrick *advertising executive*
Mancuso, Michael John *retired corporate financial executive*
Manly, Marc Edward *lawyer, energy executive*
May, Benjamin Tallman *securities specialist, administrator*
Mayopoulos, Timothy J. *lawyer, bank executive*
McAfee, Larry W. *chemistry educator*
McBryde, Neill Gregory *lawyer*
McClelland, Richard Lee *dentist*
McClure, Howard Jean, Jr. *advocate*
McCoy, Michael D. *lawyer*
McCrory, Patrick *mayor*
McFayden, Shannon W. *bank holding company executive*
McGee, Liam E. *bank executive*
McGill, John Knox *lawyer*
McKay-Wilkinson, Julie Ann *minister, marriage and family therapist*
McKinnish, Richmond D. *manufacturing executive*
McMillan, William P. *lawyer*
Mehta, Kiran H. *lawyer*
Metz, Catherine Taylor *performing arts educator*
Migoya, Carlos *bank executive*
Montague, Edgar Burwell, III, (Monty Montague) *industrial designer*
Moynihan, Brian T. *finance company executive*
Mullen, Graham C. *judge*
Myers, Robert Manson *language educator, writer*
Nedzbala, Michael *lawyer*
Neel, Richard Eugene *economist, educator*
Nelson, Thomas C. *manufacturing executive*
Newitt, John Garwood, Jr. *lawyer*
O'Connor, Thomas C. *energy executive*
Oken, Marc D. *retired bank executive*
Oliver, John William Posegate *minister*
Parrish, D. Michael *manufacturing executive*
Peacock, A(lvin) Ward *textile company executive*
Pedigo, Paul F. *lawyer*
Peppers, Julius *professional football player*
Perry, Glenn *orthopedic surgeon*
Peterson, Evonne Stewart *elementary school educator*
Plunkett, Steven R. *radiologist*
Price, Joe L. *bank executive*
Pyle, Gerald Fredric *geographer, educator*
Ragan, Robert Allison *private investment executive, financial consultant*
Rawlins, Donald Ray *lawyer*
Rhue, Monika Rivera *archivist*
Rikard, William L., Jr. *lawyer*
Roberts, David A. *manufacturing executive*
Roche, Cathy *energy executive*
Rodite, Robert R.R. *research scientist, finance and computer consultant, educator*
Rogers, James Eugene *energy executive*
Rolfe, Christopher C. *energy executive*
Rutkowski, Joseph A. *manufacturing executive*
Schafermeyer, Robert William *emergency physician, educator, health policy consultant*
Schulz, Walter Kurt *accountant, information technology consultant*
Seidel, James P. *manufacturing executive*
Shappert, Gretchen C(ecilia) F(rances) *prosecutor, lawyer*
Shaw, Ruth G. *energy company executive*
Shulstad, Andrew Robert *pediatrician*
Siegel, Samuel *metals company executive*
Simmons, Charles B., Jr. *lawyer*
Sink, Robert C. *lawyer*
Sintz, Edward Francis *librarian*
Skains, Thomas E. *gas industry executive*
Smith, B. Scott *automotive executive*
Smith, Kenneth T. *retail executive*
Smith, O. Bruton *automotive company executive*
Smith, Steve *professional football player*
Smith, Wilburn Jackson, Jr. *retired bank executive*
Spangler, Clemmie Dixon, Jr. *construction company executive*
Spiro, Robert Harry, Jr. *foundation and business executive, educator*
Squires, James Ralph *development company executive*
Staley, Dawn Michelle *professional basketball player*
Stepp, James Michael *finance company executive*
Sulg, Madis *manufacturing executive, entrepreneur*
Sutton, Cecilia (Cece Sutton) *bank executive*
Swecker, Chris (Christophe E. Swecker) *protective services official, former federal agency administrator*
Taylor, Gene *bank executive*
Taylor, R. Eugene *bank executive*
Thames, Rick *publishing executive, editor-in-chief*
Thigpen, Richard Elton, Jr. *retired lawyer*
Thompson, G. Kennedy (Ken Thompson) *bank executive*
Thompson, Jocelyn Pharr *organist, director, music educator*
Thompson, John Albert, Jr. *dermatologist*
Thompson, Sydnor, Jr., (Charles William Sydnor Thompson Jr.) *lawyer, mediator, arbitrator*
Treanor, Mark C. *lawyer, diversified financial services company executive*
Trent, B. Keith *lawyer, energy executive*
Truslow, Donald K. *bank executive*
Turner, James Lee *energy executive*
Tyson, Cynthia Haldenby *academic administrator*
Valasquez, Joseph Louis *industrial engineer*
Van Allen, William Kent *lawyer*
Van Alstyne, Vance Brownell *management consultant*
Van Hoy, Philip Marshall *lawyer*
Vazquez Rivera, Ornela Amliv *psychologist*
Vincent, Sam (James Samuel Vincent) *professional basketball coach, former professional basketball player*
Vinroot, Richard Allen *lawyer, mayor*
Voorhees, Richard Lesley *federal judge*
Wagner, Kenneth Lynn *lawyer*
Walker, Clarence Wesley *lawyer*
Walker, Jewett Lynius *clergyman, church official*
Webster, Murray Alexander, Jr. *sociologist, educator*
Weinke, Chris *professional football player*
Whitfield, Fred, Jr. *professional sports team executive*
Whitney, Frank DeArmon *federal judge, former prosecutor*
Williams, Edwin Neel *newspaper editor*
Wilson, Paul Lowell *mortgage company executive, lawyer*
Wolson, Craig Alan *lawyer*
Wood, Donald Craig *retired marketing professional*
Wood, William McBrayer *lawyer*
Woodward, James Hoyt *retired academic administrator, engineering educator*
Wright, Bonnie H. *middle school educator*
Wright, Wayne Kenneth *federal agency statistician*
Wurtz, Thomas J. *bank executive*
Wyche, James Ramage *lawyer*
Xu, Mingxin *mathematics professor*
Yorke, John Bundy *lawyer*

Cherokee

Martin, Harry Corpening *lawyer, retired state supreme court justice*

Cherry Point

Knoell, Michael David *health facility administrator, military officer*

Cherryville

Huffstetler, Palmer Eugene *lawyer*
Mayhew, Kenneth Edwin, Jr. *retired transportation executive*

Chocowinity

Castle, William Eugene *retired academic administrator*

Clemmons

Foxx, Virginia Ann *congresswoman, small business owner*

Clinton

Davis, William Maxie, Jr. *lawyer*
Griffin, Betty Lou *not-for-profit developer, educator*

Columbus

Brooks, Jerry Claude *safety engineer, educator*
Wetherby, Ivor Lois *retired librarian*

Concord

Burkard, Heather C. *prosecutorial investigator*
Howard, Vivian Amick *music educator*
Smith, Ollen Bruton *sports association executive*

Cornelius
Riou, Jean-Pierre Alain *plastic surgeon*
Schneider, Lori Beth *neurologist*

Cove City
Hawkins, Elinor Dixon (Mrs. Carroll Woodard Hawkins) *retired librarian*
Miller, Wendy A. *elementary school educator*

Creedmoor
Muller, William Albert III *retired library director*

Cullowhee
Armfield, Terri Elaine *music educator, musician*
Bardo, John William *academic administrator*
Beam, Richard Squires *theater educator*
Coulter, Myron Lee *retired academic administrator*
Reed, Alfred Douglas *retired academic administrator*
Willis, Ralph Houston *mathematics professor*

Davidson
Cole, Richard Cargill *language educator*
Dixon, Stephanie Bell *elementary school educator*
Grosch, Laura Dudley *artist, educator*
Jackson, Herb *artist, educator*
Klein, Benjamin Garrett *mathematics professor, consultant*
Palmer, Edward L. *psychologist, educator, writer*
Park, Leland Madison *librarian*
Ross, Clark Grant *economics professor*
Sprague, Raymond *music educator*

Denver
McIntosh, Anita Jane *retired administrative assistant*

Dunn
Hill, Susan Beasley *recreational therapist*
Wilson, Douglas Leonard *minister, educator*

Durham
Afshari, Natalie Adel *ophthalmologist, surgeon, educator*
Agre, Peter Courtland *medical educator*
Albala, David Mois *urologist, educator*
Aldrich, John Herbert *political science professor*
Anderson, William Banks, Jr. *ophthalmology educator*
Anlyan, William George *surgeon, educator, academic administrator*
Armstrong, Brenda Estelle *pediatrician, cardiologist*
Auld, Skip (Hampton Auld) *library director*
Barker, Ben *chef, restaurant owner*
Barker, Karen *restaurant owner, chef*
Bartlett, Katharine Tiffany *dean, law educator*
Bejan, Adrian *mechanical engineering educator*
Bennett, Peter Brian *medical researcher, educator*
Bernard, Pamela Jenks *lawyer*
Bettman, James Ross *management educator*
Blackburn, John Oliver *economist, consultant*
Blazer, Dan German, II, *psychiatrist, epidemiologist*
Blazing, Michael August *internist*
Blum, Jacob Joseph *physiologist, educator*
Bollinger, Ralph Randal *surgeon, researcher*
Borges-Neto, Salvador *radiologist, cardiologist, educator*
Bradford, William Dalton *pathologist, educator*
Brantley, Jeffrey Garland *health science association administrator*
Breeden, Douglas Tower *finance educator, consultant, former dean*
Breland-Noble, Alfiee Matiese *psychologist, researcher*
Brodhead, Richard H. *academic administrator*
Brodie, Harlow Keith Hammond *psychiatrist, educator*
Bryant, Robert Leamon *mathematics educator*
Buckley, Rebecca Hatcher *allergist, immunologist, pediatrician, educator*
Budd, Louis John *language educator*
Burks, A. Wesley *pediatrics educator*
Butters, Ronald Richard *language educator*
Cai, Xinjiang *cardiologist, researcher*
Canada, Mary Whitfield *retired librarian*
Carpenter, Charles Francis *lawyer*
Carrington, Bessie Meek *librarian*
Carrington, Paul DeWitt *lawyer, educator*
Carroll, Kenneth G. *lawyer*
Carter, Calvin H., Jr. *materials engineer*
Carter, James Harvey *psychiatrist, educator*
Case, Richard W. *sports association executive*
Casey, H(orace) Craig, Jr. *electrical engineering educator*
Cayne, Bernard Stanley *editor*
Chafe, William Henry *history professor*
Chapman, Robert Lee III *real estate developer*
Chemerinsky, Erwin *law educator*
Christie, George Custis *lawyer, educator, writer*
Cohen, Harvey Jay *geriatrician, hematologist, oncologist, educator*
Cohn, Stephen Andrew *publishing executive*
Colton, Joel *historian, educator*
Colvin, O. Michael *medical association administrator, medical educator*
Conklin, George Henry *sociologist, educator*
Cook, Philip Jackson *economist, educator*
Cook-Deegan, Robert Mullan *physician, educator*
Cox, James D. *law educator*
Crawford, Jeffrey C. *oncologist, educator*
Danner, Richard Allen *dean, law educator*
Daubert, Erik Joseph *organization administrator, consultant*
Davis, Calvin De Armond *historian, educator*
Daw, Amy W. *music educator*
Dellinger, Walter Estes III *lawyer, educator*
Demott, Deborah Ann *law educator*
Dorn, Louis Otto *retired minister*
Dowell, Earl Hugh *dean, aerospace and mechanical engineering educator*
Doyle, Gloria Thorpe *secondary school educator*
Dunshee, Melanie J. *law librarian, educator*
Dzau, Victor Joseph *cardiologist, director, researcher*
Edelsbrunner, Herbert *computer scientist, educator, mathematician*
Edmond, John *engineering company executive*
Edwards, Christopher Levon *medical association administrator*
Ekici, Kivanc *aerospace engineer, researcher*
Elliot, Jeffrey M. *political science professor, department chairman*
Everett, Robinson Oscar *federal judge, educator*
Falletta, John Matthew *pediatrician, educator*
Fisher, Stewart Wayne *lawyer*
Fisk, Catherine Laura *lawyer, educator*
Fiske, Edward B. *editor, educator, journalist, consultant*
Foreman, John William *pediatrician, educator*
Frank, Michael M. *physician*
Freemark, Michael Scott *pediatric endocrinologist, educator*
Fridovich, Irwin *biochemistry professor*
Frothingham, Thomas Eliot *pediatrician*
Fulkerson, William *hospital administrator, pulmonologist*
Gainetdinov, Raul Radikovich *pharmacologist, researcher*
Georgiade, Gregory Stephen *plastic surgeon, educator*
Giannopoulos, Athina *physician, surgeon*
Gillham, Nicholas Wright *geneticist, educator*
Gillings, Dennis B. *medical products executive*
Gilliss, Catherine Lynch *vice chancellor, dean, nursing educator*
Goodwin, Frank Erik *materials engineer*
Greenfield, Joseph Cholmondeley, Jr. *physician, educator*
Gunter, Emily Diane *communications executive, marketing professional, educator, real estate developer, writer*
Guseh, James Sawalla *public administration educator*
Guttentag, Christoph *dean*
Haagen, Paul Hess *law educator*
Hammes, Gordon G. *chemistry professor*
Hammond, Charles Bessellieu *obstetrician, gynecologist, educator*
Han, Moo-Young *physicist, educator*
Harrell, Carlton (Benjamin Carlton Harrell) *retired editor, writer*
Havighurst, Clark Canfield *law educator*
Hawkins, William E. N. *newspaper editor*
Haynes, Barton Ford *medical educator*
Hellkamp, Anne Sidlo *statistician, researcher*
Hogan, Brigid L.M. *molecular biologist*
Holder, Angela Roddey *law educator*
Holsti, Ole Rudolf *political scientist, educator*
Horowitz, Donald Leonard *lawyer, arbitrator, political scientist, educator*
Jakubs, Deborah *university librarian*
James, Sherman Athonia *epidemiologist, educator*
Jarvis, Erich David *neurobiologist, educator*
Jaszczak, Ronald Jack *physicist, researcher, consultant*
Jenkins, Richard Erik *lawyer*
Jennings, Robert Burgess *experimental pathologist, medical educator*
Jirtle, Randy *medical educator, geneticist*
Johnson, Kristina M. *dean*
Joklik, Wolfgang Karl *biochemist, virologist, educator*
Katz, Samuel Lawrence *pediatrician, researcher*
Keene, Jack Donald *molecular genetics and microbiology educator*
Keller, Thomas Franklin *business administration educator*
Kelley, Allen Charles *economist, educator*
Kemper, Alex R. *pediatrician, educator*
Kirkpatrick, John Paxton *oncologist, educator*
Kishnani, Priya Sunil *medical geneticist*
Klitzman, Bruce *physiologist, plastic surgery educator, researcher*
Koepke, John Arthur *hematologist, clinical pathologist*
Koepke, Tracey Lynn *marketing professional, writer*
Kort, Wesley Albert *religious studies educator, writer*
Krakowski, Jane *actress*
Krishnan, Krishnaswamy Ranga Rama R. *psychiatry educator*
Krucoff, Mitchell Wolfe *cardiologist*
Krzyzewski, Mike (Michael William Krzyzewski) *college basketball coach*
Kuniholm, Bruce Robellet *academic administrator, educator*
Ladd, Marcia Lee *medical products executive*
Lagoo, Anand Shreeram *pathologist, educator*
Land, Kenneth Carl *sociologist, educator, demographer*
Lange, Peter *academic administrator*
Lefkowitz, Robert Joseph *biomedical researcher, educator*
Leppert, Phyllis Carolyn *obstetrician, gynecologist*
Lerner, Warren *historian, educator*
Levin, Lawrence Scott *plastic surgeon*
Lieberman, Rochelle Phyllis *small business owner*
Lockhead, Gregory Roger *retired psychology professor*
Maar, Rosina *medical products executive*
MacIntyre, Neil Ross, Jr. *medical educator*
Malling, Heinrich Valdemar *retired geneticist*
Mark, Daniel Benjamin *cardiologist*
Marsh, William Andrew III *lawyer*
Masand, Prakash S. *psychiatrist, researcher*
Matchar, David B. *physician, researcher*
Maxwell, Richard Callender *retired lawyer, educator*
McBane, Sarah Elizabeth *pharmacist, educator*
McCallie, Joanne P. *women's college basketball coach*
McClain, Paula Denice *political scientist, educator*
McMahon, John Alexander *law educator*
McNamara, James O. *physician, scientist*
Meyer, Horst *physics professor*
Meyers, Eric Mark *religion educator*
Michener, James Lloyd *medical educator*
Mikhailov, Stepan Fedorovich *physicist, researcher*
Miller, David Edmond *physician*
Modrich, Paul L. *biochemistry professor*
Moehring, Amanda J. *geneticist*
Mushak, Paul *toxicologist, consultant*
Nakarai, Charles Frederick Toyozo *music educator*
Nowicki, Stephen *dean, biology professor*
Ohman, E. Magnus *cardiologist, educator*
Olsen, Elise *dermatologist, researcher*
O'Neal, Cynthia Ann *lawyer*
Ortel, Thomas Lee *oncologist, hematologist, educator*
Ostbye, Truls *medical researcher, educator*
Otterbourg, Robert Kenneth *public relations consultant, writer*
Parker, William *education educator*
Pearsall, George Wilbur *materials scientist, mechanical engineer, consultant, educator*
Pearsall, Samuel Haff III *ecologist, geographer, foundation administrator*
Petroski, Henry *engineering educator, writer*
Pimm, Stuart L. *ecology educator*
Pinnell, Sheldon Richard *dermatologist, researcher, retired educator*
Pirrung, Michael Craig *chemistry professor, consultant*
Pizzo, Salvatore Vincent *pathologist*
Plonsey, Robert *electrical and biomedical engineer*
Quin, Louis DuBose *chemist, educator*
Quinn, Jarus William *physicist, former association executive*
Rabinovich, Egla Consuelo *pediatrician, rheumatologist*
Raetz, Christian R. H. *biochemistry professor*
Robboy, Stanley J. *pathologist, educator*
Robertson, Horace Bascomb, Jr. *retired law educator*
Rondinelli, Dennis A(ugust) *business administration educator, researcher*
Rossiter, Alexander, Jr. *publishing executive, editor*
Rouse, Doris Jane *physiologist, research scientist*
Rowe, Thomas Dudley, Jr. *law educator*
Sabiston, David Coston, Jr. *surgeon, educator*
Schmalbeck, Richard Louis *dean, lawyer*
Schwarcz, Steven Lance *lawyer, educator*
Scott, Anne Byrd Firor *history professor*
Seewaldt, Victoria L. *medical educator, researcher*
Semans, Mary Duke Biddle Trent *foundation administrator*
Sharma, Anand *manufacturing executive*
Shelburne, John Daniel *pathologist*
Sheppard, Blair H. *dean, finance company executive, educator*
Simons, Elwyn LaVerne *physical anthropologist, primatologist, paleontologist, educator*
Sloan, Maceo Kennedy *lawyer, investment company executive*
Smith, Grover C(leveland) *language educator*
Smith, Harmon Lee, Jr. *clergyman, theology studies educator*
Staddon, John Eric Rayner *psychology professor, neurobiology professor, zoology professor*
Staelin, Richard *business administration educator*
Steinmetz, David Curtis *religious studies educator*
Stiff-Roberts, Adrienne D. *electrical engineer, educator*
Story, Tyler James *psychologist, educator*
Surwit, Richard Samuel *psychology professor*
Talley, Joseph Eugene *psychologist*
Taylor, James Francis *marketing professional*
Tedder, Thomas Fletcher *immunology educator, researcher*
Thompson, James Howard *historian, librarian*
Thompson, William Moreau *radiologist, educator*
Toloza, Eric M. *thoracic surgeon*
Tselev, Alexander *physicist, researcher*
Utku, Senol *civil engineer, computer science educator*
Voynow, Judith Ann *pediatric pulmonologist, educator*
Ward, Robert *composer, educator, conductor*
Weiner, Richard David *psychiatrist, researcher*
Wilcox, Allen James *epidemiologist*
Wilkins, Robert Henry *neurosurgeon, educator, editor*
Williams, George Walton *language educator*
Williams, Redford Brown *medical educator*
Wilson-Whitaker, Portia Elaine *school system administrator*
Young, Terri L. *ophthalmologist*
Yu, Bing *researcher*
Zenn, Michael Robert *plastic and reconstructive surgeon*

Efland
Weinberg, Gerhard Ludwig *history professor*

Elizabeth City
Boyle, Terrence W. *federal judge*
Griffin, Gladys Bogues *critical care nurse, educator*
Storie, Eric Duane *science administrator*
Williams, Rita Carroll *protective services official, language educator, poet, librarian*

Ellerbe
Rankin, Pressley Robinson, Jr. *physician*

Elon
Arcaro, Thomas E. *sociologist, educator*
Buckmaster, Matthew Tobe *musician, educator*
Nash, Katie C. *archivist*
Powell, William Council, Sr. *service company executive*
Tolley, Jerry Russell *academic administrator*

Fairmont
Byrne, James Frederick *banker*
Spencer, Melissa Johanna *psychotherapist, special education educator*

Fairview
Brown, Gregory Neil *academic administrator, forester, educator*

Fayetteville
Barnicle, Mary Anne *music educator, piano accompanist*
Batts, Dorothy Marie *clergywoman, educator, writer*
Bunting, John Charles *pastoral associate, youth minister*
Carney, Karen Rose *music educator, pianist*
Curry, Virginia Frances *retired language educator*
Hagans, Valerie Mae Gee *special education educator*
Jansen, Michael John *health facility administrator*
Jones, Villie *music educator*
Jordan, Karla Salge *retired primary school educator*
Lowe, James Edward, Jr. *plastic and reconstructive surgeon*
MacRae, Elizabeth (Elizabeth MacRae Halsey) *counselor, actor*
McLaurin, Jocee Elizabeth *elementary school educator*
Mitchell, Ronnie Monroe *lawyer, educator*
Redding, Bobbie Newman *lawyer*
Richardson, Emilie White *manufacturing, investment company executive, educator*
Roe, Kathryn Jane *elementary school educator*
Ruppe, Arthur Maxwell *retired lawyer*
Shaffer, Denny Richard *small business owner*
Soderberg, Herman Albert *minister, educator*
Townsend, William Jackson *lawyer*
Truong, Dothang *information scientist, educator*

Fearrington Village
Cell, Gillian Townsend *retired historian, educator*

Flat Rock
Bailey, Louise Howe *columnist, educator*
Childress, Richard Thomas *international business consultant*
Oliver, Ann Breeding *secondary school educator, art dealer*
Weill, Hans *medical educator*

Fletcher
Hill, Ronald Charles *surgeon, educator*
Seagle, J. Harold *lawyer*

Fort Bragg
Anderson, Curtis Thorwald, II, *military officer*
Fishback, Ian *military officer*
Laney, Patricia Ann *elementary school educator*
Stafford, C. Stewart *educational consultant, educator*

Four Oaks
Jordan, Lyndon Kirkman *physician*

Franklin
Earhart, Eileen Magie *retired elementary school and child and family life educator*
Johnson, Herbert Alan *historian, lawyer*
Kinard, Cynthia Cochran *artist, writer*

Franklinton
Elmore, Cenieth Catherine *music educator*

Gastonia
Burns, Judith O'Dell *library assistant, educator*
Crissman, Katherine Kolb *counseling administrator*
Easter, Willie, Jr. *artist, writer*
Fayssoux, Patricia Ann Paysour *music educator*
Kimbrell, Willard Duke *textiles executive*
Lawson, William David III *retired cotton company executive*
Patterson, Elaine Wilcox *art educator*
Stott, Grady Bernell *lawyer*
Teem, Paul Lloyd, Jr. *bank executive*

Goldsboro
Strickland, Donald Bennett *lawyer*

Granite Falls
Humphreys, Kenneth King *engineer, educator, professional society administrator*

Greensboro
Allen, Jesse Owen III *organizational behavior specialist*
Blackwell, William Ernest *broadcast executive*
Bolick, Ronnie Lee *mechanical engineer*
Brotherton, Joseph Faler *lawyer*
Bullock, Frank William, Jr. *lawyer, retired federal judge*
Chandler, Austin Grace *psychologist*
Chow, Anthony Shong-yu *library sciences educator*
Clark, Clifton Bob *physicist*
Clark, David McKenzie *lawyer*
Cole, Johnnetta Betsch *former academic administrator, educator*
Cummings, Candace S. *lawyer, apparel company executive*
Cushman, Keith *English professor*
Davis, Ferd Leary, Jr. *law educator, consultant*
Davis, Herbert Owen *lawyer*
Deere, James Dickson *singer, pianist, voice and music educator, writer*
Detschel, William Frederick *information scientist*
Englar, John David *finance educator, textiles executive, lawyer*
Eromon, David Ighogboya *electronics engineer, educator*

Evans, Jonathan Christopher *social worker*
Floyd, Jack William *lawyer*
French, Lenny Sue *elementary school educator*
Fujino, Michimasa *aeronautical engineer*
Gause, Charles Phillip *education educator*
Goldman, Bert Arthur *psychologist, educator*
Goulder, Gerald Polster *retail executive, management consultant, lawyer*
Hammond, David Alan *stage director, educator*
Hanson, Randall A. *lawyer*
Harris-Offutt, Rosalyn Marie *counselor, consultant, mental health nurse, writer*
Helms-VanStone, Mary Wallace *anthropology educator*
Houston, Frank Matt *dermatologist*
Hunter, Bynum Merritt *retired lawyer*
Jellicorse, John Lee *communications and theatre educator*
Johnson, Marshall Hardy *investment company executive*
Jones, Thomas Owen, Jr. *finance educator, military officer*
Knesel, Ernest Arthur, Jr. *health facility administrator, chemicals executive*
Koonce, Neil Wright *lawyer*
Lloyd, Robert Blackwell, Jr. *lawyer*
Locke, John R. *music educator, director*
Lou, Jianzhong *chemical engineer, educator*
Malveaux, Julianne Marie *academic administrator, economist, writer*
McDaniel, James Mark, Jr. *health care executive*
McDonald, Mackey J. *apparel executive*
Medford, James A. *lawyer*
Melvin, Charles Edward, Jr. *lawyer*
Michalak, Sarah C. *university librarian*
Middleton, Herman David, Sr. *retired theater educator*
Miller, Robert Louis *dean, chemistry professor*
Mozell, Herbert Lee *mental health services professional*
Neerman, Sandra M. *library director*
Noble, Ralph C. *animal scientist, department chairman*
Oliver, Donna H. *academic administrator, former secondary school educator*
Oliver, Terry James *retired electronics engineer, communications engineer*
Osteen, William L. *federal judge*
Penley, Virginia Long *social worker*
Penninger, Frieda Elaine *retired literature educator*
Reed, Robert Alan *lawyer*
Revell, Henry, Jr. *social services administrator, retired education educator*
Ryan, John R. *educational association administrator, former academic administrator, career military officer*
Schell, Braxton *lawyer*
Schunk, Dale Hansen *dean*
Schwenn, Lee William *retired health facility administrator*
Semmler, Carl D. *lawyer*
Seong, Younho *engineering educator*
Shaw, Robert Gilbert *retired state legislator, food service executive*
Shearer, Robert K. *apparel executive*
Shelton, David Howard *economics professor*
Slaughter, James H. *lawyer*
Smith, Lanty L(loyd) *lawyer, corporate financial executive*
Staab, Thomas Robert *consumer product company financial executive*
Stocks, William L. *federal judge*
Sullivan, Patricia A. *academic administrator*
Swan, George Steven *law educator*
Tilley, Norwood Carlton, Jr. *federal judge*
Tucker, Robert Rand *lawyer*
Wagoner, Anna Mills S. *prosecutor*
Wang, Jie *computer science educator*
Ward, Charles A. *federal agency administrator*
Ward Black, Janet *lawyer*
Watson, Robert Winthrop *poet*
Wiseman, Eric C. *apparel executive*
Zopf, Evelyn LaNoel Montgomery *retired guidance counselor*

Greenville
Aziz, Shahnaz *psychology professor*
Babb, Joseph Dolby *physician*
Ballard, Steven C. *academic administrator*
Bearden, James Hudson *university official*
Beers, Burton Floyd *historian, educator*
Colombo, Michael Allen *lawyer*
Dixon, Phillip Ray, Sr. *lawyer*
Duffy, Michael *art educator*
Eakin, Richard Ronald *academic administrator, mathematics educator*
Gilham, Hanna Kaltenbrunner *writer*
Habal, Nizar *oncologist, surgeon, educator*
Howard, Malcolm Jones *federal judge*
Jackson, Bobby Rand *minister*
James, James Franklin *psychiatrist, educator, academic administrator*
Johnson, Cynda Ann *physician, educator*
Jones, Walter Beaman, Jr. *congressman*
Khuri, Soumaya Makdissi *mathematics professor*
Knighten, Christopher Blair *conductor, educator*
Lee, Kenneth Stuart *neurosurgeon, educator*
Meggs, William Joel *toxicologist, allergist, emergency physician, educator*
Pories, Walter Julius *surgeon, educator*
Stanfield, Charles Freeman *chemist*
Stevens, David Boyette *law educator*
Tingelstad, Jon Bunde *retired pediatrician, educator*
Wallin, Leland Dean *artist, educator*
Waugh, William Howard *physician, research scientist*
White, Larry Nash *library and information scientist*
Wiley, John Edwin *cytogeneticist*
Wilkerson, William Holton *banker*

Hampstead
Snyder, Clair Allison *banker*
Walters, Sherwood George *management consultant, educator*

Harrisburg
Economaki, Chris Constantine (Christopher) *publishing executive*
Hendrick, Joseph Riddick, III, (Rick) *race team owner*
Patchen, Kelly A. *elementary school educator*

Hayesville
Galloway, David Craig *chemist*

Henderson
Serafin, Donald *plastic surgeon, educator*

Hendersonville
Blount, Cindy Karen *web site designer, web programmer*
Brittain, James Edward *science and technology educator, researcher*
Carney, Robert Arthur *restaurant executive*
Franks, Stephen Field *retired judge*
Harris, James Braxton *retired humanities educator, freelance/self-employed writer*
Jefferson, Letitia Gibson *rehabilitation counselor*
Reinhart, John Belvin *retired child and adolescent psychiatrist, educator*
Roberts, James Allen *retired urologist, educator*
Saby, John Sanford *physicist, consultant*
Tatreau, (Dolores) Maxine *artist*
Tatsch, Jacki Lynn *music educator, diversified financial services company executive*
Trexler, Edgar Ray *minister, editor*

Hertford
Johnson, Donald Lee *retired agricultural materials processing company executive*
McClung, Kenneth Austin, Jr. *training executive, performance consultant*

Hickory
Ballenger, Cass (Thomas Cass Ballenger) *former congressman, retired plastics company executive*
Beasley, Diana F. *biology educator*
Drendel, Frank Matthew *cable company executive*
George, Boyd Lee *consumer products company executive*
Lefler, Wade Hampton, Jr. *ophthalmologist*
Smith, Young Merritt, Jr. *lawyer*

High Point
Bardelas, Jose Antonio *allergist*
Burton, Ward *professional race car driver*
Chavis, Glenn Romero *retired historian, writer*
Corey, James William *political scientist, educator*
Draelos, Zoe Diana *dermatologist, consultant*
Fenn, Ormon William, Jr. *furniture company executive*
Kandt, Raymond S. *neurologist*
Keever, Mary Moore *elementary school educator*
McAllister, Kenneth Wayne *lawyer*
Palmer, Pamela Murrill *educator*
Pate, William Patrick *city manager*
Phillips, Earl Norfleet, Jr. *diplomat, financial services executive*
Scearse, Patricia Dotson *nursing educator, dean*
Sheahan, Robert Emmett *lawyer, consultant*
Weatherford, Carole Boston *publications specialist*

Highlands
Shaffner, Randolph Preston *shop owner, educator, writer, publisher*

Hillsborough
Adams, Rex *dean*
Goodwin, Craufurd David *economics professor*
Johnston, William Webb *pathologist, educator*
Piper, Don Courtney *political scientist, educator*

Holly Springs
Booth, Penelope Partridge *secondary school educator, writer, principal*

Horse Shoe
Roskoski, Robert, Jr. *biochemist, educator, author*

Huntersville
Atrak, Taisser M. *pediatrician, director*
Nowlin, Connie Blackwell *artist*
Stamey, Derrick *management consultant*
Stewart, Tony *professional race car driver*

Indian Trail
Brewer, James Timothy *music educator, director*

Iron Station
Wise, Kimberly Anne (Schillaci) *musician, educator*

Jacksonville
Guyer, Charles Grayson, II, *psychologist*
Kimball, Lynn Jerome *historian*

Jamestown
Schmitt, William Allen *lawyer*

Jefferson
Franklin, Robert McFarland *book publisher*
Merrion, Arthur Benjamin *mathematics professor, tree farmer*

Kannapolis
Brown, Bachman Storch, Jr. *lawyer*
Thigpen, Alton Hill *transportation executive*

Kinston
Baker-Gardner, Jewelle *interior designer, business consultant*
Petteway, Samuel Bruce *college president*

Kitty Hawk
Sjoerdsma, Albert *research and development company executive*
Tucker, Don Eugene *retired lawyer*

Kure Beach
Wiebe, Richard Herbert *reproductive endocrinologist, educator*

Lake Junaluska
Martinson, Jacob Christian, Jr. *academic administrator*
Stanton, Donald Sheldon *retired academic administrator*
Tullis, Edward Lewis *retired bishop*

Lake Toxaway
Raynolds, Elaine Spalding *sales executive, photojournalist*

Laurinburg
Deegan, John, Jr. *academic administrator, educator, researcher*
Gilbert, Marie Rogers *poet*

Leasburg
Treacy, Sandra Joanne Pratt *retired art educator, illustrator*

Leicester
Entzi, Karen Russell *orchestra educator*

Leland
Karch, Jacqueline *artist*

Lexington
Carlton, Robbin Briley *elementary school educator*
Cuthrell, Carl Edward *retired clergyman, lawyer, educator*
Frontz, Leslie Kay *art educator*
Snyder, James Eugene, Jr. *lawyer*

Lillington
O'Brien, Eileen Kathryn *art educator*

Littleton
Skinner, Sue Dossett *retired vocational director*

Louisburg
Miller, Brian Daniel *music educator, organist*

Lumberton
Johnson, Judy Van *minister, educator*
Tolar, Anne Melton *minister, music educator*

Maiden
Peeler, Forrest Edwards *retired physician*

Manteo
Irby, Katherine Scott Roche *educational association administrator*

Marion
Burgin, Charles Edward *lawyer*

Mars Hill
Greene, Tena Lorraine *singer, educator, actor*
Newton, Paul George *musician, retired librarian*

Matthews
Kocsis, Joan Bosco *elementary school educator*
Twisdale, Harold Winfred *dentist*
Veyera, Jeffrey Alan *bank executive*

Maxton
Ellis, Hubert Lee *retired secondary school educator*

Mebane
Langley, Ricky Lee *occupational medicine physician*

Midland
Voncannon, Brian Everett *writer, scriptwriter, radio personality, naturopath*

Mill Spring
Saunders, Barry Wayne *state official*

Monroe
Casstevens, Charles Franklin, Jr. *music educator, minister*
Kyle, John Emery *retired religious organization administrator*
Taylor, Jimmy Lynn *retired family practice physician, administrator*

Mooresville
Badr, Gamal Moursi *legal consultant*
Black, Kenneth W., Jr. *retail executive*
Busch, Kurt *race car driver*
Castroneves, Hélio *race car driver*
Earnhardt, Dale, Jr. *race car driver*
Earnhardt, Teresa *race team owner*
Edwards, Carl *race car driver*
Faires, Ian Matthew *music educator*
Johnston, James Wesley *retired consumer products company executive*
Mabry, Joseph M.(Mike), Jr. *consumer products company executive*
Martin, Mark *race car driver*
McCanless, Ross William *lawyer, retail executive*
Münter, Leilani Maaja *race car driver*
Niblock, Robert A. *consumer home products company executive*
Waltrip, Michael Curtis *professional race car driver*

Morehead City
Beattie, Elise Meredith *artist*
Wainwright, George L., Jr. *retired state supreme court justice*

Morganton
Baden, Thomas James *dermatologist*
Carpenter III, Harry Everett *social sciences educator, history professor*
Stevenson, C. Donald *youth organization executive, folk artist*

Morrisville
Baumann, Karsten *engineer, researcher*
Bolognesi, Dani Paul *virologist, educator*
Harker, Brian J. *tobacco company executive*
Harrison, Pete (Robert E. Harrison) *tobacco company executive*
Melby, Thomas Edwin *clinical virologist, medical writer*

Morven
Lowe, David Wayne *elementary school and education educator*

Mount Airy
Thoppil, Cecil Koshey *pediatrician, consultant, educator*
Woltz, Howard Osler, Jr. *retired metal products executive*

Mount Gilead
Culyer, Richard C. III *education educator, consultant*

Mount Olive
Marbais, Peter Christian *language educator*
Raper, William Burkette *retired college president*

Murfreesboro
White, Martin Christopher *academic administrator*

Murphy
Bata, Rudolph Andrew, Jr. *lawyer*
Holcomb, Linda Laine *elementary school educator, director*
Pezzella, Jerry James, Jr. *investment and real estate company executive*

Nashville
High, (Mary) Elizabeth Hilley *retired art educator*
Penick, Angela Lucas *elementary school educator*

New Bern
Davis, James Lee *lawyer*
Jones, Victor Thomas, Jr. *librarian*
Linkonis, Suzanne Newbold *retired probation officer, retired counselor*
McKee, Francis John *medical association consultant, lawyer*
Moeller, Dade William *environmental engineer, educator*
Overholt, Hugh Robert *lawyer, retired military officer*
Painter, Jack Timberlake *civil engineer*
Sinning, Mark Alan *thoracic and vascular surgeon*
Whitehurst, Brooks Morris *chemical engineer*

Newland
Campany, Kay Hudkins *biology educator, assistant principal*
Lustig, Susan Gardner *occupational therapist*

North Wilkesboro
Keener, Gaither McDonald, Jr. *corporate lawyer*
Parsons, Irene Adelaide *management consultant*
Stone, Larry Dean *consumer products company executive*

Pembroke
Curtis, Anthony R. *communications educator*
Curtis, Judith Genevicz *communications educator*
Meadors, Allen Coats *health facility and academic administrator, educator*

Pfafftown
Wood, Stephen Wray *minister, educator, legislator, singer, songwriter*

Pilot Mountain
Slomanski-Ward, Patricia Ann *minister*

Pine Knoll Shores
Graham, Gloria Flippin *dermatologist*

Pinehurst
Carroll, Kent Jean *retired naval officer*
Heim, Lori Joan *physician*
Huizenga, John Robert *nuclear chemist, educator*
Linville, Ray Pate *English educator, retired military officer, editor, writer*
McDannald, Clyde Elliott, Jr. *management consultation company executive*
Nordloh, David Joseph *literature and language professor, dean*
O'Neill, John Joseph, Jr. *retired chemicals executive*
Rees, Clifford Harcourt, Jr., (Ted Rees) *consulting company executive, retired trade association administrator, military officer*
Swanson, Richard Everett *physics professor, dean*

Pisgah Forest
Albyn, Richard Keith *retired architect*

Pittsboro
Boyce, Emily Stewart *retired library and information scientist, educator*
Cotter, Michael William *retired ambassador*
Griffith, Katherine Scott *retired communications executive, librarian, reporter*
Kachergis, Joyce W. *book designer*
Richardson, Richard Judson *retired political science professor*
Squire, Alexander *management consultant*

Raleigh
Aiken, Clay (Clayton Holmes Aiken) *singer*
Allen, Steven Glen *economics and business professor*
Aronson, Arthur Lawrence *retired veterinarian, toxicologist, educator, pharmacologist*

Aspnes, David Erik *physicist, researcher*
Atkinson, June St Clair *school system administrator*
Baker, Stanley Beckwith *education educator*
Banker, Maureen Joyce *artist, educator*
Bar, Roselyn R. *legal association administrator, lawyer, executive secretary*
Barish, Charles Franklin *internist, gastroenterologist, researcher*
Barnhardt, Robert Alexander *retired dean*
Barrett, Rolin Farrar, Jr. *mechanical engineer, consultant*
Bateman, Angela Anderson *anesthetist*
Batson, Jonathon Kingsley *composer, singer*
Baynes, Ronald Edward *pharmacologist, educator*
Beatty, Kenneth Orion, Jr. *chemical engineer, educator*
Bernholc, Jerzy *physicist, educator*
Bitzer, Donald Lester *electrical engineer, educator, retired lab administrator*
Blackburn, James B. III *lawyer*
Boone, Mary L. *library director*
Boyette, Richard T. *lawyer*
Brady, Edward Thomas *state supreme court justice*
Brind'Amour, Rod *professional hockey player*
Brown, Robert Dale *wildlife science educator, dean*
Brown, William Harris *editor*
Burkholder, JoAnn M. *botany educator*
Burris, Craven Allen *retired college administrator, educator*
Carlton, Alfred Pershing, Jr. *lawyer*
Carter, Jean Gordon *lawyer*
Case, Charles Dixon *lawyer*
Chou, Wushow *retired computer scientist*
Chukwu, Ethelbert Nwakuche *mathematics professor*
Clapp, Allen Linville *electric supply and communications utility consultant, mediator/arbitrator*
Clarke, Lewis James *landscape architect*
Cole, Erik *professional hockey player*
Cook, Maurice Gayle *soil science educator, consultant*
Cooper, Arthur Wells *retired ecologist, educator*
Cooper, Roy Asberry III *state attorney general*
Cunningham, Michael *lawyer*
Davey, Charles Bingham *soil scientist, educator*
Davis, Egbert Lawrence III *lawyer*
Davis, Janice *school system administrator*
Doherty, Robert Cunningham *retired advertising executive*
Dolce, Carl John *education administration educator*
Donadio, Donald A. *lawyer*
Dorsett, James K. III *lawyer*
Doyle, Kevin Michael *otolaryngologist*
Dunphy, Edward James *science educator, crop extension specialist*
Eagles, Sidney Smith, Jr. *retired judge*
Easley, Michael F. *governor*
Eberly, Harry Landis *retired communications company executive*
Edens, Frank Wesley *physiologist*
Edmunds, Robert Holt, Jr. *state supreme court justice*
Edwards, (Mary) Elizabeth *lawyer, writer*
Effron, Seth Alan *editor, journalist*
Ellis, Lester Neal, Jr. *lawyer*
Ellis, Richard W. *lawyer*
Evans, Margaret Griffin *music educator*
Fantz, Janet Nelsen *school psychologist*
Fedewa, Michael Joseph *school system administrator*
Flournoy, William Louis, Jr. *landscape architect*
Francis, Ron *professional sports team executive, retired professional hockey player*
Freeman, Franklin Edward, Jr. *government agency administrator*
Gale, James L. *lawyer*
Gardner, Robin Pierce *engineering educator*
Garriss, Phyllis Weyer *music educator, performer*
Gillette, Dale Alan *retired research scientist*
Glass, Fred Stephen *lawyer*
Goodman, Major Merlin *botanical sciences educator*
Gordon, Morris Aaron *medical mycologist*
Gould, Christopher Robert *physics professor*
Graham, William Edgar, Jr. *lawyer, utilities executive*
Hall, Carol K. *chemical engineering educator, researcher*
Hansley, Lee *art dealer*
Hardin, Eugene Brooks, Jr. *bank executive*
Hardin, James W. *botanist, educator, herbarium curator*
Hardison, Cynthia Ann Stoltze *retired hematologist, oncologist*
Harrison, Cecil W., Jr. *lawyer*
Hartford, Maureen A. *academic administrator*
Havlin, John Leroy *soil scientist, educator*
Hawkins, Eleanor Carroll *veterinary educator*
Hedican, Bret *professional hockey player*
Hoch, Paul Frederick, Jr. *history educator*
Hodgson, Ernest *toxicologist, educator*
Holton, William Coffeen *electrical engineering executive*
Hudson, Robin E. *state supreme court justice*
Huff, Ann Linnea *music educator*
Huggard, John Parker *lawyer*
Hughes, Francis P. *medical association administrator*
Hunt, James Baxter, Jr. *lawyer, former governor*
Hunter, Richard Samford, Jr. *lawyer*
Imade, Lucky Osagie *political scientist, educator*
Jarrett, Polly Hawkins *retired secondary school educator*
Jessen, David Wayne *accountant*
Johnson, Mary Pauline (Polly Johnson) *nursing administrator*
Johnson, William Dean *power company executive*
Joyner, Walton Kitchin *lawyer*
Kapp, Michael Keith *lawyer*
Karmanos, Peter, Jr. *computer company executive, professional sports team executive*
Kirk-Duggan, Michael Allan *retired law, economics and computer sciences educator*
Kolbas, Robert Michael *electrical engineering educator*
Kuhler, Renaldo Gillet *retired museum director, medical illustrator*
Lancaster, H(arold) Martin *congressman, academic administrator*
Larsen, Ralph Irving *retired environmental engineer*
Laviolette, Peter *professional hockey coach*
Leak, Robert Edwards *economic development consultant*
Lee, Howard N. *educational association administrator*
Lenard, Mary Jane *finance educator*
Lilliston, Andrew Wilson, Jr. *lawyer*
Littleton, Isaac Thomas III *retired library director*
Loboa, Elizabeth Grace *biomedical engineer, educator*
Long, David W. *lawyer*
Loper, Johnny M. *lawyer*
Lowe, Sidney *men's college and former professional basketball coach*
Lynch, John Christopher *lawyer*
Lynema, Emily *library and information scientist, university librarian*
Mac Cormac, Earl Ronald *retired education educator*
Maidon, Carolyn Howser *director*
Malecha, Marvin John *architect, academic administrator*
Markoff, Brad Steven *lawyer*
Marshall, Elaine Folk *state official*
Martin, John Charles *judge*
Martin, Mark D. *State Supreme Court Justice*
Masnari, Nino Antonio *electrical engineer, educator*
McArthur, John R. *utilities executive, lawyer*
McGee, Linda Mace *judge, lawyer*
McGehee, Robert B. *energy executive*
McKinney, Donald Lee *magazine editor*
McNish, Susan Kirk *retired lawyer*
Memory, Jasper Durham *academic administrator, physics professor*
Michielsen, Stephen *chemistry professor*
Millberg, John C. *lawyer*
Mitchell, Burley Bayard, Jr. *lawyer*
Mitchell, Gary Earl *physicist, researcher*
Mitchell, Memory Farmer *retired communications executive*
Moore, Nancey Fay *history educator*
Moore, Richard Hancock *lawyer, state official*
Moore, Thomas Lloyd *library director*
Moreland, Donald Edwin *physiologist*
Morris-Bryant, Edye Darlene *principal*
Murray, Raymond Le Roy *nuclear engineering educator*
Neely, Charles B., Jr. *lawyer*
Nelson, Larry A. *statistics educator, consultant*
Newby, Paul Martin *state supreme court justice*
Newman, Slater Edmund *psychologist, educator*
Nutter, Susan K. *librarian, academic administrator*
Oblinger, James L. *academic administrator*
Odum, Jeffery Neal *mechanical engineer*
Osteryoung, Janet Gretchen *chemistry professor*
Ozturk, Mehmet Cevdet *engineering educator*
Pace, Andrew K. *information technology library director*
Paesler, Michael *physics professor, department chairman*
Parker, John Hill *lawyer*
Parker, Joseph Mayon *retired publishing executive*
Parker, Sarah Elizabeth *state supreme court chief justice*
Parramore, Barbara Mitchell *education educator*
Parsons, William Jonathan *cardiologist*
Patterson, William S. *lawyer*
Pendry, Pattie Louise *writer*
Penick, John E. *education educator*
Perdue, Beverly Eaves *lieutenant governor, geriatric consultant*
Phillips, Oliverio Michelsen *retired chemical engineer*
Pittman, James Morris (Jack Pittman) *cartoonist, illustrator, character designer, consultant*
Poe, Terry Lynn *music educator*
Powell, Durwood Royce *lawyer*
Prior, William Allen *electronics company executive*
Rahmani, Carol Hipp *retired school system administrator, psychologist*
Reeves, Ralph Bernard III *publishing executive*
Reynolds, C. Lewis, Jr. *materials scientist, educator*
Rhodes, Donald Robert *musicologist, educator, retired electrical engineer*
Riggs, Wayne *artist, photographer*
Risher, James A. *electronics executive*
Riviere, Jim Edmond, Jr. *pharmacologist, toxicologist, educator*
Roach, Wesley Linville *lawyer, insurance executive*
Robinson, Charlotte Hill *artist*
Robinson, Prezell Russell *academic administrator*
Rusher, Mary Nash Kelly *lawyer*
Rutherford, Jim *professional sports team executive*
Sanders, Douglas Charles *horticulturist, researcher, educator*
Sanford, Jo Anne *state agency administrator*
Scott, Peter M. III *utility company executive*
Scott, Stephen Carlos *academic administrator*
Simpson, Steven Drexell *lawyer*
Sloan, O. Temple, Jr. *automotive equipment executive*
Smith, Joseph A., Jr. *state agency administrator*
Smith, Sherwood Hubbard, Jr. *retired electric utilities executive*
Sneed, Ronald Ernest *retired project engineer, engineering educator*
Spearman, Robert Worthington *lawyer*
Speer, Kevin Paul *surgeon*
Spruill, W. Murray *lawyer*
Staal, Eric *professional hockey player*
Stevens, Richard Yates *state senator*
Stillman, Cory *professional hockey player*
Stroup, Richard Lyndell *economist, educator, writer*
Stuber, Charles William *retired genetics educator, researcher, director*
Sudhakar, Nori *materials scientist, researcher*
Suhr, Paul Augustine *lawyer*
Sun, Ying-Hsuan *research scientist*
Sutton, Ronnie Neal *state legislator, lawyer*
Swaisgood, Harold Everett *biochemist, educator*
Szulik, Matthew J. *information technology executive*
Tally, Lura Self *state legislator*
Thompson Cornwall, Lonieta Aurora *music educator, consultant*
Timmons, Sean Abbott *lawyer*
Timmons-Goodson, Patricia *state supreme court justice*
Tucker, Helen Welch *writer*
Turinsky, Paul Josef *nuclear engineer, educator*
Valois, Robert Arthur *lawyer*
Ward, Cam *professional hockey player*
Wehring, Bernard William *nuclear engineering educator*
Weisel, Michael Lloyd *lawyer, educator*
Wesley, Glen *professional hockey player*
Wetsch, John Robert *information scientist*
Wetsch, Laura Johnson *lawyer*
Whitney, Ray *professional hockey player*
Whitten, Jerry Lynn *chemistry professor*
Willer, Edward Herman *real estate broker*
Williams, Hugh Alexander, Jr. *retired mechanical engineer, consultant*
Wilson, Donald Hurst III *biopharmaceutical industry executive*
Windham, Donald Eric *bioinformatics analyst*
Winstead, Nash Nicks *academic administrator, plant pathologist*
Wynne, Johnny Calvin *dean, plant pathologist, researcher*
Yim, Man-Sung *engineering educator, consultant*
Youngman, Lola Jeanne *music educator*
Yow, Kay (Sandra Kay Yow) *women's college basketball coach*
Zelnak, Stephen P., Jr. *construction materials company executive*
Zorowski, Carl Frank *engineering educator, academic administrator*

Randleman
Jordan, Lillian B. *judge*
Petty, Richard *retired race car driver*

Research Triangle Park
Advani, Deepak *computer company executive*
Atkins, John L. III *architect*
Bolen, M. Christopher *lawyer*
Bond, Enriqueta Carter *science administrator*
Bottomley, Gregory E. *electrical engineer, researcher*
Everett, LaTonya Michelle *computer engineer*
Fisher, Robert Perry *environmental scientist, researcher*
Gentzsch, Wolfgang *grid computing and networking service company executive*
Haynes, Victoria F. *science administrator*
Hornberger, Keith Robert *chemist*
Isler, Raymond Earl *engineer*
Mumford, Stephen Douglas *research scientist*
Reynolds, Peter James *physicist*
Roses, Allen David *neurologist, educator*
Schwartz, David A. *federal agency administrator*
Selkirk, James Kirkwood *biochemist, researcher*
Wani, Mansukhlal Chhaganlal *chemist*
Welborn, Reich Lee *lawyer*
Whichard, Willis Padgett *lawyer, retired educator, judge*
Zeng, Ming *molecular biologist, researcher*

Rich Square
Baugham, Samuel McCoy *actor, painter*

Robbinsville
Ginn, Ronn *architect, urban planner, general contractor*

Rockingham
Robertson, Ralph S. *secondary school principal*

Rocky Mount
Ellis, J(ames) Nicholas *lawyer*
Killoran, Thomas M. *mathematics professor, department chairman*
Stubbs, Will, Jr. *pharmaceutical company manager*
Wordsworth, Jerry L. *wholesale distribution executive*
Zipf, Robert Eugene, Jr. *legal medicine consultant, pathologist*

Rougemont
Holeman, Betty Jean *counseling administrator*

Rutherfordton
Crummie, Ann Vaughn *mental health services professional*

Salisbury
Candler, Faxon David *small business owner*
Higbee, Dale (Strohe) *musician, retired psychologist*
Jenkins, Jimmy Raymond *academic administrator*
McKinzie, James S. *librarian*
Troxler, Willie Thomasene *retired elementary school educator*
Tseng, Howard Shih Chang *business educator, investment company executive, economics professor*
Watkins, Kellee Dillard *literature and language educator*

Saluda
Cutright, Phillips *sociologist, educator*
McCutcheon, John Tinney, Jr. *retired journalist*

Sanford
Brown, Eva Everlean *business executive*
Decker, Roger Walter *biologist, researcher*
Harrington, Anthony Ross *radio announcer, educator*
Higgins, George Edward *sculptor*
Raisig, Paul Jones, Jr. *lawyer*
Sodini, Peter J. *food service executive*

Seven Lakes
Reilly, David Henry *retired university dean*

Shelby
Oliver, Jeffrey Michael *protective services official*

Smithfield
McClain, Gregory David *chaplain*

Snow Hill
Stevens, JoAnn A. *textile, political leader, author, minister*

Southern Pines
Cooper, Kevin R. *materials scientist*
Funderburk, David Britton *retired congressman, ambassador, consultant*
Owings, Malcolm William *retired management consultant*
Toon, Malcolm *former ambassador*
Warren, Donald William *medical and dental educator*

Southern Shores
Kegel, William George *mining company executive*

Southport
Kahai, Jugta *pediatrician*
Pepper, Jeffrey Mackenzie *publishing executive*

Spindale
Howard, Elizabeth Ann Blanton *transportation executive*

Spring Hope
Hildreth, James Robert *retired air force officer*

Statesville
Allred, Susan G. *school system administrator*
Elliott, Carolyn Cole *secondary school educator, department chairman*
Grogan, David R. *work saver company executive*
Kahne, Kasey *race car driver*
Redman, William Walter, Jr. *retired realtor*

Tabor City
Jorgensen, Ralph Gubler *lawyer, accountant*

Tarboro
Hopkins, Grover Prevatte *lawyer*

Taylorsville
Bolick, Katie N. *elementary school educator*
Lewczyk, David C. *military officer*
Ross, David Edmond *church official*

Thomasville
Hinkle, William Paul *mechanical and electrical engineer, consultant*
Sprinkle, Robert Lee, Jr. *podiatrist*

Todd
Cole, Susan Stockbridge *retired theater educator*

Trinity
McIlquham, David J. *consumer products company executive*
Walker, Kenneth Lynn *lawyer*

Tryon
Flynn, Kirtland, Jr. *accountant*
Mellberg, James Richard *retired dental research chemist*

Vale
Chandonnet, Ann Fox *journalist, poet*

Vass
Glassman, Edward *public relations executive, educator, journalist*

Vilas
Stolberg, Mary Margaret *historian*

Wadesboro
Hamby, Kristie Lynne *director*

Wake Forest
Buchanan, Edward A. *education educator*
Gamble, Michael F. *human resources generalist*
Kimrey, Karen Goss *secondary school educator*

Warsaw
Thompson, Eugene Cebron III *lawyer*

Washington
Rader, Steven Palmer *lawyer*

Waxhaw
Edwards, Irene Elizabeth (Libby) *dermatologist, educator, medical researcher*

Waynesville
Cole, James Yeager *foundation administrator*
Hale, Joe (Joseph Rice) *church organization executive*
McKinney, Alexander Stuart *retired neurologist*
Stokes, Mack Boyd (Marion Boyd Stokes) *bishop*

Weaverville
Edwards, Otis Carl, Jr. *theology studies educator*

Flaxman, Fred *broadcast producer, host*
Hauschild, Douglas Carey *optometrist*

Welcome
Harvick, Kevin *race car driver*

Weldon
Barringer, Paul Brandon, II, *lumber company executive*

West End
Krallinger, Joseph Charles *entrepreneur, consultant, writer*

Whispering Pines
Kuhn, Matthew *retired engineering company executive*

Whiteville
Council, James Braxton, Jr. *school system administrator*

Wilkesboro
Bridgeford, Gregory M. *consumer products company executive*
Brown, Michael K. *retail executive*
Canter, Charles W. (Nick) *retail executive*
Hull, Robert F., Jr., (Bob) *consumer products company executive*

Willow Spring
Valvo, Barbara-Ann *lawyer, surgeon*

Wilmington
Ao, Qi *nuclear engineer, research scientist*
Askew, Jennifer P. *pharmacist*
Buckland, Wendy *medical products executive*
Cameron, Kay *conductor, composer*
Conser, Walter Hurley, Jr. *religion and philosophy educator*
De Maria, Alfred Anthony *neurologist*
Fox, James Carroll *federal judge*
Fuller, Melvin Stuart *botany educator*
Herman, Russell Leland *mathematics, physics professor*
Hines, Elizabeth *geographer, educator*
Jones, Lucian Cox *lawyer*
Kelley, Patricia Hagelin *geology educator*
Maness, Eleanor Palmer *researcher*
McCauley, Cleyburn Lycurgus *lawyer*
Medlock, Donald Larson *lawyer*
Mintzes, Joel J. *biology professor, researcher*
Palmer, Liza Jane *librarian*
Pickett, Alicia Euliss *environmental scientist*
Richey, Luke Merritt *otolaryngologist, researcher*
Seapker, Janet Kay *museum administrator, architectural historian, history consultant*
Snowden, Lynne *sociologist, educator*
Stratas, Byron Aristotle *ophthalmologist*
Wall, James J. *lawyer*
Wilkins, Lucien Sanders *gastroenterologist*

Wilson
Kushner, Michael James *neurologist, consultant, educator*
Ladwig, Harold Allen *neurologist*
Leonard, J. Rich *federal judge, educator*
McCain, Betty Landon Ray (Mrs. John Lewis McCain) *political party and state official*
Stewart, Burton Gloyden, Jr. *retired banker*
Wyatt, Edward Avery, V, *city manager*

Wingate
Dodd, John Robert *non-profit organization administrator*

Winston Salem
Adams, Alfred Gray *lawyer*
Adams, Reid C., Jr. *lawyer*
Allison, John Andrew, IV, *bank executive*
Applegate, William Brown *dean, researcher, medical educator, department chairman*
Atala, Anthony John *surgeon*
Baker, R. Scott *education educator*
Barnett, Richard Chambers *historian, educator*
Barnhill, Henry Grady, Jr. *lawyer*
Beardsley, Charles Mitchell *retired insurance company executive*
Beaty, James Arthur, Jr. *federal judge*
Blynn, Guy Marc *lawyer*
Borwick, Susan Harden *musicologist, educator*
Bourne, Henry Clark, Jr. *electrical engineer, educator, retired academic administrator*
Brewster, Daryl G. *food products executive*
Capps, Richard Henry *retired minister*
Chaden, Lee A. *apparel and former food products executive*
Chilson, John A. *lawyer, military officer*
Clinard, Keith A. *lawyer*
Cook, Sharon Warren *social worker, educator*
Copenhaver, W. Andrew *lawyer*
Donofrio, Peter Daniel *neurology educator*
Dyer, Raymond B. *diagnostic radiology physician*
Early, James H., Jr. *lawyer*
Edwards, Charles Archibald *lawyer*
Ehle, John Marsden, Jr. *writer*
Eldridge, J. Charles *endocrinologist, educator, researcher*
Eliason, Russell Allen *judge*
Faccinto, Victor Paul *artist, gallery administrator*
Ferree, Carolyn Ruth *retired radiation oncologist, educator*
Fleischer, Alan Bernard, Jr. *dermatologist, educator*
Foy, Herbert Miles III *lawyer, educator*
Gitter, Allan Reinhold *lawyer*
Gordon, William Charles *academic administrator*
Graham, William Thomas *lawyer*
Graybeal, Barbara *editor, writer*
Greason, Murray Crossley, Jr. *lawyer*
Gregg, Ellen M. *lawyer*
Griffin, Andrew Steven *urologist*
Grillo, Henry R. *theater educator, technical director*
Grobe, Jim *college football coach*
Gunter, Michael Donwell *lawyer*
Gunzenhauser, Gerard Ralph, Jr. *management consultant, investor*
Hammon, John William, Jr. *medical educator, thoracic surgeon*
Hanes, Frank Borden *writer, former business executive, farmer*
Hanes, Ralph Philip, Jr. *retired textiles executive, horse breeder*
Harle, Thomas Stanley *radiologist*
Harrelson, Walter Joseph *minister, educator*
Hatch, Nathan Orr *academic administrator*
Hearn, Thomas K., Jr. *academic administrator*
Heckelman, Jac C. *economics professor*
Hendricks, J(ames) Edwin *historian, educator, consultant, author*
Herrington, David McLeod *cardiologist, educator*
Holton, Walter Clinton, Jr. *lawyer*
Howell, Charles Maitland *dermatologist*
Humphrey, Dudley *lawyer*
Hunt, Ellen *minister, evangelist*
Ivey, Susan M. *tobacco company executive*
James, Francis Marshall III *anesthesiologist*
Jenkins, Barbara Alexander *pastor, overseer*
Johnson, Frank William *marketing professional*
Kaur, Mandeep *dermatologist, educator*
Kerr, William C. *physics professor*
King, Roberta B. *lawyer*
King, Wayne Edgar *journalist, educator*
Kohut, Robert Irwin *otolaryngologist, educator*
Lambeth, Judy (E. Julia Lambeth) *tobacco company executive, lawyer*
Laxminarayana, Dama *geneticist, researcher, educator*
Leonard, R. Michael *lawyer*
Lipscomb, Lewis D. *obstetrician, gynecologist*
Little, George L. *lawyer*
Ludolf, Marilyn Marie Keaton *lay worker*
Marino, Nancy A. *marketing professional*
Maselli, John Anthony *food products executive*
Maynard, Charles Douglas *radiologist*
McKnight, Gregory Richard *research director*
Mclorie, Gordon Arthur *urologist, educator*
Mecimore, Charles Douglas *retired accounting educator*
Medlin, John Grimes, Jr. *banker, director*
Meis, Paul Jean *retired obstetrics and gynecology educator*
Michel, Sandra K. *lawyer, food products executive*
Miller, Richard Harry *philosopher, educator*
Mokrasch, Lewis Carl *neurochemist, educator*
Moody, Dixon McGuire *radiologist*
Moser, Kenneth Allen *lawyer*
Mueller, Margaret S. *musician, educator*
Muir, Douglas R. *food service executive*
Neal, Dianne M. *consumer products company executive*
Noll, Richard A. *apparel executive*
O'Donovan, Cormac A. *neurologist, educator*
Oldaker, Guy Brooklyn III *lawyer*
Oliver, Patricia *lawyer*
Osborn, Malcolm Everett *lawyer*
O'Steen, Wendall Keith *anatomist, neurologist, educator*
Parker, Marian F. *law librarian, educator*
Patel, Ajay *dean*
Podgorny, George *emergency physician*
Pollock, Jeffrey *neuroscientist, radiologist*
Poovey, Mark Nixon *lawyer*
Powell, Bayard Lowery *oncologist, educator*
Preslar, Len Broughton, Jr. *hospital administrator*
Price, Henry Escoe *broadcast executive*
Quick, Elizabeth L. *lawyer*
Ragland, George A. *lawyer*
Rauschenberg, Bradford Lee *museum program director*
Rights, Graham Henry *retired minister*
Robinson, Edward Norwood *lawyer*
Rodgman, Alan *chemist, consultant*
Roth, Marjory Joan Jarboe *special education educator*
Sandresky, Margaret Vardell *retired composer*
Sandridge, William Pendleton, Jr. *lawyer*
Sawyer, John Wesley *retired mathematics and computer science educator, consultant*
Schollander, Wendell III *lawyer*
Schollander, Wendell Leslie, Jr. *lawyer*
Schroeder, Thomas D. *lawyer*
Shapere, Dudley *philosophy educator*
Sharpe, Keith Yount *retired lawyer, writer*
Simon, Jimmy Louis *pediatrician, educator*
Sink, Kaycee M. *geriatrician, medical educator*
Smith, David Coventry *lawyer*
Smith, Ronald G. *music educator*
Spach, Jule Christian *church executive*
Stein, Barry Edward *medical educator*
Strickland, Robert Louis *retired retail executive*
Sullivan, William Beaumont *lawyer*
Sutton, Lynn Sorensen *librarian*
Tannu, Nilesh Suresh *medical researcher*
Taylor, Daniel Russell, Jr. *lawyer*
Toole, James Francis *medical educator*
Torti, Frank Michael *internist, health facility administrator*
Vaughan, Keith W. *lawyer*
Vaughn, Robert Candler, Jr. *lawyer*
Walker, George Kontz *law educator*
Walsh, Robert K. *dean*
Wanders, Hans Walter *banker*
Weller, Robert Stephen *anesthesiologist*
Whittington, Stephen Lunn *museum director*
Wiley, C. Mark *lawyer, department chairman*
Wilson, Grover Gray *lawyer*
Winn, Albert Curry *clergyman*
Womble, William Fletcher *lawyer*
Zagoria, Sam D(avid) *reporter, educator, federal agency administrator*
Zhang, Lei *physics professor*

Winton
Williams, Sue Darden *library director*

Woodland
Wilson, Lloyd Lee *registrar, educator*

Wrightsville Beach
Mc Ilwain, William Franklin *newspaper editor, writer*

Zebulon
Privette, Janet Brown *elementary school educator*
Ruffing, Anne Elizabeth *artist*

NORTH DAKOTA

Ashley
Kretschmar, William Edward *state legislator, lawyer*

Bisbee
Keller, Michelle R. *science educator*

Bismarck
Crothers, Daniel J. *state supreme court justice*
Dalrymple, Jack *lieutenant governor, former state legislator*
Evanson, Barbara Jean *middle school education educator*
Gilbertson, Joel Warren *lawyer*
Hildestad, Terry D. *energy executive*
Hoeven, John *governor*
Jaeger, Al (Alvin A. Jaeger) *state official*
Joersz, Fran Woodmansee *secondary school educator*
Kapsner, Carol Ronning *state supreme court justice*
Karsky, Timothy J. *state agency administrator*
King, Lawrence Edmund *lawyer*
Klemin, Lawrence R. *lawyer*
Knoll, Gloria Jean *music educator*
Leidenix, Monte John *ophthalmologist, researcher*
Lundberg, Susan Ona *musical organization administrator*
Maring, Mary Muehlen *state supreme court justice*
Moore, Sherry Mills *lawyer*
Murry, Charles Emerson *lawyer, federal official*
Nelson, Carolyn *state legislator*
Neumann, William Allen *retired state supreme court justice*
Newborg, Gerald Gordon *state archives administrator*
Niksic, Gwen M. *biology professor*
Ott, Doris Ann *librarian*
Potts, Robert Leslie *academic administrator*
Rettig, Pam *literature educator*
Sandness, Paul K. *lawyer, energy executive*
Sandstrom, Dale Vernon *state supreme court justice*
Sanstead, Wayne Godfrey *school system administrator*
Schmidt, Kelly *state official*
Spagnolia, Thomas Nickolas *neurosurgeon, consultant*
Stenehjem, Wayne Kevin *state attorney general, lawyer*
Tornow, L. William *musician*
VandeWalle, Gerald Wayne *chief justice*

Cando
Jorde, Terry J. *bank executive*

Devils Lake
Rygg, Glenn *retired music educator*

Dickinson
Kessel, Lloyd R. *nursing administrator, educator*

Edgeley
Schimke, Dennis J. *former state legislator*

Elgin
Hintz, Pam K. *secondary school and science educator*

Ellendale
Schlieve, Hy C. J. *school administrator*

Erie
Pueppke, Glenn Howard *farmer, agricultural products executive*

Fargo
Bright, Myron H. *federal judge*
Bye, Kermit Edward *federal judge, lawyer*
Foss, Richard John *bishop*
Hektner, Joel Martin *psychology professor*
Herman, Sarah Andrews *lawyer*
Littlefield, Robert Stephen *communications educator, training consultant*
Magill, Frank John *federal judge*
Marcil, William Christ, Sr. *publisher, broadcast executive*
Meester, Holly *elementary school educator, music educator, sales executive*
Mitchell, James Edward *physician, educator*
Morey, Charlotte Ann *elementary school educator, music educator*
Nasrullah, Mohammed Jaleel *research scientist*
Reitan, Daniel Kinseth *electric and computer engineering educator*
Riley, Thomas Joseph *anthropologist, academic administrator*
Schmidt, Claude Henri *retired science administrator*
Tallman, Dennis Earl *chemistry professor, research scientist*
Tharaldson, Gary Dean *hotel developer, owner*
Unhjem, Michael Bruce *lawyer*
Wagner, Alexander Johannes *physicist, educator*
Williams, Michael James *lawyer*
Wrigley, Drew H. *prosecutor, lawyer*
Yadav, Om Prakash *reliability engineer, educator*

Grand Forks
Bradley, April Rain *psychology professor*
Carlson, Edward C. *anatomy educator, cell biologist, department chairman*
Davis, W. Jeremy *retired lawyer, dean*
Gaul, Gerald *ophthalmologist*
Gjovig, Bruce Quentin *entrepreneur, consultant*
Glassheim, Eliot Alan *editor, state legislator*
Haskins, James P. *finance educator, consultant*
Hoffmann, Mark R. *physical chemist, educator*
Huang, Xiaozhao *language educator*
Jackson, Jon *medical educator, consultant*
Jones, Arthur Frederick *art university administrator, educator*
Kupchella, Charles Edward *academic administrator, author, educator*
Maddock, Patrick Jerome *lawyer*
Mondry, Diane *secondary school educator*
Nielsen, Forrest Harold *research nutritionist*
Nordlie, Robert Conrad *biochemistry educator*
Page, Sally Jacquelyn *university official, management educator*
Patton, Gregory Kenneth *management educator*
Russell, Sue Ann *clinical psychologist*
Seelan, Santhosh Kumar *science educator*
Sharma, Sushil K. *medical educator*
Swanson, Zona Luciel *retired elementary school educator*
Towne, Gary Spaulding *music educator*
Wakefield, Mary Katherine *medical association administrator, medical educator*
Widdel, John Earl, Jr. *lawyer*
Wogaman, George Elsworth *insurance company executive, financial consultant*
Yoshida, Glen Yoshio *otolaryngologist*

Hatton
Strand, Fred P. *mathematics educator*

Mandan
Bair, Bruce Blythe *lawyer*
Heick, Leon Joseph *data processing executive*

Mayville
Champion, Kathleen Ann *mathematics professor*
Karaim, Betty June *retired librarian*
McMahon, Dalton Edward *history professor, social sciences educator, department chairman*
Pederson, John Martin *education educator*
Sorteberg, Ann Marie *education educator*

Minot
Eadens, Ethan Ennis *minister, writer*
Jermiason, John Lynn *elementary school educator, farmer, investor*
Kerian, Jon Robert *retired judge*
Srock, Marlene *elementary school educator*
Tollefson, Ben C. *state legislator, retired utilities executive*
Watne, Darlene Claire *county official*

Valley City
Stillings, Dennis Otto *research association administrator, consultant*

Wahpeton
Donahe, Peggy Yvonne *gifted and talented educator, librarian*
Reubish, Gary Richard *English language educator*

West Fargo
Schneider, Dennis Eugene *manufacturing executive*

Williston
Adducci, Joseph Edward *obstetrician, gynecologist*
Yockim, James Craig *foundation administrator*

OHIO

Ada
Allison, Jeffery Clay *pharmacist, educator*
Baker, Kendall L. *academic administrator*
Boyadzhiev, Khristo Nonev *mathematician, educator, researcher*
Cooper, Ken Errol *retired management educator*
Durkin, Keith Francis *sociologist, researcher*
Estell, John K. *computer science and engineering educator, department chair*
Fenton, Howard Nathan III *lawyer, educator*
Stockert, Amy L. *chemistry professor*

Akron
Ahn, Dae Up *polymer engineer, researcher*
Alexander, Anthony J. *electric power industry executive*
Allen, Marc Kevin *emergency physician, educator*
Barker, Harold Kenneth *former university dean*
Barlowe Bodman, Amy *violinist, composer*
Bartlo, Sam D. *lawyer*
Bell, Samuel H. *federal judge, educator*
Bishop, Christy B. *lawyer, researcher*
Borowiec, Andrew *art educator, photographer*
Brake, Yvonne Marie *not-for-profit developer*
Brown, David Rupert *engineering executive*
Burbach, Mike *editor*
Buzzelli, Charlotte Grace *special education educator*
Castronovo, Thomas Paul *architect, consultant*
Cherpas, Christopher Theodore *lawyer*
Cody, Daniel Schaffner *lawyer*
Collier, Alice Elizabeth Becker *retired social services administrator*
Crawford, Robert John *credit company executive*
Daniels, Christopher *mechanical engineer, educator*
Emmett, John Colin *retired inventor, consultant*
Evans, Douglas McCullough *surgeon, educator*
Fisher, James Lee *lawyer*
Garbrandt, Gail Elaine *political science professor, consultant*
Geier, Kathleen T. *human resources specialist*
Gent, Alan Neville *physicist, researcher*
Glinsek, Gerald John *lawyer*
Grigg, Richard R. *energy executive*
Haines, Terry L. *plastics company executive*
Harvie, Crawford Thomas *lawyer*
Henry, Jed William *urologist*

Holloway, Donald Phillip *lawyer*
Ichilov, Nehemia *principal, consultant*
Isayev, Avraam Isayevich *polymer engineer, educator*
Jana, Sadhan C. *engineering educator, researcher*
Jennings, David C. *library director, educator*
Kahan, Mitchell Douglas *museum director*
Kaufman, Donald Leroy *building products executive*
Keegan, Robert J. *manufacturing executive*
Kennedy, Joseph Paul *chemist, researcher*
Knepper, George W. *historian, educator*
Kramer, Richard J. *manufacturing executive*
Lee, Brant Thomas *lawyer, educator, federal official*
Lim, Edward Chol *chemistry professor, researcher*
Linberger, Peter *school librarian*
Lombardi, Frederick McKean *lawyer*
Malone, Alicia Jane *minister, theologian*
Marsh, Richard H. *energy executive*
Martin, Jack *educational services company executive, former federal agency administrator*
Milsted, Amy *biomedical educator*
Moriarty, John Timothy *transportation consultant, writer*
Phares, James Kenneth *retired electronics engineer*
Plusquellic, Donald L. *mayor*
Ramsey, Sally Judith Weine *chemist, research and development company executive*
Rebenack, John Henry *retired librarian*
Reilly, Elizabeth Ann *law educator, dean*
Richert, Paul *law educator*
Rouvas, Sakas *singer, gymnast*
Schoenfeld, Andrew Jason *orthopedist, surgeon*
Schrader, Alfred Eugene *lawyer*
Seiberling, John Frederick *retired congressman, lawyer, educator*
Shea-Stonum, Marilyn *federal bankruptcy judge*
Smart, George M. *energy executive, former packaging company executive*
Sonnecken, Edwin Herbert *management consultant*
Stewart, Mizell III *editor*
Taormina, Charles Anthony *writer, editor, artist*
Taylor, E. Jane *lawyer*
Timmons, Gerald Dean *pediatric neurologist*
Tipping, Harry A. *lawyer*
Trotter, Thomas Robert *lawyer*
Vespoli, Leila L. *lawyer, energy executive*
von Spiegel, Janice Krieger *mathematics educator*
West, Michael Alan *retired hospital administrator*
Williams, William Proctor *literature educator*
Wolfe, John Leslie *lawyer*
Wright, Bradley Abbott *lawyer*
Yardeni, Edward *economist, investment advisor*

Alpha
James, Francis Edward, Jr. *investment advisor*

Amelia
Hayden, Joseph Page, Jr. *finance company executive*
Kahles, Cheryl Mary *elementary school educator*

Archbold
Henry, Dinah D. *science educator*

Ashland
Ford, Lucille Garber *economist, educator*
Gearhart, Randall F. *healthcare educator*
Watson, JoAnn Ford *theology studies educator*

Ashtabula
Carrell, Janeen Brown *retired psychologist*
Morisue, Glenn T. *graphics designer*

Athens
Bacal, Kira *emergency physician, educator*
Borchert, Donald Marvin *philosopher, educator*
Brobst, Peter John *history professor*
Bruning, James Leon *academic administrator, educator*
Cooper-Chen, Anne *journalism educator, researcher*
Crist, Richard Le Roy *voice educator*
Crowl, Samuel Renninger *retired dean, language educator*
Ehrlich, Philip *philosophy educator*
Hedges, Richard Houston *lawyer, epidemiologist*
Hogan, Terrence James *academic administrator, consultant*
Irwin, Richard Dennis *electrical engineering educator*
Krendl, Kathy *dean*
Kurz, David Bryan *web site designer*
Lavelle, William Ambrose *lawyer, judge*
Lazuka, Robert *artist, art educator*
Matthews, Jack (John Harold Matthews) *language educator, writer*
McDavis, Roderick J. *academic administrator*
McNamara, John Regis *psychology educator*
Metters, Thomas Waddell *sportswriter*
Nance, Richard Damian *geologist, consultant*
Pasic, Hajrudin *mathematician, educator*
Scott, Charles Lewis *retired photojournalist*
Stempel, Guido Hermann III *journalism educator*
Stump, Earl Spencer *psychologist*
Torres, Daniel *literature educator*
Vedder, Richard Kent *economics professor*
Wen, Shih-Liang *mathematics professor*
Whealey, Lois Deimel *humanities scholar*

Aurora
Berry, Dean Lester *lawyer*
Eakin, Thomas Capper *sports promotion executive*
Kirchner, James William *retired electrical engineer*
Lawton, Florian Kenneth *artist, educator*
Ross, Violet Bica *retired elementary school educator, retired psychologist*
Su, Sunyu *physicist*

Austintown
Hill, Thomas Allen *lawyer*

Avon Lake
Morton, David Ray *sales and marketing executive*
Newlin, Stephen Dore *chemicals executive*
Parke, M(argaret) Jean *retired business owner, editor*
Pascarella, Perry James *editor, writer*
Patient, William F. *chemicals executive*
Poblete, J. Vicente *medical director*
Shiba, Wendy C. *lawyer*

Bannock
Gentile, Anthony *coal company executive*

Barberton
Kitto, John Buck, Jr. *mechanical engineer*
Zufra, Mindy Marie *mathematics educator*

Batavia
Meek, David Jason *recreational facility executive, real estate developer*
Siddiqi, Munawar *anesthesiologist, consultant*

Bath
Coyne, Thomas Joseph *economics and finance professor*

Bay Village
Berry, Edgar Allen *music educator*
Hook, John Burney *investment company executive*
Kapp, C. Terrence *lawyer*

Beachwood
Budish, Armond David *state legislator, lawyer, journalist*
Clegg, Christopher R. *lawyer*
Demetriou, Steven J. *metal products executive*
Friedman, Arnold Bernard *retired pediatrician*
Fufuka, Natika Njeri Yaa *retail executive*
Krieger, Irvin Mitchell *retired chemistry professor*
Moskowitz, Roland Wallace *internist*
Robertson, Ned *dentist*
Sullivan, John E. III *lawyer*
Varner, Arthur E. *allergist, researcher*

Beavercreek
Pasupuleti, Venumadhav *information technology executive*
Stadnicar, Joseph William *lawyer*

Bedford
Klukan, Joseph Frank *aerospace transportation executive, manufacturing executive*

Bellaire
Kniesner, John Thomas *librarian*

Bellevue
Aigler, William Frank *lawyer*
Davenport, Thomas Herbert *small business owner*

Bellville
Hooker, James Todd *manufacturing executive*

Beloit
Barnett, Robert James *music educator, musician*

Berea
Crennel, Romeo *professional football coach*
Durst, Richard Wayne *academic administrator*
Kennelly, Laura Ballard *literature educator, writer*
Lewis, Jamal *professional football player*
Little, Richard Allen *mathematics professor, computer science educator*
Quinn, Brady (Brady Tyler Quinn) *professional football player*
Zeitlin, Louise R. *music educator*

Bexley
Yashon, David *neurosurgeon, educator*

Bloomingdale
Calabrese, Charles *radio station official*

Bluffton
Dudley, Durand Stowell *retired librarian*

Boardman
Skinner, William Philip, Jr. *manufacturing executive*

Bowling Green
Baird, Alice Knar *retired education educator*
Baird, James Abington *retired judge*
Berger, Bonnie G. *sport psychologist, educator*
Browne, Ray Broadus *popular culture educator*
Clark, Eloise Elizabeth *biologist, educator*
Goza, Franklin William *sociology educator*
Guion, Robert Morgan *psychologist, educator*
Hakel, Milton Daniel, Jr. *psychologist, educator, writer, consultant*
Krane, Vikki *psychology educator*
Lunde, Harold Irving *retired management educator*
McCaghy, Charles Henry *retired social sciences educator*
Middleton, Charles Ronald *history educator*
Nagi, Lillian S. *biology professor*
Ocvirk, Otto George *artist*
Singer, Carol Ann *librarian, researcher*
Versteeg, Robert John *minister, actor, writer*

Bratenahl
Dunn, Horton, Jr. *organic chemist*
Jones, Trevor Owen *biomedical industry executive, management consultant*

Brecksville
Pappas, Effie Vamis *language educator, finance educator, writer, poet, artist*

Brookfield
Manos, Thomas G. *investment company executive*

Brookpark
Heil, Michael Lloyd *military officer, academic administrator*

Brunswick
Kuchynski, Marie *physician*
Sandvick, Janet Rose *history educator*

Bryan
Carrico, Virgil Norman *physician*
Oberlin, Earl Clifford III *securities brokerage company executive*
Shaffer, Wayne Eugene *lawyer*

Bucyrus
Cooper, April Helen *family practice nurse practitioner*

Cadiz
Thompson, Sandra Lee *library administrator*

Cambridge
Reisner, Andrew Douglas *psychologist*

Canfield
Scurich, Kelly Lemos *music director*

Canton
Barkan, John Martin, Jr. *architect*
Bennington, Ronald Kent *lawyer*
Burkhart, William R. *lawyer*
Carson, Harry *retired professional football player*
Covert, Susan Jane *rehabilitation services professional, director*
Griffith, James W. *manufacturing executive*
Howland, Willard J. *radiologist, educator*
Krider, Patricia Ann *library director*
Mann, John Martin *minister*
McFarren, Leland Cullen *educational association administrator, educator*
Metzger, Janet *librarian*
Mitchell, Jan L. *advocate, writer*
Moon, Warren *professional football player*
Nadas, John Adalbert *psychiatrist, educator*
Peck, Douglas Caton *dean, educator*
Perry, Stephen A. *museum administrator, former federal agency administrator*
Schauer, Thomas Alfred *insurance company executive*
Swidarski, Thomas W. *manufacturing executive*
Timken, Ward J., Jr. *manufacturing executive*
Tyburski, Charles J. *lawyer*
Wright, Rayfield *professional football player*

Cardington
Linscott, Ross Edward *school psychologist*

Cedarville
Firmin, Michael Wayne *psychology professor*

Celina
Fanning, Ronald Heath *architect, engineer*

Centerburg
Reynolds, Don William *geologist*

Centerville
Giffen, Daniel Harris *lawyer, educator*

Chagrin Falls
Brophy, Jere Hall *manufacturing executive*
Brown, Jeanette Grasselli *retired director*
Deihl, Charles L. *former college president*
Heckman, Henry Trevennen Shick *retired steel executive*
Lingl, Friedrich Albert *psychiatrist*
Miller, John Robert *oil industry executive*
Shakley, Elaine M. *organist, department chairman*
Smith, Barbara Jean *lawyer*
Stec, John Zygmunt *retired real estate company officer*
Vail, Iris Jennings *civic worker*

Chardon
Columbro, Madeline M. *education educator*
Dobyns, Brown McIlvaine *retired surgeon, educator*
Horvath, Madelon Toft *secondary school educator*
Kellis, Michael John *osteopathic physician*

Chesterland
Aster, Ruth Marie Rhydderch *business owner*
Ruble, Bernard Roy *minister, educator, human resources specialist, labor relations consultant*
Wood, Kenneth Anderson *small business owner, display designer*

Chippewa Lake
Javorek, Richard Alan *history educator, consultant*

Cincinnati
Abate, Anne Katherine *librarian, consultant, educator*
Adams, Edmund John *lawyer*
Agrawal, Dharma Prakash *engineering educator*
Aguirre, Fernando *food products executive*
Albainy-Jenei, Stephen R. *lawyer*
Alexander, James Wesley *surgeon, educator*
Alexander, John Kurt *history professor*
Allison, Jon B. *lawyer*
Anderson, James Milton *lawyer, hospital administrator*
Anderson, Jerry William, Jr. *diversified financial services company executive, educator*
Anderson, Joan Balyeat *theology studies educator, minister*
Anderson, William Hopple *lawyer*
Anning, Robert Doan Hopkins *brokerage company executive*
Anstaett, Jennifer Griffin *lawyer*
Anthony, Thomas Dale *lawyer*
Antoine, Richard L. *human resources specialist, consumer products company executive*
Arb, Carrie Samantha *adult education educator*
Arnold, Susan E. *consumer products company executive*
Artzt, Edwin Lewis *consumer products company executive*
Ashley, Lynn *social sciences educator, consultant*
Auttonberry, Sheri E. *lawyer*
Auyang, Grace Chao *education educator, consultant*
Bahlman, William Thorne, Jr. *retired lawyer*
Bahr, Donald Walter *retired chemical engineer*
Baldwin, William D.G. *lawyer*
Barrett, John F. *insurance company executive*
Barrett, Michael Ryan *federal judge*
Baskett, Mary Welsh *art dealer, consultant*
Bateman, Sharon Louise *public relations executive*
Beckwith, Barbara Jean *journalist*
Beckwith, Sandra Shank *federal judge*
Bell, Ronald A. *lawyer*
Bell, Sandra Elizabeth *corporate financial executive*
Bellet, Paul Sanders *pediatrician, educator*
Bergeron, Pierre H. *lawyer*
Besier, James Louis *pharmacist, educator*
Betsky, Aaron *art museum director*
Bieliauskas, Vytautas Joseph *psychologist, educator*
Bilionis, Louis D. *dean, law educator*
Birmingham, Stephen *writer*
Biro, Frank M. *pediatrics educator*
Bishop, George Franklin *political scientist, educator*
Bishop, Jerome C. *lawyer*
Bissinger, Mark Christian *lawyer*
Bissler, John Joseph *nephrologist, educator*
Black, Stephen L. *lawyer*
Blandford, Colleen M. *lawyer*
Blaske, Nathan H. *lawyer*
Bleznick, Donald William *Romance languages educator*
Blickensderfer, Matthew C. *lawyer*
Bluestein, Venus Weller *retired psychologist, educator*
Boat, Thomas Frederick *pediatrician, pulmonologist, researcher, educator*
Boyd, Deborah Ann *pediatrician*
Braun, Joseph J. *lawyer*
Brehm-Heeger, Paula *library director, library association executive*
Bride, Nancy J. *lawyer*
Briggs, Henry Payson, Jr. *headmaster*
Briskin, Madeleine *oceanographer, paleontologist*
Britt, Kent A. *lawyer*
Brod, Stanford *graphics designer, educator*
Broderick, Dennis John *lawyer, retail executive*
Bronson, Michael J. *lawyer*
Brown, Dale Patrick *retired advertising executive*
Brown, Daniel *curator, executive secretary*
Bryant, Irene Melba *retired elementary school educator, artist*
Buchanan, Margaret E. *publishing executive*
Buncher, Charles Ralph *epidemiologist, educator, biostatistician*
Burdette, Robert Bruce *retired lawyer*
Burke, Rachel E. *lawyer*
Burleigh, William Robert *media executive*
Byrnes, Bruce L. *consumer products company executive*
Cabezas, Heriberto *chemical engineer, researcher*
Callinan, Tom *editor-in-chief*
Cappel, Harry W. *lawyer*
Carmichael, Greg D. *bank executive*
Cathey, Christopher D. *lawyer*
Cawood, James M. III *lawyer*
Chalkley, Roger *mathematics professor*
Chambliss, Carroll Christopher *professional baseball coach*
Chapman, Jamie L. *pharmacist*
Chatterjee, Jayanta *architecture and planning educator*
Chesley, Stanley Morris *lawyer*
Childs, Erin C. *lawyer*
Ching, Ho *surgeon*
Christensen, Paul Walter, Jr. *retired gear manufacturing company executive*
Christenson, Gordon A. *law educator*
Christopher, John E. *lawyer*
Ciani, Alfred Joseph *dean*
Cioffi, Michael Lawrence *lawyer*
Cissell, James Charles *lawyer*
Clay, Eric L. *federal judge*
Cloyd, G. Gil *information technology executive*
Coberly, LeAnn *internist*
Cobey, John Geoffrey *lawyer, consultant*
Cody, Thomas Gerald *retail executive, lawyer*
Coffaro, Steven C. *lawyer*
Coffey, Lela *advertising executive*
Cole, Thomas L. *retail executive*
Combs, Eric K. *lawyer*
Conaton, Michael Joseph *diversified financial services company executive*
Cook, Deborah L. *federal judge, former state supreme court justice*
Cooney, Kevin L. *lawyer*
Cors, Jeanne Marie *lawyer*
Craig, L. Clifford *lawyer*
Crew, Spencer *museum administrator*
Cunningham, Pierce Edward *lawyer, city planner*
Curtis-Francis, Kelley Ann *pharmacist*
Daley, Clayton Carl, Jr. *consumer products company executive*
Davis, Robert Lawrence *lawyer*
de Courten-Myers, Gabrielle Marguerite *retired neuropathologist*
Dehner, Joseph Julnes *lawyer*

Denton, D. Brock *lawyer*
Derstadt, Ronald Theodore *health facility administrator*
Desai, Deepak K. *lawyer*
De Witt, Jeanette Marie *physical therapist*
Dick, Barry Lee *surgeon*
Diller, Edward Dietrich *lawyer*
Dillon, David Brian *retail grocery executive*
Diwan, Abhinav *medical educator, researcher*
Dlott, Susan Judy *judge, lawyer*
Do, Twee T. *orthopedist*
Dornette, W(illiam) Stuart *lawyer, educator*
Dougherty, Charlotte Anne *financial planner, insurance and securities representative*
Dougherty, David Francis *business process outsourcing executive*
Draper, Sharon M. *writer, elementary school educator*
Duffy, Virginia *minister*
Dunn, Adam *professional baseball player*
Dunsker, Stewart B. *neurosurgeon*
Eckner, Shannon F. *lawyer*
Ehrnschwender, Arthur Robert *former utility company executive*
Ellerman, Paige L. *lawyer*
Erhart, Sue A. *lawyer*
Esamann, Douglas F. *utilities executive*
Evans, James E. *lawyer*
Everson, Jean Watkins Dolores *librarian, media consultant, educator*
Faller, Susan Grogan *lawyer*
Farmer, Richard T. *uniform rental and sales executive*
Farmer, Scott D. *apparel executive*
Farrell, Pamela Christine *secondary school educator*
Faulkner, Laura R. *lawyer*
Feichtner, Douglas J. *lawyer*
Fender, Kimber L. *library director, educator*
Ficke, Gregory C. *utilities executive*
Fink, Jerold Albert *lawyer*
Fitzsimmons, Becky Barlow *lawyer*
Flamm, Justin D. *lawyer*
Flick, Thomas Michael *mathematician, educator, educational association administrator*
Florez, Mary A. *artist*
Foley, Cheryl M. *electric power industry executive*
Francis, Marion David *consulting chemist*
Friedman, Penny *lawyer, not-for-profit developer*
Fronduti, John S. *lawyer*
Frooman, Thomas E. *lawyer*
Garfinkel, Jane E. *lawyer*
Garretson, Matthew Lee *lawyer*
Gates, Katherine A. *accountant, writer*
Gaunt, Karen Kreider *lawyer*
Gehrig, Michael Ford *lawyer*
Geoppinger, Jeffrey D. *lawyer*
Gettler, Benjamin *lawyer, manufacturing company executive*
Ghassomian, Kevin R. *lawyer*
Ghia, Kirti N. *fluid mechanics engineer, aerospace educator*
Giannella, Andrew R. *lawyer*
Gilbert, Jay *radio personality*
Giles, Brian T. *lawyer*
Glass, Joanne Wissman *lawyer*
Glendening, Everett Austin *architect*
Goebel, Jens *physician*
Goetzman, Bruce Edgar *architecture educator*
Goldstein, Sidney *pharmacist*
Goodman, Bernard *physics professor*
Goodman, Stanley *lawyer*
Goodwin, John P. *treasurer*
Greenberg, David Bernard *chemical engineering educator*
Greengus, Samuel *academic administrator, theology studies educator*
Griffey, Ken, Jr., (George Kenneth Griffey Jr.) *professional baseball player*
Griffin, Richard Allen *federal judge*
Grove, Janet E. *retail executive*
Guard, Roger *information technology executive*
Habel, Christopher S. *lawyer*
Hale, Nathan Kelly *music educator, artist*
Harding, Warren Gamaliel III *surgeon*
Hardy, Thomas Cresson *insurance company executive*
Hardy, William Robinson *lawyer*
Harmon, Patrick *historian, retired editor, commentator*
Harrington, Jeremy Thomas *priest, publishing executive*
Harris, Irving *lawyer*
Harrison, Donald Carey *academic administrator, cardiologist, educator*
Hastings, Kerry P. *lawyer*
Hawkins, Lawrence Charles *management consultant, educator*
Hawkins, William H., II, *lawyer*
Hayden, Jeremy A. *lawyer*
Heaton, Charles Lloyd *dermatologist, educator*
Heiliger, Robert Lee *minister*
Heimlich, Henry J. *physician, surgeon, educator*
Heldman, James Gardner *lawyer*
Heldman, Paul W. *lawyer, food service executive*
Henney, Jane Ellen *health facility administrator, educator, oncologist*
Hensgen, Herbert Thomas *medical technologist*
Hermanies, John Hans *retired lawyer*
Heschel, Michael Shane *retail food products executive*
Hess, Ashley W. *lawyer*
Hess, Evelyn Victorine *medical educator*
Hicks, Drew M. *lawyer*
Hicks, Sarah Ellington *lawyer*
Hillard, James Randolph *psychiatry educator*
Hill-Cook, Patricia Ann *social services administrator*
Hinegardner, Laura A. *lawyer*
Hinners, Stacy Chubak *lawyer*
Hodge, Bobby Lynn *mechanical engineer, manufacturing executive*
Hodge, Robert Joseph *retail executive*
Hoefle, H. Frederick *lawyer*
Hoffheimer, Daniel Joseph *lawyer*
Hoffman, Bridget C. *lawyer*
Hoffman, Lawrence A. *rabbi*
Hoguet, Karen M. *retail executive*
Holschuh, John David, Jr. *lawyer*
Hopkins, Jeffery P. *federal judge*
Horrell, Karen Holley *insurance company executive, lawyer*
Howington, John *thoracic surgeon, educator*
Huenefeld, Thomas Ernst *financial consultant, retired banker*
Hust, Bruce Kevin *lawyer*
Hutton, Edward Luke *medical products executive*
Hylander, Jessica S. *lawyer*
Iroh, Jude Onwuegbu *chemistry professor*
Irwin, Miriam Dianne Owen *publishing executive, writer*
Jackson, Kory A. *lawyer*
Jarvi, Paavo *conductor, music director*
Jenkins, Paul Owen *library director, educator*
Jensen, Elwood Vernon *biochemist*
Joffe, Craig P.R. *personal care industry executive*
Joffe, Stephen Neal *surgeon, medical educator*
Johnson, Chad *professional football player*
Johnson, James J. *lawyer*
Jones, Daniel W. *construction executive*
Jurs, Peter B. *lawyer*
Kabat, Kevin Thomas *bank executive*
Kallas, Hani R. *lawyer*
Kane, Scott A. *lawyer*
Katz, Reuven J. *lawyer*
Keck, Paul E., Jr. *psychiatrist*
Kelley, John Joseph, Jr. *lawyer*
Kereiakes, Dean James *cardiologist*
Kern, David Graham *lawyer*
Kernan, Jerome Bernard *retired marketing educator, researcher*
Kessinger, Thomas Anthony *education educator, social studies educator, researcher, consultant*
Kiel, Frederick Orin *lawyer*
Kilgore, Jenny A. *education educator*
Kindt, Monica V. *lawyer*
Kircher, Christopher *neurologist, consultant*
Klein, Jerry Emanuel *insurance planning and financial planning executive*
Klein, Sophia H. *entrepreneur*
Kleindorfer, Dawn Olson *medical educator, neurologist*
Kordons, Uldis *lawyer*
Kotchka, Claudia B. *consumer products company executive, accountant*
Kowel, Stephen Thomas *electrical engineer, educator*
Kronick, Susan D. *retail executive*
Kuhn, Keith C. *library director*
Kuntz, Charles, IV, *neurosurgeon*
Laffitte, Larry James *industrial organizational psychologist, consultant*
Lafley, Alan G. *consumer products company executive*
Laney, Sandra Eileen *information technology executive*
Langston, Malinda L. *lawyer*
Lauer, Richard T. *lawyer*
Lawrence, James Kaufman Lebensburger *lawyer*
Lawrence, Jennifer L. *lawyer*
Lawson, Randall Clayton, II, *finance company executive*
Lee, Eric McCauley *museum director, art historian*
Lehmann, Corinne E. *medical educator*
Levinson, Joseph E. *retired internist, rheumatologist, educator*
Lewis, Marvin *professional football coach*
Lichtin, Leon (Judah Leon Lichtin) *retired pharmaceutical educator*
Lindberg, Charles David *lawyer*
Lindell, Andrea Regina *dean, nurse*
Lindner, Carl H. III *insurance company executive*
Lindner, Carl Henry, Jr. *insurance company executive, professional sports team owner*
Lindner, S(tephen) Craig *insurance company executive*
Liss, William J. *lawyer*
Lockwood, Bert Berkley, Jr. *law educator*
Loftus, Jean M. *plastic surgeon*
Loggie, Jennifer Mary Hildreth *retired physician, educator*
Long, Don Scott *physiatrist*
Long, Phillip Clifford *retired museum director*
Longenecker, Mark Hershey, Jr. *lawyer*
Lorentz, Joshua A. *lawyer*
Love, Lisa A. *lawyer*
Lowe, Kenneth W. *multimedia executive*
Lower, Elyse E. *physician, educator*
Lucke, Robert Vito *investment company executive*
Luckner, Herman Richard III *interior designer*
Lundgren, Terry J. *retail company executive*
Lundrigan, Nicole M. *lawyer*
Lutz, James Gurney *lawyer*
Maeder, Michael C. *endocrinologist*
Mahon, Stephen C. *lawyer*
Mallory, Mark L. *mayor, former state legislator*
Malof, Kevin K. *lawyer*
Maltz, Robert *surgeon*
Mann, David Scott *lawyer*
Mantel, Samuel Joseph, Jr. *management educator, consultant*
Marshall, Christopher G. *bank executive*
Martin, John Bruce *chemical engineer*
Mason, Jeremy R. *lawyer*
Mason, Rachel J. *lawyer*
Maxwell, Robert Wallace, II, *lawyer*
McAusland, Randolph Melville Neal *writer, art consultant*
McClain, William Andrew *lawyer*
McCluskey, Laurie A. *lawyer*
McDaniels, Audrey Evelyn *microbiologist*
McDonald, Robert Alan (Bob McDonald) *consumer products company executive*
McEwen, Bob *former congressman*
McGavran, Frederick Jaeger *lawyer*
McGeorge, Don W. *retail executive*
McHenry, Powell *lawyer*
McKay, Bernard L. *lawyer*
McMullen, W. Rodney *financial officer*
McMullin, Ruth Roney *retired publishing executive*
McPeek, Bradley *lawyer*
Meal, Larie *chemistry professor, researcher, consultant*
Mechem, Charles Stanley, Jr. *retired broadcast executive*
Medina, Krista Lisdahl *neuropsychologist, educator*
Mehta, Parinda Apurva *pediatrician, medical educator, hematologist, oncologist*
Meister, Julia B. *lawyer*
Meller, Jaroslaw *biotechnologist, information scientist, educator*
Meyers, Karen Diane *lawyer, educator*
Meyers, Pamela Sue *lawyer*
Miles, John Bill *retired accountant, tax specialist*
Miller, W. Timothy *lawyer*
Moeddel, Michael J. *lawyer*
Montavon, Victoria A. *university librarian, dean*
Mordino, Joseph T. *lawyer*
Morgan, Victoria *performing company executive, choreographer*
Morgan, William Richard *mechanical engineer*
Motch, Marjorie McCullough *service organization executive*
Moyo, Kimya Maunda *elementary school educator*
Munir, Muhammad *pain medicine physician, director*
Murphy, Theodore R., II, *utilities executive*
Nakata, Akinori *epidemiologist, psychologist, researcher*
Nalbandian, John B. *lawyer*
Nebert, Daniel Walter *molecular geneticist, research administrator*
Nechemias, Stephen Murray *lawyer*
Nester, William Raymond, Jr. *retired academic administrator*
Newman, Danny Merril *lawyer*
Nielsen, George Lee *architect*
Nussbaum, Michael Scot *physician, medical educator*
Oberhaus, Geoffrey Luther *lawyer*
O'Grady, Michael J. *lawyer*
O'Guinn, M. Dave III *lawyer*
O'Hara, Sara Marie *radiologist*
O'Reilly, James Thomas *lawyer, educator, writer*
Orr, James Francis *business process outsourcing executive*
Pacheco, Bryan E. *lawyer*
Painter, Mark Philip *judge*
Palmer, Carson *professional football player*
Panioto, Ronald Angelo *judge*
Parker, R. Joseph *lawyer*
Pathak, Sanjeev *psychiatrist, researcher*
Paulson, Eric J. *literacy education educator*
Pepper, John Ennis, Jr. *former consumer products company, historical museum executive*
Perlman, Burton *judge*
Petrie, Bruce Inglis *lawyer*
Pilarczyk, Daniel Edward *archbishop*
Pomerantz, Wendy Jane *pediatrician, educator*
Porotsky, Richard D., Jr. *lawyer*
Porter, Robert Carl, Jr. *lawyer*
Preiser, Wolfgang Friedrich Ernst *architect, educator, consultant, researcher*
Proffitt, Kevin *archivist*
Rahnfeld, Vincent D. *counseling administrator*
Rammes, Lisa M. *lawyer*
Ramsey, Jamie M. *lawyer*
Ramundo, Kimberly E. *lawyer*
Randman, Barry I. *real estate developer*
Randolph, Leonard McElroy, Jr. *career officer*
Ratliff, Thomas Asbury, Jr. *retired engineer*
Reddy, Likith V. *maxillofacial surgeon, director*
Reichert, David *lawyer*
Relyea, Carl Miller *retired hydrologist*
Reuter, Mark F. *lawyer*
Reynolds, Paul L. *lawyer, bank executive*
Rich, Robert Edward *lawyer*
Richardson, Eric W. *lawyer*
Roach, Adrienne J. *lawyer*
Rogers, Brie S. *lawyer*
Rogers, John Marshall *judge, educator*
Rohner, Nicholas K. *lawyer*
Rose, Donald McGregor *retired lawyer*
Ross, Lori A. *lawyer*
Rowe, Rachael A. *lawyer*
Rucker, Fanon A. *lawyer*
Ruh, Michael A., Jr. *lawyer*
Rumberg, Orly Robin *lawyer*
Runk, Fred J. *retired insurance company executive*
Ruthman, Thomas Robert *manufacturing executive*
Ruwe, Bradley N. *lawyer*
Ryan, James Joseph *retired lawyer*
Saal, Howard Max *clinical geneticist, pediatrician, educator*
Sakkab, Nabil Yaqub *research and development company executive*
Sallquist, Gary Ardin *minister, non-profit executive*
Samson, Carl J. *artist*
Sarembock, Ian Joseph *internist, cardiologist*
Schaefer, Frank William III *microbiologist, researcher*
Schaefer, George A., Jr. *bank executive*
Schatz, Brett A. *lawyer*
Scheineson, Irwin Bruce *insurance and investment company executive*
Schiff, John Jefferson, Jr. *finance company executive*
Schlotman, J. Michael *food products executive*
Schreiner, Albert William *internist, educator*
Schrier, Arnold *historian, educator*
Schubert, William Kuenneth *hospital medical center executive*
Schuck, Thomas Robert *lawyer, farmer*
Schwartz, Robert Terry *industrial designer, director*
Scott, Jim *radio personality*
Senhauser, John Crater *architect*
Shaffer, Robert M.M. *lawyer*
Shearer, David A., Jr. *lawyer*
Shipley, Tony L(ee) *software company executive*
Shore, Thomas Spencer, Jr. *retired lawyer*
Siekmann, Donald Charles *accountant*
Sies, Timothy Ray *music educator*
Silbersack, Mark Louis *lawyer*
Silberstein, Edward Bernard *nuclear medicine educator, oncologist, researcher*
Simpson, Lisa Ann *physician, educator*
Sinha, Sunil K. *aerospace engineer, consultant*
Smith, Gregory Allgire *academic administrator*
Smith, Leroy Harrington, Jr. *mechanical engineer, consultant*
Smith, Sheila Marie *lawyer*
Smittle, Nelson Dean *military analyst, artist*
Smyth, Robery M. *lawyer*
Souter, Philip Frank *research scientist*
Sowder, Fred Allen *foundation administrator, alphabet specialist*
Sprecher, Christina M. *lawyer*
Sprecher, Kevin S. *lawyer*
Stern, David Mark *dean, educator*
Stern, Joseph Smith, Jr. *former footwear manufacturing company executive*
Stern, Noah J. *lawyer*
Stewart, John Patrick *art educator, researcher*
Stinson, Mary Florence *retired nursing educator*
Storrs, Glenn William *museum administrator, paleontologist*
Sublett, Roger H. *academic administrator*
Sullivan, James F. *physicist, researcher*
Sundberg, Ruth Dorothy *hematologist, educator*
Sung, Hou-mei *curator, researcher*
Sutton, Jeffrey S. *federal judge*
Swigert, James Mack *lawyer*
Tan, Ming *research scientist*
Teeters, Jeffrey R. *lawyer*
Ten Eyck, Dorothea Fariss *real estate agent*
Tepe, Thomas M., Jr. *lawyer*
Thompson, James E. *lawyer*
Tobias, Paul Henry *lawyer*
Tocco, James *pianist*
Tomain, Joseph Patrick *law educator, retired dean*
Trokhan, Paul Dennis *technologist, researcher*
Tsibulsky, Vladimir Lvovich *psychologist, researcher*
Tsuneoka, Yutaka *molecular geneticist*
Uhi, Judd R. *lawyer*
Ure, Colin *research scientist*
Valentine, Lona J. *lawyer*
Vander Laan, Mark Alan *lawyer*
Visscher, Marty Orrico *biomedical researcher*
Vogel, Cedric Wakelee *lawyer*
Wagner, Thomas Edward *academic administrator, educator*
Wales, Ross Elliot *lawyer*
Wall, Della *human resources specialist, manufacturing executive*
Weber, H. Patrick *lawyer*
Weber, Herman Jacob *senior district judge*
Weeks, Steven Wiley *lawyer*
Wei, Heng *engineering educator*
Weinstein, Anna *music educator*
Weisenberger, Andrew *lawyer*
Weisman, Joel *retired engineering educator*
Welsh, George Franklin *plastic surgeon, educator*
Wesloh, Steven M. *lawyer*
West, Clark Darwin *pediatric nephrologist, educator*
Westbrook, Lynda A. *financial consultant*
Wheatley, Christine S. *lawyer*
Whitsett, Jeffrey Allen *pediatric educator*
Wilkowski, E. Todd *lawyer*
Wilson, Christopher J. *lawyer*
Winfrey, Marcellene Sedetta *music educator, church musician*
Winkler, Henry Ralph *retired academic administrator, historian*
Wiot, Jerome Francis *radiologist*
Wisler, David Charles *aerospace engineer*
Witten, Louis *physics professor*
Wood, Robert Emerson *pediatrics educator*
Woods, Carol Smith *private school educator*
Woodside, Frank C. III *lawyer, educator, physician*
Wuebbling, Donald J. *lawyer, insurance company executive*
Wulker, Laurence Joseph *portfolio manager, educator, financial planner*
Wygant, Foster Laurance *art educator*
Yalamanchili, Surya *advertising executive*
Yi, Michael *internist, pediatrician*
Zahneis, Leona Beth *lawyer*
Zahniser, Rachel S. *lawyer*
Zamary, Kimberly Kyle *lawyer*
Zaring, Allen G. *homebuilding company executive*
Zavatsky, Michael Joseph *lawyer*
Zimmerman, James M. *retail company executive*
Zimmerman, James M. *lawyer*
Zimpher, Nancy Lusk *academic administrator*
Zola, Gary Phillip *rabbi, historian*

Circleville

Conley, John Wallace *academic administrator*
Smith, James Leslie *minister, educator, counselor*

Cleveland

Abramson, Alexis R. *mechanical engineering educator*
Adamo, Kenneth Robert *lawyer*
Adams, Albert T. *lawyer*
Adams, Henry *art educator*
Agani, Faton Hilmi *anatomist, educator*
Aldrich, Ann *judge*
Anderson, James M. *pathologist*
Andorka, Frank Henry *lawyer*
Andrews, Oakley V. *lawyer*
Angus, John Cotton *chemical engineering educator*
Appleby, Stuart *professional golfer*
Arnold, Craig *manufacturing executive*
Ashmus, Keith Allen *lawyer*
Austin, Arthur Donald, II, *lawyer, educator*
Awais, George Musa *obstetrician, gynecologist*

Bacon, Brett Kermit *lawyer*
Baker, Saul Phillip *geriatrician, cardiologist, internist*
Barnett, Gene Henry *neurosurgeon*
Barrie, Dennis Ray *museum director*
Baskind, Samantha *art historian*
Bays, James C. *lawyer*
Beall, Cynthia *anthropologist, educator*
Bell, James R. III *bank executive*
Bellamy, Gail Anne Ghetia *magazine editor, author, speaker*
Berger, Melvin *allergist, immunologist*
Berger, Nathan Allen *medical educator, academic administrator*
Berick, James Herschel *lawyer*
Bethoux, François Andre *physiatrist, researcher*
Bhadra, Narendra *biomedical engineer, researcher*
Bibb, Paul E. (Buck Bibb) *bank executive*
Bidelman, William Pendry *astronomer, educator*
Binford, Gregory Glenn *lawyer*
Binstock, Robert Henry *public policy educator, writer*
Blackwell, John *science educator*
Blum, Arthur *social worker, educator*
Boboc, Marius *education educator*
Bodner, Donald Roger *urologist, medical educator*
Bowen, Richard Lee *architect*
Bowerfind, Edgar Sihler, Jr. *internist, educator, retired medical association administrator*
Boyd, Arthur Bernette, Jr. *surgeon, clergyman, beverage company executive*
Boyko, Christopher Allan *federal judge*
Boyle, Kammer *financial planner, investment advisor, research analyst, options trader*
Brandt, John Reynold *editor, journalist*
Braverman, Herbert Leslie *lawyer*
Bravo, Kenneth Allan *lawyer*
Brazdil, James Frank *chemist, researcher*
Brennan, Maureen *lawyer*
Brentlinger, Paul Smith *venture capital executive*
Brody, Robert *dermatologist, educator*
Brown, Mike *professional basketball coach*
Brucken, Robert Matthew *lawyer*
Bruner, William Evans, II, *ophthalmologist, educator, researcher*
Buente, Stephen M. *manufacturing executive*
Buhrow, William Carl *religious organization administrator*
Burge, David Alan *lawyer, writer*
Burghart, James Henry *electrical engineer, educator*
Burke, Kathleen B. *lawyer*
Burke, Lillian Walker *retired judge*
Burns, Michael Kent *retired educator, chemical dependency counselor*
Burton, Jay H. *sports management executive*
Cahn, James *lawyer, educator*
Cairns, James Donald *lawyer*
Calkins, Benjamin *lawyer*
Calkins, Hugh *foundation executive*
Callahan, Thomas James *lawyer*
Callesen-Gyorgak, Jan Elaine *special education educator*
Campbell, Jane Louise *former mayor*
Carey, Paul Richard *biophysicist*
Carfagna, Peter A. *lawyer*
Carlson, James R. *lawyer*
Carlsson, Bo Axel Vilhelm *economics professor*
Carrabba, Joseph A. *mining executive*
Carrol, Edward Nicholas *psychologist*
Carson, Randy W. *manufacturing executive*
Carson, Van *lawyer*
Carter, E. Kennedy, Jr. *bank executive*
Carter, John Dale *organizational development coordinator*
Cassill, Herbert Carroll *artist*
Castele, Theodore John *radiologist*
Cavanagh, Matthew John *lawyer*
Cerone, David *academic administrator*
Cerqueira, Manuel DeCastro *nuclear medicine physician*
Chak, Amitabh *gastroenterologist, researcher*
Chamis, Christos Constantinos *aerospace scientist, educator*
Charnas, Michael (Mannie) *investment company executive*
Christopher, William F. *metal products executive*
Chung, Anita *curator*
Chvetsov, Alexei V. *medical physicist, educator*
Ciccia, Angela Hein *speech educator, speech pathology/audiology services professional*
Cirincione, Ross Joseph *mathematician, educator*
Clapp, Kent W. *insurance company executive*
Clark, Paul G. *bank executive*
Clark, Robert Arthur *mathematician, educator*
Clarke, Charles Fenton *lawyer*
Coffey, Thomas William *lawyer*
Coleman, Deborah Ann *lawyer*
Collin, Thomas James *lawyer*
Collins, Duane E. *manufacturing executive*
Colussi, Valdir Carlos *physicist*
Conner, William Herbert *lawyer*
Connor, Christopher M. *manufacturing executive*
Connors, Alfred Francis *internist, researcher*
Conrad, Robert David *broadcast executive, educator*
Cooper, Gregory Scott *epidemiologist, gastroenterologist, educator*
Copelan, Edward A. *medical educator*
Copeland, Sharon *reporter*
Coquillette, William Hollis *lawyer*
Cosgrove, Delos M. (Toby Cosgrove) *health facility administrator, surgeon*
Couture, Jon N. *bank executive*
Cowan, Dale Harvey *internist, lawyer*
Creasey, Graham Harold *surgeon, researcher*
Crist, Paul Grant *lawyer*
Cronquist, Robert Lee *conductor*
Crosby, Fred McClellan *retail executive*
Crowl, Robert B. *bank executive*
Cudak, Gail Linda *lawyer*
Currivan, John Daniel *lawyer*
Cutler, Alexander MacDonald *manufacturing executive*
Cutler, Timothy Spence *music educator, composer*
Daberko, David A. *bank executive*
Danco, Léon Antoine *management consultant, educator*
Dancyger, Ruth *art historian*
Dannemiller, John C. *transportation company executive*
Daroff, Robert Barry *neurologist, educator*
Davis, Pamela Bowes *pediatric pulmonologist*
Deal, William Thomas *retired school psychologist*
Decker, John William *metal products executive*
DeGroote, Michael G. *management consulting company executive*
Deissler, Robert George *fluid dynamics researcher*
DeKaser, Richard J. *bank executive*
Dell'Osso, Louis Frank *neuroscience educator*
DeMetz, Kathleen Susan *lawyer*
Deming, David Lawson *art educator*
Demitrack, Thomas *lawyer*
Deschenes, Isabelle *medical educator, researcher*
Detterman, Douglas Kenward *psychologist, researcher*
Dicken, Eric L. *academic administrator*
DiSilvio, Marilena *lawyer*
Distelhorst, Garis Fred *trade association administrator*
DiVenere, Anthony Joseph *lawyer*
Domeck, Brian C. *insurance company executive*
Domenzain, Antonio *statistician, consultant*
Domiano, Joseph Charles *lawyer*
Doris, Alan S(anford) *lawyer*
Downey, Kay *librarian*
Dreicer, Robert *oncologist, director, medical educator*
Drinko, John Deaver *lawyer*
Dugan, Patrick J. *lawyer*
Dunbar, Mary Asmundson *communications executive, public information officer, consultant, investor*
Duncan, Ed Eugene *lawyer*
Dunham, J. Andrew *bank executive*
Duvin, Robert Phillip *lawyer*
Eagleeye-Lord, Amy *writer, editor*
Eastwood, Gregory Lindsay *former academic administrator*
Eberhard, William Thomas *architect*
Egger, Terrance C.Z. *publishing executive*
Eiben, Robert Michael *pediatric neurologist, educator*
Ellis, Lloyd H., Jr. *emergency physician, art historian*
Elston, Robert C. *medical educator*
Emrick, Charles Robert, Jr. *lawyer*
Eng, Charis Eu Li *oncologist, geneticist*
Erb, Donald *composer*
Eustis, Joanne D. *university librarian*
Fabens, Andrew Lawrie III *lawyer*
Falcone, Tommaso *reproductive endocrinologist*
FallCreek, Stephanie Jean *non-profit organization executive*
Fallon, Pat *artist, educator*
Falsgraf, William Wendell *retired lawyer*
Fay, Regan Joseph *lawyer*
Fazio, Victor Warren *physician, colon and rectal surgeon*
Fearon, Richard H. *manufacturing executive*
Feinberg, Paul H. *retired lawyer*
Felty, Kriss Delbert *lawyer*
Ferry, Danny *professional sports team executive, retired professional basketball player*
Finn, Robert *writer, educator*
Fischer, Michelle K. *lawyer*
Fletcher, Robert *retired lawyer*
Fountain, Ronald Glenn *management consultant, corporate financial executive, entrepreneur, educator*
Frate, Daniel J. *bank executive*
Freire, Gloria Medonis *social worker*
Friedman, Barton Robert *language educator*
Friedman, Harold Edward *lawyer*
Friedman, James Moss *lawyer*
Fu, Zhenghong Alex *medical educator*
Fung, John Julian *transplant surgeon, immunologist*
Gallagher, Patrick Francis Xavier *public relations executive*
Gardner, Richard Kent *retired librarian, educator, editor*
Gentile Sachs, Valerie Ann *lawyer*
Geraghty, Paul D. *bank executive*
Giannetti, Louis Daniel *film critic, educator*
Gibans, James David *architect, consultant*
Gildea, Thomas Robert *pulmonologist*
Gillespie, Robert Wayne *banker*
Glaser, Robert Edward *lawyer*
Glickman, Carl David *banker*
Goetz, Kenneth M. *bank executive*
Goffman, William *mathematician, educator*
Goins, Frances Floriano *lawyer*
Gold, Gerald Seymour *lawyer*
Goldberg, Jerold S. *academic administrator*
Goldberg, Susan *editor*
Goldfarb, Bernard Sanford *lawyer*
Goldman, Steven Andrew *plastic surgeon, educator*
Goldstein, Marvin Emanuel *aerospace scientist*
Goler, Michael David *lawyer*
Gooden, Drew *professional basketball player*
Goodman, David S. *lawyer*
Gorney, Jon L. *bank executive*
Grabow, Raymond John *mayor, lawyer*
Grebenc, Jane *bank executive*
Greppin, John Aird Coutts *philologist, editor, educator*
Groedel, Caryn G. *lawyer*
Grossman, Mary Margaret *retired elementary school educator*
Grossman, Theodore Martin *lawyer*
Gulick, James P. *bank executive*
Haeck, James F. *manufacturing executive*
Hafner, Travis Lee *professional baseball player*
Haiman, Irwin Sanford *lawyer*
Hajj-Ali, Rula Adel *rheumatologist, researcher*
Hardy, Richard Allen *mechanical engineer, engineering executive*
Harris, Paul N. *lawyer*
Hastings, Susan C. *lawyer*
Henes, Samuel Ernst *lawyer*
Henman, Tim *professional tennis player*
Hennessy, Sean P. *corporate financial executive*
Henry, Edward Frank *retired data processing executive*
Heresi, Gustavo A. *physician*
Hermann, Robert Ewald *retired surgeon*
Hochman, Kenneth George *lawyer*
Hoerner, Robert Jack *lawyer*
Hoffman, Sharona *law educator*
Hogg, James Stuart *lawyer*
Hokenstad, Merl Clifford, Jr. *social work educator*
Hollington, Richard Rings, Jr. *lawyer*
Holmes, Arthur S. *manufacturing executive*
Holzbach, Raymond Thomas *gastroenterologist, educator, writer*
Horner, John Atlee *educational association administrator*
Horst, J. Robert *lawyer*
Horvitz, Michael John *lawyer*
Hundert, Edward M. *former academic administrator, educator*
Iannotti, Joseph Patrick *orthopedic surgeon*
Ivy, Conway Gayle *paint company executive*
Jackson, Frank G. *mayor*
Jacobs, Leslie William *lawyer*
Jacobs, Richard E. *real estate company executive, sports team owner*
James, LeBron *professional basketball player*
Janke, Ronald Robert *lawyer*
Jelinek, Gregory M. *bank executive*
Jensen, Kathryn Patricia (Kit) *broadcast executive*
Jenson, Jon Eberdt *metal products executive*
Jerse, Edward *state representative*
Jeyakumar, Anita *pediatrician, otolaryngologist*
Jindra, Christine *editor*
Jorgenson, Mary Ann *lawyer*
Kahrl, Robert Conley *lawyer*
Kaouk, Jihad *urologist*
Karp, Marvin Louis *lawyer*
Kass, Lawrence *hematologist, oncologist, educator*
Katcher, Richard *lawyer*
Katz, Lewis Robert *law educator*
Kelly, Dennis Michael *lawyer*
Kelly, Jeffrey D. *bank executive*
Kestner, Robert Steven *lawyer*
Khayat, Clark *bank executive*
Kilbane, Thomas Stanton *lawyer*
Kinsella, Timothy J. *radiation oncologist*
Kirsch, James F. *materials executive*
Klopman, Gilles *chemistry professor*
Knerly, Stephen John, Jr. *lawyer*
Ko, Wen-Hsiung *electrical engineering educator*
Koch, Charles John *credit agency executive*
Koenig, Jack L. *chemist, educator*
Kohn, Mary Louise Beatrice *nurse*
Kohn, William Irwin *lawyer*
Kolb, David Allen *psychologist, educator*
Kolda, Thomas Joseph *non-profit organization executive*
Komoroski, Len *professional sports team executive*
Korngold, Gerald *law educator, former dean*
Kovel, Ralph Mallory *writer, antique expert*
Kovel, Terry Horvitz *writer, antiques authority*
Kowalski, Kenneth Lawrence *physicist, researcher*
Kraay, Matthew Joseph *orthopedist, educator*
Kramer, Edward George *lawyer*
Kramer, Eugene Leo *lawyer*
Krasuski, Richard *cardiologist*
Krauss, Lawrence Maxwell *physicist, astronomy educator, researcher, author*
Kuehn, Richard Arthur *telecommunications consultant*
Kurit, Neil *lawyer*
Lamm, Michael Emanuel *pathologist, immunologist, educator*
Lando, Jerome Burton *macromolecular science educator*
Lathe, Timothy J. *bank executive*
Lawniczak, James Michael *lawyer*
Lease, Robert K. *lawyer*
Leavitt, Jeffrey Stuart *lawyer*
Lefferts, William Geoffrey *internist, educator*
LeGrand, Susan Buchanan *palliative medicine physician, educator*
Leiken, Earl Murray *lawyer*
Lenkoski, Leo Douglas *retired psychiatrist, educator*
Lennox, Heather *lawyer*
Lerner, Randolph D. *finance company executive*
Levitan, Nathan *internist, hematologist, medical oncologist*
Lewine, Mark Saul *anthropology professor*
Lewis, John Bruce *lawyer*
Lewis, John Francis *lawyer*
Lewis, Peter Benjamin *insurance company executive*
Lopez, Nancy *retired professional golfer*
Lord, James Gregory *organizational, community and philanthropic counsel*
Lowe, James Allison *lawyer, educator*
Lowe, John Burton *medical association administrator, molecular biologist, educator, pathologist*
Lowe, Mark J. *physicist*
Luke, Randall Dan *retired manufacturing executive, lawyer*
Lyons, Janis E. *bank executive*
Lytle, Bruce Whitney *cardiovascular surgeon*
Machaskee, Alex *retired newspaper publishing company executive*
Mack, Richard G. *mathematician, consultant*
Macklis, Roger Milton *physician, educator, researcher*
Madden, James D. *forensic engineer*
Madison, Robert Prince *architect*
Malangoni, Mark Alan *surgeon, educator*
Mandel, Jack N. *manufacturing executive*
Manning, W. Robert, Jr. *bank executive*
Markus, Richard M. *judge, arbitrator*
Martinez, Victor Jesus *professional baseball player*
Marting, Michael G. *lawyer*
Mason, Thomas Albert *retired lawyer*
Mates, Barbara T. *librarian, library association executive*
Matia, Paul Ramon *lawyer*
Mawardi, Osman Kamel *retired plasma physicist*
Mayland, Kenneth Theodore *economist*
Mayne, Lucille Stringer *finance educator*
McArdle, Richard Joseph *retired academic administrator*
Mc Cartan, Patrick Francis *lawyer*
McCarthy, Mark Francis *lawyer*
McCartin, Joseph T. *bank executive*
McCrodden, Bruce A. *bank executive*
McCullough, Joseph *retired academic administrator*
McFadden, John Volney *retired manufacturing company executive*
McGinty, Alan J. *real estate company executive*
McGuire, Mark M. *lawyer, manufacturing executive*
McHale, Vincent Edward *political science professor*
McHenry, Martin Christopher *physician, educator*
McKee, Thomas Frederick *lawyer*
McLaughlin, Patrick Michael *lawyer*
Meador, Michael Anthony *chemist, researcher*
Mehlman, Maxwell Jonathan *law educator*
Meissner, Michael G. *lawyer*
Messinger, Donald Hathaway *lawyer*
Meyer, G. Christopher *lawyer*
Miller, Genevieve *retired medical historian*
Millisor, Kenneth Ray *lawyer*
Millstone, David Jeffrey *lawyer*
Moceanu, Dominique *retired Olympic athlete*
Molyneaux, David Glenn *newspaper travel editor*
Montague, Drogo K. *urologist*
Mood, Girish Rudra Naik *physician*
Mooney, Beth *bank executive*
Moore, Karen Nelson *judge*
Moore, Kenneth Cameron *lawyer*
Morgenthaler, David Turner *venture capitalist*
Morikis, John G. *manufacturing executive*
Morrical, Glenn Edwin *lawyer*
Musallam, Samer Makram *lawyer*
Myers, Eddie Earl *psychologist*
Nance, Frederick *lawyer*
Naraine, Chameli *bank executive*
Neal, Carolyn V. *librarian*
Nelson, Sue Grodsky *humanities educator, consultant*
Neuhauser, Duncan vonBriesen *medical educator*
Newman, John M., Jr. *lawyer*
Nickerson, Gary Lee *educational consultant*
Nicols, Howard J.C. *lawyer*
Nissen, Steven E. *cardiologist, researcher*
Novick, Andrew Carl *urologist*
Oakar, Mary Rose *congresswoman*
O'Hara, Thomas Patrick *managing editor*
Okada, Ronald Shig *lawyer*
O'Keefe, Francis Ronald *lawyer*
Ollinger, W. James *lawyer*
Olness, Karen Norma *medical educator*
Ornt, Daniel B. *physician*
Osborne, Frank R. *lawyer, educator, lecturer*
Owendoff, Stephen Peter *lawyer*
Pallam, John James *lawyer*
Paris, Zachary T. *lawyer*
Parobek, Drew Thomas *lawyer*
Parry, Michael *not-for-profit fundraiser, singer, actor*
Pearlman, Samuel Segel *lawyer, educator*
Penman, Robbie Mae *volunteer, political organization worker*
Perkovic, Robert Branko *retired international management consultant*
Perry, George Williamson *lawyer*
Pianalto, Sandra *bank executive*
Pierce, Mary *professional tennis player*
Pietrzen, Julie Lynn *lawyer*
Pike, Kermit Jerome *cultural organization administrator*
Pilla, Anthony Michael *bishop*
Piraino, Thomas Anthony, Jr. *lawyer*
Podboy, Alvin Michael, Jr. *law librarian, director*
Pogue, Richard Welch *lawyer*
Pollock, R. Jeffrey *lawyer*
Prahl, Joseph Markel *mechanical engineering educator*
Price, T. Michael *bank executive*
Pugh, David L. *manufacturing executive*
Putka, Andrew Charles *lawyer*
Queen, Joyce *elementary school educator*
Quigney, Theresa Ann *special education educator*
Raaf, John Hart *surgeon, educator, health facility administrator*
Raghavan, Derek *oncologist, medical researcher, educator*
Rains, M. Neal *lawyer*
Rakita, Louis *retired cardiologist*
Ransohoff, Richard Milton *neurologist, researcher*
Rao, Shaoqi *medical educator*
Rapp, Robert Neil *lawyer*
Raskind, Peter E. *bank executive*
Rawson, Rachel L. *lawyer*
Rawson, Robert H., Jr. *lawyer*
Remick, Scot Clifton *oncologist, clinical investigator, educator*
Reminger, Richard Thomas *lawyer, artist*
Renwick, Glenn M. *insurance company executive*
Reppert, Richard Levi *lawyer*
Resnick, Martin I. *urologist, educator*
Rhew, Perry James *federal judge*
Rice, Philip L. *bank executive*
Richlovsky, Thomas Andrew *bank executive*
Rickert, Jeanne Martin M. *lawyer*
Roberts-Mamone, Lisa A. *lawyer*

Robinson, William H. *curator, art historian, educator*
Rogers, Charles Edwin *physical chemistry and polymer science professor*
Rome, Ellen S. *physician*
Roop, James John *public relations executive*
Rosenbaum, Jacob I. *retired lawyer*
Rothstein, Fred C. *health facility administrator*
Rowe, Robert C. *bank executive*
Rub, Timothy F. *museum director*
Ruben, Alan Miles *law educator*
Ruff, Robert Louis *neurologist, physiologist, researcher*
Saada, Adel Selim *civil engineer, educator*
Sabathia, C.C. (Carsten Charles Sabathia) *professional baseball player*
Salomon, Roger Blaine *retired language educator*
Sande, Theodore Anton *architect, educator, foundation executive*
Sanislo, Paul Steve *lawyer*
Santisi, Terri M. (Theresa M. Santisi) *multi-media company executive*
Savinell, Robert Francis *engineering educator*
Sawyer, Raymond Terry *lawyer, consultant, theater producer*
Schaefer, David Arnold *lawyer*
Schecter, William H. *bank executive*
Schneider, Richard Durbin *art educator*
Schreckengost, Viktor *artist*
Schuele, Donald Edward *retired physics professor, dean*
Schwieg, Frederic P. *lawyer*
Seger, Thomas M. *lawyer*
Seifert, Shelley Jane *bank executive*
Seles, Monica *professional tennis player*
Shapiro, Fred David *lawyer*
Shapiro, Mark *professional sports team executive*
Shatila, Ahmad Hussain *surgeon, oncologist*
Sheeran, Timothy J. *lawyer*
Sherry, Paul Henry *minister, religious organization administrator*
Sibley, Willis Elbridge *anthropology educator, consultant*
Sicherman, Marvin Allen *lawyer*
Siedlecki, Sandra Lee *nursing educator, researcher*
Simmons, Clinton Craig *human resources executive*
Simson, Gary Joseph *dean, law educator*
Sizemore, Grady III *professional baseball player*
Slinger, Michael Jeffery *law librarian, director*
Slobozhanin, Lev Arkadievich *fluid mechanics engineer, researcher*
Smith, Jerome (Dr. Jerome Smith) *not-for-profit developer, film producer, writer*
Smith, Mark Anthony *neuroscientist, educator*
Smith, N. Lindsey *lawyer*
Snyder, Barbara Rook *academic administrator*
Sobonya, Stephanie Jean N'Cole *mathematics educator*
Sogg, Wilton Sherman *lawyer*
Solomon, Randall Lee *lawyer*
Soltis, Katherine *editor*
Stanley, Hugh Monroe, Jr. *lawyer*
Stanton, R. Thomas *lawyer*
Stanton-Hicks, Michael D'Arcy *anesthesiologist, pain medicine specialist*
Stauffer, Thomas George *retired hotel executive*
Stavitsky, Abram Benjamin *immunologist, educator*
Stellato, Louis Eugene *lawyer*
Stern, Robert C. *pediatrician, medical educator*
Stevens, Thomas Charles *lawyer*
Stewart, William James *cardiologist*
Stokes, Louis *lawyer, former congressman*
Stone, James Merrill *lawyer*
Stone, Karin L. *bank executive*
Stornes, Mark *professional sports team executive*
Stratton-Crooke, Thomas Edward *financial consultant*
Strauch, John L. *lawyer*
Striefsky, Linda A(nn) *lawyer*
Strimbu, Victor, Jr. *lawyer*
Stropki, John M., Jr. *electric power industry executive*
Stuhan, Richard George *lawyer*
Summers, William B., Jr. *brokerage house executive*
Summers, William Lawrence *lawyer*
Swartzbaugh, Marc L. *lawyer*
Sweetenham, John W. *medical educator*
Sweetnam, James E. *manufacturing executive*
Swetland, David Wightman *real estate company executive, investment company executive*
Szarek, Stanislaw Jerzy *mathematics professor*
Taw, Dudley Joseph *sales executive, director*
Taylor, Harris C. *endocrinologist, consultant*
Taylor, Margaret Wischmeyer *retired language educator*
Taylor, Nellie Ruby *artist, poet*
Taylor, Steve Henry *zoologist*
Tengel, Jeffrey J. *bank executive*
Terburg, Bart Paul *physicist, industrial engineer*
Thimmig, Diana Marie *lawyer*
Thomas, David Manning *secondary school educator*
Thomas, Dynda A. *lawyer*
Thomas, Richard Stephen *construction executive*
Thompson, Paul C. *labor union administrator*
T'ien, James Shaw-Tzuu *engineering educator*
Toohey, Brian Frederick *lawyer*
Toomajian, William Martin *lawyer*
Topol, Eric Jeffrey *academic administrator, cardiologist, educator*
Ubogu, Eroboghene Ekamereno *physician*
Vande Steeg, Nickolas W. *manufacturing executive*
Venable, Andrew A., Jr. *library director*
von Mehren, George M. *lawyer*
Waldeck, John Walter, Jr. *lawyer*
Waldo, Albert Leon *internist, educator*
Wallach, Mark Irwin *lawyer*
Walters, Mark Douglas *obstetrician, gynecologist, director*
Wang, Run *research scientist*
Warren, Russell James *investment banker, consultant*
Washkewicz, Donald E. *manufacturing executive*
Watson, Richard Thomas *lawyer*
Weaver, Robin Geoffrey *lawyer, educator*
Webster, Leslie Tillotson, Jr. *pharmacologist, educator*
Wedge, Eric *archbishop*
Weeden, Jeffrey Blane *bank executive*
Weidenthal, Maurice David (Bud) *academic administrator, journalist*
Weiler, Jeffry Louis *lawyer*
Weir, Dame Gillian Constance *musician*
Weiss, Morry *greeting card company executive*
Weiss, Zev *corporate financial executive*
Weitzner, Ronald Philip *special education educator*
Wells, Lesley *federal judge*
Welser-Möst, Franz *conductor, music director*
Wertheim, Sally Harris *director, academic administrator, dean, education educator, consultant*
White, Gregory A. *prosecutor*
Whitney, Richard Buckner *lawyer*
Wilson, Jack *aeronautical engineer*
Wish, Jay Barry *nephrologist, specialist*
Wolinsky, Emanuel *internist, educator*
Wong, Margaret Wai *lawyer*
Woods, Jacqueline F. *public relations executive*
Woyczynski, Wojbor Andrzej *mathematician, educator*
Wykle, May L. *dean, educator, researcher*
Yanoti, Timothy *bank executive*
Yetman, Randall John *plastic surgeon*
Young, James Edward *lawyer*
Young, Jess Ray *retired internist*
Zambie, Allan John *lawyer*
Zhang, Nengli *research scientist*
Zoeller, David Louis *lawyer, bank executive*
Zung, Thomas Tse-Kwai *architect*
Zwick, Gary Alan *lawyer*

Cleveland Heights

Challenger, Vicki Lee *elementary school educator*
Chilcote, Lee A. *lawyer*
Close, Carole Lynne *education educator, consultant*
Sandburg, Helga *author*

Columbia Station

Goll, Paulette Susan *education educator*
Yearley, Barbara Ellen *music educator*

Columbus

Acker, Alan Scott *lawyer*
Adams, Marty E. *diversified financial services company executive*
Adeli, Hojjat *engineer, educator, computer scientist*
Adelson, Edward *physicist, educator, musician*
Agbemabiese, Padmore Enyonam *educator*
Agnew, Gary *professional hockey coach*
Akers, Saundra Ruth *retired disability rights advocate*
Akins, Nicholas K. *electric power industry executive*
Alexander, Carl Albert *materials engineer, engineering educator*
Alger, Chadwick Fairfax *political scientist, educator*
Allen, Lois Arlene Height *musician*
Altan, Taylan *engineering educator, director*
Anand, Jaideep *management educator, consultant*
Anderson, Jon Mac *lawyer, educator*
Arvia, Anne L. *bank executive*
Ash, Thomas Phillip *school system administrator*
Aukland, Duncan Dayton *lawyer*
Ayers, James Cordon *lawyer*
Babcock, Charles Luther *classics educator*
Bagnoli, Dannelle M. *school psychologist*
Bailey, Daniel Allen *lawyer*
Baird, Leonard Lynn *social scientist, educator, researcher, editor*
Baker, J. Craig *electric power industry executive*
Balcerzak, Stanley Paul *retired hematologist, oncologist, director, medical educator*
Balkrishnan, Rajesh *education educator*
Barlow-Ware, Jacqueline Sue *music educator*
Barnes, Wallace Ray *retired lawyer*
Barnett, Robert B., Jr. *lawyer*
Barry, James P(otvin) *editor, writer*
Bartels, Robert Louis *retired physical education educator, coach*
Barth, Rolf Frederick *pathologist, educator*
Barthelmas, Ned Kelton *brokerage house executive*
Battersby, James Lyons, Jr. *language educator*
Beck, Paul Allen *dean, political science professor*
Behrman, Edward Joseph *biochemistry educator*
Beja, Morris *English literature educator*
Bell, Karen A. *dean*
Belton, John Thomas *lawyer*
Bennett, Robert Thomas *lawyer, professional athletics manager*
Berndt, Ellen German *lawyer*
Berntson, Gary Glen *psychiatry, psychology and pediatrics educator*
Berry, William Lee *business administration educator*
Beversdorf, David Quentin *neurologist, researcher*
Bhushan, Bharat *mechanical engineer*
Billings, Charles Edgar *physician*
Blackburn, John D. (John David Blackburn) *lawyer, educator*
Blanco, Humberto *soil scientist, researcher*
Bloomfield, Clara Derber *oncologist, educator, medical institute administrator*
Blum, William George *hematologist, clinical researcher educator*
Booker, James Douglas *retired lawyer, government official*
Boué, Daniel Robert *pediatric pathologist, neuropathologist, educator*
Boyle, Kevin Gerard *historian, educator, writer*
Branin, Joseph J. *library director*
Bridgman, G(eorge) Ross *lawyer*
Brodkey, Robert Stanley *chemical engineering educator*
Brooke, John L. *history professor*
Brooks, Richard Dickinson *lawyer*
Brown, Philip Albert *lawyer*
Brown, Rowland Chauncey Widrig *library and information scientist, consultant*
Brubaker, Robert Loring *lawyer*
Brunner, Jennifer Lee *state official, lawyer*
Brust, Frederick William, Jr. *structural and mechanical engineer*
Buchenroth, Stephen Richard *lawyer*
Budler, Joanne *library director*
Buehrer, Stephen *state senator*
Bullock, Joseph Daniel *pediatrician, educator*
Burgdoerfer, Stuart *retail executive*
Burke, Kenneth Andrew *advertising executive*
Bush, Margaret Eileen *elementary school educator*
Caniano, Donna Anne *surgeon, educator*
Capen, Charles Chabert *veterinary pathology educator*
Caragine, Louis Philip, Jr. *neurosurgeon*
Carnahan, John Anderson *retired lawyer*
Carpenter, Michael H. *lawyer*
Carter, William H. *chemicals executive*
Cenname, August *investment advisor*
Chandrasekaran, Balakrishnan *computer scientist, educator*
Chappelear, Stephen Eric *lawyer*
Charles, Gerard *performing company executive, choreographer*
Cheap, Richard A. *lawyer, bank executive*
Cheesman, Kerry Lee *biology educator, researcher*
Chester, John Jonas *lawyer, educator*
Chisholm, Malcolm Harold *chemistry professor*
Christoforidis, A. John *radiologist, educator*
Cocchi, Wayne Paul *special education educator*
Cole, Clarence Russell *college dean*
Cole, Ransey Guy, Jr. *federal judge*
Coleman, Michael Bennett *mayor*
Collier, David Alan *management educator*
Coopersmith, Jeffrey Alan *real estate developer*
Corbato, Charles Edward *geology educator, academic administrator*
Cordell, Philip Granvile *music educator, musician*
Cordray, Richard A. *state legislator*
Cornwell, David George *biochemist, educator*
Cottingham, Richard Sumner *paper company executive*
Cox, Mitchel Neal *editor*
Crowder, Marjorie Briggs *lawyer*
Cruz, Jose Bejar, Jr. *engineering educator*
Culbertson, Jack Arthur *education educator*
Cupp, Robert Richard *state supreme court justice, former state senator, attorney*
Curtin, Michael Francis *publishing executive*
Cvetanovich, Dan L. *lawyer*
Daab-Krzykowski, Andre *pharmaceutical and nutritional manufacturing company administrator*
Daehn, Glenn Steven *materials scientist*
Dann, Marc *state attorney general, former state senator*
Darling, George Curtis *minister, administrator*
Davis, Julia A. *lawyer, retail executive*
Davis, Steven A. *restaurant company executive*
Denlinger, David Landis *insect biology educator*
DeRousie, Charles Stuart *lawyer*
Di Lorenzo, John Florio, Jr. *retired lawyer*
Dimmick, John W. *communications educator*
Doolittle, Kenneth Herbert *retired urologist*
Dowling, Thomas Allan *mathematics professor*
Drvota, Mojmir *retired cinema educator, author*
Duckworth, Winston Howard *researcher*
Dunlay, Catherine Telles *lawyer*
Duryee, Harold Taylor *insurance consultant*
Edwards, Jennifer Lynn *adult education educator, researcher*
Elliot, David Hawksley *geologist, educator*
Ellison, Edwin Christopher *surgeon, educator*
Elsharydah, Ahmad *anesthesiologist*
English, Carl L. *electric power industry executive*
Epstein, Arthur Joseph *physics and chemistry educator*
Evans, Daniel E. *manufacturing executive, restaurant chain company executive*
Everhart, Velma Vizedom *retired home economics educator, retired real estate agent*
Fahey, Richard Paul *lawyer*
Fan, Liang-Shih *chemical engineering educator*
Faure, Gunter *geology educator*
Fawcett, Sherwood Luther *lab administrator*
Fay, Terrence Michael *lawyer*
Fedorov, Sergei *professional hockey player*
Fenton, Robert Earl *electrical engineering educator*
Ferguson, Gerald Paul *lawyer*
Findley, Carter Vaughn *historian, educator*
Fingerhut, Eric D. *academic administrator, former state legislator and congressman, lawyer*
Fisher, Lee I. *lieutenant governor, former state attorney general*
Fisher, Lloyd Edison, Jr. *lawyer*
Fishman, Steven S. *retail executive*
Flanagan-Soulen, Mary Susan *secondary school educator, adult education educator*
Floyd, Gary Leon *plant cell biologist*
Foland, Kenneth A. *geological sciences educator*
Foster, Jim (James S. Foster) *women's college basketball coach*
Foster, Woodbridge A. *medical entomologist, educator*
Fried, Samuel P. *lawyer*
Friedman, Avner *mathematician, educator*
Fry, Donald Lewis *physiologist, educator*
Frye, Richard Arthur *judge*
Galantowicz, Mark Edward *cardiothoracic surgeon*
Gall, John Ryan *lawyer*
Ganschinietz, Deepa *elementary school educator*
Gee, Elwood Gordon *academic administrator*
Geiger, Heather L. *lawyer*
Ghafourifar, Pedram *pharmacologist, director*
Gibson, Rick J. *lawyer*
Gilliom, Morris Eugene *social studies and global educator*
Gillmor, Karen Lako *state agency administrator*
Glaser, Ronald *microbiologist, educator*
Glenn, John Herschel, Jr. *former senator, astronaut*
Grauer, David W. *lawyer*
Gribble, Charles Edward *editor, language educator*
Griffith, Dennison W. *academic administrator, artist, educator*
Gross, James Howard *lawyer*
Grossberg, Michael Lee *film critic, writer*
Guglielmi, Rhonda E. *nursing administrator*
Hagan, Thomas M. *electric power industry executive*
Hamm, Paul *Olympic athlete*
Haque, Malika Hakim *pediatrician*
Hardymon, David Wayne *lawyer*
Hare, Robert Yates *musicologist, educator*
Harmon, Phillip Louis *lawyer*
Harris, Donald *composer*
Harris, Ronald David *chemical engineer*
Hatler, Patricia Ruth *lawyer*
Haubiel, Charles W., II, *lawyer*
Hengst, Linda Ruth *library director*
Henkin, Tina M. *science educator, researcher*
Herbst, Eric *physicist, astronomer, chemist*
Heremans, Joseph Pierre *physicist*
Hildreth, James David *musician, educator*
Hirokami, Junichi *conductor, music director*
Hitchcock, Ken *professional hockey coach*
Hoaglin, Thomas E. *savings and loan association executive*
Hollenbaugh, H(enry) Ritchey *lawyer*
Holschuh, John David *federal judge*
Houser, Donald Russell *mechanical engineering educator, consultant*
Howard, Marilyn Kaye *political science professor*
Howson, Scott *professional sports team executive*
Huheey, Marilyn Jane *ophthalmologist, educator*
Hutson, Jeffrey Woodward *lawyer*
Iammartino, Nicholas R. *corporate communications executive*
Jackson, Reginald W. *lawyer*
Jarvis, Gilbert Andrew *humanities educator, writer*
Jebsen, Harry Alfred Arthur, Jr. *history professor*
Johnson, Bruce S. *law librarian, educator*
Johnson, David Lee *lawyer*
Johnson, Mark Alan *lawyer*
Johnson, Martha (Marty) Junk (Marty Johnson) *psychology professor*
Johnson, Neal Frederick *psychologist, educator*
Jolly, Daniel Ehs *dental educator*
Jurgensen, William G. *insurance company executive*
Kapral, Frank Albert *microbiologist and immunology educator*
Kasulis, Thomas Patrick *humanities educator*
Keane, John B. *lawyer, electric power industry executive*
Kefauver, Weldon Addison *publishing executive*
Kennedy, Lawrence Allan *mechanical engineering educator*
Kessel, John Howard *political scientist, educator*
Ketcham, Richard Scott *lawyer*
Kidder, C. Robert *finance company executive*
Kiecolt-Glaser, Janice Kay *psychologist*
Kinzer, Allen Shawn *lawyer*
Kirila, Jill S. *lawyer*
Kirk, Ballard Harry Thurston *architect*
Knilans, Michael Jerome *retired food products executive*
Koblentz, Robert Alan *lawyer*
Koenigsknecht, Roy A. *dean*
Koeppel, Holly Keller *electric power industry executive*
Kohrt, Carl Fredrick *research and development company executive*
Kresty, Laura Ann *medical researcher, educator*
Kronmiller, Jan E. *dean, academic administrator*
Kuehnle, Kenton Lee *lawyer*
Kuhn, Albert Joseph *language educator*
Kurtz, Charles Jewett III *lawyer*
LaLonde, Bernard Joseph *finance educator*
Lancione, Bernard Gabe *lawyer*
Lander, Ruth A. *medical association administrator*
Lanzinger, Judith Ann *state supreme court justice*
Larsen, Clark Spencer *anthropology educator*
Lashutka, Gregory S. *mayor, lawyer*
Lazar, Theodore Aaron *retired manufacturing executive, lawyer*
Lee, Kichoon *animal scientist, educator*
Leeman, Stacy N. *artist, education educator*
Leier, Carl Victor *internist, cardiologist*
Lewis, Richard Phelps *cardiologist, educator*
Ling, Ta-Yung *physicist*
Lisko (Dozer), Bonnie Lee *education educator*
Liston, Jefferson Edward *lawyer*
Long, Sarah Elizabeth Brackney *physician*
Long, Teresa C. *city health department administrator*
Long, Thomas Leslie *lawyer*
Losinski, Patrick A. *library director*
Lowe, Clayton Kent *radio film critic, educator*
Madia, William Juul *chemist*
Magliocca, Larry Anthony *education educator*
Mahoney, Kimberly Lynne *event and facility executive*
Mann, William Craig *lawyer*
Margolis, Jay M. *clothing executive*
Marrison, Benjamin J. *editor-in-chief*
Mason, Raymond E., Jr. *distributing company executive*
Matta, Thad Michael *men's college basketball coach*
McClain, Thomas Emerson *retired communications executive*

McConnaughey, George Carlton, Jr. *retired lawyer*
McConnell, John P. *metal products executive*
Mc Cormac, John Waverly *judge*
McCoy, John Bonnet *retired bank executive*
McCutchan, Gordon Eugene *retired lawyer, insurance company executive*
McDermott, Kevin R. *lawyer*
McInturff, Floyd M. *retired state agency administrator*
McKenna, Alvin James *lawyer*
Meezan, William Alan *social work educator, consultant*
Milford, Frederick John *retired research and development company executive*
Miller, Don Wilson *nuclear engineering educator*
Miller, Terry Alan *chemistry professor*
Miller, Terry Morrow *lawyer*
Millett, Stephen Malcolm *futurist, consultant, historian*
Min, David Byong *chemist, educator, research scientist*
Minor, Robert Allen *lawyer*
Mirman, Joel Harvey *lawyer*
Mirzaie, Ida A. *economics professor*
Modin, Fredrik *professional hockey player*
Moloney, Thomas E. *lawyer*
Moncrief, Jacqueline C. *retired state agency administrator*
Morganstern, James *art history educator*
Morris, Michael G. *electric power industry executive*
Morrison, Craig O. *chemicals executive*
Morrow, Grant III *medical research director, pediatrician*
Moul, William Charles *lawyer*
Moulton, Edward Quentin *civil engineer, educator*
Moyer, Thomas J. *state supreme court chief justice*
Mrozek, Lawrence James *director*
Mueller, Charles Frederick *radiologist, educator*
Mueller, John Ernest *political science professor, dance critic*
Muller, Mervin Edgar *computer scientist, consultant, statistician, educator*
Nathan, Jerry E. *lawyer*
Naylor, James Charles *psychologist, educator*
Needham, Glen Ray *entomology and acarology educator, researcher*
Newman, Diana S. *foundation administrator, consultant*
Newsom, Gerald Higley *astronomy educator*
Newton, William Allen, Jr. *pediatrician, pathologist*
Nissl, Colleen Kaye *lawyer*
Norris, Alan Eugene *federal judge*
Nwomeh, Benedict C. *pediatric surgeon*
Ockerman, Herbert W. *agricultural studies educator*
O'Connor, Maureen *state supreme court justice*
O'Donnell, Terrence *state supreme court justice*
O'Hanlon, Nancyanne *school librarian, educator*
Olson, Ray Alan *librarian*
Oman, Richard Heer *retired lawyer*
Osgood, Robert T., Jr. *architect, strategic planner*
Otte, Paul John *academic administrator, consultant*
Otterson, Gregory Alan *oncologist, educator*
Ozkan, Umit Sivrioglu *chemical engineering professor*
Pease, William Stoess *physiatrist, educator*
Peca, Michael *professional hockey player*
Peterle, Tony John *zoologist, educator*
Peters, Leon, Jr. *retired engineering educator*
Peterson, Gale Eugene *historian*
Peterson, Ruth D. *sociologist*
Petricoff, M. Howard *lawyer, educator*
Pfeifer, Paul E. *state supreme court justice*
Pfening, Frederic Denver III *manufacturing executive*
Phillips, James Edgar *lawyer*
Pigman, Jack Richard *lawyer*
Pizzuti, Ronald A. *real estate developer*
Potter, Michael J. *retail stores executive*
Powers, Robert P. *electric power industry executive*
Pressley, Fred G., Jr. *lawyer*
Pryce, Deborah Denine *congresswoman*
Pyatt, Leo Anthony *retired real estate broker*
Quigley, John Bernard *law educator*
Raabe, William Alan *tax writer, business educator*
Radnor, Alan T. *lawyer*
Ramey, Denny L. *bar association executive director*
Rapp, Robert Anthony *metallurgical engineering educator*
Rasmussen, Stephen S. *insurance company executive*
Ray, Frank Allen *lawyer*
Reardon, John B. III *state agency administrator*
Reasoner, Willis Irl III *lawyer*
Rector, Susan Darnell *lawyer*
Redgrave, Martyn Robert *retail executive*
Reibel, Kurt *physicist, researcher*
Ress, Charles William *management consultant*
Ridgley, Thomas Brennan *lawyer*
Robinson, Barry R. *lawyer*
Robol, Richard Thomas *lawyer*
Rogers, Douglas L. *lawyer*
Rogers, Nancy Hardin *dean, law educator*
Rose, Michael Dean *retired lawyer, educator*
Rosenstock, Susan Lynn *orchestra administrator*
Rosholt, Robert A. *diversified financial services company executive, insurance company executive*
Roth, Robert Earl *ecologist, educator*
Rouda, Harley, Jr. *real estate company executive*
Ruberg, Robert Lionel *surgery educator*
Rund, Douglas Andrew *emergency physician*
Russell, Nas'Naga R. *illustrator*
Ryan, James M. *cardiologist, educator*
Saad, Michael D. *lawyer*
St. Pierre, George Roland, Jr. *materials scientist, engineering executive, educator*
Sanfilippo, Alfred Paul *dean, medical educator, pathologist*
Sawyers, Elizabeth Joan *librarian, director*
Saxbe, William Bart *lawyer, former United States attorney general*
Sayers, Martin Peter *pediatric neurosurgeon*
Scanlan, James Patrick *philosophy and Slavic studies educator*
Schneider, Cindy E. Gower (Lones) *financial advisor*
Schottenstein, Jay L. *retail executive*
Schrag, Edward A., Jr. *lawyer*
Schricker, Scott Raymond *dental educator*
Schuler, Robert Leo *appraiser, consultant*
Schuller, David Edward *cancer center administrator, otolaryngologist*
Sebo, Stephen Andrew *electrical engineer, educator, researcher, consultant*
Sedmak, Daniel D. *academic administrator*
Selby, Diane Ray Miller *fraternal organization administrator*
Setzer, Arlene J. *state representative, retired secondary school educator*
Shane, Peter Milo *law educator*
Sharma, Manu *risk management consultant, researcher*
Sharp, Paul David *institute administrator*
Sherrill, Thomas Boykin III *retired newspaper publishing executive*
Sheward, Richard S. *lawyer*
Shinkel, Bernie (Bernard Albert Shinkel) *investment advisor*
Shisler, Arden L. *insurance and transportation company executive*
Shore, Sheldon G. *chemist, educator*
Shumate, Alex *lawyer*
Sidman, Robert John *lawyer*
Sims, Richard Lee *retired hospital administrator*
Simson, Bevlyn *artist*
Singh, Rajendra *mechanical engineering educator, director*
Sites, Richard Loren *lawyer, educator*
Smead, William Lewis *surgeon, educator*
Smith, Gene *athletic director*
Smith, George Curtis *judge*
Smith, Shirley A. *state legislator, state representative*
Soloway, Albert Herman *medicinal chemist*
Sostaric, Joe Zeljko *research scientist*
Sowald, Heather Gay *lawyer*
Spoerry, Robert F. *manufacturing executive*
Sporleder, Thomas Lynn *economist, researcher*
Stefanescu, Doru Michael *metallurgical engineer, educator*
Stein, Arland Thomas *lawyer*
Stephan, Alexander Friedrich *German language and literature educator*
Stephens, Thomas M(aron) *education educator*
Stern, Geoffrey *lawyer*
Stevenson, Joanne Sabol *nursing educator, consultant, retired dean*
Stinehart, Roger Ray *lawyer*
Stoner, Gary David *cancer researcher*
Stratton, Evelyn Lundberg *state supreme court justice*
Strickland, Ted *governor, former congressman*
Studer, William Joseph *library director*
Sully, Ira Bennett *lawyer*
Sunami, John Soichi *designer*
Swarlis, Linda *library and information scientist*
Swetnam, Daniel Richard *lawyer*
Swift, David A. *lawyer*
Tadesse, Mesfin *botanist, consultant, biology professor, researcher*
Taggart, Thomas Michael *lawyer*
Tait, Robert E. *lawyer*
Tarpy, Thomas Michael *lawyer*
Taylor, Celianna Isley *information systems specialist*
Taylor, Joel Sanford *government agency administrator, retired lawyer*
Terakedis, John, Jr. *lawyer*
Thompson, Harold Lee *lawyer*
Thompson, Lonnie G. *glaciologist, educator*
Thresher, Mark R. *insurance company executive*
Tian, Fei-Ran *mathematician, educator*
Tiberi, Patrick Joseph *congressman, former state legislator*
Tipton, Clyde Raymond, Jr. *communications and resources development consultant*
Todd, William Michael *lawyer*
Tollifson, Thomas Gerald *retired art education consultant, educator*
Tomasky, Susan *electric power industry executive*
Tomczak, Rodney Louis *retired surgeon, medical educator*
Trent, Elton Roger *educational assessment administrator, writer*
Tressel, Jim (James Patrick Tressel) *college football coach*
Triplehorn, Charles A. *entomologist, educator*
Tripp, Thomas Neal *lawyer, political scientist*
Turano, David A. *lawyer*
Turner, Elvin L. *retired school system administrator*
Turney, Sharen Jester *apparel executive, cosmetics executive*
Turney, Sharon Jester *retail executive*
Tyack, Thomas Michael *lawyer*
Tybout, Richard Alton *economics professor*
Valdivia Arenas, Martin A. *pulmonary and critical care physician*
Vasseur, Dominique Henri *curator*
Velayutham, Murugesan *research scientist*
Vogel, Thomas Timothy *surgeon, educator, lay worker*
Vorys, Arthur Isaiah *lawyer*
Voss, Jerrold Richard *architecture educator*
Wachtmann, Lynn R. *state legislator*
Wagner, Robert Walter *photographer, communications educator, film producer, consultant*
Wali, Mohan Kishen *environmental scientist, forester, educator*
Walker, Charles Henri *lawyer*
Wang, Deliang *computer scientist, educator*
Warner, Charles Collins *lawyer*
Wasserman, Karen Boling *clinical psychologist, nursing consultant*
Weisberg, Herbert Frank *political science professor*
Welch, Dennis E. *electric power industry executive*
Westman, Judith Ann *clinical geneticist, dean*
Wexner, Abigail *apparel executive*
Wexner, Leslie Herbert *retail executive*
Whipps, Edward Franklin *lawyer*
Wightman, Alec *lawyer*
Wigington, Ronald Lee *retired chemical information services executive*
Wilansky, Heywood *retail executive*
Wild, Earl *musician, composer*
Wilkins, John Warren *physics professor*
Williams, Douglas Leonard *lawyer*
Williams, James Case *metallurgist*
Williams, Susan Shidal *language educator*
Willke, Thomas Aloys *academic administrator, statistician, educator*
Winkler, John Frederick *lawyer, educator*
Wise, William Edward, Jr. *colon and rectal surgeon, oncologist*
Wojcicki, Andrew Adalbert *chemist, educator*
Wood, Jackie Dale *physiologist, educator, researcher*
Yeazel, Keith Arthur *lawyer*
Yenkin, Bernard Kalman *coatings and resins company executive*
Yu, Chack Yung *pediatrics educator, molecular biologist*
Zakin, Jacques Louis *chemical engineering educator*
Zartman, David Lester *retired zoology educator, researcher*
Zelman, Susan Tave *school system administrator*
Zex, Damon *artist*
Zweben, Stuart Harvey *information scientist, educator, dean*
Zweibel, Alan *writer*

Concord
Ulsenheimer, Dean *language educator*

Copley
Weil, Edward David *chemist, researcher, consultant, inventor*

Coshocton
Freund, Carol Louise *social services consultant*
McGinnis, Tammy Marie *health services manager*

Crooksville
Childers, Susan Lynn Bohn *special education educator, school system administrator, human resources and transition specialist, consultant*

Cuyahoga Falls
Barsan, Robert Blake *dentist*
Butcher, Jack Robert (Jack Risin) *manufacturing executive, film producer, actor, artist*
Curtis, Carolyn Ann *musician, educator*
Haag, Everett Keith *architect*
Jones, John Frank *retired lawyer*
Moses, Abe Joseph *financial planner, consultant*
Roth, Gregory Edward *social studies educator*

Dayton
Abueida, Atif *mathematics professor*
Ambalavanan, Siva *nephrologist, educator*
Ballal, Dilip Ramchandra *mechanical engineering educator*
Battino, Rubin *retired chemistry professor*
Burick, Lawrence T. *lawyer*
Chernesky, Richard John *lawyer*
Chin, Hong Woo *oncologist, educator, researcher*
Conway, Mark Allyn *lawyer*
Coutu, Ronald Armand, Jr. *electrical engineer, program manger*
Curran, Daniel J. *academic administrator, sociologist, educator*
Daley, Robert Emmett *retired foundation executive*
Daoud, George Jamil *hotel and motel consultant*
Dorn, Jacob Henry *history professor*
Farquhar, Robert Nichols *lawyer*
Faruki, Charles Joseph *lawyer*
Geswein, Gregory T. *software company executive*
Gillig, Paulette Marie *psychiatry educator, researcher*
Gladden, Robert Wiley *healthcare executive*
Gomez-Cambronero, Julian *cell biologist, biochemist, educator*
Gregor, Clunie Bryan *geology educator*
Guan, Shan *materials scientist*
Haddad, Freddie Duke, Jr. *resource development professional*
Hadley, Robert James *lawyer*
Hanna, Marsha L. *artistic director*
Harden, Oleta Elizabeth *literature educator, academic administrator*
Harlan, Norman Ralph *construction executive*
Hayes, Stephen Kurtz *writer*
Heath, Mariwyn Dwyer *writer, legislative staff member*
Heyman, Ralph Edmond *lawyer*
Hoge, Franz Joseph *accounting firm executive*
Hopkins, David R. *academic administrator, educator*
Houpis, Constantine Harry *retired electrical engineering educator*
Isaacson, Milton Stanley (Jim) *research and development company executive, engineer*
Jackson, Jason M. *military officer, educator*
Jenks, Thomas Edward *lawyer*
Johnson, C. Terry *lawyer*
Kazimierczuk, Marian Kazimierczuk *electrical engineer, educator*
Klinck, Cynthia Anne *library director*
Knapp, James Ian Keith *judge*
Krebs, Leo Francis *lawyer*
Kumar, Binod *materials engineer, educator*
Lair, Vickie Sue *mathematics professor*
Lashley, William Bartholomew *county official*
Lasley, Thomas J., II, *education educator*
Lieb, Peter *lawyer*
Lockhart, Gregory Gordon *prosecutor*
Macklin, Crofford Johnson, Jr. *lawyer*
Matheny, Ruth Ann *editor*
Mathile, Clayton Lee *pet food company executive*
McDonald, Bronce William *community activist, advocate*
McIlroy, Alan F. *manufacturing executive*
McLin, Rhine Lana *mayor, former state legislator*
McWhorter, Stanley Bruce *retired language educator*
Meister, Mark Jay *museum director, professional society administrator*
Mohler, Stanley Ross *preventive medicine physician, educator*
Monk, Susan Marie *pediatrician, educator*
Mosier, William Arthur *psychiatrist, psychotherapist, director, medical educator, researcher*
Mues, Robert Leighton *lawyer*
Mukhopadhyay, Sharmila Mitra *materials engineer, educator*
Nanagas, Maria Teresita Cruz *pediatrician, educator*
Neltner, Michael Martin *lawyer*
Nielsen, Philip Edward *physicist, research manager*
Nixon, Charles William *retired acoustician*
Nuti, William R. *computer services company executive*
O'Keefe, Linda Lee *physical education educator*
Part, Howard Mitchell *dean*
Pestello, Fred P. *academic administrator*
Petrick, Joseph Anthony *small business owner, management consultant, educator*
Phillips, Chandler Allen *biomedical engineer, human factors engineer*
Prayson, Michael J. *orthopedic surgeon, medical educator, director*
Riley, David Richard *retired management consultant, military officer*
Ringler, James M. (James M. Ringler) *computer services company executive*
Rion, John Hayes *lawyer*
Ruegsegger, Donald Ray, Jr. *radiological physicist, educator*
Saul, Irving Isaac *lawyer*
Schmitt, George Frederick, Jr. *materials engineer*
Seon, Yvonne *cultural educator, minister*
Singhvi, Surendra Singh *financial consultant*
Spicer, John Austin *physicist*
Suwyn, Mark A. *paper company executive*
Tatar, Jerome F. *business products executive*
Taylor, Edward McKinley, Jr. *lawyer*
Taylor, Elisabeth Coler *retired secondary school educator*
Thomas, Marianna *volunteer community activist, writer, speaker*
Vaughn, Noel Wyandt *lawyer*
Vice, Roy Lee *history professor*
Vukelich, Sharon Irene *aerospace engineer, consultant*
Watts, Steven Richard *lawyer*
Weinberg, Sylvan Lee *cardiologist, educator, editor, writer*
Wertz, Kenneth Dean *real estate company officer*
Williams, Walker Richard, Jr. *social services administrator*
Wilson, William Campbell McFarland *gastroenterologist*
Wyllie, Stanley Clarke *retired librarian*
Zahner, Mary Anne *art educator*

Delaware
Bahrick, Harry Phillip *science educator, researcher*
Ciochetty, John Bryan *protective services official*
Eells, William Hastings *retired automobile company executive*
Gardner, Bonnie Milne *theater educator, playwright*
Garner, Harvey Louis *computer scientist, consultant, engineering educator*
Huml, Donald Scott *manufacturing executive*
Jamison, Roger W. *pianist, educator*
Lemke, Stacy J. *secondary school educator*
Martz, Gary R. *lawyer*
Schlichting, Catherine Fletcher Nicholson *librarian, educator*

Delta
Miller, Beverly White *former college president, educational consultant*

Dover
Haggis, Mary Ripley *nurse, genealogist*

Doylestown
Morton, Sallie W. *music educator*

Dublin
Anderson, Kerrii B. *food service executive*
Baker, Mary Evelyn *retired librarian*
Bird, Shelley *communications executive*
Borror, Douglas G. *construction company executive*
Clark, R. Kerry (Kerry Clark) *health products executive*
Clement, Henry Joseph, Jr. *diversified building products executive*
Davids, Jody R. *information technology executive*
Dempsey, Lorcan *library and information scientist*
Dolch, Gary D. *health products executive*
Fitzsimmons, Jay (Joseph J. Fitzsimmons) *food service executive*
Fong, Ivan Kenneth *health products executive, lawyer*
Ford, Brendan A. *health facility administrator*
Henderson, Jeffrey W. *health products executive*

Heneman, Robert Lloyd *management educator*
Inzetta, Mark Stephen *lawyer*
Jordan, Robert (Jay) L. *computer library service and research organization executive*
Kinman, Gary W. *landscape company executive*
Labrum, Ronald K. *health facility administrator*
Lamp, Benson J. *tractor company executive*
Li, Chenglong *biophysicist, educator*
Lynch, Michael A. *health products executive*
Maloon, Jerry L. *lawyer, physician*
McCorkle, Leon Marshall, Jr. *lawyer, educator*
Meek, Violet Imhof *retired dean*
Needham, George Michael *association executive*
Papa, Joseph C. *pharmaceutical executive*
Parrish, Mark *health products executive*
Pickett, James V. *food service executive*
Redman, Janis F. *special education educator, department chairman*
Rishel, James Burton *manufacturing executive, director*
Rosenbaum, Mark E. *health products executive*
Schlotterbeck, David L. *health products executive*
Slagle, Tom *medical products executive*
Smith, K(ermit) Wayne *computer company executive*
Tenuta, Luigia *lawyer*
Troup, Gordon A. *health products executive*
Vassell, Gregory S. *electric utility consultant*
Walsh, Daniel J. *health products executive*
Walter, Robert D. *health products executive*
Wang, Andrew Hsing-Jen *marketing professional, information technology executive, journalist, librarian*
Warmbrod, Catharine Phelps *educational researcher, consultant*
Watkins, Carole S. *human resources specialist, medical products executive*
Wilkins, Jeffrey M. *computer company executive*
Winstead, Dwight *medical products executive*
Wu, Junxian *chemist, researcher*

East Cleveland
England, Diana Whitten *elementary school educator*

East Palestine
Rohrbaugh, Lisa Anne *librarian*

Eastlake
Suchanek, Wojciech Lukasz *materials scientist, researcher*

Eaton
Kisling, Fanny *counselor, educator*
Thomas, James William *lawyer*

Edon
Wilson, Wayne Maurice *real estate broker, auctioneer*

Elyria
Foote, Nathan Maxted *retired physical science educator*
Mixon, Aaron Malachi III *medical products executive*
Myers, John T. *physical therapist, educator*
Patton, Thomas James *marketing executive, sales executive*
Sanders, Phyllis May *musician*

Euclid
Adrine-Robinson, Kenyette *writer, educator, poet, artist, photographer*
Dowell, Michael Brendan *chemist*
Howson, James G. *photographer*
Linderman, Eric Graham *librarian*
Miller, Demetra Fay Pelat *elementary school educator, city official*
Obloy, Leonard Gerard *priest*
Ramsey, Charles *retired government agency administrator*

Fairborn
Combs, Eric A. *social studies educator*
Goetz, Douglas Neil *contract management educator*
Gupta, Vijay Kumar *retired chemistry professor*
Szucs, Andrew Eric *freelance/self-employed writer*

Fairfield
Benoski, James E. *insurance company executive*
Carmichael, Dan R. *insurance company executive*
Glass, Linda L. *elementary school educator*
Hubbard, Michele Masanek *secondary school educator, soccer coach*
McHenry, Kathryn *forensic specialist*
Robertson, Oscar Palmer (Big O Robertson) *chemical company executive, former professional basketball player*
Sheehan, Samantha *gymnast*
Stecher, Kenneth W. *financial corporation executive*
Wilson, James Miller, IV, *cardiovascular surgeon, educator*
Zierolf, Mary Louise *nurse anesthetist*

Fairlawn
Kitchen, Charles William *lawyer*

Fairview Park
Flynn, Patricia M. *director, special education and gifted and talented educator*
Fordyce, James Stuart *non-profit organization executive*

Findlay
Armes, Roy V. *manufacturing executive*
Freed, DeBow *academic administrator*
Fry, Charles George *theologian, educator*
Hanson, David Alan *music educator*
Kline, James Edward *lawyer*
Kostyo, John Francis *lawyer*
Peters, Milton Eugene *retired educational psychologist*
Stephani, Nancy Jean *social worker, journalist*
Yammine, Riad Nassif *retired oil industry executive*

Fostoria
Howard, Kathleen *computer company executive*

Fremont
Hill, Becky (Rebecca Baker Hill) *librarian*
Ruble, Amanda L. *elementary school educator*
Smart, Judith Ann *mathematics professor*

Gahanna
Majtenyi, Steven Istvan *retired civil engineer, consultant*

Galena
Berggren, Ronald Bernard *surgeon, retired educator*
Greek, Darold I. *lawyer*

Galion
Cobey, Ralph *industrialist*

Gallipolis
Senthil Nathan, Selvaraj *internist, geriatrician*

Gambier
Holdener, Judy Ann *mathematics professor, researcher*
Leech, Charles Russell, Jr. *lawyer*
Nugent, S. Georgia *academic administrator*
Spaid, Gregory P. *academic administrator, art educator*

Garrettsville
Diskin, Michael Edward *plastics company and food service executive*

Gates Mills
Abbott, James Samuel III *marketing executive*
Enyedy, Gustav, Jr. *chemical engineer*
Reitman, Robert Stanley *management consultant, not-for-profit advisor*
Veale, Tinkham, II, *retired chemicals executive, engineer*

Geneva
Carrel, Marianne Eileen *music educator*

Georgetown
Fite, Tom W. *retired mathematics educator, farmer*
Ruthven, John A. *wildlife artist*

Glendale
Strom, Kristina Chase *writer, consultant*

Granville
Knobel, Dale Thomas *historian, educator, university president*
Lisska, Anthony Joseph *humanities educator, philosopher*
Santoni, Ronald Ernest *philosophy educator*

Greenville
Alexander, Paul Richard *illustrator*
Thieme, Jean Louise *retired art association administrator*

Grove City
Kilman, James William *surgeon, educator*
Kimethu, Susan Wanja *computer specialist, database manager*
Rudy, Monica Elaine *small business owner, music educator*

Groveport
Motts, Warren Earl *museum director*

Hamilton
Epp, Mary Elizabeth *retired technologies consultant*
Gruenwald, James Howard *association executive, consultant*
Kerestan, Kitty Wilde *music educator*
Moore, Michael Robert *music educator, band director*
Munson, Richard Howard *horticulturist*

Harrison
Kocher, Juanita Fay *retired auditor*

Hemlock
Johnson, George Warner *gifted and talented educator, consultant*

Highland Hills
Brathwaite, Ormond Dennis *chemistry professor*
Kharina, Nina Yurievna *science educator*

Hilliard
Craig, Steve A. *lawyer*
Cupp, David Foster *photographer, journalist*
Jungeberg, Thomas Donald *lawyer*
Riggle, Blair Andrew *educational association administrator, consultant, psychologist, educator*

Hiram
Chema, Thomas V. *government official, consultant, academic administrator, lawyer*

Holland
Conlin, Thomas *conductor*
D'Anniballe, Priscilla Lucille *contracting company executive*
Matthews, Christian William, Jr. *minister*
Sacksteder, Thomas Michael *corporate financial executive, entrepreneur, writer*

Howard
Lee, William Johnson *lawyer*

Hubbard
Trucksis, Theresa A. *retired library director*

Hudson
Carducci, Judith Weeks Barker *artist, retired social worker*
Clark, Robert Phillips *editor, consultant*
Frank, John V. *foundation administrator*
Goheen, Janet Moore *counseling administrator, sales executive*
Lambacher, Kathleen Hartwell *retired education educator*
Webb, Darrell D. *retail executive*
Withers, Carl Raymond *lawyer*

Huron
Leser, Anne Elizabeth *education educator*

Independence
Kola, Arthur Anthony *lawyer*
Lanigan, John *radio personality*
Malone, Jimmy *radio personality*
Van Kirk, Robert John *nursing case manager, educator*

Ironton
Allen, Craig Adams *lawyer, director*
Cremeans, James L. *minister*
Curry, Estella Roberta *education educator, school psychologist, consultant*

Jackson
Benson, Steven Clark *management and engineering executive*
Dallura, Sal Anthony *physician*
Lewis, Richard M. *lawyer*

Jackson Center
Thompson, Wade Francis Bruce *manufacturing executive*

Kent
Baeseman, Jenny L. *environmental scientist, educator*
Bansal, Arvind Kumar *computer scientist, educator*
Beer, Barrett Lynn *historian*
Bissler, Richard Thomas *mortician*
Buttlar, Rudolph Otto *retired college dean*
Cartwright, Carol Ann *retired academic administrator*
Dahl, Peter Steffen *geologist, educator*
Feinberg, Richard *anthropologist, educator*
Gaston, Paul Lee *academic administrator, language educator*
Gosnell, Davina J. *dean, nursing educator*
Hassler, Donald Mackey, II, *English language educator, writer*
Lefton, Lester Alan *academic administrator, psychology professor*
Lovejoy, Claude Owen *anthropologist, educator*
Marovitz, Sanford Earl *English language and literature educator*
Paschen, Stephen H. *archivist, historian*
Phillips, Matthew Todd *history educator*
Reid, S.W. *language educator*
Ryans, John Kelley, Jr. *marketing educator*
Varga, Richard Steven *retired mathematics professor*
Weber, Mark W. *library director, dean*
Williams, Donald R. *social sciences educator*
Williams, Harold Roger *economist, educator*

Kettering
Cline, Allen Lee *endocrinologist, medical educator*
De Guzman, Ricardo D. *retired physician*
Eubank, David Lynn *lawyer, consultant*
Kell, Joseph William *materials scientist*
Kent, Lawrence *retired association executive, education and mental health director*
Meckstroth, Wilma Jean *piano and organ educator, accompanist*
Peres, Frank J. *healthcare administrator*
Porter, Walter Arthur *retired judge*

Kirtland
Asnien, Phyllis Arline *humanities educator, writer*
Basich, Richard B. *mathematics professor*
Johnston, Stanley Howard, Jr. *curator*
Petrone, John R. *retired music educator, composer*

Lakeside Marblehead
Haering, Edwin Raymond *chemical engineering educator, consultant*

Lakewood
Condon, George Edward *journalist*
Kucinich, Dennis John *congressman*
McAndrews, James Patrick *retired lawyer*

Lancaster
Katlic, John Edward *management consultant*
Libert, Donald Joseph *lawyer*
Phillips, Edward John *consulting firm executive*
Varney, Richard Alan *health facility administrator*

Lewis Center
Heinlen, Daniel Lee *alumni organization administrator, consultant*
Thomason, Sandra Lee *elementary school educator*

Lima
Jacobs, Ann Elizabeth *lawyer*
MacBenn, Joseph Vernon *director*
Pranses, Anthony Louis *retired electric power industry executive*
Robenalt, John Alton *lawyer*
Rogers, Richard Michael *judge*

Lisbon
Dailey, Coleen Hall *magistrate*

London
Hughes, Clyde Matthew *religious denomination executive*

Lorain
Murrell, Jill Pongracz *music educator, director*

Louisville
Faigley, Joseph Raymond *social studies educator*

Loveland
Voluse, Charles Rodger III *retired education educator*

Lucasville
Reno, Ottie Wayne *former judge*

Lyndhurst
Harper, Williard Flemmett *language educator*

Madison
Stafford, Arthur Charles *medical association administrator*

Mansfield
Capaldo, Guy *obstetrician, gynecologist*
Converse, Sandra *city finance director, financial planner*
Gibson, David Mark *biochemist, educator*
Gorman, James Carvill *manufacturing executive*
Gregory, Deirdre Dianne *secondary school educator*
Gregory, Thomas Bradford *mathematics professor*
Houston, William Robert Montgomery *ophthalmologist, surgeon*
Riedl, John Orth *retired university dean*
Shah, James M. *actuary*
Sheridan, Mark William *mechanical engineer, financial planner*
Wolf, Marcus Alan *lawyer*

Mantua
Wallingford, Jack W. *secondary school educator*

Marblehead
Lis, David Joseph *priest*

Marietta
Fields, William Albert *lawyer*
Jache, Albert William *retired chemistry professor, academic administrator, research scientist*
Putnam, Robert Ervin *chemist, consultant*
Wilbanks, Jan Joseph *retired philosopher*

Marion
Barker, Tamara Elizabeth *music educator*

Marysville
Aronowitz, David M. *lawyer, chemicals executive*
Hagedorn, James *landscape company executive*
Hamilton, Robert Otte *lawyer*
Kelly, Thomas N., Jr. *telecommunications industry executive*

Mason
Beary, John Francis III *rheumatologist, pharmaceutical executive, medical researcher*
Clements, Michael Craig *health services consulting executive, retired renal dialysis technician*
Cuff, Virginia Evelyn *architectural firm executive, consultant*
Kohlhepp, Robert J. *apparel executive*
Smith, C. LeMoyne *retired publishing executive*
Wilson, Frederic Sandford *pharmaceutical company executive*

Massillon
Eckhart, Marylouise Christine Santilli *pre-school educator*

Maumee
Burchinow, Naran U. *lawyer*
Fallat, Dale William *lawyer*
Konopinski, Virgil James *retired industrial hygienist, safety consultant*
Marsh, Benjamin Franklin *lawyer*
Tuschman, James Marshall *lawyer*
Witherell, Dennis Patrick *lawyer*

Mayfield
Jarrett, Charles Elwood *lawyer, insurance company executive*

Mayfield Heights
Bittenbender, Charles A. *lawyer*
Grants, Valdis *engineering manager*
Newman, Joseph Herzl *advertising executive, consultant*
Rankin, Alfred Marshall, Jr. *manufacturing executive*

Mc Donald
Daigle, Barbara Dianne *elementary school educator*

Medina
Ballard, John Stuart *retired mayor, lawyer, educator*
Matejka, Robert *chemicals executive*
Rog, Joseph W. *engineering company executive*
Smith, Richey *manufacturing executive*
Sullivan, Frank C. *manufacturing executive*
Sullivan, Thomas Christopher *coatings company executive*
Tompkins, P. Kelly *lawyer, manufacturing executive*

Mentor
Callsen, Christian Edward *health products executive*
Hale, Jeffrey L. *economics educator*

Miamisburg
Byrd, James Everett *lawyer*

Miamiville
Franz, (Iris) Vivian *dean, director*

Middleburg Heights
Maciuszko, Kathleen Lynn *librarian, educator*

Middlefield
Hullihen, Karen A. *chemist*

Middletown
Gordon, Sandy Gale Combs *medical/surgical nurse*
Horn, David C. *lawyer*
Marine, Susan Sonchik *analytical chemist, educator*
Newby, John Robert *metallurgical engineer*
Powell, Stephen Walter *judge*
Rathman, William Ernest *retired lawyer, minister*
Schaefer, Patricia Ann *retired librarian*
Wainscott, James Lawrence *steel industry executive*

Milan
Henry, Joseph Patrick *chemicals executive*

Milford
Arnest, Richard T. *composer, consultant*
Creath, Curtis Janssen *pediatric dentist*

Millersburg
Trubee, R. Eldon *minister, writer*

Minerva
Grunder, Stuart Edwin *social studies educator*
Martin, Robert Dale *lawyer*

Montpelier
Deckrosh, Hazen Douglas *retired state agency educator and administrator*

Moreland Hills
Groetzinger, Jon, Jr. *lawyer, pharmaceutical executive, educator*
Tolchinsky, Paul Dean *organization design psychologist*

Mount Healthy
Scheffel, Kenneth Paul *retired archivist*

Mount Vernon
Miller, Joyce Catherine *chemistry professor, research scientist*
Rose, Kim Matthew *lawyer, educator*
Shriver, William Russell *secondary school educator*

Napoleon
Meekison, MaryFran *writer*

Nashport
Gilmore, Clare Mae *writer*

New Albany
Duggan, Thomas Patrick *management consultant*
Jeffries, Michael S. (Mike Jeffries) *apparel executive*
Page, Linda Kay *bank executive*
Schlesinger, Leonard Arthur *retail executive*
Stevens, Kenneth T. *retail executive*

New Bremen
Dicke, James Frederick, II, *manufacturing executive*

New Concord
Boggs, Bennett Gibson *academic administrator*

New Matamoras
Brown, Blanche Y. *secondary school educator, genealogist, researcher*

New Philadelphia
Doughten, Mary Katherine (Molly) *retired secondary school educator*

Newark
Black, Boyd Carson *small business owner*
Federspiel, Howard M. *political science professor*
Hite, David L. *lawyer*
Mantonya, John Butcher *lawyer*
McConnell, William Thompson *bank executive*
Mencer, Jetta *lawyer*
Meyer, Christopher Richard *lawyer*
Sharrock (Wrentmore), Anita Kay *management and program analyst*

North Canton
Burns, Andrew E. *chemistry professor, researcher*
Cooney, Sondra Miley *literature and language educator*
Dettinger, Warren Walter *lawyer*
Dishong, Morris William *forensic specialist, nurse*
Di Simone, Robert Nicholas *radiologist, educator*
Fernandez, Kathleen M. *cultural organization administrator*
Lynham, C(harles) Richard *manufacturing executive*
Vazzano, Frank Paul *historian, educator*

North Olmsted
Bluford, Guion Stewart, Jr. *engineering company executive*
Janson, Patrick *vocalist, educator, actor*
Semple, Jane Frances *health facility director*

North Ridgeville
Cobbledick, Susie Diane *librarian*
Stewart, Arden Ruth *retired automotive executive*

North Royalton
Fast, Henryk *mathematician, educator*

Northfield
Arndt, Charles Richard *educational consultant*
Stavole, Janet M. *librarian, director*

Norwalk
Brewer, Clair Herbert, Jr. *retired minister*
Germann, Richard P(aul) *pharmaceutical company chemist, chemicals executive*
Gutowicz, Matthew Francis, Jr. *radiologist*

Norwood
Wright, Creighton Bolter *cardiovascular surgeon, educator*

Oak Harbor
Randels, David George *retired secondary school educator*

Oberlin
Benzing, David Hill *biologist, educator*
Brown, John Lott *former university president, retired educator*
Carlton, Terry Scott *retired chemist, educator*
Cartier, Brian Evans *consumer products company executive*
English, Ray *library administrator*
Greenberg, Eva Mueller *retired librarian*
Koppes, Clayton R. *academic administrator*
Krislov, Marvin *academic administrator, lawyer, educator*
Luck, Dennis Noel *retired biologist, educator, researcher*
McGuire, Charles Edward *musicology educator*
Moore, Jane Ross *librarian, educator*
Mumford, Jeffrey *composer, educator*
Taylor, Richard Wirth *retired political science professor*
Taylor, Robert Larry *freelance/self-employed writer*

Olmsted Falls
Faller, Dorothy Anderson *training services executive, consultant*
Mercer, John Lee *secondary school educator, department chairman*

Orrville
Daniel, Deckler *engineering educator*
Harlan, Mary Ann *lawyer*
Hennell, Robert William III *secondary school educator*
Smucker, Richard K. *food products executive*
Smucker, Timothy P. *food products executive*
Warner, Patricia Ann *secondary school educator*

Orwell
Strong, Marcella Lee *music specialist, educator*

Owensville
Seifert, Caroline Hamilton *community health nurse*

Oxford
Bergen, Doris *psychologist, educator*
Dawisha, Adeed *political science professor*
Eshbaugh, W(illiam) Hardy *botanist, educator*
Ewing, Susan R. *artist, educator*
Gordon, Gilbert *chemist, educator*
Gupta, Barnali *economics professor*
Macklin, Philip Alan *retired physics professor*
Miller, Norman Calvin *economist*
Miller, Robert James *educational association administrator*
Pont, John *football coach, educator*
Pratt, William Crouch, Jr. *literature and language professor, writer*
Rejai, Mostafa *political science professor*
Sanders, Gerald Hollie *communications educator*
Sessions, Judith Ann *dean, university librarian*
Shriver, Phillip Raymond *academic administrator*
Thompson, Bertha Boya *retired education educator*
Ward, Roscoe Fredrick *engineering educator*
Yamauchi, Edwin Masao *history professor*

Painesville
Davis, Barbara Snell *education educator*
Dean, J. Thomas *lawyer*
Filson, Ronald Coulter *architect, educator, dean*
Kutz, Alexandra Ellen *prosecutor*
LaTourette, Steven C. *congressman*
McQuaid, Kim *historian, educator, writer*

Parma
Feldman, Sari *library director*
Musat, Katherine Gadus *retired music educator*
Petrus, Sally A. *elementary school educator*
Romanovich, Patricia M. *parochial school educator*
Tener, Carol Joan *retired secondary school educator, consultant*

Pataskala
Ripley, Randall Butler *political scientist, educator*

Pemberville
King, Laura Jane *librarian, genealogist*

Peninsula
Shaw, Doris Beaumar *film and video producer, executive recruiter, management consultant*
Sigler, Theresa Jane *school system administrator*

Pepper Pike
Cohen, Judith R. *realtor*
Mc Call, Julien Lachicotte *banker*
Schnell, Carlton Bryce *lawyer*
Stano, Sister Diana *academic administrator*
Vail, Thomas Van Husen *retired publishing executive*

Perrysburg
Autry, Carolyn *artist, educator*
Baehren, James W. *lawyer*
Catalano, Dominic *art educator, illustrator*
King, John Joseph *manufacturing executive*
Stockner, Linda Ann *elementary school educator*
Weaver, Richard L., II, *writer, educator*

Williamson, John Pritchard *retired utilities executive*

Pickerington
Callander, Kay Eileen Paisley *business owner, retired education educator, writer*
Collins, Arlene *secondary school educator*

Pomeroy
Brockert, Joseph Paul *government executive, writer, editor, designer*

Port Clinton
Ewersen, Mary Virginia *retired school system administrator, poet*
Woodson, Riley Donald *thoracic and cardiovascular surgeon, lawyer*

Portsmouth
Gerlach, Franklin Theodore *lawyer*

Powell
Emanuelson, James Robert *retired insurance company executive*
Hanna, Jack Bushnell *zoo director*
Mitchell, Cathy (C.C.) Christine *art educator*

Randolph
Pecano, Donald Carl *automotive manufacturing executive*

Ravenna
Nolfi, Edward Anthony *lawyer*
Turcotte, Margaret Jane *retired nurse*

Reynoldsburg
Neal, Diane L. *retail executive*
Odor, Richard Lane *mental health administrator, psychologist*

Richfield
Lewis, Sylvia Davidson *foundation executive*

Rio Grande
Hatfield, Barbara Scott *academic administrator*

Ripley
Curtis, Russell Glenn *social studies educator*

Rocky River
O'Brien, John Feighan *investment banker*
Shively, Daniel Jerome *retired transportation executive*

Rootstown
Chiang, John Young Ling *biochemistry professor, researcher*
Nora, Lois Margaret *neurologist, educator, academic administrator, dean*

Sagamore Hills
Miller, Susan Ann *retired school system administrator*

Saint Marys
Dicke, Candice Edwards *librarian, educator*
Huber, William Evan *lawyer*
Kemp, Barrett George *lawyer*
VanderHorst, Monica S. *physical education educator*

Salem
Barcey, Harold Edward Dean (Hal) *real estate consultant*
Fehr, Kenneth Manbeck *retired computer company executive*
Goll, Geoffrey Steven *lawyer*
Ronshausen, Nina Lorraine *retired mathematics professor, genealogist*

Sandusky
Bailey, K. Ronald *lawyer*
Runner, Jack Charles *health facility executive*
Stacey, James Allen *retired judge*

Sardinia
Evans, C(aroline) Sue *education educator*

Seaman
Young, Vernon Lewis *retired lawyer*

Sebring
Doty, James Edward *minister, psychologist*
Kelley-Hall, Maryon Hoyle *retired social worker*

Seven Hills
Stanczak, Julian *artist, educator*

Shadyside
Weeks, Nancy Kay *psychologist, educator*

Shaker Heights
Bates, Walter Alan *retired lawyer*
Brachna, Gabor (Samuel) *elementary school educator*
de Coningh, Lise N. *language educator*
Ludwig, L(owell) Mark *social studies educator*
Miller, Holly Dara *hospital administrator, physician*
Siegel, Robert *heat transfer engineer*
Smith, Jonathan David *medical educator*
Solganik, Marvin *real estate executive*
Trefts, Joan Landenberger *retired principal*

Shandon
Wilson, James Ray *small business owner*

Shelby
Phelan, Martha Armstrong *retired realtor*

Sidney
Leffler, Carole Elizabeth *retired women's and mental health nurse*
Menz, Robert L. *psychotherapist, minister*
Seitz, James Eugene *retired college president, freelance writer*
Stevens, Robert Jay *magazine editor*

Solon
Gallo, Donald Robert *retired literature educator*
Kratche, Richard P. *physician*
Rosica, Gabriel Adam *retired manufacturing executive, electrical engineer*
Williams, Jeffery Lynn *secondary school educator, consultant, writer*

South Euclid
Greenman, Steven Mark *musician*

Springboro
Saxer, Richard Karl *metallurgical engineer, retired military officer*

Springfield
Davis, Robert Leigh *language educator*
Hobson, David Lee *congressman, lawyer*
Humphries, Jimmy *set designer, educator*
Kinnison, William Andrew *retired university president*
Kurian, Pius *nephrologist, educator*
Lagos, James Harry *lawyer, small business owner*
Ryu, Kyoo-Hai Lee *physiologist*
Seifert, Shelley Elizabeth *psychologist*
Stelzer, Patricia Jacobs *retired secondary school educator*
Todd, Carol *music educator*

Steubenville
Reddy, Vardhan Jonnala *surgeon*
Scanlan, Michael *priest, academic administrator*
Sheldon, Gilbert Ignatius *clergyman*

Stow
Castillo, Katherine Lynn *secondary school educator, writer, translator, business owner*
Eiber, Carol Shattuck *language educator*
Rao, Balakrishna *plant pathologist, mycologist, botanist*

Streetsboro
Cielec, Greg J. *literature and language educator*
Cravcenco, Ludmila *academic administrator*

Strongsville
Blumer, Frederick Elwin *retired philosophy educator*
Cameron, David Ronald *entrepreneur, historian, researcher*
Myers, Jack Fredrick *artist, educator, writer*
Pinkerton, Richard LaDoyt *retired management educator*
Yates, Patricia Lawrence *elementary school educator*

Sugar Grove
Dombrowski, Karen S. *social studies and education educator*

Sylvania
Block, Allan James *communications executive*
Burkhart, Craig Garrett *dermatologist, researcher*
Camp, Alice Ann *medical transcriptionist*
Garrison, Linda *retired foundation administrator*
Heuschele, Sharon Jo *dean*
Kastner, Michael James *dentist*
Masten, Barbara Jean *education educator, department chairman*
Ring, Herbert Everett *retired management executive*
Sampson, Earldine Robison *education educator*

Tallmadge
Kaul, Mohan Lal *retired social worker, educator, writer*

Terrace Park
Naylor, Paul Donald *retired lawyer*

Tiffin
Gridley, Mark Charles *psychologist*
Hillmer, Margaret Patricia *library director*

Tipp City
Glassmeyer, James Milton *aerospace, computer, and electronics engineer*
Hartland, James Robert *retired minister*
Tighe-Moore, Barbara Jeanne *electronics executive*

Toledo
Anspach, Robert Michael *lawyer*
Averill, Bruce Alan *chemistry professor*
Ayoub, Judith Lorene *retired nursing educator*
Bacigalupi, Don *museum director*
Barrett, Michael John *anesthesiologist*
Bixler, R. Jeffrey *lawyer*
Block, John Robinson *newspaper publisher, editor-in-chief*
Block, William K., Jr. *media executive*
Brower, James Calvin *graphic artist, painter*
Brown, David T. *manufacturing executive*
Brown, Nancy J. *literature educator*
Burns, Michael J. *automotive executive*
Campbell, James *philosopher, educator*
Carr, James Gray *federal judge*
Carroll, William J. *municipal official*
Carson, Samuel Goodman *retired bank executive*
Cavanaugh, Steven M. *healthcare company executive*
Chakraborty, Joana *physiologist, educator, science administrator*
Chambers, Virginia Anne *music educator*
Chen, Jiquan *ecologist, educator*
Closius, Phillip J. *dean, law educator*
Comerota, Anthony James *vascular surgeon, biomedical researcher*
Cosentino, Mary Jane *retired science educator*
Cousino, Joe Ann *sculptor*
Dalrymple, Thomas Lawrence *retired lawyer*
DeBacker, Michael Lee *automotive executive, lawyer*
Dukkipati, Rao Venkateswara *engineering educator, researcher, scientist*
Ebraheim, Nabil Anwar *orthopedist, surgeon*

Elmer, Lawrence William *neurologist, researcher*
Francis, Barbara Joan *nurse, paralegal*
Funk, Jeanne B. *psychology professor*
Geisler, Nathan David *financial consultant*
Girgis-Hanna, Mary Fahim *music educator*
Glaab, Charles Nelson *historian, educator*
Gouttiere, John P. *lawyer*
Grundish, Lee Anne *small business owner, writer*
Gutteridge, Thomas G. *academic administrator, consultant, arbitrator*
Harter, James Lester *academic administrator, consultant*
Hartmann, Ann Wilson *financial planner*
Heintz, Carolinea Cabaniss *retired home economist, educator*
Herring, Katherine L. *historian*
Hiltz, Kenneth A. *corporate financial executive*
Jackson, Reginald Sherman, Jr. *lawyer, educator*
Jacobs, Lloyd A. *vascular surgeon*
Kaatz, Forrest H. *physicist, educator*
Kanjwal, Mohammed Y. *cardiologist*
Kaptur, Marcia Carolyn (Marcy Kaptur) *congresswoman*
Kona, Martha Mistina *librarian*
Konwinski, Jacqueline Marie Koralewski *secondary school educator*
Koo, Benjamin Hai Chang *structural engineer, educator*
Koppus, Betty Jane *retired savings and loan association executive*
Krull, Stephen Keith *lawyer*
Kunze, Ralph Carl *retired savings and loan association executive*
La Rue, Carl Forman *lawyer*
Lessick, Mira Lee *nursing educator*
Maiwald, Diane Cecile *dermatologist*
Martin, Robert Edward *architect*
McGlauchlin, Tom *artist*
Mrak, Robert Emil *neuropathologist, educator*
Mulrow, Patrick Joseph *medical educator*
O'Connell, Maurice Daniel *lawyer*
Ormond, Paul A. *healthcare company executive*
Page, Jutta Annette *curator*
Paquette, Jack Kenneth *management consultant, writer, historian*
Perz, Sally *former state legislator, former academic administrator*
Pham, David Lan *secondary school educator, writer*
Pletz, Thomas Gregory *lawyer*
Reichert, Christine Edwards *academic administrator*
Rejent, Marian Magdalen *retired pediatrician*
Romanoff, Marjorie Reinwald *retired education educator*
Romanoff, Milford Martin *retired building contractor*
Royhab, Ronald *journalist, editor*
Scoles, Clyde Sheldon *library director*
Seubert, Lori A. *elementary school educator*
Shaikh, Bahu Sultan *physician, educator*
Shelley, Walter Brown *dermatologist, educator*
Skiver, Stephen Allen *lawyer, physician*
~~Smith, Robert Freeman *history professor*~~
Spitzer, John Brumback *lawyer*
Strobel, Martin Jack *lawyer, manufacturing and distribution company executive*
Stroucken, Albert P. L. *consumer products company executive, former chemical company executive*
Talmage, Lance Allen *obstetrician, gynecologist, military officer*
Thaman, Michael H. *building material systems executive*
Webb, Thomas Irwin, Jr. *lawyer, director*
Wicklund, David Wayne *lawyer*
Wolff, Edwin Ray *retired construction engineer, consultant*
Zouhary, Jack *federal judge*

Trotwood
Oluyitan, Emmanuel Funso *communications educator*

Troy
Bazler, Frank Ellis *retired lawyer*
Puthoff, Mark Allen *lawyer*

Uniontown
France, Dorothy Daniel *minister*
Krabill, Robert Elmer *osteopathic physician*

University Heights
Cook, Alexander Burns *curator, artist, educator*
Eslinger, Kenneth Nelson *social sciences educator*
Murphy, Paul Regis, Jr. *business educator*
Seaton, Shirley Smith *academic administrator, consultant*
Whelan, John Joseph *education educator*

Upper Arlington
Bordelon, Carolyn Thew *elementary school educator*
Relle, Ferenc Matyas *chemist*

Upper Sandusky
Baker, Harrison Scott *application developer, consultant*

Urbana
Phillips, Julieanne Appleson *history professor*

Valley View
Petroski, James *thermal engineer*

Vincent
Meek, Barbara Susan *elementary school educator*

Wadsworth
McIlvaine, James Ross *lawyer*
Neumann, Jeffrey Jay *photographer, minister*
Wilhelm, Cathy S. *elementary school educator*

Walton Hills
Elliott, Stanley B. *chemist, researcher*

Wapakoneta
Wirth, Tamara L. *music educator*

Warren
Dinh, Hai Quang *mathematics professor, researcher*
He, Min *mathematics professor*
Nader, Robert Alexander *judge, lawyer*
Rossi, Anthony Gerald *lawyer*
Ryan, Timothy J. *congressman*

Wauseon
Stutzman, Donna J. *minister*

West Chester
Arasakesari, Subramaniam *chemical engineer, researcher, consultant*
End, William Thomas *marketing executive*
Mack, Mark Philip *chemical company executive*
Macks, Ryan Jeffrey *psychologist*
Tanov, Romil R. *mechanical engineer, researcher*

West Farmington
Smith, Agnes Monroe *history professor*

Westerville
Barr, John Michael *investor, management consultant*
Brombacher, Bruce E. *mathematics educator*
DeVassie, Terry Lee *retired publishing executive*
DeVore, C. Brent *college president, educator*
Helvey, Edward Douglas *lawyer*
Husarik, Ernest Alfred *educational administrator*
Kerr, Thomas Jefferson, IV, *academic administrator*
St. Pierre, Ronald Leslie *public health and medical educator, academic administrator*
Schultz, Arthur LeRoy *clergyman, educator*
Young, Bette Ann *writer*
Young, Sheldon Mike *lawyer, author*

Westlake
Doane, Tim *travel company executive*
Kuhn, Edwin P. *travel company executive*
Lee, Steven C. *lawyer*
Ohno, Apolo Anton *Olympic athlete*
Skulina, Thomas Raymond *lawyer*
Whitehouse, John Harlan, Jr. *systems software consultant, diagnostician*

Whitehouse
Boyle, Daniel Robert *musician, delivery service executive*

Wickliffe
Barnes, Lili Darnelle *music educator, director*
Bauer, Joseph W. *lawyer, chemicals executive*
Cooley, Charles P. *chemicals executive*
Crehore, Charles Aaron *lawyer*
Fisher, Nancy DeButts *library director*
Hambrick, James L. *chemicals executive*
~~Kidder, Fred Dockstater *retired lawyer*~~
Krause, Marjorie N. *biochemist*
Pevec, Anthony Edward *bishop*

Wilberforce
Habash, Khalil M. *computer engineer, educator*
Hargraves, William Frederick, II, *mathematics and computer science professor*
Williamson, Vikki Lyn *university official, financial executive*

Willoughby
Baker, Charles Stephen *music educator*
Carter, John Robert *retired physician*
Corrigan, Faith *journalist, educator, historian*
Driggs, Charles Mulford *lawyer*
Linsenmeier, Carol Vincent *music educator*
Vokic, Heather Maureen *artist, educator*

Wilmington
Evans, Elizabeth Ann West *retired real estate agent*
Hete, Joseph C. *air transportation executive*

Winchester
Koford, Stuart Keith *electronics executive*

Wooster
August, Robert Olin *retired journalist*
Geiser, Robert Neil *computer scientist*
Hales, Raleigh Stanton, Jr. *retired mathematics professor, academic administrator*
Hoy, Casey William *ecologist, educator*
Kennedy, Charles Allen *lawyer*
Schilling, W. A. Hayden *history professor*
Schmitt, Wolf Rudolf *consumer products executive*
Schreiber, Clare Adel *journalist*
Zink, Harry A. *ophthalmologist*

Worthington
Albert, Robert Hamilton *lawyer*
Bernhagen, Lillian Flickinger *retired school health consultant*
Brinkman, Dale Thomas *lawyer*
Compton, Ralph Theodore, Jr. *electrical engineering educator*
Fisher, Fredrick Lee *lawyer*
Lentz, Edward Allen *consultant, retired health administrator*
Luck, James I. *foundation executive*
Speck, Samuel Wallace, Jr. *state official*
Vladem, Steven Allen *writer, film producer, motivational speaker*
Winter, Chester Caldwell *surgeon, educator, historian, writer*
Wu, Tien Hsing *civil engineering educator, consultant*

Wright Patterson Afb
Banda, Siva S. *research scientist*
Cranston, Stewart E. *career officer*
Fernelius, Nils Conard *physicist*
Garscadden, Alan *physicist*
Mall, Shankar *engineering mechanics educator, researcher*
Meccia, Neil Rocco *health facility administrator, physician*
Ray, James Lee *military officer*
Rizzetta, Donald P. *aerospace engineer*

Wyoming
Cooley, William Edward *research scientist, consultant*

Xenia
Bigelow, Daniel James *aerospace executive*
Chappars, Timothy Stephen *lawyer*
Nutter, Zoe Dell Lantis *retired public relations executive*
Wolaver, Stephen Arthur *judge*

Yellow Springs
Cawood, Albert McLaurin (Hap Cawood) *retired newspaper editor*
Fogarty, Robert Stephen *historian, educator, editor*
Spokane, Robert Bruce *biophysical chemist*
Trolander, Hardy Wilcox *engineering executive, consultant*
Von Gierke, Henning Edgar *biomedical science educator, former government official, researcher*
Webb, Paul *physiologist, educator, researcher, consultant*

Yorkville
Estrada, Erik (Henry Enrique Estrada) *actor*

Youngstown
Amin, Isam Eldin *science educator, researcher*
Ausnehmer, John Edward *lawyer*
Binning, William Charles *political science professor*
Bowers, Bege Kaye *literature and communications educator, academic administrator*
Briach, George Gary *lawyer, consultant*
Brown, Steven Ray *language professional*
Camacci, Michael A. *real estate broker and developer, consultant*
Carlin, Clair Myron *lawyer*
Catoline-Ackerman, Pauline Dessie *small business owner*
Cernica, John N. *engineering educator, civil engineer, consultant*
DeBartolo, Edward John, Jr. *real estate developer, former professional football team owner*
Dunlap, Catherine Mary *clergywoman*
Edirisooriya, Gunapala *finance educator*
Estrin, Melvyn J. *computer products company executive*
Fok, Thomas Dso Yun *civil engineer*
Green, Adele C. *educator*
Itts, Elizabeth Ann Dunham *retired psychotherapist, consultant*
Kessler, Ronald N. *plastics company executive*
Miller, Kenneth Lee *counselor, educator*
Petrony, John Francis *lawyer*
Roth, Daniel Benjamin *lawyer, company executive*
Zorn, Robert Lynn *education educator*

Zanesville
Holdren, Susan *literature and language professor, foundation administrator*
Istok, Christine Markward *retired executive director social service agency, consultant*
McLaughlin, James Lee *musician, director*
Micheli, Frank James *lawyer*
Ray, John Walker *otolaryngologist, educator, broadcast commentator*
Strahm, Mary Ellen *music educator*

OKLAHOMA

Ada
Anoatubby, Bill *governor of Chickasaw Nation*
Baggech, Melody A. *music educator*
Baker, Judith Ann *retired computer technician*
Biles, Charles Lee *plant pathologist, physiologist, educator*
Daniel, Arlie V. *speech education educator*
Stafford, Donald Gene *chemistry professor*
Wang, Mingyu *hydrologist, environmental scientist*

Alva
Batalha da Conceicao, Jose Joao *chemistry professor, researcher*
Mitchell, Allan Edwin *lawyer*
Vandewalker, Richard Edward *music educator*

Ardmore
Cawley, Michael A. *foundation administrator, lawyer*
Dixon, Richard Arthur *botanist, educator, researcher*

Bartlesville
Baker-Morris, Kay *special education educator*
Connor, James William *lawyer*
Doty, Donald D. *retired bank executive*
Hankinson, Risdon William *retired chemical engineer*
Hogan, John Paul *chemistry researcher, consultant*
Jackson, Brian Kelly *economics professor*
Price, Joe D. *pipeline developer*
Roff, Alan Lee *retired lawyer, consultant*
Silas, Cecil Jesse *retired petroleum company executive*
Sweem, Billy Don *bishop, religious organization administrator*

Bethany
Alexander, Patrick Byron *hospital administrator*
Arbuckle, Averil Dorothy (Cookie Arbuckle) *healthcare facility administrator*
Leggett, James Daniel *bishop*
McGowan, Bernard Wayne (Bernie) *venture capitalist, writer*

Bixby
Walker, Jerald Carter *academic administrator, minister*

Bristow
Caudle, Letha Grace *secondary school educator*

Broken Arrow
Huff, Melinda Louise *art educator*
Jones, Ronald Lee *lawyer, writer*
Muller, Patricia Ann *nursing administrator, educator*
Smith, Jeffrey Andrews *musician, educator, sound recording engineer*
Stewart, Murray Baker *retired lawyer*

Calera
Parker, Marilla J. *school psychologist*

Chandler
Swanson, Robert Lee *lawyer*

Cherokee
Stein, Sam Lee *lawyer*

Chickasha
Hanson, Dan Lewis *music educator, composer*

Choctaw
Uselton, Bill W. *secondary school educator*

Claremore
Heidlage, Patsy Jo *physical education educator*
Steidley, Juan Dwayne *lawyer, judge*
Vargas, Traci Junelle *special education educator*
Whinery, Michael Albert *physician*
Wittenberg, Henry Taylor, Jr. *physician, surgeon*
Woller, Kevin Marc Peter *psychology professor, researcher*

Cleveland
Henry, Kathleen Marie *marketing executive*

Disney
Hamilton, Carl Hulet *retired academic administrator*

Durant
Rice, Stanley Arthur *biology professor*

Edmond
Adams, Donald E. *physiatrist*
Angel, Steven Michael *retired lawyer*
Coyne, Wayne *musician*
Harryman, Rhonda L. *special education educator*
Hayes, Kevin J. *literature educator*
Hopwood, Howard Hoppy Perry *military officer*
~~Ivins, Michael Lee *musician*~~
Laughlin, Monique Myrtle Weant *mental health counselor*
Lester, Andrew William *lawyer*
Loman, Mary LaVerne *retired mathematics professor*
Loving, Susan Brimer *lawyer, former state official*
Morris, Donna *library director*
Myster, Randall Walton *education educator, researcher*
Sanchez, Cindi Asbury *physical education educator*
Sibley, William Arthur *retired academic administrator, physics professor, consultant*
Smock, Donald Joe *real estate analyst, political scientist*
Wilson, Julia Ann Yother *lawyer*

Enid
Jones, Stephen *lawyer*
Marquardt, Shirley Marie *retired management consultant*
Taveggia, Thomas Charles *management consultant*
Ward, Llewellyn Orcutt III *oil industry executive*

Fort Towson
Pike, Thomas Harrison *plant chemist*

Frederick
Evans, Michael D. *lawyer*
Stone, Voye Lynne *women's health nurse practitioner*

Grove
Trippensee, Gary Alan *retired aerospace executive*

Guthrie
Brooks, Larry Roger *judge*
Davis, Frank Wayne *lawyer*

Hodgen
Brower, Janice Kathleen *library and information scientist*

Inola
Paul, Gary Wayne *music educator*

Jennings
Nixon, Arlie James *gas and oil company executive*

Jones
Dean, Bill Verlin, Jr. *lawyer*

Kingfisher
Buswell, Arthur Wilcox *physician, surgeon*

Lamont
Covalt, Edna Irene *retired medical/surgical nurse*

Langston
Haysbert, JoAnn Wright *academic administrator*

Showalter, Betsy S. *mathematics educator*

Lawton
Bonnell-Mihalis, Pamela Gay Scoggins *library director*
Carraher, Shawn Michael *investment company executive, management educator*
Davis, Ellen Marie *business educator*
Detweiler, Stanley Bruce *music educator*
Hooper, Roy B. *lobbyist*
Kroll, Connie Rae *librarian, information services consultant*
Mays, Quincey *art educator*
Moore, Roy Dean *retired judge*
Riley, Robert Shean *writer, publishing executive, retired army officer*
Thomlinson, Vivian Aytes *literature and language professor*
Webb, Orville Lynn *retired physician, pharmacologist, educator*

Mcalester
Cornish, Richard Pool *lawyer*

Mcloud
Goats, Debbie *elementary school educator*

Miami
George, Barbara M. *theater educator, department chairman, actor, director*

Midwest City
Cheek, Norma Jean *retired elementary school educator*
Gonzalez, Richard Theodore *photographer*
Harrell, Beverly Ellen *mathematics professor*
Wier, Leanne M. *life sciences educator*

Monkey Island
Vanatta, Chester B. *management consultant, educator*

Moore
Chiles, Mary Jane *secondary school educator*
Lee, Myung Woo *accountant, financial secretary*

Mounds
Fellows, Esther Elizabeth *musician, educator*
Halsey, James Albert *entertainer, theater producer*

Muskogee
Hasler-Reid, Linda *elementary school educator*
Heck, Jennifer Leigh *neonatal clinical nurse specialist, educator*
Hilbern, Sandra J. *library director*
Kang, Heesam *investment analyst, educator*
Kent, Bartis Milton *retired physician*
Robinson, Adelbert Carl *lawyer, judge*
Sperling, Sheldon J. *prosecutor*
Swanson, Jacqueline V. *academic administrator, educator, women's health nurse practitioner*
Williams, Betty Outhier *lawyer*
Woods, Stuart Henry *environmental scientist, educator*

Mustang
Hutter, Teresa Ann *art educator*
Laurent, Jerry Suzanna *communications executive*

Nichols Hills
Trost, Louis Frederick, Jr. *banker, financial planner*

Noble
Winchell, Michael George *lawyer*

Norman
Affleck, Marilyn *retired sociology educator*
Altan, M(ustafa) Cengiz *mechanical engineering educator*
Ambrosini, Armand Anthony *music educator*
Apanasov, Boris N. *mathematics professor, researcher*
Beasley, William H. *meteorology professor*
Bert, Charles Wesley *mechanical and aerospace engineer, educator*
Biscoe, Belinda P. *academic administrator, psychologist*
Bluestein, Howard Bruce *meteorology educator*
Boren, David Lyle *academic administrator, former senator*
Brown, Sidney DeVere *history professor*
Campbell, John Morgan *retired chemical engineer*
Corr, Edwin Gharst *ambassador*
Cowan, John James *physicist, astronomer, educator*
Croft, Janet Brennan *academic librarian*
Dille, John Robert *retired physician*
Dorrough, Vicki Lee *theater educator*
Droegemeier, Kelvin K. *meteorologist, educator*
Dryhurst, Glenn *retired chemistry professor*
Fairbanks, Robert Alvin *lawyer*
Fears, Jesse Rufus *historian, educator, academic dean*
Gollahalli, Subramanyam Ramappa *engineering educator*
Gourley, Jonathan Joseph *hydrologist*
Harjo, Pattipeg Snyder *language educator*
Hastie, John Douglas *lawyer*
Henderson, Arnold Glenn *architect, educator*
Henderson, George *educational sociologist, educator*
Hutchison, Victor Hobbs *biologist, educator*
Kessler, Edwin *meteorology educator, consultant*
Khoury, Naji *engineering educator*
Koshkin-Youritzin, Victor *art educator*
Lai, Feng Chyuan *engineering educator*
Lamb, Peter James *meteorology educator, researcher, consultant*
Landers, Thomas Lee *dean, educator*
Lee, Sul Hi *library administrator, dean*
Lester, June *library and information scientist, educator*
Levy, David William *history educator*
Lowitt, Richard *history professor*
Lura, Susan *librarian*
MacFarland, Miriam Katherine (Mimi) *computer engineer, consultant, writer, educator*
Masters, Anne *library director*
Mergler, Nancy L. *academic administrator*
Miller, Fred Heins *lawyer, retired law educator*
Mooneyham, Bobby R. *educational association administrator*
Oliver, Dean S. *petroleum engineer, educator*
Pappas, James Pete *university administrator*
Pigott, John Dowling *geologist, geophysicist, geochemist, educator, consultant*
Provine, Lorraine *retired mathematics educator*
Roller, Chad B. *research and development company executive*
Savage, William Woodrow, Jr. *historian, consultant, social sciences educator*
Sharp, Paul Frederick *retired academic administrator, educational consultant*
Sherman, Mary Angus *public library administrator*
Stoops, Bob *college football coach*
Talley, Richard Bates *lawyer*
Trimble, Preston Albert *retired judge*
Trytten, Deborah Anne *computer scientist, educator*
Tussing, Marilee Appleby *music educator*
Van Fleet, Connie Jean *library and information scientist, educator*
Van Horn, Richard Linley *academic administrator*
Vaughn, Caryn Carpenter *zoologist, educator*
Wallace, Danny P. *library and information scientist, educator*
Winters, Martha P. *history and language educator*
Wood, Betty Jean *conceptual artist, art educator*
Yi, Myongho *library and information scientist*
Zapffe, Nina Byrom *retired elementary school educator*
Zelby, Leon Wolf *electrical engineer, educator, consultant*
Zhang, Liang *research scientist*
Zrnic, Dusan S. *research scientist, educator*

Ochelata
Hitzman, Donald Oliver *microbiologist*

Oklahoma City
Adams, R. Scott *lawyer*
Adams, Russell Lee *neuropsychologist*
Alaupovic, Alexandra Vrbanic *artist, educator*
Alaupovic, Petar *biochemist, educator*
Allen, Robert Dee *lawyer*
Andrews, Mitchell Dewayne *internist, educator, dean*
Askins, Jari *lieutenant governor, former state representative*
Bamgbola, Oluwatoyin Fatai *pediatric renal physician, researcher*
Beltran, Eusebius Joseph *archbishop*
Binning, Bette Finese (Mrs. Gene Hedgcock Binning) *athletic association official*
Binning, Gene Barton *real estate company executive*
Blackwell, John Adrian, Jr. *computer company executive*
Bogardus, Carl Robert, Jr. *radiologist, educator*
Boston, Billie *costume designer and history educator*
Bower, Jeff *professional sports team executive*
Bowlby, Leymond Ambrose *linguist, translator*
Bozalis, John Russell *physician*
Bradford, Dennis Doyle *real estate broker and developer*
Branch, John Curtis *biology professor, lawyer*
Brooks, Gene (Leslie Gene Brooks) *cultural organization administrator*
Busey, Phil Gordon *lawyer*
Butnev, Viktor Yurievich *research scientist*
Campbell, David Gwynne *petroleum executive, geologist*
Carballo, Bernard A. *computer company executive*
Carey, Susan R. *lawyer*
Cauthron, Robin J. *federal judge*
Claflin, James Robert *pediatrician, allergist*
Coats, Andrew Montgomery *dean, lawyer, former mayor*
Colbert, Thomas *state supreme court justice*
Collins, William Edward, Jr. *aeromedical administrator, researcher, psychologist*
Comp, Philip Cinnamon *medical researcher*
Conger, J. William *lawyer*
Cornett, Mick *mayor*
Court, Leonard *lawyer, educator*
Craig, George Dennis *economics professor, consultant*
Crawford, James Leroy *minister, retired theology studies educator*
Crites, Carl D. *auditor*
Culkin, Daniel Joseph *urologist, educator, department chairman*
Cunningham, Stanley Lloyd *lawyer*
Decker, Michael Lynn *lawyer, judge*
Derrick, Gary Wayne *lawyer*
Dezhnyuk, Sergey Fedorovich *business executive, minister*
Dubowski, Kurt Max *toxicologist, educator, consultant*
Edmondson, Drew (William Andrew Edmondson) *state attorney general*
Edmondson, James E. *state supreme court justice*
Fallin, Mary Copeland *congresswoman, former lieutenant governor*
Feng, Chengde *mathematician, educator*
Fenton, Elliott Clayton *lawyer*
Fernandez, Lisa *softball player*
Filley, Warren Vernon *allergist*
Foerster, David William *plastic surgeon*
Ford, Michael Raye *lawyer*
Forni, Patricia Rose *nursing educator*
George, Hardy *curator*
Gibson, Keith Russell *lawyer, educator*
Gigantelli, James William *ophthalmic plastic surgeon*
Gordon, Kevin Dell *lawyer*
Gourley, James Leland *editor, publishing executive*
Greiner, Kenneth Donald, Jr. *retired management consultant, health facility administrator*
Grupe, Robert Charles *corporate communications specialist*
Gunter, James T. *research scientist*
Hageman, Dale *alternative staffing company executive*
Halpin, Anna Marie *retired architect*
Halverstadt, Donald Bruce *urologist, educator*
Hampton, Carol McDonald *priest, educator, historian*
Hampton, James Wilburn *hematologist, oncologist*
Hanna, Terry Ross *lawyer, small business owner*
Harding, Susan M. *language educator*
Hargrave, Rudolph *state supreme court justice*
Harolds, Jay Alan *radiologist, nuclear medicine physician*
Harrington, Gary Burnes *retired controller*
Hefner, William Johnson, Jr., (W. John Hefner Jr.) *oil and gas industry executive*
Henry, Brad (C. Brad Henry) *governor*
Henry, Robert Harlan *federal judge, former attorney general*
Hilger, Robyn *music educator*
Holloway, William Judson, Jr. *federal judge*
Holt, Karen Anita Young *language educator*
Homsey, Joseph Richard, Jr. *lawyer*
Hood, Henry J. *lawyer, energy executive*
Houpt, Jeff *energy management executive*
Ille, Bernard Glenn *insurance company executive, director*
Isaacs, Garvin Alfred *lawyer*
Jemison, Major Lewis *pastor, religious organization administrator*
Johnson, Robert Max *lawyer*
Jones, Renee Kauerauf *health facility administrator*
Jones, Tad *state representative*
Kauger, Yvonne *state supreme court justice*
Kelley, Ed *editor-in-chief*
Kelly, Vicky Leloie *music educator*
Kenney, John Arthur *lawyer*
Kerr, Lou C. *foundation administrator*
Kline, David Adam *lawyer, educator, writer*
Kriesel, Deanna *education educator*
LaMotte, Janet Allison *retired management consultant*
Langton, Jackson Maurice *mining executive, geologist*
Lavender, Robert Eugene *state supreme court justice*
Legg, William Jefferson *lawyer*
Leonard, Timothy Dwight *judge*
Lowe, Lyle Justin *lawyer*
MacDougall, Vicki Lawrence *law educator, writer*
Maddux, Vernon Ray *retired history professor*
Mallonee, Sue *epidemiologist, researcher*
Mass, Michael Don *state legislator*
Mather, Stephanie June *lawyer*
Matsumoto, Hiroyuki *biochemistry professor, researcher*
McCampbell, Robert Garner *lawyer, former prosecutor*
McClellan, Mary Ann *pediatric nurse practitioner*
McClendon, Aubrey K. *energy executive*
McEwen, Irene Ruble *physical therapy educator*
McVey, Susan C. *library director*
Meacham, Scott *state official*
Mildren, Jack *bank executive, retired state official*
Miller, Herbert Dell *petroleum engineer*
Moler, Edward Harold *retired lawyer*
Moore, Steven E. *energy executive*
Morgan, Catherine Marie *psychologist, writer*
Mustion, Alan Lee *pharmacist*
Nakagawara, Van B. *optometrist, researcher*
Necco, Alexander David *lawyer, educator*
Nelon, Robert Dale *lawyer*
Neville, Jack L. (Drew), Jr. *lawyer*
Nour, Bakr M. *surgeon, health facility administrator*
Ogle, James David *lawyer*
Opala, Marian Peter *state supreme court justice*
Pain, Betsy M. *lawyer*
Parke, David Wilkin, II, *ophthalmologist, educator, health facility administrator*
Paul, Chris *professional basketball player*
Paul, William George *lawyer*
Payne, Gareld Gene *vocal music educator, medical transcriptionist*
Peace, H. W., II, *small business owner, retired oil industry executive*
Perez-Cruet, Jorge *geriatric psychiatrist, researcher*
Pfefferbaum, Betty Jane *psychiatrist, educator*
Poole, Richard William *economist*
Price Boday, Mary Kathryn *choreographer, small business owner, educator*
Ragsdale, Frank Wayne *voice educator, singer*
Reed, Willis *professional sports team executive*
Reich, Richard Allen *bank executive*
Reimer, Dennis J. *retired career military officer*
Resman-Targoff, Beth Holly *pharmacist, educator*
Rhoades, Everett Ronald *medical educator*
Richels, John *energy executive, lawyer*
Richter, John Charles *prosecutor*
Ridley, Betty Ann *theology studies educator*
Riley, Nancy C. *state legislator*
Risser, Paul Gillan *academic administrator, botanist*
Rockett, D. Joe *lawyer, director*
Ross, William Jarboe *lawyer*
Rossavik, Ivar Kristian *obstetrician, gynecologist*
Ruffin, Richard A. *orthopedic surgeon*
Russell, David L. *federal judge*
Savage, Susan M. *state official, former mayor*
Schimek, John Bradley *music educator, musician*
Schroeder, David J. Dean *psychologist*
Schwabe, George Blaine III *lawyer*
Scott, Byron *professional basketball coach, retired professional basketball player*
Shelite, Leslie Michelle *middle school educator*
Shillingburg, Herbert Thompson, Jr. *dental educator*
Smith, (Carl) Michael *lawyer, former federal agency administrator*
Spencer, Melvin Joe *retired health facility administrator, retired lawyer, retired consultant*
Stanley, Brian Jordan *lawyer*
Steinhorn, Irwin Harry *lawyer, educator, corporate financial executive*
Stong, Roger Alan *lawyer*
Stringer, L. E. (Dean) *retired lawyer*
Taylor, Lyndon C. *lawyer, energy executive*
Taylor, Steven W. *state supreme court justice*
Taylor-White-Grigsby, Queen Deloris *minister, consultant*
Thadani, Udho *physician, cardiologist*
Thompson, David *publishing executive*
Thompson, Mick *state agency administrator*
Thompson, Ralph Gordon *federal judge*
Tompkins, Raymond Edgar *lawyer*
Towery, Curtis Kent *lawyer*
Triplett, E. Eugene *editor*
Tuck-Richmond, Doletta Sue *prosecutor*
Turner, Eugene Andrew *manufacturing executive*
Voth, Douglas W. *dean, educator*
Walke, Geary Lynn *judge*
Walsh, Lawrence Edward *lawyer*
Ward, Tom L. *energy executive*
Watson, Brenda Bennett *insurance company executive*
Watt, Joseph Michael *state supreme court justice*
Weber, Hugh *professional sports team executive*
Weddington, Stacey Lee *not-for-profit developer*
Weigel, Paul Henry *biochemistry educator, researcher, consultant*
Welsh, Jack Daryl *retired medical educator, writer*
West, Lee Roy *federal judge*
Wheeler, Jane Frances *protective services official*
Williamson, Marvel *dean, nursing administrator, sexologist, educator*
Winchester, James R. *state supreme court justice*
Wisdom, Peggy Jean *neurologist*
Wolraich, Mark Lee *pediatrician, educator*
Woods, Harry Arthur, Jr. *lawyer*
Woods, Pendleton *college director, author*
Wynn, Brenda Reneau *former trade association executive*
Xu, Jiaqiong *research scientist, statistician*
Young, Stephen K. *dean, academic administrator*
Zuhdi, Nazih *retired surgeon*

Okmulgee
Mitcham, Julius Jerome *accountant*

Owasso
Reed, Walter George, Jr. *retired osteopath*

Park Hill
Yeager, Debra Lyn *science educator*

Pawhuska
Strahm, Samuel Edward *retired veterinarian*

Ponca City
Gallagher, Gary W(ayne) *educational services executive*
Northcutt, Clarence Dewey *lawyer*
Raley, John Wesley, Jr. *lawyer*
Rice, Sue Ann *retired dean, psychologist*
Wann, Laymond Doyle *retired petroleum research scientist*
Wood-Warren, Maxine *artist, art educator*

Poteau
Long, Sheila Joan *academic administrator*
Sanders, Douglas Warner, Jr. *lawyer, judge*

Pryor
Stinson, Marion Dennis *lawyer, land use planner, judge*

Ripley
Chlouber, Dale Edward *curator*

Sallisaw
Crowson, Watie Dee *foundation administrator, poet, lyricist*

Sand Springs
Quinn, Art Jay *retired veterinarian, educator*

Sapulpa
Claussen, Alex *music educator*

Sayre
Brooks, David Eugene *lawyer*

Seminole
Elsener, G. Dale *lawyer*

Shawnee
Farrand, James Clinton *minister, consultant*
Sharp, Ron *secondary school educator*
Stoddard, Allan Lee *writer, musician*

Skiatook
Harwell, Kenneth E. *chemist, researcher, consultant*

Sperry
Dunn, Albert Edgar *electrical engineer*

Stillwater
Anderson, Cokie Gaston *computer educator, humanities educator*
Binegar, Birne *mathematics professor*
Case, Kenneth Eugene *industrial engineering educator*
Chakraborty, Goutam *marketing educator*
Chung, Chanjin *economics professor, researcher*
Clark, Gary Carl *lawyer*

Confer, Anthony Wayne *veterinary pathologist, educator*
Cooper, Donald Lee *physician*
Darcy, Robert Emmett *political science and statistics professor*
DeLacerda, Melissa Griner *lawyer*
Dunlap, Riley Eugene *sociologist*
Ewing, Sidney Alton *veterinary medical educator, parasitologist*
Finchum, George Allen, II, *geography educator*
Fischer, LeRoy Henry *historian, educator*
Fischer, Richard Samuel *lawyer*
French, Donald P. *zoologist, educator*
Fried, Vance Hoyt *entrepreneur, educator*
Grischkowsky, Daniel Richard *research scientist, educator*
Halligan, James Edmund *academic administrator, chemical engineer*
Hubbard, Todd Philip *aerospace scientist*
Jaco, William H. *mathematics professor, researcher*
Lucas, Frank D. *congressman*
Luebke, Neil Robert *philosophy educator*
Maddox, Robert Nott *chemical engineer, educator*
Max, Elizabeth *retired language educator*
Mize, Joe Henry *industrial engineer, educator*
Royer, Tom A. *entomologist, educator*
Sarangan, Venkatesh *computer scientist, educator*
Strathe, Marlene I. *academic administrator*
Thompson, David Russell *engineering educator, dean*
Zhang, Guolong *immunologist, educator*

Tahlequah
Stowers, Lela M. *retired academic administrator*

Tecumseh
Moser, Glenda Faye *media specialist*

Terlton
Bender, John Henry, Jr., (Jack) *editor, cartoonist*

Tinker AFB
Foote, Wayne C. *military officer*
Goodman, Ernest Monroe *military officer*
Heinz, Jeremy David *military officer*

Tonkawa
Ackerson, Rex David *science educator, museum director*

Tulsa
Abbott, William Thomas *private investigator*
Abrahamson, A. Craig *lawyer*
Ahmed, Ramadan *engineering educator, educator*
Alexander, Adrian W. *library director, dean*
Angelini, Marcello *performing company executive*
Arrington, John Leslie, Jr. *lawyer*
Azar, J. J. *engineering educator*
Ball, Rex Martin *urban planner, architect*
Barker, John Roy *lawyer, gas industry executive*
Belsky, Martin Henry *law educator, dean*
Bender, James J. *lawyer, oil industry executive*
Berlin, Steven Ritt *oil industry executive*
Bidwell, Duane R. *religious studies educator*
Biolchini, Robert Fredrick *lawyer*
Blais, Roger Nathaniel *physics professor, academic administrator*
Bransford-Young, Angharad Ann *counselor, educator*
Braumiller, Allen Spooner *gas industry executive, geologist*
Bryant, Hubert Hale *lawyer*
Buckley, Thomas Hugh *historian, educator*
Busch, Daniel Adolph *geologist, educator*
Buthod, Mary Clare *school administrator*
Butkin, Robert A. *former state treasurer, law educator*
Cadieux, Chester *retail executive*
Carney, Timothy Alan *lawyer*
Carpenter, Nancy J. *health science association administrator*
Carter, Terry *retail executive*
Chappel, Donald R. *petroleum pipeline company executive*
Cherry, Andrew Lawrence, Jr. *social work educator, researcher*
Clark, Joseph Francis, Jr. *lawyer*
Clement, Evelyn Geer *librarian, educator*
Collins, Laura Jane *music educator, singer*
Cooper, Richard Casey *lawyer*
Cox, William Jackson *retired bishop*
Davis, Lourie Irene Bell *retired computer education and information systems specialist*
Deihl, Michael Allen *federal agency administrator*
Dinan, Curtis L. *gas industry executive*
Donaldson, Robert Herschel *university administrator, educator*
Dotson, George Stephen *retired oil industry executive*
Eagan, Claire Veronica *chief district court judge*
Eagleton, Edward John *lawyer*
Engel, David Wayne *lawyer, federal official*
Farrell, John L., Jr. *lawyer, consultant, corporate financial executive*
Fielding, Peggy Lou Moss *writer*
Frasier, Nikki *sales executive*
Frey, Martin Alan *lawyer, educator*
Frizzell, Gregory Kent *federal judge*
Gabbard, Douglas, II, (James Gabbard) *judge*
Gaberino, John Anthony, Jr. *lawyer*
Gardner, Dale Ray *lawyer*
Gentry, Bern Leon, Sr. *management consultant*
Gibson, John W. *gas industry executive*
Givens, Jack Rodman *lawyer*
Goodman, Jerry L(ynn) *judge*
Gottschalk, Sister Mary Therese *nun, hospital administrator*
Haring, Robert Westing *newspaper editor*
Hatfield, Jack Kenton *lawyer, accountant*
Haynie, Tony Wayne *lawyer*
Henneke, Ben Graf *retired humanities educator*
Hess, Stanley O. *retired art educator*
Hoe, Richard March *insurance and securities consultant, writer*
Holmes, Jerome A *federal judge*
Hong, Jianhui *chemical engineer*
Horkey, William Richard *retired oil industry executive*
Howard, Gene Claude *lawyer, retired state senator*
Huckin, William Price, Jr. *prosecutor*
Huffman, Robert Allen, Jr. *lawyer*
Imel, John Michael *lawyer*
Ingram, Charles Clark, Jr. *energy executive*
Johnson, Cornelius Raymond *prosecutor*
Kaiser, George B. *corporate financial executive*
Kalbfleisch, John McDowell *cardiologist, educator*
Kern, Terry C. *judge*
Kihle, Donald Arthur *lawyer*
Kneale, James C. *gas company executive*
Kozhevnikov, Vladimir F. *physicist, researcher, educator*
Kronfeld, Edwin *natural gas company executive*
Kyle, David L. *gas industry executive*
LaButti, Ronald Stephan *orthopedist*
Lawhorn, Caron A. *gas industry executive*
Lewis, Patricia Mohatt (Patty) *special education educator*
Liu, Xiaofan Sophie *engineering educator*
Luthey, Graydon Dean, Jr. *lawyer, educator*
Ma, Xiaomin *communications educator*
Madison, Eddie Lawrence, Jr. *public relations consultant, editor, writer*
Malcolm, Steven J. *petroleum pipeline company executive*
Marlar, Donald Floyd *lawyer*
Matthies, Mary Constance T. *lawyer*
McCullough, Robert Dale, II, *osteopath*
Moffett, J. Denny *lawyer*
Murphy, Lawrence R. *lawyer*
Neas, John Theodore *investment company executive*
Nedom, H. Arthur *petroleum consultant*
Nettles, John Barnwell *obstetrics and gynecology educator*
Newell, David L. *curator*
Norvell, John Edmondson III *retired neuroscientist, educator*
Nyikos, Stacy Ann *publishing executive*
O'Meilia, David E. *prosecutor, lawyer*
Osborn, La Donna Carol *clergywoman*
O'Sullivan, Cindy Marie *mathematics professor*
Owens, Jana Jae *entertainer*
Paxton, Gary L. *auto rental company executive*
Plumb, Charles Sumner III *lawyer*
Plunket, Daniel Clark *pediatrician, educator*
Rahja, Virginia H. *retired art educator, artist*
Randle, Rodger A. *human relations professor, political science professor*
Roberts, (Granville) Oral *clergyman*
Roger, Jerry Lee *academic administrator*
Rooney, Laurence Francis III *ambassador to the Vatican, construction executive*
Russell, Irma S. *lawyer, educator*
Rutter, Frances Tompson *retired publisher*
Say, Burhan *retired physician*
Seymour, Stephanie Kulp *federal judge*
Singer, George Alan *oil and gas company executive, arts association administrator*
Slicker, Frederick Kent *lawyer*
Sowell, Laven *retired music educator*
Steltzlen, Janelle Hicks *lawyer*
Strecker, David Eugene *lawyer*
Stuart, Harold Cutliff *lawyer, business executive*
Sturdivant, James M. *lawyer*
Taylor, Joe Clinton *judge*
Taylor, Kathy *mayor*
Thomas, Robert Eggleston *retired manufacturing executive*
Thornton, Charlie Mae *secondary school educator*
Tremblay, Ronald Joseph *minister, religious studies educator*
Trennepohl, Gary Lee *academic administrator, finance educator*
Tucker, John *lawyer*
Upham, Steadman *academic administrator, anthropologist, educator*
Upton, Howard B., Jr. *writer, lawyer*
Valero, Maria Teresa *photographer, art educator*
Williams, John Horter *civil engineer, energy industry executive*
Williamson, Walter Bland *lawyer*
Womack, Lee Ann *country musician*
Wood, Donald Euriah *retired lawyer*
Wood, Emily Churchill *special education and social studies educator, consultant*

Vinita
Johnston, Oscar Black III *lawyer*
Neer, Charles Sumner, II, *orthopedic surgeon, educator*
Wright, Jo Anne *priest*

Wagoner
Hadley, Charline A. *protective services official*

Warr Acres
Engle, Richard Victor *publishing executive*
Weir, Richard Dale *elementary school educator*

Weatherford
Beam, Stephen D. *lawyer*
Boggs, Lisa Lynn *biology professor*

Wewoka
Rains, Mary Jo *banker*
Trimble, Vance Henry *retired newspaper editor*

Wilburton
Carey, Levenia Marie *counselor*

Woodward
Fisher, Deena Kaye *social studies education administrator*
Riffel, Loren Darrel *retired entrepreneur*

OREGON

Albany
Oakley, Carolyn Le *state legislator, city manager, director*
Wood, Kenneth Arthur *retired editor, writer*
Yu, Kitson Szewai *computer science educator*

Ashland
Abrahams, Sidney Cyril *physicist, crystallographer*
Bornet, Vaughn Davis *social sciences educator, historian, researcher*
Christianson, Roger Gordon *biology professor, department chairman*
Cullinan, Mary Patricia *academic administrator, literature and language professor*
Grover, James Robb *chemist, editor*
Kreisman, Arthur *higher education consultant, retired humanities educator*
Masters, Robert Edward Lee *psychotherapist, sexologist*
Mularz, Theodore Leonard *architect*
Risser, James Vaulx, Jr. *journalist, educator*
Schachter-Shalomi, Zalman *rabbi*

Astoria
Haskell, Donald McMillan *lawyer*
LaMear, Arline Joan *librarian, writer*

Aurora
Meulemans, William Charles *political science professor*

Bandon
Handley, Louise Patricia *artist*
Lindquist, Louis William *artist, researcher, writer*

Beatty
Nettelbeck, Fred Arthur *poet*

Beaverton
Bird, Lewis L. III *apparel executive*
Blair, Donald W. *apparel executive*
Burson-Dyer, Lorraine *library executive*
Campbell, Richard Lynn *research engineer*
Carter, James C. *lawyer, apparel executive*
Chartier, Vernon Lee *electrical engineer*
Clarke, Thomas E. *apparel executive*
Denson, Charles D. *apparel executive*
de Sá e Silva, Elizabeth Anne *secondary school educator*
DeStefano, Gary M. *apparel executive*
Duncan, Richard Fredrick, Jr. *retired secondary school educator, consultant*
Edwards, Trevor *apparel executive*
Frank, Sister Ruth M. *principal, educator*
Hatfield, Tinker L. *architect, apparel designer, product designer*
Knight, Philip Hampson *apparel executive*
Nathanson, David *communications executive*
Parker, Mark G. *apparel executive*
Pond, Patricia Brown *library and information scientist, educator*
Shimojima, Chris *retail executive*
Stewart, Lindsay D. *lawyer, apparel executive*
Temple, Mike *software company executive*
Torvalds, Linus Benedict *application developer*
Vardavas, Stephanie J. *lawyer*
Wall, Brian Raymond *forest economist, business consultant, researcher*
Wedlake, Martine *application developer*

Bend
Brooke, Sandra Lee *painter*
Denton, Jody *chef*
Evers-Williams, Myrlie Beasley *advocate, cultural organization administrator*
Knitowski, David Alan *civil engineer, urban planner*
Moss, Patricia L. *bank executive*
Singletary, DeJuan Theresa *child and adolescent psychiatrist*
Whitcomb, Brian *sports association executive*

Brookings
Maxwell, William Stirling *retired lawyer*
Shepherd, William Michael *music educator, musician*

Cannon Beach
Greaver, Harry *artist*
Hellyer, Constance Anne (Connie Anne Conway) *writer, musician, educator*
Hillestad, Charles Andrew *lawyer*
Wismer, Patricia Ann *retired secondary school educator*

Central Point
Brown, Christopher Patrick *health care administrator, educator*
Ingraham, Laura *lawyer, political commentator*
Richardson, Dennis Michael *lawyer, educator*

Chiloquin
Reed, David George *entrepreneur*

Clackamas
George, Oakie Lee *mechanic*
Kostow, Kathryn E. *conservation biologist*
Woods, Dennis Oliver *headmaster, market and political research analyst*

Coos Bay
Hanlin, Shawn *academic administrator*

Corvallis
Baird, William McKenzie *chemical carcinogenesis researcher, biochemistry professor*
Benoit Bird, Kelly J. *science educator*
Byers, William D. *engineering executive*
Byrne, John Vincent *educational consultant*
Casey, Pat *college baseball coach*
Castle, Emery Neal *economist, educator*
Chambers, Kenton Lee *botany educator*
Cho, Jang-Cheon *microbiologist, researcher*
Chung, Woon-Gye *toxicologist, researcher*
Coakley, James A. *atmospheric science educator*
Dalrymple, Gary Brent *research geologist*
Davis, John Rowland *academic administrator*
Dennis, John Davison *minister*
Drake, Charles Whitney *physicist*
Engelbrecht, Rudolf *electrical engineering educator*
Frakes, Rodney Vance *plant geneticist, educator*
Frohnmayer, John Edward *lawyer, writer*
Gillis, John Simon *retired psychologist, educator*
Hall, Don Alan *editor, writer*
Holman, Robert Alan *oceanography educator*
Lee, Yun-Shik *physics professor*
Levine, Shepard *painter, educator*
Loper, Joyce E. *plant pathologist, educator*
Lubchenco, Jane *environmental scientist, marine ecologist, science association director*
Main, Michael Dee *information developer*
Mathews, Christopher King *biochemist, educator*
Morita, Richard Yukio *microbiology and oceanography educator*
Neumann, Nancy Ruth *film studio educator*
Oldfield, James Edmund *retired nutrition educator*
Parks, Harold Raymond *mathematician, educator*
Perry, David Anthony *ecologist*
Poinar, George Orlo, Jr. *entomologist, science educator*
Ray, Edward John *economics professor, academic administrator*
Temes, Gabor Charles *electrical engineering educator*
Tyavnagimatt, Shanthakumar R. *research scientist, pharmacist*
Van Holde, Kensal Edward *biochemistry educator*
Verts, Lita Jeanne *academic administrator*
Westwood, Melvin Neil *horticulturist, pomologist*
Wilkins, Caroline Hanke *advocate, political organization worker*
Yeats, Robert Sheppard *geologist, educator*
Young, Roy Alton *university administrator, educator*
Zhang, Eugene *engineering educator*

Culver
Siebert, Diane Dolores *author, poet*

Dallas
Brown, James Chandler *retired university administrator*
Nathan, Gerald Dale *retired psychologist, researcher, writer*

Dayton
Anderson, Herbert Hatfield *lawyer, farmer*

Depoe Bay
Eaton, Leonard Kimball *retired architecture educator*

Eugene
Acker, Martin Herbert *psychotherapist, educator*
Aldave, Barbara Bader *lawyer, educator*
Bailey, Exine Margaret Anderson *soprano, educator*
Baker, Alton Fletcher III *editor, publishing executive*
Baker, Bridget *publishing executive*
Bascom, Ruth F. *retired mayor*
Bellotti, Mike *football coach*
Bennett, Robert Royce *engineering and management consultant*
Bergquist, Peter *retired music educator*
Bichsel, Ruth J. *psychologist, educator*
Briston, Heather Irene *archivist*
Camp, Delpha Jeanne *counselor*
Cawood, Elizabeth Jean *public relations executive*
Collis, Dennis K. *orthopedic surgeon*
Crasemann, Bernd *physicist, researcher*
Csonka, Paul L. *theoretical physicist, educator*
Deshpande, Nilendra Ganesh *physics professor*
Donnelly, Russell James *physicist, educator*
DuPriest, Douglas Millhollen *lawyer*
Edwards, Ralph M. *librarian*
Freyd, Jennifer Joy *psychology professor*
Frohnmayer, David Braden *academic administrator*
Gall, Meredith (Mark) Damien *retired education educator, writer*
Graziano, Margaret A. *chaplain, recreational therapist, educational consultant, volunteer*
Griffith, Osbie Hayes *retired chemistry professor*
Hildreth, Richard G. *lawyer, educator*
Horn, John Harold *lawyer*
Hunt, Elizabeth Hope *psychologist*
Jacobson, Jon L. *law educator*
Jewell, Mark Laurence *plastic surgeon*
Kent, Ernie *men's college basketball coach*
Khang, Chulsoon *economics professor*
Kimball, Reid Roberts *psychiatrist*
Langfedlt, Andrew *engineer*
Lindholm, Richard Theodore *economics and finance educator*
Littman, Richard Anton *psychologist, educator*
Loescher, Richard Alvin *retired gastroenterologist*
Matthews, Brian W. *molecular biology educator*
Maurer, Robert Distler *retired industrial physicist*
Mazo, Robert Marc *retired chemistry professor*
McCrea, Shaun S. *lawyer*
Miner, John Burnham *industrial relations educator, writer*
Moseley, John Travis *academic administrator, physicist, researcher*
Neville, Helen J. *psychology professor, neuroscientist*
Pascal, C(ecil) Bennett *classics educator*
Peterson, Donna Rae *health facility administrator, gerontologist, director*
Pickett, Stephen Wesley *academic administrator, consultant*

Retallack, Gregory John *geologist, educator*
Richmond, Geraldine Lee *chemist, educator*
Roe, Thomas Leroy Willis *retired pediatrician*
Roesler, Robert Harry *media consultant*
Sanders, Jack Thomas *religious studies educator*
Scoles, Eugene Francis *lawyer, educator*
Sygall, Susan E. *international educational exchange director*
Toolson, Kay *transportation executive*
Tykeson, Donald Erwin *broadcast executive*
von Hippel, Peter Hans *chemistry professor, researcher*
Walters, Martha Lee *state supreme court justice*
Weiss, Marianna Shrenger *psychotherapist*
White, Patricia Marie *psychology professor, researcher*
Wickes, George *English literature educator, writer*
Wilhelm, Kate (Katy Gertrude) *author*
Wilhite, Tamara Sue *public health service officer*
Womack, James Errol *college president*
Woolley, Donna Pearl *lumber company executive*
Youngquist, Walter Lewellyn *geologist, consultant*

Florence
Ericksen, Jerald Laverne *retired science engineering educator*
Marble, Duane Francis *geography educator, researcher*
Van Horn, O. Frank *retired counselor, consultant*

Forest Grove
Carson, William Morris *manpower planning and development advisor*
Fuiten, Helen Lorraine *small business owner*
Gibby-Smith, Barbara *psychologist, nurse*
Marvin, Monica Louise Wolf *lawyer*

Gladstone
Beals, Herbert Kyle *urban planner, historian, consultant*

Gleneden Beach
Parker, Edwin Burke *communications executive*

Grants Pass
Murdock, Doris Dean *special education educator, program developer*
Smith, Barnard Elliot *management educator*

Gresham
Cooke, Jackie (Jacqueline Marie Cooke) *elementary school educator*
Lazenby, Justin Wyatt *forensic scientist*
Light, Betty Jensen Pritchett *retired dean*
Waagen, Linda Louise *elementary school educator*
Webb, Donna Louise *academic director, educator*
Zook, John Edwin *surgeon*

Hermiston
Lampkin, Toni K. *elementary school educator*

Hillsboro
Barnes, Keith Lee *electronics executive*
Berger, Otto *engineer*
Blackburn, Terry L. *systems administrator*
Bohr, Mark T. *architectural engineer*
Dubrulle, Françoise M. *architect, painter, interior designer*
Ferguson, James Clarke *mathematician, algorithmist*
Heath, Matthew W. *engineer*
Hiranandani, Manish Ashok *electrical engineer*
Pixley, Carl Preston *mathematician*
Rueda, Guillermo *architect, researcher*

Jacksonville
Hennion, Reeve Lawrence *communications executive*
O'Connor, Karl William (Goodyear Johnson) *retired lawyer*

John Day
Tuttle, Kenneth Lewis *retired engineering educator, consultant, researcher*

Joseph
Coppin, Caryl Mary *retired librarian*
Gilbert, David Erwin *academic administrator, physicist*

Keizer
Stevens, Sharon Cox *lawyer*

Kimberly
Fremd, Theodore J. *paleontologist, regional science advisor*

Klamath Falls
Dow, Martha Anne *academic administrator, biology professor*
Klepper, Carol Herdman *mental health therapist*
Koch, Margaret Rau *writer, artist, historian*
Wendt, Richard L. *manufacturing executive*
Woodall, David Monroe *engineer, researcher, dean*

La Grande
Espinosa, Leandro *composer, conductor, educator*
Fatemi, Khusrow *academic administrator, economics educator*
Joseph, Steven Jay *lawyer*
Thompson, Jo(an) *anthropologist*

Lake Oswego
Bruce, John Allen *retired foundation executive, educator*
Byczynski, Edward Frank *lawyer, corporate financial executive*
Campbell, Colin Herald *former mayor*
Gehrig, Edward Harry *electrical engineer, consultant*
Hill, Gary D. *lawyer*
Hutchens, Tyra Thornton *pathologist, educator*
Julien, Robert Michael *anesthesiologist, writer*
Kuntz, Joel Dubois *lawyer*
McDonald, Wilson *lawyer*
McKay, Laura L. *bank executive, consultant*
McPeak, Merrill Anthony *retired military officer, investor, company director*
Parrick, Gerald Hathaway *communications and marketing executive*
Rasmussen, Richard Robert *lawyer*
Wicklund, Lee Arthur *retired school system administrator*

Lincoln City
Arant, Eugene Wesley *lawyer*
Morrow, James Thomas *energy executive*

Lowell
Boyle, John Howard *history educator*

Madras
Ramsey, Jarold William *literature and language professor, writer*

Marylhurst
Hatfield, Mark Odom *former senator*

Mcminnville
Nelson, Donna Gayle *state representative*
Ramsay, Violeta *language educator, consultant*
Thompson, Robert Samuel *retired lawyer*
Walker, Charles Urmston *retired university president*

Medford
Carter, William G. *lawyer*
Deatherage, William Vernon *lawyer*
De Boer, Sidney B. *automotive executive*
Dixon, Andrew Derart *retired academic administrator*
Entorf, Richard Carl *retired management consultant*
Franklin, Darlene Kay *elementary school educator*
Frost, Orcutt William *historian, educator*
Hall, Roger V. *cardiac surgeon*
Heimann, M.L. (Dick Heimann) *auto dealership executive*
Hennion, Carolyn Laird (Lyn) *investment executive*
Panner, Owen M. *federal judge*
Rogers, Gardner Spencer *railroad company executive*
Schubert, Ruth Carol Hickok *artist, educator*
Shekhar, Stephen S. *obstetrician, gynecologist*
Straus, David A. *architectural firm executive*
Thierolf, Richard Burton, Jr. *lawyer*

Milton Freewater
Agidius, Michael Gregory *music educator*
Gipson, Stephen Richard *journalist, construction executive*

Milwaukie
Eichinger, Marilynne Katzen *museum administrator*
Orloff, Barbara-Lee Marguerite Hewitt *retired social worker*
Sklovsky, Robert Joel *naturopathic physician, pharmacist, educator*

Monmouth
Cannon, Beverly J. *deaf education educator, interpreter*
Henderson, Jessica *science educator*
Minahan, John P. *academic administrator*
White, Donald Harvey *retired physics professor*

Mount Angel
Petrik, F. A. *music educator*

Myrtle Point
Walsh, Don *engineer, consultant*

Newberg
Adams, Wayne Verdun *pediatric psychologist, educator*
Johnson, Thomas Floyd *former academic administrator, educator*
Keith, Pauline Mary *artist, illustrator, writer*
Terry, Mark *art educator*
Warford, Patricia *psychologist*

Newport
Gilhooly, David James III *artist*
Kennedy, Richard Jerome *writer*
Pavlish, Catherine Ann *language educator, writer*
Peterson, William T. *oceanographer*
Sonnier, Patricia Bennett *business management educator*

North Plains
Wood, James Anderson *cardiac surgeon*

Oceanside
Wadlow, Joan Krueger *retired academic administrator, construction executive*

Oregon City
Burke, William Romney *urologist*
Lounsbury, Steven Richard *lawyer*
Ringle, Philip Hamilton, Jr. *lawyer*
Vasquez, Paul I. *director*

Pendleton
Klepper, Elizabeth Lee *retired physiologist*
Machado, Stephen *science educator*
Smiley, Richard Wayne *researcher*

Port Orford
Drinnon, Richard *retired historian*

Portland
Abel, William Edward *applied physicist, consultant*
Abravanel, Allan Ray *lawyer*
Ahuja, Jagdish Chand *mathematics professor*
Aldridge, LaMarcus Nurae *professional basketball player*
Allen, Rex Whitaker *retired architect*
Almers, Wolfhard *physiology and biophysics educator*
Al-Rabadi, Anas Naser Essa *electrical and computer engineer*
Anastasiou, Harry *international peace and conflict studies professor*
Arthur, Michael Elbert *financial advisor, lawyer*
Attig, Rick *editor*
Bacon, Vicky Lee *lighting services executive*
Baker, Diane R.H. *dermatologist*
Baker, William I. *application developer*
Balkowiec, Agnieszka Zofia *science educator, researcher*
Ball, Melvyn *medical educator*
Barbeau, Monique Andrée *chef*
Barry, John Maynard *urologist*
Bartlett, Thomas Alva *retired educational administrator*
Bates, Doug *editor*
Beatty, John Cabeen, Jr. *judge*
Beauchamp, E(dward) William *priest, lawyer, university administrator, management educator*
Beer, Tomasz M. *physician*
Bennett, William Michael *internist, educator, nephrologist*
Berentsen, Kurtis George *music educator, conductor*
Bhatia, Peter K. *editor, journalist*
Blank, Eugene *pediatrician, radiologist, educator*
Blanke, Charles D. *medical educator*
Bloom, Joseph D. *psychiatrist, medical educator*
Blumenauer, Earl *congressman*
Bodin, Kate *dean*
Boulot, Philippe *chef*
Boutwell, Anne Dielschneider *artist, painter*
Boyle, Gertrude *sportswear company executive*
Bragdon, Paul Errol *retired academic administrator, educator*
Brashier, Kenneth E. *humanities educator*
Braun, Stephen Baker *academic administrator*
Brenneman, Delbert Jay *lawyer*
Browne, Joseph Peter *retired librarian*
Bunza, Linda Hathaway *editor, writer, composer, director*
Cable, John Franklin *lawyer*
Cady, Sherry L. *astrobiologist, educator*
Campbell, John Richard *pediatric surgeon*
Carter, Charles Conrad *medical educator*
Carter, John D. *recycling company executive*
Casey, Daniel E. *psychiatrist, educator*
Chevis, Cheryl Ann *lawyer*
Claycomb, Cecil Keith *biochemist, educator*
Clinton, Jack W. *dean*
Cohen, Norm *chemist*
Cohen, Stuart F. *investment company executive*
Coleman, Debi (Deborah Ann) *investment and former computer company executive*
Colwell, Robert L. *computer architect, consultant*
Conkling, Roger Linton *management consultant, business administration educator, retired utilities executive*
Conlin, Michael Joseph *physician*
Cook, Nena *lawyer*
Crawshaw, Ralph *psychiatrist*
Crowell, John B., Jr. *lawyer, former government official*
Curtis, Michael *lawyer*
Dailey, Dianne K. *lawyer*
Daim, Tugrul Unsal *technology management specialist, educator*
Davis, Raymond P. *bank executive*
Dean, E. Joseph *lawyer*
Denson, Bryan *reporter*
Diver, Colin S. *academic administrator, educator*
Donegan, Mark *metal products executive*
Drinkward, Cecil *construction company executive*
Druker, Brian Jay *medical educator, researcher*
Dubanevich, Keith Scott *lawyer*
Dunn, Randall Lawson *judge*
Ebert, Leslie *artist*
Eifler, Karen Elizabeth *language educator*
Englert, Walter George *classics and humanities educator*
English, Stephen Francis *lawyer*
Epperson, Eric Robert *finance executive, film producer*
Epstein, Edward Louis *lawyer*
Ernst, David A. *lawyer*
Fan, Lee Siu *business executive and vocational training program administrator*
Farner, Darla A. *artist*
Feuerstein, Howard M. *lawyer*
Finley, Lewis Merren *financial consultant*
Foley, Ridgway Knight, Jr. *lawyer, writer*
Francis, Steve *professional basketball player*
Franzke, Richard Albert *lawyer*
Fraunfelder, Frederick Theodore *ophthalmologist, educator*
Friesen, David Douglas *musician, music educator, composer*
Fulsher, Allan Arthur *lawyer*
Furse, Elizabeth *retired congressman, small business owner*
Glanville, Jerry *college football coach, former professional football coach*
Glasgow, William Jacob *lawyer, venture capitalist, business executive*
Golub, Mike *professional sports team executive*
Goodman, Richard H. *biomedical researcher*
Gordly, Avel Louise *state legislator, political organization worker*
Graber, Susan P. *federal judge*
Graves, Earl William, Jr. *journalist*
Greene, Herbert Bruce *lawyer, investor, entrepreneur*
Greer, Monte Arnold *endocrinologist, educator*
Grossmann, Ronald Stanyer *lawyer*
Hagenstein, William David *forester, consultant*
Hall, Howard Pickering *engineering and mathematics educator*
Hamilton, Bronwyn Elizabeth *radiologist*
Hanna, Harry Mitchell *lawyer*
Harnden, Edwin A. *lawyer*
Harris, Cynthia Viola *principal*
Hart, John Edward *lawyer*
Harter, Lafayette George, Jr. *retired economics professor*
Hayward, Lani *bank executive*
Hedges, Jerris *medical educator, health services researcher*
Hinckley, Gregory Keith *software industry executive*
Hinkle, Charles Frederick *lawyer, educator*
Hirshon, Robert Edward *lawyer*
Hochstettler, Thomas John *academic administrator, historian*
Holt, Mavis Murial *social services administrator*
Horowitz, David A. *history professor, writer*
Houser, Douglas Guy *lawyer*
Hudson, Jerry E. *foundation administrator*
Huggett, Monica *performing company executive, musician*
Iamratanakul, Supachart *educational consultant*
Immergut, Karin J. *prosecutor*
Jackson, Roberta Q. *music educator*
Jacob, Stanley Wallace *surgeon, educator*
Jarvis, Peter R. *lawyer*
Jensen, J. Alan *lawyer*
Jiang, Bin *mathematician, educator*
Johnson, Mark Andrew *lawyer*
Johnston, David Frederick *lawyer*
Johnston, Virginia Evelyn *retired editor*
Jolles, Bernard *lawyer*
Jones, Robert Edward *federal judge*
Josephson, Richard Carl *lawyer*
Kalmar, Carlos *conductor, music director*
Kanter, Stephen *lawyer, educator, dean*
Katz, Vera *former mayor, college administrator, state legislator*
Kendall, John Walker, Jr. *internist, researcher, dean*
Kennedy, Jack Leland *lawyer*
Kennedy, R(obert) Evan *engineering executive, consultant, retired structural engineer*
Kester, Randall Blair *lawyer*
Khalil, Mohammad Aslam Khan *environmental science educator, engineering educator, physics professor*
King, Garr Michael *federal judge*
Kirk, Jill *management consultant*
Knoll, James Lewis *lawyer*
Koblik, Steven S. *academic administrator*
Kocaoglu, Dundar F. *engineering management educator, industrial engineer, civil engineer*
Kohne, Heidi Ann *church musician*
Koon, Theresa Helen *voice educator, singer*
Korb, Christine Ann *music therapist, researcher, educator*
Kosseff, Jeff *reporter, news correspondent*
Krahmer, Donald Leroy, Jr. *lawyer*
Kristof, Ladis Kris Donabed *political scientist, writer*
Lang, Philip David *retired state legislator, insurance company executive*
Larpenteur, James Albert, Jr. *retired lawyer*
Larson, Wanda Z. *writer, poet*
Leavy, Edward *federal judge*
Leupp, Edythe Peterson *retired education educator*
Liem, Timothy K. *surgeon*
Linstone, Harold Adrian *management consultant, educator*
Livingston, Louis Bayer *lawyer*
Lorenz, Nancy *artist*
Love, Edith Holmes *theater producer*
Love, William Edward *lawyer*
Loveless, Peggy Ann *social work administrator*
Lovett, Richard A. *writer, photographer*
Lum, Gregory *high school librarian*
Machida, Curtis A. *research molecular neurobiologist, educator*
Maloney, Robert E., Jr. *lawyer*
Mandel, Gail *immunologist*
Matarazzo, Joseph Dominic *psychologist, educator*
Matarazzo, Ruth Gadbois *retired psychology professor*
McClave, Donald Silsbee *academic administrator*
McMahon, Paul Francis *finance company executive*
McMillan, Nathaniel (Nate McMillan) *professional basketball coach*
Menashe, Albert Alan *lawyer*
Meng, Linda *lawyer*
Miller, Larry G. *professional sports team executive*
Miller, William Richey, Jr. *lawyer*
Milton, Catherine Higgs *entrepreneur*
Moore, Thomas Scott *lawyer*
Mosman, Michael W. *federal judge, former prosecutor*
Mowe, Gregory Robert *lawyer*
Neavoll, George Franklin *writer*
Ng, John Daniel *ophthalmologist, educator*
Njoku, Scholastica Ibari *retired college librarian, writer*
Noonan, William Donald *lawyer, physician*
Nunn, Robert Warne *lawyer*
Oden, Greg *professional basketball player*
Orloff, Chet *historian*
O'Scannlain, Diarmuid Fionntain *federal judge*
Packard, Robert Goodale III *urban planner*
Paley, Vitaly *chef, food service executive*
Pamplin, Robert Boisseau, Sr. *retired textile manufacturing executive*
Pamplin, Robert Boisseau, Jr. *manufacturing company executive, minister, writer*
Parsons, Eric E. *insurance company executive*
Patterson, James Randolph *physician*
Paulson, Jane *lawyer*
Pearson, David Petri *chemist*
Pham, Kinh Dinh *electrical engineer, executive, educator*
Phillips, Vicki L. *school system administrator*
Pine, William Charles *foundation executive*
Porter, Elsa Allgood *writer, educator*

Potter, Tom *mayor*
Prendergast, William John *ophthalmologist*
Pritchard, Kevin *professional sports team executive*
Purcell, John F. *lawyer*
Ramsby, Mark Delivan *lighting designer, consultant*
Raphael, Molly (Mary E. Raphael) *library director*
Redden, James Anthony *federal judge*
Rees, Nina Shokraii *educational association administrator, former federal agency administrator*
Richardson, Campbell *retired lawyer*
Richter, Peter Christian *lawyer*
Riggs, R. William *retired state supreme court justice*
Robertson, Joseph E., Jr. *academic administrator, ophthalmologist, educator*
Rooks, Charles S. *foundation administrator*
Rosen, Steven O. *lawyer*
Rosenblum, Ellen F. *judge*
Rowe, Sandra Mims *editor*
Roy, Brandon Dawayne *professional basketball player*
Rucker, Gabriel *chef*
Rushanaedy, Agustinus *urologist*
Rutherford, William Drake *investment executive*
Ruzicka, Alexander Marion *geologist, educator*
Ryan, John Duncan *lawyer*
Ryberg, William A. *orchestra executive*
Savage, John William *lawyer*
Schmidt, Stanley Eugene *retired speech educator*
Schmidt, Waldemar Adrian *pathologist, educator*
Schuster, Philip Frederick, II, *lawyer, writer, educator*
Scott, John D. *pharmacologist*
Shangraw, Robert Edward *medical educator, researcher*
Shireman, Joan Foster *social work educator*
Showalter, Marilyn Grace *trade association administrator, director*
Shumway, Holly Ann *art educator*
Simpson, Robert Glenn *lawyer*
Skopil, Otto Richard, Jr. *federal judge*
Sokol, Larry Nides *lawyer, educator*
Stanton, John W. *communications executive*
Steinman, Lisa Malinowski *English literature educator, writer*
Stewart, Marlene Metzger *financial planning practitioner, insurance agent*
Stewart, Milton Roy *lawyer*
Stickel, Frederick A. *publishing executive*
Stone, Richard James *lawyer*
Stott, Peter Walter *investment company executive*
Stowell, Christopher R. *performing company executive, choreographer, retired dancer*
Strader, Timothy Richards *lawyer*
Street, Terry M. *artist, educator*
Sullivan, Edward Joseph *lawyer*
Sutherland, Donald Wood *retired cardiologist*
Swanstrom, Lee Leray *surgeon*
Swenson, Constance Rae *lawyer*
Sylvester, Robert *dean, musician*
Taylor, J. Mary (Jocelyn Mary Taylor) *museum director, educator, zoologist*
Taylor, James Gilbert *protective services official*
Taylor, Robert Brown *physician, educator, writer*
Tucker, Roy W. *lawyer*
Tuska, Jon *writer, publishing executive*
Urbanowski, John Richard *lighting systems company official*
Vanderslice, Ellen *architect, composer*
Van Exel, Nickey Maxwell *professional basketball player*
Van Hoomissen, George Albert *state supreme court justice*
Van Valkenburg, Edgar Walter *lawyer*
Vaughan, Thomas James Gregory *historian, writer*
Waggoner, James Clyde *lawyer*
Watne, Donald Arthur *retired accountant, educator*
Weber, George Richard *financial and internet marketing executive, writer*
Weeks, Wilford Frank *retired geophysics educator, glaciologist*
Westwood, James Nicholson *lawyer*
Whinston, Arthur Lewis *lawyer*
White, Douglas James, Jr. *lawyer*
White, Roberta Lee *financial analyst*
Wieden, Dan G. *advertising executive*
Wiens, Arthur Nicholai *psychology professor*
Williamson, Charles Ready III *lawyer*
Wilson, Owen Meredith, Jr. *lawyer, mediator, arbitrator*
Wilson, William Harwell *psychiatrist, educator*
Wood, Cynthia Wilder *elementary school educator*
Wood, Marcus Andrew *lawyer*
Wu, David *congressman*
Yoshida, Stephen P. *lawyer*
Yugler, Richard S. *lawyer*
Zaitz, Leslie Lee *reporter*
Zalutsky, Morton Herman *lawyer*
Zerbe, Kathryn Jane *psychiatrist*

Redmond
Blue, Frederick Judd *retired history professor, writer*
Dey, Charlotte Jane *retired community health nurse*

Roseburg
Oliphant, Charles Romig *retired physician*
Reenstjerna, Frederick Roberts *librarian, writer*
Tilson, Daniel *elementary school educator*

Salem
Abrams, Marc *lawyer, political organization worker*
Balmer, Thomas Ancil *state supreme court justice*
Benson, Steven Donald *marketing professional, mechanical engineer, writer*
Bradbury, Bill (William Chapman Bradbury III) *state official*
Breen, Richard F., Jr. *law librarian, educator*
Brown, Eden Rose *lawyer*
Burdick, Ginny Marie *state senator*
Carter, Margaret L. *legislator*
Castillo, Susan *school system administrator*
Clark, David Scott *law educator, consultant*
De Muniz, Paul J. *state supreme court chief justice*
Dmytryshyn, Basil *historian, educator*
Durham, Robert Donald, Jr. *state supreme court justice*
Edge, James Edward *health care administrator*
Edwards, Randall *state official*
Erickson, Ray Charles *retired wildlife biologist*
Frank, Gerald Wendel *advocate, journalist*
Gillette, P. Roger *physicist, systems engineer*
Gillette, W. Michael *state supreme court justice*
Haselton, Rick Thomas *lawyer*
Kistler, Rives *state supreme court justice*
Kulongoski, Ted (Theodore Ralph Kulongoski) *governor, former state supreme court justice*
Linde, Hans Arthur *state supreme court justice*
Linder, Virginia Lynn *state supreme court justice*
Mainwaring, William Lewis *publishing company executive, author*
Mannix, Kevin Leese *lawyer, school system administrator*
Myers, Hardy *state attorney general*
Nafziger, James Albert Richmond *law educator*
Nicholson, Bradley James *lawyer*
Page, Cheryl Miller *elementary school educator*
Pelton, M. Lee *academic administrator*
Peterson, Edwin J. *retired judge, mediator, educator*
Robertson, Marian Ella (Marian Ella Hall) *small business owner, handwriting analyst*
Scheppke, Jim *library director*
Swaim, Michael E. *lawyer, former mayor*
Tatman, David C. *state agency administrator*
Tomei, Carolyn *state representative*
Warnath, Maxine Ammer *psychologist, arbitrator*
Yih, Mae Dunn *state legislator*
Zeller, Kurt-Alexander *vocalist, actor, stage director, voice educator*
Zumwalt, Roger Carl *hospital administrator, consultant*

Sandy
Jensen, Judy Dianne *psychotherapist, consultant*
Rosier, David Lewis *retired investment banker*

Spray
Fussner, F. Smith *history professor, retired rancher*

Springfield
Davis, George Donald *executive land use policy consultant*
Lutes, Donald Henry *architect*

Summerville
Hopkins, Gerald Frank *trade association administrator*

Sutherlin
Gugel, Merilynn Sue *artist*

Talent
MacMillen, Richard Edward *biological sciences educator, researcher*

The Dalles
Hayden, I. Jill *secondary school educator*

Troutdale
Unis, Richard L. *judge*

Tualatin
Brown, Robert Wallace *mathematics professor, educator*
Hick, Kenneth William *marketing executive*
Peters, Robert Wayne *small business owner*
West, Michael G. *electric power industry executive*
Yavorsky, William D. *semiconductor company executive*

Turner
Ratzlaff, Ruben Menno *theology studies educator, minister*

Waldport
Ginter, Carolyn Augusta Romtvedt *retired underwriter*

Wallowa
Wizard, Brian *publisher, author*

Welches
Merrill, William Dean *retired architect, medical association administrator*

West Linn
Luchterhand, Ralph Edward *financial advisor*

Wilsonville
Giesbrecht, F. Bruce *entertainment company executive*
Gordon, John Charles *forestry educator*
Humphrey, Lois Ellen *librarian*
Langrock, Karl Frederick *writer, retired academic administrator*

Yachats
Robeck, Mildred Coen *retired education educator, writer*

PENNSYLVANIA

Aaronsburg
Teeple, Bruce Jeffery *historian, writer*

Abington
Anderson, Valerie B. *actress, writer*
Bildersee, Robert Alan *lawyer*

Acme
Babcock, Marguerite Lockwood *addictions treatment therapist, educator, writer*

Akron
Dickinson, Margery Elsie *missionary, clinical psychologist*
Leithmann, David Edward *music educator*

Aldan
Stegmuller, Agnes Leonore *physical education educator*

Aliquippa
Drobac, Nikola (Nick) *education educator, consultant*
Forringer, Letitia Marie *music educator*

Allentown
Abel, James E. *treasurer*
Baker, Dexter Farrington *manufacturing executive, director*
Barraco, Robert Don *surgeon*
Beck, Glenn E. *information technology executive*
Beltzner, Gail Ann *music educator*
Brown, Robert Wayne *lawyer*
Brown, W(illiam) Douglas *lawyer*
Chang, Chris C.N. *pediatric surgeon*
Chowdary, Raj P. *plastic surgeon*
Clemmer, Richard L. *electronics executive*
Cullen, Edward Peter *bishop*
Dickson, John T. *information technology executive*
Doughty, George Franklin *airport administrator*
Farr, Paul A. *electric power industry executive*
Flautz, Nancy A. *librarian*
Foster, Edward Paul (Ted Foster) *process industries executive*
Gaylor, Donald Hughes *surgeon, educator*
Gewartowski, James Walter *retired electrical engineer*
Graham, Kenneth Robert *psychologist, educator*
Grey, Robert J. *lawyer, electric power industry executive*
Heitmann, George Joseph *business educator, consultant*
Helm, Peyton Randolph *academic administrator, history professor*
Hill, John Andrew *protective services official*
Holt, Leon Conrad, Jr. *lawyer, chemicals executive*
Hutton, William Michael *manufacturing executive*
Jones, John P. III *chemicals executive*
Kocsis, James Paul *artist*
Lovett, John Robert *retired chemical company executive*
Maffeo, Alphonse A. *anesthesiologist*
McGinley, Paul Anthony, Jr. *lawyer*
McGlade, John E. *chemicals executive*
Miller, James H. *electric power industry executive*
Orphanides, Gus George *licensing executive*
Palumbo, Robert Craig *sports medicine physician, director, not-for-profit developer*
Pavelich, Judith *retired secondary school educator*
Platt, William Henry *judge*
Saab, Deanne Keltum *real estate broker, appraiser*
Sacks, Patricia Ann *librarian, consultant*
Spence, William H. *electric power industry executive*
Szwerc, Michael Francis *thoracic surgeon*
Valero-Lopez, Ari Yakov *electrical engineer*

Allison Park
Backus, John King *former chemical company research administrator*
Dodani, Sunita *physician, educator*
Ewalt, Henry Ward *lawyer*
Herrington, John David III *retired lawyer, director*
Hollerman, Charles Edward *retired pediatrician*
LaDow, C. Stuart *financial consultant*
Ries, William Campbell *lawyer*
Rulis, Christopher C. *lawyer*
Sullivan, Neil Maxwell *oil and gas company executive*
Toerge, Lynn *athletic trainer*

Altoona
Anthony, Bertha M. *minister*
Gurman, Andrew William *orthopedist, educator*
Kinney, Janis Marie *librarian, consultant*
McKibbin, Ralph David *gastroenterologist, consultant*
Moffitt, Charles William *art gallery director*
Sheetz, Stanton R. *grocery retail executive*
Shurin, Leonard Joseph *school system administrator*
Tormey, Brian B. *environmental geomorphologist, aerial mapping consultant*

Ambler
Carey, Francis James *investment banker*
Hilty, James Walter *historian, educator, media consultant*

Annville
Foley, Brian Joseph *philosophy educator*
Kiehl, Kraig Robert *military officer, law educator*
Lou, Manza *psychology professor*
McGill, William James, Jr. *academic administrator, writer*
Tezanos-Pinto, Rosa *Hispanic American literature educator*
Verhoek, Susan Elizabeth *botany educator*

Apollo
Musselman, Larry L. *chemical engineer*

Ardmore
Heinzen, Bernard George *lawyer*
Levy, Rochelle Feldman *artist*
Silvers, Willys Kent *geneticist*
Speakman, Joseph M. *retired history professor*
Waetzman, Larry Samuel *diversified financial services company executive*

Armagh
Gongaware, Acey M. *music educator*

Ashland
Polyakov, Yuriy Sergeyevich *engineer, researcher*

Aston
DiMarco, David *mathematician, educator*

Atglen
Curiel, Judith Rea *language educator*

Audubon
Tanis, James Robert *library director, history professor, clergyman*

Avondale
Friel, Daniel Denwood, Sr. *manufacturing executive*

Avonmore
Smith, Luella Margaret *special education educator*

Bakerstown
Beachley, Michael Charles *radiologist*

Bala Cynwyd
Aziz, Adnan *manufacturing engineer, marketing products engineer*
Chovanes, Eugene *lawyer*
Cohen, Rachel Rutstein *financial planner*
Corliss, John Ozro *zoology educator*
Dorwart, Bonnie Brice *historian, retired rheumatologist*
Garrity, Vincent Francis, Jr. *lawyer*
Glat, Paul Mitchell *plastic surgeon*
Kane-Vanni, Patricia Ruth *lawyer, paleontologist, educator*
Masket, Samuel *medical association administrator*
Mattison, Priscilla Jane *lawyer*
McGill, Dan Mays *insurance business educator*
Mezrow, Craig *plastic surgeon*
Miller, L. Martin *accountant, financial planner*
Murphey, Murray Griffin *history professor*
Oswald, James Marlin *education educator, researcher*
Peret, Karen Krzyminski *health facility administrator*
Schwartz, Jeffrey Byron *lawyer*
Shepard, Geoffrey Carroll *insurance company executive*
Shore, Eric Eugene *internist, consultant, lawyer*
Staley, Kenneth Bernard *civil engineer*
Weisberg, Richard Charbourn *lawyer*
Wheatley, William Arthur *consulting firm executive*
Wiener, Thomas Eli *lawyer*

Bangor
Schiavone, John *state agency administrator*

Beach Lake
Chatlos, William Edward *management consultant*

Beaver
High, Keith B. *information scientist*
Petrush, John Joseph *lawyer*
Strock, Robert S. *retired education educator*

Beaver Falls
Copeland, Robert Marshall *music educator, department chairman*
Miller, Albert Jay *retired library director*

Belle Vernon
Wapiennik, Carl Francis *manufacturing executive, planetarium and science institute administrator*

Bensalem
Bern, Dorrit J. *apparel executive*
Kang, Benjamin Toyeong *journalist, minister*
Long, Robert C. *retired military officer, management consultant*
O'Toole, Michael Anthony *academic administrator*
Stern, Colin D. *lawyer, retail executive*

Bentleyville
Blasko, Barbara Ann *secondary school educator*

Berwick
Pasukinis, Cheryl Renee *elementary school educator*

Berwyn
Bluestone, Ellen Hope *literature, writing, and women's studies professor, writer*
Burch, John Walter *mining equipment company executive*
Devlin, Thomas McKeown *biochemist, educator*
Fry, Clarence Herbert *retired retail executive*
Hambrecht, William R. *investment banking firm executive*
Seidel, Arthur Harris *lawyer*
Watters, Edward McLain III *lawyer*
Wood, Thomas E. *lawyer*

Bethel Park
Korchynsky, Michael *metallurgical engineer*
Menees, Katherine Determan *parochial school educator*
Tranovich, Michael A. *orthopedist*
Willard, John Gerard *communications executive, consultant, writer, educator*

Bethlehem
Agbeh, Anthony Odey *education educator, consultant*
Allen, Beatrice *music educator, pianist*

Aronson, Jay Richard *economics professor, researcher, academic administrator*
Barnette, Curtis Handley *steel company executive, lawyer*
Barsness, Richard Webster *management educator, academic administrator*
Beidler, Peter Grant *retired language educator*
Caskie, Grace I. L. *statistics professor*
Cole, Jack Eli *physician*
Dent, Charles Wieder (Charlie Dent) *congressman*
Diggs, David B. *music educator*
Donnangelo, David Michael *artist*
El-Aasser, Mohamed S. *engineering educator, academic administrator*
Gardiner, Keith Mattinson *engineering executive, educator*
Gast, Alice Petry *academic administrator, chemical engineering educator*
Ghosh, Bhaskar Kumar *statistics educator, researcher*
Hartmann, Robert Elliott *retired manufacturing executive*
Heindel, Ned Duane *chemistry professor*
Herman, Richard Gerald *research chemist, consultant, educator*
Hittinger, William Charles *electronics company executive*
Hobbs, James Beverly *business administration educator, writer, academic administrator*
King, Jane Connell *mathematics professor*
Koch, Thomas L *engineering educator*
Kodama, Kenneth Philip *science educator, academic administrator*
Koel, Bruce Edward *chemist, educator, researcher*
Lyman, Charles Edson *materials scientist, educator*
Marsh, Robert Harry *chemicals executive*
Parmet, Harriet Abbey L. *literature educator*
Paustian, Paul Robert *librarian*
Pense, Alan Wiggins *metallurgical engineer, academic administrator*
Rambo, Kelly Clifford *lawyer*
Saeger, James Schofield *history professor, writer*
St. John, Anthony Paul *retired manufacturing executive*
Schattschneider, Doris Jean *retired mathematics professor*
Scheirer, William Kenneth *economist, consultant*
Schwartz, Eli *retired economics professor, writer*
Sengupta, Arup Kumar *engineering educator, researcher*
Sircar, Shivaji *chemical engineer, researcher*
Smolansky, Bettie Moretz *sociology educator*
Smolansky, Oles M. *retired humanities educator*
Smyth, Donald Morgan *chemistry professor, researcher*
Spillman, Robert Arnold *architect*
Spry, Donald Francis, II, *lawyer*
Steffen, Lloyd Howard *minister, religious studies educator*
Stella, John Anthony *financial executive*
Styer, Jane M. *computer scientist, consultant*
Taggart, Bruce M. *library administrator*
Tuzla, Kemal *mechanical engineer, researcher*
Wetcher-Hendricks, Debra Elizabeth *social sciences educator*

Beyer
Cornell, William Harvey *clergyman*

Bloomsburg
Kozloff, Jessica S. *academic administrator*
Leitzel, Jeffrey Dale *psychology professor*
Trapane, Ruth *educator, artist*

Blue Bell
Brendlinger, LeRoy R. *academic administrator*
Carrow, John C. *computer company executive*
Dillman, Frederick *information technology executive*
Elliott, John Michael *lawyer*
Giordano, Nicholas Anthony *brokerage house executive*
Gregson, Nigel Christopher *pharmaceutical executive, consultant*
Halas, Cynthia Ann *business information specialist*
Haugen, Janet B. *corporate financial executive*
Kalinsky, Michael *management consultant*
Maddox, David M. *management consultant, career military officer*
McAdam, Will *electronics executive, consultant*
McGrath, Joseph W. *computer services company executive*
Potash, Charles *lawyer*
Rounick, Jack A. *lawyer, clothing retail executive*
Siedzikowski, Henry Francis *lawyer*
Sun, Hun H. *retired electrical and biomedical engineering educator*
Sundheim, Nancy Straus *lawyer, computer company executive*
Swansen, Samuel Theodore *lawyer*

Boalsburg
Gettig, Martin Winthrop *retired mechanical engineer*

Boyertown
Fortes, Brenda Joyce *language educator*

Braddock
Slack, Edward Dorsey III *financial systems professional, consultant*

Bradford
Cox, J. Arthur *minister*
Ewert, Kevin *theater educator*
Hauser, Christopher George *lawyer*
Laroche, Roger Renan *psychiatrist*
Rice, Lester *electronics company executive*

Breinigsville
Darden, Joseph Samuel, Jr. *health educator*

Bristol
Card, Wesley Roy *apparel and footwear company executive*
Kimmel, Sidney *apparel company executive, film producer*
McClain, John T. *corporate financial executive*
Murphy, Patrick J. *congressman*

Brockway
Ball, Karen Elaine *elementary school educator*

Brookville
Smith, Sharon Louise *lawyer, consultant*

Broomall
DiRosa, Steven Joseph *primary and secondary school educator*

Brownsville
Miner, Brad C. *secondary school educator*

Bryn Mawr
Ackoff, Russell Lincoln *social systems designer, educator*
Anderson, Eric Edward *psychologist, consultant, healthcare educator*
Baird, John Absalom, Jr. *retired academic administrator*
Braha, Thomas I. *oil industry executive*
Brunt, Manly Yates, Jr. *psychiatrist*
Crawford, Maria Luisa Buse *geology educator*
Dudden, Arthur Power *historian, educator*
Frank, Edward David, II, *history educator*
Frick, Benjamin Charles *lawyer*
Gaisser, Julia Haig *classics educator*
Giese, William Herbert *tax accountant*
Godinez, Marye H. *anesthesiologist*
Goutman, Lois Clair *retired drama educator*
Hegedus, L. Louis *chemical engineer, consultant, retired research and development company executive*
Hirsh, Sharon Latchaw *academic administrator, art history educator*
Huth, Edward Janavel *internist, educator, editor*
Krausz, Michael *philosopher, educator*
Lane, Barbara Miller (Barbara Miller-Lane) *humanities educator*
Lang, Mabel Louise *classics educator*
Levitt, Robert E. *gastroenterologist*
Liu, Hans Hamilton *infectious disease physician, educator*
McCabe, Louise Beachboard *language educator*
Moyer, F. Stanton *financial executive*
Narin, Stephen B. *lawyer*
Newhall, Jane Ward *psychologist*
Noone, R. Barrett *plastic surgeon*
Peters, Douglas Scott *health care executive*
Pew, Robert Anderson *retired real estate and equipment leasing corporation officer*
Porter, Judith Deborah Revitch *sociologist*
Price, Trevor Robert Pryce *psychiatrist, educator*
Vickers, Nancy J. *academic administrator*

Buffalo Mills
Duppstadt, William Homer *retired botanist, educator, lay worker*

Bushkill
Garretto, Leonard Anthony, Jr. *insurance company executive*

Butler
Walsh, Joy Irene *literature educator, language educator*

California
Crawford, Paul Fleming *historian*

Camp Hill
Beasley, Ed *retail executive*
Blouch, Timothy Craig *food company executive*
Brandow, Theo *architect*
Cardinale, Gerald P. *retail executive*
Crider, Rudyard Lee *psychotherapist*
Crist, Christine Myers *consulting executive*
Davis, Don P. *retail executive*
de Bruin, Jerry Mark *retail executive*
Donley, Douglas E. *retail executive*
Easley, Robert J. *retail executive*
Ellis, Stephen A. *engineering executive, consultant*
Fazzolari, Salvatore D. *mining products executive*
Gibbons, Miles Joseph, Jr. *foundation administrator*
Hall, Christopher S. *retail executive*
Hathaway, Derek C. *mining products executive*
Johnston, Thomas McElree, Jr. *retired church administrator*
Keough, Philip J., IV, *retail executive*
Kimmel, Mark E. *lawyer*
Learish, John *retail executive*
Lester, Wilson A., Jr. *retail executive*
Lovett, Keith W. *retail executive*
Mackin, Charles Philip, Jr. *lawyer*
Mastrian, James P. *retail executive*
McCarty, Todd *retail executive*
Mead, James Matthew *insurance company executive*
Miller, Robert G. *drug store chain company executive*
Panzer, Mark *retail executive*
Rowe, Michael Duane *artist*
Rugen, Karen *retail executive, corporate communications specialist*
Sammons, Mary F. *retail executive*
Sari, Robert B. *lawyer, retail executive*
Shirtliff, Bryan *retail executive*
Todd, Murray *retail executive*
Tokuhata, George K. *retired medical educator, epidemiologist, consultant*
Twomey, Kevin *retail executive*
Yates, James Arthur *plastic surgeon*

Canonsburg
Coury, Robert J. *pharmaceutical executive*
Mascetta, Joseph Anthony *principal*
Puskar, Milan *pharmaceuticals executive*
Southern, David *history professor*

Carlisle
Asimakakis, Panagiota *mathematics educator*
Bergeron, Arthur William, Jr. *historian, writer*
Butler, William Elliott *lawyer, educator*
Crane, Conrad C. *history professor*
Durden, William G. *academic administrator*
Fish, Chester Boardman, Jr. *retired editor*
Fox, Arturo Angel *Spanish language educator*
Huntoon, Maj. Gen. David H., Jr. *military officer*
Jones, Oliver Hastings *consulting economist*
Laws, Kenneth L. *physics professor*
Long, Howard Charles *retired physics professor*
McConnaughay, Philip J. *dean, law educator*
Robinson, Ronald Michael *financial executive, consultant*
Shrader, Charles Reginald *historian*
Turo, Ron *lawyer*
Vickery, Jon Livingstone *neurologist*
Wyn-Jones, Alun (William Wyn-Jones) *software developer, mathematician*

Center Valley
Gambet, Daniel G(eorge) *academic administrator, minister*
Risher, William Henry *cardiothoracic surgeon, educator*
Smillie, Douglas James *lawyer*
Wehr, Matthew *music educator*

Chadds Ford
Cohen, Felix Asher *lawyer*
Duff, James Henry *museum director, environmental services administrator*
Isakoff, Sheldon Erwin *chemical engineer*
Lee, David A.H. *pharmaceutical executive*
Strawhecker, Kenneth Edward *research scientist*
Swensson, Evelyn Dickenson *conductor, composer, librettist*

Chalfont
Ashley, Kathleen Labonis *elementary school educator*
Hetherington, John Joseph *lawyer*
Wilson, Jean Louise *retired state legislator*

Chambersburg
Bitner, Betty L. *education educator*
Furr, Quint Eugene *marketing executive*
O'Connor, John Morris III *retired humanities educator*
Rumler, Robert Hoke *agricultural products executive, consultant, retired trade association administrator*
Yeun, Paul Lorenzo *clergy member*

Cheltenham
Weinstock, Walter Wolfe *systems engineer*

Chester
Buck, Lawrence Paul *history professor, former academic administrator*
Harris, James Thomas III *college administrator, educator*
Huang, Zhongping *engineering educator*

Chesterbrook
Chou, John G. *lawyer*
DiCandilo, Michael D. *corporate financial executive, accountant*
Hilzinger, Kurt John *health products executive*

Cheyney
Bagley, Edythe Scott *theater educator*

Clairton
Brodland, David G. *dermatologist, surgeon*
Mina, John Louis (Ivan Minea) *religious studies educator, archivist*

Clarion
Canaday, Doris Charlene *retired traffic representative*
Foreman, Thomas Alexander *dentist*
Harry, Vickie Diane *education educator*

Clarks Green
Bourcier, Richard Joseph *retired French language and literature educator*
Kubic, Charles Richard *civil engineer*

Clarks Summit
Beemer, John Barry *lawyer*
Cagley, Susan A. *history professor*
Janoski, Henry Valentine *investment advisor, former banker*

Claysville
Stewart, Pamela Widdup *language educator, musician*

Clinton
Talbot, Mary Lee *minister*

Coatesville
Ainslie, George William *psychiatrist*
Albrecht, Thomas Charles III *computer technician*
Bell, Robert Lloyd *retired neurosurgeon*
Lee, Daniel *retired physician, public health service officer*
Makous, Norman *retired internist, cardiologist, educator*
Sauer, James Leslie *librarian, educator*

Cochranville
Sazegar, Morteza *artist*

Collegeville
Butz, Geneva Mae *pastor*
Sharifi, Azalea A. *orthodontist and general dentist*
Stiles, Gary Lester *cardiologist, molecular pharmacologist, educator*

Conneaut Lake
Parmiter, Karen Lynn *retired education educator*

Connellsville
Humbert, Kimberly Ramsay *secondary school educator*
Shearer, Linda Rae *English educator*

Conshohocken
Bramson, Robert Sherman *lawyer*
Glazer, William H. *real estate developer*
Lotman, Herbert *food processing executive*
Naples, Ronald James *manufacturing executive*
Spaeth, Karl Henry *retired chemicals executive, lawyer*
Thompson, Pamela Padwick *public relations executive*

Coopersburg
Bednar, Charles Sokol *political science professor*
Bolle, Donald Martin *retired engineering educator*
Peserik, James E. *electrical engineer, consultant, safety engineer, computer engineer*
Siess, Alfred Albert, Jr. *engineering executive, management consultant*

Cooperstown
Hogg, James Henry, Jr. *retired education educator*

Coplay
Briggs, Chad Michael *political science professor*
Norbeck, Jack Carl *library exhibitor*

Coraopolis
Beaver, William R. *sociology professor*
Kay, George Paul *environmental engineer*
Koepfinger, Joseph Leo *retired utilities executive*
Stout, Alastair *music director, composer*

Corry
Chaffee, Philip *retired military officer, retired small business owner*

Corsica
Elza, Betty Ann *retired librarian*

Coudersport
Kysor, Daniel Francis *psychologist*

Cranberry Township
Hauck, Lindsay Beth *elementary school educator*
Lorenz, John George *librarian, consultant*
McNamara, Michael Lee Perry *automation engineer*
Patten, Charles Anthony *management consultant, retired manufacturing company executive, writer, publisher*
Tiller, Olive Marie *retired church worker*
Walsh, Arthur Campbell *retired psychiatrist*

Cresco
Upright, Kirby Grant *lawyer*

Crum Lynne
Metzger, Scott *information technology executive*

Danville
Blankenship, James Colegrove *cardiologist*
Chan, Yiumo *biochemist*
Gubbiotti, Christine M. *lawyer*
Pierce, James Clarence *surgeon, educator*
Ramdas, Jagadeesh *physician*

Darby
Eiser, Arnold Robert *physician executive, bioethicist, nephrologist, internist*

Delmont
Thompson, Paul A. *business consultant, performance improvement expert*

Delta
Withrow, James A. *music educator*

Denver
Milner, Charles Fremont, Jr. *manufacturing executive*

Derry
Baltzer, Cynthia Louise *music educator*

Devon
Boehne, Edward George *banker*
Earley, Laurence Elliott *retired medical educator*
Porter, Roger John *research and development company executive, neurologist, pharmacologist*
Wilson, Malcolm Campbell *investment trust management executive*

Dillsburg
Bowers, Glenn Lee *retired professional society administrator*
Jackson, George Lyman *retired nuclear medicine physician*
Smith, William Raymond *farmer, horse breeder*

Dover
Butterfield, Andrea Christine *elementary school educator*
Hover, Carl Arthur *retired minister*
Moul, Brian E. *music educator*

Downingtown
Deb, Arun Kumar *environmental engineer*
Sweeney, Sarina Marie *psychologist, consultant*
Wusinich, Joseph F. III *lawyer, educator*

Doylestown
Bowers, Nell S. *psychologist*
Elliott, Richard Howard *lawyer*
Ginsberg, Barry Gavrille *psychologist, marriage and family therapist*
Kropp, Edward H. *education educator, consultant*

McCafferty, Barbara Jean (BJ McCafferty) *sales executive*
Mishler, John Milton (Yochanan Menashsheh ben Shaul) *science educator, artist*
Solly, Richard Peter *music educator*
Thomas, Ellen Louise *school system administrator*

Dresher
Faust, Carrissima Washington *educational consultant*
Levicoff, Valerie Ann *music educator*

Drexel Hill
Benglian, Barbara Mason *music educator*
Martino, Michael Charles *entertainer, musician, actor*
Schiazza, Guido Domenic (Guy Schiazza) *educational association administrator*
Thompson, William David *minister, educator*

Du Bois
Blakley, Benjamin Spencer III *lawyer*
Emmer, Barbara Louise *librarian*
Forsythe, Velma Brown *accountant, consultant, literature educator*
Forthun, Larry F. *social sciences educator, consultant*

Duncansville
Smith, D. Brooks *federal judge*

Dunmore
Krogh-Jespersen, Mary-Beth *academic administrator*
Sebastianelli, Mario Joseph *internist, nephrologist, health facility administrator*
Timlin, James Clifford *bishop*

East Petersburg
Pedrow, Brenda M. *retired language educator*

East Stroudsburg
Braithwaite, Barbara Jo *retired secondary school educator*
Henley, Richard James *health facility administrator*
Kansfield, Norman J. *former seminary president*
Smith, Elizabeth Leigh *literature and language professor*
Switzer, Sharon Cecile *language educator, researcher*

Easton
Bellissimo, Mary E. *art educator*
Bose, Ajay Kumar *retired chemistry professor*
Brown, Robert Carroll, Jr. *lawyer*
Grunberg, Robert Leon Willy *nephrologist, educator*
Holmes, Larry, Sr. *retired boxer*
Kincaid, John *political science professor, editor*
Lamb-Faffelberger, Margarete Barbara *foreign language educator*
Milgrim, Roger Michael *lawyer*
Murphy, Bruce Allen *government educator, law educator, writer*
Noel, Nicholas III *legal company executive, lawyer*
Schlueter, June Mayer *literature educator, writer*
Schott, Michael J. *library director*
Stitt, Dorothy Jewett *journalist*
Stull, Frank Walter *elementary school educator*
Sun, Robert Zu Jei *manufacturing company executive, inventor, educator*
Teboh-Ewungkem, Miranda Ijang *education educator*
Traldi, Lorenzo *mathematician, educator*
Trigiano, Lucien Lewis *physician*
Van Antwerpen, Franklin Stuart *federal judge*
Weiss, Daniel H. *academic administrator, former dean*

Ebensburg
Wojcik, Jason Paul *history professor*

Edgemont
Davis, Scott Charles *music educator, political activist*

Edinboro
Mahmood, Akhtar Hasan *physicist, educator, researcher*

Eighty Four
Hardy, Joseph A., Sr. *wholesale distribution executive*
Magerko, Margaret Hardy (Maggie) *lumber company executive*

Elizabethtown
Bartoli, Jill Sunday *reading and language arts educator*
Brown, Dale Weaver *clergyman, theology studies educator*
Dickel, David I. III *financial analyst*
Garber, Margaret Mary *elementary school educator*
Gordon, Laurie Anne *academic director*
Kenley, David Lynn *history professor*
Ritsch, Frederick Field *academic administrator, historian*
Sample, Frederick Palmer *former college president*

Elkins Park
Burnley, June Williams *secondary school educator*
Davidson, Abraham Aba *art historian, educator, photographer*
Erlebacher, Martha Mayer *artist, educator*
Hart, William C. *underwriter, educator, writer*
Myers, Kenneth Raymond *lawyer*
Pak, Hyung Woong *community advocate*
Stinnett, Hester *art school administrator, educator*

Emlenton
Berg, Janice Carol *elementary school educator*

Emmaus
Bowers, Klaus D(ieter) *electronics executive, researcher*
Bricklin, Mark Harris *magazine editor, publisher*
Rodale, Ardath Harter *publishing executive*
Rodale, Maria *publishing executive*
Vaccariello, Liz *editor-in-chief*

Ephrata
Reed, Galen K. *music educator*

Erdenheim
Schiff, Lawrence Alan *dentist*

Erie
Ayrault, Evelyn West *psychologist, writer*
Bennett, Charles Andrew *economics professor, department chairman*
Breckenridge, James G. *dean, consultant*
Daly, Mary *college administrator*
Dockstader, Emmett Stanley *civil engineer, construction executive*
Garcia, Philip A. *insurance company executive*
Gottschalk, Frank Klaus *real estate company executive*
Hagen, Thomas Bailey *business owner, former state official, retired insurance company executive*
Hirt, F. William *insurance company executive*
Ludrof, Jeffrey A. *insurance company executive*
Mason, Gregg Claude *orthopedic surgeon, researcher*
Michaelides, Doros Nikita *internist, medical educator*
Miller, Virginia Louise *director*
Orton, Geraldine Leitl *psychologist, mental health therapist, educator, author*
Renkis, Alan Ilmars *plastics formulating company executive*
Tanous, James Joseph *lawyer, insurance company executive*
Trautman, Donald W. *bishop*
Vanco, John L. *art museum director*
Van Gorder, Jan Reid *lawyer, insurance company executive*
Woodard, Jon L. *lawyer*
Wykoff, Gary Lee *writer*
Zamboldi, Richard Henry *lawyer*
Zelazny, Catherine *retired elementary school educator*

Etters
Steps, Barbara Jill *lawyer*

Evans City
Pagonis, William Gus *retired army general*

Everett
Whetstone, Joni Lee *music educator*

Exeter
Flickinger, Donald E. *mathematics educator*
Stocker, Joyce Arlene *retired secondary school educator*

Exton
Ashton, Mark Randolph *lawyer*
Berry, Matthew M. *aerospace engineer*
Hidalgo, Ismael J. *pharmaceutical scientist*
Roth, William McKinley *psychologist*
Smith, Joseph Lorenzo, II, *otolaryngologist*
Webber, Helen *artist*

Fairfield
Freund, John Richard *former English educator*

Fairless Hills
Frazier, Brett W. *waste management executive*
Rosella, John Daniel *clinical psychologist, educator*
Steckroat, Patricia A. *special education educator*

Fairview
Stern, Marilyn Jean *special education educator*

Farrell
Patton-Newell, Janet Lavelle *minister*

Fayetteville
Daywalt, Lee Eric *minister, museum administrator*
Etchison, Bruce *retired museum director, conservator*
Molitor, Graham Thomas Tate *lawyer*

Feasterville Trevose
Dickstein, Jack *chemist*
Osterhout, Richard Cadwallader *lawyer*

Flourtown
Christy, John Gilray *diversified financial services company executive*
Cooke, Sara Mullin Graff *daycare provider, kindergarten educator, medical assistant*
Lee, Adrian Iselin, Jr. *journalist*

Fogelsville
Yadush, John G *musician, real estate investor, educator*

Fort Washington
Pappas, Charles Engelos *plastic surgeon*
Pezick, Patricia *music educator*

Fountainville
Brown, Madeline Morgan *internist*

Franklin
Sauer, Mary Julia *special education educator*

Frazer
Baldino, Frank, Jr. *biopharmaceutical executive*
Osborn, John Edward *lawyer, pharmaceutical industry executive, former government official*

Freeport
Smits, Ronald Francis *language educator, poet*

Friendsville
Babb, Harold *psychologist, educator*

Gaines
Beller, Martin Leonard *retired orthopaedic surgeon*

Galeton
Bull, Inez Stewart *retired curator, director, singer, writer, musician, educator*

Gap
Beiler, Anne F. *food company executive*
Burton, Mary Louise Himes *information technology executive*
Klinefelter, Hylda Catharine *retired obstetrician, gynecologist*

Gettysburg
Coughenour, Kavin Luther *career officer, military historian*
Gritsch, Ruth Christine Lisa *editor*
Hallberg, Budd Jaye *management consulting firm executive*
Hendrix, Sherman Samuel *biology professor, researcher*
Roach, James Clark *federal agency administrator*
Will, Katherine Haley *academic administrator*

Gibsonia
Benson, Stuart Wells III *lawyer*
Krause, Helen Fox *retired otolaryngologist*

Girardville
Dempsey, Thomas Joseph *retired postmaster*

Gladwyne
Acton, David *lawyer*
Booth, Harold Waverly *lawyer, finance company executive*
Cooney, Patricia Ruth *civic worker*
Fletcher, Marjorie Amos *librarian*
Geisel, Cameron Meade, Jr. *retired bank executive*
Katz, Julian *gastroenterologist, educator*
Kaye, Donald *internist, educator*
Morrison, Gail *internist, nephrologist, educator*
Patten, Lanny Ray *gas industry executive*
Pendergrass, Henry Pancoast *radiologist, nuclear medicine physician*
Stearns, Milton Sprague, Jr. *financial executive*
Webber, John Bentley *orthopedic surgeon*

Glen Mills
Churchill, Stuart Winston *chemical engineering educator*
Kaufman, Antoinette Dolores *information technology manager*
Turner, Janet Sullivan *painter, sculptor*

Glenmoore
Fix, Irene M. *pianist*

Glenshaw
Guentner, James Francis, Jr. *artist, educator*
Wilkes, John Michael *military officer, auditor*

Glenside
Block, Isaac Edward *professional society administrator*
Carr, Scott *technology educator*
Doman, Janet Joy *professional society administrator*
Jones, Elaine F. *psychologist, educator*
Medel, Rebecca Rosalie *artist*
Mermelstein, Jules Joshua *lawyer, educator, commissioner*
Ralston, Steven Philip *portfolio manager, financial analyst*
Rawlins, W. Scott *art educator*
Reiss, George Russell, Jr. *physician*
Willig, Barbara Adele *music educator*

Greencastle
Scott, Leighton Reeves *interior designer, artist, writer*
Wertime, Timothy Ray *music educator*

Greensburg
Duck, Patricia Mary *librarian*
Evanson, Paul John *utilities executive*
Ference, Edward W. *engineering executive, structural engineer*
Gebrosky, Norman Paul *urologist*
Goulding, Philip L. *energy executive*
Gounley, Dennis Joseph *lawyer*
Langer, Alois *biomedical engineer*
Lu, Shu Jiang *literature and language professor*
Neff, Mary Ellen Andre *retired elementary school educator*
Ramm, Douglas Robert *psychologist*
Spaeder, Francis Xavier *forensic electrical engineer*

Greentown
Forcheskie, Carl S. *former apparel company executive*

Grove City
Brenner, Frederic James *biology professor, ecologist, consultant*
Kochems, Robert Gregory *lawyer*
McBride, Milford Lawrence, Jr. *lawyer*

Gwynedd Valley
Owens, Kathleen C. *academic administrator*

Hamburg
Schappell, Abigail Susan *retired speech, language and hearing specialist, massage therapist, Reiki master*

Hanover
Clark, Sandra Marie *school administrator*
Kline, Donald *food company executive*

Harleysville
Browne, Michael L. *insurance company executive*
Browne, Michael Leon *lawyer*
Kauffman, Robert A. *lawyer*
Smagalski, Carolyn M. *publishing executive, webmaster, director*

Harmony
O'Shea, Patrick Alan *elementary school educator*

Harrisburg
Adams, Barbara *lawyer*
Angino, Richard Carmen *lawyer*
Bailey, Diandrea Michelle *rehabilitation services professional*
Baker Knoll, Catherine *lieutenant governor*
Barasch, David M. *lawyer, former prosecutor*
Batts, Barbara Jean *academic administrator, director*
Bottini, David William *artist, educator*
Breslin, Michael Joseph III *social services administrator, educator*
Brown, John Walter *vocational education supervisor*
Burcat, Joel Robin *lawyer*
Burns, Rebecca Ann *elementary school educator, librarian*
Buss, George Edward, Jr. *museum program director*
Cadieux, Roger Joseph *geriatrics services professional*
Clark-Jones, Thomas Rees *musician*
Cline, Andrew Haley *lawyer*
Corbett, Thomas Wingett, Jr. *state attorney general, lawyer*
Cortés, Pedro A. *state official*
DeKok, David *writer, reporter*
Diehm, James Warren *lawyer, educator*
Dinniman, Andrew Eric *international studies and history professor, state senator*
Downey, Brian Patrick *lawyer*
Emerick, John L. *library director*
Fenstermacher, Joyce Doris *real estate agent, real estate appraiser*
Fine, David R. *lawyer*
Fontana, Mark Allan *lawyer*
Frankel, Carl Abbott *ophthalmologist*
Fulmer, Deborah Lee *education educator, oncological nurse*
Gover, Raymond Lewis *retired newspaper executive*
Hafer, Barbara *state official*
Hafer, Joseph Page *lawyer*
Hample, Judy G. *academic administrator*
Kane, Yvette *lawyer, judge*
Kelly, Robert Edward, Jr. *lawyer*
Khanzhina, Helen P. *language and literature educator, translator*
Klein, Michael D. *lawyer*
Knackstedt, Mary V. *interior designer*
Kraus, David Robert *lawyer*
Kulicki, John M. *structural engineer*
Lappas, Spero Thomas *lawyer*
Logue, James Nicholas *epidemiologist*
Mahey, John Andrew *retired museum director*
Meilton, Sandra L. *lawyer*
Miller, Leslie Anne *lawyer*
Moritz, Milton Edward *security consultant*
O'Brien, Dennis M. *state legislator*
Pearson, Ronald K. *mathematical data analyst*
Perzel, John Michael (Jay Perzel) *state legislator*
Pileggi, Dominic F. *state senator*
Pizzingrilli, Kim *state official*
Popnik, Marlene Alita *retired school librarian*
Rambo, Sylvia H. *federal judge*
Ramirez, Eneida Sarahi *biology professor*
Reider, Victoria A. *state agency administrator*
Rendell, Edward Gene *governor, retired mayor, lawyer*
Renner, William Scott *retired military officer*
Rudy, Frank R. *pathologist*
Saylor, Thomas G. *state supreme court justice*
Scarnati, Joseph B. III *state senator*
Sheldon, J. Michael *lawyer, educator*
Smith, Eric Ledell *historian*
Stanley, Edward Alexander *geologist, paleontologist, researcher, retired director, forensic specialist*
Stefanon, Anthony *lawyer*
Strouss, Carleton O. *lawyer*
Sullivan, John Cornelius, Jr. *lawyer*
Torres, Maribel *social welfare administrator*
Vance, Patricia H. *state senator*
Van Zile, Philip Taylor III *lawyer, educator*
Warshaw, Allen Charles *lawyer*
Wentzel, Paul H., Jr. *state agency administrator*
West, James Joseph *lawyer*
Weston, R. Timothy *lawyer, government administrator*
Williams, Constance *state senator*
Willow, Judith Ann Loye *tax preparer*
Wolfe, Gary Donald *commissioner, retired librarian*
Zahorchak, Gerald Lee *school system administrator*
Zales, Mary Clare *library director*
Zavacky, Susan Kline *law librarian*

Hatboro
Carroll, Lucy Ellen *theater director, educator*
John, Robert McClintock *lawyer*
Nicholson, Bruce Allen *lawyer*
Quigley, Robert Charles *insurance industry consultant*

Hatfield
Jesberg, Robert Ottis, Jr. *educational consultant, science educator*

Haverford
Aronson, Carl Edward *pharmacology and toxicology educator*

Bean, Philip Albert *dean, historian*
Brand, Charles Macy *history professor*
DiBerardino, Marie Antoinette *developmental biologist, educator*
Emerson, Stephen G. *academic administrator, oncologist, hematologist, educator*
Gollub, Jerry Paul *physics professor*
Goppelt, John Walter *physician, psychiatrist*
Gutwirth, Marcel Marc *literature educator*
Jorden, Eleanor Harz *linguist, educator*
Kee, Howard Clark *religion educator*
Mathews, Timothy Newlyn *lawyer*
Northrup, Herbert Roof *economist*
Palmer, Richard Ware *retired lawyer*
Stiller, Jennifer A. *lawyer*
Stroud, James Stanley *retired lawyer*
Tritton, Thomas Richard *former academic administrator, biologist, educator*
Williams, William Earle *artist, educator, curator*

Havertown
Bala, Gary Ganesh *lawyer*
Brinker, Thomas Michael *finance company executive*
Evarts, Mary H. *mathematics educator*
Hendrickson, Paul Joseph *journalist, writer, educator*
Wright, Cecilia Powers *gifted and talented educator*

Hazleton
Kraynak, Marcelle Georgeann *not-for-profit developer*
Lawler, Gary M. *academic administrator*
Libonati-Ritz, Genene Marie *lawyer*
Schiavo, Pasco Louis *lawyer*

Henryville
Salmon, Thomas P. *musician*

Hermitage
English, Philip Sheridan *congressman*
Gurgovits, Stephen J. *financial executive*

Hershey
Buck, Michele *food products executive*
Caputo, Gregory Michael *internist, educator*
Cherry, Robert A. *surgeon*
Davis, Dwight *cardiologist, educator*
Eyster, Mary Elaine *hematologist, educator*
Jones, Marshall Bush *education educator, researcher*
Kauffman, Gordon Lee, Jr. *surgeon, educator*
Lenny, Richard Herbert *food products executive, marketing professional*
Lim, Jung Yul *biomedical engineer*
Madewell, John Edward *radiologist*
Marks, James Garfield, Jr. *dermatologist*
Moskowitz, Jay *health science association administrator, educator, dean*
Naeye, Richard L. *pathologist, educator*
Paz, Harold Louis *hospital administrator, internist, educator*
Pierce, William Schuler *cardiac surgeon*
Quraishi, Sadeq Ali *anesthesiologist, educator*
Reese, Carl Thomas *urologist*
Rohner, Thomas John, Jr. *urologist*
Severs, Walter Bruce *pharmacology educator, researcher*
Snyder, Burton Harold *lawyer*
Tan, Tjiauw-Ling *psychiatrist, educator*
Thomas, Andrea B. *food products executive*
Thomas, Patrick Robert Maxwell *oncologist, educator, academic administrator*
Uhde, Thomas Whitley *psychopharmacology, psychiatrist*
Undar, Akif *research scientist, biomedical engineer, educator*
Vender, Robert Louis *medical educator*
Vesell, Elliot Saul *pharmacologist, educator*
Waldhausen, John Anton *retired surgeon, editor*
Wassner, Steven Joel *pediatric nephrologist, educator*
Zagon, Ian Stuart *neuroscience and anatomy educator, researcher, inventor*
Zelis, Robert Felix *cardiologist, educator*

Hollidaysburg
Bloom, Lawrence Stephen *retired clothing company executive*
Shuster, William (Bill Shuster) *congressman*

Homestead
King, Richard Wayne *principal*
Mandel, Herbert Maurice *civil engineer*

Honesdale
Barbe, Walter Burke *education educator*

Horsham
Barzilay, Zvi *real estate developer*
Best, Franklin Luther, Jr. *lawyer*
Christian, Mildred Stoehr *health products executive*
DeHoratius, Raphael Joseph *rheumatologist*
Luby, Michael J. *research and development company executive*
Rassmann, Joel H. H. *corporate financial executive*
Sachs, Keith L. *manufacturing executive*
Toll, Bruce Elliot *real estate developer*
Toll, Robert Irwin *home construction company executive*

Hulmeville
Jackson, Mary L. *health services executive*

Hummelstown
Biebuyck, Julien Francois *anesthesiologist, medical administrator, educator*

Huntingdon
Kepple, Thomas Ray, Jr. *college administrator*
Stiffler, Stuart Alden *retired library director*

Huntingdon Valley
Cohen, Michael R. *health facility administrator, pharmacist*

DiBello, Joseph Nicholas *plastic surgeon*
Edelman, Janice *artist, educator*
Godfrey, John Carl *medicinal chemist*
Krzyzanowski, Richard L. *lawyer*
Leibholz, Stephen Wolfgang *physicist, information technology executive, entrepreneur*
Sadoff, Joan Handleman *film producer, social worker*
Verrant, John Alan *engineering executive*
Vollum, Robert Boone *management consultant*
West, A(rnold) Sumner *chemical engineer*

Immaculata
Fadden, Sister R. Patricia *academic administrator, nun*
Grimes, Diane Spellman *art educator, department chairman, sculptor*

Indiana
Barbor, John Howard *lawyer*
Bencloski, Joseph W. *geography educator*
Black, Lynanne *psychologist, educator*
Ciano-Federoff, Lynda *psychologist, educator*
Falcone, Thomas William *finance educator*
Kenning, Gregory George *physicist, educator*
Mc Cauley, R. Paul *criminologist, educator*
Pidgeon, John Anderson *headmaster*
Reynolds, Virginia Edith *sociologist, anthropologist, educator, artist*
Salser, Scott A. *music educator*
Thibadeau, Eugene Francis *education educator, consultant*

Irwin
Kuhn, Howard Arthur *engineering executive, educator*
Perich, Terry Miller *retired secondary school educator*

Jamison
Touhill, C. Joseph *environmental engineer*

Jefferson Hills
Smith, Leslie Edgar *vocational school administrator*

Jenkintown
Bales, John Foster III *retired lawyer*
Black, Thomas Donald *retired religious organization administrator*
Booker, Alvin Eugene *publishing executive, consultant*
Friedman, Ralph David *lawyer*
Greenspan-Margolis, June E. *psychiatrist*
Hidalgo, Alfreda Edith *elementary school educator*
Oh, Soojin Susan *elementary school educator*
Sadoff, Robert Leslie *psychiatrist, educator*
Worthington, Sandra Boulton *lawyer*

Jim Thorpe
Meneeley, Edward Sterling *artist*

Johnstown
Borkow, Mary P. *small business owner, consultant*
Kaharick, Jerome John *lawyer*
Miloro, Protopresbyter Frank *religious organization administrator, theology studies educator*
Smisko, Nicholas Richard *bishop, educator*

Kelton
Gulick, Walter Lawrence *psychologist, educator, retired academic administrator*

Kennett Square
Bell, Philip Wilkes *accountant, economist, educator*
Brooks, Joae Graham *psychiatrist*
Conard, Alfred Fletcher *legal educator*
Hager, George V., Jr. *health services executive*
Hennes, Robert Taft *former management consultant, investment executive*
Landstrom, Elsie Hayes *retired editor*
Martin, George (Whitney) *writer*
Richardson, Dean Wheeler *equine surgeon, veterinary educator*
Smith, Virginia Eleanore *psychologist, educator*
Wilson, Armin *retired chemist*

Kimberton
Williams, Lawrence Soper, Jr. *photographer*

King Of Prussia
Broido, Arnold Peace *music publishing company executive*
Burda, Steven *financial analyst and manager*
Clauson, Sharyn Ferne *consulting company executive, educator*
Fardone, Guy *communications executive*
Gallis, John Nicholas *retired military officer, executive leadership training consultant*
Gilbert, Bruce Rits *lawyer*
Goldsmith, Eleanor Jean *retired hospital administrator*
Greenberg, Lon Richard *energy executive, lawyer*
Hallman, Patricia L. *musician, educator*
Helmetag, Diana *music educator*
Katz, Arnold Martin *insurance brokerage firm executive*
Liebermann, Lowell *composer, conductor, pianist*
Miller, Alan B. *hospital management executive*
Rubin, Michael G. *sports internet company executive*
Schneider, Pam Horvitz *lawyer*
Schumann, Paula M. L. *writer*
Volpe, Ralph Pasquale *retired insurance company executive*
Walsh, John L. *energy executive*
Webb, Richard Stephen *manufacturing executive*
Yeo, Mark Andrews *diversified financial services company executive*

Kingsley
McNabb, Corrine Radtke *librarian*

Kingston
Meyer, Martin Jay *lawyer*
Weisberger, Barbara *artistic director, advisor, educator*

Kintnersville
Barnes, Francis V. *school system administrator*

Knox
Rupert, Elizabeth Anastasia *retired dean*

Kresgeville
Beckley, Roberta Ann *elementary school educator*

Kutztown
Ballas, Dean James *graphics designer, educator*
Gupta, Venu Gopal *psychology professor*
Ogden, James Russell *marketing educator, consultant, lecturer, writer*
Vasko, Francis Joseph *mathematics professor*
Weber, Michael Allen *school librarian*

La Plume
Boehm, Edward Gordon, Jr. *college administrator, educator*

Lafayette Hill
Delacato, Carl Henry *education educator*
Delacato, Janice Elaine *special education educator, consultant*
Edwards, JoAnn Louise *human resources executive*
King, Leon *investment advisor*
Miller, Nancy Lois *senior pastor*

Lake Harmony
Polansky, Larry Paul *legal association administrator*

Lancaster
Ashby, Richard James, Jr. *bank executive, lawyer*
Binkley, Luther John *philosophy educator*
Brunner, Lillian Sholtis *nurse, writer*
Burlingame, Mark Wayne *cardiothoracic surgeon*
Carlisle, James Patton *entrepreneur*
Dodge, Arthur Byron, Jr.
Ebersole, J. Glenn, Jr. *engineering, marketing, management, public relations and strategic planning executive*
Ebersole, Mark Chester *emeritus college president*
Fry, John Anderson *academic administrator*
Glick, Garland Wayne *retired theological seminary president*
Graffis, Leister F. *retired engineering executive*
Heil, Paul Samuel *radio producer*
High, S. Dale *construction executive*
Kelly, Robert Lynn *advertising executive*
Kendall, Leigh Wakefield *surgeon, hospital administrator*
Kermes, Constantine John *artist, industrial designer*
Kneedler, (Alvin) Richard *academic administrator*
Kornhauser, Barry Paul *playwright, theater director*
Lewis, Alvin Bower, Jr. *lawyer*
Liddell, W. Kirk *specialty contracting company executive*
Lockhart, Michael D. *manufacturing executive*
Minney, Michael Jay *lawyer*
Nast, Dianne Martha *lawyer*
Pavlatos, Arthur L. *retired social studies educator*
Pyfer, John Frederick, Jr. *lawyer, director*
Rigas, John Nicholas *lawyer*
Shaw, Charles Raymond *journalist*
Shenk, Lois Elaine Landis *writer*
Snelson, Pamela *librarian, association executive, researcher*
Steiner, Robert Lisle *retired language educator*
Taylor, Ann *writer, educator*
Veitch, Boyer Lewis *printing company executive*
Zeager, Lloyd *librarian*
Zimmerman, Donald Patrick *lawyer*

Langhorne
DiPasquale, John *real estate developer*
Fitzpatrick, Michael G. *former congressman, lawyer*
Isensee, Paul Ralph *music educator, minister*
Neff, Amy Hancock *elementary school educator*

Lansdale
Bierman, Arnold *optometrist*
Fawley, John Jones *retired banker*
Hargens, Charles William III *electrical engineer, consultant*
Nithoo, Rovindranath *pharmacist*
Schwartz, Louis Winn *ophthalmologist*
Sensenig, David Martin *retired surgeon*
Strohecker, Leon Harry, Jr. *orthodontist*
Sultanik, Jeffrey Ted *lawyer*

Lansdowne
Geist, Lorraine Pinnelli *music educator, director*
Purcell, Mary Hamilton *speech educator*

Latrobe
Cardoso, Carlos M. *metal products executive*
Daughenbaugh, Terry L. *metal products executive*
Greenfield, David W. *lawyer*
Hupe, Donna Marie *education educator*
Porembka, Michael Richard *assistant principal, supervisor*
Rhodes, Michael E. *biologist, educator*
Tambakeras, Markos I. *machine tool manufacturer*
Towey, Jim (H. James Towey) *academic administrator, former federal official*
Will, James Fredrick *academic administrator, former steel company executive*

Lebanon
Deysher, Paul Evans *retired management consultant*
McMindes, Roy James *aggregate company executive*

Leesport
Jackson, Eric Allen *philatelist*

Lehighton
Perkins, David L. *music educator*

Lehman
Novrocki, Michael W. *secondary school educator*
Williams, Thomas Alan *elementary school educator, small business owner*

Lemoyne
Custer, John Charles *portfolio manager*
Stewart, Richard Williams *lawyer*

Levittown
Henshaw, Jonathan Cook *retired manufacturing executive*
Lombardi, Michael *application developer*
Marable, Simeon-David *artist*

Lewisburg
Aldrich, Robert Adams *agricultural engineer, consultant*
Candland, Douglas Keith *psychology professor*
Dively, Justin Matthew *psychologist*
Fernsler, John Paul *lawyer*
Hauck, William Edward *retired education educator*
Jump, Chester Jackson, Jr. *clergyman, church official*
Kinnaman, Thomas Christopher *economics professor, researcher*
Mitchell, Brian Christopher *academic administrator*
Muller, Riana Ricci *musician, educator*
Neuman, Nancy Adams Mosshammer *civic leader*
Payne, Michael David *English language educator*
Rote, Nelle Fairchild Hefty *management consultant*

Lewistown
Levin, Allen Joseph *lawyer*
Varner, Vance Sieber *principal*

Liberty
Nelson, Thomas John *music educator, musician*

Ligonier
Mellon, Seward Prosser *brokerage house executive*
Pilz, Alfred Norman *manufacturing executive*
Vogelsang, Eric R. *language educator, basketball and soccer coach*

Lincoln University
Nelson, Ivory Vance *academic administrator*
Norris, Jo Anne Wareham *school counselor*
Nwachuku, Levi Akalazu *social sciences and behavioral studies educator*
Venerable, Grant Delbert, II, *chemist, educator, systems scientist*
Williams, Willie, Jr. *physicist, researcher*

Line Lexington
Kuehne, Tracy Elizabeth *music educator*

Linwood
Johnson, John George, Jr. *industrial services executive*

Lititz
Lehman, Richard William *electrical engineer*
McGlynn, James Francis *chemistry educator, chemical engineer*
Sandercox, Robert Allen *academic administrator, minister*

Little Meadows
Staby, Dorothy Louise *elementary school educator*

Lock Haven
Almes, June *retired education educator, librarian*
Chang, Shirley Lin (Hsiu-Chu Chang) *librarian, educator*
Jamieson, Cynthia Kay *military specialist*
Jia, Dongdong *nanoscience educator, physics professor*
Kerszberg, Annik Doquire *language educator*
Snowiss, Alvin L. *lawyer*
Story, Julie Ann *language educator*

Loretto
Jareb, Jerome *history professor, researcher*

Lower Gwynedd
Pendleton, Robert Grubb *pharmacologist*

Lumberville
Katsiff, Bruce *artist*

Lykens
Sultzbaugh, John Stephan *historian, educator*

Lyon Station
Breidegam, DeLight Edgar, Jr. *battery company executive*

Macungie
Moore, Joyce Kristina *financial planner, director*
Rubin, Arthur Herman *retired academic administrator*

Malvern
Bhaskar, K.S. *information technology executive*
Brighton, Ruth Louise *lay worker, educator*

Cameron, John Clifford *lawyer, health science association administrator*
Dixon, E. A., Jr. *lawyer*
Dohan, Andrew H. *lawyer*
Espe, Matthew J. *manufacturing executive*
Hershey, Mark A. *lawyer*
Liang, Jianming *computer scientist, researcher*
Miller, Richard Stanley *music educator*
Paul, Gerald D. *electronics executive*
Saruk, Michael *dermatologist, educator*
Stetson, John Batterson, IV, *construction executive*
Zaleski, John R. *medical researcher*
Zandman, Felix *electronics executive*

Manns Choice
Braendel, Douglas Arthur *hotel executive*

Mansfield
Donahue, Martha *retired librarian*
Haner, Matthew S. *mathematics professor, statistician*
Loeschke, Maravene S. *academic administrator, theater educator*
Schmid, Mark Daniel *music educator*

Maple Glen
Weaver-Stroh, Joanne Mateer *education educator, consultant*

Marion Center
Purdy, David Lawrence *medical products executive*

Marshalls Creek
Svoboda, Joanne Dzitko *artist, educator*

Martinsburg
Neff, Robert Wilbur *academic administrator, educator, minister*

Marysville
Trigilio, John Patricio *pastor*

Mc Elhattan
Garner, Charles William *retired educational administration educator, consultant*

Mc Kees Rocks
Wardell, Tamara Lynn *critical care nurse*

Mc Keesport
Lodor, Marci Ann *dietitian*
Micale, Frank Jude *lawyer*

Mc Murray
Brzustowicz, John Cinq-Mars *lawyer*
Celento, Florence M. *librarian*
Langenberg, Frederick Charles *manufacturing executive*
Mortimer, James Winslow *chemist*
Sherry, John Sebastian *lawyer*

Mc Veytown
Crosby, Edward George *psychologist*

Meadowbrook
Johnson, Victor Lawrence *banker, director*

Meadville
Adams, Earl William, Jr. *retired economics professor*
Cook, Richard James *academic administrator*
Dixon, Armendia Pierce *school program administrator*
Steen, John *health policy company executive, consultant*

Mechanicsburg
Derr, William James *retired non-commissioned officer*
Eakin, J. Michael *state supreme court justice*
Feaser, Deborah Ellen *mathematics educator*
Ortenzio, Robert A. *health and medical products executive*
Ortenzio, Rocco Anthony *health facility administrator*
Sutherly, Curtis Kent *civilian military employee, journalist, writer*

Media
Barnett, Samuel Treutlen *consultant*
Brobeck, John Raymond *physiology educator*
D'Amico, Andrew J. *lawyer*
Durham, James W. *lawyer*
Emerson, Sterling Jonathan *lawyer*
Garvin, Florence Ward *management consultant*
Leiby, Bruce Richard *retired secondary school educator, writer*
Li, Weiye *ophthalmologist, educator, biochemist*
Sestak, Joe (Joseph A. Sestak Jr.) *congressman, retired military officer*
Tomlinson, Herbert Weston *lawyer, defender*
Turner, Letitia Rhodes *artist*
Voltz, Sterling Ernest *physical chemist, researcher*

Mendenhall
Reinert, Norbert Frederick *lawyer, retired chemicals executive*

Mercer
DaCosta, Caroline Lee *small business owner*

Mercersburg
Owen, Lindsay Alexander *music director*

Merion Station
Gillman, Derek A. *museum director, academic administrator*
Littell, Marcia Sachs *Holocaust and genocide studies professor*

Middletown
Walters, Marian R. *research administrator*

Mifflinburg
Messimer, Donald McKee, Jr. *language educator*

Mifflinville
Farber, Phillip Andrew *retired biological and allied health sciences educator*

Milford
Le Guin, Ursula Kroeber *writer*

Millersville
Farkas, Kerrie R.H. *literature and language professor*
Miller, Steven Max *humanities educator*

Minersville
Eisenhuth, Edward George *social studies educator*

Monessen
Vivian, Cassandra *museum administrator, writer, photographer*

Monongahela
Yovanof, Silvana *physician*

Monroeville
Cohen, Laura *lawyer*
Skolnick, Marilyn *civic worker*

Mont Alto
Achampong, Francis Kofi *academic administrator*

Montgomeryville
Detwiler, Christine Wendler *special education educator*

Montoursville
Hunter, Corey Ryan *secondary school educator*

Moon Township
Alstadt, Lynn Jeffery *lawyer*
Rabosky, Joseph George *engineering consulting company executive*

Morgantown
Dierwechter, David C. *retired elementary school educator, theater director*

Mount Bethel
Carpenter, Carolyn *elementary school educator*

Mount Gretna
Agudo, Mercedes Engracia *psychiatrist*

Mount Joy
Lodde, Gordon Maynard *health physics consultant*

Mount Pleasant
Collins, Frederick George *music educator, secondary school educator*
Dangelo, Eugene Michael *elementary school educator*
Morgan, Joyce Kaye *social worker*
Roadman, Joseph Peter *engineering consultant*

Mountainhome
Buttz, Charles William *outdoor advertising executive*

Murrysville
Ferri, Karen Lynn *lawyer*
Yang, Wen-Ching *chemical engineer*

Nanticoke
Eddy, Carl F. *engineering educator*
Pajka, R. Bonnie *language educator*

Narberth
Nathanson, Neal *virologist, epidemiologist, educator*
Newhall, John Harrison *retired business executive, management consultant*
Strom, Brian Leslie *internist, educator*

Natrona Heights
Maleski, Cynthia Maria *lawyer*

Nazareth
Bast, Kimberly Ann *social studies educator*
Ferraro, Margaret Louise (Peg) *secondary school educator*
Stitt, Thomas Paul, Sr. *lawyer*

Nelson
Kyofski, Bonelyn Lugg *retired education educator*

New Alexandria
Sehring, Hope Hutchison *library science educator*

New Buffalo
Cramer, John McNaight *lawyer*

New Castle
Panella, Michael Joseph *pathologist, lawyer*

New Cumberland
Peters, Ralph Edgar *architectural firm, engineering executive*

New Freedom
Eikenberg, John Robert *retired electronics executive*
Sedlak, Valerie Frances *retired English language and literature educator, academic administrator*

New Holland
Fanus, Pauline Rife *librarian*
Papadakis, Emmanuel Philippos *physicist, consultant*
Roesch, Clarence Henry *banker*
Wagner, Bradley Jeremiah *agricultural engineer*

West, Daniel Charles *dentist*

New Hope
Coyle, Diane Bonanomi *special education educator*
Ecker, Sidney Wolf *urologist, consultant*
Hover, John Calvin, II, *banker*
Raabe, Gerhard Karl *epidemiologist*
Sergey, John Michael, Jr. *investment company executive, consultant*

New Kensington
Gilley, Jennifer R. *librarian*
Ray, Siba Prasad *materials scientist, ceramics scientist*
Wallace, Henry Jared, Jr. *lawyer*
Zaidi, Mohammad A. *metal products executive*

New Kingstown
DiSipio, Rocco Thomas *writer*

New Milford
Cunningham, Mary Ann Michael *secondary school educator*

New Stanton
Black, Cora Jean *evangelist, wedding consultant*

New Tripoli
Hess, Darla Bakersmith *cardiologist, educator*

Newmanstown
Hertzog, Noel Kent *retired elementary school educator*

Newtown
Bernstine, Daniel O'Neal *educational association administrator, law educator*
Booraem, Hendrik, V, *education educator, historian*
Brennan, Thomas John *city and state official, consultant, educator*
Duncan, Stephen Robert *elementary school educator*
Godwin, Robert Anthony *lawyer*
Paghdiwala, Abid F *dentist*
Rao, Sudhakar *aerospace engineer, researcher*
Ross, Edwin William *rubber company executive*
Sheridan, John J. *musician, music educator*
Somers, Anne Ramsay *retired medical educator*

Newtown Square
Benenson, James, Jr. *manufacturer*
Bertolet, Caroline Lynne Georgeanne *special education educator, labor union administrator*
Cordes, Eugene Harold *retired pharmacy and chemistry educator*
DeLuca, Jennie M. *English educator*
de Rivas, Carmela Foderaro *retired psychiatrist, health facility administrator*
Garthwaite, Thomas Leonard *medical officer*
Grubb, Gary S. *pharmaceutical executive*
Kendall, Robert Louis, Jr. *lawyer*
Lewis, James Earl *investor*
Mestre, Oscar Luis *financial consultant*
Perrone, Nicholas *engineering company executive*
Reiley, T(homas) Phillip *consultant*
Staats, Dean Roy *retired reinsurance executive*
Swing, Elizabeth Sherman *education educator*

Norristown
Aman, George Matthias III *lawyer*
Britt, Earl Thomas *lawyer*
Brown, Patrick Alan *systems analyst*
DeMedio, Kathleen Marie *chemistry educator*
Gold-Bikin, Lynne Z. *lawyer*
Gregg, John Pennypacker *lawyer*
Marzewski, Janeen Lynette *elementary school educator*
Steinberg, Arthur Irwin *periodontist, educator*

North Huntingdon
Huszar, Carl George *social studies educator*

North Versailles
King, Cheryl Brea *elementary, secondary and music educator*

North Wales
Calder, Robert Austin *preventive medicine physician, administrator*
Gorby-Schmidt, Martha Louise *pharmacologist, researcher*
Kim, Peter Sungbai *pharmaceutical and research and development company executive, educator*
Vietri, Linda Smith *gifted and talented educator*

Northern Cambria
Fisher, Connie Marie *physical therapist*

Nottingham
White, Richard Edmund *human resources specialist*

Oaks
Marland, Alkis Joseph *leasing company executive, computer scientist, educator, financial planner*
West, Alfred Paul, Jr. *financial services executive*

Orefield
Armor, John N. *chemical company scientist, consultant, research manager*
Langman, Peter Fabbri *psychologist, poet, playwright*

Orwigsburg
Mason, Joan Ellen *nurse*

Palmyra
Singer, William Harry *retired artificial intelligence application developer, retired research scientist*

Paoli
Burget, Dean Edwin, Jr. *plastic surgeon*

Denny, William Murdoch, Jr. *investment management executive*
Hermance, Frank S. *electronics executive*

Pen Argyl
Martocci, Lewis Nicholas III *writer*

Pennsburg
Shuhler, Phyllis Marie *physician*

Pequea
Sandt, Carol Hargis *microbiologist, researcher*

Perkasie
Dillingham, Lee *social studies educator*

Philadelphia
Aaron, Kenneth Ellyot *lawyer*
Abramowitz, Robert Leslie *lawyer*
Acker, Michael A. *thoracic surgeon, educator*
Adamany, David Walter *law and political science educator, former academic administrator*
Adawi, Nadia Sharon *energy executive*
Adetunji, Babatunde Abayomi *forensic psychiatrist*
Adler, Martin William *neuropharmacologist*
Ajzenberg-Selove, Fay *physicist, researcher*
Akiyama, Cliff *forensic science educator, criminologist, researcher, consultant*
Albert, Jeffrey B. *lawyer*
Alchin, John Reginald *cable tv company executive*
Alexander, William Herbert *business educator, former construction executive*
Alford, Larry P. *university librarian*
Allen, Julian Lewis *medical educator, researcher*
Altschuler, Steven M. *health facility executive, pediatrician, gastroenterologist*
Ammon, Gary D. *lawyer*
Ances, Beau M. *neurologist*
Anders, Jerrold P. *lawyer*
Anderson, Rolph Ely *finance educator*
Angel, Marina *law educator*
Angelakis, Michael J. *communications executive*
Angell, Mary Faith *federal magistrate judge*
Arce, A. Anthony *psychiatrist, educator*
Arem, Lawrence Jay *lawyer*
Armstrong, C. Michael *retired communications executive*
Armstrong, Clay *physiology educator*
Arnold, Lee *library director, archivist*
Asbury, Arthur Knight *neurologist, educator*
Auten, David Charles *lawyer*
Auten, Donald R. *lawyer*
Aversa, Dolores Sejda *educational administrator*
Azzolina, David Sean *librarian*
Babbel, David Frederick *finance and insurance educator*
Bachman, Arthur *lawyer*
Backstrom, C. Stephen *communications executive*
Badler, Norman Ira *computer and information science educator*
Baker, Stephen C. *lawyer*
Baldwin, Cynthia Ackron *state supreme court justice*
Baltuch, Gordon Hirsh *neurosurgeon*
Banerji, Ranan Bihari *mathematics professor*
Banse, Amy L. *communications executive, lawyer*
Bantel, Linda Mae *former museum curator, consultant*
Barchi, Robert Lawrence *clinical neurologist*
Barker, Clyde Frederick *surgeon, educator*
Barnett, Bonnie Allyn *lawyer*
Barnett, Jonathan *urban planner, educator, architect*
Barrett, J. Patrick *manufacturing executive*
Barrett, John J(ames), Jr. *lawyer*
Bartlett, Allen Lyman, Jr. *retired bishop*
Bartlett, Scott Paul *plastic surgeon*
Barton, Thomas J. *lawyer*
Baserga, Renato Luigi *pathology educator*
Bass, Aaron *school system administrator*
Bates, James Earl *academic administrator*
Baum, Stanley *radiologist, educator*
Baxt, William Gordon *medical educator*
Beck, Aaron Temkin *psychiatrist, educator*
Beck, John Robert *pathologist, information scientist*
Beck, Stuart Edwin *lawyer*
Becker, Lance B. *medical educator*
Beeman, Richard Roy *historian, educator*
Behrman, Jere Richard *economics professor*
Bell, Michael W. *insurance company executive*
Bell, Steven J. *school librarian, educator, writer*
Benson, Hande Yurttan *adult education educator*
Berenato, Mark Anthony *lawyer, insurance company executive*
Berger, Harold *lawyer, electrical engineer*
Berger, Lawrence Douglas *lawyer*
Berger, Lawrence Howard *lawyer*
Berkley, Emily Carolan *lawyer*
Berkman, Richard Lyle *lawyer*
Berlin, Norman B. *lawyer*
Bernabeo, Gregory S. *lawyer*
Bernard, John Marley *lawyer, educator*
Berney, David J. *lawyer*
Bernheim, Daniel S. *lawyer*
Bernstein, Charles *poet, writer, educator*
Berry, Mary Frances *history professor, former federal agency administrator*
Bershad, Jack R. *retired lawyer*
Betancourt, Philip P. *art historian, archaeologist, educator*
Beyer, Aaron Jay *lawyer*
Bibbo, Marluce *physician, educator*
Bilaniuk, Larissa Tetiana *neuroradiologist, educator*
Bilgutay, Nihat Mustafa *engineering educator, associate dean*
Biron, Martin *professional hockey player*
Black, Allen Decatur *lawyer*
Black, Creed C., Jr. *lawyer*
Blakely, Kevin M. *management association executive*

Blavat, Jerry (Gerald Joseph Blavat) *television personality, actor*
Blaze, Matthew *computer science educator, researcher*
Block, Arthur R. *communications executive, lawyer*
Bloom, Joel N. *science museum director*
Blumberg, Baruch Samuel *research scientist, educator*
Blume, Fred *lawyer*
Blume, Marshall Edward *finance educator*
Blumstein, Edward *lawyer*
Bochetto, George Alexander *lawyer*
Boden, Guenther *endocrinologist*
Boggia, Eugene Stephen *lawyer*
Bogutz, Jerome Edwin *lawyer, educator*
Bonella, Michael J. *lawyer*
Booth, Anna Belle *accountant*
Bordogna, Joseph *engineering educator, former science foundation executive*
Borislow, Alan Jerome *hospital dental department chairman*
Bortnick, Newman Mayer *research chemist*
Boruch, Robert Francis *educator, consultant*
Boss, Amelia Helen *lawyer, educator*
Boucher, Brian *professional hockey player*
Bovaird, Brendan Peter *lawyer*
Bove, Alfred Anthony *medical educator*
Bower, John Arnold, Jr. *architect*
Bowman, Marjorie Ann *physician, educator*
Brady, Luther W., Jr. *radiologist, educator*
Brandt, Jennifer Anne *lawyer*
Breslow, Tina *public relations executive*
Bressler, Barry E. *lawyer*
Brier, Bonnie Susan *lawyer*
Briere, Daniel *professional hockey player*
Brinster, Ralph Lawrence *biologist, educator*
Briscoe, Jack Clayton *lawyer*
Brookman, Marc D. *lawyer*
Brooks, John Samuel Joseph *pathologist, researcher*
Brooman, David J. *lawyer*
Brown, Dave *professional sports team executive*
Brown, Denise Scott *architect, urban planner*
Brown, Larry (Lawrence Harvey Brown) *professional sports team executive, former professional basketball coach*
Brown, Stephen D. *lawyer*
Brown, William Hill III *lawyer*
Browne, Stanhope Stryker *lawyer*
Brozena, Susan C. *cardiologist*
Brucker, Paul C. *academic administrator, physician*
Brunk, Samuel Frederick *oncologist*
Bryans, Henry S. *lawyer*
Bryce, Teresa Audrey *lawyer*
Buccino, Ernest John, Jr. *lawyer*
Buchholz, Carl M. *lawyer*
Buckwalter, Ronald Lawrence *federal judge*
Budin, Beverly R. *lawyer*
Burbank, Stephen Bradner *law educator*
Burch, Francis Floyd *clergyman*
Burdumy, Stephen T. *lawyer*
Burke, Brother Daniel *museum director, educator*
Burke, Stephen B. (Steve Burke) *communications company executive*
Burling, Stacy *reporter*
Burstein, Elias *physicist, researcher*
Butler, Marie Gladys *nursing educator*
Byler, Anthony J. *lawyer*
Callahan, James Michael *physician, educator*
Calman, Robert Frederick *mining executive*
Calvert, Jay H., Jr. *lawyer*
Camardo, Michael F. *retired aerospace transportation executive*
Camp, Donald Eugene *experimental photographer, educator*
Cannon, John III *lawyer, insurance company executive*
Capers, Gregg *secondary school educator, musician*
Caplan, Arthur Leonard *university program director, educator*
Carey, Arthur Bernard, Jr. *editor, columnist*
Carroll, Mark Thomas *lawyer*
Cartmell, Elizabeth Bayley (Liza) *hospitality and food services executive*
Carven, John Winslow *priest*
Cashman, Wayne *professional athletics coach*
Casper, Charles B. *lawyer*
Cassel, Christine Karen *physician*
Castille, Ronald D. *state supreme court justice*
Chagares, Michael Arthur *federal judge*
Chanin, Bernard *lawyer*
Charney, Natalie J. *mental health services professional, educator, researcher*
Cheeks, Maurice Edward *professional basketball coach, retired professional basketball player*
Chen, Lan X. *physician, educator*
Cherken, Harry Sarkis, Jr. *lawyer*
Childress, Scott Julius *medicinal chemist*
Chimples, George *lawyer*
Chiu, Alexander G. *otolaryngologist, educator*
Chopko, Mark E. *lawyer*
Christenbury, T. Daniel *lawyer*
Chrysikou, Evangelia G. *psychology professor*
Clark, John J. *economist, finance educator*
Clark, Peter S., II, *lawyer*
Clark, William H., Jr. *lawyer*
Clarke, Robert Earle (Bobby Clarke) *professional sports team executive*
Clarkin, John Francis *health care management executive*
Clauss, Peter Otto *lawyer*
Clearfield, Harris Reynold *physician*
Clothier, Robert Clarkson *lawyer*
Coché, Judith *psychologist, educator*
Cohen, David Louis *communications executive*
Cohen, David Walter *academic administrator, educator, periodontist*
Cohen, Ira Myron *retired aeronautical and mechanical engineering educator*
Cohn, Mildred *retired biochemist, educator*
Coleman, Gerald Charles *judge, educator*
Coleman, Robert J. *lawyer*
Colli, Bart Joseph *lawyer*
Collings, Robert L. *lawyer*
Colman, Robert Wolf *hematologist, educator*
Colson, Rosemary *music educator*
Comisky, Hope A. *lawyer*
Congdon, Charles B. *lawyer*
Conn, Rex Boland, Jr. *pathologist, educator*
Conway, John W. *manufacturing executive*
Cooney, J(ohn) Gordon, Jr. *lawyer*
Cooper, Edward Sawyer *cardiologist, internist, educator*
Cooper, Frank G. *lawyer*
Cooper, Richard Alan *health policy consultant*
Corbin, Theodore J., Jr. *emergency physician*
Cortès, Luis *religious organization administrator*
Corzo, Miguel Angel *academic administrator*
Cotsarelis, George *dermatologist, educator*
Coulson, Zoe Elizabeth *retired consumer marketing executive*
Cox, Roger Frazier *lawyer*
Coyne, Charles Cole *lawyer*
Cozen, Stephen Allen *lawyer*
Cramer, Harold *lawyer*
Crawford, James Douglas *lawyer*
Crocker, John C. *chemical and biomolecular engineer, educator*
Croisetiere, Jacques M. *chemicals executive*
Cross, Milton H. *lawyer*
Cruess, Dean *psychologist, educator*
Crumb, George Henry *composer, educator*
Cunningham, Jacqueline Lemmé *psychologist, educator, researcher*
Dabrowski, Doris Jane *lawyer*
Daemmrich, Horst Sigmund *German language and literature educator*
Dagit, Charles Edward, Jr. *architect, educator*
Dalinka, Murray Kenneth *radiologist, educator*
Dalton, David Robert *chemistry professor*
Daly, John M. *surgeon, educator*
Damsgaard, Kell Marsh *lawyer*
D'Angelo, Christopher Scott *lawyer*
D'Angio, Giulio John *radiologist, educator*
Danien, Elin C. *archaeologist, researcher*
Dasgupta, Indranil *physician, educator*
Daugherty, F(rancis) Mark *music educator, conductor, theater director*
Davey, Adam *gerontologist, researcher*
Davidoff, Joanne Malatesta *multi-media specialist*
Davis, Alan Jay *lawyer*
Davis, Allen Freeman *history professor, writer*
Davis, Glenn Craig *psychiatrist*
Davis, Paige (Mindy Paige Davis) *television personality and host*
Days, Michael *editor*
deBenedet, Rachel *actress*
DeBunda, Salvatore Michael *lawyer*
de Cani, John Stapley *retired statistician, educator*
Delacato, Carl Henry *lawyer*
Delaney, Terence (Terry) P. *gas industry executive*
Del Raso, Joseph Vincent *lawyer*
Dennis, Roger J. *dean, law educator*
Devlin, John Gerard *lawyer, writer*
DeVoe, Andrew *healthcare system executive*
Dewan, Vikram H. *zoological park administrator*
Diamantis, Jennifer *lawyer*
Diamond, Paul Steven *federal judge, lawyer, educator*
Diaz, Magna M. *librarian*
Diaz, Nelson A. *lawyer*
Diaz, Romulo L., Jr. *lawyer*
Di Benedetto, C. Anthony *marketing educator*
Dichter, Marc Allen *physician*
Dichter, Mark S. *lawyer*
Diebold, Francis X. *economist, educator*
Di Falco, Gerard A. *artist*
DiLeo, Tony *professional sports team executive*
DiPalma, Joseph Rupert *pharmacology educator, dean*
Director, Stephen William *electrical and computer engineering educator, academic administrator*
Djerassi, Isaac *medical researcher*
Donaldson, Thomas *business educator*
Donnelly, Gloria Ferraro *university dean*
Donohue, James J. *lawyer*
Donohue, John Patrick *lawyer*
Dooner, Marlene S. *communications executive*
Dorfman, John Charles *lawyer*
Doty, Richard L. *medical researcher*
Dougherty, Brian James *lawyer*
Dougherty Buchholz, Karen *communications executive*
Douglas, Steven Daniel *immunologist, educator, director*
Drake, William Frank, Jr. *lawyer*
Driver, Robert Baylor, Jr. *opera company director*
Drosdick, John Girard *oil industry executive*
Dubin, Leonard *lawyer*
Duffy, Seamus C. *lawyer*
Dugan, Brendan J. *bank executive*
Dunn, Mary Maples *academic administrator*
Dunphy, Fran *men's college basketball coach*
Durant, Marc *lawyer*
Dutton, P(eter) Leslie *biochemist, educator*
Dworetzky, Joseph Anthony *lawyer, city manager*
Eaker, Seth A. *financial consultant*
Ehrlich, George Edward *rheumatologist, consultant*
Eiberson, Jeffrey Lawrence *psychologist, consultant*
Eisen, Howard Joel *internist, researcher*
Eisenberg, Ted Steven *plastic and reconstructive surgeon*
Eisenstein, Toby K. *microbiology professor*
Eiswerth, Barry Neil *architect, educator*
Englander, Sol Walter *biochemistry and biophysics educator, medical educator*
Epstein, Alan Bruce *lawyer*
Erdmann, James Bernard *educational psychologist*
Esser, Carl Eric *lawyer*
Evan, William Martin *sociologist, educator*
Ewald, William Bragg III *law educator, philosopher*
Fader, Henry Conrad *lawyer*
Fala, Herman Camillo *lawyer*
Falkie, Thomas Victor *mining engineer, engineering executive*
Farley, Richard John *architect, engineer*
Fegley, Kenneth Allen *systems engineering educator*
Feirson, Steven B. *lawyer*
Feldman, Arthur M. *cardiologist*
Feldman, Eric Adam *law educator, academic administrator*
Feldman, Jeffrey Mark *anesthesiologist*
Feninger, Claude *retired hotel executive*
Fernandez, Happy Craven (Gladys) *academic administrator*
Fickler, Arlene *lawyer*
Fiebach, H. Robert *lawyer*
Fielding, Allen Fred *oral and maxillofacial surgeon, educator*
Finck, Christine M. *pediatric surgeon, educator*
Fineman, S. David *lawyer*
Finkelstein, Joseph Simon *lawyer*
Finney, Graham Stanley *management consultant*
Fischer, Bruce G. *gas industry executive*
Fisher, Aron Baer *physiology educator*
Fisher, Lane J. *lawyer*
Fisher, Robert *gastroenterologist, health facility administrator*
Fishman, Alfred Paul *physician*
Fitts, Donald Dennis *chemist, educator*
Fitts, Michael Andrew *dean, law educator*
Flanagan, Joseph Patrick, Jr. *retired lawyer*
Floyd, Michael O'S. *lawyer*
Foley, Regina M. *lawyer*
Foo, Susanna *chef*
Foti, Margaret *medical association administrator, editor, consultant*
Fox, Renée Claire *sociology educator*
Fox, Richard L. *lawyer*
Frank, Barbara Balis *gastroenterologist, educator*
Frank, Barry H. *lawyer*
Frank, George Andrew *lawyer*
Frankel, Francine Ruth *political science professor*
Frankel, Sherman *physicist, educator*
Freeman, Ellen Wood *research professor*
Friedman, Harvey Michael *infectious diseases educator*
Fromm, Eli *engineering educator*
Frucher, Meyer S. (Sandy Frucher) *stock exchange executive*
Furth, John Jacob *molecular biologist, educator, pathologist*
Fusco, Richard *English literature educator*
Fussell, Paul *writer, literature educator*
Gagné, Simon *professional hockey player, Olympic athlete*
Gaillard, Theodore Lee, Jr. *literature and language educator, writer*
Gaiser, Robert Raymond *obstetric anesthesiologist, educator*
Gallagher, William T. *lawyer, manufacturing executive*
Galván, Gary *small business owner, educator*
Garcia, Rudolph *lawyer*
Garnier, Jean-Pierre *pharmaceutical executive*
Garonzik, Sara Ellen *stage producer*
Gartland, John Joseph *physician, writer*
Gausas, Roberta Elisabeth *oculoplastic and orbital surgeon*
Gavrin, Jonathan Robert *medical educator, internist*
Gelles, Richard James *sociology and psychology professor, academic administrator*
Genkin, Barry Howard *lawyer*
George, Paul M. *law librarian, director*
Gerhart, Frederick John *lawyer*
Gerner, Edward William *medical educator*
Gershenfeld, Matti Kibrick *psychologist*
Gershenson, Alan C. *lawyer*
Gilberg, Kenneth Roy *lawyer*
Gilbert, Charles *performing arts educator, writer*
Gillick, Patrick
Girard-diCarlo, David Franklin *lawyer*
Givens, Janet Eaton *writer*
Glandt, Eduardo Daniel *chemical engineering educator*
Glass, Dennis Robert *insurance company executive*
Glick, Jane Mills *biomedical researcher, educator*
Glick, John H. *oncologist, medical educator*
Glickman, Sallie A. *professional society administrator*
Glusker, Jenny Pickworth *chemist*
Godley, Joanne *city health department administrator*
Gogotsi, Yury *materials scientist, educator*
Goldberg, Joseph *lawyer*
Goldberg, Marvin Allen *lawyer, consultant*
Goldberg, Richard Robert *lawyer*
Golden, Thomas M. *federal judge*
Goldfarb, Stanley *internist, educator*
Goldman, Gary Craig *lawyer*
Goldman, Jerry S. *lawyer*
Goldstein, William Marks *lawyer*
Gonzalez-Scarano, Francisco Antonio *neurologist, virologist*
Goodenough, Ward Hunt *anthropologist, educator*
Goodman, Stephen Murry *lawyer*
Goon, Arthur David *academic administrator, educator*
Gorberg, David J. *lawyer*
Gordon, Anne Kathleen *editor*
Goschke, Linda Fry *artist*
Gough, John Francis *lawyer*
Gowa, Andrew *investor, lawyer*
Graffman, Gary *academic administrator, pianist, music educator*
Granger, Randy William *art educator, consultant*
Grant, M. Duncan *lawyer*
Greenstein, Jeffrey Ian *neurologist*
Grove, David Lavan *lawyer*
Gueson, Emerita Torres *obstetrician, gynecologist*
Guillen, Mauro Federico *sociology and management educator*
Gupta, Rajiv Lochan *chemicals executive*
Gutmann, Amy *academic administrator, political science and philosophy educator*
Hack, Gary Arthur *dean*
Hackney, (Francis) Sheldon *history professor, former academic administrator*
Hadjiliadis, Denis *physician*
Hagan, Mary Ann *lawyer*
Hahn, Steven *history professor, writer*
Haimm, Neil Keith *lawyer*
Haines, Clifford E. *lawyer*
Haley, Vincent Peter *retired lawyer*
Halpern, Eric Franklin *university publishing director*
Hameka, Hendrik Frederik *chemistry professor*
Hamels, Cole (Colbert Michael Hamels) *professional baseball player*
Hamilton, Samuel C. *not-for-profit fundraiser*
Hamilton, Stephen David Derwent *lawyer*
Hammond, Benjamin Franklin *microbiologist, educator*
Hangley, William Thomas *lawyer*
Hansen-Flaschen, John Hyman *medical educator, researcher*
Hanway, H. Edward *insurance company executive*
Harbater, David *mathematician*
Hardiman, Thomas Michael *federal judge*
Harkins, John Graham, Jr. *lawyer*
Harris, A. Brooks *physicist, researcher*
Harris, Judith E. *lawyer*
Harris, Raymond Jesse *retired federal official*
Hart, Ann Weaver *academic administrator*
Hartley, Paul E. *insurance company executive*
Harvey, Gregory Merrill *lawyer*
Harvey, John Adriance *psychologist, educator, pharmacologist, researcher*
Hatch, Denny (Alden Denison) *publishing executive, writer*
Hayes, John Freeman *architect*
Heber-Katz, Ellen *research scientist, educator*
Hemphill, John Lindsay III *administrative assistant*
Henisz, Witold Jerzy *social sciences educator*
Herling, Irving Marc *internal medicine educator, cardiologist*
Hickok, D. Alicia *lawyer*
Hickok, Robert L. *lawyer*
Hillen, John Francis *think-tank executive, former federal agency administrator*
Hindelang, Thomas Joseph *finance educator, dean*
Hirschmann, Ralph Franz *chemist*
Hochstrasser, Robin M. *chemist, educator*
Hoelscher, Robert James *lawyer*
Hoffman, Alan Jay *lawyer*
Hofmann, Thomas W. *oil industry executive*
Hoke-Scedrov, Bonnie Carol *music educator, soprano*
Holmgren, Paul *professional sports team executive, retired professional hockey player*
Horwitz, Eric M. *radiation oncologist*
Hossain, Murshed *physicist, researcher*
Hou, J. Steve *pathologist*
Houstoun, Feather O'Connor *foundation administrator*
Howard, David Miles *lawyer*
Howard, Ryan James *professional baseball player*
Hua, Xianxin *cell and cancer biology educator*
Hunter, James Austen, Jr. *lawyer*
Hynes, Virtner Gilmore *rehabilitation services professional*
Iglewicz, Boris *statistician, educator*
Ingolfsson-Fassbind, Ursula G. *music educator*
Ivey, Stephen David *lawyer*
Jackson, Harold *journalist*
Jacobs, Jonathan Mark *parliamentary consultant*
James, Jennifer DuFault *lawyer*
Jaron, Dov *biomedical engineer, educator*
Jayadevappa, Ravishankar *science educator*
Jeffcoat, Marjorie K. *dean, dental educator*
Jenkins, Marc Delano *music educator*
Jennings, Richard *communications executive*
Jessup, Mariell *physician, director*
Jimenez, Sergio A. *internist, educator, rheumatologist*
Johnson, Joseph Eggleston III *physician, educator*
Johnson, Sylvester *police commissioner*
Jones, Robert Jeffries *lawyer*
Jordan, Kent A. *federal judge*
Jordan, Michael B. *lawyer*
Jordan, V. Craig *endocrine pharmacologist, educator*
Josephs, Babette *legislator*
Joyner, J(ames) Curtis *judge*
Kadison, Richard Vincent *mathematician, educator*
Kaestner, Klaus H. *genetics educator*
Kahn, James Robert *lawyer*
Kaier, Edward John *lawyer*
Kaiser, Larry Robert *thoracic surgeon*
Kaiser, Roy *performing company executive*
Kaji, Akira *microbiology scientist, educator*
Kamp, R. Stephen *finance educator*
Kang, Ju-Seop *medical educator, consultant, medical researcher*
Kang, Yoogoo *anesthesiologist, educator*
Kaplan, Keith Eugene *insurance company executive, lawyer*
Kassner, Andrew Charles *lawyer*
Katherine, Robert Andrew *chemicals executive*
Kaufman, Russel Eugene *hematologist, oncologist*
Kazazian, Haig Hagop, Jr. *pediatrician, researcher, educator*
Keene, John Clark *lawyer, educator*
Kefalides, Nicholas Alexander *physician, educator*
Keim, Donald Bruce *finance educator*
Kelley, William Nimmons *physician, educator, science administrator, dean*
Kelly, Robert Francis *federal judge*

Stonecipher, David A. *insurance company executive*
Stoopler, Eric T. *dentist, dental educator*
Strasbaugh, Wayne Ralph *lawyer*
Strazzella, James Anthony *lawyer, educator*
Street, John F. *mayor*
Strickler, Matthew M. *lawyer*
Stuart, Glen R(aymond) *lawyer*
Stuart, Marie Jean *physician, hematologist, researcher*
Stunkard, Albert James *psychiatrist, educator*
Stuntebeck, Clinton A. *lawyer*
Sugrue, Thomas J. *history professor, social sciences educator*
Suh, Byungse *medical educator*
Sulyk, Stephen *retired archbishop*
Summers, Anita Arrow *finance educator*
Summers, Clyde Wilson *law educator*
Summers, Robert *economics professor*
Suplee, Dennis Raymond *lawyer*
Sutherland, L(ewis) Frederick *food products executive*
Suzuki, Jon Byron *medical educator, periodontist, microbiologist*
Swain, Clifford H. *lawyer*
Sweet, James M. *lawyer*
Taney, Francis Xavier, Jr. *lawyer*
Taniguchi, Tadatsugu *biology professor, researcher*
Tannen, Richard Laurence *nephrology educator*
Tansy, Martin F. *dean*
Temin, Michael Lehman *lawyer*
Terry, John Joseph *transportation investor*
Testa, Joseph R. *geneticist*
Thomas, Glen R. *lawyer*
Thompson, Craig B. *physician*
Tiger, Ira Paul *retired lawyer*
Tileston, Jackie *artist, educator*
Tooker, John Phillip *internist, educator, medical association administrator*
Torg, Joseph Steven *orthopaedic surgeon, educator*
Tourtellotte, Charles Dee *internist, rheumatologist, educator*
Tractenberg, Craig R. *lawyer*
Tran, Judith Thuha *psychiatrist*
Trojanowski, John Q. *medical educator, health facility administrator*
Tuan, Kailin *management consultant, educator*
Utley, Chase Cameron *professional baseball player*
Vaira, Peter Francis *lawyer*
Van Arsdalen, Keith Norman *urologist*
Vanarsdall, Robert Lee, Jr. *orthodontist, educator*
vanBemmelen, Paul S. *surgeon, educator*
van Rhyn, Jacqueline J. *curator*
Velazquez, Omaida Caridad *vascular surgeon, researcher*
Venturi, Robert *architect*
Verlin, Jonathan R. *secondary school educator*
Virelli, Louis James, Jr. *lawyer*
Vitek, Vaclav *materials scientist*
Vitez, Michael *reporter*
Vogel, Warren *lawyer*
Volgin, Denys V. *medical researcher*
von Seldeneck, Judith Metcalfe *career planning administrator*
Wachman, Marvin *retired academic administrator*
Wachter, Michael L. *law and finance educator*
Wachter, Susan Melinda *finance educator*
Wajert, Sean Peter *lawyer*
Wales, Walter D. *physicist, researcher*
Walker, Allen Lyon *engineer*
Walker, Danielle *engineering executive*
Wallace, Anthony Francis Clarke *anthropologist, educator*
Wallace, Emily Mitchell *writer, editor, educator*
Walter, William G. *consumer products company executive*
Wang, Jiongjiong *neuroscientist, educator*
Waskow, Arthur Ocean *theologian, educator*
Webb, William Yerick *lawyer*
Webber, Ross Arkell *management educator*
Weil, Jeffrey George *lawyer*
Wein, Alan Jerome *urologist, educator, researcher*
Weisberg, Morris L. *retired lawyer*
Weitz, Howard Hy *cardiologist, educator*
Weller, Elizabeth Boghossian *child and adolescent psychiatrist*
Wellington, Ralph Glenn *lawyer*
Welsh, Diane M. *federal judge*
Whinston, Stephen Alan *lawyer*
Whitaker, Linton Andin *plastic surgeon*
White, Howard D. *information science educator*
White, Nicholas John *musician, director, composer*
Whiteside, William Anthony, Jr. *retired lawyer*
Wickstrom, Eric *biophysical chemist, educator*
Wiener, Morris Jay *air transportation executive*
Wiener, Ronald Martin *lawyer*
Wild, Richard P. *lawyer*
Wilde, Norman Taylor, Jr. *investment banking company executive*
Wilkinson, Signe *cartoonist*
Willet, E. Crosby (Everett Crosby Willet) *artist*
Willi, Steven Matthew *physician, educator, researcher*
Williams, Sankey Vaughan *health services researcher, internist*
Winkler, Gail Caskey *historian, writer*
Winkler, Jeffrey D. *chemist*
Winston, Flaura K. *engineering researcher*
Wint, Dennis Michael *museum director*
Wittels, Barnaby Caesar *lawyer, writer*
Wolf, Bruce *lawyer*
Wolfe, John Hall *medical researcher, educator, consultant*
Wolff, Deborah H(orowitz) *lawyer*
Wood, Roger F. *lawyer*
Woodside, Lisa Nicole *humanities educator*
Woody, George Edward *psychiatrist, educator*
Woosnam, Richard Edward *venture capitalist, lawyer*
Wright, Minturn Tatum III *retired lawyer*
Wu, Hong *pathologist*
Wysocki, Charles Joseph *neuroscientist*
Yang, Shu *materials scientist*
Yanoff, Myron *ophthalmologist*
Yaros, Constance Gregory *painter, sculptor*
Yaruss, Howard Seth *lawyer*
Yoh, William C. *outsourcing company executive*
Yohn, William H(endricks), Jr. *federal judge*
Young, Donald Stirling *clinical pathology educator*
Young, John Paul *accountant*
Young, Robert Crabill *medical researcher, science administrator, internist*
Zderic, Stephen Anthony *urologist, surgeon*
Ziegler, Donald Robert *accountant*
Zubernis, Lynn Smith *psychologist, counselor*
Zuckerman, Brian David *lawyer*
Zuckerman, Marvin *retired psychologist*
Zweiman, Burton *allergist, immunologist, educator*

Phoenixville
Brundage, Russell Archibald *retired data processing executive*
Hanlon, Barbara Jean *family and consumer sciences educator*
Lukacs, John Adalbert *historian, retired educator*

Pipersville
McNutt, Richard Hunt *manufacturing executive*

Pittsburgh
Abbott, Kevin Charles *lawyer*
Acheson, Amy J. *lawyer*
Adelson, P. David *pediatric neurosurgeon*
Aderson, Sanford M. *lawyer*
Aggarwal, Shushma *anesthesiologist, educator*
Allen, Rachel Lorey *lawyer*
Allen, Thomas E. *obstetrician, gynecologist*
Amara, Susan *neuroscientist*
Ambrose, Donetta W. *federal judge*
Amon, Cristina Hortensia *mechanical engineering educator, researcher*
Anderson, Scott Richard *geologist, consultant*
Aneja, Rajesh *medical educator, pediatrician*
Anthony, Edward Mason *linguistics educator*
Apone, Carl Anthony *journalist*
Arac, Jonathan *literature and language professor*
Aronson, Mark Berne *retired lawyer, advocate*
Artz, John Curtis *lawyer*
Asher, Sanford Abraham *chemist, educator*
Baer, Max *state supreme court justice*
Balas, Edith *art historian, educator*
Balas, Egon *mathematician, educator*
Baldauf, Kent Edward *lawyer*
Bardyguine, Patricia Wilde *dancer, performing company executive*
Barkus, Bruce E. *health products executive*
Barry, Herbert III *psychologist, educator*
Bartley, Burnett Graham, Jr. *oil industry executive*
Basinski, Anthony Joseph *lawyer*
Bates, Beverly Jo-Anne *artist, educator*
Becherer, Richard John *architecture educator*
Beck, Paul A. *lawyer*
Belda, Alain J. P. *metal products executive*
Bellisario, Domenic *lawyer*
Bender, Charles Christian *retail home center executive*
Berkman, Louis *steel company executive*
Bernt, Benno Anthony *entrepreneur, investor*
Berry, Guy Curtis *polymer science educator, researcher*
Bicchieri, Cristina *science educator*
Biegler, Lorenz Theodor *chemical engineering educator*
Biondi, Manfred Anthony *physicist*
Bissoon, Cathy *lawyer*
Bleier, Michael E. *lawyer, director*
Blenko, Walter John, Jr. *lawyer*
Bloom, William Millard *furnace design engineer*
Blum, Eva Tansky *lawyer*
Blum, Lenore *mathematician, computer scientist, educator*
Blum, Manuel *computer science educator*
Blumstein, Alfred *urban and public affairs educator*
Bobby, Theodore N. *lawyer, food products executive*
Bochicchio, Vito Salvatore *lawyer*
Bodine, William Beekman, Jr. *museum director*
Bodnar, Lisa M. *medical educator*
Bohlin, Peter Quarfordt *architect*
Booker, Daniel I. *lawyer*
Boswell, William Paret *lawyer*
Bothner-By, Aksel Arnold *chemist*
Boyce, Doreen Elizabeth *foundation administrator, educator*
Bradley, James P. *orthopedist*
Braun, Thomas W. *dean, academic administrator*
Brauner, Ronald Allan *theology studies educator*
Breault, Theodore E(dward) *lawyer*
Brendel, John S. *lawyer*
Brent, David A. *psychiatrist, medical educator*
Brosky, John G. *retired judge*
Brown, David Ronald *lawyer*
Brown, James Benton *lawyer, department chairman*
Brownlee, David A. *lawyer*
Bruno, Audrei Ann *nurse educator, administrator*
Buchanan, Bruce G. *computer scientist, educator*
Buchanan, Mary Beth *prosecutor*
Bunch, Charles E. *manufacturing executive*
Burger, Herbert Francis *retired advertising agency executive*
Burgess, David Lowry *artist*
Burkoff, John Michael *law educator*
Caginalp, Gunduz *mathematician, educator, researcher*
Cagney, William Robert *psychologist*
Cahouet, Ann P. *lawyer*
Cameron, Douglas E. *lawyer*
Candris, Laura A. *lawyer*
Cappy, Ralph Joseph *state supreme court chief justice*
Carbo, Toni (Toni Carbo Bearman) *information scientist, educator*
Cardenes, Andres Jorge *musician, educator*
Carelli, Mario Domenico *nuclear engineer*
Carley, Kathleen M. *computer scientist, educator*
Carr, Walter James, Jr. *research physicist, consultant*
Carr, Winifred Walker *artist, historian*
Carrau, Ricardo L. *otolaryngologist, educator*
Casasent, David Paul *electrical engineer, educator, data processing executive*
Cassidy, William Arthur *geology and planetary science educator*
Charap, Stanley Harvey *electrical engineering educator*
Cheever, George Martin *lawyer*
Chelly, Jacques E. *anesthesiologist*
Chi, David H. *otolaryngologist*
Cho, Sung K. *education educator*
Choset, Howie *engineering educator, researcher*
Choyke, Wolfgang Justus *physicist*
Cicero, J. Deborah *management consultant*
Cindrich, Robert James *lawyer, retired federal judge*
Clack, Jerry *classics educator*
Clarke, Edmund M. *computer scientist, educator*
Cohen, Bernard Irvin *plastic surgeon*
Cohen, Bernard Leonard *physicist, researcher*
Cohen, Sheldon *psychologist, psychology professor*
Cohill, Maurice Blanchard, Jr. *federal judge*
Cohon, Jared L. *academic administrator*
Colen, Frederick Haas *lawyer*
Collins, Bobby McManus, II, *dental educator*
Coltman, John Wesley *physicist*
Coney, Aims C., Jr. *lawyer, labor-management negotiator*
Connelly, John J. *metal products executive*
Connors, Eugene Kenneth *lawyer, educator*
Conti, Joy Flowers *judge*
Cooper, Thomas Louis *lawyer*
Corcoran, John Paul *lawyer, educator*
Cowan, Barton Zalman *lawyer*
Cox, Richard James *information science educator*
Crosby, Sidney *professional hockey player*
Crossely, Mary A. *dean, law educator*
Cubbage, Bobbie Danielle *pre-school administrator, educator*
Curry, Nancy Ellen *psychologist, psychoanalyst, educator*
Dabrishus, Michael John *librarian*
Damianos, Sylvester *architect, sculptor*
Damico, David A. *lawyer*
Daniel, Robert Michael *lawyer*
Davis, Larry E. *academic administrator*
Davis, Lewis U., Jr. *lawyer*
Dawes, Robyn Mason *psychology professor*
Dawson, Mary Ruth *curator, educator*
DeGroat, William Chesney *pharmacology educator*
DeKosky, Steven Trent *neurologist*
Demchak, William S. *bank executive*
Demetri, Kathryn J. *civil engineer*
Dempsey, Jerry Edward *retired service company executive*
DeNinno, David L. *lawyer*
Denys, Sylvia *lawyer, researcher*
Desiree, Laura *dancer*
Diamond, Gustave *federal judge*
Dixit, Balwant Narayan *pharmacology and toxicology educator*
Dixon, Jamie (P.), (II) *men's college basketball coach*
Doft, Bernard Harvey *ophthalmologist*
Dolfi, Chip *publishing executive*
Donahue, John Francis *investment company executive*
Doty, Robert Walter *lawyer*
Dougherty, Charles John *academic administrator*
Drawbaugh, Daniel *information technology executive, biomedical engineer*
Drennan, Robert D. *archeology educator, researcher*
Drescher, Seymour *historian, educator, writer*
Druckenmiller, Stanley F. *investment company executive*
Druzdzel, Marek Jozef *information systems educator, researcher*
Dugan, John F. *lawyer*
Dunn, Kenneth B. *dean*
Dutt, Varun *systems and software engineer*
Dzombak, David Adam *environmental engineering educator*
Eaton, Joseph W. *sociology educator*
Eckert, Jean Patricia *elementary school educator*
Ehrenwerth, David Harry *lawyer*
Ehrlich, Garth David *molecular biologist*
Einhorn, Jerzy *internist, endocrinologist, consultant*
Ellsworth, Laura E. *lawyer*
Emmerich, Werner Sigmund *physicist, educator*
Evans, Bruce Dwight *lawyer*
Faneca, Alan *professional football player*
Fararo, Thomas John *sociologist, educator*
Fawcett, David B. III *lawyer*
Feingold, David Sidney *microbiology and biochemistry educator, researcher*
Feller, Robert Livingston *chemist, art conservation scientist*
Fernstrom, John Dickson *pharmacology and nutrition researcher, educator*
Ferrara, Albert E. *corporate executive*
Fetterolf, Donald Edward *physician executive, consultant*
Fiaschi-Taesch, Nathalie Madeleine *medical educator*
Fienberg, Stephen Elliott *statistician*
Fine, Milton *hotel company executive, lawyer*
Finegold, Alan H. *lawyer*
Fireman, Philip *pediatrician, allergist, immunologist*
Fischer, Nora Barry *federal judge, lawyer*
Fischhoff, Baruch *psychologist, educator*
Fisher, Bernard *surgeon, educator*
Fisher, D. Michael *judge*
Fitzgerald, James J. III *state supreme court justice*
Fitzgerald, Judith Klaswick *federal judge*
Flaherty, John Paul, Jr. *chief justice emeritus*
Flechtner, Harry Marshal *law educator*
Flinn, Michael James *lawyer*
Fontes, Paulo A. *surgeon, educator*
Fowler, Fred Joseph *human services manager*
Fox, Debra L. *educational association administrator, business owner*
Frank, Alan I W *manufacturing executive*
Frank, Ronald William *lawyer*
Franklin, Kenneth Ronald *management consultant*
Friday, Gilbert Anthony, Jr. *pediatrician*
Frolik, Lawrence Anton *lawyer, educator, consultant*
Fu, Weinong *electrical engineer*
Gale, Robert Lee *retired literature educator, critic*
Garraux, James D. *lawyer, metal products executive*
Geeseman, Robert George *lawyer*
Geibel, Sister Grace Ann *university president*
George, John Anthony *health corporation executive*
Gerard, Leo W. *labor union executive*
Gerjuoy, Edward *physicist*
Geskin, Larisa *dermatologist, researcher*
Giel, James Arthur, Jr. *employee benefits management*
Goldberg, Mark Joel *lawyer*
Goldstein, Bernard David *public health service officer, educator*
Goldstein, Donald Maurice *historian, educator*
Gollin, Susanne Merle *cell biologist, researcher*
Good, Candace R. *psychiatrist, educator*
Goodish, John H. *metal products executive*
Granati, Diane Alane *retired ophthalmic nurse*
Greenamyre, John Timothy *medical educator*
Grossmann, Ignacio Emilio *chemical engineering educator*
Grupp, Edward A. *arbitrator, prosecutor*
Guadagnino, Frank T. *lawyer*
Gulley, Joan Long *banker*
Gupta, Anil K. *philosophy professor*
Gurtin, Morton Edward *mathematics professor*
Guyaux, Joseph C. *corporate financial executive*
Hackett, Mary J. *lawyer*
Hackett, Stephanie R. *educational association administrator*
Haggerty, Gretchen R. *metal products executive*
Haley, Roy W. *finance company executive*
Hall-Stoodley, Luanne *science educator, researcher*
Halpern, Richard I. *lawyer*
Hansen, Stephen Christian *banker*
Hardesty, Robert Lynch *surgeon, educator*
Harrell, Edward Harding *wine festival executive*
Harris, Ann Birgitta Sutherland *art historian*
Harrold, Ronald Thomas *research scientist*
Harth, Sidney *musician, educator*
Hartman, Ronald G. *lawyer*
Harty, James Quinn *lawyer*
Harvey, J. Brett *energy executive*
Hassey, L. Patrick *metal products executive*
Hatfull, Graham F. *microbiologist, educator*
Heckler, Frederick Roger *plastic surgeon*
Heilman, Marlin Stephen *medical products executive*
Hellman, Arthur David *law educator, consultant*
Helminiak, Daniel Albert *theologian, counselor*
Helmrich, Joel Marc *lawyer*
Hendrickson, Chris Thompson *civil and environmental engineering educator, researcher*
Herberman, Ronald Bruce *medical association administrator, immunologist*
Hernandez, William H. *chemical company executive*
Herring, David John *dean, law educator*
Herrington, Howard Ray *artist*
Hershey, Dale *lawyer, educator*
Hershey, Nathan *lawyer, educator*
Hicks, Wendell *history professor, political scientist, publishing executive*
Higgs, C. Fred III *mechanical engineer, educator*
Hill, John Howard *retired lawyer*
Hillenbrand, David M. *museum administrator*
Hillman, Henry Lea *investment company executive*
Hitt, Leo N. *lawyer, educator*
Hoburg, James Frederick *electrical engineering educator*
Hollingsworth, Samuel Hawkins, Jr. *bassist*
Hollis, Ralph L. *science educator*
Holzner, Burkart *retired sociologist, educator*
Horowitz, Carole Spiegel *landscape contractor*
Hull, John Daniel, IV, *lawyer, writer*
Humphrey, Watts Sherman *information technology executive, writer*
Hunker, Jeffrey *dean*
Huntington, James Cantine, Jr. *retired equipment manufacturing company executive*
Hurnyak, Christina Kaiser *lawyer*
Ijiri, Yuji *finance educator*
Jacoud, Adriana *art director*
Janis, Allen Ira *retired physicist, educator*
Jannetta, Peter Joseph *neurosurgeon, educator*
Jarrett, Fredric *surgeon, educator*
Jefferson, Joseph Murray *banker*
Jenkins, Georgann Klaus *librarian*
Jeremiah, Barbara S. *metal products executive*
Jin, Tao *research scientist*
Johnson, Richard J. *bank executive*
Johnson, Robert Alan *lawyer*
Johson, Michael Pennington *finance educator, consultant*
Jones, Craig Ward *retired lawyer*
Jones, Elizabeth Winifred *biology professor*
Jones, James M. *lawyer*
Jordan, Angel Goni *electrical and computer engineering educator*
Jordan, Gregory B. *lawyer*
Josey, E(lonnie) J(Unius) *librarian, retired state agency administrator*
Joyce, Judith Marie *radiologist*
Kalis, Peter John *lawyer*
Kamienska-Carter, Eva Hanna *designer, artist*
Kassam, Amin B. *neurosurgeon, educator*

Kelly, Edward J. III *diversified financial services company executive*
Kenrick, Charles William *lawyer*
Kerber, Frank John *retired diplomat*
Ketter, David Lee *lawyer*
Khosla, Pradeep Kumar *engineering educator*
Kiger, Robert William *botanist, science historian, educator, researcher*
Kilkeary, Kevin P. *hospitality executive*
Kim, Yongbok *physicist*
King, Elaine A. *curator, art historian, critic*
King, Robert Alan *lawyer*
King, William Richard *business educator, writer, consultant*
Klatzky, Roberta Lou *psychologist, educator*
Klett, Edwin L. *lawyer*
Knox, Charles Graham *lawyer*
Kochanek, Patrick Michael *pediatrician, educator*
Koedel, Robert Craig *minister, historian, educator*
Krasik, Carl *lawyer, bank executive*
Krebs, Robert Alan *lawyer*
Kriebel, Charles Hosey *management sciences educator*
Kryder, Mark Howard *computer and electrical engineering executive, educator, consultant*
Kuehm, Julie K. *nurse, educator*
Kupfer, David J. *psychiatry professor*
Kutka, J. James, Jr. *metal products executive*
Kydland, Finn E. *economics professor*
LaJohn, Lawrence Anthony *research scientist*
Lally-Green, Maureen Ellen *judge, educator*
Larsen, Ronald L. *dean, information scientist, educator*
Laughlin, David Eugene *materials scientist, educator, metallurgist, consultant*
Lave, Judith Rice *economics professor*
Lazo, John Stephen *science educator, director*
LeBeau, Dick *professional football coach and retired player*
Leech, Frederick C. *lawyer*
Lego, Paul Edward *retired manufacturing executive*
Lehoczky, John Paul *statistics educator*
Leibowitz, Marvin *lawyer*
Lemieux, Mario *professional sports team executive and retired hockey player*
Leney, George Willard *retired consulting engineer*
Lenhart, Cheryl Hayes *nursing administrator, consultant*
Leo, Peter Andrew *columnist, educator*
Letwin, Jeffrey William *lawyer*
Levin, Golan *artist, composer, engineer*
Levine, Arthur Samuel *pediatric hematologist, dean, educator, oncologist, researcher*
Levine, Macy Irving *physician*
Levine, T. Barry *cardiologist, educator*
Li, Ching-Chung *electrical engineering educator*
Litman, Roslyn Margolis *lawyer*
Lopes, Jerry *broadcast executive*
Lorensen, Frederick Hamilton *educational administrator, consultant*
Lovett, Robert G. *lawyer*
Lunsford, Lawrence Dade *medical educator*
Lyjak Chorazy, Anna Julia *pediatrician, educator, retired health facility administrator*
Magovern, James Anthony *thoracic surgeon*
Maher, James Vincent, Jr. *physics professor, academic administrator*
Mahone, Glenn R. *lawyer*
Malkin, Evgeni *professional hockey player*
Maly, Wojciech P. *engineering educator, researcher*
Marazita, Mary Louise *genetics researcher*
Mason, Matthew Thomas *robotics researcher*
Mason-Hipkins, Patricia *minister*
Massalski, Thaddeus Bronislaw *materials scientist, educator*
Matyjaszewski, Krzysztof *chemist, educator*
Mazzaferro, Kathryn E. *statistician, researcher*
McAvoy, Bruce Ronald *engineer, consultant*
McCafferty, Leo Raymond *plastic surgeon*
McCallum, Bennett Tarlton *economist, educator*
McCartney, Robert Charles *retired lawyer*
McClendon, Michele Rosalind *literature educator*
McConnell-Serio, Suzie Theresa *women's college basketball coach, retired professional basketball player*
McDevitt, Jerry S. *lawyer*
McDuffie, Keith A. *literature educator*
McGough, Walter Thomas, Jr. *lawyer*
McGuire, Timothy William *economics and management educator, dean*
McKinney, Donald Joseph *music educator, musician*
McLaughlin, John Sherman *lawyer*
Means, Dwight Bardeen, Jr. *financial consultant, educator*
Mehalik, Matthew M. *industrial engineer, educator*
Meisel, Alan *law educator*
Melani, Kenneth R. *insurance company executive*
Mello-Thoms, Claudia *medical educator, researcher*
Meltzer, Allan H. *economist, educator*
Messner, Robert Thomas *lawyer, bank executive*
Meyers, Jerry Ivan *lawyer*
Mickle, Marlin Homer *electrical engineer, educator*
Miller, David William *historian, educator*
Miller, Ronald Lynn *director*
Miller, Rush Glenn, Jr. *library director*
Miller, William Charles *theological educator, minister*
Milnes, Arthur George *electrical engineer, educator*
Milsom, Robert Cortlandt *banker, director*
Minnaugh, Mark J *food products/retail grocery executive*
Minnigh, Joel Douglas *library director*
Mistick, Barbara Knaus *library director*
Mitchell, George Charles *diplomat, international consultant, mediator, educator, writer*
Moore, Pearl B. *retired nursing educator*
Moore, Robert Yates *neuroscience educator*
Morgan, M(illett) Granger *electrical engineering educator, researcher*
Morningstar, Colin Jon *physicist, researcher*
Mosesso, Vincent Nicholas, Jr. *emergency physician, health facility administrator*
Muder, Robert Richard *physician, epidemiologist*
Mulsant, Benoit Henri *psychiatrist, educator, medical researcher*
Muluk, Satish Chandra *vascular surgeon*
Münck, Eckard *chemistry professor*
Murdoch, David Armor *lawyer*
Murdoch, Robert Whitten *lawyer*
Murrin, Regis Doubet *retired lawyer*
Mutale, Christian Thales *research scientist*
Mutterperl, William Charles *lawyer, corporate financial executive*
Myers, Eugene Nicholas *otolaryngologist, educator*
Nagle, John Frederick *physicist*
Naugle, Louis A. *lawyer*
Navetta, Christopher J. *metal products executive*
Needleman, Herbert Leroy *psychiatrist, pediatrician*
Neel, John Dodd *cemetery executive*
Neufeld, Ronald David *environmental engineer, educator*
Neuman, Charles P. *electrical and computer engineering educator*
Newlin, William Rankin *lawyer*
Nielsen, Paul Douglas *engineering executive, retired military officer*
Noeckert, Robert J. *ophthalmologist, educator*
Nogay, Arlie R. *lawyer*
Nollen, Meg (Margaret Roach Nollen) *food products executive*
Nordenberg, Mark Alan *academic administrator, law educator*
Norris, James Harold *lawyer*
Ober, Russell John, Jr. *lawyer*
O'Connor, Edward Gearing *lawyer*
O'Donnell, William James *engineering executive*
Oeler, Robert P. *bank executive*
Ogul, Morris Samuel *political science professor, consultant*
Olson, Stephen M(ichael) *lawyer*
Omiros, George James *medical foundation executive*
O'Neill, Paul Henry *former secretary of the treasury*
Orenstein, David M. *medical educator*
Orr, Terrence S. *dancer, ballet master, artistic director*
Orsatti, Ernest Benjamin *lawyer*
Packard, Rochelle Sybil *retired elementary school educator*
Palevsky, Paul Marc *nephrologist, educator*
Pardini, James Christopher *musician, conductor, composer*
Partanen, Carl Richard *biology professor*
Paul, Robert Arthur *steel company executive*
Paulston, Christina Bratt *linguistics educator*
Pennell, Daniel Mark *researcher*
Perel, James Maurice *pharmacology and psychiatry educator, researcher*
Perloff, Robert *psychologist, educator*
Perry, Jon Robert *lawyer*
Peterman, Donna Cole *communications executive*
Petersen, Jean Snyder *educational association administrator*
Peterson, Robert Scott *electrical engineer*
Pettit, Frederick Sidney *metallurgical engineering educator, department chairman*
Phelps, Daniel Christopher *information scientist, researcher*
Phillips, Larry Edward *lawyer*
Picadio, Anthony Peter *lawyer*
Plazek, Donald John *materials scientist, educator*
Plowman, Jack Wesley *lawyer*
Pohl, Paul Michael *lawyer*
Polamalu, Troy *professional football player*
Pollack, Ian Fredric *physician, researcher*
Post, Peter David *lawyer*
Posvar, Mildred Miller *opera singer*
Powderly, William H. III *lawyer*
Pudlin, Helen Pomerantz *lawyer*
Pusateri, David P. *lawyer*
Quigley, Matthew Richard *neurosurgeon*
Quinn, Clark Nives *psychologist, consultant*
Rago, John Thomas *law educator*
Randolph, Robert DeWitt *lawyer*
Rathke, Sheila Wells *strategic planning and marketing executive*
Ravenstahl, Luke R. *mayor*
Rawski, Evelyn Sakakida *history professor*
Raynovich, George, Jr. *retired lawyer*
Rebei, Adnan *physicist, researcher*
Rebich, Lois J. *elementary school educator*
Recchi, Mark *professional hockey player*
Reddy, Raj *science educator, academic administrator*
Reed, W. Franklin *lawyer*
Reichblum, Audrey Rosenthal *public relations and publishing executive*
Rescher, Nicholas *philosopher, author, educator*
Resnick, Robert *physicist, researcher*
Restivo, James John, Jr. *lawyer*
Richardson, J. William *hotel executive*
Richey, Cynthia K. *library director*
Richey, P. Jerome *lawyer, energy executive*
Ritchey, Patrick William *lawyer*
Roberts, Gary *professional hockey player*
Roethlisberger, Ben *professional football player*
Rogers, Robert Mark *physician*
Rohr, James Edward *diversified financial services company executive*
Rollett, Rebecca A. *musician, director*
Romoff, Jeffrey Alan *healthcare executive*
Roof, Robert L. *broadcast executive, sales executive*
Rooney, Daniel M. *professional sports team executive*
Rosen, Richard David *lawyer*
Rosenberg, Jerome Laib *chemist, educator*
Rosenberger, Bryan David *lawyer*
Ross, Eunice Latshaw *retired judge*
Ross, Madelyn Ann *academic administrator, newspaper editor*
Roth, Loren H. *psychiatrist*
Rudy, Ellen Beam *nursing educator*
Ruh, Edwin *ceramic engineer, consultant, researcher*
Ruskin, Ryan Scott *packaging company executive*
Russell, Richard A. *lawyer*
Russo, Linda M. *pediatric cardiologist*
Saaty, Thomas Lorie *science educator*
St. Clair, Gloriana Strange *librarian, dean*
Sanfilippo, Joseph Salvatore *gynecologic endocrinologist, educator*
Savvides, Marios *electrical and computer engineer, research professor*
Saykiewicz-Sajkiewicz, Jan Napoleon *marketing educator*
Schatten, Gerald Phillip *stem cell biologist, reproductive biologist, educator*
Schaub, Marilyn McNamara *theology studies educator*
Scheinholtz, Leonard Louis *lawyer*
Schorr-Ribera, Hilda Keren *psychologist*
Schwab, Arthur James *lawyer*
Schwass, Gary L. *utilities executive*
Schwendeman, Paul William *lawyer*
Sekerka, Robert Floyd *physics and mathematics professor*
Seol, Dai-Wu *geneticist, educator*
Shea, John Joseph *electrical engineer*
Sheon, Aaron *art historian, educator*
Sherman, Frederick Scott *pediatric cardiologist*
Shero, Ray (Rejean Shero) *professional sports team executive*
Shin, Sungjae *nutritionist*
Shribman, David Marks *editor*
Shuman, Joseph Duff *lawyer*
Sieg, Wilfried *philosophy educator*
Siker, Ephraim S. *anesthesiologist*
Silverman, Arnold Barry *lawyer*
Simaan, Marwan *electrical engineering educator*
Simmons, Richard L. *surgeon*
Simon, Jacob Matthew *lawyer*
Simpson, Daniel H. *ambassador*
Singer, Paul Meyer *lawyer*
Skwaryk, Robert Francis *judge*
Smartschan, Glenn Fred *educational consultant*
Smorey-Giger, Marcy *lawyer*
Snoke, David Wayne *physicist, researcher*
Snyderman, Carl Henry *otolaryngologist*
Sokulski, Gary A. *lawyer*
Solano, Francis X., Jr. *internist*
Soran, Z. Ozlem *medical educator*
Spector, Alfred Zalmon *computer specialist, educator, consultant*
Stack, Edward W. *retail executive*
Stahl, Laddie L. *engineering company executive*
Standish, William Lloyd *judge*
Star, Alexander *chemist, educator*
Stein, Adam Matthew *military officer*
Stein, Bradley Daniel *child and adolescent psychiatrist, researcher*
Stepanian, Steven Arvid, II, *lawyer, financial consultant*
Sterling, Thomas W. *metal products executive*
Stevens, William Talbert *financial services executive*
Stirewalt, John Newman *coal company executive*
Strader, James David *lawyer*
Straub, Terrence D. *metal products executive*
Strauss, Robert Philip *economics professor*
Stroyd, Arthur Heister, Jr. *lawyer*
Surma, John P., Jr. *metal products executive*
Sussna, Edward *economist, educator*
Sweeney, Clayton Anthony *lawyer, business executive*
Sykora, Petr *professional hockey player*
Symons, Edward Leonard, Jr. *lawyer, educator, investment advisor*
Tarasi, Louis Michael, Jr. *lawyer*
Tarr, Joel Arthur *historian, educator*
Therrien, Michel *professional hockey coach*
Thomas, Paul D. *metal products executive, human resources specialist*
Thompson, Thomas Martin *lawyer*
Thorne, John Reinecke *finance educator, venture capitalist*
Thurman, Andrew Edward *lawyer*
Tomlin, Mike *professional football coach*
Tracy, Jim (James Edward Tracy) *professional baseball manager*
Trotter, Joe William, Jr. *history professor, writer*
Turner, Harry Woodruff *lawyer*
Ubinger, John Walter, Jr. *lawyer*
Udler, Rubin Yakovlevich *linguist*
Ummer, James Walter *lawyer*
Unkovic, John Clark *lawyer*
Valdés-Pérez, Raul E. *computer scientist, researcher*
Van Dusen, Albert Clarence *academic administrator*
Van Kirk, Thomas L. *lawyer*
Vater, Charles J. *lawyer*
Veeder, Peter Greig *lawyer*
Vo, Evanly *organic chemist*
Vogel, Victor Gerald *medical educator, researcher*
Vogrin, Joseph Edward III *lawyer*
von Ahn, Luis *computer science educator, computer scientist*
von Waldow, Arnd N. *lawyer*
Wabby, James Patrick *quality assurance professional, educator*
Wald, Niel *public health educator*
Walls Perry, J(oyce) Lorraine *elementary school educator*
Walton, James Mellon *investment company executive*
Walton, Jon David *lawyer*
Wannstedt, David Raymond *college football coach, former professional football coach*
Ward, Hines, Jr. *professional football player*
Warman, Guy Lee *lawyer*
Wedhsler, Lawrence Richard *neurologist, educator*
Weidman, John Carl, II, *education and sociology educator, consultant*
Weingartner, Rudolph Herbert *philosophy educator*
Weis, Joseph Francis, Jr. *federal judge*
Wessels, Daniel L. *lawyer*
Westerberg, Arthur William *retired chemical engineering professor*
Wetzel, Amanda Grace *secondary school educator*
White, Robert Marshall *retired physicist, educator, government official, consultant*
Whitehead, Paul *lawyer, labor union administrator*
Whittaker, William L. (Red Whittaker) *engineering educator, research scientist*
Wilkins, David George *fine arts educator*
Wilkinson, James Allan *lawyer, healthcare executive*
Willard, Louis Charles *librarian*
Willke, Theodore Lawrence *research facility director*
Wilson, Frances Helen *retired occupational therapist*
Wilson, Mark Lowell *philosopher, educator*
Winkleblack, Arthur B. *food products executive*
Winter, Peter Michael *anesthesiologist, educator*
Wohleber, Lynne Farr *archivist, librarian*
Woo, Savio Lau-Yuen *bioengineering educator*
Woods, Allan P. *information technology executive*
Wycoff, William Mortimer *lawyer*
Xia, Yunkai *engineer*
Yang, Wesley *lawyer*
Yellon, Robert Forrest *surgeon, medical educator*
Yorsz, Stanley *lawyer*
Young, Hugh David *physics professor, writer*
Zafonte, Ross D. *physiatrist*
Zanardelli, John Joseph *healthcare organization executive*
Zanic, Michael G. *lawyer*
Zappala, Stephen A. *state supreme court justice*
Zeevi, Adriana *microbiologist, immunologist*
Zeolla, Kim Anne *minister*
Ziegler, Arthur P., Jr. *foundation executive*
Ziegler, Donald Emil *retired federal judge*
Zoffer, H. Jerome *business educator, dean*

Pittston Township
Renfer, James Allen *elementary school educator*

Plymouth
Musto, Joseph John *lawyer*

Plymouth Meeting
McCausland, Margaret A. *lawyer, educator*
Nobel, Joel J. *biomedical researcher*
Siegal, Jacob J. *management and financial consultant*
Spiers-Lopez, Pernille (Pernille Lopez) *consumer products company executive*

Pocono Summit
Yorke-Viney, Sally Anne *elementary school educator*

Port Matilda
Holt, Frieda M. *nursing educator, retired academic administrator*

Port Royal
Wert, Jonathan Maxwell, II, *management consultant*

Portland
Groff, Arthur M. *controller*

Pottstown
Coulter, Kathleen Marie *psychotherapist, consultant*
Hergert, Herbert Lawrence *retired consultant*
Hylton, Thomas James *author*
Mitchell, Eric Ehrman *photographer, stock broker*
Nash, William Lewis III *retired music educator*
Nestler, Patricia C. *English professor*

Pottsville
Tamulonis, Frank Louis, Jr. *lawyer*

Presto
Moeller, Audrey Carolyn *retired energy company executive, corporate secretary*
Pfaff, Robert James *retired lawyer*

Punxsutawney
Dinsmore, Roberta Joan Maier *library director*

Quakertown
Babb, Lisa Marie *physical education educator*

Quarryville
Harris, Robert Laird *minister, theology educator emeritus*

Radnor
Bertolino, Dean A. *lawyer*
Buck, James Mahlon, Jr. *venture capitalist*
Cunningham, James Gerald, Jr. *transportation company executive*
Eagleson, William Boal, Jr. *banker*
Hemphill, James S. *investment management executive, financial advisor*
Liang, Bailin *immunologist*
Paier, Adolf Arthur *management consultant*
Rosnow, Ralph Leon *psychologist, educator*
Sicoli, Mary Louise Corbin *psychologist, educator*
Silvestry, Frank E. *cardiologist*
Simon, David Frederick *lawyer*

Reading
Ayala, Joe Serrano *marketing professional, personal trainer*
Bell, Frances Louise *medical technologist*
Brightbill, David John *lawyer, former state legislator*

Carlino, Peter M. *gaming company executive*
DeEsch, Vasti F. *museum registrar*
Dietrich, Bruce Leinbach *museum administrator, astronomer, educator*
Duff, Michael A. *lawyer, transportation executive*
Garrison, Matthew Moore *artist, educator*
Hart, LeRoy Banks *systems administrator, director*
Hornish, Sam, Jr. *race car driver*
Kiehne, Frank Charles, Jr. *foundation administrator*
Kraras, Gust C. *hotel executive*
Linton, Jack Arthur *lawyer*
Lusch, Charles Jack *oncologist, director*
Mack, Sara Rohrbach *librarian, educator*
McCullough, Eileen (Eileen McCullough LePage, Elli McCullough) *financial consultant, writer, editor, educator*
Moriarty, John Klinge *electrical engineer, consultant*
Pumariega, Andres Julio *medical administrator, educator, researcher*
Pumariega, JoAnne Buttacavoli *mathematics educator*
Rochowicz, John Anthony, Jr. *mathematician, mathematics educator, physics educator*
Rodgers, Lana Loretta Lusch *retired elementary school educator*
Sauer, Elissa Swisher *nursing educator*
Shin, Dong-Hee *communication technology educator*
Shultz, Lois Frances Casho *nursing supervisor*
Watcke, Thomas C. *art educator*
Zug, Elizabeth E. *concert pianist, educator*

Red Lion
Hartman, Charles Henry *transportation and not-for-profit executive, educator*

Richboro
Burtt, Larice Annadel Roseman *artist*
Dott, John R. *marine life administrator*
Higginbotham, Kenneth James *finance company executive*
Maholic, Nancy L. *nurse*

Ridgway
Aiello, Gennaro C. *insurance company executive*

Ridley Park
Walls, William Walton, Jr. *management consultant*

Riegelsville
Banko, Ruth Caroline *retired library director*

Rimersburg
Rush, Kevin Arland *music educator*

Royersford
Black, Jeffrey P. *manufacturing executive*
Jennings, Kris *music educator*
Krell-Morris, Cheri Lee *psychologist*
Rhoads, Michael Dennis *sales executive*

Russellton
Curtis, Paula Annette *elementary and secondary education educator*

Rutledge
Senior, Robert Thomas *retired military officer*

Rydal
Boreen, Henry Isaac *computer company executive*
Fernberger, Marilyn Friedman *not-for-profit developer, consultant, volunteer*
Heebner, Albert Gilbert *retired economist, educator, bank executive*
Johnson, Waine Cecil *dermatologist, educator*
Reese, Francis Edward *retired chemical company executive, consultant*

Sadsburyville
Gellman, Gloria Gae Seeburger Schick *marketing professional*

Saegertown
Ralph, NancyJo *retired music educator*

Saint Davids
Bertsch, Frederick Charles III *appraiser, finance company executive*
Denenberg, Herbert Sidney *journalist, lawyer, educator, retired state official*
Sheftel, Roger Terry *merchant banker*

Saint Marys
Johnson, J. M. Hamlin *manufacturing executive*

Saint Peters
Detterline, Milton E., Jr. *minister*

Sayre
Ali, Arshad *medical researcher*
Bentley, Dianne H. Glover *minister, consultant*
Dinich, Michael Andrew *financial planner*
Moody, Robert Adams *neurosurgeon*

Schnecksville
Hansel, James Gordon *retired engineer, educator*
Labbiento, Julianne Marie *mathematics professor*
Malozzi, Jason Anthony *mathematics professor*
Molano, Charles Hernando *Spanish professor, consultant*
Schillow, Ned William *mathematics professor*

Scottdale
Lee, John Lawrence, Jr. *educational administrator*

Scranton
Blewitt, Thomas Michael *chief US magistrate judge*
Brandreth, Elizabeth Anne *library director*
Browning, William J. *child protective service director*
Burke, Henry Patrick *lawyer*
Conaboy, Richard Paul *federal judge*
De Celles, Charles Edouard *theologian, educator*
Elvidge, Christina Marie *director*
Gross, Patricia A. *education educator*
Haggerty, James Joseph *lawyer*
Howley, James McAndrew *lawyer*
Kosik, Edwin Michael *federal judge*
Lawhon, Patricia Patton *literature and language professor, writer educator*
Lynett, William Ruddy *publishing and broadcast executive*
Marino, Thomas A. *prosecutor, lawyer*
McKenna, Ann K. *nutritionist, educator*
Nealon, William Joseph *federal judge*
O'Malley, Carlon Martin *judge*
Panuska, Joseph Allan *retired academic administrator*
Parente, William Joseph *political science professor*
Passon, Richard Henry *retired academic administrator, language educator*
West, Daniel Jones, Jr. *health care consultant, educator*
Yamanouchi, Midori *social sciences educator*
Zaydon, Jemille Ann *language educator, communications educator*

Selinsgrove
Lemons, L. Jay *academic administrator*
Viker, Erik *theater educator*

Sellersville
Rilling, David Carl *surgeon*

Sewickley
Bly, James Charles, Jr. *finance company executive*
Bouchard, James Paul *metal products executive*
Fells, Charles Dayton *civil engineer, educator*
Grubba, Matthew John *journalist*
Jehle, Michael Edward *financial advisor, lawyer*
Kornetchuk, Elena *curator, art dealer*
Maurer, Richard Michael *investment company executive*
Milne, Christopher *photographer, journalist, educator*
Swann, Lynn Curtis *sportscaster, former professional football player*

Sharon
Kovac, Shirley Ann *retired elementary school educator*

Sharpsburg
Drango, Mark A. *mechanical services specialist*

Shavertown
Simon, Herbert Bernheimer *sculptor*

Shillington
Blum, Robin N. *elementary school educator*

Shippensburg
Basler, Linda Gerber *retired elementary school educator*
Cart, Jon Robert *music educator, musician*
Ceddia, Anthony Francis *university administrator*
France, Olin Kenneth, Jr. *psychologist*
Vaughan, Elizabeth Jean *education educator*

Shiremanstown
Nesbit, William Terry *small business owner, consultant*

Silverdale
Carney, Shannon Maureen *small business owner, educator*

Sinking Spring
Bausher, Verne C(harles) *retired bank executive*

Slippery Rock
Iossifova, Albena Roumenova *business educator, researcher*
McIlvaine, Robert Morton *literature educator*
Payne, Ursula Octavia *choreographer, educator*

Solebury
Anthonisen, George Rioch *sculptor, artist*
Cross, Robert William *lawyer, venture capitalist*
Keep, Charles Russell, Jr. *foundation administrator*
Valentine, H. Jeffrey *legal association executive*

Somerset
Kline, Eva Jane *library services administrator, educator*
Nair, Velupillai Krishnan *cardiologist*
Rose-Deal, Mary Frances *language educator*

Souderton
Hoeflich, Charles Hitschler *banker*

South Canaan
Herman, *archbishop, head of Orthodox Church in America*

South Park
Furman, L. Robert *principal, music educator*
Lotze, Barbara *retired physicist*

Southampton
Bendiner, Robert *writer, editor*
Gniewek, Debra Lyman *school librarian, consultant*
Lenox, Gina Marie *music educator*

Southeastern
Amichetti, Dennis Joseph *advertising and marketing executive*
Rassbach, Herbert David *marketing executive*

Spring City
Britcher, Michael *music educator*

Spring House
Payn, Clyde Francis *technology company executive*
Rosoff, William A. *lawyer*
van Steenwyk, John Joseph *healthcare plan consultant*

Springfield
Maclay, Donald Merle *retired lawyer*
Sing, Robert Fong *physician*

State College
Aberg, Gilbert S. *retired writer*
Albright, Gifford Harry *retired architectural engineering educator, consultant*
Barash Coppersmith, Marian Ungar *magazine publisher*
Barnoff, Robert Mark *civil engineering educator*
Book, Edward Raymond *retired trade association administrator*
Boone, Tracy Marie *mathematics professor*
Brault, Gerard Joseph *French language educator*
Brown, John Lawrence, Jr. *electrical engineering educator*
Byrom, Fletcher Lauman *chemical manufacturing company executive*
Dupuis, Victor Lionel *retired curriculum and instruction educator*
Foderaro, Anthony Harolde *nuclear engineering educator*
Garrett, Steven Lurie *physicist*
Goldschmidt, Arthur Eduard, Jr. *historian, educator, writer*
Grimes, Dale Mills *physics and electrical engineering educator*
Haas, John C. *architect*
Hettche, L. Raymond *engineering educator, retired research scientist*
Huck, John Lloyd *pharmaceutical executive*
Isenberg, Ann Marie *psychologist*
Katok, Anatole *mathematics professor*
Klein, Philip Alexander *economist*
Lamb, Robert Edward *retired diplomat, professional society administrator*
Madjid, A. Hamid *retired science educator*
Olson, Donald Richard *mechanical engineering educator*
Parsonage, K. Susan *artist*
Phillips, Janet Colleen *retired educational association administrator, editor*
Redford, Donald Bruce *historian, archaeologist*
Remick, Forrest Jerome, Jr. *former university official*
Robinett, Betty Wallace *linguist, educator*
Schaie, K(laus) Warner *human development and psychology educator*
Schmalstieg, William Riegel *retired Slavic languages educator*
Sibul, Leon Henry *electrical engineer*
Subler, Edward Pierre *advertising executive*
Xu, Jinchao *mathematics professor*

Strasburg
Bell, Kurt Robert *archivist*
Lindsay, George Carroll *former museum director*
Morton, D. Holmes *physician*

Sugarloaf
Waldron, Theodore Charles *physician*

Sunbury
Ely, Donald J(ean) *retired clergyman, secondary school educator*
Rich, Norman S. *food service executive*
Saylor, Charles Horace *lawyer, judge*
Weis, Robert Freeman *supermarket company executive*

Swarthmore
Bilaniuk, Oleksa Myron *physicist, researcher*
Bloom, Alfred Howard *academic administrator, educator*
Carey, William Bacon *pediatrician, educator*
Devin, Lee (Phillip) *researcher, consultant, dramaturg, author*
Elman, Gerry Jay *lawyer*
Field, Dorothy Maslin *minister*
Frost, Jerry William *religious studies educator, history professor, retired library director, researcher*
Gilbert, Scott Frederick *biologist, educator, author*
Hungerford, Constance Cain *art educator*
Keith, Jennie *anthropology educator, academic administrator, writer*
Kelemen, Charles F. *computer science educator*
Krendel, Ezra Simon *systems and human factors engineering consultant*
Krizek, Edwin John *marketing professional*
Marecek, Jeanne *psychologist, educator*
North, Helen Florence *classicist, educator*
O'Connell, Virginia Adams *sociologist*
Ostwald, Martin *retired classicist*
Pasternack, Robert Francis *chemistry professor*
Redden, Taylor Tilghman *musician*

Swiftwater
Brooks, Joyce Maria *music educator*
Bybel, Michael John *medical researcher*
Nalli, Sandro *research scientist, consultant*
Shirazi, Arash *research scientist*

Tarentum
Koharchik, Thomas David *music educator*

Telford
Boughter, Barbara B. *retired mathematics educator*

Temple
Denaro, Anthony Thomas *psychiatrist*
Stump, Richard Carl *environmental services administrator, consultant*

Thorndale
Hodess, Arthur Bart *cardiologist*

Tioga
Sullins, Ken *mathematics, science and computer science educator*

Titusville
Campasino, Ellen Marie *elementary school educator*

Tobyhanna
Lapidus, Arnold *mathematician, educator*

Tower City
Adams, Susan L. *art educator*

Townville
Rudy, Elaine Kim *elementary school educator*

Tunkhannock
Sherwood, Donald Lewis *former congressman*

Union City
Thomas, Paul Milton *retired science educator*

Uniontown
Coldren, Ira Burdette, Jr. *lawyer*
Duvall, Hollie Jean *music educator*

Unionville
De Marino, Donald Nicholson *federal agency administrator, diversified financial services company executive*
Pitts, Joseph R. (Joe Pitts) *congressman*

University Park
Allcock, Harry R. *chemistry professor*
Andrews, George Eyre *mathematics professor*
Antle, Charles Edward *statistics educator*
Askov, Eunice May *adult education educator*
Azmy, Yousry Youssef *computational scientist*
Badding, John Victor *chemistry professor*
Barlow, Jesse Louis *computer scientist, educator*
Barnes, Hubert Lloyd *geochemistry educator*
Blackadar, Alfred Kimball *meteorologist, educator*
Bose, Nirmal Kumar *electrical engineer, mathematics educator*
Brenchley, Jean Elnora *microbiologist, researcher, science administrator*
Buskirk, Elsworth Robert *physiologist, educator*
Cahir, John Joseph *meteorologist, educator, educational administrator*
Castleman, Albert Welford, Jr. *physical chemist, educator*
Chan, Moses Hung Wai *physicist, researcher*
Coleman, Michael Murray *polymer science educator*
Cosgrove, Daniel Joseph *biology educator*
Cross, Leslie Eric *electrical engineering educator*
Davids, Norman *engineering educator, researcher*
De Jong, Gordon Frederick *demography professor, director*
Dugda, Mulugeta Tuji *education educator*
Dutton, John Altnow *meteorologist, educator*
Eaton, Nancy Ruth Linton *librarian, dean*
Ebitz, David MacKinnon *art historian, educator, museum director*
Fedoroff, Nina Vsevolod *research scientist, consultant, educator*
Ford, Donald Herbert *psychologist, educator*
Garoian, Charles Richard *artist, educator*
Garrison, Barbara Jane *chemistry professor*
Grenfell, Bryan Thomas *biology professor*
Halsey, Martha Taliaferro *Spanish language educator*
Hammes-Schiffer, Sharon *chemist, educator*
Hammond, J. D. *retired academic administrator*
Hedges, Stephen Blair *biology professor, researcher*
Holl, John William *engineering educator*
Hosler, Charles Luther, Jr. *meteorologist, educator*
Howell, Benjamin Franklin, Jr. *geophysicist, educator*
Humphrey, Craig Reed *social studies educator*
Irwin, Mary Jane *engineering educator*
Jackman, Lloyd Miles *chemistry professor*
Joyce, William Leonard *librarian*
Kabel, Robert Lynn *chemical engineering professor*
Kadir, Djelal *literature educator*
Knott, Kenneth *industrial engineering educator, consultant*
Lima, Robert *language educator*
Liu, Zi-Kui *materials engineer, educator*
Mahan, Gerald Dennis *physicist, researcher*
Manbeck, Harvey B. *agricultural and biological engineer, educator*
Mann, Michael E. *physicist, educator, climatologist*
Mayers, Stanley Penrose, Jr. *public health service officer, educator*
McCormick, Barnes Warnock *aerospace engineering educator*
McKeown, James Charles *finance educator, consultant*
Muhlert, Jan Keene *art museum director*
Naydan, Michael M. *foreign language educator*
Osseo-Asare, Kwadwo *engineering educator*
Paterno, Joe (Joseph Vincent Paterno) *college football coach*
Ramani, Raja Venkat *engineering educator*
Ray, William Jackson *psychologist*
Roy, Della Martin *materials science educator, researcher*
Roy, Rustum *citizen scientist*
Scanlon, Andrew *structural engineering educator*
Sen, Ayusman *chemistry professor*
Spanier, Graham Basil *academic administrator*
Stern, Robert Morris *gastroenterologist, psychologist, researcher*
Stout, Leon James *archivist, librarian*
Thatcher, Sanford Gray *publishing executive*
Thomas, James B. *dean, management educator*
Tittmann, Bernhard Rainer *engineering science and mechanics educator*

Todd Copley, Judith A. *engineering educator*
Vannice, M. Albert *chemical engineering professor, researcher*
Varghese, Oomman Kulathinthekkethil *materials scientist, researcher*
Vrentas, James Spiro *chemical engineering professor*
Weiss, Paul Storch *chemistry educator*
White, William Blaine *geochemist, researcher*
Winograd, Nicholas *chemist*
Wormley, David Neal *engineering educator*
Wysk, Richard A. *engineering educator, researcher*
Zabel, Diane Marion *school librarian*
Zhang, Qiming *engineering educator, researcher*

Upper Black Eddy
Wechsler, Gil *lighting designer*

Upper Darby
Crouse, Carol K. Mavromatis *elementary school educator*
Hudiak, David Michael *academic administrator, lawyer*
Pittman, Mia N. *educational association administrator, entrepreneur*

Upper Saint Clair
Raymond, Bruce Allen *retired surgeon, medical association administrator*

Valley Forge
Barton, R. Gregory *lawyer, investment company executive*
Bogle, John Clifton *investment company executive*
Brennan, John Joseph *mutual fund company executive*
Combs, Ann Laine *investment company executive, former federal agency administrator*
Dachowski, Peter Richard *manufacturing executive*
Erb, Robert Allan *physical scientist*
Kelly, Peter *energy executive*
Knauss, Robert H. *lawyer*
LaBoon, Lawrence Joseph *human resources specialist, consultant*
Mesher, John R. *lawyer*
Miller, Betty Brown *freelance writer*
Phelizon, Jean Francois *finance company executive*
Sprague, William Douglas *lawyer*
Stam, Heidi *lawyer*

Vandergrift
Aikins, Candace Sue *music educator, consultant*

Verona
Bruno, Louis Vincent *principal*
Demmler, John Henry *retired lawyer*

Villanova
Beck, Robert Edward *computer scientist, educator*
Bergquist, James Manning *history professor*
Bersoff, Donald Neil *lawyer, psychologist, educator*
Deshmukh, Venkatesh Suresh *education educator*
Dobbin, Edmund J. *former academic administrator*
Donohue, Peter M. *academic administrator, priest, theater educator, director*
Edwards, John Ralph *retired chemist, educator*
Fitzpatrick, M. Louise *dean, nursing educator*
Friend, Theodore Wood III *foundation executive, historian, writer*
Haynor, Patricia Manzi *nursing educator, consultant*
Heitzmann, Ray *education educator, athletic coach*
Helmetag, Charles Hugh *foreign language educator*
Hunt, John Mortimer, Jr. *classical studies educator*
Johannes, John Roland *political science professor, dean*
Langran, Robert Williams *political scientist, educator*
Lewis, Wayne H. *investment company executive*
Maule, James Edward *law educator*
McLaughlin, Philip VanDoren, Jr. *mechanical engineering educator, researcher, consultant*
Murphy, John Francis *law educator, consultant*
Nawrocki, David Norman *finance educator*
Norton, Douglas Evatt *mathematician, educator*
Papaefthymiou, Georgia C. *physicist, educator*
Phares, Alain Joseph *physicist, researcher*
Sahmoudi, Mohamed *computer scientist*
Sargent, Mark A. *dean, law educator*
Tomlinson, J. Richard *retired engineering services company executive*
Wright, Jay *men's college basketball coach*
Zearfoss, Herbert Keyser *retired lawyer*

Wallingford
Adamiec, Jean Kraus *retired advertising executive*
Cook, Harvey Carlisle *law enforcement official*
Morrison, Donald Franklin *statistician, educator*
Severdia, Anthony George *chemistry researcher*

Wapwallopen
Cardimona, Kimberly Marie *language educator*

Warminster
Ciao, Frederick J. *school system administrator, educator*
Hostovich, John Larry *lawyer*
Hull, Lewis Woodruff *manufacturing executive*
Kan, Kevin S. *automotive executive*
Thorne, John Watson III *advertising and marketing executive*

Warren
Ristau, Mark Moody *lawyer, consultant*

Warrendale
O'Donnell, James V. *apparel executive*

Rumbaugh, Max Elden, Jr. *professional society administrator*
Savitt, Kathy *marketing, apparel executive*

Warrington
Hostert, Leona Teressa *retired librarian, researcher*
Sigety, Elizabeth Donnem *lawyer*
Vosik, Wayne Gilbert *lawyer*
Ward, Hiley Henry *journalist, educator*

Washington
Erdner, Jon W. *small business owner, securities trader*
Haring-Smith, Tori *academic administrator*
Kastelic, Robert Frank *aerospace transportation executive*
Lerner, William C. *lawyer*
Richman, Stephen I. *lawyer*

Washington Boro
Snyder, John Jacob *researcher*

Washington Crossing
Kozlowski, Thomas Joseph, Jr. *lawyer, wealth management executive*
Roche, Gail Connor *editor*

Wayne
Annenberg, Leonore A. *foundation administrator*
Binder, David Franklin *lawyer, writer*
Carroll, Robert W. *retired management consultant*
Cole, Charles Chester, Jr. *academic administrator*
Conde, Cristobal I. *computer company executive*
Etris, Samuel Franklin *trade association research consultant*
Fabbri, Anne R. *critic, curator*
Freyer, Charles C. *lawyer*
Garrison, Guy Grady *librarian, educator*
Guerette, Susan M. *lawyer*
Kolar, Erik E. *real estate company executive*
Krutsick, Robert Stanley *retired science administrator*
Kyung, Yun Seung *biochemist, researcher*
Lefevre, Thomas Vernon *retired utilities executive*
Patel, Niraj B. *information technology executive*
Patterson, Scott David *lawyer*
Rabii, Patricia Berg *retired church administrator*
Rubley, Carole A. *state legislator*
Rush, James Edward *retired information scientist*
Salinas, Eliseo *research and development company executive, psychiatrist, researcher*
Silbey, Victoria E. *lawyer*
Sims, Robert John *financial planner*
Stayton, William Ralph *psychologist, educator*
Thelen, Edmund *research executive*
Ward, Keca B. *small business owner, consultant*
Wilson, Bruce Brighton *lawyer, retired transportation executive*
Wilson, James Lawrence *retired chemical company executive*
Yoskin, Jon William, II, *insurance company executive*
Yost, R. David (David Yost) *pharmaceutical executive*

Waynesboro
Coles, Robert Nelson, Sr. *religious organization administrator*
Cryer, Theodore Hudson *ophthalmologist, educator*
Martin, Harold G. *engineering consultant*

Waynesburg
Maguire, Mildred May *retired chemistry professor*

Weatherly
Molnar, Michael J. *artist, educator*

Wellsboro
Driskell, Lucile G. *artist*

Wernersville
Koenig, Robert Emil *clergyman*

West Chester
Archbold, William Cornell, Jr. *lawyer*
Babcock, Charles Witten, Jr. *lawyer*
Ballbach, John M. *wholesale distribution executive*
Blasiotti, Robert Vincent *accountant, consultant*
Bove, Patrice Magee *elementary school educator*
Burton, John Bryan *music educator*
Carter, Shawn David *protective services official*
Cox, Karen Michelle *finance educator, computer company executive*
Donatoni, Robert J. *lawyer*
Dunlop, Edward Arthur *computer company executive*
Ewing, Joseph Neff, Jr. *retired lawyer*
Gadsby, Robin Edward *chemicals executive*
Gallagher, Terrence Vincent *editor*
Gougher, Ronald Lee *language educator*
Griffith, Edward *judge*
Handzel, Steven Jeffrey *accountant*
Hanna, Colin Arthur *management consultant, political organization worker, consultant*
Heaps, Marvin Dale *retired food services company executive*
Heston, Thomas J. *historian, educator*
Hipple, Walter John *language educator*
Lamb, William H. *lawyer, former state supreme court justice*
Mahoney, William Francis *editor, writer*
McFarland, Ann Louise *music educator*
Meystel, Michael A. *Internet company executive*
Murray, Lawrence *management consultant*
Shaffer, Leigh S. *psychology professor*
Teti, Louis Nicholas *lawyer*
Zlotowski, Martin *psychologist*

West Conshohocken
Boenning, Henry Dorr, Jr. *investment banker*

Klimczuk, Stephen John *business executive, foundation director*
Lenfest, Harold FitzGerald *former cable television executive, lawyer*
Mullen, Eileen Anne *human resources executive*
Odell, Herbert *lawyer*
Sager, Margaret E.W. *lawyer*
Saul, Ralph Southey *diversified financial services company executive*
Savadove, Daniel C. *broadcast executive*
Schneider, John K. *financial advisor*
Teillon, Louis Pierre, Jr. *lawyer*
Templeton, John Marks, Jr. *retired pediatric surgeon, foundation administrator*

West Grove
Allman, Margo Hutz *sculptor, painter*
Allman, William Berthold *musician, engineer, consultant*
Olson, Leroy Calvin *retired educational administration educator*
Snow, James Byron, Jr. *otolaryngologist, research administrator, educator*

West Mifflin
Ardash, Garin *mechanical engineer*
Rosko, Maryann A. *nurse*

West Point
Buckland, Barry Christopher *chemical engineer*
Choi, Dennis W. *pharmaceutical executive, neurologist, educator*
Grabenstein, John Douglas *pharmacist, military officer*

West Reading
Sutherland, Robert D. *orthopedist, surgeon*

Wexford
Bossart, Paul Nathaniel, Jr. *geologist, geophysicist, consultant*
Stover, Richard L. *investor*

Whitehall
Tcherviakova, Olga A. *language educator*

Wilkes Barre
Baranoski, Joseph Thomas *music educator*
Casale, Alfred Stanley *thoracic and cardiovascular surgeon*
Hayes, Wilbur Frank *retired biology professor*
Hepp, John Henry, IV, *historian, lawyer*
Horoszy, Albert John *mathematics educator*
Lindemann, George L. *gas industry executive*
Loomis, Richard Morgan *literature and language educator*
McHale, Maureen Bernadette Kenny *controller*
Mech, Terrence Francis *library director*
O'Donnell, Catherine Rose *lawyer*
O'Hara, Thomas J. *priest, academic administrator, educator*
Roth, Eugene *lawyer*
Schwartz, Roger Alan *judge*
Ufberg, Murray *lawyer*
Yarmey, Richard Andrew *investment manager*

Williamsport
Buckman, Debra Ann *science educator*
Carlucci, William Philip *lawyer*
Jones, John E. III *judge*
Knecht, William L. *lawyer*
Largen, Joseph *retail executive, purchasing agent*
Martin, Thomas John *pediatrician, sports medicine physician*
Mason, Ardis J.P. *elementary school educator*
McClure, James Focht, Jr. *federal judge*
McDonald, Peyton Dean *brokerage house executive*
Muir, Malcolm *federal judge*
Rosebrough, Carol Belville *cable television company executive*
Trometter, Mary Gionta *chef, educator*
Vonada, Nicholas Andrew *information technology educator*
Wright, David C. *school system administrator*

Willow Grove
Asplundh, Christopher B. *tree service company executive*
Ohama, Gary Louis *dental ceramist*
Schiffman, Louis F. *management consultant*
Suer, Marvin David *architectural consultant*

Willow Hill
Dorand, Freda J. *music educator*

Willow Street
Blevins, William Edward *management consultant*
Coleman, Ernest Albert *plastics and materials consultant*
Henderson, Joseph Ralston *educator*
Jones, Joseph Louis *retired manufacturing executive*
Keiser, Paul Harold *retired hospital administrator*
Reese, Harry Edwin, Jr. *electronics executive*
Wesbury, Stuart Arnold, Jr. *health science association administrator, educator*
Yrigoyen, Charles, Jr. *retired church denomination executive*

Wilmerding
Kirk, Linda Louise *elementary school educator*

Wormleysburg
Cherewka, Michael *lawyer*
Grass, Alexander *retail executive*

Wyncote
Davis, Robert, Jr. *art educator, artist*
Ehrenkrantz, Dan *rabbi*
Koppel, Ross *sociology professor, researcher*
Wolfson, Ivan Richard *management consultant*

Wyndmoor
Brown, Gary Christian *ophthalmologist, director*
Pfeffer, Philip Elliot *biophysicist*

Strobaugh, Terence Philip, Jr. *molecular biologist, microbiologist*

Wynnewood
Alter, Milton *retired neurologist*
Anyanwu, Chukwuma Uchenna *clinical pharmacist, biomedical researcher*
Belinger, Harry Robert *retired business executive*
Camp, Kimberly N. *museum administrator, artist*
Frankl, William Stewart *cardiologist, educator*
Marks, Gerald *surgeon, educator*
Meyers, Mary Ann *foundation administrator, consultant, writer*
Robinson, Robert L. *retired diversified financial services company executive, lawyer*
Rosefsky, Jonathan Benensohn *pediatrician*
Rosen, Gerald Harris *physicist, consultant, educator*
Sanyour, Michael Louis, Jr. *diversified financial services company executive*
Sider, Ronald J. *theology educator, author*
Wadden, Thomas Anthony *psychologist, educator*
Zoler, Mitchel L. *journalist*

Wyomissing
Doherty, Edmond John *retired librarian*
Gebbia, Robert James *tax executive*
Gordon, Mildred Harriet Gross *hospital executive*
Hildreth, Eugene A. *physician, educator*

Yardley
Breitenfeld, Frederick, Jr. *retired educational consultant, broadcast executive*
Fraser, David William *epidemiologist*
Gilmour, D(avid) James *financial and systems analyst*
Hochreiter, Joseph Christian, Jr. *engineering company executive*
Huret, Barry S. *marketing professional, consultant*
Makadok, Stanley *management consultant*
Minter, Philip Clayton *retired communications company executive*
Newsom, Carolyn Cardall *management consultant*
Newsom, John Harlan *physician*
Soultoukis, Donna Zoccola *library director*
Weaver, William Clair, Jr., (Mike Weaver) *human resources development executive*

York
Addison, Brian Michael *lawyer*
Alcon, Sonja L. *retired medical social worker*
Bartels, Bruce Michael *health facility administrator*
Bergren, Byron L. *retail executive*
Buzzendore, Robert L. *lawyer*
Davis, Jane G. *lawyer*
Day, Ronald Richard *retired financial executive*
Foster, Timothy Edward *educational association administrator*
Grossman, Robert Allen *transportation executive*
Gyenes, Scott Matthew *history professor*
Hoffmeyer, William Frederick *lawyer, educator*
Horn, Russell Eugene *engineering executive, consultant*
Horn, Russell Eugene, Jr. *engineering executive*
Kennedy, Christopher Robin *ceramics engineer, director*
Livingston, Pamela A. *corporate image and marketing management consultant*
Rebert, Jephrey Lee *urban planner, musician*
Rhoads, Jonathan Evans, Jr. *surgeon, medical educator*
Rosen, Raymond *health facility executive*
Thomas, Tracey Williams *researcher*
White, Timothy Paul *brokerage house executive*
Wiles, Lessley Decker *foundation administrator, preservationist*
Wiles, William Wharton *retired federal government official*
Wise, Bret W. *chemical company executive*
Wise, Charles William III *financial advisor*
Wittmer, Elyse Marie *academic administrator*
Yeater, Kathleen Wecker *musician, educator*

Youngstown
Love, George H., Jr. *lawyer*
Palmer, Arnold Daniel *professional golfer*

Zelienople
Efaw, Cary Ross *manufacturing executive*

RHODE ISLAND

Barrington
Carpenter, Charles Colcock Jones *internist, educator*
Hjerpe, Edward Alfred III *finance and banking executive*
Mihaly, Eugene Bramer *management consultant*
Soutter, Thomas Douglas *retired lawyer*

Bristol
Bogus, Carl Thomas *law educator*
Danzberger, Alexander Harris *retired chemical engineer, consultant*
Hendrix, John Shannon *architecture educator*
McMullen, Susan Taylor *librarian*

Charlestown
Rohm, Robert Hermann *sculptor, educator*

Chepachet
Jubinska, Patricia Ann *ballet instructor, choreographer, artist, anthropologist, archaeologist*

Coventry
Schweinsburg, Jane Duberg *librarian*

Cranston
Alston, Jametta O. *lawyer*

Burge, David Russell *concert pianist, composer, educator*
Langlois, Michael A. *financial consultant*
Livingston, Carolyn Harris *music educator*
Parravano, Amelia Elizabeth (Amy Beth Parravano) *recording industry executive*

Cumberland

Clemente, Alice Rodrigues *language educator*
Rossi, Joseph Anthony *film and television make-up artist, educator*

East Greenwich

Carlson, Shawn Eric *physicist, educator*
Dence, Edward William, Jr. *retired lawyer, bank executive*
Greene, Jack Phillip *historian, educator*

East Providence

Spina, Douglas John *priest, educator*
Tripp, Michael Windsor *accountant*

Foster

Sawyer, Mildred Clementina *retired real estate agent*

Greenville

Carter, Wilfred Wilson *retired finance company executive, controller*

Harmony

Fogarty, Charles Joseph *former lieutenant governor*

Hope

Stadtmueller, Claire Louise *soprano, performing arts educator*

Hope Valley

Laub, Sandra *secondary school educator*

Jamestown

Parks, A. Lauriston *lawyer*
Tinker, Thomas Eaton *retired headmaster*
Ullrich, Robert Albert *academic administrator*
Worden, Katharine Cole *sculptor*
Wright, Harrison Morris *historian, educator*

Johnston

Pomeroy, John J. *lawyer, insurance company executive*
Subramaniam, Shivan Sivaswamy *insurance company executive*
Torelli, Anthony-Alexander *musician, educator, conductor*

Kingston

Alexander, Lewis McElwain *retired geographer, educator*
Blissmer, Bryan *medical researcher, educator*
Caldwell, Naomi Rachel *library and information scientist, educator, writer*
Carothers, Robert Lee *academic administrator*
Fastovsky, David E. *geoscientist, educator*
Hufnagel, Linda Ann *biology professor, researcher*
Kim, Yong Choon *philosopher, theologian, educator*
LaPlante, Kerry L. *pharmacist, educator*
Markin, Karen Mary *research scientist, journalist*
Mazze, Edward Mark *marketing educator, consultant*
Molloy, David Scott, Jr. *labor relations educator*
Newman, Barbara Miller *psychologist, educator*
Reshetnyak, Yana K. *physics professor*
Sundlun, Bruce *former governor*
Turnbaugh, William Arthur *archaeologist, educator*

Lincoln

Barlow, August Ralph, Jr. *minister*
DiMuccio, Robert A. *insurance company executive*
Marsden, Herci Ivana *classical ballet artistic director*
Morrissey, Thomas F. *art educator*

Little Compton

Caron, Wilfred Rene *retired lawyer*
Middendorf, J. William, II, *investment banker*

Middletown

Carroll, Rosemary Frances *historian, educator, lawyer*
Demy, Timothy James *military chaplain*
Ellison, William Theodore *marine engineer*
Jackson, John Edward *adult education educator, retired military officer*
Leighton, Charles Milton *retired specialty consumer products executive*

Narragansett

Goos, Roger Delmon *retired mycologist*
Nixon, Scott West *oceanography science educator*
Pilson, Michael Edward Quinton *oceanography educator*
Rossby, Hans Thomas *oceanographer, educator*
Stark, Dennis Edwin *private investor, retired bank executive*

Newport

Brown, David William *economist, educator, consultant*
Burgin, William Lyle *architect*
Carpenter, Stanley Dean MacDonald *military officer, educator*
Chace, Jameson Fales *ecologist, educator*
Cicilline, J. Clement *mental health services professional, state legislator*
Cray, Benjamin A. *mechanical engineer*
Ellsworth, James Byron *national security educator*
Englander, Roger *television producer, director*
Haas, William Paul *humanities educator, retired academic administrator*
Hence, Jane Knight *interior designer*
Koch, Robert Michael *research scientist, consultant, educator*
Malkovich, Mark Paul III *musician, performing company executive*
McConnell, David Kelso *lawyer*
Mooshagian, Mark Nishan *education educator*
Morris, Betty Ann *artist*
Peterson, Eric F. *headmaster*
Raum, Mary Beth *performing arts educator*
Roos, Casper *actor*
Rous, Stephen Norman *urologist, educator*
Ruffa, Anthony Armand *mechanical engineer*
Sands, Harold Winthrop *banker, financial planner*
Shuford, Jacob L. *academic administrator, career military officer*
Woods, Donald E. *healthcare executive*

North Kingstown

Jarvis, William David *pharmacologist, researcher*
Knowles, Charles Timothy *lawyer, state legislator, military officer, educator*
Kullberg, Gary Walter *advertising agency executive*
Mellor, Kathy *English as a second language educator*
Morse, Barbara *mathematics educator*
Novich, Bruce Eric *chemicals executive*

Pawtucket

Cheever, James Jefferson *counselor*
Chopra, Pradeep *physician, educator*
Crowley, James Patrick *hematologist, medical educator, immunologist*
Glicksman, Arvin S(igmund) *radiation oncologist*
Hassenfeld, Alan Geoffrey *consumer products company executive*
Kranseler, Lawrence Michael *lawyer*
Lepore, Lisa *principal*
Nagler, Barry *lawyer*
Orson, Barbara Tuschner *actress*
Palav, Anjali *neuropsychologist*
Trueb, Martin R. *toy company executive*
Verrecchia, Alfred Joseph *toy company executive*

Portsmouth

Bergstrom, Albion Andrew *retired military officer, educator*
Levie, Howard S(idney) *lawyer, educator*
Needham, Richard Lee *magazine editor*
Parker, Nancy Knowles (Mrs. Cortlandt Parker) *publishing executive*

Providence

Ackerman, Felicia Nimue *philosophy educator, writer*
Adu-Gyamfi, R. Siisi *multi-industry company executive*
Algiere, Dennis Lee *state legislator*
Amaral, Joseph Ferreira *surgeon*
Anderson, James Alfred *cognitive science professor*
Aronson, Stanley Maynard *physician, educator*
Authelet, Keith A. *information technology executive*
Avery, Donald Hills *metallurgist, educator*
Barnhill, James Orris *theater educator*
Barnum, William Milo *architect*
Bensmaia, Reda *French studies educator, researcher*
Berkelhammer, Robert Bruce *lawyer*
Besdine, Richard William *medical educator, researcher*
Biron, Christine Anne *medical science educator, researcher*
Blasing, Mutlu Konuk *English language educator*
Blazar, Andrew S. *reproductive endocrinologist*
Block, Bartley Cavanough *biologist, educator*
Block, Stanley Hoyt *pediatrician, allergist*
Bohlen, Kenneth C. *multi-industry company executive*
Boksenbaum, Howard *library director*
Borts, George Herbert *economist, educator*
Bready, Richard Lawrence *manufacturing executive*
Breece, Elliott *network administrator, Internet entrepreneur*
Briant, Clyde Leonard *metallurgist, educator*
Brown, Larry K. *psychiatrist, researcher*
Bulman, John *lawyer*
Butler, John D. *multi-industry company executive*
Cady, Blake *surgical oncologist*
Campbell, James T. *history professor*
Campbell, Lewis B. *multi-industry company executive*
Caprio, Frank Thomas *state official, lawyer*
Carcieri, Donald L. *governor*
Carlotti, Stephen Jon *lawyer*
Carpenter, Gene Blakely *crystallography and chemistry educator*
Chafee, Lincoln Davenport *political science professor, former senator*
Chlebus, Andrew J. *lawyer*
Choquette, Paul Joseph, Jr. *construction company executive*
Conley, Patrick T. *lawyer, writer, historian, educator, real estate developer*
Cooper, Leon N *physicist, researcher*
Corrente, Robert Clark *prosecutor*
Curran, Joseph Patrick *lawyer*
Dafermos, Constantine Michael *applied mathematics professor*
Dahlberg, Albert Edward *biochemistry professor*
Degroot, Leslie Jacob *medical educator*
Dempsey, Raymond Leo, Jr. *radio and television producer, moderator, writer*
Donahue, John Edward *physician*
Donnelly, Kevin William *lawyer*
Donoghue, John Phillip *neuroscience educator, neurotechnology company executive*
Donovan, Bruce Elliot *literature educator, dean*
Dowben, Robert Morris *physiologist, researcher*
Duffy, Kevin *dean*
Dujardin, Richard Charles *journalist*
Easton, J(ohn) Donald *neurologist, educator*
Elbaum, Charles *physicist, educator, researcher*
Enteman, Willard Finley *retired philosopher*
Erikson, G(eorge) E(mil) (Erik Erikson) *information specialist, anatomist, archivist, science historian*
Estrup, Peder Jan *physics and chemistry professor*
Ewing, John Harwood *mathematics professor, department chairman, professional society administrator*
Faraone, Philip *organist, director, consumer products company executive*
Farmer, Susan Lawson *retired broadcast executive, former secretary of state*
Farrell, Margaret Dawson *lawyer*
Feldman, Allan Maurice *economist*
Feldman, Walter Sidney *artist, educator*
Ferruolo, Stephen Carl *lawyer, historian*
Fessler, Ann Helene *artist, photography educator*
Fish, Lawrence Kingsbaker *bank executive*
Fishman, Bernard Philip *museum director*
Flaherty, Francis Xavier *state supreme court justice*
Fleming, Wendell Helms *mathematician, educator*
Fogarty, Edward Michael *lawyer*
Fornara, Charles William *historian, classicist, educator*
Forsyth, Donald William *geophysics educator*
Freiberger, Walter Frederick *mathematics professor*
French, Ted R. *multi-industry company executive*
Frerichs, Ernest Sunley *religious studies educator*
Freund, Lambert Ben *engineering educator, researcher, consultant*
Gamboli, Michael A. *lawyer*
Gasbarro, Pasco, Jr. *lawyer*
Gass, Jennifer S. *oncologist, surgeon*
Gerritsen, Hendrik Jurjen *physics professor, researcher*
Gibbs, June Nesbitt *state senator*
Gilbane, Thomas F., Jr. *construction executive*
Gilmore, Judith Marie *physician*
Gleason, Abbott *history professor*
Glicksman, Maurice *engineering educator, retired dean, provost*
Gohh, Reginald Yuchengco *nephrologist*
Goldberg, Maureen McKenna *state supreme court justice*
Goldstein, Sidney *sociologist, educator, demographer*
Gottlieb, David *mathematics professor*
Grace, Richard John *history professor*
Green, Angel Yvonne *literature educator*
Greer, David Steven *dean, educator, physician*
Grossi, Linda Marie *elementary school educator*
Guggenheim, Frederick Gibson *psychiatrist, educator*
Guggenmos, Karl J. *dean*
Hamerly, Michael T. *librarian, historian*
Harleman, Ann *literature educator, writer*
Hazeltine, Barrett *electrical engineer, educator*
Head, James William III *geological sciences educator*
Heath, Dwight Braley *anthropologist, educator*
Hedlund, Ellen Louise *state agency administrator, educator*
Helfand, Stephen L. *biomedical researcher, educator*
Hemmasi, Harriette Ann *university librarian*
Heyman, Lawrence Murray *printmaker, painter*
Hopmann, Philip Terrence *political science educator*
Houston, Stephen D. *anthropologist, educator*
Howes, Lorraine de Wet *fashion designer, educator*
Jenny, Carole *physician, researcher*
Johnson, Vahe Duncan *lawyer*
Jones, Lauren Evans *lawyer*
Joukowsky, Artemis A. W. *private investor*
Kane, Agnes Brezak *pathologist, educator*
Kean, John Vaughan *retired lawyer*
Kenna, George Anthony *pharmacist, researcher*
Kim, Jaegwon *philosophy educator*
Klyberg, Albert Thomas *historical society administrator*
Knopf, Paul Mark *immunologist*
Konstan, David *classics and comparative literature professor, researcher*
Kosterlitz, J. Michael *physics professor*
Kraemer, Michael Frederick *lawyer*
Kramer, Peter David *psychiatrist, psychology professor*
Kushner, Harold Joseph *mathematics professor*
LaFrance, William Curt Phillip, Jr. *neuropsychiatrist, educator, medical researcher*
Lagueux, Ronald Rene *federal judge*
Lanou, Robert Eugene, Jr. *physicist, researcher*
Lawal, Taiwo Munir *civil engineer*
Lee, Eugene *theatrical set designer*
Lenox, William F. *literature and language professor*
Lesko, Leonard Henry *historian, educator, writer*
Levin, Frank S. *physicist, educator*
Lewis, David Carleton *medical educator, academic administrator*
Licht, Richard A. *lawyer*
Lipsey, Howard Irwin *lawyer, educator*
Lisi, Mary M. *federal judge*
López-Morillas, Frances (Mapes) *translator*
Lynch, Patrick C. *state attorney general*
Lynch, William Joseph *lawyer*
Marcello, Matthew T. III *lawyer*
Marsh, Robert Mortimer *sociologist, educator*
Marshall, Jason P. *lawyer*
Mayer, Kenneth Hugh *physician*
McAndrew, Thomas Joseph *lawyer*
McCann, Gail Elizabeth *lawyer*
McCleary, Benjamin Ward *investment banker*
Mc Donald, Charles J. *dermatologist, educator*
McElroy, Michael Robert *lawyer*
McIntyre, Jerry L. *lawyer*
McWalters, Peter *school system administrator*
Medeiros, Matthew Francis *lawyer*
Mello, Kerry L. *pharmacist*
Miller, Linda B. *political scientist*
Mollis, Ralph (A. Ralph Mollis) *state official, former mayor*
Monteiro, George *language educator, writer*
Mumford, David Bryant *mathematics professor*
Needleman, Alan *mechanical engineering educator*
Nelson, Jonathan M. *finance capital executive*
Nurmikko, Arto Veikko *engineering educator*
O'Donnell, Terrence *lawyer, multi-industry company executive*
Oh, William *physician*
Olson, Jeannine Evelyn *history professor*
Paolino, Ronald Mario *clinical psychologist, consultant, psychopharmacologist, pharmacist*
Papitto, Ralph Raymond *manufacturing executive*
Paster, Benjamin G. *lawyer*
Price, William Walley, Jr. *counselor, artist*
Pueschel, Siegfried M. *pediatrician, educator*
Putnam, Michael Courtney Jenkins *classics educator*
Putterman, Louis G. *economics professor*
Raaflaub, Kurt Arnold *classics educator*
Reilly, Charles James *lawyer, educator, accountant*
Rhodes, Ramona Lagiers *medical educator, researcher*
Ribbans, Geoffrey Wilfrid *language educator*
Richman, Marc Herbert *engineer, forensic specialist, educator*
Rizzo, Christie J. *psychologist*
Roberts, Elizabeth H. *lieutenant governor, former state legislator*
Robinson, William Philip III *state supreme court justice*
Rohr, Donald Gerard *history professor*
Roney, John M. *lawyer*
Ryder, Harl Edgar *economist, educator*
Saint-Amand, Pierre Nemours *humanities educator*
St. Florian, Friedrich Gartler *architect, educator*
Salter, Lester Herbert *lawyer*
Salvadore, Guido Richard *lawyer*
Savage, John Edmund *computer science educator, researcher*
Schevill, James Erwin *poet, playwright*
Schoenfeld, Barbara Braun *executive recruiter, lawyer, consultant*
Schulz, Juergen *art historian, educator*
Schwartz, Richard Evan *mathematician, educator*
Selya, Bruce Marshall *federal judge*
Shapiro, Ronald Gary *psychologist*
Sherman, Deming Eliot *lawyer*
Shu, Chi-Wang *mathematics professor, researcher*
Silverman, Joseph Hillel *mathematics professor*
Simmons, Ruth J. *academic administrator*
Siqueland, Einar *psychologist, educator*
Sosa, Ernest *philosopher, educator*
Steinbach, Meredith Lynn *writer, educator*
Stratt, Richard Mark *chemistry researcher, educator*
Stultz, Newell Maynard *retired political science professor*
Suttell, Paul Allyn *state supreme court justice*
Suuberg, Eric Michael *chemical engineering educator*
Tobin, Thomas J. *bishop*
Torres, Ernest C. *federal judge*
Townley, Hugh *sculptor, educator*
Treaba, Diana Olguta *physician*
Tucci, Joseph Ralph *endocrinologist, educator*
Upfal, Eliezer (Eli Upfal) *computer scientist, educator*
Valles, James M., Jr. *physics professor*
Vezeridis, Michael Panagiotis *surgeon, educator*
Vogel, Paula Anne *playwright*
Walker, Corey David Bazemore *humanities educator*
Weiner, Jerome Harris *mechanical engineering educator*
Weinstein, Philip Merrill *lawyer*
Weisberger, Joseph Robert *retired state supreme court justice*
Weitberg, Alan Barry *physician, researcher*
Wetle, Terrie Fox *gerontologist, educator, dean*
Wideman, John Edgar *English literature educator, novelist*
Williams, Frank J. *state supreme court chief justice, historian, writer*
Wolf, Geralyn *bishop*
Wood, Craig Breckinridge *paleobiologist, natural sciences educator*
Wood, Gordon Stewart *historian, educator, writer*
Wright, Carolyn D. *language educator, poet*
Yap, George S. *immunologist, educator*
Yates, Richard L. *multi-industry company executive*
Ziroli, Dennis F. *state agency administrator*

Riverside

Lekas, Mary Despina *retired otolaryngologist*
Schwegler, Nancy Ann *librarian, writer*

Rockville

Walker, Howard Ernest *lawyer*

Saunderstown

Knauss, John Atkinson *retired federal agency administrator, oceanographer, educator, retired dean*
Leavitt, Thomas Whittlesey *retired museum director, educator*
Waters, Chris Harold *literature and language professor, poet*

Scituate

Gorham, Bradford *lawyer*
Neves, David *musician, educator*

Smithfield

Joseph, Antoine L. *sociologist, educator*

Litoff, Judy Barrett *history professor*
Morahan-Martin, Janet May *psychologist, educator*

Wakefield
Alexander, Jacqueline Peterson *retired librarian*
Boothroyd, Geoffrey *industrial and manufacturing engineering educator*
Leete, William White *retired artist*
Mason, Scott MacGregor *entrepreneur, inventor, consultant*
Moore, George Emerson, Jr. *geologist, educator*
Phipps, Lynne Bryan *interior architect, educator, minister*
Reed, LoriJean Kinsey *anesthesiologist*
Rosenberg, Alan Gene *editor*
Wyman, James Vernon *retired publishing executive*

Warren
Mehlman, Edwin Stephen *endodontist*

Warwick
Halperson, Michael Allen *publishing executive*
Hayes, Catherine Davis *elementary school educator*
Horn, Donna M. *pharmacist, medical association administrator*
Izzi, John *mathematics educator, writer, actor*
Kelley, James Edward *actor, writer*
Losek, Darren Thomas *property manager, sales manager*
McNeil, Paul Joseph, Jr. *financial analyst*
Reilly, John B. *lawyer*
Revens, John Cosgrove, Jr. *state legislator, lawyer*
Richards, Priscilla Ann *medical/surgical nurse*
St. Pierre, Michael A. *lawyer*

West Kingston
Dowdell, Rodger B., Jr. *electronics executive*

Westerly
Crowley, Cynthia Warner Johnson *secondary school educator*
Moore, Edwin J.T. *retired obstetrician, gynecologist*
Walsh, Robert Anthony *lawyer*

Woonsocket
Bodine, Chris W. *retail executive*
Coady, Michael Anthony *surgeon, department chairman*
Crawford, (Edwin) Mac *pharmaceutical company executive*
Crowley, Rosa Quinonez *literature and language educator*
Ferdinandi, V. Michael *retail executive*
Frappier, Pearl Peters *retired bookkeeper*
Lankowsky, Zenon P. *lawyer, retail executive*
McLure, Howard A. *pharmaceutical executive*
Merlo, Larry J. *retail executive*
Rickard, David B. *retail executive*
Roszkowski, Joseph John *lawyer*
Ryan, Thomas M. *pharmaceutical company executive*
Sgarro, Douglas A. *pharmaceutical executive, lawyer*
Spalding, William R. *lawyer, pharmaceutical executive*
Stubbs, Donald Clark *retired secondary school educator*
Walker, Suzanne Ross *mathematics and education educator*
Wanebo, Harold J. *surgeon, educator*

SOUTH CAROLINA

Abbeville
Cellura, A(ngele) Raymond *psychologist*

Adams Run
Stewart, Shirley S. *retired elementary school educator*

Aiken
Bertsch, Paul M. *ecologist, director*
Bransome, Edwin Dagobert, Jr. *internal medicine educator*
Chelberg, Robert Douglas *military officer*
Dewberry, Raymond Allen *research scientist, combat engineer*
Dickson, Paul Wesley, Jr. *physicist*
Ely, Duncan Cairnes *social services administrator*
Fadimba, Koffi Baana *mathematics professor*
Hallman, Cecilia Ann *real estate consultant*
Hootman, Harry Edward *English professor, retired nuclear engineer*
Jefferson, Helen Butler *public health service officer*
Li, Rao *mathematician, computer scientist*
Naifeh, Steven Woodward *writer*
Pearce, Richard Lee *lawyer*
Rudnick, Irene Krugman *lawyer, educator, former state legislator*
Seabrook, John Martin *retired food products executive, chemical engineer*
Snyder, Robert Ellis *retired music educator, minister*
Sykes, Richard Nesbit *retired history professor, department chairman*
Wright, G. Todd *lab administrator, director*

Anderson
Anderson, George Ross, Jr. *federal judge*
Barrett, James Gresham *congressman*
Chipman, Dennis Clarence, Jr. *forensic psychiatrist, consultant*
Diekhoff, Billy Herman *retired music educator*
Kaiser, Louise Martin *elementary school educator*
Williford, Sandra Simmons *music educator*
Williford, Velma Jean *minister*

Beaufort
Harvey, William Brantley, Jr. *lawyer, retired lieutenant governor*
Parisi, Leah Evans *dean, nursing educator, lawyer*
Pinkerton, Robert Bruce *mechanical engineer*

Bennettsville
Kinney, William Light, Jr. *editor, publishing executive*

Bishopville
Miller, Blondell Stephenson *social worker, minister*

Bluffton
Brown, Dallas Coverdale, Jr. *retired military officer, historian, educator*
Cann, Sharon Lee *retired health science librarian*
Croft, George T. *physicist*
Jerger, Edward William *engineering educator, dean*
Pendley, William Tyler *military officer, educator*
Powell, Robert Ellis *mathematics professor, dean*
Reuben, Alvin Bernard *communications and entertainment executive*

Blythewood
Daniels, James Douglas *retired academic administrator*

Camden
Daniels, John Hancock *agricultural products company executive*
Jacobs, Rolly Warren *judge*

Cayce
McElveen, William Lindsay *broadcasting executive, lecturer*

Charleston
Allen, Robert Johnson *plastic surgeon*
Appleget, Terri Lynn *elementary school educator*
Austin, Linda S. *psychiatrist*
Barrett, Michael Baker *historian, educator*
Behre, Robert Fuller *journalist*
Bell, James L. *lawyer*
Bell, Norman Howard *retired endocrinologist, educator*
Benson, P. George *academic administrator, finance educator*
Bowman, C. Michael *physician*
Bowman, Daniel Oliver *retired psychologist*
Branham, C. Michael *lawyer*
Cantwell, Don *artistic director*
Carek, Donald J(ohn) *child psychiatry educator*
Chardon, Marc d'Estournelles *software company executive*
Chiaramida, Salvatore *cardiologist, educator, health facility administrator*
Cordova, Maria Asuncion *dentist*
Cox, Walter Thompson III *lawyer, federal judge, educator*
Crawford, Fred Allen, Jr. *cardiothoracic surgeon, educator*
Daniell, Herman Burch *pharmacologist*
De Wolff, Louis *management consultant*
Dobson, Richard Lawrence *dermatologist, educator*
Dominick, Paul Allen *lawyer*
Donnem, Sarah Lund *financial analyst, non-profit and political organization consultant*
Egelson, Pauline C. *director*
Farr, Charles Sims *lawyer*
Fei, James Robert *engineering executive, consultant*
Fenno, Edward Thorndike *lawyer*
Festa, Conrad *academic administrator*
Finn, Albert Frank, Jr. *physician*
Fragile, Patrick Christopher *physics professor, astrophysicist, researcher*
Freer, Robert Elliott, Jr. *lawyer*
Garr, David Ross *physician, educator*
Glassman, Armand Barry *physician, educator, scientist, administrator, pathologist*
Grant, J. Kirkland *lawyer, educator*
Greenberg, Raymond Seth *academic and health facility administrator, educator*
Grinalds, John Southy *military officer, retired academic administrator*
Gunn, Morey Walker, Jr. *director, musician, educator*
Gupta, Monika *nephrologist, researcher*
Haemmerich, Dieter *biomedical engineer*
Hartsock, Langdon All *medical educator, department chairman, physician*
Hoel, David Gerhard *statistician, science educator*
Hoffman, Brenda Joyce *gastroenterology educator*
Hughes, Blake *retired professional society administrator, retired publishing executive*
Jaffa, Ayad A. *medical educator, researcher*
Jaffe, Murray Sherwood *retired surgeon*
Jones, Vivian Eilene *music educator*
Kahn, Ellis Irvin *lawyer*
Khan, Mushfiquddin *neuropharmacologist, researcher*
Kraveka, Jacqueline Maria *pediatrician, oncologist, researcher, scientist*
Lader, Philip *corporate financial executive, lawyer, academic administrator, diplomat*
Lazarchick, John *hematologist, educator*
Leonard, Guy Meyers, Jr. *international holding company executive*
Long, Angus Quentin *lawyer, art association administrator*
Long, J. Grahame *curator*
Margolius, Harry Stephen *pharmacologist, physician*
Maria, Bernard L. *pediatric neurologist*
Martin, Roblee Boettcher *retired cement manufacturing executive*
Martin, Thomas Rhodes *communications executive, writer, educator*
McConnell, Bright III *orthopaedic surgeon*
McCullough, Ralph Clayton, II, *law educator*
McCurdy, Layton *medical educator*
Mohr, Lawrence Charles *physician*
Mowry, Maxwell Reed *language educator*
Nixon, Daniel Walker *oncologist, researcher*
Ogretmen, Besim *science educator, molecular biologist, researcher*
Osguthorpe, John David *otolaryngologist, educator*
Othersen, Henry Biemann, Jr. *surgeon, physician, educator*
Pan, Bing *information technology educator, researcher*
Patrick, Charles William, Jr. *lawyer*
Plichta, Thomas Edward *software engineering company executive*
Polson, Shawn William *microbiologist, molecular biologist*
Poole, Roger Cliff *retired academic administrator, finance educator, retired military officer*
Prewitt, William Chandler *finance company executive*
Reves, Joseph Gerald (Jerry Reves) *anesthesiology educator, dean*
Richardson, Anne Worsham *art gallery owner, artist*
Robinson, Neil Cibley, Jr. *lawyer*
Rollins, John Maxwell *mathematics professor, disc jockey*
Rosa, John William *academic administrator, career military officer*
Ruggiero, Kenneth Joseph *psychologist*
Saifan, Chadi *physician*
Salmon, Edward Lloyd, Jr. *bishop*
Schreadley, Richard Lee *newswriter, retired editor*
Sharpe, Kathryn Moye *retired psychologist*
Simms, Lois Averetta *retired secondary school educator*
Simpson, William M., Jr. *family medicine educator*
Sloan, Mark Hamilton *art gallery director, educator, author*
Smail, Karen Mary *physical education educator, consultant*
Spitz, Hugo Max *retired lawyer*
Strauch, Katina Parthemos *college librarian, publishing executive*
Stuart, Robert Kenneth *internist, hematologist, oncologist, educator*
Underwood, Paul Benjamin *gynecologist, oncologist, educator*
Waller, John Louis *anesthesiologist, educator*
Waring, Bradish J. *lawyer*
Watts, Claudius Elmer III *retired military officer*
Wen, Xuejun *biomedical engineer, educator*
Williams, Barbara Stambaugh *editor*
Wilson, Frederick Allen *gastroenterologist, health facility administrator, educator*
Winter-Switz, Cheryl Donna *travel company executive*
Wyrick, Charles Lloyd, Jr. *editor, writer*
Yu, Shan Ping *neuroscientist, educator*

Clemson
Bailey, Beatrice Naff *language educator, researcher*
Barker, James F. *academic administrator*
Bartley, Abel Alphonso *history professor*
Bowden, Tommy *college football coach*
Clausen, Hugh Joseph *retired army officer*
Cox, Headley Morris, Jr. *lawyer, educator*
DesMarteau, Darryl Dwayne *chemistry professor*
Greenstein, Joel Sandor *industrial engineering educator*
Halfacre, Robert Gordon *ombudsman, landscape architect, horticulturist, educator*
Jalili, Nader *mechanical engineer, educator*
Kelly, John William, Jr. *academic administrator*
Lander, Ernest McPherson, Jr. *history and economics professor*
Lewis, Barbara Sue *chemist*
Luo, Jian *engineering educator, researcher*
Melton, Gary Bentley *psychologist, educator*
Purnell, Oliver Gordon, Jr. *men's college basketball coach*
Pursley, Michael Bader *engineering educator, communications systems researcher, consultant*
Riley, Helene Maria Kastinger *Germanist*
Sluss, Dorothy Louise *education educator, researcher*
Underwood, Richard Allan *English language educator*
Wall, Kay *librarian, dean*
Wilson, Paul W. *economics professor*
Zielinski, Paul Bernard *grant program administrator, civil engineer*
Zumbrunnen, David Arnold *engineering educator*

Clinton
Adams, Joanne Nelson *special education educator*
Cornelson, George Henry, IV, *retired textile company executive*
Griffith, John Vincent *academic official*
Roth, Dale Davis *music educator, religious organization administrator*

Columbia
Adams, John Hurst *bishop*
Aelion, C. Marjorie *science educator*
Almond, Carl Herman *surgeon, physician, educator*
Amidon, Roger Lyman *public health service officer, educator*
Anderson, Charles Hill *lawyer*
Anderson, William H. *architect*
Averyt, Gayle Owen *retired insurance executive*
Babcock, Keith Moss *lawyer*
Barnes, Gail VanAernum *music educator*
Barnum, Mary Ann Mook *information management manager*
Barnum, William Douglas *retired communications executive*
Baskin, C. R. *civil engineer*
Bauer, R. Andre *lieutenant governor*
Bedenbaugh, Allyn Purvis *retired elementary school educator*
Bernstein, Barry Joel *lawyer*
Bjontegard, Arthur Martin, Jr. *foundation executive*
Blanton, Hoover Clarence *lawyer*
Boggs, Jack Aaron *banker, mayor, publisher, municipal government official*
Boyce, Corrie Mosby *music educator*
Breedin, Berryman Brent *journalist, consultant, historian, public relations executive*
Briggs, Ward Wright *classics educator*
Bristow, Walter James, Jr. *retired judge*
Brockelsby, Jeffrey Lind *investment executive*
Brooker, Jeff Zeigler *retired cardiologist*
Bryan, Charles Stone *internist, educator*
Burnett, E. C. III *state supreme court justice*
Calk, Stephen Hamilton *environmentalist*
Carpenter, Charles Elford, Jr. *lawyer*
Carter, Kathryn Gibson *education educator, consultant*
Conrad, Paul Ernest *transportation consultant*
Courson, John Edward *state legislator, insurance company executive*
Cuervo-Cazurra, Alvaro *finance educator*
Currie, Cameron McGowan *federal judge*
da Silva, Ercio Mario *physician*
Day, Richard Earl *lawyer, educator*
Dobrasko, Rebekah *cultural organization administrator, historian*
Dohohue, John Francis *secondary school educator*
Donald, Alexander Grant *psychiatrist, educator*
Duggan, Kevin *information technology professional*
Edgar, Walter Bellingrath *historian, educator*
Edge, Ronald Dovaston *physics professor*
Edwards, James Benjamin *accountant, educator*
Ellis, F. Earl, Jr. *lawyer*
Ellison, Henry Phillips *military officer*
Ezell, Elizabeth Anne *music educator*
Finkel, Gerald Michael *lawyer*
Flanagan, Clyde Harvey, Jr. *psychiatrist, psychoanalyst, educator*
Friedman, Myles Ivan *education educator*
Gaffney, Thomas Edward *physician*
Gandy, James Thomas *meteorologist, entrepreneur*
Gasser, Jonathan S. *prosecutor*
Geckle, George Leo III *language educator*
Gibbes, William Holman *lawyer*
Gibbons, Joseph Harrison *engineering educator, farmer*
Glad, Betty *political scientist, educator*
Goble, David S. *library director*
Graulty, Robert Thomas *engineer, consultant*
Gray, Elizabeth Van Doren *lawyer*
Hamilton, Clyde Henry *federal judge*
Hammond, Mark *state official*
Handel, Richard Craig *lawyer*
Harvey, Jonathan Matthew *lawyer*
Hastings, Samantha Kelly *library and information science professor, director*
Helmuth, Brian *marine biologist, educator*
Helsley, Alexia Jones *archivist*
Hollis, Charles Eugene, Jr. *finance company executive*
Houston, Kevin Todd *speech and language pathologist*
Hudson, Carolyn Brauer *application developer, educator*
Humphries, John O'Neal *cardiologist, educator, dean*
Jacobs, Louie A. *state agency administrator*
Johnson, Lawrence Wilbur, Jr. *lawyer*
Johnson, William Woodward (Hootie Johnson) *bank executive, retired sports association executive*
Kegley, Charles William, Jr. *political science professor*
Kendler, Bernhard *retired editor*
Kiker, Billy Frazier *economics professor*
Koley, Goutam *science educator*
Ladmer, William Edward *food product engineering executive*
Lambert, Lanneau William, Jr. *lawyer*
Land, John Calhoun III *lawyer, state legislator*
Leader, Jonathan M *archaeologist, researcher*
Leatherman, Hugh Kenneth, Sr. *state legislator, engineering executive*
Limehouse, Harry Bancroft, Jr. *real estate developer, transportation consultant*
Lloyd, Reginald Ivan *prosecutor, former judge*
Logan, Sandra Jean *retired economics and business professor*
Long, Eugene Thomas III *philosophy educator, academic administrator*
Martin, John Randolph *judge*
Martin, Robert William *econometrician*
Mason, Thomasine Grayson *judge*
Matthews, Steve Allen *lawyer*
McCaslin, Elizabeth Ann *athletic trainer*
McLendon, Brian Andrew *lab administrator, educator*
McLeod, Walton James *lawyer, state legislator*
McMaster, Henry Dargan *state attorney general*
McNeely, Patricia Gantt *communications educator*
Monahan, Thomas Paul *accountant*
Mood, Francis P., Jr. *lawyer, utilities executive*
Moore, James E. *state supreme court justice*
Nagi, Samuel Njuguna *psychotherapist, director*
Newton, Rhonwen Leonard *writer, data processing executive, consultant*
Nexsen, Julian Jacobs *lawyer*
Outin, Mary Louise *business, multi-cultural history and geneology educator*
Page, Randall *state official*
Paleologos, Evangelos *hydrologist, educator*
Palms, John Michael *academic administrator, physicist*
Pleicones, Costa M. *state supreme court justice*
Porchea, Sameano Francisco *educational association administrator, systems analyst*

Powell, Donald Ashmore *clinical research psychologist*
Pritchett, Samuel Travis *finance and insurance educator, researcher, consultant*
Rawlinson, Helen Ann *librarian*
Rex, Jim *school system administrator*
Robbins, Emmalee Elizabeth *theater director, speech professional*
Roberts, Pamela J. *lawyer*
Rucker, Darius *musician*
Samuel, May Linda *environmental scientist*
Sanford, Marshall (Mark Sanford) *governor, former congressman*
Schilit, Matthew Todd *assistant principal*
Seigler, Ruth Queen *college nursing administrator, educator, consultant, nurse*
Sepulveda, Sonja Marian Atkinson *choral director, accompanist*
Shafer, John Milton *hydrologist, consultant, data processing executive*
Shedd, Dennis W. *federal judge*
Sheppe, Joseph Andrew *surgeon*
Shmunes, Edward *dermatologist*
Shuler, Ellie Givan, Jr. *retired military officer, museum administrator*
Silver, Rick *marketing professional*
Sinclair, Linda Drumwright *educational consultant*
Smith, Theresa Joanne *research scientist, educator*
Sorensen, Andrew Aaron *academic administrator*
Sowell, Thornwell F. (Biff) *lawyer*
Sproat, Ruth C. *retired director, consultant*
Spurrier, Steve(n) (Orr) *college football coach*
Still, Charles Neal *retired neurologist, medical educator, consultant*
Synnott, Marcia Graham *history professor*
Tate, Harold Simmons, Jr. *lawyer*
Timmerman, William B. *utilities executive, accountant*
Toal, Jean Hoefer *state supreme court chief justice*
Toombs, Kenneth Eldridge *librarian*
Towns, Evelyn *state government educational administrator*
Turk, John Cobb *retired architect, educator*
Waller, John Henry, Jr. *state supreme court justice*
Warren, Charles David *library administrator*
Watabe, Norimitsu *marine biologist, educator*
Wideman, Ida Devlin *science educator*
Wilder, Ronald Parker *economics professor*
Wright, Harry Hercules *psychiatrist*
Zimmerman, Nancy Picciano *library and information scientist, educator*

Conway
Bachman, Maria K. *English professor*
Flaten, Arne R. *art educator*
Martin, Gregory Keith *lawyer, mayor*
McMillan, Michael Reid *retired orthopedic surgeon*
Sinclair, Frances Teresa *music educator, musician*
Suggs, Michael Edward *lawyer*

Daniel Island
Gillespie, John David *political science educator*

Darlington
Gough, Herbert Frederick, Jr. *minister*

Denmark
Bendidi, Rachid *dean, educator*

Due West
Carlock, John Bruce, Jr. *language educator*

Duncan
Calloway, Stephanie Michelle *secondary school educator*

Easley
Howe, Linda Arlene *nursing educator, writer*
Sustar, T. David *religious organization administrator*

Edisto Island
Van Metre, Margaret Cheryl *performing company executive, dancer, educator*

Florence
Baroody, Albert Joseph, Jr. *pastoral counselor*
DeMichele, Domenic John *neurologist, neuroradiologist*
Foster, Jackie Green *voice educator*
Havens, Timothy John *physicist*
Imbeau, Stephen Alan *allergist*
Reay-Jones, Francis Peter Fortnum *entomologist, researcher*
Waddill, Cynthia Kay *orthopaedic nurse practitioner*
West, Jesse Michael *pediatric neuropsychologist*
Wurster, Abigail Michelle *theater educator, costume designer*

Fort Mill
Bowles, Crandall Close *textiles executive*

Gaffney
Griffin, Penni Oncken *social worker, educator*
Griffin, Walter Roland *academic administrator, historian, educator*
Hill, Harry Hoffman, Jr. *musician, educator*
Wilde, Edwin Frederick *retired mathematics professor*

Georgetown
Ahearn, Arthur Mason *orthopedist, surgeon, consultant*
Bazemore, Trudy McConnell *librarian*
Howard, Thomas Joseph, Sr. *editor*
Schumaker, William Thomas *retired insurance company executive*

Gilbert
Padget, Barbara Johnson *elementary school educator*

Goose Creek
Vogt, Kathleen Cunningham *musician, educator*

Graniteville
Learnard, James Michael *special education educator, retired collections and bad debt manager*

Greenville
Axelson, Linda Rae *business director, event planning specialist*
Baker, Harriet Kugley *elementary school educator*
Bauknight, Clarence Brock *construction and retail executive, consultant*
Baur, Michael L. *information technology executive*
Belanger, Laura Hewlette *environmental scientist, consultant*
Bonner, Jack Wilbur III *psychiatrist, educator, administrator*
Castle, Carey William *dean*
Christina, Thomas Michael *lawyer*
Crawford, William David *real estate broker, consultant*
Cureton, Claudette Hazel Chapman *retired biology professor*
Davis, Joan Carroll *retired museum director*
DeBloom II, James Robert *surgeon*
DeMint, Jim (James Warren DeMint) *senator, former congressman*
Dorman, D. Douglas *human resources specialist, hospital administrator*
Dreskin, Jeanet Steckler *painter, medical artist, educator*
Edwards, Harry LaFoy *lawyer*
Estridge, Larry D. *lawyer*
Ferguson, Donald Littlefield *retired lawyer*
Fitzgerald, Eugene Francis *management consultant*
Forrest, Daniel Ernest *composer, music educator*
Herlong, Henry Michael, Jr. *federal judge*
Hipp, William Hayne *broadcast executive*
Holleman, Frank Sharp III *lawyer*
Horton, James Wright *retired lawyer*
Hultstrand, Charles John *architect*
Hutson, Melvin Robert *lawyer*
Jones, Bob III *academic administrator*
Jones, Robert Thaddues *retired principal*
Kalbaugh, Corey Andrew *bioengineering researcher*
Kilgore, Donald Gibson, Jr. *pathologist*
Kupferer, James Leo, Jr. *biotechnologist*
Lindsay, Ronald Thomas *lawyer, paper company executive*
Manly, Sarah Letitia *retired state legislator, ophthalmic photographer, angiographer*
Mann, James Robert *former congressman*
Massey, Raymond David *lawyer*
Mauldin, John Inglis *public defender*
Mebane, William deBerniere *newspaper publisher*
Newman, R. Donald *paper company executive*
Oxner, George Dewey, Jr. *lawyer*
Oxner, Glenn Ruckman *financial executive*
Paterson, David J. *paper company executive*
Payne, George Frederick *academic administrator*
Pepper, Latongia Kenyetta *physicist, curator*
Phillips, Joseph Brantley, Jr. *lawyer*
Porter, Charles Michael (Mike Porter) *diversified financial services company executive*
Riley, Richard Wilson *lawyer, former secretary of education*
Ringenberg, Donna Lou *music educator, conductor*
Scales, Pat R. *library association executive, library director*
Schoonmaker, Gail Graham *voice educator, director*
Shi, David E. *academic administrator, historian*
Simmons, Charles Bedford, Jr. *judge*
Smith, Philip Daniel *academic administrator, education educator*
Smoak, Lewis Tyson *lawyer*
Talley, Michael Frank *lawyer*
Todd, John Dickerson, Jr. *retired lawyer*
Townes, Bobby Joe *travel agency executive*
Traxler, William Byrd, Jr. *federal judge*
Trevillian, Wallace Dabney *retired economics professor, dean*
Varin, Roger Robert *textile executive*
Walters, Johnnie McKeiver *lawyer*
Westrope, Martha Randolph *psychologist, consultant*
White, Daniel Bowman *lawyer*
Wilkins, William Walter *federal judge*
Wyche, Cyril Thomas *lawyer*
Wyche, Madison Baker III *lawyer*

Greenwood
Boiter, Kevin Ernest *electronics and electrical educator*
Hughes, Christopher Adam *conductor, educator*
Jackson, Larry Artope *retired college president*
Marino, Louis J(ohn) *mathematics educator*
Marino, Sheila Burris *education educator*
Nexsen, Julian Jacobs, Jr. *lawyer*

Greer
Hu, Yiping *metallurgical engineer*
McAbee, Thomas Allen *psychologist*
McKenzie, Kathleen Julianna *artist*
Moore, Gareth *human resources specialist*
Sundstrom, Harold Walter *public relations executive*

Hardeeville
Kadar, Karin Patricia *librarian*

Hartsville
Cecil, Allan *corporate communications executive*
DeLoach, Harris E.(Eugene), Jr. *manufacturing executive, lawyer*
Menius, Espie Flynn, Jr. *electrical engineer*

Hilton Head Island
Adams, William Hensley *ecologist, educator*
Balkin, Alfred *music educator, composer*
Becker, Karl Martin *retired lawyer*
Birk, Robert Eugene *retired internist*
Brock, Karena Diane *dancer, educator*
Brown, Arthur Edmon, Jr. *retired army officer*
Conn, Margaret Elbow *human resources specialist*
Cunningham, William Henry *retired food products executive*
Davis, Mary Martha (Marty Davis) *small business owner, consultant*
Duvall, Charles Patton *internist, retired oncologist*
Engelman, Karl *physician*
Esposito, John Vincent *lawyer*
Field, James Bernard *internist, educator*
Gruchacz, Robert S. *real estate company officer*
Hagoort, Thomas Henry *retired lawyer*
Harty, James D. *former manufacturing company executive*
Hewes, Robert Charles *radiologist*
Huckins, Harold Aaron *chemical engineer*
Jarvis, William Robert *epidemiologist, educator*
Lattimer, Gary Lee *physician*
Lefer, Allan Mark *physiologist*
Levy, Maurice *education educator, researcher*
Lewis, Gene Evans *retired medical equipment company executive*
McKeldin, William Evans *management consultant*
Mersereau, Hiram Stipe *wood products company consultant*
Ostergard, Paul Michael *not-for-profit executive*
Patton, Joseph Donald, Jr. *management consultant*
Pritchard, Dalton Harold *retired electronics executive*
Reed, Frances Boogher *writer, actress*
Roehrig, C(harles) Burns *internist, consultant*
Rulis, Raymond Joseph *manufacturing executive, consultant*
Russell, Allen Stevenson *retired metal products executive*
Selvy, Barbara *dance instructor*
Wesselmann, Glenn Allen *retired health facility administrator*
Windman, Arnold Lewis *retired mechanical engineer*
Woodrum, Robert Lee *executive search consultant*
Wright, Marshall *manufacturing executive, diplomat*

Hopkins
Garrett, Robin Scott *health facility administrator*

Inman
D'Ambrosio, Jody (Gigi) Lynn *art educator*
Fogarty, Charles Michael *pulmonologist, researcher*

Irmo
Branham, Jennie Jones *artist*
Branham, Mack Carison, Jr. *retired religious organization administrator, minister*
Murphy, Jennifer H. (Buffy Murphy) *elementary school educator*
Parks, Garry Lee *military officer*

Isle Of Palms
Elliott, Larry Paul *radiologist, educator*
Horger, Edgar Olin III *retired obstetrics and gynecology educator*
Wohltmann, Hulda Justine *pediatrician, endocrinologist*

Jackson
Smith, Mark Eugene *nuclear engineering service company executive*

Johns Island
Cameron, Thomas William Lane *investment company executive*
Carter, Mary Andrews *paralegal*
Norton, Norman James *retired exploration geologist, educator*
Silveston, Peter Lewis *engineering educator, consultant*
Tarr, Robert Joseph, Jr. *publishing executive, retail executive*

Johnsonville
Davis, Aquilla *diversified financial services company executive*

Kiawah Island
Korb, William Brown, Jr. *retired manufacturing executive*
Warren, Russell Glen *educational consultant*

Lake Wylie
Buggie, Frederick Denman *management consultant*
Sanford, James Kenneth *public relations executive*

Lancaster
Bundy, Charles Alan *retired foundation executive*

Laurens
Gordon, Bobby G. *civilian military employee*

Lexington
Calloway, Gary R. *choral director, music director*
Lide, Vinton DeVane *lawyer*
Wilkins, Robert Pearce *writer, lawyer*

Marion
Jameson, Darrell P. *social studies educator*
Kirkpatrick, Donald Robert *secondary school educator*

Mauldin
Wood, Myra Linden Frank *consultant*

Mc Cormick
Soni, Jayshri *science educator, director*

Mount Pleasant
Bilas, Richard A. *economist*
Brewerton, Timothy David *psychiatrist*
Gilbert, James Eastham *academic administrator*
Glenn, Edward Vernon Ferrell *lawyer, consultant*
Hill, Larkin Payne *jewelry designer, manufacturer*
Macdonald, Robert Rigg, Jr. *retired museum director*
Maize, John Christopher *dermatologist, educator*
Royall, Mary-Julia C. *church organist, historian*
Scott, Jeffrey Ryan *music educator*
Thordarson, William *retired hydrogeologist*

Murrells Inlet
Justice, Franklin Pierce, Jr. *oil industry executive*
Kelly, Gerald Wayne *chemical coatings company executive*

Myrtle Beach
Feck, Asmus Wilhelm *retired mechanical engineer*
Gravely, Mary Jeane *volunteer*
Harwell, David Walker *retired judge*
McCollum, M. Gregory *lawyer*
Schwartz, Steve Wendelin *physician*

Nesmith
Pressley, Deloris N. *literacy educator*

New Zion
Gibbons, Robert Butler, Jr. *retired military officer*

Newberry
Lander, James Albert *retired military officer, controller*
McGinnis, Barry Eugene *music educator, musician*
Partridge, William Franklin, Jr. *lawyer*

North Augusta
Rowland, Arthur Ray *librarian*

North Charleston
Davidson, Margaret A. *federal agency administrator, lawyer*
Heyward, Willie Bruce *lawyer, advocate*
Laddaga, Lawrence Alexander *lawyer*
Wigger, Jarrel L. *lawyer*
Zucker, Jerry *chemical manufacturing executive*

North Myrtle Beach
Wheless, Albert Eugene *lawyer*

Orangeburg
Barnwell, Charles Brison, Jr. *lawyer*
Bozinovski, Stevo *computer science educator, researcher*
Byers, Keith Thomas *librarian*
Dalton, Cheryl Renee *entrepreneur*
Hill, Howard Darnell *retired education educator, educational consultant*
Hong, Jae-Dong *industrial engineering educator*
Hunter, Terry K. *artist, educator, director*
McIver, Barbara Basore *language educator*
Sims, Edward Howell *editor, writer*
Smoak, Randolph Duncan, Jr. *surgeon*
Staley, Alvin *artist, educator*
UmBayemake, Linda *library branch manager, rehabilitation services professional*

Pacolet
Hartell, Holly *school librarian*

Pageland
Simon, Kindra Lee *language educator, translator*

Pawleys Island
Grubb, William Francis Xavier *consumer products company executive, marketing professional*
Kay, Thomas Oliver *agricultural consultant*
Matelic, Candace Tangorra *museum director, educator*
Noble, Joseph Veach *retired museum director*
Proefrock, Carl Kenneth *academic medical administrator*

Pendleton
Marshall, Gerald Lee *mathematician, educator*

Pickens
Hardin, Janet Becker *gifted and talented educator, music educator*
Lofink, Glenda Jean *science educator*

Prosperity
Long, William McMurray *physiology educator*

Rembert
Woodward, Margaret Newbern *language educator*

Ridge Spring
Livingston, Kimberly R. *elementary school educator*

Rock Hill
Bristow, Robert O'Neil *writer, educator*
Cornick, Michael F(rederick) *accounting educator*
Ford, Mary (Polly) Wylie *retired physical education educator*
Hardin, James Carlisle III *lawyer, educator*
MacInnis, John Christian *music educator*
Maheswaranathan, Ponn *physicist, educator*
Manetta, Ameda Avrill *social sciences educator*
Witzel, Bradley Steven *special education educator*

Roebuck
McShane, Bernard *purchasing agent*
Smith, Alan Wade *music educator*

Saint Helena Island
Tarr-Whelan, Linda *policy center executive*
Yates-Williams, Linda Snow *real estate broker*

Seabrook
Bower, Philip Jeffrey *cardiologist*

Seneca
Hodges, Marlane Fairleigh *retired management educator*
Strong-Tidman, Virginia Adele *marketing professional*

Simpsonville
Kanzler, George *journalist, music critic*
Munley, William Edward *health services administrator*
Pratt, Harry Davis *retired entomologist*

Spartanburg
Belenchia, Elizabeth C. *international corporate realtor*
Bullard, John Moore *religious studies educator, church musician*
Colloms, Vergene Jenkins *music educator, composer, musician, music producer, arranger*
Deku, Afrikadzata *African studies professor, writer*
Dent, Frederick Baily *retired textiles executive, ambassador*
Dunlap, Benjamin Bernard *academic administrator*
Fouillade, Jean-Paul Eric *management consultant*
Grummel, John Arne *political science professor*
Hilton, Theodore Craig *computer scientist, Internet company executive*
Hodge, Gameel Byron *retired surgeon*
Jones, William Osborne, II, *physician assistant, nephrologist*
Leonard, Walter Raymond *retired biology professor*
McCraw, William Gary *music educator, director, musician*
McGehee, Larry Thomas *retired academic administrator*
Milliken, Roger *textile/chemical company executive*
Moyer, Terry T. *lawyer*
Parmley, Richard Turner *pediatric hematologist, oncologist*
Smithart-Oglesby, Debra Lynn *food service executive*
Stephens, Bobby Gene *college administrator, consultant*

Sullivans Island
Romaine, Henry Simmons *retired investment company executive, consultant*
Selby, John Bayne, Sr. *retired radiologist, medical educator*

Summerville
Bell, Benjamin Harrison, Jr. *solicitor*
Brooks, Jeffrey Martin *marketing and sales executive*
Burke, Rhonda Williams *counselor*
Deavers, James Frederick *optometrist, clinical nutritionist*
Reisman, Rosemary Moody Canfield *writer, humanities educator*

Sumter
Blakely, Delores Phinella *financial consultant, business advisor, evangelist*
Ford, Peter Hilary *music educator*
Leavell, Elizabeth Boykin *retired pediatrician*
McFadden, Lee Vernon *religious organization administrator*
Olsen, Thomas Richard, Sr. *air force officer*
Powers, Thomas Lynwood *professor, military reserve officer*
Van Bulck, Hendrikus Eugenius *accountant*

Sunset
Brodbeck, William Jan *marketing professional*

Surfside Beach
Favaro, Mary Kaye Asperheim *pediatrician, writer*

Swansea
Inabinet, George Walker, Jr. *retired state agency administrator*

Taylors
Smith, Morton Howison *religious organization administrator, educator*

Tigerville
NeSmith, Richard A. *education educator, consultant*

Townville
Wright, George Cullen *retired electronics company executive*

Travelers Rest
Bailey, Helen McShane *historian, consultant*

Union
Whitener, Martha Sarratt *retired history educator*
Whitener, William Jackson *retired military officer, retired dean*

Walterboro
Armentrout, Charles Edward *secondary school educator*
Cone, George Wallis *lawyer*
Refinetti, Roberto *biopsychologist*

Wedgefield
McLaurin, Hugh McFaddin III *military officer, museum program director*

Wellford
Seay, Stephanie *elementary school educator*

West Columbia
Byars, Merlene Hutto *accountant, artist, writer*
Harmon, Horace Elmer, Jr. *museum director, consultant*
Klutzow, Friedrich Wilhelm *neuropathologist*
Phillips, Karen Diane *surgeon*
Witherspoon, Walter Pennington, Jr. *orthodontist*

White Rock
Aull, James Stroud *retired bishop*

Whitmire
Hall, Joye *elementary school educator*

Winnsboro
Meyer, Jack Allen *historian, consultant*

Woodruff
Childers, Bob Eugene *educational association executive*

Yemassee
Olendorf, William Carr, Jr. *small business owner*

York
Blackwell, Paul Eugene, Sr. *military officer*

SOUTH DAKOTA

Aberdeen
Hedges, Mark Stephen *clinical psychologist*
Hollingsworth, John Arthur *business educator*
Maier, Karen Marie *school librarian*
Richards, Carlyle Edward *lawyer*
Stoia, Viorel G. *life underwriter*

Britton
Farrar, Frank Leroy *lawyer, former governor*

Brookings
Cervantes Laurean, Daniel *biochemist*
Chicoine, David Lyle *academic administrator*
Eischen, Michelle Robin *art educator*
Evans, David Allan *language educator*
Gilbert, Howard Alden *retired economics professor*
Hardwidge, Philip Ross *microbiologist, educator*
Jenks, Jonathan Alden *biologist, educator*
Moldenhauer, William Calvin *soil scientist*
Perumal, Omathanu Pillai *research scientist, medical researcher, educator*
Qian, Li *engineering educator*
Vanderpan, Norma *retired elementary school educator*

Canton
Perkinson, Robert Ronald *psychologist, consultant*

Dakota Dunes
Leman, Eugene D. *meat industry executive*

Eagle Butte
Webb, Yvonne M. *secondary school educator*

Freeman
Ries, Edward Richard *petroleum geologist, consultant*

Gettysburg
Burge, Steven Donald *city administrator*

Hot Springs
Hook, William Franklin *radiologist*

Ipswich
Beck, Vaughn Peter *lawyer*

Kadoka
Stout, Maye Alma *retired secondary school educator*

Lennox
Brendtro, Larry Kay *psychologist*

Miller
Morford, JoAnn (JoAnn Morford-Burg) *state senator, investment company executive*

Mission
Jackson, Lori Lee *secondary school educator, elementary school educator*
MacKichan, Margaret Anna *artist, art educator*

Mitchell
Padrnos, Diane E. *language arts educator*

Mobridge
Hall, Jo(sephine) Marian *editor*

Mud Butte
Ingalls, Marie Cecelie *former state legislator, retail executive*

Parker
Zimmer, John Herman *lawyer*

Pierre
Daugaard, Dennis M. *lieutenant governor, former state senator*
Gerdes, David Alan *lawyer*
Gilbertson, David *state supreme court justice*
Johnson, Julie Marie *lawyer, lobbyist, judge*
Konenkamp, John K. *state supreme court justice*
Larsen, Wallace Lawrence *retired transportation engineer, county official*
Larson, Vern L. *state official*
Liegl, Dorothy M. *library director*
Long, Larry *state attorney general*
Meierhenry, Judith Knittel *state supreme court justice*
Melmer, Rick *school system administrator*
Nelson, Chris A. *state official*
Novotny, Roger *state agency administrator*
Pederson, Gordon Roy *state legislator, retired military officer*
Riter, Robert C., Jr. *lawyer*
Rogers, Darla Pollman *lawyer*
Rounds, Mike (Marion Michael Rounds) *governor*
Sabers, Richard Wayne *state supreme court justice*
Thompson, Charles Murray *lawyer*
Zinter, Steven L. *state supreme court justice*

Platte
Pennington, Beverly Melcher *financial services company executive*

Rapid City
Bang, Sangchul *engineering educator*
Brookes, Leslie Joan *retired maternal/surgical nurse*
Cleveland, Herbert Bruce *minister, consultant*
Corwin, Bert Clark *optometrist*
Daughenbaugh, Randall Jay *retired chemical company executive, consultant*
Duhamel, Judith Reedy Olson *public information officer, former state senator*
Foye, Thomas Harold *lawyer*
Gowen, Richard Joseph *electrical engineer, educator, retired academic administrator*
Hamilton, Douglas Warren *real estate executive*
Hefling, Debra L. *financial representative*
Palmer, J. Crisman *lawyer*
Pillay, Gautam *chemical engineer, chemist, academic administrator*
Ramakrishnan, Venkataswamy *civil engineer, educator*
Schleusener, Richard August *college president*
Schreier, Karen Elizabeth *judge*
Scofield, Gordon Lloyd *mechanical engineer, educator*
Smith, Paul Letton, Jr. *geophysicist*
Viken, Linda Lea Margaret *lawyer*
Voyles, C. Robert *electronics executive*
Wishard, Della Mae *former newspaper editor*

Saint Lawrence
Lockner, Vera Joanne *farmer, rancher, state legislator*

Sioux Falls
Ashworth, Julie *elementary school educator*
Balcer, Charles Louis *college president emeritus, educator*
Bjerkaas, Carlton Lee *information technology executive*
Carlson Aronson, Marilyn A. *language educator*
Carpenter, Paul Lynn *cardiologist*
Casas-Melley, Adela Teresa *pediatrician, surgeon*
Christensen, David Allen *retired manufacturing executive*
Dowling, Barbara R. *elementary school educator*
Fenton, Lawrence Jules *medical educator*
Garson, Arnold Hugh *publishing executive*
Gerdes, Anthony Martin *research scientist, health science association administrator*
Giri, Chandra Prasad *research scientist*
Himler, Thomas Charles *psychologist*
Huseboe, Arthur Robert *American literature educator*
Jackley, Martin J. (Marty Jackley) *prosecutor*
Jaqua, Richard Allen *pathologist*
Johnson, Richard Arlo *lawyer*
Knapp, Thomas Joseph *lawyer*
Marshall, Mark F. *lawyer*
Narendranath, Neelakantam V. *microbiologist, researcher*
Piersol, Lawrence L. *federal judge*
Piper, Kathleen *former political organization administrator*
Richards, George Alvarez *psychiatrist, educator*
Rogers, David Hughes *banking and financial service professor, dean, real estate company executive*
Rosenthal, Joel *manufacturing executive*
Sanford, T. Denny (Thomas Denny Sanford) *bank executive*
Staggers, Kermit LeMoyne, II, *history and political science professor, state legislator, municipal official*
Stowers, Mark David *chemicals executive*
Talley, Robert Cochran *academic administrator, cardiologist*
Tapken, Michelle G. *prosecutor*
Thompson, Ronelle Kay Hildebrandt *library director*
Travis, Richard L. *lawyer*
VanDemark, Michelle Volin *critical care, neuroscience nurse*
Viste, Arlen Ellard *chemistry professor*
Wagoner, Ralph Howard *academic administrator*
Welk, Thomas John *lawyer*
Wollman, Roger Leland *federal judge*
Zawada, Edward Thaddeus, Jr. *physician, educator*

Spearfish
Addy, Alva Leroy *mechanical engineer*
Ellis, Mary Louise Helgeson *retired healthcare technology company executive*
Erickson, Richard Ames *physicist, emeritus educator*
Reznikov, Andrey *linguist, educator*

Vermillion
Avoseh, Mejai Bola Mike *adult education educator, researcher*
Clem, Alan Leland *retired political scientist, educator*
Maney, Jack Logan *mathematician, educator*
Sevening, Diane Kay *alcohol/drug abuse studies educator, researcher*

Wessington Springs
Mohling, Charlotte *middle school educator*

Yankton
Foster, James Caldwell *dean, historian*
Ranney, Brooks *gynecologist, educator*

TENNESSEE

Alamo
Finch, Evelyn Vorise *financial planner*

Alexandria
Thomas, Deona Lee *music educator*

Allardt
Copeland, Patricia Ruth *elementary school educator*

Antioch
Brown, Katherine Yvonne *occupational therapist, educator*
Mattice, Debora J. *special education educator, consultant*
Worthington, Melvin Leroy *minister, writer*

Athens
Trent, Henry Gibson, Jr. *insurance company executive, educator*

Bartlett
Huffman, D. C., Jr. *pharmacist, educator, health science association administrator*
Huffman, Delton Cleon, Jr. *pharmacy association executive*

Big Sandy
Chastain, Kenneth Duane *retired foreign language educator, writer*

Blaine
Bull, James C. *poet*

Blountville
Wells, H. Greeley, Jr. *prosecutor*

Bluff City
Arnold, SaBrina Nicole *secondary school educator*

Bolivar
Boyle, Candyace *psychologist*

Brentwood
Carpenter, William F. III *hospital management company executive, lawyer*
Chapdelaine, Perry Anthony, Jr. *public health service officer, preventive medicine physician, educator*
Chappell, Charles Richard *space scientist*
Clevenger, William Thomas *electrical engineer*
Davis, James Richard *software engineer, consultant*
Grant, Amy *singer, songwriter*
Hearn, Billy Ray *recording industry executive*
Heiser, Arnold Melvin *astronomer*
Lee, Robert Erich *Internet company executive, information technology consultant, biomedical imaging researcher*
Lodowski, Charles Alan *trade association administrator, lobbyist*
Lyon, Sharron *retired church organist*
Mc Creary, James Franklin *lawyer, mediator*
Provine, John Calhoun *retired lawyer*
Seifert, Rachel A. *lawyer*
Smith, Wayne Thomas *healthcare company executive*
Swenson, Kathleen Susan *music educator, art educator*
Taylor, Nicole Renée (Niki Taylor) *model, shop owner*
Tucker, Tanya Denise *singer*
Vance, Kim *lawyer*
Walker Bonner, Linda Carol *music educator*
Wright, James F. *agricultural products executive*

Bristol
Hill, Kenneth Clyde *clergyman*
Markison, Brian A. *pharmaceutical executive*
Werner, Dawn Heterick *elementary school educator*

Brownsville
Banks, Webb Follin *mayor*
Kalin, Robert *retired mathematics professor*

Camden
Jasper, Doris J. Berry *nurse*

Chattanooga
Bahner, Thomas Maxfield *lawyer*
Brooks, Ellyn Hersh *retired special education educator*
Campbell, Paul III *lawyer*
Campbell, William O'Neal *retired physician*
Cooper, Gary Allan *lawyer*
Copeland, Floyd Dean *insurance company executive, lawyer*
Derthick, Alan Wendell *architect, architectural firm executive*
Duckworth, Jerrell James *electrical engineer*
Edgar, R(obert) Allan *federal judge*
Franks, Herschel Pickens *judge*
Gartman, Max Dillon *language educator*
Glick, Charles L. *lawyer, insurance company executive*
Greving, Robert C. *insurance company executive*
Lutgen, Robert Raymond *newspaper editor*
Marler, B. Evonne *not-for-profit fundraiser*
Marshall, Willis Henry *psychiatrist*
Martin, Chester Y. *sculptor, painter*
Mattice, Harry Sandlin, Jr. *federal judge, former prosecutor*
Mills, Olan, II, *photography company executive*
Milton, Michael Anthony *minister, writer*
Moore, Hugh Jacob, Jr. *lawyer*
Obear, Frederick Woods *academic administrator*
Pate, Lisa M. *transportation services executive, lawyer*
Phillips, John Bomar *lawyer*
Quinn, Patrick *transportation executive*
Rabin, Alan A. *economics professor*
Ramsey, Stephanie Denise *medical transcriptionist*

Resnick, Irven Michael *philosophy educator*
Rutledge, Valerie Copeland *education educator*
Shannon, Jerry Wayne *mathematician, educator*
Shuck, Edwin Haywood III *surgeon*
Stacy, Bill Wayne *academic administrator*
Steele, Shirley Sue *retired special resource educator*
Summers, Gerald Howard (Jerry) *lawyer*
Vital, Patricia Best *lawyer*
Watjen, Thomas Ros *insurance company executive*
Wilson, Richard Lee *political science professor*

Clarksville
Gold, Moniqueka E. *education educator*
Hoppe, Sherry Lee *academic administrator*
King, Thomas Roy *voice educator, music educator, director*
Mitchell, John Gerald *educational administrator*
Newby, Earl Fernando *education educator*
Staivisky, Jeanne Louise *counselor, alcohol/drug abuse services professional*
Stoddard, Peter Hawkins *education educator, consultant*
Winters, David Douglas *lawyer*

Cleveland
Harper, James Edward, Jr. *academic administrator*
Hughes, Ray Harrison *minister, religious organization administrator*
Kraus, Ruby Jean *art educator*
Preston, Forrest L. *healthcare executive*
Renfro, Zoe Vaughan *principal*
Rhodes, Arthur Delano *benefits administrator*
Taylor, William Al *church administrator*
Wittenburg, Michael Shane *concert pianist, music educator*

College Grove
Battle, William Robert (Bob) *retired publishing executive*

Collegedale
Clark, Ann Rorabaw *English professor, consultant, writer*
McKee, Ellsworth R. *food products executive*

Collierville
Boswell, Rupert Dean, Jr. *retired academic administrator, mathematician, educator*
Mann, Clifton *secondary school educator*
Springfield, James Francis *retired lawyer, banker*
Tesreau, Cynthia Lynn *elementary school educator*

Columbia
Cantrell, Sharron Caulk *principal*

Cookeville
Airhart, Douglas L. *horticulturist, educator*
Chang, Wei Tsun *music educator*
Chowdhuri, Pritindra *retired electrical engineer, educator*
Hossain, Faisal *engineering educator*
Mohr, Benjamin John *engineering educator*
Reynolds, Barbara C. *retired mental health educator, dean*
Sissom, Leighton Esten *engineering educator, dean, consultant*
Smolenski, Lisabeth Ann *physician*
Ting, Kwun-Lon *engineer, educator, consultant*
Volpe, Angelo Anthony *retired academic administrator, chemist, educator*
Wilson, Terrence Raymond *manufacturing executive*

Cordova
Floyd, John David *theology studies educator, minister*
Jacobs, M. Louise *secondary school educator*
Pugh, Dorothy Gunther *performing company executive*

Covington
Gordon, J. Houston *lawyer, political organization worker*
Wright, Bonnie Shankle *assistant principal, choir director*

Crab Orchard
McBee, Christy Dawn *art educator, pre-school educator*

Crossville
Bell, Charles Eugene, Jr. *retired industrial engineer*
Frazier, June Marie *retired public relations executive*
Lansford, Edwin Gaines *accountant*
Marlow, James Allen *lawyer*

Cunningham
Mince, Carol Kirkham *history educator*

Dandridge
Coley, Jan Brumback *biology educator*

Dayton
Cornelius, Richard Meredith *literature and language professor*
Ketchersid, William Lester *history professor*

Dyersburg
Wilder, James Sampson III *lawyer, judge*

Eads
Bogan, John C. *real estate appraiser*

Englewood
Brown, Helen Dodson *retired librarian*

Fayetteville
Bone, Lawson Mitchell *songwriter, poet*
Esslinger, Eric Jason *web site designer*
Wolfhard, Hans Georg *retired research scientist*

Franklin
Andrews, William Frederick *manufacturing executive*
Bull, Sandy (Alexander Benjamin Bull) *musician, composer*
Fink, Robert Michael *pharmacist*
Miller, Dennis Edward *health medical executive*
Rosen, William Warren *lawyer*
Thornsberry, Clyde *microbiologist*
White, David R. *healthcare company executive*

Gallatin
Bradley, Nolen Eugene, Jr. *retired personnel executive, educator*
Brett, John Brendan, Jr. *retired advertising and public relations executive*
Durham, Walter Thomas *historian, researcher*
Ellis, Joseph Newlin *retired wholesale distribution executive*
Ritter, Renee D. *theater educator*

Gatlinburg
Cave, Kent R. *parks director*

Germantown
Depperschmidt, Thomas Orlando *economist, consultant*
Frantzikinakis, Nikos *mathematics professor*
Loper, Linda Sue *librarian*
Mowry, Robert Wilbur *pathologist, educator*
Waddell, Phillip Dean *lawyer*

Goodlettsville
Beré, David L. *retail executive*
Lanigan, Susan S. *lawyer*
Perdue, David A., Jr. *retail executive*
Vatandoost, Nossi Malek *art school administrator*

Gray
Combs, Stephen Paul *pediatrician, health facility administrator*

Greenbrier
Ault, Andrew Jared *music educator, disc jockey*
Newell, Paul Haynes, Jr. *engineering educator*

Greeneville
Corey, Mark *historic site director*
Hull, Thomas Gray *federal judge*
Smith, Myron John, Jr. *librarian, author*

Harriman
Pierce, Patricia Ann *retired university administrator*

Henderson
Gardner, Elmer Claude *academic administrator*

Hendersonville
Burt, Alvin Miller III *anatomist, educator, cell biologist, writer*
McCaleb, Joe Wallace *lawyer*
Spain, Mary Ann *realtor, educator, historian, writer*

Hermitage
Burkett, Gerald Arthur *lawyer, musician*
Thompson, Fred Dalton *actor, former senator*

Hickory Valley
Weaver, Peggy (Marguerite McKinnie Weaver) *plantation owner*

Hixson
Segler, Christopher Paige *surgeon, researcher*

Huntingdon
King, Tracy Lynn *science educator*

Huntland
Burton, Janet Ruth Wisner *music educator*

Jackson
Agee, Bob R. *academic administrator, educator, minister*
Boswell, G(eorge) Harvey *federal judge*
Britt, Timothy *mathematics professor*
Cole, John Frankland *electrical engineer, educator*
Dale, Karen McCall *music educator*
Evans, Sean *political science professor*
Hoyle, Shetina Yevette *librarian*
Seaton, Robert Lamar *pharmacist*
Swaim, Mark Wendell *physician, molecular biologist, gastroenterologist, photographer*
Todd, James Dale *federal judge*
Wallis, Edwin E., Jr. *lawyer*

Jefferson City
Baumgardner, James Lewis *history professor*
Muncy, Estle Pershing *physician*

Jellico
Hausman, Keith Lynn *health facility administrator, physical therapist*
Walden, James William *accountant, educator*

Johnson City
Coogan, Philip Shields *pathologist*
Epps, James Haws III *lawyer*
Franks, Ronald Dwyer *dean, psychiatrist, educator*
Freeman, Michael Byron *protective services official, consultant*
Gerhardt, E. Alvin, Jr. *retired museum director*
Giorgadze, Tamar Afred *pathologist, physician*
Hamdy, Ronald Charles *geriatrician*
Jenrette, Thomas Shepard, Jr. *music educator, choral director*
Lyle, Valarie Gay *art educator, artist*
Olsen, Martin E. *obstetrician, educator*
Pandian, Shantha G. *psychiatrist*
Rahmani, Ramin Khosravi *mechanical engineer, researcher*
Rush, Daniel Scott *vascular surgeon, educator*
Snyder-Sowers, Mary Anne Sarah *performing arts educator, performing company executive, choreographer*
Taylor, Grant David *urologist*
Tollefson, Terrence Alfred *education educator, consultant*

Jonesborough
Jenkins, Ronald Wayne *lawyer, mediator, engineer*
Kiener, John Leslie *retired judge*

Kingsport
Coover, Harry Wesley *manufacturing executive*
Crockett, Frank McClung *retired arts and music educator*
Ferguson, J. Brian *chemicals executive*
Findley, Don Aaron *manufacturing executive*
Hale, Jerry B. *information technology executive*
Head, William Iverson, Sr. *retired chemical company executive*
Lee, Theresa K. *lawyer, chemicals executive*
Ogbonnaya, Chuks Alfred *entomologist, agronomist, environmentalist*
Rigsby, Mary Sue *retired elementary school educator, adult education educator*
Siirola, Jeffrey John *chemical engineer*
Smith, JoAnn Carroll *library and information scientist*
Solomon, Joseph Alphous *physician*
Tant, Martin Ray *chemical engineer, biomedical engineer*

Knoxville
Abidi, Besma Roui *information scientist, educator*
Adams, Gerald Dwayne *medical technician*
Alexeff, Igor *retired electrical engineering educator*
Bass, William Marvin III *anthropology educator*
Beavers, James Earl *engineer, director, consultant*
Beeler, Sandra Gillespie *realtor*
Bell, James A.H. *lawyer*
Bell, Linda R. *writer, photographer*
Blake, Gerald Rutherford *retired banker*
Boling, Edward Joseph *retired academic administrator*
Bose, Bimal Kumar *electrical engineering educator*
Brantley, Andy (Anthony G.) *educational association administrator*
Brown, Deanna G. *marketing executive*
Brown, Patricia Ann *child health nurse*
Campbell, Michael L. *recreational facility executive*
Chen, James Pai-fun *biology professor, researcher*
Cleland, Charles Leslie *sociologist, educator*
Coleman, Shannon DeShae *lawyer, educator*
Cottrell, Jeannette Elizabeth *retired librarian*
Cox, Anna Lee *retired administrative assistant*
Crabtree, Loren William *academic administrator, history professor*
Creasia, Joan Catherine *dean, nursing educator*
Cremins, William Carroll *lawyer*
Cutler, Everette Wayne *history professor*
Davis, John Kerr *philosopher, educator, lawyer*
Dedrick, James R. *prosecutor*
Dewey, Barbara I. *librarian, dean*
Dillard, W. Thomas *lawyer*
Drinnon, Janis Bolton *artist, poet, volunteer*
Felder-Hoehne, Felicia Harris *librarian, researcher*
Filston, Howard Church *pediatric surgeon*
Froula, James DeWayne *honor society administrator*
Fu, Joshua S. *environmental engineer, educator, research scientist*
Fulmer, Phillip *university football coach*
Galligan, Thomas C., Jr. *law educator*
Garrison, Arlene Allen *academic administrator, engineering educator*
Gentry, Mack A. *lawyer*
Gentry, Robert Vance *physicist, researcher, writer*
Giordano, Lawrence Francis *lawyer*
Harris, Diana Koffman *sociologist, educator*
Hatcher, Robert Dean, Jr. *geologist, educator*
Holt, Dawn Lizabeth *paralegal*
Hooper, William Edward *writer, broadcast journalist*
Howard, Lewis Spilman *lawyer*
Infante, Isa Maria *political scientist, educator, lawyer, writer*
Irick, David Kim *engineering educator, consultant*
Jarvis, James Howard, II, *judge*
Jones, Sherman J. *cultural organization administrator, financial consultant, educator*
Jordan, Robert Leon *judge*
Joseph, Pamela A. *bank executive*
Kennedy, Alfred Parker, Jr. *pediatrician, surgeon*
Kliefoth, A. Bernhard III *neurosurgeon*
Kulikowski, Michael *history professor*
Lawson, Fred Raulston *banker*
Levy, Robert A. *academic administrator*
Lloyd, Francis Leon, Jr. *lawyer*
Lowe, Alan Conner *library director*
Mankel, Francis Xavier *retired principal, priest*
Markert, Cynthia Allin *artist*
Martin, James Robert *identification company executive*
Matteson, Karla J. *health science association administrator*
Mayfield, T. Brient, IV, *media and computer executive*
Mazur, Peter *physiologist, cryobiologist*
McCall, Jack Humphreys, Jr. *lawyer*
McCullough, Glenn L., Jr. *electric power industry executive*
Mc Dow, John Jett *biosystems engineering educator*
McElroy, Gloria Freels *secondary school educator*
McGuire, Sandra Lynn *nursing educator*
Mc Hargue, Carl Jack *lab administrator*
Mise, Jesse Sherden *structural engineer, consultant*
Moore, Marvelene C. *music educator*
Moore, Richard Wayne *electric power industry executive, former prosecutor*
Murrian, Robert Phillip *retired federal judge, educator*
Naoumov, Viatcheslav I. *mechanical engineer, educator*
Naoumova, Irina Yevgenievna *business educator, consultant*
Nukala, Sirisha Saripalli *research scientist, educator*
Oakes, Thomas Wyatt *environmental engineer, computer engineer*
Oberman, Steven *lawyer*
Pace, Elizabeth Barber *elementary school educator*
Paul, Jerald S. *former federal agency administrator, state legislator*
Petersen, John D. *academic administrator*
Phillips, Thomas Wade *judge, lawyer*
Pjesivac-Grbovic, Jelena *computer scientist, researcher*
Plummer, E. Ward *physics professor*
Prados, John William *retired engineering educator*
Purcell, Aaron D. *archivist, historian*
Qiu, Wulin *chemist, materials scientist, materials engineer*
Reath, David Brooke *plastic surgeon*
Renshaw, Amanda Frances *retired physicist, nuclear engineer*
Reynolds, Glenn Harlan *law educator, blogger*
Richards, Stephen Harold *engineering educator*
Ritchie, Albert *lawyer*
Roach, Jon Gilbert *lawyer*
Roth, John Reece *electrical engineer, educator, researcher, inventor*
Routh, John William *lawyer*
Rukeyser, William Simon *journalist*
Russell, Rodney E. *school system administrator*
Sansom, William B. *consumer products executive*
Schuler, Theodore Anthony *retired civil engineer*
Schweitzer, George Keene *chemistry professor*
Simberloff, Daniel *biologist, educator*
Stephens, Otis Hammond, Jr. *political science professor, law educator*
Summitt, Patricia Head *women's college basketball coach*
Swanson, Charles Walter *lawyer*
Taylor, Jackie A. *educational association administrator*
Teeter, Dwight Leland, Jr. *journalism educator*
Trout, Monroe Eugene *health facility administrator*
Uhrig, Robert Eugene *nuclear engineer, educator*
Wade, Gary R. *state supreme court justice*
Wallace, Lorraine Silver *medical educator, researcher*
Wang, Peiling *information scientist, educator*
Wawrzyniak, Cynthia *biology professor*
Wheeler, John Watson *lawyer*
White, Edward Gibson, II, *lawyer*
Worthington, Robert Fletcher, Jr. *lawyer*
Wu, Jie *electronics engineer, educator*
Wunderlich, Bernhard *retired physical chemistry professor*
Ye, Xiaofei *education educator*
Zhong, Qixin *physical chemist, chemistry professor*
Ziegler, Dhyana *broadcasting educator, academic administrator*

Kodak
Keller, Daniel Sylvester *director*

La Follette
Eads, Ora Wilbert *clergyman, church administrator*
Watson, S. Michele *school nurse*

La Vergne
Ingram, David B. *entertainment company executive*

Lawrenceburg
Hayes, Sylvia Richmond *music educator*

Lebanon
Burns, George Franklin *archivist, retired English language educator*
Daniels, Charlie *musician, lyricist*
Eaton, Harvill Carlton *academic administrator*
Evins, Dan W. *food products executive*
Shoaf, Forrest *lawyer*
White, Lawrence Edward *finance executive*
Woodhouse, Michael A. *restaurant holdings company executive*

Lenoir City
Edwards, C. Karen *consultant company executive*
Sproul, Harvey Leonard *lawyer*

Linden
Mitchell, Elizabeth Marelle *family practice nurse practitioner, medical/surgical nurse, nursing educator*

Loudon
Hallstrand, Sarah Laymon *denomination executive*
Hicks, Betty Harris *real estate broker, company executive*
Horst, Teresa Dale *music educator*
Jones, Robert Gean *religion educator*
Randall, Marilyn Mae *writer*
Stafford, William Franklin *veterinarian, educator*

Madison
Collins, Joyce A.P. *minister, librarian, educator, realtor*
Hadley, John Livingston, V, *management executive, writer*

Manchester
Westberry, Anita Parrish *education educator*

Martin
Howard, Nathan Dale *history professor*
Parker, Henry Herbin *humanities educator*
Wade, Reba *musician, educator*
Wheeler, Edward *engineering educator*

Maryville
Bradford, Tutt Sloan *retired publisher*
Howard, Cecil Byron *retired pediatrician*
Oakes, Lester Cornelius *retired electrical engineer, consultant*
Tabor, Curtis Harold, Jr. *retired librarian, minister*
Weeks, Robert Andrew *materials science researcher, educator*

Mason
Wilder, John Shelton *state senator, former lieutenant governor*

Mc Ewen
Williams, John Lee *lawyer*

Memphis
Abston, Dunbar, Jr. *management consultant*
Adsit, Russell Allan *landscape architect*
Allen, David Mark *psychiatrist, educator, director*
Allen, Newton Perkins *lawyer*
Amonette, Rex. A. *physician*
Anghelescu, Doralina Lucia *anesthesiologist*
Baker, Gerald L. *bank executive*
Bargagliotti, Lillian Antoinette *nursing educator*
Barone, Tony, Sr. *professional basketball coach*
Battier, Shane *professional basketball player*
Battle, Allen Overton, Jr. *psychologist, educator*
Beranova-Giorgianni, Sarka *biomedical researcher, educator*
Berman, Jeffrey Scott *psychology professor*
Bhagat, Shaum P. *speech educator*
Bhattacharya, Syamal Kanti *biomedical scientist, educator*
Bobango, John Allen *lawyer*
Born, Robert Heywood *consulting civil engineer*
Brandon, Elvis Denby, Jr. *financial planner*
Brandon, Elvis Denby III *financial planner*
Brandon, Raymond Wilson *financial planner, securities principal*
Broadhurst, Jerome Anthony *lawyer*
Broffitt, Joyce Cassandra *judge*
Brown, R. Larry *human resources specialist, transportation executive*
Buckner, Thomas Randolph *lawyer*
Butts, Herbert Clell *retired dentist, educator*
Calipari, John V. *men's college basketball coach*
Cannon, Joe Louis *retired orthodontist*
Carr, Oscar Clark III *lawyer*
Carter, Michael Allen *nursing educator*
Carter, Robert B. *delivery service executive*
Chesney, Russell Wallace *pediatrician*
Ching, James Michael *performing company executive, composer, conductor*
Clippard, Richard F. *prosecutor*
Cook, August Joseph *lawyer, accountant*
Cox, Clair Edward, II, *urologist, medical educator*
Crane, Laura Jane *retired chemist*
Crawford, Sheila Jane *librarian, reading specialist*
Crye, Harold *real estate company executive*
Currey, Thomas Arthur *ophthalmologist*
Daughdrill, James Harold, Jr. *academic administrator*
Daugherty, James Albert *retired aeronautical engineer*
Desiderio, Dominic Morse, Jr. *chemistry and neurochemistry professor*
deWitt, Charles Benjamin III *lawyer, educator*
Diggs, Walter Whitley *health science facility administrator*
Doggrell, Henry Patton *lawyer*
Dolich, Andrew Bruce *professional sports team executive*
Drescher, Judith Altman *library director*
Dreyfus, Susan Kahn *middle school educator*
Dunathan, Harmon Craig *college dean*
Dunnigan, T. Kevin *retired electrical and electronics manufacturing company executive*
Edwards, Martin *real estate company executive*
Evans, James Mignon *architect*
Fain, John Nicholas *biochemistry educator*
Ford, Harold Eugene *retired congressman*
Franceschetti, Donald Ralph *physicist, educator*
Freeman, Bob A. *retired microbiology educator, retired dean*
Gay, Rudy Carlton, Jr. *professional basketball player*
Gerald, Barry *retired radiology educator, neuroscientist*
Gibbons, Julia Smith *federal judge*
Giles, William (Bill) T. *retail executive*
Gilman, Ronald Lee *federal judge*
Gilpatrick, Russell O. *dean, dental educator*
Glenn, T. Michael *delivery/messenger service executive*
Goldsmith, Harry Louis *lawyer*
Gourley, Dick R. *college dean*
Graf, Alan B., Jr. *delivery service executive*
Griffin, Clement M. *information technology executive*
Haltom, William H. *lawyer*
Harris, Terrell Lee (Terry Harris) *delivery services company executive, former prosecutor*
Harvey, Albert C. *lawyer*
Hayes, Michael J. *retail executive*
Heimberg, Murray *pharmacologist, biochemist, physician*
Heiter, Matthew Stephen *lawyer*
Helton, Kathleen Jacobson *neuroradiologist*
Herenton, Willie W. *mayor*
Herrod, Henry Grady III *pediatrics professor, allergist, immunologist*
Holder, Janice Marie *state supreme court justice*
Howe, Martha Morgan *microbiologist, educator*
Hughes, Walter Thompson *pediatrician, educator*
Hunt, James Calvin *physician, academic administrator*
Iavaroni, Marc (Marcus John) *professional basketball coach, retired professional basketball player*
Iles, Roger Dean *business educator*
Jackson, Thomas Francis III *lawyer*
Jalenak, Peggy Eichenbaum *volunteer*
Johnson, Harry A. III *lawyer, finance company executive*
Johnson, Johnny *research psychologist, consultant*
Johnson, Joseph Erle *mathematician*
Kelly, Aleda Mae *retired secondary education educator*
Knight, H. Stuart *law enforcement official, consultant*
Korones, Sheldon Bernarr *pediatrician, educator*
Krieger, Robert Lee, Jr. *human resource/management consultant, educator, writer, travel/meeting planner, political analyst, internet marketing consultant*
Kustoff, David F. *prosecutor*
Lazar, Rande Harris *otolaryngologist*
Ledbetter, Paul Mark *lawyer, writer*
Madlock, Yvonne *city health department administrator*
Manire, James McDonnell *lawyer*
Mantey, Elmer Martin *food company executive*
Masterson, Kenneth Rhodes *lawyer*
McDaniel, A. Stephen *lawyer*
McLean, Robert Alexander *lawyer*
McPherson, Larry Eugene *photographer, educator*
Morgan, Colby Shannon, Jr. *lawyer*
Morreim, E. Haavi *medical ethics educator*
Nance, Libba L. *elementary school educator*
Nemec, Christopher E. *music educator*
Nesin, Jeffrey David *academic administrator*
Nienhuis, Arthur Wesley *physician, researcher*
Noel, Randall Deane *lawyer*
Norris, Charles Head *lawyer, manufacturing executive*
O'Hagan, William D. *metal products manufacturing executive*
Ouzts, David Perry *church music director, organist*
Owen-Leinert, Susan Huff *voice educator, vocalist*
Patton, Charles Henry *lawyer, educator*
Person, Curtis S., Jr. *judge, former state legislator, lawyer*
Philipp, Karla Ann *music educator, conductor, musician*
Pileggi, Dominic J. *electronics executive*
Pope, Thaddeus Mason *law educator*
Pourciau, Lester John, Jr. *retired librarian*
Presley, Lisa Marie *singer*
Pruitt, Rosalyn Jolena *science educator*
Raines, Jim Neal *lawyer*
Raines, Shirley Carol *academic administrator*
Razzouk, Bassem Ibrahim *hematologist, oncologist*
Reid, Karen Denise *aerospace transportation executive, writer*
Rhodes, William C. III *automotive executive*
Rice, George Lawrence, III, (Larry) *lawyer*
Richards, Christine P. *delivery service executive, lawyer*
Riely, Caroline Armistead *gastroenterologist, educator*
Robertson, James Thomas *neurosurgeon*
Rue, Douglas Michael *solutions engineer*
Russell, James Franklin *lawyer*
Rutledge, Roger Keith *lawyer*
Schoech, Stephan James *biology professor*
Scroggs, Larry Kenneth *lawyer, state legislator*
Sherr, Charles J. *immunologist, researcher*
Shochat, Stephen Jay *pediatrician, surgeon*
Shulkin, Barry *health facility administrator*
Smith, Frederick Wallace *delivery service executive*
Smith, Maura Abeln *lawyer, paper company executive*
Stagg, Louis Charles *English language and literature educator*
Steib, James Terry *bishop*
Steinhauer, Gillian *lawyer*
Tate, Stonewall Shepherd *lawyer*
Terry, Joseph Ray, Jr. *retired lawyer*
Thompson, Jerome Walter *otolaryngologist*
Tibbs, Martha Jane Pullen *civic worker, retired social worker*
Todd, Virgil Holcomb *clergyman, theology studies educator*
Tonkin, Ina Lynn Dyer *physician, cardiovascular radiologist, educator*
Trammell, Bradley Ellis *lawyer*
Troutt, William Earl *academic administrator*
Umholtz, Clyde Allan *financial analyst*
Van Middlesworth, Lester *physiology, biophysics and medicine educator, internist*
Vaughn, Cary Edward *minister, director*
Walker, Randolph Meade *minister*
Wallace, Chris *professional sports team executive*
Waller, Robert Rex *ophthalmologist, educator, foundation administrator*
Wallis, Carlton Lamar *librarian*
Webster, Robert G. *virologist, educator*
Wheless, James Warren *neurologist*
White, Nicholas L. *law educator*
Wilcox, Harry Hammond *retired anatomist*
Willet, John *lawyer*
Williams, David Russell *retired music educator*
Winchester, Richard Lee, Jr. *lawyer*
Wright Carrier, J. T. *business owner*

Millington
Gray, Barbara L. *assistant principal, tax specialist*
Jones, Lawrence Andrew *research scientist, retired military officer*
Thomas-Harris, Yvonne Anita *writer, poet*

Morristown
Johnson, Evelyn Bryan *airport terminal executive*

Mount Juliet
Chester, Thomas Wayne *state agency administrator*

Murfreesboro
Breault, Kevin D. *social studies educator, researcher*
Coleman, Jack Andrew, Jr. *otolaryngologist*
Corlew, Robert Ewing *history professor, academic administrator*
Doyle, Delores Marie *retired principal*
Flanagan, Van Kent *journalist*
Ford, William F. *banker*
Gregory, Brenda Kay *music educator*
Hemby-Grubb, Virginia *education educator, consultant*
Jih, Wen-Jang *information scientist, educator*
Klein, Christopher Carnahan *economist*
Locke, Gregory Duane *evangelist*
Phillips, Philip Edward *English professor*
Rankins, Darren Barnard *poet*
Reed, Angelica Denise *sculptor, writer, illustrator*
Walker, David Ellis, Jr. *communications educator, minister, consultant*
Weller, Martha Riherd *physics and astronomy professor, consultant*

Nashville
Abram, Monroe J. *athletic trainer, educator*
Adams, Kenneth Stanley, Jr., (Bud) *energy executive, professional sports team executive*
Adams, Ryan (David Ryan Adams) *musician*
Allbritton, Cliff *personal and organizational consultant*
Allen, George Sewell *neurosurgery educator*
Allison, Fred, Jr. *internist, retired medical educator*
Archibald, Chestina Mitchell *minister*
Armistead, M. Kathryn *editor*
Arnott, Jason *professional hockey player*
Arteaga, Carlos Luis *medical researcher, director*
Ascencao, Erlete Malveira *psychologist, educator*
Atkins, Rodney *musician*
Autry, Philip Earl *music educator, musician*
Bailey, Stephanie B.C. *city health department administrator*
Balcomb, Melanie S. *women's college basketball coach*
Baldwin, Harold Scott *pediatrician, educator*
Balzary, Michael Peter (Flea) *musician, recording artist, actor*
Barfield, Henry Lee, II, *lawyer*
Barker, William M. *state supreme court justice*
Barnett, Bruce Edwin *lawyer*
Barrett, George Edward *lawyer*
Bass, James Orin, Sr. *lawyer*
Bates, George William *obstetrician, gynecologist, educator*
Beach, Margaret Smith *retired language educator*
Beck, Robert Beryl *real estate executive*
Belton, Robert *law educator*
Benbow, Camilla Persson *dean, psychology professor*
Bennett, Marc Logan *otolaryngologist*
Benson, Edwin Welburn, Jr. *trade association executive*
Bentley, Dierks *country singer, songwriter*
Bernard, Louis Joseph *surgeon, educator*
Bigham, Wanda Durrett *religious organization administrator*
Bird, Caroline *author*
Blackstock, James Fielding *lawyer*
Blair, Margaret Mendenhall *economist, consultant, law educator*
Blake, Randolph *psychology professor*
Blumstein, James Franklin *lawyer, educator, consultant*
Bolian, George Clement *healthcare executive, psychiatrist*
Boorman, Howard Lyon *history professor*
Bostick, Charles Dent *retired lawyer*
Bottorff, Dennis C. *banker*
Boyd, Theophilus Bartholomew III *publishing company executive*
Bracken, Richard M. *healthcare company executive*
Bradford, James C., Jr. *brokerage house executive*
Bradford, James Warren, Jr. *dean, finance educator*
Bramlett, Paul Kent *lawyer*
Bredesen, Philip Norman *governor*
Brewer, Clint *editor*
Bridges, Lewis David *elementary school educator*
Brigham, Nicolette Bainbridge *special education services professional*
Brill, Aaron Bertrand *nuclear medicine educator*
Brooks, Kix (Leon Eric Brooks) *musician*
Brophy, Jeremiah Joseph *retired finance company executive, military officer*
Brown, Joe Blackburn *judge*
Brown, Tommie Florence *social work educator*
Brown, Wendy Weinstock *nephrologist, educator*
Brukardt, Gary A. *health facility administrator*
Buckles, Stephen Gary *economist, educator*
Buerhaus, Peter I. *nursing administrator*
Burch, John Christopher, Jr. *investment banker*
Burnett, Lonnie Sheldon *obstetrics and gynecology educator*
Burnett, Michael Bruce *benefits compensation analyst*
Butler, William Blaine *dean, dental educator*
Byrd, Andrew Wayne *investment company executive*
Cantrell, Luther E., Jr. *lawyer*
Capdevila, Jorge H. *medical educator, biochemistry educator*
Carmack, Catherine Elise *archives administrator*
Carr, Davis Haden *lawyer*
Carroll, Frank Edward, Jr. *radiologist, researcher*
Catania, Kenneth C. *neuroscientist, educator*
Cerjan, Martin *law librarian, educator, dean*
Chandler, Nettie Johnson *artist*
Chang, Sam S. *urologist, surgeon, educator*
Chapman, Morris Hines *denominational executive*
Chari, Ravi S. *surgeon*
Chesney, Kenny *country singer, songwriter*
Christie, William Gary *finance educator*
Chytil, Frank *biochemist*
Clark, Cornelia A. *state supreme court justice*
Clemens, Peter J., IV, *corporate financial executive*
Cobb, Stephen A. *lawyer*
Cohen, William Mark *lawyer*
Collins, Joe Lena *retired secondary school educator*
Collins, Kerry *professional football player*
Compton, John Joseph *philosophy educator*
Conkin, Paul Keith *history professor*
Conner, Lewis Homer, Jr. *lawyer*
Cook, Ann Jennalie *literature educator, cultural organization administrator*
Cook, E. Gary *manufacturing executive*
Cooney, Charles Hayes *lawyer*
Cooper, Robert Elbert, Jr. *state attorney general*
Cornfield, Daniel Benjamin *sociology educator*
Covington, Robert Newman *law educator*
Cowart, Richard G. *lawyer*
Cundiff, Lou Willie *artist, sculptor, writer*
Cyrus, Cynthia J. *dean, music educator*
Daane, James Dewey *banker*
Dalton, James Edgar, Jr. *health facility administrator*
Darnell, Riley Carlisle *state official, lawyer*
Daughtrey, Martha Craig *federal judge*
Davis, Kelvisha Lashae *forensic specialist*
Davis, Stephen N. *endocrinologist*
Demarcus, Jay (Stanley Demarcus) *country musician, songwriter*
Dennen, Keith Cameron *lawyer*
Diaz, José J. *surgeon*
Dickerson, Dennis Clark, Sr. *historian, educator*
Dillehay, Tom D. *anthropologist, educator*
Dmochowski, Roger *urologist, educator*
DuBois, Raymond N. *medical educator, researcher*
Dunn, Ronnie Gene *musician*
Dupont, William Dudley *biostatistician, educator*
Echols, Robert L. *federal judge*
Epps, Anna Cherrie *immunologist, educator, dean*
Estrin, Kari (Karen Ruth Estrin) *music producer, agent, consultant*
Etherington, Carol A. *medical association administrator*
Evans, Sara *country singer, songwriter*
Fanning, Ellen *biology professor, research scientist*
Feldman, Leonard Cecil *physicist*
Fields, James Perry *dermatologist, dermatopathologist, allergist, pharmacologist, pharmacist*
Fisher, Jeff *professional football coach*
Fitzgerald, Edmund Bacon *electronics executive*
Fleischer, Arthur C. *medical educator, radiologist*
Ford, Gerald J. (Jerry) *finance company executive*
Forlines, Franklin Leroy *minister, educator*
Fort, Tomlinson *chemist, chemical engineering educator*
Frensley, Susanne H. *history educator*
Frist, Thomas Fearn, Jr. *hospital management company executive*
Frost, Richard W. *manufacturing executive*
Frost, Rick *manufacturing executive*
Frusciante, John Anthony *musician*
Fuchs, Mark *lawyer*
Fulmer, Douglas Alan *political scientist, consultant, journalist*
Gabbe, Steven Glenn *dean, educator, obstetrician, gynecologist*
Gallagher, Martin Joseph *neurologist, neuroscientist*
Galloway, Kenneth Franklin *engineering educator*
Gannon, John Sexton *lawyer, management consultant, arbitrator, mediator*
George, Eddie (Edward Nathan George) *former professional football player*
Gherman, Paul M. *university librarian*
Giles, Joe W. *music educator*
Gillmor, John Edward *lawyer*
Girgus, Sam B. *English literature educator*
Glenn, Christopher Mark *music educator*
Gmeiner, Timothy J. *music librarian, music director*
Gonzales, Greg *state agency administrator*
Goodman, Joe M. *lawyer*
Gore, Steven Lowell *accountant*
Gore, Tipper (Mary Elizabeth Gore) *wife of the former Vice President of the United States*
Green, Lisa Cannon *editor*
Griffith, James Leigh *lawyer*
Griffith, Nanci *singer, songwriter*
Grimes, R. Dale *lawyer*
Guha, Sujata *education educator*
Guinsburg, Philip Fried *alcohol and substance abuse counselor*
Habermann, Ted Richard *lawyer*
Hagan, Kevin F. *plastic surgeon, educator*
Hahn, George Thomas *materials engineering educator, researcher*
Hall, Taffey Rena *archivist*
Halperin, John William *English literature educator*
Hamilton, Joseph Hants, Jr. *physicist, researcher*
Hanselman, Richard Wilson *entrepreneur*
Hargrove, Erwin Charles, Jr. *political science professor*
Harris, Emmylou *singer*
Harris, J. George (Jacob George Harris) *health products executive*
Harris, Raymond Clement *nephrologist, educator*
Harrison, Clifford Joy, Jr. *banker*

Hart, Richard Banner *lawyer*
Hartley, Michael J. *travel company executive*
Havens, Murray Clark *political scientist, educator*
Hays, Stephen Robert *pediatrician*
Heard, Edwin Anthony *banker*
Henderson, Milton Arnold *professional society administrator*
Hercules, David Michael *chemistry professor, consultant*
Hill, Faith *musician*
Hillenmeyer, Henry Reiling, Jr. *restaurant company executive*
Hinshaw, Carroll Elton *economics professor*
Howell, John Floyd *insurance company executive*
Hueneke, Michael *plastic surgeon*
Hwang, Jae-Kwang *physicist, researcher*
Ike, Justus *biology professor*
Inagami, Tadashi *biochemistry professor*
Ingram, Martha Rivers *publishing executive*
Ingram, Orrin Henry, II, *transportation executive*
Jackson, Alan *musician, lyricist*
Jakes, William Bryan III *lawyer*
Jarman, Mark Foster *language educator*
Jarquin Valdivia, Adrian Alberto *internist, neurologist, researcher*
Jennings, Henry Smith III *cardiologist*
Jiang, Xiaomo *engineering researcher*
Johnson, David Horton *oncologist*
Johnson, Melvin N. *academic administrator, economist*
Johnson, R. Milton *healthcare executive*
Johnston, William P. *health facility administrator*
Jones, George *country music singer, songwriter*
Judd, Wynonna Ellen (Christina Claire Ciminella) *vocalist, musician*
Juszkiewicz, Henry Edward *musical instrument company executive*
Kaiser, Allen Bernard *health facility administrator*
Kaufman, Martin Keplinger *landscape artist*
Kiedis, Anthony *vocalist, recording artist, actor*
King, David A. *lawyer*
King, Ed *musician*
Koch, William C., Jr. *state supreme court justice*
Kohan, Betsy Burns *lawyer*
Krauss, Alison *country musician*
Kuhn, Paul Hubert, Jr. *investment advisor*
Lambert, Miranda *vocalist*
Land, Richard Dale *minister, religious organization administrator*
Lane, Cornell D. *psychology professor, director*
Lazar, Irving *psychologist*
Ledyard, Robins Heard *lawyer*
Lee, Donald Han *surgeon, orthopedist*
Lee, Douglas A. *musicologist*
Leipold, Craig L. *professional sports team executive*
LeVan, Martin Douglas *chemical engineering professor*
Levox, Gary (Gary Wayne Vernon Jr.) *country/rock singer*
Lodge, J. Richard *lawyer*
Longhurst, Robert Russell *retired secondary school educator*
Lukehart, Charles Martin *chemistry professor*
Lynch, John Brown *plastic surgeon, educator*
Lynn, C(harles) Stephen *franchising company executive*
Lyon, Philip Kirkland *lawyer*
Mandrell, Barbara Ann *singer, entertainer, actress, producer, writer*
Manning, Charles W. *university chancellor*
Marney, Samuel Rowe, Jr. *allergist, immunologist, educator*
Maron, David Joel *cardiologist, educator*
Martin, Charles Neil, Jr. *health care management company executive*
Martin, Henry Alan *public defender*
Martin, James Larence *dentist, educator*
Martin, Peter Robert *psychiatrist, pharmacologist*
Masys, Daniel Richard *medical educator, department chairman*
Maxwell, George Patrick *plastic surgeon*
May, James M. *medical educator, researcher*
May, Joseph Leserman (Jack May) *retired lawyer*
Mayden, Barbara Mendel *lawyer*
Mayer, John *musician*
Mayhew, Aubrey *music industry executive*
McAndrew, Mark Philip *orthopaedic surgeon, educator, clinical researcher*
McBride, Martina *vocalist*
McCarty, Richard Charles *psychology professor, dean*
McDonald, Michael Eugene *lawyer, educator, clergyman*
McKenzie, Ralph Nelson *mathematician, educator*
McMurry, Idanelle Sam *educational consultant*
McNutt, Mona Belle *social worker*
Medwedeff, Fred M. *retired dentist*
Merritt, Gilbert Stroud *federal judge*
Mitchell, Angela Carol *elementary school educator*
Montgomery, Dillard Brewster *musician, educator*
Moore, William Grover, Jr. *management consultant, retired military officer*
Morrow, Jason Drew *pharmacologist, medical researcher*
Morton, Linda June *academic administrator*
Morton-Young, Tommie *psychology professor, writer*
Moses, Harold L. *oncologist*
Neilson, Eric Grant *physician, educator, health facility administrator*
Nelson, Edward Gage *brokerage house and bank executive, consultant*
Nicely, Donna D. *library director*
Oates, John Alexander III *medical educator*
O'Neill, James Anthony, Jr. *pediatric surgeon, educator*
Orgebin-Crist, Marie-Claire *retired biology professor, department chairman*
Ossoff, Robert Henry *otolaryngologist, surgeon*
Page, Frank S. *head of religious order*
Pagnani, Michael Joseph *orthopaedic surgeon*
Paisley, Brad *musician*
Partain, Clarence Leon *radiologist, nuclear medicine physician, educator, health facility administrator*
Passman, Marc A. *vascular surgeon*
Pearson, Sela *poet, speaker*
Perlin, Jonathan Brian *health services company executive, former federal agency administrator*
Petrie, William Marshall *psychiatrist*
Pfanner, Helmut Franz *German language educator*
Phillips, John A(tlas) III *geneticist, educator*
Pinson, Charles Wright *surgeon, educator, academic administrator*
Pitz, Robert Wendell *professor mechanical engineering*
Poile, David Robert *professional sports team executive*
Policinski, Eugene Francis *syndicated columnist, editor, radio and television personality, producer*
Polk, David Brent *pediatrician, educator*
Powell, Billy *musician*
Price, David Taylor *college baseball player*
Quinlan, J(oseph) Michael *lawyer*
Radcliff, Joyce B. *librarian*
Raj, Satish Ramnarayan *cardiologist, researcher*
Ramer, Hal Reed *retired academic administrator*
Ramsaur, Allan Fields *legal association administrator, lobbyist*
Ramsey, Ronald L. *lieutenant governor, state senator, realtor*
Reinfeldt, Mike (Michael Ray Reinfeldt) *professional sports team executive, former professional football player*
Reschly, Daniel J. *education educator, psychologist*
Ridley, Carolyn Fludd *retired social studies educator*
Riley, Wayne Joseph *academic administrator, medical educator*
Risko, Victoria J. *language educator*
Roberts, John Robert *cardiothoracic surgeon, consultant*
Roberts, Kenneth Lewis *investor, lawyer, foundation administrator*
Robertson, David *neurologist, educator*
Robinson, Nathaniel David, Jr. *physician, consultant*
Rooney, Joe Don *country musician*
Ross, Joseph Comer *pulmonologist, educator, academic administrator*
Rossington, Gary *musician*
Rothenberg, Mace L(awrence) *physician, medical educator*
Royal, Brenda Campbell *biology educator*
Rubin, Edward *dean, law educator*
Saff, Edward Barry *mathematics professor, dean*
Sargent, Mildred Crow *retired history educator, writer*
Sartor, David P. *composer*
Schaffner, William *medical educator*
Schnelle, Karl Benjamin, Jr. *chemical engineering professor, consultant, researcher*
Schoggen, Phil H(oward) *psychologist, educator*
Schreiber, Kurt Gilbert *lawyer*
Schroeder, Joni Lynn *secondary school educator*
Seivers, Lana C. *school system administrator*
Seligson, Mitchell A. *political science educator*
Sergent, John Stanley *rheumatologist, educator*
Sevin, Dieter Hermann *literature and language professor*
Shack, R. (Robert) Bruce *plastic surgeon, department chairman*
Sharp, Julie Ervin *communications educator*
Shaw, Carole *editor, publisher*
Sheik, Duncan *singer, songwriter*
Shell, Owen G., Jr. *retired bank executive*
Sherborne, Robert *editor*
Shockley, Ann Allen *librarian, writer*
Silberman, Enrique *physicist, director*
Sims, Dale *state official*
Sims, Wilson *lawyer*
Smith, Bradley E. *anesthesiologist*
Smith, Chad Gaylord *musician, recording artist*
Smith, Donnie Kay *state agency administrator, retired military officer*
Snoddy, Chris Raymond *athletic trainer*
Snyder, Barbara Lou *retired educational association administrator*
Soltman, Ronald P. *lawyer*
Speece, Richard Eugene *civil engineer, educator*
Spengler, Dan Michael *orthopedic surgery educator, surgeon*
Stahlman, Mildred Thornton *pediatrician, pathologist, educator, researcher*
Starkey, Thomas D. *surgeon*
Stead, William Wallace *medical educator, researcher, department chairman*
Sternberg, Paul *ophthalmologist, researcher*
Stewart, David Marshall *librarian*
Stone, Lawrence Mynatt *publishing executive*
Sugg, Jeanne D. *library director*
Summers, Paul G. *lawyer, former state attorney general*
Surowiec, Andrew Julius *biophysicist, researcher*
Swensson, Earl Simcox *architect*
Takahashi, Takamune *medical researcher, educator*
TeSelle, Eugene Arthur, Jr. *religion educator*
Thomas, Hazel Beatrice *state official*
Thomas, Randall Stuart *lawyer, educator*
Thomas, Robert Paige *lawyer*
Thompson, Dean Allan *cattleman*
Torrey, Claudia Olivia *lawyer*
Trauger, Aleta Arthur *judge*
Trotz, Barry *professional hockey coach*
Tuke, Robert Dudley *lawyer, educator*
Turk, Thomas Liebig *arts consultant*
Twain, Shania (Eilleen Regina Edwards) *musician*
Ullestad, Merwin Allan *tax specialist, director*
Urban, Keith *country singer, songwriter*
Urmy, Norman B. *hospital administrator*
Van Mol, Louis John, Jr. *public relations executive*
Viscusi, W(illiam) Gregory Kip *law and economics educator*
Voegeli, Victor Jacque *historian, educator, dean*
Waterman, Robert A. *lawyer*
Weingartner, H(ans) Martin *finance educator*
Weinger, Matthew B. *anesthesiologist, educator*
Westfield, Fred Meinhard *economics professor*
Williams, Anthony Ervin *music educator*
Williams, Hank, Jr., (Randall Hank Williams) *country music singer, songwriter*
Williams, Marsha Rhea *computer scientist, educator, researcher, consultant*
Williams, Noel Brown *information technology executive*
Winstead, George Alvis *law librarian, director*
Wire, William Shidaker, II, *retired apparel and footwear manufacturing company executive*
Wiseman, Craig *song writer, publisher*
Wiseman, Thomas Anderton, Jr. *federal judge*
Wonders, Pamela Kim *music educator*
Young, Vince Paul, Jr. *professional football player*
Yuspeh, Alan Ralph *lawyer, health company executive*
Zavalin, Andrey I. *optics scientist, educator*
Zeppos, Nicholas S. *academic administrator*
Zhang, Mingzhi *nephrologist, educator*
Zibart, Michael Alan *wholesale book company executive*

Newport
Ball, Travis, Jr. *editor, retired school administrator*
Bell, John Alton *lawyer, judge*
Myers, John William *lawyer*
Porter, James Kenneth *retired judge*

Oak Ridge
Bhuiyan, Shafiqur Rahman *materials scientist*
Boatner, Lynn Allen *research physicist*
Borie, Bernard Simon, Jr. *retired physicist, educator*
Carlsmith, Roger Snedden *chemistry and energy conservation researcher*
Colston, Freddie Charles *political science professor*
Han, Qingyou *research scientist, metallurgist*
Harvey, John Arthur *nuclear physicist*
Holloway, Jacqueline *county commissioner*
Hu, Zhiyu *research scientist, educator*
Jones, Virginia McClurkin *retired social worker*
Katoh, Yutai *materials scientist*
Krause, Manfred Otto *physicist*
Kronenberg, Andreas *nuclear chemist, radiochemist, nuclear technology consultant*
Larson, Bennett Charles *solid state physicist, researcher*
Liu, C(hain)-T(suan) *materials scientist, researcher*
Maienschein, Fred *retired physicist*
McNeilly, Kathy Eden *librarian, library director*
Melnichenko, Yuri B. *physicist*
Nephew, Edmund A. *physicist, retired mayor*
Painter, Gayle Stanford *research physicist, consultant*
Pannala, Sreekanth *aerospace engineer*
Plasil, Franz *physicist*
Poutsma, Marvin L. *retired chemical research administrator*
Raridon, Richard Jay *retired computer scientist*
Regan-Stanton, Christa Maria *artist*
Schwenterly, Stanley William *physicist, researcher*
Shapiro, Selma *retired museum director*
Spray, Paul Ellsworth *retired surgeon*
Wadsworth, Jeffrey *metallurgist, educator*
Zinkle, Steven John *engineer, researcher*

Old Hickory
Reid, Donna Joyce *small business owner*

Ooltewah
Birch, Lorna May *geriatrician*

Paris
Maskas, Auba Sue *elementary school educator*
Prehm, Mary Elizabeth *elementary school educator*

Pigeon Forge
Catron, Stephen Barnard *lawyer, real estate developer, director*
Parton, Dolly Rebecca *singer, composer, actress*

Pleasant Hill
Hull, Charles William *retired special education educator*

Powell
Hyman, Roger David *lawyer*

Ripley
Hartman, Joan Evans *educational consultant*
Klutts, William Alonzo *editor*

Rockford
Nesbit, Sandi Michelle *corporate financial executive*

Savannah
Flanagan, Judy *director, special events consultant*

Sevierville
Koff, Shirley Irene *writer*
Rogers, Edna Loveday *elementary school educator*
Waters, John B. *lawyer*

Sewanee
Croom, Frederick Hailey *academic administrator, mathematician, educator*
Cunningham, Joel Luther *academic administrator*
Parsley, Henry Nutt, Jr. *bishop, academic administrator*
Patterson, William Brown *dean, history professor*
Poe, George Wilkinson *literature and language professor*
Williamson, Samuel Ruthven, Jr. *historian, educator*
Winton, Calhoun *literature educator*
Yeatman, Harry Clay *biologist, educator*

Seymour
Steele, Ernest Clyde *retired insurance company executive*

Shiloh
Allen, Stacy Dale *historian, parks director*

Signal Mountain
Cooper, Robert Elbert *state supreme court justice*
Howe, Lyman Harold III *chemist, researcher*
Swann, Nat Henderson, Jr. *physician*

Soddy Daisy
Bice, Edna Jewel *artist, educator*
Leitner, Paul Revere *lawyer*
Randall, Kay Temple *accountant, retired real estate agent*

Somerville
Macdonald, Sally Polk Bowers *retired addictions therapist*

Sparta
Lentini, Joseph Charles *retired webmaster, systems analyst*

Springfield
Wilks, Larry Dean *lawyer*

Townsend
Sundquist, Don *retired governor, retired congressman, sales executive*

Trenton
Smith, Jeffrey A. *lawyer*

Tullahoma
Daniel, Donald Clifton *academic administrator, aerospace engineer*
Jackson, William David *research and development company executive*

Union City
Graham, R(ichard) Newell *soft drink bottling company executive*

Washburn
Romeo, Joanne Josefa Marino *mathematics educator, department chairman*

Waverly
Peeler, William James *lawyer*

Whites Creek
Coleman, John Daniel *political strategist*

Williamsport
Dysinger, Paul William *preventive medicine physician, educator*

Winchester
Miller, Monte Baldwin *retired internist*
Whetsel, Roger Girton *retired aerospace engineer*

TEXAS

Abilene
Armstrong, Randy Lee *communications educator*
Ashford, Kecia A. *voice educator, vocalist*
Bentley, Clarence Edward *savings and loan association executive*
Betts, Joe Delton *retired religious studies educator*
Boone, Billy Warren *lawyer, retired judge*
Boyll, David Lloyd *retired broadcast executive*
Flores, Kathryn Louise *mathematics educator*
Kirby, D'Lyla *speech pathology/audiology services professional, educator*
McCaleb, Gary Day *university official*
Morgan, Clyde Nathaniel *dermatologist*
Pender, Martha Helen *retired dramatic soprano*
Perry, Troy D. *minister, religious organization administrator*
Robinson, Vianei Lopez *lawyer*
Sartain, James Edward *lawyer*
Specht, Alice Wilson *university libraries dean*
Suttle, Stephen Hungate *lawyer*
Trimble, Celia Denise *lawyer*
Tucker, John Mark *librarian, educator*
Turner, Willard Craig *academic administrator*

Addison
Beck, Charles Wesley, II, *lawyer*
Epstein, Brooke C. *lawyer*
Goldmann, James Allen *healthcare consultant*
Grote, Dick (Richard Charles) *management consultant, educator, writer, radio commentator*
Holl, David B. *cosmetics company executive*
Kimbler, Larry Bernard *real estate executive, accountant*
Mackie, Landon Keller *lawyer*
McKinney, Melissa A. *lawyer*
Rinehart, Neil *financial consultant*
Rogers, Richard Raymond *cosmetics company executive*
Staubach, Roger Thomas *real estate executive, former professional football player*
Wolf, Brandon B. *lawyer*
Zientz, Michael Wayne *lawyer*

Aledo

Barton, David *activist organization administrator, writer*
Reilly, Michael Atlee *finance company executive, venture capital investor*

Alice

Taylor, Bryce B. *music educator, consultant*
Tetlie, Harold *soldier, priest*

Allen

Biard, James Robert *retired electrical engineer, consultant*
Fornadel, Martha Sue *elementary school educator*
Martin, Patrick Michael *physicist, director*

Alpine

Chambers Tucker, Johnnie L. *elementary school educator, rancher*
Cullins, Robert Carlton *academic administrator*
Kittlitz, Rudolf Gottlieb, Jr. *chemical engineer, researcher*
Morgan, Raymond Victor, Jr. *mathematics professor*

Alvin

Lyons, Phillip Michael, Sr. *insurance accounting and real estate executive*

Amarillo

Arnold, Winnie Jo *retired mental health nurse*
Attebury, William Hugh *construction company executive*
Berry, Jacob Obadiah *not-for-profit developer, rancher*
Burnette, Susan Lynn *lawyer*
Carter, Edythe L. (Edie Carter) *mathematics educator*
Fisher, Timothy Roy *protective services official*
Laur, William Edward *retired dermatologist*
Madden, Wales Hendrix, Jr. *lawyer*
Marupudi, Sambasiva Rao *surgeon, educator*
McDonough, Raenell *musician, educator*
McGrath, Daniel Andrew *hydrologist*
Meloro, Peggy Arm-Bosley *retired rehabilitation nurse, small business owner*
Mojtabai, Ann Grace *author, educator*
Parker, Gerald M. *osteopath, researcher*
Parker, Lynda Michele *psychiatrist*
Pratt, Donald George *physician*
Robertson, Pauline Durrett *publishing executive*
Robinson, Mary Lou *federal judge*
Robinson, Ola Mae *accountant*
Saadeh, Constantine Khalil *internist, educator, health facility administrator*
Siddiqui, Afzal A. *medical educator*
Von Eschen, Robert Leroy *electrical engineer, consultant*

Angleton

Fu, Cary T. *electronics executive*
Nigbor, Donald E. *electronics executive*

Argyle

Pettit, John Douglas, Jr. *management educator*
Stallings, Frank, Jr. *realtor, director*

Arlington

Adam, Thomas *humanities educator*
Brainerd, Charles J(on) *psychologist, mathematics professor*
Buckner, Joyce *psychologist, educator*
Cole, Richard Louis *political scientist, educator*
Copeland, Anita Bob *director, retired elementary school educator, senior consultant*
Dasgupta, Purnendu Kumar *chemist, educator, department chairman*
de Jong, Pieter Johannes *finance educator, physical therapist*
Dollar, David *chemistry professor*
English, Marlene Cabral *management consultant*
Ferrier, Richard Brooks *architect, educator*
Goodman, Toby Ray *lawyer*
Graca, Thomas John *education educator, lawyer*
Han, Chien-Pai *statistics educator*
Hoefer, Richard A. *social work educator, non-profit management consultant*
Howell, Holly Lyn *athletic trainer*
Huang, Junmin *chemist, researcher*
Jensen, John Robert *lawyer*
Joohi, Lee *early childhood educator*
Jordan, Robert Randy *music educator*
Lewis, Frank Leroy *electrical engineer, educator, researcher*
Lingerfelt, B. Eugene, Jr. *minister*
Liu, Hanli *biomedical engineer, educator*
Malorzo, Thomas Vincent *lawyer*
Massah, Cherilyn *retired auditor*
McCuistion, Robert Wiley *hospital administrator, management consultant, lawyer*
Mc Keen, Chester M., Jr. *retired manufacturing executive*
Minnerly, Robert Ward *retired headmaster*
Moore, Herff Leo, Jr. *management educator*
Moore, Marion E. *retired mathematics professor*
Munoz, Celia Alvarez *artist*
Oehler, Judith Jane Moody *retired counselor*
Pierson, Grey *lawyer*
Pomerantz, Martin *chemistry educator, researcher*
Ramsey, Charles Eugene *sociologist, educator*
Ray, Asok Kumar *physicist, researcher*
Rollins, Albert Williamson *civil engineer, consultant*
Rosenberry, William Kenneth *lawyer, educator*
Sawyer, Dolores *motel chain executive*
Shanmugam, Ganapathy *geologist, researcher*
Siegfried, Cary Ann *library director*
Smith, Charles Isaac *geology educator*
Sosa, Sammy (Samuel Sosa) *professional baseball player*
Stevens, Gladstone Taylor, Jr. *retired industrial engineer, retired educator*
Stripling, Betty Keith *artist, retired medical/surgical nurse*
Swanson, Peggy Eubanks *finance educator*
Thomas, Lois C. *musician, educator, religious organization administrator, composer*
Tingley, Floyd Warren *retired internist*
Washington, Ron *professional baseball manager*
Weekley, Frederick Clay, Jr. *lawyer*
Wiig, Karl Martin *knowledge management expert and consultant*
Willoughby, Sarah-Margaret C. *retired chemist, educator, chemical engineer, consultant*
Wright, C(arroll) Lee, Jr. *architecture educator*
Young, Michael Brian *professional baseball player*

Athens

Geddie, Thomas Edwin *retired small business owner*

Aubrey

Denny, Mary Craver *retired state legislator, business owner*
Pizzamiglio, Albert Theodore (Al Pierson) *conductor*

Austin

Aadnesen, Christopher *rail transportation executive, consultant*
Abbott, Greg *state attorney general, former state supreme court justice*
Abraham, Jacob A. *computer engineering educator, consultant*
Akins, Vaughn Edward *retired engineering company executive*
Alexander, Drury Blakeley *retired architecture educator*
Alofsin, Anthony *architect, art historian, writer, educator*
Alpert, Mark Ira *marketing educator*
Anderson, David Arnold *law educator*
Anderson, Mo *real estate company executive*
Anderson, Urton Liggett *accounting educator*
Antokoletz, Elliott Maxim *music educator*
Armstrong, Lance *retired professional cyclist*
Armstrong, Nak *jewelry designer*
Armstrong, Neal Earl *academic administrator*
Ashworth, Kenneth Hayden *public information administrator*
Aubery, Stephen Royston Edmund *film producer*
Ayres, Robert Moss, Jr. *retired university president*
Babuska, Ivo Milan *mathematics professor*
Bae, Sungkoo *aeronautical engineer, aerospace engineer, researcher*
Baker, Lee Edward *biomedical engineering educator*
Baker, Mark Bruce *lawyer, educator*
Baltzer, Rebecca A. *musicologist, researcher, consultant*
Banks, Virginia Anne (Ginger) *association administrator*
Barbara, Paul Frank *chemistry professor*
Barnes, Rick (Richard Dale Barnes) *men's college basketball coach*
Barnes, Thomas Joseph *writer*
Barrera, Elvira Puig *retired counselor, academic administrator*
Bash, Frank Ness *astronomer, educator*
Baumgartner, Robert *investment company executive, consultant*
Beazley, Hamilton *writer, educator*
Beckner, William *mathematician*
Benavides, Fortunato Pedro (Pete Benavides) *federal judge*
Bengtson, Roger Dean *physicist, department chairman*
Biesele, John Julius *biologist, educator*
Billings, Harold Wayne *retired library director, editor, writer*
Bishop, Robert Harold *aerospace engineering educator*
Blodgett, Warren Terrell *public affairs educator*
Blunck, Tedde *lawyer, engineer, engineering company executive*
Bobbitt, Philip Chase *law educator, writer*
Bode, Joyce Scruggs *lawyer*
Boggs, James Ernest *chemistry professor*
Bordin, Cristina Stadolny *academic administrator*
Bost, Jane Morgan *psychologist*
Botsford, David L. *lawyer*
Branch, Brenda Sue *library director*
Brannon-Peppas, Lisa *chemical engineer, researcher*
Breen, John Edward *civil engineer, educator*
Brewer, Thomas Bowman *retired university president*
Brister, Scott Andrew *state supreme court justice*
Brock, James Rush *chemical engineering professor*
Brockett, Oscar Gross *theater educator*
Bronaugh, Edwin Lee *retired electrical engineer*
Brown, Frank Beverly, IV, *lawyer*
Brown, Mack *college football coach*
Brown, Norman Donald *history professor*
Brown, Samuel Paul *biologist*
Buchanan, Bruce, II, *political science professor*
Buell, Samuel W. *law educator, lawyer*
Burgess, Kevin L. *lawyer*
Burnham, Walter Dean *political science professor*
Burns, Ned Hamilton *civil engineering educator*
Byars, Samuel D. *lawyer*
Caffarelli, Luis Angel *mathematician, educator*
Cantú, Norma V. *law educator, former federal official*
Carleton, Don Edward *academic administrator, writer*
Carlton, Donald Morrill *retired research, development and engineering executive*
Carpenter, Delbert Stanley *educational administration educator*
Carson, Loftus C., II, *law educator*
Causey, Robert Louis *philosopher, educator, consultant*
Chae, Seung-Hyun *research scientist*
Charles, Michael Ray *artist*
Clark, Charles T(aliferro) *retired statistician*
Clark, Pat English *lawyer*
Cole, Scott L. *lawyer*
Combs, Susan *state agency administrator*
Conine, Ernest *columnist*
Connor, Geoffrey Scott *former state official, lawyer*
Conradt, Jody *retired women's college basketball coach*
Contador Velasco, Alberto *professional cyclist*
Cook, J(ohn) Rowland *lawyer*
Cook, Michael L. *lawyer*
Cooke, Carlton Lee, Jr. *mayor*
Cooper, William Wager *economics, accounting and finance professor, dean*
Corredor, Mary B. *director, language educator*
Crenshaw, Ben *professional golfer*
Cruz, Ted *lawyer*
Culp, Joe C(arl) *electronics executive*
Cundiff, Edward William *retired marketing educator*
Cunningham, Judy Marie *lawyer*
Cunningham, Julia Woolfolk *author*
Cunningham, William Hughes *retired academic administrator, marketing professional, educator*
Curle, Robin Lea *computer company executive*
Cywar, Adam Walter *engineering executive*
Davis, Creswell Dean *lawyer, consultant*
Davis, Donald Robert *nutritionist, researcher, consultant*
Davis, Morris *lawyer*
Davis, Robert Larry *lawyer*
Decaro, Angelo Anthony, Jr. *data processing executive*
Deisler, Paul Frederick, Jr. *retired oil company executive*
Demond, Walter Eugene *lawyer*
Dewhurst, David *lieutenant governor*
DeWitt-Morette, Cécile *physicist*
Dickie, Martha S. *lawyer*
Dillon, Andrew Patrick *dean, library and information science educator*
Doluisio, James Thomas *dean, pharmacy educator*
Dougal, Arwin Adelbert *electrical engineer, educator*
Doyle, Marcus H. *computer technology educator*
Drummond Borg, Lesley Margaret *geneticist*
DuBose, Gaylan Ray *elementary school educator, musician, writer*
Dubose, Kathryn Michaud *secondary school educator*
Duke, Carol Michiels *health products executive*
Dulles, John Watson Foster *history professor*
Dumas, Sara Lee *psychologist*
Duncombe, Raynor Lockwood *astronomer*
Durbin, Richard Louis, Sr. *health facility administrator, consultant*
Dusansky, Richard *economist, educator*
Dyer, Cromwell Adair, Jr. *lawyer, legal association administrator*
Elequin, Cleto, Jr. *retired physician*
Ersek, Robert Allen *plastic surgeon*
Erskine, James Lorenzo *physics professor*
Ewell, Gary L. *lawyer*
Fair, James Rutherford, Jr. *engineering educator, consultant*
Farkas, Gavril *mathematics professor*
Farrell, Edmund James *retired English language educator, writer*
Fearing, William Kelly *art educator, artist*
Feazell, Vic *lawyer*
Fernandes, Edward F. *lawyer*
Firey, Walter Irving, Jr. *retired sociologist*
Fisher, William Lawrence *geologist, educator, dean*
Fleeger, David Clark *colon and rectal surgeon*
Fleming, Francine Faye *legal nurse consultant*
Flowers, Betty Sue *library director, educator*
Foley, Neal T. *cardiovascular surgeon*
Folk, Robert Louis *geologist, educator*
Fonken, Gerhard Joseph *retired chemistry professor, academic administrator*
Forbath, William E. *law educator*
Fowler, David Wayne *architectural engineering educator*
Freeman, Robert Schofield *musicologist, educator, pianist*
Friedman, Alan Warren *humanities educator*
Friedman, Kinky (Richard Friedman) *writer, musician*
Fryxell, Greta Albrecht *marine botany educator, oceanographer*
Fyfe, Steven Trey *otolaryngologist*
Galinsky, Gotthard Karl *classicist, educator*
Gallerano, Andrew John *lawyer*
Gangopadhyay, Abhijit *geophysicist*
Gangstad, John Erik *lawyer*
Garwood, William Lockhart *federal judge*
Gary, James M. *lawyer*
Gau, George W. *dean*
Gavenda, J(ohn) David *physicist*
Gehm, Amy K. *lawyer*
Gentle, Kenneth William *physicist*
George, Timothy Merrill *neurosurgeon, educator*
George, Walter Eugene, Jr. *architect*
Georgiou, George *chemical engineer, educator*
Giblin, Pamela M. *lawyer*
Gibson, Jerry Leigh *oil industry executive*
Giddings, Helen *state representative, personnel management director*
Gillespie, Danny, Jr. *management consultant, music foundation administrator*
Gilliand, Tom *chef, Restaurant Owner*
Gillman, Leonard *mathematician, educator*
Glade, William Patton, Jr. *economics professor*
Goestenkors, Gail Ann *women's college basketball coach*
Golden, Kimberly Kay *critical care nurse*
Golemon, Ronald Kinnan *lawyer*
Gonzalez-Gerth, Miguel *literature and language educator, writer*
Goode, Steven *law educator*
Goodenough, John Bannister *engineering educator, physicist, researcher*
Gracy, David Bergen, II, *archivist, information science educator, writer*
Graglia, Lino Anthony *lawyer, educator*
Graham, Lawrence Sherman *political science educator, management consultant*
Graham, Seldon Bain, Jr. *lawyer, engineer*
Granof, Michael H. *finance educator, department chairman*
Grant, Verne Edwin *biology professor*
Green, Paul Warren *state supreme court justice*
Green, Shirley Moore *retired communications executive, public information officer*
Greenhill, Joe Robert *retired judge, lawyer*
Greig, Brian Strother *lawyer*
Griffy, Thomas Alan *physics professor*
Groat, Charles George *geologist, former federal agency administrator*
Groten, Barnet *energy executive*
Gurasich, Stephen William, Jr. *advertising executive*
Haas, Joseph Marshall *retired petroleum consultant*
Hackert, Marvin LeRoy *chemistry professor, biophysical researcher*
Hamermesh, Daniel Selim *economics professor*
Hancock, Gerre Edward *musician, educator*
Hardin, Dale Wayne *political science professor*
Harms, Robert Thomas *linguist, educator*
Harris, Ben M. *education educator*
Harris, Richard Lee *engineering executive, retired military officer*
Harrison, Richard Wayne *lawyer*
Hassibi, Arjang *engineering educator, director*
Hatgil, Paul Peter *artist, sculptor, educator*
Hayden, Tim *marketing executive*
Hayes, Patricia Ann *health facility administrator*
Heath, Fred Milton *library director, educator*
Hecht, Nathan Lincoln *state supreme court justice*
Helman, Stephen Jody *lawyer*
Henderson, George Ervin *lawyer*
Henley, Paul Thomas *music educator, researcher*
Hernandez, Mack Ray *lawyer*
Hester, Thomas Roy *anthropologist, educator*
Hetzler, Susan Elizabeth Savage *educational administrator*
Higginbotham, Patrick Errol *federal judge*
High, Timothy Griffin *artist, educator, curator, writer*
Himmelblau, David Mautner *chemical engineer*
Hinojosa-Smith, Roland *language educator, writer*
Hitchcock, Joanna *publisher*
Hixson, Elmer L. *retired engineering educator*
Holmquist, Darrel Vernon *geotechnical engineer, arbitrator, mediator*
Holtzman, Joan King *musician, composer*
Holtzman, Wayne Harold *psychologist, educator*
Holz, Robert Kenneth *retired geography educator*
Hopkins, Antony Gerald *history professor*
Hopkins, Bill Everitt *lawyer*
Hornaday, Jon Russell *professional association administrator*
Houston, Ron *professional society administrator*
Howell, John Reid *mechanical engineering educator, director*
Hubbs, Clark *zoologist, researcher*
Hughes, Thomas Joseph Robert *mechanical engineering educator, consultant*
Hull, David George *aerospace engineering educator, researcher*
Ikard, Frank Neville, Jr. *lawyer*
Immroth, Barbara *library and information scientist*
Ingram, Jack *musician*
Inman, Bobby Ray *retired electronics executive*
Ivy, John L. *medical educator, researcher*
Jacobson, Antone Gardner *retired zoology educator*
James, Randall S. *state agency administrator*
Janes, Brandon Chaison *lawyer*
Jansen, Donald Orville *lawyer*
Jastrow, Kenneth M. *forest products, real estate and financial company executive*
Jefferson, Wallace B. *state supreme court chief justice*
Jensen, Paul Allen *mechanical engineer*
Jentz, Gaylord Adair *law educator*
Johnson, Philip Wayne *state supreme court justice*
Johnson, Sandra K. *electrical engineer*
Jordan, Bryce *retired university president*
Justice, William Wayne *federal judge*
Kalmykov, Serguei *physicist*
Keasler, Michael Edward *judge*
Kelley, Henry Paul *academic administrator, psychology educator*
Kendrick, David Andrew *economist, educator*
Keys, Jerry Malcom *lawyer, educator*
Killough, David E. *lawyer*
Kimberlin, Sam Owen, Jr. *financial consultant*
Kirk, Lynda Pounds *biofeedback therapist, neurotherapist, counselor*
Kirk, Terrence *lawyer*
Knapp, Mark Lane *communications educator, consultant*
Knepp, Christopher A. *lawyer*
Knowles, Harry Jay *internet personality, blogger, film critic*
Koen, Billy Vaughn *mechanical engineering educator*
Kolar, Mary Jane *trade and professional association executive*
Krische, Michael J. *chemistry professor*
Kyriakides, Stelios K. *aerospace engineer, educator*
Lam, Simon Shin-Sing *computer science educator*
Lamb, Jamie Parker, Jr. *retired mechanical engineer*
Lambert, David L. *astronomer, educator*
Lambowitz, Alan Marc *biochemistry educator*
Lamis, Leroy *artist, retired art educator*
Lang, Roberta Lynn *food products company executive, lawyer*
Lansford, James Lowell *technologist*
Larkam, Beverley McCosham *social worker, marriage and family therapist*
Larson, Kermit Dean *finance educator*

Lary, Banning Kent *film producer, writer*
Laubach, Stephen Ernest *research scientist*
Lawrence, Mell *architect*
Leeman, Daniel J. *otolaryngologist*
LeFebvre, Julie Aguilar *not-for-profit fundraiser*
Lemens, William Vernon, Jr. *banker, finance company executive, lawyer*
Lenoir, Gloria Cisneros *secondary school educator, consultant*
Lindsay, Leslie *packaging engineer*
Liu, Hung-wen (Ben) *science educator, researcher*
Livingston, William Samuel *retired academic administrator, political scientist, educator*
Lochridge, Lloyd Pampell, Jr. *lawyer*
Lochridge, Patton G. *lawyer*
Loehlin, John Clinton *psychologist, educator*
Loo, Lynn (Yueh-Lin) *chemical engineer*
Lorenz, Ted R. *lawyer*
Louis, William Roger *historian*
Lowry, Alaire Howard *psychologist*
Mackey, John P. *food products executive*
Magee, Stephen Pat *economics professor, finance professor*
Mark, Hans Michael *physicist, former federal agency administrator*
Marshall, Richard Paul, Jr. *lawyer*
Martin, Stephen F. *chemist, educator, researcher*
Martin, Thomas Brooks, Jr. *computer company executive*
Mathias, Reuben Victor (Vic Mathias) *organization executive, real estate investor*
Mathis, Marsha Debra *customer service administrator*
May, Robert George *dean, accounting educator*
Mayer, Michel *computer company executive*
Mayes, Wendell Wise, Jr. *former broadcasting company executive*
McBride, Earle F. *geologist, educator*
McCullough, Frank Witcher III *lawyer*
McFadden, Dennis *psychologist, educator*
McKeown-Moak, Mary Park *educational consultant*
Mc Ketta, John J., Jr. *chemical engineering professor*
McKetta, John J. III *lawyer*
Medina, David *state supreme court justice*
Mersky, Roy Martin *legal association administrator, educator*
Meyers, Lawrence Edward *state judge*
Middleton, Christopher *Germanic languages and literature educator*
Mills, Stephen *performing company executive*
Moag, Rodney Frank *language educator, country and bluegrass singer, musician, record producer*
Montoya, Rudy, Jr. *volunteer*
Mooney, John Bradford, Jr. *oceanographer, engineer, consultant*
Moore, J. Strother *computer scientist, educator*
Morton, R. Steven *lawyer*
Moss, Bill Ralph *lawyer*
Moss, Logan Vansen *lawyer*
Mountain, Janet M. *foundation administrator, former computer company executive*
Mueller, Peggy Jean *dance educator, choreographer, rancher*
Mulconrey, Brian George *management consultant, futurist*
Mullen, Ron *insurance company executive*
Mullenix, Linda Susan *law educator*
Nasta, Deep *real estate agent and broker*
Neavel, Celia Beth *medical association administrator*
Neeley, Shirley J. *school system administrator*
Neely, Stephanie *librarian*
Nichols, Steven Parks *mechanical engineer, educator, academic administrator, lawyer*
Novak, Gordon S., Jr. *computer scientist, educator*
Nowlin, James Robertson *federal judge*
Oden, John Tinsley *engineering educator, mathematician, consultant*
O'Neill, Harriet *state supreme court justice*
Oram, Robert W. *library administrator*
Osborne, Duncan Elliott *lawyer*
Oshinsky, David M. *history professor, writer*
Otto, Byron Leonard *retired lawyer, state agency administrator*
Owen, Priscilla Richman *federal judge, former state supreme court justice*
Painter, Theophilus Shickel, Jr. *internist, allergist*
Parrish, William M. *lawyer*
Patterson, Donald Eugene *research scientist*
Payne, John Ross *archivist, educator, library and information scientist, educator*
Payne, Tyson Elliott, Jr. *retired insurance executive*
Pearson, Jim Berry, Jr. *human resources specialist*
Pena, Richard *lawyer*
Peppas, Nicholas Athanassiou *chemical and biomedical engineering educator, consultant*
Perry, Rick *governor*
Phillips, Joseph Daniel *geophysicist, oceanographer*
Phillips, Thomas Royal *lawyer, former state supreme court chief justice*
Pickett, Sandra *archivist, information scientist*
Pirkey, Louis Thomas *lawyer*
Pope, Andrew Jackson, Jr., (Jack) *retired judge*
Powers, William Charles, Jr. *academic administrator, law educator*
Prior, David B. *academic administrator*
Ramirez Garza, Elizabeth Ann *biology professor, researcher*
Rascoe, Paul Stephen *librarian, researcher*
Ravago, Miguel *chef, Restaurant Owner*
Ray, Cread L., Jr. *retired judge*
Reese, Lymon Clifton *civil engineering educator*
Reible, Danny David *environmental chemical engineer, educator*
Reid, Jackson Brock *psychologist, educator*
Reiter, David S. *engineering company executive, lawyer*
Rich, John Martin *humanities educator, researcher*
Richards-Kortum, Rebecca Rae *biomedical engineering educator*
Roach, James Robert *retired political science professor*
Roan, Forrest Calvin, Jr. *lawyer*
Robertson, Damon D. *lawyer*
Rossky, Peter Jacob *chemistry professor, chemical engineer, researcher*
Rostow, Elspeth Davies *political science professor*
Roueche, John Edward, II, *education educator, director*
Roy, Loriene *library association executive, library and information scientist*
Royal, Darrell K. *university official, retired football coach*
Rudd, Peggy D. *library director*
Rylander, Henry Grady, Jr. *mechanical engineering educator*
Sager, Lawrence Gene *dean, law educator*
Sampson, John J. *law educator*
Sandberg, Irwin Walter *retired electrical and computer engineering educator*
Sawyer, Margo Lucy *artist, educator*
Sawyer, William Dale *internist, educator, dean, foundation administrator*
Schechter, Robert Samuel *chemical engineer, educator*
Schleuse, William *retired psychiatrist, psychoanalyst*
Schmitt, Karl Michael *retired political scientist*
Schneider, James M. *bank executive, former computer company executive*
Schulze, Eric William *lawyer*
Schuring, Elizabeth *lawyer*
Schuurman, Willem Gerhard *lawyer*
Schwartz, Aaron Robert *lawyer, former state legislator*
Schwitters, Roy Frederick *physicist, researcher*
Sciance, Carroll Thomas *chemical engineer, educator*
Serafine, Mary Louise *psychologist, educator, lawyer*
Sessler, Jonathan Lawrence *chemistry professor*
Seung, Thomas Kaehao *philosophy educator*
Shapiro, David L. *lawyer*
Shapiro, Florence *state legislator, advertising and public relations executive*
Shilling, Roy Bryant, Jr. *academic administrator*
Simpson, Beryl Brintnall *botany educator*
Smith, Jeffrey Chipps *art educator*
Smith, Patricia H. *library association director*
Sparks, Sam *federal judge*
Spence, Roy Milam, Jr. *advertising executive*
Spicer, Beverly White *writer, photojournalist, artist*
Springer, David William *dean, social sciences educator*
Starbird, Michael *mathematics professor*
Steinfink, Hugo *chemical engineering professor*
Stephen, John Erle *lawyer, consultant*
Stewart, Kent Kallam *analytical biochemistry educator*
Stokoe, Kenneth H., II, *civil engineer, educator*
Stoner, James Lloyd *retired foundation administrator, clergyman*
Strassels, Scott A. *pharmacist, researcher*
Strauser, Robert Wayne *lawyer*
Streetman, Ben Garland *electrical engineering educator*
Sturley, Michael F. *law educator*
Stutts, William Floyd, Jr. *lawyer, educator*
Sutherland, William Owen Sheppard *retired language educator, consultant*
Sutton, Beverly Jewell *psychiatrist*
Sutton, Harry Eldon *geneticist, educator*
Sutton, John F., Jr. *lawyer, educator, dean*
Swartzlander, Earl Eugene, Jr. *engineering educator, former electronics company executive*
Swinney, Harry Leonard *physics professor*
Tate, John Torrence *mathematics professor, researcher*
Temple, Larry Eugene *lawyer*
Thornton, Joseph Scott *research and development company executive, materials scientist*
Thurston, George Butte *mechanical and biomedical engineering educator*
Todaro, Julie Beth *libraries dean, association executive*
Torres, Gerald *law educator*
Torres, John D. *lawyer*
Tottenham, Terry Oliver *lawyer*
Townsend, Justin C. *lawyer*
Trabulsi, Judy *advertising and marketing executive*
Trafton, Laurence Munro *astronomer, researcher*
Truchard, James J. *engineering executive*
Tucker, Richard Lee *civil engineer, educator*
Uhlenbeck, Karen Keskulla *mathematician, educator*
Vande Hey, James Michael *retired air force officer*
van Otteren, Juliet *photographer*
Velz, John William *retired literature educator*
Volk, William R. *lawyer*
Vykukal, Eugene Lawrence *pharmaceutical executive, director*
Wahl, William Bryan *marketing professional, real estate company officer*
Wahlberg, Philip Lawrence *former bishop*
Wainwright, Dale V. *state supreme court justice*
Walter, Virginia Lee *psychologist, educator*
Walton, Charles Michael *civil engineering educator*
Watkins, Joe Bill *lawyer*
Weddington, Sarah Ragle *lawyer, educator*
Weinberg, Louise *law educator, writer*
Weintraub, Russell Jay *lawyer, educator*
Welch, Ashley James *engineering educator*
Wentworth, Earl Jeffrey *lawyer, realtor, state legislator*
West, Royce *lawyer, state legislator*
Westbrook, Jay Lawrence *law educator*
Wheeler, John Craig *astrophysicist, writer*
Whitbread, Thomas Bacon *language educator, writer*
Willett, Don R. *state supreme court justice*
Williams, Anna Lassiter *psychologist, researcher*
Williams, Jerome Denean *advertising educator*
Williams, Mary Pearl *judge*
Williams, Roberton Capell III *economics professor*
Williamson, Barry Scott *conductor, performing arts educator*
Williamson, Thomas Arnold *publishing executive*
Willson, C. Grant *chemical engineering and chemistry professor*
Wilson, Clark R. *geophysicist, educator*
Wilson, Margaret Scarbrough *retail executive*
Wilson, Phil (Samuel Philip Wilson) *state official*
Winegar, Bradford Charles *otolaryngologist, surgeon, researcher*
Winters, Sam *lawyer*
Wise, Gary Lamar *electrical engineer, educator, mathematician, researcher*
Wohlers, Teresa Dahmus *lawyer*
Wood, Donald F. *lawyer*
Wurzbach, Linda *educational consultant*
Wynn, Will *mayor*
Xin, Jack *mathematician, educator*
York, Candace A. *marketing professional, writer*
Young, Harrison, II, *software development and marketing executive*
Young, Phyllis Casselman *music educator*
Yudof, Mark George *academic and federal agency administrator, law educator*
Zeng, Hongliu Henry *geophysicist, geologist*

Bacliff
Bacani, Nicanor-Guglielmo Vila *civil and structural engineer, consultant*

Baird
Rodenberger, Charles Alvard *aerospace engineer, consultant*

Bandera
Bartley, Dee Gray *information technology executive*

Bastrop
Clemons, Barbara Gail *history educator*
Johanning, Gary Lee *medical educator*
Phillips, Joseph Michael *historian, writer*
Reaves, Melvin Junior *retired small business owner*

Baytown
Harrison, Paula Jean *church musician*
Lee, Gordon Kay *humanities educator*
Leiper, Robert Duncan *local government official*
Williams, Drew Davis *surgeon*

Beaumont
Alter, Nelson Tobias *retail executive, wholesale distribution executive*
Baden, Sheri Louise *primary school educator*
Bahrim, Cristian *physicist, educator, researcher*
Black, Robert Allen *lawyer*
Bradley, Jerry Wayne *language educator, department chairman*
Brentlinger, William Brock *college dean*
Brooks, Jack Bascom *former congressman*
Davis, Gloria Whittie *educational association administrator*
Dowell, James Dale *lawyer*
Dryden, Woodson E. *lawyer*
Hopper, Jack Rudd *chemical engineering professor*
Kemble, Joe David *mathematics professor*
Koehn, Enno *engineering educator, researcher*
Lord, Evelyn Marlin *mayor*
Lozano, Jose *nephrologist*
Needham, Keith Alan *language educator*
Payne, Elton Curtis, Jr. *adult education educator*
Peirce, Dwight A(lexander), Jr. *music educator*
Roth, Lane *communications educator*
Scofield, Louis M., Jr. *lawyer*
Sooudi, Matthew M. *retired surgeon*
Tarpley, Lee *botanist, educator*

Bedford
Dawes, Robert Leo *mathematician, consultant*

Beeville
Freeman, Patsy L. *director*
Littlejohn, John Joseph *petroleum engineer*

Bellaire
Crayton, Arnell *secondary school educator*
Haywood, Theodore Joseph *physician, educator*
Jacobus, Charles Joseph *lawyer, title company executive, writer*
Lundy, Victor Alfred *architect, educator*
Mayo, Clyde Calvin *psychologist, educator*
Soffar, William Douglas *lawyer*

Belton
Erlund, Cecilia Wharton *psychology professor, small business owner*
Shoemaker, Robert Morin *retired military officer, commissioner*

Bertram
Albert, Susan Wittig *writer*

Big Spring
Fryrear, Donald William *agricultural engineer, researcher*

Boerne
Daugherty, Linda Hagaman *real estate company executive*
Goode, Bobby Claude *retired secondary school educator*
Price, John Randolph *writer*
Richmond, James Ellis *retired restaurant company executive*
Tom, James Robert *accountant*
Vaughan, Edward Gibson *lawyer*
Wittmer, James Frederick *preventive medicine physician, educator*

Bogata
Marris, Roy O. *agriculturist, consultant*

Booker
Doerrie, Bobette *secondary school educator, consultant*

Borger
Edmonds, Thomas Leon *lawyer, management consultant*
Strecker, Judy Ellen *music educator*

Breckenridge
Jones, Karen Annette *civic volunteer*

Brenham
Dalrymple, Christopher Guy *chiropractor*
Moorman, Richard Hal, IV, *lawyer*
Pipes, Paul Ray *county commissioner*

Brooks City-Base
Miller, Carolyn Lyons *microbiologist, military officer*
Villarreal, Roberto Escamilla *retired political science researcher, educator, administrator*

Brownsville
Britten, Thomas Anthony *history professor*
Emilio, Garrido Sanabria Rafael *science educator, researcher*
Fleming, Tommy Wayne *lawyer*
Garcia, Juliet Villarreal *academic administrator*
Holkup, Linda Patricia *music educator*
Imperial, Henry L. *internist*
Pena, Raymundo Joseph *bishop*
Ray, Mary Louise Ryan *lawyer*
Rodriguez, Eduardo Roberto *lawyer*
Santa-Coloma, Bernardo *retired secondary school educator*
Soldan, Angelika *political science educator, philosopher*
Weisfeld, Sheldon *lawyer*
Yi, Taeil *mathematician, educator*

Brownwood
Bell, Mary E. Beniteau *accountant*
Bell, William Woodward *lawyer*
DeHay, Jerry Marvin *business educator, small business owner*
Weeks, Patsy Ann Landry *librarian, educator*

Bryan
Bigham, Robert Eric *engineer*
Bryant, Keith Lynn, Jr. *history professor*
Buckley, John Joseph, Jr. *healthcare executive*
Dirks, Kenneth Ray *medical educator, army officer*
Fields, Sheila Crain *elementary school educator*
Julson, Amanda Palmer *science educator*
Koehler, Myron *retired secondary school educator*
McIntyre, John Armin *physics professor*
Milford, Murray Hudson *retired soil science educator*
Miller, Thomas Eugene *lawyer, writer*
Owens, Harold B. *former state agency consultant*
Samson, Charles Harold, Jr., (Car Samson) *retired engineering educator, consultant*
Soonthornpoct, Punnee *biology professor*

Bullard
Mote, Clyde A *lawyer*

Burleson
Hunter, Louis G. *retired aerospace engineer*

Burton
Knauss, Robert Lynn *corporate financial executive*

Bushland
Howell, Terry Allen *agricultural engineer*
Payne, William Albert, Jr. *agronomist, educator*

Calvert
Alemán, Marthanne Payne *environmental scientist, consultant*

Canyon
Atchison, Timothy B. *education educator, neuropsychologist*
Hueston, Harry Raymond, II, *criminal justice educator, researcher*
Long, Russell Charles *retired academic administrator*
Stuntz, Jean Allison *history professor*
Thoman, Roy Edward *political scientist, educator*
Trela, Richard Joseph *conservator, educator*

Canyon Lake
Bowden, Virginia Massey *librarian*

Carrollton
Barland, Sarah Elizabeth *secondary school educator*
Illes, George Maximilian *retired food products executive*
Lieberman-Cline, Nancy *sports commentator, former professional basketball coach and player*
Riggs, Arthur Jordy *retired lawyer*
Wilson, Kristen Ellen *psychologist*
Withrow, Lucille Monnot *nursing home administrator*

Cat Spring
Ramsey, Mary Catherine *mechanical engineer, consultant*

Cedar Hill
Findley, Milla Jean *nutritionist*

Hickman, Traphene Parramore *retired library director, consultant*
Jackson, Jewel *retired state agency administrator*
Jackson, Robert Roscoe *education educator*
Stowers, Carlton Eugene *writer*

Cedar Park
Albin, Leslie Owens *biology professor*
Lam, Pauline Poha *library director*
Love, Ben Howard *retired organization executive*

Channelview
Dunn, Donald Glenn *electrical engineer, consultant*
Nyberg, Donald Arvid *oil industry executive*

Chillicothe
Brock, Helen Rachel McCoy *retired mental health and community health nurse*

Chireno
Mayhar, Ardath Frances (Frank Cannon, John Killdeer, Frances Hurst) *writer*

Cisco
Johnson, Cynthia Zuckernick *history educator*

Cleburne
MacLean, John Ronald *lawyer*

Cleveland
Campbell, Selaura Joy *lawyer*

Coldspring
Bunch, Robert Craig *librarian*

College Station
Adkisson, Perry Lee *university system chancellor*
Akin, Bilal *electrical engineer*
Armstrong, Robert Beall *physiologist, educator*
Arnold, J(ames) Barto III *marine archaeologist*
Arnowitt, Richard Lewis *retired physics professor*
Bass, George Fletcher *retired archaeology educator*
Basu, Shabari *research scientist*
Beaver, Bonnie Veryle *veterinarian, educator*
Bennett, G(eorge) Kemble *engineering educator*
Borlaug, Norman Ernest *agricultural scientist*
Bowen, Ray Morris *academic administrator, engineering educator*
Boyd, Lorraine Alison *finance educator*
Buchanan, Walter Woolwine *electrical engineer, educator, academic administrator*
Butenko, Sergiy *engineering educator*
Butler-Purry, Karen L. *electrical engineer, educator*
Cannon, Garland *linguist, educator*
Carlton, Paul Kendall, Jr. *physician*
Cocanougher, Arthur Benton *academic administrator*
Cook, C. Colleen *librarian, dean*
Cook, Violetta Burke *university administrator*
Dasgupta, Sumantra *education educator, researcher*
Davis, Eddie Joe *academic and foundation administrator*
Dessler, Alexander Jack *astrophysicist, educator*
Dethloff, Henry Clay *historian, educator*
Dickey, Nancy Wilson *chancellor, physician*
Duce, Robert Arthur *atmospheric chemist, oceanographer, educator*
Eaton, Gordon Pryor *geologist, consultant*
Edwards, George Charles III *political science professor, writer*
Ehsani, Mehrdad (Mark) *electrical engineering educator, consultant*
Erlandson, David Alan *education administration educator*
Ewing, Richard Edward *mathematics, chemical and petroleum engineering educator*
Ezell, Margaret M. *language educator*
Finch, Warren L., Jr. *library director, archivist*
Fletcher, Leroy Stevenson *mechanical engineer, educator*
Franchione, Dennis *university football coach*
Furubotn, Eirik Grundtvig *economics professor*
Gan, Jianbang *agricultural studies educator, economist*
Godfrey, Cullen Michael *lawyer, academic administrator*
Goodman, David Wayne *research chemist, educator*
Greenhut, Melvin Leonard *economist, educator*
Gunn, Clare Alward *travel consultant, writer, retired educator*
Hall, Kenneth Richard *chemical engineering professor, consultant*
Hammond, Tracy Anne *computer scientist, educator*
Hann, Roy William, Jr. *civil engineer, educator*
Hardy, John Christopher *physicist, researcher, educator*
Harner, James Lowell *language educator*
Hise, Richard Todd *marketing professional, educator, consultant*
Holzweiss, Robert F. *archivist, educator*
Hooton, James G. *academic administrator*
Jackson, Thomas O. *real estate appraiser, urban planner*
Kier, Ann B. Burnette *pathology educator*
Kuhn, Beverly Thompson *transportation engineer*
Laane, Jaan *chemistry professor*
Lancaster, Sarah *research scientist*
Lee, William John *petroleum engineering educator, consultant*
Lu, Mi *computer engineer, educator*
Lynn, Laurence Edwin, Jr. *academic administrator, educator*
Lytton, Robert Leonard *civil engineer, educator*
MacOpiyo, Laban Adero *geographer, researcher, ecologist*
Mahajan, Arvind *finance educator*
Martin, Carol Jacquelyn *artist, educator*
Mathewson, Christopher Colville *engineer, geologist, educator*
McCrady, James David *veterinarian, educator*
McIntyre, Peter Mastin *physicist, researcher*
Meier, Kenneth John *political scientist*
Monroe, Haskell Moorman, Jr. *chancellor emeritus, retired history professor, dean*
Moroney, John Rodgers *economist, educator*
Murano, Elsa A. *academic and former federal agency administrator*
Nachman, Ronald James *chemist, researcher*
Neill, William Harold, Jr. *science educator, researcher*
Ntaimo, Lewis *engineering educator, researcher*
O'Connor, Rod *chemist, consultant, inventor*
Ory, Marcia Gail *social science researcher*
Page, Robert Henry *retired engineering educator, researcher*
Painter, John Hoyt *engineer*
Patton, Alton DeWitt *electrical engineering consultant*
Phillips, Charles David *gerontologist, researcher, medical educator*
Piscitelli, Felicia Ann *librarian, musician, musicologist*
Prescott, John Mack *biochemist, retired university administrator*
Radovic, Miladin *engineering educator, researcher*
Reddy, J. N. *mechanical engineering educator*
Reinschmidt, Kenneth Frank *engineering and construction executive, educator*
Richardson, Herbert Heath *retired mechanical engineer, educator, dean, academic administrator*
Riskowski, Gerald Lee *engineering educator*
Saric, William Samuel *aerospace engineering educator*
Schunicht, Shannon Anthony *retired military officer, political scientist*
Shepley, Mardelle McCuskey *architect, educator*
Solymosy, Edmond Sigmond Albert *marketing professional, retired military officer*
Strawser, Jerry R. *dean*
Stroustrup, Bjarne *computer science and engineering professor*
Sun, Yuefeng *research scientist, educator*
Swaggerty, Christina L. *microbiologist, researcher*
Tai-Seale, Ming *science educator, consultant*
Turgeon, Mark *men's college basketball coach*
Ullman, Gerald Lee *transportation engineer*
Van Riper, Paul Pritchard *political science professor*
Wenger, Scott Andrew *orthopedist, surgeon*
Wichern, Dean William *business educator*
Wild, James Robert *biochemistry and genetics professor*
Woodcock, David Geoffrey *architect, educator*
Xie, Rui-Hua *physicist, researcher*
Zheng, Qi *statistician, biomathematician*

Colleyville
Donnelly, Barbara Schettler *retired medical technologist*
Hennessey, Audrey Kathleen *computer researcher, educator*
Whittenberg, Ira Orville *lawyer*

Commerce
Justice, Madeline Carol *education educator*
Linck, Charles Edward, Jr. *English language educator*
Scott, Joyce Alaine *academic administrator*
Vornberg, James Alvin *education educator*

Conroe
Bowersox, Thomas H. *lawyer*
Fleming, Michael Paul *lawyer*
Gray, Janet Ethel *elementary school educator*
Johnson, Raymond K. *information technology manager*
Steed, Theresa Jean *manufacturing executive*

Coppell
Aikman, Troy *sportscaster, retired professional football player*
McCally, Charles Richard *construction company executive, consultant, mathematician, educator*
Owen, Cynthia Carol *sales executive*

Copperas Cove
Hardin, Ann *marriage and family therapist*

Corpus Christi
Abdelsamad, Moustafa Hassan *dean*
Al-Akash, Samhar I. *pediatrician, nephrologist*
Allison, Joan Kelly *music educator, pianist*
Ayar, Divyang *radiologist*
Beller, Stephen Mark *retired academic administrator*
Benepe, Virginia Lynn *medical/surgical nurse, oncological nurse, educator*
Benner, Richard Walter *oil industry executive, petroleum engineer, geologist*
Blankenship, Billy Jim *surgeon*
Branscomb, Harvie, Jr. *lawyer*
Breecher, Maury Martin *writer, small business owner*
Canales, Herbert Glenn *library director*
Cassidy, Jack *academic administrator, educator*
Cook, Kenneth Ray *radiologist*
Coover, Ann E. *lawyer*
Cutlip, Randall Brower *retired psychologist, university president emeritus*
Fancher, Rick *lawyer*
Finley, George Alvin III *wholesale executive, oil industry executive*
French, Dorris Towers Bryan *volunteer*
Furgason, Robert Roy *academic administrator, director, retired engineering educator*
Haas, Paul Raymond *petroleum company executive*
Head, Hayden Wilson, Jr. *federal judge*
Hepner, Jon R. *investment company executive*
Hunter, Jack E. *retired judge*
Jack, Janis Graham *judge*
Kane, Sam *meat company executive*
Killebrew, Flavius Charles *academic administrator, biology professor*
Klein, Melvyn Norman *lawyer, investment executive*
Lim, Alexander Rufasta *neurologist, clinical investigator, clinical neurophysiologist, educator, writer*
Locke, Michelle Ivy *curator*
McDowell, Barbara *artist*
Merritt, Paul *neuroscientist, educator*
Miller, Carroll Gerard, Jr., (Gerry Miller) *lawyer*
Norman, Wyatt Thomas III *landman, consultant*
Paulson, Bernard Arthur *oil industry executive, consultant*
Potter, Allan L. *lawyer*
Rotta, Alexandre Tellechea *pediatrician, educator*
Salazar, Laura Ann *education educator*
Sisley, Nina Mae *physician, public health service officer*
Snouffer, Nancy Kendall *literature and language educator*
Stukenberg, Michael Wesley *lawyer*
Susser, Sam L. *oil industry executive, consumer products company executive*
Wilken, Jimmy Louis *radio news director, radio station manager, professional photographer*
Wilkinson, Malcolm Doyle *retired pharmacist*
Wooster, Robert *history professor*

Corsicana
Carroll, Ray Dean, Sr. *retired veterinarian*
Dyer, James Mason, Jr. *investment company executive*
McSpadden, Jody Sodd *lawyer*
Smerge, Raymond G. *finance company executive*

Crockett
Gibbs, James Howard *broadcast executive*
LaClair, Patricia Marie *physical education director, paramedic*

Crosby
King, Vernon Dale *art educator*

Crowley
Kemp, Thomas Joseph *retired electronics executive*
Sizemore, Deborah Lightfoot *writer, editor*

Daingerfield
Bruster, Anthony K. *lawyer*
Smith, D. Neil *lawyer*

Dale
LittleDog, Pat *writer*

Dallas
Abdo, Virginia Richie *retired secondary school educator*
Acker, Rodney *lawyer*
Ackerman, Deborah *lawyer*
Adams, John Lewis *transportation executive*
Adams, Richard Lloyd *lawyer*
Ajlouni, Raed Fakhry *dentist, educator*
Albright, Michael *construction executive*
Anderson, Barbara McComas *lawyer*
Anderson, E. Karl *lawyer*
Angelilli, Lawrence *construction executive*
Anglin, Michael Williams *lawyer*
Antich, Peter *radiologist, educator*
Arpey, Gerard J. *air transportation executive*
Ashby, Danny S. *lawyer*
Ashfaq, Raheela *pathologist, educator*
Askew, Kim Juanita *lawyer*
Attanasio, John Baptist *dean, law educator*
Auchus, Richard J. *internist, endocrinologist*
Augur, Marilyn Hussman *distribution executive*
Babcock, Charles Lynde, IV, *lawyer*
Baggett, Steven Ray *lawyer*
Baggett, W. Mike *lawyer*
Bailon, Gilbert *newspaper executive*
Baker, Tom *utilities executive*
Bangs, Nelson A. (Tony Bangs) *lawyer*
Barbour, David A. *lawyer*
Barnes, Madge Lou *physician*
Barnes, Robert Vertreese, Jr. *construction executive*
Baron, Frederick M. *lawyer*
Barrett, Colleen Crotty *air transportation executive*
Bartlett, Richard Chalkley *writer, conservationist*
Baxter, Richard Henry Geoffrey *research scientist*
Bayne, James Elwood *investor*
Beam, Justin *chef*
Beard, Bruce H. *retired psychiatrist*
Becker, Jeffrey M. *lawyer*
Becker, Nancy Woolverton *public relations executive, event planner*
Beer, James A. *information technology executive, former air transportation executive*
Benkowitz, Kevan I. *lawyer*
Bergner, John F. *lawyer*
Bergstresser, Paul Richard *dermatologist, educator*
Berry, James F. (Jim Berry) *engineering executive*
Best, Robert Wayne *gas transmission company executive, lawyer*
Betts, Dianne Connally *economist, educator*
Beuttenmuller, Rudolf William *lawyer*
Bick, Rodger Lee *hematologist, researcher, oncologist, educator*
Bickel, John W., II, *lawyer*
Biegler, David W. *energy executive*
Biermacher, Kenneth Wayne *lawyer*
Birkeland, Bryan Collier *lawyer*
Bishop, Gene Herbert *corporate financial executive*
Black, Robert W. *health products executive*
Blair, Gary Wesley *pharmacist*
Blessen, Karen Alyce *freelance/self-employed journalist, artist*
Blessing, Edward Warfield *petroleum company executive*
Bliss, Robert Harms *lawyer*
Blodgett, Lynn R. *information technology company executive*
Blount, Charles William III *lawyer*
Blue, John Ronald (J. Ronald Blue) *evangelical mission executive*
Bockstruck, Lloyd DeWitt *librarian*
Bombaci, Anthony *chef*
Bondy, Joanne *chef*
Bonte, Frederick James *radiologist, educator, physician*
Boone, Michael Mauldin *lawyer*
Bosch, Joseph A. *construction executive*
Boswell, George Marion, Jr. *orthopedist, health facility administrator*
Boyle, Jane J. *federal judge, lawyer*
Bradford, William Edward *oil field equipment manufacturing company executive*
Bradley, John Andrew *health facility administrator*
Brainin, Stacy L. *lawyer*
Bramblett, George, Jr. *lawyer*
Brandt, Carole *theater educator, department chairman*
Brekhus, Melvin G. *construction executive*
Brin, Royal Henry, Jr. *lawyer*
Brinker, Nancy Goodman *social services administrator, former ambassador*
Brinker, Norman E. *restaurant company executive*
Bristol, Murray L. *lawyer*
Bromberg, Alan Robert *lawyer, educator*
Bromberg, John E. *lawyer*
Brooker, Chip *lawyer*
Brooks, Ben A. *lawyer*
Brooks, Douglas H. *food service executive*
Brooks, James Elwood *geologist, educator*
Brown, Benjamin A. *investment advisor*
Brown, Colleen *broadcast executive*
Brown, Michael Stuart *geneticist, educator, science administrator*
Brown, Stephen F. *health facility administrator*
Buchholz, Donald Alden *stock brokerage company executive*
Budner, Craig W. *lawyer*
Bumpas, Stuart Maryman *lawyer*
Burke, Carla Michelle *lawyer*
Burke, William Temple, Jr. *lawyer*
Burns, Alton Jay *plastic surgeon*
Burns, Sandra *lawyer, educator*
Burns, Scott *columnist*
Buthman, Mark A. *health products executive*
Byrd, Henry Stephenson (Steve) *plastic surgeon, educator*
Caetano, Raul *psychiatrist, educator*
Cain, David H. *lawyer, former state legislator*
Caldwell, Bradley W. *lawyer*
Callahan, Jack F., Jr. *food products executive*
Campbell, David *lawyer, utilities executive*
Campbell, Kevin P. *oil industry executive*
Campbell, Raymond III *publication director*
Canada, W. Ralph, Jr. *lawyer*
Cantrell, Scott *newspaper music critic*
Cantrill, Thomas H. *lawyer*
Carl, Robert E. *retired marketing company executive*
Carnes, Joseph Sydney *clergyman*
Carrozza, Vincent A. *investment company executive*
Casada, Hilaree A. *lawyer*
Case, Thomas Louis *lawyer*
Cassel, Marc *chef*
Castillo, Christine Lynn *pediatric neuropsychologist*
Cavanagh, Harrison Dwight *ophthalmologist, educator*
Cave, Ellis *information technology executive*
Charboneau-McInnis, Janine Joyce *veterinary animal behaviorist*
Charlton, Michael Thomas *surgeon*
Chavez, John Richard *historian, educator*
Chawner, Lucia Martha *language educator*
Cheatum, Don Elwood *rheumatologist*
Cherry, William Speakman *real estate consultant*
Cho, Ho Soon Michelle L. *adult education educator*
Clancy, Denyse Finn *lawyer*
Clapner, Katherine *chef*
Clark, Robert Murel, Jr. *lawyer*
Clements, Jerry K. *lawyer*
Clifton, Matthew P. *petroleum refining company executive*
Cline, Bobby James *insurance company executive*
Cloud, Robert Royce *surgeon*
Cloutman, Edward Bradbury III *lawyer*
Cobb, Melanie H. *biomedical researcher*
Cochran, Mona Sheinfeld *retired economics professor*
Cockerham, Sidney Joe *professional society administrator*
Coggins, Paul Edward, Jr. *lawyer*
Cohen, Harlan P. *lawyer*
Cole, James S. *dean, dental educator*
Coleman, Robert Winston *lawyer*
Collins, Bruce W. *lawyer*
Collins, Philip A. *management consultant*
Colson, Randall Elwin *lawyer*
Comini, Alessandra *art historian, educator*
Conner, Terry W. *lawyer*
Cook, Gary Raymond *academic administrator, minister*
Cook, Virginia *real estate company executive*
Cooper, Daniel E. *orthopedic surgeon*
Copley, Edward Alvin *lawyer*
Countryman, Edward Francis *historian, educator*
Cowan, Barry W. *lawyer*
Cowart, T(homas) David *lawyer*
Cowles, Jim E. *lawyer*
Cowling, Terianne *medical researcher*
Cox, Rody P(owell) *internist, educator*
Crain, John Walter *historian, educator*
Crain, Russell Jon *lawyer*
Creel, Luther Edward III *lawyer*
Crichton, Thomas, IV, *lawyer*
Crockett, Dodee Frost *brokerage house executive*
Crotty, Robert Bell *retired lawyer*
Crowley, James Worthington *retired lawyer, investor, financial consultant*

Cuban, Mark *professional sports team owner, Internet company executive*
Cummins, James Duane *retired news correspondent*
Curran, Charles Edward *theology studies educator, priest*
Daley, Jennifer *internist, educator*
Dalton, Harry Jirou, Jr., (Jerry Dalton) *public relations executive*
Daly, Gail M. *law librarian, educator, dean*
Dao, Kathryn H. *rheumatologist*
Daves, Don Michael *minister*
Davis, Barry E. *energy executive*
Davis, Clarice McDonald *lawyer*
Davis, Joe A. *lawyer*
Davis, Robert Edwin *lawyer*
Dawson, Edward Joseph *merger and acquisition executive*
Dawson, William B. *lawyer*
Dealey, Lynn Townsend *artist*
Deason, Darwin *information technology executive*
Decherd, Robert William *newspaper and broadcasting executive*
Deckelman, William L., Jr. *lawyer*
Dederich-Pejovich, Susan Russell *harpist*
Dee, Ronda *poet, photographer, small business owner, journalist*
Deisenhofer, Johann *biochemistry professor, researcher*
Delagi, Greg *electronics executive*
de Lemos, James Andrew *cardiologist, researcher*
Dell, Susan *foundation administrator, apparel designer*
Demarest, Sylvia M. *lawyer*
Dillon, David Anthony *editor, educator*
Dinkins, Jane Poling *management consultant, application developer*
Dir, Dave *professional soccer coach*
Doke, Marshall J., Jr. *lawyer*
Donnell, Carolyn Faye *music educator*
Doran, Mark Richard *real estate financial executive*
Dorrill, Jeff W. *lawyer*
Dossett, Andrew Bienvenu *orthopedic and spine surgeon*
Doty, Elmer *aeronautical engineer*
Dozier, David Charles, Jr. *advertising and public relations executive*
Drapkin, Dennis B. *lawyer*
Duddlesten, Kevin M. *lawyer*
Dumerer, Lorraine JoAnne Lori *secondary school educator, consultant*
Durham, Michael Jonathan *investment professional*
Dutton, Diana Cheryl *lawyer*
Dyess, Bobby Dale *lawyer*
Dykeman, Alice Marie *public relations executive*
Eads, John A. *accountant*
Eaton, Michael William *lawyer, educator*
Eberhart, Robert Clyde *biomedical engineering educator, researcher*
Edmondson, James Howard *investor, former insurance executive*
Eichman, John C. *lawyer*
Einspruch, Burton Cyril *psychiatrist*
Ellenbogen, Paul H. *radiologist*
Eller, Timothy R. *construction and real estate company executive*
Ellis, Alfred Wright (Al Ellis) *lawyer*
Emery, Herschell Gene *lawyer*
Engibous, Thomas James *electronics executive*
England, Julie Spicer *computer company executive*
Engles, Gregg L. *food products executive*
Esserman, Sander L. *lawyer*
Estep, Robert Lloyd *lawyer*
Etgen, Ann *performing arts educator, choreographer*
Ethridge, Joseph Alfred *manufacturing executive*
Evangelist, Shane *advertising executive*
Evans, Laurie A. *library director*
Evans, Roger *lawyer*
Everbach, Otto George *lawyer*
Fagin, Stephen Andrew *historian*
Fairbairn, Ursula Farrell *human resources executive*
Falk, Robert Hardy *lawyer*
Falk, Thomas J. *health products executive*
Fankhauser, Mark A. *lawyer*
Fanning, Barry Hedges *lawyer*
Farell, Dan *utilities executive*
Farquhar, Robert Michael *lawyer*
Fegan, Jeffrey P. *airport executive*
Feld, Alan David *lawyer*
Fenner, Suzan Ellen *lawyer*
Fetter, Trevor *healthcare industry executive*
Fielder, Charles Robert *retired oil industry executive*
Figari, Ernest Emil, Jr. *lawyer, educator*
Fijolek, Richard M. *lawyer*
Fillmore, Robert M. *lawyer*
Fisher, Richard Welton *bank executive*
Fishman, Edward Marc *lawyer*
Flanagan, Christie Stephen *lawyer*
Flatt, Adrian Ede *surgeon*
Flegle, Jim L. *lawyer*
Fleming, Tom *chef*
Flood, Joan Moore *paralegal*
Fontana, Robert Edward *electrical engineer, educator, retired military officer*
Forbess, Joseph Matthew *thoracic surgeon, educator*
Fordtran, John Satterfield *physician*
Forshey, Michael S. *lawyer*
Fortado, Michael George *lawyer*
Foster, Daniel Willett *medical educator*
Fox, Stephen E. *lawyer*
France, Newell Edwin *retired health facility administrator*
Francisco, Glen Leif *engineer, engineering executive*
Franklin, Kirk *singer*
Franze, Laura Marie *lawyer*
Frazier, Charles T., Jr. *lawyer*
Free Hosford, Mary Moore *biological and medical anthropologist*
Freidel, David Alan *archaeologist, anthropologist, educator*
Freling, Richard Alan *lawyer*
French, Joseph Jordan, Jr. *lawyer*
Frenkel, Eugene Phillip *physician*
Freytag, Sharon Nelson *lawyer*
Friedberg, Errol Clive *pathology educator, researcher*
Friedheim, Jan V. *educational association administrator*
Friedheim, Stephen Bailey *educational consultant*
Frieling, Scott R. *lawyer*
Frisbie, Curtis Lynn, Jr. *lawyer*
Fritz, Terrence Lee *investment banker, strategic consultant*
Fuller, Kenneth D. *lawyer*
Fuller, Kevin Rice *lawyer*
Fyfe, Alistair Ian *cardiologist, scientist, educator*
Gafford, Ronald J. *construction executive*
Galvin, Charles O'Neill *retired law educator*
Gant, Norman Ferrell, Jr. *obstetrician, gynecologist, educator*
Gardner, Stephen Henry *lawyer*
Garner, Bryan Andrew *law educator, consultant, writer*
Garner, Daniel C. *lawyer*
George, Arthur L. *electronics executive*
Gerberding Cowart, Greta Elaine *lawyer*
Gibbs, James Alanson *geologist*
Gibby, Diane Louise *physician, plastic surgeon*
Gilbert, David *chef*
Gilchrist, Henry *lawyer*
Gillett, Grover *author*
Gilman, Alfred Goodman *pharmacologist, educator*
Girards, James Edward *lawyer*
Glancy, Walter John *lawyer*
Glendenning, Don Mark *lawyer*
Glick, Gina Phillips Moran *retired physician*
Glines, Carroll Vane, Jr. *magazine editor*
Godwin, Donald Everett *lawyer*
Goldstein, Joseph Leonard *molecular biologist, educator*
Goodstein, Barnett Maurice *lawyer*
Goolsby, Bryan L. *lawyer*
Goolsby, Michelle P. *lawyer, food products executive*
Gores, Christopher Merrel *lawyer*
Gottlich, Scott *chef*
Goyne, Roderick A. *lawyer*
Grahmann, Charles V. *bishop*
Granowsky, Alvin *writer, educator*
Grant, Joseph Moorman *finance company executive*
Gratton, Patrick John Francis *oil industry executive*
Gray, James Larry *international business executive*
Greef, Charles E. (Stormy Greef) *lawyer*
Gregory, Louis P. *lawyer, gas industry executive*
Griffeth, Landis King *nuclear medicine physician*
Grimes, David Lynn *communications executive*
Gross, Gary Neil *allergist, physician*
Guerin, Dean Patrick *metal products executive*
Gumbiner, Anthony Joseph *investment banker, lawyer*
Guthrie, M. Philip *corporate financial executive*
Haayen, Richard Jan *academic administrator, insurance company executive*
Hage, Sharon *chef*
Haggar, J. M. III *retail executive*
Hale, Earl F., Jr. *lawyer*
Hamas, Robert Steven *plastic surgeon*
Hames, Michael J. *electronics executive*
Hamilton, David Lee *sports association administrator, retired environmental company executive*
Hammond, Herbert J. *lawyer, arbitrator, mediator*
Hankinson, Deborah G. *former state supreme court justice*
Harbin, Duane *library and information science director, theology educator*
Harless, Katherine J. *telecommunications industry executive*
Harris, Curtis Dean *financial consultant*
Harris, Hazel Lynn *medical/surgical nurse*
Harrison, Frank *former university president*
Hartnett, Will Ford *lawyer*
Hartt, Grover III *lawyer*
Hawkins, H. Ralph *architectural firm executive*
Hay, Jess Thomas *retired finance company executive*
Heacock, David *electronics executive*
Hedrick, Chad *Olympic athlete*
Hegi, Frederick B., Jr. *wholesale distribution executive*
Helfand, Marcy Caren *lawyer*
Henkel, Kathryn Gundy *lawyer*
Hennessy, Daniel Kraft *lawyer*
Henry, Vic Houston *lawyer*
Hensley, Noel M. B. *lawyer*
Hesse, Gregory Getty *lawyer*
Hester, Linda Hunt *dean, retired sociology and physical education professor*
Heydrick, Linda Carol *consulting company executive, editor*
Hicks, Marion Lawrence, Jr., (Larry Hicks) *lawyer*
Hinshaw, Chester John *lawyer*
Hirsch, Laurence Eliot *construction executive, investment banker*
Hirschman, Karen L. *lawyer*
Hitt, David Hamilton, Sr. *retired health facility administrator*
Hobbs, Helen Haskell *medical geneticist*
Hoffman, Marguerite Steed *former art gallery director*
Hoglund, Forrest Eugene *retired petroleum company executive*
Holben, David *chef*
Holman, James *allergist*
Holmes, Bert Otis E., Jr. *retired editor*
Holmes, James Hill III *lawyer*
Hopkins, Michael B. *lawyer*
Horchow, S(amuel) Roger *marketing consultant*
Horvat, Vashti *principal*
Houpt, Karen Rae *dermatologist*
Howard, Josh *professional basketball player*
Howland, Grafton Dulany *financial counselor*
Huang, Yen Ti *civil engineer*
Hubach, Joseph F. *lawyer, electronics executive*
Hudel, Chestella Alvis *athletics educator*
Huff, Dann *musician, producer, singer*
Huffman, Gregory Scott Combest *lawyer*
Hughes, Vester Thomas, Jr. *lawyer*
Humble, Monty Garfield *lawyer*
Hunt, Ray Lee *petroleum company executive*
Hunter, Robert Charles *entertainment executive*
Hunter, Robert Grams *retired language educator*
Hurwitz, Ann *lawyer*
Huston, Angela C. *lawyer*
Hutchison, Ray Ray (E. Ray) *lawyer*
Ibach, Robert Daniel, Jr. *library director*
Irwin, Ivan, Jr. *lawyer*
Jakes, T(homas) D(exter) *bishop*
Jayson, Melinda Gayle *lawyer*
Jennings, James Burnett *oil industry executive*
Jillson, Andrew E. *lawyer*
Jobe, Larry Alton *finance company executive*
Johnson, Avery *professional basketball coach, retired professional basketball player*
Johnson, James Joseph Scofield *lawyer, educator, writer, judge*
Johnson, Mary Elizabeth *musician, educator*
Johnson, Murray H. *optometrist, researcher, consultant, lecturer*
Johnson, Robert Lee, Jr. *physician, educator, researcher*
Johnston, Stephen C. *lawyer*
Jolas, Paul M. *lawyer, diversified financial services company executive*
Jones, Everett Riley, Jr. *oil industry executive*
Jones, James Alton *lawyer*
Jones, Lindy Don *lawyer*
Jordan, Charles C. *lawyer*
Jordan, William Davis *lawyer*
Joyner, Tom *radio personality*
Jung, Peter Michael *lawyer*
Kaiser, Fran Elizabeth *endocrinologist, gerontologist*
Kangas, Edward A. *healthcare company and former diversified financial services company executive*
Kaplan, E. Paul *urologist*
Katz, Karen W. *retail executive*
Keithley, Bradford Gene *lawyer*
Kelleher, Herbert David *air transportation executive, lawyer*
Kelly, Gary C. *air transportation executive*
Kemp, Mark D. *construction executive*
Kemper, Robert Van *anthropologist, educator, minister*
Kennedy, Marc J. *lawyer*
Kent, David Charles *lawyer*
Keown, Michael H. *food products executive*
Keyes, James Willard *film rental company executive*
King, Clifford Thomas *protective services official, martial arts instructor, educator*
King, Raymund Camilo *lawyer, physician*
Kinnebrew, Jackson Metcalfe *lawyer*
Kinzie, Jack L. *lawyer*
Kitner, David N. *lawyer*
Kneese, Kyle Calvin *lawyer*
Kneipper, Richard Keith *lawyer*
Knott, Jennifer W. *lawyer*
Kobdish, George Charles *lawyer*
Kober, John A. *lawyer*
Koeppel, Peter Stafford *advertising executive*
Koning, Paul Matthew *lawyer*
Kovacevic, Radovan *mechanical engineering educator*
Kruse, Ann Gray *computer programmer*
Kryder, George M. III *lawyer*
Kuhn, Willis Evan, II, *lawyer, mediator*
Kunkle, David M. *police chief*
Kutner, Janet *art critic, book reviewer*
Lacy, John Ford *retired lawyer*
Ladik, Steven M. *lawyer*
Laettner, Christian Donald *professional basketball player*
Lake, Joseph Edward *ambassador*
Lakhanpal, Sharad *physician*
Lan, Donald Paul, Jr. *lawyer*
Landry, Jane Lorenz *architect*
Lane, John Rodger *museum director*
Laney, David M. *railroad industry executive, lawyer*
Lang, Douglas Stewart *judge*
Lawrence, Annette *artist*
Layton, Kennith F. *neuroradiologist*
Leatherbury, Thomas Shawn *lawyer*
LeBlanc, Jennifer Dawn *lawyer*
Lee, Carl B. *lawyer*
Lee, George Terry, Jr. *lawyer*
Leedom, John Nesbett *manufacturing executive, state legislator*
Leppert, Thomas C. *mayor, former construction executive*
Lerman, Mark Jeffrey *nephrologist, medical administrator*
Lesmes, Stephanie Brooks *lawyer*
Levenson, Stanley Richard *public relations and advertising executive*
Levin, Hervey Phillip *lawyer*
Levy, I. Richard *lawyer*
Lewis, Jerry M. *psychiatrist, educator*
Lichliter, Warren Eugene *surgeon, educator*
Lilyhorn, Gregory Dean *security firm executive*
Lindley, Hamilton P. *lawyer*
Liskow, Frederic Cullen (Ric) *printing company executive*
Lister, George *pediatrician*
Littlejohn, James R. *lawyer*
Litton, Andrew *conductor, music director*
Lockridge, Deborah Ann *minister, educator, small business owner*
Long, Sarah Holley *lawyer*
Lotan, Yair *urologist*
Lovett, Melendy *electronics executive*
Lowe, Gregg A. *electronics executive*
Lowe, John Stanley *law educator*
Lowery, David J. *lawyer*
Lumpkin, John O. *news organization executive*
Lynch, William Wright, Jr. *investment company executive, engineer*
Madden, Teresa Darleen *insurance agency owner*
Maddrey, Willis Crocker *medical educator, internist, academic administrator, consultant, researcher*
Madzik, Elizabeth May *hospital administrator*
Makel, Larry A. *lawyer*
Malouf, Mark E. *structural engineer, consultant*
Malouf, Stephen Ferris *lawyer*
Mankoff, Ronald Morton *retired lawyer*
Manteuffel, Robert Lee *lawyer*
March, Kevin P. *electronics executive*
Mareiniss, Darren Peter *lawyer, physician*
Maris, Stephen S. *lawyer, educator*
Marlow, Patricia Bair Bond *realtor*
Marshall, John Harris, Jr. *geologist, oil industry executive*
Martin, Boe Willis *lawyer*
Martin, Jack *physician*
Mason, Thomas P. *lawyer*
Massman, Richard Allan *lawyer*
Mathis-Thorton, Dianna Dawn *protective services official, writer, publishing executive, not-for-profit developer*
Maxey, Kevin *chef*
May, Kenneth Austin *consumer products company executive*
Mayo, Thomas William *law educator*
McAleenan, Donald F. *lawyer, construction executive*
McAtee, David Ray *lawyer*
Mc Clelland, Robert Nelson *surgeon, educator*
McCombs, David Louis *lawyer*
McCombs, Gillian M. *library director, dean*
McConnell, John Dowling *urologist, educator*
McCormack, William Arthur *lawyer*
McCurley, Carl Michael *lawyer*
McCurley, Mary Johanna *lawyer*
McDonald, Michael Scott *lawyer*
McDowell, John Henry, Jr. *lawyer*
Mc Elhaney, John Hess *lawyer*
McElvain, David Plowman *retired manufacturing, finance company executive*
McGowan, Patrick Francis *lawyer*
McKnight, Joseph Webb *lawyer, educator, historian*
McKnight, Steven Lanier *molecular biologist*
McKool, Mike, Jr. *lawyer*
McLane, William Delano *mechanical engineer*
McNamara, Lawrence John *lawyer*
McNamara, Martin Burr *lawyer, former gas industry executive*
McNeil, Barry *lawyer*
McPherson, Gail *publishing, real estate executive*
McTee, Cindy *classical musician, educator*
McWhorter, Kathleen *orthodontist*
McWilliams, Mike C. *lawyer*
Medlin, Homer Lewis *engineering executive*
Melançon, Renée M. *lawyer*
Melin, Stacy M. *literature and language educator*
Melsheimer, Thomas M. *lawyer*
Mendez, Michelle Annette *lawyer*
Menter, M(artin) Alan *dermatologist*
Meyerson, Morton Herbert *investor, real estate company executive*
Micciche, Daniel John *lawyer*
Miers, Harriet Ellan *lawyer, former federal official*
Migdol, Marvin Jacob *public relations and marketing executive, consultant*
Mighell, Kenneth John *lawyer*
Miller, Charles P. *lawyer*
Miller, Jo Carolyn Dendy *family and marriage counselor, educator*
Miller, Norman Richard *lawyer*
Miller, R. Terry *lawyer*
Mills, Jerry Woodrow *lawyer*
Mitchell, Patrick E. *lawyer*
Mitchell, Teddy Lee *physician*
Moneypenny, Edward William *retail executive*
Mong, Robert William, Jr. *publishing executive*
Montgomery, Matthew L. *lawyer*
Montgomery, Will S. *lawyer*
Moore, Cheryl (Milkes) Jerome *lawyer*
Moore, Edward Warren *lawyer*
Moore, Thomas Joseph *finance company executive*
Morgan, Gregory Paul *financial investment advisor*
Moroney, James M. III *publishing executive*
Mow, Robert Henry, Jr. *lawyer*
Mueller, Mark Christopher *lawyer*
Mukherjee, Ann (Anindita Mukherjee) *advertising executive*
Murphy, John Joseph *manufacturing executive*
Murphy, Kathryn J. *lawyer*
Muse, John R. *investment company executive*
Musselman, P. Weston *lawyer*
Nabors, Marion Carroll *retired English educator*
Nassar, Susan D. *lawyer*
Nelson, Donnie *professional sports team executive*
Nelson, Elaine Edwards *lawyer*
Nemunaitis, John J. *oncologist, medical association administrator*
Nevins, William J. *oil and gas brokerage executive, consultant*
Newman, Keith David *surgeon*
Newman, Steven L. *health care executive*
Niccol, Brian *marketing executive*
Nichols, Henry Louis *lawyer*
Nikaidoh, Hisashi *pediatric cardiac surgeon, professor*
Nikopoulos, Beth *educational association administrator*
Nolan, John Michael *lawyer*
Norman, Bobby Don *artist, writer, research scientist*

Nowitzki, Dirk Werner *professional basketball player*
Nye, Erle Allen *electric power industry executive, lawyer*
Odom, Floyd Clark *surgeon*
Orwig, Matthew Dane *lawyer, former prosecutor*
Osborne, Burl *publishing executive, editor*
Oualline, Viola Jackson *psychologist, consultant*
Owen, Daniel Thomas *entrepreneur, venture capitalist*
Pace, Carolina Jolliff *communications executive, investor*
Palmer, Anthony J. *health products executive*
Palmer, Christine (Clelia Rose Venditti) *vocalist, educator, musician*
Panatier, Christopher J. *lawyer*
Parada, Luis Fernando *science educator*
Parameswara, Vinay Kumar *medical educator*
Parks, J. Michael *data processing executive*
Pauley, Shirley Stewart *religious organization executive*
Payne, Brett H. *lawyer*
Pearce, Ronald *retired cosmetic company executive*
Pearson, Robert Lawrence *executive recruiter*
Pell, Jonathan Laurence *performing company executive*
Pelletier, Sho-mei *musician, educator*
Pennington, Karen Harder *lawyer*
Perkins, Thomas P., Jr. *lawyer*
Perry, George Wilson *oil and gas company executive*
Peterson, Edward Adrian *lawyer*
Pew, John Glenn, Jr. *lawyer*
Phelan, Robin Eric *lawyer*
Phillips, Betty Lou (Elizabeth Louise Phillips) *writer, interior designer*
Pickens, Boone (T. Boone Pickens, Thomas Boone Pickens Jr.) *oil industry executive*
Pickton, Robert (Bob) J. *information technology executive*
Pingree, Bruce Douglas *lawyer*
Pinson, William Meredith, Jr. *pastor, writer, administrator*
Pleasant, James Scott *lawyer*
Poole, David P. *lawyer, utilities executive*
Porter, Biggs C. *corporate financial executive*
Porter, J. Reid *lawyer*
Portman, Glenn Arthur *lawyer*
Powers, Timothy Eugene *lawyer*
Prather, Robert Charles, Sr. *lawyer*
Price, John Aley *lawyer*
Price, Robert Eben *judge*
Proud, Robert Donald (Robert Payton) *broadcast executive*
Pruessner, David Morgan *lawyer*
Pullen, Timothy L. *corporate financial executive*
Purnell, Maurice Eugene, Jr. *lawyer*
Pyles, Stephen *chef*
Quinones, Marissa Escobar *pharmacist*
Rabun, Daniel W. *oil and gas industry executive*
Rachofsky, Howard *retired investor, art collector, patron*
Raggio, Thomas Louis *lawyer*
Rainwater, R. Steven *systems engineer*
Rathburn, Kent *chef*
Rather, Dan *news correspondent, former network news anchor*
Ray, Bradley Stephen *petroleum geologist*
Ray, Hillol Kumar *environmental engineer, poet*
Reddy, J. Patrick *gas industry executive*
Redman, Gary Lon, II, *lawyer*
Rees-Jones, Trevor D. *oil industry executive*
Reid, Langhorne III *merchant banker*
Reid, Rust Endicott *lawyer*
Reinert, James A. *entomology educator*
Rexford, John H. *information technology company executive*
Ribman, James W. *lawyer*
Rice, John S. *lawyer*
Richards, Stanford Harvey *advertising agency and design studio executive*
Richmond, John Revere *physician, educator*
Riddle, Michael Lee *lawyer*
Ringle, Brett Adelbert *lawyer, oil and gas industry executive*
Ritchie, Kevin *electronics executive*
Roach, John D. *building products company executive*
Roberts, Harry Morris, Jr. *lawyer*
Roberts, William Clifford *medical association administrator*
Robertson, Beverly Carruth *retired steel company executive*
Robertson, Rose Marie *cardiologist, educator*
Robison, Brian E. *lawyer*
Rodgers, John Hunter *lawyer*
Rodriguez, Raul Pedro *plastic surgeon*
Rohrich, Rod(ney) James *plastic surgeon, educator*
Roper, Richard B. III *prosecutor*
Rosenberg, Roger Newman *neurologist, educator, department chair*
Rosenblatt, Randall Lee *internist*
Rosson, Glenn Richard *building products and furniture company executive*
Roth, James Frank *chemicals executive, chemist*
Rudolph, William Keyse *curator*
Rush, Augustus John *psychiatrist*
Russell, David W. *molecular geneticist*
Ryan, Dennis Neil *lawyer*
Sagalowsky, Arthur I. *urologist, educator*
Sallee, Wanda Jean *music educator*
Salyer, Kenneth E. *surgeon*
Samuel, Greg R. *lawyer*
Sanders, Harold Barefoot, Jr. *judge*
Satarino, F. Michael (Michael Satarino) *principal*
Schaeffler, Georg *lawyer, manufacturing executive*
Schaffer, Joseph Ira *physician, educator*
Schecter, Arnold Joel *public health physician, researcher*
Schiller, Joan Hoff *oncologist, educator*
Schochet, Barry P. *health care executive*
Schreiber, Howard E. *lawyer*
Schreiber, Sally Ann *lawyer*
Schulze, Richard Hans *environmental engineering executive*
Schwartz, Charles Morris *lawyer*
Scott, John Roland *business law educator*
Self, Scott W. *lawyer*
Selinger, Jerry Robin *lawyer*
Sengupta, Chaitali *computer engineer*
Shambaugh, Irvin Calvin, Jr. *aptitude test firm executive*
Shank, Mark A. *lawyer*
Sharry, Janice Vyn *lawyer*
Shaw, Curtis S. *lawyer, chemicals executive*
Shepherd, Jon Glen *lawyer*
Shepherd, Nick P. *film rental company executive*
Sherman, Floyd F. *construction executive*
Sherrod, Danny Troy *writer, educator*
Shimer, Daniel Lewis *finance company executive*
Showalter, Buck (William Nathaniel Showalter III) *former professional baseball team manager*
Simmons, Harold C. *investment company executive, sugar company executive*
Simmons, Terry L. *lawyer*
Sims, William D., Jr. *lawyer*
Sinak, David Louis *lawyer*
Sizer, Phillip Spelman *gas industry executive, retired oil industry executive*
Slawter, John David, Jr. *oil industry executive*
Sloman, Marvin Sherk *lawyer*
Smith, Catherine R. *construction executive*
Smith, Patsy Juanita *financial executive*
Smith, Sue Frances *newspaper editor*
Solender, Robert Lawrence *retired real estate company executive, retired publishing executive*
Solomon, Risa Greenberg *clinical social worker, child and family therapist, former entertainment industry executive*
Solomon, William Tarver *general construction company executive*
Sonsteby, Charles M. *food service executive*
Spiegel, Lawrence Howard *advertising executive*
Stackhouse, Jerry *professional basketball player*
Stacy, Dennis William *architect*
Stalcup, Joe Alan *retired lawyer, dean*
Steinberg, Lawrence Edward *lawyer*
Sterin, Steven M. *chemicals executive*
Stern, Andrew Milton *public relations executive*
Stewart, Daniel Clark *lawyer*
Stewart, Kenneth L. *lawyer*
Stewart, Robert S. *construction executive*
Stinnett, Mark Allan *lawyer*
Stockard, James Alfred *lawyer*
Stoffel, Paul T. *investment company executive*
Stone, Marvin Jules *hematologist, oncologist, educator*
Storey, Charles Porter *lawyer*
Strock, William C. *lawyer*
Sucato, Daniel J. *orthopaedic surgeon*
Sudhof, Thomas Christian *molecular genetics educator*
Suter, Robert Eduard *emergency physician, educator*
Swindle, Shannon *chef*
Szuwalski, Andre Michael *lawyer*
Szygenda, Stephen A. *electrical and computer engineering educator, researcher*
Tansky, Burton M. *department store executive*
Tapscott, William Ken, Jr. *lawyer*
Templeton, Richard K. *electronics executive*
Templin, Donald C. *lawyer*
Terry, Marshall Northway, Jr. *language educator, writer*
Thiele, Dwain Louis *medical educator, department vice chairman*
Thomas, Paul Lindsley *composer, musician, director*
Thomas, Sarah Elaine *music educator*
Thompson, B. Lolana *archivist*
Thompson, James Nicholas *medical association administrator*
Thompson, Keith F. MacKechnie *geochemist, consultant*
Thompson, Zachary *city health department administrator*
Thomson, Basil Henry, Jr. *lawyer*
Thomson, Roger F. *lawyer*
Thorne, Carl F. *gas industry executive*
Timpa, Vicki Ann *government health program administrator*
Tompkins, Alan W. *lawyer*
Tran, Quoc-Hung *psychiatrist*
True, Roy Joe *lawyer*
Tubb, James Clarence *lawyer*
Tucker, J. Walter, Jr. *manufacturing executive*
Tucker, Keith A. *investment company executive*
Tucker, Kevin W. *curator*
Turley, Linda *lawyer*
Turner, R(obert) Gerald *academic administrator*
Udashen, Robert Nathan *lawyer*
Urbanowicz, E(ugene) Peter, (Jr.) *lawyer*
Ussery, Terdema L., II, *professional sports team executive*
Valentine, Foy Dan *clergyman*
Vanden Eykel, Ike *lawyer*
Vandermeer, Robert D. *orthopedic surgeon*
Vanderveld, John, Jr. *diversified financial services company executive*
Van Scoter, John C. *electronics executive*
van Zweden, Jaap *conductor*
Veach, Robert Raymond, Jr. *lawyer*
Vetter, James George, Jr. *lawyer*
Villareal, Patricia J. *lawyer*
Villarreal, Christie M. *lawyer*
Vitetta, Ellen S. *microbiologist, immunologist, educator*
Voyles, Robb Lawrence *lawyer*
Waddell, Douglas Howard *family physician*
Wagner, Todd *Internet company executive*
Walker, Gordon Beverley Moore, Jr. *business educator*
Walkowiak, Vincent Steven *lawyer*
Wallace, Anderson, Jr. *lawyer, educator*
Wallace, Timothy R. *manufacturing executive*
Walsh, David M., IV, *lawyer*
Wang, Xiaodong *biomedical researcher, educator*
Warman, Lynnette R. *lawyer*
Warren, Kelcy L. *energy executive*
Wassenich, Linda Pilcher *retired health policy analyst, social worker*
Watkins, Craig *prosecutor*
Watler, Paul C. *lawyer*
Watson, Claude Armstead *counselor*
Watson, Steven L. *investment company executive*
Weakley, Clare George, Jr. *insurance company executive, theologian, entrepreneur*
Weber, David J. *history educator*
Weidman, David N. *chemicals executive*
Welch, Frank D. *architect*
Welch, Gerald Thomas *lawyer, electrical engineer*
Werbner, Mark S. *lawyer*
West, Teresa L. (Terri West) *electronics executive*
Westfall, Constance Courtney *lawyer*
Wheeler, M. Cass *health science association administrator*
Whitaker, Darla *electronics executive*
Whitaker, Elizabeth D. *lawyer*
White, James Richard *lawyer*
Whitman, Jeffrey *ophthalmologist*
Wiegand, Robert C. *lawyer*
Wilcox, Tre *chef*
Wildenthal, C(laud) Kern *physician, educator*
Wilder, C. John (John Wilder) *energy executive*
Wiles, Charles Preston *minister*
Wilk, Stuart *publishing executive*
Will, Clark Bradford *lawyer*
Williams, Michael Edward, Sr. *dean*
Willingham, Clark Suttles *lawyer*
Wilson, Angela Lynn *theater producer, playwright*
Wilson, Claude Raymond, Jr. *lawyer*
Wilson, Jean Donald *endocrinologist, educator*
Wilson, Jonathan C. *lawyer*
Wilson, Morgan *chef*
Wilson, Richard A. *oil and gas industry support services executive*
Wilson, Robert E. *lawyer*
Wilson, Taylor *lawyer*
Witte, Robert Jay *lawyer*
Wolford, Larry M. *surgeon*
Wolin, Robert Everett *lawyer*
Wommack, Ron *architect*
Woram, Brian J. *lawyer, construction executive*
Wortley, Micahel D. *lawyer*
Wright, Alan *lawyer*
Wright, Laura L. *air transportation executive*
Wrucke-Nelson, Ann C. *elementary school educator*
Wu, Kathleen J. *lawyer*
Wyant, Clyde W., Jr. *manufacturing executive*
Wyly, Charles Joseph, Jr. *entrepreneur*
Xiu, Liming *electrical engineer*
Yaeger, Evelyn Ann *lawyer*
Yanagisawa, Masashi *geneticist, educator, researcher*
Yang, Emeline *lawyer*
Yeffeth, Glenn Barry *publishing executive, management consultant*
Young, Barney Thornton *lawyer*
Young, Julia Anne *librarian, elementary school educator*
Young, William D. *lawyer*
Zahn, Donald Jack *lawyer*
Zeitlin, Laurie *printing company and information technology executive*
Zhou, Desheng *petroleum engineer*
Zine, Larry Joseph *film rental company executive*
Zumwalt, Richard Dowling *flour mill executive*

Dayton
Davis, Kelli Ansley *social studies educator*

Decatur
Boyd, Derrick S. *lawyer*

Del Rio
Prather, Gerald Luther *management consultant, retired judge, military officer*

Dell Computers
Jarvis, Mark *information technology executive*

Denison
Cameron, Frances Marilyn *elementary school educator*

Denton
Alatzas, George *delivery service company executive*
Alexander, Jim R. *social sciences educator*
Bataille, Gretchen *academic administrator*
Belfiglio, Valentine John *political science professor*
Bertine, Dorothy Wilmuth *artist, educator, accountant, genealogist, poet, writer*
Brewer, Louie George, Jr. *blood bank specialist*
Brock, Horace Rhea *finance educator*
Gabriel, Eberhard John *lawyer, bank executive*
Garcia, Oscar Nicolas *computer science educator*
Golden, Richard M. *history professor*
Gough, Clarence Ray *retired designer, educator*
Greenlaw, Marilyn Jean *retired adult education educator*
Hurley, Alfred Francis *historian, academic administrator emeritus, retired air force officer*
Kesterson, David Bert *language educator, dean, academic administrator*
Kim, Hansoo *materials scientist, researcher*
Kougianos, Elias *engineering educator, consultant*
Krokhin, Arkadii *physics professor*
Lawhon, John III *lawyer, retired county official*
Lawhon, Tommie Collins Montgomery *humanities educator*
McCaslin, Richard Bryan *history educator*
McDonald-West, Sandi MacLean *director, consultant*
Mears, Michelle Morgan *archivist*
Mihalcea, Rada Flavia *language educator*
Newell, Charldean *public administration educator*
Nievar, M. Angela *social sciences professor*
Novak, Rynell Stiff *retired academic administrator*
Peters, Juanita Teal *music educator*
Poole, Eva Duraine *librarian*
Simpson, Carol Mann *librarian, educator, editor*
Smith, Howard Wellington *education educator, retired dean*
Snapp, Elizabeth *librarian, educator*
Snapp, Harry Franklin *historian, educator*
Surprise, Juanee *chiropractor, nutrition consultant*
Swigger, Keith *library and information scientist, educator*
Thompson, Frances McBroom *mathematics professor, writer*
Totten, Herman Lavon *dean, library and information science educator*
Turner, Philip Michael *academic administrator, writer*
Ver Duin, D'Arlene K. *sociologist, researcher*
Wodnicki, Adam Juliusz *pianist, educator*
Yang, Philip Q. *sociologist*

Detroit
Cates, Sue Sadler *special education counselor*

Devine
Passty, Jeanette Nyda *literature and language professor, writer*

Diboll
Fisher, Richard Forrest *research scientist, editor-in-chief*
Harbordt, Charles Michael *forest products executive*

Dickinson
Neves, Kerry Lane *lawyer*

Dripping Springs
Baker, III, Rex Gavin *lawyer, educator*
Daly, Stephen Jeffrey *artist, educator*

Duncanville
Fewel, John Gerrard *government agency administrator, director*
Lang, James Devore, Jr. *ministry executive*

Early
Ross-Parsons, Donna Michelle *counselor, small business owner*

Edinburg
Ayala, Kara J. *speech educator, researcher*
Benham, Grant *psychologist, researcher*
Carrera, Victor Manuel *lawyer*
Lowdermilk, John Lloyd *special education educator, special education services professional*
Lozano, Karen *engineering educator*
Manuella, Frank *art and design educator*
Mollick, Andre Varella *economics professor, researcher*
Munn, Vivian Carole *music educator, conductor*
Pecina, Julie H. *education educator*
Vasquez, Horacio *mechanical engineer, educator*
Wilson, Bruce Keith *men's health nurse*

Egypt
Wynn, John Thomas *retired academic administrator, farming executive, economic consultant, oil and gas producer*

El Campo
Fisher, Robert Bruce *priest*

El Lago
Chase, Jeanette Knapp *music educator*

El Paso
Ambriz, Lorely *library and information scientist*
Barfield, Lowry *lawyer*
Boyd, Dana Kristin *elementary school educator*
Brey-Casiano, Carol A. *library director*
Briones, David *judge*
Cadena, Frederico Eduardo *finance company executive*
Cardwell, James A., Sr. *service company executive*
Casas, Martha *education educator*
Cook, John *mayor*
Cox, Sanford Curtis, Jr. *lawyer*
Cross, Clinton Ferguson *lawyer*
Cuartas, Beatriz H. *humanities educator*
Curie, Roger Kent *adult education educator, consultant*
Edmonds, Velma McInnis *nursing educator*
Erskine, William Crawford *retired academic and health facility administrator, accountant*
Feuille, Richard Harlan *lawyer, director*
Flores, Yolanda *speech pathology/audiology services professional, consultant*
Foged, Leslie Owen *mathematician, educator*
Foster, Paul L. *oil industry executive*
Gardner, Kerry Ann *librarian*
Gibson, Sidney Kay *retired lawyer*
Gill, Thomas Edward *science educator*
Gladstein, Mimi Reisel *theater and literature educator*
Goldfarb, William D. *underwriter, investor*
Goodman, Gertrude Amelia *civic worker*
Hanbali, Fadi *neurosurgeon, educator*
Harlass, Frederick E. *obstetrician, gynecologist*
Hedrick, Wyatt Smith *pharmacist*
Heide, John Wesley *engineering executive*
Jarvis, Richard S. *academic administrator*
Jordan, Shannon Collen *medical/surgical nurse*
Juarez, Antonio *psychotherapist, consultant, counselor, educator*
Kelley, Sylvia Johnson *financial services firm executive*
Lujan, Rosa Emma *bilingual specialist, trainer, consultant, assistant principal*
Marshall, Richard Treeger *lawyer*
Mitchell, Paula Rae *nursing educator, dean*
Morton, Fred J. *lawyer*
Moya, Eva M. *health services executive*

Müller, Gene Alan *historian, consultant*
Natalicio, Diana Siedhoff *academic administrator*
Olisa, Nzedegwu Robert III *information technology executive, manufacturing executive*
Paxson, Sam M. *judge*
Penley, Julie Anne *psychologist, educator*
Peralta-Videa, Jose R. *environmental scientist, researcher*
Quevedo, Hector Adolf *operations research specialist, environmental scientist*
Riter, Stephen *academic administrator, electrical engineer*
Roberts, Ernst Edward *marketing consultant*
Salas, Guillermo *biologist, educator, medical technician*
Saul, Charlie *small business owner, investor*
Sipiora, Leonard Paul *retired museum director, art appraiser*
Sisney, Philip Lynn *retired pilot*
Smith, Tad Randolph *lawyer*
Stanley, Duffy B. *architect, planner*
Taber, David O. *urological surgeon*
Torres, Richard *literature and language educator*
Wardy, Joe *former mayor*
Williams, Darryl Marlowe *medical educator*
Yetter, Richard *lawyer*
Zaloznik, Arlene Joyce *retired oncologist, military officer*
Zopfi, Emma G. *elementary school educator*

Eldorado

Kosub, James Albert *lawyer*

Elgin

Jordan, Charlene Hanson *writer*
Shelby, Nina Claire *special education educator*

Ennis

Swanson, Wallace Martin *lawyer*

Euless

Halter, Jon Charles *retired magazine editor, writer*
Paran, Mark Lloyd *retired lawyer*
Self, Mark Edward *communications consultant*

Falfurrias

Cantu, Imelda M. *theater educator*

Farmers Branch

Blachly, Jack Lee *lawyer*
Reyes, Czarina Suzanne *mathematics educator*
Walsh, Elizabeth Jameson *musician*

Flower Mound

Hunt, David Ford *lawyer*
Kolodny, Stanley Charles *oral surgeon, retired military officer*
Kumar, Surinder *food products executive*
Lowe, J. Allen *minister*
Marrs, Carol Faye *performing arts educator, writer*
Ross, Lesa Moore *quality assurance professional*

Fort Hood

Metz, Thomas Frederic *career military officer*
Sorenson, Kenneth Raymond *military officer, chaplain*

Fort Sam Houston

Betancourt, Jose A. *dean, public health service officer*
Blueitt, Odis R. *financial analyst, military officer*
Fallert, David Orval *military officer, military analyst*
Goetschius, James Brian *military officer, urban planner*
Hewitson, William Craig *physician, career officer*
Hutton, Robert Lee *pathologist*
McNeil, Christopher Ryan *emergency physician, military officer*
Wojcik, Barbara Elzbieta *statistician, researcher*

Fort Worth

Adams, Lavonne Marilyn Beck *critical care nurse, educator*
Appel, Bernard Sidney *marketing professional, consultant, retired electronics executive*
Ard, Harold Jacob *library administrator*
Astrup, Jens Leo *retired civil engineer*
Auping, Michael G. *curator*
Bailey, Susan Rudd *physician*
Bass, Robert Muse *financier*
Bass, Sid Richardson *investment company executive*
Berce, Daniel Eugene *financial services company executive, accountant*
Berenson, William Keith *lawyer*
Bernard, Robert William *language educator, theology studies educator, humanities educator*
Blackburn, Wyatt Douglas *insurance executive*
Blanck, Ronald Ray *academic administrator, internist, military officer*
Bonderman, David *investment company executive, lawyer*
Boschetti, Philip J. *oil industry executive*
Boschini, Victor John, Jr. *academic administrator*
Brennan, Edward A. *air transportation and former retail executive*
Brown, C. Harold *lawyer*
Brown, Richard Lee *lawyer*
Brumley, Jon S. *oil industry executive*
Brundage, Jeffrey J. *human resources specialist, air transportation executive*
Caldwell, Billy Ray *geologist*
Chalk, John Allen, Sr. *lawyer*
Clark, Emory Eugene *diversified financial services company executive*
Cliburn, Van (Harvey Lavan Cliburn Jr.) *concert pianist*
Colaluca, Beth *pediatric neurpsychologist*
Corbusier, Drue *apparel and home furnishings executive*
Cox, James Sidney *physician*
Crumley, John Walter *lawyer*
Culbertson, Richard Donell *oil industry executive, lawyer*
Cunningham, Atlee Marion, Jr. *aeronautical engineer*
Currier, Mike *elementary school educator, writer*
Curts, Harold Layne *construction executive*
Day, Julian C. *retail executive*
Dean, Beale *lawyer*
Dees, Sandra Kay Martin *psychologist, research scientist*
DeLotto, Jeffrey Daniel *language educator, writer*
de Toledo, Catherine Holt *medical writer*
de Tonnancour, Paul Roger Godefroy *library administrator*
Dominiak, Geraldine Florence *retired accounting educator*
Donovan, Nowell *academic administrator*
Doran, Robert Stuart *mathematician, educator*
Dunleavy, Willa Gill *music educator, director*
Durham, Jo Ann Fanning *artist*
Dwyer, Stacey H. *construction executive*
Elkins-Elliott, Kay *law educator*
Elliott, Frank Wallace *lawyer, educator*
Endres, Arthur P. (Skip Endres) *rail transportation executive*
Faherty, David Miles *musical instrument repairman*
Friedman, Walker C. *lawyer*
Fuller, Samuel R. *construction executive*
Gilbert, James Cayce *minister*
Gilderhus, Mark Theodore *historian, educator*
Gillette, Paul Crawford *pediatric cardiologist*
Goldberg, David *lawyer, retail executive*
Hahn, Marc B. *physician, dean*
Hall, Randy Jarvis *lawyer*
Harbour, Ted Ira *lawyer, construction executive*
Harcrow, Edward Earl *lawyer*
Hart, John Clifton *lawyer*
Harth-Bedoya, Miguel *conductor*
Hoferer, Paul R. *lawyer, rail transportation executive*
Horton, Donald R. *construction executive*
Horton, Thomas W. *air transportation and former telecommunications company executive*
Hund, Thomas N. *rail transportation executive*
Hyde, Clarence Brodie, II, *oil industry executive*
Ice, Carl R. *rail transportation executive*
Ingram, Denny Ouzts, Jr. *lawyer, educator*
Jackson, Donald Wilson *political science professor, lawyer*
Johnson, Melody *school system administrator*
Keith, Courtney S. *lawyer*
Kelly, Dee J. *lawyer*
Kelly, Janet *science educator*
Kelly, Raymond Boone III *lawyer*
Kennedy, Gary F. *air transportation executive, lawyer*
King, Steve Mason *judge, lawyer*
Kowalski, Debra Atkisson *physician*
Lale, Cissy Stewart (Lloyd Lale) *freelance writer*
Lancarte, Lanny P., II, *chef*
Lanigan, John P., Jr. *rail transportation executive*
Larimore, Tom L. *lawyer*
Laughlin, Christel Renate *translator, consultant*
Lawson, Carole Jean *religious educator, author, poet*
Li, Richard T. *retired library director, secondary school educator*
Lichtman, David Michael *orthopedist, health facility administrator, educator, retired military officer*
Lipkin, Seymour *musician, conductor, educator*
Lowseth, Lisa Anne *veterinarian*
Mack, Theodore *lawyer*
Maldonado, Francisco Javier *electrical research engineer*
Mayyas, Mohammad A. *mechanical engineer, researcher*
McBryde, John Henry *federal judge*
McConnell, Michael Arthur *lawyer*
McDonald, Frank G. *lawyer, energy executive*
Means, Terry Robert *federal judge*
Miller, Kleber C. *lawyer*
Minton, Jerry Davis *lawyer, consultant, retired banker*
Moncrief, Michael Joseph *mayor, former state legislator*
Moncrief, William Alvin, Jr. *oil and gas producer*
Mullendore, Walter Edward *retired economist*
Munday, Stephen Dale *writer, artist*
Munn, Cecil Edwin *lawyer*
Nazarian, Manucher *surgeon*
Nicholas, Nicholas Constantine *retired military officer*
Nichols, James Richard *civil engineer, consultant*
Nober, Roger *rail transportation executive*
Patterson, Gary *college football coach*
Potts, Timothy F. *museum director*
Quarles, Carroll Adair, Jr. *physicist, researcher*
Quinn, Francis Xavier *arbitrator, mediator, writer, law educator*
Rainwater, Richard Edward *financial consultant, investor*
Record, Phillip Julius *journalist*
Reinecke, Manfred G. *chemistry professor*
Reuter, Frank Theodore *historian, educator*
Roach, John Vinson, II, *retail company executive*
Robin, Clara Nell (Claire Robin) *English language educator*
Robinson, Gleniece Armstrong *library director*
Robinson, Nell Bryant *nutrition educator*
Rogers, Charles Ray *minister, religious organization administrator*
Rogers, Dale Craig *finance company executive*
Roland, Billy Ray *electronics company executive*
Rollins, Kevin B. *former computer company executive*
Rose, Matthew K. *rail transportation executive*
Saenz, Michael *college president*
Saenz, Nancy Elizabeth King *civic worker*
Schussler, Irwin *psychiatrist, educator*
Scott, P. Mark *musician, educator*
Searcy, Marshall Mayes, Jr. *lawyer*
Shade, Joseph *law educator*
Shannon, Joe, Jr. *lawyer*
Sharpe, James Shelby *lawyer*
Shehan, Geraldean Harrison *ESL educator*
Shupe, Dwight A. (Ike) *lawyer*
Sikes, Mary Taggart *librarian*
Simmons, Jean Byers *academic administrator, director*
Simpson, Bob R. *energy executive*
Simpson, Dennis Dwayne *psychologist, educator*
Smith, Alexander W. *retail executive*
Stevenson, Ben *performing company executive*
Streck, Frederick Louis III *lawyer*
Sullenberger, Ara Broocks *mathematics professor*
Thornton, Charles Victor *metals executive*
Tillman, Massie Monroe *mediator, arbitrator, art gallery owner, retired judge*
Tobey, Martin Alan *cardiologist*
Tomnitz, Donald J. *construction executive*
Tucker, William Edward *academic administrator, minister*
Turner, Wesley R. *publishing executive*
Tyler, Ronnie Curtis *museum director, art historian*
Wallace, R. H., Jr. *lawyer*
Wallach, David Michael *lawyer*
Wampler, Wesley Allen *chemist*
Warner, Malcolm John *curator*
Warren, Peter Gigstad *financial planner*
Watson, Robert Francis *lawyer*
Weaber, Terry Lee *information scientist*
West, Robert Grady *lawyer*
West, Sylvia Wandell *small business owner, director, educator, researcher*
Wheat, Bill W. *construction executive*
Wicker, Dorothy Baldwin *physicist*
Wilkie, Valleau, Jr. *foundation executive*
Willard, Ralph Lawrence *retired surgeon, physician, academic administrator, educator*
Wilson-Webb, Nancy Lou *educational association administrator*
Wise, Charla Kamm *aeronautics company executive*
Witt, Jim *executive editor*
Yacante, Maria Lucy *music educator, researcher*
Yanni, John Michael *pharmacologist*

Franklin

Perry, Anne Marie Litchfield *secondary school educator*

Fredericksburg

Arnold, George Lawrence *retired advertising company executive*
Chase, John David *retired dean, internist*
Manhart, Marcia Y(ockey) *art museum director*
Vinson, David Berwick *neuropsychologist*

Freeport

Gresham, Karen Renee *elementary school educator, singer*
Stevens, James C. *chemist*

Friendswood

Youngdahl, Jay Thomas *lawyer*

Frisco

Armstrong, Doug *professional sports team executive*
Bloskas, John D. *retired finance company executive*
Culpepper, Guy Lee *physician*
Gajraj, Noor *anesthesiologist, educator*
Hawk, Phillip Michael *service corporation executive*
Hicks, Thomas O. *professional sports team executive, real estate developer*
Hull, Brett A. *retired professional hockey player, former commentator*
Lindros, Eric *professional hockey player*
Lites, James R. *professional hockey team executive*
Mackenzie, John *retired oil industry executive*
Mihm, John Clifford *chemical engineer*
Modano, Mike *professional hockey player*
Smith, Neil *former professional sports team executive*
Taylor, Dave *professional sports team executive, retired professional hockey player*
Tippett, Dave *professional hockey coach*

Fulton

Lamb, Richard *cultural organization administrator*

Gainesville

Brooks, Jerry Robert *small business owner*
McCormack, Lowell Ray *oil industry executive, corporate financial executive, consultant*

Galena Park

Fierro, Robert, Jr. *librarian*

Galveston

Anderson, Garland D. *dean, obstetrician, gynecologist, educator*
Baker, Robert Ernest, Jr. *retired foundation executive*
Balaban, Alexandru T. *chemistry professor, researcher*
Bloomfield, Maxwell Herron III *retired history and law professor*
Burris, Chester Ray *retired medical educator*
Caldwell, Garnett Ernest *lawyer*
Chonmaitree, Tasnee *pediatrician, educator, epidemiologist*
Dawson, Earl Bliss *medical educator*
Esenaliev, Rinat Orozbekovich *science educator, lab administrator*
Estes, Ernest L. *geologist, educator*
Foster, William Edwin (Bill Foster) *nonprofessional basketball coach*
Frederickson, Christopher John *neuroscientist*
Gonzalez, Emilio Bustamante *rheumatologist, educator*
Goodwin, Jean McClung *psychiatrist*
Gorenstein, David G. *chemistry and biochemistry professor*
Hawkins, Hal K(enneth) *pathologist*
Ingole, Sudeep Prabhakar *engineering educator, researcher*
Ismail, Nahed *microbiologist, immunologist*
James, Thomas Naum *cardiologist, educator*
Kanuth, Michelle Susan *science educator*
Kaplan, Cheryl L. *theater educator*
Keeney, Susan E. *pediatrician, educator*
Klein, Gordon Leslie *pediatrician, educator*
Kumar, Santosh *medical educator, research scientist*
Leary, James Francis *biomedical research scientist, educator*
Makino, Shinji *virologist, educator*
Markides, Kyriakos Socrates *gerontology educator*
McLeod, E. Douglas *real estate developer, lawyer*
Moody, Robert Lee *insurance company executive*
Munsell, Debra S. *physician assistant, educator*
Murphy, Frederick Augustus *virologist, researcher*
Otis, John James *civil engineer*
O'Toole, Austin Martin *lawyer, mediator*
Powell, Don Watson *gastroenterologist, educator*
Protas, Elizabeth J. *physical therapist, academic administrator*
Riall, Taylor Sohn *surgeon, researcher*
Rosanio, Salvatore *cardiologist, educator*
Salch, Steven Charles *lawyer, mediator, arbitrator*
Sandstead, Harold Hilton *physician, researcher, educator, director*
Shelton, Kenneth R., Jr. *real estate company executive, artist*
Simmons, Anthony *virology educator, physician, researcher*
Smith, David English *pathologist, educator*
Snyder, Ned *gastroenterologist, medical educator*
Stobo, John David *academic administrator, physician*
Szauter, Karen *gastroenterologist*
Thompson, Edward Ivins Bradbridge *biological chemistry and genetics educator, endocrinologist*
Townsend, Courtney M. *surgeon*
Tyson, Kenneth Robert Thomas *surgeon, educator*
Vedernikov, Yuri P. *pharmacologist, educator*
Vie, George William III *lawyer*
White, Robert Brown *medical educator*
Willis, William Darrell, Jr. *neuroscientist, educator*
Zimmerman, Roger Joseph *fishery biologist*

Garland

Bausch, Claire *library director*
Christensen, Allan Robert *electrical engineer, financial consultant, social services counselor*
Driver, Joe Luther *state legislator, consultant, insurance agent*
Irby, Holt *lawyer*
Kemp, Pamela Jean *marriage and family therapist*
LeDoux, Ellen G. *music educator*
McGill, Maurice Leon *corporate financial executive*
McGrath, James Thomas *real estate investment company executive*
Quinn, Peggy Armstrong *elementary school educator, writer*
Sparks, Raymond Fredrick *protective services official*

Georgetown

Brody, Gerald David *academic administrator*
Bryce, William Delf *lawyer*
Busfield, Roger Melvil, Jr. *retired trade association executive, educator*
Deviney, Marvin Lee, Jr. *science administrator, director*
Gerding, Thomas Graham *medical products executive*
Hartman, Thomas Bennett *mechanical engineer*
Lopreato, Joseph *evolutionary sociologist, writer*
Lovin, Keith Harold *retired academic administrator, philosopher, educator*
Manning, Robert Thomas *internist, educator*
Moore, Pat Howard *engineering and construction executive, educator*
Netsiri, Chaiyapoj *research scientist*
Olson, Dean A. *lawyer*
Purdy, Jesse E. *psychology professor*
Schrum, Jake Bennett *academic administrator*
Sellers, Fred Evans *accounting educator*
Shelby, Roselle Price *writer, retired special education educator*
Smith, John Brewster *library administrator*
Smitheram, Margaret Etheridge *health facility administrator, director*

Giddings

Dismukes, Carol Jaehne *county official*
Walker, Hershel O. *history educator*

Glen Rose

Lane, Willa Joan Manes *retired psychologist*

Glenn Heights

Rowe, Nancie E. *director, minister*

Gonzales

Ince, Laurel T. *music educator*
Mosher, Kenneth Vester, II, *property tax appraiser*

Graham

Lovell, Lisa Inez *special education educator*
Richie, Boyd Lynn *lawyer*

Granbury

Adams, Christopher Steve, Jr. *retired electronics executive, military officer*

Curl, Samuel Everett *retired dean, agriculturist, consultant*

Grand Prairie
Ebozue, Benson Obian *financial analyst*
Puckett, Mary Alice *primary school educator, consultant*
Solomon, Arthur Charles *pharmacist*

Grapevine
Ansohn, John Hugo *emergency physician, educator*
Fontaine, R. Richard *computer game company executive*
Franks, Jon Michael *lawyer, mediator*
Hirsh, Cristy J. *principal*
Stack, George Joseph *philosopher, writer*

Guthrie
Marion, Anne Windfohr *rancher, museum administrator*

Hale Center
Courtney, Carolyn Ann *school librarian*

Happy
Bloodworth, Rick Keith *minister*

Hardin
Ringer, Paula Denise Hollenshead *secondary school educator*

Harlingen
Klein, Garner Franklin *cardiologist, internist*
Lytle, Michael Allen *forensic criminologist, consultant*
Martin, Leland Morris (Pappy) *historian, educator*
Matz, James Richard *municipal official*
Maupin, Alan Rodger *science educator*
Pope, William L. *lawyer, judge*
Salcedo-Dovi, Hector Eduardo *anatomist, educator, surgeon*

Heath
Kolodey, Fred James *lawyer*

Helotes
Rojo, Ruth M. *nutritionist, consultant, director*
Yamin, Sonya *music educator, voice educator*

Hempstead
Propst, Catherine Lamb *biotechnology and pharmaceutical company executive*

Henderson
Adkison, Ron *lawyer*

Hereford
Yavornik, Barbara Ann *pre-school educator*

Hewitt
Walbesser, Henry Herman *computer science educator*
Wilson, Thomas W. *pharmacist*

Highland Village
Lawrence, William Clarence *lawyer, mediator*
Richardson, K. Scott *sales executive*

Hillsboro
Haddaway, James David *retired insurance company official*
McClendon, Fred Vernon *real estate professional, equity and realty appraiser, financial consultant*

Hitchcock
Shaffer, Richard Paul *financial planner, real estate company executive, military officer*

Hockley
Williams, James Lee *finance company executive*

Horseshoe Bay
Anderson, Kenneth Ward *investor, consultant*
Jorden, James Roy *oil industry executive, consultant*
Simpson, H. Richard (Dick Simpson) *retail buyer*

Houston
Aardsma, David A. *waste management executive*
Abbey, George W. S. *space center executive*
Achenbaum, W(ilbert) Andrew *historian, gerontologist*
Adams, C. Lee *marketing executive*
Adams, Yolanda Yvette *singer*
Addison, Linda Leuchter *lawyer, writer, commentator, columnist*
Adelman, Rick (Richard Leonard Adelman) *professional basketball coach*
Adrogue, Horacio Esteban *nephrologist, educator*
Adrogué, Sofia *lawyer*
Aguirre, Sarah K. *lawyer*
Ahmad, Farrukh *environmental engineer, chemist*
Akers, William Walter *chemical engineering educator*
Alexander, Leslie Lee *professional sports team owner*
Alexanian, Raymond *hematologist*
Alfini, James Joseph *dean, educator, lawyer*
Alford, Bobby Ray *otolaryngologist, educator, academic administrator*
Allen, Frank Clinton, Jr. *lawyer, chemical engineer*
Allen, Steven Jeffrey *anesthesiologist, educator*
Allender, John Roland *lawyer*
Altman, William Carl *health facility administrator, industrial relations specialist, investment company executive, consultant*
Amann, Leslie Kiefer *lawyer, educator*
Amdur, Arthur R. *lawyer*
Anani, Tarig *lawyer*
Anderson, Claire W. *gifted and talented educator*
Anderson, Clayton C. *astronaut*
Anderson, D(arryl) Kent *bank executive*
Anderson, Doris Ehlinger *lawyer*
Anderson, Eric Severin *lawyer*
Anderson, Nick *editorial cartoonist*
Anderson, Paul Milton *energy executive*
Anderson, Richard Carl *geophysical exploration company executive*
Anderson, William (Albion), Jr. *management consultant*
Anderson-Lehman, Ron *air transportation executive*
Appel, Stanley Hersh *neurologist, educator*
Archambault, Lee Joseph *astronaut*
Arcilla, Juanita R. *physical therapist*
Armstrong, Greg L. *oil industry executive*
Arnold, Ken E. *engineering company executive*
Arnot, William G. III *lawyer*
Ashby, Jeffrey S. *astronaut*
Asmus, David F. *lawyer*
Asselin, Heather E. *lawyer*
Athanasiou, Kyriacos A. *biomedical engineer*
Atlas, Scott J. *lawyer*
Ayadi, Mary Olufemi *health economist, educator*
Ayers, Howard T. *lawyer*
Ayus, Juan Carlos *nephrologist*
Bachmann, Richard H. *lawyer, energy executive*
Backus, Marcia Ellen *lawyer*
Bahl, Saroj Mehta *nutritionist, educator*
Bai, Yong *engineering executive, educator*
Bailey, Harold Randolph *surgeon, educator*
Bailey, Kelley *foundation administrator*
Bair, Royden Stanley *retired architect*
Baker, C. Mark *lawyer*
Baker, Ellen Shulman *astronaut, physician*
Baker, James Addison, III, (Jim Baker) *lawyer, former secretary of state*
Baker, Robert W. *lawyer*
Baker, Stephen Denio *physics professor*
Baker, Vincent Lamont *professional basketball player*
Bakulin, Andrey *geophysicist*
Ball, George L. *investment banker*
Ballanfant, Richard Burton *lawyer*
Ballo, Matthew T. *radiation oncologist, educator*
Bally, Albert W. *retired geologist, geology educator*
Bankhead, Sherry L. *lawyer*
Barbour, Larry Gregory *lawyer*
Bargfrede, James Allen *lawyer*
Barlow, Jim B. *retired columnist, writer*
Barnett, Donald Blake *corporate financial executive*
Barnett, Edward William *lawyer*
Barracano, Henry Ralph *retired oil company executive, management consultant*
Barrere, Clem Adolph *business brokerage company executive*
Barrere, Jamie Newton *real estate company executive*
Barrett, Bernard Morris, Jr. *plastic and reconstructive surgeon*
Barton, Sarah Muriel *lawyer*
Bates, Gwen Lee *health facility administrator, consultant*
Batsakis, John George *pathology educator*
Battin, R. Ray (Rosabell Harriet Ray) *audiologist, neuropsychologist*
Beauchamp, Robert E. *information technology executive*
Beaudet, Arthur L. *medical genetics researcher*
Bech, Douglas York *retired lawyer, resort executive*
Bechtol, J. Currie *lawyer, oil industry executive*
Beckingham, Kathleen Mary *education educator, researcher*
Beirne, Martin Douglas *lawyer*
Belk, Joan Pardue *language and literature educator*
Bellatti, Lawrence Lee *lawyer*
Benefield, Janis Wilson *school librarian, media specialist*
Bennett, Olga Salowich *civic worker, graphic arts researcher, consultant*
Bentsen, Kenneth Edward *architect*
Berg, Amie G. *lawyer*
Berg, David Howard *lawyer*
Bergsrud, Mark *air transportation executive*
Berkman, Lance *professional baseball player*
Berry, William B. *oil industry executive*
Bethea, Louise Huffman *allergist*
Betts, Nicole Lavette *elementary school educator, consultant*
Bevers, Therese Bartholomew *physician, educator*
Beyoncé, (Beyoncé Giselle Knowles) *singer*
Biery, Evelyn Hudson *lawyer*
Biggio, Craig *professional baseball player*
Bigwood, David P. *librarian, writer*
Bikram, Malavosklish *medical educator*
Bilger, Bruce R. *lawyer*
Bischoff, Susan Ann *newspaper editor*
Black, Donna Lord *psychologist*
Blackburn, Sadie Gwin Allen *conservation executive*
Blackshear, A. T., Jr. *lawyer*
Blakemore, Amy *photographer*
Bland, John Lloyd *lawyer*
Blanton, Jack Sawtelle *oil industry executive*
Blickwede, Donald Johnson *retired metal products executive*
Blodgett, J. Kevin *lawyer*
Bodey, Gerald Paul *retired medical educator*
Bogard, Donald Dale *planetary geochemist*
Bomba, John Gilbert *civil engineer, consultant*
Bonds, Michael P. *air transportation executive*
Bonner, Billy Edward *physics professor*
Bonneville, Richard Briggs *retired gas industry executive*
Bookout, John Frank, Jr. *oil industry executive*
Boren, William Meredith *manufacturing executive*
Bott, Simon Gregory *chemistry educator, researcher*
Boule, Michelle L. *librarian, writer*
Boulware, Margaret A. *lawyer*
Boutros, Sean *plastic surgeon*
Bovay, Harry Elmo, Jr. *retired engineering company executive*
Bowden, M. Gabriela *biomedical researcher, educator*
Bowen, William Jackson *retired gas industry executive*
Bowron, Edgar Peters *art museum curator, administrator*
Boyce, Maria Wyckoff *lawyer*
Bradley, Melvin LeRoy *communications executive*
Bramanti, Frank J. *insurance company executive*
Brandenstein, Daniel Charles *astronaut, retired military officer*
Brann, Richard Roland *lawyer*
Bridges, David Manning *lawyer*
Brinkley, Douglas G. *historian, writer, educator*
Brinson, Gay Creswell, Jr. *retired lawyer*
Brito, Dagobert Llanos *economics professor*
Brodsky, Donald W. *lawyer*
Brody, Baruch Alter *medical educator, academic administrator*
Brooks, Philip Russell *chemistry educator, researcher*
Brotzen, Franz Richard *materials scientist, educator*
Brown, David M. *surgeon, researcher*
Brown, Glenda Ann Walters *ballet director*
Brown, Jacqueline Elaine *obstetrician, gynecologist*
Brown, Thaddeus B. *professional sports team executive*
Brunson, John Soles *lawyer, investor*
Bryant, John Bradbury *economics professor, consultant*
Buckingham, Edwin John III *lawyer*
Buckley, Vincent H. *lawyer*
Bue, Carl Olaf, Jr. *retired federal judge*
Buja, L. Maximilian *pathologist, academic administrator, educator*
Bungo, Michael William *cardiologist, educator, science administrator*
Burbank, Daniel C. *astronaut*
Burch, Voris Reagan *mediator, arbitrator, retired lawyer*
Burg, Brent Lawrence *lawyer, judge*
Burgert, David Lee *lawyer*
Burke, Kevin Charles Antony *geologist*
Burman, Darryl Michael *lawyer*
Burnett, Susan Walk *personnel service company owner*
Burns, David Alan *lawyer*
Burrus, (Charles) Sidney *electrical engineering educator*
Burton, Joseph Randolph *lawyer*
Burzynski, Stanislaw Rajmund *internist*
Bush, George Herbert Walker *41st President of the United States*
Buster, John Edmond *obstetrician, medical researcher*
Butel, Janet Susan *virologist, department chairman, research scientist*
Butler, William Thomas *academic administrator, physician, educator*
Bux, William John *lawyer*
Cabana, Robert D. *aerospace transportation executive, astronaut*
Cabaniss, John Trigg *lawyer*
Caddell, Lynn M. *waste management executive*
Caddy, Michael Douglas *lawyer*
Cagle, Yvonne Darlene *astronaut*
Caldwell, Barry H. *waste management executive*
Caldwell, Richard H. *lawyer*
Caldwell, Tracy Ellen *surface chemist, researcher*
Caligur, Matthew W. *lawyer*
Callender, Norma Anne *counselor, public relations executive*
Camarda, Charles J. *astronaut*
Campbell, Eileen M. *oil industry executive*
Carabin, Dana A. *lawyer*
Caram, Dorothy Farrington *educational consultant*
Carman, Carol A. *psychologist, educator*
Carnes, Tara Lea Barker *music educator*
Carr, Edward A. *lawyer*
Carrig, John A. *oil industry executive*
Carrig, Kenneth J. *food products executive*
Carroll, Charles A. *manufacturing executive*
Carroll, Milton *oil industry executive*
Carter, John Francis, II, *lawyer*
Carter, John Loyd *lawyer*
Caruso, Nick J. *energy executive*
Casarez, Rueben Charles *lawyer*
Caskey, Caroline T. *lab administrator*
Castañeda, James Agustín *language educator, golf coach*
Catlin, Francis Irving *physician*
Caudill, William Howard *lawyer*
Cazalot, Clarence P., Jr. *oil industry executive*
Cazenave, Anita Washington *secondary school educator*
Chalmers, David B. *petroleum executive*
Chambers, Norman C. *manufacturing executive*
Chamillionaire, (Hakeem Seriki) *rap artist, recording industry executive*
Chance, Jane *English literature educator*
Chandler, Richard E., Jr. *lawyer*
Chandler-Munson, Cynthia *elementary school educator*
Chang, Chung-Che *hematopatholgist, medical researcher, medical educator*
Chang, Nancy T. *pharmaceutical executive*
Chao, Albert *chemicals executive*
Chapman, Alan Jesse *engineering educator*
Chapman, Cynthia B. *lawyer*
Chavez, Brenda G. *construction executive, real estate agent*
Chavez, J. Anthony *lawyer*
Cheatham, John Bane, Jr. *retired mechanical engineering educator*
Cheavens, Joseph D. *lawyer*
Cheung, Min Rex *medical educator*
Chevray, Pierre M. *medical educator*
Chiao, Leroy *astronaut*
Chiou-Tan, Faye *physician, educator*
Chu, Paul Ching-Wu *physicist, director, academic administrator, educator*
Chu, Wei-Kan *physicist, researcher*
Clark, James R. *oil industry executive*
Clark, Janet F. *oil industry executive*
Clarke, Douglas E. *lawyer*
Clarke, Robert Logan *lawyer*
Cleeland, Charles S. *medical educator, researcher*
Clifton, Guy L. *neurosurgeon, educator*
Clore, Lawrence Hubert *lawyer*
Cochran, Fielding B. III *lawyer*
Cockrell, Kenneth Dale *astronaut*
Coghlan, Kelly Jack *lawyer*
Cohen, Jeff *editor, publishing executive*
Cohn, William Ettlinger *cardiologist, thoracic surgeon, product designer*
Colbert, Kevin LeRoy *lawyer*
Coleman, Catherine G. *astronaut*
Coleman, Gregory S. *lawyer*
Coley, Randolph C. *lawyer*
Collings, Chris D. *lawyer*
Colson, John R. *electric power industry executive*
Colvin, Vicki Leigh *chemistry professor, educator*
Compton, James E. *air transportation executive*
Condit, Linda Faulkner *retired economist*
Conlon, Michael William *lawyer*
Constantine, Kevin *professional hockey coach*
Cooley, Denton Arthur *surgeon, educator*
Cooper, Valerie Gail *minister*
Corken, Heather Marie *lawyer*
Corley, Larry Steven *chemist*
Cornelison, Albert Otto, Jr., (Bert Cornelison) *lawyer*
Couch, Jesse Wadsworth *retired insurance company executive*
Couch, Robert Barnard *physician, medical researcher, microbiologist, immunologist, educator*
Coverdale, John Howard *psychiatrist*
Covey, Richard Oswalt (Dick Covey) *aerospace transportation executive, former astronaut*
Cox, James D. *radiologist*
Cox, James Talley *lawyer*
Crain, Alan Rau, Jr. *lawyer, oil industry executive*
Crane, James R. *delivery service executive*
Creel, Michael Allen *energy executive*
Crinion, Gregory Paul *lawyer*
Crispin, Andre Arthur *diversified financial services company executive*
Cunningham, Tom Alan *lawyer*
Cupp, Aneta Joan *music educator*
Cupp, B. Garland *computer company executive*
Curbeam, Robert L., Jr. *astronaut*
Curl, Robert Floyd, Jr. *chemistry professor*
Currie, John Thornton (Jack Currie) *retired investment banker*
Currie, Nancy Jane *astronaut*
Curtiss, Jeff *consumer products company executive, lawyer*
Cuthbertson, Gilbert Morris *political science professor*
Cutler, John Earl *landscape architect*
Cyrus, Jamal D. *artist*
DaCunha, Jeffrey J. *oil industry executive, researcher*
D'Agostino, James Samuel, Jr. *corporate financial executive*
Dameris, Thad Thano *lawyer*
Dang, Kimberly Allen *energy executive*
D'Arche, Douglas D. *lawyer*
Dasari, Ganeswara R. *oil industry executive*
Davidson, Chandler *sociologist, educator*
Davidson, Charles D. *energy executive*
Davis, Leon *oil industry executive*
Davis, (Alice) Marlece *secondary school educator, director*
Davis-Lewis, Bettye *nursing educator*
Dawson, Carroll *professional sports team executive*
Day, Jonathan S. *lawyer*
Day, Twila M. *food service executive*
Dean, Robert Franklin *insurance company executive*
Deaton, Chad C. *oil and gas industry executive*
De Bremaecker, Jean-Claude *geophysics educator*
DeGeurin, George Michael, Jr., (Mike DeGeurin) *lawyer*
DeGeurin, Mike *lawyer*
DeGuerin, Dick *lawyer*
Del Valle, Teresa Jones *lawyer*
DeMent, James Alderson, Jr. *lawyer*
Demory-Luce, Debby Kay *dietician, consultant*
DeMoss, Harold Raymond, Jr. *federal judge*
Demouy, Alyson M. *social studies educator*
DeNicola, T. Kevin *chemicals executive*
Deter, Russell Lee, II, *obstetrical ultrasonographer*
DeVault, John Lee *oil industry executive, geophysicist*
Devlin, Francis James *lawyer*
De Wree, Eugene Ernest *manufacturing executive*
Diamond, Pamela M. *science educator*
Dice, Bruce Burton *gas industry executive*
Dilg, Joseph Carl *lawyer*
Dillard, Michael E. *lawyer*
Dillard, Stephen C. *lawyer*
DiNardo, Daniel N. *archbishop*
Dinkins, Carol Eggert *federal official, lawyer*
Djerejian, Edward Peter *academic administrator, retired diplomat*
Dodd, Gerald Dewey, Jr. *radiologist, educator*
Dodd, Jeff C. *lawyer*
Donnelly, Rosemarie *lawyer*
Dorman, Margaret K. *corporate financial executive*
Doubleday, Charles William *dermatologist, educator*
Douglas, Frank Fair *architect, graphic designer*
Douglas, James Matthew *law educator, dean*
Douglass, John Jay *lawyer, educator*
Downing, Margaret Mary *newspaper editor*

Drew, Benjamin Alvin, Jr. *astronaut*
Drew, Katherine Fischer *history professor*
Dreyer, Alec Gilbert *electric power industry executive*
Dronamraju, Krishna Rao *geneticist*
Drumheller, Anthony D. (Andy) *lawyer*
Drury, Leonard Leroy *retired oil company executive*
Drutz, Jan Edwin *pediatrics educator*
Duerr, David *civil engineer*
Duncan, Charles William, Jr. *investor, retired federal official*
Duncan, Dan L. *energy executive*
Duncan, Robert D. *real estate company executive*
Dunham, Archie Wallace *petroleum company and chemicals executive*
Dunlop, Fred Hurston *lawyer*
DuPont, Herbert Lancashire *medical educator, researcher*
Dykes, Osborne Jefferson III *lawyer*
Eckhardt, William Rudolf III *lawyer*
Efendi, Riad *biochemist*
Eiland, Gary Wayne *lawyer*
Eisner, Diana *pediatrician*
Elkins, James Anderson III *financial consultant*
Ellis, Raymond Clinton, Jr. *retired hotel executive*
Eng, Cathy *oncologist, educator*
Engelhardt, Hugo Tristram, Jr. *physician, educator*
Engerrand, Kenneth G. *lawyer, educator*
Englesmith, Tejas *actor, television producer, curator*
Erikson, Sheldon R. *oil industry executive*
Erwin, Mark A. *air transportation executive*
Espree, Mildred Michelle *language educator, writer*
Essmyer, Michael Martin *lawyer*
Estes, Mary K. *virologist, researcher*
Esteva, Francisco Javier *physician, researcher*
Eubank, J. Thomas *lawyer*
Evans, Harry Launius *pathology educator*
Evans, Karen Ann *social studies educator*
Evans, Kenya *artist*
Ewing, Patrick Aloysius *professional basketball coach*
Fanchi, John Richard *physicist, educator, consultant*
Farenthold, Frances Tarlton *lawyer*
Farner, Wendy Mineau *lawyer*
Farnsworth, T. Brooke *lawyer*
Farrell, John Marshall *architect*
Farris, G. Steven *energy executive*
Faulkner, Larry Ray *foundation and former academic administrator*
Feigon, Judith Tova *ophthalmologist, educator, surgeon*
Ferguson, Christopher J. *astronaut*
Fiese, Richard Kelly *music educator*
Filipp Beseda, Carolyn Francine *music educator, insurance agent*
Finch, Michael Paul *lawyer*
Fincke, Edward Michael (Mike) *astronaut*
Fiorenza, Joseph A. *retired archbishop*
Fishman, Marvin Allen *pediatric neurologist, educator*
Fladung, Richard Denis *lawyer*
Flaitz, Catherine M. *dean, dental educator*
Flato, William Roeder, Jr. *software development company executive*
Florian-Lacy, Dorothy *psychologist, educator*
Focht, John Arnold, Jr. *engineer*
Foger, Frances Murchison *minister*
Ford, Thomas W., Jr. *lawyer*
Ford III, Don D. *lawyer*
Foreman, Michael J. *astronaut*
Fornage, Bruno Denis *radiologist, educator*
Forney, Jan Lynette *geophysicist*
Forrester, Patrick G. *astronaut*
Foshee, Douglas L. *gas industry executive*
Foss, Michelle Michot *think-tank executive, economist*
Fossum, Michael E. *astronaut*
Foster, Charles Crawford *lawyer, educator*
Foster, Dale Warren *political scientist, educator, real estate agent, accountant, management consultant*
Fowler, Fred J. *energy executive*
Fowler, W. Randall *energy executive*
Francis, James Stephen, Jr. *psychology professor, psychologist*
Frank, Karen Denise *aerospace engineer*
Frederickson, Philip L. *oil industry executive*
Freireich, Emil J. *hematologist, educator*
Freud, Anthony Peter *opera company director*
Friedkin, Thomas H. *automotive executive*
Friedman, Paul M. *dermatologist*
Frost, John Elliott *minerals company executive*
Fuglesang, Christer *astronaut*
Fullenweider, Donn Charles *lawyer*
Fulwiler, Robert Neal *oil industry executive*
Furbacher, Stephen A. *energy executive*
Gabbard, Glen Owens *psychiatrist, psychotherapist*
Gaelens, Albert Robert *retired director, educational administrator, priest*
Gagnon, Stewart Walter *lawyer*
Gale, Stephen C. *surgeon, educator*
Gallogly, James Lawrence *oil industry executive, lawyer*
Galvin, Kerry A. *lawyer, chemicals executive*
Gardner, Everette Shaw, Jr. *information sciences educator, consultant, author*
Gates, Stephen Frye *lawyer, oil industry executive*
Gaut, C. Christopher *oil industry executive*
Gelb, Morris *chemicals executive*
George, Deveral D. *editor, journalist, advertising consultant*
Gerachis, George Matthew *lawyer*
Gertzbein, Stanley David *orthopedic surgeon*
Getz, Lowell Vernon *financial advisor*
Gibbs, James R. *oil industry executive*
Gibson, Everett Kay, Jr. *aerospace scientist, geochemist*
Gibson, Rex Hilton *lawyer*
Gigli, Irma *dermatologist, educator, academic administrator*
Gilbert, Jill Barson *management consultant*
Gilbert, Keith Thomas *lawyer, consultant*
Girouard, Peggy Jo Fulcher *ballet educator*
Gladden, Dean Robert *arts administrator, educator, consultant*
Glassell, Alfred Curry, Jr. *investor*
Glick, William H. *dean*
Glowinski, Roland *mathematics professor*
Goff, Robert Burnside *retired food company executive*
Goldman, Nathan Carliner *lawyer, educator*
Goldman, Stanford Milton *medical educator*
Goldsmith, Billy Joe *real estate broker, rancher*
Golinkin, Webster Fowler *healthcare executive, media consultant*
Goloby, George William, Jr. *environmental scientist, editor, ornithologist*
Golubitsky, Martin Aaron *mathematician, educator*
Gonçalves, C. Lourenço *metal products executive*
Gonynor, Francis James *lawyer*
Gonzalez, Antonio *academic administrator, educator, title company executive*
Goode, Coralyn *lawyer*
Goodman, Barry Michael *lawyer*
Goodman, Herbert Irwin *petroleum company executive*
Goodman, John B. *heating/air conditioning manufacturing executive*
Gould, Kenneth Lance *cardiologist, researcher, educator*
Grace, James Martin, Jr. *lawyer*
Graf, Hans *conductor, music director*
Graham, David Yates *gastroenterologist*
Graves, Daniel Edward *medical association administrator, researcher*
Graving, Richard John *law educator*
Gray, Robert F., Jr. *lawyer*
Gray, Robert Steele *publishing executive, editor, writer*
Green, Ahman Rashad *professional football player*
Green, Linda Kathleen *pathologist, educator*
Greenberg, Angela Barmby *lawyer*
Greene, Alison de Lima *curator*
Grigore, Alina M. *anesthesiologist*
Grizzle, J. David *air transportation executive*
Grossberg, Marc Elias *lawyer*
Grossett, Deborah Lou *psychologist, consultant*
Grossman, Herbert Barton *urologist, researcher*
Grossman, Robert George *neurosurgeon, department chairman*
Guest, Floyd Emory, Jr. *lawyer*
Gunn, Albert Edward, Jr. *internist, health facility administrator, lawyer, educator*
Gunn, Joan Marie *health facility administrator*
Gunter, Joseph Clifford III *lawyer*
Gupta, Monesha *pediatrician, educator*
Gupta, Shefali *internist, nephrologist*
Gutheinz, Joseph Richard, Jr. *criminal justice educator, consultant, lawyer*
Guynn, Robert William *psychiatrist, educator*
Haden-Pinneri, Kathryn *pathologist*
Haensly, Patricia Anastacia *psychology professor*
Hafner, Joseph A., Jr. *food products executive*
Hale, C. Robert, III, (Bob) *real estate company executive*
Hall, Charles Washington *lawyer*
Hall, Robert Joseph *internist, educator*
Hamel, Douglas E. *lawyer*
Hamid, Basem *neurologist, consultant*
Hamill, Marshall Bowes *medical educator*
Hamilton, Carlos Robert, Jr. *endocrinologist, consultant, academic administrator*
Hamilton, Jacqueline *arts consultant*
Handy, Beverly C. *medical educator*
Hanks, George Carol, Jr. *state judge*
Hanrahan, Lawrence Martin *healthcare consultant*
Harper, A(lfred) J(ohn), II, *lawyer*
Harrington, Bruce Michael *lawyer, investor*
Harris, Venita Van Caspel *retired financial planner*
Harris, Warren Wayne *lawyer*
Hartrick, Janice Kay *lawyer*
Harvin, David Tarleton *lawyer*
Hasen, Michael *engineering company executive, civil engineer*
Hattaway, Karen Ann *literature and language professor*
Hawes, Clay Erik *lawyer*
Hawes, William Kenneth *communication educator, author*
Hawkins, Barbara Reed *mental health nurse*
Hayes, Elvin Ernest *retired basketball player*
Haynes, Richard (Racehorse Haynes) *lawyer*
Haynie, Thomas Powell III *physician*
Hazelip, Linda Ann *musician, small business owner, executive assistant*
Heard, Larry *real estate company executive*
Hebert, Adelaide *dermatologist, pediatrician*
Heeg, Peggy A. *lawyer, former gas industry executive*
Heinrich, Randall Wayne *lawyer*
Helland, George Archibald, Jr. *manufacturing executive, federal official*
Hellerstein, Lewis Jan *hematologist, oncologist, consultant*
Heminger, Gary R. *oil industry executive*
Hemminghaus, Roger Roy *energy company executive, chemical engineer*
Hempel, John P. *mathematics professor*
Hempfling, Linda Lee *nurse*
Henington, David Mead *retired library director*
Henley, Ernest Justus *retired chemical engineering professor*
Hesterberg, Earl J. *automotive executive*
Heuser, Mark Charles *military officer, educator*
Hewitt, Lester L. *lawyer*
Higginbotham, Joan E. *astronaut*
Higgins, Ryan K. *lawyer*
Hilborn, Marilyn Ann *educational consultant*
Hildebrand, Jeffrey D. *oil industry executive*
Hilfman, David L. *air transportation executive*
Hinton, Paula Weems *lawyer*
Hittner, David *federal judge*
Hlavinka, Paul Thomas *lawyer*
Hobaugh, Charles O. *astronaut*
Hobby, William Pettus *retired broadcast executive*
Hodgess, Erin Marie *statistics educator*
Hoeg, Matthew *lawyer*
Hoffman, Philip Guthrie *former university president*
Hoffman, Ronald Bruce *biophysicist, consultant, life scientist*
Hollingsworth, Derek S. *lawyer*
Hollingsworth, Lara Hudgins *lawyer*
Holloway, Gordon Arthur *lawyer*
Hollyfield, John Scoggins *lawyer*
Holmes, Ann Hitchcock *journalist*
Holmes, Harry Dadisman *health care administrator*
Holstead, John Burnham *retired lawyer*
Honeycutt, George Leonard *retired photographer*
Hong, Waun Ki *oncologist, researcher*
Hook, Harold Swanson *former management consulting executive*
Horowitz, Scott Jay *astronaut, military officer*
Horrigan, Joseph Stewart *lawyer*
Horton, Donald J. *lawyer*
Horton, Thomas Edward, Jr. *mechanical engineering educator*
Horvitz, Paul Michael *finance educator*
Hossain, Anwar *molecular biologist, educator*
Howell, Jefferson Davis, Jr. *aerospace transportation executive, retired military officer*
Hoyt, Mont Powell *lawyer*
Hsu, Sylvia *dermatologist, educator*
Hsu, Thomas Tseng-Chuang *civil engineer, educator*
Huang, Beiqing *mechanical engineer, educator*
Huang, Hsien-Lu *electrical engineer*
Huang, Shawn Shaoping *engineer*
Hudson, Franklin *lawyer, real estate developer*
Hudspeth, Chalmers Mac *lawyer, educator*
Huff, Danny W. *paper products executive*
Huffington, Roy Michael *business executive, former ambassador*
Hughes, Lynn Nettleton *federal judge*
Hulet, Randall Gardner *physics professor*
Hull, Robert Joe *lawyer*
Hunsaker, Barry, Jr. *lawyer*
Hurley, R. Bruce *lawyer*
Hussain, Moinuddin Syed *geologist, engineer, consultant*
Hutchens, Jerome Enos *psychiatrist*
Hynes, Thomas N. (Toby) *automotive company executive*
Ifft, Lewis George III *company administrator*
Innes, Deborah *bank executive*
Irvin, Michael P. *lawyer*
Irwin, John Robert *oil and gas industry executive*
Ivanov, Lyuben Dimitrov *naval architecture researcher, educator*
Ivey, Jack Todd *lawyer*
Jackson, John E. *gas industry executive*
Jackson, Michael Lynn *civil and structural engineer, sales executive*
Jacobs, Mark M. *energy executive*
Jacobs, Tonya A. *lawyer*
Jaffe, Amy Myers *energy executive, educator*
Jamail, Joseph Dahr, Jr. *lawyer*
Jankovic, Joseph *neurologist, educator*
Janssens, Joe Lee *accountant*
Jean, Raymond A. *manufacturing executive*
Jenkins, Sheila Alnita *psychologist*
Jeske, Charles Matthew *lawyer*
Jett, Brent W., Jr. *astronaut, military officer*
Jewell, Robert V. *lawyer*
Jines, Michael L. *lawyer, energy executive*
Johnson, Arnold J. *lawyer, energy executive*
Johnson, Craig M. *real estate company executive*
Johnson, Marilyn *retired obstetrician, gynecologist*
Johnson, Sandra Ann *counselor, educator*
Johnson, Wayne D. *gas industry executive*
Joiner, Jamie A. *lawyer*
Jolibois, Marcus *professional sports team executive*
Jolivet, Joselyn DeVez *music company executive*
Jones, Edith Irby *internist*
Jones, Florence M. *music educator*
Jones, Frank Griffith *lawyer*
Jordan, Charles Milton *lawyer*
Jordan, W. Carl *lawyer*
Jordon, Robert Earl *physician*
Joyce, James Daniel *clergyman*
Jurtshuk, Peter, Jr. *microbiologist, educator*
Justice, (David) Blair *psychology educator, writer*
Justino, Henri *pediatric cardiologist*
Kagle, Joseph Louis, Jr. *artist, arts administrator, historian and educator*
Kahan, Barry Donald *surgeon, educator*
Kakadiaris, Ioannis *computer science educator*
Kanellos, Nicolás *language and liberal studies educator*
Kaplan, Lee Landa *lawyer*
Karff, Samuel Egal *rabbi*
Karner, Stephen Leslie *geophysicist*
Karnes, John Herbert, Jr. *corporate financial executive, lawyer*
Katopodis, Louis *supermarket chain executive*
Katrana, David John *plastic and reconstructive surgeon*
Katta, Rajani *dermatologist*
Katz, Barry Jay *geologist, researcher*
Kaufman, Raymond Henry *retired physician, retired educator*
Kavandi, Janet Lynn *aerospace power engineer, chemist*
Kavraki, Lydia *computer scientist, educator*
Kay, Joel Phillip *lawyer*
Kean, Steven J. *energy executive*
Kellner, Lawrence W. (Larry Kellner) *air transportation executive*
Kelly, Hugh Rice *lawyer, retired energy executive*
Kelly, James M. *astronaut, military officer*
Kelly, Janet Langford *oil industry executive, lawyer*
Kelly, Mark E. *astronaut*
Kelly, Scott J. *astronaut, military officer*
Kelly, T. Mark *lawyer*
Kelly, William Franklin, Jr. *lawyer*
Kennedy, John Edward *lawyer*
Kerr, Baine Perkins *oil industry executive*
Ketchand, Robert Lee *lawyer*
Kevan, Larry *chemistry professor*
Key, James Everett *ophthalmologist*
Kilrain, Susan *astronaut*
Kim, Pyung-Soo *martial arts educator*
Kimyai-Asadi, Arash *surgeon*
Kinder, Richard Dan *natural gas pipeline, oil and gas company executive*
King, Carolyn Dineen *federal judge*
Kinnear, Peter D. *energy executive*
Kinsey, James Lloyd *chemist, educator*
Kirkland, John David *oil and gas company executive*
Kit, Saul *retired biochemist, educator*
Klausmeyer, David Michael *scientific instruments manufacturing company executive*
Klein, Nora J. *pediatrician*
Kline, Allen Haber, Jr. *lawyer*
Kline, Mark Wendel *pediatric medicine educator*
Knapp, David Hebard *retired banker*
Kneese, Carolyn Calvin *retired education educator*
Knesek, Michael John *energy executive*
Knickel, Carin S. *oil industry executive*
Kobayashi, Riki *retired chemical engineer, educator*
Kochi, Jay Kazuo *chemist, educator*
Koenig, Rodney Curtis *lawyer, rancher*
Kollaer, Jim C. *real estate executive, architect*
Komaki Cox, Ritsuko U. *medical educator*
Komanduri, Krishna V. *physician, research scientist*
Kors, R. Paul *search company executive*
Kosten, Thomas R. *psychiatrist, educator*
Kotov, Oleg Valerievich *cosmonaut*
Koul, Dimpy *biology professor, cell biologist, researcher*
Kouri, Donald Jack *chemist, educator*
Kraft, Irvin Alan *psychiatrist*
Krajewski, Michael *conductor*
Kramer, Phillip D. *oil industry executive*
Kramm, Deborah Ann *information technology executive*
Kratochvil, L(ouis) Glen *lawyer*
Kraus, Gary Edward *neurosurgeon*
Krause, William Austin *engineering executive*
Krebs, Arno William, Jr. *lawyer*
Kregel, Kevin R. *astronaut*
Kridel, Russell William Hayes *plastic surgeon, educator*
Krieger, Paul Edward *lawyer*
Krishen, Kumar *research technologist*
Krishnan, Sunil *radiologist, educator, oncologist, researcher*
Kristiansen, Eric W. *lawyer*
Krohn, Tracy W. *oil industry executive, gas industry executive*
Kruse, Layne E. *lawyer*
Kubiak, Gary *professional football coach*
Kuehn, Ronald L., Jr. *natural resources company executive*
Kuntz, Hal Goggan *petroleum exploration company executive, rancher*
Kurrass, Lisa *real estate company executive*
Lacy, Terri *lawyer*
Laderman, Gerald *air transportation executive*
LaFuze, William L. *lawyer*
Lake, Kathleen Cooper *lawyer*
Lakkis, Nasser *cardiologist, educator*
Lamb, Sydney MacDonald *linguistics educator*
Lamont, Gene *professional baseball coach and former team manager*
Landrum, Brian *energy executive*
Lane, Andrew *oil industry executive*
Lane, Neal Francis *physics professor, retired federal agency administrator*
Lannie, Paul Anthony *lawyer, energy executive*
Lanoue, Elaine Rose *visual artist, painter*
Lapsley, Andrea Ricards *marketing and development professional, librarian*
Larin, Kirill V. *biomedical engineer, educator*
Larkin, Lee Roy *retired lawyer*
Larkin, William Vincent, Jr. *corporate financial executive*
Lassetter, Scott D. *lawyer*
Lawrence, Wendy B. *astronaut*
Lawson, Rhea Brown *library director*
Lee, Carlos Noriel *professional baseball player*
Lee, Donghyung *psychologist*
Lee, Janie C. *curator*
Lee, Soo-Kyung *molecular biologist, educator*
Leebron, David Wayne *academic administrator, law educator*
Leguillon, Rolande Lucienne *French educator*
Lehrer, Kenneth Eugene *economic consulting company executive*
Lemmer, William C. *lawyer*
LeNôtre, Marie *dean*
Leonard, Charles H. (Chuck Leonard) *air transportation executive*
Lesar, David J. *oil industry executive*
Leslie, Mae Sue *writer*
Levin, Bernard *physician*
Levit, Max *wholesale distribution and food service executive*
Levy, Eugene Howard *planetary sciences and astrophysics educator, researcher*
Lewandowski, Jerome L. *physicist*
Lewis, Chip *lawyer*
Lewis, Kevin Paul *lawyer*
Liang, Edison Parktak *astrophysicist, plasma physicist, educator, researcher*
Liberato, Lynne *lawyer*
Lidge, Brad *professional baseball player*
Lienhard, John Henry, IV, *mechanical engineer, educator*
Limbacher, Randy L. *energy executive*

Lindemulder, Laurie piano educator, concert pianist
Lindsey, John H. former insurance agency executive
Lindsey, Steven W. astronaut, military officer
Listengart, Joseph lawyer, energy executive
Liu, Jing pathologist, educator
Liu, Jinsong pathologist
Locke, Gene L. lawyer
LoMonaco, John Joseph, Jr. plastic surgeon
Long, Meredith J. art dealer
Looper, Marcia Lynn elementary school educator, consultant
Looser, William Gregory lawyer
Lopez, David Tiburcio lawyer, arbitrator, mediator, educator
Lopez-Alegria, Michael Eladio astronaut
Lott, Marley lawyer
Love, Scott Anthony lawyer
Lowe, John E. oil industry executive, accountant
Lowenberg, Michael J. lawyer
Lowman, Sara Allison library director
Lowry, Montecue Judson military historian
Lu, Edward Tsang astronaut
Lucid, Shannon W. biochemist, astronaut
Lukens, Max L. manufacturing executive
Luss, Dan chemical engineering professor
Lynch, John F. lawyer
Macdonald, Sheila L. manufacturing executive
Mackwell, Stephen Joseph geophysicist, educator
MacLean, Steve(n) G. astronaut
Mahadeva, Manoranjan financial executive, accountant
Malki, Heidar A. dean
Mallett, Edward A. lawyer
Mallia, Marianne medical writer
Mallow Corbett, Stephanie pharmacist, educator
Mampre, Virginia Elizabeth communications executive
Mangieri, Mark Louis computer engineer
Manias, William G. oil industry executive
Mansell, Joyce Marilyn retired special education educator
Mao, Li molecular biologist, educator
Marcotte, Michael Steven municipal official
Marek, Joycelyn publishing executive
Mariotto, Marco Jerome dean, psychology educator, researcher
Marlow, Orval Lee, II, lawyer
Marston, Edgar Jean III lawyer
Martin, J. Clark lawyer
Martin, James Kirby historian, educator
Martin, Jay Griffith lawyer
Martin, Paul Edward lawyer
Martin, William C. social studies educator, writer
Martinez, David Roger chemist, researcher
Marzetta, Dante R., II, air transportation executive
Marzio, Peter Cort museum director
Mason, Dwayne L. lawyer
Massad, Stephen Albert lawyer
Massoud, Yehia science educator
Mastracchio, Richard A. (Rick) astronaut
Matheny, Kenneth L. oil industry executive
Mathers, Paula Janecek lawyer
Mathis, James Forrest retired petroleum company executive
Matthews, Charles Sedwick petroleum engineer, consultant
Matthews, Kathleen Shive biochemistry educator
Mattox, Sharon M. lawyer
Mawhood, Aristide Roscoe mechanical engineer
Max, Ernest surgeon
Mays, Randall T. communications company executive
McArthur, William Surles, Jr. astronaut, retired military officer
McCarter, Louis Eugene lawyer
McClanahan, David M. energy executive
McClure, Daniel M. lawyer
McClure, Jeffrey B. lawyer
McCollam, Marion Andrus consulting firm executive, educator
McCreary, Frank E. III lawyer
McDaniel, Jarrel Dave lawyer
McDavid, George Eugene (Gene Mc David) retired newspaper executive
McEachern, Stephen Mathew accountant
McFall, Donald Beury lawyer
McFarland, Marcie Allred lawyer
Mc Ginty, John Milton architect, consultant
McGrady, Tracy professional basketball player
McKee, Rae Ellen (Rae Ellen McKee-Doucette) special education educator
McLeod, Chanse L. lawyer
McLeod, Harry O'Neal, Jr. retired petroleum engineer, consultant
McPherson, Alice Ruth ophthalmologist, educator
McQuarrie, Claude Monroe III lawyer
McShane, Michael manufacturing executive
Medeiros, L. Jeffrey hematologist, educator
Meehan, William A. air transportation executive
Melroy, Pamela Ann astronaut
Melton, Stephen Reid lawyer
Mendelsohn, John oncologist, hematologist, educator, health facility executive
Mendelson, Robert Allen polymer scientist, rheologist
Meng, Ru-Ling research scientist
Menscher, Barnet Gary steel company executive
Mentz, Henry A. III plastic surgeon
Miele, Angelo engineering educator, researcher, consultant, author
Milam, John Daniel pathologist, educator
Miller, Barry Rixmann lawyer
Miller, Charles Rickie systems analyst, engineering executive
Miller, Gary C. lawyer
Miller, Gary Evan psychiatrist, mental health services professional
Miller, Gray Hampton federal judge, lawyer
Miller, Harry Freeman university administrator
Miller, Janel Howell psychologist
Miller, Merrill Anthony, Jr. energy executive
Miller, Robert Harold otolaryngologist, educator
Miller, Sabrina Wares librarian
Millican, Elliot Stephen mechanical engineer
Milstead, Terry Lee secondary school educator
Ming, Yao professional basketball player
Minor, Sterling Arthur lawyer
Minter, David Lee English literature educator
Mintz-Hittner, Helen Ann physician, researcher
Mire, Weldon J. oil industry executive, human resources specialist
Misner, Jeffrey J. air transportation executive
Mitch, William Evans nephrologist
Moehlman, Michael Scott lawyer
Mohan, Sameer Vijay lawyer
Moncure, John Lewis lawyer
Montgomery, Cleothus minister
Montgomery, Denise Karen nurse
Montoya, Delilah Marie artist, educator
Moore, Barry M. architect, educator
Moore, Lois Jean health science facility administrator
Moore, Tim lawyer
Moorhead, Gerald Lee architect
Moran, Mark J. air transportation executive
Morey, Daryl professional sports team executive
Morgan, Barbara R. astronaut
Morgan, Richard Greer lawyer
Moroney, Linda L.S. (Muffie) lawyer, educator
Morris, Malcolm Stewart title company executive, lawyer
Morris, Owen Glenn engineering corporation executive
Morris, Stephen Jay music educator
Morris, Stewart, Jr. title insurance company executive
Moulds, Eric Shannon professional football player
Moya, Olga Lydia law educator
Mulva, James Joseph oil industry executive
Munisteri, Joseph George construction executive
Murad, Ferid physician
Murphy, Ewell Edward, Jr. lawyer
Murphy, William Alexander, Jr. diagnostic radiologist, educator
Mutombo, DiKembe (Dikembe Mutombo Mpolondo Mukamba Jean Jacque Wamutombo) professional basketball player
Myers, James Clark advertising and public relations executive
Nacol, Mae lawyer
Nathan, Arthur M. lawyer
Nations, Howard Lynn lawyer
Nelson, David Loren geneticist, educator
Nelson, Joelle Grace Kenney lawyer
Nesbitt, DeEtte DuPree small business owner, investor
Neslage, John E. lawyer
Nespoli, Paolo Angelo astronaut
Netherland, Joseph H. manufacturing executive
Neuhaus, Philip Ross investment banker
Neumann, Henry W., Jr. energy executive
Nichols, Michael Cooper food products executive, lawyer
Nickens, Jacks Clarence lawyer
Niebruegge, Michael E. lawyer
Nielsen, Niels Christian, Jr. retired religious studies educator
Noguchi, Soichi astronaut
Noland, Mary Richerson retired management consultant
Nolen, Roy Lemuel retired lawyer
Norris, Chuck (Carlos Ray) actor
Nosé, Yukihiko surgeon, educator
Nugent, Paul C. lawyer
Oakes, Pamela R. retired elementary school educator
Ochoa, Ellen astronaut
O'Connor, Ralph Sturges investment company executive
O'Donnell, Lawrence III waste management executive
Oefelein, William A. astronaut, military officer
O'Geary, Dennis Traylor retired engineering company executive
Oh, Junghwan biomedical scientist, researcher
Oldham, Darius Dudley lawyer
Oldham, John Michael physician, psychiatrist, educator
Olivas, John D. (Danny) astronaut
Onn, Amir medical educator, researcher
O'Quinn, John M. lawyer
Oren, Bruce Clifford editor, artist
Orengo-Nania, Silvia ophthalmologist
Orr, Carole artist
Osteen, Joel minister
Ostendorf, Lance Stephen lawyer, financial consultant, educator
Osterberg, Edward Charles, Jr. lawyer
Oswalt, Roy E. professional baseball player
Owens, Betty Ruth lawyer
Palmer, Willard Aldrich III magician, writer, actor
Pannill, William Presley lawyer
Papa, Mark Gary oil and gas industry executive
Parazynski, Scott E. astronaut
Parle, Bertha Ibarra writer
Parnas-Simpson, Marianna chorus director, singer
Parsons, Edmund Morris investment company executive
Pate, Stephen Patrick lawyer
Patrick, Nicholas J.M. astronaut
Patten, Robert Lowry language educator
Paul, Gordon Lee behavioral scientist, psychologist
Peabody, Arlene L. Howland Bayar retired enterostomal therapy nurse
Pearson, Michael P. lawyer
Pector, Michelle D. lawyer
Pefanis, Harry N. oil industry executive
Peng, Liang-Chuan mechanical engineer
Perich, Thomas J. lawyer
Pete, Eric E. writer, claims representative
Peterson, Terry Norris lawyer
Pettit, Donald R. astronaut, flight engineer, researcher
Phung, Nguyen Dinh medical educator
Pickering, James Henry III academic administrator, educator
Pierce, Frank Powell lawyer, judge
Pierce, Jesse R. lawyer
Pilibosian, Michele Mason lawyer
Pitts, Gary Benjamin lawyer
Plaeger, Frederick Joseph, II, lawyer
Plank, Raymond energy executive
Plank, Roger B. energy executive
Polansky, Mark L. astronaut
Port, P. Allan lawyer
Porter, Thomas William III lawyer
Pospisil, JoAnn historian, archivist
Potluri, Venkateswara Rao medical facility administrator
Powell, Alan engineering educator, research scientist
Powers, William Edward emergency physician, medical educator, flight surgeon
Prats, Michael petroleum engineer, educator
Pravel, Bernarr Roe lawyer
Pruitt, Robert A. artist
Pryor, William Daniel Lee humanities educator
Pugh, William Whitmell Hill III lawyer
Qiao, Fengxiang transportation engineer, educator
Quiros-Tejeira, Ruben Eloy pediatrician, educator, researcher
Radoff, Leonard Irving librarian, consultant
Ragauss, Peter A. oil industry executive
Raijman, Isaac gastroenterologist, educator
Rakel, Robert Edwin physician, educator
Raley, John Wesley III lawyer
Ramirez, Mari Carmen curator
Ramsey, Michael W. lawyer
Rapini, Ronald Peter dermatology educator
Rapp, Robert David lawyer
Rappaport, Norman Harvey plastic surgeon
Raspino, Louis A. energy executive
Rawson, Jim Charles finance company executive
Ray, Hugh Massey, Jr. lawyer
Ray, Hugh Massey III lawyer
Rayala, Suresh Kumar medical educator
Read, Michael Oscar editor, consultant
Ream, James B. (Jim Ream) air transportation executive
Reasoner, Barrett Hodges lawyer
Reasoner, Harry Max lawyer
Reavley, Thomas Morrow federal judge
Reece, Gregory Paul plastic surgeon, educator
Reed, Kathlyn Louise occupational therapist, educator
Reid, Katherine Louise artist, educator, writer
Reiff, Patricia Hofer space physicist, educator
Reso, Anthony geologist, educator, earth resources economist
Rettig, Dwight W. lawyer
Reynolds, John Terrence oil industry executive
Ribble, John Charles medical educator
Richards, Leonard Martin investment executive, consultant
Rider, Roger Alan lawyer
Riedel, Alan Ellis manufacturing executive, lawyer
Rigdon, Kevin Leigh theater educator, lighting designer, set designer
Riggenbach, Jeff journalist
Riley, William John neurologist
Risin, Semyon Aaron pathologist, educator
Roach, Robert Michael, Jr., (Randy) lawyer
Robb, Geoffrey Lawrence plastic surgeon
Robbins, Susan Paula social work educator
Roberts, Charles Murray retired publishing executive, writer
Roberts, David E., Jr. oil industry executive
Robin, Alan Jay lawyer
Rock, Douglas Lawrence manufacturing executive
Rodríguez, Félix M. oil industry executive
Roff, J(ohn) Hugh, Jr. energy executive
Romans, Jay waste management executive
Rommel, A. Ross, Jr. lawyer
Roos, Sybil Friedenthal retired elementary school educator
Rose, Beatrice Schroeder harpist, educator
Rosenthal, Gary L. lawyer
Rosenthal, Lee H. federal judge
Ross, Jerry L. astronaut
Ross, Michael Wallis public health educator
Ross, Patti Jayne obstetrics and gynecology educator
Ross, R. Dale medical products executive
Rowe, Zane Conrad air transportation executive
Rowland, Kelly (Kelendria Trene Rowland) singer
Rowland, Robert Alexander III lawyer
Rozzell, Scott Ellis lawyer, energy executive
Rudolph, Andrew Henry dermatologist, educator
Rudolph, Richard L. medical products executive, physician
Ruiz, Pedro psychiatrist
Runco, Mario, Jr. astronaut, meteorologist, researcher
Runnels, David G. lawyer
Russell, John Francis retired librarian
Rustay, Jennifer Beth lawyer
Ryan, Jason Michael lawyer
Ryan, Stephen M. lawyer
Ryan, Thomas L. funeral company executive
Ryan, Thomas William lawyer
Ryan, Vince lawyer
Saavedra, Abelardo school system administrator
Saizan, Paula Theresa business consultant
Sales, James Bohus lawyer
Sanderson, Mary Louise medical association administrator
Sandman, Bradford Aaron coach, educator
Sargent, John psychiatrist
Sarne, Andrew J. lawyer
Sarofim, Fayez Shalaby finance company executive
Saunders, Charles Albert lawyer
Saunders, William Arthur management consultant
Sawh, Ravi-Persad lab administrator, researcher
Schaffer, Randy lawyer
Schaffer, Stuart F. lawyer
Scharold, Mary Louise psychoanalyst, psychiatrist, educator
Schechter, Arthur Louis lawyer
Schick, Robert Michael lawyer
Schneiders, Richard J. food service company executive
Schnieders, Richard J. food products executive
Schnoebelen, Anne Mary musicologist, educator
Schoolar, Joseph Clayton psychiatrist, pharmacologist, educator
Schumacher, Diane Kosmach manufacturing executive, lawyer
Schusterman, Mark A. surgeon, plastic surgeon
Schwartz, Charles Walter lawyer
Schwartzel, Charles Boone lawyer
Schwind, William F., Jr. lawyer, oil industry executive
Scoggins, Brenda Carol language educator, department chairman
Scott, Danny Eugene metal products executive, metallurgical engineer
Scott, David Warren statistics educator
Scuseria, Gustavo Enrique theoretical chemist
Seale, Robert Arthur lawyer
Secrest, George McCall, Jr., (Mac Secrest) lawyer
Segal, Steven E. retired lawyer
Segner, Edmund Peter III natural gas company executive
Sellers, Piers J. astronaut
Severance, Diana Lynn curator
Shackouls, Bobby S. oil and gas industry executive
Shaddock, Carroll Sidney lawyer
Shaffer, Anita Mohrland counselor, educator
Shafiei-Sararodi, Majoud language educator
Shan, Kesavan cardiologist, researcher
Shannon, Holden E. air transportation executive
Shannon, Margaret Barrett lawyer
Shaper, C. Park energy executive
Shapirov, Salizhan Shakirovich cosmonaut
Shearer, William Thomas pediatrician, educator
Sheinfeld, Myron M. lawyer, educator
Shelley, Clyde Burton artist
Shely, John B. lawyer
Sheppard, Ben H., Jr. lawyer
Sher, George Allen philosophy educator
Sherer, Jeffrey Todd pharmacist, educator
Sherman, Mike (Michael Francis Sherman) professional football coach
Shetty, Gunapala biologist, researcher, educator
Shiao, Shyang-Yun Pamela K. nursing educator, researcher
Shouse, August Edward lawyer
Shu, Glen lawyer
Shulman, Robert Jay pediatrician, nutritionist, gastroenterologist, educator
Siegler, Kelly R. lawyer
Silva, Eugene Joseph lawyer
Simmons, Stephen Judson lawyer
Simpson, Robert G. waste management executive
Simpson, Robert Louis music educator
Sing, William Bender lawyer
Skalka, Michael B. insurance company executive, lawyer
Smisek, Jeffery A. air transportation executive
Smith, Alison Leigh lawyer
Smith, Arthur Kittredge, Jr. academic administrator, political scientist, educator
Smith, Dan F. chemicals executive
Smith, David Kingman retired oil company executive, consultant
Smith, E. Ashley lawyer, insurance company executive
Smith, Jerry Edwin federal judge
Smith, Martha Lee lawyer
Smith, Rick professional sports team executive
Smith, Roland Blair, Jr. university administrator
Smith, Walter John lawyer
Smith, William Ashley lawyer, investment banker, energy executive
Smythe, Cheves McCord internist, geriatrician, educator, dean
Sondock, Ruby Kless retired judge
Sonfield, Robert Leon, Jr. lawyer
Sorrels, Randall Owen lawyer
Sostman, Dirk physician, clinical researcher, medical educator
Spalding, Andrew Freeman lawyer
Spikes, Patricia White medical technologist
Spira, Melvin plastic surgeon
Spudich, John Lee biochemist, molecular biologist, chemistry professor
Staff, Joel V. energy executive
Steele, James Harlan retired veterinarian
Stefanyshyn-Piper, Heidemarie M. astronaut
Steiner, David P. waste management executive
Steiner, Uwe language educator
Stephens, Sidney Dee human resources specialist, retired chemical manufacturing company executive
Stewart, David James oncologist, educator
Stewart, J.W. energy executive, lawyer
Stone, Robert G., Jr. water transportation executive
Stradley, William Jackson lawyer
Strauss, Cindi curator
Streng, William Paul lawyer, educator
Stryker, Steven Charles lawyer
Stubblefield, John K., Jr. food products executive
Sturckow, Frederick W. (Rick) astronaut
Sugars, Janeal M. opera singer, vocal educator
Sullivan, Charles, Jr. retired lawyer
Sullivan, John F. III lawyer
Sullivan-Szuts, Betty Anne academic administrator, educator
Susman, Stephen Daily lawyer
Sutton, Jeffrey Paul physician, scientist
Sutton, Neal S. lawyer
Swan, Michael K. lawyer
Swanson, Roy Joel lawyer
Swanson, Steven R. astronaut
Swartz, Michael D. statistical geneticist
Sweeney, Jack publishing executive
Swick, Todd J. medical association administrator
Swift, Robert J. lawyer

Swisher, Stephen G. *thoracic surgeon*
Swoopes, Sheryl Denise *professional basketball player*
Sydow, Michael David *lawyer*
Szalkowski, Charles C. *lawyer*
Taheri, Marshall M. *lawyer, educator*
Talwani, Manik *geophysicist, educator*
Tanner, Joseph Richard *astronaut*
Tanous, Helene Mary *radiologist, educator*
Tapia, Richard Alfred *mathematics professor*
Tartt, Blake *lawyer*
Taylor, Cindy B. *oil industry executive*
Tervalon, Josephine M. *psychotherapist, social worker*
Thirsk, Robert Brent *astronaut*
Thomas, Andrew S.W. *astronaut*
Thomas, Byron Andrew *lawyer*
Thompson, Jerry E. *oil industry executive*
Thompson, Jon L. *retired oil industry executive*
Thompson, Karleen *professional basketball coach*
Thompson, Sandra Guerra *lawyer, educator*
Thompson, Tina Marie *professional basketball player*
Thompson-Draper, Cheryl L. *electronics and real estate company executive*
Tomson, Mason B. *environmental engineer, educator*
Tong, Louis Lik-Fu *information scientist*
Totten, Patricia A. *lawyer*
Touchy, Deborah K.P. *lawyer, accountant*
Tour, James M. *chemistry educator, researcher*
Townsend, Roger Dale *lawyer*
Trauber, Stephen M. (Steve Tauber) *investment banker*
Trice, David A. *oil industry executive*
Tripp, Karen Bryant *lawyer*
Tsai, Tom Chunghu *chemical engineer*
Tsui, Stephen Alan *researcher*
Tucker, Anne Wilkes *curator, historian, photographer, critic*
Tweardy, David John *physician, educator*
Ulmer, Gregory C. *lawyer*
Urbina, Manuel, II, *legal research historian, history professor*
Usher, Thomas James *metal products executive*
Utt, William P. (Bill Utt) *construction executive*
Vallbona, Carlos *physician*
Vallbona, Rima-Gretel Rothe *retired foreign language educator, writer*
Vanderploeg, James M. *preventive medicine physician*
Van Dyke, Gene *oil industry executive*
Van Eeckhoudt, Marc Victor Celestin *oil industry executive*
Van Fleet, George Allan *lawyer*
Van Kerrebrook, Mary Alice *lawyer*
Van Wagenen, Paul G. *gas industry executive*
Varma, Datla G.K. *radiologist, researcher*
Varner, David Eugene *lawyer*
Vassar, Claudia Sue Gee *lawyer*
Vassilopoulou-Sellin, Rena *researcher*
Vaughan, Eugene H. *investment company executive*
Vaughan, Jack M. *lawyer*
Veech, William Austin *mathematics professor*
Vittori, Roberto *astronaut*
Vladimirovich, Vinogradov Pavel *cosmonaut*
Vogel, Jennifer L. *lawyer, air transportation executive*
von der Mehden, Fred R. *political science professor*
Wagener, Christine Elizabeth *psychotherapist, educator*
Wagner, Charlene Brook *secondary school educator*
Wagner, Leslie *lawyer*
Wagner, Paul Anthony, Jr. *education educator*
Walker, Charles D. *astronaut*
Walker, John E. (Ned Walker) *air transportation executive*
Walker, William Easton *surgeon, educator, lawyer*
Wall, Kenneth E., Jr. *lawyer*
Wallace, Mark Allen *hospital administrator*
Walls, Martha Ann Williams (Mrs. B. Carmage Walls) *publishing executive*
Walters, Richard B. *lawyer*
Walton, Conrad Gordon, Sr. *retired architect*
Walton, Dan Gibson *lawyer*
Waltrip, Robert L. *environmentalist, funeral company executive*
Wang, Chao-Cheng *mathematician, engineer*
Ward, Robin A. *mathematics professor*
Warren, Tommy Melvin *petroleum engineer*
Watson, John Allen *lawyer*
Webb, Jack M. *lawyer*
Webb, Marty Fox *principal*
Weber, Fredric Alan *lawyer*
Weiner, Bradley Kenneth *surgeon, researcher*
Weiner, Sanford Alan *lawyer*
Weinstein, Roy *physics professor*
Weinstock, George Matthew *biology educator, researcher*
Weitzel, Amy Ragan *not-for-profit developer*
Welch, Stanton *performing company executive*
Wells, Damon *investment company executive*
Welsh, H. Ronald *lawyer*
Westby, Timothy Scott *lawyer, researcher*
Wheelan, R(ichelieu) E(dward) *lawyer*
Wheelock, Douglas H. *astronaut, military officer*
Whilden, Robert Harral, Jr. *lawyer*
White, Bill (William Howard White) *mayor*
White, Ronald Joseph *biomedical researcher, physiologist, educator*
Whiting, Hugh Richard *lawyer*
Whiting, Martha Countee *retired secondary school educator*
Whiting, S. Carol *music educator*
Whitlock, Gary L. *energy executive*
Wiater, Richard M. *manufacturing executive*
Wiglesworth, Michael Bland *advertising executive*
Wilburn, John *editor*
Wiley, Michael E. *oil industry executive*
Wilkin, Alana Zimmer *elementary school educator*
Wilkinson, Bruce W. *construction executive*
Williames, Lee John *academic administrator, history professor*
Williams, Clay C. *energy executive*
Williams, David R. (Dafydd Rhys Williams) *astronaut*
Williams, Edward Earl, Jr. *entrepreneur, educator*
Williams, Ella *healthcare educator*
Williams, Lowell Craig *lawyer, employee relations executive*
Williams, Mario *professional football player*
Williams, Michelle (Tenitra Michelle Williams) *singer*
Williams, O'Banion III *lawyer*
Williams, Robert Henry *oil industry executive*
Williams, Sunita L. *astronaut*
Williamson, Bruce A. *gas industry executive*
Williamson, Peter David *lawyer*
Willis, Arthur William *ophthalmologist*
Wilson, Carl Weldon, Jr. *construction company executive, civil engineer*
Wilson, Edward Converse, Jr. *oil and natural gas production company executive*
Wilson, Floyd C. *oil industry executive*
Wilson, Gerald Everette *funeral services company executive*
Wilson, Stephanie D. *astronaut*
Wilson, Thomas Leon *physicist, researcher*
Winston, Leland A. *orthopedic surgeon, educator*
Wittenbraker, Rick L. *lawyer, waste management executive*
Wong-Liang, Eirene Ming *psychologist*
Woo, Stanley Y. *medical educator, director, optometrist*
Wood, Michael W *lawyer*
Woodhouse, John Frederick *retired wholesale distribution executive*
Woods, Ronald G. *lawyer, former prosecutor*
Worthing, Louie Fabian III *plastic surgeon*
Worthington, William Albert III *lawyer*
Wray, Thomas Jefferson *lawyer*
Wren, Robert James *aerospace engineering manager*
Wright, Clark Phillips *computer systems specialist*
Wuori, Stephen J. *energy executive*
Wyatt, Oscar Sherman, Jr. *energy company executive*
Wynne, John Carlton *lawyer*
Wyrsch, Martha B. *lawyer, energy executive*
Yatsenko, Yuri Petrovich *economics professor, mathematician*
Yeates, Marie R. *lawyer*
Yeh, Edward Tu-Hsing *cardiologist, educator, medical researcher*
Yeoman, Lynn Chalmers *medical educator*
Yetter, R. Paul *lawyer*
Yokubaitis, Roger T. *lawyer*
Young, David *anesthesiologist, educator*
Young, Wayne C. *lawyer*
Yuen, Benson Bolden *air transportation and software executive, consultant*
Zacharias, Nikolaos Marios *obstetrician, gynecologist, perinatologist*
Zager, Steven Mark *lawyer*
Zamka, George D. *astronaut*
Zeigler, Ann dePender *lawyer*
Zhou, Min *geophysicist*
Zoghbi, Huda Y. *neurologist, geneticist, educator*

Humble
Ellis, James Otto *secondary school educator*
Pickle, George Edward *lawyer*
Trowbridge, John Parks *physician*

Hunt
Gambrell, James Bruton III *lawyer, educator*

Huntsville
Conwell, Halford Roger *physician*
Daniel, Kathryn Hutchins *musician, educator*
Hanssen, Kristina Schirm *costume designer, educator*
Lea, Stanley E. *artist, educator*
Payne, David Emer *university administrator*
Raymond, Kay E(ngelmann) *Spanish language educator, consultant*
Russell, George Haw *video production company executive*
Sower, Victor Edmund *management educator*
Stowe, Charles Robinson Beecher *management consultant, educator, lawyer*
Vaughn, Michael S. *law educator*
Ward, Richard Hurley *education educator, writer*
Wells, William *criminal justice educator*

Hurst
Bishara, Amin Tawadros *management and consulting firm executive*
Mabry, Philip T. *political scientist, consultant*

Hutto
Hamilton, Elizabeth Ann *elementary school educator*

Industry
Huitt, Jimmie L. *rancher, oil and gas industry executive, real estate developer*

Ingram
Hughes, David Michael *oil industry executive, rancher*

Iola
Nelson, John Harrison *mathematics educator*

Iowa Park
Wright, Sabra Dell *music educator*

Irving
Albers, Mark W. *oil industry executive*
Ali, Ashraf *psychiatrist*
Barnard, Ray F. *engineering and construction management company executive*
Beach, Charles Addison *lawyer*
Beasley, Mark V. *lawyer*
Berg, Mark S. *lawyer, oil industry executive*
Boeckmann, Alan L. *engineering and construction management company executive*
Brown, Linda Harper *bookkeeping company executive*
Burton, Betsy (Mary Elizabeth) *retail executive*
Cavanaugh, Lucille J. *oil industry executive*
Cherri, Mona Y. *computer scientist, educator, computer scientist, consultant*
Conger, Sue Ann *computer information systems educator*
Cornell, Brian C. *food service executive, retail executive*
Dingle, Philip *retired oil industry executive*
Eaker, Charles William *chemistry professor*
Flowers, Garry W. *engineering and construction management company executive*
Gilbert, H. Steven *engineering and construction management company executive*
Glenn, Terry *professional football player*
Hawkins, William David *marketing executive*
Humphreys, Donald D. *oil industry executive*
Jones, Jerry (Jerral Wayne Jones) *professional sports team executive*
Jones, Julius *professional football player*
Kling, Lewis M. *multi-industry executive*
Lambert-Saul, Beth *real estate company executive*
Lang, Laura Smith *lawyer*
LaSala, Stephen R. *lawyer, oil industry executive*
Longwell, Harry J. *retired oil industry executive*
Martin, Thomas Lyle, Jr. *academic administrator*
Matthews, Charles W., Jr. *oil industry executive, lawyer*
McClean, Murray R. *metal products executive*
Mc Cray, Ronald David *lawyer, health products executive*
Molay, Hilary S. *lawyer*
Mulva, Patrick T. *oil industry executive*
Nugent, John Hilliard *communications executive*
Olson, Gary Robert *banker*
Olson, Herbert Theodore *trade association executive*
Owens, Terrell Eldorad *professional football player*
Pascal, Tracey Michele *software engineer, director*
Phillips, Wade *professional football coach*
Plaskett, Thomas George *transportation executive, director*
Potter, Robert Joseph *technical and business executive*
Rabin, Stanley Arthur *metal products manufacturer*
Rees, Frank William, Jr. *architect*
Romo, Tony (Antonio Ramiro Romo) *professional football player*
Rouleau, R. Michael *retail executive*
Sheffield, Scott D. *oil industry executive*
Shuff, Ronald F. *lawyer*
Simon, J. Stephen *oil industry executive*
Sommerfeldt, John Robert *historian, educator*
Sudbury, David Marshall *lawyer*
Tidwell, James *Sommelier*
Tillerson, Rex W. *oil company executive*
Walley, James Marvin, Jr. *engineering executive, management consultant, real estate company executive*
Wenetschlaeger, Patty Strader *lawyer*
Wicks, William Withington *retired public relations executive*
Williams, Roy L. *fraternal organization administrator*
Wood, Robert E. *philosopher, educator*
Wyly, Samuel E. *retail executive*
Young, J. Warren *magazine publisher*
Zisman, Barry Stuart *retired lawyer*

Jacksboro
Patterson, Ronald R(oy) *management consultant*

Jacksonville
Blaylock, James Carl *clergyman, librarian*
Thrall, Gordon Fish *publishing executive*

Joaquin
Gill, Madeline Kay *school and youth counselor*

Junction
Evans, Jo Burt *communications executive, rancher*

Katy
Sadowski, Chester Philip, Jr. *real estate executive*
Vickery, Edward Downtain *lawyer*

Kaufman
Hausler, Rudolf Heinrich *research chemist*
Tygrett, Howard Volney, Jr. *judge, lawyer*

Keene
Doroftei, Mugur Gideon *music educator, conductor, composer, musician*
Taroy-Valdez, Lolita B. *nursing educator, nurse*

Keller
Smith, Eleanor Jane *retired university chancellor, consultant*

Kemp
Melton, Kathy A. *medical transcription educator*
Shugart, Jill *academic administrator*

Kerrville
Freeny, Katherine H. *adult education educator, chemist, researcher*
Frudakis, Evangelos William *sculptor*
Shaw, Alan Bosworth *geologist, retired paleontologist*

Kilgore
Rorschach, Richard Gordon *lawyer*

Killeen
Jenkins, Sharon Leigh *special education educator*
Lane, Penelope Diane *special education educator*
Peronto, Janice Lynn *principal*

Kingsville
Bleidt, Barry Anthony *pharmacy educator*
Hunter, Leslie Gene *history educator*
Nutan, Mohammad Tawhidul Haque *pharmacy educator, researcher*
Sethi, Rajat *cardiologist, educator*
Stanford, (Frances) Jane Herring *dean, management consultant, educator, writer*

Kingwood
Hagen, Barbara C. *music educator*
Hearn, Jackson *church musician, educator*
Spartz, Alice Anne Lenore *retired retail executive*
van Beem, Janny *geneticist, researcher*

Kyle
Saunders, Patricia Gene Knight *freelance writer, editor*

La Feria
Zamarripa, Victor Manuel *sound recording engineer, purchasing agent*

La Marque
Disher, David Alan *lawyer, consultant*

La Porte
Fotsch, George Bernard III *chemical addiction counselor*

Lackland Afb
Fadare, Oluwole *pathologist, researcher, director*
Perry, William Brian *colorectal surgeon*

Lake Jackson
Hill, Diane Louise *educator*
Tarrant, Sasha Ranae Adams *history professor*

Lakehills
Spears, Diane Shields *retired art director, elementary school educator*

Laredo
Black, Clifford Merwyn *academic administrator, sociologist, educator*
Cai, Gangshu *finance educator*
Chavez, Mary Rose *counselor, educator*
Heimes, Charmaine Marie *elementary school educator, poet, writer*
Hudson, Robert Donald *dermatologist*
Kazen, George Philip *federal judge*
Ortiz, Jaime *business educator*
Riggs, William W. *social sciences educator*
Soto, Gilberto D. *music educator*
Weber, Janice Ann *library director, grant writer*
Wu, Fuming *computer science educator*
Zaffirini, Judith *state legislator, small business owner*

Laughlin A F B
Files, Douglas Scott *surgeon, military officer*

League City
Dupuy, Christopher Michael *lawyer*
Kanuth, James Gordan *chemical engineer*

Leander
Fraley, Linda Williams Darnell *music educator*
Ramirez, Ciro *mechanical engineer, consultant*

Lewisville
Ferguson, R. Neil *computer scientist, consultant*
Hirschhorn, Robert B. *lawyer*
Nickon, Alex *chemist, educator*
Whitney, Sharry Jan *science educator*
Wrenn, Susan Stroud *language educator*

Lindale
Beckerley, Robert M. *realtor, consultant*
Carter, Thomas Smith, Jr. *retired rail transportation executive*

Littlefield
Muller, Janice Elaine *secondary school educator*

Livingston
Davidson, John Robert *retired dentist*
Rauscher, Richard Conrad *psychotherapist, writer*
Stovall, Jerry Coleman *insurance company executive*

Llano
Wallis, Olney Gray *lawyer*
Wilson, Dena Suzette *elementary school educator*

Lockney
Williams, Jamie Gaye *medical transcriptionist*

Longview
Harrison, Guy Newell *lawyer*
Mann, Jack Matthewson *bottling company executive*
Mann, True Sandlin *psychologist, consultant*
McKinley, Jimmie Joe *small business owner*
Udy, Rae *columnist, writer*
Welge, Jack Herman, Jr. *lawyer*
Williams, Willie Alvin *retired literature educator*

Lubbock
Adamcik, Joe Alfred *retired chemistry professor, lawyer*
Aker, Suzanne Deverse *physical movement educator*
Archer, James Elson *engineering educator*
Beck, George Preston *anesthesiologist, educator*
Beyer, Gerry Wayne *lawyer, educator*
Blevins, Stanley Nance *minister, educator*
Brimée, Jean-Michel *physical therapist, educator*
Broselow, Linda Latt *medical office technician, aviculturist*

Bullock, James Jefferson, II, *literature and language professor, director*
Chiriva Internati, Maurizio *immunologist, researcher*
Clausen, Jane *library director*
Conover, William Jay *statistics educator*
Craighead, Owen Lindsay *writer*
Dennison, Daniel Thomas *environmental compliance and lab administrator*
Dudek, Richard Albert *engineering educator*
Feola, Mario *researcher*
Fontenot, Andrea Dean *communications executive*
Frezza, Eldo E. *surgeon, educator*
Gill, Gurdev S. *orthopaedic surgeon*
Hance, Kent Ronald *academic administrator, former congressman*
Haragan, Donald Robert *academic administrator, geologist, educator*
Hartwell, William Gersham III *retired music educator*
Hentges, David John *microbiology educator*
Huffman, Walter B. *retired army officer, dean, law educator*
Illner-Canizaro, Hana *physician, researcher, oral surgeon*
Jackson, Raymond Carl *cytogeneticist*
Jugenheimer, Donald Wayne *advertising executive, communications educator, academic administrator*
Ketner, Kenneth Laine *philosopher, educator*
Kiesling, Ernst Willie *civil engineering educator, dean*
Knight, Bobby (Robert Montgomery Knight) *men's college basketball coach*
Kristiansen, Magne *electrical engineer, educator*
Leach, Mike *college football coach*
Martin, Clyde F. *engineering educator*
May, Donald Robert Lee *ophthalmologist, educator, academic administrator, farmer*
Mehta, Kishor Chandulal *civil engineering educator*
Mittemeyer, Bernhard Theodore *urology and surgery educator*
Morton, Harvey Leon *lawyer*
Moseley, Patricia Ann *lawyer*
Phelan, Marilyn Elizabeth *law educator*
Punyanunt-Carter, Narissra *communications educator*
Purdom, Thomas James *lawyer*
Riley, Jennifer Bell *finance educator*
River, Sandra A. *university librarian*
Sabatini, Sandra *physician*
Skoog, Gerald Duane *science educator*
Stuart, Frank Adell *county official*
Wendt, Charles William *soil scientist, educator*
White, Alice Virginia *academic administrator*
Whitmore, Jon Scott *academic administrator, play director*
Wilhelm, Jennifer Anne *mathematics and science professor*
Wolfe, Verda Nell *pension consultant, financial planner*
Wood, Richard Courtney *library director, educator*
Yoder-Wise, Patricia Snyder *nursing educator*

Lufkin
Haas, Sally Marie *mathematician, educator*
Mott, Earl *artist, poet, writer*
Thames, William Dennis, Jr. *physician*

Magnolia
Bradie, Peter Richard *lawyer, engineer*
Girard, Louis Joseph *retired ophthalmologist, educator*
Tarver, Betty Gail *music educator*

Mansfield
Parnell, Charles L. *speechwriter*

Marshall
Branscome, Eric Eugene *music educator, writer*
Fogle, Sheryl Kay *voice educator, music educator*
Magrill, Rose Mary *library director*
Sudhivoraseth, Niphon *pediatrician, immunologist, allergist*

Mc Kinney
Albano, Christine Grace *lawyer*
Dorff, Barbara L. *elementary and secondary school educator*
Dowdy, William Clarence, Jr. *retired lawyer*
Frank, Steven Neil *chemist*
Gill, David bRIAN *electrical engineer, educator*
Harris, Andrew Bennett *artist, writer, producer*
Kessler, John Paul, Jr. *financial planner*
McAndrew, Mark S. *insurance company executive*
Roessler, P. Dee *lawyer, educator, mediator, former judge*
Sundaram, Shankar M. *surgeon*
Wright, Thomas Parker *artist*

Mcallen
Arredondo, Jenna Dolores *speech pathology/audiology services professional*
Casso, Ramiro Raul *physician, academic administrator*
Connors, Joseph Aloysius III *lawyer*
Conrad, Philip Jefferson *social worker*
Gonzalez, Rolando Noel *secondary school educator, theology studies educator, photographer*
Hinojosa, Federico Gustavo, Jr. *retired judge*
Hinojosa, Ricardo H. *federal judge*
Huber, Melba Stewart *dance studio owner, educator, historian, writer, retailer*
McGee, William Howard John *library director*
Ramirez, Leo Armando, Sr. *mathematics educator*
Ramirez, Linda Manning *counselor*
Ramirez, Mario Efrain *physician*
Rebuelta, Avelino Luis *public administration educator*
Rodriguez, Maria Dolores *librarian*

Spyker, Leola Edith *missionary*
Tupper, Ron *public health service officer, finance educator*
von Kuster, Lee Norman *retired mathematics professor*

Meadowlakes
Blackmon, Willie Edward Boney *judge, military officer*
Nussbaum, Paul Stowell *retired urologist*

Memphis
Gerkey, Stephen J. *management consultant, writer, speech educator*

Mesquite
Budd, Rose Antoinette *language educator*
Byrd, Kathryn Susan *psychologist, educator*
Vaughan, Joseph Lee, Jr. *education educator, consultant, director, academic administrator*
Wenrich, John William *college president*

Midland
Abney, William K. *lawyer*
Berner, Leo De Witte, Jr. *retired oceanographer*
Bridges, Judy Cantrell *gifted and talented education educator*
Celia, George *composer, writer*
Estes, Andrew Harper *lawyer*
Groce, James Freelan *financial adviser*
Grover, Rosalind Redfern *oil and gas company executive*
MacDonald, Leland Lloyd *lawyer*
Meyers, Alan Hoge *lawyer*
Morrow, William Clarence *judge, lawyer, arbitrator*
Rowe, Mary R. *lawyer*
Sherpa, Fran Magruder *geography educator*
Syed, Elizabeth Chance *health facility administrator, critical care nurse*
Truitt, Robert Ralph, Jr. *lawyer*

Mineola
Stevenson, David Wayne *municipal official*

Mineral Wells
Braun, Gustav Milan *otolaryngologist, surgeon*
Mei, Anhua *mechanical engineer, researcher*
Warfield, Gerald Alexander *composer, writer*

Mission
Eyre, Pamela Catherine *retired career officer*

Missouri City
de Kanter, Ellen Ann *retired English and foreign language educator*
Hodges, Jot Holiver, Jr. *retired lawyer, corporate financial executive*
Rathnau, Heather Hearn *music educator, writer*
Weber, Katie *retired special education educator*

Montgomery
Kelsey, Clyde Eastman, Jr. *philosophy educator, psychology professor*

Mount Pleasant
Vaughn, William Preston *retired historian, educator*

Murchison
Taweel, Janice M. *artist, educator*

Murphy
Rathmell, Robert D. *physicist*

Nacogdoches
Bias, Dana G. *lawyer*
Bowen, Donald Edgar *physics professor, former academic administrator*
Campo, David Wayne *conductor, educator, composer*
Carter, Evelyn *retired elementary school educator*

Navasota
Coffey, Sharon Marie *music educator*

New Braunfels
Barragān, Celia Silguero *elementary school educator*
Benfield, Marion Wilson, Jr. *law educator*
Dugger, Roy Wesley *academic administrator, retired military officer*
Krueger, Robert Charles *former ambassador, congressman, senator*
Oestreich, Charles Henry *retired university president*
Pharis, Ruth McCalister *retired bank executive*
Rush, W.M. (Rusty) *trucking executive*
Wilson, James Lee *retired geology educator, consultant*
Zipp, Ronald Duane *judge, real estate broker, clergyman*

New Caney
Hayes, Ann Carson *computer company executive*

Normangee
Cox, Jack Ronald, Jr. *finance educator*
Stork, Vera Lee *retired elementary school educator*

North Richland Hills
Gedwed, William J. *insurance company executive*
Reed, Glenn W. *lawyer*

Odessa
Hendrick, Benard Calvin, VII, *lawyer*
Reed, James Michael *church musician*

Odonnell
Saleh, John *lawyer*

Olney
Timmons, Gordon David *economics professor, farmer*

Paige
Trevino, Jerry Rosalez *retired secondary school principal*

Palestine
Williams, Franklin Cadmus, Jr. *bibliographer*

Pampa
Willingham, Jeanne Maggart *performing arts educator and company executive*

Panhandle
Sherrod, Lloyd Bruce *retired nutritionist*

Paris
McCuen, Maureen E. *history educator*

Pasadena
Austin, Pamela Kay *voice educator*
Azuonye, Felix O. *pharmacist*
Blue, Monte Lynn *college president*
Gilley, Mickey Leroy *musician*
Gross, Cynthia Sue *petrochemicals manufacturing executive*
Kenagy, Cheri Lynn *nurse*
Martinez, Fernando V. *civil engineer*
Moon, John Henry, Sr. *banker*
Mullins, Jack Allen *cardiologist, educator*
Ruiz, Miriam *secondary school educator*
Russell, Yvonne Williams *history educator*
Scott, William Floyd *accountant*
Shapiro, Edward Muray *dermatologist*

Pearland
Hammond, Raymond William *pharmacotherapy specialist*
Johnson, Hugh James *retired music educator*
Liles, Clifton Roy *retired application developer*
Shurtleff, Malcolm C. *plant pathologist, consultant*
Würsig, Bernd Gerhard *marine biology educator*

Pharr
Medina, Jesse James *protective services official, educator*

Pittsburg
Cogdill, Richard A. *food products executive*
Goolsby, O. B., Jr. *food products executive*
Pilgrim, Lonnie (Bo Pilgrim) *food products executive*

Plainview
Belshaw, Gary D. *music educator, composer*

Plano
Altabef, Peter Anthony *lawyer*
Ansari, Amir *digital home and multimedia management technology company executive*
Ansari, Anousheh *digital home and multimedia management technology company executive, first female civilian space traveler*
Ansari, Hamid *digital home and multimedia management technology company executive*
Bain, Travis Whitsett, II, *manufacturing and retail executive*
Baumbach, Joyce *library director*
Becker, Doreen Doris *medical/surgical nurse*
Bober, Joanne L. *lawyer, retail executive*
Bonet, Frank Joseph *retired lawyer*
Bravard, Jean-Louis *diversified financial services company executive*
Cavanaugh, Robert B. *department store executive*
Chopra, Anil *oil industry executive*
Day, Kevin Thomas *retired business executive, investment banker, foundation administrator*
Dillon, Donald Ward *management consultant*
Dougherty, F(rancis) Kelly *data processing executive*
Emerson, Roger Hill, Jr. *orthopeadist*
Evans, Pat *mayor*
Gallardo, Henrietta Castellanos *writer*
Galloway, Marianne Thérèse *performing company executive*
Glenn, Marshall Andrew *psychologist*
Gordon, Storrow Moss *lawyer, information technology executive*
Haggard, Geraldine Langford *primary school, adult education educator, consultant, writer*
Heller, Jeffrey M. *data processing executive*
Hilton, Steven J. *real estate executive*
Hu, Mei Melvin *interventional physiatrist*
Hurley, Rebecca *lawyer*
James, Michael Thames *information technology executive, consultant*
Korst, Christopher A. *lawyer, rental company executive*
Landon, John R. *real estate developer*
MacAlpine, Michelle Lewis *neuroscientist*
McClaskey, Michael Keith *information technology executive*
Miller, Waenard Livingston *cardiologist*
Mondul, Donald David *patent lawyer*
Naor, Daniel *food products executive*
Neppl, Walter Joseph *retired retail executive*
O'Loughlin-Brooks, Jennifer L. *psychology professor*
Papalia, Rocco Dominic *food products executive*
Perot, Ross (H. Ross Perot, Henry Ross Perot) *real estate company, investment company, data processing executive*
Perot, Ross, Jr., (Henry Ross Perot Jr.) *real estate developer, professional sports team executive*
Rittenmeyer, Ronald Allen *information technology executive*
Robertson, Richard L. *lawyer*
Ryu, Manho *application developer*
Schuh, Frank Joseph *oil industry executive, consultant*
Scott, Terry Lee *communications executive*
Shapiro, Todd D. *lawyer*
Shelton, James D. (Denny Shelton) *hospital management company executive*
Shepherd, Karen Schiller *biology educator*
Sivinski, Tina M. *human resources specialist*

Speese, Mark E. *rental company executive*
Suleman, Amer *internist, cardiologist*
Taylor, Paul Peak *pediatric dentist, educator*
Theilmann, Michael T. *human resources specialist*
Vargo, Ronald Paul *information technology executive*
Vempati, Rajan K. *research scientist, educator*
Warburton, Ralph Joseph *architect, educator, engineer*
Wayne, Jeanette Marie *auditor*
Worsfold, Victor Leonard *retired social sciences educator*
Wyman, Richard Thomas *information technology manager, researcher*

Port Aransas
Lehmann, William Leonardo *electrical engineer, educator*
Schake, Lowell Martin *zoology educator, writer*
Turner, Elizabeth Adams Noble (Betty Turner) *real estate company executive, writer*
Van Baalen, Donna Gale *artist, retired pharmacist*

Port Arthur
Munoz, Andrea Lee *human resources specialist*
Vinecour, Oneida Agnes *nurse*

Portland
Soliz, Eusebio *military officer*

Post
Earl, Lewis Harold *economist, consultant, lawyer*
Neff, Marie Taylor *museum director, artist*

Pottsboro
Hanning, Gary William *utilities executive, consultant, water transportation executive*
Jackson, Nona Armour *writer, illustrator*
Thomas, Ann Van Wynen *retired law educator*

Prairie View
Ciftja, Orion *physicist, researcher*
Cuero, Raul G. *microbiologist, researcher, educator*
Hritonenko, Natali *mathematics professor, researcher*
Prestage, Jewel Limar *political science professor*

Quitaque
Herrington, Patsy Jean Stark *music educator*

Rancho Viejo
Garza, Roberto Jesus *retired education educator*

Randolph Afb
Brennan-Bergmann, Bridget Catherine *special education educator*
Ellis, Edward R. *career officer*
Looney, William R. III *career military officer*

Red Oak
Jones, Genia Kay *critical care nurse, consultant*
Shaw, Sue Ann *medical transcriptionist*

Richardson
Acosta, Eduardo G. *physiatrist, director*
Al-Dhahir, Naofal *engineering educator*
Andrews, Melinda Wilson *human development researcher*
Atzori, Marco *neuroscientist, educator*
Austin, Ann Sheree *lawyer*
Berry, Brian Joe Lobley *geographer, educator, urban planner, political economist*
Bluedorn, Todd M. *manufacturing executive*
Burke, Thomas William *benefits compensation analyst*
Carlson, Catherine Kossan *secondary school educator*
Conkel, Robert Dale *lawyer, consultant*
Cox, David Leon *telecommunications industry executive*
Daniel, David Edwin *academic administrator, civil engineer*
Dian, Jianwei *mathematician*
Easttom, Chuck *computer scientist, educator*
Goodspeed, Linda A. *manufacturing executive*
Gray, Donald Melvin *molecular and cell biology educator*
Griffith, Daniel Alva *geography educator*
Hicks, Donald Albert *economics professor*
Holmen, Orrie Jeffrey *electronics company executive*
Ishak-Boushaki, Mustapha *research scientist, physicist*
Krauss, Henry Frederick, Jr. *optometrist*
Lee, Jimmy Che-Yung *urban planner*
Martin, Richard Kelley *lawyer*
McMechan, George *science educator*
Monti, Paolo *research scientist*
Oliff, Michael D. *finance educator*
Olson, Dennis Oliver *lawyer*
Overall, Theresa Lynne *computer professor*
Redman, Timothy Paul *language educator, writer*
Rutford, Robert Hoxie *geologist, educator*
Safka, Jim *information technology executive*
Salamon, Myron Ben *physicist, educator, dean*
Sall, Larry David *library director*
Sandler, Todd Michael *economist, political scientist, educator*
Schjerven, Robert E. *manufacturing executive*
Smith, Mark P. *foundation administrator*
Sowers, Wesley Hoyt *lawyer, management consultant*
Stoll, William Frederick, Jr. *lawyer*
Williams, James Francis, Jr. *religious organization administrator*
Wiorkowski, John James *mathematics professor*

Richland Hills
Haynes, Ruth Elaine *accountant*

Richmond
Elliott, Brady Gifford *judge*

Roanoke
Kleinkort, Joseph Alexius *physical therapist, ergonomist, consultant*

Rockport
Berkebile, Charles Alan *geology educator, hydrogeology researcher*
Minor, Joseph Edward *civil engineer, educator*
Porter, Charles Raleigh, Jr. *retired lawyer*

Rockwall
Fisher, Gene Jordan *retired chemical company executive*
Johnston, Nicklett Rose *research nurse, clinical perfusionist*
Kotas, Robert Vincent *pediatrician, educator*
Tucker, Kimberly Joan *music educator, director*
White, Todd William *lawyer, educator*

Rosenberg
Haygood, Eithel Marinella *artist, educator*
Lefler, Sherry LynettE *elementary school educator*
Slack, Molly Johanna *theater educator*
White, Gretchen Nance *education educator, writer*

Rosharon
Jenkins, Judith Alexander *bank consultant*
Lopez, Placida Ramos *elementary school educator*
Marya, Manuel Paul Claude *metallurgical and materials engineer*

Round Rock
Bell, Paul D. *computer company executive*
Cannon, Michael R. *computer company executive, former electronics executive*
Carty, Donald J. *computer company and former air transportation executive*
Dell, Michael Seth *computer company executive*
Garriques, Ron G. *computer company executive*
Hudson, Michel Colette *management consultant*
Khalid, Humayun *computer scientist, consultant*
O'Connor, Clint Haynie *electrical engineer*
Puri, Rajendra Kumar *business and tax specialist, consultant*
Ricklefs, Dale Lynne *library director*
Ryan, Nolan *former professional baseball player*
Schneider, Dennis Ray *microbiology professor, research and development company executive*
Schuckenbrock, Steve (Stephen Francis Schuckenbrock) *computer company executive, former information technology executive*
Sheskey, Susan E. *computer company executive*
Tu, Lawrence P. *lawyer, computer company executive*

Round Top
Vernon, Karen *art gallery owner, educator*

Rowlett
Bell, Ronald *secondary school educator*

Sachse
Eichelberger, Charles Bell *retired career officer*
Rogers, Mal David, Jr. *chemical engineer*

Salado
Parks, Lloyd Lee *oil industry executive*

San Angelo
Chatfield, Mary Van Abshoven *retired librarian*
Fischer, Duncan Kinnear *neurosurgeon*
Mobley, Nancy Elizabeth *artist, educator*

San Antonio
Abramson, Hyman Norman *engineering and science research executive*
Ammann, Lillian Ann Nicholson *writer, editor, small business owner*
Anderson, Anita L. *psychology professor*
Angel, Luis F. *pulmonologist, director*
Armstrong, William Tucker III *lawyer*
Artemov, Vladimir Nikolaevich *gymnastics coach*
Arthur, Gary L., Jr. *energy executive*
Aust, Joe Bradley *surgeon, educator*
Austin, Catherine Deady *retired school librarian, musician*
Austin, Lola Houston *psychologist*
Avant, Patricia Kay *nursing educator*
Aycock, James J. *lawyer*
Baker, Floyd Wilmer *surgeon, retired military officer*
Barilleaux, Rene Paul *curator*
Barton, James Cary *lawyer*
Becker, Quinn Henderson *orthopedic surgeon, military officer*
Beckmann, Charles Henry *cardiologist, educator*
Behrens, Kay S. *lawyer*
Bellows, Thomas John *political scientist, educator*
Bennett, Steven Alan *lawyer, insurance company executive*
Bettac, Robert Edward *lawyer*
Blank, Steven A. *energy executive*
Blokzyl, Matthew Augustus *respiratory therapist*
Blystone, Robert Vernon *cell biologist, educator*
Bookbinder, Russ *professional sports team executive*
Bowen, Bruce *professional basketball player*
Bowers, Kim *lawyer, energy executive*
Bramble, Ronald Lee *lawyer, consultant*
Branton, James LaVoy *lawyer*
Breit, William *economist, educator, writer*
Brewster, Olive Nesbitt *retired librarian*
Brown, Mary Rose *energy executive*
Browning, Jay D. *energy executive*
Budalur, Thyagarajan Subbanarayan *chemistry professor*
Buford, R.C. *professional sports team executive*
Burch, James Leo *science research institute executive*
Burden, W. Eugene *oil industry executive*
Burzik, Catherine M. *health products executive*
Butt, Charles Clarence *food service executive*
Callaway, James W. (Jim) *telecommunications industry executive*
Campbell, Robert Murray, Jr. *surgeon, researcher*
Castleberry, James Newton, Jr. *retired law educator, dean*
Catto, Henry Edward *former government official, retired ambassador*
Chasnoff, Barry A. *lawyer*
Chiego, William J. *museum director*
Cicconi, James William *lawyer, telecommunications industry executive*
Ciskowski, Michael S. *energy executive*
Cisneros, Henry G. *homebuilding and broadcast executive, retired federal official*
Clark, Wendy *advertising executive*
Claus, Christopher W. *insurance company executive*
Collins, Kevin Lloyd *lawyer*
Colyer, Kirk Klein *insurance and real estate investment executive*
Condos, Barbara Seale *real estate broker, developer, investor*
Condos, J. Alexander *mortgage company executive*
Condrill, Jo Ellaresa *freelance/self-employed small business owner, writer, consultant*
Conklyn, Elizabeth D. *insurance company executive*
Corrigan, Helen González *retired cytologist*
Coughlin, Cathy M. *telecommunications industry executive*
Crabtree, Ben C. *neuromuscular therapy clinic director*
Cragnolino, Gustavo Adolfo *research scientist*
Crichton, Flora Cameron *volunteer, foundation administrator*
Croft, Harry Allen *psychiatrist*
Crownover, Mike *energy executive*
Cura, Marco Antonio *interventional radiologist, educator*
Daley, William M. *bank executive, former federal government official*
Danney, Mark Maxwell *pediatrician*
Darling, John Rothburn *business educator*
Datta, Rupali *geochemist, educator*
Davis, George Edward *industrial designer*
Davis, Robert G. *insurance company executive*
de la Garza, Luis Adolfo *automotive executive, lawyer*
DeNice, Marcella Louise *counselor*
Digicaylioglu, Murat Haydar *medical educator*
Dorman, David W. *former telecommunications industry executive*
Downing, Jane Katherine *psychiatric nurse, lawyer*
Dumitru, Daniel *physiatrist*
Duncan, A. Baker *investment banker*
Duncan, Tim *professional basketball player*
Duron, Robert J. *school system administrator*
Edwards, Gene *energy executive*
Edwards, S. Eugene *energy executive*
Ellis, James D. *telecommunications industry executive, lawyer*
Estep, Myrna Lynne *systems analyst, philosophy educator*
Evans, Betty Vaughn *minister*
Evans, Richard W., Jr., (Dick) *bank executive*
Farrell, Michael Lynn *medical educator*
Faules, Barbara Ruth *retired elementary school educator*
Fehrenbach, T.R. (Theodore Reed Fehrenbach) *writer*
Finley, Michael *professional basketball player*
Finnerty, William J. *oil industry executive*
Flagg, C.A. (Chuck Flagg) *oil industry executive*
Flores, Belinda Bustos *bilingual educator, administrator*
Fonseca, Joseph Mojica, Jr. *political science professor*
Forgione, Dana Anthony *accounting educator*
Foster, Nancy Haston *columnist, writer*
Frazer, Robert Lee *retired landscape architect*
Frigerio, Charles Straith *lawyer*
Fruth, Roman Martin *piano technician, musician*
Fuhrmann, Charles J., II, *financial consultant, educator*
Furgeson, William Royal *federal judge*
Furino, Antonio *economist, educator*
Garcia, Henry Frank *supply and project management consultant*
Garrison, David H. *insurance company executive*
Garza, Ed *former mayor*
Garza, Emilio Miller *federal judge*
Gates, Mahlon Eugene *retired research and development company executive, retired military officer*
Gibbons, Robert Ebbert *university official*
Ginobili, Manu *professional basketball player*
Goksel, Tamer *oral surgeon, director*
Golden, Stephen L. *lawyer*
Goldstein, Gerald H. *lawyer*
Goldstein, Jerry *physicist, educator*
Gomez, José H. *archbishop*
Gonzalez, Hector Hugo *nursing educator*
Gonzalez-Marrero, Virnalisis M. *dermatologist*
Gorder, Joseph W. *energy executive*
Gracy, Robert *science educator*
Graff, Harvey J. *history and humanities educator*
Greenbaum, Yvonne Lee *medical/surgical nurse*
Grimshaw, James Albert, Jr. *retired language educator*
Gruber, John Balsbaugh *physics professor*
Guenther, Jack Egon *lawyer*
Gwathmey, Joe Neil, Jr. *retired broadcast executive*
Hammon, Becky (Rebecca Lynn Hammon) *professional basketball player*
Hardberger, Phillip Duane *mayor, judge, lawyer, journalist*
Hardy, Harvey Louchard *retired lawyer*
Hare, Henry Phillip, Jr. *psychiatrist*
Haywood, J. William *oil industry executive*
Heidelberg, Paul *writer*
Heloise, *columnist, writer*
Henderson, Connie Chorlton *retired city planner, artist, writer*
Henderson, Dwight Franklin *dean, educator*
Henry, Peter York *lawyer, mediator*
Hermann, Robert Charles, Jr. *neurologist, educator*
Holt, Peter M. *professional sports team owner, agricultural products executive*
Hsieh, Pei-Hsuan (Peggy) *education educator*
Hudspeth, Almetra Kavanaugh *retired elementary school educator*
Hughes, Dan *professional basketball coach*
Hughes, Philip S. H. *dermatologist*
Irving, George Washington III *veterinarian, researcher, small business executive*
Jackson, Carlayne E. *neurologist, educator*
Jary, Mary Canales *business owner*
Javore, Gary William *lawyer*
Jennings, Karen *telecommunications industry executive*
Jones, Daniel Hare *librarian, consultant*
Jones, James Richard *business administration educator*
Kahan, James S. *telecommunications industry executive*
Kalkwarf, Kenneth Lee *dean, dental educator*
Kasinath, Balakuntalam S. *medical researcher*
Kellman, Steven G. *literature educator, author*
Killinger, Clayton *energy executive*
Klaerner, Curtis Maurice *gas industry executive*
Kline, John William *retired military officer, management consultant*
Kotecki, Kevin *beer company executive*
Koziol, John Craig (Craig Koziol) *career military officer*
Labenz-Hough, Marlene *mediator*
Lalwani, Ashok K. *marketing educator*
Langland, Olaf Elmer *retired dental educator*
Lefeber, Edward James, Jr. *internist, educator*
Leighton, Albert Chester *history professor*
LeMaistre, Charles Aubrey *retired internist, epidemiologist, educator*
Lenke, Joanne Marie *publishing executive*
Leon, Robert Leonard *psychiatrist, educator*
Levin, Andrew W. *lawyer, communications executive*
Lewis, Everett D. *oil industry executive*
Lindner, Richard G. *telecommunications industry executive*
Loeffler, Tom (Thomas Gilbert Loeffler) *lobbyist, former congressman*
Luby, Michael A. *insurance company executive*
Ludzik, Steve *professional hockey coach*
Lutter, Charles William, Jr. *lawyer*
Lyle, Robert Edward *chemist*
Maloney, Marynell *lawyer*
Mamtani, Manju Rameshlal *geneticist, researcher*
Marbut, Robert Gordon *communications, electronic security and broadcast executive, investor*
Marcogliese, Richard J. *energy executive*
Martin, James Charles *physician*
Matus, Kristi Ann *insurance company executive*
Maxwell, Diana Kathleen *education educator, primary school educator*
Mays, L(ester) Lowry *broadcast executive*
Mays, Mark Pitman *communication company executive*
Mc Allister, Gerald Nicholas *retired bishop, minister*
McComas, David John *science administrator, space physicist*
McCoy, Reagan Scott *oil industry executive, lawyer*
McFadden, Robert Stetson *hepatologist*
McFee, Arthur Storer *physician*
McGill, Henry Coleman, Jr. *pathologist, educator, researcher*
McGuire, William Dennis *healthcare consultant*
McIntosh, Dennis Keith *veterinarian, consultant*
Meffert, Jeffrey John *dermatologist*
Michaels, Willard A. (Bill Michaels) *retired broadcasting executive*
Miller, Forrest E. *telecommunications industry executive*
Mohammed, Nazr *professional basketball player*
Monroe, Joseph M. *oil industry executive*
Montemayor, Carlos Rene *advertising agency executive*
Moynihan, John Bignell *retired lawyer*
Myers, Ellen Howell *historian, educator*
Myers, Paul Walter *military officer, researcher, retired neurosurgeon*
Newton, Virginia *archivist, historian, librarian*
Nichols, Sharon Louise *educator, researcher*
Ognibene, Andre John *internist, educator, retired military officer*
Oppenheim, Martha Kunkel *pianist, educator*
O'Rourke, Robert A. *cardiologist, educator*
Orr, Joseph Newton *recreational guide, outdoor educator*
Parker, Stuart Blain *insurance company executive*
Parker, Tony (William Anthony Parker II) *professional basketball player*
Parrish, Charles S. *lawyer, oil industry executive*
Patrick, Dane Herman *lawyer*
Patterson, Jan Evans *epidemiologist, educator*
Pawel, Nancy Emma Ray *oil industry executive, educator, artist*
Peacock, S. Wayne *insurance company executive*
Perry, George *neuroscientist, educator*
Perry, Robert Michael *lawyer, consultant, rancher*
Persellin, Robert Harold *physician*
Pestana, Carlos *surgeon, retired dean, educator*
Pfeiffer, Philip John *lawyer*
Pipkin, Marvin Grady *lawyer*
Pitluk, Ellen Eidelbach *lawyer, mediator*
Popovich, Gregg *professional basketball coach*
Porter, Daniel J. *oil industry executive*
Pruitt, Basil Arthur, Jr. *surgeon, retired military officer*
Putman, (James) Michael *lawyer*
Pych, Rick *professional sports team executive*
Reams, Bernard Dinsmore, Jr. *law educator*
Redfield, Carol Ann Luckhardt *computer scientist, educator*
Renfro, Norm *energy executive*
Restrepo, Ruben Dario *physician, educator*
Reuter, Stewart Ralston *retired radiologist*
Ribble, Ronald George *psychologist, educator, writer, behavioral consultant*
Rivard, Robert *newspaper executive*
Robertson, Samuel Luther, Jr. *psychotherapist, educator*
Robertson, Sterling Clifton *music educator, musician*
Robinson, Glenn *professional basketball player*
Robles, Josue, Jr. *insurance company executive*
Rollin, Michael Fredrick *history professor*
Route, Candace *elementary school educator*
Rush, Kent Thomas *art educator, artist*
Rush, W. Marvin *trucking executive*
Ruttenberg, Frank Z. *lawyer*
Sakai, Peter A. *lawyer*
Salazar, Ramiro S. *library director*
Salvucci, Linda *history professor*
Schenker, Steven *internist, educator*
Schlueter, David Arnold *law educator*
Schmutz, John Francis *lawyer*
Schwethelm, Otto C. *oil industry executive*
Sculley, Patrick David *retired army officer, director*
Shanklin, Kenneth Dale *plastic surgeon*
Silantien, John Joseph *music educator*
Smith, Bruce Alfred *oil industry executive*
Smith, Rebecca Lynn *language educator*
Smith, Reginald Brian Furness *retired anesthesiologist, educator*
Spears, Sally *lawyer*
Spiro, Herbert John *political scientist, ambassador*
Stankey, John T. *information technology executive*
Steen, John Thomas, Jr. *lawyer*
Stephenson, Randall L. *telecommunications industry executive*
Stephenson, Thomas A. *publishing executive*
Stevens, Dennis Max *auditor*
Strong, Wendi Ellen *insurance company executive*
Sutton, Johnny Keane *prosecutor, lawyer*
Swansburg, Russell Chester *retired nursing educator, writer, consultant*
Synek, Miroslav *physicist, chemist, world affairs consultant*
Tallon, Michael *language educator*
Taylor, Ishmael Jay *environmental scientist*
Terracina, Roy David *entrepreneur*
Trent, Joyce Miller *librarian*
Upton, Wade *energy executive*
Urbach, Adam Robert *chemistry professor*
Vadlamudi, Ratna K. *healthcare educator*
Villavazo, Kristen Lee *language educator*
von Raffler-Engel, Walburga (Walburga Engel) *retired language educator*
Wahl, Rosemarie *biologist, educator*
Wallis, Ben Alton, Jr. *lawyer*
Walsh, Nicolas Eugene *rehabilitation services professional, educator*
Wang, Yufeng *science educator*
Watts, Mikal C. *lawyer*
Weber, William Wesley *accountant*
Weiner, Marcia Myra *justice of the peace*
Welch, Billy E. *retired government agency administrator, retired management consultant*
Wellberg, Edward Louis, Jr. *insurance company executive*
Wells, Tullos *lawyer*
Welmaker, Forrest Nolan *lawyer*
Westfall, Lynn D. *oil industry executive*
Wheatley, Seagal V. *lawyer, legal association administrator*
Whitacre, Edward E., Jr. *retired telecommunications industry executive*
Whitesell, Stephen Ernest *parks director*
Wilkins, Christopher Putnam *conductor*
Wilkins, Rayford, Jr. *telecommunications industry executive*
Williams, Docia Schultz *small business owner*
Williams, Thomas Eugene *pediatric hematologist, pediatric oncologist, pharmaceutical executive*
Williamson, Fletcher Phillips *real estate broker*
Williams-Perry, Brenda Lee *pre-school educator*
Wilson, Martha C. *physician*
Wiskocil, Angiolina *telecommunications industry executive*
Wright, Gregory A. *oil industry executive*
Wright, Wayne E. *education educator*
Yates, Norris William, Jr. *lawyer*
Young, James Julius *academic administrator, retired military officer*
Zachry, Henry Bartell, Jr. *construction executive*
Zesch, Hal *energy executive*
Zieres, Carol Lynne *military officer*
Zilveti, Carlos Benjamin *preventive medicine physician, pediatrician*

San Marcos
Allsup, Roxane Cuellar *curriculum and instruction educator*
Fischer, Joyce Faye *engineering educator*
Huber, John D. *psychologist, consultant*
Imel, Elizabeth Carmen *retired physical education educator*
Moore, Patsy Sites *food service consultant*
Palmer, Roger Raymond *finance educator*
Ronan, Clifford John *literature and language professor*
Schmidt, John Charles *music educator*
Stovall, Frances Middagh *journalist, preservationist*
Taylor, Ruth Arleen Lesher *marketing educator*

Schulenburg
Clark, I. E. *publisher*

Seabrook
Fischer, Craig Leland *physician*
Patten, Bernard Michael *neurologist, writer, educator*
Spears, James Grady *small business owner*

Seguin
Robinson, Ronald Alan *manufacturing executive*

Sheppard Afb
Cook, Sharla J. *career officer*

Sherman
Brown, Paul Neeley *federal judge*
Page, Oscar C. *academic administrator*
Schell, Richard A. *federal judge*

Smithville
Clark, LaVerne Harrell *writer*
Dearmin, Christopher Carl *medical technician*
Scofield, Virginia Lee *research scientist*

Snyder
Gray, Donna Lea *small business owner*
Siegel, Mark S. *energy executive*
Talbott, Cloyce A. *energy executive*

Southlake
Arafat-Johnson, Danyah *secondary school educator, director*
Bogdan, Michael Andrew *plastic surgeon*
Gilliland, Michael S. (Sam Gilliland) *travel company executive*
Glueck, Jeffrey *travel company executive*
Herrmann, Debra McGuire *chemist, educator*
Peluso, Michelle *Internet company executive, travel company executive*
Schwarte, David A. *lawyer, travel company executive*
Sorge, Karen Lee *printing company executive, consultant*

Spring
Ciancimino, Joseph Andrew *data processing executive*
Corbett, Luke R. *former energy company executive*
Farley, Andrew Newell *lawyer, consultant*
Howard, Richard Carl *minister*
Hunt, T(homas) W(ebb) *retired religion educator*
Kehoe, John Kimball *finance educator, consultant*
Randazzo, Gary Wayne *newspaper executive*
Rex, Lonnie Royce *religious organization administrator*
Szymczak, Edward Joseph *mechanical engineer*
Woodward, Clifford Edward *chemical engineer*

Spring Branch
Barban, Arnold Melvin *advertising executive, educator, writer*

Spur
Warren, Jennifer Elizabeth *family nurse practitioner*

Stafford
Krenek, Mary Louise *political scientist, researcher*
Le, Duy-Loan *electrical engineer*
Mills-Horton, Cynthia Marie *art educator*

Stephenville
Bane, Alma Lynn *data research administrator*
Little, Bertis Britt *medical research scientist, obstetrician educator, university administrator*
McElroy, Linda Sue *retired elementary school educator*
Schmelzer, Janet L. *history professor, researcher*

Sugar Land
Downs, Hartley H. III *chemist*
Goodwin, Anthony Robert Holmes *chemist, editor*
Greer, Raymond White *lawyer*
Harribance, Sean Lalsingh *parapsychologist*
Heitzenrater, James F *hospital administrator*
Hitchcock, Bion Earl *lawyer*
Huston, Daniel Cliff *geophysicist*
Keefe, Carolyn Joan *retired tax accountant*
Martinez, Antonio *choir director, art director*
Ritzen, Horst Reinhold *retired pharmacist*
Theys, Philippe Paul *data quality professional*
Victor, Ann Michele *musician, educator*
Wagner, Donald Bert *health facility administrator*

Sulphur Springs
Hadlow, Vivian Jean *elementary school educator*

Sweetwater
Taylor, Martha Sue *librarian*

Taylor Lake Village
Jenicek, Alicia Joanne *nursing consultant*

Temple
Asea, Alexzander *research scientist*
Bumpus, Floyd David, Jr. *microcomputer analyst*
Dehmer, Gregory Joseph *cardiologist*
Donner, Ludvik Rafael *pathologist, educator*
Dostal, David Eugene *education educator, researcher*
Feldtman, Robert *surgeon*
Hayward, Ronald Hamilton *surgeon*
Hoffer, John Lee *health facility administrator, medical educator*
Holleman, Vernon Daughty *internist, educator*
Lynch, Dennis James *plastic surgeon*
Matush, William Joe *educational association administrator*
McLane, Robert Drayton, Jr. *food products company executive*
Meshack, Geneva Tucker *retired elementary school educator*
Pickle, Jerry Richard *lawyer*
Rohack, John James *cardiologist*

Texarkana
Bertrand, Betty Harleen *nurse*
Calhoun, John C., Jr. *academic administrator*
Mojiri, Ahmad *mathematics professor*
Peck, Leonard Warren, Jr. *lawyer*
Presley, James Wright *writer, environmentalist*

Texas City
Fuchs, Owen George *chemist*
Hammett, Beth A. *language educator*
Hodges, Richard Dean *instrument and electrical technician*
Mitchell, Susan Elaine *pharmacist*
Robertson, Paul Francis *mathematician, educator*

The Colony
Culver, Jennifer Lynn *secondary school educator*
Mitchell, Melvin Clifford *music educator*

The Woodlands
Benedetto, Anthony R. *religious mediator*
Bohannon, Paul M. *lawyer*
Brenneman, Gregory D. *food service executive*
Cagle, Melinda Reeves *editor*
Desjardins, Raoul *medical association administrator, financial consultant*
Evans, Walter Reed *retired engineering executive, consultant*
Glenn, Gerald Marvin *marketing, engineering and construction executive*
Graham, James Michael *orthopedic spine surgeon, educator*
Griffith, James William *systems engineer, consultant*
Hackett, James T. *oil industry executive*
Hagerman, John David *lawyer, investment advisor*
Jones, Lincoln III *military officer*
Kalish, Bob *lawyer*
Kurz, Karl F. *oil industry executive*
Logan, Mathew Kuykendall *journalist*
Machle, Edward Johnstone *religious studies educator, philosopher*
Morrison, Scott David *management consultant, small business owner*
Pickelman, John E. *academic administrator*
Reeves, Robert K. *lawyer, oil industry executive*
Ripley, Charlene A. *lawyer*
Schott, Sally Maria *music publisher, arts education consultant*
Shannon, Thomas O. *plastic surgeon*
Sharman, Richard Lee *telecommunications executive, consultant*
Stahl, Craig L. *lawyer*
Stolle, Russell Robert *chemicals executive*
Walker, R. A. *oil industry executive*
Wilcox, Raymond I. *oil industry executive*

Tomball
Frideres, Steffani Anne *art educator*

Trinidad
Conant, Allah B., Jr. *lawyer*

Trophy Club
Holley, Cyrus Helmer *management consulting service executive*

Tyler
Albertson, Christopher Adam *librarian*
Alworth, Charles Wesley *lawyer, engineer*
Bailey, Nan Hutchins *mathematician, educator*
Brock, Dee Sala *television executive, educator, writer, consultant*
Brookshire, Bruce G. *retail grocery store executive*
Dacus, Deron R. *lawyer*
Davidson, Jack Leroy *academic administrator*
Edwards, D. M. *retail, wholesale distribution and real estate company executive*
Ellis, Donald Lee *lawyer*
Green, Douglas Alvin *retired library director*
Guthrie, Judith K. *federal judge*
Hadden, Arthur Roby *lawyer, retired judge*
Harrison, Preston Ershel, Jr. *neurologist*
Hester, Sean W. *lawyer*
Hughes, Arthur Hyde *accountant, energy industry executive, accountant*
Kronenberg, Richard Samuel *physician, educator*
Layton, Robert E., Jr. *retired aeronautical engineer*
Mastern, Dean Scott *personal growth and development consultant*
McGoff, William Stanley *speech educator, consultant*
Neuenschwander, Pierre Fernand *medical educator*
Patterson, Donald Ross *lawyer, educator*
Peters, Robert K. *dean, newscaster, newswriter, journalist*
Prater, Emma Lou *retired academic administrator*
Presley, Lucinda Hanks *art educator*
Sanchez, Heliodoro Torres, Jr. *education educator*
Sathyamoorthy, Muthukrishnan *engineering educator, associate provost*
Smith, Howard Thompson *manufacturing executive*
Thames, E. Glenn, Jr. *lawyer*
Waller, Wilma Ruth *retired secondary school educator, librarian*
Wrenn, Christopher Jay *physician*
Wright, Mary Ellen *theater educator*

Uvalde
Barrett, James Bruce *systems engineer*
Graham, Robert Albert *physicist, researcher, curator*
Ramsey, Frank Allen *veterinarian, retired army officer*

Valley Mills
Odell, Patrick Lowry *retired mathematics professor*

Valley Spring
Bonner, Herbert Dwight *construction management educator*

Valley View
Wallace, Donald John III *rancher*

Van Alstyne
Hornbeck, Larry J. *physicist, researcher*

Vernon
Malinowski, Dariusz Piotr *horticulturist, educator*

Victoria
Fellhauer, David E. *bishop*
Harrington, Rick *psychology professor*
McKay, Robert Connally *lawyer*

Vidor
Nye, Betty Ann *professional society administrator*

Waco
Albrecht, Karen Elizabeth *voice educator, theater director*
Belew, John Seymour *academic administrator, chemist*
Brooks, Roger Leon *retired academic administrator*
Farison, James Blair *electrical engineer, biomedical engineer, educator*
Grinols, Earl Leroy III *economist, educator*
Hair, William Bates III *librarian, dean*
Hunt, Maurice Arthur *language educator, researcher*
Jeffrey, David Lyle *literature and language professor, writer*
Kvanvig, Jonathan Lee *philosophy educator*
Lilley, John Mark *academic administrator*
Lindsey, Jonathan Asmel *academic administrator, school librarian, educator*
McKinney, Timothy Richmond *music educator*
Mc Swain, Angus Stewart, Jr. *retired law educator*
Morrison, Michael Dean *lawyer, law educator*
Murray, Kathleen Sarah-Jane *literature and language professor*
Page, Jack Randall *lawyer*
Pedrotti, Leno Stephano *physics professor*
Quarles, Brandon *law librarian*
Richie, Rodney Charles *critical care and pulmonary medicine physician*
Riemer, Michael Paul *educational association administrator*
Rolf, Howard Leroy *mathematician, educator*
Rose, John Thomas *finance educator*
Rusling, Barbara N(eubert) *real estate broker*
Sheng, Qin *mathematics professor*
Slaughter, Michael Wayne *education educator*
Sloan, Robert Bryan, Jr. *academic administrator*
Smith, Cullen *lawyer*
Stratton, Margaret Anne *minister*
Talbert, Charles Harold *theologian, educator*
Toben, Bradley J. B. *dean, law educator*
Voight, Carolyn Jean *administrative assistant*

Waller
Evans, Nancy Peltier *behavioral specialist, educator*

Warda
Kunze, George William *retired soil scientist*

Waxahachie
Johnson, Ronald Kay *retail company executive*
Kiser, Colin Lee *military officer, government contractor*

Weatherford
Fisk, Doris Rosalie Scanlan *volunteer*
Houchin, Shannon Marie *secondary school educator*
King, Douglas Michael *lawyer, accountant*

Webster
Farnam, Jafar *allergist, immunologist, pediatrician*
Kobayashi, Herbert Shin *electrical engineer*

Weslaco
Yang, Chenghai *agricultural engineer, researcher*

West
Bills, Peggy Nannette *parochial school educator*

West Lake Hills
Burns, Thomas Patrick *orthopedic surgeon*

Wharton
George, Lila Gene Plowe Kennedy *music educator*
Maxfield, Rose Mary *retired government official*

Whitewright
Burg, John Parker *electric power industry executive*

Wichita Falls
Altman, William Kean *lawyer*
Fowler, Robert Martin *oil industry executive, consultant*
Hamlin, Don Auer *retired military officer, financial health care executive*
Hancock, Carole Patricia *academic administrator*
Lowrance, Muriel Edwards *retired educational specialist*
Parker, Eva Annette *librarian*
Scherler, Kathy Louise *music educator, researcher*

Willis
Rappaport, Martin Paul *internist, nephrologist, educator*
Snider, Robert Larry *management consultant*
Thomas, Orville C. *retired allergist*

Wimberley
Brinsmade, Lyon Louis *retired lawyer*
Ellis, John *retired school system administrator, writer*
Jennett, Joseph Charles *retired academic administrator, engineering educator*
McCoy, John Denny *artist*
Skaggs, Wayne Gerard *retired diversified financial services company executive*

Woodway
Packard, Joyce Hornaday *retired counselor*

Wylie
Carson, Charles Michael *composer, musician*

Yoakum
Williams, Walter Waylon *lawyer, agricultural products supplier*

Zavalla
Devlin, Cynthia M. *air transportation executive, consultant*

Zephyr
Lancaster, Carroll Townes, Jr. *health services executive*

UTAH

Boulder
Gove, Walter R. *sociology educator*

Bountiful
Burningham, Kim Richard *educational association administrator, former state legislator*
Callister, Louis Henry, Jr. *lawyer*
Clay, Orson C. *insurance company executive, director*
Mangum, Garth Leroy *retired economist*
Ross, Gerald Harvey *family practice and environmental medicine physician*

Brigham City
Hepworth, John Leonard *chemist, researcher*

Brookside
McMahon, James Patrick *ecologist, consultant*

Castle Valley
Zavada, Barbara Johanna *artist, educator*

Cedar City
Benson, Michael T. *academic administrator*
Mayron, Lewis Walter *clinical ecology consultant*
Modesitt, Leland Exton, Jr., (L.E. Modesitt Jr.) *writer, poet, consultant*
Slack, Jeffery E *lawyer*

Cedar Hills
Ashton, Dawne Belinda *retired secondary school educator*

Centerfield
Parkin, Fern Agnes Marvel *medical/surgical nurse, nursing educator*

Centerville
Schwartz, Heidi K. *science educator*

Corinne
Ferry, Miles Yeoman *state legislator*

Draper
Escobar, Anthony *marketing professional, consultant*
Walz, Angela *retired secondary school educator*
Wright, Stuart I. *materials scientist, materials engineer*

Dugway
Benson, Morgan *energy engineer, retired military officer*
Davis, Vernon Thomas *military officer, researcher*
Phan, Richard Man *chemist*

Hill AFB
Bergren, Scott C. *career officer*
Lohman, Arthur Grover *civilian military employee*

Hinckley
Riding, Randy Lynn *welder*

Holladay
McKell, Cyrus M. *retired dean, plant physiologist, consultant*
O'Halloran, Thomas Alphonsus, Jr. *retired physicist, retired researcher*
Silver, Barnard Joseph Stewart *mechanical and chemical engineer, consultant, inventor*

Hurricane
Green, Peter Carlyle *retired physician, farmer*

Ivins
Theurer, Byron W. *aerospace engineer, business owner*

Kaysville
Houtz, Randy L. *music educator*

Layton
Woodbury, Lark Karin *secondary school educator*
Yates, York J. *plastic surgeon*

Lindon
Osmond, Donald Clark (Donny Osmond) *singer*

Logan
Albrecht, Stan LeRoy *academic administrator, sociologist, educator*
Aust, Steven Douglas *biochemistry, biotechnology and toxicology educator*
Bowles, David Stanley *engineering educator, consultant*
Culver, Milton Lawrence *historian, educator*
Daines, N. George *lawyer*
Davis, Daniel M. *curator, librarian*

Dethier, C. Brock *humanities educator, writer*
Hargreaves, George Henry *civil and agricultural engineer, researcher*
Hruby, George Geoffrey *writer, educator*
Keller, Jack *agricultural engineering educator, consultant*
McNeal, Lyle Glen *science educator, rancher, consultant*
Oladi, Reza *education educator*
Qi, Xiaojun *engineering educator*
Rasmuson, Brent J. *photographer, small business owner*
Rasmussen, Harry Paul *horticulture and landscape educator*
Ren, Wei *control systems educator*
Roberts, Donald Wilson *pathologist, consultant*
Schunk, Robert Walter *space physics research administrator*
Shaver, James Porter *retired education educator, dean*
West, Stephen Allan *lawyer*
Zhu, Lie *physics professor*

Manti
Funk, William Henry *retired environmental engineering educator*
Petersen, Benton Lauritz *paralegal*

Mapleton
Hillyard, Ira William *retired pharmacologist, educator*

Midvale
Smith, Mary Ellen *educational program facilitator*
Teerlink, J. Leland (Joseph Leland Teerlink) *real estate developer*

Midway
Zenger, John Hancock *training company executive*

Moab
Tallman, Eve *library director*

Montezuma Creek
Schaefer, Kim *high school music educator*

Murray
Twitchell, E(rvin) Eugene *retired lawyer*
Volberg, Herman William *electronics engineer, consultant*

North Ogden
Heap, Joan S. *elementary school educator*

North Salt Lake
Bouley, Joseph Richard *pilot*
Johnson, Frank *educator, retired state official*
Malan, Chris J. *lawyer*

Ogden
Adams, J. Phillip *oil industry executive*
Amsel, Eric David *psychology professor*
Buckner, Elmer La Mar *retired insurance company executive*
Davidson, Thomas Ferguson *retired chemical engineer*
Harrington, Mary Evelina Paulson (Polly) *writer, educator*
Mecham, Glenn Jefferson *lawyer, mayor*
Millner, F. Ann *academic administrator*
Pappas, Leah Aglaia *foundation administrator, political organization worker, secondary school educator*
Seager, Dauna Gayle Olson-Stokes *speech therapist*
Sharpes, Donald Kenneth *graduate program educator*
Sullivan, Kevin Patrick *lawyer*

Orem
Clark, Bruce Budge *humanities educator*
Hall, Blaine Hill *retired librarian*
Hunt, H(arold) Keith *retired business management educator, marketing consultant*
Jackman, Roderick Victor *distance learning educator*
Moore, Hal G. *mathematician, educator*
Sawyer, Thomas Edgar *management consultant*
Schofield, Anthony Wayne *lawyer*
Sederburg, William Albert *academic administrator, former state senator*
Segelman, Alvin Burton *pharmaceutical executive, educator, research scientist*
Snow, Marlon O. *trucking executive, state agency administrator*
Takke, Karyn Coppock *social worker, educator*

Park City
Armstrong, Roger L. *lawyer*
Becker, William Watters *theater producer*
Chin, Augustus G. *lawyer*
Edwards, Howard Lee *retired oil and gas industry executive, lawyer*
Gallivan, John William *retired publishing executive*
Mancuso, Julia *skier, Olympic athlete*
Miller, Bode (Samuel Bode Miller) *professional skier*
Milner, Harold William *hotel executive*
Montgomery, James Fischer *savings and loan association executive*
Shea, Jim *Olympic athlete*
Vance, Dianne Sanchez *mathematician, educator*
White, Shaun Roger *Olympic athlete, professional snowboarder, professional skateboarder*
Young, Steven *retired professional football player*

Price
King, Carrie Anne *publishing executive, advertising executive*

Providence
Vest, Hyrum Grant, Jr. *retired horticultural sciences educator*

Provo
Ashworth, Brent Ferrin *lawyer*
Bartlett, Leonard Lee *retired communications educator, advertising executive*
Baum, Kerry Robert *retired military officer, director*
Blake, George Rowland *soil scientist, educator, environmental scientist, researcher*
Bott, Jay Cordell *oncologist, hematologist*
Boyter, Scott M. *academic administrator*
Bradshaw, Jerald Sherwin *chemistry educator, researcher*
Brown, Ralph Browning *sociologist, educator*
Bullough, Robert Vernon, Jr. *educational studies professor*
Bywater, Duncan *biologist, educator*
Cheney, Brigham Vernon *physical chemist, consultant*
Creer, Thomas Laselle *psychologist, educator, writer*
Crookston, R. Kent *agronomy educator*
Deng, Shenglou *chemistry professor*
Densley, Colleen T. *principal*
Draper, Roni Jo *literature and language professor*
Fielding, Eric *set designer, educator*
Gantt, Edwin ElRay *psychology professor*
Gray, Campbell *museum director*
Hansen, H. Reese *law educator, former dean*
Hart, Edward LeRoy *poet, educator*
Hastriter, Michael Wayne *medical entomologist*
Henderson, Douglas James *physicist, chemist, educator, researcher*
Hill, Ned Cromar *dean, finance educator, consultant*
Hill, Richard Lee *lawyer*
Hopkins, Ramona O. *psychologist, neuroscientist*
Hughes, (Robert) John *journalist, educator*
Jackson, James F. *nuclear engineer, educator*
Jensen, Clayne R. *retired academic administrator*
Jensen, Michael Allen *engineering educator*
Jensen, Richard Dennis *librarian*
Jones, Steven Earl *physics educator, researcher*
Luthy, Karlen E. *adult nurse practitioner, educator*
Lyon, James Karl *German language educator*
McArthur, Eldon Durant *geneticist, researcher*
Murphy, John Joseph *literature educator, critic, editor*
Nokes, Jeffery D. *history professor*
Olsen, Randy J. *university librarian*
Pedersen, Darhl Max *psychology professor*
Peer, Larry Howard *literature educator*
Porter, Blaine Robert Milton *sociology professor, psychology professor*
Prater, Mary Anne *special education educator, researcher*
Randle, Cammon C. *filmmaker*
Samuelson, Cecil O., Jr. *academic administrator*
Sawyer, Melvin Wayne *psychologist*
Seipel, Michael *social sciences educator*
Staheli, Kory D. *law librarian*
Thomas, David Albert *law educator, director*
Valentine, John Lester *state legislator, lawyer*
Willes, Mark Hinckley *media specialist*
Worthen, Kevin *dean, law educator*
York, Neil Longley *history professor*
Youd, T. Leslie *retired civil engineer*
Young, Bruce Wilson *language educator*

Saint George
Atkin, Jerry C. *air transportation executive*
Beesley, H(orace) Brent *bank executive*
Bondanella, Peter *literature and language professor, writer*
Gallian, Russell Joseph *lawyer*
Martinez, Dennis J. *art educator*
Pearce, Carole Ann *poet*
Terry, Gary A. *lawyer, director, former trade association executive*

Salt Lake City
Adams, Joseph Keith *lawyer*
Allen, Ronald Carl *commissioner, artist, consultant, former state senator, computer company executive*
Alter, Edward T. *treasurer*
Amaechi, John *retired professional basketball player*
Anderson, Charles Ross *civil engineer*
Anderson, Robert Monte *lawyer*
Anderson, Ross Carl *mayor, lawyer*
Anderson, Stephen Hale *federal judge*
Atkinson, Geoff *marketing executive*
Bacon, Marlene Parkinson *dean, nursing educator*
Balasubramonian, Rajeev *computer science educator*
Baldwin, John *legal association administrator, lawyer*
Barney, Kline Porter, Jr. *engineering company executive, consultant*
Barusch, Lawrence Roos *lawyer*
Bass, Brenda L. *biochemist, educator*
Bassis, Michael Steven *academic administrator*
Baucom, Sidney George *lawyer*
Bauer, A. Robert, Jr., (August Robert Bauer Jr.) *surgeon*
Beall, Burtch W., Jr. *architect*
Bendinger, Gary Frederick *lawyer*
Benjamin, Lorna Smith *psychologist*
Bennion, John Warren *urban education educator*
Benson, Dee Vance *federal judge*
Berman, Daniel Lewis *lawyer*
Betz, A. Lorris *pediatrician, educator*
Bilginsoy, Cihan *economics professor*
Bird, David R. *lawyer*
Black, Wilford Rex, Jr. *retired state legislator*
Blackburn, Michael Dale *lawyer, educator*
Blair, David F. *biochemist, educator*
Boozer, Carlos Austin, Jr. *professional basketball player*
Bossard, Robert Lee *biologist, educator*
Brady, Rodney Howard *diversified financial services and broadcast company executive, retired academic administrator, federal official*
Brems, David Paul *architect*
Bromley, Benjamin C *physics professor*
Burke, John Patrick *internist, educator*
Call, Charles H., Jr. *civil engineer*
Capecchi, Mario Renato *genetics educator*
Carey, John Clayton *pediatrician, educator, medical geneticist*
Carnahan, Orville Darrell *retired state legislator, academic administrator*
Cash, Roy Don *retired gas and petroleum company executive*
Chillingworth, Lori *bank executive*
Chodosh, Hiram *dean, law educator*
Chong, Richard David *architect*
Christensen, Patricia Anne Watkins *lawyer*
Christensen, Ray Richards *lawyer*
Christopher, James Walker *architect, educator*
Clark, Deanna Dee *volunteer*
Clark, Glen Edward *judge*
Colessides, Nick John *lawyer*
Coley, Phyllis Dewing *biology professor*
Conard, Jane Reister *lawyer*
Conway, Nancy Ann *newspaper editor*
Cornaby, Kay Sterling *lawyer, retired state senator*
Covey, Stephen Merrill Richards *business consultant, speaker, author*
Curtis, D. Jay *lawyer*
Davis, Gene *public relations executive, state legislator*
Davis, Loyd Evan *defense industry marketing professional*
DeVries, Kenneth Lawrence *mechanical engineer, educator*
Dewsnup, Ralph L. *lawyer*
Dick, Bertram Gale, Jr. *physics professor*
Dole, Janice Gail Arnold *literacy educator*
Drew, Clifford James *dean, psychologist, educator*
Durham, Christine Meaders *state supreme court chief justice*
Durrant, Matthew B. *state supreme court justice*
Elkins, Glen Ray *retired diversified management services company executive*
Emerson, Norene Rogers *music educator*
Esplin, J. Kimo *chemicals executive*
Eyring, Henry Bennion *bishop*
Fehr, John William *newspaper editor*
Fields, Debbi (Debra Fields Rose) *cookie franchise executive*
Firmage, Edwin Brown *lawyer, educator*
Foltz, Rodger Lowell *chemistry professor*
Frank, Thomas *construction executive, management and design executive*
Fujinami, Robert Shin *neurology educator*
Gandhi, Om Parkash *electrical engineer*
Gathogo, Patrick Nduru *geologist, researcher*
George, Sarah B. *museum director*
Ghosh, Sambhunath (Sam) *environmental engineer, educator*
Gifford, Thomas Owen *physician*
Gleich, Gerald Joseph *immunologist, researcher, educator*
Gortatowski, Melvin Jerome *retired chemist*
Gray, Douglas D. *child and adolescent psychiatrist*
Greene, John Thomas *judge*
Greenwood, David A. *lawyer*
Gregersen, R(oald) George *newspaper publishing executive*
Grosser, Bernard Irving *psychiatrist, educator*
Hankins, Anthony P. *chemicals executive*
Harrington, Patti *school system administrator*
Haslam, Dennis V. *professional sports team executive, lawyer*
Hatch, George Clinton *television executive*
Hembree, James D. *retired chemical company executive*
Herbert, Gary Richard *lieutenant governor*
Hinckley, Gordon B. *religious organization administrator*
Holding, R(obert) Earl *oil industry executive*
Holland, Jeffrey R. *religious organization administrator*
Holtkamp, James Arnold *lawyer, educator*
Horne, Benjamin Davies *epidemiologist*
Howell, Scott Newell *computer company executive, state legislator*
Huelskamp, Willamarie Ann *artist*
Hulme, Paul G. *chemicals executive*
Huntsman, Jon Meade *chemicals executive*
Huntsman, Jon Meade, Jr. *governor, former federal agency administrator*
Huntsman, Peter R. *chemicals executive*
Hutchinson, Douglas Truman *surgeon*
James, Brent Carl *health care executive, biomedical sciences educator*
Jenkins, Bruce Sterling *federal judge*
Jensen, Dallin W. *lawyer*
Jepperson, Thomas C. *lawyer*
Johnson, Auston Gilbert III *auditor*
Johnson, Xan Stuart *performing arts educator*
Julander, Paula Foil *retired foundation administrator*
Keefe, Maureen Ruth *dean*
Keenan, Thomas J. *chemicals executive*
Kern, Michael J. *chemicals executive*
Kim, Sung Wan *chemistry professor*
Kirkham, John Spencer *lawyer, director*
Kumpfer, Karol Linda *research psychologist*
Laursen, Thomas E. *lawyer*
Leary, G. Edward *state agency administrator*
Liu, Gang *education educator, researcher*
Livne, Nava Levia *psychologist, researcher*
Livne, Oren Eliezer *mathematician, educator*
Louie, Janis *chemistry professor*
Madsen, Brigham Dwaine *history professor*
Manning, Brent V. *lawyer*
Matsumori, Douglas *lawyer*
Mattis, Daniel Charles *physicist, researcher*
McCleary, Lloyd E(verald) *education educator*
McConnell, Michael W. *federal judge, law educator*
McKay, Monroe Gunn *federal judge*
Melton, Arthur Richard *public health administrator*
Mendenhall, Robert W. *information technology executive*
Meyers, Rebecka Louise *pediatric general surgeon*
Miller, Jan Dean *metallurgy educator*
Miller, Joel Steven *inorganic and organic materials chemist, educator*
Miller, Larry H. *professional sports team owner, auto dealer, broadcast executive*
Miller, William Charles *architect, educator*
Mogren, Paul Andrew *librarian*
Monson, Thomas Spencer *religious organization administrator, retired publishing executive*
Moore, James R. *lawyer*
Morris, Donna Jones *library director*
Moser, Royce, Jr. *preventive medicine physician, educator*
Murphy, Michael R. *federal judge*
Nehring, Ronald E. *state supreme court justice*
Nelson, John C. *obstetrician, gynecologist*
Nelson, Roger Hugh *corporate financial executive, educator, consultant*
Nelson, Russell Marion *surgeon, educator*
Newmark, William D. *conservation biologist*
Niederauer, George H. *bishop*
Ninow, Kevin J. *chemicals executive*
Nydegger, Rick D. *lawyer*
Ockey, Ronald J. *lawyer*
O'Connell, James F. *anthropologist, educator*
O'Connor, Kevin *professional sports team executive*
Ogburn, Joyce L. *library director*
Okur, Mehmet *professional basketball player*
Olivera, Baldomero M. *biology professor*
Olson, Ferron Allred *metallurgist, educator*
Osherow, Jacqueline Sue *poet, English language educator*
Palmer, David Keith *otolaryngologist*
Parkinson, Justin Paul *urologist*
Parrish, Jill Niederhauser *state supreme court justice*
Patterson, M. Brett *musician*
Paulsen, Vivian *editor*
Poulter, Charles Dale *chemist, educator, consultant*
Prince, William B. *lawyer*
Pysher, Theodore James *pathologist, medical educator*
Rasmussen, Thomas Val, Jr. *lawyer, small business owner*
Rattie, Keith O. *gas industry executive*
Reeder, F. Robert *lawyer*
Ridd, Brian V. *chemicals executive*
Robbins, Sherri Lynn *quality assurance professional*
Roens, Steven Thomas *music educator, associate dean*
Romney-Manookin, Elaine Clive *retired music educator, composer*
Rosenberg, Thomas D. *orthopedic surgeon*
Salisbury, Frank Boyer *botanist, educator, writer*
Salomonson, Vincent Victor *meteorologist, educator*
Sam, David *federal judge*
Sandquist, Gary Marlin *engineering educator, researcher, consultant, writer, military officer*
Scruggs, Samuel D. *lawyer, chemicals executive*
Shepherd, Karen *retired congresswoman*
Shurtleff, Mark L. *state attorney general*
Sigal, Jill Lea *nuclear energy industry executive, former federal agency administrator*
Sillars, Malcolm O. *communications educator*
Simmons, Harris H. *bank executive*
Sklute, Adam *performing company executive, dancer*
Sloan, Jerry (Gerald Eugene Sloan) *professional basketball coach*
Smith, Donald E. *broadcast engineer*
Smith, Eldred Gee *church leader*
Smith, Janet Hugie *lawyer*
Sohn, Hong Yong *chemical and metallurgical engineer, educator*
Sorensen, John B. *surgeon*
Sorenson, James LeVoy *research and development company executive*
Sorenson, Stephen Jay *lawyer*
Sparks, Mildred Thomas *state agency administrator, educator*
Speer, Susan H. *bank executive*
Stang, Peter John *organic chemist*
Stanutz, Donald J. *chemicals executive*
Stitley, James Walter, Jr. *food manufacturing executive*
Straight, Richard Coleman *photobiologist, natural philosopher*
Stringfellow, Gerald B. *engineering educator*
Swinton, Jeffrey Cheever *lawyer*
Tani, Lloyd Yasuo *pediatrician, educator*
Thomas, David Snow *plastic surgeon*
Thompson, Neil Daniel *retired lawyer*
Threedy, Debora Lynn *law educator*
Tolman, Brett L. *prosecutor*
Tomsic, Peggy A. *lawyer*
Trapa, Peter Engel *mathematics professor*
Urie, Alan T. *bank executive*
Velick, Sidney Frederick *research biochemist, educator*
Virkar, Anil V. *materials engineer, educator*
Walker, Carlene Martin *state senator*
Walker Neve, Diana *singer, voice educator*
Warner, Paul Michael *federal judge, former prosecutor*
Watt, Ronald G. *archivist*
Wickman, Lance B. *lawyer*
Wikstrom, Francis M. *lawyer*
Wilberg, Mack J. *conductor, composer*
Wilkins, Michael Jon *state supreme court justice*
Wingate, Thomas Russell *writer*
Wirthlin, Richard Bitner *researcher*
Witty, Christine (Chris Witty) *speed skater*
Wolf, Harold Herbert *pharmacy educator*
Wolfinger, Nicholas H. *educator*
Wright, Larry Jan *epidemiologist*
Young, Michael Kent *academic administrator, law educator*
Zimmerman, Michael David *lawyer*
Zipser, Edward J. *meteorologist, educator*

Sandy
Smith, Willard Grant *psychologist*

Santa Clara
Llewellyn, Linda J. *motivational speaker, consultant, writer*

South Jordan
Jacobsen, Laren *retired programmer*
Larson, Bryan Alan *lawyer*

Springville
Francis, Rell Gardner *artist, photographer, writer*

St George
Snow, Vanburen Lowry *lawyer*

Tooele
Jansen, Lambertus *retired state agency administrator, judge, criminal justice educator*

Tremonton
Eakle, Arlene Haslam *genealogist*

Vernal
Judd, Dennis L. *lawyer*

Washington
De Vany, Arthur Stacy *economics professor*

West Jordan
Betenson, Gaye Brinton *secondary school educator*
James, Linda Coates *elementary school educator*

West Valley City
Peterson, Millie M. *state senator*
Shah, Saurabh B. *surgeon*

Woods Cross
Blackley, Cheryl Ann *musician, freelance/self-employed educator*
Hendriksen, Neil Evan *music educator*

VERMONT

Arlington
Pond, Thomas Alexander *physics professor, academic administrator*

Barnard
Duckworth, Ruth *sculptor*
Larson, John Hyde *retired utilities executive*

Barre
Heath, Karen *secondary school educator*
Koch, Thomas Frederick *lawyer*

Bennington
Bernard, April *poet, literature educator*
Burkhardt, Frederick Henry *editor*
Coleman, Elizabeth *college president*
Franklin, Jamie *curator, consultant*
Lum, Mary *artist, educator*
Williams, Robert Joseph *retired museum director, educator*

Bethel
West, Jessamyn Charity *librarian, blogger*

Brandon
Farnsworth, Frank Albert *retired economics professor*
Konwin, Thor Warner *financial executive*

Brattleboro
Abrams, Jackie *artist, educator*
Agallianos, Dennis Dionysios *psychiatrist*
Ames, Adelbert III *neuroscientist, educator*
Bellamy, Carol *international organization administrator*
Gorman, Robert Saul *architect*
Reid, David G. *lawyer*
Steffens, Annie Laurie *sign language educator, interpreter*

Brownsville
Olderman, Gerald *retired medical device company executive*

Burlington
Allard, Judith Louise *retired secondary school educator*
Anderson, Jon Timothy *lawyer*
Anderson, Thomas D. *prosecutor*
Angell, Kenneth Anthony *bishop*
Bongard, Josh Clifford *computer scientist, educator*
Burton, Jake (Jake Burton Carpenter) *sports apparel executive*
Cooper, Sheldon Mark *immunologist, rheumatologist, educator, researcher*
Cutler, Stephen Joel *sociologist, educator*
Daniels, Robert Vincent *history professor, former state senator*
Davis, Christopher Lee *lawyer*
Dinitz, Susan Marie *language educator*
Dinse, John Merrell *lawyer*
Donahoo, William Troy *medical educator*
Drizo, Aleksandra *researcher, educator*
(Kahn) Fogel, Daniel Mark *academic administrator, literature educator, writer*
Gabriel, Diane Augusta *artist, educator*
Gennari, F(rank) John *medical educator*
Grunberg, Steven Marc *medical educator*
Hall, Robert William *philosophy religious studies educator*
Hearon, Shelby *writer, educator*
Heinrich, Bernd *biologist, educator*
Hennessey, John William, Jr. *academic administrator, educator*
Hoar, Samuel Neil, Jr. *lawyer*
Keeton, William Scott *ecologist, educator*
Kelly, Sister Marie *school system administrator*
Kirby, David V. *prosecutor*
Kunin, Madeleine May *former ambassador to Switzerland, former governor*
Lawson, Robert Bernard *psychology professor*
Lucey, Jerold Francis *pediatrician*
Marshall, Jeffrey Scott *mechanical engineer, educator*
Naylor, Magdalena Raczkowska *psychiatrist, educator*
Nyborg, Wesley Lemars *physics professor*
Outwater, John Ogden *mechanical engineering educator*
Pinder, George Francis *engineering educator, research scientist*
Post, Peter L. *marketing executive, writer*
Rendall, Donald James, Jr. *lawyer*
Riddick, Daniel Howison *obstetrician, gynecologist, priest*
Sampson, Samuel Franklin *sociology educator*
Saule, Mara *librarian, dean*
Sessions, William K. III *federal judge*
Shattuck, Gary G. *lawyer*
Tampas, John P. *radiologist*
Thompson, Ellen Ann *elementary school educator*
Warneck, Robert Townsend *religious studies educator*
Zhao, Feng-Qi *endocrinologist, educator*

Castleton
Leenman, Willem P. *mental health services professional, director*
Meloy, Judith Marie *humanities educator*
Roper, Scott Christopher *geographer, researcher*

Charlotte
Hamilton, Lawrence Stanley *environmental consultant*
Melby, Edward Carlos, Jr. *veterinarian*
Naylor, Thomas Herbert *economist, educator, consultant*
Robinson, Sally Winston *artist*
Sim, Craig Stephen *retired investment banker*

Chester
Coleman, John Royston *writer*

Colchester
Blacketor, Paul Garber *minister*
Lawton, Lorilee Ann *small business owner, accountant*
Mindich, David T.Z. *journalist, educator*
Niemi, Robert James *adult education educator, writer*
Sobel, Burton Elias *cardiologist, educator*

Concord
Norsworthy, Elizabeth Krassovsky *lawyer*

Corinth
Bellamy, John Stark, II, *librarian, historian, writer*

Danby
Peel, Harris *retired small business owner*

Dorset
Bamford, Joseph Charles, Jr. *gynecologist, obstetrician, educator, medical missionary, author*
Hittle, Richard Howard *gas and oil industry executive, consultant*
Marron, Pamela Anne *artist*

East Calais
Low, Anthony *language educator*

East Dummerston
Bertone, Thomas Lee *management consultant*

East Montpelier
Christiansen, Andrew P. *website designer, historic archives digitilizer*

East Thetford
Cummings Rockwell, Patricia Guilbault *psychiatric nurse*

Enosburg Falls
Svendsen, Alf *artist, educator*

Essex Junction
Bisson, Roger *middle school educator*
Jin, Zhenrong *electrical engineer, researcher*
Sweetser, Susan W. *lawyer, advocate, retired state legislator*

Greensboro
Gilpin, Robert George, Jr. *political science professor*
Hill, Lewis Reuben *horticulturist, nursery owner, writer*

Guildhall
Resden, Ronald Everett *medical devices product development engineer*

Hartland Four Corners
Brady, Upton Birnie *editor, literary agent*

Hinesburg
Fay, Glenn Mills, Jr. *science educator*

Hyde Park
Sanford, Dianne H. *lawyer*

Jacksonville
Dell, Ralph Bishop *retired pediatrician, researcher*
Hein, Karen Kramer *pediatrician, epidemiologist*

Johnson
Whitehill, Angela Elizabeth *artistic director*

Lincoln
Kompass, Edward John *consulting editor*

Lyndon Center
Dame, William Page III *bank executive, educational administrator*

Lyndonville
Atkins, Nolan Thomas *meteorologist, educator*
Moore, Carol A. *academic administrator*

Manchester
Carey, James Henry *banker*
Kouwenhoven, Gerrit Wolphertsen *retired museum director*

Manchester Center
Carr, Gerald Paul *retired astronaut, engineer, marketing professional, military officer*

Marlboro
Stevenson, Laura Caroline *writer, educator*

Middlebury
Albers, Jan Maria *historian, museum director*
Bergesen, Robert Nelson *transportation consultant*
Bumbeck, David *artist, retired educator*
Colander, David Charles *economist, educator*
Ferm, Robert Livingston *religion educator*
Forman, Michele *secondary school educator*
Geier, Philip Otto III *foundation executive, consultant, director, academic administrator*
Jacobs, Travis Beal *historian, educator*
Katz, Michael Ray *Slavic languages educator*
Lamberti, Marjorie *retired social studies educator*
Liebowitz, Ronald D. *academic administrator*
MacDonald, Kenneth R., Jr. *author, artist*
Monod, Paul Kleber *history professor*
Nuovo, Betty A. *state representative*
O'Brien, George Dennis *retired academic administrator*
Pardee, Scott Edward *securities dealer*
Robbins, Stephen J. M. *lawyer*
Vail, Van Horn *German language educator*
Winkler, Paul Frank, Jr. *astrophysicist, educator*

Milton
Rivero, Marilyn Elaine Keith *state legislator*

Montgomery Center
Oktavec, Eileen M. *anthropologist, artist*

Montpelier
Barbieri, Christopher George *professional society administrator*
Burgess, Brian Louis *state supreme court justice*
Cate, Richard H. *school system administrator*
Diamond, M. Jerome *lawyer, retired state attorney general*
Dooley, John Augustine III *state supreme court justice*
Douglas, Jim (James Holley) *governor*
Dubie, Brian E. *lieutenant governor*
Dumville, John P. *historic site director*
Gibson, Ernest Willard III *retired state supreme court justice*
Guild, Alden *retired lawyer*
Johnson, Denise Reinka *state supreme court justice*
MacLeay, Thomas H. *insurance company executive*
Markowitz, Deborah Lynn *state official*
McShane, Sybil Brigham *library director*
Paquin, Edward H., Jr. *retired state legislator, not-for-profit developer*
Putter, David Seth *lawyer*
Reiber, Paul L. *state supreme court chief justice*
Skoglund, Marilyn *state supreme court justice*
Sorrell, William H. *state attorney general*
Spaulding, George B. *state official*
Thabault, Paulette J. *state agency administrator*
Thwaites, Christian William *investment company executive*
Valerio, Matthew F. *lawyer*
Voigt, Francis *academic administrator*

Morrisville
Besser, Gretchen Rous *writer, educator*
Lechevalier, Hubert Arthur *microbiology educator*
Lechevalier, Mary Pfeil *retired microbiologist, educator*
Simonds, Marshall *retired lawyer*

Newbury
Doig, Jameson Wallace *political science professor*
McGarrell, James *artist, educator*

Newport
Pepyne, Edward Walter *lawyer, psychologist, educator*

North Bennington
Adler, Irving *mathematician*

North Clarendon
Freed, Walter Everett *petroleum company executive, state representative*

North Pomfret
Crowl, John Allen *retired publishing company executive*
Shepherd, Gaal *artist*

Northfield
Farkas, Meredith G. *librarian*
Wick, William Shinn *clergyman, chaplain, pastor*

Norwich
Foster, Michael Kirk *anthropologist, linguist*
Katz, Arnold Martin *medical educator*
Paine, Walter Cabot *journalist, consultant*
Snapper, Ernst *mathematics professor*
Stamelman, Richard Howard *French and humanities educator*
Stevenson, Josiah, IV, *management consultant*

Pawlet
Buechner, Carl Frederick *minister, author*

Peacham
Barnes, Harry G., Jr. *advocate, consultant*
Engle, James Bruce *ambassador*

Perkinsville
Harris, Christopher *editor, writer, illustrator, graphics designer*

Plainfield
Jervis, Jane Lise *academic administrator, historian*

Proctorsville
Harper, Jennifer *elementary school educator*

Putney
Gill, Jane Roberts *retired psychotherapist, clinical social worker*
Keil, John Mullan *advertising executive, artist*

Quechee
DeRouchey, Beverly Jean *investment company executive*
Dorsey, Jeremiah Edmund *pharmaceutical company executive*
Vitty, Roderic Bemis *retired financial planner, publishing executive*
Wood, R. Stewart, Jr. *retired bishop*

Randolph
Minsinger, William Elliott *orthopedist, surgeon*

Randolph Center
Sax, Daniel Saul *neurologist, educator*

Reading
Dike, Rad (Edward Conrad Dike) *artist*

Rutland
Carroll, La Shun La Rue *dentist*
Chapman, Silas Stacy III *lawyer*
Crowley, Arthur Edward, Jr. *lawyer*
Faignant, John Paul *lawyer, educator*
Ferraro, Betty Ann *retired state senator*
Haley, John Charles *retired bank executive*
Norris, Richard Anthony *accountant*

Saint Albans
Keenan, Kathleen *state legislator*

Saint Johnsbury
Gallagher, James C. *lawyer*
Marshall, John Henry *lawyer*

Shelburne
Anderson, Richard Louis *electrical engineer*
Canfield, Andrew Trotter *lawyer, writer*
Mead, Philip Bartlett *healthcare administrator, educator, retired obstetrician*
Ryerson, William Newton *non profit organization executive*
Weiger, John George *foreign language educator*
White, William North *retired chemistry professor*

South Burlington
Pizzagalli, James *construction executive*
Shinozaki, Tamotsu *retired physician, retired anesthesiologist*

South Londonderry
Spiers, Ronald Ian *diplomat*

South Royalton
Dycus, Stephen *law educator*
Goodenough, Oliver Ramsdell *lawyer, educator*
Powers, Thomas Moore *writer*
Wroth, L(awrence) Kinvin *law educator*

Springfield
Guité, J. C. Michel *telephone company owner*
Putnam, Paul Adin *federal agency administrator*

Stamford
Stevens, Lauren Rogers *writer, environmentalist*

Stowe
Siegel, David Burton *lawyer*
Whiteman, Joseph David *retired lawyer, manufacturing company executive*

Strafford
Williams, William Magavern *headmaster*

Swanton
Suitor, Dorcas P. *elementary school educator*

Thetford
Hoagland, Mahlon *biochemist, educator*

Tunbridge
Childs, Marilyn Carlson *journalist, educator*

Underhill
Danforth, Elliot, Jr. *medical educator*

Vergennes
Eric, Bechhoefer Robert *technologist*
Grant, Edwin Randolph *retail executive, manufacturing executive*

Waitsfield
Dodds, Judy B. *curator, consultant, artist*
Esty, David Cameron *marketing and communications executive*

Wallingford
Gutmann, David Leo *psychology professor*

Warren
Raphael, Albert Ash, Jr. *retired lawyer*
Sullivan, Kathleen *elementary school educator*

Waterbury
Hilton, Linda D. *academic administrator*

West Burke
Van Vliet, Claire *artist*

West Danville
Pollack, Irwin William *psychiatrist, educator*

West Glover
Weaver, John Borland *musician, department chairman, composer*

Weston
Kasnowski, Chester Nelson *artist, educator*
Stettler, Stephen F. *performing company executive*

White River Junction
Berman, Stephen Alan *neurologist*
Kainen, Michael Roland *lawyer, state representative*
Myers, Warren Powers Laird *internist, educator*
Xie, Chi *transportation engineer, researcher*

Whiting
Jacobson, Edward *retired elementary school educator, principal*

Williston
Essman, Robert Norvel *artist, graphics designer*
Laskarzewski, Debra Sue *language educator*

Wilmington
Little, Thomas M. *public relations executive*

Wolcott
Fisher, Neal Floyd *religious organization administrator*

Woodstock
Billings, Franklin Swift, Jr. *federal judge*
Goulazian, Peter Robert *retired broadcasting executive*
Hoyt, Coleman Williams *postal consultant*
Killian, Edward James *retired pediatrician*
Matlins, Stuart M. *management consultant, publisher*
Zonay, Thomas A. *lawyer*

VIRGINIA

Abingdon
Jones, James Parker *federal judge*
Jones, Mary Trent *endowment fund trustee*
Moore, Suzan E. *lawyer*
Quillen, Michael J. *energy executive*
Ramos-Cano, Hazel Balatero *caterer, chef, innkeeper, restaurateur, entrepreneur*
Shortridge, Judy Beth *lawyer*

Afton
Stefanovic, Victor R. *electrical engineer, consultant*

Aldie
Weaver, Kitty Dunlap *author*

Alexandria
Adams, Ranald Trevor, Jr. *retired air force officer*
Allen, Ernie (Ernest Eugene Allen) *non-profit organization executive, lawyer*
Anderson, Maynard Carlyle *security firm executive*
Anderson, Steven C. *pharmaceutical association executive*
Apperson, Bernard James *lawyer*
Armstrong, Cathal *chef*
Arundel, John Howard *journalist, publisher*
Bailey, Tracey L. *educational association administrator*
Baker, Brent Harold *foundation executive, blogger*
Balch, Charles M. *surgeon, educator*
Barnes, John D. *health science association administrator*
Baroody, Michael Elias *trade association executive*
Barry, Lance Leonard *judge*
Bartels, Teresa Hall *non-profit organization administrator*
Bartlett, Elizabeth Susan *audio-visual specialist*
Berger, Patricia Wilson *retired librarian*
Bezold, Clement *futurist*
Birely, William Cramer *investment banker*
Blair, Dennis Cutler *career officer*
Blue, Catherine Anne *lawyer*
Boisi, Geoffrey T. *investment company executive*
Bolger, Robert Joseph *retired trade association administrator*
Bombardt, John Nicholas *research scientist*
Borum, Olin Henry *retired research scientist*
Bostetter, Martin V. B., Jr. *bankruptcy court judge*
Bowman, Richard Carl *defense consultant, retired air force officer*
Bozell, Brent (L. Brent Bozell III) *communications executive*
Brickhill, William Lee *international finance consultant*
Brinkema, Leonie Milhomme *federal judge*
Brown, Frederic Joseph *military officer*
Bryant, Anne Lincoln *educational association administrator*
Burch, John Thomas, Jr. *lawyer*
Burke, Kelly Howard *retired military officer, entrepreneur, philanthropist*
Butler, Susan Lowell *educational association executive, writer*
Byrne, John Edward (JEB Byrne) *retired federal official*
Carter, Gene Raymond *professional association executive*
Carter, Richard Dennis *lawyer, educator*
Carter, William Harold, Sr. *physicist, researcher, electrical engineer*
Carville, James, Jr., (Chester James Carville) *political scientist, consultant*
Chapman, Anthony Bradley *psychiatrist*
Chen, Fen *mathematician, educator, researcher*
Collins, Cardiss *retired congresswoman*
Connell, Mary Ellen *diplomat*
Connelly, Gail *educational association administrator*
Cook, Charles William *aerospace engineer, consultant, educator*
Coons, Barbara Lynn *public relations executive, librarian*
Copulos, Milton Russell *energy executive*
Corrothers, Helen Gladys *criminal justice official*
Costagliola, Francesco *retired government official*
Cottrell, James Ray *lawyer*
Cross, Dorothy Abigail *retired librarian*
Cross, Eason, Jr. *architect*
Crundwell, Duncan James *electronics executive*
Dennison, Donald Lee *lawyer*
Devantier, Paul W. *religious organization administrator, broadcast executive*
Dowling, Dean Edward *information scientist, educator*
Drennan, Joseph Peter *lawyer*
Dubin, Martin Steven *principal*
Dunn, Bernard Daniel *former naval officer, consultant*
Edmonds, Albert J. *career officer*
Ellison, Pamela Ion *secondary school educator, consultant*
Engler, Brian David *professional society administrator*
Esslinger, John Thomas *lawyer*
Fainberg, Anthony *physicist*
Fedorochko, William, Jr. *retired military officer, military analyst*
Fisher, Donald Wayne *medical association administrator*
Fitton, Harvey Nelson, Jr. *former government official*
Flater, Morris Eugene *lawyer*
Fleming, Douglas Riley *journalist, publishing executive, consultant*
Fliflet, Arne Woolsey *research scientist*
Fosdick (Beebe), Cora Prifold *management consultant*
Foster, Robert Francis *communications executive*
Foster, Serrin Marie *non-profit organization executive*
Frommer, Lawrence Julian *retired travel company executive*
Gallagher, Anne Porter *communications executive*
Geary, Patrick Joseph *security and emergency planning administrator, writer*
Georges, Peter John *lawyer*
Gernand, Bradley Elton *archivist, librarian*
Ginsburg, Charles David *lawyer*
Goldfarb, Ronald Lawrence *lawyer, writer, literary agent*
Goolrick, Robert Mason *management consultant*
Gormley, Dennis Michael *research scholar*
Gould, Charles W. *foundation administrator, lawyer*
Gould, Phillip *engineer*
Grachek, Marianna Kern *healthcare administrator*
Greenstein, Ruth Louise *think-tank executive, lawyer*
Greigg, Ronald Edwin *lawyer*
Gurke, Sharon McCue *career officer*
Gutsch, William Anthony, Jr. *astronomer*
Gwadosky, Dan A. *former state official, federal agency administrator*
Hale, Robert Fargo *federal association executive*
Hammad, Alam E. *international business consultant, educator*
Hansen, Jacob Bernard *military officer*
Hark, William Henry *retired federal agency administrator, aerospace physician*
Harris, Dale William *systems engineer*
Harris, David Ford *management consultant, retired federal official*
Harting, Harry Lloyd, Jr. *government agency administrator, retired military officer*
Havens, Harry Stewart *retired federal official, management consultant*
Haygood, Alma Jean *elementary school educator*
Helman, Gerald Bernard *diplomat*
Hesterberg, Larry Allen *aerospace engineer*
Hilferty, Bryan Carey *public relations specialist*
Hilton, Claude Meredith *federal judge*
Hirsch, Robert Louis *energy analyst, consultant*
Hirschkop, Philip Jay *lawyer, educator*
Hobbs, Michael Edwin *broadcast executive*
Hobson, James Richmond *lawyer*
Huckabee, Harlow Maxwell *lawyer, writer*
Hudgins, David Drake *lawyer*
Hughes, Grace-Flores *federal agency administrator*
Hurtado, Rodrigo Claudio *allergist*
Ikossi, Kiki *electrical and computer engineer*
Jenkins, John Smith *retired dean, lawyer*
Johnson, Edgar McCarthy *psychologist*
Johnson, JoAnn Mardelle *federal agency administrator*
Kaplan, Richard Alan *government official*
Kelly, Nancy Frieda Wolicki *lawyer*
Kim, Sook Cha *artist*
Knowlton, William Allen *federal agency administrator, educator*
Kohlberg, Ira *physicist, mathematician*
Kopp, Eugene Paul *lawyer*
Kotlarchuk, Ihor O.E. *lawyer*
Kratovil, Jane Lindley *think tank associate, not-for-profit developer*
Kroesen, Frederick James *retired army officer, consultant*
Krueger, Gerald Peter *psychologist*
Lachance, Janice Rachel *professional association and federal agency administrator, lawyer*
Lantz, Phillip Edward *security firm executive, consultant*
Lasser, Howard Gilbert *chemical engineer, consultant*
Laurent, Lawrence Bell *communications executive, retired journalist*
Leahy, Pat (P. Patrick Leahy) *geologist, former federal official*
Leestma, Robert *retired federal agency administrator, educational association administrator*
Lenz, Edward Arnold *trade association administrator, lawyer*
Leonhart, Michele Marie *federal agency administrator*
Lindsey, Sara Ann *sociologist, educator*
Lipnick, Anne Ruth *advocate*
Lipnick, Robert Louis *chemist, toxicologist*
Loren, Donald Patrick *federal official, retired military officer*
Lundeberg, Philip Karl Boraas *curator, historian*
Lusk, Cody *auto association executive*
MacLaren, William George, Jr. *engineering executive*
Maehara, Paulette V. *fundraising executive*
Maloof, Farahe Paul *lawyer*
Malott, John Raymond *writer, consultant, not-for-profit executive*
Masterson, Kleber Sanlin, Jr. *physicist*
Matalin, Mary *political consultant*
McConville, Judy Allen *social studies educator*
McDowell, Charles Eager *lawyer, retired military officer*
McMillan, Charles William *consulting company executive*
McNicol, David Leon *retired federal official, researcher*
Meisinger, Susan *human resources specialist*
Montague, Robert Latane III *lawyer*
Mossinghoff, Gerald Joseph *lawyer, educator*
Muir, Warren Roger *chemist, educator*
Murray, Russell, II, *aeronautical engineer, security consultant*
Nelson, David Leonard *data processing executive*
Nicholas, Lynn B. *medical association administrator*
Nodeen, Janey Price *information technology executive*
Nutile, David Albert *retired information security and systems consultant*
O'Brien, Patrick Michael *library administrator*
O'Hara, John Patrick *lawyer, consultant*
Pastin, Mark Joseph *health science association administrator, educator*
Patel, Manu V. *physics educator*
Paturis, E(mmanuel) Michael *lawyer*
Paulson, Gwen O. Gampel *government relations consultant, life and leadership coach*
Pearson, Lynda Ann *music educator*
Piecuch, Diane Marie *music educator*
Plitt, Jeanne Given *librarian*
Poehlein, Gary Wayne *retired chemical engineering professor*
Powell, Colin Luther *former secretary of state, former Chairman of the Joint Chiefs of Staff*
Pringle, Robert Maxwell *diplomat*
Pyle, Howard *lawyer, consultant*
Rabun, John Brewton, Jr. *criminal justice agency administrator*
Rae, Jeneanne *new product development and innovation consultant, educator*
Rahming, John Christopher *investment company executive, consultant*
Rayman, Russell Barry *physician*
Rector, John Michael *pharmaceutical association executive, lawyer*
Revere, Virginia Lehr *psychologist*
Richards, Darrie Hewitt *investment company executive*
Romney, Carl F. *seismologist*
Roof, Michael Kitching *demographer, researcher*
Rosenberg, Chuck (Charles P.) *prosecutor*
Safier, Pedro N. *physicist, contractor*
Sapp, Eric *religious organization executive*
Sheffield, Greg *media blogger*
Sheffield, Matthew *media blogger*
Shern, David Len *mental health services professional, former dean*
Shosky, John Edwin *media consultant, speechwriter*
Signorovitch, Dennis J. *communications executive, educator*
Simmons, Richard De Lacey *mass media executive*
Smith, Jeffrey Greenwood *retired military officer*
Snyder, Larry *priest, social services administrator*
Spencer, George Henry *lawyer*
Spencer, James R. *federal judge*
Stempler, Jack Leon *aerospace executive*
Stevens, Ron A. *lawyer, advocate, surveyor*
Stone, Ann Elizabeth *marketing agency executive, consultant, entrepreneur, volunteer*
Straub, Peter Thornton *lawyer*
Sturtevant, Brereton *retired lawyer, federal official*
Swift, Stephen Christopher *lawyer*
Tandy, Karen P. *federal agency administrator*
Thrasher, Todd *bar chef*
Toulmin, Priestley *retired geologist*
Tucker, Alvin Leroy *retired government official*
Tucker, Howard McKeldin *investment banker, consultant*
Vanderslice, Mara *religious organization executive*
Verburg, Edwin Arnold *management consultant*
Von Drehle, Ramon Arnold *lawyer*
Vosbeck, Elizabeth Just *retired geneticist*
Vosbeck, William Frederick, Jr. *architect*
Walker, Edward Keith, Jr. *retired management consultant, retired military officer*
Walkup, Charlotte Lloyd *lawyer*
Watta, David Anthony *product manager*
Weisberg, Leonard R. *retired engineering executive, researcher*
Welburn, Brenda Lilienthal *educational association administrator*
Whitaker, Mary Fernan *lawyer*
Whitson, Elizabeth Temple *graphics designer*
Wilcox, David Eric *electrical engineering, educator, consultant, business owner*
Wilhide, Stephen D. *medical association administrator*
Williams, John Edward *lawyer*
Wilson, Tyler J. *medical association administrator*
Winzer, P.J. *lawyer*
Wolfe, Thad Allison *air force officer*
Woolley, Mary Elizabeth *science administrator, advocate*
Wynn, Robert E. *electronics executive, retired military officer*
Yoder, Edwin Milton, Jr. *columnist, educator, editor, writer*

Amherst
Campbell, Catherine Lynn *elementary school educator*

Amissville
Hunter, Beverly Claire *research scientist, educator*

Annandale
Abdellah, Faye Glenn *retired public health service officer*
Armstrong, Henry Jere *retired judge*
Bragg, Cheryl Fuller *psychologist*
Brotton, Joyce Dupras *English language educator*
Carvalho, Julie Ann *psychologist*
Christianson, Geryld B. *government agency administrator, consultant*
Freeman, Baba Foster *editor*
Gioconda, Thomas F. *program manager, retired military flag officer*
Greinke, Everett Donald *management consultant*
Hulbert, Mark J. *financial analyst, columnist*
Hutcheon, Wallace Schoonmaker *historian, educator*
Jarvis, Elbert, II, (Jay Jarvis) *employee benefits specialist*
Jollie, Susan Barbara *lawyer*
Khim, Jay Wook *information technology executive*
Matuszko, Anthony Joseph *research chemist, administrator, educator*
Nelson, Harold E. (Bud Nelson) *fire protection engineer*
Ochs, Walter J. *civil engineer, consultant*
Passut, Christine Diana *special education educator*
Piscitelli, Emile James *philosopher, educator*
Raab, Harry Frederick, Jr. *retired physicist*
Rogers, Stephen Hitchcock *retired ambassador*
Samuelson, Douglas Alan *information technology executive*
Shamburek, Roland Howard *physician*
Southern, Kimberly Elaine *art historian, educator*
Tencer, John G. *military officer*

Appomattox
Beatson, LeGrande Guerry *environmental health specialist*

Arlington
Ablard, Charles David *administrative judge*
Adams, Hunter (Patch Adams) *internist, health facility administrator*
Adams, Jimmie Vick *communications systems company executive, retired military officer*
Aggrey, Orison Rudolph *former ambassador, consultant, academic administrator*
Alcalde, Hector *public relations executive*
Allard, Dean Conrad *historian, retired historical center director*
Allen, David *systems engineer*
Anthony, Robert Armstrong *lawyer, educator*
Arehart-Treichel, Joan *writer*
Arnold, Gary Howard *film critic*
Askey, Thelma J. *federal agency administrator*
Baginski, Maureen A. *former federal agency administrator*
Baker, Russell Wayne *columnist, writer*
Bakke, Dennis W. *energy company executive*
Bement, Arden Lee, Jr. *engineering educator, government agency administrator*
Bennett, Christopher Lawrence *hotel executive, lawyer*
Bentsen, Kenneth E., Jr. *trade association administrator, former congressman*
Bigeleisen, Jacob *chemist, educator*
Blum, Steven (H. Steven Blum) *career military officer*
Bolster, Archie Milburn *retired foreign service officer*
Bond, Phillip J. *technology association executive, former advertising executive*
Boorstein, Laurence *economist, educator*
Brenner, Edgar H. *legal association administrator*
Brighton, John A. *mechanical engineer, academic administrator*
Bromley, Marilyn Modlin *librarian*
Buchanan, Louise *political organization worker, consultant*
Buckley, Francis H. *economist, lawyer, educator*
Burgess, David *lawyer*
Calland, Albert M. III *information technology executive, former federal official, retired military officer*
Caplan, Mitchell H. *diversified financial services company executive*
Cehelsky, Marta *scientific organization executive*
Chamot, Joshua Andrew *science administrator*
Chatfield, William Austin *federal agency administrator*
Chipman, Susan Elizabeth *psychologist, researcher*
Choksi, Mary Claire *investment company executive*
Chubb, Talbot Albert *physicist, consultant*
Clapman, Leah Meredith *public television editor*
Claussen, Eileen Barbara *environmental services administrator, former federal agency administrator*
Clayton, James Edwin *journalist*

Clump, Michael Aden *psychologist, educator*

Coe, Doug *religious organization administrator*

Cofoni, Paul Michael *information technology executive*

Cohen, Sheldon Irwin *lawyer*

Covington, James Edwin *government agency administrator, psychologist*

Cox, Henry *engineer, researcher*

Crosby, Michael P. *science administrator*

Crouch, Richard Edelin *lawyer*

Culligan, Thomas M. *electronics executive*

David, Ruth A. *public-service research institute executive*

Davis, Lynn Etheridge *political scientist, educator*

DeFeo, Charles Joesph *Internet company executive*

DeFilippi, George *retired air force officer*

Demetrion, James Thomas *retired museum director, consultant*

Dobbins, Jim (James Francis Dobbins Jr.) *think-tank executive, former federal agency administrator*

Dodgen, Larry J. *career military officer*

Dorman, Janet Lee Vosper *elementary school educator*

Doyle, Gerard Francis *lawyer*

Drayton, Bill (William Drayton) *social entrepreneur, lawyer, management consultant*

Dudas, Jonathan W. *federal agency administrator*

Dunlap, William *artist, educator, art critic, educator*

Dunn, Michael M. *military association executive, retired military officer*

Earl, Sister Patricia Helene *religious studies educator, director*

Eddy, John Joseph *diplomat*

Edmondson, William Brockway *retired foreign service officer*

Elsberg, John William *publishing executive, writer*

England, Robert Stowe *writer*

Erb, Karl Albert *physicist, government official*

Erwin, Frank William *human resources consultant*

Fay, Kevin J. *public relations executive*

Feerick, John Paul *neurologist, researcher, military officer*

Ferraz, Francisco Marconi *neurological surgeon*

Finta, Frances Mickna *secondary school educator*

Fischer, Ivan *conductor*

Flinn, Charles Gallagher *lawyer, priest*

Foster, Michael T. *architect*

Franklin, Jude Eric *electronics executive*

Fuchs, Roland John *geography educator, academic administrator*

Futrell, John William *environmental agency executive, lawyer*

Gainer, Ronald Lee *lawyer*

Galloway, William Jefferson *retired foreign service officer*

Gergely, Tomas Esteban *astronomer*

Gifford, Jonathan Lewis *transportation policy researcher, educator*

Glaser, Gerard R. *science administrator*

Glass, Andrew James *newspaper editor*

Gracey, James Steele *manufacturing executive, director, management consultant*

Gravel, Mike (Maurice Robert Gravel) *former senator*

Graves, Ernest, Jr. *retired army officer, consultant, engineer*

Green, Richard Alan *retired lawyer*

Gunn, Joseph Ridgeway III *consulting economist*

Gurian, Elaine Heumann *museum consultant*

Haggett, Rosemary Romanowski *academic administrator*

Haig, Alexander Meigs, Jr. *former secretary of state, retired military officer*

Hall, Carl William *agricultural and mechanical engineer*

Hamilton, Anthony *singer*

Hanrahan, Paul Thaddeus *utilities executive*

Hansen, Kenneth D. *lawyer, ophthalmologist*

Harker, Victoria D. *electric power industry executive*

Harrington, George Fred *retired air transportation executive*

Harris, John F. *editor-in-chief*

Harris, William James, Jr. *retired science administrator*

Harrison, Emmett Bruce, Jr. *public relations counselor*

Hassett, Valerie Jane *interior designer, architect, educator*

Hawley, Edmund S. (Kip) *federal agency administrator*

Hazelrigg, George Arthur, Jr. *systems engineer, educator*

Heineken, Frederick George *biochemical engineer*

Heivilin, Donna Mae *retired government executive*

Held, Joe Roger *retired veterinarian*

Hellmuth, George William *architect*

Herbst, Robert LeRoy *organization executive*

Hewitt, Thomas Francis *hotel executive*

Hickman, Elizabeth Podesta *retired counselor*

Hinton, Thomas Allen *government agency administrator*

Hokborg, Sven-Olof *military officer*

Holovaty, Adrian *editor, web site designer*

Houston, Paul David *educational association administrator*

Howlett, Clifford Theodore, Jr., (Kip Howlett) *chemicals executive*

Hullin, Tod Robert *aerospace transportation executive*

Hunter, J(ohn) Robert *insurance consumer advocate*

Ifill, Gwen *moderator, political reporter*

Jacoby, Lowell Edwin (Jake Jacoby) *information technology executive, retired military officer*

Johnson, Charles Owen *retired lawyer*

Junker, Bobby Ray *research and development company executive, physicist*

Katzen, Jay Kenneth *retired diplomat, state legislator, government agency administrator*

Keene, Deborah M. *law librarian*

Kelly, John James *lawyer*

Kerger, Paula Arnold *broadcast executive*

Kerns, Wilmer Lee *researcher*

Kicklighter, Claude Milton (Mick Kicklighter) *federal agency administrator*

Kleinman, Katie (Katherine Miller Kleinman) *public television editor*

Korman, James William *lawyer*

Kosarin, Jonathan Henry *lawyer, consultant*

Kozlov, Viktor *professional hockey player*

Krys, Sheldon Jack *retired diplomat*

Lakefield, Bruce R. *air transportation executive*

Lala, Jaynarayan Hotchand *computer engineer*

Langley, Harold David *historian, educator*

Langworthy, Everett Walter *professional society administrator, natural gas exploration company executive*

Lauderdale, Katherine Sue *lawyer*

Lease, Mary Mundy *literature and language professor*

Legum, Judd *think-tank executive, editor*

Lehrer, James Charles *reporter, journalist*

Leland, Marc Ernest *trust company executive, consultant, lawyer*

Leslie, Gregg P. *lawyer*

Lilenfeld, Lisa Rachelle *psychology professor, psychologist*

Lohr, Michael F. *lawyer*

London, J. Phillip (Jack London) *information technology executive*

Luraschi, William R. *utilities executive, lawyer*

MacDougall, William Lowell *magazine editor*

MacNeil, Robert Breckenridge Ware *retired journalist, writer*

Mainwaring, Thomas Lloyd *transportation executive, director*

Malone, William Grady *retired lawyer*

Markessini, Joan *research scientist, psychologist*

Martin, Harry C. *lawyer*

Matthews, Allan Freeman *geologist*

McCaffrey, Barry Richard *retired military officer*

McDermott, Francis Owen *retired lawyer*

McDonald, Bernard Robert *retired federal agency administrator*

Mc Donald, Gail Faber *musician, educator*

Mc Donald, John Warlick *diplomat*

McKinley, Craig R. *career military officer*

McKinnon, Russell F. *professional society administrator*

McTigue, Maurice P. *director*

Meadows, Vickers B. *federal agency administrator*

Meisel, Michael J. *lawyer*

Mellor, Chip (William H. Mellor) *lawyer*

Miller, Kenneth Gregory *retired air force officer*

Milton-Jones, DeLisha *professional basketball player*

Moore, Guy Will *retired public information officer, historian, writer*

Muñoz, George *investment company executive, former federal agency administrator*

Nagin, Lawrence M. *lawyer*

Nash, Anthony J. *military analyst*

Nash, Bob J. *political organization worker*

Neikirk, William Robert *journalist*

Newburger, Beth Weinstein *communications executive*

Nguyen-Dinh, Thanh *internist, geriatrician, acupuncturist*

Niccolls, Wesley Oliver, Sr. *retired electronics engineering technician*

Nirschl, Robert Phillip *orthopedic surgeon*

Ochmanek, David Alan *defense analyst*

Ochoa-Brillembourg, Hilda Margarita *investment banker*

O'Connor, Christopher John *information technology manager, consultant*

O'Day, Paul Thomas *trade association executive*

Oliver, Robert M. *engineer*

Olsen, Kathie Lynn *science foundation director*

O'Neill, Brian *science administrator*

Ordway, Frederick Ira III *science educator, consultant, researcher, writer*

O'Sullivan, Lynda Troutman *lawyer*

Page, Harry Robert *business administration educator*

Palmer, Larry Leon *foundation administrator, former ambassador*

Parker, Jeffrey Scott *law educator*

Pelton, Erik Michael *lawyer*

Pendleton, Mary Catherine *retired foreign service officer*

Polsby, Daniel D. *dean, law educator*

Powell, Edward A., Jr., (Ned Powell) *nonprofit organization executive*

Price, Donald Ray *academic administrator, researcher, agricultural engineer*

Price, Joseph Maurice *retired military officer*

Putnam, George W., Jr. *retired army officer*

Pyatt, Everett Arno *federal official*

Quinn, John Collins *publishing executive, editor*

Rabaut, Thomas W. *defense industry executive*

Rahman, Muhammad Abdur *mechanical engineer*

Raizen, Senta Amon *educational association administrator, researcher*

Reagan, Lawrence Paul, Jr. *engineering executive, consultant*

Regnery, Alfred Scattergood *publishing executive*

Reiss, Susan Marie *editor, writer*

RisCassi, Robert W. *communications systems company executive, retired military officer*

Robb, Chuck (Charles Spittal) *law educator, former senator*

Rockefeller, Sharon Percy *broadcast executive*

Rogers, Alan Victor *former career officer*

Rogers, James Frederick *banker, management consultant*

Rotunda, Ronald Daniel *law educator, consultant*

Rousselot, Peter Frese *lawyer, consultant*

Rudolph, Lawrence *lawyer*

Rymer, Jon T. *federal agency administrator*

Salmon, William Cooper *mechanical engineer, company executive*

Samburg, A. Gene *security company executive*

Sanz, Luis E. *gynecologist, educator*

Scarborough, Robert Henry, Jr. *entrepreneur*

Schmidt, Paul Wickham *lawyer*

Schultz, Roger C. *career military officer*

Shannon, Thomas Alfred *retired educational association administrator emeritus*

Sharp, Barry J. *school system administrator*

Shepherd, Mildred Roof *retired secondary school educator, art restorer*

Siddayao, Corazón Morales *economist, educator, consultant*

Simonson, David C. *retired newspaper association executive*

Singstock, David John *military officer*

Sloan, Clifford M. *lawyer, publishing executive*

Smith, Louis John *historian*

Solis Doyle, Patti *political campaign worker*

Spaulding, Wallace Holmes *retired federal agency professional*

Sterner, Robert Warner *ecologist, science administrator*

Stevens, Donald King *retired aeronautical engineer, consultant*

Stickler, Richard E. *federal agency administrator*

Stokes, B. R. *transportation executive, consultant*

Stone, Stuart Lee Morrison *librarian, language educator*

Sullivan, Gordon R. *military association executive, retired military officer*

Sundquist, James Lloyd *retired political scientist*

Sundquist, M. Alexandra (Alix Sundquist) *diplomat, consultant*

Surko, Stephen William *systems engineer*

Swetnam, Michael S. *think-tank executive*

Tafoya, Joe *school system administrator*

Thompson, Geraldine Kelleher Richter *retired orthopedist*

Thompson, Wayne Wray *historian*

Tichenor, Charles Beckham III *operations research analyst*

Timperlake, Edward Thomas *writer*

Tolchin, Susan Jane *political science professor, writer*

Tyrrell, Robert Emmett, Jr. *editor-in-chief, writer*

VandeHei, Jim W. (James W. VandeHei) *political executive editor*

Vaughn, Clyde A. *career military officer*

Vitz, Paul Clayton *psychologist, educator*

von Furstenberg, George Michael *economics professor, researcher*

Vuono, Carl E. *communications systems company executive, retired military officer*

Wahlquist, Andrew Folkman *government affairs executive*

Walcher, Greg E. *government agency administrator, small business owner*

Walker, Woodrow Wilson *retired lawyer, real estate investor, farmer*

Warshawsky, Mark Joel *human resources specialist, former federal agency administrator*

Watkins, Birge Swift *real estate investment executive*

Wheeler, Gerald F. *educational association administrator*

Whetsell, Paul W. *hotel executive*

Whitcomb, James Hall *geophysicist, foundation administrator*

Whitfield, Margaret Denny *retired music educator*

Whittier, Barbara J (Bobbie) *retired biology educator, retired chemistry educator*

Wilcox, Shirley Jean Langdon *genealogist*

Wilderotter, James Arthur *lawyer*

Witort, Janet Lee *lawyer*

Yates, Allison A. *medical association administrator*

Zorthian, Barry *communications executive*

Ashburn

Bawa, Raj *biotechnology educator, nanotechnologist*

Bennett, Lawrence Herman *physicist*

Boyne, Walter James *writer, retired museum director*

Gibbs, Joe (Joseph Jackson Gibbs) *professional football coach*

Gold, George Myron *lawyer, editor, writer, consultant*

Haymon, Chadron Zonelle *music educator, minister*

Hershey, Paul Christian *engineer*

Moss, Santana *professional football player*

Nickle, Dennis Edwin *electronics engineer, consultant, deacon*

Pavsek, Daniel Allan *banker, educator*

Portis, Clinton *professional football player*

Riddiford, Lynn Moorhead *biologist, educator*

Rubin, Gerald Mayer *biochemistry researcher, educator*

Sanfelici, Arthur H(ugo) *editor, writer*

Smoot, Fred *professional football player*

Snyder, Daniel *professional sports team and communications executive*

Ashland

Inge, Milton Thomas *American literature and culture educator, author*

Lindgren, Robert R. *academic administrator*

Axton

Bestler, J. Michael *columnist, retired surgeon*

Baskerville

Boyd, John W., Jr. *farmer, association executive*

Bassett

Spilman, Robert Henkel *furniture company executive*

Basye

Amolsch, Arthur Lewis *publishing executive*

Bedford

Brooks, Robin C. *food products executive*

Day, Mark Ronald *history educator, reenactor*

Ramsey, Forrest Gladstone, Jr. *retired engineering company executive*

Blacksburg

Agah, Masoud *electrical engineer, educator*

Aref, Hassan *fluid mechanics engineer, educator*

Arnold, Jesse Charles *retired statistician*

Asryan, Levon V. *physicist, electronics engineer, materials scientist*

Bailey, Annette F. *librarian*

Barksdale, Mary Alice *education educator*

Batra, Romesh Chander *engineering educator, researcher*

Beamer, Frank *college football coach*

Bliznakov, Milka Tcherneva *architect, educator*

Brown, Gary Sandy *electrical engineering educator*

Bryant, Clifton Dow *sociologist, educator*

Burkhart, Harold Eugene *forester, educator*

Campbell, Joan Virginia Loweke *secondary school and language educator*

Chatfield, Dean Charles *business professor*

Cowles, Joe Richard *biology professor*

Dautartas, Minodaugas (Mino) Fernand *physical chemist*

de Wolf, David Alter *physicist, educator*

Disney, Ralph L(ynde) *retired industrial engineering educator*

Doswald, Herman Kenneth *language educator, retired academic administrator*

Gablik, Suzi *art educator, writer*

Glasser, Wolfgang Gerhard *science researcher, educator*

Good, Irving John *statistician, educator, philosopher*

Gray, Festus Gail *electrical engineer, educator, researcher*

Graybeal, Jack Daniel *chemist, educator*

Grover, Norman LaMotte *theologian, philosopher*

Hanowski, Richard Joseph *transportation engineer, director*

Hirt, Joan B. *education educator*

Hitchingham, Eileen *librarian, dean*

Hovakimyan, Naira *mathematician, educator*

Jannuzi, F. Tomasson *economics professor*

Jensen, Walter Edward *retired lawyer, educator*

Kelly, James Michael *plant and soil scientist*

Lamb, Ashley Brooks *entomologist*

Lee, Fred C. *electrical engineering educator*

McCue, Leigh Shaw *aerospace engineer, educator*

McNamee, Mark *academic administrator*

Mitchell, James Kenneth *civil engineer, educator*

Mo, Luke Wei *physicist, researcher*

Moore, Laurence John *business educator*

Patterson, Douglas MacLennan *finance educator*

Perez, Miguel A. *industrial engineer, researcher*

Phadke, Arun G. *engineering educator*

Poole, Scott *architect, educator*

Posey, Eldon Eugene *mathematician, educator*

Price, Dennis Lee *industrial engineer, educator*

Randall, Clifford Wendell *civil engineer, educator*

Rodriguez-Camilloni, Humberto Leonardo *architect, historian, educator*

Salinas, Orlando Franco *physician*

Schetz, Joseph Alfred *aerospace engineer, educator*

Schmittmann, Beate *physics professor*

Squires, Arthur Morton *chemical engineer, educator*

Steger, Charles William *academic administrator*

Sukkariyah, Beshr *soil scientist*

Torgersen, Paul Ernest *academic administrator, educator*

Varadarajan, Srinidhi *computer scientist*

Weaver, Pamela Ann *education educator*

Blue Ridge

Elmore, Walter A. *electrical engineer, consultant*

Bluemont

Kobetz, Richard William *criminologist, consultant*

Boston

Fisher, John Morris *association official, business executive, educator*

Bristol

Creger, David Lee *financial planner, insurance executive*

Bristow

Schrock, Simon *retail executive*

Bumpass

Hoyt, John Arthur *cultural organization administrator, minister*

Burgess

Burch, Michael Ira *public relations executive, retired federal agency administrator*

Harris, Paul Lynwood *retired aerospace transportation executive*

Krebs, Rockne *artist*

Burke

Bishop, Alfred Chilton, Jr. *lawyer*

Hipfel, Steven J. *lawyer*

Lynch, Charles Theodore, Sr. *materials science engineering researcher, consultant, educator*

Shen, Weixing *meteorologist*

Woodruff, C(harles) Roy *retired professional association executive, consultant*

Catlett

Broderick, Anthony James *air transportation executive*

Centreville

De Gennaro, Eida Mendoza *interpreter, real estate agent*

Etters, Ronald Milton *retired lawyer, former government official*

Fells, Robert Marshall *lawyer*
Kendall, William Melvin *lawyer*
Malouff, Frank Joseph *health care association executive*

Chantilly
Austin, Wanda Murry *systems engineer*
Becker, James Richard *lawyer*
Carlson, Robert Charles *financial planner, writer*
Costello, Daniel Brian *lawyer, consultant*
DeLeon, Charles *lawyer*
Fitzgerald, Dennis D. *federal agency administrator*
Kerr, Donald MacLean, Jr. *federal agency administrator, physicist*
Sroka, John Walter *trade association executive*
Ward, George Truman *architect*

Charlottesville
Abbot, William Wright *history professor*
Abraham, Henry Julian *retired political science professor*
Abraham, Kenneth Samuel *law educator*
Adams, Reid *physician*
Andrews, Minerva Wilson *retired lawyer*
Andrews, William Lester Self *chemistry educator*
Arnold, Albert James *foreign language educator*
Aylor, James Hiram *engineering educator*
Balogun, Rasheed Abiodun *medical educator*
Battestin, Martin Carey *retired literature and language professor*
Bednar, Michael John *architecture educator*
Belanger, Terry *historian, educator*
Beller, George A. *cardiologist, educator*
Berger, Toby *electrical engineer, educator*
Biltonen, Rodney Lincoln *biochemistry and pharmacology educator*
Blankfein-Tabachnick, David H. *philosophy educator*
Bloomfield, Louis Aub *physicist, researcher*
Bonnie, Richard Jeffrey *lawyer, educator, consultant*
Brown, Holmes *public relations executive*
Bull, George Albert *retired banker*
Cantrell, Robert Wendell *otolaryngologist, head and neck surgeon, educator*
Carey, Robert Munson *physician, educator*
Carter, William Walton *physicist, researcher*
Casey, John Dudley *writer, language educator*
Casteen, John Thomas III *academic administrator*
Chandler, Lawrence Bradford, Jr. *lawyer*
Chapel, Robert Clyde *theater director, educator*
Cherry, Kenneth Jerome, Jr. *surgeon*
Chevalier, Roger Alan *astronomy educator, consultant*
Click, Patricia C. *historian, educator*
Cornell, Dewey Gene *psychologist*
Crackel, Theodore Joseph *historian*
Crutchfield, William Gayle, Jr. *retail executive*
Davidson, Hugh MacCullough *French language and literature educator*
Davis, Edward Wilson *business administration educator*
DeMong, Richard Francis *finance and investments educator*
Dooley, Michael P. *law educator*
Dorning, John Joseph *nuclear engineering, physics, and applied mathematics educator*
Dotson, Donald L. *lawyer*
Dove, Rita Frances *poet, language educator*
Ellett, John Spears, II, *retired taxation educator, accountant, lawyer*
Elzinga, Kenneth Gerald *economics professor*
Epstein, Robert Marvin *anesthesiologist, educator*
Fink, Lester Harold *retired engineering company executive, educator*
Finley, Robert Van Eaton *minister*
Fitchett, Taylor *law librarian*
Flickinger, Charles John *anatomist, educator*
Forbes, John Douglas *architectural and economic historian*
Forrest, Patricia Anne *publishing executive, editor*
Fox, Charles Dunsmore, IV, *lawyer*
Fraser, Cassandra Lynne *chemist, educator*
Fredrick, Laurence William *astronomer, educator*
Gaden, Elmer Lewis *retired engineering educator*
Garber, Nicholas Jack *civil engineer, educator*
Garrett, George Palmer, Jr. *language educator, writer*
Garrett, Reginald Hooker *biology professor, researcher*
Garson, Arthur, Jr. *dean, medical educator*
Gaskin, Felicia *biochemist, educator*
Goetz, Charles John *law and economics educator*
Good, Richard Standish *geologist*
Graebner, Norman Arthur *historian, educator*
Grimes, Russell Newell *inorganic chemist, educator*
Grosh, William W. *internist*
Guerrant, Richard Littleton *medical educator*
Gunter, Bradley Hunt *capital management executive*
Haj-Hariri, Hossein *engineering educator, department chairman*
Handler, Jerome Sidney *anthropology educator*
Hanft, Ruth S. Samuels *economist, consultant*
Harris, Robert Shields *finance educator*
Harrison, John Collier *law educator*
Hecht, Sidney Michael *chemistry professor*
Henderson, Stanley Dale *lawyer, educator, arbitrator*
Henry, Laurin Luther *public affairs educator*
Hine, Jonathan Trumbull, Jr. *translator, educator*
Hirsch, Eric Donald, Jr. *language educator*
Hochberg, Bayard Zabdial *retired lawyer*
Hodous, Robert Power *lawyer*
Hoel, Lester A. *civil engineering educator, department chairman*
Hoffman, Paul Stokes *microbiologist, researcher*
Horgan, Cornelius Oliver *applied mathematics and mechanics professor, engineering educator*
Hornberger, George Milton *environmental science educator*
Howard, Arthur Ellsworth Dick *law educator*
Howell, Robert Edward *hospital administrator*
Hudson, John Lester *chemical engineering professor*
Humphreys, Paul William *philosophy educator, consultant*
Hunt, Donald Frederick *chemistry professor*
Hunt, William B. *pulmonologist*
Hurd, Nicole Farmer *director*
Hymes, Dell Hathaway *anthropologist, educator*
Inigo, Rafael Madrigal *retired electrical engineering educator*
Jeffries, John Calvin, Jr. *dean, law educator*
Jevtovic-Todorovic, Vesna *physician, researcher*
Johnson, Deborah G. *philosopher, educator*
Johnson, Richard Marc *civics educator*
Johnston, Margaret Schuster *volunteer, retired language educator*
Jolly, Bruce Dwight *manufacturing executive*
Jones, Rayford Scott *surgeon, educator*
Jordan, Daniel Porter, Jr. *foundation administrator, historian, educator*
Kaiserlian, Penelope Jane *publishing executive*
Kalantarinia, Kambiz *medical educator*
Kassell, Neal Frederic *neurosurgery educator*
Kattwinkel, John *pediatrician, educator*
Keats, Theodore Eliot *radiologist, educator*
Keen, Rachel *psychology professor*
Kelly, Thaddeus Elliott *medical geneticist*
Kennedy, Cornelius Bryant *retired lawyer*
Kensington, Andrew Justus *litigation specialist*
Kitch, Edmund Wells *law educator*
Kraehe, Enno Edward *history professor*
Krzysztofowicz, Roman *systems engineering and statistical science educator, consultant*
Kudravetz, David Waller *lawyer*
Landess, Fred Stone *retired lawyer*
Lane, Ann Judith *history and women's studies educator, director*
Lane, Mark *lawyer, educator, writer*
Langbaum, Robert Woodrow *language educator*
Laurencin, Cato Thomas *biomedical engineer, orthopaedic surgeon*
Laws, Edward Raymond, Jr. *neurological surgery educator*
Leffler, Melvyn P. *history professor*
Levenson, Jacob Clavner *language educator*
Lin, Kant *plastic surgeon, educator*
Linden, Peppy G. *museum director*
Little, Wm. A. (William Alfred Little) *language educator, researcher, musicologist*
Lo, Kwok-Yung *astronomer, educator, researcher, administrator*
Long, Charles Farrell *insurance company executive*
MacDonald, Timothy Lee *chemistry professor*
Marshall, James Arthur *chemistry professor*
Marshall, John Crook *internal medicine educator, researcher*
Martin, David Alan *law educator*
McCrimmon, Barbara Smith *writer, librarian*
McDonough, William Andrews *architect, former dean*
McGann, Jerome John *language educator*
Meador, Daniel John *law educator*
Megill, Allan *historian*
Menaker, Michael *biology professor*
Menefee, Samuel Pyeatt *lawyer, academic*
Middleditch, Leigh Benjamin, Jr. *lawyer, educator*
Midelfort, Hans Christian Erik *history professor*
Mikalson, Jon Dennis *classics educator*
Minehart, Jean Besse *retired tax accountant*
Molhoek, Kerrington Ramsey *research scientist*
Monahan, John T. *law educator, psychologist*
Moore, John Norton *lawyer, educator, diplomat*
Moreno, Jonathan *bioethicist*
Morgan, Raymond F. *plastic surgeon*
Muller, William Henry, Jr. *retired surgeon, educator*
Nelson, Caleb Edward *law educator*
Nelson, Raymond John *language educator, dean*
Newsom, David Dunlop *ambassador, educator*
Nohrnberg, James Carson *language educator*
Nolan, Stanton Peelle *surgeon, educator*
O'Brien, David Michael *law educator*
O'Connell, Jeffrey *law educator*
Owen, John Atkinson, Jr. *internist, educator*
Parrish, David Walker, Jr. *legal publishing company executive*
Parshall, Karen Virginia Hunger *mathematician*
Pate, Robert Hewitt, Jr. *counselor educator*
Perkowski, Jan Louis *language, literature and folklore educator*
Pertzoff, Margaret Henderson *history professor*
Peterson, Kent Wright *physician*
Peterson, Merrill Daniel *historian, educator*
Peura, David *medical educator*
Pierce, Shayn *biomedical engineer, educator*
Platts-Mills, Thomas Alexander E. *immunologist, educator, researcher*
Plog, Stephen E. *anthropologist, educator*
Powers, Robert David *physician*
Quandt, William Bauer *political scientist*
Rehm, Patrice Koch *radiologist, educator*
Reppucci, Nicholas Dickon *psychologist, educator*
Reynolds, Albert Barnett *nuclear engineer, educator*
Reynolds, Robert Edgar *academic administrator*
Rhoads, Steven Eric *political science professor*
Rich, Tyvin Andrew *radiation therapist*
Riley, Margaret Foster (Mimi) *law educator*
Rini, Joel *language educator, linguist*
Robinson, Mildred Wigfall *law educator*
Root, James Benjamin *landscape architect*
Roseberry, Edwin Southall *retired state agency administrator*
Ross, Walter Beghtol *music educator, composer*
Rowlingson, John Clyde *anesthesiologist, physician, educator*
Rubin, David Lee *humanities educator, critic, editor*
Ryan, Debbie (Deborah A. Ryan) *women's college basketball coach*
Sabato, Larry Joseph *political science professor, director*
Sahr, Morris Gallup *financial planner*
Sanders, Robert Hawver *systems administrator*
Sarazin, Craig Leigh *astronomer*
Scheld, William Michael *internist, educator*
Schneider, Edward Martin *retired internist, medical educator*
Schuker, Stephen Alan *historian, educator*
Scott, Nathan Alexander, Jr. *minister, educator, critic*
Sedgwick, Alexander *retired historian, educator*
Seidelmann, Paul Kenneth *astronomer, educator*
Setear, John K. *law educator*
Shaw, Donald Leslie *Spanish language educator*
Sheehan, Jason *neurosurgeon*
Shenkir, William Gary *business educator*
Sihler, William Wooding *finance educator*
Skrutskie, Michael F. *science educator*
Slaughter, Edward Ratliff, Jr. *lawyer*
Smith, Clyde Ray *dean*
Spearing, Anthony Colin *English literature educator*
Stocker, Arthur Frederick *classics educator*
Stroud, Robert Edward *lawyer*
Sundberg, Richard Jay *chemistry professor*
Sykes, Gresham M'Cready *sociologist, educator, artist*
Theodoridis, George Constantin *biomedical engineering educator, researcher*
Thomas, Lawrence Eldon *mathematics professor*
Thorner, Michael Oliver *medical educator*
Thornhill, Arthur H., Jr. *retired publishing executive*
Townsend, Miles Averill *aerospace and mechanical engineering educator*
Turner, Robert Foster *law educator, writer*
Tuttle, Jeremy Ballou *neuroscientist*
Vaidhyanathan, Siva *journalist, educator*
Vanden Bout, Paul Adrian *astronomer, physicist, educator*
Wadlington, Walter James *law educator*
Wagner, Roy *anthropology educator, researcher*
Wagoner, Jennings Lee, Jr. *historian, educator*
Warren, Russ C. *artist, educator*
Weary, Peyton Edwin *retired medical educator*
Weber, Hans Jürgen *physics professor*
Weinberger, Adrienne *artist, art appraiser*
Wenger, Larry Bruce *law librarian, educator*
Whitaker, John King *retired economics professor*
White, George Edward *lawyer, educator*
Whitehead, John Wayne *lawyer, educator, writer*
Wiggins, Barbara Sue *pharmacist, educator*
Wilkinson, J(ames) Harvie III *federal judge*
Winston, David Charles *pathologist*
Wittenborg, Karin *university librarian*
Wolcott, John Winthrop III *retired manufacturing executive*
Wright, Charles Penzel, Jr. *writer, educator*
Wulf, William Allan *foundation administrator, information scientist, educator*
Yates, John Thomas, Jr. *chemistry professor, research scientist*
Zelikow, Philip David *public policy educator, former federal official*
Zunz, Olivier Jean *history professor*

Charlottesvle
Goodrich, George Herbert *retired judge*

Chase City
Caknipe, Christopher Howard *environmental health specialist*

Chesapeake
Bockwoldt, Todd Shane *nuclear engineer*
Brock, Macon F., Sr. *retail company executive*
Brock, Macon F., Jr. *retail company executive*
Gorry, James A. III *lawyer*
Hudgins, Paul Granville *health facility administrator*
Jackson, Cynthia Ann *medical association administrator, health consultant*
Locke, L. Muriel *mathematician, educator*
Myrick, Bismarck *diplomat, history professor*
Notti, Donna Betts *special education educator*
Owens, Susan Elizabeth *realtor*
Sari, Dana *psychologist*
Sasser, Robert *retail executive*
Stillman, Margaret (Peggy Stillman) *library director*
Webb, Julia Jones *elementary school educator, minister*

Chester
Connelly, Colin Charles *lawyer*
Gray, Charles Robert *lawyer*
Gray, Frederick Thomas, Jr., (Rick Gray) *journalist, actor, educator*
Law, Thomas Melvin *academic administrator*
Roane, David James, Jr. *information technology auditor*
Walton, G. Clifford *physician*

Chesterfield
Congdon, John Rhodes *transportation executive*
Davis, Bonnie Christell *judge*
Garnett, Douglas Acree *financial analyst, researcher*
Love, Dana Francis Ignatius *telecommunications industry executive*
Tate, Wendy K. *insurance company executive, risk management consultant*
Young, Kenneth Wayne *environmental health specialist*

Christiansburg
Blanchard, Dorothy Hardt *academic administrator, volunteer*
Hawley, Rollin James *neurologist*

Clifton
Hennesy, Gerald Craft *artist*
Hoffman, Karla Leigh *mathematician, educator*

Clifton Forge
Miller, Catherine H. *nursing administrator, property manager*

Cobbs Creek
Crum, John Kistler *management consultant*

Coeburn
Hopkins, Alisa Dawn *small business owner*

Colonial Heights
Grizzard-Barham, Barbara Lee *artist*
Morgan, Barbara M. *psychotherapist, educator*

Courtland
Minor, Edward Colquitt *paper company executive, lawyer*

Covesville
Williams, Patricia Anne *philosopher, writer*

Covington
Rohr, Dwight Mason *news director, radio marketing consultant*
Stephenson, Roscoe Bolar, Jr. *state supreme court justice*

Crozet
Detmer, Don Eugene *health informatics, management and policy researcher*
Reswick, James Bigelow *former government official, biomedical engineer*

Culpeper
Bahl-Moore, Elizabeth Ann *artist, educator*
Dulaney, Richard Alvin *lawyer*

Dahlgren
Bressler, Barry Lee *physicist, systems analyst*

Dale City
Baxter, Ruth Howell *educational administrator, psychologist*

Daleville
Butler, Manley Caldwell *retired lawyer*

Danville
Aaron, Larry Gene *secondary school educator, writer, minister*
Abreu, Luis Alberto *lawyer*
Hayes, Jack Irby *historian, educator*
Kiser, Jackson L. *federal judge*
Lea, Robert Lee III *social sciences educator*
Pfau, Richard Anthony *university president*
Regan, Michael Patrick *lawyer*
Talbott, Frank III *lawyer*

Deltaville
Koedel, John Gilbert, Jr. *retired metal products executive*

Drakes Branch
Locke, Thomas Edward, Jr. *retired industrial engineer*

Dublin
Billaud, Louise Ann *musician, educator*
Douthat, Rebecca Arlene *retired secondary school educator*
Linzey, Juanita Bird *biology professor*

Dulles
Balis, Janet *Internet company executive*
Desmond, Ned *editor, writer*
Dodson, Carl Edward *nuclear engineer, real estate agent, minister, assistant superintendent*
Elias, Antonio L. *aerospace transportation executive*
Falco, Randy (Randel A.) *Internet company executive, former broadcast executive*
Glacel, Robert Allan *retired military career officer*
Grant, Ronald E. *Internet company executive*
Jacobs, Janice Lee *ambassador*
Kumar, Nisha *Internet company executive*
McKinley, John *information technology executive*
Parker, Ira H. *Internet company executive, lawyer*
Perry, June Carter *ambassador*
Skodon, Emil Mark *ambassador*
Wood, William Braucher *ambassador*

Dumfries
Avrit, Richard Calvin *defense consultant, career officer*
Locigno, Paul Robert *public relations executive*

Dutton
Washburn, John Rosser *entrepreneur*

Earlysville
Bartoes, Richard Alan *agricultural products executive*
Brownell, Blaine Allison *educational association and academic administrator, history professor*

Eastville
Williams, Ida Jones *consumer and home economics educator, writer*

Edinburg
Rhodes, Stephen Michael *poultry company executive*
Trindal, Wesley Steele *mechanical engineer*

Emory
Jones, Jerry Lee *computer educator*

Fairfax
Aharonov, Yakir *physicist, researcher*
Anderson, David Lawrence *lawyer*
Arnold, William McCauley *lawyer*
Arntson, Peter Andrew *lawyer*
Baghi, Heibatollah *medical educator*
Baird, Charles Bruce *lawyer, consultant*
Baker, Daniel Richard *computer company executive*
Barth, Michael Carl *economist*
Bennett, James Thomas *economics professor*

Bobzien, David P. *lawyer*
Bohan, Gloria *travel company executive*
Boone, James Virgil *retired engineering executive, researcher*
Buchanan, James McGill *economist, educator*
Chalasani, Venkat *management consultant*
Chen, Chun-Hung *engineering educator*
Clay, Edwin S. III *library director*
Codding, Frederick Hayden *lawyer*
Colvin, Donald Bernard *surgeon*
Cook, Gerald *electrical engineering educator*
Cosing, Arthur Paul, Jr. *writer, artist*
Cowen, Tyler *economics professor*
Dennis, Rutledge M. *sociologist, educator*
Dowlut, Robert *lawyer*
Downey, Richard Lawrence *lawyer*
Edelman, Ric *investment advisor*
Fagan, John Ernest *lawyer*
Felsburg, David F. *engineering executive, educator*
Fitzgerald, Helen Teresa *social worker, writer*
Folk, Thomas Robert *lawyer*
Foster, (Paul) Wesley, Jr. *real estate broker*
Fox, Donna M. *dean, biology professor*
Gertler, Janos John *electrical engineer, educator*
Hackleman, Kelly Ker *music educator*
Hale, Thomas Morgan *professional services executive*
Harrison, Robert Allen *retired operations research analyst*
Haskett, Dianne Louise *retired mayor, lawyer, consultant*
Hollans, Irby Noah, Jr. *retired trade association administrator*
Hopson, Everett George *retired lawyer*
Horton, Lois Elaine *history professor*
Houck, Mark Hedrich *engineering educator*
Hussam, Abul *chemistry professor*
Jones, George Fleming *international consultant*
Kash, Don Eldon *political science professor*
Keith, John A(ugustine) C(hilton) *lawyer*
Kendall Hull, Margarida *art educator, painter*
Kettlewell, Gail Biery *academic administrator, research professor*
Kieffer, Jarold Alan *publishing executive, writer*
King, James Cecil *retired language and literature educator, medievalist*
Knee, Ruth Irelan *social worker, health care consultant*
Ko, Jang Wan *research scientist, educator*
LaPierre, Wayne R., Jr. *lobbyist*
Larranaga, Jim *men's college basketball coach*
Lavine, Thelma Zeno *philosophy educator*
Lillard, Mark Hill III *engineering consultant, retired military officer*
Lomax, Michael Lucius *non-profit association administrator*
Longin, Thomas Charles *retired academic administrator*
Mackall, Henry Clinton *lawyer*
Mann, Laura Ann *soprano*
McAllister, William Howard III *newspaper reporter, columnist, public affairs consultant*
McGavin, John David *lawyer*
Meamber, Laurie Ann *marketing educator*
Merten, Alan Gilbert *academic administrator*
Miller, Emilie F. *former state senator, consultant*
Miller, Patricia A. *music educator, opera and concert artist*
Morowitz, Harold Joseph *biophysicist, educator*
Morrison, Ann M. *not-for-profit fundraiser*
Mulvaney, Mary Frederica *systems analyst*
Nicogossian, Anrauld E.T. *education educator*
Palmer, James Daniel *information technology educator*
Pfiffner, James Price *political science professor*
Pruitt, Dean Garner *psychologist, educator*
Pugh, Arthur James (Jay Pugh) *retired retail executive*
Raizer, Victor *physicist, researcher*
Rieger, Michael Ira *lawyer*
Roberts, Cecil Edward, Jr. *labor union administrator*
Robinson, Kayne B. *lobbyist, former political organization officer*
Rosenkranz, Robert Bernard *military officer*
Rust, John Howson, Jr. *lawyer, state legislator*
Sage, Andrew Patrick *systems engineering and management educator*
Sanderson, Douglas Jay *lawyer*
Schulman, Joseph Daniel *physician, health facility administrator, medical geneticist, educator*
Selk, Stephen Jeffrey *chemical engineer*
Siddons, Joy Garbee *music educator*
Silcox, Gordon Bruce *executive coach*
Simpson, Carter B. *lawyer*
Sklarow, Mark Howard *educational association administrator*
Smith, Vernon Lomax *economist, researcher*
Stage, Thomas Benton *psychiatrist*
Stearns, Peter Nathaniel *history professor, academic administrator*
Steele, Howard Loucks *economic development consultant, author*
Steger, Edward Herman *retired chemist*
Stitt, David Tillman *judge*
Sun, Donglian *meteorologist*
Susko, Carol Lynne *lawyer, accountant, educator*
Travis, Toni-Michelle C. *political scientist, educator*
Umbel, Tammie *cosmetics executive*
Villarreal, Carlos Castañeda *engineering executive*
Wagner, Richard E. *economist, educator*
Williams, Marcus Doyle *judge*
Witek, James Eugene *retired public relations executive*
Zhou, Qiuping *nursing educator, director*

Fairfax Station
Barringer, Joan Marie *counselor, educator, artist, writer*
Carver, George Allen, Jr. *retired lawyer*
Duff, William Grierson *electrical engineer, educator*
Kaminski, Paul Garrett *former federal agency administrator, investment banker*
Randell, Cortes W. *news service executive*
Szczublewski, Wendy Sue *small business owner, musician, freelance/self-employed writer*

Falls Church
Akkara, Joseph Augustine *chemist, educator*
Aukofer, Frank Alexander *journalist*
Barkley, Paul Haley, Jr. *architect*
Benton, Nicholas Frederick *publisher*
Bingman, Charles Franklin *government executive, educator*
Boehm, Kenneth *legal association administrator*
Brady, Rupert Joseph *retired lawyer*
Bruck, Bill *educational association administrator*
Burroughs, Benton, Jr. *lawyer*
Calkins, Susannah Eby *retired economist*
Cazan, Sylvia Marie Buday (Mrs. Matthew John Cazan) *retired real estate company executive*
Chabraja, Nicholas D. *equipment manufacturing executive, lawyer*
Christman, Bruce Lee *lawyer*
Clizbe, John Anthony *psychologist, social services administrator*
Courtney, William Harrison *security firm executive*
Cromley, Allan Wray *retired journalist*
Dao, Thuy Dinh *personal care industry executive*
DeMuro, Gerard J *information technology executive*
Dewey-Balzhiser, Anne Elizabeth Marie *lawyer*
Diamond, Robert Michael *lawyer*
Elliott, Virginia F. Harrison *retired anatomist, publisher, educator, investment advisor, kinesiologist, philanthropist*
Evans, Peter Yoshio *ophthalmologist, educator*
Fink, Charles Augustin *behavioral systems scientist*
Flaherty, Peter *legal association administrator*
Golden, Wilson *lawyer*
Gosnell, Nanci Little *information technology executive, nurse*
Graif, Joseph Nicholas *musician*
Gray, D'Wayne *retired marine corps officer*
Green, James Wyche *sociologist, anthropologist, consultant, psychotherapist*
Hall, Charles M. *manufacturing executive*
Hammerman, Herbert *retired economist*
Hardin, Mark A. *legal association administrator*
Hart, C(harles) W(illard), Jr. *zoologist, curator*
Hibbs, Ernest G. *computer scientist, engineering executive*
Honigberg, Carol Crossman *lawyer*
Johnson, William David *retired academic administrator*
Jones, Linda R. Wolf *consulting company executive*
Jones, Russel Cameron *civil engineer, educator*
Kaplow, Herbert Elias *journalist*
Klingman, Charles David *health services researcher*
Klopfenstein, Rex Carter *electrical engineer*
Kurtzke, John Francis, Sr. *neurologist, epidemiologist*
Lanese, Herbert J. *multi-industry executive*
Lefrak, Edward Arthur *cardiovascular and thoracic surgeon*
Lorenzo, Michael *engineer, real estate broker, government official*
Luchini, Joseph S. *lawyer*
May, Carol Lee *mechanical engineer*
McCue, David J. *information systems specialist, entrepreneur*
McGinly, William C. *healthcare association executive*
Meserve, Richard Andrew *lawyer, administrator*
Michelsen, Cleo *retired education educator, writer*
Middleton, J. Howard, Jr. *lawyer*
Morrison, H. Robert *small business owner, photographer, retired municipal official*
Mukherjee, Dipankar *surgeon*
Nason, Charles Tuckey *retired diversified financial services company executive*
Nathan, Steven D. *pulmonologist*
Oliver, Walter M. *human resources specialist*
Orben, Robert *scriptwriter, writer*
Perkins, Jack Edwin *lawyer*
Pischke, Vail W. *lawyer, judge*
Poza, Hugo Bernardo *aerospace company executive*
Redd, L. Hugh *manufacturing executive*
Rodgers, Kirk Procter *international environmental consultant*
Rooney, Kevin Davitt *federal agency administrator*
Rosenberg, Theodore Roy *finance company executive*
Rostker, Bernard *civilian military employee*
Roussel, Lee Dennison *economist*
Savner, David A. *lawyer*
Schoonover, Stanley R. *music educator, consultant*
Scott, Hugh Patrick *former surgeon, military officer, medical advisor*
Shipko, Janet M. *program director*
Sveinsson, Linda Rodgers *engineering company executive*
Tether, Anthony John *aerospace executive*
Thomas, William Griffith *lawyer*
Van Cleve, Ruth Gill *retired lawyer*
Ward, George Frank, Jr. *international programs executive, ambassador*
Ward, Joe Henry, Jr. *retired lawyer*
Waxman, Bruce I. *lawyer*
Weiss, Armand Berl *economist, association management executive*
Whitehead, Kenneth Dean *writer, translator, retired federal agency administrator*
Wood, John Martin *lawyer*
Yoshimura, Yoshiko *librarian*

Farmville
Dorrill, William Franklin *political scientist, educator*
Lu, Lucia Y. *education educator*
Terry, Wayne Gilbert *healthcare educator, hospital administrator*

Flint Hill
Dietel, William Moore *former foundation executive*
Williamson, Richard Hall *federal agency administrator*

Forest
Ehrhorn, Richard William *electronics executive*

Fort Belvoir
Anderson, Frank J., Jr. *retired career officer*
Crenshaw, Horace, Jr. *military officer*
Harms, John Kevin *lawyer*
Kiechel, Walter, Jr. *lawyer*
O'Kane, Barbara Lynn *research psychologist*
Parrish-St. John, Florence Tucker *writer, retired federal agency administrator*
Tegnelia, James A. *federal agency administrator*
Thompson, Carlynn Jean *information scientist*
Wooten, Michael Eric *academic administrator*

Fort Lee
Chumley, Perry Ray *veterinarian, military officer*
Leppo, Lisa Marie *forensic anthropologist*
Sterling, Keir Brooks *historian, educator*

Franklin
Watkins, Thomas Linnane *lawyer*

Franktown
Kellam, Caramine *volunteer*

Fredericksburg
Arnn, Nancy Shank *secondary school educator*
Billingsley, Robert Thaine *lawyer*
Braxton, Herman Harrison, Jr. *lawyer*
Dorman, John Frederick *genealogist*
Edmunds, Jeffrey Garth *librarian*
Eslinger-Brown, Vanessa Pauline *humanities educator*
Gill, Milvi Kosenkranius *artist, photographer*
Hajek, Otomar *mathematician, educator*
Hasenfus, Harold Joseph *retired mechanical engineer, naval technical director*
Jones, Harry Edward *diplomat, writer*
Kusserow, Richard Phillip *federal agency administrator, corporate financial executive*
McCrary, Lisa Hooper *secondary school educator*
McGhee, Jay D. *ecologist, educator*
McWilliams, Dallas *technical educator*
Medding, Walter Sherman *retired environmental engineer*
Mellinger, Keith E. *mathematician, educator*
Mezo, Richard Eugene *literature and language professor, writer*
Rampersad, Peggy A. Snellings *sociologist, consultant*
Schmutzhart, Berthold Josef *sculptor, educator*
Sisk, Fred Dean *retired cartographer*
Somma, Thomas P. *art historian, museum director*

Front Royal
Andes, Larry Dale *minister*
Bonzagni, Vincent Francis *lawyer*
Stevens, Loretta Marie *special education educator*

Gainesville
Ferrara, Peter Joseph *federal official, lawyer, author, educator*
French, Dorothy Marie *music educator*
Lee, Won Jay *radiologist*
Levell, Edward, Jr. *retired airport director, aviation consultant*
Lukowsky, Gerhard Hans *internist*
Tuck, Russell R., Jr. *college president emeritus*

Galax
Dunson, William Albert *biology professor, ecological consultant*

Garrisonville
Emely, Charles Harry *trade association executive, consultant*

Glen Allen
Anderson, James Frederick *clergyman*
Batzli, Terrence Raymond *lawyer*
Cornwell, Patricia Daniels *writer*
den Hartog, Grace Robinson *lawyer*
Gulling, Mark V. *consumer products company executive*
Harter, John J. *economic analyst*
Kirshner, Alan I. *insurance company executive*
Levit, Jay J(oseph) *lawyer*
Rajkowski, E. Mark *corporate financial executive*
Rogal, Andrew L. *insurance company executive*
Weaver, Mollie Little *lawyer*

Gloucester
Hicks, C. Flippo *lawyer*

Gloucester Point
Bush, Elizabeth Olney *marine lab technician*

Goochland
Parsons, Donna Lynn *artist*

Gordonsville
Wells, Mary Elizabeth Thompson *deacon, chaplain, spiritual director, iconographer*

Great Falls
Andrews, Betty Bauserman *retired secondary school educator, real estate manager*
Bachner, John Philip *business consultant*
Cass, Ronald Andrew *lawyer, former dean*
Castro-Klaren, Sara *Latin American literature professor*
Cowhill, William Joseph *retired naval officer, consultant*
DiBona, Charles Joseph *retired trade association administrator*
Drummond, Alexander R. *priest*
Garrett, Wilbur (Bill) *magazine editor*
Minikes, Stephan Michael *ambassador, lawyer, banker*
Mitchell, Roy Shaw *lawyer*
Neidich, George Arthur *lawyer*
Preston, Charles George *lawyer*
Shay-Byrne, Olivia *lawyer*
Turner, Stansfield *former CIA director, retired military officer*

Greenbackville
Lewis, Kay *interior designer, consultant*

Greenville
Todd, John Edward *retired farmer*

Grundy
McGlothlin, Michael Gordon *lawyer*
Shinn, Clinton Wesley *lawyer*

Gum Spring
Dilworth, Robert Lexow *career military officer, educator*

Hampden Sydney
Arieti, James Alexander *classics educator, writer*
Bortz, Walter M. III *academic administrator*
Porterfield, William Wendell *chemist, educator*
Wilson, Samuel V. *academic administrator*

Hampton
Abner, Harold Loyd *military officer, consultant*
Barrow, Irene Marie *speech pathology educator*
Bartels, Robert Edwin *aerospace engineer*
Bell, Gladys Smiley *university librarian*
Brauer, Harrol Andrew, Jr. *broadcast executive*
DeCuir, Bryan Jude *automotive technician, computer engineer*
Divers, Kevin Samuel *aerospace physiologist*
Enriquez, Manuel Hipolito *physician*
Goode, Constance Loper *elementary school principal*
Harris, Carl G. *music educator*
Harvey, William Robert *university president*
Holmes, Leonard George *psychologist*
Johnson, Leona Melissa *psychology professor, researcher*
Joshi, Suresh Meghashyam *engineer, researcher*
Lawson, Donna Yvette *special education educator*
McAdaragh, Raymon Michael *aerospace engineer, researcher*
Nazaryan, Hovakim *mathematician, researcher, atmospheric scientist*
Nazaryan, Vahagn *physics researcher, consultant*
Refaat, Tamer F. *electrical engineer, researcher*
Roe, Lesa B. *federal agency administrator*
Smith, Stephen Mark *lawyer*
Sobieski, Jaroslaw *aerospace engineer*
Sun, Rensheng *electrical engineer, educator*
Sypolt, Shirley Rae *elementary school educator*
Thengumthara, Kunhikrishnan *meteorologist*
Tripathi, Ram Kishore *physicist, researcher*
Verma, Arun K. *mathematician, educator*
Walsh, Brian M. *physicist*
Yamakov, Vesselin Ivanov *aerospace scientist, researcher*

Hardyville
White, Gordon Eliot *historian, writer*

Harrisonburg
Baker, George Harold III *physicist, educator*
Carrier, Ronald Edwin *academic administrator, director*
Choi, In Dal *music educator*
Frazier, Chapman Hood *literature and language professor*
Fritz, Diane P. *controller*
Gill, Gerald Lawson *librarian*
Grayson, Joann Hess *psychology professor*
Harper, Steven R. *finance educator*
Pappas, Eric Charles *director*
Ramsey, Jackson Eugene *management educator*
Wallinger, M(elvin) Bruce *lawyer*

Hartfield
Johnson, Carl Randolph *chemist, educator*

Hayes
Casson, Richard Frederick *lawyer, hotel executive*
Phillips, Elizabeth Jason *lawyer, state agency administrator*

Haymarket
Crafton-Masterson, Adrienne *real estate company executive*
Doolittle, Warren T. *retired federal official*
Frank, Jacob *lawyer*
Katz, Alan Charles *toxicologist*
Seely, James Michael *retired military officer, defense consultant, small business owner*

Heathsville
McKerns, Charles Joseph *lawyer*
Winkel, Raymond Norman *aerospace scientist, consultant, retired military officer*

Herndon
Bridges, Roy Dubard, Jr. *former federal agency administrator*
Burns, Patrick Owen *venture capital company executive*
Draper, William David *systems engineer*
Economon, Paul David *lawyer, management consultant*
Gilbert, Douglas Brainerd *telecommunications industry executive*
Golden, John Joseph, Jr. *information technology executive*

Hermansen, John Christian *application developer, linguist, consultant*
Hollis, Katherine Mary *information scientist, consultant*
Huntoon, Nancy *security manager*
Jones, Reba (Becki) Pestun *elementary school and music educator*
Nolan, Leslie Marian *artist*
Roof, Joseph A. *educational association administrator*
Simanski, Claire Dvorak *art educator*

Independence
Craig, James Hicklin *fine arts consultant*

Irvington
Ritchie, George G., Jr. *retired psychiatrist*

Isle Of Wight
Huber, Janet Barlow *librarian*

Ivy
Lord, Richard Dennis *photographer*
Ubben, Donald Thomas *lawyer*
Wilcox, Harvey John *lawyer*

Jamestown
Kelso, William M. *archaeologist*

Jeffersonton
Armor, David J. *sociologist*

Keswick
Hawkins, Edward J. *retired lawyer*
IRafajko, Robert Richard *science administrator*
Pochick, Francis Edward *financial consultant*
Rowe, William Joseph *internist*
Woods, Reginald Foster *management consulting executive*

Kilmarnock
Ibañez, Alvaro *museum director, patent design company executive, artist*

King George
Agnew, Christopher Mack *minister, historian*
Newhall, David III *retired federal official*
Revercomb, Horace Austin III *judge*

Lake Ridge
Ingrassia, Anthony Frank *human resource specialist*
Stottlemyer, David Lee *federal official*

Langley Afb
Blalock, Thomas Sullivan, Jr. *military officer*
Corley, John D. W. *career military officer*
Smail, Leslie Anne *librarian*

Lansdowne
Colson, Charles Wendell *lay minister, writer*
Miller, Dorothy Anne Smith *retired cytogenetics educator*
Quinn, Matthew J. *educational association administrator*

Leesburg
Beach, Barbara Purse *lawyer*
Brown, James Robert *retired air force officer*
Budiansky, Stephen Philip *writer*
De Barbieri, Mary Ann *not-for-profit management consultant*
Ink, Dwight A. *government agency administrator*
Kushner, Gordon Peter *lawyer*
Levin, Mark Reed *radio personality, legal foundation administrator*
Lobanov-Rostovsky, Oleg *management consultant*
Mahood, Ken *music educator*
Petranek, Stephen Lynn *editor*

Leon
Han, Nong *artist, sculptor, painter*

Lexington
Barrett, John Gilchrist *retired historian*
Beckley, Harlan R. *religious studies educator*
Cline, Philip Lee *business and economics educator*
DeVogt, John Frederick *management science and business ethics educator, consultant*
Elmes, David Gordon *psychologist, educator*
Gaines, James Edwin, Jr. *retired librarian*
Jarrard, Leonard Everett *psychologist, educator*
John, Lewis George *political science educator*
Kirgis, Frederic Lee *law educator*
Koeniger, Alfred Cash *history professor*
Koons, Kenneth Edward *historian, educator, historian, consultant*
Krantz, Linda Law *librarian*
Kricorian, Mary Jo Geyer *biology instructor, environmental scientist, consultant*
Leach, Maurice Derby, Jr. *librarian, educator*
Luecke, Pamela *editor, educator*
McGuire, Katherine Ann *academic administrator, voice educator*
Peay, J.H. Binford III *academic administrator, career military officer*
Phillips, Charles Franklin, Jr. *retired economist*
Ruscio, Kenneth Patrick *academic administrator, political science professor*
Ryan, Halford Ross *speech educator*
Solod, Lisa *writer*
Spencer, Edgar Winston *geology educator*
Stephens, Laurence David, Jr. *linguist, investor, oil industry executive*
Stuart, Dabney *poet, language educator*
Taylor, Wesley Bayard, Jr. *retired army officer*
Tierney, Michael John *mathematics professor*
Wiant, Sarah Kirsten *law librarian, educator, director*
Williams, H. Thomas (Tom Williams) *academic administrator, physicist, educator*
Winfrey, John Crawford *economist, educator*

Linden
Martin, Joseph Bryan *application developer*

Locust Grove
Cordray-Van de Castle, Karen *elementary school educator*
Gulya, Aina Julianna *retired medical association administrator*
Huntsman, Lawrence Darrow *lawyer, director*

Lorton
Celentano, Suzanne *movement educator*
Fulmer, Ashlee Susan *forensic specialist*
Hunter, Cherye Renee *counselor*
Jackson, Gary Lee *security consultant*
Mastromarco, Dan Ralph *lawyer, consultant*
Ricci, Lisa A. *geneticist, researcher*

Louisa
Small, William Edwin, Jr. *association and recreation executive*

Lovettsville
Flannery, John Philip *lawyer*
Foard, Douglas W. *historian*

Lynch Station
Skeen, David Ray *systems engineer, consultant, engineering executive, educator*

Lynchburg
Angel, James Joseph *lawyer*
Bowman, Kathleen Gill *academic administrator*
Burnette, Ralph Edwin, Jr. *judge*
Coates, Ardith Williams *language educator*
Duff, Ernest Arthur *political scientist, educator*
Elson, James Martin *retired landmark director*
Healy, Joseph Francis, Jr. *lawyer, retired air transportation executive*
Henderson, Horace Edward *World War II historian, peace advocate*
Howell, Peggy Haas *musician*
Hudson, Walter Tiree *artist*
Johnson, Robert Bruce *historic preservationist, director, small business owner*
LaHaye, Timothy F. *pastor, writer*
Marra, Anthony Tullio *audio visual specialist*
McClenon, John Raymond *retired chemistry professor*
McRorie, William Edward *retired insurance company executive*
Melton, Brian Christopher *history professor, writer*
Moon, Norman K. *judge*
Morgan, Evan *retired chemist*
Packert, G(ayla) Beth *retired lawyer*
Partie, David John *language educator*
Pursley, Frank James *retired personal development specialist*
Snead, George Murrell, Jr. *military officer, research scientist, consultant*
Solyom, Antal Endre *retired psychiatrist*
Stephens, Bart Nelson *former foreign service officer*
Sullivan, Gregory Paul *secondary school educator*
Wang, Kaihong *mechanical engineer, researcher*
Womack, Edgar Allen, Jr. *energy executive, nuclear technology consultant*
Worden, Virginia Hill *academic administrator, lawyer*

Lyndhurst
Dieter, Melvin Easterday *retired minister, educator*

Manakin Sabot
Bright, Craig Bartley *lawyer*

Manassas
Archer, Chalmers, Jr. *retired education educator*
Bruno, Irene Evelyn *mathematician, educator*
Cooper, James Nelson *medical educator*
Haddad, Nadim Fawzi *engineer, researcher*
Hayes, Linda Marie *middle school educator*
Isbister, Jenefir Diane Wilkinson *microbiologist, researcher, educator, consultant*
Jong, Shung-Chang *mycologist*
Livingston, Jo Ellen Brooks *music educator*
Lowther, Edward Glenn *school system administrator, educator*
Parrish, Frank Jennings *retired food products executive*
Schlechte, Deborah Whitley *music educator*
Storing, Paul Edward *retired foreign service officer*

Manquin
Osgood, Nancy Jean *medical educator, writer*

Marion
Armbrister, Douglas Kenley *surgeon*
Groseclose, Joanne Stowers *special education educator*
Johnson, Douglas Blaikie *lawyer*

Martinsville
Frith, Douglas Kyle *retired lawyer*
Van Oeveren, Edward Lanier *lawyer, biologist, physician*

Mason Neck
Mc Curdy, Patrick Pierre *editor*

Mathews
Akaike, Hiroko *music educator, conductor*

Mc Dowell
Harkleroad, Jo-Ann Decker *special education educator*

Mc Lean
Alexander, Fred Calvin, Jr. *lawyer*
Appler, Thomas L. *lawyer*
Aucutt, Ronald David *lawyer*
Auerbach, Anita L. *clinical psychologist*
Bailar, Gregor S. *finance company executive*
Baker, Keith Leon *lawyer*
Bitsberger, Timothy S. *finance company executive, former federal agency administrator*
Black, Ginger Elizabeth *elementary school educator*
Bostrom, Robert Everett *lawyer, finance company executive*
Boyd, Ralph F., Jr. *finance company executive, former federal agency administrator*
Brady, Phillip Donley *lawyer*
Brown, Margaret Ann *lawyer*
Brown, Thomas Cartmel, Jr. *lawyer*
Burke, Sheila P. *federal agency administrator*
Byrnes, William Joseph *lawyer*
Cahill, Harry Amory *diplomat, educator*
Calhoun, John Alfred *social services administrator*
Callahan, Vincent Francis, Jr. *state legislator, publishing executive*
Cannon, Mark Wilcox *retired government official*
Carnicero, Jorge Emilio *aeronautical engineer, transportation executive*
Cawley, Thomas J. *lawyer*
Chang, Michael *professional tennis player*
Chase, Ernest Frank, Jr. *retired federal agency administrator*
Checchi, Alfred A. *air transportation executive, financial consultant*
Church, Randolph Warner, Jr. *lawyer*
Claringbould, John *lawyer*
Clark-Johnson, Susan *publishing executive*
Cook, Patricia L. *finance company executive*
DeGiovanni-Donnelly, Rosalie Frances *biologist, educator*
Dempsey, James Raymon *manufacturing executive*
Dobson, Donald Alfred *retired electrical engineer*
Donovan, David P. *lawyer*
Doyle, Frederick Joseph *retired government research scientist*
Dubow, Craig A. *publishing executive*
Duvall, Richard Osgood *lawyer*
Ellison, Earl Otto *computer scientist*
Estren, Mark James *communications executive, television producer, writer*
Ethell, Judy A. *consulting company executive*
Fairbank, Richard D. *diversified financial services company executive*
Felman, Marc David *air force officer*
Filerman, Gary Lewis *medical educator*
Finneran, John G., Jr. *lawyer, diversified financial services company executive*
Fleischer, Walter Hersch *lawyer*
Forman, Lee Lavinthal *museum administrator*
Forster, Jonathan M. *lawyer*
Frazier, Walter Ronald *real estate investment company executive*
Fritz, Thomas Vincent *business executive*
Frostic, Frederick Lee *strategic planning and defense policy consultant*
Gallagher, Brian *editor*
Gammon, James Alan *lawyer*
George, Paul G. *finance company executive*
Giallombardo, Leslie *publishing executive*
Giragosian, C. Christopher *lawyer*
Glassman, M. Melissa *lawyer*
Goktepe, Janet Rose *retired financial analyst*
Gotts, Lawrence J. *lawyer*
Graham, Thomas, Jr. *lawyer*
Healy, Theresa Ann *retired ambassador*
Herge, J. Curtis *lawyer*
Hess, Adam R. *lawyer*
Hewitt, Lleyton Glynn *professional tennis player*
Horan, Richard T., Jr. *lawyer*
Hudson, William L. *conductor*
Ingersoll, William Boley *lawyer, real estate developer*
Jackson, Juanita Wallace *educational consultant*
Jackson, William Paul, Jr. *lawyer*
Jayne, Edward Randolph, II, *executive search consultant*
Johnson, Omotunde Evan George *economist*
Kanas, John Adam *bank executive*
Kappaz, Michael H. *engineering executive, energy executive*
Kautt, Glenn Gregory *financial planner, consultant*
Klaassen, Paul J. *personal care industry executive*
Knebel, John Albert *lawyer, retired government agency administrator*
Koehler, Robert H. *lawyer*
Kondracki, Edward John *lawyer*
Krugman, Stanley Liebert *science administrator, geneticist*
Laning, Robert Comegys *retired physician, retired military officer*
Layman, Lawrence *naval officer*
Leiter, Michael E. *government agency administrator*
LeSourd, Nancy Susan Oliver *lawyer, writer*
Lewis, James (Jim) M. *lawyer*
Lion, Linda N. *retired federal agency administrator*
Mahan, Clarence *federal agency administrator, writer*
Main, David C. *lawyer*
Mars, Forrest E., Jr. *candy company executive*
Mars, Jacqueline Badger *food products executive*
Mars, John Franklyn *candy company executive*
Martore, Gracia *publishing company executive*
Mathews, Linda McVeigh *newspaper editor*
Mazzarella, David *editor*
McCorkindale, Douglas Hamilton *publishing executive*
McInerney, James Eugene, Jr. *trade association executive*
McLean, Robert III *real estate company executive*
McQuade, Eugene M. *finance and former bank executive*
Meltzer, Steven Lee *lawyer*
Miller, David L. *lawyer*
Miller, Donald Eugene *lawyer*
Molineaux, Charles Borromeo *lawyer, arbitrator, columnist, poet*
Moon, Craig A. *publishing executive*
Morlan, Merwyn Eugene *retired music educator*
Morris, James Malachy *lawyer*
Mortensen, Robert Henry *landscape and golf course architect*
Murphy, Mary *retired librarian*
Murphy, Thomas Patrick *lawyer*
Nobil, James Howard, Jr. *real estate investor, developer, broker, consultant*
Nothaft, Frank Emile *economist*
O'Brien, Morgan Edward *communications executive, lawyer*
Olson, Walter Justus, Jr. *management consultant*
Olson, William Jeffrey *lawyer*
Orkand, Donald Saul *management consultant*
Parshall, Gerald *journalist*
Paschall, Lee McQuerter *retired communications executive*
Paul, Andrew Robert *defense and government consultant*
Paulson, Kenneth Alan *editor-in-chief*
Perlin, Gary Laurence *diversified financial services company executive*
Persavich, Warren Dale *diversified manufacturing company executive*
Pilling, Donald L. *management consultant, retired military officer*
Piszel, Anthony S. (Buddy Piszel) *finance company executive*
Porter, Philip Drew *lawyer*
Price, Ilene Rosenberg *lawyer*
Prichard, Peter S. *newspaper editor*
Rath, Manik K. *lawyer*
Reiff, Laura Foote *lawyer*
Rose, Susan Porter *management and governmental affairs consultant*
Rosenbaum, David Mark *engineering executive, consultant, educator*
Russell, Theodore Emery *diplomat*
Sack, James M. *lawyer*
Safer, John *artist*
Schauer, Franz Peter *civil and nuclear engineer, educator*
Schneider, Peter Raymond *political scientist*
Schubert, Richard Francis *social services administrator, consultant*
Shapiro, Nelson Hirsh *lawyer*
Shortal, Terence Michael *systems company executive*
Shrader, Ralph W. *management consultant*
Singh, K. Paul *telecommunications industry executive*
Sirilla, George M. *lawyer*
Smialowski, Joseph A. *finance company executive*
Smith, Esther Thomas *communications executive*
Smith, Russell Jack *diplomat, consultant*
Stackpole, Kerry Clifford *association executive*
Stine, John Andrew *communications engineer, researcher*
Stowe, Alexis Mariani *accountant, consultant*
Stump, John Sutton *retired lawyer*
Syron, Richard F. (Richard Francis Syron) *finance company executive, economist*
Talbot, Lee Merriam *ecologist, educator, director*
Talbot, Martha Hayne *conservationist, biologist*
Tansill, Frederick Joseph *lawyer*
Theon, John Speridon *meteorologist, researcher*
Townsend, Christopher Gordon *lawyer*
Trout, Maurice Elmore *diplomat*
Vandemark, Robert Goodyear *retired retail executive*
Van Lare, Wendell John *lawyer, director*
Wallace, Barbara Brooks *writer*
Wallace, Robert Bruce *retired surgeon*
Walsh, Marie Leclerc *nurse*
Watson, Jerry Carroll *advertising executive*
Webber, Diana L. *management consultant executive, engineering educator*
Wellings, Tom *chef*
Wilchins, Howard Martin *lawyer*
Wilhour, Brian Edward *composer, music director*
Wilton, Elisabeth Starr *management consultant*
Wimmer, Kurt A. *lawyer*
Woolsey, R(obert) James *lawyer, former CIA director*
Wright, William Evan *physician, consultant*
Yancik, Joseph John *retired government official*
Yarborough, William Glenn, Jr. *military officer, forester, international business executive*
Youngs, William Ellis *photographer, electronics engineer*
Zakheim, Dov Solomon *economist, former federal agency administrator*
Zirkle, Warren E. *lawyer*

Meadowview
Kingsolver, Barbara Ellen *writer*

Mechanicsville
Bierman, James L. *health products executive*
Combee, Susan *assistant principal*
Gerrish, Brian Albert *theologian, educator, retired minister*
Higday, Paul T. *medical products distribution company executive*
Hinkle, Barton Leslie *retired electronics company executive*
Minor, George Gilmer III *drug and hospital supply company executive*
Smith, Craig R. *health products executive*
Wells, Mary Julia *psychologist*

Melfa
Harmon, Patricia Marie *retired special education educator*

Merrifield
Earner, William Anthony, Jr. *naval officer*

Middleburg
Beddall, Thomas Henry *lawyer*
Boardman, Harold Frederick, Jr. *lawyer, retired corporate financial executive*
Grove, Noel Randall *writer*
Langley, Rolland Ament, Jr. *engineering and management consultant*
McNichols, Gerald Robert *consulting company executive*
Paige, Wayne Leo *visual arts educator, artist*

Parkinson, James Thomas III *investment consultant*
Sodolski, John *retired professional society administrator*
vom Baur, Daphne de Blois *artist*
Yovanovich, Robyn Dobson *theater educator, department chairman*

Midlothian
Chapman, Gilbert Whipple, Jr. *publishing executive*
Crutchfield, George Thomas *journalism educator*
Friedel, Robert Oliver *physician*
Hall, Franklin Perkins *lawyer, bank executive, state official*
Lamont-Gordon, Melissa Lynne *orchestra director, music educator*
Nuckols, Otis Wills *lawyer, educator*
Stringham, Luther Winters *retired economist, retired health facility administrator*
Wadsworth, Robert David *advertising executive*

Millboro
Minetree, James Lawrence III *retired military officer, educator*

Mineral
Donald, James Robert *federal agency administrator, writer, economist*
Mayo, Louis Allen *diversified financial services company executive*
Speer, Jack Atkeson *publisher*

Monterey
Tabatznik, Bernard *retired cardiologist*

Montross
Fountain, Robert Roy, Jr. *retired engineering company executive, farmer, military officer*

Mount Vernon
Belden, David Leigh *professional society administrator, engineering educator*

Newington
Robertson, Jean Elizabeth *sociology educator*

Newport News
Abbott, Beverly Stubblefield *artist*
Behlmar, Cindy Lee *medical association administrator, management consultant*
Cardman, Lawrence Santo *physics professor, researcher*
Donaldson, Coleman duPont *retired aeronautical engineer, aerospace engineer, consultant*
Drummond, Neil Hiden *retired secondary school educator*
Duskin, J. Eric *history professor*
Eastman, John Robert *education educator*
Forbes, Sarah Elizabeth *gynecologist, real estate company officer*
Goldberg, Stanley Irwin *real estate company executive*
Hubbard, Harvey Hart *aeroacoustician, noise control engineer, consultant*
Inman, Jonathan Russell *mechanical engineer*
Kamp, Arthur Joseph, Jr. *lawyer*
Le Mons, Kathleen Ann *securities company executive, portfolio manager, investment officer*
Mazur, Rhoda Himmel *community volunteer*
McDougall, Heather Renee *political science professor*
Santoro, Anthony Richard *history professor*
Saunders, Bryan Leslie *lawyer*
Segall, James Arnold *lawyer*
Sheaks, Barclay *artist*
Summerville, Richard M. *mathematician, academic administrator*
Trible, Paul Seward, Jr. *former United States senator*
Waller, George Darryl *music educator*
Warren, Daniel Churchman *health facility administrator*

Norfolk
Adams, David Huntington *judge*
Adams, Kevin MacGregor *military officer, educator*
Addis, Kay Tucker *newspaper editor*
Albert, Alan Dale *lawyer*
Baird, Edward Rouzie, Jr. *retired lawyer*
Barry, Richard Francis III *media executive*
Batten, Frank *newspaper publisher, cable broadcaster*
Baysal, Oktay *dean, educator*
Bishop, Bruce Taylor *lawyer*
Blount, Robert Haddock *management consultant, retired military officer*
Bonney, Hal James, Jr. *federal judge*
Brown, Mary Wilkes *secondary school educator*
Byrne, William Andrew *historian, educator*
Callahan, Kim Versprille *special education educator*
Combs, Charles Donald *academic administrator*
Corcoran, Andrew Patrick, Jr. *lawyer*
Cranford, Page Deronde *lawyer*
Crenshaw, Francis Nelson *retired lawyer*
Davis, Russell Haden *psychotherapist, consultant*
Davis, Terry Hunter, Jr. *lawyer*
DeVenny, Lillian Nickell *trophy company executive*
Dimino, Joseph C. *lawyer*
Donohue, David Patrick *engineering executive, retired military officer*
Drescher, John Webb *lawyer*
Dungan, William Joseph, Jr. *insurance agent, educator, economist*
Earl, Archie William, Sr. *mathematician, educator*
Farmer, Evan R. *dermatologist, researcher*
Faulconer, Robert Jamieson *pathologist, educator*
Gómez, Edwin *social sciences educator*
Grierson, Kevin William *lawyer*
Haoudi, Abdelali *science educator*
Hartman, Deanna Mears *retired family counselor, addiction counselor*
Heck, Henry D'Arcy *retired toxicologist, consultant*
Hirrel, Leo P. *historian, retired military officer*
Hixon, James A. *lawyer, rail transportation executive*
Holloway, John Early *lawyer*
Hood, Antoinette Foote *dermatologist*
Isekeije, Solomon Rowland *artist, educator*
Jackson, Raymond A. *federal judge*
James, Gus John, II, *lawyer*
Jamison, Joi Nichole *media specialist, performing company executive, educator*
Javaheri, Ashkan *physician*
Karakla, Daniel W. *otolaryngologist, surgeon*
Karim, Mohammad Ataul *electrical engineering educator, researcher*
Kennedy, Douglas Ayers *education educator, dean*
Kern, David Jeffery *military officer*
Koch, James Verch *academic administrator, economist*
Kreger, David Lawrence *gastroenterologist*
Lester, Richard Garrison *radiologist, educator*
Lowe, Eric Jeffrey *hematologist, oncologist, director*
Maas, Norman Lewis *library director*
Magee, Kathleen S. *foundation executive*
Magee, William Preston, Jr. *plastic surgeon*
Maly, Kurt John *computer science educator*
Mark, Peter *performing company executive, conductor*
Martin, Howard W., Jr. *lawyer*
McDemmond, Marie Valentine *academic administrator, consultant*
McKee, Timothy Carlton *taxation educator*
McKinnon, Arnold Borden *retired transportation company executive*
Meyers, Carolyn Winstead *academic administrator, mechanical engineer, educator*
Miller, Khadijah Olivia *education educator*
Moorman, Charles W. *transportation executive*
Morgan, Henry Coke, Jr. *judge*
Musgrave, Thea *composer, conductor*
Myers, Richard Brad *pharmacist, director*
Neumann, Serina Ann Louise *psychologist, researcher*
Newby-Alexander, Cassandra Lynn *history professor*
Newkirk, Ingrid *animal rights activist*
Nicholson, Myreen Moore *artist, researcher*
Nixon, Patricia Saunders *music educator, actress*
Noginov, Mikhail A. *physicist, researcher, educator*
Oelberg, David George *neonatologist educator, researcher*
Padgett, John David *lawyer*
Panneton, Jean M. *vascular surgeon*
Parker, Richard Wilson *lawyer, retired rail transportation executive*
Pearson, John Yeardley, Jr. *lawyer*
Platsoucas, Chris Dimitrios *immunologist*
Poston, Anita Owings *lawyer*
Poyner, Kenneth G. *systems engineer, writer*
Quinlan, Kenneth J., Jr. *military officer*
Qureshi, Faiqa *pediatric emergency physician*
Reason, J. Paul *naval officer*
Rephan, Jack *lawyer*
Reynolds, Sheri *writer*
Rohn, Reuben David *medical educator, director*
Roughead, Gary *career military officer*
Runte, Roseann *academic administrator*
Russell, C. Edward, Jr. *lawyer*
Ryan, John Morgan *lawyer*
Shannon, John Sanford *lawyer, retired rail transportation executive*
Sizemore, William Howard, Jr. *journalist*
Smith, Lance L. *career military officer*
Squires, James A. *rail transportation executive*
Steele, James Eugene *retired school system administrator*
Stillman, Gregory N. *lawyer*
Taylor, Gail Singleton *education educator*
Teal, Gilbert Earle, II, *lawyer, coast guard officer*
Tobias, Stephen C. *rail transportation executive*
Train, Harry Depue, II, *retired naval officer*
Van Buren, William Ralph III *lawyer*
Ware, Guilford Dudley *lawyer*
Weinberg, Jerrold Gladstone *lawyer*
Wilson, Harold Stacy *history professor, writer*
Wiltse, James Clark *civil engineer*
Wolcott, Hugh Dixon *obstetrics and gynecology educator*

North Garden
Moses, Hamilton III *neurologist, hospital administrator, author*

Norton
Jessee, Roy Mark *lawyer*
Vest, Steven Lee *gastroenterologist, hepatologist, internist*
Wells, Charles Rayburn *retired insurance company executive*

Oak Hill
Okay, John Louis *management consultant*

Oakton
Duesenberg, Robert H. *retired lawyer*
Entzminger, John Nelson, Jr. *federal agency administrator, electrical engineer*
Frost, S. David *retired naval officer*
Levin, Warren Mayer *family practice physician*
MacCracken, Thomas Gregg *musicologist*
Randolph, Christopher Craven *lawyer*

Occoquan
Nemecek, Albert Duncan, Jr. *retail executive, investment banker, management consultant*
Vercauteren, Richard Frank *career officer*

Orange
Thompson, Louis Milton, Jr. *investment company executive, consultant*

Paeonian Springs
Sloyan, Patrick Joseph *journalist*

Painter
Lubs, Herbert Augustus *retired genetics educator, administrator*

Palmyra
Levy, Bern *communications executive, optical applications consultant*

Penhook
Hahn, John William *retired insurance company executive*

Petersburg
Abbott-Ryan, Pat *painter, writer*
Baskervill, Charles Thornton *lawyer*
Benn, Candace Marilea *elementary school educator*
Burns, Cassandra Stroud *prosecutor*
Dance, Gloria Fenderson *dance studio executive, ballet administrator*
Everitt, Alice Lubin *labor arbitrator*
Garrott, Carl Lee *foreign language educator*
Gosciewski, Robert Louis *logistician*
Johnson, Cherlyn Ann *education educator*
Lakew, Dejenie Alemayehu *mathematician*
Spero, Morton Bertram *retired lawyer*
Stronach, Carey Elliott *physicist, researcher*

Philomont
Kok, Frans Johan *investment banker*

Poquoson
Holloway, Paul Fayette *retired aerospace transportation executive*
Tai, Elizabeth Shi-Jue Lee *library director*

Port Royal
Clarke-Hall, Deborah Renay *elementary school educator*

Portsmouth
Buxton, Margaret Rose *human resources specialist, director*
DeMaio, Marlene *orthopedist, surgeon*
Duke, Betsy (Elizabeth A.) *bank executive*
Mapp, Alf Johnson, Jr. *writer, historian, educator*
Monroe, Evelyn Jones *retired librarian*
Moody, Willard James, Sr. *lawyer*
Ojeda, Ana Maria *therapist, clinical caseworker*
Paquette, William Arthur *historian, educator*
Rampersaud Lundy, Sheryll *special education educator*
Wolf, Jeffrey Stephen *physician*
Yarbrough, Terry Pinckney *physician*

Potomac Falls
Trainor, Bernard Edmund *retired military officer*

Powhatan
Eberle, Charles Edward *paper and consumer products executive*

Prince George
Brown, Del M. Mauhrine *lawyer, educator*

Prospect
Picotte, Leonard Francis *naval officer*
Shield, Julie Marie Karst *artist, educator*

Pulaski
McCarthy, Thomas James, Jr. *lawyer*

Purcellville
Davenport, Aaron Christopher *military officer*
Grow, Robert Theodore *economist, trade association executive*
Sharples, Winston Singleton *automobile importer and distributor*
Sweeny, Peter Michael *lawyer*

Quantico
Dones, Darvis Darell *government agency administrator*
Dotto, Peter Attilius *retired marine corps officer, defense consultant*
Mangan, Terence Joseph *retired federal agency administrator*
Stout, Mary Webb *dean*

Quinton
Hinkle, Douglas Paddock *retired languages educator*

Radford
Boyd, Donna Catherine *physical anthropologist, educator*
Davis, Richard Waters *lawyer*
Dunaway, Marsha Landrum *special education educator*
James, Clarity (Carolyne Faye James) *mezzo soprano*
McNeil, Ramsey English *religious studies educator*
Radford, James H. *retired military officer, political science professor*
Shell, Robert Edward Lee *photographer, writer*
Taylor, William Irving *retired chemicals executive*
Turk, James Clinton, Jr. *lawyer*
Zweifel, Paul Frederick *retired physics professor*

Rapidan
Grimm, Ben Emmet *library director, consultant*

Reston
Abraham, Magid M. *Internet company executive*
Ancell, Robert Manning *leadership organization executive*
Anderson, Charles Anthony *lawyer*
Andrews, C(harles) E(lliot), (Jr.) *finance company executive*
Angelino, Mark E. *telecommunications industry executive*
Autor, Robert S. *finance company executive*
Bradley, Murray L(ee) *librarian*
Bredehoft, Elaine Charlson *lawyer*
Brennan, Norma Jean *professional society administrator, director*
Burgujian, Richard V. *lawyer*
Choi, Michael Kamwah *aerospace and mechanical engineer, researcher*
Choudhary, Abdur Rahim *physics professor*
Christian, Eliot Jordan *information technology manager, consultant*
Conway, William E., Jr. *telecommunications industry executive, venture capitalist*
Cowan, Keith O. *telecommunications industry executive*
Dickman, Robert S. *aerospace institute administrator, retired military officer*
Dziak, Jack *telecommunications industry executive*
Easton, Glenn Hanson, Jr. *management consultant, federal official, military officer*
Fernandez, Raul J. *data processing executive*
Foley, Christopher P. *lawyer*
Foosaner, Robert Stephen *telecommunications industry executive, lawyer*
Forsee, Gary D. *telecommunications industry executive*
Fowler, David Lucas *corporate lawyer*
Frankel, Kenneth M. *lawyer*
Fulgoni, Gian Marc *Internet company executive*
Gates, James David *retired professional society administrator*
Gregory, John Forrest *information technology specialist*
Grey, Jerry *science educator*
Grivner, Carl J. *telecommunications industry executive*
Gude, Atish *telecommunications industry executive*
Harrison, William Henry *retired medical educator*
Harvey, Aubrey Eaton III *industrial engineer*
Hill, David Warren *lawyer*
Hirsch, Robert Maurice *hydrologist*
Hope, Samuel Howard *accreditation organization executive*
Icahn, Carl Celian *investor*
Kahn, Robert E. *electrical engineer*
Keefe, James Washburn *educational writer, researcher, consultant*
Kelly, Timothy E. *communications executive*
Kennedy, Leonard Jervey *telecommunications industry executive, lawyer*
Kirsch, Mark A. *lawyer*
Kramish, Arnold *physicist, historian, writer*
Kreyling, Edward George, Jr. *retired railroad executive*
Lavet, Robert *lawyer*
LeFave, Richard T.C. *telecommunications industry executive*
Lipsey, Charles E. *lawyer*
Lord, Albert L. *finance company executive*
Lowell, Bret *lawyer*
Lynch, Monique Christine *mathematics educator*
Madry-Taylor, Jacquelyn Yvonne *educational association administrator*
Maher, David Willard *Internet company executive*
McBride, Andrew Gerald *prosecutor*
McJunkin, John G. *lawyer*
Miller, John Edward *military officer, educational association administrator, information technology executive*
Minton, Joseph Paul *retired safety organization executive*
Mogge, Harriet Morgan *educational association executive*
Montoni, Richard A. *management consultant*
Myers, Mark D. *federal official, geologist*
Myerson, Jay Barry *lawyer*
Naeser, Nancy Dearien *geologist, researcher*
Natale, Patrick J *professional society administrator*
Naylon, Michael Edward *retired army officer*
Payne, Roger Lee *geographer*
Pendergraft, David *management consultant*
Plave, Lee Jonathan *lawyer*
Pocalyko, Michael Nicholas *investment banker, venture capitalist*
Polemitou, Olga Andrea *accountant*
Powell, Anne Elizabeth *editor-in-chief*
Rastogi, Anil Kumar *health products executive*
Rau, Lee Arthur *lawyer*
Reeve, Deborah B. *art association administrator, art educator*
Rosendhal, Jeffrey David *federal agency administrator, educator, astronomer, consultant*
Rubillo, James M. *educational association administrator*
Saleh, Paul N. *telecommunications industry executive*
Sarreals, Sonia *data processing executive, consultant*
Sato, Motoaki *geologist, researcher*
Saville, Paul C. *construction executive*
Schar, Dwight C. *construction executive*
Scharff, Joseph Laurent *lawyer*
Scheeler, James Arthur *architect*
Schick, Michael William *public relations executive*
Shank, Fred Ross *food scientist*
Shindler, Steven M. *telecommunications industry executive*
Smith, Ralph Lee *writer, musician*
Tifford, John Mark *lawyer*
Tirozzi, Gerald N. *educational association administrator*
West, Barry J. *telecommunications industry executive*
Westermeier, John Thomas, Jr. *lawyer, educator*
Witt, Ruth Hutt *management consultant*

Richlands
Surles, Harold Brady *history professor*

Richmond
Agee, G. Steven *state supreme court justice*

Aiken, Peter Haynes *systems engineer, educator, architect, consultant, data engineer*
Alewine, Betty *retired telecommunications executive*
Allen, Jeffrey Rodgers *lawyer*
Anderson, Bette (Bonnie) Ferguson *music educator*
Arango-Lasprilla, Juan Carlos *medical educator*
Atkinson, Richard Lee, Jr. *internal medicine educator*
Austin, John D. *corporate financial executive*
Austin, Terry Lee *director, conductor*
Ayers, Edward L. *academic administrator, history professor*
Bagley, Philip Joseph III *lawyer*
Bagley, Terrence M. *lawyer*
Ballentine, Ron *pharmacist, educator*
Balster, Robert Louis *alcohol/drug abuse services professional, researcher*
Barker, Thomas Carl *retired health facility administrator*
Bates, John Wythe III *lawyer*
Beales, Randolph A. *lawyer, former state attorney general*
Belcher, Dennis Irl *lawyer*
Bell, Gregory James *information technology manager*
Betts, James Edward *lawyer*
Bing, Richard McPhail *lawyer*
Black, Robert Perry *bank executive*
Blake, Peter A. *state agency administrator*
Blankenship, Don L. *energy executive*
Blumberg, Michael Zangwill *allergist*
Boadle-Biber, Margaret Clare *physiologist, educator*
Bohannon, Sarah Virginia *personnel professional*
Bolling, Bill (William T. Bolling) *lieutenant governor, former state senator*
Booker, Lewis Thomas *lawyer*
Bovender, Jack Oliver, Jr. *hospital management company executive*
Brackenridge, N. Lynn *not-for-profit developer*
Brasfield, Evans Booker *lawyer*
Brissette, Martha Blevins *lawyer*
Broadbent, Peter Edwin, Jr. *lawyer*
Brockenbrough, Henry Watkins *lawyer*
Brown, Marilyn Branch *retired educational administrator*
Browning, Keith D. *automotive executive*
Bryan, John Stewart III *newspaper publisher*
Bryson, William Hamilton *law educator*
Buckley, Kevin Joseph *lawyer*
Buford, Robert Pegram *lawyer*
Bukszár, József *mathematics professor*
Bunzl, Rudolph Hans *retired manufacturing executive*
Burke, John K(irkland), Jr. *lawyer*
Burrus, Robert Lewis, Jr. *lawyer*
Buttery, Christopher Malcolm Gedda *medical educator*
Campbell, Mary Elizabeth *retired primary school educator*
Cannaday, Billy K., Jr. *school system administrator*
Capps, Thomas Edward *utilities company executive, lawyer*
Carlton, Buzz (Clyde Gordon Carlton Jr.) *singer, songwriter, entertainer, recording artist*
Carrell, Daniel Allan *lawyer*
Carrico, Harry Lee *retired judge*
Casini, Jane Sloan *wholesale distribution executive*
Catlett, Richard H., Jr. *retired lawyer*
Chandler, Theodore Lindy, Jr. *title insurance company executive, lawyer*
Charlesworth, Arthur Thomas *mathematics professor*
Chewning, Thomas N. *energy executive*
Christian, David A. *energy executive*
Christie, Laurence Glenn, Jr. *surgeon, educator*
Coalter, Milton J., Jr. *library director, educator*
Cogbill, John Valentine III *lawyer*
Compton, Olin Randall *consulting electrical engineer, researcher*
Cooper, William Edwin *former academic administrator*
Cramer, Jackie Rae *information technology executive*
Cutchins, Clifford Armstrong, IV, *lawyer*
Dan, Michael T. *security firm executive*
Denny, Collins III *lawyer*
Derry, William R., Jr. *lawyer*
Dhindsa, Harinder Singh *emergency physician, educator*
Dias, Fiona P. *retail executive*
DiLorenzo, Francis X. *bishop*
Dohnal, Dennis William *judge*
Dostart, Thomas J. *lawyer*
Doswell, Mary Cummings *energy executive*
Drain, Cecil B. *dean, nursing educator, retired military officer*
Dray, Mark Stanley *lawyer*
Dunn, Leo James *obstetrician, gynecologist, educator*
Dunn, Linda Baugh *middle school educator*
Dunn, Philip J. *retail executive*
Edmonds, Thomas Andrew *legal association administrator*
Ellis, Andrew Jackson, Jr. *lawyer*
Epstein, David Stanley *educator, consultant*
Face, E. Joseph, Jr. *state agency administrator*
Fairman, Ralph Paul *physician, medical educator*
Farquhar, Doris Irene Davis *academic administrator*
Farrell, Thomas Francis, II, *energy executive*
Fauls, Thomas E. (Ted Fauls) *lawyer*
Feinstein, Brett *political scientist, consultant*
Fenn, John Bennett *chemist, educator*
Fierro, Marcella Farinelli *forensic pathologist, educator*
Flippen, Edward L. *lawyer*
Folliard, Thomas J. *automotive executive*
Foster, Charles H. *title insurance company executive*
Fox, Sandra Gail *insurance marketing executive*
Fraizer, Michael D. *insurance company executive*
Framme, Lawrence Henry III *political organization administrator, lawyer*
Freed, David Clark *artist*
Freeman, Edward Carl, Jr. *music minister*
Freeman, George C. III *tobacco company executive, lawyer*
Freeman, George Clemon, Jr. *lawyer*
Freund, Emma Frances *technologist*
Gad-el-Hak, Mohamed *aerospace and mechanical engineering educator, researcher*
Gandy, Gerald Larmon *rehabilitation counseling educator, psychologist, writer*
Gary, Richard David *lawyer*
Geary, David Patrick *criminal justice educator, consultant, writer*
Gluck, Michelle H. *lawyer*
Goodpasture, Philip Henry *lawyer*
Goolsby, Allen Cunningham III *lawyer*
Gottwald, Floyd Dewey, Jr. *chemicals executive, director*
Gottwald, William M. *chemicals executive*
Gould, Karen A. *lawyer*
Gregory, Roger Lee *federal judge*
Grey, Robert J., Jr. *lawyer*
Griffith, William Herbert *retired psychotherapist, minister*
Gu, Xing *semiconductor engineer, researcher*
Gulbis, Natalie Anne *professional golfer, television personality*
Hackney, Virginia Howitz *lawyer*
Hager, John Henry *political organization, former federal agency administrator, former lieutenant governor*
Hall, James Curtis *business professor*
Hall, James H(errick), Jr. *philosophy educator, writer*
Hall, Stephen Charles *lawyer*
Hamel, Dana Bertrand *academic administrator*
Hanley, Katherine Keith *state official*
Hardy, Eva Teig *energy executive*
Hardy, Richard Earl *rehabilitation counseling educator*
Hassell, Leroy Rountree, Sr. *state supreme court chief justice*
Heaton, Stuart Alan *lawyer*
Hedgebeth, Reginald D. *lawyer, retail executive*
Helwig, Arthur Woods *retired chemical company executive*
Henderson, Harriet *librarian, director*
Hettrick, George Harrison *lawyer*
Hetzer, G. Scott *energy executive*
Hughes, Mike *advertising executive*
Hunt, Ronald J. *dean, dental educator*
Hutcher, Neil Edward *surgeon*
Irwin, Donald Paulding *lawyer*
Jacobs, Harry Milburn, Jr. *advertising executive*
Jagdmann, Judy (Judith Williams Jagdmann) *commissioner, former state attorney general*
Jamgochian, Victoria *interior designer*
Joel, William Lee, II, *interior and lighting designer*
Johnson, Jay L. *energy executive*
Johnson, Katherine Anne *health facility administrator, lawyer*
Johnston, Francis Claiborne, Jr. *lawyer*
Jones, Jeanne Pitts *pre-school administrator*
Joynes, Barbara Cole *marketing executive*
Kaine, Timothy Michael *governor*
Kaplowitz, Lisa Glauser *physician, educator*
Kearfott, Joseph Conrad *lawyer*
Keenan, Barbara Milano *state supreme court justice*
Kelleher, Patrick B. *insurance company executive*
Kendler, Kenneth S. *medical educator*
Kennedy, Patricia Berry *retired music educator*
Kevorkian, Richard *artist*
Kilgore, Jerry Walter *lawyer, former state attorney general*
King, Allen B. *tobacco company executive*
King, Robert Leroy *business administration educator*
King, William H., Jr. *lawyer*
Kinser, Cynthia D. *state supreme court justice*
Kissam, Luther C., IV, *lawyer, chemicals executive*
Konvicka, Jason Wade *lawyer*
Koonce, Paul D. *energy executive*
Koontz, Lawrence L., Jr. *state supreme court justice*
Kornstein, Susan G. *medical educator*
Kozlowski, Ronald Stephan *retired librarian*
Kum-Nji, Philip *pediatrician, educator*
Lacker, Jeffrey Malcolm *bank executive, economist*
Lacy, Elizabeth Bermingham *state supreme court justice*
Landin, David Craig *lawyer*
Laskin, Daniel M. *oral and maxillofacial surgeon, educator*
Lawrence, Walter, Jr. *surgeon, educator*
Ledbetter, David Oscar *lawyer*
Lee, Peter James *bishop*
Leggett, Gloria Jean *minister*
Lemons, Donald W. *state supreme court justice*
Leshner, Robert Theodore *neurologist*
Levit, Héloïse B. (Ginger Levit) *art historian, journalist, art dealer, consultant*
Lutz, Jacob A., III, (Jake Lutz) *lawyer*
Lyons, Curtis A. *archivist*
Malone, Nicholas Sherlon *systems analyst, consultant*
Manjili, Masoud H. *immunologist, educator*
Marshall, Gary S. *lawyer*
Martin, Ann McCarthy *library-media specialist, library association executive*
Mathews, Roderick Bell *lawyer*
Mattauch, Robert Joseph *retired electrical engineering educator, retired dean*
McCall, Shedrick Dwight *psychologist*
McClard, Jack Edward *lawyer*
McCorey, William E., Jr. *retail executive*
McCune, John Brian *broadcast engineer*
McDaid, Jennifer Davis *archivist*
McDermid, Margaret E. (Lyn McDermid) *information technology executive, engineer*
McDonnell, Bob (Robert Francis) *state attorney general, former state legislator*
McElligott, James Patrick, Jr. *lawyer*
McFarlane, Walter Alexander *lawyer, educator*
McGee, Henry Alexander, Jr. *academic administrator*
McGettrick, Mark F. *energy executive*
Meath, James V. *lawyer*
Melcher, Elizabeth *musician*
Merrell, Ronald Clifton *surgeon, educator*
Miller, Stephen Wiley *lawyer*
Mims, William Cleveland *lawyer*
Minardi, Richard A. (Rick), Jr. *lawyer*
Mollen, Edward Leigh *pediatrician, allergist, clinical immunologist*
Moore, Andrew Taylor, Jr. *banker*
Moore, T. Justin III *lawyer*
Moore, Thurston Roach *lawyer*
Morkoç, Hadis *electrical engineer, educator*
Morris, James Carl *architect*
Morris, James Watson III *lawyer*
Moskowitz, William B. *cardiologist*
Mullinax, Perry Franklin *rheumatologist, immunologist, allergist*
Murphey, Robert Stafford *pharmaceutical executive*
Neal, Gail Fallon *physical therapist, educator*
Neal, Marcus Pinson, Jr. *radiologist, educator*
Nestler, John Edwin *endocrinology educator*
Nyerges, Alexander Lee *museum director*
O'Leary, Elizabeth Lokey *curator*
Owen, Duncan Shaw, Jr. *internist, retired educator*
Pagan, John Ruston *law educator*
Palen, J(oseph) John *social sciences educator*
Pearsall, John Wesley *lawyer*
Peart, Sandra Joan *dean*
Phillips, Thomas Edworth, Jr. *financial advisor, investment management consultant*
Pinckney, Charles Cotesworth *lawyer*
Plack, Vernon C. *financial analyst, investment advisor*
Pollard, Overton Price *retired lawyer*
Pope, Robert Dean *lawyer*
Powell, J. Braxton *state official*
Powell, Lewis Franklin III *lawyer*
Pulley, (J.) Waverly. (III) *lawyer*
Radtke, Duane C. *energy executive*
Rainey, Gordon Fryer, Jr. *lawyer*
Rasmussen, William Meade Stith *curator, historian*
Ravenal, John B. *curator*
Redmond, David Dudley *lawyer*
Reshchikov, Michael A. *physics professor, researcher*
Rettig, James R. *university librarian, library association executive*
Rhoads, Mark B. *lawyer*
Richardson, David L. *lawyer*
Richardson, David Walthall *cardiologist, educator, consultant*
Rigsby, Linda Flory *lawyer, director*
Rilling, John Robert *history professor*
Rinaca, James M. *lawyer*
Ritter, Robert T. *diversified financial services company executive*
Robertson, Gregory B. *lawyer*
Roday, Leon E. *lawyer, finance company executive*
Rogers, Steven A. *energy executive*
Rohman, Thomas P. *lawyer*
Rohr, Mark C. *chemicals executive*
Rolfe, Robert Martin *lawyer*
Rowe, William L. S. *lawyer*
Rucker, Douglas Pendleton, Jr. *lawyer*
Ryland, Walter H. *lawyer*
Salley, John Jones *retired academic administrator, oral pathologist*
Sanderlin, James L. *energy executive*
Savedge, Anne Creery *artist, educator*
Schoonover, Philip J. *retail executive*
Schwarzschild, Jane L. *lawyer*
Scott, George Cole III *investment advisor*
Scott, Sidney Buford *finance company executive*
Sharer, John Daniel *lawyer*
Shiembob, Mark S. *lawyer*
Shipman, Jean Pugh *medical librarian*
Sirica, Alphonse Eugene *pathology educator*
Slater, Thomas Glascock, Jr. *lawyer*
Slaughter, Alexander Hoke *lawyer*
Sledd, Robert C. *food products executive*
Slemp, Dennett Clinton *priest, counselor*
Smith, R. Gordon *lawyer*
Smolla, Rodney Alan *dean, law educator*
Spahn, Gary Joseph *lawyer*
Spindler, Judith Tarleton *elementary school educator*
Spinner, Steven L. *food products executive*
Sprinkle, William Melvin *acoustical engineer, engineering executive*
Starke, Harold Eugene, Jr. *lawyer*
Starr, Edward H., Jr. *lawyer*
Sterling, Anne D. *library association executive*
Stone, Jacquelyn Elois *lawyer*
Stover, Jill S. *school librarian, writer*
Strauss, Jerome Frank III *reproductive endocrinologist, educator*
Strickland, William Jesse *lawyer*
Stutts, James F. *lawyer, energy executive*
Sutherland, Page Hamilton *retired government relations executive*
Talley, Charles Richmond *retired bank executive*
Terry, Robert Meredith *foreign language educator*
Thomas, John Charles *lawyer*
Thompson, Paul Michael *lawyer*
Thro, William Eugene *lawyer*
Tice, Douglas Oscar, Jr. *federal bankruptcy judge*
Torres Filho, Ivo *medical educator*
Toscan, Richard Eric *dean, theater educator*
Traficanti, Joseph J. *lawyer*
Trani, Eugene Paul *university president, educator*
Treadway, Sandra Gioia *library director*
Trott, Sabert Scott, II, *marketing professional, consultant*
Troy, Anthony Francis *lawyer*
Tuck, Grayson Edwin *real estate agent, gas industry executive*
Turner, Elaine S. *allergist, immunologist*
Vann, John Daniel III *library consultant, historian*
Van Neste, Karen Lane *librarian, editor*
Vaughan, C. Porter III *lawyer*
Waddell, William Robert *lawyer*
Wagner, Jody M. *treasurer*
Walsh, James Hamilton *lawyer*
Walsh, William Arthur, Jr. *lawyer*
Ward, Harry Merrill *history professor*
Warthen, Harry Justice III *lawyer*
Watkins, Hays Thomas *retired railroad executive*
Watts, Robert Glenn *retired pharmaceutical executive*
Watts, Stephen Hurt, II, *lawyer*
Weaver, Michael F. *internist, researcher*
Weedfald, Peter C. *retail executive*
Wellford, Hill B., Jr. *lawyer*
Whitehurst, Lucinda Snyder *school librarian*
Whittemore, Anne Marie *lawyer*
Wigner, Preston Douglas *lawyer*
Wilder, L(awrence) Douglas *mayor, former governor*
Wilkinson, David Stanley *pathologist, consultant, researcher, educator*
Williams, Amy McDaniel *lawyer*
Williams, Karen Johnson *federal judge*
Williams, Richard Leroy *federal judge*
Winslett, Stoner *artistic director*
Witt, Walter Francis, Jr. *lawyer*
Womack, Robert Robinson *artist*
Wright, Wiley Reed, Jr. *lawyer, retired judge, mediator*
Xi, Lei *medical educator*
Yelich, Nolan T. *library director*
Yeudall, William Andrew *biochemist, molecular oncologist*

Roanoke
Al-Zubaidi, Amer Aziz *physicist, researcher*
Anderson, Phillip Verne *lawyer*
Barnhill, David Stan *lawyer*
Bates, Harold Martin *lawyer*
Brouillard, John Charles (Jack) *automotive parts and former grocery company executive*
Brownlee, John L. *prosecutor*
Crumley, James Robert, Jr. *retired bishop*
Densmore, Douglas Warren *lawyer*
Edwards, Lacy Lee, Jr. *real estate agent*
Fishwick, John Palmer *retired lawyer, railroad executive*
Fitzgerald, Mary Eileen *museum program director*
Glenn, Robert Eastwood *lawyer*
Gray, Nancy Ann Oliver *academic administrator*
Hutcheson, Jack Robert *hematologist, medical oncologist*
Kinzer, Donald Marshall *banker*
Kinzie, Brenda Asburry *counselor*
Klein, Deborah Rae *nurse*
Landis, John William *retired engineering executive, consultant, government advisor*
Lemon, William Jacob *lawyer*
Margolin, Eric Mitchell *lawyer*
Marshall, Heman Alexander III *lawyer*
McGarry, Richard Lawrence *lawyer*
Miller, Deborah Brewster *educational consultant*
Mundy, Gardner Marshall *lawyer*
Pace, G. Michael, Jr. *lawyer*
Schumm, Darla Yzonne *religious studies educator*
Steele, (Margaret) Anita Martin *law librarian, law educator*
Sweaton, Cheryl Anne *bank customer service specialist*
Thomas, Radford *art educator, painter*
Thomson, Paul Rice, Jr. *lawyer*
Turk, James Clinton *federal judge*
Waldron, Karen *development, construction and management company executive*
Wallace, Linda Kay *mathematics professor*
Werner, Mark J. *healthcare executive, pediatrician*
Woodrum, Clifton A. III *lawyer, retired state legislator*

Rockbridge Baths
Glidden, Robert Burr *academic administrator, consultant, music educator*

Rose Hill
Lane, Mary Winston *retired secondary school educator*

Roseland
Stemmler, Edward Joseph *physician, retired health facility administrator, dean*

Round Hill
Hannes, Martin Roy *telecommunications company executive*
Hillis, John David *broadcast executive, television producer, newswriter*
Schleede, Glenn Roy *marketing professional, consultant*
Tice, Raphael Dean *military officer*

Rural Retreat
Evans, Susan W. *mathematics educator*

Salem
Brand, Edward Cabell *retail executive*
Cirasunda, Esther Bond *librarian*
Day, John T. *academic administrator, dean*
Griffith, H(oward) Morgan *lawyer*
Sailer, Rachel Ann *secondary school educator*
Shaffner, Patrick Noel *retired architectural engineering executive*

Sandston
Manson, Zynora Davis *music educator, minister*

Sandy Point
Douglas, Daisy Howard *retired elementary school educator, writer, consultant*

Scottsville
Griebenauw, Liza-Marie *secondary school educator*

Seaford
Jenkins, Margaret Bunting *human resources executive*

Smithfield
Cole, Michael H. *food products executive*
Luter, Joseph Williamson III *meat packing and processing company executive*
Manly, Robert W., IV, *food products executive*
Pope, C. Larry *food products executive*
Zadeh, Mansour T. *food products executive*

South Riding
Murray, Michael Patrick *lawyer*

Spotsylvania
Goforth, Deborah S. *school librarian, educator*
Hardy, Dorcas Ruth *business and government relations executive*
Hill, Jimmie Dale *retired federal agency administrator*
Manthei, Richard Dale *retired lawyer, health products executive*
Singleton, Tanya *nursing educator*

Springfield
Bartlow, Gene Steven *professional society executive, retired military officer*
Benson, William Edward (Barnes) *geologist*
Brown, Margaret Catherine *artist*
Bruen, John Dermot *management consultant*
Campbell, Francis James *retired chemist*
Casazza, John Andrew *electrical engineer, energy executive*
Chatelier, Paul Richard *aviation psychologist*
Dake, Marcia Allene *retired nursing educator, dean*
de Haan, Henry John *research psychologist*
D'Elosua, Jennifer Dawn *music educator*
Doran, Doris Jeanne *librarian*
Englert, Roy Theodore *lawyer*
Ferrante, Jon Visconti *leadership and technology transfer executive, consultant*
Furst, Eric Jonathan *physician, surgeon*
Ginn, Richard Van Ness *retired military officer, healthcare executive*
Greer, Mark Francis *information technology executive*
Hart, Herbert Michael *military officer*
Kalkwarf, Leonard V. *minister*
Kurth, Ronald James *retired academic administrator, military officer*
Larson, Reed Eugene *foundation administrator*
Meikle, Philip G. *engineer, retired government agency executive*
Myers, Elissa Matulis *publishing executive, professional society administrator*
Quick, Danny Richard *computer systems engineer*
Sonnemann, Harry *electrical engineer, consultant*
Williams, Cecilia Lee Pursel *optometrist*

Stafford
Sedlak, James William *organization administrator*
Williams, Carlisle M., Jr. *municipal official, insurance company executive*

Stanardsville
Anns, Arlene Eiserman *publishing company executive*
Anns, Philip Harold *brokerage house and pharmaceutical executive*
Gladstone, Arthur M. *artist, writer, aerospace engineer*
Keel, Alton Gold, Jr. *ambassador*

Staunton
Balsley, Philip Elwood *entertainer*
Cochran, George Moffett *retired judge*
Jolloff, Nilda Elizabeth *artist, educator*
Vettel, Eric J. *library director*

Stephenson
Johnson, Eva Maria *retired translator*

Sterling
Blum, John Curtis *agricultural economist*
Chavez, Linda *civil rights organization executive*
Clegg, Roger Burton *lawyer*
Cleveland, Harlan *political scientist, public affairs executive*
Fiacco, Anthony Vincent *educator, researcher*
Foster, Mark D. *information technology executive*
Friedheim, Jerry Warden *museum consultant*
Jaffe, Russell Merritt *pathologist, research director*
Jefferson, Sandra Traylor *choreographer*
Lacey, Aaron Michael *actor, director, film producer, scriptwriter*
Martin, Roger John *computer scientist*
Oller, William Maxwell *retired energy executive, retired military officer*
Piper, Thomas Samuel *minister, consultant*
Potts, Martha Wilburn *elementary school educator*
Steffens, Brian Douglas *elementary school educator, music director*
Thompson, David Walker *astronautics company executive*

Stuart
Clark, Martin F(illmore), Jr. *judge*

Suffolk
Baker, Timothy Louis *retired naval officer*
Birdsong, George Yancy *manufacturing executive*
Bollinger, Michael *artistic director*
Bowman, Dorothy Marie *retired librarian*
Burd, Joyce Ann *librarian*
Carroll, George Joseph *pathologist, educator*
Diehl, Richard Paul *lawyer*
Hall, Wayne Michael *management consultant*
Hines, Angus Irving, Jr. *petroleum marketing executive*
Holloway, Christopher Matthew *brokerage house executive*
Matson, Virginia Mae Freeberg (Mrs. Edward J. Matson) *retired special education educator, author*
Noblitt, Nancy Anne *aerospace engineer*

Sumerduck
McCamy, Sharon Grove *English educator*

Susan
Ambach, Dwight Russell *retired foreign service officer*

Sweet Briar
Miller, Reuben George *retired economics professor*
Muhlenfeld, Elisabeth Showalter *academic administrator, literature educator, writer*
Piepho, Lee (Edward Lee Piepho) *humanities educator*
Shea, Brent Mack *social sciences educator*
Wassell, Stephen Robert *mathematics professor, researcher*

Swoope
Avery, Robert Newell *sculptor*

Tabb
Budd, Richard Wade *academic administrator, dean, priest*

Tazewell
Weeks, Ross Leonard, Jr. *museum executive*

The Plains
Gibbons, John Howard (Jack Gibbons) *federal official, physicist*

Triangle
Thomas, Lindsey Kay, Jr. *research ecology biologist, educator, consultant*

Upperville
Johnson, Manuel Holman, Jr. *government official, economics educator, business executive*

Verona
MacTavish, Susanne Hanna *retired library and information scientist*

Vienna
Anderson, Eric C. *aerospace transportation executive*
Beyer, Barbara Lynn *transportation executive, consultant*
Bhide, Manohar Gopal *nuclear scientist, educator*
Burr, Ronald Edwin *publisher*
Chandler, Hubert Thomas *former army officer*
Cochran, Deborah Donick *lawyer*
DeWitt, Charles Barbour *federal official*
Dolan, William D. III *lawyer*
Drumheller, Linda Blocher *language educator*
Edwards, Phillip Milton *retired import/export company executive*
Farrace, Melissa Anne *language educator, secondary school educator*
Gardenier, John Stark *statistician, philosopher, researcher, writer*
Gardenier, Turkan Kumbaraci *statistician, researcher*
Gary, Stuart Hunter *lawyer*
Higginbotham, Wendy Jacobson *legislative staff member, writer*
Holland, Joel Kent III *entrepreneur*
Isaac, William Michael *brokerage house executive, retired government agency administrator*
Jenkins, Robert Gordon *retired military officer, federal official*
Jones, Terrence Dale *foundation executive, consultant*
Kader, Nancy Stowe *nursing consultant, bioethicist, philosopher*
Keiser, Bernhard Edward *engineering executive, communications engineer, consultant*
Kumar, Verinder *accountant, financial executive*
Liu, Cejun *science educator, researcher, program analyst*
Mackesey, Daniel R. *lawyer*
Maguire, Margaret Louise *lawyer*
Maiwurm, James John *lawyer*
Marx, Gary Dean *educational consultant, futurist, think-tank executive*
McElveen, Joseph James, Jr. *journalist, writer, newscaster, educator*
Monroe, Robert Rawson *national security consultant*
Mujumdar, Vilas Sitaram *structural engineer, researcher*
Olshaker, Mark Bruce *scriptwriter, filmmaker*
Patrick, Susan D. *educational association administrator, former federal agency administrator*
Peters, Geoffrey Wright *lawyer, fundraising executive*
Rogers, Raymond Jesse *retired federal railroad associate administrator*
Salah, Sagid *retired nuclear engineer*
Schwartz, Philip *lawyer*
Schwartz, Richard Harvey *pediatrician*
Stearns, Frank Warren *lawyer*
Titus, Bruce Earl *lawyer*
Townsend, Irene Fogleman *accountant, tax specialist*
Vaughan, Patrick J. *lawyer*
Walker, William Woodard, Jr. *management consultant, telecommunications technology executive*
Walsh, William L., Jr. *lawyer*
Webb, William Loyd, Jr. *retired military officer*
Whitaker, Thomas Patrick *lawyer*
Wiesnet, Donald Richard *retired hydrologist*
Woodward, Kenneth Emerson *retired mechanical engineer*
Yamaguchi, Yuriko Fujita *artist*
Yurow, Michael Jay *lawyer*

Virginia Beach
Adams, David Franklyn *music educator*
Alexander, William Powell *business advisor*
Antol, Joseph J. *artist*
Apperson, Jack Alfonso *retired army officer, management executive*
Baldwin, Stanley Forrest *lawyer, insurance company executive*
Barney, Michael E. *lawyer*
Bradshaw, Denis James *engineer, graphic designer*
Buzard, David Andrew *lawyer*
Carlson, James G. *healthcare services executive*
Carlston, John A. *allergist*
Choe, Kyle Seung *facial plastic surgeon*
Christiansen, Margaret Louise *law librarian, lawyer*
Christy, Larry Todd *publisher*
DeFord, Nancy T. *retired educational association and school system administrator*
Dixon, John Spencer *performing arts association administrator*
Felts, Margaret Jean *secondary school educator*
Fletcher, Margaret Ann *religious studies educator*
Fraser, Ruth Hodges *city clerk*
Friedman, Andrew Mitchell *director housing and neighborhood preservation*
Gardner, Karen High *special education educator*
Goffigan, Christopher Wayne *research associate*
Hajek, Francis Paul *lawyer*
Hamilton, George Henry, Jr. *geologist, consultant*
Harrell, Charles Lydon, Jr. *retired lawyer*
Hatt, Clifford Van *school system administrator, psychologist*
Hilgers, John Jack William *management and transportation consultant*
Hodapp, Heidi Francine *middle school educator*
Jones, Robert Clair *middle school educator*
Jones, Robert Griffith *law educator, mayor*
Lewis, Donald Sykes, Jr. *artist*
Lowe, Cameron Anderson *dentist, endodontist, educator*
Lutsyshyn, Oksana *concert pianist, organist*
McDonald, Linda L. *massage therapist*
McWaters, Jeffrey L. *healthcare executive*
Melsheimer, Mel P(owell) *venture capitalist*
Melvin, Carole Ramey *educational consultant*
Morgan, Raymond Franklin *education educator*
Oberndorf, Meyera E. *mayor*
Pickett, Owen Bradford *lawyer, former congressman*
Prescott, David L. C., Jr. *music educator*
Reece-Porter, Sharon Ann *international human rights educator*
Robbins, Reginald L. *mathematician, educator*
Robertson, Pat (Marion Gordon Robertson) *religious broadcasting executive, university president and chancellor*
Roy, Laura Godfrey *history educator, artist*
Schreiber, Mark Traudt *psychiatrist*
Sekulow, Jay Alan *lawyer*
Selig, William George *academic administrator*
Sims, Marcy (Martha J. Sims) *library director*
Spitzli, Donald Hawkes, Jr. *lawyer*
Stansberry, James Wesley *air force officer*
Stanton, Pamela Freeman *interior designer, writer*
Swope, Richard McAllister *retired lawyer*
Thomas, Jimi Elizabeth *elementary school educator*
Trach, Sherry Lynn *elementary school educator*
Tuskey, Laura Jeanne *music educator, pharmacologist*
Watkins, Brenda L. *music educator*
Wick, Robert Thomas *retired supermarket executive*
Williams, J.(John) Rodman *theologian, educator, clergyman*
Ziegler, Rochelle Elizabeth *special education educator*

Wallops Island
Krause, David John *aerospace engineer*

Ware Neck
McVey, Henry Hanna III *retired lawyer*
Tabb, Waller Crockett *retired allergist, immunologist*

Warrenton
Gullace, Marlene Frances *systems engineer, consultant*
Holt, Linda Louise *elementary school educator*
Howard, Blair Duncan *lawyer*
Malmgren, Harald Bernard *economist*
Pribram, Karl Harry *neuroscience and psychology educator, brain researcher*

Washington
Arbelbide, C(indy) L(ea) *librarian, historian, author*
Potts, Richard Bruce *paleoanthropologist*

Waynesboro
Alexander, William Woodward, Jr. *military officer*
Dillon, William Henry *retired secondary school educator*
Edwards, William Bennett *firearms industry consultant, gun dealer*
Lane, Lawrence Jubin *retired electrical engineer, consultant*

Weems
Martin, William Raymond *retired financial manager*

Weyers Cave
Bell, John Malcolm *art educator*

White Stone
Kingsbury, Ellen Ann Dagon *anesthesiologist, general practitioner*
Sparks, Kenneth R. *association executive*

Williamsburg
Aaron, Bertram Donald *engineering executive, management consultant*
Ackerman, Lennis Campbell *retired management consultant*
Axtell, James Lewis *history professor*
Ball, Donald L. *retired language educator*
Barausky, Kenneth P. *aerospace company executive*
Brooks, Philip Coolidge, Jr. *archivist, curator, historian*
Calver, Richard Allen *retired dean*
Campbell, Colin Goetze *foundation president*
Cauthen, Charles Edward, Jr. *retired retail executive, management consultant*
Chandler, Kimberley Lynn *educational association administrator*
Chappell, Miles Linwood, Jr. *art historian, educator*
Christison, Muriel Branham *retired museum director, art history educator*
Church, Dale Walker *lawyer*
Clark, Morton Hutchinson *lawyer*
Coakley, Richard Walker *retired chemical engineer*
Cohen, Lewis Carroll *sculptor, educator*
Coleman, Henry Edwin *artist, educator*
Connell, Alastair McCrae *physician*
Crapol, Edward P. *history professor*
Davis, Richard Bradley *pathologist, educator, internist*
Eliason, Nancy Carol *education consultant*
Farrar, John Thruston *health facility administrator*
Finn, A. Michael *corporate communications specialist*
Flanders, Raymond Alan *dentist, governmental health agency administrator, author*
Gavaler, Joan Susan *dance educator*
Gentry, James William *retired state agency administrator*
Gordon, Baron Jack *stockbroker*
Gottfried, Mark Ellis *accountant, consultant*
Graham, David Browning *lawyer*
Griffith, Melvin Eugene *entomologist, public health service officer*
Guastaferro, Angelo *space science administrator, consultant*
Heller, James Stephen *law librarian, educator*
Herbert, Albert Edward, Jr. *interior and industrial designer*
Herrmann, Benjamin Edward *former insurance executive*
Hight, Orian Langley *retired education educator*
Hoffman, Ronald *historian, educator*
Holmes, David Lynn *religion educator*
Holstein, William Kurt *business administration educator*
Hoving, John Hannes Forester *consulting firm executive*
Jacoby, William Jerome, Jr. *internist, retired military officer*
Kerns, Virginia B. *anthropologist, writer*
Kottas, John Frederick *business administration educator*
Krakauer, Sarah Yael *psychologist*
Landen, Robert Geran *retired historian, academic administrator*
Lange, Carl James *retired psychology professor*
Lorenz, Hans Ernest *photographer*
Maloney, Milford Charles *retired internal medicine educator*
Marcus, Paul *law educator*
Margolin, Robert Jeremy *lawyer*
McCarthy, Connie Kearns *university librarian*
McGarvie, Blythe J. *management consultant*
McGiffert, Michael *retired historian*
McLennan, Barbara Nancy *tax specialist*
Merritt, James Edward *lawyer*
Montgomery, Joseph William *financial consultant*
Moorman, John A. *librarian*
Morris, Robert Louis *management consultant*
Nettels, Elsa *English language educator*
Nichol, Gene Ray, Jr. *academic administrator, law educator*
O'Connell, William Edward, Jr. *retired finance educator*
Paige, Hilliard Wegner *corporate financial executive, consultant*
Pearson, Roy Laing *business administration educator*
Reiss, Mitchell B. *academic administrator, law educator, former ambassador*
Reveley, Walter Taylor III *dean, law educator*
Ringlesbach, Dorothy Louise *retired nurse, writer*
Roberson, Robert S. *investment company executive*
Robinson, Jay (Thurston) *artist*
Rodman, Leiba *mathematician*
Sherman, Richard Beatty *historian, educator*
Smith, Roger Winston *retired political theory educator*
Smith, William Henry Preston *freelance/self-employed writer, editor, former telecommunications industry executive*
Spitzer, Cary Redford *avionics consultant, electrical engineer*
Starnes, Sofia Molina *writer, editor*
Starnes, William Herbert, Jr. *chemist, educator*
Starry, Donn Albert *retired aerospace corporate executive, retired military officer*
Strikwerda, Carl James *dean*
Sullivan, Timothy Jackson *museum and retired academic administrator, educator*
Trott, Barry *librarian*
Turnage, Martha Allen *academic administrator*
Van Tassel-Baska, Joyce Lenore *education educator*
Wallach, Alan *art historian, educator*

Winchester
Aiosa, Charlotte Nelson *music educator*
Bechamps, Gerald Joseph *surgeon*
Behr, Ken *religious organization administrator*
Bonometti, Robert John *technology management and strategy executive*
Byrd, Harry Flood, Jr. *publishing executive, retired senator*
Conteh, Nabie Y. *information systems and computer technology educator*
Engelage, James Roland *management consultant*
Gaither, George Manney *marketing consultant*
Helentjaris, Diane *physician*
Holland, James Tulley *retired plastics company executive*
Ludwig, George Harry *retired physicist, electrical engineer*
Meschutt, David Randolph *historian*
Moore, Richard Carroll, Jr. *physician*
Nelson, Paul D. *retired religious organization administrator*
Ojeda Eiseley, Jaime de *former Spanish ambassador, educator*
Tisinger, Catherine Anne *retired history professor*
Yancey, Cheryl Lynn *apparel designer, educator*

Wise
Benke, Robin Paul *librarian*
Rogers, Leonard David *lawyer*
Smiddy, Joseph Charles *retired academic administrator*

Woodberry Forest
Campbell, Dennis Marion *academic administrator, educator, theologian*

Woodbridge
Andrews, Michael William *library and information scientist*
Binder, L. James *retired magazine editor, journalist*
Brittain, Lara Michelle *music educator*
Flori, Anna Marie DiBlasi *health facility administrator, nurse, anesthesiologist*
Garon, Richard Joseph, Jr. *political organization worker*
Halagao, Avelino Garabiles *lawyer*
Hollingsworth, Bobby G. *career officer*
Hood, Ronald Chalmers III *historian, writer*
Kreipke, Merrill Vincent *civil engineer, consultant*
Messerschmidt, William Harclerode *retired non-commissioned officer, musician*
Monaco, Anthony John *retired health facility administrator, writer*
Roberts, Charles Bren *lawyer*
Sandler, Betty Moore *lawyer*

Woodford
Orrock, Robert Dickson *agricultural educator, state legislator*

Woodstock
Mrosko, Matthew L. *music educator*
Sharp, Wayne David *retired military officer*
Walton, Morgan Lauck III *lawyer*

Wytheville
Linzey, Donald Wayne *biologist, educator, researcher*

Yorktown
Gross, Leroy *retired sugar company executive*
Kirsch, Darren Matthew *music educator*
Laurier, Maurice Josef *marine architect, engineer, consultant*
Romjue, John Lawson *historian, writer*
Wood, James Edward, Jr. *religion educator, author*

WASHINGTON

Anacortes
Cavanaugh, Michael Everett *lawyer, arbitrator, mediator*
Cook, Don W. *human resources specialist, retired military officer, risk management consultant*
Felger, Ralph William *education educator, retired military officer*
Glein, Richard Jeriel, Sr. *lawyer*
Higgins, Robert (Walter) *career officer, physician*
Hoffmann, Manfred Walter *consulting company executive*
Mc Cracken, Philip Trafton *sculptor*
Randolph, Carl Lowell *chemicals executive*

Arlington
Bullington, Gayle Rogers *writer, researcher*
Gerwick-Brodeur, Madeline Carol *marketing and timing professional*
Hedman, Zoe Ann *retired literature and language educator, artist*

Auburn
Nazaire, Michel Harry *physician*
Rohlff, Geri *secondary school educator*
Sims, Marcie Lynne *language educator, writer*
Whitmore, Donald Clark *retired engineer*

Bainbridge Island
Berg, Walter Louis *retired history professor*
Bowden, William Darsie *retired interior designer*
Carlson, Robert Michael *artist*
Cosgrove, Theresa Margaret *museum director*
Gibbons, Franklin (Chip) Arthur *application developer, systems analyst, writer*
Harrison, Cynthia L. *librarian*
Hubbard, Stephen *cardiologist, consultant*
Skotheim, Robert Allen *retired academic administrator, educator*

Battle Ground
Ezelle, Robert Eugene *diplomat*
Hansen, James Lee *sculptor*

Belfair
Hager, Robert Worth *retired aerospace executive*

Bellevue
Andersen, James A. *retired state supreme court justice*
Anderson, David Coryell *lawyer, automotive executive*
Armstrong, Ronald E. *corporate financial executive*
Arnold, Ronald Henri *nonprofit organization executive, consultant*
Berkley, James Donald *clergyman*
Cardillo, James G. *automotive executive*
Carlson, Curtis Eugene *orthodontist, periodontist*
Connors, John G. *former computer software company executive*
Dean, Scott P. *music educator, director*
Gangl, Kenneth R. *automotive executive*
Gope, Dipanjan *computer engineer*
Graham, John Robert, Jr. *financial executive*
Grosvenor, Allan Dace *engineer*
Hackett, Carol Ann Hedden *physician*
Hackett, John Peter *dermatologist*
Hall, Eleanor Williams *public relations executive*
Hannah, Lawrence Burlison *lawyer*
Kari, Donald G. *lawyer*
Khosrowshahi, Dara *travel company executive*
King, Elizabeth Maureen *business systems executive*
Landau, Felix *lawyer*
Marosan, George *plastic surgeon*
McReynolds, Neil Lawrence *management consultant*
Morie, G. Glen *lawyer, manufacturing executive*
Myhrvold, Nathan P. *technology executive*
Mylnechuk, Larry Herbert *financial executive*
Olson, Robert William *writer, retired counselor*
Page, Roy Christopher *periodontist, scientist, educator*
Parks, Donald Lee *mechanical engineer, human factors engineer*
Phillips, Zaiga Alksnis *pediatrician*
Pigott, Charles McGee *transportation equipment manufacturing executive*
Pigott, Mark C. *automotive executive*
Plimpton, Thomas E. *automotive executive*
Rand, Richard P. *plastic surgeon*
Reynolds, Stephen Philip *utility company executive*
Rice, Kay Diane *elementary school educator, consultant*
Schroder, Sigrid Caroline *lawyer, consultant*
Scott, J. Lennox *real estate company executive*
Sebris, Robert, Jr. *lawyer*
Shifrin, Donald Lee *pediatrician*
Simonyi, Charles *software engineer*
Smith, Bruce Cameron *physician*
Sweeney, David Brian *lawyer*
Tembreull, Michael A. *automotive executive*
Thompson, Winston Mark Obed *entomologist, consultant, writer*
Tian, Hongqi *application developer, researcher*
Warren, James Ronald *retired museum director, journalist*
Wells-Henderson, Ronald John *investment counselor*
Westergaard, George Henry *secondary school educator*
Whatmore, George Bernard *research scientist, writer, internist*
Williamson, Charles R. *retired energy company executive*

Bellingham
Adelstein, Steven Paul *lawyer*
Anderson, David Bowen *lawyer*
Bourm, Roger Michael *real estate broker, investor, property manager*
Brakke, Myron Kendall *retired research chemist, educator*
Burdge, Rabel James *sociology educator*
Clark-Langager, Sarah Ann *curator, academic administrator*
Cox, David Jackson *biochemistry professor*
Davis, Brantley Pierce *physician, researcher*
Dooley, Kathleen Ann *elementary school educator*
Feodorov, John *artist*
Howe, Warren Billings *physician*
Jansen, Robert Bruce *consulting civil engineer*
Morse, Karen Williams *academic administrator*
Nelson, George Driver *astronomer, educator, former astronaut*
Packer, Mark Barry *lawyer, financial consultant, foundation official*
Raas, Daniel Alan *lawyer*
Ross, June Rosa Pitt *biologist, educator*
Whyte, Nancy Marie *performing arts educator*

Benton City
Omel, June M. *elementary school educator*

Blaine
Miller, Ronald *journalist, critic*
Steward, David John *retired anesthesiologist, educator, researcher*

Bothell
Anders, Harley Dillon, Sr. *retired federal agency administrator*
Boynton, Alton L. *pharmaceutical executive*
Constantino, Karen Marie *elementary school educator*
Grewal, Iqbal S. *immunologist, biotechnology company executive*
Gustafson, Alice Fairleigh *lawyer*
Watts, Linda Susan *humanities educator*

Bremerton
Cunningham, Gary Allen *lawyer*

Brush Prairie
Edlich, Richard French *biomedical engineer, educator*
Zawodny, LaRae Jean *artist, secondary school educator*

Burien
Burgess, Charles Orville *history professor*
McClean, Patrick H. *otolaryngologist*
Risse, Guenter Bernhard *physician, historian, educator*

Burton
Dyer, Carolyn Price *artist, writer*

Camano Island
Clowes, Garth Anthony *electronics executive, consultant*
de Vries, Rimmer *economist*
Hartley, Celia Love *retired nursing educator, administrator, consultant, writer*
O'Connor, Thomas Edward *petroleum geologist, management consultant*
Thayer, Thomas Manor, Jr. *artist*

Camas
Kotsovos, Jerry Frank *retired secondary school educator*

Carnation
Beshur, Jacqueline E. *retired animal trainer, farmer, writer*

Centralia
Buzzard, Steven Ray *lawyer*
Gay, Larry Kenneth *artist, automotive executive, consultant*
Gimbel, Hervey Willis *public health physician, medical administrator*

Chehalis
Burrows, Robert Paul *optometrist*

Cheney
Smith, Grant William *language educator, volunteer*

Clarkston
Torgerson, Linda Belle *music educator*

Clinton
Holtby, Kenneth Fraser *retired manufacturing executive*
Powers, David Richard *educational administrator*

Clyde Hill
Condon, Robert Edward *surgeon, educator, consultant*

Colville
Culton, Sarah Alexander *psychologist, educator*
Forman, Robert Edgar *retired sociology professor*

Coupeville
Lotzenhiser, George William *musician, educator, academic administrator, composer*
Mayhew, Eric George *medical researcher, educator, consultant*
Piercy, Gordon Clayton *bank executive, educator*
Thom, Richard David *retired electronics executive*

Des Moines
McMannon, Timothy J. *history professor*
Tuell, Jack Marvin *retired bishop*

Dupont
Pettit, Ghery St. John *electronics engineer*

East Wenatchee
Hanna, Harold B. *retired lawyer*

Eastsound
de Boor, Carl-Wilhelm R. *mathematician*
Hoagland, Karl King, Jr. *lawyer*
Murray, Michael Kent *lawyer*

Edmonds
Bell, Nancy Lee Hoyt *real estate investor, middle school educator, volunteer*
Laico, Colette *artist*
Monroe, James Walter *retired corporate financial executive*
Owen, John *retired newspaper editor*
Peckol, James Kenneth *consulting engineer*
Schmit, Lucien André, Jr. *retired structural engineer*
Thyden, James Eskel *diplomat, educator, lecturer*
Yoon, Jay Myoung *oncologist, hematologist, internist*

Ellensburg
Carrothers, Carol Ann *special education services professional, educator*
Hoover, Amy Lynn *pilot, educator*
McIntyre, Jerilyn Sue *academic administrator*
Miller, Maxine Lynch *retired home economist, retired interior designer, educator*
Panerio, Robert Major, Sr. *music educator, composer*
Rosell, Sharon Lynn *physics and chemistry professor*

Everett
Bowden, George Newton *judge*
Brown, Frederick Calvin *retired physics professor*
Byrne, Patrick J. *information technology company executive*
Jewell, Judy Ann *funeral director, counselor*
Mestel, Mark David *lawyer*
Nelson, Carol Kobuke *bank executive*
O'Keefe, Kathleen Mary *state official*
Oliver, William Donald *orthodontist*
Ostergaard, Joni Hammersla *lawyer*
Simmons, Eileen *librarian*
Valentine, Mark Conrad *dermatologist*

Federal Way
Ballard, Ernesta *lumber company executive*
Blywise, Barbara *mental health services professional*
Corbin, William R. *wood products executive*
Cunningham, John Randolph *project manager*
Fulton, Daniel S. *corporate real estate executive*
Hanson, Richard E. *paper company executive*
Hogans, Mack L. *paper company executive*
McDade, Sandy D. *lawyer, paper company executive*
Mersereau, Susan *information systems company, data processing executive*
Muzyka-McGuire, Amy *marketing professional, nutritionist, consultant*
Nance, John Joseph *lawyer, writer, air traffic controller, announcer, consultant*
Pitts, Melissa Dawn *underwriter*
Rogel, Steven R. *forest products company executive*
Rossi, Ruth Harris *special education educator*
Taggart, Richard J. *forest products company executive*
Weyerhaeuser, George H., Jr. *paper manufacturing company executive*

Fort Lewis
Beekley, Alec C. *surgeon, researcher*
Lubbers, Alice Dianne *operating room nurse*

Freeland
Calio, Anthony John *research scientist, operations specialist*

Friday Harbor
Agosta, William Carleton *chemist, educator*
Daum, David Ernest *machinery manufacturing company executive*
Geyman, John Payne *physician, educator*
MacGinitie, Walter Harold *psychologist, educator*

Gig Harbor
Bernard, Lowell Francis *retired academic administrator, educator*
Stover, Miles Ronald *management consultant*
Thompson, Ronald Edward *lawyer*

Goldendale
Skillern, Michael Phillip *museum administrator*

Granite Falls
Hamilton, Pamela Jane *psychologist, special education educator*
Peterson, Andrea *elementary school educator*

Hansville
Blalock, Ann Bonar *evaluation researcher*

Hoquiam
Kessler, Keith Leon *lawyer*

Hunts Point
Ebsworth, Barney A. *retired travel company executive*

Issaquah
Barchet, Stephen *obstetrician, gynecologist, retired military officer*
Benoliel, Joel *lawyer*
Brotman, Jeffrey H. *wholesale distribution executive*
Cain, Coleen W. *writer, educator*
DiCerchio, Richard D. *wholesale distribution executive*
Drazdoff, Nola Gay *psychologist*
Evans, Ersel Arthur *engineering executive, consultant*
Galanti, Richard A. *wholesale business executive*
Hilst, Glenn Rudolph *environmental sciences administrator, researcher*
Matthews, John *human resources specialist, wholesale distribution executive*
Oles, Stuart Gregory *lawyer*
Parker-Fairbanks, Dixie *artist*
Ptacek, William H. *library director*
Reid, John Mitchell (Jack Reid) *biomedical engineer, researcher, consultant*
Sinegal, James D. *wholesale distribution executive*
von Speyer, Jacques *financier*
Wainwright, Paul Edward Blech *construction company executive*
Wright, Theodore Otis *forensic engineer*

Kelso
Janke, John Eric *secondary school educator*

Kenmore
Guy, Arthur William *electrical engineering educator, researcher*
Jennerich, Edward John *academic administrator, dean*
Sobolewski, John Stephen *computer scientist, director, consultant*
Sokol, Jennifer Marie *musician, writer*
Springer, Floyd Ladean *architect*

Kennewick
Brewton, Wesley Hopkins (Wes Brewton) *retired chef, retired real estate manager*
Cochran, James Alan *mathematics professor, department chairman, dean*
Hames, William Lester *lawyer*
Merkel, Patricia Mae *retired school system administrator*

Kent
Goo, Abraham Meu Sen *retired manufacturing executive*
Hebeler, Henry Koester *retired electronics executive, aerospace engineer*
Pierce, Danny Parcel *artist, educator*

Keyport
Treacy, Gerald Bernard, Jr. *lawyer*

Kirkland
Aikawa, Jerry Kazuo *internist, educator*

Alexander, Shaun *professional football player*
Argue, Don Harvey *college president, minister*
Barto, Deborah Ann *physician*
Chapple, John H. *telecommunications industry and former professional sports team executive*
Dunn, Jeffrey Edward *neurologist*
Gilleland, John Rogers *technology company executive*
Holmgren, Mike *professional football coach*
McCaw, Craig O. *communications executive*
McDonald, Joseph Lee *insurance broker*
Mitchell, Joseph Patrick *architect*
Mora, Jim (James Lawrence Mora) *professional football coach*
Pope, Deborah Renaye *literature and language professor*
Rich, Clayton *retired academic administrator, educator*
Ryles, Gerald Fay *investor, finance company executive*
Szablya, Helen Mary *writer, language educator*
Teeley, Kevin *educational association administrator*
Tyllia, Frank Michael *academic administrator, educator*
Welke, Elton Grinnell, Jr. *publisher, writer*

La Conner
Garcia, John *psychologist, educator*
Knopf, Kenyon Alfred *economist, educator*
Robbins, Thomas Eugene *writer*

La Push
Krueger, Katherine Kamp *lawyer*

Lacey
Breytspraak, John, Jr. *management consultant*
Louis, Glen *music educator*
Mata, Linda Sue Proctor *writer, consultant*
Spangler, David Robert *academic administrator, engineer, educator*

Lake Forest Park
Adams, Hazard Simeon *retired language educator, writer*
Angell, Tony *artist, writer*

Lake Stevens
Durden, Rome L. *aircraft manufacturing company executive*

Lakewood
Gilchrist, Debra L. *college librarian*
McEwen, Doris Ann *education educator*
Owen, Thomas Walker *banker, portfolio manager*

Longview
Altman, Bernie *retired secondary school educator, editor*
Foster, Virginia *retired botany educator*
Uthmann, Richard W. *retired music educator*
Walston, Rick Lyle *clergyman, seminary executive, educator*

Lopez Island
Brownstein, Barbara Lavin *geneticist, educator, director*

Lummi Island
Ewing, Benjamin Baugh *environmental engineer, educator, consultant*
Hanson, Polly (Pauline) Mae Early *librarian*

Lynden
Hibbs, Clair M. *retired pathologist*

Lynnwood
Bear, Gregory Dale *writer, illustrator*
Jenes, Theodore George, Jr. *retired military officer*
Lynch, Juneann M. *medical/surgical nurse, nursing educator*
Olsen, Kenneth Harold *geophysicist, astrophysicist, historian*
Tebbs, Carol Ann *secondary school educator, academic administrator*

Manchester
Fearon, Lee Charles *chemist*

Manson
Stager, Donald K. *retired construction company executive*

Maple Valley
Brown, Thomas Andrew *retired aircraft/weaponry manufacturing executive*
Willson, David Allen *retired reference librarian, writer*

Marysville
Kell, Lyle Nicholas *retired minister, retired real estate broker*

Medical Lake
Grub, Phillip Donald *business educator*

Medina
Dagnon, James Bernard *human resources executive*
Lucas, Patricia Latourette *writer*
Schlotterbeck, Walter Albert *manufacturing executive, lawyer*

Mercer Island
Anderson, Peter MacArthur *retired lawyer*
Bridgforth, Robert Moore, Jr. *aerospace engineer*
Dunner, David Louis *medical educator*
Dykstra, David Charles *management executive, consultant, accountant, author, educator*
Elgee, Neil Johnson *retired internist, endocrinologist, educator*
Gould, Alvin R. *manufacturing executive*
Levenson, Robert Montie *retired physician*
Medved, Robert Allen *lawyer*
Noe, James Alva *retired judge*

Mill Creek
Latta, Diana Lennox *retired interior designer*

Mount Vernon
Klein, Henry *architect*
Langworthy, William Clayton *retired college official*

Mountlake Terrace
Schweyen, Stephen Gregory *engineering company executive*

Mukilteo
Atal, Bishnu Saroop *retired speech research executive, educator*
Bohn, Dennis Allen *engineering executive*
Brown, Bruce Baden *accountant*
White, Lowell Elmond, Jr. *retired medical educator*

Naches
Assink, Nellie Grace *agricultural executive*

Newcastle
Erxleben, William Charles *lawyer, data processing executive*

Nordland
Kramnicz, Rosanne *freelance writer*

North Bend
Brumbaugh, Harley Aaron *retired music educator, conductor, composer, poet*

Oak Harbor
Daugherty, Kenneth Earl *research company executive, educator*
Meaux, Alan Douglas *retired computer technician, artist*
Miller, Robert Scott *clinical social worker, psychiatric hospital surveyor*

Ocean Park
Lee, Martha *artist, writer*

Olympia
Alexander, Gerry L. *state supreme court justice*
Bergeson, Teresa *school system administrator*
Bloomquist, Rodney Gordon *geologist*
Bridge, Bobbe Jean *state supreme court justice*
Bruce, Robert Vance *historian, educator*
Chambers, Thomas Jefferson *state supreme court justice*
Coontz, Stephanie Jean *history professor, writer*
Esbeck, Edward S. *retired education educator*
Fairhurst, Mary E. *state supreme court justice*
Fisher, Nancy Louise *pediatrician, geneticist, retired nurse*
Gregoire, Christine O. *governor, former state attorney general*
Harmon, Lynn Astrid *announcer, writer*
Haseltine, James Lewis *artist, consultant*
Haugen, Mary Margaret *state legislator*
Hutchins, Diane Elizabeth Rider *librarian*
Isaki, Lucy Power Slyngstad *lawyer*
Jackson, Thelma Harrison *educational consultant, researcher*
Jarvis, Scott *state agency administrator*
Johnson, Charles William *state supreme court justice*
Johnson, James Martin *state supreme court justice, lawyer*
Jun, Heesoon *psychology professor*
Long, Jeanine Hundley *retired state legislator*
Macduff, Ilone Margaret *music educator*
Madsen, Barbara A. *state supreme court justice*
Markham, J. David *secondary school educator, writer, historical consultant*
McKenna, Rob *state attorney general, former councilman*
Miller, Allen Terry, Jr. *lawyer*
Murphy, Michael Joseph *state official*
Myers, Sharon Diane *auditor*
Nadkarni, Nalini Moreshwar *biology professor, researcher*
Oberbillig, Molly Castleman *utilities executive*
Owen, Bradley Scott *lieutenant governor*
Owens, Susan *state supreme court justice*
Randlett, Mary Willis *photographer*
Reed, Sam *state official*
Roach, Pam *state legislator*
Roe, Charles Barnett *lawyer*
Sanders, Richard Browning *state supreme court justice*
Sesonske, Alexander *nuclear and chemical engineer*
Smith, Charles Z. *retired state supreme court justice*
Spanel, Harriet *state legislator*
Walker, Francis Joseph *lawyer*
Walsh, Jan *library director*
Zussy, Nancy Louise *librarian*

Orcas
Greever, John *retired mathematics professor*

Parkland
Johnson, LuAn K. *disaster management consultant*

Port Angeles
Brewer, John Charles *journalist*
Gay, Carl Lloyd *lawyer*
Muller, Carolyn Bue *physical therapist, volunteer*
Muller, Willard C(hester) *writer*
Taylor, S. Brooke *lawyer*

Port Ludlow
Krugman, Stanley Lee *international management consultant*

Port Orchard
Thoman, Mark Edward *pediatrician*

Port Townsend
Hiatt, Peter *retired library and information scientist*
Jones, John Wesley *entrepreneur*
Kooser, Ted (Theodore J. Kooser) *poet*
MacLean, Barbara Hutmacher *retired journalist, writer*
Woolf, William Blauvelt *retired association executive*

Poulsbo
Romaine, Grant Hirsch *protective services official*

Prosser
Cooper, Lynn Dale *retired minister, retired navy chaplain*
Proebsting, Edward Louis, Jr. *retired horticulturist*

Pullman
Arthur, Linda Louise *sociologist, educator*
Banas, Emil Mike *physicist, researcher*
Bates, Robert C. *academic administrator*
Bennett, Dick *college basketball coach*
Bennett, Tony (Anthony G. Bennett) *men's college basketball coach*
Berge, Anna Catharina Björnsdotter *veterinarian, epidemiologist*
Clement, Stephen Le Roy *agricultural researcher*
Condon, William Francis, Jr. *literacy educator*
Elstad, Catherine Ann *dean*
Floyd, Elson Sylvester *academic administrator*
Hinman, George Wheeler *physics professor*
Hosick, Howard Lawrence *cell biology professor, academic administrator*
Ibekwe, Abasiofiok Mark *soil scientist, educator*
Jussaume, Raymond Adelard *political science professor*
Kallaher, Michael Joseph *mathematics professor*
Katona, Michael George *civil engineer, educator*
Kohler, Timothy A. *social sciences educator*
Lewis, Norman G. *academic administrator, researcher, consultant*
McSweeney, Frances Kaye *psychology professor*
Paznokas, Lynda Sylvia *elementary school educator*
Rawlins, V. Lane *economics professor, retired academic administrator*
Ryan, Clarence Augustine, Jr. *biochemistry professor*
Savage, David William *lawyer*
Stock, David Earl *mechanical engineering educator*
Streamas, John *ethnic and American studies professor*
Swan, Susan Linda *history professor*
Thomashow, Linda Suzanne *microbiologist*
Warner, Dennis Allan *psychology professor*

Puyallup
Hwang, Chan S. *physiatrist, consultant*
Saxey, Roderick *radiologist, writer*

Redmond
Allard, J. *computer scientist*
Ayala, Orlando *information technology executive*
Bach, Robert J. (Robbie Bach) *information technology executive*
Balakrishnan, Radhesh *marketing professional*
Ballmer, Steven Anthony *computer software company executive*
Boyle, Alan *editor*
Bradford, Joanne K. *computer software company executive*
Brod, Frank H. *computer company executive, accountant*
Burt, Thomas William *lawyer*
DelBene, Kurt *information technology executive*
DeVaan, Jon S. *information technology executive*
Fiske, Neil S. *retail executive*
Flake, Gary William *computer software company executive*
Flessner, Paul *information technology executive*
Freedman, Michael Hartley *mathematician, educator*
Gates, Bill (William Henry Gates III) *computer software company executive*
Grebnev, Igor *application developer*
He, Xiaodong *application developer*
Leblond, Antoine *computer company executive*
Liddell, Christopher P. *computer software company executive*
Lomet, David Bruce *computer scientist*
Markezich, Ron *information technology executive*
Martinez, Maria *computer software company executive*
Mathews, Mich *computer company executive*
Mattrick, Donald A. *interactive entertainment software company executive*
Meshii, Masahiro *materials science educator*
Mundie, Craig James *computers software company executive*
Nadella, Satya *information technology executive*
Nelson, Kimberly Terese *computer software company executive, former federal agency administrator*
Oliver, Nuria Maria *computer science researcher*
Ozzie, Ray (Raymond E. Ozzie) *computer software company executive*
Raikes, Jeff *information technology executive*
Shirley, Jon Anthony *software company executive*
Smith, Bradford Lee *information technology executive, lawyer*
Smith, Burton Jordan *computer designer*
Sobey, Edwin J. C. *museum director, oceanographer, consultant*
Sowder, Robert Robertson *architect*
Troberman, Gayle Deborah *marketing executive*
Turner, Kevin (B. Kevin Turner) *information technology executive*
Vaskevitch, David *information technology executive*
Willard, H(arrison) Robert *electrical engineer*

Renton
Barber, Mark Edward *lawyer*
Reitz, Jennifer Lee *financial company managing partner*
Sun, Zuo *aerospace engineer, researcher*

Republic
Chambers, Milton Warren *retired architect*

Richland
Bair, William J. *retired radiobiologist*
Bevelacqua, Joseph John *physicist, researcher*
Blumenkranz, David Benjamin *chemical engineer, consultant*
Brashear, Karen Kathleen *elementary school educator*
Chou, Charissa J. *staff scientist*
Elderkin, Charles Edwin *retired meteorologist*
Garrett, Bruce C. *materials scientist, researcher*
Glennen, Robert Eugene, Jr. *retired academic administrator*
Harvey, Scott Douglas *chemist, researcher*
Kathren, Ronald Laurence *health physicist*
Kim, Jin Yong *research scientist*
Miller, James Vince *university president*
Moore, Emmett Burris, Jr. *physical chemist, educator*
Onishi, Yasuo *environmental researcher*
Peters, Leonard K. *environmental scientist*
Petrini, Fabrizio *computer scientist, researcher*
Powell, David Charles *music educator, meteorologist*
Roop, Joseph McLeod *economist*
Shin, Yongsoon *research scientist*
Singhal, Subhash C. *engineer*
Stenner, Robert David *environmental and health research engineer, toxicologist*
Trent, Donald Stephen *thermo fluids engineer*
Westergard, Billie *project engineer*

Sammamish
Gaboriau, Henri P. *plastic surgeon*
Yocam, Eric Wayne *engineer*

Seatac
Wells, Roger Stanley *software engineer*

Seattle
Abu-Raddad, Laith Jamal *mathematical epidemiologist, educator*
Alberg, Tom Austin *investment company executive, lawyer*
Alkire, John D. *lawyer, arbitrator, mediator*
Allen, Paul Gardner *professional sports team and computer company executive*
Allen, Scott D. *architect*
Allison, Kimberly Heller *pathologist, educator*
Alsdorf, Robert Hermann *lawyer*
Alvord, Chase *lawyer*
Andersen, Niels Hjorth *chemistry professor, biophysicist, consultant, researcher*
Andrews, J. David *lawyer*
Andrews, Richard Otis *museum director*
Ansell, Julian S. *urologist, educator*
Appelbaum, Frederick Ray *oncologist*
Aprikyan, Andranik Andrew Goorgen *molecular biologist, biomedical researcher*
Arnold, Robert Morris *banker*
Arthur, William Lynn *environmental and political program director*
Aspaas, Jennifer *lawyer*
Atwater, Brian F. *geologist, educator*
Ayer, William S. *air transportation executive*
Bagshaw, Bradley Holmes *lawyer*
Bain, William James, Jr. *architect*
Baker, David *biochemist*
Baker, Roland Jerald *finance educator*
Baker-Johnson, Marcia J. *dental hygienist*
Banks, James Albert *research director, educator*
Barlow, Tani E. *history and women's studies professor*
Barth, Danny *professional sports team executive*
Baruffi, Kumi Yamamoto *lawyer*
Bassingthwaighte, James Bucklin *physiologist, educator, medical researcher*
Batalov, Leo *lawyer*
Bates, Charles Walter *human resources executive, lawyer*
Baum, William Alvin *astronomer, educator*
Beighle, Douglas Paul *aerospace transportation executive*
Beirne, Owen Ross *dental educator, researcher*
Bell, William C. *foundation administrator*
Benedict, Tim *lawyer*
Bennett, Clayton Ike *professional sports team owner*
Berger, Paul Eric *artist, photographer*
Berman, Steve William *lawyer, author*
Bernard, Eddie Nolan *oceanographer*
Berni, Rosemarian Rauch *rehabilitation and oncology nurse*
Beyers, William Bjorn *geography educator*
Bezos, Jeffrey Preston *multimedia company executive*
Bianco, James A. *research and development executive*
Bichsel, Hans *physicist, consultant, researcher*
Bigelow, Reba Seetin *artist*
Bird, Sue (Suzanne Brigit Bird) *professional basketball player*
Birk, Ian *lawyer*
Birmingham, Richard Joseph *lawyer*
Bishop, Virginia Wakeman *retired librarian, humanities educator*
Bladen, Edwin Mark *judge, lawyer*
Blair, M. Wayne *lawyer*
Blake-Inada, Louis Michael *cardiologist, researcher*
Blethen, Frank A. *newspaper publisher*
Bley, John L. *financial executive*
Blom, Daniel Charles *lawyer, investor, retired insurance company executive*
Blumenfeld, Charles Raban *lawyer*
Boal, Peter Cadbury *performing company executive*
Boardman, David *editor-in-chief*
Bocian, Peter *corporate financial executive*

Bodansky, David *physicist, researcher*
Boeder, Thomas L. *lawyer*
Boersma, P. Dee *conservation biologist, educator*
Boggs, Paula Elaine *lawyer, food service executive*
Borgatta, Edgar F. *sociologist, educator*
Bornstein, Paul *medical educator, biochemist*
Bosworth, Thomas Lawrence *architect, retired educator*
Boulware, Michael *professional football player*
Bowden, Douglas McHose *neuropsychiatric scientist, foundation director*
Bowen, Jewell Ray *chemical engineering professor*
Boylan, Merle Nelson *librarian, educator*
Brammer, Lawrence Martin *psychologist, educator*
Breslow, Norman Edward *biostatistics educator, researcher*
Bridge, Herbert Marvin *retail executive*
Bridge, Jonathan Joseph *lawyer, retail executive*
Bridgman, Geoff *lawyer*
Bringman, Joseph Edward *lawyer*
Brock, Isaac *musician*
Brooks, Alfred R. *bank executive*
Brown, Michael Jay *lawyer*
Brown, Robert Alan *geophysicist, educator*
Brownlee, Donald Eugene, II, *astronomer, educator*
Bruce, Harry *dean, library and information science educator*
Bruner, Nancy J. *publishing executive*
Brunett, Alexander J. *archbishop*
Buck, Linda B. *medical educator*
Buckner, Philip Franklin *newspaper publisher*
Bufano, Ralph A. *retired museum executive*
Bunting, Kenneth Freeman *newspaper editor*
Burke, Jane *software company executive*
Burke, William Thomas *lawyer, educator*
Burrows, Elizabeth MacDonald *religious organization executive, educator*
Cahn, John Werner *metallurgist, educator*
Campbell, Charles Taylor *chemistry educator*
Campbell, Robert Hedgcock *investment banker, lawyer*
Carlesimo, P.J. (Peter J. Carlesimo) *professional basketball coach*
Carlson, Dale Arvid *retired dean*
Carpenter, Stephen Hayes, Jr. *lawyer*
Carr, Thomas A. *lawyer*
Carsberg, Scott *chef*
Carson, Scott E. *aerospace transportation executive*
Casey, Tom (Thomas W. Casey) *bank executive*
Catterall, William A. *pharmacology, neurobiology educator*
Cha, Junho *medical researcher*
Chapman, Fay L. *lawyer, bank executive*
Char, Patricia Helen *lawyer*
Charlson, Robert Jay *atmospheric sciences educator*
Chatard, Peter Ralph Noel, Jr. *aesthetic plastic surgeon*
Chew, Ron Alpha *museum director*
Chicoine, Nicole *lawyer*
Chin, Simon H. *plastic surgeon*
Chong, Arthur *lawyer*
Christian, Gary D. *chemistry professor*
Claflin, Arthur Cary *lawyer*
Clausen, Mark A. *lawyer*
Coburn, Robert Craig *philosopher, educator*
Cochran, Wendell Albert *science editor*
Cogan, Tom (Thomas J. Cogan) *aerospace engineer*
Coldewey, John Christopher *English literature educator*
Coles, Martin *beverage company executive*
Collier, Tom Ward *musician, educator*
Corcoran, James B. *bank executive*
Corey, Lawrence *medical educator*
Corning, Nicholas F. *lawyer*
Coughenour, John Clare *federal judge*
Cox, Frederick Moreland *retired dean, social worker*
Creager, Joe Scott *geology and oceanography educator*
Crego, Mary *lawyer*
Crenshaw, Edward Lee, Sr. *aviation electronics technician*
Criminale, William Oliver, Jr. *applied mathematics professor*
Cross, Bruce Michael *lawyer*
Cullen, Jack Joseph *lawyer*
Cunningham, Janis Ann *lawyer*
Dale, David C. *physician, educator*
Dalzell, Rick *information technology executive*
Dang, Chinh *information scientist*
Daniel, Thomas L. *zoology educator*
Davidson, Ernest Roy *chemist, educator*
Davidson, Robert William *not-for-profit executive*
Davies, Katherine Stefanie *environmental scientist, educator*
Davis, Earl James *chemical engineering professor emeritus*
Davis, John MacDougall *lawyer*
Davis, Susan Rae *lawyer*
Dawson, Patricia Lucille *surgeon*
Day, Robert Winsor *preventive medicine physician, researcher*
De Alessi, Ross Alan *lighting designer*
Dear, Ronald Bruce *retired social work educator*
Dehmelt, Hans Georg *physicist, educator*
Deines, Katrina *architecture educator*
Deming, Jody Wheeler *oceanography educator*
Denke, Conrad William *motion picture producer*
Denny, Brewster Castberg *retired university dean*
Desouza, Kevin Clyde *application developer, educator*
de Tornyay, Rheba *nursing educator, retired dean*
DeVore, Paul Cameron *lawyer*
Dial, Ellen Conedera *lawyer*
Diamond, Josef *lawyer*
Dickenson, Larry *aerospace transportation executive*
Dillard, Marilyn Dianne *property manager*
Dillon, Matthew *chef*
Dillow, John David *lawyer*
Dimmick, Carolyn Reaber *federal judge*
Distad, B. Jane *neurologist*
Domke, David S. *communications educator*
Donald, James L. *food service executive*
Dong, Nelson G. *lawyer*
Donovan, Anne *professional basketball coach*
Doran, Charles Francis, Jr. *mathematician, mathematics professor*
Dotten, Michael Chester *lawyer*
Dunbar, Jeffrey *lawyer*
Durant, Kevin Wayne *professional basketball player*
Duryee, David Anthony *management consultant*
Eastham, John D. *marketing executive*
Eaton, Philip W. *academic administrator*
Eggers, Susan J. *computer science educator*
Eigsti, Roger Harry *retired insurance company executive*
Eisenberg, Michael Bruce *library and information scientist, educator*
Elgin, Ron Alan *advertising executive*
Eller, Marlin *security firm executive*
Ellis, Georgiana Kehr *internist, oncologist*
Ellison, Herbert Jay *historian, educator*
El-Moslimany, Ann Paxton *paleoecologist, educator, writer*
Elyn, Mark *retired vocalist*
Emmert, Mark Allen *academic administrator, educator*
Engel, Thomas Walter *chemistry professor*
Eschbach, Joseph Wetherill *nephrology educator*
Estes, Kenneth William *history professor, military officer*
Evans, Bernard William *geologist, educator*
Fancher, Michael Reilly *editor, publishing executive*
Farr, Ross *lawyer*
Farris, Jerome *federal judge*
Favard, Kristi *lawyer*
Feldman, Roger Lawrence *artist, educator*
Ferencz, Garrett R. *lawyer*
Fidel, Raya *information science educator*
Fiedler, Fred Edward *retired organizational psychology educator, consultant*
Fine, Arthur I. *philosopher, educator*
Fine, James Stephen *physician*
Finlayson, Bruce Alan *retired chemical engineering professor*
Fischer, Edmond Henri *biochemistry educator*
Fischer, Fred Walter *physicist, engineer, educator*
Fischer, Thomas Covell *law educator, consultant, writer*
Fisher, Jeffrey L. *lawyer*
Fletcher, Betty Binns *federal judge*
Fluke, Lyla Schram (Mrs. John M. (Lyla) Fluke Sr.) *publisher*
Forbes, David Craig *musician*
Foster, Barry Alan *cultural organization researcher, educator*
Franklin, Jerry Forest *forest ecologist, educator*
Friedman, Alexander Stephen *foundation administrator, investment banker*
Friend, Stephen H. *biotechnology company executive*
Gaffney, Joseph M. *lawyer*
Galloway, Patricia Denese *civil engineer*
Gao, Dayong *science educator*
Gardiner, John Jacob *writer, educator, philosopher*
Gardiner, T(homas) Michael *artist*
Gartman, David Miner *cardiothoracic surgeon*
Garvens, Ellen Jo *artist, educator*
Gass, Michelle Petkers *advertising executive*
Gates, Melinda French *foundation administrator*
Gates, Mimi Gardner *museum director*
Gerberding, William Passavant *retired university president*
Gerrard, Keith *lawyer*
Giblett, Eloise Rosalie *retired hematologist*
Gilbert, Paul H. *engineering executive, consultant*
Giles, Robert Edward, Jr. *lawyer*
Gillispie, Steven Brian *systems analyst, researcher*
Gittinger, D. Wayne *lawyer*
Glaser, Robert *communications executive*
Glover, Karen Elaine *lawyer*
Goff, Barbara Ann *obstetrician, gynecologist, gynecologic oncology*
Goodkin, Robert *neurosurgeon, educator*
Goodlad, John Inkster *education educator, writer*
Gores, Thomas C. *lawyer*
Gormèzano, Keith *small business advisor, arbitrator, writer, web site designer*
Gorton, Slade (Thomas Slade Gorton III) *lawyer, former senator*
Gottlieb, Daniel Seth *lawyer*
Gottlieb, Jourdan *plastic surgeon*
Gould, Ronald Murray *federal judge*
Gouldthorpe, Kenneth Alfred Percival *state official, editor*
Grace, Ryan Thomas *lawyer*
Gradel, James D. *lawyer*
Graham, Stephen Michael *lawyer*
Gray, Marvin Lee, Jr. *lawyer*
Green, Joshua III *foundation administrator, retired bank executive*
Green, William L. *lawyer*
Greenberg, E. Peter *microbiologist*
Greenwald, Anthony Galt *psychology educator*
Gross, Edward *retired sociologist*
Groudine, Mark Terry *oncologist*
Guntheroth, Warren Gaden *pediatrician, educator*
Gustafson, Seth *lawyer*
Gwinn, Mary Ann *editor*
Halvarsson, Misha *business development strategist, entrepreneur*
Halver, John Emil *nutritional biochemist*
Haman, Raymond William *retired lawyer*
Hampton, Shelley Lynn *hearing impaired educator*
Hansen, Thomas Nanastad *hospital administrator, pediatrician*
Hansen, Wayne W. *lawyer*
Harmon, Daniel Patrick *classics educator*
Hartwell, Leland Harrison (lee hartwell) *geneticist, educator*
Hasselbeck, Matt *professional football player*
Hawrylycz, Michael *information scientist*
Hazelton, Penny Ann *law librarian, educator*
Hazzard, William Russell *geriatrician, educator*
Heath, George Ross *oceanographer*
Heath, Richard Raymond *retired investment company executive*
Heer, Nicholas Lawson *language educator*
Hellström, Ingegerd *medical researcher*
Hellström, Karl Erik *science educator, researcher*
Henderson, Maureen McGrath *medical educator*
Hendrickson, Anita Elizabeth *biology professor*
Henikoff, Steven *research scientist, educator*
Henley, Ernest Mark *physics professor, retired dean*
Hermsen, James R. *lawyer*
Hernandez, Felix Abraham *professional baseball player*
Hill, Chrystie R. *library and information scientist*
Hill, G. Richard *lawyer*
Hille, Bertil *physiology educator*
Hills, Regina J. *journalist*
Hilpert, Edward Theodore, Jr. *retired lawyer*
Himma, Kenneth Einar *philosophy educator*
Hineline, Curt Roy *lawyer*
Hirschman, Charles, Jr. *sociologist, educator*
Hirschmann, Franz Gottfried *aerospace executive*
Hoffman, Allan Sachs *chemical engineer, educator*
Holburn, Andrea *lawyer*
Hollender, Lars Gösta *dental educator*
Holley, Rick R. *lumber company executive*
Hollinrake, John D., Jr. *lawyer*
Holmes, King Kennard *medical educator*
Holtan, Ramer B., Jr. *lawyer*
Hood, Leroy Edward *molecular biologist, educator*
Hornbein, Thomas Frederic *anesthesiologist*
Horsey, David *editorial cartoonist*
Horvath, Debora *bank executive*
Houston, Janeanne Currier *vocalist, educator*
Howshar, Erin *lawyer*
Huey, Raymond B. *zoologist, educator*
Huston, John Charles *law educator*
Hutcheson, Mark Andrew *lawyer*
Hutton, Winfield Travis *management consultant, educator*
Ishimaru, Akira *electrical engineering educator*
Isik, Frank *plastic surgeon*
Israel, Allen D. *lawyer*
Jackson, Dylan E. *lawyer*
Jackson, Lauren *professional basketball player*
Jacobs, Deborah L. *library director*
Jacobson, Phillip Lee *architect, educator*
Jaffe, Robert Stanley *lawyer*
Jenkins, Speight *opera company director, writer*
Jensen, Jessica *lawyer*
Jessen, Joel Anne *not-for-profit executive, art educator*
Jiambalvo, James *dean*
Johnson, Bruce Edward Humble *lawyer*
Johnson, Darryl Norman *former ambassador*
Jonassen, James O. *architect*
Jones, Allan *medical research organization executive*
Jones, Grant Richard *landscape architect*
Jones, Randal R. *lawyer*
Jorgensen, Jens Erik *mechanical engineer, educator*
Judson, C(harles) James (Jim Judson) *lawyer*
Jurevicius, Joe *professional football player*
Kahn, Steven Emanuel *medical educator*
Kalet, Ira Joseph *medical computer scientist*
Kane, Alan Henry *lawyer*
Kaplan, Robert David *lawyer*
Kapur, Kailash Chander *industrial engineering educator*
Kareiva, Peter Michael *zoology educator, research ecologist*
Kari, Ross *insurance company executive*
Kates, Carolyn Louise *physical therapist*
Katon, Wayne J. *psychiatrist, researcher*
Katz, Treuman P. *health facility administrator*
Kaufman, Joel Daniel *medical educator, medical researcher*
Keegan, John E. *lawyer*
Kelman, Glenn *Internet company executive, entrepreneur*
Kennedy, Mary Virginia *retired diplomat*
Kenny, George Edward *pathobiology educator*
Kevorkian, Jirair *aeronautics and astronautics engineering educator*
Keyt, David *philosophy and classics educator*
Killinger, Kerry Kent *bank executive*
Kilpatrick, John Aaron *construction and development company executive*
Kim, Yongmin *electrical engineer, educator, biomedical engineer*
Kimball, Harry Raymond *medical association administrator, educator*
King, Ivan Robert *astronomy educator*
King, Jeffrey J. *lawyer*
King, Mary-Claire *geneticist, educator*
Kirby, Ronald Eugene *fish and wildlife research administrator*
Kirk, Judd *real estate development executive*
Kirschner, Marc Alan *neuroscientist*
Klebanoff, Seymour Joseph *medical educator*
Klee, Victor La Rue *mathematician, educator*
Klein, Jonathan D. *finance company executive*
Klein, Otto George III *lawyer*
Knight, Christopher L. *medical educator*
Knight, W. H., Jr., (Joe Knight) *law educator, former dean*
Kobayashi, Albert Satoshi *mechanical engineering educator*
Koehler, Reginald Stafford III *lawyer*
Koh, Steve Y. *lawyer*
Kolb, Keith Robert *architect, educator*
Koppel, Michael G. *retail executive*
Korg, Jacob *English literature educator*
Kraft, George Howard *physician, educator*
Kraft, James Allen *lawyer*
Krebs, Edwin Gerhard *biochemistry educator*
Krochalis, Richard F. *federal agency administrator*
Krohn, Kenneth Albert *radiologist, educator*
Kruckeberg, Arthur Rice *botanist, educator*
Kruse, Stein *cruise line executive*
Kuhl, Patricia K. *science educator*
Kuhrau, Edward W. *lawyer*
Kundig, Tom *architect*
Kunkel, Georgie Bright *freelance writer, retired counselor*
Kusunose, Taro *lawyer*
Kwiram, Alvin L. *retired chemistry professor, academic administrator*
Lacitis, Erik *journalist*
Landefeld, Stewart M. *lawyer*
Larrabee, Wayne Fox, Jr. *facial plastic surgeon*
Larson, Eric B. *medical educator, director, internist*
Lazowska, Edward Delano *computer science educator*
Leale, Olivia Mason *small business owner, import marketing executive*
Lee, Cheegwan *environmental engineer, consultant*
Lee, John Marshall *mathematics professor*
Lein, Ed *research scientist*
Leitzell, Terry Lee *lawyer*
Lemire, Ronald John *pediatrician, educator*
Lemly, Thomas Adger *lawyer*
Lendvay, Thomas Sean *pediatric urologist, medical educator*
Lidstrom, Mary E. *chemical engineering and microbiology professor*
Lincoln, Howard *manufacturing company and sports team executive*
Lisbakken, James Robert *lawyer*
Locke, Gary F. *lawyer, former governor*
Loftus, Thomas Daniel *lawyer*
Lombard, Kenneth T. *beverage and music company executive*
Longbrake, William Arthur *bank executive*
Loveless, Keith *lawyer, air transportation executive*
Lovett, Wendell Harper *architect, educator*
Loyer Nelson, Edith Merilynn *retired social worker*
Lubatti, Henry Joseph *physicist, researcher*
Lundin, Norman Kent *artist, educator*
MacLachlan, Douglas Lee *marketing educator*
Madis, Eric Stephen *musician*
Maier, Ronald Vitt *surgeon, educator*
Malone, Thomas William *lawyer*
Manning, J. Richard *lawyer*
Marchese, Lisa Marie *lawyer, educator*
Marshall, Donald E. *mathematics professor*
Marshall, Toby *lawyer*
Martínez, Yolanda R. *social services administrator*
Mason, Marilyn Gell *library administrator, writer, consultant*
Mason, Robert McSpadden *information scientist, educator, dean*
Matchett, William H(enry) *English literature educator*
Matsen, Frederick Albert III *orthopedic educator*
Mayo, Robert N. *computer science researcher*
McAndrews, Brian *digital marketing executive*
McCann, Richard Eugene *lawyer*
McClure, R. Dale *physician*
McCracken, Peter H. *librarian*
McCune, Philip Spear *lawyer*
Mc Feron, Dean Earl *mechanical engineer, educator*
McKay, John *former prosecutor, lawyer, law educator*
McKay, Michael Dennis *lawyer*
Melo, Welton *professional soccer player*
Michael, Ernest Arthur *mathematics professor*
Miles, Anthony R. *lawyer*
Miles, Don Clifford *architect*
Miller, Crystal Ann *respiratory therapist*
Mines, Michael *retired lawyer*
Monsen, Elaine Ranker *nutritionist, educator, editor*
Moore, Cori *lawyer*
Moore, Daniel Charles *retired anesthesiologist*
Motulsky, Arno Gunther *internist, geneticist, educator*
Moya, Cynthia Ann *small business owner, librarian*
Murdock, Tullisse Antoinette (Toni Murdock) *academic administrator*
Mussehl, Robert Clarence *lawyer*
Nash, Cynthia Jeanne *journalist*
Nelson, Allen F. *proxy solicitation company executive*
Nelson, Christina Gerrish *lawyer*
Nelson, James Alonzo *radiologist, educator*
Netterfield, Kyle *lawyer*
Neu, David C. *lawyer*
Neukom, William H. *lawyer*
Nickels, Greg *mayor*
Niemi, Janice *retired lawyer, state legislator, judge*
Ning, Xue-Han (Hsueh-Han Ning) *physiologist, researcher*
Nordstrom, Blake W. *retail executive*
Nunn, Todd L. *lawyer*
Nutting, Maureen Murphy *historian, educator*
O'Brien, Kevin D. *medical educator*
O'Brien, Kristiana *lawyer*
Oehler, Richard William *lawyer*
Oelschlager, Brant Kurt *surgeon, researcher*
Ojemann, Jeffrey G. *neurosurgeon*
Olmstead, Marjorie Ann *physics professor*
Olsen, Harold Fremont *lawyer*
Olson, David John *political science professor*
Olson, James William Park *architect*
Olstad, Roger Gale *science educator*
Oman, Henry *retired electrical engineer, engineering executive*
Orth, Andrea *lawyer*
Ostrom, Katherine (Kate) Elma *retired secondary school educator*

Ostrow, Jay Donald *gastroenterology educator, researcher*
Overstreet, Karen A. *federal bankruptcy judge*
Pace, David A. *human resources specialist, retail executive*
Paget, Joel Hathaway *lawyer*
Pagon, Roberta Anderson *pediatrician, educator*
Palmer, Douglas S., Jr. *lawyer*
Parks, Michael James *editor*
Parks, Patricia Jean *lawyer*
Parris, Mark S. *lawyer, professional athletes consultant*
Patrick, Donald Lee *sociologist, educator*
Patton, Jody *management company executive*
Paul, Thomas Frank *lawyer*
Pauwels, Judith *physician, medical educator*
Pearl, Nancy Linn *librarian*
Pedersen, Jamie D. *lawyer*
Perrin, Edward Burton *biomedical researcher, public health educator*
Perthou, Alison Chandler *interior designer*
Peterson, Jan Eric *lawyer*
Petrie, Gregory Steven *lawyer*
Petry, Don D. *educational association administrator*
Phillips, William Robert *physician*
Pierson, David John *medical educator*
Piven, Peter Anthony *architect, management consultant*
Platt, Thomas E. *lawyer*
Plotnick, Robert David *economic consultant, educator*
Plough, Alonzo L. *city health department administrator*
Porter, Stephen Cummings *geologist, educator*
Prentke, Richard Ottesen *lawyer*
Pressly, Thomas James *history professor*
Presti, Sam *professional sports team executive*
Price, John R. *lawyer, educator*
Pritchard, Llewelyn George *lawyer*
Putz, J.J. (Joseph Jason Putz) *professional baseball player*
Rabak, David William *retired family practice physician, educator, consultant*
Rabinovitch, Benton Seymour *chemist, educator emeritus*
Raese, David Senna *aerospace and mass properties engineer, consultant*
Raghu, Ganesh *physician, educator*
Ramsey, Paul Glenn *dean, internist*
Ravenholt, Reimert Thorolf *epidemiologist, researcher*
Ray, Charles Kendall *retired dean*
Redman, Eric *lawyer*
Reese, Pokey *professional baseball player*
Reeves, Joan Hutchins *painter*
Reid, Frances A. *music educator*
Reinhardt, William Parker *chemical physicist, educator*
Reskin, Barbara F. *sociologist*
Reynvaan, Michael Thomas *lawyer*
Riccobono, Richard M. *bank executive, former federal administrator*
Rice, Norman B. *bank executive, former mayor*
Rieke, Paul Victor *lawyer*
Riley, Jessica *lawyer*
Ritter, Daniel Benjamin *lawyer*
Rivara, Frederick Peter *pediatrician, educator*
Robb, John Wesley *religion educator*
Roberts, Frank Alan *periodontist, researcher, dental educator*
Robertson, William Osborne *physician*
Robinson, Jeffery P. *lawyer*
Robinson, Lawrence R. *medical educator, vice-dean, director*
Rojas, Eddy M. *engineering educator*
Romm, Daniel F. *writer, retired computer technician*
Rondeau, George Charles, Jr. *lawyer*
Rose, Peter J. *delivery service executive*
Rosen, Jon Howard *lawyer*
Rosenblum, Jeffrey Ira *consulting economist*
Rosenthal, Gabriel *lawyer*
Rosput Reynolds, Paula Gail (Paula Rosput Reynolds) *energy executive*
Rotella, Stephen J. *bank executive*
Ruckelshaus, William Doyle *investment company executive, former federal agency administrator*
Rule, Ann *writer*
Rummage, Stephen Michael *lawyer*
Russell, Francia *retired ballet director, educator*
Sale, George Edgar *pathologist*
Samiljan, Katriana *lawyer*
Sandstrom, Alice Wilhelmina *accountant*
Saneto, Russell Patrick *pediatric neurologist, epileptologist, neurobiologist*
Sarason, Irwin G. *psychology professor*
Sasaki, Tsutomu (Tom Sasaki) *real estate company executive, trade association administrator, consultant*
Sasenick, Joseph Anthony *consumer products company executive*
Savage, Daniel Keenan *columnist, editor-in-chief*
Schiffrin, Milton Julius *physiologist*
Schimmelbusch, Werner Helmut *psychiatrist*
Schmidt, Peter Gustav *marine engineer*
Schneider, David C. *bank executive*
Schneider, Harry H., Jr. *lawyer*
Schoenfeld, Walter Edwin *manufacturing executive*
Schultheis, Patrick Joseph *lawyer*
Schultz, Howard *beverage service executive*
Schwab, Evan Lynn *lawyer*
Schwartz, Irwin H. *lawyer*
Schwartz, Pepper Judith *sociologist, educator*
Scott, Brian David *lawyer*
Scott, Cheryl M. *foundation administrator, healthcare educator*
Scott, Rachel E. *lawyer*
Segal, Jack *mathematics professor*
Sellick, Kathleen A. *hospital administrator*
Senczuk, Anna Maria *cell biologist, researcher*
Sher, Bartlett *theater director*
Silver, Michael *education educator*
Sinanan, Mika Narad *surgeon, educator*
Skinner, Joan *dancer, choreographer, educator*
Smith, Orin C. *retired food products executive*
Smith, Orville Auverne *physiology educator*
Smith, Scott A. *lawyer*
Snow-Smith, Joanne Inloes *art history educator*
Soltys, John Joseph *lawyer*
Somerman, Martha J. *dean, dental educator*
Spafford, Michael Charles *artist*
Spindel, Robert Charles *electrical engineering educator*
Spitzer, Hugh D. *lawyer*
Spoor, Rhys *dentist*
Squires, William Randolph III *lawyer*
Stamper, Norman H. *protective services official*
Starr, Isidore *law educator*
Staryk, Steven Sam *violinist, concertmaster, educator*
Stearns, Susan Tracey *lighting design company executive, lawyer*
Steichen, Randall R. *lawyer*
Steiner, Robert Alan *neuroendocrinologist, educator*
Stenchever, Morton Albert *obstetrician, gynecologist*
Stern, Edward Abraham *physics professor*
Stifelman, Marc Lee *toxicologist, risk management consultant*
Stoebuck, William Brees *law educator*
Stokke, Diane Rees *lawyer*
Stolov, Walter Charles *medicine physiatrist, educator*
Stonesifer, Patty (Patricia Q. Stonesifer) *foundation administrator*
Storey, Mitchel D. *sports medicine physician*
Stowell, Kent *retired ballet director*
Strahilevitz, Meir *inventor, researcher, psychiatry educator*
Stricherz, Vincent C. *journalist*
Stringer, William Jeremy *university official*
Stross, Cynthia *lawyer*
Strunz, Kai *research scientist, educator*
Sullivan, Daniel J. *artistic director*
Sun, Yilin *language educator*
Sundberg, Richard *architectural firm executive*
Sundborg, Stephen V. *academic administrator*
Sundstrom, Johnathan *chef*
Sutter, Joseph F. *aeronautical engineer, consultant, retired air transportation executive*
Suzuki, Ichiro *professional baseball player*
Szkutak, Tom *corporate financial executive*
Takenaka, Toshiko *lawyer, educator*
Tallman, Richard C. *federal judge, lawyer*
Tanzi, Ronald Thomas *artist, educator*
Taucher, Fred Horace *data procesing company executive*
Teemer, Carey *physiologist, medical researcher*
Terwilliger, Molly *lawyer*
Tessier, Dennis Medward *paralegal, writer*
Thirlby, Richard Coller *surgeon*
Thomas, Edward Donnall *internist, hematologist, retired medical educator*
Thomas, Irv *writer, journalist*
Thomas, John Val *architect*
Thomassen, Pauline Frances *medical and surgical nurse*
Thouless, David James *retired physicist, educator*
Tift, Mary Louise *artist*
Tilden, Bradley Douglas *air transportation executive*
Todaro, George Joseph *pathologist, researcher*
Tousley, Russell Frederick *lawyer*
Treiger, Irwin Louis *lawyer*
True, William L. (Bill True) *retired real estate company executive*
Tschernisch, Sergei P. *academic administrator*
Tune, James Fulcher *lawyer*
Turnovsky, Stephen John *economics professor*
Tuthill, Oliver W., Jr. *psychologist, consultant, independent film producer, director*
Ulrich, Cornelia (Neli) *research scientist*
Vallières, Eric *thoracic surgeon*
van den Berghe, Pierre Louis *sociologist*
Vander Ark, Tom *foundation administrator*
Vater, Youri L. *medical educator*
Vuoto, Anthony F. *corporate financial executive*
Wagoner, David Everett *lawyer, arbitrator*
Wagoner, David Russell *writer, educator*
Walker, Walter Frederick *professional basketball team executive*
Walker, William O., Jr. *pediatrician*
Walter, Michael Charles *lawyer*
Ward, Ronald R. *lawyer*
Wayne, Robert Jonathan *lawyer, educator*
Weaver, Lois Jean *physician, educator*
Wechsler, Mary Heyrman *lawyer*
Weinberg, John Lee *federal judge*
Welk, Richard Andrew *plastic surgeon*
Wenk, Edward, Jr. *civil engineer, educator, writer, policy analyst*
Whittaker, James Kevin *retired social sciences educator*
Whorton, James Clifton *history professor*
Wilets, Lawrence *physicist, educator*
Williams, J. Vernon *retired lawyer*
Williams, Nancy *lawyer*
Williams, Rebecca Lynn *lawyer, nurse*
Williams-Derry, Amy *lawyer*
Wilson, Jason *chef*
Wilson, L. Michelle (Michelle Wilson) *lawyer, information technology executive*
Wilson, Lizabeth Anne (Betsy) *dean, library director*
Wilson, Richard Randolph *lawyer*
Woods, James Sterrett *toxicologist*
Woods, Nancy Fugate *dean, women's health nurse, educator*
Wright, Bagley *venture capitalist, entrepreneur, art collector*
Wurster, Charles Frederick *environmental scientist, educator*
Yarington, Charles Thomas, Jr. *surgeon, educator, health facility administrator*
Yue, Agnes Kau-Wah *otolaryngologist*
Zapolsky, David A. *lawyer*
Zhou, Yong-Pin *finance educator*
Zilly, Thomas Samuel *federal judge*

Seaview
McNeil, Helen Jo Connolly *nursing educator, public health administrator*

Sequim
Huntley, James Robert *government official, international affairs scholar*
Jackson, Patrick Joseph *real estate company officer*
Kretschmer, Keith Hughes *investor*
Laube, Roger Gustav *retired banker*
Meacham, Charles Harding *federal agency administrator*

Shelton
Barnard, Susan *literature and language educator*
Leverich, Denis *protective services official, educator*
McNabb, David E. *business educator, writer*
Milander, Henry Martin *educational consultant*

Shoreline
Bailey, Sandra *secondary school educator, department chairman*
Dolacky, Susan K. *music educator*
Hanson, Kermit Osmond *business administration educator, retired dean*
Matesky, Nancy Lee *music educator*
Merendino, K. Alvin *surgeon, educator*

Silverdale
Balcomb, Mary Nelson *small business owner*
Shaw, Annita Louise *art educator*
Walske, M(ax) Carl, Jr. *physicist*

Snohomish
Ellis, Stephen Charles *lawyer*

Spanaway
Loete, Steven Donald *pilot*
Parker, Lynda Christine Rylander *secondary school educator*

Spokane
Baker, Danial Edwin *pharmacist, educator*
Barnes, Ned Maclin *lawyer*
Baugh, Bradford Hamilton *occupational and environmental health advisor*
Bender, Betty Wion *librarian*
Brock, Randall J. *poet*
Bulan, Liana *dentist*
Bunker, Nancy A(nn) *librarian, researcher*
Burton, Robert Lyle *accounting firm executive*
Bynagle, Hans Edward *library director, philosophy educator*
Cameron, Alex Brian *accountant, educator*
Carriker, Robert Charles *history professor*
Chamberlain, Barbara Kaye *communications executive*
Clarke, Judy *lawyer*
Cohen, Arnold Norman *gastroenterologist*
Connolly, Kenneth Thomas *lawyer*
Cope, Kathleen Adelaide *critical care nurse, parish nurse, educator*
Covey, Michael J. *forest products and real estate executive*
Cowles, William Stacey *newspaper publisher*
Crosby, Glenn Arthur *chemistry professor*
Danke, Virginia *educational administrator, travel consultant*
Edwards, James Robert *minister, educator*
Eliassen, Jon Eric *retired corporate financial and utilities executive*
Ely, Gary G. *utilities company executive*
Eymann, Richard Charles *lawyer*
Garrison, Mark W. *medical educator*
Gibson, Melvin Roy *retired pharmacology educator*
Grant, William Joseph *retired judge*
Hakan, Kaya *oncologist, hematologist*
Harbaugh, Daniel Paul *lawyer*
Herzer, Marian Day *not-for-profit developer, educator*
Horton, Susan Pittman *bank executive*
Houseman, Gerald L. *political science professor, writer*
Iltz, Jason L. *pharmacist, educator*
Imbrogno, Cynthia *judge*
Kafentzis, John Charles *journalist, educator*
Koegen, Roy Jerome *lawyer*
Kovacevich, Robert Eugene *lawyer*
Kunkel, Richard Lester *public radio executive*
Lee, Hi Young *physician, acupuncturist*
Lee, Richard Francis James *evangelical clergyman, media consultant, lawyer*
Leighton, Jack Richard *retired small business owner, education educator*
Linn, Diana Patricia *retired elementary school educator*
Lollis, Blake David *physician, military officer*
MacKay, Alexander Russell *neurosurgeon*
Main, Jack *military officer*
May, Richard B. *psychology professor*
McCulloh, Thayne Martin *university administrator, consultant*
McDevitt, James A. *prosecutor, lawyer*
McWilliams, Edwin Joseph *banker*
Mielke, Clarence Harold, Jr. *hematologist*
Migliazzo, Arlin C. *history professor*
Mobley, Karen Ruth *art director*
Moon, Loretta Marie *recreational therapist*
Murray, James Michael *librarian, lawyer*
Novak, Terry Lee *dean, educator*
Polley, Harvey Lee *retired missionary, math and science educator*
Pontarolo, Michael Joseph *lawyer*
Quackenbush, Justin Lowe *federal judge*
Robinson, Herbert Henry III *psychotherapist, educator*
Robinson, William P. *academic administrator, consultant, speaker*
Sayre, Richard Layton *lawyer*
Siegel, Louis Pendleton *retired forest products executive*
Sines, Randy Dwain *retail executive*
Spitzer, Robert J. *academic administrator*
Stackelberg, John Roderick *history professor*
Stanley, Heidi *bank executive*
Steele, Karen Dorn *journalist*
Storey, Francis Harold *business consultant, retired bank executive*
Teets, Walter Ralph *accounting educator*
Ueberroth, Peter Victor *former baseball commissioner*
Van Sickle, Frederick L. *federal judge*
Weatherhead, Leslie R. *lawyer*
Wirt, Michael James *library director*

Stanwood
Birkestol, Annabelle Mollie Elsie *retired elementary school educator*

Sumas
Hemry, Larry Harold *former federal agency official, writer, inventor*

Sunnyside
Capener, Regner Alvin *minister, electronics engineer, writer*

Tacoma
Archangelsky, Dmitry A. *application developer, researcher*
Bartlett, Norma Thyra *retired administrative assistant*
Baxter, Sheila R. *career military officer*
Bryan, Robert J. *federal judge*
Callan, Josi Irene *museum director*
Carlisle, Dale L. *lawyer*
Dressel, Melanie J. *bank executive*
Feroz, Ehsan Habib *accounting educator, researcher, writer*
Frantz, Dale Nelson *automobile import processing company executive*
George, Nicholas *lawyer, entrepreneur*
Gordon, Joseph Harold *lawyer*
Holt, William E. *lawyer, department chairman*
Homan, Jean P. *lawyer*
Hostnik, Charles R. *lawyer*
Hudson, Edward Voyle *retired apparel executive*
Hutchings, George Henry *food company executive*
Krueger, James A. *lawyer*
Leitz, Paula Helen *education educator*
Lent, Michael Stephen *artist, curator*
Liddle, Alan Curtis *retired architect*
Lind, Eric Hawthorn *sales executive*
Magden, Ronald Earnest *education educator*
Maloney, Patsy Loretta *nursing educator*
Mowery, Gerald Eugene *publishing executive, writer*
Mungia, Salvador Alejo *lawyer*
Parikh, Neel *library director*
Quinn, Jennifer J. *mathematics professor*
Settle, Benjamin Hale *federal judge*
Stewart, Susan Marie *psychologist, educator*
Stuart, Jeffrey L. *mathematics professor, consultant*
Taylor, Peter van Voorhees *advertising and public relations consultant*
Thomas, Ronald Robert *English literature educator, writer*
Waldo, James Chandler *lawyer*
Wang, Arthur Ching-li *judge, educator*
Wesch, Angelia DeAn *lawyer*
Wiegman, Eugene William *minister, academic administrator*
Zeeck, David A. *newspaper editor*

Toppenish
Ross, Kathleen Anne *academic administrator*

Trout Lake
Anderson, Douglas Del *retired music educator, recording industry executive*

Tukwila
Fitzpatrick, Thomas Mark *lawyer*
Robinson, Howard Arthur, Jr. *minister*
Talmadge, Philip Albert *retired judge, state senator*
Weidner, Mark *environment research executive*

Tumwater
Edmondson, Frank Kelley, Jr. *lawyer, legal administrator*

University Place
Bourgaize, Robert G. *economist*
Henterly, Mary B. *biology educator*
Pliskow, Vita Sari *anesthesiologist*
Seiber, Richard Allan *retired minister*

Vancouver
Archer, Stephen Hunt *economist, educator*
Bridgewater, Rachel *library and information scientist*
Crews, William Odell, Jr. *religious organization administrator*
Cushwa, William *biology professor*
Dettman, Donald Reese *loss control inspector*
Dodds, Michael Bruce *lawyer*
Donovan, Thomas John *retired humanities educator*
Engelker, Lynsey L. *athletic trainer, professional athletics manager*
Harris, Robert L(ee) *judge*
Ogden, Daniel Miller, Jr. *public official, educator*
Ogden, Valeria Munson *management consultant, state representative*
Robertson, Joel Thomas *railroad executive*
Scott, Gary LeRoy *small business owner, photographer*
Smith, Linda A. *retired congresswoman*
Vossler, Deborah J. *mathematics and science educator*

Vashon
Cushman, Karen Lipski *writer*
Moser, Sarah Gunning *manufacturing engineer, small business owner*

Veradale
Keating, Eugene Kneeland *animal scientist, educator*

Walla Walla
Bridges, George S. *academic administrator, sociology educator*
Carlsen, James Caldwell *retired musicologist*
Chaidarun, Sushela Songtanin *endocrinologist, researcher*
Hayner, Herman Henry *lawyer*
Krebs, Keith Ervin *minister*
Krizan, Kelly Joe *physician, leather craftsman*
Lords, Traci Elizabeth (Nora Louise Kuzma) *actress, singer*
McIlvaine, Patricia Morrow *physician*
Perry, Louis Barnes *retired insurance company executive*
Potts, Charles Aaron *management, publishing executive, writer*
Simon, Nancy Lynn *performing arts educator, director*
Wade, Leroy Grover, Jr. *chemistry educator*

Washougal
Guillory, Richard John *retired science educator*
Harness, William Edward *tenor*
Semke-Fox, Suzanne Marie *retired middle school educator*

Wenatchee
Bastian, Stanley A. *lawyer*
Elfving, Don C. *horticulturist, educator*
Gotthold, William Eugene *emergency physician*
Primm, Richard Kirby *physician*
Schrader, Lawrence Edwin *plant physiologist, educator*

Woodinville
Couser, William Griffith *nephrologist, academic administrator, educator*
Love, Keith Sinclair *communications executive*
Sanders, Richard Kinard *actor*

Woodland
Hansen, Walter Eugene *insurance executive*

Yakima
Beehler, Tobi Lorraine *elementary school educator, education educator*
Jongeward, George Ronald *retired systems analyst*
Larson, Paul Martin *lawyer*
Meshke, George Lewis *retired drama and humanities educator*
Newland, Ruth Laura *small business owner*
Scott, David Irvin *minister*
Simonson, Susan Kay *hospital clinical care coordinator*
Suko, Lonny Ray *judge*
Wright, J(ames) Lawrence *lawyer*

WEST VIRGINIA

Athens
Marsh, Joseph Franklin, Jr. *retired academic administrator*

Bakerton
Allen, Elizabeth Frater *artist*

Beckley
Rehbein, Edward Andrew *minister, geologist, consultant*
Rhoades, Marye Frances *paralegal*

Berkeley Springs
Morris, Sarah *literature and language educator*
Yoho, Billy Lee *lawyer*

Bethany
Smith, G(odfrey) T(aylor) *college president*

Bluefield
Chryssikos, Alexandra Gianelos *secondary school educator*
Kantor, Isaac Norris *lawyer*
Reid, William James *mining executive*

Bruceton Mills
Butcher, Fred R. *biochemistry professor, academic administrator*

Bunker Hill
Marple, Thomas Franklin *columnist, reporter*

Chapmanville
Wilson, Terilyn Barrett *elementary school educator*

Charles Town
McDonald, Angus Wheeler *farmer*
Na, Tsung Shun (Terry Na) *Chinese studies educator, writer*
Starks, Doris N. *retired nursing educator, administrator*

Charleston
Albright, Joseph P. *state supreme court justice*
Arrington, Carolyn Ruth *school system administrator, consultant*
Benjamin, Brent D. *state supreme court justice, lawyer*
Betts, Rebecca A. *lawyer*
Boland, James Pius *surgeon, educator*
Brewer, Lewis Gordon *judge, educator*
Brown, James Knight *lawyer*
Chapman, John Andrew *retired chamber of commerce executive*
Chilton, Elizabeth Easley Early *newspaper executive*
Cline, Michael Robert *lawyer*
Combs, Philip Judson *lawyer*
Cook, Debra Jo *counseling administrator, elementary school educator*
Cunningham, Kimberly Ellen *medical transcriptionist*
Davis, Billie Johnston *school counselor*
Davis, Robin Jean *state supreme court chief justice*
DiPino, Raymond Kim *psychologist*
Dissen, James Hardiman *lawyer*
Faber, David Alan *federal judge*
Goins, Michael Roy *otolaryngologist*
Goodwin, Joseph Robert *judge*
Haught, James Albert, Jr. *journalist, editor*
Hechler, Ken *retired state official, retired congressman, writer, political science professor*
Horswell, Bruce Brian *facial surgeon*
Ireland, Betty *state official*
Jenkins, Evan H. *state legislator, medical association administrator, lawyer*
King, Robert Bruce *federal judge*
Lamb, Patrick John *retired financial consultant, state official*
Larimer, Phyllis Miller *artist, art gallery director*
Lewis, Charles Raymond, II, *traffic engineer, consultant*
Love, Charles Marion III *lawyer*
Manchin, Joe, III, (Joseph Manchin III) *governor, former state official*
Marland, Melissa Kaye *judge*
Maynard, Elliott E. *state supreme court justice*
McCabe, Brooks Fleming, Jr. *state legislator*
Mc Gee, John Frampton *communications company executive*
Mc Graw, Darrell Vivian, Jr. *state attorney general*
McHugh, Thomas Edward *state supreme court justice*
Mellert, Lucie Anne *writer, photographer*
Michael, M. Blane *federal judge*
Miller, Charles T. *prosecutor*
Mills, Brad *computer technician*
Neely, Richard *lawyer*
Paine, Steven L. *school system administrator*
Pasinetti, Nina Denton *dance educator, choreographer*
Perdue, John D. *state official*
Prichard, John David *minister*
Richardson, Sally Keadle *academic administrator*
Robinson, E. Glenn *lawyer*
Rowe, Larry Linwell *lawyer, former state senator*
Scott, Olof Henderson, Jr. *priest*
Starcher, Larry Victor *state supreme court justice*
Stark, Larry A. *state agency administrator*
Teare, John Richard, Jr. *lawyer*
Tomblin, Earl Ray *state legislator, lieutenant governor*
Victorson, Michael Bruce *lawyer*
Waggoner, James D. (J.D. Waggoner) *library director*
Ward, Ken, Jr. *journalist*
Zak, Robert Joseph *lawyer*

Clarksburg
Keeley, Irene Patricia Murphy *federal judge*
Leuliette, Connie Jane *secondary school educator*
Payne, Johnny F. *minister*
Sarino, Edgardo Formantes *radiologist, physician*
West, James C., Jr. *lawyer*

Cottageville
Clark, Paul M. *retired protective services official*

Dunbar
Russell, James Alvin, Jr. *college administrator*

Elkins
Bailey, John Preston *federal judge, lawyer*
Maxwell, Robert Earl *federal judge*
Payne, Gloria Marquette *business educator*

Fairmont
Aloi, Michael John *lawyer*
Fulda, Michael *political scientist, educator, space policy researcher*
Hardway, Wendell Gary *retired academic administrator*
Huffman, Valarie *music educator*
Swiger, Elizabeth Davis *chemist, educator*

Fairview
Bunner, William Keck *lawyer*

Fayetteville
Cook, Lewis Anderson *physician, anthropologist*

Frankford
Mazzio-Moore, Joan L. *retired radiology educator, physician*

Gassaway
Jones, Jeniver James *lawyer*

Glenville
Tubesing, Richard Lee *library director*

Greenville
Warner, Kenneth Wilson, Jr. *editor, publishing executive*

Harpers Ferry
Boucher, Wayne Irving *policy analyst*

Harrisville
Harper, George Daniel *retired art educator*
White, Kathleen Ann *elementary school educator*

Hedgesville
Boland, Gerald Lee *health facility administrator*

Huntington
Aluthge, Ariyadasa *mathematics professor, researcher*
Cocke, William Marvin, Jr. *plastic surgeon, educator*
Foster, Earl James *orthopedist*
Gould, Alan Brant *academic administrator*
Hayes, Robert Bruce *former college president, educator*
Johnson, Pamela *music educator, director*
Jones, Donnie *men's college basketball coach*
Joyce-Norris, Elaine Rozelle *elementary school educator*
Kent, Calvin Albert *academic administrator*
Kopp, Stephen James *academic administrator*
Locascio, Joseph A. *surgeon, educator*
McKown, Charles Henry *dean*
Molina, Rafael Evencio *retired urologist*
Mufson, Maurice Albert *infectious diseases physician, educator*
Oakley, Gerard Joseph *gynecologist*
Reynolds, Marshall Truman *printing company executive*
Wenzel, Loren Alvin *finance educator*

Hurricane
Blair, Paul Alex *otolaryngologist, plastic surgeon*
Chaney, Robin White *secondary school educator, consultant*
Hage, Lillian C. *religious organization administrator, director, dean*
Hill, David Lawrence *lawyer*

Jane Lew
Turner, Linda Jeannette Chapman *artist, historian*

Kearneysville
Biggs, Alan Richard *plant pathologist, educator*
Williams, Solomon Joseph III *military officer*

Kingwood
Campbell, Casey Joseph *chaplain*
Moyers, Sylvia Dean *retired medical librarian*

Lewisburg
Ford, Richard Edmond *lawyer*

Martinsburg
Ayers, Anne Louise *small business owner, consultant, counselor*
Day, Michael Gordon *information technology executive, educator*
Dugger, Debra Martin *school counselor*
Hayes, Carol Sue *elementary school educator*
Hill, Philip Bonner *lawyer*
Rice, Lacy I., Jr. *lawyer*

Matewan
Call, Bridget Kay *literature and language educator*

Morgantown
Albrink, Margaret Joralemon *medical educator*
Alkadry, Mohamad G. *public administration educator*
Allamong, Betty Davis *retired academic administrator, biology professor*
Bajura, Richard Albert *academic administrator, mechanical engineer, educator*
Bell, Lewis Clay *economics professor, government administrator*
Bender, Nathan Edward *librarian, archivist*
Blaydes, Sophia Boyatzies *English language educator*
Bucklew, Neil S. *former academic administrator, educator*
Bush, Carletta Ann *historian, educator*
Chisholm, Lionel Donald John *ophthalmologist*
Cochrane, Robert Lowe *biologist*
Collins, James William *health science association administrator, director, epidemiologist, mechanical engineer*
D'Alessandri, Robert M. *academic administrator, retired dean*
De Vore, Paul Warren *technology educator*
Ducatman, Alan Marc *physician*
Fisher, John Welton, II, *lawyer, educator, academic administrator*
Fleming, William Wright, Jr. *pharmacology educator, department chairman*
Fusco, Andrew G. *lawyer*
Garrison, Michael S. *academic administrator, lawyer, educator*
Gladfelter, Wilbert Eugene *physiology educator*
Glover, Douglas Dennis *obstetrics, gynecology and pharmacology educator*
Griffith, Charles T. *accountant, consultant*
Gustafson, Robert Allen *pediatric cardiothoracic surgeon*
Halabe, Udaya Bhatta *civil engineering educator, researcher*
Han, Runlin *biochemist, researcher*
Hardesty, David Carter, Jr. *law educator, former academic administrator*
Hayes, Angela Mariw *psychologist*
Huggins, Bob *former college basketball coach*
Kim, Hong Nack *political science professor*
Koelbl, James J. *dean*
Kuo, Ying Ying *instructional designer*
Morris, William Otis, Jr. *lawyer, educator*
Moxley, Roy Anthony *early childhood educator*
Nath, Joginder *genetics and biology educator, researcher*
Peng, Syd S. *mining engineer, educator*
Pinheiro, Germania Araujo *physician, researcher*
Pyles, Rodney Allen *archivist, county official*
Rieder, Keith Lee *psychologist*
Ringer, Darrell Wayne (Dan) *lawyer*
Rodriguez, Rich *college football coach*
Scudiere, Debra Hodges *lawyer*
Seehra, Mohindar Singh *physics professor, researcher*
Talukder, Jamil *physiologist, researcher*
Waller, Stacey *psychologist*
Wenger, Sharon Louise *cytogeneticist, researcher, educator*
Wiedebusch, Mary Kathryne *dance educator*
Wilson, Mary Alice *musician, educator*
Witt, Tom *economics researcher, educator*

Mullens
McGhee, William Cleveland *retired military officer, retired transportation engineer*

Oak Hill
Hamilton, Pat R. *retired lawyer, state representative*

Parkersburg
Branch, Michael Lee *social studies educator, consultant*
Dennis, James L. *history educator*
Francis, Lynne Ann *elementary school and music educator*
McClung, Mary Denise *psychology professor*
McClung, Phil Oran *psychology professor*
McKenzie, Lawrence J. *composition educator*
Sperati, Carleton Angelo *retired chemist*
Wilson, Roberta Bush *retired psychotherapist, accountant*
Zeck, Van *federal agency administrator*

Pennsboro
Poling, Kermit William *minister*

Philippi
Markwood, Stephen Ernest *academic administrator, educator*

Point Pleasant
Rerych, Stephen Karl *surgeon*

Ranson
Rudacille, Sharon Victoria *medical technician*

Reedsville
Williford, Drury Fisher, Jr. *retired historical researcher, writer, editor*

Romney
Saville, Royce Blair *lawyer*

Ronceverte
Hooper, Anne Dodge *pathologist, educator*

Saint Albans
Smith, Robert Carlisle *department administrator, welding educator*

Salem
Raad, Virginia *pianist, educator*

Shepherdstown
Elliott, Jean Ann *retired library director*
Snyder, Joseph John *editor, lecturer, consultant, historian, writer*
Summerford, Ben Long *retired artist, educator*
Wilson, Miriam Janet Williams *publishing executive*

Shinnston
Ford, Alma Regina *retired union official, educator*
Spears, Jae *state legislator*

South Charleston
Bhasin, Madan Mohan *research scientist*
Fishkin, Anne Sonya *retired special education educator*

Spencer
Parker, Theresa Ann Boggs *retired special education educator, retired music educator*

Summit Point
Taylor, Harold Allen, Jr. *industrial minerals consultant*

Teays
Lamb, Carl Vernon *writer, retired engineer*

Triadelphia
McCullough, John Phillip *management consultant, educator*

Weirton
Fahey, William Thomas, II, *lawyer*

Wellsburg
Viderman, Linda Jean *legal assistant, corporate financial executive*

Weston
Billeter, Robert James *newspaper publisher*

Wheeling
de Paulo, Craig J. N. *priest, philosopher, educator*
Duffy, Norman Vincent *chemistry professor*
Good, Laurance Frederic *hospital administrator*
Hickcox, Leslie Kay *education educator, consultant*
Hill, Barry Morton *lawyer*
Johnston, Thomas E. *judge*
Phillis, Marilyn Hughey *artist*
Potter, Sharon Lynn *prosecutor*
Stamp, Frederick Pfarr, Jr. *federal judge*
Thurston, Bonnie Bowman *religious studies educator, minister, poet*

WISCONSIN

Algoma
Golomski, William Arthur Joseph *consulting company executive*

Appleton
Beck, Jill *academic administrator, dancer, educator*
Boldt, Oscar Charles *construction executive, director*
Boren, Clark Henry, Jr. *general and vascular surgeon*
Chaney, William Albert *retired history professor*
Froehlich, Harold Vernon *judge, retired congressman*
Geller, Scott A. *management consultant*
Goldgar, Bertrand Alvin *historian, educator*
Grayson, David S. *paper company executive*
Luther, Thomas William *retired dermatologist*

Malaney, Stephanie J. *reading specialist*
Maravolo, Nicholas C. *biology professor*
Petinga, Charles Michael *transportation executive*
Seifert, Kathi P. *manufacturing executive*
Spiegelberg, Harry Lester *retired paper company executive*
Stellmacher, Jon Michael *corporate financial executive*
Warrick, Paul David *otolaryngologist*

Argyle
Daley, Ron(ald Eugene) *playwright, poet, theater director, theater producer*

Ashland
Beever, Erik Alan *ecologist, biologist*
Schulte, Melanie Ann *athletic trainer*
Smith, Jane Schneberger *retired city administrator*

Baileys Harbor
Schultz, Richard Otto *ophthalmologist, educator*

Baraboo
Lang, Gregory P. *music educator*
Umhoefer, Aural M. *retired dean, educational consultant*

Barneveld
Kolb, Victoria L. *retired mathematics educator*

Barron
Kienbaum, Janice Mae *reading specialist*

Beaver Dam
Butterbrodt, John Ervin *real estate company officer*
Manthe, Cora De Munck *real estate company executive*

Belgium
Sullivan, Patricia W. (Terry Sullivan) *real estate trainer*

Beloit
Burris, John Edward *academic administrator, biologist, educator*
Davis, Harry Rex *political science professor*
Hendricks, Kenneth *wholesale distribution executive*
Knueppel, Henry W. *manufacturing executive*
Wheeler, Karla *education educator*

Black Earth
Klug, Scott Leo *former congressman*

Black River Falls
Lister, Thomas Edward *lawyer*

Bloomer
Prenzlow, Elmer John-Charles, Jr. *minister*

Boscobel
Young, Gary William *minister, educator, retired military officer*

Bowler
Bartholomaus, Brett William *small business owner*

Brookfield
Bauer, Chris Michael *banker*
Carter, Charlene Ann *psychologist*
Curfman, Floyd Edwin *retired engineering educator*
Dillon, Donald F. *data processing executive*
Lavender, Cheryl Ann *music educator, composer, writer*
Nielsen, Leon *animal scientist*
Olson, David Carl *physician*
Rettmann, Robert D. *corporate communications specialist*
Schmitz, John J. *writer, educator*
Sprague, Charles W. *lawyer, finance company executive*
Sullivan, Owen *employment services executive*
Thomas, John *mechanical engineer, artist*
Walters, Ronald Ogden *mortgage banker*
Winsten, Saul Nathan *lawyer*
Yabuki, Jeffrey W. *data processing company executive, former accounting company executive*
Zander, Gaillienne Glashow *psychologist*

Bryant
Sutherland, Marion Ida *music educator*

Campbellsport
Klein, David P. *painter*

Cascade
Baumann, Carol Edler *retired political scientist*

Cashton
Haas, James Wayne *accountant*

Cassville
Tubbs, Christopher Charles *music educator*

Clintonville
Johnson, Edward C. *literature and language educator, social sciences educator*
Primmer, Lillian Juanda *science educator*
Reinke, Sussanah Hope *music educator, coach*
Simpson, Vinson Raleigh *manufacturing executive, director*

Colgate
Earl, Marcia Hunt *music educator, director*

Columbus
Brinkman, Michael Owen *health care consultant, educator*

Cottage Grove
Baird, Robert Dahlen *retired theology studies educator*
Lund, Daryl Bert *retired food science educator*

Darien
Miller, Malcolm Henry *manufacturing sales executive, real estate developer*

De Forest
O'Neil, J. Peter (James Peter O'Neil) *elementary school educator, computer scientist*

De Pere
Kersten, Frederick Irving *retired philosopher, educator*
Patterson, Wayne K. *historian, educator*

Deerfield
Pappas, David Christopher *lawyer*

Delafield
Haugner, Carolyn M. *elementary school educator*
Hausman, C. Michael *lawyer*

Delavan
Julius, Scott David *music educator*

Dodgeville
Dentinger, Ronald Lee *comedian, speaker, freelance writer*

Dousman
Petersen, Jonathan Christian *elementary school educator, music educator*

Eagle
Kalnes, Donna M. Simondet *retired principal, alcohol and drug abuse education program director*

Eagle River
Agre, James Courtland *physiatrist*

Eau Claire
Brill, Donald Maxim *researcher, educator*
Dick, Raymond Dale *psychologist, educator*
Field, Barbara Kay *elementary school educator*
Frank, John LeRoy *commissioner, lawyer, educator*
King, Frederick W. *chemistry professor, researcher*
Kirkhorn, Lee-Ellen Charlotte *community health nurse, educator*
Knight, Robert Michael *music educator, department chairman*
Menard, John R., Jr. *home improvement retail executive*
Rusch, Gerald Allen *financial representative*
Sands, Dawn M. *lawyer*
Tiefel, Virginia May *librarian*
Weil, D(onald) Wallace *business administration educator*

Elkhorn
Dunn, Walter Scott, Jr. *writer, museum director, consultant*
Eberhardt, Daniel Hugo *lawyer*
Reinke, Doris Marie *retired elementary school educator*
Sostarich, Mark Edward *lawyer*
Sweet, Lowell Elwin *lawyer, writer*

Ferryville
Tedeschi, John Alfred *historian, educator, librarian*

Fish Creek
Abegg, Martin Gerald *retired academic administrator*

Fitchburg
Bhargava, Ashok *retired economics professor*
Zolot, Marvin Mitchell *internist*

Fond Du Lac
Boelhower, Patricia Lee *history educator*
Christie, Jacqueline Ann *nurse*
Shipe, Dale Allen *music educator*
Treffert, Darold Allen *psychiatrist, writer, hospital administrator*
Witte, Dale Andrew *choral director, educator*

Fort Atkinson
Jones, Alan Porter, Jr. *food manufacturing executive*
Lorman, Barbara K. *retired state senator*

Franklin
Schutte, Richard David *diversified financial services company executive*
Stenzel, Mary Francis *social worker*
Wheaton, Douglas B. *city manager, lawyer*

Franksville
Palecek, Michael R. *information technology manager*

Genesee Depot
Kaldhusdal, Terry Lee *elementary school educator*

Genoa
Parkyn, John Duwane *nuclear engineer*

Germantown
Ehlinger, Ralph Jerome *lawyer*
Rudebeck, Carol A. *school system administrator*

Glendale
Brosio, Richard Anthony *social studies educator*
Feitler, Robert *shoe company executive*
Schenker, Eric *university dean, economist*

Grafton
Jakubowski, Jennifer Sara *music educator*

Maynard, John Ralph *lawyer*

Green Bay
Alesch, Daniel James *social sciences educator, researcher*
Beideman, Paul S. *bank executive*
Burnett, Ralph George *lawyer*
Conley, William Cleland *statistician, educator*
Daley, Arthur James *retired magazine publisher*
Erickson, Ruth Alice *poet, artist*
Favre, Brett Lorenzo *professional football player*
Geisendorfer, James Vernon *religious writer, researcher*
Hardy, Deborah Lewis *dean, educator, dental hygienist*
Harlan, Robert Ernest *professional football team executive*
Harris, John T., IV, *religious organization administrator*
Hawk, A.J. *professional football player*
Kress, William F. *manufacturing executive*
LaRue, Lillian Jayne *electrical engineer, educator*
Lofgren, Christopher B. *trucking executive*
Lynch, Matthew J. *information technology executive, retail executive*
McCarthy, Mike *professional football coach*
McIntosh, Elaine Virginia *nutrition educator*
Milson, Bertram Irving *surgeon*
Nixon, Timothy Francis *lawyer*
Oshefsky, Carol Ann *retired elementary school educator*
Pukel, Clifford Stuart *physician*
Reinke, Mark Kevin *otolaryngologist*
Schneider, Donald J. *trucking company executive*
Thill, Linda Susan *secondary school educator*
Vandenberg, Thomas E. *lawyer, transportation services executive*
Vandenhouten, Peter G. *lawyer*
Vannieuwenhoven, Vicki *professional sports team executive*
Weyers, Larry Lee *energy executive*

Greendale
Kaiser, Ann Christine *magazine editor*
Patterson, Amanda Margaret *music educator*
Pohl, Kathleen Sharon *editor*
Vinent-Cantoral, Aida R. *mediator*

Greenfield
Mayr, James Francis *physician*
McKillip, Patricia Claire *operatic soloist*

Hales Corners
Case, Karen Ann *lawyer*
Kuwayama, S. Paul *physician, immunologist, allergist*
McNally, Vincent Joseph *historian, educator*

Hartford
Aubuchon, Richard E. *engineering executive*
Falkenstein, Sara André *retired elementary school educator*

Hartland
Atlee, John Light *retired physician, consultant*
Burrus, Daniel Allen *research and development company executive, consultant*
Stamsta, Jean F. *artist*

Hayward
Tabbert, James Lee *music educator*

Hazel Green
Amweg, Eric Paul *music educator*

Hilbert
Postell, Shawn T. *music educator, school disciplinarian*

Hollandale
Colescott, Warrington Wickham *artist, printmaker, educator*

Holmen
Meyer, Karl William *retired university president*

Hortonville
Forton, Gregory A. *secondary school educator*
Juhl, Stacy Marie *music educator, director*

Hudson
Anderson, Gregory Shane *insurance executive*
Dahle, Carol Jo *secondary school educator, director*
Dahle, Johannes Upton *retired academic administrator*
Meincke, Carl Russell *music educator, director*
Sanders, Travis Allen *health facility administrator, director*

Iola
Krause, Chester Lee *publishing executive*
Mishler, Clifford Leslie *publisher*

Jackson
Goede, Michael Jon *secondary school educator*

Janesville
Butters, John Patrick *travel company executive, educator*
Fitzgerald, James Francis *broadcast executive*
Gianitsos, Anestis Nicholas *surgeon*
Kubina, June M. *elementary school educator, music educator*
Steil, George Kenneth, Sr. *lawyer*

Jefferson
Smith, Dena Michele *physical education educator*

Kenosha
Adler, Seymour Jack *social services administrator*
Campbell, F(enton) Gregory *academic administrator, historian*
Cook, Leslie Pam *music educator*

Cyr, Arthur I. *political science and economics professor*
Gustin, Brenda Sue *retired art educator, painter*
Higgins, John Patrick *lawyer, mediator, lobbyist, educator*
Iaquinta, Leonard Phillip *academic administrator, writer, consultant, not-for-profit fundraiser*
Kolb, Vera M. *chemist, educator*
Kollatz, Rebecca Lynn *music educator*
Kummings, Donald Dale *language educator*
Marrinan, Susan Faye *lawyer*
Michaelis, Karen Lauree *law educator*
Pinchuk, Nicholas Thomas *manufacturing executive*
Potente, Eugene, Jr. *interior designer*

Kohler
Kohler, Herbert Vollrath, Jr. *diversified manufacturing company executive*
Kohler, Laura E. *human resources executive*
Kukla, Wendy Jo *music educator*
Wells, Richard A. *manufacturing executive*

La Crosse
Bouri, Anil K. *neurologist, director*
Clark, Malcolm Gene, Sr. *artist, consultant, historian, writer, conservator, researcher*
Davy, Michael Francis *civil engineer, consultant*
Gorman, Kathleen Jean *performing arts educator, choreographer*
Gow, Joe *academic administrator*
Klos, Jerome John *lawyer, director*
Luckner, Brian William *choir director, organist, composer*
Medland, William James *university chancellor*
Rademacher, Dana Ellis *urologist*
Rude, Brian David *utilities executive*
Sleik, Thomas Scott *lawyer*
Smith, Martin Jay *physician, biomedical research scientist*
Webster, Stephen Burtis *dermatologist, educator*

Lake Geneva
Braden, Berwyn Bartow *lawyer*
Dobray, Alan Michael *theoretical physicist, research scientist*
Lemke, Sherry Ellen *therapist*

Lake Mills
Lazaris, Pamela Adriane *community planning and development consultant*

Lancaster
Croft, Candace Ann *psychology professor, academic administrator, small business owner*
Halferty, James Burkhardt *lawyer*

Madison
Abrahamson, Shirley Schlanger *state supreme court chief justice*
Adler, Julius *biochemist, educator, biologist*
Albers, Sheryl Kay *state legislator*
Albert, Daniel Myron *ophthalmologist, educator*
Aldag, Ramon John *management and organization educator*
Amasino, Richard M. *plant physiologist*
Anderson, David R. *insurance company executive*
Anderson, Louis Wilmer, Jr. *physicist, researcher*
Anderson, Michael Steven *lawyer*
Andreano, Ralph Louis *economist, educator*
Arndt, George Arthur *anesthesiologist, consultant*
Askey, Richard Allen *mathematician, educator*
Bablitch, William A. *lawyer, retired state supreme court justice*
Barger, Amy J. *astronomer, educator*
Barger, Vernon Duane *physicist, educator*
Barish, Lawrence Stephen *nonpartisan legislative staff administrator*
Barkan, Steven M. *law librarian, educator*
Barnhill, Charles Joseph, Jr. *lawyer*
Barnick, Helen *retired judicial clerk*
Bartell, Angela Gina Baldi *judge*
Bartley, Linda L. *musician, music educator*
Basting, Thomas J., Sr. *lawyer*
Bauman, Susan Joan Mayer *mayor, lawyer, commissioner*
Beachley, Norman Henry *mechanical engineer, educator*
Beatty, Mark A. *librarian*
Beck, Anatole *mathematician, educator*
Behnke, Michelle A. *lawyer*
Bennett, Kenneth Alan *retired biological anthropologist*
Berg, William James *language educator, writer, translator*
Berghahn, Klaus Leo *German and Jewish studies educator*
Berven, Norman Lee *counselor, psychologist, educator*
Beyer-Mears, Annette *physiologist*
Bielema, Bret *university football coach*
Bird, Robert Byron *chemical engineering educator, author*
Bisbee, Joyce Evelyn *retired utility company executive*
Blackwell, Helen E. *chemistry professor*
Bochert, Linda H. *lawyer*
Bogue, Allan George *historian, educator*
Botez, Dan *physicist*
Boucher, Joseph W(illiam) *lawyer, educator, accountant, writer*
Boykoff, Thomas M. *retired lawyer*
Boyle, William Charles *engineering educator*
Bradley, Ann Walsh *state supreme court justice*
Bremer, Howard Walter *lawyer, consultant*
Brennan, Robert Walter *association executive*
Bridges, Alan J. *physician*
Brock, Thomas Dale *retired microbiology professor*
Brock, William Allen III *economist, educator*
Bruch, Ludwig W. *physicist, researcher*
Bugge, Lawrence John *lawyer, educator*
Bunge, Charles Albert *library science educator*
Burgess, James Edward *publishing executive*

Burgess, Richard Ray *oncologist, molecular biologist, biotechnologist, educator, researcher, consultant*
Burish, Andrew D. *investment advisor*
Burmaster, Elizabeth *school system administrator*
Burns, Elizabeth Murphy *media executive*
Burris, Robert Harza *biochemist, educator*
Busby, Edward Oliver *retired dean*
Butler, Louis Bennett, Jr. *state supreme court justice*
Callen, James Donald *plasma physicist, nuclear engineer*
Cao, Guoping *research scientist*
Carnell, Kent I. *lawyer*
Carroll, Sean B. *geneticist, biologist, educator, researcher, writer*
Cassinelli, Joseph Patrick *astronomy educator*
Chandler, Richard Gates *lawyer*
Chapman, Loren J. *psychology professor*
Charo, Robin Alta *law educator*
Choi, Hongseok *mechanical engineer, researcher*
Christensen, Nikolas Ivan *geophysicist, educator*
Churchwell, Edward Bruce *astronomer, educator*
Ciplijauskaite, Birute *humanities educator*
Clay, Clarence Samuel *acoustical oceanographer*
Cleland, W(illiam) Wallace *biochemistry educator*
Cohen, Marcus *allergist, immunologist*
Conniff, Gregory *photographer*
Connors, Kenneth Antonio *retired pharmacy educator*
Cooper, Peggy (Mary Margaret) *artist, educator, poet, composer, choreographer*
Coppersmith, Susan Nan *physicist*
Crabb, Barbara Brandriff *federal judge*
Crim, Forrest Fleming, Jr. *chemist, educator*
Cripps, Derek J. *dermatologist, educator*
Cronon, William *history professor*
Crooks, Neil Patrick *state supreme court justice*
Crow, James Franklin *retired genetics educator*
Culbertson, Frances Mitchell *psychology professor*
Curtis, Charles G., Jr. *lawyer*
Curtiss, Charles Francis *retired chemist, educator*
Dahl, Lawrence Frederick *chemistry professor*
Darling, Alberta Helen *state legislator, art gallery director, marketing professional*
Davidson, Richard J. *psychology and psychiatry professor, researcher*
Davis, Kenneth Boone, Jr. *dean, law educator*
DeBruin, Donald J. *church musician*
DeMain, John *opera company director*
DeMets, David L. *medical educator, biomedical researcher*
Derzon, Gordon M. *hospital administrator*
DeWerd, Larry Albert *medical physicist, educator*
DeWitt, David J. *computer scientist*
Dierauf, Leslie Ann *wildlife veterinarian, conservation biologist, consultant*
Dietmeyer, Donald Leo *retired electrical engineering educator*
Dimick, Barbara L. *library director*
Dott, Robert Henry, Jr. *geologist, educator*
Doyle, Jim (James Edward) *governor, former state attorney general*
Draper, Norman Richard *statistician, educator*
Drechsel, Robert Edward *journalism educator*
Drewal, Henry John *art historian, educator*
Dubrow, Heather *literature educator*
DuRose, Stanley Charles, Jr. *retired insurance company executive*
Earl, Anthony Scully *retired governor, lawyer*
Easterday, Bernard Carlyle *veterinary medicine educator*
Eldridge, James Francis *lawyer, insurance company executive*
Emmert, Gilbert Arthur *retired engineering educator*
Evan, Amato Tomas *climate scientist*
Evenson, Merle Armin *chemist, educator*
Evert, Ray Franklin *botany educator*
Fahien, Leonard August *physician, educator*
Farrar, Thomas C. *chemist, educator*
Farrell, Patrick V. *academic administrator*
Farrell, Philip M. *physician, dean, educator, researcher*
Faulkner, Julia Ellen *opera singer*
Field, Henry Augustus, Jr. *lawyer*
Fitchen, Allen Nelson *publisher*
Fleming, Michael F. *medical educator*
Ford, Charles Nathaniel *otolaryngologist, educator*
Fox, Michael Vass *theology studies educator*
Frautschi, W. Jerome (Jerry Frautschi) *foundation administrator, retired manufacturing executive*
Frazier, Kenneth L. *university librarian*
Frey, Perry A. *biochemistry educator*
Frykenberg, Robert Eric *historian, educator*
Ganetzky, Barry S. *geneticist, science educator*
Garver, Thomas Haskell *curator, consultant, writer*
Garvre, Fanny P. *art gallery owner*
Gellman, Samuel Helmer *chemist, educator*
Goldberger, Arthur Stanley *economics professor*
Golovkin, Igor *physicist*
Goodrich, James A. *veterinarian, researcher*
Graf, Truman Frederick *agricultural economist, educator*
Graziano, Frank Michael *medical educator, researcher*
Greaser, Marion Lewis *science educator*
Greenfield, Norman Samuel *psychologist, educator*
Greenler, Robert George *physics professor, researcher*
Greer, Frank Roland *pediatrician, neonatologist*
Griffin, Martin P.A. *research scientist*
Grobschmidt, Richard A. *school system administrator*
Gruber, John Edward *editor, historian, photographer*
Gustafson, David Harold *industrial engineering and preventive medicine educator*
Hamerow, Theodore Stephen *historian, educator*
Hamers, Robert J. *chemistry educator, researcher*
Handelsman, Jo *plant pathologist, educator*
Hansen, Sherri M. *psychiatrist*
Hansen, W. Lee *economics professor*
Hanson, David James *lawyer*
Harvey, William D. *utilities executive, lawyer*
Haslanger, Philip Charles *journalist*
Hawkinson, Lorraine A. *librarian*
Heatley, Gregg Alan *ophthalmologist*
Hempe, A. Henry *labor relations specialist, labor arbitrator, lawyer*
Heymann, S. Richard *lawyer*
Hibbard, William Louis *computer scientist*
Hildebrand, Daniel Walter *lawyer*
Hill, Charles Graham, Jr. *chemical engineering educator*
Himpsel, Franz Josef *physicist, researcher*
Hokin, Lowell Edward *biochemist, educator*
Hopen, Herbert John *horticulture educator*
Hopson, James Warren *publishing executive*
Horning, Kathleen T. *library director*
Howell, Roberta F. *lawyer*
Hoyt, James Lawrence *journalism educator, writer*
Iltis, Hugh Hellmut *botanist, educator, environmental advocate*
Jacobsen, Kendra *health facility administrator*
Javid, Manucher J. *retired neurosurgeon, educator*
Jeanne, Robert Lawrence *entomologist, educator*
Jefferson, James Walter *psychiatrist, educator*
Jiang, Eric Y *research scientist, marketing executive*
Johnson, Jean Elaine *nursing educator*
Johnson, Maryl Rae *cardiologist*
Johnson, Millard Wallace, Jr. *mathematics and engineering professor*
Johnson, Richard Arnold *statistics educator, consultant*
Kaesberg, Paul Joseph *virology researcher*
Kastenmeier, Robert William *congressman*
Kawaoka, Yoshihiro *virologist, educator*
Keating Heinemann, Lorrie T. *state agency administrator*
Kemnitz, Joseph William *physiologist, researcher*
Khazins, David Mikhailovich *research scientist*
Kiessling, Laura Lee *chemist, researcher*
Kingdon, Robert McCune *historian, educator*
Kleinhenz, Christopher *foreign language educator, researcher, director*
Knetter, Michael Mark *dean*
Knowles, Richard Alan John *language educator*
K-Turkel, Judith Leah Rosenthal (Judi K-Turkel) *writer, editor, publisher*
Kutler, Stanley Ira *historian, lawyer, educator*
Kutzbach, John E. *climate scientist*
Ladson-Billings, Gloria J. *education educator*
Laessig, Ronald Harold *preventive medicine and pathology educator, state official*
La Follette, Douglas J. *state official*
Lagally, Max Gunter *physics professor*
Lakes, Roderic Stephen *biomedical engineering educator*
Langer, Richard J. *lawyer*
Lardy, Henry A(rnold) *biochemistry professor*
Larson, John David *insurance company executive, lawyer*
Lasseter, Robert Haygood *electrical engineering educator, consultant*
Lautenschlager, Peggy A. *former state attorney general*
Lawler, James Edward *physics professor*
Lawton, Barbara *lieutenant governor*
Lemanske, Robert F., Jr. *allergist, immunologist*
Levine, Steven Alan *lawyer*
Li, Kai *chemist, research scientist*
Lightfoot, Edwin Niblock, Jr. *retired chemical engineering educator*
Lillesand, Thomas Martin *engineer, educator*
Lin, Chun Chia *research physicist, educator*
Linstroth, Tod Brian *lawyer*
Linzer, Mark *medical educator, internist*
Little, George Daniel *clergyman*
Lovell, Edward George *mechanical engineering educator*
Ma, Zhenqiang *education educator*
MacDougall, Priscilla Ruth *lawyer*
Macfarlane, Alastair Iain Robert *manufacturing executive, consultant*
MacKinney, Archie Allen *physician*
Maher, Louis James, Jr. *geologist, educator*
Maki, Dennis G. *epidemiology educator*
Malkus, David Starr *mathematician*
Malter, James Samuel *pathologist, educator*
Marlett, Judith Ann *nutritional sciences educator, researcher*
Marrett, Cora B. *science educator*
Martin, Robert David *judge, educator*
Mash, Donald J. *college president*
Mau, Bob *statistician*
McCallum, Laurie Riach *state government lawyer*
McNelly, John Taylor *retired journalist, educator*
Mehta, Minesh P. *oncologist, educator*
Melli, Marygold Shire *law educator*
Miller, Paul Dean *breeding consultant, geneticist, educator*
Moore, Lorrie *writer, English professor*
Morton, Stephen Dana *chemist, consultant*
Mowris, Gerald William *lawyer*
Mueller, Willard Fritz *economics professor*
Mukerjee, Pasupati *chemistry professor*
Nevin, John Robert *business educator, consultant*
Newcomb, Eldon Henry *retired botany educator*
Ney, Peter Ernest *mathematician, educator*
Nichols, Donald Arthur *economist, educator*
Nordby, Eugene Jorgen *orthopedic surgeon*
Novotny, Donald Wayne *electrical engineer, educator*
Odden, Allan Robert *education educator*
Olson, Norman Fredrick *not-for-profit developer, retired food science educator*
Peercy, Paul Stuart *engineering educator*
Pella, Milton Orville *science educator*
Perepezko, John H. *engineering educator*
Peterson, Erik Charles *prosecutor*
Peterson, H. Dale *lawyer*
Pitot, Henry Clement III *pathologist, educator*
Pitzner, Richard William *lawyer*
Pondrom, Lee Girard *physicist, researcher*
Post, Jeffrey H. *insurance company executive*
Powell, Barry Bruce *classicist, educator*
Prange, Roy Leonard, Jr. *lawyer*
Pray, Lloyd Charles *geologist, educator*
Prosser, David Thomas, Jr. *state supreme court justice and former legislator*
Ragatz, Thomas George *lawyer*
Rakel, David Paul *sports medicine physician, director*
Rankin, Gene Raymond *lawyer*
Ranney, Joseph Austin *lawyer*
Record, M. Thomas, Jr. *biochemist, educator*
Reilly, Kevin P. *academic administrator*
Reynolds, Ernest West *retired internist, educator*
Reynolds, Ronald J. *astronomer, educator*
Rice, Joy Katharine *psychologist, education educator*
Rich, Daniel Hulbert *retired chemistry professor*
Rikkers, Layton Frederick *surgeon*
Ring, Gerald J. *real estate developer, insurance company executive*
Rioult, Fabien Andre *research scientist*
Roberts, Leigh Milton *psychiatrist*
Robinson, Stephen Michael *mathematician, educator*
Roessler, Carol Ann *state legislator*
Rogers, Joel Edward *law, sociology and political science educator*
Roggensack, Patience Drake *state supreme court justice*
Rosser, Annetta Hamilton *composer*
Rueckert, Roland Rudyard *retired virologist, educator*
Rusi, Eduard *engineering educator*
Russell, Jeffrey Scott *engineering educator*
Ryan, Bo (William F. Ryan Jr.) *men's college basketball coach*
Sack, Robert David *geography professor*
Salzwedel, Jack C. *insurance company executive*
Sapiro, Virginia *academic administrator, political science professor*
Sass, Dawn Marie *state official*
Sauer, Jeff *university hockey coach*
Sazhin, Sergey Victorovich *electrochemist, researcher*
Scarano, Francisco A. *humanities educator*
Scheller, John C. J. *lawyer*
Scherdin, Mary Jane Liskovec *retired librarian, researcher*
Scherer, Victor Richard *physicist, computer scientist, consultant, musician*
Schmid, John Henry, Jr. *lawyer*
Schott, Donald Karl *lawyer*
Schultz, Daniel R. *insurance company executive*
Schutta, Henry Szczesny *neurologist, educator*
Sewell, Richard Herbert *retired historian, retired educator*
Shabaz, John C. *judge*
Shafer, Byron Edwin *American government educator*
Shain, Irving *retired chemicals executive, academic administrator*
Sharkey, Thomas David *botanist, educator*
Shohet, Juda Leon *electrical and computer engineering educator, researcher, information technology executive*
Skiles, James Jean *electrical and computer engineer, educator*
Skilton, John Singleton *lawyer*
Skinner, James Lauriston *chemist, educator*
Skochelak, Susan E. *dean*
Smith, Michael James *industrial engineering educator*
Sondel, Paul Mark *pediatric oncologist, educator*
Sonnedecker, Glenn Allen *pharmaceutical historian, educator*
Spencer, Cheryl L. *literature and language educator*
Spencer, Christopher S. *lawyer, insurance company executive*
Stein, James Howard *medical educator, researcher*
Steingass, Susan R. *lawyer*
Stites, Susan Kay *writer, human resources specialist, consultant*
Strier, Karen Barbara *anthropologist, educator*
Susman, Millard *geneticist, educator*
Swan, Barbara J. *lawyer, utilities executive*
Temkin, Harvey L. *lawyer*
Thomas, J. Mark *sociologist, educator, minister*
Thompson, Barbara Storck *state official*
Thomson, James Alexander *molecular biologist, educator*
Tishler, William Henry *landscape architect, educator*
Turner, Monica Goigel *ecologist*
Turner, Robert Lloyd *state legislator*
Turng, Lih-Sheng *education educator*
Uttal, Lynet *education educator*
Van Hollen, J(ohn) B(yron) *state attorney general, former prosecutor*
Vaughan, Michael Richard *lawyer*
Vaughan, Worth Edward *retired chemistry professor*
Viscovich, Nancy Anne *psychologist*
Voight, Jack C. *state official*
Vowles, Richard Beckman *literature educator*
Wald, Arnold *gastroenterologist*
Waldo, Robert Leland *retired insurance company executive*
Walker, Duard Lee *medical educator*
Walsh, David Graves *lawyer*
Webster, John Goodwin *biomedical engineering educator, researcher*
Weinbrot, Howard David *language educator*
Westman, Jack Conrad *child psychiatrist, educator*
Whiffen, James Douglass *surgeon, educator*
White, William Fredrick *lawyer*
Wilcox, Jon P. *state supreme court justice*
Wiley, John D. *academic administrator*
Wilson, Franklin D. *sociology educator*
Wineke, William Robert *reporter, minister*
Wink, Andre *history professor*
Wolfe, Barbara L. *economics professor, researcher*
Yevzlin, Alexander Sasha *nephrologist, medical products executive*
Young, Merwin Crawford *political science professor*
Young, Rebecca Mary Conrad *retired state legislator*
Yu, Hyuk *chemist, educator*
Yu, Jae-Hyuk *geneticist, educator*
Zell, Josephine May *retired language educator*
Ziegler, Annette Kingsland *state supreme court justice*
Zimmerman, Howard Elliot *chemist, educator*
Zinder, Newton Donald *investment advisor, consultant*
Zweifel, David Alan *newspaper editor*

Manitowoc
Growcock, Terry D. *manufacturing executive*
Jones, Maurice D. *lawyer*
Meyer, Kelly Lee *music educator*
Muchin, Arden Archie *lawyer, director*
Nelson, Robert Louis *education educator, consultant*
Tellock, Glen E. *manufacturing executive*
Trader, Joseph Edgar *orthopedic surgeon*

Markesan
Chamberlain, Robert Glenn *retired tool manufacturing executive*
Kastenschmidt, Betty M. *elementary school educator, director*

Marshfield
Kuehner, Marvin Ernest *surgeon*
Vidaillet, Humberto J., Jr. *physician, administrator, researcher*

Mayville
Kruger, Todd M. *music educator*

Mc Naughton
Bradshaw, Glenn Raymond *art educator*

Menasha
Kroening, K. Dubear *biology professor, researcher*
Walter, Thomas Bernard *music educator, conductor*

Menomonee Falls
Bonning, Kenneth *retail executive*
Boyle, Jack H. *retail executive*
Brennan, Donald A. *retail executive*
Chicorel, Ralph *librettist, composer, playwright*
Eskenasi, Peggy *retail executive*
Gardner, Julie *retail executive*
Hinnrichs-Dahms, Holly Beth *elementary school educator*
Janzen, Norine Madelyn Quinlan *clinical laboratory scientist*
Jeffries, Telvin *retail executive*
Kingsbury, Tom (Thomas A. Kingsbury) *retail executive*
Lesko, John J. *retail executive*
Mansell, Kevin B. *retail executive*
McDonald, Wesley S. *retail executive*
Montgomery, Larry (R. Lawrence Montgomery) *retail executive*
Nordeen, Jon K. *retail executive*
Schepp, Richard D. *lawyer, retail executive*
Woger, John Allen *band director, department chairman*
Worthington, John M. *retail executive*

Menomonie
Asthana, Rajiv *engineering educator, researcher*
Cutnaw, Mary-Frances *retired communications educator, writer, editor*
Lueder, Dianne Carol *library director*
Steans, Phillip Michael *lawyer*

Mequon
Andritzky, Joseph George *law educator*
Bloom, James Edward *commodity trading and financial executive*
Braun, Michael Andrew *radiologist*
Elias, Paul S. *retired marketing executive*
Ellis, William Grenville *academic administrator, management consultant*
Gettel, James Joseph *lawyer, consultant*
O'Shaughnessy, James Patrick *lawyer, consultant*
Richman, Stephen Erik *retired lawyer, consultant*
Sisney, Ned *education educator*
Terry, Leon Cass *neurologist, educator*
Whyte, George Kenneth, Jr. *lawyer*

Merrill
Goessl, Celine *head of religious order*
Schram, Jeffrey Scott *music educator*

Middleton
Bass, Bill *apparel executive*
Berman, Ronald Charles *lawyer, accountant*
Crawford, Mark E. *chemist*
Dorner, Peter Paul *retired economist, educator*
Lee, Leslie Warren *marketing executive, educator*
O'Brien, James Aloysius *foreign language educator*
Taylor, Fannie Turnbull *art association administrator, educator*

Milton
Enlow, Donald Hugh *retired anatomist, dean*

Milwaukee
Abraham, William John, Jr. *lawyer*
Adami, Norman J. *brewery executive*
Alred, Gerald James *literature and language professor*
Alverson, William H. *lawyer*
Aman, Mohammed Mohammed *dean, library and information science professor*

Arbit, Bruce *direct marketing executive, consultant*
Arkless, David *employment services executive*
Attanasio, Mark L. *investment banker, professional sports team executive*
Babler, Wayne E., Jr. *lawyer*
Bader, Alfred Robert *chemist*
Baez, JoAnne Marie *school psychologist*
Bailey, Thomas Anthony *lawyer*
Ballman, Patricia Kling *lawyer*
Bannen, John Thomas *lawyer*
Barrett, Thomas M. *mayor, former congressman*
Barth, John M. *manufacturing executive*
Barth, Karl Luther *retired seminary president*
Baumgardner, Dennis J. *physician, researcher, educator*
Beals, Vaughn Le Roy, Jr. *retired motorcycle manufacturing executive*
Beck, Barbara J. *employment services executive*
Behrendt, David Frogner *retired journalist*
Berdan, Robert J. *lawyer, insurance company executive*
Bergmann, Thomas E. *corporate financial executive*
Berkoff, Marshall Richard *lawyer*
Biehl, Michael Melvin *lawyer, writer*
Biller, Joel Wilson *lawyer, retired diplomat*
Biskupic, Steven M. *prosecutor, lawyer*
Blain, Peter Charles *lawyer*
Bleustein, Jeffrey L. *motorcycle company executive*
Boer, Ralf Reinhard *lawyer*
Boese, Gil Karyle *cultural organization administrator*
Bogut, Andrew *professional basketball player*
Bowen, Michael Anthony *lawyer, writer*
Branch, Joseph C. *lawyer*
Bremer, John M. *lawyer*
Brenner, Elizabeth (Betsy Brenner) *publishing executive*
Bruce, Peter Wayne *lawyer, insurance company executive*
Burch, Thaddeus Joseph, Jr. *physics professor, priest*
Busch, John Arthur *lawyer, business executive*
Buss, Daniel Frank *environmental scientist*
Cannon, David Joseph *lawyer*
Casey, John Alexander *lawyer*
Casper, Richard Henry *lawyer*
Chan, Carlyle Hung-lun *psychiatrist, educator*
Chandler, Edward William *communication systems engineer, electrical engineer, electrical engineering educator*
Cheatham, Wallace McClain *music educator*
Chen, Qinghua *engineering educator*
Chitambar, Christopher Rajiv *internist, oncologist, hematologist*
Christiansen, Keith Allan *lawyer*
Clark, James Richard *lawyer*
Coffman, Terrence J. *retired academic administrator*
Colbert, Virgis W. *food products executive*
Connelly, Mark *writer, educator*
Connolly, Gerald Edward *lawyer*
Cordero, Francisco Javier *professional baseball player*
Cowley, Allen Wilson, Jr. *physiologist*
Crocker, Ray Dean *musician, musical director*
Culver, Curt S. *diversified financial services company executive*
Cutler, Richard W. *lawyer*
Cutler, Verne Clifton *engineering educator, consultant*
Czarnezki, Mary Elaine *media specialist*
Daily, Frank J(erome) *lawyer*
D'Amato, Sandy *chef*
Daniels, John W., Jr. *lawyer*
Davidson, Rick *employment services executive*
Davis, Don H., Jr. *multi-industry high-technology company executive*
Davis, Susan F. *human resources specialist*
Delfs, Andreas *conductor, musical director*
Demerdash, Nabeel Aly Omar *electrical engineer*
Dionisopoulos, George Allan *lawyer*
Dolan, Timothy Michael *archbishop*
Donahue, John Edward *lawyer*
Dunn, Michael J. *dean*
Ellis, Dwight Holmes III *lawyer*
Emanuel, John F. *lawyer*
Erickson, Randall J. *lawyer*
Eshetu, Gwendelbert Lewis *retired social worker*
Evans, Terence Thomas *federal judge*
Farrell, Patrick *artist*
Farris, Trueman Earl, Jr. *retired newspaper editor*
Feinsilver, Donald Lee *psychiatry professor*
Fielder, Prince Semien *professional baseball player*
Fink, Jordan Norman *allergist, educator*
Florsheim, Richard Steven *lawyer*
Foldy, Seth Leonard *physician, educator*
Fournelle, Raymond Albert *engineering educator*
Fraser, Alexander Paul *lawyer*
Frauen, Kurt Herman *lawyer*
Frautschi, Timothy Clark *lawyer*
Friebert, Robert Howard *lawyer*
Friedman, James Dennis *lawyer*
Friedman, Paula Sopkin *literature educator*
Furlong, Mark Francis *diversified financial services company executive, bank executive*
Gaggioli, Richard Arnold *mechanical engineering educator*
Gaines, Irving David *lawyer*
Galanis, John William *lawyer*
Gallagher, Richard Sidney *lawyer*
Gallop, Jane (Jane Anne Gallop) *women's studies educator, writer*
Garcia, Astrid J. *newspaper executive*
Gefke, Henry Jerome *lawyer*
Geilfuss, C. Frederick, II, *lawyer*
Gemignani, Joseph Adolph *lawyer*
Gershan, William M. *pediatrician, educator*
Geske, Janine Patricia *law educator*
Ghiardi, James Domenic *lawyer, educator*
Giacinti, Louis Anthony *science educator, writer*
Goodkind, Conrad George *lawyer*
Goodstein, Aaron E. *federal magistrate judge*
Grabowski, Michael Joseph *financial executive*
Grade, Jeffery T. *manufacturing executive*
Graef, Luther William *civil engineer*
Greenstreet, Robert Charles *architect, educator*
Griffith, Owen Wendell *biochemistry professor*
Guerin, D. Michael *lawyer*
Haberman, F. William *lawyer*
Habush, Robert Lee *lawyer*
Hackbarth, Donald A., Jr. *medical educator, orthopedist*
Hagerman, Douglas M. *consumer products company executive, lawyer*
Hanson, John Nils *industrial high technology manufacturing company executive*
Harbeck, William H. *lawyer*
Harrington, John Timothy *retired lawyer*
Harris, Larry *professional sports team executive*
Hase, David John *lawyer*
Hatch, Michael Ward *lawyer*
Haworth, Daniel Thomas *chemistry professor*
Heinen, James Albin *electrical engineering educator*
Hirsh, Annette Marie *artist*
Hoffman, Nathaniel A. *lawyer*
Holz, Harry George *lawyer*
Horsman, Lenore Lynde (Eleanora) *soprano, actress, voice educator*
Hubbard, John M. *library and information scientist*
Hunter, Victor Lee *marketing executive, consultant*
Hur, Su-Ryong *physician, anesthesiologist*
Iding, Allan Earl *lawyer*
Jackson, Tamara Nicole *lawyer*
Janavitz, Kurt L. *insurance company executive*
Jaspan, Stanley S. *lawyer*
Joerres, Jeffrey A. *employment services executive*
Johannes, Kay L. *insurance company executive*
Johns, Tammy *employment services executive*
Jones, Paul W. *manufacturing executive*
Jordan, Ruth Ann *retired physician*
Jost, Lawrence John *lawyer*
Kaiser, Martin *editor-in-chief*
Kampine, John P. *anesthesiology and physiology educator*
Karkheck, John Peter *physics professor, researcher*
Karp, David Barry *lawyer*
Kearney, Joseph D. *dean, law educator*
Kennedy, John Patrick *lawyer, corporate financial executive*
Keshvala, Seelpa H *secondary school educator*
Kessler, Joan F. *judge, lawyer*
Keyes, James Henry *manufacturing executive*
Kiely, Paula *city librarian*
Kircher, John Joseph *law educator*
Klappa, Gale E. *energy executive*
Kopell, Brian Harris *neurosurgeon, director*
Kringel, Jerome Howard *lawyer*
Kritzer, Paul Eric *publishing executive, lawyer*
Kroft, Steven Howard *hematopathologist, medical educator*
Krueger, Raymond Robert *lawyer*
Krystkowiak, Larry Brett *professional basketball coach*
Ksobiech, Kate *sociologist, educator*
Kubale, Bernard Stephen *lawyer*
Kuester, Dennis J. *diversified financial services company and bank executive*
Kurtz, Harvey A. *lawyer*
Kushner, Beth *lawyer*
LaBudde, Roy Christian *lawyer*
Lane, Jeffrey H. *lawyer*
Langley, Grant F. *municipal lawyer*
Larson, David Lee *surgeon*
Laughlin, Steven L. *advertising executive*
Lee, Jack (Jim Sanders Beasley) *broadcast executive*
Levine, Herbert *lawyer*
Levit, William Harold, Jr. *lawyer*
Levy, Alan M. *lawyer*
Levy, Stuart Arthur *pulmonologist, consultant*
Lione, Gail Ann *lawyer*
Liu, Qingmin *software engineer, materials engineer*
Lobb, William K. *dean, dental educator*
Long, Tom *brewery executive*
Lueders, Wayne Richard *lawyer*
Lynch, Michael *lawyer, staffing company executive*
Manning, Kenneth Paul *specialty chemical company executive*
Mariano, Robert A. *retail executive*
Marquis, William Oscar *lawyer*
Masterson, Joseph D. *lawyer, partner*
Matusiak, Krystyna K. *school librarian, translator*
McDonald, R. Bruce *corporate financial executive*
McGaffey, Jere D. *retired lawyer*
McGinnity, Maureen Annell *lawyer*
McKeown, James T. *lawyer*
McSweeney, Maurice J. (Marc McSweeney) *lawyer*
Meldman, Robert Edward *lawyer*
Melin, Robert Arthur *lawyer*
Mitten, Matthew John *law educator, lawyer*
Mortimer, Norma Sue *music educator*
Mulcahy, Robert William *lawyer*
Murphy, Judith Chisholm *trust company executive*
Myers, C. David *manufacturing executive*
Namdari, Bahram *surgeon*
Neumann, Donald A. *physical therapist, educator*
Nissen, Varina *employment services executive*
Noonan, Timothy Paul *musicologist, educator*
Nosbusch, Keith D. *multi-industry high-technology company executive*
Okarma, Jerome D. *lawyer, manufacturing executive*
Olson, John Marshall *lawyer*
O'Meara, Stephen Charles *lawyer*
O'Toole, Robert Joseph *retired manufacturing executive*
Otto, Jean Hammond *journalist*
Pagel, Paul Stanley *anesthesiologist*
Paulson, Belden Henry *political scientist, educator*
Peckerman, Bruce Martin *lawyer*
Peltz, Cissie Jean *art gallery director, cartoonist*
Peng, Zhong-Ren *education educator*
Phillips, Thomas John *lawyer*
Pindyck, Bruce Eben *lawyer, corporate financial executive*
Pink, Michael *performing company executive*
Poliner, Gary A. *corporate financial executive*
Porter, Richard H. *lawyer*
Prising, Jonas *employment services executive*
Quereshi, Mohammed Younus *retired psychology professor*
Ransom, Randy *marketing executive*
Redd, Michael *professional basketball player*
Reyer, Steven E. *engineering educator*
Rheams, Annie Elizabeth *education educator*
Richer, Marc-Hans *marketing executive*
Rivera-Velazquez, Maria *marketing professional*
Roell, Stephen A. *manufacturing executive*
Runkel, Phillip M. *archivist*
Ryan, Patrick Michael *lawyer*
Saam, Robert Harry *human resources specialist, consultant*
Samson, Richard Max *theater director, investment company executive*
Sanfilippo, Jon *lawyer, court clerk*
Sankovitz, James Leo *retired development director, lobbyist*
Santelle, James Lewis *prosecutor*
Sato, Thomas T. *surgeon, educator*
Schneider, Thomas Paul *non-profit agency administrator*
Schnoll, Howard Manuel *financial consultant, investment company executive*
Schnur, Robert Arnold *lawyer, educator*
Schoenfeld, Howard Allen *management consultant, lawyer*
Schott, Sarah E. *lawyer*
Schroeder, John H. *university chancellor*
Schwartz, Carl R. *lawyer*
Schwister, Jay Edward *portfolio manager*
Scrivner, Thomas William *lawyer*
Sennett, Nancy J. *lawyer*
Shapiro, James Edward *judge*
Shapiro, Robyn Sue *lawyer, educator*
Sheets, Ben M. *professional baseball player*
Sherman, Daniel James *history professor, director*
Shetty, Kaup Rajmohan *endocrinologist, educator*
Shiely, John Stephen *manufacturing executive, lawyer*
Shriner, Thomas L., Jr. *lawyer*
Siegel, Kristi Ellen *language educator*
Siegel, Robert Harold *English literature educator, writer*
Simmons-Welburn, Janice *dean, library director*
Simoneau, Daniel Robert *application developer, accountant, educator, artist*
Simpson, Deborah *medical educator*
Sinclair, Stephen Lawrence Rabehl *psychologist, educator*
Slavik, Donald Harlan *lawyer*
Soergel, Konrad Hermann *physician*
Spore, Keith Kent *newspaper executive*
Steinmiller, John F. *professional sports team executive*
Stemper, Brian D. *biomedical engineer, educator*
Sterner, Frank Maurice *manufacturing executive*
Stokes, Kathleen Sarah *dermatologist, educator*
Sturm, William Charles *lawyer*
Surridge, Stephen Zehring *lawyer, writer*
Sutherlin, Michael W. *paper company executive*
Swan, Mara E. *employment services executive*
Swanson, Roy Arthur *classicist, educator*
Sykes, Diane S. *federal judge, former state supreme court justice*
Terschan, Frank Robert *lawyer*
Theis, Peter George *retired classicist*
Thrall, Arthur Alvin *artist, educator*
Towne, Jonathan Baker *vascular surgeon*
Treuden, Terry S. *music educator, director*
Trytek, David Douglas *insurance company executive*
Tully, Catherine T. *lawyer*
Tyson, Joseph B., Jr. *lawyer*
Uecker, Bob *actor, radio announcer, former baseball player, television personality*
Ullman, Pierre Lioni *retired Spanish educator*
Valance, Marsha Jeanne *library director, storyteller*
Van Handel, Michael J. *employment services executive*
Van Vugt, Eric J. *lawyer*
Velez, William *education educator*
Wake, Madeline Musante *academic administrator, nursing educator*
Waller, Mary Bellis *educational consultant, researcher*
Wandell, Keith E. *manufacturing executive*
Warejcka, Debra J. *research scientist*
Weakland, Rembert G. *retired archbishop*
Weiner, Wendy L(ou) *elementary school educator, writer*
Widera, Georg Ernst Otto *mechanical engineering educator, consultant*
Wild, Robert Anthony *academic administrator*
Wiley, Edwin Packard *retired lawyer*
Will, Trevor Jonathan *lawyer*
Williams, Allen W., Jr. *lawyer*
Williams, Clay Rule *lawyer*
Winters, Jill Mary *nursing educator, director*
Wynn, Stanford Alan *lawyer*
Yancey, Kim Bruce *dermatology researcher*
Yeh, Chia-Chou *electrical engineer, researcher*
Yi, Jianlian *professional basketball player*
Yost, Ned *professional baseball player*
Youker, James Edward *radiologist*
Yu, Hong *humanities educator*
Yue, Xiaohang *finance educator*
Ziemer, James L. *motorcycle company executive*
Zore, Edward John *financial services executive*

Monona
Jensen, Jill Susan *music educator*

Monroe
Figi, Matthew L. *secondary school educator*
Frantz, John A. *physician, writer*
Kittelsen, Rodney Olin *lawyer*
Rogerson, Anthony Richard *otolaryngologist*

Montello
Scheele, Adam *music educator*

Mosinee
Dul, Carla Marie *music educator*

Mount Horeb
Becker, David *artist, retired educator*

Nashotah
Hollister, Winston Ned *pathologist*
Neumann, Mark W. *former congressman, real estate developer*
Vincent, Norman L. *retired insurance company executive*

Neenah
Kalmanson, Steven R. *health products executive*
Orm, Sally S. *music educator, consultant*

New Berlin
Belich, Kay S. *music educator*
Gebhard, LaVerne Elizabeth *retired accounting educator*
Totten, Charles Arthur *sales executive*

New Glarus
Sippy, David Dean *dentist*

New Richmond
Schwan, LeRoy Bernard *artist, retired art educator*
Zuberbier, Jo Ann *elementary school educator*

Oak Creek
Gagliani, William Dennis *school librarian*
Giblin, Louis *lawyer*

Oconomowoc
Bleke, Diane K. *music educator, director*
Conrader, Constance Ruth *artist, writer*
Kneiser, Richard John *accountant*
Peebles, Allene Kay *manufactured housing company executive*
Sieckert, Kristine Ellen *school psychologist, consultant*

Oconto Falls
Dolibois, John Michael *surgeon*

Onalaska
Waite, Lawrence Wesley *osteopathic physician, educator*

Oshkosh
Barwig, Regis Norbert James *priest*
Blankfield, Bryan J. *lawyer, automotive executive, accountant*
Bohn, Robert G. *transportation company executive*
Cheng, Theresa *neurosurgeon*
Cooper, Janelle Lunette *neurologist, educator*
Curtis, George Warren *lawyer*
Earns, Lane Robert *academic administrator, historian, educator*
Gruberg, Martin *political science professor*
Hu, Li *art educator*
Kelly, John Martin *lawyer*
Olejniczak, Bernard Charles *education educator*
Rainwater, Terry I. *counseling administrator*
Ristow, Thelma Frances *retired elementary school educator*
Siepmann, James Patrick *research and development company executive, retired physician*
Wilde, William Richard *lawyer*

Pepin
Seymour, Mary Frances *lawyer*

Pewaukee
Farrow, Margaret Ann *former lieutenant governor*
Ward, James A. *lawyer*

Pickerel
Cook, Barbara K. *music educator*

Pittsville
Bayerl, Scott Lee *animal welfare organization administrator, web programmer*

Platteville
Alcalay, Eugene Christian *pianist*

Pleasant Prairie
Biland, Alan Thomas *computer integrated manufacturing executive*
Cherry, Peter Ballard *electrical products corporation executive*
Morrone, Frank *electronics executive*

Plover
Loteyro, Corazon Bigata *physician*

Plymouth
Gentine, Lee Michael *marketing professional*

Prairie Du Sac
Seltzner, Rachel *curator, science educator*

Pulaski
Kozlovsky, Timothy Francis *music educator*
Stangel, Philip David *secondary school educator, band instructor*

Racine
Baumgardt, George Francis *bank executive, musician, director*
Bean, S. Craig *minister, consultant*
Campbell, Edward Joseph *retired machinery company executive*
Coates, Glenn Richard *lawyer*
Du Rocher, James Howard *lawyer*
Gasiorkiewicz, Eugene Anthony *lawyer*
Hecker, David *lawyer*
Johnson, H(erbert) Fisk *manufacturing executive*
Johnson-Leipold, Helen P. *outdoor recreation company executive*
Johnson-Marquart, Winnie *consumer products company executive*
Klein, Gabriella Sonja *retired communications executive*
Konz, Gerald Keith *retired manufacturing executive*
MacNair, David Cameron *marketing executive*
McCollum, W. Lee *chemical company executive*
Rayburn, David B. *manufacturing executive*
Rodrigues-Pavao, Antonio *vocal music teacher*
Rosso, Jean-Pierre *electronics executive*
Rudebusch, Alice Ann *lawyer*
Sahakian, Lillian Zarouhi *artist, designer*
Stephens, James Linton *mechanical engineer*
Stewart, Richard Donald *internist, educator, writer*
Taragin, Davira Spiro *curator*
Wambold, Richard Lawrence *manufacturing executive*
Wright, Betty Ren *children's book writer*

Reedsburg
Bruer, Scott Vincent *music educator*
Mockler, Jolee Marie *art educator*

Rhinelander
Saari, John William, Jr. *lawyer*

Rice Lake
Mueller, Philip Kearns *retired minister*

Richland Center
Gollata, James Anthony *library director, educator*
Heinen, John Timothy *environmental engineer*

Ripon
Jeffries, Paul Franklin *philosophy professor*
Prissel, Barbara Ann *paralegal, law educator*

River Falls
Fry, Blake Edward *academic administrator*
Hedahl, Gorden Orlin *theater educator, dean*
Krey, DeAn Marie *retired education educator*
LeCapitaine, John Edward *counseling psychology educator, researcher, writer*
Smith, Clyde Curry *historian, educator*
Thibodeau, Gary A. *academic administrator*

Rudolph
Heywood, Gail Anne *musician, educator*

Saukville
Gulan, Bonnie Marion *writer, researcher*

Shawano
Mutter, John J., Jr. *writer, researcher*
Swetlik, William Philip *orthodontist*

Sheboygan
Abler, Ronald Francis *geography educator*
Biró, Marcel *chef*
Fritz, Kristine Rae *retired secondary school educator*
Navis, Timothy James *music minister*
Yurk, Todd Michael *retired health products executive*

Sheboygan Falls
Potter, Calvin J. *retired library director*

Shell Lake
Aderman, Oscar Darrell *retired music educator*

Shorewood
Bowers, Jane Meredith *retired music educator*
Lietz, Jeremy Jon *educational administrator, writer*

Soldiers Grove
Ewing, Brian Kim *retired engineering executive, writer*

Solon Springs
Swanson, Jean Laurie *music educator*

South Milwaukee
Kitzke, Eugene David *research and development company executive*
Schwantes, Brianne Catherine *marketing professional*

Spooner
Frey, Paul Howard *chemical engineer, engineering consultants company executive*

Spring Green
Day, Sarah Jane *actor*

Stevens Point
Barjis, Joseph *computer scientist, educator*
Cwiertniak, Robert L. *psychologist, educator, consultant*
Drew, Richard Allen *retired electrical engineer*
Droske, John P. *chemistry professor*
Mertz, Paul Eric *retired history professor, writer*
O'Reilly, William M. *lawyer, insurance company executive*
Schuh, Dale R. *insurance company executive*
Sheftz, Stephen Walter Robert *music educator, director, conductor*

Stoughton
Mason, Craig Alan *clinician*

Sturgeon Bay
Maher, Virginia Jones *art historian, educator*
Van Duyse, Francis Donald (Fritz Van) *publisher*

Sturtevant
Brandes, JoAnne *lawyer*
Johnson, S. Curtis *chemicals executive*
Lonergan, Edward F. *manufacturing executive*

Sun Prairie
Eustice, Francis Joseph *lawyer*

Superior
Carroll, David William *psychology professor*
DuBois, Robert Bradford *natural resources research scientist*
Erlenbach, Julius E. *academic administrator, musician*
Jacobs, Laura Elizabeth *school librarian, educator, archivist*
McKnight, Patricia Gayle *musician, artist, writer, educator*
Morden, Annette Sonja Knudson *retired education educator*
Robek, Mary Frances *business education educator*
Taylor, Winnifred Jane *psychologist*
Vance, Mary Lee *academic administrator*

Sussex
Losee, John Frederick, Jr. *manufacturing executive*
Stromberg, Gregory *printing ink company executive*
Waite, Jon Philip *music educator*

Thiensville
Roselle, William Charles *librarian*

Three Lakes
Bauknecht, Barbara Belle *retired pre-school educator*

Tomah
Neurohr, Shirley Ann *retired special education educator*

Union Grove
Dawson, Rose Dorothy *retired elementary school educator*
Stern, Walter Wolf III *lawyer*

Verona
Bell Swanson, Katie J. *music educator*

Washburn
Nutt, Sandra Kay *elementary school educator*

Washington Island
Raup, David Malcolm *paleontology educator*
Schweikert, Norman Carl *retired musician*

Waterford
Hanson, Jody Elizabeth *special education educator*
Karraker, Louis Rendleman *retired corporate executive*

Watertown
Malmanger, Curtis A. *mathematician, educator*

Waukesha
Arenz, Dale Wesley *lawyer, law educator*
Bonnett, James W. *engineer*
Cauley, James Robert *lawyer*
Day, Natalie Marie *music educator, director*
Dreyfus, Lee Sherman *international speaker*
Franze, Robert Dennis *social studies educator*
Graham, George Andrew, Jr. *psychologist, consultant*
Gustafson, Mardel Emma *secondary school educator, writer*
Hastad, Douglas Noel *academic administrator, physical education educator*
Hogan, Joseph M. *health products executive*
Lightfoot, Alfred J. *retired education educator*
Maas, Duane Harris *distilling company executive*
McCoy, John V. *lawyer*
Meyer, Debora Lynn *music educator*
Stringham, Phyllis Joan *retired music educator*

Waupaca
Feldt, Mary *elementary school educator*
Hansen, Louise Hill *music educator, retired application developer*

Waupun
Wendt, Thomas *finance company executive*

Wausau
Drengler, William Allan John *lawyer*
Etten, Stewart Louis *lawyer*
Grischke, Alan Edward *lawyer*
Loftus, Stephen Edward *elementary art educator*
Orr, San Watterson, Jr. *lawyer*
Rusch, Denise Marie *school system administrator*
Veninga, James Frank *humanities educator, editor, writer*
Wadzinski, Mary Beth *administrative assistant*

Wauwatosa
Alexander, Robert Gardner *lawyer*
Franke, Brent Douglas *real estate/insurance executive*
Heath, Robert F. *lawyer*
Kalogjera, Ikar Jaksa *psychiatrist, educator*
Mancuso, Joseph Edward *medical psychotherapist*
Savage, Thomas Ryan *lawyer*
Stubbe, Ray William *minister, writer*
Verdoni, Shawn Marie *not-for-profit fundraiser*

West Bend
Ackley, Daniel *music educator, conductor, composer*
Dittmer, H. Robert *music educator, director*
Gehl, William D. *manufacturing executive*
Schaefer, Gordon Emory *food products executive*
Van Treeck, Jennifer Lynn *music educator*

Weyauwega
Maasch, Lloyd Palmer *physician*

Whitefish Bay
Hawkins, Brett William *retired political science professor*
Hendee, William Richard *medical physics educator, academic administrator, radiologist*
Miotke, Anne Elizabeth *artist, educator*

Whitewater
Baica, Malvina Florica *mathematician, educator, researcher*
Busse, Eileen Elaine *special education educator*
Chapman, Stephanie Lynn *education educator*
Connor, James Richard *retired academic administrator*
Jennings, Robert Lee *retired music educator*
Kolb, Sharon Marie *education educator, director, consultant*
Kumpaty, Hephzibah J. *chemistry professor*
Nam, Ki-Bong *mathematics professor*
Norgard, Karen-Sam *art educator*

Williams Bay
Hobbs, Lewis Mankin *astronomer*

Wisconsin Rapids
Engelhardt, LeRoy A. *retired paper company executive*
Olson-Hellerud, Linda Kathryn *elementary school educator*

Woodruff
Polasek, Edward John *retired electrical engineer, consultant*

WYOMING

Afton
Nethercott, Mark A. *physics educator*

Buffalo
Kirven, Timothy J. *lawyer*

Casper
Anderson, Kevin Stuart *archivist, librarian*
Bennion, Scott Desmond *physician*
Combs, W(illiam) Henry III *lawyer*
Cotherman, Audrey Mathews *educational association administrator, management consultant*
Downes, William F. *federal judge*
Durham, Harry Blaine III *lawyer*
Elliott, Marian Kay *real estate manager*
Eskew, Sandra Caye *elementary school educator*
Foster, Vicki Anne *secondary school educator*
Keim, Michael Ray *dentist*
Kilts, Laurie Dawn *elementary school educator*
Lowe, Robert Stanley *lawyer*
Ptasynski, Harry *geologist, oil industry executive*
Rickabaugh, René Lane *principal*
Scaling, Sam T. *obstetrician, gynecologist*
Stroock, Thomas Frank *oil and gas company executive*
Sullivan, Michael John *lawyer, former ambassador*
Wieder, Brian H. *neurosurgeon*
Wildman, Peter Roberts *mathematics professor*
Wold, John Schiller *geologist, former congressman*

Cheyenne
Boughton, Lesley D. *library director*
Brimmer, Clarence Addison *federal judge*
Brorby, Wade *federal judge*
Burke, E. James *lawyer, state supreme court justice*
Carlson, Kathleen Bussart *law librarian*
Crank, Patrick J. (Pat Crank) *state attorney general*
Freudenthal, Dave (David D. Freudenthal) *governor*
Freudenthal, Steven Franklin *lawyer, political organization worker*
Golden, T. Michael *state supreme court justice*
Hill, William U. *state supreme court justice, former state attorney general*
Kite, Marilyn S. *state supreme court justice, lawyer*
Knight, Robert Edward *bank executive, educator*
Kunz, April Brimmer *state legislator, lawyer*
Lanier, Robert Lewis *oncologist*
Laycock, Anita Simon *psychotherapist*
Lummis, Cynthia Marie *former state official, lawyer*
Maxfield, Max R. *state official*
McBride, James M. *school system administrator*
Mockler, Esther Jayne *state senator*
Moore, Mary French (Muffy Moore) *potter, advocate*
Myers, Rolland Graham *investment counselor*
Newman, Steven David *psychologist, consultant*
Noe, Guy *retired social services administrator*
O'Brien, Terrence Leo *federal judge*
Palma, Jack D. *lawyer*
Sansonetti, Thomas L. *lawyer, former federal agency administrator*
Speight, John Blain *lawyer*
Thomson, Thyra Godfrey *former state official*
Vogel, Jeffrey C. *state agency administrator*
Voigt, Barton R. *state supreme court chief justice*
Weigner, Brent James *secondary school educator*
White, Daniel Eugene *lawyer*
Wolfe, Lawrence J. *lawyer*
Woodhouse, Gay Vanderpoel *former state attorney general, lawyer*

Cody
Donoghue, Ann Marie *museum administrator, consultant*
Garry, James B. *historian, naturalist, storyteller, writer*
Jackson, Harry Andrew *artist*
Price, B. Byron *historian*
Simpson, Alan Kooi *retired senator, lawyer*

Dubois
Glasser, Pamela Jean *musician, educator*

Evanston
Harris, Mark W. *mayor, lawyer*

Fairview
Luginbuehl, Marsha Lee *psychologist*

Gillette
Bailey, Daniel B. *lawyer, entrepreneur*
Lubnau, Thomas Edwin, II, *lawyer*

Green River
Albers, Dolores M. *secondary school educator*

Jackson
Cox, Paul Alan *ethnobotanist, educator*
Herrick, Gregory Evans *computer company executive*
Hirschfield, Alan James *entrepreneur*
Law, Clarene Alta *small business owner, retired state legislator*
Massy, William Francis *education educator, consultant*
Reiniger, Douglas Haigh *lawyer*
Schuster, Robert Parks *lawyer*
Shockey, Gary Lee *lawyer*
Spence, Gerry (Gerald Leonard Spence) *lawyer, writer*

Jackson Hole
Farkas, Carol Garner *nurse, administrator*

Kelly
Knowles, William Standish *retired chemist*

Lander
Field, Francis Edward *electrical engineer, educator*
Raynolds, David Robert *buffalo breeder, writer*
Stevens, Sufjan *musician*

Laramie
Allen, John Logan *geographer, department chairman*
Arnold, Joseph Patterson *artist, small business owner*
Boresi, Arthur Peter *writer, educator*
Buchanan, Tom *academic administrator*
Chai, Winberg *political science professor, foundation administrator*
Chisum, Emmett Dewain *historian, researcher, archaeologist*
Crocker, Thomas Dunstan *economics professor*
Darnall, Roberta Morrow *educational association administrator*
Dickman, Francois Moussiegt *former foreign service officer, educator*
Farrell, Mary M(aggie) *Dean of Libraries*
Gill, George Wilhelm *retired anthropologist*
Guerin, Charles Allan *museum director, artist*
Hansen, Matilda *former state legislator*
Kelley, Robert Otis *anatomist, educator*
Kinney, Lisa Frances *lawyer*
Kirkwood, Carol *literature and language educator*
Lauer, Warren A. *lawyer*
Lewis, Randolph Vance *molecular biologist, researcher*
Maxfield, Peter Charles *state legislator, lawyer, educator*
Meyer, Edmond Gerald *energy scientist, retired chemistry professor, academic administrator, entrepreneur*
Mingle, John Orville *engineer, educator, lawyer, consultant*
Moldenhauer, Susan *museum director, curator*
Nye, Eric W. *English language and literature educator*
Rechard, Paul Albert *retired civil engineering company executive, consultant*
Reif, David (Frank David Reif) *artist, educator*
Roark, Terry Paul *astronomer, educator*
Shaffer, Sherrill Lynn *economist*
Smith, Thomas Shore *retired lawyer*
Spiegelberg, Emma Jo *business education educator, academic administrator*
Stefanovic, Margareta *science educator*
Towler, Brian Francis *petroleum engineer, educator*
Williams, Roger Lawrence *historian, educator*
Yamamoto, Masahiro *adult education educator*

Newcastle
Engle, Kathleen Faye *elementary education educator*

Pinedale
Barlow, John Perry *writer, former rancher, advocate*

Powell
LaRowe, Miles *academic administrator*
Myers, Rex Charles *historian, educator, retired dean*
Patrick, H. Hunter *retired judge, lawyer*

Riverton
Bebout, Eli Daniel *oil industry executive*
Girard, NettaBell *lawyer*
Peck, Robert A. *publishing executive, state legislator*

Rock Springs
Thompson, Josie *nurse*

Sheridan
Aguirre Batty, Mercedes *Spanish, English and literature educator*
Cannon, Kim Decker *lawyer*

Ryan, Michael Louis *controller*

Teton Village
Conrad, Donald Glover *insurance executive*

Torrington
Lewis, Mary Jane *retired elementary school educator*

Wheatland
Hunkins, Raymond Breedlove *lawyer, rancher*

Wilson
Breitenbach, Mary Louise McGraw *psychologist, chemical dependency counselor*
Chrystie, Thomas Ludlow *investor*
Gordon, Stephen Maurice *manufacturing company executive, rancher*
Harrell, Samuel Macy *agribusiness executive*
Sage, Andrew Gregg Curtin, II, *former investment banking house executive*

Worland
Berryman, Carl *veterinarian, retired epidemiologist*
Woods, Lawrence Milton *airline company executive*

Yellowstone National Park
Lewis, Suzanne *parks director*
Cohen, David John *cardiothoracic surgeon*
Patterson, Sally Jane *communications executive, consultant*

TERRITORIES OF THE UNITED STATES

AMERICAN SAMOA

Pago Pago
Fung-Chen-Pen, Emma Talauna Solaita *librarian, director*
Jyothibhavan, Joserose S. *chemistry educator*
Kruse, F. Michael *judge*
Poumele, Claire Tuia *school system administrator*
Richmond, Lyle L. *judge*
Ripley, Afa, Jr. *attorney general*
Sunia, Aitofele Toese F. *lieutenant governor*
Tulafono, Togiola T.A. *governor*
Weitzel, John Quinn *bishop*

FEDERATED STATES OF MICRONESIA

Chuuk
Samo, Amando *bishop*

GUAM

Barrigada
French, Jennifer Suzanne *language educator*
Ilagan, Artemio B. *territorial agency administrator*
McDonald Terlaje, Patricia *counselor*

Hagatna
Artero, Margaret T. *academic administrator, military officer*
Camacho, Felix Perez *governor*
Carbullido, F. Philip *judge*
Cruz, Michael W. *lieutenant governor, surgeon*
Gutierrez, Carl T. C. *former governor*
Leon-Guerrero, Jillette Torre *nonprofit organization executive, consultant, writer*
Limtiaco, Alicia Garrido *attorney general, former prosecutor*
Manibusan, Joaquin V.E., Jr. *magistrate judge*
Maraman, Katherine Ann *judge*
Torres, Robert J., Jr. *judge*
Tydingco-Gatewood, Frances Marie *federal judge*
Unpingco, John Walter Sablan *federal judge*
Weeks, Janet Healy *retired supreme court justice*

Mangilao
Dames, Vivian Loyola *social sciences educator*
Duenas, Laurent Flores *health and nursing consultant*
Inoue, Yukiko *educational research educator*
Strauch, Edward Hugo *writer, retired literature and language professor*

Talofofo
Taylor, James John *finance educator*

Tamuning
Aguigui, Ignacio Cruz *lawyer*

NORTHERN MARIANA ISLANDS

Saipan
Borja, David M. *school system administrator*
Camacho, Charlotte DLG *principal, elementary school educator*
Castro, Alexandro C. *commonwealth supreme court justice*
Dela Cruz, Acelia Castro *elementary school educator*
Demapan, Miguel S. *commonwealth supreme court justice*
Fitial, Benigno Repeki *governor*
Gregory, Matthew T. *attorney general*
Lamkin, Celia Belocora *physician*
Manglona, John A. *commonwealth supreme court justice*
Munson, Alex Robert *judge*
Rapadas, Leonardo M. *prosecutor, lawyer*
Villagomez, Timothy P. *lieutenant governor*

PUERTO RICO

Aguadilla
Gómez-Jiménez, Carlos *science educator, microbiologist, geneticist*

Arecibo
Kerr, Robert B. *astronomer, atmospheric scientist*

Barceloneta
Rosado, Jose Elias *religious organization administrator, priest*

Bayamon
Berio, Blanca *editor, writer*
Cabrera-Otero, Sylvia *physician*
Carro, Eric F. *neurosurgeon*
Ortiz, William *composer, music educator*

Cabo Rojo
Rivera-Martinez, Socorro *retired elementary school educator, assistant principal*

Caguas
Aviles Miranda, Maximo *insurance company executive*
Ortiz, Víctor Raúl *parochial school educator*

Dorado
Glickman, Marlene *non-profit organization administrator*
Spector, Michael Joseph *agribusiness executive*

Guaynabo
Guisasola Gamez, Elina *psychologist*
Lasa-Ferrer, Armando *lawyer*

Hatillo
Santos, Isabel Rodriguez *high school marketing educator*

Hato Rey
Carrion, Richard L. *bank executive*
Cerezo, Carmen Consuelo *judge*
Ferrer, Miguel Antonio *brokerage house executive*
Gelpi, Gustavo Antonio *federal judge*

Humacao
MacDonald, Gordon Rhodes *retired urologist, military officer*

Manati
Martinez, Heriberto *human resources professional*

Mayaguez
Aguero, Joseph Edward *psychologist, educator*
Collins, Dennis Glenn *mathematics professor*
Coriano, Irmarie *mathematics educator, department chairman*
Hepperly, Paul Reed *plant pathologist*
Ruiz-Vargas, Yolanda *finance educator*
Sahai, Hardeo *medical statistics educator*
Suarez, Luis Edgardo *civil engineering educator*

Old San Juan
Weinstein-Bacal, Stuart Allen *lawyer, educator*

Ponce
Hernandez, Carlos I. *historian, educator*

San Juan
Acevedo-Vilá, Aníbal *governor, former congressional representative*
Acosta, Raymond Luis *federal judge*
Almodovar, Edna *pharmacist, educator*
Aponte Martinez, Luis Cardinal *retired archbishop*
Aponte Samalot, Myrelis *neuroscientist, psychologist, consultant*
Bacelo, Daniel Enrique *chemist, educator*
Besosa, Francisco Augusto *federal judge*
Bonilla, Fernando J. *Puerto Rican government official*
Carreras, Francisco José *retired academic and foundation administrator*
Casiano, Kimberly *publishing executive*
Cordero, Jose Fernando *pediatrician, dean*
Corrada del Rio, Baltasar *lawyer, retired former state supreme court justice*
Daddy Yankee, (Raymond Ayala) *musician*
Delgado-Colon, Aida M. *federal judge*
Del Toro Soto, Jaime *psychiatrist*
Dominguez, Daniel R. *judge*
Espino, Ana M. *parasitology and immunology educator, researcher*
Ferre, Antonio Luis *newspaper publisher*
Fiol Matta, Liana *judge*
Folch-Serrano, Karen D. *psychologist, consultant*
Fusté, José Antonio *federal judge*
Fuster Berlingeri, Jaime B. *judge*
Gil, Guillermo *prosecutor*
González Nieves, Roberto Octavio *archbishop*
Hernández Denton, Federico *judge*
Hoglund, Heath *lawyer*
Joglar, Francisco *academic administrator*
Lockwood-Benet, Mildred M. *language educator*
Marcano, Mariano *mathematics professor*
Martin, Ricky (Enrique Martin Morales IV) *vocalist, actor, producer, composer*
Marvel, Thomas Stahl *architect*
Matheu, Federico Manuel *university chancellor*
Muñoz-Solá, Haydeé Socorro *library administrator*
Negron-Garcia, Antonio S. *law educator, former territory supreme court justice*
Ocasio-Melendez, Marcial Enrique *history professor*
Oms, Luis J. *physician*
Padilla, Alfredo *state agency administrator*
Padrón, Luije *writer*
Pierluisi, Pedro R. *lawyer*
Quinones-Burgos, Dayna *pharmacist, educator*
Rebollo López, Francisco *judge*
Rey-Hernandez, Cesar A. *school system administrator*
Rivera Pérez, Efraín E. *judge*
Rodriguez, Annabelle *judge, former attorney general*
Rodriguez-Diaz, Juan E. *lawyer*
Rodriguez-Velez, Rosa Emilia *prosecutor*
Rossello, Pedro Juan *legislator, former governor*
Sanchez-Ramos, Roberto J. *attorney general*
Santini, Jorge *mayor*
Santos de Alvarez, Brunilda *lawyer*
Santos Pico, Jose V. *neurosurgeon*
Wexler, David B. *law educator*

Santa Isabel
Lugo-Paoli, Luz Minerva *counselor, educator*

Santurce
Residante, El (René Pérez) *singer, composer*
Visitante, El (Eduardo Cabra) *singer, musician*

Trujillo Alto
Crespo de Sanabia, María Milagros *retired education educator*

Vega Alta
Matos, Cruz Alfonso *environmental consultant*

Viejo San Juan
Casellas, Salvador E. *judge*

VIRGIN ISLANDS

Charlotte Amalie
Barnard, Geoffrey W. *judge*
Feuerzeig, Henry Louis *lawyer*
Francis, Georgia *music educator*
Garfield, Winifred L. *nursing administrator*
Stapleton, Marylyn Alecia *diplomat*

Christiansted
Bland, James Theodore, Jr. *lawyer*
Christian, Cora L.E *health facility administrator, physician*
Finch, Raymond Lawrence *judge*
Francis, Gregory R. *lieutenant governor*
Hewlett, Joycelyn Janice *lawyer*
McIntosh, Maxwell David *lawyer*

Frederiksted
Birbahadur, Dindial *secondary school educator*

Kingshill
Bryson, Valrica *high school music educator*

St Croix
Cannon, George W., Jr. *judge*
Charles, Sharon Patricia *elementary school educator*
Lee, Sidney Phillip *chemical engineer, state senator*

St John
Campbell, Thomas Douglas *business executive*
Walker, Ronald R. *editor, educator, writer*

St Thomas
Berry, Lorraine Ledee *state senator*
Caffee, Lorren Dale *lawyer*
Carty, Amos W. *lawyer*
de Jongh, John P., Jr. *governor, real estate company executive*
Frazer, Vincent F. *attorney general*
Gomez, Curtis V. *judge*
Jenkins, Anthony Jerome *prosecutor*
Larsen, Lauren *school system administrator*
Michael, Noreen *academic administrator*
O'Bryan, James A. *communications specialist, political organization administrator*
Prior, Cornelius Bernard, Jr. *utilities executive, financial consultant*
Turnbull, Charles Wesley *former governor*

MILITARY ADDRESSES OF THE UNITED STATES

EUROPE

APO
Bowker, Rayanne Sones *elementary school educator*
Cejas, Paul L. *diplomat, executive*
Crocker, Ryan Clark *ambassador*
Leibrecht, Murl Edwin *preventive medicine physician, consultant, retired military officer*
Lietzau, William Kendall *career officer, lawyer*
Marshall, Brian Laurence *federal official*
Mason, Kevin George *military analyst and officer*
Morella, Constance Albanese *ambassador, former congresswoman*
Prendergast, Kenneth Lee Michael, Jr. *career officer*
Salerno, Patricia J. *elementary school educator*
Simpson, Sandra Kay *operations research specialist*
Untermeyer, Charles Graves (Chase Untermeyer) *ambassador, diplomat*
Wagner, Mary S. *education center administrator*
Walsh, Douglas Shawn *medical association administrator, dermatologist, director, military officer*
Yates, John Melvin *ambassador*
Yates, Mary Carlin *civilian military employee, former ambassador*

FPO
Tuttle, Robert Holmes *ambassador, former federal official*

PACIFIC

APO
Gordon, Carey Nathaniel *lawyer, federal agency administrator*
Stanton, William Anthony *diplomat*

FPO
Ecker, Robert Doniger *neurosurgeon*

CANADA

ALBERTA

Calgary
Anderson, J.C. *oil and gas industry executive, rancher*
Arledge, David A. *energy executive*
Campbell, Finley Alexander *geologist, consultant*
Cumming, Thomas Alexander *brokerage house executive*
Daniel, Patrick D. *energy executive*
Fleming, Wayne *professional hockey coach*
Glockner, Peter G. *civil and mechanical engineering educator*
Grand-Maitre, Jean *performing company executive*
Haskayne, Richard Francis *retired petroleum company executive*
Holman, J(ohn) Leonard *retired manufacturing corporation executive*
Horton, William Russell *retired utilities executive*
Hotchkiss, Harley N. *professional hockey team owner, oil industry executive*
Hovdestad, Wayne Roy *petroleum engineer*
Hume, James Borden *foundation administrator, director*
Jones, Geoffrey Melvill *physiology research educator*
Keenan, Mike (Micheal Edward Keenan) *professional hockey coach, former professional sports team executive*
Kiprusoff, Miika *professional hockey player*
Lam, Galen Ka-Ron *electrical engineer*
Lougheed, Peter *lawyer, former Canadian premier*
Major, John Charles *judge*
Malik, Om Parkash *electrical engineering educator, researcher*
McDaniel, Roderick Rogers *petroleum engineer, consultant*
McEwen, Alexander Campbell *legal association administrator, consultant, cadastral studies educator, former Canadian government official, land use planner*
McKinnon, F(rancis) A(rthur) Richard *utilities executive*
Monk, Allan James *baritone*
Neale, Ernest Richard Ward *retired university official, consultant*
Phillips, Robert Alexander Bell *management consultant*
Playfair, Jim *professional hockey coach*
Pourbaix, Alexander *energy executive*
Raeburn, Andrew Harvey *performing arts consultant, recording industry executive*
Robottom, David T. *lawyer, energy executive*
Seaman, Daryl Kenneth *oil industry executive*
Serletis, Apostolos *finance educator*
Smith, Eldon *cardiologist, physiologist, educator*
Smith, Rowland James *educational administrator*
Southern, Nancy C. *utilities executive*
Stebbins, Robert Alan *sociology educator*
Sutter, Darryl John *professional sports team executive, former professional hockey coach*
Swartout, Hank B. *oil and gas industry executive*
Walker, Roger Geoffrey *geology educator, consultant*
Watanabe, Mamoru *internist, researcher*
White, Terrence Harold *academic administrator, sociologist*

Canmore
Janes, Robert Roy *museum director, archaeologist, editor*

Edmonton
Beaulieu, Norman C. *engineering educator, writer*
Davis, Wayne Alton *computer science educator*
Fields, Anthony Lindsay Austin *health facility administrator, oncologist, educator*
Freeman, Milton Malcolm Roland *anthropology educator*
Gough, Denis Ian *geophysics educator*
Gyenes, Gábor *physician, educator*
Halloran, Philip Francis *nephrologist, immunologist*
Harris, Walter Edgar *chemistry professor*
Hiruki, Chuji *plant pathologist, educator*
Hughes, Linda J. *newspaper publisher*
Ingles, Ernie Boyce *academic administrator, library director*
Kay, Cyril Max *biochemist, educator*
Keown, Lauriston Livingston, Jr. *consulting psychologist*
Kratochvil, Byron George *chemistry educator, researcher*
Lock, Gerald Seymour Hunter *retired mechanical engineering educator*
Lowe, Kevin Hugh *professional sports team executive, former hockey player and coach*
MacTavish, Craig *professional hockey coach, former professional hockey player*
Oberg, Lyle *physician, academic administrator*
Offenberger, Allan Anthony *retired electrical engineering educator*
Otto, Fred Douglas *chemical engineering professor*
Penner, Dustin *professional hockey player*
Rutter, Nathaniel Westlund *geologist, educator*
Stelck, Charles Richard *geology educator*

Stevenson, William Alexander *retired justice of Supreme Court of Canada*
Tyrrell, D. Lorne J. *university dean*

Lethbridge
Rand, Duncan Dawson *retired librarian*

Red Deer
Donald, Jack C. *gas industry executive*

Saint Albert
Randhawa, Bikkar Singh *retired psychologist, retired educator*

BRITISH COLUMBIA

Burnaby
Brantingham, Paul Jeffrey *criminologist, educator*
Brinkman, Fiona Susan *bioinformaticist, educator, molecular biologist*
Kimura, Doreen *psychology professor, researcher*
Kitchen, John Martin *historian, educator*
Switlo, Janice Georgina Alice E. *barrister, solicitor, mediator, consultant*
Wainwright, David Stanley *patent agent*

Cobble Hill
Cox, Albert Reginald *retired dean, retired cardiologist*

Coquitlam
Hainsworth, Melody May *library and information scientist, researcher*

Cowichan Station
Grauer, Sherrard *artist*

Delta
Russell, Richard Doncaster *geophysics educator, academic administrator*

Fernie
McFarlin-Kosiec, Barbara Ann *secondary school educator, literature and language professor, small business owner*

Heriot Bay
Bringhurst, Robert *poet*

Kelowna
Basdeo, Sahadeo *government official, educator, politician*

Lake Country
Muggeridge, Derek Brian *engineering executive, consultant*

Langley
Thomas, Howard Paul *civil engineer, consultant*

Lions Bay
Bartholomew, Gilbert Alfred *retired physicist*

North Saanich
Saddlemyer, Ann (Eleanor Saddlemyer) *humanities educator, critic, theater historian*

Parksville
Weir, Bryce Keith Alexander *neurosurgeon, neurologist, educator*

Richmond
Durrant, Geoffrey Hugh *retired language educator*

Salt Spring Island
Raginsky, Nina *artist*

Sidney
Bigelow, Margaret Elizabeth Barr (M.E. Barr) *retired botany educator*
Kendrick, William Bryce *biologist, consultant, editor, writer*
Mann, Cedric Robert *retired science administrator, oceanographer*
van den Bergh, Sidney *astronomer*

Sooke
Howard, John Lindsay *lawyer*

Surrey
Igali, Baraladei Daniel *Olympic athlete, coach, motivational speaker*
Lee, Jeong-Kyu *education educator, researcher, academic administrator*

Vancouver
Affleck, Ian Keith *physics educator*
Baird, Patricia Ann *physician, educator*
Batts, Michael Stanley *retired language educator*
Bentley, Thomas Roy *retired language educator, writer*
Bonifacho, Bratsa *artist*
Bowering, George Harry *writer, consultant, language educator*
Campbell, Bruce Alan *corporate coach*
Clark, Colin Whitcomb *mathematics professor*
Clarren, Sterling Keith *pediatrician*
Cohen, Leonard (Norman Cohen) *poet, writer, musician*
Conway, John S. *history professor*
Cynader, Max Sigmund *psychology and physiology professor, researcher*
Donaldson, Edward Mossop *research scientist, marine biologist, consultant*
Doyle, Patrick John *otolaryngologist, department chairman*
Eaves, Allen Charles Edward *hematologist, health facility administrator*
Erickson, Arthur Charles *architect*
Feaver, George Arthur *political science professor*
Feldman, Joel Shalom *mathematician*
Finnegan, Cyril Vincent *retired dean, zoology educator*
Friedland, Robert M. *mining executive*
Friedman, Sydney M. *anatomist, educator, medical researcher*
Granirer, Edmond Ernest *mathematician, educator*
Hardwick, David Francis *pathologist*
Hardy, Walter Newbold *physics professor, researcher*
Holsti, Kalevi Jacque *political scientist, department chairman*
Jones, David Robert *retired zoology educator*
Jones, Norah (Geethali Norah Jones Shankar) *singer*
Keevil, Norman B. *mining executive*
Kesselman, Jonathan Rhys *economics professor, public policy researcher*
Krall, Diana *musician, singer*
Laponce, Jean A. *political scientist, educator*
Lavigne, Avril *singer*
Lindsey, Casimir Charles *zoologist, educator*
Ling, Victor *oncologist, educator*
Luongo, Roberto *professional hockey player*
Lyons, Terrence Allan *mining executive*
Marchak, Maureen Patricia *anthropology and sociology educator, academic administrator*
Mattessich, Richard Victor (Alvarus) *business administration researcher*
McCaw, John E., Jr. *investment company, professional sports team executive*
McEachern, Allan *lawyer*
McGeer, Edith Graef *retired neurological science educator*
McLachlan, Sarah *musician, composer*
Mc Lean, Donald Millis *microbiologist, educator, pathologist, pediatrician*
McNeill, John Hugh *pharmaceutical sciences educator*
McWhinney, Edward Watson *Canadian government legislator*
Mizgala, Henry F. *physician, consultant, retired medical educator*
Murray, Anne *singer*
Nemetz, Peter Newman *economist, researcher, policy analysis educator*
Newman, Murray Arthur *aquarium administrator*
Newmeyer, Frederick Jaret *linguist, educator*
Nonis, David *professional sports team executive*
Nosco, Peter Erling *humanities educator, consultant*
Olsen, Inger Anna *retired psychologist*
Overmyer, Daniel Lee *humanities educator*
Pacheco-Ransanz, Arsenio *language educator, historian, educator*
Penikett, Tony *mediator, negotiator, writer*
Peterson, Leslie Raymond *barrister*
Phillips, Anthony George *neurobiology researcher*
Phillips, John Edward *zoologist, educator*
Piternick, Anne Brearley *librarian, educator*
Rennie, Paul Steven *research scientist, surgeon*
Rothstein, Samuel *librarian, educator*
Salcudean, Martha Eva *mechanical engineer, educator*
Saunders, Peter Paul *investor*
Shaw, Michael *biologist, educator*
Shearer, Ronald Alexander *economics professor*
Sinclair, Alastair James *geology educator*
Singer, Sue *academic administrator*
Sion, Maurice *mathematics professor*
Smolinski, Bryan *professional hockey player*
Suedfeld, Peter *psychologist, educator*
Tees, Richard Chisholm *psychology professor, researcher*
Unger, Richard Watson *history professor*
Vigneault, Alain *professional hockey coach*
Vogt, Erich Wolfgang *physicist, academic administrator*
Walker, Michael Angus *economist, director*
Wellington, William George *entomologist, ecologist, educator*
Willson, John Michael *retired mining company executive*
Yaffe, Barbara Marlene *journalist*
Young, Lawrence *electrical engineering educator*

Victoria
Antoniou, Andreas *electrical engineering educator*
Batten, Alan Henry *astronomer*
Best, Melvyn Edward *geophysicist*
Finlay, James Campbell *retired museum director*
Fuller, James Chester Eedy *retired chemical company executive*
Garrett, Christopher J.R. *oceanographer*
Harvey, Donald *artist, educator*
Hollis, Reginald *archbishop*
Hutchings, John Barrie *astronomer, researcher*
Israel, Werner *physicist, educator*
Leffek, Kenneth Thomas *retired chemist, educator*
Manning, Eric *computer scientist, educator, dean, researcher*
Meadow, Charles *information scientist, writer*
Morton, Donald Charles *astronomer*
Nuttall, Richard Norris *management consultant, physician*
Rathore, Akshay Kumar *electrical engineer, researcher*
Richards, Vincent Philip Haslewood *librarian*
Shaw, Timothy Milton *political science professor*
Turpin, David Howard *biologist, educator, academic administrator*
Wiles, David McKeen *chemist*

West Vancouver
Copes, Parzival *economist, researcher*
Wynne-Edwards, Hugh Robert *geologist, educator, entrepreneur*

Westbank
Wedepohl, Leonhard Martin *electrical engineering educator*
Ribary, Urs *neuroscientist, educator*

MANITOBA

Winnipeg
Anderson, David Trevor *law educator*
Cohen, Albert Diamond *retail executive*
Curtis, Charles Edward *Canadian government official*
Edwards, Clifford Henry Coad *law educator*
Eyre, Ivan *artist*
Haworth, James Chilton *pediatrics educator*
Jamieson, James Chilles *biochemist, educator*
Kuffel, Edmund *electrical engineering educator*
Lewis, André Leon *performing company executive*
MacKenzie, George Allan *medical products executive*
Mufti, Aftab A. *civil engineering educator*
Persaud, Trivedi Vidhya Nandan *anatomy educator, researcher, consultant*
Poettcker, Henry *retired academic administrator*
Rozumnyj, Jaroslav *literature educator*
Schacter, Brent Allan *oncologist, health facility administrator*
Schaefer, Theodore Peter *retired chemistry professor*
Schnoor, Jeffrey Arnold *lawyer*
Smith, Ian Cormack Palmer *biophysicist*
Turner, Robert Comrie *composer*

NEW BRUNSWICK

Fredericton
Bray, Dale Irving *civil engineering educator*
Grotterod, Knut *retired paper company executive*
Kenyon, Gary Michael *gerontologist, educator*
Saunders, Gary William *biology educator, phycology researcher*
Strange, Henry Hazen *judge*

Rothesay
Fairweather, Robert Gordon Lee *retired lawyer*

Saint Andrews
Anderson, John Murray *operations research specialist, consultant, retired academic administrator*

Saint John
Condon, Thomas Joseph *university historian*

NEWFOUNDLAND AND LABRADOR

Corner Brook
Payne, Sidney Stewart *retired archbishop*

Saint John's
Clark, Jack Ivor *civil engineer, researcher*
Gibbons, Rex Vincent *geologist*
May, Arthur W. *retired academic administrator, educator*
Rochester, Michael Grant *geophysics educator*

Torbay
Dabinett, Diana Frances *artist*

NOVA SCOTIA

Bayfield
Blair, Rosemary Miles *retired art educator, environmentalist*

Bedford
Birdsall, William Forest *retired librarian*
Hennigar, David John *portfolio manager, director*

Chester Basin
Parr-Johnston, Elizabeth *economist, consultant*

Dartmouth
Horrocks, Norman *librarian, educator, editor*
Mann, Kenneth Henry *marine ecologist*

Glasgow
Williams, Edna Aleta Theadora Johnston *journalist*

Halifax
Chowdhury, Dhiman *physician, consultant*
Dahn, Jeff Raymond *physics professor*
Dexter, Robert Paul *lawyer*
Fillmore, Peter Arthur *mathematician, educator*
Fowler, Charles Allison Eugene *retired architect, civil engineer*
Glube, Constance Rachelle *retired judge*
Gratwick, John *management consulting executive, writer, consultant*
Gray, James *English literature educator*
Hall, Brian Keith *biology professor, writer*
Hiltz, Arnold Aubrey *retired chemist*
Jaeger, Leslie Gordon *academic administrator*
Kulyk, Karen Gay *artist*
Langley, George Ross *medical educator*
Laursen, Finn *political science professor*
Matta, Chérif Farid *chemistry professor*
Murray, Thomas John (Jock Murray) *physician, neurologist, educator*
Renouf, Harold Augustus *retired transportation executive*
Stairs, Denis Winfield *political science professor, department chairman*
Tonks, Robert Stanley *pharmacologist, educator, retired dean*

Harbourville
Forsyth, George Lionel *psychotherapist, author*

Lower Sackville
Ortlepp, Bruno *marine navigation educator, master mariner*

Mahone Bay
Collins, John Alfred *retired obstetrician, gynecologist, educator*

North Sydney
Nickerson, Jerry Edgar Alan *business executive*

Stellarton
Sobey, David Frank *food company executive*
Sobey, Donald Creighton Rae *real estate developer*

Tatamagouche
Roach, Margot Ruth *retired biophysicist, educator*

Wolfville
Ogilvie, Kelvin Kenneth *academic administrator, chemist, educator*

ONTARIO

Aurora
Cellucci, (Argeo) Paul *former ambassador, governor*
Lanthier, Ronald Ross *retired manufacturing executive*

Bolton
Coffey, Paul *retired professional hockey player*

Bracebridge
Evans, John David Daniel *judge*

Brampton
Bastian, Donald Noel *retired bishop*
Kraemer, Philipp *manufacturing company executive, inventor*
Malhi, Gurbax Singh *Canadian government official*
Paikeday, Thomas M. *lexicographer, linguistic consultant*

Brantford
Hanna, William Brooks *publishing executive, literary agent*

Brockville
Spalding, James Stuart *retired telecommunications industry executive*

Burlington
Harris, Philip John *retired engineering educator*

Callander
Haig, Susan *conductor*

Cambridge
MacBain, William Halley *minister, theology studies educator, academic administrator*
White, Joseph Charles *manufacturing and retailing company executive*

Chatham
McKeough, William Darcy *supply company executive*

Deep River
Davies, John Arthur *retired physics professor, engineering educator, research scientist*
Milton, John Charles Douglas *nuclear physicist, researcher*

Don Mills
French, William Harold *retired newspaper editor*

Dorchester
Fanning, William James *professional sports team executive, commentator*

Downsview
Forer, Arthur H. *biology professor, researcher, editor*

Etobicoke
McIntyre, John George Wallace *real estate developer, management consultant*
Scholefield, Peter Gordon *health facility administrator*

Flamborough
Lee, Alvin A. *literary educator, scholar, author*

Freelton
Sonnenberg, Hardy *data processing executive, researcher, electrical engineer*

Gloucester
Malouin, Jean-Louis *adult education educator*

Greely
Lister, Earle Edward *retired research executive*

Guelph
Beveridge, Terrance James *microbiology professor, researcher*
Bewley, John Derek *botany researcher, educator*
Dickinson, William Trevor *hydrologist, educator*
Kasha, Kenneth John *agriculturist, educator*
Land, Reginald Brian *library administrator*

Hamilton
Bandler, John William *electrical engineering educator, consultant*
Bienenstock, John *pathologist, educator, health facility administrator*
Blajchman, Morris Aaron *science educator, physician*
Campbell, Colin Kydd *electrical and computer engineering educator, researcher*
Crowe, Cameron Macmillan *chemical engineering professor*
Datars, William Ross *physicist, researcher*
Garland, William James *nuclear engineer, educator*
George, Peter James *economist, educator*
Gillespie, Ronald James *chemistry professor, researcher, writer*
Hirsh, Jack *medical researcher*
Jonasson, Ralph George *chemist, researcher*
McKay, Alexander Gordon *classics educator*
Mott, Rodney B. *metal products executive*

Roland, Charles Gordon *physician, medical educator, historian*
Ryan, Ellen Bouchard *psychology professor, gerontologist*
Spenser, Ian Daniel *chemistry professor*
Wong, Kon Max *electrical engineer educator*

Harrow
Kurtz, James P. *retired judge*

Kanata
Emery, Ray *professional hockey player*
Heatley, Dany *professional hockey player*
Melnyk, Eugene N. *professional sports team executive, retired pharmaceutical executive*
Murray, Bryan Clarence *professional sports team executive, former professional hockey coach*
Spezza, Jason *professional hockey player*

Kingston
Akenson, Donald Harman *historian, educator*
Batchelor, Barrington de Vere *civil engineer, educator*
Ewan, George Thomson *physicist, researcher*
Kaliski, Stephan Felix *economics professor*
Kaufman, Nathan *retired pathologist, educator*
Leggett, William C. *biology professor, academic administrator*
Lewis, William John *aerospace engineer*
Low, James A. *physician*
MacKinnon, James Gordon *economist, educator*
Meisel, John *political scientist*
Spencer, John Hedley *biochemistry educator*
Stewart, Alec Thompson *physicist, educator*
Szarek, Walter Anthony *chemist, educator*
Wyatt, Gerard Robert *biology professor, researcher*

Kitchener
Coles, Graham *conductor, composer*
Eldred, Gerald Marcus *performing company executive*
Winger, Roger Elson *retired church administrator*

London
Bancroft, George Michael *chemical physicist, educator*
Bauer, Michael Anthony *computer scientist, educator*
Borwein, David *mathematics professor*
Davenport, Alan Garnett *civil engineer, educator*
Davenport, Paul *economics professor*
Dreimanis, Aleksis *emeritus geology educator*
Fyfe, William Sefton *geochemist, educator*
Gerber, Douglas Earl *classics educator*
Inculet, Ion I. *electrical engineer, educator, science association director, consultant*
Kang, Chil-Yong *virologist, immunology educator*
Laidler, David Ernest William *economics professor*
Lala, Peeyush Kanti *research scientist, educator*
Marotta, Joseph Thomas *medical educator*
Osbaldeston, Gordon Francis *finance educator, retired federal agency administrator*
Poole, Nancy Geddes *art gallery curator, writer*
Rudnick, Abraham *psychiatrist, philosopher*
Stewart, Harold Brown *biochemist*
William, David *theater director, actor*
Wonnacott, Ronald Johnston *retired economics professor*

Manotick
Hobson, George Donald *retired geophysicist*
Osmond, Dennis Gordon *anatomist, researcher, medical educator*

Markham
Are, Ayokunnu Olanrewaju *financial advisor, investment banker*
Gulden, Simon *lawyer, management consultant, consultant*

Mississauga
Foda, Rabiz Nasir *industrial and electrical engineer*
Gupta, Rajesh *engineer, consultant*
Shivji, Khushnooda Amin *hospital administrator*
Tully, Mary Jean *travel company executive*

Nepean
Chudobiak, Walter James *electronics executive*
Kallmann, Helmut Max *musicologist, retired librarian*

Niagara-on-the-Lake
Nielsen-Jones, Ian Richard *lottery and gaming executive, consultant*
Olley, Robert Edward *economist, educator*

Nobleton
Embleton, Tony Frederick Wallace *retired Canadian government official*

North York
Adelman, Howard *philosophy educator*
Blundell, William Richard Charles *retired electric company executive*
Buzacott, John Alan *engineering educator*
Davey, Kenneth George *biologist, educator, academic administrator*
Flock, Howard *psychology professor*
Gasparrini-Etheridge, Claudia *publishing executive, research scientist, writer*
Nicholls, Ralph William *physicist, researcher*
Regan, David *neuroscientist*
Thomas, Clara McCandless *retired literature educator*
Tse, Philip Kui *airport engineering maintenance consultant*

Ohawa
Day, Stockwell Burt *government official*

Oshawa
Zhang, Dan *engineering educator, researcher*

Ottawa
Ahmadi, Mojtaba *engineering educator, consultant*
Alper, Howard *chemistry professor*
Altman, Samuel Pinover *mechanical engineer, research consultant*
Armstrong, Henry Conner *former Canadian government official, consultant*
Austin, Jacob (Jack Austin) *Canadian government official*
Baum, Bernard Rene *research scientist*
Beare-Rogers, Joyce Louise *retired research and development executive*
Beatty, Perrin *business association executive*
Bélisle, Paul Charles *Canadian government official*
Bevilacqua, Maurizio *member of Canadian parliament*
Bozozuk, Michael *civil engineer*
Brooks, David Barry *resource economist*
Buchanan, John MacLennan *Canadian provincial official*
Carty, Arthur John *science policy advisor, research administrator*
Cools, Anne C. *Canadian senator*
Copps, Sheila *former Canadian government official, political journalist, commentator*
Courtois, Bernard Andre *communications executive*
Csörgö, Miklós *mathematics and statistics educator*
d'Aquino, Thomas *lawyer, educator, entrepreneur*
Davey, Clark William *newspaper publisher*
de Bold, Adolfo J. *pathologist, educator, physiologist, researcher*
de Chastelain, A(lfred) John G(ardyne) D(rummond) *Canadian army officer, diplomat*
Dlab, Vlastimil *mathematics professor, researcher*
Dray, William Herbert *philosophy educator*
Dryden, Ken *legislator, former sports team executive, retired professional hockey player*
Fairbairn, Joyce *Canadian government official*
Fellegi, Ivan Peter *statistician*
Fitzpatrick, Brian *Canadian legislator*
Georganas, Nicolas D. *electrical engineering educator, academic administrator*
Gillingham, Bryan Reginald *music educator*
Gold, Lorne W. *Canadian government official*
Griller, David *management consultant*
Guarnieri, Albina *Canadian legislator*
Hagen, Paul Beo *pharmacologist*
Halliday, Ian *astronomer*
Harb, Mac *Canadian senator*
Harington, Charles Richard *vertebrate paleontologist*
Hervieux-Payette, Céline *Canadian senator*
Holmes, John Leonard *retired chemistry professor*
Hughes, Stanley John *retired mycologist*
Hurteau, Gilles David *retired obstetrician, gynecologist, educator, dean*
Ingold, Keith Usherwood *chemist, educator*
Kates, Morris *biochemist, educator*
Kilgour, David *Canadian member parliament*
Kingsley, Jean-Pierre *federal official*
Krechetnikov, Rouslan *mathematician, educator*
Labarge, Margaret Wade *medieval history professor, historian, writer*
Lavoie, Lionel A. *physician, health science association administrator*
Lay, Marion *sports association executive*
MacDonald, Flora Isabel *Canadian government official*
MacFarlane, John Alexander *retired federal agency administrator*
MacKay, William Andrew *judge*
Macklem, Michael Kirkpatrick *publisher*
Margeson, Theodore Earl *judge*
Maxwell, Judith *think-tank executive, economist*
McAvity, John Gillis *museum director, association executive, museologist*
McLachlin, Beverley *Canadian supreme court chief justice*
McLure, John Douglas *management consultant, former Canadian government official*
Mills, Bob *member of Canadian parliament*
Murray, Lowell *Canadian senator*
Pal, Prabir Kumar (Sunny Pal) *lawyer*
Penner, Keith *former Canadian government official*
Perry, Malcolm Blythe *biologist, researcher*
Peterson, James Scott (Jim Peterson) *Canadian government official*
Philogene, Bernard J. R. *academic administrator, science educator*
Plumptre, Tim *think-tank executive*
Prevost, Roxane Lise *music theory educator*
Ramsay, Donald Allan *physical chemist*
Roland, Anne *registrar Supreme Court of Canada*
Ryan, William Francis *priest*
Scott, Marianne Florence *retired librarian, educator*
Shiari, Behrouz *mechanical engineer, researcher*
Silverman, Ozzie *consulting strategist*
Southam, G(ordon) Hamilton *former Canadian government official*
Squire, Anne Marguerite *retired humanities educator*
Staines, David McKenzie *language educator*
Stanford, Joseph Stephen *diplomat, lawyer, educator*
St-Onge, Denis Alderic *geologist, research scientist, educator*
Storey, Kenneth Bruce *biology professor*
Strayer, Barry Lee *retired judge*
Sylvestre, Jean Guy *former national librarian*
Tassé, Roger *lawyer, former Canadian government official*
Telegdi, Andrew *member of parliament*
Tellier, Henri *retired Canadian military officer*
Vassilyadi, Michael *pediatric neurosurgeon*
Veizer, Ján *geology educator*
Vellacott, Maurice *legislator*
Volpe, Joseph *Canadian government official*
Wallot, Jean-Pierre *archivist, historian*
Whitehead, J. Rennie *science administrator, consultant*
Yalden, Maxwell Freeman *Canadian diplomat*
Yelich, Lynne *member of parliament*
Yeomans, Donald Ralph *Canadian government official, consultant*

Owen Sound
Morley, Lawrence Whitaker *geophysicist, consultant*

Paris
Hooper, Wayne Nelson *retired clergy member*

Peterborough
Burwick, David *beverage company executive*
Dumas, Michael Godfrey Joseph *artist*
Hutchinson, Thomas Cuthbert *ecology and environmental educator*
Theall, Donald Francis *retired university president*

Richmond Hill
Fong, Maryanne T.P. *telecommunications industry executive, researcher*

Saint Catharines
Ayanso, Anteneh Wondimu *information systems educator*
Bergevin, V. Réal *customer relationship management executive*
Miller, Jack (John Peter Miller) *journalist*
Sivell, John Norman *language educator*

Sault Sainte Marie
Ferris, Ronald Curry *bishop*

Scarborough
Cetin, Anton *artist*
White, Calvin John *zoo executive, zoological association executive, financial manager*

Stittsville
MacLeod, Robert Angus *microbiology educator, researcher*

Thorold
O'Mara, John Aloysius *retired bishop*

Toronto
Ames, Steven *management consultant*
Arthurs, Harry William *lawyer, educator, academic administrator*
Astman, Barbara Ann *artist, educator*
Augustine, Jerome Samuel *merchant banker*
Bandeen, Robert Angus *management consultant*
Bandrowczak, Steven J. *communications executive*
Bargnani, Andrea *professional basketball player*
Bartleman, James K. *lieutenant governor*
Baxendale, Sonia A. *diversified financial services company executive*
Beckwith, John *musician, composer, educator*
Blewett, David Lambert *English literature educator*
Bohme, Diethard Kurt *chemistry professor*
Boland, Janet Lang *judge*
Bolley, Andrea *artist*
Bosh, Chris *professional basketball player*
Brook, Adrian Gibbs *chemistry professor*
Bryant, Josephine Harriet *library executive*
Budrevics, Alexander *landscape architect*
Carrothers, Gerald Arthur Patrick *environmental and city planning educator*
Chandra, Ranjit Kumar *research scientist, educator, physician*
Chester, Robert Simon George *lawyer*
Clark, Maura J. *oil and gas industry executive*
Clarkson, Adrienne *former Governor General of Canada*
Cleghorn, John Edward *bank executive*
Cockwell, Jack Lynn *finance company executive*
Colangelo, Bryan *professional sports team executive*
Colgrass, Michael Charles *composer*
Connell, Philip Francis *food industry executive*
Cook, Stephen Arthur *mathematics and computer science educator*
Cook-Bennett, Gail *pension fund administrator*
Cornies, Larry Alan *journalist, educator*
Cunningham, Gordon Ross *finance company executive*
Curlook, Walter *management consultant*
Dale, Robert Gordon *investment company executive*
Davis, Antonio Lee *professional basketball player*
Davison, Edward Joseph *electrical engineering educator*
Dean, Geoffrey *book publisher*
Dimma, William Andrew *real estate executive*
Dobson, Wendy Kathleen *economics professor*
Dooher, Donna *chef*
Dubin, Charles Leonard *lawyer*
Dunlop, David John *geophysics educator, researcher*
Eagles, Stuart Ernest *real estate company officer*
Egoyan, Atom *film director*
Elder, Richard Bruce *artist, writer*
Endrenyi, Janos *research engineer, educator*
Evans, John Robert *academic administrator, cardiologist*
Farkas, Leslie Gabriel *plastic surgeon*
Farquharson, Gordon MacKay *lawyer, director*
Fatt, William Robert *hotel executive*
Ferguson, John, Jr. *professional sports team executive*
Ferguson, Kingsley George *retired psychologist*
Fierheller, George Alfred *communications executive*
Fife, Edward H. *landscape architecture educator*
Finlay, Terence Edward *retired archbishop*
Fox, Wayne C. *stock exchange and corporate financial executive*
Fraser, William Neil *retired government agency administrator*
Friedlander, John Benjamin *mathematician, educator*
Fullerton, R. Donald *banker*
Furtado, Nelly Kim *vocalist*
Garbajosa (Chaparro), Jorge *professional basketball player*
Gilbert, Greg *professional hockey coach, retired professional hockey player*
Glaus, Troy *professional baseball player*
Godsoe, Peter Cowperthwaite *retired banker*
Goh, Chan Hon *ballerina*
Goold, Douglas *think-tank executive*
Gordon, Harold Sonny *bank executive*
Goring, David Arthur Ingham *chemist, educator*
Gotlieb, Allan E. *former ambassador*
Gotlieb, Calvin Carl *computer scientist, educator*
Granatstein, Jack Lawrence *historian*
Grayson, Albert Kirk *social studies educator*
Gregor, Tibor Philip *retired management consultant*
Halladay, Roy (Harry Leroy Halladay) *professional baseball player*
Hayhurst, James Frederick Palmer *career and business consultant, inspirational speaker, writer*
Helleiner, Gerald Karl *economics professor*
Hofmann, Theo *biochemist, educator*
Holyday, Douglas Charles *city councillor*
Hore, John Edward *retired commodity futures educator*
Hutchison, Andrew Sandford *archbishop*
Janischewskyj, Wasyl *electrical engineering educator*
Jaworska, Tamara *artist*
Kain, Karen Alexandria *ballet dancer*
Kaufman, Donna Soble *lawyer, director*
Kerr, David Wylie *corporate financial executive, director*
Knowlton, Thomas A. *retired dean, food products executive*
Kramer, Burton *graphic designer, educator*
Kresge, Alexander Jerry *chemistry professor*
Kudelka, James *choreographer, artistic director*
Kushner, Eva *academic administrator, educator, author*
Lawson, Jane Elizabeth *retired bank executive*
Leech, James William *investment company executive*
Lindsay, Roger Alexander (Baron of Craighall) *investment executive*
Lindsay, William Kerr *surgeon*
Litherland, Albert Edward *physics professor*
Liversage, Richard Albert *cell biologist, educator*
Macdonald, Donald Stovel *public policy advisor*
Macdonald, Hugh Ian *economics professor, public policy professor, academic administrator*
MacDougall, Hartland Molson *retired bank executive*
MacLaren, Roy *retired Canadian government official*
MacLennan, David Herman *research scientist, educator*
Maidment, Karen E. *bank executive*
Mann, George Stanley *diversified financial services company executive, real estate company officer*
Martin, Robert William *retired utilities executive*
Masui, Yoshio *zoology educator*
Maurice, Paul *professional hockey coach*
Mc Culloch, Ernest Armstrong *internist, educator*
McMurtry, R. Roy *federal judge*
Meagher, George Vincent *mechanical engineer*
Mercier, Eileen Ann *pension fund chairman*
Millgate, Michael (Michael Henry Millgate) *retired literature educator*
Mintz, Jack Maurice *think-tank executive, economics professor*
Mitchell, Sam *professional basketball coach*
Moore, Carole Irene *librarian*
Moore, Christopher Hugh *writer*
Morey, Carl Reginald *musicologist*
Morneau, William *pension and benefits company executive*
Mulholland, William David, Jr. *retired bank executive*
Munk, Peter *mining executive*
Munro, John Henry Alexander *economics professor, writer*
Naylor, C. David *academic administrator*
Nesbitt, Richard *stock exchange executive*
Nguyen, San Duy *psychiatrist, educator*
Novak, David *theology studies educator, rabbi*
Ogilvie, Richard Ian *clinical pharmacologist*
Osler, Gordon Peter *retired utilities executive*
Ostry, Sylvia *academic administrator, economist*
Oundjian, Peter *conductor, music director*
Palozzi, Dina *bank executive*
Pawson, Anthony J. *molecular biologist*
Peacock, Molly *poet, educator*
Peddie, Richard *professional sports team executive*
Peterson, David Robert *lawyer, former Canadian government official*
Polanyi, John Charles *chemist, educator*
Poon, Alan Ming Wang *sports association executive, director*
Poprawa, Andrew *diversified financial services company executive, accountant*
Poulsen, Jens Kristian *ultrasonics researcher*
Pratt, Robert Cranford *political scientist, educator*
Price, Timothy R. *accountant*
Pritchard, Huw Owen *chemist, educator*
Rasky, Harry *producer, director, writer*
Regan, Francis Vincent *lawyer*
Ricciardi, J.P. *professional sports team executive*
Rogers, Edward Samuel *communications company executive*
Rooney, Paul George *mathematics professor*
Rose, Jeffrey Raymond *retired economist, public servant, trade unionist*
Salama, C. Andre Tewfik *electrical engineering educator*
Schramek, Tomas *ballet dancer, educator*

Schwartz, Gerald Wilfred *business executive*
Seiersen, Nicholas Steen *management consultant*
Semak, Michael William *photographer, educator*
Sessle, Barry John *adult education educator, researcher*
Shepherd, Gordon Greeley *space physics educator, researcher*
Silk, Frederick C.Z. *financial consultant*
Skvorecky, Josef Vaclav *literature educator, writer*
Slemon, Gordon Richard *electrical engineering educator*
Smith, Peter William Ebblewhite *electrical engineer, educator, research scientist, physicist*
Sole, Michael Joseph *cardiologist*
Staines, Mavis Avril *performing company executive*
Stoicheff, Boris Peter *physicist, researcher*
Storey, Susan *investment banker*
Stymiest, Barbara *stock exchange executive*
Sues, Hans-Dieter *paleontologist, zoologist, educator*
Sundin, Mats Johan *professional hockey player*
Tanenbaum, Joey *real estate developer*
Taylor, Allan Richard *retired banker*
Taylor, Kathleen P. *hotel executive*
Techar, Frank J. *bank executive*
Thall, Burnett Murray *retired newspaper executive*
Thein, Hla-Hla *research scientist*
Thomas, Frank Edward *professional baseball player*
Thomson, David Kenneth Roy *publishing executive*
Thomson, Richard Murray *retired bank executive*
Till, James Edgar *medical educator, researcher*
Tobe, Stephen Solomon *zoology educator*
Tolmie, Kenneth Donald *artist, writer*
Tsubouchi, David H. *Canadian provincial official*
Turnbull, John Cameron *retired pharmacist, consultant*
van Ginkel, Blanche Lemco *architect, educator*
Venetsanopoulos, Anastasios Nicolaos *electrical engineer, educator*
Verschuren, Annette *retail executive*
Webb, Anthony Allan *banker, director*
Weston, W. Galen, Sr., (Galen Weston) *diversified financial services company executive*
Wevers, John William *retired Semitic languages educator*
Whitfield, Simon *Olympic athlete*
Williams, Ricky (Errick Lynne Williams) *professional football player*
Wilson, Lynton Ronald *retired telecommunications industry executive*
Wleugel, John Peter *manufacturing executive*
Wonham, Walter Murray *electrical engineer, educator*
Zeng, Hong *audio system architect, researcher*

Waterloo
Aczél, János Dezsö *mathematician*
Balsillie, Jim *information technology executive*
Berczi, Andrew Stephen *academic administrator, educator*
Fallding, Harold Joseph *sociology educator*
Gladwell, Graham Maurice Leslie *mathematician, civil engineering educator*
Haworth, Lawrence Lindley *philosophy educator*
Lazaridis, Mike *information technology executive, entrepreneur*
Morgan, Alan Vivian *geologist, educator*
Paldus, Josef *mathematics professor*
Penlidis, Alexander *chemical engineering professor*
Sedra, Adel Shafeek *engineering educator, academic administrator*
Smolin, Lee *physicist, researcher, writer*
Sprott, David Arthur *statistician, educator, psychologist, educator*
Suits, Bernard Herbert *philosophy educator*
Urquhart, Tony *artist, educator*
Van Seters, John *retired biblical literature educator*
Vlach, Jiri *electrical engineering educator, researcher*
Warner, Barry Gregory *ecologist, educator*

West Toronto
Iacobucci, Frank *lawyer, judge, former academic administrator*

Willowdale
Goldberg, David Meyer *retired biochemist*
Irwin, John Wesley *publisher*
MacDonald, Brian Scott *management consultant*
Sze, Michael Ming-Chih *actuary, consultant*
Winter, Frederick Elliot *fine arts educator*

Windsor
Ferguson, John Duncan *medical research educator*
Hackam, Reuben *electrical engineering educator*
La Rocque, Eugene Philippe *retired bishop*
Thibert, Roger Joseph *clinical chemist, educator*
Mohler, Brian Jeffery *diplomat*

PRINCE EDWARD ISLAND

Charlottetown
Sanborn, George Freeman, Jr. *genealogist*

QUEBEC

Beaconsfield
Harder, Rolf Peter *graphic designer, painter*

Beauharnois
Lebel, Robert *retired bishop*

Gatineau
Wilson, Ian Edwin *cultural organization administrator, archivist*

Ile Perrot
Lalonde, Marc *lawyer, former Canadian government official*

Jonquière
Couture, Jean Guy *bishop*

Kirkland
Baroudy, Bahige Mourad *biochemist, researcher*

Laval
Bourget, Edwin Robert *marine ecologist, educator*
Talbot, Pierre Joseph *microbiologist, researcher*

Leclercville
Morin, Pierre Jean *retired management consultant, social services administrator*

Montpellier
Poirier, Louis Joseph *neurology educator*

Montreal
Aguayo, Alberto Juan *neuroscientist*
Barrette, Jean *physicist, researcher*
Beaudoin, Laurent *train manufacturing company executive*
Beauregard, Luc *public relations executive*
Beugnot, Bernard Andre Henri *literature educator*
Brecher, Michael *political science professor*
Bruemmer, Fred *writer, photographer*
Burgess, John Herbert *cardiologist, educator*
Carbonneau, Guy *professional hockey coach, former professional hockey player*
Carroll, Robert Lynn *biology professor, paleontologist, curator, museum director*
Cedraschi, Tullio *investment company executive*
Chang, Thomas Ming Swi *research scientist, biotechnologist, educator*
Charney, Melvin *artist, architect, educator*
Cruess, Richard Leigh *orthopedic surgeon, dean*
Cyr, J. V. Raymond *telecommunications industry executive*
Das Gupta, Subal *physics professor, researcher*
Davidson, Colin Henry *architect, educator*
Dealy, John Michael *chemical engineer, educator*
Desmarais, Paul *diversified management and holding company executive*
Ducharme, Francine Carole *nursing educator, researcher*
Eisenberg, Adi *chemist*
Freedman, Samuel Orkin *university official*
Freeman, Carolyn Ruth *oncologist*
Gabbour, Iskandar *city and regional planning educator*
Gainey, Bob (Robert Michael) *professional sports team executive, retired professional hockey player*
Genest, Jacques *nephrologist, clinical scientist, science administrator*
Gillespie, Thomas Stuart *investment company executive*
Gillett, George Nield, Jr. *professional sports team executive, communications executive*
Girard, Francois *film director*
Gold, Phil *immunologist, educator, researcher*
Goldbloom, Victor Charles *pediatrician*
Goltzman, David *endocrinologist, educator, researcher*
Gonthier, Charles Doherty *retired judge*
Gratton, Robert *diversified financial services company executive*
Haccoun, David *electrical engineering educator*
Ikawa-Smith, Fumiko *anthropologist, educator*
Johnstone, Rose Mamelak *biochemistry educator*
Jolicoeur, Paul *molecular biologist*
Jones, Barbara Ellen *neurologist, educator*
Kinsley, William Benton *literature educator*
Koivu, Saku *professional hockey player*
Kovalev, Alexei *professional hockey player*
Kramer, Michael Stuart *pediatric epidemiologist*
Labadie, Bernard *performing company executive*
Lacombe, Jacques *conductor*
Ladanyi, Branko *civil engineer, educator*
Lamarre, Bernard *engineering executive*
Large, John Andrew *library and information service professor*
Laurin, Pierre *finance company executive*
Leroy, Claude *physics professor, researcher*
Lock, Edouard *performing company executive*
Macaulay, Ann C. *physician*
Mac Lean, Lloyd Douglas *surgeon*
Matziorinis, Kenneth N. *economist*
Melzack, Ronald *psychology professor*
Milic-Emili, Joseph *physiologist, educator*
Molson, Eric H. *brewery company executive*
Moser, William Oscar Jules *mathematics professor*
Moss, David *music company executive*
Mulder, David S. *cardiovascular surgeon*
Mulroney, Brian (Martin Brian Mulroney) *former Prime Minister of Canada*
Mysak, Lawrence Alexander *oceanographer, climatologist and mathematics educator*
Nattel, Stanley *cardiologist, research scientist*
Nayar, Baldev Raj *political science professor*
Ngo, Van Tan (Tan Van) *financial planner, poet*
Normandeau, Andre Gabriel *criminologist, educator*
Paidoussis, Michael Pandeli *mechanical engineering educator*
Pankov, Gradimir Krunislav *performing company executive*
Pasternac, André *cardiologist, educator*
Paul, T. V. *social sciences educator*
Perlin, Arthur Saul *chemistry professor*
Podgorsak, Ervin B. *medical physicist, educator, administrator*
Popovici, Adrian *law educator*
Pound, Richard William Duncan *lawyer, accountant*
Ramachandran, Venkatanarayana Deekshit *electrical engineering educator*
Raynauld, Andre *economist, educator*
Robb, James Alexander *lawyer*
Rochette, Louis *water transportation executive*
Rolland, Lucien Gilbert *paper company executive, director*
Romanov, Volodymyr Alexeevich *computer science educator, researcher*
Saint-Pierre, Guy *engineering executive*
Scriver, Charles Robert *medical researcher, human geneticist, retired medical educator*
Selvadurai, Antony Patrick Sinnappa *civil engineer, mathematician, educator, consultant*
Sirois, Charles *communications executive*
Snell, Linda S. *internist, educator*
Solomon, Samuel *biochemistry educator, administrator*
Sourkes, Theodore Lionel *biochemistry professor*
Speirs, Derek James *diversified financial services company executive*
Stewart, Jane *psychology professor*
Suen, Ching Yee *computer scientist, educator, researcher*
Szabo, Denis *criminologist, educator*
Taras, Paul *physicist, researcher*
Thompson, John Douglas *corporate financial executive*
Torrey, David Leonard *investment banker*
Turcotte, Jean-Claude Cardinal *archbishop*
Vaillancourt, Jean-Guy *sociology educator, researcher*
Vinet, Luc *physicist, educator*
Waller, Harold Myron *political science professor*
Webster, Norman Eric *journalist, foundation administrator*
Whitehead, Michael Anthony *chemistry professor*

Mount Royal
Elie, Jean André *investment banker*

North Hatley
Jones, Douglas Gordon *retired literature educator*

Outremont
Dufour, Jean-Marie *economist, statistician, educator*
Gulkin, Harry *arts administrator, film producer*
Letourneau, Jean-Paul *professional society administrator*

Pointe-Claire
Bachynski, Morrel Paul *physicist*
Lapointe, Lucie *research institute executive*

Quebec City
Belanger, Gerard *economics professor*
Bonnelly, Claude *library director*
Dinan, Robert Michael *lawyer*
Habashi, Fathi *retired metallurgy professor, consultant*
LeMay, Jacques *lawyer*
Morin, Louis *lawyer*
Potvin, Pierre *physiologist, educator*
Prothro, Jerry Robert *lawyer*
Roy, Patrick *professional sports team executive, coach, retired professional hockey player*
Stavert, Alexander Bruce *archbishop*
Thibault, Lise *Canadian lieutenant governor*
Verge, Pierre *legal educator*

Rimouski
Blanchet, Bertrand *archbishop*

Rosemere
Hopper, Carol *incentive program and trade association administrator*

Saint Jean Sur Richelieu
Trudel, Marc J. *botanist, educator*

Saint Lambert
Clermont, Yves Wilfrid *anatomy educator, researcher*

Saint-Sauveur
Hanigan, Lawrence *retired rail transportation executive*

Sainte-Foy
Normand, Robert *retired lawyer*
Tremblay, Marc Adélard *anthropologist, educator*

Sherbrooke
Tremblay, André-Marie *physicist*

Varennes
Bartnikas, Raymond *electrical engineer, educator*

Verdun
Lessard, Michel M. *finance company executive*

Westmount
Coolidge, Robert Tytus *deacon, historian, educator*
Fortier, L. Yves *barrister*
Rothman, Melvin L. *retired judge*

SASKATCHEWAN

Regina
Barber, Lloyd Ingram *retired university president*
Bayda, Edward Dmytro *retired chief justice*
MacKay, Harold Hugh *lawyer*
Mollard, John Douglas *engineering and geology executive*
Phillips, Roger *retired steel company executive*
Symes, Lawrence Richard *computer science educator, university dean*

Saskatoon
Babiuk, Lorne Alan *virologist, immunologist, researcher*
Blakeney, Allan Emrys *Canadian government official, lawyer, educator*
Bornstein, Eli *artist, sculptor*
Houston, C(larence) Stuart *radiologist, educator*
Huang, Pan Ming *soil science educator*
Ish, Daniel Russell *law educator, academic administrator*
Kennedy, Marjorie Ellen *librarian*
Kerrich, Robert *geologist, educator*
Knott, Douglas Ronald *dean, agricultural sciences educator, researcher*
Smith, C. D. *civil engineering educator*
Sowa, Artur *mathematician, researcher*

YUKON TERRITORY

Whitehorse
Couchman, Robert George James *foundation executive*

Calgary
Amonte, Tony (Anthony Lewis Amonte) *professional hockey player*
Maier, Gerald James *gas industry executive*
McCarty, Darren *professional hockey player*

Hamilton
Etches-Johnson, Amanda *library and information scientist*

Kanata
Paddock, John (Alvin John Paddock) *professional hockey coach*

Montreal
Bertrand, Luc *stock exchange executive*
Johnston, Donald James *lawyer, educator*
Lowy, Frederick Hans *academic administrator, psychiatrist*
Pierre, Samuel J. *engineering educator*

Niagara Falls
Watson, George W. *energy executive*

North Hatley
Salt, Alfred Lewis *priest*

Ontario
Babulak, Eduard *computer scientist, educator, researcher, consultant*
MacKenzie, Lewis Wharton *military officer*
Warren, Jack Hamilton *retired diplomat, banker, trade policy advisor*

Saint Catharines
Bordonaro, Karen Elizabeth *school librarian, educator*

Sainte Anne de Bellevue
Grant, William Frederick *geneticist, educator*

Saskatoon
Casson, Alan Graham *thoracic surgeon, researcher*

Sherbrooke
Deslongchamps, Pierre *chemistry professor*

Toronto
Angel, Aubie *endocrinologist, academic administrator*
Armstrong, Robin Louis *physics professor, physicist*
Katchanovski, Ivan G. *political scientist, researcher*
Polley, Sarah *actress*
Pollock, Bruce Godfrey *psychiatrist, educator*
Scardamalia, Marlene *education educator, researcher*
Stanley, Deirdre *lawyer*
Wells, Vernon III *professional baseball player*

Vancouver
Packer, James Innell *priest, professor of theology*

Whistler
Rae, Barbara Joyce *employee placement company executive*

Windsor
Van Den Brande, Rene Albert *retired accountant*

ARGENTINA

Buenos Aires
Gondolesi, Gabriel Eduardo *transplant surgeon*
Lopez-Murphy, Ricardo Hipolito *economist*
Montes, Leopoldo Feliciano *dermatologist, educator*
Walker, Ignacio Jose *lawyer*

Córdoba
Cabrera, Angel Leopoldo *professional golfer*

District Capital
Frasch, Alberto Carlos C. *molecular genetics educator*

ARMENIA

Yerevan
Adamyan, Tsovinar *medical educator*
Sargsyan, David *library director*

AUSTRALIA

Altona
Daniel-Dreyfus, Susan B. Russe *information technology executive*

Armadale
Neil, Sandra Eilleen Silverberg *psychologist*

Brighton
Bellin, Howard *management consultant*

Camberwell
Base, Graeme Rowland *illustrator, author*
Peterson, Douglas Pete (Pete Peterson) *former ambassador, retired congressman*

Cammeray
Besley, Morrish Alexander (Tim Besley) *civil engineer*

Camperdown
Zobras, Helen *gynecologist, director*

Canberra
Taylor, Stuart Ross *geochemist, writer*

Darlinghurst
Davis, Judy *actress*

Double Bay
Guerin, Didier *magazine executive*
Peacock, Penne Korth *ambassador*

Hackett
Leigh, Andrew Keith *economist, researcher*

Malanda
Cooper, William Thomas *natural history artist*

Melbourne
Batrouney, Clive M. *finance company executive*
Browne, Jeffrey Francis *lawyer*
Fahour, Ahmed *investment company executive*
Searby, Richard Henry *academic administrator, lawyer*
Wolfram, David Anthony *information technology manager*

Milsons Point
Foster, Milo George *manufacturing executive*

Nedlands
Marshall, Barry James *gastroenterologist*
Oxnard, Charles Ernest *anatomist, anthropologist, biologist, educator*

Norfolk Island
McCullough, Colleen *author*

North Sydney
Crowe, Russell *actor*
Scott, Brian Walter *management consultant*

Paddington
Keneally, Thomas Michael *author*

Parkville
Denton, Derek Ashworth *medical researcher, foundation administrator*
Metcalf, Donald *biomedical researcher*

Perth
Dow, Simon *artistic director, choreographer*

Queensland
Ho, Yik Hong *colon and rectal surgeon*

Redfern
Campion, Jane *film director, screenwriter*

Springfield
Spalvins, Janis Gunars *steamship company executive*

Sydney
Gomes, Ivan Joaquim *computer network designer*
Hora, Heinrich *physicist*
Miller, George *film director*

Woollahra
Hall, Peter Francis *retired physiologist*

AUSTRIA

Graz
Weisstein, Ulrich Werner *English literature educator*

Grossgmain
Mueller, Christa *radiologist*

Vienna
Higgins, William Woods *painter, art educator*

Wien
Reichl, Peter *computer scientist, researcher*

THE BAHAMAS

Nassau
Beck, Jan Scott *lawyer*
Harrison, Johnnie Sheppard *religious organization administrator*
Templeton, John Marks *investment counsel, financial analyst*

BAHRAIN

Manama
Sarhan, Mansoor Mohamed *library director*

BANGLADESH

Dhaka
Brooks, W. Abdullah *pediatrician, researcher*

Kushtia
Latifur Rahaman, Rasul Boaksh *legal association administrator*

BELGIUM

Antwerp
Snyders, Dirk Johan *electrophysiologist and biophysicist educator*

Brussels
Baptiste, Thomas L. *career military officer*
Barnum, John Wallace *lawyer*
Boon, Thierry *biomedical researcher*
Buysse, Paul Henri Maria *manufacturing executive*
Ciarka, Agnieszka *internist, researcher*
Craddock, Bantz John (John Craddock) *career military officer*
de Duve, Christian René *chemist, educator*
Freizer, Louis A. *radio producer*
Gray, C. Boyden (Clayland Boyden Gray) *ambassador, lawyer*
Lewis, Jesse *editor*
Nuland, Victoria *ambassador*

Diegen
Dörken, Uwe R. *finance company executive*

Genappe
Williams, Jody *political organization administrator*

La Louviere
Dragone, Franco *performing company executive*

Liège
Mosora-Stan, Florentina Ioana *physics professor*

BELIZE

Belize City
Brown, Sir George Noel *judge*

BERMUDA

Hamilton
McCormick, Hugh Thomas *lawyer*

Pembroke
Freimark, Jeffrey Philip *corporate financial executive*
Spector, Phillip Louis *lawyer*
Stempel, Ernest Edward *insurance executive*

Tuckers Town
Heizer, Edgar Francis, Jr. *venture capitalist*

BOSNIA-HERZEGOVINA

Sarajevo
Lozančić, Niko *President of Federation of Bosnia and Herzegovina*

BRAZIL

Rio de Janeiro
Davidovich, Luiz *physics professor*
de Araújo, Aloisio Pessoa *mathematics professor*

Rio deJaneiro
Sluberski, Thomas Richard *international educator, journalist, theologian*

Santa Catarina Florianopolis
da Costa, Newton Carneiro Affonso, Jr. *engineering educator, researcher*

Sorocaba
Martins, Nelson *physics professor*

São Paulo
Riecken, Claudia *researcher, director*

BRITISH VIRGIN ISLANDS

Tortola
Chalwell-Brewley, Lavon Patricia *biology educator*

BULGARIA

Blagoevgrad
Stefanov, Stefan Minev *mathematics professor, researcher*

Sofia
Alexiev, Borislav Alexandrov *pathologist*
Lazarov, Raicho Dimitrov *mathematician, educator*

CHILE

Santiago
Wilkey, Malcolm Richard *retired ambassador, retired judge*

Valdivia
Teitelboim, Claudio *academic administrator*

CHINA

Beijing
Akeley, Kurt Barton *computer graphics company executive, engineer*
Bai, Chunli *professional society administrator, educator*
Cheng, Josephine *computer scientist, educator*
Christianson, Jon L. *lawyer*
Christianson, Wei Sun *diversified financial services company executive*
Dingman, Michael David *manufacturing executive, investor*
Duan, Zhenhao *geochemist, educator, editor*
Hsieh, Din-Yu *applied mathematics professor*
Jiabao, Wen *Chinese government official*
Lin, James K. *communications executive, educator*
Ma (Xuezheng), Mary *retired computer company executive*
Thornton, John L. *former diversified financial services company executive*
Wu, Ying *telecommunications industry executive*
Yang, Chen Ning Franklin *physicist, educator*
Yao, Andrew Chi-Chih *engineering educator*
Yuan, Longping *agronomist*
Zhou, Bang Rong *physicist, researcher*

Chengdu
Ma, Shijun *engineering educator*

Hong Kong
Halperin, David Richard *lawyer*
Li, Ka-Shing *international entrepreneur*
Nelson, Steven Craig *lawyer*
Pacter, Paul Allan *accounting standards researcher*

Shanghai
Chueh, Chun Fei *import/export company executive*
Jiang, Jason Nanchun *advertising executive*
Lin, Maria C.H. *lawyer*
Lu, Bao-Liang *computer scientist, educator*
Prosser, Michael Hubert *communications educator*
Yun, Liang *marine engineer, educator*

Tianjin
Leyden, Michael Joseph, II, (Lei Jie Ming) *finance educator, entrepreneur, writer*

Wuhan
Cao, Hanqiang *science educator, researcher*

Xi'an
Zhao, Wenming *retired biochemistry and molecular biology educator*

COLOMBIA

Bogotá
Reina, Carrillo José Gabriel *physician, surgery educator*

COSTA RICA

San José
Hoffman, Irwin *orchestra conductor*
Leon Azofeifa, Pedro *molecular biologist*

CYPRUS

Nicosia
Aloneftis, Andreas *business executive*
Elias, Kyriakides *electrical engineer, educator, researcher*

CZECH REPUBLIC

Brno
Klapka, Jindřich Ludvík *mathematician, physicist, educator, researcher*

Prague
Čejka, Jiří *retired chemist, researcher*
Cusumano, James Anthony *filmmaker, vocalist, retired pharmaceutical, hotel, and recording industry executive*
Kalkus, Stanley *librarian, administrator, consultant*
Kotrla, Miroslav *physicist*
Sebek, Michael *research scientist, entrepreneur, educator*
Tuma, Stanislav Josef *radiologist*
Turková, Helga *librarian*

Pribram
Kuba, John Albert *mortician*

DENMARK

Charlottenlund
Garner, Fradley Hamilton *freelance/self-employed writer, editor*

Copenhagen
Elmer, Michael Bendik *legal administrator*
Jacobsen, Stine *veterinarian, educator*
Kurrild-Klitgaard, Peter *political science professor*
Mottelson, Ben Roy *physicist*
Olgaard, Anders *economics professor*
Pethick, Christopher John *physicist*

Farum
Larsen, Poul Steen *retired information science educator*

Horsholm
Sørensen, Erik *retired diversified financial services company executive*
Svensson, Sven Eilif *civil engineer, consultant*

ECUADOR

Quito
Del Pino, Eugenia M. *biology professor*
Wesberry, James Pickett, Jr. *retired anti-corruption specialist, management consultant, speaker, author*

EGYPT

Assiut
Abdel-Hakim M. Aly, Alaa El-Din *engineer, researcher*

Cairo
Elaraby, Nabil A. *former judge, former diplomat*
Fahmy, Ibrahim Mounir *hotel executive*
Hawass, Zahi *archaeologist, educator, writer*
Lesch, Ann Mosely *political scientist, educator*
Sallam, Ismail Awad-Allah *government agency administrator, educator*

Giza
Digham, Fadel *research and development company executive, director*

Kafr el Sheikh
Saad, Fawzy Ali *molecular geneticist*

ENGLAND

Askett Bucks
Irons, Jeremy John *actor*

Beaconsfield
Lindley, David *mechanical engineer*

Beckenham
Lader, Malcolm Harold *pharmaceutical consultant*

Berkshire
Everitt-Newton, Katherine Evelyn *international management consultant*

Beverley
Edles, Gary Joel *lawyer, educator*

Brentford
Bondy, Rupert *pharmaceutical executive, lawyer*
Gersappe, Sunil *marketing executive*

Cambridge
Buckingham, Amyand David *chemistry professor*
Edwards, Sir Samuel Frederick *physicist, researcher*
Garrow, David Jeffries *historian, author*
Gurdon, John Bertrand *cell biologist*
Hawking, Stephen William *astrophysicist, mathematician, educator*
Hawthorne, Sir William Rede *aerospace and mechanical engineer, educator*
Hogwood, Christopher Jarvis Haley *music educator*
Huxley, Sir Andrew (Fielding) *physiologist, educator*
Kermode, Frank (John Kermode) *literary critic, educator*
Klug, Aaron *molecular biologist*
Lawson, Peter Roderick *physicist, researcher*
Mirrlees, Sir James Alexander *economics professor*
Ramakrishnan, Venkatraman (Venki Ramakrishnan) *scientist*
Rees, Martin John *astronomy educator*
Renfrew, Andrew Colin (Lord Renfrew of Kaimsthorn) *archaeologist, educator, director*
Richard, Alison Fettes *anthropology educator, academic administrator*
Steiner, George (Francis Steiner) *author, educator*
Walker, John Ernest *molecular biologist, researcher*

Canterbury
Holwell, Peter *management consultant*

Charlbury
Belkin, Boris David *violinist*

Cheltenham Gloucestershire
Winwood, Stephen Lawrence *musician, composer*

Cheshunt Hertfordshire
Leahy, Sir Terry *food products executive, marketing professional*

Coulsdon
Vijayaratnam, Kanapathipillai *civil and environmental engineer, consultant, director, educator*

Coventry
Feelisch, Martin *research scientist, consultant*
Thomas, Howard *business educator*

East Sussex
Baker, James Barnes *architect*
Katin, Peter Roy *pianist*

Essex
Collins, Joan Henrietta *actress*

Falmer
Cornforth, Sir John Warcup *chemist*

Headington
Bell, John Irving *medical researcher, educator*

Henley on Thames
Bullock, Peter Bradley *company director, consultant*

Isle of Wight
Stigwood, Robert Colin *film producer, television producer, radio producer, theater producer*

Kent Cranbrook
Hattersley-Smith, Geoffrey Francis *retired government research scientist*

Leavesden
Watson, Emma *actress*

Leeds
Ichino, Yoko *ballerina*
Nixon, David *dancer*
Phillips, Oliver *tropical forest ecologist, researcher*
Pillay, Anand *education educator, researcher*
Slechta, Jiri *theoretical physicist*

Leicester
Harijan, Ram *technology transfer researcher*
Jeffreys, Sir Alec John *geneticist, educator*
Valente, Giorgio *finance educator*

Liverpool
Osetsky, Yuri Nicolai *physicist, researcher*

London
Abu-Deeb, Kamal Mikha'il *humanities educator*
Alexeev, Dmitri Konstantinovich *pianist*
Andsnes, Leif Ove *concert pianist*
Arman Gelenbe, Deniz *concert pianist*
Ashkenazy, Vladimir Davidovich *concert pianist, conductor*
Assousa, George Elias *information technology executive, physicist, corporate executive*
Auerbach, Frank *artist*
Bailey, Christopher *apparel designer*
Baird, Dugald Euan *automotive executive*
Barnevik, Percy Nils *electrical company executive*
Batla, Raymond John, Jr. *lawyer*
Beckinsale, Kate *actress*
Bell, Joshua *musician*
Bertolucci, Bernardo *film director*
Binney, Robert Harry *bank executive*
Bloom, Orlando *actor*
Blunt, Emily Olivia L. *actress*
Blunt, James Hillier *singer*
Bono, (Paul David Hewson) *singer, songwriter*
Boucher, Bruce Ambler *art historian, art critic*
Bourne, Matthew *performing company executive, artistic director*
Bravo, Rose Marie *apparel executive*
Brennan, David R. *pharmaceutical executive*
Butler, Geezer (Terence Michael Joseph Butler) *musician*
Butler, Peter E. *plastic surgeon*
Carroll, Cynthia B. *mining executive*
Chadwick, Derek James *foundation administrator*
Chang, Sarah *violinist*
Chevalier, Tracy Rose *writer*
Clark, Cynthia Zang Facer *federal agency administrator*
Clay, Clifton Ford *motion picture producer, writer*
Cleese, John Marwood *writer, comedian*
Codron, Michael Victor *theater producer*
Collins, Paul John *banker*
Cope, Wendy *poet*
Cowell, Simon *television personality, music producer*
Curtis, Richard *author, screenwriter*
Dahrendorf, Lord Ralf Gustav *sociologist, educator*
Daughtry, Christopher Adam *singer*
Davis, Crispin *publishing company executive*
Day-Lewis, Daniel Michael Blake *actor*
Deighton, Len *author*
Desai, Nitin Dayalji *international organization official*
de Savorgnani, Adriane Aldrich *healthcare administrator, nurse*
Dohnányi, Christoph von *musician, conductor*
Drabble, Margaret *writer*
Duffy, Simon P. *telecommunications industry executive*
Duke, Lawrence Kenneth *banker*
Duncan, Lindsay *actress*
Dyson, Tim *public relations executive*
Edwards, Sylvia Ann *artist*
Elizabeth, , II, (Elizabeth Alexandra Mary) *By the Grace of God of the United Kingdom of Great Britain and Northern Ireland and of Her Other Realms and Territories Queen, Head of the Commonwealth, Defender of the Faith*
Enya, (Eithne Ni Bhraonain, Enya Brennan) *musician*
Eustace, Dudley Graham *diversified financial services company executive*
Fabricant, Arthur E. *lawyer, corporate financial executive*
Fiennes, Joseph *actor*
Fine, Anne *writer*
Flint, Douglas J. *investment company executive*
Flor, Claus Peter *conductor*
Forst, Edward C. *investment company executive*
Forsyth, Stephen A. *venture capitalist, department chairman*
Frayn, Michael *playwright*
Freud, Lucian Michael *painter*
Fuller, Simon *music company executive, television producer*
Galloway, Janice *writer, editor*
Gambon, Michael John *actor*
Gelenbe, Sami Erol *computer scientist, engineering educator*
Gervais, Ricky *actor, scriptwriter*
Glazer, Barry David *lawyer*
Glocer, Thomas Henry *publishing executive*
Goosen, Retief *professional golfer*
Gottesman, A(rthur) Edward *lawyer*
Graubard, Stephen Richards *historian, educator, editor*
Gray, Simon James Holliday *writer, educator*
Greener, Sir Anthony *educational association administrator*
Habgood, Anthony John *wholesale distribution executive*
Haitink, Bernard J. H. *conductor*
Hall, Sir Peter Geoffrey *urban and regional planning educator*
Hallissey, Michael *retired management consultant*
Hare, David *playwright*
Harney, Kathryn Ann *opera singer*
Harris, Thomas *writer*
Hicks, Taylor Reuben *singer*
Hoskins, Bob (Robert William Hoskins) *actor*
Hudson, Manley O., Jr. *lawyer*
Hunter Blair, Pauline Clarke *author*
Hurt, John Vincent *actor*
Ioannou, Constantinos Elia *accountant*
Iommi, Tony (Frank Anthony Iommi) *musician*
Ischinger, Wolfgang *ambassador, diplomat*
James, P(hyllis) D(orothy) (Baroness James of Holland Park of Southwold in County of Suffolk) *author*
John, Sir Elton Hercules (Reginald Kenneth Dwight) *musician*
Jourdren, Marc Henri *investment banking company executive*
Junz, Helen B. *economist*
Kallakis, His Excellency Achilleas Michalis S. (His Excellency Ambassador Achilleas M. Kallakis of the Republi *transportation executive, real estate company executive*
Kapranos, Alexander (Franz Ferdinand) *singer, musician*
Kingsley, Sir Ben *actor*
Knightley, Keira *actress*
Kuper, Adam Jonathan *anthropologist, educator*
Leaf, Robert Stephen *public relations executive*
Lee, Janet *professional tennis player*
Leigh, Mike *film director*
Lessing, Doris (Doris May) *writer*
Lloyd Webber, Lord Andrew (Baron of Sydmonton) *composer*
Lowenthal, David *historian, geographer*
Lynch, John Edward, Jr. *lawyer*
Mackerras, Sir Charles (Alan Maclaurin) *conductor*
Masur, Kurt *conductor, music director*
May, Robert McCredie (Lord May of Oxford) *biology educator*
McCowen, Alec *actor*
McGregor, Ewan Gordon *actor*
McKellen, Sir Ian *actor*
McPhee, Katharine Hope *singer*
Mellon, Tamara *apparel executive*
Mendes, Sam (Samuel Alexander Mendes) *film director, theater director*
Meyer, Sir Christopher J.R. *former ambassador*
Miller, Jonathan Wolfe *theater and film director, physician*
Minnick, Mary E. *investment company executive, former beverage company executive*
Minton, Yvonne Fay *mezzo-soprano*
Mirren, Helen (Ilynea Lydia Mironoff) *actress*
Mizumura, Megumi *conservator*
Montgomery, John Warwick (Baron of Kiltartan and Lord of Morris, Comte de St. Germain de Montgommery) *law educator, theologian*
Moody, Ron *actor, writer*
Mooney, James F. *telecommunications industry executive*
Morris, Desmond (John) (Desmond John Morris) *zoologist, writer, artist*
Moss, Kate *model*
Mosselmans, Carel Maurits *investment banker*
Muir-Taylor, Douglas James *ophthalmologist*
Murdoch, Elisabeth *media company executive*
Murray, Robin MacGregor *psychiatrist, educator, consultant*
Nagano, Kent George *conductor, music director*
Nelson, Elizabeth Hawkins *not-for-profit association administrator*
Newell, Mike *film director*
Nighy, Bill Francis *actor*
Oliver, Diane Frances *publisher, writer*
Oliver, Jamie *chef, television personality*
Ormsby, Eric Linn *writer, educator*
Palahniuk, Chuck (Charles Michael Palahniuk) *writer, journalist*
Paton Walsh, Jill *writer*
Pessl, Marisha *writer, artist*
Phocas, George J. *lawyer*
Plapinger, William A. *lawyer*
Polk, George Washington *telecommunications executive, entrepreneur*
Portes, Richard David *economics professor*
Pryce, Jonathan *actor*
Quillen, Cecil Dyer III *lawyer*
Quint, David Paul *investment banking executive*
Ralston, Anthony *computer scientist, mathematician, educator*
Read, Piers Paul *author*
Rice, Sir Timothy Miles Bindon *lyricist*
Richardson, Miranda *actress*
Rickman, Alan *actor*
Rowling, J.K. (Joanne Kathleen Rowling) *writer*
Rutter, Michael Llewellyn *child psychology educator*
Sarkis, Ziad Joseph *private equity executive*
Scardino, Dame Marjorie Morris *publishing executive*
Scott, Raymond Peter William *chemistry professor, writer*
Shakira, (Shakira Isabel Mebarak Ripoll) *musician*
Shankar, Ravi *composer, musician*
Sher, Sir Antony *actor, author*
Smith, Dame Maggie (Margaret Natalie Smith Cross) *actress*
Smith, Zadie (Sadie Smith) *writer*
Spacey, Kevin *actor*
Spillane, Mary Catherine *television producer*
Staunton, Imelda (Imelda Mary Philomena Bernadette Staunton) *actress*
Stella, Frank Philip *artist*
Stelle, Kellogg Sheffield *physicist*
Stevens, Robert Bocking *lawyer*
Stojkovic, Dusan *lawyer*
Stoppard, Tom (Tomas Straussler) *playwright*
Studzinski, John Joseph Paul *investment banking executive*
Thomas, Allen Lloyd *lawyer, private investor*
Uchida, Mitsuko *pianist*
Verwaayen, Ben J.M. *communications company executive*
Walsh, Paul S. *beverage executive*
Ward, Bill *musician*
Warner, Scott Dennis *investment banker*
Winner, Michael Robert *film director, film producer, writer*
Zonana, Victor *lawyer, educator*

Manchester
Wilson, Keith Dudley *media and music educator, consultant, dean*

Milton Keynes
Throdahl, Mark Crandall *medical products executive*

North Wales
Hands, Terence David (Terry) *theater and opera director*

North Yorks
Swan, Robert *explorer, adventurer, foundation administrator*

Norwich
Baulcombe, David C. *virologist*

Old Windsor
Marsh, Donna M. *sales executive, consultant*

Oxford
Bell Burnell, S. Jocelyn (Susan Jocelyn Bell) *astrophysicist, physics professor*
Carey, John *language educator, critic*
Dawkins, Richard (Clinton Richard Dawkins) *ethologist, evolutionary biologist, educator, writer*
Harvey, Paul H. *evolutionary biologist, researcher*
Krebs, John Richard *zoologist, science administrator*
Peto, Sir Richard *medical researcher*
Raz, Joseph *philosophy and law educator*
Shaw, Dennis Frederick *former library director, chartered physicist, consultant*
Thomas, Sarah E. *university librarian*
Vaisey, David George *librarian, archivist*
Varese, Federico *sociology professor*

Reading
Dunning, John Harry *economics educator*
Spencer, David Anthony *geologist, researcher, educator*
Thacker, Charles P. *computer engineer, engineering executive*

Redhill
Donaldson, David *pathologist*

Richmond
Armfield, Diana Maxwell *artist, educator*

Richmond-upon-Thames
Smith, Norman Raymond *academic administrator*

Saint Margaret's
Attenborough, Baron Richard Samuel *actor, film director, producer, ambassador*

Southampton
Brebbia, Carlos Alberto *engineering educator, consultant*

Stevenage
Follett, Kenneth Martin *author*

Stoke-on-Trent
Kim, Do Kyung *science educator*

Stroud
Robinson, John Beckwith *development management consultant*

Surrey
Holm, Sir Ian *actor*
Immelman, Trevor *professional golfer*
Weston, Sir John (Sir Philip John Weston) *retired diplomat*

Westminster
Broers, Lord Alec Nigel *engineering educator*

Whitchurch
Adams, Richard George *writer*

Wiltshire
Dyson, Sir James *manufacturing executive, inventor*
Sherwin, James Terry *lawyer*
Ahrendts, Angela J. *apparel executive*
Aufhauser, David D. *lawyer, former federal agency administrator*

ESTONIA

Tallinn
Kõõrna, Arno *economist, educator*

FINLAND

Espoo
Hari, Riitta Kyllikki *neuroscientist*

Helsinki
Juhani, Erma *lawyer, former stock exchange executive*
Liewendahl, Bo Kristian *retired pathologist, nuclear medicine physician*

Tampere
Andriano, Kirk Patrick *pharmaceutical executive*

FRANCE

Antony
Dahling, Gerald Vernon *lawyer, director*

Arles
Clergue, Lucien Georges *photographer*

Besancon
Boillat, Guy Maurice Georges *mathematical physicist*

Biarritz
Friedman, Richard Everett *curator, art appraiser*

Chatenay-Malabry
Evesque, Pierre Henri *physics researcher*

Collonges
Morgenstern, Sheldon Jon *symphony orchestra conductor*

Compiegne
Dubuisson, Bernard Louis *science educator, administrator*

Creteil
Renoux, André *physicist, researcher*

Fontainebleau
Demers, Elizabeth Anne *education educator*

Gif-sur-Yvette
Duplessy, Jean Claude *research scientist*

Issy Les Moulineaux
Pouzilhac, Alain Duplessis de *advertising executive*

Lacoste
Strauss, Gwen B. *writer, editor*

Le Vesinet
Fourt, Bernard-Francois P. *retired engineer*
Hillion, Pierre Théodore Marie *mathematical physicist*

Levallois-Perret
Filipacchi, Daniel *publishing executive*

Lyon
Robertson, David *conductor, music director*

Malaucene Vaucluse
Langenkamp, Mary Alice (M.A. Langenkamp) *artist, educator*

Marseille
Boutterin, Emmanuel *public relations executive*

Noisy-le-Grand
Le Quéré, Jean François Marie *scientific instrumentation researcher*

Orleans
Price, David Cecil Long *physicist, researcher*

Orsay
Friedel, Jacques *retired physics professor*

Paris
Alaïa, Azzedine *fashion designer*
Baum, Axel Helmuth *lawyer*
Bergé, Pierre *apparel design executive*
Burke, Michael *apparel executive*
Cagle, William Rea *retired librarian*
Cardin, Pierre *fashion designer*
Cherkaoui, Mohamed *sociologist*
Choay, Patrick Henri *pharmaceutical executive*
Constantin, Emilia *physicist, researcher*
Courtaud, Bernard Jean-Jacques *human resource consulting executive*
Courtois, Jean-Philippe *information technology executive*
Dean, John Gunther *diplomat*
de Havilland, Olivia Mary *actress*
de Menil, Georges *economist, educator*
Deneuve, Catherine (Catherine Dorleac) *actress*
Elbaz, Alber *apparel designer*
Fitoussi, Jean-Paul Samuel *economics professor*
Gaultier, Jean-Paul *fashion designer*
Gontier, Jean Roger *medicine and physiology educator*
Horovitz, Israel Arthur *playwright*
Jacob, François *biologist, educator*
Jolas, Betsy *composer, educator*
Kammerer, Kelly Christian *lawyer*
Kourilsky, François Michel *research scientist*
Lagarde, Christine *French government official, lawyer*
Lagardere, Arnaud *media company executive*
Lagerfeld, Karl Otto *fashion designer*
Lehn, Jean-Marie Pierre *chemistry professor*
Littell, Jonathan *writer*
Marcus, Claude *advertising executive*
Mortier, Gerard *opera director*
Myerson, Jacob Myer *retired diplomat*
Oliver, Louise V. *ambassador*
Payri, Joel *pharmaceutical marketing executive*
Piano, Renzo *architect*

Raharinaivo, André Léon *research scientist, educator*
Raimondi, Ruggero *opera singer*
Rawlings, Boynton Mott *lawyer*
Renouf, Edda *artist*
Reynolds, Stephen Robert *lawyer*
Ricol, Rene Jean *accountant*
Robuchon, Joël *restaurateur*
Ross, Charles *artist*
Saint Laurent, Yves (Henri Donat Mathieu) *couturier*
Salans, Carl Fredric *lawyer*
Serre, Jean-Pierre *mathematician, scholar*
Tapponnier, Paul *physics professor*
Vandame, Jean-Marie Richard *diversified financial services company executive*
Yuechiming, Roger Yue Yuen Shing *mathematics professor*

Port-Fréjus
Crapon de Caprona, Count Noël François Marie *retired senior United Nations official*

Roques
White, Norval Crawford *architect*

Saint Ceols
Saisselin, Remy Gilbert *fine arts educator*

Saint Etienne
Vergnaud, Jean-Maurice *science educator, researcher*

Valbonne
Junker, Ulrich *computer scientist, researcher*

Vandoeuvre-les-Nancy
Blazy, Pierre François *science educator*

Vence
Polk, William Roe *historian*

Villefranche-sur-Mer
Legendre, Louis *oceanographer, educator, research scientist*

Villeneuve d'Ascq
Allain, Louis *literature educator*

GEORGIA

Tbilisi
Noghaideli, Zurab *Prime Minister of Georgia*

GERMANY

APO
Adams, Julian Timothy *psychologist*
Schall, David Gordon *military officer, surgeon*

Aachen
Pischinger, Franz Felix *engineer, researcher, engineering educator*

Alstadt
Richter, Gerhard *artist*

Augsburg
Kunes, Jan *physicist*

Bad Homburg
Klatten, Susanne Quandt *pharmaceutical executive*

Bad Nauheim
Engel, Felix Benedikt Salomon *cell biologist, researcher*

Bavaria Murnau
Trapp, Oliver Marcus *surgeon, consultant*

Berlin
Barenboim, Daniel *conductor, pianist, music director*
Eichler, Hans Joachim *physics professor*
Jahnke, Kristoph *internist, hematologist, oncologist, researcher*
Jochmann, Frank *mathematician*
Köhler, Horst *President of Federal Republic of Germany*
Mantsch, Henry Horst *chemistry professor*
Piper, Adrian Margaret Smith *philosopher, artist, educator*
Simon, Hans-Joerg Walter *lawyer*

Bonn
Rampacher, Hermann Hans *writer, consultant*

Braunschweig
Diethelm, Kai *mathematician, researcher*
Leseberg, Dieter Wolfgang Michael *mathematician*

Bremen
Fahle, Manfred *ophthalmology researcher*
Wells, Raymond O'Neil, Jr. *mathematics professor, researcher*

Cologne
Korenkov, Michael *surgeon*
Neisser, Horst *library director, writer*

Damstadt
McNeill, Dan K. *career military officer*

Dresden
Gluch, Steffen *company executive*
Schreier, Peter *tenor*
Wartenberg, Katja Eltriede *neurologist*

Düsseldorf
Andre, Carl *sculptor*
Schulz, Ekkehard *metal products executive*

Frankfurt
Ammann, Jean-Christophe *art director*
Greiner, Walter Albin Erhard *physicist*
Michel, Hartmut *biochemist*
Papademos, Lucas *bank executive*
Simitis, Spiros *legal educator*
von Rosen, Rüdiger *stock exchange executive*

Freiberg
Zabecki, David Tadeusz *engineer, educator, military historian, military officer*

Fulda
Beckman, James Wallace Bim *management consultant, educator*

Furth
Rau, Magda *ophthalmologist*

Garching
Cesarsky, Catherine *astrophysicist*

Göttingen
Starck, Christian Walter *retired judge, law educator*
Toennies, Jan Peter *research chemical physicist*

Halle
Schmoll, Hans Joachim *hematology and oncology educator*
Thamm, Jochen Walter *library director*

Hamburg
Lüst, Reimar *foundation president*
Neumeier, John *choreographer, ballet company director*

Hannover
Allen, Bruce *physicist*

Koln
Lee, Catherine *sculptor, painter*

Korschenbroich
Engau, Alexander *research scientist*

Leipzig
Pääbo, Svante *molecular biologist, biochemist*

Lübeck
Fligge, Jörg *librarian, library director*

Mannheim
Solz, Hermann *plastic surgeon*

Mayen
Gartz, Rolf F. *foundation administrator*

Munich
Araiza, Francisco (José Francisco Araiza Andrade) *opera singer*
Bangle, Christopher Edward (Chris Bangle) *automotive company car designer*
Heywang-Koebrunner, Sylvia H. *radiologist, educator*
Huber, Robert *biochemist, educator*
Loescher, Peter Hans *electronics executive*
Schmidt, Stefan *mechanical engineer, economist*
Viermetz, Kurt F. *banker*

Münster
Spevack, Marvin *language educator*

Neu Isenburg
Hoare-Temple, Piers Howard *building maintenance executive*

Nuremberg
Doerries, Reinhard René *historian, educator*

Obbornhofen
Edwards, Grey Holt, Jr. *academic administrator, adult education educator*

Ottilienstr
Clarke, Ingrid Gadway *retired academic ombudsman, consultant*

Paderborn
Thim, Frank *physicist, astronomer*

Regensburg
Eisenmann-Klein, Marita *plastic surgeon*

Rostock
Vaupel, James W. *demographer*

Schleusingen-Gethles
Frank, Dieter *retired chemicals executive*

Seeheim-Jugenheim
Halama, Niels *physician, researcher*

Sonnenberg-Wiesbaden
Lynch, Lucia *language educator*

Starnberg
Huber, Franz *retired research director*

Stutensee
Barbian, Otto Alfred *physicist*

Stuttgart
Anderson, Reid Bryce *performing company executive*
Cardona, Manuel *physics professor*
Geh, Hans-Peter *retired library director, consultant*
von Klitzing, Klaus *research facility administrator, physicist*
Ward, William E. (Kip Ward) *career military officer*
Zetsche, Dieter *automotive executive*

Tübingen
Nüsslein-Volhard, Christiane *medical researcher*

Witten
Gaengler, Peter Wolfgang *dentist, researcher*

Wuppertal
Schubert, Guenther Erich *pathologist*

GHANA

Accra
Jones, Monty P. *science administrator*

GIBRALTAR

DeLeon, Russ *Internet company founder*

GREECE

Athens
Boudoulas, Harisios *cardiologist, researcher, medical educator*
Kalamotousakis, George John *economist, merchant banker, educator*
Kenourgios, Dimitris *finance educator*
Larounis, George Philip *manufacturing executive, director*
Miliotis, Demitrios *physics professor*
Papadakis, Panagiotis Agamemnon *corporate financial executive*
Zevgolis, Ioannis *geotechnical engineer, researcher*

Larisa
Zacharoulis, Dimitris *surgeon, researcher*

Marousi
Joannou, Dakis *businessman*

Piraeus
Papachristou, Costas John *physicist, researcher*

GUANA ISLAND

Barrigada
Perez, Annie Rivera *elementary school educator*

GUATEMALA

Antigua
Rodgers, Frank *librarian*

Guatemala City
Herrera-Llerandi, Rodolfo Eduardo *surgeon, educator*
Mayora-Alvarado, Eduardo Rene *lawyer, educator*
Mishaan, Emilio *transplant surgeon, educator*

HAITI

Port-au-Prince
Pape, Jean William *physician, researcher*

HONG KONG

Central
Bing, Xu *artist*

Cheung Sha Wan
Dyer, David F. *apparel company executive*
Hilfiger, Tommy (Thomas Jacob Hilfiger) *apparel designer*

Hong Kong
Kao, Charles Kuen *electrical engineer, educator*
Laurie, James Andrew *broadcast executive, consultant, director, television executive producer, journalist*
Lee, Shau Kee *real estate developer*
Leung, Ka-Cheong *engineering educator*
Podd, Ann *newspaper editor*
Tse, Edmund Sze-Wing *insurance company executive*
Tsui, Lap-Chee *academic administrator, molecular genetics educator*

Kowloon
Fung, Victor K. (Victor Fung Kwok King) *consumer products trading company executive*
Wu, Daniel *actor*

New Territories
Lau, Lawrence Juen-Yee *academic administrator, economics professor, consultant*

Wanchai
Paulus, Michael John *government official, economist, bank executive*
Roach, Stephen S. *economist*

HUNGARY

Budapest
Gotsch, John Warren *contemporary arts house director*
Poprády, Géza *librarian*
Rakos, Balázs *physicist, researcher*
Szigeti, János *physicist*

Debrecen
Csikai, Gyula *physicist, researcher*

Sopron
Sitkei, György *engineer, educator*

ICELAND

Reykjavik
Leitner, James *finance company executive*

INDIA

Baner Pune
Ohri, Sangeeta Jean Mary *social studies educator*

Bangalore
Gadagkar, Raghavendra *ecologist, educator, entomologist*
Siddiqi, Obaid *retired geneticist*

Calcutta
Kothari, Hemraj *mechanical engineer, management consultant*

Chandigarh
Pattipati, Sreenivasulu Naidu *science educator*

Delhi
Mitra, Asoke Nath *retired physicist, educator*

Gurgaon Haryana
Katariya, Kushagra *cardiothoracic surgeon, educator*

Haryana Rohtak
Chauhan, Ashok Kumar *medical educator*

Hyderabad
Gummaraju, Srinivas Chakravarthy *oncologist, hematologist*
Shanmugasundaram, Anantharaman *geologist, consultant*

Jaipur
Gupta, V. P. *economist, academic administrator*

Kanpur
Joglekar, Satish Dinkar *physicist, educator*

Karnataka
Ravish, I. R. *urologist, surgeon*

Lucknow
Kumar, Raj *medical educator*
Mohan, Dinesh *research scientist*

Manipal
Pai, Satish Upendra *publishing executive*

New Delhi
Gupta, Vijay *mathematics professor*
Malone, David Michael *diplomat, educator*
Mashelkar, Raghunath Anant *chemical engineer*
Reddy, K. Srinath *cardiologist*
Watson, Paul *photojournalist, correspondent*

Noida
Jain, Prem Chand *mechanical engineer*

Tiruchirappalli
Ramesh, Srikrishnaperumal Thanga *engineering educator*

INDONESIA

Jakarta
Hsi, Edward Yang *lawyer, venture capitalist, industrialist*
Tilaar, Henry A.R. *social sciences educator*

IRELAND

Cork
Lyons, Nona Mary *adult education educator*

County Kildare
Kabdebo, Thomas George *library director*

Donegal
Friel, Brian (Bernard Patrick Friel) *author*

Dublin
Coey, John Michael David *physicist, educator*
Dooge, James Clement Ignatius *civil engineer, hydrologist*
Foley, Thomas Coleman *ambassador, investor*
O'Reilly, Sir Anthony John Francis *media company executive, former food products company executive*
Sheridan, Jim *film director, screenwriter*

Galway
Hynes, Garry *theater director*

Mullingar
Donleavy, James Patrick *writer, artist*

ISRAEL

Arad
Hollander, Samuel *economist, educator*

Be'er Sheva
Brosilow, Coleman Bernard *chemical engineering educator*
Carmeli, Moshe *theoretical physicist*
Frenkel, David Arie *law professor*

Givat Brener
Tritter, Richard Paul *strategic consultant*

Haifa
Ziv, Jacob *communications engineer*

Jerusalem
Abramsky, Oded *neurologist*
Hazboun, Viveca *psychiatrist*
Hrushovski, Ehud *mathematics professor*
Menses, Jan *artist, draftsman*
Rozett, Robert Bernard *library director, historian*

Kiryat Shmone
Gophen, Moshe *research scientist*

Netanya
Tsitverblit, Naftali Anatol *physicist, fluid mechanics engineer, researcher*

Ra'anana
Hayon, Elie M. *chemist, educator*

Ramat Aviv
Bernstein, Joseph *mathematician, researcher, educator*

Ramat-Gan
Aron, Roberto *lawyer, writer, educator*

Rehovot
Sachs, Leo *geneticist, educator*
Shamir, Adi *computer scientist*

Savyon
Bushinsky, Jay (Joseph Mason) *journalist, news correspondent*

Tel Aviv
Gross, Joseph H. *lawyer, educator*
Jortner, Joshua *physical chemist, educator*
Rosenne, Meir *lawyer, federal agency administrator*

ITALY

Bologna
Eco, Umberto *semiotics educator, author*
Keller, Kenneth Harrison *engineering educator*

Ciserano di Zingonia
Vieri, Christian *professional soccer player*

Como
Casati, Fabio *engineer*
Casati, Giulio *theoretical physics professor*

Cremia
Malipiero, Victoria Schneider *opera singer*

Florence
Cecil, Charles Harkless *artist, educator*
Giannini, Frida *apparel designer*

Maranello
Schumacher, Michael *retired race car driver*

Milan
Berlusconi, Marina *publishing executive*
Cavalli, Roberto *fashion designer*
Dolce, Domenico *fashion designer*
Gabbana, Stefano *fashion designer*
Honegger, Federico *artist*
Prada, Miuccia Bianca *fashion designer*
Versace, Donatella *fashion designer*

Naples
Tarro, Giulio *virologist*

Padua
Pozzan, Tullio *medical educator*
Shea, William Rene *historian, history and philosophy professor*

Palermo
Fiumara, Ettore *neurosurgeon*

Pisa
Labardi, Massimiliano *research scientist*
Settis, Salvatore *archaeologist, art historian*

Rieti
Truini Palomba, Maria Giuseppina *supreme court lawyer, judge*

Rome
Balducci, Alessandro *nephrologist, educator*
Benedict XVI, His Holiness Pope (Joseph Alois Ratzinger) *Pope of Roman Catholic Church, Bishop of Rome*
Gros-Pietro, Gian Maria *economics professor*
Kolvenbach, Peter Hans *priest, head of religious order*
Levada, William Joseph Cardinal *archbishop emeritus, cardinal*
Levi-Montalcini, Rita *neurobiologist, researcher*
Maraviglia, Bruno *physicist, researcher*
McGurn, William Barrett III *lawyer*
Scognamiglio Pasini, Carlo *economics and finance professor, senator*
Shiner, Josette Sheeran (Josette Sheeran) *international organization official, former federal agency administrator*
Sisulu, Sheila Violet Makate *international organization official, diplomat*
Stigliano, Jose Maria *information technology executive, computer scientist*
Valentino, (Valentino Garavani) *fashion designer*
Westley, John Richard *economist*

Siena
Rappuoli, Rino *immunologist*

Turin
Elia, Michele *mathematics professor*
Rossi, Guido A(ntonio) *mathematics professor, researcher*

Vatican City
Foley, John Patrick *archbishop*
Stafford, J. Francis Cardinal *Cardinal*
Stafford, James Francis *cardinal*
Szoka, Edmund Casimir Cardinal *archbishop*

Venice
Pasinetti, Pier Maria *author*

Verona
Pozzo, Riccardo *philosophy educator*
Spogli, Ronald P. *ambassador*

JAMAICA

Mona
Harris, Eon Nigel *dean, rheumatologist, internist*

JAPAN

Chiba
Arai, Toshihiko *retired microbiology and immunology educator*
Hattori, Naozo *science educator*

Fukuoka
Ishibashi, Akira *mechanical engineer, educator*

Gifu
Hatada, Kazuyuki *mathematician, educator*

Gunma
Hironaka, Heisuke *mathematics professor, academic administrator*
Okada, Ryozo *medical educator, researcher*

Gyoda
Shibasaki, Yoshio *chemistry professor, researcher*

Hamamatsu
Kaneko, Masao *radiology educator, researcher, specialist*

Hirakata
Shigemitsu, Toshiro *ophthalmologist, researcher*

Hirosaki
Sato, Hiroyuki *materials engineer, researcher*

Ibaraki
Urabe, Tohsuke *mathematics professor, researcher*

Kanagawa
Fukatsu, Tanefusa *retired classicist, educator*

Kashiwara
Hori, Keiko *English literature educator*

Kasugai
Miyake, Yasuji *computer science educator*

Kinokawa-shi
Yamawaki, Nobuyuki *engineering educator, biomedical engineer, researcher*

Kobe
Inoue, Shun *sociologist*
Shrestha, Manoj Lal *economics professor, policy studies researcher*

Kushimoto
Akura, Junsuke *ophthalmologist, researcher*

Kyoto
Kashida, Jeffrey Shinji *diversified financial services company executive*
Tsuji, Toshizo *hospital administrator, educator*

Mie
Isshiki, Masayuki *sociologist, educator, dean*
Kitashirakawa, Michihisa *head of religious order*

Mitaka
Kazama, Toshio *retired humanities educator*

Mito
Kobayashi, Susumu *retired computer company executive*

Nagoya
Kajitani, Motohisa *sociology educator*
Sakai, Toshihiko *engineer*
Sendo, Takeshi *mechanical engineering educator, researcher, writer*

Okayama
Morooka, Hiroshi *neurosurgeon*
Nii, Shiro *director, virologist, educator*
Okada, Shigeru *medical educator*
Ubuka, Toshihiko *biochemist, educator, academic administrator*

Osaka
Akase, Masako *humanities educator*
Horii, Reiichi *library director, educator*
Ikeda, Kazuyosi *physicist, poet*

Saitama
Hozumi, Motoo *medical educator, researcher*

Sapporo
Asari, Eikichi *information sciences educator, researcher*
Nakagawa, Koji *retired endocrinologist, educator*
Sakai, Yu *pathologist*

Shizuoka
Anma, So *engineer, consultant*

Tochigi
Honma, Koichi *pathologist, researcher*
Hyodo, Haruo *radiologist, educator*

Tokorozawa
Nakamura, Hiroshi *urology educator*

Tokushima
Kinno, Hitoshi *mechanical engineer, educator*

Tokyo
Chang, Steve *internet security company executive*
Chiba, Machiko *cooking advisor*
Esaki, Leo (Esaki Leona) *physicist, foundation executive, university president*
Eto, Hajime *retired information scientist, educator*
Farrar, Stanley F. *lawyer*
Fukushima, Kiyohiko *economist*
Gyohten, Toyoo *economist*
Hakoshima, Shin-ichi *publishing executive*
Harada, Norio *software engineer, researcher, educator*
Hirai, Kazuo (Kaz) *electronics executive*
Hirayama, Eiji *psychologist, educator*
Hori, Yukio *engineering educator, scientific association administrator*
Iida, Shuichi *physicist, educator*
Ishii, Akira *parasitologist, allergist, malariologist*
Kaneko, Isao *air transportation executive*
Kato, Shuichi *information scientist, educator*
Kobayashi, Noritake *business educator*
Koshiba, Masatoshi *physicist, educator*
Krisher, Bernard *foreign correspondent*
Maki, Atsushi *economics professor*
Matsuda, Masatake *rail transportation executive*
Mukaiyama, Teruaki *chemist, educator*
Nakajima, Hiroshi *education educator*
Nishiyama, Chiaki *economist, educator*
Ohga, Norio *retired electronics executive*
Ono, Eiichi *engineering educator, researcher*
Ozawa, Seiji *conductor, music director*
Petersen, Barry Rex *news correspondent*
Saba, Shoichi *electronics executive, director*
Sakurada, Yutaka *retired chemist*
Sakuta, Manabu *neurologist, educator*
Shirai, Shun *law educator, lawyer*
Suzuki, Akira *physics professor*
Toyoshima, Chikashi *structural biologist, educator*
Wakumoto, Yoshihiko *electronics company executive, grants executive*
Yaku, Takeo T. *computer scientist, educator*

Toyama
Sumiyoshi, Tomiki *psychiatrist, researcher*

Toyota
Toyoda, Shoichiro *automotive executive*

Tsukuba
Hanaki, Nobuyuki *economics professor*
Shimizu, Kazuhiko *education educator*

Utsunomiya
Yorikawa, Hiroharu *physicist, researcher*

Yokohama
Ito, Noboru *electric power industry executive*
Taketomi, Susamu *physicist, researcher*

JORDAN

Amman
Saadeh, Sherif Nabil *gastroenterologist, hepatologist, researcher*

Zarka
Abu-Khader, Nabil *electrical engineer, educator*

Zarqa
Al-Bataineh, Osama Mohammad *biomedical engineer*

KAZAKHSTAN

Almaty
Sadykova, Vera Philippovna *librarian, educator*

KENYA

Mombasa
Harrell, Jerry DeWitt *ophthalmologist, director*

Nairobi
Maathai, Wangari *environmentalist, consultant*

LATVIA

Riga
Lācis, Aris *health facility administrator, cardiac surgeon*
Strautins, Vilnis *music educator, retired performing company executive*

LEBANON

Beirut
Khatib, Rustom Atfat *gynecologist, researcher, endocrinologist, consultant, economist*
Waterbury, John *academic administrator, political science professor, writer*

MADAGASCAR

Antananarivo
Rakotoarisoa, Jean Aimé *director museum*

MALAWI

Lilongwe
Eastham, Alan Walter, Jr. *foreign service officer, lawyer*

MALAYSIA

Cyberjaya
Lai, Ming-Ming *finance educator*

Perak
Yussuf Izzuddim, Shah Ghafraullah Sultan *Sultan of Perak*

Petaling Jaya
Wong, Kuok-Shoong Daniel *research scientist*

Selangor
Azer, Samy Aziz *gastroenterologist, educator*

Skudai
Ruzairi, Abdul Rahim *engineer, educator, director*

MEXICO

Aguascalientes
Godinez Flores, Ramon *bishop*

Alvaro Obregon
Sepúlveda Amor, Jaime *public health service officer*

Caolniatizapan
Ramirez-Mireles, Fernando *electrical engineer*

Ciudad Juarez
Tabuenca-Cordoba, Maria-Socorro *education educator, researcher*

Colonia Cuauhtemoc
Garza, Antonio O., Jr. *ambassador*

Cuernavaca
Palacios, Rafael *geneticist*

Guadalajara
Durand, Jorge *anthropologist*
Yashima, Mutsuo *language educator*

Mexico City
Aramburúzabála, Maria Asunción *food products executive*
Bruton, John Macaulay *trade association executive, consultant*
Carreto-Chavez, Gerardo *lawyer*
de la Fuente Ramirez, Juan Ramon *academic administrator*
De La Riva, Myriam Ann *artist*
Leon-Portilla, Miguel *historian, educator*
Ortiz, Guillermo *banker*
Trevino, Guillermo Prieto *stock exchange executive*
Vargas Legaspi, Juan *manufacturing executive*

Saltillo
Anderson, Brooks Doran, II, *geologist, consultant*

Tijuana
Chayet, Arturo S. *ophthalmologist, surgeon, consultant*
Carabias Lillo, Julia *government official*
Téllez Kuenzler, Luis *former government official, investment banker*

MOLDOVA

Kishinev
Pyshkin, Sergei L. *physics professor, researcher*

MONACO

Monte Carlo
Lovett, Laurence Dow *retired real estate and steamship executive*

MONGOLIA

Ulaanbaatar
Mandel, Leslie Ann *investment advisor, writer*

MOROCCO

Rabat
Rafi, Mostafa *ophthalmologist*

Tangier
Ashler, Philip Frederic *international trade and development advisor*

NEPAL

Kathmandu
Baker, Ian Archbald *explorer, educator, writer, photographer*

NETHERLANDS

Amsterdam
Dahan, Rene *retired oil industry executive*

Kolko, Gabriel *historian, educator*
Martinez, Arthur C. *bank executive, retired retail executive*
Vinken, Pierre Jacques *publishing executive*

Maastricht
Van Praag, Herman Meir *psychiatrist, educator, researcher*

Rotterdam
van Wachem, Lodewijk Christiaan *petroleum company executive*

Schiphol Rijk
Enders, Thomas *air transportation executive*

The Hague
Aldrich, George Hoover *judge, arbitrator*
Allison, Richard Clark *judge*
Boed, Roman A. *legal administrator*
Buergenthal, Thomas *judge*
Cook, Linda Z. *utilities executive*
Higgins, Dame Rosalyn *judge*
Jiuyong, Shi *judge*
Koroma, Abdul G. *judge*
Mocumbi, Pascoal Manuel *former prime minister of Mozambique*
Owada, Hisashi *judge*
Parra-Aranguren, Gonzalo *judge*
Tomka, Peter *diplomat, arbitrator, judge, lawyer*

Utrecht
't Hooft, Gerardus (Gerard 't Hooft) *physicist, researcher*
Tielman, Rob A.P. *social sciences educator*

Vlaardingen
Smith, Arlan Robert *plastic and reconstructive surgeon*

NEW ZEALAND

Auckland
Gluckman, Peter *endocrinologist, fetal physiologist*

Palmerston North
Krone, Cheryl A. *research scientist, consultant*

Wellington
Jackson, Peter *film director*
Paquin, Anna *actress*
Gould, Wayne *application developer, retired judge*

NIGERIA

Enugu
Ozumba, Benjamin Chukwuma *obstetrician, gynecologist, educator*

NORWAY

Kjeller
Maeland, Arnulf Julius *research scientist*

Lilleström
Gjessing, Dag Trygveson *physicist*

Oslo
Birketvedt, Grethe Støa *medical scientist, writer, musician*
Fitzpatrick, Whitfield Westfeldt *lawyer*
Gjønnes, Jon Kjell *physics professor*
Karlsen, Paul Johan *psychologist, researcher, writer*
Pettersen, Suzann *professional golfer*

PANAMA

Balboa
Piperno, Dolores *research scientist*

PARAGUAY

Asuncion
Cason, James Caldwell *ambassador*

PERU

Lima
Kuczynski, Pedro-Pablo *Prime Minister of Peru*
Struble, James Curtis *ambassador*
Yardley, Jonathan *journalist*

Trujillo
Ungaro, Mario *pathologist, educator*

PHILIPPINES

Cebu City
Bate, Brian R. *retired psychologist*

Makati
Mabilangan, Felipe Hugo, Jr. *diplomat*

Mondaluyong City
Abiera, Roberto *mechanical engineer*

Quezon City
Padlan, Eduardo Agustin *retired immunologist*

POLAND

Bydgoszcz
Czajkowski, Gerard Zygfryd *physicist, researcher*

Gdansk
Mokrzecki, Lech Marian *history of education educator*

Szczecin
Wierzcholski, Wunschik Christoph *mechanical engineer, mathematician, information scientist*

Warsaw
Abakanowicz, Magdalena *artist, sculptor*
Klemens, Rudolf Henryk *mechanical engineer*
Koscielak, Jerzy *research scientist*

Wroclaw
Golinski, Joseph Antoni *mechanical engineer*

PORTUGAL

Algés
Horta, José Carlos de Oliveira Sousa *civil engineering consultant*

Lisbon
Campos, Luís Manuel Braga da Costa *mathematics, physics, acoustics and aeronautics educator*
Hansen-Nord, Jørgen *Danish agency administrator*
Portela, Antonio Gouvea *retired mechanical engineer, researcher*

REPUBLIC OF KOREA

Busan
Ha, Chang Sik *polymer science educator*
Lee, Heesoo *engineering educator*
Lee, Young Woo *neurosurgery educator*
Sung, Gyung Tak *urologist, department chairman*

Cheonan
Shin, Hyun Joon *industrial engineering professor*

Chuncheon
Lee, Won Gyu *chemical engineer, educator*

Daegu
Yim, Man Bin *neurosurgeon, educator*

Daejeon
Choi, Yong-Seok *communications engineer, researcher*
Jeong, Seong-Il *aerospace engineer, researcher*
Ryu, Ho Jin *materials researcher*
Shin, Myung-Ki *computer scientist, researcher*

Gwangju
Kim, Kwang Seog *medical educator*

Gyeonggi Yongin
d'Auriol, Brian J. *engineering educator, researcher*

Gyeonggi-do Suwon
Lee, Byoung-Kuk *engineering educator*

Gyeongsan
Shamsuzzoha, M. D. *research scientist, chemical engineer*

Gyumggi-do
Yoon, Hyung-Doo *publisher, educator*

Incheon
Cho, Chongdu *mechanical engineer, educator*
Gerson, Donald Franklin *pharmaceutical executive*
Hwang, Beongbok *engineering educator*

Seoul
Cha, Suk Won *engineering educator, researcher*
Chi, Je Geun *retired pathologist*
Choi, Won Il *entomologist, researcher*
Chun, Jang Ho *science educator, researcher*
Han, Oksoo *musician, educator*
Hong, Seungkwan *engineering educator*
Jee, Won-Hee *radiologist, educator*
Jeong, Ji-Hoon (Rain) *singer*
Ju, Se-Jong *research scientist*
Keum, Jong-Hae *mathematician, educator*
Kim, Chul Sung *physicist, educator*
Kim, Won *architect*
Kim, Yong-Hak *microbiologist*
Kwon, Yang *neurosurgeon, medical educator*
Lee, Il-Ok *anesthesiologist, education educator*
Lee, Sungho H. *education educator, consultant, academic administrator*
O'Brien, Timothy James *lawyer*
Oh, Myoungho *computer scientist, educator*
Oh, Sangyoon *research scientist*
Park, Myungkark *publishing company owner, physicist*
Seong, Byeongchan *mathematics professor*
Sohn, Jungyul *education educator*
Song, Mi-Yeon *education educator, physician*
Yoo, Vak Yeong *health facility administrator*
Zi, Goangseup *engineering educator*

Suwon
Chang, Seunghyuk *physicist, electrical engineer*
Lee, Tong Hun *economics professor*

Taegu
Seok, Jaewook *materials scientist, polymer scientist*

Wonju
Jeon, Byong-Hun *environmental engineer, educator*

Yuseung
Lee, Kwangil *electrical engineer, researcher*

ROMANIA

Bucharest
Badic, Mihai *research scientist*
Zamfir, Nicolae Victor *physicist, researcher*

RUSSIA

Biysk
Efimov, Valerey Grigorijevich *physicist, researcher*

Kazan
Yulmetyev, Renat Muzipovich *physicist, educator*

Moscow
Braginsky, Vladimir Borisovich *physics professor, department chairman*
Grigoriev, Sergei Aleksandrovich *political scientist, researcher*
Karasev, Vladimir *physicist, researcher*
Kirpilenko, Grigory Grigor'evich *engineer, researcher*
Kogan, Pavel *conductor*
Krikalev, Sergei Konstantinovich *flight engineer, cosmonaut, researcher*
Novikov, Sergei Petrovitch *mathematician*
Padalka, Gennady Ivanovich *cosmonaut*
Romanovski, Mikhail Rem *mathematician*
Saltykov, Boris Georgievich *economist, politician*
Tillett, Samuel Raymond *lawyer*
Zubritsky, Alexander Nickolaevich *pathologist*

Yurga
Apasov, Alexander Mikhailovich *physicist, educator*

SAUDI ARABIA

Dhahran
Muqaibel, Ali Hussein *engineer, educator*

Jeddah
Basfar, Hassan Omar *communications educator*

Riyadh
Alsaud, Prince Alwaleed Bin Talal Bin AbdulAziz *investment company executive, investor, entrepreneur*
Olayan, Lubna S. *finance company executive*
Wagoner, Michael D. *ophthalmologist*

SCOTLAND

Aberdeenshire
Talbot, Nyna Lucille *psychologist, writer*

Cellardyke Fife
Roff, William Robert *historian, educator, writer*

Edinburgh
Atiyah, Sir Michael Francis *mathematician*
Macneil, Ian Roderick *lawyer, educator*

Saint Andrews
Dover, Sir Kenneth James *chancellor, retired classicist*

St Andrews
Lee, Thomas Alexander *accountant, educator*

Stirling
Lenman, Bruce Philip *historian, educator*

SERBIA

Belgrade
Anderson, Joshua Douglas *military officer*

SIERRA LEONE

Freetown
Rapp, Stephen John *international prosecutor*

SINGAPORE

Singapore
Herbold, Patricia Louise *ambassador*
Kong, Adams Wai Kin *electrical engineer, researcher*
Lau, John Hon Shing *electronics scientist*
McNamara, Michael *electronics executive*
Soon, Boon Yi *engineer*
Henretta, Deborah A. *consumer products company executive*
Hill, Gregory Paul *oil industry executive*
Hunter, Howard Owen *academic administrator, law educator*

SLOVENIA

Maribor
Strojnik, Tadej *neurosurgeon, researcher*

SOUTH AFRICA

Bloemfontein
Stulting, Andries Andriessen *ophthalmologist*

Cape Town
Cleary, Sean Michael *risk management executive*
Tutu, Desmond Mpilo *retired archbishop*

Johannesburg
Berk, Philip Woolf *journalist*

Lesotho
Davis, Sarah Frances *management consultant, bishop*

Pretoria
Stocks, Rundell Kingsley *management, construction, education and general consultant*

Thohoyandou
Samie, Amidou *microbiologist, educator, molecular biologist*

SPAIN

Adeje
Grindley, Bruce Alan *real estate agency executive*

Barcelona
Nadal, Rafael (Rafael Nadal Parera) *professional tennis player*
Ronaldinho, (Ronaldo de Assis Moreira) *professional soccer player*

Betlem
Cecchini, Leo *entrepreneur*

Canary Islands
Wells, Melissa Foelsch *retired ambassador*

Madrid
Abellan, José Luis *humanities educator*
Botín, Ana Patricia *bank executive*
Feltenstein, Harry David, Jr. *chemicals executive*
Frühbeck de Burgos, Rafael *conductor*
Herrero Rodriguez de Miñon, Miguel *lawyer, legislator, consultant*
Pérez-Díaz, Víctor Miguel *sociology educator*

Pamplona
Masdeu, Jose Cruz *neurologist, health facility administrator*

Seville
Sanchez, Leonedes Monarrize Worthington (His Royal Highness Duke de Leonedes of Spain Sicily Greece) *fashion designer*

Valencia
Bañuelos, Enrique *real estate company executive*

Zaragoza
Yadav, Prashant *economics educator*

SRI LANKA

Colombo
Spain, James William *political scientist, writer*

SUDAN

Malakal
Wieu, Andrew W. Riang *government agency administrator*

SWEDEN

Bralanda
Emilson, Henry Bertil *artist*

Göteborg
Norrby, Klas Carl Vilhelm *pathology educator*
Svensson, Robert Charles Wilhelm *physicist, researcher*

Leksand
Belfour, Ed *professional hockey player*

Lerum
Borei, Sven Hans Emil *translator, writer, educator*

Saltsjö-Duvnäs
Gyll, John Sören *marketing executive*

Solna
Fleisher, Frederic Elliott *communications executive*

Stockholm
Johnson, Antonia Axson *food products executive*
Lidman, Tomas Erik *national archivist*
Sohlman, Michael *foundation administrator*
Stewart, S. Jay *automotive executive*
van den Bosch, Margareta *apparel company executive*
Wachtmeister, Count Wilhelm H.F. *diplomat*
Wastberg, Olle M. *cultural organization administrator*

Uppsala
Champion, Margrét Gunnarsdóttir *literature and language educator*

Västerås
Xiong, Ning *computer scientist*

Örebro
Persliden, Jan R. G. *physicist*

Österskär
Bolin, Bert Richard Johannes *atmospheric physicist, meteorologist, researcher*

SWITZERLAND

Aargau
Bodis, Stephan B. *radiologist, oncologist, educator*

Alpnach
Bocker, Hans Jurgen *editor-in-chief, consultant, finance educator*

Baar
Rich, Marc David *commodities trader*

Basel
Arber, Werner *microbiologist*
Eriksen, Erik Fink *endocrinologist, internist, researcher*
Gehring, Walter Jakob *biology professor, geneticist*
Nidecker, Andreas Cornelis *radiologist, educator*

Bern
Abe, Nobuyasu *ambassador*
Carlson, Dale Bick *writer*

Chateau d'Oex
Berman, Joshua Mordecai *lawyer, manufacturing executive*

Geneva
Aaronson, Robert Jay *air transportation executive*
Bader, William Banks *historian, former corporate executive, foundation executive*
Ballin, William Christopher *international shipping and investment advisor*
Brown, Kent Newville *ambassador*
Charpak, Georges *physicist, nuclear scientist*
Evans, Timothy Grant *international organization administrator*
Farman-Farmaian, Ghaffar *investment company executive*
Gueudet, Edouard Philippe *financial consultant*
Heymann, David L. *public health service officer*
Jacquesson, Alain L. *librarian*
Kim, Jim Yong *public health service officer, preventive medicine physician*
Maglacas, A. Mangay *nursing researcher, educator*
Peskov, Vladimir Dmitrievich *physicist, consultant, physics professor*
Piot, Peter *international organization administrator*
Ross, Eleanor *retired medical association administrator*
Sommaruga, Cornelio *foundation administrator, diplomat*
Steinberger, Jack *physicist, researcher*

Gland
Leape, James P. *science foundation director*

Hombrechtikon
Landis, Floyd *professional cyclist*

Lausanne
Bloemsma, Marco Paul *investor*
Swartz, Melody A. *biomedical engineer, educator*

Meggen
Galway, Sir James *flutist*

Versoix
Mahler, Halfdan Theodor *physician, health organization executive*

Yverdon-les-Bains
Egolf, Peter William *physicist*

Zurich
Calatrava, Santiago *architect, structural engineer, artist*
Domingue, Gerald James *medical researcher, microbiologist, immunologist, educator, clinical bacteriologist*
Dougan, Brady W. *diversified financial services company executive*
Ernst, Richard Robert *chemist, educator*
Eschenmoser, Albert *chemist*
Hammesfahr, Robert Winter *lawyer*
Morari, Manfred *chemical engineer, educator*
Wassmer, Rudolf Andreas *entrepreneurial engineer*
Wüthrich, Kurt *molecular biologist, biophysicist, educator*
Zinkernagel, Rolf Martin *immunology educator*

TAIWAN

Hsinchu
Wang, David *finance educator*

Kaohsiung
Lambert, Marianne T. *retired elementary school educator*
Liang, Tyng-Yeu *engineering educator*
Wang, Gwo Jaw *orthopedic surgery educator*

Kaohsiung Hsien
Lin, Yusen Eason *microbiologist, educator*

Pingtung
Fan, Tai-Sheng Allen *social scientist in computer education and computing, educator*

Taichung
Liang, Chenju *engineering educator*

Tainan
Chen, Chun-Jen *lawyer, educator*
Hsiao, Shih Wen *mechanical engineer, educator*
Huang, Ting-Chia *chemical engineering professor, researcher*
Lin, Jiin-Huey Chern *engineering educator*

Taipei
Chen, Ding-Shinn *gastroenterologist, educator*
Chuang, Yii-Der *retired manufacturing executive, diplomat*
Lai, Shu-Fen *language educator*
Lee, Yuan Tseh *chemistry professor*
Wu, Maw-Kuen *physicist*

TANZANIA

Moshi
Pomfret, David B. *medical educator, internist*

THAILAND

Bangkok
McMillion, Margaret Kim *foreign service officer*

Northaburi
Austermann, Christopher Brent *language educator*

Phuket
Pianko, Theodore A. *lawyer*

TUNISIA

Carthage
Sehili, Mahmoud *artist*

TURKEY

Adana
Diler, Rasim Somer *psychiatrist, researcher*

Konya
Unusan, Cagatay *finance educator*

UNITED ARAB EMIRATES

Abu Dhabi
Cleaves, Peter Shurtleff *foundation administrator*

UNITED STATES

APO
Carner, George *foreign service executive, economic strategist*

VENEZUELA

Caracas
Chang-Mota, Roberto *electrical engineer*

VIETNAM

Ho Chi Minh City
Israel, Barry John *lawyer*

WALES

Cardiff
Jiles, David Collingwood *physicist, materials science educator*

ADDRESS UNPUBLISHED

Aall, Christian Bergengren *entrepreneur*
Aamodt, Roger Louis *retired federal agency administrator*
Abbas Borhan, Richat *research and development company executive*
Abbe, Elfriede Martha *sculptor, graphics designer*
Abbett, Robert Kennedy *artist, writer*
Abbott, Charles Favour *lawyer*
Abbott, Edward Leroy *finance executive*
Abbott, George Lindell *retired librarian*
Abbott, Lawrence E. *lawyer*
Abbott, Rebecca Phillips *art historian, consultant, photographer, director*
Abbott, Regina A. *neurodiagnostic technologist, consultant, business owner*
Abdelrahman, Talaat Ahmad Mohammad *financial executive*
Abdullaev, Yalchin *neuroscientist, educator*
Abel, Barbara Ellen *photographer*
Abeles, Kim Victoria *artist*
Abeles, Sigmund M. *painter, sculptor, printmaker*
Aberlin, Betty Kay *actor, poet*
Abernathy, Jennifer P. *music educator*
Abetti, Pier Antonio *electrical engineer, management consultant, educator*
Abid, Ann B. *art librarian*
Abizaid, John Philip *retired military officer*
Able, Kenneth Paul *biology professor*
Ablow, Keith Russell *writer*
Aboufakher, Rabeea *cardiologist*
Aboussie, Marilyn *retired judge*
Abraham, Alfred Jude *lawyer*
Abraham, F. Murray (Fahrid Murray Abraham) *actor, educator*
Abraham, Nathan Samuel *advertising agency and public relations executive, marketing and management consultant*
Abram, Ruth Jacobeth *museum administrator and founder*
Abramowitz, Morton I. *former ambassador*
Abrams, Arthur Jay *retired physician*
Abrams, Fredrick Ralph *physician, clinical ethicist*
Abu-Khalaf, Murad *researcher*
Abu-Mostafa, Ayman Said *application developer, consultant*
Accordino, Frank Joseph *architect*
Accorsi, Ernie (Ernest William Accorsi Jr.) *retired professional sports team executive*
Acerra, Michele (Mike Acerra) *engineering and construction company executive*
Achauer, Bruce Michael *plastic surgeon*
Achi, May Ifeoma *pharmacist, consultant*
Achord, James Lee *retired gastroenterologist*
Achorn, Robert Comey *retired newspaper publisher*
Acker, Robert Flint *retired microbiologist*
Ackerman, Jack Rossin *investment banker*
Ackerman, Melvin *investment company executive*
Ackerman, Raymond Basil *advertising executive*
Ackerman, Valerie B. *former sports association executive*
Ackermann, Barbara Bogel *counselor*
Adaikkalavan, Raman *computer scientist, educator*
Adair, Irmalee Traylor *social worker*
Adair, Stefan Rene *plastic surgeon*
Adam, John, Jr. *insurance company executive emeritus*
Adams, Arlin Marvin *lawyer, retired judge, arbitrator, mediator*
Adams, Daniel Fenton *law educator*
Adams, David Parrish *historian, epidemiologist, educator*
Adams, Edwin Melville *retired diplomat, actor, writer*
Adams, Forrest H. *retired pediatrician*
Adams, James Thomas *surgeon*
Adams, Jennifer *medical products executive*
Adams, John Carter, Jr. *retired insurance executive*
Adams, Kevin *lighting designer*
Adams, Leocadia Donat *secondary school educator, writer*
Adams, Margaret Bernice *retired museum official*
Adams, Phyllis Yewell *foreign language educator*
Adams, Robert McCormick *anthropologist, educator*
Adams, Sharon Butler *minister, philosopher, researcher*
Adams, Thomas Lawrence *lawyer*
Adams, Thomas Lynch, Jr. *lawyer*
Adams, Timothy D. *former federal agency administrator*
Adams, Weston *former diplomat, military officer, lawyer*
Addo, Charles Kwame *science educator*
Adkins, Thomas Samuel *library director*
Adkinson, Brian Lee *manufacturing executive*
Adler, Jack Saul *retired accountant*
Adler, Raphael *retired humanities educator, speech pathology/audiology services professional*
Adler, Richard Melvin *architect, planner*
Adler, Samuel Hans *retired conductor, composer*
Adolph, Kathryn Ann *passenger service employee*
Adsumilli, Chowdary B. *research scientist*
Adu, Freddy *professional soccer player*
Adubato, Richard Adam (Richie Adubato) *former professional basketball coach*
Aduen, Javier Francisco *physician, researcher*
Adzick, Nick Scott *surgeon, educator*
Aehlert, Barbara June *health facility administrator*
Africa, Colby Tait *information technology executive, poet*
Agarwal, Sanjiv *nutritionist, researcher*
Agarwal, Suman Kumar *editor*
Aghdashloo, Shohreh *actress*
Aguilar-Bryan, Lydia *medical educator, researcher*
Aguilera, Christina *singer*
Aguinsky, Richard Daniel *electrical engineer, engineering executive*
Ahearne, John Francis *science foundation director, researcher*
Ahmad, Syeda Sultana *physician*
Ahmed, Syed Z. *anthropologist*
Ahmed, Walid Khairy Mohamed *electrical engineer*
Aho, Melissa Kay *librarian, educator, writer*
Ahrens, Franklin Alfred *veterinary pharmacology educator*
Ahrens, Kent *museum director, art historian*
Ahrens, Thomas H. *communications executive*
Aiken, Michael Thomas *former academic administrator*
Aikman, Albert Edward *lawyer*
Aisen, Ari *economist, researcher*
Aja-Herrera, Manuel Angel *art educator*
Akindemowo, Olujoke Eniola *law educator, researcher*
Akinnuoye-Agbaje, Adewale *actor*
Akiyama, Carol Lynn *motion picture industry executive*
Akiyoshi, Toshiko *jazz composer, pianist*
Akkor, Gundogdu *retired architectural firm executive, engineering executive, foundation administrator*
Akos, Francis *retired violinist, conductor*
Alaimo, Terry M. *financial consultant*
Alba, Jessica *actress*
Alba, Lois *singer, educator*
Albanese, Thomas *entrepreneur*
Albano, Pasquale Charles *finance educator, management consultant*
Alberger, William Relph *lawyer, former legislative staff, government official*
Albers, Charles Edgar *retired investment company executive*
Alberti-Chappell, Roxana Dearing *psychologist*
Alberts, Renée Miller *counselor, alcohol/drug abuse services professional*
Albin, Barry G. *lawyer, rabbi*
Albrecht, Rebekah S. *mathematician, educator*
Albritton, William Harold III *federal judge*
Alden, Ingemar Bengt *pharmaceuticals executive*
Alderfer, Clayton Paul *organizational consultant, writer*
Alderson, Sandy (Richard Lynn Alderson) *major league baseball executive*
Alderson, Vanessa *administrative assistant*
Aldous, Charla G. *lawyer*
Aldredge, Theoni Vachliotis *costume designer*
Aldrich, David Alan *accountant, consultant*
Aldrich, Franklin Dalton *medical researcher, consultant*
Aldrich, Patricia Anne Richardson *retired magazine editor*
Aldridge, Adrienne Yingling *accountant, financial analyst, writer*
Aldridge, Christopher D. *biotechnology executive, consultant*
Aldridge, Donald O'Neal *military officer*
Aldrin, Buzz *retired astronaut*
Aldrow-Liput, Priscilla Reese *retired elementary school educator*
Alemneh, Daniel Gelaw *information technology manager, educator*
Alemu, Fitsum Achamyeleh *lawyer, researcher*
Aleshire, Joan Allan *poet, creative writing educator*
Alexander, Ascencion (Cency) H. *school psychologist, educator*
Alexander, Barbara Toll *financial consultant*
Alexander, Faith Dorothy *retired training services executive*
Alexander, George Jonathon *lawyer, educator, dean*
Alexander, James H. *industrial designer*
Alexander, Jason (Jay Scott Greenspan) *actor*
Alexander, Jeremiah Roy *molecular biologist, researcher*
Alexander, Jessica Aronow *anesthesiologist*
Alexander, Jon M. *contractor, consultant*
Alexander, Jonathan *cardiologist, consultant*
Alexander, Judd Harris *retired paper company executive*
Alexander, Lora Kay *writer, composer*
Alexander, Marjorie Anne *artist, consultant*
Alexander, Nancy A. *information technology manager, consultant*
Alexander, Richard Elmont *lawyer*
Alexandratos, Spiro Dionisios *chemistry professor, dean*
Alexiades-Armenakas, Macrene Renee *dermatologist, scientist, researcher, educator, consultant*
Alfano, Robert R. *science and engineering educator*
Alfonso-Bica, Kristy Lynn *elementary school educator*
Alford, Renee Marie *speech pathology/audiology services professional, educator*
Alfred, Stephen Jay *retired lawyer*
Alfriend, Kyle Terry *aerospace engineer*
Al-Hajj, Muhammad *biologist*
Ali, Mohammed Zamshed *information technology executive, researcher*
Ali, Muhammad (Cassius Marcellus Clay) *retired boxer*
Aliber, Robert Z. *economist, educator*
Alinder, Mary Street *writer, educator*
Allday, Martin Lewis, Jr. *retired lawyer*
Allemang, Arnold A. *chemicals executive*
Allen, Bennie Carnel *employee relations specialist*
Allen, Betty Noldon *education educator, consultant*
Allen, Bruce Templeton *retired economics professor*
Allen, Carol E. *retired elementary school educator*
Allen, Charles E. *federal agency administrator*
Allen, Charles Eugene *university administrator, agriculturist, educator*
Allen, Charlotte *secondary school educator*
Allen, Claude Alexander *former federal official*
Allen, Donald Vail *investment company executive, pianist*
Allen, Frances Elizabeth *computer scientist*
Allen, George Felix, Jr. *former senator, governor*
Allen, Jane Folger *psychologist*
Allen, Louis Alexander *management consultant*
Allen, Marilyn Myers Pool *theater director, video specialist*
Allen, Norma Ann *librarian, educator*
Allen, Pamela Smith *retired psychologist, writer*
Allen, Patricia J. *retired library director*
Allen, Philip *artist*
Allen, Ralph Carnell *retired assistant principal*
Allen, Richard S. *engineering company executive*
Allen, Richard Vincent *international business consultant, former national security advisor*
Allen, Roberta *writer, photographer, conceptual artist*
Allen, Toni K. *lawyer*
Allen, William Hayes *lawyer, educator*
Allen, William Sheridan *retired social sciences educator*
Allen, Woody (Allen Stewart Konigsberg) *director, actor, writer*
Allender, Julie Ann *psychologist*
Alley, Kirstie *actress*
Allison, Andrew Marvin *church administrator*
Allred, Dawn Peterman *adult education educator*
Allston, Charita Capers *music educator*
Alm, John Richard *beverage company executive*
Almeida, Richard Joseph *finance company administrator*
Almodovar, Pedro *filmmaker*

Almore-Randle, Allie Louise *special education educator, academic administrator*
Aloff, Mindy *writer*
Alou, Felipe Rojas *former professional baseball team manager*
Alpen, Edward Lewis *biophysicist, educator*
Alper, Andrew Michael *former investment banker*
Alper, Merlin Lionel *corporate financial executive*
Alpern, Andrew *lawyer, architect, historian*
Alpher, Ralph Asher *physicist, educator*
Alpher, Victor Seth *clinical psychologist, consultant*
Al-Shawwa, Bahauddin A. *pediatrician, medical educator*
Altekruse, Joan Morrissey *retired preventive medicine physician*
Alters, Jeremy W. *lawyer*
Altman, Irwin *psychologist, educator*
Altman, Louis *lawyer, author, educator*
Altman, Robert Alan *lawyer*
Altschaeffl, Adolph George *retired civil engineering educator*
Altshuler, Kenneth Z. *psychiatrist, educator*
Altsuler, Kent *lawyer*
Alutto, Joseph Anthony *academic administrator, former dean, management educator*
Alvare, Charles Daguerre *financial advisor, educator*
Alvarez, Aida M. *former federal agency administrator*
Alvarez-Corona, Marti *school psychologist, educator*
Alves, Kyrin Jean *cultural organization administrator, educator*
Alvis, Joel Lawrence, Jr. *minister*
Amabile, Celene *pharmacist*
Amabile, John Louis *lawyer*
Amacher, Arthur Loren *neurosurgeon*
Amann, Charles Albert *mechanical engineer, researcher*
Amar, Akhil Reed *law educator*
Amara, Lucine *vocalist*
Amato Chiaramonte Bordonaro, Baron Carlo Camillo *ambassador, consultant*
Ambach, Gordon Mac Kay *educational association executive*
Ambersound, Rochelle Lillian *retired social worker*
Ambrose, Daniel Michael *publishing executive*
Ambrozic, Aloysius Cardinal (His Eminence Aloysius Cardinal Ambrozic) *archbishop emeritus*
Ament, Kyle Tyler *director*
Ames, Donald Paul *retired air research director*
Ames, Marc L. *retired lawyer*
Ames, Stephen Michael *professional golfer*
Amestoy, Jeffrey Lee *former state supreme court chief justice, educator*
Amiel, Howard *ophthalmologist, corneal surgeon*
Amin, Iran Arbabi *language educator*
Amis, Edward Stephen, Jr. *radiologist, retired military officer*
Amisano, Joseph *architect*
Amling, Frederick *economist, educator, investment advisor*
Amorello, Matthew John *former state agency administrator, state senator*
Amoroso, Richard Louis *psychologist, educator*
Amos, Linda K. *academic administrator*
Amos, Wally (Famous Amos) *entrepreneur*
Amparado, Keith D. *communications company executive*
Amstutz, Curtis J. *music educator*
Amstutz, Daniel Gordon *agricultural products executive, consultant, retired federal agency administrator, grain company executive*
Amundson, John Kay *electrical engineer*
Amussen, Susan Dwyer *history professor*
An, Chungming *telecommunications industry executive*
Anand, Sanjay *training services executive, consultant, entrepreneur, educator*
Anaya, Richard Alfred, Jr. *financial consultant*
Anbar, Michael *biophysics professor*
Ancker-Johnson, Betsy *physicist, engineer, retired automotive executive*
Ancona, George Efrain *photographer, author*
Anderberg, Roy A. *journalist*
Anderegg, Karen Klok *business executive*
Anderer, Joseph Henry *textile company executive*
Anders, George Charles *journalist, writer*
Andersen, Kurt Byars *writer*
Anderson, Allamay Eudoris *retired health educator, home economist*
Anderson, Bernard E. *economist*
Anderson, Carlen Joseph *city agency administrator*
Anderson, Christine Marlene *software engineer*
Anderson, Dawolu Jabari *illustrator*
Anderson, Dean William *museum consultant*
Anderson, Edgar Ratcliffe, Jr. *career officer, physician, health facility administrator*
Anderson, Edward Riley *retired state supreme court justice*
Anderson, Geraldine Louise *medical researcher*
Anderson, Gillian *actress*
Anderson, Gregory Thomas *secondary school educator, researcher, historian*
Anderson, Herschel Vincent *retired librarian*
Anderson, Hugh George *bishop*
Anderson, Jack Roy *healthcare company executive*
Anderson, Jacqueline Annette *information technology specialist*
Anderson, James Francis *lawyer*
Anderson, James George *sociologist, educator, communications educator*
Anderson, Jeffrey Elton *history professor*
Anderson, Jerry Maynard *retired speech educator*
Anderson, Joan R. *secondary school educator*
Anderson, John Firth *retired religious organization administrator, retired librarian*
Anderson, John Gaston *electrical engineer, consultant*
Anderson, Jon Eric *lawyer*
Anderson, Jon Stephen *newswriter*
Anderson, Joseph Norman *retired food products executive, academic administrator*
Anderson, Linda Jean *critical care nurse, psychiatric nurse practitioner*
Anderson, Lisa D. *graphics designer, educator*
Anderson, Marcie *communications executive*
Anderson, Mark Robert *data processing executive, biochemist*
Anderson, Maurice Elton *minister*
Anderson, M.T. *children's book writer and illustrator*
Anderson, N. Christian III *former newspaper publisher*
Anderson, Ned, Sr. *Apache tribal chairman*
Anderson, Paul Irving *management executive*
Anderson, Paul Wayne *assistant principal*
Anderson, Paulette Elizabeth *real estate developer, entrepreneur, retired elementary school educator*
Anderson, Rachael Keller (Rachael Keller) *retired library director*
Anderson, Richard McLemore *internist*
Anderson, Robert Orville *oil and gas company executive*
Anderson, Ruth Lucille *interior designer, educator, artist, librarian, archivist*
Anderson, Shawn Renee *director*
Anderson, Tom *Internet company executive*
Anderson, Wayne Carl *public information officer, retired corporate financial executive*
Anderson-Spivy, Alexandra *arts correspondent, editor, critic, writer, historian*
Andersson, Bo I. *automotive executive*
Andersson, Craig Remington *retired chemical company executive*
Andjaba, Martin *ambassador*
Ando, Kunitake *consumer products company executive*
Andrade, Edna *artist, educator*
Andreas, David Lowell *retired banker*
Andreas, Dwayne Orville *agricultural products executive*
Andreasson, Kim J. *writer, consultant*
Andreoli, Thomas Eugene *physician*
Andretti, Mario *retired race car driver*
Andreu, Helene C. *dancer, educator*
Andrew, Dudley *film and comparattive literature professor*
Andrews, Byllie D'Amato *retired mathematics professor*
Andrews, David Ralph *lawyer*
Andrews, Dame Julie (Julia Elizabeth Wells) *actress, singer*
Andrews, Karen Leigh *language educator*
Andrews, Marion E. *artist, calligrapher*
Andrews, Naveen William Sidney *actor*
Andrews, Richard Vincent *physiologist, educator*
Andrews, William Cooke *physician*
Andreychuk, David *former professional hockey player*
Andrisani, John Anthony *editor, writer*
Andrus, Jennifer Gail *otolaryngologist, surgeon, educator, educational consultant*
Angel, Carlos Alberto *pediatric surgeon, urologist*
Angeles, Rodolfo B. *elementary school educator*
Angula, Helmut Kangulohi *Prime Minister of Namibia*
Anjulis, Stanley Joseph *retired church administrator*
Annesi, Adele Mary *editor*
Annus, John Augustus *artist*
Ansbro, John Joseph *philosopher, educator*
Anschutz, Philip F. *communications and professional sports team executive*
Anselmo, Robert Louis *writer*
Ansley, Shepard Bryan *lawyer*
Antezano, Antonio *investment company executive*
Antezzo, Matthew J. *artist*
Anthony, Joan Caton *administrative judge*
Anthony, Wilma Tylinda *retired customer service administrator*
Anthony-Perez, Bobbie Cotton Murphy *retired psychology professor*
Antioco, John F. *former film rental company executive*
Antonelli, Judith Sarah *writer*
Antonelli, Rosemary *writer*
Antonishek, Joseph John *chef*
Antoun, Mikhail *medicinal chemistry and pharmacognosy educator*
Antreasian, Garo Zareh *artist, lithographer, educator*
Anversa, Piero *medical educator*
Aon, Frank Joseph Garcia *lab administrator, materials scientist*
Apel, Robert William *actor*
Aponte, Frances *psychologist, educator*
Appelbaum, Yonatan Asher *administrative assistant, city manager*
Appell, Louise Sophia *retired consulting company executive*
Appella, Daniel *biochemist, researcher*
Appenzeller, Otto *neurologist, researcher*
Apple, Gary Winston *writer, educational consultant*
Applebaum, Edward Leon *otolaryngologist, educator*
Applegate, Christina *actress*
Appleton, Kevin *academic administrator*
Apps, Jerold Willard *writer*
Apted, Michael David *film director*
Araujo, Ilka Vasconcelos *musicologist, pianist*
Arbaugh, Jon Halbert *legal assistant*
Arbuckle, John Finley, Jr. *retired investment advisor*
Archer, Lillian Patricia *academic administrator, dean*
Archibald, Nolan D. *household and industrial products company executive*
Arciniega, Armando *mathematics professor*
Arcos, Cresencio S. *ambassador*
Arcus, Sam George *social worker, educator, writer*
Arden, Bruce Wesley *retired computer scientist, retired engineering educator*
Areen, Judith Carol *law educator*
Arehole, Shalini *audiologist, educator*
Arenal, Julie (Mrs. Barry Primus) *choreographer*
Arenberg, Irving Kaufman Karchmer *otolaryngologist*
Arenberg, Julius Theodore, Jr. *retired accounting company executive*
Argers, Helen *writer, playwright*
Argiris, Athanassios *oncologist, researcher*
Argyros, George L. *real estate company executive, former ambassador*
Arifi, Fatana Baktash *artist, educator*
Arimilli, Ravi K. *computer engineer*
Ariola, Dante *television commercial and video director*
Ariyoshi, George Ryoichi *lawyer, business consultant, former governor*
Arkin, Alan Wolf *actor*
Arking, Lucille Musser *nurse, epidemiologist, consultant*
Arking, Robert *geneticist, gerontologist, educator*
Arlen, Michael J. *writer*
Arlidge, John Walter *retired utilities executive*
Arlotta, John J. *pharmaceutical executive*
Armacost, Mary-Linda Sorber Merriam *educational consultant*
Armaingaud, Franck *engineer*
Armanios, Daniel Erian *mechanical engineer, political science scholar*
ArmeN, Margaret Meis *lawyer*
Armistead, Katherine Kelly (Mrs. Thomas B. Armistead III) *interior designer, travel consultant, civic worker*
Armitage, Richard Lee *former federal agency administrator*
Armstrong, Anne Legendre *retired ambassador*
Armstrong, Billie Joe *singer, musician*
Armstrong, Douglas Dean *journalist*
Armstrong, Edward Bradford, Jr. *oral and maxillofacial surgeon, educator*
Armstrong, F(redric) Michael *retired insurance company executive, consultant*
Armstrong, Jacque *pre-school educator*
Armstrong, (Arthur) James *minister, educator, consultant, writer*
Armstrong, Sonya M. *mathematics professor, researcher*
Armstrong, Thomas Newton III *landscape artist*
Armstrong-Law, Margaret *school administrator*
Arndt, Dianne Joy *artist, photographer*
Arndt, Laura Denise Lyons Bodeen *mathematics educator*
Arndt, Matthew *scriptwriter*
Arndt, Michael *scriptwriter*
Arnesen, Norman Howard *pastor, educator*
Arnett, David Leslie *former diplomat, speaker, writer*
Arnett, Edward McCollin *chemistry educator, researcher*
Arnold, Alanna S. Welling *lawyer*
Arnold, Charlotte S. *criminal justice agency executive, activist*
Arnold, Henri *cartoonist*
Arnold, Janet Nina *health facility administrator, consultant*
Arnold, Jerome Gilbert *lawyer*
Arnold, Marygwen Suella *language educator, medical/surgical nurse*
Arnott, Howard Joseph *biology professor, dean*
Arnquist, Carol Anne *humanities educator*
Aronson, Jason *publisher*
Arora, Sandeep *cardiologist*
Arp, Arlene *elementary school educator*
Arrington, LaVar *professional football player*
Arrington, (Jack) Michael *web publishing company executive, blogger, lawyer*
Arrott, Patricia Graham *artist, educator*
Arrowood, Catharine Biggs *lawyer*
Arrowood, Deborah Messer *medical transcriptionist*
Arscott, R. Lyndon (Raymond Lyndon Arscott) *management consultant*
Arsic, Antoinette *information specialist*
Arthur, Beatrice *actress*
Arthur (II), Hugh Thomas *lawyer*
Arthur, John Morrison *retired utilities executive*
Asadorian, Diana C. *electrical engineer, educator*
Asai-Sato, Carol Yuki *retired lawyer*
Asato, Evan Masami *artist, architect, designer*
Aschauer, Charles Joseph, Jr. *retired health products executive*
Aschheim, Eve Michele *artist, educator*
Aschheim, Joseph *retired economist, educator*
Asensi, Gustavo *advertising executive, cinematographer*
Ash, Dorothy Matthews *civic worker*
Ash, Roy Lawrence *former federal official*
Ashanti, Baron James *poet, educator*
Ashby, Franklin Charles, Jr. *corporate financial executive, educator*
Ashcraft, David John *secondary school music educator*
Ashcroft, John David *law educator, former United States attorney general*
Ashe, Bernard Flemming *arbitrator, lawyer, educator*
Ashkin, Rajasperi Maliapen *marketing executive*
Ashton, Betsy Finley *artist, broadcast journalist, author, lecturer*
Ashton, Harris John *lawyer*
Ashton, Thomas Walsh *investment banker*
Ashworth, Bessie *benefits compensation analyst, writer*
Asiabanpour, Bahram *engineering educator*
Asirvatham, Angela Lily *science educator*
Askew, Rilla *author*
Askey, William Hartman *United States magistrate judge*
Askins, Nancy Ellen Paulsen *training services executive*
Aslan, Madalyn *writer, educator*
Asma, Evren *medical researcher*
Asman, Bub (Henry B. Asman) *sound editor*
Astin, Sean Patrick *actor, film director, film producer, writer*
Astriab, Steven Michael *military officer*
Astroth, Michael Patrick *military officer*
Atcheson, Sue Hart *business educator*
Atchison, Doug *film director, writer*
Atchison, Joseph Edward *pulp and paper industry consultant*
Atchison, Richard Calvin *trade association director*
Atchison, Rodney Raymond *retired lawyer, arbitrator*
Ater, Al *former state official*
Atherton, Barbara Klein *elementary school educator*
Atherton, William *actor*
Atilgan, Timur Faik *retired structural engineer*
Atkin, J. Myron *science educator*
Atkins, Veronica *philanthropist*
Atkins, Victor Kennicott, Jr. *private investor*
Atkins, William Paul *lawyer*
Atkinson, Holly Gail *physician, journalist, educator, human rights activist, writer*
Atkinson, Tracey Blake *artist, educator*
Atlas, David *meteorologist, research scientist*
Attebery, Louie Wayne *language educator*
Atwater, Phyllis Y. *municipal official*
Atwood, Donna Elaine *retired financial manager*
Aubrey, Douglas P. *ecologist, researcher*
Auden, Bruce James *chef, restauranteur, consultant*
Auerbach, Andrew Daniel Tretter *consulting executive*
Auerbach, Ernest Sigmund *lawyer, insurance company executive, writer*
Augustine, Norman Ralph *not-for-profit executive, business executive, educator, government agency administrator*
Aulbach, George Louis *retired real estate company executive*
Aumann, Robert John *economics professor*
Aune, Debra Bjurquist *lawyer*
Aurin, Robert James *entrepreneur*
Aurora, Sheena Kaur *neurologist*
Austan, Frank Acosta *clinician, educator*
Austin, Grant William *real estate appraiser*
Austin, John DeLong *retired judge*
Austin, John H. *health care administrator*
Austin, Johnta *musician*
Austin, Philip Edward *economics professor, former academic administrator*
Austin, Robert Clarke *naval officer*
Auston, David Henry *former academic administrator, electrical engineer, educator*
Autrey, Wesley *Construction Worker*
Autry, Lola Mae *music educator*
Avant, Gayle *political scientist, educator*
Avant, Robert Frank *retired physician*
Avery, Mary Ellen *pediatrician, educator*
Avery, Stephen Neal *playwright, writer*
Avila, Charlie A. *physics researcher, inventor*
Aviles, Alice Alers *psychologist*
Awazu, Yukika *corporate executive, researcher, consultant, writer*
Awomoyi, Agnes Abiola *microbiologist, researcher*
Axford, Roy Arthur *nuclear engineering educator*
Axilrod, Stephen Harvey *global economic consultant, economist*
Ayad, Joseph Magdy *retired psychologist*
Aydin, Levent *electrical engineer*
Ayedun, Kehinde Peter *information systems executive*
Azad, Nilofer Saba *oncologist*
Azadpur, Mohammad *philosopher, educator*
Azar, Alex Michael, II, *former federal agency administrator, lawyer*
Aziz, Faisal *surgeon*
Baab-Hohman, Roberta (Robin) *artist, scriptwriter, state manager*
Baba, Marietta Lynn *anthropologist, academic administrator*
Babao, Donna Marie *retired community health and psychiatric nurse, educator*
Babar, Sardar Ijlal *pulmonologist*
Babauta, Juan Nekai *former governor, congressional representative*
Babb, Roberta Joan *educational administrator*
Babbin, Jed Lloyd *lawyer, former deputy undersecretary of defense*
Babbitt, Samuel Fisher *retired university official*
Babitzke, Theresa Angeline *health facility administrator*
Baca, Jim *mayor*
Baca, Joseph Francis *retired judge*
Bacas, Andrew R. *data processing executive*
Bach, Jan Morris *composer, educator*
Bach, Mary Irene *music educator*
Bacharach, Melvin Lewis *venture capitalist*
Bachelder, Cheryl Anne *former food service company executive*
Backus, Elaine Athene *entomologist, educator*
Backus, Keriann M. *chemistry scholar, Latin American studies scholar*
Bacon, Caroline Sharfman *investor, consultant*
Bacon, Leslie Edward *operations analysis manager*
Bacon, Phillip *geographer, author, consultant*
Baddour, Anne Bridge *pilot*
Badger, William John *urologist, surgeon*
Badgley, Theodore McBride *retired psychiatrist, neurologist*
Badham, John MacDonald *motion picture director*
Baer, Harold, Jr. *senior federal judge*
Baerwald, Susan Grad *television broadcasting company executive, producer*
Baez-Feliciano, Doris V. *demographer, educator*
Baggett, Donnis Gene *newspaper publisher*
Bagley, William Thompson *lawyer*
Bagwill, John Williams *retired pension fund administrator*
Bahbah, Bishara Assad *investment company executive, consultant*

Bahr, Jane Marie *writer, retired language educator*
Bai, Zongwu *polymer engineer*
Baier, Edward John *retired public health service officer, industrial hygiene engineer, consultant*
Bailar, Barbara Ann *retired statistician*
Bailey, Charles-James Nice *linguistics educator*
Bailey, Jami Lea *pharmacist*
Bailey, Janet Dee *publishing executive*
Bailey, Rita Maria *investment advisor, psychologist*
Bailey, Robert C. *opera company executive*
Bailey, William Waddell *writer, communications executive*
Bain, Douglas G. *retired aerospace transportation executive, lawyer*
Bain, William Donald, Jr. *lawyer, chemicals executive*
Bains, Harrison MacKellar, Jr. *retired corporate financial executive*
Bainton, Donald J. *diversified manufacturing company executive*
Bajaj, Mandeep *medical researcher, educator*
Bakeman, Carol Ann *travel writer, singer*
Baker, Carolyn Simmons *library director, consultant, researcher*
Baker, D. James *oceanographer, administrator, science and management consultant*
Baker, Daniel Paul *advertising executive, entrepreneur*
Baker, Deborah *medical educator*
Baker, Donald *lawyer, director*
Baker, Dusty (Johnnie B. Baker Jr.) *former professional baseball team manager, retired professional baseball player*
Baker, Edward Kevin *retail executive*
Baker, Eva Lee *education educator, researcher*
Baker, Henry S., Jr. *retired bank executive*
Bákér, J. A., II, *executive management advisor and consultant, monetary architect, financial engineer emeritus*
Baker, James Edward *city planner*
Baker, Katherine June *elementary school educator, minister, artist*
Baker, Leslie David *actor*
Baker, Marjane L. *social studies educator*
Baker, Nathan Adam *music theorist*
Baker, Patricia *health foundation administrator*
Baker, Paul Thornell *anthropology educator*
Baker, Richard *physician, consultant*
Baker, Robert (Robbie) Michael *protective services official*
Baker, Ronald James *language educator, academic administrator*
Baker, William Franklin *retired broadcast executive*
Baker, William Thompson, Jr. *lawyer*
Baker, Zachary Moshe *librarian*
Bakht, Baidar *civil engineer, researcher, educator*
Bakke, Merlin Russell *application developer*
Bakken, Gordon Morris *law educator*
Bakkensen, John Reser *lawyer*
Baktir, Selcuk *electrical and computer engineer, researcher*
Bakula, Scott *actor*
Balaban, Bob *actor, film director*
Balachandran, Priya *environmental scientist*
Balaji, Rengarajan V. *grant specialist*
Balakrishnan, P. V. (Sundar) *marketing educator*
Baldassano, Corinne Leslie *radio executive*
Baldrige, Letitia *writer, management consultant*
Baldwin, Donovan A. *marketing professional, writer*
Baldwin, George Curriden *physicist, researcher*
Baldwin, Ralph Belknap *retired manufacturing executive, astronomer*
Baldwin, William Russell *optometrist, foundation administrator*
Baldyga, Leonard J. *retired diplomat, consultant*
Bale, Christian *actor*
Balick, Kenneth D. *international business development consultant*
Baliga, Radhakrishna *pediatrician, educator, nephrologist, director*
Baliga, Ragavendra Ramakrishna *cardiologist, researcher*
Ball, Carroll Raybourne *anatomist, researcher, medical educator*
Ball, Clyde Curtis *journalist, public information officer, public relations executive*
Ball, Howard Guy *association administrator, educator*
Ball, James Herington *retired lawyer*
Ball, John Robert *healthcare executive*
Ballard, David M. *elementary school educator*
Balser, Robert Edward *animation film producer, director*
Balstad, Roberta *social scientist*
Baltake, Joe *film critic*
Baltazzi, Evan Serge *retired engineering research consulting company executive*
Balter, Frances Sunstein *civic worker*
Bamberger, Gerald Francis *plastics marketing consultant*
Bamberger, Phylis Skloot *lawyer, educator, retired judge*
Bana, Eric *actor*
Bandar, Prince bin Sultan bin Abd al-Aziz Al Saud *former ambassador*
Bandow, Douglas Leighton *editor, columnist, consultant*
Bandy, Jack D. *lawyer*
Bandyopadhyay, Ram Shyamal *molecular biologist, researcher*
Banerjee, Gaurab *research scientist*
Baney, Richard Neil *retired physician, internist*
Bank, Roy J. *television producer*
Banker, Rajiv D. *finance educator, consultant*
Banks, Carolyn Duty *retired history educator*
Banks, Charles Augustus III *distribution executive*
Banks, Deirdre Margaret *retired church organization administrator*
Banks, Robert Kaley *real estate and food products executive, lawyer*
Bankston, Elaine *artist*
Bannister, Robert Corwin, Jr. *historian, educator*
Bansak, Stephen A., Jr. *investment banker, financial consultant*
Bantry, Bryan *entrepreneur, air transportation executive*
Baptista, Robert Charles, Jr. *federal official, lawyer*
Baptiste, La Verne Johnson *retired secondary school educator*
Baquet, Charles R. III *former federal agency administrator, international studies educator*
Bar, Robert S. *endocrinologist, educator*
Barahona, Francisco *researcher*
Baramova, Irina Antonova *investment banker*
Baranyi, Lajos *research scientist*
Barash, Anthony Harlan *lawyer*
Barbachyn, Michael R. *chemist*
Barber, Gary *motion picture company executive*
Barber, James Alden *navy officer, educator*
Barbisch, Donna F. *retired military officer*
Barbo, Dorothy Marie *obstetrician, gynecologist, educator*
Barbour, Doris LaJune *editor*
Barca, George Gino *international winery executive, financial investor, consultant*
Barca, Kathleen *marketing executive*
Barclay, Paris *television director, television producer*
Bar-Cohen, Avram *mechanical engineering educator*
Bardin, Clyde Wayne *biomedical researcher*
Barefoot, Aldos Cortez, Jr. *retired forester, educator*
Barefoot, Tommy Dean *retired boat captain*
Barfield, Tim *manufacturing executive*
Barger, William James *management consultant, educator*
Barger Johnson, Jennifer *law educator, judge*
Barham, Charles Dewey, Jr. *electric power industry executive, lawyer*
Barham, Warren Sandusky *horticulturist*
Barker, Bruce Crichlow *barrister, solicitor*
Barker, Richard Alexander *organizational psychologist*
Barker, Virginia Lee *nursing educator*
Barkley, Terrell Wayne *archivist, curator, school librarian*
Barkmeier, Wayne W. *dentist, researcher, educator*
Barlow, John Sutton *neuroscientist, lexicographer*
Barlow, Lou *painter*
Barlowe, Dorothea *art educator, illustrator*
Barnard, Donald Roy *medical and veterinary entomologist*
Barner, Mark E. *minister, consultant*
Barnes, Joy Chappell *lawyer*
Barnes, Robert F *agronomist*
Barnes, Robert Vincent *retired elementary and secondary school art educator*
Barnes, Samuel Henry *political science professor*
Barnes, Wesley Edward *energy and environmental executive*
Barnes-Kempton, Isabel Janet *retired microbiologist, dean*
Barnett, Amy DuBois *editor-in-chief*
Barnett, Benjamin Lewis, Jr. *retired physician, educator*
Barnett, Elizabeth Hale *organizational consultant*
Barnett, Michael *former professional sports team executive*
Barnett, Patricia Ann *development professional*
Barnewall, Marilyn MacGruder *retired banker*
Barney, Austin Dunham, II, *real estate developer*
Barnhardt, Zeb Elonzo, Jr. *lawyer, mediator, arbitrator*
Barnhart, Charles Elmer *zoology educator*
Baron, Jeffrey *retired pharmacologist*
Baron, Stanley N. *retired electrical engineer*
Baron, Susan *former publishing executive*
Baron Cohen, Sacha (Ali G, Borat) *actor, comedian*
Barr, Adam *biology educator*
Barr, Charles F. *lawyer, insurance company executive*
Barr, James III *telecommunications company executive*
Barr, John Baldwin *chemist, research scientist*
Barr, Michael Charles *research director, lawyer*
Barram, David J. *federal agency administrator*
Barranger, Milly Slater *theater educator, writer*
Barrett, Barbara McConnell *ranch owner, lawyer*
Barrett, Beverly Frances *public relations specialist*
Barrett, Katherine *writer, columnist*
Barrett, Lida Kittrell *mathematics professor*
Barretto, Anjali *education educator*
Barros, Colleen *federal agency administrator*
Barrow, Charles Herbert *investment banker*
Barrow, Robert Earl *retired agricultural fraternal executive*
Barrow, Thomas Davies *retired oil and mining company executive, consultant*
Barrow, Thomas Francis *artist, educator*
Barry, Dave *columnist, writer*
Barry, Phillip Owen *college president*
Barsalona, Frank Samuel *retired theatrical agent*
Barsun, Hans Frederick *engineer*
Bartel, Arthur Gabriel *retired principal, alderman, culinary arts instructor*
Bartelt, William E. *historian, educator*
Barth, David Keck *retired wholesale distribution executive, consultant*
Barth, Frances *artist*
Bartlett, Arthur Eugene *real estate company executive*
Bartlett, Dan (Daniel Joseph Bartlett) *former federal official*
Bartlett, David *management consultant*
Bartlett, Dede Thompson *association executive*
Bartlett, Desmond William *engineering company executive*
Bartlett, John *fashion designer*
Bartlett, Richard Allan *finance company executive*
Bartlett, Shirley Anne *accountant*
Barton, Gregory Mark *Olympic athlete*
Barton, Mischa *actress*
Barton, Robert H. III *automotive executive*
Bartosiak, Stan Theodore *secondary school educator*
Bartrem, Duane Harvey *retired military officer, residential designer, consultant*
Bartz, David John *lawyer*
Bartzatt, Ronald Lee *research biochemist, consultant*
Baruch, Hurd *retired lawyer*
Barud, Stephanie *pharmacist, educator*
Barzun, Jacques *writer, literary agent*
Basch, Richard Vennard *photographer, producer, writer, director*
Basham, W. Ralph *federal agency administrator*
Bashaw, Daniel James *investigator*
Bashi, Vilna Francine *sociology professor*
Basinger, Kim (Kimila Ann Basinger) *actress*
Baskins, Ann O'Neil *lawyer, former computer company executive*
Basmajian, John Varoujan *medical researcher, educator*
Basova, Yulia *chemical engineer, researcher*
Bass, Charles Foster *former congressman*
Bass, Lynda D. *retired medical/surgical nurse, nursing educator*
Bass, Steven Craig *computer science educator*
Bassano, C. Louis *state legislator, fuel oil company executive*
Bassett, Angela *actress*
Bassett, Elizabeth Ewing (Libby Bassett) *writer, editor, consultant*
Bassett, Leslie Raymond *composer, educator*
Bassford, Lynn Foster *physicist, engineer manager*
Bassin, Jules *foreign service officer*
Bast, Kenneth George *healthcare executive*
Bastin, Thoma *educational consultant*
Batalden, Paul Bennett *pediatrician, educator*
Batarseh, Amani Musa *chemist, researcher*
Batchelder, Alice M. *federal judge*
Bateman, David Alfred *lawyer*
Bateman, John Jay *classics educator*
Bateman, Robert McLellan *artist*
Bates, Barbara J. Neuner *retired municipal official*
Bates, Kathy *actress*
Bates, Margaret P. *historian*
Bateson, Mary Catherine *retired anthropology educator, writer, lecturer*
Batt, James Murray *retired financial consultant*
Batt, Nick *property and investment executive*
Battie, David Anthony *art appraiser*
Battin, Patricia Meyer *librarian*
Battle, Vincent M. *former ambassador*
Battocchi, Ronald Silvio *lawyer*
Batts, Warren Leighton *retired manufacturing executive*
Bauer, Barbara Ann *marketing consultant*
Bauer, Henry Hermann *chemistry and science educator*
Bauer, James Monie *aerospace scientist*
Bauer, Richard Carlton *nuclear engineer*
Bauer, Virginia Samaras *state agency administrator*
Baughman, R(obert) Patrick *lawyer*
Bauhan, Hobart Baker *retired mining engineer, retired farmer*
Baum, Jules Leonard *ophthalmologist, educator*
Baum, Roger S. *writer*
Baum, Stanley David *lawyer*
Bauman, Frederick Carl *lawyer*
Baumann, Martin F. *former finance company executive*
Baumgarten, Jon A. *lawyer*
Baumgartner, Andrew C. *retired elementary school educator*
Baumgartner, Brian *actor*
Baumgartner, John H. *gas industry executive*
Baumhart, Raymond Charles *religious organization administrator*
Baxley, Lucy *former lieutenant governor*
Baxter, Cecil William, Jr. *retired academic administrator*
Baxter, John Darling *internist, endocrinologist, educator, health facility administrator*
Baxter, Nevins Dennis *bank consultant*
Baxter, Stephen Bartow *retired historian*
Bayer, Robert Edward *retired federal agency administrator*
Bayes, Beverley Joan *retired pediatrician*
Bayko, Emil Thomas *lawyer*
Bayley, Suzanne Ludey *civic volunteer*
Baym (Stillinger), Nina *literature educator, researcher, writer*
Baymiller, Lynda Doern *social worker*
Bayne, David Cowan *priest, educator, lawyer*
Bazar, Jill A. *music educator*
Beach, Harry Lee, Jr. *mechanical engineer, aerospace engineer*
Beachy, Philip Arden *molecular biology educator*
Beadle, Elizabeth Ahrens *retired elementary school educator*
Beagrie, George Simpson *dentist, educator, retired dean*
Beal, Merrill David *conservationist, museum director*
Beals, Nancy Farwell *former state legislator*
Bean, Bruce Winfield *lawyer*
Beane, Clyde Earl *reporter, political organization worker*
Bear, Geraldine M. *nursing assistant, poet*
Beard, Ann Southard *diplomat, oil industry executive*
Beard, Leo Roy *retired civil engineer*
Beasley, Barbara Starin *sales executive, marketing professional*
Beasley, David Muldrow *former governor, consultant*
Beattie, George Chapin *retired orthopedist, surgeon*
Beatts, Anne Patricia *writer*
Beatty, Frances *civic worker*
Beatty, Judy Iola Spencer *library director*
Beauprez, Bob (Robert L. Beauprez) *former congressman*
Beaver, Barbara Leann *elementary school educator, writer*
Beavers, Karen Marjorie *small business owner*
Beavers, Roy Lackey *retired utilities executive, volunteer, writer*
Becchetti, Frederick Daniel, Jr. *physicist, researcher*
Becerra, Rosina Madeline *social welfare educator*
Becerra Ibanez Pelliza, Julio C. *psychologist, consultant*
Bechkoff, Jennifer "Kat" *business educator*
Becht, Lawrence John *elementary school educator*
Bechtel, Stephen E. *mechanical engineer, educator*
Beck, Albert *manufacturing executive*
Beck, Barbara Nell *elementary school educator*
Beck, Jane *dance educator, choreographer*
Beck, Robert James *editor, writer, economist, consultant*
Beck, Timothy Daniel *human resources specialist, consultant*
Beck, William Harold, Jr. *lawyer*
Becker, Allienne R. *education educator, writer*
Becker, JoAnn Elizabeth *retired insurance company executive*
Becker, John Alphonsis *retired bank executive*
Becker, Nancy May *nursing educator*
Becker, Robert A. *advertising executive*
Beckett, Faye Trumbo *school psychologist*
Beckett, Victoria Ling *physician*
Beckford, Omar Marien *researcher*
Beckjord, Eric Stephen *nuclear engineer, researcher*
Beckson, Mace *psychiatrist*
Beckwith, Steven Van Walter *astronomy educator*
Bedrij, Orest *physicist, investment banker*
Bedsworth, William W. *judge*
Beegle, Amy *music educator, researcher*
Beeler, Charles Alan *retired music educator*
Beezer, Robert Renaut *federal judge*
Beggs, William H. *microbiologist, researcher*
Behlmer, Rudy H., Jr. *retired director, writer, film educator, scriptwriter*
Behnava, Shahriyar *management consultant*
Behr, Marion Ray *artist*
Behrendt, John Charles *geophysicist, researcher, writer*
Behrens, James William *physicist, administrator, author*
Behrmann, Joan Gail *editor*
Beider, Marlys Anna *hotel executive, writer*
Beighey, Lawrence Jerome *packaging company executive*
Beilman, Teresa Marie *artist, poet*
Beitler, Stephen *investment company executive, venture capitalist*
Bejanishvili, Saba *neurologist*
Bekavac, Nancy Yavor *retired academic administrator, lawyer*
Bekkers, John *former food products executive*
Belafonte, Harry (Harry George Belafonte Jr.) *singer, concert artist, actor*
Belanger, Cherry Churchill *elementary school educator*
Belco, Karen Marie *cardiology nurse*
Beldock, Donald Travis *investor*
Beldock, Myron *lawyer*
Beldon, Sanford T. *publisher*
Belfer, Inna *research scientist, medical educator*
Belk, Leotis S. *language educator*
Bell, Albert Atwood, Jr. *history professor, writer*
Bell, Albert Jerome *lawyer*
Bell, Angela *music educator*
Bell, Haney Hardy III *lawyer*
Bell, Janet S. *interior designer, developer, event producer*
Bell, John William *lawyer*
Bell, Larry Stuart *artist*
Bell, Phillip Jackson *federal agency administrator*
Bell, Susan Jane *nurse*
Bellamy, James Carl *retired insurance company executive*
Beller, Luanne Evelyn *retired accountant*
Belleville, Philip Frederick *lawyer*
Bellini, Francesco *chemist*
Bellm, Joan *civic worker*
Bellon, Venetia Rochelle *retired financial consultant*
Bellotti, Robert Michael *coach, educator*
Bellows, Charles Frederick III *surgeon, educator*
Bellows, Howard Arthur, Jr. *corporate financial executive*
Belluomini, Frank Stephen *accountant*
Bell-White, Patricia *photographer, artist, writer*
Belnick, Mark Alan *lawyer*
Belski, Keith Christopher *computer technician*
Belvis, Renee Magdalena *elementary school educator*
Belzberg, Edet *filmmaker*
Benatar, Pat (Pat Andrzejewski) *rock singer*
Benbow, Joel Joshua *minister*
Bencardino, Jenny Teresa *musculoskeletal radiologist*
Bencini, Sara Haltiwanger *concert pianist*
Bender, Ross Thomas *minister*
Bender, Virginia Best *computer scientist, educator*
Benedict, Stewart H. *writer, playwright*
Benefield, Emily Anne *nurse, human services manager*
Benfield, Ann Kolb *retired lawyer*
Benfield, John Richard *surgeon, educator*
Benjamin, Arlin James *physicist*
Bennet, Douglas Joseph, Jr. *former academic administrator*
Bennett, Amanda *former editor*
Bennett, Bryce Hugh, Jr. *lawyer*
Bennett, Charles Leonard *astrophysicist, educator*
Bennett, Edward Virdell, Jr. *surgeon*
Bennett, Lerone, Jr. *retired magazine editor, author*

Bennett, Matthew Damon *entrepreneur, researcher*
Bennett, Peter Dunne *retired marketing educator*
Bennett, Richard Edward *lawyer*
Bennett, Robert LeRoy *computer software development company executive*
Bennett, Tony (Anthony Dominick Benedetto) *entertainer*
Bennett, Velma Joyce (Joyce Williams) *writer, poet*
Bennett, William Ralph, Jr. *physicist, researcher*
Bennett Spector Greenfield, Veronica (Ronnie Spector) *singer*
Benney, Douglas Mabley *direct marketing executive, consultant*
Benoit, Philip Grosvenor *communications executive, educator, writer*
Benor, Sarah Bunin *language educator, religious studies educator*
Benseler, David P. *foreign language educator*
Benson, Allen B. *chemist, educator, consultant*
Benson, Craig Robert *former governor*
Benson, Donald Erick *finance company executive*
Benson, James *aerospace transportation executive*
Benson, James M. *investment company executive*
Benson, Joanne E. *retired lieutenant governor*
Benson, Lucy Wilson *historian, consultant*
Benson, Terry *stage manager*
Bentley, Charles Raymond *geophysics educator*
Bentley, Charmaine Clark O'Fallon *secondary school educator*
Bentley, Donald Lyon *mathematics professor, minister*
Bentley, Kenneth Chessar *oral and maxillofacial surgeon, educator*
Benton, Robert *film director, screenwriter*
Benway, Heather *oceanographer, researcher*
Benzle, Curtis Munhall *artist, educator*
Bercovitch, Sacvan *English language professional, educator*
Bercu, Barry Bernard *pediatric endocrinologist*
Berenson, Abbey Belina *gynecologist, educator*
Berg, Peter *actor*
Bergan, Edmund Paul, Jr. *lawyer*
Bergan, William Luke *lawyer*
Bergau, Frank Conrad *real estate, commercial and investment properties executive*
Bergen, Candice *actress, writer, photojournalist*
Berger, Arthur Seymour *organization executive, former city official*
Berger, Barbara *special education educator, consultant*
Berger, Carl Brendt *art educator*
Berger, Deborah Kornbluth *educator, consultant, real estate agent*
Berger, Frank Stanley *management consultant*
Berger, Miriam Roskin *dance therapist, educator*
Berger, Robert Bertram *lawyer*
Berger, Sanford Jason *retired lawyer, securities dealer, real estate broker*
Berger, Steven R. *retired lawyer, state official*
Berger, William Ernest *newspaper publisher*
Bergeron, Earleen Fournet *actress*
Bergeron, Elmo P. *chemical engineer, consultant*
Bergeron, Patricia Ann *education educator, consultant*
Bergeson-Dana, Tonya *psychologist, researcher*
Berglund, Robin G. *psychiatrist, management consultant*
Bergman, Hermas John (Jack) *retired college administrator*
Bergmann, Donald Gerald *pharmaceutical company executive*
Bergquist, Rick *software company executive*
Bergquist, Sandra Lee *claims consultant*
Bergstein, Daniel Gerard *lawyer*
Bergsten, C. Fred *economist*
Bergstrom, Sheryl Lindsey *jet propulsion administrator*
Beringer, William Ernst *mediator, arbitrator, lawyer, retired manufacturing executive*
Berka, Marianne Guthrie *health and physical education educator*
Berkhoudt, Thomas Walter *director*
Berkley, Erma Van Meter *retired librarian*
Berkley, Peter Lee *lawyer*
Berkley, Stephen M. *entrepreneur, investor*
Berkowitz, Henry *artist*
Berlin, Howard Richard *investment company executive, retired portfolio manager*
Berlin, Kenneth Darrell *chemistry professor, consultant, researcher*
Berlin, Robert Harry *historian, educator*
Berlind, Roger Stuart *stage and film producer*
Berliner, Ruth Shirley *real estate company executive*
Berlinger, Warren *actor*
Berman, Gail *former film company executive*
Berman, Miriam Naomi *librarian*
Berman, Mona S. *actress, playwright, theater director, theater producer*
Berman, Richard Angel *health facility administrator*
Berman, Richard Bruce *lawyer*
Berman, Richard Keith *television producer, film producer*
Berman, Russell Scott *oncologist, educator*
Berman, Sanford *librarian*
Berman, Saul J. *rabbi*
Berman, Shari Springer *film director, scriptwriter*
Berman, Tony *lawyer*
Berman, William H. *retired publishing company executive*
Bernard, Cathy S. *management corporation executive*
Bernard, Michael Mark *lawyer, city planning consultant*
Bernath, John Charles, Jr. *electronics engineer*
Bernhardt, Arthur Dieter *urban planner, consultant*
Bernheimer, Martin *music critic*
Bernsen, Harold John *political scientist, educator, retired military officer*
Bernstein, Carl *writer, journalist*
Bernstein, Edward Charles *rabbi*
Bernstein, I. Melvin *dean, materials scientist*
Bernstein, Merton Clay *law educator, arbitrator*
Bernstein, Stuart A. *former ambassador*
Bernthal, Harold George *health products executive, director*
Berra, P. Bruce *computer science educator*
Berrey, Robert Forrest *lawyer*
Berry, Gail W. *psychiatrist, educator*
Berry, Phil Hunter, Jr. *orthopedic surgeon*
Berry, Richard Lewis *information technology manager, writer, magazine editor, lecturer, programmer*
Berry, Robert Vaughan *retired electrical manufacturing company executive*
Berry, Sharon *medical/surgical nurse, legal nurse consultant*
Berry, Wendell *farmer, author*
Berry, William Willis *retired utilities executive*
Bers, Abraham *electrical engineering and physics educator*
Bershad, Neil Jeremy *electrical engineering educator*
Bersin, Richard Lewis *physicist*
Bert, Clara Virginia *retired secondary school educator, administrator*
Bertelsman, William Odis *federal judge*
Bertin, John Joseph *aeronautical engineer, educator, researcher*
Bertram, Jean DeSales *writer*
Bertram, Manya M. *retired lawyer*
Bertrand, Frederic Howard *retired insurance company executive*
Bertucelli, Robert Edward *accountant, educator*
Beschloss, Michael *historian, writer, lecturer, commentator*
Besing, Ray Gilbert *lawyer, educator*
Best, Eve (Emily Best) *actress*
Best, Laurence Edward *lawyer*
Best, Lawrence C. *retired medical products executive*
Beswick, Ellen J. *research scientist*
Beswick, Kurt F. *artist, graphic designer*
Bethea, Elizabeth *social sciences educator, psychologist, minister*
Bethke, Louise Virginia *music educator, writer*
Betti, John Anso *federal official, retired automotive executive*
Beukema, John Frederick *lawyer*
Beumer, Richard Eugene *retired engineering executive*
Beuthien, Gayle Dawn *special education educator, swim coach*
Beutler, Arthur Julius *manufacturing executive*
Beutler, Ernest *physician, research scientist*
Bevan, Tim *film producer*
Bevelhymer, Darlene Pearl *lawyer, retired secondary school educator*
Be Vier, William A. *retired religious studies educator*
Bevington, Edmund Milton *electrical machinery manufacturing company executive*
Bewley, Peter David *lawyer*
Beyeler, Julia *retired academic administrator*
Beyene, Nahom Minassie *aerospace engineer*
Beyer, Lisa *journalist*
Beyer, Marcus Paul *lawyer*
Beyman, Jonathan Eric *investment company executive*
Bhada, Rohinton Khurshed *chemical engineering educator*
Bhadra, Jayanta *computer scientist, electrical engineer*
Bhaloo, Salim *otolaryngologist*
Bhangale, Tushar *biomedical engineer, researcher*
Bhatia, Rajan *engineer, physicist, researcher*
Bhatnagar, Abha *school system administrator, department chairman*
Bhavsar, Dhaval *medical researcher*
Biagiotti, Guy A. *urologist, medical association administrator, director*
Bianchi, Matt *neurologist, researcher*
Bibby, Douglas Martin *mortgage association executive*
Bick, Katherine Livingstone *neuroscientist, educator, researcher*
Bickford, Margaret Wyatt *minister*
Biddle, Judith Ann *retired writer*
Bidwell, James Truman, Jr. *lawyer*
Bidwell, Roger Grafton Shelford *biologist, educator*
Bieber-Roberts, Peggy Eilene *communications educator, editor, journalist, researcher*
Biederman, Edwin Williams, Jr. *retired geologist*
Biegel, David Eli *social worker, educator*
Bier, Karla *manufacturing engineer, chemical engineer, educator*
Bierig, Jack R. *lawyer, educator*
Bierman, Sandra *artist*
Bierstedt, Peter Richard *entertainment industry consultant, lawyer*
Bies, Susan Schmidt *former federal official*
Bigby, JudyAnn *medical educator*
Bigelow, Robert P. *lawyer, arbitrator, mediator, journalist*
Bigelow, Sharon Lee *elementary school educator*
Bigelow, Vivian Lou *elementary school educator, secondary school educator*
Biggs, Arthur Edward *retired chemicals executive, social services administrator*
Bijur, Peter I. *retired petroleum company executive*
Bikales, Norbert M. *chemist, science administrator*
Biklen, Stephen Clinton *retired diversified financial services company executive*
Bilancia-Vittum, Denise *secondary school educator*
Bilbo, Thomas Earl *biology professor*
Bilbray, James Hubert *retired congressman, lawyer, consultant*
Bilecki, Ronald Allan *financial planner*
Biles, Gloria C. *historian, educator*
Bilirakis, Michael *former congressman, lawyer, corporate financial executive*
Billion, John Joseph *surgeon, retired state representative*
Bin, Joo Won *physician*
Binder, Amy Finn *public relations company executive*
Bingham, Jinsie Scott *broadcast company executive*
Bingham, Marian *artist, printmaker*
Binienda, John J. *state legislator*
Binkley, David Martin *electrical engineer, educator, musician*
Binkley, Timothy *computer graphics designer, educator*
Binns, Jane Camille *humanities educator*
Binoche, Juliette *actress*
Binsfeld, Connie Berube *former state official*
Binzen, Peter Husted *journalist*
Birch, Adolpho A., Jr. *retired state supreme court justice*
Bird, Mary Lynne Miller *professional society administrator*
Birdsong, Alta Marie *volunteer*
Birk, John Richard *management consultant*
Birky, John Edward *banker, financial consultant*
Birnbaum, Robby H. *lawyer*
Birne, Kenneth Andrew *lawyer*
Bishop, Budd Harris *retired museum director*
Bishop, C. Diane *state agency administrator, educator*
Bishop, Charles Edwin *academic administrator, economist, educator*
Bishop, Charles Joseph *retired manufacturing executive*
Bishop, Gordon Bruce *journalist*
Bishop, Ina Sue Marquis (Ina Sue Marquis Bishop) *retired dean*
Bishop, Kim Irene *pharmaceutical consultant, psychopharmacologist*
Bishop, Mark D. *finance company executive, director*
Bishop, Oliver Richard *retired state official*
Bishop, William Peter *management consultant, rancher, musician*
Bisignano, Frank *diversified financial services company executive*
Bissell, James Dougal III *motion picture production designer*
Bitner, John William *banker*
Biziou, Peter *cinematographer*
Blachman, Michael Joel *lawyer*
Black, Bud (Harry Ralston Black) *professional baseball manager*
Black, David *writer, educator*
Black, Hillel Moses *publisher*
Black, Kris Susan Lynn *marketing company executive, speaker, author, poet*
Black, Shirley Temple (Mrs. Charles A. Black) *retired ambassador, retired actress*
Black, Susan Harrell *federal judge*
Black, William Rea *lawyer*
Blackbourn, David Gordon *history professor*
Blackburn, Joy Martin *retired librarian*
Blackburn, Larry H. *builder*
Blacker, Deborah *epidemiologist, educator, psychiatrist*
Blackford, Robert Newton *lawyer, director*
Blackledge, David William *retired academic administrator*
Blackmun, Barbara Winston *art historian, educator, academic administrator*
Blackstone, Dara *music educator, conductor*
Blackwell, F. Oris *environmental scientist, educator*
Blackwell, Ken (John Kenneth Blackwell) *former state official, former mayor*
Blackwell, Lois Moore *fashion designer, educator, visual artist*
Blagojevic, Goran *electrical engineer, consultant*
Blaine, Davis Robert *valuation consultant, investment banker*
Blair, David Clark *information scientist, educator*
Blair, Fred Edward *social services administrator*
Blair, Philippa Mary *artist, educator*
Blake, Elizabeth K. *lawyer*
Blake, Kimberly Bosworth *pharmacist*
Blake, King Charles *humanities educator, writer*
Blake, Simone Elaise *retired school librarian*
Blakely, Jesse Alan *military officer*
Blakely, William D. *lawyer*
Blake Ramos, Debra Barbara *writer*
Blakesley, Wayne Lavere, Jr. *retired production engineer*
Blakey, G(eorge) Robert *law educator*
Blalock, Louise *librarian, public administrator*
Blamer, Steven W. *former advertising executive*
Blanchard, MaryAnn N. *state legislator*
Blanchard, Richard Frederick *construction executive*
Blanchard, Townsend Eugene *retired service companies executive*
Blanco, Laura *interior designer*
Blank, Rebecca Margaret *economist*
Blankenship, J. Richard *former ambassador*
Blankfein, Robert Jerome *retired neurologist*
Blatt, Gregory R. *lawyer*
Blatz, Kathleen Anne *former state supreme court justice*
Blatz, Linda Jeanne *sales manager*
Blazina, Janice Fay *pathologist*
Blech, Ilan Asriel *retired technology company executive*
Bleicher, Samuel Abram *law educator, consultant*
Bleicher, Sheldon Joseph *endocrinologist, medical educator*
Bleszinski, Cliff (Clifford Michael Bleszinski) *game designer*
Blevins, James Ray *lawyer, insurance company claims executive*
Blevins, Jeffrey Alexander *lawyer*
Blige, Mary Jane *singer*
Bliss, Donald Tiffany, Jr. *ambassador*
Blissett, William Frank *English literature educator*
Blitt, Rita Lea *artist*
Blix, Hans Martin *retired international organization official*
Blixt, Charles A. *lawyer*
Bloch, Anthony Michael *mathematician, educator*
Bloch, Erich *retired electrical engineer, science foundation director*
Bloch, Julia Chang *not-for-profit developer*
Bloch, Stuart Marshall *lawyer, banker*
Block, Emil Nathaniel, Jr. *retired air force officer*
Block, Gene David *academic administrator, biologist, educator*
Block, Lawrence *writer*
Bloes, Richard K. *audio-visual specialist, artist*
Blomquist, Alan Charles *film producer*
Blomstrand, Doreen Kathryn *retired physician assistant*
Blondin, C. J. *trade association administrator, lawyer*
Blonz, Edward Robert *nutritionist, biochemist*
Bloodworth, Gladys Leon *elementary school educator*
Bloom, Gary L. *data processing executive*
Bloom, Hyman (Chaim Melamed) *artist*
Bloomer, Harold Franklin, Jr. *retired lawyer*
Bloomfield, Lincoln Palmer *political scientist*
Bloomquist, Kenneth Gene *music educator, director*
Bloomquist, Paul Frederick *music educator, director, secondary school educator, musician*
Blooston, Roselee *cultural organization administrator, writer*
Blos, Joan Windsor *writer, critic, educator*
Blossom, Beverly *choreographer, educator*
Blount, Benroe Wayne *physician, department chairman*
Blow, George *lawyer*
Bluh, Bonnie *scriptwriter, actress, novelist, playwright*
Blum, Barbara Davis *investor*
Blum, Bradley D. *former food service executive*
Blum, Gerald Henry *retired retail executive*
Blum, Samuel *retired research scientist*
Blumberg, Mark Stuart *health service researcher, scientist, director*
Blumenthal, W. Michael (Werner Michael Blumenthal) *retired manufacturing company executive, former secretary of the treasury*
Blumin, Stuart M. *history professor*
Bluth, B. J. (Elizabeth Jean Catherine Bluth) *sociologist, aerospace technologist*
Blyth, Myrna Greenstein *publishing executive*
Boal, Dean *retired arts center administrator, educator*
Boal, Ellis *lawyer*
Boardman, Elizabeth Drake *computer security professional*
Boardman, Eunice *retired music educator*
Boatwright, Charlotte Jeanne *marketing professional, public relations executive*
Bobbitt, Juanita Crawford *international organization executive*
Bobrow, Susan Lukin *retired lawyer*
Boch, David Paul *engineering technical specialist*
Bock, Janine Schmelzer *music educator*
Bockius, Ruth Bear *nursing educator*
Bodanszky, Miklos *chemist, educator*
Boddie, Arthur Walker, Jr. *surgeon, cancer researcher*
Bodensteiner, Lisa M. *former utilities executive, lawyer*
Bodey, Richard Allen *minister, educator*
Bodner, Bruce Ira *ophthalmologist*
Bodsworth, Fred *writer, ecologist*
Bodwell, Lori *lawyer*
Boe, David Stephen *musician, educator, dean*
Boehlert, Sherwood Louis *former congressman*
Boehnen, David Leo *food service executive, lawyer*
Boesch, Diane Harriet *retired elementary school educator*
Boff, Kenneth Richard *engineering research psychologist*
Bogden, Daniel G. *former prosecutor*
Bogle, Jane E. *medical transcriptionist*
Bogosian, Eric *actor, writer*
Bogren, Carol Ferrer *secondary school educator*
Bohanon, Kathleen Sue *neonatologist*
Bohm, Henry Victor *physicist*
Bohrman, Catherine Leuchs *sculptor*
Bohrman, David Ellis *television news producer*
Boiler, Elizabeth Anne *literature and language educator*
Boise, Audrey Lorraine *retired special education educator*
Boitano, Brian *Olympic athlete*
Bokat, Stephen Arthur *lawyer, former business association executive*
Boldt, Kimberly L. *lawyer*
Bolen, David Benjamin *former ambassador*
Bolie, Victor Wayne *molecular biologist, researcher*
Bollapragada, Ramesh *information scientist, educator*
Bolliger, Eugene Frederick *former surgeon*
Bolnick, Howard Jeffrey *insurance company executive, educator, investor*
Bolsterli, Margaret Jones *English professor, farmer*
Bolt, Dawn Maria *financial planner*
Bolton, John Robert *former ambassador, federal agency administrator*
Bonanno, Bruce Brian *emergency physician*
Bonazzi, Elaine Claire *mezzo soprano*
Bond, Julian *civil rights association executive*
Bond, Victoria Ellen *conductor, composer*
Bondi, Harry Gene *lawyer*
Bondi, Joseph Charles, Jr. *education educator, consultant*
Bone, Henry Grady III *physician, clinical researcher*
Boner, Eleanor Katz *lawyer*
Bonesio, Woodrow Michael *lawyer*
Bonifati, Louis M. *music educator*
Bonilla, Henry *former congressman, broadcast executive*

Bon Jovi, Jon (John Francis Bongiovi Jr.) *musician, singer, songwriter, actor, professional sports team executive*
Bonnard, Raymond *theater director*
Bonnell, Victoria Eileen *sociologist, educator*
Bonner, John Tyler *biology professor*
Bonney, Jo *theater director*
Bonnie, Shelby W. *Internet company executive*
Bonsack, Rose Mary Hatem *state legislator, physician*
Boo, Katherine *newswriter*
Booher, Alice Ann *lawyer*
Booker, Nana Laurel *art gallery owner, honorary consul*
Boone, Charles W. *physician, pathologist*
Boone, Donna Clausen *physical therapist, statistician, researcher*
Boone, Stephen Christopher *retired neurosurgeon*
Booth, Margaret A(nn) *communications company executive*
Boothe, Leon Estel *academic administrator emeritus, consultant*
Boothe, Nancy Nancy *construction executive*
Booton, Carolyn Ann *mathematics educator*
Borda, Richard Joseph *retired insurance company executive*
Bordelon, Suzanne Mackie *writing and rhetoric educator*
Borden, Ernest Carleton *oncologist, educator*
Borenstein, Mark A. *lawyer*
Boresi, Joy Suzanne *pharmacist*
Borg, Ruth I. *home nursing care provider*
Borges, William III *management consultant*
Boriboonsomsin, Kanok *transportation engineer*
Borisy, Gary G. *molecular biology professor*
Bork, Robert Heron *law educator, retired federal judge*
Borkowski, Francis Thomas *music educator*
Borkowski, John Joseph *lawyer*
Bormann, Marie L. *medical transcriptionist, small business owner*
Bornhorst, Kenneth Frank *electromagnetics and systems engineer*
Bornstein, Steven M. *former broadcast executive*
Borowitz, Albert Ira *lawyer, writer*
Borschel, Debaroti Mullick *internal medicine physician*
Borum, Rodney Lee *corporate financial executive*
Borysewicz, Mary Louise *editor*
Boschmann, Erwin *chemistry professor*
Boscia, Jon Andrew *insurance company executive*
Bosco, Anthony Gerard *bishop*
Bosco, Philip Michael *actor*
Bose, Anjan *electrical engineering educator, academic administrator*
Bose, Santanu *virologist, educator*
Boskovich, Nick F. *artist, art educator*
Bosl, Phillip L. *retired lawyer*
Bosmajian, Haig Aram *speech communication educator*
Bosson, Richard Campbell *state supreme court justice*
Bostrom, Carl Otto *physicist, research facility administrator*
Bosworth, Dale N. *former federal agency administrator*
Botelho, Bruce Manuel *mayor, retired state attorney general*
Bothwell, John Charles *retired archbishop*
Botkin, Monty Lane *computer company executive*
Botsford, Mary Henrich *retired ophthalmologist*
Bottolfson, Wahnita Joan *parochial school educator*
Bottone, Edward Joseph *microbiologist, educator*
Bottone, JoAnn *health services executive*
Boudreau, Daniel J. *retired state supreme court justice*
Boudreaux, John *marketing and public relations executive*
Bougas, James Andrew *physician, surgeon, educator*
Boulez, Pierre *composer, conductor*
Boultbee, John Arthur *former publishing executive*
Bourdain, Anthony *chef, writer*
Bourguignon, Erika Eichhorn *anthropologist, educator*
Bourque, Boyd D. *secondary school educator*
Bouth, Michael T. *marketing executive*
Bouvier, Linda Fritts *publishing executive*
Bouvier, Marshall Andre *lawyer*
Bouvier, Monica Renee *traffic director*
Bova, Benjamin William *writer, editor*
Bow, Stephen Tyler, Jr. *business executive*
Bowa, Lawrence Robert (Larry Bowa) *former professional baseball manager*
Bowden, Mark Robert *writer*
Bowden, William P., Jr. *lawyer, finance company executive*
Bowen, James Thomas *career officer*
Bowen, Jean *retired librarian, consultant*
Bowen, Otis Ray *former secretary of health and human services, former governor*
Bowen, Richard Lee *retired academic administrator, political scientist, educator*
Bowen-Forbes, Jorge Courtney *artist, poet*
Bower, James Mason *neuroscientist, educator, science administrator*
Bower, Jean Ramsay *lawyer, writer*
Bowers, Christi C. *mediator, lawyer, writer, poet*
Bowers, Richard Philip *manufacturing executive*
Bowes, Frederick III *publishing executive, consultant*
Bowes, Henry Edward *retired communications executive*
Bowick, Susan D. *retired computer company executive*
Bowles, Barbara Landers *investment company executive*
Bowling, John C. *academic administrator*
Bowman, Bruce Alan *civil engineer*
Bowman, David Frederick *music educator*
Bowman, John J. *judge*
Bowman, Patricia Lynn *lawyer*
Bowne, Shirlee Pearson *credit manager*
Box, Thadis Wayne *university dean emeritus, educator*
Boyatt, Thomas David *retired ambassador*
Boyce, Joseph Nelson *retired journalist, consultant, educator*
Boyd, Joseph Arthur, Jr. *lawyer*
Boyd, Mary Frances *retired school nurse, pastor*
Boyd, Todd *cinematic arts educator*
Boyd, William Sprott *lawyer*
Boyer, Herbert Wayne *retired biochemist, biotechnology company executive*
Boyer, Robert Allan *finance company executive*
Boykin, Robert Heath *retired banker*
Boyle, Lara Flynn *actress*
Boyle, Richard John *art historian, author*
Boyle, Tatiana Gennadievna *research scientist*
Boyle, T.C. *writer, literature educator*
Boyle, Tim *apparel executive*
Boyles, James Kenneth *retired banker*
Boynes, Sean G. *dental anesthesiologist, researcher*
Boysen, Jonea Gene *marketing executive, copywriter*
Braasch, John William *retired surgeon, consultant*
Brach, Paul Henry *artist*
Bracken, Peg *writer*
Brackett, Colquitt Prater, Jr. *judge, lawyer*
Bradbeer, Clive *biochemistry educator*
Bradburn, Norman M. *behavioral science educator*
Bradbury, Steven G. *federal agency administrator*
Braddock, Richard S. *Internet company executive*
Braden, Thomas Wardell *news correspondent*
Bradford, Louise Mathilde *social work administrator*
Bradford, Marlene Kay *history educator, writer*
Bradford, Susan Anne *management consultant, writer*
Bradley, Amelia Jane *lawyer*
Bradley, Elizabeth Clay *financial planner, educator*
Bradley, Jeb (Joseph E. Bradley) *former congressman*
Bradley, Jennette B. *former state official, lieutenant governor*
Bradley, Slater *artist*
Bradley, William Bryan *cable television regulator*
Bradshaw, John Robert Covington III *Internet company executive*
Bradsher, Keith Vinson *journalist*
Brady, Donna Elizabeth *sales, marketing and performing company executive*
Brady, Edmund Matthew, Jr. *lawyer*
Brady, Edward Thomas, Jr. *lawyer, writer*
Brady, Jean Stein *retired librarian*
Brady, Mary Rolfes *music educator*
Brady, M(uriel) Jane *judge, former state attorney general*
Brady, Nicholas Frederick *investment company executive, former secretary of the treasury*
Brady, Terrence Joseph *mediator, arbitrator, retired judge*
Brady-Borland, Karen *retired reporter, columnist*
Braff, Zach *actor, director, scriptwriter*
Brafford, William Charles *lawyer*
Bragg, Michael Ellis *lawyer, insurance company executive*
Brainard, Melissa *accountant*
Brakeley, George Archibald, Jr. *fundraising consultant*
Braker, William Paul *retired aquarium executive, ichthyologist*
Bram, Leon Leonard *publishing company executive*
Branagan, James Joseph *lawyer*
Branagh, Kenneth *actor, film director*
Brancato, Leo John *manufacturing executive*
Branch, Felecia Ann-Seldon *elementary school educator*
Brandeis, Barry *retired apparel executive*
Brandon, Liane *filmmaker, educator*
Brandt, Robert Frederic III *retired editor, journalist*
Brandt, Ronald Stirling *retired editor, researcher*
Brandt-Soetermans, Valerie Louise *dancer, educator*
Branson, Harley Kenneth *finance company executive*
Branstetter, Cecil Dewey, Sr. *lawyer*
Brantz, George Murray *retired lawyer*
Braswell, Daniel Edwin *military officer*
Bratt, Benjamin *actor*
Bratt, Nicholas *investment and research and development company executive*
Bratton, William Edward *electronics executive, management consultant*
Braude, Robert Michael *retired medical librarian*
Brauer, Rhonda Lyn *publishing executive, lawyer*
Braun, Jerome Irwin *lawyer*
Braun, Lilian Jackson *writer*
Braun, Lloyd *Internet company executive*
Braun, Mary Lucile Dekle (Lucy Braun) *psychotherapist, consultant, counseling administrator, educator*
Braun, Stanley *orthodontist, educator*
Braunstein, Diane Karen *non-profit association executive, government administrator, government relations professional*
Brawner, Gerald Andre *paralegal*
Braxton, Frederick *music educator*
Brazile, Francisco LaRue *management consultant*
Brazinski, Frank William *composer, educator*
Breakstone, Joshua Scott *musician, educator, composer*
Breathed, Berkeley *cartoonist*
Breault, Robert Lee *music educator*
Brechtel, Unda Jurka *retired library director*
Breda, John Alexander *physician, musician*
Bredehoft, John Michael *lawyer*
Bredfeldt, John Creighton *economics educator, writer, retired military officer*
Breece, Robert William, Jr. *lawyer*
Breeden, Richard C. *investment company executive, former federal agency administrator*
Brehl, James William *lawyer*
Bremer, (L.) Paul (Lewis Paul Bremer III) *former diplomat*
Bremer, Ronald Allan *genealogist, editor*
Bremer Martino, Juan Jose *former ambassador*
Bremner, John McColl *agronomy and biochemistry educator*
Brenes, Jeremy *homeopath, researcher*
Brennan, Donna Lesley *public relations company executive*
Brennan, Gerald D. (Jerry) *biotechnology company executive*
Brennan, James Joseph *lawyer, bank executive*
Brennan, Lawrence Edward *retired electronics engineer*
Brenneis, Anne Schaack *religious studies educator*
Brennen, Stephen Alfred *management consultant*
Brent, Robert Leonard *medical educator*
Breon, April Michelle *music educator*
Breslin, Abigail Kathleen *actress*
Bresse-Rodenkirk, Robert Francis *journalist*
Brett, Thomas Rutherford *federal judge*
Bretthauer, Erich Walter *chemist, educator*
Brett-Major, David Michael *physician, military officer*
Breuer, William Bentley *author*
Brewer, Angela Sue *middle school educator*
Brewer, Barbara Bagdasarian *nursing administrator*
Brewer, Carey *retired academic administrator*
Brewer, Roy Edward *lawyer*
Brewer, Timothy Francis III *retired cardiologist*
Brewster, Elizabeth Winifred *literature educator, poet, writer*
Brewster, Jamie Susan *theater educator*
Brewster, Mary Moorhead *retired educational association administrator*
Briccetti, Albert B. *physician, consultant*
Brice, Jacqueline (Jackie Brice) *landscape artist*
Brick, Arline Roth *education educator*
Brickell, Charles Hennessey, Jr. *marine engineer, retired military officer*
Bricker, Harvey Miller *retired anthropology educator*
Bricker, Ruth *national foundation administrator, real estate developer*
Bricker, Victoria Reifler *anthropologist, educator*
Brickner, Steven J. *chemist*
Bridger, Baldwin, Jr. *electrical engineer*
Bridges, Leonard Hal *retired history educator, writer*
Briggle, Gary Lee *singer, actor, director, educator*
Briggs, Hazen Spencer Pingree III *air traffic controller, educator*
Briggs, Philip *insurance company executive*
Briggs, Philip James *political science professor, writer*
Brigham, Henry Day, Jr. *retired lawyer*
Briles, Judith *writer, consultant*
Brill, Kenneth C. *federal official, former ambassador*
Brim, Orville Gilbert, Jr. *former foundation administrator, writer*
Brin, Foster Blake *psychiatrist*
Brinberg, Herbert Raphael *publishing executive*
Brinn, Louis Bernard *radiologist*
Brisbane, Arthur Seward *newspaper publisher*
Briskin, Jacqueline Elizabeth *author*
Brister, Bill H. *lawyer, former bankruptcy judge*
Bristow, William Harvey, Jr. *psychiatrist*
Britt, John Roy *banker*
Britt, Joseph John *religious studies educator*
Britt, Ronald Leroy *retired manufacturing company executive*
Brixiova, Zuzana *economist*
Brizio-Molteni, Loredana *surgeon, educator*
Broadrick-Allen, Sandra Carol *retired city manager, civic worker, consultant*
Broadwater, James E. *publisher*
Brobston, Stanley Heard *music educator, writer*
Brock, William Emerson *former secretary of labor*
Broderick, B. Michael, Jr. *state legislator, banker*
Broderick, James Allen *painter, art educator, etcher*
Broderson, Thelma Sylvia *retired marketing professional*
Brodhead, David Crawmer *lawyer*
Brodie, Alice Velma *health and ethics advocate*
Brodsky, Beverly Anne *writer, consultant, editor*
Brodsky, Marc Herbert *physicist, research and publishing executive*
Brody, Adrien *actor*
Brodzik, Lester Leonard *artist, retired occupational therapist*
Brogliatti, Barbara Spencer *retired television and motion picture executive, consultant*
Brokaw, Tom (Thomas John Brokaw) *former network news anchor*
Brokke, Catherine Juliet *retired mission executive*
Broman, Per Fredrik *education educator*
Bromund, Alice A. *retired elementary school educator*
Bromwell, Linda Anne *librarian, writer*
Bronfman, Edgar Miles, Sr. *retired liquor company executive*
Bronkar, Eunice Dunalee *artist, educator*
Brook, Scott Jonathan Bradley *mayor, lawyer*
Brooke, Edward William III *lawyer, retired senator*
Brooke, Francis John III *retired academic administrator*
Brooke, Ralph Ian *dental educator*
Brooker, Robert Elton, Jr. *retired manufacturing company executive*
Brooks, Andrée Aelion *journalist, educator, writer*
Brooks, Babert Vincent *publisher*
Brooks, Darius *music company executive*
Brooks, Garth (Troyal Garth Brooks) *musician, singer*
Brooks, Geraldine *writer, reporter, news correspondent*
Brooks, Jeffrey James *environmental services administrator, educator*
Brooks, Kathleen *journalist*
Brooks, Kenneth N. *forestry educator*
Brooks, Linton Forrestall *former federal agency administrator*
Brooks, Lorraine Elizabeth *retired music educator*
Brooks, Lynda Barbara *psychologist*
Brooks, Michael Paul *retired urban planning educator*
Brooks, Patrick William *lawyer, researcher*
Brooks Shoemaker, Virginia Lee *librarian*
Brooks-Turner, Myra *music educator*
Broome, Claire Veronica *epidemiologist, researcher*
Broome, Oscar Whitfield, Jr. *finance educator*
Brosda von Kupferberg, Baron Alexander Christian *investment banker*
Brosnan, Pierce *actor*
Brosz, Margaret Headley *pediatrics nurse*
Brothers, John Alfred *retired oil company executive, chemicals executive*
Brotman, David Joel *architectural firm executive, consultant*
Brotman, Stuart Neil *management consultant, law educator, communications executive*
Brott, Walter Howard *retired cardiac surgeon, educator, military officer*
Broude, Ronald *music publisher*
Broughton, Phillip Charles *lawyer, director*
Browder, Felix Earl *mathematician, educator*
Brown, Alice Elste *artist*
Brown, Amira Khalila *neuropsychologist, researcher*
Brown, Amy Christine *art educator*
Brown, Ashley *actress*
Brown, B. Andrew *lawyer*
Brown, Barbara June *hospital and nursing administrator*
Brown, Billye Jean *retired nursing educator*
Brown, Britt *retired publishing company executive*
Brown, Bruce Maitland *philanthropy consultant*
Brown, Bruce P. *radiologist*
Brown, Candia Post *psychologist*
Brown, Carol Ann *librarian, director*
Brown, Carol Rose *artist*
Brown, Charles Dodgson *lawyer*
Brown, Charles Samuel *singer, composer, educator*
Brown, Dale Susan *retired federal agency and academic administrator, consultant, writer, learning disabilities website manager*
Brown, David Richard *school system administrator, minister*
Brown, Denise Marie *elementary school educator*
Brown, Donald Douglas *transportation executive, consultant, retired military officer*
Brown, Elizabeth Eleanor *retired librarian*
Brown, Frank R. *judge*
Brown, George W. *social psychiatrist*
Brown, Geraldine *nurse, freelance writer*
Brown, Harley Procter, Jr. *zoology educator, entomologist, researcher*
Brown, Herbert Graham *entrepreneur*
Brown, Herbert Russell *lawyer, writer*
Brown, J. E. (Buster Brown) *lawyer, consultant*
Brown, James Nelson, Jr. *retired accountant*
Brown, Jerry Milford *health products executive*
Brown, John Robert *lawyer, priest*
Brown, June Gibbs *retired government official*
Brown, Kay (Mary Kathryn Brown) *retired state official, consultant, political organization worker*
Brown, Laima Adomaitis *art therapist, artist, writer*
Brown, Lee Patrick *retired mayor, federal official, protective services official, educator*
Brown, Les (Lester Louis) *journalist*
Brown, Lora Alice *entertainment company executive, educator*
Brown, Mary Ellen *former state legislator, accountant*
Brown, Michael DeWayne *former federal agency administrator, lawyer*
Brown, Michael Robert *healthcare corporation executive*
Brown, Pamela S. *former attorney general*
Brown, Pearlie Murray *retired school librarian*
Brown, Peter Megargee *lawyer, educator, writer*
Brown, Raymond M. *lawyer, television personality*
Brown, Robert Baldwin III *lawyer*
Brown, Robert E. *transportation executive*
Brown, Robert Laidlaw *state supreme court justice*
Brown, Sandra *writer*
Brown, Seth M. *otolaryngologist*
Brown, Stephen S. *telecommunications industry executive*
Brown, Steven Harry *engineering executive*
Brown-Barton, Grace Olive *music educator*
Browne, Frederick Douglas *physiologist, educator*
Browne, Jackson *singer, songwriter*
Browne, John Charles *physicist, researcher, lab administrator*
Browne, Ray *insurance agent, retired congressman*
Browne, Thomas Jeffrey *healthcare executive*
Brownell, Blanche Parisi *retired secondary school educator*
Brownell, Nora Mead *former commissioner*
Brownfield, William R. *former ambassador*
Brown Leatherberry, Thomas Henry *performing company executive, clergyman*
Brownlee, Les (Romie Leslie Brownlee) *former civilian military employee*
Brownlee, Paula Pimlott *higher education consultant*
Brownlee, Robert Calvin *pediatrician, educator*

Brownrigg, Walter Grant *cartoonist*
Brown Spitzmueller, Janiece Marie *lawyer*
Broyles, William Dodson, Jr. *author, editor, scriptwriter*
Brozowski, Laura Adrienne *mechanical engineer*
Bru, Abelardo E. *retired food products executive*
Brubaker, Crawford Francis, Jr. *federal agency administrator, aerospace scientist, consultant*
Brubaker, James Edward *mechanical engineer*
Brubaker, William W., Jr. *federal agency administrator, civil engineer*
Bruce, David Lionel *retired anesthesiologist, educator*
Bruce, James Edmund *retired utilities executive*
Bruess, Charles Edward *lawyer*
Brugger, David John *media consultant*
Bruland, Gregory Lee *agricultural studies educator*
Brumback, Charles Tiedtke *retired newspaper executive*
Brungraber, Robert J. *civil engineer, educator*
Bruning, Earl H. *music educator*
Brunner, Kathleen Marie *humanities educator*
Bruns, David Eugene *medical educator, researcher*
Bryan, Billie Marie (Mrs. James A. Mackey) *retired biologist*
Bryan, J(ames) P(erry), Jr. *energy executive*
Bryan, Lawrence Dow *college president*
Bryan, Robert E. *editor*
Bryant, Bertha Estelle *retired medical/surgical nurse*
Bryant, Jennifer Campbell *mathematics educator*
Bryant, La Kesha Joy *physical education educator*
Bryant, Melissa Lee *elementary school educator*
Bryson, Nancy Southard *lawyer, former federal agency administrator*
Bubrick, Melvin Phillip *surgeon*
Buchanan, Carolee Horstman *special education educator, consultant*
Buchanan, John Lynn *retired broadcast executive*
Buchanan, J(ohn) Robert *physician, educator*
Buchanan, Pat (Patrick Joseph Buchanan) *journalist, political commentator*
Buchanan, William H., Jr. *retired lawyer, venture capitalist*
Buchbinder, Darrell Bruce *lawyer*
Buchholz, Todd *journalist, social sciences educator, consultant*
Buchin, Jean *psychologist, educator*
Bucholz, Robert Orland *history professor, writer*
Buchwald, Naomi Reice *federal judge*
Buck, Earl Wayne *private investigator, motel owner*
Buckels, Marvin Wayne *savings and loan association executive*
Buckingham, David Cowan *judge*
Buckler, Marilyn Lebow *school psychologist, educational consultant*
Buckley, Eleanor Jane *retired elementary school educator*
Buckley, Frederick Jean *lawyer*
Buckley, Joseph Paul III *computer technician*
Buckley, Kristy Loraine *lawyer, accountant*
Buckman, Raymond William, Jr. *engineering educator*
Bucknum, Michael John *chemist, crystallographer, educator*
Bucksbaum, Philip Howard *physicist*
Buckwalter, Roger Jerome *editor, columnist*
Bucove, Arnold David *psychiatrist*
Bucy, J. Fred, Jr. *retired electronics company executive*
Buda, Thaddeus J., Jr. *retired lawyer*
Budnick, Ernest Joseph *recording industry executive*
Budnicki, Michael J. *nurse*
Buell, Lawrence Ingalls *language educator*
Buhagiar, Marion *editor, writer*
Buhain, Wilfrido Javier *medical educator*
Buhl, Cynthia Maureen *advocate, educator*
Buhler, Jill Lorie *editor, writer*
Buia, Calin Ioan *neuroscientist*
Buist, Neil Robertson MacKenzie *pediatric educator, medical association administrator*
Buker, Robert Hutchinson, Sr. *army officer, thoracic surgeon*
Bulkley, Gregory Bartlett *fisheries biologist, retired research scientist, academic surgeon, educator, cattle rancher*
Bull, Bergen Ira *retired equipment manufacturing company executive*
Bullard, Ervin Trowbridge *horticulturist*
Bullard, Judith Eve *psychologist, systems engineer*
Bullock, Mary Brown *adult education educator*
Bullock, Molly *retired elementary school educator*
Bullock, Sandra (Sandra Annette Bullock) *actress*
Bullough, John Donovan *information scientist, educator*
Bulow, Jack Faye *retired library director*
Bumbry-Bronson, Venetta *music educator*
Bunch, Jennings Bryan, Jr. *retired electrical engineer*
Bunkowske, Eugene Walter *religious studies educator*
Bunyan, Ellen Lackey Spotz *retired chemist*
Burack, Michael Leonard *lawyer*
Burch, Annetta Jane *writer*
Burchard, Ellen Williams *actress, film producer, artist, writer*
Burchard, John Kenneth *retired chemical engineer*
Burchell, Kenneth Wayne *historian, appraiser*
Burchman, Leonard *federal official, journalist*
Burch-Martinez, Berkeley Alison *primary school educator*
Burden, Ordway Partridge *investment banker*
Burgdoerfer, Jerry J. *marketing and distribution executive*
Burge, Constance M. *television producer*
Burge, John Wesley, Jr. *management consultant*
Burgess, Donna Angele *researcher*
Burgess, Hayden Fern (Poka Laenui) *lawyer*
Buritz, Robert Samson *retired electrical engineer*
Burk, Raymond Franklin, Jr. *internist, educator, medical researcher*
Burk, Robert S. *lawyer*
Burkart, Walter Mark *retired manufacturing company executive*
Burke, Brooke *actress, model*
Burke, Joseph C. *former university official*
Burke, Karen A. *medical/surgical nurse*
Burke, Linda Beerbower *lawyer, mining executive, metal products executive*
Burke, Michael Desmond *pathologist, educator*
Burke, Paul Norman *publishing executive, automotive executive*
Burkes, Lionel Seaton *science educator, writer, researcher*
Burket, John McVey *retired dermatologist*
Burkett, Lawrence V. *retired insurance company executive, lawyer*
Burkey, Lee Melville *lawyer*
Burkhart, Catherine Ray *retired secondary school educator*
Burki, Fred Albert *labor union official*
Burkle, Ronald W. *entrepreneur, retired food service executive*
Burman, Kenneth Dale *physician*
Burnett, Iris Jacobson *corporate communications specialist*
Burnham, Christopher Bancroft *former international organization official, former federal agency administrator*
Burnham, J. V. *retired sales executive*
Burns, Edward J., Jr. *actor, film director*
Burns, James William *financial executive*
Burns, Joseph M. *economist*
Burns, Kathleen Adley *educational consultant*
Burns, Marcelline *retired psychologist, researcher*
Burns, Max *former congressman*
Burns, Michael Joseph *operations and sales-marketing executive*
Burns, Toni Anthony *artist*
Burns, William Earl *historian*
Burnstein, Daniel *lawyer*
Burrell, Orville Richard (Shaggy) *popular musician*
Burris, Kelly L. *lawyer*
Burris, Steven Michael *lawyer*
Burroughs, Augusten Xon *advertising executive*
Burrow, Harold *retired gas industry executive*
Burrows, Donald Albert *artist, painter, photographer, dean*
Burrows, Edwin Gladding *retired broadcaster, writer, poet*
Burrows, James *television and motion picture director, producer*
Burson, Betsy Lee *librarian*
Burson, Charles W. *retired agricultural products executive, former federal official, state attorney general*
Bursten, Stuart Lowell *physician, biochemist*
Burt, Richard *lawyer*
Burtley, Calvin *art director*
Burton, Bruce Arthur *education educator*
Burton, John Campbell *accounting educator, former dean*
Burton, Kate *actress*
Burton, Lawrence DeVere *agriculturist, educator*
Burton, Richard Jay *lawyer*
Buscaglia, Robert M. *financial analyst*
Buscemi, Steve *actor*
Busch, August Adolphus III *retired brewery company executive*
Busch, David Dennis *writer, photographer*
Busch, J. Herbert *electrical contractor, writer*
Busch, Joyce Ida *small business owner*
Busch, Kyle *race car driver*
Bush, Barbara Pierce *former First Lady of the United States, volunteer*
Bush, Eileen Shanin *voice educator*
Bush, Ellen D. *music educator*
Bush, Frederick Morris *former federal agency administrator*
Bush, Jeb (John Ellis Bush) *former governor*
Bush, Norman *research and development company executive*
Bush, Sarah Lillian *historian*
Busquet, Anne M. *Internet company executive*
Bussan, James A. *tax specialist*
Busse, Leonard Wayne *banker, financial consultant*
Busse, Paul Lawrence *science educator*
Bustreo, Flavia *epidemiologist*
Butchko, Harriett Hays *physician*
Butenis, Patricia A. *ambassador*
Butki, Brian David *psychologist, educator*
Butler, Debra Yvonne *special education educator, small business owner*
Butler, Denise Elizabeth *primary school educator*
Butler, Donald Philip *electrical engineer, educator*
Butler, Donna Marcia *retired mathematics educator*
Butler, Douglas John *physician*
Butler, Jack Fairchild *electric power industry executive*
Butler, James Newton *retired chemist, educator*
Butler, John Musgrave *financial consultant*
Butler, J(ohn) S(cott) *economist, educator*
Butler, Leslie Ann *artist, writer, editor*
Butler, Orton Carmichael *retired climatologist, educator*
Butler, Robert Leonard *retired sales executive*
Butler, Robert Thomas *retired advertising executive*
Butler, William Joseph *lawyer, educator*
Butterfield, Bruce Scott *executive, editor, author, educator, consultant*
Butterfield, Deborah Kay *sculptor*
Buttrey, Donald Wayne *lawyer*
Butz, Earl Lauer *former secretary of agriculture, consultant*
Butz, Jami Lipan *psychiatric pharmacy specialist*
Butz, Norbert Leo *actor*
Buzard, James Albert *healthcare management consultant*
Buzzi, Ruth *comedienne*
Byerly, Steven Lee *educational consultant*
Bynes, Amanda *actress*
Bynes, Frank Howard, Jr. *physician*
Byrd, Janice Adele *elementary school educator*
Byrd, Joan Eda *retired librarian*
Byrd, Lloyd Garland *retired civil engineer*
Byrd, Marc Robert *floral designer*
Byrne-Dempsey, Cecelia (Cecelia Dempsey) *journalist*
Byrnes, Hope Huska *singer, volunteer*
Byun, Youngjoo *research scientist*
Cabcabin, Diana M. *elementary school educator, consultant*
Cable, Charles Allen *mathematician*
Cabot, Hugh III *painter, sculptor*
Cacciatore, Ronald Keith *lawyer*
Cáceres, Franklin Thomas *retired writer*
Cacioppo, John Terrance *psychologist, educator, researcher*
Cades, Stewart Russell *lawyer, communications executive*
Cafferty, Jack *news anchor*
Cage, Jack Hays *executive search consultant*
Cagle, Roger E. *physician*
Cahill, Charles L. *retired academic administrator, chemistry professor*
Cai, Ming Zhi *chemist, researcher, film producer*
Cai, Zhijun *mechanical engineer*
Caicedo, Patricia *singer, musicologist, physician*
Cain, David Lee *retired corporate executive*
Cain, Russell M. *psychiatrist, educator, administrator*
Cain, William Howard *secondary school educator*
Caine, Arnold *pharmaceutical executive*
Caine, Raymond William, Jr. *retired public relations executive*
Cakir, Hasan *research analyst*
Calabrese, Kirk Robert *medical transcriptionist*
Calamar, Gloria *artist*
Calame, Byron Edward *journalist*
Calarco, Vincent Anthony *specialty chemicals company executive*
Calder, Iain Wilson *publishing executive*
Caldera, Louis Edward *former academic administrator, former federal official*
Calderón, Sila Maria *former governor*
Caldwell, Ann Wickins *academic administrator*
Caldwell, Benjamin Dale *corporate financial executive, consultant*
Caldwell, Elwood Fleming *food scientist, educator*
Caldwell, Louise Phinney *historical researcher, community volunteer*
Calegari, Maria *ballerina*
Calfano, Brian Robert *education educator*
Calhoun-Senghor, Keith *lawyer*
Calise, William Joseph, Jr. *lawyer*
Calissi, Jeffrey Luke *music educator*
Callahan, Sonny (H.L. Callahan) *former congressman*
Callahan, Vivian *broadcast executive*
Callahan Kern, Gene Marie C. *soprano, music educator*
Callander, Bruce Douglas *journalist, freelance writer*
Callard, David Jacobus *investment company executive*
Calleo, David Patrick *history professor, political scientist*
Calley, John *former motion picture company executive, film producer*
Callow, William Grant *retired judge*
Calman, Craig David *actor, writer*
Calore, Paul *writer, retired government agency administrator*
Calvert, Jack George *atmospheric chemist, educator*
Calvert, William Preston *radiologist*
Camara, David John *school librarian*
Camara, Vincent Antonin Reginald *statistician, educator, researcher*
Camargo, Anthony *jewelry designer*
Cambone, Stephen Anthony *former federal agency administrator*
Cambrice, Robert Louis *lawyer*
Cameron, Jeffrey M. *lawyer*
Cameron, Joseph Alfred III *pharmacist*
Cameron, Kirk MacGregor Drummond *statistician*
Cameron, Lucille Wilson *retired dean*
Camilleri, Michael *lawyer, educator*
Campbell, Alan *actor*
Campbell, Andrew William *immunotoxicology physician*
Campbell, Arthur Andrews *retired federal agency administrator*
Campbell, Ben Nighthorse *former senator*
Campbell, Byron Chesser *newspaper publishing executive*
Campbell, Demarest Lindsay *artist, writer, interior designer*
Campbell, Edward Wallace *nutritionist*
Campbell, Edwin Denton *educational association administrator, consultant, accountant*
Campbell, Frederick Hollister *retired lawyer, historian, retired military officer*
Campbell, George Emerson *lawyer*
Campbell, Henry Cummings *librarian*
Campbell, James P. *manufacturing executive*
Campbell, Janet Coral *architect*
Campbell, John *former ambassador*
Campbell, Joseph John *technology and financial company executive*
Campbell, Joyce S. *language educator, department chairman*
Campbell, Mary Stinecipher *retired chemist*
Campbell, Melissa Lynnsimmons *music educator*
Campbell, Neal Franklin *music educator*
Campbell, Vincent Bernard *judge, lawyer*
Campion, Thomas Francis *lawyer*
Campos-Orrego, Nora Patricia *lawyer, consultant*
Candlish, Malcolm *manufacturing executive*
Canelas, Dale Brunelle *retired library director*
Canelli, Jeanne *early childhood educator*
Canes-Wrone, Brandice *political scientist, educator*
Cannavale, Bobby (Roberto Cannavale) *actor*
Cannizzaro, Linda Ann *geneticist, researcher*
Canterbury-Counts, W. Douglas *psychologist*
Canu, William Henry *psychology professor*
Caparro, James *entertainment industry executive*
Capasso, Federico *physicist*
Capice, Philip Charles *retired broadcast executive*
Caplin, Olga Yeryomina *psychiatrist*
Caplow, Theodore *sociologist*
Capon, Edwin Gould *retired religious organization administrator, minister*
Caraway, Stephanie Schankerman *prosecutor*
Carballo, Juan-Antonio *research scientist*
Card, Andy (Andrew Hill Card Jr.) *former White House Chief of Staff*
Carder, Paul Charles *retired advertising executive*
Cardona, Julio Jose *student affairs director, educational researcher*
Cardone, Bonnie Jean *freelance/self-employed photojournalist*
Cardoso, Anthony Antonio *artist, educator*
Cardwell, Nancy Lee *editor, writer*
Carell, Steve *comedian, actor*
Carey, David P. *judge, career military officer*
Carey, Drew *actor*
Carey, Edward John *insurance company executive*
Carey, Jana Howard *lawyer*
Carey, Kathryn Ann *retired foundation administrator, editor, consultant*
Carey, Stephanie L. *systems engineer, educator*
Carfora, John Michael *economics professor, academic administrator*
Carides, George Warren *health economic statistics director*
Carley, Kurt *actor*
Carlile, Janet Louise *artist, educator*
Carlin, George Denis *comedian, actor*
Carlin, John William *educator, retired governor*
Carlin, Marian P. *secondary school educator*
Carliner, Geoffrey Owen *economist, director*
Carlisle, Rick (Richard Preston Carlisle) *former professional basketball coach, retired professional basketball player*
Carlock, Sandra Lynn *musician, educator*
Carls, Alice Catherine *history professor*
Carlsen, Mary Baird *clinical psychologist*
Carlson, Burford Arlen *retired military officer, pilot*
Carlson, Devon McElvin *architect, educator*
Carlson, Donald Otto *magazine publisher, editor*
Carlson, Janet Frances *psychologist, educator*
Carlson, Natalie Traylor *publisher*
Carlson, Richard Warner *journalist, broadcast executive, federal agency administrator, diplomat*
Carlson, Robert Codner *industrial engineering educator*
Carlson-Rukavina, Patricia Ann *small business owner*
Carlucci, Frank Charles III *former secretary of defense*
Carlyle, Bobbie Kristine *sculptor*
Carlyon, David James *writer, theater director*
Carmack, Mildred Jean *retired lawyer*
Carman, Judith Elaine *music educator, writer*
Carmichael, Judy Lea *record industry executive, concert jazz pianist*
Carmona, Richard Henry *former Surgeon General of the United States*
Carnahan, Brice *chemical engineer, educator*
Carner, Dorothy Ann *financial advisor*
Carnesale, Albert *engineering educator, former academic administrator*
Carney, Timothy Michael *ambassador*
Carnwath, Squeak *artist, educator*
Caroleo, Linn E. *mathematician, writer*
Carone, Nicolas *artist*
Carp, Daniel A. *former consumer products company executive*
Carpenter, David Erwin *retired county official, land use planner*
Carpenter, Derr Alvin *retired landscape architect*
Carpenter, Michael A. *diversified financial services company executive*
Carpenter, Robert C. *state legislator, retired banker*
Carpenter, Susan Karen *defender*
Carpenter-Mason, Beverly Nadine *quality assurance professional, medical/surgical nurse, pediatric nurse practitioner, consultant, writer*
Carpentieri, Sarah C. *neuropsychologist, researcher, clinical psychologist*
Carr, E. Barbara *librarian*
Carr, Harold Noflet *investment company executive*
Carr, Larry Dean *not-for-profit executive*
Carradine, Keith Ian *actor, singer, composer*
Carraher, Mary Lou Carter *art educator*
Carrera, Jaganath *acupuncturist, yoga educator*
Carrigan, David Owen *history educator*
Carroll, John Millar *computer science and psychology educator*
Carroll, John Sawyer *educator, former newspaper editor*
Carroll, Joseph J(ohn) *lawyer*
Carroll, Karen Colleen *pathologist, epidemiologist*
Carroll, Marie-Jean Greve *retired artist, educator*
Carroll, Mary Colvert *not-for-profit developer, consultant*
Carson, Alice Hines *secondary school educator*
Carson, Andrew Doyle *applied psychologist*
Carson, Brad Rogers *former congressman*
Carson, Christopher Leonard *retired lawyer*
Carson, Denise Wilkinson *retired gifted and talented educator*
Carson, James Wood *psychologist*
Carson, John Robert *lobbyist, secondary school educator*
Carson, Mary Kay *writer*

Carson, Regina E. *healthcare administrator, pharmacist, educator, geriatric specialist*
Carson, Wallace Preston, Jr. *retired state supreme court justice*
Carstairs, Sharon *legislator*
Carstens, David Henry *military officer*
Carswell, Jane Triplett *retired family physician*
Carter, Betsy L. *editor, writer*
Carter, Cynthia (Cindy) Lynn *writer*
Carter, Dennis Lee *marketing professional*
Carter, Henry Moore, Jr. *retired foundation executive*
Carter, Hodding, III, (William) *retired foundation executive, journalist, commentator, educator*
Carter, Jaine M(arie) *human resources specialist, director*
Carter, Jeanne Wilmot *lawyer, publishing executive*
Carter, Jeffrey Richard *music educator*
Carter, Kathy Deonne *language educator*
Carter, Kenneth Charles *geneticist*
Carter, Melva Jean *retired medical technician*
Carter, Nanette Carolyn *artist*
Carter, Rosalynn Smith (Eleanor Rosalynn Carter) *former First Lady of the United States*
Carter, Scott *television producer*
Carter, Tonya M. *science educator*
Carter, Yvonne Breaux *retired librarian*
Carter-Miller, Jocelyn *former retail executive*
Carton, Lonnie Caming *educational psychologist*
Cartwright, Talula Elizabeth *leadership consultant, educator*
Carver, Kendall Lynn *insurance company executive*
Carvey, Dana *actor, stand up comedian*
Casadesus, Penelope Ann *advertising executive, film producer*
Casanova, Aldo John *sculptor*
Case, Elizabeth Joy *psychology and educational assessment director*
Casei, Nedda *mezzo soprano*
Caseiras, Jo Ann Striga *artist, educator*
Casele, Holly *obstetrician*
Casella, Peter F(iore) *patent and licensing executive*
Casella, Russell Carl *physicist*
Casey, Dwane L. *former professional basketball coach*
Casey, Micheal William *portfolio manager*
Cash, Joseph Carl *history educator, government educator*
Cash, Mary Frances *minister, retired civilian military employee*
Cash, W. Larry *health products executive*
Casillas, Mark *lawyer*
Caskey, Charles Thomas *biotechnology executive, biology and genetics educator*
Cassara, Frank *artist, educator, printmaker*
Cassel, Robert Uriah *chemist*
Cassell, Eric Jonathan *physician*
Cassell, Kay Ann *librarian*
Casselman, William E., II, *lawyer*
Casserly, Charley *former professional football team executive*
Cassidy, James Mark *construction company executive*
Cassidy, John Harold *lawyer*
Castagna, Vanessa J. *retail executive*
Castagna, William John *federal judge*
Castaldi, David Lawrence *health products executive*
Castel, Jean Gabriel *lawyer, educator, international arbitrator*
Castellano, Mark Joseph *music educator*
Castiglia, Patricia Anne Thorson *dean, nursing educator*
Castile, Rand (Jesse Randolph III) *retired museum director*
Castle, Howard Blaine *retired religious organization administrator*
Castle, James Cameron *information technology executive*
Caston, J(esse) Douglas *retired medical educator*
Castor, Jon Stuart *electronics executive*
Castro, Maria Graciela *medical educator, geneticist, researcher*
Castro, Raul Hector *lawyer, retired governor, ambassador*
Castro, Teresa Jacira *small business owner*
Castronova, John *special education educator*
Caswell, Dorothy Ann Cottrell *performing arts association administrator*
Catalano, Louis William, Jr. *neurologist*
Cates, Dennis Lynn *minister*
Cates, Matt *actor, writer*
Cathou, Renata Egone *chemist, consultant*
Caucia, Louisa B. *retired elementary school educator*
Cauthorne-Burnette, Tamera Dianne *family practice nurse practitioner, consultant*
Cavallini, Donna Francesca *law librarian*
Cavanagh, Richard Edward *corporate executive director*
Cavill, Ronald William *financial planner*
Cavin, Susan Elizabeth *sociologist, writer*
Cawley, Joseph Douglas *retired reading professor*
Cazalas, Mary Rebecca Williams *lawyer, nurse*
Ceasor, Augusta Casey *medical technician, microbiologist, clinical laboratory scientist*
Cecil, Alex Thomson *travel executive*
Cecil, David Rolf *mathematician, educator*
Cecil, Elizabeth Jean *writer*
Cefalo, Robert Charles *obstetrician, gynecologist*
Celentano, Francis Michael *artist, educator*
Cellarius, Richard Andrew *biology professor*
Censullo, Michael *radiologist*
Centafont, Lucy Ann Alexander *occupational therapist, consultant*
Cep, Casey Nicole *writer, theology scholar*
Cermak, Josef Rudolf Cenek *lawyer, director*
Cerny, Louis Thomas *civil and transportation engineer, consultant*
Cerny, William *retired education educator, musician*
Cesnik, James Michael *retired labor union administrator, publishing executive*
Cezar, Gabriela *research scientist, entrepreneur*
Cha, Soyoung Stephen *mechanical engineer, educator*
Cha, Stephen S. *emergency physician*
Chacko, George Kuttickal *management science educator, consultant*
Chadsey, Harold A. *astronomer, physicist*
Chafel, Judith Ann *education educator*
Chafkin, Rita M. *retired dermatologist*
Chaifetz, David Harvey *lawyer*
Chalcraft, Elena Marie *actress, singer*
Chalif, Ronnie *medical association administrator, artist*
Chalikian, Alice Beatrice *chiropractor*
Challis, Richard Bracebridge *art dealer, educator*
Chalupsky, Mary Etta Griffith *health products executive*
Chamberlain, William Edwin, Jr. *management consultant*
Chamberlin, Michael Meade *lawyer*
Chambers, Elenora Strasel *artist*
Chan, Jackie *actor, film director*
Chan, KitYu Evan *civil engineer*
Chance, Steven Kent *lawyer*
Chandiwal, Amito *research scientist*
Chandler, Alice *retired academic administrator, educational consultant*
Chandler, Jeffrey *family trust and agricultural products executive*
Chandler, Robert Leslie *public relations executive*
Chandra, Abhijit *engineering educator*
Chandra, Subodh *lawyer*
Chang, Chong Hyuck *engineer*
Chang, Clarence Dayton *retired chemist*
Chang, David Z. *oncologist*
Chang, Debbie I-Ju *health programs and research executive, director*
Chang, Helen Chung-Hung Hsiang *music educator*
Chang, Hernan Robert *infectious disease consultant*
Chang, Runzi *electrical engineer*
Chang, Samuel Henry *computer scientist, educator*
Chang, Susan Marina *neuroscientist*
Chang, Victor Tsu-Shih *oncologist, researcher, educator*
Chang, Won *economist*
Chang, Ying Chih *engineering educator, researcher*
Changeri, Michael Dennis *contractor, protective services official*
Chang-Yong, Nam *engineer, researcher*
Chanos, George J. *former state attorney general*
Chansley, Deborah Lynn *education educator*
Chao, James Min-Tzu *architect*
Chao, Ruth *psychologist, researcher*
Chapman, Geneva Joyce *entrepreneur, educator, writer*
Chapman, Linda Lee *computer company executive, consultant*
Chapman, Robert Foster *federal judge*
Chapman, Thomas William *hospital executive*
Chapman, William *baritone*
Chappell, Annette M. *educational consultant, minister*
Chappell, Fred Davis *language educator, poet*
Chappell, Wallace *performing company executive*
Chappelle, Emmett W. *physical scientist*
Chapple, Thomas Leslie *lawyer*
Chaput, Eugene Michael *advertising executive*
Charles, Luenda E. *public health service officer, researcher*
Charles, Marilyn Kay *secondary school educator*
Charles, Robert Bruce *lawyer, former federal agency administrator*
Charles, Walter *actor*
Charleton, Margaret Ann *child care administrator, consultant*
Charlton, Jesse Melvin, Jr. *retired management educator, lawyer*
Charlton, Paul K. *former prosecutor, lawyer*
Charnveja, Pat S. *civic leader, former oil and gas industry executive*
Charron, Paul Richard *retail executive*
Charwat, Andrew Franciszek *engineering educator*
Chase, Barbara Landis *headmaster*
Chase, Francis Marvin, Sr. *education educator, consultant*
Chase, J. Vincent *property manager*
Chase, James Richard *retired college president*
Chase, Will *actor*
Chase, William Robert *television executive*
Chaseman, Joel *communications consultant*
Chassin, Jameson Lewis *retired surgeon*
Chassman, Leonard Fredric *retired labor union administrator*
Chast, Roz *cartoonist*
Chasteen, Beverly Joan *parochial school educator, retired secondary school educator*
Chati, Mandar Kalidas *operations research specialist*
Chatterjee, Anindya *economist, researcher*
Chatterton, Raymond Edward *economics educator*
Chattman, Raymond Christopher *association executive*
Chave, Carol *arbitrator, retired lawyer*
Chaves-Carballo, Enrique *neuropediatrician*
Chaykin, Robert Leroy *manufacturing and marketing executive*
Cheadle, Don *actor*
Cheatham, Robert William *retired lawyer*
Checketts, Dave (David Wayne Checketts) *professional sports team executive*
Cheddie, Denver Faron *engineering educator, researcher*
Cheeger, Jeff *mathematics educator*
Cheek, Michael Carroll *lawyer*
Cheek, William Shields, Jr. *protective services official*
Cheesman, John Michael *corporate financial executive*
Cheever, Susan *freelance/self-employed writer*
Chelle, Robert Frederick *electric power industry executive, educator*
Chem, Widhya *ambassador*
Chen, Del-Min Amy *lawyer*
Chen, Di *electronics executive, optical engineer, consultant*
Chen, Eric Yen-Po *accountant, consultant*
Chen, Feng *adult education educator, researcher*
Chen, Ho-Hong H.H. *industrial engineering executive, educator*
Chen, Kenichi *chef*
Chen, Kuen Hai *physician*
Chen, Philip Minkang *strategic consultant*
Chen, Qiang *engineer*
Chen, Qiming *engineer*
Chen, Shoei-Sheng *retired mechanical engineer*
Chen, Shuang *computer science professional*
Chen, Steve Shih *Internet company executive*
Cheney, Mary Claire *Internet company executive*
Cheng, Liang *video architect, researcher*
Cheng, Wan-Lee *mechanical engineer, educator*
Cheng, Yue *molecular geneticist, pathologist*
Chercover, Murray *television executive*
Cher-Killigm, Beatrice M. *history professor, art educator*
Chernavsky, George Y. *composer, producer, song writer*
Chernichaw, Mark *broadcast, cable television, corporate communications and advertising executive, television producer, director, media consultant, educator*
Chernow, Ron *writer, journalist*
Cherovsky, Erwin Louis *lawyer, writer*
Cherry, Robert Steven III *municipal official*
Cherry, Sabrina *psychiatrist*
Chesler, Doris Adelle *real estate broker*
Chessa, Luciano *composer, musicologist, educator*
Chesson, Michael Bedout *history professor, writer*
Chevalier, Denise Ann *director*
Chevalier, Paul Edward *retired retail executive, lawyer*
Chevins, Anthony Charles *retired advertising agency executive*
Chiang, I-Ting *engineering educator*
Chiang, Michael Fred *physician*
Chiang, Mung *engineering educator, consultant*
Chiang, Wen-Chyuan *operations management educator*
Chiara, Margaret Mary *former prosecutor, lawyer*
Chiaramonte, Christine Loren *elementary school educator*
Chihorek, John Paul *electronics company executive*
Chihuly, Dale Patrick *artist*
Chiklis, Michael *actor*
Childers, Charles Eugene *mining company executive*
Childs, John David *retired computer company executive*
Chilvers, Derek *insurance company executive*
China, Daniel William *lawyer*
Chirico-Elkins, Ursula *retired librarian*
Chirinos, Julio Alonso *physician, researcher*
Chisholm, Tommy *lawyer, utilities executive*
Chitnis, Ashay *research scientist*
Chitre, Subodh Subhash *computer company executive*
Chittum, Anthony *chef*
Chittum, Heather *chef*
Chiu, Bella Chao *astrophysicist, writer*
Chiu, Dorothy *retired pediatrician*
Chmielinski, Edward Alexander *retired electronics company executive*
Cho, Alfred Yi *electrical engineer*
Chock, Clifford Yet-Chong *family practice physician*
Chocola, Chris (Joseph Christopher Chocola) *former congressman, lawyer*
Choi, Stephen Sukjun *physicist*
Choi, Youngok *information science educator*
Chojnowski, Donna Applegate *cardiac nursing administrator, heart failure nurse practitioner*
Cholewka, Patricia Anne *nursing educator*
Chong, James Tzeh-min *finance educator, researcher*
Chopin, Christopher Allen *lawyer*
Chopra, Samir *pharmaceutical and real estate company executive*
Chou, Chung-Kwang *bio-engineer*
Chou, Sunlin *retired computer company executive*
Chouery, Farid Alexandre *electrical and structural engineer, consultant*
Choukas-Bradley, Melanie *writer, photographer*
Chouteau, Kristin N. *engineer*
Chow, Rita Kathleen *nursing consultant*
Chow, Stephen (Sing-Chi Chow) *actor*
Chow, Timothy Yi-Chung *mathematician, systems engineer*
Chow, Winston *engineering executive, researcher*
Chow, Yun-fat (Chow Yun-Fat) *actor*
Chowitz Placzek, Gail Louise *school psychologist*
Chretien, Jane Henkel *internist*
Chretien, Paul Bernard *oncologist, medical researcher*
Chrétien, Raymond A.J. *retired ambassador*
Chrisanthopoulos, Peter *advertising executive*
Christensen, Karen Kay *lawyer*
Christenson, Gregg Andrew *bank executive*
Christenson, William Newcome *retired occupational and internal medicine physician*
Christian, James Wayne *economist*
Christiansen, Richard Dean *retired newspaper editor*
Christiansen, Richard Louis *orthodontist, educator, dean*
Christin, Nicolas *computer scientist, researcher*
Christine, Chan B. *educational consultant, researcher*
Christoffersen, Ralph Earl *chemist, researcher, director*
Christopher, Russell Lewis *baritone*
Christopher, Sharon A. Brown *bishop*
Christopher, William Garth *lawyer*
Christopherson, Myrvin Frederick *college president*
Christy, Nicholas Pierson *physician*
Chryssakis, Christos *mechanical engineer*
Chu, Ellin Resnick *librarian, consultant*
Chu, Jack J. (Jack J. Zhu) *electrical engineer*
Chu, James *electronics executive*
Chu, Katherine K. *music educator*
Chulack, Christopher M. *television director, television producer*
Chun, Asaph Y. *research scientist*
Chun, Jacqueline Clibbett *artist, educator*
Chung, Benjamin Inbeh *urologist*
Chung, Caroline *marketing professional*
Chung, Doo-ri *apparel designer*
Chung, Woo Cheol *electrical engineer*
Church, Eugene Lent *physicist, consultant*
Church, Thomas Haden *actor*
Churchill, Robert Wilson *state legislator, lawyer*
Ciampaglio, Jeff William *sculptor*
Cibes, William Joseph, Jr. *retired academic administrator*
Cibull, Michael Lee *pathologist, educator*
Cicero, Carmen Louis *artist, educator*
Cichello, Samuel Joseph *architect*
Cicolani, Angelo George *research and development company executive, operating engineer*
Cikovsky, Nicolai, Jr. *retired curator, art historian, educator*
Cilella, Salvatore George, Jr. *museum director*
Ciofalo, Linda *vocalist, educator*
Ciraolo, Debra *sign language interpreter, consultant*
Citron, Beatrice Sally *law librarian, educator*
Citron, Diane *lawyer*
Citron, Richard Ira *management consultant*
Claes, Gayla Christine *writer, editor, consultant*
Claflin, Bruce L. *software company executive*
Claiborne, Kenya Wynette *secondary school educator*
Clancy, Mathew P. *chemical engineer*
Clancy, Patrick L. *lawyer*
Clancy, Thomas L., Jr. *novelist, producer*
Claridge, Elmond Lowell *retired engineering educator*
Clarizio, Josephine Delores *retired foundation administrator, manufacturing and engineering company executive*
Clark, Alicia Garcia *political party official*
Clark, Beverly Ann *retired lawyer*
Clark, Caleb Morgan *political scientist, educator*
Clark, Candy *actress*
Clark, Celia Rue *lawyer*
Clark, David Joseph *pharmacist*
Clark, Donald Otis *lawyer*
Clark, Edgar Sanderford *insurance broker, consultant*
Clark, Edward Eugene *academic administrator, educator, lawyer*
Clark, Eve Vivienne *linguist, educator*
Clark, James Covington *journalist, historian*
Clark, James Milford *retired college president*
Clark, Jim (James H.) *entrepreneur, real estate company and former computer software company executive*
Clark, John F. *federal agency administrator*
Clark, Karen Heath *lawyer*
Clark, Mary Higgins *writer, communications executive*
Clark, Matt *writer*
Clark, Nancy Lucinda Brown *retired music educator*
Clark, Peter Bruce *retired publishing executive*
Clark, Philip Hart *retired urban and regional planner*
Clark, Ramsey (William Ramsey Clark) *lawyer, former United States attorney general*
Clark, Richard Eugene *music educator*
Clark, Thomas Carlyle *retired banker*
Clark, Wesley Kanne *emergency management executive, educator, retired military officer*
Clark, Wesley M. *manufacturing executive*
Clark, William, Jr. *diplomat*
Clark, William Arthur V. *geographer*
Clarke, Sir Arthur Charles *author*
Clarke, Ciana Bernadine Bennett *education educator, researcher*
Clarke, Henry Lee *foreign service officer, ambassador*
Clarke, Janet Morrison *marketing executive*
Clarke, Richard Alan *former federal official*
Clarke, Terence Michael *public relations and advertising executive*
Clarke, Victoria C. (Torie Clarke) *former federal agency administrator*
Clarno, Kevin Taylor *nuclear engineer*
Clausen, Jerry Lee *psychiatrist*
Claver, Robert Earl *television producer, director*
Clawson, John Addison *investment company and retired chemicals executive*
Clayton, David A(lvin) *biology professor*
Clayton, Julia B. *academic administrator, musician*
Clayton, Raymond Edward *municipal official*
Clayton, Richard Reese *retired diversified financial services company executive*
Clayton, Robert Norman *chemist, educator*
Claytor, Richard Anderson *retired federal agency administrator*
Clear, Albert F., Jr. *retired hardware manufacturing company executive*
Cleary, Jane M. *not-for-profit developer, consultant*
Cleary, Manon Catherine *artist, retired educator*
Cleary, Meagan Bayless *ecologist, educator, researcher*
Cleave, Mary L. *environmental engineer, former astronaut*
Cleaver, James Edward *radiologist, educator*
Cleland, Max (Joseph Maxwell Cleland) *former senator*
Clemendor, Anthony Arnold *obstetrician, educator, gynecologist, educator*
Clement, Bill *hockey analyst*

Clement, Hope Elizabeth Anna *retired librarian*
Clement, John Edward Strausz *retired minister, retired religious organization administrator*
Clement, Yvonne Madeline *librarian*
Clements, Thomas Frank *writer*
Clemmensen, Larry P. *investment company executive*
Clewett, Raymond Winfred *mechanical design engineer*
Clifford, Brother Peter *academic administrator, religious studies educator*
Clifton, Douglas C. *retired newspaper editor*
Clifton, Russell B. *retired mortgage company executive, consultant*
Climer, Karen Elise *not-for-profit fundraiser*
Clinkscale, Martha Novak *music educator, researcher*
Clogan, Paul Maurice *English language and literature educator*
Closen, Michael Lee *retired law educator*
Cloud, Bruce Benjamin, Sr. *retired construction executive*
Clough, Ray William, Jr. *civil engineering educator*
Clouston, Ross Neal *retired food and related products company executive*
Clubb, Bruce Edwin *retired lawyer*
Clymer, Adam *journalist, writer*
Coar, Richard John *mechanical engineer, aerospace transportation executive, consultant*
Cobabe, Alvin Fred *retired surgeon, small business owner*
Cobb, John Boswell, Jr. *clergyman, educator*
Cobb, Miles Alan *retired lawyer*
Cobb, Virginia Horton *artist, educator*
Cobbs, Charles Glenn *retired medical educator*
Cobey, Virginia Branum *artist, actress, art collector*
Coburn, D(onald) L(ee) *playwright*
Coburn, Steven D. *composer, musicologist, educator, pianist*
Coccia, Michel Andre *retired lawyer*
Cochetti, Roger James *international communications and internet company executive*
Cochran, John P. *economics professor*
Cochran, Kathy Holcombe *music educator, conductor*
Cochran, Robert Lee *music educator*
Cochrane, Walter E. *academic administrator, conductor, music supervisor, clarinet soloist*
Cockram, Suzanne M. *elementary school educator*
Cockrum, William Monroe III *investment banker, educator*
Codo, Christina *securities executive*
Cody, Aldus Morrill *retired editor, journalist, typographer*
Cody, Frank Joseph *education educator, consultant*
Coe, Emma A. *finance educator*
Coe, Rodney Michael *medical educator*
Coffee, Joseph Denis, Jr. *retired college chancellor*
Coffey, John Louis *federal judge*
Coffin, Bertha Louise *retired telecommunications industry executive*
Coffin, Frank Morey *retired federal judge*
Cohane, Heather Christina *publishing executive, editor*
Coheleach, Guy Joseph *artist*
Cohen, Allan Richard *broadcast executive*
Cohen, Aryell *music educator*
Cohen, Betty L. *former broadcast executive*
Cohen, Carolyn A. *healthcare educator*
Cohen, Christopher B. *lawyer*
Cohen, Claire Gorham *investment company executive*
Cohen, Gloria Ernestine *elementary school educator*
Cohen, Jay M. *federal agency administrator, retired military officer*
Cohen, Joel J. *lawyer, investment banker*
Cohen, Larry *film director, producer, screenwriter*
Cohen, Lawrence Alan *health facility administrator*
Cohen, Mark Herbert *broadcast executive*
Cohen, Michael *urologist*
Cohen, Michael Paul *statistician*
Cohen, Murray *aerospace engineer, consultant*
Cohen, Nelson Craig *lawyer*
Cohen, Philip N. *sociologist, educator*
Cohen, Roberta Jane *think-tank associate*
Cohen, Rosalie *civic worker*
Cohen, Stanley *retired biochemistry educator*
Cohen, William Nathan *radiologist*
Cohen-Schwartz, Dawn Sheri *radiologist*
Cohn, Avern Levin *district judge*
Cohn, Gary Dennis *journalist, educator*
Cohn, Marianne Winter Miller *civic activist*
Coker, Larry E. *former college football coach*
Colacello, Bob (Robert John Colacello) *magazine editor, writer*
Colaianni, Joseph Vincent *judge*
Colbern, Steven Garrett *chemist, researcher*
Colbert, Stephen *comedian, actor*
Colburn, David R. *academic administrator*
Colburn, Kenneth Hersey *retired financial executive*
Cole, Nancy Stooksberry *educational research executive*
Cole, Nikki Jo *music educator*
Coleman, Claire Kohn *public relations executive*
Coleman, Claudia L. *marketing executive*
Coleman, Dabney W. *actor*
Coleman, Douglas *research scientist, educator*
Coleman, Earl Maxwell *publishing company executive*
Coleman, Gary William *retired elementary school educator*
Coleman, George Edward *musician*
Coleman, James Edwin, Jr. *lawyer*
Coleman, John Michael *lawyer, consumer products company executive*
Coleman, Mary Sue *academic administrator*
Coleman, Richard William *retired lawyer*
Coleman, Robert Lee *retired lawyer*
Coleman, Ronald Lee *insurance claims executive*
Colette, S. *artist*
Coletti, John Anthony *lawyer, retail and real estate company executive*
Colgate, Stephen *small business owner*
Colker, David A. *former stock exchange executive*
Colker, Edward *artist, educator*
Collens, Lewis Morton *retired academic administrator, law educator*
Collier, Herman Edward, Jr. *retired college president*
Collier, William Gayle *psychology professor, researcher*
Collins, Allen Howard *psychiatrist*
Collins, Caron Lee *music educator*
Collins, Eileen Marie *astronaut*
Collins, Elsie Martha *apparel designer, costume designer*
Collins, Frank, Jr. *dentist, educator*
Collins, Gail *former newspaper editor*
Collins, Harker *retired economist, manufacturing and publishing executive*
Collins, Izola E. *retired music educator*
Collins, J. Michael *retired public broadcasting executive*
Collins, James Duffield *marine engineer, editor*
Collins, Jean Katherine *language educator*
Collins, Jeffrey G. *lawyer, former prosecutor*
Collins, Kathleen Anne *artistic director*
Collins, Martha *English language educator, writer*
Collins, Michael *aerospace consultant, astronaut*
Collins, Richard Stratton (Dick Collins) *retired public relations executive*
Collins, Stephen *actor*
Collins, Steve Anthony *oil industry executive*
Collins, Theodore John *lawyer*
Collins, Walter Lloyd George *editor*
Collins, William J. (Billy Collins) *poet, educator*
Collischan, Judy Kay *art gallery director, museum director, critic, artist*
Collmer, Robert George *retired language educator*
Colman, Jenny Meyer *psychiatrist*
Colodny, Edwin Irving *lawyer, retired air transportation executive*
Colombo, Rose Marie *freelance/self-employed newswriter, television personality*
Colonnier, Marc Leopold *retired anatomist*
Colton, John P. *nuclear scientist, engineering executive*
Colton, Mindy Zimmerman *artist, art director, consultant*
Colton, Sterling Don *retired lawyer, hotel executive*
Colwell, Bryan York *private investor, philanthropist*
Combs, Holly Marie *actress*
Combs, Sean (Diddy) *record company executive, producer*
Comer, Clarence C. *gas industry executive*
Comer, Evan Philip *manufacturing executive*
Comisky, Ian Michael *lawyer*
Commander, Clayton W. *computer scientist*
Common, (Lonnie Rashid Lynn, Common Sense) *rap artist*
Compton, Allen T. *retired state supreme court justice*
Compton, Diane Groat *professional counselor, researcher*
Compton, Norma Haynes *retired dean, artist*
Compton, R. Brian *finance company executive*
Compton, Robert H. *lawyer*
Compton, W. Dale *physicist, researcher, engineer*
Compton, William F. *retired air transportation executive*
Compton, William Thomas *real estate investor*
Comstock, Dale Robert *mathematics professor*
Con, Adam Jonathan *choral conductor, music educator*
Conaway, Margaret Grimes (Peggy Conaway) *library administrator*
Condayan, John *foreign service officer*
Condra, Allen Lee *retired lawyer, state official*
Condry, Robert Stewart *retired hospital administrator*
Conger, Harry Milton *mining company executive*
Conklin, William Frank *writer*
Conley, Ruth Irene *poet*
Conn, Richard Lee *computer scientist, educator*
Conn, Sallee J. *minister, educator*
Connell, Carol Matheson *corporate communications specialist, consultant*
Connell, George Edward *retired academic administrator, research scientist*
Connell, Shirley Hudgins *public relations professional*
Connell, William D. *lawyer*
Connelly, Mary Jo *lawyer, nurse*
Connelly, Sharon Rudolph *lawyer*
Conner, Lindsay Andrew *lawyer*
Conner, William J. III *diversified financial services company executive*
Connolly, Violette M. *small business owner*
Connor, Laurence Davis *retired lawyer*
Connor, Roger Arthur *retired dermatologist*
Connor, William Edwin, II, *finance company executive*
Conomy, John Paul *neurologist, educator, lawyer*
Conover, Lloyd Hillyard *retired research scientist*
Conover-Carson, Anne *writer*
Conquest, Claire M. *secondary school counselor*
Conrad, David Williams *retired lawyer*
Conrad, Harold Theodore *psychiatrist*
Conrad-England, Roberta Lee *pathologist*
Conrath, Barney Jay *astrophysicist*
Conroy, Tamara Boks *artist, retired special education educator*
Conroy, Thomas Francis *insurance company consultant*
Consoli, Marc-Antonio *composer*
Constantine, Larry L. *software designer, design and consultanting company executive*
Conte, Julie Villa *nurse, administrator*
Conti, Indalicio Palomar *finance educator*
Contiguglia, Joseph Justin *preventive medicine physician, internist*
Conway, Jill Kathryn Ker *historian, writer, former academic administrator*
Conway, William Gaylord *zoologist, zoo director, conservationist*
Cook, Charles Wilkerson, Jr. *bank executive, retired municipal official*
Cook, Eddie Walton *army chaplain, military officer*
Cook, Edward Joseph *college president*
Cook, Sister Mary Mercedes *school system administrator, director*
Cook, Myrtle *special education and elementary school educator*
Cook, Quentin LaMar *lawyer, church administrator, healthcare executive*
Cook, Richard Kelsey *aerospace transportation executive*
Cook, Robin *writer*
Cook, Stephen Champlin *retired shipping company executive*
Cooke, Robert William *retired science journalist*
Cooley, James William *retired executive researcher*
Cooney, John Thomas *retired banker*
Cooning, Craig R. *career officer*
Coop, Frederick Robert *retired city manager*
Cooper, Austin Morris *chemist, consultant, chemical engineer, researcher*
Cooper, Brett D. *mathematician, educator*
Cooper, Charles Donald *military association executive, editor, retired military officer*
Cooper, Charles Gordon *retired insurance company executive*
Cooper, Charles Howard *retired photojournalist, retired publishing executive*
Cooper, Elva June *artist*
Cooper, Eugene Bruce *speech pathology/audiology services professional, educator*
Cooper, Hal *television director*
Cooper, Hal Dean *lawyer*
Cooper, Jacquelyn Barber *librarian*
Cooper, James Michael *education educator*
Cooper, John Arnold *financial analyst*
Cooper, Josephine Smith *trade association and public affairs executive*
Cooper, Judith Kase *retired theater educator, playwright*
Cooper, Kathleen Bell *dean, former federal agency administrator*
Cooper, Michael Wayne *graphics designer*
Cooper, Norton J. (Sky) *liquor, wine and food company executive*
Cooper, Rebecca *art dealer*
Cooper, Roger Merlin *information technology executive, school system administrator, federal agency administrator*
Cooper, Russell John III *lawyer*
Cooper, William S. *retired state supreme court justice*
Cooperman, Barry S. *academic administrator, chemist, educator*
Coors, Jeffrey H. *technology manufacturing executive*
Cope, Jeannette Naylor *minister*
Cope, Kenneth Wayne *retail executive*
Cope, Laurence Brian *financial, energy and strategic consulting executive*
Cope, Melba Darlene *volunteer, photographer*
Copeland, Bonnie S. *former school system administrator*
Copeland, Charlene Carole *lawyer*
Copeland, Henry Jefferson, Jr. *former college president*
Copeland, Phillips Jerome *retired academic administrator, military officer*
Copperfield, David (David Kotkin) *illusionist, director, producer*
Coppie, Comer Swift *retired state official*
Coppola, Francis Ford *film director, producer, writer*
Coppola, Michael N. *former automotive parts executive*
Coppola, Sofia Carmina *film director, film producer, scriptwriter*
Copus, David Allen *lawyer*
Corace, Joseph Russell *automotive executive*
Corbet, Kathleen A. *former financial information company executive*
Corbet, Richard Hugh *trade policy specialist, writer*
Corbett, Alice Catherine *investor*
Corbett, Gordon Leroy *minister*
Corbett, Lenora Meade *mathematician, community college educator*
Corbin, Veronica L. *secondary school educator, information scientist, consultant*
Corderman, Douglas George *retired non-profit organization executive*
Cordes, Brett McCormack *otolaryngologist*
Cordes, Jill *chef*
Cordova, Barbara Joy *activities director*
Cordova, Ruben Charles *art historian, curator, photographer*
Corey, Judith Ann *retired elementary school educator*
Corey, Kenneth Edward *urban planning and geography educator, researcher*
Corkery, James Caldwell *retired Canadian government executive, mechanical engineer*
Corkins, Bob *school system administrator*
Corkran, Virginia B. *retired real estate agent*
Corle, James Thomas *lawyer*
Cormie, Donald Mercer *investment company executive*
Cornell, Robert Arthur *federal official*
Cornett, Gregg *publishing and computer company executive, editor*
Cornish, Jay, Jr., (Thelbert Bernard) *Internet company executive*
Corona, Joseph Anthony *operations research analyst, mathematician, educator*
Correa-de-Araujo, Rosaly Lia *medical researcher, medical educator*
Correll, Alston Dayton, Jr., (Pete) *forest products company executive*
Corrigan, Brian Jay *literature educator, writer*
Corry, Aline Lahusen *art educator*
Cortese, Richard Anthony *computer company executive*
Corts, Thomas Edward *academic administrator*
Corwell, Ann Elizabeth *public relations executive*
Cosby, Bill *actor, television producer*
Cosell, Bernard *retired computer systems architect*
Cosman, Francene Jen *former government official*
Costa, Kathy *retired librarian*
Costa, Mary *soprano*
Costa-Gavras, (Constantin Gavras) *film director, writer*
Costandi, Wisam Emile *application developer, biomedical researcher, consultant*
Costello, Elvis (Declan Patrick McManus) *musician, songwriter, singer*
Costner, Kevin *actor*
Cothran, Anne Jennette *academic administrator*
Cotrubas, Ileana *opera singer, retired lyric soprano*
Cotruvo, Joseph Alfred *water, environmental and public health consultant*
Cotsakos, Christos Michael *retired internet financial services company executive*
Cottam, Keith M. *librarian, educator, administrator*
Cotten, Annie Laura *psychologist, educator*
Cotter, Robert F. *hotel executive*
Cotter, William Reckling *foundation administrator*
Cotting, James Charles *manufacturing executive, director*
Cotton-Cobb, Robin Leeanne *music educator*
Cottongame, W. Brice *lawyer*
Cottrell, Mary-Patricia Tross *bank executive*
Couch, Daniel Michael *healthcare executive*
Coughlan, Kenneth L. *lawyer*
Coughlin, Jack *printmaker, sculptor, art educator*
Coughlin, Shaun R. *research scientist*
Cougill, Roscoe McDaniel *retired military officer*
Coukis, Peter George *musician, composer*
Coullard, Chad *information systems specialist*
Coulter, Jack Benson, Jr. *financial planner*
Coulter, William Kirk *lawyer*
Countryman, Gary Lee *retired insurance company executive*
County, Janis Emerson *school counselor*
Courtenay, William James *historian, educator*
Courtés, Joseph Jean-Marie *humanities educator, writer*
Courtnay, Wiliam Gerard *osteopathic physician*
Courtney, Edward *retired classics educator*
Coutifaris, Christos *gynecologist, research scientist*
Covassin, Tracey *athletic training educator*
Cowan, Andrew Glenn *television writer, producer, performer*
Cowher, Bill (William Laird Cowher) *sportscaster, former professional football coach*
Cowles, Robert Lawrence *lawyer*
Cowles, Roger E. *computer consultant*
Cowper, Stephen Cambreleng *international business consultant, former governor*
Cowperthwait, Lindley Murray *lawyer*
Cowser, Danny Lee *lawyer, mental health specialist*
Cox, Beulah Elizabeth *violinist, music educator*
Cox, Chapman Beecher *retired lawyer, charitable organization and aerospace executive*
Cox, Courtland *minority business administrator*
Cox, Gary Walter *political science professor*
Cox, James Elmer *medical educator, department chairman*
Cox, John Curtis *health facility administrator*
Cox, John Francis *retired cosmetic company executive*
Cox, Linda Smoak *real estate broker*
Cox, Marshall *lawyer*
Cox, Robert *retired landscape company executive*
Cox, Robert Hames *chemist, consultant*
Cox, Wilford Donald *retired food company executive*
Cox, William Andrew *cardiovascular thoracic surgeon*
Coyle, Martin Adolphus, Jr. *lawyer*
Coyne, Brian J(oseph) *pharmaceutical researcher*
Coyne, William Joseph *former congressman*
Crabbs, Roger Alan *publishing executive, director, small business owner, military officer, educator*
Crabtree, Davida Foy *minister*
Crabtree, Jacquelynn Kay *elementary school educator*
Crabtree, Robert Howard *chemistry professor, consultant*
Craft, Edmund Coleman *retired manufacturing executive*
Crahalla, Jacqueline R. *state representative*
Crahan, Elizabeth Schmidt *librarian*
Craig, Daniel *actor*
Craig, Larry Edwin *former senator*
Craighead, John Edward *pathology educator*
Craiglow, James Hawkins *academic administrator*
Craik, Mary Bernice *artist, art gallery owner*
Cramer, James Dale *physicist, scientific company executive*
Cramer, Robert Vern *retired college administrator, consultant*
Cramp, John Franklin *retired lawyer*
Crandall, Albert Earl *retail executive, accountant, entrepreneur*
Crandall, Elizabeth Walbert *retired home economics professor*
Crandall, John Alfred *corporation official*
Crane, Barry D. *former federal agency administrator*

Cranney, Marilyn Kanrek *retired lawyer*
Cravats, Monroe *science educator*
Craven, Wes *film director*
Craver, Earlene *historian, educator*
Crawford, Bruce Edgar *advertising executive*
Crawford, Carol Tallman *law educator*
Crawford, James Dee *chemical distribution executive*
Crawford, Kenneth Charles *retired academic administrator*
Crawford, Muriel Laura *lawyer, educator, writer*
Crawford, Richard Eben, Jr. *retired investment advisor*
Crawford, Stephen S. *investment banker*
Crawford, William Walsh *retired consumer products company executive*
Crawley, Cheryl K. *school system administrator*
Crebbin, Anthony Micek *retired lawyer, military officer*
Creech, John Lewis *botanist, consultant*
Creenan, Katherine Heras *lawyer*
Cremeens, Joanne *medical researcher*
Cremer, Leon E. *retired federal agency administrator, lawyer*
Cremins, James Smyth *lawyer*
Creswell, Dorothy Anne *computer consultant*
Cretara, Domenic Anthony *artist, educator*
Crewdson, John Mark *journalist, writer*
Crewson, Wendy Jane *actress*
Crino, Marjanne Helen *anesthesiologist*
Crisci, Mathew G. *financial consultant, writer*
Croan, Robert James *music critic*
Crocker, Saone Baron *lawyer*
Crocker, Suzanne *painter*
Cromar, Michael Earl *information and finance executive, distribution and transportation, oil and gas exploration and production executive*
Cromer, Donald L. *aerospace and electrical engineer*
Cromwell, Florence Stevens *occupational therapist*
Cromwell, James *actor*
Cronce, Paul Calvin *retired dermatologist*
Cronson, Robert Granville *lawyer*
Crook, Robert Wayne *retired portfolio manager*
Crosby, Norman Lawrence *comedian*
Croskell, Madelon Byrd *music educator, classical vocalist*
Cross, Kathryn Patricia *education educator*
Cross, Robert Louis *retired realtor, landscape architect, land use planner, writer, real estate appraiser*
Crossley, Nancy Ruth *retired federal agency administrator*
Crotts, Carolyn Pearl *school librarian*
Crouch, J.D. (Jack Dyer Crouch II) *former federal official, former ambassador*
Crow, Sheryl *singer, songwriter, musician*
Crowder, Richard Morgan *pilot*
Crowe, James Joseph *lawyer*
Crowell, Craven H., Jr. *retired federal agency administrator*
Crowl, Steven Craig *aerospace engineer*
Crowley, Bob *scenic designer, costume designer, director*
Cruikshank, Thomas Henry *energy services and engineering executive*
Cruise, Tom (Thomas Cruise Mapother IV) *actor*
Crumley, Martha Ann *charity fundraising executive*
Crumpton, Henry A. (Hank Crumpton) *former federal agency administrator*
Crutcher, Michael Bayard *lawyer, retired consumer products company executive*
Crutchfield, James N. *publishing executive*
Crutchfield, Marjorie Alice *retired elementary school educator, director*
Cruver, Suzanne Lee *communications executive, writer*
Cruz-Connerton, Mayra *elementary school educator*
Cruz-Romo, Gilda *soprano*
Crystal, Billy *actor, comedian*
Cuarón, Alfonso *film director, film producer*
Cuatrecasas, Pedro Martin *research biochemist, pharmaceutical executive*
Cuddihy, Robert Vincent, Jr. *finance and marketing executive*
Cuetter, Albert Cayetano *neurologist*
Cui, Hongliang *engineering company executive, researcher*
Culcasi, Karen *geographer, researcher*
Culkin, Macaulay *actor*
Cullari, Salvatore Santino *clinical psychologist, educator, writer*
Cullen, James G. *telecommunications industry executive*
Cullen, Shawn Paul *emergency physician, military officer*
Culligan, Patrick John *obstetrician, urogynecologist, surgeon, researcher*
Culliton, Barbara J. *publishing executive*
Cullum, John *actor, singer*
Cullum, Lee Brooks *journalist*
Culmo, Tom A. *lawyer*
Culp, Mildred Louise *corporate financial executive*
Culpepper, Daunte *professional football player*
Culton, Paul Melvin *retired counselor, educational administrator, professor, interpreter*
Culwell, Charles Louis *retired manufacturing executive*
Culy, Steven Wayne *application developer, physicist*
Cumming, Robert Hugh *artist, photographer*
Cummings, David William *artist, retired educator*
Cummins, Bud *former prosecutor*
Cummins, Charles Fitch, Jr. *lawyer*
Cummins, Nancyellen Heckeroth *electronics engineer*
Cummins, Wilma Jeanne *actress, comedienne*
Cunard, Derek *academic administrator*
Cunningham, Alice Welt *law and mathematics educator*
Cunningham, Andrea Lee *public relations executive*
Cunningham, James Blair *ambassador*
Cunningham, Jessie Jerome *real estate investor, import/export company executive, entrepreneur, small business owner*
Cunningham, Kathy *artist, educator*
Cunningham, Michael Gerald *composer, writer, music educator emeritus*
Cunningham, Ronnie Walter *venture capitalist*
Cunningham, Terence Thomas III *hospital administrator*
Cunningham, William Francis, Jr. *literature and language professor, academic administrator*
Cupp, Lucy Paschall *retired elementary school educator, minister*
Cupp, Robert Erhard *golf course architect, land use planner*
Curatola, Daniel L. *retired sales executive*
Curie, Charles G. *former federal agency administrator*
Curley, Elmer Frank *librarian*
Curnutte, Mary E. *artist*
Curran, Michael J. *finance company executive*
Currie, Steven Ray *artist*
Currier, Nathan K. *composer, educator*
Curry, Carlton E. *broadcast and waterworks executive, councilman*
Curry, Daniel Francis Myles *filmmaker*
Curry, Goldie *elementary school educator*
Curry, John Michael *investment banker*
Curry Scott, Shirley Goodman *retired director*
Curson, Theodore *musician*
Curtis, Arnold Bennett *retired lumber company executive*
Curtis, Edward Joseph, Jr. *gas industry executive, management consultant*
Curtis, Mary E. (Mary Horowitz) *publishing executive*
Curtis, Robert Allen *lawyer*
Curtis, Susan Grace *lawyer*
Curtis, Thomas Pelham, II, *artist, educator, small business owner*
Cushing, Mark L. *lawyer*
Cussler, Clive Eric *author*
Custer, Beth *composer, musician*
Cutler, Karan Davis *writer, columnist*
Cutler, Laurence Jeffrey *lawyer*
Cutting, Heyward *designer, planner*
Cutting, Sean Eugene *aeronautical engineer*
Cyford, Janet Irene *Spiritualist medium, meditation consultant*
Cyr, Conrad Keefe *federal judge*
Czarnecki, Gerald Milton *investment banker, venture capitalist*
Czinger, Kevin Robert *entrepreneur, venture capitalist*
Czop, Andrew Paul *electrical engineer*
Dable, Carol M. *primary school educator*
D'Abruzzo, Stephanie *actress*
Daffron, MaryEllen *retired librarian*
Dafoe, Willem *actor*
Dagenais, Simon *chiropractor, epidemiologist*
Daglis, Lisa Genine *deputy attorney general*
Daher, Edouard *cardiologist*
Dahlburg, John-Thor Theodore *news correspondent*
Dahlgren, Carl Herman Per *performing company executive, educator*
Dahlman, Simon Jacques *journalist, educator*
Dahlstrom, Becky Joanne *journalist*
Dahse, Kenneth William *photographer, writer, educator*
Dailey, Daniel Owen *artist, educator, product designer*
Dailey, Franklyn Edward, Jr. *electronic image technology company executive, analyst, consultant*
Dailey, Janet *writer*
Dailey, Jim *former mayor*
Daily, Deirdre Lynn *systems analyst*
Daily, Thomas A. *lawyer*
Dajnowicz, Jan *software and hardware designer, researcher*
Dakin, Christine Whitney *dancer, educator*
Dale, T.D. *architectural firm executive*
D'Alesandro, Philip Anthony *parasitologist, immunologist, retired medical educator*
D'Alessandro, David Francis *insurance company executive*
D'Alessio, Valaida Corrine *artist, consultant*
Daley, Sandra *retired artist, filmmaker, photographer*
Dallek, Robert *historian, professor, writer*
Dallmann, Daniel F. *artist, educator*
Dally, James William *mechanical engineering educator, consultant*
Dal Santo, Diane *retired judge, writer, arbitrator, mediator*
Daly, Carson Jones *television personality*
Daly, Donald F. *retired engineering company executive*
Daly, Miriam Shamer *retired family physician*
Daly, Paul Sylvester *former mayor, retired academic administrator, management consultant*
Dame, Richard Franklin *marine biology educator*
Damon, Matt (Matthew Paige Damon) *actor*
Dampf, Beth Ann *music educator*
Damsgaard, Patricia Rae *artist, educator*
Dana, Edward Runkle *retired physician*
Danaher, Mallory Millett (Mallory Jones) *actress, photographer, film and theater producer*
Danehy, Robert Joseph *aquatic biologist*
Danelo, David Joseph *writer, editor*
Danes, Claire *actress*
Danforth, Arthur Edwards *finance executive*
D'Angelo, Vincent A. *diversified financial services company executive, consultant*
Dangoor, David Ezra Ramsi *consumer goods company executive*
Dangremond, David W. *art history educator*
Dani, *sculptor, painter*
Daniel, Coldwell III *economist, educator, entrepreneur*
Daniel, Jonathan Alexander *chiropractor, educator*
Daniel, Marilyn S. *lawyer*
Daniel, William Walter, Jr. *retired radiologist*
Daniele, Graciela *choreographer*
Daniels, Daniel Baker *information technology manager, small business owner*
Daniels, Diana M. *lawyer, retired publishing executive*
Daniels, Edgar Roth *educator*
Daniels, James Maurice *retired physicist*
Daniels, Lydia M. *health care administrator*
Daniels, Mary P. *academic administrator, technologist*
Daniels, Ronald George *theater director*
Daniels, Sydney Robert *theater director, educator*
Daniels, William Burton *retired physicist, educator*
Danielsen, Albert Leroy *economics professor, energy and utilities consultant*
Danner, Blythe *actress*
Danner, Bryant Craig *lawyer*
Danner, Patsy Ann *former congresswoman*
Danni, F. Robert *town official*
Dano, Paul Franklin *actor*
Danse, Ilene Homnick Raisfeld *physician, educator, toxicologist, sculptor*
Danzig, Frederick Paul *newspaper editor*
Danzig, Voleen H. *marketing professional, educator*
Danziger, Glenn Norman *retired chemicals executive*
Da Pena, Eileen *psychologist*
Daram, Sumanth Reddy *medical educator*
D'Arbanville, Patti *actress*
Darby, Joseph M. *reservist*
Darden, Derrick Carolyle *civilian military employee, educator*
Darden, Lauretta *elementary school educator*
Daren, Sylvia *poet*
Dargan, Pamela Ann *systems engineer, consultant*
Dargel, Corey *composer, singer*
Darien, Steven Martin *management consulting company executive*
Darling, Robert Edward *theater director, designer*
Darrow, William Richard *retired pharmaceutical company executive, consultant*
Darsie, Richard Floyd, Jr. *medical entomologist*
Darvarova, Elmira *musician, concertmaster*
Daschle, Thomas Andrew *former senator*
Dash, Sanford Mark *aerospace scientist*
Date, Elaine Satomi *physiatrist, educator*
Dattilo, Thomas A. *retired manufacturing executive*
Davatzes, Nickolas *retired broadcast executive*
Davenport, Ann Adele Mayfield *retired home care agency administrator*
Davenport, Lawrence Franklin *academic administrator*
DaVerne, Steven Richard *advertising director, artist, illustrator, behavior analyst, marketing professional, consultant*
Daves, Glenn Doyle, Jr. *science educator, chemist, researcher*
David, Clive *events executive*
David, Larry *television scriptwriter and producer, actor*
David, Martin Heidenhain *economics professor*
Davids, Robert Norman *retired petroleum exploration geologist*
Davidson, Bonnie Jean *gymnastics educator, sports management consultant*
Davidson, Diane (Marie Davidson) *publisher*
Davidson, Jeannie *costume designer*
Davidson, John Kenneth, Sr. *sociologist, educator, researcher, writer, consultant*
Davidson, Mayer B. *endocrinologist, educator, researcher*
Davidson, Richard J. *retired medical association administrator*
D'Avignon, Roy Joseph *lawyer*
Davis, Anna Jane Ripley *elementary school educator*
Davis, C. VanLeer III *lawyer*
Davis, Charles Memath, Sr. *non-commissioned officer*
Davis, Clarence Clinton, Jr. *lawyer*
Davis, Darrell L. *retired automotive executive*
Davis, Donald Alan *news correspondent, writer, lecturer*
Davis, Donald Glenn *lawyer*
Davis, Elizabeth Eileen *education educator*
Davis, Frederick Benjamin *retired law educator*
Davis, Gordon Richard Fuerst *retired biologist, translator*
Davis, Harley Cleo *retired military officer*
Davis, Hiram Joe *public school administrator*
Davis, J. Alan *writer, film and television producer*
Davis, Jack Wayne, Jr. *retired publishing executive*
Davis, James Allan *gerontologist, educator*
Davis, Jimmy Frank *prosecutor*
Davis, John Warren *real estate broker, consultant*
Davis, Joseph Lloyd *academic administrator, consultant*
Davis, June Fiksdal *medical facility owner, floral designer*
Davis, Lanita Irene *secondary school educator*
Davis, Luther *writer, theater producer, motion picture producer*
Davis, Mamie (Denise Davis) *writer*
Davis, Margaret Thacker *retired critical care, medical and surgical nurse*
Davis, Marguerite Herr *judge*
Davis, Martha Frances *lawyer*
Davis, Mary Byrd *conservationist, researcher*
Davis, Mary Helen *psychiatrist, educator*
Davis, Mellar Pilgrim *oncologist*
Davis, Osceola A. *opera singer*
Davis, Rex Lloyd *insurance company executive*
Davis, Robert W. *computer company executive*
Davis, Roger Edwin *lawyer, retired retail executive*
Davis, Ruth Margaret *information technology executive*
Davis, Samuel *hospital administrator, educator, consultant*
Davis, William Allison, II, *retired lawyer*
Davis, William C., Jr. *judge*
Davison, Helen Irene *secondary school educator, counseling administrator*
Dawdy, Doris Ostrander *writer*
Dawson, Geraldine *medical educator, social worker*
Dawson, Rosario *actress, singer*
Dawson, Suzanne Stockus *lawyer*
Dawson, Virginia Sue *retired editor*
Day, Donald Lee *retired engineering educator*
Day, John Denton *small business owner, animal breeder*
Day, Kahlil Amyn *mediator, lawyer*
Day, Richard Allen *retired chemistry professor*
Day, Roland Bernard *retired judge*
Dayton, Mark Brandt *former senator*
Dea, Peter Allen *gas industry executive, geologist*
Deacon, David Emmerson *advertising executive*
Dean, Carole Lee *film company executive*
Dean, Edwin Becton *entrepreneur*
Dean, Edwin Robinson *economist, educator, consultant*
Dean, John Wesley III *investment banker, former federal official*
Dean, Kaseem *music producer*
Dean, Leslie Alan (Cap Dean) *international economic, social and political development consultant, interagency and defense analyst*
Dean, Michael M. *lawyer*
Dean, Patricea Louise *lawyer, educator, small business owner*
Dean, Richard N. *lawyer*
Dean, Rosemarie Denise *medical transcription supervisor*
Dean, Thompson *diversified financial services company executive, investment banker*
DeAndrade, Kristy A. *elementary school educator*
De Angelis, Rosemary Eleanor *actress*
DeAngelo, LeAnna Marie *research health psychologist, writer*
De Antoni, Edward Paul *lab administrator*
Deats, Suzanne *writer, editor, artist*
DeBakey, Michael Ellis *surgeon, educator*
DeBakey, Selma *communications educator, writer, editor*
deBear, Richard Stephen *library planning consultant*
DeBerry, Donna *retail executive*
De Blasi, Tony (Anthony Armando De Blasi) *artist*
de Blasis, James Michael *performing company executive, theater producer*
DeBock, Ronald Gene *real estate company executive*
Debraski, Sarah Cornish *librarian*
DeBrincat, Susan Jeanne *nutritionist*
deCastro, Cristina L. *secondary school educator*
de Champeaux de Laboulaye, Dennis *computer scientist*
Dechant, Virgil C. *retired fraternal organization administrator*
Dechar, Peter Henry *artist*
Dechene, Arthur C., Jr. *philosopher, religious studies educator*
Deckard, Steve Wayne *science educator, academic administrator*
Decker, Mark Jonathan *radiologist*
Decker, Walter Johns *toxicologist*
De Cou-Landberg, Michelle V. *retired language educator*
DeDio, Robert *otolaryngologist*
Dedman, Bill *journalist*
Deems, Sherran Ellen (Sherry) *artist, educator, editor*
Deer, (Richard) Alan *lawyer*
Dees, Bowen Causey *retired institute executive*
De Fabo, Edward Charles *photobiologist, research scientist, educator, photoimmunologist*
De Felitta, Frank Paul *film producer, writer*
Degabrielle, Donald J., Jr. *prosecutor*
De Gette, Diana Louise *congresswoman, lawyer*
DeGiulio, Lucas *artist*
Degn, Douglas J. *retired retail executive*
DeHoff, Valerie S. *music educator*
Deiro, Judith Anne *chemical dependency educator*
DeJarnatt, Kitty M. *special education educator*
De Jesus, Veronica *artist, educator*
Dejud, Carlos *psychologist*
Dela Cruz, Jose Santos *retired commonwealth supreme court justice*
Delahanty, Rebecca Ann *school system administrator*
Delaney, John *protective services official*
Delaney, Wayne Edward *retired surgeon*
DeLapp, Tina Davis *retired nursing educator*
de la Rocha, Zack *singer, musician*
de La Sabliere, Jean-Marc *former international organization official*
DeLaTorre, Phillip Eugene *law educator*
Delaty, Simone *retired language educator*
De Laurentiis, Dino *motion picture producer*
De Laurentiis, Giada *chef*
de Lavallade, Carmen *dancer, choreographer*
DeLay, Tom (Thomas Dale DeLay) *former congressman*
Delehant, Joseph Henry *lawyer*
Delffs, Dudley J. *writer, educator*
Delgado, Roger Rodriguez *surgeon, educator*
Delgado Guay, Marvin Omar *internist, geriatrician*
DeLillo, Don *author*
Dell, Charlene Elizabeth *music educator*
Dellagloria, John Castle *lawyer, educator*
DellaVecchia, Michael Anthony *ophthalmologist, pathologist, educator*
Delli, Bertrun H. *art historian*
Deloatch, Cheryl Lee *writer*
DeLonge, Thomas Matthew, Jr. *musician*

De Lorenzo, William E. *retired foreign language educator*
Delpy, Julie *actress*
Del Rio, Kathleen O. *language educator*
del Toro, Guillermo *film director*
De Lutis, Donald Conse *investment advisor, consultant*
Dely, Steven *retired aerospace company executive*
Demant, Margaret H. *retired interior designer*
de Margitay, Gedeon *acquisitions and management consultant*
DeMartini, Richard Michael *retired bank executive*
DeMartino, Anthony Gabriel *cardiologist, internist*
DeMary, Jo Lynne *retired school system administrator, former elementary school educator*
de Matteo, Drea *actress*
Demere, Robert Houstoun, Jr. *oil industry executive*
DeMille, Nelson Richard *writer*
Deming, Rust M. *ambassador*
DeMitchell, Terri Ann *law educator*
Demme, Jonathan *director, producer, writer*
de Molina, Alvaro G. *former bank executive*
Dempsey, Edward Joseph *lawyer*
Demson, Philip Henry *military officer*
Dench, Judi *actress*
de Neufville, Pierre *retired brokerage house executive*
Denevan, William Maxfield *geographer, historical ecologist, educator*
Deng, Li *computer scientist, researcher, electrical engineer*
Denham, Earl Lamar *lawyer*
Denious, Sharon Marie *retired publishing executive*
DeNisi, Angelo *dean*
Denman, David *actor*
Denn, Cyril Joseph *retired financial advisor*
Denneen, John Paul *lawyer*
Dennehy, Brian *actor*
Dennick, Lori Ann (L. Anne) *publicist, actress, journalist*
Dennis, Anthony James *lawyer*
Dennis, Gigi (Ginette E. Dennis) *former state official*
Dennis, Patricia Diaz *lawyer*
Dennison, Shirley Ann *publishing executive*
Dent, Julie *executive director*
Denver, Eileen Ann *retired editor*
Deoul, Kathleen Boardsen *publishing executive*
DePalma, Ralph George *surgeon, educator*
De Palma-Iozzi, Frances M. *music educator, conductor*
DePaul, Michael *music educator*
DePinto, David J. *public relations executive*
de Planque, E. Gail *physicist*
Dergarabedian, Paul *environmental services administrator, consultant*
Der-Houssikian, Haig *linguist, educator*
Derickson, Sandy (Sandra L.) *bank executive*
Dermanis, Paul Raymond *architect*
Dern, Laura *actress*
Deromedi, Roger K. *food products executive*
Derrick, Kathryn Thill *secondary school educator*
Der Torossian, Papken *engineering executive*
Deryuga, Vyacheslav O. *nuclear physicist*
Desbarats, Peter Hullett *journalist, educator, academic administrator*
Deschanel, Mary Jo *actress*
Desilets, Alicia R. *pharmacist, educator*
Desio, Delores Jean *writer, artist, retired elementary school educator*
Desmond, Susan Fahey *lawyer*
Desnoyers, Megan Floyd *retired archivist, educator*
Despommier, Dickson Donald *microbiology educator, parasitologist*
DeStafeno, John J. *ophthalmologist*
Detert, Miriam Anne *chemical analyst*
DeThomas, Joseph Michael *former ambassador*
Detweiler, David Kenneth *veterinary physiologist, educator*
Deutsch, Alin Bernard *computer scientist, educator*
Deutsch, Didier (Delaunoy) *music producer, writer*
Deutsch, Herbert Arnold *music educator*
Deutsch, James I. *curator*
Deutsch, Kathleen Pilarcik *artist*
Deutschman, Louise Tolliver *curator*
DeVaris, Jeannette Mary *psychologist*
deVeer, Robert Kipp, Jr. *investment banker*
DeVita, Vincent Theodore, Jr. *oncologist*
DeVivo, Ange *retired small business owner*
Devlin, Michael Coles *bass-baritone*
DeVore, Daun Aline *lawyer*
DeVries, Robert Allen *foundation administrator*
DeVylder, Edgar Paul, Jr. *lawyer*
Dewar, James McEwen *marketing, aerospace and defense executive, developing nations consultant*
Dewey, Arthur Eugene *former federal agency administrator*
deWilde, David Michael *management consultant, lawyer, finance company executive, retired recruiter*
DeWine, Mike (Richard Michael DeWine) *former senator, lawyer*
DeWolfe, John Chauncey, Jr. *lawyer*
Dews, P(eter) B(ooth) *retired pharmacology educator, physician*
Dey, Moul *molecular biologist, researcher*
DeYoung, Marilyn Brant-Chandler *retired urban planner, farmer*
Dhara, Venkata Ramana *physician, educator*
Di, Francine *music educator, writer*
Diakos, Stephen Samuel *billing and insurance specialist*
Diakunchak, Ihor S. *retired mechanical engineer*
Diamant, Anita *writer*
Diamond, Richard *retired educator*
Diamond, Robert Mach *higher education administrator*
Diamond, Stuart *lawyer, educator, business executive, writer*
Diamond, Susan Zee *management consultant*
Diaz, Cameron *actress*
Diaz, Fernando Gustavo *neurosurgeon*
Diaz, Nina Isabel *industrial engineer*
Diaz-Verson, Salvador, Jr. *investment advisor*
Di Benedetto, Stephen Anthony *performing arts educator*
Dibner, David Robert *architect, writer*
DiBuono, Eileen Elizabeth *artist*
DiCaprio, Leonardo *actor*
Di Carlo, Armando *Italian language educator*
Di Cecco, James *real estate company executive*
DiCello, Carmen Charles *health educator*
Dick, James Cordell *concert pianist*
Dickens, Joyce Rebecca *addictions therapist, educator*
Dickens, Justin Kirk *nuclear physicist*
Dickerson, Claire Moore *lawyer, educator*
Dickerson, John Robert *retired automotive engineer*
Dickeson, Robert Celmer *retired foundation administrator, management consultant*
Dickey, Betty C. *former state supreme court justice*
Dickey, Joseph William *utilities executive, engineer*
Dickie, Renee *physiologist, researcher*
Dickinson, Donald Charles *library science professor*
Dickinson, Gail Krepps *library science educator*
Dickman, James Bruce *photojournalist*
Dicksheet, Sharadkumar *plastic surgeon*
Dickson, Constance Pierce *retired law librarian*
Dickson, James Francis III *surgeon*
Dickstein, Michael Ethan *mediator, arbitrator, lawyer*
Dickstein, Morris *language educator, writer*
Dickstein, Sidney *lawyer*
DiDomenico, Mauro, Jr. *communications executive*
Diederichs, Janet Wood *public relations executive*
Diefenderfer, Dan *filmmaker*
Diehl, Deborah Hilda *lawyer*
Diehl, Louis F. *hematologist*
Diehl, Stephen Anthony *human resources consultant*
Diemer, Emma Lou *composer, educator*
Diener, Erwin *immunologist*
Diener, Royce *retired health products executive*
Dierickx, Constance Ricker *psychologist, management consultant*
Dietel, James Edwin *lawyer, consultant*
Dietrich, William Alan *reporter, writer*
Dietz, Arthur Townsend *investment counseling company executive*
DiFiore, David Gerard *musician*
Di Giacomo, Fran *artist*
Di Giovanni, Anthony *retired coal mining company executive*
DiGregorio, Amanda Elizabeth *medical products executive*
Dillard, Suzanne *interior designer, actress*
Dillon, Francis Patrick *retired human resources specialist*
Dillon, Robert Sherwood *retired diplomat*
Dillon Rydman, Linda Gay *nurse, consultant*
Dills, James Arlof *retired publishing executive*
Dimaira, Ann B. *medical/surgical nurse*
Dimancescu, Mihai D. *neurosurgeon, researcher, educator*
Di Massa, Ernani Vincenzo, Jr. *communications executive, television producer, writer*
Dincecco, Jennie Elizabeth Williams Swanson *healthcare administrator, mentor, educator, volunteer*
Ding, Jinwen *biomedical researcher*
Dingle, Carol A. *state agency administrator, writer*
Dinkel, John George *automotive executive, consultant*
DiNovi, Denise *producer*
Diorio, Eileen Patricia *retired medical technologist, philosophy educator*
DiPentima, Renato Anthony *information technology executive*
DiPiazza, Michael Charles *insurance company executive*
DiPietro, Joseph A. *dermatologist*
Dipko, Thomas Earl *retired minister, religious organization administrator*
DiPrima, Richard Joseph *neuropsychologist*
Di Rita, Larry (Lawrence T.) *bank executive, former federal agency administrator*
Dirks, Roger L. *mathematics educator*
Dirnt, Mike (Michael Ryan Pritchard) *musician, singer*
Dirvin, Gerald Vincent *retired consumer products company executive*
DiSantis, Linda Katherine *lawyer*
Dishy, Bob *actor*
Disney, Roy Edward *broadcasting company executive*
Dispenza, Mary Catherine *director, educator, photographer*
DiSpirito, Rocco *restaurant owner, chef*
DiStefano, Philip *academic administrator*
Di Suvero, Mark *sculptor*
Ditka, Mike (Michael Keller Ditka Jr.) *sports commentator, former professional football coach*
Dittenhafer, Brian Douglas *banker, economist*
Dittenhafer, Daniel Webster, II, *computer scientist*
Ditter, J. William, Jr. *federal judge*
Divakaran, Vijay Ganesh *medical researcher*
Diviney, Nancy Lynn *elementary school educator*
Dixit, Avinash Kamalakar *economics professor*
Dixner, Arne Wilfred *environmental services administrator*
Dixon, Albert Truman *mathematician, educator*
Dixon, Ben Harold *musician, educator*
Dixon, Gordon Henry *biochemist, educator*
Dixon, Harry D., Jr., (Donnie Dixon) *lawyer, former prosecutor*
Dixon, Jane Frazier *elementary school educator, consultant*
Dixon, John Morris, Jr. *retired judge, lawyer*
Dixon, William Robert *musician, educator*
Djang, David S.W. *physician*
Djordjevic, Dimitrije *historian, educator*
Dluhos, Andre *artist*
Doan, Mary Frances *advertising executive*
Dobbs, Lou (Louis Earl Dobbs) *commentator, former broadcast executive*
Dobbs, Micheal W. *lawyer*
Doberenz, Alexander R. *retired nutrition educator, chemist*
Dobler, Donald William *retired procurement and materials executive, dean*
Dobriansky, Lev Eugene *economics professor, diplomat*
Dobson, Dorothy Lynn Watts *retired elementary school educator*
Dobson, Robert Albertus III *lawyer, volunteer*
Dockery, J. Lee *retired medical school administrator*
Dockstader, Deborah Ruth *minister*
Doctor, Kenneth Jay *digital content consultant*
Doctorow, Cory *blogger, writer*
Dodge, R(alph) Edward, Jr. *physician*
Dodin, Ilya *research scientist*
Dodson, Daryl Theodore *ballet administrator, consultant*
Dodson, Samuel Robinette III *retired investment banker*
Doebler, Bettie Anne *language educator, researcher, poet*
Doerper, John Erwin *journal editor, publishing executive*
Dogançay, Burhan C. *artist, photographer, sculptor*
Doherty, Charles Vincent *investment advisor*
Doherty, Evelyn Marie *data processing consultant*
Doherty, Peter Charles *immunologist*
Dohmen, Mary Holgate *retired primary school educator*
Dohrmann, Russell William *retired manufacturing executive*
Dokurno, Anthony David *lawyer*
Dolan, Edward Francis *writer*
Dolan, Louise Ann *physicist*
Dolan, Michael J. *former multi media company and advertising executive*
Dolan, Peter Brown *lawyer*
Dole, Arthur Alexander *former psychology professor, department chairman*
Dolenz, Mickey (George Michael Dolenz, Mickey Braddock) *entertainer, actor, television producer*
Dolev, Jacqueline *physician, researcher*
Dolezal, Dale Francis *truck manufacturing company executive*
Dolgen, Jonathan L. *former motion picture company executive*
Doligosa, Annie Lumampao *elementary school educator, researcher*
Dollens, Ronald W. *pharmaceutical executive*
Dolman, John Phillips, Jr., (Tim Dolman) *communications company executive*
Dolph, Wilbert Emery *lawyer*
Doman, Elvira *retired science administrator*
Dominguez, Cari M. *former federal official*
Dominguez, Eddie *artist*
Dominguez, Michael L. *federal agency administrator, former civilian military employee*
Domjan, Laszlo Karoly *journalist*
Domzella, Janet *retired library director*
Donahue, Ann M. *television producer*
Donahue, J. Kevin *electrophysiologist, researcher*
Donahue, John Joseph *parks director*
Donahue-Mathov, Sara Heather *radiologist, educator*
Donald, Aida DiPace *retired publishing executive*
Donaldson, Eva G. *chemist, writer*
Donaldson, Myrtle Norma *musician, educator*
Donaldson, William Henry *investment banker, former federal agency administrator*
Donaldson, Wilma Crankshaw *elementary school educator*
Donberger, Karen Shepard *special education and elementary school educator*
Donley, Russell Lee III *small business owner, former state legislator*
Donlon, William James *retired lawyer*
Donnally, Patricia Broderick *writer*
Donnell, Harold Eugene, Jr. *retired professional society administrator*
Donnelley, Strachan *philosopher*
Donoff, R. Bruce *dean, oral surgeon, dental educator*
Donoghue, John Francis *archbishop*
Donohoe, Jerome Francis *lawyer*
Donohue, George L. *mechanical engineer, educator*
Donohue, Marc David *chemical engineering professor*
Donohue, Susan K. *information technology executive, researcher*
Donovan, Brian *freelance/self-employed journalist*
Donovan, Dennis Dale *priest*
Donovan, Gerald Alton *retired academic administrator, dean*
Donovan, James Robert *business equipment company executive*
D'Ooge, Benjamin Wayne *emergency physician*
Dooley, Brendan David *criminologist, researcher*
Doppmann, William *composer, pianist*
Dorado, Marianne Gaertner *retired lawyer*
Dore, Patricia Ann *psychologist*
Doret, Peter *state agency administrator, lawyer*
Dorkin, Frederic Eugene *lawyer*
Dorman, Richard Frederick, Jr. *association executive, consultant*
Dorn, Gordon Joseph *artist, educator*
Dornbush, K. Terry *former ambassador, consulting company executive, educator*
Dorsey, Dolores Florence *retired corporate treasurer, finance company executive*
Dorsky, Nathaniel *filmmaker*
Doss, Delia L. *mathematics educator*
Doss, Jessica Yarina *financial analyst*
Dossin, Ernest Joseph III *credit manager*
Doto, Paul Jerome *retired accountant*
Doucet, Jennifer *research scientist*
Doud, Guy R. *motivational speaker, former secondary education educator*
Doud, Wallace C. *retired information technology executive*
Dougherty, John Chrysostom III *retired lawyer*
Douglas, Diane Miriam *museum director*
Douglas, James (Buster) *boxer*
Douglas, Janice Green *physician, educator*
Douglas, Karin Nadja *engineer*
Douglas, Kirk (Issur Danielovitch) *actor, motion picture producer*
Douglas, P C *producer, director, reporter, editor*
Douglas, Victoria Jean *marketing professional, communications executive, educator*
Douglass, Frank Russell *lawyer*
Douglass, Jane Dempsey *retired theology educator*
Dow, David Sontag *retired ophthalmologist*
Dow, Garnett McCormick *geologist, consultant*
Dow, Mary Alexis *auditor*
Dow, Peter Anthony *advertising executive*
Dowd, Morgan Daniel *retired political science professor, dean*
Dowdy, Robert Alan *retired lawyer, director*
Dowers, Lois Ann *writer*
Dowley, Joseph Kyran *lawyer, congressman*
Dowling, Edward Thomas *economics professor*
Dowling, Michael Paul *think-tank executive*
Dowling, Vincent John *retired lawyer*
Downen, Robert Lynn *international affairs analyst and political consultant, editor, writer*
Downes, Rackstraw *artist*
Downey, Robert, Jr. *actor, singer, musician*
Downing, Daniel Leon *agricultural studies educator*
Downing, Hudson Uroquhart *retired securities trader, bank executive*
Downing, Kathryn M. *former newspaper publishing executive, lawyer*
Downs, Dorothy Rieder *art historian, consultant, writer*
Downs, Jon Franklin *drama educator, director, writer*
Dowtin, Amanda Elizabeth *elementary school educator*
Doyle, Christine Ellen *museum researcher, educator*
Doyle, Gillian *actress*
Doyle, L. F. Boker *retired trust company executive*
Doyle, Tom *sculptor*
Dozier, James Lee *former army officer*
Dozier, Therese Knecht *department of education advisor, former education association administrator*
Drabkin, Murray *lawyer*
Dracos, Theodore Michael *journalist, television producer*
Dragoi, George *research scientist*
Dragon, William, Jr. *footwear and apparel company executive*
Dragoumis, Paul *electric utility company executive*
Dragushanskaya, Lyudmila *language educator, department chairman*
Drahos, Sandra P. *retired chemist*
Drake, Donald Charles *journalist, playwright*
Drake, Evelyn Downie *retired secondary school educator*
Drake, George Albert *retired academic administrator, historian, educator*
Drake, Miriam Anna *retired librarian, educator, writer, consultant*
Drake, Patti Linn *retired consumer products company executive*
Drake, Rodman Leland *investment company executive, consultant*
Drakeman, Donald Lee *venture capitalist*
Drance, Stephen Michael *ophthalmologist, educator*
Draper, Edgar *psychiatrist*
Draper, E(rnest) Linn, Jr. *retired electric utility executive*
Draper, Gerald Linden *retired lawyer*
Drasler, Gregory John *artist*
Drechsler, Beatrice Krain *lawyer*
Drennen, William Miller, Jr. *cultural organization administrator, film producer, writer*
Dreskin, Stephen Charles *immunologist, allergist*
Dressler, Christy Anna *elementary school educator*
Dressler, David Charles *retired aerospace transportation executive*
Drew, Walter Harlow *retired paper company executive*
Drews, Jürgen *pharmaceutical researcher*
Drexler, Clyde *retired professional basketball player*
Drexler, Richard Allan *manufacturing executive*
Dreyer, Jeffrey S. *parochial school educator*
Dreyfuss, Richard Stephan *actor*
Driscoll, Kimberlee Marie *lawyer*
Driskill, Thomas K. *transportation executive*
D'Rivera, Paquito *clarinetist, saxophonist, conductor, composer*
Drohan, David F. *medical products company executive*
Drost, Marianne *lawyer*
Drowota, Frank F. III *retired state supreme court justice*
Drozd, Leszek Stanislaw *film producer, composer, musician*
Drucker, Alan Steven *mechanical engineer*
Drucker, Mitchell David *physician, educator*
Drue, Kerry Erica *former attorney general*
Druffel, Ann Bernice *researcher, writer*

Drum, Alice *academic administrator, educator*
Drummond, Carol Cramer *voice educator, lyricist, writer, artist*
Drummond, Dixie Dale *retired adult education educator*
Drummond, Dorothy Weitz *geography education consultant, educator, author*
Drummond, Sally Hazelet *artist*
Dryman, Amy *epidemiologist*
Duarte, Prospero Villacin *retired entrepreneur*
Dubik, James M. *career military officer*
Dubin, David Meyer *lawyer, educator*
Dubin, Howard Victor *dermatologist*
Dubin, Stephen Victor *lawyer*
Dublon, Dina *former bank executive*
Du Boff, Michael H(arold) *lawyer*
Dubuc, Carroll Edward *lawyer*
Duckworth, Angela Lee *psychology professor*
Duckworth, Tara Ann *insurance company executive*
Dudden, Alexis *history professor*
Duderstadt, James Johnson *academic administrator, engineering educator*
Dudley, Craig *actor*
Dudley, Thora Louise *rehabilitation services professional*
Dudman, Richard Beebe *journalist*
Duduit, Michael *editor, academic administrator*
Duel, Ward Calvin *retired healthcare consultant*
Duelfer, Charles Alfred *aerospace transportation executive, weapons inspector, director*
Duerksen, George Louis *music therapist, educator*
Duerr, Herman George *retired publishing executive*
Duff, Patricia *civic activist*
Duffy, Ann Patricia *retired elementary school educator*
Duffy, Dan *computer company executive*
Duffy, John Joseph *retired academic administrator, historian, educator*
Duffy, Martin Edward *management consultant, economist*
Dufour, Jack Edward *small business owner, retired special education educator*
Dugan, Charles Clark *retired physician, surgeon*
Dugan, Patrick Raymond *microbiologist, educator, dean*
DuHaime, Michael *political organization worker*
Duhl, Olga Anna *literature educator, researcher*
Duke, George *jazz keyboardist, composer*
Duke, Robin Chandler Tippett *retired public relations executive, former ambassador*
Duke, William Edward *public affairs executive*
Dulin, Eric D. *archivist*
Dull, William Martin *retired engineering executive*
Dumanoski, Dianne *journalist, writer*
Dumas, Sandra Lee *medical technician, microbiologist*
Duminuco, Vincent Joseph *academic administrator, educator*
Dumont, Allan Eliot *retired physician, educator*
Dunagin, William G. *dermatologist*
Dunaway, Faye (Dorothy Dunaway) *actress*
Dunaway, Frank Rosser III *emergency physician*
Dunbar, Diana (Diane) L. *educator, dancer, artist, writer, storyteller*
Dunbar, Maurice Victor *language educator*
Duncan, Allyson K. *federal judge*
Duncan, David Ewing *editor, writer*
Duncan, Robert Bannerman *dean, strategy and organizations educator*
Dune, Steve Charles *retired lawyer*
Dunfee, Thomas Wylie *law educator*
Dunham, Benjamin Starr *editor, art association administrator*
Dunham, Elizabeth Grace *librarian*
Duniphan, J. P. *state legislator, small business owner*
Dunlap, F. Thomas, Jr. *lawyer, retired electronics executive*
Dunlap, Loren Edward *painter, educator*
Dunlap, Patricia C. *state legislator*
Dunn, Arnold Samuel *biochemistry educator*
Dunn, Helen Elizabeth *retired secondary school educator*
Dunn, Jack Newton *urologist*
Dunn, Jennifer Blackburn *former congresswoman*
Dunn, John Raymond, Jr. *stockbroker*
Dunn, Linda Kay *retired physician*
Dunn, Melvin Edward *retired judge*
Dunn, Richard Joseph *retired investment advisor*
Dunn, Robert Lawrence *lawyer*
Dunst, Kirsten *actress*
Duong, Anh *artist, actress*
Duplessis, Audrey Joseph *school system administrator*
Dupuis, Russell Dean *electrical engineer, researcher*
Dur, Philip Alphonse *retired shipbuilding executive, military officer*
Durant, John Ridgeway *retired oncologist, health facility administrator, consultant*
Durek, Dorothy Mary *retired language educator*
Durell, Jack *psychiatrist*
Durell, Viviane G. *psychologist, small business owner*
Durham, Jimmie *artist, poet*
Duringer, David Robert *lawyer*
Durio, William Henry *lawyer*
Durr, Robert Joseph *construction executive, mechanical engineer*
Durrani, Sajjad Haidar *retired aerospace and communications engineer*
Dusenbury, Ruth Ellen Cole *business owner*
Duteil, Hervé Pierre *bank executive*
Dutile, Fernand Neville *law educator*
Dutson, Thayne R. *dean*
Dutta, Sanjeev *surgeon*
Duval, Olivia Blackmon *music educator*
Duvall, Robert (Robert Selden Duvall) *actor*
Dvorson, Natalya *lawyer*
Dwan, Dennis Edwin *broadcast executive, photographer*
Dworzan, Helene Liberman *writer, poet, playwright*
Dwyer, Gerald Paul, Jr. *economist, bank executive*
Dwyer, John P. *law educator*
Dwyer, William H. *real estate company executive*
Dyar, Kathryn Wilkin *pediatrician*
Dybner, Ruben *urologist*
Dyck, Walter Peter *gastroenterologist, educator, academic administrator*
Dycus, Elizabeth Rasmussen *academic administrator*
Dye, Nancy Schrom *historian, educator, former academic administrator*
Dye, Robert Harris *retired manufacturing company executive*
Dyer, Ira *ocean engineering educator, consultant*
Dyer, Susan Kristine *editor, librarian*
Dyer, Wayne Walter *psychologist, writer, radio and television personality*
Dykas, Matthew J. *psychologist*
Dykstra, Gretchen *not-for-profit developer*
Dykstra Lynch, Mary Elizabeth *library and information scientist, educator*
Dy-Liacco, Gabriel S. *psychotherapist, social sciences educator*
Dysart, Benjamin Clay III *conservationist, consultant, engineer*
Dyson, Allan Judge *retired librarian*
Dyson, Esther *editor-in-chief*
Dzapo, Kyle Jean *musician, educator*
Dzhandzhulyan, Lev *business analyst, consultant*
Dziewanowska, Zofia Elizabeth *pharmaceutical executive*
Eachempati, Soumitra R. *surgeon*
Eadie, John William *historian, educator*
Eads, Paul Bryan *production designer*
Eaglet, Robert Danton *electrical engineer, aerospace scientist, consultant, retired military officer*
Earenfight, Theresa Marie *education educator*
Earle, Timothy Keese *anthropology educator*
Early, Bert Hylton *retired lawyer, consultant*
Eastman, Francesca Marlene *volunteer, art historian*
Easton, Charles Clement, Jr. *corporate financial executive*
Easton, James L. *International Olympic Committee Member, sports equipment company executive*
Easton, Roger L. *former operations research specialist, consultant*
Eaton, Joe Oscar *federal judge*
Eaton, Katherine Girton *retired library educator*
Eaton, Larry Ralph *lawyer*
Eaton, Shirley M. *medical/surgical nurse*
Ebbs, George Heberling, Jr. *university executive*
Eberhart, Steven Wesley *psychologist*
Eberly, Joseph Henry *physics professor, consultant, quantum optics scientist*
Ebersole, Christine *actress*
Eberstein, Arthur *former biomedical engineering educator, researcher*
Ebert, Robert Peter *German language professor*
Ebie, William D. *retired museum director*
Ebrahim, Arbin *electrical engineer, researcher*
Echols, Mary Evelyn *training services executive, writer*
Echols, Robert L. *emergency physician*
Eck, Robert Edwin *retired physicist*
Eckmann, Rory Albert *telecommunications industry executive*
Eckstein, Jerome *philosopher, retired educator*
Ecton, Donna R. *business executive*
Eddy, David Maxon *health policy and management advisor*
Eddy, Don *artist*
Eddy, Kelly J. *history educator*
Edelman, Norman Herman *dean, medical educator, academic administrator*
Edelsberg, Sally Comins *retired physical therapist, educator*
Edelson, Mary Beth *artist, educator*
Edelson, Zelda Sarah Toll *retired editor, artist*
Edelstein, Rosemarie (Hublou) *medical, surgical and geriatric nurse, educator*
Eden, Katreina *lawyer*
Edens, Betty Joyce *reading recovery educator*
Edgar, Robert S. *biology professor*
Edgar, Thomas Flynn *chemical engineering professor*
Edgett, William Maloy *lawyer, arbitrator*
Edgren, Gretchen Grondahl *magazine editor*
Edmo, Jean Umiokalani *artist, poet*
Edmonds, Anne Carey *librarian*
Edmonds, Crystal D. *language educator, distance learning coordinator*
Edmunds, Darryl B. *mathematics professor*
Edwards, Adrien *business executive*
Edwards, Annmarie Monica *language educator, career coach, entrepreneur*
Edwards, Anthony *actor*
Edwards, Ardis Lavonne Quam *retired elementary education educator*
Edwards, Blaine Douglass *lawyer*
Edwards, Charles *neuroscientist, educator*
Edwards, Daniel Paul *lawyer, educator*
Edwards, Geoffrey Hartley *newspaper publisher*
Edwards, Helen Thom *physicist*
Edwards, James D. *accounting company executive*
Edwards, John Allen *physician, director*
Edwards, Larry David *internist, educator, dean*
Edwards, Mark U., Jr. *academic administrator, history professor, writer*
Edwards, Patrick Ross *retail executive, lawyer, management consultant*
Edwards, Priscilla Ann *small business owner*
Edwards, Richard Alan *retired lawyer*
Edwards, Robert Hazard *retired college president*
Edwards, Victor Henry *chemical engineer*
Eerkens, Jeff W. *nuclear scientist, educator, laser engineer*
Efird, Frank Kimball, Jr. *archivist*
Efird, Jimmy Thomas *statistician*
Egan, Edward Michael Cardinal *archbishop, cardinal*
Egan, Richard John *retired information technology executive, former ambassador*
Egan, Timothy K. *writer, journalist*
Egan, Wesley William *former ambassador*
Egas, Eric *artist*
Eger, Joseph *conductor*
Eggers, William D. *retired lawyer*
Eglee, Charles Hamilton *scriptwriter, film and television producer*
Egnaczak, Raymond Charles *design educator, graphics designer*
Eguchi, Miharu *chemist, researcher*
Ehigie, Benjamin Odion *radiographer, technologist*
Ehle, Jennifer *actress*
Ehlers, Kathryn Hawes (Mrs. James D. Gabler) *physician*
Ehrenfeld, John Roos *environmental policy educator*
Ehrenreich, Barbara *writer*
Ehret, Megan J. *pharmacist, educator*
Ehrlich, Stephen Richard *lawyer*
Eibeler, Paul G. *former computer game company executive*
Eichenwald, Heinz Felix *physician*
Eickhorst, Kristin Michele *research scientist*
Eimers, Jeri Anne *retired counselor*
Einhorn, Martin B. *physicist, educator*
Einoder, Camille Elizabeth *retired secondary school educator*
Einsel, Naiad June *illustrator, graphics designer*
Eire, Carlos *historian, educator, writer*
Eischen, Donald F. *psychologist, educator, writer*
Eisenberg, Alan *retired professional society administrator*
Eisenberg, Carola *psychiatrist, educator*
Eisenberg, Jay Lynn *marketing research professional*
Eisenhower, John Sheldon Doud *former ambassador, writer*
Eisenstat, Theodore Ellis *colon and rectal surgeon, educator*
Eisner, Peter Norman *journalist, writer*
Eisold, John Francis *physician*
Elam, Fred Eldon *retired military officer*
Elam, Matthew *industrial engineer, educator*
Elble, Joseph M. *computer scientist, researcher*
Elcik, Elizabeth Mabie *fashion illustrator*
Eldard, Ron (Ronald J. Eldard) *actor*
Elder, Mary Louise *retired librarian*
Electra, Carmen (Tara Leigh Patrick) *actress*
Eley, Lynn W. *political science professor, retired mayor*
Elgart, Edward Guerry *civilian military employee*
Elgart, Larry Joseph *orchestra leader*
Elgart, Mervyn L. *retired dermatologist, educator*
Elias, Lori Anne *music educator, journalist, photojournalist*
Elicker, Gordon Leonard *retired lawyer*
Eliot, Charles William John *former university president*
Eliot, Theodore Lyman, Jr. *former ambassador, consultant*
Elise, Kimberly (Kimberly Elise Trammel, Kimberly Elise Oldham) *actress*
Elisha, Larisa *musician, performer, educator*
Elix, Douglas Thorne *computer company executive*
Elizondo, Hector *actor*
Elkie, Kimberly K. *medical editor*
Elkind, Mort William *management consultant*
Elledge, Stephen Joseph *medical educator*
Ellenberger, Jack Stuart *law librarian*
Ellenberger, Lon Karl *singer, music educator*
Ellett, Alan Sidney *real estate developer*
Ellickson, Donald Lien *retired economist, county official*
Ellig, Bruce Robert *retired personnel director*
Ellington, Mildred L. *retired librarian*
Elliot, Jared *financial management consultant*
Elliott, Bill *race car driver*
Elliott, David LeRoy *mathematics and engineering educator*
Elliott, Edward *investment executive, financial planner*
Elliott, Kenneth Yates *theater educator*
Elliott, Stuart Jay *editor, journalist*
Ellis, Anne Elizabeth *fundraiser*
Ellis, John Hubert *retired history professor*
Ellis, Joseph John Michael III *historian, professor*
Ellis, Laurel Glynn *retired entrepreneur*
Ellis, Lawrence Dobson *internist, educator*
Ellis, Lynn Webster *retired finance educator, telecommunications consultant*
Ellis, Robert Harry *retired broadcast executive, academic administrator*
Ellis, Sophia (Lugene) Holley *retired secondary school educator*
Ellis, Steven George *public relations/corporate communications executive*
Ellner, Paul Daniel *retired microbiologist*
El-Moursy, Magdy *electronics engineer*
Elrick, Donald *retired literature educator*
Elrod, Deborah Lee *special education educator*
Else, Carolyn Joan *retired library director*
Elsey, George McKee *retired foundation administrator*
Elson, Edward Elliott *diplomat*
Eltayeb, Emil *pharmacist, researcher*
Elverum, Gerard William, Jr. *retired electronics and aerospace transportation executive*
Elwin, James William, Jr. *lawyer*
Elwood-Akers, Virginia Edythe *librarian, retired archivist*
Elzay, Richard Paul *retired dean, dental educator, department chairman*
Embry, Stephen Creston *lawyer*
Emek, Sharon Helene *risk management consultant*
Emerling, Carol G. *management consultant*
Emerson, Claudia *poet, language professor*
Emerson, Daniel Everett *retired communications company executive*
Emery, Nancy Beth *lawyer*
Emmett, James Robert *retired lawyer*
Emmett, Rita *professional speaker*
Emmons, Robert Duncan *diplomat*
Encarnación, Jose M. Izquierdo *construction executive, former Puerto Rico secretary of state*
Endicott, William F. *journalist*
Eng, Adrienne Rose *corporate financial executive*
Engel, Bernard Theodore *psychologist, educator*
Engel, Richard L. *career officer*
Engelbreit, Mary *art licensing entrepreneur*
Engelhardt, John Hugo *lawyer, bank executive*
Engelman, Rosalyn Ackerman *artist*
Engels, Beatrice Ann *artist, poet, retired real estate company executive*
Engels, Lawrence Arthur *retired metal products executive*
Enger, Edward Henry, Jr. *retired editor, writer*
Enger, Shelley McClelland *epidemiologist, researcher*
Engle, Howard A. *retired pediatrician*
Engle, Mary Allen English *retired physician*
Engle, Steve Eugene *artist*
Engle, Steven B. *biotechnology company executive*
Engler, John M. *trade association administrator, former governor*
English, Bruce Vaughan *environmentalist, consultant*
English, Floyd Leroy *telecommunications industry executive*
English, Patricia Dorzell *women's health nurse practitioner*
English, Stephen Raymond *lawyer*
English-Anderson, San Dei *minister*
Englund, Robert *actor, director, producer*
Engstrom, Marlene Mae *volunteer*
Enhorning, Goran *obstetrician, gynecologist*
Eno, Amos Stewart *natural resource foundation administrator*
Enoch, Craig Trively *retired judge*
Enomoto, Daisuke (Dice-K) *entrepreneur, investor*
Ensminger, John Jay *writer, poet, minister, counselor, playwright*
Ensminger, Luther Glenn *retired chemist*
Epcar, Richard Michael *actor, writer, film director*
Ephron, Nora *writer*
Epp, Dianne Naomi *secondary school educator*
Epp, Eldon Jay *religion educator*
Eppolito, Mary *assistant principal, educator*
Epps, Charles Harry, Jr. *retired orthopaedic surgery educator, dean*
Epstein, Adam *theater producer*
Erb, James Bryan *conductor, musicologist, educator*
Erb, Richard Louis Lundin *resort and hotel executive*
Erb, Thomas Owen *education educator*
Erbay, Nazli *radiologist*
Erdmann, Joachim Christian *retired physicist*
Erenberg, Samuel Joseph *artist*
Erenstein, Alan *emergency nurse practitioner, nursing consultant*
Erickson, Alan Eric *librarian*
Erickson, Carol Jean *literature and language professor*
Erickson, Edward Leonard *biotechnologist, consultant*
Eriksson, Steven *social studies educator*
Erkonen, William Edward *radiologist, medical educator*
Erlebacher, Arlene Cernik *retired lawyer*
Erlicht, Lewis Howard *broadcasting company executive*
Ernst, Edward Willis *retired electrical engineering educator*
Eron, Leonard David *retired psychology professor*
Erskine, Rodney D. *oil industry executive*
Ervin, Kathleen Gwen *journalist*
Erwin, Donald Carroll *plant pathology educator*
Erwin, Douglas Hamilton *museum director, paleobiologist*
Erwin, Elmer Louis *vintager, consultant*
Erwin, Gregory Scott *lawyer*
Erwin, Linda McIntosh *retired librarian*
Erwin, Mary R. *investment advisor*
Escalante, Juan *performing company executive*
Esher, Brian Richard *manufacturing executive*
Eskew, Henry Lawrence, Jr. *economist, consultant*
Esparza, Raul *actor*
Espenlaub, Margo Linn *women's studies educator, writer, artist*
Espiricueta, Sylvia *counseling administrator*
Esposito, Jennifer *actress*
Esquivel, Agerico Liwag *retired research physicist*
Esrey, William Todd *telecommunications company executive*
Esterly, Nancy Burton *retired physician*
Estes, Carl Lewis, II, *lawyer*
Estes, Elaine Rose Graham *retired librarian*
Estes, Jack Charles *entrepreneur, oil industry executive, research scientist*
Estes, Leslie Karen *educator*
Estrin, Deborah Perry *human resources executive*
Estrin, Herbert Alvin *financial consultant, film company executive*
Estrin, Richard William *real estate and business broker, retired editor*
Esty, John Cushing, Jr. *writer, educator, not-for-profit counsel*
Etchegoyen Lynch, Martin *lawyer, consultant*
Etheridge, Diana Carol *internet business executive*
Etra, Lionel *lawyer*
Ettinger, Harry Joseph *retired industrial hygiene engineer, consultant*
Ettinger, Joseph Alan *lawyer*
Ettore, Joseph R. *retired discount department store chain executive*
Euster, Joanne Reed *retired librarian*

Eustis, Albert Anthony *lawyer, diversified financial services company executive*
Euwer, Rebecca L. *dermatologist*
Evangelista, Anita Loretta *freelance/self-employed writer, publishing executive, psychologist, nurse*
Evangelista, Nick Forrest *fencing master, writer, illustrator, publisher*
Evans, Allan Joseph *research scientist, educator*
Evans, Barton, Jr. *retired analytical instrument company executive*
Evans, Daniel A. *pediatrician, educator*
Evans, Dennis Hyde *chemist, educator*
Evans, Eric Alan *retired lawyer*
Evans, Faith *singer*
Evans, Frank Bernard *retired historian*
Evans, Gerald William *engineering educator, consultant*
Evans, Geraldine Ann *former academic administrator*
Evans, Jack R. (J. Glenn) *writer, poet*
Evans, James Handel *academic administrator, architect*
Evans, James Hurlburt *retired transportation and natural resources executive*
Evans, John Derby *telecommunications industry executive*
Evans, Lane Allen *retired congressman*
Evans, Linda Kay *publishing executive*
Evans, Mari *author*
Evans, Marsha Johnson *former non-profit association administrator, retired military officer*
Evans, Philip G. *former sports association executive*
Evans, Richard Austin *education educator, consultant*
Evans, Rosemary Hall *civic worker*
Evans, Tony *language educator*
Evans, Wayne *obstetrician, perinatologist*
Everdell, William *retired lawyer*
Everett, Mark Allen *dermatologist, educator*
Everett, Rupert *actor*
Everett, Tom *actor*
Everhart, Gloria Elaine *music educator*
Evert, Chris (Christine Marie Evert) *retired professional tennis player*
Eviatar, Lydia *pediatrician, neurologist*
Ewald, Laura Anne *school librarian*
Ewald, Roberta Grant *artist, writer*
Ewen, H. I. *physicist*
Ewing, Diane *medical transcriptionist*
Ewing, Elisabeth Anne Rooney *priest*
Ewing, James E. *priest*
Ewing, Raymond Charles *retired ambassador*
Exner, Frank Kepler *information scientist, indexer*
Eyler, John H., Jr. *retail toy and game company executive*
Eyman, Earl Duane *electrical science educator, consultant*
Faber, Michael Warren *lawyer*
Fabiano, Nicola *physicist, researcher*
Fabio, Jim *television producer, film producer, television director, film director, film editor*
Fa'Bos, Julius Gyuda *retired horticulturist, educator*
Fabricatore, Carol Diane *artist, educator*
Fabunan, Ruben G. *physician, research scientist, inventor*
Fackner, Robert E. *protective services official, consultant*
Fadiman, Anne *writer, educator*
Fagan, Drew Stephen *language educator*
Fagin, David Kyle *mining executive*
Fagles, Robert *classicist, educator, translator*
Fahey, Jeff *actor*
Fahmy Hudome, Randa *lawyer*
Fahn, Larry *former environmental organization administrator*
Fahrenkrog, Eugene Henry, Jr. *lawyer*
Fahringer, Catherine Hewson *retired savings and loan association executive*
Fair, Jean Everhard *retired education educator*
Fairfield, Paula Kathleen *sound recording engineer*
Fake, Caterina *Internet company executive*
Falcon, Armando, Jr. *financial consultant, lawyer*
Fales, Haliburton, II, *lawyer*
Faller, Keith *healthcare insurance company executive*
Fan, Jiang *manufacturing executive*
Fanos, Kathleen Hilaire *osteopathic physician, podiatrist*
Fanwick, Ernest *lawyer*
Fargo, Thomas Boulton *retired career military officer*
Farha, Todd S. *health products executive*
Faria, Me'Shell Anita *special education educator*
Farias, Brian K. *music educator*
Faricy, John Hartnett, Jr. *lawyer*
Faris, James Vannoy *cardiologist, educator, health facility administrator*
Fariss, Bruce Lindsay *endocrinologist, consultant*
Farkas, Daniel Frederick *food science and technology educator*
Farley, Barbara Suzanne *lawyer*
Farmakides, John Basil *lawyer*
Farmer, Christopher J. *political scientist, writer*
Farmer, Cornelia Griffin *lawyer, consultant, county hearings official*
Farmer, Crofton Bernard *atmospheric physicist*
Farnsworth, Elizabeth *broadcast journalist*
Farquhar, Robin Hugh *educational consultant, former university president*
Farr, Barry Miller *physician, epidemiologist*
Farr, Ivanne Estelle *small business owner, consultant, artist, sculptor*
Farrall, Harold John *retired accountant*
Farrar, David Holleman *investor*
Farrar, Elaine Willardson *artist*
Farrar, John Edson, II, *finance company executive, consultant, investment advisor*
Farrell, Jeffrey Michael *electrical engineer, consultant*
Farrell, Mike *actor*
Farrell, Suzanne (Roberta Sue Ficker) *ballerina*
Farrell, W. James *metal products manufacturing company executive*
Farrell, William Edgar *sales executive, management consultant*
Farrelly, Peter John *screenwriter*
Farrington, Gregory C. *former academic administrator*
Farris, Ronald M. *retired intelligence officer*
Fasick, Adele Mongan *library and information scientist, educator*
Fasman, Marjorie Lesser *artist, writer*
Faso, John J. *lawyer, former state legislator*
Fassel, Jim (James E. Fassel) *former professional football coach*
Fatemi, Faramarz Saifpour *history and political science professor, consultant*
Faucette, Gloria Marie *accountant, educator*
Faulkner, Frances Mayhew *retired federal agency administrator*
Faulkner, James Vincent, Jr. *lawyer*
Faunce, Sarah Cushing *retired curator*
Fawcett, John Thomas *archivist*
Faxon, Alicia Craig *art educator, department chairman*
Fay, Conner Martindale *retired marketing executive*
Fay, Craig Alan *engineering executive*
Fay, Donald P. *lawyer*
Fay, Miriam Soler *school counselor, educator*
Fay, Peter Thorp *federal judge*
Fay, William Frederick *film producer*
Fazio, Evelyn M. *publisher, writer, agent, editor*
Fearon, Charlene O'Brien *special education educator*
Fearrington, Ann Peyton *writer, illustrator, news correspondent*
Feather, Gloria Anne *language educator*
Federer, Roger *professional tennis player*
Federing, Eric K. *legislative staff member, public information officer*
Feeney, Maryann McHugh *not-for profit professional*
Feeney, Matthew Edward *linguist, educator*
Feeser, Larry James *retired civil engineering educator, researcher*
Feidler, Mark L. *telecommunications industry executive*
Feigenbaum, David Louis *lawyer*
Feigin, Barbara Sommer *marketing consultant*
Fein, Seymour Howard *pharmaceutical executive*
Feinberg, David M. *energy executive, lawyer*
Feiner, Ava Sophia *public affairs consultant, management consultant, economist*
Feinstein, Robert P. *dermatologist*
Feir, Dorothy Jean *entomologist, educator, physiologist*
Feld, Carole Leslie *marketing executive*
Feldkamp, John Calvin *retired lawyer, educator*
Feldman, Eva Lucille *neurology educator*
Feldman, H. Larry *lawyer*
Feldman, Marc David *psychiatrist*
Feldman, Roger David *lawyer*
Feldman, Shana Madigan *legal assistant*
Feldstein, Joshua *educational administrator*
Feldt, Gloria A. *social services administrator*
Felgar, Raymond Eugene *pathologist, educator*
Felicetti, Daniel A. *academic administrator*
Felix, Arthur Martin *chemistry educator, researcher*
Felix, Cheryl A. *air transportation executive*
Fell, Elizabeth P. *education educator*
Feller, Avi *political science scholar*
Feller, Robert William Andrew *public relations executive, retired professional baseball player*
Fellers, Rhonda Gay *lawyer*
Fels, Rendigs *economist, educator*
Felsted, Carla Martindell *librarian, writer, editor*
Felt, Mark (Deep Throat, William Mark Felt Sr.) *former federal agency administrator*
Felton, Helen Martin *retired adult education educator, writer*
Fenech, Daniel Thomas *cartoonist*
Fenech, Joseph Charles *lawyer*
Feng, Jianhua *education educator*
Fenimore, George Wiley *management consultant*
Fenn, Daniel Jonathan *organist*
Fenton, Thomas Trail *journalist*
Fenwick, James Henry *editor, writer, columnist*
Ferber, Samuel *publishing executive*
Ferencz, Charlotte *pediatrician, epidemiologist, preventive medicine physician, educator*
Fergie, (Stacy Ann Ferguson) *singer*
Ferguson, Bradford Lee *lawyer*
Ferguson, Emmet Fewell, Jr. *retired surgeon*
Ferguson, Gary Lee *public relations and security management executive*
Ferguson, John D. *cardiovascular surgeon, researcher, retired military officer*
Ferguson, Lloyd Elbert *retired manufacturing engineer*
Fergusson, Frances Daly *former academic administrator*
Fernald, Harold Allen *publishing executive*
Fernandes, Jane K. *former academic administrator, sign language professional*
Fernandes, Verônica Rolim S. *cardiologist, researcher*
Fernandez, Antonio S. *investment company executive*
Fernandez, Fernando Lawrence *aeronautical engineer, research and development company executive*
Fernandez, Margaret J. *pharmacist*
Fernández-Velazquez, Juan Ramon *university chancellor*
Ferreira, Armando Thomas *sculptor, educator*
Ferreira, Jo Ann Jeanette Chanoux *management consultant, delivery service executive*
Ferris, Roger Patrick *architect*
Ferry, Joan Evans *school counselor*
Ferry, Martha Morton *non-profit executive*
Fetkovich, Michael J. *retired petroleum engineer*
Fetters, Doris Ann *retired secondary education educator*
Fetters, Norman Craig, II, *retired banker*
Fey, John Theodore *retired insurance company executive*
Fey, Willard *global environmental researcher, educator*
Fibiger, John Andrew *life insurance company executive*
Fichtner, William *actor*
Fiddick, Paul William *public official, broadcast executive*
Fiedler, Tom (Thomas Edward Fiedler) *retired editor*
Field, Arthur Norman *lawyer*
Field, Sally Margaret *actress*
Field, (William) Todd *actor, film director, scriptwriter*
Fields, C(lara) Virginia *former city manager*
Fields, Douglas Philip, Sr. *building supply wholesale company executive*
Fields, Velma Archie *medical/surgical nurse*
Fields, Victor Lee *music educator*
Fields-Harris, Deborah Carol *mathematician, educator*
Fiene, Brian D. *protective services official, retired military officer*
Fiennes, Ralph (Ralph Nathaniel Twisleton-Wykeham Fiennes) *actor*
Fierman, Ella Yensen *retired psychotherapist*
Fiero-Maza, Lorraine Doris *music educator*
Fietsam, Robert, Jr. *physician*
Fife, Jonathan Donald *education educator*
Figa, Phillip S. *judge*
Filchock, Ethel *education educator*
Filer, Emily Symington Harkins *retired foundation administrator, writer, non-profit consultant, associate chaplain*
Filerman, Michael Herman *television producer*
Filley, Christopher Mark *neurologist, researcher*
Fillmore, John Dillon *artist*
Finale, Frank L. *retired elementary school educator, writer*
Finch, Christopher Robin *writer*
Finch, Janet Buswell *musician*
Finckenauer, James O. *criminal justice educator, researcher*
Finder, Joseph Alan *writer*
Fine, Frederick L. *computer company and health products executive*
Fine, Lawrence B. *lawyer*
Fine, Roger Seth *lawyer, educator, former pharmaceutical executive*
Finelsen, Libbi June *lawyer*
Finestone, Sheila *senator, retired legislator*
Finger, Harold Ben *nuclear energy industry executive, consultant, government agency administrator*
Finger, Jason Roy *food service executive, internet entrepreneur*
Fingerson, Leroy Malvin *engineering executive, mechanical engineer*
Fink, Daniel Julien *management consultant*
Fink, Matthew Pollack *retired trade association administrator, lawyer*
Fink, Mitchell Phillip *surgeon, researcher*
Fink, Norman Stiles *lawyer, educational administrator, fundraising consultant*
Fink, Raymond *medical educator*
Finkelstein, Daniel *ophthalmologist*
Finlay, Robert Derek *food products executive*
Finlayson, John Sylvester *retired biochemist*
Finley, Harry *artist, museum director*
Finley, Sarah Maude Merritt *retired social worker*
Finn, Charlotte Kaye *interior designer*
Finn, Jane E. *education educator*
Finnberg, Elaine Agnes *psychologist, editor*
Finnegan, Sara Anne (Sara F. Lycett) *publisher*
Finneran, Katie (Kathleen) *actress*
Finney, Albert *actor, theater director*
Finnigan, Robert Emmet *retired small business owner*
Finocchiaro, Alfonso G. *bank executive*
Fiore, Joseph Albert *artist*
Fiorenza, Lisa A. *music educator*
Fiorina, Carly (Cara Carleton Sneed Fiorina) *former computer company executive*
Fiorito, Edward Gerald *lawyer*
Fire, Edward *retired labor union administrator*
Fischer, Carl Robert *retired health facility administrator*
Fischer, David Charles *lawyer*
Fischer, David J. *retired mayor*
Fischer, David Jon *lawyer*
Fischer, Jenna (Regina Marie Fischer) *actress*
Fischer, Maxim *electronics engineer*
Fischer, Michael Ludwig *environmental executive*
Fischer, Russell Leonard *public relations executive*
Fischer, William Samuel *composer, lecturer*
Fischer, Zoe Ann *real estate, property and marketing company executive*
Fiscus, Thomas J. *former judge, career military officer*
Fish, Howard Math *aerospace transportation executive*
Fish, Janet Isobel *artist*
Fishburn, Janet Forsythe *dean*
Fisher, Ann Lewis *judge*
Fisher, Barbara A. *former broadcast executive*
Fisher, Carrie Frances *actress, writer*
Fisher, Charles Harold *chemistry educator, researcher*
Fisher, Dale Dunbar *animal scientist, dairy nutritionist*
Fisher, Derek *former professional basketball player*
Fisher, Isla Lang *actress*
Fisher, Linda J. *former federal agency administrator*
Fisher, Robert Charles Haru *publishing executive, editor*
Fisher, Seymour *psychologist, educator*
Fishman, Bernard *mechanical engineer*
Fishman, Joshua Aaron *sociolinguist, educator*
Fisk, Edward Ray *retired civil and structural engineer, author, educator*
Fisk, Jean Bauder *music educator, director*
Fisk, Scott *graphics designer, educator*
Fiszer-Szafarz, Berta (Berta Safars) *research scientist*
Fitch, Frank Wesley *pathologist, immunologist, dean, educator*
Fitch, Robert McLellan *research and development company executive, consultant*
Fitts, Catherine Austin *investment advisor*
Fitz-Enz, David G. *retired military officer, television producer*
Fitzgerald, Joan V. *artist*
FitzGerald, John Edward III *lawyer*
FitzGerald, Kyriaki Antonia *theologian, psychologist*
Fitzgerald, Peter Gosselin *former senator, lawyer*
Fitzgerald, William Allingham *savings and loan association executive, director*
Fitzmaurice, Laurence Dorset *social services administrator*
Fitzpatrick, Nancy Hecht *editor*
Fitzpatrick, Raymond John *retired urologist*
Fitzroy, Nancy deLoye *engineering executive, mechanical engineer*
Fiumefreddo, Charles A. *brokerage house executive*
Fix, John Neilson *banker*
Flaherty, William E. *chemicals executive, metal products executive*
Flanagan, James Loton *electrical engineer, educator, researcher*
Flanagan, Nancy A. *nursing educator, researcher*
Flanagan, Norman Patrick *lawyer*
Flanders, Robert G., Jr. *lawyer, educator, association administrator*
Flaster, Donald J. *retired pharmaceutical executive*
Fleck, Bela *country musician*
Fleetwood, Mary Annis *education association executive*
Fleischer, Ari (Lawrence Ari Fleischer) *former White House press secretary*
Fleischman, Herman Israel *lawyer*
Fleishman, Philip Robert *internist*
Fleksher, Cassandra C. *psychology and research rehabilitation professional*
Fleming, Gavin John *lawyer*
Fleming, Horace Weldon, Jr. *academic administrator*
Fleming, John Jacob *music educator, director*
Fleming, Rhonda *actress, singer*
Fleming, Thomas A. *retired administrative assistant*
Fleming, Thomas James *writer*
Flemming, David Paul *biologist*
Fletcher, Denise Koen *strategic and financial consultant*
Fletcher, Donald Rodgers *writer, religious studies educator*
Fletcher, Norman S. *retired state supreme court justice*
Fletcher, Ronald Darling *microbiologist educator*
Fletcher, Vernon Jerome *dental association administrator, director*
Fleury, Paul Aimé *dean, physicist*
Flick, Carl *electrical engineer, consultant*
Flick, John Edmond *retired lawyer*
Flickinger, Harry Harner *management consultant*
Flickinger, Joe Arden *telecommunications educator, department chairman*
Flinn, Paul Anthony *materials scientist*
Flint, John E. *retired historian*
Flipse, John Edward *naval architect, mechanical engineer*
Flitcraft, Richard Kirby, II, *former chemical company executive*
Florescu, John Maurice *broadcast executive*
Flory, Peter Cyril Wyche *federal agency administrator*
Flournoy, John Craig *journalism educator*
Flowers-Schoen, Marylu Utley *art educator*
Floyd, Otis Henry *retired military officer, adult education educator*
Floyd, William R. *former health facility administrator*
Fluharty, David Arthur *automotive executive, statistician, consultant*
Fluhr, Jeff *Internet company executive*
Fluth, John Adam *medical educator*
Flye, Carolyn Marie *minister*
Flynn, Paul Bartholomew *foundation executive*
Flynt, Larry Claxton, Jr. *publisher*
Fobert, Pamela Hart *music educator*
Fodera, Leonard V. *lawyer*
Fodiman, Aaron Rosen *publishing executive*
Fogel, Esther Marian (Esther Marian Roseig) *veterinary researcher*
Fogelman, Ann Florence *nutrition consultant, educator, researcher*
Fogelnest, Robert *lawyer*
Fogg, Richard Lloyd *food products executive*
Fogleman, Guy Carroll *physicist, mathematician, educator*
Foglesong, James Staton (Jim) *retired music company executive*
Foldi, Andrew Harry *retired vocalist*
Foley, Gary J. *chemical engineer, researcher, computer scientist, federal agency administrator*
Foley, Mark Adam *former congressman*
Follit, Evelyn V. *former retail executive*
Folsom, Tyler Cleveland *computer engineer, educator*
Fomon, Samuel Joseph *pediatrician, educator*
Fonda, Bridget *actress*
Fonda, Peter *actor, director, producer*
Fondiller, Shirley Hope Alperin *nursing educator, journalist, historian*
Fons, Eric Wallace *physics professor*
Fontana, Mario H. *nuclear engineer*
Fontane, Emily *physician, educator*
Fontes, Manuel Lopes *medical educator, researcher*
Fontes, Patricia J. *psychologist*
Foote, Evelyn Patricia *retired military officer*
Foote, Horton *playwright, scriptwriter*
Foote, William Chapin *manufacturing executive*

Foran, Jessica Lea *veterinary technician, educator*
Forbes, Mary Allison *psychology educator*
Forbes, Michael Patrick *former congressman*
Forbes-Richardson, Helen Hilda *state agency administrator*
Ford, Barbara Jean *librarian, educator*
Ford, Christopher Ashley *federal official, lawyer*
Ford, Ford Barney *retired federal official*
Ford, George Burt *retired lawyer*
Ford, Gregory Ray *investment banker*
Ford, Harrison *actor*
Ford, Judith Ann Tudor *retired natural gas distribution company executive*
Ford, Kenneth William *physicist*
Ford, Loretta C. *retired dean, educator, consultant, nurse*
Ford, Ralph Lee *academic administrator*
Ford-Reed, Lillie Mae *geriatrics services professional*
Foreman, Edward Rawson *retired lawyer*
Foreman, George Edward *retired boxer, minister, boxing commentator*
Foreman, Spencer (Spike Foreman) *pulmonologist, retired hospital administrator*
Forese, James John *business machine company executive*
Forget, Mark Alan *educational consultant, educator*
Foriest, JoAnn M. *education educator*
Forman, Edgar Ross *mechanical engineer*
Forman, Leonard P. *former publishing executive*
Forman, Sydney *finance company executive*
Fornari, Victor M. *psychiatrist*
Forrester, Jay Wright *management consultant, educator*
Forry, John Ingram *lawyer*
Forry, Steven *not-for-profit fundraiser*
Forsberg, Peter *professional hockey player*
Forson, Heather Leah *physician assistant*
Forster, Merlin Henry *foreign languages educator, writer, researcher*
Forster, Robert *actor, educator*
Forstmann, Theodore J. *investment firm executive*
Forsyth, Ben Ralph *retired academic administrator, medical educator*
Forsyth, Richard J. *chemist*
Fort, Robert Bradley *minister*
Fortenbaugh, Samuel Byrod III *lawyer*
Fortmann, Stephen Paul *medical educator, researcher, epidemiologist*
Fortner, Hueston Gilmore *lawyer, writer, composer*
Fortner, Rosanne White *environmental scientist, educator*
Foss, Lukas *composer, conductor, pianist*
Fossum, Robert Merle *mathematician, educator*
Foster, Charles Henry Wheelwright *former foundation officer, consultant, author*
Foster, David Lee *lawyer*
Foster, Judith Christine *lawyer, writer*
Foster, Ken *writer, educator*
Foster, Martha Tyahla *pre-school administrator*
Foster, Mary Christine *film producer, writer*
Foster, Roseanne H. *business educator*
Fotopoulos, Sophia Stathopoulos *medical research scientist, administrator*
Fountain, Karen Schueler *retired physician*
Fountain, Linda Kathleen *health science association executive*
Fournier, Dudley John *surgeon*
Fournier, R. E. Keith *biologist*
Foust, Robert Schmertz *retired legislative staff member, educator*
Fowke, Benjamin G.S. III *energy executive*
Fowler, Alan Bicksler *retired physicist*
Fowler, Beth *actress*
Fowler, Flora Daun *retired lawyer*
Fowler, James D., Jr. *leadership executive*
Fox, Daniel Michael *foundation executive, writer*
Fox, Edward Alan *retired finance company executive*
Fox, Eleanor Mae Cohen *lawyer, educator, writer*
Fox, Galen W. *state representative*
Fox, Joan Phyllis *environmental engineer, engineering executive*
Fox, Lawrence J. *lawyer*
Fox, Michael Wilson *veterinarian, animal scientist*
Fox-Clarkson, Anne C. *fundraising company executive*
Foxman, Abe (Abraham Henry Foxman) *advocacy organization administrator*
Foxworthy, Jeff *comedian, writer, actor*
Foy, Betty Lou Jones *educational administrator*
Foy, Charles Daley *retired soil scientist*
Foyouzi-Youssefi, Reyhaneh *pharmacologist*
Foyston, Frederick L. (Rick Foyston) *literature and language educator, coach*
Frackman, Noel *art critic*
Fradkin, David Milton *physicist, researcher*
Fragen, Andrew J. *surgeon*
Fralix Gold, Carolyn M. *medical/surgical nurse, educator, consultant*
France, Jennifer Jean *lawyer, educator*
Francis, Jerome Leslie *lawyer*
Francis, Karen *painter, television producer, writer*
Francis, Norman C. *academic administrator*
Francis, Philip Hamilton *management consultant*
Francis, Warren William *retired surgeon, educator*
Francke, Linda Bird *journalist*
Franco, Adolfo Alberto *former federal agency administrator*
Francoeur, Christina *special education educator*
Francois, William Armand *lawyer*
Frangos, Spiros G. *medical educator*
Frank, Charles Raphael, Jr. *financial consultant, director*
Frank, Dennis *psychotherapist, educator*
Frank, Edgar Gerald *retired finance company executive*
Frank, Larry James *library director*
Frank, Linda Maria *science educator*
Frank, Michael Victor *risk assessment engineer*
Frank, Ronald Edward *marketing educator*
Franke, John Charles *retired human resources executive*
Franke, Wayne Thomas *retired government affairs director, consultant*
Frankel, Diane *former museum institute administrator*
Frankel, James Burton *retired lawyer*
Frankel, Jennie Louise *writer, composer, playwright*
Frankel, Mary Ann (Kate Frankel) *librarian, educator*
Frankel, Terrie Maxine *writer, composer, playwright*
Frankenberger, Bertram, Jr. *investor, consultant*
Frankenstein, John *international management educator, consultant*
Franklin, Aretha Louise *singer*
Franklin, Bonnie Gail *actress*
Franklin, Carl *director*
Franklin, Edward Ward *international investment consultant, lawyer, actor*
Franklin, John Hope *historian, writer*
Franklin, Margery Bodansky *psychology professor, researcher*
Franklin, Michael Harold *arbitrator, lawyer, consultant*
Franklin, William Price *information technology manager*
Frankowiak, James Raymond *public relations executive*
Franks, Robert D. (Bob Franks) *former congressman*
Franks, Tommy Ray *retired military officer*
Frankson-Kendrick, Sarah Jane *publisher*
Frankston, Robert M. *computer software executive, developer*
Frantz, Ray William, Jr. *retired librarian*
Franz, Elizabeth *actress*
Franz, John E. *bio-organic chemist, researcher*
Franz, Judy R. *physics professor*
Frasca, Gabriel *chef*
Fraser, Donald MacKay *retired mayor, congressman*
Frasier, Ralph Kennedy *lawyer, bank executive*
Fratello, Mike (Michael Robert Fratello) *former professional basketball coach*
Frazier, Eloise M. *minister*
Frazier, Henry Bowen III *retired federal agency administrator*
Frears, Stephen *film director*
Fredeman, Betty Coley (Betty Coley) *retired librarian, editor*
Frederick, Elizabeth Eleanor Tatum *watercolor artist, retired educator*
Frederick, John *retired actor, writer*
Frederick, Virginia Fiester *state legislator*
Frederick-Mairs, T(hyra) Julie *administrative health services official*
Frederickson, Christine Magnuson *reporter, researcher, editor, writer*
Freed, Eva Praeger *investment advisor*
Freed, Michael J. *lawyer*
Freed, Richard (Donald) *music critic*
Freedman, Aaron David *retired medicine and biochemistry educator, dean*
Freedman, Joseph *retired sanitary and public health engineering consultant*
Freedman, Russell Bruce *author*
Freeh, Louis Joseph *lawyer, former FBI director*
Freeland, Richard Middleton *former academic administrator, historian*
Freeman, Charles E. *state supreme court justice*
Freeman, Herbert *retired computer engineering educator*
Freeman, John Arthur *theater educator*
Freeman, Morgan *actor*
Freeman, Theodore Monroe *physician*
Frei, Brent R. *computer software executive*
Freilicher, Jane *artist*
Freiman, Charles Visvald *retired engineering foundation administrator*
French, Arthur (Arthur Wellesley French Jr.) *actor, theater director*
French, Clarence Levi, Jr. *retired shipbuilding company executive*
French, Julia McAllister (Judy) *environmental consultant*
French, Laurence Armand *social sciences educator*
French, Marilyn *writer, critic, historian*
French, Mary B. *editor, photographer, poet, retired literature educator*
French, Roderick Stuart *university chancellor*
French, Stephanie Taylor *grantmaking and philanthropy expert*
Frenzel, Frances Johnson *nurse, educator, real estate broker, poet*
Freston, Tom (Thomas E. Freston) *former broadcast executive*
Frey, Charles Frederick *surgeon, educator*
Frey, Glenn *songwriter, vocalist, guitarist*
Freyermuth, Virginia Karen *art educator*
Fri, Robert Wheeler *retired museum director*
Frick, David Rhoads *lawyer, retired insurance company executive*
Frick, Ivan Eugene *retired academic administrator, educational consultant*
Friday, Elbert Walter, Jr. *federal agency administrator, meteorologist*
Friday, Katherine Orwoll *artist*
Fridley-Hereford, Vivian Suzanne *secondary school educator*
Fried, Charles *law educator*
Friedensohn, Henry *retired physician*
Friedlander, Charles Douglas (Chuck Friedlander) *aerospace scientist, consultant*
Friedlander, Lee N. *photographer*
Friedman, Howard W. *retired real estate company executive*
Friedman, James Winstein *economist, educator*
Friedman, Jared *realtor*
Friedman, Joan M. *retired accountant, educator*
Friedman, Kenni *health facility administrator, councilman*
Friedman, Kent Parks *nuclear medicine physician, educator*
Friedman, Martin *museum director, arts adviser*
Friedman, Mildred *architecture educator, design educator, curator*
Friedman, Miles *trade association and financial services company executive, university lecturer*
Friedman, Paul Richard *lawyer*
Friedman, Tully Michael *finance company executive*
Friedmann, Theodore *physician*
Frieling, Gerald Harvey, Jr. *specialty steel company executive*
Friend, William Benedict *bishop*
Frisbee, Don Calvin *retired utilities executive*
Frisby, Herbert Russell *lawyer*
Frisch, Sidney, Jr. *lawyer, real estate and insurance broker*
Frisco, Louis Joseph *retired electronics executive, electrical engineer*
Friskey, Edwin Robert, Jr. *former military specialist*
Frist, Bill (William Harrison Frist) *retired senator, thoracic surgeon*
Fristoe, Macalyne *speech pathology/audiology services professional, psychologist, educator, writer*
Fritz, Rene Eugene, Jr. *manufacturing executive*
Froberg, Brent Malcolm *classics educator*
Fromm, Joseph *retired editor, foreign correspondent, foreign affairs consultant*
Fross, Roger Raymond *lawyer*
Frost, Ellen Louise *political economist*
Frost, Rita Kenton *special education and education educator*
Frost, Sue Emmons *art educator*
Frowner, Byron *retired electrical engineer, researcher*
Frudakis, Zenos Antonios *sculptor, artist*
Frue, William Calhoun *lawyer*
Fry, Hedy *Member of Parliament*
Frye, Channing *professional basketball player*
Fryer, Thomas Waitt, Jr. *writer*
Frymer, Murry *writer, film and theater critic*
Fu, Yan Cindy *psychologist*
Fudge, Ann Marie *former advertising executive*
Fuentes, Beatriz Pastor *language educator, department chairman*
Fuentes, Carlos *writer, retired ambassador*
Fuerstner, Fiona Margaret Anne *ballet company executive, educator*
Fugate-Wilcox, Tery *artist*
Fugett, Roberta Lynn *special education educator*
Fuke, Dawn C. *clinical pharmacy specialist*
Fukuda, Atsuo *physicist, materials science researcher, educator*
Fukuda, Keiji *epidemiologist*
Fuller, Cynthia L. *biologist, researcher*
Fuller, David Randall *retired music educator*
Fuller, Jack William *writer, retired publishing executive*
Fuller, Kathryn Scott *former environmental services administrator*
Fuller, Maxine Compton *retired secondary school educator*
Fuller, Millard Dean *foundation administrator, lawyer*
Fuller, Robert Ferrey *retired lawyer, investor*
Fuller, Samuel Ashby *retired lawyer, mining executive*
Fuller, Sandra Vivian *oil and gas industry executive*
Fulmer, Vincent Anthony *retired college president*
Fulton, Amy Lou *artist, former realtor*
Fulton, Conchetta White *pharmacist, educator*
Fulton, William *mathematics professor*
Funk, Edith Kay *retired minister, psychotherapist, social worker*
Funseth, Robert Lloyd Eric Martin *international consultant, retired diplomat*
Furlong, George Morgan, Jr. *museum program director, retired military officer*
Furlotti, Alexander Amato *real estate company executive, investment company executive*
Furman, Howard *arbitrator, lawyer, mediator*
Furnas, David William *plastic surgeon, educator*
Furst, E. Kenneth *accountant*
Furth, Karen J. *artist*
Futrell, Steven *psychologist*
Gabel, Connie *chemist, educator*
Gabel, Katherine *retired academic administrator*
Gabel, Ronald Glen *telecommunications executive*
Gaber, Robert *psychologist*
Gaberman, Harry *retired lawyer*
Gable, Carl Irwin *writer, investor, retired lawyer*
Gable, Karen Elaine *retired healthcare educator*
Gabor-Hotchkiss, Magda *research scientist, librarian*
Gabriel, Jeanette Hanisee *curator, art historian*
Gabriel, Judith A. *bodywork therapist, educator, writer*
Gaddis, John Lewis *history professor*
Gaddy, Sidney Warren *government agency administrator*
Gadiesh, Orit *management consulting executive*
Gadomski, Robert Eugene *consulting and retired gas industry executive*
Gadsden, James Irvin *ambassador*
Gaffin, David Morris *meteorologist, researcher*
Gaffney, Thomas *retired banker*
Gage, Patrick (Leonard Patrick Gage) *biotechnology & pharmaceutical industry consultant*
Gagnon, Robert *application developer*
Gahagan, Thomas Gail *obstetrician, gynecologist*
Gaiber, Lawrence Jay *financial company executive*
Gaillard, George Siday III *architect*
Gaines, Boyd *actor*
Gaines, Brenda J. *retired financial services company executive*
Gainey, Lilah Leigh *librarian*
Gainor, Thomas Edward *bank executive*
Gajl-Peczalska, Kazimiera J. *retired surgeon, pathologist, educator*
Galagan, Carol Anne *special education educator*
Galante, Jane Hohfeld *musician, historian*
Galbraith, William Bruce *internist, educator*
Galda, Dwight William *finance company executive*
Gale, Stanley William *psychiatrist*
Galiardo, Christopher James Francis *language educator, political organization worker*
Gall, Mary Sheila *former federal agency administrator*
Gallagher, Edward Peter *foundation executive*
Gallagher, Michael Robert *retired consumer products company executive*
Gallaher, Frederick Blake *emergency mgmt. specialist*
Gallant, Stephen Laurie *librarian*
Gallops, R. Wayne *music educator*
Galloway, Eilene Marie *space and astronautics consultant*
Gallucci-Breithaupt, Adrianne *psychologist, social worker*
Galvin, Anthony J. *auditor*
Galvin, Matthew Reppert *psychiatry educator*
Galvis, Camilo Andres *real estate company executive, researcher*
Gamache, Claudette Theresa *artist, nurse*
Gamble, Desirata *artist, poet*
Gamble, E. James *lawyer, accountant*
Gamble, Vanessa Northington *historian, healthcare educator, bioethicist*
Gambrell, Luck Flanders *corporate financial executive*
Gamer, Carlton Edwin *composer, music educator*
Gammon, Samuel Rhea III *retired association executive, former ambassador*
Gamroth, Arthur Paul *small business owner*
Gan, Chenny Quan *musician, educator, artist*
Gan, Juis *interior designer*
Gandhi, Sandip R. *pharmacist*
Gandhi, Shaan-Chirag C. *biochemistry and chemistry scholar*
Gandolf, Raymond L. *media correspondent*
Gangopadhyay, Arup *research scientist*
Ganguly, Ananda Roop *business management educator*
Ganske, J. Greg *former congressman, plastic surgeon*
Gantz, Carroll Melvin *industrial design consultant, consumer product designer*
Ganz, Lowell *scriptwriter, television producer*
Garber, Aaron Matthew *performing company executive, music director*
Garber, Helen Kolikow *photographer, artist*
Garber, Victor *stage and film actor*
Garcia, Humberto Sigifredo *former prosecutor, lawyer*
Garcia, Jorge *actor*
Garcia, Julia Theresa *secondary school educator*
Garcia, Luis F. *photographer*
Garcia-Granados, Sergio Eduardo *portfolio manager, writer, historian*
Garcia y Carrillo, Martha Xochitl *pharmacist*
Gardiner, Hobart Clive *petroleum company executive*
Gardiner, Lester Raymond, Jr. *retired lawyer*
Gardner, Elizabeth Ann Hunt *artist, poet, genealogist*
Gardner, Emerson N., Jr. *military officer*
Gardner, John Howland III *neurologist*
Gardner, Wilford Robert *physicist, researcher*
Gardom, Garde Basil *former lieutenant governor of British Columbia*
Gareau, Jean L. *application technology executive*
Garfield, Robert Edward *journalist*
Garfield-Woodbridge, Nancy *writer*
Garfinkle, Elaine Myra *writer*
Gariepy, Carole Jane *writer, retired elementary school educator*
Garland, Elsie M. *counselor*
Garland, James C. *retired academic administrator*
Garman, David Kline *former federal agency administrator*
Garmany, Catharine Doremus *astronomer*
Garner, Algean, II, *healthcare company administrator, consultant*
Garner, Carlene Ann *not-for-profit fundraiser, consultant*
Garner, Jay Montgomery *retired military officer*
Garner, Jennifer Anne *actress*
Garniss, Joan Brewster *musician, educator*
Garrett, Brad *actor, comedian*
Garrett, Marshall Lee *anesthesiologist, educator*
Garriott, Owen Kay *astronaut, scientist*
Garrison, Robert Frederick *astronomer, educator*
Garrison, William Lloyd *retired cemetery executive, social worker*
Garruto, John Anthony *cosmetics executive*
Garruto, Ralph Michael *biomedical anthropologist, biologist, educator*
Gartenberg, Seymour Lee *retired recording industry executive*
Gartner, Lawrence Mitchell *pediatrician, medical educator*
Gartner, Mike (Michael Alfred Gartner) *former sports association administrator, retired professional hockey player*
Garwin, Richard Lawrence *physicist*
Gary, Marc *lawyer, former telecommunications industry executive*
Garypie, Rudolph Renwick *retired library director*
Garza, Cutberto *nutrition educator*
Gasper, Jo Ann *social services administrator, consultant*
Gasper, Ruth Eileen *real estate executive*
Gasser, Michael J. *consumer products company executive*
Gatch, Milton McCormick, Jr. *library director, clergyman, educator*
Gatewood, Willard Badgett, Jr. *retired historian, writer*
Gathright, John Byron, Jr. *colon and rectal surgeon, educator*
Gatlin, Justin *Olympic track and field athlete*
Gatria, America I *retired writer*
Gaudio, Bob *composer, musician*
Gaudio, Maxine Diane *biofeedback therapist, stress management consultant*

Gaulke, Mary Florence *retired library administrator*
Gaunt, Janet Lois *arbitrator, mediator*
Gauss, John A. *former federal agency administrator, retired naval officer*
Gaustad, Edwin Scott *historian, educator*
Gavin, Donald Glenn *lawyer, educator*
Gavin, Maria *television producer, writer*
Gavin, Mary Jane *retired medical/surgical nurse*
Gavril, Jean (Jean Van Leeuwen) *writer*
Gay, William Ingalls *veterinarian, retired health science association administrator*
Gayles, Joseph Nathan, Jr. *fundraiser, chemist*
Gaylin, Willard *physician, educator*
Gaynes, Thomas Edward, Jr. *retired judge, lawyer, educator, mediator*
Geake, Raymond Robert *psychologist*
Geary, Stephen R. *engineer, educator, engineering executive*
Gebauer, Kurt Manfred *management executive*
Gebelein, Richard Stephen *judge, former state attorney general*
Gechtoff, Sonia *artist*
Geddes, Robert *architect, educator*
Gee, Robert Neil *law librarian*
Geha, Alexander Salim *cardiothoracic surgeon, educator*
Gehring, Frederick William *mathematician, educator*
Geiger, Beth C. *freelance/self-employed journalist*
Geisel, Harold Walter *diplomat*
Geisler, Thomas Milton, Jr. *law educator, lawyer*
Geissinger, Frederick Wallace *finance company executive*
Geistfeld, Ronald Elwood *retired dental educator*
Geithner, Paul Herman, Jr. *retired banker*
Gelber, Robert Cary *law librarian*
Gelberg, Lillian *family medicine physician, educator*
Gelboin, Harry Victor *biochemistry educator, researcher*
Gellar, Sarah Michelle *actress*
Geller, Glenn *broadcast executive*
Geltzer, Sheila Simon *public relations executive*
Gemignani, Michael Caesar *clergyman, retired mathematics professor*
Genaro, Donald Michael *industrial designer*
Gendell, Gerald Stanleigh *retired public relations executive*
Gendron, George *magazine editor*
Genesoni, Jacqueline *mathematics educator*
Genét, Barbara Ann *accountant, travel company executive*
Gengler, Richelle Ruth *musician, educator*
Genia, James Michael *lawyer*
Genieser, Nancy Branom *radiologist*
Genis, Sean A. *philosophy, politics and economics scholar*
Genkins, Gabriel *physician*
Gens, Ralph Samuel *electrical engineering consultant*
Genser, Jared Matthew *lawyer*
Gentilcore, Eileen Marie Belsito *principal*
Gentry, Donald William *engineering executive, mining engineer*
George, Alfred L., Jr. *medical educator, researcher*
George, Donald *opera and concert singer*
George, Gay *lawyer*
George, Gerald William *writer*
George, Jennifer M. *management professor, psychology professor*
George, Joey Russell *lawyer*
George, Kiranraj *electrical engineer, researcher*
Geraghty, Elizabeth *food products executive*
Geraghty, James D. *health science association administrator*
Gerald, Michael Charles *pharmacy educator, dean*
Gerard, Gary *neurologist*
Gerard, Roy Dupuy *retired oil company executive*
Gerber, Milo Phil *urologist*
Gerber, Murry S. *gas, oil and utilities executive*
Gere, James Monroe *civil engineering educator*
Gere, Richard *actor*
Gerges, Rafik Refaat Wessa *structural engineer*
Gerhardt, Carol *artist*
Gerlach, Jeanne Elaine *English language educator*
Germolus, Penny Lynn *music educator*
Gerou, Phillip Howard *architect*
Gerras, Stephen Joseph *military officer, psychologist*
Gerritsen, Mary Ellen *vascular and cell biologist*
Gerry, Debra Prue *psychotherapist, recording artist, writer*
Gerson, Donald Jerome *computer scientist, consultant, photographer, small business owner*
Gerson, Elliot Francis *foundation administrator*
Gerstein, Mordicai *illustrator, writer*
Gerstner, Jonathan Neil *religious studies educator*
Gerstner, Mary Jane *nurse*
Gerwin, Leslie Ellen *lawyer, consultant, public relations executive*
Geschke, Charles M. *computer company executive*
Gessaman, Margaret Palmer *mathematician, educator, retired dean*
Gettleman, Marvin E. *retired history professor*
Gettner, Alan Frederick *retired lawyer*
Getty, Balthazar *actor*
Getty, Estelle (Estelle Scher) *actress*
Getzendanner, Susan *lawyer*
Gewitz, Michael Harold *pediatric cardiologist*
Gharabawi Garibaldi, George Milad *psychiatrist, neuroscientist*
Ghausi, Mohammed Shuaib *retired dean, electrical engineer, educator*
Ghavamian, Taghi *orthopedist, surgeon*
Ghebrhiwet, Freweiny Wendy *real estate broker, consultant*
Gherardi, Gherardo Joseph *pathologist*
Ghesquière, Nicolas *apparel designer*
Ghogawala, Zoher *neurosurgeon*
Ghovanloo, Maysam *engineer, educator*
Giacchino, Michael *composer*
Giaccio, Anthony *lawyer*
Giampietro, Wayne Bruce *lawyer*
Gianturco, Delio Emanuele *management consultant, educator, author*
Gibb, Ginari Rene *psychiatrist*
Gibb, Roberta Louise *lawyer, artist*
Gibbons, Sam Melville *retired congressman, government agency administrator*
Gibbs, David Richard *musician, journalist, photographer, writer*
Gibbs, Frederick Winfield *lawyer, communications executive*
Gibbs, Leonard (Doc Gibbs) *musician*
Giberson, Joan Alyne *retired school nurse practitioner*
Giblin, Patrick David *retired bank executive*
Gibran, Kahlil *sculptor*
Gibson, Ben S. *art educator*
Gibson, Lisette L. *elementary school and music educator*
Gibson, Mel *actor, film director and producer*
Gibson, Milton Eugene *cardiologist*
Gibson, Pamela Hemenway *elementary school educator*
Gibson, Robert Lee *astronaut*
Gibson, William Willard, Jr. *law educator*
Giebel, Miriam Catherine *librarian, genealogist*
Giesey, Ralph Edwin *retired historian*
Gieszl, Louis Roger *mathematician*
Gifford, John Irving *retired agricultural equipment company executive*
Gifford, Marjorie Fitting *mathematician, educator, consultant*
Gift, James Joseph *aquatic toxicologist*
Gilbert, Charles D. *neurobiologist*
Gilbert, Elayne Rhoda *writer*
Gilbert, Frederick E. *development planner, Africanist, consultant*
Gilbert, Harriette Gurley *retired music educator*
Gilbert, Jack *poet*
Gilbert, Melissa *former actors guild executive, actress*
Gilbert, Ronald Rhea *lawyer*
Gilbert, Stanley Dean *history educator*
Gilchrest, Thornton Charles *retired association executive*
Gilchrist, Gerald Seymour *pediatric hematologist, oncologist, educator*
Gile, Carole S. *retired education educator*
Giles, William Elmer *editor*
Gill, Henry Herr *photojournalist*
Gill, Thomas James III *pathologist, educator*
Gillespie, Gary Don *physician*
Gillespie, Gerald Ernest Paul *comparative literature educator, writer*
Gillett, James Warren *retired ecotoxicology educator*
Gillett, Mary Caperton *military historian*
Gilliam, Terry Vance *film director, actor, writer, illustrator*
Gilliar, Beate C. *educator*
Gillice, Sondra Jupin *sales and marketing executive*
Gilliland, Richard *actor*
Gilmartin, Geoffrey Scott *physician, researcher*
Gilmore, Kathi *former state treasurer*
Gilmore, Marshall *bishop*
Gilroy, Frank Daniel *playwright*
Gimenes, Sonia Regina Rosendo *family therapist, psychologist*
Ginley, Thomas H., Jr. *urologist*
Ginsberg, Ernest *lawyer, banker*
Ginsburg, Lynn *writer*
Ginsburg, Norton Sydney *retired geographer*
Giocomo, Lisa *research scientist*
Giovinazzo, Vivian Curry *writer*
Gipstein, Milton Fivenson *lawyer, psychiatrist, health facility administrator*
Girgis, Michael M. *physician*
Girouard, Marvin J. *retired retail executive*
Gist, John Montfort *publishing executive, educator*
Gist, William Claude, Jr. *retired dentist*
Gitelson, Susan Aurelia *corporate executive, philanthropist*
Gitner, Gerald L. *air transportation executive, investment banker*
Giuliani, Judith Ann *not-for-profit executive*
Giuliano, Neil Gerard *civil rights organization executive, former mayor*
Giusti, Joseph Paul *retired academic administrator, consultant*
Givenchy, Hubert James Marcel Taffin de *fashion designer*
Givens, Robin *actress*
Glacel, Barbara Pate *management consultant*
Gladden, Joseph Rhea, Jr. *lawyer*
Gladden, Vivianne Cervantes *healthcare consultant, writer*
Glantz, Lawrence G. *special education and social studies educator*
Glasberg, Laurence Brian *investment company executive*
Glaser, Patricia L. *lawyer*
Glaser, Peter Edward *retired mechanical engineer, consultant, educator*
Glaser, Robert Joy *retired internist, foundation administrator*
Glashow, Sheldon Lee *physicist, researcher*
Glass, Dorothea Daniels *physiatrist, educator*
Glass, Ira *radio producer, radio personality*
Glass, Kenneth Edward *management consultant*
Glass, Noah N. *entrepreneur*
Glass, William Robert *history professor*
Glasser, Ira Saul *former civil liberties organization administrator*
Glassheim, Jeffrey Wayne *allergist, immunologist, pediatrician*
Glassick, Charles Etzweiler *foundation administrator*
Glasson, Lloyd *sculptor, educator*
Glatter, Rebecca Jan *secondary school educator*
Glaze, Lynn Ferguson *pre-school administrator*
Glazer, Robert Boyd *musician, educator*
Gleaves, Leon Rogers *marketing and sales executive*
Gleijeses, Mario *holding company executive*
Glen, Niki *artist, sculptor*
Glendening, Terry Sky *psychologist*
Glenister, Brian Frederick *geologist, educator*
Glenn, Chance Michael *engineering educator, researcher, singer, writer*
Glenn, Constance White *art museum director, educator, consultant*
Glenn, James Francis *urologist, educator*
Glenn, Morton Bernard *retired internist*
Glenn, Norval Dwight *sociologist, educator*
Glenn, Roland Douglas *chemical engineer*
Glennon, Charles Edward *retired judge, lawyer*
Gletherow, Jamie *computer scientist*
Glick, J. Leslie *entrepreneur*
Glick, Ruth Burtnick *literature educator, writer*
Glindeman, Henry Peter, Jr. *real estate developer*
Glismann, Clementine *retired elementary school educator*
Glosser, Jeffrey Mark *lawyer*
Glover, Crispin Hellion *actor*
Glover, David Lloyd *artist*
Glover, James Todd *manufacturing executive*
Glover, Melvin (Melle Mel, Grandmaster Melle Mel) *rap artist*
Glück, Louise Elisabeth *poet, educator*
Gluckstern, Robert Leonard *physics professor*
Gluys, Charles Byron *retired marketing management consultant*
Glynn, Carlin (Carlin Masterson) *actress*
Glynn, Edward *retired academic administrator*
Glynn, Kevin Peltier *pulmonologist*
Glysch, Randall Lee *research scientist*
Goach, Kenneth Edmund *professional counselor*
Gobel, John Henry *lawyer*
Goble, Paul *writer, illustrator, artist*
Godager, Jane Ann *retired social worker*
Goddard, Claude Philip, Jr. *lawyer*
Goddess, Lynn Barbara *real estate investor*
Godfrey, Norman V. *plastic surgeon*
Godhardt, Karen *information technology executive*
Godin, Seth Warren *video production executive, writer, entrepreneur, blog website writer*
Godinez, Joshua Ray *social sciences educator*
Godwin, Pamela June *financial services executive*
Godwin, Ralph Lee, Jr. *real estate executive*
Goebel, William Horn *lawyer*
Goel, Karan *entrepreneur*
Goeltz, Richard Karl *finance company executive*
Goen, Bob *television show host*
Goerz, Mary Elizabeth Larsen *civic worker*
Goff, Renee Rosenstock *gifted and talented educator*
Goffman, Thomas Edward *radiation oncologist*
Goforth, Jill Hastings *principal*
Gogbashian, Andrew *surgeon, researcher*
Goines, Leonard *music educator, consultant*
Gold, Harold Arthur *lawyer*
Gold, Judith Hammerling *psychiatrist*
Gold, Leonard Singer *librarian, translator, curator*
Goldberg, David Alan *investment banker, lawyer*
Goldberg, Edwin *rehabilitation specialist, interfaith clergyman*
Goldberg, Lee Dresden *endocrinologist, educator*
Goldberg, Lee Winicki *furniture company executive*
Goldberg, Lois D. *health facility administrator, disability analyst*
Goldberg, Lucianne *literary agent*
Goldberg, Mark Arthur *neurologist*
Goldberg, Martin *internist, educator*
Goldberg, Michael Ellis *neurologist, neuroscientist*
Goldberg, Samuel *retired mathematician, foundation administrator*
Goldberg, Victor Joel *retired data processing company executive*
Goldberg, Whoopi (Caryn Elaine Johnson) *actress, comedienne*
Goldberger, Arthur Earl, Jr. *information technology executive*
Goldberger, George Stefan *finance company executive*
Goldblum, Jeff *actor*
Golden, Bryan *management consultant, writer*
Golden, Charles Edward *retired pharmaceutical company executive*
Golden, David Edward *physicist*
Golden, Gerald Samuel *retired national medical board executive*
Golden, Hal *artist, consultant*
Golden, Joseph Aaron *lawyer*
Golden, Judith Greene *artist, educator*
Golden, Louis Joseph *retired editor, publishing executive*
Golden, Olivia Ann *state official, human services administrator*
Golden, Sheila S. *retired special education educator*
Goldenberg, Kim *retired academic administrator, internist, consultant*
Goldfarb, Muriel Bernice *marketing and advertising consultant*
Goldfarb, Ruth *poet, educator*
Goldin, Leon *artist*
Golding, Carolyn May *former government senior executive, consultant*
Goldman, Alan Ira *brokerage house executive*
Goldman, Alvin Ira *philosopher, educator*
Goldman, Judith *writer, editor, curator, consultant, publisher*
Goldman, William *writer, scriptwriter*
Goldmann, Morton Aaron *cardiologist, educator*
Goldner, Sheldon Herbert *retired import/export company executive*
Goldsborough, Robert Gerald *publishing executive, author*
Goldschmidt, Lynn Harvey *lawyer*
Goldsmith, Jeff Charles *management consultant*
Goldsmith, Willis Jay *lawyer*
Goldspiel, Arnold Nelson *real estate executive*
Goldstein, Alfred George *consumer products company executive*
Goldstein, Avram *pharmacology educator*
Goldstein, Bernard *transportation and hotel executive*
Goldstein, Burton Jack *psychiatrist*
Goldstein, Debra Holly *judge*
Goldstein, Dora Benedict *pharmacologist, educator*
Goldstein, Irving Solomon *chemistry professor, consultant*
Goldstein, Jerome Arthur *mathematics professor*
Goldstein, Leonard Barry *dentist*
Goldstein, Michael I. *ecologist*
Goldstein, Norman Ray *international trading company executive, consultant*
Goldstein, Tamara Beth *musician*
Goldstein, Walter Elliott *biotechnology executive*
Goldston, Stephen Eugene *community psychologist, educator, consultant*
Goldthwait, Christopher E. *ambassador*
Goleman, Daniel Jay *psychologist, journalist*
Golston, Allan C. *foundation administrator*
Golub, Sharon Bramson *retired psychologist, educator*
Gomez, Jaime Luis (Taboo) *rap artist*
Gomez, Melissa Mordell *trial consultant*
Goncharov, Viktor *biochemist, researcher*
Gonder, Daryl William *art and literature educator*
Gonnering, Russell Stephen *ophthalmic plastic surgeon*
Gonsalves, Philip *music educator*
Gonzales, Alberto R. *former United States attorney general, former state supreme court justice*
Gonzales, Ernesto Luis B. *bank executive*
Gonzales, Richard Robert *counselor*
Gonzales, Ron *mayor, former county supervisor*
Gonzalez, Fredi *professional baseball manager*
Gonzalez, Gabriela *history professor*
Gonzalez, Gabriela Ines *physics professor*
Gonzalez, Karen Eileen *middle school educator*
Gonzalez, Richard *maritime safety officer*
Gonzalez, Rose Marie Juarez *retired education executive*
Gonzalez-del-Valle, Luis Tomas *Spanish language educator*
Good, Walter Raymond *investment company executive*
Goodall, Jane *zoologist*
Goode, Stephen Hogue *publishing executive*
Goodenow, Robert W. *lawyer, former sports association administrator*
Goodfellow, Robin Irene *surgeon*
Goodkin, Michael Jon *publishing company executive*
Goodling, Monica Maria *former federal official*
Goodman, Bennett J. *hedge fund executive*
Goodman, Charles David *physicist, researcher*
Goodman, Cynthia Diane *public health physician*
Goodman, Elizabeth Ann *retired lawyer*
Goodman, Frederick Denis *retired environmental scientist*
Goodman, Robert Mark *dean, educator*
Goodnough, Robert Arthur *artist*
Goodrich, Kenneth Paul *retired dean*
Goodsell, Charles True *public administration educator, researcher*
Goodwin, Andrew Wirt, II, *radiologist*
Goodwin, Irwin *journalist, writer*
Goodwin, Robert Keer *foundation administrator*
Gootee, Jane Marie *lawyer*
Gopalakrishnan, Kasthurirangan *civil engineer, research scientist*
Gora, Susannah Porter Martin *journalist, poet*
Gorbaty, Martin Leo *chemist, researcher*
Gorbaty, Norman *graphics designer, artist*
Gorden, David Lee *surgeon, educator*
Gordis, David Moses *academic administrator, rabbi*
Gordon, David Zevi *retired lawyer*
Gordon, Ezra *architect, educator*
Gordon, Leonard H(erman) D(avid) *history educator*
Gordon, Lonny Joseph *artist, educator, dean*
Gordon, Marjorie *lyric-coloratura soprano, music educator, opera producer*
Gordon, Sharon Ann *mathematics and pre-school educator*
Gordon, William Edwin *physicist, educator, electrical engineer, academic administrator*
Gore, Tushar *marketing professional*
Gorence, Patricia Josetta *judge*
Goreniuc, Mircea C. Paul *sculptor*
Gorham, Robin Wilson *biology professor*
Gorman, Charlotte A. *business executive*
Gorman, Michael Joseph *retired library director, educator*
Gornick, Loni Erin *music educator*
Gorny, Jacob Aaron *religious organization administrator, researcher*
Gorske, Robert H. *lawyer*
Gorski, Waldemar *chemist, educator*
Gorsline, Stephen Paul *security specialist*
Gorsuch, Edward Lee *former chancellor*
Gorton-Horan, Ann Hilbert *vice principal*
Gosavi, Sucheta *internist*
Goss, Jerome Eldon *craftsman, retired cardiologist*
Goss, Joel Francis *writer*
Goss, Porter Johnston *former CIA director, former congressman*
Gossard, Marcia Nadine *writer*
Gotman, John Andrew *freelance/self-employed journalist*
Gottfried, Eugene Leslie *physician, educator*
Gottlieb, Alan Merril *advertising, fundraising and broadcasting executive, writer*
Gottlieb, Gary L. *hospital administrator*
Gottlieb, Lynn *engineer*
Gottlieb, Robert Adams *editor, dance critic, writer*
Gottschalk, Charles M. *international energy consultant*
Gougar, Hans David *nuclear engineer, director*
Gould, Howard Richard *retired physician*

Gould, Martha Bernice *retired librarian*
Goulet, Charles Ryan *retired insurance company executive*
Goulet, Lorrie *sculptor*
Gourley, Sara J. *lawyer*
Gourvitz, Elliot Howard *lawyer*
Gouse, S. William, Jr. *mechanical engineering executive, researcher*
Gouw, Julia Suryapranata *bank executive*
Govan, Gladys Vernita Mosley *retired critical care nurse, medical/surgical nurse*
Govindjee, *biophysics, biochemistry, and biology professor*
Gowans, Sir James Learmonth *science administrator, immunologist*
Goyol, Apollos Bitrus *education educator*
Gozon, Richard C. *retired paper distribution executive*
Grab, Frederick Charles *lawyer*
Graber, Samuel David *environmental and water resources engineer, consultant*
Graber, William Raymond *former pharmaceutical executive*
Grabitske, David M. *historian*
Grabstald, Harry *urologist, oncologist*
Grace, Marcia Bell *advertising executive*
Grace, Topher *actor*
Grady, Lee Timothy *pharmaceutical chemist*
Grady, Sandra C. *minister, counselor*
Grady, Wayne Joseph *retired government official*
Graebner, James Herbert *transportation executive*
Grafton, Beth P. *music educator*
Graham, Bob (Daniel Robert Graham) *former senator, former governor*
Graham, David F. *lawyer*
Graham, David G. *preventive medicine physician, psychiatrist*
Graham, Garth N. *public health service officer, medical educator*
Graham, Howard Lee, Sr. *finance company executive*
Graham, James Herbert *retired dermatologist*
Graham, Jewel Freeman *social worker, lawyer, educator*
Graham, K(athleen) M. (K. M. Graham) *artist*
Graham, Lanier *art historian, curator*
Graham, Laurie *editor, writer*
Graham, Michael Haw *orthopedist*
Graham, Olive Jane *retired medical/surgical nurse*
Graham, Stuart Edward *construction company executive*
Graham, Susette Ryan *retired English educator*
Graham, Vicary M. *trust company executive*
Graham, Wallace Karl *chemicals executive*
Graham, William Henry *lawyer*
Gralla, Lawrence *publishing company executive*
Gralla, Milton *retired publisher*
Grames-Lyra, Judith Ellen *artist, educator, municipal official*
Granato, Catherine (Cammi Granato) *former olympic athlete, sports association executive*
Grandi, Attilio *engineering consultant*
Grandy, Walter Thomas, Jr. *physicist, researcher*
Granik, Russ (Russell T. Granik) *financial advisory firm executive, former sports association executive*
Grann, Phyllis E. *editor, former publisher executive*
Granott, Nira *psychologist, researcher*
Grant, Alexander Marshall *retired ballet director*
Grant, Brian Wade *professional basketball player*
Grant, Carmen Hill *psychologist, psychotherapist*
Grant, Daniel Gordon *information technology executive*
Grant, Isabella Horton *retired judge*
Grant, Leonard Tydings *clergyman*
Grant, Mark Antonio *organization administrator*
Grant, Merrill Theodore *television producer*
Grant, Richard Earl *retired medical and legal consultant*
Grant, Walter Matthews *retired lawyer*
Grantham, Joyce Carol *small business owner, music educator*
Grasso, Dick (Richard A. Grasso) *former stock exchange executive*
Graves, John William *state supreme court justice*
Graves, Lorraine Elizabeth *dancer, educator, coach*
Graves, Wallace Billingsley *retired university executive*
Graves, William Preston *former governor*
Gravitte, Debbie Shapiro (Lynn Shapiro) *singer, actress, dancer*
Gray, Amy Castle *lawyer*
Gray, Francine du Plessix *writer*
Gray, Gloria Meador *librarian*
Gray, Gordon L. *communications educator*
Gray, Hazel Irene *retired special education educator, counselor, consultant*
Gray, James N. *computer scientist*
Gray, Luke Alexander *artist*
Gray, Mary Jane *retired obstetrician, gynecologist*
Gray, Richard Alexander, Jr. *retired chemical company executive*
Gray, Richard Arden *retired transportation executive*
Gray, Richard Moss *retired college president*
Gray, Robert Ward *art association administrator*
Gray, Shawn Scott *social services administrator*
Gray, Thomas Stephen *writer*
Graziani, Leonard Joseph *pediatric neurologist, researcher*
Greaser, Constance Udean *communications executive, researcher*
Grebstein, Sheldon Norman *academic administrator*
Greco, Christopher Jon *musician, composer, educator*
Greco, Richard, Jr. *former civilian military employee*
Gredzens, Sandra May Pillsbury *art educator*
Greehey, William Eugene (Bill Greehey) *energy executive*
Greeley, Andrew Moran *sociologist, writer*
Green, Carol H. *lawyer, educator*
Green, Carole L. *lawyer*
Green, David *hematologist*
Green, Dennis E. *former professional football coach*
Green, Eva Gaelle *actress*
Green, Grant S., Jr. *former federal agency administrator*
Green, John *radio broadcast editor and author*
Green, Mark Andrew *former congressman*
Green, Morris *retired pediatrician, educator*
Green, Patricia Pataky *school system administrator, consultant*
Green, Richard C. *lawyer*
Greenberg, Albert *art director*
Greenberg, Carolyn Phyllis *retired anesthesiologist*
Greenberg, Gary Howard *lawyer*
Greenberg, Hinda Feige *library director*
Greenberg, Ira Arthur *psychologist*
Greenberg, Irving *rabbi*
Greenberg, Jack M. *former food products executive*
Greenberg, Maurice Raymond (Hank) *retired insurance company executive*
Greenberg, Morton Paul *lawyer, consultant, life settlement broker*
Greenberg, Ronald David *lawyer, educator*
Greenburg, Dan *author*
Greene, Alvin *management consultant*
Greene, Donald Richard *dermatologist, educator*
Greene, Frank Sullivan, Jr. *investment company executive*
Greene, Jerry George *retired physician*
Greene, Jo *school system administrator*
Greene, John Colton *retired historian*
Greene, John Joseph *lawyer*
Greene, Jule Blounte *lawyer*
Greene, Robert (Bob) Bernard, Jr. *news correspondent, journalist, writer*
Greene, Warner Craig *medical educator, administrator*
Greenebaum, Leonard Charles *retired lawyer*
Greenfield, Linda Sue *nursing educator*
Greenfield, Val Shea *ophthalmologist*
Greengrass, Paul *film director*
Greenslade, Thomas Boardman, Jr. *physics educator*
Greenspan, Alan *former Chairman of the Board of Governors of the Federal Reserve System, economist*
Greenstein, Merle Edward *import/export company executive*
Greenwald, Alice Marian *museum director*
Greenwald, John Edward *publishing executive, journalist*
Greenway, Joan M. *dean*
Greenwood, Jane *costume designer, educator*
Greenwood, Janet Kae Daly *psychologist, academic administrator, marketing professional*
Greenwood, William Warren *journalist*
Greer, Carl Crawford *petroleum company executive*
Greer, Germaine *author*
Greer, Jean Reese *music educator*
Greer, K. Gordon *banker*
Greer, Robert Bruce III *orthopedist, educator*
Greer, Suzanne Michelle *music educator*
Greetham, Elizabeth M. *former health products executive*
Greever, Margaret Quarles *retired mathematics educator*
Gregerson, Daniel P. *retired computer company executive*
Greggs, Elanora *social worker*
Gregor, Dorothy Deborah *retired librarian*
Gregory, Bettina Louise *retired journalist*
Gregory, Claire Distelhorst *television producer*
Gregory, David Steven *physician*
Gregory, Frederick Drew *federal agency administrator*
Gregory, James Alexander *editor, writer, film producer*
Gregory, Nelson Bruce *retired motel owner, naval officer*
Gregory, Peggy J. *music educator*
Gregory, Sara Susan (Sudie) *musician, singer, lyricist, poet, recording industry executive, sound recording engineer, archivist*
Greif, Joseph *lawyer*
Greiner, Nicole K. Hudak *physical education educator*
Grendell, James Henry *medical educator*
Grenier, Laura Margiotta *medical/surgical nurse*
Greuner, David A. *surgeon*
Grew, Raymond Edward *mechanical engineer*
Grey, Ruthann E. *corporate communications specialist, director*
Gribbon, Deborah *museum director*
Griego, Linda *entrepreneur*
Grier, David Alan *actor*
Griffin, Campbell Arthur, Jr. *retired lawyer*
Griffin, Carleton Hadlock *accountant, educator*
Griffin, James Anthony *bishop*
Griffin, Leann Creasy *science educator*
Griffin, Robert H. *career military officer*
Griffin, Tim (John Timothy Griffin) *former prosecutor*
Griffith, B(ezaleel) Herold *retired plastic surgeon, retired educator*
Griffith, Melanie *actress*
Griffith, Monica *psychologist*
Griffith, Rosita Denise *elementary school educator*
Griffiths, Phillip A. *mathematician, retired academic administrator*
Griffiths, Rachel *actress*
Griffiths, Yolanda W. *occupational therapist, educator*
Griggs, Joyce L. *secondary school educator*
Grim, Patricia Ann *retired banker*
Grimaldi, David *financial advisor*
Grimes, James Gordon *geologist*
Grinell, Sheila *museum director*
Griner, Paul Francis *physician*
Grinnell, Helen Dunn *musicologist, arts administrator*
Griswold, Frank Tracy III *retired bishop*
Grodsky, Jamie Anne *law educator*
Grody, Donald *actor, judge, lawyer*
Groenheim, Henri Arnold *psychologist, consultant*
Groetken, Troy Alan *lawyer, pharmacist*
Groh, Sebastien Stephane *materials scientist, researcher*
Grohl, David Eric *musician*
Grolli, Frank Thomas *retired pharmacist*
Gromacki, Susan Jean *optometrist*
Grooms, Henry Randall *retired civil engineer*
Grosbard, Ulu *film director*
Groskopf, Aubrey Bud *broadcast executive, lawyer*
Grosland, Emery Layton *retired banker*
Grosman, Alan M. *retired lawyer*
Gross, Geoffrey Fries *systems architect*
Gross, Laura Ann *marketing and communications professional, herbalist, acupuncturist*
Gross, Mark *lawyer, food products executive*
Gross, Pamela H. *editor*
Grossman, Carolyn Sylvia Cort *retired elementary school educator*
Grossman, Cissy *curator, art historian, appraiser*
Grossman, Edward Jerome *music educator, composer*
Grossman, Ginger Scheflin *advocate*
Grossman, Jonathan Lee *sports agent, law educator*
Grossman, Joyce Renee *pediatrician, internist*
Grosso, Doreen Elliott *management consultant*
Grosso, Sue Jane Rivas *radiologist*
Grothendieck, Alexandre *retired mathematician*
Grove, Richard Charles *retired power tool company executive*
Groves, Bernice Ann *retired elementary and secondary school coordinator, educator*
Growick, Philip *advertising executive*
Grubb, Donald Hartman *paper industry company executive*
Gruber, Ira Dempsey *historian, educator*
Grudzielanek, Mark James *professional baseball player*
Gruen, Margaret *actress*
Gruen, Shirley Schanen *artist*
Gruetzmacher, Nancy Lynn *retired middle schoool educator*
Grunder, Fred Irwin *retired industrial hygienist, consultant*
Grunder, Hermann A. *science administrator, director, research scientist*
Gruneich, Jeffrey Alan *biotechnologist, director*
Grunt, Jerome Alvin *retired pediatric endocrinologist*
Grupe, Scott M. *management consultant*
Grushow, Sandy *broadcast executive*
Grutman, Jewel Humphrey *lawyer, writer*
Gruver, William Rolfe (Bill Gruver) *finance educator, retired investment banker*
Guarascio, Philip *advertising executive*
Gubbins, Keith Edmund *chemical engineering educator*
Guber, Peter *executive producer*
Gubser, Peter Anton *political scientist, writer, educator*
Gudenberg, Harry Richard *arbitrator, mediator*
Gudmundsson, Finnbogi *library administrator*
Guerra, Alma Del Rosario *music educator*
Guerrero, Lisa (Lisa Guerrero-Coles) *former sports reporter*
Gugel, Craig Thomas *advertising executive*
Gui, James Edmund *architect*
Guild, Jeffrey K. *mathematics professor*
Guillama-Alvarez, Noel Jesus *merchant banker, healthcare executive*
Guilmartin, Eugenia Katherine *military officer*
Guinn, Kenny C. (Kenneth Carroll Guinn) *former governor*
Guinn, Theodore *retired mathematics professor, research scientist*
Guinther, Christine Louise *special education educator*
Gulay, Robert Roman *epidemiologist, educator*
Gulbrandsen, Patricia Hughes *physician*
Gulcher, Robert Harry *aerospace transportation executive*
Gulick, Sidney (Denny) L. III *mathematics professor, writer*
Gulledge, Sandra Smith *publishing executive, film producer*
Gulotta, Stephen J. *cardiologist*
Gumpert, Carolyn L. *secondary school educator*
Gund, Ann *art association administrator*
Gundelfinger, Benjamin Fremont *military officer*
Gundersheimer, Werner Leonard *library director*
Gunderson, Judith Keefer *golf association executive*
Gunderson, Ted Lee *security consultant*
Gundian, Julio Cesar *urologist*
Gunger, Richard William *lawyer*
Gunning, Carolyn Sue *dean, provost, nursing educator*
Gunsaulis, Linda C. *elementary school educator*
Gunter, William Dayle, Jr. *physicist, consultant*
Guo, Dongbai *application developer*
Guo, Mingruo *food scientist, educator*
Gupta, Kuldip Chand (KC) *retired electrical and computer engineering educator, researcher*
Gupta, Sanju *education educator, researcher*
Gupta, Yash *dean*
Gurian, Mal *telecommunications executive*
Gurstel, Norman Keith *lawyer*
Gurudu, Suryakanth R. *gastroenterologist, educator*
Gurvich, Victor Alexander *physicist, engineer*
Gurwitch, Arnold Andrew *communications executive*
Guskin, Alan E. *university president*
Guskov, Sergey *security firm executive*
Gussow, Sue Ferguson *artist, educator*
Gustafson, Craig Thomas *theater director, playwright, graphics designer*
Gustafson, Richard Alrick *retired university president*
Gustafsson, Lars Erik Einar *writer, educator*
Gutheinz, James O'Leary *military officer, law clerk*
Gutheinz, Jean *public relations executive*
Guthridge, Bill *university basketball coach*
Guthrie, Janet *professional race car driver*
Guthrie, Wallace Nessler, Jr. *naval officer*
Gutknecht, Gil (Gilbert William Gutknecht Jr) *former congressman, former state legislator*
Gutman, Richard Edward *lawyer*
Gutstein, Carol Feinhandler *realtor*
Guttau, Michael K. *state agency administrator, banker*
Guy, Eleanor Bryenton *retired writer*
Guymon, Gary LeRoy *civil engineering educator*
Guynn, Jack (George C. Guynn) *retired bank executive*
Guyon, John Carl *retired university administrator*
Gyemant, Robert Ernest *diversified financial services company executive, merchant banker*
Ha, Chong Wan *information technology executive*
Haaland, Gordon Arthur *retired academic administrator*
Haas, Aaron C. *sales executive*
Haas, Charlie *screenwriter*
Haas, Edward Lee *management consultant*
Haas, Frederick Carl *retired paper company executive, retired chemicals executive*
Haas, Howard Green *retired bedding manufacturing company executive*
Haas, Mark Richard *management consultant researcher*
Haas, Suzanne Alberta *elementary and secondary school educator*
Habeck, Christian Georg *medical educator*
Habeck, James Roy *judge*
Habecker, Eugene Brubaker *academic administrator*
Haber, Ann *biology professor, physiologist*
Haber, Geoffrey John *rabbi*
Haber, Pierre-Claude *psychologist*
Haber, Ralph Norman *psychology consultant, researcher, educator*
Haberman, Charles Morris *mechanical engineer, educator*
Habermann, Helen Margaret *botanist, educator*
Habicht, Frank Henry *retired manufacturing executive*
Hackel-Sims, Stella Bloomberg *lawyer, former government official*
Hackett, Robert John *lawyer*
Hackett, Wesley Phelps, Jr. *lawyer*
Hackleman, Phyllis Ann *artist, genealogist*
Hackney, Hugh Edward *lawyer*
Hackney, James Acra III *industrial engineer, consultant, retired manufacturing executive*
Hadda, Janet Ruth *language educator, lay psychoanalyst*
Haddad, Edmonde Alex *public affairs executive*
Haddady, Shirin *medical educator*
Haddock, Raymond Earl *retired career officer*
Haddock, Robert Lynn *information services entrepreneur, writer*
Haddy, Theresa Brey *pediatrician, educator, hematologist, oncologist*
Haden, Clovis Roland *retired academic administrator, engineering educator*
Hadl, John *marketing executive*
Hadley, Leila Eliott-Burton (Mrs. Henry Luce III) *writer*
Hadley, William Melvin *retired dean*
Haeske, Ron A. *financial analyst, singer*
Hafemeister, Beverly Rae *consumer products company executive*
Hafez, Mahmoud A. *orthopedic surgeon*
Haft, Gail Klein *pediatrician*
Haga, Kazunori *medical researcher*
Hagan, Joseph Henry *educational consultant*
Hagberg, Chris Eric *lawyer*
Hagel, John III *management consultant*
Hagel, Raymond Charles *publishing company executive, educator*
Hagelstein, Robert Philip *publisher*
Hageman, Richard Philip, Jr. *educational administrator*
Hagenlocker, Edward E. *retired automobile company executive*
Hagerman, Michael Charles *lawyer, arbitrator, mediator*
Haggerty, Robert Johns *pediatrician, educator*
Haggis, Paul Edward *scriptwriter, television producer, television director*
Hahn, Frank Horace *economics professor*
Hahn, Mary Downing *writer*
Haile, L. John, Jr. *journalist, publishing executive*
Hain, Pamela Chase *historian, writer*
Haines, David Harry *consulting executive*
Haines, Richard Foster *retired psychologist*
Haining, Jeane *psychologist*
Hairfield-Marrs, Judy L. *elementary school educator*
Haisch, Bernard Michael *astronomer, researcher*
Hait, Patrick David *elementary school music educator*
Hajek, Robert J., Sr. *lawyer, real estate broker*
Hakala, Karen Louise *retired real estate specialist*
Hake, Ralph F. *former appliance manufacturing executive*
Hakeem, Muhammad Abdul *artist, educator*
Hakim, Besim Selim *architecture and urban design educator, researcher, consultant, urban planner*
Hakim-Elahi, Enayat *obstetrician, gynecologist, educator*
Hakimoglu, Ayhan *electronics executive*
Halada, Richard Stephen *physics educator*
Halasyamani, P. Shiv *inorganic chemist, researcher*
Halasz, Stephen Joseph *retired electro-optical systems engineer*
Halberstam, Heini *mathematics professor*

Haldeman, Joe William *writer*
Hale, Nancy Annette Bills *kindergarten educator*
Hale, Wesley Raymond *research associate, chemical engineer, polymer scientist*
Haley, George Brock, Jr. *retired lawyer*
Haley, Jackie Earle *actor, film director*
Haley, Johnetta Randolph *music educator*
Halfen, David *retired publishing executive*
Halitsky, Steve *data analyst, statistician, researcher*
Hall, Adrienne A. *international marketing communications executive*
Hall, Charles Worth Leo *college administrator*
Hall, Christopher George Longden *academic administrator*
Hall, Donald *poet*
Hall, Donald Joyce, Jr. *consumer products company executive*
Hall, Gregory *composer, engineer*
Hall, Hansel Crimiel *communications executive*
Hall, James Evan *lawyer*
Hall, James Stanley *jazz guitarist, composer*
Hall, James William *university chancellor*
Hall, Jay *social psychologist*
Hall, John Fry *retired psychologist*
Hall, John Hopkins *retired lawyer*
Hall, Miles Lewis, Jr. *lawyer*
Hall, Milton Reese *retired oil company executive, accountant, controller*
Hall, Monty *television producer, actor*
Hall, Peggy Craft *poet, retired secondary school educator*
Hall, Richard Clyde, Jr. *retired religious educational administrator*
Hall, Robert L. *curator, educator*
Hall, Susan Laurel *artist, educator, writer*
Hall, Teresa Ruth *publishing executive*
Hall, Tom T. *retired country singer, songwriter*
Hall, Tony P. *former ambassador, retired congressman*
Hall, Zach Winter *former health science association administrator*
Halleck, Charles White *lawyer, photographer, former judge*
Haller, Jordan D. *cardiovascular surgeon*
Halliburton, Lloyd *retired Romance philology educator*
Halliday, William Ross *retired physician, speleologist, writer*
Hallman, Linda D. *medical association administrator*
Halmrast, Lynn James *psychologist*
Halperin, Jerome Arthur *retired pharmaceutical executive*
Halpern, Alvin Michael *retired physicist, educator, consultant*
Halpern, James Bladen *lawyer*
Halpin, Daniel William *engineering educator, consultant*
Halprin, Lawrence *landscape architect, urban planner*
Halverstadt, Robert Dale *mechanical engineer, metal products executive*
Ham, Sommy L. *publisher, writer*
Hambidge, Douglas Walter *archbishop*
Hamblen, Lapsley Walker, Jr. *retired judge*
Hamblin, Terry Robert, Jr. *historian, educator*
Hamecs, Francella Cheslock *elementary and secondary school educator*
Hamed, Martha Ellen *retired small business owner*
Hamel, Louis Reginald *retired systems analyst*
Hamel, Rodolphe *retired lawyer, pharmaceutical executive*
Hamelin, Marcel *historian, educator*
Hamil, Burnette Wolf *science educator*
Hamill, Pete (William Pete Hamill) *newspaper columnist, author, editor*
Hamilton, Charles Edward *information technology consultant, military officer*
Hamilton, Dagmar Strandberg *lawyer, retired educator*
Hamilton, David Eugene *minister, educator*
Hamilton, Jean *financial services executive, e-commerce and software executive*
Hamilton, Laird John *professional surfer*
Hamilton, Robert Woodruff *retired legal association administrator, educator*
Hamilton, Thomas Michael *marketing executive*
Hamilton, Virginia Van der Veer *historian, educator*
Hamit, Francis Granger *novelist, playwright*
Hamlen, Kevin William *computer scientist, educator*
Hamlin, Dan William *accountant, management consultant*
Hamlin, Sonya B. *communications specialist*
Hammam, M. Shawky *electrical engineer, educator*
Hammann, Gregg C. *fitness equipment executive*
Hammar, Sherrel Leyton *medical educator*
Hammer, Joyce Mae *retired gifted and talented educator*
Hammer, Wade Burke *retired oral and maxillofacial surgeon, educator*
Hammer, (Stanley Kirk Burrell) *musician*
Hammerschmidt, John Paul *retired congressman, lumber company executive*
Hammond, Ann P. *retired elementary. high school and college educator, poet*
Hammond, Caleb Dean III *publishing executive*
Hammond, Glenn Barry, Sr. *judge, electrical engineer*
Hammond, Graeme Lord *surgeon, educator*
Hammond, Harmony *artist, educator*
Hammond, Paul Young *political science professor*
Hammond, Robie Lee *health science association administrator*
Hampton, Lori Beth *psychologist*
Hancock, Artemus Ward, Sr. *music educator*
Hancock, Charles R. *education educator*
Hancock, Patricia Ann *artist*
Hand, Herbert Hensley *finance educator, writer, entrepreneur*
Hand, Maryanne Kelly *artist, educator*
Hand, Peter James *neurobiologist, educator*
Hand, Roger *physician, educator*
Handford, H. Allen *retired psychiatrist, medical educator*
Handler, Harold Robert *lawyer*
Hands, Eric William *civil engineer, researcher*
Handschu, Barbara Ellen *lawyer*
Handschumacher, Robert Edmund *biochemistry professor*
Handy, Edward Otis, Jr. *retired diversified financial services company executive*
Handy, Rollo Leroy *philosopher, researcher*
Hanford, George Hyde *retired educational association administrator*
Hangen, Terra *librarian, writer*
Hanket, Mark John *lawyer*
Hanks, Alan R. *retired chemistry professor*
Hanlon, Michael Gregory *lawyer*
Hanmer, Stephen Read, Jr. *retired federal official*
Hanna, Duke Ellsworth *retired neurological surgeon*
Hanna, Michael George, Jr. *immunologist, pharmaceutical executive*
Hanna, Noreen Anelda *adult education educator, consultant*
Hannaman, Alberta Anna *artist*
Hanneman, Rodney Elton *metallurgical engineer*
Hansell, John Royer *retired pathologist*
Hansen, Nick Dane *lawyer*
Hanson, Arnold Philip *retired lawyer*
Hanson, Carey B. *costume designer, educator*
Hanson, Harold Palmer *physicist, editor, academic administrator, government official*
Hanson, Jo *artist, educator, writer*
Hanson, John M. *civil engineering and construction educator*
Hantman, Barry G. *software engineer*
Hanushek, Eric Alan *economics professor*
Hanvy, Phillip Wayne *benefits compensation analyst*
Hao, Lawrence Kaholo *state official, clinical hypnotherapist*
Hapner, Mary Lou *securities trader, writer*
Haque, Rezaul *design engineer*
Harari, Eli *computer company executive*
Haratani, Joan Mei *lawyer*
Harbaugh, Janice M. *counselor, consultant*
Harbert, Ted (Edward W. Harbert III) *broadcast executive*
Hardage, Page Taylor *elementary school educator*
Hardaway, Robert Morris III *retired surgeon*
Hardaway, Timothy Duane *professional basketball player*
Hardcastle, Marcia E. (Marcia E. Temme) *retired journalist*
Harden, Mary Louise *human resources consultant, real estate broker, real estate appraiser*
Harden, Patrick Alan *journalist*
Harder, Robert Clarence *state official*
Hardie, James Hiller *retired lawyer*
Hardie, Michael Howard *mathematician, educator*
Hardin, Bridgette Everhart *educational research analyst*
Hardin, Edward Lester, Jr. *lawyer*
Hardin, Hal D. *lawyer, judge, former US attorney*
Hardin, James Neal *language educator, writer*
Hardin, Mary L. *interior designer*
Hardin, Paul III *law educator*
Harding, Ray Murray, Jr. *retired judge*
Hardis, Stephen Roger *retired manufacturing company executive*
Hardison, Kadeem *actor*
Hardwicke, Catherine Helen *film director, set designer*
Hardy, Chester Alfred *engineer*
Hardy, Clarence Earl, Jr. *government, nonprofit and corporate sector executive*
Hardy, Michele *literature and language professor*
Hardy, Ralph W. F. *biochemist*
Hardy, Richard Allen, Jr. *psychologist, educator*
Hare, Norma Q. *retired school system administrator*
Haren, Elizabeth Gaye *counselor*
Harff, Charles Henry *retired lawyer, manufacturing executive*
Harford, Robert R. *dermatologist*
Hargadon, Bernard Joseph, Jr. *retired consumer goods company executive*
Hargrove, Mike (Dudley Michael Hargrove) *former professional baseball team manager*
Haring, Ellen Stone *philosophy educator*
Haring-Smith, Whitney *political science scholar*
Hariton, Lorraine Jill *information technology executive*
Harlan, Raymond Carter *special investigator, writer, retired communication executive, educator, and military officer*
Harler, Donna *voice educator*
Harley, Ruth *artist, educator*
Harlin, Marilyn Miler *marine botany educator, researcher, consultant*
Harlin, Renny (Renny Lauri Mauritz Harjola) *film director*
Harman, Jennifer (Jennifer Harman-Traniello) *professional poker player*
Harman, Maryann Whittemore *artist, educator*
Harman, Rebecca Howard *educator*
Harman, Wallace Patrick *lawyer*
Harmatuk, Frances A. *retired psychiatrist, anesthesiologist*
Harmel, Merel Hilber *anesthesiologist, educator*
Harmon, Gail McGreevy *lawyer*
Harms, Nancy Ann *nursing educator*
Harnack, Don Steger *retired lawyer*
Harnedy, Joan Catherine Holland *retired systems analyst*
Harper, Charles Michel *food products executive, director*
Harper, Conrad Kenneth *lawyer*
Harper, Henry H. *retired military officer*
Harper, James Weldon III *finance consultant*
Harper, Marsha Wilson *religious organization administrator*
Harper, Richard Henry *film producer, director*
Harr, Lucy Loraine *public relations executive*
Harrell, Henry Howze *tobacco company executive*
Harrell, John Michael *military officer*
Harrell, Richard Godwin *alcohol/drug abuse services professional*
Harrigan, Anthony Hart *author*
Harrigan, Rosanne Carol *medical educator*
Harriman, John Howland *retired lawyer*
Harrington, Jean Patrice *academic administrator*
Harrington, John Tolan *medical educator, internist, nephrologist, retired dean*
Harrington, Robert Dudley, Jr. *retired printing company executive*
Harris, Carla Ann *investment company executive*
Harris, Cyril Manton *physicist, acoustical engineer, engineering and architecture educator*
Harris, Dale Hutter *retired judge*
Harris, Dolores M. *retired academic administrator, adult education educator*
Harris, Elaine K. *medical consultant*
Harris, Erica Renee *researcher*
Harris, Harriet *actress*
Harris, Jeremy *former mayor*
Harris, Joe Frank *former governor*
Harris, Katherine H. *former congresswoman, former state official*
Harris, Margaret T. *school system administrator*
Harris, Mark R. *film producer*
Harris, Merle Wiener *college administrator, educator*
Harris, Nancy Lee *special education educator, behavior analyst*
Harris, Nicholas George *publisher*
Harris, Paul Smith *human resources professional*
Harris, Richard Eugene Vassau *lawyer*
Harris, Robert A. *retired music educator*
Harris, Robert Norman *advertising executive, educator*
Harris, Rogers Sanders *bishop*
Harris-Barber, Daisy *elementary school educator*
Harrison, Andre L. *education educator, director*
Harrison, Charles Maurice *retired lawyer, communications executive*
Harrison, Gordon Ray *engineering executive, consultant, research scientist*
Harrison, John Raymond *foundation administrator, retired publishing executive*
Harrison, William Burwell, Jr. *retired diversified financial services company executive*
Harrison-Jervay, Evelyn Yvonne *publishing executive*
Harrold, Thomas J., Jr. *lawyer*
Harrop, Daniel Smith III *psychiatrist*
Harrop, Thomas *publishing company executive*
Harrow, Jeffrey John *spinal cord injury physician*
Harshbarger, Richard B. *retired economics professor*
Harstad, Carolyn Audrey *writer, educator, photographer*
Hart, Arthur Alvin *historian, author*
Hart, Cecil William Joseph *otolaryngologist, surgeon*
Hart, Gary W. *retired senator, lawyer*
Hart, James Warren *retired athletic administrator, professional football player*
Hart, Karen E. *psychologist, consultant*
Hart, Marnie R. *art educator*
Hart, Melissa Anne *former congresswoman*
Hart, Paul Vincent, Jr. *emergency and acute care physician, inventor*
Harte, John Herman *artist*
Hartger, Barbara J. *marketing professional*
Hartley, James R. *musician, writer*
Hartman, David G. *actuary*
Hartman, Earl Kenneth *writer*
Hartman, George M. *retired engineering contracts manager*
Hartman, Rosemary Jane *retired special education educator*
Hartmann, George Herman *retired manufacturing executive*
Hartsock, Linda Sue *retired management consultant*
Hartstein, Harold Herman *psychology educator, consultant*
Hartwig, Robert Paul *insurance institute executive, economist*
Hartzell, Irene Janofsky *retired psychologist*
Hartzell, Karl Drew *retired dean, historian*
Harvey, Birt *retired pediatrician, educator*
Harvey, Douglass Coate *retired photographic company executive*
Harvey, Francis J. *former civilian military employee*
Harvey, Glenn Francis *management consultant*
Harvey, Lynne Cooper *broadcast executive, civic worker*
Harvey, Marc S(an) *lawyer, historian, educator*
Harvey, Richard Dudley *marketing consultant*
Harwell, Denise *researcher*
Harwell, William Earnest (Ernie Harwell) *retired commentator*
Harwit, Martin Otto *astrophysicist, writer, educator, museum director*
Harwood, Robert Bernard, Jr. *former state supreme court justice*
Haryono, Ignatius Wibisono *writer*
Hasanyan, Davresh *research scientist, educator*
Hasen, Burton Stanley *painter*
Hasija, Sameer *finance educator, consultant*
Haskell, Anne *secondary school educator*
Hasko, Judith Ann *lawyer*
Haslett, Jared Wooddell *physicist, educator*
Hassan, Ibne *lawyer, diplomat, political philosopher, international strategist*
Hassan, Sayed Mohammed *chemist*
Hasse, John Edward *music curator*
Hasselhoff, David *actor*
Hasselmeyer, Eileen Grace *medical researcher*
Hasselmo, Nils *retired academic administrator, linguist*
Hastings, John Jacob *writer, lyricist, consultant, activist*
Hastings, Lindsay Marie *industrial engineer*
Hastings, L(ois) Jane *architect, educator*
Hatch, Richard *actor*
Hatfield, Julie Stockwell *journalist*
Hatfield, Stacey *elementary school educator*
Hathaway, Anne *actress*
Hathcock, John Edward *vocalist*
Hathorne, Gayle Gene *musician, family historian*
Hatkoff, Craig Mitchell *real estate executive, educator*
Hatton, Barbara R. *academic administrator*
Hauck, Frederick Hamilton *retired military officer, retired astronaut, aerospace executive*
Hauer, Erwin Franz *sculptor, educator*
Haugland, Susan Warrell *education educator, consultant*
Hauner, David *economist*
Haupt, Roger A. *advertising executive*
Hauptmann, Randal Mark *biotechnologist*
Hausdorfer, Gary Lee *management consultant*
Hauser, Joyce Roberta *marketing professional*
Hausman, Arthur Herbert *electronics company executive*
Hausman, Harriet Seceley *administrator*
Hausmann, Charles Stewart *retired funeral director*
Hautman, Pete (Peter Murray) *writer*
Hauver, Constance Longshore *lawyer*
Havemann, Joel *editor*
Havens, Arnold I. *lawyer*
Haver-Allen, Ann *communications director*
Hawes, Bess Lomax *retired folklorist*
Hawes, Sue *lawyer*
Hawke, John Daniel, Jr. *former federal official*
Hawkes, Mary Newgeon *retired minister, educator*
Hawkins, Ellis Delano *manufacturing, insurance company, gaming executive*
Hawkins, Harold Stanley *pastor, school director, police chaplain*
Hawkins, Mary Ellen Higgins *retired state legislator, public relations executive*
Hawthorne, Bruce N. *lawyer, former telecommunications industry executive*
Hawthorne, Roy John *retired music educator*
Hay, Austin (George A. Hay) *actor, artist, musician, writer*
Hayakawa, Kan-Ichi *retired food scientist*
Hayden, Paul Allan *speech pathology educator, consultant, researcher*
Hayek, Carolyn Jean *financial consultant, retired judge*
Hayes, Byron Jackson, Jr. *retired lawyer*
Hayes, Charles Franklin III *retired museum director*
Hayes, Colleen Ballard *journalist, photographer, writer*
Hayes, Cynthia Ann (C.A. Hayes) *writer*
Hayes, Daun L. *music educator*
Hayes, David Ryan *mathematics professor*
Hayes, David Vincent *sculptor*
Hayes, Janet Gray *retired management consultant, mayor*
Hayes, John Patrick *retired manufacturing company executive*
Hayes, Patricia Thornton *music educator, retired director*
Hayes, Paula Freda *federal agency administrator*
Hayes, Reggie *actor*
Hayes, Sean (Sean Patrick Hayes) *actor, comedian*
Hays, Dennis K. *former ambassador*
Hays, Patrick Gregory *healthcare executive*
Haywood, H(erbert) Carl(ton) *psychologist, educator*
Hayworth, J.D. (John David Jr.) *former congressman*
Hazard, Christopher Wedvik *international business executive*
Hazard, Geoffrey Cornell, Jr. *law educator*
Hazard, Robert Culver, Jr. *hotel executive*
Hazekamp, Phyllis Wanda Alberts *retired library director*
Hazel, Mary Belle *university administrator*
Hazeltine, Joyce *former state official*
H'Doubler, Francis Todd, Jr. *surgeon*
He, Pingan *systems engineer*
He, Shouling *engineering educator*
Healey, Kerry Murphy *former lieutenant governor*
Healy, Bernadine P. *physician, educator, former federal official*
Healy, Patricia Colleen *social worker*
Healy, Steven Michael *accountant, city official*
Heaney, Gerald William *retired federal judge*
Heanue, Anne Allen *retired librarian*
Heard, James Henry *lawyer, educator, historian*
Heard, Ronald Roy *motion picture producer, lawyer*
Hearn, Joyce Camp *retired state legislator, educator, consultant*
Heath, Charles Dickinson *lawyer, telecommunications industry executive*
Heath, John Robert *music educator*
Heath, Joseph Nounnan *retired literature and language educator, writer*
Heath, Patti *art educator, musician*
Heath, Richard Eddy *lawyer*
Heath, Ross Bradley *consulting company executive*
Heatherley, James Lawrence *psychotherapist, educator*
Hebert, William N. *lawyer*
Heche, Anne (Anne Celeste Heche) *actress*
Hecht, Laurence M. *editor, political organization worker*
Heck, Debra Upchurch *information technology, procurement professional*
Heck, James Baker *retired education educator*
Heckadon, Robert Gordon *plastic surgeon*
Heckel, John Louis (Jack Heckel) *aerospace management executive*
Hecker, Michael Hanns Louis *retired electrical engineer, speech scientist*
Heckler, Gerard Vincent *lawyer*
Heckman, Gary Walter *military career officer*

Heckmann, Richard J. *sporting goods company executive*
Hedberg, Paul Clifford *broadcast executive*
Heddings, Raymond Eugene *military officer*
Hedien, Colette Johnston *lawyer*
Hedley-Whyte, Elizabeth Tessa *neuropathologist*
Hedreen, Richard C *real estate developer*
Hedrich, Cleda Pollard *real estate broker, writer*
Heed, Peter W. *former state attorney general*
Heeschen, David Sutphin *astronomer, educator*
Hefeman, Mark *real estate broker*
Hefferan, Colien Joan *economist*
Heffernan, James Anthony Walsh *language and literature educator*
Heffernan, Thomas Carroll *English literature and American studies educator*
Heffron, Howard A. *lawyer*
Hefley, Joel Maurice *former congressman*
Hegamin-Younger, Cecilia *statistician, consultant, educator*
Hegar, Rebecca L. *social worker, educator, consultant*
Heider, Jon Vinton *retired lawyer*
Heidt-Dunwell, Debra Sue *vocational school educator*
Heiligenstein, Christian Enric *lawyer*
Heilmann, Christian Flemming *manufacturing executive*
Heilmeier, George Harry *electrical engineer, researcher*
Heimbinder, Isaac *lawyer*
Heimbold, Charles Andreas, Jr. *former ambassador*
Heimbold, Margaret Byrne *publisher, poet, consultant, realtor*
Heineman, Andrew David *retired lawyer*
Heiney, John Weitzel *former utilities executive*
Heinicke, Ralph Martin *science administrator, consultant*
Heinsohn Kropp, Holly Lynn *educational consultant, history professor, researcher*
Heinze, Mark William *elementary school educator*
Heirman, Donald Nestor *training engineering company executive, consultant, educator, director, research scientist*
Heise, John Irvin, Jr. *lawyer*
Hel, Zdenek *immunologist, educator*
Helfand, Arthur Erwin *podiatrist*
Helfer, Michael Stevens *lawyer, insurance company executive*
Helfer, Ricki Tigert *banking consultant*
Helfgott, Roy B. *economist, educator*
Helgenberger, Marg *actress*
Helgeson, John Paul *plant pathology and botany educator*
Heller, Adam *chemist, researcher*
Heller, Arthur *advertising executive*
Heller, Jules *artist, educator, writer*
Heller, Robert *financial executive, economist*
Hellerstein, David Joel *psychiatrist, researcher, writer*
Hellmers, Norman Donald *retired historic site director*
Helm, DeWitt Frederick, Jr. *professional society administrator, consultant*
Helm, Lewis Marshall *communications executive*
Helm, Steven M *lawyer*
Helman, Alfred Blair *retired academic administrator, educational consultant*
Helms, J. Lynn *retired federal agency administrator*
Helms, Jesse *retired senator*
Helpern, Joan (Joan Marshall) *fashion designer, entrepreneur*
Helprin, Mark *author*
Hemann, Raymond Glenn *research company executive*
Hemby, James Benjamin, Jr. *college president*
Hemingway, Richard William *law educator*
Hemmingsen, Barbara Bruff *retired microbiologist*
Hemon, Aleksander *writer*
Hendershott, Anna Lorraine *educational director*
Henderson, Charles Brooke *research and development company executive*
Henderson, Cynthia *medical librarian*
Henderson, Florence *actress, singer*
Henderson, John Drews *architect*
Henderson, Melford J. *epidemiologist, molecular biologist, chemist*
Henderson, Thomas Henry, Jr. *lawyer, former legal association executive*
Hendricks, David Wesley *engineering executive*
Hendricks, James Powell *artist*
Hendrix, Scott Norton *history professor*
Hendrix, Stephen C. *financial executive, consultant*
Hendry, Jean Sharon *psychopharmacologist*
Hendry, Robert Ryon *lawyer*
Henes, Donna *artist, writer*
Heng, Donald James, Jr. *lawyer*
Henikoff, Leo M., Jr. *academic administrator, medical educator*
Henke, Robert Joseph *federal agency administrator*
Henke, Tracy Ann *federal official*
Henley, Patricia Joan *consultant, former superintendent*
Henley, Robert Lee *school system administrator*
Henneman, Richard Bruce *counselor, pastor*
Henneman, Stephen Charles *psychotherapist*
Hennessey, Patrick Daniel *musician, educator, musicologist*
Hennessey, Robert John *pharmaceutical company executive*
Hennessey, William Joseph *physician*
Hennessy, Dean McDonald *lawyer, municipal official, director*
Henney, Christopher Scot *immunologist*
Henning, George Thomas, Jr. *retired steel company executive*
Henrikson, Mary Ida *artist, educator*
Henry, Dale *artist*
Henry, Frances Ann *retired journalist, educator*
Henry, Martin Daniel *military academy vice president*
Henry, Philip Lawrence *marketing professional*
Henry, Rene Arthur *writer, consultant*
Henry, Robert John *lawyer*
Henry, Sherrye P. *political advisor, radio personality*
Henry, Stephen Lewis *retired lieutenant governor, orthopedic surgeon, educator*
Henry, Sue *retired social worker, educator*
Henry, William Ray *business administration educator*
Henselmeier, Sandra Nadine *retired training services executive*
Hensleigh, Howard Edgar *lawyer*
Hensley, Patricia Drake *principal*
Hensley, Ralph Henry III *federal management analyst*
Henson, Robert Frank *retired lawyer*
Hepper, Carol *artist, educator*
Heptinstall, Robert Hodgson *physician*
Herbert, Adam William, Jr. *former academic administrator, educator*
Herbert, Gavin Shearer *health care products company executive*
Herbert, James Alan *writer*
Herbert, James Charles *academic administrator*
Herbst, Jurgen *historian, educator*
Herch, Frank Alan *law librarian, lawyer*
Heresniak, Marty *music educator, actor*
Hereguth, Robert John *retired columnist*
Hering, Doris Minnie *dance critic*
Herley, Daveen Dorothy *artist, educator*
Herlik, Ed *military officer, pilot, small business owner, entrepreneur*
Herman, Alexis M. *retired labor union administrator*
Herman, Andrea Maxine *newspaper editor*
Herman, David Jay *orthodontist*
Herman, Ellen Rombs *retired literature and language educator, painter*
Herman, George Adam *writer, literature educator*
Herman, Hank *writer*
Herman, Lynn Briggs *state legislator*
Herman, Martin Neal *neurologist, educator*
Herman, Michelle *writer*
Herman, Rayna S. *pharmaceutical consultant*
Herman, Robert Lewis *cork company executive*
Herman, William Arthur *engineering and physics laboratory director*
Hermann, Donald Harold James *law educator*
Hermann, Kelly A. *music educator*
Hermann, Robert Bell *physical chemist, consultant*
Hernandez, David N(icholas) *lawyer*
Hernandez, Michelle A. *lawyer*
Hernandez, Ramon Robert *retired minister, school librarian*
Herod, Charles Carteret *Afro-American studies educator*
Herold, Jeffrey Roy Martin *retired library director*
Herold, Rochelle Snyder *early childhood educator*
Herr, Dwight L. *lawyer*
Herrera, Guillermo Antonio *pathologist, educator, researcher*
Herriford, Robert Levi, Sr. *retired military officer*
Herring, Jerone Carson *retired lawyer, bank executive*
Herring, Joan Sanders *secondary school educator*
Herringer, Maryellen Cattani *lawyer*
Herrmann, Jeffrey William *engineering educator*
Herrmann, Thomas Francis *systems administrator*
Herrnkind, Hilda Marie *writer, military volunteer*
Herron, Edwin Hunter, Jr. *energy consultant*
Herron, Orley R. *college president*
Hershatter, Richard Lawrence *lawyer, writer*
Herson, Arlene *television producer, journalist, television personality, radio commentator*
Herstand, Theodore *retired theatre artist, educator*
Hertel, Suzanne Marie *musician*
Hertz, Kenneth Theodore *healthcare executive*
Herwig, Nelson Gene *retired curator, retired counselor*
Herz, Irene Laurel *web site design company executive, librarian*
Herzberg, Thomas *artist, educator, illustrator*
Herzfeld, Charles Maria *physicist, educator*
Herzfeld, Siegfried *manufacturing executive, consultant*
Herzog, Jennifer A. *biology professor*
Herzog, Peter Emilius *retired legal educator*
Hess, Wendi Elizabeth *secondary school educator*
Hesser, Elise L. *retired elementary school educator*
Hester, James McNaughton *retired foundation administrator, artist*
Hester, Nancy Elizabeth *county government official*
Hester, Thomas Patrick *lawyer*
Hetland, James Lyman, Jr. *banker, lawyer, educator*
Heuer, Martin *retired human resources specialist*
Hewitt, Don S. *television news producer*
Hewitt, Ruth Price *retired librarian, elementary school educator*
Hewlett, Jamie *graphics designer, animator, cartoonist*
Hey, Robert Pierpont *retired editor*
Heyer, Stephanie *science educator*
Heyer, Steven J. *former hotel and beverage company executive*
Heyman, Ira Michael *federal agency administrator, law educator, museum executive*
Heymann, Philip Benjamin *law educator*
Heyrman, Laura Gardner *art historian, educator*
Heyward, Andrew John *former broadcast executive*
Heywood, Harriett *lawyer, consultant*
Hiatt, Arnold *apparel and retail executive*
Hickerson, Glenn Lindsey *leasing company executive*
Hickey, Joseph Michael *investment banker*
Hickey, Kevin Francis *software company executive*
Hickey, Robert Joseph *research scientist, educator*
Hickey, Win E(spy) *former state legislator, social worker*
Hickman, Lucille *physical therapist*
Hickok, Eugene Welch *former federal agency administrator*
Hicks, Allen Morley *retired hospital administrator*
Hicks, Paul B. *psychiatrist, director*
Hicks, Ritchie B. *physical education educator*
Hickson, Ernest Charles *financial executive*
Hidden-Dodson, Nancy *retired psychologist, consultant, educator*
Hietala, Valerie Grace *realtor, environmentalist, educator*
Higbee, Beth *communications executive*
Higbee, Donna Good *writer, researcher*
Higdon, Hal *sportswriter*
Higdon, Pamela Leis *writer*
Higginbotham, Edith Arleane *radiologist, researcher*
Higginbotham, John Taylor *lawyer*
Higginbottom, Samuel Logan *retired air transportation executive*
Hightower, Jack English *retired judge, former congressman*
Hightower, John Brantley *retired museum administrator*
Hijazi, Yazan S. *research scientist, educator*
Hildebrand, Verna Lee *human ecology educator*
Hildebrandt, Frederick Dean, Jr. *management consultant*
Hiler, Edward Allan *agricultural and engineering educator*
Hilgraves, Rebekkah *singer, consultant*
Hill, Antony J. deV. *headmaster, history educator*
Hill, Bob (Robert G. Hill) *former professional basketball coach*
Hill, Brian A. *former professional basketball coach*
Hill, David Lawrence *research corporation executive*
Hill, (Karim) Dulé *actor, dancer*
Hill, Edwin D. *trade association administrator*
Hill, Emita Brady *academic administrator, consultant*
Hill, Harold Nelson, Jr. *lawyer*
Hill, Jerry Dean *secondary school educator*
Hill, John Sylvester *allergist*
Hill, Laban Carrick *writer*
Hill, Lowell Dean *agricultural marketing educator*
Hill, Mark C. *lawyer*
Hill, Martha N. *dean, community health nurse*
Hill, Patricia Francine *information technology executive, educator*
Hill, Virgil Lusk, Jr. *academic administrator, military officer*
Hillenbrand, Shea Matthew *professional baseball player*
Hillenburg, Stephen *writer, television producer, animator*
Hillerman, Tony *writer, journalist, educator*
Hilliard, Sam Bowers *geography educator*
Hillis, William Daniel *biology professor*
Hills, Kendell Lenar *music educator*
Hilton, Andrew Carson *investment company and retired manufacturing executive, management consultant*
Hilton, Nicky (Nicholai Olivia Hilton) *apparel designer*
Hilton, Paris *actress*
Hiltzik, Michael *journalist*
Himes, Diane Adele *buyer, fundraiser, actress, lobbyist*
Himes, John Harter *medical researcher, educator*
Himmelfarb, Gertrude *writer, educator*
Hincks, Marcia Lockwood *retired insurance company executive*
Hind, Harry William *pharmaceutical company executive*
Hinderliter, Richard Glenn *electrical engineer*
Hindery, Leo Joseph, Jr. *communications executive*
Hinds, Edward Dee *insurance and investment professional, financial planner*
Hines, Andrew Hampton, Jr. *utilities executive*
Hines, Cheryl *actress*
Hines, Colleen M. *clinical nurse specialist*
Hingle, Pat *actor*
Hinshaw, Edward Banks *retired broadcast executive*
Hinshaw, Ernest Theodore, Jr. *private investor, retired Olympic team official, retired finance company executive*
Hinshaw, Mark Larson *architect, urban planner*
Hintz, Scott Raymond *investor, financial consultant*
Hinz, William Max *retired pediatrician, military officer*
Hirahara, Patti *public relations executive*
Hires, William Leland *psychologist, consultant*
Hirose, Teruo Terry *surgeon, educator*
Hirsch, George Aaron *publishing executive*
Hirsch, Horst Eberhard *metal products executive, consultant*
Hirsch, Judd *actor*
Hirsch, Larry Joseph *retired retail executive, lawyer*
Hirsch, Lawrence Leonard *physician, retired educator*
Hirsh, Bernard *supply company executive, consultant*
Hitchcock, Jane Stanton *playwright, novelist*
Hitchcock, Walter Anson *retired educational consultant*
Hitz, Frederick Porter *public and international affairs educator*
Hixson, Harry F., Jr. *health products executive*
Hjerpe, Carl William *retired mechanical engineer, banker*
Hjort, Howard Warren *economist, consultant*
Ho, Chih-Ming *physicist, researcher*
Ho, Eric Caleb *lawyer*
Hobson, Jade *journalist, consultant*
Hochhalter, Gordon Ray *advertising communications executive*
Hochheimer, Frank Leo *brokerage and financial industry executive*
Hochschild, Adam *journalist*
Hock, Frederick Wyeth *retired lawyer*
Hockeimer, Henry Eric *engineering executive*
Hodge, Shawna Marie *nutritionist, consultant, researcher*
Hodge, Verne Antonio *judge*
Hodgen, Maurice Denzil *retired history professor, writer*
Hodges, Adele E. *career military officer*
Hodges, Ann *retired television editor, columnist*
Hodges, Ann *actress, singer, dancer*
Hodges, Heather M. *ambassador*
Hodgson, Joseph *education educator*
Hodsoll, Francis Samuel Monaise *government official*
Hodson, Sara Suzanne *manuscripts curator*
Hoeben, Barbara J. *pharmacist*
Hoeg, Donald Francis *chemist, consultant, research and development company executive*
Hoenig, Steven Lawrence *chemist*
Hoeppner, David William *mechanical engineering educator*
Hoerder, Dirk *history educator*
Hofer, Stephen Robert *lawyer*
Hoff, Benjamin Lloyd *writer, scriptwriter*
Hoff, Charles Worthington III *retired banker*
Hoff, Peter Sloat *academic administrator, educator*
Hoffheimer, Michael Harry *law educator*
Hoffheimer, Minette Goldsmith *community service volunteer*
Hoffman, Alan Craig *lawyer, consultant*
Hoffman, Basil *actor, educator*
Hoffman, Daniel (Gerard) *literature educator, poet*
Hoffman, Darnay Robert *management consultant*
Hoffman, Edward Ted Charles III *director, educator*
Hoffman, Franklin Thomas *artist, printmaker, retired army officer*
Hoffman, Jerry Irwin *retired dental educator*
Hoffman, Jill M. *neuroscientist, researcher*
Hoffman, John Fletcher *retired lawyer*
Hoffman, John Raymond *lawyer*
Hoffman, Jonathan Frederick *military officer*
Hoffman, Judy Greenblatt *preschool director*
Hoffman, Marian Ruth *singer, voice educator*
Hoffman, S. David *lawyer, engineer, military officer, educator*
Hoffman, Sharon Lynn *adult education educator*
Hoffman, William *writer*
Hoffmann, Christoph Ludwig *lawyer*
Hoffmann, Frances Porter *librarian*
Hoffschneider, Gertrude Delores *pre-school educator*
Hofmann, Andreas G. *engineer, researcher*
Hofmann, Paul Bernard *healthcare consultant*
Hogan, Neville John *mechanical engineering educator, consultant*
Hogan, Robert Henry *trust company executive*
Hogan, Thomas Francis *federal judge*
Hogan, William T. *retired academic administrator*
Hogg, Virginia Lee *retired medical educator*
Hogle, Ann Meilstrup *painter, art educator*
Hohlt, Richard Frederick *lobbyist*
Hoke, Sheila Wilder *retired librarian*
Holben, Sharie Cecilia *small business owner*
Holbrook, Jay Mack *publishing company executive*
Holbrook, Karen Ann *retired academic administrator, biologist*
Holch, Gregory John *editor, writer*
Holcomb, Gene Ann *federal loan officer*
Holdaway, Phillip Wayman *retired environmental planner*
Holdaway, Ronald M. *retired federal judge*
Holden, Betsy D. *former food products company executive*
Holden, Donald *artist, writer*
Holden, William Willard *insurance executive*
Holdridge, Barbara *book editor, writer, consultant*
Holdsclaw, Chamique Shaunta *retired professional basketball player*
Holeman, Russell Kent *civil engineer, director, construction executive*
Holford, Theodore Richard *biostatistician, educator*
Holiday, Edith Elizabeth *former presidential adviser, cabinet secretary*
Holifield-Kennedy, Linda R. *physician*
Holland, Beth *actress*
Holland, Branti Latessa *science educator*
Holland, David Thurston *former editor*
Holland, Joseph John *retired financial executive*
Holland, Michael James *computer services administrator*
Holland, Rosemary Sheridan *program evaluation consultant*
Holland, Ruby Mae *social welfare administrator*
Hollander, Anne *writer*
Hollander, Lawrence Jay *retired marketing executive*
Holle, Reginald Henry *retired bishop*
Holleb, Doris B. *urban planner, economist*
Hollerbach, Serge *artist*
Holli, Melvin George *retired history professor*
Holliday, Robert Kelvin *retired state legislator, publishing executive*
Hollinger, Peggy Louise *elementary school counselor*
Hollings, Fritz (Ernest Frederick) *former senator*
Hollis, Deborah D. *systems analyst, application developer*
Holloran, Thomas Edward *business educator*
Holloway, Ernest Leon *retired university president*
Holloway, James Lemuel III *foundation executive, retired military officer*
Hollowell, John W. *retired urologist*

Jablonski, Robert Leo *architect*
Jabs, Aura Lee *minister, educator*
Jackman, Hugh *actor*
Jackson, Brian Matthew *musician, educator*
Jackson, Charles Ian *writer, consultant*
Jackson, Deborah Cheryl *mathematician*
Jackson, Edwin Atlee *retired physicist, educator*
Jackson, Eric Michael *marketing executive, writer, media specialist*
Jackson, Felicity Anne *performing arts organization administrator*
Jackson, Guida Myrl *writer, editor, literature educator*
Jackson, Hunter *health products executive*
Jackson, John Wyant *biotechnology company executive*
Jackson, Kenneth Arthur *physicist, researcher*
Jackson, Michael Joseph *musician*
Jackson, Miles Merrill *retired university dean*
Jackson, Nagle *stage director, playwright*
Jackson, Raymond Sidney, Jr. *lawyer*
Jackson, Robert Howard *food company executive, scientist*
Jackson, Robert William *retired utilities executive*
Jackson, Susan Marie *lawyer*
Jackson, Thomas Penfield *federal judge*
Jackson, Victoria Lynn *actress, comedienne*
Jackson, William Elmer, Jr. *retired packaging company administrator*
Jackson, William J. (Bill Jackson) *lawyer*
Jackson-Leslie, Llenda Diane *media consultant*
Jackson-Tkac, Stephanie Ann *nurse*
Jackson Wright, Adrienne A. *educational consultant*
Jacobowitz, Ellen Sue *curator, museum administrator*
Jacobs, Arthur Dietrich *health services executive, educator, researcher*
Jacobs, Bradley S. *former rental company executive*
Jacobs, Christopher L. *real estate developer, former state official*
Jacobs, Gretchen Huntley *psychiatrist*
Jacobs, John Patrick *lawyer*
Jacobs, Michael Roy *microbiologist, researcher*
Jacobs, Nancy Carolyn Baker *writer*
Jacobs, Richard Alberto *mechanical engineer*
Jacobsen, Diane DeMell *foreign policy specialist*
Jacobson, Eugene Donald *medical educator, academic administrator, researcher*
Jacobson, James Bassett *retired insurance and financial services company executive*
Jacobson, Matthew Frye *historian, educator*
Jacobson, Norman L. *retired agricultural educator, researcher*
Jacobson, Norman Maron *computer science educator*
Jacoby, Erika *social worker*
Jaffe, Charles J. *allergist*
Jaffé, Ernst Richard *medical educator, dean*
Jaffee, Annette Williams *novelist*
Jain, Archana *medical educator*
Jain, Rachna D. *psychologist, consultant, small business owner*
Jakubauskas, Edward Benedict *college president*
Jalba, Mihai Sergiu *epidemiologist, pulmonologist, physician, researcher*
Jallins, Richard David *lawyer*
Jambor, Robert Vernon *lawyer*
James, Allix Bledsoe *retired university president*
James, Bruce Richard *publishing executive*
James, Charles Franklin, Jr. *retired engineering educator*
James, Estelle *economist, educator*
James, Kay Coles *former federal agency administrator*
James, Kevin *actor*
James, Sharpe *state senator, former mayor*
Jameson, Patricia Marian *government agency administrator*
Jamison, Daniel Oliver *lawyer*
Jamison, John Callison *business educator, investment banker*
Jamison, Philip *artist*
Jan, Yuh Nung *biochemistry and physiology educator*
Janak, Peter Harold *retired automotive company executive*
Janda, Christopher Crisco *actor*
Janeway, Richard *retired academic administrator*
Janicak, Philip Gregory *psychiatrist, educator*
Janis, Conrad *actor, musician, art dealer*
Janke, Norma E. *legal nursing consultant*
Janney, Allison *actress*
Janney, Kay Print *retired performing arts educator, theater director*
Jansen, Angela Bing *artist, educator*
Jansen, Daniel Ervin *former professional speedskater, marketing professional, former olympic athlete*
Jaquith, George Oakes *ophthalmologist*
Jarmusch, Jim *film director, actor*
Jarrell, Charles Michael *bishop*
Jarrett, Jeffrey D. *energy companies association executive, former federal agency administrator*
Jarsma, Cynthia Lynn *secondary school educator*
Järvi, Neeme *conductor, music director*
Jasper, Norman Hans *engineer*
Javernick, Amy Sue *special education educator*
Javits, Eric Moses *ambassador, lawyer*
Javits, Joshua Moses *lawyer*
Javitt, Daniel C. *psychiatrist, researcher*
Javitt, Jonathan C. *ophthalmologist*
Jaw, Andrew Chung-Shiang *software analyst*
Jay, Norma Joyce *artist*
Jean, Claudette R. *retired elementary school educator*
Jefferson, Daisy M. *social studies educator*
Jefferson, Marvin Kazembe *actor, theater educator*
Jefferson, Monica Louise *neuroscientist, psychologist*
Jeffords, James Merrill *former senator*
Jelinek, John Joseph *public relations executive*
Jen, Joseph Jwu-Shan *academic administrator, former federal agency administrator*
Jenai, Marilyn *psychotherapist*
Jenerette, Joyce Williams *elementary school educator, educational consultant*
Jenkin, James Thomas *video editor*
Jenkins, Bill (William Lewis Jenkins) *former congressman*
Jenkins, Brenda Gwenetta *pre-school administrator, special education educator*
Jenkins, Charles H., Jr. *retail company executive*
Jenkins, Darrell Lee *librarian*
Jenkins, Jeffery A. *mathematics professor*
Jenkins, Lawanna *elementary school educator*
Jenkins, Melanie Shun *dietician, counselor*
Jenkins, Richard Dale *actor, theater director*
Jenkins, William L. *former academic administrator*
Jenkyn, Adrian John *computer company executive*
Jenness, Muriel Whitlock *reading specialist*
Jennings, Bojan Hamlin *chemist, former educator*
Jennings, Byron *actor*
Jennings, Jeffrey Scott *government agency administrator*
Jennings, Joseph Ashby *banker*
Jennings, Thomas Parks *lawyer*
Jennings, Toni (Antoinette Lee Jennings) *former lieutenant governor, former state senator*
Jennison, Brian (Lester) *environmental specialist*
Jensen, Eva Marie *medical/surgical nurse*
Jensen, Marvin Eli *retired agricultural engineer, science administrator*
Jensen, Michael Charles *journalist, lecturer, author*
Jensen, Nancy Daggett *music educator*
Jeong, Jinho *writer*
Jepson, Robert Scott, Jr. *bank executive*
Jerrytone, Samuel Joseph *financial property broker*
Jessup, Nancy Jean *music educator*
Jeswald, Joseph *artist*
Jetley, Karun *software company executive, consultant*
Jett, Stephen Clinton *geography and textiles educator, researcher*
Jetton, C. Loring, Jr. *lawyer*
Jeyaretnam, Benjamin S. *science administrator*
Jiang, Tianyi *computer company executive*
Jiang, Wei *adult education educator*
Jimenez, Dawn Marie *judge*
Jimenez, Joseph *management executive*
Jimenez, Marcos Daniel *former prosecutor*
Jin, Byoungho *retail executive, educator*
Jin, Helena *research scientist*
Jinks, Robert Larry *retired newspaper publisher*
Jo, Mi-Yeoung *neuropsychologist*
Joanou, Phillip *advertising executive*
Jocelyn, Marthe Mary *writer*
Jochner, Michele Melina *lawyer*
Jodry, Louis Frederick, V, *music educator*
Joel, Katie (Katie Lee Joel, Katherine Lee) *television personality*
Joelson, Mark René *lawyer*
Joffe, Barbara Lynne *business transformation architect*
Johansen, John MacLane *architect*
Johanson, David Richard *lawyer*
Johansson, Alicia Barbara *musician*
John, Sarah *physicist*
Johns, Warren LeRoi *retired lawyer*
Johnson, Albert Wesley *retired political science professor, public official*
Johnson, Anita Louise *artist, art director*
Johnson, Arthur William, Jr. *retired research scientist*
Johnson, Barbara Elizabeth *lawyer*
Johnson, Benjamin F., VI, *economist, consultant*
Johnson, Brenda LaGrange *ambassador*
Johnson, Bruce E. *former lieutenant governor, state legislator*
Johnson, Charles *political blogger*
Johnson, Clifton Herman *archivist, retired professional society administrator*
Johnson, Craig N. *management consultant*
Johnson, David Wilfred, Jr. *ceramics engineer, researcher*
Johnson, Deborah Lorraine *not-for-profit developer, consultant*
Johnson, Doris Jean *social worker*
Johnson, Dorothy Jean *retired secondary school educator*
Johnson, Edward Michael *lawyer, small business owner*
Johnson, Elizabeth *communications executive, interpreter*
Johnson, Elizabeth Diane Long *retired lawyer*
Johnson, Eugene Laurence *lawyer*
Johnson, Francis Severin *physicist*
Johnson, Frank Edward *surgeon educator*
Johnson, Freda S. *financial analyst, consultant*
Johnson, Glendon E. *retired insurance company executive*
Johnson, Gordon Gilbert *theology studies educator, minister*
Johnson, Hansford Tillman *former civilian military employee*
Johnson, Hazel Winifred *nurse, retired army officer*
Johnson, Henry Louis *former federal agency and school system administrator*
Johnson, Herbert Frederick *sales executive, retired academic administrator, librarian*
Johnson, Hiroko *art history educator*
Johnson, Irving Stanley *pharmaceutical executive, research scientist*
Johnson, James Terence *lawyer, educator, writer, minister*
Johnson, Janet Hovey *English language educator*
Johnson, J(anet) Susan *psychologist*
Johnson, Jay Withington *former congressman*
Johnson, Jeanne Jordan *music educator, department chairman*
Johnson, Jennie *chaplain, social worker, poet*
Johnson, Jerrilyn Jenkins *academic administrator*
Johnson, Jimmy *sports broadcaster, former professional football coach*
Johnson, John *broadcast journalist, artist*
Johnson, John Henry *film director, producer, photographer, educator*
Johnson, John Prescott *retired philosophy educator*
Johnson, Joyce *retired military officer*
Johnson, June Alexis *counselor, social worker*
Johnson, Karen A. *legal association administrator*
Johnson, Kay Durbahn *real estate manager, consultant*
Johnson, Kevin *computer software company executive*
Johnson, Kimberly Cassandra *psychologist*
Johnson, Lael Frederic *lawyer*
Johnson, Laymon, Jr. *management analyst*
Johnson, Lennart Ingemar *materials engineering consultant*
Johnson, Leonard Hjalma *lawyer*
Johnson, Leonard Morris *retired pediatric surgeon*
Johnson, Marc Robert *music educator, director*
Johnson, Margaret Heller *artist, educator*
Johnson, Maryann Elaine *educational administrator*
Johnson, Matilee Howard *retired headmistress*
Johnson, Maurice Verner, Jr. *agricultural research and development executive*
Johnson, Michael Warren *international relations specialist*
Johnson, Nichole Sharese *school nurse practitioner, basketball coach*
Johnson, Noel Lars *biomedical engineer*
Johnson, Norman Terry *public relations executive, writer*
Johnson, Pam Clarene *radiographer, bone densitometrist, consultant*
Johnson, Randall Clyde *mortgage company executive*
Johnson, Richard Tenney *lawyer*
Johnson, Robert D. *aerospace transportation executive*
Johnson, Sally A. *nurse, educator*
Johnson, Sandra Kay *music educator*
Johnson, Scott William *lawyer, manufacturing executive*
Johnson, Silas R., Jr. *retired military officer*
Johnson, Stewart Willard *civil engineer*
Johnson, Suzanne Nora *former diversified financial services company executive, lawyer*
Johnson, Sylvia Sue *university administrator, educator*
Johnson, Trina Lynn *special education educator*
Johnson, W. Clayton *lawyer*
Johnson, Wayne Harold *librarian, retired municipal official*
Johnson, William G. *neurologist, educator*
Johnson, William Potter *publishing executive, director*
Johnson, William R. *food products executive*
Johnson, Yvonne Thomas *elementary school educator*
Johnson-Moran, Kelly Kathleen *health facility administrator, writer*
Johnsrud, Brian C. *literature educator, scholar*
Johnston, Carolyn S. *elementary school educator, reading specialist*
Johnston, Catherine Viscardi *former magazine publisher*
Johnston, John Devereaux, Jr. *retired law educator*
Johnston, Kristen *actress*
Johnston, Laurance Scott *foundation director, healthcare educator*
Johnston, Lawrence R. *former food products executive*
Johnston, Oliver Martin, Jr., (Ollie Johnston) *animator*
Johnston, Paul Warren *retired surgeon*
Johnstone, D. Bruce *education educator, academic administrator*
Johnstone, Douglas Inge *retired state supreme court justice, lawyer*
Johnstone, Iain Murray *statistician, educator, consultant*
Johnstone, John William, Jr. *retired chemical company executive*
Johnstone, Martin E. *retired state supreme court justice*
Johnstone, Stowell *former state agency administrator*
Joines, Sharon Melissa Bennett *design educator, researcher*
Jolly, Meenakshi *rheumatologist*
Jolowsky, Christene Marie *pharmaceutical executive, director*
Jones, Andrew Zimmerman *editor, writer*
Jones, Anita Katherine *computer scientist, educator*
Jones, Carleton Shaw *information technology executive, lawyer*
Jones, Carter Ruthven, Jr. *sculptor, educator*
Jones, Charles Hill, Jr. *banker*
Jones, Christine Massey *retired furniture company executive*
Jones, Claire Burtchaell *artist, educator, writer*
Jones, Cleopatra Celeste *retired gerontologist, sociologist, educator*
Jones, Constance Coralie *retired music educator*
Jones, David A. *former consumer products company executive*
Jones, David Allen *retired health benefits company executive*
Jones, David Charles *retired air force officer, former chairman Joint Chiefs of Staff*
Jones, David Rhodes *editor, consultant*
Jones, Donya *elementary school educator*
Jones, Edith Hollan *federal judge*
Jones, Edward Paul *writer, editor*
Jones, Elaine R. *former legal association administrator, civil rights advocate*
Jones, Ervin E. *physician, educator*
Jones, Eugene Gordon *pharmaceutical company executive*
Jones, Harold Antony *retired banker*
Jones, Jack Bristol *education educator*
Jones, Joe Kenley *journalist*
Jones, Joel Mackey *academic administrator*
Jones, John Harding *photographer*
Jones, Jolene Rebecca *medical transcriptionist, educator*
Jones, Julie Ann *elementary school educator, choreographer*
Jones, Keith Alden *lawyer*
Jones, Leonade Diane *media publishing company executive*
Jones, Lisa Maria Draper *counselor*
Jones, Louis, Jr., (Bucky Jones) *academic administrator*
Jones, Lupe Sirena *insurance agent*
Jones, Marvin Lamar *histologist*
Jones, Peter d'Alroy *historian, writer, retired educator*
Jones, Phyllis Gene *judge*
Jones, Richard Melvin *bank executive, director, former retail executive*
Jones, Robert Henry *automotive distribution executive*
Jones, Roslyn Joyce *secondary school educator*
Jones, Ruth A. *secondary school educator*
Jones, Sarah B. *psychologist*
Jones, Shirley *actress, singer*
Jones, Sylvanus Benson *legal association administrator, consultant*
Jones, Thomas Claburn *poet, educator*
Jones, Thomas Owen *computer company executive*
Jones, Thornton Keith *chemist, researcher*
Jones, Walton Linton *internist, retired government agency administrator*
Jones, Wayne Allen *psychotherapist, publisher*
Jones, William Adrian *musician, educator, program developer*
Jones, William Augustus, Jr. *retired bishop*
Jones, William Rex *law educator*
Jones-Ketner, Elizabeth Brown *writer*
Jones Tergeoglou, Beverly Gloria *special education services professional*
Joosten, Kathryn (Kathryn Joostyn) *actress*
Jorapur, Vinod *physician, researcher*
Jorda, Merce Maria *pathologist*
Jordan, Carrie Grayson (Carrie Grayson-Jordan) *writer, poet, drama designer*
Jordan, Daniel Porter III *federal judge*
Jordan, Deovina Nasis *nursing administrator*
Jordan, Howard Emerson *retired engineering executive, consultant*
Jordan, I(rving) King *former academic administrator*
Jordan, Janine *interior designer, consultant, small business owner*
Jordan, Jerry Dale *lawyer, gas industry executive*
Jordan, John Frederick *farmer, consultant*
Jordan, Katherine D. (Kate Jordan) *lawyer*
Jordan, Kenneth D. *chemistry professor*
Jordan, Lisa Anne *dancer, educator*
Jordan, Marvin Evans, Jr. *record company executive, vocalist, actor, composer*
Jordan, Michael Hugh *information technology executive*
Jordan, Michelle Denise *judge*
Jordan, Rickey Woodrow *retired automobile manufacturer technician*
Jordan, Robert Reed *retired geologist, educator*
Jordan, Robert Smith *political science professor, civilian military employee*
Jordan, Thomas Fredrick *physics professor*
Jorden, William John *writer, retired diplomat*
Joseph, Eleanor Ann *retired health science association administrator, consultant*
Joseph, J. Jonathan *interior designer*
Joseph, Michael Thomas *broadcast consultant*
Joseph, Ramon Rafael *internist, educator*
Joseph, Robert G. *former federal agency administrator*
Josephson, Kenneth Bradley *artist, retired educator*
Joshi, Madhukar *statistician, consultant*
Josten, Katherine A. *artist*
Jourdan, Toni Christina *small business owner, actress, writer*
Joyce, Joseph James *lawyer, food products executive*
Joyce, William Robert *textile machinery company executive*
Joyner Kersee, Jackie (Jacqueline Joyner Kersee) *retired track and field athlete*
Judd, Scott Randall *information technology manager*
Judge, Mike *animator*
Judge, Nancy Elizabeth *obstetrician, gynecologist*
Judge, Rajinder *psychiatrist*
Judy, Cheryl D. *art educator, artist*
Jugulum, Rajesh *engineer, researcher*
Jumper, John Phillip *retired military officer*
Jung, Kwan Yee *artist*
Jung, Sangwook *neurobiologist*
Jungbluth, Connie Carlson *private banker*
Juran, Sylvia Louise *retired editor*
Juricic, Davor *engineering educator*
Jurkiewicz, Carole Lynn *education educator*
Juskowiak, Terry Eugene *career military officer, computer company executive*
Just, Ward Swift *author*
Juviler, Peter Henry *political scientist, educator*
Kaback, Keith Ross *emergency physician, educator*
Kabakov, Ilya *artist*
Kaculi, Xhemal T. *oil industry analysis/design engineer*
Kaczmarek, Jane *actress*
Kadel, Lee A. *information technology manager, systems analyst*
Kadhim, Estelle Beverly *retired librarian*
Kadonsky, Christine Elaine *historian, educator*
Kadota, Takashi Theodore *mathematician, electrical engineer*
Kaemper, Laura Jean *medical transcriptionist*
Kageyama, Mariko *collections manager*
Kahana, Eva Frost *sociology educator*
Kahmann, Sarah Stuber *retired foundation administrator*
Kahn, Alfred Joseph *social services researcher, educator*

Kahn, Herta Hess (Mrs. Howard Kahn) *retired investment company executive*
Kahn, James Steven *retired museum director*
Kahn, Laurence Michael *lawyer, management consultant*
Kahn, Susan *artist*
Kahn, Victoria Elaine Hopkins *special education educator*
Kahol, Kanav *researcher*
Kahwash, Eiad B. *medical educator, poet*
Kaim, Samuel C. *retired psychiatrist*
Kaiser, Nina Irene *healthcare consultant*
Kaiser, Robert A. *telecommunications industry executive*
Kaiser, Suzanne Billo *investment banker, writer*
Kaler, Eric William *chemical engineer, educator*
Kalina, Richard *artist*
Kaling, Mindy *actress, scriptwriter, television producer*
Kaliski, Mary *psychologist*
Kallay, Michael Frank, II, *medical products executive*
Kallenberg, John Kenneth *retired librarian*
Kallewaard, Susan L. *elementary school educator*
Kalof, Alexandra N. *pathologist, educator*
Kamalasadan, Sukumar *electrical and computer engineering educator, researcher*
Kamanu, Uchemadu Chee *chemist*
Kambutu, John *adult education educator*
Kamen, Paula *journalist, playwright*
Kamerin, Kim K. *music educator*
Kamin, Blair Douglass *architecture critic*
Kaminsky, Alice Richkin *retired literature educator*
Kampe, Carolyn Jean *elementary school educator, special education educator, art educator*
Kampmeier, Curt *management consultant*
Kampouris, Emmanuel Andrew *retired corporate executive*
Kamrin, Michael Arnold *toxicology educator*
Kan, Yue-Sai *journalist, writer, television personality, entrepreneur, humanitarian*
Kanagy, Steven Albert *foundation administrator*
Kander, John Harold *composer*
Kane, Cynthia A. *special education educator*
Kane, Jennifer Lynn *pharmacist, medical/surgical nurse*
Kane, Karen Marie *public affairs consultant*
Kane, Margaret Brassler *sculptor*
Kane, Mary Deely *former state official*
Kane, Michael Barry *social science research executive*
Kane Hittner, Marcia Susan *bank executive*
Kang, Bann C. *immunologist*
Kang, Hyun Wook *research scientist*
Kantor, Harvey Sherwin *medical educator*
Kantor, Mark Alan *lawyer, arbitrator*
Kantrowitz, Susan Lee *lawyer*
Kanuk, Leslie Lazar *management consultant, educator*
Kapany, Narinder Singh *physicist*
Kaplan, Barbara Jane *retired city planner*
Kaplan, Barry Martin *lawyer*
Kaplan, David L. *retired communications educator, actor, artist, sculptor*
Kaplan, Edward L. *retired electronics executive*
Kaplan, Gabriela Diana *radiologist*
Kaplan, Gerson Nathaniel *retired radiologist*
Kaplan, Helene Lois *lawyer*
Kaplan, Leonard Eugene *accountant*
Kaplan, Paul Elias *physiatrist, writer, educator*
Kaplan, Richard James *film producer and director, educator, consultant, scriptwriter*
Kaplan, Robert B. *linguistics educator, consultant, researcher*
Kaplan, Robert David *journalist*
Kaplowitz, Neil *gastroenterologist, educator*
Kapner, Lewis *lawyer*
Kapnick, Richard Bradshaw *lawyer*
Kapnick, Stewart *investment banker*
Kappner, Augusta Souza *academic administrator*
Kaprielian, Walter *advertising executive*
Kapur, Vishesh *medical educator, epidemiologist*
Karakey, Sherry JoAnne *real estate company executive, interior designer*
Karalekas, Anne *media executive*
Karalis, John Peter *computer company executive, lawyer*
Karasik, Miriyam Beth *artist, writer*
Karayan, Ani A. *psychologist, consultant*
Karayanis, Plato Steven *opera company executive*
Karben, Shelley Valerie *elementary and special education school educator*
Karcz, Andrzej *literature educator*
Kari, Daven Michael *English and religious studies professor*
Karim, Jawed *application developer*
Karim, Muhammad Bazlul *political scientist, educator*
Karlinsky, Simon *language educator, writer*
Karnas, Fred G., Jr. *poverty and homeless specialist*
Karnaugh, Maurice *computer scientist, educator*
Karnauskas, Kristopher Benson *research scientist*
Karnazes, Dean (Constantine Karnazes) *endurance athlete, writer*
Karns, Elizabeth (Libby) A. *retired daycare administrator*
Karol, Michael Alan *editor*
Karon, Sheldon *lawyer*
Karp, Gerald Charles *biologist, educator, writer*
Karp, Rosanne *oncology and women's health nurse*
Karplus, Paul Andrew *biochemistry educator*
Karr, James Richard *ecologist, educator, research director*
Karr, Stephen William *retired judge*
Karson, Samuel *psychologist, educator*
Kartchner, Gayla L. *elementary school educator*
Kasdan, Lawrence Edward *film director, screenwriter*
Kaser, David *retired librarian, educator, consultant*
Kasich, John R. *former congressman*
Kaskowitz, Edwin *social services executive*
Kaslick, Ralph Sidney *dentist, educator*
Kaslow, Florence Whiteman *psychologist, educator, family business consultant*
Kasprzak, Lucian Alexander *physicist, researcher, materials scientist*
Kass, David Norman *accountant, lawyer*
Kass, Jerome Allan *writer*
Kassewitz, Ruth Eileen Blower *retired public relations executive*
Kasten, Stanley Harvey *professional sports team executive*
Kaster, Laura A. *lawyer*
Kastner, Marc Aaron *physics professor*
Kastor, Frank Sullivan *language educator*
Katen, Karen L. *retired pharmaceutical company executive*
Katona, Peter Geza *biomedical engineer, educator*
Katz, Andrues U. *surgeon*
Katz, Jeff *television personality*
Katz, Lawrence Sheldon *lawyer*
Katz, Natasha *lighting designer*
Katz, Sanford Noah *lawyer, educator*
Katz, William Loren *author*
Katzenbach, Nicholas deBelleville *former United States attorney general*
Kauffman, B. Suzanne *historian, genealogist*
Kauffman, David Lin *lawyer*
Kauffold, Ruth Elizabeth *psychologist*
Kaufman, James Jay *lawyer*
Kaufman, Luna Amalia *musicologist*
Kaufman, Stephen Lawrence *radiologist, educator*
Kaushik, Prashant *rheumatologist, educator*
Kavalek, Lubomir *chess expert*
Kavanaugh, Frank James *film producer, educator*
Kaveeshwar, Ashok G. *former federal agency administrator*
Kavli, Fred *retired manufacturing and engineering executive*
Kawamoto, Keith Hitoshi *protective services official*
Kawamura, Kenji *aerospace scientist*
Kaye, Debra *composer, music educator*
Kaye, Edward Michael *biotechnologist, physician, neurogeneticist*
Kaye, Gordon Israel *pathologist, anatomist, educator*
Kaye, Stuart Martin *lawyer*
Kaylan, Howard Lawrence *musical entertainer, screenwriter, composer*
Kayse, Kathleen *publishing executive*
Kayser, Brian D. *retired psychologist, writer*
Kaz, Nathaniel *sculptor*
Kazakov, Aleksey V. *product designer*
Kazanchyan, Gevork *public health educator*
Kazanci, Deniz *mathematician*
Kazemitabar Amirkolaie, Seyed Javad *engineer, researcher*
Kazi, Sumaya *entrepreneur*
Keala, Francis Ahloy *security executive*
Kean, Thomas Howard *former academic administrator, governor*
Keane, Jeffry Robert *secondary school educator*
Kear, Rebecca JoAnn *retired librarian*
Kearney, Douglas Charles *lawyer, journalist*
Kearns, James Joseph *artist*
Kearns, Merle Grace *state agency administrator*
Keating, Mark Taylor *physician, medical educator*
Keatinge, Robert Reed *lawyer*
Keaton, Diane *actress*
Keaton, Michael *actor, comedian*
Keaty, Robert Burke *lawyer, business consultant*
Kebert, Kent Lerdy *ophthalmologist*
Keck, Leonhard *retired small business owner*
Kedes, Laurence Herbert *biochemistry professor, physician, researcher*
Keech, Elowyn Ann *interior designer*
Keegan, James Joseph *entrepreneur*
Keegan, John Charles *former mayor, retired military officer, former state legislator*
Keehn, Robin *community program specialist*
Keehner, Rebecca Lynn *interior designer*
Keeler, James Leonard *food products executive*
Keeler, William Henry Cardinal *retired cardinal*
Keeling, J(ohn) Michael *lawyer, trade association executive*
Keen, Constantine *retired manufacturing executive*
Keenan, Anthony Lee *trucking executive*
Keene, Mary Ellen *federal agency executive*
Keene-Burgess, Ruth Frances *military official*
Keeney, Virginia T. *retired child psychiatrist*
Keevil, Philip Clement *investment banker*
Keffer, Charles Joseph *retired physics professor, academic administrator*
Kegerreis, Robert James *management consultant, marketing professional, educator*
Kehew, George Mansir *artist*
Kehlmann, Robert *artist, critic*
Kehoe, L. Paul *state judge*
Keil, M. David *retired international association executive*
Keill, Stuart Langdon *psychiatrist*
Keim, Betty Lou *actress, literary consulant*
Keir, Gerald Janes *banker*
Keith, Brian Thomas *automotive executive*
Keith, Robert William *banker*
Keith, Toby (Toby Keith Covel) *country singer, songwriter, producer*
Keith, William Douglas *lawyer*
Kelder, Dorothy Mae *science educator*
Kell, Michael Jon *physician, researcher*
Kelleher, Timothy John *retired publishing company executive*
Keller, Paul *advertising executive, researcher*
Keller, Roberta Lynn *physician, researcher*
Kelley, A. Benjamin *writer, educator, consultant*
Kelley, Edward Allen *publisher*
Kelley, James Francis *lawyer*
Kelley, Patrick Alan *neurologist, educator*
Kellner, Irwin L. *economist*
Kellogg, Peter R. *securities dealer*
Kellum, Donald Arthur *military officer*
Kelly, Anthony Odrian *textiles executive*
Kelly, Beverly Ann *elementary school educator*
Kelly, James Andrew *former federal agency administrator, policy research executive*
Kelly, Kathleen Dennis *international government affairs consultant*
Kelly, Lucie Stirm Young *retired nursing educator*
Kelly, Nancy Folden *art association administrator*
Kelly, Paul Vincent *retired military officer, former federal agency administrator*
Kelly, Raymond Crain *toxicologist*
Kelly, Sue (Susan Weisenbarger Kelly) *former congresswoman*
Kelly, Timothy Johnston *secondary school educator*
Kelly, Timothy William *lawyer*
Kelm, Bonnie G. *art museum director, educator, art appraiser, consultant*
Kelman, Ari *history professor, educator*
Kelso, Charlotte Elizabeth *elementary school educator, health and physical education specialist*
Kelso, John Hodgson *retired federal agency administrator*
Kelton, Elmer Stephen *novelist*
Kemper, John Dustin *mechanical engineering educator*
Kempf, Donald G., Jr. *retired lawyer*
Kempner, Maximilian Walter *dean, lawyer*
Kendall, Charles Terry *librarian*
Kendall, Dorothy Irene *secondary school educator*
Kendall, Harry Wesley *playwright, writer*
Kenderian, Shant *engineer, consultant*
Kendig, William Lamar *retired federal official, accountant*
Kendrick, Budd Leroy *psychologist*
Kendrick, Peter Murray *communications executive, investor*
Kendzior, Robert Joseph *marketing executive*
Kennard, Lydia H. *former airport terminal executive*
Kennedy, Charles *retired neuroscientist, retired medical educator*
Kennedy, David *musician*
Kennedy, Harold Edward *lawyer*
Kennedy, Jerrie Ann Preston *public relations executive*
Kennedy, Karen Syence *advertising agency executive*
Kennedy, Leo Raymond *engineering executive*
Kennedy, Mark Raymond *former congressman*
Kennedy, Megan Catherine *music educator*
Kennedy, Thomas J. *lawyer*
Kennerly, David Hume *photographer, writer, producer*
Kennett, Lee Boone, Jr. *historian, educator*
Kenney, Estelle Koval *artist, educator*
Kenney, Melissa A. *environmental scientist, educator*
Kenny, Deborah *marketing professional, finance educator*
Kenny, James Casey *former ambassador, construction company executive*
Kenny, Robert Wade *social sciences and humanities educator, writer*
Kenrich, John Lewis *retired lawyer*
Kenseth, Matt *race car driver*
Kent, Georgia L. *obstetrician, gynecologist, healthcare executive, educator*
Kent, Matthew *law clerk*
Kent, Philip I. *broadcast executive, communications executive*
Kenton, Edgar Jackson III *neurologist*
Kenworthy, Scott *humanities educator*
Kenworthy, William Eugene *judge*
Kenyon, Daphne Anne *economist*
Keohane, Nannerl Overholser *political scientist, academic administrator*
Kerber, Ronald Lee *industrial corporation executive*
Kercher, David Max *retired mechanical engineer*
Kercheval, John William III *finance professor, aerospace and defense executive, vulture capitalist, former investment banker*
Kerins, Francis Joseph *college president*
Kern, Charles William *retired academic administrator, chemist, educator*
Kern, Irving John *retired food company executive*
Kern, Ronald Paul *dean, consultant*
Kernan, Barbara Desind *federal official*
Kernan, Joseph Eugene III *former governor*
Kerner, Michael Philip *lawyer*
Kerr, Frederick Hohmann *retired health facility and academic administrator*
Kertzer, David Israel *academic administrator, anthropology educator, writer*
Kerwin, Walter Thomas, Jr. *career officer, consultant*
Kesler, Theodore B. *educational consultant*
Kesseler, Matthew John *librarian*
Kesselring, Debbie Anne *systems engineer*
Kessler, Gale Suzanne *psychologist, educator*
Kessler, Roslyn Marie *financial analyst*
Kestenbaum, Harold L. *lawyer*
Kester, Helen Mary *minister*
Kettelkamp, Donald Benjamin *retired orthopedist*
Kettimuthu, Rajkumar *computer scientist*
Kevles, Bettyann Holtzmann *writer, historian, educator*
Key, Ted *cartoonist*
Keyes, Joan Ross Rafter *education educator, writer*
Keys, Alicia (Alicia Augello Cook) *vocalist, musician, songwriter*
Keys, John W. III *former federal agency administrator*
Keyworth, George Albert *physicist, consulting company executive*
Kezlarian, Nancy Kay *marriage and family therapist*
Khan, Ahmed Mohiuddin *insurance company executive*
Khan, Arfa *radiologist, educator*
Khan, Jamil Akber *chemical company executive*
Khan, Junaid H. *surgeon*
Khasawneh, Shadi Turki *computer scientist*
Khatib, Kathy *school administrator, educator*
Khavari, Khalil Akhtar *psychology professor*
Khidiatova, Alia *transportation executive*
Khosla, Ved Mitter *oral and maxillofacial surgeon, educator*
Khuong, Loc Huu *finance educator*
Khuri, Fadlo Raja *oncologist, educator*
Khvost-Vostrikova, Natalia S. *art educator, consultant*
Kibler, William Westcott *French language and literature educator*
Kice, John Edward *engineer, educator, consultant*
Kidder, Tracy (John Tracy Kidder) *writer*
Kidney, William Leslie *retired secondary school educator*
Kieback, Dirk Guenter *gynecologist, researcher*
Kiefer, Anselm Karl Albert *artist*
Kienitz, LaDonna Trapp *lawyer, librarian, municipal official*
Kierscht, Marcia Selland *academic administrator, psychologist*
Kiesler, Charles Adolphus *psychologist, academic administrator*
Kiffmeyer, Mary *former state official*
Kikareas, Panagiotis *foundation administrator, retired military officer*
Kilbane, Kathleen Ann *stage manager*
Kilbourn, William Douglas, Jr. *law educator*
Kile, Robert Merlin *emergency physician*
Kiley, Kevin Christopher *retired military officer*
Kilgus, Edward Chip *singer, actor, writer, poet*
Kilinc-Balci, Fatma Selcen *textile engineer, researcher*
Killeen, Michael John *lawyer*
Killian, Lawrence Harding, II, (Larry H. Killian) *sculptor*
Killian, William Paul *manufacturing executive*
Kilmann, Ralph Herman *business educator*
Kilmer, Val *actor*
Kilpatrick, James Jackson, Jr. *columnist, writer*
Kilts, James M. *investment banker, former consumer products company executive*
Kim, Charles Wesley *microbiology educator*
Kim, Daniel Dae *actor*
Kim, Deok-Ho *biomedical researcher*
Kim, Heather *director*
Kim, Michael S. *lawyer*
Kim, Robert J. *cardiologist*
Kim, Soongun *educational consultant*
Kim, Wan J. *former federal agency administrator, lawyer*
Kim, Won Gyu *research scientist*
Kim, Wonsuk *mechanical engineer, researcher*
Kimball, George Edward III *sports columnist*
Kimball, Richard Arthur, Jr. *retired lawyer*
Kimbrell, Deborah Ann *geneticist, educator*
Kimbrell, Grady Ned *writer, educator, retired school system administrator*
Kim-Farley, Robert James *epidemiologist, educator*
Kimmel, Mark *author, venture capital company executive*
Kincaid, Jamaica *writer*
Kincaid, Steven Randall *marketing professional*
Kindberg, Shirley Jane *pediatrician*
Kinder, Suzanne Fonay Wemple *retired historian, retired educator*
King, Alfred Meehan *financial executive*
King, Algin Braddy *retired marketing educator*
King, Amy Cathryne Patterson *retired mathematics educator, researcher*
King, Cynthia Bregman *writer*
King, David Alan *ecologist*
King, David Roy *lawyer*
King, Glen (Lenard Glen King) *broadcasting educator, composer*
King, Graham *film producer*
King, Gregory C. *energy executive*
King, Gundar Julian *retired dean*
King, Hueston Clark *retired otolaryngologist, educator*
King, Imogene M. *retired nursing educator*
King, Jack A. *lawyer*
King, James Calvin *mathematics educator*
King, Jane Cudlip Coblentz *volunteer educator*
King, Jeff *dog musher*
King, John Charles Peter *editor, writer*
King, John Ethelbert, Jr. *retired academic administrator*
King, Joy Riemer *art educator, linguist*
King, Larry L. *playwright, actor*
King, Megan Christine *cell biologist*
King, Michael Howard *lawyer*
King, Quintin L. *trade association administrator, lobbyist*
King, Rebecca J. *lawyer, consultant*
King, Robert Lucien *retired lawyer*
King, Robert Thomas *editor, writer*
King, Ronald Lee *retired accountant, government agency administrator*
King, Rosalyn Mercita *social sciences educator, researcher, psychologist*
King, Royce Arthur *retired farm equipment executive*
King, Sheldon Selig *health facility administrator, educator*
King, Sheryl Jayne *retired secondary school educator, counselor*
King, Susan Bennett *retired glass company executive*
King, William *sculptor*
King, William Collins *retired oil industry executive*
Kingsbery, Walton Waits, Jr. *retired accounting firm executive*
Kingston, Maxine Hong *writer, educator*
Kinnear, Greg *actor, film producer*
Kinsey, Angela *actress*
Kinsley, Michael E. *newspaper columnist*
Kinslow, Margie Ann *volunteer*
Kinter, Kerri Anne *elementary school educator*
Kinzie, Jeannie Jones *radiation oncologist, nuclear medicine physician*

Kipke, Michele Diane *education and social services administrator, former hospital director*
Kipniss, Robert *artist*
Kipniss MacDonald, Betty Ann *artist, educator*
Kipper, Barbara Levy *wholesale distribution executive*
Kirakosyan, Arman *physicist, researcher*
Kiraz, Bahri *plastics and mechanical engineer, consultant*
Kirby, Lisa Anne *literature educator*
Kirby, Odell *retired small business owner, newswriter, writer*
Kirchman, Eric Hans *lawyer*
Kirchner, Lisa Beth *actress, vocalist*
Kirchner, Peter Thomas *nuclear medicine physician, educator, consultant*
Kirk, Carmen Zetler *data processing executive*
Kirk, Connie Ann *writer*
Kirk, Donald Evan *electrical engineering educator, dean*
Kirk, John Robert, Jr. *retired lawyer, consultant*
Kirk, Rea Helene (Rea Helene Glazer) *special education educator*
Kirkby, Maurice Anthony *oil industry executive*
Kirkland, Geoffrey Alan *motion picture production designer*
Kirkland, Rebecca Trent *endocrinologist*
Kirkland, Richard Ide (Rik), Jr. *magazine editor*
Kirkland, Virgil Wayne *retired electrical engineer*
Kirkpatrick, Charles Harvey *immunologist, researcher*
Kirkpatrick, Garland Penn *retired pediatrician*
Kirsch, Roslyn Ruth *artist, educator, painter, printmaker*
Kirschenmann, Henry George, Jr. *management consultant, retired government official, accountant*
Kirschner, William Steven *lawyer*
Kirshbaum, Jon Alan *systems analyst, consultant, retired systems administrator*
Kirshenbaum, Ari P. *engineering educator*
Kirsteuer, Ernst Karl Eberhart *biologist, curator*
Kiselik, Paul Howard *manufacturing executive*
Kiser, Nagiko Sato *retired librarian*
Kisiel, Ida Marie *education educator, writer*
Kisker, Carl Thomas *pediatrician, educator*
Kisor, Henry Du Bois *retired editor, columnist, critic, writer*
Kissinger, Henry Alfred *international consulting company executive, former secretary of state*
Kistiakowsky, Vera *physical researcher, educator*
Kitchen, Paul Howard *hockey historian*
Kitt, Eartha Mae *actress, singer*
Kittrell, Pamela R. *lawyer*
Kitzmiller, Howard Lawrence *retired lawyer*
Kivikoski, Asko Ilmari *retired obstetrician, gynecologist*
Kizilisik, Aydin Tarik *surgeon, researcher*
Klaehne, Eberhard O.W. *pharmaceutical executive, chemist*
Klafter, Cary Ira *lawyer*
Klahr, Lewis *film director*
Klamon, Lawrence Paine *lawyer*
Klanderman, Bruce Holmes *retired chemist*
Klarich, David John *lobbyist, lawyer*
Klauberg, William Joseph *information technology executive*
Klaus, Charles *retired lawyer*
Klausner, Richard Daniel *cell biologist, researcher*
Klayman, Larry Elliott *lawyer, legal association administrator*
Kleiman, Alan Boyd *artist*
Klein, Charlotte Conrad *public relations executive*
Klein, Charlotte Feuerstein *art consultant*
Klein, Chuck *retired private investigator, writer*
Klein, Edward *writer*
Klein, Eugene *lawyer*
Klein, James Edgar *actor*
Klein, Linda Ann *lawyer*
Klein, Lynn Ellen *artist*
Klein, Martin *ocean engineering consultant*
Klein, Mary Ann *special education educator*
Klein, Paul E. *lawyer*
Klein, Stephen Thomas *performing arts executive*
Klein, Susan Elaine *librarian*
Kleinberg, Howard J. *newswriter*
Kleinlein, Kathy Lynn *training and development executive*
Klein-Seetharaman, Judith *biochemist*
Kleinsorge, William Peter *metallurgical engineer*
Klema, Ernest Donald *nuclear physicist, educator*
Klement, Vera *artist*
Klesko, Ryan *professional baseball player*
Klesse, William R. (Bill Klesse) *energy executive*
Klett, Gordon A. *retired savings and loan association executive*
Kliebard, Herbert Martin *education educator, writer*
Kliebhan, Sister M(ary) Camille *academic administrator*
Kline, Norman Douglas *retired judge*
Kline, Richard C. *oncologist*
Klinghoffer, Judith Apter *historian, consultant*
Klippert, Richard Hobdell, Jr. *engineering executive*
Kliszus, Edward A., Jr. *school system administrator*
Klob, Hans Rudolph *economist, consultant*
Klobe, Tom *retired art gallery director*
Kloepfer, William, Jr. *retired public relations executive*
Klohn, Earle Jardine *retired engineering company executive, consultant*
Klotman, Robert Howard *retired music educator*
Klott, David Lee *lawyer*
Klughart, Toni Anne *musician, educator, singer*
Knable, Michael *medical researcher*
Knauer, Virginia Harrington *advocate, retired federal agency administrator*
Knecht, Ben Harrold *retired surgeon*
Knecht, David Freemont *pastor*
Knecht, James Herbert *retired lawyer*
Knechtmann, James Allen *archivist, researcher*
Kneller, John William *academic administrator, retired literature and language educator*
Knight, Eric A. *aerospace executive, entrepreneur, inventor*
Knight, Gary *lawyer, writer, educator*
Knight, Patricia Marie *biomedical engineer, consultant*
Knight, Shirley *actress*
Knighten, Latrenda *elementary school educator, consultant*
Knobloch, Ferdinand J. *psychiatrist, educator*
Knobloch, Marcia M. (Marta Knobloch) *writer*
Knodt, Jean Amelia Sausele *artist, educator*
Knott, Wiley Eugene *retired electronics engineer*
Knotts, Robert Spencer (Bob Knotts) *writer, playwright*
Knowles, Elizabeth Pringle *museum director*
Knowles, William Leroy (Bill Knowles) *television news producer, journalism educator*
Knox, Lance Lethbridge *venture capitalist*
Knox, Simmie Lee *artist*
Ko, Kyungduk *statistician, educator*
Kobak, Alfred Julian, Jr. *obstetrician, gynecologist*
Kocel, Katherine Merle *psychology professor, researcher*
Koch, John Michael *psychiatrist*
Koch, Kathleen Day *lawyer*
Koch, Molly Brown *retired parent educator*
Koch, Virginia Greenleaf (Virginia M. Greenleaf) *painter*
Koelmel, Lorna Lee *data processing executive*
Koenig, Allen Edward *higher education consultant*
Koenig, Kristi L. *emergency physician*
Koenig, Maureen Catherine *science educator*
Koenig, Robert Louis *writer*
Koepke, Allen Henry *music educator, composer*
Kogan, Esther *education educator, director*
Kogan, Richard J. *former pharmaceutical company executive*
Koglin, Terry Lee *mechanical engineer, consultant*
Kogut, John Anthony *wholesale distribution executive*
Kogut, Lior *mechanical engineer, researcher*
Kohan, Dennis Lynn *finance educator*
Kohler, Peter Ogden *retired academic administrator, internist, educator*
Kohlstedt, James August *lawyer*
Kohn, Jean Gatewood *retired health facility administrator, pediatrician*
Kohrman, Arthur Fisher *pediatrics educator*
Kojima, Takeshi *law educator, arbitrator, writer, dean*
Koken, M. Diane *former state official, insurance company executive*
Kokkeler, Fay Esther *music educator*
Kolarik, William Joel, II, *accountant*
Kolb, Dorothy Gong *elementary school educator*
Kolb, Gloria Ro *medical products executive*
Kolb, Harold Hutchinson, Jr. *language educator*
Kolb, James A. *science foundation director, writer*
Kolbe, Jim (James Thomas Kolbe) *retired congressman*
Kolbert, Jack *language educator*
Kolbert, Kathryn *lawyer, educator*
Koldenhoven, Dean *former mayor*
Kolenda, Joanne L. *elementary school educator, secondary school educator, volunteer*
Kolesnikov, Evgeni *surgeon, scientist, consultant*
Kolff, Willem Johan *retired internist, medical educator*
Kollar, Edward James *retired biology educator*
Koller, Loren D. *veterinary medicine educator*
Kollias, Jim Harry *music educator*
Kolodny, Stephen Arthur *lawyer*
Kolokythas, Antonia *oral surgeon, oncologist*
Koltun, Frances Lang *editor, publisher, broadcaster*
Komar, Vitaly *artist*
Komisar, David Daniel *retired academic administrator*
Komisarjevsky, Christopher P.A. *retired public relations executive*
Konate, Dialla *mathematician, educator*
Konchitsky, Alon *electronics engineer, communications executive*
Kondas, Nicholas Frank *retired shipping company executive*
Konecni, Vladimir J. J. Ch. S. (Graf Konecni) *psychologist, educator, writer*
Kong, Xuan *electrical engineer, educator*
Konigsburg, Elaine Lobl *writer*
Konner, Joan Weiner *academic administrator, writer, educator, television producer and retired executive*
Konnyu, Ernest Leslie *former congressman*
Konstantinova, Irina Vital'evna *immunologist, researcher*
Kooijmans, Pieter Hendrik *former judge*
Kooken, John Frederick *retired bank holding company executive*
Kooluris Dobbs, Linda Kia *artist, photographer*
Kope, Shane Brien *lawyer*
Kopelson, Arnold *film producer*
Kopielski, Camille Ann *counseling administrator, volunteer*
Kopko, Kimberly Ann *psychologist, researcher*
Koplan, Stephen *former federal official*
Koplowitz, Stephan *choreographer*
Kord, Victor George *artist, educator*
Koreman, Dorothy Goldstein *physician, dermatologist*
Koren, Edward Benjamin *cartoonist, educator*
Koren, Michael *elementary school educator*
Korenic, Lynette Marie *librarian*
Kormondy, Edward John *retired academic administrator, science educator*
Korn, Jessica Susan *research scientist, educator, program manager*
Korn, Michael Jeffrey *lawyer*
Korn, Peter A. *arbitrator, mediator, educator*
Kornblatt, M. David *corporate financial executive*
Kornbluth, Jesse *editor, writer*
Kornel, Ludwig *medical educator, physician, scientist*
Kornhaber, Donna Marie *theater educator*
Korobkin, Barry Jay *architect*
Korologos, Ann McLaughlin *communications executive, former secretary of labor*
Korologos, Tom Chris *former ambassador*
Koros, William John *chemical engineering educator*
Korot, Beryl *artist*
Korotkov, Roman Y. *engineer, research scientist*
Korshunov, Vyacheslav Slava A. *pharmacist, educator*
Korten, David C. *writer*
Kos, Paul *artist*
Kosner, Edward A(lan) *editor*
Kosslyn, Stephen M. *psychologist, educator*
Kostere, Kim Martin *psychologist, consultant*
Kostic, Dina *musician, music educator*
Koszarski, Richard *art historian, curator*
Koszegi, Kathleen A. *elementary school educator*
Kotcher, Shirley J.W. *lawyer*
Kotin, Paul *pathologist*
Kotler, Steven *investment banker*
Kotlowitz, Alex *writer, journalist*
Kotter, John Paul *organizational behavior educator, management consultant*
Kottkamp, Jeffrey Dean *lieutenant governor, lawyer*
Kotz, Nathan Kallison (Nick Kotz) *news correspondent, author*
Kovach, Andrew Louis *human resources specialist, consultant*
Kovach, Bill *educational foundation administrator*
Kovacs, William Joseph *physician, educator*
Kovarik, Madeline *education educator*
Kowalchick, Edward M. *headmaster*
Kozak, Alexander L. *engineer*
Koziara, Eugene Harry *retired aerospace engineer*
Kozlowski, Damian Mark *diversified financial services company executive*
Krabbe, Thomas Joseph *music educator*
Kraemer, Alfred Robert *school librarian*
Kraft, Henry Robert *lawyer*
Kraft, Yvette *art educator*
Kraichnan, Robert Harry *physicist, consultant*
Krakaur, Linda E. *language educator*
Krakosky, Norah *historic site staff member*
Krakower, Bernard Hyman *management consultant*
Krakower, Terri Jan *biochemist, researcher*
Krall, Lisa Kristina *education educator*
Krall, Todd *program manager*
Kramer, Dale Vernon *retired language educator*
Kramer, Kenneth Bentley *retired federal judge, former congressman*
Kramer, Mary Elizabeth *ambassador, former state legislator*
Kramer, Paul R. *lawyer*
Kramer, Peter Robin *computer company executive*
Kramer, Richard Jay *gastroenterologist, educator*
Kramp, Suzan Marie *systems programmer*
Krantz, Michael Scott *protective services official, educator*
Krantz, Steven George *mathematics professor, writer*
Kranzow, Ronald Roy *lawyer*
Krasinski, John *actor*
Kraslow, David *retired publishing executive, writer, consultant, reporter*
Krasnow, Kenneth *real estate company executive*
Kratt, Peter George *lawyer*
Kraus, Jill Gansman *former jewelry industry marketing executive*
Kraus, Naomi *retired biochemist*
Krause, Edward Charles *priest, educator*
Krause, Sonja *chemistry professor*
Krauthammer, Charles *columnist, editor*
Kravetz, Katharine *education educator*
Kravitch, Phyllis A. *federal judge*
Kravitz, Ellen King *musicologist, educator*
Kravitz, Rubin *chemist*
Krawetz, Stephen Andrew *molecular medicine and genetics scientist, educator*
Kreer, Irene Overman *association and meeting management executive*
Kreider, Clement Horst, Jr. *neurosurgeon*
Kreith, Frank *research engineer, consultant*
Kreitlow, Burton William *retired adult education educator*
Kreitzburg, Marilyn June *academic librarian*
Kreitzer, Lois Helen *investor*
Kreizinger, Loreen I. *lawyer*
Krell, Rebecca Dawn *music educator*
Kremer, Honor Frances (Noreen Kremer) *real estate broker, small business owner*
Krenicki, John, Jr. *manufacturing executive*
Krens, Thomas *museum director*
Kresa, Kent *retired aerospace executive*
Kretchmar, Leslie *medical/surgical nurse*
Kretschmer, Frank Frederick, Jr. *electrical engineer, researcher, consultant*
Kribel, Robert Edward *consultant, retired physicist, academic administrator*
Krieg, Kenneth Joseph *former federal agency administrator*
Kriegsman, Sali Ann *performing arts executive, consultant, writer*
Kriesberg, Irving *painter*
Krim, Mathilde *medical educator*
Kring, Tim (Richard Timothy Kring) *television producer, writer*
Krishnamurthy, Kathiravan *research associate*
Kristiansen, Kai de Lange *physicist*
Krivoshia, Eli, Jr. *lawyer*
Kriz, George James *retired agricultural research administrator*
Krohnke, Duane W. *retired lawyer*
Krominga, Lynn *cosmetics executive, lawyer*
Kroto, Harold Walter *chemistry researcher, educator*
Kruck, Donna Jean *special education educator, consultant*
Krueger, Arlin James *physicist*
Kruesi, Frank Eugene *transportation executive, former federal agency administrator*
Kruger, Mollee Coppel *writer*
Krulik, Barbara S. *production manager, curator, art director, writer*
Krulitz, Leo Morrion *financial planner, publishing executive, director*
Krupp, James Arthur Gustave *management consultant*
Krylov, Dmitri *biologist*
Kubo, Edward Hachiro, Jr. *prosecutor*
Kucera, Daniel William *retired bishop*
Kucij, Timothy Michael *engineer, minister, musician*
Kudo, Toshifumi *surgeon, researcher*
Kudrow, Lisa (Lisa Marie Diane Kudrow) *actress*
Kuehn, James Marshall *newspaper editor*
Kuehni, Norman Arnold *small business owner*
Kuhler, Deborah Gail *grief therapist, retired state legislator*
Kuhlmann-Wilsdorf, Doris *materials scientist, inventor, retired educator*
Kuhn, James Paul *management consultant*
Kula, Irwin James *religious education educator*
Kulenovic, Dzafer Jeff *bank executive, advocate*
Kulesha, Kevin John *investment banker*
Kulesza, Chester Stephen (Bud Kulesza) *financial executive*
Kulik, Rosalyn Franta *food company executive, consultant*
Kull, Bryan Paul *business consulting executive*
Kulnane, Laura Shapiro *geneticist*
Kulstad, Guy Charles *public works official*
Kultermann, Udo *architectural and art historian, educator, writer*
Kumako, Kuami Mawunyo *agricultural scientist*
Kumar, Ramya *academic administrator*
Kumar, Vikas *neuropharmacologist, researcher*
Kumble, Steven Jay *lawyer*
Kumin, Maxine Winokur *poet, writer*
Kundel, Harold Louis *radiologist, educator*
Kung, Douglas C. *systems engineer*
Kung, Patrick Chung-Shu *biotechnologist*
Kunkle, William Joseph *judge, lawyer*
Kunstadter, Geraldine Sapolsky *foundation executive*
Kunze, Otto Robert *retired agricultural engineering educator*
Kuo, Chun-Fang Frank *counselor, educator*
Kupelian, Louise Paulson *musician, educator*
Kupersmith, Joel *internist, medical school dean*
Kuriansky, Judy *television and radio personality, reporter, clinical psychologist, writer, educator*
Kuritsyn, Alexey *physicist, researcher*
Kurnick, Nathaniel Bertrand *retired oncologist, hematologist*
Kurnick, Robert H., Jr. *automotive executive, lawyer*
Kuroda, Yasumasa *political science professor, researcher*
Kurth, Donald James, Jr. *medical educator, mayor*
Kusama, Yayoi *sculptor, painter*
Kushlan, James Anthony *science administrator, educator, conservationist, writer*
Kushner, Harvey David *management consultant*
Kushner, Todd Roger *computer scientist, application developer*
Kushner, Tony *playwright, scriptwriter*
Kusma, Kyllikki *retired lawyer*
Kussrow, Nancy Esther *educational association administrator*
Kusterer, Thomas *program director*
Kustin, Kenneth *chemist*
Kutrzeba, Joseph S. *theater producer, director*
Kutscher, Ronald Earl *retired federal agency administrator*
Kutyna, Donald Joseph *air force officer*
Kuznetsova, Natalia P. *music educator*
Kvint, Vladimir Lev *economist, mining engineer, finance educator*
Kvitko, Arkady *mathematician, researcher*
Kwan, David Chung Man *business executive*
Kwik, Christine Irene *physician, retired military officer, retired foreign service officer*
Kwon, O-Mun *electrical engineer, researcher*
Kwon, Taek *Internet company executive*
Kwong, Eva *artist, educator*
Kyesmu, Pius Michael *biology professor, researcher*
Kyle, Gene Magerl *merchandise presentation artist*
Kylstra, Johannes Arnold *physician*
Kyriakides, Elias *electrical engineer, educator*
LaBarre, Carl Anthony *retired federal agency administrator*
LaBeouf, Shia *actor*
La Blanc, Robert Edmund *information technology executive*
Labor, Earle Gene *literature and language professor*
Laborde, Enrique *retired communications engineer*
Labore, Brian Edward *computer animator, artist*
Labrecque, Richard Joseph *retired industrial executive*
Lacer, Alfred Antonio *lawyer, educator*
Lacey, Cloyd Eugene *retired insurance company executive*
Lacey, Trudi *professional athletics coach*
Lachapelle, Cleo Edward *retired social worker, real estate broker*
Lachey, Nick (Nicholas Scott Lachey) *singer, actor*
Lackenmier, James Richard *academic administrator, priest*
Lackland, John *lawyer, nurseryman*
LaCrue, Alexis Nichole *parasitologist*
Lacy, Bill *former academic administrator, architect*

add, Diane *actress, writer, film director, film producer*
add, Joseph Carroll *retired insurance company executive*
adewig, Anita C. *elementary school educator, researcher*
adewig Goodman, Jeanne Margaret *artist*
adjevardi, Habib *historian*
adner, Benjamin *former academic administrator*
afever, Howard Nelson *botanist, educator, geneticist*
affer, Arthur Betz *economist*
aGanke, Allyson Ann *psychologist*
agna, Giorgio *molecular biologist, researcher*
ago, Rodrigo M. *internist*
agomasino, Maria Elena *investment company and retired bank executive*
agow, Richard James *chemistry professor*
aHood, Marvin John *retired language educator*
ai, Feng-Qi *instructional designer, educator*
aidlaw, Robert Richard *retired publishing executive*
aird, Cheryl F. *mental health services professional, paralegal*
aiskonis, Michael *chef*
ai-Yuen, Susana *engineering educator*
ake, Carol Lee *anesthesiologist, physician, educator*
ake, I. Beverly, Jr. *retired state supreme court justice*
ala, Dominick Joseph *manufacturing executive*
aliberte, Brian J. *prosecutor*
ally, John Patrick *investment company executive*
aMantia, Charles Robert *management consulting company executive*
amarre, Meaghan *internet communications specialist*
amb, Michael Donald *secondary school educator*
ambert, Daniel Michael *retired academic administrator*
ambert, George H. *physician, director*
ambert, John Walton *music educator*
ambert, Kirsten Schnoor *public relations executive, writer*
ambert, LeClair Grier *writer, lecturer, consultant, former state government public information administrator*
ambert, Richard Bowles, Jr. *freelance writer*
amberton, Jacquelyn Edmunds *retired psychotherapist*
amborn, LeRoy Leslie *law educator*
amel, Linda Helen *lawyer, arbitrator, professional society and retired insurance company executive, college president*
amont, Edward Miner, Jr. *telecommunications industry executive*
amont, Lee *music company and communications executive*
aMorte, Joyce E. *music educator*
ampert, Eleanor Verna *retired human resources specialist*
ampert-Shepel, Elina *education educator*
ampman, Richard H. (Dick Lampman) *former computer company executive*
ampson, Butler Wright *computer scientist*
amy, M. Rebecca (Mary Rebecca Lamy) *consultant, land developer, government official*
anahan, Daniel Joseph *lawyer*
ancaster, Jeanette (Barbara Lancaster) *dean, nursing educator*
ancaster, Kirsten Kezar *psychologist*
ancaster, Rogers *retired minister*
and, Jennifer Rebekah *mathematics educator, science educator*
Land, Susan Kathleen *application developer*
Landau, Emily Fisher *art collector, foundation administrator*
Landeck, Carl *corporate financial executive*
Lander, Howard *entertainment newspaper publisher*
Landes, George Miller *biblical studies educator*
Landes, William-Alan *film company executive*
Landesberg, Steve *actor*
Landis, Donna Marie *nursing administrator, women's health nurse*
Landon, John William *retired minister, social worker, educator*
Landon, Robert Gray *retired manufacturing company executive*
Landon, Susan N. *humanitarian, arts and environmental advocate, poet*
Landon, William J. *retired intelligence officer*
Landry, Paul Leonard *lawyer*
Landy, Lisa Anne *lawyer*
Lane, Laura Alice *retired librarian*
Lane, Richard Allan *preventive medicine physician, educator*
Lane, Shawn Lanard *journalist, motivational speaker*
Lane, Ted A. *music educator, musician*
Lane, William W. *electronics executive*
Laney, Marti Olsen *psychoanalyst, researcher*
Laney, Michael L. *manufacturing executive*
Lang, Michael *mathematics professor*
Lang, Richard Gordon *physician*
Lang, William Charles *retail executive*
Langbo, Arnold Gordon *former food company executive*
Langdale, Noah Noel, Jr. *retired education educator, academic administrator*
Lange, Frederick Edward, Jr. *computer information systems architect*
Lange, Jessica Phyllis *actress*
Langell, John Thomas *surgeon, researcher*
Langenkamp, R. Dobie *lawyer, educator*
Langenkamp, Sandra Carroll *retired human services administrator*
Langer, Dennis Henry *pharmaceutical company executive*
Langer, Glenn Arthur *cellular physiologist, educator*
Langer, Ralph Ernest *journalist, retired editor*
Langer, Ray Fritz *retired insurance executive*
Langston, James Leland *electronics engineer*
Langton (Tomasiewicz), Dawn Theresa *literature and language educator*
Lanham, Richard J. *oncologist, educator*
Lanier, W. Mark *lawyer*
Lannon, Paul G. *lawyer*
Lanoue, David J. *political science professor, department chairman*
Lanpher, Katherine *radio personality, columnist*
Lansing, Sherry Lee *foundation administrator, former film company executive*
Lanterman, Jennifer L. *researcher, educator*
Lantz, Joanne Baldwin *retired academic administrator*
Lao, Debang *electrical engineer, researcher*
LaPaglia, Anthony *actor*
Lape, Robert Cable *broadcast journalist*
LaPidus, Jules Benjamin *educational association administrator*
Lapin, Daniel *rabbi*
Lapine, James Elliot *playwright, director*
Lapinsky, Joseph F. *manufacturing executive*
Lapiz-Bluhm, Maria Danet Sanchez *neuroscientist, medical/surgical nurse*
Laporte, Leo Frederic *geologist, educator, paleontologist*
LaPorte, Leon Joseph *retired military officer*
Lapuz-De La Pena, Erlinda Laron *retired pathology professor*
Laqueur, Walter *history professor, writer*
Larkin, Joan *poet, literature and language educator*
Larkin, John Edward, Jr. *orthopedic surgeon*
LaRobardier, Genevieve Krause *lawyer*
La Rocca, Isabella *artist, educator*
Larr, Peter *retired bank executive*
Larsdotter, Anna-Lisa *retired translator, artist*
Larsen, Donald E. *education educator*
Larson, Charles Fred *management consultant*
Larson, Erik *writer*
Larson, Janice Talley *application developer*
Larson, Joan Isbell *musician, educator*
Larson, Larry *retired librarian*
Larson, Richard Smith *pathologist, researcher*
Larson, Robert Craig *real estate company officer*
Larson, Robert William *education educator, consultant*
Larson, Roger Keith *physician, writer*
Larson, Vicki Lord *academic administrator, communication disorders educator*
Lasher, Lara Elaine *epidemiologist, researcher*
Lashley, Felissa Rose *dean, nursing educator, researcher*
Laskawy, Philip Alan *retired accounting and management consulting firm executive*
Lasky, David *lawyer*
Lasky, Richard Donald *psychoanalyst, educator*
Lasky, William M. *manufacturing executive*
La Spata, Michelle Gayle *school psychologist*
Lass, Diane *marriage and family therapist*
Lasser, Lawrence J. *former investment company executive*
Laszewski, Boleslaw Tadeusz *civic volunteer*
Lathrope, Daniel John *law educator*
Latimer, James Harold *musician, conductor, composer, music educator*
Latiolais, Minnie Fitzgerald *retired nurse, health facility administrator*
La Torre, Carissa Danitza *counselor*
Latta, George Haworth III *neonatal/perinatal nurse practitioner*
Latta, Thomas Albert *lawyer*
Lauderdale, Vance, Jr. *anesthesiologist*
Laudone, Anita Helene *lawyer*
Lauer, Jeanette Carol *dean, history educator, writer*
Lauer, Len J. *former telecommunications executive*
Laughlin, Louis Gene *economic analyst, consultant*
Laurent, Pierre-Henri *retired history professor*
Lauterbach, Edward Charles *psychiatric educator*
Lauterstein, Joseph *cardiologist*
LaVerdiere, Claudette Marie *nun, head of religious order*
Lavezzi, John Charles *retired art history educator, archaeologist*
Lavidge, Robert James *marketing research executive*
Lavin, Bernice E. *cosmetics executive*
Law, Marcia Elizabeth *rehabilitation services professional*
Lawer, Betsy *banker, small business owner, vintner, director*
Lawler, John A. *publishing executive*
Lawless, Lucy (Lucille Francis Ryan) *actress*
Lawless, Michael Rhodes *pediatrics educator*
Lawless, Robert William *retired academic administrator*
Lawless, Thomas William *lawyer*
Lawlor, LynnAnn Jennifer *reading educator*
Lawrence, David Long *radiologist*
Lawrence, Glenn Robert *arbitrator, mediator, lawyer*
Lawrence, Margery H. (Margery Hulings Lawrence) *marketing consultant*
Lawrence, Mary Josephine (Josie Lawrence) *artist, retired library official*
Lawrence, Sally Clark *retired academic administrator*
Lawson, Carolina Donadio *language educator, translator*
Lawson, John Joseph *vocational educator, consultant*
Lawson, Trent *artist*
Lawton, Kelly Marie Lee *secondary school educator, performing arts director*
Lax, Philip *land developer, space planner*
Layne, James Nathaniel *retired vertebrate biologist*
Layton, Robert Glenn *radiologist*
Layton, William George *consultant, retired human resources and import/export company executive*
Lazar, Zoe L. *psychologist*
Lazarus, Bruce I. *restaurant and hotel management educator*
Lazovsky, Lorna Deane *minister*
Lea, Lorenzo Bates *lawyer*
Leach, Brenda Lee *special education educator*
Leach, Howard H. *former ambassador, former health care products company executive*
Leach, Jim (James Albert Smith Leach) *former congressman*
Leachman, Russell DeWitt *lawyer*
Leaf, Paul *film producer, writer*
Leahy, Jeannette (Jeannette Oliver Leahy Tinen Kaehler) *actress*
Leahy, T. Liam *business development and technology investor*
Leali, Bradford Charles *musician, educator*
Lear, M. Kathleen *artist, music educator, small business owner*
Leary, Margaret A. *law library director*
Leary, Thomas Barrett *lawyer, former federal agency administrator*
Leath, Cheryl Lynn *retired pre-school educator, poet, painter*
Leath, Kenneth Thomas *plant pathologist, educator, agriculturist, consultant*
Leather, Victoria Potts *college librarian*
Leatherdale, Douglas West *insurance company executive*
Leaver, Betty Lou *educational administrator, writer*
Leavy, Herbert Theodore *publisher*
Leazer, William *retired biomedical consultant*
LeBlanc, Daniel G. *state official*
LeBlanc, Hugh Linus *political science professor, consultant*
LeBlanc, Jonathan M. *lawyer*
LeBlanc, Leonard Joseph *retired electronics company executive*
LeBlanc, Matt (Matthew Steven LeBlanc) *actor*
LeBlond, Paul Henri *oceanographer, educator*
Leboeuf, Edmond Arthur *human resources specialist*
Lebon, Rachel L. *musician, educator*
Lebowitz, Catharine Koch *state legislator*
Lebras, Paul J. *retired career military officer*
LeBrecht, Thelma Jane Mossman *retired reporter*
Lecat, Robert J. *retired aeronautical engineer*
LeClair, John Clark *professional hockey player*
Ledbetter, Jennifer Lynn *anthropologist, educator*
Lederer, Edith Madelon *journalist*
Lederer, Peter David *lawyer*
Lederman, Leon Max *physicist, researcher*
Ledford, Janet Marie Smalley *real estate appraiser, consultant*
Ledogar, Stephen J. *retired diplomat*
Ledoux, John Lance *military officer*
Ledwig, Donald Eugene *association executive, consultant, retired broadcast executive, military officer*
Lee, Bobby *actor, comedian*
Lee, Bovey *artist, educator*
Lee, Bryan *information technology executive*
Lee, Burton Hoyt *aerospace engineer*
Lee, Cathy *emergency physician*
Lee, Charles Sung Chull *otolaryngologist*
Lee, Chava Cherta *psychotherapist, consultant*
Lee, Conrad S. *councilman*
Lee, Dan M. *retired state supreme court chief justice*
Lee, Eunice *music educator*
Lee, Gavin *actor, choreographer*
Lee, Harrison Hon *librarian, consultant*
Lee, Hwan-Soo *materials scientist, researcher*
Lee, Jonathan Owen *financial services company executive, lawyer*
Lee, Joseph William *sales executive*
Lee, Katie N. *biochemistry and chemistry scholar*
Lee, Katrina LaShawn *health insurance business consultant*
Lee, Marilyn Modarelli *lawyer, retired law library director*
Lee, Mordecai *political scientist, educator*
Lee, Nelda S. *art appraiser, art dealer, film producer*
Lee, Pali Jae (Polly Jae Stead Lee) *retired librarian, writer*
Lee, Paul P. *ophthalmologist, educator, lawyer*
Lee, Richard Kenneth *software company executive*
Lee, Seokwoo S. *periodontist, educator*
Lee, Soo-Hoon *human resources specialist*
Lee, Steve Chi Kong *bank executive*
Lee, Tabia (T. Lee) *social studies educator*
Lee, Thomas E. *emergency physician*
Lee, Thomas H. *investment company executive*
Lee, Thomas Tehwen *neurosurgeon*
Lee, Tonïa Reneé *entertainer, former government agent, educator*
Lee, Vanilla R. *school system administrator, educational consultant*
Lee, William Franklin III *composer, musician*
Lee, Winnie Sita *dentist*
Leeds, Douglas Brecker *advertising executive, theater producer*
Leeds, Jennifer Alyson *bacteriologist, researcher*
Leeds, Nancy Brecker *sculptor, lyricist*
Leek, Anne Carlin *music educator*
Leeper, Kathleen Marie *elementary school educator*
Leetch, Brian Joseph *retired professional hockey player*
Lefar, Marc P. *former telecommunications industry executive*
Leff, Ilene J(afnel) *corporate executive, federal official*
Leff, Joseph Norman *yarn manufacturing company executive*
Lefferts, George *television producer*
Lefkowitz, Alan Zoel *retired lawyer*
Legge, Charles Alexander *federal judge*
Leggett, Roberta Jean (Bobbi Leggett) *retired social services administrator*
Lehane, Dennis *writer*
Lehman, Jeffrey Sean *academic administrator*
Lehman, Joan Alice *real estate company executive*
Lehman, John F., Jr. *private equity executive*
Lehmann, Doris Elizabeth *retired elementary school educator*
Lehner-Quam, Alison Lynn *library administrator*
Leiber, Judith Maria *designer, manufacturer*
Leibler, Kenneth Robert *finance company executive*
Leiby, Arthur Daniel *accountant*
Leidel, Katherine *journalist, newscaster*
Leidy, Charlotte *military officer*
Leifert, Terence *engineer*
Leigh, Vincenta M. *health administrator*
Leijonhufvud, Axel Stig Bengt *economics professor*
Leipzig, Arthur *photographer, retired educator*
Leistner, Mary Edna *retired secondary school educator*
Leitzel, Joan Ruth *retired academic administrator*
Lelyveld, Joseph Salem *former newspaper editor, news correspondent, writer*
LeMaire, Elizabeth Griffin *parochial school educator*
Leman, Loren Dwight *former lieutenant governor, civil engineer*
LeMarbe, Edward S. *marketing and engineering executive*
Lembark, Connie Wertheimer *art consultant*
Lemieux, Jacob E. *biochemist*
Lemke, Carol Ann *music educator, pianist, accountant*
Lemke, James Underwood *physicist*
Lemlich, Robert *chemical engineer, educator*
Lemos, Arthur *retired music educator*
Lempert, Richard Owen *lawyer, educator*
Lenhart, Cynthia Rae *conservation organization executive*
Lennix, Harry Joseph III *actor*
Lennon, Joseph Luke *retired academic administrator, priest*
Lennox, Donald D(uane) *retired automotive and housing components company executive*
Lennox, William James, Jr. *retired military officer*
Leno, Jay (James Douglas Muir Leno) *talk show host, comedian, writer*
Lentini, Francine *retired physical education educator*
Lentz, Mary A. *lawyer, educator*
Lenz, Henry Paul *management consultant*
Leon, Nellie *health educator*
Leonard, Sister Anne C. *school system administrator*
Leonard, Elmore John *writer, scriptwriter*
Leonard, Hasse A. *psychologist, educator*
Leonard, Richard Hart *journalist, educator*
Leong, Stephanie Mei *financial planner*
Leonhardt, Thomas Wilburn *librarian, library director*
Leoni, Tea (Elizabeth Tea Pantaleoni) *actress*
Lepage, Robert *actor, playwright*
L'Eplattenier, Nora Sweeny Hickey *nursing educator*
Lepley, Rick Allen *consumer products company executive*
Leppard, Stephanie Jean *systems analyst, artist*
Lerner, Beth M. *non-profit consultant*
Lerner, Herbert J. *tax consultant*
Lerner, Laurence M. *college administrator*
Lerner, Vladimir Semion *computer scientist, educator*
Lerner-Lam, Eva I-Hwa *transportation executive*
LeRoy, G. Palmer *art dealer*
Lesch, Michael *cardiologist*
Lescroart, John Thomas *writer, composer, singer*
Le Shana, David Charles *retired academic administrator*
Lesher, John Lee, Jr. *consulting services company executive*
Leslie, Alfred *painter, filmmaker*
Leslie, Maureen Heelan *university director*
Lester, Alicia Louise *financial analyst*
Lester, Bill (William Alexander Lester) *race car driver*
Lester, Julius B. *author*
Lester, Mark Charles *neurosurgeon*
Lester, Robin Dale *historian, educator, writer, former headmaster*
Lester, Virginia Laudano *academic administrator*
Lethem, Jonathan Allen *writer*
Letterie, Kathleen *broadcast executive*
Letterman, David *talk show host, producer, comedian, writer*
Leupold, Herbert August *physicist*
LeValley, Amber Noel *school psychologist*
LeVasseur, Lee Allan *artist*
Levchin, Max *Internet company executive*
Leveille, Gilbert Antonio *food products executive*
Level, Leon Jules *investor, director*
Leven, Stephen H. *retired human resources specialist*
Levenback, Karen L. *librarian, archivist, educator, writer, editor*
Levens, Dorsey (Herbert Levens) *professional football player*
Levenson, Marc David *optics and lasers specialist, editor*
Leventhal, Ellen Iris *portfolio manager*
Levermore, Monique A. *psychologist, educator*
Levey, Robert Frank *columnist, not-for-profit fundraiser*
Levi, Danilo *sociologist, educator, director*
Levi, Josef Alan *artist*
Levick, Richard Scott *communications executive, lawyer, consultant, educator*
Levien, Roger Eli *strategy and innovation consultant*
Levin, A. Leo *law educator, retired government official*
Levin, Alan Scott *pathologist, allergist, immunologist, lawyer*
Levin, Gilbert Victor *biotechnology company executive*
Levin, Ian *radiologist*
Levin, Jack *physician, biomedical investigator, educator*
Levin, Michael Stuart *steel company executive*

Levin, Morton D(avid) *artist, printmaker, educator*
Levin, Richard I. *dean, cardiologist, researcher*
Levin, Steven Jonathan *physician*
Levin, William Edward *lawyer*
Levine, Alan *lawyer*
Levine, Arthur Elliott *former academic administrator, educator*
Levine, Jack *artist*
Levins, John Raymond *investment advisor, educator, management consultant*
Levinsky, Frieda Libby *language educator*
Levinsohn, Gary *producer*
Levinson, Herbert Sherman *civil and transportation engineer*
Levinson, Peter Joseph *retired lawyer*
Levinson, Stephen Eliot *electrical engineer, educator*
Levitt, Brian Michael *consumer products company executive, lawyer*
Levitt, Seymour Herbert *radiologist, educator*
Levy, Arthur James *public relations executive, writer*
Levy, David *retired lawyer, insurance company executive, consultant*
Levy, Leah Garrigan *federal official*
Levy, Leslie Ann *application developer*
Levy, Louis Edward *retired accounting firm executive*
Levy, Norman B. *psychiatrist, educator*
Levy, Robert Edward *retired management consultant*
Levy, Stephen H. *computer scientist, educator*
Levy, Todd Robert *musician, educator*
Lew, Ginger Ehn *investment company executive, lawyer*
Lew, Roger Alan *manufacturing executive*
Lewie, Reva Goodwin *artist, educator*
Lewin, Tamar (Katherine Lewin) *reporter*
Lewins, Steven *financial analyst, investment company executive, legislative staff member, retired military officer*
Lewis, Andrew Lindsay, Jr., (Drew Lewis) *former transportation and natural resources executive*
Lewis, Anthony *columnist, educator*
Lewis, Brian Kreglow *retired physiologist, computer scientist*
Lewis, Brock *investment company executive*
Lewis, Charles Leonard *psychologist*
Lewis, Christa Marie *music educator*
Lewis, David L. *lawyer*
Lewis, Dennis Carroll *writer, publishing executive*
Lewis, Douglas *retired art historian*
Lewis, Emanuel Raymond *historian, psychologist, retired librarian*
Lewis, Floyd Wallace *former electric utility executive*
Lewis, George Ralph *consumer goods company executive*
Lewis, Homer Dick *retired nuclear engineer*
Lewis, Hunter *investment advisor, writer*
Lewis, James Kevin *music educator*
Lewis, James Lee, Jr. *actuary*
Lewis, Leslie Joy *music company executive, consultant*
Lewis, Martin Edward *transportation executive, oil trader, foreign government concessionary*
Lewis, Martin R. *paper company executive, consultant*
Lewis, Ned Lehmon *secondary school educator*
Lewis, Perry Joshua *investment banker*
Lewis, Rita Hoffman *plastic products manufacturing company executive*
Lewis, Samuel Winfield *retired federal agency administrator, diplomat*
Lewis, Sharyn Lee *sculptor*
Lewis, Suford *computer scientist, consultant*
Lewitt, Miles Martin *computer engineering company executive*
Li, Gong *actress*
Li, Jet (Li Lian Jie, Lei Lin-Git) *actor*
Li, Jianliang *engineer*
Li, Lide *mathematician, econometrician, consultant*
Li, Maria *neurosurgeon*
Li, Ming *oceanographer*
Li, Qin *news anchor, reporter, television director and producer*
Li, Tingye *electrical engineer*
Li, Xiang-Yang *science educator*
Liang, Junxiang *retired aeronautics and astronautics engineer, educator*
Liang, Qingqing *electronics engineer*
Libassi, Frank Peter *lawyer*
Liberati, Maria Theresa *lifestyle company executive, cooking expert, writer*
Liberman, Gail Jeanne *editor*
Lichtblau, John H. *retired economist*
Lichtenbaum, Peter *lawyer, former federal agency administrator*
Lichtenstein, Harvey *performing arts association administrator*
Lichtenstein, Natalie G. *lawyer*
Lichtman, Emily Ann *radiologist*
Licke, Wallace John *lawyer*
Liden, Hanna *photographer*
Lidsky, Ella *retired law librarian*
Liebeler, Susan Wittenberg *lawyer*
Lieberfarb, Warren N. *digital media pioneer*
Lieberman, Anne Marie *retired financial executive*
Lieberman, Gail Forman *financial consultant*
Lieberman, Louis (Karl Lieberman) *artist*
Lieberson, Peter *composer*
Liebman, Sarah *artist, educator*
Liebowitz, Daniel S.F. *retired medical educator*
Liebrandt, Paul *chef*
Liess, Benjamin D. *otolaryngologist*
Lifson, Kalman Alan *retired retail and bank executive, portfolio manager*
Lifton, Paul Samuel *theater educator*
Ligety, Ted *Olympic athlete*
Light, Arthur Heath *bishop*
Lightman, Alan Paige *writer, physicist, educator*
Lightman, Harold Allen *marketing executive*
Lightstone, Ronald *lawyer*
Ligon, Duke R. *lawyer*
Liguori, Robert *lawyer, insurance company executive*
Likins, Peter William *retired academic administrator*
Likins, Rose Marie *former federal agency administrator, ambassador*
Li-lan, *artist*
Lilienstern, O. Clayton *lawyer, educator*
Liljegren, Frank Sigfrid *art association administrator, artist, educator*
Lillehoff, Piper *psychiatrist*
Lilley, William III *business executive, consultant*
Lilly, Edward Guerrant, Jr. *retired utilities executive*
Lilly, Thomas Gerald *retired lawyer*
Lilly-Hersley, Jane Anne Feeley *nursing researcher*
Limburg-Santistevan, Ellen H. *retired geologist, artist*
Limerick, Dianne A. *mathematics educator, athletic trainer*
Limpus, Charles Everett III *non-commissioned officer*
Lin, Edward C. *engineering educator*
Lin, Henry C. *physician, researcher*
Lin, Maya *architect, sculptor*
Lin, Qiuyun *education educator*
Lin, Ray-Qing *physicist, researcher*
Lin, Ronghui *chemist, researcher*
Lincicome, David Richard *biomedical scientist, animal scientist*
Lind, Niels Christian *civil engineering educator*
Linda, Gerald *advertising and marketing executive*
Lindberg, Francis Laurence, Jr. *management consultant*
Linde, Armando Steven *economist*
Linde, Maxine Helen *lawyer, corporate financial executive, investor*
Linde, Ronald Keith *investor*
Lindegren, Cecile Keyser *music educator*
Lindeman, Barry James *internal auditor, nurse, minister*
Lindenberger, Herbert Samuel *writer, literature educator*
Lindenmayer, Elisabeth *international organization administrator*
Lindgren, William Dale *librarian*
Lindo, Allen Pineda (Apl.de.ap) *rap artist*
Lindquist, Michael Adrian *career military officer*
Lindsey, Lawrence Benjamin *economist*
Lindsey, Roberta Lewise *music researcher, historian, educator*
Lindsley, Joyce Lillian *music educator*
Lindstrom, Rosetta Arline *retired medical technician*
Lineen, Edward M. *lawyer, information technology executive*
Linett, David *retired lawyer*
Ling, Bai *actor*
Lingle, Marilyn Felkel *journalist, columnist, writer*
Link, George Hamilton *retired lawyer*
Link, Phoebe Forrest *education educator, writer, social worker, poet*
Link, Phyllida Korman *artist, educator*
Linn, Richard *federal judge*
Linster, Michelle Lynn *education educator, consultant*
Linton, Michael Alan *food products executive*
Linville, Randal L. *agricultural company executive*
Linz, Anthony James *osteopathic physician, consultant, educator*
Lioi, Sara Elizabeth *judge*
Liotta, Lance Allen *pathologist*
Lipinski, Tara Kristen *retired professional figure skater*
Lipinski, William Oliver *former congressman*
Lipkin, David Lawrence *physician*
Lipman, David *retired journalist, multi-media consultant*
Lipman, Hannah Ilene *medical educator*
Lippard, Lucy Rowland *writer, educator, critic, curator*
Lippes, Richard James *lawyer*
Lippincott, James Andrew *retired biochemistry and biological sciences educator*
Lippincott, Philip Edward *retired paper company executive*
Lipsey, Joseph, Jr. *wholesale distribution executive*
Lipsey, Richard George *economist, educator*
Lipsitt, Lewis Paeff *psychology professor*
Lipsky, Burton G. *lawyer*
Lipsman, Richard Marc *lawyer, educator*
Lipson, Abigail *psychologist*
Lipson, Allen S. *former entertainment company executive, lawyer*
Lipton, Bob *music educator, composer*
Lipton, Glenn E. *orthopaedic surgeon*
Lipton, Robert Steven *lawyer*
Lisio, Donald John *historian, educator*
Lister, Harry Joseph *financial company consultant*
Lithgow, John Arthur *actor, film director*
Litman, Harry Peter *lawyer, educator*
Litrownik, Alan Jay *psychologist, educator*
Little, Arthur Dehon *investor*
Little, Charlotte Louise *poet, writer*
Little, Dallas *minister*
Littleford, William Donaldson *retired publishing executive*
Little Gurley Brady O'Little, Cassandra Oneda *education educator*
Littler, Gene Alec *professional golfer*
Little Richard, (Richard Wayne Penniman) *musician, lyricist, minister*
Littleton, Harvey Kline *artist*
Littman, Earl *advertising and public relations executive*
Litwin, Todd *software engineer*
Litwinowicz, Anthony *information scientist, researcher*
Liu, Katherine Chang *artist, art educator*
Liu, Songtao *medical researcher*
Liu, Wei *telecommunications industry executive, researcher*
Liu, Yong Cheng *chemist, educator*
Livengood, Scott A. *former food products executive*
Liverman, Betty Jean *elementary school educator*
Livermore, Ann Martinelli *computer company executive*
Livingston, Vernon *retired health facility administrator*
Livingstone, Susan Morrisey *management consultant, former federal agency administrator*
Livingstone, Trudy Dorothy Zweig *dancer, educator*
Lloyd, David Livingstone, Jr. *lawyer*
Lloyd, Ray Dix *retired health physicist*
Loarie, Thomas Merritt *healthcare executive*
Lobdell, Frank *artist*
Lober, Irene Moss *educational consultant*
Lober, Lionel M. *scriptwriter, film producer*
Lobrano, Mary Elizabeth *radiologist, director*
Lobue, Ange *psychiatrist, author*
Lochner, Philip Raymond *retired communications executive, former commissioner*
Locke, Edwin Allen III *retired psychologist, educator*
Locke, Norton *hotel and construction executive*
Locke, William Henry *lawyer*
Locklear, Heather *actress*
Lockwood, Robert W. *management consultant*
Lockwood, Theodore Davidge *retired academic administrator*
Locricchio, Matthew *actor, writer*
Loddenkemper, Tobias *neurologist*
Löe, Harald *retired dentist, educator, researcher*
Loesch, Arthur Z. *environmental scientist, educator*
Loew, Brenda *publisher*
Lofton, Kevin Eugene *medical facility administrator*
Loftus, Elizabeth F. *psychology professor*
Logan, David Bruce *health facility administrator, nurse*
Logan, James Kenneth *lawyer, retired judge*
Logan, Kent *retired securities industry executive*
Logue, Jean Evelyn *music educator*
Lohman, Gordon Russell *retired manufacturing executive*
Lohmann, Christoph Hubertus *orthopaedic surgeon, researcher*
Lohmann, George Young, Jr. *neurosurgeon, health facility administrator, artist*
Lohmuller, Martin Nicholas *retired bishop*
Loiello, John Peter *diplomat, international consultant*
Loizos, Dimitrios *electrical engineer, researcher*
Loken, Barbara *marketing educator, social psychologist*
Lokmer, Stephanie Ann *international business development consultant*
Lolley, William Randall *minister*
Lollis, Stuart Scott *neurosurgeon*
Lombard, Richard Spencer *lawyer*
Lombardi, Mary Luciana *musician, historian*
Lonchyna-Lisowsky, Maria *music educator*
Lonegan, Thomas Lee *retired restaurant corporation executive*
Long, Charles Thomas *lawyer, history professor*
Long, Clarence Dickinson III *lawyer*
Long, Elaine *writer, editor*
Long, James Jay *lawyer*
Long, Peter Avard Chipman *retired military officer*
Long, Ralph Stewart *clinical psychologist*
Long, Roger Leonard *artist*
Long, Shelley (Shelley Lee Long) *actress*
Longaberger, Tami *home decor accessories company executive*
Longfield, William Herman *health products executive*
Longobardo, Anna Kazanjian *engineering executive*
Longobardo, Guy Alfred *lawyer, department chairman*
Longstreet, John Charles *retired computer scientist*
Longsworth, Robert Morrow *language educator*
Loomis, Salora Dale *psychiatrist*
Looney, Gerald Lee *medical educator, administrator*
Looser, Donald William *academic administrator*
Loper, Carl Richard, Jr. *metallurgical engineer, educator*
Loper, James Leaders *broadcasting executive*
Lopera, Gustavo Adolfo *cardiologist, electrophysiologist*
Lopez, Barry Holstun *writer*
Lopez, Soledad *actress*
Loppnow, Milo Alvin *clergyman, former church official*
Lord, George Frank *educational director*
Lord, Jerome Edmund *education administrator, writer*
Lorelli, Elvira Mae *artist, art educator*
Lorelli, Michael Kevin *consumer products company executive*
Loren, Allan Z. *former financial services company executive*
Loren, Norman James *lawyer*
Loring, Gloria Jean *vocalist, actress, writer*
Lorne, Simon Michael *lawyer*
Los, Marinus *retired agrochemical researcher*
Loscalzo, Anthony Joseph *lawyer*
Loschen, Earl Lee *psychiatrist, educator*
Loser, Joseph Carlton, Jr. *dean, retired judge*
Losi, Maxim John *medical communications executive*
Loss, John C. *architect, retired educator*
Lotas, Judith Patton *advertising executive*
Lotchin, Roger Williams *history professor, writer*
Lotsch, Alexander *scientist*
Lotspiech, Jeffrey *computer scientist, consultant*
Lott, Ronnie (Ronald Mandel Lott) *retired professional football player, television broadcaster*
Lotter, Charles Robert *retired lawyer*
Louargand, Marc Andrew *real estate executive, financial consultant*
Louie, Steven Gwon Sheng *physics professor, researcher*
Love, Courtney *singer, actress*
Love, Michael Joseph *lawyer*
Love, Robert Lyman *retired education educator, consultant*
Love, Shirley *mezzo-soprano*
Lovelace, Julianne *former library director*
Lovelace, Rose Marie Sniegon *federal space agency administrator*
Loveland, Eugene Franklin *retired gas industry executive*
Loveland, Sylvia Marie *translator*
Lovell, Carl Erwin, Jr. *lawyer*
Lovell, Malcolm Read, Jr. *public information officer, educator, retired trade association administrator, federal official*
Lovett, Clara Maria *retired academic administrator, historian*
Lovick, Norma McGinnis *social studies educator*
Lovinger, Andrew Joseph *polymer scientist*
Lovins, Amory Bloch *physicist, energy consultant*
Low, Eugene Jensen *pathologist*
Low, Harry William *judge*
Low, Morton David *retired neuroscientist, healthcare educator*
Lowden, John L. *retired manufacturing executive*
Lowe, John III *consulting civil engineer*
Lowe, John C. *medical researcher, director*
Lowe, Patricia A. *psychologist, educator*
Lowell, Virginia Lee *retired librarian*
Lowenthal, Constance *art historian, consultant*
Lowery, Daniel Louis *publishing executive*
Lowrie, William G. *former oil company executive*
Lowry, Julie Royal *music educator*
Loy, Frank Ernest *retired federal agency administrator*
Loy, Richard Franklin *civil engineer*
Loye, Estelle C. *contractor, travel consultant*
Lozano, Monica Cecilia *publishing executive*
Lu, Erdong *research scientist*
Lu, Natalie *federal agency administrator*
Lubell, Ellen *writer*
Lubezki, Emmanuel *cinematographer*
Lubic, Ruth Watson *health facility administrator, nurse midwife*
Lubick, Donald Cyril *lawyer*
Lubin, Steven *concert pianist, musicologist*
Lubner, Mary F. *retired elementary school educator*
Lucander, Henry *investment banker*
Lucas, Janet Marie *language educator*
Lucas, Josh (Josh Maurer) *actor*
Lucas, Katherine E. *epidemiologist*
Lucas, Michele Angelyn *learning consultant, special education educator*
Lucas, Teri Kathleen *secondary school educator*
Lucas, William Ray *aerospace scientist, consultant*
Lucca, David Alan *money manager*
Luce, Donald Sanders *social worker*
Luce, Edward Andrew *plastic surgeon*
Luce, Priscilla Mark *public relations executive*
Luce, Thomas Warren III *former federal agency administrator*
Lucht, Orren Jesse *retired mechanical engineer*
Lucier, P. Jeffrey *publishing executive*
Lucker, Jay K. *library consultant*
Luckey, Doris Waring *civic volunteer*
Ludden, John Franklin *retired economist*
Ludwig, Christa *retired mezzo soprano*
Ludwig, Stephen *pediatrics and emergency medicine educator*
Luedeman, Gerald Warren *radiologist*
Luening, Robert Adami *retired agricultural studies educator*
Luetkehoelter, Gottlieb Werner (Lee Luetkehoelter) *retired bishop, clergyman*
Lufty, JoyBeth *minister*
Lugenbeel, Edward Elmer *publisher*
Luger, Donald R. *engineering company executive*
Lukacs, Michael Edward *electro-optics researcher*
Luke, David Lincoln III *retired paper company executive*
Luke, Karen *chemist, researcher*
Luke, Robert George *nephrologist, medical educator*
Lumsden, Rachel Lee *musician*
Luna, Pedro P. *academic administrator*
Lund, Rita Pollard *aerospace engineer, consultant*
Lundgren, Colleen Bowling *elementary school educator, consultant*
Lundgren, Gail M. *lawyer*
Lundin, Benjamin W. *religious studies scholar, political science scholar*
Lundstedt, Sven Bertil *behavioral and social scientist, educator*
Lupin, Louis Martin *lawyer*
Lupu, Radu *pianist*
Lurie, Alvin David *lawyer*
Luskin, Frederic Michael *psychologist, educator*
Lustyk, Mary Kathleen *neuroscientist, educator*
Lusztig, Peter Alfred *dean, educator*
Lutes, Jim G. (James Lutes) *artist*
Luthy, Richard Godfrey *environmental engineering educator*
Luti, Bill (William Joseph Luti) *federal official, retired military officer*
Lutts, Ralph Herbert *scholar, educator, museum administrator*
Lutz, Jeanne V. *elementary school educator*
Lutz, Matthew Charles *oil industry executive, geologist*
Lutz, Tamara Jean *nursing consultant*
Luviano, Damien M. *ophthalmologist*
Lyall, Katharine Culbert *former academic administrator, economist, educator*

Lyford, Ronald Lee *music educator*
Lyles, Mark Bradley *advanced technology company executive, military officer*
Lyn, Jean *interior designer*
Lynch, Charles Andrew *chemicals executive*
Lynch, Charlotte Andrews *retired communications executive, consultant*
Lynch, Harry James *retired biologist*
Lynch, Jessica *military officer*
Lynch, John Thomas *retired science administrator, physicist*
Lynch, Robert Berger *retired lawyer, judge*
Lynch, Robert Emmett *mathematics professor*
Lynch, Thomas Peter *retired investment company executive*
Lynch, Thomas Wimp *lawyer*
Lynds, Gayle Hallenbeck *writer*
Lyne, Dorothy-Arden *secondary school educator*
Lyngbye, Jørgen *hospital advisor, researcher*
Lynn, Naomi B. *academic administrator*
Lyon, Bruce Arnold *lawyer, educator*
Lyon, Martha Sue *research engineer, retired military officer*
Lyons, Champ, Jr. *state supreme court justice*
Lyons, Charles M. *education educator, former academic administrator*
Lyons, John David *literature and language professor*
Lyons, John W(inship) *retired civilian military employee, chemist, consultant*
Lyons, Richard Kent *dean, finance educator*
Lyons, Susanne D. *former finance company executive*
Lysne, Allen Bruce *laboratory director*
Ma, Vu *chemist*
Maarbjerg, Mary Penzold *retired office equipment company executive*
Maatman, Gerald Leonard *insurance company executive*
Maben, Hayward Clinton, Jr. *cardiothoracic surgeon*
Mabey, Ralph R. *lawyer*
Mabus, Raymond Edwin, Jr. *former ambassador, governor*
Mac Alister, Robert James *executive recruiter*
Macarol, Victor George *artist*
MacArthur, Marcia *primary school educator*
Macaulay, David Alexander *author, illustrator*
MacAulay, Lawrence A. *former Canadian government official, member of Parliament*
MacAvoy, Thomas Coleman *manufacturing executive, educator*
MacCarthy, John L. *lawyer*
MacCarthy, Talbot Leland *civic volunteer*
MacCormack, Jean F. *academic administrator*
MacCracken, Michael Calvin *atmospheric scientist*
MacDevitt, Brian *lighting designer*
MacDonald, Alan Hugh *academic administrator*
MacDonald, Donald Paul *lawyer*
Macdonald, Lenna Ruth *lawyer, business advisor*
MacDonald, Priscilla Ann *history professor*
MacDonald, Ronald Francis *diversified financial services company executive*
MacDonough, Robert Howard *consulting engineer, tax specialist, consultant*
Macedo de la Concha, Rafael *former Mexican government official*
Macera, Michelle Heffner *marriage and family therapist*
MacFarlane, Cathy M. *federal agency administrator*
MacFarlane, John Charles *utilities executive*
Macha, Ken *former professional baseball coach*
MacHovec, Frank J. *psychologist*
Mackay, Leo Sidney, Jr. *healthcare company executive, former federal agency administrator*
MacKenzie, Donald Murray *health facility administrator*
Mackey, Jeffrey Allen *priest*
Mackey, Nathaniel *poet and poetry professor*
Mackey Catoe, Margaret Emmie *library media specialist*
MacKinnon, John Alexander *lawyer*
MacKinnon, Kevin Scott *lawyer*
MacLean, Doug *former professional hockey coach, former sports team executive*
MacLennan, Beryce Winifred *psychologist*
Macleod, Angus *retired internist*
Maclin, Amy *editor*
MacMillan, Whitney *retired food products and import/export company executive*
MacNeill, James William *environmental energy and management consultant*
MacQueen, Robert Moffat *solar physicist*
MacWilliams, Kenneth Edward *investment banker*
MacWilliams, Michael L., Jr. *environmentalist, educator*
Macy, Bill (William Macy Garber) *actor*
Madden, Richard Blaine *forest products executive*
Maddin, Robert *metallurgist, educator*
Maddox, Nadana *secondary school educator*
Maddux, Gregory Alan *professional baseball player*
Madeira, Francis King Carey *conductor, educator*
Madison, Anne Conway *marketing, public relations professional*
Madison, Deborah Leafy *writer, chef*
Madix, Robert James *chemical engineer, educator*
Madonna, (Madonna Louise Veronica Ciccone) *singer, actress, producer*
Madrid, Cirilo L. *health facility administrator*
Madsen, Virginia *actress*
Maeda, J. A. *data processing executive, consultant*
Maehl, William Harvey *retired historian*
Maehr, Martin Louis *psychology professor*
Maestrone, Frank Eusebio *diplomat*
Maffei, Frank Anthony *pediatrician, educator*
Magana, Melanie G *psychologist, consultant*
Magaw, John W. *former federal agency administrator*
Magazine, Alan Harrison *association executive, consultant*
Mage, Rose Goldman *immunologist, educator*
Magee, Alan *artist*
Magee, John Francis *research and development company executive*
Maginn, John Leo *retired insurance company executive*
Magnano, Salvatore Paul *retired finance company executive, treasurer*
Magner, Marjorie J. (Marge Magner) *investment company executive*
Magnes, Harry Alan *physician*
Magor, Louis Roland *conductor*
Magrill, Joe Richard, Jr. *religious organization administrator, minister*
Magro, Cynthia Maria *pathologist*
Magruder, Jack *retired academic administrator*
Maguire, James Harvey *physician*
Maguire, Martie (Martha Elenor Erwin Maguire) *musician*
Maguire, Robert Francis III *real estate investor*
Magurno, Richard Peter *lawyer*
Mahaffey, Marcia Hixson *retired educational administrator*
Mahajan, Ashutosh *library and information scientist*
Maharidge, Dale Dimitro *journalist, educator, writer*
Mahesh, Virendra Bhushan *endocrinologist*
Mahle, Christoph Erhard *electrical engineer*
Mahmood, Nafeesa F. *physician, consultant*
Mahmoodi, Hamid *engineer*
Mahmud, Shireen Dianne *photographer*
Mahoney, Ann Dickinson *fundraiser*
Mahoney, George LeFevre *lawyer*
Mahoney, George R., Jr. *lawyer*
Mahoney, John *actor*
Mahoney, John L. *English literature educator*
Mahoney, Michael Robert Taylor *art historian, educator*
Mahoney, Robert William *electronic and security systems manufacturing executive*
Maikish, Charles John *engineer, lawyer*
Mailer, Norman Kingsley *writer, playwright, film director*
Main, Robert Gail *communications educator, training services executive, television and film producer, retired military officer*
Mainella, Fran (Frances P. Mainella) *educator, former federal agency administrator*
Maines, Natalie Louise *musician*
Maiolini, Gloria J. *nursing case manager, poet, writer*
Maioriello, Richard Patrick *retired otolaryngologist*
Mair, Bruce Logan *interior designer, architectural firm executive*
Maisto, John F. *former ambassador*
Majeed, D. Hadayai S. *publishing executive, writer*
Major, Patrick Webb III *principal*
Majors, Nelda Faye *physical therapist*
Mak, Linda L. *dermatologist*
Makarov, Iouri *advertising executive*
Makepeace, Mary Lou *foundation administrator, former mayor*
Makimura, Yasuhiro *history professor*
Makki, S. Kami *education educator*
Makrogiannis, Sokratis *physicist, researcher*
Mala, Theodore Anthony *physician, consultant*
Malach, Monte *physician*
Malaro, Marie C. *retired museum administrator, lawyer*
Malatesta, Mary Anne *lawyer*
Malek, Marlene Anne *foundation administrator*
Maley, Abigail Joy *zoologist, researcher*
Mali, Paul *publisher, retired management educator*
Malik, Om *former venture capitalist, blog website company executive, journalist*
Malin, Robert Abernethy *retired investment company executive*
Maling, George Croswell, Jr. *physicist*
Malins, Donald Clive *biochemist, researcher*
Malishenko, Timothy Peter *aerospace company executive*
Malkin, Michael M. *lawyer*
Malkovich, John *actor*
Malks, Betty F. *social worker*
Malley, Raymond Charles *retired foreign service official, industrial executive*
Mallison, Howard Danford *retired corporate communications specialist*
Mallory, Arthur Lee *dean, retired state official*
Malloy, John Richard *lawyer, chemicals executive*
Malloy, Michael Terrence *journalist, reporter*
Malluche, Hartmut Horst *nephrologist, medical educator*
Malone, Claudine Berkeley *management consultant*
Malone, Robert Wallace *surgeon*
Maloney, James Henry *community development executive, former congressman*
Maloney, Therese Adele *retired insurance company executive*
Malphurs, Roger Edward *biomedical marketing executive*
Maltas, Carla Jo *music educator, education educator*
Maltby, Florence Helen *library science educator*
Malter-Hoffman, Kelly A. *finance company executive, consultant*
Manas, Gerald Bennett (Jerry Manas) *information technology manager*
Manchester, Kenneth Edward *electronics executive, consultant*
Mandel, Adrienne Abramson *state legislator*
Mandelbrot, Benoit B. *mathematician, research scientist, educator*
Mandell, Gerald Lee *internist, educator*
Mandile, Michael Angelo *investment advisor*
Mandyam, Giridhar Dhati *electronics engineer*
Maneker, Roberta S(ue) *public relations executive*
Manfredi, Zachary-John A. *political scientist*
Mangasarian, Olvi Leon *research scientist, educator*
Mangelsdorf, Thomas Kelly *psychiatrist, consultant*
Mangino, Christine *academic administrator*
Mangla, Sundeep *radiologist, research scientist*
Manglona, Ramona V. *judge, former attorney general*
Mangold, John Frederic *manufacturing executive, retired military officer*
Mangold, Sylvia Plimack *artist*
Manion, Bonnie J. *volunteer, poet, composer*
Mankiewicz, Thomas Frank *screenwriter, director, producer*
Mankin, Henry Jay *orthopedist, educator, health facility administrator*
Mankin, Robert Stephen *diversified financial services company executive*
Mankoff, David Abraham *nuclear medicine physician*
Manley, Joan A(dele) Daniels *retired publishing executive*
Manley, John Hugo *computer company executive, educator*
Manley, Judith L. *director*
Manley, Kelli Jo *writer, photographer*
Mann, Clarence Charles *retired realtor*
Mann, Eric Louis *retired military officer, mathematics professor, researcher*
Mann, Merlin Dean III *blogger*
Mann, Sally *photographer*
Manne, Henry Girard *lawyer, consultant, economist, educator, retired dean*
Mannelli, Paolo *psychiatrist, educator*
Mannelly, Patrick J. *former beverage company executive*
Mannes, Elena Sabin *film and television producer, television director*
Manninen, Peter R. *chemist*
Manning, John Warren III *retired surgeon, medical educator*
Manning, Michael Nicholas *actor, singer, guitarist, broadcaster, journalist*
Manning, William Dudley, Jr. *retired specialty chemical company executive*
Manos, Christopher Lawrence *lawyer, mediator*
Manson, Harold Craig *former federal agency administrator, former judge*
Mantei, Lorraine E. *school system administrator*
Mantione, Kirk John *research scientist, consultant*
Mantz, Arlan W. *physics professor*
Manuel, Ralph Nixon *retired private school executive*
Manville, Greta Craig *writer*
Manyam, Bala Venkatesha *medical researcher, neurology educator*
Mao, Aiwu *physician, radiologist*
Mapes, William W. *auditor*
Maplesden, Carol Harper *marriage and family therapist, music educator*
Mapp, Edward Charles *speech educator*
Marano, Thomas J. *marketing professional*
Marcdante, Karen Jean *medical educator*
Marceau, Judith Marie *retired elementary school educator, small business owner*
March, Michael F. *propulsion systems analyst, consultant*
Marchenko, Tamara G. *music educator*
Marchi, Sergio Sisto *Canadian government official*
Marco, Cura A. *medical educator*
Marcopoulos, George John *history professor*
Marcoux, Julia A. *midwife*
Marcus, Bernard *foundation administrator, retired retail executive*
Marcus, Edward *economist, educator*
Marcus, Greil Gerstley *critic*
Marcuse, Dietrich *retired physicist*
Marcy, Kevin Michael *film producer, lawyer*
Mare, Jennifer Le *medical technician*
Maready, William Frank *lawyer*
Margolis, Daniel Herbert *lawyer*
Margoshes, Miriam Kagan *information specialist*
Margules, Cecelia *composer, poet*
Mariano, Ana Virginia *retired pathologist*
Marier, Robert L. *dean, hospital administrator*
Marinetti, Guido V. *biochemistry professor*
Maring, Donald George, Jr. *electrical engineer*
Marini, Frank Nicholas *political science and public administration educator*
Marinis, Thomas Paul, Jr. *lawyer*
Marino, Giovanni *surgeon*
Marion, John Louis *former fine arts auctioneer and appraiser*
Marion, Marjorie Anne *English language educator, educational consultant*
Mariucci, Steve *professional football coach, former college football coach*
Mark, Hon Fong Louie *cytogeneticist*
Mark, Michael Laurence *retired music educator*
Marken, William Riley *editor-in-chief*
Marker, Marc Linthacum *lawyer, investor, entrepreneur*
Markey, Randolph David *marketing professional*
Markham, Charles Henry *neurologist*
Markham, Reed B. *education educator, consultant*
Markovich, Alexandria *assistant principal*
Markovich, Patricia H. *economist*
Marks, Bruce *performing company executive, choreographer*
Marks, John *engineer, consultant*
Marks, Martha Alford *writer*
Marks, Roberta Barbara *artist, educator*
Marley, Damian Robert Nesta (Jr. Gong) *reggae artist*
Marlow, Edward A. *former army officer*
Marlowe, Willie *artist, fine arts educator*
Marmer, Nancy *editor*
Maron, Marc *comedian, actor, writer*
Maroni, Donna Farolino *biologist, researcher*
Marquand, Jean MacMurtry *educational association administrator*
Marrin, Charles Ainsworth Staveley *cardiovascular and thoracic surgeon, educator*
Marro, Anthony James *retired newspaper editor*
Marsalis, Wynton *musician*
Marschall, Nicole *music educator*
Marse, Melissa J. *music educator, concert pianist*
Marsee, Susanne Irene *vocalist*
Marsh, Don Ermal *supermarket executive*
Marsh, Jack, Jr., (John Otho Marsh) *lawyer, former federal agency administrator, congressman*
Marsh, Joan Knight *educational film company executive, video company executive, publishing executive*
Marsh, Merrilyn Delano *sculptor, artist, painter*
Marshak, Robert Reuben *retired dean, medical educator, veterinarian*
Marshall, Charles Noble *rail transportation executive*
Marshall, Conrad Joseph *entrepreneur*
Marshall, Dale Rogers *former academic administrator, political scientist, educator*
Marshall, Dante *lawyer*
Marshall, Deborah Jill *immunologist*
Marshall, Edith *veterinarian*
Marshall, Frank W. *film producer, director*
Marshall, John Paul *broadcast engineer*
Marshall, Jonathan *foundation administrator, journalist*
Marshall, Kathleen Ann *elementary school educator*
Marshall, Kathryn Sue *lawyer*
Marshall, Kenneth Robert *retired music educator*
Marshall, Marilyn Josephine *retired lawyer*
Marshall, Robert Charles *computer company executive*
Marshall, Wayne Keith *anesthesiology educator*
Marte-Bautista, Helen I. *retired performing arts educator*
Martin, Albert Charles *manufacturing executive, lawyer*
Martin, Alice Howze *prosecutor*
Martin, Andrea Louise *actress, comedienne, writer*
Martin, Bruce J. *elementary school educator*
Martin, Clyde Verne *psychiatrist*
Martin, Daniel C. *surgeon, gynecologist, educator*
Martin, Donald Walter *editor, writer, publisher*
Martin, Edwin Wilson *corporate director, columnist, educational consultant, webmaster*
Martin, Elliot Edwards *theatrical producer*
Martin, George Monroe *pathologist, gerontologist, educator*
Martin, George Raymond Richard *writer*
Martin, Jacqueline Briggs *writer*
Martin, James Kay *management consultant*
Martin, James William *lawyer*
Martin, John F. *academic administrator*
Martin, John Joseph *journalist*
Martin, John William, Jr. *retired lawyer, automotive executive*
Martin, Johnny Benjamin *accountant*
Martin, Joseph Vinson *neuroscientist, educator*
Martin, Karen Siebenthal *community health nurse*
Martin, Marcia D. *science educator*
Martin, Marilyn Mann *retired media specialist*
Martin, Martha Ann *secondary school educator*
Martin, Michael John *journalist, editor*
Martin, Noel *graphics designer, educator*
Martin, Paul *former Prime Minister of Canada*
Martin, Robert Sidney *librarian, educator*
Martin, Sally *singer, voice educator*
Martin, Sarah Michael *pharmacist, educator*
Martin, Trisa *education and human development educator*
Martin, William Collier *hospital administrator*
Martin, William Edwin *lawyer*
Martineau, Robert John *retired law educator*
Martinez, Matthew Gilbert *former congressman*
Martin-Lowry, Beverly Anne *writer, columnist*
Martino, Joseph Paul *research scientist, researcher*
Martin Patterson, Connie Ruth *retired lawyer*
Mártonyi, Csaba Lászlo *retired ophthalmic photographer*
Marty, Martin Emil *theology studies educator*
Martyl, (Mrs. Alexander Langsdorf Jr.) *artist*
Martyn, Evi *music educator, musician*
Maruoka, Jo Ann Elizabeth *retired information systems manager*
Maruyama, Magoroh *business educator, researcher, consultant*
Marvin, Laura Lynn *art educator*
Marx, Darrelyn Madonna *music and drama educator*
Marx, Jeff *composer, lyricist, lawyer, writer*
Marx, Michael William *language educator, writer*
Maryks, Robert A. *history professor*
Masa, George John *retired bank executive*
Masagutov, Vakhid Erkinjonovich *application developer*
Mascheroni, Eleanor Earle *marketing communications executive*
Mashnik, Stepan G. *physicist*
Masi, Julia A. *elementary school educator*
Masiello, Rocco Joseph *air transportation executive, consultant*
Masket, Edward Seymour *television executive*
Maslanka, Daniel Chester *percussionist and music educator*
Mason, Connie Jeanne *writer*
Mason, Deirdre Dianne *secondary school educator*
Mason, Frank Henry III *automotive and rental company executive*
Mason, George Henry *retired business educator*
Mason, John Latimer *engineering executive*
Mason, John Oliver *freelance journalist, community activist, poet*
Mason, Linda *physical education educator, coach*
Mason, Lois E. (J. Day Mason) *painter, poet, actress, educator*
Mason, Marsha *actress, theater director, writer*
Massey, Robert Unruh *internist, educator, dean*
Massey, Stephen Charles *rare book dealer, consultant*

Massey, Thomas Benjamin *retired university president*
Massey, William Walter, Jr. *sales executive*
Massoudi, Bahram Barry *management consultant*
Mastandrea, Linda Lee *lawyer*
Masten, Jacqueline Gwendolyn *small business owner*
Masters, George Windsor, Jr. *electrical engineer, educator*
Masterson, Peter *actor, film producer*
Mastrian, Stacey Lynn *singer, educator*
Mastro, Christopher P. *secondary school educator*
Masuda, Michele Michi *statistician*
Mataré, Herbert F. *physicist, consultant*
Matasar, Ann B. *retired dean, finance educator*
Matema, Zsun-nee Kimball (Annette K. Miller) *social sciences educator*
Matera, Frances Lorine *retired elementary school educator*
Materia, Kathleen Patricia Ayling *nurse*
Materson, Richard Stephen *physician, educator*
Mates, Lawrence A., II, *medical company executive, consultant*
Mates, Robert Edward *mechanical engineering educator*
Matheny, Adam Pence, Jr. *child psychologist, educator, consultant, researcher*
Mathes, Rachel Clarke *voice educator, singer*
Mathew, Trini Ann *internist*
Mathews, Mary Kathryn *retired government official*
Mathewson, George Atterbury *retired lawyer*
Mathieu, Gail Dennise *ambassador*
Mathieu, Georges Victor Adolphe *artist*
Mathieu, Michele Suzanne *grant writer, computer scientist, consultant*
Mathis, John Prentiss *lawyer*
Mathis, Stephanie Charlotte *veterinarian*
Matlock, John Hudson *science administrator, materials engineer*
Matlock, Kent *advertising and public relations executive*
Matschullat, Robert W. *former consumer products company executive*
Matsen, John Martin *academic administrator, pathologist*
Matsuda, Fujio *retired academic administrator*
Matsuda, Paul Kei *literature and language professor*
Matsushima, Akira Paul *manufacturing executive*
Mattar, Philip *writer*
Matterson, Joan McDevitt *physical therapist*
Matthew, Lyn *sales executive, consultant, marketing professional*
Matthews, Norman Stuart *retail executive*
Matthews, Paul Aaron *lawyer*
Matthews, Rondra J. *publishing executive*
Mattice, Howard LeRoy *education educator*
Mattingly, Mack Francis *former ambassador, senator, entrepreneur*
Mattoon, Scott Alexander *private school educator*
Mattox, Johnny Lynn *biologist, educator*
Mattson, Stephen Joseph *retired lawyer*
Mauch, Robert Carl *energy and financial services executive*
Maudlin, Robert V. *economics and government affairs consultant*
Mauger, Thomas F. *ophthalmologist, department chairman*
Maul, Ronald Allen *surgeon*
Maunder, Addison Bruce *agronomic research company executive*
Maurer, Trent W. *humanities educator*
Mauskopf, Seymour Harold *history professor*
Mavilio, Domenico *medical researcher, physician*
Maxfield, Louise Fonda Gribble *executive secretary*
Maxwell, Jerome Eugene *corporate executive*
Maxwell, Robert William *investment banker, financial analyst*
Maxwell, Sara Elizabeth (Sally) *psychologist, educator, speech pathology/audiology services professional, recording industry executive, director*
May, Christopher N. *retired law educator*
May, Edgar *former state legislator*
May, Gary Stephen *electrical engineer*
May, Henry Stratford, Jr. *lawyer*
May, Ingrid Barbara *elementary school educator*
May, Janet Sue *playwright, lyricist*
May, Phyllis Jean *financial executive*
Mayaram, Kartikeya *electrical engineer, educator*
Mayer, Allan *communications consultant, writer*
Mayer, Anthony John *investment company executive*
Mayer, James Joseph *retired corporate lawyer*
Mayer, Michael *theater director*
Mayer, Robert Anthony *retired college president*
Mayer, Susan Martin *art educator*
Mayfield, Robert Charles *academic administrator, geographer, educator*
Maynard, Natalie Ryshna *pianist, educator*
Mayo, Henry P. *surveyor*
Mayoras, Donald Eugene *corporate executive, writer, consultant, educator*
Mayro, Karl R. *realtor*
Mays, Jefferson *actor*
Mayuga, Kenneth A. *physician*
Mazankowski, Donald Frank *Canadian government official*
Mazumder, Sandip *engineer, researcher*
Mazza, David S. *pediatrician*
Mazzilli, Lee *sportscaster, former professional baseball manager*
McAbee, Gary *neurologist, lawyer*
McAleese Dube, Eileen Marie *retired secondary school educator*
McAlonis, Christopher M. *engineer*
McAmis, Edwin Earl *lawyer*
McAniff, Nora P. *former publishing executive*
McAnuff, Des *artistic director*
McAuley, Van Alfon *aerospace mathematician*
McAuliffe, Terry (Terence Richard McAuliffe) *former political organization administrator*
McAvoy, John Joseph *lawyer*
McBride, Brian *professional soccer player*
McBride, Brian F. *biomedical researcher, consultant*
McBride, Mildred Maylea *retired elementary school educator*
McBride, Thomas Dwayne *management consultant*
McBurney, Margot B. *retired librarian*
McCabe, Linda Jean *elementary school educator*
McCabe, Thomas Edward *lawyer, financial software executive*
McCaleb, Neal A. *former federal agency administrator*
McCall-Rodriguez, Leonor *healthcare services company executive, entrepreneur*
McCambridge, John James *retired civil engineer*
McCandless, Carolyn Keller *retired human resources specialist*
McCann, Diana Rae *secondary school educator*
McCann, Elizabeth Ireland *theater, television and film producer*
McCann, Jim (James F. McCann) *consumer products company executive*
McCann, June Vivian *retired physical education educator*
McCann, Peter Paul *biology researcher, educator*
McCardell, John Malcolm, Jr. *history professor, academic administrator*
McCarey, Wilma Ruth *retired lawyer*
McCarney, Dan *former college football coach*
McCarrick, Theodore Cardinal *archbishop emeritus*
McCarthy, Daniel William *management consultant*
McCarthy, Harold Charles *retired insurance company executive*
McCarthy, J. Thomas *lawyer, educator*
McCarthy, Karen P. *former congresswoman, former state legislator*
McCarthy, Kathy *actress, writer*
McCarthy, Paul Fenton *aerospace transportation executive, retired military officer*
McCarthy, Rhoda Ann *retired nursing administrator, retired medical/surgical nurse*
McCarthy, Vincent Paul *lawyer*
Mc Carthy, Walter John, Jr. *retired utilities executive*
McCarthy-Allen, Mary Frances *medical foundation administrator, not-for-profit fundraiser, consultant*
McCartney, Sir Paul (James Paul McCartney) *musician*
McCarty, Thomas Joseph *publishing executive*
McCash, June Hall *writer, retired language educator*
McCaslin, David E. *hotel executive*
McCauley, Harold Homer *retired mechanical engineer*
McCauley, John *music educator*
McCausland, Peter *technology company executive*
McCausland, Thomas James, Jr. *retired brokerage house executive*
McClain, Lena Alexandria *protective services official*
McClanahan, Rue (Eddi-Rue McClanahan) *actress*
McClane, Robert Sanford *entrepreneur, bank executive*
McClatchy, Kevin S. *professional sports team executive*
McCleary, William E(rnest) *retired school librarian, historian*
Mc Clellan, Catharine *anthropologist, educator*
McClellan, Larry Allen *minister, educator*
McClellan, Roger Orville *toxicologist*
McClellan, Scott K. *former White House press secretary*
Mc Clendon, William Hutchinson III *retired lawyer*
McClennen, Miriam J. *former state official*
McClintock, William Thomas *healthcare consultant*
McClinton, Donald George *retired diversified holding company executive*
McClinton, James Leroy *city administrator*
McCloskey, J(ohn) Michael *retired environmental services administrator*
McCloy, Shirley *physical education educator*
McClure, Ann Crawford *judge, lawyer*
McCobb, John Bradford, Jr. *lawyer*
McColgan, Ellyn A. *diversified financial services company executive*
McCollum, Pamela Rae *music educator*
McConaughey, Matthew *actor*
McConnell, Edward Bosworth *legal association administrator, lawyer*
McConnell, Jack Baylor *retired corporate executive, physician*
McConnell, John William, Jr. *lawyer*
McCormack, Douglas P. *lawyer*
Mc Cormack, Francis Xavier *lawyer, former oil company executive*
McCormick, David Arthur *lawyer*
McCormick, Donald Bruce *retired biochemist, educator*
McCormick, Heather N. *mathematics educator*
McCormick, Homer L., Jr. *lawyer*
McCormick, John Owen *retired comparative literature educator*
McCormick, Robert Junior *former federal agency administrator*
McCoy, Dorothy Eloise *writer, educator*
McCoy, John Joseph *lawyer*
McCoy, Mary Jane *retired principal*
Mc Coy, Tidal Windham *former government official*
McCracken, Edward R. *electronics executive*
McCrary, Jonathan Mark *mathematician, educator*
McCready, Kenneth Frank *former electric utility executive*
McCready, Sam *theater educator, actor, theater director*
McCue, Howard McDowell III *lawyer, educator*
McCuistion, Peg Orem *retired health facility administrator*
McCullough, David Legarde *urologist*
McCullough, Laurence Bernard *medical educator, consultant*
McCully, Emily Arnold *illustrator, writer*
McCurdy, Larry Wayne *automotive parts company executive*
McCurdy, Michael Charles *illustrator, author*
McCurley, Robert Lee, Jr. *lawyer, educator*
McCurry, Eddie Joe *entertainer*
McCutchan, William M. *banker*
McCutchen, William Walter, Jr. *retired management educator*
McDade, James Russell *management consultant*
McDaniel, Sara Sherwood (Sally McDaniel) *trainer, consultant*
McDarrah, Gloria Schoffel *editor, writer*
McDermott, Agnes Charlene Senape *philosophy educator*
Mc Dermott, John Francis *psychiatrist, physician*
McDermott, Kathleen E. *lawyer*
McDiarmid, Lucy *literature educator, writer*
McDonald, April D. *writer*
McDonald, Bradley G. *lawyer*
McDonald, Douglas Robert *non profit agency executive*
McDonald, Mark Douglas *electrical engineer*
McDonald, Natasha L. *school psychologist, educator*
McDonald, Peter D. *air transportation executive*
McDonald, William Henry *manufacturing executive*
McDonell, Horace George, Jr. *instrument company executive*
McDonnell, Joseph B. *lawyer*
McDonough, Richard Michael *philosophy educator*
McDonough, William J. *diversified financial services company executive*
McDougall, Donald Blake *retired provincial official, librarian*
McDougall, Ronald Alexander *restaurant executive*
McDowell, Elaine *retired federal government executive, educator*
McDowell, Elizabeth Mary *retired pathology educator*
McDowell, Malcolm *actor*
McElhatten, Betty Shreve *writer, illustrator*
McElwreath, Sally Chin *corporate communications executive*
McEnroe, John Patrick, Jr. *professional tennis player*
McEntire, Reba Nell *musician, actress*
McEvoy, Lorraine Katherine *oncology nurse*
McEvoy, Michael Joseph *economist*
McEvoy, Pamela T. *clinical psychologist*
Mc Fadden, George Linus *retired army officer*
Mc Fadden, Joseph Michael *historian, educator*
McFadden, Peter William *retired mechanical engineering educator*
McFadden, Robbyn Kilbane *interior designer, public policy specialist, artist, advocate*
McFarlane, Donovan Anthony *finance educator, poet, researcher*
McFarlane, Seth *animator, director*
McFarling, Usha Lee *journalist*
McFate, Kenneth Leverne *trade association administrator*
McFate, Patricia Ann *foundation executive, science educator*
McFeatters, Ann Carey *journalist*
McFerren, Martha Dean *writer, librarian*
McGann, Lisa B. Napoli *language educator*
McGarry, Marcia *retired community service coordinator*
McGarvie-Munn, Iain Lachlan *real estate agent, curator, writer*
McGee, Harold Johnston *former academic administrator*
McGee, Humphrey Glenn *retired architect*
McGee, Jane Marie *retired elementary school educator*
McGinnis, Jon David *philosopher, educator*
McGlashan, Thomas Hamel *psychiatrist, educator*
McGlohon, Susan Marie *educational association administrator*
McGlothlen, John M. *librarian*
McGoldrick, John Lewis *lawyer*
McGough, Brian Edward *investment banker, lawyer*
McGough, Duane Theodore *economist, consultant, retired federal official*
McGovern, George Stanley *former senator*
McGowan, Bruce Edward *social studies educator, secondary school educator*
McGowan, Rose *actress*
McGowan, Susan *gifted and talented educator*
McGrath, J. Paul *lawyer*
McGrath, Mary Helena *plastic surgeon, educator*
McGraw, Donald Jesse *biologist, science historian, writer*
McGraw, Susan Catherine *interior designer*
McGreevey, Jim (James Edward McGreevey) *former governor*
McGreevey, Lisa S. *investment company executive*
McGuinn, Edwin J. *chemicals executive*
McGuinn, Martin Gregory *retired bank executive, lawyer*
McGuire, Amy Catherine *school psychologist*
McGuire, John W., Sr. *advertising executive, marketing professional, writer*
McGuire, Michael John *environmental engineer*
McGuirk, Ronald Charles *retired bank executive, economic advisor*
McGuirk, Terrence *former broadcasting company executive*
McGurk, Christopher Jamie *film company executive*
McGwire, Mark David *retired professional baseball player*
McHale, George T. *mathematics and computer science educator*
McHale, Judith A. (Judith Ottalloran) *former broadcast executive, lawyer*
McHale, Paul F., Jr. *federal agency administrator, former congressman*
McInnes, Robert A. *archivist*
McIntosh, Terrie Tuckett *lawyer*
McIntyre, Bruce Herbert *media consultant, marketing professional*
McIntyre, Virgie M. *retired elementary school educator*
McKagan, Duff (Michael Andrew McKagan) *bassist*
McKay, John Douglas *lawyer*
McKay, Kenneth Gardiner *retired physicist, electronics company executive*
McKay, Melinda *hotel executive*
McKay, Michael Kevin *nurse, priest*
McKay, Paul Patrick *healthcare executive*
McKay, Renee *artist*
McKeachnie, Gayle F. *former lieutenant governor*
McKean, Robert Jackson, Jr. *retired lawyer*
McKee, Betty Davis *English language educator*
McKee, Roger Curtis *retired federal judge*
McKelvey, Andrew J. *former advertising executive*
McKendrick, John *director*
McKendrick, Ryan Parker *music educator, conductor*
McKenna, Margaret Anne *former academic administrator*
McKenna, Terence Patrick *retired insurance company executive*
McKenna, William John *retired textile products executive*
McKennon, Keith Robert *chemical company executive*
McKeown, Lorraine Laredo *travel company executive, writer*
McKeown, William P. *retired lawyer*
McKinley, Ellen Bacon *priest*
McKinley, James Frank, Jr. *retired manufacturing executive*
Mc Kinney, David E(wing) *retired information processing products company executive, museum administrator*
McKinney, Mark A. *finance educator*
McKinney, William T. *psychiatrist, educator*
McKinnon, Karl Luther *museum director*
McKinstry, Ronald E. *retired lawyer*
McKnight, Thomas Frederick *artist*
McLaughlin, John Edward *former federal agency administrator*
McLaughlin, Joseph *lawyer*
McLaughlin, Leighton Bates, II, *retired journalist, reporter, educator*
McLaughlin, Michael John *retired insurance company executive*
McLaughlin, William Irving *space technical manager, writer*
McLawhon, Ronald William *pathology educator, biochemist*
McLean, Craig Elliott *retired non-commissioned officer*
McLean, Walter Franklin *government agency administrator, business consultant, legislator, minister*
McLellon, Richard Steven *aerospace engineer, consultant*
Mclendon, Roger Edwin *neuropathologist, educator*
McLendon, Susan Michelle *lawyer*
McLeskey, Charles Hamilton *anesthesiologist, educator, pharmaceutical executive*
McMahon, James E. *lawyer, former prosecutor*
McMahon, Julian *actor*
McManus, Jason Donald *retired editor-in-chief*
McManus, Joanna Quilala *medical device sales manager, physician assistant*
McManus, Patrick Francis *editor, educator, writer*
McManus, Richard Philip *lawyer, agricultural products executive*
McManus, Sean Joseph *broadcast executive*
McManus, William Paul *police chief*
McMaster, Belle Miller *religious organization administrator*
McMaster, Brian John *artistic director*
McMaster, Juliet Sylvia *English language educator*
McMeen, Albert Ralph III *writer, technical trainer, multimedia programmer, financial services executive*
McMennamin, Michael J. *savings and loan executive, investment banker*
McMillan, Robert Ralph *lawyer*
McMillan, Terry L. *writer, educator*
McMillen, Elizabeth Cashin *artist*
McMinn, J. B. *retired philosophy educator, composer*
McMorrow, Mary Ann Grohwin *retired state supreme court justice*
McMurray, Jamie *race car driver*
McNair, John William, Jr. *civil engineer*
McNamara, Brenda Norma *retired secondary school educator*
McNamara, Ted (Thomas Edmund McNamara) *federal official, former ambassador*
McNamara, Tom *scientific consulting corporation executive*
McNeil, Edward Warren *real estate company executive*
McNeill, Robert Patrick *investment advisor*
McNitt, Willard Charles *food products executive*
McNulty, Kathleen Anne *social worker, consultant, psychotherapist*
McPeters, Sharon Jenise *artist, writer*
McPhee, John Angus *writer*
McPheeters, Edwin Keith *architect, educator*
McPherson, Bruce A. *former state official, former state legislator*
McPherson, Donald Scott *labor and employment arbitrator/mediator*
McPherson, Elizabeth Wright *clinical geneticist*
McPherson, James Alan *writer, educator*
McPherson, James E. *judge*

McPherson, John Edwin, Jr. *zoologist, educator, entomologist, researcher*
McPherson, Ted R. (Edward Russell McPherson) *former federal agency administrator*
Mc Quade, Lawrence Carroll *lawyer, investment company executive*
McQuerry, Patricia Ann *painter, retired secondary school educator*
McQuilkin, John Robertson *theology studies educator, writer, academic administrator*
McRaney, Gerald *actor*
McShane, Ian *actor*
McShefferty, John *retired research scientist, personal care industry executive, consultant*
McSorley, Rita Elizabeth *adult education educator*
McSwain, Byrdie Engle *laboratory scientist, immunohematologist*
McSwain, Larry Lee *religious studies educator*
McSweeny, William Francis *petroleum company executive, author*
McTaggart, Timothy Robert *state agency administrator, lawyer*
McTague, John Paul *materials scientist, educator, chemist, researcher*
McTeer, Robert D., Jr. *former academic administrator, bank executive*
McVeigh-Pettigrew, Sharon Christine *communications consultant*
McWethy, John Fleetwood *journalist*
McWethy, Patricia Joan *educational association administrator*
McWhorter, Diane *writer*
McWilliams, Karen Joan *writer*
McWilliams, Michael *writer, publisher*
Mead, Jean Henry *freelance/self-employed photojournalist*
Mead, Matthew Hansen *former prosecutor*
Meadors, Howard Clarence, Jr. *electrical engineer*
Meads, Donald Edward *management services company executive*
Means, Elizabeth-Rose Thayer *financial planner, lawyer, writer*
Means, Marianne *columnist*
Meany, Philip Augustus *retired library director*
Meara, Anne *actress, playwright, writer*
Mears, Walter Robert *retired journalist*
Mecham, Steven Ray *school system administrator*
Mecklenburg, Gary Alan *hospital executive*
Medavoy, Mike *film company executive, producer*
Medina, Jane S. *music educator*
Mednick, Robert *accountant*
Medoff, Mark Howard *playwright, scriptwriter*
Meek, Forrest Burns *retired trading company executive*
Meeker, Guy Bentley *banker*
Meerow, Alan William *geneticist, horticulturist, botanist*
Meerschaert, Joseph Richard *retired physician*
Meffert, Roland Matthew *periodontist, educator*
Megiddo, Nimrod *mathematician, computer scientist*
Megna, Steve Allan *retired secondary school educator*
Mehan, George Tracey III *former federal agency administrator*
Mehiel, Dennis *investment company executive*
Mehltretter, Kathleen M. *former prosecutor*
Mehringer, Richard Patrick *design educator, artist*
Mehta, Ariz Ruyintan *physiatrist, researcher*
Mehta, Jatin Vinodrai *biomedical engineer*
Mehta, Mausmi *oceanographer*
Mehta, Ravi Ravinder Singh *commodities trader, consultant*
Mehta, Shailesh J. *banker*
Meier, George Karl III *minister, lawyer*
Meigher, S. Christopher III *communications and media executive, publisher*
Meiksin, Zvi H. *electrical engineering educator*
Meilan, Celia *food products executive*
Meilman, Edward *physician*
Meinwald, Jerrold *retired chemistry professor*
Meisels, Judith A. *pianist, music educator*
Melanson, Dorothy *political organization administrator*
Melczek, Dale J. *bishop*
Melder, Keith E. *retired curator*
Melendez, Sonia Ivette *counselor*
Meli, Salvatore Andrew *lawyer*
Melillo, Joseph Vincent *theater producer*
Mellanby, Scott Edgar *retired professional hockey player*
Mellema, Donald Eugene *retired radio news reporter and anchor*
Mellette, Julian Ramsey, Jr. *dermatologist, dermatologic surgeon*
Mellins, Claude Ann *psychologist*
Mellins, Harry Zachary *radiologist, educator*
Mellits, Marc Andrew *composer*
Mellon, Matthew J. *urologist*
Melody, Michael Edward *publishing company executive*
Melrose, Ian Paul Ellis *music educator, director, secondary school educator*
Melton, Emma Alexander *educational consultant, retired elementary school educator*
Melton, William Everett *retired music educator*
Meltzer, Jay H. *lawyer, consultant*
Melvin, Billy Alfred *clergyman*
Melvin, Peter Joseph *astrophysicist, educator*
Memik, Gokhan *engineering educator*
Menachem, Andrew *financial advisor*
Menachery, Elizabeth P. *physician*
Menaker, Daniel *former publishing executve*
Menaker, Ronald Herbert *retired bank executive*
Mench, John William *retail executive, electrical engineer*
Mende, Robert Graham *retired engineering association executive*
Mendels, Joseph *psychiatrist, educator*
Mendelson, Sol *physical science educator, consultant*
Mendis, Patrick *diplomat, writer, educator*
Mendoza, George *poet, author*
Mendoza, Karen Lynn *special education educator*
Menefee, Linnea-Norma *antique dealer*
Meng, Anne L. *pediatric nurse practitioner*
Meng, Yu-Ju Gloria *research scientist*
Mengel, Charles Edmund *internist, educator*
Menges, Martha *special education educator*
Menken, Alan *composer*
Menn, Julius Joel *retired research scientist, consultant*
Menna, Sári *artist, educator*
Menon, Jai M. *information technology manager*
Mentz, Lawrence *lawyer*
Menzel, Marybelle Proctor *volunteer*
Mercer, Edwin Wayne *lawyer*
Mercuri, Joan B. *museum administrator*
Mercurio, Renard Michael *real estate company executive*
Meredith, Wendi Sue *music educator*
Meriwether, Heath J. *newspaper consultant, retired publisher, educator*
Mermelstein, Hope Leah *educational consultant*
Merriam, Robert W. *engineering executive, educator*
Merrick, George Boesch *aerospace transportation executive*
Merrill, Abel Jay *retired lawyer*
Merrill, Frank Harrison *data processing executive, consultant*
Merrill, Jean Fairbanks *writer*
Merring, Robert Alan *lawyer, arbitrator, mediator*
Merritt, Bruce Gordon *lawyer*
Merritt, Nancy-Jo *lawyer*
Merritt, Susan Mary *computer science educator, dean*
Merriweather, Freda E. *education educator*
Mertz, Aaron F. *physicist*
Meshel, Harry *former state senator, political party official*
Mesrobian, Arpena Sachaklian *publishing executive, consultant, editor*
Messenkopf, Eugene John *real estate developer, hotel executive*
Messer, Donald Edward *theology educator, administrator*
Messerle, Judith Rose *retired medical librarian, public relations executive*
Messier, Mark Douglas *retired professional hockey player*
Messier, Pierre *lawyer, manufacturing executive*
Messmer, Donald Joseph *business management educator, marketing consultant*
Messner, Howard Myron *former professional association executive*
Mestres, Ricardo A. III *film company executive*
Metcalf, Karen *retired foundation executive*
Metcalf, Wayne C. III *retired insurance company executive*
Metcalf, William Edwards *museum curator, educator*
Metcalfe, Robert Davis III *lawyer*
Metoyer, Pamela Paradis *scientific editor, writer*
Metz, Steven William *small business owner*
Metz, T(heodore) John *librarian, educator*
Metz, Werner Adam *physicist*
Metzger, James W. *career military officer*
Metzger, Jeffrey Paul *lawyer*
Metzger, Paul Louis *theologian, director*
Metzler, Ruth Horton *genealogical educator*
Metzner, Charles Miller *federal judge*
Mewani, Rajshree R.(amchand) *researcher*
Meyer, Andreas S. *architect, consultant*
Meyer, Carol Frances *retired pediatrician, allergist*
Meyer, Daniel Kramer *real estate executive*
Meyer, Donald Robert *state agency administrator, lawyer*
Meyer, Edward Henry *retired advertising executive*
Meyer, Frances Margaret Anthony *educational consultant*
Meyer, Gabriel R. *writer*
Meyer, Henry Lewis III *bank executive*
Meyer, Joseph B. *state official*
Meyer, Max Earl *lawyer*
Meyer, Pucci *editor*
Meyer, Roger Jess Christian *pediatrics educator*
Meyerink, Victoria Paige *film producer, actress*
Meyers, Christine Laine *marketing and media executive, consultant*
Meyers, Jan *retired congresswoman*
Meyers, John Allen *magazine publisher*
Meyerson, Ivan D. *lawyer, former corporate financial executive*
Mezacapa, Edna S. *music educator, elementary school educator*
Michael, George T. *real estate manager, developer*
Michael, Jerrold Mark *public health service officer, educator, retired dean*
Michael, Mark Dixwell *lawyer*
Michaels, Andrew David *medical educator, cardiologist*
Michaels, Jack D. *manufacturing executive*
Michaels, Marion Cecelia *newswriter, editor, news syndicate executive*
Michaud, Georges Joseph *physics professor*
Michelle, Cadieux M. *writer*
Michlik, John F. *engineer*
Micozzi, Marc Stephen *medical educator, writer*
Middaugh, Robert Burton *artist*
Middleman, Raoul Fink *artist*
Middleton, James Arthur *oil and gas company executive*
Middleton, James Boland *retired lawyer*
Miekka, Jeanette Ann *retired science educator*
Miele, Joel Arthur, Sr. *civil engineer*
Miftahof, Roustem Narimanovich *science educator, researcher*
Migue, Jean Luc *economics professor*
Mikhelson, Sergei *mathematician, educator*
Mikiewicz, Anna Daniella *marketing and international business export manager*
Mikitka, Gerald Peter *brokerage house executive, consultant*
Miksis, Christina Barbara *psychologist*
Milberg, Joachim *retired automotive executive*
Miles, Donald F. *lawyer*
Miles, Frank Charles *retired newspaper executive*
Miles, Laveda Ann *advertising executive*
Miles, Mary Ellen *retired human resources specialist*
Miles, Michael Arnold *consumer products executive*
Milewski, Barbara Anne *pediatrics nurse, neonatal/perinatal nurse practitioner, critical care nurse*
Millane, Lynn *retired municipal official*
Millar, John Donald *physician, environmental services administrator, essayist, consultant, musician*
Millard, Charles Warren III *museum director, writer*
Millard, Donald Rex *financial executive*
Millea, Thomas Francis *photographer*
Miller, Alan J. *retired financial company executive*
Miller, Anthony Bernard *physician, researcher*
Miller, Arjay *retired university dean*
Miller, Bernard Joseph, Jr. *advertising executive*
Miller, Beverly A(nn) *reference librarian*
Miller, Charles Allen *politics educator*
Miller, Charles Leland *pediatrician*
Miller, Conrad S. *emergency physician, writer*
Miller, Darcy M. *publishing executive*
Miller, Donald Kenneth *engineering consultant*
Miller, Donald LeSessne *publishing executive*
Miller, Donald Muxlow *accountant*
Miller, Ellen S. *marketing executive*
Miller, Gay Davis *lawyer*
Miller, Geoffrey *child neurologist*
Miller, Harold Edward *retired manufacturing conglomerate executive, consultant*
Miller, Henry Forster *architect*
Miller, Ilana Deborah *history professor*
Miller, Jack Conway *small business owner, landscape company executive*
Miller, Jack David R. *radiologist, physician, educator*
Miller, Jacqueline Winslow *library director*
Miller, Jerry Huber *retired university chancellor*
Miller, Judith A. (Judy Miller) *retired journalist*
Miller, Kerry Lee *lawyer*
Miller, Laura M. *former mayor, journalist*
Miller, Linda Karen *retired secondary school educator, social studies educator, law educator*
Miller, Lisa Ann *lawyer*
Miller, Louis Howard *biologist, researcher*
Miller, Marilyn Lea *library and information scientist, educator*
Miller, Norman Charles, Jr. *editor, reporter*
Miller, Patricia Louise *state legislator, nurse*
Miller, Patrick William *research scientist, educator*
Miller, Paul David *aerospace transportation executive, retired admiral*
Miller, Penelope Ann (Penolope Andrea Miller) *actress*
Miller, Phillip Edward *environmental scientist*
Miller, R. Charles *lawyer*
Miller, Richard Steven *lawyer*
Miller, Robert Joseph *lawyer, former governor*
Miller, Roberta Doris *elementary school educator*
Miller, Ross Hays *retired neurosurgeon*
Miller, Shannon *Olympic athlete*
Miller, Thomas J. *former ambassador*
Miller, Thormund Aubrey *lawyer*
Miller, W. Kievit *writer*
Miller, Walter James *retired literature educator, writer*
Miller, Warren Lloyd *lawyer*
Milligan, Sister Mary *theology studies educator, consultant*
Milligan, Victor *consulting engineer*
Millikan, Clark Harold *physician*
Millimet, Erwin *lawyer*
Mills, Charles N. *healthcare supplies and products company executive*
Mills, Dale Douglas *journalist*
Mills, Douglas L. *physics professor*
Mills, Elizabeth Shown *historical writer, genealogist*
Mills, Eugene Sumner *academic administrator*
Mills, Helene Audrey *retired education educator*
Mills, Kevin Lee *computer scientist, researcher*
Millsaps, William Hobart, Jr. *retired editor*
Milner, Irvin Myron *retired lawyer*
Milnor, Hazel *nurse*
Milnor, William Robert *physician*
Milstein, Monroe Gary *retail executive*
Milunas, J. Robert *health care organization executive*
Minahan, Daniel Francis *lawyer, retired manufacturing executive*
Minarik, Stephen Joseph III *communications executive, former political organization administrator*
Mindlin, Paula Rosalie *retired reading educator*
Minehan, Cathy Elizabeth *retired bank executive*
Ming, Jenny J. *former retail executive*
Mingle, James John *lawyer*
Minna, Anthony Joseph *financial planner, lawyer*
Minners, Howard Alyn *federal agency administrator, researcher, preventive medicine physician*
Minnix, Bruce Milton *television and theatre director*
Minshall, Greg *computer programmer*
Mintz, M. J. *lawyer*
Mintz, Morton Abner *writer, reporter*
Miquelon, Miriam F. *former prosecutor, lawyer*
Mirabile, Thomas Keith *lawyer*
Miracle, Doris Jean *retired medical/surgical nurse*
Miracle, Nancy *foundation administrator, writer*
Miranda-Levi, Jason *film producer, writer*
Mirk, Judy Ann *retired elementary school educator*
Mirza, Zakir Hussain *aerospace company consultant*
Miscella, Maria Diana *humanities educator*
Mischke, Carl Herbert *retired religious association executive*
Miselson, Alex J. (Jacob Miselson) *portfolio manager, securities analyst, investment theorist*
Miskimen, Theresa Marie *psychiatrist, educator*
Miskus, Michael Anthony *electrical engineer*
Mislow, Kurt Martin *chemist, educator*
Misner, Charlotte Blanche Ruckman *retired community organization administrator*
Misrach, Richard Laurence *photographer*
Missan, Richard Sherman *lawyer, educator*
Mistry, Percy Shiavak *investment banker*
Mitchard, Jacquelyn *writer*
Mitchell, Brian Stokes *actor*
Mitchell, Carol Ann *nursing educator*
Mitchell, Carol Ann *lawyer*
Mitchell, David Benjamin *lawyer, arbitrator, mediator*
Mitchell, George Phydias *gas and petroleum company executive*
Mitchell, Jerry *choreographer, actor*
Mitchell, John Charles *marketing professional*
Mitchell, John Daniel *taxonomist, ecologist*
Mitchell, John Laurin Amos *biological science educator*
Mitchell, Lucille Anne *retired elementary school educator*
Mitchell, Marcia Jeanne *writer*
Mitchell, Rick *journalist, writer*
Mitchell, Steve Harold *psychologist*
Mitchell, William Graham Champion *lawyer, corporate officer*
Mitzner, Kenneth Martin *electrical engineer, consultant*
Miyagawa, George Robert *retired military officer*
Miyata, Sachiko *social scientist, researcher*
Moazed, Khosrow L. *retired engineering educator*
Mobley, William Hodges *management consultant, educator, writer, researcher*
Modny, Cynthia Jean *dermatologist*
Moe, Lonn Andre *state revenue official*
Moffat, MaryBeth *consulting company executive*
Moffatt, Joyce Anne *performing company executive*
Moffatt, Katy (Katherine Louella Moffatt) *musician, lyricist, vocalist*
Moglewer, Sarah Anne *music educator*
Mohamed, Joseph, Sr. *real estate broker, developer, farmer*
Mohan, Tungesh Nath *television and film producer, film educator*
Mohieldin, Ahmed Nader *electrical engineer*
Mohler, Ronald Rutt *electrical engineering educator*
Molaison, Elaine Fontenot *dietician, nutritionist, educator*
Molholm, Kurt Nelson *retired federal agency administrator*
Molina, Kevin *social studies educator*
Molinaro, Joseph Daniel *dentist, director*
Molinaro, Thomas J. *lawyer*
Molitor, Michael A. *entrepreneur, consultant*
Moll, David Carter *civil engineer*
Moll, Lloyd Henry *retired bank executive*
Moll, Maryann Elizabeth *education educator*
Molland, Maria U. *Internet company executive*
Mollenauer, Linn Frederick *retired physicist, writer*
Molloy, Sylvia *language educator*
Moloff, Alan Lawrence *retired military officer, physician*
Molz, Redmond Kathleen *public affairs educator*
Momah, Ethel Chukwuekwe *retired women's health nurse*
Monacelli, Gianfranco *publishing executive*
Monaco, Daniel Joseph *lawyer*
Monaghan, Craig Thomas *former retail and automotive executive*
Monck, Maureen F. *psychoanalyst*
Mondlin, Marvin *publisher, appraiser, consultant*
Monheit, Molly Jane *artist*
Monk, Debra *actress*
Monroe, Frederick Fales *geologist, oceanographer*
Monroe, William Lewis *human resources executive*
Monson, David Carl *school system administrator, state legislator, farmer*
Monteith, Larry King *chancellor emeritus*
Montelongo, Michael D. *marketing executive, former civilian military employee*
Montgomery, Betty Dee *former state attorney general, retired state legislator*
Montgomery, Cliff Wilson *journalist, writer, researcher*
Montgomery, Hubert Theron, Jr. *physician, health care administrator*
Montgomery, Lani Lynn *art educator*
Montgomery, Roy Delbert *retired gas industry executive*
Montoya, Regina T. *association executive, lawyer*
Montrone, Paul Michael *former scientific instruments company executive*
Moog, Matthew *Internet company executive*
Moon, Il-Ju *marine biologist, educator*
Mooney, John Joseph *chemical engineer*
Mooney, Michael Joseph *university professor*
Mooney, Thomas Robert *lawyer*
Mooney, Thomas T. *history educator, geography educator*
Moore, Betty Jo *legal assistant*
Moore, Cornell Leverette *financial services executive, lawyer*
Moore, Daniel Alton, Jr. *retired state supreme court justice*
Moore, Donald Walter *retired academic administrator*
Moore, Fay Linda *systems engineer*
Moore, Jean E. *social worker, academic administrator, educator, radio personality*
Moore, John Eddy *former lieutenant governor*
Moore, John Ronald *manufacturing executive*

Moore, Juel Ann *retired elementary school educator*
Moore, Malcolm Frederick *manufacturing executive*
Moore, Mike (Michael C.) *lawyer, former state attorney general*
Moore, Oliver Semon III *publishing executive, consultant*
Moore, Pamela Gay *retired music educator*
Moore, Richard Alan *landscape architect*
Moore, Robert Henry *writer, editor, communications consultant*
Moore, Robert Lowell, Jr., (Robin Moore) *author*
Moore, Robert William *professional organization executive*
Moore, Stanley Wayne *retired political science professor*
Moore, Thomas Andrew *biotechnology executive*
Moore, Thomas David *academic administrator*
Moore, Thomas Paul *retired broadcast executive*
Moore, Tirin *neuroscientist, educator*
Moore, William Henry *radiologist*
Moore, William Leroy, Jr. *career officer, internist*
Moore-Wleklinski, Patricia Marie *secondary school educator*
Moorhead, Lucy Galpin *writer*
Moossy, John *neurologist, consultant, pathologist*
Mora, Antonio Gonzalez III *broadcast journalist*
Mora, Pat *writer, speech professional*
Moradi, Ahmad F. *software company executive*
Morales, Diane K. *former federal agency administrator*
Moran, Charles A. *security firm executive, educator*
Moran, Thomas Harry *retired academic administrator*
Moran, Wendi K *biology educator*
Morano, Gerard John *marketing executive*
Morden, John Reid *security-business intelligence consultant*
Morden, Robert Dean *biology professor*
Morehead, Richard Scott *medical educator*
Morelan, Paula Kay *choreographer*
Moreland, Richard Paul *musician, educator*
Morello, Joseph Albert *musician, educator*
Morello, Tom *musician*
Moretti, August Joseph *pharmaceutical executive, lawyer*
Morfopoulos, V. *metallurgical engineer, materials engineer*
Morgan, Anne Marie G. *broadcast journalist, educator*
Morgan, Arlene Notoro *university administrator*
Morgan, Bethanye Branch *biology professor*
Morgan, Edmund Sears *retired history professor*
Morgan, Elizabeth K. *retired critical care nurse*
Morgan, James Durward *retired computer company executive*
Morgan, James John *environmental engineering educator*
Morgan, Jane Hale *retired library director*
Morgan, Linda Gail *theater producer*
Morgan, M. Jane *computer systems consultant*
Morgan, Marianne *corporate professional*
Morgan, Mary Lou *retired education educator, volunteer*
Morgan, Owain David *investment company executive*
Morgan, Robin Evonne *poet, writer, journalist, editor*
Morgan, Ronald Brian *retired aerospace engineer, advocate, writer, lecturer*
Morgan, Ruth Prouse *academic administrator, educator*
Morgan, Thomas Rowland *retired marine corps officer*
Morgan, Timi Sue *lawyer*
Morgan, William J. *retired accounting company executive*
Morgenroth, Earl Eugene *entrepreneur*
Morgenstein, William *shoe company executive*
Moriarty, Donald William, Jr. *bank executive*
Morin, Lynn P. *music educator, director, secondary school educator*
Moritz, Chad Henry *research scientist*
Morley, James Everitt, Jr., (Jay Morley Jr.) *retired academic and educational association administrator*
Morley, Lloyd Albert *electrical engineering educator*
Morman, Dean Smith *accountant, consultant*
Morof, Jeffrey W. *lawyer*
Moroz, Pavel Emanuel *retired research scientist*
Morrell, Gene Paul *gas industry executive, consultant*
Morrill, Penny Chittim *art historian*
Morris, Brenda Denise *music educator, director*
Morris, Daniel S. *computer scientist, researcher*
Morris, Donald George *engineering company executive*
Morris, G. Ronald *automotive executive*
Morris, Jack Austin, Jr. *art gallery executive*
Morris, James Thomas *former international organization official*
Morris, John Woodland, II, *retired engineering consultant, military officer*
Morris, Mary Elizabeth *pastor*
Morris, Colonel Robert *songwriter, musician, music educator*
Morris, Robert Gemmill *retired foreign service officer*
Morris, Roy Leslie *lawyer, electrical engineer, venture capitalist*
Morris, Tammy Kay *bank executive*
Morris, Thomas Bateman, Jr. *lawyer*
Morrish, Thomas Jay *golf course architect*
Morrison, Denise M. *sales executive*
Morrison, Donald William *lawyer*
Morrison, John M. *bank executive*
Morrison, Margaret Anne *literature educator*
Morrison, Martin *writer*
Morrison, Rey Eileen *history educator, writer*
Morrison, Richard Drury *health policy consultant, medical educator*
Morrison, Robert Scheck *former manufacturing, food marketing processing company executive*
Morrison, Sarah Lyddon *author*
Morrison, Shelley *actress*
Morrison, Toni (Chloe Anthony Wofford) *writer, educator, editor*
Morrissey, Edward T., II, *conservative political blogger, nationally-syndicated radio co-host, columnist*
Morrissey, Thomas Paul *medical educator, physician*
Morrow, Barry Nelson *screenwriter, producer*
Morrow, Nana Kwasi Scott Douglas *choreographer, director, writer, filmmaker, educator*
Morse, Gayle Skawennio *psychologist, consultant*
Morse, Joseph Grant *chemistry educator*
Morse, Robert Harry *lawyer*
Morse-McNeely, Patricia *poet, writer, retired secondary school educator*
Mortensen-Say, Marlys *retired school system administrator*
Mortimer, Richard Walter *mechanical engineer, educator*
Morton, Donald John *librarian*
Morton, James Carnes, Jr. *automotive executive*
Morton, M. Juanita *writer, accountant*
Mosallaei, Hossein *science educator*
Moseley, James R. *former federal agency administrator, farmer*
Mosemann, Lloyd Kenneth, II, *retired research and development company executive*
Moser, Barry *artist*
Moser, Jeffery Richard *real estate manager*
Moser, Robert Lawrence *pathologist, health facility administrator*
Moses, Jeffrey Warren *cardiologist, educator*
Moses, Michael James *insurance company executive, small business owner*
Moses, Shelia P. *writer, poet, playwright, producer*
Mosiman, Rita Esther *music educator, performing artist*
Moskovitz, Jackob *biology professor*
Moskow, Michael H. *retired bank executive*
Mosner, Lawrence J. *retired financial administration company executive*
Mospaw, Kathan J. *retired social studies educator*
Moss, Carrie-Anne *actress*
Moss, Thomas Henry *science foundation director, physicist*
Mossawir, Harve H., Jr. *retired lawyer*
Mosteller, Darla Brooks *singer*
Motsenbocker, Rex Alan *construction company executive*
Mott, Stewart Rawlings *food products executive, political organization worker*
Motto, Jerome Arthur *psychiatrist, educator*
Mottola, Tommy (Thomas D. Mottola) *recording industry executive*
Moulitsas Zúniga, Markos *former military officer, blog writer*
Moulthrop, Rebecca Lee Stilphen *retired elementary school educator*
Moulton, Grace Charbonnet *retired physicist*
Mount, Thomas H(enderson) *motion picture and stage producer*
Mow, Van C. *engineering educator, researcher*
Moya, Patrick Robert *lawyer*
Moyer, Craig Alan *lawyer*
Moyer, J. Keith *former publishing executive*
Moyer, R. Charles *finance company executive, educator, retired dean*
Moynahan, John Daniel, Jr. *retired insurance executive*
Moyse, Hermann III *banker*
Mracky, Ronald Sydney *marketing executive, tourism consultant, media specialist*
Mramor, Marti *engineer, linguist*
Mruthinti, Shyamala *pharmacologist, educator*
Muchmore, Don Moncrief *retired cultural organization administrator, retired museum director, foundation administrator*
Muckerman, Norman James *priest, writer*
Muckler, John E. *former professional sports team executive, former professional hockey coach*
Mudavanhu, Blessing *research scientist*
Mudd, John O. *lawyer*
Mudd, Roger Harrison *newscaster, educator*
Mudry, Michael *pension and benefit consultant*
Muegge, Uwe *terminology professor*
Mueller, Gary Alfred *software engineer*
Mueller, Robert Louis *manufacturing executive*
Mueller-Heubach, Eberhard *medical educator*
Mugridge, David Raymond *lawyer, educator, writer*
Muhammad, Claudette Marie *religious organization administrator*
Muhn, Judy Ann *psychologist, genealogist, trainer*
Muir, Patricia Allen *professional association administrator*
Mujica, Mauro E. *architect*
Mukamal, David Samier *sign manufacturing company executive*
Mularkey, Mike *professional football coach*
Mulcahy, Gabriel M. *pathologist*
Mulcahy, Robert Edward *management consultant*
Mullen, Terri Ann *retired special education educator*
Mullen, William Joseph III *military analyst, retired army career officer*
Muller, Henry Nicholas III *retired foundation administrator*
Muller, Peter *lawyer, film company and retail executive*
Muller, Scott William *lawyer*
Mullet, Robin M. *retired accountant*
Mulligan, Brian C. *film company executive*
Mulligan, David Keith *consulting company executive, securities arbitrator*
Mulligan, Robert *film director, producer*
Mullin, Leo Francis *airline executive*
Mullins, Charles Brown *physician, academic administrator*
Mullins, Eustace Clarence *writer*
Mullis, Kary Banks *biochemist*
Mulvee, Robert Edward *bishop*
Mumma, Albert Girard, Jr. *architect*
Munger, Paul R. *engineering educator*
Munitz, Barry A. *former foundation administrator*
Muñiz, Olga M. *language educator, consultant*
Muñoz, Carlos Ramón *retired bank executive*
Munoz, Cheryl Ann *portfolio manager*
Munoz, Laura A. *foundation administrator*
Munoz, Mario Alejandro *civil engineer, retired consultant*
Muñoz Dones De Carrascal, Eloisa (Eloise Munoz Dones) *hospital administrator, pediatrician, educator*
Munro, Donald William, Jr. *non-profit organization executive*
Munsell, Elsie Louise *retired lawyer*
Munsey, Virdell Everard, Jr. *retired utilities executive*
Munt, Janet Staples *state senator*
Muntz, David S. *information technology executive*
Munzner, Robert Frederick *biomedical engineer*
Murarka, Shyam Prasad *science and engineering educator, administrator*
Murat, William M. *legislative staff member*
Murat, Yusef J. *plastic surgeon*
Murchison, David Claudius *lawyer*
Murdock, Pamela Ervilla *travel and advertising company executive*
Murguia, Janet *non-profit organization administrator*
Murillo, Jose R., Jr. *pharmacist*
Murnion, William Edward *philosopher*
Murphey, Sheila Ann *infectious diseases physician, educator, researcher*
Murphy, Alexis D. *auditor*
Murphy, Daniel Ignatius *lawyer*
Murphy, Eddie *actor, comedian*
Murphy, Evelyn Frances *economist*
Murphy, Francis *language educator*
Murphy, Gerald *retired federal official*
Murphy, Kathleen M. *lawyer*
Murphy, Margaret A. *nursing educator, adult nurse practitioner*
Murphy, Marion Colucci *writer, poet*
Murphy, Michael George *actor*
Murphy, Randall Kent *writer, educator, consultant*
Murphy, Robert James *language educator, consultant, pianist, pipe organ performer*
Murphy, Sandra Robison *lawyer*
Murphy, Timothy W. *music educator*
Murr, James Coleman *retired federal agency administrator*
Murray, Alan Robert *sound editor*
Murray, Carla Mary *sound effects artist, artist*
Murray, David George *architect*
Murray, Elizabeth Davis Reid *writer, researcher*
Murray, Julia Kaoru (Mrs. Joseph E. Murray) *occupational therapist*
Murray, Robert Gray *sculptor*
Murray, Roderick Charles *manufacturing executive*
Murray, Sabina *writer*
Murray, Stephen Sanford *composer, lyricist, playwright*
Murray, Timothy Patrick *lieutenant governor, former mayor*
Murray, William Michael *lawyer*
Murray Shaw, Juleen *actress*
Murugan, Thirumagal Anandhi *medical researcher*
Musa, Samuel Albert *university executive*
Musante, Tony (Anthony Peter Musante Jr.) *actor*
Musgrave, Story *design educator, astronaut, physiologist, surgeon*
Mushlin, Alvin I. *medical educator, researcher*
Musick, Robert Lawrence, Jr. *lawyer*
Muson, Howard Henry *writer, consultant*
Musselman, Eric *former professional basketball coach*
Mustard, Lewis Williams *management consultant, educator*
Mutalipassi, Louis Richard *psychologist, educator*
Myer, Donald Beekman *architect*
Myerowitz, P(aul) David *cardiac surgeon, educator, writer*
Myers, Alison Kay *assistant principal*
Myers, Allen Richard *rheumatologist*
Myers, Angela Michelle *music educator, department chairman*
Myers, Charles Edwin *child therapist, educator*
Myers, Dorothy Roatz *artist*
Myers, Franklin *oil industry executive*
Myers, Jeffrey Daniel *concert pianist, music educator*
Myers, Jesse Jerome *lawyer*
Myers, Julie L. *federal agency administrator*
Myers, Michele Tolela *former academic administrator*
Myers, Mike *actor, scriptwriter, film producer*
Myers, Phillip Fenton *corporate financial, information technology executive*
Myers, Robert David *judge*
Myers, Sophia M. *writer, researcher, artist, cartographer, translator*
Myerson, Alan *television director, film director*
Myles, LaToya *research scientist*
Myren, Richard Albert *criminologist, consultant*
Myrie, Leslie Rolce, Jr. *marketing executive*
Nabers, Claude Lowrey *retired periodontist, writer*
Nabers, Drayton, Jr. *retired state supreme court chief justice, insurance company executive*
Nabors, Robert L. *military officer*
Nachman, Gerald Weil *columnist, critic, writer*
Nacht, Sergio *biochemist*
Nackhla, G. Habib *retired physician*
Nadeau, Joseph P. *retired state supreme court justice*
Nadel, Elliott *investment company executive*
Nadelman, Martin Hershel *college president*
Nadelson, Sandra G. *nursing educator*
Nadolski, Dora J. *social sciences educator, researcher*
Naeve, Milo Merle *retired curator, director*
Nagel, Sidney Robert *physics professor*
Nagel, Thomas *philosopher, lawyer, educator*
Nagler, Leon Gregory *retired management consultant*
Nagler, Stewart Gordon *retired insurance company executive*
Nagra, Parminder *actress*
Nagy, Donna M. *dean, law educator*
Nagy, Elizabeth Garver *artist*
Nahman, Norris Stanley *electrical engineer*
Nahmias, Maria Lynn *education educator*
Naidorf, Louis Murray *architect*
Nakayama, Wataru *engineering educator, consultant*
Nakazato, Takuya *ecological geneticist*
Nam, Seung Yeob *network technician, researcher*
Nance, Mary Joe *retired secondary school educator*
Nanda, Navreet K. *research scientist*
Nanda, Ved Prakash *law educator, director, academic administrator*
Nangle, John Francis *federal judge*
Nanos, George Peter, Jr. *science administrator, military officer, physicist*
Nanula, Richard D. *former heath products company executive*
Naples, Caesar Joseph *lawyer, educator*
Napoli, Joseph Stephen *horticulturist, conductor*
Naqvi, Tasneem Zehra *cardiologist, researcher, consultant*
Naraev, Boris G. *physician*
Nardell, Edward Anthony *pulmonologist, researcher*
Nardozzi, Peter Michael *pharmacist, clinical educator, lecturer, entrepreneur*
Narita, Hiro *cinematographer*
Narron, Jerry Austin *former professional baseball manager*
Nasgaard, Roald *museum curator*
Nash, Melvin Samuel *lawyer*
Nash, Richard Edin *publishing executive*
Nason, Dolores Irene *computer company executive, social welfare administrator, minister*
Nassau, David L. *engineer*
Nasseripour, Mohammad Michel *artist, architect*
Natcher, Stephen Darlington *retired lawyer, electronics executive*
Nation, David Arthur *retired computer scientist, sculptor*
Nativi Nicolau, Juan Jose *industrial engineer*
Naughton, Eileen T. *Internet company executive*
Naughton, James *actor*
Naulty, Susan Louise *archivist*
Naumer, Carola *art historian, educator*
Navab, Aphrodite Desiree *artist, educator, writer*
Navarrete, Jorge Eduardo *ambassador*
Navarro, Guillermo *cinematographer*
Navasky, Victor Saul *publisher*
Navratilova, Martina *professional tennis player*
Ndura, Elavie *literature and language educator*
Neal, Dennis Melton *elementary school educator*
Nearine, Robert James *educational psychologist*
Neary, Patricia Elinor *ballet director*
Neblett, Carol *soprano*
Nederlander, James Laurence *theater producer*
Neel, Judy Murphy *management consultant*
Neely, Mark Edward, Jr. *writer*
Neff, Donald Lloyd *news correspondent, writer*
Neff, John Brown *financial portfolio manager*
Neidich-Ryder, Carole Louise *curator, educator*
Neldner, Summer D. *athletic trainer*
Nelligan, William David III *professional association executive*
Nelp, Wil B. *physician, medical educator*
Nelsen, William Cameron *educational consultant*
Nelson, Alice Carlstedt *retired nursing educator*
Nelson, Allyson Lyn *lawyer*
Nelson, Bruce (Murray Bruce Nelson) *former consumer products company executive*
Nelson, Carl Roger *retired lawyer*
Nelson, Carol Evelyn *retired pre-school educator*
Nelson, Christopher Grant *dermatologist*
Nelson, Craig T. *actor*
Nelson, David Aldrich *former federal judge*
Nelson, Frederick Dickson *judge*
Nelson, Geralda *language educator*
Nelson, Glen David *health products executive, physician*
Nelson, John Woolard *neurology educator, physician*
Nelson, Norman Daniel *government official*
Nelson, Reginald (Bob) Wenon, Jr. *minister*
Nelson, Ron *composer, educator, conductor*
Nelson, Roy Hugh, Jr. *mediator, arbitrator, lawyer*
Nelson, Sandra E. *information technology executive*
Nelson, Thomas Adams *electrical engineer, consultant*
Nelson, Walter Gerald *retired insurance company executive*
Nemec, Josef *retired organic chemist, researcher*
Nemfakos, Charles Panagiotis *defense industry executive, strategic consultant*
Nemiroff, Maxine Celia *small business owner, art historian*
Nenstiel, Susan Kisthart *fundraising professional*
Nephew, Julia Anne *language educator*
Neri, Manuel *sculptor, educator*
Néron, Martin *musician*
Nesbitt, Charles Rudolph *lawyer, energy executive, consultant*
Nesbitt, John Arthur *recreational therapist, writer, educator, researcher*
Nesbitt, Mitzi Evalee *voice educator, director*
Ness, Bernice Hagie *retired music educator*
Ness, Norman Frederick *retired astrophysicist, educator, administrator*

Outten, Kristina Marie *secondary school educator*
Ouyang, Norma M. *psychologist*
Owen, Amy *library director*
Owen, Tony Quinn *investment company executive, horse trainer*
Owens, Charles Vincent, Jr. *pharmaceutical executive, consultant*
Owens, Gail Frances *pharmaceutical executive*
Owens, Major Robert Odell *former congressman*
Owens, William Arthur (Bill Owens) *telecommunications industry executive, retired military officer*
Owen-Towle, Carolyn Sheets *clergywoman*
Oxnam, Philip Linton *small business owner*
Özalp, Nesrin *mechanical engineer, research scientist*
Ozick, Cynthia *writer*
Paavola, Fred G. *pharmacist*
Pace, Charles Robert *psychologist, educator*
Pace, Stephen Shell *artist, educator*
Pacheco, Manuel Trinidad *retired academic administrator*
Pacholski, Richard Francis *securities trader, financial consultant*
Pachter, Lee M. *pediatrician*
Paci, Ruth A. *freelance/self-employed writer*
Pacifico, Albert Dominick *cardiovascular surgeon*
Pack, Michael *television producer, writer, director*
Pack, Susan Joan *writer*
Packard, John Mallory *physician, researcher*
Packard, Stephen Michael *legal association administrator, lawyer*
Padden, Anthony Aloysius, Jr. *retired federal government official*
Paderewski, Sir Clarence Joseph *architect*
Padian, Nancy *medical educator, epidemiologist*
Padilla, James Jerome (Jim Padilla) *retired automotive executive*
Paganelli, Charles Victor *physiologist, educator*
Page, Amanda Lee *secondary school educator*
Page, Barbara Rose *primary school educator*
Page, Patricia (Patty) Newton *real estate broker, real estate company executive*
Page, Rodney Fred *lawyer*
Pagels, Elaine Hiesey *theology studies educator, writer*
Paige, Vivian Jo-Ann *accountant*
Paik, Ji Hye *research scientist*
Paik, John Kee *structural engineer*
Paikowsky, Samuel G. *civil engineering educator*
Paine, Alan *poet*
Painter, Richard William *lawyer, educator*
Painton, Russell Elliott *retired lawyer, mechanical engineer*
Pakala, James Cotton *library director, minister*
Pakenham, Rosalie Muller Wright *magazine and newspaper editor*
Pal, Pratapaditya *curator*
Palacio, Carlos *physician, medical educator*
Palade, George Emil *research scientist, educator*
Paladino, Albert Edward *venture capitalist*
Palii, Sergiu Petru *chemist, researcher*
Palisi, Anthony Thomas *psychologist, educator*
Pallin, Samuel Lear *ophthalmologist, educator, medical director*
Pallot, Joseph Wedeles *lawyer*
Palmer, Dave Richard *retired military officer, academic administrator*
Palmer, Grant *medical products executive*
Palmer, Irene Sabelberg *retired dean, retired nursing educator, genealogist*
Palmer, Jessica A. *former diversified financial services company executive*
Palmer, John Anthony III *language professor, secondary school educator, music educator*
Palmer, Marilyn Joan *English composition educator*
Palmieri, Dora Ann *retired language educator*
Palms, Roger Curtis *writer, educator, minister*
Palola, Harry Joel *retired international affairs executive, consultant*
Palow, James Alexander *real estate company executive*
Palter, Robert Monroe *humanities educator*
Palumbo, Matthew Aloysius *marketing executive*
Palumbo, Michael *investment company executive*
Pamela, Taylor K. *writer, editor*
Pan, Deming *chemistry professor*
Pan, Ya-Hui Laurie *toxicologist, director*
Pan, Yue *finance educator*
Panagiotopoulos, Athanassios Zois *chemical engineering educator*
Panchyk, Richard Robert *writer*
Panettiere, Hayden *actress*
Panko, George *application developer*
Pantaleo, Jack *playwright, composer, educator*
Panzer, Mary Caroline *historian, museum curator*
Panzer, Milton *retired orthodontist, volunteer*
Paolucci, Anne Attura *playwright, poet, literature educator, educational consultant*
Papa, Vincent T. *insurance company executive*
Paparella, Leon Ralph *psychotherapist, consultant*
Papathomas, Georgia Nikolakopoulou *technology executive*
Pappas-Speairs, Nina *financial planner, educator*
Paps, Betty Lou *nursing educator*
Paquin, Gerald Chester *retired military officer, retired registrar*
Parameswaran, Raju *accountant*
Paranjpe, Pankaj Vinaykumar *research scientist*
Parcells, Bill (Duane Charles Parcells) *sportscaster, retired professional football coach*
Pardue, Dwight Edward *venture capitalist*
Paredes, James Anthony *anthropologist, educator*
Pareene, Alex E. *political blog editor*
Parent, Rodolphe Jean *retired Canadian air force officer, pilot*
Parham, Ellen Speiden *nutrition educator*
Parins, Robert James *professional football team executive, judge*
Paris, David Andrew *dentist*
Paris, Gordon A. *investment banker*
Paris, Steven Mark *application developer*
Paris-De Monte, Ileana M. *assistant principal*
Parish, Thomas Scanlan *psychology professor*
Parisi, Valerie Marie *former dean, medical educator*
Park, John Thornton *retired academic administrator*
Park, Maria *artist, educator*
Park, Myung Kun *medical educator*
Park, Naeun *statistician*
Park, Won Kuk *foundation administrator*
Parkel, James G. *former health association administrator*
Parker, Brent Mershon *retired medical educator, internist, cardiologist*
Parker, Joel Louise *nursing administrator*
Parker, Mel *editor*
Parker, Melissa Epley *psychologist*
Parker, Michael J. *editor, writer, researcher*
Parker, Michael Seth *technical development manager*
Parker, Robert Chauncey Humphrey *clergyman, publishing executive*
Parker, Sara Ann *librarian, consultant*
Parker, Susan Brooks *government agency administrator*
Parker, Towana D. *entrepreneur, director*
Parkin, James Lamar *retired otolaryngologist, educator*
Parks, Jane deLoach *retired law librarian, legal assistant*
Parks, Jean Anne *retired acute care nurse*
Parks, Judith Tyler *business executive, consultant*
Parkyn, John William *editor, writer, columnist*
Parmenter, Kelli Denise *middle school educator, small business owner*
Parode, Ann *lawyer*
Parr, Royse Milton *retired lawyer, writer*
Parra, Ro (Rosendo G. Parra) *former computer company executive*
Parrette, Leslie Jackson *lawyer*
Parrish, Edward Alton, Jr. *electrical and computer engineering educator, academic administrator*
Parrish, Matthew Denwood *psychiatrist*
Parsons, Alexandra Clare *literature and language educator*
Parsons, Vinson Adair *retired computer company executive*
Partridge, Bruce James *lawyer, educator, writer*
Pascale, Daniel Richard *lawyer*
Pasco, Hansell Merrill *retired lawyer*
Pascoe, Patricia Hill *former state legislator*
Pascu, Dan *astronomer*
Pasek, Mark Edward *manufacturing executive*
Pasnicu, Cornel *mathematician, educator*
Pasquier, Joël *music educator*
Passaro, Paul Charles *strategic planning consultant*
Pasternack, Robert Harry *former federal agency administrator*
Pastizzo, Frank Anthony *writer, educator*
Pasupathy, Kalyan Sunder *education educator, consultant*
Patchett, Arthur Allan *medicinal chemist, pharmaceutical executive*
Patchin, Rebecca J. *anesthesiologist, educator, administrator*
Patel, Nima P. *surgeon*
Patel, Snehal Raman *oral surgeon*
Patel, Tillian K. *critical care nurse*
Patel, Uptal Dinesh *nephrologist, researcher*
Paterson, Robert E. *retail executive*
Pathak, Anant Madhav *retired anesthesiologist*
Patience, Gregory Scott *chemical engineer, educator*
Patino-Brandfon, Sylvia *retired psychologist*
Patki, Kiran C. *pharmacologist, researcher*
Patrick, Brenda Jean *educational consultant*
Patrick, Craig *former professional hockey team executive*
Patrick, Dan *sportscaster*
Patrick, Danica Sue *race car driver*
Patrick, Pauline Margaret *secondary school educator*
Patrick, Victor Phillip *lawyer, construction executive*
Patrusky, Ben *writer*
Patterson, Dennis Joseph *retired management consultant*
Patterson, Edward Palmer *retired physicist*
Patterson, Elizabeth Johnston *retired congresswoman*
Patterson, Jim *economist, writer*
Patterson, Richard North *writer, lawyer*
Patterson, Samuel C. *retired political science professor*
Patterson, Steve *former professional sports team executive*
Pattillo, Manning Mason Calvert *academic administrator*
Patton, James Richard, Jr. *lawyer*
Patton, Kassie (Kathleen Moroney Patton) *former principal, director*
Patton, Susan Oertel *clinical social worker, educator*
Pauken, Thomas Weir *venture capital executive, mediator*
Paul, Arthur *artist, illustrator, graphics designer, design consultant*
Paul, Bipul C. *research scientist*
Paul, Debajyoti *geologist, educator*
Paul, Eve W. *retired lawyer*
Paul, Kenneth *newspaper editor*
Paul, Norman Leo *psychiatrist, educator*
Paul, Richard Wright *lawyer*
Paul, Ronald Ernest *congressman*
Pauley, Bruce Frederick *retired history professor*
Pauley, Jane *newscaster, journalist*
Paulsen, Brian Oliver *art educator, artist*
Paulsen, Frank Robert *college dean emeritus*
Paulsen, Serenus Glen *retired architect, educator*
Pauly, John Edward *retired anatomist*
Paup, Martin Arnold *securities investor, real estate investor*
Pavarini, Peter Alfred *lawyer*
Paxton, J. Willene *retired academic administrator*
Payne, Alexander *film director, writer*
Payne, Anita Hart *reproductive endocrinologist, researcher*
Payne, Barbara Ann *artist, educator*
Payne, Daniel Harold (Harold Payne) *real estate developer, small business owner*
Payne, Ladell *retired academic administrator*
Payne, Leland Howard *lawyer*
Payne, Mary Libby *retired judge*
Payton, Thomas William *finance company executive*
Peach, Robert Westly *retired small business owner, engineer*
Peacock, Mary Willa *magazine editor, consultant*
Peapples, George Alan *retired automotive executive*
Pear, Charles E., Jr. *lawyer*
Pearce, Jody Ann *mathematics educator*
Pearce, Paul Francis *retired electronics executive, aerospace engineer*
Pearce-Moses, Richard *librarian*
Pearl, Laurence Dickson *retired federal government executive*
Pearl, Sharrona Hyla *science educator*
Pearlstein, Philip *artist*
Pearson, Henry Clyde *retired judge*
Pearson, Jennie Sue *retired government administrator*
Pearson, Paul Holding *insurance company executive*
Pearson, Richard Joseph *archaeologist, educator*
Pearson, W(illiam) Robert *former federal agency administrator, former ambassador*
Pease, Edward A. *former congressman*
Pease, Neal *history professor*
Pease-Pretty On Top, Janine B. *community college administrator*
Pecha, Brian S. *physician*
Peck, Arthur John, Jr. *retired manufacturing executive, lawyer*
Peck, Douglas Edward *lawyer*
Peck, Ernest James, Jr. *academic administrator*
Peck, Mira P. *lawyer*
Peck, Paul Lachlan *minister*
Pecker, David J. *magazine publishing company executive*
Peckham, Ellen *artist, poet*
Pecora, David Victor *retired surgeon*
Peden, Keith J. *human resources specialist*
Pedersen, Karen Sue *electrical engineer*
Pedersen, Knud George *retired economics professor, academic administrator*
Pederson, Sally J. *former lieutenant governor*
Pederson, William Christopher *plastic surgeon*
Pedini, Egle Damijonaitis *radiologist*
Pedini, Kenneth *radiologist*
Peduzzi, Claudia Claire *elementary school educator*
Peebles, Peyton Zimmermann, Jr. *electrical engineer, educator*
Peeples, Mary Anne Baumann *science educator*
Pefley, Norman Gordon *bank executive*
Pei, I.M. (Ieoh Ming Pei) *architect*
Peiris, Suhithi Mahesica *chemist, researcher*
Peixoto Neto, Jose Ulysses *internist, researcher*
Peleg, Avner *physicist, mathematician*
Pelikan, Donna Mae *retired secondary school educator*
Pell, Claiborne *former senator*
Pellegrino, Peter *retired surgeon*
Pelletier, Louis Conrad *surgeon, educator, health facility administrator*
Pence, Ira Wilson, Jr. *engineering executive, researcher*
Pence, Jean Virginia (Jean Pence) *retired real estate broker*
Pencola, Annamaria Regina *elementary school educator*
Pendleton, Austin *actor, theater director*
Pendleton, Florence Howard *former shadow senator*
Penney, Alexandra *magazine editor-in-chief, writer*
Penny, Roger Pratt *retired management consultant*
Penrod, Marian Penuel *wellness consultant, retired school librarian*
Penwell, Rebecca Ann *science educator*
Peoples, John Arthur, Jr. *former university president, consultant*
Peper, Charlotte Ann *educational consultant*
Pépin, Jacques G. *chef*
Pepper, Joline Romano *psychologist, educator*
Pepper, Jonathon L. *media executive*
Pepper, Maury *computer consultant*
Pepper, Pamela Poe *psychologist*
Peralta, Luis Francisco *language educator*
Percy, Lee Edward *motion picture film editor*
Perdigó, Luisa Marina *foreign language and literature educator*
Perenchio, Andrew Jerrold *film and television executive*
Peretti, Peter Oral *psychology professor, researcher*
Pereyra-Suarez, Charles Albert *lawyer*
Perez, Antonio M. *imaging company executive*
Perez, Paul Ignatius *prosecutor, lawyer*
Perger, Donna Spagnoli *retired secondary school mathematics educator*
Peringian, Lynda Ann *dietician, writer*
Perkiel, Mitchel H. *lawyer*
Perkins, Cheryl A. *paper company executive*
Perkins, Eddie *boxer*
Perkins, Edward A., Jr. *secondary school educator*
Perkins, Jon Douglas *accountant, educator*
Perkins, Leeman Lloyd *musicologist, educator*
Perkins, Lucian *photographer*
Perkins, Nancy Jane *industrial designer*
Perkins, Raymond Lamont *retired government official*
Perkins, Samuel Swenson *education educator*
Perkner, Stanislav *academic administrator, educator*
Perko, Francis Michael *church administrator, researcher*
Perl, Harold *neonatologist, pediatrician*
Perle, George *composer*
Perlingieri, Ilya Sandra *art historian, writer*
Perlman, Itzhak *violinist*
Perlmutter, Barbara S. *retired public relations executive*
Perlmutter, David H. *physician, educator*
Perlmutter, Diane F. *marketing executive*
Perrin, Michael Warren *lawyer*
Perrineau, Harold *actor*
Perrot, Paul Norman *museum director*
Perrotta, Antonio *trust company executive*
Perry, Chris Nicholas *retired advertising executive*
Perry, James Benn *former casino and hotel executive*
Perry, James E. *marketing executive, consultant*
Perry, Matthew *actor*
Perry, Nancy Bland *accountant*
Perry, Tyler *playwright, actor, theater director, theater producer*
Persad, Anand Bhopraj *entomologist*
Persad, Chadee *information technology manager*
Persico, Joseph Edward *historian, biographer*
Persoff, Nehemiah *actor, artist*
Person, Tammy *psychologist*
Peruzzo, Albert Louis *actuary, accountant*
Pescatore-Shirey, Hope Jean *middle school reading educator*
Pesch, Ellen P. *lawyer*
Pesci, Joe *actor*
Peshkin, Samuel David *retired lawyer*
Pesin, Ella Michele *journalist, public relations executive*
Pesola, Gene Raymond *physician*
Peszke, Michael Alfred *psychiatrist, writer*
Peters, Carol Ann Dudycha *counselor*
Peters, Christopher Allen *systems analyst, consultant*
Peters, Connie Jane *librarian, media specialist*
Peters, Douglas Alan *risk management and compliance consultant*
Peters, LeRoy Richard *materials management consulting company executive*
Peters, Robert Woolsey *retired architect*
Peters, Sammy *artist*
Petersen, Arne Joaquin *chemist, consultant*
Petersen, Dorothy Virginia *investment company executive*
Petersen-Frey, Roland *manufacturing executive*
Peterson, Ann Sullivan *physician, consultant*
Peterson, Anne Elizabeth Wallace *music educator, composer*
Peterson, Betty W. *language educator, writer*
Peterson, Bruce D. *lawyer, energy executive*
Peterson, Carl Eric *metal products executive, banker*
Peterson, Clark C. *announcer, writer, poet, speaker*
Peterson, David Maurice *retired physiologist*
Peterson, Dawn Michelle *entrepreneur, writer*
Peterson, Donald Kent *former telecommunications industry executive*
Peterson, Howard Cooper *lawyer, accountant*
Peterson, Robert Austin *retired manufacturing executive*
Peterson, Rosetta Hicks *retired music educator*
Peterson, Walter Fritiof *retired academic administrator*
Petit, Emmanuel J. *architecture educator*
Petit-Phare, Vanessa *secondary school educator*
Petkovic, Lucia M. *research scientist*
Petkovska, Iva *medical researcher*
Petrequin, Harry Joseph, Jr. *foreign service officer*
Petriashvili, Marina *physician*
Petrillo, Leonard Philip *lawyer, retired investment company executive*
Petro, Jim (James Michael) *former state attorney general*
Petru, Suzanne Mitton *retired health care finance executive*
Petrulis, Alan Joseph *artist*
Pett, John Lyman *banker*
Pettiette, Alison Yvonne *lawyer*
Pettigrew, L. Eudora *retired academic administrator*
Pettis-Roberson, Shirley McCumber *retired congresswoman*
Pettit, Erin *glaciologist*
Pettit, Ghery DeWitt *retired veterinary medicine educator*
Pettitt, Jay S. *architect, consultant*
Petz, Thomas Joseph *internist*
Petzold, Carol Stoker *state legislator*
Pevear, Roberta Charlotte *retired state legislator*
Pewitt, James Dudley *retired academic administrator*
Peyton, John *mayor*
Pezeshk, Violet *psychologist, educator*
Pfaffenroth, Peter Albert *lawyer*
Pfantz, Craig D. *farmer*
Pfeifer, Edward C. *secondary school educator*
Pfeiffer, Gary M. *chemicals executive*
Pfeiffer, Michelle *actress*
Pfeister, Raymond Lynn *diversified financial services company executive*
Pfennig, Dennis Joseph *secondary school educator*
Pflanze, Otto Paul *history professor*
Pflum, Barbara Ann *retired allergist*
Phair, Joseph Baschon *lawyer*
Pham, Lee *literature and language professor, consultant*
Phelps, Bonnie Noreen *retired secondary school educator*
Phelps, Michael Edward *biophysics professor*
Philander, Samuel George Harker *oceanographer*
Philippon, Thomas *finance educator*
Philips, Laura Alma *former pharmaceutical executive*
Phillips, Caroline L. *lab administrator*
Phillips, Dorothy K. *lawyer*
Phillips, Glynda Ann *editor*
Phillips, James Dickson, Jr. *retired federal judge*

Phillips, James Harold *retired lawyer*
Phillips, Jill Meta *writer, critic, astrologer*
Phillips, John P(aul) *retired neurosurgeon*
Phillips, Joyce Martha *human resources executive*
Phillips, Julia Mae *physicist*
Phillips, Kathleen Gay *small business owner*
Phillips, Leo Harold, Jr. *lawyer*
Phillips, Michelle Gilliam *actress, writer*
Phillips, Richard A. *retired literature and language educator*
Phillips, Robert James, Jr. *lawyer, corporate financial executive*
Phillips, Shay E. *pharmacist, educator*
Phillips, Stone (Lester Stockton Phillips) *newscaster*
Phillips, Tikera Monique *elementary school educator*
Phillips, Todd *film director, film producer*
Phillips, William *real estate company executive*
Phillips, Winifred Patricia *composer*
Philson, Richard Michael *academic administrator*
Phipard, Nancy Midwood *retired special education educator, poet*
Pickering, Thomas Reeve *retired aerospace transportation executive, diplomat*
Pickett, Cecil B. *pharmaceutical executive*
Pickett, Cecil Bruce *cell biologist*
Pickford, Rollin, Jr. *artist*
Pickrel, Paul *language educator*
Picower, Warren Michael *editor*
Pieper, Darold D. *lawyer*
Pierangeli, Silvia Susana *medical educator, consultant*
Pierce, David Hyde *actor*
Pierce, Donald Shelton *retired orthopedic surgeon, educator*
Pierce, Hilda (Hilda Herta Harmel) *painter*
Pierce, John Thomas *physician, industrial hygienist, clinical toxicologist*
Pierce, Lawrence Warren *retired federal judge*
Pierce, Lisa Margaret *telecommunications industry executive, marketing professional, educator*
Pierce, Michael Norman *internist*
Pierce, Ponchitta Ann *TV host, television producer, journalist, writer, consultant*
Pierce, Stephen D. *oceanographer, researcher*
Pierce, Susan Resneck *academic administrator, literature educator, consultant*
Pierce, Tamora *writer*
Pierog, Margaux Marie *food service executive, restaurant manager*
Pifer, Scott Thomas *mathematics educator*
Piga, Stephen Mulry *retired lawyer*
Pike, Anastasia *music educator, artist*
Pilisuk, Marc *psychology educator*
Pilous, Betty Scheibel *medical/surgical nurse*
Pinaud, Raphael *research scientist*
Pinchak, Ann Simcha *lawyer*
Pinchot, Bronson *actor*
Pindyck, Frank *surgeon*
Ping-Robbins, Nancy Regan *musician, writer, artist*
Pinkel, Gary *university football coach*
Pinkerton, A. Louise *vocalist, music educator*
Pinkett-Smith, Jada *actress*
Pinkins, Tonya *actress*
Pinkney, D. Timothy *investment company executive*
Pino, Richard Edmund *corporate financial executive*
Pinter, Gabriel George *retired physiology educator*
Pinto, Rosalind *retired secondary school educator, volunteer*
Piontkowski, Stephen Robert *environmental services administrator*
Pipchick, Margaret Hopkins *advance practice psychiatric nurse, marriage and family therapist*
Piper, Ervin Leonard *retired information technology manager, consultant*
Piper, George Chilton *lawyer*
Pippen, Scottie *professional basketball player*
Pirkle, Earl Charnell *retired geologist*
Pirkle, George Emory *photographer, instructional media producer*
Pirodsky, Donald Max *psychiatrist, educator*
Pirro, Alfred Anthony, Jr. *emergency physician*
Pirsch, Carol McBride *retired county official, state senator, community relations manager*
Pitcher, Griffith Fontaine *lawyer*
Pitman, Angelia Dee *web site design company executive*
Pitman, LaVern Frank *librarian*
Pitman-Gelles, Bonnie Louise *museum administrator, educator*
Pitofsky, Robert *federal agency administrator, law educator*
Pittman, Jonathan *computer scientist*
Pittman, Lisa *lawyer*
Pittman, Roy Clinton, Jr. *neurosurgeon, theologian, lawyer, philosopher*
Pitts, Allie Faye *retired elementary school educator*
Pitts, Gregory Scott *corporate financial executive*
Piven, Jeremy *actor*
Place, Mary Kay *actress*
Plame, Valerie Elise *former intelligence agent*
Plant, Jackson Vaughn *minister*
Plants, Walter Dale *retired elementary school educator, minister*
Platis, James George *secondary school educator*
Plauche, Nancy Caroline *retired counselor*
Plautz, Kimberly Ann *music educator*
Pletcher, Eldon *retired cartoonist*
Pleuger, Guenter *diplomat*
Plimpton, Martha *actress*
Plomp, Teunis (Tony Plomp) *minister*
Plotkin, Stanley Alan *virologist*
Plottel, Gloria Susanne Stone *marketing professional*
Plummer, Ahmed *professional football player*
Plummer, Jake (Jason Steven Plummer) *professional football player*
Plummer, Leonard Niel *geochemist*
Pniakowski, Andrew Frank *structural engineer*
Poad, Flora Virginia *retired librarian, retired elementary school educator*
Podbilski, Lisa Lyn *Mandarin Chinese educator*
Podichetty, Vinod Kumar *medical researcher*
Poe, Laura *nursing educator, administrator*
Poehling, Katherine *pediatrician*
Poehner, Raymond Glenn *retired bank executive*
Pohlhaus, Tess *theater educator*
Poitier, Sidney *actor, film director*
Pokras, Sheila Frances *retired judge*
Polascik, Mary Ann *ophthalmologist*
Polen-Dorn, Linda Frances *communications executive*
Poleway, Christopher J. *former publishing executive*
Polfliet, Sarah Jean *physician*
Policy, Carmen A. *professional sports team executive*
Polimeni, Rebecca H. *special education educator*
Poll, Martin Harvey *film producer*
Pollack, Gerald Alexander *economist, educator, federal agency administrator*
Pollack, Gerald Leslie *physicist, researcher, educator*
Pollack, Marsha *secondary school educator*
Pollak, Kevin *actor*
Pollard, Dennis Bernard *lawyer, educator*
Pollard, Henry *arbitrator, mediator*
Pollard, Samuel D. *film producer, director and editor*
Pollock, Karen Anne *computer analyst*
Polman, Jerry R. *choral director, singer*
Polon, Ira H. *lawyer*
Polsby, Allen Isaac *retired lawyer*
Polster, James *writer, film producer*
Polzonetti, Pierpaolo *musicologist, music educator*
Pombo, Richard William *former congressman, rancher, farmer*
Pomeroy, Gregg Joseph *lawyer*
Pomfret, Bonnie *music educator*
Ponce, Mary Helen *writer*
Pond, Byron O., Jr. *retired manufacturing executive*
Ponitz, David H. *former academic administrator*
Ponnapalli, Ramachandra Murty *retired statistician, researcher*
Pontius, Stanley N. *bank holding company executive*
Pont Marchese, Marisara *former Puerto Rican government official*
Pool, Philip Bemis, Jr. *investment banker*
Poor, Janet Meakin III *landscape designer*
Pope, Dale Allen *investment company executive*
Pope, Ingrid Bloomquist *sculptor, poet, painter*
Pope, John Charles *former airline company executive*
Popp, Lilian Mustaki *writer, educator*
Poppe, Laurie Catherine *matrimonial lawyer, social worker, real estate executive*
Poppel, Seth Raphael *entrepreneur*
Poppers, Paul Jules *anesthesiologist, educator*
Poppler, Doris Swords *lawyer*
Poritz, Deborah Tobias *former state supreme court justice and attorney general*
Portal, Gilbert Marcel Adrien *oil industry executive*
Porter, Dixie Lee *retired insurance company executive, consultant*
Porter, J. Ridgely III *lawyer*
Porter, James Morris *retired judge*
Porter, John Wilson *educational association administrator, director*
Porter, Michael Pell *lawyer*
Porter, Philip Thomas *retired electrical engineer*
Porter, Walter Thomas, Jr. *retired bank executive*
Portis, Alan Mark *physicist, researcher*
Portland, Rene (Maureen Portland) *retired women's college basketball coach*
Portman, Robert Jones *former federal official, former ambassador*
Portnoy, Sara S. *lawyer*
Portoveltsky, Simcha *musician, cellist*
Poser, Ernest George *psychologist, educator*
Posner, Kenneth *lighting designer*
Posner, Sidney *advertising executive*
Posner, Sylvie Pérez *lawyer*
Pospelov, Dmitriy *transportation executive*
Poss, Jeffery Scott *architect, educator*
Post, Avery Denison *retired church official*
Post, Gaines, Jr. *retired history professor, dean, academic administrator*
Post, Mike *lighting designer*
Post, Richard Bennett *retired human resources executive*
Post, Stephen Garrard *theologian, philosopher, educator*
Potash, Stephen Jon *public relations executive*
Potter, Bill R. *business executive*
Potter, J. Stewart *property manager*
Potter, James Earl *retired international hotel management company executive*
Potter, Robert Daniel *federal judge*
Potter, Tanya Jean *lawyer*
Potts, Gerald Neal *manufacturing executive*
Potvin, Alfred Raoul *engineering executive*
Pound, Frank R., Jr. *lawyer*
Pound, Robert Vivian *physics professor*
Poundstone, William Nicholas, Jr. *writer*
Povich, Lynn *journalist, Internet executive, editor*
Powell, Alma Johnson *writer, advocate, foundation administrator*
Powell, Ardal *music company executive, editor*
Powell, Kathleen Lynch *lawyer, real estate executive*
Powell, Thomas Edward III *biological supply company executive, physician*
Power, Mary Susan *political scientist, educator*
Power Anderson, Vanessa L. *dean*
Powers, Elizabeth Whitmel *lawyer*
Powers, John T., Jr. *former mayor*
Pozzatti, Rudy Otto *artist*
Prado, Edward Charles *federal judge*
Pradzynski, Andrzej Henryk *chemist*
Prakapas, Eugene Joseph *art gallery director*
Prange, Hilmar Walter *neurology educator*
Prasad, Navin *ophthalmologist*
Prather, Lenore Loving *former state supreme court chief justice*
Prather, William C. III *lawyer, writer*
Pratt, Robert Windsor *lawyer*
Preddy, Raymond Randall *retired newspaper publisher, educator*
Preer, Joan C. *retired assistant principal, retired science educator*
Prem, F. Herbert, Jr. *retired lawyer*
Prema, Nitya *marriage and family therapist, artist*
Premack, David *psychologist*
Prescott, Barbara Lodwich *educational association administrator*
Prescott, Richard Chambers *writer*
Presley, Arthur Henry *writer, artist*
Press, Aida Kabatznick *retired editor, poet, writer*
Press, Anthony L. *lawyer*
Pressler, Larry *former senator, lawyer*
Pressman, Jacob *retired rabbi*
Preston, Seymour Stotler III *chemicals executive*
Preston, Thomas Ronald *language educator, researcher*
Preus, David Walter *bishop, minister*
Prevatt, David O. *civil engineer, researcher*
Previte, Robert (Bobby) *composer, musician*
Prewitt, Kenneth *political science professor, foundation administrator*
Prewoznik, Jerome Frank *retired lawyer*
Price, Alfred Lee *lawyer, mining executive*
Price, Betty Jeanne *chimes musician*
Price, Bruce Deitrick *advertising executive, author*
Price, Charles Gower *music educator*
Price, Clifford Warren *retired metallurgist, researcher*
Price, Jason Todd *director*
Price, Joseph Sterling *retired air force officer*
Price, Michael Howard *journalist, critic, composer*
Price, Nelson (John Nelson Price) *author, journalist*
Price, Robert Ira *coast guard officer*
Price, Thomas Frederick *theater educator*
Price, Tom *journalist*
Price, William James, IV, *investment banker*
Pride, Benjamin David *sales executive*
Pridmore, Roy Davis *retired federal official*
Priest, Jessie Shaw *media specialist*
Priestley, Jason (Jason Bradford Priestley) *actor*
Primosch, James Thomas *music educator, composer, musician*
Prince, Andrew Steven *lawyer, retired government agency administrator*
Prince, Anna Lou *composer, music publisher, construction executive*
Prince, George Edward *retired pediatrician*
Priory, Richard Baldwin *former electric power industry executive*
Pristoop, Simon Morris *retired physicist, systems engineer, consultant*
Pritchard, Claudius Hornby, Jr. *retired university president*
Pritchard, Kathleen Jo *not-for-profit association administrator*
Pritchett, Meri Katherine *filmmaker*
Proctor, Richard James *geologist, consultant*
Proctor, Robert Neel *history educator*
Proenza, Bill (Xavier William Proenza) *meteorologist, former federal agency administrator*
Profeta, Salvatore, Jr. *chemist, educator*
Prokasy, William Frederick *academic administrator*
Propp, Steven H. *personnel director*
Propst, Anthony Mark *obstetrician, gynecologist*
Propst, Harold Dean *retired academic administrator*
Prosper, Pierre-Richard *former federal agency administrator*
Proulx, (Edna) Annie *writer*
Provencio, Linda Kay *music educator*
Provensen, Alice *artist, writer*
Provitt, Linda K. *forensic specialist, mental health services professional, consultant*
Pruden, Ann Lorette *chemical engineer, researcher, management consultant*
Pruehsner, William Robert *biomedical engineer*
Pruis, John J. *manufacturing executive*
Pruitt, Anne Loring *academic administrator, education educator*
Pruitt Lemley, Cynthia Kaye *computer educator*
Prusiner, Stanley Ben *neurologist, biochemist, virologist, educator*
Pruter, Robert Douglas *librarian*
Pruzan, Irene *musician, educator, public relations executive, art association administrator*
Pryor, Harold S. *retired college president*
Pryor, Richard Walter *telecommunications executive, retired air force officer*
Puck, Wolfgang *chef*
Pugliese, Stanislao *history educator, researcher*
Pulhamus, Marlene Louise *retired elementary school educator*
Pulitzer, Emily Rauh (Mrs. Joseph Pulitzer Jr.) *art historian, consultant*
Pullen, Bruce Reed *retired pastor*
Pullen, Penny Lynne *non-profit organization administrator, retired state legislator*
Pulley, Brett A. *communications executive*
Pullman, Jennifer King *art educator, artist*
Pullman, Philip Nicholas *writer, educator*
Pulwers, Jack Edward *news executive, writer, historian, journalism educator, lecturer, broadcaster*
Purcell, Bill *mayor*
Purcell, George Richard *artist*
Purcell, Philip James *retired diversified financial services company executive*
Purdy, Kevin Moore *estate planner*
Pursey, Derek Lindsay *retired physics professor*
Purtle, John Ingram *lawyer, former state supreme court justice*
Purves, William Kirkwood *biologist, educator*
Purvez, Akhtar *interventional pain management specialist, writer, speaker, advocate*
Puryear, James Burton *college administrator*
Puryear, Martin *artist, educator*
Pust, Ronald E. *physician, educator*
Pustilnik, David Daniel *lawyer*
Putman, Carol Jean *photographer, artist*
Pyatt, Kedar Davis, Jr. *research and development company executive*
Pyle, Robert Milner, Jr. *financial consultant*
Pylipow, Stanley Ross *retired manufacturing company executive*
Pynchon, Thomas Ruggles, Jr. *author*
Pytell, Robert Henry *retired lawyer, former judge*
Pytlewski, Laura Jean *chemistry professor*
Pytlinski, Jerzy Teodor *physicist, educator, research scientist*
Pytte, Agnar *physicist, retired academic administrator*
Qi, Xiaoning *electrical engineer, electronics engineer, researcher*
Qi, Zhigang *materials scientist, chemist*
Qian, Zifen *artist, editor-in-chief*
Qiu, Xiangjun *mining engineer*
Quade, Vicki *editor, writer, playwright, theater producer*
Qualls, Robert L. *manufacturing and bank executive, educator, retired state official*
Qualls, Roxanne *mayor*
Quan, Gang *engineering educator*
Quant, Harold Edward *retired financial services company executive, rancher*
Quarles, James Linwood III *lawyer*
Quarles, Randal Keith *former federal agency administrator, lawyer*
Quay, Thomas Emery *lawyer*
Quencer, Robert Moore *neuroradiologist, researcher*
Query, Lois A. *elementary school educator*
Quiala, Maribel *psychotherapist, consultant*
Quick, Adam D. *neurologist*
Quigley, Martin Schofield *writer, educator*
Quillen, Cecil Dyer, Jr. *lawyer, consultant*
Quillen, Lloyd Douglas *oil and gas executive*
Quillen, William Tatem *retired judge, lawyer, educator*
Quinlan, Kathleen *actress*
Quinn, Charles Nicholas *journalist*
Quinn, Eugene Frederick *diplomat, minister*
Quinn, Helen Rhoda Arnold *physicist*
Quinn Trank, Christine *education educator*
Quinonez, Tasha Marie *elementary school educator*
Quintana-Allenson, Ana M. *government agency executive*
Quintero, Elias Matthew *biomedical researcher*
Quirk, Kenneth Paul *accountant*
Quirk, Mary *writer, consultant*
Quist, Roxanne Genevieve *middle school teacher*
Qutub, Amina Ann *biomedical researcher, entrepreneur*
Qutub, Musa Yacub *hydrogeologist, educator, consultant*
Rabideau, Marilyn Ann *elementary school educator*
Rabinowitz, Yaron Gil *psychologist, military officer*
Rabó, Jule Anthony *research scientist, consultant*
Rabon, Anthony Perez *protective services official*
Rabon, William James, Jr. *architect*
Race, George Justice *pathology educator*
Raciti, Cherie *artist*
Radcliffe, Daniel *actor*
Radcliffe, Redonia (Donnie Radcliffe) *journalist, writer*
Radde, Bruce *retired architecture educator*
Rader, Dotson Carlyle *writer, journalist*
Radford, R. S. *lawyer, law educator*
Radhakrishnan, Ravi *science educator*
Radkowsky, Karen *advertising research specialist*
Radlauer, Steve *freelance writer, journalist, producer*
Radmilovic, Velimir *materials scientist, researcher*
Radzik, Albin F. *federal analyst, military consultant*
Raffegeau, Jean Michel *audit and consulting company executive*
Ragans, Rosalind Dorothy *writer, artist, retired educator*
Ragent, Boris *physicist*
Raghavan, Rajagopal S. *retired petroleum engineer*
Ragheb, Samia *immunologist, educator*
Ragland, Kathryn Marie *dancer, educator*
Rago, Dorothy Ashton *retired elementary school educator*
Ragone, David Vincent *former university president*
Ragone, Tara Adams *lawyer*
Ragsdale, Sandra Russell *special education educator*
Raguckas, Sarah *pharmacist, educator*
Rahal, Imad *computer science educator*
Rahe, Maribeth Sembach *investment management executive*
Rahimi, Hessam *dentist*
Rahman, Abu Tayeb Rafiqur *former United Nations official*
Rahming, Etta Lorraine *social worker, consultant, psychotherapist, school psychologist*
Raichle, Marcus Edward *radiology, neurology educator*
Railsback, Sherrie Lee *management consultant, educator*
Raimi, Samuel M. *film director*
Rainer, Rex Kelly *civil engineer, educator*
Raines, Franklin Delano *former finance company executive*
Raines, Howell Hiram *former newspaper editor, journalist*

Raines, Jeff *biomedical scientist, medical research director*
Rainville, Allison M. *language educator*
Rainville, Christina *lawyer*
Rairdin, Craig Allen *software company executive, software developer*
Raitt, Bonnie Lynn *singer, musician*
Rajani, Prem Rajaram *transportation company financial executive*
Raje, Sachin *information technology manager*
Raju, Minnie M. *application analyst, critical care nurse*
Rajupalepu, Rahi K. *technologist, consultant*
Rakes, Ganas Kaye *retired finance and banking educator*
Rako, Susan *psychiatrist, writer*
Raley, Bennett William *former federal agency administrator*
Rallo, Harry *architectural firm executive*
Ralston, Susan Bonzon *former federal official*
Ram, Chitta Venkata *physician*
Ramakrishnan, Kannan *mechanical engineer*
Ramer, James LeRoy *civil engineer*
Ramey, Eudora Malois *minister*
Ramirez, Evangeline Rose *elementary school educator*
Ramirez, Martin Ruben *engineering educator*
Ramirez, Ronaldo Victor *science educator*
Ramirez Nafarrate, Adrian *industrial engineer*
Ramirez-Rivera, Jose *physician*
Ramo, Virginia M. Smith *civic worker*
Ramsay, J. Russell *psychologist*
Ramsay, Karin Kinsey *publisher, educator*
Ramser, Wanda Tene *librarian, educator*
Ramsey, Charles H. *former police chief*
Rand, Calvin Gordon *art educator, educational consultant*
Rand, Joella Mae *retired nursing educator, counselor*
Randall, Peter *retired plastic surgeon*
Randall, Richard Rainier *geographer*
Randazzo, Marisa R. *psychologist*
Randinelli, Tracey Anne *magazine editor*
Randolph, Judson Graves *pediatric surgeon*
Randolph, Virgella *retired federal official*
Ranjan, Rahul *engineer, researcher*
Rankin, Scott David *artist, educator*
Ranney, Helen Margaret *retired internist, hematologist, educator*
Ranney, Richard Raymond *periodontist educator, researcher, dean*
Ransom, Margaret Palmquist *public relations executive*
Ransom, Tasha Elana *news production assistant, producer*
Rao, Rama Krishna R. *pharmaceutical company executive*
Raoufi, Azadeh *music educator*
Raphael, Carol *health care administrator*
Rapoport, Ronald Jon *journalist*
Rappaport, Irving S. *entrepreneur, lawyer, consultant*
Rappaport, James Wyant *lawyer, real estate developer*
Rascon, Alfred V. *former federal agency administrator*
Rash, David C. *lawyer*
Rashad, Phylicia *actress, singer, dancer*
Rasi, Humberto Mario *editor, educator*
Raskin, Fred Charles *retired transportation and utility holding company executive, educator*
Raskin, Michael A. *retail executive, director*
Rasor, Dina Lynn *journalist, private investigator*
Rastogi, Shipra *cell biologist*
Ratliff, William *former state senator, lieutenant governor, civil engineer*
Ratner, Buddy Dennis *biomedical engineer, educator*
Ratner, Michael D. *lawyer*
Ratterree, John Eric *academic administrator*
Raucher, Herman *screenwriter, novelist*
Rauh, Joshua D. *finance educator*
Rausher, David Benjamin *internist, gastroenterologist*
Raven, Francis Harvey *mechanical engineer, educator*
Raven, Patricia Elaine (Penny Raven) *real estate broker, developer, columnist*
Ravetch, Irving *screenwriter*
Ravinsky, Anthony *music educator*
Rawls, Frank Macklin *lawyer*
Rawnsley, Howard Melody *pathologist, educator*
Rawson, Richard J. *telecommunications industry executive, lawyer*
Ray, Jane Zimrude *retired machine shop executive*
Ray, Marilyn Anne *nursing educator, researcher*
Ray, Marjorie *retired financial planner*
Ray, Susan Elaine *principal*
Raymond, David Walker *lawyer*
Raymond, Lisa *professional tennis player*
Raymond, Ural Wayne *retired retail executive*
Rayner, William Alexander *retired newspaper editor, author*
Rea, Anne E. *lawyer*
Read, Richard Eaton *newspaper reporter*
Read, Tony John *information scientist, consultant*
Read, Virginia Hall *retired biochemistry professor*
Reader, George G. *retired internal-public health medicine educator*
Readey, Marijo *artist, educator*
Reagan, Nancy Davis (Anne Francis Robbins) *former First Lady of the United States, volunteer*
Reams, Patricia Lynn *retired elementary school educator*
Reath, George, Jr. *lawyer, mediator, arbitrator*
Reaves, Ray Donald *civil engineer*
Reavis, Charles Benton *choir director, educator*
Reavis, Hubert Gray, Jr. *retired metal products executive*
Reay, Stefanie *application developer, educator*
Rebay, Luciano *language educator, literary critic*
Rebhun, Joseph *allergist, immunologist, medical educator*
Rech, Lindsay Faith *writer*
Rechy, John Francisco *writer*
Reck, Elizabeth Torre *social worker, educator*
Rector, Donna Lynn *writer, photographer, vocalist*
Redd, Scott (John Scott Redd) *federal official, retired military officer*
Redding, Rogers Walker *physics professor, academic administrator*
Reddy, Ravinder *medical educator, director*
Reddy, Shyam K. *lawyer*
Redfield, Pamela A. *state legislator*
Redgrave, Vanessa *actress*
Redman, Clarence Owen *lawyer*
Redman, John Fletcher *urologist, educator*
Redmon, Larry Allen *agronomist, educator*
Redmont, Bernard Sidney *dean, communications educator*
Redstone, Shari Ellin *amusement company executive*
Reece, David Bryson *information systems administrator*
Reece, Julia Ruth *systems analyst, entrepreneur*
Reece, Karyn Lynn *business owner, consultant*
Reed, Adam Victor *psychologist, engineer, information scientist*
Reed, Anne F. Thomson *management consultant*
Reed, Austin F. *lawyer*
Reed, Betty Jamerson *historian, educator*
Reed, Dale F. *computer scientist, educator*
Reed, David Patrick *information scientist*
Reed, Diane Marie *retired psychologist*
Reed, H. Owen *retired music educator*
Reed, John Shedd *former railway executive*
Reed, John Shepard *former stock exchange executive*
Reed, Leon Samuel *secondary school educator, photographer*
Reed, Mary Carolyn Camblin *retired music educator, retired county official*
Reed, Robert N., Jr. *retired announcer*
Reed, Susan J. *elementary school educator*
Reeder, James Arthur *lawyer*
Reeder, Robert Harry *retired lawyer*
Rees, Raymond F. *military officer*
Reese, Hayne Waring *psychologist, educator*
Reeves, Daniel Edward *former professional football coach*
Reeves, Hallie Lawson *retired music educator, retired chaplain*
Reeves, Kathleen Walker *English language educator*
Reeves, Lucy Mary *retired elementary school educator*
Reeves, Michael Spencer *investment company executive*
Reeves, Richard *writer, historian*
Regal, Randall Nathaniel *policy analyst*
Regan, Judith Terrance *former publishing executive*
Regan, Paul Jerome, Jr. *manufacturing company executive, consultant*
Regan, Peter Francis III *physician, medical educator*
Regan, Susan Wright *dance educator, small business owner, choreographer*
Regel, Teresa Diamond *elementary school educator*
Regelbrugge, Roger Rafael *steel company executive*
Regenstreif, Herbert *lawyer*
Reggio, Vito Anthony *retired management consultant*
Rehak, James Richard *orthodontist*
Rehnke, Mary Ann *academic administrator*
Rehth, Ann *counselor*
Reich, Laurence *lawyer*
Reiche, Frank Perley *lawyer, former federal commissioner*
Reichenbach, Linda Louise *mathematician, language educator*
Reichmanis, Elsa *chemist*
Reichs, Kerry E. *lawyer*
Reid, Andrew Ernest *composer*
Reid, Geraldine Wold (Geraldine Reid Skjervold) *artist*
Reid, Helen Veronica *provost*
Reid, Ivonne Figueroa *language educator*
Reid, Robert Lelon *engineering educator, dean*
Reidy, Thomas Michael *financial executive*
Reiff, Jay *political organization worker*
Reilley, Dennis H. *retired chemicals executive*
Reilly, Charles Edmund, Jr. *communications executive*
Reilly, David N. (Nick Reilly) *automotive executive*
Reilly, John C. *actor*
Reilly, Robert Joseph *counselor*
Reiman, Donald Henry *language educator*
Reims, Clifford Waldemar *music educator*
Reinardy, Scott Robert *science educator*
Reinhard, Joao Pedro *chemicals company executive*
Reinhardt, John Edward *former international affairs specialist*
Reinhardt, Stephen Roy *federal judge*
Reinhart, Charles Lawrence *performing company executive*
Reinhart, Richard Paul *lawyer*
Reinhold, Judge (Edward Ernest Reinhold Jr.) *actor*
Reinike, Irma *retired civilian military employee, writer, artist, poet, lyricist*
Reinke, Ralph Louis *retired academic administrator*
Reinleitner, Katherine Mindlin *psychologist, foundation administrator*
Reinoehl, Richard Louis *artist, scholar, martial artist*
Reisman, Judith Ann Gelernter *media communications executive, educator*
Reiss, Jerome *retired lawyer*
Reiss, Robert Francis *physician*
Reiter, Glenn Mitchell *lawyer*
Remes, Robin Eva *secondary school educator, cartographer*
Remkus, Connie Elaine *nutritional consultant*
Rempt, Rodney P. *retired academic administrator, career military officer*
Ren, Xing Jian *physician*
Renard, Paul Steven *music educator*
Renaud, Bernadette Marie Elise *author*
Rendich, Ana *painter, collage artist*
Rendl-Marcus, Mildred *artist, economist*
Rendu, Jean-Michel Marie *mining executive*
Renfro, Charles Gilliland *economist*
Renfro, Patricia Elise *library director, academic administrator*
Renfro, William Leonard *futurist, lawyer, inventor, entrepreneur*
Renkes, Gregg D. *former state attorney general*
Renne, Paul F. *retired food products executive*
Reno, Janet *former United States attorney general*
Reno, Joseph Harry *retired orthopedist*
Renouf, Anne *corporate financial executive, consultant*
Renshaw, Charles Lucius *retired surgeon*
Rent, Clyda Stokes *academic administrator*
Renyi, Thomas A. *bank executive*
Repinski, Sara *library director*
Repnikova, Maria *international migration scholar*
Resch, Rita Marie *retired music educator*
Reschke, Michael W. *real estate company officer*
Resnick, Alice Robie *retired state supreme court justice*
Resnick, Kirsten Fay Markuson *history professor*
Resnick, Myron Jay *retired insurance company executive, lawyer*
Reuber, Grant Louis *banking insurance company executive*
Reuther, Ronald Theodore *museum director*
Reveal, Ernest Ira III *retired lawyer*
Rew, Lawrence Boyd *lawyer*
Rewcastle, Neill Barry *neuropathologist*
Reynik, Robert John *materials scientist, consultant, science educator*
Reynolds, Clark Winton *economist, educator*
Reynolds, Donald Martin *art historian, foundation administrator, educator*
Reynolds, Frank Miller *retired government agency administrator*
Reynolds, Karen Ann *retired elementary school educator*
Reynolds, Lewis Dayton *pastor*
Reynolds, Patricia Ellen *artist*
Reynolds, Robert *artist, educator*
Reynolds, William Bradford *lawyer*
Reza, Shahed *electrical engineer*
Rezek, Francisco *former judge, former supreme court justice*
Reznikov, Vladimir Lvovich *historian, playwright*
Rhea, Jerry Dwaine *consumer lending director*
Rheney, Susan O. *paper company executive*
Rhoads, James Berton *archivist, consultant, federal official, educator*
Rhodes, Lawrence *artistic director*
Rhodes, Linda Jane *psychiatrist*
Rhodes, Melvin Frank *minister, writer*
Rhodes, Peter Edward *label company executive*
Rhyne, James Jennings *condensed matter physicist*
Rhyne, Sidney White *retired lawyer*
Riasanovsky, Nicholas Valentine *retired historian, educator*
Ribonson-Smith, Sonia Anthonette *counselor, mental health services professional*
Riccio, Angela *science educator*
Ricco, Donna *fashion designer*
Rice, Claretha Mayes *medical/surgical nurse, educator*
Rice, Ferill Jeane *writer*
Rice, Gary Russell *retired special education educator*
Rice, Jerry Lee *retired professional football player*
Rice, Joseph Albert *retired bank executive*
Rice, Kenner Cralle *medicinal chemist*
Rice, Patricia Oppenheim Levin *retired special education educator, consultant*
Rice, Richard Lee *retired architect*
Rice, Stuart Alan *chemist, educator*
Rich, Jeffrey A. *former information technology company executive*
Rich, Laura *columnist*
Rich, Michael Joseph *lawyer*
Rich, Norman Minner *surgeon*
Richard, Candace L. *music educator*
Richard, Edward H. *manufacturing executive, retired municipal official*
Richard, Robert Carter *retired psychologist*
Richards, Austin Ames *physicist, artist*
Richards, Carmeleete A. *computer company executive, network administrator, consultant*
Richards, David Gleyre *German language educator*
Richards, Herbert East *retired minister, commentator*
Richards, John Pickford *musician, educator*
Richards, Martin *theatrical producer*
Richards, Michael *actor, comedian*
Richardson, Arthur Wilhelm *lawyer*
Richardson, Charles Clifton *biochemist, educator*
Richardson, Desmond *dancer*
Richardson, Edward R. *former academic administrator*
Richardson, Gerald B. *hearing officer, lawyer*
Richardson, Jeffrey Carl *public relations executive*
Richardson, John Carroll *lawyer, financial consultant*
Richardson, Margaret Ann *art historian, educator*
Richardson, Margaret Milner *retired lawyer*
Richardson, Paul Joseph *food scientist, researcher*
Richardson, Robert *cinematographer*
Richardson, Robert Dale, Jr. *language educator*
Richardson, Thomas Andrew *business executive, educator*
Richardson, Veta Teresa *professional society administrator, lawyer*
Richardson, William Chase *retired foundation executive*
Richardson, Willie Forrest, Jr. *physician, consultant*
Richardson-Bowman, Lequetta Devera *finance company executive, consultant*
Richburg, Billy Keith *healthcare manager, consultant, entrepreneur*
Richey, Ellen *credit card company executive*
Richey, Mary Ellen *lawyer*
Richgels, Glen William *mathematics professor*
Richman, Alan *magazine editor, educator*
Richman, Paul *semiconductor industry executive, educator*
Richman, Peter *electronics executive*
Richmond, Anthony Henry *sociologist, emeritus educator*
Richmond, Julius Benjamin *retired pediatrician, former Surgeon General of the United States, health policy educator*
Richter, Robert C. *retired automotive executive*
Richter, W.D. *screenwriter, director, producer*
Rick, Roseleen P. *lawyer*
Rickard, Ruth David *retired history and political science professor*
Rickel, Annette Urso *psychology and psychiatry researcher, educator*
Rickert, Jonathan Bradley *retired foreign service officer*
Ricketson, Mary E. *former dean, lawyer*
Rickett, Carolyn Kaye Master *artist, small business owner*
Ricketts, Sondra Lou *librarian*
Ricks, Joycia Camilla *retired lawyer*
Ricks, Mark G. *former lieutenant governor, former state senator*
Ricks, Thomas Miller *historian, academic administrator*
Riden, Michael David *nuclear engineer*
Ridenhour, Marilyn Housel *retired accountant*
Ridge, Davy-Jo Stribling *retired school librarian*
Ridge, Tom (Thomas Joseph) *former secretary of homeland security, governor*
Ridgway, James Mastin *retired government agency administrator*
Ridgway, Rozanne LeJeanne *corporate director, retired ambassador*
Ridings, Dorothy Sattes *former association executive*
Ridolfi, Dorothy Porter Boulden *nurse, real estate broker*
Ridolfi, Patrick Murphy *music educator, tenor*
Ridout, Susan Ramp *education educator*
Rief, Michelle M. *cultural studies educator*
Riehecky, Janet Ellen *writer*
Riekki, Lee William *musician, educator*
Ries, Charles P. *ambassador*
Riffenburgh, Gerrye H. *artist, educator*
Riffenburgh, Robert Harry *biostatistician, researcher*
Rifka, Judy *artist, educator*
Rifkin, Ron *actor*
Rifkin, Stephen *nephrologist*
Rigaud, Edwin Joseph *museum administrator*
Rigby, Perry Gardner *medical association administrator, internist, medical educator*
Rigdon, David Tedrick *military officer, geneticist, director*
Rigg, Carol Margaret Elizabeth Ruth *retired art educator*
Rigg, Charles Andrew *pediatrician*
Rigg, Lyle D. *headmaster*
Riggio, Kerry Kerstin *elementary school worker, researcher*
Riggs, Michael David *editor, writer*
Righini, Marilou Mausteller *editor, consultant*
Righter, Kathleen Anne *language educator*
Righter, Walter Cameron *retired bishop*
Rihanna, (Robyn Rihanna Fenty) *singer, actress*
Riley, Cheryl M. *prosthodontist, military officer*
Riley, James Clifford *military career officer*
Riley, Monica *microbiologist, educator*
Riley, Rebecca Michelle *music educator*
Rimel, Ira Wesley *writer, US Navy supply officer, real estate specialist, real estate appraiser, real estate broker*
Rimler, Anita A. *former state official*
Rimsza, Skip *former mayor*
Rindone, Joseph Patrick *clinical pharmacist, educator*
Rinebold, Alice June *environmental scientist*
Ring, Nancy Gail *artist, writer, art educator*
Ring, Renee Etheline *lawyer*
Ringel, Judy G. *writer*
Ringler, Kenneth J., Jr. *former state agency administrator*
Rino, Barbara Elizabeth *musician, educator*
Riordan, John Thomas *trade association executive, consultant*
Riordan, Richard J. *former state official, former mayor*
Ripert, Eric *food service executive*
Riposo, Joseph *music educator, director*
Rippert, Eric Theodore *oral and maxillofacial surgeon, healthcare consultant*
Rips, Lance Jeffrey *psychology professor*
Risdon, Michael Paul *manufacturing executive*
Rishel, Richard Clinton *retired bank executive*
Riskin, Victoria *former trade association administrator*
Risley, Todd Robert *psychologist, educator*
Rissman, Burton Richard *lawyer*
Ritchey, Samuel Donley, Jr. *retired retail executive*
Ritman, Barbara Ellen *counselor*
Ritter, Ann Marie *pediatric neurosurgeon*
Ritter, Elise Dawn *therapist, clinical social worker, writer, artist, photographer*
Rivadeneira, David Edward *colon and rectal surgeon, researcher*
Rivera, Oscar R. *lawyer, educator*
Rivera, Richard Edwin *former restaurant chain executive*
Rivers, Beverly D. *former district secretary*
Rivet, Dennis James *neurosurgeon*
Rivlin, Rachel *lawyer*

Rizowy, Carlos Guillermo *lawyer, educator, political analyst*
Rizzo, Jeffrey F. *corporate financial executive*
Roach, James W. *orthopedist, surgeon*
Roaden, Arliss Lloyd *retired academic administrator*
Roark, Barbara Ann *librarian*
Robards, Thomas Frederick *banker*
Robart, James Louis *federal judge, lawyer*
Robbins, Alice Elizabeth *musician*
Robbins, Christiane Patricia *media director, artist, designer, educator*
Robbins, Norman Nelson *lawyer*
Robbins, Ray C. *retired manufacturing executive*
Robe, Thurlow Richard *retired engineering educator, dean*
Roberson, James O. *foundation executive*
Roberts, Alan Silverman *orthopedic surgeon*
Roberts, Albert Dee *internist*
Roberts, Carter S. *environmental services administrator*
Roberts, David Glen *prospector, investor*
Roberts, David Lowell *journalist, educator*
Roberts, Delmar Lee *editor*
Roberts, Doris *actress*
Roberts, Edwin Albert, Jr. *editor, journalist*
Roberts, Judith Marie *librarian, educator*
Roberts, Kathleen Mary *retired school system administrator*
Roberts, Katrina M. *real estate agent*
Roberts, Lawrence Gilman *telecommunications industry executive*
Roberts, Margaret Harold *editor, publisher*
Roberts, Melville Parker *neurosurgeon*
Roberts, Michael Joseph *journalist*
Roberts, Patricia Lee *education educator*
Roberts, Patricia Lee *small business owner, consultant*
Roberts, Philip John *history professor, editor*
Roberts, Rodney R. *systems analyst, educator*
Roberts, Stanley Dwayne *physician, educator, academic administrator*
Roberts, Susan Sturgeon *art educator, writer*
Roberts, Suzanne Catherine *artist*
Roberts, Thomas George *retired physicist*
Roberts, William H. *lawyer*
Robertson, A. Haeworth *actuary, foundation executive, benefits consultant*
Robertson, Charles James *museum director emeritus*
Robertson, Cliff *actor, writer, director*
Robertson, Jack Clark *accounting educator*
Robertson, John Archibald Law *nuclear scientist*
Robertson, LaVerne *minister*
Robertson, Robert Graham Hamish *physicist*
Robertson, Wyndham Gay *university official, journalist*
Robins, Norman Alan *management consultant, retired metal products executive*
Robinson, Aminah Brenda Lynn *artist, illustrator*
Robinson, David Bradford *writer, poet*
Robinson, David Brooks *retired naval officer*
Robinson, David Zav *not-for-profit consultant*
Robinson, Davis Rowland *lawyer, international arbitrator*
Robinson, Devette Lorraine *music educator*
Robinson, Frank *former professional baseball manager, retired professional baseball player*
Robinson, Gail Patricia *retired mental health counselor*
Robinson, Harlow Loomis *language educator, historian, writer*
Robinson, Hugh Granville *consulting management company executive*
Robinson, James Alfred *middle school educator*
Robinson, James Arthur *political scientist*
Robinson, Linda Gosden *communications executive*
Robinson, Marguerite Stern *anthropologist, educator, consultant*
Robinson, Mary Elizabeth Goff *retired historian, researcher*
Robinson, Molly Jahnige *statistician, educator*
Robinson, Rebecca Lynne *medical researcher*
Robinson, Verna Cotten *retired librarian, real estate manager*
Robinson, William I. *sociologist*
Robison, Emily Burns *musician*
Robison, Paula Judith *flutist*
Roble, Carole Marcia *accountant*
Robles, Rosalie Miranda *elementary school educator*
Rocca, Christina B. *ambassador, former federal agency administrator*
Roche, James Gerard *former civilian military employee*
Roche, Pauline Jennifer *artist*
Rochelle, Lugenia *academic administrator*
Rochlin, Paul R. *lawyer*
Rock, Chris *actor, comedian*
Rock, John Aubrey *gynecologist, obstetrician, educator, administrator, retired chancellor*
Rock, Mary Ann *artist, educator*
Rockburne, Dorothea Grace *artist*
Rockwell, Elizabeth Dennis *retirement specialist, financial planner*
Rockwood, Frederick Whitney *insurance company executive*
Rodbell, Clyde Armand *retired distribution executive*
Roddick, Andy Stephen *professional tennis player*
Rodecker, Stephen Bailey *science specialist, secondary school educator*
Roden, Michael Frank *geochemist, educator, director*
Rodenburg, Clifton Glenn *lawyer*
Rodgers, Bruce Alan *government agency administrator, psychologist*
Rodgers, Lawrence Rodney *internist, educator*
Rodgers, Lois Eve *secondary school educator*
Rodgers, Robert Aubrey *physicist*
Rodin, Eugene *aerospace scientist, researcher, engineering educator*
Rodino, Vincent Louis *insurance company executive*
Roditti, Esther C(laire) *lawyer, writer*
Rodman, Sue A. *wholesale company executive, artist, writer*
Rodnunsky, Sidney *lawyer, educator*
Rodriguez, Angel Luis *electrical engineer*
Rodriguez, Carlos A. *lawyer*
Rodriguez, Carlos Augusto *lawyer*
Rodriguez, Elena Garcia *retired pension fund administrator*
Rodriguez, Michelle (Mayte Michelle Rodriguez) *actress*
Rodriguez, Robert *filmmaker*
Rodriguez, Timothy Allen *language educator*
Rodriguez, Vivian N. *lawyer, accountant*
Rodriguez, William Julio *physician*
Roe, Mark J. *law educator*
Roe, Mary Ann *retired postmaster*
Roe, Thomas Coombe *former utility company executive*
Roe, Thomas F. *retired endocrinologist*
Roeg, Nicolas Jack *film director*
Roehm, Julie A. *marketing executive*
Roeller, Herbert Alfred *biology professor*
Roemer, Carol Kaluga *art educator*
Roemer, James Paul *data processing executive, writer*
Roenigk, Martin Allen *insurance company executive*
Roesner, Peter Lowell *manufacturing executive*
Rogaczewski, Sherrie Reece *small business owner, singer*
Rogalski, Lois Ann *speech and language pathologist*
Rogan, Robert *management educator, consultant, osteopath, psychiatrist, lawyer*
Rogen, Seth *actor*
Rogers, Alice Louise *retired bank executive, writer, researcher*
Rogers, Bernard William *military officer*
Rogers, David *playwright, actor*
Rogers, Dorothea May *education educator*
Rogers, Elizabeth London *retired geriatrics services professional*
Rogers, Jack David *plant pathologist, educator*
Rogers, Justin Towner, Jr. *retired utility company executive*
Rogers, Katharine Munzer *English literature educator*
Rogers, Margaret Ellen Jonsson *civic worker*
Rogers, Mark Charles *physician, entrepreneur, anesthesiologist, pediatrician, educator*
Rogers, Ruth Frances *retired microbiologist*
Rogers, Sally J. *psychologist, educator*
Rogers, Wanda Faye *vocalist*
Rohde, Joe (Joseph Martin Rohde) *theme park executive, designer*
Rohr, Davis Charles *aerospace consultant, retired military officer*
Rohrbach, Heidi A. *lawyer*
Roitman, Judith *mathematician, educator*
Rojany, Lisa Adrienne *publishing company executive, writer*
Rojas, Victor Hugo Macedo *retired vocational education educator*
Rokhvarger, Anatoly Efim *materials science and ceramic technology scientist*
Roland, Donald Edward *advertising executive*
Roller, David Isaac *financial services company executive*
Roller, Pamela Jo *elementary school educator*
Rollins, Alfred Brooks, Jr. *historian, educator*
Rollins, Carole Ann *writer, artist*
Rollins, Diann Elizabeth *occupational health nurse, educator, primary school educator*
Rollins, Faye Lorraine *medical transcriptionist*
Roman, Alfred Victor *science education educator*
Roman, Nancy Grace *astronomer, consultant*
Roman, Stanford Augustus, Jr. *medical educator, dean*
Romano, Gaetano *research scientist, educator*
Romano, Joseph Anthony *healthcare education and marketing consultant*
Romano, Louis George *education educator*
Romano, Ray *actor, comedian*
Romanow, Josh *lawyer*
Romanowski, Thomas Andrew *physicist, educator*
Romanucci-Ross, Lola *anthropologist, educator*
Romer, Denise Patrice *lawyer*
Romer, Roy R. *retired school system administrator, former governor*
Romig, Thomas J. *judge, career military officer*
Romo, Randulfo *physiologist, educator*
Ronalter, Chelsea Maria *artist, graphic designer*
Ronan, Mark A. *mathematician, writer*
Roncal, Rogelio *psychiatrist*
Rondepierre, Edmond Francois *insurance executive, lawyer*
Rook, Judith Rawie *television producer, writer*
Rook, Vicki Lynn *safety specialist*
Rooney, Andrew Aitken *writer, journalist*
Roorda, John Francis, Jr. *manufacturing executive, consultant*
Rooth, Signe Alice *editor, consultant*
Roper, Sally Ann *health facility administrator*
Rosati, Diane Claire *epidemiologist, educator, artist*
Rose, Arthur Royal *financial planner, tax consultant*
Rose, Elihu Isaac *lawyer*
Rose, James Turner *aerospace engineer, consultant*
Rose, Margarete Joyce *musician, interpreter*
Rose, Marian Henrietta *physics researcher*
Rose, Michael Elvin *oil and gas exploration company executive*
Rose, Michael Leonard *film, television and video producer*
Rose, Michael Robertson *evolutionary biology educator, consultant*
Rose, Paul Edward *systems administrator, educator*
Rose, Robert Edgar *retired state supreme court justice*
Rose, Sarah Elizabeth *genealogist, writer, counselor, web site designer*
Roseanne, (Roseanne Barr) *actress, comedienne, television producer, writer*
Rosellon, Juan *economist, researcher*
Roseman, Jack *computer services company executive*
Rosen, Arthur Marvin *advertising executive*
Rosen, Judah Ben *computer scientist*
Rosen, Myor *harpist, educator*
Rosen, Paul Peter *pathologist*
Rosenberg, Alison P. *public policy officer*
Rosenberg, David Alan *military historian, strategic analyst*
Rosenberg, Raymond David *special education educator, consultant*
Rosenberg, Rudy *chemical company executive*
Rosenberg, Sheli Zysman *retired finance company executive*
Rosenblatt, Roger *writer*
Rosenblum, Estelle H. *retired dean, nursing educator*
Rosenblum, Mindy Fleischer *pediatrician*
Rosenfeld, Albert Hyman *science and medical writer*
Rosenfeld, Nachman *plastic surgeon*
Rosenfield, James Harold, Sr. *communications executive*
Rosenhouse, Howard *retired lawyer*
Rosenkilde, Carl Edward *retired physicist*
Rosenkranz, E. Joshua *lawyer*
Rosenn, Harold *lawyer*
Rosenow, Mitchell Paul *sound recording engineer, studio owner, musician, music producer*
Rosenquist, James Albert *artist*
Rosensaft, Lester Jay *management consultant, lawyer*
Rosenstein, Robert Alan *scientific consultant*
Rosenthal, James D. *retired federal official, retired ambassador*
Rosenthal, Joel *chemist, researcher*
Rosenthal, Michael Ross *academic administrator, consultant*
Rosenthal, Susan Barbara *retired librarian*
Rosenthal, Tony (Bernard) *sculptor*
Rosett, Daniel J. *film company executive*
Rosha, Uzi *lawyer*
Roshan, Daniel *obstetrician, gynecologist*
Rosky, Burton Seymour *lawyer*
Rosmus, Anna Elisabeth *writer*
Rosner, Seth *lawyer, educator*
Ross, Bobby (Robert Joseph Ross) *retired college football coach*
Ross, Carol *retired women's college basketball coach*
Ross, Christopher Wade Stelyan *diplomat*
Ross, Dennis E. *retired automotive executive, lawyer*
Ross, Gerald Fred *electrical engineering executive, researcher*
Ross, Harold Anthony *lawyer*
Ross, Ivy E. *apparel executive, artist*
Ross, John T. *artist, educator*
Ross, Leonard Lester *retired academic administrator*
Ross, Michael Aaron *lawyer*
Ross, Molly Owings *small business owner, sculptor*
Ross, Tracey *actress*
Rosser, Essie *minister, counselor, marketing professional*
Rossi, Dino J. *former state legislator*
Rossin, Lawrence George *ambassador*
Roster, Michael *lawyer*
Roszkowski, Stanley Julian *retired federal judge*
Rotenberg, Marc Steven *advocate, lawyer*
Rotermund, Donald O. *musician, minister*
Roth, Harvey Paul *retired publishing executive*
Roth, Michael *lawyer*
Roth, Paul Barry *dean, educator, emergency medicine physician*
Roth, Philip Milton *writer*
Roth, Richard *news correspondent*
Rothenberg, Albert *psychiatrist, educator*
Rothman, Howard Joel *lawyer*
Rothschild, Rick *entertainment company executive*
Rothstein, Gerald Alan *investment consultant*
Rothwell, Timothy *pharmaceutical executive*
Rottenstein, Jessica Brooke *biology educator, earth science educator, researcher*
Rotunda, Adam Michael *dermatologist*
Roudebush, James Gordon *career military officer*
Roukema, Margaret Scafati *congresswoman*
Rouman, James Christ *anesthesiologist*
Rouman, John Christ *classics educator*
Rourke, Mickey (Philip Andre Rourke Jr.) *actor*
Rouse, Roscoe, Jr. *retired librarian, educator*
Rouse, Terrie Suzitte *museum director*
Rousseau, Eugene Ellsworth *musician, music educator, consultant*
Rouxel, Olivier *geochemist, research scientist*
Rove, Karl Christian *former federal official*
Rowe, Audrey *paralegal*
Rowe, Ernest Ras *education educator, academic administrator*
Rowe, John Wallis (Jack Rowe) *retired insurance company executive, education educator*
Rowe, Melinda Grace *public health service officer*
Rowe, William Davis *finance company executive*
Rowell, Barbara Caballero *retired academic administrator*
Rowell, Lester John, Jr. *retired insurance company executive*
Rowen, Henry Stanislaus *retired economist, former federal agency administrator*
Rowland, Allen R. *former retail executive*
Rowlands, Gena *actress*
Rowley, Maxine Lewis *education educator, retired academic administrator*
Roy, Michelle E. *musician, information technology consultant*
Roy, Rachel *fashion designer*
Royce, Paul Chadwick *healthcare administrator*
Ruan, Jiening *literature and language professor, director, director, writer*
Rubbert, Paul Edward *retired engineering executive*
Rubello, David Jerome *artist*
Ruben, Jeffrey M. *finance company executive, lawyer*
Rubenfeld, Stanley Irwin *lawyer, director, mediator, arbitrator*
Rubenstein, Allen Ira *lawyer*
Rubenstein, Atoosa Behnegar *former editor-in-chief*
Rubenstein, David Aaron *military officer, healthcare administrator*
Rubin, Bruce Joel *screenwriter, director, producer*
Rubin, Ellen *education/access consultant*
Rubin, Louis Decimus, Jr. *retired language educator, writer, publishing executive*
Rubin, Martin N. *meeting planner, consultant*
Rubin, Michael P. *surgeon, researcher*
Rubin, Phyllis Getz *health association executive*
Rubin, Richard Allan *lawyer*
Rubin, Robert Joseph *internist, nephrologist, consultant*
Rubin, Sandra Mendelsohn *artist*
Rubin, Vera Cooper *astronomer, researcher*
Rubin, Zick *lawyer, writer, psychology professor*
Rubino, Stephen John *secondary school educator*
Rubinstein, Eva (Anna) *photographer*
Rubinstein, Jonathan J. *computer company executive*
Rubottom, George Milton *foundation administrator, chemist*
Rudd, D(ale) F(rederick) *chemical engineering professor*
Ruddy, Kathy Aakre *paralegal*
Ruder, Tia L. *music educator*
Rudin, Anne *retired mayor, nursing educator*
Rudner, Sara *dancer*
Rudolph, James Robert *psychologist*
Rudolph, Wallace Morton *law educator*
Rudy, Raymond Bruce, Jr. *retired food company executive*
Ruegg, Donald George *retired rail transportation executive*
Ruffin, Herbert George, II, *history professor*
Ruffner, Charles Louis *lawyer*
Ruffo, Michael *painter*
Rugaber, Walter Feucht, Jr. *retired publishing executive, academic administrator*
Ruggiero, David L. *music educator, accountant*
Ruggiero, Matthew John *bassoonist*
Ruggles, Rudy Lamont, Jr. *international security advisor*
Ruhl, Sarah *playwright*
Ruhm, Thomas Francis *retired lawyer*
Ruiz-Deya, Gilberto *urologist*
Rukeyser, Robert James *manufacturing executive*
Ruland, Mildred Ardelia *retired retail executive, retail buyer*
Rumney, Helene Vosburgh *retired poet, peace activist*
Rump, Marjorie *library director*
Rumschitzki, David Sheldon *chemical engineering educator*
Rumsfeld, Donald Henry *former secretary of defense*
Runge, Jeffrey William *former federal agency administrator*
Runkle, Martin Davey *library director*
Runner, Jeffrey Thomas *linguist*
Ruoff, A. LaVonne Brown *language educator*
Rush, Julia Ann Halloran (Mrs. Richard Henry Rush) *artist, writer*
Rush, Norman *author*
Rush, Richard Henry *finance company executive, educator, writer*
Rushforth, Ann Fay *artist, educator*
Rushing, John Alan *business educator*
Rushnell, Squire Derrick *writer, speaker, television executive*
Rushworth, Michele D. *artist*
Russ, Edmond Vincent, Jr. *marketing professional*
Russ, Joanna *author*
Russack, John A. *federal official*
Russell, Andrew Benjamin *historian, educator*
Russell, Bill *former professional basketball team executive, former professional basketball player*
Russell, Carol Ann *city council member, retired company executive*
Russell, Florence L. *elementary school educator*
Russell, James Benjamin *microbiologist, educator, research scientist*
Russell, James Brian *broadcast executive, media consultant*
Russell, Liane Brauch *retired geneticist*
Russell, Maryanne *photographer*
Russell, Michael K. *psychology professor, consultant*
Russell, Theresa Lynn *actress*
Russell, Walter Dallas, Jr. *diversified financial services company executive*
Russo, Jose *pathologist*
Russo, Richard *writer*
Russo, Roy Lawrence *retired electronics engineer*
Russo, Vincent Joseph *surgeon*
Rutan, Charles R. *musician*
Rutgard, Lorraine Levin *hearing impaired educator*
Rutherford, John Sherman, III, (Johnny Rutherford) *professional race car driver*
Rutsala, Vern A. *poet, writer, language educator*
Ruud, Clayton Olaf *engineering educator*
Ruviella-Knorr, Jeanne L. *music educator, consultant, clinician*
Ryan, Daniel John *university administrator*
Ryan, George William *manufacturing executive*
Ryan, James *insurance company executive*
Ryan, John Joseph *physician*
Ryan, John William *educational association administrator*
Ryan, Joyce Ethel *writer, artist*
Ryan, Leo Vincent *business educator*
Ryan, Marleigh Grayer *language educator*

Ryan, Melbagene T. *retired food service and nutrition director*
Ryan, Timothy Patrick *investment company executive*
Rybczyk, Joseph Anthony *physicist, researcher, writer, inventor*
Rydén, Bengt Gunnar *retired stock exchange executive*
Ryder, Winona (Winona Laura Horowitz) *actress*
Rydholm, Ralph Williams *advertising executive*
Rymar, Julian W. *manufacturing executive, director*
Ryskamp, Charles Andrew *museum director, educator*
Ryther, Stephen Glenn *military officer, protective services official*
Rytkonen, Juha Kalevi *corporate financial executive*
Ryun, Jim (James Ronald Ryun) *former congressman*
Saalfeld, Fred Erich *science educator, researcher*
Sabatini, David Domingo *cell biologist, biochemist*
Sabatini, Nelson John *healthcare executive*
Sabatino, Thomas Joseph, Jr. *lawyer, pharmaceutical executive*
Sabb, Annmarie Louise *retired chemist*
Sabbatini, Marcello *journalist, motor sports weekly director*
Sabeti, Mike A. *endodontist, periodontist, educator*
Sablik, Martin John *research physicist*
Sabo, Martin Olav *former congressman*
Sabol, Steve *film company executive*
Sabundayo, Beulah Perdue *pharmacist, researcher*
Sack, Sylvan Hanan *lawyer*
Sackett, Susan Deanna *writer*
Sacks, Temi J. *public relations executive*
Sacripanti, Peter John *lawyer*
Sadinsky, Rachael *curator, art appraiser*
Sadoh, Godwin Simeon *music educator*
Sadow, Harvey S. *healthcare company executive*
Saeks, Richard Ephraim *engineering executive*
Saenz, Cecilia Sonia *education educator*
Saenz, Silvia Patricia *special education educator*
Safford, Florence Viray Sunga *travel agent, consultant*
Safian, Shelley Carole *advertising executive*
Safren, Cheryl *artist, art educator*
Sagan, M. J. *architectural firm executive*
Sager, Donald Jack *librarian, consultant, retired publishing executive*
Sahai, Akhil *computer scientist, researcher*
Sahl, Jacob *retired technologist, secondary school educator, researcher*
Sahner, Christian C. *historian*
Sahrakorpi, Seppo *physicist, researcher*
Saiah, Sue Lynn *linguist, educator*
Saindon, Michael *music educator*
Saint, Eva Marie *actress*
St. Clair, Donald David *lawyer*
St. Clair, Jesse Walton, Jr. *retired savings and loan association executive*
St. Clair, Thomas McBryar *mining and manufacturing company executive*
St. Claire, Frank Arthur *lawyer*
St. Germain, Fernand Joseph *retired congressman*
Saint-Girard, Christian *theater director, actor, educator, choreographer, theater producer*
Saint-Jacques, Bernard *linguistics educator*
St. John, Kristoff *actor*
Saito, Robert Shunichi *writer, poet*
Sajak, Pat *television game show host*
Sak, Gilbert *music educator*
Saks, Gene *theater and film director, actor*
Saks, Judith-Ann *artist*
Saks, Stephen Howard *accountant, health organization executive*
Salahuddin, Parveen *information scientist, researcher*
Salamone, Joseph Charles *polymer chemistry professor*
Salant, Nira L. *geographer, educator*
Salapatek, John (John Franklin) *literature and language educator, writer*
Salari Sander, Sherry *artist, sculptor*
Salat, Cristina *writer*
Salathe, John, Jr. *retired manufacturing executive*
Salazar, Omar Mauricio *radiation oncologist, educator*
Saleh, Brian Behrooz *aerospace transportation executive*
Salerno, Frederic V. *retired telecommunications company executive*
Salerno, Sister Maria *advanced practice nurse, educator*
Saligman, Harvey *retired consumer products and services company executive*
Salinas, Rodney Jay C. *media company executive*
Salins, Peter D. *political science professor, academic administrator*
Salisbury, Micheal Wayne *education educator*
Saliterman, Richard Arlen *lawyer*
Salkind, Michael Jay *science administrator, metallurgical engineer*
Sallis, James *writer*
Salmen, Charles R. *medical research scholar*
Salom, Roberto *retired finance company executive*
Salpeter, Shelley *medical educator*
Saltzman, Philip *television producer, writer*
Saluko, Ayodelo V. *hospital administrator*
Salvan, Sherwood Allen *lawyer*
Salvatore, Diane J. *editor-in-chief*
Salzman, Arthur George *architect, consultant*
Salzman, Stanley P. *lawyer*
Samblis, Kelley C. *educator, researcher*
Sambora, Richie (Richard Stephen Sambora) *musician, singer, songwriter*
Samec, Diane Patricia *retired elementary school educator*
Samenuk, George C. *former software security company executive*
Samer, Bill Fred Carl *writer, filmmaker*
Samolyk, Keith Andrew *cardiovascular perfusionist, director*
Samples, Mark Christopher *music editor*
Samples, Phil Lovin *pharmacist, military officer*
Sampson, Donna Rene *mathematics educator*
Sampson, Robert Neil *professional society administrator, consultant*
Samuels, Janet Lee *lawyer*
Samuels, Maurice Anthony *French literature educator*
Samuelson, Robert Jacob *journalist*
Sanchez, Alita Cassandra *physical education educator, personal trainer*
Sanchez, Fausto H. *advertising executive*
Sanchez Mills, Peggy *women's association executive*
Sandage-Mussey, Elizabeth Anthea *retired market research executive*
Sanders, Barry *retired professional football player*
Sanders, Charles Franklin *energy executive, consultant*
Sanders, Franklin D. *retired insurance company executive*
Sanders, Jackie Wolcott *ambassador*
Sanders, Linda E. *psychologist, educator*
Sanders, Marlene *news correspondent, journalism educator*
Sanders, Shannon Kay *professional society administrator*
Sanders, Vanessa *journalist, writer*
Sanders, Walter Jeremiah, III, (Jerry Sanders) *retired computer company executive*
Sanderson, James Richard *retired naval officer, financial consultant*
Sandhu, Sukhminder Kaur *epidemiologist, researcher*
San Diego, Armando G. *retired military officer, pathologist, consultant*
Sandkuhler, Kevin M. *military officer*
Sandler, Adam *actor*
Sandler, Harold *retired cardiologist, research scientist, consultant*
Sandman, Dan D. *lawyer*
Sandorsen, Cassiopeia *public health service officer*
Sandwell, Kristin Ann *special education educator*
Sanford, Irene W. *lawyer*
Sanger, Frederick *retired molecular biologist*
Sanger, Lawrence Mark *editor-in-chief*
Sangster, Paul Edward *radiologist*
San Miguel, Manuel *painter, historian, composer, poet*
Santiago, Jose E. *film producer, writer, director, educator*
Santina, Dalia *nutritionist, writer, skin care specialist*
Santman, Leon Duane *lawyer, former federal government executive*
Santomero, Anthony M. *financial consultant, former bank executive, public policymaker*
Santora, Ellen Durrigan *education educator*
Santos, Arthur Magno *thoracic cardiovascular surgeon*
Santos, Nicole Marie *elementary school educator*
Santry, Barbara Lea *venture capitalist*
Sapiano, Mathew Raymond Paul *meteorologist*
Sapienza, Madeline *historian, researcher*
Sapoff, Meyer *retired electronics executive*
Sapp, John Raymond *lawyer*
Sapsowitz, Sidney H. *entertainment and media company executive*
Saravolatz, Louis Donald *epidemiologist, medical educator*
Sarbanes, Paul Spyros *former senator*
Sardegna, Verónica Gabriela *language educator*
Sargent, Thomas Andrew *retired political science professor*
Sargent, William Winston *retired anesthesiologist*
Sarich, Drew *actor*
Sarkar, Malancha *research scientist, educator*
Sarma, Pallav *research scientist*
Sarno, Maria Erlinda *lawyer, chemist*
Sarris, Andrew George *film critic*
Sarry, Christine *ballerina*
Sass, Mary Martha *freelance writer, artist*
Sathaye, Jayant *research scientist*
Satinover, Jeffrey B. *physicist, psychiatrist, writer*
Satterfield, David Michael *ambassador*
Satterthwaite, Helen Foster *retired state legislator*
Satterwhite, R. Scott *computer company executive*
Sattler, Bruce Weimer *lawyer*
Sattler, Rolf *retired plant morphologist, educator*
Satz, Louis K. *publishing executive*
Saucier, Gene Duane *retired state legislator, import/export company executive*
Saucier, Guylaine *corporate financial executive*
Sauerhaft, Stan *retired public relations executive, consultant*
Saul, Mark E. *secondary school educator, consultant*
Saunders, James Allen *secondary school educator*
Saunders, Lonna Jeanne *lawyer, newscaster*
Saunders, Richard Henry III *museum director*
Saunders, Stacy Dawn *journalist, music educator, vocalist*
Saunders, Terry Rose *lawyer*
Sava, Vasyl *education educator*
Savage, Kim I. *academic administrator*
Savedra-Schroeder, Jeannine Evangeline *artist, educator*
Savercool, Susan Elisabeth *elementary school educator*
Savin, Ronald Richard *chemicals executive*
Savini, Tom *make-up artist, actor, director*
Savitt, Susan Schenkel *lawyer, mediator*
Savitz, Maxine Lazarus *retired aerospace transportation executive*
Savoy, Suzanne Marie *nursing educator*
Sawai, Dahleen Emi *language educator*
Sawczuk, Ihor S. *urologist*
Sawicki, Mikolaj Ziemislaw *physicist*
Sax, Joseph Lawrence *lawyer, educator*
Saxon, Burton Roy *humanities educator*
Saxon, Wolfgang Erik Georg *journalist, writer*
Sayles, Leonard Robert *management educator, consultant*
Sayre, David *physicist*
Sayre, Donna *elementary school educator*
Sayre, Robert Freeman *language educator*
Saywell, William George Gabriel *business development and management consultant*
Sazant, Neil S. *real estate investor and developer*
Scacchetti, David J. *lawyer*
Scacchi, Greta *actress*
Scaife, Richard Mellon *philanthropist*
Scala, James *health facility administrator, consultant, writer*
Scandary, E. Jane *special education educator, consultant*
Scanlon, Peter Redmond *retired accountant*
Scannell, Herb *broadcast executive*
Scannell, William Edward *aerospace transportation executive, consultant, psychologist*
Scarborough, Ann Barlow *secondary school educator*
Scarchuk, Lynn Nettleton *retired music educator*
Scardino, Peter T. *urologic oncologic surgeon*
Scaringello, Nina Maria *literature and language professor*
Scarwid, Diana Elizabeth *actress*
Scerno, Joseph Benedict *management consultant executive, arbitrator*
Schadow, Karen E. *public speaking trainer, educator*
Schadt, James Phillip *investment and software executive*
Schaechter, Moselio *microbiology educator*
Schaefer, C. Barry *rail transportation executive, investment company executive*
Schaefer, William Goerman *lawyer*
Schallert, William Joseph *actor*
Schanfield, Fannie Schwartz *community volunteer*
Scharf, Michael Paul *law educator*
Scharf, William *artist*
Scharlemann, Robert Paul *theology studies educator, minister*
Schatz, Wayne Ardale *district technology coordinator, educator*
Schauf, Victoria *pediatrician, educator*
Schaupp, Joan Pomprowitz *trucking executive, writer*
Schaut, Joseph William *retired bank executive*
Scheel, Nels Earl *corporate financial executive, accountant*
Scheetz, Bernadette Estelle *elementary mathematics educator*
Scheffler, Stuart Jay *lawyer*
Schefter, Ed Queen *minister*
Scheiber, Stephen Carl *psychiatrist, director*
Scheiberg, Susan L. *librarian*
Scheier, Ivan Henry *volunteer, writer, retired cultural organization administrator*
Schein, Edgar Henry *management educator*
Schein, Virginia Ellen *psychologist*
Scheinberg, Phyllis F. *federal agency administrator*
Scheinman, Nancy Jane *psychologist*
Schell, Allan Carter *retired electrical engineer*
Schell, Melvin Frank, Jr. *real estate agent*
Schellenberger, Robert Earl *retired management educator, department chairman*
Schellman, John A. *chemistry professor*
Schenck, Jack Lee *retired electric utility executive*
Schenker, Marc Benet *preventive medicine physician, medical educator, department chairman*
Schenkkan, Robert Frederic *playwright, scriptwriter*
Schenkman, Walter Allen *retired music educator*
Schepartz, Alanna *biochemist, educator*
Scher, Jordan Mayer *pharmacologist, psychiatrist, alcohol/drug abuse services professional*
Scherer, Ronald Callaway *voice scientist, educator*
Scherger, Joseph Edward *family physician, educator*
Scheuerman, Walter George *retired neurologist, retired surgeon*
Schexnayder, Brian Edward *vocalist, educator*
Schexnayder, Charlotte Tillar *state legislator*
Schexnider, Virginia Reeves *school psychologist*
Scheyer, Daniel *lawyer*
Schifano, Kath M. *artist*
Schiff, Martin *physician, surgeon*
Schiff, Molly Jeanette *artist, researcher*
Schiff, Richard *actor*
Schiff, Stacy *writer*
Schiffer, Claudia *model*
Schild, Raymond Douglas *lawyer*
Schiller, Robert E. *former school system administrator*
Schlafly, Hubert Joseph, Jr. *communications executive*
Schlagel, Richard H. *retired philosophy educator*
Schlageter, Robert William *museum administrator*
Schlenker, Gary Chris *landscape company executive*
Schlesinger, Deborah Lee *retired librarian*
Schless, Phyllis Ross *investment banker*
Schley, Reeve III *artist*
Schlosser, Anne Griffin *librarian*
Schlothauer, Shirley Norton *retired media consultant, writer*
Schlozman, Bradley J. *former prosecutor*
Schlueter, Linda Lee *law educator*
Schmalz, Carl Nelson, Jr. *artist, educator, art appraiser, printmaker*
Schmandt-Besserat, Denise *archaeologist, educator*
Schmidly, David J. *academic administrator, biology professor*
Schmidt, Albert John *retired history professor*
Schmidt, Hans R. *retired history educator*
Schmidt, Hildred Doris *music educator*
Schmidt, Karl A. *lawyer*
Schmidt, Kathleen Marie *lawyer*
Schmidt, L. Lee, Jr. *retired university official*
Schmidt, Robert *retired mechanics and civil engineering educator*
Schmidt, Ruth Ann *retired academic administrator*
Schmidtke, Suzanne de Fine *retired social worker*
Schmit, Randall *painter*
Schmitz, Barbara *art preservationist*
Schmitz, Dennis Mathew *retired language educator*
Schmitz, Joseph Edward *lawyer, former federal agency administrator*
Schmoll, Harry F., Jr. *lawyer, educator*
Schmults, Edward Charles *lawyer*
Schnackenberg, Gjertrud Cecelia *poet*
Schneck, Stuart Austin *retired neurologist, educator*
Schneider, Calvin *physician*
Schneider, Carl Edward *law educator*
Schneider, Carl Stanley *retired physics professor, researcher*
Schneider, Carolyn Alice Brauch *elementary school educator*
Schneider, Catherine Chemin *occupational therapist, consultant*
Schneider, Edgar Rolf Gottfried *retired mathematician, application developer, writer*
Schneider, Howard Stewart *former newspaper editor*
Schneider, Jan *retired obstetrics and gynecology educator*
Schneider, Janet M. *museum administrator, painter, curator*
Schneider, Karen G. *freelance writer*
Schneider, Kirk J. *psychologist, writer*
Schneider, Mary Louise *retired elementary school educator*
Schneider, Phyllis Leah *writer, editor*
Schneider, Sharon M. *systems administrator, information technologist*
Schneider, Thomas Aquinas *surgeon, educator, retired surgeon*
Schneider, Valerie Lois *retired speech educator*
Schneider, William George *chemist, research consultant*
Schneiderman, David Abbott *former publishing executive*
Schneidler, Jon Gordon *lawyer*
Schnepf, Harry Ernest *microbiologist, consultant*
Schnitzer, Iris Taymore *diversified financial services company executive, lawyer, arbitrator, mediator*
Schock, Robert Norman *geophysicist*
Schoen, Allen Harry *retired aerospace engineering executive*
Schoen, William Jack *finance company executive*
Schoenberg, Mark George *government agency administrator*
Schoenberger, James Edwin *retired federal agency administrator*
Schoener, Allon *museum and organization consultant*
Schoettler, Gail Sinton *former ambassador*
Schofield, Robert E. (Robert Edwin Schofield) *historian, educator, academic administrator*
Scholes, Edison Earl *military officer*
Schonberg, Alan Robert *personnel director*
Schonhorn, Harold *chemist, researcher*
Schoomaker, Peter Jan *retired military officer*
Schoonmaker Powell, Thelma *film editor*
Schor, Joseph Martin *pharmaceutical executive, biochemist*
Schor, Laura Strumingher *historian*
Schor, Suzi *lawyer, psychologist*
Schorr, Daniel Louis *broadcast journalist, author, lecturer*
Schottenheimer, Marty (Martin Edward Scottenheimer) *former professional football coach*
Schowalter, William Raymond *college dean, educator*
Schrader, William L. *communications executive*
Schrag, Philip Gordon *law educator*
Schrage, Rose *retired academic administrator*
Schram, Ronald Byard *lawyer*
Schramm, Bernard Charles, Jr. *retired advertising agency executive*
Schrand, Richard Henry, Sr. *broadcast executive, advertising bureau owner, educator*
Schreckinger, Sy Edward *advertising executive, consultant*
Schreiber, Paul Solomon *lawyer*
Schroder, Rick *actor*
Schroeder, Brian S. *philosopher, educator*
Schroeder, Gerald Frank *retired state supreme court justice*
Schroeder, LaVerne *medical/surgical nurse*
Schroeder, W(illiam) Widick *retired religion educator*
Schubert, Barbara Schuele *retired performing arts association administrator*
Schubert, Helen Celia *public relations executive*
Schuchard, Robert L. *lawyer*
Schuelke, John Paul *religious organization administrator*
Schuessler, John T. (Jack Schuessler) *retired food service executive*
Schull, Natasha Dow *anthropologist, educator*
Schulman, Alan *lawyer*
Schulman, Harold *obstetrician, gynecologist*
Schulman, Sidney *neurologist, educator*
Schultz, Albert Barry *engineering educator*
Schultz, Clarence John *minister*
Schultz, Dennis Bernard *lawyer*
Schultz, Eileen Hedy *creative director*
Schultz, Louis William *retired judge*
Schultz, Marian Starr *musician, educator*
Schultz, Robert Jordan *orthopaedic surgeon, educator*
Schultz, Stanley George *physiologist, educator, dean*

Schulz, Raymond Alexander *medical marketing professional, consultant*
Schulz, William Frederick *human rights scholar and advocate*
Schulzke, Margot Seymour *artist, author, educator*
Schumacher, Barret *motion picture propman, writer*
Schumacher, Cynthia Jo *retired elementary and secondary education educator*
Schumann, Nicholas M. *elementary school educator*
Schupp, Russ *computer professor, web site designer*
Schurenberg, Eric *magazine editor*
Schur Kaufman, Susan *retired public affairs consultant*
Schuster, Carol Joyce *special education educator, consultant*
Schuster, Elaine *retired civil rights professional*
Schutz, Donald Frank *geochemist, environmental corporate executive*
Schutzer, Karen Ann *nurse*
Schuur, Diane Joan *vocalist*
Schuurs, Marieke E. *singer, educator, small business owner*
Schwab, Eileen Caulfield *lawyer, educator*
Schwab, John H. *psychologist*
Schwab, Judith *artist, educator, sculptor*
Schwabe, John Bennett, II, *lawyer*
Schwantes, Carlos Arnaldo *history professor, consultant*
Schwartz, Bernard Leon *retired space and communications company executive*
Schwartz, Brian Michael *philosopher, think-tank executive*
Schwartz, Carol Levitt *government official*
Schwartz, Daniel Bennett *artist*
Schwartz, Eleanor Brantley *academic administrator*
Schwartz, Judy Ellen *thoracic surgeon*
Schwartz, Leon *foreign language educator*
Schwartz, Leonard Jay *retired lawyer*
Schwartz, Lillian Feldman *artist, filmmaker, critic, nurse, writer*
Schwartz, Lyle Howard *materials scientist, science administrator*
Schwartz, Michael Robinson *management consultant*
Schwartz, Shirley E. *retired chemist, researcher*
Schwartz, Sima M. *music educator*
Schwartz, Stephen Blair *retired information technology executive*
Schwartz, Stephen Lawrence *composer, lyricist*
Schwary, Ronald Louis *motion picture producer*
Schwarz, Joe (John J.H. Schwarz) *former congressman, physician*
Schwarz, M. Roy *physician, administrator*
Schweiker, Richard Schultz *former trade association administrator, former secretary of health & human services, former senator*
Schwerdtner, Frederick Howard *lawyer, retired police commander, real estate broker*
Schwimmer, David *actor*
Sciuva, Margaret W. *counselor*
Scogin, Troy Pope *publishing executive, finance company executive*
Scoppetta, Nicholas *fire commissioner*
Scorsese, Martin *film director, film producer*
Scott, Benjamin *retired electrical engineer*
Scott, Bradford *surgeon*
Scott, Campbell *actor*
Scott, Carol Seeley *retired librarian, researcher*
Scott, Catherine Dorothy *librarian, library and information scientist, consultant*
Scott, Charles David *chemical engineer, consultant*
Scott, Gloria Randle *former college president*
Scott, Isadore Meyer *retired energy executive*
Scott, Jacqueline Delmar Parker *educational association administrator, consultant*
Scott, Joyce *writer*
Scott, Karen Elizabeth *advocate*
Scott, Michael Dennis *lawyer*
Scott, Sherie René *actress*
Scott, T. Gordon *chemistry and math educator, writer*
Scrivner, B(arbara) E. *piano educator*
Scruggs, Earl Eugene *entertainer*
Scully, Marlan Orvil *physics professor*
Sczudlo, Walter Joseph *lawyer*
Seabold, Danielle *educational association administrator*
Seabolt, Robert D. *lawyer*
Seaden, George *civil engineer*
Seader, Junior DeVere (Bob Seader) *retired chemical engineering professor*
Seagal, Steven *actor*
Seale, James Millard *retired religious organization administrator, minister*
Seals, Margaret Louise Crumrine *retired journalist*
Seaman, Natasha *art historian, educator*
Seamans, William *writer, retired reporter, commentator*
Searl, Stanford Jay, Jr. *language educator*
Searle, Philip Ford *banker*
Searle, Rodney Newell *state legislator, farmer, insurance agent*
Searles, Edna Lowe *artist, illustrator, composer, poet*
Sears, Mary Helen *lawyer*
Sears, Sandra Jones *medical/surgical nurse, consultant*
Sease, Gene Elwood *communications executive*
Seawell, Thomas Robert *artist, retired art educator*
Sebastian, Peter *political scientist, consultant, retired diplomat*
Sebolt-George, Alberta *retired museum administrator*
Secchiutti, Ronald *electrical engineering designer*
Sechrist, Chalmers Franklin, Jr. *electrical engineering educator*
Secrest, Glenda *music educator*
Sedaris, David Raymond *writer*
Sedas, D(anna) Michelle *editor*
Seddon, Priscilla Tingey *painter*
Sedelmaier, John Josef *filmmaker*
Sedighi, Artin *application developer, researcher*
Seeds, Sharon Lynn *bank processor*
Seelig, Gerard Leo *management consultant*
Seemann, Rosalie Mary *international business and foreign policy association executive*
Seff, Richard *actor, writer*
Segal, Phyllis Nichamoff *mediator*
Segel, Karen Lynn Joseph *lawyer, tax specialist*
Segger, Martin Joseph *museum director, educator, art historian*
Seggerman, Anne Crellin *foundation executive*
Seib, Billie McGhee Rushing *nursing administrator, consultant*
Seible, Frieder *structural engineer, educator*
Seidel, Frederick Lewis *poet*
Seidel, Selvyn *lawyer, educator*
Seidenman, Neil Arnold *interpreter*
Seidman, Ellen Shapiro *lawyer, government official*
Seidman, Glenn Elliott *sales executive, marketing professional, consultant*
Seiff, Stephen S. *ophthalmologist*
Seigenthaler, John Michael *newscaster*
Seinfeld, Jerry *comedian, actor, television producer, scriptwriter*
Seiple, John W., Jr. *corporate financial executive*
Seitz, Henry W. *information technology manager*
Sekula-Gibbs, Shelley *former congresswoman, dermatologist*
Selders, Jean E. *retired psychology professor*
Seldin, David C. *internist, medical educator*
Seldman, Neil Norman *cultural organization administrator*
Seldner, Betty Jane *environmental engineer, consultant, aerospace transportation executive*
Seli, Emre Utku *reproductive endocrinology and infertility specialist, physician researcher*
Seligman, Joel *academic administrator*
Seligman, Nicole K. *broadcast executive, lawyer*
Seligson, Carl Harold *corporate financial executive*
Selin, Nina Evvie *museum director, electric power industry executive, volunteer*
Selkowitz, Arthur *retired advertising executive*
Sell, LeeLou *retired elementary school educator*
Sellmann, Meinolf *computer science educator*
Sells, Boake Anthony *private investor*
Seltser, Raymond *epidemiologist, educator, oncologist*
Seltzer, Leo *cinematographer, educator*
Sembler, Melvin F. *former ambassador, real estate developer*
Seminara, Lynda Anne *editor*
Semler, William Ludwig *retired obstetrician, retired gynecologist*
Semple, Susan *early childhood educator*
Semrod, T. Joseph *banker*
Sena, Charalena *dental office executive*
Senechal, Alice R. *federal magistrate judge, lawyer*
Sengupta, Abhijit *molecular and optical physicist*
Seniors, Paula Marie *history professor, researcher*
Sennema, David Carl *arts consultant*
Sentenne, Justine *corporate ombudsman consultant*
Senty, James A. *energy executive*
Serdari, Thomaï *architect, historian*
Serenbetz, Robert *manufacturing executive, financial planner*
Serkes, Jeffrey D. *former energy executive*
Serling, Joel Martin *educational psychologist*
Serrie, Hendrick *retired anthropology and international business educator*
Servien, Louis-Marc (Comte De Boisdauphin, Lord of Quendon) *finance company, import/export company executive*
Setser, Carole Sue *food scientist, educator*
Sever, John Louis *medical researcher, educator*
Severino, Elizabeth Forrest *consulting company executive, animal communicator, spiritual healer*
Severo, Richard *writer*
Sewell, John Williamson *research association executive*
Sewell, Michael E. *music educator, musician*
Sexton, Carol Burke *finance company executive, consultant*
Seymour, Barbara Laverne *lawyer*
Seymour, Claudia Hultgren *painter*
Sfekas, Stephen James *lawyer, educator*
Sha, William T. *nuclear scientist, consultant*
Shabot, Myron Michael *critical care educator*
Shackelford, Scott Addison *retired chemist, researcher*
Shader, Richard Irwin *psychiatrist, pharmacologist, educator*
Shaeffer, John Nees *historian, educator*
Shaevitz, Geoff *film company executive*
Shafer, L. M. *writer*
Shaffer, Bernard William *mechanical and aerospace engineering educator*
Shaffer, Richard James *lawyer, retired manufacturing executive*
Shaffert, Kurt *retired lawyer, chemical engineer*
Shafipour, Pouya *physician, dermatologist*
Shagan, Steve *scriptwriter, film producer*
Shah, Bipin Chandra *banker*
Shah, Nandlal Chimanlal *retired physiatrist*
Shah, Y. T. *academic administrator*
Shaheen, George T. *software company executive*
Shaheen, Shaheen Azeez *minister, textiles executive*
Shahied, Ishak I. *science educator*
Shain, Kenneth Stephen *management consultant, executive, writer*
Shaker, William Haygood *marketing professional, public policy reformer*
Shakow, Alexander *economist, government official*
Shalikashvili, John Malchase *former Chairman of the Joint Chiefs of Staff*
Shamatava, Irma *physicist, researcher*
Shambaugh, Stephen Ward *lawyer*
Shamberg, Michael *film producer*
Shane, John Marder *endocrinologist*
Shank, Maurice Edwin *aerospace engineer, consultant*
Shankar, Maya *research scientist*
Shannon, Mary Lou *adult health nursing educator*
Shannon, W. Patrick *telecommunications industry executive*
Shapira, David S. *food products and retail grocery executive*
Shapiro, Amir *mechanical engineer, researcher*
Shapiro, Donald P. *retired otolaryngologist*
Shapiro, Edwin Stanley *lawyer, judge*
Shapiro, Harvey *poet*
Shapiro, Leo J. *social researcher*
Shapiro, Marc Robert *retail executive*
Shapiro, Richard Charles *publishing executive, sales executive, marketing professional*
Shapiro, Sander Wolf *retired lawyer*
Shapiro, Zalman Mordecai *chemist, consultant*
Sharansky, Natan (Anatoly Sharansky) *human rights activist, former Israeli government official*
Sharbaugh, Thomas J. *lawyer*
Sharick, Merle Dayton, Jr. *sales executive*
Sharkey, Leonard Arthur *automobile company executive*
Sharkey, Robert Emmett *lawyer*
Sharkey, Vincent Joseph *finance company executive*
Sharma, Avanti *physician*
Sharma, Martha Bridges *geography educator*
Sharma, Padmanee *immunologist, oncologist*
Sharman, William *professional basketball team executive*
Sharp, Anne Catherine *artist, educator*
Sharp, Dan Steven *epidemiologist*
Sharpe, William Forsyth *economics professor*
Sharples, Ruth Lissak *communications executive*
Sharpton, Alfred Charles, Jr. *minister, political activist*
Shartle, Stanley Musgrave *engineering executive, consultant, surveyor*
Shasteen, Donald Eugene *retired government official, small business consultant*
Shastry, Suresh *research scientist*
Shatin, Judith *composer, educator*
Shattuck, Cathie Ann *lawyer, former government official*
Shaughnessy, Allen F. *pharmacist, educator*
Shaughnessy, Marie Kaneko *artist*
Shavender, Marilyn Faye *retired elementary school educator*
Shaw, Cecelia *retired chef*
Shaw, (Eugene) Clay, (Jr.) *former congressman*
Shaw, David Robert *secondary school educator, theater director*
Shaw, Elizabeth Orr *retired lawyer*
Shaw, Harold *retired performing arts association administrator*
Shaw, Helen Lester Anderson *nutrition educator, researcher, retired dean*
Shaw, Jack Allen *communications company executive*
Shaw, John Frederick *retired naval officer*
Shaw, Joseph Thomas *Slavic languages educator*
Shaw, Kathleen M. Troutner *retired librarian*
Shaw, L. Edward, Jr. *lawyer*
Shaw, Melvin Phillip *physicist, engineering educator, psychologist*
Shaw, Nina L. *lawyer*
Shaw, Richard Thomas *humanitarian, retired federal agent, retired military officer*
Shaw, Ronald Ahrend *physician, educator*
Shaw, Thomas *conductor, director*
Shayman, James Alan *nephrologist, educator*
Shea, Bernard Charles *retired pharmaceutical executive*
Sheaffer, Richard Allen *electrical engineer*
Shearer, Charles Livingston *academic administrator*
Shearing, Miriam *retired state supreme court chief justice*
Sheeder, Robert Elwood *lawyer*
Sheedy, John Thomas (Jack) *writer*
Sheehan, D'eane *biology professor*
Sheehan, Robert James, II, *management and market research consultant*
Sheen, Charlie (Carlos Irwin Estevez) *actor*
Sheen, Martin (Ramon Estevez) *actor*
Sheen, Michael *actor*
Sheesley, Mary Frank *art educator*
Sheffey, Ruthe T. *language educator*
Sheikh, Aatif Manzoor *military officer, pharmacist*
Sheikh, Fazal *photographer, writer*
Sheils, Paul T. *lawyer*
Sheindlin, Judith (Judge Judy) *television personality, judge*
Sheinin, Rose *biochemist, educator*
Sheldon, Robert *composer*
Sheldon, Stephen *pediatric sleep medicine educator, researcher*
Sheldon, Terry Edwin *lawyer, investment advisor*
Shell, Art (Arthur Shell Jr.) *former professional football coach*
Shelley, Kevin Francis *former state official*
Shellman-Lucas, Elizabeth C. *special education educator, researcher*
Shelly, Nicholas J. *military officer, international relations scholar*
Shelton, Hugh (Henry Hugh Shelton) *former Chairman of the Joint Chiefs of Staff*
Shelton, James Douglas *banker*
Shelton, Robert Warren *marketing professional*
Shelton, Stephani *broadcast journalist, consultant*
Shemonsky, Natalie Kaplin *physician, lawyer*
Shen, Yu-Chu *economics professor*
Shenderov, Kevin *immunologist*
Shepard, Christy J. *special education educator*
Shepard, Michael J. *prosecutor*
Shepard, Richard Blount *surgeon, educator*
Shepard, Sam (Samuel Shepard Rogers) *playwright, actor*
Shepard, Sara Lynette *elementary school educator*
Shepherd, Bobby E. *federal judge*
Shepherd, Cybill Lynne *actress, singer*
Shepherd, Douglas *hospital administrator*
Shepherd, Mark, Jr. *retired electronics company executive*
Shepp, Bryan Eugene *psychologist, educator*
Sheppard, Gayle Teresa *software executive*
Sheppard, Jennifer Modlin *retired genealogist*
Sheppard, John Wilbur *computer research scientist*
Sher, Leo *psychiatrist*
Sherbell-Na, Rhoda *artist, sculptor*
Shere, Dennis *lawyer, writer, retired publishing executive*
Sheridan, Patrick Michael *retired finance company executive*
Sheridan, Sonia Landy *artist, retired educator*
Sheriff, Seymour *retired lawyer*
Sherin, Edwin *theater director, film director, television director, actor*
Sherling, Fred W. *lawyer*
Sherman, George M. *former food products executive*
Sherman, Howard D. *financial consultant*
Sherman, Jimmie Lee *mathematician, educator*
Sherman, John Foord *biomedical consultant*
Sherman, Joseph Owen *pediatric surgeon*
Sherman, Patsy O'Connell *retired manufacturing executive, chemist*
Sherman, Roger Talbot *surgeon, educator*
Sherpa, Donna M. *history educator*
Sherrell-Leo, Cindy *retired museum administrator*
Sherrer, Charles David *dean, clergyman*
Sherris, David Allan *surgeon, researcher, educator*
Sherry, George Leon *political science professor*
Sherwood, Gloria N. *graphics designer, genealogist, small business owner*
Shetty, Mulki Radhakrishna *retired oncologist*
Shevitz, Mark H. *sales promotion and marketing executive*
Shi, Jiaqi *medical educator*
Shi, Stone D.H. *research scientist*
Shieh, Eric Y. *music educator*
Shields, Cynthia Rose *college administrator*
Shields, Portia Holmes *former academic administrator*
Shier, Gloria Bulan *mathematics professor*
Shifrin, Harris David *physician*
Shikler, Aaron A. *artist*
Shikuma, Eugene Yujin *travel company executive*
Shillingsburg, Miriam Jones *literature educator, academic administrator*
Shils, Maurice Edward *physician, educator, research scientist*
Shimoda, Jerry Yasutaka *retired national historic park manager*
Shimpock, Kathy Elizabeth *lawyer, writer*
Shindle, William Richard *retired musicologist, educator*
Shinn, George Latimer *investment banker, consultant, finance educator*
Shinolt, Eileen Thelma *artist*
Shinseki, Eric Ken *retired military officer*
Shipley, Andrew G. *psychology scholar*
Shire, Talia Rose (Talia Rose Coppola) *actress*
Shirley, Bryan Douglas *lawyer*
Shirley, David Arthur *chemistry professor, science administrator*
Shirley-Quirk, John *singer, educator*
Shiue, Chyng-Yann *research director, educator*
Shivers, Mitchell Everett *diplomat*
Shochet, Melvyn Jay *physicist*
Shockley, Edward Julian *retired air transportation executive*
Shoemaker, Bobby Jean (B.J. Foster) *writer*
Shoemaker, Elizabeth Ellen *retired military officer*
Shoemaker, William C. *journalist*
Shohet, Stephen Byron *medical educator*
Shoop, Glenn Powell *investment consultant*
Shore, Eleanor Gossard *retired medical school dean*
Shore, Stephen *photographer*
Short, Ray Everett *minister, sociologist, educator, writer*
Short, William Frederick *gynecologist*
Shorter, Nicholas Andrew *pediatric surgeon*
Shotwell, Malcolm Green *minister*
Shoun, Ellen Llewellyn *retired secondary school educator*
Shoup, Andrew James, Jr. *retired oil industry executive*
Shreve, Susan Richards *writer, educator*
Shrum, Robert Matthew *political strategist, educator, journalist*
Shubb, William Barnet *judge*
Shuchart, Eugene Joseph *retired accountant*
Shuler, Caroletta Alexis *criminal justice educator*
Shuler, Jon Emmett *securities industry professional*
Shulgasser-Parker, Barbara *critic, writer*
Shull, Claire *documentary film producer, casting director*
Shulman, Mildred *artist*
Shulman, Yechiel *engineering educator*
Shultis, Robert Lynn *finance educator, consultant, retired professional society administrator*
Shultz, Delray Franklin (Lucky Shultz) *business coach, consultant*
Shultz, Stephen A. *secondary school educator*
Shumacker, Harris B., Jr. *retired surgeon, educator, author*
Shuman, Ann *investment company executive*
Shuman, Samuel Irving *lawyer, educator*
Shuman, Stanley S. *investment banker*
Shuster, Bud *business executive, former congressman*
Shuster, Frederick *retired internist, gastroenterologist*

Shuster, Robert G. *electronics executive, consultant*
Shute, Richard Emil *federal agency administrator, engineer*
Shutler, Mary Elizabeth *retired academic administrator*
Shutt, Elsie G. *systems analyst, application developer, consultant*
Siavosh-Haghighi, Ali *physical chemist, researcher*
Sibbernsen, Richard *telecommunications industry executive*
Sibo, Elsa Lynette *secondary school educator*
Sicart, Pierre-Alexandre Serge Henry *writer*
Siddeeq, Baiyinah Nawal Rubye *secondary school educator*
Siddons, (Sybil) Anne Rivers *writer*
Sidebottom, William George *communications executive*
Sides, Jack Davis, Jr. *lawyer*
Sidhu, Jay S. *former bank executive*
Sidnam, Alan Northcote *retired advertising executive, venture capitalist*
Sidney, Corinne Entratter *retired journalist, actress*
Siebel, Thomas M. *software company executive*
Sieburth, Richard *literature educator, interpreter*
Siefers, Robert George *banker*
Siefert, David Michael *research and development company executive*
Siefert-Kazanjian, Donna *corporate librarian*
Siegal, Allan Marshall *journalist, consultant*
Siegal, Rita Goran *engineering company executive*
Siegel, George Henry *management consultant*
Siegel, Jack Morton *retired pharmaceutical executive*
Siegel, Mary Ann Garvin *writer*
Siegel, Sarah Ann *lawyer*
Siegel, Vivian *biomedical editor*
Siekman, Thomas Clement *lawyer*
Sielicki-Korczak, Boris Zdzislaw *political educator, investigative consultant*
Siemer, Deanne Clemence *lawyer*
Siemon, Joyce Marilyn *lawyer, writer*
Siems, Bennett A. *composer, performing company executive*
Siffert, Robert Spencer *orthopedic surgeon*
Sifton, David Whittier *retired magazine editor*
Siganga, Walter *physics professor*
Sigety, Charles Edward *lawyer, financial planner*
Sigmon, J. Lewis, Jr. *medical educator*
Sikes, Michelle M. *health sciences scholar*
Sikorski, James Alan *research chemist*
Silano, Lawrence *music educator*
Silberman, H. Lee *public relations executive, consultant*
Silberman, Larry (Laurence Hirsch) *federal judge*
Silberstein, Alan Mark *financial services executive*
Silianoff, David *secondary school educator, educator, mathematics educator*
Siljak, Dragoslav D. *engineering educator, researcher*
Sill, Robert Michael *curator*
Sillman, Amy *painter, art educator*
Silver, Audrey Wilma *nurse, educator, writer*
Silver, George *metal trading and processing company executive*
Silver, Malcolm David *pathologist, educator*
Silverberg, Mark Victor *lawyer, educator*
Silverman, Burton Philip *artist*
Silverman, Ira Norton *news producer*
Silverman, Kenneth Eugene *language educator, writer*
Silverman, Stanley Wayne *chemical company executive*
Silverstein, Barbara Ann *conductor, artistic director*
Silvestri, Alan Anthony *film composer*
Silvestri, Gina *lawyer*
Silvey, Anita Lynne *editor*
Sim, Jai-hoon *electronics researcher*
Simecka, Betty Jean *marketing executive*
Simendinger, Theodore John *writer, publishing executive*
Simeral, William Goodrich *retired chemical company executive*
Simmonds, Robert Maurer *education educator*
Simmons, Debra Adams *editor*
Simmons, Deidre Warner *retired performing company executive, arts consultant*
Simmons, Lynda Merrill Mills *retired principal*
Simmons, Mark Isaac *voice educator, director*
Simmons, Richmond Hogle *retired obstetrician, gynecologist*
Simmons, Russell *recording industry executive*
Simmons, Timothy F. *military officer*
Simms, Maria Ester *health facility administrator*
Simon, Bernece Kern *retired social worker*
Simon, David Judah *reporter*
Simon, Donald John *financial planner, small business owner*
Simon, John Douglas *academic administrator*
Simon, Melvin I. *molecular biologist, educator*
Simon, Neil *playwright, screenwriter, television writer*
Simon, Norma Plavnick *psychologist*
Simon, Peter E. *publishing executive*
Simon, Robert G. *lawyer*
Simon, Ronald Isaac *financial executive*
Simon, Trevor *management consultant, educator, human resources specialist*
Simon, William Leonard *scriptwriter, television producer, writer, film producer*
Simonian, Simon John *surgeon, scientist, educator, health science association administrator*
Simons, Anneke Prins *artist, educator*
Simons, Lewis Martin *journalist*
Simons, Lynn Osborn *educational consultant*
Simonson, Lee Stuart *broadcast executive*
Simpson, Andrea Lynn *communications executive*
Simpson, Frederick James *retired science administrator*
Simpson, Hugh L. *news correspondent, newswriter*
Simpson, Jack Benjamin *medical technologist, business executive*
Simpson, John Noel *health facility administrator*
Simpson, Michael Marcial *science specialist, consultant*
Simpson, Murray *electrical engineer, consultant*
Simpson, Robert Homer *meteorologist, consultant*
Sims, Elizabeth LaNeal *retired healthcare association executive*
Sims, John R. *lawyer*
Sims, Kent Otway *economist*
Sims, Lowery Stokes *museum curator and administrator, writer, educator*
Sims, Pamela Jan (Cerussi) *writer, minister*
Simson, Jo Anne *retired anatomy and cell biology educator*
Sinagra, Jack G. *former state senator*
Sinai, Allen Leo *economist, educator*
Sinclair, Carole *publishing executive, editor*
Sincoff, Michael Z. *human resources and marketing executive, educator*
Singer, David Michael *marketing and public relations executive*
Singer, Donna Lea *writer, editor, educator*
Singer, Markus Morton *retired trade association administrator*
Singer-Chang, Gail Leslie *medical and social sciences educator, consultant*
Singer-Granick, Carol J. *pediatric endocrinologist, educator*
Singh, Meenakshi *pathologist, educator*
Singleton, John *director, screenwriter*
Singleton, Jonetta Williams *poet, retired special education educator*
Singleton, Robert Culton *academic administrator, theology studies educator*
Sinha, Rakesh Kumar *computer scientist, researcher*
Sinha, Sunil Kumar *physicist*
Sinkford, Jeanne Craig *dental association administrator, retired dentist, dean, educator*
Sinn, Ryan *musician*
Sinor, Howard Earl, Jr. *lawyer*
Sirna, Gail Carolyn *artist, educator, writer*
Sisk, Eileen Victoria *writer, journalist*
Sisk, Jane Elizabeth *economist, educator*
Siska, John Edward *foundation administrator, publishing executive*
Sisley, Emily Lucretia *psychologist, writer*
Sissel, George Allen *manufacturing executive, lawyer, engineer*
Sissman, Liron *artist, painter*
Sisto, Jeremy Merton *actor*
Sites, Kevin *news correspondent, journalist, web blogger*
Sitnyakovsky, Roman Emmanuil *scientist, writer, inventor, translator*
Sittig, James Christopher *art dealer, painter, sculptor, landscape artist, poet*
Siu, Wang-Ngai *solicitor*
Sivak-Callcott, Jennifer A. *ophthalmologist*
Sivill, Jason Ryan *music educator*
Sjostrand, Fritiof Stig *biologist, educator*
Skaff, Joseph John *state agency administrator, retired military officer*
Skaggs, Bebe Rebecca Patten *college dean, clergywoman*
Skala, Gary Dennis *management consultant*
Skiena, Steven Sol *computer scientist, educator*
Skigen, Patricia Sue *lawyer*
Skinner, Daniel Thomas *language educator*
Skinner, Jonathan Snowden *economics educator*
Skinner, Knute Rumsey *poet*
Skinner, Patricia Morag *state legislator*
Skinner, Thomas *broadcast executive*
Sklar, Eric B. *neurologist*
Skolnick, Lawrence *neonatal physician, medical association administrator*
Skolnik, Barnet David *retired lawyer*
Skotzko, Christine *psychiatrist, department chairman*
Skov, Arlie Mason *petroleum engineer, consultant*
Skowronski, Vincent Paul *musician, recording industry executive*
Skramstad, Harold Kenneth, Jr. *museum consultant*
Skrocki, Edmund Stanley, II, *health fair promoter, executive*
Skromme, Lawrence H. *consulting agricultural engineer*
Skwarczyński, Henryk Adam (Henryk Skwar) *writer*
Slade, John Danton *lobbyist*
Slash, (Saul Hudson) *guitarist*
Slater, Eve E. *former federal agency administrator*
Slater, Jeffrey Keith *banker*
Slaugh, Lynn H. *retired chemist*
Slaughter, Djuanique Naté *healthcare analyst, project manager, consultant*
Slaughter, Freeman Cluff *retired dentist*
Slavens, Thomas Paul *library science educator*
Slavit, David Hal *otolaryngologist*
Slavitt, David Walton *retired lawyer*
Slayman, Carolyn Walch *geneticist, educator*
Sledjeski, Eve Mary *psychologist, researcher*
Sliger, Herbert Jacquemin, Jr. *lawyer*
Slim, Michel S. *surgeon, educator, health facility administrator*
Sloan, Carolyn *music educator, composer, lyricist*
Sloan, Michael Allan *neurologist*
Sloane, Neil James Alexander *mathematician, researcher*
Slonaker, Norman Dale *lawyer*
Sloop, Joseph C. *chemistry professor*
Slosberg, Mike *advertising executive*
Slover, William Lewis *lawyer*
Sloyan, Gerard Stephen *theology studies educator, priest*
Slusser, Eugene Alvin *electronics executive, consultant*
Slutz, Pamela Jo Howell *ambassador*
Small, Lawrence M. *former museum executive*
Small, Melvin D. *physician, educator*
Small, Sarah Mae *volunteer*
Smally, Donald Jay *consulting engineering executive*
Smaragdis, Paris *audiologist, researcher*
Smart, James Anthony *music educator*
Smart, Jill Bellavia *financial consultant*
Smeallie, Kevin Wayne *engineering company executive, consultant*
Smelser, Neil Joseph *sociologist*
Smith, A. Robert *editor, author*
Smith, Alan Michael *music educator, musician*
Smith, Alvy Ray *computer graphics designer*
Smith, Amy B. *mechanical engineer, educator*
Smith, Anne Day *writer*
Smith, Anne Marie Schoefer *application developer*
Smith, Barbara Barnard *music educator*
Smith, Barbara Jeanne *retired librarian*
Smith, Barbara Roderick *health and social services administrator, nursing consultant*
Smith, Brad M. *political science scholar*
Smith, Carole Dianne *retired lawyer, editor, writer, product developer*
Smith, Catherine H. *bank executive*
Smith, Catherine Marie *science educator*
Smith, Charles Haddon *geologist, consultant, retired federal agency administrator*
Smith, Charles Hyde *librarian, historian, geographer*
Smith, Charlotte Reed *retired music educator*
Smith, Christopher T. *environmental health officer*
Smith, Connie *hospital administrator*
Smith, D. Jason *music educator, composer*
Smith, D(aisy) Mullett *publisher*
Smith, Dan *chef*
Smith, David Horton *retired social sciences educator*
Smith, Deirdre O'Meara *lawyer*
Smith, Diana Barker *music educator*
Smith, Elise Fiber *international non-profit development agency administrator*
Smith, Elmer *telecommunications industry executive*
Smith, Fern M. *judge*
Smith, Floyd Leslie *insurance company executive*
Smith, Frederick Coe *retired manufacturing executive*
Smith, George Drury *publishing executive*
Smith, George Patrick, II, *lawyer, educator*
Smith, Goff *industrial equipment manufacturing executive*
Smith, H. Morgan *environmental scientist, educator*
Smith, Hamilton Othanel *molecular biologist, educator*
Smith, Harold Charles *pension fund administrator*
Smith, Jack David *lawyer*
Smith, Jackson Barkley, Jr. *retired judge*
Smith, James A. *lawyer*
Smith, Jean Kennedy *former ambassador*
Smith, John W(esley), Jr. *data processing executive, consultant*
Smith, Jules Louis *lawyer*
Smith, Julious Perry, Jr. *lawyer*
Smith, Karen Ann *visual artist*
Smith, Kelly M. *pharmacist, educator, researcher*
Smith, Kevin *film director, writer, actor*
Smith, Leila Hentzen *artist*
Smith, Leonore Rae *artist*
Smith, Lois Arlene *actress, writer*
Smith, Margaret Taylor *volunteer*
Smith, Marie F. *lobbyist, small business owner, writer*
Smith, Martin Bernhard *retired journalist*
Smith, Martin Cruz *author*
Smith, Martin Henry *retired pediatrician*
Smith, Michelle Rene *elementary school educator*
Smith, Morton Alan *retired lawyer*
Smith, Nancy Angelynn *federal agency administrator*
Smith, Nick H. *former congressman, archivist, farmer*
Smith, Ozzie (Osborne Earl Smith) *retired professional baseball player*
Smith, Pamela Hyde *ambassador*
Smith, Patricia (Pat) Ann *elementary school educator*
Smith, Patricia Lynne *artist*
Smith, Patti *vocalist, poet, lyricist*
Smith, Paul Vergon, Jr. *retired gas industry executive*
Smith, Peter Plympton *former international organization official, former academic administrator, former congressman*
Smith, Phyllis *actress*
Smith, Rae *artist*
Smith, Raymond Leigh *retired plastic surgeon*
Smith, Richard Alan *publishing and specialty retailing executive*
Smith, Robert Hugh *retired engineering construction company executive*
Smith, Robert J., Jr. *real estate executive*
Smith, Robert Michael *lawyer, mediator, arbitrator, writer*
Smith, Robert Powell *former ambassador, retired foundation administrator*
Smith, Stanley Roger *retired professional tennis player*
Smith, Stuart Lyon *psychiatrist, corporate financial executive*
Smith, Theodore Glenn *technology educator, researcher*
Smith, Thomas Eugene *investment company executive, financial consultant*
Smith, Vincent Milton *Feng Shui consultant, educator, writer*
Smith, Vme Edom (Verna Mae) *social sciences educator, freelance photographer, freelance writer*
Smith, Wayne Calvin *chemical engineer, consultant*
Smith, Wendy L. *foundation executive*
Smith, Will *actor, rap artist*
Smith, William Charles *retired lawyer*
Smith, Yolanda Ippolito *law educator, researcher, writer*
Smith, Zannie O. *retired career officer*
Smith-Epstein, Mary Kathleen *dancer*
Smither, Howard Elbert *musicologist, educator*
Smitherman, Todd A. *psychologist, researcher*
Smits, Helen Lida *medical association administrator, educator*
Smock, Raymond William *historian*
Smouse, H(ervey) Russell *lawyer*
Smukal, Michael William *musician, educator, composer*
Snare, Carl Lawrence, Jr. *retired accountant, financial planner*
Sneeringer, Stephen Geddes *lawyer*
Sneider, Joyce Pappachristou *dietician, educator*
Snelling, Barbara W. *retired state legislator*
Snider, George Runyon, Jr. *retired franchising company executive*
Snider, L. Britt *federal official*
Snider, Scott William *civilian military employee*
Snipes, Wesley *actor, film producer*
Snortland, Howard Jerome *financial consultant*
Snow, Claude Henry, Jr. *information services executive, consultant*
Snow, Joel Alan *research director*
Snow, Marina *writer*
Snow, Tony *former White House press secretary, political commentator, analyst*
Snow, Tower Charles, Jr. *lawyer*
Snowden, Lawrence Fontaine *retired air transportation executive, retired military officer*
Snyder, Alan Carhart *finance company executive*
Snyder, Jean Maclean *lawyer*
Snyder, John Millard *travel company executive, educator*
Snyder (Mackley), Louise Marie *speech pathology/audiology services professional, consultant*
Snyder, Marvin *neuropsychologist*
Snyder, Michael F. *telecommunications industry executive*
Snyder, Nathan *entrepreneur, investor*
Snyder, William Burton *insurance company executive*
Snyderman, Ralph *medical educator, physician*
Sobell, Nina R. *artist*
Sobkowicz, Hanna Maria *retired neurologist*
Soble, Mark Richard *lawyer*
Sobolev, Alexandre Andreevich *physicist*
Socolow, Elizabeth Anne *poet, educator, artist, writer*
Socolow, Robert Harry *engineering educator, physicist*
Sodders, Michael Andrew *application developer*
Soderberg, Leif G. *electronics company executive*
Soderbergh, Steven Andrew *filmmaker*
Sodrel, Michael Eugene *former congressman, small business owner*
Soeteber, Ellen *journalist, editor*
Soileau, Monica Marie *economist*
Sojka, Gary Allan *biologist, educator, academic administrator*
Sokal, Robert Reuven *biology professor, writer*
Sokol, Jan D. *lawyer*
Sokolow, Marvin Joel *antiques dealer, appraiser*
Sola, Augusto *pediatrician, educator*
Solano, Julio Rafael *priest, educator*
Solberg, Ronald Louis *investment adviser, portfolio manager*
Soliemanzadeh, Peyman *plastic surgeon, otolaryngologist*
Solkoff, Jerome Ira *lawyer, educator*
Sollender, Joel David *management consultant, financial executive, accountant*
Soller, Elaine Rita *psychologist, artist*
Solls, Mark A. *lawyer*
Solman, Joseph *artist*
Solmssen, Peter *retired academic administrator*
Solo, Joyce Rubenstein *volunteer*
Solomon, Andrew Wallace *author*
Solomon, Elizabeth Ann *mathematics educator*
Solomon, Jack David *investment banker*
Solomon, Neal Edward *management consultant, executive recruiter, social theorist, entrepreneur, author*
Solomon, Susan *chemist, scientist*
Solon, Leonard R(aymond) *retired physicist, educator, consultant*
Soltero-Harrington, Luis Rubén *retired surgeon, educator*
Somasundaran, Ponisseril *surface and colloid engineering educator*
Somers, Emmanuel *retired pathologist*
Somers, Louis Robert *retired food company executive*
Somers, Suzanne Marie (Suzanne Marie Mahoney) *actress, writer, singer*
Somes, Joan Marie *emergency nurse practitioner*
Somide, Adegboyega Adesina *financial analyst, state official, educator, writer*
Sondheim, Stephen Joshua *composer, librettist, lyricist*
Sonnenschein, Hugo Freund *academic administrator, writer, economist, educator*
Sonntag, Bernard H. *agronomist, researcher, public information officer*
Sontag, James Mitchell *oncologist, researcher*
Sopranos, Orpheus Javaras *manufacturing executive*
Sorber, Charles Arthur *academic administrator*
Soregaroli, A(rthur) E(arl) *mining executive, geologist*
Sorel, Edward *artist*
SoRelle, Ruth Doyle *writer, journalist*
Sorensen, Murray Jim *lawyer*
Sorgenfrei, Robert L. *retired trust company executive*
Sorger, Stephan Gunther *marketing professional, educator*
Sorrell, Rozlyn *singer, actress, theater director, educator*

Sturr, James William, Jr. *bandleader, recording industry executive, clarinetist, saxophonist, small business owner*
Stutz, Pearl Hewlett *retired photojournalist*
Styer, Denise Marie *psychologist*
Su, Fei *electrical engineer, researcher*
Su, Kendall Ling-Chiao *engineering educator*
Suber, Robin Hall *former medical and surgical nurse*
Subotnick, Ali *curator, writer*
Subramanian, Tirunelveli Satyanandam *physicist*
Sudan, Ravindra Nath *electrical engineer, physicist, educator*
Sudarsky, Jerry M. *industrialist*
Suders, Joan Mary *elementary school educator*
Sugintas, Nora Maria *healthcare executive*
Suglia, Joseph Vincent *writer, educator*
Suh, Jung Sook Ky *personnel consultant*
Sui, Anna *fashion designer*
Sui, Haichang *electrical engineer, researcher*
Suissa, David *advertising executive*
Sullivan, Charles *dean, educator, author*
Sullivan, Daniel Joseph *theater critic*
Sullivan, Dennis James, Jr. *retired hospitality and music executive*
Sullivan, Eugene John Joseph *manufacturing executive, director*
Sullivan, Eugene Raymond *federal judge*
Sullivan, G. Craig *household products executive*
Sullivan, George Edward *writer*
Sullivan, James Leo *organization executive*
Sullivan, Jeremy R. *psychologist, educator*
Sullivan, John Dominic *theater producer, writer*
Sullivan, Kathryn D. *geologist, former astronaut, former science association executive*
Sullivan, Kevin B. *former lieutenant governor, state legislator*
Sullivan, Mary Ann *artist*
Sullivan, Mary Rose *retired English language educator*
Sullivan, Neil Samuel *physicist, researcher, educator, former dean*
Sullivan, Nicholas G. *science educator*
Summerfield, John Robert *textile curator*
Summers, Carol *artist*
Summers, Cathleen *film producer*
Summers, David Stewart *neurologist, consultant*
Summers, Lorraine Dey Schaeffer *retired librarian*
Summers, Marc *TV host, TV personality*
Sun, Chenghua *composer, music educator*
Sun, Nilaja *playwright, actress*
Sun, Ruidong *petroleum engineer*
Sund, Rick (Richard W. Sund) *former professional sports team executive*
Sunde, Douglas *plastic surgeon*
Sunderman, Duane Neuman *chemist, research and development company executive*
Sundquist, David Hall *voice educator*
Sundstrom, Aileen Lois *speech educator*
Sunley, Emil McKee *economist, consultant*
Sunward, Justin Hugo *artist*
Supino, Phyllis Gail *medical researcher, educator*
Suppes, Patrick *statistician, philosopher, psychologist, educator*
Suput, Ray Radoslav *librarian*
Surawicz, Borys *physician, educator*
Surface, James Louis, Sr. *trust officer, lawyer*
Surles, Richard Hurlbut, Jr. *retired law librarian*
Surplus, Robert Wilbur *retired music educator*
Susman, Morton Lee *lawyer*
Sussman, Andrew Louis *research scientist*
Sussman, Barry *writer, demographer, editor*
Sussman, Howard Sivin *lawyer*
Sussman, Janet I. *social sciences educator*
Sutin, Norman *retired chemist, researcher*
Sutnick, Alton Ivan *internist, educator, researcher, consultant, dean*
Sutro, Edmund J. *secondary school educator, consultant*
Sutter, Laurence Brener *lawyer*
Suttie, John Weston *biochemist*
Sutton, Dolores *actress, writer*
Sutton, Julia *musicologist, dance historian*
Sutton, Lee *biology professor*
Sutton-Creech, Donna Lynn *gifted and talented educator*
Suzuki, Hidetaro *violinist*
Suzuki, Kunihiko *biomedical educator, researcher*
Suzuki, Nobutaka *chemistry professor*
Svensson, Lars Georg *cardiovascular and thoracic surgeon*
Svoboda, Janice June *nurse*
Swacker, Frank Warren *lawyer*
Swager, Cleo Marie *secondary school educator*
Swailes, William E. *counseling administrator*
Swalm, Thomas Sterling *retired military officer, aviations systems consultant*
Swan, Annalyn *writer*
Swank, Hilary *actress*
Swann, Charena Rai *psychotherapist, social worker*
Swanson, Victoria Clare Heldman *lawyer*
Swanstrom, Thomas Evan *economist*
Swartz, Jon David *psychologist, educator*
Swartz, Renee Becker *library advocate, civic volunteer*
Sweatman, Kelly *information technology executive*
Sweeney, Deidre Ann *lawyer*
Sweeney, Don Patrick *music coordinator, conductor, writer*
Sweeney, John E. *former congressman*
Sweetland, Loraine Fern *librarian, educator*
Swensen, David Frederick *investment advisor*
Swenson, Jack G. *writer, consultant*
Swerdlow, Amy *historian, educator, writer*
Swerdlow, Martin Abraham *pathologist, educator*
Swett, Richard Nelson (Dick Swett) *diplomat, former congressman*
Swinburn, Carol Ditzler *retired state and municipal agency administrator*
Swinburn, Charles *retired rail transportation executive*
Swint, Kerwin *political science professor*
Switzer, Maurice Harold *journalist*
Swoap, David Bruce *government and state agency administrator, consultant, art director*
Swoap, Thomas Frank, Jr. *history educator*
Swope, Donald Downey *retired banker*
Sykiotis, Gerasimos *biomedical researcher*
Symchowicz, Samson *retired biochemist*
Synclair, Larry Ross *news correspondent, educator, advocate*
Sypolt, Diane Gilbert *retired judge*
Syverud, Kent Douglas *dean, law educator*
Szakal, Andras Kalman *immunologist, anatomist, educator*
Sze, Sarah *sculptor*
Szelenyi, Ivan *adult education educator*
Szeliga, Victoria I. *retired social studies educator*
Taati, Poopak *media director*
Tabazadeh, Azadeh *environmental scientist, researcher*
Taber, Geoffrey Alexander *industrial engineer, quality assurance professional*
Tack, Theresa Rose *women's health nurse*
Tackett, Stephen Douglas *retired education services specialist*
Tackett, Viti Lee *writer*
Taddei, Lois Annette Magowan *artist, interior designer*
Tadepalli, Srikanth *mechanical engineer, researcher*
Tadros, Fawzi M. *educator*
Taft, Bob (Robert Alphonso Taft II) *former governor*
Taft, Sheldon Ashley *retired lawyer*
Tagiuri, Consuelo Keller *child psychiatrist, educator*
Tagliabue, Paul John *retired national football league commissioner*
Tagliente, Josephine Marlene *artist*
Tague, John Patrick *air transportation executive*
Taiebat, Mahdi *civil engineer*
Taiganides, E. Paul *agricultural and environmental engineer, consultant*
Talamo, Jonathan Haskell *ophthalmologist, educator*
Talent, James Matthes *former senator, congressman, lawyer*
Talese, Nan Ahearn *freelance/self-employed publishing executive*
Taliaferro, Philip III *lawyer*
Talis, Esther R. *educator, writer*
Tallet, Jorge Antonio *philosopher, writer*
Tallett, Elizabeth Edith *biopharmaceutical company executive*
Tallman, Ami Renee *artist*
Tallman, Ann Marie *lawyer*
Talmage, David Wilson *retired microbiologist, educator, dean*
Tam, Sunny Wing Yee *physicist*
Tamaro, George John *retired consulting engineer*
Tamborlane, William V., Jr. *pediatrician, educator*
Tambs, Lewis Arthur *diplomat, historian, educator*
Tamen, Harriet *lawyer*
Tamkus, Daniel *writer, advertising executive*
Tammeus, William David *journalist, columnist*
Tamte-Horan, Michael William *music educator, conductor*
Tan, Soo Chuen *financial analyst, researcher*
Tanaka, J(eannie) E. *lawyer*
Tancs, Linda Ann *lawyer*
Tandler, Bernard *cell biology educator*
Tandon, Rajiv *psychiatrist, educator*
Tane, Susan Jaffe *retired manufacturing company executive*
Tanenbaum, Jay Harvey *lawyer*
Tang, Ching Wan *research scientist*
Tang, Yue *financial analyst*
Tangherlini, Frank Robert *physics educator*
Tanguay, Jeanne Marie *social worker*
Tannenberg, Dieter E.A. *retired manufacturing executive*
Tanner, Laurel Nan *education educator*
Tanner, W(alter) Rhett *lawyer*
Tansey, Mark *painter*
Tao, Jing *environmental scientist*
Tao, Mariano *biochemistry educator*
Taqueti, Viviany R. *immunologist*
Taranta, Angelo (Visca Taranta) *physician, educator*
Tarantino, David A., Jr. *military officer, emergency physician*
Tarbi, William Rheinlander *secondary education curriculum consultant, researcher*
Tarbutton, Lloyd T. *hotel executive, consultant*
Taren, James Arthur *neurosurgeon, educator*
Tarn, Nathaniel *poet, educator, translator*
Tarnopol, Michael Lazar *bank executive*
Tarr, Curtis W. *management consultant, educator*
Tarr, David Gerald *economist*
Tarr, Kenneth J. *retired investment company executive*
Tarrance, Vernon Lance, Jr. *research and development company executive*
Tarrant, Christine Gloria *music educator*
Tarses, Jamie *television producer, former television network executive*
Tartaglia, John *actor, puppeteer*
Tarver, Antonio *professional boxer*
Tasman, Alice Lea Mast *not-for-profit fundraiser*
Tata, Giovanni *publishing executive*
Tatavarthy, Aparna *biologist, researcher*
Tate, Larenz *actor*
Tatlock, Anne M. *retired trust company executive*
Tatum, Valorie *elementary school educator, pharmacist*
Taub, Alan I. *automotive executive, researcher*
Taub, Eli Irwin *arbitrator, mediator, lawyer, judicial hearing officer*
Taub, Stephen Richard *lawyer*
Taubman, A. Alfred *real estate developer*
Tauc, Jan *retired physics professor*
Tauscher, Ellen O. *congresswoman*
Tavalin, Fern *educational consultant*
Tavares, Samia Costa *economics professor*
Tavella, Elise Shannon *librarian*
Tavrow, Richard Lawrence *lawyer*
Taw, James S. *history professor*
Tayler, Irene *retired English literature educator*
Taylor, Anthony Baldwin *civil engineer*
Taylor, Carolyn Roberts *small business owner, chef*
Taylor, Carson William *retired electrical engineer*
Taylor, Charles Hart *former congressman*
Taylor, Charles Henry *psychoanalyst, educator*
Taylor, Corinna Lorrainne *artist, small business owner*
Taylor, David George *retired banker*
Taylor, Diana Lancaster *investment company executive, former state official*
Taylor, Edna Jane *retired employment program counselor*
Taylor, Francis X. *former federal agency administrator, retired military officer*
Taylor, George Frederick *newspaper publisher, editor*
Taylor, Henry Splawn *retired literature educator, poet*
Taylor, Holly Ann *music educator*
Taylor, Jim *scriptwriter, film director*
Taylor, Job III *lawyer*
Taylor, John Brian *economist, educator, former federal agency administrator*
Taylor, John Calvin *dentist*
Taylor, John Jackson (Jay Taylor) *writer, retired diplomat*
Taylor, June Ruth *retired minister*
Taylor, Kathleen (Christine Taylor) *physical chemist, researcher*
Taylor, Nathalee Britton *retired nutritionist, freelance/self-employed writer*
Taylor, Peyton Troy, Jr. *oncologist, educator*
Taylor, Regina *actress*
Taylor, Robert Morgan *electronics executive*
Taylor, Ronald Lewis *sociology educator*
Taylor, Roy Lewis *botanist, educator*
Taylor, Sara Marie *former federal official*
Taylor, William Colton *physician, educator*
Taylor-Anderson, Jill *reading specialist*
Taylor Claud, Andrea *retired educational consultant*
Teagan, John Gerard *publishing executive*
Teasdale, Brent *sociologist, educator*
Teater, Dorothy Seath *retired county official*
Tebedo, MaryAnne *state legislator*
Tecco, Romuald Gilbert Louis Joseph *violinist, concertmaster*
Tedesco, Paul Herbert *humanities educator*
Teel, Patricia Jo *English language educator*
Teets, Peter B. *former civilian military employee*
Te Kanawa, Kiri *opera and concert singer*
Teleman, Silviu *mathematician, educator*
Telushkin, Joseph *rabbi*
Temerlin, Liener *advertising executive*
Templeman, Lydia *retired assistant principal*
Templin, Kenneth Elwood *paper company executive*
Tenenbaum, Inez Moore *former school system administrator*
TenHoeve, Thomas *academic administrator*
Tenney, Frank Putnam *marketing executive*
Teplow, Theodore Herzl *retired valve company executive*
Tepper, Lloyd Barton *preventive medicine physician, educator*
Tepper, Morris *retired health science association administrator, mathematics professor*
Ter Horst, Jerald Franklin *public affairs counselor*
Termini, Roseann Bridget *law educator*
Terp, Thomas Thomsen *lawyer*
Terpeluk, Peter G., Jr. *former ambassador*
Terr, Lenore Cagen *psychiatrist, writer*
Terracciano, Antonio *psychologist, researcher*
Terrell, G. Irvin *lawyer*
Terrell, Hellenna L. *education educator*
Terris, Susan *physician, cardiologist, researcher*
Terry, Carole Cosgrove *retired small business owner, historian, researcher*
Terry, Clifford Lewis *journalist*
Terry, Edwin Wellington *college librarian*
Terry, Frances Jefferson *retired psychiatric nurse practitioner*
Terry, Mickey Thomas *music educator, director*
Terzic, Petar *mathematician, educator*
Tesarek, Dennis George *retired business consultant, writer, educator*
Teubner, Ferdinand Cary, Jr. *retired publishing executive*
Teuscher, Simon Hans *history professor, researcher*
Tevault, David Earl *chemist, researcher*
Tew, E. James, Jr. *management services company executive*
Teweleit, Russ *music educator*
Texter, John *physical chemist consultant*
Textor, Robert Bayard *cultural anthropology educator, writer, consultant*
Thacker, Thomas James *surveyor*
Thackston, Edward Lee *civil engineering educator*
Thaler, Richard Winston, Jr. *investment banker*
Tharoor, Shashi *former international organization official, writer*
Tharp, Stephen John *organist and pianist, artist*
Tharp, Twyla *dancer*
Tharpe, Frazier Eugene *journalist*
Thayer, Robert Wilcox *music educator*
Theodorescu, Dan *urologic oncologist, molecular biologist*
Theroux, Paul Edward *author*
Thiara, Parvinder Singh *chemistry scholar*
Thie, Joseph Anthony *nuclear engineer*
Thiel, Philip *design educator*
Thiele, Howard Nellis, Jr. *lawyer*
Thiemens, Mark H. *chemistry professor*
Thiessen, Delbert Duane *psychologist*
Thistlethwaite, David Richard *architect*
Thoman, Henry Nixon *lawyer*
Thomas, Adrian Wesley *research scientist, director, retired science educator*
Thomas, Betty *director, actress*
Thomas, Beverly Irene *special education educator, counseling administrator, educational diagnostician*
Thomas, Brooke C. *assistant principal*
Thomas, David Lindsey *lawyer, former state senator*
Thomas, Franklin Augustine *lawyer, consultant*
Thomas, James Edward, Jr. *brokerage house executive*
Thomas, Janet Y. *political science professor, researcher*
Thomas, Jo *journalist, educator*
Thomas, Joe Carroll *retired human resources director*
Thomas, John Howard *astrophysicist, mechanical engineer, educator*
Thomas, Kenneth Glyndwr *mining executive*
Thomas, Melissa Ann *lawyer*
Thomas, Patricia Anne *retired law librarian*
Thomas, Patricia Goodnow *journalist*
Thomas, Ralph Charles III *federal official*
Thomas, Regena L. *former state official*
Thomas, Teresa Ann *retired microbiologist, educator*
Thomas, Tom *retired plastics company executive*
Thomas-Robinson, Gregory Leon *sales executive*
Thompson, Alan Eric *economics professor*
Thompson, Andrea *television personality, retired newscaster, actress*
Thompson, Claire Louisa *nurse, educator, consultant, human services manager*
Thompson, Craig Snover *corporate communications executive*
Thompson, David O'Neal *retired basketball player*
Thompson, Dean M., II, *marketing executive*
Thompson, Ewa M. *foreign language educator*
Thompson, Herbert Alden *microbiologist, public health scientist*
Thompson, Holley Marker *lawyer, consultant, marketing professional*
Thompson, J. Andy *bank executive*
Thompson, Jack Edward *mining company executive*
Thompson, James Alexander, Jr. *lawyer*
Thompson, Jane *writer*
Thompson, Jennifer B. *Olympic swimmer*
Thompson, Jonathan Sims *business executive*
Thompson, Kenneth *software engineer*
Thompson, Kenneth W(infred) *educational association administrator, writer, editor, social sciences educator*
Thompson, Martin Christian *retired news executive*
Thompson, Mary Koleta *small business owner, not-for-profit developer*
Thompson, Philip C. *lawyer, investment advisor, educator*
Thompson, Ralph Newell *former chemical corporation executive*
Thompson, Richard Leon *pharmaceutical executive, lawyer*
Thompson, Richard Lloyd *retired pastor*
Thompson, Richard Stephen *management consultant*
Thomson, Caroline Helen *artist*
Thomson, Keith Stewart *biologist, author*
Thomson, Todd Stuart *former diversified financial services company executive*
Thomson, Virginia Winbourn *humanities educator, writer*
Thoreen, Mary Louise *elementary school educator, consultant*
Thoreson, Ryan R. *social anthropology scholar*
Thorn, Terence Hastings *energy executive, consultant, writer*
Thorne, William Albert *retired lawyer*
Thornell, Patricia L. *elementary school educator*
Thornhill, Harlen Webster *retired aircraft engineer*
Thornton, Felicia D. *food service company executive*
Thornton, Michael Albert *information technology manager*
Thornton, Rita Louise *environmental scientist, lawyer*
Thornton, Thomas Noel *former publishing executive*
Thornton, Yvonne Shirley *obstetrician, writer, musician*
Thorp, Benjamin A. III *retired paper company executive*
Thorsen, Marie Kristin *radiologist, educator*
Thorson, Connie Capers *library educator*
Thorstenberg, (John) Laurence *oboe and English horn player*
Thrall, Richard Cameron, Jr. *broadcast executive*
Thrasher, Rose Marie *critical care and community health nurse*
Threlkeld, Richard Davis *retired broadcast journalist*
Thueme, William Harold *secondary school educator, counselor, travel coordinator*
Thulean, Donald Myron *symphony conductor*
Thumma, Samuel Anderson *lawyer*
Thurmond, George Murat *judge*
Thurmond, J. Strom, Jr. *lawyer, former prosecutor*
Thurmond, John Peter, II, *bank executive, rancher, archaeologist*
Tian, Li *computer company executive, educator*
Tiano, Anthony Steven *television producer, publishing executive*
Tice, Bradley Scott *humanities educator*
Tidmore, Bryce William *retired secondary school educator*
Tidswell, Mark *medical researcher*
Tiefenbrun, Jonathan *surgeon*
Tiemeyer, Kayla Sue *music educator*
Tienken, Arthur T. *retired foreign service officer*
Tierney, Brian Patrick *publishing executive, former advertising and public relations executive*
Tilford, Terry Trent *translator*

Vessey, John William, Jr. *military officer*
Vest, Charles Marstiller *engineering educator, former academic administrator*
Vest, Gayle Southworth *obstetrician, gynecologist*
Vichiola, Christopher Michael *writer, educator*
Vicino, Thomas Joseph *political science professor*
Viegas, Jennifer *journalist, writer*
Viest, Ivan Miroslav *structural engineer, consultant*
Vieth, Christopher W. *former publishing executive*
Vigil-Giron, Rebecca *former state official*
Vila, Adis Maria *lawyer, business government executive*
Vilenchik, Michael Marc *radiobiologist, biophysicist, bio-oncologist*
Villaire, Holly Hennen Hood *theater producer, director, actress, educator*
Villa-Komaroff, Lydia *molecular biologist, educator, academic administrator*
Villanueva, Benito *physician, educator*
Villavaso, Stephen Donald *lawyer, urban planner*
Villella, Edward Joseph *dancer, choreographer, performing arts association administrator*
Villforth, John Carl *engineer, health physicist*
Villines, Bobby T. *environmental services administrator, information technology manager*
Villoch, Kelly Carney *art director*
Vilma, Jonathan Polynice *professional football player*
Vilsack, Tom (Thomas James) *former governor*
Vinar, Benjamin *lawyer*
Vincent, Charles Eagar, Jr. *sportswriter*
Vincent, Francis Thomas, Jr., (Fay Vincent) *former baseball commissioner*
Vincent, Hal Wellman *retired military officer, investor*
Vincent, James Louis *biotechnology company executive*
Vines, John R. *career military officer*
Vinkey, Rachel Burdick *psychiatrist*
Viorst, Judith Stahl *writer*
Viorst, Milton *writer*
Virani, Shanil *data analyst*
Virkhaus, Taavo *conductor*
Viscardi, Peter G. *risk management and environmental affairs executive*
Vishniac, Ethan Tecumseh *astronomy educator*
Visocki, Nancy Gayle *information services consultant*
Vita, Steven *poet*
Vitale, Ruth Ann *former film company executive*
Vitt, David Aaron *health products executive*
Vittetoe, Marie Clare *retired clinical laboratory science educator*
Vladeck, Bruce Charney *healthcare educator, former academic administrator*
Vlahos, Efstratios G. *retired cardiologist*
Vlasak, Brian Emerson *composer*
Vlazny, John George *archbishop*
Voegtlin-Anderson, Mary Margaret *music educator, small business owner*
Vogel, H. Victoria *psychotherapist, educator, writer, stress disorder and addiction recovery counselor*
Vogel, Susan Carol *nursing administrator*
Vohs, James Arthur *health plan administrator*
Voight, Jon *actor*
Voigt, Cynthia *writer*
Voigt, Karl Albert *electrical engineer, military officer*
Voitier, Doris *school system administrator*
Vojnovic, Igor Zoran *geographer, urban planner, educator*
Voketaitis, Arnold Matthew *bass-baritone, educator*
Volcker, Paul A(dolph) *economist, former Chairman of the Board of Governors of the Federal Reserve System*
Volk, Austin N. *retired insurance company executive*
Volk, Patricia Gay *writer, essayist*
Volkay, Chris John *investment company executive*
Volkers, Nancy Elaine *writer*
Volkhardt, John Malcolm *retired food products executive*
Volkman, Alvin *retired physician, research scientist, educator*
Volpe, Doris *artist*
Volpe, Edmond L(oris) *retired college president*
Volpi, Mike (Michelangelo A. Volpi) *internet television service company executive*
Von Brandenstein, Patrizia *production designer*
Vonderhaar, Steven Paul *counseling administrator*
von Furstenberg, Betsy *actress, writer*
von Furstenberg, Diane *fashion designer, writer, entrepreneur*
von Hake, Margaret Joan *librarian*
von Hoffman, Nicholas *writer, retired reporter*
von Kaenel, Howard J. *army officer*
von Sauers, Joseph F. *lawyer*
Vook, Frederick Ludwig *physicist, consultant*
Vosk, Ted W. *lawyer*
Voss, Omer Gerald *farm equipment executive*
Voss, Regis Dale *agronomist, educator*
Vost, Kevin Gerard *psychologist*
Voytek, Mary Sullivan *sculptor*
Vreeland, Russell Glenn *tax manager, accountant, consultant*
Vu, Joseph Duong *financial educator*
Vuckovic, Vladeta D *retired mathematics professor*
Vugmeister, Boris *physicist, writer*
Vuitton, Henry-Louis *designer*
Vyas, Nisha Anne *physician*
Wachtell, Esther *non-profit management executive, consultant*
Wachtman, Jeanette Marie *art educator, artist, writer*
Wackernagel, Mathis *engineering company executive, director*
Wade, June Booth *secondary school educator*
Wadley, M. Richard *consumer products executive*
Waggoner, Kathleen Alice *psychotherapist*
Wagman, Robert John *journalist, writer*
Wagner, Anthony E. *academic administrator, former state official*
Wagner, Arthur Ward, Jr. *lawyer*
Wagner, Cheri J. *business owner*
Wagner, Cheryl Jean *elementary school educator*
Wagner, John Edward *equity specialist*
Wagner, Lindsay Jean *actress*
Wagner, Robert *actor*
Wahl, Donald J. *counseling administrator*
Wahweah, Linda McNeil *insurance agent, writer*
Waite, Dennis Vernon *brokerage house executive, consultant*
Waitkus, Jay *writer*
Waitt, Theodore W. (Ted Waitt) *venture capitalist, former computer company executive*
Wald, Ingeborg *librarian, translator*
Waldman, Barry Howard *film producer*
Waldmeir, Peter Nielsen *retired journalist*
Waldon, Alton Ronald, Jr. *judge*
Waldrep, B. Dwain *education educator*
Walk, Barbra Denise *customer service administrator, tutor*
Walker, Annette *retired counseling administrator*
Walker, Antoine Devon *professional basketball player*
Walker, Bernice Baker *artist*
Walker, Carolyn Mae *retired secondary school educator*
Walker, Clarence Eugene *psychology professor*
Walker, Craig Michael *lawyer*
Walker, Donald Barclay *retired criminal justice educator, consultant, researcher, writer*
Walker, Donald Burke *retired music educator, retired archivist, composer*
Walker, Fred Elmer *broadcast executive*
Walker, George Herbert III *former ambassador, retired investment banking company executive*
Walker, George W. *bishop*
Walker, Gloria Lee *training services executive*
Walker, Gordon Davies *government official, writer, lecturer, consultant*
Walker, Henry Gilbert *health care executive, consultant*
Walker, Linda Lee *lawyer*
Walker, Lorenzo Giles *surgeon, educator*
Walker, Margaret Smith *real estate company executive*
Walker, Mark A. *lawyer*
Walker, Michael Charles, Sr. *retired services executive*
Walker, Olene S. *former governor*
Walker, Pamela *mathematics educator*
Walker, Philip Doolittle *retired literature and language professor, composer*
Walker, Richard Henry *lawyer*
Walker, Ronald Tracy *retired personnel director*
Walker, Roslyn Adele *retired museum director*
Walker, Ruth Charlotta *language educator, real estate broker*
Wall, Frederick Theodore *retired chemistry professor*
Wall, M. Danny *finance company executive*
Wallace, Ardelia Leslene *elementary school educator*
Wallace, Arthur, Jr. *retired college dean*
Wallace, David K. *musician, composer*
Wallace, Dee *actress*
Wallace, Douglas C. *geneticist, educator*
Wallace, F. Blake *retired aerospace transportation executive, retired mechanical engineer*
Wallace, Jane House *retired geologist*
Wallace, Michele *writer, educator*
Wallace, Mike (Myron Leon Wallace) *newscaster, television personality*
Wallace, Nicolle (Nicolle Devenish) *former federal official*
Wallach, Patricia *councilman, retired mayor*
Wallack, Rina Evelyn *lawyer*
Waller, Eunice McLean *retired elementary school educator*
Waller, Steven R. *engineer*
Wallingford, Anne *freelance/self-employed writer, marketing professional, consultant*
Wallis, Diana Lynn *artistic director*
Wallison, Frieda K. *lawyer*
Wallpher, Luis Antonio *small business owner, painter, writer*
Wallskog, Joyce Marie *nursing educator, retired psychologist*
Walmer, Edwin Fitch *retired lawyer*
Walmsley, Priscilla Helen *computer company executive*
Walpole, Jim (James R.) *lawyer*
Walsh, Diana Chapman *former academic administrator, sociologist, educator*
Walsh, Diane *pianist*
Walsh, George William *publishing company executive, editor, author*
Walsh, Joseph Thomas *retired state supreme court justice*
Walsh, M. Emmet *actor*
Walsh, Michael P. *mechanical engineer*
Walsh, Michael Thomas *historian, musician*
Walsh, Nan *artist, painter, sculptor, consultant*
Walsh, Russell W. *director tutorial services*
Walsh, William Albert *management consultant, retired military officer*
Walsh, William Desmond *investor*
Walter, Carmel Monica *writer*
Walter, J. Jackson *management consultant, foundation administrator*
Waltermire, Thomas Allen *finance company executive*
Walters, Farah M. *health services company administrator, former hospital administrator*
Walters, Glen Robert *retired banker*
Walters, Robert Ancil *physicist, mathematician*
Walther, Adriaan *retired physics professor*
Waltner, Beverly Ruland *artist*
Walton, Alice Louise *bank executive*
Walton, Andre Pierre *psychologist, consultant*
Walton, Cedar *musician*
Walton, Christy R. *philanthropist*
Waltrip, Darrell Lee *race car driver*
Walz, Edward George *protective services official*
Wan, Guofang *education professor*
Wan, Julia Chang *retired science educator*
Wang, Chen-ku *retired library director*
Wang, Elise *political science scholar*
Wang, Fen *adult education educator, researcher*
Wang, Jian *materials scientist, researcher*
Wang, Nancy *pathologist, educator*
Wang, Xiubin *transportation educator*
Wang, Yinmin *materials scientist, educator*
Wang, Yu-Ping *computer science educator, engineering educator*
Wanger, Eugene Gilkison *retired lawyer*
Wangsness, Genna Stead *retired hotel executive, innkeeper*
Wannier, Mario Marc-Antoine *oil industry executive, multi-media specialist, director*
Wantland, William Charles *retired bishop, lawyer*
Warberg, Willetta *concert pianist, music educator*
Warcken, Nancy B. *elementary school educator*
Ward, Charlie *professional basketball player*
Ward, Chester Lawrence *physician, consultant*
Ward, Thomas *research scientist*
Warder, Richard Currey, Jr. *dean, mechanical aerospace engineering educator*
Wardlow, Benjamin Franklin III *sales executive*
Ware, D. Clifton *vocalist, educator*
Ware, Gwendolyn C. *retired counseling administrator*
Warfel, M(artha) Kay *speech pathology/audiology services professional*
Warian, Christine Barbara *elementary school educator*
Warman, Linda K. *retired secondary school educator*
Warner, Karl K. *former prosecutor*
Warner, William Hamer *mathematician*
Warnock, William Reid *lawyer*
Warren, John William *professional society administrator*
Warren, Rosanna *poet*
Warrington, George D. *former transportation executive*
Warshaw, Carole Klein *retired education educator*
Wartluft, David Jonathan *retired librarian, minister*
Washburn, Donald Arthur *retired transportation executive, investor*
Washburn, Gladys Rice *photojournalist, educator*
Washington, Denzel *actor*
Washington, James Winston, Jr. *artist, sculptor*
Washington, Kerry *actor*
Washington, Michele *educational consultant*
Wasmuth, Carl Erwin *retired physician, lawyer*
Watanabe, Ken *actor*
Waterhouse, Keith *urologist, educator, retired surgeon*
Waters, Betty Lou *newspaper reporter, writer*
Waters, Jack *artist, filmmaker*
Waters, Lou *news correspondent*
Waters, William Carter III *retired internist, educator*
Waterston, Robert Hugh *medical educator, researcher, medical geneticist, department chairman*
Watkins, Ann Esther *mathematics professor*
Watkins, Dean Allen *electronics executive, educator*
Watkins, George Daniels *physics professor*
Watkins, James David *federal official, military officer*
Watkins, Wesley Wade *retired congressman*
Watrous, Robert Thomas *academic director*
Watson, Bernard Charles *foundation administrator, educator*
Watson, Catherine Elaine *journalist*
Watson, Donald Charles, Jr. *cardiothoracic surgeon, educator*
Watson, Easter Jean *psychotherapist, financial program consultant*
Watson, George Henry, Jr. *broadcaster, journalist*
Watson, Patricia Pullums *school system administrator*
Watson, Patty Jo *anthropology educator*
Watson, Robert Joe *retired health facility administrator, retired career officer*
Watt, Stephanie Denise *musician, educator, department chairman*
Watters, Ann Oliva *psychologist, educator*
Watters, Raymond Wendell *family medicine physician*
Watts, Anthony Lee *bank executive*
Watts, Doris Earlene *retired librarian*
Watts, Ginny (Virginia C. Watts) *artist*
Watts, Mary Ann *retired elementary school educator*
Waud, Roger Neil *economist, educator*
Wavle, James Edward, Jr. *pharmaceutical company executive, lawyer*
Waxman, Ronald *computer engineer*
Way, Barbara Haight *retired dermatologist*
Way, Jacob Edson III *museum director*
Wayne, Kyra Petrovskaya *writer*
Weatherburn, Stephen James *humanities educator*
Weathersby, George Byron *management company executive*
Weaver, Delbert Allen *retired lawyer*
Weaver, Franklin Thomas *retired newspaper executive*
Weaver, Howard C. *newspaper executive*
Weaver, William Charles *manufacturing executive*
Weaver, William Schildecker *retired electric power industry executive*
Webb, Carl B. *banker*
Webb, O. Glenn *retired farm supplies company executive*
Webb, Wellington Edward *political organization administrator, former mayor*
Webb, William Timothy *mobile communications professional*
Webel, Charles Peter *human science and psychology educator*
Weber, Bruce Edward *art historian*
Weber, Carl *publishing executive, retail bookstore executive, writer*
Weber, Donald B. *advertising executive, marketing professional*
Weber, Frederick D. *information technology executive*
Weber, Gloria Richie *retired minister, retired state legislator*
Weber, Idelle *artist, educator*
Weber, Jean Macphail *museum director*
Weber, John Walter *insurance company executive*
Weber, Kenneth J. *hotel executive*
Weber, Susan A. *lawyer*
Weber, Thomas William *chemical engineering professor*
Webster, Christopher White *foreign service officer*
Webster, Harold Frank *physicist*
Webster, John Crosby Brown *minister, educator*
Webster, Larry Russell *artist*
Webster, Owen Wright *chemist*
Webster, Robert Kenly *lawyer*
Webster, Ronald D. *diversified financial services company executive*
Webster, William G., Jr. *career military officer*
Wechsler, Sergio *automotive executive, consultant*
Wedgeworth, Ann *actress*
Weeks, Clifford Myers *musician, academic administrator*
Weeks, Jeffrey R. *mathematician, researcher, educator*
Weeks, Lori D. *elementary school educator*
Weeks, William Rawle, Jr. *oil industry executive*
Wegman, William George *artist*
Wehn, Karen Swaney *education educator, consultant*
Weickert, Wanda Opal *child welfare and attendance counselor, psychotherapist, educator*
Weida, Johnny A. *career military officer*
Weiherer, Patricia Dee *retired librarian*
Weihmuller, Patricia Ann *minister, artist, retired executive secretary*
Weil, Lynne Amy *communications executive, writer*
Weil, Peter Henry *lawyer*
Weil, Randolph Allen *engineering executive*
Weil, Rolf Alfred *economist, retired university president*
Weil, Susan Ellen *dietician, consultant*
Weil, Thomas P. *retired health services consultant*
Weiland, Scott Richard *singer*
Weinberg, Steven *physics professor*
Weinberger, Arnold *retired electrical engineer*
Weinbrenner, George Ryan *aeronautical engineer*
Weiner, Anne Lee *social worker*
Weiner, Ferne *psychologist*
Weiner, H. Richard *internist*
Weiner, Richard *public relations executive*
Weingand, Darlene Erna *librarian, educator*
Weingarten, Joseph Leonard *aerospace engineer*
Weinkauf, Mary Louise Stanley *retired clergywoman, educator*
Weinman, Glenn Alan *lawyer*
Weinreb, Herbert L. *physician*
Weinreb, Michael Philip *physicist*
Weinshall, Iris *academic administrator*
Weinshenker, Naomi Joyce *clinical psychiatrist, educator, researcher*
Weinstein, Arthur Gary *lawyer*
Weinstein, Marta *packaging services company executive*
Weinstein, Michael P. *marine scientist, administrator*
Weinstein, Milton Charles *decision scientist, educator*
Weintraub, Sam *retired reading educator*
Weir, Sir William H. *lawyer, judge, educator*
Weis, Margaret Edith *writer, editor*
Weisberg, Barbara *writer, editor*
Weisberg, David Charles *lawyer*
Weisbrod, John *former professional sports team executive*
Weisburger, Elizabeth Kreiser *retired chemist*
Weisman, Gary *sculptor, educator*
Weisman, Paul Howard *lawyer*
Weismantel, Gregory Nelson *management consultant, computer company executive*
Weiss, Alvin Harvey *chemical engineer, educator, research scientist, consultant*
Weiss, Jerry Kenneth *sales executive, consultant, marketing professional*
Weiss, Kenneth Andrew *lawyer, educator*
Weiss, Lyn Denise *physician*
Weiss, Michael Allen *retired retail executive*
Weiss, Rainer *physics educator*
Weiss, Stefan Craig *dermatologist, director*
Weiss, Steven Gary *physician*
Weissman, Jack (George Anderson) *retired editor*
Weiss Newton, Joanne Marion *writer*
Weiswasser, Stephen *electronics executive*
Weisz, Paul B(urg) *physicist, researcher, chemical engineer*
Welburn, Edward T. *automotive executive*
Welch, Martin E. III *investor, retail executive*
Welch, Oliver Wendell *retired pharmaceutical executive*
Welch, Richard L. *priest, lawyer*
Weldon, Charles Jauverni *actor*
Weldon, Curt (Wayne Curtis Weldon) *former congressman*
Weldon, Jeffrey Alan *lawyer*
Weldon, William Forrest *electrical and mechanical engineer, educator*
Weller, Milton Webster *wetland ecologist, educator*
Weller, Peter *actor*
Weller, Sol William *chemical engineering professor*
Weller, Thomas Huckle *physician, retired medical educator*
Wellisz, Stanislaw *economics professor*

Wellner, Marcel Nahum *research scientist, educator*
Wells, Don *artist*
Wells, John Calhoun *retired physics professor*
Wells, Kitty (Ellen Muriel Deason) *musician*
Wells, Lynton Alfred *artist*
Wells, Peter Scoville *retired marketing professional*
Welna, Cecilia *retired mathematics professor, dean*
Welnak, Llowell A. *retired lawyer*
Welsh, Dorothy Dell *columnist, writer*
Welsh, John Beresford, Jr. *retired lawyer*
Welsh, Louis Ward *otolaryngologist*
Welsome, Eileen *journalist, writer*
Weltchek, Robert Jay *lawyer*
Welz, Rebecca Beall *sculptor, educator*
Wen, Leana S. *epidemiologist*
Wen, Yunfei *research scientist*
Wendlinger, Robert Matthew *communications and memory consultant*
Wendt, E. Allan *international affairs consultant*
Wendt, George Robert *actor*
Wenger, James L. *education educator*
Wentworth, LaVerne Wellborn *curriculum consultant*
Wentworth, Murray Jackson *artist, educator*
Wentz, Jeffrey Lee *information systems executive*
Wentz, Sidney Frederick *insurance company executive, foundation administrator*
Wentz, William Henry, Jr. *aerospace engineer, educator*
Werman, Thomas Ehrlich *record producer*
Werner, Stuart Lloyd *computer services company executive*
Werner-Jacobsen, Emmy Elisabeth *developmental psychologist*
Wernick, Richard Frank *composer, conductor, educator*
Werthan, Jeffrey Michael *lawyer*
Wertsman, Vladimir Filip *librarian, writer, library and information scientist, translator*
Weselak, Anna Marie Schmidt *educational association administrator, media consultant*
Wesley, Norman H. *consumer products company executive*
Wessel, Morris Arthur *retired pediatrician*
Wessel, Peter *lawyer*
Wesselink, David Duwayne *finance company executive*
Wessling, Gregory Jay *retail executive*
Wessling, Robert Bruce *retired lawyer*
West, Catherine G. *former retail executive*
West, Jerry Alan *former professional sports team executive, retired professional basketball player*
West, Rexford Leon *retired bank executive*
West, W. Richard *museum director*
Westerfield, Holt Bradford *retired political scientist*
Westergard, Sue Benzel *elementary education educator*
Westerhoff, John Henry III *priest, theologian, educator*
Westerhout, Gart *retired astronomer*
Westernoff, Trent H. *surgeon*
Westfall, David *lawyer, educator*
Weston, Michael C. *retired lawyer*
Wetherbe, Herbert John *pharmacist*
Wetherell, Albert A. *secondary school educator*
Wetherill, Eikins *lawyer, investment company executive*
Wexler, Haskell *film producer*
Wexler, Sandra M. *artist, medical illustrator*
Weyman, Steven Aloysius *retired military officer*
Weymouth, Elizabeth (Lally) Graham *editor, columnist*
Whalen, Charles William, Jr. *writer, retail executive, congressman, educator*
Whaley, Ross Samuel *environmentalist, educator*
Wheatland, Richard, II, *fiduciary services executive, museum executive*
Wheaton, M. Gene *investigator, consultant*
Wheeler, Albin Gray *retired military officer, retail executive, educator*
Wheeler, Burton M. *language educator, dean*
Wheeler, David Laurie *university dean*
Wheeler, George Charles, Jr. *materials engineer, process engineer*
Wheeler, John Oliver *retired geologist*
Wheeler, R(ichard) Kenneth *lawyer, educator*
Wheeler, Stephen Frederick *legal administrator*
Whelan, Colm T. *physicist, researcher*
Whelan, James Robert *investor, mining company executive*
Whelan, Joseph L. *neurologist*
Whelan, Stephen Thomas, Jr. *lawyer*
Whelchel, Sandra Jane *writer*
Whipple, Judith Roy *retired editor*
Whippo, Scott Dean *consultant*
Whisler, James Steven *retired mining executive, lawyer, rancher*
Whitaker, Bruce Ezell *college president*
Whitaker, Pernell (Sweet Pea Whitaker) *retired boxer*
Whitaker, Thomas O'Hara *theater educator, theater director*
Whitburn, Merrill Duane *English literature educator*
Whitcomb, Richard Travis *aeronautical consultant*
White, Bertram Milton *chemicals executive*
White, Charles Olds *aeronautical engineer*
White, Charles Sidney John *retired humanities educator*
White, Dawn Marie *elementary school educator*
White, Eugene Vaden *retired pharmacist*
White, Florence May *retired special education educator*
White, Helene Nita *federal judge*
White, Jan Tuttle *information technology executive*
White, Jill Carolyn *lawyer*
White, John Joseph III *lawyer*
White, John Wesley, Jr. *retired academic administrator*
White, Julie *actress*
White, Kendred Alan *lawyer*
White, Kerr Lachlan *retired physician, foundation administrator*
White, Lonnie Joe *retired history educator*
White, Loray Betty *TV talk show host, writer, television producer, director, vocalist, actress*
White, Margit Triska *financial advisor*
White, Pamela Jo *elementary school educator*
White, Ralph Paul *automotive executive, consultant*
White, Rebecca E. *advocate*
White, Richard Thomas *radiologist*
White, Ronald Leon *retired business executive*
White, Stanley Archibald *electrical engineer, researcher*
White, W. Robin *writer*
White, William Dudley *safety engineer*
White, William Nelson *lawyer*
White, Yonsenia S. *artist, educator*
Whitehead, Edgar Douglas *urology educator*
Whitehead, John Cunningham *former bank executive*
Whitehead, Tanya Dianne Grubbs *psychologist, educator, researcher*
Whitehorn, Clark Allan *retired urologist*
Whitehurst, Jim (James M. Whitehurst) *former air transportation executive*
Whiteley, Benjamin Robert *retired insurance company executive*
Whitener, Carolyn Raye *artist*
Whitesell, John Edwin *retired motion picture company executive*
Whiting, Brian Christopher *hospitality consultant*
Whitman, Christine Todd *former federal agency administrator, governor*
Whitman, Gregory Theodore *neurologist*
Whitman, Kathy Velma Rose (Elk Woman Whitman) *artist, painter*
Whitmore, Bruce G. *lawyer*
Whitney, Edward Bonner *retired investment banker*
Whitney, Ralph Royal, Jr. *financial executive*
Whitsell, John Crawford, II, *general surgeon*
Whitsitt, Bob (Robert James Whitsitt) *former professional football team executive*
Whittell, Polly (Mary Kaye Whittell) *editor, journalist*
Whittemore, Brian *media consultant, advertising executive*
Whittingham, Kenneth *television director*
Whittington-Brown, Vanessa Elizabeth *secondary school educator*
Whouley, Kate *writer, consultant*
Wichman, Karen Lin *medical transcriptionist*
Wicker, Thomas Carey, Jr. *retired judge*
Wickman, Leslie *research scientist, science administrator*
Wicks, David O., Jr. *communications executive*
Wickstrom, Jon Alan *telecommunications executive, consultant*
Widener, Hiram Emory, Jr. *judge*
Widner, Ralph Randolph *retired public administrator*
Widner, Roberta Ann *accountant, artist*
Wiebenson, Dora Louise *architectural historian, editor, writer*
Wiehl, Lis W. *legal analyst, educator*
Wieland, Gilbert Darryl *medical researcher, anthropologist, gerontologist*
Wieland, William Dean *healthcare consulting executive*
Wiener, Jon *history professor*
Wies, Barbara *publishing executive, editor*
Wiesen, Donald Guy *retired diversified manufacturing company executive*
Wiessler, David Albert *news correspondent*
Wiest, Dianne *actress*
Wigand, Robert Charles, Jr. *retired civil engineer, retired aerospace engineer*
Wiggins, Charles Henry, Jr. *lawyer*
Wiggins, Samuel Paul *education educator*
Wilbur, Marcia Kaoru *writer*
Wilburn, Mary Nelson *lawyer, writer, poet, translator*
Wilcox, Hugh Edward *plant physiologist*
Wilcox, Mark Dean *lawyer*
Wilde, Daniel Underwood *computer engineering educator*
Wilder, Gene *actor, film director, writer*
Wilder, Janet Mary *performing company executive*
Wilder, Ksenia A. *systems analyst*
Wildhack, William August, Jr. *lawyer*
Wilds, Daniel O. *health products executive*
Wileman, George Robert *retired lawyer*
Wiley, Carl Ross *timber company executive*
Wiley, Richard Arthur *lawyer*
Wilhelmi, Cynthia Joy *information technology manager, information scientist, consultant*
Wilhelmsen, Harold John *accountant*
Wilk, Ronald *physician*
Wilkening, Laurel Lynn *academic administrator, aerospace scientist*
Wilkens, Lenny (Leonard Randolph Wilkens Jr.) *sportscaster, former professional sports team executive, retired professional basketball player*
Wilkerson, Matha Ann *retired oil company executive*
Wilkin, Richard Edwin *clergyman, religious organization administrator*
Wilkins, Barratt (George Wilkins) *librarian*
Wilkins, Fred Clayton *physician, educator, engineer*
Wilkinson, Claude Henry *writer, artist, English literature educator*
Wilkinson, Doris *medical sociology educator*
Wilkinson, Harry Edward *management educator, consultant*
Will, Roland Tracy, II, *writer, editor, journalist, publisher, television producer*
Willard, Atom (Adam Willard) *musician*
Willard, Richard Kennon *lawyer, former pharmaceutical company executive*
Willauer, Whiting Russell *retired manufacturing executive, systems engineer*
Wille, Wayne Martin *retired editor*
Willenbecher, John *artist*
Williams, Alfred B. *retired management educator*
Williams, Anthony Allan (Tony) *former mayor*
Williams, B. John, Jr. *retired federal agency administrator, lawyer*
Williams, Bernard *film producer*
Williams, C(harles) K(enneth) *poet, educator, literature educator*
Williams, Charles Wesley *retired engineering executive, consultant, researcher*
Williams, Clara A. *sculptor*
Williams, Darcel Patrice *writer, editor*
Williams, Dorothy Standridge *retired food products manager, civic worker*
Williams, Doyle Z. *finance educator*
Williams, Elizabeth *human services administrator*
Williams, Ervin Eugene *religious organization administrator*
Williams, Freda Videll *speech pathology/audiology services professional*
Williams, George Christopher *biologist, ecology and evolution educator*
Williams, Howard Walter *aerospace engineer, engineering executive*
Williams, Ian George *writer*
Williams, James Buchanan *retired surgeon*
Williams, Jatika *social worker, educator*
Williams, JoBeth *actress*
Williams, Lisa A. *special education educator*
Williams, Louis Clair, Jr. *public relations executive*
Williams, Michael Richard *protective services official*
Williams, Neville *solar power company executive*
Williams, Patricia Badia *retired counseling administrator*
Williams, Patterson Bouic *museum program director*
Williams, Paul Robert *lawyer, foreign policy analyst*
Williams, Paul Stratton *executive recruiter*
Williams, Phyllis Cutforth *retired realtor*
Williams, Robert Chadwell *history professor*
Williams, Robert Leon *retired psychiatrist, neurologist, educator*
Williams, Robert Sanders (Sandy Williams) *dean, academic administrator, educator, researcher*
Williams, Robin *actor, comedian*
Williams, Roger (J. Roger Williams) *former state official*
Williams, Ronald Oscar *mathematician*
Williams, Shannon Renee *mental health services professional*
Williams, Stephen Edward *retired lawyer*
Williams, Steven D. *plastic surgeon*
Williams, Sue M. *federal agency administrator, writer*
Williams, Terrie Michelle *public relations executive*
Williams, Thelma B. *retired principal*
Williams, Thomas W. *electrical engineer*
Williamson, Richard Salisbury *ambassador*
Willig, Karl Victor *computer company executive*
Willingham, Mary Maxine *fashion retailer*
Willis, Beverly Ann *architect*
Willis, Clayton *broadcaster, former government official, educator, arts consultant*
Willis, Paul Allen *retired librarian, retired dean*
Willis, Ruth *freelance/self-employed theater director, actress*
Willis, Selene Lowe *electrical engineer, application developer, consultant, information technology manager*
Willis, Solomon Lee *mathematics educator*
Willison, Bruce Gray *dean*
Willner, Kenneth M. *lawyer*
Willock, Marcelle Monica *retired medical educator*
Wills, Charles Francis *retired religious organization administrator*
Wills, J. Robert *retired academic administrator, theater educator, writer*
Wills, John Elliot, Jr. *retired historian, writer*
Wills, William Ridley, II, *retired insurance company executive, historian*
Wilmore, Douglas Wayne *surgeon, educator*
Wilmut, Ian *biologist*
Wilner, Alan M. *retired judge*
Wilner, Thomas Bernard *lawyer*
Wilpon, Fred *professional sports team executive*
Wilson, Carolyn Ross *retired school system administrator*
Wilson, Cheryl Yvonne *elementary and secondary school educator*
Wilson, Colin Henry *writer*
Wilson, Don Matthew III *corporate banking executive*
Wilson, Gretchen *vocalist*
Wilson, James Reid, Jr. *publishing executive*
Wilson, Jane *artist*
Wilson, John Pasley *retired law educator*
Wilson, Joseph Charles, IV, *former ambassador*
Wilson, Karen Lee *museum staff member, researcher*
Wilson, Karen Wilkerson *paralegal*
Wilson, Kathy Kay *former foundation administrator, consultant*
Wilson, Kenneth Geddes *physics research administrator*
Wilson, Lanford *playwright*
Wilson, Lois M. *minister*
Wilson, Martin D. *pharmaceutical executive*
Wilson, Mary Elizabeth *epidemiologist, physician, educator*
Wilson, Melvin Edmond *retired civil engineer*
Wilson, Myron Robert, Jr. *retired psychiatrist*
Wilson, Patricia Potter *library and information science educator*
Wilson, Peggy Mayfield *retired chemist*
Wilson, Rainn D. (Rainn Dietrich Wilson) *actor*
Wilson, Ralph Cookerly, Jr. *professional football team executive*
Wilson, Rhys Thaddeus *lawyer*
Wilson, Rita *actress*
Wilson, Robert M. *diversified financial services company executive*
Wilson, Robert Woodrow *radio astronomer*
Wilson, Roberta Louise *writer, editor, journalist, activist*
Wilson, Robin Scott *retired academic administrator, writer*
Wilson, Ronald A. *judge*
Wilson, Scott Thomas *psychologist, researcher*
Wilson, Troy Lynn *technologist*
Wilson, Virgil James III *lawyer, judge*
Wilson, Walter Clinton *retired oil and gas industry executive*
Wilson, Wanda Lee Davis *retired casting director*
Wilson, Warren Samuel *clergyman*
Wilson, Wendy Marie *elementary school educator, consultant*
Wimmer, Kathryn *retired elementary school educator*
Wimpffen, Otto Rudolph *mathematics professor*
Wimpress, Gordon Duncan, Jr. *management consultant, foundation administrator*
Winder, Robert Owen *mathematician, computer engineer, geophysicist*
Windhauser, John William *retired journalism educator, consultant*
Wingate, Robert Lee, Jr. *internist*
Winkenwerder, William, Jr. *former federal agency administrator*
Winkler, Agnieszka M. *marketing executive*
Winkler, Joseph Conrad *former recreational products manufacturing executive*
Winkler, Lee B. *business consultant*
Winn, Carolyn Pautke *librarian, consultant*
Winn, Joseph Lampher *retired electronics executive*
Winn, Morris X. *former federal agency administrator*
Winnowski, Thaddeus Richard (Ted Winnowski) *investment banker, consultant*
Winokur, Marissa Jaret *actress*
Winslet, Kate *actress*
Winslow, David Allen *chaplain, retired military officer*
Winslow, John Franklin *lawyer*
Winslow, Walter William *psychiatrist, educator*
Winter, Harvey John *retired government official*
Winter, Jeffrey B. *elementary school educator*
Winter, Judy Elaine *freelance/self-employed journalist, speaker*
Winter, Leigh Ellen *artist, educator*
Winter, Roger Paul *former federal agency administrator*
Winter, Terence *writer*
Winter-Neighbors, Gwen Carole *special education and art educator, consultant*
Winters, Jonathan *actor*
Wintersheimer, Donald Carl *retired state supreme court justice*
Winterstein, James Fredrick *academic administrator*
Wirth, Kelley K. *state representative*
Wise, Patricia *opera singer, educator*
Wisehart, Mary Ruth *retired religious organization administrator*
Wiseman, Douglas Carl *education educator, department chairman, dean*
Wish, LeslieBeth Berger *psychotherapist, writer, management consultant*
Wishnick, Marcia Margolis *pediatrician, geneticist, educator*
Wisniewski, Thomas Joseph *music educator*
Wissel-Littmann, Jeffrey G. *health facility executive*
Wiswall, Dorothy Roller *language educator*
Witcher, Michael H. *homeland and national security expert*
Witcover, Jules Joseph *columnist, writer*
Withrow, Mary Ellen *federal agency administrator*
Witt, Alicia *actress*
Witt, Hugh Ernest *manufacturing executive, consultant*
Witte, Owen Neil *microbiologist, molecular biologist, educator*
Wittich, John Jacob *retired academic administrator, finance company executive*
Wittig, Raymond Shaffer *lawyer, intellectual property technology manager*
Wittmann, Marshall *political organization worker*
Wittry, Diane Marie *conductor, musician*
Wivel, Nelson Auburn *physician, medical researcher, educator, biotechnology consultant*
Wixen, Joan Saunders *journalist*
Wizda, Christine Anne *history professor*
Wodlinger, Mark Louis *broadcast executive*
Woerner, Robert Eugene *retired editor, writer*
Woestendiek, John, Jr., (William John Woestendiek) *newspaper reporter*
Woldman, Sherman *pediatrician*
Wold-Olsen, Per *pharmaceutical executive*
Woldt, Harold Frederick, Jr. *newspaper publishing executive*
Wolf, Alan Steven *lawyer*
Wolf, Dale Edward *state official*
Wolf, Jacqueline L. *gastroenterologist*
Wolf, Stephen M. *consumer products company executive, former airline executive*
Wolf, William Martin *computer company executive, consultant*
Wolfberg, Melvin Donald *optometrist, educational association administrator, consultant*
Wolfe, Charles Morgan *electrical engineering educator*
Wolfe, Gregory Baker *international relations educator*
Wolfe, Linda *writer*
Wolfe, Margaret Ripley *historian, educator, consultant*
Wolff, Brian Richard *metal products executive*
Wolff, Eleanor Blunk *actress*
Wolff, Manfred Ernst *chemist, pharmaceutical executive*

Wolfman, Ira Joel *editor, writer*
Wolfson, Michael George *retired lawyer*
Woll, Harry J. *electrical engineer*
Wollert, Gerald Dale *retired food products executive, securities trader*
Wolpert Richard, Chava *artist*
Woltering, Margaret Mae *retired educational association administrator*
Wonders, William Clare *geography educator*
Wong, Ah-San *planetary scientist, musician, writer*
Wong, B.D. (Bradley Darryl Wong) *actor*
Wong, Liliane *architect, educator*
Wong, Richard *music educator*
Wong, Stova *law firm executive*
Wong, Yanyi Liu *physicist, researcher*
Wong-Diaz, Francisco Raimundo *lawyer, educator*
Wong Smith, Helen Mei Lin *librarian, archivist, consultant*
Woo, Benjamin Kai Pan *psychiatrist*
Woo, Derek *electrical and computer engineer*
Woo, Kenneth Roger *urologist*
Wood, Cheryl Raley *minister, musician*
Wood, Corinne Gieseke *former lieutenant governor*
Wood, Evan Rachel *actress*
Wood, Frances Diane *medical secretary, artist*
Wood, Frank *actor*
Wood, Janis Louise *retired assistant principal*
Wood, Margaret *performing company executive*
Wood, Marian Starr *publishing executive*
Wood, Maurice *medical educator*
Wood, Robert Charles *lawyer, real estate developer*
Wood, Vivian Poates *mezzo soprano, educator*
Wood, William Preston *writer, lawyer*
Wood, Willis Bowne, Jr. *retired utilities executive*
Woodard, Catherine *arts patron*
Woodard, Joseph Lamar *law librarian, emeritus professor*
Woodbridge, John Dunning *history professor*
Wooden, John Robert *former college basketball coach*
Woodland, N. Joseph *retired optical engineer, retired mechanical engineer*
Woodruff, Judy Carline *broadcast journalist*
Woodruff, Truman O(wen) *physicist, emeritus educator*
Woodruff, Virginia *broadcast journalist, writer*
Woodrum, Patricia Ann *librarian*
Woods, Dan *information technology manager, consultant*
Woods, J. P. *religious organization administrator*
Woods, Sandra Kay *real estate executive*
Woods, Willie E. *information specialist*
Woodson, Jacqueline *writer*
Woodsworth, Anne *retired academic administrator, librarian*
Woodward, James Franklin *science educator*
Woodward, Ralph Barclay *music educator, small business owner*
Woodward, Ralph Lee, Jr. *retired historian, educator*
Woodward, Thomas Morgan *actor*
Wookey, Sara Hastings *artist*
Wooldridge, Sue Ellen *former federal agency administrator, lawyer*
Wooldridge, William Charles *lawyer*
Woolston-Catlin, Marian *retired psychiatrist*
Woolworth, Susan Valk *primary school educator*
Woosnam, Ian Harold *professional golfer*
Wooten, Cecil Aaron *retired religious organization administrator*
Wooten, Frank Thomas *retired research facility executive*
Wooten, James Terrell *journalist*
Worboys, Roger Dick *retired communications executive*
Worenklein, Jacob Joshua *lawyer*
Workman, John Mitchell *chemist*
Workman, John P., Jr. *marketing professor*
Worley, April Cole *artist, grant writer*
Worley, Richard B. *financial consultant*
Worner, Theresa Marie *internist, educator*
Woronov, Mary Peter *actress*
Worrell, Stewart Phillip *lawyer, diversified financial services company executive*
Worth, Gary James *communications executive*
Worthington, Daniel Glen *lawyer, educator*
Worthington, Tracy *retired operations research specialist*
Woteki, Catherine Ellen *nutritionist*
Wott, John Arthur *retired arboretum and botanical garden executive, horticulture educator*
Wozencraft, John McReynolds *retired communications engineer*
Wray, Wilson E., Jr. *lawyer*
Wreghitt, Randall L. *theater producer*
Wright, Barbara Clare *business librarian*
Wright, David John *telecommunications systems specialist, educator*
Wright, David L. *food and beverage company executive*
Wright, Dell *residential care and treatment facility executive*
Wright, Douglas Tyndall *former university administrator*
Wright, Frances Mary *principal*
Wright, Franz Paul *poet, writer, translator*
Wright, Gladys Stone *music educator, writer, composer*
Wright, James Ralph *retired lawyer*
Wright, Joan L. *artist*
Wright, Josephine Rosa Beatrice *musicologist, educator*
Wright, Kevin Dale *medical researcher*
Wright, Kristopher *biology professor*
Wright, Lawrence George *writer*
Wright, Lori Dunkle *musician, educator*
Wright, Randolph Earle *retired petroleum company executive*
Wright, Richard Stevens *film producer*
Wright, Robert Payton *lawyer*
Wright, Sylvia *government agency administrator*
Wright, Theodore Robert Fairbank *biologist, educator*
Wright, Virginia *art collector, curator*
Wright, Will *computer game designer*
Wriston, Kathryn Dineen *corporate director, consultant*
Wrobel, Bruce J. *energy and utilities company executive*
Wroble, Arthur Gerard *judge*
Wrong, Dennis Hume *retired sociologist, educator*
Wroth, James Melvin *retired military officer*
Wruble, Bernhardt Karp *lawyer*
Wruble, Brian Frederick *investor*
Wruck, Erich-Oskar *retired foreign language educator, administrator*
Wu, Benjamin H. *federal agency administrator, lawyer*
Wu, Jonathan T. H. *science educator*
Wu, Li-Tzy *alcohol/drug abuse services professional, researcher*
Wu, Min *computer and electrical engineer*
Wu, Xin *electrical engineer, researcher, educator*
Wu, Yider *research scientist*
Wuensche, Vernon Edgar *construction company executive*
Wunsch Cox, Kathryn Sutherland *retired lawyer*
Wurm, Jan *artist, educator*
Wyatt, Robert Lee, IV, *lawyer*
Wyatt, Thomas Csaba *lawyer*
Wyker, Kenneth E. *lawyer*
Wylan, Barbara *artist*
Wynalda, Eric *professional soccer player*
Wynar, Bohdan Stephen *retired librarian, writer, editor*
Wyngaarden, James Barnes *retired physician*
Wyrtki, Klaus *oceanography educator*
Wyse, Jason LaMar *music educator, director*
Xi, Cecilia Q. *research scientist*
Xia, Guohua *scientist, psychiatrist, psychologist*
Xia, Yusen *education educator*
Xiang, Hui *biochemist, researcher*
Xiong, Liufeng *research scientist*
Xoubi, Ned *nuclear engineer*
Xu, Dongming *engineer, researcher*
Xue, Yibin *metallurgist, educator*
Yack, Patrick Ashley *editor*
Yackel, James William *mathematician, academic administrator*
Yadeka, Theophilus Adeniyi *hospital administrator*
Yadrick, Robert Martin *occupational analyst*
Yaffe, Sumner Jason *pediatrician, educator, science administrator*
Yalam, Arnold Robert *allergist, immunologist, consultant*
Yale (Yeleyenide-Yale), Melpomene Fotine *researcher, anthropologist, archaeologist, art historian, conservator*
Yamaguchi, Kenneth Steven *chemistry professor*
Yamamoto, Joe *retired psychiatrist, educator*
Yampolsky, Phyllis *artist*
Yandle, Stephen Thomas *dean*
Yang, Bing-Shiang *engineering educator*
Yang, Schuman Chuo *music educator*
Yannella, Donald *literature and language professor*
Yao, Frances *music educator, small business owner*
Yarbrough, Kathryn Davis *public health nurse*
Yarbrough, Matthew E. *lawyer*
Yarchoan, Robert *clinical immunologist, researcher*
Yarrow, Peter *folksinger*
Yarymovych, Michael Ihor *retired manufacturing company executive*
Yastine, Barbara A. *former diversified financial services company executive*
Yates, David John C. *chemist, researcher*
Yates, Ronald Eugene *newspaper editor, educator, author, journalist*
Yates, Steven A. *curator, artist*
Yau, Siu-Tung *physics professor*
Yawney, Trent *former professional hockey coach, retired professional hockey player*
Yeadon, Tammy Pamela *information specialist*
Yeager, Dennis Randall *lawyer*
Yeager, Kurt Eric *research and development company executive*
Yeager, Phillip Charles *transportation company executive*
Yearwood, Trisha *country music singer, songwriter*
Yee, Henry Chan Myint *cardiologist*
Yeh, Ying-Yu Emily *music educator*
Yeliseev, Alexei Arkadievich *biochemist, researcher*
Yerrick, Randy Kregg *science educator*
Yglesias, Rafael Jose *novelist*
Yielding, K. Lemone *physician*
Ying, Jinfa *chemist*
Ying, John L. *manufacturing executive*
Yingling, Phyllis Stuckey *writer*
Yiotis, Gayle *archivist, researcher, anthropologist, writer*
Yocam, Delbert Wayne *retired software products company executive*
Yodaiken, Ralph E. *pathologist, occupational health physician, educator*
Yoder, Kristine E. *molecular biologist, educator*
Yoder, Randall D. *music educator*
Yohe, Harry Edward, Jr. *special education educator*
Yollick, Bernard Lawrence *otolaryngologist, surgeon*
Yong, Raymond Nen-Yiu *civil engineering educator*
Yontz, Kenneth Fredric *medical and chemical company executive*
Yoon, Bogum *literacy educator*
Yoon, E. Yul *retired career officer*
Yoon, Jeong Whan *research scientist, educator*
Yopconka, Natalie Ann Catherine *secretary officer, computer specialist, educator, entrepreneur, small business owner*
York, David P. *former prosecutor*
York, Herbert Frank *university official*
York, James Wesley, Jr. *theoretical physicist, educator*
York, Jerome B. *investment company executive, former computer retail executive*
York, Joan Elizabeth Smith *psychologist*
Yoshizumi, Marc O. *ophthalmologist, educator*
Yost, William Albert *psychology professor*
Youmans, Julian Ray *neurosurgeon, educator*
Young, Alfred Byron *neurosurgeon*
Young, Andrew Jackson, Jr. *civil rights leader, pastor, retired mayor, ambassador, congressman*
Young, Barry Harrison *retired mathematician, mechanical engineer*
Young, Burt *actor*
Young, Charles Edward *former academic administrator*
Young, David Michael *biochemist, molecular biologist, internist, educator*
Young, Dona Davis Gagliano *insurance company executive, lawyer*
Young, Edwin S. W. *federal agency official*
Young, Elizabeth Bell *organization consultant*
Young, Frank Edward *retired federal agency and religious organization administrator*
Young, Gail Diane *secondary school educator*
Young, George Haywood III *investment banker*
Young, Jacqueline Eurn Hai *former state legislator, consultant*
Young, James E. *real estate company executive, consultant, engineer*
Young, Jay Maitland *health products executive, consultant*
Young, Jeremy Edward *systems engineer*
Young, John Hardin *lawyer*
Young, John Watts *retired astronaut*
Young, Judith Anne *animal conservationist*
Young, Marlene Annette *lawyer*
Young, Patrick *editor, writer*
Young, Richard Alan *association executive*
Young, Robert Bond *lawyer*
Young, Ruth Brooks *retired elementary school educator*
Young, Sherilyn Burnett *lawyer*
Young, Teresa Gail Hilger *retired adult education educator*
Young, Thomas Lee *lawyer*
Young, Tzay Y. *electrical and computer engineering educator*
Youngblood, Sandra Lea *retired secondary school educator*
Youngblood, Sylvia T. *counselor*
Youngs, Diane Campfield *learning disabilities specialist, educator*
Younker, Kathleen Teuber *pianist, music educator*
Youst, David Bennett *career development educator*
Yu, Jessica *director, producer, writer, editor*
Yu, Robert Kuan-jen *biochemistry professor*
Yu, Tian-En *musician, music educator*
Yue, Alfred Shui-Choh *metallurgical engineer, consultant*
Yuen, Stanley Manfung *engineering company executive, electrical engineer*
Yuksel, Murat *computer scientist, educator*
Yun, James Kyoon *electrical engineer*
Yung, Patsy P. *lawyer*
Yunis, Jorge Jose *anatomy, pathology, and microbiology educator*
Yurasko, Frank Noel *judge*
Yurechko, John Joseph *federal agency administrator, director*
Yuriko, (Yuriko Kikuchi) *dancer, choreographer*
Yzaguirre, Raul Humberto *civil rights leader*
Zabetakis, Paul Michael *nephrologist, educator*
Zacarías, Fernando R. K. *physician*
Zacharias, Donald Wayne *retired academic administrator*
Zachary, Je'Quita Yvette *elementary school educator, singer*
Zack, Daniel Gerard *library consultant*
Zaferson, William S. *philosophy educator, publisher*
Zaffino, Michael J. *social studies educator*
Zaghloul, Dina Amal *quality assurance professional, consultant*
Zahn, Paula *newscaster*
Zahner Kraeft, Dorothy Simkin *retired elementary school educator, school librarian*
Zahran, Mohamed Mostafa *electrical engineer, educator*
Zaidi, Asad R. *medical products executive, biomedical engineer*
Zais, Mitchell M. *career military officer*
Zajac, John *semiconductor equipment company executive*
Zakim, David *biochemist*
Zakim, Tom Edward *history professor*
Zaktsman, Yona R. *business owner*
Zaleski, Jan Franciszek *biochemist*
Zaleski, Jean *artist*
Zaltman, Mark Allen *federal agency administrator*
Zanetti, Teresa A. *state representative*
Zanjacomo, Paulo Regis *engineering executive*
Zapf, Hermann *book and type designer*
Zappa, Gail *record producer*
Zappe, John Paul *city editor, newspaper executive, educator*
Zarb, Frank Gustave *investment company executive*
Zarins, Bertram *orthopedic surgeon*
Zaros, Wendy Cecilia *soprano, educator*
Zarro, Janice Anne *lawyer*
Zatsiorsky, Vladimir Moiseevich (Michailovich) *biomechanics educator, researcher*
Zauder, Gail S. *investment banker*
Zawacki, Bruce Edwin *surgeon, educator, ethicist*
Zazzali, James R. *retired state supreme court justice*
Zdanis, Richard Albert *academic administrator*
Zebroski, Edwin Leopold *risk management consultant*
Zeffren, Eugene *cosmetics executive*
Zehr, Norman Robert *retired association administrator*
Zeiger, Mikhail *composer, concert pianist*
Zeigler, George Gavin *painter, sculptor*
Zeilberger, Doron *mathematics professor, researcher*
Zeilig, Nancy Meeks *writer, editor*
Zekman, Terri Margaret *graphic designer*
Zelaya, Ian A. *biologist, consultant*
Zelazny, Gary A. *dermatologist*
Zelinski, Joseph John *engineering educator, consultant*
Zelinsky, Paul O. *illustrator, artist, writer*
Zelizer, Julian E. *historian, educator*
Zeller, Joseph Paul *advertising executive*
Zeller, Michael Eugene *lawyer*
Zellers, Robert Charles *materials engineer, consultant, speaker*
Zerger, Kirsten Louise *mediator, lawyer*
Zerman, Melvyn Bernard *retired publishing executive, writer*
Zgaljardic, Dennis Joseph *clinical neuropsychologist*
Zhang, Guili *statistician, educator*
Zhang, Jiawei *finance educator*
Zhang, Li *engineer, researcher, educator*
Zhang, Ming *business and management consultant*
Zhang, Shibao *electrical engineer*
Zhang, Yanwen *physicist*
Zhao, Hong *biomedical engineer, educator*
Zhao, Kezhong *electrical engineer*
Zhao, Xueheng *research scientist*
Zhao, Zhen *music educator*
Zharikov, Alexander Nikolaevich *trade union federation executive*
Zhdanov, Boris *research scientist*
Zheng, Lingyi Albert *materials scientist, materials engineer, researcher*
Zhou, Dazhuang *aerospace scientist, researcher*
Zhou, Pengbo *medical educator*
Zhou, Shao Man *chemist, researcher*
Zhou, Yiqun *humanities educator*
Zhu, Yingwu *application developer, educator*
Zhu, Yong *research scientist*
Ziegler, Gwendolyn Woods *minister, consultant*
Ziegler, Jack (Jack Denmore) *cartoonist*
Ziegler, James L. *marketing executive*
Ziegler, John Augustus, Jr. *lawyer*
Ziegler, William Alexander *lawyer*
Ziemba, Karen *actress*
Zien, Chip *actor*
Zierler, Neal *retired mathematician*
Zilbert, Allen Bruce *education educator, computer scientist, consultant*
Zilkha, Ezra Khedouri *banker*
Zimet, Lloyd *sport psychologist, health educator, program planner and administrator*
Zimmatore, John Joseph *information technology manager*
Zimmer, Markus Bernhard *legal association administrator*
Zimmerman, Harold Samuel *retired state legislator, publishing executive, state agency administrator*
Zimmerman, Helene Loretta *retired business educator*
Zimmerman, Jean *lawyer*
Zimmerman, Jo Ann *retired health science association administrator, educator, retired lieutenant governor*
Zimmerman, Marlin U., Jr. *chemical engineer*
Zimmerman, Phyllis Elaine *music educator, composer, director*
Zimmerman, William Edwin *editor, writer*
Zimmermann, Philip R. *software engineer, consultant*
Zimmermann, Thomas Callander Price *retired historian, educator*
Zimmern-Reed, Annette Wacks *psychologist*
Zimny, Max *labor union administrator, lawyer, arbitrator*
Zimov, Bruce Steven *software engineer*
Zinn, Howard *historian, educator, playwright*
Zinnen, Robert Oliver *management consultant, consultant*
Zinser, Elisabeth Ann *former academic administrator*
Zipf, Jennifer E. *marketing professional*
Zischke, Douglas Arthur *foreign service officer*
Zischke, Michael Herman *lawyer*
Zivelonghi, Kurt Daniel *painter, computer graphics artist, designer*
Zoe, Rachel (Rachel Zoe Rosenzweig) *fashion stylist*
Zoeller, Donald J. *lawyer*
Zohn, Martin Steven *lawyer*
Zou, Dekun *research scientist*
Zsigmond, Vilmos *cinematographer, film director*
Zuber, Catherine *costume designer*
Zubov, Sergei *professional hockey player*
Zuck, Alfred Miller *public administration educator*
Zucker, Alexander *physicist, researcher*
Zuckerberg, Mark Elliot *Internet company executive, entrepreneur, programmer*
Zuckerman, Harriet *sociologist, educator*
Zufryden, Fred S. *academic administrator, finance educator, researcher*
Zuiches, James Joseph *sociologist, educator*
Zuick, Ernest Ronald, Jr. *career officer, advertising executive*
Zuker, Charles S. *neuroscientist, biology professor*
Zulauf, Sander (Sander William Zulauf) *poet, educator, editor*
Zumwalt, Ross Eugene *forensic pathologist, educator*
Zupsic, Matthew Michael *insurance company executive*
Zwerling, Gary Leslie *retired investment company executive*
Zwick, Edward M. *director, producer, scriptwriter*
Zwislocki, Jozef John *neuroscience educator, researcher*

Professional Index

AGRICULTURE

UNITED STATES

ALABAMA

Auburn University
Mosjidis, Jorge *agricultural studies educator, researcher*

ARKANSAS

Fayetteville
Kellogg, David Wayne *agricultural studies educator, researcher*

CALIFORNIA

Fresno
Epperson, Robert Dale *farmer*

Livingston
Foster, Ron *agricultural products supplier and executive*

Modesto
Gallo, Joseph E. *vintner*

Napa
Chiarella, Peter Ralph *vintner*

Pacific Palisades
Jennings, Marcella Grady *rancher, investor*

San Francisco
Hills, Austin Edward *vineyard executive*

San Jose
D'Arrigo, Stephen, Jr. *agricultural company executive*

COLORADO

Denver
McFarlane, Willis McKee *buffalo company executive*

Fort Collins
Hughes, Harrison G. *horticulture educator*

Montrose
Kontny, Vincent L. *rancher, retired engineering executive*

Springfield
Wessler, Melvin Dean *farmer, rancher*

FLORIDA

Gainesville
Hochmuth, George J. *horticultural educator*
Nair, Ramachandran P.K. *agroforestry educator, researcher*
Seale, James Lawrence, Jr. *agricultural studies educator, trade association administrator, researcher*

Ocala
Ray, Ruth Alice Yancey *retired rancher, real estate developer*

HAWAII

Honolulu
Ching, Chauncey Tai Kin *agricultural studies educator, economist*

ILLINOIS

Chicago
McCutcheon, Jennifer Lynne *horse breeder, lawyer*

Deerfield
Wilson, Stephen Ray *fertilizer manufacturing company executive*

Pleasant Plains
Thomas, Evelyn B. *agricultural products supplier*

Urbana
Hoeft, Robert Gene *agricultural studies educator*
Spitze, Robert George Frederick *agricultural studies educator*

INDIANA

Fort Wayne
Marine, Clyde Lockwood *agricultural products supplier, consultant*

Indianapolis
Hegel, Carolyn Marie *farm owner and organization executive*

West Lafayette
Lechtenberg, Victor L. *agricultural studies educator*

IOWA

Akron
Hultgren, Dennis Eugene *farmer, management consultant*

Ames
Retallick, Michael S. *agricultural studies educator, director*
Topel, David Glen *agricultural studies educator*

Indianola
Mapel, Patricia Jolene *farmer, consultant*

KANSAS

Chetopa
Reid, William R. *agricultural studies educator*

Claflin
Burmeister, Paul Frederick *farmer*

Iola
Strickler, Ivan K. *dairy farmer*

Manhattan
McKee, Richard Miles *retired agricultural studies educator*

KENTUCKY

Princeton
McNeill, Samuel Gaither *farm management extension agent, educator, engineering educator*

MICHIGAN

Ann Arbor
Heydon, Peter Northrup *farmer, educator, philanthropist*

MINNESOTA

Canby
Larson, Gary Arthur *farmer, financial consultant*

Goodridge
Hanson, Norma Lee *farmer*

MISSISSIPPI

Ackerman
James, Lee J. *agriculture educator*

Starkville
Gregg, Billy Ray *seed industry executive, consultant*

MISSOURI

Sturgeon
Fashing, Edward Michael *ranch owner, physical science educator*

NEBRASKA

Chadron
Younglove, Georgia A. *agricultural studies educator*

NEVADA

Yerington
Scatena, Lorraine Borba *retired rancher, women's rights advocate, researcher*

NEW YORK

Pine Island
Rogowski, Cheryl *farmer*

NORTH DAKOTA

Erie
Pueppke, Glenn Howard *farmer, agricultural products executive*

OHIO

Columbus
Ockerman, Herbert W. *agricultural studies educator*

PENNSYLVANIA

Dillsburg
Smith, William Raymond *farmer, horse breeder*

SOUTH DAKOTA

Saint Lawrence
Lockner, Vera Joanne *farmer, rancher, state legislator*

TENNESSEE

Hickory Valley
Weaver, Peggy (Marguerite McKinnie Weaver) *plantation owner*

Nashville
Thompson, Dean Allan *cattleman*

TEXAS

College Station
Gan, Jianbang *agricultural studies educator, economist*

Guthrie
Marion, Anne Windfohr *rancher, museum administrator*

Industry
Huitt, Jimmie L. *rancher, oil and gas industry executive, real estate developer*

Valley View
Wallace, Donald John III *rancher*

VIRGINIA

Baskerville
Boyd, John W., Jr. *farmer, association executive*

Greenville
Todd, John Edward *retired farmer*

WASHINGTON

Pullman
Clement, Stephen Le Roy *agricultural researcher*

WEST VIRGINIA

Charles Town
McDonald, Angus Wheeler *farmer*

WYOMING

Lander
Raynolds, David Robert *buffalo breeder, writer*

ADDRESS UNPUBLISHED

Barrett, Barbara McConnell *ranch owner, lawyer*
Berry, Wendell *farmer, author*
Brooks, Kenneth N. *forestry educator*
Bruland, Gregory Lee *agricultural studies educator*
Downing, Daniel Leon *agricultural studies educator*
Erwin, Elmer Louis *vintager, consultant*
Jacobson, Norman L. *retired agricultural educator, researcher*
Johnson, Maurice Verner, Jr. *agricultural research and development executive*
Jordan, John Frederick *farmer, consultant*
Kriz, George James *retired agricultural research administrator*
Luening, Robert Adami *retired agricultural studies educator*
Pfantz, Craig D. *farmer*
Stimpert, Michael Alan *retired agricultural products company executive*
Voss, Omer Gerald *farm equipment executive*
Webb, O. Glenn *retired farm supplies company executive*

ARCHITECTURE & DESIGN

UNITED STATES

ALABAMA

Auburn
Millman, Richard George *architect, educator*

Birmingham
Barrow, Richard Edward *architect*
Gilchrist, William Aaron *architect*

ALASKA

Anchorage
Maynard, Kenneth Douglas *architect*

ARIZONA

Green Valley
Johnson, Charles Foreman *architectural firm executive*

Payson
Hershberger, Robert Glen *architect, educator*

Phoenix
Elmore, James Walter *architect, educator, retired dean*
Gwozdz, Kim Elizabeth *interior designer, furniture designer*
Hawkins, Jasper Stillwell, Jr. *architect*
Jones, Eddie *architect*
Schiffner, Charles Robert *architect*

Scottsdale
Brown, Shirley Margaret Kern (Peggy Brown) *interior designer*
Lloyd-Lee, Beverly *interior designer*
Wong, Joe Bing *retired architect*

Sonoita
Cook, William Howard *architect*

Tempe
Thums, Charles William *designer, consultant*

Tucson
Nelson, Edward Humphrey *architect*
Robles, Maricela *architect*
Seehausen, Richard Ferdinand *architect*
Wallach, Leslie Rothaus *architect*

ARKANSAS

Little Rock
Chilcote, Lugean Lester *retired architect, researcher*
Levy, Eugene Pfeifer *architectural firm executive, architect*
Truemper, John James, Jr. *retired architect*

Winslow
Burggraf, Frank Bernard, Jr. *landscape architect, retired educator*

CALIFORNIA

Bakersfield
McAlister, Michael H. *architect*

Belvedere
Hugenberg, Patricia Ellen Petrie *product designer*

Berkeley
Brocchini, Ronald Gene *architect*
Cardwell, Kenneth Harvey *architect, educator*
Cranz, Galen *architecture educator, sociologist*
Stoller, Claude *architect*
Walker, Peter *landscape architect*

Chula Vista
Weiss-Cornwell, Amy *interior designer*

Corona Del Mar
Jacobs, Donald Paul *architect*
Yeo, Ron *architect*

Culver City
Ehrlich, Steven David *architect*
Moss, Eric Owen *architect*
Sussman, Deborah Evelyn *interior designer, small business owner*

El Cerrito
Burger, Edmund Ganes *architect*

El Segundo
Jones, Wes *architect*

Fresno
Darden, Edwin Speight, Sr. *architect*
Patnaude, William Eugene *architect*
Pings, Anthony Claude *architect*

Greenbrae
Tyng, Anne Griswold *architect*

Huntington Beach
Foose, Chip *automotive designer, television personality*

Irvine
Kraemer, Kenneth Leo *architect, urban planner, educator*

Laguna Niguel
Axon, Donald Carlton *architect*

Laguna Woods
Badgley, John Roy *architect*

Los Angeles
Dworsky, Daniel Leonard *architect, educator*
Fickett, Edward Hale *architect, educator, arbitrator*
Gehry, Frank Owen *architect*
Landry, Richard *architect*
Maltzan, Michael Thomas *architect*
Man, Lawrence Kong *architect, art dealer*
Moe, Stanley Allen *architect, consultant*
Neutra, Dion *architect*
Noble, Douglas *architecture educator*
Phelps, Barton Chase *architect, educator*

Manhattan Beach
Blanton, John Arthur *architect, writer*

Mill Valley
D'Amico, Michael *architect, urban planner*

Mojave
Rutan, Burt (Elbert Leander Rutan) *aircraft designer, aircraft company executive*

Monterey Park
Goei, Bernard Thwan-Poo (Bert Goei) *retired architectural and engineering firm executive*

Mountain View
Kobza, Dennis Jerome *architect*

Newport Beach
Bissell, George Arthur *architect*
Blankenship, Edward G. *architect*
Richardson, Walter John *architect*

Novato
Thompson, Peter Layard Hailey, Sr. *landscape and golf course architect, architectural firm executive*

Oxnard
O'Connell, Hugh Mellen, Jr. *retired architect*

Palo Alto
Lucente, Sam *industrial designer*

Pasadena
Thomas, Joseph Fleshman *retired architect*

Riverside
Deal, Kevin Paul *furniture designer*

Sacramento
Lionakis, George *architect*
Wasserman, Barry L(ee) *architect*

Saint Helena
Backen, Howard J. *architect*

San Diego
Delawie, Homer Torrence *retired architect*
Quigley, Rob Wellington *architect*
Stepner, Michael Jay *architect*

San Francisco
Béhar, Yves *industrial designer*
Bull, Henrik Helkand *architect*
Del Campo, Martin Bernardelli *architect*
Ellis, John *urban designer*
Field, John Louis *architect*
Gensler, M. Arthur, Jr. *architect*
Jennings, Jim *architect*
Judd, Bruce Diven *architect*
Kriken, John Lund *architect*
Minar, Paul G. *interior designer, consultant*
Moris, Lamberto Giuliano *architect*
Raeber, John Arthur *architect, construction consultant*
Warnecke, John Carl *architect*

San Jose
Tanaka, Richard Koichi, Jr. *architect, planner*

San Luis Obispo
Deasy, Cornelius Michael *retired architect*

San Marcos
Harmon, Harry William *architect, former university administrator*

San Mateo
Pfeffer, Patrick *architect*

San Rafael
Manny, Carter Hugh, Jr. *architect, foundation administrator*

Santa Barbara
Burgee, John Henry *architect*
Cung, Thiep H. *architectural firm executive*
Kruger, Kenneth Charles *architect*
Pochini, Judy Hay *interior designer, writer, editor*

Santa Monica
Appleton, Marc *architect*
Mayne, Thom *architect*
Ruble, John *architect*
Yudell, Buzz (Robert Yudell) *architect*

Sausalito
Sinclair, Cameron *architect*

South Pasadena
Girvigian, Raymond *architect*

Stanford
Eustis, Robert Henry *design company executive, mechanical engineer*

Tarzana
Smith, Mark Lee *architect*

Turlock
Shirvani, Sir Hamid *architect, educator, philosopher, writer, university president*

Walnut Creek
Costa, Walter Henry *architect*
Hassid, Sami *architect, educator*

COLORADO

Broomfield
Williams, John James, Jr. *architect*

Denver
Abo, Ronald Kent *freelance/self-employed architect*
Anderson, John David *architect*
Brownson, Jacques Calmon *architect*
Dominick, Peter Hoyt, Jr. *architect*
Fuller, Robert Kenneth *architect, urban designer*
Hoover, George Schweke *architect*
Prosser, John Martin *architecture educator*

Fort Collins
Grandin, Temple *industrial designer, science educator*

Fort Garland
Boyer, Lester Leroy, Jr. *architecture educator, consultant*

Grand Junction
Burdick, Margaret Seale (Marge Burdick) *interior designer*

Littleton
Shepherd, Donna Lou *interior designer*

Vail
Vosbeck, Robert Randall *architect*

CONNECTICUT

Centerbrook
Grover, William Herbert *architect*

Cheshire
Rowland, Ralph Thomas *retired architect*

Greenwich
Matthaei, Gay Humphrey *interior designer*
Wharton, Bernard Mapes *architect*

Hamden
Roche, (Eamonn) Kevin *architect*

Hartford
Amatuli, Robert Alexander *architect*

New Britain
Mooney, Kenneth Frank *design educator*

New Canaan
Dean, Robert Bruce *architect*
Papp, Laszlo George *retired architect*
Risom, Jens *furniture designer, consultant, manufacturing executive*

New Haven
Bloomer, Kent Cress *architecture educator*
Chilton, William David *architect*
Newick, Craig David *architect*
Pelli, Cesar *architect*
Roth, Harold *architect*

Niantic
Butler, Jonathan Putnam *architect*
Danos, Harry John *architect, educator, artist*

Northford
Gregan, Edmund Robert *landscape architect*

South Kent
Baker, John Milnes *architect*

Stonington
Stoddard, Alexandra *interior designer, educator, writer*

Trumbull
Watson, Donald Ralph *architect, dean, writer, artist*

DELAWARE

Newark
Stick, Thomas Howard Fitchett *architect, construction litigation consultant*

DISTRICT OF COLUMBIA

Washington
Bagnoli, David Christopher *architect*
Birnbaum, Charles A. *landscape architect*
Coffin, Beatriz de Winthuysen *landscape architect*
Cox, Warren Jacob *architect*
Gentner, Paul LeFoe *architect, consultant*
Greene, Thomas Hardy *architect*
Hartman, George Eitel *architect*
Holladay, Wilhelmina Cole *interior designer, museum director*
Jacobsen, Hugh Newell *architect*
Kulski, Julian Eugeniusz *architect, writer*
Lewis, Anne McCutcheon *architect*
Lewis, Roger Kutnow *architect, educator, author*
Liebenson, Gloria Krasnow *interior design executive, freelance writer*
Miller, Ewing Harry *retired architect*
Murray, Christopher Charles III *architect*
Oehme, Wolfgang Walter *landscape architect*
Ramberg, Walter Dodd *architect*
Schlesinger, B. Frank *architect, educator*
Shepherd, Leslie L. *architect*
Siegel, Lloyd Harvey *architect, real estate developer, consultant*
Woofter, Vivien Perrine *interior designer, consultant*
Yerkes, David Norton *architect*

FLORIDA

Bal Harbour
Spiegel, Siegmund *architect*

Boca Raton
Harris, S. Buddy *architect, interior designer*

Coral Gables
Heisenbottle, Richard John *architect*

Daytona Beach
Amick, William Walker *golf course architect*

Delray Beach
Rippeteau, Darrel Downing *retired architect*

Fort Myers
Sappenfield, Charles Madison *architect, educator*
Trudnak, Stephen Joseph *landscape architect*

Gainesville
Kohen, Martha *architecture educator*

Jacksonville
Morgan, William Newton *architect, educator*

Miami
Arango, Jorge Sanin *architect*
Chisholm, Robert E. *architect*
Feito, Jose *architect*
Hampton, Mark Garrison *architect*
Shulman, Allan T. *architect*
Spear, Laurinda Hope *architect*

Miramar
Stewart Simpson, Donnamay Angela *interior designer*

Naples
Bradley, Charles MacArthur *retired architect*
Lewis, Gordon Gilmer *golf course architect*
Lickhalter, Merlin *architect*

Orlando
Hsu, C.T. *architect*

Oviedo
Duda, Richard Frank *architect, engineering executive*

Palm Beach
Smith, Jeffery W. *architect*

Pensacola
Bullock, Ellis Way, Jr. *architect*
Woolf, Kenneth Howard *architect*

Saint Augustine
Wilkes, Delano Angus *architect*

Saint Petersburg
Wedding, Charles Randolph *architect*

Sebastian
Lagin, Neil *landscape designer, consultant*

Stuart
Ankrom, Charles Franklin *golf course architect, consultant*

Tallahassee
Lewis, Tom E., Jr. *architect*

Tampa
Howey, John Richard *architect, writer*
Jennewein, James Joseph *architect*

Vero Beach
Ahrens, William Henry *architect*
Gibson, James Elliott *architect*

West Palm Beach
Marshall-Beasley, Elizabeth *landscape architect*
Ross, Edward Joseph *architect*

Winter Haven
Burns, Arthur Lee *architect*

GEORGIA

Atlanta
Bainbridge, Frederick Freeman III *architect*
Bull, Frank James *retired architect*
Cooper, Jerome Maurice *architect*
Diedrich, Richard Joseph *architect*
Guest, Rita Carson *interior designer*
Hatch, Helen Davis *architect*
Lewcock, Ronald Bentley *architect, educator*
Peponis, John *architect, educator*
Portman, John C., Jr. *architect, developer*
Pulgram, William Leopold *architect, space designer*
Sizemore, Michael Maynard *architectural firm executive*

Augusta
Woodhurst, Robert Stanford, Jr. *architect*

Decatur
Mc Intosh, James Eugene, Jr. *interior designer*

Hiram
Stevens, Charles Thomas, Sr. *drafting technology educator*

Kingsland
Huygens, Remmert William *architect*

Macon
Dunwody, Eugene Cox *architect*

Saint Simons Island
Webb, Lamar Thaxter *architect*

HAWAII

Honolulu
Botsai, Elmer Eugene *architect, educator, retired dean*
Hamada, Duane Takumi *architect*
Steinmann, John Colburn *architect*
Yeh, Raymond Wei-Hwa *architect, educator*

Waipahu
Chang, Walter Tuck, Sr. *draftsman, real estate agent, religious studies educator*

IDAHO

Boise
Hunsucker, (Carl) Wayne *architectural firm executive, educator*

ILLINOIS

Bloomington
Switzer, Jon Rex *architect*

Champaign
Baker, Jack Sherman *architect, educator*
Boubekri, Mohamed *architecture educator*
Hopkins, Lewis Dean *architecture educator*
Riley, Robert Bartlett *landscape architect*

Chicago
Balasi, Mark Geoffrey *architect*
Barney, Carol Ross *architect*
Belluschi, Anthony C. *architect*
Brininstool, David *architect*
Epstein, Sidney *architect, civil engineer*
Gang, Jeanne *architect*
Garofalo, Douglas *architectural firm executive, educator*
Gold, Allan Harold *architect, structural engineer, educator*
Hackl, Donald John *architect*
Holabird, John Augur, Jr. *retired architect*
Kerbis, Gertrude Lempp *architect*
Kerwin, Thomas P. *architect*
Legge Kemp, Diane *architect, landscape consultant*
Mack, Alan Wayne *interior designer*
Matthei, Edward Hodge *architect*
McCullagh, Grant Gibson *retired architect*
McCurry, Margaret Irene *architect, furniture, interior designer, educator*
Phillips, Frederick Falley *architect*
Robertson, Donna Virginia *architect, educator, dean*
Ronan, John *architect*
Schroeder, Douglas Fredrick *architect*
Smith, Adrian Devaun *architect*
Tigerman, Stanley *architect, educator*
Torgersen, Torwald Harold *architect, consultant*
VanderBeke, Patricia K. *architect*
Weber, Hanno *architect*
Weese, Benjamin Horace *architect*
Wheeler, Daniel Harding *architect, educator*
Whitney, Patrick Foster *design educator*
Wimer, Ross *architect*
Zheng, James *architectural firm executive*

Evanston
Grunsfeld, Ernest Alton III *architect*
Macsai, John *retired architect*

Highland Park
Dirsmith, Ronald *architect*
Dubin, Arthur Detmers *retired architect*
Tobin, Calvin Jay *retired architect*

Hinsdale
Unikel, Eva Taylor *interior designer*

Kenilworth
Schneider-Criezis, Susan Marie *architect*

Lake Zurich
Krolopp, Rudolph William *retired industrial designer, consultant*

Peoria
Budzinski, Ronald J. *architect*
Golan, Kim Marie *facility interior designer*

Plainfield
Vargo, Louise Ann *landscape artist, music educator*

Schaumburg
Otis, James, Jr. *architect*

Skokie
Siegal, Burton Lee *product designer, consultant, inventor*

Tinley Park
Lobes, Mark Robert *graphic design educator, coach*

Wheaton
Martin, Marcia Gray *retired architecture educator, artist, designer*

Winnetka
Piper, Robert Johnston *retired architect, urban planner*
Schlossman, John Isaac *architect*

INDIANA

Bloomington
Lim, Youn-kyung *design educator*

Carmel
Eden, Barbara Janiece *commercial and residential interior designer*
McLaughlin, Harry Roll *architect*

Indianapolis
Elvin, George *architecture educator*

Mishawaka
Ponko, William Reuben *architect*
Troyer, LeRoy Seth *architect*

Notre Dame
Stamper, John W. *architecture educator, academic administrator*

South Bend
Horsbrugh, Patrick *architect, educator, environologist*
Smith, Thomas Gordon *architect*

IOWA

Ames
Lewis, Calvin Fred *architect, educator*
Palermo, Gregory Sebastian *architect*

Clear Lake
Broshar, Robert Clare *retired architect*

Iowa City
Neumann, Roy Covert *architect*

KANSAS

Lawrence
Grabow, Stephen Harris *architecture educator*

Manhattan
Foerster, Bernd *architecture educator*

Overland Park
Cummings, Jan Norman *interior designer, educator*

Topeka
Karst, Gary Gene *retired architect*
Slemmons, Robert Sheldon *architect*

KENTUCKY

Lexington
Romanowitz, Byron Foster *architect, engineer*

LOUISIANA

Baton Rouge
Reich, Robert Sigmund *landscape architect*

Bogalusa
Gallaspy, Dixie *interior designer, innkeeper*

Metairie
Fuhrmann, Emile Frederick *architect*

New Orleans
Ball, F. Macnaughton, Jr. *architect*
Bookhardt, Fred Barringer, Jr. *architect*
Dumez, Steve *architect*
Frantz, Phares Albert *architect*
Klingman, John Philip *architect, educator*
Mathes, Edward Conrad *architect*
Waggonner, Joseph David III *architect*

MAINE

Edgecomb
Carlson, Suzanne Olive *architect*

New Gloucester
Jaccaci, August Thayer, Jr. *social architect, educator*

New Harbor
Fradley, Frederick Macdonell *retired architect*

Seal Harbor
Forbes, Peter *architect*

York
Lyman, William Welles, Jr. *retired architect*

MARYLAND

Annapolis
Jansson, John Phillip *architect, consultant*
Miller, Richards Thorn *naval architect, engineer*

Baltimore
Adams, Harold Lynn *architect*
Askew, Laurin Barker, Jr. *architect*
Brodie, Menasha Jacob (Jay) *architect, city planner, government executive*
Donkervoet, Richard Cornelius *architect*
Snead, James Arrington *architect*

Bowie
Stone, Edward Harris, II, *landscape architect*

Chevy Chase
Auerbach, Seymour *architect*

Olney
Delmar, Eugene Anthony *architect*

Rockville
Morgan, William Bruce *naval architect*

Severna Park
Allison, John Langsdale *naval architect, marine engineer*

Takoma Park
DeVaris, Panayotis Eric *architect*

MASSACHUSETTS

Amherst
Cornish, Geoffrey St. John *golf course architect*

Bedford
Payne, Harry Morse, Jr. *architect*
Shepley, Hugh *architect*

Boston
Collins, James H., Jr. *architectural firm executive*
Costa, Daniel Lawrence *architect*
Finegold, Maurice Nathan *architect*
Goody, Joan Edelman *architect*
Harkness, John Cheesman *retired architect*
Klema, Donald David *architect*
Pisani, Anthony Michael *architect*
Ponce de Leon, Monica *architect*
Rawn, William Leete III *architect*
Stull, Donald LeRoy *architect*
Sullivan Stemberg, Maureen *interior designer*
Tappé, Albert Anthony *architect*
Tehrani, Nader *architect*

Cambridge
Anderson, Stanford Owen *architect, architectural historian, educator*
Campbell, Robert *architect, writer*
Gund, Graham *architectural firm executive*
Hamner, W. Easley *architect*
Kobus, Richard Lawrence *architect*
Kruger, Kenneth *architect*
Porter, William Lyman *architect, educator*
Rabbat, Nasser O. *architecture educator*
Ratti, Carlo Filippo *architect, researcher, educator*
Santos, Adèle Naudé *architect, educator*
Tsoi, Edward Tze Ming *architect, urban planner, interior designer*

Concord
Brooker, Richard I. *architect*

Edgartown
Rosenfeld, Walter David, Jr. *architect, writer*

Marblehead
Green, Richard John *architect*

North Andover
Goldstein, Charles Henry *architect, consultant*

Springfield
Engebretson, Douglas Kenneth *architect, interior designer*

Waltham
Notkin, Leonard Sheldon *architect*

Wellesley
Birkerts, Gunnar *architect*

Weston
Wood, Jeremy Scott *architect, urban designer*

Woods Hole
Newman, John Nicholas *naval architect educator*
Suchy, Albert Francis *marine architect*

MICHIGAN

Ann Arbor
Beckley, Robert Mark *architect, educator*
Chaffers, James A. *architect, educator*
Metcalf, Robert Clarence *architect, educator*

Chelsea
Fry, Richard E. *architectural firm executive*
Kendall, Kay Lynn *interior designer, consultant*

Detroit
Francis, Edward D. *architect*
Frank, Richard Calhoun *architect*
Roehling, Carl David *architect*

Flint
Tomblinson, James Edmond *architect*

Flushing
Demankowski, Lisa Renee *architect, educator*

Kalamazoo
Carver, Norman Francis, Jr. *architect, photographer*

South Haven
LaRocque, Linda Lou *interior designer, educator, playwright*

MINNESOTA

Duluth
Salmela, David Daniel *architect*
Whiteman, Richard Frank *architect*

Minneapolis
Clemence, Roger Davidson *landscape architect, educator*
Fulop, Laszlo G. *architect*
Jacob, Bernard Michel *architect*
Martin, Roger Bond *landscape architect*
Swenson, Mark Gregory *architect*

Northfield
Sovik, Edward Anders *architect, consultant*

MISSISSIPPI

Biloxi
Zocchi, Louis Joseph *product designer, game company executive*

Columbus
Kaye, Samuel Harvey *architect, educator*
Rood, Cynthia Hooper *landscape architect, consultant*

Jackson
Burns, Robert, Jr. *retired architect, painter*

Mississippi State
Martin, Edward Curtis, Jr. *landscape architect, educator*

Starkville
Ford, Robert MacDonald III *architect, educator*

MISSOURI

Branson
Ownby, Jerry Steve *landscape architect, educator*

Kansas City
Seligson, Theodore H. *architect, interior designer, urban planner*
Spear, Joseph E. *architect*

Saint Louis
Bextermiller, Theresa Marie *architect, computer engineer*
Cotton, W(illiam) Philip, Jr. *architect*
Lovelace, Eldridge Hirst *retired landscape architect, city planner, civil engineer*
Marti, Paul Edgar, Jr. *architect, educator*
Michaelides, Constantine Evangelos *architect, educator*
Thalden, Barry *architect*
Weese, Cynthia Rogers *architect, educator*

Springfield
Hancock, Timothy Daniel *architect, musician*

Webster Groves
Becker, Rex Louis *architect*

MONTANA

Bozeman
DeHaas, John Neff, Jr. *retired architecture educator*

Great Falls
Davidson, David Scott *retired architect*

NEBRASKA

Lincoln
Stange, James Henry *architect*
Steward, Weldon Cecil *architecture educator, architect, consultant*

Omaha
Polsky, Donald Perry *architect*
Ryan, Mark Anthony *architect, lawyer*

NEVADA

Las Vegas
Marnell, Anthony Austin, II, *architect*

NEW HAMPSHIRE

Hanover
Brooks, H. Allen *architectural educator, author, lecturer*

NEW JERSEY

Bound Brook
Shive, Richard Byron *architect*

Cape May Point
Jordan, Joe J. *architect*

East Orange
Fielo, Muriel Bryant *interior designer*

Englewood
Schmidt, Ronald Hans *architect*

Jersey City
Adlershteyn, Leon *retired marine architect, retired engineering educator and researcher*

Morristown
Nadaskay, Raymond *architect*

Newark
Goldman, Glenn *architect, educator*

Princeton
Allen, Stanley T. *architect, dean, educator*
Diller, Elizabeth E. *architect, educator, artist*
Ford, Jeremiah III *architect*
Graves, Michael *architect, educator*
Hillier, J(ames) Robert *architect*

Somerdale
Botka, Betsy Jean *industrial arts and career awareness instructor*

Sussex
Hoyt, Earl Edward, Jr. *industrial designer*

Trenton
Jones, Sophia LaShawn *architect*

NEW MEXICO

Albuquerque
Foster, Judi *interior designer, artist*
Pirkl, James Joseph *industrial designer, educator, writer*
Predock, Antoine Samuel *architect, educator*
Prince, Bart *architect*

Corrales
Hooker, Van Dorn *architect, educator, artist*

Santa Fe
Franzen, Ulrich J. *architect*
Leon, Bruno *architect, educator*
Mazria, Edward *architectural firm executive*

NEW YORK

Ardsley On Hudson
Guise, David Earl *architect, educator*

Binghamton
Bearsch, Lee Palmer *architect, urban planner*

Bridgehampton
Cook, Peter Halsey *architect*

Bronx
Gaveras, Harry *architect*

Bronxville
Frost, A. Corwin *architect, consultant*

Brooklyn
Rice, John Thomas *architecture educator*

Buffalo
Coles, Robert Traynham *architect*

Cranberry Lake
Glavin, James Edward *landscape architect*

Cross River
Thorn, Susan Howe *interior designer*

Cutchogue
Schulze, Paul *industrial designer, educator*

Dobbs Ferry
Guggenheimer, Tobias Immanuel Simon *architect*

East Hampton
Damaz, Paul F. *architect*
Delson, Sidney Leon *architect*

Hastings On Hudson
Weinstein, Edward Michael *architect, consultant*

Jamaica
Gati, William Eugene *architect, educator, industrial designer*

Kew Gardens
Aldea, Patricia *architect*

Locust Valley
Bentel, Frederick Richard *architect, educator*
Bentel, Paul Louis *architect, educator*

Long Island City
Sadao, Shoji *architect*

New Rochelle
Menzies, Henry Hardinge *architect*

New York
Arad, Michael Sahar *architect*
Aranda, Benjamin *architect*
Baird, Penny Drue *interior designer*
Balmori, Diana *landscape designer*
Bartlett, Elizabeth Easton *interior designer*
Bergdoll, Barry G. *architectural historian, educator*
Bland, Frederick Aves *architect*
Bond, James Max, Jr. *architect, academic administrator*
Borrelli, John Francis *architect*
Brennan, Henry Higginson *architect*
Buatta, Mario *interior designer*
Buttrick, Harold *architect*
Carlson, Richard A. *interior designer*
Chan, Lo-Yi Cheung Yuen *architect*

Childs, David M. *architectural firm executive*
Cobb, Henry Nichols *architect*
Cohn, Ian J. *architect*
Cushing, Charles R. *architectural firm executive*
Cutler, Laurence Stephan *architect, museum administrator, writer, advertising executive, educator*
Czajka, James Vincent *architect*
David, Theoharis Lambros *architect, educator*
Dennis, Diane Joy Milam *retired architect*
De Vido, Alfredo Eduardo *architect*
Edelman, Judith H. *architect*
Eisenman, Peter David *architect, educator*
Fowle, Bruce S. *architect*
Fox, Robert Frederick, Jr. *architect*
Galan, Leonidez Vindollo *architect*
Gatje, Robert Frederick *architect, writer*
Giddens-Jones, Emily Jane *architectural and interior designer, consultant*
Ginsberg, David Lawrence *architect*
Gluck, Peter L. *architect*
Gorlin, Alexander *architect*
Gwathmey, Charles *architect*
Halsband, Frances *architect*
Hardy, Hugh *architect*
Hinz, Theodore Vincent *architect*
Holl, Steven Myron *architect, educator*
Holub, Martin *architect*
Ivy, Robert Adams, Jr. *architect, editor-in-chief*
Kligerman, Thomas Alexander *architect*
Kliment, Robert Michael *architect*
Kliment, Stephen Alexander *architect, editor, journalist*
Kohn, A. Eugene *architect*
Krebs, Carl F. *architectural firm executive*
Lasch, Christopher *architect*
Leavitt, David Livingstone *architect*
Lefferts, Gillet, Jr. *architect*
Libeskind, Daniel *architect*
Liebman, Theodore *architect*
Marino, Peter *architect*
Marvel, Jonathan J. *architect*
Masey, Jack *exhibition designer*
Meier, Richard Alan *architect*
Minskoff, Edward *architectural firm executive*
Pennoyer, Peter Morgan *architect*
Perkins, Lawrence Bradford, Jr. *architect*
Pokorny, Jan Hird *architect, educator*
Polshek, James Stewart *architect*
Pomeroy, Lee Harris *architect*
Prince-Ramus, Joshua *architect*
Quennell, Nicholas *landscape architect, educator*
Robertson, Jaquelin Taylor *architect, educator*
Rogers, Robert M. *architect*
Shamamian, Oscar *architect*
Slomanson, Lloyd Howard *architect, musician, photographer*
Smith-Miller, Henry Houck *architect*
Smotrich, David Isadore *architect*
Solomonoff, Galia *architect*
Sono, Masayuki *architect, artist*
Stern, Robert Arthur Morton *architect, educator, writer*
Taylor, Marilyn Jordan *architectural firm executive*
Tsien, Billie *architect*
Varney, Carleton Bates, Jr. *interior designer, columnist, educator*
Viñoly, Rafael *architectural firm executive*
Voorsanger, Bartholomew *architect*
Wanzenberg, Alan *architect*
Wedlick, Dennis *architect, writer*
Wexler, Allan *architect, educator*
Williams, Tod Culpan *architect, educator*
Wilson, Robin *interior designer*
Woods, Lebbeus *theoretical architect, educator*

Nyack
Degenshein, Jan *architect, planner*

Penfield
Kraft, Donald Eugene *architecture and engineering company executive*

Rye
Rolland, Peter George *landscape architect*

Syracuse
Skoler, Louis *architect, educator*
Smardon, Richard Clay *landscape architect, environmental studies professor*

Troy
Haviland, David Sands *retired architectural educator, researcher, administrator*

Wappingers Falls
Johnson, Jeh Vincent *architect*

Westhampton Beach
Flood, Angela *interior designer, artist*

NORTH CAROLINA

Asheville
King, Joseph Bertram *architect*

Boone
Oelberg, Robert Nathan *landscape architect*

Chapel Hill
Dixon, Frederick Dail *architect*
Godschalk, David Robinson *architect, urban development planner, educator*
Stipe, Robert Edwin *retired design educator*

Charlotte
Ferebee, Stephen Scott, Jr. *retired architect*
Gantt, Harvey B. *architect, former mayor*
Huberman, Jeffrey Allen *architect*
Montague, Edgar Burwell, III, (Monty Montague) *industrial designer*

Kinston
Baker-Gardner, Jewelle *interior designer, business consultant*

Pisgah Forest
Albyn, Richard Keith *retired architect*

Raleigh
Clarke, Lewis James *landscape architect*
Flournoy, William Louis, Jr. *landscape architect*
Malecha, Marvin John *architect, academic administrator*

Research Triangle Park
Atkins, John L. III *architect*

Robbinsville
Ginn, Ronn *architect, urban planner, general contractor*

OHIO

Akron
Castronovo, Thomas Paul *architect, consultant*

Canton
Barkan, John Martin, Jr. *architect*

Celina
Fanning, Ronald Heath *architect, engineer*

Cincinnati
Chatterjee, Jayanta *architecture and planning educator*
Glendening, Everett Austin *architect*
Goetzman, Bruce Edgar *architecture educator*
Luckner, Herman Richard III *interior designer*
Nielsen, George Lee *architect*
Preiser, Wolfgang Friedrich Ernst *architect, educator, consultant, researcher*
Schwartz, Robert Terry *industrial designer, director*
Senhauser, John Crater *architect*

Cleveland
Bowen, Richard Lee *architect*
Eberhard, William Thomas *architect*
Gibans, James David *architect, consultant*
Madison, Robert Prince *architect*
Sande, Theodore Anton *architect, educator, foundation executive*
Zung, Thomas Tse-Kwai *architect*

Columbus
Kirk, Ballard Harry Thurston *architect*
Osgood, Robert T., Jr. *architect, strategic planner*
Voss, Jerrold Richard *architecture educator*

Cuyahoga Falls
Haag, Everett Keith *architect*

Mason
Cuff, Virginia Evelyn *architectural firm executive, consultant*

Painesville
Filson, Ronald Coulter *architect, educator, dean*

Toledo
Martin, Robert Edward *architect*

OKLAHOMA

Norman
Henderson, Arnold Glenn *architect, educator*

Oklahoma City
Halpin, Anna Marie *retired architect*

OREGON

Ashland
Mularz, Theodore Leonard *architect*

Beaverton
Hatfield, Tinker L. *architect, apparel designer, product designer*

Depoe Bay
Eaton, Leonard Kimball *retired architecture educator*

Hillsboro
Dubrulle, Françoise M. *architect, painter, interior designer*
Rueda, Guillermo *architect, researcher*

Medford
Straus, David A. *architectural firm executive*

Portland
Allen, Rex Whitaker *retired architect*
Vanderslice, Ellen *architect, composer*

Springfield
Lutes, Donald Henry *architect*

Welches
Merrill, William Dean *retired architect, medical association administrator*

PENNSYLVANIA

Bethlehem
Spillman, Robert Arnold *architect*

Camp Hill
Brandow, Theo *architect*

Greencastle
Scott, Leighton Reeves *interior designer, artist, writer*

Harrisburg
Knackstedt, Mary V. *interior designer*

New Cumberland
Peters, Ralph Edgar *architectural firm, engineering executive*

Philadelphia
Bower, John Arnold, Jr. *architect*
Brown, Denise Scott *architect, urban planner*
Dagit, Charles Edward, Jr. *architect, educator*
Eiswerth, Barry Neil *architect, educator*
Farley, Richard John *architect, engineer*
Hayes, John Freeman *architect*
Lawson, John Quinn *architect*
Magaziner, Henry Jonas *architect, writer*
Maxman, Susan Abel *architect*
Mertins, Detlef *architect, educator*
Olin, Laurie Dewar *landscape architect, educator*
Rauch, John Keiser, Jr. *architect*
Rybczynski, Witold Marian *architect, educator, writer*
Saylor, Peter M. *architect*
Venturi, Robert *architect*

Pittsburgh
Becherer, Richard John *architecture educator*
Bohlin, Peter Quarfordt *architect*
Damianos, Sylvester *architect, sculptor*
Horowitz, Carole Spiegel *landscape contractor*

State College
Haas, John C. *architect*

Willow Grove
Suer, Marvin David *architectural consultant*

RHODE ISLAND

Bristol
Hendrix, John Shannon *architecture educator*

Newport
Burgin, William Lyle *architect*
Hence, Jane Knight *interior designer*

Providence
Barnum, William Milo *architect*
St. Florian, Friedrich Gartler *architect, educator*

Wakefield
Phipps, Lynne Bryan *interior architect, educator, minister*

SOUTH CAROLINA

Clemson
Halfacre, Robert Gordon *ombudsman, landscape architect, horticulturist, educator*

Columbia
Anderson, William H. *architect*
Turk, John Cobb *retired architect, educator*

Greenville
Hultstrand, Charles John *architect*

Mount Pleasant
Hill, Larkin Payne *jewelry designer, manufacturer*

TENNESSEE

Chattanooga
Derthick, Alan Wendell *architect, architectural firm executive*

Memphis
Adsit, Russell Allan *landscape architect*
Evans, James Mignon *architect*

Nashville
Kaufman, Martin Keplinger *landscape artist*
Swensson, Earl Simcox *architect*

TEXAS

Arlington
Ferrier, Richard Brooks *architect, educator*
Wright, C(arroll) Lee, Jr. *architecture educator*

Austin
Alexander, Drury Blakeley *retired architecture educator*
Alofsin, Anthony *architect, art historian, writer, educator*
George, Walter Eugene, Jr. *architect*
Lawrence, Mell *architect*

Bellaire
Lundy, Victor Alfred *architect, educator*

College Station
Shepley, Mardelle McCuskey *architect, educator*
Woodcock, David Geoffrey *architect, educator*

Dallas
Hawkins, H. Ralph *architectural firm executive*
Landry, Jane Lorenz *architect*
Stacy, Dennis William *architect*
Welch, Frank D. *architect*
Wommack, Ron *architect*

Denton
Gough, Clarence Ray *retired designer, educator*

El Paso
Stanley, Duffy B. *architect, planner*

Houston
Bair, Royden Stanley *retired architect*
Bentsen, Kenneth Edward *architect*
Cutler, John Earl *landscape architect*
Douglas, Frank Fair *architect, graphic designer*
Farrell, John Marshall *architect*
Ivanov, Lyuben Dimitrov *naval architecture researcher, educator*
Mc Ginty, John Milton *architect, consultant*
Moore, Barry M. *architect, educator*
Moorhead, Gerald Lee *architect*
Walton, Conrad Gordon, Sr. *retired architect*

Irving
Rees, Frank William, Jr. *architect*

Plano
Warburton, Ralph Joseph *architect, educator, engineer*

San Antonio
Davis, George Edward *industrial designer*
Frazer, Robert Lee *retired landscape architect*

UTAH

Salt Lake City
Beall, Burtch W., Jr. *architect*
Brems, David Paul *architect*
Chong, Richard David *architect*
Christopher, James Walker *architect, educator*
Miller, William Charles *architect, educator*

VERMONT

Brattleboro
Gorman, Robert Saul *architect*

VIRGINIA

Alexandria
Cross, Eason, Jr. *architect*
Vosbeck, William Frederick, Jr. *architect*

Arlington
Foster, Michael T. *architect*
Hassett, Valerie Jane *interior designer, architect, educator*
Hellmuth, George William *architect*

Blacksburg
Bliznakov, Milka Tcherneva *architect, educator*
Poole, Scott *architect, educator*
Rodriguez-Camilloni, Humberto Leonardo *architect, historian, educator*

Chantilly
Ward, George Truman *architect*

Charlottesville
Bednar, Michael John *architecture educator*
McDonough, William Andrews *architect, former dean*
Root, James Benjamin *landscape architect*

Falls Church
Barkley, Paul Haley, Jr. *architect*

Greenbackville
Lewis, Kay *interior designer, consultant*

Mc Lean
Mortensen, Robert Henry *landscape and golf course architect*

Reston
Scheeler, James Arthur *architect*

Richmond
Jamgochian, Victoria *interior designer*
Joel, William Lee, II, *interior and lighting designer*
Morris, James Carl *architect*

Virginia Beach
Stanton, Pamela Freeman *interior designer, writer*

Williamsburg
Herbert, Albert Edward, Jr. *interior and industrial designer*

Yorktown
Laurier, Maurice Josef *marine architect, engineer, consultant*

WASHINGTON

Bainbridge Island
Bowden, William Darsie *retired interior designer*

Kenmore
Springer, Floyd Ladean *architect*

Kirkland
Mitchell, Joseph Patrick *architect*

Mill Creek
Latta, Diana Lennox *retired interior designer*

Mount Vernon
Klein, Henry *architect*

Redmond
Sowder, Robert Robertson *architect*

Republic
Chambers, Milton Warren *retired architect*

Seattle
Allen, Scott D. *architect*
Bain, William James, Jr. *architect*
Bosworth, Thomas Lawrence *architect, retired educator*
Deines, Katrina *architecture educator*
Jacobson, Phillip Lee *architect, educator*
Jonassen, James O. *architect*

Jones, Grant Richard *landscape architect*
Kolb, Keith Robert *architect, educator*
Kundig, Tom *architect*
Lovett, Wendell Harper *architect, educator*
Miles, Don Clifford *architect*
Olson, James William Park *architect*
Perthou, Alison Chandler *interior designer*
Piven, Peter Anthony *architect, management consultant*
Sundberg, Richard *architectural firm executive*
Thomas, John Val *architect*

Tacoma
Liddle, Alan Curtis *retired architect*

WEST VIRGINIA

Morgantown
Kuo, Ying Ying *instructional designer*

Summit Point
Taylor, Harold Allen, Jr. *industrial minerals consultant*

WISCONSIN

Kenosha
Potente, Eugene, Jr. *interior designer*

Madison
Tishler, William Henry *landscape architect, educator*

Milwaukee
Greenstreet, Robert Charles *architect, educator*

TERRITORIES OF THE UNITED STATES

PUERTO RICO

San Juan
Marvel, Thomas Stahl *architect*

CANADA

BRITISH COLUMBIA

Vancouver
Erickson, Arthur Charles *architect*

NOVA SCOTIA

Halifax
Fowler, Charles Allison Eugene *retired architect, civil engineer*

ONTARIO

Toronto
Budrevics, Alexander *landscape architect*
Fife, Edward H. *landscape architecture educator*
van Ginkel, Blanche Lemco *architect, educator*

QUEBEC

Montreal
Davidson, Colin Henry *architect, educator*

ENGLAND

East Sussex
Baker, James Barnes *architect*

FRANCE

Paris
Piano, Renzo *architect*

Roques
White, Norval Crawford *architect*

REPUBLIC OF KOREA

Seoul
Kim, Won *architect*

SWITZERLAND

Zurich
Calatrava, Santiago *architect, structural engineer, artist*

ADDRESS UNPUBLISHED

Accordino, Frank Joseph *architect*
Adler, Richard Melvin *architect, planner*
Akkor, Gundogdu *retired architectural firm executive, engineering executive, foundation administrator*
Alexander, James H. *industrial designer*
Amisano, Joseph *architect*
Anderson, Ruth Lucille *interior designer, educator, artist, librarian, archivist*
Armistead, Katherine Kelly (Mrs. Thomas B. Armistead III) *interior designer, travel consultant, civic worker*
Armstrong, Thomas Newton III *landscape artist*
Bell, Janet S. *interior designer, developer, event producer*
Blanco, Laura *interior designer*
Brice, Jacqueline (Jackie Brice) *landscape artist*
Brotman, David Joel *architectural firm executive, consultant*
Campbell, Janet Coral *architect*
Carlson, Devon McElvin *architect, educator*
Carpenter, Derr Alvin *retired landscape architect*
Chao, James Min-Tzu *architect*
Cheng, Liang *video architect, researcher*
Cichello, Samuel Joseph *architect*
Cupp, Robert Erhard *golf course architect, land use planner*
Cutting, Heyward *designer, planner*
Dale, T.D. *architectural firm executive*
Demant, Margaret H. *retired interior designer*
Dermanis, Paul Raymond *architect*
Dibner, David Robert *architect, writer*
Dillard, Suzanne *interior designer, actress*
Egnaczak, Raymond Charles *design educator, graphics designer*
Ferris, Roger Patrick *architect*
Finn, Charlotte Kaye *interior designer*
Flipse, John Edward *naval architect, mechanical engineer*
Friedman, Mildred *architecture educator, design educator, curator*
Gaillard, George Siday III *architect*
Gan, Juis *interior designer*
Gantz, Carroll Melvin *industrial design consultant, consumer product designer*
Geddes, Robert *architect, educator*
Genaro, Donald Michael *industrial designer*
Gerou, Phillip Howard *architect*
Gordon, Ezra *architect, educator*
Gui, James Edmund *architect*
Hakim, Besim Selim *architecture and urban design educator, researcher, consultant, urban planner*
Halprin, Lawrence *landscape architect, urban planner*
Hardin, Mary L. *interior designer*
Hastings, L(ois) Jane *architect, educator*
Henderson, John Drews *architect*
Hinshaw, Mark Larson *architect, urban planner*
Hooper, Roger Fellowes *retired architect*
Hutchins, Robert Ayer *architectural consultant*
Jablonski, Robert Leo *architect*
Joffe, Barbara Lynne *business transformation architect*
Johansen, John MacLane *architect*
Joines, Sharon Melissa Bennett *design educator, researcher*
Jordan, Janine *interior designer, consultant, small business owner*
Joseph, J. Jonathan *interior designer*
Kazakov, Aleksey V. *product designer*
Keech, Elowyn Ann *interior designer*
Keehner, Rebecca Lynn *interior designer*
Korobkin, Barry Jay *architect*
Lai, Feng-Qi *instructional designer, educator*
Lin, Maya *architect, sculptor*
Loss, John C. *architect, retired educator*
Lyn, Jean *interior designer*
Mair, Bruce Logan *interior designer, architectural firm executive*
McFadden, Robbyn Kilbane *interior designer, public policy specialist, artist, advocate*
McGee, Humphrey Glenn *retired architect*
McGraw, Susan Catherine *interior designer*
McPheeters, Edwin Keith *architect, educator*
Mehringer, Richard Patrick *design educator, artist*
Meyer, Andreas S. *architect, consultant*
Miller, Henry Forster *architect*
Moore, Richard Alan *landscape architect*
Morrish, Thomas Jay *golf course architect*
Mujica, Mauro E. *architect*
Mumma, Albert Girard, Jr. *architect*
Murray, David George *architect*
Musgrave, Story *design educator, astronaut, physiologist, surgeon*
Myer, Donald Beekman *architect*
Naidorf, Louis Murray *architect*
Odermatt, Robert Allen *architect*
Oles, Paul Stevenson (Steve Oles) *architect, educator*
Omholt, Bruce Donald *product designer, mechanical engineer, consultant*
Orr, Frank Howard III *architect*
Paderewski, Sir Clarence Joseph *architect*
Paulsen, Serenus Glen *retired architect, educator*
Pei, I.M. (Ieoh Ming Pei) *architect*
Perkins, Nancy Jane *industrial designer*
Peters, Robert Woolsey *retired architect*
Petit, Emmanuel J. *architecture educator*
Pettitt, Jay S. *architect, consultant*
Poor, Janet Meakin III *landscape designer*
Poss, Jeffery Scott *architect, educator*
Rabon, William James, Jr. *architect*
Radde, Bruce *retired architecture educator*
Rallo, Harry *architectural firm executive*
Rice, Richard Lee *retired architect*
Rohde, Joe (Joseph Martin Rohde) *theme park executive, designer*
Sagan, M. J. *architectural firm executive*
Salzman, Arthur George *architect, consultant*
Serdari, Thomaï *architect, historian*
Smith, Vincent Milton *Feng Shui consultant, educator, writer*
Speck, Lawrence W. *architect, educator*
Strombom, David Glen *designer*
Strong, Annsley Chapman *interior designer, volunteer*
Thiel, Philip *design educator*
Thistlethwaite, David Richard *architect*
Tomasi, Donald Charles *architect*
Twomey, Timothy *architect*
Van Dine, Harold Forster, Jr. *architect, artist*
Van Housen, Thomas Corwin III *architect*
Willis, Beverly Ann *architect*
Wong, Liliane *architect, educator*

ARTS: LITERARY *See also* COMMUNICATIONS MEDIA

UNITED STATES

ALABAMA

Montgomery
Greenhaw, (Harold) Wayne *writer*
Leventhal, William E. (Willy) Siegel *writer*

Selma
Fitts, Alston III *writer*

ALASKA

Anchorage
Strohmeyer, John *writer, retired editor*
Thomas, Lowell, Jr. *writer, retired military officer, state senator*

North Pole
McGee, Michael Vanhook *writer, playwright*

ARIZONA

Avondale
Chan, Kathleen Ann *writer, social worker*

Mesa
St. Cyr, Margaret Ann (Peggy St. Cyr) *writer*

Phoenix
Duyck, Kathleen Marie *poet, musician, retired social worker*

Tempe
Boudreau, Diane *writer*
Raby, William Louis *writer, consultant*

Tucson
Butcher, Russell Devereux *writer, photographer*
Martin, Marci *writer, former advertising specialist*
Nord, Myrtle Selma *writer, researcher*
Stitt, Mari Leipper *poet*

ARKANSAS

Fayetteville
Williams, Miller *retired poet, writer, translator*

Little Rock
Nunn, Patarica Dian *poet*

Malvern
Selix, Karen Elizabeth *writer, artist, vocalist*

North Little Rock
Jackson, Willie *writer, researcher*

CALIFORNIA

Alameda
Rubin, Charles Alexis *writer*

Altadena
Burden, Jean Prussing *retired poet, editor*

Aromas
Fleischman, Paul *children's author*

Atascadero
Locke, Virginia Otis *writer*

Berkeley
Brooke, Tal (Robert Taliaferro) *writer*
Callenbach, Ernest *writer, editor*
Chetin, Helen Campbell *writer*
Katzen, Mollie *writer*
Kluger, Richard *writer, editor*
Knox, Helene Margrethe *poet, editor*
Ofteness, Ove (O.V. Michaelsen) *writer, musician*
Ruppenthal, Karl M. *author, educator*
Smith, Charles Lee *writer*

Beverly Hills
Apatow, Judd *scriptwriter, television and film producer*
Ball, Alan *screenwriter*
Basichis, Gordon Allen *writer, scriptwriter, novelist, marketing consultant, media consultant*
Bass, Ronald *screenwriter*
Bergman, Andrew *scriptwriter, film director*
Chase, David (David DeCaesare) *scriptwriter, television director and producer*
Crowe, Cameron *screenwriter, film director*
Farrelly, Bobby (Robert Leo Rarrelly Jr.) *scriptwriter, film director and producer*
Gaghan, Stephen *scriptwriter, film director*
Gelbart, Larry *scriptwriter, television and theater producer*
Groening, Matthew (Abram) *writer, cartoonist*
Lloyd, Christopher *television writer and producer*
Mandel, Babaloo *scriptwriter*
Mendelsohn, Daniel *writer, humanities professor*
Meyers, Nancy Jane *screenwriter, producer, director*
Pezzullo, Ralph Michael *writer, playwright*
Quinn, Patricia K. *literary agent*
Rosenthal, Mark David *screenwriter*
Roth, Eric *screenwriter*
Schaffer, Akiva *writer, director*
Schulian, John (Nielsen Schulian) *screenwriter, author*
Shanley, John Patrick *playwright, screenwriter*
Sorkin, Aaron *scriptwriter, television producer, playwright*
Steinem, Gloria *writer, editor, advocate*
Taccone, Jorma *writer, director*
Ward, David Schad *scriptwriter, film director*

Cameron Park
Vorce-Tish, Helene R. *writer*

Carlsbad
Farrell, Warren Thomas *author*

Carmel
Creighton, John Wallis, Jr. *writer, former management educator, consultant, small business owner*

Castro Valley
Wycoff, Charles Coleman *writer, retired anesthesiologist*

Chico
Livingston, Myran Jay *author, film writer, director and producer*

Chula Vista
Nelson, Carl Alfred *writer, international business educator*
Ryan, Candace I. *writer, director, editor*

Citrus Heights
Daves, Sandra Lynn *poet, lyricist*

Claremont
Tilden, Wesley Roderick *writer, retired application developer*
Wachtel, Albert *writer, educator*
Wallace, David Foster *writer*

Clovis
Shields, Allan Edwin *writer, photographer*

Colton
Allen, Blair Hamilton *writer, poet, artist, editor, photographer*

Compton
Shiloh, Allen *writer*

Cotati
Hill, Debora Elizabeth *writer, journalist, screenwriter*

Cromberg
Kolb, Ken Lloyd *writer*

Cypress
Edmonds, Ivy Gordon *retired writer*

Davis
Bunch, Richard Alan *writer, educator, poet, philosopher*
Major, Clarence Lee *writer, painter, poet, educator*
Rooks, George Malcolm *writer, educator, small business owner*

Del Mar
Morton, Frederic *author*

Fresno
Garrison-Finderup, Ivadelle Dalton *writer, educator*
Lanter, Lanore *writer, educator*

Garden Valley
Price, Lew Paxton *writer, engineer*

Glendale
Spring, Carl Chaffee, Jr. *writer*

Grass Valley
Cheney, Margaret *writer, retired editor*
Washington, Allyn Jarvis *writer*

Healdsburg
Myers, Robert Eugene *writer, educator*

Hermosa Beach
Battles, Roxy Edith *novelist, consultant, educator*

Hollywood
Melchior, Ib Jorgen *scriptwriter, author, film director*

Huntington Beach
Flakes, Susan *playwright, theater director*

Idyllwild
Schneider, Paul *writer*

Kensington
Littlejohn, David *writer*

La Jolla
Antin, David *poet, critic*

Laguna Beach
Chevli, Lyn *writer*

Lompoc
Jack, Morgann Tayllor *writer, artist*

Los Angeles
Baumbach, Noah *screenwriter*
Corwin, Norman *scriptwriter, film producer, film director*
Daniels, Gregory Martin *screenwriter*
Golden, Arthur *writer*
Good, Edith Elissa (Pearl Williams) *writer*
Gordon, David *writer, educator*

Horowitz, David Joel *author*
Horta, Silvio *scriptwriter*
Kaplan, Nadia *writer*
Noguchi, Thomas Tsunetomi *writer, pathologist*
Patrick, Robert *playwright*
Schulberg, Budd *author*
Schwimmer, George *writer, film producer*
Sedaris, Amy *writer, actress*
Shapiro, Mel *playwright, educator, theater director*

Menlo Park
Heller, Esther A. *writer, educator*

Morgan Hill
Singh, Loren Chan *writer, educator*

Newport Beach
Koontz, Dean Ray *writer*
Wentworth, Diana von Welanetz *author*

North Hollywood
Campos, Luis *puzzle writer*

Northridge
Boberg, Dorothy Kurth *author*

Oakland
Foley, Jack (John Wayne Harold Foley) *poet, writer, editor-in-chief*
Haiman, Franklyn Saul *writer, communications educator*
Schacht, Henry Mevis *writer, consultant*
Silverberg, Robert *writer*

Oceano
Scott, Donald Michael *writer, educator*

Ontario
Kloepfer, Marguerite Fonnesbeck *writer*

Orinda
Strong, Susan Clancey *writer, communications executive, editor*

Pacific Grove
Yep, Laurence Michael *author*

Palm Desert
Benn, Theodore Alexander (Alec Benn) *writer*

Palm Springs
Nelson, K. Bonita *literary agent*
Wouk, Herman *writer*

Pasadena
Brogden-Stirbl, Shona Marie *writer, researcher*
Yeager, Caroline Hale *writer, retired radiologist, consultant*

Penngrove
Haslam, Gerald William *writer, educator*

Petaluma
Hass, Robert L. *writer, literature educator*
Laporte, Leo *writer, blogger, radio personality*
Pronzini, Bill John (William Pronzini) *writer*
Sebold, Alice *writer*
Spiegelman, Art *writer, cartoonist*

Placerville
Wilkinson, Rosemary Regina Challoner *poet, writer*

Playa Del Rey
McNeill, Daniel Richard *writer*

Pomona
Mezey, Robert *poet*

Rancho Santa Fe
Byrd, Betty Rantze *writer*

Rancho Santa Margarita
Shusterman, Neal Douglas *writer, scriptwriter*

Ross
Godwin, Sara *writer*

Sacramento
Gerringer, Elizabeth (The Marchioness de Roe Devon, Poet Julie de Vontine) *writer, lawyer*

San Bernardino
Hansen, Anne Katherine *poet*

San Diego
Lederer, Richard Henry *writer, educator, columnist*
Robbins, Tony (Anthony Robbins) *writer*
Skwara, Erich Wolfgang *writer, poet, critic, literature educator*

San Francisco
Blaise, Clark Lee *writer, educator*
Cohn, Kathleen Mandry *writer*
Eggers, Dave *fiction writer, magazine editor*
Emery, Vince *writer, educator*
Ferlinghetti, Lawrence *poet*
Ferris, Russell James, II, *writer*
Field, Carol Hart *writer, news correspondent, journalist*
Glueckman, Alan Jay *writer, producer, director*
Rivlin, Gary *writer, reporter*
Rusher, William Allen *writer, commentator, columnist*
Sachs, Marilyn Stickle *writer, educator, editor*
Saunders, Sally Love *poet, educator*
Talbot, David Lyle *online magazine publisher, former editor*

San Jose
Fitzgerald, Timothy K. *writer, political organizer, non-profit administrator*
Loventhal, Milton *writer, playwright, lyricist*
Prestine, Joan Singleton *writer, educator, editor*

San Luis Obispo
Bunge, Russell Kenneth *writer, poet, educator*

San Marcos
Snow, Tiffany *writer, healer, composer*

San Marino
Sherwood, Midge *writer*

San Rafael
Nelson, James Carmer, Jr. *writer, editor, advertising executive*

Santa Barbara
Behrens, June Adelle *writer*
Canfield, Jack *writer, speaker, trainer*
Mitchell, Shawne Maureen *author*
Ramsay, William Charles *writer, composer*

Santa Clara
Simmons, Janet Bryant *writer, publishing executive*

Santa Cruz
Davis, Angela Yvonne *political activist, educator, writer*

Santa Monica
Crichton, Michael (John Michael Crichton) *writer, film director*
Huffington, Arianna (Arianna Stassinopoulos) *writer*
Mora, Philippe *screenwriter, producer, director, painter*
Scott, Jill *poet, musician*
Shiffrin, Nancy *writer, educator*

Sebastopol
Marler, Joan *writer, educator*

Somis
Premack, Ann J. *writer*

Sonoma
Kizer, Carolyn Ashley *poet, educator*

Stanford
Conquest, Robert (George Robert Acworth Conquest) *writer, historian, poet*
Djerassi, Carl *writer, retired chemistry professor*
Steele, Shelby *writer, educator*
Wolff, Tobias (Jonathan Ansell Wolff) *writer*

Studio City
Parish, James Robert *writer, cinema historian*

Sun Valley
Casey, Paul Arnold *writer, producer, photographer, composer, director*

Van Nuys
Becker, Frawley *writer, dialogue director, location manager*

Venice
Eliot, Alexander *writer*

Vernon
Kim, Ho Gill *poet*

Walnut Creek
Chu, Valentin Yuan-ling *author*

West Hills
Alexander, Sue *writer*

West Hollywood
Slade, Bernard *playwright*

Westminster
Amalsad, Meher Dadabhoy *writer, speaker, seminar leader*

Woodland Hills
Jason, Sonya *writer*

Yorba Linda
Medland, Maurice Blue *writer*

COLORADO

Bayfield
Korns, Leota Elsie *writer, mountain land developer, insurance broker*

Colorado Springs
Lyddane, Anne Alexandra *retired writer*
Rhodes, Daisy Chun *writer, researcher, historian*

Denver
Avi, (Avi Wortis) *author*
Buckstein, Caryl Sue *writer*
Dallas, Sandra *writer*
Ducker, Bruce *writer, lawyer*
MacGregor, George Lescher, Jr. *freelance/self-employed writer, brokerage house executive*
Nemiro, Beverly Mirium Anderson *author, educator*

Englewood
As-Salaam, Jamaal (William Louis Williams Jr.) *poet, film producer, writer*

Greeley
Willis, Connie (Constance E. Willis) *writer*

Lakewood
Peters, Julie Anne *writer*

Littleton
Norman, Marcia Macy *writer, realtor*

Lyons
Spring, Kathleen *writer*

Montrose
Gates, Viola R. *writer*

Wheat Ridge
Morriss, Frank *writer, educator*

CONNECTICUT

Avon
Nagel, Miriam Carlson *freelance/self-employed writer*

Clinton
Adler, Peggy Ann *writer, illustrator, consultant, protective services official*

Danbury
Kavasch, Elizabeth Barrie *writer, educator, illustrator*

East Hampton
Tucceri, Clive Knowles *writer, science educator, consultant*

Easton
Maloney, John Joseph *writer*

Greenwich
Ewald, William Bragg, Jr. *writer, consultant*
Hoberman, Mary Ann *author*
Wallach, Magdalena Falkenberg (Carla Wallach) *writer*

New Canaan
Fredericks, Jeanne Maria Judson *literary agent*

New Haven
Applegate, Debby *biographer*
Hayden, Dolores *author, architecture educator*
Phillips, Caryl *writer*
Sommer, Miriam Goldstein (Mimi G. Sommer) *writer, photographer*

New London
Morgan, John Richard *writer, publishing executive*

Roxbury
Gurney, Albert Ramsdell *playwright, educator*

Sharon
Lisle, Laurie *author*

Stamford
Herlands, E. Ward *poet, printmaker*

Storrs Mansfield
Rimland, Lisa Phillip *writer, composer, lyricist*

Waterford
Commire, Anne *playwright, writer, editor*

West Hartford
Calip, Roger *writer, educator*

Weston
Diforio, Robert George *literary agent*
Kilty, Jerome Timothy *playwright, theater director, actor*
Wiseman, Carter Sterling *writer, educator*

Westport
Hotchner, Aaron Edward *author*

DELAWARE

Hockessin
Mertz, Anne Morris *writer, researcher, journalist, educator*

Wilmington
Ziolkowska-Boehm, Aleksandra *writer*

DISTRICT OF COLUMBIA

Washington
Alperovitz, Gar *author, educator*
Angell, Lois Louise *writer, actor, comedienne, poet*
Arndt, Richard Tallmadge *writer, consultant, cultural administrator*
Atlas, Liane Wiener *writer*
Birnbaum, Norman *writer, humanities educator*
Burnham, David Bright *writer, educator*
Burns, David Mitchell *writer, retired diplomat*
Carroll, Andrew Patrick Keating *writer*
Coulter, Ann *writer, political columnist, lawyer*
Cox, Ana Marie *writer, former political blogger*
Dunbar, Leslie Wallace *writer, consultant*
Easterbrook, Gregg Edmund *writer*
Furgurson, Ernest Baker, Jr., (Pat Furgurson) *writer*
Gallo, Anthony Ernest *playwright, economist*
Gioia, Dana (Michael Dana Gioia) *poet, critic, cultural organization administrator*
Hiebert, Ray Eldon *writer, educator*
Kramer, Simon Paul *writer*
Leamer, Laurence Allen *writer*
Lynn, Karyl Charna (Karyl Lynn Kopelman Zietz) *writer, filmmaker, critic, television producer*
Mallon, Thomas *writer*
May, Stephen *writer, federal official, historian*
McCrary Anthony, Crystal *writer, producer, lawyer*
McGurn, William Joseph *speechwriter, editor*
Murphy, Joanne Becker *writer*
Nash, James Lee *poet, security official*
Robb, Lynda Johnson *writer*
Shakir, Faiz *writer, political blogger*
Shaw, Russell Burnham *writer, journalist*
Smith, Stuart Seaborne *writer, government and union official*

Tannen, Deborah Frances *writer*
Zacarías, Karen *playwright*

FLORIDA

Aventura
Meltzer, Brad *writer*

Babson Park
Morrison, Kenneth Douglas *writer, columnist*

Belleair Beach
Fuentes, Martha Ayers *playwright*

Boca Raton
Keyes, Daniel *author*

Bradenton
Blanchard, Leonard Albert *writer, consultant, educator*

Brandon
Pantano, Daniele *poet, educator*

Cape Canaveral
Hess, Terry Lee *writer, educator, logistician*

Cape Coral
Hopkins, Lee Bennett *writer, educator*

Daytona Beach
Mc Collister, John Charles *writer, minister, educator*

Eustis
Chorosinski, Eugene Conrad *writer, poet, author*

Fort Lauderdale
Schneider, Ursula Wilfriede *author*

Gainesville
Carlson, David Edward *jounalism educator, journalist, consultant*
Smith, Jo Anne *writer, retired communications educator*

Hallandale Beach
Geller, Bunny Zelda *poet, writer, publisher, sculptor, artist*

Highland Beach
Tolf, Robert Walter *writer*

Hobe Sound
Houser, Constance (Connie) W. *writer, artist*

Homosassa
Carmichael, Roberta Kay *writer*

Key Biscayne
Cardozo, Arlene Rossen *writer*
Clay, Cynthia Joyce *writer, editor-in-chief*

Key West
Mathews, Harry Burchell *poet, writer, educator*

Longboat Key
Hazan, Marcella Maddalena *writer, educator, consultant*

Miami
Alperin, Stanley I. *writer, editor, consultant*
Alschuler, Al *freelance/self-employed writer*
Benestante, Vincenzo *writer*
Morgan, Marabel *writer*

Miramar
Abbott, Paul Scott *writer, public relations executive, consultant*

Naples
Alpert, Hollis *writer*
Capelle-Frank, Jacqueline Aimee *writer*
Mills, Dorothy Jane (Dorothy Z. Seymour) *writer, editor, consultant*

Oldsmar
Craft Davis, Audrey Ellen *writer, educator*

Orlando
Comfort, Iris Tracy *writer*

Palm Beach
Javits, Joan (Zeeman) *writer, inventor*
Kay, Marcia Chellis *writer*

Panama City
Schafer, John Stephen *poet*

Placida
McClister, Michael *writer*

Sarasota
Boersma, June Elaine (Jalma Barrett) *retired writer, photographer*
Jones, Sally Daviess Pickrell *writer*
Kessler, Leonard *writer, illustrator*
Weeks, Albert Loren *writer, educator, journalist*
Wilson, Kenneth Jay *writer*

Tallahassee
Butler, Robert Olen *writer, educator*
Johnson, Margaret Anderson *writer, publishing and agricultural products executive*
Tourtet, Christiane Andrée *writer, photojournalist, reporter, advocate*

The Villages
Oetjen, David L. (Jon David Douglas) *writer, film producer*

Vero Beach
Massey, Howard Clayland *writer*
Proctor, William Gilbert, Jr. *writer*

West Palm Beach
Bergmann, Arthur M. *writer, retired journalist, retired county official*
Passy, Charles *writer*

Winter Park
Rooks, Linda *writer*

GEORGIA

Atlanta
Cleage, Pearl Michelle *writer, playwright, journalist*
Moore, Philip Nicholas *author*
Rushdie, Salman (Ahmed Salman Rushdie) *writer, educator*
Trethewey, Natasha *poet, literature educator*

Barnesville
Brown, Angelia *poet*

Hoschton
Campbell, Leslie Caine (Caine Campbell) *writer, historian*

Loganville
Smelser, Thelma Ann *writer, tax specialist*

Pine Mountain
Bishop, Michael *writer*

Savannah
Coffey, Thomas Francis, Jr. *retired writer*
Thomas, Dwight Rembert *writer*

Stone Mountain
Allen (Irvin M.N.), Georgianne Lydia Christian *writer, poet*

Woodstock
Furuta, Soichi *poet, art consultant, educator*

HAWAII

Honolulu
Halloran, Richard Colby *writer, reporter, communications executive, editor*

Kailua
Bone, Robert William *writer*

IDAHO

Moscow
Anderson, Clifton Einar *writer, corporate communications specialist*

ILLINOIS

Belleville
Pounds, Regina Dorothea *writer*

Chicago
Blackman, Everett Allan *writer*
Camper, John Jacob *writer, academic administrator*
Carroll, David *writer, illustrator*
Lach, Alma Elizabeth *food and cooking writer, consultant*
Lerner, Barbara *writer, researcher*
Madsen, Dorothy Louise (Meg) *writer*
Manelli, Donald Dean *scriptwriter, film and television producer*
McKinney, Megan *writer*
Melnick, Jane Fisher *writer, educator, photographer*
Muller, Leon *writer*
Paley, Vivian Gussin *writer*
Plotnik, Arthur *writer, columnist*
Stacey, James Henry *writer, columnist*
Terkel, Studs (Louis Terkel) *writer, journalist*
Turow, Scott F. *writer, lawyer*
Verschoor, Curtis Carl *writer, consultant*

Crystal Lake
Fleming, Marjorie Foster *freelance writer, artist*

Evanston
Gibbons, William Reginald, Jr. *poet, writer, translator, editor*
Kertész, Imre *writer*

Highland Park
Greenblatt, Miriam *writer, editor, educator*

Lake Forest
Swanton, Virginia Lee *writer, publisher*
Taylor, Barbara Ann Olin *writer, educational consultant*

Marengo
Mrkvicka, Edward Francis, Jr. *writer, finance company executive*

Morton Grove
Vega, Steve *poet, protective services official*

Northfield
Mamet, David Alan *playwright, scriptwriter*

Oak Lawn
Sullivan, Michael *writer, retired mathematics professor*

Oakland
Eriksen, Barbara Ann *writer, researcher*

Ottawa
Ballowe, James *writer, educator*

Palatine
Pohl, Frederik *freelance/self-employed writer*

Peoria
Grebner, Bernice Prill *author, astrological counselor*

Prospect Heights
Mooney, Timothy *playwright, actor, theater director*

Rochester
Petterchak, Janice A. *writer*

South Barrington
Kissane, Sharon Florence *writer, consultant, educator*

Stoy
Rhoten, Kenneth Dale *writer*

University Park
Alozie, Emmanuel C. *writer, educator*
Patton, June Odessa *writer, consultant, educator, researcher*

Urbana
Dovring, Karin Elsa Ingeborg *writer, poet, playwright, media specialist*
Lieberman, Laurence *poet, educator*
Powers, Richard S. *writer, educator*

Wilmette
Miripol, Jerilyn Elise *poet, writer, writing therapist*

INDIANA

Bloomington
Kibbey, Hal Stephen *science writer*

Carmel
Fadely, James Philip *writer, educator*

Chesterton
Petrakis, Harry Mark *author*

Elkhart
Eddy, Darlene Mathis *poet, educator*

Fort Wayne
Frost, Helen Marie *writer*
Langhinrichs, Ruth Imler *playwright, writer*

Frankfort
Borland, Kathryn Kilby *writer*

Howe
Bowerman, Ann Louise *writer, secondary school educator, genealogist*

Muncie
Thornbro, William Graden *writer*

Westfield
Basil, Douglas Constantine *writer, educator*

IOWA

Cedar Falls
Skaine, Rosemarie Keller *writer, consultant, publisher*

Iowa City
Bell, Marvin Hartley *poet, language educator*
Johnson, Nicholas *writer, lawyer, educator*
Merrill, Christopher Lyall *writer*
Stein, Robert A. *writer, educator, military officer*

Sioux City
Hassenger, James Michael *writer, retired small business owner*

Windsor Heights
Beadel, Stephen Jay *author*

KANSAS

Leawood
Garwood, Julie *writer*
Gray, Thomas Alva, Jr. *writer, minister, retired protective services official*

KENTUCKY

Covington
McQueen, Regenia *writer*

Frankfort
Embry, Michael Dale *writer, editor, educator*

Lexington
Bell, Randall Keith *writer*
Johnson, Jane Penelope *freelance/self-employed writer*

Madisonville
May, Richard Warren *writer*

LOUISIANA

Baton Rouge
La Carna, John Edward *writer, social worker*
Madden, David *author*
Mueller, Lisel *writer, poet*

Eunice
Attole, Mary Bertha *writer*

Lafayette
Gaines, Ernest James *author*

Metairie
Grau, Shirley Ann (Mrs. James Kern Feibleman) *writer*

New Orleans
Friedmann, Patricia Ann *writer*
Tetlow, Elisabeth Meier *writer, researcher, lawyer*

Shreveport
Kendrick, Rhonda Lynn *poet, small business owner*

MAINE

Bangor
King, Stephen Edwin *novelist, scriptwriter*

Bristol
Sabin, William Albert *writer*

Dixmont
Cummings, James William *poet*

East Boothbay
Ford, Richard *writer*

Gardiner
Dunbar, Robert Everett *writer, educator*

Milbridge
Enslin, Theodore Vernon *poet*

New Harbor
Carr, James Revell *writer, curator, retired museum director*

Portland
Thompson, William Irwin *writer, educator*
Weir, Anne *writer*

Saint Francis
Hafford, Faye O'Leary *writer*

South Portland
Manuel, Peter Jay *poet, singer/songwriter, dramatist, language professor, librettist*

Stonington
Pitts, Edgar Thurlow *writer, retired educator*

MARYLAND

Annapolis
Miller, John Grider *writer*

Baltimore
Barth, John Simmons *writer, educator*
Epstein, Daniel Mark *poet, dramatist, biographer*
Fisher, Alan Hall *guidebook writer*
Schultheis, Patricia Ann *writer, editor*
Tyler, Anne (Mrs. Taghi M. Modarressi) *writer*
Van Riper, Robert Austin *writer, retired public relations executive*

Bethesda
Kingsley, Mary Lee *writer, researcher, consultant, retired marketing executive*
Schaeffer, Charles Perry *writer, editor*

Chevy Chase
Bacon, Donald Conrad *writer, editor*

College Park
Whittemore, Edward Reed, II, *poet, retired educator*

Easton
Chambers, Will Earl *retired freelance writer*

Fort Washington
Cameron, Rita Giovannetti *writer, publishing executive*

Frederick
Randall, Frances *technical writer*

Fulton
Hamlin, George L. *writer*

Gaithersburg
Naylor, Phyllis Reynolds *writer*

Potomac
Kessler, Ronald *author*
Pastan, Linda Olenik *poet*

Rockville
Madle, Robert Albert *writer*

Saint Marys City
Clifton, Lucille Thelma *author*

Salisbury
Booker, Betty Mae *poet*

Severna Park
Davis, Clayton *writer, pilot, photographer*
Windsor, Patricia (Katonah Summertree, Perrin Winters, Anna Seeling) *author, educator, lecturer*

Silver Spring
Whitten, Leslie Hunter, Jr. *writer, poet, reporter*

Upper Marlboro
Zane, *writer, publishing executive*

MASSACHUSETTS

Amherst
Sandweiss, Martha Ann *writer, history professor*
Tate, James Vincent *poet, English educator*

Barre
Sullivan, James Edward *poet*

Belmont
Rand, Peter *writer, editor, educator*

Boston
Angelou, Maya (Marguerite Annie Johnson) *writer, actress*
Appelbaum, Diana Karter *author*
Foer, Jonathan Safran *writer*
Lahiri, Jhumpa (Nilanjana Sudeshna) *writer*
Lowry, Lois (Lois Hammersberg) *writer*
Say, Allen *writer, illustrator*
Schlosser, Eric *writer*
Shearer, Harry Julius *scriptwriter, actor, television director*
Simpson, Bennett *art critic, art museum curator*
Strothman, Wendy Jo *literary agent*
Terrill, Ross Gladwin *writer, educator*
Van Allsburg, Chris *writer, artist*
Wiesel, Elie *writer, educator*
Zelnick, Carl Robert *writer, educator*

Brighton
Valianti, Deborah L. *playwright*

Byfield
Kozol, Jonathan *writer*

Cambridge
DiCamillo, Kate *writer*
Dyck, Martin *literary theorist, mathematics historian*
Graham, Jorie *writer, educator*
Hughes, Libby *writer*
Kaplan, Justin *author*
Ladd, Florence Cawthorne *writer*
Rhoda, Janice Tucker *writer, educator, musician*
Yergin, Daniel Howard *writer, consultant*

Chestnut Hill
Valette, Jean Paul *writer*

Cohasset
Whipple, Jacqueline Conant *writer, media specialist*

Cummington
Smith, William Jay *author*
Wilbur, Richard Purdy *writer, educator*

Hatfield
Yolen, Jane *writer*

Lexington
Kennedy, X.J. (Joseph Kennedy) *writer*

Lincoln
Donald, David Herbert *writer, history professor*

Medford
Sarno, Christopher Ed *writer*

North Chelmsford
Erkkila-Ricker, Barbara Howell *writer, photographer*

Northampton
Newman, Lesléa *writer*

Pelham
Fetler, Andrew *author, educator*

Provincetown
Oliver, Mary *poet*

Revere
Recupero-Faiella, Anna Antonietta *poet*

Southborough
Mylotte, John Arnold *writer, educator*

Uxbridge
Zeis, Joanne A. *medical writer*

Wellesley
Jacobs, Ruth Harriet *poet, playwright, sociologist, gerontologist*
Lloyd-Jones, Sir (Peter) Hugh (Jefferd) *writer*

Wellfleet
Piercy, Marge *poet, writer*

West Newbury
Dooley, Ann Elizabeth *freelance writers cooperative executive, editor*

West Roxbury
Ellenbogen, George *poet, educator*

Worcester
Vick, Susan *playwright, educator, director, actress*

MICHIGAN

Ann Arbor
Gregerson, Linda Karen *poet, language educator, critic*
Perkins, George *writer, educator*

Belleville
Schaefer, James Theodore *writer, editor, educator*

Burton
Farmer, Philip José *writer*

Charlotte
Coirolo, Christina *writer, author representative*

Detroit
Madgett, Naomi Long *poet, editor, publisher, educator*

East Lansing
Perrin, Robert *writer, consultant*
Wakoski, Diane *poet, educator*

Holland
Nieuwsma, Milton John *writer, journalist*

Idlewild
Wooley, Geraldine Hamilton *poet, writer*

Kalamazoo
Light, Christopher Upjohn *freelance/self-employed writer, photographer*

Mount Pleasant
Smallwood, Carol *writer*

Okemos
Klunzinger, Thomas Edward *writer, actor, film director*

Quinnesec
Opolka, Jayme Lyn *medical writer, researcher*

Republic
Wixtrom, Donald Joseph *translator*

Sodus
Handy, Virginia Mae *writer*

Ypsilanti
Lottie, Adrian Jerome *writer, educator, consultant*

MINNESOTA

Anoka
Lindbergh, Reeve *writer, poet*

Minneapolis
Baker, John Stevenson (Michael Dyregrov) *writer*
Erdrich, Louise (Karen Erdrich) *writer, poet*
Hampl, Patricia *writer, educator*
Korotkin, Fred *writer, philatelist*
Miller, Alan M. *writer, educator, television host*
Tatlock, Ann *writer*
Walker, Sally M. *writer*

Mounds View
Wang, Aixue *translator, writer*

Saint Paul
Bly, Carol McLean *writer, educator*
Doermann, Humphrey *writer, consultant*
Keillor, Garrison Edward *writer, radio personality*

Shakopee
Gertis, Neill Allan *writer*

MISSISSIPPI

Jackson
Redmon, Cynthia Ann *poet, songwriter*

MISSOURI

Bloomfield
Ferrell, Paul Cleveland *writer*

Jefferson City
McDaniel, Sue Powell *writer*

Kansas City
Kirch, Donald Allen *writer, composer*
Martin-Bowen, Lindsey *freelance writer*

Maryville
Tennihill, Sally Kay *writer, music educator*

Saint Louis
Burgin, Richard Weston *writer, educator, editor*
Gass, William H. *writer, educator*
Lubbock, James Edward *retired writer, photographer, media consultant*
Lutz, John Thomas *author*
Miller, Judith Braffman *writer*
Schlafly, Phyllis Stewart *writer*
Swinson, Sara Hope *writer, chaplain*

MONTANA

Bigfork
Wetzel, Betty Preat *writer*

Bonner
Smith, Annick *writer*

Helena
Benyus, Janine M. *writer*

Missoula
Haines, John Meade *poet, translator, writer*
Yee, Albert Hoy *writer, retired psychologist, educator*

NEBRASKA

Lincoln
Magorian, James *poet, writer*

NEVADA

Cold Springs
Turner VanLydegraf, Claudia Beth *writer, researcher*

Las Vegas
Gardner, Grace Joely *writer, consultant, psychologist*
Palmer, Lynne *writer, astrologer*

Pahrump
Noble, Alice L. *writer, researcher*

Reno
Feinhandler, Edward Sanford *writer, photographer, art dealer*
Scrimgeour, Gary James *writer, educator*

NEW HAMPSHIRE

Cornish
Atkinson, James Blakely *writer, editor*

Durham
Ford, Daniel (Daniel Francis Ford) *writer*

Etna
Picoult, Jodi *writer*

Greenville
Talbot, Franis *writer*

Peterborough
Thomas, Elizabeth Marshall *writer*

NEW JERSEY

Bergenfield
Clark, Fred *writer, editor*
Davidson, Marilyn Copeland *writer, musician, educator*

Cape May Court House
Cohen, Daniel Edward *writer*
Cohen, Susan Lois *writer*

Cherry Hill
Gardner, Joel Robert *writer, historian*

Elizabeth
Barnes, Marjorie *poet, educator*
Lucco, James Perry *writer*

Jackson
Heck, Roberta M. *poet, writer*

Leonardo
Bianchi, Hollis Dolce *writer, poet, artist*

Long Branch
Lagowski, Barbara Jean *writer, editor*

Maplewood
Lally, Michael David *writer, actor*

Medford
Henderson, Rita Elizabeth *literary agent, journalist*

Metuchen
Smyth, David *writer, editor*

Monroe Township
Allen, Katherine Spicer *writer, former chemist*

Montclair
Delgado, Ramon Louis *theater educator, author, director, playwright, lyricist*

New Brunswick
Jenkins, Alyce Mitchem *writer, educator*
Martínez, Tomás Eloy *writer, journalist*

Newark
Dickson, Jim *writer, theater producer*

Pine Hill
Albee, Gloria *playwright*

Princeton
Cheiten, Marvin Harold *playwright, manufacturing executive*
Harford, James *writer*
Muldoon, Paul *poet, educator*
Waters, Robyn *writer, marketing consultant*

Princeton Junction
Norback, Craig Thomas *writer*

Saddle River
Roes, Nicholas A. *writer, artist*

South Orange
Riordan, Rick *writer*

Teaneck
Wallmann, Jeffrey Miner *author*

Trenton
Obed, Leonora Rita Villegas *writer*

Warren
Baxter, Nancy *medical writer*

Whiting
Willis, Ben *writer, artist*

NEW MEXICO

Albuquerque
Anaya, Rudolfo *writer, educator*
Anderson, Kristina Elizabeth *writer*
Gahala, Estella Marie *writer, consultant*
Harden, Neva Ninette *writer, consultant*
Priem, Richard Gregory *writer, executive*

Las Vegas
Howard, Leland William *writer*

Ranchos De Taos
Dickey, Robert Preston *writer, educator, poet*

Rio Rancho
Stevens, Roger Templeton *writer*

Santa Fe
Ferguson, Glenn Walker *writer, educator, retired ambassador*

Silver City
Parent, Annette Richards *free lance writer, artist*

NEW YORK

Albany
Kennedy, William Joseph *novelist, educator*

Annandale On Hudson
Achebe, Chinua *writer, humanities educator*
Manea, Norman *writer, educator*
Sourian, Peter *writer, language educator, educator*

Ardsley
Silman, Roberta Karpel *writer, critic*

Ballston Spa
Barba, Harry *writer, publisher, educator*

Briarcliff Manor
Windham, Revish *poet*

Brightwaters
North, E(dward) Lee *retired writer, former aerospace company professional*

Bronx
Bingham, June *playwright*
Kornfeld, Robert Jonathan *playwright, photographer*

Bronxville
Rosenthal, Lucy Gabrielle *writer, editor, educator*

Brooklyn
Chambers, William Edmond *writer*
Cummings, Josephine Anna *writer, consultant, advertising executive*
Donaldson, Stephen Reeder *author*
Garrett, Nancy Fales *playwright, educator*
Gioseffi, Daniela (Dorothy Daniela Gioseffi) *poet, writer, playwright, critic*
Reynolds, Nancy Remick *writer, researcher, editor*
Rogers, Michael Alan *writer*

Buffalo
Feldman, Irving *poet*

Cairo
Ludwig, Laura Lonshein *poet*

Catskill
Philp, Richard Nilson *writer, editor, journalist, historian*

Chappaqua
George, Jean Craighead *author, illustrator*

Chatham
Kherdian, David *writer*

Copake
Johnson, Paul Edward *poet, writer*

Croton Falls
Jakes, John *author*

Dobbs Ferry
Fritz, Jean Guttery *writer*

Flushing
Goldsmith, Howard *writer, consultant*
Zinnes, Harriet Fich *poet, fiction writer, retired English educator, literary and art critic*

Forest Hills
Henley, Arthur *writer, editor*

Fulton
Long, Robert Emmet *author*

Garden City
Hecht, Jennifer Michael *poet, historian*

Garnerville
Evers, Gene *writer*

Great Neck
Hurwitz, Johanna (Johanna Frank) *writer*

Greenfield Center
Bruchac, Joseph *writer, storyteller*

Hamilton
Berlind, Bruce Peter *poet, educator*

Henrietta
Byfield, Bert A. *conservative humanitarian novelist*

Interlaken
Bleiler, Everett Franklin *writer, publishing company executive*

Ithaca
Morgan, Robert *writer, poet, educator*

Katonah
McCauley, Gerard Francis *literary agent*

Medusa
Groom, Winston Francis, Jr. *writer*

Munnsville
Carruth, Hayden *poet*

New Paltz
Robinson, Anthony Christopher *novelist, educator*

New Rochelle
Branch, William Blackwell *playwright, producer*
Saperstein, David *writer, film director, television personality*
Sommer, Jay *writer, literature and language educator*

New York
Albee, Edward Franklin *playwright, writer*
Allen, Oliver E. *writer*
Alvarez, Julia *writer*
Angell, Roger *writer, magazine editor*
Ashdown, Marie Matranga *writer, educator, cultural organization administrator*
Ashton, Dore *writer, educator*
Atwood, Margaret Eleanor *writer*
Auster, Paul *writer*
Baitz, Jon Robin *playwright*
Baldacci, David *writer*
Bank, Melissa S. *writer*
Bauer, Marion Dane *writer*
Bawden, Nina (Mary Bawden) *author*
Beattie, Ann *writer, educator*
Begley, Louis *writer, lawyer*
Beim, Norman *playwright, actor, theater director, writer*
Bell, Hilari *writer, former librarian*
Bell, Theodore Augustus, III, (Ted Bell) *writer, former advertising executive*
Bentley, Eric *writer, playwright, literature educator*
Berendt, John Lawrence *writer, editor*
Berg, A(ndrew) Scott *writer*
Berger, Thomas Louis *author*
Berkow, Ira Harvey *writer, journalist*
Birstein, Ann *writer, educator*
Block, Francesca Lia *writer*
Blume, Judy *author*
Bradbury, Ray Douglas *writer*
Bradford, Barbara Taylor *writer, journalist*
Bradley, Richard (Richard Blow) *writer*
Branch, Taylor *writer*
Brashares, Ann *writer*
Brathwaite, Edward Kamau (Kamau Brathwaite, Lawson Edward Brathwaite) *poet, educator*
Braudy, Susan Orr *writer*
Broad, William J. *science writer*
Brown, Dan *writer*
Brown, Rita Mae *writer*
Brown, Stuart F. *writer*
Bujold, Lois McMaster *writer*
Burros, Marian Fox *writer*
Cabalquinto, Luis Carrazcal *freelance writer*
Caldwell, Ian *writer*
Callo, Joseph Francis *writer*
Caputo, Philip Joseph *writer, journalist*
Card, Orson Scott (Byron Walley) *writer*
Carey, Peter Philip *writer*
Carlson, P(atricia) M(cElroy) *writer*
Carter, Lonnie Tyrone *playwright, educator*
Castro, Jan Garden *writer, art educator, consultant*
Chabon, Michael *writer*
Cherryh, C. J. *writer*
Christopher, Nicholas *poet, writer*
Cleary, Beverly Atlee (Mrs. Clarence T. Cleary) *writer*
Coben, Harlan *writer*
Connelly, Michael *writer*
Conroy, Pat (Donald Patrick Conroy) *writer*
Coupland, Douglas Campbell *writer*
Crittenden, Danielle Ann *writer, journalist*
Cronin, Doreen *writer, former lawyer*
Crouch, Stanley *writer, musician*
Curry, Jane Louise *writer*
Danto, Arthur Coleman *writer, philosopher, critic*
Davis, Patti *writer*
Decter, Midge *writer*
Denker, Henry *playwright, author, director*
Desai, Kiran *writer*
Deveraux, Jude (Jude Gilliam White) *writer*
Diamonstein-Spielvogel, Barbaralee *writer*
Didion, Joan *writer*
Dillard, Annie *writer*
Dobell, Byron Maxwell *magazine consultant*
Doctorow, E.L. (Edgar Lawrence) *writer, English educator*
Dowling, Danielle *writer*
Duffy, James Henry *writer, retired lawyer*
Duncan, Pearl Rose *writer*
Dunne, Dominick *writer*
Earling, Debra Magpie *writer, educator*
Eckert, Allan Wesley *writer*
Eichenwald, Kurt *writer*
Eisenberg, Lee B. *writer*
Ellis, Bret Easton *writer*
Ellison, Nicholas Howell *literary agent*
Ellroy, James *writer*
Ensler, Eve *playwright, actress*
Evanovich, Janet *writer*
Fagin, Dan *science and environmental writer, reporter*
Fast, Julius *writer, editor*
Ferguson, Kitty Gail *writer, educator*
Fielding, Helen *writer*
Fitch, Janet *writer*
Fleischman, Albert Sidney (Sid Fleischman) *writer*
Flory, Marjorie Anne *writer, editor*
Fox, Paula *writer*
Frank, Elizabeth *writer, educator*
Franzen, Jonathan *writer*
Frazier, Charles Robinson *writer*
Friedman, B(ernard) H(arper) *writer*
Gelb, Leslie Howard *writer, lecturer, consultant*
George, Elizabeth (Susan Elizabeth George) *writer*
Giblin, James Cross *writer, publishing executive*
Gladwell, Malcolm *writer*
Glass, Julia *writer*

Goddard, Donald Letcher *writer, editor*
Goldman, Peter Louis *writer*
Golomb, Susan L. *literary agent*
Gonnerman, Jennifer *writer, journalist*
Goodman, Allegra *writer*
Goodman, George Jerome Waldo (Adam Smith) *writer, television journalist, consultant*
Gordimer, Nadine *writer*
Gordon, David *playwright, theater director, choreographer*
Goulden, Joseph Chesley *author*
Gourevich, Philip *writer, editor*
Grafton, Sue *novelist*
Grant, Cynthia D. *writer*
Greenwald, Sheila Ellen *writer, illustrator*
Grisham, John *writer*
Grogan, John *writer*
Hackbarth, Steven Lyle *writer, educator, audio-visual specialist*
Hadas, Rachel *poet, educator*
Hague, William Edward *writer*
Haigh, Jennifer *writer*
Hamilton, Laurell K. *writer*
Handler, Daniel (Lemony Snicket) *writer*
Hardwick, Elizabeth *writer*
Hathaway, Robin *writer*
Hazzard, Shirley *author*
Heinemann, Larry C. *writer*
Hesse, Karen (Karen Sue Hesse) *writer, educator*
Heymann, C(lemens) David *author*
Hiaasen, Carl *writer, reporter*
Hillenbrand, Laura *writer*
Hjortsberg, William Reinhold *writer*
Hoffman, Alice *writer*
Hosseini, Khaled *writer*
Hotz, Robert Lee *writer, editor*
Howard, Richard (Joseph) *poet, literary translator*
Hwang, David Henry *playwright, screenwriter*
Iglauer, Edith *writer, reporter*
Iles, Greg *writer*
Ishiguro, Kazuo *writer, scriptwriter*
Jacker, Corinne Litvin *playwright, writer*
Jacobs, Arnold Stephen *writer, commentator*
Jhabvala, Ruth Prawer *writer*
Johnson, Charles Richard *writer, teacher*
Jones, Diana Wynne *writer*
Jong, Erica Mann *writer*
Josephson, Marvin *literary agent*
Kafka, Barbara Poses *writer, chef*
Kauffmann, Stanley Jules *author*
Kaufman, Bel *author, educator*
Keene, Donald *writer, translator, language educator*
Kehret, Peg *writer*
Kellerman, Jonathan Seth *writer, pediatric psychologist, educator*
Kelley, Kitty *writer*
Kennedy, Adrienne Lita *playwright*
Kinnell, Galway *poet, translator*
Klein, T(heodore) E(ibon) D(onald) *writer*
Koch, Stephen Bayard *writer, language educator*
Koke, Richard Joseph *writer, curator*
Kostelanetz, Richard *writer, artist*
Kostova, Elizabeth *writer*
Kotlowitz, Robert *writer, editor*
Kotzwinkle, William *writer*
Krantz, Judith Tarcher *novelist*
Lamb, Wally *writer*
Lamm, Donald Stephen *literary agent*
Lapierre, Dominique *writer, historian, philanthropist*
Lawson, Nigella *cookbook writer, celebrity chef*
Lee, Helie *writer*
L'Engle, Madeleine (Mrs. Hugh Franklin) *writer*
Levin, Gail *writer, educator, photographer*
Levin, Ira *writer, playwright*
Levine, Gail Carson *writer*
Levoy, Myron *author*
Levy, Shawn Anthony *writer*
Lewis, Michael *writer, journalist*
Lindsay-Abaire, David *playwright*
Lippman, Laura *writer*
Lorch, Maristella De Panizza *writer, educator*
Lurie, Alison *writer*
Macer-Story, Eugenia Ann *writer*
MacLachlan, Patricia *author*
Maguire, Gregory *writer*
Manning, Martha Mary *writer, psychologist*
Mason, Bobbie Ann *writer*
Maupin, Armistead Jones, Jr. *writer*
McCarthy, Cormac (Charles Joseph McCarthy) *writer*
McCourt, Frank (Francis McCourt) *writer*
McCullough, David *writer, educator*
McDermott, Alice *writer*
Mcdonald, Gregory Christopher *author*
McInerney, Jay *writer*
McMurtry, Larry Jeff *writer*
McNally, Terrence *playwright*
McQuown, Judith Hershkowitz *writer, consultant, financial planner*
Meltzer, Milton *author*
Menza, Claudia Marcella *literary agent*
Milch, David *screenwriter, producer*
Mills, Stephanie Ellen *writer*
Minarik, Else Holmelund (Bigart Minarik) *author*
Moehringer, J. R. *writer*
Mooney, Richard Emerson *writer*
Moore, Christopher *writer*
Mosley, Walter *writer*
Navarra, Tova *writer, artist*
Neier, Aryeh *author, human rights organization administrator*
Newberg, Esther *literary agent*
Nicol, Dominik *writer, photographer*
Noonan, Peggy *writer*
Oates, Joyce Carol *writer*
O'Doherty, Brian *writer*
Offit, Sidney *writer, educator*
O'Toole, Patricia Ellen *writer, educator*
Packer, George *writer*
Pall, Ellen Jane *writer*
Palmer, Michael *poet*
Papell, Helen Gertrude *poet, retired librarian*
Paretsky, Sara N. *writer*
Paterson, Katherine Womeldorf *writer*
Patterson, James Brendan, Jr. *writer, former advertising executive*
Perez-Firmat, Gustavo Francisco *writer, language educator*
Pérez-Rivera, Francisco (Frank Rivera) *writer*
Phillips, Reneé *writer*
Pomerantz, Charlotte *writer*
Pool, Mary Jane *writer, editor*
Poole, William Daniel *writer, editor*
Powell, Julie *writer*
Prelutsky, Jack *author*
Price, Reynolds *writer, educator*
Quin-Harkin, Janet Elizabeth (Rhys Bowen) *writer*
Rapp, Adam *writer, playwright*
Rathmann, Peggy *writer, illustrator*
Reig, June Wilson *scriptwriter, television director and producer*
Renehan, Edward John *writer*
Revkin, Andrew C. *writer, reporter*
Rhodes, Richard (Lee) *writer*
Rice, Luanne *writer*
Rich, Adrienne *poet*
Roberts, Nora *writer*
Robinson, Kim Stanley *science fiction author*
Robinson, Marilynne *writer*
Rollin, Betty *writer, television journalist*
Rollins, James (Jim Czajkowski, James Clemens) *writer, veterinarian*
Ronde, John Herman *writer, translator*
Rothenberg, Jerome *writer, literature educator*
Rubell, Jennifer *writer, hotelier*
Rumaker, Michael *writer, language educator*
Sachar, Louis *writer*
Salinger, J(erome) D(avid) *author*
Salter, James *writer*
Salter, Mary Jo *poet*
Sandford, John (John Roswell Camp) *writer, journalist*
Sargent, Pamela *writer*
Schisgal, Murray *playwright*
Seaman, Barbara (Ann Rosner) *author*
Segal, Lore *writer*
Sendak, Maurice Bernard *writer, illustrator*
Shaffer, Peter (Sir Peter Shaffer) *playwright*
Shao, Wei *writer, educator*
Shawn, Wallace *playwright, actor*
Sheehan, Susan *writer*
Shriver, Lionel (Margaret Ann Shriver) *writer*
Shulevitz, Uri *writer, illustrator*
Silbersack, John Walter *literary agent*
Silva, Daniel Joseph *writer*
Silverman, Allison *scriptwriter, television producer, actress*
Smiley, Jane Graves *author, educator*
Smith, Betty *writer, not-for-profit developer*
Smith, Ian K. *writer, columnist, physician*
Smith, Warren Allen *writer, director, columnist*
Solnit, Rebecca *writer, critic*
Steel, Danielle Fernande *author*
Stevenson, William Henri *author*
Swann, Brian *writer, humanities educator*
Sykes, Plum *writer*
Sypher, Francis J. *writer, editor, educator*
Talese, Gay *writer*
Tan, Amy Ruth *writer*
Taylor, Mildred D. *author*
Teachout, Terry *writer, critic*
Tomkins, Calvin *writer*
Toobin, Jeffrey Ross *writer, legal analyst*
Trillin, Calvin *writer, journalist*
Tuck, Lily *writer*
Urban, Amanda (Binky Urban) *literary agent*
Vidal, Gore (Eugene Luther Gore Vidal) *writer*
Vorhees, Mark *writer*
Walker, Alice *writer*
Waller, Robert James *writer*
Ward, Geoffrey Champion *writer, editor*
Wasserman, Steve *literary agent*
Watt, Douglas (Benjamin Watt) *writer, drama critic*
Wender, Phyllis Bellows *literary agent*
Weschler, Lawrence Michael *writer, journalist*
West, Paul Noden *writer, playwright*
Westlake, Donald Edwin (Tucker Coe, Richard Stark) *writer*
Wilds, Bonnie *writer, volunteer*
Wilson, Edwin *writer, playwright, educator, theater director*
Wolf, Naomi *writer*
Wolfe, Tom (Thomas Kennerly Wolfe Jr.) *writer, journalist*
Wolff, Virginia Euwer *writer*
Woods, Stuart *writer*
Wren, Gayden *playwright, theater director*
Wright, Douglas *playwright*
Wright, Gwendolyn *writer, architecture educator, historian*
Yaffe, James *writer*
Yglesias, Helen Bassine *author, educator*

North Tonawanda
Powers, Bruce Raymond *writer, language educator, consultant*

Nyack
Hendin, David Bruce *literary agent, writer, numismatist, educator*

Olivebridge
Osborne, Seward Russell *writer*

Palisades
Davis, Dorothy Salisbury *writer*
Polk, Milbry Catherine *writer*

Pawling
Lester, Helen Doughty *writer*

Plandome
Sherwood, James Webster III *writer*

Poughkeepsie
Willard, Nancy Margaret *writer, educator*

Purchase
Phillips, Carly *writer*

Rhinebeck
Sloane, Beverly LeBov *writer, instructor, consultant*

Rochester
Hoch, Edward Dentinger *writer*
Rothberg, Abraham *writer*

Rockville Centre
Mazzucelli, Colette Grace Celia *author, educator*
Schwartz, Arthur *playwright, poet*

Rye
Hurwitz, Sol *writer, consultant*
Ketchum, William Clarence *author, educator*

Sag Harbor
Pashman, Susan Ellen *writer*

Sagaponack
Cedering, Siv *poet, writer*

Saratoga Springs
Sainer, Arthur *writer, theater educator*

Scarsdale
Holmes, Rupert *playwright, singer, writer*
Topping, Seymour *writer*

Shelter Island
Mayer, Martin Prager *writer*

Staten Island
Foster, Paul *playwright*
Porter, Darwin Fred *writer*

Syracuse
Luft, Eric V.D. *writer, educator, publisher*
Staples, Heidi L *poet, writer*

Tivoli
Ratcliff, Carter Goodrich *writer, critic, poet*

Valley Stream
Rachlin, Harvey Brant *writer*

Wainscott
Herzog, Arthur III *author*

Warwick
Linnéa, Sharon *writer, playwright*

West Nyack
Pringle, Laurence Patrick *writer*

Woodstock
Godwin, Gail Kathleen *writer*

Yonkers
Baumel, Joan Patricia French *writer, educator*

NORTH CAROLINA

Chapel Hill
Berne, Suzanne *writer, educator*
Spencer, Elizabeth *writer*

Charlotte
Ethridge, Mark Foster III *writer, publishing executive, consultant*
Finley, Glenna *writer*

Greensboro
Watson, Robert Winthrop *poet*

Greenville
Gilham, Hanna Kaltenbrunner *writer*

Laurinburg
Gilbert, Marie Rogers *poet*

Midland
Voncannon, Brian Everett *writer, scriptwriter, radio personality, naturopath*

Raleigh
Pendry, Pattie Louise *writer*
Tucker, Helen Welch *writer*

Vale
Chandonnet, Ann Fox *journalist, poet*

Winston Salem
Ehle, John Marsden, Jr. *writer*
Hanes, Frank Borden *writer, former business executive, farmer*

OHIO

Akron
Taormina, Charles Anthony *writer, editor, artist*

Cincinnati
Birmingham, Stephen *writer*
Draper, Sharon M. *writer, elementary school educator*
McAusland, Randolph Melville Neal *writer, art consultant*

Cleveland
Eagleeye-Lord, Amy *writer, editor*
Finn, Robert *writer, educator*
Kovel, Ralph Mallory *writer, antique expert*
Kovel, Terry Horvitz *writer, antiques authority*

Cleveland Heights
Sandburg, Helga *author*

Columbus
Zweibel, Alan *writer*

Dayton
Hayes, Stephen Kurtz *writer*
Heath, Mariwyn Dwyer *writer, legislative staff member*

Euclid
Adrine-Robinson, Kenyette *writer, educator, poet, artist, photographer*

Fairborn
Szucs, Andrew Eric *freelance/self-employed writer*

Glendale
Strom, Kristina Chase *writer, consultant*

Napoleon
Meekison, MaryFran *writer*

Nashport
Gilmore, Clare Mae *writer*

Oberlin
Taylor, Robert Larry *freelance/self-employed writer*

Perrysburg
Weaver, Richard L., II, *writer, educator*

Westerville
Young, Bette Ann *writer*

Worthington
Vladem, Steven Allen *writer, film producer, motivational speaker*

OKLAHOMA

Lawton
Riley, Robert Shean *writer, publishing executive, retired army officer*

Shawnee
Stoddard, Allan Lee *writer, musician*

Tulsa
Fielding, Peggy Lou Moss *writer*
Upton, Howard B., Jr. *writer, lawyer*

OREGON

Beatty
Nettelbeck, Fred Arthur *poet*

Cannon Beach
Hellyer, Constance Anne (Connie Anne Conway) *writer, musician, educator*

Culver
Siebert, Diane Dolores *author, poet*

Eugene
Wilhelm, Kate (Katy Gertrude) *author*

Klamath Falls
Koch, Margaret Rau *writer, artist, historian*

Newport
Kennedy, Richard Jerome *writer*

Portland
Larson, Wanda Z. *writer, poet*
Lovett, Richard A. *writer, photographer*
Neavoll, George Franklin *writer*
Porter, Elsa Allgood *writer, educator*
Tuska, Jon *writer, publishing executive*

PENNSYLVANIA

Erie
Wykoff, Gary Lee *writer*

Kennett Square
Martin, George (Whitney) *writer*

King Of Prussia
Schumann, Paula M. L. *writer*

Lancaster
Kornhauser, Barry Paul *playwright, theater director*
Shenk, Lois Elaine Landis *writer*
Taylor, Ann *writer, educator*

Milford
Le Guin, Ursula Kroeber *writer*

New Kingstown
DiSipio, Rocco Thomas *writer*

Pen Argyl
Martocci, Lewis Nicholas III *writer*

Philadelphia
Bernstein, Charles *poet, writer, educator*
Fussell, Paul *writer, literature educator*
Givens, Janet Eaton *writer*
Kinsella, Thomas *poet*
Nickels, Thom *writer, journalist*
Paglia, Camille *writer, humanities educator*
Wallace, Emily Mitchell *writer, editor, educator*

Pottstown
Hylton, Thomas James *author*

Southampton
Bendiner, Robert *writer, editor*

State College
Aberg, Gilbert S. *retired writer*

Valley Forge
Miller, Betty Brown *freelance writer*

RHODE ISLAND

Providence
López-Morillas, Frances (Mapes) *translator*
Schevill, James Erwin *poet, playwright*
Steinbach, Meredith Lynn *writer, educator*
Vogel, Paula Anne *playwright*

SOUTH CAROLINA

Aiken
Naifeh, Steven Woodward *writer*

Columbia
Newton, Rhonwen Leonard *writer, data processing executive, consultant*

Hilton Head Island
Reed, Frances Boogher *writer, actress*

Lexington
Wilkins, Robert Pearce *writer, lawyer*

Rock Hill
Bristow, Robert O'Neil *writer, educator*

Summerville
Reisman, Rosemary Moody Canfield *writer, humanities educator*

TENNESSEE

Blaine
Bull, James C. *poet*

Knoxville
Bell, Linda R. *writer, photographer*
Hooper, William Edward *writer, broadcast journalist*

Loudon
Randall, Marilyn Mae *writer*

Millington
Thomas-Harris, Yvonne Anita *writer, poet*

Murfreesboro
Rankins, Darren Barnard *poet*

Nashville
Bird, Caroline *author*
Pearson, Sela *poet, speaker*
Wiseman, Craig *song writer, publisher*

Sevierville
Koff, Shirley Irene *writer*

TEXAS

Amarillo
Mojtabai, Ann Grace *author, educator*

Austin
Barnes, Thomas Joseph *writer*
Beazley, Hamilton *writer, educator*
Cunningham, Julia Woolfolk *author*
Friedman, Kinky (Richard Friedman) *writer, musician*
Spicer, Beverly White *writer, photojournalist, artist*

Boerne
Price, John Randolph *writer*

Cedar Hill
Stowers, Carlton Eugene *writer*

Chireno
Mayhar, Ardath Frances (Frank Cannon, John Killdeer, Frances Hurst) *writer*

Corpus Christi
Breecher, Maury Martin *writer, small business owner*

Crowley
Sizemore, Deborah Lightfoot *writer, editor*

Dale
LittleDog, Pat *writer*

Dallas
Bartlett, Richard Chalkley *writer, conservationist*
Dee, Ronda *poet, photographer, small business owner, journalist*
Gillett, Grover *author*
Granowsky, Alvin *writer, educator*
Phillips, Betty Lou (Elizabeth Louise Phillips) *writer, interior designer*
Sherrod, Danny Troy *writer, educator*

Elgin
Jordan, Charlene Hanson *writer*

Fort Worth
de Toledo, Catherine Holt *medical writer*
Lale, Cissy Stewart (Lloyd Lale) *freelance writer*
Laughlin, Christel Renate *translator, consultant*
Munday, Stephen Dale *writer, artist*

Georgetown
Shelby, Roselle Price *writer, retired special education educator*

Houston
Leslie, Mae Sue *writer*
Mallia, Marianne *medical writer*
Parle, Bertha Ibarra *writer*
Pete, Eric E. *writer, claims representative*

Lubbock
Craighead, Owen Lindsay *writer*

Mansfield
Parnell, Charles L. *speechwriter*

Plano
Gallardo, Henrietta Castellanos *writer*

Pottsboro
Jackson, Nona Armour *writer, illustrator*

San Antonio
Ammann, Lillian Ann Nicholson *writer, editor, small business owner*
Fehrenbach, T.R. (Theodore Reed Fehrenbach) *writer*
Heidelberg, Paul *writer*

Smithville
Clark, LaVerne Harrell *writer*

Texarkana
Presley, James Wright *writer, environmentalist*

UTAH

Cedar City
Modesitt, Leland Exton, Jr., (L.E. Modesitt Jr.) *writer, poet, consultant*

Logan
Hruby, George Geoffrey *writer, educator*

Provo
Hart, Edward LeRoy *poet, educator*

Saint George
Pearce, Carole Ann *poet*

Salt Lake City
Osherow, Jacqueline Sue *poet, English language educator*
Wingate, Thomas Russell *writer*

Santa Clara
Llewellyn, Linda J. *motivational speaker, consultant, writer*

VERMONT

Bennington
Bernard, April *poet, literature educator*

Burlington
Hearon, Shelby *writer, educator*

Chester
Coleman, John Royston *writer*

Marlboro
Stevenson, Laura Caroline *writer, educator*

Middlebury
MacDonald, Kenneth R., Jr. *author, artist*

Morrisville
Besser, Gretchen Rous *writer, educator*

South Royalton
Powers, Thomas Moore *writer*

Stamford
Stevens, Lauren Rogers *writer, environmentalist*

VIRGINIA

Aldie
Weaver, Kitty Dunlap *author*

Alexandria
Malott, John Raymond *writer, consultant, not-for-profit executive*

Arlington
Arehart-Treichel, Joan *writer*
England, Robert Stowe *writer*
Timperlake, Edward Thomas *writer*

Ashburn
Boyne, Walter James *writer, retired museum director*

Charlottesville
Casey, John Dudley *writer, language educator*
Dove, Rita Frances *poet, language educator*
Hine, Jonathan Trumbull, Jr. *translator, educator*
McCrimmon, Barbara Smith *writer, librarian*
Wright, Charles Penzel, Jr. *writer, educator*

Fairfax
Cosing, Arthur Paul, Jr. *writer, artist*

Falls Church
Orben, Robert *scriptwriter, writer*
Whitehead, Kenneth Dean *writer, translator, retired federal agency administrator*

Fort Belvoir
Parrish-St. John, Florence Tucker *writer, retired federal agency administrator*

Glen Allen
Cornwell, Patricia Daniels *writer*

Leesburg
Budiansky, Stephen Philip *writer*

Lexington
Solod, Lisa *writer*
Stuart, Dabney *poet, language educator*

Mc Lean
Wallace, Barbara Brooks *writer*

Meadowview
Kingsolver, Barbara Ellen *writer*

Middleburg
Grove, Noel Randall *writer*

Norfolk
Reynolds, Sheri *writer*

Portsmouth
Mapp, Alf Johnson, Jr. *writer, historian, educator*

Reston
Smith, Ralph Lee *writer, musician*

Stephenson
Johnson, Eva Maria *retired translator*

Vienna
Olshaker, Mark Bruce *scriptwriter, filmmaker*

Williamsburg
Smith, William Henry Preston *freelance/self-employed writer, editor, former telecommunications industry executive*
Starnes, Sofia Molina *writer, editor*

WASHINGTON

Arlington
Bullington, Gayle Rogers *writer, researcher*

Bellevue
Olson, Robert William *writer, retired counselor*

Issaquah
Cain, Coleen W. *writer, educator*

Kirkland
Szablya, Helen Mary *writer, language educator*

La Conner
Robbins, Thomas Eugene *writer*

Lacey
Mata, Linda Sue Proctor *writer, consultant*

Lynnwood
Bear, Gregory Dale *writer, illustrator*

Medina
Lucas, Patricia Latourette *writer*

Nordland
Kramnicz, Rosanne *freelance writer*

Port Angeles
Muller, Willard C(hester) *writer*

Port Townsend
Kooser, Ted (Theodore J. Kooser) *poet*

Seattle
Gardiner, John Jacob *writer, educator, philosopher*
Kunkel, Georgie Bright *freelance writer, retired counselor*
Romm, Daniel F. *writer, retired computer technician*
Rule, Ann *writer*
Thomas, Irv *writer, journalist*
Wagoner, David Russell *writer, educator*

Spokane
Brock, Randall J. *poet*

Vashon
Cushman, Karen Lipski *writer*

WEST VIRGINIA

Charleston
Mellert, Lucie Anne *writer, photographer*

Teays
Lamb, Carl Vernon *writer, retired engineer*

WISCONSIN

Argyle
Daley, Ron(ald Eugene) *playwright, poet, theater director, theater producer*

Brookfield
Schmitz, John J. *writer, educator*

Elkhorn
Dunn, Walter Scott, Jr. *writer, museum director, consultant*

Green Bay
Erickson, Ruth Alice *poet, artist*

Madison
K-Turkel, Judith Leah Rosenthal (Judi K-Turkel) *writer, editor, publisher*
Moore, Lorrie *writer, English professor*
Stites, Susan Kay *writer, human resources specialist, consultant*

Milwaukee
Connelly, Mark *writer, educator*

Racine
Wright, Betty Ren *children's book writer*

Saukville
Gulan, Bonnie Marion *writer, researcher*

Shawano
Mutter, John J., Jr. *writer, researcher*

WYOMING

Laramie
Boresi, Arthur Peter *writer, educator*

Pinedale
Barlow, John Perry *writer, former rancher, advocate*

TERRITORIES OF THE UNITED STATES

GUAM

Mangilao
Strauch, Edward Hugo *writer, retired literature and language professor*

PUERTO RICO

San Juan
Padrón, Luije *writer*

CANADA

BRITISH COLUMBIA

Heriot Bay
Bringhurst, Robert *poet*

Vancouver
Bowering, George Harry *writer, consultant, language educator*
Cohen, Leonard (Norman Cohen) *poet, writer, musician*

ONTARIO

Toronto
Moore, Christopher Hugh *writer*
Peacock, Molly *poet, educator*

QUEBEC

Montreal
Bruemmer, Fred *writer, photographer*

AUSTRALIA

Norfolk Island
McCullough, Colleen *author*

Paddington
Keneally, Thomas Michael *author*

DENMARK

Charlottenlund
Garner, Fradley Hamilton *freelance/self-employed writer, editor*

ENGLAND

Cambridge
Steiner, George (Francis Steiner) *author, educator*

London
Chevalier, Tracy Rose *writer*
Cleese, John Marwood *writer, comedian*
Cope, Wendy *poet*
Curtis, Richard *author, screenwriter*
Deighton, Len *author*
Drabble, Margaret *writer*
Fine, Anne *writer*
Frayn, Michael *playwright*
Galloway, Janice *writer, editor*
Gray, Simon James Holliday *writer, educator*
Hare, David *playwright*
Harris, Thomas *writer*
Hunter Blair, Pauline Clarke *author*
James, P(hyllis) D(orothy) (Baroness James of Holland Park of Southwold in County of Suffolk) *author*
Lessing, Doris (Doris May) *writer*
Ormsby, Eric Linn *writer, educator*
Palahniuk, Chuck (Charles Michael Palahniuk) *writer, journalist*
Paton Walsh, Jill *writer*
Pessl, Marisha *writer, artist*
Read, Piers Paul *author*
Rowling, J.K. (Joanne Kathleen Rowling) *writer*
Smith, Zadie (Sadie Smith) *writer*
Stoppard, Tom (Tomas Straussler) *playwright*

Stevenage
Follett, Kenneth Martin *author*

Whitchurch
Adams, Richard George *writer*

FRANCE

Lacoste
Strauss, Gwen B. *writer, editor*

Paris
Horovitz, Israel Arthur *playwright*
Littell, Jonathan *writer*

GERMANY

Bonn
Rampacher, Hermann Hans *writer, consultant*

IRELAND

Donegal
Friel, Brian (Bernard Patrick Friel) *author*

Mullingar
Donleavy, James Patrick *writer, artist*

ITALY

Venice
Pasinetti, Pier Maria *author*

SWITZERLAND

Bern
Carlson, Dale Bick *writer*

ADDRESS UNPUBLISHED

Aleshire, Joan Allan *poet, creative writing educator*
Alexander, Lora Kay *writer, composer*
Alinder, Mary Street *writer, educator*
Allen, Roberta *writer, photographer, conceptual artist*
Aloff, Mindy *writer*
Andersen, Kurt Byars *writer*
Anderson, M.T. *children's book writer and illustrator*
Andreasson, Kim J. *writer, consultant*
Anselmo, Robert Louis *writer*
Antonelli, Judith Sarah *writer*
Antonelli, Rosemary *writer*
Apple, Gary Winston *writer, educational consultant*
Apps, Jerold Willard *writer*
Argers, Helen *writer, playwright*
Arlen, Michael J. *writer*
Arndt, Matthew *scriptwriter*
Arndt, Michael *scriptwriter*
Ashanti, Baron James *poet, educator*
Askew, Rilla *author*
Aslan, Madalyn *writer, educator*
Avery, Stephen Neal *playwright, writer*
Bahr, Jane Marie *writer, retired language educator*
Bailey, William Waddell *writer, communications executive*
Bakeman, Carol Ann *travel writer, singer*
Baldrige, Letitia *writer, management consultant*
Barrett, Katherine *writer, columnist*
Barzun, Jacques *writer, literary agent*
Bassett, Elizabeth Ewing (Libby Bassett) *writer, editor, consultant*
Baum, Roger S. *writer*
Beatts, Anne Patricia *writer*
Benedict, Stewart H. *writer, playwright*
Bennett, Velma Joyce (Joyce Williams) *writer, poet*
Bernstein, Carl *writer, journalist*
Bertram, Jean DeSales *writer*
Biddle, Judith Ann *retired writer*
Black, David *writer, educator*
Blake Ramos, Debra Barbara *writer*
Block, Lawrence *writer*
Blos, Joan Windsor *writer, critic, educator*
Bluh, Bonnie *scriptwriter, actress, novelist, playwright*
Bodsworth, Fred *writer, ecologist*
Bova, Benjamin William *writer, editor*
Bowden, Mark Robert *writer*
Boyle, T.C. *writer, literature educator*
Bracken, Peg *writer*
Braun, Lilian Jackson *writer*
Breuer, William Bentley *author*
Briles, Judith *writer, consultant*
Briskin, Jacqueline Elizabeth *author*
Brodsky, Beverly Anne *writer, consultant, editor*
Brooks, Geraldine *writer, reporter, news correspondent*
Brown, Sandra *writer*
Burch, Annetta Jane *writer*
Busch, David Dennis *writer, photographer*
Cáceres, Franklin Thomas *retired writer*
Calore, Paul *writer, retired government agency administrator*
Carlyon, David James *writer, theater director*
Carson, Mary Kay *writer*
Carter, Cynthia (Cindy) Lynn *writer*
Cecil, Elizabeth Jean *writer*
Cep, Casey Nicole *writer, theology scholar*
Cheever, Susan *freelance/self-employed writer*
Chernow, Ron *writer, journalist*
Choukas-Bradley, Melanie *writer, photographer*
Claes, Gayla Christine *writer, editor, consultant*
Clancy, Thomas L., Jr. *novelist, producer*
Clark, Mary Higgins *writer, communications executive*
Clark, Matt *writer*
Clarke, Sir Arthur Charles *author*
Clements, Thomas Frank *writer*
Coburn, D(onald) L(ee) *playwright*
Collins, William J. (Billy Collins) *poet, educator*
Conklin, William Frank *writer*
Conley, Ruth Irene *poet*
Conover-Carson, Anne *writer*
Cook, Robin *writer*
Cowan, Andrew Glenn *television writer, producer, performer*
Cussler, Clive Eric *author*
Cutler, Karan Davis *writer, columnist*
Dailey, Janet *writer*
Danelo, David Joseph *writer, editor*
Daren, Sylvia *poet*
David, Larry *television scriptwriter and producer, actor*
Davis, J. Alan *writer, film and television producer*
Davis, Luther *writer, theater producer, motion picture producer*
Davis, Mamie (Denise Davis) *writer*
Dawdy, Doris Ostrander *writer*
Deats, Suzanne *writer, editor, artist*
Delffs, Dudley J. *writer, educator*
DeLillo, Don *author*
Deloatch, Cheryl Lee *writer*
DeMille, Nelson Richard *writer*
Desio, Delores Jean *writer, artist, retired elementary school educator*
Diamant, Anita *writer*
Dolan, Edward Francis *writer*
Donnally, Patricia Broderick *writer*
Dowers, Lois Ann *writer*
Druffel, Ann Bernice *researcher, writer*
Dworzan, Helene Liberman *writer, poet, playwright*
Egan, Timothy K. *writer, journalist*
Eglee, Charles Hamilton *scriptwriter, film and television producer*
Ehrenreich, Barbara *writer*
Emerson, Claudia *poet, language professor*
Ensminger, John Jay *writer, poet, minister, counselor, playwright*
Ephron, Nora *writer*
Esty, John Cushing, Jr. *writer, educator, not-for-profit counsel*
Evangelista, Anita Loretta *freelance/self-employed writer, publishing executive, psychologist, nurse*
Evans, Jack R. (J. Glenn) *writer, poet*
Evans, Mari *author*
Fadiman, Anne *writer, educator*
Farrelly, Peter John *screenwriter*
Fearrington, Ann Peyton *writer, illustrator, news correspondent*
Finch, Christopher Robin *writer*
Finder, Joseph Alan *writer*
Fleming, Thomas James *writer*
Fletcher, Donald Rodgers *writer, religious studies educator*
Foote, Horton *playwright, scriptwriter*
Foster, Ken *writer, educator*
Frankel, Jennie Louise *writer, composer, playwright*
Frankel, Terrie Maxine *writer, composer, playwright*
Freedman, Russell Bruce *author*
French, Marilyn *writer, critic, historian*
Fryer, Thomas Waitt, Jr. *writer*
Frymer, Murry *writer, film and theater critic*
Fuentes, Carlos *writer, retired ambassador*
Fuller, Jack William *writer, retired publishing executive*
Gable, Carl Irwin *writer, investor, retired lawyer*
Ganz, Lowell *scriptwriter, television producer*
Garfield-Woodbridge, Nancy *writer*
Garfinkle, Elaine Myra *writer*
Gariepy, Carole Jane *writer, retired elementary school educator*
Gatria, America I *retired writer*
Gavril, Jean (Jean Van Leeuwen) *writer*
George, Gerald William *writer*
Gilbert, Elayne Rhoda *writer*
Gilbert, Jack *poet*
Gilroy, Frank Daniel *playwright*
Ginsburg, Lynn *writer*
Giovinazzo, Vivian Curry *writer*
Glück, Louise Elisabeth *poet, educator*
Goble, Paul *writer, illustrator, artist*
Goldberg, Lucianne *literary agent*
Goldfarb, Ruth *poet, educator*
Goldman, Judith *writer, editor, curator, consultant, publisher*
Goldman, William *writer, scriptwriter*
Goss, Joel Francis *writer*
Gossard, Marcia Nadine *writer*
Gray, Francine du Plessix *writer*
Gray, Thomas Stephen *writer*
Greenburg, Dan *author*
Greer, Germaine *author*
Gustafsson, Lars Erik Einar *writer, educator*
Guy, Eleanor Bryenton *retired writer*
Haas, Charlie *screenwriter*
Hadley, Leila Eliott-Burton (Mrs. Henry Luce III) *writer*
Haggis, Paul Edward *scriptwriter, television producer, television director*
Hahn, Mary Downing *writer*
Haldeman, Joe William *writer*
Hall, Donald *poet*
Hall, Peggy Craft *poet, retired secondary school educator*
Hamit, Francis Granger *novelist, playwright*
Harrigan, Anthony Hart *author*
Harstad, Carolyn Audrey *writer, educator, photographer*
Hartman, Earl Kenneth *writer*
Hastings, John Jacob *writer, lyricist, consultant, activist*
Hautman, Pete (Peter Murray) *writer*
Hayes, Cynthia Ann (C.A. Hayes) *writer*
Helprin, Mark *author*
Hemon, Aleksander *writer*
Henry, Rene Arthur *writer, consultant*
Herbert, James Alan *writer*
Herman, George Adam *writer, literature educator*
Herman, Hank *writer*
Herman, Michelle *writer*
Herrnkind, Hilda Marie *writer, military volunteer*
Higbee, Donna Good *writer, researcher*
Higdon, Pamela Leis *writer*
Hill, Laban Carrick *writer*
Hillenburg, Stephen *writer, television producer, animator*
Hillerman, Tony *writer, journalist, educator*
Himmelfarb, Gertrude *writer, educator*
Hitchcock, Jane Stanton *playwright, novelist*
Hoff, Benjamin Lloyd *writer, scriptwriter*
Hoffman, William *writer*
Hollander, Anne *writer*
Homes, A. M. *writer*
Hornby, Nick *writer*
Horsman, David A. Elliott *writer, finance company executive, educator*
Houze, Herbert George *writer*
Howes, Sophia DuBose *writer*
Howland, Bette *writer*
Hoyt, Mary Finch *writer, media consultant, retired federal official*
Hu, Hua-ling Wang *writer, historian*
Hughey, Richard Kohlman *writer, lawyer*
Innis, Pauline *writer, publishing company executive*
Irving, John Winslow (John Wallace Blunt Jr.) *writer*
Isaacs, Susan *writer, scriptwriter*
Isenberg, Jane Frances *writer, retired language educator*
Jackson, Charles Ian *writer, consultant*
Jackson, Guida Myrl *writer, editor, literature educator*
Jacobs, Nancy Carolyn Baker *writer*
Jaffee, Annette Williams *novelist*
Jeong, Jinho *writer*
Jocelyn, Marthe Mary *writer*
Jones, Edward Paul *writer, editor*
Jones, Thomas Claburn *poet, educator*
Jones-Ketner, Elizabeth Brown *writer*
Jordan, Carrie Grayson (Carrie Grayson-Jordan) *writer, poet, drama designer*
Jorden, William John *writer, retired diplomat*
Just, Ward Swift *author*
Kass, Jerome Allan *writer*
Katz, William Loren *author*
Kelley, A. Benjamin *writer, educator, consultant*
Kelton, Elmer Stephen *novelist*
Kendall, Harry Wesley *playwright, writer*
Kevles, Bettyann Holtzmann *writer, historian, educator*
Kidder, Tracy (John Tracy Kidder) *writer*
Kimbrell, Grady Ned *writer, educator, retired school system administrator*
Kimmel, Mark *author, venture capital company executive*
Kincaid, Jamaica *writer*
King, Cynthia Bregman *writer*
King, Larry L. *playwright, actor*
Kingston, Maxine Hong *writer, educator*
Kirk, Connie Ann *writer*
Klein, Edward *writer*
Knobloch, Marcia M. (Marta Knobloch) *writer*
Knotts, Robert Spencer (Bob Knotts) *writer, playwright*
Koenig, Robert Louis *writer*
Konigsburg, Elaine Lobl *writer*
Korten, David C. *writer*
Kotlowitz, Alex *writer, journalist*
Kruger, Mollee Coppel *writer*
Kumin, Maxine Winokur *poet, writer*
Kushner, Tony *playwright, scriptwriter*
Lambert, LeClair Grier *writer, lecturer, consultant, former state government public information administrator*
Lambert, Richard Bowles, Jr. *freelance writer*
Lapine, James Elliot *playwright, director*
Larkin, Joan *poet, literature and language educator*
Larsdotter, Anna-Lisa *retired translator, artist*
Larson, Erik *writer*
Lehane, Dennis *writer*
Leonard, Elmore John *writer, scriptwriter*
Lescroart, John Thomas *writer, composer, singer*
Lester, Julius B. *author*
Lethem, Jonathan Allen *writer*
Lewis, Dennis Carroll *writer, publishing executive*
Lightman, Alan Paige *writer, physicist, educator*
Lindenberger, Herbert Samuel *writer, literature educator*
Lippard, Lucy Rowland *writer, educator, critic, curator*
Little, Charlotte Louise *poet, writer*
Lober, Lionel M. *scriptwriter, film producer*
Long, Elaine *writer, editor*
Lopez, Barry Holstun *writer*
Loveland, Sylvia Marie *translator*
Lubell, Ellen *writer*
Lynds, Gayle Hallenbeck *writer*
Macaulay, David Alexander *author, illustrator*
Mackey, Nathaniel *poet and poetry professor*
Madison, Deborah Leafy *writer, chef*
Mailer, Norman Kingsley *writer, playwright, film director*
Mankiewicz, Thomas Frank *screenwriter, director, producer*
Manley, Kelli Jo *writer, photographer*
Manville, Greta Craig *writer*
Marks, Martha Alford *writer*
Martin, George Raymond Richard *writer*
Martin, Jacqueline Briggs *writer*
Martin-Lowry, Beverly Anne *writer, columnist*
Mason, Connie Jeanne *writer*
Mathieu, Michele Suzanne *grant writer, computer scientist, consultant*
Mattar, Philip *writer*
May, Janet Sue *playwright, lyricist*
McCash, June Hall *writer, retired language educator*
McCoy, Dorothy Eloise *writer, educator*
McDonald, April D. *writer*
McElhatten, Betty Shreve *writer, illustrator*
McFerren, Martha Dean *writer, librarian*
McMeen, Albert Ralph III *writer, technical trainer, multimedia programmer, financial services executive*
McMillan, Terry L. *writer, educator*
McPhee, John Angus *writer*
McPherson, James Alan *writer, educator*
McWhorter, Diane *writer*
McWilliams, Karen Joan *writer*
McWilliams, Michael *writer, publisher*
Medoff, Mark Howard *playwright, scriptwriter*
Mendoza, George *poet, author*
Merrill, Jean Fairbanks *writer*
Meyer, Gabriel R. *writer*
Michelle, Cadieux M. *writer*
Miller, W. Kievit *writer*
Mills, Elizabeth Shown *historical writer, genealogist*
Mintz, Morton Abner *writer, reporter*
Mitchard, Jacquelyn *writer*
Mitchell, Marcia Jeanne *writer*
Moore, Robert Henry *writer, editor, communications consultant*
Moore, Robert Lowell, Jr., (Robin Moore) *author*
Moorhead, Lucy Galpin *writer*
Mora, Pat *writer, speech professional*
Morgan, Robin Evonne *poet, writer, journalist, editor*
Morrison, Martin *writer*
Morrison, Sarah Lyddon *author*
Morrison, Toni (Chloe Anthony Wofford) *writer, educator, editor*
Morrow, Barry Nelson *screenwriter, producer*
Morse-McNeely, Patricia *poet, writer, retired secondary school educator*
Morton, M. Juanita *writer, accountant*
Moses, Shelia P. *writer, poet, playwright, producer*
Mullins, Eustace Clarence *writer*
Murphy, Marion Colucci *writer, poet*
Murphy, Randall Kent *writer, educator, consultant*
Murray, Elizabeth Davis Reid *writer, researcher*
Murray, Sabina *writer*
Muson, Howard Henry *writer, consultant*
Myers, Sophia M. *writer, researcher, artist, cartographer, translator*
Neely, Mark Edward, Jr. *writer*
Nevai, Lucia *writer*
Noëldechen, Joan Marguerite *writer*
Norman, Kristy West *writer*
Nova, Craig *writer*
Nurick, Carl J. *writer, consultant, poet*
O'Brien, Charles Harold *writer, priest*
O'Connor, Patrick Joseph *writer, musician, university educator*
Oglesby, Joseph Woodson (Mike English) *writer, publishing executive*
Ognibene, Peter John *writer*
Oransky, Ivan *writer, editor*
Orkin, Jenna *writer*
Ostriker, Alicia Suskin *poet*
Ozick, Cynthia *writer*
Paci, Ruth A. *freelance/self-employed writer*
Pack, Susan Joan *writer*
Paine, Alan *poet*
Pamela, Taylor K. *writer, editor*
Panchyk, Richard Robert *writer*
Pantaleo, Jack *playwright, composer, educator*
Paolucci, Anne Attura *playwright, poet, literature educator, educational consultant*
Pastizzo, Frank Anthony *writer, educator*
Patrusky, Ben *writer*
Patterson, Richard North *writer, lawyer*
Perry, Tyler *playwright, actor, theater director, theater producer*
Phillips, Jill Meta *writer, critic, astrologer*
Pierce, Tamora *writer*
Polster, James *writer, film producer*
Ponce, Mary Helen *writer*
Popp, Lilian Mustaki *writer, educator*
Poundstone, William Nicholas, Jr. *writer*
Powell, Alma Johnson *writer, advocate, foundation administrator*
Prescott, Richard Chambers *writer*
Presley, Arthur Henry *writer, artist*
Proulx, (Edna) Annie *writer*
Pullman, Philip Nicholas *writer, educator*
Pynchon, Thomas Ruggles, Jr. *author*
Quigley, Martin Schofield *writer, educator*
Quirk, Mary *writer, consultant*
Rader, Dotson Carlyle *writer, journalist*
Ragans, Rosalind Dorothy *writer, artist, retired educator*
Raucher, Herman *screenwriter, novelist*
Ravetch, Irving *screenwriter*
Rech, Lindsay Faith *writer*
Rechy, John Francisco *writer*
Rector, Donna Lynn *writer, photographer, vocalist*
Reeves, Richard *writer, historian*
Renaud, Bernadette Marie Elise *author*
Rice, Ferill Jeane *writer*
Richter, W.D. *screenwriter, director, producer*
Riehecky, Janet Ellen *writer*
Rimel, Ira Wesley *writer, US Navy supply officer, real estate specialist, real estate appraiser, real estate broker*
Ringel, Judy G. *writer*
Robinson, David Bradford *writer, poet*
Rogers, David *playwright, actor*
Rollins, Carole Ann *writer, artist*
Rooney, Andrew Aitken *writer, journalist*
Rosenblatt, Roger *writer*
Rosenfeld, Albert Hyman *science and medical writer*
Rosmus, Anna Elisabeth *writer*
Roth, Philip Milton *writer*
Rubin, Bruce Joel *screenwriter, director, producer*
Ruhl, Sarah *playwright*
Rumney, Helene Vosburgh *retired poet, peace activist*
Rush, Norman *author*
Russ, Joanna *author*
Russo, Richard *writer*
Rutsala, Vern A. *poet, writer, language educator*
Ryan, Joyce Ethel *writer, artist*
Sackett, Susan Deanna *writer*
Saito, Robert Shunichi *writer, poet*
Salat, Cristina *writer*
Sallis, James *writer*
Samer, Bill Fred Carl *writer, filmmaker*
Schenkkan, Robert Frederic *playwright, scriptwriter*
Schiff, Stacy *writer*
Schnackenberg, Gjertrud Cecelia *poet*
Schneider, Karen G. *freelance writer*
Schneider, Phyllis Leah *writer, editor*
Scott, Joyce *writer*

Seamans, William *writer, retired reporter, commentator*
Sedaris, David Raymond *writer*
Seidel, Frederick Lewis *poet*
Severo, Richard *writer*
Shafer, L. M. *writer*
Shagan, Steve *scriptwriter, film producer*
Shapiro, Harvey *poet*
Sheedy, John Thomas (Jack) *writer*
Shepard, Sam (Samuel Shepard Rogers) *playwright, actor*
Shoemaker, Bobby Jean (B.J. Foster) *writer*
Shreve, Susan Richards *writer, educator*
Sicart, Pierre-Alexandre Serge Henry *writer*
Siddons, (Sybil) Anne Rivers *writer*
Siegel, Mary Ann Garvin *writer*
Simendinger, Theodore John *writer, publishing executive*
Simon, Neil *playwright, screenwriter, television writer*
Simon, William Leonard *scriptwriter, television producer, writer, film producer*
Sims, Pamela Jan (Cerussi) *writer, minister*
Singer, Donna Lea *writer, editor, educator*
Singleton, Jonetta Williams *poet, retired special education educator*
Sisk, Eileen Victoria *writer, journalist*
Skinner, Knute Rumsey *poet*
Skwarczyński, Henryk Adam (Henryk Skwar) *writer*
Smith, Anne Day *writer*
Smith, Martin Cruz *author*
Snow, Marina *writer*
Socolow, Elizabeth Anne *poet, educator, artist, writer*
Solomon, Andrew Wallace *author*
SoRelle, Ruth Doyle *writer, journalist*
Spada, James *writer, photographer, publishing executive*
Sparks, Nicholas *writer*
Spencer-Fleming, Julia *writer*
Spies, Karen Bornemann *writer, educational consultant*
Stashower, Daniel Meyer *writer*
Steele, Judith McConnell *writer*
Stepak, Asa Martin *writer, linguist*
Stern, Richard Gustave *writer*
Stevens, Shane *novelist*
Stockwell, John *screenwriter, director, actor*
Stone, Elaine Murray *writer, composer, television producer*
Strand, Mark *poet*
Straub, Peter Francis *novelist*
Strong, Virginia Wilkerson *freelance writer, former special education educator*
Stroud, Patricia Tyson *writer*
Strouse, Jean *writer*
Suglia, Joseph Vincent *writer, educator*
Sullivan, George Edward *writer*
Sun, Nilaja *playwright, actress*
Sussman, Barry *writer, demographer, editor*
Swan, Annalyn *writer*
Swenson, Jack G. *writer, consultant*
Tackett, Viti Lee *writer*
Tamkus, Daniel *writer, advertising executive*
Tarn, Nathaniel *poet, educator, translator*
Taylor, Jim *scriptwriter, film director*
Taylor, John Jackson (Jay Taylor) *writer, retired diplomat*
Theroux, Paul Edward *author*
Thompson, Jane *writer*
Tilford, Terry Trent *translator*
Todd, Catherine Jackson *writer*
Toibin, Colm *writer, journalist*
Tower, Mollie Gregory *writer, educator, consultant*
Towler, Katherine *writer*
Treichel, Dixie Ann *writer, composer*
Trubo, Richard M. *writer*
Truman, Margaret *writer*
Twichell, Chase *poet*
Ucko, Barbara Clark *writer*
Ulin, David Lawrence *writer, editor, educator*
Unger, Barbara *poet, writer, retired literature and language professor*
Updike, John Hoyer *writer*
Valentine, Jean *poet, educator, writer*
Vaughan, Brian K. *writer, scriptwriter*
Vaz, Katherine Anne *writer*
Verlich, Jean Elaine *writer, public relations executive, consultant*
Vichiola, Christopher Michael *writer, educator*
Viorst, Judith Stahl *writer*
Viorst, Milton *writer*
Vita, Steven *poet*
Voigt, Cynthia *writer*
Volk, Patricia Gay *writer, essayist*
Volkers, Nancy Elaine *writer*
von Hoffman, Nicholas *writer, retired reporter*
Waitkus, Jay *writer*
Wallace, Michele *writer, educator*
Wallingford, Anne *freelance/self-employed writer, marketing professional, consultant*
Walter, Carmel Monica *writer*
Warren, Rosanna *poet*
Wayne, Kyra Petrovskaya *writer*
Weis, Margaret Edith *writer, editor*
Weisberg, Barbara *writer, editor*
Weiss Newton, Joanne Marion *writer*
Whalen, Charles William, Jr. *writer, retail executive, congressman, educator*
Whelchel, Sandra Jane *writer*
White, W. Robin *writer*
Whouley, Kate *writer, consultant*
Wilbur, Marcia Kaoru *writer*
Wilkinson, Claude Henry *writer, artist, English literature educator*
Will, Roland Tracy, II, *writer, editor, journalist, publisher, television producer*
Williams, C(harles) K(enneth) *poet, educator, literature educator*
Williams, Darcel Patrice *writer, editor*
Williams, Ian George *writer*
Wilson, Colin Henry *writer*
Wilson, Lanford *playwright*
Wilson, Roberta Louise *writer, editor, journalist, activist*
Winter, Terence *writer*
Wolfe, Linda *writer*
Wood, William Preston *writer, lawyer*
Woodson, Jacqueline *writer*
Wright, Franz Paul *poet, writer, translator*
Wright, Lawrence George *writer*
Yglesias, Rafael Jose *novelist*
Yingling, Phyllis Stuckey *writer*
Zeilig, Nancy Meeks *writer, editor*
Zulauf, Sander (Sander William Zulauf) *poet, educator, editor*

ARTS: PERFORMING

UNITED STATES

ALABAMA

Auburn
Turner, Louise (Lee) Kreher *retired dance educator*
Vasquez, Ramon Francisco *music educator*

Birmingham
Laeger, Therese Roach *performing arts educator*
Reynolds, Jeffrey Warren *music educator*

Daphne
Kauffman, Carl Herbert *retired music educator*

Florence
Lee, Soojeong *music educator, soprano*

Huntsville
Contreras, Frank R. *musician*

Jacksonville
Wight, Nathan *music educator*

Jasper
Stallsmith, Becki Laughlin *music educator*

Marion
Gosselin, Karen Chowning *music educator*

Millbrook
Boartfield, Ernest William *music educator*

Montgomery
Copeland, Jacqueline Turner *music educator*
Petty, Willie Clifford *musician, composer, educator*

Point Clear
Englund, Gage Bush *dancer, educator*

Talladega
Lanier, Anita Suzanne *musician, educator*
McKinney, John Paul *performing company executive*

Troy
Allard, Catherine *music educator, musician*

ALASKA

Auke Bay
d'Armand, John Berger *music educator*

Fairbanks
Celaire, Jaunelle Roberta *music educator*

ARIZONA

Chandler
Simon, Diane Rose *music educator, writer, poet*

Cottonwood
Masters, Arlene Elizabeth *singer*

Florence
Mosby, Nora Jane *music educator*

Fountain Hills
Tyl, Noel Jan *retired vocalist, astrologer, writer*

Glendale
Cotton, Sally Jean *retired music educator*
Pang, Darren *hockey analyst, retired professional hockey player*

Mesa
Skoldberg, Phyllis Linnea *musician, educator*

Phoenix
Altiere, Lauren M. *music educator, consultant*
Andersen, Ib *performing company executive*
Cooper, Alice (Vincent Damon Furnier) *popular musician*
Farney, Charlotte Eugenia *musician, educator*
Hernandez, Heather Marie *organist, music director*
Hooper, Daniel Lee *music educator, composer*
Kirkland, Joseph *voice educator*
Long, Michael Alan *musician, writer*
Nijinsky, Tamara *actress, puppeteer, author, librarian, educator*
Walker, Thomas Carlton *music educator*
Wheaton, Marilyn *musician*

Prescott Valley
Shelley, Bonnie J. *retired voice educator*

Scottsdale
Newman, Ursula Irene *music educator*

Sierra Vista
Boughan, Zanetta Louise *music educator*

Surprise
Eastman, Donna Kelly *composer*

Tempe
Bradford, Steven Paul *film educator, department chairman*
Bush, Jeffrey E. *music educator, art association administrator*
Lombardi, Eugene Patsy *retired conductor, musician, educator*
Nagrin, Daniel *dancer, educator, choreographer, writer*

Tucson
Aurand, Charles Henry, Jr. *music educator*
Bluemer, Bevan *acrobatics company executive*
Moeckel, Steven *concertmaster*
Powell, Winona *music educator*
Seaman, Arlene Anna *retired musician*

ARKANSAS

Conway
Johnson, David Randall *radio director*

Fort Smith
Bailey, Donald Keith *music educator, composer, musician*

Gravette
Legler, Kristin M. *music educator*

Greers Ferry
Robbins, Etta Jo *music educator*

Hot Springs Village
Philpott, Larry La Fayette *retired horn player*

Jonesboro
Bartee, Neale *music educator, musician, conductor*
Groves, Mark *music director*

Little Rock
Davis, Suanna Jeanette *mezzo-soprano, retired music educator*
Raney, Miriam Day *actress*

Russellville
Vance, Sue Ann *musician, educator*

Siloam Springs
Wubbena, Jan Helmut *music professor*

West Memphis
Peoples, Johnny Ray *music educator*

CALIFORNIA

Alameda
LaRose, Katherine Stencel *music educator*

Altadena
Klages, Karen Louise *musician, educator*
Wilson, Nancy *singer*

Anaheim
Browne, Autumn Lee *theater educator, actress, theater director*

Antioch
Adams, Liliana Osses *music performer, harpist*

Arcadia
Chih, Luke *music educator, conductor*

Bakersfield
Provencio, Roberto Enrique *music educator, music minister*

Belmont
Musmann, Lois S. *conductor, music educator*

Belvedere Tiburon
McFarland, Ronald G. (Ron McFarland) *composer, music educator, musician*

Berkeley
Campion, Edmund Joseph *composer, educator*
Dudley, Anna Carol *singer, voice educator*
Hagar, Sammy *musician, vocalist, composer*
Imbrie, Andrew Welsh *composer, educator*
Medak, Susan Lee *performing company executive*
Reid, Frances Evelyn Kroll *freelance/self-employed cinematographer, film director, communications executive*
Zaentz, Saul *film producer, former record company executive*

Beverly Hills
Abdul, Paula (Paula Julie Abdul) *singer, dancer, choreographer*
Abrams, J.J. (Jeffrey Jacob Abrams) *television producer, scriptwriter*
Affleck, Ben *actor*
Allen, Joan *actress*
Allen, Ted *television personality*
Allen, Tim (Timothy Allen Dick) *actor, comedian*
Ambrose, Lauren (Lauren Anne D'Ambruoso) *actress*
Anderson, Pamela Denise *actress*
Anderson, Wes (Wesley Wales Anderson) *film director*
Aniston, Jennifer *actress*
Ann-Margret, (Ann-Margret Olsson) *actress, performer*
Arnold, Tom *actor, comedian, television producer*
Arquette, Patricia *actress*
Avary, Roger Roberts (Frank Brauner) *film director, producer, writer*
Aykroyd, Daniel Edward *actor, writer*
Azaria, Hank *actor*
Bacon, Kevin *actor*
Bader, Diedrich *actor*
Baldwin, Alec (Alexander Rae Baldwin III) *actor*
Banderas, Antonio *actor*
Barkin, Ellen *actress*
Barrymore, Drew *actress*
Bateman, Jason *actor*
Bay, Michael Benjamin *film director*
Beatty, Warren *actor, film director, film producer*
Bell, Zoë *stunt-woman, actress*
Bello, Maria Elana *actress*
Belushi, James A. *actor*
Bening, Annette *actress*
Benjamin, Andre Lauren (Dre, André 3000) *vocalist, actor*
Berenger, Tom (Thomas Michael Moore) *actor*
Berg, Jeffrey Spencer *talent agency executive*
Berkus, James *talent agent*
Biel, Jessica *actress, model*
Bisset, Jacqueline *actress*
Black, Jack (Thomas Black) *actor*
Blaine, David *magician*
Blanchett, Cate (Catherine Elise Blanchett) *actress*
Bogdanovich, Peter *film director, writer, producer, actor*
Bonham-Carter, Helena *actress*
Bosworth, Kate *actress*
Bridges, Beau (Lloyd Vernet Bridges III) *actor*
Bridges, Jeff *actor*
Brillstein, Bernie J. *producer, talent manager*
Broderick, Matthew *actor*
Brokaw, Norman Robert *talent agency executive*
Brown, Clancy *actor, publishing executive*
Buckland, Marc *television director*
Burnett, Carol *actress, comedienne, singer*
Burnham, John Ludwig *agent*
Burstyn, Ellen (Edna Rae Gillooly) *actress*
Bush, Sophia *actress*
Bymel, Suzan Yvette *talent manager, film producer*
Byrne, Gabriel *actor*
Campbell, Neve *actress*
Capshaw, Kate (Kathy Sue Nail) *actress*
Carpenter, John Howard *director, screenwriter*
Carrey, Jim *actor*
Caruso, David *actor*
Casey, Sue (Suzanne Marguerite Philips) *actress, real estate broker*
Castellaneta, Dan (Daniel Louis) *actor*
Castle-Hughes, Keisha *actress*
Caton-Jones, Michael *film director, film producer*
Cattrall, Kim *actress*
Caviezel, James Patrick *actor*
Channing, Carol *actress*
Chappelle, Dave (David Chappelle) *actor, comedian*
Christensen, Hayden *actor*
Chritton, George A. *theater producer*
Clarkson, Kelly Brianne *singer*
Clooney, George *actor*
Close, Glenn *actress*
Coates, Anne V. *film editor*
Collette, Toni *actress, singer*
Columbus, Chris J. *film director, screenwriter*
Condon, Tom *sports agent*
Condon, William (Bill) *director, writer, producer*
Congdon, Amanda *actress, web video blogger, writer*
Connelly, Jennifer *actress*
Connery, Sir Sean (Thomas Sean Connery) *actor*
Cook, Dane (Dane Jeffrey Cook) *comedian, actor*
Corbett, John *actor*
Corbin, Barry *actor, writer*
Cox Arquette, Courteney *actress*
Cristofer, Michael *actor, writer, playwright, scriptwriter*
Croll, Tony *cinematographer, television director*
Cronenberg, David *film director*
Cruz, Penelope *actress*
Curry, Tim *actor*
Curtis, Jamie Lee *actress*
Cusack, Joan *actress*
Cusack, John *actor*
Daly, Tyne *actress*
Daniels, Jeff *actor, playwright*
Danson, Ted (Edward Bridge Danson III) *actor*
Davis, Geena (Virginia Davis) *actress*
DeGeneres, Ellen *actress, comedienne, talk show host*
Delaney, Kim *actress*
De Niro, Robert *actor, film producer and director, restaurant owner*
Depp, Johnny *actor*
Dern, Bruce MacLeish *actor*
DeVito, Danny Michael *actor, film director*
Diesel, Vin (Mark Vincent) *actor*
Donner, Richard *film director, producer*
Dorff, Stephen *actor*
Dourdan, Gary *actor*
Drescher, Fran *actress*
Driver, Minnie *actress*
Duchovny, David *actor*
Duhamel, Josh David *actor*
Duke, Patty (Anna Marie Duke) *actress*
Duncan, Michael Clarke *actor*
Eastwood, Clint (Clinton Eastwood Jr.) *actor, film director and producer*
Elfman, Jenna (Jennifer Mary Butala) *actress*
Elliott, Sam *actor*
Emanuel, Ari (Ariel Z. Emanuel) *talent agent*
Epps, Omar *actor*
Estevez, Emilio *actor, writer, director*
Eyre, Chris *film director*
Falco, Edie *actress*
Fallon, Jimmy *actor*
Favreau, Jon *actor, film director, film producer*
Ferguson, Craig *actor*
Ferrell, Conchata Galen *actress, performing arts educator*
Ferrell, Will (John William Ferrell) *actor*
Fey, Tina *actress*
Fincher, David *film director and producer*

Flaum, Marshall Allen *television producer, writer, director*
Fleder, Gary *film director, producer*
Flockhart, Calista *actress*
Foch, Nina *actress, creative consultant, film director, educator*
Foley, James *film director*
Fonda, Jane *actress*
Forsythe, William *actor*
Fox, Michael J. (Michael Andrew Fox) *actor*
Fox, Vivica *actress*
Foxx, Jamie (Eric Bishop) *actor, comedian*
Franken, Al (Alan Stuart Franken) *comedian, writer, actor*
Fraser, Brendan *actor*
Friendly, David T. *film executive, producer*
Futterman, Dan *actor, scriptwriter*
Gandolfini, James *actor*
Garofalo, Janeane *actress, comedienne*
Garr, Teri (Ann) *actress*
Gilpin, Peri *actress*
Glenn, (Theodore) Scott *actor*
Glover, John *actor*
Glover, Savion *actor, dancer*
Gooding, Cuba, Jr. *actor*
Goodman, John *actor*
Gossett, Louis, Jr. *actor*
Graham, Heather *actress*
Graham, Lauren *actress*
Grant, Hugh *actor*
Gray, Thomas Knox *film producer*
Grenier, Adrian *actor*
Griffin, Kathy *comedienne, actress*
Griffith, Andy (Andrew Samuel Griffith) *actor*
Guest, Christopher *actor, director, screenwriter*
Gugino, Carla *actress*
Gyllenhaal, Jake *actor*
Gyllenhaal, Maggie *actress*
Hackford, Taylor *film director*
Hackman, Gene (Eugene Alden Hackman) *actor*
Hallstrom, Lasse *film director*
Hamilton, Linda *actress*
Hamlin, Harry Robinson *actor*
Hanks, Tom *actor, film producer, film director*
Hannah, Daryl *actress*
Hanson, Curtis *film director, scriptwriter*
Harden, Marcia Gay *actress*
Harrelson, Woody *actor*
Harris, Mel (Mary Ellen Harris) *actress*
Harris, Neil Patrick *actor*
Hart, Melissa Joan Catherine *actress*
Hartnett, Josh *actor*
Hawke, Ethan Green *actor*
Hawn, Goldie *actress*
Hayek, Salma *actress*
Haysbert, Dennis *actor*
Heasley, Thomas Allen *composer, musician*
Heaton, Patricia *actress*
Heder, Jon *actor*
Herrmann, Edward Kirk *actor*
Heston, Charlton (John Charlton Carter) *actor*
Hewitt, Jennifer Love *actress, singer*
Hoffman, Dustin Lee *actor*
Holmes, Katie (Katherine Noelle Holmes) *actress*
Hopkins, Sir Anthony (Philip) *actor*
Hopkins, Stephen *film director, producer*
Hopper, Dennis *actor, writer, photographer, film director*
Howard, Ron *film director*
Hughes, John W. *film producer, director, screenwriter*
Hunt, Bonnie *actress*
Hunt, Helen (Helen Elizabeth Hunt) *actress*
Hurd, Gale Anne *film producer*
Hurley, Elizabeth (Liz Hurley) *actress, model*
Hurt, William *actor*
Huston, Anjelica *actress*
Hutton, Timothy *actor*
Idle, Eric *actor, scriptwriter, film producer, lyricist*
Imperioli, Michael *actor*
Jackson, Janet (Damita Jo) *vocalist, dancer*
Janseen, Famke *actress*
Johansson, Scarlett *actress*
Jolie, Angelina *actress*
Jones, Cherry *actress*
Jordan, Glenn *film, television and theater director*
Jordan, Neil Patrick *film director, writer*
Josephson, Nancy *talent agency executive*
Judd, Ashley *actress*
Kavner, Julie *actress*
Keach, Stacy, Jr. *actor, theater director and producer, musician, composer*
Keener, Catherine *actress*
Keitel, Harvey *actor*
Kelly, Moira *actress*
Kerns, Joanna de Varona *actress, writer, director*
Khan, Chaka (Yvette Marie Stevens) *singer*
Kidman, Nicole *actress*
Kingston, Alex (Alexandra Kingston) *actress*
Klum, Heidi *model, actress*
Knight, Theodore Raymond (T.R. Knight) *actor*
Knoxville, Johnny (Philip John Clapp) *actor*
Krause, Peter *actor*
Kressley, Carson *television personality*
Lahti, Christine *actress*
Lake, Ricki (Ricki Pamela Lake) *talk show host, actress*
Lane, Diane *actress*
Lane, Nathan (Joseph Lane) *actor*
Langella, Frank *actor*
Lansbury, Angela Brigid *actress*
Laurie, Hugh *actor*
Law, Jude (David Jude Law) *actor*
Lawrence, Martin *actor, comedian*
Lear, Norman Milton *producer, writer, director*
Leder, Mimi *television and film director, producer*
Lee, Ang *film director*
Lee, Jason *actor*
Lee, Jason Scott *actor*
Leguizamö, John *actor, comedian*
Lehmann, Michael Stephen *film director*
Leigh, Jennifer Jason (Jennifer Leigh Morrow) *actress*
Levant, Brian *film director*
Levinson, Barry L. *film director*
Levy, Eugene *actor, film director, screenwriter*
Lewis, Juliette *actress*
Limato, Edward Frank *talent agent*
Lindo, Delroy *actor*
Linney, Laura *actress*
Liotta, Ray *actor*
Liu, Lucy *actress*
Lloyd, Christopher *actor*
Lohan, Lindsay Dee *actress*
Lord, Marjorie *actress*
Lovett, Richard *talent agency executive*
Lowe, Rob *actor*
Lynch, David K. *film director, writer*
Mac, Bernie *actor, comedian*
MacLaine, Shirley *actress*
Macy, William H. *actor*
Madsen, Michael *actor*
Maher, Bill *television personality and producer, comedian*
Malick, Terrence (David Whitney II) *film director*
Mandel, Howie *actor, comedian*
Manheim, Camryn *television and film actress*
Mann, Michael Kenneth *film director, producer*
Mantello, Joseph *theater director*
Margulies, Julianna *actress*
Marsden, James (James Paul Marsden) *actor*
Martin, Steve *actor, comedian*
Martinson, Constance Frye *television personality and producer*
Masterson, Mary Stuart *actress*
Mastrantonio, Mary Elizabeth *actress*
Matheson, Tim *actor*
McAdams, Rachel *actress*
McCarthy, Jenny *actress*
McDermott, Dylan *actor*
McKean, Michael *actor*
Meirelles, Fernando *film director*
Mendes, Eva *actress*
Messing, Debra *actress*
Metcalf, Laurie (Lauren Ophelia Metcalfe) *actress*
Meyer, Breckin *actor*
Miller, Bennett *film director*
Miller, Sienna *actress*
Miller, Wentworth *actor*
Mol, Gretchen *actress*
Molina, Alfred *actor*
Moore, Demi (Demi Guynes, Demetria Gene Guynes) *actress*
Moore, Julianne (Julie Anne Smith) *actress*
Moore, Mandy (Amanda Leigh Moore) *actress, singer*
Moore, Mary Tyler *actress*
Moore, Michael *film director, writer*
Mortensen, Viggo *actor, writer*
Morton, Samantha *actress*
Moynahan, Bridget (Kathryn Bridget Moynahan) *actress*
Mullally, Megan *actress*
Mulroney, Dermot *actor*
Muniz, Frankie (Francisco James Muniz IV) *actor*
Murphy, Brittany *actress*
Murphy, Cillian *actor*
Murray, Bill *actor, writer*
Najimy, Kathy *actress*
Neville, Aaron *musician*
Nicita, Rick *agent*
Nixon, Cynthia *actress*
O'Donnell, Chris *actor*
Olmos, Edward James *actor*
Owen, Clive *actor*
Pacino, Al (Alfredo James Pacino) *actor, film director, film producer*
Paltrow, Gwyneth *actress*
Pantoliano, Joe *actor*
Parker, Mary-Louise *actress*
Parker, Sarah Jessica *actress*
Patinkin, Mandy *actor, singer*
Patton, Antwan Andre (Big Boi) *vocalist*
Paxton, Bill *actor, film director*
Peet, Amanda *actress*
Pepper, Barry *actor*
Phillippe, Ryan *actor*
Pitt, Brad *actor*
Platt, Oliver *actor*
Plummer, Christopher (Orme) (Arthur Plummer) *actor*
Polanski, Roman *film director, writer, actor*
Pollack, Sydney *film director*
Pompeo, Ellen *actress*
Portman, Natalie *actress*
Posey, Parker *actress*
Pressman, Edward R. *motion picture producer*
Prinze, Freddie, Jr. *actor*
Pullman, Bill *actor*
Quaid, Dennis *actor*
Rai, Aishwarya *actress*
Reese, Della (Deloreese Patricia Early) *singer, actress*
Reeves, Keanu *actor*
Reiner, Carl *director, actor, writer*
Reiner, Rob *film director, actor*
Rhames, Ving (Irving) *actor*
Rhys-Meyers, Jonathan *actor*
Ricci, Christina *actress*
Richardson, Patricia *actress*
Richie, Nicole *television personality*
Ringwald, Molly *actress*
Rivers, Joan *entertainer*
Roberts, Julia Fiona *actress*
Robinson Peete, Holly *actress, writer*
Rogers, Mimi *actress*
Rose, Jessica Lee *actress*
Ross, Tracee Ellis (Tracee Joy Silberstein) *actress, model, fashion editor*
Rossellini, Isabella *actress, model*
Rudd, Paul *actor*
Ruffalo, Mark *actor*
Rush, Geoffrey *actor*
Russell, Keri *actress*
Russell, Kurt *actor*
Russo, Anthony *film director*
Russo, Joe *film director*
Ryan, Meg (Margaret Mary Emily Ann Hyra) *actress, film producer*
Saget, Bob *actor, comedian, writer, television director*
Samberg, Andy *actor*
Sambery, Andy *actor*
Sandrich, Jay H. *television director*
Sarsgaard, Peter *actor*
Schneider, Rob *actor*
Scott, Ridley *film director*
Scott-Thomas, Kristin *actress*
Seacrest, Ryan (Ryan John Seacrest) *television and radio personality, entrepreneur*
Sedgwick, Kyra *actress*
Sevigny, Chloë *actress*
Sewell, Rufus *actor*
Seymour, Jane *actress*
Shadyac, Thomas *film director, producer*
Shalhoub, Tony *actor, television producer*
Shatner, William *actor*
Short, Martin *actor, comedian, film critic*
Shue, Elisabeth *actress*
Shuler Donner, Lauren *film producer*
Shyamalan, M. Night (Manoj Nelliyattu Shyamalan) *film director*
Silverman, David *film director, television producer, television director, animator*
Silverman, Sarah *comedian, actress*
Simmons, Gene (Chaim Witz, Gene Klein) *musician*
Simpson, Jessica Ann *singer, actress*
Simpson, Mike *talent agent*
Singer, Bryan *film producer, director, writer, actor*
Sinise, Gary *actor*
Skerritt, Tom *actor*
Slater, Christian *actor*
Smith, Jaclyn *actress*
Smith, Yeardley *actress*
Sommers, Stephen *film director, producer, scriptwriter*
Sonnenfeld, Barry *director, cinematographer*
Spacek, Sissy (Mary Elizabeth Spacek) *actress*
Spader, James *actor*
Spelling, Tori (Victoria Davey Spelling) *actress*
Spielberg, Steven (Allan) *film director, producer*
Stamos, John *actor*
Statham, Jason *actor*
Stefani, Gwen (Gwen Renee Steafani) *singer*
Stern, Sandor *film director, writer*
Stiles, Julia *actress*
Streep, Meryl (Mary Louise Streep) *actress*
Sutherland, Donald *actor*
Sutherland, Kiefer *actor*
Suvari, Mena *actress*
Swayze, Patrick *actor, dancer*
Sykes, Wanda *comedienne, actress*
Symone, Raven (Raven-Symoné Christina Pearman) *actress, singer*
Tamblyn, Amber Rose *actress*
Tambor, Jeffrey *actor, theater director, educator*
Taylor, Christine *actress*
Taylor, Lili *actress*
Theron, Charlize *actress*
Thompson, Emma *actress*
Thompson, Larry Angelo *film and television producer, lawyer, motivational speaker, writer*
Thurman, Uma Karuna *actress*
Tilly, Jennifer *actress*
Tomei, Marisa *actress*
Traugott, Peter *television producer*
Travolta, John *actor*
Tripplehorn, Jeanne *actress*
Tucci, Stanley *actor*
Tucker, Chris *comedian, actor*
Turner, Kathleen *actress*
Turturro, Nicholas *actor*
Tyler, Liv *actress*
Underwood, Blair *actor, television producer*
Van Dyke, Dick *actor, comedian*
Van Zandt, Steven *actor, musician, radio personality*
Vardalos, Nia *actress, screenwriter*
Vaughn, Vince *actor*
Visnjic, Goran *actor*
Wachowski, Andy *film director*
Wachowski, Larry *film director*
Ward, Sela *actress*
Watts, Naomi *actress*
Wayans, Marlon *actor, film producer, writer*
Wayans, Shawn *actor, film producer, writer*
Weaver, Sigourney (Susan Alexandra Weaver) *actress*
Weir, Peter Lindsay *film director*
Weisz, Rachel *actress*
Whaley, Frank *actor*
White, Betty *actress, comedienne*
White, Meg(an) (Martha) *musician, vocalist*
Whitford, Bradley *actor*
Wiatt, James Anthony *theatrical agency executive*
Williams, Michelle *actress*
Williams-Paisley, Kimberly *actress*
Willis, Walter Bruce (Bruce Willis) *actor, vocalist*
Wilson, Luke *actor*
Wilson, Owen *actor*
Winkler, Henry Franklin *actor, film producer, director*
Winkler, Irwin *motion picture producer*
Wirtschafter, David *talent agency executive*
Wood, Elijah *actor*
Woods, James *actor*
Wright, Jeffrey *actor*
Wright Penn, Robin *actress*
Wu, Yusen (John Woo) *film director*
Yorn, Rick *talent agent*
Zane, Billy *actor*
Zellweger, Renee *actress*

Bonita
Ling, Jahja Wang-Chieh *conductor*

Brisbane
Baadh, Valerie *choreographer, movement educator, theater producer, production designer*

Burbank
Baker, Rick *make-up artist*
Bender, Jack *television producer, television director, actor*
Berman, Bruce *entertainment company executive, television producer*
Big Boy, (Kurt Alexander) *radio personality, actor*
Branch, Michelle (Michelle Jaquet DeSevren Branch) *musician*
Bublé, Michael *singer*
Buck, Peter *musician, guitarist*
Burk, Bryan *television producer*
Bush, Billy *television personality*
Chiarelli, Robert Charles *audio engineer*
Clapton, Eric *musician, singer*
Clark, Dick *performer, producer*
Connelly, Mary *television producer*
Crane, David *producer*
de Ravin, Emilie *actress*
Fishburne, Laurence III *actor*
Fogerty, John Cameron *musician, composer*
Franco, James *actor*
Glavin, Edward P. *television producer*
Handel, William Wolf *radio personality*
Henley, Don *singer, drummer, songwriter*
Higgins, Jean *television producer*
Howard, James Newton *composer*
Jovovich, Milla (Natasha Militza Jovovich) *model, actress*
Kilgariff, Karen *television producer*
Kingsley, Bob *radio personality*
Lakshmi, Padma *actress, television host, model*
Lang, K. D. (Katherine Dawn Lang) *country music singer, composer*
Lassner, Andy *television producer*
Lindelof, Damon *television producer, scriptwriter*
McGraw, Tim *country music singer*
Mitchell, Joni (Roberta Joan Anderson) *singer, songwriter, artist*
Moore, Ryan Natalie *creative director*
Navarro, Dave (David Michael Navarro) *musician, recording artist*
O'Quinn, Terry (Terrance Quinn) *actor*
Petty, Tom (Thomas Earl Petty) *musician, composer*
Piddock, James Anthony *actor*
Remini, Leah *actress*
Rhimes, Shonda *producer, director, writer*
Rivera, Miluka *actress, journalist, poet*
Rzeznik, Johnny *singer, musician*
Shore, Howard Leslie *composer*
Silver, Joel *film producer*
Stewart, Rod (Roderick David Stewart) *singer*
Weiskopf, Wanda *mezzo soprano, writer, poet*
Wells, John Marcum *producer, writer*
Wonder, Stevie (Steveland Hardaway Judkins, Stevland Morris) *musician*
Zimmer, Hans Florian *composer*

Carlsbad
Missett, Judi Sheppard *dancer, jazzercise company executive*

Carmel
Gordon, David Jamieson *tenor*

Castro Valley
West, Doyle Thomas *retired music educator*

Chatsworth
Cassar, Jon Francis *television director, film director*

Chico
Reinhardt, Deborah Ann *music educator*

Claremont
Bennett, William John (Bill Bennett) *radio personality, former secretary of education*
Cramer, Alfred William *musician, educator*
Huang, Hao H. *music educator, department chairman*
Nelson, Mark D. *music educator, arts education administrator*

Clovis
Badgley, Clifford W. *music educator*
Kawashima, Hope Nozomi *musician*
van der Paardt, Tamara Ann *music educator*

Concord
Accatino, Steven C. *instrumental music educator, orchestra conductor*
Blair, Virginia Devoto *music educator*
Randle, Ellen Eugenia Foster *opera and classical singer, educator*

Corona
Holt, Chifra *dancer, educator, choreographer, artist*

Corona Del Mar
Khurgel, Tatiana *music educator, director*

Costa Mesa
Mumford, Lawrence R. *composer, educator*

Culver City
Brooks, James L. *film producer, director*
Brooks, Mel *film producer and director, actor, scriptwriter*
Chaffin, Ceán *producer*
Davidson, Gordon *theater producer and director*
Evans, Linda (Linda Evanstad) *actress*
Finkelman Cox, Penney *film producer*
Fisher, Lucy *film producer*
Kaufman, Richard Stuart *conductor*
Mark, Laurence Maurice *film producer*
Marshall, Garry K. (Garry Kent Marsciarelli) *film producer, director, writer*
Sebastian, Joan (José Manuel Figueroa) *musician*
Thomas, Marlo (Margaret Julia Thomas) *actress*
Trebek, Alex *television game show host*
Wick, Douglas *producer*
Ziskin, Laura *television producer, film producer*

Cupertino
Gallegos, Vernon David *theater educator*

Davis
Bauer, Ross *composer, music educator*

Diamond Bar
Snoop Dogg, (Calvin Broadus) *vocalist, actor*

Downey
Achon, Raquel Andrea *music educator, consultant*

El Centro
Gaede, Robert Matthew *music educator*

El Cerrito
Ma, L. Eve Armentrout *television producer, television director, educator*

Emeryville
Anderson, Darla K. *animated film producer*

Encino
Bright, Kevin S. *producer*
Ehrlich, Kenneth James *television producer*
Ingels, Marty *agent, broadcast executive*
Shire, David Lee *composer*
Taylor, Renee *actress, writer*
Westmore, Michael George *make-up artist, writer*

Escondido
Rockwell, Elizabeth Goode *dance company director, consultant, educator*

Fairfield
Ornellas, Maile Louise *filmmaker, educator*

Fort Bragg
Gjerde, Rosalie Carolyn *music educator, conductor*

Fountain Valley
Treadway-Dillmon, Linda Lee *actress, stuntwoman, dancer, dispatcher, athletic trainer*

Fremont
Yamamoto, Masako *music educator, director*

Fresno
Riggs, Krista Dyonis *music educator, librarian*

Glendale
Gedjeyan, Gaiane Diana (Astvatsatrian) *pianist, physical therapist*
Gibbons, Leeza *television and radio talk show host, entertainment reporter*
Grillo, Leo *actor, photographer*
Jacobson, Nina R. *film producer and former company executive*
Lund, John Richard *entertainment company executive*
Robinson, Smokey (William Robinson) *singer, composer*
Sotelo, Eduardo (El Piolín) *radio personality*

Grass Valley
Lynn, David Lawrence *music educator*

Hat Creek
Shepard, David Haspel *film restoration specialist*

Hercules
Tandy, Carla M. *dancer, educator*

Hollywood
Adams, William James, Jr., (Will.i.am) *rap artist*
Berryman, Guy *musician*
Buckland, Jon *musician*
Champion, Will *musician*
Diamond, Mike (Mike D) *recording artist*
Greenwood, Jonathan Richard Guy (Jonny Greenwood) *musician*
Lewis, Huey (Hugh Anthony Cregg III) *singer, composer, bandleader*
Lynne, Shelby (Shelby Lynn Moorer) *country singer*
Martin, Chris *vocalist*
Michaels, Mia *choreographer, dancer*
Miles, Joanna *actress, playwright, director*
Minnelli, Liza *singer, actress*
Roberts, Mel (Melvin Richard Kells) *retired film editor*
Warren, Diane *lyricist*
Yauch, Adam Nathaniel (MCA) *recording artist*
Yorke, Thomas Edward *musician, vocalist*

Huntington Beach
Carter, Henrietta McKee *music educator, department chairman*

Irvine
Avzaradel, Bob *music educator*
Ruyter, Nancy Lee Chalfa *dance educator*

Kentfield
Halprin, Anna Schuman (Mrs. Lawrence Halprin) *dancer*

La Crescenta
Purcell, Lee (Lee Jeune Williams) *actress, film producer*

La Habra Heights
Agajanian, Gilda *pianist*

La Jolla
Ashley, Christopher *performing company executive*
Reynolds, Roger Lee *composer, educator*

La Mesa
Canzoneri, Lois H. *retired church musician*

La Palma
Levy, Elaine Ann *music educator*

Laguna Beach
Challis, Diane Leslie *theater director*

Laguna Woods
McClure, Hal H. *film producer*

Lancaster
Wooster, Larry D. *music educator*

Livermore
Darter, Thomas Eugene, Jr. *composer, musician, writer*

Lodi
Tan, Robert C. *music educator*

Lompoc
Lyra, Jon Robert *music educator, artist*

Long Beach
Engle, Robert Irwin *music educator, translator*

Los Altos Hills
Archibeque, Charlene Paullin *retired music educator*

Los Angeles
Abdy, Pamela *film producer*
Alexander, Erika *actress*
Anka, Paul *singer, composer*
Annaud, Jean-Jacques *film director, producer, scriptwriter*
Arnett, Will *actor*
Arney, Randall *artistic director*
Bacharach, Burt *composer, conductor*
Bain, Conrad Stafford *actor*
Banks, Tyra (Tyra Lynne Banks) *retired model, television personality*
Barker, Bob (Robert William Barker) *television personality*
Beatty, Ned *actor*
Beaver, James Norman, Jr., (Jim Beaver) *actor, writer*
Beck, (Beck Hansen) *musician, songwriter*
Begley, Ed, Jr. *actor*
Bell, Lee Phillip *television personality, producer*
Bell, William J., Jr. *television producer*
Berger, Albert *film producer*
Bergman, Marilyn Keith *lyricist, writer*
Biggs, Jason *actor*
Bing, Steve *film producer*
Black, Lewis *comedian, actor*
Bloom, Claire *actress*
Bosley, Tom *actor*
Brolin, James (James Brunderlin) *actor*
Brown, Jason Robert *composer, arranger*
Brown, Pat Crawford *actress*
Buonemani, James Paul *church musician, director, composer*
Burnett, T-Bone (Henry John Burnett) *music producer, musician*
Burton, Brian Joseph (Danger Mouse) *sound recording engineer, musician*
Burton, Tim (Timothy William Burton) *film director, film producer*
Caine, Michael *actor*
Campbell, Christian Bethune *actor*
Carrillo, Elpidia *actress*
Cassavetes, Nick *film director, actor*
Cates, Gilbert *television and film producer, theater director*
Cee-Lo, (Thomas DeCarlo Callaway) *singer*
Chambers, Justin *actor*
Champlin, Charles Davenport *television personality, critic, writer*
Charisse, Cyd (Tula Ellice Finklea) *actress, dancer*
Cooper, Chris *actor*
Corman, Julie Ann *producer, director*
Corman, Roger William *film director*
Cox, Brian *actor*
Crockett, Donald Harold *composer, music educator*
Crumm, Max (Aaron Maximillian Crumm) *actor*
Cyrus, Billy Ray *country music performer, actor*
D'Accone, Frank Anthony *music educator*
Dane, Eric *actor*
Daniels, William David (Bill Daniels) *actor*
Davis, John A. *film producer*
Dee, Ruby (Ruby Dee Davis) *actress, writer, film director*
Del Toro, Benicio *actor*
DeMann, Freddy *film, play and television producer*
Dempsey, Patrick *actor*
Denson, Nikkole *film producer, company executive*
Diehl, Dolores *performing company executive*
Dr. Dre, (Andre Young) *rapper, record producer*
Duke, Margaret Joyce *sound recordist, broadcast engineer*
DuMont, James Kelton, Jr. *actor, theater producer*
Duritz, Adam *musician*
Eckhart, Aaron *actor*
Edwards, Blake *film director*
Efron, Zac *actor, singer*
Elrod, Lu *music educator, actress*
Elswit, Robert *cinematographer*
Engvall, Bill *comedian, actor*
Fairchild, Morgan (Patsy McClenny) *actress*
Farrell, Joseph *film producer and company executive, financial analyst, writer, sculptor*
Feinstein, Michael Jay *singer, pianist, musicologist, actor*
Ferrera, America Georgine *actress*
Flanagan, Fionnula Manon *actress, writer, theater director*
Fleischmann, Ernest Martin *performing arts executive, consultant*
Foster, Sutton *actress*
Franz, Dennis *actor*
Garrett, Spencer *actor, writer, director*
Gaviola, Karen Z. *television director*
Gengaro, Christine Lee *music educator*
Gifford, Kathie Lee *television personality, vocalist*
Gondry, Michel *film director*
Gordon, Allen Barry *musician, composer*
Gordon, Mark, II, *film producer*
Gosling, Ryan (Ryan Thomas Gosling) *actor*
Gould, Elliott *actor*
Grammer, Kelsey *actor*
Greenberg, Barry Michael *talent executive*
Gronnier, Henry Maurice *violinist, educator*
Hancock, Herbert Jeffrey (Herbie Hancock) *composer, pianist, publisher*
Harper, Hill (Frank Harper) *actor*
Hart, Mary *television talk show host*
Heigl, Katherine Marie *actress*
Henkel, Kathy *composer*
Hershey, Barbara (Barbara Herzstein) *actress*
Hoblit, Gregory *film director, television executive*
Hoffman, Philip Seymour *actor*
Holbrook, Hal (Harold Rowe Holbrook Jr.) *actor*
Horovitz, Adam Keefe (Adrock, King Ad-Rock) *recording artist*
Hudson, Jennifer *singer, actress*
Ice Cube, (O'Shea Jackson) *rap artist, actor*
Ice-T, (Tracy Marrow) *rap artist, actor*
Ireland, Kathy *actress, apparel designer*
Jackson, Samuel L. *actor*
Jagger, Sir Mick (Michael Philip Jagger) *singer, musician*
Jones, Sir Tom (Thomas Jones Woodward) *singer*
Keith, David *symphony orchestra conductor*
Kellerman, Sally Claire *actress*
Kelley, David E. *producer, writer*
Kelley, Malcolm David *actor*
Klauss, Kenneth Karl *composer, music educator*
Kyles, Cedric Antonio (Cedric the Entertainer) *comedian, actor*
Landers, Audrey *actress, singer*
Larry the Cable Guy, (Daniel Lawrence Whitney) *comedian, radio personality*
LeBeau, Mary Delle *dancer, educator, writer*
Ledger, Heath *actor*
Leeves, Jane *actress*
LeGros, James *actor*
Lennon, Sean Taro Ono *musician*
Leto, Jared Joseph *actor, singer*
Lew, Joycelyne Mae *actress*
Linkletter, Arthur Gordon *radio and television broadcaster*
London, Andrew Barry *film editor*
Lopez, George *actor, comedian*
Lopez, Jennifer *actress, singer, dancer*
Lunden, Joan *television personality*
MacLachlan, Kyle *actor*
Maguire, Tobey (Tobias Vincent Maguire) *actor*
Malden, Karl (Mladen Sekulovich) *actor*
Malone, Nancy *actress*
Margolin, Stuart *actor, director*
McQueen, Justice Ellis (L. Q. Jones) *actor, television director*
Milchan, Arnon *film producer*
Minor, Rickey *composer, television producer, music director*
Moore, Shemar *actor*
Moreno, Rita (Rosita Dolores Alverio) *actress*
Morton, Joe *actor*
Mueller, Carl Richard *theater arts educator, author*
Muldaur, Diana Charlton *actress*
Murphy, Elaine (Frances Elaine Murphy) *musician, harpist, flutist*
Nazarian, Sam *film producer*
Newhart, Bob (George Robert Newhart) *entertainer*
Nicholson, Jack *actor*
Nilles, Laila Padorr *musician, music company executive*
Noble, James Wilkes *actor*
Ohlmeyer, Donald Winfred, Jr. *film and television producer*
Oldman, Gary *actor*
Palmer, Keke (Lauren Keyana Palmer) *actress*
Penn, Sean *actor*
Phoenix, Joaquin Raphael *actor*
Pickens, James T., Jr. *actor*
Pittman, Amanda Nelson *music educator*
Pritzker, Jean *film producer*
Rando, John *theater director*
Ratzenberger, John Deszo *actor, writer, film director*
Reynolds, Burt *actor, film director*
Richards, Keith *musician*
Rickles, Donald Jay *comedian, actor*
Roberts, Emma Rose *actress*
Roberts, Eric *actor*
Rodriguez, Daniel *tenor, former protective services official*
Rogers, Wayne M. *actor, investor, investment strategist, consultant*
Rohrer, Susan Earley *film producer, film director, scriptwriter*
Rosenberg, Alan *actors guild executive*
Ross, Marion *actress*
Roth, Tim *actor*
Rowell, Victoria *actress*
Rubin, Stanley Creamer *television producer, film producer*
Ruskin, Joseph Richard *actor, director*
Russo, Rene *actress*
Santaolalla, Gustavo *musician, composer, record producer*
Schlesinger, Adam *musician*
Schreiber, Liev (Isaac Liev Schreiber) *actor*
Schulman, Cathy *film producer*
Scott, Tony *film director*
Selleck, Tom *actor*
Shaiman, Marc *composer, arranger, orchestrator*
Shay, Anthony Victor *choreographer, dance historian*
Smiley, Tavis *radio talk show host, writer*
Smits, Jimmy *actor*
Soria, Samuel Salvador *musician*
Springsteen, Bruce (Bruce Frederick Joseph Springsteen) *musician, singer*
Stanton, Harry Dean *actor*
Stapleton, Jean (Jeanne Murray) *actress*
Stevenson, Robert Murrell *music educator*
Streisand, Barbra Joan *singer, actress, film director*
Swofford, Beth *agent*
Takei, George Hosato *actor*
Taymor, Julie *theater, film and opera director, designer*
Thomas, John David *composer, musician, compact disc artist, photographer, music and arts business owner*
Tomlin, Lily *actress*
Trembly, Dennis Michael *musician*
Ullman, Tracey *actress, singer*
Underwood, Carrie Marie *singer*
Valentine, Dean *film producer*
Waits, Thomas Alan *composer, actor, singer*
Walken, Christopher *actor*
Walsh, Kate *actress*
Walter, Jessica *actress*
Washington, Isaiah *actor*
Waterston, Samuel Atkinson *actor*
Whitaker, Forest *actor*
Wilson, Chandra Danette *actress*
Winters, Barbara Jo *musician*
Witherspoon, Reese (Laura Jean Reese Witherspoon) *actress*
Wyle, Noah *actor*
Yerxa, Ron *film producer*
Yoakam, Dwight *country western musician*
York, Michael (Michael York-Johnson) *actor*
Young, Christopher *composer*
Zemeckis, Robert L. *film director*

Los Osos
Kreitzer, Jacalyn Bower *vocalist, voice educator*

Malibu
Almond, Paul *film director, film producer, scriptwriter, writer*
Bush, Kristian *musician*
Dowd, Ned *film producer*
Harris, Ed (Edward Allen Harris) *actor*
LaChanze, (R. LaChanze Sapp, Rhonda Sapp) *actress*
Nettles, Jennifer *singer*
Vereen, Ben *actor, singer, dancer*

Menlo Park
Baez, Joan Chandos *vocalist*

Mill Valley
Padula, Fred David *filmmaker*

Modesto
Jones, Mary Cunningham *music educator*

Mountain View
Isaacs, Nicholas Stephen *music educator, director*

Nevada City
Clausen, Jeanne Lorraine *musician*

Newport Beach
Boras, Scott D. *professional sports agent*
Landau, Martin *actor*
Steinberg, Leigh William *sports agent*

North Hollywood
Calva, Robert Baraquiel *music educator*
Fanning, Dakota *actress*
Holmes, Michael *performing arts company executive, educator*
Krayzie Bone, (Anthony Henderson) *rap artist*
Newton-John, Olivia *singer, actress*
Roth, David Lee *singer*
Sacco, Tony *cinematographer, television director, film director*
Smothers, Tom *actor, singer*
Stone, Sharon *actress*
Toplitt, Gloria H. *music educator, actress, vocalist*

Northridge
Cartwright, Nancy *actress, television producer*
Haskell, Peter Abraham *actor, director*
Loudon, Craig Michael *video specialist*
Luedders, Jerry Duane *music educator, academic administrator*

Oakland
DeFazio, Lynette Stevens *dancer, choreographer, violinist, actress, educator*
Glover, Danny *actor*
Lake, Suzanne *singer, music educator*
Robinson, Ellen M. *vocalist, educator*
Zschau, Marilyn *singer*

Ojai
Paxton, Glenn Gilbert *composer*

Oxnard
Woolsey, Robert Paul *church musician*

Pacific Palisades
Ritter, Jason *actor*
Wales, Ken *film producer*

Pacifica
Latham, Benjamin Erwin *music educator*

Palo Alto
Lo, Yee On *composer*

Palo Cedro
Haggard, Merle Ronald *songwriter, recording artist*

Pasadena
Halsted, Margo *music educator, carillonneur*
Horak, Jan-Christopher *filmmaker, educator, curator*
Menefee, John William III *cinematographer, film producer*
Vance, Rodney *film producer, writer*

Petaluma
Bailey, Preston Edward *music educator*

Phillips Ranch
Chambers-Belida, Candace R. *radio personality, writer, television producer, educator*

Port Hueneme
Schneider, Arthur Paul *retired videotape and film editor, author*

Porterville
Kusserow, James *music educator*

Rancho Cucamonga
Squires, Kelley Elizabeth *music educator*

Rancho Palos Verdes
Gordon, Stewart Lynell *musician, educator*

Redondo Beach
Richards, Denise *actress*

Reedley
Walter, Burl Leroy, Jr. *retired music educator*

Riverside
Ballantyne, Ryan Johns *pipe organ builder, small business owner*
Lee, Raejin *music educator, soprano*

Sacramento
Giles, Scott Marcus Anthony *composer, artist*
Mazzaferro, James Joseph *music educator*
McCann, Kim Lou M. *theater educator, director*
Nice, Carter *conductor*
Piper, Jami Kathleen *music educator, composer, musician*
Rainwater, Eric *composer, music educator*

Salinas
Rosen, Jacqueline I. *musician, educator*

San Diego
Adler, Christopher Alan *composer, educator*
Bates-Romeo, Delores Alvenia *music educator, consultant*
Campbell, Ian David *opera company director*
Flettner, Marianne *opera administrator*
Herriman, Darleen Ann *music educator*
Latherow, Robert L. *retired music educator*
Murphy, Mary *choreographer, dancer*
O'Brien, Jack George *artistic director*
Overton, Marcus Lee *performing arts association administrator, actor, writer*
Pagan, Keith Areatus *music educator, academic administrator*
Pfiffner, Patrick Meehan *musician, educator*
Pordon, William Philip *music educator*

San Francisco
Anastacia, (Anastacia Lyn Newkirk) *singer*
Caniparoli, Val William *choreographer, dancer*
Etheridge, Melissa Lou *singer, lyricist*
Gockley, (Richard) David *opera company director*
Griggs, Lewis Brown *executive producer, speaker, trainer*
Guggenheim, Davis *film and TV director, producer*
Hastings, Edward Walton *theater director*
Lau, Jenny Kwok Wah *theater educator, consultant, film educator, consultant*
LeBlanc, Tina *dancer*
Macahilig, Suzanne *pianist, educator*
McGuire, Kathleen Alison *conductor*
Muren, Dennis E. *special effects expert*
Osborne, Donald Eugene *performing company executive*
Owens, Ronald Stephen (Ronn Owens) *radio talk show host*
Rosenberg, Pamela *opera director, conductor*
Runnicles, Donald *conductor*
Savage, Michael Alan (Michael Weiner) *radio personality, commentator*
Tomasson, Helgi *dancer, choreographer, company executive*
Van Dyck, Wendy *dancer*
Wang, Wayne *film director*

San Jose
Collins, Alison *opera singer, music educator*
Dalis, Irene *mezzo soprano, performing arts association administrator*
Hughes, Daniel David *performing company executive*
Nahat, Dennis F. *performing company executive, choreographer*
Near, Timothy *theater director*

San Marcos
Houk, Benjamin Noah *performing company executive, choreographer*

San Mateo
Burton, Al *television producer, television director, writer*

San Rafael
Brubeck, David Warren *musician*
Lucas, George Walton, Jr. *film director, producer, scriptwriter*
Marsh, Marian E. *voice educator*
Santana, Carlos *guitarist*

Santa Barbara
Brodhead, James E(aston) *actor, writer*
Feigin, Joel *composer, educator*
Horne, Marilyn Berneice *mezzo-soprano*
Howorth, David *producer, director*

Santa Clarita
Feldman Nebenzahl, Bernardo *composer, educator*
Plew, Paul Timothy *music educator, dean*

Santa Cruz
Carson, Benjamin Leeds *composer, educator*
Winston, George *solo pianist, guitarist, harmonica player*

Santa Monica
Almqvist, Pelle *singer*
Bruckheimer, Jerry Leon *producer*
Cameron, James *film director, screenwriter, producer*
Carrabba, Christopher Ender *singer*
Cornell, Chris (Christopher John Cornell) *singer, musician*
Curran, Leigh *actress, playwright*
Doran, Lindsay *film producer, executive*
Eminem, (Marshall Mathers III) *rap artist*
Eve, (Eve Jihan Jeffers) *rap artist, actress*
Fisher, Frances *actress*
Grace, Maggie *actress*
Hannigan, Alyson *actress*
Hu, Kelly *actress*
Kanin, Josh David *film studies educator*
Katina, Elena Sergejevna *singer*
Kennedy, Kathleen *film producer*
Lohner, Henning *composer, filmmaker*
Louis-Dreyfus, Julia *actress*
Manson, Marilyn (Brian Hugh Warner) *singer, musician*
Peña, Michael Anthony *actor*
Redford, Robert (Charles Robert Redford) *actor, film director*
Stewart, Patrick *actor*
Summer, Donna (La Donna Adrian Gaines) *singer, songwriter, actress*
Suschitzky, Peter *cinematographer*
The Edge, (David Howell Evans) *musician*
Watros, Cynthia *actress*
Watson, Doc (Arthel Lane Watson) *vocalist, guitarist, banjoist, recording artist*
Welker, Kara *agent*

Sherman Oaks
Beck, Glenn *radio personality*
Clark, Susan (Nora Goulding) *actress*
Elfman, Danny *composer*
Gibbs, Antony (Tony Gibbs) *film editor*
Heffner, Daniel Jason *film producer*
Jordan, Bonnie *television producer*
Karras, Alex *actor, retired professional football player*
Lorber, Jeffrey H. *jazz musician, composer*
Norwood, Brandy Rayana (Brandy) *singer, actress*
Powell, John *composer*
Schlessinger, Laura *radio talk show host*
Taylor, Elizabeth (Dame Elizabeth Rosemond Taylor) *actress*

Stanford
Cohen, Albert *musician, educator*
Smith, Anna Deavere *actress, playwright, educator*

Stevenson Ranch
Krainin, Julian Arthur *film director, producer, cinematographer, writer*

Stockton
Wilcox, Helena Marguerita (Helena Rita Wilcox) *music educator*

Studio City
Boyett, Joan Reynolds *performing company executive*
Carradine, David *actor, director*
Kenney, H. Wesley, Jr., (Harry Wesley Kenney Jr.) *television producer, television director*
King, Carole (Carole Klein) *lyricist, singer*
Lewis, Dawnn *actress*
Najee, (Jerome Najee Rasheed) *musician*
Silver, Jeffrey *film producer*
Steinberg, Roy Bennett *television producer, director, educator*
Werner, Tom *television producer, professional baseball team executive*

Sun City
Schmoll, Edith Margaret *music educator*

Sunnyvale
Lanaro, Clara Marrama *music educator, writer*

Sylmar
Foster, Dudley Edwards, Jr. *musician, educator*

Tarzana
Richman, Peter Mark *actor, painter, film producer*

Temecula
Ojeda, Nelson A., II, *musician*

Templeton
Girolo, Nella Sue *retired voice educator*

Thousand Oaks
Kroeger, Chad *musician*
Loren, Sophia *actress*
Peake, Ryan *musician*
Rooney, Mickey (Joe Yule Jr.) *actor*
Sloane, J.P. *television producer, theologian, entertainer, writer*

Toluca Lake
Nunez, Oscar *actor*

Universal City
Bowen, Andrea *actress*
Chavira, Ricardo Antonio *actor*
Cross, Marcia *actress*
Denton, James *actor*
Hatcher, Teri *actress*
Huffman, Felicity (Flicka Huffman) *actress*
Longoria, Eva (Eva Jacqueline Longoria, Eva Longoria Christopher) *actress*
McCormack, Eric *actor*
Merkerson, S. Epatha *actress*
Reitman, Ivan *film director, producer*
Savant, Doug *actor*
Sheridan, Nicollette *actress*
Strong, Brenda *actress*
Wolf, Dick (Richard A. Wolf) *television producer*
Woodard, Alfre *actress*

Valencia
Millar, Michael William *musician*
Windsor, William Earl *consulting engineer, sales representative*

Valley Center
Camp, Joseph Shelton, Jr. *film producer, director, writer*

Valley Village
Barkin, Elaine Radoff *composer*
Diller, Phyllis (Phyllis Ada Driver Diller) *actress, writer*
Oka, Masi (Masayori Oka) *actor*

Van Nuys
Boone, Deborah Ann (Debby Boone) *singer*
Walsh, Thomas Francis, Jr. *producer, writer, director*

Venice
Bill, Tony *producer, director*
Chartoff, Robert Irwin *film producer*

Ventura
Turturro, John *actor*

Visalia
Porterfield-Pyatt, Chaumonde R. *music educator, advocate*

Walnut
Karr, Joanne Fern *theater educator*

Walnut Creek
Grandi, Lois A. *theater director, choreographer, actor*

Weed
Schaefer, M. Elaine *music educator, conductor*

West Hollywood
Annakin, Kenneth Cooper *film director, writer*
Berry, Halle Maria *actress*
Burke, Clem *musician*
Cage, Nicolas (Nicolas Coppola) *actor*
Cole, Natalie Maria *singer*
Destri, Jimmy *musician*
Franklyn, Audrey Pozen *talent promoter, television personality*
Harper, Robert *actor*
Harry, Deborah Ann *singer*
Holloway, Josh *actor*
Jackson, Randy *music producer, television personality, musician*
Krabbe, Jeroen Aart *actor*
Presley, Priscilla (Pricilla Ann Wagner, Priscilla Beaulieu Presley) *actress*
Romijn, Rebecca *actress, model*
Routh, Brandon *actor*
Sackett, Barnard (Barney) *actor, film producer, director, scriptwriter*
Stein, Ben(jamin) (Jeremy) *television personality, writer, lawyer, economist*
Stein, Chris *musician*
Tarantino, Quentin Jerome *film director, scriptwriter*
Thornton, Billy Bob *actor, film producer*

Westlake Village
Dotrice, Roy Louis *actor*

Westminster
Pieper, Michael Joseph *television producer, actor, talk show host*

Whittier
Korf, Jean Prinz *retired theater educator*

Woodland Hills
O'Connor, Brian D.A. *music educator, French horn musician*

COLORADO

Arvada
Bett, Robert Scott *music educator*

Aspen
Berkeley, Edward *performing arts association administrator, music educator*

Aurora
Roberts-Ramsbotham, Hazel Ruth *piano educator*

Boulder
Fink, Robert Russell *music educator and theorist, retired dean*
Kotter, Rita Joan *theatre educator, design consultant*
Mooney, William Piatt *actor*
Sable, Barbara Kinsey *retired music educator*
Sarson, John Christopher *television producer, director, writer*

Castle Rock
Wolfer, Dale *retired music educator*

Centennial
Heath, Jayne Marie *music educator*

Colorado Springs
Ansorge, Iona Marie *musician, educator, real estate agent*
Baack, Paula D. *music educator, director*
Roberts, John, II, *television producer, writer*
Scott, Carla Anne *musician, educator*

Denver
Boggs, Gil *principal ballet dancer*
Fredmann, Martin *ballet company artistic director, educator, choreographer*
Kahane, Jeffrey *conductor, pianist*
McClinton, David Anthony *performing company executive*

Elizabeth
Brownson, Sue McPherson *music educator*

Englewood
Rowe, Mike *television personality*

Estes Park
Varilek, Julie *music educator*

Greeley
Murray, Robert Patrick *music educator, musician*
Womble, Ken *theater educator, film director, writer, actor*

Gunnison
Wacker, John M. *music educator, director*

Highlands Ranch
Scalfari, Larry Alan *music educator, director*
Snell, Michael Steven *music educator*

Lafayette
Lee, Robert Anthony *church musician, accompanist*

Littleton
Alykova, Valentina *musician, music educator*
Asbjörnson, Kevin Donald *musician, small business owner*
Day, Susan Marie *music educator, composer*
Keats, Donald Howard *composer, educator*
Reinker, Mary Stefanich *musician, educator*

Loveland
Balsiger, David Wayne *television director, writer, television producer, television director, researcher*

Northglenn
Kappler, Karen L. *musician, educator*

Sedalia
Bean, Sharon Louise *music educator*

U S A F Academy
Galema, Joseph M. *music director*

Westminster
Kopperud, Marilyn Sue *music educator*
White, John David *composer, musician*

Wheat Ridge
Hockenberry, E'Rena *music educator*

Woodland Park
Critchlow, Bryan Douglas *music educator*

CONNECTICUT

Bloomfield
Mamlok, Walter Joseph *music educator, musician*

Bridgeport
Richard, Ellen *theater executive*

Bristol
Jaworski, Ron *sports analyst*
Levy, Steve *sports anchor, studio host*
Mayne, Kenny *sports anchor*
Mortensen, Chris *sports analyst, reporter*

Brookfield
Vladimiroff, Maxim *music educator, composer*

Canaan
Thorne, Francis *composer*

Canton
Richardson, Dana Roland *technology consultant*

Colchester
Bartkowski, Kathleen Susan *musician*

Cromwell
Donohue, Richard William *musician, conductor*

Danbury
Nelson, Willie Hugh *musician, lyricist*

East Haddam
Borton, John Carter, Jr., (Terry Borton) *theatrical producer*
Frost, Susan Beth *theater producer*

Farmington
Treggor, Josef Philip *music educator, composer, researcher*

Greenwich
Shimchick, Marie *music educator*

Hartford
Mardinly, Susan J. *musician, music educator*
Mills, Corinne C. *music educator*

Meriden
Curran, Louis Jerome, Jr. *choral master*

Middletown
Ebrecht, Ronald *musician*

New Fairfield
Price, Richard Galen *sound recording engineer, music producer, conductor*

New Haven
Bresnick, Martin *composer, educator*

Bundy, James Abbott *performing company executive*
Fassler, Margot Elsbeth *music educator, religious studies educator*
Feldman, Grace A. *music educator*
Lehman, Robert Wylie *music educator*
Nolan, Victoria *theater director*
Quinn, Ian *music educator*
Tirro, Frank Pascale *music educator, composer, writer*
Van Cleve, Libby (Elizabeth W. Van Cleve) *music educator, writer*
Warshaw, Marvin D. *conductor, educator, musician*

New Preston
Grizzard, George *actor*

Newington
Anderson, Kathryn Parks *music educator*
Cohen, Fern K. *music educator*

Norwalk
Eagan, Sherman G. *producer, communications executive*
Greene, Karen Sandra *actress, educator, singer*

Oakville
Carroll, Constance Marie *pianist, music educator*

Ridgefield
Taylor, Edwin R. *music director*

Southbury
Bergen, Polly *actress*

Stamford
Johnson, Dwayne Douglas (The Rock) *actor, professional wrestler*
Karp, Steve *agent*
Macurdy, John Edward *bass*

Storrs Mansfield
Rose, Dale A.J. *performing arts educator*

Torrington
Rolfe, Ellen Mary *retired music educator*

Wallingford
Velentine, Ralph Burnet *music educator, department chairman*

Washington Depot
Tracy, Michael Cameron *choreographer, educator*

West Cornwall
Engel, Jeffrey Mark *musician, music educator*

West Hartford
Braus, Ira L. *music educator, researcher*

Weston
Fredrik, Burry *theater producer, director*

Westport
Feliciano, José *entertainer*
Newman, Paul *actor, food products executive, race car driver*
Smith, Andrew James Thomas *music educator*
Solum, John Henry *flutist, educator, author*

DELAWARE

Bear
Hudson, Kelly Marie *music educator*

Camden Wyoming
Pfeuffer, Robert John *musician*

Greenville
Parets, Paul L. *music educator*

Millville
Zinman, David Joel *conductor*

Wilmington
Wesler, Ken *performing arts company executive*

DISTRICT OF COLUMBIA

Washington
Ames, Frank Anthony *musician, film producer*
Begala, Paul Edward *television personality, political scientist, consultant*
Crawford-Mason, Clare Wootten *television producer, journalist*
Damjanovich, Chaslav M. (Casey Diamond) *filmmaker, television producer, writer*
Day, Doris (Doris von Kappelhoff) *singer, actress*
Dhue, Stephanie *television producer, reporter*
Domingo, Placido *tenor, opera company director*
Donlon, Claudette *performing company executive*
Elliott, Graham John *music educator, director*
Fischer, Elizabeth (Betsy) *television producer*
Geimann, Steve *radio producer*
Grundstrom, Brian Wilbur *composer*
Hamlisch, Marvin *composer, conductor, musician, entertainer*
Harpham, Virginia Ruth *violinist*
Inskeep, Steve *radio personality*
Kahn, Michael *stage director*
Kaiser, Michael M. *performing company executive*
Kendall, Peter Landis *television news executive*
Leavitt, Paul David *director music arts, pianist, composer*
Lelyveld, Gail Annick *actress*
Massey, Jeanne Kelly *performing company executive*
Royle, David Brian Layton *television producer, journalist*
Russell, Mark *comedian*
Saylor, Maurice Michael *composer, director, music librarian*
Schwarz, Gerard *conductor, musician, music director*
Slatkin, Leonard Edward *musician, conductor, director*
Smith, Molly D. *theater director*
Stamberg, Susan Levitt *radio personality*
Stone, Florence Smith *film presenter and film festival producer, consultant*
Walsh, John *television show host, missing children and victims' rights advocate*
Webre, Septime *performing company executive, choreographer*
Weidenfeld, Sheila Rabb *television producer, writer*

FLORIDA

Cape Coral
Wendel, Joan Audrey *music educator*

Clearwater
Cross, Beverly Jean *music educator*

Coral Gables
De Sena, Ferdinando *composer, educator*

Coral Springs
Kristofferson, Kris *singer, lyricist, actor*

Davie
Walkinshaw, Nicole M. *performing arts educator*

Daytona Beach
Poitier, Constance Rena *music specialist, educator*

Deerfield Beach
Allaire, Gaston George *music educator, researcher*

Deland
Musco, Lynn Ann *music educator*
Niemann, Chester S., Jr. *retired band director, customer service administrator*

Fort Lauderdale
LeRoy, Miss Joy *model, apparel designer*
Randi, James (Randall James Hamilton Zwinge) *magician, educator*
Stayton, James Michael *music educator*
Webster, Ernest Wesley *musician, educator*

Fort Myers
Canham, Pruella Cromartie Niver *music educator*

Gainesville
DesForges, Deborah Waln *music educator*
Jones, Gregory R. *theater educator*
Keebaugh, Aaron Christopher *music educator, historian*
Lowe, John Thomas, Jr. *church and concert musician*
Paul, Ouida Fay *music educator*

Graceville
Moon, Kimberle Irene *voice educator*

Green Cove Springs
Davidson, Joy Elaine *retired mezzo soprano*

Jacksonville
Homsley, Denise Louise *music educator*
Marks, Dennis *music educator, musician, composer*
Page, Willis *conductor*
Smith, Stephen Mark *music educator*
Stanley, Helen Camille *composer, musician*

Key West
Buffett, Jimmy (James William Buffett) *vocalist, songwriter, writer*

Lakeland
Jacobson, Barbara Dinger *music educator*

Largo
Benoit, Christopher Louis *music educator*

Lecanto
Max, Buddy (Boris Max Pastuch) *musician*
Wheatley, Deborah A. *music educator*

Lynn Haven
Birdwell, Jamie *music educator, department chairman*

Maitland
Nelson, Stephen D. *music educator*

Mary Esther
McTyeire, Robert Adams *sound engineer, music company executive, consultant*

Merritt Island
Yoh, William Harry, Jr. *music educator*

Miami
Allen, Charles Norman *television, film and video producer*
DJ Craze, (Aristh Delgado) *disc jockey*
Feinberg, Wendie *television producer*
Floyd, Suzanne Elvira Izzo *music educator*
Galatas, Ruth Ann *musician, publishing executive, educator*
Harmon, Monica Renee *music educator*
Heuer, Robert Maynard, II, *opera company executive*
Kahn, Jack Merrill *television producer*
Moody, Jacqueline Elaine *music educator*
Pilafian, Audrey Kalenian *music educator*
Walz, Leo R. *conductor*

Miami Beach
Gardiner, Pamela Nan *performing company executive*
Lawson, Eve Kennedy *dancer*
Rosenhaus, Drew *professional sports agent*

Naples
Kirby, Charles William, Jr. *dancer, choreographer*
White, Roy Bernard *performing arts association administrator*

Neptune Beach
Palmer, Jane G. *music educator*

North Miami
Stills, Stephen *musician, vocalist, composer*

North Palm Beach
Hayman, Richard Warren Joseph *conductor*

Ocala
Hammes, C. Leslie Greene *musician, educator*
Hudson, Ann Elizabeth *music educator*

Orlando
Atwell, George Michael *composer, conductor, musician*
Beckner, Cynthia Byrd *music and elementary school educator*
Caracciolo, Joseph M. *film producer*
Jordan, Grace Carol *music educator*
McMahon, Ed *television and radio personality*
Pyle, Artimus (Thomas Delmar Pyle) *musician*
Rosene, Paul Earl *music educator*
Schultz, Victoria L. *harpist, entertainer, music educator*
Weaver, Earl D. *theater educator*

Ormond Beach
Hodkinson, Sydney Phillip *composer, educator, musician, conductor*

Palm Harbor
Katzen-Guthrie, Joy *performance artist, engineering executive*

Panama City
Fejer, T. William *musician, composer, architect, furniture designer*

Panama City Beach
Birdwell, Michelle Marie *music educator*

Pensacola
Rubardt, Peter Craig *conductor, educator*

Port Orange
DeMarsico, Jonnette M. *theater educator, consultant*

Port Saint Lucie
Rothschild, Mary Ann *music educator*

Punta Gorda
Stratas, Teresa (Anastasia Strataki) *soprano*

Saint Augustine
Gilmore, H. James *film producer, educator*

Saint Petersburg
Carroll, Charles Michael *music educator*

Sanford
Terrell, Maurice L., Sr. *music educator*

Sarasota
Allen, Charles Franklin *music educator*
Edwards, Michael Donald *artistic director, drama educator*
Faron, Sally Rogers *performing arts association administrator, consultant*
McCollum, John Morris *tenor*
McMaster, Gloria (Gloria Bugni Juhn) *mezzo-soprano, educator*
Sarakatsannis, Leonidas Nicholas *musician, concert pianist, music educator, composer, conductor*
Stewart, Donald George *musician, composer, music industry executive*

Summerfield
Lynne-O'Brien, Vincent *theater director, actor*

Tallahassee
Coleman, Robert Hemphill III *theater educator*
Corzine, Jennifer Jean *music educator*
Delp, Roy Edward *music educator, singer*
Harrison, Luvada A. *voice educator, singer*
Harsanyi, Janice *retired soprano, educator*
Shaftel, Matthew Robert *music educator, tenor, conductor*
Streem, James Kenneth *musician, educator*
Zwilich, Ellen Taaffe *composer*

Tampa
Hankenson, E(dward) Craig, Jr. *performing arts executive*
Leopold, Blake *music educator*
Stefanov, Ivanka *music educator*

Tarpon Springs
Jones, Marshall David *musician, minister*

Temple Terrace
Reynolds, Jerald M. *music educator*

Treasure Island
Dunn, Craig Andrew *entertainer, conductor, writer, composer, educator*

Valparaiso
Merritt, Phyllis June *music educator, director*

Venice
Tausan, Carol A. *music educator*

West Palm Beach
Hale, Marie Stoner *performing company executive*
Robinson, Raymond Edwin *conductor, music educator, writer*

Weston
Berry, Becky *music educator*

Winter Garden
Ellis, Missie Lynne *music educator*

Winter Park
Bagley, Priscilla Annette *music educator, performing arts association administrator*
Wallace, Curtis Wilbern, Jr. *music director, organist*
Wrancher, Elizabeth Ann *music educator, opera singer*

GEORGIA

Albany
Rodriguez, Sergio Raul *music educator, conductor*

Athens
Mills, Mike *popular musician*
Staub, August William *theater producer, educator*
Stipe, Michael *musician, film producer*

Atlanta
Alexander, Alonzo III *music educator, composer*
Grant, Susan *television executive*
Harris, Clifford Joseph, Jr., (T.I., Tip Harris) *rap artist*
Kingsbury, Michael Bryant *organist, retired elementary school educator, retired secondary school educator*
McFall, John *performing company executive*
Raymond, Usher, IV, (Usher) *vocalist, actor*
Slade, Scott *radio personality*
Spano, Robert *conductor, music director*
Vulgamore, Allison *performing arts association administrator*
Wallace, Peter Marsden *radio personality and producer, commentator, writer*
Woodard, Diane E. *music educator*
Zeliazkova, Mariona Georgieva V. *music educator*

Augusta
Champion, Susan Michele *music educator*

Austell
Pope, Jacqueline Privette *music educator*

Cartersville
Kordecki, Don Harry *theater director*

Columbus
Golden, Joseph David *music educator*
Hiatt, Florence Ellen *musician*
Norah, Patricia Ann *retired music educator*

Conyers
Skipper, James Hulett, Jr. *music educator*

Cordele
Bell, Andrew C. *music educator*

Decatur
Hamilton, Frank Strawn *musician, composer, educator*
Ray, Amy *vocalist, guitarist*
Saliers, Emily *singer, musician*

Duluth
Moss, Shad Gregory (Bow Wow, Lil' Bow Wow) *rap artist*

East Point
Bridgewater, Herbert Jeremiah, Jr. *radio personality*

Fitzgerald
Newsome, John David, Jr. *music educator*

Hartwell
Rushing, Tonnie Austin Page *musician, educator*

Hephzibah
Smith, Charles Joe, Sr. *music educator*

Kennesaw
Adams, Dean (Lewis Adams) *theater director*

Lagrange
Gittinger, Laurie Ellen *music educator, elementary school educator*

Lawrenceville
Folds, Frank Elliott *music educator*

Leesburg
Hilley, Mary Kay *music educator*

Lyons
Eernisse, Susan Freeman *music educator*

Mableton
Reeves, Denise Moseley *dancer, educator*

Marietta
Roach, Carole Hyde *music educator*
Sigler, Paulette Terry *music educator*
Smith, Irene Helen-Nordine *music educator*

Martinez
Meyers, Nicholaus *music educator*

Mcdonough
Wilson, Russell Edward *music educator*

Mount Berry
Davis, John Edward *music educator, musician*

Nashville
Haywood, Mary Gwendolyn *music educator*

Oakwood
Phillips, Ernie Howard *music educator*

Peachtree City
Day, Annette J. *music educator*

Rome
Davis, Susan Lynn *musician, educator*

Roswell
Ludacris, (Chris Bridges) *musician, actor*
Siepi, Cesare *opera singer*
Welch, Robert Bennett *retired music educator, retired conductor*

Savannah
Holland, Robert D. *music educator*

Stone Mountain
Fairweather, Daniel Edward *music educator*

Toccoa Falls
Council, Thomas Maurice *music educator*
Stufft, William David *music educator*

Villa Rica
Abney, Martha McEachern *music educator*

Young Harris
Richardson, Vernal Edward *retired music educator*
Wolfersteig, Eloise Smith *retired music educator*

HAWAII

Ewa Beach
Lewis, Mary Jane *film producer, film director, scriptwriter*

Honolulu
Langhans, Edward Allen *drama and theater educator*
Tanner, Jerré E. *composer, retired publishing executive*

Kaneohe
Young-Pohlman, Colette Lisa *music educator*

Waianae
Bourke-Faustina, Marlene Frances *music educator*

IDAHO

Boise
Aitken, Paul Arthur *composer, conductor*
Hofflund, Mark *theater director*
Holt, Isabel Rae *radio program producer*

Burley
Little, Glen Gordon *retired circus clown, educator*

Moscow
Kreutzer, Natalie Ruth Jones *music educator*

Post Falls
Hasalone, Annette Leona *radio personality, research and development company executive*

Rexburg
Barrus, Charles LaMar, Jr. *music educator*

Sandpoint
Daarstad, Erik *cinematographer*

Twin Falls
Cowger, Shari Ann *music educator*

ILLINOIS

Algonquin
Wise, Jack Ronald *music educator*

Aurora
Pappas, Margene *retired music educator*

Barrington
Carter, Jeanie *performing company executive*

Belleville
Jones, Donald Leigh *retired music educator*

Bloomington
Brown, Jared *theater director, educator, writer*
Vayo, David Joseph *composer, music educator*

Bolingbrook
Tot, Zvonimir *musician, composer, music educator*

Bourbonnais
Dalton, Martha Gomer *music educator*
Woodruff, Neal *music educator*

Cary
Irey, Robin Elizabeth *performing company executive, performing arts educator*

Champaign
Fredrickson, L(awrence) Thomas *composer*
McKay, JoAnn *retired musician, composer*

Charleston
Daum, John LaVern *retired band director, educator*

Chicago
Arpino, Gerald Peter *performing company executive*
Barber, Bruce Jackson, II, *musician*
Basden, Cameron *dancer*
Byrne, Rhonda *television producer*
Card, Deborah R. *orchestra administrator*
Dabrowski, Edward John *television technical director*
Daniel, T. *mime performer, theater director, choreographer*
Eisenberg, Daniel *filmmaker*
Falls, Robert Arthur *artistic director*
Farina, Dennis *actor*
Florine, Jane L. *musicology educator*
Heider, Anne Harrington *music educator*
Janners, Erik Nikolas *music educator, conductor*
Jeff, Kevin Iega *choreographer, performing company executive*
Jelsema, Jerry Richard *music director*
Lazar, Ludmila *concert pianist, music educator*
Lombardo, Robert *composer, educator*
Mason, William *opera company director*
May, Aviva Rabinowitz *music educator, musician, linguist*
McIntyre, Sarah Elizabeth *soprano*
Noel, Carol Adele *music educator, opera singer*
Padberg, Helen Swan *violinist*
Pollak, Lisa *radio producer*
Robinson, Reginald R. *musician*
Savage, Terry *television personality, journalist, stockbroker*
Scott, Stephen Brinsley *theater producer*
Springer, Jerry (Gerald Norman Springer) *television talk show host, radio personality*
Stratman, Deborah *filmmaker, film and video educator*
Thomas, Eddie *composer, recording industry executive, producer, promoter*
Vincent, Jim *performing company executive*
Wang, Albert James *violinist, educator*
Wasson, Jeffrey *music educator*
Winfrey, Oprah *television talk show host, actress, television producer*
Zajicek, Jeronym *retired music educator*

Chicago Heights
Reed, Scott C. *musician, educator, writer*

Decatur
Coryell, Sandra Kay *music educator*

Dekalb
Gelman, Alexander *theater director, educator*
Goldenberg, William Bruce *musician, educator*

Downers Grove
Hornish, Ronald Frederick *music educator*
Roselieb, Craig Alan *band director*

East Peoria
Twitty, Susan Kay *music educator*
Wadsworth Walker, Cherilee *music educator*

Edwardsville
Anderson, Mary Jane *music educator*
Schultz, Norbert J. *retired music educator*
Stranc, Cathleen L. *music educator*

Eureka
Henry, Joseph Dean *music educator, director*

Evanston
Eberley, Helen-Kay *opera singer, recording industry executive, poet*
Galati, Frank Joseph *stage and opera director, educator, screen writer, actor*
Hall, Bruce A. *music educator*
Hemke, Frederick L. *academic administrator*
Kujala, Walfrid Eugene *musician, educator*
McDonough, Bridget Ann *music theatre company director*
Peters, Gordon Benes *retired musician*
Zimmerman, Mary Alice *performing arts educator*

Forreston
Braker, William Paul *music educator*
Harn, Amy Helen *music educator, director*

Franklin Park
Miller, Bryan Michael *music educator*

Galesburg
Polay, Bruce *musician, conductor, educator*

Glen Carbon
Jarabak, Phyllis A. *music educator*

Grayslake
Cayari, Christopher *music educator*

Griggsville
Evans, H. Todd *music educator*

Highland Park
Hobson, Stephen Gilbert *conductor, music educator*

La Grange
Zethmayr-Lolakos, Ellen *music educator, writer*

Lake Zurich
Juknelis, Nick *music educator*

Loves Park
Dixon, John James *music educator*

Macomb
Kim, Chung-Ha *music educator*
Walker, Tammie Leigh *music educator*
Wehrman, Elizabeth Ann *music educator*

Mattoon
Black, Todd Ronald *music educator*

Moline
Stodt, F. Chloe *piano educator*

North Barrington
Hogan, Harlan Robert *voice-over actor*

Northfield
Zupko, Mischa Sarché *composer, church music director*

Palatine
Cotsakis, Patricia Joan *music educator*

Park Forest
Billig, Etel Jewel *theater director, actress*

Peoria
Inman, Samantha Mae *music educator*
Peters, Margaret Myrl *retired music educator*
Vroman, David Cole *music educator*

Plainfield
Serna, Phillip Woodrow *music educator, musician*

Schaumburg
Janssen, Carron Joyce *music educator*
Riffel, Karen Sheffer *music educator*

Springfield
Cobb-Myers, Janet Lea *music educator*

Urbana
Hedlund, Ronald *baritone*

Waterloo
Hoffmann, Mary Jukich *voice educator*

Waukegan
Houle, Jeanne Larson *retired music educator*

West Chicago
Noonan, Josette Marie *music educator*

Wheaton
Schwanda, Grace Elaine *music educator*

Wilmette
Hurley, Andrew John *musician*
Jampole, Michael *music educator, composer*
Stump, Patrick Martin *musician*
Trohman, Joseph Mark *musician*
Wentz, Peter (Peter Lewis Kingston Wentz III) *musician*

Winnetka
Ladd, David Scott *music educator*

INDIANA

Bloomington
Brown, Keith *musician, educator*
Effron, David Louis *conductor, performing company executive*
Kiesgen, Paul *music educator*
Mac Watters, Virginia Elizabeth *singer, music educator, actress*
Mellencamp, John (John Cougar) *singer, lyricist*
Phillips, Harvey G. *musician, performing arts educator*
Spera, Dominic Gregorio *music educator, writer*
Svetlova, Marina *ballerina, retired choreographer*
Tsutsumi, Tsuyoshi *musician, educator*
Ward-Steinman, David *composer, music educator, pianist*

Carmel
Rund, Rex Benjamin *music director*

Columbus
Bowden, David *conductor*
Lim, Yoon-Mi *muisc director, organist*

Crown Point
Shaffer, Peggy S. *music educator*

Elkhart
Carnall, Timothy W. *music educator*

Evansville
Reed, R. Douglas *music educator*

Fort Wayne
Tucker, Dale Keith *church musical director, organist*

Greencastle
Phang, May *music educator*

Hammond
Hansen, Jack Winsor *musician, educator*

Hanover
Batchvarova, Madlen Todorova *music educator, conductor*

Indianapolis
Anderson, Walter Ernest *church musician*
Burgomaster, Frederick *music director*
Everly, Jack *conductor*
Griswold, Tom *radio personality*
Ilgen, Dorothy L. *arts foundation executive*
Kevoian, Bob *radio personality*
Murphy, Meissa Bleu *music educator, behaviorist*
Pockrass, Joseph Craig *music educator*
Schmid, John A. *musician, voice educator*
Sorley, Rebecca Ellen *music educator*
Venzago, Mario *conductor, music director*
Westra, Mitzi Sue *music educator*

Knox
Weiss, Randall A. *television and radio producer, supermarket executive, television station owner*

Marion
Lessly, Chris Ann *music educator, director, conductor*
Miller, Peter Karl *music educator*

Michigan City
Wiegand, Elizabeth Grieger *musician, educator*

Muncie
Maurer, Kathleen Marie *music educator, vocalist*

South Bend
Bell, Wishart Bryan *music educator, conductor*
Muniz, Jorge *composer, music educator*

Valparaiso
Pritchett, Daniel R. *music educator*

Waterloo
Johnson, George Axil III *television producer*

Zionsville
Garfunkel, Art *singer, actor*

IOWA

Alden
Oliver, Kerryn Hinrichs *music educator, religious studies educator*

Algona
Aboud, John Anthony *music educator*

Bettendorf
Myatt, William Howard *theater educator, director, actor*
Schulz, Sally Ann *pastoral musician, conductor, educator*

Cedar Falls
Chesnutt, Rod Martin *music educator*
Fanelli, Michael Paul *musician, educator, writer*

Cedar Rapids
Dangerfield, Joseph Allen *composer, educator*
Rohr, Carol Ann *composer, pianist, music educator*

Cherokee
Gordon, Roma Dianne *music educator*

Council Bluffs
Kurt, Johnny Thomas *music educator*
Lippoldt, Vaughn Arthur *retired music educator*

Davenport
Dcamp, Charles Barton *music educator*

Decorah
Martin, Spencer L. *musician, educator*
Monson, Larry Lee *music educator*

Indianola
Larsen, Robert LeRoy *artistic director*

Iowa City
Kottick, Edward Leon *musician, educator*
Mather, Roger Frederick *retired music educator, writer*
Preucil, Doris Bogen *music educator*

Mason City
Backlin, William Wayne *music educator, composer*

Mount Pleasant
Crane, Frederick Baron *retired music educator*
Edwards, Jason Ray *music educator, musician*

Orange City
Barker, Jeff *theater and speech educator*

Sheffield
VanHorn, Bradley Kent *musician*

Storm Lake
Safley, Holli Ewoldt *music educator*

Tipton
Farwell, Walter Maurice *vocalist, educator*

Waverly
O'Konski, Marjorie Katherine *music educator*

KANSAS

Chanute
Smith, David *music educator*

Emporia
Bartruff, Jim *theater educator, director*

Hutchinson
Brewer, William Thomas *theater educator, theater director*
Widener, Charlene *theater director, educator*

Iola
Tebbets, Gary Duane *music educator*

Lawrence
Hilding, Jerel Lee *music and dance educator, retired dancer*
Mattila, Edward Charles *music educator*
Pozdro, John Walter *retired music educator, composer*
Tsubaki, Andrew Takahisa *theater director, educator*

Lenexa
Warenskjold, Dorothy *singer, educator*

Lindsborg
Mahraun, Daniel Allen *musician, director*

Manhattan
Mortenson, Kristin Oppenheim *musician*

Mcpherson
Tomlison, Rondal Scott *music educator*

Olathe
Epp, Garrett Wayne *music educator*

Ottawa
Davidson, Medora Lea *dance educator*

Parsons
Walker, Robert R. *music educator*

Topeka
Dunning, John Wilson, II, *music educator, vocalist*
Schellman, Elizabeth Turney *vocalist, educator*
Schultz, LeAnne *violinist, performer, music educator*

Wichita
Johnson, C. Nicholas *dance company executive*
Racer, William Eugene *retired music educator*

KENTUCKY

Bowling Green
Berry, Mark Sean *music educator*

Burlington
Mitchell, Timothy Lynn *music educator*

Campbellsville
Martin, J(ames) Kenneth *music educator*
McArthur, Lisa R. *music educator, musician*

Florence
Hartman, Rome *television producer*

Frankfort
Fletcher, Winona Lee *theater educator*

Hopkinsville
Wilkinson, Daniel Melvin *music educator*

Lexington
Cameron-Mickens, Vertrelle Diane *singer, conductor, voice educator*
O'Hurley, John *actor*
Pollack, Rhoda-Gale *theater educator, director*
Sogin, David Warren *music educator*

Louisville
Lin, Stephen Houng Tze *music educator*

Monticello
Sexton, Scotty Eugene *music educator, gifted and talented educator*

Morehead
Detweiler, Greg Jeffrey *music educator*

Paris
Gallardo, Sandra Silvana *television producer, actress*

Richmond
Machado-Echezuria, Marianella Perpetua *composer, writer, educator*

LOUISIANA

Baton Rouge
Buchmann, Molly O'Banion *choreographer, educator*
Lusted, Dona Sanders *music educator, consultant, organist*
Mathews, Sharon Walker *performing company executive, secondary school educator*
McCoy, Wesley Lawrence *musician, educator, conductor*
Nave, J. L. *performing company executive*
Norem, Richard Frederick, Sr. *musician, educator*
Smith, Richard James *retired music educator*
Tandberg, Gerilyn Gay *theater educator, costume designer*
Yarbrough, Martha Cornelia *music educator*

Franklin
Rouly, Ellie Arceneaux *dancer, educator*

Iowa
Kuykendall, Richard G. *music educator*

Lafayette
Stravinska, Sarah *dance educator*

Lake Charles
Batchelor, Karen Sue *music educator*

Mandeville
Childress, Joel M. *music educator*

Metairie
Grotkowski, Edward Michael *music educator, director*

Monroe
Huntington, Lisa Lynee *music educator*
Trapp, A. C. *retired music educator*

New Orleans
St. Julien, Thais Mary *soprano, musician*

Pineville
Hamlett, Curt *music educator, director*

Sulphur
Fuller, Betty Stamps *music educator*

MAINE

Brunswick
Schwartz, Elliott Shelling *composer, writer, music educator*

Castine
Davis, Peter Frank *filmmaker, writer*

Deer Isle
Wheeler, Gerald *church musician, educator*

Gorham
Chaulet, (Frédérique) Emmanuelle *performing company executive, actress, educator, writer*

Portland
Miller, Buffy *dancer*

Sullivan
Davis-Wexler, Ginia *singer, director*

Waterville
Benissan, Jordan Messan *music educator*

MARYLAND

Annapolis
Seep, Dorothy M. *music educator*

Arnold
Marder, Barbara Hermling *theater educator, department chairman*

Baltimore
Alsop, Marin *conductor, violinist, music director*
Constantine, Andrew *conductor*
Harrison, Michael *opera company director*
Huggins, Amy Branum *music educator*
Hulbert, Jarl O. *music educator*
Jacobson, Katherine Louise *musician, educator*
Otal, Monica D. *music educator*
Skirpan, Richard Michael *conductor, music educator*
Sutherland, Donald Sinclair *music educator, musician*
Temirkanov, Yuri Khatuevich *conductor, music director*

Bel Air
Kramer, Keith Allan *music educator, composer*

Bethesda
Burkhalter, Susan Shively *music educator, organist*

Bowie
Hillsman, Joan Rucker *music educator*

Chestertown
Clarke, Garry Evans *composer, educator, academic administrator, musician*

College Park
Montgomery, William Layton *music educator, educator, musician*

Columbia
Carter, Karen Zepp *music educator, elementary school educator*
Kearns, Ronald Edwin *music educator, performance artist*
Weems, Helen Rachel *musician, educator*

Crofton
Mahaffey, Redge Allan *movie producer, director, writer, actor, scientist, business executive*

Frostburg
Bauman, Jon Ward *retired music educator*
Horner, Ronald George *musician, educator*

Germantown
Harris, William Norman *music educator*

Great Mills
Bufis, Matthew Peter *music educator*

Gwynn Oak
Hughes, Catherine L. (Cathy Hughes) *radio personality, broadcast executive*

Kensington
Forrest, Sidney *clarinetist, music educator*

La Plata
Herdman-Fisher, Carolyn A. *music educator*

Owings
O'Neill, Patricia Tydings *performing arts educator, language educator*

Owings Mills
Swartz, Eugene Robert, Jr. *music educator, minister*

Potomac
Tressel, George Walter *TV producer, science educator, consultant*

Reisterstown
Stefano, Toni Amanda *voice educator*

Saint Marys City
Froom, David *composer, music educator*

Salisbury
Bowden, Derek Thomas *orchestra director, educator*

Silver Spring
Brandt, Elsa Lund Erickson *music educator*
Secular, Sidney *actor, writer, fundraiser, business consultant*

Towson
Ahearn, Elizabeth Lowe *performing arts educator*
Crawford, Leneida Marie *singer, educator*
Forrest, Juliet *dancer, educator, choreographer*
Jothen, Michael Jon *music educator, composer, conductor*

MASSACHUSETTS

Allston
Cort, Julia *television director, television producer, scriptwriter*
Liota, Vincent *television producer*
Spencer, Lara *television personality, journalist*

Amherst
Donohue, Therese Brady *artistic director, choreographer, costume and set designer*
Spratlan, Lewis *composer, educator*

Andover
Warner, Sally Slade *musician*

Arlington
Eastburn, Christopher Amers *composer, choral director*

Auburn
Giannini, Antoinette Frances *music educator, researcher*

Boston
Bacon, A. Smoki *television host*
Barker, Edwin Bogue *musician*
Bourque, Louise *film director, film instructor*
Del Sesto, Janice Mancini *opera company executive*
Firth, Everett Joseph *timpanist*
Harvey, Mark Sumner *composer, educator, retired minister, musician*
Hoffman, Stanley Marc *composer, editor*
Hoyt, Herbert Austin Aikins *television producer*
Jochum, Veronica *pianist*
Lesser, Laurence *musician, educator*
Liotta, Jeanne *film director, educator*
Lockhart, Keith Alan *conductor, music director*
Lowell, Richard Lee *music educator, musician*
MacCombie, Bruce Franklin *composer, college administrator*
Marsh, Milton R.W. *composer*
McPhee, Jonathan *music director, conductor, composer, interim artistic coordinator*
Mitchell, Jon Ceander *music educator, conductor*
Moriarty, John *opera administrator, artistic director*
Nissinen, Mikko Pekka *dancer, performing arts company executive, artistic director*
Rochinski, Stephen James *musician, educator*
Schwartz, Lloyd *music critic, poet*
Simone, Renata *television producer*
Sonnenschein, David *music educator, composer, conductor*
Street, Tison *music educator*
Vila, Robert Joseph *television personality, real estate developer, space designer*
Ward, Wayne Conrad *music educator, conductor*
Warshaw, Dalit Hadass *composer, educator*
Wheeler, W(illiam) Scott *composer, conductor, music educator*
Williams, John Towner *composer, conductor*
Young, Laura *choreographer, educator*

Braintree
Hallenbeck, Rachel Kirsten *music educator, director*

Cambridge
Cleary, David Michael *composer, critic, library assistant*
Connick, Harry, Jr. *musician, actor, vocalist, composer, lyricist*
de Varon, Lorna Cooke *choral conductor*
Gibbons, Joe *filmmaker*
Harbison, John *composer*
Holmberg, Arthur Carl *performing arts educator, theater critic*
Kraus, Rozann B. *performing company executive*
Morris, Errol M. *filmmaker*
Orchard, Robert John *theater producer, educator*
Parker, Lisa Frederick *music educator, Dalcroze specialist*
St. Clair, Richard Collins *composer, administrative assistant*
Sims, Ezra *composer*
Wood, Pamela Sharon *music educator, soprano*

Concord
Gorny, Marina Dubinsky *music educator*

Dedham
Magner, Jerome Allen *performing company executive*

Dorchester
Jackson, Jimmie L. *retired music educator, organist*

Eastham
Tipton, Noel Martin, Jr. *musician, writer, composer*

Falmouth
Brock, Nancy Jeanne *music educator, writer*
Maness, George Andrew *music educator*

Framingham
Bogard, Carole Christine *soprano*

Great Barrington
Curtin, Phyllis *music educator, dean, vocalist*

Hingham
Noel, Barbara Hughes McMurtry *retired music educator*

Holyoke
Damon, Steven William *music educator*
Dower Gold, Catherine Anne *music history educator*

Hopkinton
Moran, Wendy Jacqueline *music educator, musician*

Lincoln
Giles, Allen *pianist, composer, music educator*
Stathos, Margaret Moreland *musician*

Marblehead
Kennedy, Elizabeth Mae *musician*

Mashpee
Jamison, John L. *musician, educator*

Monterey
Swan, William *actor*

Nantucket
Byrne, Laura G. *music educator, theater educator, vocal coach*
Rorem, Ned *composer, writer*

Needham
Di Domenica, Robert Anthony *musician, composer*

Newton
Osborne, Charles David *singer, composer, conductor*
Wahlberg, Mark *actor*

Newton Center
Schuller, Gunther Alexander *composer*

North Adams
McConnell, Matthew Stephen *composer, educator*

Northampton
Naegele, Philipp Otto *musician, educator*

Orleans
Patterson, Elizabeth C. *choir director*

Pittsfield
Guzzo, Jessica Ann *music educator*

Plymouth
Gregory, Dick *comedian, volunteer*

Roslindale
Girard, Jonathan Richard *conductor*

Salem
Melby, John B. *composer, educator*

Shirley
Hoffmann, Micheal Joseph *theater director*

Somerville
Ballman, Chris *public radio reporter*
Curwood, Steve *television producer, host*
Fitzpatrick, Terry *public radio reporter, producer*
Suhrstedt, Barbara Lynn *concert pianist, voice educator*

Vineyard Haven
Breuer, Joann Green *theater director*

Waltham
Boykan, Martin *composer, music educator*
Wyner, Yehudi *composer, pianist, conductor, educator*

Weston
Tenney, Sarah G. *music educator*

Worcester
Delorey, John Francis *music educator*
Hagar, Richard Joseph *music educator, musician*
Hatfield, Renee S.J. *music educator*

MICHIGAN

Adrian
Dodson, John Thomas *orchestra conductor*

Ann Arbor
Bolcom, William Elden *composer, educator, musician*
Kunzel, Erich, Jr. *conductor, arranger, educator*
Peng Chen, Hsiu-Hui *music educator*
Pierce, John Charles *singer*
Scavarda, Donald Robert *composer, artist*

Battle Creek
Matthews, Wyhomme S. *retired music educator, academic administrator*

Belleville
Van Tassel, Michael L. *music educator*

Benton Harbor
Schults-Berndt, Elfie *music educator*

Birch Run
Warnick, Howard James *retired church musician, educator*

Bloomfield Hills
Haidostian, Alice Berberian *concert pianist, volunteer, not-for-profit fundraiser*
Swift, Jonathan *television personality, educator*

Burton
Johnson, Jolene Carole *music educator*

Commerce Township
Thibideau, Carolyn C. *musician, educator*

Dearborn
Popovich, George Lee *theater educator*

Detroit
DiChiera, David *opera company director*
Duensing, Dorothy Jean *music educator, vocalist*
Dworkin, Aaron P. *violinist, educator*
Walls, Amos Louis III *music educator*

East Lansing
Kirk, Edgar Lee *retired musician, educator*

Farmington Hills
Goslin, Gerald Hugh *concert pianist, educator*
Purdy, Jan Rae *music educator*

Flint
Czinder, Thomas Bradley *musician, director*

Frankfort
Storrer, William Allin *theater educator, consultant*

Grand Rapids
Crowell, Gregory F. *musician, director*
Horn, Joyce Elaine *retired music educator*
Metzler, James Robert *musician*
Webb, Mark Russell *music educator*

Holland
DeBruyn, Maxine *performing arts educator*

Jackson
Nugent, Ted (Theodore Anthony Nugent) *musician, radio personality*

Kalamazoo
Ratner, Carl Joseph *opera stage director, baritone*

Lake Orion
Berger, Laura Ann *dance studio owner*

Lansing
Kluge, Len H. *director, actor, theater educator*

Livonia
Nelson, Troy Alan *music educator, church musician*

Mason
Yoakam, Kelly Lynn *harpist, educator*

Northport
Scripps, Douglas Jerry *musician, educator, conductor*

Norway
Hunt, Gregory C. *music educator*

Richland
Nott, Robin K. *theater educator, theater director*

Rochester Hills
Parker, Catherine L. *theater educator*

Romeo
Tsukamoto, Daniel *piano instructor, church organist*

Saginaw
Coughlin, Jeannine Marie *music educator*

South Haven
Tyrrell, Cole Brooks *music educator*

Swartz Creek
Packer, Matthew James *musician, educator, advertising executive*

Traverse City
Faulmann, Roger Ray *retired music educator*

Warren
Cutter, Jeffrey S. *music educator*

Waterford
Pronovost, Amy Lynne *dancer, educator*

Ypsilanti
Bengtsson, Erling Blöndal *musician, educator*

MINNESOTA

Anoka
Chamberlain, Sonja Kay *music educator*

Arden Hills
Lahann, Jon Clifford *retired music educator*

Bemidji
McKee, Marcy D'Ette *voice educator*

Bloomington
Smith, Henry Charles III *symphony orchestra conductor*

Caledonia
Kranz, Kimberly Renee *elementary music educator*

Chanhassen
Prince, (Prince Rogers Nelson) *musician, actor*

Coon Rapids
Vogel, Scott Charles *music educator*
Wilson, Sylvia Alyce *musician, educator*

Duluth
Morath, Max Edward *entertainer, composer, writer*

Fridley
Ellison, Cynthia Kuehl *music educator, musician*

Golden Valley
Spake, Mary Barbara *music educator*

Hastings
Mahlen, Tatum L. *voice educator*

Inver Grove Heights
Rone, James Stephen *performing arts association administrator*

Milaca
Wig, Robert Curtis *retired music educator, conductor*

Minneapolis
Barnard, Tom *radio personality*
Crabtree, Vicki Gail *musician*
Fetler, Paul *retired composer*
Hyslop, David Johnson *retired arts administrator*
Severinsen, Doc (Carl H. Severinsen) *conductor, musician*
Vanska, Osmo *music director*
Wollan, Curtis Noel *theater producer, theater director*

Moorhead
Rothlisberger, Rodney John *music educator*

Mound
Whaley, Roger Glenn *music educator*

New Ulm
Schubkegel, Joyce Catherine *music educator, composer*

Plymouth
Trump, Stephanie *music educator, choral director*

Saint Paul
Dahlberg, Eric Ross *music educator*
Kent, Patricia Anne *music educator, singer*
McGegan, Nicholas *music director*
You, Yali *music educator*

Vadnais Heights
Martinez, Kathryn Marie *music educator*

Wayzata
Skrowaczewski, Stanislaw *conductor, composer*

MISSISSIPPI

Cleveland
Wojcik, John Casimir *music educator, director*

Columbus
Kantack, Catherine Margaret *retired music educator, retired international and bank broker*

Greenwood
Horn, Lawrence Charles *retired music educator*

Grenada
Thomas, Ouida Power *music educator*

Hattiesburg
Stockstill, David H. *musician, research historian, lecturer*

Jackson
Smith, Carnice *music educator, director*

Mccomb
Chamberlin, Mary Ellen *music educator*

Natchez
Wynn, Bobbye Faye *music educator*

University
Dor, George W. K *music educator*

MISSOURI

Alton
Scott, Lori Denise *music educator, musician*

Blue Springs
Washburn, Gladys Haase *retired church musician, educator, director*

Butler
Turner, Vicky Jo *music educator*

Columbia
Burgoyne, Suzanne *theater educator, writer*
Vale, Patrice J. *musician, consultant*

Creve Coeur
Randle, Bernadette *musician, composer, graphics designer*

Dearborn
McInnis, Robin Lynn *voice educator*

Doniphan
McCann, Lawrence Alton *music educator*

Festus
Auchly, Christopher M. *music educator*

Hannibal
Corkern, David E. *music educator*

Hillsboro
Jackson, Candine Lee *performing arts, English and speech educator*

Independence
Pinick, Sariah Kay *music educator*

Joplin
Wostal, Holly Ann *music educator*

Kansas City
Kuenn, Marjorie Asp *music educator*
Londré, Felicia Mae Hardison *theater educator*
Meilink, Jacqueline Rae *music educator*
Myers, Betty J. *retired music specialist*
Robertson, Kenneth Carl *music educator*
Setser, Patricia A. *music educator*
Whitener, William Garnett *dancer, choreographer*

Kirksville
Weerts, Richard Kenneth *music educator*

Liberty
Harriman, Richard Lee *performing arts association administrator, educator*

Marshall
Sayer, Ronald J. *composer, educator*

Maryville
Kling, Carl Andrew *music educator*
Schultz, Patricia Bowers *vocal music educator, conductor*

Pacific
Hogan, Kurt Avery *music educator*

Platte City
Jones, Jay Robert *music educator*
Shier, Susan Lynne *music educator*

Rogersville
Hover, Tryphena Machael *music educator*

Saint Charles
Fitzpatrick, Karey Rose *music educator, director*
Quiggins, Larry Dale *theater educator*

Saint James
Stevens, Helen Jean *music educator*

Saint Joseph
Bacon, Brian James, Jr. *music and liturgy director*

Saint Louis
Hoy, Dawn Riske *musician, director*
Schindler, Laura Ann *piano teacher, accompanist*
Schweizer, Gregory Paul *music educator*
Sims, Gary Wayne *music educator*
Smith, C. Grant *film producer, scriptwriter*
Stewart, John Harger *music educator*
Stookesberry, Denise *music educator, musician*
Turner-Richard, Lana R. *musician, director, composer*
Woolf, Steven Michael *artistic director*

Saint Peters
Ranner, Shanna *music educator*

Springfield
Blake, Loretta L. *music educator*
Cassity, Michael David *music therapy educator*
Dissmore, Larry David *musician, educator, conductor*
Moulder, T. Earline *musician*
Spicer, Holt Vandercook *retired theater educator*

Trenton
Gentry, Shirley *music educator, writer*

Wentzville
Berry, Chuck (Charles Edward Anderson Berry) *musician, composer*

MONTANA

Bozeman
Biegel, Debra Jeanne *music educator*
Vick, Jeffrey Harrison *musician, educator*

Butte
Clark, Gloria A. *music educator*

Eureka
Atherton, Michael Ward *music educator*
Kessler-Hodgson, Lee Gwendolyn *actress, performing company executive*

Great Falls
Hugg, Harold J. *music educator, director*
Johnson, Gordon James *performing company executive, conductor*

Kalispell
Slater, Allen J. *music educator*

Whitefish
DeFranco, Boniface Ferdinand Leonard (Buddy DeFranco) *clarinetist, bandleader*

NEBRASKA

Crete
Runestad, Kurt S. *music educator*

Grand Island
Hesterman, Phillip Karl *music educator*

Lincoln
Blanke, Henry H., Jr. *retired theater educator*
Collier, Nathan Morris *musician, educator*
Dixon, Wheeler Winston *film and video studies educator, writer*
Fawcett-Yeske, Maxine Ann *music educator*
Koch Johns, Patricia A. *theater educator*
Salyards Burton, Shannon Marie *voice educator, singer*
White, Tyler Goodrich *composer, conductor*

Lyons
Rose, Dwight Dean *music educator*

Mc Cook
Regier, Bryan L. *music educator*
Watts, Susan Helene *theater educator*

Omaha
Johnson, James David *concert pianist, organist, educator*
Seitz, Carole Jane *composer, educator*

Sidney
Zigweid, Richard Neil *music educator*

NEVADA

Boulder City
Schultheis, Adam John *music educator, consultant*

Carson City
Theiss, Jane I. *music educator*

Indian Springs
Dvorak, DeLyle Dennis *music and early childhood educator, consultant*

Las Vegas
Baker, Anita *singer*
Bernstein, Maureen Ann *theater educator, director*
Frances, Marie Cecilia *theater producer, television producer*
Jackson, Charles Anthony *music educator, radio personality*
Kendell, Ken *music educator*
Knight, Gladys (Gladys Maria Knight) *singer*
Lewis, Jerry (Joseph Levitch) *comedian*
Muhlenbruck-Fleischer, Deborah Lynn *music educator*
Rothrock, Carson *music educator*
Sakugawa, June Elizabeth *music educator*
Wiemer, Robert Ernest *film and television producer, writer, director*

North Las Vegas
Janzen, Donna Lee (Bricker) *music educator, singer*
Nisbett, Robert F. *music educator, consultant*

Reno
Aldrich, Gary O. *singer, educator*
Daniels, Ronald Dale *conductor*

Sandy Valley
Viscuglia, Jenny Lou *music educator*

NEW HAMPSHIRE

Alstead
Holloway, Robert Charles *musician, composer*

Hanover
Dong, Kui *music educator, composer*
Ehrlich, David Gordon *film director, educator*

Orford
Karol, John J., Jr. *producer, filmmaker*

Walpole
Burns, Ken *documentary filmmaker*

NEW JERSEY

Allendale
Ruth, Rodney *musician, music consultant, contractor, educator*

Allenhurst
Tognoli, Era M. *performing company executive, artistic director*

Allentown
Sulyok, Paul David *music educator, composer*

Bergenfield
Glazer, Gilda F. *musician, educator*

Cherry Hill
Clauser, Donald Roberdeau *retired musician*

Cinnaminson
Edwin, Robert *voice educator*

Clayton
Bertenshaw, William Howard III *radio and television producer*

Cliffside Park
Perhacs, Marylouise Helen *musician, educator*

Delanco
Lane, Carrie Belle (Hairston) *retired music educator*

Denville
Veech, Lynda Anne *musician, educator*

East Brunswick
Braun, Anna M. *music educator*

Edison
Chen-Maxham, Li-Chan *soprano*
Fan, Shirley Tsui-Yu *music educator*

Elizabeth
de la Viña-Sierra, Diana Maria *music educator*

Far Hills
Burns, Amy Margaret *music educator*

Fort Lee
Thomopoulos, Michael *music educator*

Glassboro
Gephardt, Donald Louis *music educator*

Hillside
Wilson, Bertina Iolia *retired music educator*

Jersey City
Bolcar, Katherine Elizabeth *music educator*
Hayes, Isaac *rhythm and blues singer, composer*
Queen Latifah, (Dana Elaine Owens) *actress, musician*
Warren, Maredia Delois *music educator*

Lakewood
Appello, Patrick Paul *guitarist, lutenist, educator*

Leonia
Deutsch, Nina *pianist, vocalist*

Lincroft
Benham, Helen *music educator*

Madison
Monte, Bonnie J. *performing arts company executive, director, educator*

Matawan
Cohen, Robert L. *film producer*

Medford
Nicholas, Leonard G. *music educator*
Sheffer, James Thomas *music educator*

Monmouth Junction
Lien, Ting-Ting *music educator*

Montclair
Walker, George Theophilus, Jr. *composer, music educator, pianist*

Mount Laurel
Jones, Marian C. *music educator*

Newark
Macal, Zdenek *conductor, music director*

Newton
Boulware, Bobbie L. *music educator*

Northfield
McNeal, Jane Erskine *music educator, musician*

Paramus
Gordon, Scott (Harry Scott Buehlmeier) *entertainer, actor*
Marcel-Calderon, Linda *music educator*
Saltzman, Jared *performing arts educator, lighting designer*

Perth Amboy
Richardson-Melech, Joyce Suzanne *music educator, singer*

Piscataway
Sumner, Floyd G. *retired music educator*

Princeton
Branker, Anthony Daniel John *music educator, researcher, composer*
Levy, Kenneth *music educator*
Lustig, Graham *performing company executive*
Orphanides, Nora Charlotte *ballet educator*
Tymoczko, Dmitri *music educator, composer*

Ridgefield
Tracey, Matthew Sean *music educator, musician*

Rivervale
Moderacki, Edmund Anthony *music educator, conductor*

Rockaway
Steier, Audrey Keller *music educator*

Rutherford
Baker, Don L. *band director*

Scotch Plains
Kraemer, Ira B. *symphony conductor*

Secaucus
Diggs, Taye (Scott Diggs) *actor*

Sicklerville
Simpson, Eugene Thamon *music educator, singer*

South Orange
Nowik, John David *music educator, musician*

Southampton
Saltus, Phyllis Borzelliere *music educator*

Sparta
Jacobs-Quam, Vivien Marie *retired music educator*

Summit
Falletta, Jo Ann *conductor*

Teaneck
Bullough, John Frank *musician, educator*
Carter, Regina *jazz violinist*
Graham, Janet Lorraine *music educator*

Tenafly
Tall, Susan Porter *music educator*

Trenton
Cole, Richie Thomas *musician, composer, educator*
Demitry, Elpis Hope *music educator*

Warren
Maull, George Marriner *conductor, educator*

Wayne
DeRosa, Richard Jerome *composer, musician, educator*
Sullivan, Glenn D. *music educator*

West Orange
Atkins, Richard Bart *film and television producer*
Mazur, Thomas A. *music educator*

Whippany
Willans, Joanne Joy *music educator*

NEW MEXICO

Albuquerque
Kierst, Debra B. *theater educator, director, actor*
Liotta, William A. *theater educator*
Mock, Joan Bodet *music educator*
Quinn, Iain *musician*
Rasmussen, Kerrie L. *theater educator*
Thévenot, Maxine Rachael *musician, educator*
Wild, Richard *music educator, musician*

Artesia
Jensen, Eric Reinhard *music educator*

Belen
Jolly, Jeffrey Russell *musician, educator*

Edgewood
Hamilton, Jerald *musician*

Las Cruces
Fitzgearld, Gayl *musician, educator*

Portales
Carr, Tracy A. *musician, educator*
Dal Porto, Mark Daniel *music educator*
Paschke, Donald Vernon *music educator*

Santa Fe
Ballard, Louis Wayne *composer*
Gaddes, Richard *opera company director*
Gilbert, Alan T. *conductor*
Knight, Kenneth Hugh *conductor*
Ovitsky, Steven Alan *musician, classical music executive*
Rubenstein, Bernard *orchestra conductor*
Zlatoff-Mirsky, Everett Igor *violinist*

Tesuque
MacGraw, Ali *actress*

NEW YORK

Addison
Vona, John David *music educator*

Albany
Eppink, Joseph A. *music educator*

Angola
Ross, Sue Hoisington *music educator*

Annandale On Hudson
Miyagawa, Chiori *theater educator, playwright*
Tower, Joan Peabody *composer, educator*

Astoria
Francesca, Mike *radio personality*
Sirignano, Monica Ann *performing company executive, playwright*

Attica
Rogers, Donald L. *music educator, department chairman, animal breeder*

Bayside
Mullany, Kevin Fergus *music educator, director*
Zinn, William *musician, composer*

Bedford
Chase, Chevy (Cornelius Crane Chase) *comedian, actor, writer*

Binghamton
Lee, Wendy Wan-Ki *music educator*
Wildoner, Nancy Schamu *music educator, fine arts department chairman*

Bohemia
Grandmaster Flash, (Joseph Saddler) *disc jockey*

Boiceville
Thomas, David Clifton *music educator*

Briarcliff Manor
Wheeler, Margaret Jane *actress, soprano, voice educator*

Brockport
McGhee, Diane Baumann *dance instructor, consultant*

Bronx
Ask-Nanko, Lorraine Charlotte *music educator*
Baker, Blanche *actress*
Fletcher, Judith Ellen *music educator*
Lagares, Portia Octavia *music educator*
Mittler, Diana (Diana Mittler-Battipaglia) *music educator, pianist*
Rubensky, Mitchell *band director*
Sherman, Judith Dorothy *theater producer, engineer, recording industry executive*

Bronxville
Biscardi, Chester *composer, educator*

Brooklyn
Armstrong, John Wallace *film producer*
Epstein, Alvin *actor, performance artist, theater director, make-up artist*
Gatten, David *filmmaker*
Hopkins, Karen Brooks *performing arts executive*
Latif-Zade, Alisher *composer*
Lee, Spike (Shelton Jackson Lee) *film director and producer*
McQuiggan, John A. *theater producer, writer*
Morris, Mark William *choreographer*
Niesen, James Louis *theater director*
Rathbun, Andrew J. *music educator*
Richmond, Eero *composer, music librarian*
Sahlene, *singer*
Skrobela, Katherine Creelman *music producer, data processing executive*
Stevens, Aleksei Reuben *music educator, composer*
Vidal, Maureen Eris *theater educator, actress*

Buffalo
DiFranco, Ani *music executive, musician*
Lombardo Appleby, Linda Rose *music educator*
Manes, Stephen Gabriel *concert pianist, educator*
Zawadzki-Janusz, Stacy Lynn *music educator, performing arts educator*

Central Islip
Brown, Alton C. *television personality, chef*
Voigt, Philip Kenneth *music educator*

Cheektowaga
Kipler, James Michael *musician, educator*

Cicero
Pink, (Alecia B. Moore) *singer*

Clifton Park
Nair, Laura *retired music educator*

Cortland
Lyman, Kristin M. *music educator*

Croton On Hudson
Norman, Jessye *soprano*
Sayre, Susan Kathryn Greenwald *musician, educator*

Deer Park
Chapman, Ronald Thomas *musician, educator*

Derby
Cuomo, Rivers *singer, songwriter*

Dunkirk
Flaherty, Cynthia Mead *music educator*

East Amherst
Ennis, Carol Robbins *retired music educator*

East Greenbush
Quenelle, Susannah Sherman *music educator*

East Hampton
Dello Joio, Norman *composer*

Floral Park
Daloia, Rachel Rosemary *music educator*
Kolb, Lisa Marie *music educator*

Flushing
Evens, Lucie Ann *music educator*
Hart, Antonio Maurice *musician, educator*
Smaldone, Edward Michael *composer*

Forest Hills
Cerveris, Michael *actor*
Mathieu Byers, Deborah Anne *performing company executive*
Polakoff, Abe *baritone*

Freeport
Zurcher, Zean William *retired music educator, musician*

Fulton
Jennings, Meghan Young *music educator*

Garden City
Einenkel, Robert Herbert *theater educator, actor, director*
Gray, Phil R. *band director, musician*
Pereira, John William Miller *theater educator*
Wetherill-Smith, Linda Marie *musician, educator, performing arts association administrator*

Germantown
Farberman, Harold *conductor, composer*

Glenford
Matalon, Vivian *theatrical director*

Greenvale
Senft, Mason George *musician*
Sugar, Joseph Robert *music educator, conductor, musician*

Hastings On Hudson
D'Antoni, Philip *television producer*
Sharpe, Robert Kent *writer, director, producer, photographer*

Hawthorne
Hodge, Timothy *performing company executive, actor*

Hempstead
Coleman, Benjamin Joseph *music educator*
Graffeo, Mary Thérèse *music educator, performer*
Heuermann-Nowik, Patricia Calhoun *theater director*
Schechtman, Saul *conductor*

Hewlett
Williams, Tyler James *actor*

Hicksville
Garner, Bert L. *music educator*

Howard Beach
Leiter, Samuel L. *theater educator*

Hunter
Khanzadian, Vahan *tenor*

Hurley
Culver, Michael Patrick *music educator, composer*

Ithaca
Arquit, Nora Harris *retired music educator, writer*
Fonder, Mark Leslie *music educator*
Husa, Karel *composer, conductor, educator*

Kenmore
Kuhn, William Andrew *music educator*

Kings Park
LaFantano, Elizabeth *music educator*

Liverpool
Federico, Josephine A.M. *music educator*
Landers, Mary Dean J. *music educator*

Long Eddy
Hoiby, Lee *composer, concert pianist*

Manhasset
Brand, Oscar *folk singer, writer, educator*
Sirooni, Anahid Alice *composer, musician*

Massapequa
Turk, Elizabeth Ann *music educator*

Melville
Sobol, Elise Schwarcz *music educator*

Millerton
Hastings, Donald Francis *actor, writer*

Mineola
Olsen, Dorothy S. *music educator*

Monroe
Furman-Markowitz, Joanna Florence *dance educator*

Montgomery
Teutul, Paul, Sr. *television personality, mechanic*

Narrowsburg
Krause, Gloria Rose *music educator*

New Hartford
Weiss, Holly Anne *music educator, singer*

New York
Abelson, Robert Paul *cantor, singer*
Adams, Bryan *vocalist, composer, photographer*
Adams, John Coolidge *composer, conductor*
Addison, Anne Simone Pomex *television director, consultant, commentator*
Adler, Richard *composer, lyricist*
Ahrens, Lynn *lyricist*
Akon, (Aliaune Thiam) *singer*
Alda, Alan *actor, film director, scriptwriter*
Alexander, Jane (Jane Quigley) *actress, theater educator, writer*
Allen, Betty (Mrs. Ritten Edward Lee III) *mezzo-soprano*
Alpert, Jon *television producer, director, reporter*
Alt, Carol A. *actress, model, entrepreneur, writer*
Amos, Tori *musician, singer*
Andersen, Mark *musician*
Andrade, Andres *vocalist, educator*
Arroyo, Martina *soprano*
Asakawa, Takako *dancer, choreographer, educator, director*
Ashanti, (Ashanti Shequoiya Douglas) *vocalist*
Asner, Edward *actor*
Ax, Emanuel *pianist*
Bacall, Lauren (Betty Joan Perske) *actress*
Baker, Susan L. *performing company executive, retired investment banker*
Barbour, Catherine Jean *actress, set designer, director, mime*
Bart, Roger *actor*
Bashkow, Jack Simon *musician*
Bednar, Rudy *television producer, director*
Bee, Samantha *comedian, actress*
Beeson, Jack Hamilton *composer, educator, writer*
Belzer, Richard *actor, comedian*
Besterman, Douglas *composer, orchestrator*
Bikel, Theodore *actor, singer*
Birkenhead, Thomas Bruce *theater producer, educator*
Björk, (Björk Guðmundsdóttir) *singer, composer*
Bledel, Alexis (Kimberly Alexis Bledel) *actress*
Bolotowsky, Andrew Ilyitch *flutist, composer*
Bolton, Michael *singer, songwriter*
Boston, Gretha *actress, vocalist*
Boston, Lloyd *television personality*
Bracco, Lorraine *actress*
Brant, Henry *composer*
Brinkley, Christie *model, spokesperson, designer*
Brohn, William David *conductor, orchestrator, arranger*
Brothers, Joyce Diane *television personality, psychologist*
Brown, Chris (Christopher Maurice Brown) *singer*
Brown, David *motion picture producer, writer*
Brown, Trisha *dancer*
Bundchen, Giselle *model*
Burnett, Mark *television producer*
Butler, Kerry *actress*
Byer, Diana *performing company executive*
Byrd, Debra Ann *actor, theater producer, performing company executive*
Caldwell, L. Scott *actress*
Caldwell, Zoe *actress, film director*

Campbell, Naomi *model*
Cantrell, Lana *actress, lawyer, singer*
Capalbo, Carmen *theater director, producer*
Caples, Richard James *performing company executive, lawyer*
Carlson, Marvin Albert *theater educator*
Carmichael, Jesse Royal *musician*
Carmona, Wayne *television producer*
Carter, Elliott Cook, Jr. *composer*
Cash, Rosanne *singer, songwriter*
Cavenaugh, Matt *actor*
Cazeaux, Isabelle Anne Marie *retired music educator*
Cesar, Kamala *dancer, educator*
Chang, Marian S. *filmmaker, composer*
Channing, Stockard (Susan Antonia Williams Stockard) *actress*
Chenoweth, Kristin *actress*
Chong, Ping *performing company executive*
Christensen, Dieter *ethnomusicologist*
Chusid, Martin *musicologist, educator*
Ciara, (Ciara Princess Harris) *R&B performer*
Clark, Victoria *actress*
Coleman, Ornette *jazz musician*
Collins, Phil (Philip David Charles Collins) *singer, songwriter, drummer, record producer*
Conway, Kevin *actor, performing company executive*
Corddry, Rob *comedian, actor*
Corgan, Billy (William Patrick Corgan) *musician*
Corigliano, John Paul *composer*
Corsaro, Frank Andrew *theater director*
Cowing, Charles Ogden *talent agency executive*
Cunningham, Merce *performing company executive, dancer*
Curtin, Jane Therese *actress, writer*
Curtis, Paul James *performance artist, director*
Daltrey, Roger Harry *singer*
d'Amboise, Jacques Joseph *former dancer, choreographer, educator, director*
Danitz, Marilynn Patricia *choreographer, video specialist*
Dano, Linda *actress*
Danza, Tony *actor*
David, Hal *lyricist*
Davidovsky, Mario *retired composer*
Davis, Christopher James *television producer*
Davison, Bruce *actor*
Deen, Paula H. *television personality, restaurant owner, chef*
de Kenessey, Stefania Maria *composer*
Del Forno, Anton *classical guitarist, recording artist, composer, educator*
DePreist, James Anderson *conductor*
DeWoody, Beth Rudin *film producer*
DiBiasio, Adolf R. *entertainment company executive*
Dinnerstein, Simone *pianist*
Dobrin, Tory *performing company executive, dancer*
Domino, Fats (Antoine Domino) *pianist, singer, songwriter*
Downs, Hugh Malcolm *retired radio and television broadcaster*
Doyle, John *artistic director, designer*
Dratch, Rachel *comedienne, actress*
Du Boff, Jill Bonnie Candise *sound effects artist*
Duchin, Peter Oelrichs *musician*
Duff, Hilary Ann *singer, actress*
Dukakis, Olympia *actress*
Dulaine, Pierre *ballroom dancer*
Dullea, Keir *actor*
Du Prez, John *composer*
Durang, Christopher *actor, playwright*
Dusick, Ryan Michael *musician*
Dylan, Bob (Robert Allen Zimmerman) *singer, musician*
Eisler, Edith *violinist, educator*
Ellin, Doug *film producer, television producer, television director, writer*
Ellington, Mercedes *performing company executive, choreographer, director, producer, educator*
Elliott, David J. *music educator*
Elliott, Missy (Melissa Arnette Elliot) *musician*
Ellis, Scott *theatrical director*
Emme, (Emme Aronson) *model, apparel designer*
Epstein, Matthew *opera company director*
Eschenbach, Christoph *conductor, musician, music director*
Fantasia, (Fantasia Monique Barrino) *singer*
Farino, Julian *television director, film director, television producer*
Farley, Carole *soprano*
Feit, Barberi Paull *composer, lyricist, psychotherapist, writer*
Feld, Eliot *dancer, choreographer, performing company executive*
Fields, Felicia P. *actress*
Fifty Cent, (Curtis James Jackson) *rap artist*
Fisher, Joely *actress*
Flack, Roberta *singer*
Flaherty, Stephen *composer, orchestrator*
Flannery, Kate *actress*
Fleming, Renée L. *opera singer*
Flowers, Brandon Richard *singer*
Fogler, Dan *actor*
Fontana, Thomas Michael *television producer, scriptwriter*
Ford, Eileen Otte (Mrs. Gerard W. Ford) *modeling agency executive*
Foreman, Richard *theater director, playwright*
Formento, Daniel *radio company executive, writer*
Fox, Andrew *entertainment productions executive*
Fox, Matthew *actor*
Friedman, Debbie *singer, songwriter, religious studies educator*
Garcia, Andy *actor*
Gazzara, Ben *actor*
Gelb, Peter *performing company executive*
Giannini, Giancarlo *actor, director, screenwriter*
Gibney, Alex *producer, director, writer*
Gillinson, Sir Clive Daniel *music executive, former musician*
Giraldi, Robert Nicholas *film director*
Glass, Philip *composer, musician*
Glück, Sebastian M. *pipe organ builder*
Goldsmith, Merwin *actor, theater director*
Goldston, James *television producer*
Gordon, Wycliffe *trombonist, jazz musician, music educator, composer*
Goto, Midori *classical violinist*
Graff, Randy *actress*
Greenberg, Mark *television producer*
Greenfield, Lucille Jean *music educator, composer*
Griffel, L. Michael *music educator, researcher*
Grunschlag, Toni *pianist, researcher*
Haggerty, Luane Ruth Davis *theater director, educator, actress*
Hall, Michael C. *actor*
Halmi, Robert, Sr. *film, television producer*
Hamilton Jackson, Marilyn J. *dancer, educator, choreographer*
Hammett, Kirk Lee *musician*
Hammond, Darrell *actor*
Hardin, Melora *actress*
Hargitay, Mariska Magdolina *actress*
Harmon, Jane *theater producer*
Harrell, Ray Evans *performing company executive, conductor, educator*
Harris, Julie (Ann) *actress*
Harter, Theo C. *music educator, composer*
Hastings, Deborah *bass guitarist*
Hearn, George *actor*
Hebert, Bliss Edmund *opera director*
Helm, Lenora Zenzalai *musician, educator*
Herrera, Paloma *dancer*
Herron, Cindy *actress, vocalist*
Herzog, Werner (Werner Stipetic) *film director*
Hetfield, James *singer*
Ho, Betty Juenyü Yülin *retired musician, physiologist, educator*
Holmes, Anna-Marie *ballerina*
Hughes, Doug *theater director*
Hurlin, Dan *theater director*
Hutchinson, Lynda Ronette (Billie Holiday Jr., Princess of Jazz, Munchie) *vocalist, musician, comedian, actress*
Hylton, Kevin Nathaniel *musician, composer*
Imus, Don (John Donald Imus Jr.) *radio personality*
Ivory, James Francis *film director*
Jackson, Anne (Anne Jackson Wallach) *actress*
Jackson, Cheyenne *actor*
Jacobs, Jim *actor, composer, librettist, playwright*
Jacobs, Paul A. *music educator*
Jaffe, Susan *ballerina*
Jamison, Judith *performing company executive, dancer*
Jean, Wyclef *musician, recording industry executive*
Jefferson, Denise *dance school director*
Johnson, A. Paul *composer*
Jones, Bill T. *dancer, choreographer*
Jones, Sarah *actress, playwright, poet*
Jung, Doris *soprano*
Kamlot, Robert *performing arts executive*
Kanakaredes, Melina *actress*
Karchin, Louis Samuel *composer, educator*
Kassel, Virginia Weltmer *television producer, scriptwriter*
Keating, Isabel *actress*
Kelly, R. (Robert Sylvester Kelly) *musician, recording industry executive*
Kenny, Tom *actor*
Kent, Julie *dancer, actress, model*
Kent, Linda Gail *dancer*
Kid Rock, (Robert James Ritchie) *singer*
Kilik, Jon *film producer*
Kinberg, Judy *television producer and director*
King, B.B. (Riley B. King) *singer, guitarist*
Klein, Robert *comedian, actor*
Kline, Kevin Delaney *actor*
Kozak, Harley Jane *actress, writer*
Kudisch, Marc *actor*
Kurman, Juta *music educator*
Kya-Hill, Robert *actor, educator*
La Barbara, Joan *composer, musician, singer*
LaBelle, Patti (Patricia Louise Holte) *singer, entertainer*
Lane, Kenneth Robert *producer, distributor*
Lang, Pearl *dancer, choreographer*
Lang, Stephen *actor*
Lansbury, Edgar George *theatrical producer*
Lansner, Gabrielle *choreographer, dancer, performing company executive, actress*
Lauer, Matt *television personality*
Lee, Amy *singer*
Legrand, Michel Jean *composer*
Lennon, Thomas Furneaux *television producer, writer*
Lenox, Adriane *actress*
Leppard, Raymond John *conductor, musician*
Leritz, Lawrence R. *choreographer, singer, dancer*
Levine, Adam Noah *singer*
Levine, James *conductor, music director, pianist*
Levinson, Stephen *television producer*
Lewis, Jerry Lee *country-rock singer, musician*
Libin, Paul *theater producer and director*
LiBretto, John Charles *television director*
Lilly, Evangeline *actress*
Lima, Adriana Francesca *model*
Limbaugh, Rush Hudson III *radio talk show host*
Loeb, Lisa *singer, lyricist*
Loney, Glenn Meredith *theater educator*
Losier, Marie *film director*
Lowe, Nick *vocalist, musician, producer*
Lubovitch, Lar *dancer, choreographer*
Lucas, James E(vans) *operatic director*
LuPone, Patti *actress*
Lyman, Peggy *artistic director, dancer, choreographer, educator*
Ma, Yo-Yo *cellist*
Maazel, Lorin *conductor, composer, violinist, music director*
Madden, Mickey *musician*
Maddow, Rachel *radio personality, political activist*
Malkin, Barry *film editor, consultant*
Mandabach, Caryn *television producer*
Manilow, Barry (Barry Alan Pincus) *singer, composer*
Mansouri, Lotfollah (Lotfi Mansouri) *retired performing company executive*
Maraynes, Allan Lawrence *filmmaker, television producer*
Marceau, Yvonne *ballroom dancer, educator*
Mardirosian, Tom *actor, playwright*
Margolis, Mark Neal *actor*
Marshall, Kathleen *choreographer, theater director*
Marshall, Robert *film, television and theater director, choreographer*
Martini, Richard K. *theatrical producer*
Martins, Peter *ballet master, choreographer, dancer*
Mason, Marshall W. *theater director, educator, author*
Matthews, Dave *singer, musician*
Maxwell, Carla Lena *dancer, choreographer, educator*
Maysles, Albert H. *filmmaker*
Mazzo, Kay *ballet dancer, educator*
Mazzola, John William *retired performing company executive, consultant*
McDonald, Audra Ann *actress, vocalist*
McGrady, Phyllis *television producer*
McKenzie, Kevin Patrick *performing company executive*
Mc Lean, Don *singer, instrumentalist, composer*
Meadow, Lynne (Carolyn Meadow) *theater producer*
Melnick, Peter Rodgers *composer*
Michaels, Lorne *television producer*
Miller, Dennis *comedian*
Miller, Stephanie *radio personality*
Miller-Sydney, Audrey Yvonne *music educator*
Mitchell, Arthur *dancer, choreographer, performing company executive, educator*
Mitwell, Jill *television director*
Mohr, Jay *comedian, actor*
Monaghan, Dominic *actor*
Monk, Meredith Jane *artistic director, composer, choreographer, filmmaker*
Moore, Michael Watson *musician, educator*
Moore, Rachel Suzanne *performing company executive, dancer*
Muller, Jennifer *choreographer, dancer*
Muradian, Vazgen *composer*
Murphy, Donna *actress*
Murphy, Karen *film producer*
Murphy, Rosemary *actress*
Nair, Mira *film director, film producer*
Nederlander, James Morton *theater executive*
Nelly, (Cornell Haynes Jr.) *rap artist*
Neuman, Maxine Darcy *cellist, educator*
Newman, Randy *singer, songwriter, musician*
Nugent, Nelle *theater, film and television producer*
Nussbaum, Jeffrey Joseph *musician*
O'Brien, Conan *talk show host, writer, performer*
O'Neal, Hank *entertainment producer, small business owner*
O'Neill, Matthew *film producer*
Oremus, Stephen *composer*
Osborne, Joan Elizabeth *singer, songwriter*
Ostwald, David F. *theater director, educator*
Oz, Frank (Frank Richard Oznowicz) *entertainer, film director*
Parker, Alice *composer*
Parsons, Estelle *actress, director, theater producer*
Paul, George *television director*
Paul, Les *entertainer*
Pavarotti, Luciano *lyric tenor*
Payton-Wright, Pamela *actress*
Perlmutter, Alvin Howard *television and film producer*
Perry, Douglas *opera singer*
Peters, Bernadette (Bernadette Lazzara) *actress*
Peters, Roberta *soprano*
Phair, Liz *vocalist*
Philbin, Regis (Francis Xavier) *television personality*
Plant, Robert Anthony *singer, composer*
Poehler, Amy *comedienne, actress*
Poor, Peter Varnum *television producer and director*
Posin, Kathryn Olive *choreographer*
Powers, Scott *television producer, actor*
Previn, André (Ludwig) *composer, conductor, pianist*
Price, (Mary Violet) Leontyne *retired concert and opera singer, soprano*
Prince, Harold *theatrical director, producer*
Pulos, Virginia Kate *actress, consultant*
Queler, Eve *conductor*
Quivers, Robin *radio personality*
Rainer, Yvonne *choreographer, filmmaker*
Ramirez, Sara *actress*
Ramirez, Tina *performing company executive*
Randolph, David *conductor*
Reams, Lee Roy *actor*
Reeves, Dianne *singer*
Reeves, Jennifer Todd *filmmaker*
Reich, Steve *composer*
Reinking, Ann H. *dancer, actress*
Renick, Kyle *artistic director*
Reuben, Gloria *actress, singer*
Rhodes, Randi *radio personality*
Rhodes, Samuel *violist, educator*
Rice, Barbara Lynn *stage manager*
Rigg, Dame Diana *actress*
Ripa, Kelly Maria *television personality, actress*
Rivera, Chita (Conchita del Rivero) *actress, singer, dancer*
Rivera, Geraldo *television personality, journalist*
Robbins, Tim (Timothy Francis Robbins) *actor, film director*
Rodriguez, Freddy *actor*
Rollins, Sonny (Theodore Rollins) *composer, musician*
Ronstadt, Linda Marie *singer*
Rosen, Nathaniel Kent *cellist*
Ross, Diana (Diana Ernestine Earle Ross) *singer, actress, entertainer, fashion designer*
Ross, Jerrold *music educator*
Rothfeld, Michael B. *theatrical producer, investor*
Rothschild, Amalie Randolph *filmmaker, film producer, film director, photographer*
Roumain, Daniel Bernard *composer, violinist*
Rouse, Christopher Chapman III *composer, educator*
Rubin-Vega, Daphne *actress*
Rudavsky, Oren *film producer, cinematographer, film director*
Rudel, Julius *conductor*
Rudin, Scott *film and theatre producer*
Russell, David O. *film director, film producer, scriptwriter*
Saddler, Donald Edward *choreographer, dancer*
Salerno-Sonnenberg, Nadja *violinist*
Salonen, Esa-Pekka *conductor, music director*
Salonga, Lea *actress, singer*
Santos, Nadine *music director*
Sarandon, Susan Abigail *actress*
Schafer, Milton *composer, pianist, educator*
Schechner, Richard *theater director, educator*
Scheeder, Louis *theater producer, director, educator*
Schoenfeld, Gerald *performing company executive*
Schorer, Suki *ballet teacher*
Schrade, Robert Warren *classical pianist, educator*
Schwantner, Joseph *composer, educator*
Seal, *musician*
Sean Paul, (Sean Paul Henriques) *singer*
Seary, Lawrence Anthony *cinematographer, television producer*
Sedaka, Neil *singer, songwriter*
Seder, Sam *radio personality*
Seeger, Pete *folk singer, songwriter*
Seidler, Alan Richard *composer, musician, music company executive*
Seldes, Marian *actress*
Serebrier, José *musician, composer, conductor*
Severs, William Floyd *actor*
Shelley, Carole *actress*
Sherman, Arthur *theater educator, writer, actor, composer, sculptor*
Shuman, Earl Stanley *songwriter, music publisher*
Siegel, Marc Monroe *television producer, scriptwriter, director*
Silver, Joan Micklin *film director, screenwriter*
Silvers, Sally *choreographer, performing company executive*
Simmons, Joseph (Run Simmons, Reverend Run) *musician*
Simon, Joel *music producer, advertising executive*
Sitomer, Sheila Marie *television producer and director*
Sliwa, Curtis *radio personality, volunteer*
Smith, Malcolm Sommerville *bass*
Solís, Marco Antonio *singer, composer*
Solomons, Gus, Jr., (Gustave Martinez) *choreographer, dancer, writer*
Somerhalder, Ian Joseph *actor*
Soyer, David *cellist, music educator*
Spears, Britney *singer*
Speller, Robert Ernest Blakefield, Jr. *choreographer*
Spinney, Caroll *entertainer, educator*
Sporn, Michael V. *producer, director*
Stang, Arnold *actor, writer, film director*
Stang, Rolf Kristian *vocalist, educator, actor, advertising executive, writer*
Stern, Howard Allan *radio personality, television show host*
Stevens, Risë *performing arts association administrator*
Stewart, Ellen D. *theater producer*
Stewart, Jon (Jonathan Stewart Leibowitz) *comedian, actor*
Stiefel, Ethan *dancer, performing company executive*
Sting, (Gordon Matthew Sumner) *musician, songwriter, actor*
Stokes, William James *musician*
Stoltzman, Richard Leslie *clarinetist*
Storch, Arthur *theater director*
Strasfogel, Ian *stage director, playwright*
Stroman, Susan *choreographer, theater director*
Stucky, Steven (Edward) *composer, conductor*
Studdard, (Christopher) Ruben *singer*
Talmi, Yoav *conductor, composer*
Taylor, Paul B. *choreographer*
Thomas, Richard *actor*
Thompson, Donald Raymond *film producer, playwright*
Thompson, Jewel Taylor *music educator*
Tilson Thomas, Michael *conductor, music director*
Timberlake, Justin *singer*
Tokunaga, Emiko *dancer*
Tomassi Lindman, Sarah *television producer*
Torres, Dalys E. *music educator, consultant*
Travis, Sarah *orchestrator*
Tree, Michael *violinist, violist, educator*
Trujillo, Robert *musician*
Turtletaub, Marc *film producer*
Ulrich, Lars *musician*
Valentine, James Burgon *musician*
Valletta, Amber *actress, model*
Van Halen, Alex *musician*
Van Halen, Eddie (Edward Lodewijk Van Halen) *musician*
Vega, Suzanne *singer, songwriter*
Vieira, Meredith *television personality*
Wagner, Alan Cyril *television and film producer, consultant, performing arts educator*
Wainwright, Rufus *musician, singer*
Walden, Shelton Harrison *radio personality, educator*
Walker, Charles Dodsley *conductor, organist*
Wallach, Eli *actor*
Waters, Sylvia *dance company artistic director*
Waxman, Anita *theater producer*
Wek, Alek *model*
West, Kanye *rap artist*

Wheeldon, Christopher *dancer, choreographer*
White, George Cooke *theater director, foundation administrator*
White, Jack (John Anthony Gillis) *musician, producer*
White, Lillias *actress*
Wile, Joan *composer, lyricist, singer*
Wiley-Hart, Debra *musician, educator*
Williams, Montel *television talk show host*
Williams, Vanessa (Vanessa Lynn Williams) *recording artist, actress*
Williams, Wendy *radio personality, writer*
Wittstein, Edwin Frank *theater director, set designer*
Wolfe, George C. *theater director, producer, playwright*
Wong, Elizabeth Hung *organist, choirmaster*
Wood, Ronald *musician*
Woodward, Joanne Gignilliat *actress*
Woodward, Kirk *theater director*
Wuorinen, Charles Peter *composer*
Yamaguchi, Masaya *musician, educator*
Young, John Lloyd *actor*
Zambello, Francesca *opera and theater director*
Zbornak, Kent *television producer*
Zirinsky, Susan *television producer*
Zombie, Rob (Robert Cummings) *musician, filmmaker*
Zorn, John *composer, musician*
Zosike, Joanie Fritz *theater director, actress*
Zucker, Stefan *tenor, writer, editor, commentator*
Zukerman, Pinchas *concert violinist, violist, conductor*

Nyack
Sussman, Richard *music educator, composer*

Oakdale
Poppiti, Kimberly D. *performing arts educator*

Orchard Park
Carducci, Donald Joseph *music educator*

Oyster Bay
Joel, Billy (William Martin Joel) *musician*

Pawling
Jones, James Earl *actor*

Peekskill
Black, Carolyn Rebecca *music educator*

Penn Yan
Stempien, Joseph Jeffrey *music educator*

Pine Bush
Shepard, Ricahrd *film director, producer, writer*

Port Washington
Feuss, Judith Farrar *musician, educator*
Starr, Ringo (Richard Starkey) *musician, actor*

Poughkeepsie
Levine Simon, Sarah Ann *music educator*
Wilson, Richard Edward *composer, music educator, pianist*

Purchase
Magaziner, Elliot Albert *musician, conductor, educator*
McElwaine, James William *music educator*

Red Hook
Gudenzi-Ruess, Ida Carmen V. *music educator, artist*

Rochester
Gauldin, Robert L. *music educator, composer*
Günter-McCoy, Jane Hutton *singer*
Kaupa, Mike *musician, educator*
Terefenko, Dariusz *music educator*

Rocky Point
Knapp, Craig Brian *musician, educator*

Rome
Walther, Peter C. *church musician*

Roslyn
Rosegarten, Rory *personal manager, television producer, theater producer, film producer*

Saint Regis Falls
O'Bryan, Margaret Sundberg *music educator*

Saratoga Springs
Porter, David Hugh *musician, classicist, academic administrator, music educator*

Scarsdale
Carrick, Richard David *composer, performing company executive, music educator*

Schenectady
Hermance, Myron E., Jr. *conductor, educator*
Szokody, Aniko *pianist, educator*

Sea Cliff
Popova, Nina *dancer, choreographer, director*

Sparkill
Dahl, Arlene *actress, writer, designer, cosmetics executive*

Sparrow Bush
Murray, William Bruce *opera singer*

Staten Island
Fusco, Jo Ellen *music educator*
Shively, Sarah Elizabeth *actress*
Trogan, Roland Bernard *composer, educator*

Sunnyside
Gil Orrios, Angel *theater director, lighting designer, translator*

Syracuse
Caravan, Ronald L. *music educator, composer*
Elms, Ben *actor, theater director*
Orentlicher, John *video research educator, artist*
Wolff, Catherine Elizabeth *opera company executive*

Uniondale
Sanchez, Laura Ann *music educator*

Valhalla
Fachnie, H(ugh) Douglas *film manufacturing company official*

Valley Stream
Eisenberg, Michael James *music educator*

Walden
Murphy, Pamela Ann *music educator, actress, musician*

Wallkill
Strauser, Susan Parkyn *performing arts educator, singer*

Wantagh
Berk, Adele L. *composer, music educator*

Washingtonville
Fontana, Adam Vincent *music educator, musician*
Marcialis, Angelo Vincent *musician, educator*

West Hurley
Martucci, Vincent James *composer, pianist*

West Point
Williams, Craig Stewart *organist, music educator, director*

White Plains
Chase, Jenny Wei-Lang Kao *singer, music educator*
Sedelmaier, J. J. *filmmaker*
Wedge, Chris *animation director, studio executive*

Williamsville
Whitcomb, James Stuart *videographer, photographer, production company executive*

Willow
Bley, Carla Borg *composer*

Windham
Manno, Robert *composer, conductor*

Yonkers
Baumel, Herbert *violinist, conductor*
Senator, Ronald Paul *composer, writer, retired music educator*

NORTH CAROLINA

Black Mountain
Belue, Janie A. *music educator*

Boone
Mills, Susan Wilson *music educator*

Chapel Hill
Huff, Daniel M. *music educator*
Neff, Severine *music educator*
Powell, Carolyn Wilkerson *retired music educator*

Charlotte
Aycock, Joseph William *music educator, auto racing official*
Bennett, R. Monty *church organist*
Bonnefoux, Jean-Pierre *choreographer, dancer*
Herring, Rebecca Royce *music educator, consultant*
Metz, Catherine Taylor *performing arts educator*
Thompson, Jocelyn Pharr *organist, director, music educator*

Concord
Howard, Vivian Amick *music educator*

Cullowhee
Armfield, Terri Elaine *music educator, musician*
Beam, Richard Squires *theater educator*

Davidson
Sprague, Raymond *music educator*

Durham
Daw, Amy W. *music educator*
Krakowski, Jane *actress*
Nakarai, Charles Frederick Toyozo *music educator*
Ward, Robert *composer, educator, conductor*

Elon
Buckmaster, Matthew Tobe *musician, educator*

Fayetteville
Barnicle, Mary Anne *music educator, piano accompanist*
Carney, Karen Rose *music educator, pianist*
Jones, Villie *music educator*

Franklinton
Elmore, Cenieth Catherine *music educator*

Gastonia
Fayssoux, Patricia Ann Paysour *music educator*

Greensboro
Deere, James Dickson *singer, pianist, voice and music educator, writer*
Hammond, David Alan *stage director, educator*
Locke, John R. *music educator, director*
Middleton, Herman David, Sr. *retired theater educator*

Greenville
Knighten, Christopher Blair *conductor, educator*

Hendersonville
Tatsch, Jacki Lynn *music educator, diversified financial services company executive*

Indian Trail
Brewer, James Timothy *music educator, director*

Iron Station
Wise, Kimberly Anne (Schillaci) *musician, educator*

Leicester
Entzi, Karen Russell *orchestra educator*

Louisburg
Miller, Brian Daniel *music educator, organist*

Mars Hill
Greene, Tena Lorraine *singer, educator, actor*
Newton, Paul George *musician, retired librarian*

Monroe
Casstevens, Charles Franklin, Jr. *music educator, minister*

Mooresville
Faires, Ian Matthew *music educator*

Raleigh
Aiken, Clay (Clayton Holmes Aiken) *singer*
Batson, Jonathon Kingsley *composer, singer*
Evans, Margaret Griffin *music educator*
Garriss, Phyllis Weyer *music educator, performer*
Huff, Ann Linnea *music educator*
Poe, Terry Lynn *music educator*
Thompson Cornwall, Lonieta Aurora *music educator, consultant*
Youngman, Lola Jeanne *music educator*

Rich Square
Baugham, Samuel McCoy *actor, painter*

Salisbury
Higbee, Dale (Strohe) *musician, retired psychologist*

Todd
Cole, Susan Stockbridge *retired theater educator*

Weaverville
Flaxman, Fred *broadcast producer, host*

Wilmington
Cameron, Kay *conductor, composer*

Winston Salem
Grillo, Henry R. *theater educator, technical director*
Mueller, Margaret S. *musician, educator*
Sandresky, Margaret Vardell *retired composer*
Smith, Ronald G. *music educator*

NORTH DAKOTA

Bismarck
Knoll, Gloria Jean *music educator*
Lundberg, Susan Ona *musical organization administrator*
Tornow, L. William *musician*

Devils Lake
Rygg, Glenn *retired music educator*

Grand Forks
Towne, Gary Spaulding *music educator*

OHIO

Akron
Barlowe Bodman, Amy *violinist, composer*
Rouvas, Sakas *singer, gymnast*

Athens
Crist, Richard Le Roy *voice educator*

Bay Village
Berry, Edgar Allen *music educator*

Beloit
Barnett, Robert James *music educator, musician*

Berea
Zeitlin, Louise R. *music educator*

Canfield
Scurich, Kelly Lemos *music director*

Chagrin Falls
Shakley, Elaine M. *organist, department chairman*

Cincinnati
Gilbert, Jay *radio personality*
Hale, Nathan Kelly *music educator, artist*
Jarvi, Paavo *conductor, music director*
Morgan, Victoria *performing company executive, choreographer*
Scott, Jim *radio personality*
Sies, Timothy Ray *music educator*
Tocco, James *pianist*
Weinstein, Anna *music educator*
Winfrey, Marcellene Sedetta *music educator, church musician*

Cleveland
Cronquist, Robert Lee *conductor*
Cutler, Timothy Spence *music educator, composer*
Erb, Donald *composer*
Weir, Dame Gillian Constance *musician*
Welser-Möst, Franz *conductor, music director*

Columbia Station
Yearley, Barbara Ellen *music educator*

Columbus
Allen, Lois Arlene Height *musician*
Barlow-Ware, Jacqueline Sue *music educator*
Charles, Gerard *performing company executive, choreographer*
Cordell, Philip Granvile *music educator, musician*
Drvota, Mojmir *retired cinema educator, author*
Harris, Donald *composer*
Hildreth, James David *musician, educator*
Hirokami, Junichi *conductor, music director*
Rosenstock, Susan Lynn *orchestra administrator*
Wild, Earl *musician, composer*

Cuyahoga Falls
Curtis, Carolyn Ann *musician, educator*

Dayton
Hanna, Marsha L. *artistic director*

Delaware
Gardner, Bonnie Milne *theater educator, playwright*
Jamison, Roger W. *pianist, educator*

Doylestown
Morton, Sallie W. *music educator*

Elyria
Sanders, Phyllis May *musician*

Findlay
Hanson, David Alan *music educator*

Geneva
Carrel, Marianne Eileen *music educator*

Hamilton
Kerestan, Kitty Wilde *music educator*
Moore, Michael Robert *music educator, band director*

Holland
Conlin, Thomas *conductor*

Independence
Lanigan, John *radio personality*
Malone, Jimmy *radio personality*

Kettering
Meckstroth, Wilma Jean *piano and organ educator, accompanist*

Kirtland
Petrone, John R. *retired music educator, composer*

Lorain
Murrell, Jill Pongracz *music educator, director*

Marion
Barker, Tamara Elizabeth *music educator*

Milford
Arnest, Richard T. *composer, consultant*

North Olmsted
Janson, Patrick *vocalist, educator, actor*

Oberlin
Mumford, Jeffrey *composer, educator*

Parma
Musat, Katherine Gadus *retired music educator*

Peninsula
Shaw, Doris Beaumar *film and video producer, executive recruiter, management consultant*

South Euclid
Greenman, Steven Mark *musician*

Springfield
Todd, Carol *music educator*

Toledo
Chambers, Virginia Anne *music educator*
Girgis-Hanna, Mary Fahim *music educator*

Wapakoneta
Wirth, Tamara L. *music educator*

Whitehouse
Boyle, Daniel Robert *musician, delivery service executive*

Wickliffe
Barnes, Lili Darnelle *music educator, director*

Willoughby
Baker, Charles Stephen *music educator*
Linsenmeier, Carol Vincent *music educator*

Yorkville
Estrada, Erik (Henry Enrique Estrada) *actor*

Zanesville
McLaughlin, James Lee *musician, director*
Strahm, Mary Ellen *music educator*

OKLAHOMA

Ada
Baggech, Melody A. *music educator*

Alva
Vandewalker, Richard Edward *music educator*

Broken Arrow
Smith, Jeffrey Andrews *musician, educator, sound recording engineer*

Chickasha
Hanson, Dan Lewis *music educator, composer*

Edmond
Coyne, Wayne *musician*
Ivins, Michael Lee *musician*

Inola
Paul, Gary Wayne *music educator*

Lawton
Detweiler, Stanley Bruce *music educator*

Miami
George, Barbara M. *theater educator, department chairman, actor, director*

Mounds
Fellows, Esther Elizabeth *musician, educator*
Halsey, James Albert *entertainer, theater producer*

Norman
Ambrosini, Armand Anthony *music educator*
Dorrough, Vicki Lee *theater educator*
Tussing, Marilee Appleby *music educator*

Oklahoma City
Hilger, Robyn *music educator*
Kelly, Vicky Leloie *music educator*
Payne, Gareld Gene *vocal music educator, medical transcriptionist*
Price Boday, Mary Kathryn *choreographer, small business owner, educator*
Ragsdale, Frank Wayne *voice educator, singer*
Schimek, John Bradley *music educator, musician*

Sapulpa
Claussen, Alex *music educator*

Tulsa
Angelini, Marcello *performing company executive*
Collins, Laura Jane *music educator, singer*
Owens, Jana Jae *entertainer*
Sowell, Laven *retired music educator*
Womack, Lee Ann *country musician*

OREGON

Brookings
Shepherd, William Michael *music educator, musician*

Corvallis
Neumann, Nancy Ruth *film studio educator*

Eugene
Bailey, Exine Margaret Anderson *soprano, educator*
Bergquist, Peter *retired music educator*

La Grande
Espinosa, Leandro *composer, conductor, educator*

Milton Freewater
Agidius, Michael Gregory *music educator*

Mount Angel
Petrik, F. A. *music educator*

Portland
Berentsen, Kurtis George *music educator, conductor*
Friesen, David Douglas *musician, music educator, composer*
Huggett, Monica *performing company executive, musician*
Jackson, Roberta Q. *music educator*
Kalmar, Carlos *conductor, music director*
Kohne, Heidi Ann *church musician*
Koon, Theresa Helen *voice educator, singer*
Love, Edith Holmes *theater producer*
Ryberg, William A. *orchestra executive*
Stowell, Christopher R. *performing company executive, choreographer, retired dancer*

Salem
Zeller, Kurt-Alexander *vocalist, actor, stage director, voice educator*

PENNSYLVANIA

Abington
Anderson, Valerie B. *actress, writer*

Akron
Leithmann, David Edward *music educator*

Aliquippa
Forringer, Letitia Marie *music educator*

Allentown
Beltzner, Gail Ann *music educator*

Armagh
Gongaware, Acey M. *music educator*

Beaver Falls
Copeland, Robert Marshall *music educator, department chairman*

Bethlehem
Allen, Beatrice *music educator, pianist*
Diggs, David B. *music educator*

Bradford
Ewert, Kevin *theater educator*

Bryn Mawr
Goutman, Lois Clair *retired drama educator*

Center Valley
Wehr, Matthew *music educator*

Chadds Ford
Swensson, Evelyn Dickenson *conductor, composer, librettist*

Cheyney
Bagley, Edythe Scott *theater educator*

Coraopolis
Stout, Alastair *music director, composer*

Delta
Withrow, James A. *music educator*

Derry
Baltzer, Cynthia Louise *music educator*

Dover
Moul, Brian E. *music educator*

Doylestown
Solly, Richard Peter *music educator*

Dresher
Levicoff, Valerie Ann *music educator*

Drexel Hill
Benglian, Barbara Mason *music educator*
Martino, Michael Charles *entertainer, musician, actor*

Edgemont
Davis, Scott Charles *music educator, political activist*

Ephrata
Reed, Galen K. *music educator*

Everett
Whetstone, Joni Lee *music educator*

Fogelsville
Yadush, John G *musician, real estate investor, educator*

Fort Washington
Pezick, Patricia *music educator*

Glenmoore
Fix, Irene M. *pianist*

Glenside
Willig, Barbara Adele *music educator*

Greencastle
Wertime, Timothy Ray *music educator*

Harrisburg
Clark-Jones, Thomas Rees *musician*

Hatboro
Carroll, Lucy Ellen *theater director, educator*

Henryville
Salmon, Thomas P. *musician*

Huntingdon Valley
Sadoff, Joan Handleman *film producer, social worker*

Indiana
Salser, Scott A. *music educator*

King Of Prussia
Hallman, Patricia L. *musician, educator*
Helmetag, Diana *music educator*
Liebermann, Lowell *composer, conductor, pianist*

Kingston
Weisberger, Barbara *artistic director, advisor, educator*

Lancaster
Heil, Paul Samuel *radio producer*

Langhorne
Isensee, Paul Ralph *music educator, minister*

Lansdowne
Geist, Lorraine Pinnelli *music educator, director*

Lehighton
Perkins, David L. *music educator*

Lewisburg
Muller, Riana Ricci *musician, educator*

Liberty
Nelson, Thomas John *music educator, musician*

Line Lexington
Kuehne, Tracy Elizabeth *music educator*

Malvern
Miller, Richard Stanley *music educator*

Mansfield
Schmid, Mark Daniel *music educator*

Mercersburg
Owen, Lindsay Alexander *music director*

Mount Pleasant
Collins, Frederick George *music educator, secondary school educator*

Newtown
Sheridan, John J. *musician, music educator*

Philadelphia
Blavat, Jerry (Gerald Joseph Blavat) *television personality, actor*
Colson, Rosemary *music educator*
Crumb, George Henry *composer, educator*
Daugherty, F(rancis) Mark *music educator, conductor, theater director*
Davis, Paige (Mindy Paige Davis) *television personality and host*
deBenedet, Rachel *actress*
Driver, Robert Baylor, Jr. *opera company director*
Garonzik, Sara Ellen *stage producer*
Gilbert, Charles *performing arts educator, writer*
Hoke-Scedrov, Bonnie Carol *music educator, soprano*
Ingolfsson-Fassbind, Ursula G. *music educator*
Jenkins, Marc Delano *music educator*
Kaiser, Roy *performing company executive*
Myers Brown, Joan *performing company executive*
Pasternak, Jill Margot *radio producer, host, musician, educator*
Prischmann Gryniewicz, Deborah Anne *voice educator, vocalist*
Quinn, Susan Nicodemus *theater educator, director*
Sawallisch, Wolfgang *conductor*
Smith, Lloyd *musician*
White, Nicholas John *musician, director, composer*

Pittsburgh
Bardyguine, Patricia Wilde *dancer, performing company executive*
Cardenes, Andres Jorge *musician, educator*
Desiree, Laura *dancer*
Harth, Sidney *musician, educator*
Hollingsworth, Samuel Hawkins, Jr. *bassist*
McKinney, Donald Joseph *music educator, musician*
Orr, Terrence S. *dancer, ballet master, artistic director*
Pardini, James Christopher *musician, conductor, composer*
Posvar, Mildred Miller *opera singer*
Rollett, Rebecca A. *musician, director*

Pottstown
Nash, William Lewis III *retired music educator*

Reading
Zug, Elizabeth E. *concert pianist, educator*

Rimersburg
Rush, Kevin Arland *music educator*

Royersford
Jennings, Kris *music educator*

Saegertown
Ralph, NancyJo *retired music educator*

Selinsgrove
Viker, Erik *theater educator*

Shippensburg
Cart, Jon Robert *music educator, musician*

Slippery Rock
Payne, Ursula Octavia *choreographer, educator*

Southampton
Lenox, Gina Marie *music educator*

Spring City
Britcher, Michael *music educator*

Swarthmore
Redden, Taylor Tilghman *musician*

Swiftwater
Brooks, Joyce Maria *music educator*

Tarentum
Koharchik, Thomas David *music educator*

Uniontown
Duvall, Hollie Jean *music educator*

Vandergrift
Aikins, Candace Sue *music educator, consultant*

West Chester
Burton, John Bryan *music educator*
McFarland, Ann Louise *music educator*

West Grove
Allman, William Berthold *musician, engineer, consultant*

Wilkes Barre
Baranoski, Joseph Thomas *music educator*

Willow Hill
Dorand, Freda J. *music educator*

York
Yeater, Kathleen Wecker *musician, educator*

RHODE ISLAND

Chepachet
Jubinska, Patricia Ann *ballet instructor, choreographer, artist, anthropologist, archaeologist*

Cranston
Burge, David Russell *concert pianist, composer, educator*
Livingston, Carolyn Harris *music educator*

Cumberland
Rossi, Joseph Anthony *film and television make-up artist, educator*

Hope
Stadtmueller, Claire Louise *soprano, performing arts educator*

Johnston
Torelli, Anthony-Alexander *musician, educator, conductor*

Lincoln
Marsden, Herci Ivana *classical ballet artistic director*

Newport
Englander, Roger *television producer, director*
Malkovich, Mark Paul III *musician, performing company executive*
Raum, Mary Beth *performing arts educator*
Roos, Casper *actor*

Pawtucket
Orson, Barbara Tuschner *actress*

Providence
Barnhill, James Orris *theater educator*
Dempsey, Raymond Leo, Jr. *radio and television producer, moderator, writer*
Faraone, Philip *organist, director, consumer products company executive*

Scituate
Neves, David *musician, educator*

Warwick
Kelley, James Edward *actor, writer*

SOUTH CAROLINA

Aiken
Snyder, Robert Ellis *retired music educator, minister*

Anderson
Diekhoff, Billy Herman *retired music educator*
Williford, Sandra Simmons *music educator*

Charleston
Cantwell, Don *artistic director*
Jones, Vivian Eilene *music educator*

Clinton
Roth, Dale Davis *music educator, religious organization administrator*

Columbia
Barnes, Gail VanAernum *music educator*
Boyce, Corrie Mosby *music educator*
Ezell, Elizabeth Anne *music educator*
Robbins, Emmalee Elizabeth *theater director, speech professional*
Rucker, Darius *musician*
Sepulveda, Sonja Marian Atkinson *choral director, accompanist*

Conway
Sinclair, Frances Teresa *music educator, musician*

Edisto Island
Van Metre, Margaret Cheryl *performing company executive, dancer, educator*

Florence
Foster, Jackie Green *voice educator*
Wurster, Abigail Michelle *theater educator, costume designer*

Gaffney
Hill, Harry Hoffman, Jr. *musician, educator*

Goose Creek
Vogt, Kathleen Cunningham *musician, educator*

Greenville
Forrest, Daniel Ernest *composer, music educator*
Ringenberg, Donna Lou *music educator, conductor*
Schoonmaker, Gail Graham *voice educator, director*

Greenwood
Hughes, Christopher Adam *conductor, educator*

Hilton Head Island
Balkin, Alfred *music educator, composer*
Brock, Karena Diane *dancer, educator*
Selvy, Barbara *dance instructor*

Lexington
Calloway, Gary R. *choral director, music director*

Mount Pleasant
Royall, Mary-Julia C. *church organist, historian*
Scott, Jeffrey Ryan *music educator*

Newberry
McGinnis, Barry Eugene *music educator, musician*

Rock Hill
MacInnis, John Christian *music educator*

Roebuck
Smith, Alan Wade *music educator*

Spartanburg
Colloms, Vergene Jenkins *music educator, composer, musician, music producer, arranger*
McCraw, William Gary *music educator, director, musician*

Sumter
Ford, Peter Hilary *music educator*

TENNESSEE

Alexandria
Thomas, Deona Lee *music educator*

Brentwood
Grant, Amy *singer, songwriter*
Lyon, Sharron *retired church organist*
Swenson, Kathleen Susan *music educator, art educator*
Taylor, Nicole Renée (Niki Taylor) *model, shop owner*
Tucker, Tanya Denise *singer*
Walker Bonner, Linda Carol *music educator*

Clarksville
King, Thomas Roy *voice educator, music educator, director*

Cleveland
Wittenburg, Michael Shane *concert pianist, music educator*

Cookeville
Chang, Wei Tsun *music educator*

Cordova
Pugh, Dorothy Gunther *performing company executive*

Fayetteville
Bone, Lawson Mitchell *songwriter, poet*

Franklin
Bull, Sandy (Alexander Benjamin Bull) *musician, composer*

Gallatin
Ritter, Renee D. *theater educator*

Greenbrier
Ault, Andrew Jared *music educator, disc jockey*

Hermitage
Thompson, Fred Dalton *actor, former senator*

Huntland
Burton, Janet Ruth Wisner *music educator*

Jackson
Dale, Karen McCall *music educator*

Johnson City
Jenrette, Thomas Shepard, Jr. *music educator, choral director*
Snyder-Sowers, Mary Anne Sarah *performing arts educator, performing company executive, choreographer*

Knoxville
Moore, Marvelene C. *music educator*

Lawrenceburg
Hayes, Sylvia Richmond *music educator*

Lebanon
Daniels, Charlie *musician, lyricist*

Loudon
Horst, Teresa Dale *music educator*

Martin
Wade, Reba *musician, educator*

Memphis
Ching, James Michael *performing company executive, composer, conductor*
Nemec, Christopher E. *music educator*
Ouzts, David Perry *church music director, organist*
Owen-Leinert, Susan Huff *voice educator, vocalist*
Philipp, Karla Ann *music educator, conductor, musician*
Presley, Lisa Marie *singer*
Williams, David Russell *retired music educator*

Murfreesboro
Gregory, Brenda Kay *music educator*

Nashville
Adams, Ryan (David Ryan Adams) *musician*
Atkins, Rodney *musician*
Autry, Philip Earl *music educator, musician*
Balzary, Michael Peter (Flea) *musician, recording artist, actor*
Bentley, Dierks *country singer, songwriter*
Brooks, Kix (Leon Eric Brooks) *musician*
Chesney, Kenny *country singer, songwriter*
Demarcus, Jay (Stanley Demarcus) *country musician, songwriter*
Dunn, Ronnie Gene *musician*
Estrin, Kari (Karen Ruth Estrin) *music producer, agent, consultant*
Evans, Sara *country singer, songwriter*
Frusciante, John Anthony *musician*
Giles, Joe W. *music educator*
Glenn, Christopher Mark *music educator*
Griffith, Nanci *singer, songwriter*
Harris, Emmylou *singer*
Hill, Faith *musician*
Jackson, Alan *musician, lyricist*
Jones, George *country music singer, songwriter*
Judd, Wynonna Ellen (Christina Claire Ciminella) *vocalist, musician*
Kiedis, Anthony *vocalist, recording artist, actor*
King, Ed *musician*
Krauss, Alison *country musician*
Lambert, Miranda *vocalist*
Levox, Gary (Gary Wayne Vernon Jr.) *country/rock singer*
Mandrell, Barbara Ann *singer, entertainer, actress, producer, writer*
Mayer, John *musician*
McBride, Martina *vocalist*
Montgomery, Dillard Brewster *musician, educator*
Paisley, Brad *musician*
Powell, Billy *musician*
Rooney, Joe Don *country musician*
Rossington, Gary *musician*
Sartor, David P. *composer*
Sheik, Duncan *singer, songwriter*
Smith, Chad Gaylord *musician, recording artist*
Twain, Shania (Eilleen Regina Edwards) *musician*
Urban, Keith *country singer, songwriter*
Williams, Anthony Ervin *music educator*
Williams, Hank, Jr., (Randall Hank Williams) *country music singer, songwriter*
Wonders, Pamela Kim *music educator*

Pigeon Forge
Parton, Dolly Rebecca *singer, composer, actress*

TEXAS

Abilene
Ashford, Kecia A. *voice educator, vocalist*
Pender, Martha Helen *retired dramatic soprano*

Alice
Taylor, Bryce B. *music educator, consultant*

Amarillo
McDonough, Raenell *musician, educator*

Arlington
Jordan, Robert Randy *music educator*
Thomas, Lois C. *musician, educator, religious organization administrator, composer*

Aubrey
Pizzamiglio, Albert Theodore (Al Pierson) *conductor*

Austin
Antokoletz, Elliott Maxim *music educator*
Aubery, Stephen Royston Edmund *film producer*
Brockett, Oscar Gross *theater educator*
Hancock, Gerre Edward *musician, educator*
Henley, Paul Thomas *music educator, researcher*
Holtzman, Joan King *musician, composer*
Ingram, Jack *musician*
Lary, Banning Kent *film producer, writer*
Mills, Stephen *performing company executive*
Mueller, Peggy Jean *dance educator, choreographer, rancher*
Williamson, Barry Scott *conductor, performing arts educator*
Young, Phyllis Casselman *music educator*

Baytown
Harrison, Paula Jean *church musician*

Beaumont
Peirce, Dwight A(lexander), Jr. *music educator*

Borger
Strecker, Judy Ellen *music educator*

Brownsville
Holkup, Linda Patricia *music educator*

Corpus Christi
Allison, Joan Kelly *music educator, pianist*
Wilken, Jimmy Louis *radio news director, radio station manager, professional photographer*

Dallas
Brandt, Carole *theater educator, department chairman*
Dederich-Pejovich, Susan Russell *harpist*
Donnell, Carolyn Faye *music educator*
Etgen, Ann *performing arts educator, choreographer*
Franklin, Kirk *singer*
Huff, Dann *musician, producer, singer*
Johnson, Mary Elizabeth *musician, educator*
Joyner, Tom *radio personality*
Litton, Andrew *conductor, music director*
McTee, Cindy *classical musician, educator*
Palmer, Christine (Clelia Rose Venditti) *vocalist, educator, musician*
Pell, Jonathan Laurence *performing company executive*
Pelletier, Sho-mei *musician, educator*
Sallee, Wanda Jean *music educator*
Thomas, Paul Lindsley *composer, musician, director*
Thomas, Sarah Elaine *music educator*
van Zweden, Jaap *conductor*
Wilson, Angela Lynn *theater producer, playwright*

Denton
Peters, Juanita Teal *music educator*
Wodnicki, Adam Juliusz *pianist, educator*

Edinburg
Munn, Vivian Carole *music educator, conductor*

El Lago
Chase, Jeanette Knapp *music educator*

El Paso
Gladstein, Mimi Reisel *theater and literature educator*

Falfurrias
Cantu, Imelda M. *theater educator*

Farmers Branch
Walsh, Elizabeth Jameson *musician*

Flower Mound
Marrs, Carol Faye *performing arts educator, writer*

Fort Worth
Cliburn, Van (Harvey Lavan Cliburn Jr.) *concert pianist*
Dunleavy, Willa Gill *music educator, director*
Faherty, David Miles *musical instrument repairman*
Harth-Bedoya, Miguel *conductor*
Lipkin, Seymour *musician, conductor, educator*
Scott, P. Mark *musician, educator*
Stevenson, Ben *performing company executive*
Yacante, Maria Lucy *music educator, researcher*

Galveston
Kaplan, Cheryl L. *theater educator*

Garland
LeDoux, Ellen G. *music educator*

Gonzales
Ince, Laurel T. *music educator*

Helotes
Yamin, Sonya *music educator, voice educator*

Houston
Adams, Yolanda Yvette *singer*
Beyoncé, (Beyoncé Giselle Knowles) *singer*
Brown, Glenda Ann Walters *ballet director*
Carnes, Tara Lea Barker *music educator*
Chamillionaire, (Hakeem Seriki) *rap artist, recording industry executive*
Cupp, Aneta Joan *music educator*
Englesmith, Tejas *actor, television producer, curator*
Fiese, Richard Kelly *music educator*
Filipp Beseda, Carolyn Francine *music educator, insurance agent*
Freud, Anthony Peter *opera company director*
Girouard, Peggy Jo Fulcher *ballet educator*
Gladden, Dean Robert *arts administrator, educator, consultant*
Graf, Hans *conductor, music director*
Hazelip, Linda Ann *musician, small business owner, executive assistant*
Jones, Florence M. *music educator*
Krajewski, Michael *conductor*
Lindemulder, Laurie *piano educator, concert pianist*
Morris, Stephen Jay *music educator*
Norris, Chuck (Carlos Ray) *actor*
Palmer, Willard Aldrich III *magician, writer, actor*
Rigdon, Kevin Leigh *theater educator, lighting designer, set designer*
Rose, Beatrice Schroeder *harpist, educator*
Rowland, Kelly (Kelendria Trene Rowland) *singer*
Simpson, Robert Louis *music educator*
Sugars, Janeal M. *opera singer, vocal educator*
Welch, Stanton *performing company executive*
Whiting, S. Carol *music educator*
Williams, Michelle (Tenitra Michelle Williams) *singer*

Huntsville
Daniel, Kathryn Hutchins *musician, educator*
Russell, George Haw *video production company executive*

Iowa Park
Wright, Sabra Dell *music educator*

Keene
Doroftei, Mugur Gideon *music educator, conductor, composer, musician*

Kingwood
Hagen, Barbara C. *music educator*
Hearn, Jackson *church musician, educator*

La Feria
Zamarripa, Victor Manuel *sound recording engineer, purchasing agent*

Laredo
Soto, Gilberto D. *music educator*

Leander
Fraley, Linda Williams Darnell *music educator*

Lubbock
Aker, Suzanne Deverse *physical movement educator*
Hartwell, William Gersham III *retired music educator*

Magnolia
Tarver, Betty Gail *music educator*

Marshall
Branscome, Eric Eugene *music educator, writer*
Fogle, Sheryl Kay *voice educator, music educator*

Mcallen
Huber, Melba Stewart *dance studio owner, educator, historian, writer, retailer*

Midland
Celia, George *composer, writer*

Mineral Wells
Warfield, Gerald Alexander *composer, writer*

Missouri City
Rathnau, Heather Hearn *music educator, writer*

Nacogdoches
Campo, David Wayne *conductor, educator, composer*

Navasota
Coffey, Sharon Marie *music educator*

Odessa
Reed, James Michael *church musician*

Pampa
Willingham, Jeanne Maggart *performing arts educator and company executive*

Pasadena
Austin, Pamela Kay *voice educator*
Gilley, Mickey Leroy *musician*

Pearland
Johnson, Hugh James *retired music educator*

Plainview
Belshaw, Gary D. *music educator, composer*

Plano
Galloway, Marianne Thérèse *performing company executive*

Quitaque
Herrington, Patsy Jean Stark *music educator*

Rockwall
Tucker, Kimberly Joan *music educator, director*

Rosenberg
Slack, Molly Johanna *theater educator*

San Antonio
Fruth, Roman Martin *piano technician, musician*
Oppenheim, Martha Kunkel *pianist, educator*
Robertson, Sterling Clifton *music educator, musician*
Silantien, John Joseph *music educator*
Wilkins, Christopher Putnam *conductor*

San Marcos
Schmidt, John Charles *music educator*

Sugar Land
Martinez, Antonio *choir director, art director*
Victor, Ann Michele *musician, educator*

The Colony
Mitchell, Melvin Clifford *music educator*

Tyler
Wright, Mary Ellen *theater educator*

Waco
Albrecht, Karen Elizabeth *voice educator, theater director*
McKinney, Timothy Richmond *music educator*

Wharton
George, Lila Gene Plowe Kennedy *music educator*

Wichita Falls
Scherler, Kathy Louise *music educator, researcher*

Wylie
Carson, Charles Michael *composer, musician*

UTAH

Kaysville
Houtz, Randy L. *music educator*

Lindon
Osmond, Donald Clark (Donny Osmond) *singer*

Montezuma Creek
Schaefer, Kim *high school music educator*

Park City
Becker, William Watters *theater producer*

Provo
Randle, Cammon C. *filmmaker*

Salt Lake City
Emerson, Norene Rogers *music educator*
Johnson, Xan Stuart *performing arts educator*
Patterson, M. Brett *musician*
Roens, Steven Thomas *music educator, associate dean*
Romney-Manookin, Elaine Clive *retired music educator, composer*
Sklute, Adam *performing company executive, dancer*
Walker Neve, Diana *singer, voice educator*
Wilberg, Mack J. *conductor, composer*

Woods Cross
Blackley, Cheryl Ann *musician, freelance/self-employed educator*
Hendriksen, Neil Evan *music educator*

VERMONT

Johnson
Whitehill, Angela Elizabeth *artistic director*

West Glover
Weaver, John Borland *musician, department chairman, composer*

Weston
Stettler, Stephen F. *performing company executive*

VIRGINIA

Alexandria
Pearson, Lynda Ann *music educator*
Piecuch, Diane Marie *music educator*

Arlington
Clapman, Leah Meredith *public television editor*
Fischer, Ivan *conductor*
Hamilton, Anthony *singer*
Kleinman, Katie (Katherine Miller Kleinman) *public television editor*
Mc Donald, Gail Faber *musician, educator*
Whitfield, Margaret Denny *retired music educator*

Ashburn
Haymon, Chadron Zonelle *music educator, minister*

Charlottesville
Chapel, Robert Clyde *theater director, educator*
Ross, Walter Beghtol *music educator, composer*

Dublin
Billaud, Louise Ann *musician, educator*

Fairfax
Hackleman, Kelly Ker *music educator*
Mann, Laura Ann *soprano*
Miller, Patricia A. *music educator, opera and concert artist*
Siddons, Joy Garbee *music educator*

Falls Church
Graif, Joseph Nicholas *musician*
Schoonover, Stanley R. *music educator, consultant*

Gainesville
French, Dorothy Marie *music educator*

Hampton
Harris, Carl G. *music educator*

Harrisonburg
Choi, In Dal *music educator*

Leesburg
Levin, Mark Reed *radio personality, legal foundation administrator*
Mahood, Ken *music educator*

Lorton
Celentano, Suzanne *movement educator*

Lynchburg
Howell, Peggy Haas *musician*
Marra, Anthony Tullio *audio visual specialist*

Manassas
Livingston, Jo Ellen Brooks *music educator*
Schlechte, Deborah Whitley *music educator*

Mathews
Akaike, Hiroko *music educator, conductor*

Mc Lean
Hudson, William L. *conductor*
Morlan, Merwyn Eugene *retired music educator*
Wilhour, Brian Edward *composer, music director*

Middleburg
Yovanovich, Robyn Dobson *theater educator, department chairman*

Newport News
Waller, George Darryl *music educator*

Norfolk
Mark, Peter *performing company executive, conductor*
Musgrave, Thea *composer, conductor*
Nixon, Patricia Saunders *music educator, actress*

Petersburg
Dance, Gloria Fenderson *dance studio executive, ballet administrator*

Radford
James, Clarity (Carolyne Faye James) *mezzo soprano*

Richmond
Anderson, Bette (Bonnie) Ferguson *music educator*
Carlton, Buzz (Clyde Gordon Carlton Jr.) *singer, songwriter, entertainer, recording artist*
Freeman, Edward Carl, Jr. *music minister*
Kennedy, Patricia Berry *retired music educator*
Melcher, Elizabeth *musician*
Winslett, Stoner *artistic director*

Sandston
Manson, Zynora Davis *music educator, minister*

Springfield
D'Elosua, Jennifer Dawn *music educator*

Staunton
Balsley, Philip Elwood *entertainer*

Sterling
Jefferson, Sandra Traylor *choreographer*
Lacey, Aaron Michael *actor, director, film producer, scriptwriter*

Suffolk
Bollinger, Michael *artistic director*

Virginia Beach
Adams, David Franklyn *music educator*
Dixon, John Spencer *performing arts association administrator*
Lutsyshyn, Oksana *concert pianist, organist*
Prescott, David L. C., Jr. *music educator*
Tuskey, Laura Jeanne *music educator, pharmacologist*
Watkins, Brenda L. *music educator*

Williamsburg
Gavaler, Joan Susan *dance educator*

Winchester
Aiosa, Charlotte Nelson *music educator*

Woodbridge
Brittain, Lara Michelle *music educator*

Woodstock
Mrosko, Matthew L. *music educator*

Yorktown
Kirsch, Darren Matthew *music educator*

WASHINGTON

Bellevue
Dean, Scott P. *music educator, director*

Bellingham
Whyte, Nancy Marie *performing arts educator*

Clarkston
Torgerson, Linda Belle *music educator*

Coupeville
Lotzenhiser, George William *musician, educator, academic administrator, composer*

Ellensburg
Panerio, Robert Major, Sr. *music educator, composer*

Kenmore
Sokol, Jennifer Marie *musician, writer*

Lacey
Louis, Glen *music educator*

Longview
Uthmann, Richard W. *retired music educator*

North Bend
Brumbaugh, Harley Aaron *retired music educator, conductor, composer, poet*

Olympia
Macduff, Ilone Margaret *music educator*

Richland
Powell, David Charles *music educator, meteorologist*

Seattle
Boal, Peter Cadbury *performing company executive*
Brock, Isaac *musician*
Collier, Tom Ward *musician, educator*
Denke, Conrad William *motion picture producer*
Elyn, Mark *retired vocalist*
Forbes, David Craig *musician*
Houston, Janeanne Currier *vocalist, educator*
Jenkins, Speight *opera company director, writer*
Madis, Eric Stephen *musician*
Reid, Frances A. *music educator*
Russell, Francia *retired ballet director, educator*
Sher, Bartlett *theater director*
Skinner, Joan *dancer, choreographer, educator*
Staryk, Steven Sam *violinist, concertmaster, educator*
Stowell, Kent *retired ballet director*
Sullivan, Daniel J. *artistic director*

Shoreline
Dolacky, Susan K. *music educator*
Matesky, Nancy Lee *music educator*

Trout Lake
Anderson, Douglas Del *retired music educator, recording industry executive*

Walla Walla
Lords, Traci Elizabeth (Nora Louise Kuzma) *actress, singer*
Simon, Nancy Lynn *performing arts educator, director*

Washougal
Harness, William Edward *tenor*

Woodinville
Sanders, Richard Kinard *actor*

WEST VIRGINIA

Charleston
Pasinetti, Nina Denton *dance educator, choreographer*

Fairmont
Huffman, Valarie *music educator*

Huntington
Johnson, Pamela *music educator, director*

Morgantown
Wiedebusch, Mary Kathryne *dance educator*
Wilson, Mary Alice *musician, educator*

Salem
Raad, Virginia *pianist, educator*

WISCONSIN

Baraboo
Lang, Gregory P. *music educator*

Brookfield
Lavender, Cheryl Ann *music educator, composer, writer*

Bryant
Sutherland, Marion Ida *music educator*

Cassville
Tubbs, Christopher Charles *music educator*

Clintonville
Reinke, Sussanah Hope *music educator, coach*

Colgate
Earl, Marcia Hunt *music educator, director*

Delavan
Julius, Scott David *music educator*

Dodgeville
Dentinger, Ronald Lee *comedian, speaker, freelance writer*

Eau Claire
Knight, Robert Michael *music educator, department chairman*

Fond Du Lac
Shipe, Dale Allen *music educator*

Grafton
Jakubowski, Jennifer Sara *music educator*

Greendale
Patterson, Amanda Margaret *music educator*

Greenfield
McKillip, Patricia Claire *operatic soloist*

Hayward
Tabbert, James Lee *music educator*

Hazel Green
Amweg, Eric Paul *music educator*

Hilbert
Postell, Shawn T. *music educator, school disciplinarian*

Hortonville
Juhl, Stacy Marie *music educator, director*

Hudson
Meincke, Carl Russell *music educator, director*

Kenosha
Cook, Leslie Pam *music educator*
Kollatz, Rebecca Lynn *music educator*

Kohler
Kukla, Wendy Jo *music educator*

La Crosse
Gorman, Kathleen Jean *performing arts educator, choreographer*
Luckner, Brian William *choir director, organist, composer*

Madison
Bartley, Linda L. *musician, music educator*
DeBruin, Donald J. *church musician*
DeMain, John *opera company director*
Faulkner, Julia Ellen *opera singer*
Rosser, Annetta Hamilton *composer*

Manitowoc
Meyer, Kelly Lee *music educator*

Mayville
Kruger, Todd M. *music educator*

Menasha
Walter, Thomas Bernard *music educator, conductor*

Menomonee Falls
Chicorel, Ralph *librettist, composer, playwright*

Merrill
Schram, Jeffrey Scott *music educator*

Milwaukee
Cheatham, Wallace McClain *music educator*
Crocker, Ray Dean *musician, musical director*
Delfs, Andreas *conductor, musical director*
Horsman, Lenore Lynde (Eleanora) *soprano, actress, voice educator*
Mortimer, Norma Sue *music educator*
Pink, Michael *performing company executive*
Samson, Richard Max *theater director, investment company executive*
Treuden, Terry S. *music educator, director*
Uecker, Bob *actor, radio announcer, former baseball player, television personality*

Monona
Jensen, Jill Susan *music educator*

Montello
Scheele, Adam *music educator*

Mosinee
Dul, Carla Marie *music educator*

Neenah
Orm, Sally S. *music educator, consultant*

New Berlin
Belich, Kay S. *music educator*

Oconomowoc
Bleke, Diane K. *music educator, director*

Pickerel
Cook, Barbara K. *music educator*

Platteville
Alcalay, Eugene Christian *pianist*

Pulaski
Kozlovsky, Timothy Francis *music educator*

Reedsburg
Bruer, Scott Vincent *music educator*

River Falls
Hedahl, Gorden Orlin *theater educator, dean*

Rudolph
Heywood, Gail Anne *musician, educator*

Sheboygan
Navis, Timothy James *music minister*

Shell Lake
Aderman, Oscar Darrell *retired music educator*

Shorewood
Bowers, Jane Meredith *retired music educator*

Solon Springs
Swanson, Jean Laurie *music educator*

Spring Green
Day, Sarah Jane *actor*

Stevens Point
Sheftz, Stephen Walter Robert *music educator, director, conductor*

Superior
McKnight, Patricia Gayle *musician, artist, writer, educator*

Sussex
Waite, Jon Philip *music educator*

Verona
Bell Swanson, Katie J. *music educator*

Washington Island
Schweikert, Norman Carl *retired musician*

Waukesha
Day, Natalie Marie *music educator, director*
Meyer, Debora Lynn *music educator*
Stringham, Phyllis Joan *retired music educator*

Waupaca
Hansen, Louise Hill *music educator, retired application developer*

West Bend
Ackley, Daniel *music educator, conductor, composer*
Dittmer, H. Robert *music educator, director*
Van Treeck, Jennifer Lynn *music educator*

Whitewater
Jennings, Robert Lee *retired music educator*

WYOMING

Dubois
Glasser, Pamela Jean *musician, educator*

Lander
Stevens, Sufjan *musician*

TERRITORIES OF THE UNITED STATES

PUERTO RICO

Bayamon
Ortiz, William *composer, music educator*

San Juan
Daddy Yankee, (Raymond Ayala) *musician*
Martin, Ricky (Enrique Martin Morales IV) *vocalist, actor, producer, composer*

Santurce
Residante, El (René Pérez) *singer, composer*
Visitante, El (Eduardo Cabra) *singer, musician*

VIRGIN ISLANDS

Charlotte Amalie
Francis, Georgia *music educator*

Kingshill
Bryson, Valrica *high school music educator*

CANADA

ALBERTA

Calgary
Grand-Maitre, Jean *performing company executive*
Monk, Allan James *baritone*
Raeburn, Andrew Harvey *performing arts consultant, recording industry executive*

BRITISH COLUMBIA

Vancouver
Jones, Norah (Geethali Norah Jones Shankar) *singer*
Krall, Diana *musician, singer*
Lavigne, Avril *singer*
McLachlan, Sarah *musician, composer*
Murray, Anne *singer*

MANITOBA

Winnipeg
Lewis, André Leon *performing company executive*
Turner, Robert Comrie *composer*

ONTARIO

Callander
Haig, Susan *conductor*

Kitchener
Coles, Graham *conductor, composer*
Eldred, Gerald Marcus *performing company executive*

London
William, David *theater director, actor*

Ottawa
Gillingham, Bryan Reginald *music educator*
Prevost, Roxane Lise *music theory educator*

Toronto
Beckwith, John *musician, composer, educator*
Colgrass, Michael Charles *composer*
Egoyan, Atom *film director*
Furtado, Nelly Kim *vocalist*
Goh, Chan Hon *ballerina*
Kain, Karen Alexandria *ballet dancer*
Kudelka, James *choreographer, artistic director*
Oundjian, Peter *conductor, music director*
Rasky, Harry *producer, director, writer*
Schramek, Tomas *ballet dancer, educator*
Staines, Mavis Avril *performing company executive*

QUEBEC

Montreal
Girard, Francois *film director*
Labadie, Bernard *performing company executive*
Lacombe, Jacques *conductor*
Lock, Edouard *performing company executive*
Pankov, Gradimir Krunislav *performing company executive*

Toronto
Polley, Sarah *actress*

AUSTRALIA

Darlinghurst
Davis, Judy *actress*

North Sydney
Crowe, Russell *actor*

Perth
Dow, Simon *artistic director, choreographer*

Redfern
Campion, Jane *film director, screenwriter*

Sydney
Miller, George *film director*

BELGIUM

Brussels
Freizer, Louis A. *radio producer*

La Louviere
Dragone, Franco *performing company executive*

COSTA RICA

San José
Hoffman, Irwin *orchestra conductor*

CZECH REPUBLIC

Prague
Cusumano, James Anthony *filmmaker, vocalist, retired pharmaceutical, hotel, and recording industry executive*

ENGLAND

Askett Bucks
Irons, Jeremy John *actor*

Cambridge
Hogwood, Christopher Jarvis Haley *music educator*

Charlbury
Belkin, Boris David *violinist*

Cheltenham Gloucestershire
Winwood, Stephen Lawrence *musician, composer*

East Sussex
Katin, Peter Roy *pianist*

Essex
Collins, Joan Henrietta *actress*

Isle of Wight
Stigwood, Robert Colin *film producer, television producer, radio producer, theater producer*

Leavesden
Watson, Emma *actress*

Leeds
Ichino, Yoko *ballerina*
Nixon, David *dancer*

London
Alexeev, Dmitri Konstantinovich *pianist*
Andsnes, Leif Ove *concert pianist*
Arman Gelenbe, Deniz *concert pianist*
Ashkenazy, Vladimir Davidovich *concert pianist, conductor*
Beckinsale, Kate *actress*
Bell, Joshua *musician*
Bertolucci, Bernardo *film director*
Bloom, Orlando *actor*
Blunt, Emily Olivia L. *actress*
Blunt, James Hillier *singer*
Bono, (Paul David Hewson) *singer, songwriter*
Bourne, Matthew *performing company executive, artistic director*
Butler, Geezer (Terence Michael Joseph Butler) *musician*
Chang, Sarah *violinist*
Clay, Clifton Ford *motion picture producer, writer*
Codron, Michael Victor *theater producer*
Cowell, Simon *television personality, music producer*
Daughtry, Christopher Adam *singer*
Day-Lewis, Daniel Michael Blake *actor*
Dohnányi, Christoph von *musician, conductor*
Duncan, Lindsay *actress*
Enya, (Eithne Ni Bhraonain, Enya Brennan) *musician*
Fiennes, Joseph *actor*
Flor, Claus Peter *conductor*
Gambon, Michael John *actor*
Gervais, Ricky *actor, scriptwriter*
Haitink, Bernard J. H. *conductor*
Harney, Kathryn Ann *opera singer*
Hicks, Taylor Reuben *singer*
Hoskins, Bob (Robert William Hoskins) *actor*
Hurt, John Vincent *actor*
Iommi, Tony (Frank Anthony Iommi) *musician*
John, Sir Elton Hercules (Reginald Kenneth Dwight) *musician*
Kapranos, Alexander (Franz Ferdinand) *singer, musician*
Kingsley, Sir Ben *actor*
Knightley, Keira *actress*
Leigh, Mike *film director*
Lloyd Webber, Lord Andrew (Baron of Sydmonton) *composer*
Mackerras, Sir Charles (Alan Maclaurin) *conductor*
Masur, Kurt *conductor, music director*
McCowen, Alec *actor*
McGregor, Ewan Gordon *actor*
McKellen, Sir Ian *actor*
McPhee, Katharine Hope *singer*
Mendes, Sam (Samuel Alexander Mendes) *film director, theater director*
Miller, Jonathan Wolfe *theater and film director, physician*
Minton, Yvonne Fay *mezzo-soprano*
Mirren, Helen (Ilynea Lydia Mironoff) *actress*
Moody, Ron *actor, writer*
Moss, Kate *model*
Nagano, Kent George *conductor, music director*
Newell, Mike *film director*
Nighy, Bill Francis *actor*
Pryce, Jonathan *actor*
Rice, Sir Timothy Miles Bindon *lyricist*
Richardson, Miranda *actress*
Rickman, Alan *actor*
Shakira, (Shakira Isabel Mebarak Ripoll) *musician*
Shankar, Ravi *composer, musician*
Sher, Sir Antony *actor, author*
Smith, Dame Maggie (Margaret Natalie Smith Cross) *actress*
Spacey, Kevin *actor*
Spillane, Mary Catherine *television producer*
Staunton, Imelda (Imelda Mary Philomena Bernadette Staunton) *actress*
Uchida, Mitsuko *pianist*
Ward, Bill *musician*
Winner, Michael Robert *film director, film producer, writer*

Manchester
Wilson, Keith Dudley *media and music educator, consultant, dean*

North Wales
Hands, Terence David (Terry) *theater and opera director*

Saint Margaret's
Attenborough, Baron Richard Samuel *actor, film director, producer, ambassador*

Surrey
Holm, Sir Ian *actor*

FRANCE

Collonges
Morgenstern, Sheldon Jon *symphony orchestra conductor*

Lyon
Robertson, David *conductor, music director*

Paris
de Havilland, Olivia Mary *actress*
Deneuve, Catherine (Catherine Dorleac) *actress*
Jolas, Betsy *composer, educator*
Mortier, Gerard *opera director*
Raimondi, Ruggero *opera singer*

GERMANY

Berlin
Barenboim, Daniel *conductor, pianist, music director*

Dresden
Schreier, Peter *tenor*

Hamburg
Neumeier, John *choreographer, ballet company director*

Munich
Araiza, Francisco (José Francisco Araiza Andrade) *opera singer*

Stuttgart
Anderson, Reid Bryce *performing company executive*

HONG KONG

Kowloon
Wu, Daniel *actor*

IRELAND

Dublin
Sheridan, Jim *film director, screenwriter*

Galway
Hynes, Garry *theater director*

ITALY

Cremia
Malipiero, Victoria Schneider *opera singer*

JAPAN

Tokyo
Ozawa, Seiji *conductor, music director*

LATVIA

Riga
Strautins, Vilnis *music educator, retired performing company executive*

NEW ZEALAND

Wellington
Jackson, Peter *film director*
Paquin, Anna *actress*

REPUBLIC OF KOREA

Seoul
Han, Oksoo *musician, educator*
Jeong, Ji-Hoon (Rain) *singer*

RUSSIA

Moscow
Kogan, Pavel *conductor*

SPAIN

Madrid
Frühbeck de Burgos, Rafael *conductor*

SWITZERLAND

Meggen
Galway, Sir James *flutist*

ADDRESS UNPUBLISHED

Aberlin, Betty Kay *actor, poet*
Abernathy, Jennifer P. *music educator*
Abraham, F. Murray (Fahrid Murray Abraham) *actor, educator*
Adler, Samuel Hans *retired conductor, composer*
Aghdashloo, Shohreh *actress*
Aguilera, Christina *singer*
Akinnuoye-Agbaje, Adewale *actor*
Akiyoshi, Toshiko *jazz composer, pianist*
Akos, Francis *retired violinist, conductor*
Alba, Jessica *actress*
Alba, Lois *singer, educator*
Alexander, Jason (Jay Scott Greenspan) *actor*
Allen, Marilyn Myers Pool *theater director, video specialist*
Allen, Woody (Allen Stewart Konigsberg) *director, actor, writer*
Alley, Kirstie *actress*
Allston, Charita Capers *music educator*
Almodovar, Pedro *filmmaker*
Amara, Lucine *vocalist*
Amstutz, Curtis J. *music educator*
Anderson, Gillian *actress*
Andreu, Helene C. *dancer, educator*
Andrew, Dudley *film and comparative literature professor*
Andrews, Dame Julie (Julia Elizabeth Wells) *actress, singer*
Andrews, Naveen William Sidney *actor*
Apel, Robert William *actor*
Applegate, Christina *actress*
Apted, Michael David *film director*
Arenal, Julie (Mrs. Barry Primus) *choreographer*
Ariola, Dante *television commercial and video director*
Arkin, Alan Wolf *actor*
Armstrong, Billie Joe *singer, musician*
Arthur, Beatrice *actress*
Asman, Bub (Henry B. Asman) *sound editor*
Astin, Sean Patrick *actor, film director, film producer, writer*
Atchison, Doug *film director, writer*
Atherton, William *actor*
Austin, Johnta *musician*
Autry, Lola Mae *music educator*
Bach, Jan Morris *composer, educator*
Bach, Mary Irene *music educator*
Badham, John MacDonald *motion picture director*
Baerwald, Susan Grad *television broadcasting company executive, producer*
Bailey, Robert C. *opera company executive*
Baker, Leslie David *actor*
Baker, Nathan Adam *music theorist*
Bakula, Scott *actor*
Balaban, Bob *actor, film director*
Bale, Christian *actor*
Balser, Robert Edward *animation film producer, director*
Bana, Eric *actor*
Bank, Roy J. *television producer*
Barclay, Paris *television director, television producer*
Baron Cohen, Sacha (Ali G, Borat) *actor, comedian*
Barranger, Milly Slater *theater educator, writer*
Barsalona, Frank Samuel *retired theatrical agent*
Barton, Mischa *actress*
Basinger, Kim (Kimila Ann Basinger) *actress*
Bassett, Angela *actress*
Bassett, Leslie Raymond *composer, educator*
Bates, Kathy *actress*
Baumgartner, Brian *actor*
Bazar, Jill A. *music educator*
Beck, Jane *dance educator, choreographer*
Beegle, Amy *music educator, researcher*
Beeler, Charles Alan *retired music educator*
Behlmer, Rudy H., Jr. *retired director, writer, film educator, scriptwriter*
Belafonte, Harry (Harry George Belafonte Jr.) *singer, concert artist, actor*
Bell, Angela *music educator*
Belzberg, Edet *filmmaker*
Benatar, Pat (Pat Andrzejewski) *rock singer*
Bencini, Sara Haltiwanger *concert pianist*
Bennett, Tony (Anthony Dominick Benedetto) *entertainer*
Bennett Spector Greenfield, Veronica (Ronnie Spector) *singer*
Benton, Robert *film director, screenwriter*
Berg, Peter *actor*
Bergen, Candice *actress, writer, photojournalist*
Bergeron, Earleen Fournet *actress*
Berlind, Roger Stuart *stage and film producer*
Berlinger, Warren *actor*
Berman, Mona S. *actress, playwright, theater director, theater producer*
Berman, Richard Keith *television producer, film producer*
Berman, Shari Springer *film director, scriptwriter*
Best, Eve (Emily Best) *actress*
Bethke, Louise Virginia *music educator, writer*
Bevan, Tim *film producer*
Binoche, Juliette *actress*
Bissell, James Dougal III *motion picture production designer*
Biziou, Peter *cinematographer*
Blackstone, Dara *music educator, conductor*
Blige, Mary Jane *singer*
Blomquist, Alan Charles *film producer*
Bloomquist, Kenneth Gene *music educator, director*
Bloomquist, Paul Frederick *music educator, director, secondary school educator, musician*
Blossom, Beverly *choreographer, educator*
Boardman, Eunice *retired music educator*
Bock, Janine Schmelzer *music educator*
Boe, David Stephen *musician, educator, dean*
Bogosian, Eric *actor, writer*
Bohrman, David Ellis *television news producer*
Bonazzi, Elaine Claire *mezzo soprano*
Bond, Victoria Ellen *conductor, composer*
Bonifati, Louis M. *music educator*
Bon Jovi, Jon (John Francis Bongiovi Jr.) *musician, singer, songwriter, actor, professional sports team executive*
Bonnard, Raymond *theater director*
Bonney, Jo *theater director*
Borkowski, Francis Thomas *music educator*
Bosco, Philip Michael *actor*
Boulez, Pierre *composer, conductor*
Bouvier, Monica Renee *traffic director*
Bowman, David Frederick *music educator*
Boyd, Todd *cinematic arts educator*
Boyle, Lara Flynn *actress*
Brady, Mary Rolfes *music educator*
Braff, Zach *actor, director, scriptwriter*
Branagh, Kenneth *actor, film director*
Brandon, Liane *filmmaker, educator*
Brandt-Soetermans, Valerie Louise *dancer, educator*
Bratt, Benjamin *actor*
Braxton, Frederick *music educator*
Brazinski, Frank William *composer, educator*
Breakstone, Joshua Scott *musician, educator, composer*
Breault, Robert Lee *music educator*
Breon, April Michelle *music educator*
Breslin, Abigail Kathleen *actress*
Brewster, Jamie Susan *theater educator*
Briggle, Gary Lee *singer, actor, director, educator*
Brobston, Stanley Heard *music educator, writer*
Brody, Adrien *actor*
Brooks, Garth (Troyal Garth Brooks) *musician, singer*
Brooks, Lorraine Elizabeth *retired music educator*
Brooks-Turner, Myra *music educator*
Brosnan, Pierce *actor*
Brown, Ashley *actress*
Brown, Charles Samuel *singer, composer, educator*
Brown, Lora Alice *entertainment company executive, educator*
Brown-Barton, Grace Olive *music educator*
Browne, Jackson *singer, songwriter*
Brown Leatherberry, Thomas Henry *performing company executive, clergyman*
Broyles, William Dodson, Jr. *author, editor, scriptwriter*
Bruning, Earl H. *music educator*
Bullock, Sandra (Sandra Annette Bullock) *actress*
Bumbry-Bronson, Venetta *music educator*

Burchard, Ellen Williams *actress, film producer, artist, writer*
Burge, Constance M. *television producer*
Burke, Brooke *actress, model*
Burns, Edward J., Jr. *actor, film director*
Burrell, Orville Richard (Shaggy) *popular musician*
Burrows, James *television and motion picture director, producer*
Burton, Kate *actress*
Buscemi, Steve *actor*
Bush, Eileen Shanin *voice educator*
Bush, Ellen D. *music educator*
Butz, Norbert Leo *actor*
Buzzi, Ruth *comedienne*
Bynes, Amanda *actress*
Byrnes, Hope Huska *singer, volunteer*
Caicedo, Patricia *singer, musicologist, physician*
Calegari, Maria *ballerina*
Calissi, Jeffrey Luke *music educator*
Callahan Kern, Gene Marie C. *soprano, music educator*
Calman, Craig David *actor, writer*
Campbell, Alan *actor*
Campbell, Melissa Lynnsimmons *music educator*
Campbell, Neal Franklin *music educator*
Cannavale, Bobby (Roberto Cannavale) *actor*
Caparro, James *entertainment industry executive*
Carell, Steve *comedian, actor*
Carey, Drew *actor*
Carley, Kurt *actor*
Carlin, George Denis *comedian, actor*
Carlock, Sandra Lynn *musician, educator*
Carman, Judith Elaine *music educator, writer*
Carmichael, Judy Lea *record industry executive, concert jazz pianist*
Carradine, Keith Ian *actor, singer, composer*
Carter, Jeffrey Richard *music educator*
Carter, Scott *television producer*
Carvey, Dana *actor, stand up comedian*
Casei, Nedda *mezzo soprano*
Castellano, Mark Joseph *music educator*
Caswell, Dorothy Ann Cottrell *performing arts association administrator*
Cates, Matt *actor, writer*
Chalcraft, Elena Marie *actress, singer*
Chan, Jackie *actor, film director*
Chang, Helen Chung-Hung Hsiang *music educator*
Chapman, William *baritone*
Chappell, Wallace *performing company executive*
Charles, Walter *actor*
Chase, Will *actor*
Cheadle, Don *actor*
Chernavsky, George Y. *composer, producer, song writer*
Chessa, Luciano *composer, musicologist, educator*
Chiklis, Michael *actor*
Chow, Stephen (Sing-Chi Chow) *actor*
Chow, Yun-fat (Chow Yun-Fat) *actor*
Christopher, Russell Lewis *baritone*
Chu, Katherine K. *music educator*
Chulack, Christopher M. *television director, television producer*
Church, Thomas Haden *actor*
Ciofalo, Linda *vocalist, educator*
Clark, Candy *actress*
Clark, Nancy Lucinda Brown *retired music educator*
Clark, Richard Eugene *music educator*
Claver, Robert Earl *television producer, director*
Clement, Bill *hockey analyst*
Clinkscale, Martha Novak *music educator, researcher*
Coburn, Steven D. *composer, musicologist, educator, pianist*
Cochran, Kathy Holcombe *music educator, conductor*
Cochran, Robert Lee *music educator*
Cohen, Aryell *music educator*
Cohen, Larry *film director, producer, screenwriter*
Colbert, Stephen *comedian, actor*
Cole, Nikki Jo *music educator*
Coleman, Dabney W. *actor*
Coleman, George Edward *musician*
Collins, Caron Lee *music educator*
Collins, Izola E. *retired music educator*
Collins, Kathleen Anne *artistic director*
Collins, Stephen *actor*
Combs, Holly Marie *actress*
Common, (Lonnie Rashid Lynn, Common Sense) *rap artist*
Con, Adam Jonathan *choral conductor, music educator*
Consoli, Marc-Antonio *composer*
Cooper, Hal *television director*
Cooper, Judith Kase *retired theater educator, playwright*
Copperfield, David (David Kotkin) *illusionist, director, producer*
Coppola, Francis Ford *film director, producer, writer*
Coppola, Sofia Carmina *film director, film producer, scriptwriter*
Cosby, Bill *actor, television producer*
Costa, Mary *soprano*
Costa-Gavras, (Constantin Gavras) *film director, writer*
Costello, Elvis (Declan Patrick McManus) *musician, songwriter, singer*
Costner, Kevin *actor*
Cotrubas, Ileana *opera singer, retired lyric soprano*
Cotton-Cobb, Robin Leeanne *music educator*
Coukis, Peter George *musician, composer*
Cox, Beulah Elizabeth *violinist, music educator*
Craig, Daniel *actor*
Craven, Wes *film director*
Crewson, Wendy Jane *actress*
Cromwell, James *actor*
Crosby, Norman Lawrence *comedian*
Croskell, Madelon Byrd *music educator, classical vocalist*
Crow, Sheryl *singer, songwriter, musician*
Cruise, Tom (Thomas Cruise Mapother IV) *actor*
Cruz-Romo, Gilda *soprano*
Crystal, Billy *actor, comedian*
Cuarón, Alfonso *film director, film producer*
Culkin, Macaulay *actor*
Cullum, John *actor, singer*
Cummins, Wilma Jeanne *actress, comedienne*
Cunningham, Michael Gerald *composer, writer, music educator emeritus*
Currier, Nathan K. *composer, educator*
Curry, Daniel Francis Myles *filmmaker*
Curson, Theodore *musician*
Custer, Beth *composer, musician*
D'Abruzzo, Stephanie *actress*
Dafoe, Willem *actor*
Dahlgren, Carl Herman Per *performing company executive, educator*
Dakin, Christine Whitney *dancer, educator*
Daly, Carson Jones *television personality*
Damon, Matt (Matthew Paige Damon) *actor*
Dampf, Beth Ann *music educator*
Danaher, Mallory Millett (Mallory Jones) *actress, photographer, film and theater producer*
Danes, Claire *actress*
Daniele, Graciela *choreographer*
Daniels, Ronald George *theater director*
Daniels, Sydney Robert *theater director, educator*
Danner, Blythe *actress*
Dano, Paul Franklin *actor*
D'Arbanville, Patti *actress*
Dargel, Corey *composer, singer*
Darling, Robert Edward *theater director, designer*
Darvarova, Elmira *musician, concertmaster*
Davis, Osceola A. *opera singer*
Dawson, Rosario *actress, singer*
Dean, Kaseem *music producer*
De Angelis, Rosemary Eleanor *actress*
de Blasis, James Michael *performing company executive, theater producer*
De Felitta, Frank Paul *film producer, writer*
DeHoff, Valerie S. *music educator*
de la Rocha, Zack *singer, musician*
De Laurentiis, Dino *motion picture producer*
de Lavallade, Carmen *dancer, choreographer*
Dell, Charlene Elizabeth *music educator*
DeLonge, Thomas Matthew, Jr. *musician*
Delpy, Julie *actress*
del Toro, Guillermo *film director*
de Matteo, Drea *actress*
Demme, Jonathan *director, producer, writer*
Dench, Judi *actress*
Denman, David *actor*
Dennehy, Brian *actor*
De Palma-Iozzi, Frances M. *music educator, conductor*
DePaul, Michael *music educator*
Dern, Laura *actress*
Deschanel, Mary Jo *actress*
Deutsch, Didier (Delaunoy) *music producer, writer*
Deutsch, Herbert Arnold *music educator*
Devlin, Michael Coles *bass-baritone*
Di, Francine *music educator, writer*
Diaz, Cameron *actress*
Di Benedetto, Stephen Anthony *performing arts educator*
DiCaprio, Leonardo *actor*
Dick, James Cordell *concert pianist*
Diefenderfer, Dan *filmmaker*
Diemer, Emma Lou *composer, educator*
DiFiore, David Gerard *musician*
DiNovi, Denise *producer*
Dirnt, Mike (Michael Ryan Pritchard) *musician, singer*
Dishy, Bob *actor*
Dixon, Ben Harold *musician, educator*
Dixon, William Robert *musician, educator*
Dodson, Daryl Theodore *ballet administrator, consultant*
Dolenz, Mickey (George Michael Dolenz, Mickey Braddock) *entertainer, actor, television producer*
Donahue, Ann M. *television producer*
Donaldson, Myrtle Norma *musician, educator*
Doppmann, William *composer, pianist*
Dorsky, Nathaniel *filmmaker*
Douglas, Kirk (Issur Danielovitch) *actor, motion picture producer*
Douglas, P C *producer, director, reporter, editor*
Downey, Robert, Jr. *actor, singer, musician*
Downs, Jon Franklin *drama educator, director, writer*
Doyle, Gillian *actress*
Dreyfuss, Richard Stephan *actor*
D'Rivera, Paquito *clarinetist, saxophonist, conductor, composer*
Drozd, Leszek Stanislaw *film producer, composer, musician*
Drummond, Carol Cramer *voice educator, lyricist, writer, artist*
Dudley, Craig *actor*
Duke, George *jazz keyboardist, composer*
Dunaway, Faye (Dorothy Dunaway) *actress*
Dunst, Kirsten *actress*
Duval, Olivia Blackmon *music educator*
Duvall, Robert (Robert Selden Duvall) *actor*
Dzapo, Kyle Jean *musician, educator*
Eads, Paul Bryan *production designer*
Ebersole, Christine *actress*
Edwards, Anthony *actor*
Eger, Joseph *conductor*
Ehle, Jennifer *actress*
Eldard, Ron (Ronald J. Eldard) *actor*
Electra, Carmen (Tara Leigh Patrick) *actress*
Elgart, Larry Joseph *orchestra leader*
Elias, Lori Anne *music educator, journalist, photojournalist*
Elise, Kimberly (Kimberly Elise Trammel, Kimberly Elise Oldham) *actress*
Elisha, Larisa *musician, performer, educator*
Elizondo, Hector *actor*
Ellenberger, Lon Karl *singer, music educator*
Elliott, Kenneth Yates *theater educator*
Englund, Robert *actor, director, producer*
Epcar, Richard Michael *actor, writer, film director*
Epstein, Adam *theater producer*
Erb, James Bryan *conductor, musicologist, educator*
Escalante, Juan *performing company executive*
Esparza, Raul *actor*
Esposito, Jennifer *actress*
Evans, Faith *singer*
Everett, Rupert *actor*
Everett, Tom *actor*
Everhart, Gloria Elaine *music educator*
Fabio, Jim *television producer, film producer, television director, film director, film editor*
Fahey, Jeff *actor*
Fairfield, Paula Kathleen *sound recording engineer*
Farias, Brian K. *music educator*
Farrell, Mike *actor*
Farrell, Suzanne (Roberta Sue Ficker) *ballerina*
Fay, William Frederick *film producer*
Fenn, Daniel Jonathan *organist*
Fergie, (Stacy Ann Ferguson) *singer*
Fichtner, William *actor*
Field, Sally Margaret *actress*
Field, (William) Todd *actor, film director, scriptwriter*
Fields, Victor Lee *music educator*
Fiennes, Ralph (Ralph Nathaniel Twisleton-Wykeham Fiennes) *actor*
Fiero-Maza, Lorraine Doris *music educator*
Filerman, Michael Herman *television producer*
Finch, Janet Buswell *musician*
Finneran, Katie (Kathleen) *actress*
Finney, Albert *actor, theater director*
Fiorenza, Lisa A. *music educator*
Fischer, Jenna (Regina Marie Fischer) *actress*
Fischer, William Samuel *composer, lecturer*
Fisher, Carrie Frances *actress, writer*
Fisher, Isla Lang *actress*
Fisk, Jean Bauder *music educator, director*
Fleck, Bela *country musician*
Fleming, John Jacob *music educator, director*
Fleming, Rhonda *actress, singer*
Fobert, Pamela Hart *music educator*
Foldi, Andrew Harry *retired vocalist*
Fonda, Bridget *actress*
Fonda, Peter *actor, director, producer*
Ford, Harrison *actor*
Forster, Robert *actor, educator*
Foss, Lukas *composer, conductor, pianist*
Foster, Mary Christine *film producer, writer*
Fowler, Beth *actress*
Foxworthy, Jeff *comedian, writer, actor*
Franklin, Aretha Louise *singer*
Franklin, Bonnie Gail *actress*
Franklin, Carl *director*
Franz, Elizabeth *actress*
Frears, Stephen *film director*
Frederick, John *retired actor, writer*
Freeman, John Arthur *theater educator*
Freeman, Morgan *actor*
French, Arthur (Arthur Wellesley French Jr.) *actor, theater director*
Frey, Glenn *songwriter, vocalist, guitarist*
Fuerstner, Fiona Margaret Anne *ballet company executive, educator*
Fuller, David Randall *retired music educator*
Gaines, Boyd *actor*
Galante, Jane Hohfeld *musician, historian*
Gallops, R. Wayne *music educator*
Gamer, Carlton Edwin *composer, music educator*
Gan, Chenny Quan *musician, educator, artist*
Garber, Aaron Matthew *performing company executive, music director*
Garber, Victor *stage and film actor*
Garcia, Jorge *actor*
Garner, Jennifer Anne *actress*
Garniss, Joan Brewster *musician, educator*
Garrett, Brad *actor, comedian*
Gaudio, Bob *composer, musician*
Gavin, Maria *television producer, writer*
Gellar, Sarah Michelle *actress*
Gengler, Richelle Ruth *musician, educator*
George, Donald *opera and concert singer*
Gere, Richard *actor*
Germolus, Penny Lynn *music educator*
Getty, Balthazar *actor*
Getty, Estelle (Estelle Scher) *actress*
Giacchino, Michael *composer*
Gibbs, David Richard *musician, journalist, photographer, writer*
Gibbs, Leonard (Doc Gibbs) *musician*
Gibson, Mel *actor, film director and producer*
Gilbert, Harriette Gurley *retired music educator*
Gilliam, Terry Vance *film director, actor, writer, illustrator*
Gilliland, Richard *actor*
Givens, Robin *actress*
Glass, Ira *radio producer, radio personality*
Glazer, Robert Boyd *musician, educator*
Glover, Crispin Hellion *actor*
Glover, Melvin (Melle Mel, Grandmaster Melle Mel) *rap artist*
Glynn, Carlin (Carlin Masterson) *actress*
Godin, Seth Warren *video production executive, writer, entrepreneur, blog website writer*
Goen, Bob *television show host*
Goines, Leonard *music educator, consultant*
Goldberg, Whoopi (Caryn Elaine Johnson) *actress, comedienne*
Goldblum, Jeff *actor*
Goldstein, Tamara Beth *musician*
Gomez, Jaime Luis (Taboo) *rap artist*
Gonsalves, Philip *music educator*
Gordon, Marjorie *lyric-coloratura soprano, music educator, opera producer*
Gornick, Loni Erin *music educator*
Grace, Topher *actor*
Grafton, Beth P. *music educator*
Grant, Alexander Marshall *retired ballet director*
Grant, Merrill Theodore *television producer*
Graves, Lorraine Elizabeth *dancer, educator, coach*
Gravitte, Debbie Shapiro (Lynn Shapiro) *singer, actress, dancer*
Greco, Christopher Jon *musician, composer, educator*
Green, Eva Gaelle *actress*
Greengrass, Paul *film director*
Greer, Jean Reese *music educator*
Greer, Suzanne Michelle *music educator*
Gregory, Claire Distelhorst *television producer*
Gregory, Peggy J. *music educator*
Gregory, Sara Susan (Sudie) *musician, singer, lyricist, poet, recording industry executive, sound recording engineer, archivist*
Grier, David Alan *actor*
Griffith, Melanie *actress*
Griffiths, Rachel *actress*
Grody, Donald *actor, judge, lawyer*
Grohl, David Eric *musician*
Grosbard, Ulu *film director*
Grossman, Edward Jerome *music educator, composer*
Gruen, Margaret *actress*
Guber, Peter *executive producer*
Guerra, Alma Del Rosario *music educator*
Gustafson, Craig Thomas *theater director, playwright, graphics designer*
Haley, Jackie Earle *actor, film director*
Haley, Johnetta Randolph *music educator*
Hall, Gregory *composer, engineer*
Hall, James Stanley *jazz guitarist, composer*
Hall, Monty *television producer, actor*
Hall, Tom T. *retired country singer, songwriter*
Hammer, (Stanley Kirk Burrell) *musician*
Hancock, Artemus Ward, Sr. *music educator*
Hardison, Kadeem *actor*
Hardwicke, Catherine Helen *film director, set designer*
Harler, Donna *voice educator*
Harlin, Renny (Renny Lauri Mauritz Harjola) *film director*
Harper, Richard Henry *film producer, director*
Harris, Harriet *actress*
Harris, Mark R. *film producer*
Harris, Robert A. *retired music educator*
Hartley, James R. *musician, writer*
Hasselhoff, David *actor*
Hatch, Richard *actor*
Hathaway, Anne *actress*
Hathcock, John Edward *vocalist*
Hathorne, Gayle Gene *musician, family historian*
Hawthorne, Roy John *retired music educator*
Hay, Austin (George A. Hay) *actor, artist, musician, writer*
Hayes, Daun L. *music educator*
Hayes, Patricia Thornton *music educator, retired director*
Hayes, Reggie *actor*
Hayes, Sean (Sean Patrick Hayes) *actor, comedian*
Heard, Ronald Roy *motion picture producer, lawyer*
Heath, John Robert *music educator*
Heche, Anne (Anne Celeste Heche) *actress*
Helgenberger, Marg *actress*
Henderson, Florence *actress, singer*
Hennessey, Patrick Daniel *musician, educator, musicologist*
Heresniak, Marty *music educator, actor*
Hermann, Kelly A. *music educator*
Herson, Arlene *television producer, journalist, television personality, radio commentator*
Herstand, Theodore *retired theatre artist, educator*
Hertel, Suzanne Marie *musician*
Hewitt, Don S. *television news producer*
Hilgraves, Rebekkah *singer, consultant*
Hill, (Karim) Dulé *actor, dancer*
Hills, Kendell Lenar *music educator*
Hilton, Paris *actress*
Hines, Cheryl *actress*
Hingle, Pat *actor*
Hirsch, Judd *actor*
Hodges, Ann *retired television editor, columnist*
Hodges, Ann *actress, singer, dancer*
Hoffman, Basil *actor, educator*
Hoffman, Marian Ruth *singer, voice educator*
Holland, Beth *actress*
Hooper, Robert Alexander *television producer, educator*
Hooper, Tom *film and television director*
Horne, Marjorie *production stage manager, event consultant*
Hornyak, Roy Robert *music educator, minister*
Hosman, Sharon Lee *retired music educator*
Hotopp, Alice Claudine *music educator, soprano*
Houghton, Katharine *actress*
Hounsou, Djimon Gaston *actor*
Howard, David *ballet master, school administrator*
Howard, Terrence Dashon *actor*
Hsu, Apo (Ching Hsin) *conductor*
Huang, Verna D. *music educator*
Hubbard, Elizabeth *actress*
Hubbs, Violet Elizabeth Shamblin *retired filmmaker, retired photographer*
Hudson, Kate *actress*
Huffman, Cady (Catherine Elizabeth) *actress*
Hunter, Frances Ellen Croft *music educator*
Hunter, Holly *actress*
Hurtado Lee, Clara Isabelle *voice educator, singer*
Husarik, Stephen *music educator*
Hutchison, Barbara Bailey *singer, songwriter*
Hwang, Jason Kao *composer, violinist, music educator*
Iman, (Iman Abudulmajid) *model*
Iñárritu, Alejandro González *film director, producer*
Irving, George Steven *actor*
Irwin, Bill *actor, clown*
Ivey, Judith *actress*
Jackman, Hugh *actor*
Jackson, Brian Matthew *musician, educator*
Jackson, Felicity Anne *performing arts organization administrator*
Jackson, Michael Joseph *musician*
Jackson, Nagle *stage director, playwright*
Jackson, Victoria Lynn *actress, comedienne*
James, Kevin *actor*

Janda, Christopher Crisco *actor*
Janis, Conrad *actor, musician, art dealer*
Janney, Allison *actress*
Janney, Kay Print *retired performing arts educator, theater director*
Jarmusch, Jim *film director, actor*
Järvi, Neeme *conductor, music director*
Jefferson, Marvin Kazembe *actor, theater educator*
Jenkin, James Thomas *video editor*
Jenkins, Richard Dale *actor, theater director*
Jennings, Byron *actor*
Jensen, Nancy Daggett *music educator*
Jessup, Nancy Jean *music educator*
Jodry, Louis Frederick, V, *music educator*
Joel, Katie (Katie Lee Joel, Katherine Lee) *television personality*
Johansson, Alicia Barbara *musician*
Johnson, Jeanne Jordan *music educator, department chairman*
Johnson, John Henry *film director, producer, photographer, educator*
Johnson, Marc Robert *music educator, director*
Johnson, Sandra Kay *music educator*
Johnston, Kristen *actress*
Jones, Constance Coralie *retired music educator*
Jones, Shirley *actress, singer*
Jones, William Adrian *musician, educator, program developer*
Joosten, Kathryn (Kathryn Joostyn) *actress*
Jordan, Lisa Anne *dancer, educator*
Kaczmarek, Jane *actress*
Kaling, Mindy *actress, scriptwriter, television producer*
Kamerin, Kim K. *music educator*
Kander, John Harold *composer*
Kaplan, Richard James *film producer and director, educator, consultant, scriptwriter*
Karayanis, Plato Steven *opera company executive*
Kasdan, Lawrence Edward *film director, screenwriter*
Katz, Jeff *television personality*
Kavanaugh, Frank James *film producer, educator*
Kaye, Debra *composer, music educator*
Kaylan, Howard Lawrence *musical entertainer, screenwriter, composer*
Keaton, Diane *actress*
Keaton, Michael *actor, comedian*
Keim, Betty Lou *actress, literary consulant*
Keith, Toby (Toby Keith Covel) *country singer, songwriter, producer*
Kennedy, David *musician*
Kennedy, Megan Catherine *music educator*
Keys, Alicia (Alicia Augello Cook) *vocalist, musician, songwriter*
Kilbane, Kathleen Ann *stage manager*
Kilgus, Edward Chip *singer, actor, writer, poet*
Kilmer, Val *actor*
Kim, Daniel Dae *actor*
King, Graham *film producer*
Kinnear, Greg *actor, film producer*
Kinsey, Angela *actress*
Kirchner, Lisa Beth *actress, vocalist*
Kirkland, Geoffrey Alan *motion picture production designer*
Kitt, Eartha Mae *actress, singer*
Klahr, Lewis *film director*
Klein, James Edgar *actor*
Klein, Stephen Thomas *performing arts executive*
Klotman, Robert Howard *retired music educator*
Klughart, Toni Anne *musician, educator, singer*
Knight, Shirley *actress*
Knowles, William Leroy (Bill Knowles) *television news producer, journalism educator*
Koepke, Allen Henry *music educator, composer*
Kokkeler, Fay Esther *music educator*
Kollias, Jim Harry *music educator*
Kopelson, Arnold *film producer*
Koplowitz, Stephan *choreographer*
Kornhaber, Donna Marie *theater educator*
Kostic, Dina *musician, music educator*
Krabbe, Thomas Joseph *music educator*
Krasinski, John *actor*
Krell, Rebecca Dawn *music educator*
Kriegsman, Sali Ann *performing arts executive, consultant, writer*
Kring, Tim (Richard Timothy Kring) *television producer, writer*
Kudrow, Lisa (Lisa Marie Diane Kudrow) *actress*
Kupelian, Louise Paulson *musician, educator*
Kuriansky, Judy *television and radio personality, reporter, clinical psychologist, writer, educator*
Kutrzeba, Joseph S. *theater producer, director*
Kuznetsova, Natalia P. *music educator*
LaBeouf, Shia *actor*
Lachey, Nick (Nicholas Scott Lachey) *singer, actor*
Ladd, Diane *actress, writer, film director, film producer*
Lambert, John Walton *music educator*
LaMorte, Joyce E. *music educator*
Landesberg, Steve *actor*
Lane, Ted A. *music educator, musician*
Lange, Jessica Phyllis *actress*
Lanpher, Katherine *radio personality, columnist*
LaPaglia, Anthony *actor*
Larson, Joan Isbell *musician, educator*
Latimer, James Harold *musician, conductor, composer, music educator*
Lawless, Lucy (Lucille Francis Ryan) *actress*
Leaf, Paul *film producer, writer*
Leahy, Jeannette (Jeannette Oliver Leahy Tinen Kaehler) *actress*
Leali, Bradford Charles *musician, educator*
LeBlanc, Matt (Matthew Steven LeBlanc) *actor*
Lebon, Rachel L. *musician, educator*
Lee, Bobby *actor, comedian*
Lee, Eunice *music educator*
Lee, Gavin *actor, choreographer*
Lee, William Franklin III *composer, musician*
Leek, Anne Carlin *music educator*
Lefferts, George *television producer*
Lemke, Carol Ann *music educator, pianist, accountant*
Lemos, Arthur *retired music educator*
Lennix, Harry Joseph III *actor*
Leno, Jay (James Douglas Muir Leno) *talk show host, comedian, writer*
Leoni, Tea (Elizabeth Tea Pantaleoni) *actress*
Lepage, Robert *actor, playwright*
Letterman, David *talk show host, producer, comedian, writer*
Levinsohn, Gary *producer*
Levy, Todd Robert *musician, educator*
Lewis, Christa Marie *music educator*
Lewis, James Kevin *music educator*
Li, Gong *actress*
Li, Jet (Li Lian Jie, Lei Lin-Git) *actor*
Lichtenstein, Harvey *performing arts association administrator*
Lieberson, Peter *composer*
Lifton, Paul Samuel *theater educator*
Lindegren, Cecile Keyser *music educator*
Lindo, Allen Pineda (Apl.de.ap) *rap artist*
Lindsey, Roberta Lewise *music researcher, historian, educator*
Lindsley, Joyce Lillian *music educator*
Ling, Bai *actor*
Lipton, Bob *music educator, composer*
Lithgow, John Arthur *actor, film director*
Little Richard, (Richard Wayne Penniman) *musician, lyricist, minister*
Livingstone, Trudy Dorothy Zweig *dancer, educator*
Locklear, Heather *actress*
Locricchio, Matthew *actor, writer*
Logue, Jean Evelyn *music educator*
Lombardi, Mary Luciana *musician, historian*
Lonchyna-Lisowsky, Maria *music educator*
Long, Shelley (Shelley Lee Long) *actress*
Lopez, Soledad *actress*
Loring, Gloria Jean *vocalist, actress, writer*
Love, Courtney *singer, actress*
Love, Shirley *mezzo-soprano*
Lowry, Julie Royal *music educator*
Lubezki, Emmanuel *cinematographer*
Lubin, Steven *concert pianist, musicologist*
Lucas, Josh (Josh Maurer) *actor*
Ludwig, Christa *retired mezzo soprano*
Lumsden, Rachel Lee *musician*
Lupu, Radu *pianist*
Lyford, Ronald Lee *music educator*
Macy, Bill (William Macy Garber) *actor*
Madeira, Francis King Carey *conductor, educator*
Madonna, (Madonna Louise Veronica Ciccone) *singer, actress, producer*
Madsen, Virginia *actress*
Magor, Louis Roland *conductor*
Maguire, Martie (Martha Elenor Erwin Maguire) *musician*
Mahoney, John *actor*
Maines, Natalie Louise *musician*
Malkovich, John *actor*
Maltas, Carla Jo *music educator, education educator*
Mannes, Elena Sabin *film and television producer, television director*
Manning, Michael Nicholas *actor, singer, guitarist, broadcaster, journalist*
Marchenko, Tamara G. *music educator*
Marcy, Kevin Michael *film producer, lawyer*
Margules, Cecelia *composer, poet*
Mark, Michael Laurence *retired music educator*
Marks, Bruce *performing company executive, choreographer*
Marley, Damian Robert Nesta (Jr. Gong) *reggae artist*
Maron, Marc *comedian, actor, writer*
Marsalis, Wynton *musician*
Marschall, Nicole *music educator*
Marse, Melissa J. *music educator, concert pianist*
Marsee, Susanne Irene *vocalist*
Marshall, Frank W. *film producer, director*
Marshall, Kenneth Robert *retired music educator*
Marte-Bautista, Helen I. *retired performing arts educator*
Martin, Andrea Louise *actress, comedienne, writer*
Martin, Elliot Edwards *theatrical producer*
Martin, Sally *singer, voice educator*
Martyn, Evi *music educator, musician*
Marx, Darrelyn Madonna *music and drama educator*
Marx, Jeff *composer, lyricist, lawyer, writer*
Maslanka, Daniel Chester *percussionist and music educator*
Mason, Marsha *actress, theater director, writer*
Masterson, Peter *actor, film producer*
Mastrian, Stacey Lynn *singer, educator*
Mathes, Rachel Clarke *voice educator, singer*
Mayer, Michael *theater director*
Maynard, Natalie Ryshna *pianist, educator*
Mays, Jefferson *actor*
McAnuff, Des *artistic director*
McCann, Elizabeth Ireland *theater, television and film producer*
McCarthy, Kathy *actress, writer*
McCartney, Sir Paul (James Paul McCartney) *musician*
McCauley, John *music educator*
McClanahan, Rue (Eddi-Rue McClanahan) *actress*
McCollum, Pamela Rae *music educator*
McConaughey, Matthew *actor*
McCready, Sam *theater educator, actor, theater director*
McCurry, Eddie Joe *entertainer*
McDowell, Malcolm *actor*
McEntire, Reba Nell *musician, actress*
McGowan, Rose *actress*
McKagan, Duff (Michael Andrew McKagan) *bassist*
McKendrick, Ryan Parker *music educator, conductor*
McMahon, Julian *actor*
McMaster, Brian John *artistic director*
McRaney, Gerald *actor*
McShane, Ian *actor*
Meara, Anne *actress, playwright, writer*
Medina, Jane S. *music educator*
Meisels, Judith A. *pianist, music educator*
Melillo, Joseph Vincent *theater producer*
Mellits, Marc Andrew *composer*
Melrose, Ian Paul Ellis *music educator, director, secondary school educator*
Melton, William Everett *retired music educator*
Menken, Alan *composer*
Meredith, Wendi Sue *music educator*
Meyerink, Victoria Paige *film producer, actress*
Mezacapa, Edna S. *music educator, elementary school educator*
Miller, Penelope Ann (Penolope Andrea Miller) *actress*
Minnix, Bruce Milton *television and theatre director*
Miranda-Levi, Jason *film producer, writer*
Mitchell, Brian Stokes *actor*
Mitchell, Jerry *choreographer, actor*
Moffatt, Joyce Anne *performing company executive*
Moffatt, Katy (Katherine Louella Moffatt) *musician, lyricist, vocalist*
Moglewer, Sarah Anne *music educator*
Mohan, Tungesh Nath *television and film producer, film educator*
Monk, Debra *actress*
Moore, Pamela Gay *retired music educator*
Morelan, Paula Kay *choreographer*
Moreland, Richard Paul *musician, educator*
Morello, Joseph Albert *musician, educator*
Morello, Tom *musician*
Morgan, Linda Gail *theater producer*
Morin, Lynn P. *music educator, director, secondary school educator*
Morris, Brenda Denise *music educator, director*
Morris, Colonel Robert *songwriter, musician, music educator*
Morrison, Shelley *actress*
Morrow, Nana Kwasi Scott Douglas *choreographer, director, writer, filmmaker, educator*
Mosiman, Rita Esther *music educator, performing artist*
Moss, Carrie-Anne *actress*
Mosteller, Darla Brooks *singer*
Mount, Thomas H(enderson) *motion picture and stage producer*
Mulligan, Robert *film director, producer*
Murphy, Eddie *actor, comedian*
Murphy, Michael George *actor*
Murphy, Timothy W. *music educator*
Murray, Alan Robert *sound editor*
Murray, Carla Mary *sound effects artist, artist*
Murray, Stephen Sanford *composer, lyricist, playwright*
Murray Shaw, Juleen *actress*
Musante, Tony (Anthony Peter Musante Jr.) *actor*
Myers, Angela Michelle *music educator, department chairman*
Myers, Jeffrey Daniel *concert pianist, music educator*
Myers, Mike *actor, scriptwriter, film producer*
Myerson, Alan *television director, film director*
Nagra, Parminder *actress*
Narita, Hiro *cinematographer*
Naughton, James *actor*
Navarro, Guillermo *cinematographer*
Neary, Patricia Elinor *ballet director*
Neblett, Carol *soprano*
Nederlander, James Laurence *theater producer*
Nelson, Craig T. *actor*
Nelson, Ron *composer, educator, conductor*
Néron, Martin *musician*
Nesbitt, Mitzi Evalee *voice educator, director*
Ness, Bernice Hagie *retired music educator*
Neuwirth, Bebe (Beatrice Neuwirth) *dancer, actress*
Nevelle, Phyn *actress, judge*
Neville, Phoebe *choreographer, dancer, educator*
Nevins, Sheila *television producer*
Newhouse, Benjamin Reed *composer, educator*
Newmar, Julie Chalene *actress, dancer, real estate businesswoman*
Newton, Wayne (Carson Wayne Newton) *entertainer, actor, recording industry executive*
Newtown, Thandie *actress*
Nichols, Mike *stage and film director*
Nigro, Kenneth Michael *music educator, musician*
Niguidula, Kathleen Ann *music educator, musician*
Nixon, Marni *singer*
Nolker, David Brett *music educator*
Noll, Jeanne C. *retired music educator*
Nolte, Nick *actor*
Norton-Jackson, Diana A. *organist, choirmaster*
Nugent, Gratian MacRae *music educator*
Oberlin, Russell *tenor, retired music educator*
O'Brien, Orin Ynez *musician, educator*
O'Donnell, Rosie *television personality, actress, comedienne*
Odya, Gregory Matthew *music educator, musician*
Oh, Sandra *actress*
O'Hara, Catherine *actress, comedienne*
O'Hare, Denis *actor*
Ohman, Franklin Eric *ballet educator, choreographer*
O'Keefe, Gary Raymond *actor*
Olyphant, Timothy *actor*
Opel, Doug *composer, arranger*
Orbit, William (William Wainwright) *record producer*
Ormond, Julia *actress*
Ortega, Kenny *television director, choreographer*
Osbourne, Ozzy (John Osbourne) *singer*
O'Shea, Anna Belle Marie *music educator, liturgy administrator*
Osmond, Marie *singer*
Osnes, Laura *actress*
Ossello, Kristie *music educator*
Ostrow, Stuart *theatrical producer, educator, author*
Pack, Michael *television producer, writer, director*
Panettiere, Hayden *actress*
Pasquier, Joël *music educator*
Payne, Alexander *film director, writer*
Pendleton, Austin *actor, theater director*
Percy, Lee Edward *motion picture film editor*
Perle, George *composer*
Perlman, Itzhak *violinist*
Perrineau, Harold *actor*
Perry, Matthew *actor*
Persoff, Nehemiah *actor, artist*
Pesci, Joe *actor*
Peterson, Anne Elizabeth Wallace *music educator, composer*
Peterson, Clark C. *announcer, writer, poet, speaker*
Peterson, Rosetta Hicks *retired music educator*
Pfeiffer, Michelle *actress*
Phillips, Michelle Gilliam *actress, writer*
Phillips, Todd *film director, film producer*
Phillips, Winifred Patricia *composer*
Pierce, David Hyde *actor*
Pierce, Ponchitta Ann *TV host, television producer, journalist, writer, consultant*
Pike, Anastasia *music educator, artist*
Pinchot, Bronson *actor*
Ping-Robbins, Nancy Regan *musician, writer, artist*
Pinkerton, A. Louise *vocalist, music educator*
Pinkett-Smith, Jada *actress*
Pinkins, Tonya *actress*
Piven, Jeremy *actor*
Place, Mary Kay *actress*
Plautz, Kimberly Ann *music educator*
Plimpton, Martha *actress*
Pohlhaus, Tess *theater educator*
Poitier, Sidney *actor, film director*
Poll, Martin Harvey *film producer*
Pollak, Kevin *actor*
Pollard, Samuel D. *film producer, director and editor*
Polman, Jerry R. *choral director, singer*
Pomfret, Bonnie *music educator*
Portoveltsky, Simcha *musician, cellist*
Previte, Robert (Bobby) *composer, musician*
Price, Betty Jeanne *chimes musician*
Price, Charles Gower *music educator*
Price, Thomas Frederick *theater educator*
Priestley, Jason (Jason Bradford Priestley) *actor*
Primosch, James Thomas *music educator, composer, musician*
Prince, Anna Lou *composer, music publisher, construction executive*
Pritchett, Meri Katherine *filmmaker*
Provencio, Linda Kay *music educator*
Pruzan, Irene *musician, educator, public relations executive, art association administrator*
Quinlan, Kathleen *actress*
Radcliffe, Daniel *actor*
Ragland, Kathryn Marie *dancer, educator*
Raimi, Samuel M. *film director*
Raitt, Bonnie Lynn *singer, musician*
Ransom, Tasha Elana *news production assistant, producer*
Raoufi, Azadeh *music educator*
Rashad, Phylicia *actress, singer, dancer*
Ravinsky, Anthony *music educator*
Reavis, Charles Benton *choir director, educator*
Redgrave, Vanessa *actress*
Reed, H. Owen *retired music educator*
Reed, Mary Carolyn Camblin *retired music educator, retired county official*
Reeves, Hallie Lawson *retired music educator, retired chaplain*
Regan, Susan Wright *dance educator, small business owner, choreographer*
Reid, Andrew Ernest *composer*
Reilly, John C. *actor*
Reims, Clifford Waldemar *music educator*
Reinhart, Charles Lawrence *performing company executive*
Reinhold, Judge (Edward Ernest Reinhold Jr.) *actor*
Renard, Paul Steven *music educator*
Resch, Rita Marie *retired music educator*
Rhodes, Lawrence *artistic director*
Richard, Candace L. *music educator*
Richards, John Pickford *musician, educator*
Richards, Martin *theatrical producer*
Richards, Michael *actor, comedian*
Richardson, Desmond *dancer*
Richardson, Robert *cinematographer*
Ridolfi, Patrick Murphy *music educator, tenor*
Riekki, Lee William *musician, educator*
Rifkin, Ron *actor*
Rihanna, (Robyn Rihanna Fenty) *singer, actress*
Riley, Rebecca Michelle *music educator*
Rino, Barbara Elizabeth *musician, educator*
Riposo, Joseph *music educator, director*
Robbins, Alice Elizabeth *musician*
Roberts, Doris *actress*
Robertson, Cliff *actor, writer, director*
Robinson, Devette Lorraine *music educator*
Robison, Emily Burns *musician*
Robison, Paula Judith *flutist*
Rock, Chris *actor, comedian*
Rodriguez, Michelle (Mayte Michelle Rodriguez) *actress*
Rodriguez, Robert *filmmaker*
Roeg, Nicolas Jack *film director*
Rogen, Seth *actor*
Rogers, Wanda Faye *vocalist*
Romano, Ray *actor, comedian*
Rook, Judith Rawie *television producer, writer*
Rose, Margarete Joyce *musician, interpreter*
Rose, Michael Leonard *film, television and video producer*
Roseanne, (Roseanne Barr) *actress, comedienne, television producer, writer*
Rosen, Myor *harpist, educator*
Rosenow, Mitchell Paul *sound recording engineer, studio owner, musician, music producer*
Ross, Tracey *actress*
Rotermund, Donald O. *musician, minister*
Rothschild, Rick *entertainment company executive*
Rourke, Mickey (Philip Andre Rourke Jr.) *actor*

Rousseau, Eugene Ellsworth *musician, music educator, consultant*
Rowlands, Gena *actress*
Roy, Michelle E. *musician, information technology consultant*
Ruder, Tia L. *music educator*
Rudner, Sara *dancer*
Ruggiero, David L. *music educator, accountant*
Ruggiero, Matthew John *bassoonist*
Russell, Theresa Lynn *actress*
Rutan, Charles R. *musician*
Ruviella-Knorr, Jeanne L. *music educator, consultant, clinician*
Ryder, Winona (Winona Laura Horowitz) *actress*
Sadoh, Godwin Simeon *music educator*
Saindon, Michael *music educator*
Saint, Eva Marie *actress*
Saint-Girard, Christian *theater director, actor, educator, choreographer, theater producer*
St. John, Kristoff *actor*
Sajak, Pat *television game show host*
Sak, Gilbert *music educator*
Saks, Gene *theater and film director, actor*
Saltzman, Philip *television producer, writer*
Sambora, Richie (Richard Stephen Sambora) *musician, singer, songwriter*
Samples, Mark Christopher *music editor*
Sandler, Adam *actor*
Santiago, Jose E. *film producer, writer, director, educator*
Sarich, Drew *actor*
Sarry, Christine *ballerina*
Savini, Tom *make-up artist, actor, director*
Scacchi, Greta *actress*
Scarchuk, Lynn Nettleton *retired music educator*
Scarwid, Diana Elizabeth *actress*
Schallert, William Joseph *actor*
Schenkman, Walter Allen *retired music educator*
Schexnayder, Brian Edward *vocalist, educator*
Schiff, Richard *actor*
Schiffer, Claudia *model*
Schmidt, Hildred Doris *music educator*
Schoonmaker Powell, Thelma *film editor*
Schroder, Rick *actor*
Schubert, Barbara Schuele *retired performing arts association administrator*
Schultz, Marian Starr *musician, educator*
Schumacher, Barret *motion picture propman, writer*
Schuur, Diane Joan *vocalist*
Schuurs, Marieke E. *singer, educator, small business owner*
Schwartz, Sima M. *music educator*
Schwartz, Stephen Lawrence *composer, lyricist*
Schwary, Ronald Louis *motion picture producer*
Schwimmer, David *actor*
Scorsese, Martin *film director, film producer*
Scott, Campbell *actor*
Scott, Sherie René *actress*
Scrivner, B(arbara) E. *piano educator*
Scruggs, Earl Eugene *entertainer*
Seagal, Steven *actor*
Secrest, Glenda *music educator*
Sedelmaier, John Josef *filmmaker*
Seff, Richard *actor, writer*
Seinfeld, Jerry *comedian, actor, television producer, scriptwriter*
Seltzer, Leo *cinematographer, educator*
Sewell, Michael E. *music educator, musician*
Shamberg, Michael *film producer*
Shatin, Judith *composer, educator*
Shaw, Harold *retired performing arts association administrator*
Shaw, Thomas *conductor, director*
Sheen, Charlie (Carlos Irwin Estevez) *actor*
Sheen, Martin (Ramon Estevez) *actor*
Sheen, Michael *actor*
Sheindlin, Judith (Judge Judy) *television personality, judge*
Sheldon, Robert *composer*
Shepherd, Cybill Lynne *actress, singer*
Sherin, Edwin *theater director, film director, television director, actor*
Shieh, Eric Y. *music educator*
Shire, Talia Rose (Talia Rose Coppola) *actress*
Shirley-Quirk, John *singer, educator*
Shull, Claire *documentary film producer, casting director*
Siems, Bennett A. *composer, performing company executive*
Silano, Lawrence *music educator*
Silverman, Ira Norton *news producer*
Silverstein, Barbara Ann *conductor, artistic director*
Silvestri, Alan Anthony *film composer*
Simmons, Deidre Warner *retired performing company executive, arts consultant*
Simmons, Mark Isaac *voice educator, director*
Singleton, John *director, screenwriter*
Sinn, Ryan *musician*
Sisto, Jeremy Merton *actor*
Sivill, Jason Ryan *music educator*
Skowronski, Vincent Paul *musician, recording industry executive*
Slash, (Saul Hudson) *guitarist*
Sloan, Carolyn *music educator, composer, lyricist*
Smart, James Anthony *music educator*
Smith, Alan Michael *music educator, musician*
Smith, Barbara Barnard *music educator*
Smith, Charlotte Reed *retired music educator*
Smith, D. Jason *music educator, composer*
Smith, Diana Barker *music educator*
Smith, Kevin *film director, writer, actor*
Smith, Lois Arlene *actress, writer*
Smith, Patti *vocalist, poet, lyricist*
Smith, Phyllis *actress*
Smith, Will *actor, rap artist*
Smith-Epstein, Mary Kathleen *dancer*
Smukal, Michael William *musician, educator, composer*
Snipes, Wesley *actor, film producer*
Soderbergh, Steven Andrew *filmmaker*
Somers, Suzanne Marie (Suzanne Marie Mahoney) *actress, writer, singer*
Sondheim, Stephen Joshua *composer, librettist, lyricist*
Sorrell, Rozlyn *singer, actress, theater director, educator*
Sorum, Matt *drummer*
Sorvino, Mira *actress*
Spade, David (David Wayne Spade) *actor*
Sparks, Jordin Brianna *singer*
Spengler-Miller, Janet Taylor *retired music educator, choral director*
Sprecher, Baron William Gunther *pianist, composer, conductor, diplomat*
Spurlock, Morgan *television producer, film producer*
Sronce, Ashley Randall *comedian, writer*
Stahl, Nick *actor*
Stallone, Sylvester Enzio *actor, film director, scriptwriter*
Stanbridge, Bryan Scott *music educator, composer*
Stanek, Jim *actor*
Stanley, Margaret King *performing arts association administrator*
Stanley, Ralph *bluegrass musician*
Stark, Le A., Jr. *music educator*
Starkey, Cliff *musician*
Steinberg, Russell *composer, secondary education educator*
Sternhagen, Frances *actress*
Stevens, Connie *actress, singer*
Stevens, Warren *actor*
Stevenson, Amanda (Sandy Stevens) *librettist, composer, songwriter*
Stewart, Timothy Glen *organist*
Stiers, David Ogden *actor, conductor*
Stiller, Ben *actor, television producer*
Stiller, Jerry *actor*
Stone, Joss (Joscelyn Eve Stoker) *singer*
Stone, Oliver *film director, producer, scriptwriter*
Stookey, Noel Paul *folksinger, composer*
Story, Timothy Kevin (Tim Story) *film director*
Stoytcheva, Lilia Stefanova *concert pianist, educator*
Strait, George *musician*
Strathairn, David *actor*
Strevig, Janice Lee *music educator*
Strickholm, Jean *musician, music company executive, retired elementary school educator*
Stringfield, Sherry *actress*
Stritch, Elaine *singer, actress*
Strukoff, Rudolf Stephen *retired music educator*
Sturner, Lynda *performing company executive*
Sturr, James William, Jr. *bandleader, recording industry executive, clarinetist, saxophonist, small business owner*
Sullivan, John Dominic *theater producer, writer*
Summers, Cathleen *film producer*
Summers, Marc *TV host, TV personality*
Sun, Chenghua *composer, music educator*
Sundquist, David Hall *voice educator*
Surplus, Robert Wilbur *retired music educator*
Sutton, Dolores *actress, writer*
Suzuki, Hidetaro *violinist*
Swank, Hilary *actress*
Sweeney, Don Patrick *music coordinator, conductor, writer*
Tamte-Horan, Michael William *music educator, conductor*
Tarrant, Christine Gloria *music educator*
Tarses, Jamie *television producer, former television network executive*
Tartaglia, John *actor, puppeteer*
Tate, Larenz *actor*
Taylor, Holly Ann *music educator*
Taylor, Regina *actress*
Tecco, Romuald Gilbert Louis Joseph *violinist, concertmaster*
Te Kanawa, Kiri *opera and concert singer*
Terry, Mickey Thomas *music educator, director*
Teweleit, Russ *music educator*
Tharp, Stephen John *organist and pianist, artist*
Tharp, Twyla *dancer*
Thayer, Robert Wilcox *music educator*
Thomas, Betty *director, actress*
Thompson, Andrea *television personality, retired newscaster, actress*
Thorstenberg, (John) Laurence *oboe and English horn player*
Thulean, Donald Myron *symphony conductor*
Tiano, Anthony Steven *television producer, publishing executive*
Tiemeyer, Kayla Sue *music educator*
Tillman, Mercia V. *musician*
Tingler, Marlene Johannsen *music educator, insurance agent*
Tolbert, Cornelia Emma *music educator*
Tom, Lauren *actress, singer*
Torn, Rip (Elmore Rual Torn Jr.) *actor, theater director*
Townshend, Pete (Peter Dennis Blandford Townshend) *musician, composer*
Travis, Randy Bruce *musician*
Tre Cool, (Frank Edwin Wright, III) *musician*
Trythall, Harry Gilbert *music educator, composer*
Tubb, Betty Freeze *music educator*
Tubman-Reichhoff, Denise Christine *music educator*
Turner, Amy *music educator*
Turner, Tina (Anna Mae Bullock) *singer*
Turok, Paul Harris *composer, commentator, music critic*
Twitchell, Theodore Grant *music educator, composer*
Uggams, Leslie *entertainer*
Unruh, Gary Lee *retired music educator*
Upbin, Shari *agent*
Upchurch, Leslie Purcell *music educator*
Vacano, Jost *cinematographer*
Vaccaro, Brenda *actress*
Van Otterloo, Janice Helene *musician, educator*
Velarde, Rachel Day *voice educator, vocalist, educator, small business owner*
Verbinski, Gore *film director*
Villaire, Holly Hennen Hood *theater producer, director, actress, educator*
Villella, Edward Joseph *dancer, choreographer, performing arts association administrator*
Virkhaus, Taavo *conductor*
Vlasak, Brian Emerson *composer*
Voegtlin-Anderson, Mary Margaret *music educator, small business owner*
Voight, Jon *actor*
Voketaitis, Arnold Matthew *bass-baritone, educator*
Von Brandenstein, Patrizia *production designer*
von Furstenberg, Betsy *actress, writer*
Wagner, Lindsay Jean *actress*
Wagner, Robert *actor*
Waldman, Barry Howard *film producer*
Walker, Donald Burke *retired music educator, retired archivist, composer*
Wallace, David K. *musician, composer*
Wallace, Dee *actress*
Wallis, Diana Lynn *artistic director*
Walsh, Diane *pianist*
Walsh, M. Emmet *actor*
Walton, Cedar *musician*
Warberg, Willetta *concert pianist, music educator*
Ware, D. Clifton *vocalist, educator*
Washington, Denzel *actor*
Washington, Kerry *actor*
Watanabe, Ken *actor*
Watt, Stephanie Denise *musician, educator, department chairman*
Wedgeworth, Ann *actress*
Weeks, Clifford Myers *musician, academic administrator*
Weiland, Scott Richard *singer*
Weldon, Charles Jauverni *actor*
Weller, Peter *actor*
Wells, Kitty (Ellen Muriel Deason) *musician*
Wendt, George Robert *actor*
Wernick, Richard Frank *composer, conductor, educator*
Wexler, Haskell *film producer*
Whitaker, Thomas O'Hara *theater educator, theater director*
White, Julie *actress*
White, Loray Betty *TV talk show host, writer, television producer, director, vocalist, actress*
Whittingham, Kenneth *television director*
Wiest, Dianne *actress*
Wilder, Gene *actor, film director, writer*
Wilder, Janet Mary *performing company executive*
Willard, Atom (Adam Willard) *musician*
Williams, Bernard *film producer*
Williams, JoBeth *actress*
Williams, Robin *actor, comedian*
Willis, Ruth *freelance/self-employed theater director, actress*
Wilson, Gretchen *vocalist*
Wilson, Rainn D. (Rainn Dietrich Wilson) *actor*
Wilson, Rita *actress*
Wilson, Wanda Lee Davis *retired casting director*
Winokur, Marissa Jaret *actress*
Winslet, Kate *actress*
Winters, Jonathan *actor*
Wise, Patricia *opera singer, educator*
Wisniewski, Thomas Joseph *music educator*
Witt, Alicia *actress*
Wittry, Diane Marie *conductor, musician*
Wolff, Eleanor Blunk *actress*
Wong, B.D. (Bradley Darryl Wong) *actor*
Wong, Richard *music educator*
Wood, Evan Rachel *actress*
Wood, Frank *actor*
Wood, Margaret *performing company executive*
Wood, Vivian Poates *mezzo soprano, educator*
Woodward, Ralph Barclay *music educator, small business owner*
Woodward, Thomas Morgan *actor*
Woronov, Mary Peter *actress*
Wreghitt, Randall L. *theater producer*
Wright, Gladys Stone *music educator, writer, composer*
Wright, Lori Dunkle *musician, educator*
Wright, Richard Stevens *film producer*
Wyse, Jason LaMar *music educator, director*
Yang, Schuman Chuo *music educator*
Yao, Frances *music educator, small business owner*
Yarrow, Peter *folksinger*
Yearwood, Trisha *country music singer, songwriter*
Yeh, Ying-Yu Emily *music educator*
Yoder, Randall D. *music educator*
Young, Burt *actor*
Younker, Kathleen Teuber *pianist, music educator*
Yu, Jessica *director, producer, writer, editor*
Yu, Tian-En *musician, music educator*
Yuriko, (Yuriko Kikuchi) *dancer, choreographer*
Zappa, Gail *record producer*
Zaros, Wendy Cecilia *soprano, educator*
Zeiger, Mikhail *composer, concert pianist*
Zhao, Zhen *music educator*
Ziemba, Karen *actress*
Zien, Chip *actor*
Zimmerman, Phyllis Elaine *music educator, composer, director*
Zsigmond, Vilmos *cinematographer, film director*
Zwick, Edward M. *director, producer, scriptwriter*

ARTS: VISUAL

UNITED STATES

ALABAMA

Alexander City
Towery, Sarah Carlisle *artist, retired educator*

Auburn
Hatfield, Donald Gene *retired art educator*

Birmingham
Keller, Armor *artist, arts advocate*

Fairfield
McCaslin, LaTanya *art educator*

Florence
Knight, Karen Anne McGee *artist, educator, educational research administrator*

Mobile
Clausell, Deborah Deloris *artist*
Conlon, James Edward *retired art educator, sculptor*
Goff, William M., Jr. *art director, graphics designer, animator, artist*

Montevallo
Stephens, Scott *art educator*

Normal
Journey, G. Edward *art educator*

ALASKA

Cordova
Bugbee-Jackson, Joan *sculptor, educator*

Fairbanks
Freer, Fred-Christian *artist*
Nakoneczny, Michael Martin *artist*

ARIZONA

Benson
Erden, Sybil Isolde *artist*

Chinle
Coor, Caren Barbara *art educator*

Mesa
Doyle, Matthew Brian *computer graphics designer*

Oracle
Rush, Andrew Wilson *artist*

Paradise Valley
Quinn, Brian Grant *sculptor, art educator*

Patagonia
La Noue, Terence David *artist, educator*

Peoria
Bailey, Claudia Jean *artist, retired librarian*
Willard, Garcia Lou *artist*

Phoenix
Stone, Hazel Anne Decker *artist*
Tyus, Gordon *graphics designer, educator*

Scottsdale
Afsary, Cyrus *artist*

Sedona
Coleman, M.L. (Michael Lee) *artist*

Sun City
Blanchet, Jeanne Ellene Maxant *artist, educator, performer*

Tempe
Lewis, William Raymond *art educator, artist*

Tucson
Conant, Howard Somers *artist, educator*
Crooks, Roselyn June *artist, writer*
Flint, Willis Wolfschmidt (Willi Wolfschmidt) *artist, sculptor*
Goltz, Pat *artist, web site designer*
Koerber, Erica *photographer*
Matthew, Neil Edward *artist, educator*
Neff, Terry Ann R. *art director, consultant*
Paravano, Dino *artist*

ARKANSAS

Ashdown
Edmonson, Phyllis Denty *artist*

Berryville
Brown, Frances Louise (Grandma Fran) *artist, art gallery director*

Fayetteville
Wilson, Charles Banks *artist*

Little Rock
Cawood, Gary Kenneth *photography educator*
Martin, Floyd W. *art educator*

Palestine
Taylor, Barbara Mae Helm *artist, educator*

CALIFORNIA

Alta Loma
Maloof, Sam *woodworker*

Anaheim
Bennett, Genevieve *artist*
Nelipovich, Sandra Grassi *artist*

Arcata
Land-Weber, Ellen *photography professor*

Auburn
Rothwell, Elaine B. *artist*

Bakersfield
Reep, Edward Arnold *artist*
Stone, Shelley Clyde III *art educator, archaeologist*

Berkeley
Genn, Nancy *artist*
Hartman, Robert Leroy *artist, educator*
Miyasaki, George Joji *artist*
Simpson, David William *artist, educator*

Beverly Hills
Ford, Tom *apparel designer and executive*
Guggenheim, Barbara Sue *art consultant*

Bolinas
Harris, Paul *sculptor*
Okamura, Arthur Shinji *artist, educator*

Camarillo
Bowman, Bruce *art educator*

Cambria
Harden, Marvin *artist, educator*

Carmel
Hobbs, C. Fredric *artist, filmmaker, writer*
Jacobs, Ralph, Jr. *artist*
Winfield, Rodney M. *artist, retired art educator*

Carmichael
Ryan, Gretchen Margarete Frieda *art educator*

Carson
Hirsch, Gilah Yelin *artist, writer*

Chatsworth
Strieby, B. Lorraine *artist*

Chico
Golightly, Douglas Raymond *artist*
Hornaday, Richard H. *artist, retired educator*

Claremont
Benjamin, Karl Stanley *artist, educator*
Blizzard, Alan *artist*
Dunye, Cheryl *artist, filmmaker*
Furman, David Stephen *artist, educator*
Rankaitis, Susan *artist*
Zehr, Connie *sculptor, art educator*
Zornes, Milford *artist*

Concord
Broadbent, Amalia Sayo Castillo *graphic arts designer*

Corona Del Mar
Delap, Tony *artist*

Costa Mesa
Muller, Jerome Kenneth *photographer, art director, editor*

Cottonwood
Stewart, John Norman *scenic artist*

Crestline
Noble, Lawrence Alan *artist*

Crockett
Sexton, Randall C. *art educator*

Culver City
Gordon, Florence Irene *graphics designer, illustrator*
Grant, Joan Julien *artist*
Simmons, Kimora Lee *apparel designer, television personality, model*

Cupertino
Carnie, Kay C. *artist, educator*

Davis
DePaoli, Geri M. (Joan DePaoli) *artist, historian*

Desert Hot Springs
Laws, Maurice Wesley *set decorator, museum exhibit designer*

Elmira
Montoya, Malaquias *art educator, artist*

Encino
Kempisty, Michael *artist, writer, actor*

Fair Oaks
Potter, George Kenneth *artist*

Fallbrook
Ragland, Jack Whitney *artist*

Folsom
Terranova, Elizabeth (Elisa) Jo *artist*

Garberville
Nyokka, Suzette *artist, natural health educator*

Glen Ellen
Haslag, Karen Christine *art educator, musician*

Greenbrae
Blatt, Morton Bernard *medical illustrator*

Healdsburg
Wunderlich, Alfred Leon *artist, educator*

Irvine
Penny, Simon *art educator*

La Jolla
Hawkinson, Tim *sculptor*
Imana, Jorge Garron *artist*
Jensen, Henrik Wann *computer graphics designer, educator*
Low, Mary Louise (Molly) *documentary photographer*

La Puente
Vetter, Lawrence Anthony *art educator, consultant*

Lafayette
Shurtleff, Akiko Aoyagi *artist, consultant*

Lagunitas
Holman, Arthur Stearns *artist*

Lincoln
Johnson, Ursula Anne *artist*

Long Beach
Barron, (Mary Lou) Slater *artist, retired educator*
Viola, Bill *artist, writer*

Los Angeles
Apple, Jacki (Jacqueline B.) *artist, educator, writer*
Apt, Charles *artist*
Brendel, Bettina *abstract artist*
Caroompas, Carole Jean *artist, educator*
Collier, Anna *photographer*
Couturier, Darrel J. *art dealer, director*
Curran, Darryl Joseph *photographer, educator*
De Larios, Dora *artist*
Devereux, Mara *sculptor, artist*
Fredericks, Beverly Magnuson *artist*
Grinnan, Katie *artist*
Grotjahn, Mark *painter*
Hamilton, Patricia Rose *art dealer*
Hockney, David *artist*
Johnston, Ynez *artist, educator*
Layton, Harry Christopher *art director*
LeMay, Harry Adrian *artist, educator*
Lhuillier, (Diane) Monique *apparel designer*
Loomis, Rick *photographer*
Park, Lee (Lee Parklee) *artist*
Poledna, Mathias *video artist*
Sinner, Steve *sculptor*
Verdi, Robert *jewelry designer, fashion expert, television personality*
Verreos, Nick *apparel designer*
Wayne, June Claire *artist*
Weisberg, Ruth *artist*
Wells, Annie *photographer*

Los Gatos
Carson, Sol Kent *artist, educator*
Mintz, Marilyn D. *artist, writer*

Los Osos
Kreitzer, David Martin *artist*

Mariposa
Bruce, John Anthony *artist*
Rogers, Earl Leslie *artist, educator*

Moraga
O'Brien, Bea Jae *artist*

Morgan Hill
Freimark, Robert (Bob) *artist*

Mountain View
Hwang, Dennis (Dennis Hwang-Jung-moak) *graphic computer artist*

Newport Beach
Belić Weiss, Zoran *artist, design educator, director*
Spitz, Barbara Salomon *artist*

Northridge
Bassler, Robert Covey *artist, educator*

Novato
McNamara, John Stephen *artist, educator*

Oakdale
Saletta, Mary Elizabeth (Betty Saletta) *sculptor*

Oakhurst
Cantwell, Christopher William *artist*

Oakland
Beasley, Bruce Miller *sculptor*
Gonzalez, Arthur Padilla *artist, educator*
Kimpton, Laura *artist*
Rath, Alan T. *sculptor*
Saunders, Raymond Jennings *artist, educator*

Orange
Banning, Donna Rose *art educator*

Orinda
Migdale, Lawrence D. *photographer*

Pacific Palisades
Chesney, Lee Roy, Jr. *artist*

Palm Desert
Anderson, R. Christian *photographer, media consultant, art director*

Palo Alto
Richardson, Tom (Edward Thompson Richardson) *artist*

Panorama City
Janis, Elinor Raiden *artist, educator*

Pasadena
Liashkov, Peter *artist, educator*
Pashgian, Margaret Helen *artist*

Pebble Beach
Mortensen, Gordon Louis *artist, printmaker*

Penn Valley
Sands, Sharon Louise *graphics designer, artist*

Petaluma
McChesney, Robert Pearson *artist*
Skalagard, Hans Martin *artist*

Pleasant Hill
Schrank, Shirley Ann *artist*

Pomona
Fetterly, Barbara Louise *artist*
Wilson, Stanley Charles *artist, educator, curator, art gallery director, consultant*

Quartz Hill
McAllister, Bruce Richard *art educator*

Rancho Mirage
Novak, Joe *artist*

Rancho Palos Verdes
Mac Innes, David Harold *artist, small business owner*
Works, Margaret Elizabeth *retired art educator*

Redding
Matenaer, Tegwin A. *artist, retired educator, consultant*

Redlands
Goto, Toshiko *retired art educator*
Ristau, Jacob Robert *art educator, graphics designer*

Richmond
Wessel, Henry *photographer*

Ridgecrest
Miears-Cutsinger, Mary Ellen *artist, art gallery owner*

Riverside
Bell, Helen Lavin *artist*
Smith, Dorothy Ottinger *apparel designer, volunteer*

Rosemead
Jin, Jing Yi *photographer, film director*

Ross
Pierce, Carole Jean *artist*

Sacramento
Allan, William George *artist, educator*
Byer, Renee C. *photographer*
Hull, Frederick Albert *artist, writer*

Salinas
Borgman, Sylvia *artist, activist*
Puckett, Richard Edward *artist, consultant, former recreation executive*

San Carlos
Oliver, Nancy Lebkicher *artist, retired elementary school educator*

San Diego
Gregoire, Mathieu *artist, consultant*
Moore, Linda A. *art dealer, curator*
Raczka, Tony Michael *artist*

San Francisco
Babcock, Jo *artist, educator*
Baker, Joy Doreen *art educator, artist*
Beall, Dennis Ray *artist, educator*
Bechtle, Robert Alan *artist, educator*
Chin, Sue Soone Marian (Suchin Chin) *artist, photojournalist*
DeSoto, Lewis Damien *artist, educator*
Dickinson, Eleanor Creekmore *artist, educator*
Donnelly, Trisha *artist*
Eurich, Judith *art appraiser, printmaker*
Fullerton, Dorothy Mallan *artist*
Goldstein, Sydney Rachel *photographer, writer, radio producer*
Goldstine, Stephen Joseph *art educator*
Honig, Al *artist*
Huntting, Cynthia Cox *artist*
Ireland, David *artist*
Lauterbach, Michael Alan *artist*
Martin, Fred *artist, academic administrator*
McClintock, Jessica *fashion designer*
Petersen, Roland *artist, printmaker*
Pfaff, Laura King *auction house executive*
Presniakov, Alexander *artist, sculptor, inventor, writer*
Robinson, Patrick *apparel designer*
Sherratt, Holly *art appraiser*
Smith, Jennie *artist*
Ternar, Mine Y. *artist, art educator*
Thiebaud, Wayne Morton *artist*
Toney, Anita Karen *printmaker*
Van Hoesen, Beth Marie *artist, printmaker*
Wonner, Paul John *painter*

San Jose
Ellner, Michael William *art educator*
Estabrook, Reed *artist, educator*

San Juan Bautista
Nutzle, Futzie (Bruce John Kleinsmith) *artist, writer, animator*

San Juan Capistrano
Ealy, Cynthia Pike *artist, real estate agent*

San Luis Obispo
Nicholson, Bernice Loughran *art educator*

San Mateo
Huxley, Mary Atsuko *artist*

San Pedro
Parkhurst, Violet Kinney *artist*

San Rafael
Tosti, Annette Brewer *artist*

Santa Barbara
Eguchi, Yasu *artist*
Hayward, Jean *artist, musician, interior designer*
Rosenthal, Earl Edgar *art history educator*

Santa Clara
Hofstetter, Jane Robinson *artist, educator*
Lane, Holly Diana *artist*

Santa Monica
Alexander, Peter Houston *artist*
Bosman, Richard *artist, printmaker*
Giannulli, Mossimo *designer, apparel business executive*
Masucci, Michael James *artist*

Shadow Hills
Bangs, Cate (Cathryn Margaret Bangs) *film production designer, interior designer*

Somis
Kehoe, Vincent Jeffré-Roux *photographer, cosmetics executive*

Sonoma
Fellows, Alice Combs *artist*

South Pasadena
Askin, Walter Miller *artist, educator*

Stanford
Corn, Wanda Marie *art educator*

Stinson Beach
Schwarm, Harold Chambers *artist*

Stockton
Oak, Claire Morisset *artist, educator*
Sumida, Gregory Zio *artist, photographer, musician, astronomer*

Studio City
Easterson, Sam *artist*

Sun Valley
Sweet, Harvey *set and lighting designer*

Sylmar
Scheib, Gerald Paul *art educator*

Templeton
Foster-Wells, Karen Margaret *artist*

Thousand Oaks
McCarter, Nancy R. *graphics designer, educator, artist, small business owner*
Miller, Elizabeth Joan *artist, guidance counselor*

Universal City
Bismuth, Pierre *artist*

Valencia
Buchanan, Nancy Page *artist, educator*

Van Nuys
Cook, Jenik Esterm (Jenik Esterm Cook Simonian) *artist, educator*
Graham, Roger John *photography and journalism professor*
Vasilyeva, Anna *artist, writer*

Venice
Alf, Martha Joanne *artist*
Binns, Tom *jewelry designer*
Eversley, Frederick John *sculptor, engineer*

Walnut Creek
Reimann, Arline Lynn *artist*

West Hollywood
Barker, Clive *artist, film director and producer, scriptwriter*

COLORADO

Arvada
Halley, Diane Esther *artist*

Aspen
Fischl, Eric *artist*
Mitchell, Karen Frances *artist, jewelry designer*

Aurora
D'Amico, Sandra Hathaway *art educator*

Boulder
Bolomey, Roger Henry *sculptor*
Charteris, Frances I.A. *art educator, artist*
Matthews, Eugene Edward *artist*

Colorado Springs
Goehring, Kenneth *artist*

Cortez
Kristin, Karen *artist*

Denver
Graham, Pamela Smith *artist, educator*
Shwayder, Elizabeth Yanish *sculptor*

Dolores
Rice, Wayne *artist, educator, small business owner*
Winterer-Schulz, Barbara Jean *graphics designer, writer*

Durango
Balas-Whitfield, Susan *artist*

Lake George
Norman, John Barstow, Jr. *graphics designer, educator*

Laporte
Riba, Shirley *artist*

Loveland
Bierbaum, Janith Marie *artist*

Montrose
Radovich, Donald *painter, illustrator, retired art educator*

Paonia
Noonan, Robert Harry *art and music educator*

Salida
Strawn, Melvin Nicholas *artist, educator*

Woodland Park
Cockrille, Stephen *art director, business owner*

CONNECTICUT

Brooklyn
McIlvane, Edward James *stained glass artist, educator*

Danbury
Grimes, Margaret Whitehurst *artist, educator*
Saghir, Adel Jamil *art educator, painter, sculptor*

East Haddam
Conant, Jan Royce *artist*

Falls Village
Cronin, Robert Lawrence *painter*

Gaylordsville
Dunn, Virginia *artist*

Georgetown
Julian, Alexander, II, *menswear designer*

Guilford
Pease, David Gordon *artist, educator*

Hartford
Hammer, Alfred Emil *artist, educator*

Litchfield
Mullins, Patty *artist*

Meriden
Tamburine, Jean Helen *sculptor, painter, illustrator*

Milford
Curt, Denise Morris *painter, photographer*
Fagan, Alanna *artist, printmaker*

Mystic
Rooney, Maria Dewing *photographer*

Naugatuck
Mannweiler, Mary-Elizabeth *painter*

New Canaan
Kovatch, Jak Gene *artist*
Richards, Glenora *artist*

New Haven
Bailey, William Harrison *artist, educator*
Feinstein, Rochelle *artist, educator*
Grausman, Philip *sculptor*
Johnson, Lester Fredrick *artist*
Lindroth, Linda (Linda Hammer) *artist, writer, curator*
Yeargan, Michael *scenic designer*

Newtown
Cottingham, Robert *artist*

Norwalk
Perry, Charles Owen *sculptor*

Old Lyme
Osborne, Judith Barbour *artist*

Old Saybrook
Neal, Irene Collins *artist, educator*

Sharon
Johns, Jasper *artist*

Stamford
Babson, Jane Frances *artist, writer*
Cassidy, Denis Andrew *artist, architect*

Stonington
Elliott, Inger McCabe *apparel designer, consultant, textiles executive*

Storrs Mansfield
Jones, Clyde Adam *artist, educator*

Voluntown
Caddell, Foster *artist*

Wallingford
Lauttenbach, Carol *artist*

Waterbury
Johnson, Lorelei Marie *artist*

West Cornwall
Estern, Neil Carl *sculptor*
Simont, Marc *artist*

Weston
Bleifeld, Stanley *sculptor*

Westport
Chernow, Ann Levy *artist, educator*
Fisher, Leonard Everett *artist, educator, writer*
Reilly, Nancy (Anne Caulfield Reilly) *painter*
Siff, Marlene Ida *artist, designer*

DELAWARE

Dagsboro
Davis, Marica Nanci Ella Riggin *retired artist*
Hanna, Anne Marie *artist*

Greenville
Reynolds Cooch, Nancy D. *sculptor*

Lewes
Costigan, Constance Frances *artist, educator*

New Castle
Almquist, Don *illustrator, artist*

Newark
Brown, Hilton *artist, educator, writer*
Homer, William Innes *art history educator, expert, writer*
Korber, Louise Ann *artist*
Rowe, Charles Alfred *artist, graphics designer, educator*

Wilmington
Bounds-Seemans, Pamella J. *artist*
Messina, Charles *artist*

DISTRICT OF COLUMBIA

Washington
Blair, James Pease *freelance photographer*
Bowman, Dorothy Louise *artist*
Brown, Pamela Wedd *artist*
Carroll, M(argaret) Lizbeth Carr *art educator, graphics designer, photographer*
Clark, Michael *artist*
Colton Skolnick, Judith A. *artist*
DiPerna, Frank Paul *photographer, educator*
Fujimara, Makota *painter*
Gilliam, Sam *artist*
Gumpert, Gunther *artist*
Hogan, Felicity *artist*
Jecklin, Lois Underwood *art corporation executive, consultant*
Kapikian, Catherine Andrews *artist*
Kimes, Don Mark *artist, educator*
Koller, Shirley Leavitt *sculptor*
Kushnir, Andrei *artist, consultant*
Parish, Norman *artist, gallery director*
Stovall, Lou *printmaker*
Tacha, Athena *sculptor, artist, educator*
Wasko-Flood, Sandra Jean *artist, educator*

FLORIDA

Atlantic Beach
Gartland, Alice Johnson *artist*

Boca Raton
Lampasona, Eydi M. *art educator*
Wertheimer, Esther *sculptor*

Bonita Springs
Elliott, Donna Louise *artist*

Bradenton
Dryden, Stephen David *artist, product designer*
Voorhees, Stephanie Robin Faught *retired art educator*

Clearwater
Christ, Karyn Lynn *apparel designer, poet*
Slade, Roy *artist, college president, museum director*

Dania Beach
Satin, Claire Jeanine *sculptor, artist*

Daytona Beach
Alvarez, Marianne *artist, photographer, educator*

Delray Beach
St. George, Elaine *art educator*

Elfers
Milana-Panopoulos, Maria *artist, inventor, model*

Fort Lauderdale
Moorhead, Rolande Annette Reverdy *artist, educator*

Fort Myers
Schwartz, Carl Edward *artist, printmaker*

Fort Pierce
Jefferson, Zanobia Bracy *artist, educator*
Swenson, Ada Perez *artist*

Gainesville
Favini, Paul Furey *costume designer, educator*

Hobe Sound
Houser, Jim (James Cowing Houser Jr.) *artist*

Hollywood
Sadowski, Carol Johnson *artist*

Indialantic
Pavlakos, Ellen Tsatiri *sculptor*

Indian Harbor Beach
Traylor, Angelika *stained glass artist*

Jacksonville
Eden, F. Brown *artist*

Jensen Beach
Skrupky, Elaine Charlotte *art educator*

Jupiter
Secrest, Glenn James *artist*

Key Biscayne
de la Cruz, Rosa *art collector*

Key West
McIntosh, Jon Charles *illustrator, graphics designer, painter*

Kissimmee
McCann, Jean Friedrichs *artist, educator*

Lake Mary
Bachmann, Bill *photographer*

Lakeland
Rogers, James Gordon, Jr. *art educator*
Stark, Bruce Gunsten *artist*

Land O Lakes
O'Connell, Carmela Digristina *appraisal executive, consultant*

Marathon
Giffen, Lois Key *artist, psychotherapist*

Melbourne
King, Virginia Shattuck *painter, retired school nurse, educator*

Miami
Bannard, Walter Darby *artist, art critic*
Cano, Margarita *artist, consultant, retired librarian*
Kislak, Jean Hart *art director*
Pelton, Margaret Marie Miller *retired art educator, academic administrator, artist*
Pfeiffer, Mary Louise *artist, educator*
Steinbaum, Bernice *art dealer*

Miami Beach
Carnase, Thomas Paul *graphics designer, consultant*
Rut, Wanda E. *artist, educator, writer*

Mount Dora
Kirton, Jennifer Myers *artist*

Naples
Badash, Sandi B. *artist, art educator*
Eldridge, David Carlton *art and antique appraiser*
Vickrey, Robert Remsen *artist*
York, Tina *painter*

North Palm Beach
Kaplan, Muriel Sheerr *sculptor*

Orange Park
Hunt, J(ulian) Courtenay *artist*

Orlando
Lorenz, Mathias *art director*
Wade, David Allen *graphics designer*
Warren, Dean Stuart *artist*

Ormond Beach
Sugiyama, Akiko *artist*

Palm Beach Gardens
Samuels, Fern Jacqueline *artist, educator*
Squier, Jack Leslie *sculptor, retired art educator*

Pensacola
Larson, Barbara Jean *art history professor*
Maki, Hope Marie (Countess Hope Marie Maki) *artist, educator*

Ponte Vedra Beach
Scott, Marie Claudine *ceramic artist, writer*

Port Saint Lucie
Staub, Carol Anne *artist*

Punta Gorda
Pollard, Herschel Newton *artist, psychologist*
Sehring, Adolf *artist, sculptor*

Safety Harbor
Banks, Allan Richard *artist, art historian, researcher*

Saint Petersburg
Andruk, Marjorie Dean *artist, educator*

Sarasota
Burkett, Helen *artist*
Lengyel, Alfonz *art history, archeology and museology educator*
Wendlandt, Dorothea Schnepf *artist, writer*

Satellite Beach
Rains, Baxter Smith *sculptor, consultant*

Sebastian
Pieper, Patricia Rita *artist*

Tampa
de Lama, Alberto *artist*
Sopher, Vicki Elaine *appraiser*
Wujcik, Theo Frank *artist*

Titusville
Samuelson, Fred Binder *artist, educator*

Venice
Girman, Dee-Marie *retired artist, singer*

Vero Beach
Ferrell, Catherine K. *sculptor, painter*

Weston
Napp, Gudrun F. *artist*

Windermere
Cerri, Robert Noel *photographer*

Winter Haven
Schepis, Anthony Joseph *artist, educator*

GEORGIA

Alpharetta
Bolton, Robin Jean *artist, painter*

Athens
Dunham, Richard E. III *lighting designer, consultant, set designer, educator*
Herbert, James Arthur *retired art educator, artist, filmmaker*
Kaufman, Glen Frank *art educator*
Olsen, Richard James *artist, educator*
Paul, William Dewitt, Jr. *retired art educator, photographer, videographer, museum director*
Smith, Susan Carlton (Susan Carlton Smith Cavanagh) *artist, illustrator, sculptor*

Atlanta
Guberman, Sidney *painter, writer*
Malone, James Hiram *graphics designer, journalist, writer*
McLean, James Albert *artist, educator*
Rodríguez, Rocío *artist*
Wilmer, Mary Charles *artist*

Augusta
Schultz, Nancy Jansson *artist*

Cochran
Agnew, Charlie Martin *art educator, artist*

Decatur
Moore, Wayland D. *artist*

Dunwoody
Hendrix, Jane Galloway *art educator*

Greensboro
Copelan, Ann Hanson *artist, psychologist*

Hawkinsville
Whipple, Woodrow Thomas *artist, educator*

Hiawassee
Davis, Nighta J. *photographer, artist*

Macon
Weaver, Jacquelyn Kunkel Ivey *artist, educator*

Marietta
Lahtinen, Silja Liisa *artist*

Mount Berry
Mew, Thomas Joseph, III, (Tommy Mew) *artist, educator*

Roswell
Christopher, Lin *artist*

Savannah
Aja-Herrera, Marie *fashion designer, educator*
Foley, Marilyn Lorna *artist*
Hung, Chin-Cheng *artist, educator*

Wildwood
Dombrowski, Bob *artist, writer*

HAWAII

Honolulu
Betts, Barbara Stoke *artist, educator*
Guthrie, Edgar King *artist*
Nguyen, Thanh Truc Thi *computer animator, educator*
Pickens, Frances Jenkins *artist, educator*
Uhl, Philip Edward *artist, photographer, cinematographer*

Kapaau
Jankowski, Theodore Andrew *artist*

Kihei
Galesi, Deborah Lee *artist*

Makawao
Huff, Harriet *artist, educator*

IDAHO

Coeur D' Alene
Clabby, Michael *computer graphics designer, educator*

Gooding
Larson, Lynn Wood *artist, musician*

Harrison
Carlson, George Arthur *artist*

Yellow Pine
Auth, Robert Ralph *art educator*

ILLINOIS

Bourbonnais
Wilkey, Elmira Smith *illustrator, artist, writer, educator*

Champaign
Kotoske, Roger Allen *artist, educator*
Young, Paul *graphic designer, edcator*

Chicago
Alcantara, Anita Luisa *community arts administrator*
Anderson, Craig Allen *retired art educator, artist*
Aubin, Barbara Jean *artist*
Barazani, Morris *artist, educator*
Bowman, Leah *fashion designer, consultant, photographer, educator*
Burroughs, Margaret Taylor Goss *artist*
Castillo, Mario Enrique *artist, educator*
Coffey, Susanna Jean *artist, educator*
Crane, Barbara Bachmann *photographer, educator*
Dunning, Jean *artist*
Edelstein, Teri J. *art educator, director, consultant*
Fotopoulos, James *artist*
Gunning, Tom *art educator*
Himmelfarb, John David *artist*
Hunt, Richard *sculptor*
Kearney, John Walter *sculptor, painter*

King, Andre Richardson *architectural graphic designer*
Marshall, Kerry James *artist*
Martin, Ionis Bracy *artist, educator*
McElheny, Josiah G. *sculptor*
McGrail, Jeane Kathryn *artist*
Michod, Susan Alexander *artist, painter*
Pallasch, Magdalena Helena (Mrs. Bernhard Michael Pallasch) *artist*
Paterakis, Angela Gregory *art educator, writer*
Postiglione, Corey M. *artist, critic, art educator*
Preciado, Pamela *artist*
Steinberg, Rubin *retired art educator, artist*
Tessing, Louise Scire *graphic designer*

Cissna Park
McCullough, Edward L. *artist, educator*

Crystal Lake
Chechopoulos, Peter *photographer, educator*
Salvesen, B. Forbes *artist*

Des Plaines
Henrikson, Arthur Allen *political cartoonist, educator*

Dixon
Huber, Marianne Jeanne *art dealer and appraiser*

Edwardsville
Hampton, Phillip Jewel *artist, educator*
Malone, Robert Roy *artist, art educator*

Evanston
Conger, William Frame *artist, educator*

Glencoe
Siske, Regina *artist*

Glenview
Hough, Winston *artist*

Highland Park
Slavick, Ann Lillian *retired art educator*

Hudson
Mills, Frederick VanFleet *art educator, watercolorist*

Lake Forest
Weston, Dawn Thompson *artist, researcher*

Lebanon
Ottinger, David *art educator, artist*

Lombard
Ahlstrom, Ronald Gustin *artist*

Mchenry
Chisu, Ioan *artist*

Mount Prospect
Eliason, Birdell *painter, educator*

Naperville
Finzer, Carolyn Lauing *artist*

Oak Brook
Klinger, Gail Greaves *art educator, illustrator*

Oak Lawn
Jachna, Joseph David *photographer, educator*

Quincy
Gehrich, Leonora Suppan *artist, musician, German literature educator*

Rockford
Heflin, Tom Pat *artist*

Saint Charles
Malinowski, MaryEllen *photographer, artist*

Skokie
Sahagian, Arthur H. *artist*

Table Grove
Thomson, Helen Louise *artist*

Vermont
Datcu, Ioana *artist*

Waukegan
Miller, Helen Elizabeth *art educator, adult education educator, artist*

Winnetka
Plowden, David *photographer*

Yorkville
Freese, Carolyn Lee *art educator*

INDIANA

Albany
Patrick, Alan K. *artist*

Bloomington
Connally, Sandra Jane Oppy *freelance/self-employed artist, educator*
O'Hearn, Robert Raymond *stage designer*

Dyer
Crnkovich, Ruth Anne *art appraiser, museum director*

Evansville
Baker, Gloria Marie *artist*

Fort Wayne
Skinner, Jauneth *art educator, graphic artist*

Fortville
Ramanathan, Chitra *artist, art educator*

Indianapolis
Rutledge, Joanne *artist, consultant*

Seymour
Lewis, Judith Susanna *artist*

South Bend
Larkin, Eugene David *artist, educator*

Valparaiso
Olson, Lynn *sculptor, painter, writer*

West Lafayette
Ichiyama, Dennis Yoshihide *art educator, educational association administrator*
Lord, Victoria Lynn *artist*

Winamac
Ligocki, Gordon Michael *artist, educator*

IOWA

Ankeny
Stahr, Curtis Brent *photographer, art association administrator, educator*

Cedar Falls
Blakesley, Kimberly Kay *art educator, consultant*

Cresco
Fontes, Edward Michael *graphics designer*

Des Moines
Reece, Maynard Fred *artist, writer*

Iowa City
Myers, Virginia Anne *art educator*
Schmidt, Julius *sculptor*
Scott, John Beldon *art history educator, writer*

Johnston
Vawter, Toni Valentine *artist*

Mason City
Leet, Richard Eugene *artist, museum director*

Toledo
Lyon, Norma Duffield *sculptor, agriculturist*

KANSAS

Chase
Stull, Evalyn Marie *artist*

Hays
Kuksi, Kris M. *artist*

Lawrence
Dooley, Patrick John *graphic designer, educator*

Overland Park
Amundson, Beverly Carden *artist*

Topeka
Peters, Barbara Waterman *artist, educator*

KENTUCKY

Fort Wright
Sullivan, Connie Castleberry *artist*

Franklin
Law, Jerriann Marcella *artist, poet, writer*

Lexington
Girard, C. Jack *artist, educator*
Sandoval, Arturo Alonzo *artist, educator*

Murray
Guy, Sallie T. *artist*

Wickliffe
Frueh, Deborah K.A. (Debi Frueh) *artist, poet*

Winchester
Snowden, Ruth O'Dell Gillespie *artist*

LOUISIANA

Baton Rouge
Baron, Stuart *artist, art educator, director*

Choudrant
Ford, John Charles *artist*

Lafayette
Barry, Mildred Castille *artist*

Metairie
Banton, Kathleen Ariatti *artist, educator*
Casselli, Henry Calvin, Jr. *artist, painter*
Crosby, Deborah Berry *artist*

New Orleans
Liljeberg, Genevieve Brocato *artist*

Shreveport
Hughes, Mary Sorrows *artist*
Morelock, Jasmine Crawford *artist*
Wray, Geraldine Smitherman (Jerry Wray) *artist*

Westwego
Brehm, Loretta Persohn *retired art educator, librarian, consultant*

MAINE

Alna
Beerits, Janet Penrose Robinson *sculptor*

Farmington
Barigar, Elizabeth Gayle *painter, art educator*

Gorham
Chen, Ray Gow Hwei *artist, educator, department chair*
Wallace, David Eric *craftsman, retired military officer*

Kennebunk
Betts, Edward *artist*

New Harbor
Lyford, Cabot *sculptor*

Ogunquit
West, Norman Ellsworth *artist*

Vinalhaven
Indiana, Robert (Clark) *artist*

Wiscasset
Leslie, Seaver *artist*

York
Hallam, Beverly (Beverly Linney) *artist*
Roché, Robert Richard *artist*

MARYLAND

Annapolis
Fry, Virginia Milne *artist, poet*
Markman, Ronald *artist, educator*

Baltimore
Klitzke, Theodore Elmer *arts consultant, retired college dean*
Tenser, Beth Hillary *graphics designer, art director*
Tucker, James L., Jr. *artist, educator*

Bethesda
Benson, Elizabeth Polk *art specialist*
Dignac, Geny (Eugenia M. Bermudez) *sculptor*
Elliott, George Armstrong III *artist, journalist*
Fleming, Patricia Stubbs (Patsy Fleming) *artist*
Sarnoff, Lili-Charlotte (Lolo Sarnoff) *artist*

Boyds
Bu, Rulei *artist, educator*

Brentwood
Kaskey, Raymond John *sculptor*

Chestertown
Amos, James Lysle *photographer*

Chevy Chase
Kranking, Margaret Graham *artist, retired educator*

College Park
Richardson, W. C. *painter*

Galena
Hunsperger, Elizabeth Jane *art and design consultant, educator*

Landover
Rogers, Joseph Shepperd *art educator*

Lothian
Messenger, Barbara Beall *artist*

Mount Airy
Swetcharnik, William Norton *visual artist, instructor, consultant*

Rocky Ridge
Rall, Priscilla *artist, educator*

Silver Spring
Aranya, Gwendalin Qi *painter, priest, educator, yoga educator*
Fitzgerald, Joseph Patrick *artist*
Peiperl, Adam *sculptor, photographer*

Trappe
Burns-Bowie, Maureen Elizabeth *sculptor*

Woodbine
Nuss, Barbara Gough *artist*

MASSACHUSETTS

Amherst
Anderson, Ronald Trent *artist, educator*
Dabrowski, Thaddeus E. *art educator, consultant, painter*
Lasch, Pat *artist, educator*
Liebling, Jerome *photographer, educator*
Reed-Penttinen, Daphne Stevenson *artist*
Yarde, Richard Foster *art educator*

Belmont
Colón, Ernie *comic book artist*

Beverly
Manning, William Frederick *retired photographer*
Roy, Robert William *artist, educator*

Billerica
DeCrosta, Susan Elyse *graphic designer*

Boston
Ablow, Roz Karol (Roselyn Karol Ablow) *painter, curator*
Fesko, Colleene *art appraiser*
Fletcher, Stephen L. *art appraiser*
Goldstein, Nathan *artist, writer*
Hershey, Nona *artist, printmaker, educator*
Parker, Olivia *photographer*
Picker, Sebastián *artist*

Weisner, David *illustrator*
Wiesner, David *illustrator, children's writer*

Brookline
Barron, Ros *artist*
Kawada, Janet Hansen *artist, educator*
Rubin-Katz, Barbara *sculptor, human services manager*
Swirnoff, Lois *artist, educator*

Cambridge
Ackerman, James *fine arts educator*
Alcalay, Albert S. *artist, design educator*
Bakanowsky, Louis Joseph *artist, architect, educator*
Chandler, Fay Martin *artist*
Dobson, Parrish *photographer, educator*
Feininger, Theodore Lux *artist*
Jonas, Joan (Joan Amerman Edwards) *artist*
Kelsey, Robin E. *art history educator*
Mazur, Michael *artist*
Slosburg-Ackerman, Jill Rose *artist, educator*
Wodiczko, Krzysztof *artist, architect, educator*

Concord
Ihara, Michio *sculptor*
MacNeill, Frederick Douglas *artist*

Dartmouth
Wisneski, Kurt *art educator*

East Orleans
Burkert, Robert Randall *artist*

Fall River
Andrade, Manuela Pestana *art educator*
Wilner, Marion Leonard *art educator*

Framingham
Aronson, Benjamin *artist*
Casselman, Frederick Lee *computer artist, printmaker*

Gloucester
Steele-Goetemann, Judith Ann *artist, educator, art gallery owner*
White, Lucette Darby *painter, sculptor*

Granville
Brown, Stephen Pat *artist*

Haydenville
Rupp, Sheron Adeline *photographer, educator*

Lexington
Coleman, Loring W. *artist*

Natick
Geller, Esther (Bailey Geller) *artist*
Law, Jan *artist*

Newtonville
Polonsky, Arthur *artist, educator*

Northampton
Schuleit, Anna *artist*

Norwell
Brett, Jan Churchill *illustrator, author*

Provincetown
Collins, Larry Richard *artist, educator, art gallery director*
Hutchinson, Peter Arthur *artist*

Reading
Frey, Joanne Alice Tupper *art educator*
Nordstrand, Nathalie Elizabeth Johnson *artist*

Rockport
Martin, Roger Hemenway *artist, educator*
Nicholas, Thomas Andrew *artist*

Sharon
Edmonds, Nick *sculptor*

Shrewsbury
Kranich, Margaret Mansley *artist*

South Hadley
Hall, Lee *artist, educator, writer*

Sudbury
Aronson, David *artist, retired educator*

Vineyard Haven
Ortlip, Paul Daniel *artist*

Wayland
Dergalis, George *artist, educator*

Wellesley
McGibbon, Phyllis Isabel *artist, educator*

Williamstown
Blair, Phyllis E. *artist*

Winchester
Ferrara, Lee *graphics designer, artist, educator*
Neuman, Robert Sterling *art educator, artist*

MICHIGAN

Ann Arbor
Curtin, Joseph *violinmaker*
Eisenberg, Marvin Julius *retired art history educator*
Lewis, William Arthur *artist, educator*

Auburn Hills
Mandiberg, David Michael *sculptor*

Birmingham
Kozlow, Richard *artist*

Bloomfield Hills
Burnett, Patricia Hill *artist, educator*

Camden
Falls, Kathleene Joyce *photographer*

Capac
Wagner, Dorothy Marie *retired senior creative designer, artist*

Dearborn
Cape, James Odies E. *fashion designer*

Detroit
Abt, Jeffrey *art educator, art historian, artist, writer*
Day, Burnis C. *artist, educator*
DuMouchelle, Ernest J. *art appraiser*
DuMouchelle, Lawrence F. *art appraiser*
Johnson, Lester Larue, Jr. *artist, educator*
Sousanis, Nick *art web site designer*

Flint
Smith, Catherine Jean *artist, educator*

Grand Rapids
Bolt, Eunice Mildred DeVries *artist*

Hillsdale
Frudakis, Anthony Parker *sculptor, educator*

Holland
Van Noord, Diane C. *artist, educator*

Holly
Stolpin, William Roger *printmaker*

Howell
Watkins, Curtis WinthroP *artist*

Kalamazoo
Light, John Richard *sculptor*
Vander Weg, Phillip Dale *art educator, academic administrator, sculptor*

Mount Pleasant
Traines, Rose Wunderbaum *sculptor, educator*

Owosso
Tompkins, Alice Angeline *artist*

Petoskey
Switzer, Carolyn Joan *artist, educator*

Plymouth
Moore-Viculin, Charlotte Anne *artist, musician*

Port Huron
Rowark, Maureen *fine arts photographer*

Troy
Michaels, Glen *artist, sculptor*

Ypsilanti
Fairfield, Richard Thomas *art educator*

MINNESOTA

Duluth
Salminen, John Theodore *artist, educator*

Harmony
Webster, Jeffrey Leon *graphic designer*

Minneapolis
Gjertson, Stephen Arthur *artist, writer*
Hallman, Gary L. *photographer, educator*
Holen, Norman Dean *artist, educator*
Marling, Karal Ann *art history educator, social sciences educator, curator*
McRoberts, Sheryl A. *art educator*
Preuss, Roger Emil *artist*
Rose, Thomas Albert *artist, educator*
Rowan, Herman T. *art educator, artist*
Stone, Harold B. *artist, educator*

Moorhead
Boggs, David Bruce *art educator*

Park Rapids
Shilson, Wayne *artist, educator*

Robbinsdale
Harrison, Christopher Eugene *graphics designer, artist, consultant*

Saint Cloud
Specht-Jarvis, Roland Hubert *fine arts and humanities educator, dean*

Saint Paul
Burke, Mary Griggs (Mrs. Jackson Burke) *art collector*
Lasansky, Leonardo *artist, educator*
Tylevich, Alexander V. *sculptor, architect*

MISSISSIPPI

Clinton
Gore, Samuel Marshall *art educator, sculptor*

Columbus
Summer, Emily Eugenia *artist, art educator*

Hattiesburg
McRaney, Joan Katherine *artist*

Jackson
Stanton, Sylvia Doucet *artist, gallery owner*

Natchez
Golden, Rolland Harve *artist*

MISSOURI

Bourbon
Heitsch, Leona Mason *artist, writer*

Cleveland
Harper, Bill J. *floral designer, consultant, educator*

Columbia
Berry, William A. *artist, educator*
Stack, Frank Huntington *painter, retired art educator*

Hermann
Mahoney, Catherine Ann *artist, educator*

Jefferson City
Craver, Charles Henry *illustrator*

Kansas City
Clancy, Patrick *artist, educator*
Lee, Margaret Norma *artist*
Mast, Kande White *artist*
Schaffer, Sandra Sue *artist, educator*
Sipho, Ella P. *artist*

Platte City
Kalin, D. Jean (Dorothy Jean Kalin) *artist, educator*

Saint Louis
Buggs, Dwayne Andre *fine arts coordinator, music educator*
Colangelo, Carmon *artist, printmaker, educator*
Fondaw, Ronald Edward *artist, educator*
Hansman, Robert G. *artist, educator*
Metcalfe, Elizabeth Brokaw *art educator*
Zonia, Dhimitri *artist*

Springfield
Armstrong, Bill Howard *artist, educator*

NEBRASKA

Lincoln
Howlett, Ray *sculptor*

Seward
Wolfram, William Ray *artist, educator*

NEVADA

Las Vegas
Garn, Susan Lynn *art educator*
Goldblatt, Hal Michael *photographer*
Martinez, Adriana *photographer*

Reno
Goin, Peter Jackson *art educator*
Johnson, Jeffrey David *artist*

NEW HAMPSHIRE

Amherst
Johnson, Daryl Diane *painter*

Concord
Resnick, Kenneth *photography director*

Durham
McConnell, Michael *art educator*

Francestown
Milton, Peter Winslow *artist*

Hancock
Pollaro, Paul Philip *artist*

Hanover
Boghosian, Varujan Yegan *sculptor, educator*

Hillsboro
Nelson, Matthew *graphics designer*

Jaffrey
Press, Fred *artist*

Keene
Hoffman, Nancy M. *painter*

Newport
Gayvoronsky, Ludmila *artist, educator*

Portsmouth
Bourgeault, Ronald *art appraiser*

Stratham
Green, Catherine Cooper *artist*
Terry, Elizabeth Hays *artist, small business owner*

Wolfeboro
Bonin, Suzanne Jean *artist*

NEW JERSEY

Atlantic Highlands
Tice, George A(ndrew) *photographer*

Avon By The Sea
Mataranglo, Robert Patrick *artist, educator*

Belmar
Swett, Stephen Frederick, Jr. *artist, educator*

Bernardsville
Spofford, Sally (Sally Hyslop) *artist*

Blairstown
Bean, Bennett *artist*

Bridgewater
Glesmann, Sylvia-Maria *artist*
Patton, Diana Lee Wilkoc *artist, educator, illustrator*

Browns Mills
DeWitt, Edward Francis *artist*

Califon
Rosen, Carol Mendes *artist*

Camden
Tan, LiQin *artist, educator*

Cherry Hill
Toogood, James Stephen *artist, educator*

East Orange
Jones-Gregory, Patricia *art educator*

Egg Harbor Township
Schreiber, Eileen Sher *artist*

Englewood
Anuszkiewicz, Richard Joseph *artist*

Franklin Lakes
Baker, Cornelia Draves *artist*

Hackettstown
Lamour, Kenol *artist, educator*

Jersey City
Gurevich, Grigory *visual artist, educator, mime*
Riley, Cheryl *artist, educator*

Keasbey
Hari, Kenneth Stephen *painter, sculptor, writer*

Lakewood
Pilgram, Suzanne *artist, art educator*

Laurel Springs
Roma, Aida Clara *artist*

Maplewood
Woods, Krystyna Janina *artist, pharmacist*

Medford
Mayer, Joyce Harris *artist*

Metuchen
Arbeiter, Joan *artist, educator*

Montclair
Williamson, Philemona *artist*

Morris Plains
Ferris, Carlisle Keith *artist*

Morristown
Prystauk, Elissa *artist*

Oakland
Dressel, Margaret Jane *artist, educator*

Oradell
Struck, Norma Johansen *artist*

Paramus
Jacobs, Helen Nichols *artist*

Passaic
Sebek, Miklós László *sculptor, educator*

Penns Grove
Reilley, James Clark *artist, cartoonist, small business owner*

Phillipsburg
Richards, Jay Claude *photographer, publishing executive, historian*

Piscataway
Mizrahi, Isaac *fashion designer*
Rosalsky, Barbara Ellen *artist, community health nurse*

Princeton
Boretz, Naomi Messinger *artist, educator*
Bunnell, Peter Curtis *retired art educator, curator*
George, Thomas *artist*
Grabar, Oleg *retired art educator*
Mc Vicker, Charles Taggart *artist, educator*
Seawright, James L., Jr. *sculptor, educator*

Ridgefield Park
Heidel, Theresa Elizabeth *artist, educator*

Ringwood
Barbour, Arthur J. *artist*

Rutherford
Petrie, Ferdinand Ralph *illustrator, artist*

Salem
Carpenter, Margaret S. (Molly Carpenter) *artist*

South Bound Brook
Weir, Sonja Ann *artist*

Sparta
Rosser, Alvin Raymon *artist*

Stockton
Mahon, Robert *photographer*
Schoenherr, John (Carl) *artist, illustrator*

Summit
Rousseau, Irene Victoria *artist*

Tenafly
Koons, Irvin Louis *graphics designer, consultant, marketing professional*

Township Of Washington
Valenti, Thomas Peter *painter*

Trenton
Leipzig, Melvin *art educator*
Miller, Ruane *artist, educator*

Ventnor City
Robbins, Hulda Dornblatt *artist, printmaker*

Verona
Ayaso, Manuel *artist*

Wayne
Cetrulo, Jerry *artist, sculptor*
Garcia, Ofelia *art educator, administrator*

NEW MEXICO

Abiquiu
Botts, Gregory *artist*

Albuquerque
Baca, Vera Jennie Schulte *art educator*
Barry, Steve *sculptor, educator*
Coleman, Barbara McReynolds *artist*
Duke, Wanda K. *artist*
Multhaup, Merrel Keyes *artist*
Nelson, Mary Carroll *artist, writer*
Qualley, Charles Albert *art educator*
Sisson, Laurence P. *artist*
Sussman, Arthur H. *artist, painter*
Truby, Betsy Kirby *artist, illustrator, photographer*
Williams, Juanita Rosalie *artist*
Witkin, Joel-Peter *photographer, poet*

Farmington
Espinosa, Nancy Sweet *artist, anthropologist, curator*

Gallup
Cattaneo, Jacquelyn Annette Kammerer *artist, educator*

Hobbs
Garey, Patricia Martin *artist*

Las Cruces
Lopez, Carol Sue *artist*

Penasco
Marx, Nicki Diane *sculptor, painter, jeweler*

Portales
YSikes, Juanita Lou *art educator*

Roswell
Peterson, Dorothy Hawkins *artist, educator*
Wiggins, Kim Douglas *artist, appraiser, dealer*

Santa Fe
Evans, Dick *artist*
Harroun, Dorothy Sumner *artist*
Karp, Diane R. *art educator*
Kingsley, Judith *artist*
Micunis, Gordon Jules *set designer*
Peña, Amado Maurilio, Jr. *artist, curator, educator*
Roybal, James R. *artist*
Sloan, Jeanette Pasin *artist*
Wotherspoon, Mary Ruth *artist, writer*

Taos
Harmon, Barbara Sayre *artist*

Tijeras
Knutson, Mark Thomas *sculptor, architectural firm executive*

NEW YORK

Albany
Carson, JoAnne *artist, educator*

Alfred
Fei, Jun *art educator, graphics designer*
Higby, Wayne (Donald) *artist, educator*
Scheer, Joseph H. *artist, education educator*

Amenia
Hale, Nathan Cabot *sculptor, artist, poet*

Ancram
Blechman, R. O. *artist, filmmaker*

Ancramdale
Weinstein, Joyce *artist*

Annandale On Hudson
LÊ, An-My *photographer, educator*
Pfaff, Judy *artist*

Batavia
Schirm, David *art educator, artist*

Beacon
Siejka, George John *artist*

Bellerose
Stecher, Pauline *painter, educator*

Belmont
Rush, Deborah L. *art educator, artist*

Bronx
Adams, Alice *sculptor*
Bacarella, Flavia *artist, educator*
Behnken, William Joseph *artist, educator*
Juszczyk, James Joseph *artist*
Kassoy, Hortense (Honey Kassoy) *artist, sculptor, painter*
Kitt, Olga *artist*
Korman, Barbara *sculptor*

Spinka, William J. *art educator*

Brooklyn
Amendola, Sal John *artist, educator, writer*
Amrhein, Joe *artist*
Anderson, Lennart *artist*
Armstrong, L. C. *artist*
Bui, Phong *painter*
Campbell, Naomi *artist*
Costello, Jeffrey *apparel designer*
Dinnerstein, Harvey *artist*
Dinnerstein, Simon Abraham *artist, educator*
Fischer, R.M. *sculptor*
Germano, Thomas *art educator*
Gianlorenzi, Nona Elena *art dealer, painter*
Gisolfi, Diana (Pechukas) *art history educator*
Grado, Angelo John *artist*
Haber, Ira Joel *artist, educator*
Jones, Susan Emily *fashion educator, administrator, educator emeritus*
Kaprov, Susan L. *artist, photographer*
Lazansky, Edward *artist, art educator*
Lieber, Lola *artist*
Lindall, Terrance *artist*
Litto, Judith Cheryl *art educator*
Munk, Loren James *painter, writer, critic*
Nii, Yuko *artist*
Padovano, Anthony John *fine arts educator, artist*
Pearlstein, Seymour *artist*
Peker, Elya Abel *artist*
Piene, Chloe *artist, filmmaker*
Pitynski, Andrzej Piotr *sculptor*
Rauschenbusch, Stephanie *artist, educator, poet*
Schaefer, Marilyn Louise *artist, writer, educator*
Shaw, Kendall (George) *artist, educator*
Tagliapietra, Robert *apparel designer*
Zakanitch, Robert Rahway *artist*
Zinnes, Alice Fich *artist, educator*

Buffalo
Joseph, Ella *artist*
Martin, Margaret M. *artist, educator*
McKibbin, William Alex *artist*

Buskirk
Johanson, Patricia Maureen *artist, architect*

Campbell Hall
Greenly, Colin *artist*

Canaan
Walker, William Bond *painter, retired librarian*

Cazenovia
Wyckoff, Sylvia Spencer *art educator, artist*

Chester
Holzer-Gargiulo, Alexandra *graphics designer, writer*

Corning
Buechner, Thomas Scharman *artist, museum director, retired glass manufacturing company executive*

Cortlandt Manor
Rosenberg, Marilyn Rosenthal *artist, poet*

Croton On Hudson
Johann, Anne Dorothy *visual and graphic artist, painter*
Wandel, Sharon Lee *sculptor*

Cutchogue
Dank, Leonard Dewey *medical illustrator, audio-visual consultant*

Dix Hills
Fouladvand, Hengameh *artist*

Dobbs Ferry
Andreadis, Constantine *art educator, therapist*

East Hampton
Jaudon, Valerie *artist*
Scott, Rosa Mae *art educator, artist*

East Rockaway
Nodiff, Jack *artist, retired pharmacist*

East Setauket
Badalamenti, Fred Leopoldo *artist, educator*

Elmira
Gordon, June Sacavage *art educator*
Miran, Patricia Marie *art educator*

Fayetteville
Hadyk-Wepf, Sonia Margaret *artist, real estate manager*

Flushing
Carlson, Cynthia Joanne *artist, educator*
Chang, Jason *artist, educator*
Feng, Ying *painter, art educator*
Shen, Ronger *artist, educator*
Yeo, Kim Eng *artist*

Fly Creek
Dusenbery, Walter Condit *sculptor*

Forest Hills
Morgan, Jacqui *illustrator, painter, art educator, writer*

Franklin Square
Indiviglia, Salvatore Joseph *artist, retired military officer*

Freeport
Golici, Nicolae *sculptor*

Garden City
Russell, Stella Pandell *artist, author, educator*

Glenford
Rieder, Naomi *artist*

Great Neck
Seidler, Doris *artist*

Hartsdale
McMann, Edith Brozak (Edith Brozak) *performing and visual artist*

Herkimer
Durham, Jeanette Randall *artist, educator*

Hopewell Junction
Sellingsloh, Hulda Knipling *retired artist*

Hudson
Chambers, William McWillie *artist, art dealer*

Hudson Falls
Leary, Daniel *artist*

Ithaca
Garrison, Elizabeth Jane *artist*
Grippi, Salvatore William *artist*
McCue, Arthur Harry *artist, educator*
Mikus, Eleanore Ann *artist*
Poleskie, Stephen Francis *retired art educator, artist, writer, publisher*
Schuler, Mary Callaghan *artist, educational association administrator*

Jackson Heights
Dacey, Paul *artist*

Jamaica
Cade, Walter III *artist, actor, musician, vocalist*

Jamesport
Curlee, F. Lynn *illustrator*

Jefferson
Sullivan, Jim *artist*

Jeffersonville
Craft, Douglas Durwood *artist*
Harms, Elizabeth Louise *artist*

Johnson City
McMillen, Marieta Louise *art educator*

Katonah
Giobbi, Edward Giacchino *artist*

Lawrence
Henriquez, Allen *artist*

Long Island City
Leggett, Ann Vaughan *artist*
Madden, Steven *footwear designer*
Yiannes, (Iordanides) *sculptor, ceramist, educator*
Young, Aaron *conceptual artist*

Lynbrook
Cangemi, Lisa Lynne *art director, graphics designer*

Mahopac
Gonzalez-Tornero, Sergio *artist*

Manhasset
Foley, Cornelia MacIntyre *retired artist*
Stevens, Thelma Kaplan *artist, educator*

Marcellus
Baker, Bruce Roy *artist, illustrator*

Merrick
Cariola, Robert Joseph *artist*

Millbrook
Della-Volpe, Ralph Eugene *artist*

Mount Vernon
Sherrill, Milton Lewis *sculptor, painter*

New Hampton
Sinnard, Elaine Janice *painter, sculptor*

New Paltz
Azank, Roberto *artist*

New Rochelle
Metz, Roxie Anne *art educator*

New York
Abboud, Joseph M. *fashion designer*
Abish, Cecile *artist*
Adrian, Barbara (Mrs. Franklin C. Tramutola) *artist*
Aitken, Doug *artist*
Allard, Linda Marie *fashion designer*
Alpert, William Harold (Bill Alpert) *artist, painter*
Amelan, Bjorn G. *sculptor, set designer*
Amenoff, Gregory *artist, educator*
Anastasi, William Joseph *artist*
Anthony, William Graham *artist*
Antonakos, Stephen *sculptor*
Aptekar, Ken *painter*
Arcangel, Cory *artist, computer technician*
Armani, Giorgio *fashion designer*
Arnold, Ann *artist, illustrator*
Ashbaugh, Dennis *artist*
Bachner, Barbara LaVerdiere *artist*
Backstedt, Roseanne Joan *artist*
Badgley, Mark *fashion designer*
Baechler, Donald *painter*
Baldessari, John Anthony *artist*
Balilty, Oded *photographer*
Banerjee, (Bimal) *artist, educator*
Banker, Amy Beth Cohen *artist, writer, educator, curator, actress, poet*
Barnes, Gregg *costume designer*
Barnet, Will *artist, educator*
Barnett, Will *painter*
Bartlett, Jennifer Losch *artist*
Becker, Jonathan *photographer*
Ben-Haim, Zigi *artist*
Berlind, Robert Elliot *artist, educator*
Berman, Ariane R. *artist*
Bernheimer, G. Max *art appraiser*
Berthot, Jake *artist, educator*
Bethel, Denise *art appraiser*
Bialler, Nancy *art appraiser*
Biddle, Flora Miller *art patron, museum administrator*
Birmelin, Robert *artist*
Blair, Dike *sculptor, painter*
Bochner, Mel *artist*
Bonino, Fernanda *art dealer*
Bontecou, Lee *artist, sculptor*
Bourgeois, Louise *sculptor*
Boutis, Tom *artist, painter, printmaker*
Bradshaw, Dove *artist*
Brody-Lederman, Stephanie *artist*
Browne, Thom *apparel designer*
Bruder, Harold Jacob *artist, educator*
Brychtova, Jaroslava *sculptor*
Buist, Kathy *artist*
Bunts, Frank Emory *artist*
Burch, Tory *apparel designer*
Burckhardt, Tom *artist*
Butterly, Kathy *sculptor*
Byron, Eric Howard *sculptor, museum researcher and administrator*
Cajori, Charles Florian *artist, educator*
Campbell, Ronald Neil *retired graphics designer*
Canonero, Milena *costume designer*
Cappellazzo, Amy *art appraiser, writer*
Cardile, Paul Julius *fine arts dealer*
Carpenter, James *glass innovator*
Castoro, Rosemarie *sculptor*
Cattelan, Maurizio *artist*
Chamberlain, John Angus *sculptor*
Chermayeff, Ivan *graphics designer*
Chin, Mel *sculptor*
Chinn, Yuen Yuey *art educator, painter*
Christensen, Anne *art director*
Chwast, Seymour *graphic artist*
Clemente, Francesco *artist*
Close, Chuck (Charles Thomas Close) *artist*
Coe, Sue *artist, journalist*
Coffin, Anne Gagnebin *arts administrator, editor*
Cohen, Cora *artist*
Colburn, Martha *animator, filmmaker, artist*
Cole, Kenneth D. *apparel designer*
Cole, Willie *artist*
Colen, Dan *artist*
Colp, Norman Barry *artist, curator*
Conelli, Maria Ann *art educator, dean, architect*
Costa, Francisco *fashion designer*
Cowles, Charles *art dealer*
Cox, Peter *artist*
Crile, Susan *artist*
Crown, Roberta *artist, educator*
Cucullu, Santiago *artist*
Cunningham, Francis *artist*
Dana, F(rank) Mitchell *theatrical lighting designer*
Davidson, Nancy Brachman *artist, educator*
DeBellevue, Lucky *sculptor*
DeCarava, Roy R. *photographer, educator*
Deem, George *artist*
de la Renta, Oscar *fashion designer*
DeMonte, Claudia Ann *artist, educator*
Dennis, Donna Frances *sculptor, art educator*
Dennison, Lisa *auction house executive*
Di Meo, Dominick *artist, sculptor, painter*
Di Mitri, Piero *fashion designer*
Dobbs, John Barnes *artist, educator*
Donneson, Seena Sand *artist*
Doonan, Simon *window dresser, creative director*
Dowell, James Thomas *artist, filmmaker*
Drum, Sydney Maria *artist*
Dubrow, John *artist*
Duff, John Ewing *sculptor*
Dunkelman, Loretta *artist*
Dyyon, Mario (LeRoy Frazier) *artist*
Egielski, Richard *illustrator*
Eins, Stefan *artist, curator, science researcher, writer*
Eisenberg, Sonja Miriam *artist*
Enders, Elizabeth McGuire *artist*
Engelberg, Gail May *fine arts patron*
English, Mark *artist*
Fasnacht, Heide Ann *artist, educator*
Fausel, Alan *art appraiser*
Feigen, Richard L. *art dealer, collector, writer*
Feltus, Alan Evan *artist*
Fernández, Teresita *sculptor*
Feuerman, Carole A. *sculptor, artist*
Findlay, Michael Alistair *art dealer, poet*
Fischer, Carl *photographer, graphic designer, actor*
Fisher, Vernon *artist, educator*
Floret, Evelyn *sculptor*
Foulkes, Llyn *artist, educator*
Frankenthaler, Helen *artist*
Frehm, Lynne *painter*
Gagosian, Larry *art dealer*
Gallagher, Ellen *artist*
Gallo, David *scenic designer*
Gaon, Simon A. *artist, painter*
Garrett, Wendell *antiques appraiser, historian, editor*
Geissbuhler, Stephan *graphics designer*
Gerdts, William Henry *art history educator*
Gibson, Ralph H. (Ralph Holmes Gibson) *photographer*
Ginzel, Andrew H. *artist*
Glaser, Milton *graphics designer, illustrator*
Gold, Sharon Cecile *artist, educator*
Gonzalez-Falla, Sondra Gilman *art collector*
Gourevitch, Jacqueline *artist*
Greely, Hannah *artist*
Griefen, John Adams *artist, educator*
Grossman, Barbara *artist, educator*
Grossman, Nancy *artist*
Gruss, Shoshanna Lonstein *apparel designer*
Gutman, Robert William *retired art educator*
Guzman, Kathleen McFadden *antiques appraiser, auctioneer*
Haacke, Hans Christoph Carl *artist, educator*
Haas, Richard John *artist*
Haessle, Jean-Marie Georges *artist*
Halaby, Samia Asaad *painter, educator, writer*
Hamoy, Carol *artist*
Hardy, John *artist*
Harrison, Rachel *artist*
Healy, Julia Schmitt *artist, educator*
Heinemann, Peter *artist, educator*
Heintz, Florent M. *art appraiser*
Henselmann, Caspar Gustav Fidelis *sculptor*
Herman, Stan *fashion designer*
Hernandez, Lazaro *apparel designer*
Herrera, Arturo *artist*
Herrera, Carolina *fashion designer*
Herring, Oliver *artist*
Highstein, Jene Abel *sculptor*
Holstad, Christian *artist*
Horn, Roni *artist*
Hort, Michael *art collector*
Hort, Susan *art collector*
Horvat, Olga *artist*
Howard, Mildred *sculptor*
Hull, Cathy *artist, illustrator*
Incandela, Gerald Jean-Marie *artist*
Ireland, Patrick *artist*
Irwin, Robert Walter *artist*
Iturbide, Graciela *photographer*
Jackson, Henry Nathaniel *clothing designer*
Jacobs, Marc *fashion designer*
Jacquette, Yvonne Helene *artist*
Jenkins, Paul *artist*
Johnson, Betsey Lee *fashion designer*
Johnson, Harmer Frederik *art appraiser*
Joo, Michael *artist, educator*
Kahn, Wolf *artist*
Kaish, Luise Clayborn *sculptor, painter, educator*
Kaish, Morton *artist, educator*
Kalisher, Simpson *photographer*
Kamali, Norma *fashion designer*
Kan, Diana Artemis Mann Shu *painter, art educator, writer*
Karan, Donna (Donna Faske) *fashion designer*
Kelley, Mike *artist*
Kelly, Ellsworth *painter, sculptor*
Kemper, Randy *fashion designer*
Keno, Leigh R. *antiques dealer, appraiser*
Keno, Leslie B. *antiques dealer, appraiser*
Kepets, Hugh Michael *artist*
Kidd, Chip *book designer, writer*
Kim, Atta *photographer*
Kimmel Cohn, Roberta *art dealer, educator*
King, Marcia Gygli *artist*
Kinstler, Everett Raymond *artist*
Klausen, Raymond *theatre set and television production designer, sculptor*
Klein, Calvin Richard *fashion designer*
Klein, Cynthia *art appraiser*
Koons, Jeff *artist*
Koppelman, Chaim *artist, educator*
Koppelman, Dorothy Myers *artist, consultant*
Kors, Michael (Karl Anderson Jr.) *fashion designer*
Krakoff, Reed D. *apparel designer*
Kramarsky, Werner H. *art collector*
Krementz, Jill *photographer, author*
Kroell, Devi *accessories designer*
Kruger, Barbara *artist*
Kutosh, Sue *artist*
Lam, Derek *apparel designer*
Lamagna, Carlo M. *art educator*
Lane, Kenneth Jay *jewelry designer*
Lange, Liz *apparel designer, director*
Lanyon, Ellen *artist, educator*
Lash, Stephen Sycle *auction company executive*
Lasker, Jonathan Lewis *artist*
Lasker, Joseph L. *artist, illustrator*
Lauren, Ralph *fashion designer*
Leech, Katharine (Kitty Leech) *costume designer, educator*
Leiber, Gerson August *artist*
Leibovitz, Annie *photographer*
Lekberg, Barbara *sculptor*
Lerner, Sandra *artist*
Levine, David *artist*
Levine, Sherrie *conceptual artist*
Lim, Phillip *apparel designer*
Lipsky, Pat *artist*
Loengard, John Borg *photographer, editor*
Loring, John Robbins *artist, writer*
Lou, Liza *artist*
Lovell, Whitfield *artist*
Lowry, Nicholas D. *art appraiser*
Lutz, Tina *apparel designer*
Maione, Donna *fashion designer*
Malandrino, Catherine *apparel designer*
Mann, Frank Bert *artist, educator*
Mann, Katinka *artist*
Marcus, Gwen Ellen *sculptor*
Marden, Brice *artist*
Masnyj, Yuri *painter, sculptor*
Mason, Frank Herbert *artist, educator*
Maury, Richard *painter*
Mayer, Rosemary *artist*
McCollough, Jack *apparel designer*
McCredie, James Robert *fine arts educator*
McDarrah, Fred William *photographer, editor, writer*
McElhinney, James Lancel *artist, educator*
McEwen, Adam *artist*
Mc Gowin, William Edward *artist*
McHugh, Caril Eisenstein Dreyfuss *art dealer, art gallery director, consultant*
McKenzie, Mary Beth *artist*
McKinley-Haas, Mary *artist*
Mehretu, Julie *artist*
Meyer, Tobias *auction house executive*
Meyers, Dale (Mrs. Mario Cooper) *artist*
Miano, Louis Stephen *arts advisor*
Milder, Jay *artist*
Miller, Nicole Jacqueline *fashion designer*
Miller, Richard Kidwell *artist, actor, educator*
Milonas, Minos *artist*
Mir, Aleksandra *artist*
Mischka, James *fashion designer*
Miyake, Issey *fashion designer*
Morosan, Ronald *artist, educator*

Cannon Beach
Greaver, Harry *artist*

Corvallis
Levine, Shepard *painter, educator*

Medford
Schubert, Ruth Carol Hickok *artist, educator*

Newberg
Keith, Pauline Mary *artist, illustrator, writer*
Terry, Mark *art educator*

Newport
Gilhooly, David James III *artist*

Portland
Boutwell, Anne Dielschneider *artist, painter*
Ebert, Leslie *artist*
Farner, Darla A. *artist*
Lorenz, Nancy *artist*
Ramsby, Mark Delivan *lighting designer, consultant*
Shumway, Holly Ann *art educator*
Street, Terry M. *artist, educator*

Sutherlin
Gugel, Merilynn Sue *artist*

PENNSYLVANIA

Allentown
Kocsis, James Paul *artist*

Ardmore
Levy, Rochelle Feldman *artist*

Bethlehem
Donnangelo, David Michael *artist*

Camp Hill
Rowe, Michael Duane *artist*

Cochranville
Sazegar, Morteza *artist*

Easton
Bellissimo, Mary E. *art educator*

Elkins Park
Erlebacher, Martha Mayer *artist, educator*

Exton
Webber, Helen *artist*

Glen Mills
Turner, Janet Sullivan *painter, sculptor*

Glenshaw
Guentner, James Francis, Jr. *artist, educator*

Glenside
Medel, Rebecca Rosalie *artist*
Rawlins, W. Scott *art educator*

Harrisburg
Bottini, David William *artist, educator*

Haverford
Williams, William Earle *artist, educator, curator*

Huntingdon Valley
Edelman, Janice *artist, educator*

Immaculata
Grimes, Diane Spellman *art educator, department chairman, sculptor*

Jim Thorpe
Meneeley, Edward Sterling *artist*

Kimberton
Williams, Lawrence Soper, Jr. *photographer*

Kutztown
Ballas, Dean James *graphics designer, educator*

Lancaster
Kermes, Constantine John *artist, industrial designer*

Levittown
Marable, Simeon-David *artist*

Lumberville
Katsiff, Bruce *artist*

Marshalls Creek
Svoboda, Joanne Dzitko *artist, educator*

Media
Turner, Letitia Rhodes *artist*

Philadelphia
Camp, Donald Eugene *experimental photographer, educator*
Di Falco, Gerard A. *artist*
Goschke, Linda Fry *artist*
Granger, Randy William *art educator, consultant*
Lewis, E(arl) B(radley) *artist, illustrator*
Newman, Libby *painter, printmaker, curator*
Oh, Alice *art educator*
Paone, Peter *artist*
Spandorfer, Merle Sue *artist, educator, writer*
Tileston, Jackie *artist, educator*
Willet, E. Crosby (Everett Crosby Willet) *artist*
Yaros, Constance Greenberg *painter, sculptor*

Pittsburgh
Bates, Beverly Jo-Anne *artist, educator*
Burgess, David Lowry *artist*
Carr, Winifred Walker *artist, historian*
Herrington, Howard Ray *artist*
Jacoud, Adriana *art director*
Kamienska-Carter, Eva Hanna *designer, artist*
Levin, Golan *artist, composer, engineer*
Wilkins, David George *fine arts educator*

Pottstown
Mitchell, Eric Ehrman *photographer, stock broker*

Reading
Garrison, Matthew Moore *artist, educator*
Watcke, Thomas C. *art educator*

Richboro
Burtt, Larice Annadel Roseman *artist*

Sewickley
Milne, Christopher *photographer, journalist, educator*

Shavertown
Simon, Herbert Bernheimer *sculptor*

Solebury
Anthonisen, George Rioch *sculptor, artist*

State College
Parsonage, K. Susan *artist*

Swarthmore
Hungerford, Constance Cain *art educator*

Tower City
Adams, Susan L. *art educator*

University Park
Garoian, Charles Richard *artist, educator*

Upper Black Eddy
Wechsler, Gil *lighting designer*

Weatherly
Molnar, Michael J. *artist, educator*

Wellsboro
Driskell, Lucile G. *artist*

West Grove
Allman, Margo Hutz *sculptor, painter*

Wyncote
Davis, Robert, Jr. *art educator, artist*

RHODE ISLAND

Charlestown
Rohm, Robert Hermann *sculptor, educator*

Jamestown
Worden, Katharine Cole *sculptor*

Lincoln
Morrissey, Thomas F. *art educator*

Newport
Morris, Betty Ann *artist*

Providence
Feldman, Walter Sidney *artist, educator*
Fessler, Ann Helene *artist, photography educator*
Heyman, Lawrence Murray *printmaker, painter*
Howes, Lorraine de Wet *fashion designer, educator*
Lee, Eugene *theatrical set designer*
Townley, Hugh *sculptor, educator*

Wakefield
Leete, William White *retired artist*

SOUTH CAROLINA

Conway
Flaten, Arne R. *art educator*

Greenville
Dreskin, Jeanet Steckler *painter, medical artist, educator*

Greer
McKenzie, Kathleen Julianna *artist*

Inman
D'Ambrosio, Jody (Gigi) Lynn *art educator*

Irmo
Branham, Jennie Jones *artist*

Orangeburg
Hunter, Terry K. *artist, educator, director*
Staley, Alvin *artist, educator*

SOUTH DAKOTA

Brookings
Eischen, Michelle Robin *art educator*

Mission
MacKichan, Margaret Anna *artist, art educator*

TENNESSEE

Chattanooga
Martin, Chester Y. *sculptor, painter*
Mills, Olan, II, *photography company executive*

Cleveland
Kraus, Ruby Jean *art educator*

Crab Orchard
McBee, Christy Dawn *art educator, pre-school educator*

Johnson City
Lyle, Valarie Gay *art educator, artist*

Kingsport
Crockett, Frank McClung *retired arts and music educator*

Knoxville
Drinnon, Janis Bolton *artist, poet, volunteer*
Markert, Cynthia Allin *artist*

Memphis
McPherson, Larry Eugene *photographer, educator*

Murfreesboro
Reed, Angelica Denise *sculptor, writer, illustrator*

Nashville
Chandler, Nettie Johnson *artist*
Cundiff, Lou Willie *artist, sculptor, writer*

Oak Ridge
Regan-Stanton, Christa Maria *artist*

Soddy Daisy
Bice, Edna Jewel *artist, educator*

TEXAS

Arlington
Munoz, Celia Alvarez *artist*
Stripling, Betty Keith *artist, retired medical/surgical nurse*

Austin
Armstrong, Nak *jewelry designer*
Charles, Michael Ray *artist*
Fearing, William Kelly *art educator, artist*
Hatgil, Paul Peter *artist, sculptor, educator*
High, Timothy Griffin *artist, educator, curator, writer*
Lamis, Leroy *artist, retired art educator*
Sawyer, Margo Lucy *artist, educator*
Smith, Jeffrey Chipps *art educator*
van Otteren, Juliet *photographer*

College Station
Martin, Carol Jacquelyn *artist, educator*

Corpus Christi
McDowell, Barbara *artist*

Crosby
King, Vernon Dale *art educator*

Dallas
Dealey, Lynn Townsend *artist*
Lawrence, Annette *artist*
Norman, Bobby Don *artist, writer, research scientist*

Denton
Bertine, Dorothy Wilmuth *artist, educator, accountant, genealogist, poet, writer*

Dripping Springs
Daly, Stephen Jeffrey *artist, educator*

Edinburg
Manuella, Frank *art and design educator*

Fort Worth
Durham, Jo Ann Fanning *artist*

Houston
Blakemore, Amy *photographer*
Cyrus, Jamal D. *artist*
Evans, Kenya *artist*
Hamilton, Jacqueline *arts consultant*
Honeycutt, George Leonard *retired photographer*
Kagle, Joseph Louis, Jr. *artist, arts administrator, historian and educator*
Lanoue, Elaine Rose *visual artist, painter*
Long, Meredith J. *art dealer*
Montoya, Delilah Marie *artist, educator*
Orr, Carole *artist*
Pruitt, Robert A. *artist*
Reid, Katherine Louise *artist, educator, writer*
Shelley, Clyde Burton *artist*

Huntsville
Hanssen, Kristina Schirm *costume designer, educator*
Lea, Stanley E. *artist, educator*

Kerrville
Frudakis, Evangelos William *sculptor*

Lakehills
Spears, Diane Shields *retired art director, elementary school educator*

Lufkin
Mott, Earl *artist, poet, writer*

Mc Kinney
Harris, Andrew Bennett *artist, writer, producer*
Wright, Thomas Parker *artist*

Murchison
Taweel, Janice M. *artist, educator*

Port Aransas
Van Baalen, Donna Gale *artist, retired pharmacist*

Rosenberg
Haygood, Eithel Marinella *artist, educator*

San Angelo
Mobley, Nancy Elizabeth *artist, educator*

San Antonio
Rush, Kent Thomas *art educator, artist*

Stafford
Millis-Horton, Cynthia Marie *art educator*

Tomball
Frideres, Steffani Anne *art educator*

Tyler
Presley, Lucinda Hanks *art educator*

Wimberley
McCoy, John Denny *artist*

UTAH

Castle Valley
Zavada, Barbara Johanna *artist, educator*

Logan
Rasmuson, Brent J. *photographer, small business owner*

Provo
Fielding, Eric *set designer, educator*

Saint George
Martinez, Dennis J. *art educator*

Salt Lake City
Huelskamp, Willamarie Ann *artist*

Springville
Francis, Rell Gardner *artist, photographer, writer*

VERMONT

Barnard
Duckworth, Ruth *sculptor*

Bennington
Lum, Mary *artist, educator*

Brattleboro
Abrams, Jackie *artist, educator*

Burlington
Gabriel, Diane Augusta *artist, educator*

Charlotte
Robinson, Sally Winston *artist*

Dorset
Marron, Pamela Anne *artist*

East Montpelier
Christiansen, Andrew P. *website designer, historic archives digitilizer*

Enosburg Falls
Svendsen, Alf *artist, educator*

Middlebury
Bumbeck, David *artist, retired educator*

Newbury
McGarrell, James *artist, educator*

North Pomfret
Shepherd, Gaal *artist*

Reading
Dike, Rad (Edward Conrad Dike) *artist*

West Burke
Van Vliet, Claire *artist*

Weston
Kasnowski, Chester Nelson *artist, educator*

Williston
Essman, Robert Norvel *artist, graphics designer*

VIRGINIA

Alexandria
Kim, Sook Cha *artist*
Whitson, Elizabeth Temple *graphics designer*

Arlington
Dunlap, William *artist, educator, art critic, educator*

Blacksburg
Gablik, Suzi *art educator, writer*

Burgess
Krebs, Rockne *artist*

Charlottesville
Warren, Russ C. *artist, educator*
Weinberger, Adrienne *artist, art appraiser*

Clifton
Hennesy, Gerald Craft *artist*

Colonial Heights
Grizzard-Barham, Barbara Lee *artist*

Culpeper
Bahl-Moore, Elizabeth Ann *artist, educator*

Fairfax
Kendall Hull, Margarida *art educator, painter*

Fredericksburg
Gill, Milvi Kosenkranius *artist, photographer*
Schmutzhart, Berthold Josef *sculptor, educator*

Goochland
Parsons, Donna Lynn *artist*

Herndon
Nolan, Leslie Marian *artist*
Simanski, Claire Dvorak *art educator*

Independence
Craig, James Hicklin *fine arts consultant*

Ivy
Lord, Richard Dennis *photographer*

Leon
Han, Nong *artist, sculptor, painter*

Lynchburg
Hudson, Walter Tiree *artist*

Mc Lean
Safer, John *artist*
Youngs, William Ellis *photographer, electronics engineer*

Middleburg
vom Baur, Daphne de Blois *artist*

Newport News
Abbott, Beverly Stubblefield *artist*
Sheaks, Barclay *artist*

Norfolk
Isekeije, Solomon Rowland *artist, educator*
Nicholson, Myreen Moore *artist, researcher*

Petersburg
Abbott-Ryan, Pat *painter, writer*

Prospect
Shield, Julie Marie Karst *artist, educator*

Radford
Shell, Robert Edward Lee *photographer, writer*

Richmond
Freed, David Clark *artist*
Kevorkian, Richard *artist*
Savedge, Anne Creery *artist, educator*
Womack, Robert Robinson *artist*

Roanoke
Thomas, Radford *art educator, painter*

Springfield
Brown, Margaret Catherine *artist*

Stanardsville
Gladstone, Arthur M. *artist, writer, aerospace engineer*

Staunton
Jolloff, Nilda Elizabeth *artist, educator*

Swoope
Avery, Robert Newell *sculptor*

Vienna
Yamaguchi, Yuriko Fujita *artist*

Virginia Beach
Antol, Joseph J. *artist*
Lewis, Donald Sykes, Jr. *artist*

Weyers Cave
Bell, John Malcolm *art educator*

Williamsburg
Cohen, Lewis Carroll *sculptor, educator*
Coleman, Henry Edwin *artist, educator*
Lorenz, Hans Ernest *photographer*
Robinson, Jay (Thurston) *artist*

Winchester
Yancey, Cheryl Lynn *apparel designer, educator*

WASHINGTON

Anacortes
Mc Cracken, Philip Trafton *sculptor*

Bainbridge Island
Carlson, Robert Michael *artist*

Battle Ground
Hansen, James Lee *sculptor*

Bellingham
Feodorov, John *artist*

Brush Prairie
Zawodny, LaRae Jean *artist, secondary school educator*

Burton
Dyer, Carolyn Price *artist, writer*

Camano Island
Thayer, Thomas Manor, Jr. *artist*

Centralia
Gay, Larry Kenneth *artist, automotive executive, consultant*

Edmonds
Laico, Colette *artist*

Issaquah
Parker-Fairbanks, Dixie *artist*

Kent
Pierce, Danny Parcel *artist, educator*

Lake Forest Park
Angell, Tony *artist, writer*

Ocean Park
Lee, Martha *artist, writer*

Olympia
Haseltine, James Lewis *artist, consultant*
Landlett, Mary Willis *photographer*

Seattle
Berger, Paul Eric *artist, photographer*
Bigelow, Reba Seetin *artist*
De Alessi, Ross Alan *lighting designer*
Feldman, Roger Lawrence *artist, educator*
Gardiner, T(homas) Michael *artist*
Garvens, Ellen Jo *artist, educator*
Lundin, Norman Kent *artist, educator*
Reeves, Joan Hutchins *painter*
Spafford, Michael Charles *artist*
Stearns, Susan Tracey *lighting design company executive, lawyer*
Tanzi, Ronald Thomas *artist, educator*
Tift, Mary Louise *artist*

Silverdale
Shaw, Annita Louise *art educator*

Spokane
Mobley, Karen Ruth *art director*

Tacoma
Lent, Michael Stephen *artist, curator*

WEST VIRGINIA

Bakerton
Allen, Elizabeth Frater *artist*

Charleston
Larimer, Phyllis Miller *artist, art gallery director*

Harrisville
Harper, George Daniel *retired art educator*

Jane Lew
Turner, Linda Jeannette Chapman *artist, historian*

Shepherdstown
Summerford, Ben Long *retired artist, educator*

Wheeling
Phillis, Marilyn Hughey *artist*

WISCONSIN

Campbellsport
Klein, David P. *painter*

Hartland
Stamsta, Jean F. *artist*

Hollandale
Colescott, Warrington Wickham *artist, printmaker, educator*

Kenosha
Gustin, Brenda Sue *retired art educator, painter*

La Crosse
Clark, Malcolm Gene, Sr. *artist, consultant, historian, writer, conservator, researcher*

Madison
Conniff, Gregory *photographer*
Cooper, Peggy (Mary Margaret) *artist, educator, poet, composer, choreographer*

Mc Naughton
Bradshaw, Glenn Raymond *art educator*

Milwaukee
Farrell, Patrick *artist*
Hirsh, Annette Marie *artist*
Thrall, Arthur Alvin *artist, educator*

Mount Horeb
Becker, David *artist, retired educator*

New Richmond
Schwan, LeRoy Bernard *artist, retired art educator*

Oconomowoc
Conrader, Constance Ruth *artist, writer*

Oshkosh
Hu, Li *art educator*

Racine
Sahakian, Lillian Zarouhi *artist, designer*

Reedsburg
Mockler, Jolee Marie *art educator*

Wausau
Loftus, Stephen Edward *elementary art educator*

Whitefish Bay
Miotke, Anne Elizabeth *artist, educator*

Whitewater
Norgard, Karen-Sam *art educator*

WYOMING

Cheyenne
Moore, Mary French (Muffy Moore) *potter, advocate*

Cody
Jackson, Harry Andrew *artist*

Laramie
Arnold, Joseph Patterson *artist, small business owner*
Reif, David (Frank David Reif) *artist, educator*

CANADA

BRITISH COLUMBIA

Cowichan Station
Grauer, Sherrard *artist*

Salt Spring Island
Raginsky, Nina *artist*

Vancouver
Bonifacho, Bratsa *artist*

Victoria
Harvey, Donald *artist, educator*

MANITOBA

Winnipeg
Eyre, Ivan *artist*

NEWFOUNDLAND AND LABRADOR

Torbay
Dabinett, Diana Frances *artist*

NOVA SCOTIA

Bayfield
Blair, Rosemary Miles *retired art educator, environmentalist*

Halifax
Kulyk, Karen Gay *artist*

ONTARIO

Peterborough
Dumas, Michael Godfrey Joseph *artist*

Scarborough
Cetín, Anton *artist*

Toronto
Astman, Barbara Ann *artist, educator*
Bolley, Andrea *artist*
Elder, Richard Bruce *artist, writer*
Jaworska, Tamara *artist*
Kramer, Burton *graphic designer, educator*
Semak, Michael William *photographer, educator*
Tolmie, Kenneth Donald *artist, writer*

Waterloo
Urquhart, Tony *artist, educator*

Willowdale
Winter, Frederick Elliot *fine arts educator*

QUEBEC

Beaconsfield
Harder, Rolf Peter *graphic designer, painter*

Montreal
Charney, Melvin *artist, architect, educator*

SASKATCHEWAN

Saskatoon
Bornstein, Eli *artist, sculptor*

MEXICO

Mexico City
De La Riva, Myriam Ann *artist*

AUSTRALIA

Camberwell
Base, Graeme Rowland *illustrator, author*

Malanda
Cooper, William Thomas *natural history artist*

AUSTRIA

Vienna
Higgins, William Woods *painter, art educator*

ENGLAND

London
Auerbach, Frank *artist*
Bailey, Christopher *apparel designer*
Edwards, Sylvia Ann *artist*
Freud, Lucian Michael *painter*
Stella, Frank Philip *artist*

Richmond
Armfield, Diana Maxwell *artist, educator*

FRANCE

Arles
Clergue, Lucien Georges *photographer*

Malaucene Vaucluse
Langenkamp, Mary Alice (M.A. Langenkamp) *artist, educator*

Paris
Alaïa, Azzedine *fashion designer*
Bergé, Pierre *apparel design executive*
Cardin, Pierre *fashion designer*
Elbaz, Alber *apparel designer*
Gaultier, Jean-Paul *fashion designer*
Lagerfeld, Karl Otto *fashion designer*
Renouf, Edda *artist*
Ross, Charles *artist*
Saint Laurent, Yves (Henri Donat Mathieu) *couturier*

Saint Ceols
Saisselin, Remy Gilbert *fine arts educator*

GERMANY

Alstadt
Richter, Gerhard *artist*

Düsseldorf
Andre, Carl *sculptor*

Frankfurt
Ammann, Jean-Christophe *art director*

Koln
Lee, Catherine *sculptor, painter*

HONG KONG

Central
Bing, Xu *artist*

Cheung Sha Wan
Hilfiger, Tommy (Thomas Jacob Hilfiger) *apparel designer*

ISRAEL

Jerusalem
Menses, Jan *artist, draftsman*

ITALY

Florence
Cecil, Charles Harkless *artist, educator*
Giannini, Frida *apparel designer*

Milan
Cavalli, Roberto *fashion designer*
Dolce, Domenico *fashion designer*
Gabbana, Stefano *fashion designer*
Honegger, Federico *artist*
Prada, Miuccia Bianca *fashion designer*
Versace, Donatella *fashion designer*

Rome
Valentino, (Valentino Garavani) *fashion designer*

POLAND

Warsaw
Abakanowicz, Magdalena *artist, sculptor*

SPAIN

Seville
Sanchez, Leonedes Monarrize Worthington (His Royal Highness Duke de Leonedes of Spain Sicily Greece) *fashion designer*

SWEDEN

Bralanda
Emilson, Henry Bertil *artist*

TUNISIA

Carthage
Sehili, Mahmoud *artist*

ADDRESS UNPUBLISHED

Abbe, Elfriede Martha *sculptor, graphics designer*
Abbett, Robert Kennedy *artist, writer*
Abel, Barbara Ellen *photographer*
Abeles, Kim Victoria *artist*
Abeles, Sigmund M. *painter, sculptor, printmaker*
Adams, Kevin *lighting designer*
Aja-Herrera, Manuel Angel *art educator*
Aldredge, Theoni Vachliotis *costume designer*
Alexander, Marjorie Anne *artist, consultant*
Allen, Philip *artist*
Ancona, George Efrain *photographer, author*
Anderson, Dawolu Jabari *illustrator*
Anderson, Lisa D. *graphics designer, educator*
Andrade, Edna *artist, educator*
Andrews, Marion E. *artist, calligrapher*
Annus, John Augustus *artist*
Antezzo, Matthew J. *artist*
Antreasian, Garo Zareh *artist, lithographer, educator*
Arifi, Fatana Baktash *artist, educator*
Arndt, Dianne Joy *artist, photographer*
Arrott, Patricia Graham *artist, educator*
Arrowood, Deborah Messer *medical transcriptionist*
Asato, Evan Masami *artist, architect, designer*
Aschheim, Eve Michele *artist, educator*
Atkinson, Tracey Blake *artist, educator*
Baab-Hohman, Roberta (Robin) *artist, scriptwriter, state manager*
Bankston, Elaine *artist*
Barlow, Lou *painter*
Barlowe, Dorothea *art educator, illustrator*

Barnes, Robert Vincent *retired elementary and secondary school art educator*
Barrow, Thomas Francis *artist, educator*
Barth, Frances *artist*
Bartlett, John *fashion designer*
Basch, Richard Vennard *photographer, producer, writer, director*
Bateman, Robert McLellan *artist*
Battie, David Anthony *art appraiser*
Behr, Marion Ray *artist*
Beilman, Teresa Marie *artist, poet*
Bell, Larry Stuart *artist*
Bell-White, Patricia *photographer, artist, writer*
Benzle, Curtis Munhall *artist, educator*
Berger, Carl Brendt *art educator*
Berkowitz, Henry *artist*
Beswick, Kurt F. *artist, graphic designer*
Bierman, Sandra *artist*
Bingham, Marian *artist, printmaker*
Binkley, Timothy *computer graphics designer, educator*
Blackwell, Lois Moore *fashion designer, educator, visual artist*
Blair, Philippa Mary *artist, educator*
Blitt, Rita Lea *artist*
Bloom, Hyman (Chaim Melamed) *artist*
Bohrman, Catherine Leuchs *sculptor*
Boskovich, Nick F. *artist, art educator*
Bowen-Forbes, Jorge Courtney *artist, poet*
Brach, Paul Henry *artist*
Bradley, Slater *artist*
Broderick, James Allen *painter, art educator, etcher*
Brodzik, Lester Leonard *artist, retired occupational therapist*
Bronkar, Eunice Dunalee *artist, educator*
Brown, Alice Elste *artist*
Brown, Amy Christine *art educator*
Brown, Carol Rose *artist*
Burns, Toni Anthony *artist*
Burrows, Donald Albert *artist, painter, photographer, dean*
Burtley, Calvin *art director*
Butler, Leslie Ann *artist, writer, editor*
Butterfield, Deborah Kay *sculptor*
Byrd, Marc Robert *floral designer*
Cabot, Hugh III *painter, sculptor*
Calamar, Gloria *artist*
Camargo, Anthony *jewelry designer*
Campbell, Demarest Lindsay *artist, writer, interior designer*
Cardoso, Anthony Antonio *artist, educator*
Carlile, Janet Louise *artist, educator*
Carlyle, Bobbie Kristine *sculptor*
Carnwath, Squeak *artist, educator*
Carone, Nicolas *artist*
Carraher, Mary Lou Carter *art educator*
Carroll, Marie-Jean Greve *retired artist, educator*
Carter, Nanette Carolyn *artist*
Casanova, Aldo John *sculptor*
Caseiras, Jo Ann Striga *artist, educator*
Cassara, Frank *artist, educator, printmaker*
Celentano, Francis Michael *artist, educator*
Challis, Richard Bracebridge *art dealer, educator*
Chambers, Elenora Strasel *artist*
Chihuly, Dale Patrick *artist*
Chun, Jacqueline Clibbett *artist, educator*
Chung, Doo-ri *apparel designer*
Ciampaglio, Jeff William *sculptor*
Cicero, Carmen Louis *artist, educator*
Cleary, Manon Catherine *artist, retired educator*
Cobb, Virginia Horton *artist, educator*
Cobey, Virginia Branum *artist, actress, art collector*
Coheleach, Guy Joseph *artist*
Colette, S. *artist*
Colker, Edward *artist, educator*
Collins, Elsie Martha *apparel designer, costume designer*
Colton, Mindy Zimmerman *artist, art director, consultant*
Conroy, Tamara Boks *artist, retired special education educator*
Cooper, Elva June *artist*
Cooper, Michael Wayne *graphics designer*
Cooper, Rebecca *art dealer*
Corry, Aline Lahusen *art educator*
Coughlin, Jack *printmaker, sculptor, art educator*
Craik, Mary Bernice *artist, art gallery owner*
Cretara, Domenic Anthony *artist, educator*
Crocker, Suzanne *painter*
Crowley, Bob *scenic designer, costume designer, director*
Cumming, Robert Hugh *artist, photographer*
Cummings, David William *artist, retired educator*
Cunningham, Kathy *artist, educator*
Curnutte, Mary E. *artist*
Currie, Steven Ray *artist*
Curtis, Thomas Pelham, II, *artist, educator, small business owner*
Dahse, Kenneth William *photographer, writer, educator*
Dailey, Daniel Owen *artist, educator, product designer*
D'Alessio, Valaida Corrine *artist, consultant*
Daley, Sandra *retired artist, filmmaker, photographer*
Dallmann, Daniel F. *artist, educator*
Damsgaard, Patricia Rae *artist, educator*
Dangremond, David W. *art history educator*
Dani, *sculptor, painter*
Davidson, Jeannie *costume designer*
De Blasi, Tony (Anthony Armando De Blasi) *artist*
Dechar, Peter Henry *artist*
Deems, Sherran Ellen (Sherry) *artist, educator, editor*
DeGiulio, Lucas *artist*
De Jesus, Veronica *artist, educator*
Deutsch, Kathleen Pilarcik *artist*
DiBuono, Eileen Elizabeth *artist*
Di Giacomo, Fran *artist*
Di Suvero, Mark *sculptor*
Dluhos, Andre *artist*
Dogançay, Burhan C. *artist, photographer, sculptor*
Dominguez, Eddie *artist*
Dorn, Gordon Joseph *artist, educator*
Downes, Rackstraw *artist*
Doyle, Tom *sculptor*
Drasler, Gregory John *artist*
Drummond, Sally Hazelet *artist*
Dunlap, Loren Edward *painter, educator*
Duong, Anh *artist, actress*
Durham, Jimmie *artist, poet*
Eddy, Don *artist*
Edelson, Mary Beth *artist, educator*
Edmo, Jean Umiokalani *artist, poet*
Egas, Eric *artist*
Einsel, Naiad June *illustrator, graphics designer*
Elcik, Elizabeth Mabie *fashion illustrator*
Engelman, Rosalyn Ackerman *artist*
Engels, Beatrice Ann *artist, poet, retired real estate company executive*
Engle, Steve Eugene *artist*
Erenberg, Samuel Joseph *artist*
Ewald, Roberta Grant *artist, writer*
Ewing, Diane *medical transcriptionist*
Fabricatore, Carol Diane *artist, educator*
Farrar, Elaine Willardson *artist*
Fasman, Marjorie Lesser *artist, writer*
Faxon, Alicia Craig *art educator, department chairman*
Ferreira, Armando Thomas *sculptor, educator*
Fillmore, John Dillon *artist*
Finley, Harry *artist, museum director*
Fiore, Joseph Albert *artist*
Fish, Janet Isobel *artist*
Fisk, Scott *graphics designer, educator*
Fitzgerald, Joan V. *artist*
Flowers-Schoen, Marylu Utley *art educator*
Francis, Karen *painter, television producer, writer*
Frederick, Elizabeth Eleanor Tatum *watercolor artist, retired educator*
Freilicher, Jane *artist*
Freyermuth, Virginia Karen *art educator*
Friday, Katherine Orwoll *artist*
Friedlander, Lee N. *photographer*
Frost, Sue Emmons *art educator*
Frudakis, Zenos Antonios *sculptor, artist*
Fugate-Wilcox, Tery *artist*
Fulton, Amy Lou *artist, former realtor*
Furth, Karen J. *artist*
Gamache, Claudette Theresa *artist, nurse*
Gamble, Desirata *artist, poet*
Garber, Helen Kolikow *photographer, artist*
Garcia, Luis F. *photographer*
Gardner, Elizabeth Ann Hunt *artist, poet, genealogist*
Gechtoff, Sonia *artist*
Gerhardt, Carol *artist*
Gerstein, Mordicai *illustrator, writer*
Ghesquière, Nicolas *apparel designer*
Gibran, Kahlil *sculptor*
Gibson, Ben S. *art educator*
Givenchy, Hubert James Marcel Taffin de *fashion designer*
Glasson, Lloyd *sculptor, educator*
Glen, Niki *artist, sculptor*
Glover, David Lloyd *artist*
Golden, Hal *artist, consultant*
Golden, Judith Greene *artist, educator*
Goldin, Leon *artist*
Gonder, Daryl William *art and literature educator*
Goodnough, Robert Arthur *artist*
Gorbaty, Norman *graphics designer, artist*
Gordon, Lonny Joseph *artist, educator, dean*
Goreniuc, Mircea C. Paul *sculptor*
Goss, Jerome Eldon *craftsman, retired cardiologist*
Goulet, Lorrie *sculptor*
Graham, K(athleen) M. (K. M. Graham) *artist*
Grames-Lyra, Judith Ellen *artist, educator, municipal official*
Gray, Luke Alexander *artist*
Gredzens, Sandra May Pillsbury *art educator*
Greenberg, Albert *art director*
Greenwood, Jane *costume designer, educator*
Gruen, Shirley Schanen *artist*
Gussow, Sue Ferguson *artist, educator*
Hackleman, Phyllis Ann *artist, genealogist*
Hakeem, Muhammad Abdul *artist, educator*
Hall, Susan Laurel *artist, educator, writer*
Hammond, Harmony *artist, educator*
Hancock, Patricia Ann *artist*
Hand, Maryanne Kelly *artist, educator*
Hannaman, Alberta Anna *artist*
Hanson, Carey B. *costume designer, educator*
Hanson, Jo *artist, educator, writer*
Harley, Ruth *artist, educator*
Harman, Maryann Whittemore *artist, educator*
Hart, Marnie R. *art educator*
Harte, John Herman *artist*
Hasen, Burton Stanley *painter*
Hauer, Erwin Franz *sculptor, educator*
Hayes, David Vincent *sculptor*
Heath, Patti *art educator, musician*
Heller, Jules *artist, educator, writer*
Helpern, Joan (Joan Marshall) *fashion designer, entrepreneur*
Hendricks, James Powell *artist*
Henes, Donna *artist, writer*
Henrikson, Mary Ida *artist, educator*
Henry, Dale *artist*
Hepper, Carol *artist, educator*
Herley, Daveen Dorothy *artist, educator*
Herzberg, Thomas *artist, educator, illustrator*
Hewlett, Jamie *graphics designer, animator, cartoonist*
Hilton, Nicky (Nicholai Olivia Hilton) *apparel designer*
Hoffman, Franklin Thomas *artist, printmaker, retired army officer*
Hogle, Ann Meilstrup *painter, art educator*
Holden, Donald *artist, writer*
Hollerbach, Serge *artist*
Holtz, Laurence *artisan, photographer*
Holzer, Jenny *artist*
Horlick, Ruth *photographer*
Horton, Patricia Mathews *artist, violist and violinist*
Howard, David E. *artist*
Howe, William Hugh *artist*
Hsieh, Tsui-Hsia *artist, educator*
Huber, Colleen Adlene *artist*
Huete, Lala *costume designer*
Huffington, Anita *sculptor*
Hulburt, Lucille Hall *artist, educator*
Huo, Bonnie Kwan *artist*
Hurst, Heather *illustrator*
Jamison, Philip *artist*
Jansen, Angela Bing *artist, educator*
Jay, Norma Joyce *artist*
Jeswald, Joseph *artist*
Johnson, Anita Louise *artist, art director*
Johnson, Margaret Heller *artist, educator*
Johnston, Oliver Martin, Jr., (Ollie Johnston) *animator*
Jones, Carter Ruthven, Jr. *sculptor, educator*
Jones, Claire Burtchaell *artist, educator, writer*
Jones, John Harding *photographer*
Josephson, Kenneth Bradley *artist, retired educator*
Josten, Katherine A. *artist*
Judge, Mike *animator*
Judy, Cheryl D. *art educator, artist*
Jung, Kwan Yee *artist*
Kabakov, Ilya *artist*
Kahn, Susan *artist*
Kalina, Richard *artist*
Kane, Margaret Brassler *sculptor*
Karasik, Miriyam Beth *artist, writer*
Katz, Natasha *lighting designer*
Kaz, Nathaniel *sculptor*
Kearns, James Joseph *artist*
Kehew, George Mansir *artist*
Kehlmann, Robert *artist, critic*
Kennerly, David Hume *photographer, writer, producer*
Kenney, Estelle Koval *artist, educator*
Khvost-Vostrikova, Natalia S. *art educator, consultant*
Kiefer, Anselm Karl Albert *artist*
Killian, Lawrence Harding, II, (Larry H. Killian) *sculptor*
King, Joy Riemer *art educator, linguist*
King, William *sculptor*
Kipniss, Robert *artist*
Kipniss MacDonald, Betty Ann *artist, educator*
Kirsch, Roslyn Ruth *artist, educator, painter, printmaker*
Kleiman, Alan Boyd *artist*
Klein, Charlotte Feuerstein *art consultant*
Klein, Lynn Ellen *artist*
Klement, Vera *artist*
Knodt, Jean Amelia Sausele *artist, educator*
Knox, Simmie Lee *artist*
Koch, Virginia Greenleaf (Virginia M. Greenleaf) *painter*
Komar, Vitaly *artist*
Kooluris Dobbs, Linda Kia *artist, photographer*
Kord, Victor George *artist, educator*
Korot, Beryl *artist*
Kos, Paul *artist*
Kraft, Yvette *art educator*
Kriesberg, Irving *painter*
Krulik, Barbara S. *production manager, curator, art director, writer*
Kusama, Yayoi *sculptor, painter*
Kwong, Eva *artist, educator*
Kyle, Gene Magerl *merchandise presentation artist*
Labore, Brian Edward *computer animator, artist*
Ladewig Goodman, Jeanne Margaret *artist*
Landau, Emily Fisher *art collector, foundation administrator*
La Rocca, Isabella *artist, educator*
Lavezzi, John Charles *retired art history educator, archaeologist*
Lawrence, Mary Josephine (Josie Lawrence) *artist, retired library official*
Lawson, Trent *artist*
Lear, M. Kathleen *artist, music educator, small business owner*
Lee, Bovey *artist, educator*
Lee, Nelda S. *art appraiser, art dealer, film producer*
Leeds, Nancy Brecker *sculptor, lyricist*
Leiber, Judith Maria *designer, manufacturer*
Leipzig, Arthur *photographer, retired educator*
Lembark, Connie Wertheimer *art consultant*
LeRoy, G. Palmer *art dealer*
Leslie, Alfred *painter, filmmaker*
LeVasseur, Lee Allan *artist*
Levi, Josef Alan *artist*
Levin, Morton D(avid) *artist, printmaker, educator*
Levine, Jack *artist*
Lewie, Reva Goodwin *artist, educator*
Lewis, Sharyn Lee *sculptor*
Liden, Hanna *photographer*
Lieberman, Louis (Karl Lieberman) *artist*
Liebman, Sarah *artist, educator*
Li-lan, *artist*
Link, Phyllida Korman *artist, educator*
Littleton, Harvey Kline *artist*
Liu, Katherine Chang *artist, art educator*
Lobdell, Frank *artist*
Long, Roger Leonard *artist*
Lorelli, Elvira Mae *artist, art educator*
Lutes, Jim G. (James Lutes) *artist*
Macarol, Victor George *artist*
MacDevitt, Brian *lighting designer*
Magee, Alan *artist*
Mahmud, Shireen Dianne *photographer*
Mangold, Sylvia Plimack *artist*
Mann, Sally *photographer*
Marion, John Louis *former fine arts auctioneer and appraiser*
Marks, Roberta Barbara *artist, educator*
Marlowe, Willie *artist, fine arts educator*
Marsh, Merrilyn Delano *sculptor, artist, painter*
Martin, Noel *graphics designer, educator*
Mártonyi, Csaba Lászlo *retired ophthalmic photographer*
Martyl, (Mrs. Alexander Langsdorf Jr.) *artist*
Marvin, Laura Lynn *art educator*
Mason, Lois E. (J. Day Mason) *painter, poet, actress, educator*
Mathieu, Georges Victor Adolphe *artist*
Mayer, Susan Martin *art educator*
McCully, Emily Arnold *illustrator, writer*
McCurdy, Michael Charles *illustrator, author*
McFarlane, Seth *animator, director*
McKay, Renee *artist*
McKnight, Thomas Frederick *artist*
McMillen, Elizabeth Cashin *artist*
McPeters, Sharon Jenise *artist, writer*
McQuerry, Patricia Ann *painter, retired secondary school educator*
Menefee, Linnea-Norma *antique dealer*
Menna, Sári *artist, educator*
Middaugh, Robert Burton *artist*
Middleman, Raoul Fink *artist*
Millea, Thomas Francis *photographer*
Misrach, Richard Laurence *photographer*
Monheit, Molly Jane *artist*
Montgomery, Lani Lynn *art educator*
Moser, Barry *artist*
Murray, Robert Gray *sculptor*
Myers, Dorothy Roatz *artist*
Nagy, Elizabeth Garver *artist*
Nasseripour, Mohammad Michel *artist, architect*
Navab, Aphrodite Desiree *artist, educator, writer*
Neri, Manuel *sculptor, educator*
Neville, Elizabeth Egan *artist, educator*
Newman, Muriel Kallis Steinberg *art collector*
Newman, Stacey Clarfield *artist, curator*
Nichols, Iris Jean *retired illustrator*
Nix, Patricia *artist*
Nohr, Monica Carol *art educator, sculptor*
Noland, Kenneth Clifton *artist*
Novak, Barbara *art history educator*
Nuss, Joanne Ruth *artist*
O'Donnell, Kathleen C. *artist*
O'Gorman, James Francis *art educator, writer*
Okoshi-Mukai, Sumiye *artist*
Oldenburg, Claes Thure *artist*
Olkinetzky, Sam *artist, educator, retired museum director*
Ortman, George Earl *artist*
Pace, Stephen Shell *artist, educator*
Park, Maria *artist, educator*
Paul, Arthur *artist, illustrator, graphics designer, design consultant*
Paulsen, Brian Oliver *art educator, artist*
Payne, Barbara Ann *artist, educator*
Pearlstein, Philip *artist*
Peckham, Ellen *artist, poet*
Peters, Sammy *artist*
Petrulis, Alan Joseph *artist*
Pickford, Rollin, Jr. *artist*
Pierce, Hilda (Hilda Herta Harmel) *painter*
Pirkle, George Emory *photographer, instructional media producer*
Pope, Ingrid Bloomquist *sculptor, poet, painter*
Posner, Kenneth *lighting designer*
Post, Mike *lighting designer*
Pozzatti, Rudy Otto *artist*
Provensen, Alice *artist, writer*
Pullman, Jennifer King *art educator, artist*
Purcell, George Richard *artist*
Puryear, Martin *artist, educator*
Putman, Carol Jean *photographer, artist*
Qian, Zifen *artist, editor-in-chief*
Raciti, Cherie *artist*
Rand, Calvin Gordon *art educator, educational consultant*
Rankin, Scott David *artist, educator*
Readey, Marijo *artist, educator*
Reid, Geraldine Wold (Geraldine Reid Skjervold) *artist*
Reinoehl, Richard Louis *artist, scholar, martial artist*
Rendich, Ana *painter, collage artist*
Rendl-Marcus, Mildred *artist, economist*
Reynolds, Patricia Ellen *artist*
Reynolds, Robert *artist, educator*
Ricco, Donna *fashion designer*
Rickett, Carolyn Kaye Master *artist, small business owner*
Riffenburgh, Gerrye H. *artist, educator*
Rifka, Judy *artist, educator*
Rigg, Carol Margaret Elizabeth Ruth *retired art educator*
Ring, Nancy Gail *artist, writer, art educator*
Robbins, Christiane Patricia *media director, artist, designer, educator*
Roberts, Susan Sturgeon *art educator, writer*
Roberts, Suzanne Catherine *artist*
Robinson, Aminah Brenda Lynn *artist, illustrator*
Roche, Pauline Jennifer *artist*
Rock, Mary Ann *artist, educator*
Rockburne, Dorothea Grace *artist*
Roemer, Carol Kaluga *art educator*
Ronalter, Chelsea Maria *artist, graphic designer*
Rosenquist, James Albert *artist*
Rosenthal, Tony (Bernard) *sculptor*
Ross, John T. *artist, educator*
Roy, Rachel *fashion designer*
Rubello, David Jerome *artist*
Rubin, Sandra Mendelsohn *artist*
Rubinstein, Eva (Anna) *photographer*
Ruffo, Michael *painter*
Rush, Julia Ann Halloran (Mrs. Richard Henry Rush) *artist, writer*
Rushforth, Ann Fay *artist, educator*
Rushworth, Michele D. *artist*
Russell, Maryanne *photographer*
Safren, Cheryl *artist, art educator*
Saks, Judith-Ann *artist*
Salari Sander, Sherry *artist, sculptor*
San Miguel, Manuel *painter, historian, composer, poet*
Sass, Mary Martha *freelance writer, artist*
Savedra-Schroeder, Jeannine Evangeline *artist, educator*
Scharf, William *artist*
Schifano, Kath M. *artist*
Schiff, Molly Jeanette *artist, researcher*
Schley, Reeve III *artist*
Schmalz, Carl Nelson, Jr. *artist, educator, art appraiser, printmaker*

Schmit, Randall *painter*
Schmitz, Barbara *art preservationist*
Schulzke, Margot Seymour *artist, author, educator*
Schwab, Judith *artist, educator, sculptor*
Schwartz, Daniel Bennett *artist*
Schwartz, Lillian Feldman *artist, filmmaker, critic, nurse, writer*
Searles, Edna Lowe *artist, illustrator, composer, poet*
Seawell, Thomas Robert *artist, retired art educator*
Seddon, Priscilla Tingey *painter*
Sennema, David Carl *arts consultant*
Seymour, Claudia Hultgren *painter*
Sharp, Anne Catherine *artist, educator*
Shaughnessy, Marie Kaneko *artist*
Sheesley, Mary Frank *art educator*
Sheikh, Fazal *photographer, writer*
Sherbell-Na, Rhoda *artist, sculptor*
Sheridan, Sonia Landy *artist, retired educator*
Sherwood, Gloria N. *graphics designer, genealogist, small business owner*
Shikler, Aaron A. *artist*
Shinolt, Eileen Thelma *artist*
Shore, Stephen *photographer*
Shulman, Mildred *artist*
Sillman, Amy *painter, art educator*
Silverman, Burton Philip *artist*
Simons, Anneke Prins *artist, educator*
Sirna, Gail Carolyn *artist, educator, writer*
Sissman, Liron *artist, painter*
Sittig, James Christopher *art dealer, painter, sculptor, landscape artist, poet*
Smith, Alvy Ray *computer graphics designer*
Smith, Karen Ann *visual artist*
Smith, Leila Hentzen *artist*
Smith, Leonore Rae *artist*
Smith, Patricia Lynne *artist*
Smith, Rae *artist*
Sobell, Nina R. *artist*
Sokolow, Marvin Joel *antiques dealer, appraiser*
Solman, Joseph *artist*
Sorel, Edward *artist*
Sparrow, Alison Kidder *painter, sculptor*
Spence, Andrew *artist, painter*
Sperakis, Nicholas George *artist*
Stelluto, Sharon Renee *apparel designer, painter*
Stephen, Tse *artist, educator*
Stephenson, John Hughbanks *artist, retired art educator*
Stern, Marilyn *photographer, editor, writer*
Stevens, May *artist*
Stillman-Myers, Joyce L. *artist, educator, writer, illustrator, consultant*
Stingel, Rudolf *artist*
Stinsmuehlen-Amend, Susan *artist*
Stockar, Helena Marie Magdalena *artist*
Strider, Marjorie Virginia *artist, educator*
Strong, Karin Hjort *artist, educator*
Strong-Cuevas, Elizabeth *sculptor*
Stubbs, Lu *sculptor, educator*
Sui, Anna *fashion designer*
Sullivan, Mary Ann *artist*
Summers, Carol *artist*
Sunward, Justin Hugo *artist*
Sze, Sarah *sculptor*
Taddei, Lois Annette Magowan *artist, interior designer*
Tagliente, Josephine Marlene *artist*
Tallman, Ami Renee *artist*
Tansey, Mark *painter*
Taylor, Corinna Lorrainne *artist, small business owner*
Thomson, Caroline Helen *artist*
Tiravanija, Rirkrit *sculptor*
Torres, Rudy Arnold *artist*
Torrez, Michelle Marie *artist, educator*
Tovish, Harold *sculptor*
Tsai, Wen-Ying *sculptor, painter, engineer*
Turner, Florence Frances *ceramist*
Turney, Richard Kenneth *display designer, artist*
Turrell, James Archie *sculptor*
Tyler, Richard *fashion designer*
Ullberg, Kent Jean *sculptor*
Ulrich, Brian *photographer, educator*
Umlauf, Karl Allen *artist*
Unithan, Dolly *visual artist*
Valenti, Manuela Samantha *artist*
Van Bruggen, Coosje *artist, writer*
Vergano, Lynn (Marilynn Bette Vergano) *artist*
Vergara, Camilo José *photographer*
Versch, Esther Marie *artist*
Vespa, Ned Angelo *photographer*
Villoch, Kelly Carney *art director*
Volpe, Doris *artist*
von Furstenberg, Diane *fashion designer, writer, entrepreneur*
Voytek, Mary Sullivan *sculptor*
Vuitton, Henry-Louis *designer*
Wachtman, Jeanette Marie *art educator, artist, writer*
Walker, Bernice Baker *artist*
Walsh, Nan *artist, painter, sculptor, consultant*
Waltner, Beverly Ruland *artist*
Washington, James Winston, Jr. *artist, sculptor*
Waters, Jack *artist, filmmaker*
Watts, Ginny (Virginia C. Watts) *artist*
Weber, Idelle *artist, educator*
Webster, Larry Russell *artist*
Wegman, William George *artist*
Weisman, Gary *sculptor, educator*
Wells, Don *artist*
Wells, Lynton Alfred *artist*
Welz, Rebecca Beall *sculptor, educator*
Wentworth, Murray Jackson *artist, educator*
Wexler, Sandra M. *artist, medical illustrator*
White, Yonsenia S. *artist, educator*
Whitener, Carolyn Raye *artist*
Whitman, Kathy Velma Rose (Elk Woman Whitman) *artist, painter*
Wichman, Karen Lin *medical transcriptionist*
Willenbecher, John *artist*
Williams, Clara A. *sculptor*
Wilson, Jane *artist*
Winter, Leigh Ellen *artist, educator*
Wolpert Richard, Chava *artist*
Woodard, Catherine *arts patron*
Wookey, Sara Hastings *artist*
Worley, April Cole *artist, grant writer*
Wright, Joan L. *artist*
Wright, Virginia *art collector, curator*
Wurm, Jan *artist, educator*
Wylan, Barbara *artist*
Yampolsky, Phyllis *artist*
Zaleski, Jean *artist*
Zapf, Hermann *book and type designer*
Zeigler, George Gavin *painter, sculptor*
Zekman, Terri Margaret *graphic designer*
Zelinsky, Paul O. *illustrator, artist, writer*
Zivelonghi, Kurt Daniel *painter, computer graphics artist, designer*
Zoe, Rachel (Rachel Zoe Rosenzweig) *fashion stylist*
Zuber, Catherine *costume designer*

ASSOCIATIONS AND ORGANIZATIONS *See also* specific fields

UNITED STATES

ALABAMA

Alabaster
Harvey, James Mathews, Jr. *public relations administrator*

Birmingham
Carter, Frances Tunnell (Fran) *fraternal organization administrator*
Diasio, Ilse Wolfartsberger *volunteer*
Jones, William O. *not-for-profit fundraiser*

Selma
Calhoun-Bates, Carolyn E. *social services administrator*

Tuscaloosa
Jemison, Sandra J. *educational association administrator, educator*

ALASKA

Anchorage
Jones, Jewel *social services administrator*
Jones, Mark Logan *educational association executive, educator*
Ruedrich, Randy *political party official*
Williams, Deborah Lee *foundation administrator*

Juneau
Smith, Charles Anthony *foundation administrator, director*

Saint Marys
Alstrom-Beans, Gail *Native American tribal leader*

ARIZONA

Phoenix
King, Robert L. *foundation and former academic administrator*

Prescott
Garvey, Daniel Edward *foundation administrator, educator*

Scottsdale
Ferree, John Newton, Jr. *fundraising specialist, consultant*
Jacobson, Frank Joel *cultural organization administrator*
Mohraz, Judy Jolley *foundation administrator*
Wojcik, Martin Henry *not-for-profit executive*

Tubac
Chilcote, Samuel Day, Jr. *trade association administrator*

Tucson
Dale, Deborah *foundation executive*
Davenport, Sandra *cultural organization administrator*
Gonzales, Sarah *women's organization director*
Grand, Marcia *civic worker*
Hamner, Rome *social services administrator*
Harcleroad, Fred Farley *education administrator, consultant*
Healy, Stephanie Lemme *hospital organization administrator*
Jaramillo, Alba *community educator*
Mullen, Rod *nonprofit organization executive*
Orr, Ethan *non-profit organization executive*
Protas, Josh *non-profit organization director*
Riggs, Lew *foundation executive*
Tersigni, Jennifer M. *not-for-profit fundraiser*
Thorpe, Jason M. *non-profit organization director*
Tirrell, John Albert *organization executive, consultant*

ARKANSAS

Fayetteville
Malone, David Roy *retired educational association administrator, director*

Nashville
Martin, Marie Ann *art association administrator*

CALIFORNIA

Bakersfield
Huerta, Dolores Fernandez *labor union administrator*

Belvedere Tiburon
Collins, Dennis Arthur *retired foundation administrator*

Berkeley
Buell, Evangeline Canonizado *advocate*
Green, David *nonprofit organization administrator*
McLaughlin, Sylvia Cranmer *volunteer, environmentalist*
Myers, Miles Alvin *educational association administrator, researcher*

Beverly Hills
Ahmanson, Howard, Jr. *Philanthropist*
Ahmanson, Roberta *Philanthropist*
Schaff, Manya *foundation administrator*
Siciliano, Rocco Carmine *cultural institute executive*

Brea
Tamura, Cary Kaoru *consultant*

Burbank
Rawlinson, Joseph Eli *foundation administrator, lawyer*

Canoga Park
Lederer, Marion Irvine *cultural administrator*

Capistrano Beach
Dithridge, Elizabeth *civic worker*

Carmel
Bohannon-Kaplan, Margaret Anne *non-profit organization executive, lawyer*
Vardamis, Alex A. *foundation administrator, retired military officer*

Carmel Valley
Meckel, Peter Timothy *arts administrator, educator*

Citrus Heights
Osaki, Mark Stephen *foundation administrator, writer*

Claremont
Stokes, Anne Dorothy *retired educational association administrator*

Copperopolis
Whisnand, Rex James *association housing executive*

Culver City
Netzel, Paul Arthur *fundraising management executive, consultant*

Danville
Cross, Christopher T. *educational association administrator, consultant*

Davis
Maurer, Frank W, Jr. *land trust administrator*

Encino
Irmas, Audrey Menein *not-for-profit developer*
Pisano, A. Robert *former actors guild executive, former film company executive*

Fresno
Shmavonian, Gerald S. *political organization administrator*

Fullerton
Sadrudin, Moe *humanitarian organization executive*

Hercules
Tyson, Kathleen Hayhurst *educational association administrator*

Kentfield
Blum, Joan Kurley *not-for-profit fundraiser, marketing executive, consultant*

Lafayette
Edwards, Aura C. *political organization worker, volunteer*

Loma Linda
Pendergraft, Janice Gayle *volunteer*

Long Beach
Fischler, Sandy Lynn *charitable and informational organization executive*

Los Altos
Larson, Carol S. *foundation administrator, lawyer*
Wilbur, Colburn Sloan *foundation consultant, trustee, former executive*

Los Angeles
Alvarado, Pablo *day laborer organizer, immigrant rights activist*
Baer, Walter S. *think-tank executive*
Broad, Eli *foundation administrator, art collector*
Daly, Robert Anthony *international relief organization, former professional sports team and film company executive*
Erichsen, Peter Christian *foundation administrator*
Hernandez, Antonia *foundation administrator, lawyer*
Horowitz, David Charles *consumer advocate, radio and television commentator, newspaper columnist, director*
Im, Hyepin Christine *not-for-profit developer*
Lindley, F(rancis) Haynes, Jr. *foundation executive, lawyer*
Lizarraga, David C. *non-profit community development corporation administrator*
Mack, James Curtis, II, *cultural organization administrator*
Marrow, Deborah *foundation administrator*
Powell, James Lawrence *educational association administrator, museum director, geologist*
Prewitt, Jean *not-for-profit organization executive*
Racklin, Barbara Cohen *fundraising consultant*
Shakely, John Bower (Jack Shakely) *foundation executive*
Smith, Jean Webb (Mrs. William French Smith) *civic worker*
Wells, Bradley W. *foundation administrator*
Williams, James M. *foundation administrator*
Wlaschin, Ken *cultural organization administrator, writer*
Wood, James Nowell *foundation administrator, former museum director*

Los Gatos
Allan, Lionel M. *director for-profit and non-profit companies, educator*

Marina Del Rey
Heath, Berthann Jones *educational association administrator*

Menlo Park
Altman, Drew E. *foundation executive*
Collins, Nancy Whisnant *foundation administrator*
Pallotti, Marianne Marguerite *foundation administrator*
Smith, Marshall Savidge *foundation executive*

Mill Valley
Schreyer, Chara *foundation administrator, art collector*

Modesto
Barnes, William David *non-profit charities consultant, publisher*
Whiteside, Carol Gordon *foundation executive*

Monterey
Pinkham, Frederick Oliver *foundation executive, consultant*

Mountain View
Bills, Robert Howard *political party executive*

Novato
Peters, Thomas *foundation administrator*

Oakland
Hawkins, Robert B. *think-tank executive*
Lazar, John Edward *social services administrator, not-for-profit developer*
Macmeeken, John Peebles *foundation executive, educator*
Widener, Mary Lee *non-profit financial executive*

Oxnard
Tolmach, Jane Louise *community activist, municipal official*

Pacific Palisades
Caster, Jacqueline Jacobs *not-for-profit executive*
Hubbs, Donald Harvey *foundation executive*

Palm Springs
Ellsworth, Frank L. *not-for-profit executive*

Palmdale
Phillips, Ruthanne *special education administrator*

Palo Alto
Nichols, William Ford, Jr. *foundation, health science association administrator, educator*
Skoll, Jeffrey S. *philanthropist, former internet company executive*

Pasadena
Chen, Sandra Yi-Ting *political organization worker*
Staehle, Robert L. *foundation executive*

Placentia
Cash, Jeanie Maritta *educational association administrator*

Rancho Palos Verdes
Vanderlip, Elin Brekke *professional society administrator, volunteer*

Redwood City
Spangler, Nita Reifschneider *volunteer*

Riverside
Bosse, Mark Thomas *social services administrator*
Peterson, Arthur Laverne *foundation administrator*
Smith, Richard Charles *not-for-profit administrator, educator, consultant, advocate*

Sacramento
Hayward, Fredric Mark *social reformer*

San Andreas
Breed, Allen Forbes *social services administrator*

San Anselmo
Symington, Toby *foundation administrator*

San Diego
Ballinger, Charles Edwin *educational association administrator*
Grosser, T.J. *not-for-profit fundraiser*
Krejci, Robert Harry *not-for-profit developer, consultant*

Lane, Gloria Julian *foundation administrator*
McBrayer, Sandra L. *educational director, homeless outreach educator*
Roberts, James McGregor *retired trade association administrator*
Spira, Patricia Goodsitt *retired association executive*
Wallace, Candy *Culinary Association Administrator*

San Francisco
Barzelatto, Jose S. *social welfare organization executive*
Bereuter, Douglas Kent *foundation administrator, former congressman*
Bitterman, Mary Gayle Foley *foundation executive*
Canales, James Earl, Jr. *foundation president*
Eastham, Thomas *retired foundation administrator*
Egan, Patricia Jane *foundation administrator, retired director*
Fisher, Robert Morton *foundation and academic administrator*
Foulke, Laura Taylor *not-for-profit fundraiser*
Gibbs, Michael G. *not-for-profit fundraiser*
Giovinco, Joseph *non profit agency administrator, writer*
Goldman, Richard N. *foundation administrator*
Guttentag, Lucas *advocate, lawyer*
Kamm, John *non-profit organization administrator, human rights activist*
Masaoka, Jan *not-for-profit executive*
Mattern, Douglas James *think-tank executive*
Mitchell, Theodore Reed *educational association administrator, former academic administrator*
Osher, Bernard *philanthropist, former investment company executive*
Penhoet, Edward *foundation administrator, former biochemicals company executive, former dean*
Pipes, Sally C. *think-tank executive*
Pope, Carl *environmental organization administrator*
Tripp, Alan H. *educational association administrator, consultant*

San Pedro
Daniels, Kathleen Angela *educational association administrator*

Santa Barbara
McCoy, Lois Clark *retired social services administrator, retired county official, editor*
Obern, Vivian Marie *volunteer*
Rehm, Susan J. *social services professional*

Santa Clarita
Boyer, Carl III *not-for-profit developer, retired mayor, municipal official, secondary school educator*

Santa Monica
Foley, Jane Deborah *foundation executive*
Klowden, Michael Louis *think-tank executive*
Milken, Michael R. *think-tank executive, philanthropist*
Rich, Michael David *think-tank executive, lawyer*
Siart, William Eric Baxter *non-profit education organization administrator*
Thomson, James Alan *think-tank executive*

Stanford
Lyman, Richard Wall *foundation administrator, academic administrator, historian*
Shulman, Lee S. *educational association administrator*

Stinson Beach
Metz, Mary Seawell *retired foundation administrator, retired academic administrator*

Studio City
Frumkin, Simon *political organization worker, writer*

Sylmar
Froelich, Beverly Lorraine *foundation administrator*

Valencia
Anguiano, Lupe *advocate*

Woodside
Blum, Richard Hosmer Adams *foundation administrator, educator*

Yorba Linda
Stavropoulos, Rose Mary Grant *community activist, volunteer*

COLORADO

Aspen
Bucksbaum, Melva *foundation administrator*

Boulder
Hawkins, Brian Lee *educational association administrator*
Hayes, Richard Johnson *association executive, retired lawyer*
Heath, Josephine Ward *foundation administrator*
Hess, John Warren *professional society administrator*
Johnstone, Sally Mac *educational association administrator, psychology educator*

Broomfield
Flanders, Eleanor Carlson *community volunteer*

Canon City
Ward, Larry Thomas *social program administrator*

Centennial
Bryan, A(lonzo) J(ay) *retired service club official*
Fevurly, Keith Robert *educational administrator*
Lessey, Samuel Kenric, Jr. *foundation administrator*

Colorado Springs
Coppock, Richard Miles *retired not-for-profit administrator*
Hawley, Nanci Elizabeth *professional society administrator*
Killian, George Ernest *retired educational association administrator*
Miller, Zoya Dickins *civic worker, consultant*

Denver
Childears, Linda *foundation administrator*
Chu, Roderick Gong-Wah *educational association administrator*
Fujioka, Jo Ann Ota *educational association administrator, consultant*
Hogan, Curtis Jule *labor union administrator, industrial relations specialist, consultant*
Ibarra, Irene M. *foundation administrator*
Low, Merry Cook *civic worker*
McConnell, John *environmental activist, founder of Earth Day*
Waak, Patricia Ann *political organization administrator, environmental association executive*

Englewood
Gloss, Lawrence Robert *fundraising executive*
Keesling, Ruth Morris *foundation administrator*
Neiser, Brent Allen *foundation executive, public affairs and personal finance speaker, consultant*

Fort Collins
Eddy, Gladys Louise *retired educational administrator*

Greeley
Bond, Richard Randolph *foundation administrator*
Schrenk, Gary Dale *foundation executive*

Lakewood
Isely, Henry Philip *association and business executive, integrative engineer, writer, educator*

Littleton
Keogh, Heidi Helen Dake *advocate*

Loveland
Rodman, Alpine C. *arts and crafts company executive, photographer*

CONNECTICUT

Avon
Griggs, Julie Hinds *foundation administrator*

Branford
Resnick, Idrian Navarre *foundation administrator*

Danbury
Meyers, Abbey S. *foundation administrator*

Fairfield
Shelton, Carolyn Johnson *professional society administrator*

Falls Village
Toomey, Jeanne Elizabeth *animal activist*

Greenwich
Bjornson, Edith Cameron *foundation administrator, communications consultant*
Stauffer, Valerie Vilas *civic volunteer*

Groton
Kennedy, Evelyn Siefert *foundation executive, textiles executive*

Hartford
Apruzzese, Philip John *educational association administrator, educator*
Eshoo, Barbara Anne Rudolph *non-profit administrator*

New Britain
Stathos, Lifteria K. *retired educational association administrator*

New Haven
Anderson, Carl Albert *fraternal organization administrator, lawyer, dean*
Leo, Martha E. *advocate, counselor*
Singer, Jon Douglas *foundation administrator, writer*

Newington
Sumner, David George *trade association administrator*

Newtown
Forger, Robert Durkin *retired professional association administrator*

North Branford
Houghton, Alan Nourse *educational association administrator, consultant*
Logan, John Arthur, Jr. *retired foundation executive*

Riverside
Coulson, Robert *retired professional society administrator, arbitrator, writer*

Roxbury
Styron, Rose *human rights activist, poet, journalist*

South Windsor
Carman, Gary Olen *child welfare consultant*

Stamford
Peterson, Elizabeth Holly *art association administrator*
Stillings, Irene Ella Grace Cordiner *retired foundation executive*

Trumbull
Norcel, Jacqueline Joyce Casale *educational association administrator*

Waterbury
Harper, Barbara Clara *educational program administrator, counselor*
Ramirez, Sandra Ivelisse *case manager*

Westport
MacCormack, Charles Frederick *international relief organization executive*
Stolz, Alan Jay *youth camp executive*

Wilton
Kaskell, Peter Howard *professional society administrator, lawyer*

DELAWARE

Bethany Beach
Gale, Robert L. *retired educational association administrator, consultant*

Lewes
Spence, Sandra *retired trade association administrator*
Warden, Richard Dana *government labor union official*

Newark
Farstrup, Alan E. *educational association administrator*

Wilmington
Baxter, Beverley Veloris *economic association administrator, educator*
Emmert, Richard Eugene *retired industrial and professional association executive*

DISTRICT OF COLUMBIA

Washington
Able, Edward H. *association executive*
Arlook, Ira Arthur *advocate, communications executive*
Arnold, William Edwin *health advocate, consultant*
Aron, Nan *lawyer, association executive*
Aviv, Diana L. *public policy analyst, psychotherapist*
Babby, Ellen Reisman *educational association executive*
Ball, William Lockhart III *lobbyist, former civilian military employee*
Barreto, Hector V., Jr. *not-for-profit organization executive, former federal agency administrator*
Bartlett, Charles Leffingwell *foundation executive*
Baskerville, Lezli *educational association administrator*
Bass, Gary D. *advocate, director*
Bednash, Geraldine *educational association administrator*
Bell, Jerry Alan *science education association administrator*
Bender, David Ray *retired library association executive*
Benjamin, Ernst *educational association administrator*
Bernthal, Frederick Michael *research association executive*
Betancourt Lopez, Antonio L. *association executive*
Blair, Bruce G. *think-tank executive*
Boaz, David Douglas *foundation executive*
Boggs, George Robert *educational association administrator*
Bonosaro, Carol Alessandra *professional society and retired federal agency administrator*
Booker, Salih *human rights organization executive*
Borg, Joseph Philip *securities association administrator, lawyer*
Brobeck, Stephen James *consumer advocate*
Brosnan, Carol Raphael Sarah *retired art association administrator*
Burrus, William Henry *labor union administrator*
Calingaert, Michael *non-profit organization executive*
Callahan, Debra Jean *political organization worker*
Casserly, Michael David *educational association administrator*
Castagnetti, David A. *political strategist*
Cavaney, Red *trade association administrator*
Chan, Wing-Chi *cultural consultant and organization administrator, musicologist*
Cicerone, Ralph John *foundation administrator, research scientist*
Cino, Maria *political organization administrator, former federal agency administrator*
Clark, Jim *labor union president*
Coffey, Matthew B. *senior advisor to industry*
Cohen, Larry *labor union administrator*
Cohen, Michael *educational association administrator*
Cole, Lorraine *women's association executive*
Comstock, Amy L. *social services administrator*
Corts, Paul Richard *educational association and former federal agency administrator*
Craner, Lorne Whitney *not-for-profit institute executive, former federal agency administrator*
Cullman, Lewis B. *philanthropist*
Currie, Charles Leonard *educational association administrator*
Curris, Constantine William *educational association administrator*
Daly, Kenneth *business association executive*
Davidson, Dan Eugene *educational association administrator, director, language educator*
Davidson, Jo Ann *political organization executive, retired state legislator*
Deal, Timothy *association executive, former diplomat*
Dean, Howard Brush III *political organization administrator, former governor*
DeMuth, Christopher Clay *think-tank executive*
Derby, Susan Eileen *not-for-profit fundraiser*
DeWaal, Caroline Smith *education and advocacy organization executive, lawyer*
DiConti, Michael Andrew *not-for-profit executive*
Donahue, Thomas Reilly *trade union official*
Donohue, Thomas Joseph *business association administrator*
Dorn, Jennifer Lynn *professional association executive, former federal agency administrator*
Duggan, Juanita Donaghey *trade association administrator*
Duncan, Mike (Robert Michael) *political organization administrator, lawyer*
Dungy, Gwendolyn Jordan *educational association administrator*
Eaton, Judith Sheila *educational association administrator*
Edelman, Marian Wright *not-for-profit developer, lawyer*
Eisenberg, Pablo Samuel *non-profit organization executive*
Ekman, Richard H. *educational association administrator*
Elliott, Thomas Michael *retired association executive, educator, consultant*
Elmendorf, Steven A. *political strategist*
Emely, Mary Ann *association executive*
Ericsson, Sally Claire *not-for-profit consultant*
Evans, Donald Louis *think-tank executive, former secretary of commerce*
Evans, Joy *foundation administrator*
Everett, Ralph Bernard *think-tank executive*
Everson, Mark Whitty *international relief organization executive, former federal agency administrator*
Fernandez, (I)dalia P. *educational association administrator*
Finkle, Jeffrey Alan *professional association executive*
Flores, Antonio R. *educational association administrator*
Foreman, Carol Lee Tucker *consumer advocate*
Forkan, Patricia Ann *foundation executive*
Francois, Francis Bernard *retired professional society administrator, lawyer, transportation consultant*
Friedman, Alan Jacob *educational association administrator, former museum director*
Fritts, Edward O. *broadcasting association executive*
Fulton, Kenneth Ray *professional association administrator*
Gage, John *labor union administrator*
Gainsborough, Jenni *advocate*
Ganter, Susan Lynn *foundation administrator, retired mathematics professor*
Gardner, James Bailey *historical association administrator*
George, Warren S. *labor union administrator*
Gershman, Carl Samuel *foundation administrator*
Giblin, Vincent J. *labor union administrator*
Golodner, Jack *labor association official*
Gorham, William *organization executive*
Graham, John H., IV, *association executive*
Green, Madeleine F. *educational association administrator*
Griffenhagen, George Bernard *trade association executive*
Gunderson, Steven Craig *association executive, former congressman*
Hahn, Lorna *political organization executive, author*
Hamilton, Lee Herbert *educational association administrator, retired congressman*
Hamre, John J. *think-tank executive, former federal agency administrator*
Hansen, Charles Martin III *lobbyist*
Hansen, Joseph T. *labor union administrator*
Harman, Donna Akers *trade association administrator*
Height, Dorothy I. *former foundation administrator*
Heinz Kerry, Teresa (Maria Teresa Thierstein Simoes-Ferreira) *foundation administrator*
Henderson, Wade J. *civil rights advocate, law educator*
Hite, William P. *labor union administrator*
Hoffa, James Phillip *labor union administrator*
Hoffman, Ann Fleisher *labor lawyer, educator, consultant*
Huang, Margaret *human rights advocate*
Huband, Frank Louis *educational association administrator, electrical engineer, lawyer*
Hughes, Thomas Lowe *foundation executive*
Hunt, Wayne Robert, Sr. *non-profit organization executive*
Indyk, Martin S. *think-tank executive, former ambassador*
Insulza, José Miguel *international organization official, former Chilean government official*
Isaacs, Amy Fay *political organization executiv*
Isaacson, Walter Seff *think-tank executive, write*
Ishaq, Ashfaq *foundation administrator, economist, educator*
Jacobs, Madeleine *professional society administrator, writer*
Jacobson, Michael Faraday *consumer advocate, writer*
Janes, Jackson *research institute executive*
John, Christopher Charles *lobbyist, former congressman*
Johnson, Marlene M. *educational association administrator*

Jones, Diane Auer *government education association administrator*
Kamber, Victor Samuel *political consultant*
Katz, Irv *not-for-profit executive*
Keenan, Nancy *pro-choice association executive*
Keeny, Spurgeon Milton, Jr. *professional society administrator*
Kelley, Colleen M. *labor union administrator*
Knapp, Richard Maitland *association executive*
Kohr, Howard A. *lobbyist*
Kolb, Charles Chester *foundation administrator*
Kreig, Andrew Thomas *trade association executive*
Krueger, Keith Roger *educational association administrator*
LaHaye, Beverly *cultural organization administrator*
Langfeld, Patricia Ann *trade association administrator*
Law, Steven J. *business association and former federal agency administrator*
Leff, Deborah *foundation administrator*
Lendsey, Jacquelyn L. *foundation administrator*
Levin, George Martin *association and organization administrator, aeronautical engineer*
Levine, Felice J. *educational association administrator*
Levy, Jill Sondra *educational association administrator*
Lippincott, John *educational association administrator*
Lucas, C. Payne *development organization executive*
Lujan, Manuel, Jr. *think-tank executive, former secretary of the interior, retired congressman*
MacAlister, Rodney J. *President African Development Foundation*
Maddaloni, Martin J. *retired labor union administrator*
Magrath, C. Peter *educational association executive*
Marincola, Elizabeth Mark *nonprofit executive*
Martin, Jerry Lee *organization executive, educator*
Masters, Edward Eugene *association executive, former foreign service officer*
McCarron, Douglas J. *labor union administrator*
McConnell, Ted (Theodore) F. *not-for-profit fundraiser, director*
McCormick, Walter Bernard, Jr. *trade association administrator*
McCurdy, David Keith *trade association administrator, former congressman*
McElroy, Edward J. *labor union administrator*
McElveen-Hunter, Bonnie *international relief organization executive*
McEntee, Christine W. *architecture and former medical association administrator*
McEntee, Gerald W. *labor union administrator*
McGinnis, Patricia Gwaltney *non-profit organization executive*
McGuire, Jack (John F. McGuire) *international relief organization executive*
Mc Kay, Emily Gantz *civil rights and nonprofit professional*
McLaughlin, David *foundation administrator*
McNulty, Robert Holmes *non-profit executive*
McSweeny, Dorothy Pierce *art association administrator*
Mehlman, Bruce P. *trade association and formal federal agency administrator*
Meyers, Linda Dee *non-profit administrator, researcher*
Meyerson, Adam *foundation administrator*
Michelman, Kate *advocate*
Miller, Harris N. *educational association administrator*
Moore, Jacquelyn Cornelia *retired labor union administrator, editor*
Mueller, Sharon Lee (Sherry Mueller) *educational organization executive*
Murphy, Gerard Norris *trade association executive*
Murray, James Joseph III *association executive*
Nader, Ralph *advocate, lawyer, writer*
Narasaki, Karen Keiko *advocate, lawyer*
Natividad, Irene *women's rights advocate*
Nichols, Rob (Robert Stanley Nichols) *think-tank executive, former federal agency administrator*
Nicholson, Richard Selindh *educational association administrator*
Novelli, William Dominic *retirement association executive*
Oliphant, Martha Carmichael *civic worker*
Olson, Mark Walter *non-profit corporation administrator, former federal official*
O'Sullivan, Terence M. *labor union administrator*
Otremba, Geraldine Marie *congressional and international relations executive*
Pascual, Carlos E. *think-tank executive, former ambassador*
Pearson, Roger *organization executive*
Pelavin, Sol Herbert *research company executive*
Petito, Margaret L. *foundation president*
Plattner, Marc Florea *foundation administrator, editor*
Platts, Howard Gregory *cultural organization administrator, not-for-profit fundraiser, director*
Purohit, Rajeev *advocate, writer*
Radin, Alex *former association executive, consultant*
Rasmus, John Charles *trade association administrator, lawyer*
Reger, Lawrence Lee *trade association administrator*
Rehr, David K. *broadcast association executive*
Reinsch, William Alan *association executive, educator*
Renick, James Carmichael *educational association administrator, former academic administrator*
Retzer, Michael L. *political association executive*
Rich, Dorothy Kovitz *educational association administrator, writer*
Richardson, Ann Bishop *foundation executive, lawyer*
Riehle, B. Hudson *trade association executive*
Roberts, Gregory *educational association administrator*
Robinson, Sharon Porter *educational association administrator*
Rodgers, Clifton Eugene, Jr. *trade association administrator, lobbyist*
Roemer, Timothy John *think-tank executive, former congressman*
Ross, Donald K. *lobbyist, environmental organization administrator, lawyer*
Rother, John *association executive, lawyer*
Rothkopf, Arthur J. *association executive*
Ruskin, Robert Sterling *educational association administrator*
Russell, William Joseph *educational association administrator*
Saladini, Robert *educational association administrator*
Salyer, Stephen Lee *educational program administrator*
Sandler, Bernice Resnick *women's rights specialist*
Santora, Kathleen Curry *lobbyist, lawyer*
Satloff, Robert B. *think-tank executive*
Saunders, Harold Henry *foundation administrator*
Scanlon, Terrence Maurice *foundation administrator*
Schlickeisen, Rodger Oscar *non-profit environmental organization executive*
Schneider, Carol Geary *educational association administrator*
Schroeder, Patricia Scott *trade association administrator, former congresswoman*
Selig, William Paul *advocate, cultural organization administrator*
Shelton, Hilary O. *civil rights organization administration*
Shore, Bill *nonprofit organization executive*
Shulenburger, David Edwin *educational association administrator, economics educator, former academic administrator*
Sibolski, John Alfred, Jr. *educational association executive*
Smith, Jessie P. Dowling *retired social services administrator*
Smith, William S., Jr. *education association administrator*
Snyder, John Michael *lobbyist, public relations executive*
Solomon, Richard Harvey *think-tank executive*
Splete, Allen Peterjohn *educational association administrator, educator*
Stern, Andrew L. (Andy Stern) *labor union administrator*
Stewart, Debra Wehrle *educational association administrator, political science professor*
Stich, Roberta Lynn *not-for-profit fundraiser, social worker*
Stockman, Jennifer Blei *political organization administrator*
Stottlemyer, Todd A. *business association executive*
Sullivan, Jerome H. *educational association administrator*
Sullivan, John David *business association executive*
Sullivan, Michael J. *labor union administrator*
Sweeney, Dawn M. *trade association administrator*
Sweeney, John Joseph *labor union administrator*
Talbott, Strobe *think-tank executive*
Tauzin, Billy, II, (Wilbert Joseph Tauzin II) *trade association executive, former congressman*
Taylor, John E. *foundation administrator, lawyer*
Tedeschi, George *labor union administrator*
Teich, Albert Harris *professional society administrator*
Tharpe, Don I. *foundation administrator*
Theodore, Eustace D. *educational association administrator, consultant*
Tobias, Robert Max *labor leader, lawyer*
Tonkin, Leo Sampson *educational association administrator*
Trumka, Richard Louis *labor union administrator*
Utley, Jon Basil *think-tank executive, journalist*
Van Roekel, Dennis *educational association administrator*
Walda, John D. *educational association administrator, lawyer*
Walker, Edward S., Jr. *think-tank executive, former ambassador*
Ward, David *educational association administrator, former academic administrator*
Warren, David Liles *educational association administrator*
Weaver, Reg(inald) *educational association administrator*
Wertheimer, Fredric Michael *public policy advocate*
Weyrich, Paul Michael *think-tank executive*
White, Robert Edward *think-tank executive*
Wilhelm, John W. *labor union administrator*
Wilhoit, Gene *educational association administrator*
Williams, Eddie Nathan *retired think-tank executive*
Williams, James A. *labor union administrator*
Wilson, Charles Nesbitt *lobbyist, former congressman*
Wilson, John I. *educational association administrator*
Wirth, Timothy Endicott *foundation administrator, retired senator*
Wiseman, Laurence Donald *foundation executive*
Wolf, Craig (M. Craig Wolf) *trade association administrator*
Wolfe, Leslie R. *think-tank executive*
Yanikoski, Richard Alan *educational association and academic administrator*
Yost, Paul Alexander, Jr. *foundation executive, retired military officer*
Young, William H. *labor union administrator*

FLORIDA

Aventura
Flood, Henry *non-profit organization executive*

Boca Raton
Hayman, Harry *professional society administrator, electrical engineer*
Jessup, Jan Amis *arts volunteer, writer*
Leary, William James *educational association administrator*

Coconut Creek
Kaufmann, Vicki Marie *social services administrator*

Coral Gables
Landon, Robert Kirkwood *volunteer*

Coral Springs
Autry, Herman Allen, Sr. *lobbyist, writer, music executive*
Burg, Ralph *art association executive*

Delray Beach
Stewart, Patricia Carry *foundation administrator*

Estero
Brown, William Robert *trade association administrator, consultant*

Fort Lauderdale
Crawford, Claire Cressman *volunteer, educator*
Hills, John Merrill *educational association administrator, consultant, public relations executive, researcher*

Fort Pierce
Weingart, S. Len *foundation administrator*

Gainesville
Gets, Lispbeth Ella *retired educational administrator*

Hillsboro Beach
Donoho, Tim Mark *not-for-profit executive*

Holmes Beach
Dunne, Nancy Anne *retired social services administrator*

Jacksonville
Blount, Yolanda Denise *social services administrator, psychologist*

Lady Lake
Langevin, Thomas Harvey *retired educational association administrator, consultant*

Lake Wales
Echols, Verna K. *volunteer*

Lake Worth
Goldstein, Jerome Charles *retired professional society administrator, otolaryngologist, surgeon*
Jacobs, Roxanne *development director*

Lakeland
Ayaz, Sandra M. *educational association administrator*

Lauderdale By The Sea
Wynne, Brian James *retired professional society administrator*

Miami
Cooper, Johnnie Edward, Jr. *advocate*
Ibarguen, Alberto *foundation administrator, former newspaper executive*
Lynch, Catherine Gores *social services administrator*

Naples
Monaghan, Thomas Stephen *philanthropist*
Rowe, Herbert Joseph *retired trade association executive*

Okeechobee
Bishop, Sid Glenwood *union official*

Orlando
Murrah, Ann Ralls Freeman *historical association executive*

Palm Beach
Elson, Suzanne Goodman *social services administrator*
Floeckher, Louise Byrne Weldon *volunteer*
Hope, Margaret Lauten *retired civic worker*
Levine, Audrey Pearlstein *foundation administrator*

Palm Beach Gardens
Falk, Bernard Henry *trade association executive*

Palm Coast
Boyer, Kaye Kittle *association management executive*
Cook, Gloria Houston *civic leader*

Pembroke Pines
Maynard, Shirley *educational association administrator*

Ponte Vedra Beach
Slayton, Gus *foundation administrator*
Watson, John Lawrence III *former trade association executive*

Port Orange
Collyer, Robert B. *retired trade association administrator*

Saint Petersburg
Allshouse, Merle Frederick *educational organization administrator*

Sanibel
Ball, Armand Baer *former association executive, consultant*

Sarasota
Boersma, Lawrence Allan (Larry Allan) *animal welfare administrator, photographer*
Culkin, Charles Walker, Jr. *retired trade association administrator*
Field, Suellen R. *not-for-profit developer*

Satellite Beach
Newbold-Coco, Rain L. *social services administrator*

Tallahassee
Humphrey, Louise Ireland *civic worker, equestrienne*
Yecke, Cheri Pierson *educational researcher, administrator, policymaker, writer*

Tampa
Schumacher, Margaret Lynn *not-for-profit fundraiser, director*

Vero Beach
McNamara, Francis Joseph, Jr. *retired foundation executive, lawyer*

GEORGIA

Athens
Algeo, John Thomas *association executive, retired educator*

Atlanta
Anthony, Barbara Cox *foundation administrator*
Bankoff, Joseph R. *art association administrator*
Copenhaver, John Barns *not-for-profit executive, lawyer*
Dotson, Albert *not-for-profit fundraiser*
Finley, Michael Valton *foundation executive*
Hopping, Janet Melinda *educational association administrator*
Hough, Leslie Seldon *educational association administrator*
Lieberman, Laura Crowell *arts administrator, artist, critic*
McTier, Charles Harvey *foundation administrator*
Spillett, Roxanne *social services administrator*
Steele, Charles, Jr. *civil rights association executive, former state legislator*
Tillman, Mary Norman *urban affairs consultant*
Weatherly, Alvis Morrison, Jr. *retired association developer*
Wylly, Barbara Bentley *volunteer*

Decatur
Grace, George H. *not-for-profit fundraiser*
Wheelan, Belle S. *educational association administrator*

Fayetteville
De Revere, David Wilsen *retired professional society administrator*

Marietta
Kelly, William Watkins *educational association executive*

Peachtree City
Nix, Kemie Richards *educational association administrator, editor*

Roswell
Polatty, Rose Jackson *civic worker*

Saint Simons Island
Bell, Ronald Mack *university foundation administrator, consultant*

HAWAII

Honolulu
Hack, Randolph C. *advocate, educator, counselor*
Morrison, Charles Edward *think-tank executive*
Ramler, Siegfried *foundation administrator, researcher*
Robinson, Robert Blacque *foundation administrator*
White, Emmet, Jr. *retirement community administrator*

Kailua Kona
Iolana, Patricia Elvira *foundation administrator, consultant*

Volcano
Nicholson, Marilyn Lee *arts administrator*

IDAHO

Moscow
Fiske, Janet Murray *volunteer, elementary school educator, researcher*

ILLINOIS

Belvidere
Luhman, William Simon *community development administrator*

Chicago
Benedict, Kennette Mari *foundation executive, researcher*

Bourdon, Cathleen Jane *professional society administrator*
Brown, Elizabeth McCarthy *social services administrator*
Byther-Smith, Ida W. *social services administrator*
Cassens Weiss, Debra Sue *professional association administrator, publishing executive*
Chacko, Samuel *association official*
Craine, Thomas Knowlton *not-for-profit developer*
Crow, Steven D. *educational association administrator*
Davis, Mary Ellen K. *educational association administrator*
Dolan, Thomas Christopher *professional society administrator*
Fanton, Jonathan Foster *foundation administrator*
Frey, James Harrison *fundraising professional*
Gary, Warlene D. *educational association administrator*
Heineman, Natalie (Mrs. Ben W. Heineman) *civic worker*
Hodge, Linda M. *former educational association administrator*
Jackson, Jesse Louis *political organization worker, clergyman*
Jacoby Hurd, Jennifer *foundation administrator*
Jacoby Hurd, Jennifer Beth *not-for-profit executive*
Johnson, Gary Thomas *cultural organization administrator*
Jones, Mary Laura *not-for-profit developer*
Keenan, Barbara Byrd *professional society administrator*
Kelly, Jerry Bob *social services administrator*
Knapp, Paul Raymond *think-tank executive*
Kolata, David *advocate*
Lies, Valerie Sharp *foundation administrator*
Lurie, Ann LaSalle *foundation administrator*
MacDougal, Gary Edward *corporate board member, foundation trustee*
Maehr, Kate *social services organization executive*
Minow, Josephine Baskin *civic volunteer*
Ochoa, Juan A. *not-for-profit business association executive*
Olsen, Rex Norman *trade association executive*
Parker, Bonita M. *civil rights organization executive*
Richman, Harold Alan *social welfare policy educator*
Saylors, Charles J. *educational association administrator, construction executive*
Schiele, Michele M. *not-for-profit fundraiser, medical association administrator*
Serrano, Justin Forbes *education executive*
Shanahan, Betty *professional society administrator*
Sigmon, Joyce Elizabeth *professional society administrator*
Simmons, Adele Smith *foundation executive, former educator*
Strauss, Deborah *foundation administrator*
Tarlov, Alvin Richard *foundation administrator, physician, educator*
Weinstein, David M. *not-for-profit organization executive*
Wilson, Cleo Francine *foundation administrator*

Clarendon Hills
Choice, Priscilla Kathryn Means (Penny) *retired educational association administrator*

Crystal Lake
Chamberlain, Charles James *railroad labor union executive*

Des Plaines
Sampson, David Allan *insurance association executive, former federal agency administrator*

Evanston
Arrington, Michael Browne *foundation administrator*
Gordon, Julie Peyton *foundation administrator*
Lewis, Charles A. *foundation administrator*
Rielly, John Edward *educational association administrator*
Thrash, Patricia Ann *retired educational association administrator*

Galena
Sipiera, Paul P., Jr. *foundation administrator, retired geology and astronomy professor*

Hazel Crest
Freed, Melvyn Norris *retired educational association administrator, writer*

Lake Barrington
Worrell, Sharyn Dianne Kelley *volunteer, retired flight attendant*

Lake Forest
Morell, William Nelson, Jr. *retired foreign trade association executive, government agency administrator*

Oak Brook
John, Richard C. *enterprise development organization executive*

Oak Park
Greer, Julianna Patterson *not-for-profit administrator*

Ottawa
Thornton, Edmund B. *philanthropist*

Park Ridge
Pannke-Smith, Peggy *regional vice chairperson*

Plainfield
D'Arcy, Margaret Jeanette *volunteer*

Rock Island
Rafferty, Genevieve Kennedy *social service agency administrator*

Rockford
Egan, Terrence *foundation administrator*
King-Sturdivant, Constance Maria *social services administrator*

Rosemont
Good, William Allen *professional society executive*

Schaumburg
Little, Bruce Washington *professional society administrator*
Tompson, Marian Leonard *professional society administrator*

Skokie
Gleason, John Patrick, Jr. *trade association executive*
Polus Gerstner, Lillian *educational association administrator, director*

Springfield
Beard, Rick *cultural organization administrator*
Reed, James Walter, Jr. *educational association administrator*
Stremsterfer, John Gary *foundation administrator, consultant*

Sycamore
Stone, Van Courtright *not-for-profit developer*

Urbana
Williamson, Kent D. *educational association administrator*

Waukegan
Drapalik, Betty R. *volunteer, artist, educator*

Wilmette
Brink, Marion Francis *trade association administrator*

Winnetka
Bundy, Blakely Fetridge *advocate*

INDIANA

Bloomington
Brinkman, Paul Del(bert) *retired foundation administrator, journalist, educator*
Mobley, Tony Allen *foundation administrator, former dean, recreation educator*

Fort Wayne
Cooper, Charles Bradford III *educational association administrator*
Murray, Shaun Michael *lobbyist, consultant*

Indianapolis
Barcus, Robert Gene *retired educational association administrator*
Braun, Robert Clare *retired association and advertising executive*
Buckley, Pamela Kay *educational association administrator*
Finley, Katherine Mandusic *professional society administrator*
Harper, Terrance G. *journalism organization administrator*
Mutz, John Massie *foundation administrator, former state official, former energy executive*
Robbins, N. Clay *foundation administrator*
Smith, Curt *think tank executive, journalist*
Sweezy, John William *political party official*
Tempel, Eugene Raymond (Gene Tempel) *foundation administrator, speaker, researcher*
Vereen, Robert Charles *retired trade association administrator*

Lafayette
Scaletta, Helen Marguerite *volunteer*

Muncie
Shoemaker, Helen E. Martin Achor *civic worker*

North Manchester
Mason, Stephen Olin *not-for-profit developer*

South Bend
Hunt, Mary Reilly *organization executive*

Terre Haute
Aldridge, Sandra *civic volunteer*

Wabash
Ford, Richard Edwin *volunteer*

West Lafayette
Baumgardt, Billy Ray *professional society administrator, agriculturist*

IOWA

Ames
Ahoy, Christopher Keen *educational association administrator, architect*

Cedar Rapids
Whipple, William Perry *foundation administrator*

Creston
Lockard, Kathleen Ann *educational association administrator*

Des Moines
Oropeza, Dawn Martinez *art association administrator, artist, curator*

Iowa City
Ferguson, Richard L. *educational association administrator*

North Liberty
Brenneman, Tami K. *not-for-profit fundraiser*

Sioux City
Waller, Ephraim Everett *retired association executive*

West Branch
Forsythe, Patricia Hays *development professional*

KANSAS

Kansas City
Jones, Charles W. *labor union executive*

Lawrence
Wiechert, Allen LeRoy *educational association administrator*

Topeka
Frahm, Sheila *association executive, academic administrator, former government official*

Wichita
Vliet, Marni *foundation administrator*

Winfield
Gray, Ina Turner *fraternal organization administrator*

KENTUCKY

Corbin
Barton-Collings, Nelda Ann *retired political organization worker, retired bank executive, entrepreneur*

Florence
Gorman, Gayla Marlene Osborne *consumer affairs executive*

Lexington
Lewis, Robert Kay, Jr. *fundraising executive*
Sexton, Robert Fenimore *educational organization executive*

Louisville
Early, Jack Jones *foundation executive*
Mathews, William Gregory *social services administrator*
Zepeda, Susan Ghozeil *foundation administrator*

Madisonville
Livers, Thomas Henry *not-for-profit fundraiser, consultant*

LOUISIANA

Mandeville
Landry, Joseph L., Jr. *retired affirmative action specialist*

MAINE

Augusta
Gervais, Paul Nelson *foundation administrator, psychotherapist, writer, public relations executive*

Bangor
Coffman, Michael S. *international organization official, ecologist*

South Portland
Harris, Penny Smith *fundraising consultant*

Waterford
Stockwell, William F. *not-for-profit fundraiser, consultant*

York
Smart, Mary-Leigh Call (Mrs. J. Scott Smart) *civic worker*

MARYLAND

Baltimore
Fuentealba, Victor William *professional society administrator*
Gordon, Bruce S. *civil rights organization executive, former telecommunications company executive*
Hayes, Dennis Courtland *civil rights association executive, lawyer*
Leonard, Joseph Howard *staff specialist*
Mfume, Kweisi *civil rights association executive, former congressman*
Nelson, Douglas W. *foundation administrator*
Skolnik, Sandra J. *educational association administrator*
Wahington, Anthony William *volunteer coordinator*

Bel Air
Thursfield, Fred Falconer, II, *foundation administrator*

Bethesda
Beall, Robert Joseph *foundation executive*
Cleary, Timothy Finbar *professional society administrator*
Day, Robert Dwain, Jr. *foundation administrator, lawyer*
Dulin, Maurine Stuart *volunteer*
Grau, John Michael *trade association executive*
Holloman, Marilyn Leona Davis *lobbyist, non profit administrator, family practice nurse practitioner, new product developer*
Kavanaugh, Everett Edward, Jr. *trade association executive*
Metzger, Henry *federal research institution administrator*
Nelson, Ethelyn Barnett *civic worker*
Reed, Berenice Anne *cultural organization administrator, educator, artist*
Saunders, Charles Baskerville, Jr. *retired association executive*
Sprott, Richard Lawrence *foundation administrator, researcher*
Stone, Jeremy Judah *professional society administrator*

Bowie
Littlefield, Roy Everett III *association executive, law educator*

California
Powell, Melchior Daniel *educational administrator, lawyer*

Chevy Chase
Hunt, Frederick Talley Drum, Jr. *association executive*
Lennan, Anne Celeste *trade association and educational software company executive*

College Park
Brazile, Donna *advocate*
Khoury, Bernard V. *educational administrator*
Murdoch, Amelia Clara *educational association administrator*
Stover, Carl Frederick *foundation executive*

Columbia
Purcell, James Nelson, Jr. *cultural organization administrator*
Rogers, Thomas Francis *foundation administrator*
Scornaienchi, Joan Webb *educational association administrator, consultant*

Crofton
Ross, E(dwin) Clarke *association executive, educator*

Derwood
Crawford, Stephen *national association executive*

Greenbelt
Matthews, Darryl R., Sr. *not-for-profit fundraiser*
Miller, Alwin Vermar *educational association administrator, consultant*

Lusby
Sprague, Edward Auchincloss *retired professional society administrator, economist*

Mitchellville
Ball, Robert M. (Robert Myers Ball) *retired social security, welfare and health policy specialist, writer, lecturer*
Hammer, Jane Amelia Ross *advocate*

Potomac
Keefe, Arthur Thomas III *non-profit fund raising executive*
Rosenberg, Sarah Zacher *retired cultural organization administrator*

Rockville
Bardack, Paul Roitman *cultural organization administrator*
Kline, Raymond Adam *professional organization executive*
Marcuccio, Phyllis Rose *retired educational association administrator, editor*

Severna Park
Hall, Marcia Joy *non-profit organization administrator*
Humphreys Troy, Patricia *foundation administrator*

Silver Spring
Fockler, Herbert Hill *foundation executive*
Gunn, Will A. *foundation administrator, retired military officer, lawyer*
Smedley, Lawrence Thomas *retired organization executive*
Winston, Michael Russell *foundation executive, historian*

Stevensville
Engel, Bradford Charles *educational association administrator, secondary school educator*

Upper Marlboro
Buffenbarger, (Robert) Thomas *labor union administrator*

Waldorf
Raiman, Rosemary A. *advocate*

MASSACHUSETTS

Amesbury
Bartnicki, Karen Jo *social services administrator*

Amherst
MacKnight, Carol Bernier *educational association administrator*

Bedford
Ludes, Jacob III *educational association administrator*

Boston
Cabot, Louis Wellington *foundation trustee*
Chertavian, Gerald *nonprofit organization executive*
Deissler, Mary Alice *foundation executive*

DiGiustini, Antonetta Anna *educational association administrator, educator*
Glass, Renée *educational health foundation executive*
Katsoulomitis, Georgia *foundation administrator, lawyer*
Knight, Norman *volunteer, retired broadcast executive*
Meisner, Mary Jo *foundation administrator, former newspaper editor*
Trumbull, David Lewis Kitchen *trade association executive*

Brookfield
Couture, Ronald David *art association administrator, web site designer, consultant*

Cambridge
Berlowitz, Leslie *cultural organization administrator*
Lee, Barbara *political activist, foundation administrator*
Neill, Monty *educational association administrator*
Rensberger, Boyce *science journalism fellowship program administrator*
Schaeffer, Robert *educational association administrator*
White, Shelby *art association administrator*

Dorchester
Smith, Survilla Marie *social services administrator, artist, poet*

Fitchburg
Niemi, Beatrice Neal *social services professional*

Framingham
Harrington, Joseph Francis *educational company executive, history educator*
Welte, A. Theodore *chamber of commerce executive*

Greenfield
Hutcheson, Thomas Worthington *trade association administrator*

Hull
Anderson, Timothy Christopher *educational association administrator*

Ipswich
Wilson, Doris H. *volunteer*

Lexington
Garing, Ione Davis *civic worker*

Malden
Guild, Richard Samuel *trade association management company executive*

New Bedford
Bullard, John Kilburn *educational association administrator*

Pittsfield
Wenner, Gene Charles *arts management executive*

Plymouth
Joseph, Rodney Randy *art association administrator*

Quincy
Holway, David J. *labor union administrator*

Revere
Anthony, Sylvia *social welfare organization executive*

Southborough
Warren, John Coolidge *educational administrator*

Waltham
Bronfman, Charles Rosner *philanthropist, former distillery executive*

Wayland
Humphrey, Diana Young *fundraiser*

Westford
Geary, Marie Josephine *art association administrator*

Weston
Daly, Charles Ulick *foundation executive*

Westwood
Phillips, Marion Grumman *civic volunteer, writer*

MICHIGAN

Ann Arbor
Diana, Joseph A. *retired foundation executive*
Kennedy, David Boyd *foundation executive, lawyer*
Ryland, Jane N. *educational association administrator*
Ware, Richard Anderson *foundation executive*

Battle Creek
Davis, Laura Arlene *retired foundation administrator*
Speirn, Sterling K. *foundation administrator*

Detroit
Baytarian, P. Jeffrey *not-for-profit fundraiser*
Bell Wilson, Carlotta A. *social services specialist, state official, consultant*
Gettelfinger, Ron *labor union administrator*
Neithercut, Mark Edward *foundation consultant*
Noland, Mariam Charl *foundation executive*

Dowagiac
Murphy, Ellis *association management executive*

East Lansing
Luecke, Eleanor Virginia Rohrbacher *civic volunteer*

Flint
Belcher, Max *social services administrator, dean*
White, William Samuel *foundation executive*

Gaylord
Smith, Frank Earl *retired trade association administrator*

Kalamazoo
Petersen, Anne C. (Cheryl Petersen) *foundation administrator, educator*

Sterling Heights
Fleming, Mac Arthur *retired labor union administrator*

Troy
Hodges, Michele *chamber of commerce executive*
Rapson, Richard (Rip Rapson) *foundation administrator*

Waterford
Laing, James Thomas *retired not-for-profit developer*

MINNESOTA

Lake Lillian
Marquardt, Steve Robert *advocate*

Little Falls
Stobb, Mary Jean *retired association administrator*

Minneapolis
Binger, Erika L. *foundation administrator*
Johnson, John Warren *retired professional society administrator*
Leuchovius, Deborah *advocate, special education services professional, consultant*
Wolford, Kathryn Frances *foundation administrator*

Saint Cloud
Prout, Robert Stephen *higher education consultant, law enforcement consultant*

Saint Paul
Kurtz, Harold Paul *foundation executive*
Pampusch, Anita Marie *foundation administrator*
Pratt, Jon *not-for-profit executive*
Sisson, Bernice Belair *advocate*
Skillingstad, Constance Yvonne *social services administrator, educator*
Williams, Lynell R. *educational association administrator*

MISSISSIPPI

Clarksdale
Lucy, William (Bill Lucy) *labor union administrator*

Fayette
La Salle, Arthur Edward *historic foundation executive*

Jackson
Carmichael, Sally W. *volunteer*
Hendrix, Albert Randel *social services administrator*
Risley, Rod Alan *educational association administrator*

MISSOURI

Ballwin
Pallozola, Christine *not-for-profit executive*

Bridgeton
Kenison, Raymond Robert *fraternal organization administrator, director*

Chesterfield
Diamandis, Peter H. *foundation administrator, entrepreneur*

Earth City
Anderhalter, Oliver Frank *educational organization executive*

Kansas City
Bugher, Robert Dean *professional society administrator*
Kauk, Janet Lea *not-for-profit developer*

Kingsville
Schreiner, Donald Scott *not-for-profit fundraiser*

Lees Summit
Carter, William Gerald *non-profit corporation executive*

Rolla
Bagnall, Lindsay Lomax *not-for-profit executive*

Saint Louis
Bascom, C. Perry *retired foundation administrator*
Duhme, Carol McCarthy *civic worker*
Fletcher, Bill, Jr. *political organization executive, activist*
Hunter, Earle Leslie III *retired professional association executive*
Kimmey, James Richard, Jr. *foundation administrator*
Pope, Robert E(ugene) *fraternal organization administrator*

Winter, Mildred M. *educational administrator*

Springfield
O'Block, Robert *association, publishing executive*

MONTANA

Billings
Sample, Joseph Scanlon *foundation executive*

Bozeman
Sanddal, Nels Dodge *foundation executive, consultant*
Weller, Therese Marie *not-for-profit fundraiser*

NEBRASKA

Harrison
Coffee, Virginia Claire *civic worker, former mayor*

Lincoln
Hardin, Martha Love Wood *civic leader*
Rosenow, John Edward *foundation executive*

Omaha
Strawhecker, Paul Joseph *fundraising consultant*

NEVADA

Carson City
Ayres, Janice Ruth *social services administrator*

Henderson
Freyd, William Pattinson *not-for-profit fundraiser, director*

Incline Village
Johnston, Bernard Fox *foundation executive, writer*

Las Vegas
Manley, Edward Harry, Jr. *professional association administrator, food products executive, retired military officer*
Nicholson, R. Stephen *former cultural organization administrator*
Spencer, Carol Brown *retired educational association administrator*

NEW HAMPSHIRE

Dover
Nelson, Michael Underhill *educational association administrator*

Peterborough
Eppes, William David *arts and humanities advocate*

Pike
Teschner, Douglass Paul *project administrator*

Plymouth
Dutille, Jessica Annie Orf *social services administrator, educator*

NEW JERSEY

Atlantic City
Jamieson, John Edward, Jr. *social services administrator, minister*

Bernardsville
Cooperman, Saul *retired educational administrator*

Cherry Hill
Makous, Bruce B. *fundraiser, writer*

Glen Ridge
Pendley, Donald Lee *association executive*

Highland Park
Kolodzei, Natalia A. *art association administrator, art historian, curator*

Montclair
Campbell, Stewart Fred *foundation administrator, consultant*

Moorestown
Felcyn, Diane Annette *art association administrator*

New Brunswick
Bunch, Charlotte *advocate*

New Vernon
Dugan, John Leslie, Jr. *foundation executive*

Paramus
Noguere, Suzanne *trade association executive, poet*

Pennington
Calvo, Roque John *professional society administrator*

Plainfield
Limpert, John H., Jr. *fund raising executive*

Princeton
Balch, Stephen Howard *professional society administrator*
Bland, Calvin *foundation administrator*
De Lung, Jane Solberger *independent sector executive*
Freeman, Bruce George *fundraising consultant*
Hughes, Robert G. *foundation administrator*

Jeffers, Beverly Maynard *volunteer*
Kassof, Allen H. *foundation administrator*
Kenyon, Regan Clair *educational association administrator*
Landgraf, Kurt M. *educational association administrator*
Pechura, Constance Mary *foundation administrator*

Rumson
Brenner, Theodore Engelbert *retired trade association administrator*

Shiloh
Garrison, John Raymond *organization executive*

Skillman
Rhett, Haskell Emery Smith *educational association administrator*

Trenton
Binder, Elaine Kotell *associations consultant*
Powell, Joyce *educational association administrator, secondary school educator*
Ritchey, Kenneth William *social services administrator*

West Orange
Rinsky, Judith Sue Lynn *foundation administrator, consultant, educator*

NEW MEXICO

Albuquerque
Hunt, Bonnie Jo *art association administrator, writer, soprano*

Rio Rancho
Norman, Phyllis B. *volunteer*

Santa Fe
Miller-Engel, Marjorie *foundation administrator, commissioner, small business owner*

NEW YORK

Albany
Mondello, Joseph N. *political organization administrator*

Amherst
Clark, Donald Malin *professional association executive*

Bayside
Madden, Joseph Daniel *trade association executive*

Briarcliff Manor
Read, John Conyers *non-profit company executive*

Bronx
Yale (Yeleyenide-Yale), Serina *philanthropist, apparel designer*

Bronxville
Lee, Clement William Khan *trade association administrator*

Brooklyn
Horowitz, Sara *labor organizer*
Morgan, Mary Louise Fitzsimmons *fund raising executive, lobbyist*
Russell, Wayne Delano *activist, educator, poet*
Wilson, Robert Warne *philanthropist*

Buffalo
Bender, James Y. *not-for-profit fundraiser*
Clarkson, Elisabeth Ann Hudnut *volunteer*
Ezzo, David Albert *not-for-profit executive, anthropologist, educator*
Harvey, Steven John *not-for-profit developer*
Spengler, Paul Albert *grants and foundation administrator*

Centereach
Chassman, Karen Moss *educational association administrator*

Chappaqua
de Janosi, Peter Engel *research manager*

Clarence
Stringer, Gretchen Engstrom *consulting volunteer administrator*

Commack
Price, Amelia Ruth *not-for-profit foundation president, artist, small business owner*

Cooperstown
Petroskey, Dale Alan *cultural organization administrator, former professional society administrator*

Corning
Cicerchi, Eleanor Ann Tomb *not-for-profit fundraiser*

Dobbs Ferry
Sutton, Francis Xavier *social services administrator, consultant*

Flushing
Fichtel, Rudolph Robert *retired association executive*

Glenmont
Bellizzi, John J. *law enforcement association administrator, pharmacist, educator*

Harrison
Wadsworth, Frank Whittemore *foundation administrator, literature educator*

Hastings On Hudson
Cassella, William Nathan, Jr. *retired not-for-profit organization executive*

Hudson
Miner, Jacqueline *political consultant*

Jamestown
Thompson, Birgit Dolores *civic worker, writer*

Larchmont
Hinerfeld, Ruth G. *civic organization executive*

Manhasset
Foerst, John George, Jr. *retired fundraising executive*

Montauk
Butler, Thomas William *retired health and social services administrator*

Montour Falls
Spencer, Dawn Joyce *advocate*

New Paltz
Flood, Ralph F. *educational association administrator*

New Rochelle
Black, Page Morton *civic worker, vocalist, musician*

New York
Ackerman, Lisa Marilyn *foundation administrator, consultant*
Alex, Paula Ann *foundation administrator*
Anderson, Richard Theodore *trade association administrator, urban planner*
Arnold, Winfred Raymon *trade association administrator*
Ashley, Dwayne *not-for-profit fundraiser*
Ban, Ki-Moon (Ban Ki-Moon) *Secretary General of the United Nations, former South Korean government official*
Belknap, Norton *foundation administrator*
Bergman, Charles Cabe *foundation executive*
Berman, Greg *think-tank executive*
Berresford, Susan Vail *foundation administrator*
Bischoff, Theresa Ann *not-for-profit association executive*
Bowen, William Gordon *foundation administrator, economist*
Bowers, John M. *labor union administrator*
Brooks, Deborah W. *foundation administrator*
Brown, Terrence Charles *art association executive, researcher, lecturer*
Brownstein, Alan P. *health foundation executive, consultant*
Buckman, Thomas Richard *foundation executive, educator*
Calhoun, Craig Jackson *social scientist, educator*
Canada, Geoffrey *social welfare administrator, writer*
Caperton, (William) Gaston, (III) *educational association administrator, former governor*
Caputo, Lucio *trade company executive*
Carlson, Donna *art association administrator, director*
Carroll, David Paul *social welfare administrator*
Cassullo, Joanne Leonhardt *foundation administrator*
Catley-Carlson, Margaret *not-for-profit executive*
Chapin, Schuyler Garrison *retired cultural organization administrator, retired dean*
Chen, James Tsing-Fang *art association administrator, cultural organization administrator*
Christopher, Maurine Brooks *foundation administrator, writer, editor*
Conarroe, Joel Osborne *foundation administrator, editor, educator*
Connor, W(alter) Robert *foundation administrator, classicist, educator*
Cox, Larry *human rights organization executive*
Dajani, Virginia *art association administrator*
Dandonoli, Patricia A. *not-for-profit fundraiser*
Daniels, Joseph Carl *foundation administrator*
Dennis, Everette Eugene, Jr. *foundation executive, educator, writer*
Desai, Vishakha N. *professional society administrator*
DeVita, M. Christine *foundation administrator*
Diggins, Peter Sheehan *arts administrator*
Ellis, Ross *non-profit organization executive*
Ferraro, Geraldine Anne *lobbyist, former congresswoman*
Fontaine, John C. *foundation administrator, lawyer, former newspaper company executive*
Franklin, Jason Edward *advocate, researcher*
Frost, William Lee *foundation executive*
Gerner, Joan *foundation administrator*
Gomory, Ralph Edward *foundation administrator, mathematician*
Goodwin, Michael *labor union administrator*
Gore Schiff, Karenna *nonprofit organization administrator, lawyer, writer*
Grayer, Jonathan *education company executive*
Green, Micah S. *trade association administrator*
Greene, Frank Edward Wade *foundation administrator, writer*
Gregorian, Vartan *foundation administrator*
Gresham, George *labor union administrator*
Grimaldi, Nicholas Lawrence *fundraising executive*
Guehenno, Jean Marie *international organization official*
Harris, David Alan *not-for-profit organization executive*
Hatter, Richard Wayne *foundation administrator, artist*
Hemphill, Clara Jacobs *advocate*
Henry, Frederick B. *foundation administrator*
Hesselbein, Frances Richards *foundation administrator, writer, editor*
Hill, Janine *think-tank manager*
Hoekstra, Edward John *foundation administrator*
Hoffman, Linda R. *social services administrator*
Howard, David *retired educational association administrator, writer*
Hoye, J.D. *foundation administrator*
Hundley, James W. III *think-tank executive, consultant, researcher*
Innis, Roy Emile Alfredo *foundation executive*
Jacobsen, Theodore H. (Ted H. Jacobsen) *labor union administrator, secondary school educator*
Jian, Chen *international organization official*
Jones, David R. *not-for-profit executive*
Kaggen, Lois Sheila *non-profit organization executive, advocate*
Kahan, Marlene *professional association executive*
Kasirer, Suri *lobbyist*
Katzowitz Shenfield, Lauren *philanthropy consultant*
Kopp, Wendy *educational association administrator*
Labunski, Stephen Bronislaw *professional society administrator*
Larberg, John Frederick *retired social welfare executive, wine consultant, educator*
Lauder, Jo Carole *art association administrator*
Laurence, Michael Marshall *foundation administrator*
Lawson-Johnston, Peter Orman *foundation executive*
Lee, David Hee-Don *trade association administrator, educator*
Lee, Thomas F. *art association administrator*
Leet, Mildred Robbins *social welfare administrator, consultant*
Leffler, Marvin *foundation administrator, writer*
Loar, Peggy Ann *foundation administrator, museum administrator*
London, Nora Eleonor *foundation administrator*
Luckman, Sharon Gersten *arts administrator*
Luks, Allan Barry *executive director*
Mahoney, Margaret Ellerbe *foundation executive*
Maynard, Virginia Madden *foundation administrator*
McCrary, Eugenia Lester (Mrs. Dennis Daughtry McCrary) *civic worker, writer*
McNamara, Mary Ellen *not-for-profit executive*
McNeil, Wendy Lawson-Johnston *foundation administrator*
Michel, Nicolas *international organization official*
Migiro, Asha-Rose *international organization official*
Migro, Asha-Rose *international organization official*
Miller, Harvey S. Shipley *foundation trustee, philanthropist*
Miller, Merry *educational association administrator*
Moran, Martin Joseph *fundraising company executive*
Morial, Marc Haydel *association executive, former mayor*
Motoc, Mihnea Ioan *international organization official*
Neidich, Brooke Garber *foundation administrator, art patron*
Nicolau, Siobhan *cultural organization administrator*
O, Cao K. *cultural organization administrator*
Orr, James F. III *foundation administrator*
Otunnu, Olara A. *childrens organization official*
Oxnam, Robert Bromley *trust company advisor*
Pascoe, B. Lynn *international organization official, former ambassador*
Persichilli Keogh, Karen Mary *political organization worker*
Polin, Jane L. *foundation official*
Randel, Don Michael *foundation administrator, former academic administrator, musicologist*
Raynor, Bruce S. *labor union administrator*
Rodin, Judith Seitz *foundation administrator, former academic administrator, psychologist, educator*
Roney, Carley *wedding company executive, writer*
Rose, Joanna Semel *volunteer*
Rosenthal, Jacob (Jack Rosenthal) *foundation executive*
Roth, Kenneth *human rights advocate*
Rothman, Esther Pomeranz *social services administrator, psychologist*
Rover, Edward Frank *foundation administrator, lawyer*
Rupp, George Erik *international relief organization executive*
St. Martin, Charlotte *trade association administrator*
Sanchez, Manuel *retired social services administrator, writer*
Sard, Susannah Ellen *non-profit executive*
Sayres, Edwin J., Jr. *animal welfare organization administrator*
Schlesinger, Andrea Batista *think-tank executive*
Sidamon-Eristoff, Anne Phipps *not-for-profit developer*
Singh, Jyoti Shankar *international organization executive*
Slutsky, Lorie A(nn) *foundation executive*
Smith, Barry Hamilton *foundation administrator, physician*
Spero, Joan Edelman *foundation administrator*
Spindler, James Andrew *not-for-profit executive*
Steinberg, Milton *retired educational association administrator*
Straus, Oscar S., II, *foundation executive*
Sussman, Leonard Richard *foundation executive*
Tanner, Jonathan D. *educational association administrator*
Tenenbaum, Ann G. *art association administrator*
Tofel, Richard Jeffrey *foundation administrator*
Toussaint, Roger *labor union administrator*
Traverse, Lyn D. *not-for-profit fundraiser, communications executive*
Ungaro, Susan Kelliher *foundation administrator, former magazine editor*
Van de Bovenkamp, Sue Erpf *foundation administrator*
Veneman, Ann Margaret *international organization official, former secretary of agriculture*
Walker, Jennie Louise *not-for-profit fundraiser, consultant*
Wall Spitzer, Silda *not-for-profit developer, First Lady of New York State*
Wanner, Eric *foundation executive*
Wattleton, (Alyce) Faye *educational association administrator, advocate*
Weeks, David Frank *foundation administrator*
Weingarten, Randi (Rhonda) *labor union administrator, lawyer*
Wenegrat, Saul S. *art association administrator, educator*
Wilson, Marie C. *foundation administrator*
Wolfson, Howard *political analyst*
Wright, Sheena *not-for-profit developer*
Wylde, Kathryn S. *business organization executive*

Newark
Hemmings, Madeleine Blanchet *not-for-profit administrator, grant writer, media consultant*

Niagara Falls
Hawkins De Golier, Danielle *political activist*

Pawling
Peale, Ruth Stafford (Mrs. Norman Vincent Peale) *not-for-profit executive*

Pleasant Valley
Becofsky, Arthur Luke *arts administrator, writer*

Rochester
Klinke, Louise Hoyt *volunteer*
Lebman, Robert Richard *social services administrator*
Pacala, Leon *retired professional society administrator*
Robbins, Nancy Slinker *volunteer*

Saranac
Smith, J. Kellum, Jr. *foundation administrator, lawyer*

Saratoga Springs
Carovano, John Martin *not-for-profit developer*

Scarsdale
Port, Lilly Bruck Lieb *retired advocate, columnist, commentator*
Stamas, Stephen *not-for-profit administrator*

Schenectady
Hull, Roger Harold *foundation and former academic administrator*

Stony Brook
Brandwein, Ruth Ann *social welfare educator, social services administrator, writer*

Stony Creek
La Grasse, Carol Winter *property rights activist, retired civil engineer*

Syracuse
Colvin, Ruth Johnson *literacy organization founder*
Furze, Edward William *fundraising consultant*
Irwin, Peter C. *not-for-profit fundraiser*

Tarrytown
Bergson, Henry Paul *professional society administrator*

White Plains
Howse, Jennifer Louise *foundation administrator*

Yonkers
Neal, Leora Louise Haskett *social services administrator*

NORTH CAROLINA

Burnsville
Cullom, William Otis *retired trade association executive*

Cary
Bryant, Mynora Joyce *not-for-profit fundraiser*
Martin, William Royall, Jr. *retired professional society administrator*

Chapel Hill
Kenan, Thomas Stephen III *philanthropist*
Krasno, Richard Michael *foundation executive, educator*

Charlotte
Cochrane, Eugene W., Jr. *foundation administrator*
Locke, Elizabeth Hughes *retired foundation administrator*
McClure, Howard Jean, Jr. *advocate*
Spiro, Robert Harry, Jr. *foundation and business executive, educator*

Clinton
Griffin, Betty Lou *not-for-profit developer, educator*

Durham
Daubert, Erik Joseph *organization administrator, consultant*
Semans, Mary Duke Biddle Trent *foundation administrator*

Greensboro
Revell, Henry, Jr. *social services administrator, retired education educator*
Ryan, John R. *educational association administrator, former academic administrator, career military officer*

Manteo
Irby, Katherine Scott Roche *educational association administrator*

Morganton
Stevenson, C. Donald *youth organization executive, folk artist*

Raleigh
Lee, Howard N. *educational association administrator*

Waynesville
Cole, James Yeager *foundation administrator*

Wilson
McCain, Betty Landon Ray (Mrs. John Lewis McCain) *political party and state official*

Wingate
Dodd, John Robert *non-profit organization administrator*

NORTH DAKOTA

Grand Forks
Jones, Arthur Frederick *art university administrator, educator*

Williston
Yockim, James Craig *foundation administrator*

OHIO

Akron
Brake, Yvonne Marie *not-for-profit developer*
Collier, Alice Elizabeth Becker *retired social services administrator*

Canton
McFarren, Leland Cullen *educational association administrator, educator*
Mitchell, Jan L. *advocate, writer*

Chagrin Falls
Vail, Iris Jennings *civic worker*

Cincinnati
Hill-Cook, Patricia Ann *social services administrator*
Motch, Marjorie McCullough *service organization executive*
Sowder, Fred Allen *foundation administrator, alphabet specialist*

Cleveland
Calkins, Hugh *foundation executive*
Carter, John Dale *organizational development coordinator*
Distelhorst, Garis Fred *trade association administrator*
FallCreek, Stephanie Jean *non-profit organization executive*
Horner, John Atlee *educational association administrator*
Kolda, Thomas Joseph *non-profit organization executive*
Lord, James Gregory *organizational, community and philanthropic counsel*
Parry, Michael *not-for-profit fundraiser, singer, actor*
Penman, Robbie Mae *volunteer, political organization worker*
Pike, Kermit Jerome *cultural organization administrator*
Smith, Jerome (Dr. Jerome Smith) *not-for-profit developer, film producer, writer*
Thompson, Paul C. *labor union administrator*

Columbus
Akers, Saundra Ruth *retired disability rights advocate*
Newman, Diana S. *foundation administrator, consultant*
Selby, Diane Ray Miller *fraternal organization administrator*
Sharp, Paul David *institute administrator*
Trent, Elton Roger *educational assessment administrator, writer*

Coshocton
Freund, Carol Louise *social services consultant*

Dayton
Daley, Robert Emmett *retired foundation executive*
Haddad, Freddie Duke, Jr. *resource development professional*
McDonald, Bronce William *community activist, advocate*
Thomas, Marianna *volunteer community activist, writer, speaker*
Williams, Walker Richard, Jr. *social services administrator*

Dublin
Needham, George Michael *association executive*

Fairview Park
Fordyce, James Stuart *non-profit organization executive*

Greenville
Thieme, Jean Louise *retired art association administrator*

Hamilton
Gruenwald, James Howard *association executive, consultant*

Hilliard
Riggle, Blair Andrew *educational association administrator, consultant, psychologist, educator*

Hudson
Frank, John V. *foundation administrator*

Kettering
Kent, Lawrence *retired association executive, education and mental health director*

Lewis Center
Heinlen, Daniel Lee *alumni organization administrator, consultant*

North Canton
Fernandez, Kathleen M. *cultural organization administrator*

Oxford
Miller, Robert James *educational association administrator*

Richfield
Lewis, Sylvia Davidson *foundation executive*

Sylvania
Garrison, Linda *retired foundation administrator*

Worthington
Luck, James I. *foundation executive*

OKLAHOMA

Ardmore
Cawley, Michael A. *foundation administrator, lawyer*

Lawton
Hooper, Roy B. *lobbyist*

Norman
Mooneyham, Bobby R. *educational association administrator*

Oklahoma City
Brooks, Gene (Leslie Gene Brooks) *cultural organization administrator*
Kerr, Lou C. *foundation administrator*
Weddington, Stacey Lee *not-for-profit developer*
Wynn, Brenda Reneau *former trade association executive*

Sallisaw
Crowson, Watie Dee *foundation administrator, poet, lyricist*

OREGON

Ashland
Kreisman, Arthur *higher education consultant, retired humanities educator*

Bend
Evers-Williams, Myrlie Beasley *advocate, cultural organization administrator*

Corvallis
Wilkins, Caroline Hanke *advocate, political organization worker*

Lake Oswego
Bruce, John Allen *retired foundation executive, educator*

Portland
Holt, Mavis Murial *social services administrator*
Hudson, Jerry E. *foundation administrator*
Pine, William Charles *foundation executive*
Rees, Nina Shokraii *educational association administrator, former federal agency administrator*
Rooks, Charles S. *foundation administrator*
Showalter, Marilyn Grace *trade association administrator, director*

Salem
Frank, Gerald Wendel *advocate, journalist*

Summerville
Hopkins, Gerald Frank *trade association administrator*

PENNSYLVANIA

Camp Hill
Gibbons, Miles Joseph, Jr. *foundation administrator*

Dillsburg
Bowers, Glenn Lee *retired professional society administrator*

Drexel Hill
Schiazza, Guido Domenic (Guy Schiazza) *educational association administrator*

Elkins Park
Pak, Hyung Woong *community advocate*

Gladwyne
Cooney, Patricia Ruth *civic worker*

Glenside
Block, Isaac Edward *professional society administrator*
Doman, Janet Joy *professional society administrator*

Harrisburg
Breslin, Michael Joseph III *social services administrator, educator*
Torres, Maribel *social welfare administrator*

Hazleton
Kraynak, Marcelle Georgeann *not-for-profit developer*

Lewisburg
Neuman, Nancy Adams Mosshammer *civic leader*

Monroeville
Skolnick, Marilyn *civic worker*

Newtown
Bernstine, Daniel O'Neal *educational association administrator, law educator*

Philadelphia
Blakely, Kevin M. *management association executive*
Glickman, Sallie A. *professional society administrator*
Hamilton, Samuel C. *not-for-profit fundraiser*
Hillen, John Francis *think-tank executive, former federal agency administrator*
Houstoun, Feather O'Connor *foundation administrator*
Mallery, David *education association executive, consultant*
Mandel, Brett H. *community organization executive, writer*
Morse, Jean Avnet *educational association administrator, lawyer*
Reed, Sally Gardner *cultural organization administrator*
Rimel, Rebecca Webster *foundation administrator*

Pittsburgh
Boyce, Doreen Elizabeth *foundation administrator, educator*
Fox, Debra L. *educational association administrator, business owner*
Gerard, Leo W. *labor union executive*
Hackett, Stephanie R. *educational association administrator*
Petersen, Jean Snyder *educational association administrator*
Ziegler, Arthur P., Jr. *foundation executive*

Reading
Kiehne, Frank Charles, Jr. *foundation administrator*

Rydal
Fernberger, Marilyn Friedman *not-for-profit developer, consultant, volunteer*

Scranton
Browning, William J. *child protective service director*

Solebury
Keep, Charles Russell, Jr. *foundation administrator*

State College
Book, Edward Raymond *retired trade association administrator*
Phillips, Janet Colleen *retired educational association administrator, editor*

Upper Darby
Pittman, Mia N. *educational association administrator, entrepreneur*

Villanova
Friend, Theodore Wood III *foundation executive, historian, writer*

Warrendale
Rumbaugh, Max Elden, Jr. *professional society administrator*

Wayne
Annenberg, Leonore A. *foundation administrator*
Etris, Samuel Franklin *trade association research consultant*

West Conshohocken
Klimczuk, Stephen John *business executive, foundation director*

Wynnewood
Meyers, Mary Ann *foundation administrator, consultant, writer*

York
Foster, Timothy Edward *educational association administrator*
Wiles, Lessley Decker *foundation administrator, preservationist*

RHODE ISLAND

Kingston
Molloy, David Scott, Jr. *labor relations educator*

Providence
Klyberg, Albert Thomas *historical society administrator*

SOUTH CAROLINA

Aiken
Ely, Duncan Cairnes *social services administrator*

Charleston
Hughes, Blake *retired professional society administrator, retired publishing executive*

Clemson
Zielinski, Paul Bernard *grant program administrator, civil engineer*

Columbia
Bjontegard, Arthur Martin, Jr. *foundation executive*
Dobrasko, Rebekah *cultural organization administrator, historian*
Porchea, Sameano Francisco *educational association administrator, systems analyst*

Hilton Head Island
Ostergard, Paul Michael *not-for-profit executive*

Lancaster
Bundy, Charles Alan *retired foundation executive*

Myrtle Beach
Gravely, Mary Jeane *volunteer*

Saint Helena Island
Tarr-Whelan, Linda *policy center executive*

Woodruff
Childers, Bob Eugene *educational association executive*

SOUTH DAKOTA

Sioux Falls
Piper, Kathleen *former political organization administrator*

TENNESSEE

Brentwood
Lodowski, Charles Alan *trade association administrator, lobbyist*

Chattanooga
Marler, B. Evonne *not-for-profit fundraiser*

Knoxville
Brantley, Andy (Anthony G.) *educational association administrator*
Froula, James DeWayne *honor society administrator*
Jones, Sherman J. *cultural organization administrator, financial consultant, educator*
Taylor, Jackie A. *educational association administrator*

Memphis
Jalenak, Peggy Eichenbaum *volunteer*
Tibbs, Martha Jane Pullen *civic worker, retired social worker*

Nashville
Benson, Edwin Welburn, Jr. *trade association executive*
Henderson, Milton Arnold *professional society administrator*
Snyder, Barbara Lou *retired educational association administrator*

Whites Creek
Coleman, John Daniel *political strategist*

TEXAS

Aledo
Barton, David *activist organization administrator, writer*

Amarillo
Berry, Jacob Obadiah *not-for-profit developer, rancher*

Austin
Banks, Virginia Anne (Ginger) *association administrator*
Hornaday, Jon Russell *professional association administrator*
Houston, Ron *professional society administrator*
Kolar, Mary Jane *trade and professional association executive*
LeFebvre, Julie Aguilar *not-for-profit fundraiser*
Montoya, Rudy, Jr. *volunteer*
Mountain, Janet M. *foundation administrator, former computer company executive*
Stoner, James Lloyd *retired foundation administrator, clergyman*

Beaumont
Davis, Gloria Whittie *educational association administrator*

Breckenridge
Jones, Karen Annette *civic volunteer*

Cedar Park
Love, Ben Howard *retired organization executive*

Corpus Christi
French, Dorris Towers Bryan *volunteer*

Dallas
Brinker, Nancy Goodman *social services administrator, former ambassador*
Cockerham, Sidney Joe *professional society administrator*
Dell, Susan *foundation administrator, apparel designer*
Friedheim, Jan V. *educational association administrator*
Nikopoulos, Beth *educational association administrator*

El Paso
Goodman, Gertrude Amelia *civic worker*

Fort Worth
Saenz, Nancy Elizabeth King *civic worker*
Wilkie, Valleau, Jr. *foundation executive*
Wilson-Webb, Nancy Lou *educational association administrator*

Fulton
Lamb, Richard *cultural organization administrator*

Galveston
Baker, Robert Ernest, Jr. *retired foundation executive*

Georgetown
Busfield, Roger Melvil, Jr. *retired trade association executive, educator*

Houston
Bailey, Kelley *foundation administrator*
Bennett, Olga Salowich *civic worker, graphic arts researcher, consultant*
Faulkner, Larry Ray *foundation and former academic administrator*
Foss, Michelle Michot *think-tank executive, economist*
Ifft, Lewis George III *company administrator*
Weitzel, Amy Ragan *not-for-profit developer*

Irving
Olson, Herbert Theodore *trade association executive*
Williams, Roy L. *fraternal organization administrator*

Mcallen
Spyker, Leola Edith *missionary*

Richardson
Smith, Mark P. *foundation administrator*

San Antonio
Crichton, Flora Cameron *volunteer, foundation administrator*
Loeffler, Tom (Thomas Gilbert Loeffler) *lobbyist, former congressman*

Temple
Matush, William Joe *educational association administrator*

Vidor
Nye, Betty Ann *professional society administrator*

Waco
Riemer, Michael Paul *educational association administrator*

Weatherford
Fisk, Doris Rosalie Scanlan *volunteer*

UTAH

Bountiful
Burningham, Kim Richard *educational association administrator, former state legislator*

Ogden
Pappas, Leah Aglaia *foundation administrator, political organization worker, secondary school educator*

Salt Lake City
Clark, Deanna Dee *volunteer*
Julander, Paula Foil *retired foundation administrator*

VERMONT

Brattleboro
Bellamy, Carol *international organization administrator*

Middlebury
Geier, Philip Otto III *foundation executive, consultant, director, academic administrator*

Montpelier
Barbieri, Christopher George *professional society administrator*

Peacham
Barnes, Harry G., Jr. *advocate, consultant*

Shelburne
Ryerson, William Newton *non profit organization executive*

VIRGINIA

Alexandria
Allen, Ernie (Ernest Eugene Allen) *non-profit organization executive, lawyer*
Anderson, Steven C. *pharmaceutical association executive*
Bailey, Tracey L. *educational association administrator*
Baker, Brent Harold *foundation executive, blogger*
Baroody, Michael Elias *trade association executive*
Bartels, Teresa Hall *non-profit organization administrator*
Bolger, Robert Joseph *retired trade association administrator*
Bryant, Anne Lincoln *educational association administrator*
Butler, Susan Lowell *educational association executive, writer*
Carter, Gene Raymond *professional association executive*
Connelly, Gail *educational association administrator*
Engler, Brian David *professional society administrator*
Foster, Serrin Marie *non-profit organization executive*

Gould, Charles W. *foundation administrator, lawyer*
Greenstein, Ruth Louise *think-tank executive, lawyer*
Kratovil, Jane Lindley *think tank associate, not-for-profit developer*
Lachance, Janice Rachel *professional association and federal agency administrator, lawyer*
Lenz, Edward Arnold *trade association administrator, lawyer*
Lipnick, Anne Ruth *advocate*
Lusk, Cody *auto association executive*
Maehara, Paulette V. *fundraising executive*
Rabun, John Brewton, Jr. *criminal justice agency administrator*
Rector, John Michael *pharmaceutical association executive, lawyer*
Watta, David Anthony *product manager*
Welburn, Brenda Lilienthal *educational association administrator*

Arlington
Bentsen, Kenneth E., Jr. *trade association administrator, former congressman*
Bond, Phillip J. *technology association executive, former advertising executive*
Buchanan, Louise *political organization worker, consultant*
David, Ruth A. *public-service research institute executive*
Dobbins, Jim (James Francis Dobbins Jr.) *think-tank executive, former federal agency administrator*
Dunn, Michael M. *military association executive, retired military officer*
Futrell, John William *environmental agency executive, lawyer*
Herbst, Robert LeRoy *organization executive*
Houston, Paul David *educational association administrator*
Hunter, J(ohn) Robert *insurance consumer advocate*
Langworthy, Everett Walter *professional society administrator, natural gas exploration company executive*
Legum, Judd *think-tank executive, editor*
McKinnon, Russell F. *professional society administrator*
Nash, Bob J. *political organization worker*
O'Day, Paul Thomas *trade association executive*
Palmer, Larry Leon *foundation administrator, former ambassador*
Powell, Edward A., Jr., (Ned Powell) *nonprofit organization executive*
Raizen, Senta Amon *educational association administrator, researcher*
Shannon, Thomas Alfred *retired educational association administrator emeritus*
Solis Doyle, Patti *political campaign worker*
Sullivan, Gordon R. *military association executive, retired military officer*
Swetnam, Michael S. *think-tank executive*
Wheeler, Gerald F. *educational association administrator*

Boston
Fisher, John Morris *association official, business executive, educator*

Bumpass
Hoyt, John Arthur *cultural organization administrator, minister*

Burke
Woodruff, C(harles) Roy *retired professional association executive, consultant*

Chantilly
Sroka, John Walter *trade association executive*

Charlottesville
Johnston, Margaret Schuster *volunteer, retired language educator*
Jordan, Daniel Porter, Jr. *foundation administrator, historian, educator*
Wulf, William Allan *foundation administrator, information scientist, educator*

Earlysville
Brownell, Blaine Allison *educational association and academic administrator, history professor*

Fairfax
Hollans, Irby Noah, Jr. *retired trade association administrator*
LaPierre, Wayne R., Jr. *lobbyist*
Lomax, Michael Lucius *non-profit association administrator*
Morrison, Ann M. *not-for-profit fundraiser*
Roberts, Cecil Edward, Jr. *labor union administrator*
Robinson, Kayne B. *lobbyist, former political organization officer*
Sklarow, Mark Howard *educational association administrator*

Falls Church
Bruck, Bill *educational association administrator*
McGinly, William C. *healthcare association executive*
Rodgers, Kirk Procter *international environmental consultant*

Flint Hill
Dietel, William Moore *former foundation executive*

Franktown
Kellam, Caramine *volunteer*

Garrisonville
Emely, Charles Harry *trade association executive, consultant*

Great Falls
DiBona, Charles Joseph *retired trade association administrator*

Herndon
Roof, Joseph A. *educational association administrator*

Lansdowne
Quinn, Matthew J. *educational association administrator*

Leesburg
De Barbieri, Mary Ann *not-for-profit management consultant*

Louisa
Small, William Edwin, Jr. *association and recreation executive*

Lynchburg
Johnson, Robert Bruce *historic preservationist, director, small business owner*

Mc Lean
Calhoun, John Alfred *social services administrator*
McInerney, James Eugene, Jr. *trade association executive*
Schubert, Richard Francis *social services administrator, consultant*
Stackpole, Kerry Clifford *association executive*

Middleburg
Sodolski, John *retired professional society administrator*

Mount Vernon
Belden, David Leigh *professional society administrator, engineering educator*

Newport News
Mazur, Rhoda Himmel *community volunteer*

Norfolk
Magee, Kathleen S. *foundation executive*
Newkirk, Ingrid *animal rights activist*

Reston
Ancell, Robert Manning *leadership organization executive*
Brennan, Norma Jean *professional society administrator, director*
Gates, James David *retired professional society administrator*
Hope, Samuel Howard *accreditation organization executive*
Madry-Taylor, Jacquelyn Yvonne *educational association administrator*
Minton, Joseph Paul *retired safety organization executive*
Mogge, Harriet Morgan *educational association executive*
Natale, Patrick J *professional society administrator*
Reeve, Deborah B. *art association administrator, art educator*
Rubillo, James M. *educational association administrator*
Tirozzi, Gerald N. *educational association administrator*

Richmond
Brackenridge, N. Lynn *not-for-profit developer*
Framme, Lawrence Henry III *political organization administrator, lawyer*
Hager, John Henry *political organization, former federal agency administrator, former lieutenant governor*

Springfield
Bartlow, Gene Steven *professional society executive, retired military officer*
Larson, Reed Eugene *foundation administrator*

Stafford
Sedlak, James William *organization administrator*

Sterling
Chavez, Linda *civil rights organization executive*

Vienna
Jones, Terrence Dale *foundation executive, consultant*
Patrick, Susan D. *educational association administrator, former federal agency administrator*

White Stone
Sparks, Kenneth R. *association executive*

Williamsburg
Campbell, Colin Goetze *foundation president*
Chandler, Kimberley Lynn *educational association administrator*

Woodbridge
Garon, Richard Joseph, Jr. *political organization worker*

WASHINGTON

Bellevue
Arnold, Ronald Henri *nonprofit organization executive, consultant*

Kirkland
Teeley, Kevin *educational association administrator*

Port Townsend
Woolf, William Blauvelt *retired association executive*

Seattle
Arthur, William Lynn *environmental and political program director*
Bell, William C. *foundation administrator*
Davidson, Robert William *not-for-profit executive*
Foster, Barry Alan *cultural organization researcher, educator*
Friedman, Alexander Stephen *foundation administrator, investment banker*
Gates, Melinda French *foundation administrator*
Green, Joshua III *foundation administrator, retired bank executive*
Jessen, Joel Anne *not-for-profit executive, art educator*
Jones, Allan *medical research organization executive*
Martínez, Yolanda R. *social services administrator*
Petry, Don D. *educational association administrator*
Scott, Cheryl M. *foundation administrator, healthcare educator*
Stonesifer, Patty (Patricia Q. Stonesifer) *foundation administrator*
Vander Ark, Tom *foundation administrator*

Spokane
Herzer, Marian Day *not-for-profit developer, educator*

WEST VIRGINIA

Charleston
Chapman, John Andrew *retired chamber of commerce executive*

Shinnston
Ford, Alma Regina *retired union official, educator*

WISCONSIN

Kenosha
Adler, Seymour Jack *social services administrator*

Madison
Brennan, Robert Walter *association executive*
Frautschi, W. Jerome (Jerry Frautschi) *foundation administrator, retired manufacturing executive*
Olson, Norman Fredrick *not-for-profit developer, retired food science educator*

Middleton
Taylor, Fannie Turnbull *art association administrator, educator*

Milwaukee
Boese, Gil Karyle *cultural organization administrator*
Schneider, Thomas Paul *non-profit agency administrator*

Pittsville
Bayerl, Scott Lee *animal welfare organization administrator, web programmer*

Wauwatosa
Verdoni, Shawn Marie *not-for-profit fundraiser*

WYOMING

Casper
Cotherman, Audrey Mathews *educational association administrator, management consultant*

Cheyenne
Noe, Guy *retired social services administrator*

Laramie
Darnall, Roberta Morrow *educational association administrator*

TERRITORIES OF THE UNITED STATES

GUAM

Hagatna
Leon-Guerrero, Jillette Torre *nonprofit organization executive, consultant, writer*

PUERTO RICO

Dorado
Glickman, Marlene *non-profit organization administrator*

MILITARY ADDRESSES OF THE UNITED STATES

EUROPE

APO
Wagner, Mary S. *education center administrator*

CANADA

ALBERTA

Calgary
Hume, James Borden *foundation administrator, director*

ONTARIO

Ottawa
Maxwell, Judith *think-tank executive, economist*
Plumptre, Tim *think-tank executive*

Toronto
Goold, Douglas *think-tank executive*
Mintz, Jack Maurice *think-tank executive, economics professor*

QUEBEC

Gatineau
Wilson, Ian Edwin *cultural organization administrator, archivist*

Outremont
Gulkin, Harry *arts administrator, film producer*
Letourneau, Jean-Paul *professional society administrator*

YUKON TERRITORY

Whitehorse
Couchman, Robert George James *foundation executive*

MEXICO

Mexico City
Bruton, John Macaulay *trade association executive, consultant*

BELGIUM

Genappe
Williams, Jody *political organization administrator*

CHINA

Beijing
Bai, Chunli *professional society administrator, educator*

ENGLAND

London
Chadwick, Derek James *foundation administrator*
Desai, Nitin Dayalji *international organization official*
Greener, Sir Anthony *educational association administrator*
Nelson, Elizabeth Hawkins *not-for-profit association administrator*

GERMANY

Hamburg
Lüst, Reimar *foundation president*

Mayen
Gartz, Rolf F. *foundation administrator*

ITALY

Rome
Shiner, Josette Sheeran (Josette Sheeran) *international organization official, former federal agency administrator*
Sisulu, Sheila Violet Makate *international organization official, diplomat*

SWEDEN

Stockholm
Sohlman, Michael *foundation administrator*
Wastberg, Olle M. *cultural organization administrator*

SWITZERLAND

Geneva
Evans, Timothy Grant *international organization administrator*
Piot, Peter *international organization administrator*
Sommaruga, Cornelio *foundation administrator, diplomat*

UNITED ARAB EMIRATES

Abu Dhabi
Cleaves, Peter Shurtleff *foundation administrator*

ADDRESS UNPUBLISHED

Alves, Kyrin Jean *cultural organization administrator, educator*
Ambach, Gordon Mac Kay *educational association executive*
Anderson, Ned, Sr. *Apache tribal chairman*
Ash, Dorothy Matthews *civic worker*

Zimny, Max *labor union administrator, lawyer, arbitrator*

ATHLETICS

UNITED STATES

ALABAMA

Auburn
Housel, David *retired athletic director*
Tuberville, Tommy *college football coach*

Tuscaloosa
Saban, Nick Lou *college football coach, former professional football coach*

ALASKA

Eagle River
Cotten, Samuel Richard *fisheries consultant, former state legislator, consultant*

ARIZONA

Coolidge
Laursen, Lin L. *women's college basketball coach, educator*

Glendale
Doan, Shane *professional hockey player*
Gretzky, Wayne Douglas *retired professional hockey player, professional hockey coach*
Maloney, Don *professional sports team executive, retired professional hockey player*
Nolan, Owen *professional hockey player*

Phoenix
Barbosa, Leandro Mateus *professional basketball player*
Bell, Raja *professional basketball player*
Bidwill, William V. *professional sports team executive*
Boldin, Anquan *professional football player*
D'Antoni, Mike (Michael Andrew D'Antoni) *Professional basketball coach and sports team executive, former player*
Garagiola, Joe, Jr. *baseball team executive*
Hill, Grant *professional basketball player*
Hudson, Orlando Thill *professional baseball player*
James, Edgerrin Tyree *professional football player*
Johnson, Randy (Randall David Johnson) *professional baseball player*
Kerr, Steve (Stephen Douglas Kerr) *professional sports team executive, retired professional basketball player*
Leinart, Matt *professional football player*
Marion, Shawn *professional basketball player*
Nash, Steve *professional basketball player*
Pitman, Jim *professional sports team executive*
Rose, Jalen *professional basketball player*
Sarver, Robert G. *professional sports team owner*
Stoudemire, Amare Carsares *professional basketball player*
Taurasi, Diana Lurena *professional basketball player*
Valverde, Jose Rafael *professional baseball player*
Webb, Brandon Tyler *professional baseball player*
Welts, Rick *professional sports team executive*
Westhead, Paul *professional basketball coach*

Scottsdale
Duran, Roberto *retired boxer*
Ogilvy, Geoff *professional golfer*

Tempe
Erickson, Dennis *college football coach, former professional football coach*
Turner Thorne, Charli *women's college basketball coach*
Warner, Kurt(is) *professional football player*
Whisenhunt, Ken *professional football coach*

Tucson
Kearney, Joseph Laurence *retired athletic conference administrator*

ARKANSAS

Fayetteville
Broyles, Frank (John Franklin Broyles) *athletic director, retired college football coach*
Collen, Tom *women's college basketball coach*
Nutt, Houston *university football coach*
Pelphrey, John *men's college basketball coach*

CALIFORNIA

Alameda
Brooks, Aaron Lafette *professional football player*
Davis, Allen *professional football team executive*
Jordan, LaMont *professional football player*
Kiffin, Lane *professional football coach*
Russell, JaMarcus *professional football player*
Sapp, Warren Carlos *professional football player*

Aliso Viejo
Cohen, Sasha (Alexandra Pauline Cohen) *ice skater*

Anaheim
Bertuzzi, Todd *professional hockey player*
Burke, Brian *professional sports team executive*
Carlyle, Randy *professional hockey coach, retired professional hockey player*
Getzlaf, Ryan *professional hockey player*
Giguere, Jean-Sebastien *professional hockey player*
Green, Travis *professional hockey player*
Guerrero, Vladimir Alvino *professional baseball player*
Lackey, John Derran *professional baseball player*
Moreno, Arturo (Arte Moreno) *major league baseball team owner, former advertising executive*
Niedermayer, Scott *professional hockey player*
Pronger, Chris *professional hockey player*
Rodriguez, Francisco Jose *professional baseball player*
Schneider, Mathieu *professional hockey player*
Selanne, Teemu *professional hockey player*
Weaver, Jered *professional baseball player*

Berkeley
Tedford, Jeff *college football coach*

Beverly Hills
Fleming, Peggy Gale *professional ice skater*
Johnson, Magic (Earvin Johnson Jr.) *professional sports team and development company executive, former professional basketball coach and player*

Camarillo
Bryan, Bob Charles *professional tennis player*
Bryan, Mike Carl *professional tennis player*

Carson
Beckham, David (David Robert Joseph Beckham) *professional soccer player*
Lalas, Alexi (Panayotis Alexander Lalas) *professional sports team executive, retired professional soccer player*
Ruiz Gutierrez, Carlos Humberto *professional soccer player*
Schmid, Sigi *professional soccer coach*

Coronado
Axelson, Joseph Allen *professional sports team and publishing executive*

Danville
Wisniewski, Stephen Adam *professional football player*

El Segundo
Abdul-Jabbar, Kareem (Lew Alcindor, Lewis Ferdinand Alcindor) *professional basketball coach, retired professional basketball player*
Bryant, Kobe *professional basketball player*
Buss, Jerry (Gerald Hatten Buss) *professional sports team owner*
Kupchak, Mitchell *professional sports team executive, retired professional basketball player*
Odom, Lamar Joseph *professional basketball player*
Toler, Penny *former professional basketball player, sports team executive*

Fallbrook
Cordes, Kathleen Ann *retired physical education educator, director*

Huntington Beach
Slater, Kelly (Robert Kelly Slater) *professional surfer*

La Jolla
Bavasi, Peter Joseph *sports management executive*

Lake Forest
Cranmer, Scotty *professional trick bike rider*

Long Beach
Monson, Dan *men's college basketball coach*

Los Angeles
Baylor, Elgin Gay *professional sports team executive and retired basketball player*
Blake, Rob *professional hockey player*
Brown, Kwame *professional basketball player*
Brusa, Amilcar *boxing trainer*
Carroll, Pete *college football coach*
Cassell, Samuel James *professional basketball player*
Choudhury, Bikram *yoga instructor, writer, entrepreneur*
Colletti, Ned *professional sports team executive*
Cooper, Michael Jerome *professional basketball coach and former player*
Crawford, Marc *professional hockey coach*
De La Hoya, Oscar *boxer*
Dorrell, Karl *college football coach*
Dunleavy, Michael Joseph, Sr. *professional basketball coach*
Floyd, Tim *men's college basketball coach, former professional basketball coach*
Furcal, Rafael *professional baseball player*
Garciaparra, Nomar (Anthony Nomar Garciaparra) *professional baseball player*
Hextall, Ron *professional sports team executive, former professional hockey player*
Hopkins, Bernard *professional boxer*
Howland, Ben *men's college basketball coach*
Jackson, Philip Douglas *professional basketball coach*
Kent, Jeffrey Franklin *professional baseball player*
Lasorda, Tommy (Thomas Charles Lasorda) *professional baseball team manager*
Lavin, Stephen Michael *university basketball coach*
Lee, Jeanette *professional billiards player*
Leslie, Lisa DeShaun *professional basketball player*
Lewis, Dave *professional hockey coach, retired professional hockey player*
Lipscomb, Steven *sports association executive*
Little, (William) Grady *professional baseball coach*
Lombardi, Dean *professional sports team executive*
Maloney, Kristen *gymnast*
Martin, Russell Nathan Coltrane Jeanson, Jr. *professional baseball player*
Mobley, Cuttino Rashawn *professional basketball player*
Ng, Kim (Kimberly J. Ng) *professional sports team executive*
Olivier, Kathy Ricks *college basketball coach*
Penny, Brad (Bradley Wayne Penny) *professional baseball player*
Robitaille, Luc *sports team executive, retired professional hockey player*
Roeser, Andy *professional sports team executive*
Saito, Takashi *professional baseball player*
Scates, Allen Edward *coach*
Schmidt, Jason *professional baseball player*
Wells, David Lee *professional baseball player*

Monrovia
Stevens, Gary *retired jockey*

Monterey Park
Stankevitz, Diane Lynn *athletic trainer*

Northridge
Jumonville, Felix Joseph, Jr. *physical education educator, real estate company officer*

Oakland
Beane, Billy (William Lamar) *professional sports team executive*
Chavez, Eric *professional baseball player*
Cohan, Christopher J. *professional sports team owner*
Davis, Baron *professional basketball player*
Ellis, Monta *professional basketball player*
Geren, Bob (Robert Peter Geren) *professional baseball manager*
Haren, Dan (Daniel John Haren) *professional baseball player*
Kendall, Jason Daniel *professional baseball player*
Kotsay, Mark Steven *professional baseball player*
Mullin, Christopher Paul *professional sports team executive, retired professional basketball player*
Nelson, Donald Arvid (Nellie Nelson) *professional basketball coach*
Piazza, Mike (Michael Joseph Piazza) *professional baseball player*
Richardson, Jason Anthoney *professional basketball player*
Rowell, Robert *professional sports team executive*
Street, Huston *professional baseball player*

Pacific Palisades
Lewis, Carl (Frederick Carlton Lewis) *Olympic track and field athlete*

Sacramento
Abdur-Rahim, Shareef (Julius Shareef Abdul-Rahim) *professional basketball player*
Artest, Ron (Ronald William Artest Jr.) *professional basketball player*
Bibby, Mike *professional basketball player*
Boucek, Jenny *professional basketball coach*
Griffith, Yolanda Evette *professional basketball player*
Maloof, Gavin Patrick *professional sports team executive*
Maloof, Joseph *professional sports team owner*
Petrie, Geoffrey Michael *professional sports team executive, retired professional basketball player*
Reynolds, Jerry Owen *professional sports team executive*
Theus, Reggie Wayne *professional basketball coach, retired professional basketball player*
Thomas, John *professional sports team executive*

San Diego
Gates, Antonio *professional football player*
Giles, Brian Stephen *professional baseball player*
Hoffman, Trevor William *professional baseball player*
Peavy, Jake (Jacob Edward Peavy) *professional baseball player*
Smith, A.J. *professional sports team executive*
Tomlinson, LaDainian *professional football player*
Turner, Norv(al) (Eugene) *professional football coach*
Winfield, Dave (David Mark Winfield) *professional sports team executive, retired professional baseball player*

San Francisco
Bochy, Bruce *professional baseball team manager and retired player*
Bonds, Barry Lamar *professional baseball player*
Cepeda, Orlando *retired professional baseball player*
Magowan, Peter Alden *professional sports team and retail executive*
Sabean, Brian R. *professional baseball team executive*
Vizquel, Omar Enrique *professional baseball player*
Zito, Barry *professional baseball player*

San Jose
Carle, Matt *professional hockey player*
Cheechoo, Jonathan *professional hockey player*
Marleau, Patrick *professional hockey player*
Nabokov, Evgeni *professional hockey player*
Roenick, Jeremy *professional hockey player*
Thornton, Joe *professional hockey player*
Wilson, Douglas Frederick *professional sports team executive, retired professional hockey player*
Wilson, Ronald Lawrence *professional hockey coach*

Santa Clara
Chastain, Brandi Denise *professional soccer player*
Nolan, Mike *professional football coach*
Smith, Alex *professional football player*

Solvang
Roberts, Monty *horse trainer, writer*

Stanford
Bowlsby, Bob *athletic director*
Grousbeck, Harold Irving *professional sports team owner, management educator*
Harbaugh, Jim (James Joseph Harbaugh) *college football coach, retired professional football player*
Montgomery, Mike *professional basketball coach*
VanDerveer, Tara *women's college basketball coach*

Stockton
Murphy, Jeremiah T. *professional sports team, construction executive*

Studio City
Hamill, Dorothy Stuart *professional ice skater*

Valley Village
Bench, Johnny Lee *retired professional baseball player*

Vista
Hawk, Tony *professional skateboarder*
Way, Danny *professional skateboarder*

COLORADO

Boulder
Neinas, Charles Merrill *sports association executive, consultant*

Colorado Springs
Beard, Amanda *swimmer, Olympic athlete*
Bobek, Nicole *professional figure skater*
Cash, Swin (Swintayla Marie Cash) *professional basketball player*
Cheek, Joey *Olympic athlete*
Colangelo, Jerry John *professional sports team executive*
Coughlin, Natalie *Olympic swimmer*
Gardner, Rulon E. *Olympic athlete*
Hall, Gary, Jr. *Olympic athlete*
Hamilton, Tyler *professional cyclist, Olympic athlete*
Hayes, Joanna *Olympic track and field athlete*
Kwan, Michelle Wing *professional figure skater*
May, Misty *Olympic athlete*
Mayweather, Floyd, Jr. *professional boxer*
McCool, Courtney *Olympic athlete*
Ogrean, David William *sports association executive*
Patterson, Carly *Olympic gymnast*
Peirsol, Aaron *Olympic swimmer*
Phelps, Michael *Olympic swimmer*
Schultz, Richard Dale *national athletic organization executive*
Teter, Hannah *Olympic athlete*
Torres, Dara *Olympic athlete*
Tueting, Sarah *professional hockey player*
Walsh, Kerri Lee *Olympic athlete*
Wariner, Jeremy *Olympic track and field athlete*

Denver
Anthony, Carmelo *professional basketball player*
Balboa, Marcelo *professional soccer player*
Camby, Marcus D. *professional basketball player*
Chapman, Rex *professional sports team executive and retired basketball player*
Fuentes, Brian Christopher *professional baseball player*
Giguere, Francois *professional sports team executive*
Hejduk, Milan *professional hockey player*
Helton, Todd *professional baseball player*
Hurdle, Clint *professional athletics manager*
Iverson, Allen Ezail *professional basketball player*
Karl, George *professional basketball coach*
Knight, Greg *professional sports team executive*
Miller, Andre *professional basketball player*
Quenneville, Joel *professional hockey coach*
Sakic, Joe (Joseph Steve Sakic) *professional hockey player*
Smyth, Ryan *professional hockey player*
Theodore, Jose *professional hockey player*
Warkentien, Mark *professional sports team executive*

Englewood
Bailey, Champ *professional football player*
Lynch, John Terrence *professional football player*
Shanahan, Mike *professional football coach*
Smith, Rod *professional football player*

Greenwood Village
Elway, John Albert *retired professional football player*

U S A F Academy
Reynolds, Jeff *men's college basketball coach*

CONNECTICUT

Bristol
Corso, Lee *former football coach, football analyst*
Gwynn, Anthony Keith (Tony Gwynn) *former professional baseball player*
Kruk, John Martin *retired professional baseball player, sportscaster*
Sutcliffe, Rick (Richard Lee Sutcliffe) *professional baseball player*

Litchfield
Kennedy, Susan Orpha *physical education educator, consultant, sports official*

New Haven
Brand, Myles *sports association and former academic administrator*

Simsbury
Yagudin, Alexei *Olympic athlete, ice skater*

South Windsor
Baretta, Marsha Motyl *elementary school physical education educator*

Stamford
Goldsmith, Donna *sports association executive*
McMahon, Linda E. *sports association executive*
McMahon, Vince (Vincent Kennedy McMahon) *sports entertainment company executive*
Valentine, Bobby (Robert John Valentine) *professional baseball manager*

Storrs Mansfield
Auriemma, Geno *women's college basketball coach*
Calhoun, Jim *men's college basketball coach*

Uncasville
Douglas, Katie (Kathryn Elizabeth Douglas) *professional basketball player*
Lobo, Rebecca *professional basketball player*
Thibault, Mike *professional basketball coach*

DISTRICT OF COLUMBIA

Washington
Acta, Manny (Manuel Elias Acta) *professional baseball manager*
Arenas, Gilbert *professional basketball player*
Butler, (James) Caron *professional basketball player*
Grunfeld, Ernie *professional sports team executive, retired professional basketball player*
Hanlon, Glen *professional hockey coach*
Hernandez, Livan Eisler *professional baseball player*
Jamison, Antawn *professional basketball player*
Jordan, Eddie *professional basketball coach*
Kolzig, Olaf *professional hockey player*
McPhee, George *professional sports team executive*
Moreno, Jaime *professional soccer player*
Ovechkin, Alexander *professional hockey player*
Patrick, Richard M. *professional hockey team executive*
Robinson, Crystal LaTresa *professional basketball coach, retired professional basketball player*
Rollins, Tree (Wayne Monte Rollins) *professional basketball coach, former professional basketball player*
Shriver, Timothy Perry *sports association executive*
Thomas, Etan *professional basketball player, poet*
Thompson, John III *men's college basketball coach*
Upshaw, Gene (Eugene Upshaw) *sports association executive*
Zimmerman, Ryan Wallace *professional baseball player*

FLORIDA

Bradenton
Haas, Tommy (Thomas Mario Haas) *professional tennis player*

Clermont
Richardson, Dot (Dorothy Gay) *former Olympic softball player, physician*

Coral Gables
Harriell, Kysha *athletic trainer, educator*

Coral Springs
Becker, Benjamin *professional tennis player*

Davie
Capers, Dom (Dominic Capers) *professional football coach*
Green, Trent Jason *professional football player*
Taylor, Jason Paul *professional football player*
Thomas, Zach Michael *professional football player*

Daytona Beach
Ahn, Shi Hyun *professional golfer*
Andrews, Donna L. *professional golfer*
Bivens, Carolyn Vesper *sports association administrator, former advertising executive*
Bodine, Geoff *race car driver*
Castrale, Nicole *professional golfer*
Cavalleri, Silvia *professional golfer*
Creamer, Paula *professional golfer*
Davies, Laura *professional golfer*
DeLuca, Annette *professional golfer*
France, Brian Z. *sports association executive*
France, James C. *professional sports executive*
Han, Hee-Won *professional golfer*
Inkster, Juli *professional golfer*
Jang, Jeong *professional golfer*
Kerr, Cristie *professional golfer*
Kim, Mi Hyun *professional golfer*
Kung, Candie *professional golfer*
Lee, Seon-Hwa *professional golfer*
Lincicome, Brittany *professional golfer*
Mears, Casey *race car driver*
Ochoa, Lorena *professional golfer*
Pak, Se Ri *professional golfer*
Park, Hee-Jung (Hee Jong Park) *professional golfer*
Prammanasudh, Stacy *professional golfer*
Pressel, Morgan *professional golfer*
Rosales, Jennifer *professional golfer*
Sheehan, Patty *professional golfer*
Smith, Marilynn *retired professional golfer*
Sorenstam, Annika *professional golfer*
Steinhauer, Sherri *professional golfer*
Votaw, Ty M. *golf association commissioner*
Webb, Karrie *professional golfer*
Whitworth, Kathrynne Ann *professional golfer*
Wie, Michelle Sung *professional golfer*

Deerfield Beach
King, Don *boxing promoter*

Fort Lauderdale
Cameron, Cam (Malcolm Cameron) *professional football coach*
Mahan, Mary Hoyle *retired physical educator*

Gainesville
Brewer, Corey Wayne *college basketball player*
Donovan, Billy (William John) *men's college basketball coach*
Foley, Jeremy N. *athletic director*
Meyer, Urban *college football coach*

Jacksonville
Campo, Dave *professional football coach*
Del Rio, Jack *professional football coach, former professional football player*
Koetter, Dirk J. *professional and former college football coach*
Leftwich, Byron Antron *professional football player*
Shula, Mike (Michael John Shula) *professional football coach, former college football coach*
Taylor, Fred *professional football player*

Jupiter
Vanatta, Bob *athletic administrator*

Miami
Loria, Jeffrey H. *sports team executive*
Martin, Jacques *professional hockey coach and sports team executive*
O'Neal, Shaquille Rashaun *professional basketball player*
Payton, Gary Dwayne *professional basketball player*
Pfund, Randy (Randell Pfund) *professional sports team executive*
Ramirez, Hanley *professional baseball player*
Riley, Patrick James *professional basketball coach, professional sports team executive*
Rothstein, Ronald *professional basketball coach*
Shannon, Randy Lannard *college football coach*
Underwood, Joseph Warren *athletic trainer, educator*
Wade, Dwyane (Dwyane Tyrone Wade Jr.) *professional basketball player*
Williams, Jason Chandler *professional basketball player*
Willis, Dontrelle *professional baseball player*
Woolworth, Eric S. *professional sports team executive*

Miami Beach
Shula, Don Francis *retired professional football coach, professional sports team executive*

Miami Gardens
Cabrera, Miguel (Jose Miguel Cabrera) *professional baseball player*

Naples
Frazer, John Howard *tennis association and retired manufacturing executive*

Navarre
Bare Grounds, Patricia Kelly *athletic trainer, small business owner*

North Palm Beach
Nicklaus, Jack William *professional golfer*

Orlando
DeVos, Richard Marvin, Sr. *professional sports team owner, former network marketing company executive*
Fritz, Jim *professional sports team executive*
Howard, Dwight David, II, *professional basketball player*
Lewis, Rashard Quovon *professional basketball player*
Martins, Alex *professional sports team executive*
Redick, J.J. (Jonathan Clay Redick) *college basketball player*
Smith, Otis Fitzgerald *professional sports team executive, former professional basketball player*
Vander Weide, Bob *professional sports team executive*
Van Gundy, Stan *professional basketball coach*
Williams, Pat *professional sports team executive*

Palm Beach Gardens
Choi, K.J. (Kyung-ju Choi) *professional golfer*
Couples, Frederick Steven *professional golfer*
Daly, John Patrick *professional golfer*
Duval, David Robert *professional golfer*
Furyk, Jim (James Michael Furyk) *professional golfer*
Mickelson, Phil (Philip Alfred Mickelson Jr.) *professional golfer*
Nelson, Larry Gene *professional golfer*
Verplank, Scott Rachal *professional golfer*
Wadkins, Lanny Lanston *professional golfer*
Woods, Tiger (Eldrick Woods) *professional golfer*

Palm City
Mc Hale, John Joseph *baseball club executive*

Palm Harbor
Jordan, Patricia Colgan *physical education educator*

Ponte Vedra
Singh, Vijay *professional golfer*

Ponte Vedra Beach
Agassi, Andre Kirk *retired professional tennis player*
Azinger, Paul *professional golfer*
Blake, James Riley *professional tennis player*
Calcavecchia, Mark *professional golfer*
Campbell, Chad *professional golfer*
Cink, Stewart *professional golfer*
Coria, Guillermo *professional tennis player*
Curtis, Ben Clifford *professional golfer*
Els, Ernie (Theodore Ernest Els) *professional golfer*
Finchem, Tim *sports association executive*
Garcia, Sergio *professional golfer*
Gaudio, Gaston *professional tennis player*
Ginepri, Robby (Robert Louis Ginepri) *professional tennis player*
Green, Hubert *professional golfer*
Grosjean, Sebastien Rene *professional tennis player*
Howell, Charles III *professional golfer*
Johnson, Zach (Zachary Harris Johnson) *professional golfer*
Langer, Bernhard *professional golfer*
Montgomerie, Colin Stuart *professional golfer*
Moya, Carlos *professional tennis player*
Nalbandian, David *professional tennis player*
Novak, Jiri *professional tennis player*
Pavin, Corey Allen *professional golfer*
Rodriguez, Chi Chi (Juan Rodriguez) *professional golfer*
Scott, Adam *professional golfer*
Strange, Curtis Northrop *professional golfer*
Stricker, Steve *professional golfer*
Young, Mark V. *sports association executive*

Saint Petersburg
Allaster, Stacey *sports association executive*
Clijsters, Kim *retired professional tennis player*
Craybas, Jill *professional tennis player*
Dementieva, Elena *professional tennis player*
Huber, Liezel *professional tennis player*
Kazmir, Scott *professional baseball player*
Kuznetsova, Svetlana *professional tennis player*
Maddon, Joe *professional baseball coach*
Myskina, Anastasia *professional tennis player*
Sharapova, Maria *professional tennis player*
Shaughnessy, Meghann *professional tennis player*
Upton, B.J. (Melvin Emanuel Upton) *professional baseball player*
Young, Delmon Damarcus *professional baseball player*
Zimmer, Donald William *former professional baseball coach, professional baseball manager, retired professional baseball player*

Sunrise
Kitchen, Mike *professional hockey coach, retired professional hockey player*
Nieuwendyk, Joe *retired professional hockey player, consultant*

Tallahassee
Bowden, Bobby (Robert Cleckler Bowden) *college football coach*
Yerg, Beverly Johnson *retired physical education educator, researcher*

Tampa
Alstott, Michael Joseph (Mike Alstott) *professional football player*
Brooks, Derrick Dewan *professional football player*
Feaster, Jay *professional sports team executive*
Garcia, Jeff (Jeffrey Jason Garcia) *professional football player*
Glazer, Malcolm *professional sports team executive*
Gruden, Jon *professional football coach*
Lecavalier, Vincent *professional hockey player*
Richards, Brad *professional hockey player*
St. Louis, Martin *professional hockey player*
Tortorella, John *professional hockey coach*

Vero Beach
Fish, Mardy *professional tennis player*

Viera
Nessel, Edward Harry *swimming coach*

West Palm Beach
Floyd, Raymond Loran *professional golfer*

GEORGIA

Athens
Evans, Damon *university athletics director*
Richt, Mark *college football coach*

Atlanta
Aaron, Hank (Henry L. Aaron) *professional baseball team executive*
Andersen, Morten *professional football player*
Belkin, Steven *professional sports team owner*
Bellamy, Walter *professional basketball player*
Cox, Bobby (Robert Joe Cox) *professional baseball manager*
DePaoli, Lou *professional sports team executive*
Duffy, Bill *professional sports team executive*
Gailey, Chan, Jr., (Thomas Chandler Gailey) *college football coach*
Gearon, John Michael, Sr., (Michael Gearon) *professional sports team owner*
Gearon, John Michael, Jr., (Michael Gearon) *professional sports team owner, communications executive*
Hartley, Bob *professional hockey coach*
Johnson, Joe Marcus *professional basketball player*
Jones, Andruw Rudolf *professional baseball player*
Jones, Chipper (Larry Wayne Jones Jr.) *professional baseball player*
Knight, Billy (William R. Knight) *professional sports team executive*
Kovalchuk, Ilya *professional hockey player*
McCann, Brian Michael *professional baseball player*
Mullin, Bernard James *professional sports team executive*
Renteria, Edgar *professional baseball player*
Riccio, Felix *professional sports team owner*
Rucchin, Steve *professional hockey player*
Schuerholz, John Boland, Jr. *professional baseball executive*
Seydel, Rutherford (John), (II) *professional sports team owner, lawyer*
Smoltz, John Andrew *professional baseball player*
Teixeira, Mark Charles *professional baseball player*
Turner, Beau (Reed Beauregard Turner) *professional sports team owner, philanthropist*
Waddell, Don *professional sports team executive*
Wilkins, Dominique (Jacques Dominique Wilkins) *professional sports team executive, retired professional basketball player*
Woodson, Mike *professional basketball coach*
Zhitnik, Alexei *professional hockey player*

Fairburn
Holyfield, Evander *professional boxer*

Flowery Branch
Abraham, John *professional football player*
Blank, Arthur M. *professional sports team and retired lumber company executive*
Crumpler, Alge *professional football player*
Hall, DeAngelo *professional football player*
Harrington, Joey (John Joseph Harrington) *professional football player*
Horn, Joe *professional football player*
McKay, Richard James *professional sports team executive*
Petrino, Bobby *professional football coach*

Marietta
Devigne, Karen Cooke *retired amateur athletics executive*

Morrow
Totty, Totty Okoro *soccer coach*

HAWAII

Aiea
Manabe, Shari A *physical education educator*

IDAHO

Boise
Petersen, Chris *college football coach*

ILLINOIS

Alsip
Fournier, Maureen Mary *physical education educator*

Bridgeview
Guppy, John *professional sports team executive*

Carbondale
Lowery, Christopher M. *men's college basketball coach*

Chicago
Albright, Chris *professional soccer player*
Baines, Harold Douglass *retired professional baseball player, baseball bench coach*
Beasley, DaMarcus Lamont *professional soccer player*
Berhalter, Gregg *professional soccer player*
Bocanegra, Carlos *professional soccer player*
Bondra, Peter *professional hockey player*
Buehrle, Mark *professional baseball player*
Cherdunolo, Steve *professional soccer player*
Ching, Brian *professional soccer player*
Conrad, Jimmy *professional soccer player*
Convey, Bobby (Robert Francis Convey) *professional soccer player*
Dempsey, Clinton (Clint) Drew *professional soccer player*
Dempster, Ryan Scott *professional baseball player*
Deng, Luol *professional basketball player*
Donovan, Landon *professional soccer player*
Dudley, Rick (Richard C. Dudley) *professional sports team executive*
Dupree, Candice *professional basketball player*
Dye, Jermaine *professional baseball player*
Erkes, Jason *sports association executive*
Fawcett, Joy Lynn *retired professional soccer player*
Foudy, Julie Maurine *retired professional soccer player, Olympic athlete*
Gabarra, Carin Leslie *professional soccer player, professional soccer coach*
Gervais, Mark G. *physical education educator*
Gordon, Ben *professional basketball player*
Guillen, Ozzie (Oswaldo Jose Barrios Guillen) *professionall baseball manager*

Hahnemann, Marcus *professional soccer player*
Hamm, Mia (Mariel Margaret Hamm) *retired professional soccer player*
Heinrichs, April *soccer coach*
Howard, Tim *professional soccer player*
Hucles, Angela Khalia *professional soccer player*
Jenks, Bobby (Robert Scott Jenks) *professional baseball player*
Johnson, Eddie *professional soccer player*
Jones, Cobi *professional soccer player*
Keller, Kasey *professional soccer player*
Khabibulin, Nikolai *professional hockey player*
Konerko, Paul *professional baseball player*
Kreis, Jason *professional soccer coach, retired professional soccer player*
Lee, Derrek Leon *professional baseball player*
Lewis, Eddie *professional soccer player*
Mastroeni, Pablo *professional soccer player*
Milbrett, Tiffeny Carleen *professional soccer player*
O'Brien, John *professional soccer player*
Olsen, Ben *professional soccer player*
Onyewu, Oguchi *professional soccer player*
O'Reilly, Heather Ann *Olympic athlete*
Overton, Bo *professional basketball coach*
Paxson, John *professional sports team executive, retired professional basketball player*
Piniella, Lou (Louis Victor Piniella) *professional baseball team manager*
Pizer, Howard Charles *sports and entertainment executive*
Pope, Eddie *professional soccer player*
Prior, Mark *professional baseball player*
Ralph, Damani *professional soccer player*
Reddick, Catherine Anne (Cat Reddick) *Olympic athlete*
Reinsdorf, Jerry Michael *professional sports team owner, real estate company executive, accountant, lawyer*
Reyna, Claudio *professional soccer player*
Savard, Denis Joseph *professional hockey coach, former professional hockey player*
Schanwald, Steve *professional sports team executive*
Schwartz, Alan Gifford *sport company executive*
Scurry, Briana Collette *professional soccer player*
Skiles, Scott Allen *professional basketball coach*
Soriano, Alfonso Guilleard *professional baseball player*
Tallon, Dale *professional sports team executive*
Torchetti, John *professional hockey coach*
Trammell, Alan Stuart *professional baseball coach, retired professional baseball player*
Venturini, Tisha Lea *professional soccer player*
Wallace, Ben *professional basketball player*
Wambach, Abby (Mary Abigail Wambach) *Olympic athlete*
Westbrook, Brian *professional football player*
Wolff, Josh *professional soccer player*
Wood, Kerry *professional baseball player*
Zambrano, Carlos Alberto *professional baseball player*

Evanston
Davis, Shani *Olympic athlete*

Glenview
King, Billie Jean Moffitt *retired professional tennis player*

Lake Forest
Benson, Cedric *professional football player*
Griese, Brian *professional football player*
Grossman, Rex *professional football player*
McCaskey, Michael B. *professional football team executive*
Murphy, Karen *sports association executive*
Orton, Kyle *professional football player*
Smith, Lovie *professional football coach*
Urlacher, Brian Keith *professional football player*

Libertyville
Trzyna, Chris *physical education educator*

Lincolnshire
Schauble, John Eugene *physical education educator*

Mahomet
Thompson, Margaret M. *physical education educator*

Normal
Laudner, Kevin *athletic trainer, educator*

Park Ridge
Delany, Jim (James Edward Delany) *sports association administrator, lawyer*

Schaumburg
Colberg, Linda *physical education educator*

Springfield
Hicks, David Eric *retired sports association executive*

INDIANA

Bloomington
Sampson, Kelvin Dale *college basketball coach*

Granger
Thomas, Debi (Debra J. Thomas) *ice skater*

Indianapolis
Addai, Joseph *professional football player*
Bird, Larry Joe *professional sports team executive, retired professional basketball player*
Catchings, Tamika Devonne *professional basketball player*
Dawes, Dominique *Olympic athlete*
DeForge, Anna *professional basketball player*
Dungy, Tony *professional football coach*
Faulk, Marshall Williams *retired professional football player*
Freeney, Dwight *professional football player*
Greene, Maurice *Olympic athlete, track and field athlete*
Harrison, Marvin *professional football player*
Irsay, James Steven *professional football team owner*
Jones, Marion *track and field athlete*
Manning, Peyton Williams *professional football player*
Montoya, Juan Pablo *professional race car driver*
Morway, David S. *professional sports team executive*
O'Brien, Jim *professional basketball coach*
O'Neal, Jermaine *professional basketball player*
Stevens, Brad K. *men's college basketball coach*
Taylor, Angelo *Olympic athlete*
Vinatieri, Adam Matthew *professional football player*
Walsh, Donnie (Joseph Donald Walsh Jr.) *professional sports team executive*
Williams, Bernard *Olympic athlete*
Winters, Brian Joseph *professional basketball coach*

Notre Dame
Weis, Charlie *college football coach*

West Lafayette
Sims-Curry, Kristy *women's college basketball coach*
Versyp, Sharon *women's college basketball coach*

IOWA

Bettendorf
Hatch, Lori S. *physical education educator*

Davenport
Foster, James Franklin *professional sports management executive*

Iowa City
Ferentz, Kirk *college football coach*
Lickliter, Todd *men's college basketball coach*

KANSAS

Emmett
Byers, Walter *athletic association executive*

Lawrence
Self, Bill *men's college basketball coach*

Manhattan
Martin, Frank (Francisco J. Martin) *men's college basketball coach*
Patterson, Deb *women's college basketball coach*

Mcpherson
Coppock, Doris Ellen *retired physical education educator, retired music educator*

Mission
Trevino, Lee Buck *professional golfer*

Wichita
Marshall, Gregg *men's college basketball coach*

Yates Center
Stockebrand, Larry Dean *physical education educator, director*

KENTUCKY

Lexington
Gillispie, Billy Clyde *men's college basketball coach*
Prado, Edgar *horse racing jockey*
Zito, Nick *horse trainer, breeder*

Louisville
Evans, Robert L. *sports venue executive*
Kragthorpe, Steve *college football coach*
Pitino, Rick *men's college basketball coach*
Walz, Jeff (Jeffrey J. Walz) *women's college basketball coach*

Richmond
Inman, Larry Joe *basketball coach*

LOUISIANA

Baton Rouge
Chancellor, Van *women's college basketball coach*
Miles, Les *college football coach*
Starkey, Bob (Robert G. Starkey) *women's college basketball coach*

Metairie
Brees, Drew (Drew Christopher Brees) *professional football player*
Bush, Reggie *professional football player*
Loomis, Mickey *professional sports team executive*
Payton, Sean (Patrick Sean Payton) *professional football coach*

New Orleans
Scelfo, Chris *university football coach*
Shinn, George *professional sports team owner*
Toledo, Bob *college football coach*

MAINE

Bangor
Kelley, Barbara Bannin *retired physical education educator*

Kingfield
Wescott, Seth *Olympic athlete*

Portland
Blair, Bonnie Kathleen *former professional speedskater, former Olympic athlete*
Powers, Ross *Olympic athlete*

MARYLAND

Baltimore
Angelos, Peter G. *professional sports team executive, lawyer*
Duquette, Jim *professional sports team executive*
Lewis, Ray *professional football player*
MacPhail, Andrew B. *professional sports team executive*
McGahee, Willis Andrew *professional football player*
McNair, Steve LaTreal *professional football player*
Ogden, Jonathan *professional football player*
Palmeiro, Rafael Corrales *professional baseball player*
Ripken, Cal (Calvin Edwin Ripken Jr.) *retired professional baseball player*
Roberts, Brian Michael *professional baseball player*
Robinson, Brooks Calbert, Jr. *retired professional baseball player, sports commentator, business consultant*
Tejada, Miguel (Odalis) *professional baseball player*
Trembley, Dave *professional baseball manager*

Bethesda
Johnson, Robert Louis *professional sports team owner, former broadcast executive*
Palmer, James Alvin (Jim Palmer) *baseball commentator*

Bowie
Baker, Marshina *physical education educator*

College Park
Frese, Brenda S. *women's college basketball coach*

Owings Mills
Billick, Brian *professional football coach*
Newsome, Ozzie *professional sports team executive*
Smith, Troy *professional football player*

Rockville
Foreman, Todd Matthew *professional sports team owner, communications executive*
Levenson, Bruce *professional sports team owner, communications executive*
Peskowitz, Ed *professional sports team owner, communications executive*

MASSACHUSETTS

Boston
Ainge, Danny Ray *professional sports team executive, retired professional basketball player*
Allen, Ray (Walter Ray Allen) *professional basketball player*
Allen, Tony *professional basketball player*
Amaker, Tommy *men's college basketball coach*
Beckett, Joshua Patrick *professional baseball player*
Blendon, Robert Jay *health policy educator*
Chara, Zdeno *professional hockey player*
Chiarelli, Peter *professional sports team executive*
Crisp, Coco (Covelli Crisp) *professional baseball player*
Drew, J.D. *professional baseball player*
Duquette, Daniel F. *professional baseball team executive*
Epstein, Robert *professional sports team owner, real estate company executive*
Epstein, Theo N. *professional sports team executive*
Fernandez, Manny (Emmanuel Fernandez-Lemaire) *professional hockey player*
Francona, Terry Jon *professional baseball manager*
Gagne, Eric *professional baseball player*
Garnett, Kevin *professional basketball player*
Gomes, Ryan *professional basketball player*
Gonzalez, Juan (Alberto Vazquez) *professional baseball player*
Gotham, Richard Ernest *professional sports team executive*
Henry, John W. *professional sports team executive*
Julien, Claude *professional hockey coach*
Kessel, Phil *professional hockey player*
Loretta, Mark *professional baseball player*
Lowell, Mike *professional baseball player*
Lucchino, Lawrence *sports team executive, lawyer*
Magadan, David Joseph *retired professional baseball player*
Matsuzaka, Daisuke *professional baseball player*
Ortiz, David (David Americo Ortiz Arias) *professional baseball player*
Pagliuca, Stephen *professional sports team owner, investment company officer*
Papelbon, Jon (Jonathan R. Papelbon) *professional baseball player*
Pierce, Paul Anthony *professional basketball player*
Ramirez, Manny (Manuel Aristides Ramirez) *professional baseball player*
Rivers, Doc (Glenn Anton Rivers) *professional basketball coach*
Schilling, Curtis Montague *professional baseball player*
Sinden, Harry *professional sports team executive*
Szczerbiak, Wally *professional basketball player*
Varitek, Jason *professional baseball player*
Wakefield, Timothy Stephen (Tim Wakefield) *professional baseball player*
Ward, Aaron *professional hockey player*

Braintree
Malloy, Ellen Ann *athletic trainer*

Foxboro
Belichick, Bill (William Stephen Belichick) *professional football coach*
Brady, Tom (Thomas Edward Patrick Brady Jr.) *professional football player*
Bruschi, Tedy *professional football player*
Dillon, Corey *professional football player*
Kraft, Robert K. *professional sports team executive*
Moss, Randy Gene *professional football player*
Testaverde, Vincent Frank (Vinny Testaverde) *professional football player*

Framingham
Flutie, Doug (Douglas Richard Flutie) *retired professional football player*

Lexington
Grousbeck, Wycliffe *professional sports team owner, venture capitalist*

Lynnfield
Kerrigan, Nancy *professional figure skater, retired Olympic athlete*

MICHIGAN

Allen Park
Johnson, Calvin *professional football player*
Kitna, Jon *professional football player*
Marinelli, Rod *professional football coach*
Millen, Matt *professional sports team executive*
Pollard, Marcus *professional football player*
Williams, Roy *professional football player*

Ann Arbor
Beilein, John Patrick *men's college basketball coach*
Berenson, Red (Gordon A. Berenson) *hockey coach, retired professional hockey player*
Carr, Lloyd H. *college football coach*

Auburn Hills
Billups, Chauncey *professional basketball player*
Dumars, Joe III *professional sports team executive, retired professional basketball player*
Ford, Cheryl *professional basketball player*
Hamilton, Richard Clay *professional basketball player*
Hammond, John *professional sports team executive*
Johnson, Shannon *professional basketball player*
Laimbeer, Bill *professional basketball coach, retired professional basketball player*
Nolan, Deanna Nicole *professional basketball player*
Ostfield, Alan *professional sports team executive*
Saunders, Flip (Philip D. Saunders) *professional basketball coach*
Wallace, Rasheed *professional basketball player, marketing professional*
Webber, Chris (Mayce Edward Christopher Webber) *professional basketball player*
Wilson, Thomas S. *professional sports team executive*

Canton
Finnerty, Bryan *sports association executive*

Cheboygan
Ostrowski, Stacey *athletic trainer, educator*

Davison
West, Stacy Kathlena *athletic trainer*

Detroit
Babcock, Mike *professional hockey coach*
Bonderman, Jeremy *professional baseball player*
Bowman, William Scott (Scotty Bowman) *professional hockey coach*
Chelios, Chris (Christos K. Chelios) *professional hockey player*
Datsyuk, Pavel *professional hockey player*
Devellano, James Charles *professional hockey manager, baseball executive*
Dombrowski, David *baseball team executive*
Hasek, Dominik *professional hockey player*
Holland, Ken *professional sports team executive*
Holmstrom, Tomas *professional hockey player*
Ilitch, Marian *professional hockey team and food service executive*
Ilitch, Michael *professional hockey team and food products executive*
Leyland, Jim (James Richard Leyland) *professional baseball manager*
Lidstrom, Nicklas *professional hockey player*
Martz, Mike *former professional football coach*
Mclendon, Lloyd *professional baseball coach, retired baseball player*
Monroe, Craig *professional baseball player*
Nabozny, Heather *professional sports team groundskeeper*
Ordonez, Magglio Jose *professional baseball player*
Osgood, Chris *professional hockey player*
Polanco, Placido Enrique *professional baseball player*
Rafalski, Brian *professional hockey player*

Rodriguez, Ivan Torres *professional baseball player*
Rogers, Kenny (Kenneth Scott Rogers) *professional baseball player*
Sheffield, Gary Antonian *professional baseball player*
Verlander, Justin Brooks *professional baseball player*
Yzerman, Steve (Stephen Gregory Yzerman) *professional sports team executive, retired professional hockey player*

East Lansing
Izzo, Thomas *college basketball coach*
Merchant, Suzy *women's college basketball coach*

Livonia
Gilbert, Daniel *professional sports team owner, mortgage company executive*

MINNESOTA

Eden Prairie
Childress, Brad *professional football coach*
Johnson, Brad *professional football player*
McCombs, Billy Joe (Red McCombs) *professional football team executive*
Woods, Gary V. *professional football team executive, former professional basketball team executive, automotive executive*

Minneapolis
Augustus, Seimone *professional basketball player*
Boone, Bret Robert *professional baseball player*
Burke, Richard T., Sr. *professional sports team executive*
Foye, Randy *professional basketball player*
Gardenhire, Ronald Clyde *professional athletics manager*
Hudson, Troy *professional basketball player*
Hunter, Torii Kedar *professional baseball player*
Kelly, Tom (Jay Thomas Kelly) *retired professional sports team manager*
Lehman, Tom (Thomas Edward Lehman) *professional golfer*
Mauer, Joe *professional baseball player*
McHale, Kevin Edward *professional sports team executive, retired professional basketball player*
Moor, Rob *professional sports team executive*
Morneau, Justin Ernest George *professional baseball player*
Nanne, Louis Vincent *professional hockey team executive*
Nevin, Phillip *professional baseball player*
Ryan, Terry *professional sports team executive*
Santana, Johan Alexander *professional baseball player*
Smith, Tubby *men's college basketball coach*
Stack, Jim *professional sports team executive*
Wittman, Randy Scott *professional basketball coach*
Wright, Chris *professional sports team executive*
Zierden, Don *professional basketball coach*

Saint Paul
Ahlvers, Steven J. *athletic trainer*
Backstrom, Niklas *professional hockey player*
Demitra, Pavol *professional hockey player*
Lemaire, Jacques *professional hockey coach*
Risebrough, Doug *professional sports team executive*

MISSISSIPPI

University
Ladner, Renee *women's college basketball coach*

MISSOURI

Earth City
Holt, Torry *professional football player*

Kansas City
Brett, George Howard *baseball executive, former professional baseball player*
Cunningham, Gunther *professional football coach*
Edwards, Herman *professional football coach*
Gansler, Robert *professional soccer coach*
Gonzalez, Tony *professional football player*
Gordon, Alex Jonathan *professional baseball player*
Holmes, Priest *professional football player*
Johnson, Larry (Larry Alphonso Johnson Jr.) *professional football player*
Meche, Gil (Gilbert Allen Meche) *professional baseball player*
Shields, Will Herthie *professional football player*

Oregon
Lynn, Brenda *physical education educator*

Saint Louis
Carpenter, Chris *professional baseball player*
Davidson, John *professional sports team executive, former hockey analyst*
Eckstein, David Mark *professional baseball player*
Edmonds, James Patrick (Jim Edmonds) *professional baseball player*
Haslett, Jim *professional football coach*
Kariya, Paul *professional hockey player*
La Russa, Tony, Jr., (Anthony La Russa Jr.) *professional baseball manager*
Linehan, Scott *professional football coach*
MacInnis, Al *professional sports team executive, retired professional hockey player*
Majerus, Rick *men's college basketball coach*
Morris, Matthew Christian *professional baseball player*
Murray, Andy *professional hockey coach*
Pace, Orlando Lamar *professional football player*
Pleau, Lawrence Winslow *professional sports team executive*
Pujols, Albert (Jose Alberto Pujols) *professional baseball player*
Rolen, Scott Bruce *professional baseball player*
Tkachuk, Keith *professional hockey player*
Weight, Doug *professional hockey player*

MONTANA

Kalispell
Bledsoe, Drew *retired professional football player*

NEBRASKA

Lincoln
Callahan, Bill *college football coach*
Mulvaney, Mary Jean *retired physical education educator*

NEVADA

Las Vegas
Hellmuth, Phil (Phillip J. Hellmuth Jr.) *professional poker player*
Kruger, Lon *men's college basketball coach*
White, Dana *sports association executive*

Reno
Fox, Mark *men's college basketball coach*

NEW HAMPSHIRE

Keene
Bleam, Nancy Kay *physical education educator*

Newmarket
Jernigan, David Bruce *men's college basketball coach*

NEW JERSEY

Branchville
Pasvolsky, Richard Lloyd *retired parks, recreation, and environment educator*

Cherry Hill
Erving, Julius (Winfield), (II) *retired professional basketball player, business executive*

East Rutherford
Carter, Vince *professional basketball player*
Coughlin, Tom *professional football coach*
Frank, Lawrence *professional basketball coach*
Gilbride, Kevin *professional football coach*
Guevara, Amado *professional soccer player*
Jefferson, Richard *professional basketball player*
Kidd, Jason *professional basketball player*
Manning, Eli (Elisha Nelson Manning) *professional football player*
Mara, John Kevin *professional sports team executive*
Mashburn, Jamal *professional basketball player*
Reese, Jerry *professional sports team executive*
Shockey, Jeremy Charles *professional football player*
Stefanski, Edward *professional sports team executive*
Strahan, Michael Anthony *professional football player*
Thorn, Rodney King *professional sports team executive, retired professional basketball player*
Toomer, Amani *professional football player*
Umenyiora, Osi *professional football player*
Yormark, Brett D. *professional sports team executive*

Jersey City
Thor, Ira P. *sports director*

Little Falls
Berra, Yogi (Lawrence Peter Berra) *former professional baseball player, coach, manager*

Montclair
Chemidlin, Michele Lynn *athletic trainer, consultant*

New Brunswick
Dougherty, Neil Joseph *physical education educator, consultant*

Newark
Brodeur, Martin *professional hockey player*
Caron, Jacques *professional hockey coach*
Elias, Patrik *professional hockey player*
Gionta, Brian *professional hockey player*
Lamoriello, Lou (Louis Anthony Lamoriello) *professional sports team executive*
Langenbrunner, Jamie *professional hockey player*
Laperriere, Jacques (Joseph Hughes Laperriere) *professional hockey coach, retired professional hockey player*
MacLean, John *professional hockey coach, former professional hockey player*
Robinson, Larry Clark *professional hockey coach*
Stevens, Scott *retired professional hockey player*
Sutter, Brent Colin *professional hockey coach, retired professional hockey player*
Vanderbeek, Jeffrey *professional sports team executive*

Piscataway
Schiano, Greg *college football coach*

Princeton
Johnson, Sydney *men's college basketball coach, former professional basketball player*

Secaucus
Arena, Bruce *professional soccer coach*
Austin, Ski *sports association executive*
Bradley, Bob *professional soccer coach*
Criqui, Robert J. *sports association executive*
Denenberg, David Scott *sports association executive, lawyer*
Hellmuth, Stephen M. *sports association executive*
Koenig, William S. *sports association executive*
Meola, Tony *professional soccer player, actor*
Sakiewicz, Nick *professional sports team executive*
Sanders, Summer *Olympic athlete, news correspondent, newscaster*

NEW MEXICO

Abiquiu
Howlett, Phyllis Lou *retired athletics administrator*

Albuquerque
Alford, Steve (Steven Todd Alford) *men's college basketball coach*

NEW YORK

Brentwood
Burgess, John Thomas *physical education educator, consultant*

Bronx
Abreu, Bobby *professional baseball player*
Afterman, Jean *professional sports team executive*
Cano, Robinson Jose *professional baseball player*
Cashman, Brian M. *professional sports team executive*
Clemens, Roger (William Roger Clemens) *professional baseball player*
Damon, Johnny *professional baseball player*
Giambi, Jason Gilbert *professional baseball player*
Hughes, Phil (Philip J. Hughes) *professional baseball player*
Jackson, Reggie (Reginald Martinez Jackson, Mr. October) *retired professional baseball player*
Jeter, Derek Sanderson *professional baseball player*
Lienert, Christoph *physical education educator*
Martinez, Tino *professional baseball player*
Matsui, Hideki *professional baseball player*
Mussina, Michael Cole *professional baseball player*
Olerud, John Garrett *professional baseball player*
Pena, Antonio Francisco (Tony Pena) *professional athletics coach*
Pettitte, Andrew Eugene (Andy Pettitte) *professional baseball player*
Posada, Jorge Rafael *professional baseball player*
Rivera, Mariano *professional baseball player*
Rodriguez, Alex (Alexander Emmanuel Rodriguez) *professional baseball player*
Steinbrenner, George Michael III *professional baseball team and shipbuilding company executive*
Torre, Joe (Joseph Paul Torre) *professional baseball team manager*
Williams, Bernie (Bernabe Figueroa Williams) *professional baseball player*

Brooklyn
Ratner, Bruce C. *professional sports team owner, real estate developer*

Buffalo
Kelly, Jim (James Edward Kelly) *former professional football player*
Miller, Ryan *professional hockey player*
Regier, Darcy John *professional sports team executive*
Ruff, Lindy *professional hockey coach*

Cobleskill
Westervelt, Gayle Gaetano *physical education educator*

Cooperstown
Mays, Willie Howard, Jr., (Say Hey Kid) *retired professional baseball player*
Sutter, Bruce (Howard Sutter) *retired professional baseball player*

Corona
Beltran, Carlos *professional baseball player*

Flushing
Alou, Moises *professional baseball player*
Castillo, Luis Antonio Donato *professional baseball player*
Delgado, Carlos Juan *professional baseball player*
Glavine, Tom (Thomas Michael Glavine) *professional baseball player*
Henderson, Rickey Henley *professional baseball coach, retired professional baseball player*
Martinez, Pedro Jaime *professional baseball player*
Minaya, Omar *professional sports team executive*
Park, Chan Ho *professional baseball player*
Randolph, Willie (Willie Larry Randolph Jr.) *professional baseball team manager, retired professional baseball player*
Reyes, Jose Bernabe *professional baseball player*
Wagner, Billy (William Edward Wagner) *professional baseball player*
Wright, David Allen *professional baseball player*

Hempstead
Coles, Laveranues *professional football player*
Dyson, Andre *professional football player*
Ferguson, D'Brickashaw *professional football player*
Mangini, Eric *professional football coach*
Pennington, Chad (James Chadwick Pennington) *professional football player*
Tannenbaum, Mike (Michael B. Tannenbaum) *professional sports team executive*

Lake Placid
Grimmette, Mark *Olympic athlete*
Martin, Brian *Olympic athlete*
Rossi, Ronald Aldo *sports association administrator, Olympic athlete*

Mamaroneck
McEnroe, Patrick *former professional tennis player, sports commentator*

New Hyde Park
Esiason, Boomer (Norman Julius Esiason) *professional football player*

New York
Adelson, Kenneth I. *sports association executive*
Bantom, Michael Allen *sports association executive*
Behrens, Kathleen *sports association executive*
Bettman, Gary Bruce *national hockey league commissioner*
Brody, John *sports association executive*
Brown, Renee M. *sports association executive*
Buchanan, Richard W. *sports association executive, lawyer*
Canseco, Jose *retired professional baseball player*
Capriati, Jennifer Maria *professional tennis player*
Clark, Gordie *professional sports team executive*
Coyle, Pat *professional basketball coach*
Deutsch, Ayala *sports association executive, lawyer, educator*
Drury, Chris *professional hockey player*
DuPuy, Bob (Robert A. DuPuy) *major league baseball executive*
Garber, Donald *Major League Soccer commissioner*
Gliedman, Michael Seth *sports association executive*
Gomez, Scott *professional hockey player*
Goodell, Roger *national football league commissioner*
Gregory, Jim (James Michael Gregory) *sports association executive, former professional sports team executive*
Hanson, Paula *sports association executive*
Herbst, Steven *sports association executive*
Hernandez, Keith *retired professional baseball player*
Houston, Allan Wade *professional basketball player*
Hunter, Billy (G. William) *sports association administrator, lawyer*
Jackson, Stu *sports association executive, former university basketball coach*
Jagr, Jaromir *professional hockey player*
Kasparaitis, Darius *professional hockey player*
Kliavkoff, George *sports association executive*
LaRocca, Salvatore *sports association executive*
Litvin, Joel M. *sports association executive, lawyer*
Louganis, Greg E(fthimios) *retired Olympic athlete, actor*
Lundqvist, Henrik *professional hockey player*
Marbury, Stephon *professional basketball player*
Mariner, Jonathan D. *major league baseball executive*
Martin, Michael Townsend *sports association executive, marketing professional, consultant*
Mattson, Joe *sports marketing executive*
McIntyre, Brian P. *sports association executive*
Meiseles, Daniel *sports association executive*
Messick, Andrew *sports association executive*
O'Neil, Scott M. *sports association executive*
Orender, Donna *sports association executive*
Ozolinsh, Sandis *professional hockey player*
Perlman, Doug *sports association executive*
Renney, Tom *professional hockey coach*
Richard, Stephen O. *sports association executive*
Robinson, Dennis R. *sports association executive*
Ruta, Thomas V. *professional sports team and accounting executive*
Sampras, Pete *retired professional tennis player*
Sather, Glen Cameron *professional hockey team executive, coach*
Schoenfeld, Jim *professional sports team executive, former professional hockey coach*
Scott, Dale Allan *major league umpire*
Selig, Bud (Alan Huber Selig) *major league baseball commissioner*
Shanahan, Brendan Frederick *professional hockey player*
Silver, Adam *sports association executive*
Stern, David Joel *national basketball association commissioner*
Tatum, Mark A. *sports association executive*
Thomas, Isiah Lord III *professional basketball coach, sports team executive, retired professional basketball player*
Tolbert, Bernard *sports association executive*
Ueberroth, Heidi J. *sports association executive*
Zahnd, Richard H. *sports association executive, lawyer*

Orchard Park
Jauron, Dick (Richard M. Jauron) *professional football coach*
Levy, Marv (Marvin Daniel) *professional football team executive and retired coach*

Syracuse
Boeheim, Jim *college basketball coach*
Duerr, Dianne Marie *sports medicine consultant, educator*

Uniondale
Bossy, Michael *professional sports team executive, retired professional hockey player*
DiPietro, Rick *professional hockey player*
Guerin, Bill *professional hockey player*
Nolan, Ted (Theodore John Nolan) *professional hockey coach*
Snow, Garth *professional sports team executive, former professional hockey player*
Trottier, Bryan John *professional sports team executive, former professional hockey player and coach*
Wang, Charles B. *professional sports team executive, former computer company executive*

White Plains
Davenport, Lindsay *professional tennis player*
Frazier, Amy *professional tennis player*
Gilbert, Bradley *professional tennis coach, former professional tennis player, former Olympic athlete*
Williams, Serena *professional tennis player, apparel designer*
Williams, Ted Vaughnell *physical education educator*
Williams, Venus *professional tennis player*

NORTH CAROLINA

Carrboro
Generous, William Thomas, Jr., (Tom) *coach, educator*

Chapel Hill
Davis, Butch (Paul Hilton Davis) *college football coach*
Fox, Mike *college baseball coach*
Hatchell, Sylvia R. *women's college basketball coach*
Smith, Dean Edwards *retired men's college basketball coach*
Williams, Roy *men's college basketball coach*

Charlotte
Behrman, Michael J. *professional sports team executive*
Bickerstaff, Bernie (Bernard Tyrone Bickerstaff Sr.) *professional sports team executive, former professional basketball coach*
Carr, David *professional football player*
Davis, Stephen *professional football player*
Delhomme, Jake Christopher *professional football player*
Economou, Greg *professional sports team executive*
Fox, John *professional football coach*
Gordon, Jeff *race car driver*
Higgins, Rod (Roderick Dwayne Higgins) *professional sports team executive, retired professional basketball player*
Hinchey, Tim *professional sports team executive*
Johnson, Jimmie *race car driver*
Jordan, Michael Jeffrey *professional sports team executive, retired professional basketball player, professional baseball player*
Peppers, Julius *professional football player*
Smith, Steve *professional football player*
Staley, Dawn Michelle *professional basketball player*
Vincent, Sam (James Samuel Vincent) *professional basketball coach, former professional basketball player*
Weinke, Chris *professional football player*
Whitfield, Fred, Jr. *professional sports team executive*

Concord
Smith, Ollen Bruton *sports association executive*

Durham
Case, Richard W. *sports association executive*
Krzyzewski, Mike (Michael William Krzyzewski) *college basketball coach*
McCallie, Joanne P. *women's college basketball coach*

Harrisburg
Hendrick, Joseph Riddick, III, (Rick) *race team owner*

High Point
Burton, Ward *professional race car driver*

Huntersville
Stewart, Tony *professional race car driver*

Mooresville
Busch, Kurt *race car driver*
Castroneves, Hélio *race car driver*
Earnhardt, Dale, Jr. *race car driver*
Earnhardt, Teresa *race team owner*
Edwards, Carl *race car driver*
Martin, Mark *race car driver*
Münter, Leilani Maaja *race car driver*
Waltrip, Michael Curtis *professional race car driver*

Raleigh
Brind'Amour, Rod *professional hockey player*
Cole, Erik *professional hockey player*
Francis, Ron *professional sports team executive, retired professional hockey player*
Hedican, Bret *professional hockey player*
Laviolette, Peter *professional hockey coach*
Lowe, Sidney *men's college and former professional basketball coach*
Rutherford, Jim *professional sports team executive*
Staal, Eric *professional hockey player*
Stillman, Cory *professional hockey player*
Ward, Cam *professional hockey player*
Wesley, Glen *professional hockey player*
Whitney, Ray *professional hockey player*
Yow, Kay (Sandra Kay Yow) *women's college basketball coach*

Randleman
Petty, Richard *retired race car driver*

Statesville
Kahne, Kasey *race car driver*

Welcome
Harvick, Kevin *race car driver*

Winston Salem
Grobe, Jim *college football coach*

OHIO

Aurora
Eakin, Thomas Capper *sports promotion executive*

Berea
Crennel, Romeo *professional football coach*
Lewis, Jamal *professional football player*
Quinn, Brady (Brady Tyler Quinn) *professional football player*

Canton
Carson, Harry *retired professional football player*
Moon, Warren *professional football player*
Wright, Rayfield *professional football player*

Cincinnati
Chambliss, Carroll Christopher *professional baseball coach*
Dunn, Adam *professional baseball player*
Griffey, Ken, Jr., (George Kenneth Griffey Jr.) *professional baseball player*
Johnson, Chad *professional football player*
Lewis, Marvin *professional football coach*
Palmer, Carson *professional football player*

Cleveland
Appleby, Stuart *professional golfer*
Brown, Mike *professional basketball coach*
Burton, Jay H. *sports management executive*
Ferry, Danny *professional sports team executive, retired professional basketball player*
Gooden, Drew *professional basketball player*
Hafner, Travis Lee *professional baseball player*
Henman, Tim *professional tennis player*
James, LeBron *professional basketball player*
Komoroski, Len *professional sports team executive*
Lopez, Nancy *retired professional golfer*
Martinez, Victor Jesus *professional baseball player*
Moceanu, Dominique *retired Olympic athlete*
Pierce, Mary *professional tennis player*
Sabathia, C.C. (Carsten Charles Sabathia) *professional baseball player*
Seles, Monica *professional tennis player*
Shapiro, Mark *professional sports team executive*
Sizemore, Grady III *professional baseball player*
Stornes, Mark *professional sports team executive*

Columbus
Agnew, Gary *professional hockey coach*
Bartels, Robert Louis *retired physical education educator, coach*
Fedorov, Sergei *professional hockey player*
Foster, Jim (James S. Foster) *women's college basketball coach*
Hamm, Paul *Olympic athlete*
Hitchcock, Ken *professional hockey coach*
Howson, Scott *professional sports team executive*
Matta, Thad Michael *men's college basketball coach*
Modin, Fredrik *professional hockey player*
Peca, Michael *professional hockey player*
Smith, Gene *athletic director*
Tressel, Jim (James Patrick Tressel) *college football coach*

Dayton
O'Keefe, Linda Lee *physical education educator*

Fairfield
Robertson, Oscar Palmer (Big O Robertson) *chemical company executive, former professional basketball player*
Sheehan, Samantha *gymnast*

Oxford
Pont, John *football coach, educator*

Westlake
Ohno, Apolo Anton *Olympic athlete*

OKLAHOMA

Edmond
Sanchez, Cindi Asbury *physical education educator*

Norman
Stoops, Bob *college football coach*

Oklahoma City
Binning, Bette Finese (Mrs. Gene Hedgcock Binning) *athletic association official*
Bower, Jeff *professional sports team executive*
Fernandez, Lisa *softball player*
Paul, Chris *professional basketball player*
Reed, Willis *professional sports team executive*
Scott, Byron *professional basketball coach, retired professional basketball player*
Weber, Hugh *professional sports team executive*

OREGON

Bend
Whitcomb, Brian *sports association executive*

Corvallis
Casey, Pat *college baseball coach*

Eugene
Bellotti, Mike *football coach*
Kent, Ernie *men's college basketball coach*

Portland
Aldridge, LaMarcus Nurae *professional basketball player*
Francis, Steve *professional basketball player*
Glanville, Jerry *college football coach, former professional football coach*
Golub, Mike *professional sports team executive*
McMillan, Nathaniel (Nate McMillan) *professional basketball coach*
Miller, Larry G. *professional sports team executive*
Oden, Greg *professional basketball player*
Pritchard, Kevin *professional sports team executive*
Roy, Brandon Dawayne *professional basketball player*
Van Exel, Nickey Maxwell *professional basketball player*

PENNSYLVANIA

Aldan
Stegmuller, Agnes Leonore *physical education educator*

Allison Park
Toerge, Lynn *athletic trainer*

Breinigsville
Darden, Joseph Samuel, Jr. *health educator*

Easton
Holmes, Larry, Sr. *retired boxer*

King Of Prussia
Rubin, Michael G. *sports internet company executive*

Philadelphia
Biron, Martin *professional hockey player*
Boucher, Brian *professional hockey player*
Briere, Daniel *professional hockey player*
Brown, Dave *professional sports team executive*
Brown, Larry (Lawrence Harvey Brown) *professional sports team executive, former professional basketball coach*
Cashman, Wayne *professional athletics coach*
Cheeks, Maurice Edward *professional basketball coach, retired professional basketball player*
Clarke, Robert Earle (Bobby Clarke) *professional sports team executive*
DiLeo, Tony *professional sports team executive*
Dunphy, Fran *men's college basketball coach*
Gagné, Simon *professional hockey player, Olympic athlete*
Gillick, Patrick
Hamels, Cole (Colbert Michael Hamels) *professional baseball player*
Holmgren, Paul *professional sports team executive, retired professional hockey player*
Howard, Ryan James *professional baseball player*
King, Billy *professional sports team executive*
Manuel, Charlie (Charles Fuqua Manuel Jr.) *professional baseball manager*
McNabb, Donovan *professional football player*
Price, Lara *professional sports team executive*
Primeau, Keith *retired professional hockey player*
Reid, Andy (Andrew Walter Reid) *professional football coach*
Rollins, James Calvin (Jimmy Rollins) *professional baseball player*
Rowand, Aaron Ryan *professional baseball player*
Sanderson, Geoff *professional hockey player*
Snider, Edward Malcolm *professional sports team executive*
Spikes, Takeo *professional football player*
Stevens, John *professional hockey coach, retired professional hockey player*
Utley, Chase Cameron *professional baseball player*

Pittsburgh
Crosby, Sidney *professional hockey player*
Dixon, Jamie (P.), (II) *men's college basketball coach*
Faneca, Alan *professional football player*
LeBeau, Dick *professional football coach and retired player*
Lemieux, Mario *professional sports team executive and retired hockey player*
Malkin, Evgeni *professional hockey player*
McConnell-Serio, Suzie Theresa *women's college basketball coach, retired professional basketball player*
Polamalu, Troy *professional football player*
Recchi, Mark *professional hockey player*
Roberts, Gary *professional hockey player*
Roethlisberger, Ben *professional football player*
Rooney, Daniel M. *professional sports team executive*
Shero, Ray (Rejean Shero) *professional sports team executive*
Sykora, Petr *professional hockey player*
Therrien, Michel *professional hockey coach*
Tomlin, Mike *professional football coach*
Tracy, Jim (James Edward Tracy) *professional baseball manager*
Wannstedt, David Raymond *college football coach, former professional football coach*
Ward, Hines, Jr. *professional football player*

Reading
Hornish, Sam, Jr. *race car driver*

University Park
Paterno, Joe (Joseph Vincent Paterno) *college football coach*

Villanova
Wright, Jay *men's college basketball coach*

Youngstown
Palmer, Arnold Daniel *professional golfer*

SOUTH CAROLINA

Charleston
Smail, Karen Mary *physical education educator, consultant*

Clemson
Bowden, Tommy *college football coach*
Purnell, Oliver Gordon, Jr. *men's college basketball coach*

Columbia
McCaslin, Elizabeth Ann *athletic trainer*
Spurrier, Steve(n) (Orr) *college football coach*

Rock Hill
Ford, Mary (Polly) Wylie *retired physical education educator*

TENNESSEE

Knoxville
Fulmer, Phillip *university football coach*
Summitt, Patricia Head *women's college basketball coach*

Memphis
Barone, Tony, Sr. *professional basketball coach*
Battier, Shane *professional basketball player*
Calipari, John V. *men's college basketball coach*
Dolich, Andrew Bruce *professional sports team executive*
Gay, Rudy Carlton, Jr. *professional basketball player*
Iavaroni, Marc (Marcus John) *professional basketball coach, retired professional basketball player*
Wallace, Chris *professional sports team executive*

Nashville
Abram, Monroe J. *athletic trainer, educator*
Arnott, Jason *professional hockey player*
Balcomb, Melanie S. *women's college basketball coach*
Collins, Kerry *professional football player*
Fisher, Jeff *professional football coach*
George, Eddie (Edward Nathan George) *former professional football player*
Leipold, Craig L. *professional sports team executive*
Poile, David Robert *professional sports team executive*
Price, David Taylor *college baseball player*
Reinfeldt, Mike (Michael Ray Reinfeldt) *professional sports team executive, former professional football player*
Snoddy, Chris Raymond *athletic trainer*
Trotz, Barry *professional hockey coach*
Young, Vince Paul, Jr. *professional football player*

TEXAS

Arlington
Howell, Holly Lyn *athletic trainer*
Sosa, Sammy (Samuel Sosa) *professional baseball player*
Washington, Ron *professional baseball manager*
Young, Michael Brian *professional baseball player*

Austin
Armstrong, Lance *retired professional cyclist*
Barnes, Rick (Richard Dale Barnes) *men's college basketball coach*
Brown, Mack *college football coach*
Conradt, Jody *retired women's college basketball coach*
Contador Velasco, Alberto *professional cyclist*
Crenshaw, Ben *professional golfer*
Goestenkors, Gail Ann *women's college basketball coach*

Carrollton
Lieberman-Cline, Nancy *sports commentator, former professional basketball coach and player*

College Station
Franchione, Dennis *university football coach*
Turgeon, Mark *men's college basketball coach*

Dallas
Cuban, Mark *professional sports team owner, Internet company executive*
Dir, Dave *professional soccer coach*
Hamilton, David Lee *sports association administrator, retired environmental company executive*
Hedrick, Chad *Olympic athlete*
Howard, Josh *professional basketball player*
Hudel, Chestella Alvis *athletics educator*
Johnson, Avery *professional basketball coach, retired professional basketball player*
Laettner, Christian Donald *professional basketball player*
Nelson, Donnie *professional sports team executive*

Nowitzki, Dirk Werner *professional basketball player*
Showalter, Buck (William Nathaniel Showalter III) *former professional baseball team manager*
Stackhouse, Jerry *professional basketball player*
Ussery, Terdema L., II, *professional sports team executive*

Fort Worth
Patterson, Gary *college football coach*

Frisco
Armstrong, Doug *professional sports team executive*
Hicks, Thomas O. *professional sports team executive, real estate developer*
Hull, Brett A. *retired professional hockey player, former commentator*
Lindros, Eric *professional hockey player*
Lites, James R. *professional hockey team executive*
Modano, Mike *professional hockey player*
Smith, Neil *former professional sports team executive*
Taylor, Dave *professional sports team executive, retired professional hockey player*
Tippett, Dave *professional hockey coach*

Galveston
Foster, William Edwin (Bill Foster) *nonprofessional basketball coach*

Houston
Adelman, Rick (Richard Leonard Adelman) *professional basketball coach*
Alexander, Leslie Lee *professional sports team owner*
Baker, Vincent Lamont *professional basketball player*
Berkman, Lance *professional baseball player*
Biggio, Craig *professional baseball player*
Brown, Thaddeus B. *professional sports team executive*
Constantine, Kevin *professional hockey coach*
Dawson, Carroll *professional sports team executive*
Ewing, Patrick Aloysius *professional basketball coach*
Green, Ahman Rashad *professional football player*
Hayes, Elvin Ernest *retired basketball player*
Jolibois, Marcus *professional sports team executive*
Kim, Pyung-Soo *martial arts educator*
Kubiak, Gary *professional football coach*
Lamont, Gene *professional baseball coach and former team manager*
Lee, Carlos Noriel *professional baseball player*
Lidge, Brad *professional baseball player*
McGrady, Tracy *professional basketball player*
Ming, Yao *professional basketball player*
Morey, Daryl *professional sports team executive*
Moulds, Eric Shannon *professional football player*
Mutombo, DiKembe (Dikembe Mutombo Mpolondo Mukamba Jean Jacque Wamutombo) *professional basketball player*
Oswalt, Roy E. *professional baseball player*
Sandman, Bradford Aaron *coach, educator*
Sherman, Mike (Michael Francis Sherman) *professional football coach*
Smith, Rick *professional sports team executive*
Swoopes, Sheryl Denise *professional basketball player*
Thompson, Karleen *professional basketball coach*
Thompson, Tina Marie *professional basketball player*
Williams, Mario *professional football player*

Irving
Glenn, Terry *professional football player*
Jones, Jerry (Jerral Wayne Jones) *professional sports team executive*
Jones, Julius *professional football player*
Owens, Terrell Eldorad *professional football player*
Phillips, Wade *professional football coach*
Romo, Tony (Antonio Ramiro Romo) *professional football player*

Lubbock
Knight, Bobby (Robert Montgomery Knight) *men's college basketball coach*
Leach, Mike *college football coach*

Round Rock
Ryan, Nolan *former professional baseball player*

San Antonio
Artemov, Vladimir Nikolaevich *gymnastics coach*
Bookbinder, Russ *professional sports team executive*
Bowen, Bruce *professional basketball player*
Buford, R.C. *professional sports team executive*
Duncan, Tim *professional basketball player*
Finley, Michael *professional basketball player*
Ginobili, Manu *professional basketball player*
Hammon, Becky (Rebecca Lynn Hammon) *professional basketball player*
Holt, Peter M. *professional sports team owner, agricultural products executive*
Hughes, Dan *professional basketball coach*
Ludzik, Steve *professional hockey coach*
Mohammed, Nazr *professional basketball player*
Parker, Tony (William Anthony Parker II) *professional basketball player*
Popovich, Gregg *professional basketball coach*
Pych, Rick *professional sports team executive*
Robinson, Glenn *professional basketball player*

San Marcos
mel, Elizabeth Carmen *retired physical education educator*

UTAH

Park City
Mancuso, Julia *skier, Olympic athlete*
Miller, Bode (Samuel Bode Miller) *professional skier*
Shea, Jim *Olympic athlete*
White, Shaun Roger *Olympic athlete, professional snowboarder, professional skateboarder*
Young, Steven *retired professional football player*

Salt Lake City
Amaechi, John *retired professional basketball player*
Boozer, Carlos Austin, Jr. *professional basketball player*
Haslam, Dennis V. *professional sports team executive, lawyer*
Miller, Larry H. *professional sports team owner, auto dealer, broadcast executive*
O'Connor, Kevin *professional sports team executive*
Okur, Mehmet *professional basketball player*
Sloan, Jerry (Gerald Eugene Sloan) *professional basketball coach*
Witty, Christine (Chris Witty) *speed skater*

VIRGINIA

Arlington
Kozlov, Viktor *professional hockey player*
Milton-Jones, DeLisha *professional basketball player*

Ashburn
Gibbs, Joe (Joseph Jackson Gibbs) *professional football coach*
Moss, Santana *professional football player*
Portis, Clinton *professional football player*
Smoot, Fred *professional football player*
Snyder, Daniel *professional sports team and communications executive*

Blacksburg
Beamer, Frank *college football coach*

Charlottesville
Ryan, Debbie (Deborah A. Ryan) *women's college basketball coach*

Fairfax
Larranaga, Jim *men's college basketball coach*

Mc Lean
Chang, Michael *professional tennis player*
Hewitt, Lleyton Glynn *professional tennis player*

Richmond
Gulbis, Natalie Anne *professional golfer, television personality*

WASHINGTON

Carnation
Beshur, Jacqueline E. *retired animal trainer, farmer, writer*

Kirkland
Alexander, Shaun *professional football player*
Holmgren, Mike *professional football coach*
Mora, Jim (James Lawrence Mora) *professional football coach*

Pullman
Bennett, Dick *college basketball coach*
Bennett, Tony (Anthony G. Bennett) *men's college basketball coach*

Seattle
Allen, Paul Gardner *professional sports team and computer company executive*
Barth, Danny *professional sports team executive*
Bennett, Clayton Ike *professional sports team owner*
Bird, Sue (Suzanne Brigit Bird) *professional basketball player*
Boulware, Michael *professional football player*
Carlesimo, P.J. (Peter J. Carlesimo) *professional basketball coach*
Donovan, Anne *professional basketball coach*
Durant, Kevin Wayne *professional basketball player*
Hasselbeck, Matt *professional football player*
Hernandez, Felix Abraham *professional baseball player*
Jackson, Lauren *professional basketball player*
Jurevicius, Joe *professional football player*
Melo, Welton *professional soccer player*
Presti, Sam *professional sports team executive*
Putz, J.J. (Joseph Jason Putz) *professional baseball player*
Reese, Pokey *professional baseball player*
Suzuki, Ichiro *professional baseball player*
Walker, Walter Frederick *professional basketball team executive*

Spokane
Ueberroth, Peter Victor *former baseball commissioner*

Vancouver
Engelker, Lynsey L. *athletic trainer, professional athletics manager*

WEST VIRGINIA

Huntington
Jones, Donnie *men's college basketball coach*

Morgantown
Huggins, Bob *former college basketball coach*
Rodriguez, Rich *college football coach*

WISCONSIN

Ashland
Schulte, Melanie Ann *athletic trainer*

Green Bay
Favre, Brett Lorenzo *professional football player*
Harlan, Robert Ernest *professional football team executive*
Hawk, A.J. *professional football player*
McCarthy, Mike *professional football coach*
Vannieuwenhoven, Vicki *professional sports team executive*

Jefferson
Smith, Dena Michele *physical education educator*

Madison
Bielema, Bret *university football coach*
Ryan, Bo (William F. Ryan Jr.) *men's college basketball coach*
Sauer, Jeff *university hockey coach*

Milwaukee
Bogut, Andrew *professional basketball player*
Cordero, Francisco Javier *professional baseball player*
Fielder, Prince Semien *professional baseball player*
Harris, Larry *professional sports team executive*
Krystkowiak, Larry Brett *professional basketball coach*
Redd, Michael *professional basketball player*
Sheets, Ben M. *professional baseball player*
Steinmiller, John F. *professional sports team executive*
Yi, Jianlian *professional basketball player*
Yost, Ned *professional baseball player*

WYOMING

Newcastle
Engle, Kathleen Faye *elementary education educator*

CANADA

ALBERTA

Calgary
Fleming, Wayne *professional hockey coach*
Hotchkiss, Harley N. *professional hockey team owner, oil industry executive*
Keenan, Mike (Micheal Edward Keenan) *professional hockey coach, former professional sports team executive*
Kiprusoff, Miika *professional hockey player*
Playfair, Jim *professional hockey coach*
Sutter, Darryl John *professional sports team executive, former professional hockey coach*

Edmonton
Lowe, Kevin Hugh *professional sports team executive, former hockey player and coach*
MacTavish, Craig *professional hockey coach, former professional hockey player*
Penner, Dustin *professional hockey player*

BRITISH COLUMBIA

Surrey
Igali, Baraladei Daniel *Olympic athlete, coach, motivational speaker*

Vancouver
Luongo, Roberto *professional hockey player*
Nonis, David *professional sports team executive*
Smolinski, Bryan *professional hockey player*
Vigneault, Alain *professional hockey coach*

ONTARIO

Bolton
Coffey, Paul *retired professional hockey player*

Dorchester
Fanning, William James *professional sports team executive, commentator*

Kanata
Emery, Ray *professional hockey player*
Heatley, Dany *professional hockey player*
Melnyk, Eugene N. *professional sports team executive, retired pharmaceutical executive*
Murray, Bryan Clarence *professional sports team executive, former professional hockey coach*
Spezza, Jason *professional hockey player*

Ottawa
Lay, Marion *sports association executive*

Toronto
Bargnani, Andrea *professional basketball player*
Bosh, Chris *professional basketball player*
Colangelo, Bryan *professional sports team executive*
Davis, Antonio Lee *professional basketball player*
Ferguson, John, Jr. *professional sports team executive*
Garbajosa (Chaparro), Jorge *professional basketball player*
Gilbert, Greg *professional hockey coach, retired professional hockey player*
Glaus, Troy *professional baseball player*
Halladay, Roy (Harry Leroy Halladay) *professional baseball player*
Maurice, Paul *professional hockey coach*
Mitchell, Sam *professional basketball coach*
Peddie, Richard *professional sports team executive*
Poon, Alan Ming Wang *sports association executive, director*
Ricciardi, J.P. *professional sports team executive*
Sundin, Mats Johan *professional hockey player*
Thomas, Frank Edward *professional baseball player*
Whitfield, Simon *Olympic athlete*
Williams, Ricky (Errick Lynne Williams) *professional football player*

QUEBEC

Montreal
Carbonneau, Guy *professional hockey coach, former professional hockey player*
Gainey, Bob (Robert Michael) *professional sports team executive, retired professional hockey player*
Gillett, George Nield, Jr. *professional sports team executive, communications executive*
Koivu, Saku *professional hockey player*
Kovalev, Alexei *professional hockey player*

Quebec City
Roy, Patrick *professional sports team executive, coach, retired professional hockey player*

Calgary
Amonte, Tony (Anthony Lewis Amonte) *professional hockey player*
McCarty, Darren *professional hockey player*

Kanata
Paddock, John (Alvin John Paddock) *professional hockey coach*

Toronto
Wells, Vernon III *professional baseball player*

ARGENTINA

Córdoba
Cabrera, Angel Leopoldo *professional golfer*

ENGLAND

London
Goosen, Retief *professional golfer*
Lee, Janet *professional tennis player*

Surrey
Immelman, Trevor *professional golfer*

ITALY

Ciserano di Zingonia
Vieri, Christian *professional soccer player*

Maranello
Schumacher, Michael *retired race car driver*

NORWAY

Oslo
Pettersen, Suzann *professional golfer*

SPAIN

Barcelona
Nadal, Rafael (Rafael Nadal Parera) *professional tennis player*
Ronaldinho, (Ronaldo de Assis Moreira) *professional soccer player*

SWEDEN

Leksand
Belfour, Ed *professional hockey player*

SWITZERLAND

Hombrechtikon
Landis, Floyd *professional cyclist*

ADDRESS UNPUBLISHED

Accorsi, Ernie (Ernest William Accorsi Jr.) *retired professional sports team executive*
Ackerman, Valerie B. *former sports association executive*
Adu, Freddy *professional soccer player*
Adubato, Richard Adam (Richie Adubato) *former professional basketball coach*
Alderson, Sandy (Richard Lynn Alderson) *major league baseball executive*
Ali, Muhammad (Cassius Marcellus Clay) *retired boxer*
Alou, Felipe Rojas *former professional baseball team manager*
Ames, Stephen Michael *professional golfer*
Andretti, Mario *retired race car driver*
Andreychuk, David *former professional hockey player*
Arrington, LaVar *professional football player*

Baker, Dusty (Johnnie B. Baker Jr.) *former professional baseball team manager, retired professional baseball player*
Barnett, Michael *former professional sports team executive*
Barton, Gregory Mark *Olympic athlete*
Bellotti, Robert Michael *coach, educator*
Berka, Marianne Guthrie *health and physical education educator*
Black, Bud (Harry Ralston Black) *professional baseball manager*
Boitano, Brian *Olympic athlete*
Bowa, Lawrence Robert (Larry Bowa) *former professional baseball manager*
Bryant, La Kesha Joy *physical education educator*
Busch, Kyle *race car driver*
Carlisle, Rick (Richard Preston Carlisle) *former professional basketball coach, retired professional basketball player*
Casey, Dwane L. *former professional basketball coach*
Casserly, Charley *former professional football team executive*
Checketts, Dave (David Wayne Checketts) *professional sports team executive*
Coker, Larry E. *former college football coach*
Covassin, Tracey *athletic training educator*
Culpepper, Daunte *professional football player*
Davidson, Bonnie Jean *gymnastics educator, sports management consultant*
Douglas, James (Buster) *boxer*
Drexler, Clyde *retired professional basketball player*
Easton, James L. *International Olympic Committee Member, sports equipment company executive*
Elliott, Bill *race car driver*
Evangelista, Nick Forrest *fencing master, writer, illustrator, publisher*
Evans, Philip G. *former sports association executive*
Evert, Chris (Christine Marie Evert) *retired professional tennis player*
Fassel, Jim (James E. Fassel) *former professional football coach*
Federer, Roger *professional tennis player*
Fisher, Derek *former professional basketball player*
Foreman, George Edward *retired boxer, minister, boxing commentator*
Forsberg, Peter *professional hockey player*
Fratello, Mike (Michael Robert Fratello) *former professional basketball coach*
Frye, Channing *professional basketball player*
Gartner, Mike (Michael Alfred Gartner) *former sports association administrator, retired professional hockey player*
Gatlin, Justin *Olympic track and field athlete*
Gonzalez, Fredi *professional baseball manager*
Granato, Catherine (Cammi Granato) *former olympic athlete, sports association executive*
Grant, Brian Wade *professional basketball player*
Green, Dennis E. *former professional football coach*
Greiner, Nicole K. Hudak *physical education educator*
Grossman, Jonathan Lee *sports agent, law educator*
Grudzielanek, Mark James *professional baseball player*
Guthridge, Bill *university basketball coach*
Guthrie, Janet *professional race car driver*
Hamilton, Laird John *professional surfer*
Hardaway, Timothy Duane *professional basketball player*
Hargrove, Mike (Dudley Michael Hargrove) *former professional baseball team manager*
Harman, Jennifer (Jennifer Harman-Traniello) *professional poker player*
Hart, James Warren *retired athletic administrator, professional football player*
Hicks, Ritchie B. *physical education educator*
Hill, Bob (Robert G. Hill) *former professional basketball coach*
Hill, Brian A. *former professional basketball coach*
Hillenbrand, Shea Matthew *professional baseball player*
Holdsclaw, Chamique Shaunta *retired professional basketball player*
Jansen, Daniel Ervin *former professional speedskater, marketing professional, former olympic athlete*
Johnson, Jimmy *sports broadcaster, former professional football coach*
Joyner Kersee, Jackie (Jacqueline Joyner Kersee) *retired track and field athlete*
Karnazes, Dean (Constantine Karnazes) *endurance athlete, writer*
Kasten, Stanley Harvey *professional sports team executive*
Kavalek, Lubomir *chess expert*
Kenseth, Matt *race car driver*
King, Jeff *dog musher*
Kitchen, Paul Howard *hockey historian*
Klesko, Ryan *professional baseball player*
Lacey, Trudi *professional athletics coach*
LeClair, John Clark *professional hockey player*
Leetch, Brian Joseph *retired professional hockey player*
Lentini, Francine *retired physical education educator*
Lester, Bill (William Alexander Lester) *race car driver*
Levens, Dorsey (Herbert Levens) *professional football player*
Ligety, Ted *Olympic athlete*
Lipinski, Tara Kristen *retired professional figure skater*
Littler, Gene Alec *professional golfer*
Lott, Ronnie (Ronald Mandel Lott) *retired professional football player, television broadcaster*
Macha, Ken *former professional baseball coach*
MacLean, Doug *former professional hockey coach, former sports team executive*
Maddux, Gregory Alan *professional baseball player*
Mariucci, Steve *professional football coach, former college football coach*
Mason, Linda *physical education educator, coach*
McBride, Brian *professional soccer player*
McCann, June Vivian *retired physical education educator*
McCarney, Dan *former college football coach*
McClatchy, Kevin S. *professional sports team executive*
McEnroe, John Patrick, Jr. *professional tennis player*
McGwire, Mark David *retired professional baseball player*
McMurray, Jamie *race car driver*
Mellanby, Scott Edgar *retired professional hockey player*
Messier, Mark Douglas *retired professional hockey player*
Miller, Shannon *Olympic athlete*
Muckler, John E. *former professional sports team executive, former professional hockey coach*
Mularkey, Mike *professional football coach*
Musselman, Eric *former professional basketball coach*
Narron, Jerry Austin *former professional baseball manager*
Navratilova, Martina *professional tennis player*
Neldner, Summer D. *athletic trainer*
Newman, Ryan *race car driver*
Norman, Gregory John *professional golfer*
Norton, Lara Brooks *physical education educator, education educator*
Norwood, Jaime Griffis *personal trainer*
Nusum, John Barry *professional soccer player*
Okafor, Emeka *professional basketball player*
Olcyzk, Ed *professional athletics coach*
O'Malley, Susan *former professional sports team executive*
Parins, Robert James *professional football team executive, judge*
Patrick, Craig *former professional hockey team executive*
Patrick, Danica Sue *race car driver*
Patterson, Steve *former professional sports team executive*
Perkins, Eddie *boxer*
Pinkel, Gary *university football coach*
Pippen, Scottie *professional basketball player*
Plummer, Ahmed *professional football player*
Plummer, Jake (Jason Steven Plummer) *professional football player*
Policy, Carmen A. *professional sports team executive*
Portland, Rene (Maureen Portland) *retired women's college basketball coach*
Raymond, Lisa *professional tennis player*
Reeves, Daniel Edward *former professional football coach*
Rice, Jerry Lee *retired professional football player*
Robinson, Frank *former professional baseball manager, retired professional baseball player*
Roddick, Andy Stephen *professional tennis player*
Ross, Bobby (Robert Joseph Ross) *retired college football coach*
Ross, Carol *retired women's college basketball coach*
Russell, Bill *former professional basketball team executive, former professional basketball player*
Rutherford, John Sherman, III, (Johnny Rutherford) *professional race car driver*
Sanders, Barry *retired professional football player*
Schottenheimer, Marty (Martin Edward Scottenheimer) *former professional football coach*
Sharman, William *professional basketball team executive*
Shell, Art (Arthur Shell Jr.) *former professional football coach*
Smith, Ozzie (Osborne Earl Smith) *retired professional baseball player*
Smith, Stanley Roger *retired professional tennis player*
Spitz, Mark *Olympic athlete*
Stockton, John Houston *retired professional basketball player*
Stotts, Terry L. *former professional basketball coach*
Street, Picabo *Olympic athlete*
Stringer, C. Vivian *women's college basketball coach*
Sund, Rick (Richard W. Sund) *former professional sports team executive*
Tagliabue, Paul John *retired national football league commissioner*
Tarver, Antonio *professional boxer*
Thompson, David O'Neal *retired basketball player*
Thompson, Jennifer B. *Olympic swimmer*
Tobin, Vincent Michael *professional football coach, former sports team executive*
Tyson, Mike G. *boxer*
Van Gundy, Jeff *former professional basketball coach*
Van Horn, Keith *professional basketball player*
Vermeil, Dick (Richard Albert Vermeil) *retired professional football coach*
Vernon, Mike *retired professional hockey player*
Vilma, Jonathan Polynice *professional football player*
Vincent, Francis Thomas, Jr., (Fay Vincent) *former baseball commissioner*
Walker, Antoine Devon *professional basketball player*
Waltrip, Darrell Lee *race car driver*
Ward, Charlie *professional basketball player*
Weisbrod, John *former professional sports team executive*
West, Jerry Alan *former professional sports team executive, retired professional basketball player*
Whitaker, Pernell (Sweet Pea Whitaker) *retired boxer*
Whitsitt, Bob (Robert James Whitsitt) *former professional football team executive*
Wilpon, Fred *professional sports team executive*
Wilson, Ralph Cookerly, Jr. *professional football team executive*
Wooden, John Robert *former college basketball coach*
Woosnam, Ian Harold *professional golfer*
Wynalda, Eric *professional soccer player*
Yawney, Trent *former professional hockey coach, retired professional hockey player*
Zubov, Sergei *professional hockey player*

BUSINESS *See* FINANCE: INDUSTRY

COMMUNICATIONS *See* COMMUNICATIONS MEDIA; INDUSTRY: SERVICE

COMMUNICATIONS MEDIA *See also* ARTS: LITERARY

UNITED STATES

ALABAMA

Anniston
Ayers, Harry Brandt *editor, publisher, columnist*

Birmingham
Allen, Christopher C. *publishing executive*
Blackledge, Brett J. *reporter*
Bozzelli, Richard *publishing executive*
Culpepper, Mary Kay *editor*
Floyd, John Alex, Jr. *editor*
Francavilla, Donna T. *journalist*
Griffin, Eleanor *publishing executive, editor*
Hanson, Victor Henry, II, *newspaper publisher*
Kennedy, Joe David, Jr., (Joey Kennedy) *editor*
Powell, Larry *communications educator*
Scarritt, Thomas Varnon *newspaper editor*
Seitz, Karl Raymond *editor*
Smyth, Rich *publishing executive*
Stephens, James T. (J.T. Stepehens) *publishing executive*

Hueytown
Nelson, Susan Rhodes *media specialist, educator*

Trussville
Jacobson, James Edmund *retired newspaper editor*

Tuscaloosa
Reinhart, Kellee Connely *journalist*
Ross, Daniel J.J. *publishing executive*

ALASKA

Anchorage
Tobin, William Joseph *newspaper editor*

Homer
Graber, Elizabeth *communications educator, literature educator*

ARIZONA

Carefree
Mangouni, Norman *publishing executive*

Chandler
Goyer, Robert Stanton *retired communications educator and administrator*

Lake Montezuma
Loveland, John Bigelow *editor, writer*

Marana
Steckler, Larry *publishing executive, writer*

Phoenix
Breland, Sandy Ann *broadcast executive, director*
Bushee, Ward III *newspaper editor*
Dickey, Robert J. *publishing executive*
Edens, Gary Denton *broadcast executive*
Kenney, Thomas Frederick *broadcast executive*
Leach, John F. *editor, director, journalist, educator*
Moyer, Alan Dean *retired newspaper editor*
Reyes, Anna Maria *broadcast executive*
Steckler, Phyllis Betty *business and publishing consultant*
Zidich, John M. *publishing executive*

Prescott
Anderson, Parker Lynn *columnist, playwright*
Beatty, Jametha Ann *communications educator*

Scottsdale
Johnson, Micah William *television newscaster, director*
Joseph, Gregory Nelson *media critic, writer, actor, advocate*
Weil, Louis Arthur III *retired newspaper publishing executive*

Sedona
Sasmor, James Cecil *publishing representative, educator*

Tempe
Rankin, William Parkman *communications educator, academic administrator*
Richards, Gale Lee *communications educator*

Tucson
Allvin, Paul G. *communications educator*
Hale, William Bryan, Jr. *newspaper editor*
Martin, June Johnson Caldwell *journalist*

ARKANSAS

Arkadelphia
Taylor, Michael Ray *media specialist, educator*

Little Rock
Greenberg, Paul *editor*
Hussman, Walter E., Jr. *publishing executive*
Portis, Charles McColl *reporter, writer*
Smith, Griffin, Jr. *executive editor*

CALIFORNIA

Agoura Hills
Teresi, Joseph *publishing executive*

Alameda
Billings, Thomas Neal *computer and publishing executive, management consultant, entrepreneur, journalist, writer*

Alhambra
Duke, Donald Norman *publishing executive*

Alpine
Greenberg, Byron Stanley *newspaper and business executive, consultant*

Alta Loma
Straka, Laszlo Richard *retired publishing consultant*

Arcadia
Belnap, David F. *journalist*

Atascadero
Rios, Evelyn Deerwester *columnist, musician, artist, writer*

Belvedere Tiburon
Kramer, Lawrence Stephen *journalist*
Rosenthal, Robert Jon *newspaper editor, journalist*

Berkeley
Bagdikian, Ben Haig *journalist, educator*
Browne, G.M. Walter Shawn *journalist, publisher*
Helson, Henry Berge *publisher, educator, retired mathematician*
Hertelendy, Paul *critic, writer, poet*
Lesser, Wendy *editor, writer, consultant*
Susskind, Teresa Gabriel *publishing executive*

Beverly Hills
Bradshaw, Terry (Terry Paxton Bradshaw) *sports announcer, former professional football player*
Corwin, Stanley Joel *book publisher*
Davis, Jonathan, Jr. *broadcast executive*
Filosa, Gary Fairmont Randolph, II, *columnist, film producer*
Friedman, Robert Lee *film company executive*
Gabler, Elizabeth Brand *film company executive*
Ganis, Sidney *film company executive, producer*
Glotzer, Liz *film company executive*
Grazer, Brian *film company executive*
Heller, Paul Michael *film company executive, producer*
Hill, David *broadcast executive*
Komisar, Ken *recording industry executive*
Lond, Harley Weldon *editor, publishing executive*
Maisel, David *entertainment company executive*
Rapino, Michael *music company executive*
Schneider, Charles Ivan *newspaper executive*
Shapiro-Mathes, Angela *broadcast executive*
Sherwood, Kehela (Karen Kehela Sherwood) *broadcast executive*
Utley, Nancy *film company executive*
Wolper, David Lloyd *motion picture and television executive*
Zanuck, Richard Darryl *motion picture company executive*

Brisbane
Daniels, Caroline *publishing executive*

Burbank
Aviv, Oren R. *film company executive*
Berwick, Frances *broadcast executive*
Bird, Andy *film company executive*
Cohen, Polly *film company executive*
Cook, Richard W. (Dick Cook) *film company executive*
Downey, Susan *film company executive*
Hansen, Libby *broadcast executive*
Horn, Alan F. *film company executive*
Iger, Bob (Robert Allen Iger) *entertainment company executive*
Janollari, David *television broadcasting executive, cable and television producer*
Kadin, Heather *broadcast executive*
Kaye, Jhani *radio station executive, television producer and director*
Kroll, Sue *broadcast executive*
Kwan-Rubinek, Veronika *broadcast executive*

Marinelli, Janice *broadcast executive*
McPherson, Stephen *broadcast executive*
Meyer, Barry Michael *motion picture executive*
Michel, Donald Charles *editor*
Nelson, Diane W. *broadcast executive*
Ostroff, Dawn T. *broadcast executive*
Pedowitz, Mark *broadcast executive*
Pope, Katherine Collins *television executive*
Robinov, Jeff *film company executive*
Robinson, James G. *film production executive*
Ross, Rich *broadcast executive*
Sklar, Marty (Martin A. Sklar) *entertainment company executive*
Staggs, Thomas O. *entertainment company executive*
Sweeney, Anne M. *cable television company executive*
Taubin, Dawn *film company executive*
Wandell, Morgan *broadcast executive*
Wiseman, Jane *broadcast executive*
Younger, Laurie *broadcast executive*
Zucker, Jeffrey *broadcast executive*

Burlingame
Corcoran, Elizabeth Anne *journalist*
Mendelson, Lee M. *film company executive, producer, director, writer*

Calabasas
Rubin, Rick (Frederick Jay Rubin) *record producer*
Walling, Donovan Robert *editor, writer*

Carlsbad
Howard, Robert Staples *newspaper publisher*

Carmel
Koeppel, Gary Merle *publishing executive, art gallery owner, writer*
Mollman, John Peter *publishing executive*

Chula Vista
Blankfort, Lowell Arnold *newspaper publisher*

Culver City
Baer, Amy Bosley *film company executive*
Blake, Jeff *film company executive, lawyer*
Fischer, Bradley J. *film company executive*
Jacobs, Betty Jane Lazaroff *communications educator*
Landau, Yair *film company executive*
Lynton, Michael *film company executive*
Milano, Adam *film company executive*
Pascal, Amy Beth *film company executive*
Vollack, Lia *broadcast executive*
Wigan, Gareth *film company executive*

Daly City
Batlin, Robert Alfred *retired newspaper editor*

Del Mar
Kaye, Peter Frederic *columnist*
Marcus, Larry David *broadcast executive*

El Segundo
Carey, Chase (Charles G.) *broadcast executive*
Churchill, Bruce B. *broadcast executive*
Doyle, Patrick T. *broadcast executive*
Palkovic, Michael W. *broadcast executive*
Pontual, Romulo *broadcast executive*
Suranyi, John B. *broadcast executive*

Emeryville
Catmull, Edwin E. *film company executive, computer graphics engineer*
Lasseter, John A. *film company executive, computer animator*
Roth, Joe *motion picture company executive*

Encino
Altschul, David Edwin *record company executive, lawyer*
Glickman, Daniel Robert *motion picture association executive, former congressman*
Rawitch, Robert Joe *journalist, educator*

Escondido
Ehrhart, Joseph Edward *retired broadcast technician*

Fresno
Autry, Alan *film company executive, mayor, actor, former professional football player*
Wilson, James Ross *communications educator, broadcast executive*

Fullerton
Lewandoski, Robert Henry *editor, publisher*

Glendale
Coleman, Lewis Waldo *film company executive, former bank executive*
Daly, Ann Michelle *broadcast executive*
Enrico, Roger A. *film and retired soft drink company executive*
Fox, John *film company executive*
Geffen, David Lawrence *film company and former recording company executive*
Katzenberg, Jeffrey *film company executive*
Kelley, Jan *publishing executive, musician*
MacDonald, Laurie *film company executive*
Parkes, Walter F. *film company executive*
Snider, Stacey *film company executive*

Gold River
Shaw, Eleanor Jane *newspaper editor*

Grass Valley
Engles, Eric William *editor, writer*

Greenbrae
Cohn, Bruce *film and television company executive*
Freedman, Albert Z. *publishing executive*

Hollywood
McAdams, Frank Joseph III *communications educator*
Perth, Rod *network entertainment executive*

Huntington Beach
De Massa, Jessie G. *media specialist*

Irvine
Bartkus, Richard Anthony *magazine publisher*
Horne, Terry *publishing executive*
Lesonsky, Rieva *editor-in-chief*
Power, Francis William *newspaper publisher*
Siegel, Barry *journalist, writer, literature educator*

La Jolla
Copley, David C. *newspaper publishing company executive*
Freedman, Jonathan Borwick *journalist, writer, educator*
Hallin, Daniel Clark *communications educator*
Harris, T. George *editor*

Long Beach
Adler, Jeffrey D. *media consultant, management consultant*
Yousef, Fathi Salaama *communications educator, management consultant*

Los Altos
Collins, Gordon Dent *recording industry executive*

Los Angeles
Archerd, Army (Armand A. Archerd) *columnist, retired commentator*
Barberie, Jillian *newscaster, meteorologist*
Bart, Peter Benton *editor, film producer, writer*
Battista, Richard *entertainment company executive*
Blue, Violet (Ada Mae Johnson) *blogger*
Boyle, Barbara Dorman *film company executive*
Boyter, Cale *film company executive*
Charen, Mona *columnist*
Churgin, Amy *publishing executive*
Clarke, Peter *communications and health educator*
Cole, Carolyn *photojournalist*
Cole, K.C. *journalist, writer*
Delugach, Albert Lawrence *journalist*
Demick, Barbara *journalist*
Dolan, Mary Anne *journalist, columnist*
Dwyre, William Patrick *journalist*
Edmonds, Tracey E. *film company executive*
Fein, Irving Ashley *television and motion picture executive*
Field, Ted (Frederick) *film company and recording industry executive*
Findley, John Allen, Jr. *publishing executive*
Firstenberg, Jean Picker *film institute executive*
Flanigan, James J(oseph) *journalist*
Gianopulos, Jim *film company executive*
Gold, Jonathan *restaurant critic, columnist*
Gross, Larry Paul *communications educator*
Guider, Elizabeth Grier *editor*
Hefner, Hugh Marston *editor-in-chief*
Hicks, Christopher *music company executive*
Hiller, David Dean *publishing executive*
Hilton, Perez (Mario Armando Lavandeira Jr.) *celebrity gossip blogger*
Iovine, Jimmy *recording industry executive*
Israel, David *journalist, scriptwriter, film producer*
Jardin, Xeni *journalist, blogger*
Jones, Quincy *producer, composer, arranger, conductor, trumpeter*
Knapp, Cleon Talboys *publishing executive*
Kraft, Scott Corey *news correspondent*
Kristof, Kathy M. *journalist*
Lazarus, Mell *cartoonist*
Lee, Kwan Min *communications educator, consultant*
Lee, Stan (Stanley Martin Lieber) *cartoon publisher, writer*
Levine, Pamela *film company executive*
Lewis, Claudia *film company executive*
Liebling, Debbie (Deborah Liebling) *film company executive*
Liguori, Peter *broadcast executive*
Litewka, Albert Bernard *entertainment executive*
Lopez, Steve *journalist*
Louderback, Jim *broadcast executive*
Lowenthal, Abraham Frederic *international relations educator*
Malkin, Michelle *columnist*
Maltin, Leonard *commentator, writer*
Mashariki, Zola B. *film company executive*
McElwaine, Guy *motion picture company executive*
McRee, Lisa *television host, producer*
Miles, Jack (John Russiano) *journalist, educator*
Moss, Jerome (Jerry) S. *recording industry executive*
Myrth, Judy G. *editor*
Newman, Gary *broadcast executive*
Newton, Jim *editor*
North, Oliver Laurence (Ollie North) *syndicated columnist, retired military officer*
O'Shea, James E. *editor-in-chief*
Parks, Michael Christopher *journalist, educator*
Phillips, Geneva Ficker *academic editor*
Piller, Charles Leon *journalist*
Plate, Thomas Gordon *columnist, educator*
Raksin, Alex *reporter, writer*
Ramos, Jorge *newscaster*
Reilly, Kevin *broadcast executive*
Rich, Alan *music critic, writer*
Rosenzweig, Richard Stuart *publishing company executive*
Rush, Herman E. *television executive*
Saltzman, Joseph *journalist, educator, television producer*
Salzman, David Elliot *entertainment industry executive*
Sands, Rick (Richard Sands) *film company executive*
Sarnoff, Thomas Warren *television executive*
Shuster, Alvin *journalist, reporter*
Shuster, Beth *editor*
Singleton, Joan Vietor *publishing executive, writer, film producer*
Sloan, Harry Evans *film company executive*
Stephens, Loren M. *publishing executive, writer*
Tassler, Nina *broadcast executive*
Tellem, Nancy Reiss *broadcast executive*
Thompson, Anne Kathleen *entertainment journalist*
Trembly, Cristy *television executive*
Uva, Joe *broadcast executive*
Valdez, Jeff *broadcast executive, television producer*
Van Buren, Abigail (Jeanne Phillips) *columnist, educator*
Wagner, Paula *film company executive, film producer*
Walden, Dana *broadcast executive*
Ward, Leslie Allyson *journalist, editor*
Weiss, Kenneth R. *newswriter*
Weitz, Brett *broadcast executive*
Williams, Kenneth Scott *entertainment company executive*
Wilson, Ed *broadcast executive*
Yari, Bob *film company executive, producer*
Zacchino, Narda *newspaper editor*

Los Gatos
Hastings, Reed *film rental company executive, former education association administrator*

Marina Del Rey
Lindheim, Richard David *broadcast executive, director*

Mill Valley
Leslie, Jacques Robert, Jr. *journalist*
McNamara, Stephen *newspaper executive*

Monterey
Goldstein, Kenneth F. *entertainment and publishing company executive*

Monterey Park
Stapleton, Jean *journalism educator*

Napa
Crosthwaite, Rachel Anspach *editor*

National City
Beauchamp, Miles Philip *editor, columnist, consultant*

Newport Beach
Bryant, Thomas Lee *magazine editor*
Dean, Paul John *magazine editor*
Steelberg, Chad *broadcast advertising company executive*
Steelberg, Ryan *broadcasting advertising company executive*

Northridge
Dart, John Seward *journalist, editor*

Oakland
Dailey, Garrett Clark *publisher, lawyer*
George, Donald Warner *online columnist and editor, freelance writer*
McKinney, Judson Thad *broadcast executive*
Schrag, Peter *editor, writer*
Westergren, Tim *music company executive*
Wood, Larry (Mary Laird) *journalist, writer, public relations executive, educator, environmental consultant*

Oceanside
Beck, Marilyn Mohr *columnist*

Pacific Grove
Davis, Robert Edward *retired communications educator*

Pacific Palisades
Hadges, Thomas Richard *media consultant*
Kirkgaard, Valerie Anne *media group executive, radio host, writer, radio producer, consultant*

Pacifica
Cole, David Macaulay *journalist, consultant*
Kelly, Kevin *editor*

Palm Desert
Ayling, Henry Faithful *editor, consultant, journalist, poet*

Palm Springs
Gerard, James Wilson *publishing consultant*
Krans, Michelle M. *publishing executive*

Palo Alto
Hamilton, David Mike *publishing executive*

Pasadena
Matthews, Mildred Shapley *retired editor*
Spector, Phil (Harvey Phillip Spector) *record company executive*

Paso Robles
Brown, Benjamin Andrew *retired journalist*

Placentia
Zweifel, Donald Edwin *editor, lobbyist, consultant*

Playa Del Rey
Cairns, Diane Patricia *motion picture executive*

Rancho Palos Verdes
Hillinger, Charles *journalist, writer*

Redlands
Heiss, David James *editor*

Riverside
James, Etta (Jamesetta Hawkins) *recording artist*
Sokolsky, Robert Lawrence *journalist*

Rolling Hills Estates
Conrad, Paul Francis *cartoonist*

Sacramento
Heaphy, Janis Besler *newspaper executive*
Henson, Glenda Maria *newswriter*
Lundstrom, Marjie *editor*
Pruitt, Gary B. *publishing company executive*
Rodriguez, Rick *executive editor*
Shriver, Maria Owings *news correspondent*
Walsh, Denny Jay *reporter*
Walters, Daniel Raymond *political columnist*
Williams, Arthur Cozad *retired broadcasting executive*

San Diego
Breen, Stephen P. *editorial cartoonist*
Fike, Edward Lake *newspaper editor*
Humes, Edward *journalist, writer*
Kaufman, Julian Mortimer *broadcasting company executive, consultant*
Kim, Lee Ann *reporter, newscaster*
Klein, Herbert George *newspaper editor*
Krulak, Victor Harold *newspaper executive*
Kyle, Robert Campbell, II, *publishing executive*
Olshevsky, George *editor*
Pincus, Robert Lawrence *art critic, historian*
Rowe, Peter A. *columnist*
Steen, Paul Joseph *retired broadcasting executive*
Willis, Norman Hunt *author, writer, director, producer*
Winner, Karin E. *editor-in-chief*

San Francisco
Anderson, Chris W. *editor-in-chief*
Bronstein, Phil *publishing executive*
Cameron, Heather Anne *publishing executive*
Davidson, Keay *newswriter*
Dickey, Glenn Ernest, Jr. *sportswriter*
Duscha, Julius Carl *journalist*
Fainaru-Wada, Mark *journalist*
Falk, Steven B. *newspaper publishing executive*
Fifer, Sally Jo *broadcast executive, editor*
Fox, Steve *editor-in-chief*
Garchik, Leah Lieberman *journalist*
German, William *newspaper editor*
Graysmith, Robert *political cartoonist, author*
Hafner, Katie *reporter*
Hamilton, Joan Nice *editor-in-chief*
Klein, Marc S. *editor, publishing executive*
Lazarus, David *journalist*
Markoff, John *reporter*
McCracken, Harry *journalist*
Minor, Halsey *multimedia company executive*
Newmark, Craig Alexander *communications executive*
Pazour, Don *publishing executive*
Pereira, P.J. *media consultant*
Perlman, David *journalist*
Quittner, Josh *editor*
Richtel, Matt (Theron Heir) *reporter, cartoonist*
Rosen, Evan Mark *executive communication advisor, journalist*
Rosenheim, Daniel Edward *journalist, television news director*
Rubenstein, Steven Paul *newspaper columnist*
Russell, Sabin *newswriter*
Ryan, Joan *columnist*
Sansweet, Stephen Jay *journalist, writer, marketing executive*
Schwarz, Glenn Vernon *newspaper editor*
Vega, Frank J. *newspaper publishing executive*
Walsh, Joan *editor-in-chief*
Williams, Lance *journalist*
Winn, Steven Jay *critic*

San Jose
Carey, Peter Kevin *reporter*
Ceppos, Jerome Merle (Jerry Ceppos) *newspaper editor*
Diamond, Diana Louise *editor, journalist*
Harris, Jay Terrence *communications educator*
Hutton, Carole Leigh *executive editor*
Kiel, Jeff E. *publishing executive*
Mendoza, Martha *reporter*
Migielicz, Geralyn *photojournalist*
Ridder, P(aul) Anthony *newspaper company executive*
Riggs, George E. *newspaper publishing executive*
Trousdale, Stephen Richard *newspaper editor*

San Mateo
Sperling, Norman *editor*

San Pedro
Bowling, Lance Christopher *recording industry executive*

San Rafael
Morgan, Michael Brewster *publishing executive*

Santa Ana
Brusic, Ken *editor-in-chief*
Katz, Tonnie *newspaper editor*

Santa Barbara
Ackerman, Marshall *publishing executive*
Brilliant, Ashleigh Ellwood *cartoonist, writer*
Brown, J'Amy Maroney *journalist, media consultant, investor*
Dubroff, Henry Allen *editor, journalist, entrepreneur*
Jackson, Beverley Joy Jacobson *columnist, educator*
McCaw, Wendy Petrak *publishing executive*
Nabi, Robin *communications educator*

Santa Clarita
Sturges, Sherry Lynn *recording industry executive*

Santa Monica
Alpert, Herb *composer, recording artist, producer, painter*
Feltheimer, Jon *entertainment company executive*
Friedman, Robert Glenn *film company executive*

Greenberg, Sarah *film company executive*
Horowitz, Zachary I. *entertainment company executive*
Levin, Gerald M. (Jerry Levin) *former media and entertainment company executive*
Littlefield, Warren *television executive*
Morgenstern, Joe *film critic*
Palmatier, Malcolm Arthur *editor, consultant*
Rifkin, Arnold *film company executive*
Sacchi, John *film company executive*
Snedaker, Catherine Raupagh (Kit Snedaker) *editor*
Timbaland, (Timothy Z. Mosley) *recording industry executive, rap artist*

Santa Rosa
Callum, Myles *magazine editor, writer*
Person, Evert Bertil *retired newspaper and radio executive*
Swofford, Robert Lee *editor, journalist*

Sausalito
Battelle, John *journalist, educator, writer, entrepreneur*
Hansen, Charles Morton *editor, retired military officer*

Seaside
May, James Harvey *communications educator*

Sebastopol
O'Reilly, Tim *computer book publishing company executive, open sourcer advocate*

Sherman Oaks
Drudge, Matt *journalist, celebrity blogger*
Platus, Libby *journalist, art educator, sculptor, artist*

Sonoma
Beckmann, Jon Michael *publishing company executive*

Stanford
Andreopoulos, Spyros George *writer*
Suppes, Christine Johnson *publishing executive*

Summerland
Cannon, Louis Simeon *journalist, writer*

Sunland
Nepales, Ruben Viado *journalist*

Sunnyvale
Coleman, Gregory G. *former magazine publisher, Internet company executive*

Tehachapi
Mitchell, Betty Jo *publishing executive, writer*

Thousand Oaks
Albertson, Marty P. *music company executive*

Toluca Lake
Ragan, Ann Talmadge *media and production consultant, actor*

Torrance
Adelsman, Jean (Harriette Adelsman) *newspaper editor*

Tujunga
Loehwing, Lord Rudi Charles *publicist, radio broadcasting executive, journalist*

Universal City
Bromstad, Angela *broadcast executive*
Finkelstein, Rick *film company executive*
Gaspin, Jeff *broadcast executive*
Graboff, Marc *broadcast executive*
Hammer, Bonnie *broadcast executive*
Langley, Donna *film company executive*
Linde, David *film company executive*
Lowe, Kristin *film company executive*
Meyer, Ron *film company executive*
Parent, Mary *film company executive*
Rocco, Nikki *film company executive*
Shmuger, Marc *film company executive*
Silverman, Ben *broadcast executive, television producer*
Stuber, Scott *film company executive*
Weinberg, Teri Ellen *television executive, television producer*

Ventura
Howry, Joe R. *newspaper editor*

West Hollywood
Grey, Brad *film company executive*
Huntsberry, Frederick D. *film company executive*
Shaye, Robert Kenneth *film company executive*
Shearmur, Alli *broadcast executive*

Wilton
Harrison, George Harry, III, (Hank Harrison) *publishing executive, author*

Woodland Hills
Granger, David *editor*
Harris, Barbara S. *publishing executive, editor-in-chief*
Jacobson, Sidney *editor*
McCluggage, Kerry *film and television executive*
Russell, Anne M. *editor-in-chief*

Yreka
Smith, Vin *editor, small business owner, writer*

COLORADO

Aspen
Hayes, Mary Eshbaugh *editor, writer*

Boulder
El Mallakh, Dorothea Hendry *editor, publishing executive*
Kuhn, Timothy R. *communication educator*

Cherry Hills Village
Stapleton, Katharine Hall (Katie Stapleton) *commentator, writer*

Colorado Springs
Zapel, Arthur Lewis *book publishing executive*

Denver
Barbour, Alton Bradford *retired human communication studies educator*
Chavez, Jeanette *editor*
Clark, Gary R. *newspaper editor*
Cohen, Andrew *news analyst, lawyer*
Dance, Francis Esburn Xavier *communication educator*
Drake, Sylvie (Jurras) *theater critic*
Engdahl, Todd Philip *editor*
Heisler, Todd *photojournalist*
Landess, Mike (Malcolm Lee Landess III) *newscaster*
Moore, Gregory L. *editor*
Rothman, Paul Alan *publishing executive*
Saltz, Howard Joel *newspaper editor*
Sheeler, Jim *journalist*
Singleton, William Dean *publishing executive*
Tatum, Christine *editor*
Wolman, Jonathan Paley *journalist*

Evergreen
Dobbs, Gregory Allan *journalist*

Fort Collins
May, Stephen James *communications educator, writer*

Georgetown
Stern, Mort(imer) P(hillip) *communications educator, editor, reporter, consultant*

Golden
Baron, Robert Charles *publishing executive*
Zimmer, Larry William, Jr. *sports announcer*

Gunnison
Gelwicks, James M. *retired communications educator*

Highlands Ranch
Harris, Douglas Clay *retired newspaper executive*

Littleton
Udevitz, Norman *publishing executive*

Morrison
Myers, Harry J., Jr. *retired publisher*

Paonia
Ring, Ray *editor*

CONNECTICUT

Bethel
Shepard, Jean Heck *retired publishing consultant*

Bridgeport
Simoneau, Cynthia Lambert *editor, educator*

Bridgewater
Crooke, Robert Andrew *media consultant, writer, educator*

Bristol
Berman, Chris *sportscaster*
Bodenheimer, George *broadcast executive*
Brantley, Jeffrey Hoke *baseball analyst, retired professional baseball player*
Gammons, Peter *columnist, commentator*
Greenberg, Mike *sportscaster*
Johnson, Keyshawn *sportscaster, retired professional football player*
Kolber, Suzy *sportscaster*
Magnus, Burke *broadcast executive*
Olney, Robert Stanbury III *sportswriter and baseball analyst*
Scott, Stuart *sports anchor*
Simmons, Bill *sportswriter*
Skipper, John *publishing executive*
Smith, Emmitt (Emmitt James Smith III) *sportscaster, retired professional football player*
Theismann, Joe (Joseph Robert Theismann) *sportscaster, retired professional football player*
Tirico, Mike *sportscaster*
Vitale, Dick *commentator*
Wolff, Russell *broadcast executive*

Chester
Frost-Knappman, (Linda) Elizabeth *publishing executive, editor, writer*

Danbury
Reynolds, Jean Edwards *publishing executive*

Darien
Becker, Ralph Edward *broadcast executive, consultant*
Brooke, Avery Rogers *publisher, writer*
Workman, Sharon Joy *journalist*

Easton
Enos, Randall *cartoonist, illustrator*
Lorenz, Lee Sharp *cartoonist*

Fairfield
Kaff, Albert Ernest *reporter, writer*

Greens Farms
Deford, Frank *sportswriter, commentator, writer*

Greenwich
Brant, Peter M. *magazine publishing executive, real estate developer*
Landau, Jon *music producer, manager*
Moffly, John Wesley, IV, *magazine publishing executive*
Welling, Kathryn Marie *editor*

Hartford
Carver, Stephen D. *publishing executive, former broadcast executive*
Chedekel, Lisa *journalist*
Harden, Jon Bixby *publishing executive*
Kauffman, Matthew *journalist*
Noel, Don Obert, Jr. *retired editor, columnist*
Pach, Peter Barnard *columnist, editor*
Teutsch, Clifford L. *editor-in-chief*
Yardley, Bill *journalist*

Ivoryton
Bendig, William Charles *editor, artist*

Kensington
Murphy, Thomas John *publishing executive*

Lakeville
Estabrook, Robert Harley *journalist*

Madison
Egbert, Emerson Charles *retired publisher*

Milford
Henderson, Albert Kossack *publishing and food products executive, consultant*

Moodus
Cumming, Robert Emil *editor, writer*

New Canaan
Allen, Joseph Henry *retired publishing company executive*

New Haven
Balay, Robert Elmore *editor, librarian*
Brill, Steven *magazine editor*
Fuchs, Elinor *film critic, playwright, educator*
Leeney, Robert Joseph *newspaper editor*
Spence, Barbara E. *former publishing company executive*

Norwalk
DeCesare, Donald E. *broadcast executive*

Old Greenwich
Dixon, John Morris *magazine editor*

Old Saybrook
Purcell, Bradford Moore *publishing company executive*

Sharon
Gordon, Nicholas *broadcast and performing arts executive*

Shelton
Kantrowitz, Jonathan Daniel *publishing executive, educator, lawyer*

Sherman
Cowley, Robert William *editor, writer, consultant, lecturer*

Stamford
Britt, Glenn Alan *media company executive*
Fein, Ronnie *journalist, writer*
Lane, Hana Umlauf *editor*

Stonington
Elliott, Osborn *journalist, educator, retired dean*

Waterbury
Pape, William James, II, *newspaper publisher*

Westbrook
Gilmore, Clarence Percy *editor-in-chief, writer*

Westport
Kramer, Sidney B. *publishing executive, literary agent, lawyer*
McCormack, Donald Paul *newspaper consultant*
Stern, Robert D. *publishing executive*

Wethersfield
Osborne, Louise *publishing executive*

Wilton
Bair, Thomas J. *publishing executive*
Frank, Robert Allen *media consultant*
Seitz, Nicholas Joseph *editor, journalist*
Tarde, Jerry (Gerard Tarde) *editor-in-chief*

DELAWARE

Dover
Smyth, Joel Douglas *newspaper executive*

New Castle
Cansler, Leslie Ervin *retired newspaper editor*
von Hoelle, John Jacob Lewis *publisher, commercial developer*

Newark
DeVivo, Sal J. *newspaper executive*
Jackson, Marvin Dennis *journalism educator, writer*

DISTRICT OF COLUMBIA

Washington
Adams, Robert Edward *journalist*
Adelman, Kenneth Lee *journalist, former ambassador*
Allam, Hannah *journalist*
Allen, Henry Southworth *journalist, critic*
Amos, Deborah Susan *foreign correspondent*
Andrews, John Frank *editor, author, educator*
Angier, Natalie Marie *science journalist*
Anton, Frank A. *publishing executive*
Applebaum, Anne *journalist, writer*
Arnovitz, Benton Mayer *editor*
Arrott, Elizabeth *journalist*
Asker, James Robert *magazine editor*
Atlas, Terry *journalist*
Baquet, Dean Paul *editor*
Barber, Ben Bernard Andrew *journalist*
Barnes, Frederic Wood, Jr. *journalist, political analyst*
Barnes, Julian E. *editor*
Beinart, Peter Alexander *editor, columnist*
Bellows, Keith Adams *editor-in-chief, writer*
Bennett, Philip *editor*
Bird, Kai *journalist, historian*
Blankley, Tony *editor*
Blitzer, Wolf *news correspondent*
Bradford, Monica M. *editor*
Bradlee, Benjamin Crowninshield *former editor*
Branegan, James Augustus III *journalist*
Braverman, Jordan *columnist*
Brock, Gregory E. *editor*
Broder, David Salzer *reporter, writer*
Brown, Campbell *newscaster*
Brown, John Patrick *publishing executive, financial consultant*
Bruzelius, Nils Johan Axel *journalist*
Cameron, Carl (Karl Lamberg-Karlovsky) *political correspondent*
Cannon, Carl M. *reporter*
Centanni, Steve *national news correspondent*
Chandrasekaran, Rajiv *editor, writer*
Clift, Eleanor *news correspondent, writer*
Coleman, Milton *editor*
Coll, Stephen Wilson *journalist*
Compton, Ann Woodruff *news correspondent*
Cook, Charles Edward, Jr. *editor, political analyst*
Cook, David *editor*
Cooper, Matthew *journalist*
Cosgrove, John Patrick *editor*
Covault, Craig *editor*
Cowan, Edward *journalist, editor*
Crenshaw, Albert Burford *journalist*
Curtiss, Richard Holden *magazine editor, writer*
Cutler, Bernard Joseph *editor-in-chief, writer*
Davis, Nathaniel (Nate) A. *broadcast executive*
Day, Charles Williamson *commentator*
de Borchgrave, Arnaud *editor, writer, lecturer*
Deeb, Mary-Jane *editor, educator*
DeFrank, Thomas Michael *journalist*
Diehl, Jackson Kemper *journalist*
Dillin, John Woodward, Jr. *retired editor, reporter*
Dillon, Veronica *publishing executive, lawyer*
Dionne, E. J., Jr. *columnist*
Doan, Michael Frederick *editor*
Donaldson, Samuel Andrew *journalist*
Donohoe, Cathryn Murray *journalist*
Dorn, James Andrew *editor*
Dowd, Maureen *columnist*
Downie, Leonard, Jr. *editor, writer*
Dujack, Stephen Raymond *editor*
Eaton, Sabrina Catherine Elizabeth *journalist*
Edwards, Bob (Robert Alan Edwards) *radio news anchor*
Elfin, Mel *magazine editor*
Elsasser, Glen Robert *journalist*
Entman, Robert Mathew *communications educator, consultant*
Faherty, Robert Louis *publishing executive*
Fahey, John M., Jr. *book publishing executive*
Feld, Karen Irma *columnist, journalist, commentator, speech professional*
Fields, Suzanne Bregman *syndicated columnist*
Fineman, Howard David *columnist, news correspondent*
Finkel, David *journalist*
Foer, Franklin *editor*
Forgey, Benjamin Franklin *architecture and art critic*
Franzen, Byron T. (John Franzen) *media specialist*
Friedman, Thomas Loren *foreign correspondent, writer*
Garrels, Anne *news correspondent*
Gerson, Michael John *journalist*
Geyer, Georgie Anne *columnist, educator, commentator, writer*
Gibson, Florence Anderson *talking book company executive, narrator*
Givhan, Robin Deneen *journalist*
Glassman, James Kenneth *editor, writer, publishing executive*
Goldberg, Jonah Jacob *political columnist*
Graham, Donald Edward *publishing company executive*
Greenhouse, Linda Joyce *journalist*
Griffin, David *photojournalist*
Grimaldi, James V. *journalist*
Grosvenor, Gilbert Melville *journalist, educator, publishing executive*
Grubisich, Tom *web editor*
Gutman, Roy William *reporter*
Guzy, Carol *photojournalist*
Gwaltney, Corbin *publishing executive, editor*
Halsey, Ashley III *newspaper editor*
Hammond, Allen Lee *editor, consultant, former broadcaster, non-profit policy research center executive*
Harrison, Patricia de Stacy *broadcast executive, former federal agency administrator*
Headden, Susan M. *editor*
Hecht, Marjorie Mazel *editor*
Henry, Ed *news correspondent*
Henry, John Cooper *journalist*
Hiatt, Fred *journalist*
Hileman, Bette *journalist*
Hills, Stephen P. *publishing executive*
Hinden, Stanley Jay *newspaper editor*
Hitchens, Christopher Eric *columnist, writer*
Hoagland, Jimmie Lee *newspaper editor*
Hulse, Carl *newspaper executive*
Hume, Brit (Alexander Britton) *journalist*
Hunt, Albert R. *editor*
Ijaz, Mansoor *news correspondent*
Israelite, David M. *music publishing executive, prosecutor*

Jacobson, Louis Alan *journalist*
Jenkins, Loren B. *broadcast executive, publisher, writer*
Johns, Christopher George *editor-in-chief, photojournalist*
Johnson, Richard Kent *publishing executive*
Jones, Boisfeuillet, Jr., (Bo Jones) *publishing executive*
Joo, Douglas D.M. *newspaper and video production and aviation executive*
Joyce, Anne Raine *editor*
Kammer, Jerry *reporter*
Kelly, Brian J. *editor*
King, Colbert Isaiah *editor*
King, Larry (Larry Zeiger) *broadcaster, radio personality*
Kiplinger, Knight Austin *journalist, publishing executive*
Kirk, Donald *journalist*
Kirkpatrick, David D. *news correspondent*
Klose, Kevin *broadcast executive*
Knight, Athelia Wilhelmenia *journalist*
Kondracke, Morton Matt *journalist*
Kristol, William (Bill Krisol) *editor, political analyst*
Kurtz, Howard *journalist, author*
Labaton, Stephen *journalist, lawyer*
Lamb, Brian Patrick *broadcast executive*
Lambro, Donald Joseph *columnist*
Lardner, George, Jr. *journalist, writer*
Lasseter, Tom *journalist*
Lawson, Jennifer *broadcast executive*
Lee, Debra Louise *cable television company executive*
Leeds, Charles Alan *publishing executive*
Lehrman, Margaret McBride *broadcast executive, television producer*
Leubsdorf, Carl Philipp *publishing executive*
Lewis, Charles Joseph *journalist*
Lewis, Robert David Gilmore *retired editor*
Liasson, Mara *news correspondent*
Lichtblau, Eric *journalist*
Locker, Raymond Duncan *editor*
Loo, Beverly Jane *publishing executive*
Lubar, Jeffrey Stuart *journalist, trade association executive*
Margolis, Doris May Rosenberg *editor, writer*
Marshall, Joshua Micah *publisher, blog writer, columnist, editor, political journalist*
McBee, Susanna Barnes *retired journalist*
McCormally, Kevin Jay *editor*
McDevitt, Thomas P. *publishing executive*
McLaughlin, John J. *broadcast executive, television producer, journalist, political commentator*
McPherson, Peter (M. Peter McPherson) *publishing executive, educational association administrator*
Melendy, David Russell *newscaster, reporter*
Messiah-Jiles, Sonceria *publishing executive*
Meyerson, Harold *journalist*
Miller, Nicole *art columnist*
Mitchell, Andrea *journalist*
Moran, Terry *news correspondent*
Moss, Madison Scott *editor*
Murphy, Caryle Marie *foreign correspondent*
Myers, Lisa M. *broadcast journalist*
Naím, Moises *editor*
Novak, Robert David Sanders *columnist, commentator*
Ohanian, Bernard Jay *writer, editor*
Oka, Takashi *journalist, consultant, educator*
Padden, Preston *broadcast executive*
Page, Tim *music critic, writer, producer*
Palmer, Stacy Ella *periodical editor*
Panero, Hugh Edward *former broadcast executive*
Parsons, Gary M. *broadcast executive*
Peck, Louis Moses *editor*
Peirce, Neal R. *journalist*
Pelham, Ann *publishing executive, department chairman*
Peretz, Martin *publishing executive, educator*
Perl, Peter *editor*
Pincus, Walter Haskell *news editor*
Pratt, Dana Joseph *publishing consultant*
Priest, Dana *journalist*
Prina, L(ouis) Edgar *journalist*
Putzel, Michael *journalist, editor*
Raddatz, Martha *news correspondent*
Rankin, Robert Arthur *journalist*
Raspberry, William James *journalist*
Ratner, Ellen Faith *news analyst and correspondent, writer*
Ravenal, Earl Cedric *international relations educator, writer*
Rice, Susan Elizabeth *foreign policy analyst, former federal agency administrator*
Ricks, Thomas Edwin *journalist, writer*
Ridgeway, James Fowler *journalist*
Risen, James E. *journalist*
Roberts, Cokie (Corinne Boggs Roberts) *newscaster*
Roberts, John *news anchor*
Rosen, Gerald Robert *editor*
Russert, Timothy John *broadcast journalist and executive*
Safire, William *journalist, foundation administrator*
Salant, Jonathan D. *reporter*
Samsot, Robert Louis *editor, consultant*
Sanger, David E. *news correspondent*
Savage, Charles *news correspondent*
Scheibel, Kenneth Maynard *journalist*
Schieffer, Bob *newscaster*
Schmidt, Susan *journalist*
Schram, Martin Jay *journalist*
Scoblic, J. Peter *magazine editor*
Seidman, L(ewis) William *television commentator, publisher*
Semas, Philip Wayne *editor*
Shanks, Hershel *editor, writer*
Shannon, Donald Hawkins *retired editor*
Shapiro, Walter Elliot *columnist*
Sheehan, Neil *reporter, writer*
Shenon, Philip *journalist*
Siegel, Robert Charles *broadcast journalist*
Simpson, Cam *reporter*
Slafka, Kristi Lynne *journalist*
Slater, Jim *sportswriter, journalist*
Smith, John B. *publishing executive*
Smith, R. Jeffrey *reporter*
Smith, Stephen Grant *journalist*
Smith, Susan A. *photojournalist*
Stephanopoulos, George Robert *political reporter, former federal official*
Stephens, Joe Alan *investigative reporter*
Stern, Carl Leonard *retired news correspondent, federal official, educator*
Stern, Kenneth P. *broadcast executive*
Stern, Marcus A. *journalist*
Stolberg, Sheryl Gay *journalist*
Stossel, Scott Hanford *editor, writer*
Sullivan, Andrew M. *online journalist, editor, news blogger*
Sutherland, J.J. *journalist*
Taubman, Philip M. *editor*
Terzian, Philip Henry *journalist*
Thomasson, Dan King *newspaper executive, columnist*
Tiede, Tom Robert *journalist*
Tierney, John Marion *journalist, columnist, reporter*
Toedtman, James Smith *journalist, editor*
Tolchin, Martin *journalist, writer*
Toles, Thomas Gregory *editorial cartoonist*
Tortolani, Michelle F. *broadcast executive*
Totenberg, Nina *journalist*
Trafford, Abigail *columnist, editor, writer, public speaker*
Turner, Ted (Robert Edward Turner) *retired broadcast company executive, philanthropist*
Waldman, Amy *journalist*
Walsh, Kenneth Thomas *journalist*
Weisman, Steven Roger *newspaper editor*
Weiss, Rick *reporter*
Whitworth, William A. *magazine editor*
Williams, Earl Patrick, Jr. *retired editor, freelance writer*
Williams, Juan *news correspondent*
Winfrey, Carey Wells *journalist, editor*
Winter, Thomas Swanson *publishing executive*
Wood, James *magazine editor, literary critic*
Woodward, Bob (Robert Upshur Woodward) *newspaper reporter, writer*
Zwerdling, Daniel *news correspondent*

FLORIDA

Aventura
Perkel, Robert Simon *photojournalist, educator*

Boca Raton
Handel, Morton Emanuel *film company executive, management consultant*
Levine, Irving R. *commentator, dean, writer, educator*
McQueen, Scott Robert *broadcast executive*
Perel, David *editor*
Trunzo, Candace *editor-in-chief*

Boynton Beach
Jacobs, Wendy *editor, realtor*
Klein, Bernard *publishing executive*

Bradenton
Crouthamel, Thomas Grover, Sr. *editor, consultant*
McFarland, Richard Macklin *retired journalist*
White, Dale Andrew *journalist*

Clearwater
VanMeer, Mary Ann *publishing executive, writer, webmaster*

Cocoa Beach
Tewksbury, Russell Baird *media consultant, internet strategist, educator*

Coral Gables
Roberts, Samuel Smith *television news executive*

Daytona Beach
Davidson, Herbert M., Jr., (Tippen) *newspaper owner*

Delray Beach
Salsberg, Arthur Philip *publishing executive*

Dover
Pearson, Walter Donald *editor, columnist*

Fort Lauderdale
Greenberg, Howard *publishing executive*
Markus, Robert Michael *retired journalist*
Maucker, Earl Robert *editor, publishing executive*
Packer, Billy *sports announcer (broadcast)*
Ruffner, Frederick G., Jr. *book publisher*
Williamson, William Paul, Jr. *journalist*

Fort Myers
Barbour, William Rinehart, Jr. *retired book publisher*

Gainesville
Barber, Charles Edward *publishing executive, journalist*
Holland, Norman Norwood *critic*
Kaplan, John *photojournalist, educator, consultant*
Logan, William *poetry critic, literature and language professor, poet*

Heathrow
Argirion, Michael *editor*

Hialeah
Arrarás, Maria Celeste *newscaster, journalist*
Browne, Donald Victor *broadcast executive*

Hollywood
Lopez, Filemon *broadcast executive*

Jacksonville
Barrow, Sally Settle *retired media specialist, retired librarian*
Bedell, Elizabeth Snyder (Betty Bedell) *editor-in-chief, marketing professional*
Cannon, Carl N. *publishing executive*
Davis, Fred *journalist, educator*
Hartmann, Frederick William *newspaper editor*
Lehmbeck, John Pierce *journalist, writer*
Vincent, Norman Fuller *broadcast executive*

Key Biscayne
Pope, John Edwin *editor, columnist*

Lake Helen
Finn, Stephen Martin *media producer, venture capitalist*

Lakeland
MacDonald, Susan Priest *media specialist, writer*

Lutz
Kolb, Richard Maurice *sports writer, sportscaster*

Melbourne
Mikolajczyk, Mark S. *publishing executive*

Melrose
Burt, Alvin Victor, Jr. *journalist*

Miami
Black, Creed Carter *newspaper executive*
Cenziper, Debbie *journalist*
Chapman, Alvah Herman, Jr. *retired newspaper executive*
Cotayo, Charles *journalist, film producer, writer, critic*
de Leon, Lidia Maria *magazine editor*
Fichtner, Margaria *journalist*
Gyllenhaal, Anders *editor*
Hampton, John Lewis *retired newspaper editor*
Harrison, Stanley L. *editor, educator, writer*
Landsberg, David *publishing executive*
Lawrence, David, Jr. *journalist, early childhood advocate*
Lew, Salvador *radio station executive*
Lewis, John Milton *cable television company executive*
O'Bryon, Linda Elizabeth *broadcast executive*
Pitts, Leonard Garvey, Jr. *columnist, writer*
Russell, James Webster, Jr. *editor, columnist*
Salinas, María Elena *newscaster, columnist*
Savage, James Francis *editor*
Tsai, John Jengshyong *publishing executive*
Wax, William Edward *photojournalist*

Mount Dora
Trundle, W(infield) Scott *publishing executive newspaper, lawyer*

Naples
Blevins, Charles Russell *publishing executive*
Burdick, Robert W. *newspaper editor*
Clapp, Roger Howland *retired publishing executive*
Clarke, John Patrick *retired newspaper publisher*
Cobb, Brian Eric *broadcast executive*
Jones, Philip Howard *broadcast journalist*
Penniman, Nicholas Griffith, IV, *retired newspaper publisher*
Silvestri, Vito Nicholas *communications educator*

Niceville
Warren, J. Richard *editor, retired humanities educator*

North Palm Beach
Lavine, Alan *columnist, writer*

Orlando
Dunn, William Bruna III *journalist*
Hall, Charlotte Hauch *editor*
Maupin, Elizabeth Thatcher *theater critic*
Pierce, Jerry Earl *publishing executive*
Reese, Charles Edgar *columnist*
Waltz, Kathleen M. *publishing executive*

Palm Bay
Pattyn, Sue *publishing executive*

Palm Beach
Monath, Norman *publishing company executive*
Pryor, Hubert *editor, writer, consultant*

Palm Coast
Afflick, Gilbert Leslie *editor, journalist*

Palm Harbor
Barker, Larry Lee *communications educator*
Jones, Winona Nigels *retired media specialist*

Panama City
Lucas, Truett LaVan *retired communications technician*

Parkland
Froehlich, Fritz Edgar *communications educator, telecommunications scientist*

Pensacola
Bowden, Jesse Earle *editor, writer, cartoonist, journalist, educator*

Saint Augustine
Nolan, Joseph Thomas *journalism educator, communications consultant*

Saint Petersburg
Barnes, Andrew Earl *former newspaper executive*
Belich, John Patrick, Sr. *journalist, private investigator*
Corty, Andrew P. *publishing executive*
Haiman, Robert James *editor, journalist, educator, media consultant, expert witness, critic*
Hooker, Robert Wright *journalist*
Jenkins, Robert Norman *reporter, editor*
Johnson, Edna Ruth *editor*
Kubiet, Leo Lawrence *media consultant*
Naughton, James Martin *journalist*
Patterson, Eugene Corbett *retired editor, publishing executive*
Petty, Marty *publishing executive*
Pittman, Robert Turner *retired newspaper editor*
Tash, Paul Clifford *editor, publishing executive*

Sanford
Scott, Mellouise Jacqueline *retired media specialist*

Sarasota
Corrigan, William Thomas *retired broadcast news executive*
Hughes, Allen *music critic*
Jackel, Lawrence *publishing executive*
Marino, Eugene Louis *publishing executive, director*
North, Marjorie Mary *columnist*
Proffitt, Waldo, Jr. *newspaper editor*
Stevens, Elisabeth Goss (Mrs. Robert Schleussner Jr.) *journalist, writer, graphic artist*

Tallahassee
Clifford, Dorothy Ring *journalist*
Dadisman, Joseph Carrol *retired newspaper executive*
Morgan, Lucy Ware *news correspondent, journalist*
Pettijohn, Fred Phillips *retired publishing executive*

Tampa
Bachman, Gregg Paul *communications educator*
Coats, Janet S. (Janet Weaver) *executive editor*
Friedlander, Edward Jay *journalist, educator*
Huey, Peggy J. *communications educator, performing company executive*
Jacobus, Mary *publishing executive*
Palmer, Denise E. *publishing executive*
Reed, Donna Marie *editor*
Schueler, John R. *newspaper executive*
Tully, Darrow *newspaper publisher*

Tarpon Springs
Leisner, Anthony Baker *publishing company executive*

Vero Beach
Binney, Jan Jarrell *publishing executive, marketing professional*

West Palm Beach
Johnson, Martin Allen *publishing executive, artist*
Rukeyser, M.S., Jr. *television consultant, writer*

Weston
Marino, Dan (Daniel Constantino Marino Jr.) *sportscaster, retired professional football player*

GEORGIA

Athens
Feldman, Edmund Burke *art critic*
Fink, Conrad Charles *journalist, educator, communications executive, consultant*
Soloski, John *journalism and communications educator*

Atlanta
Albert, Marv *sportscaster, program director*
Amanpour, Christiane *news correspondent*
Barkley, Charles Wade *sportscaster, retired professional basketball player*
Berry, Dennis (G. Dennis Berry) *publishing executive*
Bisher, James Furman *journalist, writer*
Chambers, Anne Cox *publishing executive, former diplomat*
Connelly, Terrence John, Sr. *broadcast executive*
Hayes, Jimmy W. *media company executive*
Johnson, Ernie, Jr. *sportscaster*
Kennedy, James Cox *publishing and media executive*
Klein, Jonathan *broadcast executive*
Klibanoff, Hank *journalist*
Kloer, Philip Baldwin *critic*
Lazarus, Mark *broadcast executive*
Luckovich, Mike *cartoonist*
Mellott, John C. *publishing executive*
Merdek, Andrew Austin *publishing and media executive, lawyer*
Morant, Brenda White *publishing executive, small business owner, investor*
Neil, Robert F. *broadcast executive*
O'Leary, Robert C. *publishing and media executive*
Polk, James Ray *journalist*
Robelot, Jane *anchor*
Sams, Louise S. *broadcast executive, lawyer*
Scott, Marian Alexis *journalist*
Simao, Paul *news agency executive*
Sloan, Mary Jean *retired media specialist*
Teepen, Thomas Henry *editor, journalist*
Toner, Michael F. *journalist*
Tucker, Cynthia Anne *journalist*
Wallace, Julia Diane *newspaper editor*
Walton, Jim *news network executive*
Whitt, Richard Ernest *reporter*
Wussler, Robert Joseph *broadcast executive, media consultant*

Augusta
Denton, Frank M. *publishing executive*

Buford
Coakley, Deirdre *columnist, writer*

Carrollton
Wanager, Charles Raymond, Jr. *reporter, editor*

Decatur
Knight, Walker Leigh *publishing executive, minister*
Shaw, Jeanne Osborne *editor, poet*

Fayetteville
Turnipseed, Barnwell Rhett III *journalist, public relations consultant*

Jekyll Island
Bentley, James Luther *former journalist*

Mableton
Rowe, Bonnie Gordon *music company executive*

Marietta
Hays, Robert William *communications educator, consultant, writer*
Opre, Thomas Edward *retired editor, film company executive*
Williamsen, Dannye Sue *personal development educator, publisher*

Powder Springs
Creighton, Peggy Milam *media specialist, writer*

Roswell
Peterson, Donald Robert *editor, vintage automobile consultant*

Savannah
Smith, David Lee *retired editor*

Statesboro
Adhikari, Dharma Nanda *journalist, writer, educator*

HAWAII

Honolulu
Keyes, Saundra Elise *newspaper editor*
Simonds, John Edward *retired newspaper editor*
Sparks, Robert William *retired publishing executive*

Kahului
Yamamoto, Irwin Toraki *editor, publishing executive*

Pahoa
Lewis, Jack (Cecil Paul Lewis) *publishing executive, editor*

IDAHO

Boise
Gowler, Vicki Sue *editor-in-chief*
McLuskie, Ed *communications educator*

Idaho Falls
Harris, Darryl Wayne *publishing executive*

Sandpoint
Bowne, Martha Hoke *editor, consultant*

ILLINOIS

Arlington Heights
Baumann, Daniel E. *publishing executive*
Lampinen, John A. *newspaper editor*
Ray, Douglas Kent *newspaper executive*

Belleville
Hundsdorfer, Beth *reporter*
Pawlaczyk, George *reporter*

Berwyn
Forst, Edmund Charles, Jr. *communications educator, administrator, consultant*

Buffalo Grove
Kuennen, Thomas Gerard *journalist*
Samors, Neal *publishing executive, writer*

Burr Ridge
Wyatt, Robert Odell *journalism educator*

Carol Stream
Bemis, Mary Ferguson *magazine editor*
Franzen, Janice Marguerite Gosnell *magazine editor*
Yancey, Philip David *editor, author*

Champaign
Dulany, Elizabeth Gjelsness *editor*
Kroner, Fred L. *journalist*
McCulloh, Judith Marie *editor*
Meyer, August Christopher, Jr. *broadcast executive, lawyer*
Turquette, Frances Bond *editor*
Watts, Robert Allan *publisher, lawyer*

Charleston
Coutant, Mary McElwee *retired editor*

Chicago
Adams, Edward A. *legal journalist*
Anderson, Karl Stephen *editor*
Artner, Alan Gustav *art critic, journalist*
Barr, Emily L. *broadcast executive*
Barron, John *editor*
Bratcher, Juanita *journalist*
Burton, Cheryl *newscaster*
Cappo, Joseph C. *journalist, writer*
Chapman, Stephen James *columnist*
Cook, Bruce Lawrence *editor*
Cooke, Michael *editor-in-chief, publishing executive*
Cross, Robert Clark *journalist*
Cruickshank, John Douglas *publishing executive*
Curwen, Randall William *journalist, editor*
Darby, Edwin Wheeler *retired columnist*
Dee, Ivan Richard *book publisher*
DeLong, Ray *editor*
Dold, Robert Bruce *journalist*
Ebert, Roger Joseph *film critic*
Essex, Joseph Michael *visual communication planner*
Feder, Robert *columnist*
Ferrara, Annette *editor, educator*
Fetridge, Clark Worthington *publishing executive*
FitzSimons, Dennis Joseph *broadcast and publishing executive*
Fontanarosa, Phil Bernard *medical journal executive editor, emergency physician, educator*
Forbes, Dorsey Connors *commentator, journalist*
Francuch, Paul Charles *broadcast journalist*
Freidheim, Cyrus F., Jr. *publishing and former food products executive*
Grossman, Kate Nadia *journalist*
Hallinan, Joseph Thomas *journalist*
Hardin, Terrence Armstrong *former radio broadcasting manager*
Harrelson, Ken *sports broadcaster*
Harvey, Paul *commentator, writer, columnist*
Hefner, Christie Ann *publishing executive*
Hirt, Jane *editor*
Hlavacek, Roy George *publishing executive*
Huebner, Jeff *art journalist, freelance writer*
Huntley, Robert Stephen *newspaper editor*
Idol, Anna Catherine *magazine editor*
Jones, Linda *communications educator*
Judge, Bernard Martin *editor, publishing executive*
Kamyszew, Christopher D. *film executive, educator, curator*
Kelly, Curtis Hartt *retired publishing executive*
Klapthor, James *broadcast executive*
Klatt, Wayne Roy *editor, writer*
Klaviter, Helen Lothrop *magazine editor*
Klemens, Thomas Lloyd *editor*
Kniffel, Leonard John *editor, librarian*
Krashesky, Alan *newscaster*
Krueger, Bonnie Lee *editor, writer*
Larson, Roy *journalist, publishing executive*
Lipinski, Ann Marie *publishing executive*
Loesch, Katharine Taylor *communications educator, theater educator*
Longworth, Richard Cole *journalist*
Lythcott, Marcia A. *newspaper editor*
Madigan, John William *publishing executive*
Mariotti, Jay Anthony *journalist*
Martinez, Natalie *newscaster*
McNally, Andrew, IV, *publishing executive, director*
McNulty, Timothy J. *editor*
Migala, Lucyna J. *journalist, broadcast executive, artistic director*
More, José *photojournalist*
Nash, Jessie Madeleine *journalist, science writer*
Nault, William Henry *publishing executive*
Peerman, Dean Gordon *magazine editor*
Peres, Judith May *journalist*
Plotnick, Harvey Barry *publishing executive*
Pope, Kerig Rodgers *retired magazine executive*
Primm, Earl Russell III *publishing executive*
Reardon, John E. *broadcast executive*
Rice, Linda Johnson *publishing executive*
Rice, William Edward *journalist*
Robinson, Robin *newscaster*
Roeper, Richard *columnist*
Roth, Robert A. *newspaper executive*
Roy, Kevin *newscaster*
Rynkiewicz, Stephen Michael *journalist*
Salopek, Paul F. *news correspondent*
Scanlan, Thomas Cleary *publishing executive, editor*
Seaman, Donna Jean *editor, writer*
Smith, Sam *columnist, writer*
Smith, Scott Clybourn *publishing executive*
Stoklosa, Gregory A. *publishing executive*
Strauss, Mark *editor*
Suchomel, Mark *publishing executive*
Thompson, George Fletcher *editor, publishing executive*
von Rhein, John Richard *music critic, journalist, writer*
Weinberg, Lila Shaffer *editor, writer*
Weintraub, Joseph Barton *publishing executive*
Wier, Patricia Ann *publishing executive, consultant*
Wille, Lois Jean *retired editor*
Youngman, Owen Ralph *newspaper executive*

Crystal Lake
Keller, William Francis *publishing consultant*

Elgin
Turnquist, Jerry L. *communications educator, journalist*

Elmhurst
Pruter, Margaret Franson *editor*

Evanston
Borcover, Alfred Seymour *journalist*
Deming, Thomas Edward *publishing executive*
Felknor, Bruce Lester *publishing executive, consultant, writer*
Galvin, Kathleen Malone *communications educator*
Ghiglione, Loren Frank *journalism professor*
Jacobs, Norman Joseph *publishing executive*
Jones, Robert Russell *retired magazine editor*
Kuenster, John Joseph *editor*
McCarron, John Francis *editor*
Otwell, Ralph Maurice *retired newspaper editor*
Peck, Abraham *editor, writer, educator, media consultant*
Ziomek, Jonathan S. *journalist, educator*

Highland Park
Johnson, Curtis Lee *publishing executive, editor, writer*
Pattis, S. William *publishing executive*
Rutenberg-Rosenberg, Sharon Leslie *retired journalist*

Huntley
Balk, Alfred William *journalist*

Itasca
Porter, Ethel Mae *publishing executive*

Kenilworth
Cook, Stanton R. *media company executive*

Lake Bluff
Marozsan, John Robert *retired publishing company executive*
Schreiber, George Richard *publishing executive, writer*
Snader, Jack Ross *retired publishing company executive*

Lake Forest
Schulze, Franz, Jr. *critic, educator*

Lake In The Hills
Kay, Dennis Matthew *retired publishing company official*

Libertyville
True, Raymond Stephen *editor, writer*

Mount Vernon
LeMay, Nicholas K. *broadcast executive*
Withers, W. Russell, Jr. *broadcast executive*

Northbrook
Pesmen, Sandra (Mrs. Harold William Pesmen) *editor, educator*

Oak Brook
Biedron, Theodore John *publishing and advertising executive*

Oregon
Haynes, Gary Allen *photojournalist, editor*

Pekin
Dancey, Charles Lohman *retired newspaper executive*

Peoria
McConnell, John Thomas *publishing executive*
Murphy, Sharon Margaret *retired communications educator*

Peru
Carus, Milton Blouke *children's periodicals publisher*

Prospect Heights
Robinson, Martin (Marty Robinson) *television and radio broadcaster, media consultant*

Rockford
Jacobi, Fredrick Thomas *newspaper publisher*

Urbana
Christians, Clifford Glenn *communications educator*
Dash, Leon DeCosta, Jr. *journalist*
Ono, Kent Alan *communications educator*

Villa Park
Gordon, Rachel Singer *editor*

Wheaton
Taylor, Mark Douglas *publishing executive*

Wilmette
Boyle, Antonia Barnes *writer, editor*

Winnetka
Burke, John Edward *communications editor*
Quaal, Ward Louis *broadcast executive*

INDIANA

Anderson
Clanin, Douglas Edward *editor, researcher*

Bloomington
Jacobi, Peter Paul *journalism educator, writer*
Lee, Don Yoon *publishing executive, academic administrator, writer*
Pedersen, Paul Mark *sportswriter, educator, columnist*
Schurz, Scott Clark *journalist*

Fort Wayne
Klugman, Stephan Craig *newspaper editor*

Franklin
Nuwer, Henry Joseph (Hank Nuwer) *journalist, educator*

Greencastle
Hall, David *newspaper editor*

Indianapolis
Coffey, Charles Moore *communication research professional, writer*
Fine, Pamela B. *newspaper editor*
Garmel, Marion Bess Simon *retired arts journalist*
Henry, Barbara Ann *publishing executive*
McKeand, Patrick Joseph *newspaper publisher, educator*
Russell, Frank Eli *retired newspaper publishing executive*
Ryerson, Dennis *editor*
SerVaas, Cory *editor-in-chief*
Wright, David Burton *retired newspaper publishing company executive*

Inglefield
James, Marion Ray *retired publishing executive, editor*

Knightstown
Richardson, Shirley Maxine *editor*

Lafayette
Renzetti, Phyllis Jean *retired technical editor*

Michigan City
Varro, Barbara Joan *retired editor*

Muncie
Bell, Stephen Scott (Steve Bell) *journalist, educator*

Munster
Potempa, Philip Matthew *journalist, columnist, communications educator*

South Bend
Smith, E. Berry *television and radio consultant*

Terre Haute
Vincent, Richard C. *communications educator, researcher*

IOWA

Ames
Alumbaugh, JoAnn McCalla *magazine editor*

Cedar Falls
Skaine, James C. *retired communications educator*

Cedar Rapids
Keller, Eliot Aaron *broadcast executive*

Des Moines
Butler, Gayle *editor-in-chief*
DeWulf Nickell, Karol *editor-in-chief*
Gartner, Michael Gay *editor, baseball and television executive*
Graham, Diane E. *newspaper editor*
Hollingsworth, Laura L. *publishing executive*
Kerr, William T. *publishing and broadcast executive*
Lacy, Stephen M. *publishing and broadcasting executive*
MacKinnon, Douglas Jerome *retired radio and magazine publishing executive*
Myers, Mary Kathleen *publishing executive*
Stier, Mary P. *publishing executive*
Washburn, Carolyn K. *editor-in-chief*
Witke, David Rodney *retired newspaper editor, consultant*

Iowa City
Gronbeck, Bruce Elliot *communications educator*

Mason City
Collison, Jim *publishing executive*
Davis, Joe Daughtry III *communications educator, writer*

Moville
Baker, Kent Alfred *broadcasting and publishing company executive*

Waterloo
Green, Nancy Loughridge *publishing executive*

West Des Moines
Dooley, Donald John *retired publishing executive*

Zearing
Britten, William Harry *editor, publisher*

KANSAS

Hutchinson
Baumer, Beverly Belle *journalist*
Buchanan, Bruce *publishing executive*
Buzbee, Richard Edgar *retired newspaper editor*

Iola
Lynn, Emerson Elwood, Jr. *retired newspaper editor/publisher*

Lawrence
Dickinson, William Boyd, Jr. *media consultant*
Hale, Richard Lee *magazine editor*
Simons, Dolph Collins, Jr. *publishing executive, editor*

Manhattan
Jin, Hyun Seung *communications educator*
Seaton, Edward Lee *editor, publishing executive*

Mission Hills
Rose, Stephen F. *columnist*

North Newton
Snider, Marie Anna *syndicated columnist*

Olathe
Dodd, James B. *Internet executive*

Overland Park
Christian, Shirley Ann *journalist, author*

Shawnee Mission
Martin, Donna Lee *retired publishing company executive*

Wichita
Hatteberg, Larry Merle *photojournalist*

KENTUCKY

Fort Mitchell
Silvers, Gerald Thomas *retired publishing executive*

Greenville
Walters, Sue Fox *broadcast executive, accountant*

Lexington
Arrington, Michael Irvin *communications educator*
Chi, Keon Soo *editor, educator, researcher*
Cross, Alvin Miller (Al Cross) *journalist*
Keeling, Larry Dale *journalist*
Kelly, Timothy Michael *newspaper publisher*
Kissling, Fred Ralph, Jr. *publishing and insurance agency executive*

Louisville
Ivey, Denise Hassell *publishing executive*
Ivory, Bennie L. *executive editor*
Towles, Donald Blackburn *retired publishing executive*

Paducah
Stice, Dwayne Lee *broadcasting company executive*

Pewee Valley
Gill, George Norman *newspaper publishing company executive*

LOUISIANA

Alexandria
Smith, Joe Dorsey, Jr. *retired newspaper executive*

Baton Rouge
Camp, John Bliss *journalist, television producer*

La Place
Fiffie Proctor, JoAnn *media and technology specialist*

Lake Charles
Beam, James Carroll (Jim Beam) *retired newspaper editor*
Stacey, Truman *journalist, consultant*

New Orleans
Amoss, Walter James, III, (Jim) *editor*
Ball, Millie (Mildred Porteous Ball) *editor, journalist*
Crumley, David Oliver *publishing executive, writer, corporate executive*
Ferguson, Charles Austin *retired newspaper editor*
Kenney, Brigid *media company executive*
Phelps, Ashton, Jr. *newspaper publisher*
Pope, John Marvin *journalist*

Shreveport
Lazarus, Allan Matthew *retired newspaper editor*
Robinson, Garry Lewin *television news executive*

MAINE

Belfast
Griffith, Patricia King *journalist*

Cape Elizabeth
Rich, John Hubbard, Jr. *news correspondent*

Castine
Bernstein, Lester *editorial consultant*

Chebeague Island
Traina, Salvatore Albert *publishing executive*

Damariscotta
Blake, Bud (Julian Watson) *cartoonist*

East Boothbay
Gibson, Barry Joseph *editor*

Farmington
Lounsbury, Dave Edmond *medical editor, retired medical educator, military officer*

Lincoln
Kneeland, Douglas Eugene *retired newspaper editor*

Penobscot
dePaolo, Ronald Francis *editor-in-chief, writer*

Portland
Chimsky-Lustig, Mark Evan *editor, consultant*

Sedgwick
Schroth, Thomas Nolan *editor*

MARYLAND

Annapolis
Finerty, Martin Joseph, Jr. *editor, military officer*

Baldwin
Kiper, Mel, Jr. *sports commentator*

Baltimore
Blau, Robert *editor*
Broening, Walter Stephens, Jr. *journalist, history educator*
Donovan, Dianne Francys *journalist*
Dorsey, John Russell *journalist*
Franklin, Timothy A. *editor*
Hirsh, Allan Thurman, Jr. *publishing executive*
Justice, Christopher *communications and language educator*
Little, Robert *reporter*
Muccie, Mary Rose *publishing executive*
Murphy, Frances Louise, II, *retired newspaper publisher*
Rodricks, Daniel John *columnist, television commentator*
Rousuck, J. Wynn *theater critic*
Ryan, Timothy *publishing executive*
Sanders, Julius Ray *music company executive*
Shannon, Joe *art critic, painter*
Sterne, Joseph Robert Livingston *editor, educator*
Tucker, Abigail *journalist*
Wasta, Vanessa A. *media specialist, web site designer*

Bethesda
Chronister, Gregory Michael *newspaper editor*
Cornish, Edward Seymour *magazine editor*
English, Michela *entertainment company executive*
Frank, Richard Sanford *retired magazine editor*
Herman, Edith Carol *journalist*
Holmberg, Ted *journalist, consultant*
Johnson, Thomas Dale *publishing executive*
Kaplan, Marjorie *broadcast executive*
Kempster, Norman Roy *journalist*
Kresge, Nicole *editor*
Larrabee, Donald Richard *publishing executive*
Nelson, John Howard (Jack Howard Nelson) *journalist*
Olson, Lynn *editor*
Pickerell, James Howard *photojournalist*
Wagner, Cynthia Gail *editor, writer*

Cheverly
Miller, Mark Karl *journalist, editor*

Chevy Chase
Adler, James Barron *publishing executive*
Bruno, Harold Robinson, Jr. *retired journalist, writer*
Cowen, Eugene Sherman *broadcast executive*
Glaser, Vera Romans *journalist*
Kilborn, Peter Thurston *journalist*
Kriegsman, Alan M. *arts critic*
Shipler, David Karr *journalist, writer*
Shogan, Robert *news correspondent*
Smith, Hedrick Laurence *journalist, television producer*
Sperling, Godfrey, Jr. *retired journalist*
Toth, Robert Charles *retired journalist*

College Park
Beasley, Maurine Hoffman *journalism educator, historian*
Gomery, Douglas *communications educator, writer*
Johnson, Haynes Bonner *journalist, writer, commentator*

Columbia
Greyson D'Otazzo, Meaghan Regina *literary critic*

Galesville
Whaley, Garwood *music company executive*

Garrett Park
Kornberg, Warren Stanley *journalist*

Germantown
Warren, Frank *blogger, small business owner*

Havre De Grace
Wetter, Virginia Forwood Pate *broadcast executive*

Hunt Valley
Guthrie, Phillip Patrick *division production manager*

Lanham
Lyons, James Edward (Jed) *publishing executive*

Lutherville Timonium
Cedrone, Louis Robert, Jr. *retired critic*

Monkton
Parker, Robert M., Jr., (Bob Parker) *wine critic, writer*

North Potomac
Lide, David Reynolds *editor-in-chief*

Perryville
Quesenbery, Erika Lynn *media specialist, curator*

Potomac
Christian, John Kenton *publishing executive, marketing professional, consultant*
Fox, Arthur Joseph, Jr. *editor*
Karnow, Stanley *journalist, writer*
Lannan, Maura Anne Kelly *reporter*
Sundick, Sherry Small *journalist, writer, poet*

Rockville
Kohlmeier, Louis Martin, Jr. *newspaper reporter*
Miller, Claire Ellen *editor, educator, writer*

Salisbury
Kleiman, Gary Howard *broadcast, advertising and cellular communications consultant*

Silver Spring
Bennett, Carol(ine) Elise *retired reporter, actress*
Carson, Steven Lee *newspaper publisher*
Eiserer, Leonard Albert Carl *publishing executive*
Hendricks, John S. *broadcast executive*
Koppel, Ted *newscaster*
Kurata, Phillip Cedomir *journalist*
Rodgers, Johnathan *broadcast executive*
Vernon, Weston, III, (Wes Vernon) *broadcaster, writer, actor*
Whitaker, Joel *publishing executive, public official*
Zaslav, David M. *broadcast executive*

Street
Spangler, Ronald Leroy *retired television and aircraft executive, automobile consultant*

Sunderland
Franklin, Jon Daniel *writer, journalist, educator*

University Park
Beckenstein, Myron *journalist*

MASSACHUSETTS

Boston
Ainsley, P. Steven (Steve Ainsley) *publishing executive*
Baron, David Hume *science journalist*
Baron, Martin *editor*
Bennett, Clay *cartoonist*
Carroll, Jill *freelance journalist*
Cohen, Rachelle Sharon *journalist*
Cook, Gareth *reporter*
Feeney, Mark *journalist*
Flaherty, Lois Talbot *editor, psychiatrist, educator*
Godine, David Richard *publishing executive*
Golden, Daniel *journalist*
Harris, Roy Jay, Jr. *editor, business journalist*
Hillery, Thomas Hungiville *journalist, financial consultant*
Holt, Sidney Clark *journalist*
Hostetter, Amos Barr, Jr. *cable television executive*
Jacoby, Jeff *journalist, commentator*
James, Bill *baseball writer, statistician*
Klarfeld, Jonathan Michael *journalism educator*
Kuttner, Robert Louis *editor, writer, columnist*
Larkin, Michael John *editor, journalist*
Lawrence, Merloyd Ludington *editor*
Lee, Donald Young (Don Lee) *publishing executive*
Leland, Timothy *retired newspaper executive*
Loth, Renée *editor*
Purcell, Patrick Joseph *newspaper publisher*
Schulz, John Joseph *communications educator*
Seglin, Jeffrey L. *columnist, educator*
Twombly, Stephen Doane *magazine publisher*
Tyson, Peter *editor-in-chief*
Williams, Brown F *media specialist, consultant*

Brighton
Becton, Henry Prentiss, Jr. *broadcast executive*
Holley, Michael *sportswriter, sportscaster*

Brookline
Bourne, Katherine Day *journalist, educator*

Cambridge
Aronson, Michael Andrew *editor*
Giles, Robert Hartmann *journalist, educator*
Goodman, Ellen Holtz *journalist*
Jones, Alex S. *reporter, writer*
Lenger, John Richard *journalism educator*
MacKinnon, Rebecca *media consultant, researcher*
Negroponte, Nicholas *media specialist, educator*
Nordell, Hans Roderick *journalist, retired editor*
Wilcox, Maud *editor*

Cohasset
Replogle, David Robert *publishing executive*

Concord
Heinle, Beverly Diane *publishing executive*

Franklin
Maril, David C. *editor*

Hingham
Menzies, Ian Stuart *newspaper editor*

Hudson
Osoff, Jeffrey Arlin *media company executive*

Leeds
Deane, James Garner *editor, conservationist*

Lexington
Davis, Robert J. *internet company executive*

Lincoln
Nenneman, Richard Arthur *retired publishing executive*

Malden
Brooks, Kevin M. *multimedia researcher, technology storyteller*

Marblehead
Quigley, Stephen Howard *executive editor*

Natick
Darehshori, Nader Farhang *publishing sales executive*

Needham
Greenway, Hugh Davids Scott *journalist*

Needham Heights
Salhany, Lucille S. (Lucy Salhany) *broadcast executive*

Newton
Hume, Ellen Hunsberger *media analyst, educator, journalist*

North Adams
Thurston, Donald Allen *broadcast executive*

North Chelmsford
Kotelly, George Vincent *editor, writer, electrical engineer*

Pittsfield
Rich, Philip Dewey *publishing executive*

Plymouth
Flood, H. Gay (Hulda Gay Flood) *editor, consultant*

Quincy
Lippincott, Joseph P. *photojournalist, educator*

Rockport
Bissell, Phil (Charles P. Bissell) *cartoonist*

Siasconset
Smith, Harrison Harvey *journalism consultant*

Somerville
Gellerman, Bruce Edward *reporter*

South Easton
Keith, Michael Curtis *communication educator, writer*

South Hadley
Elleman, Barbara *editor*

Springfield
Starr, David *editor, publisher*

Waltham
Goodheart, Eugene *literary critic*

Wayland
Huff, William Braid *retired publishing company executive*

Wellfleet
Limpitlaw, John Donald *publishing executive, priest*

West Falmouth
King, Richard Hood *retired newspaper executive*

West Tisbury
Méras, Phyllis Leslie *journalist*

Weston
Sanzone, Donna S. *publishing executive*

Westport
Gormley, Robert John *retired publishing executive*

Westwood
Borgman, George Allan *journalist*

Winchester
Ockerbloom, Richard C. *newspaper executive*

Winthrop
Flockhart, Barbara Townsley *publishing executive*

MICHIGAN

Ann Arbor
Beaver, Frank Eugene *critic, historian*
Bedard, Patrick Joseph *editor, writer, consultant*
Csere, Csaba *editor-in-chief*
Driscoll, John *publishing executive*
Eisendrath, Charles Rice *journalism educator, farmer, consultant*
Hessler, David William *information and multimedia systems educator*
Houghtlin, Robert *publishing executive*
Lewis, Robert Enzer *editor, educator*

Baroda
Reckline, Sigmund Joseph *publishing executive, editor*

Bay City
Hiner, John Patrick *newspaper editor*

Birmingham
McCuen, John *columnist, educator, consultant on counterinsurgency operations*

Bloomfield Township
Brown, Lynette Ralya *journalist, publicist*

Dearborn
Hogan, Brian Joseph *editor*
Kiska, Timothy Olin *communications educator, radio producer*

Detroit
Albom, Mitch David *sports columnist*
Alpert, Daniel *broadcast executive*
Andrews, Caesar *editor*
Anger, Paul *newspaper editor*
Bennett, Grace *publishing executive*
Blomquist, David Wels *journalist*
Burzynski, Susan Marie *newspaper editor*
Butler, David J. *newspaper editor*
Hunke, David L. *publishing executive*
Parry, Dale D. *publisher, editor*
Smyntek, John Eugene, Jr. *editor*

East Lansing
Freedman, Eric *journalist, educator, writer*
Greenberg, Bradley Sander *communications educator*
Ralph, David Clinton *communications educator*

Ferndale
Haberman, Jeremy *music venue executive*

Grand Rapids
Bolinder, Scott W. *publishing company executive*
Bytwerk, Randall Lee *communication educator*
Kaczmarczyk, Jeffrey Allen *journalist, music and dance critic*

Grosse Pointe
Bryfonski, Dedria Anne *publishing executive*
Hill, Draper *editorial cartoonist*
Whittaker, Jeanne Evans *retired journalist*

Grosse Pointe Farms
Christian, Edward Kieren *broadcasting station executive*

Grosse Pointe Park
Elsila, David August *editor*

Grosse Pointe Woods
McWhirter, Glenna Suzanne (Nickie McWhirter) *retired columnist*

Harbor Springs
Cappel, Constance *editor, writer*

Jackson
Goldsen, Bruce I. *radio executive*

Lansing
Brown, Nancy Field *editor*

Manistee
Trussell, Charles Tait *columnist*

Mount Pleasant
Petrick, Michael Joseph *journalism educator*

Saginaw
Chaffee, Paul Charles *newspaper editor, publisher*

Southfield
Makupson, Amyre Porter *broadcast executive*
Margolis, Sherry *newscaster*
Osborne, Marie-Angela *journalist*
Timmons, Robbie *news anchor*

Sturgis
Hair, Robert Eugene *editor, writer, historian*

Troy
Hucal, Michelle *editor*

Waterford
James, William Ramsay *broadcast executive*

MINNESOTA

Bloomington
Larson, Michael Len *newspaper editor, hospital administrator, publishing executive*

Duluth
Latto, Lewis M. *broadcast executive*

Eden Prairie
Thompson, Sally Ann *editor*

Edina
Bisping, Bruce Henry *photojournalist*

Minneapolis
Ambrose, Thomas William *retired broadcast executive*
Barnes, Nancy *editor-in-chief*
Cope, Lewis *journalist*
Cowles, John, Jr. *publishing executive, women's sports promoter, philanthropist*
Crosby, Jacqueline Garton *newspaper editor, journalist*
Flanagan, Barbara *journalist*
Hebrink, Bob *publishing executive*
Laing, Karel Ann *publishing executive*
Lerner, Harry Jonas *publishing executive*
Meador, Ron *newspaper editor, writer*
Murphy, Joseph Edward, Jr. *broadcast executive*
Osadchuk, Margo *publishing executive*
Randall, Roger David *publishing executive*
Ridder, Par *publishing executive*
Scallen, Thomas Kaine *broadcast executive*
Smetanka, Mary Jane *reporter*
Steinberg, Michael *music critic, educator*
White, Robert James *retired columnist*

Minnetonka
Weisman, Eric *music company executive*

Rochester
Shampo, Marc Anthony *retired editor*

Saint Joseph
Rowland, Howard Ray *mass communications educator*

Saint Paul
Amidon, Paul Charles *publishing executive*
Bree, Marlin Duane *publisher, author*
Feinberg, David Erwin *retired publishing executive*
Fladung, Thom *editor-in-chief*
Gilmore, Guy L. *publishing executive*
Hubbard, Stanley Stub *broadcast executive*
Kling, William Hugh *broadcast executive*
Lofquist, Vicki L. *journalist*
Wehrwein, Austin Carl *freelance/self-employed reporter*
Weschcke, Carl Llewellyn *publishing executive*

West Saint Paul
Cento, William Francis *retired newspaper editor*

MISSISSIPPI

Gulfport
Biffle, Tony *editor*

Hattiesburg
Hickman, Ronald Lee *media broker, broadcast executive*

Jackson
Mitchell, Jerry *reporter*

Natchez
Kirk, Susanne Smith *editor*

MISSOURI

Carthage
McAfee, Diana Mae *media specialist, music educator*

Chesterfield
Gietschier, Steven Philip *journalist, historian*

Columbia
Loory, Stuart Hugh *journalist*
Sanders, Keith Page *journalism educator*

Joplin
Massa, Richard Wayne *retired communications educator*

Kansas City
Amend, Bill *cartoonist*
Batiuk, Thomas Martin *cartoonist*
Bridges, Constance Rose *communications educator*
Busby, Marjean (Marjorie Jean Busby) *retired journalist*
Davis, James Robert *cartoonist*
Gray, Helen Theresa Gott *editor*
Gusewelle, Charles Wesley *journalist, writer*
McGruder, Aaron *cartoonist*
Mc Meel, John Paul *newspaper syndicate and publishing executive*
McSweeney, William Lincoln, Jr. *retired publishing executive*
Palmer, Cruise *newspaper editor*
Tully, Mac *publishing executive*
Zieman, Mark *newspaper editor*

Marshall
Berry, Karen Ann *communications educator*

Saint Louis
Boddie, Don O'Mar *recording industry executive*
Ehrlich, Ava *broadcast executive*
Engelhardt, Thomas Alexander *editorial cartoonist*
Gauen, Patrick Emil *news correspondent*
Hays, Howard H. (Tim Hays) *editor, publisher*
Holt, Glen Edward *editor*
Killenberg, George Andrew *publishing executive, consultant, retired editor*
Mowbray, Kevin D. *publishing executive*
Pollack, Joe *retired columnist, critic, writer*
Randolph, Jennings, Jr., (Jay Randolph) *sportscaster*
Rice, Patricia Jane *journalist*
Robbins, Arnie *editor-in-chief*
Sproule, James Michael *communications educator, writer*
Waters, Richard *retired publishing executive*

Smithville
Johnson, Darryl Thomas *communications educator*

Springfield
Champion, Norma Jean *communications educator, state legislator*
Glazier, Robert Carl *publishing executive*

MONTANA

Billings
Larsen, Kimbert E. *journalist*

NEBRASKA

Chappell
Orr, Jim (James D. Orr) *editor, writer, publishing executive*

Friend
De Bevoise, Lee Raymond *editor, writer*

Lincoln
Dyer, William Earl, Jr. *retired newspaper editor*
Norton, Hugo Wilbert, Jr. *journalism educator, dean*

Omaha
Batchelder, Anne Stuart *retired publishing executive, political organization worker*
Derrick, Deborah Ball *editor, writer*

NEVADA

Henderson
Kelley, Michael John *newspaper editor*
Wills, Robert Hamilton *retired publishing executive*

Las Vegas
Ehrlich, Bruce Jay *media consultant, psychologist, writer*
Frigard, Monique Denise *journalist*
Huston, Joyce A. *entertainment and publishing company executive*
Miller, Valerie Carol *journalist*
Scherf, Dietmar *publishing executive, artist, minister*
Tash, Martin Elias *publishing company executive*

Reno
Hengstler, Gary Ardell *publisher, editor, lawyer*

Sparks
Boyer, Patricia W. *publishing executive, editor*

NEW HAMPSHIRE

Concord
Brown, Tom Christian *newspaper publishing executive*
Pride, Mike *editor*

Dublin
Hale, Judson Drake, Sr. *publishing executive, editor, writer*

Exeter
Wicklein, John Frederick *journalist, educator*

Hanover
Goodman, William Beehler *editor, literary agent*

Keene
Salcetti, Marianne *newswriter, educator*

Lyme
Dwight, Donald Rathbun *publishing executive, corporate communications specialist*

Manchester
Perkins, Charles III *newspaper and website editor*

Portsmouth
Hopkins, Jeannette Ethel *book publisher, editor*

Salem
Smith, Laurence Roger *journal editor*

NEW JERSEY

Belleville
Salvini, Emil Robert *publishing executive, writer, historian*

Bloomfield
Glasser, Stephen Andrew *publishing executive, lawyer*

Cape May
Fox, Matthew Ignatius *publishing executive*

Chatham
Meagher, James Proctor *editor*

Cherry Hill
Rudman, Solomon Kal *magazine publisher*

Cranbury
Yoseloff, Julien David *publishing company executive*

Cresskill
Benton, Donald Stewart *publishing company executive, lawyer*

Deal
Becker, Richard Stanley *music publisher*

Dover
Kassell, Paula Sally *editor, publisher*

East Brunswick
Meningall, Evelyn L. *retired educational media specialist*

East Rutherford
Kluge, John Werner *broadcast and advertising executive*

Edgewater
Siegel, Max Laurence *recording industry executive*

Edison
Hunter, Michael *publishing executive*

Englewood Cliffs
Bartiromo, Maria Sara *financial news correspondent*
Burnett, Erin *finance newscaster*
Dobrzynski, Judith Helen *journalist, commentator*
Fisher, Andrew, IV, *newswriter, television producer*
Haltiwanger, Robert Sidney, Jr. *book publishing executive*
Hoffman, Mark *broadcast executive*
Insana, Ronald Gerard *newscaster*
Saible, Stephanie Irene *editor-in-chief*

Flemington
Thomas, Anne Moreau *former newspaper owner*
Zulker, Charles Bates *broadcasting company executive*

Fords
Blond, Stuart Richard *magazine editor*

Fort Lee
Orman, Suze *news correspondent, writer*
Stuart, Carole *publishing executive*

Garwood
Jannotti, Gene Patrick *business consultant, telecommunications professional*
Smith, Joan Lowell *syndicated columnist, feature writer*

Gillette
Nathanson, Linda Sue *publishing executive, writer*

Glen Ridge
Addison, Herbert John *consulting editor, writer*

Hackensack
Ahearn, James *columnist*
Borg, Malcolm Austin *publishing executive*
Margulies, James Howard *editorial cartoonist*

Highland Park
Fogiel, Max *publishing executive*

Hoboken
Hakki, Ayesha *editor-in-chief*
Spring, Michael *editor, writer*
Tardiff, Jill Alexandria *publishing executive, photographer*
Ubell, Robert Neil *editor, educator, publishing executive, consultant*

Jackson
Wagner, Edward Kurt *publishing company executive*

Jersey City
Hitchcock, John C. *communications media executive*
Ingrassia, Paul Joseph *publishing executive*
Lipschutz, Neal S. *editor*
Stine, Rick D. *editor*

Lakewood
Forbes, Gordon Maxwell *sportswriter, commentator*

Lawrenceville
Ben-Asher, Daniel Lawrence *photojournalist, retired legislative staff member*
Oram, Fern Amy *editor-in-chief, director*

Leonia
Greenwald, Martin *publishing company executive*
Kitman, Marvin *journalist*

Matawan
Liggett, Twila C. *broadcast executive, educator*

Monmouth Junction
Prestbo, John Andrew *editor, writer, journalist*

Monroe Township
Reichek, Morton Arthur *retired magazine editor, writer*

Montclair
Delbourgo, Joëlle Lily *publishing executive*
Gollob, Herman Cohen *retired publishing executive*

Montvale
Politi, Beth Kukkonen *publishing services company executive*

Mountainside
Horner, Shirley Jaye *columnist, writing and publishing consultant*

New Brunswick
Horowitz, Irving Louis *publisher, educator*
Kadlec, Kim *media executive*

New Providence
Barnes, Sandra Henley *retired publishing company executive*

Newark
Aregood, Richard Lloyd *editor*
Arwady, George E. *publishing executive*
Cave, Damien *journalist*
Dauth, Frances Kutcher *journalist, editor*
Gettleman, Jeffrey *journalist*
Izenberg, Jerry *sportswriter, columnist, author*
Kelley, Tina *journalist*
Newhouse, Mark William *publishing executive*
Smothers, Ronald *journalist*
Steinbaum, Robert S. *publishing executive, lawyer*
Willse, James Patrick *newspaper editor*

Nutley
To, Stephen Edward *editor, writer*

Oakland
Keough, Daniel Emmet *retired magazine editor*

Oldwick
Snyder, Arthur *publishing executive*

Pitman
Reinfeld, George *retired communications educator*

Plainfield
Allen (Sup), Stuart *film and television company executive*

Princeton
Crawford, Franklin David *publishing executive*
Green, Claude *information company executive*
Hanks, Richard *information company executive*
Levine, Richard James *publishing executive*
Lincoln, Anna *publishing executive, language educator*
Lippincott, Walter Heulings, Jr. *retired publishing executive*
Nied, Thomas Herman *retired media specialist*
O'Donnell, Laurence Gerard *retired managing editor*
Weiss, Renée Karol *editor, musician*

Ridgefield Park
D'Avella, Bernard Johnson, Jr. *publishing executive, lawyer*

Ridgewood
Mitgang, Lee David *journalist, writer, educator, foundation administrator*
Ostling, Richard Neil *journalist*

Rockaway
Kurtz, Ellen R. *journalist*

Saddle River
Noyes, Robert Edwin *publisher, writer*

Secaucus
Abrams, Dan *broadcast executive, news correspondent*
Carlson, Tucker *political analyst, writer, television host*
Cosby, Rita Karen *newscaster*
Olbermann, Keith *news analyst, former sportscaster*

Short Hills
Austin, Danforth Whitley *media executive*

Schaefer, Eleanor Montville *retired publishing executive*
Soderlind, Sterling Eugene *newspaper industry consultant*
Winter, Ruth Grosman (Mrs. Arthur Winter) *journalist*

Skillman
Eiger, Richard William *retired publisher*

Southampton
Callaway, Ben Anderson *journalist*

Sparta
Spence, Robert Leroy *publishing executive*

Spring Lake
Krein, Catherine Cecilia *broadcast and journalism educator*

Teaneck
Solá, Victoria M. *announcer, writer*

Trenton
Chen, David *reporter*
Christopherson, Elizabeth Good *broadcast executive*
Kocieniewski, David *journalist*
Mansnerus, Laura *news correspondent*
Sullivan, John *news correspondent*

Weehawken
Hobson, Burton Harold *publishing executive*

West New York
Knopf, Claire *editor, writer*

West Orange
Petrokubi, Marilyn *film company executive, producer, writer, researcher*

Woodcliff Lake
Jacobs, Charles Nathan *editor, writer*

NEW MEXICO

Albuquerque
Hadas, Elizabeth Chamberlayne *editor*
Lang, Thompson Hughes *publishing executive*
Moskos, Harry *columnist, editor*

Los Alamos
Mendius, Patricia Dodd Winter *retired editor, educator, writer*

Raton
Carroll, William *publishing company executive*

Santa Fe
Dirks, Lee Edward *newspaper executive*
Groseclose, Everett Harrison *retired editor*
Lichtenberg, Maggie Klee *publishing executive*
Stieber, Tamar *journalist*
Stolley, Richard Brockway *journalist*

Silver City
Fryxell, David Allen *publishing executive*

NEW YORK

Albany
FitzAlan-Howard, Bennett-Thomas Henry Robert *news analyst, consultant, political scientist, theologian*
Mueller, I. Lynn *strategic planning and communications consultant*
Rosenfeld, Harry Morris *editor*
Smith, Rex William *journalist*

Ardsley On Hudson
Seaman, Alfred Barrett *journalist, writer*

Astoria
Salzberg, Russ *sportscaster*

Bayside
Li, Rowena Liu-ping *media specialist*

Beacon
Mc Keown, William Taylor *magazine editor, author*

Bedford
Bowman, James Kinsey *publishing executive, rare book dealer*

Bellport
Townsend, Terry *publishing executive*

Bethpage
Dolan, Charles Francis (Charles "Chuck" Dolan) *media and entertainment company executive*

Briarcliff Manor
Cooper, Gloria *editor, press critic*
Kennell, Richard Wayne *recording industry executive, consultant, small business owner, treasurer, finance company executive*

Bridgehampton
Phillips, Warren Henry *publishing executive*

Bronx
Ahmose, Nefertari A. *journalism educator*
Stein, Bernard L. *journalist*
Zalaznick, Sheldon *retired editor, journalist*

Bronxville
Lombardo, Philip Joseph *broadcasting company executive*

Brooklyn
Bianco, Anthony Joseph III *newswriter*
Fox, Cynthia F. *journalist, writer*
Frank, Hosea (Ze Frank) *web video blogger*

Ortner, Everett Howard *magazine editor, writer*
Sanford, David Boyer *journalist, editor*
Wiener, Hesh (Harold Frederic Wiener) *publishing executive, consultant*

Buffalo
Lipsey, Stanford *newspaper publisher*
Sullivan, Margaret M. *editor-in-chief*
Trotter, Herman Eager, Jr., (Herman Trotter) *retired music critic*
Urban, Henry Zeller *publishing executive*

Dobbs Ferry
Anbinder, Paul *publishing executive, consultant*
Simon, Lothar *publishing executive*

East Hampton
Brady, James Winston *commentator, writer, editor*
Jaroff, Leon Morton *retired magazine editor*
Metz, Robert Roy *publishing executive, media consultant*

East Syracuse
Duffy, Nancy Keogh *newscaster, broadcast executive*

Eastchester
Gottschall, Edward Maurice *editor, writer*

Elba
Kauffman, William Joseph *editor, writer*

Elmsford
Miranda, Robert Nicholas *publishing executive, director*

Flushing
Torrence-Thompson, Juanita Lee *editor, public relations executive*

Forest Hills
Brooks, Martin *electronic media company executive*
Kilgannon, Corey *journalist*
Reis, Don *publishing executive*

Garden City
Rhein, John Hancock Willing III *publishing executive*
Toy, Vivian *journalist*

Great Neck
Kahn, David *editor, author*
Panes, Jack Samuel *publishing executive*

Hamilton
Edmonston, William Edward, Jr. *retired publishing executive, writer, psychology professor*

Hastings On Hudson
Landau, Peter Edward *editor*
Reich, Herb *editor*

Hauppauge
Bender, Bruce F. *book publishing executive*

Hempstead
Masheck, Joseph Daniel *art critic, educator*

Hicksville
Horowitz, Barry Allan *music company executive*

Holmes
Conyers, Claude Brunson *publishing consultant, editor, dance historian*

Huntington
Connor, Joseph Robert *editor*
Reiner, John *cartoonist*

Irvington
Yablon, Leonard Harold *publishing executive*

Ithaca
Bourne, Russell *publisher, author*
Rinaldo, Peter Merritt *publishing executive*
Schwartz, Donald Franklin *communication scientist*

Katonah
Fry, John *magazine editor*

Kings Park
Greene, Robert William *communications educator, media consultant*

Latham
Condon, Joseph Dennis *broadcasting executive*

Levittown
Lambert, Bruce *journalist*
Massie, Clifford Michael *music company executive*
Vitello, Paul *journalist*

Locust Valley
Fairman, Joel Martin *retired broadcast executive*
Zulch, Joan Carolyn *retired medical publishing company executive*

Long Beach
Robbins, Jeffrey Howard *media consultant, research writer, educator*

Malverne
Pollio, Ralph Thomas *editor, consultant*

Manhasset
Burke, Alexander James, Jr. *publishing executive*
Evans, Bob (Robert Evans) *publishing executive*
Preston, Rob *editor-in-chief*
Weitzner, Steve *publishing executive*

Manlius
Harriff, Suzanna Elizabeth Bahner *media consultant*

Melville
Davidson, Justin *music critic*
Handelsman, Walt *cartoonist*
Hildebrand, John Frederick *columnist, educator*
Klurfeld, James Michael *journalist*
Knight, Timothy P. *publishing executive*
Krenek, Debby *newspaper editor*
Mancini, John *editor, publishing executive*
Moran, Paul James *journalist, columnist*

Middletown
Bedell, Barbara Lee *journalist*

Millbrook
Hall, Penelope Coker *editor, writer*

New City
McCullagh, James Charles *publishing executive*

New Hyde Park
Lehrer, Stanley *magazine publisher, editorial director, museum exhibitor*

New York
Abelson, Alan *columnist*
Abelson, Reed *reporter*
Abramson, Jill *newspaper publishing executive*
Adams, Cindy *journalist*
Adams, Scott *cartoonist*
Adcroft, Patti (Patrice Gabriella) *editor*
Adler, Edward I. *media and entertainment company executive*
Adler, Jerry *journalist, writer*
Adler, Margot Susanna *journalist, radio producer, correspondent, writer*
Adler, Stephen J. *editor-in-chief*
Ailes, Roger Eugene *broadcast executive*
Akselrad, Hal (Harold Eaton) *broadcast executive, lawyer*
Allan, Col *editor-in-chief*
Alter, Jonathan Hammerman *journalist*
Ambrosio, Anthony G. *broadcast executive*
Ames, Roger *recording industry executive*
Amster, Linda Evelyn *newspaper executive, consultant*
Ancier, Garth Richard *broadcast executive*
Anderson, David Poole *sportswriter*
Anderson, Gloria Brown *publishing executive*
Anderson, Walter Herman *editor, educator*
Andre, Michael (Kenneth Andre) *editor-in-chief*
Apcar, Leonard M. *online editor*
Arenson, Karen Wattel *reporter*
Arnold, Martin *editor, journalist*
Asher, Aaron *retired editor, publisher*
Asimov, Eric *wine critic*
Astley, Amy *editor-in-chief*
Astor, David Warren *journalist*
Atlas, James Robert *editor, writer*
Auletta, Ken *columnist*
Azzoli, Val *music company executive*
Bahr, Lauren S. *publishing executive*
Baier, Bret *news correspondent*
Bailey, Glenda *editor-in-chief*
Baker, Al *journalist*
Baker, Deborah *editor, writer*
Baker, Elizabeth Calhoun *magazine editor*
Baldwin, Deborah *editor*
Ball, John Paul *publishing company executive*
Bandier, Martin N. *music publisher*
Bandler, James *reporter*
Banerjee, Neela *reporter*
Bantivoglio, Barbara *broadcast executive*
Barber, Lionel *journalist*
Barber, Tiki (Atiim Kiambu Barber) *sportscaster, retired professional football player*
Barnes, Clive Alexander *drama and dance critic*
Barolini, Teodolinda *literary critic*
Barron, James Turman *journalist*
Barry, Dan *columnist*
Barry, William Garrett III *publishing company executive*
Bashir, Martin *news correspondent*
Bauer, Peter F. *publishing executive*
Bazell, Robert Joseph *science correspondent*
Beckman, Richard David *publishing and advertising executive*
Bellando, John W. *publishing executive, accountant*
Belson, Ken *reporter*
Bender, Judith *journalist, editor*
Bennack, Frank Anthony, Jr. *publishing company executive*
Berenson, Alex *reporter*
Berkowitz, Lauren M. *music company executive*
Berney, Bob *film company executive*
Berry, John Nichols III *publishing executive, editor*
Bettis, Jerome Abram *sports commentator, retired professional football player*
Bewkes, Jeffrey L. *television broadcasting company executive*
Binn, Jason *publishing executive*
Birch, Ian *editor-in-chief*
Black, Carole *broadcast executive*
Black, Cathleen Prunty *publishing executive*
Blair, William Granger *retired reporter*
Blank, Matthew C. *broadcast company executive*
Blum, David J. *former editor-in-chief*
Bodley, Harley Ryan, Jr. *sportswriter, announcer, editor*
Boffey, Philip M. *journalist*
Bogdanich, Walt *journalist*
Bogert, Jeremiah *journalist*
Boodro, Michael *editor*
Bookspan, Martin *broadcaster, writer*
Boot, Max *journalist*
Booth Corwin, Tami *publishing executive*
Borders, William Alexander *journalist*
Borland, Virginia Ann *journalist, fashion specialist, fiber company executive*
Bossert, Rex Thomas *editor-in-chief*
Bowen, Tim *recording industry executive*
Bowers, Brent *editor*

Boxer, Sarah *critic, reporter, writer*
Brant, Sandra J. *magazine publisher*
Brantley, Benjamin David *theater critic*
Bratten, Millie Martini *editor-in-chief*
Brauchli, Marcus Walker *editor*
Brecher, John *columnist*
Brenner, Beth Fuchs *publishing executive*
Brick, Michael *journalist*
Brody, Jane Ellen *journalist, researcher*
Bronfman, Edgar Miles, Jr. *recording industry executive*
Brooks, Timothy H. *broadcast executive*
Brown, Darrell James *publishing executive*
Brown, Helen Gurley *editor-in-chief*
Brown, Katie *columnist*
Browne, Arthur *newspaper editor*
Browne, Malcolm Wilde *journalist*
Brun, Henry *publishing executive*
Bruni, Frank *restaurant critic*
Bryson, Louise Henry *broadcast executive*
Buck, Joe (Joseph Francis Buck) *sportscaster*
Buckley, Christopher Taylor *editor, author*
Buckley, William Frank, Jr. *magazine editor, writer*
Burgheim, Richard *magazine editor*
Burnett, Len *publishing executive*
Burns, John F. *reporter*
Burtson, James E. *multimedia company executive*
Bushnell, Candace *columnist, writer*
Bylinsky, Gene Michael *magazine editor*
Byrne, Gerard Anthony (Gerry) *publishing executive, consultant*
Caine, Paul Jason *publishing executive*
Callahan, Robert F., Jr. *media company executive, former broadcast executive*
Campos, Fernando *editor-in-chief*
Cane, Jeffrey *editor*
Canedy, Dana *editor*
Caploe, Roberta *magazine editor*
Capolarello, Joe R. *photojournalist*
Capus, Steve *broadcast executive*
Cardwell, Diane *journalist*
Carey, David *publishing executive*
Carlson, Gretchen *news correspondent*
Carlucci, Paul V. *publishing executive*
Carr, Gladys Justin *publishing executive, consultant, editor, writer*
Carr, James T. *publishing executive*
Carter, Graydon (Edward Graydon Carter) *editor-in-chief*
Casella, Jim *publishing executive*
Cavallo, Rob *recording industry executive*
Cavuto, Neil *newscaster, business journalist, television host*
Cembalest, Robin *arts editor, critic*
Centrello, Gina *publishing executive*
Chan, Janet *editor-in-chief*
Chang, Laura *editor*
Charney, Marc D. *editor*
Chesnutt, Jane *editor-in-chief*
Chestnut, Colette *broadcast executive*
Chira, Susan *editor*
Chirico, Anthony (Tony) *publishing executive*
Chopey, Nicholas P. *editor*
Christy, John Hill III *journalist*
Chung, Jen *blog editor*
Cieply, Michael *editor, writer*
Clark, Joan Hardy *retired journalist*
Clayton, Joseph Paul *broadcast executive*
Clines, Francis X. *journalist*
Clower, Donna *music company executive*
Cobb, James G. *editor*
Coen, Jessica *blog writer, editor*
Cohen, Adam *reporter, lawyer*
Cohen, Patricia *editor, critic*
Cohen, Richard Martin *journalist*
Colan, Joanne *video blogger, television personality*
Coles, Joanna *magazine editor-in-chief*
Collins, Richard Lawrence *editor*
Collinsworth, Cris *sportscaster, retired professional football player*
Colmes, Alan *political commentator, radio personality*
Cona, Louis *publishing executive*
Conde, Yvonne M. *freelance journalist, writer*
Confessore, Nicholas *journalist*
Connolly, John Joseph *publishing executive*
Cooney, Joan Ganz *broadcast executive, director*
Cooper, Anderson Hays *news correspondent, cable news anchor*
Cooper, Helene *editor*
Cooper, Michael *journalist*
Corcoran, David *newspaper editor*
Corporon, John Robert *broadcast executive*
Cortina, Betty *magazine editor*
Costas, Bob (Robert Quinlan Costas) *sportscaster*
Cotter, Holland *art critic, writer*
Couric, Katie (Katherine Anne Couric) *newscaster, journalist*
Cramer, Douglas Schoolfield *broadcasting executive*
Creswell, Julie *reporter*
Crier, Catherine *newscaster*
Crist, Judith *film and drama critic*
Croce, Arlene *critic*
Cronin, Anne *editor*
Cronkite, Walter *radio and television news correspondent*
Cross, Theodore Lamont *publisher, author*
Crovitz, Louis Gordon *publishing executive, journalist, lawyer*
Crowdus, Gary Alan *film company executive*
Crystal, J. Scott *publishing executive*
Cuomo, Chris(topher) *newscaster, lawyer*
Cuozzo, Steven David *newspaper editor*
Curley, Thomas *newspaper executive*
Curry, Ann *correspondent, anchor*
Dahl, Jonathan *magazine editor-in-chief*
Daley, Suzanne *editor*
Dana, Will *editor*
D'Angelo, Joseph Francis *publishing executive*
Daniels, Susanne *broadcast executive*
Danziger, Lucy *editor*
Dargis, Manohla *film critic*

Dauman, Philippe P. *multi media company executive*
Dauten, Dale Alan *newspaper columnist*
Davis, Clive Jay *record company executive*
Day, James *television executive*
De Angelis, Judy *anchorwoman*
Denson, J. Russell *publishing executive*
Denton, Nick *publishing executive*
Derow, Peter Alfred *publishing executive*
Desiato, Michael *editor-in-chief*
Deutsch, Claudia *reporter*
Deutsch, Martin Bernard Joseph *editor, publishing executive*
DeVoe, David F., Sr. *publishing executive*
Dierdorf, Daniel Lee (Dan Dierdorf) *sports commentator, football analyst, former professional football player*
Dikkers, Scott *editor*
Disney, Anthea *publishing executive*
Dobkin, Jake *online publishing executive, blogger*
Dodge, Geoffrey A. *publishing executive*
Doerfler, Ronald John *publishing executive*
Dooley, Thomas E. *multi media company executive*
Dormann, Henry O. *magazine publisher*
Dotson, Robert Charles (Bob Dotson) *news correspondent*
Downes, Lawrence *editor*
Dozier, Kimberly *news correspondent*
Dreifus, Claudia *journalist, educator*
Dugger, Celia Williams *journalist*
Dukmejian, Michael *publishing executive*
Dunn, Martin *editor-in-chief*
Dunning, Jennifer *dance critic, reporter*
Dupri, Jermaine *recording industry executive, music producer*
Dwyer, Jim *reporter, columnist*
Eaker, Sherry Ellen *editor*
Ebersol, Dick (Duncan Dickie Ebersol) *television broadcasting executive*
Eckman, Fern Marja *journalist*
Edgerley, Susan *editor*
Edidin, Peter *editor*
Edmiston, Mark Morton *publishing company executive*
Edsall, Thomas Byrne *reporter*
Egen, Maureen Mahon *publishing executive*
Elder, Janet *editor*
Ellerbee, Linda (Linda Jane Smith) *reporter*
Ellingwood, Susan *editor*
Elliott, Andrea *reporter*
Ellis, Lisa *music company executive*
Ellis, Rosemary *editor-in-chief*
Elsen, Jon *editor*
Emmerich, Toby *film company executive*
Emmrich, Stuart J. *editor*
Engstrom, Erik *publishing executive*
Esposito, Richard Joseph *journalist, executive*
Essig, Jack *magazine publishing executive*
Esterow, Milton *publishing executive*
Evans, Greg *cartoonist*
Evans, Sir Harold Matthew *editor, publisher, writer*
Evans, Heidi *journalist*
Fabrikant, Geraldine *journalist*
Fager, Jeffrey *broadcast executive*
Fahim, Kareem *journalist*
Fallows, James Mackenzie *journalist*
Favorule, Denise *publishing executive*
Faxon, Roger *music company executive*
Fears, Linda *editor-in-chief*
Feder, Barnaby *reporter*
Federle, Michael *publishing executive*
Feldman, Helaine *editor, public relations associate*
Feniger, Jerome Roland, Jr. *broadcast executive*
Feretic, Eileen Susan *editor*
Fertig, Howard *publishing executive*
Feyer, Thomas *editor*
Fialkoff, Francine Susan *editor*
Filkins, Dexter Price *newspaper reporter*
Finkelstein, James A. *media executive*
Finn, Edwin Anthony, Jr. *publishing executive*
Finn, Peter Michael *broadcast executive*
Fiori, Pamela *publishing executive, writer*
Firestone, David E. *editor*
Firth, Nicholas *recording industry executive*
Fisher, Arthur *magazine editor*
Flanagan, Sean Patrick *publishing executive*
Fleisher, Michael D. *music company executive*
Flom, Jason *music company executive*
Florio, Steven T. *magazine executive*
Florio, Thomas A. *publishing executive*
Folio, James M. *publishing executive*
Forbes, Steve (Malcolm Stevenson Forbes Jr.) *publishing executive*
Forbes, Timothy Carter *publishing executive*
Ford, Mark Patrick *publishing executive*
Forden, Diane Claire *magazine editor*
Forelle, Charles *reporter*
Forsberg, Myra *editor*
Fox, Bette-Lee *journal editor*
Fox, Keith *publishing executive*
Fox, Margalit (Eve) *journalist, editor, writer*
Fox, Mitchell B. *publishing executive*
Fox, Sylvan *journalist, educator*
France, Kim *editor-in-chief*
Frankel, Max *retired journalist*
Franks, Lucinda Laura *journalist*
Franks, Martin Davis *broadcast executive*
Freeland, Chrystia *editor*
Frere, Fabrice G. *publishing executive*
Freudenheim, Milton B. *journalist*
Freyre, Fabio *publishing executive*
Friedman, Jane *publishing executive*
Friedman, Sam *editor*
Frommer, Arthur *editor-in-chief, travel writer*
Fuentez, Tania Michele *journalist*
Fuller, Bonnie *editor-in-chief*
Gabriel, Trip (Bertram Gabriel III) *editor*
Gabrielson, Charles *publishing executive*
Gaffney, Elizabeth Mallory *editor, writer, literature educator, translator*
Gainsburg, Roy Ellis *publishing executive*
Gallo, William Victor *cartoonist*
Ganzi, Victor Frederick *publishing executive*
Garcia, Nina *publishing executive*
Gardino, Vincent Anthony *broadcast executive*
Gardner, Janet Paxton *journalist, film producer*
Garrett, Laurie *journalist, global health scholar*
Geary, Hilary R. *society editor*
Geddes, John M. *editor*
Gehringer, Richard George *publishing executive*
Geiser, Elizabeth Able *publishing company executive*
Gellman, Barton David *correspondent*
Gewirtz-Friedman, Gerry *editor*
Geyer, Thomas Powick *newspaper publisher*
Gharib, Susie *newscaster*
Gialanella, Donald George *broadcast executive, sound recording engineer, sculptor*
Giannetti, Stephen P. *publishing executive*
Gibney, James S. *editor*
Gibson, Charles DeWolf *newscaster*
Gibson, John *news anchor, correspondent*
Gigot, Paul Anthony *editor*
Gilbert, Rose Bennett *journalist*
Giordano, Mary Ann *editor*
Girardi, Joe (Joseph Elliot Girardi) *sports announcer, former professional baseball manager, former professional baseball player*
Gissler, Sigvard Gunnar, Jr. *journalist, educator, retired editor*
Gladstone, Bernard *columnist*
Gladstone, Rick *editor*
Glanze, Walter D. *editor, writer, lexicographer, publishing consultant*
Glater, Jonathan D. *reporter*
Glowczewska, Klara *editor-in-chief, translator*
Goldberg, Danny *recording industry executive*
Golden, Michael *publishing executive*
Golin, Mark *editor*
Goodman, Michael B(arry) *communications educator*
Goodstein, Laurie Beth *journalist*
Goodstein, Les *newspaper publishing executive*
Gordon, Susan C. *broadcast executive*
Gotti, Victoria *columnist, writer, actress*
Gould, Emily *editor*
Gourevitch, Philip *editor*
Grace, Nancy A. *news correspondent, former prosecutor*
Graham, Alma Eleanor *editor, writer, educational consultant*
Graham, Fred Patterson *news correspondent, journalist*
Granath, Herbert A. *television industry executive*
Grant Goldman, Pamela *journalist, writer*
Graustark, Barbara *editor*
Graves, Earl G., Jr., (Butch Graves) *publishing executive*
Graves, Earl Gilbert *publishing executive*
Gray, Jerry *editor*
Green, Dan *publishing executive*
Green, George Joseph *publishing executive*
Greenberg, Peter S. *travel editor, news correspondent, writer*
Greenberg, Steve *music company executive*
Greene, Richard H. *journalist, writer, policy analyst*
Greenfield, (Henry) Jeff *news analyst*
Greenfield, Sarah *photo editor*
Greenman, Josh *editor*
Greenwald, Julie *recording industry executive*
Grenquist, Peter Carl *publishing executive, consultant*
Grimes, William *critic*
Gross, Amy *editor-in-chief*
Grueskin, William Steven (Bill Grusekin) *editor*
Grune, Steven Bryan *publishing executive*
Guiher, James Morford, Jr. *publisher, writer*
Gumbel, Bryant Charles *broadcaster*
Haberman, Clyde *columnist*
Hackett, George *editor*
Hackett, Larry *editor*
Haegele, Patricia *publishing executive*
Hall, Lisa Gersh *broadcast executive, lawyer*
Hall, Trish *editor*
Halperin, Mark Evan *editor*
Hansell, Saul Henry *reporter*
Harrow, Nancy (Mrs. Jan Krukowski) *editor, composer, singer*
Hart, Clare *information company executive*
Harty, Thomas H. *publishing executive*
Hauser, Gustave M. *media specialist*
Headlam, Bruce *editor*
Healy, Mark *editor-in-chief*
Hearst, George Randolph, Jr. *publishing executive, real estate company executive*
Heekin-Canedy, Scott H. *publishing executive*
Heffernan, Virginia *television critic*
Henriques, Diana Blackmon *journalist*
Herbert, Bob *columnist*
Herring, Hubert B. *editor*
Hersh, Seymour Myron *journalist, writer*
Herszenhorn, David *journalist*
Hertz, Leon *publishing executive*
Hesser, Amanda Lea *journalist, chef*
Hicks, Jonathan P. *journalist*
Hicks, Tyler Gregory *publishing company executive, writer*
Hilchey, Tim *editor*
Hippeau, Eric *book publishing executive*
Hodge, Roger D. *editor*
Hoffert, Barbara *editor*
Hoge, Warren M. *editor*
Holden, Stephen *film critic*
Holland, Bernard Peabody *music critic*
Holliday, Guy D. "Doc" *publishing executive*
Hondros, Chris *photojournalist*
Horyn, Cathy *newspaper editor*
Howard, Lisa Ryan *publishing executive*
Howat, Kevin John *publishing and healthcare services executive*
Hoyt, Clark Freeland *editor, journalist*
Hu, Winnie *journalist*
Huckshorn, Kristin *journalist*
Huey, John Wesley, Jr. *editor*
Hughes, Brigid *former editor*
Hurley, Cheryl Joyce *book publishing executive*
Hutchins, Traver *publishing executive*
Huxtable, Ada Louise *architecture critic*
Ianniello, Joseph R. *broadcast executive*
Ingrassia, Lawrence *editor*
Ireland, Jay *broadcast executive*
Irish, George Butler *media company executive*
Isenberg, Steven Lawrence *retired publishing executive*
Isherwood, Charles *theater critic*
Jackson, Keith MacKenzie *retired sports commentator*
Jacobs, Lawrence A. *media company executive, lawyer*
Jamieson, Wendell *editor*
Jamison, Jayne *publishing executive*
Jarvis, Jeff *journalist, former critic, news blogger*
Jay-Z, (Shawn Corey Carter) *music company executive, rap artist*
Jefferson, Margo L. *journalist*
Jellinek, George *broadcast executive, music educator, writer*
Jensen, Bill *editor*
Jesselli, Steve *journalist*
Johnson, Brooke Bailey *broadcast executive*
Johnson, Kristine *newscaster*
Johnson, Richard *editor*
Johnston, David Cay Boyle *journalist*
Jolly, Thomas Alan *journalist*
Jones, Judith *editor*
Jones, Laurie Lynn *magazine editor*
Jones, Richard M. *broadcast executive*
Jones Reynolds, Star (Starlet Marie Jones) *television host, lawyer, former prosecutor*
Kadden, Jack *editor*
Kagan, Julia Lee *magazine editor*
Kahn, Joseph F. *journalist*
Kakutani, Michiko *critic*
Kalajian-Lagani, Donna *publishing executive*
Kallman, Craig *music company executive*
Kaminer, Ariel *editor*
Kandel, Myron *newscaster, columnist*
Kane, Thomas Patrick *broadcast executive*
Kann, Peter Robert *retired publishing executive, journalist*
Kaplan, Jill Rebecca *publishing executive*
Kaplan, Peter W. *editor-in-chief*
Kaplan, Rick (Richard N. Kaplan) *broadcast executive*
Karlgaard, Rich *publishing executive*
Karmazin, Mel *broadcast executive*
Karpel, Craig S. *journalist, editor*
Karr, Jane *editor*
Kaufman, Victor A. *broadcast and retired film company executive*
Keane, Bil *cartoonist*
Keane, Jeff *cartoonist*
Keenan, Terry *anchor, correspondent*
Kelleher, Kevin *music company executive*
Kelleher, Kimberly Anderson *magazine publishing executive*
Keller, Bill *executive editor*
Kelly, James *editor*
Kenney, Brian *editor-in-chief*
Keppler, Herbert *publishing executive*
Kerrest, Jacques Dominique *broadcasting company executive*
Kessler, Eric *broadcast executive*
Keteyian, Armen *news correspondent*
Kimmelman, Michael Simon *art critic*
King, Gayle *editor, radio personality, television personality*
Kislik, Richard William *publishing executive*
Kissel, Howard William *drama critic*
Kisselgoff, Anna *dance critic*
Klein, Jason Evan *publishing executive*
Klein, Laura Colin *publishing executive*
Klein, Naomi *journalist*
Klingensmith, Michael *publishing executive*
Kluger, Jeffrey *reporter, author*
Knobler, Peter Stephen *magazine editor, writer*
Knopf, Alfred, Jr. *retired publisher*
Koepp, Stephen *editor*
Koerner, Brendan I. *columnist*
Kolata, Gina *journalist*
Kolatch, Myron *magazine editor*
Kolben, Deborah *editor*
Kolson, Ann J. *editor*
Koplovitz, Kay *television network executive*
Koppelman, Charles A. *record company executive*
Koster, Elaine *publishing executive*
Koteff, Ellen *editor*
Koten, John F. *editor-in-chief*
Kozinn, Allan *music critic, reporter*
Kramer, Marc Z. *publishing executive*
Kramon, Glenn *newspaper business editor*
Kravitz, Lee *editor*
Kristof, Nicholas Donabet *journalist*
Kroft, Steve *news correspondent, editor*
Kulish, Nicholas *reporter*
Kushner, Jared C. *publishing executive, real estate developer*
Lack, Andrew R. *music company executive*
Lafavore, Michael J. *editor-in-chief*
Lagani, Daniel *publishing executive*
Lagani, Joseph A. *publishing executive*
Lamont, Lansing *journalist, writer, public affairs and trust executive*
Landau, Sidney Ivan *lexicographer*
Landman, Jonathan *editor*
Lapham, Lewis Henry *editor, television personality, writer*
Larsen, Jonathan Zerbe *journalist*
Lawhon, Charla *editor*
Lawrence, Nina *publishing executive*
Laybourne, Geraldine B. *broadcast executive*
Leach, Bryan *music company executive*
Leahey, Lynn *editor-in-chief*
Leahy, Michael Joseph *retired newspaper editor*
Lee, Frances Helen *editor*
Lee, Jennifer *journalist*
Lee, Sally A. *editor-in-chief*
Lees, Alfred William *former magazine editor, writer*
Lehmann-Haupt, Christopher Charles Herbert *book reviewer*
Leive, Cynthia *editor-in-chief*
Leonard, John *film and literature critic*
Levin, Alan M. *television journalist*
Levine, Ellen R. *editor-in-chief*
Levinson, Warren Mitchell *broadcast journalist*
Levitz, Paul Elliot *publishing executive*
Levy, Clifford J. *reporter*
Levy, Dany *publishing executive*
Liberman, Megan Rose *editor*
Liles, Kevin *music company executive*
Lincoln, Stephen *publishing executive*
Lingeman, Richard Roberts *editor-in-chief, writer*
Lipscomb, Thomas Heber III *media company executive*
Lisanti, Mark V. *blogger, writer*
Lloyd, Kenneth L. *columnist*
Loeb, Marshall Robert *journalist*
Logan, Lara *news correspondent*
Lohr, Steve *reporter*
Longley, Marjorie Watters *newspaper executive*
Longobardi, David *editor-in-chief*
Loomis, Carol J. *journalist*
Lundberg, George David, II, *medical editor-in-chief, pathologist*
Luo, Michael *journalist*
Lupica, Mike (Michael Thomas Lupica) *sports columnist*
Lurie, Ranan Raymond *political cartoonist, artist, journalist*
Lyne, Susan Markham *multi-media company executive, former broadcast executive*
Lynne, Michael *film company executive*
Lyons, Daniel *editor, website blogger*
Lyons, Nick *publishing executive*
MacArthur, John Roderick C. G. (Rick MacArthur) *magazine publisher, journalist*
MacGowan, Sandra Firelli *publishing executive, consultant*
Macri, Theodore William *book publisher*
Madden, John *sportscaster, retired professional football coach*
Mapes, Glynn Dempsey *newspaper editor*
Maremont, Mark *reporter*
Marriott, Michel *reporter*
Marshall, Tom *publishing executive*
Martin, Judith Sylvia *journalist*
Martin, Paul Ross *editor*
Marzorati, Gerald *editor*
Maslin, Janet *critic*
Mason, Dan *broadcast executive*
Mathews, Jack Wayne *journalist, film critic*
Mathis, Catherine J. *publishing executive*
Matthews, Christopher John *political commentator, writer*
Maurer, Gilbert Charles *media specialist*
Maynard, Micheline Ann *journalist, writer*
Mazzola, Anthony Thomas *editor, graphics designer, consultant*
McCabe, Jim *publishing executive*
McCarrick, Edward R. *publishing executive*
McCarthy, Pamela Maffei *magazine editor*
McCarthy, Patrick *publishing executive*
McCarty, V. K. *publishing executive, chaplain, librarian*
McCormack, Thomas Joseph *retired publishing executive, playwright*
McCrie, Robert Delbert *editor, educator*
McDonald, John F. *publishing executive, restauranteur*
McDonell, Robert Terry *magazine editor, novelist*
McDonell, Terry *publishing executive, writer, editor*
McElroy, Kathleen O. *dining editor*
McFadden, Cynthia Graham *news correspondent, journalist*
McFadden, Robert Dennis *reporter*
McFeely, William Drake *publishing company executive*
McGill, Jay *magazine publisher*
McGrath, Eleanor Burns *editor, writer*
McGrath, Judy (Judith Ann McGrath) *broadcast executive*
McGraw, Harold Whittlesey, Jr. *publishing executive*
McIntire, Mike *journalist*
McNally, Michele *editor, photographer*
McNeil, Donald G., Jr. *journalist*
Meacham, Jon E. *editor*
Medina, Kate (Kathryn Bach Medina) *publishing executive, editor*
Mehta, Sonny (Ajay Singh Mehta) *publishing executive*
Meier, Barry *reporter*
Melloan, George Richard *editor*
Mencher, Melvin *journalist, educator*
Menicheschi, Edward John *publishing executive*
Meyer, Karl Ernest *journalist*
Michaels, Al (Alan Richard Michaels) *sportscaster*
Millard, Wenda Harris *multi-media company executive*
Miller, Michael Jeffrey *editor, columnist*
Millstein, Lincoln *media company executive*
Min, Janice Byung *editor-in-chief*
Minick, Michael *publishing executive*
Mirenburg, Barry Leonard *publishing executive, educator*
Mitchell, Alison N. *newspaper reporter, editor*
Mitchell, George John *entertainment company executive, lawyer, former senator*
Mohn, Louis *publishing executive*
Mooney, Ted (Edward Comstock Mooney) *editor, art critic, writer*
Moonves, Leslie *broadcast executive*
Moore, Ann S. *publishing executive*
Morgan, Mary E. *publishing executive*
Morgenson, Gretchen C. *reporter*
Morris, David S. *publishing executive*
Morris, Dick *columnist, political consultant*
Morris, Doug (Douglas Peter Morris) *recording industry executive*
Morrison, Stacy Lynne *editor*
Morrissey, Thomas A. *publishing executive*
Moscowitz, Todd *music company executive*
Moskin, John Robert *editor, writer*
Moss, Adam *editor*
Mullany, Gerry *editor*

Murdoch, Rupert (Keith Rupert Murdoch) *multi media company executive*
Myers, Roberta *editor-in-chief*
Nagourney, Herbert *publishing company executive*
Nantz, James William (Jim Nantz) *sportscaster*
Napack, Brian *publishing executive*
Nathan, Paul S. *retired editor, writer*
Nederlander, Robert E. *entertainment and television executive, lawyer*
Nelson, Anne *media consultant, educator, writer*
Nelson, Bill *broadcast executive*
Nelson, Carl *journalist*
Nelson, Jim *editor*
Nelson, Kathy *broadcast executive*
Nelson, Martha Jane *editor*
Newman, Andy *journalist*
Newman, Diane *publishing executive*
Nocera, Joseph *editor, writer*
Norman, Christina *broadcast executive*
Norris, Floyd Hamilton *financial journalist*
Norton, David K. *publishing executive, human resources specialist*
Novitz, Charles Richard *broadcast executive, reporter*
Novogrod, Nancy Gerstein *editor*
Nurnberg, Charles Gordon *publishing executive*
Nyren, Neil Sebastian *publishing executive, editor*
Obogeanu, Madalina Maria *reporter*
O'Connell, Maureen Elizabeteh *publishing executive*
O'Connor, Anahad S. *journalist*
Oestreich, James R. *editor*
Offutt, Brian *broadcast executive*
O'Kelley, Winnie *editor*
Okura-Marszycki, Mindy Emi *editor*
Oldfield, Barney *entertainment executive*
Olson, Peter *publishing executive*
O'Neill, Joan *editor*
O'Reilly, Bill (William O'Reilly Jr.) *commentator, writer*
Oricchio, Michael *editor*
Ortega, Tony *editor-in-chief*
Osberg, Gregory John *publishing company executive*
Osgood, Charles *news broadcaster, journalist*
Osnos, Peter Lionel Winston *publishing executive*
Ouroussoff, Nicolai *architecture critic*
Pace, Eric Dwight *retired journalist*
Pak, SuChin *newscaster*
Palsho, Dorothea Coccoli *information services executive*
Paneth, Donald Joseph *editor, writer*
Pareles, Jon *music critic*
Paul, Laurence M. *editor*
Penn, Stanley William *journalist*
Pennington, William Mark *sportswriter*
Perlmutter, Isaac *entertainment company executive*
Perram Frank, Heather *editor-in-chief*
Petronella, Michael A. *publishing executive*
Petzal, David Elias *editor, writer*
Pfeiffer, Jane Cahill *former broadcasting company executive, consultant*
Pines, Burton Yale *media executive*
Pinkwater, Julie *publishing executive*
Plepler, Richard L. *broadcast executive*
Plummer, William B. *publishing executive*
Podhoretz, John *editor, writer*
Pogue, David *journalist*
Pollak, William L. *newspaper publishing executive*
Pollock, Ellen Joan *editor*
Poltrack, David F. *broadcast executive, marketing educator*
Pope, Liston, Jr. *writer, journalist*
Porterfield, Christopher *magazine editor, writer*
Post, David Alan *broadcast executive*
Preston, Frances Williams *music company executive*
Preston, Julia *journalist*
Price, Frank *motion picture and television company executive*
Price, Hilary B. *cartoonist*
Prozes, Andrew *publishing executive*
Puris, Martin Ford *media company executive*
Putnam, Keri *film company executive*
Quindlen, Anna *journalist, writer*
Quinn, Jane Bryant *journalist, writer*
Race, Tim *editor*
Rampe, David *editor*
Rashad, Ahmad *sports broadcaster, former professional football player*
Ratliff, Ben *music critic*
Raven, Abbe *broadcast executive*
Redburn, Tom *newspaper editor*
Redstone, Sumner Murray *broadcast executive, lawyer*
Rehl, Beatrice Claire *editor*
Reichl, Ruth Molly *editor-in-chief*
Reid, Antonio (L.A. Reid) *music company executive*
Reif Cohen, Jessica *broadcast executive*
Reilly, William Francis *media company executive*
Remnick, David J. *journalist, editor-in-chief*
Rennie, John *editor-in-chief*
Reynolds, Fredric G. *broadcast executive*
Rhoads, Geraldine Emeline *editor, consultant*
Rhone, Sylvia Marie Miller *recording industry executive*
Ricca, Gregory J. *broadcast executive, management consultant*
Rich, Frank Hart *journalist, writer*
Rieff, David Sontag *editor, critic*
Rizzuto, Katherine *publishing executive*
Roach, Margaret *publishing executive*
Roberts, Fletcher *editor*
Roberts, Gene *newspaper executive*
Roberts, Jim *editor*
Roberts, Katy *editor*
Roberts, Robin *newscaster*
Robinson, Janet L. *publishing executive*
Robinson, Richard *publishing executive*
Rockwell, John Sargent *dance critic, writer, former arts administrator*
Roeding, Cyriac R. *broadcast executive*
Rogin, Gilbert Leslie *editor, author*
Roker, Al *newscaster*
Rose, Charlie (Charles Peete Rose Jr.) *television journalist*
Rose, Victoria Lasdon *publishing executive*
Rosenberg, Tina *reporter*
Rosenblum, Constance *newspaper editor*
Rosenthal, Andrew Mark *newspaper editor*
Rosenthal, Jane *film company executive*
Rosenthal, Shirley Lord *cosmetics magazine executive, novelist*
Ross, Brian Elliott *chief investigative correspondent*
Ross, Steve J. *publishing executive*
Rosset, Barnet Lee, Jr. *publishing executive*
Rothberg, Gerald *editor, publishing executive*
Rubin, Stephen Edward *publishing executive, editor, journalist*
Rule, Sheila *editor*
Rutenberg, Jim *journalist*
Ryan, Regina Claire (Mrs. Paul Deutschman) *editor, literary agent*
Sabat, Robert Hartman *magazine editor*
Safian, Robert L. *executive editor*
Salembier, Valerie Birnbaum *publishing executive*
Samuels, Dorothy J. *journalist, writer*
Sanders, Gina Susan *publishing executive*
Sandler, Irving Harry *art critic, art historian*
Saraf, Peter Nataniel *film producer, executive*
Sareyan, Andy *publishing executive*
Sarnelle, Joseph R. *publishing executive*
Sarnoff, Ann M. *publishing executive, former sports association executive*
Sasman, Irene Deak Handberg *publishing executive*
Sawyer, (L.) Diane *newscaster, journalist*
Sayre, Phil *editor*
Scarborough, Chuck (Charles Bishop Scarborough III) *newscaster*
Schachter, James Robert *editor*
Schamus, James Allan *film producer and company executive, screenwriter*
Schiesel, Seth *reporter*
Schlosser, Herbert S. *broadcasting company executive*
Schmemann, Serge *journalist*
Schmertz, Mildred Floyd *editor-in-chief, writer*
Schmidt, Stanley Albert *editor, writer*
Schmidt, William E. *editor*
Schmidt-Holtz, Rolf *music company executive*
Schneider, Daniel B. *reporter*
Schneider, Martin Aaron *photojournalist, ecologist, engineer, writer, artist, television director, filmmaker, public advocate, medical researcher, educator*
Schreiber, Jay *journalist*
Schuman, Patricia Glass *publishing company executive, educator*
Schwartz, Gil (Stanley Bing) *broadcast executive, writer*
Scott, Tom *broadcast executive*
Seelig, Jill *publishing executive*
Seligman, Daniel *editor*
Semple, Robert Baylor, Jr. *editor, journalist*
Sención, Felix *publishing executive*
Servodidio, Pat Anthony *broadcast executive*
Serwer, Andy (Andrew E. Serwer) *editor, journalist*
Sexton, Joe *editor*
Shafrir, Doree *editor, journalist*
Shah, Vivek *publishing executive*
Shank, Ron *publishing executive*
Shanks, David *publishing executive*
Shanor, Donald Read *journalism educator, writer*
Shapiro, Gary Evan *newspaper journalist*
Shapiro, Neal *broadcast executive, television producer*
Sharbel, Jean M. *editor*
Sharpe, Shannon *commentator, retired professional football player*
Shaw, Adam *broadcast executive*
Shea, Martin M. *broadcast executive*
Sheinman, Mort *editor, consultant, writer, photographer*
Shepard, Stephen Benjamin *journalist, educator, retired editor*
Shier, Shelley M. *production company executive*
Shnayerson, Robert Beahan *editor, consultant*
Shoket, Ann E. *editor-in-chief*
Shortz, Will *puzzle editor*
Sicha, Choire *online editor*
Siegel, Marvin *newspaper editor*
Siegel, Randy *publishing executive*
Sifton, Sam *editor*
Siklos, Richard *reporter*
Silvers, Robert B. *editor*
Simmons, Sue *newscaster*
Simms, Phil *sports commentator, retired professional football player*
Singer, Joy Daniels *journalist, consultant*
Singleton, Donald Edward *journalist*
Sischy, Ingrid Barbara *editor, art critic*
Slabe, James F. *publishing executive*
Sleed, Joel *columnist*
Sloan, Allan Herbert *journalist*
Smith, Brad *journalist*
Smith, Dennis (Edward Smith) *publishing executive, writer*
Smith, Liz (Mary Elizabeth Smith) *columnist, newscaster*
Smith, Richard Mills *editor-in-chief*
Smith, Roberta *art critic*
Sommer, Jeff *journalist*
Soriano, Nancy Mernit *editor-in-chief*
Sorkin, Andrew Ross *reporter, columnist*
Sott, Janny *journalist*
Spelling, Ian *columnist*
Squires, John *publishing executive*
Stanger, Ila *editor-in-chief*
Stanley, Alessandra *critic*
Stasio, Marilyn Louise *columnist*
Steiger, Paul Ernest *editor, journalist*
Stengel, Richard *editor*
Stern, Mitchell *broadcast executive*
Stern, Roslyne Paige *magazine publisher*
Stevens, Mark Whitney *art critic*
Stewart, James B. *journalist, writer*
Story, Richard David *publishing executive*
Stossel, John *news analyst*
Straka, Angeline C. *broadcast executive*
Strauss, Carolyn *broadcast executive*
Studin, Jan *publishing executive*
Sturtevant, Peter Mann, Jr. *television news executive*
Sugihara, Kenzi *publishing executive*
Sugiyama, Kazunori *music producer*
Suh, Mary *editor*
Sulzberger, Arthur Ochs *newspaper executive*
Sulzberger, Arthur Ochs, Jr. *newspaper publisher*
Suskind, Ronald Steven *journalist, writer*
Sussman, Gerald *publishing company executive*
Sweed, Phyllis *publishing executive*
Talley, André Leon *Editor-At-Large (Periodical)*
Tanenhaus, Sam *editor*
Tang, Terry *editor, lawyer*
Tavernise, Sabrina *journalist*
Taylor, Felicia *newscaster*
Taylor, Sherril Wightman *broadcast executive*
Taylor, Susan L. *magazine editor*
Taylor, Terry R. *editor, educator*
Tetzeli, Rick *editor*
Thomas, Brooks *publishing executive, director*
Thomas, Helen Amelia (Mrs. Douglas B. Cornell) *editor-in-chief, former White House correspondent*
Tober, Barbara D. (Mrs. Donald Gibbs Tober) *editor*
Toepfer, Susan Jill *editor-in-chief*
Tomlinson, James Francis *retired news agency executive*
Tommasini, Anthony *music critic, writer, musician*
Tonchi, Stefano *editor*
Tong, Kaity *anchor*
Townsend, Alair Ane *publishing executive*
Townsend, Charles H. *publishing executive*
Treaster, Joseph B(land) *journalist*
Tritch, Teresa *editor, writer*
Trump, Eric Frederick *journalist*
Tuchman, Phyllis *critic*
Turitzin, John N. *entertainment company executive, lawyer*
Turner, Alice Kennedy *editor*
Tyrangiel, Josh *editor*
Uchitelle, Louis *journalist*
Ulanoff, Lance *editor-in-chief*
Umansky, Diane *editor-in-chief*
Unger, David C. *journalist*
Vanden Heuvel, Katrina *publishing executive*
Van Susteren, Greta Conway *newscaster, lawyer*
Vargas, Elizabeth *newscaster*
Veale, Scott *editor, columnist*
Vecsey, George Spencer *sports columnist*
Vermeulen, Kevin J. *publishing executive*
Verongos, Helen *editor*
Vick, James Albert *publishing executive, consultant*
Vien, Patrick *music company executive*
Viladas, Pilar *editor*
Visser, Lesley *sports correspondent*
Vogt, Douglas *news cameraman, journalist*
Wackermann, William *publishing executive*
Wald, Richard Charles *media consultant, educator*
Waldman, Steven *editor*
Walk, Charlie *music company executive*
Walker, Mort *cartoonist*
Wallace, Alexandra *broadcast executive, television producer*
Wallace, Christopher *broadcast television correspondent*
Wallace, Thomas C. *editor, publishing executive*
Walters, Barbara Jill *broadcast journalist*
Waricha, Joan *publishing executive*
Warner, Peter David *publishing executive*
Wayne, Leslie *reporter*
Weber, Robert Maxwell *cartoonist*
Weinstein, Bob (Robert Weinstein) *film company executive*
Weinstein, Harvey *film company executive, film producer*
Weintraub, Beverly *editor*
Wemple, Erik C. *editor-in-chief*
Wenner, Jann Simon *editor, publisher*
Werner, Ryan *film company executive*
Westin, David Lawrence *broadcast executive, lawyer*
Whitaker, Mark Theis *broadcast executive, editor*
White, Kate *editor-in-chief*
Whitney, Craig Richard *journalist*
Wilford, John Noble, Jr. *science news correspondent*
Wilkins, Amy P. *publishing executive*
Williams, Ben *editorial director online magazine*
Williams, Brian *network news anchor*
Williams, Lena *sportswriter*
Williams, Marsha E. *broadcast executive*
Williams, Michael G. *publishing executive*
Wilson, Mike *journalist*
Winerip, Michael *reporter*
Winkler, Matthew Adam *editor-in-chief, reporter*
Winship, Frederick Moery *journalist*
Wintour, Anna *editor-in-chief*
Wohrle, Marta *publishing executive*
Woletz, Robert G. *editor*
Wong, Andrea J. *broadcast executive*
Woodruff, Bob (Robert Warren Woodruff) *newscaster*
Woodruff, Jay Noel *editor, writer*
Woodruff, Mark Reed *magazine editor*
Wragge, Chris *newscaster*
WuDunn, Sheryl *journalist, correspondent*
Yardley, Jim *journalist*
Young, Genevieve Leman *publishing executive, editor*
Zagat, Nina *publishing executive*
Zagat, Tim *publishing executive*
Zalaznick, Lauren *broadcast executive*
Zannino, Richard F. *publishing executive*
Zarghami, Cyma *broadcast executive*
Ziltz, Bob *publishing executive*
Zimbalist, Michael *publishing executive*
Zimmer, William *art critic*
Zinczenko, David *editor*
Zinoman, Jason *theater critic*
Zuckerman, Mortimer Benjamin *publishing executive, real estate developer*

Northport
Richards, Carol Ann Rubright *retired editor, journalist*

Nyack
Oursler, Fulton, Jr. *editor, writer*

Old Westbury
O'Brien, Adrienne Gratia *communications educator*

Ontario
Blackman, Lani Modica *copy editor*

Plattsburgh
Schueller, Gretel Helena *journalist, educator*

Pleasantville
Alston, Alyce C. *publishing executive, former diamond company executive*
Berner, Mary G. *publishing executive*
Clifton, Jean B. *publishing executive*
Dillon, Eva A. *publishing executive*
Geltzeiler, Michael S. *publishing executive*
Grimes, Suzanne *publishing executive*
Leo, Jacqueline M. *editor-in-chief*
McEwen, Laura *publishing executive*
Newborn, Andrea R. *publishing executive, lawyer*
Schrier, Eric Woodside W. *publishing executive*

Port Washington
Candido, Arthur Aldo *publishing and distribution company executive*
Jay, Frank Peter *retired writer, lexicographer, educator*
Ragan, David *publishing company executive*

Poughkeepsie
Kim, David Sang Chul *publishing executive, evangelist, retired academic administrator*

Purchase
Schmitz, Robert Allen *publishing executive, investor*

Remsenburg
Billman, Irwin Edward *publishing executive*

Richmondville
Bartholomew, Debra Lee *publishing executive*

Ridge
Carter, Sylvia *journalist*

Rochester
Fallesen, Gary David *journalist, lay worker*
Kaidy, Mitchell *retired journalist, legislative staff member*
Lank, Edith Handleman *journalist, educator*
Palvino, Jack Anthony *retired broadcasting executive*
Pitoniak, Scott Michael *sportswriter*

Rye
Nelson, Vita Joy *editor, publisher*

Sag Harbor
Brody, Jacqueline *editor*
Epstein, Jason *publishing company executive*

Sagaponack
Graham, Howard Barrett *publishing company executive*

Scarsdale
Erbsen, Claude Ernest *retired journalist*
Goodman, Jordan Elliot *journalist*
O'Neill, Michael James *editor, author*

Selkirk
Christoph, Peter Richard *historical editor, archivist*

Sleepy Hollow
Flynn-Connors, Elizabeth Kathryn *reporter, editor*
Melvin, Russell Johnston (Jay Melvin) *magazine publishing consultant*
Neill, Richard Robert *retired publishing executive*

Somers
Cohn, Howard *retired magazine editor*

South Setauket
Poli, Kenneth Joseph *editor, writer, photographer*

Staten Island
Dennery, Linda *newspaper publishing executive*
Newhouse, Donald E. *newspaper publishing executive*
Newhouse, Samuel Irving, Jr., (Si Newhouse Jr.) *publishing executive*
Prince, Danforth *publishing executive, journalist*

Stony Brook
Harvey, Christine Lynn *publishing executive*

Syracuse
Blakely, Caroline Miller *retired editor*
Bunn, Timothy David *newspaper editor*
Obbie, Mark Joseph *communications educator*

Tarrytown
Stein, Sol *publishing executive, writer*

Troy
Friedman, Sue Tyler *technical publications executive*

Wainscott
Henderson, William Charles *editor*

Warwick
Simon, Dolores Daly *copy editor*

Watertown
Brett, James Clarence *retired journalism educator*

White Plains
Foderaro, Lisa *reporter*
Leish, Kenneth William *retired publishing company executive*

Williamsville
Levite, Laurence A. *publishing executive*

Willsboro
Reuther, David Louis *retired children's book publisher, writer*

Yonkers
Kleman, Kimberly C. *editor-in-chief*
McKean, Kevin S. *publishing executive, writer*
Westphal, Carol Jean *media specialist*

Yorktown Heights
Wade, James O'Shea *editor, writer*

NORTH CAROLINA

Brevard
Phillips, Euan Hywel *publishing executive*

Cary
Swanson, David C. *publishing executive*

Chapel Hill
Bailey, Herbert Smith, Jr. *retired publisher*
Bowers, Thomas Arnold *journalism educator, dean*
Cole, Richard Ray *communications educator, former dean*
Lauder, Valarie Anne *editor, educator*
Meyer, Philip Edward *journalism educator*
Ravenel, Shannon *book publishing professional*

Charlotte
Armstrong, James David *editor, educator, minister*
Barrows, Frank Clemence *journalist*
Bauroth, Nancy Ann *journalist, former marketing executive*
Caulkins, Ann *publishing executive*
Gotta, Joseph D. *music company executive*
Haines, Kenneth H. *sports television broadcasting and marketing executive*
Thames, Rick *publishing executive, editor-in-chief*
Williams, Edwin Neel *newspaper editor*

Durham
Cayne, Bernard Stanley *editor*
Cohn, Stephen Andrew *publishing executive*
Fiske, Edward B. *editor, educator, journalist, consultant*
Harrell, Carlton (Benjamin Carlton Harrell) *retired editor, writer*
Hawkins, William E. N. *newspaper editor*
Rossiter, Alexander, Jr. *publishing executive, editor*

Flat Rock
Bailey, Louise Howe *columnist, educator*

Greensboro
Blackwell, William Ernest *broadcast executive*
Jellicorse, John Lee *communications and theatre educator*

Harrisburg
Economaki, Chris Constantine (Christopher) *publishing executive*

Hickory
Drendel, Frank Matthew *cable company executive*

High Point
Weatherford, Carole Boston *publications specialist*

Jefferson
Franklin, Robert McFarland *book publisher*

Pembroke
Curtis, Anthony R. *communications educator*
Curtis, Judith Genevicz *communications educator*

Raleigh
Brown, William Harris *editor*
Effron, Seth Alan *editor, journalist*
McKinney, Donald Lee *magazine editor*
Parker, Joseph Mayon *retired publishing executive*
Pittman, James Morris (Jack Pittman) *cartoonist, illustrator, character designer, consultant*
Reeves, Ralph Bernard III *publishing executive*

Saluda
McCutcheon, John Tinney, Jr. *retired journalist*

Sanford
Harrington, Anthony Ross *radio announcer, educator*

Southport
Pepper, Jeffrey Mackenzie *publishing executive*

Winston Salem
Graybeal, Barbara *editor, writer*
King, Wayne Edgar *journalist, educator*
Price, Henry Escoe *broadcast executive*
Zagoria, Sam D(avid) *reporter, educator, federal agency administrator*

Wrightsville Beach
Mc Ilwain, William Franklin *newspaper editor, writer*

NORTH DAKOTA

Fargo
Littlefield, Robert Stephen *communications educator, training consultant*
Marcil, William Christ, Sr. *publisher, broadcast executive*

Grand Forks
Glassheim, Eliot Alan *editor, state legislator*

OHIO

Akron
Burbach, Mike *editor*
Stewart, Mizell III *editor*

Athens
Metters, Thomas Waddell *sportswriter*
Scott, Charles Lewis *retired photojournalist*
Stempel, Guido Hermann III *journalism educator*

Avon Lake
Pascarella, Perry James *editor, writer*

Bloomingdale
Calabrese, Charles *radio station official*

Cincinnati
Beckwith, Barbara Jean *journalist*
Buchanan, Margaret E. *publishing executive*
Burleigh, William Robert *media executive*
Callinan, Tom *editor-in-chief*
Irwin, Miriam Dianne Owen *publishing executive, writer*
Lowe, Kenneth W. *multimedia executive*
McMullin, Ruth Roney *retired publishing executive*
Mechem, Charles Stanley, Jr. *retired broadcast executive*

Cleveland
Bellamy, Gail Anne Ghetia *magazine editor, author, speaker*
Brandt, John Reynold *editor, journalist*
Conrad, Robert David *broadcast executive, educator*
Copeland, Sharon *reporter*
Egger, Terrance C.Z. *publishing executive*
Giannetti, Louis Daniel *film critic, educator*
Goldberg, Susan *editor*
Jensen, Kathryn Patricia (Kit) *broadcast executive*
Jindra, Christine *editor*
Machaskee, Alex *retired newspaper publishing company executive*
Molyneaux, David Glenn *newspaper travel editor*
O'Hara, Thomas Patrick *managing editor*
Santisi, Terri M. (Theresa M. Santisi) *multi-media company executive*
Soltis, Katherine *editor*

Columbus
Barry, James P(otvin) *editor, writer*
Cox, Mitchel Neal *editor*
Curtin, Michael Francis *publishing executive*
Dimmick, John W. *communications educator*
Gribble, Charles Edward *editor, language educator*
Grossberg, Michael Lee *film critic, writer*
Kefauver, Weldon Addison *publishing executive*
Lowe, Clayton Kent *radio film critic, educator*
Marrison, Benjamin J. *editor-in-chief*
Sherrill, Thomas Boykin III *retired newspaper publishing executive*

Dayton
Matheny, Ruth Ann *editor*

Hudson
Clark, Robert Phillips *editor, consultant*

Lakewood
Condon, George Edward *journalist*

Mason
Smith, C. LeMoyne *retired publishing executive*

Oxford
Sanders, Gerald Hollie *communications educator*

Pepper Pike
Vail, Thomas Van Husen *retired publishing executive*

Sidney
Stevens, Robert Jay *magazine editor*

Toledo
Block, John Robinson *newspaper publisher, editor-in-chief*
Block, William K., Jr. *media executive*
Royhab, Ronald *journalist, editor*

Trotwood
Oluyitan, Emmanuel Funso *communications educator*

Westerville
DeVassie, Terry Lee *retired publishing executive*

Willoughby
Corrigan, Faith *journalist, educator, historian*

Wooster
August, Robert Olin *retired journalist*
Schreiber, Clare Adel *journalist*

Yellow Springs
Cawood, Albert McLaurin (Hap Cawood) *retired newspaper editor*

OKLAHOMA

Oklahoma City
Gourley, James Leland *editor, publishing executive*
Kelley, Ed *editor-in-chief*
Thompson, David *publishing executive*
Triplett, E. Eugene *editor*

Tecumseh
Moser, Glenda Faye *media specialist*

Terlton
Bender, John Henry, Jr., (Jack) *editor, cartoonist*

Tulsa
Haring, Robert Westing *newspaper editor*
Ma, Xiaomin *communications educator*
Nyikos, Stacy Ann *publishing executive*

Warr Acres
Engle, Richard Victor *publishing executive*

Wewoka
Trimble, Vance Henry *retired newspaper editor*

OREGON

Albany
Wood, Kenneth Arthur *retired editor, writer*

Ashland
Risser, James Vaulx, Jr. *journalist, educator*

Corvallis
Hall, Don Alan *editor, writer*

Eugene
Baker, Alton Fletcher III *editor, publishing executive*
Baker, Bridget *publishing executive*
Roesler, Robert Harry *media consultant*
Tykeson, Donald Erwin *broadcast executive*

Milton Freewater
Gipson, Stephen Richard *journalist, construction executive*

Portland
Attig, Rick *editor*
Bates, Doug *editor*
Bhatia, Peter K. *editor, journalist*
Bunza, Linda Hathaway *editor, writer, composer, director*
Denson, Bryan *reporter*
Graves, Earl William, Jr. *journalist*
Johnston, Virginia Evelyn *retired editor*
Kosseff, Jeff *reporter, news correspondent*
Rowe, Sandra Mims *editor*
Stickel, Frederick A. *publishing executive*
Zaitz, Leslie Lee *reporter*

Salem
Mainwaring, William Lewis *publishing company executive, author*

Wallowa
Wizard, Brian *publisher, author*

Wilsonville
Giesbrecht, F. Bruce *entertainment company executive*

PENNSYLVANIA

Bensalem
Kang, Benjamin Toyeong *journalist, minister*

Carlisle
Fish, Chester Boardman, Jr. *retired editor*

Easton
Stitt, Dorothy Jewett *journalist*

Emmaus
Bricklin, Mark Harris *magazine editor, publisher*
Rodale, Ardath Harter *publishing executive*
Rodale, Maria *publishing executive*
Vaccariello, Liz *editor-in-chief*

Flourtown
Lee, Adrian Iselin, Jr. *journalist*

Gettysburg
Gritsch, Ruth Christine Lisa *editor*

Harleysville
Smagalski, Carolyn M. *publishing executive, webmaster, director*

Harrisburg
DeKok, David *writer, reporter*
Gover, Raymond Lewis *retired newspaper executive*

Havertown
Hendrickson, Paul Joseph *journalist, writer, educator*

Jenkintown
Booker, Alvin Eugene *publishing executive, consultant*

Kennett Square
Landstrom, Elsie Hayes *retired editor*

King Of Prussia
Broido, Arnold Peace *music publishing company executive*

Lancaster
Shaw, Charles Raymond *journalist*

Philadelphia
Burling, Stacy *reporter*
Carey, Arthur Bernard, Jr. *editor, columnist*
Days, Michael *editor*
Gordon, Anne Kathleen *editor*
Halpern, Eric Franklin *university publishing director*
Hatch, Denny (Alden Denison) *publishing executive, writer*
Jackson, Harold *journalist*
Klein, Julia Meredith *freelance journalist*
Leiter, Robert Allen *journalist, editor, writer*
Lent, John Anthony *journalist, educator*
Marimow, William K. (Bill Marimow) *editor*
Othmer, David Artman *television and radio consultant*
Parry, Lance Aaron *publishing executive*
Pedersen, Darlene Delcourt *publishing executive, writer, psychotherapist*
Porter, Jill *journalist*
Rorer, John Whiteley *publisher, consultant*
Vitez, Michael *reporter*
Wilkinson, Signe *cartoonist*

Pittsburgh
Apone, Carl Anthony *journalist*
Dolfi, Chip *publishing executive*
Leo, Peter Andrew *columnist, educator*
Lopes, Jerry *broadcast executive*
Roof, Robert L. *broadcast executive, sales executive*
Shribman, David Marks *editor*

Saint Davids
Denenberg, Herbert Sidney *journalist, lawyer, educator, retired state official*

Scranton
Lynett, William Ruddy *publishing and broadcast executive*

Sewickley
Grubba, Matthew John *journalist*
Swann, Lynn Curtis *sportscaster, former professional football player*

State College
Barash Coppersmith, Marian Ungar *magazine publisher*

University Park
Thatcher, Sanford Gray *publishing executive*

Warrington
Ward, Hiley Henry *journalist, educator*

Washington Crossing
Roche, Gail Connor *editor*

Wayne
Fabbri, Anne R. *critic, curator*

West Chester
Gallagher, Terrence Vincent *editor*
Mahoney, William Francis *editor, writer*

West Conshohocken
Lenfest, Harold FitzGerald *former cable television executive, lawyer*
Savadove, Daniel C. *broadcast executive*

Williamsport
Rosebrough, Carol Belville *cable television company executive*

Wynnewood
Zoler, Mitchel L. *journalist*

RHODE ISLAND

Cranston
Parravano, Amelia Elizabeth (Amy Beth Parravano) *recording industry executive*

Portsmouth
Needham, Richard Lee *magazine editor*
Parker, Nancy Knowles (Mrs. Cortlandt Parker) *publishing executive*

Providence
Dujardin, Richard Charles *journalist*
Farmer, Susan Lawson *retired broadcast executive, former secretary of state*

Wakefield
Rosenberg, Alan Gene *editor*
Wyman, James Vernon *retired publishing executive*

Warwick
Halperson, Michael Allen *publishing executive*

SOUTH CAROLINA

Bennettsville
Kinney, William Light, Jr. *editor, publishing executive*

Cayce
McElveen, William Lindsay *broadcasting executive, lecturer*

Charleston
Behre, Robert Fuller *journalist*
Schreadley, Richard Lee *newswriter, retired editor*
Williams, Barbara Stambaugh *editor*

Wyrick, Charles Lloyd, Jr. *editor, writer*

Columbia
Breedin, Berryman Brent *journalist, consultant, historian, public relations executive*
Kendler, Bernhard *retired editor*
McNeely, Patricia Gantt *communications educator*

Georgetown
Howard, Thomas Joseph, Sr. *editor*

Greenville
Hipp, William Hayne *broadcast executive*
Mebane, William deBerniere *newspaper publisher*

Johns Island
Tarr, Robert Joseph, Jr. *publishing executive, retail executive*

Orangeburg
Sims, Edward Howell *editor, writer*

Simpsonville
Kanzler, George *journalist, music critic*

SOUTH DAKOTA

Mobridge
Hall, Jo(sephine) Marian *editor*

Rapid City
Wishard, Della Mae *former newspaper editor*

Sioux Falls
Garson, Arnold Hugh *publishing executive*

TENNESSEE

Brentwood
Hearn, Billy Ray *recording industry executive*

Chattanooga
Lutgen, Robert Raymond *newspaper editor*

College Grove
Battle, William Robert (Bob) *retired publishing executive*

Knoxville
Rukeyser, William Simon *journalist*
Teeter, Dwight Leland, Jr. *journalism educator*
Ziegler, Dhyana *broadcasting educator, academic administrator*

Maryville
Bradford, Tutt Sloan *retired publisher*

Murfreesboro
Flanagan, Van Kent *journalist*
Walker, David Ellis, Jr. *communications educator, minister, consultant*

Nashville
Armistead, M. Kathryn *editor*
Boyd, Theophilus Bartholomew III *publishing company executive*
Brewer, Clint *editor*
Green, Lisa Cannon *editor*
Ingram, Martha Rivers *publishing executive*
Mayhew, Aubrey *music industry executive*
Policinski, Eugene Francis *syndicated columnist, editor, radio and television personality, producer*
Sharp, Julie Ervin *communications educator*
Shaw, Carole *editor, publisher*
Sherborne, Robert *editor*
Stone, Lawrence Mynatt *publishing executive*
Turk, Thomas Liebig *arts consultant*

Newport
Ball, Travis, Jr. *editor, retired school administrator*

Ripley
Klutts, William Alonzo *editor*

TEXAS

Abilene
Armstrong, Randy Lee *communications educator*
Boyll, David Lloyd *retired broadcast executive*

Amarillo
Robertson, Pauline Durrett *publishing executive*

Austin
Conine, Ernest *columnist*
Knapp, Mark Lane *communications educator, consultant*
Mayes, Wendell Wise, Jr. *former broadcasting company executive*
Williams, Jerome Denean *advertising educator*
Williamson, Thomas Arnold *publishing executive*

Beaumont
Roth, Lane *communications educator*

Coppell
Aikman, Troy *sportscaster, retired professional football player*

Crockett
Gibbs, James Howard *broadcast executive*

Dallas
Bailon, Gilbert *newspaper executive*
Blessen, Karen Alyce *freelance/self-employed journalist, artist*
Brown, Colleen *broadcast executive*
Burns, Scott *columnist*
Cantrell, Scott *newspaper music critic*
Cummins, James Duane *retired news correspondent*
Decherd, Robert William *newspaper and broadcasting executive*
Dillon, David Anthony *editor, educator*
Glines, Carroll Vane, Jr. *magazine editor*
Holmes, Bert Otis E., Jr. *retired editor*
Keyes, James Willard *film rental company executive*
Kutner, Janet *art critic, book reviewer*
Lumpkin, John O. *news organization executive*
McPherson, Gail *publishing, real estate executive*
Mong, Robert William, Jr. *publishing executive*
Moroney, James M. III *publishing executive*
Osborne, Burl *publishing executive, editor*
Proud, Robert Donald (Robert Payton) *broadcast executive*
Rather, Dan *news correspondent, former network news anchor*
Shepherd, Nick P. *film rental company executive*
Smith, Sue Frances *newspaper editor*
Wilk, Stuart *publishing executive*
Yeffeth, Glenn Barry *publishing executive, management consultant*

Euless
Halter, Jon Charles *retired magazine editor, writer*

Fort Worth
Record, Phillip Julius *journalist*
Turner, Wesley R. *publishing executive*
Witt, Jim *executive editor*

Houston
Anderson, Nick *editorial cartoonist*
Barlow, Jim B. *retired columnist, writer*
Bischoff, Susan Ann *newspaper editor*
Cohen, Jeff *editor, publishing executive*
Downing, Margaret Mary *newspaper editor*
George, Deveral D. *editor, journalist, advertising consultant*
Gray, Robert Steele *publishing executive, editor, writer*
Hawes, William Kenneth *communication educator, author*
Hobby, William Pettus *retired broadcast executive*
Holmes, Ann Hitchcock *journalist*
Jolivet, Joselyn DeVez *music company executive*
Marek, Joycelyn *publishing executive*
McDavid, George Eugene (Gene Mc David) *retired newspaper executive*
Oren, Bruce Clifford *editor, artist*
Read, Michael Oscar *editor, consultant*
Riggenbach, Jeff *journalist*
Roberts, Charles Murray *retired publishing executive, writer*
Sweeney, Jack *publishing executive*
Wagner, Charlene Brook *secondary school educator*
Walls, Martha Ann Williams (Mrs. B. Carmage Walls) *publishing executive*
Wilburn, John *editor*

Irving
Young, J. Warren *magazine publisher*

Jacksonville
Thrall, Gordon Fish *publishing executive*

Kyle
Saunders, Patricia Gene Knight *freelance writer, editor*

Longview
Udy, Rae *columnist, writer*

Lubbock
Punyanunt-Carter, Narissra *communications educator*

San Antonio
Foster, Nancy Haston *columnist, writer*
Gwathmey, Joe Neil, Jr. *retired broadcast executive*
Heloise, *columnist, writer*
Lenke, Joanne Marie *publishing executive*
Marbut, Robert Gordon *communications, electronic security and broadcast executive, investor*
Mays, L(ester) Lowry *broadcast executive*
Michaels, Willard A. (Bill Michaels) *retired broadcasting executive*
Rivard, Robert *newspaper executive*
Stephenson, Thomas A. *publishing executive*

San Marcos
Stovall, Frances Middagh *journalist, preservationist*

Spring
Randazzo, Gary Wayne *newspaper executive*

The Woodlands
Cagle, Melinda Reeves *editor*
Logan, Mathew Kuykendall *journalist*
Schott, Sally Maria *music publisher, arts education consultant*

Tyler
Brock, Dee Sala *television executive, educator, writer, consultant*

UTAH

Park City
Gallivan, John William *retired publishing executive*

Price
King, Carrie Anne *publishing executive, advertising executive*

Provo
Bartlett, Leonard Lee *retired communications educator, advertising executive*
Hughes, (Robert) John *journalist, educator*
Willes, Mark Hinckley *media specialist*

Salt Lake City
Conway, Nancy Ann *newspaper editor*
Fehr, John William *newspaper editor*
Gregersen, R(oald) George *newspaper publishing executive*
Hatch, George Clinton *television executive*
Paulsen, Vivian *editor*
Sillars, Malcolm O. *communications educator*
Smith, Donald E. *broadcast engineer*

VERMONT

Bennington
Burkhardt, Frederick Henry *editor*

Colchester
Mindich, David T.Z. *journalist, educator*

Hartland Four Corners
Brady, Upton Birnie *editor, literary agent*

Lincoln
Kompass, Edward John *consulting editor*

North Pomfret
Crowl, John Allen *retired publishing company executive*

Norwich
Paine, Walter Cabot *journalist, consultant*

Perkinsville
Harris, Christopher *editor, writer, illustrator, graphics designer*

Tunbridge
Childs, Marilyn Carlson *journalist, educator*

Woodstock
Goulazian, Peter Robert *retired broadcasting executive*

VIRGINIA

Alexandria
Arundel, John Howard *journalist, publisher*
Fleming, Douglas Riley *journalist, publishing executive, consultant*
Hobbs, Michael Edwin *broadcast executive*
Shosky, John Edwin *media consultant, speechwriter*
Yoder, Edwin Milton, Jr. *columnist, educator, editor, writer*

Annandale
Freeman, Baba Foster *editor*

Arlington
Arnold, Gary Howard *film critic*
Baker, Russell Wayne *columnist, writer*
Clayton, James Edwin *journalist*
Elsberg, John William *publishing executive, writer*
Glass, Andrew James *newspaper editor*
Harris, John F. *editor-in-chief*
Holovaty, Adrian *editor, web site designer*
Ifill, Gwen *moderator, political reporter*
Kerger, Paula Arnold *broadcast executive*
Lehrer, James Charles *reporter, journalist*
MacDougall, William Lowell *magazine editor*
MacNeil, Robert Breckenridge Ware *retired journalist, writer*
Neikirk, William Robert *journalist*
Quinn, John Collins *publishing executive, editor*
Regnery, Alfred Scattergood *publishing executive*
Reiss, Susan Marie *editor, writer*
Rockefeller, Sharon Percy *broadcast executive*
Simonson, David C. *retired newspaper association executive*
Tyrrell, Robert Emmett, Jr. *editor-in-chief, writer*
VandeHei, Jim W. (James W. VandeHei) *political executive editor*

Ashburn
Sanfelici, Arthur H(ugo) *editor, writer*

Axton
Bestler, J. Michael *columnist, retired surgeon*

Basye
Amolsch, Arthur Lewis *publishing executive*

Charlottesville
Forrest, Patricia Anne *publishing executive, editor*
Kaiserlian, Penelope Jane *publishing executive*
Parrish, David Walker, Jr. *legal publishing company executive*
Thornhill, Arthur H., Jr. *retired publishing executive*
Vaidhyanathan, Siva *journalist, educator*

Chester
Gray, Frederick Thomas, Jr., (Rick Gray) *journalist, actor, educator*

Covington
Rohr, Dwight Mason *news director, radio marketing consultant*

Dulles
Desmond, Ned *editor, writer*

Fairfax
Kieffer, Jarold Alan *publishing executive, writer*
McAllister, William Howard III *newspaper reporter, columnist, public affairs consultant*

Fairfax Station
Randell, Cortes W. *news service executive*

Falls Church
Aukofer, Frank Alexander *journalist*
Cromley, Allan Wray *retired journalist*
Kaplow, Herbert Elias *journalist*

Great Falls
Garrett, Wilbur (Bill) *magazine editor*

Hampton
Brauer, Harrol Andrew, Jr. *broadcast executive*

Leesburg
Petranek, Stephen Lynn *editor*

Lexington
Luecke, Pamela *editor, educator*

Mason Neck
Mc Curdy, Patrick Pierre *editor*

Mc Lean
Clark-Johnson, Susan *publishing executive*
Dubow, Craig A. *publishing executive*
Gallagher, Brian *editor*
Giallombardo, Leslie *publishing executive*
Martore, Gracia *publishing company executive*
Mathews, Linda McVeigh *newspaper editor*
Mazzarella, David *editor*
McCorkindale, Douglas Hamilton *publishing executive*
Moon, Craig A. *publishing executive*
Parshall, Gerald *journalist*
Paulson, Kenneth Alan *editor-in-chief*
Prichard, Peter S. *newspaper editor*

Midlothian
Chapman, Gilbert Whipple, Jr. *publishing executive*
Crutchfield, George Thomas *journalism educator*

Norfolk
Addis, Kay Tucker *newspaper editor*
Barry, Richard Francis III *media executive*
Batten, Frank *newspaper publisher, cable broadcaster*
Jamison, Joi Nichole *media specialist, performing company executive, educator*
Sizemore, William Howard, Jr. *journalist*

Paeonian Springs
Sloyan, Patrick Joseph *journalist*

Reston
Powell, Anne Elizabeth *editor-in-chief*

Richmond
Bryan, John Stewart III *newspaper publisher*

Round Hill
Hillis, John David *broadcast executive, television producer, newswriter*

Springfield
Myers, Elissa Matulis *publishing executive, professional society administrator*

Stanardsville
Anns, Arlene Eiserman *publishing company executive*

Vienna
McElveen, Joseph James, Jr. *journalist, writer, newscaster, educator*

Virginia Beach
Goffigan, Christopher Wayne *research associate*
Robertson, Pat (Marion Gordon Robertson) *religious broadcasting executive, university president and chancellor*

Winchester
Byrd, Harry Flood, Jr. *publishing executive, retired senator*

Woodbridge
Binder, L. James *retired magazine editor, journalist*

WASHINGTON

Blaine
Miller, Ronald *journalist, critic*

Edmonds
Owen, John *retired newspaper editor*

Kirkland
Welke, Elton Grinnell, Jr. *publisher, writer*

Olympia
Harmon, Lynn Astrid *announcer, writer*

Port Angeles
Brewer, John Charles *journalist*

Port Townsend
MacLean, Barbara Hutmacher *retired journalist, writer*

Redmond
Boyle, Alan *editor*

Seattle
Blethen, Frank A. *newspaper publisher*
Boardman, David *editor-in-chief*
Bruner, Nancy J. *publishing executive*
Buckner, Philip Franklin *newspaper publisher*
Bunting, Kenneth Freeman *newspaper editor*
Cochran, Wendell Albert *science editor*
Domke, David S. *communications educator*
Fancher, Michael Reilly *editor, publishing executive*
Gwinn, Mary Ann *editor*

Hills, Regina J. *journalist*
Horsey, David *editorial cartoonist*
Lacitis, Erik *journalist*
Nash, Cynthia Jeanne *journalist*
Parks, Michael James *editor*
Savage, Daniel Keenan *columnist, editor-in-chief*
Strahilevitz, Meir *inventor, researcher, psychiatry educator*
Stricherz, Vincent C. *journalist*

Spokane
Cowles, William Stacey *newspaper publisher*
Kafentzis, John Charles *journalist, educator*
Kunkel, Richard Lester *public radio executive*
Steele, Karen Dorn *journalist*

Tacoma
Mowery, Gerald Eugene *publishing executive, writer*
Zeeck, David A. *newspaper editor*

WEST VIRGINIA

Bunker Hill
Marple, Thomas Franklin *columnist, reporter*

Charleston
Chilton, Elizabeth Easley Early *newspaper executive*
Haught, James Albert, Jr. *journalist, editor*
Ward, Ken, Jr. *journalist*

Greenville
Warner, Kenneth Wilson, Jr. *editor, publishing executive*

Parkersburg
McKenzie, Lawrence J. *composition educator*

Shepherdstown
Snyder, Joseph John *editor, lecturer, consultant, historian, writer*
Wilson, Miriam Janet Williams *publishing executive*

Weston
Billeter, Robert James *newspaper publisher*

WISCONSIN

Appleton
Malaney, Stephanie J. *reading specialist*

Fond Du Lac
Witte, Dale Andrew *choral director, educator*

Green Bay
Daley, Arthur James *retired magazine publisher*

Greendale
Kaiser, Ann Christine *magazine editor*
Pohl, Kathleen Sharon *editor*

Iola
Krause, Chester Lee *publishing executive*

Janesville
Fitzgerald, James Francis *broadcast executive*

Madison
Burgess, James Edward *publishing executive*
Burns, Elizabeth Murphy *media executive*
Drechsel, Robert Edward *journalism educator*
Gruber, John Edward *editor, historian, photographer*
Haslanger, Philip Charles *journalist*
Hopson, James Warren *publishing executive*
Hoyt, James Lawrence *journalism educator, writer*
McNelly, John Taylor *retired journalist, educator*
Wineke, William Robert *reporter, minister*
Zweifel, David Alan *newspaper editor*

Menomonie
Cutnaw, Mary-Frances *retired communications educator, writer, editor*

Milwaukee
Behrendt, David Frogner *retired journalist*
Brenner, Elizabeth (Betsy Brenner) *publishing executive*
Czarnezki, Mary Elaine *media specialist*
Farris, Trueman Earl, Jr. *retired newspaper editor*
Garcia, Astrid J. *newspaper executive*
Kaiser, Martin *editor-in-chief*
Kritzer, Paul Eric *publishing executive, lawyer*
Lee, Jack (Jim Sanders Beasley) *broadcast executive*
Otto, Jean Hammond *journalist*
Spore, Keith Kent *newspaper executive*

Waukesha
Dreyfus, Lee Sherman *international speaker*

WYOMING

Riverton
Peck, Robert A. *publishing executive, state legislator*

TERRITORIES OF THE UNITED STATES

PUERTO RICO

Bayamon
Berio, Blanca *editor, writer*

San Juan
Casiano, Kimberly *publishing executive*
Ferre, Antonio Luis *newspaper publisher*

VIRGIN ISLANDS

St John
Walker, Ronald R. *editor, educator, writer*

CANADA

ALBERTA

Edmonton
Hughes, Linda J. *newspaper publisher*

BRITISH COLUMBIA

Vancouver
Yaffe, Barbara Marlene *journalist*

NOVA SCOTIA

Glasgow
Williams, Edna Aleta Theadora Johnston *journalist*

ONTARIO

Brantford
Hanna, William Brooks *publishing executive, literary agent*

Don Mills
French, William Harold *retired newspaper editor*

North York
Gasparrini-Etheridge, Claudia *publishing executive, research scientist, writer*

Ottawa
Davey, Clark William *newspaper publisher*

Saint Catharines
Miller, Jack (John Peter Miller) *journalist*

Toronto
Cornies, Larry Alan *journalist, educator*
Dean, Geoffrey *book publisher*
Thall, Burnett Murray *retired newspaper executive*
Thomson, David Kenneth Roy *publishing executive*

QUEBEC

Montreal
Moss, David *music company executive*
Webster, Norman Eric *journalist, foundation administrator*

AUSTRALIA

Double Bay
Guerin, Didier *magazine executive*

BELGIUM

Brussels
Lewis, Jesse *editor*

CHINA

Shanghai
Prosser, Michael Hubert *communications educator*

ENGLAND

Cambridge
Kermode, Frank (John Kermode) *literary critic, educator*

London
Davis, Crispin *publishing company executive*
Fuller, Simon *music company executive, television producer*
Glocer, Thomas Henry *publishing executive*
Murdoch, Elisabeth *media company executive*
Oliver, Diane Frances *publisher, writer*
Scardino, Dame Marjorie Morris *publishing executive*

FRANCE

Levallois-Perret
Filipacchi, Daniel *publishing executive*

Paris
Lagardere, Arnaud *media company executive*

HONG KONG

Hong Kong
Laurie, James Andrew *broadcast executive, consultant, director, television executive producer, journalist*
Podd, Ann *newspaper editor*

INDIA

Manipal
Pai, Satish Upendra *publishing executive*

New Delhi
Watson, Paul *photojournalist, correspondent*

IRELAND

Dublin
O'Reilly, Sir Anthony John Francis *media company executive, former food products company executive*

ISRAEL

Savyon
Bushinsky, Jay (Joseph Mason) *journalist, news correspondent*

ITALY

Milan
Berlusconi, Marina *publishing executive*

JAPAN

Tokyo
Chang, Steve *internet security company executive*
Hakoshima, Shin-ichi *publishing executive*
Krisher, Bernard *foreign correspondent*
Petersen, Barry Rex *news correspondent*

NETHERLANDS

Amsterdam
Vinken, Pierre Jacques *publishing executive*

PERU

Lima
Yardley, Jonathan *journalist*

REPUBLIC OF KOREA

Gyumggi-do
Yoon, Hyung-Doo *publisher, educator*

Seoul
Park, Myungkark *publishing company owner, physicist*

SAUDI ARABIA

Jeddah
Basfar, Hassan Omar *communications educator*

SOUTH AFRICA

Johannesburg
Berk, Philip Woolf *journalist*

SWITZERLAND

Alpnach
Bocker, Hans Jurgen *editor-in-chief, consultant, finance educator*

ADDRESS UNPUBLISHED

Achorn, Robert Comey *retired newspaper publisher*
Agarwal, Suman Kumar *editor*
Akiyama, Carol Lynn *motion picture industry executive*
Aldrich, Patricia Anne Richardson *retired magazine editor*
Ambrose, Daniel Michael *publishing executive*
Anderberg, Roy A. *journalist*
Anders, George Charles *journalist, writer*
Anderson, Jon Stephen *newswriter*
Anderson, N. Christian III *former newspaper publisher*
Anderson-Spivy, Alexandra *arts correspondent, editor, critic, writer, historian*
Andrisani, John Anthony *editor, writer*
Annesi, Adele Mary *editor*
Antioco, John F. *former film rental company executive*
Armstrong, Douglas Dean *journalist*
Arnold, Henri *cartoonist*
Arrington, (Jack) Michael *web publishing company executive, blogger, lawyer*
Ashton, Betsy Finley *artist, broadcast journalist, author, lecturer*
Baggett, Donnis Gene *newspaper publisher*
Bailey, Janet Dee *publishing executive*
Baker, William Franklin *retired broadcast executive*
Baldassano, Corinne Leslie *radio executive*
Ball, Clyde Curtis *journalist, public information officer, public relations executive*
Baltake, Joe *film critic*
Bandow, Douglas Leighton *editor, columnist, consultant*
Barber, Gary *motion picture company executive*
Barbour, Doris LaJune *editor*
Barnett, Amy DuBois *editor-in-chief*
Baron, Susan *former publishing executive*
Barry, Dave *columnist, writer*
Beane, Clyde Earl *reporter, political organization worker*
Beck, Robert James *editor, writer, economist, consultant*
Behrmann, Joan Gail *editor*
Bennett, Amanda *former editor*
Bennett, Lerone, Jr. *retired magazine editor, author*
Benson, Terry *stage manager*
Berger, William Ernest *newspaper publisher*
Berman, Gail *former film company executive*
Berman, William H. *retired publishing company executive*
Bernheimer, Martin *music critic*
Beyer, Lisa *journalist*
Bieber-Roberts, Peggy Eilene *communications educator, editor, journalist, researcher*
Bierstedt, Peter Richard *entertainment industry consultant, lawyer*
Bingham, Jinsie Scott *broadcast company executive*
Binzen, Peter Husted *journalist*
Bishop, Gordon Bruce *journalist*
Blyth, Myrna Greenstein *publishing executive*
Boo, Katherine *newswriter*
Bornstein, Steven M. *former broadcast executive*
Borysewicz, Mary Louise *editor*
Boultbee, John Arthur *former publishing executive*
Bouvier, Linda Fritts *publishing executive*
Bowes, Frederick III *publishing executive, consultant*
Boyce, Joseph Nelson *retired journalist, consultant, educator*
Braden, Thomas Wardell *news correspondent*
Bradley, William Bryan *cable television regulator*
Bradsher, Keith Vinson *journalist*
Brady-Borland, Karen *retired reporter, columnist*
Bram, Leon Leonard *publishing company executive*
Brandt, Robert Frederic III *retired editor, journalist*
Brandt, Ronald Stirling *retired editor, researcher*
Brauer, Rhonda Lyn *publishing executive, lawyer*
Breathed, Berkeley *cartoonist*
Bresse-Rodenkirk, Robert Francis *journalist*
Brinberg, Herbert Raphael *publishing executive*
Brisbane, Arthur Seward *newspaper publisher*
Brogliatti, Barbara Spencer *retired television and motion picture executive, consultant*
Brokaw, Tom (Thomas John Brokaw) *former network news anchor*
Brooks, Andrée Aelion *journalist, educator, writer*
Brooks, Darius *music company executive*
Brooks, Kathleen *journalist*
Broude, Ronald *music publisher*
Brown, Britt *retired publishing company executive*
Brown, Les (Lester Louis) *journalist*
Brownrigg, Walter Grant *cartoonist*
Brugger, David John *media consultant*
Brumback, Charles Tiedtke *retired newspaper executive*
Bryan, Robert E. *editor*
Buchanan, John Lynn *retired broadcast executive*
Buchanan, Pat (Patrick Joseph Buchanan) *journalist, political commentator*
Buchholz, Todd *journalist, social sciences educator, consultant*
Buckwalter, Roger Jerome *editor, columnist*
Budnick, Ernest Joseph *recording industry executive*
Buhagiar, Marion *editor, writer*
Buhler, Jill Lorie *editor, writer*
Burke, Paul Norman *publishing executive, automotive executive*
Burrows, Edwin Gladding *retired broadcaster, writer, poet*
Byrne-Dempsey, Cecelia (Cecelia Dempsey) *journalist*
Cafferty, Jack *news anchor*
Calame, Byron Edward *journalist*
Calder, Iain Wilson *publishing executive*
Callahan, Vivian *broadcast executive*
Callander, Bruce Douglas *journalist, freelance writer*
Calley, John *former motion picture company executive, film producer*
Campbell, Byron Chesser *newspaper publishing executive*
Capice, Philip Charles *retired broadcast executive*
Cardone, Bonnie Jean *freelance/self-employed photojournalist*
Cardwell, Nancy Lee *editor, writer*
Carlson, Donald Otto *magazine publisher, editor*
Carlson, Richard Warner *journalist, broadcast executive, federal agency administrator, diplomat*
Carroll, John Sawyer *educator, former newspaper editor*
Carter, Betsy L. *editor, writer*
Chase, William Robert *television executive*
Chast, Roz *cartoonist*
Chercover, Murray *television executive*
Chernichaw, Mark *broadcast, cable television, corporate communications and advertising executive, television producer, director, media consultant, educator*
Christiansen, Richard Dean *retired newspaper editor*
Clark, James Covington *journalist, historian*
Clark, Peter Bruce *retired publishing executive*
Clifton, Douglas C. *retired newspaper editor*
Clymer, Adam *journalist, writer*
Cody, Aldus Morrill *retired editor, journalist, typographer*
Cohane, Heather Christina *publishing executive, editor*
Cohen, Allan Richard *broadcast executive*

Cohen, Betty L. *former broadcast executive*
Cohen, Mark Herbert *broadcast executive*
Cohn, Gary Dennis *journalist, educator*
Colacello, Bob (Robert John Colacello) *magazine editor, writer*
Coleman, Earl Maxwell *publishing company executive*
Collins, Gail *former newspaper editor*
Collins, J. Michael *retired public broadcasting executive*
Collins, Walter Lloyd George *editor*
Colombo, Rose Marie *freelance/self-employed newswriter, television personality*
Combs, Sean (Diddy) *record company executive, producer*
Cooke, Robert William *retired science journalist*
Cooper, Charles Howard *retired photojournalist, retired publishing executive*
Cornett, Gregg *publishing and computer company executive, editor*
Cowher, Bill (William Laird Cowher) *sportscaster, former professional football coach*
Crabbs, Roger Alan *publishing executive, director, small business owner, military officer, educator*
Crewdson, John Mark *journalist, writer*
Croan, Robert James *music critic*
Crutchfield, James N. *publishing executive*
Culliton, Barbara J. *publishing executive*
Cullum, Lee Brooks *journalist*
Curry, Carlton E. *broadcast and waterworks executive, councilman*
Curtis, Mary E. (Mary Horowitz) *publishing executive*
Dahlburg, John-Thor Theodore *news correspondent*
Dahlman, Simon Jacques *journalist, educator*
Dahlstrom, Becky Joanne *journalist*
Danzig, Frederick Paul *newspaper editor*
Davatzes, Nickolas *retired broadcast executive*
Davis, Donald Alan *news correspondent, writer, lecturer*
Davis, Jack Wayne, Jr. *retired publishing executive*
Dawson, Virginia Sue *retired editor*
Dean, Carole Lee *film company executive*
DeBakey, Selma *communications educator, writer, editor*
Dedman, Bill *journalist*
Denious, Sharon Marie *retired publishing executive*
Dennison, Shirley Ann *publishing executive*
Denver, Eileen Ann *retired editor*
Deoul, Kathleen Boardsen *publishing executive*
Desbarats, Peter Hullett *journalist, educator, academic administrator*
Dickman, James Bruce *photojournalist*
Dietrich, William Alan *reporter, writer*
Dills, James Arlof *retired publishing executive*
Disney, Roy Edward *broadcasting company executive*
Ditka, Mike (Michael Keller Ditka Jr.) *sports commentator, former professional football coach*
Dobbs, Lou (Louis Earl Dobbs) *commentator, former broadcast executive*
Doctor, Kenneth Jay *digital content consultant*
Doctorow, Cory *blogger, writer*
Doerper, John Erwin *journal editor, publishing executive*
Dolan, Michael J. *former multi media company and advertising executive*
Dolgen, Jonathan L. *former motion picture company executive*
Domjan, Laszlo Karoly *journalist*
Donald, Aida DiPace *retired publishing executive*
Donovan, Brian *freelance/self-employed journalist*
Downing, Kathryn M. *former newspaper publishing executive, lawyer*
Dracos, Theodore Michael *journalist, television producer*
Drake, Donald Charles *journalist, playwright*
Dudman, Richard Beebe *journalist*
Duduit, Michael *editor, academic administrator*
Duerr, Herman George *retired publishing executive*
Dumanoski, Dianne *journalist, writer*
Duncan, David Ewing *editor, writer*
Dunham, Benjamin Starr *editor, art association administrator*
Dwan, Dennis Edwin *broadcast executive, photographer*
Dyer, Susan Kristine *editor, librarian*
Dyson, Esther *editor-in-chief*
Edelson, Zelda Sarah Toll *retired editor, artist*
Edgren, Gretchen Grondahl *magazine editor*
Edwards, Geoffrey Hartley *newspaper publisher*
Eisner, Peter Norman *journalist, writer*
Elkie, Kimberly K. *medical editor*
Elliott, Stuart Jay *editor, journalist*
Ellis, Robert Harry *retired broadcast executive, academic administrator*
Endicott, William F. *journalist*
Enger, Edward Henry, Jr. *retired editor, writer*
Erlicht, Lewis Howard *broadcasting company executive*
Ervin, Kathleen Gwen *journalist*
Evans, Linda Kay *publishing executive*
Farnsworth, Elizabeth *broadcast journalist*
Fenech, Daniel Thomas *cartoonist*
Fenton, Thomas Trail *journalist*
Fenwick, James Henry *editor, writer, columnist*
Ferber, Samuel *publishing executive*
Fernald, Harold Allen *publishing executive*
Fiedler, Tom (Thomas Edward Fiedler) *retired editor*
Fisher, Barbara A. *former broadcast executive*
Fisher, Robert Charles Haru *publishing executive, editor*
Fitzpatrick, Nancy Hecht *editor*
Flickinger, Joe Arden *telecommunications educator, department chairman*
Florescu, John Maurice *broadcast executive*
Flournoy, John Craig *journalism educator*
Fodiman, Aaron Rosen *publishing executive*
Foglesong, James Staton (Jim) *retired music company executive*
Forman, Leonard P. *former publishing executive*
Frackman, Noel *art critic*
Francke, Linda Bird *journalist*
Frederickson, Christine Magnuson *reporter, researcher, editor, writer*
Freed, Richard (Donald) *music critic*
French, Mary B. *editor, photographer, poet, retired literature educator*
Freston, Tom (Thomas E. Freston) *former broadcast executive*
Fromm, Joseph *retired editor, foreign correspondent, foreign affairs consultant*
Gandolf, Raymond L. *media correspondent*
Garfield, Robert Edward *journalist*
Gartenberg, Seymour Lee *retired recording industry executive*
Geiger, Beth C. *freelance/self-employed journalist*
Geller, Glenn *broadcast executive*
Gendron, George *magazine editor*
Giles, William Elmer *editor*
Gill, Henry Herr *photojournalist*
Gist, John Montfort *publishing executive, educator*
Golden, Louis Joseph *retired editor, publishing executive*
Goldsborough, Robert Gerald *publishing executive, author*
Goode, Stephen Hogue *publishing executive*
Goodkin, Michael Jon *publishing company executive*
Goodwin, Irwin *journalist, writer*
Gora, Susannah Porter Martin *journalist, poet*
Gotman, John Andrew *freelance/self-employed journalist*
Gottlieb, Robert Adams *editor, dance critic, writer*
Graham, Laurie *editor, writer*
Gralla, Lawrence *publishing company executive*
Grann, Phyllis E. *editor, former publisher executive*
Gray, Gordon L. *communications educator*
Green, John *radio broadcast editor and author*
Greene, Robert (Bob) Bernard, Jr. *news correspondent, journalist, writer*
Greenwald, John Edward *publishing executive, journalist*
Greenwood, William Warren *journalist*
Gregory, Bettina Louise *retired journalist*
Gregory, James Alexander *editor, writer, film producer*
Groskopf, Aubrey Bud *broadcast executive, lawyer*
Gross, Pamela H. *editor*
Grushow, Sandy *broadcast executive*
Guerrero, Lisa (Lisa Guerrero-Coles) *former sports reporter*
Gulledge, Sandra Smith *publishing executive, film producer*
Hagel, Raymond Charles *publishing company executive, educator*
Haile, L. John, Jr. *journalist, publishing executive*
Halfen, David *retired publishing executive*
Hall, Teresa Ruth *publishing executive*
Ham, Sommy L. *publisher, writer*
Hamill, Pete (William Pete Hamill) *newspaper columnist, author, editor*
Hammond, Caleb Dean III *publishing executive*
Harbert, Ted (Edward W. Harbert III) *broadcast executive*
Hardcastle, Marcia E. (Marcia E. Temme) *retired journalist*
Harden, Patrick Alan *journalist*
Harrison-Jervay, Evelyn Yvonne *publishing executive*
Harrop, Thomas *publishing company executive*
Harvey, Lynne Cooper *broadcast executive, civic worker*
Harwell, William Earnest (Ernie Harwell) *retired commentator*
Hatfield, Julie Stockwell *journalist*
Havemann, Joel *editor*
Hayes, Colleen Ballard *journalist, photographer, writer*
Hecht, Laurence M. *editor, political organization worker*
Hedberg, Paul Clifford *broadcast executive*
Heimbold, Margaret Byrne *publisher, poet, consultant, realtor*
Henry, Frances Ann *retired journalist, educator*
Herguth, Robert John *retired columnist*
Hering, Doris Minnie *dance critic*
Herman, Andrea Maxine *newspaper editor*
Hey, Robert Pierpont *retired editor*
Heyward, Andrew John *former broadcast executive*
Higdon, Hal *sportswriter*
Hiltzik, Michael *journalist*
Hinshaw, Edward Banks *retired broadcast executive*
Hirsch, George Aaron *publishing executive*
Hobson, Jade *journalist, consultant*
Hochschild, Adam *journalist*
Holbrook, Jay Mack *publishing company executive*
Holch, Gregory John *editor, writer*
Holdridge, Barbara *book editor, writer, consultant*
Holland, David Thurston *former editor*
House, Karen Elliott *former publishing executive, editor, journalist*
Hudlin, Reginald Alan *broadcast executive, film director, writer*
Huey, Ward L(igon), Jr. *retired media executive*
Hurd, Byron Thomas *retired publishing executive*
Huston, Margo *journalist*
Idaszak, Jerome Joseph *economic journalist*
Ienner, Donald S. *former recording industry executive*
Impoco, Jim *editor*
Irvin, Michael Jerome *sportscaster, retired professional football player*
Ismach, Arnold Harvey *retired journalism educator*
Jackson-Leslie, Llenda Diane *media consultant*
James, Bruce Richard *publishing executive*
Jensen, Michael Charles *journalist, lecturer, author*
Jinks, Robert Larry *retired newspaper publisher*
Johnson, Charles *political blogger*
Johnson, John *broadcast journalist, artist*
Johnson, William Potter *publishing executive, director*
Johnston, Catherine Viscardi *former magazine publisher*
Jones, Andrew Zimmerman *editor, writer*
Jones, David Rhodes *editor, consultant*
Jones, Joe Kenley *journalist*
Jones, Leonade Diane *media publishing company executive*
Jordan, Marvin Evans, Jr. *record company executive, vocalist, actor, composer*
Joseph, Michael Thomas *broadcast consultant*
Juran, Sylvia Louise *retired editor*
Kamen, Paula *journalist, playwright*
Kamin, Blair Douglass *architecture critic*
Kan, Yue-Sai *journalist, writer, television personality, entrepreneur, humanitarian*
Kaplan, Robert David *journalist*
Karalekas, Anne *media executive*
Karol, Michael Alan *editor*
Kayse, Kathleen *publishing executive*
Kelleher, Timothy John *retired publishing company executive*
Kent, Philip I. *broadcast executive, communications executive*
Key, Ted *cartoonist*
Kilpatrick, James Jackson, Jr. *columnist, writer*
Kimball, George Edward III *sports columnist*
King, Glen (Lenard Glen King) *broadcasting educator, composer*
King, John Charles Peter *editor, writer*
King, Robert Thomas *editor, writer*
Kinsley, Michael E. *newspaper columnist*
Kirkland, Richard Ide (Rik), Jr. *magazine editor*
Kisor, Henry Du Bois *retired editor, columnist, critic, writer*
Kleinberg, Howard J. *newswriter*
Koltun, Frances Lang *editor, publisher, broadcaster*
Koren, Edward Benjamin *cartoonist, educator*
Kornbluth, Jesse *editor, writer*
Kosner, Edward A(lan) *editor*
Kotz, Nathan Kallison (Nick Kotz) *news correspondent, author*
Kraslow, David *retired publishing executive, writer, consultant, reporter*
Krauthammer, Charles *columnist, editor*
Kuehn, James Marshall *newspaper editor*
Laidlaw, Robert Richard *retired publishing executive*
Lamarre, Meaghan *internet communications specialist*
Lamont, Lee *music company and communications executive*
Lander, Howard *entertainment newspaper publisher*
Landes, William-Alan *film company executive*
Lane, Shawn Lanard *journalist, motivational speaker*
Langer, Ralph Ernest *journalist, retired editor*
Lape, Robert Cable *broadcast journalist*
Lawler, John A. *publishing executive*
LeBrecht, Thelma Jane Mossman *retired reporter*
Lederer, Edith Madelon *journalist*
Leidel, Katherine *journalist, newscaster*
Lelyveld, Joseph Salem *former newspaper editor, news correspondent, writer*
Leonard, Richard Hart *journalist, educator*
Letterie, Kathleen *broadcast executive*
Levey, Robert Frank *columnist, not-for-profit fundraiser*
Lewin, Tamar (Katherine Lewin) *reporter*
Lewis, Anthony *columnist, educator*
Lewis, Leslie Joy *music company executive, consultant*
Li, Qin *news anchor, reporter, television director and producer*
Liberman, Gail Jeanne *editor*
Lieberfarb, Warren N. *digital media pioneer*
Lingle, Marilyn Felkel *journalist, columnist, writer*
Lipman, David *retired journalist, multi-media consultant*
Lipson, Allen S. *former entertainment company executive, lawyer*
Littleford, William Donaldson *retired publishing executive*
Loper, James Leaders *broadcasting executive*
Lowery, Daniel Louis *publishing executive*
Lozano, Monica Cecilia *publishing executive*
Lucier, P. Jeffrey *publishing executive*
Maclin, Amy *editor*
Maharidge, Dale Dimitro *journalist, educator, writer*
Main, Robert Gail *communications educator, training services executive, television and film producer, retired military officer*
Majeed, D. Hadayai S. *publishing executive, writer*
Malloy, Michael Terrence *journalist, reporter*
Manley, Joan A(dele) Daniels *retired publishing executive*
Mann, Merlin Dean III *blogger*
Marcus, Greil Gerstley *critic*
Marken, William Riley *editor-in-chief*
Marmer, Nancy *editor*
Marro, Anthony James *retired newspaper editor*
Marsh, Joan Knight *educational film company executive, video company executive, publishing executive*
Martin, Donald Walter *editor, writer, publisher*
Martin, John Joseph *journalist*
Martin, Marilyn Mann *retired media specialist*
Martin, Michael John *journalist, editor*
Masket, Edward Seymour *television executive*
Mason, John Oliver *freelance journalist, community activist, poet*
Matthews, Rondra J. *publishing executive*
Mazzilli, Lee *sportscaster, former professional baseball manager*
McAniff, Nora P. *former publishing executive*
McCarty, Thomas Joseph *publishing executive*
McDarrah, Gloria Schoffel *editor, writer*
McFarling, Usha Lee *journalist*
McFeatters, Ann Carey *journalist*
McGuirk, Terrence *former broadcasting company executive*
McGurk, Christopher Jamie *film company executive*
McHale, Judith A. (Judith Ottalloran) *former broadcast executive, lawyer*
McIntyre, Bruce Herbert *media consultant, marketing professional*
McLaughlin, Leighton Bates, II, *retired journalist, reporter, educator*
McManus, Jason Donald *retired editor-in-chief*
McManus, Patrick Francis *editor, educator, writer*
McManus, Sean Joseph *broadcast executive*
McWethy, John Fleetwood *journalist*
Mead, Jean Henry *freelance/self-employed photojournalist*
Means, Marianne *columnist*
Mears, Walter Robert *retired journalist*
Medavoy, Mike *film company executive, producer*
Mellema, Donald Eugene *retired radio news reporter and anchor*
Melody, Michael Edward *publishing company executive*
Menaker, Daniel *former publishing executve*
Meriwether, Heath J. *newspaper consultant, retired publisher, educator*
Mesrobian, Arpena Sachaklian *publishing executive, consultant, editor*
Mestres, Ricardo A. III *film company executive*
Metoyer, Pamela Paradis *scientific editor, writer*
Meyer, Pucci *editor*
Meyers, John Allen *magazine publisher*
Michaels, Marion Cecelia *newswriter, editor, news syndicate executive*
Miles, Frank Charles *retired newspaper executive*
Miller, Darcy M. *publishing executive*
Miller, Donald LeSessne *publishing executive*
Miller, Judith A. (Judy Miller) *retired journalist*
Miller, Norman Charles, Jr. *editor, reporter*
Mills, Dale Douglas *journalist*
Millsaps, William Hobart, Jr. *retired editor*
Mitchell, Rick *journalist, writer*
Monacelli, Gianfranco *publishing executive*
Mondlin, Marvin *publisher, appraiser, consultant*
Montgomery, Cliff Wilson *journalist, writer, researcher*
Moore, Oliver Semon III *publishing executive, consultant*
Moore, Thomas Paul *retired broadcast executive*
Mora, Antonio Gonzalez III *broadcast journalist*
Morgan, Anne Marie G. *broadcast journalist, educator*
Mottola, Tommy (Thomas D. Mottola) *recording industry executive*
Moyer, J. Keith *former publishing executive*
Mudd, Roger Harrison *newscaster, educator*
Mulligan, Brian C. *film company executive*
Nachman, Gerald Weil *columnist, critic, writer*
Nash, Richard Edin *publishing executive*
Neff, Donald Lloyd *news correspondent, writer*
Newbauer, John Arthur, Jr. *editor*
Newman, Edwin Harold *news commentator*
Newman, Rachel *editor*
Nijhuis, Michelle *freelance journalist*
Novick, Julius Lerner *theater critic, educator*
Nye, Dorothy Mae *freelance journalist, educator*
Oakley, Andrew Arthur *journalist, educator*
Obermayer, Herman Joseph *newspaper publisher*
O'Brien, Soledad *news anchor*
O'Brien, Timothy Andrew *journalist, writer, lawyer, educator*
Ochs, Michael *editor, librarian, music educator*
Olive, David Michael *journalist, editor*
Oppedahl, John Frederick *newspaper publisher, executive*
Osmer-McQuade, Margaret *media consultant*
Pakenham, Rosalie Muller Wright *magazine and newspaper editor*
Parcells, Bill (Duane Charles Parcells) *sportscaster, retired professional football coach*
Pareene, Alex E. *political blog editor*
Parker, Mel *editor*
Parker, Michael J. *editor, writer, researcher*
Parkyn, John William *editor, writer, columnist*
Patrick, Dan *sportscaster*
Paul, Kenneth *newspaper editor*
Pauley, Jane *newscaster, journalist*
Peacock, Mary Willa *magazine editor, consultant*
Pecker, David J. *magazine publishing company executive*
Penney, Alexandra *magazine editor-in-chief, writer*
Pepper, Jonathon L. *media executive*
Perenchio, Andrew Jerrold *film and television executive*
Perkins, Lucian *photographer*
Pesin, Ella Michele *journalist, public relations executive*
Phillips, Glynda Ann *editor*
Phillips, Stone (Lester Stockton Phillips) *newscaster*
Picower, Warren Michael *editor*
Pletcher, Eldon *retired cartoonist*
Poleway, Christopher J. *former publishing executive*
Povich, Lynn *journalist, Internet executive, editor*
Powell, Ardal *music company executive, editor*
Preddy, Raymond Randall *retired newspaper publisher, educator*
Press, Aida Kabatznick *retired editor, poet, writer*
Price, Michael Howard *journalist, critic, composer*

Price, Nelson (John Nelson Price) author, journalist
Price, Tom journalist
Priest, Jessie Shaw media specialist
Pulwers, Jack Edward news executive, writer, historian, journalism educator, lecturer, broadcaster
Quade, Vicki editor, writer, playwright, theater producer
Quinn, Charles Nicholas journalist
Radcliffe, Redonia (Donnie Radcliffe) journalist, writer
Radlauer, Steve freelance writer, journalist, producer
Raines, Howell Hiram former newspaper editor, journalist
Ramsay, Karin Kinsey publisher, educator
Randinelli, Tracey Anne magazine editor
Rapoport, Ronald Jon journalist
Rasi, Humberto Mario editor, educator
Rasor, Dina Lynn journalist, private investigator
Rayner, William Alexander retired newspaper editor, author
Read, Richard Eaton newspaper reporter
Reed, Robert N., Jr. retired announcer
Regan, Judith Terrance former publishing executive
Rich, Laura columnist
Richman, Alan magazine editor, educator
Riggs, Michael David editor, writer
Righini, Marilou Mausteller editor, consultant
Roberts, David Lowell journalist, educator
Roberts, Delmar Lee editor
Roberts, Edwin Albert, Jr. editor, journalist
Roberts, Margaret Harold editor, publisher
Roberts, Michael Joseph journalist
Rojany, Lisa Adrienne publishing company executive, writer
Rooth, Signe Alice editor, consultant
Rosett, Daniel J. film company executive
Roth, Harvey Paul retired publishing executive
Roth, Richard news correspondent
Rubenstein, Atoosa Behnegar former editor-in-chief
Rugaber, Walter Feucht, Jr. retired publishing executive, academic administrator
Rushnell, Squire Derrick writer, speaker, television executive
Russell, James Brian broadcast executive, media consultant
Sabbatini, Marcello journalist, motor sports weekly director
Sabol, Steve film company executive
Salinas, Rodney Jay C. media company executive
Salvatore, Diane J. editor-in-chief
Samuelson, Robert Jacob journalist
Sanders, Marlene news correspondent, journalism educator
Sanders, Vanessa journalist, writer
Sanger, Lawrence Mark editor-in-chief
Sapsowitz, Sidney H. entertainment and media company executive
Sarris, Andrew George film critic
Satz, Louis K. publishing executive
Saunders, Stacy Dawn journalist, music educator, vocalist
Saxon, Wolfgang Erik Georg journalist, writer
Scannell, Herb broadcast executive
Schlothauer, Shirley Norton retired media consultant, writer
Schneider, Howard Stewart former newspaper editor
Schneiderman, David Abbott former publishing executive
Schorr, Daniel Louis broadcast journalist, author, lecturer
Schrand, Richard Henry, Sr. broadcast executive, advertising bureau owner, educator
Schurenberg, Eric magazine editor
Scogin, Troy Pope publishing executive, finance company executive
Seals, Margaret Louise Crumrine retired journalist
Sedas, D(anna) Michelle editor
Seigenthaler, John Michael newscaster
Seligman, Nicole K. broadcast executive, lawyer
Seminara, Lynda Anne editor
Shaevitz, Geoff film company executive
Shapiro, Richard Charles publishing executive, sales executive, marketing professional
Shelton, Stephani broadcast journalist, consultant
Shoemaker, William C. journalist
Shulgasser-Parker, Barbara critic, writer
Sidney, Corinne Entratter retired journalist, actress
Siegal, Allan Marshall journalist, consultant
Siegel, Vivian biomedical editor
Sifton, David Whittier retired magazine editor
Silvey, Anita Lynne editor
Simmons, Debra Adams editor
Simmons, Russell recording industry executive
Simon, David Judah reporter
Simon, Peter E. publishing executive
Simons, Lewis Martin journalist
Simonson, Lee Stuart broadcast executive
Simpson, Hugh L. news correspondent, newswriter
Sinclair, Carole publishing executive, editor
Sites, Kevin news correspondent, journalist, web blogger
Skinner, Thomas broadcast executive
Smith, A. Robert editor, author
Smith, George Drury publishing executive
Smith, Martin Bernhard retired journalist
Smith, Richard Alan publishing and specialty retailing executive
Soeteber, Ellen journalist, editor
Spanfeller, James John, Jr. publishing executive
Sparkman, Robin Hamilton editor-in-chief
Speerstra, Karen M. former publishing executive
Spence, James Robert, Jr. broadcast executive, educator
Sperling, Irene R. publishing executive
Spitaleri, Vernon Rosario newspaper publisher, manufacturing company executive
Stall, William Read retired newswriter
Stamaty, Mark Alan cartoonist, writer, artist
Stanley, Scott, Jr. editor
Stanton, John Jeffrey editor, director, journalist, government agency administrator, educator
Stauderman, Albert Philip, Jr. media production consultant
Stennett, William Clinton (Clint Stennett) television station executive, state legislator
Stephens, Edward Carl communications educator, writer
Stephenson, Toni Edwards publishing executive, investment company executive, communications executive
Steptoe, Sonja journalist
Stickney, John editor
Stiff, Robert Martin newspaper editor
Stock, Stephen Michael broadcast journalist
Strothman, James Edward editor-in-chief
Stuart, Nancy Rubin (Nancy Zimman Stetson) journalist, writer, television producer
Stutz, Pearl Hewlett retired photojournalist
Sullivan, Daniel Joseph theater critic
Sullivan, Dennis James, Jr. retired hospitality and music executive
Switzer, Maurice Harold journalist
Synclair, Larry Ross news correspondent, educator, advocate
Taati, Poopak media director
Talese, Nan Ahearn freelance/self-employed publishing executive
Tammeus, William David journalist, columnist
Tata, Giovanni publishing executive
Taylor, George Frederick newspaper publisher, editor
Teagan, John Gerard publishing executive
Terry, Clifford Lewis journalist
Teubner, Ferdinand Cary, Jr. retired publishing executive
Tharpe, Frazier Eugene journalist
Thomas, Jo journalist, educator
Thomas, Patricia Goodnow journalist
Thompson, Martin Christian retired news executive
Thornton, Thomas Noel former publishing executive
Thrall, Richard Cameron, Jr. broadcast executive
Threlkeld, Richard Davis retired broadcast journalist
Tierney, Brian Patrick publishing executive, former advertising and public relations executive
Toay, Thelma M. columnist, poet
Tobias, Andrew Previn columnist, educator
Triece, Anne Gallagher magazine publisher
Trudeau, Garretson Beekman (Garry Trudeau) cartoonist
Trueman, William Peter Main broadcaster, columnist
Turek, Sonia Fay journalist
Turnley, David Carl photojournalist
Twigg-Smith, Thurston newspaper publisher
Tyson Li, Laura journalist
Ulevich, Neal Hirsh photojournalist
Urbano, Juan Antonio broadcast executive, television producer, television director
Urdang, Laurence editor, publishing executive
Vafiadis, Jon recording industry executive
Vanbiesbrouck, John hockey analyst, retired professional hockey player
Vaughan, Samuel Snell editor, writer, publishing executive
Verdery, David Norwood broadcast programming executive
Viegas, Jennifer journalist, writer
Vieth, Christopher W. former publishing executive
Vincent, Charles Eagar, Jr. sportswriter
Vitale, Ruth Ann former film company executive
Wagman, Robert John journalist, writer
Waldmeir, Peter Nielsen retired journalist
Walker, Fred Elmer broadcast executive
Wallace, Mike (Myron Leon Wallace) newscaster, television personality
Walsh, George William publishing company executive, editor, author
Washburn, Gladys Rice photojournalist, educator
Waters, Betty Lou newspaper reporter, writer
Waters, Lou news correspondent
Watson, Catherine Elaine journalist
Watson, George Henry, Jr. broadcaster, journalist
Weaver, Franklin Thomas retired newspaper executive
Weaver, Howard C. newspaper executive
Weber, Carl publishing executive, retail bookstore executive, writer
Weissman, Jack (George Anderson) retired editor
Welsh, Dorothy Dell columnist, writer
Welsome, Eileen journalist, writer
Werman, Thomas Ehrlich record producer
Weymouth, Elizabeth (Lally) Graham editor, columnist
Whipple, Judith Roy retired editor
Whitesell, John Edwin retired motion picture company executive
Whittell, Polly (Mary Kaye Whittell) editor, journalist
Whittemore, Brian media consultant, advertising executive
Wies, Barbara publishing executive, editor
Wiessler, David Albert news correspondent
Wilkens, Lenny (Leonard Randolph Wilkens Jr.) sportscaster, former professional sports team executive, retired professional basketball player
Wille, Wayne Martin retired editor
Willis, Clayton broadcaster, former government official, educator, arts consultant
Wilson, James Reid, Jr. publishing executive
Windhauser, John William retired journalism educator, consultant
Winter, Judy Elaine freelance/self-employed journalist, speaker
Witcover, Jules Joseph columnist, writer
Wixen, Joan Saunders journalist
Wodlinger, Mark Louis broadcast executive
Woerner, Robert Eugene retired editor, writer
Woestendiek, John, Jr., (William John Woestendiek) newspaper reporter
Woldt, Harold Frederick, Jr. newspaper publishing executive
Wolfman, Ira Joel editor, writer
Wood, Marian Starr publishing executive
Woodruff, Judy Carline broadcast journalist
Woodruff, Virginia broadcast journalist, writer
Wooten, James Terrell journalist
Yack, Patrick Ashley editor
Yates, Ronald Eugene newspaper editor, educator, author, journalist
Young, Patrick editor, writer
Zahn, Paula newscaster
Zappe, John Paul city editor, newspaper executive, educator
Zerman, Melvyn Bernard retired publishing executive, writer
Ziegler, Jack (Jack Denmore) cartoonist
Zimmerman, William Edwin editor, writer

EDUCATION See also specific fields for postsecondary education

UNITED STATES

ALABAMA

Alabaster
McChesney, Robert Michael, Sr. retired academic administrator

Athens
Baird, Debra dean, education educator
Smith, Patricia Crawford elementary school educator

Auburn
Galbraith, Ruth Legg retired dean, home economist
Jones, Allen history educator, archivist
Miller, Wilbur Randolph academic administrator
Philpott, Harry Melvin former university president
Shippen, Margaret Ellen special education educator
Voitle, Robert Allen dean, physiologist
Zallen, Harold academic administrator, chemist

Auburn University
Dodge, Timothy de K. school librarian
Gibson, Keith E. education educator
Gogue, Jay (G. Jay Gogue) academic administrator
Strom, Paris Scott education educator
Wu, Chwan-Hwa John adult education educator

Bessemer
Garlikov, Patricia Moodie education educator
Stevens, Elizabeth McCartha secondary school educator

Birmingham
Berte, Neal Richard academic administrator
Deal, William Brown medical school dean, physician, educator
Garrison, Carol Z. academic administrator
Koomullil, Roy Paulose mechanics and engineering educator
Kreisberg, Robert A. dean, medical educator
Lisovicz, Nedra Ford director
Mc Callum, Charles Alexander academic administrator
McKinley, Cameron Sharbel elementary school educator
Morgan, Kathryn Diane criminology educator
Morgan, Michael Darold academic administrator
Morrisey, Michael A. health economics educator
Pollick, G. David academic administrator, philosopher
Rogers, Betsy elementary school educator
Thomas, Huw Francis dean, dental educator
Ward, Perry W. college president
Westmoreland, Andrew academic administrator
Wheeler, Susie Weems retired school system administrator

Brilliant
Franks, Gracie G. elementary school educator

Citronelle
Surry, Melinda Owen reading coach

Coosada
Reynolds, Linda Ann elementary school educator

Crossville
Blessing, Maxine Lindsey secondary school educator

Decatur
Julich, Nancy C. secondary school educator
Powell, Valerie Jean elementary school educator
Smith, Trina academic administrator

Dothan
Fleming, Jennie M retired education educator
Flowers, V. Anne retired academic administrator

Eufaula
Conniff, Alexandra Acosta secondary school educator

Falkville
Templeton, Richard Raymond special education educator, consultant

Grand Bay
Taylor, Anne Wilkerson elementary school educator

Hanceville
Holmes, Kristen Jones academic administrator

Helena
Coulter, Fern Goshen retired secondary school educator

Huntsville
Baird, James Kern educator, consultant, academic administrator
Franz, Frank Andrew academic administrator, physicist, educator
Hawley, Harold Patrick educational consultant
Lundquist, Charles Arthur academic administrator
Moore, Ann Roy school system administrator
Morgan, Beverly Hammersley secondary school educator, artist
Ratchford Merchant, Betty Jo retired elementary school educator
Smothers, Deloris Rice computer career educator
Turner, Mary Alice curriculum specialist

Jacksonville
Dunaway, William Preston retired school system administrator

Jasper
Rowland, David Jack retired academic administrator
Sparkman, Brandon Buster secondary school educator, consultant, writer

Leeds
Wilson, Maggie Isabelle Lovell secondary school educator

Livingston
Day, Richard M. computer educator
Green, Asa Norman academic administrator
Holland, Richard D. academic administrator

Madison
Brannan, Eulie Ross educational consultant
Gibson, John Thomas academic administrator, consultant
Jones, Christine Regina secondary school educator
Petty, Margaret elementary school educator

Marion
Cleveland, Willie Mae elementary school educator

Maylene
Copes, Marvin Lee academic administrator

Mobile
Collins, Harold R. director
Rewak, William John retired academic administrator, clergyman
Sumlin, Margaret (Margie) Brown special education educator

Montgomery
Jewell, Jason Eric adult education educator
Kennedy, Kamela Denise director
May, Cecil Richard, Jr. academic administrator
Morton, Joseph school system administrator
Tennimon, Dannie Earl academic administrator, educator

Moody
Brasher, Terrie Walker secondary school educator

Phenix City
Romey, Barbara Sassmann gifted and talented educator

Seale
Harris-Stokes, Joyce A. secondary school educator

Selma
Inge, DeAndres Gates mathematics educator

Sumiton
Rizzo, Stephen Wayne Burton secondary school educator, music minister

Troy
Davidson, Barry Sheldon academic administrator, comparative and adult education educator

Tuscaloosa
McNealey, Ernest college president
Randall, Kenneth C. dean, law educator
Rankin, Margaret McIsaac elementary school educator
Thomas, Joab Langston retired academic administrator, biologist, educator
Witt, Robert E. academic administrator

Tuskegee
Green, Elbert P. retired academic administrator

Vernon
Maddox, Frederick Lynn mathematics educator

Webb
Knowles, Julie Nall secondary school educator

ALASKA

Anchorage
Byrd, Milton Bruce academic administrator
Comeau, Carol Smith school system administrator
Davis, Bettye Jean school system administrator, state legislator
North, Douglas McKay academic administrator
Sandberg, Arlene elementary school educator

Thurber, Sharon Lee *elementary resource educator*
Ulmer, Frances Ann *academic administrator, retired state official*

Auke Bay
Waldrip, Karen Marie *career planning administrator*

Barrow
Blankenship, Trent *school system administrator, educator*

Chiniak
Griffin, Elaine B. *educator*

Dillingham
Bouker, Ina B. *elementary school educator*

Eagle River
Sparks, Jack Norman *dean*

Fairbanks
Doran, Timothy Patrick *academic administrator*
Hamilton, Mark R. *academic administrator*
Jones, Stephen B. *academic administrator*
Mayer, Sister Patricia E. *elementary school educator*

Juneau
Pugh, John Robert *academic administrator, educator, retired state official*
Sampson, Roger *school system administrator*

Wrangell
Miller, Jennifer L. *elementary school educator, small business owner*

ARIZONA

Anthem
Bennett, Sister Elsa Mary *retired secondary school educator*

Chandler
Casteel, Camille *school system administrator*
Fons, Margaret E. *elementary school educator*

Chinle
Hodson, William David *elementary school educator, consultant*

Desert Hills
Evans, Carol Ann *reading specialist*

Flagstaff
Baron, Patricia Burrell *university director*
Haeger, John Denis *academic administrator*

Fountain Hills
Sorenson, Gretchen Hartley *elementary school educator*
Wright, C. T. Enus *former academic administrator*

Glendale
Cota, Lisa Foley *secondary school educator*
Sweat, Ken Gunter *educator, consultant*

Goodyear
Molina, Tanya E. *school librarian*

Green Valley
Fuer-Davis, Beverly Jean *retired elementary school educator*
Smith, Raymond Lloyd *former university president, consultant*

Lakeside
Mack, Ina Leah *secondary school educator, pre-school administrator*
Seely, Dennis M. *secondary school educator*

Mesa
de Masi, Kenneth Forrest *secondary school educator*
Dillenberg, Jack *dean*
Duvall, Debra *school system administrator*
Hundley, Shelli *mathematics educator*
Molina-Walters, Debi Ann *education educator*
Weber, Yvonne Roebuck *research administrator, educator*

Peoria
Jenkins, Carol Anne *educator*

Phoenix
Comer, James V. *academic administrator*
Coor, Lattie Finch *university president*
Coyle, Linda Marie *elementary school educator*
Culnon, Sharon Darlene *special education educator, reading specialist*
Freeman, Stacey Vicario *director, model*
Frehner, Patricia Ann *education educator, consultant*
Lee, Barbara S. *special education educator*
McConnell, Albert Lynn *director*
Noone, Laura Palmer *academic administrator, lawyer*
Pepicello, William J. *academic administrator*
Peralta, Everett Figueroa *education educator, department chairman*
Schrader, Susan Rae *elementary school educator*
Sperling, John Glen *education company executive, educator*
Udall, Vesta Hammond *special education educator*
Yamamoto, Alice M. *secondary school educator*

Pinetop
Gilbert-Tiegs, Marion Ann *gifted and talented educator, consultant*

Prescott
Rinde, Andrea J. *mathematics educator*
Waterer, Bonnie Clausing *retired secondary school educator*

Rio Verde
Vanselow, Neal Arthur *retired academic administrator, internist*

San Luis
Kryger, Jerri Renee *elementary school educator*

Scottsdale
Hill, Louis Allen, Jr. *retired dean, civil engineer, consultant*
Phillips, Wanda Charity *secondary school educator, writer*
Stone, Alan Jay *retired academic administrator*
Wilson, Robert E. *academic administrator*

Sun Lakes
Thompson, Loring Moore *retired academic administrator, writer*

Surprise
Bradford, Mariah *elementary school educator, consultant*
Burns, Clare Marie *retired elementary school educator*
Neuman, Isabel *mathematics educator*
Sawyers, Norma Ann *elementary school educator, real estate agent, property manager*

Tempe
Colgate, Catharine Pamella *secondary school educator*
Crow, Michael M. *academic administrator*
Dustman, Patricia (Jo) Allen *elementary school educator, consultant*
Haggerson, Nelson Lionel, Jr. *education educator*
Milke, Linda Jean *elementary school educator*
Mittelstaedt, Robert E., Jr. *dean*
Thor, Linda M. *college president*
Wang, Ning *education educator*
White, Patricia Denise *dean, law educator*

Tucson
Aguilar, Darla J. *adult education educator*
Bootman, J. Lyle *pharmacy educator*
Brennan, Carrie *principal*
Carney, Kevin *principal*
Janes, Raena *private school educator*
Johnson, John Gray *retired university chancellor*
Kaltenbach, C(arl) Colin *dean, educator*
Maker, Carol June *gifted and talented education educator*
Massaro, Toni Marie *dean, law educator*
Moten, Darlene *elementary school educator*
Popson, Lucy (Maria D. Popson) *elementary school educator*
Portney, Paul Rogers *dean*
Raab, Diane *special education educator*
Roberts, J. Berry *elementary school educator, sports official*
Rollins, Tony James *organizational consultant*
Shelton, Robert Neal *academic administrator, physics professor, researcher*
Stoffle, Carla Joy *university library dean*

ARKANSAS

Arkadelphia
Dunn, Charles DeWitt *academic administrator*
Elrod, Ben Moody *academic administrator*
Futrell, Alvin *director*
Grant, Daniel Ross *retired academic administrator*

Bald Knob
Barber, Leah Adrianne *elementary school educator, literacy educator*

Conway
Cloyd, J. Timothy *academic administrator*

Earle
Swift, Peggy Lynette *elementary school educator*

Farmington
Schoppmeyer, Martin William, Jr. *school system administrator*

Fayetteville
Ferritor, Daniel E. *retired chancellor*
Schoppmeyer, Martin William *education educator*
Smith, Robert Victor *academic administrator, educator*
White, John Austin, Jr. *academic administrator, engineering educator*

Fort Smith
Gooden, Benny L. *school system administrator*

Hindsville
Peirce, Carole *elementary school educator*

Hot Springs
Farris, Jefferson Davis *university administrator*
Hugo, Janet *director*

Jonesboro
Malinsky, Marci Ann *education educator*
Smith, Eugene Wilson *retired academic administrator, education educator*

Little Rock
Banks, Alicia *elementary school educator*
Bass, Evelyn Elizabeth *elementary school educator*
Fribourgh, James Henry *retired university administrator*
James, T. Kenneth *school system administrator*
McIntyre, Nina M. *counseling administrator*
Pennington, Jodie A. *education outreach educator*
Truex, Dorothy Adine *retired university administrator*
Whitlow, Mary Ann *retired elementary school educator*
Wilson, I. Dodd *dean*

Magnolia
Harrison, Betty Carolyn Cook *retired education educator, administrator*

Pearcy
Burch, Bobby Joe *secondary school educator*

Pine Bluff
Jones-Woolfolk, Jerald Maxine *dean, educator*

Prairie Grove
Dunn, Anne Ewald Nefflen *retired elementary school educator*

Russellville
Morris, Lois Lawson *retired education educator*

Searcy
Burks, David Basil *academic administrator, educator*

Sherwood
Cantu, Jennifer St. John *gifted and talented educator*

Springdale
Holman, L. Charlene *elementary school educator*
Minkel, Justin *elementary school educator*

Texarkana
Petty, Marsha *chemistry educator*

White Hall
Scott, Vicki Sue *school system administrator*

CALIFORNIA

Agoura Hills
Kuzmanovic, Jane Violet *academic administrator*

Alameda
Robinson, Joanne Adele *retired secondary school educator, volunteer*
Verrill, Kathleen Wills *special education educator*

Alhambra
Suzuki, Bob H. *retired academic administrator*

Alta Loma
Campbell, Ellen Feyk *elementary school educator*
Haskvitz, Alan Paul *elementary school educator, consultant*

Anaheim
Barry, Sandra *school system administrator*
Goodspeed, Kathryn Ann *pre-school educator*
Guajardo, Elisa *counselor, educator*
Unan, George Vincent *adult education educator*

Antioch
Stamm, Barbara Marie Anderson *elementary school educator, interior designer*

Aptos
Boesewetter, William Lawrence *elementary school educator, artist*
Bohn, Ralph Carl *educational consultant*
Hirsch, Bette G(ross) *academic administrator, language educator*

Arcadia
Baltz, Patricia Ann (Pann) *retired elementary school educator*
Matsuura, Kenneth Ray *counseling administrator*

Arcata
McCrone, Alistair William *retired academic administrator*

Atherton
Lane, Joan Fletcher *academic administrator*

Azusa
Liegler, Rosemary Menke *dean*
Pacino, Maria Antonieta *education educator, department chairman*

Bakersfield
Zarra, Ernest Joseph III *secondary school educator, researcher*

Barstow
Gibbon, Mary-Lynn *special education educator*

Bass Lake
Park, Penny Sheran *retired elementary school educator*

Beaumont
Youngren, Delvana Hope *secondary school educator*

Berkeley
Birgeneau, Robert Joseph *academic administrator, physicist, researcher*
diSessa, Andrea A. *education educator*
Doyle, Fiona Mary *dean, metallurgical engineer, educator*
Freedman, David Amiel *statistics educator, consultant*
Freedman, Sarah Warshauer *education educator*
Heathcock, Clayton Howell *chemistry educator, researcher*
Linn, Marcia Cyrog *education educator*
Maurer, Stephen Mark *academic program director*
Miles, Raymond Edward *retired dean, organizational behavior and industrial relations educator*
Pearson, P. David *dean*
Shortell, Stephen Michael *dean, health services researcher*
Staff, Virgil Clinton *retired history educator*

Beverly Hills
Grant, Michael Ernest *educational administrator, management educator*

Bloomington
Lawrence, William, Jr. *retired elementary school educator*

Blythe
Wells, James Wayne *retired secondary school educator*

Brawley
Kinder, Joseph Donald *principal*

Brentwood
Groseclose, Wanda Westman *retired elementary school educator*

Calabasas
Hawkins, John N. *education educator, writer*

Camarillo
Arthington, Carol Ann *elementary school educator*
Rush, Richard R. *academic administrator*
Wakelee, Daniel William *academic administrator*

Capitola
Jackson, Kingsbury Temple *educational and financial consultant*

Carlsbad
Golding, Brage *university president*

Carmel
Faul, June Patricia *education specialist*
Freed, Sharon Lou *retired principal*

Carmichael
Friedman, Mary Kathleen *secondary school educator*
O'Leary, Marion Hugh *retired dean, chemist*
Oprsal, Nancy Upshaw *retired elementary school educator*

Carpinteria
Williams, Benjamin V., IV, *headmaster, history educator*

Carson
Mori, Allen Anthony *academic administrator, consultant*
Paige, Dorothy Billiard *retired secondary school educator, educational consultant*
Stuart, Nancy Giovinazzo *secondary school educator*

Chico
Hyde, Geraldine Veola *retired secondary school educator*
Zingg, Paul Joseph *academic administrator*

Chino
Wiegand, Penelope Tarleton *elementary school educator*

Chula Vista
Wyatt, Edith Elizabeth *elementary school educator*

Claremont
Alexander, John David, Jr. *college administrator*
Gann, Pamela Brooks *academic administrator*
Klawe, Maria Margaret *academic administrator, engineering and computer science educator*
Liggett, Thomas Jackson *retired seminary president*
Maguire, John David *academic administrator, educator, writer*
Oxtoby, David William *academic administrator, chemistry professor*
Platt, Joseph Beaven *former college president*
Skandera Trombley, Laura Elise *academic administrator, literature educator*
Stanley, Peter William *former academic administrator*
Strauss, Jon Calvert *retired academic administrator*
Weis, Frederick M. *academic administrator*

Clayton
Bower, Fay Louise *academic administrator, nursing educator*

Coronado
Kasbeer, Stephen Frederick *retired university official, investor*

Corte Madera
Dalpino, Ida Jane *retired secondary school educator*

Costa Mesa
Hara, Tadao *educational administrator*

Covina
Baker, Elenora Frances *retired elementary school educator*

Cupertino
Lyon, Mary Lou *retired secondary school educator*

Danville
Harks, Helene Louise *elementary school educator*

Davis
Biggart, Nicole Woolsey *dean*
Eastin, Delaine Andree *education educator*
Hinshaw, Virginia *academic administrator*
Kurlaender, Michal *education educator*
Perschbacher, Rex Robert *dean, law educator*
Pritchard, William Roy *former university systems administrator*
Springer, Sally Pearl *university administrator*
Tanno, John W. *university librarian*
Vanderhoef, Larry Neil *academic administrator*

Denair
Hale, Lois J. *retired mathematics educator*

Diamond Bar
Domeño, Eugene Timothy *elementary education educator, principal*

Downey
Brooks, Lillian Drilling Ashton (Lillian Hazel Church) *adult education educator*
Robles, Darline P. *school system administrator*

El Cajon
Thomas, Esther Merlene *elementary and adult education educator*

El Cerrito
Herzberg, Dorothy Crews *retired secondary school educator*

El Dorado Hills
Tierney, Kevin Allen *elementary school educator*

Elk Grove
Moe, Janet Anne *elementary school educator, church organist*

Encino
Church, Kathy Lynn *education educator, consultant*

Escondido
Carlson, Mary Lou *elementary school educator, sister*
Moore, Marc Anthony *retired academic administrator, writer, retired military officer*
Sanders, Adrian Lionel *retired educational consultant*
Walker, Patricia Ann *special education educator*

Fair Oaks
Hutton, Essex Clark, Sr. *adult education educator*
Lemke, Herman Ernest Frederick, Jr. *retired elementary school educator, consultant*

Fairfield
Mary, Diane Bradley *elementary school educator, secondary school educator*

Fountain Valley
Otto, Marie (Bertha Otto) *educational administrator, educational consulting company executive*

Fremont
Venturini, Judith Anne *education educator*

Fresno
Cornish, Bonita Clark *retired secondary school educator*
Genini, Ronald Walter *retired history educator, historian*
Misakian, Jo Ellen Priest *school librarian, dean*
Ortiz, John Michael *provost*
Stewart, Deborah Claire *dean*
Tudman, Cathi Graves *elementary school educator*
Welty, John Donald *academic administrator*

Fullerton
Donoghue, Mildred Ransdorf *education educator*
Fischer, Robert Blanchard *academic administrator, researcher*
Smith, Ephraim Philip *academic administrator*

Gardena
Hite, Janet Sue *elementary school educator*

Glendale
Whalen, Lucille *retired academic administrator*

Goleta
Everhart, Thomas Eugene *retired academic administrator, engineering educator*

Hawthorne
Brann, Donald Lewis, Jr. *school superintendent*

Hayward
Garcia, Melva Ybarra *counseling administrator, educator*
Rees, Norma S. *academic administrator*

Hermosa Beach
Zartman, Patrick Joseph *secondary school educator*

Huntington Beach
Davidson-Shepard, Gay *secondary school educator*
Houck, Aleda Jean *dean*
Ramphal, Julie Frances *retired secondary school educator*
Yglesias, Kenneth Dale *college president*

Indio
Houghton, Robert Charles *secondary school educator*

Irvine
Bryant, Susan V. *academic administrator*
Drake, Michael V. *academic administrator, ophthalmologist, educator*
Fleischer, Everly Borah *academic administrator, department chairman*
Jorion, Philippe *education educator*
Lin, Kwei-Jay *education educator, researcher*
McCubbin, Sharon A. *elementary school educator*
Munoff, Gerald J. *university librarian*
Policano, Andrew J. *dean, finance educator*
Schaefer, Ronald Dean *secondary school educator*

Jackson
Tyler, Clifford Ernest *director*

Kentfield
Dargel, Jan Kay *college administrator, institute president, lawyer*

La Canada Flintridge
Lamson, Robert Woodrow *retired school system administrator*

La Jolla
Atkinson, Richard Chatham *academic administrator, cognitive scientist*
Cavenee, Webster K. *director*
Chandler, Marsha *academic administrator, educator*
Colbert, James, Jr. *academic administrator*
Foxe, Marye Anne *academic administrator*
Gabay, Janis T. *literature and language educator*
Holmes, Edward Warren *dean, medical educator*
Karin, Michael *educator, molecular biologist, consultant*
Mah, Silvia Armitano *director, educator*
Miller, Carol *elementary school educator, counselor*
Miller, David R. *academic administrator*
Schottlaender, Brian E.C. *university librarian*
Sullivan, Robert S. *college dean*

La Puente
Chico, Darlene Ehrich *elementary school educator*
Pleitez, Concepcion Maria *elementary school educator*
Ver Kuilen, Marion Jane *retired instructional aide*

La Verne
Fleck, Raymond Anthony, Jr. *retired academic administrator*
Morgan, Stephen Charles *academic administrator*

Ladera Ranch
Skidmore, Michelle Marie *elementary school educator, principal*

Laguna Woods
Walker, Donald Ezzell *retired academic administrator*

Lake Elsinore
Druskoff, Barbara Therese *elementary school educator*

Lancaster
Strom, Susan G. *special education educator*

Live Oak
Spilman, Janet Lynne *special education educator*

Lodi
Reinold, Christy Diane *school counselor, consultant*

Loma Linda
Goodacre, Charles J. *dean, educator*
Kyle, James Lewis *dean, physician*

Long Beach
Alexander, F. King *academic administrator*
Burnett, Ella M. Glenn *education educator*
Cook, Karla Joan *elementary school educator*
Duran, Matias Martin *retired adult education educator*
Elston, Joan Wilma *adult education educator, real estate agent*
Fleming, Jane Williams *retired elementary school educator, writer*
Jeynes, William Hettich *education educator, religious organization administrator, minister*
Lathrop, Irvin Tunis *retired dean*
Lauda, Donald Paul *retired dean*
Reed, Charles Bass *chief academic administrator*
Rutherford, Vicky Lynn *special education educator*
Springer, Wilma Marie *retired elementary school educator*
Wollmer, Richard Dietrich *statistics and operations research educator*

Los Altos
Welsh, Doris McNeil *early childhood education specialist*

Los Angeles
Ansley, Julia E. *retired elementary school educator, poet, writer*
Armstrong, Lloyd, Jr. *academic administrator, physics professor*
Bernstein, Leslie *academic administrator, biostatistician, epidemiologist*
Bice, Scott Haas *dean, law educator*
Brewer, David L. III *school system administrator, retired military officer*
Chapman Collins, Janice *school system administrator*
Cheeseboro, Margrit *retired economics educator*
Colacurcio, Michael J. *English professor*
Cowan, Marie Jeanette *dean, nurse, educator*
Davis-Fernandes, Tina Denise *secondary school educator, coach*
Dewey, Donald Odell *dean, academic administrator*
Ellis, James G. *dean, finance educator*
Erdos, Joanna E. *school counselor, secondary school educator*
Fitz-Carter, Aleane *retired elementary school educator, composer*
Ghez, Andrea Mia *astronomy and physics educator*
Gilligan, Thomas W. *dean, finance educator*
Gothold, Stuart Eugene *school system administrator, education educator*
Guarnieri, Roberta Jean *elementary school educator, consultant*
Haley, Roslyn Trezevant *educational program director*
Henderson, Brian Edmond *dean, physician, educator*
Herscher, Uri David *academic administrator, history educator, rabbi*
Hill, Millicent E. *English educator*
Hoi, Samuel Chuen-Tsung *academic administrator*
Hubbard, John Randolph *retired academic administrator, diplomat*
Kleingartner, Archie *dean, educator, academic administrator*
Legohn, Lisa Marie *vocational school educator*
Levey, Gerald Saul *dean, internist, educator*
Lieber, David Lee *university president*
Lynch, Beverly Pfeifer *education and information studies educator*
Malone, Carolyn Lucia Marino *education educator*
Mandel, Joseph David *academic administrator, lawyer*
Martin, Shane Patrick *education educator, consultant*
McGregor, Judith Ann *education educator*
McKinney, Virginia Elaine Zuccaro *educational administrator*
Mentzer, Roslyn *academic administrator*
Moriuchi, K. Derek *secondary school educator*
Nakanishi, Don Toshiaki *Asian American studies educator, writer*
Needleman, Jack *education educator, researcher*
Oakes, Jeannine *education educator*
Olian, Judy D. *dean*
Park, No-Hee *dean, academic administrator*
Petak, William John *systems management educator*
Pierskalla, William Peter *dean, finance, engineering educator*
Prager, Susan Westerberg *academic administrator, law educator*
Quinlan, Catherine *university librarian*
Rasmussen, Robert Kenneth *dean, law educator*
Rosenstock, Linda *dean, medical educator*
Sample, Steven Browning *academic administrator*
Schill, Michael H. *dean, law educator*
Schuetze-Coburn, Marje *university librarian*
Shideler, Ross Patrick *literature and language educator, writer, translator, poet*
Slavkin, Harold Charles *dean, biologist*
Strong, Gary Eugene *university librarian*
Taylor, Leigh Herbert *dean*
Torres-Gil, Fernando M. *academic administrator*
Valladares-Barbush, Lisette Marie *mathematics educator*
Vredevoe, Donna Lou *academic administrator, microbiologist, educator, biomedical researcher*
Wagner, William Gerard *dean, information scientist, consultant, physicist, investment manager*
Waterman, Christopher *dean*
Wexler, Robert *academic administrator*
Wilkerson, LuAnn *dean, medical educator*
Zeithammer, Robert *adult education educator*

Lynwood
Sitomer, Alan Lawrence *literature and language educator*

Malibu
Benton, Andrew Keith *academic administrator, lawyer*
Phillips, Ronald Frank *academic administrator*
Roosa, Mark S. *dean, librarian*
Starr, Kenneth Winston *dean, lawyer*
Warder, Michael Young *academic administrator*

Menifee
Balow, Irving Henry *retired education educator*

Merced
Tomlinson-Keasey, Carol Ann *academic administrator*

Milpitas
Allen, Irma M. *adult education educator*
Ogawa, Joichi Raphael *director, consultant*

Mission Viejo
Lake, Jane Burford *special education educator, hypnotherapist, small business owner*

Modesto
Price, Robert William *school superintendent, consultant*
Tidball, Lee Falk *elementary school educator, writer*

Montebello
Lopez, Donald Robert *parochial school educator, writer*

Monterey
Oder, Broeck Newton *history educator, director*

Moreno Valley
Bajor, Renee Allyson *special education educator*
Marshall, Debra Lynn *secondary school educator*

Morgan Hill
Horning, Barbara Hortense Scheer *retired elementary school educator*

Murrieta
deVries-White, Donna Lynn *education educato consultant*

Napa
Schmidt, Hollie *secondary school educator*

Nicasio
Richardson, Jerome Lynn (Jerry Richardson) *secondary school educator*

North Hills
Deets, Richard M. *secondary school educator, consultant*

North Hollywood
Chang, Wung *academic administrator, investment advisor, educator*

Northridge
Curzon, Susan Carol *academic administrator*
Koester, Jolene *academic administrator*
Mitchell, James Andrew *education educator*
Rowlands, Kathleen Dudden *education educato*

Novato
Jaeger, Patsy Elaine *retired secondary school educator, artist*
Lane, Michele Jeanne *special education educat*
Patterson, W. Morgan *college president*

Oakland
Diaz, Sharon *education administrator*
Dibble, David Van Vlack *visually impaired educator, lawyer*
Dynes, Robert C. *academic administrator, physicist*
Gomes, Wayne Reginald *academic administrat*
Holmgren, Janet L. *academic administrator*
Kepner, William Raymond, Jr. *retired secondar school educator*
Stewart, John Lincoln *former academic administrator*

Oceanside
Daniel, Susan Qualls *secondary school educato*
Wright, Darcy Laureen *leadership educator, writer*

Ojai
Mulligan, Michael K. *headmaster*
Shagam, Marvin Hückel-Berri *private school educator*

Olivehurst
Green, Tim M. *mathematics educator*

Orange
Carriere, Brother William Joseph *school system administrator*
Christian-Brougham, Ruby Rosalie *education educator*
Hamilton, Harry Lemuel, Jr. *academic administrator, science educator*
Kraft, Arthur *dean*

Orinda
Counelis, James Steve *education educator*

Oxnard
Leedy, Wallace Curtis *former educator*

Pacific Grove
Longman, Anne Strickland *special education educator, consultant*

Pacific Palisades
Outcalt, David Lewis *academic administrator, mathematics professor, consultant, musician*

Palm Desert
Baxter, Betty Carpenter *academic administrator*
Owings, Thalia Kelley *elementary school educator*

Palo Alto
Chace, William Murdough *former university administrator, literature educator*
Dugger, Marguerite J. *retired special education educator*
Heneveld-Story, Christy Jean *educational researcher*

Palos Verdes Estates
Lazzaro, Anthony Derek *academic administrato*

Paradise
Barr, Donald Roy *statistics and operations research educator, statistician*

Pasadena
Arnold, Frances Hamilton *chemistry educator*
Baltimore, David *former academic administrato microbiologist, educator*
Becker, Christopher *educator, chef*
Bischoff, Rick *admissions director*
Chameau, Jean-Lou *academic administrator*
Douglas, Kimberly *university librarian*
Gilman, Richard Carleton *retired academic administrator*
Koshalek, Richard *academic administrator, former museum director, consultant*
Lingenfelter, Sherwood Galen *academic administrator, retired anthropologist*
Siemon-Burgeson, Marilyn M. *education administrator*
Winbush, Olga Joyce *education educator, consultant*

Petaluma
O'Hare, Sandra Fernandez *education educator*
Thomas, Nancy Hinckley *special education educator*

Placerville
Wessels-McCoy, Denise Wendy *pre-school administrator, consultant*

Playa Del Rey
Baker, Robert M.L., Jr. *academic administrator, research scientist*

Pleasant Hill
Bastrenta, Brigitte Elisabeth *school administrator*

Pleasanton
Roshong, Dee Ann Daniels *dean, educator, counselor*

Pomona
Ambrose, William Wright, Jr. *dean, educator, academic administrator*
Dishman, Rose Marie Rice *academic administrator, researcher*
Trotter, F(rederick) Thomas *retired academic administrator*

Poway
Conant, Kim Untiedt *retired elementary school educator*

Quartz Hill
Nettelhorst, Robin Paul *academic administrator, writer*

Rancho Cordova
Gosfield, Margaret *secondary school educator, school system administrator, consultant, editor*

Rancho Cucamonga
Kennedy, Mark Alan *secondary school educator*

Redlands
Simnjanovski, Riste *counseling administrator*
Wilson, Lois Fair *school system administrator, educator*

Redondo Beach
Crean, Maureen Rose *educational consultant*

Richmond
Sibitz, Michael William *school system administrator*

Ripon
Freeman, Janice Kalina *elementary school educator*

Riverside
Boldt, William Gregory *academic administrator, consultant*
Day, Renee Noelle *secondary school, special education educator, special education educator*
Fontana, Sandra Ellen Frankel *special education educator*
Geraty, Lawrence Thomas *academic administrator, archaeologist, educator*
Grey, Robert Dean *academic administrator, biology educator*
Jackson, Ruth Moore *university librarian*
Rainey, Susan J. *school system administrator*
Russo, Marisa Natalina *educational consultant*
Suyenaga, Elsie Sakae *retired elementary school educator*
Yacoub, Ignatius I. *dean*

Rocklin
Yates, Coleen Denise *special education educator*

Rohnert Park
Arminana, Ruben *academic administrator, educator*
Babula, William *dean, writer*

Sacramento
Amezcua, Esther Hernandez *elementary school educator*
Barankin, Joseph Paul *director, consultant*
Bass de Martinez, Bernice *academic administrator, consultant*
Block, Alvin Gilbert *academic director*
Bond, Linda Grace *educational consultant*
Clover, Haworth Alfred *elementary school educator, historian*
Drummond, Marshall Edward (Mark) *academic administrator*
Gerth, Donald Rogers *retired university president, educator*
O'Connell, Jack *school system administrator*
Opperman, Rosanna Resendez *vice principal*
Parker, Elizabeth Rindskopf *dean, law educator*
Pomeroy, Claire *dean*
Silva, Joseph, Jr. *dean, medical educator*
Zaidi, Emily Louise *retired elementary school educator*

Salinas
Bernhard, Nancy Lynn *secondary school educator*
Huston, Velvali deAyxa *elementary school and voice educator*
Mathews, Valinda Gail *elementary school educator, theater educator, gifted and talented educator*

San Diego
Adriaan, Saint Claire Marlin *elementary school educator*
Blas, Marlene Jambaro *academic administrator, educator*
Early, Teri Wilson (Denise Wilson) *elementary school educator, educator*
Hasl, Rudolph Carl *dean, law educator*
Idos, Margarita de Leon *elementary school educator*
Jellison, Beverly Irene *literature and language educator*
Lyons, Mary E. *academic administrator*
Maloney, Ellen Claire *elementary school educator*
Mayer, George Roy *education educator*
Meno, Lionel R. *academic administrator*
Rodenberg, Johanna Kristine *education educator, consultant*
Rodriguez, Daniel B. *dean, law educator*
Schwartz, Alfred *former dean*
Vega, Carolyn Jane *elementary educator, consultant, writer*
Weber, Stephen Lewis *academic administrator*

San Francisco
Abbott, Richard Lee *academic administrator*
Brand, Jeffrey S. *dean, law educator*
Bratton, Christopher Alan *academic administrator, videographer, art educator*
Butter, Karen Ann *school librarian*
Clifford, Geraldine Joncich *retired education educator*
Corrigan, Robert Anthony *academic administrator*
Davis, Patricia Margaret Alice *psychology and religion educator*
Dracup, Kathleen Anne *dean, nursing educator*
Dugoni, Arthur A. *retired dean, orthodontics educator*
Featherstone, John Douglas Bernard *dean, biochemistry educator*
Fleishhacker, David *school administrator*
Kane, Mary Kay *academic administrator, law educator*
Kessler, David Aaron *dean, medical educator*
Kozloff, Lloyd M. *dean, microbiologist, educator*
LaBelle, Thomas Jeffrey *research executive, academic administrator*
Moore, Megan M. *mathematics educator, department chairman*
Murdoch, Colin *academic administrator*
Newton, Nell Jessup *dean, law educator*
Oberman, Ida *research and evaluation director, consultant*
Peterson, Linda Lou *special education educator*
Privett, Stephen A. *academic administrator, priest*
Robertson, Merle Greene *art historian, academic administrator*
Sakamoto, Katsuyuki *retired academic administrator, psychologist, educator*
Stauffer, Thomas Michael *university president*
Stephens, Elisa *college president*
Subbiondo, Joseph L. *academic administrator*
Warner, Rollin Miles, Jr. *economics educator, real estate broker*

San Jacinto
Hert, Theresa M. *mathematics educator*

San Jose
Arvizu, Charlene Sutter *elementary school educator*
Boac, Thelma Blantucas *principal*
Dorsa, Gene J. *secondary school educator*
Haycock, Kenneth Roy *academic administrator, educator, consultant*
Lobig, Janie Howell *retired special education educator*
Okerlund, Arlene Naylor *academic administrator, writer*
Rodrigues, Margaret L. *elementary school educator, consultant*
Wesson, Kenneth Alan *educational consultant*

San Leandro
Dolgin, Stephen Mark *secondary school educator, retired social worker*

San Luis Obispo
Aiello, Michael Benjamin *secondary school educator*
Baker, Warren J(oseph) *university president*
Ericson, Jon Meyer *academic administrator, language educator*
Floyd, Barry *information systems educator, consultant*
Gardebring, Sandra S. *academic administrator*
Haile, Allen Cleveland *academic administrator*
Singh, Jay *director, researcher*

San Marcos
Lilly, Martin Stephen *retired university dean*

San Marino
Footman, Gordon Elliott *educational administrator*
Toy, Helen Guerrant *secondary school educator*

San Pedro
Gaines, Jerry Lee *retired secondary school educator*

San Rafael
Adcock, Muriel W. *special education educator*
Fink, Joseph Richard *academic administrator*
Thomas, Mary Ann McCrary *counselor, school system administrator*

Santa Ana
Lawson, Barbara Slade *elementary school educator, artist*
Moore, David Gene *academic administrator*

Santa Barbara
Boyan, Norman J. *retired education educator*
Cirone, William Joseph *educational administrator*
Lucas, Gene *academic administrator*
O'Dowd, Donald Davy *retired university president*
Sinsheimer, Robert Louis *retired academic administrator, educator*
Yang, Henry T.Y. *chancellor, educator*

Santa Clara
Goodchild, Lester Francis *higher education educator*
Locatelli, Paul Leo *academic administrator*
Polden, Donald *dean, law educator*

Santa Clarita
Lavine, Steven David *academic administrator*

Santa Cruz
Blumenthal, George *academic administrator, astronomy and astrophysics professor*
Garcia-Luna-Aceves, J.J. *education educator*
Goldenkranz, Andrew *principal, educator*
Rothwell, Wendy *biology educator*
Steel, Virginia (Ginny) *university librarian*

Santa Monica
Kemper, Tom A. *secondary school educator*
Soloff, Laura J. *academic administrator*

Santa Rosa
Webb, Charles Richard *retired university president*

Saratoga
Barna, Lillian Carattini *school system administrator*
Houston, Elizabeth Reece Manasco *correctional education consultant*

Seal Beach
Pipes, Doris Perry *secondary school educator, consultant*

Seaside
Anderson, David Louis *academic administrator, history professor*

Signal Hill
Vandament, William Eugene *retired academic administrator*

Silverado
Mamer, James Michael *secondary school educator*

Sonoma
Hobart, Billie *education educator, consultant*

South Pasadena
Fuller, Kathy J. *special education educator, consultant, researcher*

Stanford
Anderson, Theodore Wilbur *statistics educator*
Barron, Brigid *education educator*
Boaler, Jo *education educator*
Eisner, Elliot W. *education educator*
Etchemendy, John *academic administrator, educator*
Hennessy, John L. *academic administrator*
Joss, Robert L. *dean*
Kamil, Michael *education educator*
Kays, William Morrow *academic administrator, mechanical engineer*
Kramer, Larry *dean, lawyer, educator*
Laughlin, Robert B. *academic administrator, physics professor*
Loeb, Susanna *education educator*
Long, Sharon Rugel *dean, molecular biologist, educator*
Lotan, Rachel *education educator*
Palm, Charles Gilman *academic administrator*
Pea, Roy *education educator*
Raisian, John *academic administrator, economist*
Riggs, Henry Earle *academic administrator, engineering educator*
Shaw, Richard H. *dean*
Spence, Andrew Michael *former dean, finance educator*
Stone, William Edward *academic administrator, consultant*
Strober, Myra Hoffenberg *education educator, consultant*
Veinott, Arthur Fales, Jr. *university educator*
Whitney, Rodger Franklin *academic administrator*
Wotipka, Christine Min *education educator*

Stockton
Cobb, Judy Lynn *elementary school educator*
DeRicco, Lawrence Albert *retired college president*
DeRosa, Donald V. *academic administrator*
Fish, Tom *special education and vocational school educator*
Gilbertson, Philip *academic administrator*
Ren, Jianhua *education educator*
Sorby, Donald Lloyd *retired dean*

Sun Valley
Mayhue, Richard Lee *dean, minister, writer*

Sunnyvale
Schwartz, Eleanore Anita *retired elementary school educator, small business owner*

Tarzana
Zeitlin, Herbert Zakary *college administrator, real estate consultant, writer*

Tehachapi
Sprinkle, Martha Clare *elementary school educator*

Temecula
Cherrington, Pamela Jo *special education educator*

Thousand Oaks
Lieberman, Judith L. *retired special education educator*
Sladek, John R., Jr. *academic administrator, neurobiology and anatomy educator*
Venable, Diane Dailey *retired elementary school educator*

Torrance
Kuc, Joseph A. *research scientist*

Tulare
Pinto, Marie Malania *academic administrator, consultant*

Turlock
Burns, James Wesley *academic administrator, researcher, consultant*

Twentynine Palms
Clemente, Patrocinio Ablola *secondary school educator*

Union City
Lindsey, Tommie *secondary school educator*
Muñoz, Eduardo Rafael *elementary school educator*

Vallejo
Wilson, Carrie Lee Stroud *principal*
Zingale, Donald Paul *academic administrator, educator*

Valley Center
Arciniega, Tomas Abel *university president*

Valley Ford
Mulkern-Kolosey, Sandy Kathleen *college counselor, educator, realtor*

Van Nuys
Wright, Judith Ann *elementary school educator*

Venice
Beery-Polglase, Penelope (Pixie) *education educator*

Victorville
Hauk, Beth MacKenzie *elementary school educator, writer*
Scott, Deborah Elizabeth *school system administrator, poet*

Walnut
Tran, Nam Van *secondary school educator*

Walnut Creek
Lilly, Luella Jean *retired academic administrator*

Weimar
Kerschner, Lee R(onald) *academic administrator, political scientist, educator*

West Hills
Christenson, Allen Cecil *retired mathematics educator*

Westlake Village
Doerr, Patricia Marian *elementary and special education educator*

Whittier
Cruz, Denis J. *elementary school educator*
Pencall, Constance McConnell *retired secondary school educator*

Woodland Hills
Berry, Barbara Cochran *education educator, writer*

Yorba Linda
Lunde, Dolores Benitez *retired secondary school educator*

Yuba City
Leverett, Dawn R. *disability education consultant*

COLORADO

Arvada
Krohnfeldt, Gretchen Ann *secondary school educator, genealogist*

Aurora
Kellogg Fain, Karen *retired history educator*

Bayfield
Horton, Frank Elba *academic administrator, geographer, educator*

Boulder
Anderson, Ronald Delaine *education educator*
Borko, Hilda *education educator*
Landesman, Howard M. *retired academic administrator*
Peterson, G. P. (Bud Peterson) *academic administrator*
White, Cindy Hagemeier *adult education educator*
Williams, James Franklin, II, *dean, librarian*
Wilson, M. Roy *academic administrator, medical educator*

Broomfield
Parker, Bobby Douglas *secondary school educator*

Calhan
Henderson, Freda LaVerne *elementary school educator*

Colorado Springs
Adams, Bernard Schroder *retired college president*
Adams, Janelle R. *mathematics educator, gifted and talented educator*
Burdo, Amy *elementary school educator*
Celeste, Richard F. *academic administrator, retired ambassador, governor*
Fielden, C. Franklin III *early childhood education consultant*
Hinkle, Betty Ruth *retired academic administrator*
McDade, Roberta Clark *secondary school educator*
Shockley-Zalabak, Pamela Sue *academic administrator*

Denver
Albino, Judith Elaine Newsom *university president*
Allen, Nancy H. *dean, library director*
Brown, Hank *academic administrator, former senator*
Burrows, Bertha Jean *retired academic administrator*
Byyny, Richard Lee *former academic administrator, physician, educator*
Coombe, Bob (Robert D.) *academic administrator*
Emmet, Thomas Addis, Jr. *college administrator, consultant*
Fulkerson, William Measey, Jr. *college president*
Hecox, Morris B. *academic administrator*
Hegarty, George John *university president, literature and language professor*
Jarles, Ruth Sewell *education educator*
Jordan, Stephen M. *academic administrator*
Kourlis, Rebecca Love *director, former state supreme court justice*
Kraus, Joseph Roland *reference librarian*
Matkowski, Bette *academic administrator*
Mears, Carolyn Lunsford *education educator*
Meeks, Patricia Lowe *literature and language educator, consultant*
Moloney, William J. *school system administrator*
Newman, Kimberly Eileen *adult education educator*
Rubin, Cathy Ann *secondary school educator*
Slotta, Oliveann Davis *mathematics educator, consultant*
Sumner, Stephen C. *academic administrator*
Tombaugh, Dorothy Elve *retired secondary school educator, author, lecturer*
Vigil, Daniel Agustin *academic administrator*
Winn, Joan *adult education educator*

Dolores
Harper, Laura Lee *principal*

Durango
Barter, Mary F. *academic administrator*

Englewood
Kubik, Timothy Robert White *director, history educator*

Erie
Nichols, Janet Hildreth *elementary school educator, childbirth and parenting educator*

Estes Park
Ryder, Susan R. *elementary school educator*

Fort Collins
Baldwin, Lionel Vernon *retired university president*
Bloemen, Crystal Lynn *secondary school educator*
Colbert, Debora A. *director*
Harper, Judson Morse *retired university administrator, consultant, educator*
Maher, Thomas George *academic administrator, producer, media educator*
Penley, Larry Edward *academic administrator, finance educator*

Golden
Bickart, Theodore Albert *university president emeritus*
Scoggins, M. W. (Bill Scoggins) *academic administrator*
Shea, Dion Warren Joseph *academic administrator, fundraiser*
Truly, Richard H. *academic and federal agency administrator, retired pilot*

Grand Junction
Armstrong, Alden Arthur *retired elementary school educator, photographer, writer*

Greeley
Christiansen, Matthew Lane *mathematics educator*
Duff, William Leroy, Jr. *retired dean, finance educator*
Reardon, James F. *adult education educator*
Seager, Daniel Albert *university librarian*

Joes
Crawford, Dorothy Hill *retired secondary school educator, art educator, artist*

Lakewood
McBride, Guy Thornton, Jr. *college president emeritus*
Nelson, Deborah Jane *family and consumer science educator*
Reed, Joan-Marie *special education educator*
Stromberg, Patricia Roberts *retired school librarian*

Lamar
Banker, Carol Anne *elementary school educator*

Littleton
Greenberg, Elinor Miller *director, consultant*
Grounds, Vernon Carl *seminary administrator*
Tucker, James Raymond *primary school educator*

Louisville
Bravo, Adele *elementary school educator*

Mancos
Seney, Robert William *retired education educator*
Whitehead, Linda Sue *literature and language educator, history educator, special education educator*

Nederland
Lutz, Frank Wenzel *education administration educator*

Norwood
Brantingham, Andrya J. *special education educator*

Ordway
Fosdick, Jacque Janelle *literature and language educator, theater educator*

Parachute
Leonard, Betsy Ann *director, writer*

Pueblo
Becker, Charles A. *adult education educator*
Ramirez, Monica E. *education educator, consultant*
Sisson, Ray L. *retired dean, author*

Snowmass Village
DiBiaggio, John A. *university president*

U S A F Academy
Born, Dana H. *dean, career military officer*
Regni, John F. *academic administrator, career military officer*

Walsh
Lancaster, Robert Carl *secondary school educator*

Westminster
Eaves, Stephen Douglas *high school and vocational administrator, educator, consultant*

CONNECTICUT

Bloomfield
Baccus, R. Eileen Turner *retired academic administrator, educational consultant*
Nelson-Kauffman, Wendy *history educator*
Rendock, Mary Kay *elementary school educator*

Branford
Johnson, Eva Jo *educational consultant*

Bridgeport
Rahrig, Carol Ann *literature and language educator*

Bristol
LaGanga, Donna Brandeis *dean*
Vojtek, RoseAnne OBrien *principal*

Canterbury
Yaworski, James John III *elementary school educator*

Coventry
Dimmock, Virginia Ellen *literature and language educator, consultant*

Danbury
Agoora, Lammia Hasson *mathematics educator*
Hawkes, Carol Ann *academic administrator*

Enfield
Doty, Victoria Skower *elementary school educator*

Fairfield
Howell, Karen Jane *private school educator*
Miles, Leland Weber *retired academic administrator*
Paolini, Claire Jacqueline *dean, educator*

Falls Village
Purcell, Mary Louise Gerlinger *retired adult education educator*

Farmington
Deckers, Peter John *dean*
Ford, Burch Tracy *headmaster*
Robinson, Peter J. *dean, periodontal educator, pathologist*

Greenwich
Sternberg, Betty J. *school system administrator*

Groton
English, James Fairfield, Jr. *former college president*
Galbraith, Marian *elementary school educator*

Guilford
Speth, James Gustave *dean, environmental studies educator, lawyer*

Hamden
Brown, Jay Marshall *retired secondary school educator*

Hartford
Carter, David George, Sr. *academic administrator*
Coleman, George A. *school system administrator*
Frost, James Arthur *former university president*
Hay, Leroy E. *school system administrator*
Jones, James Fleming, Jr. *academic administrator, language educator*
McQuillan, Mark K. *school system administrator*
Reynolds, Scott Walton *academic administrator*

Lakeville
Mattoon, Robert H., Jr., (Skip) *headmaster*

Manchester
Daube, Jonathan Mahram *academic administrator*

Middletown
Roth, Michael S. *academic administrator, art educator*

Milford
Gallop, Sophronia Langston *elementary school educator*

New Britain
Shen, Xiaoping *geography educator*

New Canaan
Despres, Louise Fay *secondary school educator*
McKeough, Susan Anne *elementary school educator*

New Haven
Alpern, Robert J. *dean, medical educator*
Benson, Richard *dean, photographer*
Birnbaum, Irwin Morton *educational consultant, lawyer*
Brenzel, Jeffrey *dean*
Daly, Radley Hutchinson *retired academic administrator*
Degutis, Linda Christine *adult education educator, epidemiologist, researcher*
Greene, Liliane *literature and language educator, editor*
Hennah, Vivian Lisa *school system administrator*
Koh, Harold Hongju *dean, law educator*
Kronman, Anthony Townsend *dean, law educator*
Lamar, Howard Roberts *academic administrator, historian*
LaPalombara, Joseph *political science educator, industrial management educator*
Levin, Rick (Richard Charles Levin) *academic administrator, economist*
Lorimer, Linda Koch *university educator*
McNamara, Julia Mary *academic administrator, foreign language educator*
Pagani, Mark *education educator, researcher*
Podolny, Joel M. *dean, management educator*
Sykes, Gwendolyn *academic administrator, former federal agency administrator*

New London
Higdon, Leo Ignatius, Jr., (Lee) *academic administrator*

North Branford
Gasparine, Barbara Ellen *elementary school educator*

North Haven
Fuggi, Gretchen Miller *education educator*
Hudson, Richard L. *retired adult education educator, minister*
Morrissey, Charles Richard, Sr. *retired elementary school educator*

North Stonington
Keane, John Patrick *retired secondary school educator*

Norwalk
Johnson, Robert James *psychology educator*

Putnam
Ames, Sandra Cutler *secondary school educator*

Redding
Poulos, Christopher *literature and language educator*

Ridgefield
Brewster, Carroll Worcester *former academic administrator*
Lindsay, Dianna Marie *educational administrator*

South Windsor
Plummer, Daria Marie *elementary school educator*

Stamford
Dodd, Meghan P. *mathematics educator*
Handler, Evelyn *former academic administrator*

Storrs Mansfield
Baxter, Donald Leon Murray *education educator*
Hogan, Michael J. *academic administrator*
Kerr, Kirklyn M. *academic administrator, veterinarian, pathologist*
MacDonald, John Thomas *school system administrator*
Nicholls, Peter J. *academic administrator*
Price, Glenda Delores *dean, college president*
Sriram, S. *educator*
Woods, David G. *dean*

Suffield
Montalto, Paul *academic administrator*

Taconic
Medvecky, Patricia *retired elementary school educator*

Terryville
Doughty-Jenkins, Bonnie-Marie *middle school educator*

Trumbull
Nevins, Lyn (Carolyn A. Nevins) *school disciplinarian*

Wallingford
Shanahan, Edward J. *headmaster*

Waterbury
Lang, Christine JoAnn *elementary school educator*
Martone, Eric Anthony Domenic *history educator*
Sanders, Richard L. *academic administrator*

Waterford
Weidenbaum, Rhoda Sussman *history educator, researcher*

West Hartford
Alexandrin, Julie Richmond *special education educator, consultant*
Chase, Carol Johnson *mathematics educator*
Harrison, Walter Lee *university president*
Malone, Thomas Francis *academic administrator, meteorologist*
Markham, Claire Agnes (M. Clare Markham) *retired chemistry educator, consultant*
Tonkin, Humphrey Richard *academic administrator, educator*

Westport
Freedman, Judith Greenberg *retired elementary school educator, state legislator*
Kuroghlian, Gerald E. *English educator*
Warner, Kerstin Julianna *gifted and talented educator*

Willimantic
Barbuto, Leah M. *early childhood and technology educator, consultant*
Wilson, Margaret Sullivan *retired executive dean, consultant*

Wilton
Reilly, Kathleen C. *director, retired secondary school educator*

Windsor
Weigel, Russell H. *headmaster*

Windsor Locks
Coelho, Sandra Signorelli *secondary school educator, consultant, elementary school educator*

Woodbridge
Malloy, Ina Arlene *secondary school educator, photographer*

DELAWARE

Dover
Braverman, Ray Howard *secondary school educator*
Jones, Geraldine Ann Johnson *secondary school educator*
Sessoms, Allen Lee *academic administrator, physicist, educator, retired diplomat*
Sorenson, Liane Beth McDowell *director, state legislator*
Woodruff, Valerie *school system administrator*

Georgetown
Lane, William H. *education educator*

Laurel
Lydic, Garrett Walton *elementary school educator*
Selby, Cora Norwood *retired elementary school educator*

Middletown
Roach, Daniel T., Jr., (Tad Roach) *headmaster*

New Castle
Brownson, Kenneth C. *dean*
Rolland, Kathy Ann *elementary school educator*
Sanderson, Devon Lee *elementary school educator*

Newark
Bailey, Daniel Carl *higher education administrator*
Dybowski, Cecil *chemistry educator*
Harker, Patrick Timothy *academic administrator, systems engineer, educator*
Mitchell, Peter Kenneth *educational consultant*
Roselle, David Paul *retired academic administrator, mathematician, educator*
Swany, Douglas Martin *education educator*

Wilmington
Alonso, Caridad *elementary school educator*
Fullerton, Ann Elizabeth *retired biology educator*
Higgins, Roxanne Snelling *educational consultant*

DISTRICT OF COLUMBIA

Washington
Ajami, Fouad *professor of middle eastern studies*
Alatis, James Efstathios *university dean emeritus*
Aleinikoff, Thomas Alexander *dean, law educator*
Arnez, Nancy Levi *educational leadership educator*
Barrett, Richard David *university director, consultant, retired bank executive*
Bowden, Aisha L. *elementary school educator*
Burgin, Walter Hotchkiss, Jr. *retired academic administrator*
Burke-Ables, Kim S. *biology educator*
Buser, Carolyn Elizabeth *adult education educator*
Carrier, Warren Pendleton *retired university chancellor, writer*
Churchill, John Hugh *college academic administrator*
Clewell, Beatriz Chu *director, researcher*
Convey, John J. *academic administrator*
Covington, Eileen Queen *secondary school educator*
Crane, Edward Harrison III *academic administrator, financial analyst*
Crockett, Kristen Michelle *director*
Daly, George Garman *dean*
Davila, Robert R. *academic administrator*
DeGioia, John J. *academic administrator*
DePaul, Christina *dean, artist*
Duffey, Joseph Daniel *academic administrator*
Elliott, Emerson John *education consultant, policy analyst*
Evers, Williamson Moore *education policy analyst, political scientist*
Feder, Judith *dean*
Fisher, Miles Mark, IV, *education and religious studies educator, minister*
Flaherty, Sister Mary Jean *dean*

Fox, William F. *dean, law educator*
Fusco, Aurilla Marie *director*
Garrison, Gwen E. *educational researcher, consultant*
Gerety, Tom R. *former academic administrator, lawyer, educator, philosopher*
Greenhalgh, Paul *academic administrator*
Grossman, Claudio M. *dean, law educator*
Hale, Martha Larsen *dean, library and information science educator*
Harris, June Leatrice *education coordinator, administrator*
Hassan, Aftab Syed *education specialist, writer, editor*
Jarvis, Charlene Drew *academic administrator, former scientist*
Jones, Alice Samuels *elementary education educator, reading specialist*
Jones, Judith Miller *director*
Kamras, Jason *mathematics educator*
Keaney, Thomas Addis *academic administrator, management consultant, educator, military officer*
Keeley, Robert Vossler *retired academic administrator, ambassador*
Kerwin, Cornelius Martin *academic administrator, educator*
Kim, Mikyong Minsun *education educator*
Kirk, Artemis G. *university librarian*
Lazarin, Melissa Y. *director*
Luttwak, Edward Nicolae *academic administrator, policy and business consultant, senior advisor*
Malveaux, Floyd Joseph *dean*
Mantyla, Karen *distance learning consultant*
McDowell-Craig, Vanessa Dennise *supervisor, consultant*
Milman, Natalie Bordelon *education educator*
Mohrman, Kathryn j. *academic administrator*
Muller, Steven *international studies educator, academic administrator*
Natarajan, Githa *elementary school educator*
Nwagbaraocha, Joel Onukwugha *academic administrator, educator*
O'Connell, David M. *academic administrator, priest*
O'Donovan, Leo Jeremiah *former academic administrator, priest, theologian*
O'Dor, Ronald Keith *dean, biology professor, research scientist*
Phillips, Susan Meredith *academic administrator, economist*
Ranck, Edna Runnels *academic administrator, researcher*
Reddel, Carl Walter *academic administrator*
Robert, Davila R. *academic administrator*
Rouse, Leo E. *dean, dental educator*
Schmoke, Kurt Lidell *dean, former mayor*
Siggins, Jack Arthur *university librarian*
Swygert, Haywood Patrick *academic administrator*
Thomas-Razza, Constance *retired elementary school educator*
Thompson, Bernida Lamerle *principal, consultant, educator*
Trangsrud, Roger H. *dean, law educator*
Tucker, Marc Stephen *education policy analyst, author*
Vajda, Judith Parsons *psychology educator*
Van Ummersen, Claire A. *academic administrator, biologist, educator*
Weiner, Stephen Francis *academic administrator, communications educator*
Weingold, Marjorie Nassau *retired special education educator*
Weiss, Charles, Jr. *educator*
Williams, Ella Marilyn *mathematics educator*
Wise, Lorraine E. *educational consultant*
Woodson, Ruby Garrard *educational administrator, chemistry educator*

FLORIDA

Belle Glade
Grear, Effie Carter *principal*

Boca Raton
Arden, Eugene *retired university provost*
Boykin, Anne Jane *dean*
Braisted, Mary Jo *elementary school educator*
Brogan, Frank T. *academic administrator, former lieutenant governor*
Comment, Anna Mae *retired principal*
Friedland, Michael Lawrence *dean, medical educator*
Lazar, Charna L. *education educator, retired CIA officer, security consultant*
Ross, Kevin McAndrew *academic administrator*
Tennies, Robert Hunter *headmaster*
Tracy, James Frederick *media educator*

Bonita Springs
Becker, Richard Charles *retired academic administrator*
Borchers, Janet Marise *elementary school educator, counselor*
Johnson, Franklyn Arthur *academic administrator*
Knight-McDowell, Victoria *former elementary school educator, health products executive*

Bradenton
Driscoll, Constance Fitzgerald *education educator, writer, consultant*
Moore, John Hampton *academic administrator*
Pillot, Gene Merrill *retired school system administrator*
Wolf, John Michael *adult education seminar consultant*

Brooksville
Chamberlain, Daniel Robert *retired college president*

Cape Coral
Bradley, Jean Irene *elementary school educator*
Graham, Dorothy E. *elementary school educator*

Clewiston
Burroughs, Jeannette *elementary school educator*

Coconut Creek
Brenner, Egon *academic administrator, consultant*

Coral Gables
Mangravite, Ronald *education educator, writer*
Prilleltensky, Isaac *dean*
Shalala, Donna Edna *academic administrator, former secretary of health and human services*
Temares, M. Lewis *academic administrator*
Tien, James M. *dean, engineering educator, consultant*

Davie
Collins, Mary Lynn *education educator*

Daytona Beach
Green, Betty Nielsen *education educator, consultant*

Debary
Coble, Alicia Sharon *retired elementary and secondary school educator*

Deland
Dascher, Paul Edward *dean, accounting educator*
Langston, Paul T. *dean, composer, music educator*

Delray Beach
Hofman, Elizabeth Elveretta *retired mathematics educator, guidance counselor, dean*
Ross, Donald Edward *former academic administrator*
Schwartz, Diane N. *secondary school educator, researcher*
Sparrow, Kathleen Gail *retired secondary school educator*

Deltona
Marrett, Caroline Denise *special education educator*

Dunedin
Jacobs, Marilyn Arlene Potoker *gifted education educator, consultant, author*

Fort Lauderdale
Edmund, Norman Wilson *educational researcher*
Fischler, Abraham Saul *retired academic administrator, educator*
Hall, David *principal*
Hanbury, George Lafayette, II, *academic administrator*
McCan, James Lawton *education educator*
Trubey, Lillian Priscilla *retired secondary school educator*
Uchin, Robert Allen *dean, endodontist*

Fort Myers
Blanchard, Susan Manning *academic administrator, director, engineering educator*
Carothers, Douglas Edward *special education educator*
Colgate, Doris Eleanor *sailing school owner, administrator*
Drushal, Mary Ellen *retired education educator*
Harris, Connie *gifted and talented educator*
Robertson, Mary Amos *mathematics educator*

Fort Pierce
Schwenger, Wilbur John *mathematics educator, mathematics professor*

Fort Walton Beach
Hicks, Patricia J. *secondary school educator*
Moran, Kimberly Dianne *secondary school educator, artist*

Gainesville
Bartlett, Rodney J. *chemistry and physics educator*
Brodeur, Michael Stephen *dean*
Brown, Myra Suzanne *university librarian*
Bryan, Robert Armistead *academic administrator, educator*
Challoner, David Reynolds *academic administrator, endocrinologist*
Chambers, Robert Hunter III *academic administrator, consultant, historian, educator*
Cheek, Jimmy Geary *academic administrator, agricultural studies educator*
Dolan, Teresa A. *dean, educator, researcher*
Fouke, Janie M. *academic administrator, educator*
Jerry, Robert Howard, II, *dean, law educator*
Kraft, John *dean*
Lowenstein, Ralph Lynn *university dean emeritus*
Machen, James Bernard *academic administrator*
Maple, Marilyn Jean *educational media coordinator*
Marshall, Kevin A. *director*
Mills, Jon *dean emeritus, law educator*
Phillips, Winfred Marshall *academic administrator, mechanical engineer, educator, biomedical researcher*
Rosenberger, Margaret Adaline *retired elementary school educator, writer*
Saucerman, Alvera Adeline *elementary school educator*
Viessman, Warren, Jr. *dean, civil engineering educator*
York, E. Travis *retired academic administrator*

Graceville
Kinchen, Thomas Alexander *college president*

Hernando
Rodgers, John Joseph III *educational administration consultant, educator*

Hialeah
Agrawal, Piyush C. *school system administrator*
Jenkins, Dawn Paula *special education educator, dancer*

Hobe Sound
Blumengarten, Jerry *educational consultant*

Homestead
Whitehorton, Thelma *educational administrator*

Indialantic
Scrivener, Lois Doing *principal, educator*

Jacksonville
Davis, Craig Anderson *school system administrator, educator*
Delaney, John Adrian *academic administrator*
Grabowski, Rodney Michael *academic administrator, consultant*
Hughes, Carolyn Wright *elementary school educator, director*
Jamrich, John Xavier *retired university administrator*
Kinne, Frances Bartlett *academic administrator*
Main, Edna Dewey (June Main) *education educator*
Olin, Marilyn *secondary school educator*
Osborn, Marvin Griffing, Jr. *educational consultant*
Otto, Elizabeth Hall *education educator*

Jensen Beach
Dahn, Conney Colley *special education educator*
Kraynak, Helen *special education consultant*

Kennedy Space Center
Feldman, Stephen *academic administrator*

Kissimmee
Haynes, Ulric St. Clair, Jr. *retired dean*
Toothe, Karen Lee *elementary and secondary school educator*

Lake Worth
Carlisle, Ervin Frederick *university provost, educator*

Lakeland
Washington, Gloria Dunn *secondary school educator*

Land O Lakes
Mallon, Kellie Jane *special education educator*
Quackenbush, Roger E. *retired secondary school educator*

Lantana
Caughman, Patricia Ann *mathematics educator*

Leesburg
Smith, Kathy L. *elementary school educator, cosmetics executive, consultant*

Longwood
Johnson, Nancy Plattner *retired secondary school educator*

Loxahatchee
Russell-Tyson, Pearl Leonie *elementary school educator*

Melbourne
Catanese, Anthony James *academic administrator*
Fox, Thomas George *academic administrator*
Weaver, Lynn Edward *academic administrator, consultant, editor*
Zabel, Dianne Donnelly *retired elementary school educator*

Merritt Island
McClanahan, Leland *university director*

Miami
Addy, Dawn Emerson *adult education educator, consultant*
Brooten, Dorothy *retired dean, nursing educator*
Cardenas, Diana Delia *academic administrator, retired physician, educator*
Clarkson, John G. *academic administrator, ophthalmologist*
Fish, Stanley Eugene *dean, language educator*
Foote, Edward Thaddeus, II, *academic administrator, lawyer*
Glaser, Thomas William *educational administrator*
Kahn, Barbara E. *dean, marketing educator*
Kaplan, Betsy Hess *retired school board member*
Katz, Sandra *educational consultant, psychologist, education educator*
Maidique, Modesto Alex *academic administrator*
Martinez-Canas, Maria *photography educator*
McCabe, Robert Howard *college president*
McLaughlin, Margaret Brown *adult education educator, writer*
Patrie, Cheryl Christine *elementary school educator*
Rodriguez, Josefa Nieves *special education educator, language educator*
Rodriguez-Walling, Matilde Barcelo *special education educator*
Wated, Guillermo *psychology educator*

Miami Beach
Foote, Gwendolyn Sue *middle school educator, artist*
Gitlow, Abraham Leo *retired dean*

Miami Gardens
Conley, James W. *English language educator, language arts educator*
Robinson, Beatriz Gonzalez *academic administrator*

Miramar
Huang, Guiyou *dean, English studies educator, writer*

Monticello
Johnson, Artis *educational administrator, clergyman*

Montverde
Revis-Pyke, Robin Lynn *director*

Mount Dora
Scharfenberg, Margaret Ellan *retired elementary school educator*

Naples
Mahalawich, Anne Mary *retired mathematics educator*
Wedel-Cowgill, Millie Redmond *secondary school, performing arts, communication and education educator*

Nokomis
Lockledge, Jack E. *retired principal*

North Miami Beach
Clanton, Wendy McCarley *elementary school educator, assistant principal*
Sorosky, Jeri P. *academic administrator*

Ocoee
Godsell, Richard Vernon *elementary school educator, researcher*

Opa Locka
Sample, Althea Merritt *retired secondary education educator, conductor*

Orange City
Brakeman, Louis Freeman *retired university official*

Orlando
Bersia, John Cesar *political science educator, editorial writer*
Clinton, Stephen Michael *academic administrator*
Connolly, Joseph Francis, II, *academic administrator, government consultant*
Gill, Michele Gregoire *education educator*
Graham, Eleanore Davis *elementary school educator*
Hitt, John Charles *academic administrator*
Vaughn, Rosalyn Mae *academic administrator*
Wilson, Brenda Marie *secondary school educator*

Osprey
Weathermon, Sidney Earl *retired elementary school educator*

Oviedo
Gendron, Mary W. *retired educator*
MacKenzie, Charles Sherrard *academic administrator*

Palatka
Embree, Mary Evelyn *retired secondary school educator*

Palm Bay
Colman, Charles Kingsbury *academic administrator, criminologist*
Whitten, Shannon Nicole *education educator*

Palm Beach Gardens
Peck, Maryly VanLeer *retired academic administrator, chemical engineer*

Palm Harbor
Hewitt, Sarah Nichole *educational consultant, researcher*
Perkins, Robert Edward *retired secondary school educator*

Panama City
Rockhill, Marsha *special education educator*

Pembroke Pines
Embergher, Mary Louise *elementary school educator*
Poore, Paul Michael *school system administrator*

Pensacola
Brown, Ernest L. *education educator*
Di, Xu *education educator*

Plantation
Young, William Benjamin *retired special education educator*

Pompano Beach
Baslaw-Finger, Annette *education educator, consultant*
Endahl, Ethelwyn Mae *elementary education educator, consultant*
Johnson, Dorothy Curfman *elementary school educator*
Williams, Cloretta Mae *retired elementary school educator*

Ponte Vedra Beach
Patterson, Oscar III *academic administrator*

Port Charlotte
Hill, Richard Earl *academic administrator*
Norris, Dolores June *elementary school educator*

Port Orange
Chesnut, Nondis Lorine (Angel Love) *education educator, writer, learning specialist, scriptwriter*
Johnson, Susan F. *elementary school educator*

Port Saint Lucie
Earley, Deborah Loraine *education educator, researcher*

Guglielmino, Lucy Margaret Madsen *education educator, researcher, consultant*
Guglielmino, Paul Joseph *educator*
Malcolm, Edith *elementary school educator*

Punta Gorda
Klarik, Bela William James Clark *retired school system administrator*
Lynch, Constance *reading specialist*
Spaulding, Mar *retired special education educator*

Saint Augustine
Proctor, William Lee *college chancellor*
Sappington, Sharon Anne *retired school librarian*

Saint Leo
Hammond, Bruce Ray *academic administrator, consultant*

Saint Petersburg
Armacost, Peter Hayden *academic administrator*
Chapin, Lloyd Walter *academic administrator*
Coraggio, James Thomas *educational researcher, measurement consultant*
Dinsdale, Carol Ellen *special education educator*
Southworth, William Dixon *retired education educator*
Young, June Hurley *elementary school educator, writer*

Sarasota
Atwell, Robert Herron *academic administrator*
Cleland, Sherrill *college president*
Michalson, Gordon E., Jr. *academic administrator*
Miller, Peggy Gordon Elliott *retired academic administrator*
St. John, Terri *secondary school educator*
Scanlon, Janice Lynn *retired gifted and talented educator*
Thompson, Annie Figueroa *retired academic administrator*

Sebastian
Burns, Robert Edward *dean, retired history professor*
Mauke, Otto Russell *retired college president*

Sebring
Parrett, Janelle Swilley *secondary school educator*

South Daytona
Fernández, Lianne *elementary school educator, consultant*

Spring Hill
Wood, Shelton Eugene *education educator, minister, consultant*

Sugarloaf
Greenberg, Linda Garrett *education educator, volunteer, singer*

Sun City Center
Chapman, Lenora Rosamond *day care provider, social service organization director*

Tallahassee
Burkman, Ernest, Jr. *education educator*
Bye, Raymond Erwin, Jr. *academic administrator*
Dennis, Lawrence C. (Larry) *dean, physics professor*
Ervin, Charles Phifer, Jr. *education educator, retired military officer*
Grant, Sydney R. *education educator, consultant*
Keating, Kevin *academic administrator, chef*
Lick, Dale Wesley *educational leadership educator, mathematician*
Mills, Belen Collantes *early childhood education educator*
Mooney, Krista Michele *academic administrator*
Morgan, Robert Marion *educational research educator*
Rosenberg, Mark B. *academic administrator*
Scott, Fran *adult education educator*
Sliger, Bernard Francis *academic administrator, economist, educator*
Waas, Harriet Issner *elementary school educator*
Weidner, Donald J. *dean, law educator*
Wetherell, Thomas Kent *academic administrator*
Winn, John L. *school system administrator*

Tampa
Branch, Mary Fletcher Cox *secondary school educator*
Genshaft, Judy Lynn *academic administrator, psychologist, educator*
Gomes, Neil Domnic *director*
Jones, Franklin Ross *education educator*
Leto, Sharon Ann *secondary school educator, consultant*
Loiselle, Joan Brenda *elementary school educator, art educator*
Meisels, Gerhard George *academic administrator, chemist, educator*
Sanchez, Mary Anne *retired secondary school educator*

The Villages
Phillips, Patricia Jeanne *retired school system administrator*

Titusville
O'Sullivan, Patricia Ann *principal, writer*
Robinson, Christina Anne *secondary school educator*

Venice
Felker, Ouida Jeanette Weissinger *special education educator*

Vero Beach
Hardie, James Carl *academic administrator, consultant*

West Palm Beach
Grant, Joi Odom *mathematics educator*
Pantone, David *academic administrator*
Pingpank, Robert Charles *retired mathematics educator*

Wewahitchka
de Abreu, Sue *elementary school educator*

Wimauma
Shober, Amy *education educator*

Winter Garden
Gillet, Pamela Kipping *special education educator*

Winter Haven
Bennett, Samuel *elementary school educator*

Winter Park
Carpan, Ann Carolyn *school librarian, educator*
Short, Edmund Coen *retired education educator*

Winter Springs
McNeal, Mary Kay *secondary school educator*

Zephyrhills
Barron, Ilona Eleanor *elementary school educator, consultant*

GEORGIA

Albany
Forsyth, Rosalyn Moye *middle school educator*
Johnson, Debra Pope *education educator*

Alpharetta
Filliat, Elizabeth Hartley *retired secondary school educator*

Americus
Capitan, William Harry *university president emeritus*
Stanford, Henry King *college president*

Athens
Adams, Michael Fred *academic administrator, political scientist, educator*
Andrews, Grover Jene *retired adult education educator, administrator*
Baumann, Nancy *school librarian*
Castenell, Louis Anthony *academic administrator*
Crowley, John Francis III *university dean*
Hoyt, Robert E. *dean, management educator*
Potter, William Gray, Jr. *university librarian*
Smagorinsky, Peter *education educator*
White, Rebecca Hanner *dean, law educator*
Wraga, William Gerard *education educator*

Atlanta
Aaberg, Thomas Marshall, Sr. *academic administrator*
Affonso, Dyanne D. *dean*
Alexander, Cecil Abraham *academic administrator, consultant, retired architect*
Arthur, Thomas Carlton *former dean, law educator*
Bellamy, Ivory *elementary school educator, consultant*
Benveniste, Lawrence M. *dean*
Blum, Terry Christine *dean*
Bright, David Forbes *academic administrator, classicist, educator*
Broadnax, Walter D. *university president, educator*
Cilella, Mary Winifred *director*
Clough, (Gerald) Wayne *academic administrator*
Cox, Kathy *school system administrator*
Davis, Erroll Brown, Jr. *academic administrator, former utilities executive*
Ferris, James Leonard *academic administrator*
Franklin, Robert Michael, Jr. *academic administrator, theology studies educator*
Hall, Beverly L. *school system administrator*
Henry, Ronald James Whyte *academic administrator, physicist, educator*
Henry, Thomas Reid *education educator, researcher*
Hogan, John Donald *retired college dean, finance educator*
Horsley, Alex *director*
Jefferson, Jonathan Kenneth *dean*
Jolley, Samuel Delanor, Jr. *academic administrator*
Kaminshine, Steven J. *dean, law educator*
Lawley, Thomas Joseph *dean, medical educator*
Lewis, Earl *academic administrator*
Long, Leland Timothy *retired geophysics educator, seismologist*
Luce, Richard *university librarian*
Massey, Walter Eugene *retired academic administrator, physicist*
Meyer, Richard W. *university librarian*
Mogabgab, Rose-Warren Berryman *academic administrator, writer*
Partlett, David F. *dean, law educator*
Patton, Carl Vernon *academic administrator, educator*
Rogers, Brenda Gayle *educational administrator, educator, consultant*
Rojas, Carlos *literature and language educator*
Tatum, Beverly Daniel *academic administrator, writer, psychology and education educator*
Wagner, James Warren *academic administrator, engineering educator*
Yancey, Carolyn Dunbar *retired education policymaker*

Augusta
Drisko, Connie Lee Hastings *dean, dental educator*
Puryear, Joan Copeland *academic administrator*
Tedesco, Francis Joseph *retired academic administrator, medical educator*

Austell
Scott, Yvonnie Michelle *special education educator, diagnostician, paralegal*

Bainbridge
Miley, Jenna Yvonne *education educator, consultant*

Baxley
Williams, David Alfred *elementary school educator*
Williams, Sonia Kay *retired secondary school educator*

Bishop
Bower, Douglas William *counseling administrator, psychotherapist, clergyman*

Blairsville
Stainback, Susan Bray *retired education educator*

Brooklet
McCormick, Paula Shurling *elementary school educator*

Brunswick
Pittman, Catherine Sylvia *secondary school educator*

Carrollton
Hynes, Thomas John *academic administrator*
Sethna, Beheruz Nariman *academic administrator, educator, management consultant*

Cataula
Averill, Ellen Corbett *retired secondary education science educator, administrator*

College Park
Hogan, Ernestine Dearing *retired mathematics educator, retired school system administrator*

Columbus
Beall, Charles Donald *former special education educator*
Duncan, Frances Murphy *retired special education educator*
Montgomery, Anna Frances *elementary school educator*
Riggsby, Dutchie Sellers *education educator*

Conyers
Grider, Rhonda Patriece *elementary school educator, writer*

Covington
Norwood, Brandi Aisha *middle school educator*

Cumming
Johnston, Melissa *school librarian*

Dalton
Ford, Katherine Michelle *special education educator*

Dawsonville
Jorgensen, Alfred H. *retired information technology educator*

Decatur
Kiss, Elizabeth *academic administrator, philosophy educator*

Demorest
Rogers, Elizabeth (Betty) Carlisle *education educator, consultant*

Douglasville
Smith, Stephanie Renae *middle school educator*
Walker, Pam *biology educator*

Dublin
Shuman-Riley, Brenda *literature and language educator*
Yauck, F. Alan *biology educator*

Duluth
Cothrun, Thomas Keith *secondary school educator*
Guillory, Barbara Ann *elementary school educator*

Eatonton
Digby, Pamela Annette *elementary school educator*

Fairburn
Milam, Lynne Morgan *special education educator*

Flowery Branch
Coll, Edward Girard, Jr. *university president*

Forest Park
Lambert, Ethel Gibson Clark *secondary school educator*

Gainesville
Burd, John Stephen *retired academic administrator, music educator*
Floyd, Hazel McConnell *special education educator*

Ila
Greene, Sheree' Jeane *elementary school educator, consultant*

Jeffersonville
Capece, Michelle René *elementary school educator*
Hawthorne, Sarah Beck *reading educator*

Jonesboro
Perez, Maritza E. *elementary school educator*

Kennesaw
Siegel, Betty Lentz *university president*

Lake Park
Blanton, Vallye J. *elementary school educator*

Lawrenceville
Crain, Mary Ann *elementary school educator*

Lilburn
Bendelius, Bonnie Sue *elementary school educator*

Macon
Davis, David Scott *academic administrator, chemistry professor*
Floyd, Daisy Hurst *dean, law educator*
Pilcher, Christie W. *retired special education educator*
Steeples, Douglas Wayne *retired university dean, consultant, researcher*

Marietta
Bivens, Mitchel Lee *school system administrator, minister*
Bollinger, Frances L. *elementary school educator*
Hammond, Elea Anne *special education educator*
Houston, Dorothy Middleton *elementary school educator*
Laframboise, Joan Carol *middle school educator*
Overstreet, Regina Nix *mathematics educator*
Rossbacher, Lisa Ann *academic administrator*

Mcdonough
Mauney, Brandi Savage *special education diagnostician*

Milledgeville
Childre, Amy *education educator*

Peachtree City
Barnes, Marylou Riddleberger *retired academic administrator*

Pearson
Delk, Charlotte Turley *elementary school educator*

Rockmart
Vinson, Victoria Dean *middle school educator*

Roopville
Huckeba, Emily Causey *retired elementary school educator*

Saint Marys
Hall, Lois Bremer *secondary school educator, volunteer*

Saint Simons Island
Mathis, Luster Doyle *academic administrator, political scientist, educator*

Savannah
Chong, Bruce Simon *dean, broadcast executive*
Houngues, Desire Mensanh *dean*
Leighton, Richard Frederick *retired dean*
Polite, Evelyn C. *retired elementary school educator, evangelist*
Rowan, Richard G. *former academic administrator*
Siuta, Abby Mae *primary school educator*
Taggart, Helen M. *adult education educator, nurse*
Thompson, Larry James *retired gifted and social studies education educator*
Wallace, Paula S. *academic administrator*

Snellville
Blankenship, Colleen Marie-Krick *secondary school educator, writer*

Stone Mountain
Brown, Rhonda Jean *special education educator*
Dees, Julian Worth *retired academic/research administrator*
Jones, Ellen *elementary school educator*

Suwanee
Brewer, Brenda Neal *assistant principal, educator*
Stanley, Gwen G. *elementary school educator*
Williams, Terry Neal *secondary school educator*

Tifton
Waldrop, Sherry Hutchinson *elementary school educator*

Toccoa Falls
Gardner, Donna Rae (Donna Rae Diehl) *education educator*

Tucker
Stewart, Connie Ward *retired academic administrator*

Union City
Drake-Hamilton, Lillie Belle *retired secondary school educator*

Valdosta
Bailey, Hugh Coleman *academic administrator*
Burnette, Ada M. Puryear *program coordinator*

Villa Rica
Carroll, Linda Lovell *elementary school educator*

Waleska
Gustafson, Deborah Ann *mathematics educator*

Watkinsville
Vaughn, Lisa Michelle *assistant principal*

West Point
Albarado, Rebecca Hill *elementary school educator*

Whitesburg
Nicholson, Diane M. *special education educator*

Young Harris
Cox, Cathy *academic administrator, former state official*

HAWAII

Hilo
Pezzuto, John Michael *dean, pharmacology educator*
Tseng, Rose *academic administrator*

Honolulu
Castle, Alfred *administrator*
Englert, Peter *academic administrator, director*
Gee, Chuck Yim *dean*
Hamamoto, Patricia *school system administrator, educator*
Ingersoll, Caroline Yee *director*
Keith, Kent Marsteller *academic administrator, motivational speaker, lawyer, writer*
Kessler, Cristy *education educator*
Kim-Rupnow, Weol Soon *education educator*
Konan, Denise *academic administrator, economics professor*
McClain, David Stanley *academic administrator, business and management professor*
Muranaka, Jami *biology educator*
Perkins, Frank Overton *academic administrator, marine biologist*
Pickens, Alexander Legrand *retired education educator*
Silva, Mary Barnes *retired elementary school educator*
Soifer, Aviam *dean, law educator*
Uejo, Colleen Misaye *elementary school educator*
Wee, Christine Dijos *elementary school educator*
Wesselkamper, Sue *academic administrator*
Wright, Chatt Grandison *academic administrator*

Kailua Kona
Diama, Benjamin *retired secondary school educator, artist, composer, writer*
Spitze, Glenys Smith *retired teacher and counselor*

Kaneohe
Ashley, Elizabeth *dean, educator*

Kapaa
Caspillo, Carol A. *secondary school educator*

Laie
Miller, Ronald Mellado *education educator*
Shumway, Eric Brandon *academic administrator*

Pearl City
Awakuni, Gene I. *academic administrator, psychologist*

IDAHO

Boise
Andrus, Cecil Dale *academic administrator*
DeMotte, John Buck *educational consultant*
Griffin, Sylvia Gail *reading specialist*
Luna, Thomas *school system administrator*
Maloof, Giles Wilson *academic administrator, educator, author*

Caldwell
Hendren, Robert Lee, Jr. *academic administrator*
Hoover, Robert Allan *university president*

Lewiston
Marshall, Josie *secondary school educator*
Thomas, Dene Kay *academic administrator, educator*

Moscow
Abraham, Terry *school librarian*
Jankowska, Maria Anna *school librarian, educator*
White, Timothy Peter *academic administrator, physical education educator*

Nampa
Hagood, Richard A. *academic administrator, educator*

Ola
Farr, Reeta Rae *special education administrator*

Parma
Sharkey, (John) Mick *biology educator*

Pocatello
Lawson, Jonathan Nevin *academic administrator, educator*
Robinson, Evelyn Etta *principal*

Rexburg
Clark, Kim Bryce *academic administrator*

Rogerson
Boss, Marylin Jeanette *elementary school educator*

Sun Valley
Cassell, William Comyn *retired college president*

Wayan
Carney Nelson, Ellen B. *elementary school educator*

ILLINOIS

Alexander
Eck, Gail Ann *elementary school educator*

Alton
Boyle, Ann M. *dean, dental educator*

Aurora
Daugherty, Patricia Ann *retired elementary school educator*

Belleville
Hilgenbrink, Robert J. *academic administrator*
Terveer, Joyce Ann *academic administrator, English language educator*

Berwyn
Wunderlich, Dorothy Anastasia *superintendent*

Bloomington
Wilson, Richard F. *academic administrator*

Bourbonnais
Gipple, Ellen A. *elementary school educator*

Broadview
Bland, Pamela June *special education educator*

Carbondale
Dixon, Billy Gene *academic administrator, educator*
Poshard, Glenn (Glendal W. Poshard) *academic administrator, former congressman*
Scott, Shirley Clay *dean*
Snyder, Carolyn Ann *education educator, librarian, director*
Treviño, Fernando Manuel *academic administrator, medical educator*

Carlyle
Spihlmann, Kris Ann *mathematics educator*

Carol Stream
Armerding, Hudson Taylor *retired college president, consultant*

Champaign
Ghosh, Avijit *dean*
Gomez, Terrine *school director*
Herman, Richard H. *academic administrator*
Hurd, Heidi M. *dean, humanities and law educator*
Ikenberry, Stanley Oliver *education educator, director, former university president*
Justice, Patricia *academic administrator, educator*
Loeb, Jane Rupley *academic administrator, educator*
McConkie, George Wilson *education educator*
Spodek, Bernard *early childhood educator*
Summerfield, Gale *director, educator*
Unsworth, John M. *dean, library and information science educator*

Charleston
Eberly, Charles *counseling and student development educator*
O'Rourke, Kathleen Ann *education educator*
Rives, Stanley Gene *retired academic administrator*
Surles, Carol D. *academic administrator*
Thornburgh, Daniel Eston *retired university administrator, journalism educator*

Chebanse
McLaughlin, Barbara Lyn *elementary school educator*

Chicago
Adelman, Pamela Bernice Kozoll *education educator*
Anderson, John Leonard *academic administrator, chemical engineering educator*
Anderson, Thomas Caryl *dean*
Baley, Joan Marie *elementary school educator*
Behnke, Michael Clare *academic administrator*
Bindenagel, James Dale *university executive*
Binion, Celious *retired parochial school educator*
Birnbaum, Barry William *special education educator*
Boulanger, Victor *director*
Buniak, Raymond *educational professional*
Cafferty, Pastora San Juan *education educator*
Chanyungco, Delly Yangco *dean*
Chinniah, Nim *academic administrator*
Clark, Gerda Margarete *special education educator*
Cosentino, Barbara *counseling administrator*
Cueto, Rochelle E. *elementary school educator*
Culp, Kristine Ann *dean, theology studies educator*
Daniel, Elnora D. *academic administrator*
Davis, Addie L. *mathematics educator*
Driskell, Claude Evans *college director, educator, dentist*
Duncan, Arne *school system administrator*
Foley, Father John P. *school system administrator, reverend*
Garanzini, Michael J. *academic administrator, priest*
Garber, Philip Robert *academic administrator, researcher*
Graham, Bruce S. *dean, educator*
Gross, Theodore Lawrence *university administrator, author*
Hamada, Robert S(eiji) *dean, educator, economist, entrepreneur*
Harris, Shirley *elementary and secondary and adult education school educator*
Hawkins, Loretta Ann *retired secondary school educator, playwright*
Hayes, Alice Bourke *academic administrator, biologist, researcher*
Holtschneider, Dennis H. *academic administrator, priest*
Inwang, Rosie L. *education educator*
Jacobson, Michael Harold *principal*
Jenkins, John Balester *academic administrator*
Jones, Tony *academic administrator*
Keiderling, Timothy Allen *chemistry educator, researcher*
Khan, M. Wasiullah *academic administrator*
Kim, Mi Ja *dean, academic administrator*
King, Tim *charter school administrator*
Kirsch, Lloyd *academic administrator*
Krent, Harold J. *dean, law educator*
Kubistal, Patricia Bernice *educational consultant*
Kuner, Charles *retired secondary school educator*
Landerholm, Elizabeth Jane *early childhood education educator*
Landsberg, Lewis *dean, endocrinologist, medical researcher*
Levandowski, Barbara Sue *education educator*
Levmore, Saul *dean, law educator*
Lusk, Peggy June *retired counseling administrator*
Madara, James Lee *dean, pathologist, educator, epitheliologist*
Mahaley-Johnson, Hosanna *school system administrator*
Mayo, Cora Louise *educator*
McCrank, Lawrence J. *dean, school librarian*
McMath, Lula Wray *retired elementary school educator, realtor*
McPherson, Michael Steven *academic administrator, economist*
Minogue, John P. *academic administrator, educator, priest*
Mirza, Leona Lousin *elementary school educator, director*
Morris-Rogers, Cheryl-Ann *daycare provider, director, educator*
O'Brien, Gregory Michael St. Lawrence *academic administrator*
O'Reilly, Charles Terrance *university dean*
Panko, Jessie Symington *education educator*
Pappas, David Wayne *guidance counselor, consultant*
Perez, Ziomara Darlene *pre-school educator*
Petitan, Debra Ann Burke *elementary school educator, counselor, design engineer, writer*
Powers, William Bryan *academic administrator*
Pulliam, Yvonne Antoinette *gifted education educator*
Reilly, Anne Huedepohl *university educator, researcher*
Reynolds, Ruth Carmen *school administrator, secondary school educator*
Rhone, Elvie Sue *educational administrator*
Richardson, John Thomas *academic administrator, clergyman*
Royster, Lynn Christine *academic administrator, educator*
Schieser, Hans Alois *education educator*
Schubert, William Henry *curriculum studies educator*
Sessions, Joan T. *director, educator*
Shaver, Joan Louise Fowler *dean, women's health nurse*
Snyder, Edward Adams *dean, economics professor*
Steinberg, Salme Elizabeth Harju *academic administrator, historian*
Stewart, Donald M. *college president*
Sufian, Sandy M. *education educator*
Sulkin, Howard Allen *academic administrator*
Swanson, Don Richard *university dean*
Tangora, Anthony Joseph *director*
Thompson, Richard Ellis *secondary school educator*
Van Zandt, David E. *dean, law educator*
Wasan, Darsh Tilakchand *academic administrator, chemical engineer, educator*
Wham, David Buffington *secondary school educator*
White, C. Vanessa *director*
Young, Lauren Sue Jones *education educator*
Yu, Clement Tak *educator, researcher, consultant*
Zimmer, Robert Jeffrey *academic administrator, mathematician, educator*

Chicago Heights
Buishas, Kristin Maureen *elementary school educator*
Nowocin, Debra Terese *gifted and talented secondary education educator*

Country Club Hills
Snyder, Caroline Jean *secondary school educator*

Crystal Lake
Haas, Sheila Jean *secondary school educator*

Davis
Fulfer, Matrona Penny *retired school librarian, educator, columnist*

Decatur
Jones, Penny Lee *elementary school educator*
Munoz, Joseph Mark *education educator, consultant*

Deerfield
Meyer, Mara Ellice *special education educator, consultant, academic administrator*
Wrobbel, Karen *education educator, consultant*

Dekalb
Legg, J. Ivan *academic administrator*
Monat, William Robert *university official*
Piot, Philippe Regis-Guy *educator, researcher*

Des Plaines
Lee, Margaret Burke *college president, language educator*

Dow
Schuler, Dorothy R. *education educator, consultant, retired elementary school educator*

Du Quoin
Ibendahl, Jean Ayres *retired elementary and secondary educator*

East Dubuque
Kussmaul, Donald *academic administrator*

East Saint Louis
Wright, Katie Harper *educational administrator, journalist*

Elgin
Kuforiji, Pamela DeLois *school system administrator*
Mao, Ruixuan (Rick Mao) *dean*
Puotinen, Arthur Edwin *college president, minister*

Eureka
Staudenmeier, William John, Jr. *academic administrator, dean, sociology professor*

Evanston
Bienen, Henry Samuel *academic administrator, political scientist, educator*
Boye, Roger Carl *academic administrator, journalism educator*
Christian, Richard Carlton *dean, former advertising agency executive*
Dumas, Lawrence B. *academic administrator*
Jain, Dipak Chand *dean, marketing educator, consultant*
Lewis, Dan Albert *education educator*
Peterson, Penelope Loraine *dean, education educator*
Power, Peggy Ann *elementary school educator*
Sheldon, Mark *assistant dean*
Watson, Christopher *dean*
Weber, Arnold Robert *academic administrator*

Evergreen Park
Wigsmoen, Susan Catania *elementary school educator*

Flossmoor
Sayler, Donna L. *secondary school educator, director*

Fox Lake
Smith, Justin Stuart *mathematics educator*

Galesburg
Haywood, Bruce *retired academic administrator*
Taylor, Roger Lee *academic administrator, lawyer*

Glen Carbon
Lazerson, Earl Edwin *retired academic administrator*

Glen Ellyn
Bollendorf, Robert Fredrick *retired education educator, psychologist*
Finley, Claudia D. *secondary school educator, consultant*
King, Peggy Marsha *special education educator, researcher*
Neurauter, Elizabeth Strain *secondary school educator*

Glenview
Corley, Jenny Lynd Wertheim *elementary school educator*
Whipple, Matthew Robert *secondary school educator*

Granite City
Humphrey, Owen Everett *retired education administrator*

Grayslake
Fonté, Richard W. *educational consultant, former academic administrator*

Harwood Heights
Rudel, Barbara Elizabeth *elementary school educator*

Highland Park
Hershenson, Martha Bradford *history educator*
Tribbey, Fern *mathematics educator*

Hoffman Estates
McCullough, Gary E. *education company executive*

Irvington
Brown, Robert William *elementary school educator*

Jacksonville
Johns, Beverley Anne Holden *special education administrator*

Joliet
Tokatlioglu, Theresa Diaz Lopez *elementary school educator*

Justice
Casselle, Corene *pre-school educator*

Kankakee
Roy, Sudipta D. *education educator*

Ladd
Shea, Mary Frances *retired elementary school educator*

Lemont
Doebert, Sandra L. *school system administrator*

Lincolnshire
Zorc, Renee *school librarian*

Lombard
Benning, Joseph Raymond *principal*

Macomb
Chu, Felix T. *school librarian*
Goldfarb, Alvin *academic administrator*
Hayes, Paul Robert *retired field and clinical experiences coordinator*

Madison
Purdes, Alice Marie *retired adult education educator*

Maple Park
Carter, Ethel Ilene *secondary school educator*

Markham
Peacock, Marilyn Claire *retired primary school educator*

Marseilles
Nellett, Gaile H. *adult education educator*

Maywood
Lid, Glenn David *chemistry educator*

Metamora
Harbers, Rebecca Ann *physical education educator*

Moline
Maroney, Sharon A *special education educator*

Naperville
Briseno, Kathleen *education educator*
Gilmore, Brenda René *literature and language educator, theater director*
Rosenthal, Edward Leonard *secondary school educator*
Wilde, Harold Richard *college president*

New Baden
Franke, Louise Anna *early childhood educator, farmland manager*

New Lenox
Heffernan, Debra Jane *administrator*

Normal
Conant, Brian *secondary school educator*
Miller, Wilma Hildruth *education educator*
Presley, John Woodrow *academic administrator*
Ward, Dane Michael *academic administrator*

Northbrook
Ben-Arie, Ronit Peleg *elementary school educator*
Ruter, Allan J. *literature and language educator*

Oak Brook
Hoffmann, Joan Carol *retired academic dean*

Oak Lawn
McSweeney, Sean Thomas *director*
Minarik, Carol T. *elementary school educator*

Oak Park
Adelman, William John *retired academic administrator, industrial relations specialist*
Venerable, Shirley Marie *retired gifted and talented educator*
Young, Jessica S.E. *secondary school educator*

Oakbrook Terrace
Taylor, Ronald Lee *academic administrator*

Orland Park
Burfeind, Betty Ruth *retired secondary school educator, coach*

Oswego
Johnson, Dawn Sundene *chemistry educator*

Palatine
Bassi, Suzanne Howard *retired secondary school educator, volunteer*

Palos Hills
Crawley, Vernon Obadiah *academic administrator*

Park Forest
Dalke, Carl D. *school system administrator, consultant*
Orr, Marcia *primary school educator, consultant, director*

Peoria
Kelly, Grace Dentino *secondary school educator*
Sanderson, Kenneth Jerome *school system administrator, consultant*

Peotone
Kanosky, Albert Leo *history educator, small business owner*

Quincy
Tomczak, Patricia Ann *dean, archivist*

Richton Park
Pierce, Mary E. *retired elementary school educator, public relations consultant*
Piucci, Virginio Louis *academic administrator*

River Forest
Carroll, Donna M. *academic administrator*
Coe, Donald Kirk *retired academic administrator*

Riverside
Smith, Ronald Forrest *retired history educator*

Robinson
Wolfe, Ellen Darlene *school librarian, elementary school educator*

Rock Island
Bahls, Steven Carl *academic administrator, educator*
Horstmann, James Douglas *retired academic administrator*

Rockford
Homewood, Elizabeth Holmes Nash *elementary school educator*
Howard, John Addison *former academic administrator*
Johnson, Elizabeth Ericson *retired educator*
Steele, Carl Lavern *academic administrator*

Rockton
Bolger, Jacqueline E. *literature and language educator*

Round Lake Beach
Harold, Kathleen T. *elementary school educator*

Saint Charles
Larsen, David Allen *educational consultant*

Schaumburg
Maluchnik, Rosemary Pellicore *elementary school educator*

Sigel
Stapleton, Patricia Jean *elementary school educator*

Springfield
Kersten, Christian George *university administrator*
Koch, Christopher A. *school system administrator*
Kocis, Janet Kay *elementary school educator*
Poorman, Robert Lewis *retired academic administrator*
Schroeder, Raymond Ernest *educational administrator*

University Park
Keys, Paul Ross *academic administrator, educator*
Maimon, Elaine Plaskow *academic administrator*

Urbana
Kaufman, Paula T. *university librarian*
Stukel, James Joseph *academic administrator, mechanical engineer, educator*

Vernon Hills
Cho, Yong Hyo *education educator, consultant*

Waterman
Arends, Ann M. *elementary school educator, pianist*

Waukegan
Akouris, Dianne *elementary school educator*

Wheaton
Ford, Andrew Thomas *former academic administrator*
LaFrancis, Nicole Marie *secondary school educator*
Litfin, A. Duane *academic administrator*

Wilmette
Mandel, Judith Lynn *primary school educator*
Olson, Patricia Hagey *retired elementary school educator*
Smutny, Joan Franklin *academic director, educator*

Winnetka
Huggins, Charlotte Susan Harrison *retired secondary school educator, writer, travel company executive*
McKee, Judith Nelson *elementary school educator, educational consultant*

Wood River
Shelton, Michael Patrick *principal*

Woodridge
Jandes, Kenneth Michael *retired superintendent of schools*

INDIANA

Anderson
Nicholson, Robert Arthur *college president*

Bicknell
Ford, Andrea Michelle *mathematics educator*

Bloomington
Arnove, Robert Frederick *education educator*
Barnes, A. James *dean*
Bertenthal, Bennett Ira *dean, psychologist, educator*
Bornholdt, Laura Anna *academic administrator*
Chaifetz, Marshal Lawrence *educational consultant, educator*
Mehlinger, Howard Dean *education educator*
Robel, Lauren *dean, law educator*
Robinson, Jennifer Meta *academic administrator, consultant*
Ryan, John William *academic administrator*
Smith, Carl Bernard *education educator*
Smith, Daniel C. *dean, finance educator*
Webb, Charles Haizlip, Jr. *retired dean*

Brownsburg
Strahle, Ron E. *elementary school educator, social studies educator*

Carmel
Rand, Leon *academic administrator*

Clarksville
von Allmen, Dion S. *mathematics educator, department chairman, mathematics professor*

Connersville
Newton, Cindy Lynn *elementary school educator, media specialist*

Corydon
Miller, Judith Elaine *retired middle school educator, musician*

Crawfordsville
White, Patrick E. *academic administrator*

Evansville
Jennings, Stephen Grant *academic administrator*

Fishers
Shults, Anna *elementary school educator*

Fort Wayne
Snyder, Arthur E. *academic administrator*
Wartell, Michael Alan *academic administrator*

Franklin
Stone, Mary Ann *literature and language educator*

Gary
Sia, Kimberlee Jean *principal*
Smith, Vernon G. *education educator, state legislator*

Goshen
Meyer, Albert James *educational researcher*

Granger
Morgan, Ardys Nord *school improvement consultant*

Greencastle
Bottoms, Robert Garvin *academic administrator*

Griffith
Luetschwager, Mary Susan *educational consultant*

Hammond
Delph, Donna Jean (Maroc) *education educator, consultant, academic administrator*

Hobart
Hanley, Roberta Lynn *alternative education coordinator, educator*

Indianapolis
Bepko, Gerald Lewis *retired academic administrator, law educator*
Brash, Susan Kay *principal*
Brater, Donald Craig *dean, educator*
Brenner, Mark Lee *academic administrator, physiologist, educator*
Broome, Marion *dean*
Chandler, Julie Light *secondary school educator*
Clark, Charles M., Jr. *medical school administrator*
Dai, Yuan-Shun *education educator*
Floyd, James M., Jr. *adult education educator*
Goldblatt, Lawrence I. *dean, educator, researcher*
Gooldy, Patricia Alice *retired elementary school educator*
Hardin, Boniface *academic administrator*
Harrold, John Andrew *education educator, consultant*
Keaton, Margaret-Ann Coleman *education educator*
Kennedy, Russell Edward *academic administrator*
LaGrotto, Louisa *middle school educator*
Malone, Jean Hambidge *educational consultant*
Najjar, Diana *elementary school educator*
Pitts, Beverley J. *academic administrator*
Reed, Suellen Kinder *school system administrator*
Solomon, Marilyn Kay *primary school educator, consultant, small business owner*
Speth, Gerald Lennus *educational consultant, management consultant*
Sullender, Joy Sharon *retired elementary school educator*
Sykes, Linda Diane *elementary school educator, music educator*
Tribble, Hazel R. *elementary school educator*
Van Lieu, Thomas Jerry *school system administrator*
Whitfield, Erica Sharon *director, career planning administrator*
Willham, Lorann Ellyn *assistant principal*
Williams, Luida K. *retired elementary school educator*
Woody, John Frederick *retired secondary school educator*

La Porte
Johnson, Bruce Ross *elementary school educator*

Lafayette
Jischke, Martin C. *retired academic administrator*
Roush, Nadine Marie *elementary school educator*
Troutner, Joanne Johnson *director, consultant, secondary school educator*

Lizton
King, Richard Gene *superintendent*

Mishawaka
Watts, Mark Edwin *secondary school educator, professional volleyball player*

Muncie
Amman, E(lizabeth) Jean *academic administrator*
Gora, JoAnn M. *academic administrator*
Kitchens, Frederick Lynton III *education educator, researcher*
Lawhead, Victor Bernard *education educator*
Stewart, Rita Joan *academic administrator*
Van Ness, Ross Howard *education educator*

New Albany
Riehl, Jane Ellen *education educator*

New Harmony
Rice, David Lee *university president emeritus*

New Haven
Powelson, Gale Dawn *elementary school educator*

North Manchester
Switzer, Jo Young *college president*

Notre Dame
Burish, Thomas Gerard *academic administrator, psychology professor*
Crosson, Frederick James *retired dean, humanities educator*
Jenkins, John I. *academic administrator*
Malloy, Edward Aloysius *academic administrator*
Marino, Joseph Paul, Sr. *dean, chemist, researcher*
Marmion, Daniel Keith *school librarian*
O'Hara, Patricia Anne *dean, law educator*
O'Meara, Onorato Timothy *academic administrator, mathematician*
Scheidt, W. Robert *chemistry educator, researcher*
Woo, Carolyn Yauyan *dean*
Younger, Jennifer A. *university librarian*

Roanoke
Cutshall-Hayes, Diane Marion *elementary school educator*

Russiaville
Berry, Patricia A. *middle school educator*

Schererville
Platis, Chris Steven *adult education educator*

South Bend
Agbetsiafa, Douglas Kofi *academic administrator, financial and management consultant*
Harriman, Gerald Eugene *retired business administrator, economics professor*
Rodgers, Grace Anne *university official*
Shepherd, Terry Lynn *special education educator*
Storin, Matthew Victor *academic administrator, educator, retired editor*

Spencerville
Clark, Donna M. *retired elementary school educator*

Terre Haute
Benjamin, Lloyd William III *academic administrator*
Dando, William Arthur *academic administrator, geography and geology educator*
Gilman, David Alan *education educator*
Hunt, Effie Neva *retired dean, literature educator*
Leach, Ronald George *education educator, librarian*
Malooley, David Joseph *electronics and computer technology educator*
McCallister, Myrna J. *school librarian, administrator*

Upland
Kesler, Jay Lewis *retired academic administrato*

Valparaiso
Mundinger, Donald Charles *retired college president*
Schnabel, Robert Victor *retired academic administrator*

Wanatah
Moser, Sandra Kay *secondary school educator*

West Lafayette
Beering, Steven Claus *academic administrator, medical educator*
Córdova, France Anne-Dominic *academic administrator, astrophysicist*
Cosier, Richard A. *dean, finance educator*
Dyrenfurth, Michael John *education educator, academic administrator*
Gennett, Timothy *academic administrator*
Jang, SooCheong (Shawn) *education educator*
Moyars-Johnson, Mary Annis *retired academic administrator*
Namkung, Young *educator, researcher*
Ringel, Robert Lewis *academic administrator*
Rud, Anthony Gordon, Jr. *education educator*
Shertzer, Bruce Eldon *education educator*
Silva, Tony *education educator, editor*
VanFossen, Phillip J. *academic administrator*
Vitter, Jeffrey Scott *academic administrator, computer science educator, researcher*
Xin, Yan Ping *special education educator*

Westfield
Bradbury, Betty Marie *history and music educator*

IOWA

Ames
Allen, Benjamin J. *academic administrator*
Bugeja, Michael Joseph *director, educator, write*
Crabtree, Beverly June *retired dean*
Ebbers, Larry Harold *education educator*
Geoffroy, Gregory L. *academic administrator, educator*
Hoffman, Elizabeth *academic administrator, economics professor*
Jackson, George Arthur *dean, educator*
Manatt, Richard *retired education educator*

Mattila, Mary Jo Kalsem *elementary school educator, special education educator, art educator*

Ankeny
Keese, Jan *elementary school educator*

Bettendorf
Hengst, Herbert Randall *retired adult education educator*
Taylor, Paulette Ann *special education educator, educational consultant*

Cedar Falls
Cai, Mingshui *education educator*
Lettow, Lucille Jane *school librarian, education educator*
Lundy, Sherman Perry *secondary school educator*

Cedar Rapids
Brighi, Robert J. *principal*
Snell, Jennifer Sue *school system administrator, psychologist*
Urbanowski, Melena Haskovec *elementary school educator*

Creston
Dillenburg, Carolyn Eva Lauer *retired secondary school educator*

Davenport
Hudson, Celeste Nutting *education educator, consultant, reading clinic administrator*
Sheehey, Patricia Ann *secondary school educator*

Des Moines
Burn, Barbara Louise *literature and language educator*
Gaines, Ruth Ann *secondary school educator*
Jeffrey, Judy *school system administrator*
Maxwell, David E. *academic executive, educator*
Paterik, Frances Sue *secondary school educator, actress*

Dubuque
Haugen, Jane S. *elementary school educator*
Lickteig, Mary Joan *elementary school educator*
Toale, Thomas Edward *school system administrator, minister*

Epworth
Boice, Daniel Gene *college librarian*

Fort Madison
Sodey, Angela Ann *gifted and talented educator*

Grinnell
Osgood, Russell King *academic administrator*

Indianola
Dyer, Cynthia Myers *college librarian, archivist*

Iowa City
Boyd, Willard Lee *academic administrator, educator, lawyer, museum director*
Brennan, Robert Lawrence *educational director, psychometrician*
Buckwalter, Kathleen C. *academic administrator, educator*
Dreher, Melanie Creagan *dean, nursing educator*
Feldt, Leonard Samuel *academic administrator, educator*
Hunter, William Curt *dean, finance educator*
Jepsen, David Andrew *retired counselor, educator*
Johnsen, David C. *dean, dental educator*
Jones, Carolyn *dean, law educator*
Jones, Catherine Clarissa *retired secondary school educator*
Mason, Sally Kay Frost *academic administrator, biology professor*
Newell, Steven Wayne *secondary school educator, consultant*
Plapp, Bryce Vernon *biochemistry educator*
Porter, Nancy Lefgren *reading recovery educator*
Robillard, Jean Eugene *dean, pediatrician*
Schmeiser, Cynthia Board *educational organization executive*
Spriestersbach, Duane Caryl *academic administrator, speech pathology/audiology services professional, educator*

Manchester
Cook, Sharon Lee Delancey *retired elementary school educator, musician*

Maquoketa
Krum, Dee *secondary school educator*

Mount Vernon
Will, Frederic *academic administrator, educator, writer*

Muscatine
Mowl, Linda *special education educator*

Newton
Ward, Doree Maxine *secondary school educator*

Norwalk
Augspurger, Mark Christian *elementary school educator*

Oelwein
Flaucher-Falck, Velma Ruth *retired special education educator*

Oskaloosa
Burrow, Paul Irving *secondary school educator*

Ottumwa
Newquist, Judy Lynne Roos *elementary school educator, education educator*

Pella
Steele, Mildred Romedahl *educator*

Rock Valley
Bulthuis, Sidney Aaron *secondary school educator*
Ortman, Don L. *principal*

Sioux City
Clovis, Samuel Harvey, Jr. *academic administrator*
Mounts, Nancy *secondary school educator*
Rants, Carolyn Jean *academic administrator, educator*
Warnstadt, Jacqueline Rae *elementary school educator*

Storm Lake
Bochtler, Stanley Edwin *education educator*

Urbandale
Hoyt, Kenneth Boyd *education educator, writer*

Waterloo
Alfrey, Marian Antoinette *retired education educator*
Kober, Arletta Refshauge (Mrs. Kay L. Kober) *supervisor*

Waverly
Menzel, Ferol Schricker *academic administrator*
Rose, Mary Mabel *retired elementary school educator*

KANSAS

Baldwin City
Baker, Margaret Moore-Fritz *retired school librarian, humanities educator*
Long, Patricia N. *academic administrator*

Caney
Wilmoth, Marsha H. *elementary school educator*

Cottonwood Falls
Dodez, Diane M. *principal*

El Dorado
Langley, William M. *educator*

Emporia
Fowler, Barbara J. *middle school educator*
Phelps, Connie Lea *psychology and special education educator*

Eureka
Pitko, Pamela Ann *physical education educator, coach*

Frontenac
Wilson, Donald Wallin *academic administrator, communications educator*

Geuda Springs
Moore, BettyJane *elementary school educator*

Goddard
Molz, Carol Jean *elementary school educator*

Great Bend
Rittenhouse, Nancy Carol *elementary school educator*

Independence
Wright, Tami LaDonna *pre-school educator*

Kansas City
Atkinson, Barbara F. *dean, medical educator, executive vice chancellor*
Burke, Thomas Richard *community college administrator*
Caruthers, Loyce Ellenor *education educator*
Clifton, Thomas E. *academic administrator, minister*
Miller, Karen L. *dean, nursing educator*
Warne, Alan M. *continuing education educator, consultant*

Lawrence
Frederickson, Horace George *retired academic administrator, humanities educator*
Hemenway, Robert E. *academic administrator, language educator*
Lariviere, Richard Wilfred *academic administrator, educator*
Locke, Carl Edwin, Jr. *academic administrator, engineer, educator*
McAllister, Stephen Robert *dean, law educator*
Peterson, Nancy *special education educator*
Turnbull, Ann Patterson *special education educator, consultant, research director*

Leawood
Talley, Melvin Gary *academic administrator*

Liberal
Hicks, Linda Reona *elementary school educator*
Smothermon, Reba Maxine *elementary school educator*

Manhattan
Amtoft, Torben *adult education educator, researcher*
Coffman, James Richard *academic administrator, veterinarian, educator*
Hawley, Jana Marie *educator, department head*
Muir, William Lloyd III *academic administrator*
Wefald, Jon *academic administrator*

Meade
Brannan, Cleo Estella *retired elementary school educator*

North Newton
Ediger, Marlow *retired education educator*

Olathe
Anderson, Peggy C. *retired elementary school educator*
Obenhaus, Steven Lee *secondary school educator*
Stevens, Diana Lynn *elementary school educator*

Overland Park
Velicer, Janet Schafbuch *retired elementary school educator*
Voska, Kathryn Caples *consultant, facilitator*

Pomona
Gentry, Alberta Elizabeth *elementary school educator*

Pratt
Hart, Don Lee *academic administrator, writer*

Shawnee Mission
Allen, Janet Lee *special education educator*
Sweeney, Leo Joseph *university administrator*

Sublette
Swinney, Carol Joyce *secondary school educator*

Topeka
Dye, Gloria A. *education educator*
Farley, Jerry B. *academic administrator*
McFarland, William Joseph (Joe McFarland) *academic administrator*

Uniontown
Conard, Norman Dale *secondary school educator*

Wichita
Powell, Shirley Theressa *elementary school educator*

KENTUCKY

Berea
Krug, John Carleton (Tony Krug) *academic administrator, library director, consultant*

Bowling Green
Atwell, Nedra Wheeler *education educator, consultant*
Burch, Barbara G. *academic administrator*
Haynes, Robert Vaughn *retired academic administrator, historian*

Covington
Berg, Lorine McComis *retired guidance counselor*
Tenkotte, Paul Allen *history and international studies educator*

Danville
Breeze, William Hancock *academic administrator*
Roush, John A. *academic administrator*

Fort Knox
Tucker, Brenda Brunette *elementary school educator*

Fort Mitchell
Malayery, Nasrin *educational consultant*

Fort Thomas
Yelton, Dianne Burgess *secondary school educator*

Frankfort
Erwin, Barbara F. *school system administrator*
Noland, Kevin M. *school system administrator*
Sisney, Sherleen Sue *secondary school educator*

Grethel
Hughes, Cindi Baker *special education educator*

Guston
Yundt, Betty Brandenburg *elementary school educator*

Hardin
Morrow, Bruce William *academic administrator, management consultant*

Harlan
Greene, James S. III *school administrator*

Harrodsburg
Worley, Carolyn Ann Hiner *retired secondary school educator*

Hopkinsville
Redmon-Holliday, Rose Marie *secondary school educator*

Lexington
Allison, Jonathan Mackinnon *university professor, researcher*
Cole, Henry Philip *educational psychology educator*
Guskey, Thomas Robert *education educator*
Hinds, Sara Feagan *elementary school educator*
Todd, Lee Trover, Jr. *academic administrator, electrical engineer*
Turner, Sharon P. *dean, dentist, educator*
Vestal, Allan W. *dean, law educator*

Louisville
Atcher, Joseph Ray *director*
Cecil, Bonnie Susan *elementary school educator*
Choi, Namok *education educator*
Goldstein, Irvin L. *elementary school educator*
Greaver, Joanne Hutchins *mathematics educator, writer*
Jenne, Sue Oak *secondary school educator*
Kaplan, Joel A. *academic administrator*
Karwowski, Waldemar *adult education educator*
Martinez-Maldonado, Manuel *academic administrator, dean, medical and science educator*
Mohler, Richard Albert, Jr. *academic administrator, theologian*
Newell, Elizabeth Carolyn *retired secondary school educator*
Noah, Christopher Ray *history educator*
Ramsey, James R. *academic administrator*
Rothstein, Laura *dean, law educator*
Ruter, Ruth Evelyn *elementary school educator*
Swain, Donald Christie *retired academic administrator, historian, educator*
Wright, Jeffrey A. *biology, physics educator*

Madisonville
Parrent, Jonathan Vince *dean*

Midway
Critchfield, Alison *education educator*

Morehead
Kantrovich, Adam J. *education educator*
Klecker, Beverly McCauley *academic administrator*

Mount Sterling
Aileen-Donohew, Phyllis Augusta *educational consultant*

Murray
Dunn, Randy J. *academic administrator*

Newport
Clinkenbeard, James Howard *principal*

Nicholasville
Midkiff, Dinah Lee *retired elementary and middle school educator*

Paducah
Mittendorf, Kimberly Ann *secondary school educator, real estate consultant*
Talbert, Debra Kaiser *elementary school educator, artist*

Princeton
Earnest, Melissa Webb *education educator*
Faughn, Dale *biology educator*
Noffsinger, Nancy Leigh *retired special education educator*

Simpsonville
Burkhardt, Susanne M. *elementary school educator*

Somerset
Pennington, Aubrey El *director*

LOUISIANA

Alexandria
Maples, Mary Lou *elementary school educator*
Wesse, David Joseph *higher education administrator, consultant*

Angie
Kennedy, Joan Pace *school librarian, educator*

Baker
Baker, Yvonne Bell *elementary school educator*

Baton Rouge
Bensman, Stephen J. *school librarian, researcher*
Boyce, Bert Roy *university dean emeritus, library and information science educator*
Caffey, Horace Rouse *academic administrator, agricultural company executive*
Harper, Sandra Stecher *academic administrator*
Harrelson, Clyde Lee *retired secondary school educator*
Lombardi, John V. *academic administrator, historian*
Mc Cameron, Fritz Allen *retired university administrator*
O'Keefe, Sean Charles *academic administrator, former federal agency administrator*
Pastorek, Paul G. *school system administrator, lawyer*
Prestage, James Jordan *university chancellor, consultant*
Risinger, Beth N. *elementary school educator*
Smith, Michael *academic administrator*
Vallas, Paul G. *school system administrator*

Benton
Rivers, Christine D. *academic administrator*

Choudrant
Lofton, Brenda M. *secondary school educator*

Deridder
Smith, Mabel Hargis *retired secondary school educator, musician*

Franklin
Fairchild, Phyllis Elaine *school counselor*

Glenmora
Burns, Linda D. *elementary school educator*

Gonzales
Kidd, Ruth Price *retired secondary school educator*

Grambling
Judson, Horace Augustus *academic administrator, chemistry educator*
Porter, Wilma Jean *retired educational consultant*

Hammond
Parker, Clea Edward *retired university president*
Siegel, Wendy Lowe *special education educator*

Harvey
Weekley, Judy Liddington *special education educator*

Houma
Colasurdo, Irma Louise *secondary school educator, department chairman*

Lafayette
Authement, Ray Paul *college president*
Colbert-Cormier, Patricia A. *secondary school educator*
Marceaux, Linda d'Augereau *elementary school educator*

Lake Charles
Fields-Gold, Anita *retired dean*
Lee, Brandi Gremillion *elementary school educator*

Mandeville
Arrowsmith, Marian Campbell *elementary school educator, supervisor, educator*

Metairie
Blunt, Joyce Omega *special education educator*
Chambers, Thomas Edward *academic administrator, psychologist*
Crosby, Marena Lienhard *retired academic administrator*

Natchitoches
Wolfe, George Cropper *retired private school educator, artist, writer*

New Iberia
Hockless, Mary Fontenot *educational consultant*

New Orleans
Christen, Carol A. *principal*
Cody, Wilmer St. Clair *educational policy researcher*
Cowen, Scott S. *academic administrator*
Gordon, Joseph Elwell *university official, educator*
Hovland, Eric Jeffrey *dean, endodontics educator*
McCall, John Patrick *college president, educator*
Novakov, George John, Jr. *gifted and talented educator, consultant, administrative assistant*
Paradise, Louis Vincent *education educator, dean*
Pomes, Stephen Vincent *school librarian*
Ponoroff, Lawrence *dean, law educator, consultant*
Query, Lance D. *dean, university librarian*
Sherman, Edward Francis *dean, law educator*

Newllano
Boren, Lynda Sue *gifted education educator*

Opelousas
Underwood, Lorainne Ballard *literature and language educator*

Pineville
Lott, Johnnye Jo *elementary school educator, writer*

Prairieville
Biri, Toni Roppolo *elementary school educator*

Ruston
Bourgeois, Patricia McLin *academic administrator, women's health and pediatrics nurse, educator*
Freasier, Aileen W. *special education educator*
Maxfield, John Edward *retired university dean*
Nassar, Raja *statistics educator, researcher, consultant*
Taylor, Foster Jay *retired university president*

Saint Martinville
Fournet, Patricia Sibley *retired secondary school educator*

Slidell
Dabdoub, Paul Oscar *academic administrator*
Fincher, Margaret Ann *retired secondary school educator*
Ladner, Norma Foley *elementary school educator*

Springhill
Thomas, Faye Evelyn J. *elementary and secondary school educator*

Thibodaux
Harris, Rose M. *academic administrator*
Hulbert, Stephen Thompson *academic administrator*

West Monroe
Ford, Mary Ann *secondary school educator*

Westlake
Grantham, Camille Renee Theriot *high school librarian, media specialist*

Zachary
Price, Carol Leah *mathematics educator*

MAINE

Augusta
Crosby, Nathaniel Howard *elementary school educator*
Gendron, Susan Ann *school system administrator*
Randall, Richard J. *academic administrator*

Bangor
MacTaggart, Terrence Joseph *education educator, researcher, former academic administrator*
McKinnon, Carolyn Ann *retired child care center director*
Pattenaude, Richard Louis *academic administrator, educator*

Bar Harbor
Krevans, Julius Richard *academic administrator, internist*
Swazey, Judith Pound *academic administrator, science educator*

Bremen
Wilson, Linda Smith *retired academic administrator*

Brunswick
Greason, Arthur LeRoy, Jr. *retired university administrator*
Mills, Barry *academic administrator, lawyer*

Corea
Harward, Donald West *retired academic administrator*

Dennysville
Hobart, Rebecca Weston *retired elementary school educator*

Farmington
Kalikow, Theodora June *academic administrator*

Harrington
Ray, Brittany E. *literature and language educator*

Islesboro
Rogers, William Raymond *retired academic administrator, psychologist, educator*

Kennebunkport
Featherman, Sandra *retired academic administrator, political science professor*

Lewiston
Hansen, Elaine Tuttle *academic administrator*
Reich, Jill *dean*
Tardif, Donna Lynn *elementary school educator*

Newfield
Patten, Ronald James *university dean*

North Yarmouth
Fecteau, Rosemary Louise *educational administrator, educator, consultant*

Old Orchard Beach
Day, Marlene E. *elementary school educator*

Old Town
Alex, Joanne DeFilipp *elementary school educator*

Orono
Butterfield, Stephen Alan *education educator*
Kennedy, Robert Alan *educational administrator*
Szymanski, Edna Mora *provost*
Wiersma, G. Bruce *dean, forester, educator*

Portland
Dill, William Rankin *college president*
Pitegoff, Peter Robert *dean, law educator*
Vincent, Christine *academic administrator*
Wood, Joseph S. *academic administrator*

Skowhegan
Ross, James Owen *education educator, researcher*

Standish
Clements, Kathleen Kiley *education educator*

Waterville
Adams, William D. *academic administrator*
Cook, Susan Farwell *director*

Yarmouth
Bischoff, David Canby *retired university administrator*
Hart, Loring Edward *academic administrator*

MARYLAND

Accokeek
Kutchi, Judith Ann *elementary school educator*

Adamstown
Church, Martha Eleanor *retired academic administrator*

Adelphi
Kirwan, William English, II, *academic administrator, mathematics professor*
Walker, Mamie Odena *retired secondary school educator*

Annapolis
Bowen, Linnell R. *director*
Fowler, Jeffrey L. *academic administrator, career military officer*
Miller, William Charles *academic administrator, retired naval officer*
Stern, Margaret Bassett *retired special education educator, author*

Arnold
Smith, Martha A. *academic administrator*

Baltimore
Allan, Janet D. *dean*
Arrindell, Nicholas J. *academic administrator, educator*
Ball, Gregory Francis *biological psychology educator*
Ball, Marion Jokl *academic administrator*
Bjerkaas, Allan Wayne *associate dean, physicist*
Brody, William Ralph *academic administrator, radiologist, educator*
Chylinski-Polubinski, Roger *academic administrator*
Elias, Sarah Davis *retired English language educator*
Ellis, Brother Patrick (H. J.) *academic administrator*
Gifford, Donald George *dean, law educator, consultant*
Grasmick, Nancy S. *school system administrator*
Guler, Osman *education educator, researcher*
Hoehn-Saric, R. Christopher *educational organization executive*
Hrabowski, Freeman Alphonsa III *academic administrator*
Jackson, Stanley Edward *retired special education educator*
Lazarus, Fred, IV, *academic administrator*
McPartland, James Michael *academic administrator*
Oji, Pauline E. *secondary school educator*
Patel, Chintan *adult education educator*
Ross, Richard Starr *retired medical school dean, cardiologist, educator*
Rothenberg, Karen H. *dean, law educator*
Scales, Robert H., Jr. *former academic administrator, retired army officer*
Seurkamp, Mary Pat *college president*
Stohler, Christian S. *dean, dental educator*
Trombley, Edward Francis III *registrar*
Valentine, April Sue *elementary school educator, department chairman*

Bel Air
Miller, Dorothy Eloise *education educator*

Belcamp
Tapp, Mamie Pearl *educator*

Beltsville
Bruckner, Daniel Raymond *history educator*

Berlin
Hammond, Michelle *middle school educator*

Bethesda
Corn, Milton *dean, physician, consultant*
Hemming, Val G. *retired dean, educator*
Hutchins, Michael *non-profit scientific society administrator, conservation biologist*
Pemberton, S. Macpherson *government official, educator*
Solomon, Henry *university dean*

Bowie
Lowe, Calvin W. *university president*

California
Galligan, James *retired guidance counselor*

Chevy Chase
Rayburn, Wendell Gilbert, Sr. *educational consultant*
Towsner, Cynthia Merle *academic administrator, educator*

College Park
Dieter, George Elwood, Jr. *academic administrator*
Frank, Howard *dean, information technology executive*
Imig, David Gregg *education educator, retired educational association administrator*
Ingold, Catherine White *academic administrator*
Langenberg, Donald Newton *retired academic administrator, physicist*
Mote, Clayton Daniel, Jr. *academic administrator, mechanical engineer, educator*
Preece, Jennifer J. *dean, information scientist, educator*
Toll, John Sampson *retired academic administrator, physics professor*

Columbia
Jones-Wilson, Faustine Clarisse *retired education educator*
Whiting, Albert Nathaniel *former university chancellor*

Crownsville
Campbell, Walter Everett *adult education educator*

District Heights
Parham, Sheila D. *elementary school educator*

Easton
Behm, Mark Edward *academic administrator, consultant*

Edgewater
Falk, John H. *educational administrator*

Ellicott City
Bruley, Duane Frederick *academic administrator, consultant, engineer*

Essex
Bunn, Wm. Jeffrey *secondary school educator, director*

Frederick
Burkhard, Fred (Bud) *academic administrator*
Pastoor, Robertus Antonius *academic administrator*

Frostburg
Gibralter, Jonathan C. *academic administrator*
Root, Edward Lakin *education educator, academic administrator*

Gaithersburg
Bremenstuhl, David P. *elementary school educator*

Germantown
Khan, Tapan Kumar *adult education educator*

Glen Burnie
Watts, Virginia Agnes *retired special education educator*

Greenbelt
Bernstein, Kenneth J. *secondary school educator*

Hagerstown
Stonestreet, Jeannine Lee *edcuator*
Warner, Charles David III *academic administrator*

Joppa
Bates, Martha Copenhaver *elementary school educator*

Kensington
Ellwanger, Albert Thompson III *secondary school educator*

Laurel
Dorsey, John Wesley, Jr. *retired academic administrator, economist*
Stumpff, Robert Thomas *retired academic administrator*
Williams, Barbara Ivory *educational researcher*

Lusby
Ladd, Culver Sprogle *secondary school educator*

Marion Station
Handy, Mary Thomas *retired elementary school educator*

Millersville
Culver, Catherine Marie *secondary school educator*

Ocean Pines
Crawford, Norman Crane, Jr. *academic administrator, consultant*

Odenton
Lambert, Vickie Ann *retired dean, nursing consultant*

Olney
Taggarse, Jyotsna Sharad *mathematics educator*

Owings
Oring, Stuart August *audio-visual specialist, writer, photographer, researcher*

Phoenix
Hairston, Walter Albert *school system administrator*

Potomac
Bulger, Roger James *academic administrator*
Hey, Nancy Henson *retired educational administrator*
Ingram, Richard Thomas *retired president, consultant, writer*
Kuykendall, Crystal Arlene *educational consultant, lawyer*

Princess Anne
Thompson, Thelma Barnaby *university president, classical languages educator*

Riverdale
Brown, Yvonne Nardin *secondary school educator*

Rockville
Robinson, Cheryl Jeffreys *special education educator*
Stansfield, Charles W. *educational administrator*

Saint Marys City
O'Brien, Jane Margaret *academic administrator*

Saint Michaels
Feisel, Lyle Dean *retired dean, electrical engineer, educator*

Silver Spring
Burgos-Sasscer, Ruth *chancellor emeritus*
Cohen, Sharon Claire *history educator, consultant*
Coles, Anna Louise Bailey *retired dean, nurse*
Cooper, Nannie Coles *education educator, consultant*
Haynes, Leonard L. III *director*
Latson, Richard Charles *retired audio-visual specialist*
Makris, Margaret Lubbe *retired elementary school educator*
Miller, Karla Patricia *elementary school educator*
Oliver, Kimberly *primary school educator*
Whalen, John Philip *retired academic administrator, priest, lawyer*

Solomons
Wright, David Alan *environmental toxicology professor, consultant*

Swanton
Cummins, Delmer Duane *academic administrator, historian*

Towson
Caret, Robert Laurent *academic administrator*
Hoch, David Allen *athletic director*

Union Bridge
Hannah, Judy Challenger *private education tutor*

MASSACHUSETTS

Agawam
Goodwin, Beverly Ann *elementary school educator*

Amherst
Adrion, William Richards *academic administrator, computer and information sciences educator, writer*
Call, Gregory S. *academic administrator, mathematics professor*
Hartwell, Alfred Stedman (Ash Hartwell) *international relations educator, consultant*

Hexter, Ralph J. *academic administrator, literature educator*
Immerman, Neil *academic administrator, computer science educator*
Marx, Anthony W. *academic administrator*
May, Ernest Dewey *academic administrator, musician*
Prince, Gregory Smith, Jr. *retired college president*
Seymour, Charlena *academic administrator*

Ayer
Sizer, Theodore R. *education educator*

Babson Park
Rice, Mark P. *dean, management educator*

Bedford
White, Alan Frederick *academic administrator*

Beverly
Eastman, W. Dean *secondary school educator*

Bolton
Wintle, Suzanne *elementary school educator*

Boston
Alden, Vernon Roger *academic administrator*
Andrews, Nancy Catherine *dean, pediatrician, hematologist, educator*
Aoun, Joseph *academic administrator, linguistics educator, researcher*
Ash, Barbara Lee *education and human services educator*
Auger, Jessie L. *elementary school educator*
Bloom, Barry R. *dean, medical educator*
Brown, Robert Arthur *academic administrator, chemical engineering professor*
Brown, Roger H. *academic administrator*
Chang, Shan Nan *education educator, academic administrator*
DePaola, Dominick Philip *academic administrator*
Dienstag, Jules Leonard *dean, hepatologist, researcher*
Dluhy, Deborah Haigh *dean*
Elasmar, Michael *director, educator*
Federman, Daniel David *academic administrator, endocrinologist, educator*
Flier, Jeffrey S. *dean, endocrinologist*
Frankl, Spencer Nelson *dean, dentist*
Hedlund, Ronald David *academic administrator, researcher, educator*
Katzman, Lauren I. *special education educator, consultant*
Kirkpatrick, Edward Thomson *retired academic administrator, mechanical engineer*
Koh, Howard Kyongju *academic administrator, educator, former public health commissioner*
Landsmark, Ted (Theodore C. Landsmark) *academic administrator*
Lataif, Louis Edward *dean*
Le Quesne, Philip William *chemistry educator, researcher*
Maganzini, Brother John Bernard *academic administrator*
Mehra, Pushkar *director, educator*
Meissner, Walt *dean*
Morris, Robert *education educator*
Norris, Lonnie Harold *dean*
O'Rourke, Maureen A. *dean, law educator*
Penney, Sherry Hood *academic administrator, consultant*
Pereira, Julio Cesar *middle school educator*
Reede, Joan Yvonne *academic administrator, medical educator, pediatrician*
Ronayne, Michael Richard, Jr. *academic dean*
Scrimshaw, Susan Crosby *academic administrator*
Silber, John Robert *retired academic administrator, law and philosophy educator*
Simmons, Sylvia Jeanne Quarles (Mrs. Herbert G. Simmons Jr.) *academic administrator, educator*
Sloan, Katherine (Kay Sloan) *college president*
Spieler, Emily A. *dean, law educator*
Zungolo, Eileen H. *dean*

Braintree
Watts, Kisha Mann *school system administrator, secondary school educator*

Bridgewater
Tinsley, Adrian *former college president*

Byfield
Doggett, John Martin, Jr., (Marty Doggett) *headmaster*

Cambridge
Bane, Mary Jo *dean, political science professor*
Champion, Hale (Charles Hale Champion) *academic administrator, lecturer, government official, consultant*
Chernoff, Herman *statistics educator*
Clay, Phillip L. *academic administrator*
Edley, Christopher F., Jr. *dean, law educator*
Ellwood, David Tabor *dean, public policy educator*
Eurich Lazarus, Nell P. *education educator*
Faust, Drew Gilpin (Catharine) *academic administrator, historian*
Fischer, Kurt Walter *education educator*
Fitzsimmons, William R. *dean*
Fox, John Bayley, Jr. *university dean*
Graham, Patricia Albjerg *education educator*
Gray, Paul Edward *academic administrator*
Hockfield, Susan *academic administrator, medical educator*
Howitt, Arnold Martin *academic administrator, educator*
Hyman, Steven Edward *academic administrator, physiatrist, educator*
Johnson, Howard Wesley *retired academic administrator, finance company executive*
Kagan, Elena *dean, law educator*
Kelman, Steven Jay *education educator*
Khoury, Philip S. *academic administrator*
LaGuardia, Cheryl M. *school librarian, writer*
Linsky, Marty *education educator*
McCartney, Kathleen *dean, education educator*
Putnam, Robert D. *education educator*
Reif, L. Rafael *academic administrator, engineering educator*
Rowe, Mary P. *organizational ombudsman, management educator*
Schmalensee, Richard Lee *dean*
Schmill, Stuart *admissions director*
Shinagel, Michael *dean, English literature educator*
Smith, David Julian *educational consultant*
Smith, Michael D. *dean, electrical engineering and computer science professor*
Sollors, Werner *literature and language educator*
Thiemann, Ronald Frank *dean, religious studies educator*
Whitlock, Charles Preston *former university dean*

Carver
Simeone, Wendy Frances *secondary school educator, department chairman*

Chatham
Stout, Sharon Sparkes *elementary school educator, counselor*

Chestnut Hill
Altbach, Philip *director, educator*
Beaton, Albert Eugene *education educator*
Boynton, Andrew C. *dean*
Leahy, William Patrick *academic administrator, historian, educator*
Nemerowicz, Gloria *academic administrator*

Concord
Dresden, Jacob A. *headmaster*
Giles, Kathleen C. *headmaster*

Danvers
Beauregard, John *college librarian, consultant*
Clark, Sharon Jackson *private school administrator*

Dighton
Buote, Rosemarie Boschen *retired special education educator*
Foley, Gerard F. *history educator*

Douglas
Bachelder, Beverly Brandt *secondary school educator, assistant principal, director*

Duxbury
Thrasher, Dianne Elizabeth *mathematics educator, computer scientist, consultant*

East Walpole
Paul, Carol Ann *retired academic administrator, biology educator*

Everett
Blake, Margaret Mary *director*

Fiskdale
Costello, Christine Ann *fine arts director, church organist*

Framingham
Flanagan, Timothy James *academic administrator, criminal justice educator*

Franklin
Benjamin, Bernard Edward *school system administrator, director*

Groton
Commons, Richard B. *headmaster*
Wiggins, D. Scott *headmaster*

Harwich
Caretti, Ann M. *school system administrator*

Haydenville
Shallcross, Doris Jane *education educator*

Holden
O'Neil, William Francis *academic administrator*

Hyannis
O'Brien, Kathleen L. *special education educator*

Hyde Park
Harris, Emily Louise *special education educator*

Ipswich
Dion Faust, Debra *secondary school educator*
Lombardo, Ann Marie *special education educator, writer, artist*

Lancaster
Dugan, Maureen *biology educator, consultant*

Lexington
Collins, Allan Meakin *education educator*
McFarland, Philip James *secondary school educator, writer*
Wilson, Wendy Scott *history educator*

Longmeadow
Ezrin, Myer *retired director*
Katz, Barbara Stein *special education educator*
Leary, Carol Ann *academic administrator*

Lowell
Meehan, Martin Thomas (Marty Meehan) *academic administrator, former congressman, lawyer*
Ting, John M. *dean, engineering educator*

Lynn
Astuccio, Sheila Margaret *educational administrator*
Ryder, Edward Francis *secondary school educator*

Malden
Driscoll, David P. *school system administrator*

Marion
McPartland, Patricia Ann *adult education educator*

Marstons Mills
Martin, David Standish *education educator*

Medford
Bacow, Lawrence Seldon *academic administrator, environmental scientist, educator*
Bharucha, Jamshed *academic administrator*
Bosworth, Stephen Warren *dean, former ambassador*
Sternberg, Robert Jeffrey *dean, psychology professor, researcher*

Middleton
Stanley, (Malchan) Craig *school system administrator, consultant, psychologist, researcher*

Mill River
Dunsay, Charles William *elementary school educator*

Milton
Robertson, Robin Alayne *headmaster, anthropologist*
Wengler, Marguerite Marie *counseling administrator*

Monson
Webster, Ronie Ruth *secondary school educator*

Needham
Miller, Richard Keith *academic administrator, engineering educator*
Zambone, Alana Maria *special education educator, consultant*

New Bedford
Matsumoto, Carolee Setsuko *researcher, education developer and administrator*

Newburyport
Robinson, Joyce McPeake *academic administrator*

Newton
Matteson, Carol J. *academic administrator*
O'Connell, Sister Virginia M. *school librarian*
Peterson, Lloyd, Jr. *academic administrator, consultant*

Newton Center
Garvey, John Hugh *dean, law educator*

North Andover
Becker, Lawrence Wilfred *headmaster*

Northampton
Christ, Carol Tecla *academic administrator*
Mahoney, Maureen A. *academic administrator*

Northborough
Cradler, Judith A. *science educator*

Norton
Crutcher, Ronald Andrew *academic administrator, music educator*

Orange
Strunjo, Jacob Anthony *elementary school educator*

Peabody
Generazzo, Arlene Diamond *retired elementary school educator*

Pittsfield
Norris, Jeannie *headmaster*
Wood, Elizabeth Ann *special education educator*

Plymouth
Phillips, Warren G. *secondary school educator*
Woodburn, Norma Denman *biology educator, researcher*

Quincy
Adams, Ronald G. *elementary school educator*

Salem
Doran, Kathleen Brewer *dean, consultant*

Scituate
Spangler, Stanley Eugene *international relations educator*

Shrewsbury
Onorato, Nicholas Louis *retired program director, economist*

Somerset
Joseph, George Foster, Jr. *elementary school educator, historian*

Somerville
Austill, Allen *dean emeritus*

South Dartmouth
Ward, Richard Joseph *university dean, educator, author*

South Hadley
Bowie, Lee *academic administrator, philosopher, educator*
Creighton, Joanne Vanish *academic administrator*

Southborough
Stubbart, David James *elementary school educator*

Southbridge
Vasey, Ann L. *pre-school administrator, counselor*

Spencer
Robinson, Evelyn Edna *secondary school educator*

Springfield
Caprio, Anthony S. *academic administrator*
Cook, Kathryn Anne *secondary school educator*
Scibelli, Andrew M. *academic administrator*

Waltham
Adamian, Gregory Harry *academic administrator*
Edmiston, Scott *academic administrator, educator*
Klerman, Lorraine Vogel *public health educator*
Larson, Gloria Ann Cordes *academic administrator, lawyer*
Reinharz, Jehuda *academic administrator, history educator*
Sullivan, Mary E. *retired secondary educator, past state legislator*
Wawrzaszek, Susan V. *university librarian*

Wellesley
Auerbach, Jerold S. *academic administrator, educator*
Bottomly, (H.) Kim *academic administrator, biology professor, researcher*

West Roxbury
Roach, Maureen S. *primary school educator*

Williamstown
Chandler, John Wesley *educational consultant*
Niemeyer, Peter Eduard *history educator*
Schapiro, Morton Owen *academic administrator*

Winchester
Irving, Gitte Nielsen *secondary school educator*

Woburn
Winson, Ellen-Marie (Macone) *school system administrator, reading specialist*

Woods Hole
Farrington, John William *academic administrator, dean, research scientist*

Worcester
Arthur, Gwendolynne Lee *university librarian*
Bassett, John E. *academic administrator, language educator*
Berkey, Dennis Dale *academic administrator*
Brooks, John Edward *college president*
Cesareo, Francesco *academic administrator, historian, educator*
Harding, Beth Ann *middle school educator*
Indic, Premananda *education educator, researcher*
Lazare, Aaron *dean, psychiatrist*
Mardilovich, Ivan P. *education educator, researcher*
McFarland, Michael C. *academic administrator*
Stutz, Cathleen Kinsella *education educator*

Yarmouth Port
Hall, James Frederick *retired college president*

MICHIGAN

Allendale
Haas, Thomas Joseph *academic administrator, chemistry educator*

Alma
Tracy, Saundra J. *academic administrator*

Ann Arbor
Annchild, Cynthia *educational consultant*
Ball, Deborah Loewenberg *dean, education educator*
Beutler, Suzanne A. *retired secondary school educator, artist*
Boehnke, Michael *biostatistics educator*
Bryant, Barbara Everitt *academic administrator, researcher, retired marketing professional, federal agency administrator*
Caminker, Evan H. *dean, law educator*
Courant, Paul Noah *university librarian, economist, educator*
Dobranski, Bernard *dean, law educator*
Dolan, Robert J. *dean*
Fleming, Suzanne Marie *academic administrator, freelance/self-employed writer*
Hilton, James L. *university librarian*
Kalbfleisch, John David *statistics educator*
Kelch, Robert Paul *former dean, pediatric endocrinologist*
Masten, Scott Edward *economics and public policy educator, consultant*
Matthews, Rowena Green *biological chemistry educator*
Omenn, Gilbert Stanley *academic administrator, internist*
Paul, Ara Garo *university dean*
Pollack, Martha E. *dean, computer science and engineering educator*
Polverini, Peter J. *dean, dental educator*
Potempa, Kathleen M. *dean, nursing educator*
Robbins, Jerry Hal *educational administration educator*
Rogers, Bryan L. *dean*
Rogers, Bryan Leigh *dean, artist, art educator*
Schacht, Jochen Heinrich *biochemistry educator*
Sullivan, Thomas Patrick *academic administrator*
Tice, Carol Hoff *intergenerational specialist, consultant*

Warner, Kenneth E(dgar) *dean, public health educator, consultant*
Xie, Yu *adult education educator*

Armada
Kummerow, Arnold A. *superintendent of schools*

Benton Harbor
Yoder, Dale Roy *history educator*

Berrien Springs
Lesher, William Richard *retired academic administrator*
Lundgren, Dennis David *elementary school educator, secondary school educator*

Beverly Hills
Pardington, Mary Elizabeth *elementary school educator*

Big Rapids
Ryan, Ray Darl, Jr. *academic administrator*
Westman, Craig Ellery *academic administrator*

Bloomingdale
Schultheis, Ann Lucia *curriculum specialist*

Canton
Broniak, Lynn Marguerite *gifted and talented educator, technology educator*

Carleton
Ely, Deborah D. *elementary school educator*

Caro
Hile, Michele Vera *middle school educator*

Dearborn
Beyer, Roberta Bonnie *dean, education professor, writer, researcher*
Henderson, Stanley Elwood *academic administrator, consultant*
Zhu, Qiang *education educator*

Dearborn Heights
Johns, Diana *secondary school educator*

Detroit
Barrett, Nancy Smith *academic administrator*
Brown, Gloria Diane *elementary school educator*
Burnside, Wanda Jacqueline *elementary school educator*
Corbitt, Eumiller Mattie *special education educator*
Edelstein, Tilden Gerald *academic administrator, historian, educator*
Fay, Sister Maureen A. *university president*
Jones, James Allen *secondary school educator*
Kyff, Kimberly *elementary school educator*
Little, Laura Ann *elementary school educator, art educator*
Mitchell, Connie *director*
Smith, Gary Richard *technology educator*
Speegle, Laura Ann *elementary school educator*
Steiman, H. Robert *dean, dental educator*
Williams, Denise *academic administrator*

East Lansing
Brophy, Jere Edward *education educator, researcher*
Byerrum, Richard Uglow *college dean*
Harrison, Jeremy Thomas *dean, law educator*
Honhart, Frederick Lewis III *academic director*
King, Lonnie J. *dean*
Ladenson, Sharon *university librarian*
Petropoulos, Evangelos *former health institute director, educator, researcher*
Rothert, Marilyn L. *dean, nursing educator*
Simon, Lou Anna Kimsey *academic administrator*
Snoddy, James Ernest *education educator*
Strampel, William Derkey *dean, medical educator*
Yang, Lijian *educator*

Elk Rapids
Thompson, Richard Thomas *academic administrator*

Farmington Hills
Barry, Essie Marilyn *elementary school educator, writer*
Hagerty, Robert E. *academic administrator*

Flint
Simmons, Robert Randolph *principal*

Franklin
Reinhart, Anne Christine *special education educator, consultant*

Grand Rapids
Diekema, Anthony J. *college president, consultant*
Evans, Oliver H. *college administrator*
Lubbers, Arend Donselaar *retired academic administrator*
Maupin, Karin Louise *secondary school educator*

Gwinn
Lasich, Vivian Esther Layne *secondary school educator*

Hale
Lixey, Elizabeth Voulgarakis *secondary school educator*

Haslett
Warrington, Willard Glade *retired university official*

Holland
Nyenhuis, Jacob Eugene *academic administrator*
Van Wylen, Gordon John *former college president*

Holt
Wood, Mary Elizabeth *retired secondary school educator, church musician*

Houghton
Abdelkhalik, Ossama *computer science educator, researcher*
Hungwe, Kedmon Nyasha *education educator, researcher*

Interlochen
Kimpton, Jeffrey S. *academic administrator*

Jackson
Livesay, Jacqueline Ryder *elementary school educator, music educator, director*
Wingblade, Loren Charles *education educator*

Kalamazoo
Bailey, Judith Irene *academic administrator, educator, consultant*
Burns, James W. *education educator*
Dahlinger, Martha Louise *elementary school educator*
Haenicke, Diether Hans *academic administrator emeritus, educator*
Lavender, Maryann Michelle *history educator*
Palchick, Bernard S. *academic administrator, painter, educator*
Showalter, Shirley H. *former academic administrator*

Lake Orion
Leonard, Jacquelyn Ann *retired elementary school educator*

Lanse
Augustine, Henry Joseph *secondary school educator*

Lansing
Flanagan, Michael P. *school system administrator*
Straus, Kathleen Nagler *academic administrator, educator*

Lawrence
Applewhaite, Carlisle S. *special education educator, consultant*

Livonia
Kujawa, Sister Rose Marie *academic administrator*
McDowell, Richard William *academic administrator*

Ludington
Puffer, Richard Judson *retired college chancellor*

Macomb
Farmakis, George Leonard *retired education educator*

Madison Heights
Pierce, Jean Lois *elementary school educator*

Marquette
Cotter, June Ann *special education educator*
Manning, Robert Hendrick *retired audio-visual services executive*

Midland
Barker, Nancy Lepard *university official*

Moline
Grassmid, Ronald Jay *elementary school educator*

Mount Pleasant
Scott, Renay Marie *academic administrator, educator*

Muskegon
Ross, Annette Lee *educational consultant*

Novi
Serenson, Lynn Ann *mathematics educator*

Oak Park
Gardin, Hershel *academic administrator, dean, management consultant*

Okemos
Edwards, Caryn Louise *educational consultant, special education educator*

Pontiac
Anderson, Anita A. *secondary school educator*
Riley, Mary Jane Stewart *secondary school educator*

Port Huron
Ruby, Kathryn Grace *education educator*

Ravenna
Herremans, Paul William *mathematics educator*

Rochester
Packard, Sandra Podolin *education educator, consultant*

Royal Oak
Pricer, Wayne Francis *counseling consultant*

Saginaw
Scharffe, William Granville *academic administrator, educator*

Saint Clair Shores
Howe, Jennifer Lynn *secondary school educator*
Skoney, Sophie Essa *educational administrator*

Sault Sainte Marie
Youngblood, Betty J. *academic administrator*

South Haven
Llorens, Merna Gee *elementary school educator, retired music educator*

Southfield
Chambers, Charles MacKay *academic administrator, lawyer, consultant*
Lee, James Edward, Jr. *educational consultant*

Taylor
Coleman, Fay *literature and language educator, director*

Traverse City
Zimmerman, Paul Albert *retired academic administrator, minister*

University Center
Boyse, Peter Dent *academic administrator*
Gilbertson, Eric Raymond *academic administrator, lawyer*

Waterford
Anderson, Francile Mary *secondary school educator*

West Bloomfield
Simpson, Robert Lee *academic administrator, department chairman, biologist, educator*

Williamston
Johnson, Tom Milroy *dean, physician, educator*
Schab, Daniel J. *mathematics educator*

Wyoming
Couch, Katrina Denise *elementary school educator*

Ypsilanti
Lewis-White, Linda Beth *elementary school educator*
Willis, Craig Dean *academic administrator*

MINNESOTA

Ada
Sillerud, Arlen Roger *retired secondary school educator*

Alexandria
Lillestol, Jane Brush *educational consultant*

Anoka
Weidner, Jacque Goodin *educational consultant, not-for-profit developer*

Bemidji
Rogers, Patricia Louise *education educator, consultant, dean*

Cloquet
Belanger, Sharon Amling *special education educator*

Coleraine
Jones, Gail *elementary school educator*

Collegeville
Reinhart, Dietrich Thomas *academic administrator, social studies educator*

Coon Rapids
Enzenauer, Kirk Karl *elementary school educator*

Duluth
Stauber-Johnson, Elizabeth Jane *retired elementary school educator*
Wen, Shixing *school librarian*
Ziegler, Richard J. *dean, educator*

Eagan
Sievwright, Julia Ann *elementary school educator*

Eden Prairie
Knickerbocker, Vicky Ann *academic administrator*

Excelsior
Pfeifer, Polly Lee *elementary school educator*

Faribault
Collins, Ruth Ann *principal*

Little Falls
Morgan, Mary Jo *school system administrator*
Perfetti, Robert Nickolas *educational consultant*

Long Lake
Lowthian, Petrena *academic administrator*

Mankato
Nickerson, James Findley *retired education educator*

Maple Grove
Kirpes, Anne Irene *elementary school educator*

Marine On Saint Croix
Gavin, Robert Michael, Jr. *educational consultant*

Marshall
Van Overbeke, Debbie Ann *education educator*

Mendota Heights
Friedrichs, Terence Paul *special education educator*

Minneapolis
Atwood, John Brian *dean*
Bowie, Norman Ernest *university official, educator*
Bruininks, Robert H. *academic administrator, psychologist, educator*
DiGangi, Frank Edward *academic administrator*
Edwardson, Sandra *dean, nursing educator*
Huntzicker, William Edward *journalism educator, writer*
Johnson, Alex Moore *dean, law educator*
Lindell, Edward Albert *academic and religious organization administrator*
Lloyd, Patrick M. *dean, dental educator*
Loreno, Nina Louise *elementary school educator*
Lougee, Wendy Pradt *university librarian, educator*
Mengler, Thomas M. *dean*
Montgomery, Lynn Marie *educational consultant*
O'Keefe, Michael *academic administrator, physicist*
O'Keefe, Thomas Michael *academic administrator*
Schuh, G(eorge) Edward *dean, agricultural economist*
Stephens, Lee-Ann Williams *elementary school educator, educator*
Sullivan, Alfred Dewitt *academic administrator*
Svendsbye, Lloyd August *academic administrator, theologian, educator*
Warring, Douglas Franklin *education educator, psychologist*

Minnetonka
Wigfield, Rita L. *elementary school educator*

Moorhead
Dille, Roland Paul *college president*
Treumann, William Borgen *university dean*

Northfield
Oden, Robert A., Jr. *academic administrator*

Osseo
Anya, Adamma Chukwudi *special education educator*

Park Rapids
Novak, Larry Ray *secondary school educator, music educator, director*

Plymouth
Vieth, William Chapman *secondary school educator*

Richfield
Devlin, Barbara Jo *school district administrator*
Reilly, Jill Marlene *school system administrator*

Rochester
Stockwell, Linda M. *principal*

Roseville
Seagren, Alice *school system administrator, former state legislator*

Saint Cloud
Godzala, Jesse Thomas *history educator*
Huber-Warring, Tonya *education educator*
Wertz, John Alan *retired secondary school educator*

Saint Paul
Bauer, Jean Warner *family economics educator*
Brushaber, George Karl *academic administrator, minister*
Dybvig, Mary McIlvaine *educational consultant, psychologist*
Dykstra, Robert *retired education educator*
Hanna, Kathryn Lura *university administrator*
Huber, Sister Alberta *academic administrator*
King, Jack Burge *academic librarian*
Lee, Andrea Jane *academic administrator, nun*
Maxfield, Lori Rochelle *education educator*
McCormick, James Harold *academic administrator*
McNamee, Sister Catherine *educator*
Rodríguez, Liliana Cristina *mathematics educator*
Rosenberg, Brian C *academic administrator*
Skinner, Pamela J. *adult education educator*
Stelzig, Samuel Frederic *retired secondary school educator*
Tesch, Phiip C. *dean, minister*
Vecoli, Rudolph John *retired history educator, director*

Sleepy Eye
Jirak, Sarah Reed *secondary school educator*

Stillwater
Erwin, Raymond Maurice *secondary school educator*

Waseca
Frederick, Edward Charles *university official*

Waterville
Pettis, Patricia Amanda *secondary school educator, farmer*

Winona
Nasstrom, Roy Richard *educational consultant*

MISSISSIPPI

Ackerman
Coleman, Frances McLean *secondary school educator*

Alcorn State
Wyatt, Helen J. *special education educator*

Batesville
Neal, Joseph Lee *vocational school educator*

Biloxi
Brown, Sheba Ann *elementary school educator*
Manners, Pamela Jeanne *secondary school educator*

Caledonia
Reed, James Tabor *history educator, consultant*

Collins
Lamb, Connie *retired elementary school educator*

Columbus
Sumners, Sarah Elizabeth *grant manager, history professor*
Traynham, Lurene Jones *retired secondary school educator*

Crystal Springs
Nixon, Brenda Joyce *elementary school educator, small business owner*

Ecru
Mounce, Carolyn P. *retired school librarian*

Gulfport
Davis, Wynndi P. *elementary school educator*
Egland, Katherine Tatum *educational consultant, director*
Opel, Pamela Lynn *elementary school educator*

Hattiesburg
Bedenbaugh, Angela Lea Owen *chemistry educator, researcher*
Diket, Mary Read M. *academic administrator, educator*
Gunther, William David *academic administrator, economics professor*
Lucas, Aubrey Keith *retired university president*
Noonkester, James Ralph *retired college president*
Saunders, Martha Dunagin *academic administrator*

Holly Springs
Beckley, David Lenard *academic administrator*

Jackson
Anglin, Linda McCluney *retired elementary school educator*
Bounds, Hank M. *school system administrator*
Creel, Sue Cloer *retired secondary school educator*
Hupp, James R. *dean, dental educator*
Lucas, Frances *academic administrator*
Mayeaux, Anne Russell *education educator*
McLin-Bronson, Hattie Rogers *school system administrator*

Madison
Watts, Thomas Parrish *history educator, consultant*

Meridian
Leewer, William George, Jr. *education educator*

Minter City
Mitchell, Patsy Malier *religious school founder, administrator*

Mississippi State
Foglesong, Robert H. *academic administrator, career military officer*
Rabideau, Peter Wayne *dean, chemistry professor, educator*
Swafford, Jeanne *education educator*

Natchez
Foster, Evaline L. *education educator, researcher*

Olive Branch
Leary, Frances Elizabeth Cooper *secondary school educator*

Oxford
Moorhead, Sylvester Andrew *retired education educator*
Walton, Gerald Wayne *retired university official*

Philadelphia
Montgomery, Kathryn Suzainne *elementary school educator*

Ridgeland
Harmon, George Marion *academic administrator*

Saltillo
Hopkins, Betty Belinda *elementary school educator*

Senatobia
Latham, Amy Moore *academic administrator*

Starkville
Mabry, Donald Joseph *retired academic administrator, history professor*
Martin, Theodore Krinn *former university administrator*
Mosley, Mary Nell H. *retired elementary school educator*

Tupelo
Cleveland, Mary Heloise *elementary school educator*

University
Davis, Samuel Marion *dean, law educator, researcher*
Khayat, Robert Conrad *academic administrator*

Vicksburg
Keulegan, Emma Pauline *special education educator*
Pace, Carol Rebecca *elementary school educator*

Waynesboro
Crager, Ginny Lee *gifted and talented educator*

MISSOURI

Advance
Thomas, Rich L. *secondary school educator*

Arnold
Kasey, Arthur R. III *secondary school educator*

Bakersfield
Barnes, Sandra Lynn *special education educator*

Bethel
Coonrod, Delberta Hollaway (Debbie) *retired elementary school educator, consultant*

Blue Springs
Hochgrebe, Nolan Robards *secondary school educator*

Carl Junction
Pulliam, Frederick Cameron *educational administrator*

Columbia
Crist, William Miles *dean, pediatrician, educator*
Deaton, Brady J. *academic administrator*
Dessem, R. Lawrence *dean, law educator*
Flinn, Mark van Doren *education educator*
George, Melvin Douglas *retired university president*
Janda, Mark William *history educator*
Lamb, Gordon Howard *academic administrator*
Libby, Wendy B. *academic administrator*
McKinley, Lori *education educator*
Miller, Paul Ausborn *adult education educator*

Fayette
Inman, Marianne Elizabeth *academic administrator*

Florissant
Ackley, Robert Arthur *mathematics educator, retired military officer*
Conrad, Mary Trench *elementary school educator*
Kralemann, William Joseph *retired chemistry educator*
Linn, Dale E. *secondary school educator*

Forsyth
Klinefelter, Sarah Stephens *retired dean, broadcast executive*

Fulton
Lamkin, Fletcher M., Jr. *academic administrator*

Granby
Sparkman, Lyle Bruce *academic administrator, education educator*

Holt
Merrill, Donna *special education educator*

Independence
Franklin, J. Richard *principal*
House, Lianne Kay *elementary school educator*
Rees, Elaine *chemistry educator*

Jefferson City
King, D. Kent *school system administrator*
Mahoney, Carolyn Ray *academic administrator*
Novotney, Donald Francis *superintendent of schools*

Kansas City
Byers-Pevitts, Beverley *college administrator, educator*
Caulfield, Joan *director, educator*
Churchman, Michael Steele Bright *educational consultant, educator*
Collins, Kathleen *academic administrator, art educator*
Eubanks, Eugene Emerson *education educator, consultant*
Guilliland, Martha W. *academic administrator*
Hamilton, Richard Alfred *academic administrator, marketing executive*
Jonas, Harry S. *medical education consultant*
Judd, Barbara Anne *history educator, counselor*
McCollum, Clifford Glenn *college dean emeritus*
Snelling, Troy Wayne *history educator*
Suni, Ellen Y. *dean, law educator*
Swaffar, Glenda Jean *director*
Willsie, Sandra Kay *internist, educator*
Woods-Taylor, Cleora Lynesia *mathematics educator, consultant*

Kirksville
Dixon, Barbara Bruinekool *academic administrator*

Liberty
Tanner, Jimmie Eugene *retired dean*

Marshfield
Frame, Susan S. *special education educator*

Maryville
Hubbard, Dean Leon *academic administrator*

Neosho
Allman, Margaret Ann Lowrance *counseling administrator*

Nevada
Schulze, Cheryl Ranea *secondary school educator*

New Bloomfield
Luebbert, Terry Lynne *elementary school educator*

O Fallon
Reid, Lorene Frances *middle school educator*

Parkville
Breckon, Donald John *academic administrator*

Raymore
Dickerson, Jill Louise *elementary school educator*
Spainhower, James Ivan *retired college president*

Raytown
MacLeod, Linda Ann *secondary school educator*

Richmond Heights
Chandler, James Barton *international education consultant*

Rolla
Carney, John F. III *academic administrator*
Warner, Don Lee *dean emeritus*
Wray, Kent *academic administrator*
Wu, Shuo-sheng *director*

Saint Charles
Parker, Marsha Marie *dean, actress*
Segelhorst, Cindy Marie *pre-school educator*

Saint Louis
Baker, Shirley Kistler *academic administrator, university librarian*
Biondi, Lawrence *academic administrator, priest*
Blankenship, Robert Eugene *biochemistry educator*
Blanton, Elizabeth Anne *secondary school educator*
Booth, Betty Jean *retired daycare administrator, poet*
Cain, James Nelson *arts school and concert administrator*
Danforth, William Henry *retired academic administrator, physician*
Dodge, Paul Cecil *academic administrator*
Doughty, Nikedra *academic administrator*
Elder, Dee A. *literature and language educator*
George, Thomas Frederick *academic administrator*
Gilligan, Sandra Kaye *private school director*
Gupta, Mahendra R. *dean*
Hinton, Velecia Ann *academic administrator*
Hrubetz, Joan *retired dean, nursing educator*
Hughes, Jeffrey A. *art history educator*
Koff, Robert Hess *academic administrator, adult education educator*
Krasney, Rina Susan *school librarian*
Lackey, Kayle Diann *elementary school educator*
Leavitt, Lynda *school system administrator, educator*
Leonard, Judith Price *educational advisor*
Lewis, Jeffrey E. *dean, law educator*
Lewis, Jodi A. *secondary school educator, theater educator*
Lombardi, Mark Owen *academic administrator, international relations educator*
Mahan, David James *retired academic administrator*
Monteleone, Patricia L. *dean*
Muns, Raleigh Clayton *school librarian*
Ramming, Michael Alexander *retired school system administrator*
Rice, Rose Ann M. *secondary school educator*
Smith, Karen Jody *education educator*
Staines, Gail M. *university librarian*
Walker, Doretta Anita *director*
Weiss, Robert Francis *retired academic and religious organization administrator, consultant*
Welch, Michael John *chemistry educator, researcher*
Williamson, Marilyn *retired secondary school educator*
Wrighton, Mark Stephen *academic administrator, chemistry professor*

Saint Peters
Caples, Linda Griffin *retired secondary school educator*
Thornton, Girard B., Jr., (Jerry) *elementary school educator*

Springfield
Reed, Peggy Anne *education educator*
Sherman, Ruth Todd *counseling administrator, educator*
Sutton, Kim Rochell *education educator*
Toste, Anthony Paim *chemistry educator, researcher*

Troy
Bockhorst, Barbara Alice *retired secondary school educator*
Lawrence, John R. *academic administrator*

Warrensburg
Jurkowski, Odin Lech *education educator*

Washington
Chambers, Jerry Ray *school system administrator, consultant*

Webb City
James, Kathryn A. *secondary school educator*

Wildwood
Truitt, William Harvey *private school educator*

Windyville
Condron, Daniel Ralph *academic administrator, metaphysics educator*

MONTANA

Billings
Mace, Michael R. *academic administrator, real estate development consultant, mortgage executive*
Sexton, Ronald P. *academic administrator*
Tryon, Margaret A. *director, school psychologist*

Bozeman
Buonamici, April Graham *elementary school and music educator*
Gamble, Geoffrey *academic administrator*

Butte
Gilmore, W. Franklin (Frank) *academic administrator*
L'heureux, Richard Allen *academic administrator, consultant*

Dayton
Catalfomo, Philip *retired university dean*

Dillon
Storey, Richard D. *academic administrator, biology professor*

Havre
Capdeville, Alex *academic administrator*

Helena
McCulloch, Linda *school system administrator*
Pettit, Lawrence Kay *university president*
Stearns, Sheila MacDonald *academic administrator*

Lodge Grass
Rockabove, Magdalene M. *special education educator*

Missoula
Brown, Perry Joe *dean*
Dennison, George Marshel *academic administrator*
Vogelsberg, Ross Timm *education educator, researcher*

Whitefish
Carmichael, Gary Alan Alan *social studies educator*

Wolf Point
Morin, JoyAnn Hauge *education educator*

NEBRASKA

Adams
Nieveen, Teresa J. *elementary school educator*

Arlington
Moskus, Jerry Ray *retired academic administrator*

Aurora
Lockmon, Nancy *mathematics educator*

Bellevue
Kayne, Jon Barry *academic administrator, psychologist*
Muller, John Bartlett *university president*

Cedar Bluffs
Fleischman, Brian William *mathematics educator*

Kearney
Johnston, Gladys Styles *university official*

Kimball
Walker, Judy Lou *special education educator, director*

Lincoln
Bradley, Richard Edwin *retired academic administrator*
Christensen, Douglas D. *school system administrator*
Dunlap, Michael S. *student loan company executive*
Grew, Priscilla Croswell *academic administrator, geologist, educator*
Hansen-Daberkow, Michelle Len *elementary school art educator*
Kern, Jeanne Rustemeyer Wood *retired secondary school educator*
Mendola, Joseph Robert *philosophy professor, department chairman*
Milligan, Cynthia Hardin *dean, lawyer*
Nelson, Darrell Wayne *retired academic administrator, research scientist*
Obafunwa, John Oladapo *academic administrator, pathologist, educator*
Perlman, Harvey Stuart *academic administrator*
Reinhardt, John W. *dean, dental educator*
Smith, L. Dennis *former academic administrator*
Willborn, Steven L. *dean, law educator*

Neligh
Kinnan, Sharon Jo *elementary school educator*

Omaha
Baker, Gail *director, ESL educator*
Belck, Nancy Garrison *dean, educator*
Bruckner, Martha *academic administrator*
Fennell, Madaline *elementary school educator*
Foster, Betty Louise *secondary school educator*
Gerteis, Christopher *history educator*
Louis, Virgie Lee *retired secondary school educator*
Newton, John Milton *academic administrator, psychologist, educator*
Pamies, Rubens John *dean*
Ryan, Sheila A. *retired dean, nursing educator*

Seward
Bork, Ronald Dale *academic administrator*

Taylor
Brown, Kevin Paul *secondary school educator*

Waverly
Jensen, Daniel *history educator*

Winnebago
Bauer-Sanders, Katherine Ann *primary school educator*

NEVADA

Carson City
Brant, James William *educational consultant, mathematician, educator*

Eftimoff, Anita Kendall *retired educational consultant*
Rheault, Keith W. *school system administrator*

Elko
Lesbo, Paula Mae *elementary and secondary education educator*

Henderson
Keene, Richard Brian *school system administrator, educational consultant*
Maryanski, Fred J. *academic administrator*
Teemant, Melanie J. *middle school educator*
Thomas, James Patrick *special education educator*

Incline Village
Large, Larry Denton *academic administrator*

Las Vegas
Ananias, José *retired school system administrator*
Ashley, David B. *academic administrator, engineering educator*
Baloglu, Seyhmus *hospitality and tourism educator*
DeBusk, Lorraine *elementary school educator*
Edualino, Emilio Quial *school educator*
Ernst, Suzanne *academic administrator, educator*
Ferrillo, Patrick J., Jr. *dean, endodontist*
Gaspar, Anna Louise *retired elementary school educator, consultant*
Hall, Gene E. *education educator*
Levasseur, Mark *dean*
Morgan, Richard J. *dean, law educator*
Pierce, Thresia Korte (Tish Pierce) *primary school educator*
Shuman, R. Baird *academic administrator, consultant, language educator, writer*
Singer, Clifford *mathematics educator, artist*

North Las Vegas
Manley, Audrey Forbes *retired academic administrator, pediatrician, retired military officer*

Reno
Cathey-Gibson, Sharon Sue Rinn *principal, academic administrator*
Dietrich, Dean Forbes *academic administrator*
Glick, Milton Don *academic administrator, chemist*
McCarty-Puhl, J-Petrina *chemistry educator*
Perry, Jean Louise *academic administrator*

NEW HAMPSHIRE

Brentwood
Boozer-Blasco, Claudia Ruth *family and consumer resources educator*

Colebrook
Bernard, Susan Shattuck *retired secondary school educator*
Bernard, Wilbert Auguster, Jr. *retired school system administrator*

Concord
Blankenstein, Elizabeth M. *director, educator*
Hutson, John D. *dean, retired military officer*
Jillette, Arthur George, Jr. *school system administrator, educator*
Kenney, Kimberly *elementary school educator*
Matthews, William R., Jr., (Bill Matthews) *headmaster*
Tracy, Lyonel B. *school system administrator*

Dover
Pelletier, Marsha Lynn *secondary school educator, poet*

Durham
Farrell, William Joseph *university chancellor*
Huddleston, Mark Wayne *academic administrator, political scientist, educator*
Ray, Stephen Alan *academic administrator, lawyer*

Exeter
Kelley, Carolyn *biotechnology educator*
Tingley, Tyler C. *headmaster*

Gilford
Wool, Alan D. *mathematics educator*

Hanover
Danos, Paul *dean, accounting educator*
Green, Ronald Michael *bioethics educator*
Laskaris, Maria *dean*
Spielberg, Stephen Paul *dean, educator*
Wright, James Edward *academic administrator, historian, educator*

Henniker
Nitschke-Shaw, Debra Ann *education educator, dean*

Lebanon
Cole, Bernard F. *community and family medicine professor*

Manchester
Roche, John Edward *college administrator, human resources specialist, educator*

Middleton
Feyler, Carrie A. *elementary school educator*

Milford
Queeney, Deborah Ann *special education educator*

Nashua
Arthur, Rose Ann Horman *dean*
Mitsakos, Charles Leonidas *education educator, consultant*

Plaistow
Goddu, Kevin Albert *secondary school educator*

Rindge
Martin, Frederick Nichols *school system administrator*

Salem
Courtois, Michael G. *biology educator*

Sanbornville
Szugda, Sharon A. *elementary school educator*

Somersworth
Dahms, Bruce John *secondary school educator*

West Lebanon
Halperin, George Bennett *education educator, retired military officer*

NEW JERSEY

Bayonne
Lo Re, Vincent, Jr. *retired academic administrator, municipal official*

Belleville
Shuhan, Janice-Lynn Nazziola *secondary school educator*

Bellmawr
Wilke, Constance Regina *elementary school educator*

Bernardsville
Robinson, Maureen Loretta *retired secondary school educator*

Bridgewater
Hart, Karen Jean *special education educator*

Burlington
Cobb, Vanessa Wyvette *elementary school educator*

Caldwell
Savage, Joseph George *academic administrator*
Werner, Patrice (Patricia Ann Werner) *academic administrator*

Camden
Brooks, Gail Denise *school system administrator, consultant*
Gordon, Walter Kelly *retired academic administrator, retired language educator*
Solomon, Rayman Louis *dean, law educator*

Cherry Hill
Del Rossi, Christopher *elementary school educator*

Colts Neck
Crowder-Pagano, Linda Louise *special education educator*

Columbia
Timcenko, Lydia Teodora *secondary school educator, biochemist*

Denville
Doane, Eileen Maloney *learning disabilities teacher consultant*

Egg Harbor City
Farris, Vera King *former college president*

Egg Harbor Township
Carney, Michelle Catherine *assistant principal*

Englewood
DeJarnett, Rodney *headmaster*

Ewing
Gitenstein, Donna M. *academic administrator*

Flanders
Kuzma, Deborah J. *vice principal, music educator*

Fords
Ayers, Christopher James *special education educator*

Fort Lee
Sugarman, Alan William *educational consultant*
Umansky, Edith Simon *retired school librarian, retired elementary school educator*
Young, Vera Lee Hall *academic administrator, director*

Glassboro
D'Augustine, Robert *academic administrator, lawyer*

Hackensack
Jaye, Daniel *principal*
Williamson, (Eulah) Elaine *elementary school educator*

Hightstown
Elliott, Frank Nelson *retired college president*
Green, John F. *headmaster*

Hillside
Dickerson, Martin Lee *principal*

Hoboken
Korfiatis, George *academic administrator, engineering educator*
Raveché, Harold Joseph *academic administrator*

Jackson
Ranone, John Louis *school board executive*

Jersey City
Cornacchia, Eugene John *academic administrator, political science professor*
Farrior, Evan Bell *special education educator, writer*
Soo Hoo, Tsung (Bill) Yao *security studies educator, consultant*

Lakewood
Conklin, Jack L. *education educator*
Doak, Nancy Ann *mathematics educator*
Williams, Barbara Anne *retired academic administrator*

Lanoka Harbor
Lake, William Robert *school district administrator*

Lawrenceville
Jordan, Mildred Rice Loretta *education educator*
Rozanski, Mordechai *academic administrator*
Stehle, Edward Raymond *secondary education educator, school system administrator*
Tharney, Leonard John *education educator, consultant*

Layton
Seely, Maribeth Walsh *elementary school educator*

Lincroft
Ruiz Madas, Yesenia *educational counselor*

Linwood
Sutman, Francis Xavier *retired academic administrator, chemist, writer*

Madison
Bull, Vivian Ann *retired academic administrator, educator*
Weisbuch, Robert Alan *academic administrator*

Manalapan
Barratt, Donna Lee *elementary school educator*

Maplewood
Fiorito, Frank Anthony *secondary educator*

Marlboro
Kayafas, Stephanie Ann *special education educator, consultant, supervisor, actress*

Marlton
Cheney, Eleanora Louise *retired secondary school educator*

Mendham
Posunko, Barbara *retired elementary school educator*

Metuchen
Massey, Eleanor Nelson *retired school librarian, media specialist*

Middlesex
Baker, James Clifford *school system administrator*

Monmouth Beach
Ginty, Karen *elementary school educator*

Monroe Township
Treatman, Paul *retired school system administrator*

Montclair
Cole, Susan A. *academic administrator, language educator*
Cooke, Nicole *school librarian*

Montville
Birkett, Norman Myles *private school educator, writer*
Riotto, Scott M. *secondary school educator*

Morristown
Gordon, Erin Kathleen *elementary school educator*
Mertz, Francis James *university president*
Venezia, William Thomas *school system administrator, counseling consultant*

New Brunswick
Friedrich, Gustav William *dean, communications educator*
Greenberg, Michael Richard *urban studies and community health educator*
Libutti, Patricia O'Brien *university librarian*
McCormick, Richard Levis *academic administrator*
Nelson, Jack Lee *education educator*
Stanley, Jason *education educator*
Stauffer, George B. *dean, musician, historian, consultant*
Strawderman, William E. *statistics educator*
Strickland, Dorothy *education educator*
Tanner, Daniel *education educator*

New Monmouth
Santos, Sharon Lee *parochial school educator*

New Providence
Blessing, Leonard C. *secondary school educator*
Hirsch, Maxine K. *special education educator, councilman*

Newark
Altenkirch, Robert A. *academic administrator*
Arbuckle, Peggy Trawick *special education educator, consultant*
Bergen, Stanley Silvers, Jr. *retired academic administrator*
Bloom, Joel S. *academic administrator*
Bolden, Marion A. *superintendent*
Feldman, Cecile Arlene *dean, dental educator*
Fenster, Saul K. *retired academic administrator*
Gadepalli, Vijaya L. *mathematics educator*

Graycar, Adam *dean, former Australian government official*
Hobbs, Patrick Esmond *dean, law educator*
Joffe, Russell T. *former dean*
Owen, William Franklin, Jr. *academic administrator, former research and development company executive*
Petillo, John J. *former academic administrator, priest*
Vincenti, Gene A. *director, consultant*

Newton
MacMurren, Margaret Patricia *secondary school educator, consultant*

Norwood
Murburg, Thelma D. *retired elementary school educator*

Oradell
Huntington, Raymond J. *education center executive*

Paramus
Atkins, Yvette *special education educator*
Jenkins, Elaine *middle school educator*
Tamburro, Peter James, Jr. *secondary school educator*

Parsippany
Smay, Connie R. *educational media specialist, educator*

Paterson
Fields, Marvin Leon *secondary school educator*

Pennington
Townsend, Peggy (Stephanie G.) *headmaster*

Piscataway
Amaral, Andre Renato Sales *education educator, researcher*
Dill, Ellis Harold *university dean*
Lu, Yen-Wen *adult education educator*
Trontell, Marie Celestine *dean*

Plainfield
Ruiz, Pedro Javier *education educator*

Pleasantville
London, Charlotte Isabella *secondary school educator*

Pompton Plains
Pischl, Adolph John *school administrator*

Princeton
Cooper, Michael R. *dean*
Dawes, Trevor A. *school librarian*
Duncan, Dianne Walker *elementary school educator*
Goddard, Peter *academic administrator, mathematical physicist*
Hollander, Toby Edward *education educator*
Malkiel, Nancy Weiss *dean, historian, educator*
Pimley, Kim Jensen *financial training consultant*
Rapelye, Janet Lavin *dean*
Rohrer, Katherine Tinley *academic administrator*
Slaughter, Anne-Marie *dean*
Tilghman, Shirley Marie *academic administrator, biology professor*
Tumposky, Daniel L. *education assessment specialist*

Rahway
Freedman, Stanley Lewis *assistant principal*

Randolph
Ghosh, Ajit Kumar *daycare administrator*

Rockaway
Allen, Dorothea *secondary school educator*

Roselle
Di Marco, Barbaranne Yanus *principal*
Wilson, Arthur Theodore *education consultant*

Short Hills
Robbins-Wilf, Marcia *educational consultant*

Sicklerville
Miller, Audrey Thornton *retired vice principal*

South Amboy
Moskal, Anthony John *retired dean, management consultant, educator*

South Orange
Sheeran, Robert T. (Monsignor) *academic administrator*

Southampton
O'Connor, Sheryl Broderick *literature and language educator*

Teaneck
Cowen, John Edwin *education educator*
Dewey, Ralph Jay *school system administrator*
Lichtenstein, Robert *Education executive*
Smith, Susan Elizabeth *guidance director*

Tenafly
Gold, Marc J. *secondary school educator, supervisor*

Tinton Falls
Arminio, Josephine Meconi *elementary school educator*
Ostar, Allan William *educational consultant*

Trenton
Brown, Peggy Lee *academic administrator, consultant, singer*
Davy, Lucille E. *school system administrator*
Depuglio, Joseph *physics educator*
Donohue, Patricia Carol *academic administrator*
Pruitt, George Albert *college president*

Riccards, Michael Patrick *academic administrator*
Scheiring, Michael James *college official*
Smallwood, Robert Albian, Jr. *retired secondary education educator*

Union
Lederman, Susan Sturc *public administration professor*

Union City
Bozoyan, Sylvia *elementary school educator*
Englese, Damon Joseph *director*

Waldwick
Lynch, Carol *special services director, psychologist, minister*

Wall
Petrovich, Dorothy *elementary school educator*

Warren
Hennings, Dorothy Grant *education educator*

West Long Branch
Gaffney, Paul Golden, II, *academic administrator, retired military officer*
Lutz, Francis Charles *dean, civil engineering educator*
Martin, Sylvia S. *special education educator, psychology educator*
Pearson, Thomas Spencer *academic administrator*

West Orange
Bojsza, Joan E. *elementary school educator*
Thomas, Gary L. *retired academic administrator*

Whippany
Vallee, Michelle Linda *pre-school educator*

Williamstown
Heidemark, George John *elementary school educator*

Willingboro
Denslow, Deborah Pierson *primary school educator*

Woodbridge
Warren, Arthur Lee *secondary school educator, school system administrator*

NEW MEXICO

Alamogordo
Hobson, Suellen Ann Weber *retired elementary school educator*

Albuquerque
Beiler, Holly Anne *education educator*
Caplan, Edwin Harvey *retired dean, finance educator*
DelCampo, Robert Gregory *education educator*
Draper, Dorothy E. *middle school mathematics educator*
Duryea, Elias J. *education educator*
Everitt, Elizabeth M. *school system administrator*
Florez, Viola E. *academic administrator, dean*
Frias, Shirlee N. *elementary school educator*
Garcia, F. Chris *academic administrator, political scientist, educator*
Graff, Pat Stuever *secondary school educator*
Hansen, Harold B., Jr. *assistant principal*
Harris, David W. *academic administrator*
Hopfinger, Anton Joseph *education educator, consultant*
Lambert, Jeffrey Scott *secondary school educator*
Lattman, Laurence Harold *retired academic administrator*
Qi, Huaqing *special education educator*
Scarnecchia, Suellyn *dean, law educator*
Stuart, Cynthia Morgan *retired academic administrator*
Wade, Gaylia Suzanne *secondary school educator*
Zink, Lee Berkey *retired academic administrator, economist, educator*

Carlsbad
Christopherson, Ron *mathematics educator*

Cerrillos
Lutz, Nancy Cole *educational consultant*

Farmington
Anderson, Evelyn Louise *elementary school educator*
Brown, Kimleigh Clayton *special education educator, biologist*

Hobbs
Dill, Gary A. *academic administrator*

Las Cruces
Egginton, Everett *educational administrator*
Heger, Herbert Krueger *education educator*
Martin, Michael V. *academic administrator, economics professor*

Las Vegas
Fries, James A. *academic administrator*
Immerman, Michael *director*

Lordsburg
Clem, Sarah Lynn *special education educator*
Moralez, Joselyn Hope *special education educator*

Los Alamos
Benjamin, Susan Selton *elementary school educator*

Moriarty
Cox, Darlene Beth *secondary school educator*

Placitas
Watson-Boone, Rebecca A. *dean, researcher, library and information scientist, educator*

Portales
Frost, Everett Lloyd *academic administrator, anthropologist*
Howard, Carolyn F. *elementary school educator*

Prewitt
Reinhardt, Elizabeth A. *mathematics educator*

Reserve
Wiley, James Dee *retired history and biology educator, national park service ranger*

Santa Fe
Cerny, Charlene Ann *director*
Gallegos, Mary Ellen *education educator, department chairman*
Garcia, Veronica *school system administrator*

Silver City
Snedeker, John Haggner *university president*

NEW YORK

Albany
Brademas, John *retired academic administrator, former congressman*
Clark, John B. *academic administrator*
Mills, Richard Paul *school system administrator*
Mumpower, Jeryl L. *academic administrator*
Robbins, Cornelius (Cornelius Van Vorse) *educational administration educator*
Verdile, Vincent Paul *dean, emergency physician*

Annandale On Hudson
Botstein, Leon *academic administrator, conductor, historian*

Attica
Allen, Susan Diane *educator*

Aurora
Ryerson, Lisa M. *academic administrator*

Babylon
DaSilva, Lynn Judith *special education educator*
Herbst, Jane Elizabeth *school librarian*
Schwarz, Barbara Ruth Ballou *elementary school educator*

Baldwin
Aliano, Joy Caryl *retired elementary school educator*

Batavia
Steiner, Stuart *college president*

Beacon
Rousseau, Christina Jeannie *elementary school educator*

Bellerose
Roberts, Kathleen Joy Doty *secondary school educator*

Bellmore
Feldman, Harriet Ruth *dean*

Bellport
Coonerty, Mary Elizabeth *special education educator*
Schultheis, Edwin Milford *dean, business educator*

Binghamton
DeFleur, Lois B. *academic administrator*
Meador, John Milward, Jr. *dean, librarian*
Swain, Mary Ann Price *university official*

Brockport
Gemmett, Robert J. *dean, English language educator*

Brocton
Berman, Alexis Danielle *elementary school educator*

Bronx
Antwi, Ebenezer Yaw *education educator*
Bowers, Francis Robert *educational consultant, literature educator*
Chase, Martin Leslie *literature and language educator, priest*
Hauser, Bernice Worman *director*
Keating, Tedd Michael *adult education educator*
Kelley, Aloysius Paul *academic administrator, priest*
Kelly, Thomas M. *headmaster*
McCabe, James Patrick *university librarian*
McShane, Joseph Michael *academic administrator, priest*
Nathanson, Melvyn Bernard *academic administrator, mathematician, educator*
Nierva, Magdelena Lavesores *mathematics educator*
Purpura, Dominick P. *dean emeritus, neuroscientist*
Reidy, Valerie J. *principal, educator*
Robinson, Gwendolyn Niema *elementary school educator*
Sanchez-Silkman, Jennifer Christine *elementary school educator*
Scanlan, Thomas Joseph *college president, educator*
Sisson, Elisabeth Joanne *elementary school educator*
Spiegel, Allen Michael *dean, internist*
Wertheim, Mary Danielle *educational coordinator*
Wilson, Sarada Amelia Princess *elementary school educator*

Bronxville
Lawrence, Karen R. *academic administrator, literature and language professor*

Brooklyn
Bakakos, Diana *middle school educator*
Birenbaum, William M. *former university president*
Bugliarello, George *academic administrator, educator*
Chung, Ping Tsai *education educator*
D'Elia, Nicholas *secondary school educator*
Douglass, Melvin Isadore *school system administrator, humanities educator, composer*
Felder, Mira B. *dean, academic administrator*
Fletcher, Donna Angella *secondary school educator*
Frisch, Ivan Thomas *academic administrator, educator, computer and communications company executive*
Gamble, Cahtina Robyne *elementary school educator*
Gentile, Robert A. *assistant principal*
Hill, Elizabeth Anne *academic administrator, lawyer*
Hultin, Jerry MacArthur *academic administrator, former dean*
Ierardi, Eric Joseph *school system administrator*
Kimmich, Christoph Martin *academic administrator, educator*
Mc Clenney, Byron Nelson *community college administrator*
O'Connor, Sister George Aquin (Margaret M. O'Connor) *academic administrator, educator*
Panwar, Shivendra Singh *education educator, researcher*
Remsen, James F., Jr. *biology educator*
Schweikert, Mary Lou *elementary school educator*
Shivcharran, Jaigobin *secondary school educator, consultant*
Simons, Barbara *retired elementary school educator*
Taylor, Ian Logan *dean*
Wexler, Joan G. *dean, law educator*
Witherspoon, Maria Bernarda Pena *principal*
Wolfe, Ethyle Renee *academic administrator*

Brookville
Swaner, Lynn E *education educator*

Buffalo
Brathwaite, Frank B. *education educator*
Buchanan, Richard N. *dean, dental educator*
Gielow, Kathleen Louise *career planning administrator, consultant, special education educator*
Grant, S. G. *education educator*
Lee, Jaekyung *education educator, researcher*
Meshlovitz, Mary E. *educational consultant, special education educator*
Milazzo, David Anthony *mathematics educator*
Olsen, R. Nills *dean, law educator*
Paige, Susan Mary *adult education educator*
Simpson, John Barclay *academic administrator*
Swenson, William W. *retired dean, aerospace engineer, consultant*
Triggle, David John *dean, pharmacist, consultant*
Tucker, Melvin Jay *education educator, researcher*
Veronica, Debra Clarisse *principal*
Wang, Jui Hsin *biochemistry educator*

Cambria Heights
Welfare, Frederick George *secondary school educator*

Canastota
Mirante, Thomas Anthony *retired secondary education educator*

Canton
Sullivan, Daniel F. *academic administrator, sociologist, educator*

Castleton On Hudson
Kienzle, John Fred *retired history educator*

Catskill
Johnson, Deborah Jean *director*

Cedarhurst
Lagnado, Jennifer M. *assistant principal*

Central Islip
James, Sharon Ann *elementary school educator*
Taylor, Carol Fay *education educator*

Chazy
Ratner, Gayle *special education educator*

Cheektowaga
Wagle, A. Tina *education educator, researcher*

Churchville
Balch, Glenn McClain, Jr. *academic administrator, minister, writer*

Clifton Springs
Spoto, Carl Alexander, Jr. *history educator*

Clinton
Stewart, Joan Hinde *academic administrator*

Cornwall On Hudson
Peirce, Karen Patricia *education educator*

Delmar
Houghton, Raymond Carl, Jr. *education educator*

Dobbs Ferry
Postman, Robert Derek *dean, mathematics professor, writer*

Douglaston
Palatnick, Frank Sidney *educational consultant*

Dryden
Powell, Marsha *director, educator*

East Aurora
Woodard, Carol Jane *educational consultant*

East Islip
Donohue, Claire P. *retired school librarian*

East Syracuse
McGlynn, Sean Edward *secondary school educator*

Eastchester
Kravath, Alan Wolfe *retired education evaluator*

Elmira
Meier, Thomas Keith *academic administrator, language educator*
Reddick, Bryan DeWitt *academic administrator*

Endicott
Goodwin, Charles Hugh *technology education educator*

Endwell
Maliwacki, John M. *secondary school educator*

Fairport
DeMay, Michael F. *secondary school educator, small business owner*

Falconer
Halm, Nancye Studd *retired academic administrator*

Far Rockaway
Sussman, Laureen Glicklin *retired elementary school educator*

Fayetteville
Krathwohl, David Reading *retired education educator*

Floral Park
Curci, Paula *counseling educator, poet, radio personality*
Goldstein, George A. *school system administrator*

Flushing
Anderson, Michelle J. *dean, law educator*
DellaPina, Mario John *academic administrator*
Rosenberg, Deborah A. *special education educator*
Totakura, Satyanarayana Raju *secondary school educator*

Forest Hills
Buhks, Ephraim *college administrator, technology educator*
D'Addario, Alice Marie *retired school system administrator*

Fredonia
Arnavut, Ziya *educator*
Croxton, Jack Sanders *director, consultant*

Freeport
Martorana, Barbara Joan *secondary school educator*
Mitchell, Alice Joyce *retired secondary school educator, retired dietician*

Fresh Meadows
Vigoda, Paul Evan *secondary school educator*

Garden City
Scott, Robert Allyn *academic administrator*
Shuart, James Martin *retired academic administrator*
Storandt, Peter *educational consultant*

Garnerville
Chapman, Margaret Elizabeth *elementary school educator*

Geneseo
Bauer, Norman James *retired education educator*

Glen Cove
Olsen, Robert C., Jr. *academic administrator, military officer*
Rothberg, Judith *elementary school educator, researcher*

Glen Head
Martin, David S. *retired secondary school educator, administrator*

Glenwood
Chambers, Denning Jessyca *middle school educator*

Great Neck
Marcus, Philip *dean*

Greenport
Monsell, Thomas Oliver *secondary school educator, writer*

Greenvale
Lennox, Pamela Chatterton *academic administrator*
Regazzi, John James III *dean, publishing executive*
Steinberg, David Joel *academic administrator, historian, educator*

Hamilton
Chopp, Rebecca S. *academic administrator*
Johnston, Michael (William) *political science educator, university administrator*
Pagano, Jo Anne *education educator*

Hampton Bays
Bucicchia, Carolanne Stephanie *elementary school educator*
Wille, Rosanne Louise *educational consultant*

Harrison
Northcutt, Marie Rose *elementary school educator, special education educator*

Hartsdale
Aker, Susan K. *elementary school educator, assistant principal*
Lightburn, Anita Louise *dean, social work educator*

Hauppauge
Reid, Margaret Elizabeth *elementary school educator, secondary school educator*

Hempstead
Adams, Velma M. *assistant principal, consultant*
Berliner, Herman Albert *academic administrator, economist, educator, dean*
Watford, Dolores *elementary school educator*

Herkimer
Lowery, Kathleen Ann *elementary school educator*

Hicksville
Noll, Amy *secondary educator*

Holland
Loockerman, William Delmer *retired educational administrator*

Hornell
Hunter, John Orr *retired college president*

Houghton
Luckey, Robert Reuel Raphael *retired academic administrator*

Huntington Station
Stevens, Susan Seltenreich Cirillo *special education educator*

Hurley
Opdahl, Viola Elizabeth *secondary school educator*

Islip
Libert, Nancy Porta *retired elementary school educator*

Ithaca
Firebaugh, Francille Maloch *academic administrator*
Halpern, Bruce Peter *academic administrator, researcher, educator*
Kenney, Anne *university librarian*
Lovelace, Richard Van Evera *education educator, research scientist*
McConkey, James Rodney *literature and language educator, writer*
Norton, Mary Beth *history educator, writer*
Paau, Alan Shiukee *academic administrator, biotechnologist, educator*
Rhodes, Frank Harold Trevor *academic administrator, geologist*
Schwab, Stewart Jon *dean, law educator*
Scott, Norman Roy *academic administrator, agricultural engineer, educator*
Skorton, David Jan *academic administrator*
Stycos, Maria Nowakowska *adult education educator*
Swieringa, Robert Jay *dean, accounting educator*
Williams, Peggy Ryan *academic administrator*

Jackson Heights
Ryan, Judith Ann *dean*

Jamaica
Bartilucci, Andrew Joseph *university administrator*
Bunshaft, Charles Edward *elementary school educator, consultant*
Cline, Janice Claire *education educator*
Daly, Mary C. *dean, law educator*
Davis-Jerome, Eileen George *educational consultant, principal*
Faust, Naomi Flowe *education educator*
Harrington, Donald James *university president*
Kaplan, Carolyn Sue *elementary school educator*
Pratt-Johnson, Yvonne Karen *education professor*
Sciame, Joseph *university administrator*

Jamestown
Kestler, Richard Michael *mathematics educator*

Lake Placid
Johns, Sara Kelly *school librarian, library association executive*
Pappalardo, Rosa Gloria *secondary school educator*
Reiss, Paul J. *academic administrator*

Lockport
Leader, Bruce Robert *secondary school educator*

Long Beach
Shahda Geraci, Carole Anne *retired elementary school educator*

Long Island City
Belkharraz, Abderrazak Idrissi *education educator, researcher*
Dromm, Daniel Patrick *elementary school educator*
Lieberman, Janet Elaine *academic administrator*
Lucca, Louis Anthony *academic administrator*

Loudonville
Doyle, Mathias Francis *academic administrator, political scientist, educator*
Drake, Robert *academic administrator, educator*
Toal, James Francis *academic administrator*

Mahopac
McCluskey, Frank Bryce *director*

Mamaroneck
Martin, Roger Harry *retired college president*

Mendon
Munson, Harold Lewis *education educator*

Merrick
Fleischman, Francine D. *secondary school educator*
Garfinkel, Lawrence Saul *academic administrator, educator, television producer*
Harrison, Marjorie Freeman *secondary education educator, librarian*
Howard, Joyce Anne *elementary school educator*

Middle Island
Clarke, Hughette Naomi *elementary school educator*

Middleburgh
Mau, Lisa Anne *special education educator*

Minoa
Sickler, Michael Allan *educator, artist*

Montgomery
Feldman, Arlene Karp *special education educator, director*
Moore, Virginia Lee Smith *elementary school educator*

Monticello
Dutcher, Joana *elementary school educator, singer*

Mount Vernon
Addesso, Angela Joyce *school system administrator*

New Hartford
Boyle, William Leo, Jr. *educational consultant, retired academic administrator*

New Paltz
Emanuel-Smith, Robin Lesley *special education educator*
Flanagan Kelly, Anne Marie *academic administrator*
Gee, David E. *academic administrator*
Poskanzer, Steven Gary *academic administrator, lawyer*

New Rochelle
Cohen, Saul Bernard *retired academic administrator, geographer*
Gunther, Virginia F. *history educator*
Reddington, Mary Jane *retired secondary school educator*

New York
Ackerman, Arlene *education professor, former school system administrator*
Adler, Norman Tenner *psychology educator, dean*
Alfano, Michael Charles *university administrator*
Augustine, Cynthia H. *educational services company executive, lawyer*
Bearse, Carol Irene *education educator*
Benhabib, Jess *adult education educator*
Bertolami, Charles Nicholas *dean, dental educator, oral surgeon*
Best, Wanda *career planning consultant*
Bloomgarden, Karenne Jo *elementary school educator, small business owner*
Bollinger, Lee Carroll *academic administrator, law educator*
Boylan, Elizabeth Shippee *academic administrator, biologist, educator*
Brabeck, Mary Margaret *dean, psychology professor*
Brinkley, Alan David *provost, historian*
Brizendine, Ellanor N. (Bodie) *headmaster*
Brown, Joyce F. *academic administrator*
Burgess, Clara Skipwith *retired principal*
Burns, Red *academic administrator*
Campbell, Mary Schmidt *dean*
Caputo, David Armand *academic administrator, political scientist, educator*
Carnabuci, Frank J. III *headmaster*
Chernis, Mark *educational organization executive*
Clapp, Stephen Henry *dean, violinist*
Claster, Jill Nadell *academic administrator, history educator*
Consagra, Sophie Chandler *academic administrator*
Cooley, Thomas F. *dean, economist, educator*
Danielson, John M. *educational consultant, former federal agency administrator*
Daubs, James Daniel *educational assessment specialist*
Davidson, Anthony R. *education educator, consultant*
Davis, D. Lavelda *dean, academic administrator*
Durkin, Dorothy Angela *university official*
Ellenson, David *college president*
Fabian, Larry Louis *academic administrator*
Fischbach, Gerald D. *dean, neurobiology educator*
Fuhrman, Susan H. *academic administrator, education educator, researcher*
Gerberg, Judith Levine *career consultant*
Germano, William Paul *dean, former publishing executive*
Geurts, Tom Geerd *real estate educator, consultant*
Gibson, Arlene Joy *retired headmaster*
Gillespie, John Thomas *retired university administrator*
Goldberger, Paul Jesse *dean, architecture critic, writer*
Goldstein, Matthew *academic administrator*
Gottschalk, Alfred *retired academic and museum administrator*
Haffner, Alden Norman *academic administrator*
Halperin, Jonathan L. *medical school administrator*
Hamilton, Dorothy Cann *academic administrator*
Handler, Janet Bougash *elementary school educator*
Hansen, William D. *educational consultant, former federal agency administrator*
Hickey, Catherine Josephine *school system administrator*
Hoffner, Marilyn *university administrator*
Hood, Donald Charles *academic administrator, psychologist, educator*
Horowitz, Frances Degen *academic administrator, psychology educator*
Hubbard, R(obert) Glenn *dean, former federal official*
Ilchman, Warren Frederick *academic and foundation administrator, educator*
Iselin, John Jay *academic administrator*
Istomin, Marta Casals *retired school president, performing company executive*
Jansky, Jeannette Jefferson *learning disabilities specialist*
Jelinek, Vera *dean*
Jeynes, Mary Kay *college dean*
Joel, Richard Marc *academic administrator, law educator, dean*
Kase, Nathan Ginden *dean*
Katzman, John S. *educational organization executive*
Kerrey, Bob (J. Robert Kerrey) *academic administrator, former senator*
Klein, Joel Irwin *school system administrator*
Lamm, Norman *academic administrator, rabbi*
Lamster, Ira Barry *dean, academic administrator*
Lange, Phil C. *retired education educator*
Levine, Naomi Bronheim *academic administrator*
Lloyd, Jean *retired early childhood educator*
Love-Hassell, Esther Boyer *special education educator, consultant*
Macchiarola, Frank Joseph *academic administrator, educator*
Malinowska-Sempruch, Kasia *director*
Mandel, Carol *university librarian*
Marcuse, Adrian Gregory *academic administrator*
Marinaccio, Jessica *dean*
Mawhinney, Thomas Stephen *education educator, educational consultant*
Monson, Robert Joseph *education educator*
Morreale, Joseph Constantino *academic administrator, educator, economist, consultant*
Neal, James G. *university librarian*
Nurse, Sir Paul M. *academic administrator*
Oliva, Lawrence Jay *retired academic administrator, history professor*
Paige, Roderick Raynor *educational consultant, former secretary of education*
Parkin, Gerard Francis Ralph *chemistry educator, researcher*
Pawliczko, George Ihor *academic administrator*
Perik, Michael J. *educational organization executive*
Picciano, Anthony Gerade *academic administrator*
Polisi, Joseph William *academic administrator*
Pulanco, Tonya Beth *special education educator*
Rabb, Harriet Schaffer *academic administrator, lawyer*
Reutter, Eberhard Edmund, Jr. *education and law educator*
Revesz, Richard Luis *dean, law educator*
Rhodes, David *academic administrator*
Roeder, John Louis *physics educator*
Rowland, Esther E(delman) *retired dean*
Rubino, Victor Joseph *academic administrator, lawyer*
Rudenstine, David *dean, law educator*
Rudenstine, Neil Leon *former academic administrator, educator*
Schizer, David Michael *dean, law educator*
Sclafani, Susan K. *educational consultant, former federal agency administrator*
Seitz, Frederick *former university administrator*
Selby, Cecily Cannan *dean, science educator, scientist*
Sexton, John Edward *academic administrator, law educator*
Shapiro, Judith R. *academic administrator, anthropology educator*
Shields, James Joseph *academic administrator, educator, writer*
Silverman, Martin Morris Bernard *secondary school educator*
Snyder, Jon David *dean*
Southworth, Robert Alexander, Jr. *education researcher, educator*
Steiner, David M. *dean*
Street, Sharon *philosophy educator*
Teitel, Stanley *principal, science educator*
Thompson, William C., Jr. *school system administrator*
Travis, Jeremy *academic administrator*
Treanor, William Michael *dean, law educator*
Waren, Stanley Arnold *academic administrator, performing company executive*
Waterman, Millicent Adora *education educator, minister*
Weinstein, Sidney *retired university program director*
Wylie, James Malcolm *adult education educator*
Yetman, Leith Eleanor *academic administrator*
Yu, Pauline Ruth *former dean, educational association administrator*

Niagara University
Brown, Kathleen *education educator*
Foote, Chandra Jeanet *education and elementary school educator, writer*

North Tonawanda
Beach, Sandra Marie Yudichak *secondary school educator*

Northport
Weaver, Eric James *educational administrator*

Old Westbury
Christofides, Fotine *parochial school educator*
van Wie, Paul David *secondary school educator, historian*

Orangeburg
Filippelli, James Anthony *literature and language educator*

Oswego
Garruto, John *counseling administrator*
Hockey, Christopher Lawrence *academic administrator*

Ovid
Scoles, Marie Y. *elementary school educator*

Ozone Park
Bellamy, Renee Adele *secondary school educator*

Patchogue
Igneri, David Sebastian *elementary school educator*

Pittsford
Barker, Julie A. *school system administrator*
Bernstein, Paul *retired academic dean*
Sproull, Robert Lamb *retired academic administrator, physicist, director*
Thompson, Brian John *academic administrator, optics scientist, educator*

Plattsburgh
Withrow, Gregory B. *director, accountant*

Pomona
Frelow, Robert Dean *retired school system administrator, writer*

Port Jefferson Station
Shockley, Alonzo Hilton, Jr. *school system administrator*
Spahr, Clinton S., Jr. *retired elementary school educator*

Potsdam
Collins, Anthony G. (Tony Collins) *academic administrator*
Ha, Andrew Kwangho *education educator*
Rudiger, Lance Wade *secondary school educator*
Schwaller, John Frederick *academic administrator, historian, educator*
Scott, Jean A. *university president*

Poughkeepsie
Brakas, Nora Jachym *education educator*
Conklin, Donald David *academic administrator*
Hill, Catharine Bond (Cappy) *academic administrator, economics professor*
Lowden, Christine C. *school system administrator*
Opdycke, Leonard Emerson *retired elementary school educator, publishing executive, writer*
Taylor, Patricia *director*

Purchase
Schwarz, Thomas J. *academic administrator, lawyer*
West, Kazuko Ito *mathematics educator, department chairman*

Rexford
Schmitt, Roland Walter *retired academic administrator*

Rochester
Adams, Carol H. *dean*
Blanda-Holtzberg, Marianne Lourdes *education educator, consultant*
Campbell, Alma Jacqueline Porter *elementary school educator*
Chiverton, Patricia Ann *dean, nursing educator*
Cohen, Jules *former dean, internist, educator*
Colabufo, Steven James *mathematics educator*
Destler, William W. *academic administrator*
Everett, Claudia Kellam *retired special education educator*
Guzick, David S. *dean, educator*
Jackson, Thomas Humphrey *former academic administrator*
Joynt, Robert James *academic administrator, physician*
Larson, Joanne Caroline *education educator*
Shirley, Bonnie J. *retired elementary school educator*
Zupan, Mark A. *dean, business professor*

Rockville Centre
Lynch, Peter K. *education educator*

Rocky Point
Falcone, David J. *elementary school educator*
Meschi, Jennifer Margaret *technology educator*
Scalfani, Carl *secondary school educator*

Roslyn
Stracher, Dorothy Altman *education educator, consultant*

Saint James
Kelly, Michael Joseph *academic administrator, consultant*

Sanborn
Michalak, Janet Carol *childhood education educator, coordinator*
Nowak (Jarosz), Linda Therese *special education educator, consultant*

Sands Point
Cullinan, Bernice Ellinger *education educator*

Saratoga Springs
Glotzbach, Philip A. *academic administrator, philosopher, educator*

Patel, Ajay *dean*
Roth, Marjory Joan Jarboe *special education educator*
Walsh, Robert K. *dean*

Woodland
Wilson, Lloyd Lee *registrar, educator*

Zebulon
Privette, Janet Brown *elementary school educator*

NORTH DAKOTA

Bismarck
Evanson, Barbara Jean *middle school education educator*
Joersz, Fran Woodmansee *secondary school educator*
Potts, Robert Leslie *academic administrator*
Sanstead, Wayne Godfrey *school system administrator*

Elgin
Hintz, Pam K. *secondary school and science educator*

Ellendale
Schlieve, Hy C. J. *school administrator*

Fargo
Meester, Holly *elementary school educator, music educator, sales executive*
Morey, Charlotte Ann *elementary school educator, music educator*

Grand Forks
Kupchella, Charles Edward *academic administrator, author, educator*
Mondry, Diane *secondary school educator*
Nordlie, Robert Conrad *biochemistry educator*
Page, Sally Jacquelyn *university official, management educator*
Swanson, Zona Luciel *retired elementary school educator*

Hatton
Strand, Fred P. *mathematics educator*

Mayville
Pederson, John Martin *education educator*
Sorteberg, Ann Marie *education educator*

Minot
Jermiason, John Lynn *elementary school educator, farmer, investor*
Srock, Marlene *elementary school educator*

Wahpeton
Donahe, Peggy Yvonne *gifted and talented educator, librarian*

OHIO

Ada
Baker, Kendall L. *academic administrator*

Akron
Barker, Harold Kenneth *former university dean*
Buzzelli, Charlotte Grace *special education educator*
Ichilov, Nehemia *principal, consultant*
Linberger, Peter *school librarian*
Martin, Jack *educational services company executive, former federal agency administrator*
von Spiegel, Janice Krieger *mathematics educator*

Amelia
Kahles, Cheryl Mary *elementary school educator*

Athens
Bruning, James Leon *academic administrator, educator*
Cooper-Chen, Anne *journalism educator, researcher*
Crowl, Samuel Renninger *retired dean, language educator*
Hogan, Terrence James *academic administrator, consultant*
Krendl, Kathy *dean*
McDavis, Roderick J. *academic administrator*

Aurora
Ross, Violet Bica *retired elementary school educator, retired psychologist*

Barberton
Zufra, Mindy Marie *mathematics educator*

Berea
Durst, Richard Wayne *academic administrator*

Bowling Green
Baird, Alice Knar *retired education educator*

Brunswick
Sandvick, Janet Rose *history educator*

Canton
Peck, Douglas Caton *dean, educator*

Chagrin Falls
Brown, Jeanette Grasselli *retired director*
Deihl, Charles L. *former college president*

Chardon
Columbro, Madeline M. *education educator*
Horvath, Madelon Toft *secondary school educator*

Chippewa Lake
Javorek, Richard Alan *history educator, consultant*

Cincinnati
Arb, Carrie Samantha *adult education educator*
Auyang, Grace Chao *education educator, consultant*
Bilionis, Louis D. *dean, law educator*
Briggs, Henry Payson, Jr. *headmaster*
Bryant, Irene Melba *retired elementary school educator, artist*
Farrell, Pamela Christine *secondary school educator*
Greengus, Samuel *academic administrator, theology studies educator*
Harrison, Donald Carey *academic administrator, cardiologist, educator*
Kessinger, Thomas Anthony *education educator, social studies educator, researcher, consultant*
Kilgore, Jenny A. *education educator*
Lindell, Andrea Regina *dean, nurse*
Moyo, Kimya Maunda *elementary school educator*
Nester, William Raymond, Jr. *retired academic administrator*
Rahnfeld, Vincent D. *counseling administrator*
Smith, Gregory Allgire *academic administrator*
Stern, David Mark *dean, educator*
Sublett, Roger H. *academic administrator*
Wagner, Thomas Edward *academic administrator, educator*
Winkler, Henry Ralph *retired academic administrator, historian*
Woods, Carol Smith *private school educator*
Zimpher, Nancy Lusk *academic administrator*

Circleville
Conley, John Wallace *academic administrator*

Cleveland
Boboc, Marius *education educator*
Burns, Michael Kent *retired educator, chemical dependency counselor*
Callesen-Gyorgak, Jan Elaine *special education educator*
Cerone, David *academic administrator*
Dicken, Eric L. *academic administrator*
Eastwood, Gregory Lindsay *former academic administrator*
Eustis, Joanne D. *university librarian*
Goldberg, Jerold S. *academic administrator*
Grossman, Mary Margaret *retired elementary school educator*
Hundert, Edward M. *former academic administrator, educator*
McArdle, Richard Joseph *retired academic administrator*
McCullough, Joseph *retired academic administrator*
Nickerson, Gary Lee *educational consultant*
Queen, Joyce *elementary school educator*
Quigney, Theresa Ann *special education educator*
Simson, Gary Joseph *dean, law educator*
Snyder, Barbara Rook *academic administrator*
Sobonya, Stephanie Jean N'Cole *mathematics educator*
Thomas, David Manning *secondary school educator*
Topol, Eric Jeffrey *academic administrator, cardiologist, educator*
Weidenthal, Maurice David (Bud) *academic administrator, journalist*
Weitzner, Ronald Philip *special education educator*
Wertheim, Sally Harris *director, academic administrator, dean, education educator, consultant*
Wykle, May L. *dean, educator, researcher*

Cleveland Heights
Challenger, Vicki Lee *elementary school educator*
Close, Carole Lynne *education educator, consultant*

Columbia Station
Goll, Paulette Susan *education educator*

Columbus
Agbemabiese, Padmore Enyonam *educator*
Ash, Thomas Phillip *school system administrator*
Balkrishnan, Rajesh *education educator*
Beck, Paul Allen *dean, political science professor*
Bell, Karen A. *dean*
Bush, Margaret Eileen *elementary school educator*
Cocchi, Wayne Paul *special education educator*
Cole, Clarence Russell *college dean*
Culbertson, Jack Arthur *education educator*
Edwards, Jennifer Lynn *adult education educator, researcher*
Fingerhut, Eric D. *academic administrator, former state legislator and congressman, lawyer*
Flanagan-Soulen, Mary Susan *secondary school educator, adult education educator*
Ganschinietz, Deepa *elementary school educator*
Gee, Elwood Gordon *academic administrator*
Griffith, Dennison W. *academic administrator, artist, educator*
Koenigsknecht, Roy A. *dean*
Kronmiller, Jan E. *dean, academic administrator*
Lisko (Dozer), Bonnie Lee *education educator*
Magliocca, Larry Anthony *education educator*
Mrozek, Lawrence James *director*
O'Hanlon, Nancyanne *school librarian, educator*
Otte, Paul John *academic administrator, consultant*
Rogers, Nancy Hardin *dean, law educator*
Sanfilippo, Alfred Paul *dean, medical educator, pathologist*
Sedmak, Daniel D. *academic administrator*
Stephens, Thomas M(aron) *education educator*
Turner, Elvin L. *retired school system administrator*
Willke, Thomas Aloys *academic administrator, statistician, educator*
Zelman, Susan Tave *school system administrator*

Crooksville
Childers, Susan Lynn Bohn *special education educator, school system administrator, human resources and transition specialist, consultant*

Dayton
Curran, Daniel J. *academic administrator, sociologist, educator*
Hopkins, David R. *academic administrator, educator*
Lasley, Thomas J., II, *education educator*
Part, Howard Mitchell *dean*
Pestello, Fred P. *academic administrator*
Taylor, Elisabeth Coler *retired secondary school educator*

Delaware
Lemke, Stacy J. *secondary school educator*

Delta
Miller, Beverly White *former college president, educational consultant*

Dublin
Meek, Violet Imhof *retired dean*
Redman, Janis F. *special education educator, department chairman*
Warmbrod, Catharine Phelps *educational researcher, consultant*

East Cleveland
England, Diana Whitten *elementary school educator*

Euclid
Miller, Demetra Fay Pelat *elementary school educator, city official*

Fairborn
Combs, Eric A. *social studies educator*
Goetz, Douglas Neil *contract management educator*

Fairfield
Glass, Linda L. *elementary school educator*
Hubbard, Michele Masanek *secondary school educator, soccer coach*

Fairview Park
Flynn, Patricia M. *director, special education and gifted and talented educator*

Findlay
Freed, DeBow *academic administrator*

Fremont
Ruble, Amanda L. *elementary school educator*

Gambier
Nugent, S. Georgia *academic administrator*
Spaid, Gregory P. *academic administrator, art educator*

Georgetown
Fite, Tom W. *retired mathematics educator, farmer*

Hemlock
Johnson, George Warner *gifted and talented educator, consultant*

Hudson
Goheen, Janet Moore *counseling administrator, sales executive*
Lambacher, Kathleen Hartwell *retired education educator*

Huron
Leser, Anne Elizabeth *education educator*

Ironton
Curry, Estella Roberta *education educator, school psychologist, consultant*

Kent
Buttlar, Rudolph Otto *retired college dean*
Cartwright, Carol Ann *retired academic administrator*
Gaston, Paul Lee *academic administrator, language educator*
Gosnell, Davina J. *dean, nursing educator*
Lefton, Lester Alan *academic administrator, psychology professor*
Phillips, Matthew Todd *history educator*

Lewis Center
Thomason, Sandra Lee *elementary school educator*

Lima
MacBenn, Joseph Vernon *director*

Loveland
Voluse, Charles Rodger III *retired education educator*

Mansfield
Gregory, Deirdre Dianne *secondary school educator*
Riedl, John Orth *retired university dean*

Mantua
Wallingford, Jack W. *secondary school educator*

Massillon
Eckhart, Marylouise Christine Santilli *pre-school educator*

Mc Donald
Daigle, Barbara Dianne *elementary school educator*

Mentor
Hale, Jeffrey L. *economics educator*

Miamiville
Franz, (Iris) Vivian *dean, director*

Mount Vernon
Shriver, William Russell *secondary school educator*

New Concord
Boggs, Bennett Gibson *academic administrator*

New Matamoras
Brown, Blanche Y. *secondary school educator, genealogist, researcher*

New Philadelphia
Doughten, Mary Katherine (Molly) *retired secondary school educator*

North Canton
Cooney, Sondra Miley *literature and language educator*

Northfield
Arndt, Charles Richard *educational consultant*

Oak Harbor
Randels, David George *retired secondary school educator*

Oberlin
Brown, John Lott *former university president, retired educator*
Koppes, Clayton R. *academic administrator*
Krislov, Marvin *academic administrator, lawyer, educator*
McGuire, Charles Edward *musicology educator*

Olmsted Falls
Mercer, John Lee *secondary school educator, department chairman*

Orrville
Hennell, Robert William III *secondary school educator*
Warner, Patricia Ann *secondary school educator*

Orwell
Strong, Marcella Lee *music specialist, educator*

Oxford
Sessions, Judith Ann *dean, university librarian*
Shriver, Phillip Raymond *academic administrator*
Thompson, Bertha Boya *retired education educator*

Painesville
Davis, Barbara Snell *education educator*

Parma
Petrus, Sally A. *elementary school educator*
Romanovich, Patricia M. *parochial school educator*
Tener, Carol Joan *retired secondary school educator, consultant*

Peninsula
Sigler, Theresa Jane *school system administrator*

Pepper Pike
Stano, Sister Diana *academic administrator*

Perrysburg
Stockner, Linda Ann *elementary school educator*

Pickerington
Collins, Arlene *secondary school educator*

Port Clinton
Ewersen, Mary Virginia *retired school system administrator, poet*

Rio Grande
Hatfield, Barbara Scott *academic administrator*

Sagamore Hills
Miller, Susan Ann *retired school system administrator*

Saint Marys
VanderHorst, Monica S. *physical education educator*

Sardinia
Evans, C(aroline) Sue *education educator*

Shaker Heights
Brachna, Gabor (Samuel) *elementary school educator*
Trefts, Joan Landenberger *retired principal*

Sidney
Seitz, James Eugene *retired college president, freelance writer*

Solon
Williams, Jeffery Lynn *secondary school educator, consultant, writer*

Springfield
Kinnison, William Andrew *retired university president*
Stelzer, Patricia Jacobs *retired secondary school educator*

Stow
Castillo, Katherine Lynn *secondary school educator, writer, translator, business owner*

Streetsboro
Cielec, Greg J. *literature and language educator*
Cravcenco, Ludmila *academic administrator*

Strongsville
Yates, Patricia Lawrence *elementary school educator*

Sylvania
Heuschele, Sharon Jo *dean*

Masten, Barbara Jean *education educator, department chairman*
Sampson, Earldine Robison *education educator*

Toledo
Closius, Phillip J. *dean, law educator*
Gutteridge, Thomas G. *academic administrator, consultant, arbitrator*
Harter, James Lester *academic administrator, consultant*
Konwinski, Jacqueline Marie Koralewski *secondary school educator*
Pham, David Lan *secondary school educator, writer*
Reichert, Christine Edwards *academic administrator*
Romanoff, Marjorie Reinwald *retired education educator*
Seubert, Lori A. *elementary school educator*

University Heights
Seaton, Shirley Smith *academic administrator, consultant*
Whelan, John Joseph *education educator*

Upper Arlington
Bordelon, Carolyn Thew *elementary school educator*

Vincent
Meek, Barbara Susan *elementary school educator*

Wadsworth
Wilhelm, Cathy S. *elementary school educator*

Westerville
DeVore, C. Brent *college president, educator*
Husarik, Ernest Alfred *educational administrator*
Kerr, Thomas Jefferson, IV, *academic administrator*

Wilberforce
Williamson, Vikki Lyn *university official, financial executive*

Youngstown
Green, Adele C. *educator*
Zorn, Robert Lynn *education educator*

OKLAHOMA

Bartlesville
Baker-Morris, Kay *special education educator*

Bixby
Walker, Jerald Carter *academic administrator, minister*

Bristow
Caudle, Letha Grace *secondary school educator*

Choctaw
Uselton, Bill W. *secondary school educator*

Claremore
Heidlage, Patsy Jo *physical education educator*
Vargas, Traci Junelle *special education educator*

Disney
Hamilton, Carl Hulet *retired academic administrator*

Edmond
Harryman, Rhonda L. *special education educator*
Myster, Randall Walton *education educator, researcher*
Sibley, William Arthur *retired academic administrator, physics professor, consultant*

Langston
Haysbert, JoAnn Wright *academic administrator*
Showalter, Betsy S. *mathematics educator*

Mcloud
Goats, Debbie *elementary school educator*

Midwest City
Cheek, Norma Jean *retired elementary school educator*
Wier, Leanne M. *life sciences educator*

Moore
Chiles, Mary Jane *secondary school educator*

Muskogee
Hasler-Reid, Linda *elementary school educator*
Swanson, Jacqueline V. *academic administrator, educator, women's health nurse practitioner*

Norman
Biscoe, Belinda P. *academic administrator, psychologist*
Boren, David Lyle *academic administrator, former senator*
Croft, Janet Brennan *academic librarian*
Landers, Thomas Lee *dean, educator*
Mergler, Nancy L. *academic administrator*
Pappas, James Pete *university administrator*
Provine, Lorraine *retired mathematics educator*
Sharp, Paul Frederick *retired academic administrator, educational consultant*
Van Horn, Richard Linley *academic administrator*
Winters, Martha P. *history and language educator*
Zapffe, Nina Byrom *retired elementary school educator*

Oklahoma City
Coats, Andrew Montgomery *dean, lawyer, former mayor*
Hageman, Dale *alternative staffing company executive*
Kriesel, Deanna *education educator*
Risser, Paul Gillan *academic administrator, botanist*
Shelite, Leslie Michelle *middle school educator*
Voth, Douglas W. *dean, educator*
Weigel, Paul Henry *biochemistry educator, researcher, consultant*
Williamson, Marvel *dean, nursing administrator, sexologist, educator*
Woods, Pendleton *college director, author*
Young, Stephen K. *dean, academic administrator*

Ponca City
Gallagher, Gary W(ayne) *educational services executive*
Rice, Sue Ann *retired dean, psychologist*

Poteau
Long, Sheila Joan *academic administrator*

Shawnee
Sharp, Ron *secondary school educator*

Stillwater
Halligan, James Edmund *academic administrator, chemical engineer*
Strathe, Marlene I. *academic administrator*

Tahlequah
Stowers, Lela M. *retired academic administrator*

Tulsa
Buthod, Mary Clare *school administrator*
Donaldson, Robert Herschel *university administrator, educator*
Lewis, Patricia Mohatt (Patty) *special education educator*
Roger, Jerry Lee *academic administrator*
Thornton, Charlie Mae *secondary school educator*
Trennepohl, Gary Lee *academic administrator, finance educator*
Upham, Steadman *academic administrator, anthropologist, educator*
Wood, Emily Churchill *special education and social studies educator, consultant*

Warr Acres
Weir, Richard Dale *elementary school educator*

OREGON

Ashland
Cullinan, Mary Patricia *academic administrator, literature and language professor*

Beaverton
de Sá e Silva, Elizabeth Anne *secondary school educator*
Duncan, Richard Fredrick, Jr. *retired secondary school educator, consultant*
Frank, Sister Ruth M. *principal, educator*

Cannon Beach
Wismer, Patricia Ann *retired secondary school educator*

Clackamas
Woods, Dennis Oliver *headmaster, market and political research analyst*

Coos Bay
Hanlin, Shawn *academic administrator*

Corvallis
Byrne, John Vincent *educational consultant*
Coakley, James A. *atmospheric science educator*
Davis, John Rowland *academic administrator*
Verts, Lita Jeanne *academic administrator*
Young, Roy Alton *university administrator, educator*

Dallas
Brown, James Chandler *retired university administrator*

Eugene
Frohnmayer, David Braden *academic administrator*
Gall, Meredith (Mark) Damien *retired education educator, writer*
Moseley, John Travis *academic administrator, physicist, researcher*
Pickett, Stephen Wesley *academic administrator, consultant*
Sygall, Susan E. *international educational exchange director*
Womack, James Errol *college president*

Grants Pass
Murdock, Doris Dean *special education educator, program developer*

Gresham
Cooke, Jackie (Jacqueline Marie Cooke) *elementary school educator*
Light, Betty Jensen Pritchett *retired dean*
Waagen, Linda Louise *elementary school educator*
Webb, Donna Louise *academic director, educator*

Hermiston
Lampkin, Toni K. *elementary school educator*

Joseph
Gilbert, David Erwin *academic administrator, physicist*

Klamath Falls
Dow, Martha Anne *academic administrator, biology professor*

La Grande
Fatemi, Khusrow *academic administrator, economics educator*

Lake Oswego
Wicklund, Lee Arthur *retired school system administrator*

Lowell
Boyle, John Howard *history educator*

Mcminnville
Walker, Charles Urmston *retired university president*

Medford
Dixon, Andrew Derart *retired academic administrator*
Franklin, Darlene Kay *elementary school educator*

Monmouth
Cannon, Beverly J. *deaf education educator, interpreter*
Minahan, John P. *academic administrator*

Newberg
Johnson, Thomas Floyd *former academic administrator, educator*

Oceanside
Wadlow, Joan Krueger *retired academic administrator, construction executive*

Oregon City
Vasquez, Paul I. *director*

Portland
Bartlett, Thomas Alva *retired educational administrator*
Bodin, Kate *dean*
Bragdon, Paul Errol *retired academic administrator, educator*
Braun, Stephen Baker *academic administrator*
Clinton, Jack W. *dean*
Diver, Colin S. *academic administrator, educator*
Fan, Lee Siu *business executive and vocational training program administrator*
Harris, Cynthia Viola *principal*
Hochstettler, Thomas John *academic administrator, historian*
Iamratanakul, Supachart *educational consultant*
Koblik, Steven S. *academic administrator*
Leupp, Edythe Peterson *retired education educator*
McClave, Donald Silsbee *academic administrator*
Njoku, Scholastica Ibari *retired college librarian, writer*
Phillips, Vicki L. *school system administrator*
Robertson, Joseph E., Jr. *academic administrator, ophthalmologist, educator*
Sylvester, Robert *dean, musician*
Wood, Cynthia Wilder *elementary school educator*

Roseburg
Tilson, Daniel *elementary school educator*

Salem
Castillo, Susan *school system administrator*
Page, Cheryl Miller *elementary school educator*
Pelton, M. Lee *academic administrator*

The Dalles
Hayden, I. Jill *secondary school educator*

Yachats
Robeck, Mildred Coen *retired education educator, writer*

PENNSYLVANIA

Aliquippa
Drobac, Nikola (Nick) *education educator, consultant*

Allentown
Helm, Peyton Randolph *academic administrator, history professor*
Pavelich, Judith *retired secondary school educator*

Altoona
Shurin, Leonard Joseph *school system administrator*

Annville
McGill, William James, Jr. *academic administrator, writer*

Avonmore
Smith, Luella Margaret *special education educator*

Bala Cynwyd
Oswald, James Marlin *education educator, researcher*

Beaver
Strock, Robert S. *retired education educator*

Bensalem
O'Toole, Michael Anthony *academic administrator*

Bentleyville
Blasko, Barbara Ann *secondary school educator*

Berwick
Pasukinis, Cheryl Renee *elementary school educator*

Bethel Park
Menees, Katherine Determan *parochial school educator*

Bethlehem
Agbeh, Anthony Odey *education educator, consultant*
Gast, Alice Petry *academic administrator, chemical engineering educator*

Bloomsburg
Kozloff, Jessica S. *academic administrator*
Trapane, Ruth *educator, artist*

Blue Bell
Brendlinger, LeRoy R. *academic administrator*

Brockway
Ball, Karen Elaine *elementary school educator*

Broomall
DiRosa, Steven Joseph *primary and secondary school educator*

Brownsville
Miner, Brad C. *secondary school educator*

Bryn Mawr
Baird, John Absalom, Jr. *retired academic administrator*
Frank, Edward David, II, *history educator*
Hirsh, Sharon Latchaw *academic administrator, art history educator*
Vickers, Nancy J. *academic administrator*

Canonsburg
Mascetta, Joseph Anthony *principal*

Carlisle
Asimakakis, Panagiota *mathematics educator*
Durden, William G. *academic administrator*
McConnaughay, Philip J. *dean, law educator*

Center Valley
Gambet, Daniel G(eorge) *academic administrator, minister*

Chalfont
Ashley, Kathleen Labonis *elementary school educator*

Chambersburg
Bitner, Betty L. *education educator*

Chester
Harris, James Thomas III *college administrator, educator*

Clarion
Harry, Vickie Diane *education educator*

Conneaut Lake
Parmiter, Karen Lynn *retired education educator*

Connellsville
Humbert, Kimberly Ramsay *secondary school educator*
Shearer, Linda Rae *English educator*

Cooperstown
Hogg, James Henry, Jr. *retired education educator*

Cranberry Township
Hauck, Lindsay Beth *elementary school educator*

Dover
Butterfield, Andrea Christine *elementary school educator*

Doylestown
Kropp, Edward H. *education educator, consultant*
Thomas, Ellen Louise *school system administrator*

Dresher
Faust, Carrissima Washington *educational consultant*

Dunmore
Krogh-Jespersen, Mary-Beth *academic administrator*

East Stroudsburg
Braithwaite, Barbara Jo *retired secondary school educator*
Kansfield, Norman J. *former seminary president*

Easton
Stull, Frank Walter *elementary school educator*
Teboh-Ewungkem, Miranda Ijang *education educator*
Weiss, Daniel H. *academic administrator, former dean*

Elizabethtown
Garber, Margaret Mary *elementary school educator*
Gordon, Laurie Anne *academic director*
Ritsch, Frederick Field *academic administrator, historian*
Sample, Frederick Palmer *former college president*

Elkins Park
Burnley, June Williams *secondary school educator*
Stinnett, Hester *art school administrator, educator*

Emlenton
Berg, Janice Carol *elementary school educator*

Erie
Breckenridge, James G. *dean, consultant*
Daly, Mary *college administrator*
Miller, Virginia Louise *director*
Zelazny, Catherine *retired elementary school educator*

Exeter
Flickinger, Donald E. *mathematics educator*

Stocker, Joyce Arlene *retired secondary school educator*

Fairless Hills
Steckroat, Patricia A. *special education educator*

Fairview
Stern, Marilyn Jean *special education educator*

Flourtown
Cooke, Sara Mullin Graff *daycare provider, kindergarten educator, medical assistant*

Franklin
Sauer, Mary Julia *special education educator*

Gettysburg
Will, Katherine Haley *academic administrator*

Glenside
Carr, Scott *technology educator*

Greensburg
Neff, Mary Ellen Andre *retired elementary school educator*

Gwynedd Valley
Owens, Kathleen C. *academic administrator*

Hanover
Clark, Sandra Marie *school administrator*

Harmony
O'Shea, Patrick Alan *elementary school educator*

Harrisburg
Batts, Barbara Jean *academic administrator, director*
Brown, John Walter *vocational education supervisor*
Burns, Rebecca Ann *elementary school educator, librarian*
Fulmer, Deborah Lee *education educator, oncological nurse*
Hample, Judy G. *academic administrator*
Popnik, Marlene Alita *retired school librarian*
Zahorchak, Gerald Lee *school system administrator*

Hatfield
Jesberg, Robert Ottis, Jr. *educational consultant, science educator*

Haverford
Bean, Philip Albert *dean, historian*
Emerson, Stephen G. *academic administrator, oncologist, hematologist, educator*
Tritton, Thomas Richard *former academic administrator, biologist, educator*

Havertown
Evarts, Mary H. *mathematics educator*
Wright, Cecilia Powers *gifted and talented educator*

Hazleton
Lawler, Gary M. *academic administrator*

Hershey
Jones, Marshall Bush *education educator, researcher*

Homestead
King, Richard Wayne *principal*

Honesdale
Barbe, Walter Burke *education educator*

Huntingdon
Kepple, Thomas Ray, Jr. *college administrator*

Immaculata
Fadden, Sister R. Patricia *academic administrator, nun*

Indiana
Pidgeon, John Anderson *headmaster*
Thibadeau, Eugene Francis *education educator, consultant*

Irwin
Perich, Terry Miller *retired secondary school educator*

Jefferson Hills
Smith, Leslie Edgar *vocational school administrator*

Jenkintown
Hidalgo, Alfreda Edith *elementary school educator*
Oh, Soojin Susan *elementary school educator*

Kintnersville
Barnes, Francis V. *school system administrator*

Knox
Rupert, Elizabeth Anastasia *retired dean*

Kresgeville
Beckley, Roberta Ann *elementary school educator*

Kutztown
Weber, Michael Allen *school librarian*

La Plume
Boehm, Edward Gordon, Jr. *college administrator, educator*

Lafayette Hill
Delacato, Carl Henry *education educator*
Delacato, Janice Elaine *special education educator, consultant*

Lancaster
Ebersole, Mark Chester *emeritus college president*
Fry, John Anderson *academic administrator*
Kneedler, (Alvin) Richard *academic administrator*

Langhorne
Neff, Amy Hancock *elementary school educator*

Latrobe
Hupe, Donna Marie *education educator*
Porembka, Michael Richard *assistant principal, supervisor*
Towey, Jim (H. James Towey) *academic administrator, former federal official*
Will, James Fredrick *academic administrator, former steel company executive*

Lehman
Novrocki, Michael W. *secondary school educator*
Williams, Thomas Alan *elementary school educator, small business owner*

Lewisburg
Mitchell, Brian Christopher *academic administrator*

Lewistown
Varner, Vance Sieber *principal*

Lincoln University
Nelson, Ivory Vance *academic administrator*

Lititz
McGlynn, James Francis *chemistry educator, chemical engineer*
Sandercox, Robert Allen *academic administrator, minister*

Little Meadows
Staby, Dorothy Louise *elementary school educator*

Lock Haven
Almes, June *retired education educator, librarian*

Macungie
Rubin, Arthur Herman *retired academic administrator*

Mansfield
Loeschke, Maravene S. *academic administrator, theater educator*

Maple Glen
Weaver-Stroh, Joanne Mateer *education educator, consultant*

Martinsburg
Neff, Robert Wilbur *academic administrator, educator, minister*

Mc Elhattan
Garner, Charles William *retired educational administration educator, consultant*

Meadville
Cook, Richard James *academic administrator*
Dixon, Armendia Pierce *school program administrator*

Mechanicsburg
Feaser, Deborah Ellen *mathematics educator*

Media
Leiby, Bruce Richard *retired secondary school educator, writer*

Montgomeryville
Detwiler, Christine Wendler *special education educator*

Montoursville
Hunter, Corey Ryan *secondary school educator*

Morgantown
Dierwechter, David C. *retired elementary school educator, theater director*

Mount Bethel
Carpenter, Carolyn *elementary school educator*

Mount Pleasant
Dangelo, Eugene Michael *elementary school educator*

Nazareth
Ferraro, Margaret Louise (Peg) *secondary school educator*

Nelson
Kyofski, Bonelyn Lugg *retired education educator*

New Hope
Coyle, Diane Bonanomi *special education educator*

New Milford
Cunningham, Mary Ann Michael *secondary school educator*

Newmanstown
Hertzog, Noel Kent *retired elementary school educator*

Newtown
Booraem, Hendrik, V, *education educator, historian*
Duncan, Stephen Robert *elementary school educator*

Newtown Square
Bertolet, Caroline Lynne Georgeanne *special education educator, labor union administrator*
Swing, Elizabeth Sherman *education educator*

Norristown
DeMedio, Kathleen Marie *chemistry educator*
Marzewski, Janeen Lynette *elementary school educator*

North Versailles
King, Cheryl Brea *elementary, secondary and music educator*

North Wales
Vietri, Linda Smith *gifted and talented educator*

Philadelphia
Aversa, Dolores Sejda *educational administrator*
Bass, Aaron *school system administrator*
Bates, James Earl *academic administrator*
Bell, Steven J. *school librarian, educator, writer*
Benson, Hande Yurttan *adult education educator*
Boruch, Robert Francis *educator, consultant*
Brucker, Paul C. *academic administrator, physician*
Capers, Gregg *secondary school educator, musician*
Caplan, Arthur Leonard *university program director, educator*
Cohen, David Walter *academic administrator, educator, periodontist*
Corzo, Miguel Angel *academic administrator*
Dennis, Roger J. *dean, law educator*
Donnelly, Gloria Ferraro *university dean*
Dunn, Mary Maples *academic administrator*
Fernandez, Happy Craven (Gladys) *academic administrator*
Fitts, Michael Andrew *dean, law educator*
Gaillard, Theodore Lee, Jr. *literature and language educator, writer*
Goon, Arthur David *academic administrator, educator*
Graffman, Gary *academic administrator, pianist, music educator*
Gutmann, Amy *academic administrator, political science and philosophy educator*
Hack, Gary Arthur *dean*
Hart, Ann Weaver *academic administrator*
Jeffcoat, Marjorie K. *dean, dental educator*
Liacouras, Peter James *academic administrator, lawyer, arbitrator, educator*
Lynch, Douglas E. *dean*
Mazer, Toby Rotman *adminstrative director*
Means, John Barkley *director, language educator*
Nasca, Thomas Joseph *dean*
Onley, Sister Francesca *academic administrator*
Padulo, Louis *university administrator*
Papadakis, Constantine N. *academic administrator, civil engineer, educator*
Porter, Andrew Calvin *dean, psychologist, educator*
Reinstein, Robert J. *dean, law educator*
Robertson, Thomas Sinclair *dean, marketing educator*
Romer, Daniel *university official, psychologist, educator*
Rubenstein, Arthur Harold *academic administrator, dean, internist, educator*
Rudczynski, Andrew B. *academic administrator, medical researcher*
Sibolski, Elizabeth Hawley *academic administrator*
Sipe, Lawrence Robert *education educator*
Stetson, Willis J., Jr., (Lee Stetson) *dean*
Tansy, Martin F. *dean*
Verlin, Jonathan R. *secondary school educator*
von Seldeneck, Judith Metcalfe *career planning administrator*
Wachman, Marvin *retired academic administrator*

Pittsburgh
Braun, Thomas W. *dean, academic administrator*
Cho, Sung K. *education educator*
Cohon, Jared L. *academic administrator*
Crossely, Mary A. *dean, law educator*
Cubbage, Bobbie Danielle *pre-school administrator, educator*
Davis, Larry E. *academic administrator*
Dougherty, Charles John *academic administrator*
Dunn, Kenneth B. *dean*
Eckert, Jean Patricia *elementary school educator*
Geibel, Sister Grace Ann *university president*
Herring, David John *dean, law educator*
Hunker, Jeffrey *dean*
Kupfer, David J. *psychiatry professor*
Larsen, Ronald L. *dean, information scientist, educator*
Lehoczky, John Paul *statistics educator*
Lorensen, Frederick Hamilton *educational administrator, consultant*
Miller, Ronald Lynn *director*
Nordenberg, Mark Alan *academic administrator, law educator*
Packard, Rochelle Sybil *retired elementary school educator*
Rebich, Lois J. *elementary school educator*
Ross, Madelyn Ann *academic administrator, newspaper editor*
Smartschan, Glenn Fred *educational consultant*
Van Dusen, Albert Clarence *academic administrator*
Walls Perry, J(oyce) Lorraine *elementary school educator*
Weidman, John Carl, II, *education and sociology educator, consultant*
Wetzel, Amanda Grace *secondary school educator*

Pittston Township
Renfer, James Allen *elementary school educator*

Pocono Summit
Yorke-Viney, Sally Anne *elementary school educator*

Quakertown
Babb, Lisa Marie *physical education educator*

Reading
Pumariega, JoAnne Buttacavoli *mathematics educator*
Rodgers, Lana Loretta Lusch *retired elementary school educator*

Russellton
Curtis, Paula Annette *elementary and secondary education educator*

Scottdale
Lee, John Lawrence, Jr. *educational administrator*

Scranton
Elvidge, Christina Marie *director*
Gross, Patricia A. *education educator*
Panuska, Joseph Allan *retired academic administrator*
Passon, Richard Henry *retired academic administrator, language educator*

Selinsgrove
Lemons, L. Jay *academic administrator*

Sharon
Kovac, Shirley Ann *retired elementary school educator*

Shillington
Blum, Robin N. *elementary school educator*

Shippensburg
Basler, Linda Gerber *retired elementary school educator*
Ceddia, Anthony Francis *university administrator*
Vaughan, Elizabeth Jean *education educator*

South Park
Furman, L. Robert *principal, music educator*

Southampton
Gniewek, Debra Lyman *school librarian, consultant*

State College
Dupuis, Victor Lionel *retired curriculum and instruction educator*
Remick, Forrest Jerome, Jr. *former university official*

Swarthmore
Bloom, Alfred Howard *academic administrator, educator*

Telford
Boughter, Barbara B. *retired mathematics educator*

Titusville
Campasino, Ellen Marie *elementary school educator*

Townville
Rudy, Elaine Kim *elementary school educator*

University Park
Antle, Charles Edward *statistics educator*
Askov, Eunice May *adult education educator*
Dugda, Mulugeta Tuji *education educator*
Hammond, J. D. *retired academic administrator*
Spanier, Graham Basil *academic administrator*
Thomas, James B. *dean, management educator*
Zabel, Diane Marion *school librarian*

Upper Darby
Crouse, Carol K. Mavromatis *elementary school educator*
Hudiak, David Michael *academic administrator, lawyer*

Verona
Bruno, Louis Vincent *principal*

Villanova
Deshmukh, Venkatesh Suresh *education educator*
Dobbin, Edmund J. *former academic administrator*
Donohue, Peter M. *academic administrator, priest, theater educator, director*
Fitzpatrick, M. Louise *dean, nursing educator*
Heitzmann, Ray *education educator, athletic coach*
Sargent, Mark A. *dean, law educator*

Warminster
Ciao, Frederick J. *school system administrator, educator*

Washington
Haring-Smith, Tori *academic administrator*

Wayne
Cole, Charles Chester, Jr. *academic administrator*

West Chester
Bove, Patrice Magee *elementary school educator*

West Grove
Olson, Leroy Calvin *retired educational administration educator*

Wilkes Barre
Horoszy, Albert John *mathematics educator*
Loomis, Richard Morgan *literature and language educator*

Williamsport
Mason, Ardis J.P. *elementary school educator*
Wright, David C. *school system administrator*

Willow Street
Henderson, Joseph Ralston *educator*

Wilmerding
Kirk, Linda Louise *elementary school educator*

Yardley
Breitenfeld, Frederick, Jr. *retired educational consultant, broadcast executive*

York
Wittmer, Elyse Marie *academic administrator*

RHODE ISLAND

Hope Valley
Laub, Sandra *secondary school educator*

Jamestown
Tinker, Thomas Eaton *retired headmaster*
Ullrich, Robert Albert *academic administrator*

Kingston
Carothers, Robert Lee *academic administrator*

Middletown
Jackson, John Edward *adult education educator, retired military officer*

Newport
Ellsworth, James Byron *national security educator*
Mooshagian, Mark Nishan *education educator*
Peterson, Eric F. *headmaster*
Shuford, Jacob L. *academic administrator, career military officer*

North Kingstown
Morse, Barbara *mathematics educator*

Pawtucket
Lepore, Lisa *principal*

Providence
Duffy, Kevin *dean*
Greer, David Steven *dean, educator, physician*
Grossi, Linda Marie *elementary school educator*
Guggenmos, Karl J. *dean*
Hemmasi, Harriette Ann *university librarian*
McWalters, Peter *school system administrator*
Simmons, Ruth J. *academic administrator*

Warwick
Hayes, Catherine Davis *elementary school educator*
Izzi, John *mathematics educator, writer, actor*

Westerly
Crowley, Cynthia Warner Johnson *secondary school educator*

Woonsocket
Crowley, Rosa Quinonez *literature and language educator*
Stubbs, Donald Clark *retired secondary school educator*
Walker, Suzanne Ross *mathematics and education educator*

SOUTH CAROLINA

Adams Run
Stewart, Shirley S. *retired elementary school educator*

Anderson
Kaiser, Louise Martin *elementary school educator*

Beaufort
Parisi, Leah Evans *dean, nursing educator, lawyer*

Blythewood
Daniels, James Douglas *retired academic administrator*

Charleston
Appleget, Terri Lynn *elementary school educator*
Benson, P. George *academic administrator, finance educator*
Egelson, Pauline C. *director*
Festa, Conrad *academic administrator*
Greenberg, Raymond Seth *academic and health facility administrator, educator*
Gunn, Morey Walker, Jr. *director, musician, educator*
Poole, Roger Cliff *retired academic administrator, finance educator, retired military officer*
Rosa, John William *academic administrator, career military officer*
Simms, Lois Averetta *retired secondary school educator*
Strauch, Katina Parthemos *college librarian, publishing executive*

Clemson
Barker, James F. *academic administrator*
Kelly, John William, Jr. *academic administrator*
Sluss, Dorothy Louise *education educator, researcher*

Clinton
Adams, Joanne Nelson *special education educator*
Griffith, John Vincent *academic official*

Columbia
Bedenbaugh, Allyn Purvis *retired elementary school educator*
Carter, Kathryn Gibson *education educator, consultant*
Dohohue, John Francis *secondary school educator*
Friedman, Myles Ivan *education educator*
Outin, Mary Louise *business, multi-cultural history and geneology educator*
Palms, John Michael *academic administrator, physicist*
Rex, Jim *school system administrator*
Schilit, Matthew Todd *assistant principal*
Sinclair, Linda Drumwright *educational consultant*
Sorensen, Andrew Aaron *academic administrator*
Sproat, Ruth C. *retired director, consultant*
Towns, Evelyn *state government educational administrator*

Denmark
Bendidi, Rachid *dean, educator*

Duncan
Calloway, Stephanie Michelle *secondary school educator*

Gaffney
Griffin, Walter Roland *academic administrator, historian, educator*

Gilbert
Padget, Barbara Johnson *elementary school educator*

Graniteville
Learnard, James Michael *special education educator, retired collections and bad debt manager*

Greenville
Baker, Harriet Kugley *elementary school educator*
Castle, Carey William *dean*
Jones, Bob III *academic administrator*
Jones, Robert Thaddues *retired principal*
Payne, George Frederick *academic administrator*
Shi, David E. *academic administrator, historian*
Smith, Philip Daniel *academic administrator, education educator*

Greenwood
Boiter, Kevin Ernest *electronics and electrical educator*
Jackson, Larry Artope *retired college president*
Marino, Sheila Burris *education educator*

Hilton Head Island
Levy, Maurice *education educator, researcher*

Irmo
Murphy, Jennifer H. (Buffy Murphy) *elementary school educator*

Kiawah Island
Warren, Russell Glen *educational consultant*

Marion
Kirkpatrick, Donald Robert *secondary school educator*

Mount Pleasant
Gilbert, James Eastham *academic administrator*

Orangeburg
Hill, Howard Darnell *retired education educator, educational consultant*

Pacolet
Hartell, Holly *school librarian*

Pawleys Island
Proefrock, Carl Kenneth *academic medical administrator*

Pickens
Hardin, Janet Becker *gifted and talented educator, music educator*

Ridge Spring
Livingston, Kimberly R. *elementary school educator*

Rock Hill
Witzel, Bradley Steven *special education educator*

Simpsonville
Munley, William Edward *health services administrator*

Spartanburg
Deku, Afrikadzata *African studies professor, writer*
Dunlap, Benjamin Bernard *academic administrator*
McGehee, Larry Thomas *retired academic administrator*
Stephens, Bobby Gene *college administrator, consultant*

Sumter
Powers, Thomas Lynwood *professor, military reserve officer*

Tigerville
NeSmith, Richard A. *education educator, consultant*

Union
Whitener, Martha Sarratt *retired history educator*

Walterboro
Armentrout, Charles Edward *secondary school educator*

Wellford
Seay, Stephanie *elementary school educator*

Whitmire
Hall, Joye *elementary school educator*

SOUTH DAKOTA

Aberdeen
Maier, Karen Marie *school librarian*

Brookings
Chicoine, David Lyle *academic administrator*
Vanderpan, Norma *retired elementary school educator*

Eagle Butte
Webb, Yvonne M. *secondary school educator*

Kadoka
Stout, Maye Alma *retired secondary school educator*

Mission
Jackson, Lori Lee *secondary school educator, elementary school educator*

Mitchell
Padrnos, Diane E. *language arts educator*

Pierre
Melmer, Rick *school system administrator*

Rapid City
Schleusener, Richard August *college president*

Sioux Falls
Ashworth, Julie *elementary school educator*
Balcer, Charles Louis *college president emeritus, educator*
Dowling, Barbara R. *elementary school educator*
Talley, Robert Cochran *academic administrator, cardiologist*
Wagoner, Ralph Howard *academic administrator*

Vermillion
Avoseh, Mejai Bola Mike *adult education educator, researcher*

Wessington Springs
Mohling, Charlotte *middle school educator*

Yankton
Foster, James Caldwell *dean, historian*

TENNESSEE

Allardt
Copeland, Patricia Ruth *elementary school educator*

Antioch
Mattice, Debora J. *special education educator, consultant*

Bluff City
Arnold, SaBrina Nicole *secondary school educator*

Bristol
Werner, Dawn Heterick *elementary school educator*

Chattanooga
Brooks, Ellyn Hersh *retired special education educator*
Obear, Frederick Woods *academic administrator*
Rutledge, Valerie Copeland *education educator*
Stacy, Bill Wayne *academic administrator*
Steele, Shirley Sue *retired special resource educator*

Clarksville
Gold, Moniqueka E. *education educator*
Hoppe, Sherry Lee *academic administrator*
Mitchell, John Gerald *educational administrator*
Newby, Earl Fernando *education educator*
Stoddard, Peter Hawkins *education educator, consultant*

Cleveland
Harper, James Edward, Jr. *academic administrator*
Renfro, Zoe Vaughan *principal*

Collegedale
Clark, Ann Rorabaw *English professor, consultant, writer*

Collierville
Boswell, Rupert Dean, Jr. *retired academic administrator, mathematician, educator*
Mann, Clifton *secondary school educator*
Tesreau, Cynthia Lynn *elementary school educator*

Columbia
Cantrell, Sharron Caulk *principal*

Cookeville
Volpe, Angelo Anthony *retired academic administrator, chemist, educator*

Cordova
Jacobs, M. Louise *secondary school educator*

Covington
Wright, Bonnie Shankle *assistant principal, choir director*

Cunningham
Mince, Carol Kirkham *history educator*

Dandridge
Coley, Jan Brumback *biology educator*

Goodlettsville
Vatandoost, Nossi Malek *art school administrator*

Harriman
Pierce, Patricia Ann *retired university administrator*

Henderson
Gardner, Elmer Claude *academic administrator*

Jackson
Agee, Bob R. *academic administrator, educator, minister*

Johnson City
Franks, Ronald Dwyer *dean, psychiatrist, educator*
Tollefson, Terrence Alfred *education educator, consultant*

Kingsport
Rigsby, Mary Sue *retired elementary school educator, adult education educator*

Knoxville
Boling, Edward Joseph *retired academic administrator*
Crabtree, Loren William *academic administrator, history professor*
Creasia, Joan Catherine *dean, nursing educator*
Garrison, Arlene Allen *academic administrator, engineering educator*
Levy, Robert A. *academic administrator*
Mankel, Francis Xavier *retired principal, priest*
McElroy, Gloria Freels *secondary school educator*
Pace, Elizabeth Barber *elementary school educator*
Petersen, John D. *academic administrator*
Russell, Rodney E. *school system administrator*
Ye, Xiaofei *education educator*

Kodak
Keller, Daniel Sylvester *director*

Lebanon
Eaton, Harvill Carlton *academic administrator*

Manchester
Westberry, Anita Parrish *education educator*

Memphis
Daughdrill, James Harold, Jr. *academic administrator*
Dreyfus, Susan Kahn *middle school educator*
Dunathan, Harmon Craig *college dean*
Gilpatrick, Russell O. *dean, dental educator*
Gourley, Dick R. *college dean*
Kelly, Aleda Mae *retired secondary education educator*
Nance, Libba L. *elementary school educator*
Nesin, Jeffrey David *academic administrator*
Raines, Shirley Carol *academic administrator*
Troutt, William Earl *academic administrator*

Millington
Gray, Barbara L. *assistant principal, tax specialist*

Murfreesboro
Doyle, Delores Marie *retired principal*
Hemby-Grubb, Virginia *education educator, consultant*

Nashville
Benbow, Camilla Persson *dean, psychology professor*
Bradford, James Warren, Jr. *dean, finance educator*
Bridges, Lewis David *elementary school educator*
Butler, William Blaine *dean, dental educator*
Collins, Joe Lena *retired secondary school educator*
Cyrus, Cynthia J. *dean, music educator*
Frensley, Susanne H. *history educator*
Gabbe, Steven Glenn *dean, educator, obstetrician, gynecologist*
Gherman, Paul M. *university librarian*
Guha, Sujata *education educator*
Johnson, Melvin N. *academic administrator, economist*
Longhurst, Robert Russell *retired secondary school educator*
Manning, Charles W. *university chancellor*
McMurry, Idanelle Sam *educational consultant*
Mitchell, Angela Carol *elementary school educator*
Morton, Linda June *academic administrator*
Pitz, Robert Wendell *professor mechanical engineering*
Ramer, Hal Reed *retired academic administrator*
Reschly, Daniel J. *education educator, psychologist*
Riley, Wayne Joseph *academic administrator, medical educator*
Royal, Brenda Campbell *biology educator*
Rubin, Edward *dean, law educator*
Sargent, Mildred Crow *retired history educator, writer*
Schroeder, Joni Lynn *secondary school educator*
Seivers, Lana C. *school system administrator*
Seligson, Mitchell A. *political science educator*
Zeppos, Nicholas S. *academic administrator*

Paris
Maskas, Auba Sue *elementary school educator*
Prehm, Mary Elizabeth *elementary school educator*

Pleasant Hill
Hull, Charles William *retired special education educator*

Ripley
Hartman, Joan Evans *educational consultant*

Savannah
Flanagan, Judy *director, special events consultant*

Sevierville
Rogers, Edna Loveday *elementary school educator*

Sewanee
Croom, Frederick Hailey *academic administrator, mathematician, educator*
Cunningham, Joel Luther *academic administrator*
Patterson, William Brown *dean, history professor*

Tullahoma
Daniel, Donald Clifton *academic administrator, aerospace engineer*

Washburn
Romeo, Joanne Josefa Marino *mathematics educator, department chairman*

TEXAS

Abilene
Flores, Kathryn Louise *mathematics educator*
McCaleb, Gary Day *university official*
Specht, Alice Wilson *university libraries dean*
Turner, Willard Craig *academic administrator*

Allen
Fornadel, Martha Sue *elementary school educator*

Alpine
Chambers Tucker, Johnnie L. *elementary school educator, rancher*
Cullins, Robert Carlton *academic administrator*

Amarillo
Carter, Edythe L. (Edie Carter) *mathematics educator*

Arlington
Copeland, Anita Bob *director, retired elementary school educator, senior consultant*
Graca, Thomas John *education educator, lawyer*
Han, Chien-Pai *statistics educator*
Joohi, Lee *early childhood educator*
Minnerly, Robert Ward *retired headmaster*
Pomerantz, Martin *chemistry educator, researcher*

Austin
Armstrong, Neal Earl *academic administrator*
Ayres, Robert Moss, Jr. *retired university president*
Bordin, Cristina Stadolny *academic administrator*
Brewer, Thomas Bowman *retired university president*
Carleton, Don Edward *academic administrator, writer*
Carpenter, Delbert Stanley *educational administration educator*
Corredor, Mary B. *director, language educator*
Cunningham, William Hughes *retired academic administrator, marketing professional, educator*
Dillon, Andrew Patrick *dean, library and information science educator*
Doluisio, James Thomas *dean, pharmacy educator*
DuBose, Gaylan Ray *elementary school educator, musician, writer*
Dubose, Kathryn Michaud *secondary school educator*
Gau, George W. *dean*
Gonzalez-Gerth, Miguel *literature and language educator, writer*
Graham, Lawrence Sherman *political science educator, management consultant*
Harris, Ben M. *education educator*
Hetzler, Susan Elizabeth Savage *educational administrator*
Jordan, Bryce *retired university president*
Kelley, Henry Paul *academic administrator, psychology educator*
Lenoir, Gloria Cisneros *secondary school educator, consultant*
Livingston, William Samuel *retired academic administrator, political scientist, educator*
May, Robert George *dean, accounting educator*
McKeown-Moak, Mary Park *educational consultant*
Neeley, Shirley J. *school system administrator*
Powers, William Charles, Jr. *academic administrator, law educator*
Prior, David B. *academic administrator*
Roueche, John Edward, II, *education educator, director*
Royal, Darrell K. *university official, retired football coach*
Sager, Lawrence Gene *dean, law educator*
Shilling, Roy Bryant, Jr. *academic administrator*
Springer, David William *dean, social sciences educator*
Todaro, Julie Beth *libraries dean, association executive*
Wurzbach, Linda *educational consultant*
Yudof, Mark George *academic and federal agency administrator, law educator*

Bastrop
Clemons, Barbara Gail *history educator*

Beaumont
Baden, Sheri Louise *primary school educator*
Brentlinger, William Brock *college dean*
Payne, Elton Curtis, Jr. *adult education educator*

Beeville
Freeman, Patsy L. *director*

Bellaire
Crayton, Arnell *secondary school educator*

Boerne
Goode, Bobby Claude *retired secondary school educator*

Booker
Doerrie, Bobette *secondary school educator, consultant*

Brownsville
Garcia, Juliet Villarreal *academic administrator*
Santa-Coloma, Bernardo *retired secondary school educator*

Bryan
Fields, Sheila Crain *elementary school educator*
Koehler, Myron *retired secondary school educator*

Canyon
Atchison, Timothy B. *education educator, neuropsychologist*
Long, Russell Charles *retired academic administrator*

Carrollton
Barland, Sarah Elizabeth *secondary school educator*

Cedar Hill
Jackson, Robert Roscoe *education educator*

Cisco
Johnson, Cynthia Zuckernick *history educator*

College Station
Adkisson, Perry Lee *university system chancellor*
Bowen, Ray Morris *academic administrator, engineering educator*
Cocanougher, Arthur Benton *academic administrator*
Cook, Violetta Burke *university administrator*
Dasgupta, Sumantra *education educator, researcher*
Davis, Eddie Joe *academic and foundation administrator*
Dickey, Nancy Wilson *chancellor, physician*
Erlandson, David Alan *education administration educator*
Hooton, James G. *academic administrator*
Lynn, Laurence Edwin, Jr. *academic administrator, educator*
Monroe, Haskell Moorman, Jr. *chancellor emeritus, retired history professor, dean*
Murano, Elsa A. *academic and former federal agency administrator*
Strawser, Jerry R. *dean*

Commerce
Justice, Madeline Carol *education educator*
Scott, Joyce Alaine *academic administrator*
Vornberg, James Alvin *education educator*

Conroe
Gray, Janet Ethel *elementary school educator*

Corpus Christi
Abdelsamad, Moustafa Hassan *dean*
Beller, Stephen Mark *retired academic administrator*
Cassidy, Jack *academic administrator, educator*
Furgason, Robert Roy *academic administrator, director, retired engineering educator*
Killebrew, Flavius Charles *academic administrator, biology professor*
Salazar, Laura Ann *education educator*

Crockett
LaClair, Patricia Marie *physical education director, paramedic*

Dallas
Abdo, Virginia Richie *retired secondary school educator*
Attanasio, John Baptist *dean, law educator*
Cho, Ho Soon Michelle L. *adult education educator*
Cole, James S. *dean, dental educator*
Cook, Gary Raymond *academic administrator, minister*
Dumerer, Lorraine JoAnne Lori *secondary school educator, consultant*
Friedheim, Stephen Bailey *educational consultant*
Haayen, Richard Jan *academic administrator, insurance company executive*
Harrison, Frank *former university president*
Hester, Linda Hunt *dean, retired sociology and physical education professor*
Horvat, Vashti *principal*
Melin, Stacy M. *literature and language educator*
Satarino, F. Michael (Michael Satarino) *principal*
Shambaugh, Irvin Calvin, Jr. *aptitude test firm executive*
Turner, R(obert) Gerald *academic administrator*
Williams, Michael Edward, Sr. *dean*
Wrucke-Nelson, Ann C. *elementary school educator*

Denison
Cameron, Frances Marilyn *elementary school educator*

Denton
Bataille, Gretchen *academic administrator*
Greenlaw, Marilyn Jean *retired adult education educator*
McCaslin, Richard Bryan *history educator*
McDonald-West, Sandi MacLean *director, consultant*
Novak, Rynell Stiff *retired academic administrator*
Smith, Howard Wellington *education educator, retired dean*
Totten, Herman Lavon *dean, library and information science educator*
Turner, Philip Michael *academic administrator, writer*

Detroit
Cates, Sue Sadler *special education counselor*

Edinburg
Lowdermilk, John Lloyd *special education educator, special education services professional*
Pecina, Julie H. *education educator*

Egypt
Wynn, John Thomas *retired academic administrator, farming executive, economic consultant, oil and gas producer*

El Paso
Boyd, Dana Kristin *elementary school educator*
Casas, Martha *education educator*
Curie, Roger Kent *adult education educator, consultant*
Erskine, William Crawford *retired academic and health facility administrator, accountant*
Jarvis, Richard S. *academic administrator*
Natalicio, Diana Siedhoff *academic administrator*
Riter, Stephen *academic administrator, electrical engineer*
Torres, Richard *literature and language educator*
Zopfi, Emma G. *elementary school educator*

Elgin
Shelby, Nina Claire *special education educator*

Farmers Branch
Reyes, Czarina Suzanne *mathematics educator*

Fort Sam Houston
Betancourt, Jose A. *dean, public health service officer*

Fort Worth
Blanck, Ronald Ray *academic administrator, internist, military officer*
Boschini, Victor John, Jr. *academic administrator*
Currier, Mike *elementary school educator, writer*
Donovan, Nowell *academic administrator*
Johnson, Melody *school system administrator*
Saenz, Michael *college president*
Simmons, Jean Byers *academic administrator, director*
Tucker, William Edward *academic administrator, minister*

Franklin
Perry, Anne Marie Litchfield *secondary school educator*

Fredericksburg
Chase, John David *retired dean, internist*

Freeport
Gresham, Karen Renee *elementary school educator, singer*

Galveston
Anderson, Garland D. *dean, obstetrician, gynecologist, educator*
Stobo, John David *academic administrator, physician*

Garland
Quinn, Peggy Armstrong *elementary school educator, writer*

Georgetown
Brody, Gerald David *academic administrator*
Lovin, Keith Harold *retired academic administrator, philosopher, educator*
Schrum, Jake Bennett *academic administrator*

Giddings
Walker, Hershel O. *history educator*

Glenn Heights
Rowe, Nancie E. *director, minister*

Graham
Lovell, Lisa Inez *special education educator*

Granbury
Curl, Samuel Everett *retired dean, agriculturist, consultant*

Grand Prairie
Puckett, Mary Alice *primary school educator, consultant*

Grapevine
Hirsh, Cristy J. *principal*

Hale Center
Courtney, Carolyn Ann *school librarian*

Hardin
Ringer, Paula Denise Hollenshead *secondary school educator*

Hereford
Yavornik, Barbara Ann *pre-school educator*

Houston
Alfini, James Joseph *dean, educator, lawyer*
Anderson, Claire W. *gifted and talented educator*
Beckingham, Kathleen Mary *education educator, researcher*
Benefield, Janis Wilson *school librarian, media specialist*
Betts, Nicole Lavette *elementary school educator, consultant*
Bott, Simon Gregory *chemistry educator, researcher*
Brooks, Philip Russell *chemistry educator, researcher*
Butler, William Thomas *academic administrator, physician, educator*
Caram, Dorothy Farrington *educational consultant*
Cazenave, Anita Washington *secondary school educator*
Chandler-Munson, Cynthia *elementary school educator*
Davis, (Alice) Marlece *secondary school educator, director*
Djerejian, Edward Peter *academic administrator, retired diplomat*
Flaitz, Catherine M. *dean, dental educator*
Gaelens, Albert Robert *retired director, educational administrator, priest*
Glick, William H. *dean*
Gonzalez, Antonio *academic administrator, educator, title company executive*
Hilborn, Marilyn Ann *educational consultant*
Hoffman, Philip Guthrie *former university president*
Kneese, Carolyn Calvin *retired education educator*
Leebron, David Wayne *academic administrator, law educator*
LeNôtre, Marie *dean*
Looper, Marcia Lynn *elementary school educator, consultant*
Malki, Heidar A. *dean*
Mansell, Joyce Marilyn *retired special education educator*
Mariotto, Marco Jerome *dean, psychology educator, researcher*
Matthews, Kathleen Shive *biochemistry educator*
McKee, Rae Ellen (Rae Ellen McKee-Doucette) *special education educator*
Miller, Harry Freeman *university administrator*
Milstead, Terry Lee *secondary school educator*
Oakes, Pamela R. *retired elementary school educator*
Parnas-Simpson, Marianna *chorus director, singer*
Pickering, James Henry III *academic administrator, educator*
Roos, Sybil Friedenthal *retired elementary school educator*
Saavedra, Abelardo *school system administrator*
Smith, Arthur Kittredge, Jr. *academic administrator, political scientist, educator*
Smith, Roland Blair, Jr. *university administrator*
Sullivan-Szuts, Betty Anne *academic administrator, educator*
Wagner, Paul Anthony, Jr. *education educator*
Webb, Marty Fox *principal*
Whiting, Martha Countee *retired secondary school educator*
Wilkin, Alana Zimmer *elementary school educator*
Williamses, Lee John *academic administrator, history professor*

Humble
Ellis, James Otto *secondary school educator*

Huntsville
Payne, David Emer *university administrator*
Ward, Richard Hurley *education educator, writer*
Wells, William *criminal justice educator*

Hutto
Hamilton, Elizabeth Ann *elementary school educator*

Iola
Nelson, John Harrison *mathematics educator*

Irving
Martin, Thomas Lyle, Jr. *academic administrator*

Joaquin
Gill, Madeline Kay *school and youth counselor*

Keller
Smith, Eleanor Jane *retired university chancellor, consultant*

Kemp
Shugart, Jill *academic administrator*

Kerrville
Freeny, Katherine H. *adult education educator, chemist, researcher*

Killeen
Jenkins, Sharon Leigh *special education educator*
Lane, Penelope Diane *special education educator*
Peronto, Janice Lynn *principal*

Kingsville
Stanford, (Frances) Jane Herring *dean, management consultant, educator, writer*

Lake Jackson
Hill, Diane Louise *educator*

Laredo
Black, Clifford Merwyn *academic administrator, sociologist, educator*
Heimes, Charmaine Marie *elementary school educator, poet, writer*

Littlefield
Muller, Janice Elaine *secondary school educator*

Llano
Wilson, Dena Suzette *elementary school educator*

Lubbock
Conover, William Jay *statistics educator*
Hance, Kent Ronald *academic administrator, former congressman*
Haragan, Donald Robert *academic administrator, geologist, educator*
River, Sandra A. *university librarian*

White, Alice Virginia *academic administrator*
Whitmore, Jon Scott *academic administrator, play director*

Mc Kinney
Dorff, Barbara L. *elementary and secondary school educator*

Mcallen
Gonzalez, Rolando Noel *secondary school educator, theology studies educator, photographer*
Ramirez, Leo Armando, Sr. *mathematics educator*

Mesquite
Vaughan, Joseph Lee, Jr. *education educator, consultant, director, academic administrator*
Wenrich, John William *college president*

Midland
Bridges, Judy Cantrell *gifted and talented education educator*

Missouri City
Weber, Katie *retired special education educator*

Nacogdoches
Carter, Evelyn *retired elementary school educator*

New Braunfels
Barragán, Celia Silguero *elementary school educator*
Dugger, Roy Wesley *academic administrator, retired military officer*
Oestreich, Charles Henry *retired university president*

Normangee
Stork, Vera Lee *retired elementary school educator*

Paige
Trevino, Jerry Rosalez *retired secondary school principal*

Paris
McCuen, Maureen E. *history educator*

Pasadena
Blue, Monte Lynn *college president*
Ruiz, Miriam *secondary school educator*
Russell, Yvonne Williams *history educator*

Plano
Haggard, Geraldine Langford *primary school, adult education educator, consultant, writer*
Shepherd, Karen Schiller *biology educator*

Rancho Viejo
Garza, Roberto Jesus *retired education educator*

Randolph Afb
Brennan-Bergmann, Bridget Catherine *special education educator*

Richardson
Carlson, Catherine Kossan *secondary school educator*
Daniel, David Edwin *academic administrator, civil engineer*

Rosenberg
Lefler, Sherry LynettE *elementary school educator*
White, Gretchen Nance *education educator, writer*

Rosharon
Lopez, Placida Ramos *elementary school educator*

Rowlett
Bell, Ronald *secondary school educator*

San Antonio
Austin, Catherine Deady *retired school librarian, musician*
Duron, Robert J. *school system administrator*
Faules, Barbara Ruth *retired elementary school educator*
Gibbons, Robert Ebbert *university official*
Henderson, Dwight Franklin *dean, educator*
Hsieh, Pei-Hsuan (Peggy) *education educator*
Hudspeth, Almetra Kavanaugh *retired elementary school educator*
Kalkwarf, Kenneth Lee *dean, dental educator*
Maxwell, Diana Kathleen *education educator, primary school educator*
Nichols, Sharon Louise *educator, researcher*
Route, Candace *elementary school educator*
Williams-Perry, Brenda Lee *pre-school educator*
Wright, Wayne E. *education educator*
Young, James Julius *academic administrator, retired military officer*

San Marcos
Allsup, Roxane Cuellar *curriculum and instruction educator*

Sherman
Page, Oscar C. *academic administrator*

Southlake
Arafat-Johnson, Danyah *secondary school educator, director*

Stephenville
McElroy, Linda Sue *retired elementary school educator*

Sulphur Springs
Hadlow, Vivian Jean *elementary school educator*

Temple
Dostal, David Eugene *education educator, researcher*
Meshack, Geneva Tucker *retired elementary school educator*

Texarkana
Calhoun, John C., Jr. *academic administrator*

The Colony
Culver, Jennifer Lynn *secondary school educator*

The Woodlands
Pickelman, John E. *academic administrator*

Tyler
Davidson, Jack Leroy *academic administrator*
Peters, Robert K. *dean, newscaster, newswriter, journalist*
Prater, Emma Lou *retired academic administrator*
Sanchez, Heliodoro Torres, Jr. *education educator*
Waller, Wilma Ruth *retired secondary school educator, librarian*

Waco
Belew, John Seymour *academic administrator, chemist*
Brooks, Roger Leon *retired academic administrator*
Lilley, John Mark *academic administrator*
Lindsey, Jonathan Asmel *academic administrator, school librarian, educator*
Slaughter, Michael Wayne *education educator*
Sloan, Robert Bryan, Jr. *academic administrator*
Toben, Bradley J. B. *dean, law educator*

Weatherford
Houchin, Shannon Marie *secondary school educator*

West
Bills, Peggy Nannette *parochial school educator*

Wichita Falls
Hancock, Carole Patricia *academic administrator*
Lowrance, Muriel Edwards *retired educational specialist*

Wimberley
Ellis, John *retired school system administrator, writer*
Jennett, Joseph Charles *retired academic administrator, engineering educator*

UTAH

Cedar City
Benson, Michael T. *academic administrator*

Cedar Hills
Ashton, Dawne Belinda *retired secondary school educator*

Draper
Walz, Angela *retired secondary school educator*

Holladay
McKell, Cyrus M. *retired dean, plant physiologist, consultant*

Layton
Woodbury, Lark Karin *secondary school educator*

Logan
Albrecht, Stan LeRoy *academic administrator, sociologist, educator*
Oladi, Reza *education educator*
Shaver, James Porter *retired education educator, dean*

Midvale
Smith, Mary Ellen *educational program facilitator*

North Ogden
Heap, Joan S. *elementary school educator*

Ogden
Millner, F. Ann *academic administrator*
Sharpes, Donald Kenneth *graduate program educator*

Orem
Jackman, Roderick Victor *distance learning educator*
Sederburg, William Albert *academic administrator, former state senator*

Provo
Boyter, Scott M. *academic administrator*
Bradshaw, Jerald Sherwin *chemistry educator, researcher*
Bullough, Robert Vernon, Jr. *educational studies professor*
Densley, Colleen T. *principal*
Hill, Ned Cromar *dean, finance educator, consultant*
Jensen, Clayne R. *retired academic administrator*
Prater, Mary Anne *special education educator, researcher*
Samuelson, Cecil O., Jr. *academic administrator*
Worthen, Kevin *dean, law educator*

Salt Lake City
Bacon, Marlene Parkinson *dean, nursing educator*
Balasubramonian, Rajeev *computer science educator*
Bassis, Michael Steven *academic administrator*
Bennion, John Warren *urban education educator*
Chodosh, Hiram *dean, law educator*
Drew, Clifford James *dean, psychologist, educator*
Harrington, Patti *school system administrator*
Keefe, Maureen Ruth *dean*
Liu, Gang *education educator, researcher*
McCleary, Lloyd E(verald) *education educator*
Wolfinger, Nicholas H. *educator*
Young, Michael Kent *academic administrator, law educator*

West Jordan
Betenson, Gaye Brinton *secondary school educator*
James, Linda Coates *elementary school educator*

VERMONT

Barre
Heath, Karen *secondary school educator*

Bennington
Coleman, Elizabeth *college president*

Brattleboro
Steffens, Annie Laurie *sign language educator, interpreter*

Burlington
Allard, Judith Louise *retired secondary school educator*
(Kahn) Fogel, Daniel Mark *academic administrator, literature educator, writer*
Hennessey, John William, Jr. *academic administrator, educator*
Kelly, Sister Marie *school system administrator*
Thompson, Ellen Ann *elementary school educator*

Colchester
Niemi, Robert James *adult education educator, writer*

Essex Junction
Bisson, Roger *middle school educator*

Lyndonville
Moore, Carol A. *academic administrator*

Middlebury
Forman, Michele *secondary school educator*
Liebowitz, Ronald D. *academic administrator*
O'Brien, George Dennis *retired academic administrator*

Montpelier
Cate, Richard H. *school system administrator*
Voigt, Francis *academic administrator*

Plainfield
Jervis, Jane Lise *academic administrator, historian*

Proctorsville
Harper, Jennifer *elementary school educator*

Strafford
Williams, William Magavern *headmaster*

Swanton
Suitor, Dorcas P. *elementary school educator*

Warren
Sullivan, Kathleen *elementary school educator*

Waterbury
Hilton, Linda D. *academic administrator*

Whiting
Jacobson, Edward *retired elementary school educator, principal*

VIRGINIA

Alexandria
Bartlett, Elizabeth Susan *audio-visual specialist*
Dubin, Martin Steven *principal*
Ellison, Pamela Ion *secondary school educator, consultant*
Haygood, Alma Jean *elementary school educator*
Jenkins, John Smith *retired dean, lawyer*
Patel, Manu V. *physics educator*
Rae, Jeneanne *new product development and innovation consultant, educator*

Amherst
Campbell, Catherine Lynn *elementary school educator*

Annandale
Passut, Christine Diana *special education educator*

Arlington
Dorman, Janet Lee Vosper *elementary school educator*
Finta, Frances Mickna *secondary school educator*
Haggett, Rosemary Romanowski *academic administrator*
McTigue, Maurice P. *director*
Polsby, Daniel D. *dean, law educator*
Price, Donald Ray *academic administrator, researcher, agricultural engineer*
Sharp, Barry J. *school system administrator*
Shepherd, Mildred Roof *retired secondary school educator, art restorer*
Tafoya, Joe *school system administrator*
Whittier, Barbara J (Bobbie) *retired biology educator, retired chemistry educator*

Ashland
Lindgren, Robert R. *academic administrator*

Bedford
Day, Mark Ronald *history educator, reenactor*

Blacksburg
Barksdale, Mary Alice *education educator*
Campbell, Joan Virginia Loweke *secondary school and language educator*
Hirt, Joan B. *education educator*
McNamee, Mark *academic administrator*
Steger, Charles William *academic administrator*
Torgersen, Paul Ernest *academic administrator, educator*
Weaver, Pamela Ann *education educator*

Charlottesville
Biltonen, Rodney Lincoln *biochemistry and pharmacology educator*
Blankfein-Tabachnick, David H. *philosophy educator*
Casteen, John Thomas III *academic administrator*
Garson, Arthur, Jr. *dean, medical educator*
Hurd, Nicole Farmer *director*
Jeffries, John Calvin, Jr. *dean, law educator*
Smith, Clyde Ray *dean*
Wittenborg, Karin *university librarian*

Chesapeake
Notti, Donna Betts *special education educator*
Webb, Julia Jones *elementary school educator, minister*

Chester
Law, Thomas Melvin *academic administrator*

Christiansburg
Blanchard, Dorothy Hardt *academic administrator, volunteer*

Dale City
Baxter, Ruth Howell *educational administrator, psychologist*

Danville
Aaron, Larry Gene *secondary school educator, writer, minister*
Pfau, Richard Anthony *university president*

Dublin
Douthat, Rebecca Arlene *retired secondary school educator*

Fairfax
Fox, Donna M. *dean, biology professor*
Kettlewell, Gail Biery *academic administrator, research professor*
Longin, Thomas Charles *retired academic administrator*
Merten, Alan Gilbert *academic administrator*
Nicogossian, Arnauld E.T. *education educator*
Silcox, Gordon Bruce *executive coach*

Falls Church
Johnson, William David *retired academic administrator*
Michelsen, Cleo *retired education educator, writer*

Farmville
Lu, Lucia Y. *education educator*

Fort Belvoir
Wooten, Michael Eric *academic administrator*

Fredericksburg
Arnn, Nancy Shank *secondary school educator*
McCrary, Lisa Hooper *secondary school educator*

Front Royal
Stevens, Loretta Marie *special education educator*

Gainesville
Tuck, Russell R., Jr. *college president emeritus*

Great Falls
Andrews, Betty Bauserman *retired secondary school educator, real estate manager*

Hampden Sydney
Bortz, Walter M. III *academic administrator*
Wilson, Samuel V. *academic administrator*

Hampton
Bell, Gladys Smiley *university librarian*
Goode, Constance Loper *elementary school principal*
Harvey, William Robert *university president*
Lawson, Donna Yvette *special education educator*
Sypolt, Shirley Rae *elementary school educator*

Harrisonburg
Carrier, Ronald Edwin *academic administrator, director*
Pappas, Eric Charles *director*

Herndon
Jones, Reba (Becki) Pestun *elementary school and music educator*

Lexington
John, Lewis George *political science educator*
McGuire, Katherine Ann *academic administrator, voice educator*
Peay, J.H. Binford III *academic administrator, career military officer*
Ruscio, Kenneth Patrick *academic administrator, political science professor*
Williams, H. Thomas (Tom Williams) *academic administrator, physicist, educator*

Locust Grove
Cordray-Van de Castle, Karen *elementary school educator*

Lynchburg
Bowman, Kathleen Gill *academic administrator*

Sullivan, Gregory Paul *secondary school educator*
Worden, Virginia Hill *academic administrator, lawyer*

Manassas
Archer, Chalmers, Jr. *retired education educator*
Hayes, Linda Marie *middle school educator*
Lowther, Edward Glenn *school system administrator, educator*

Marion
Groseclose, Joanne Stowers *special education educator*

Mc Dowell
Harkleroad, Jo-Ann Decker *special education educator*

Mc Lean
Black, Ginger Elizabeth *elementary school educator*
Jackson, Juanita Wallace *educational consultant*

Mechanicsville
Combee, Susan *assistant principal*

Melfa
Harmon, Patricia Marie *retired special education educator*

Middleburg
Paige, Wayne Leo *visual arts educator, artist*

Midlothian
Lamont-Gordon, Melissa Lynne *orchestra director, music educator*

Newport News
Drummond, Neil Hiden *retired secondary school educator*
Eastman, John Robert *education educator*

Norfolk
Baysal, Oktay *dean, educator*
Brown, Mary Wilkes *secondary school educator*
Callahan, Kim Versprille *special education educator*
Combs, Charles Donald *academic administrator*
Kennedy, Douglas Ayers *education educator, dean*
Koch, James Verch *academic administrator, economist*
McDemmond, Marie Valentine *academic administrator, consultant*
Meyers, Carolyn Winstead *academic administrator, mechanical engineer, educator*
Miller, Khadijah Olivia *education educator*
Runte, Roseann *academic administrator*
Steele, James Eugene *retired school system administrator*
Taylor, Gail Singleton *education educator*

Petersburg
Benn, Candace Marilea *elementary school educator*
Johnson, Cherlyn Ann *education educator*

Port Royal
Clarke-Hall, Deborah Renay *elementary school educator*

Portsmouth
Rampersaud Lundy, Sheryll *special education educator*

Quantico
Stout, Mary Webb *dean*

Radford
Dunaway, Marsha Landrum *special education educator*

Reston
Keefe, James Washburn *educational writer, researcher, consultant*
Lynch, Monique Christine *mathematics educator*

Richmond
Austin, Terry Lee *director, conductor*
Ayers, Edward L. *academic administrator, history professor*
Brown, Marilyn Branch *retired educational administrator*
Campbell, Mary Elizabeth *retired primary school educator*
Cannaday, Billy K., Jr. *school system administrator*
Cooper, William Edwin *former academic administrator*
Drain, Cecil B. *dean, nursing educator, retired military officer*
Dunn, Linda Baugh *middle school educator*
Epstein, David Stanley *educator, consultant*
Farquhar, Doris Irene Davis *academic administrator*
Hamel, Dana Bertrand *academic administrator*
Hunt, Ronald J. *dean, dental educator*
Jones, Jeanne Pitts *pre-school administrator*
McGee, Henry Alexander, Jr. *academic administrator*
Peart, Sandra Joan *dean*
Rettig, James R. *university librarian, library association executive*
Salley, John Jones *retired academic administrator, oral pathologist*
Smolla, Rodney Alan *dean, law educator*
Spindler, Judith Tarleton *elementary school educator*
Stover, Jill S. *school librarian, writer*
Toscan, Richard Eric *dean, theater educator*
Trani, Eugene Paul *university president, educator*
Whitehurst, Lucinda Snyder *school librarian*

Roanoke
Gray, Nancy Ann Oliver *academic administrator*
Miller, Deborah Brewster *educational consultant*

Rockbridge Baths
Glidden, Robert Burr *academic administrator, consultant, music educator*

Rose Hill
Lane, Mary Winston *retired secondary school educator*

Rural Retreat
Evans, Susan W. *mathematics educator*

Salem
Day, John T. *academic administrator, dean*
Sailer, Rachel Ann *secondary school educator*

Sandy Point
Douglas, Daisy Howard *retired elementary school educator, writer, consultant*

Scottsville
Griebenauw, Liza-Marie *secondary school educator*

Spotsylvania
Goforth, Deborah S. *school librarian, educator*

Springfield
Kurth, Ronald James *retired academic administrator, military officer*

Sterling
Fiacco, Anthony Vincent *educator, researcher*
Potts, Martha Wilburn *elementary school educator*
Steffens, Brian Douglas *elementary school educator, music director*

Suffolk
Matson, Virginia Mae Freeberg (Mrs. Edward J. Matson) *retired special education educator, author*

Sweet Briar
Muhlenfeld, Elisabeth Showalter *academic administrator, literature educator, writer*

Tabb
Budd, Richard Wade *academic administrator, dean, priest*

Vienna
Marx, Gary Dean *educational consultant, futurist, think-tank executive*

Virginia Beach
DeFord, Nancy T. *retired educational association and school system administrator*
Felts, Margaret Jean *secondary school educator*
Gardner, Karen High *special education educator*
Hatt, Clifford Van *school system administrator, psychologist*
Hodapp, Heidi Francine *middle school educator*
Jones, Robert Clair *middle school educator*
Melvin, Carole Ramey *educational consultant*
Morgan, Raymond Franklin *education educator*
Roy, Laura Godfrey *history educator, artist*
Selig, William George *academic administrator*
Thomas, Jimi Elizabeth *elementary school educator*
Trach, Sherry Lynn *elementary school educator*
Ziegler, Rochelle Elizabeth *special education educator*

Warrenton
Holt, Linda Louise *elementary school educator*

Waynesboro
Dillon, William Henry *retired secondary school educator*

Williamsburg
Calver, Richard Allen *retired dean*
Eliason, Nancy Carol *education consultant*
Hight, Orian Langley *retired education educator*
McCarthy, Connie Kearns *university librarian*
Nichol, Gene Ray, Jr. *academic administrator, law educator*
Reiss, Mitchell B. *academic administrator, law educator, former ambassador*
Reveley, Walter Taylor III *dean, law educator*
Strikwerda, Carl James *dean*
Turnage, Martha Allen *academic administrator*
Van Tassel-Baska, Joyce Lenore *education educator*

Winchester
Conteh, Nabie Y. *information systems and computer technology educator*

Wise
Smiddy, Joseph Charles *retired academic administrator*

Woodberry Forest
Campbell, Dennis Marion *academic administrator, educator, theologian*

WASHINGTON

Anacortes
Felger, Ralph William *education educator, retired military officer*

Arlington
Hedman, Zoe Ann *retired literature and language educator, artist*

Auburn
Rohlff, Geri *secondary school educator*

Bainbridge Island
Skotheim, Robert Allen *retired academic administrator, educator*

Bellevue
Rice, Kay Diane *elementary school educator, consultant*
Westergaard, George Henry *secondary school educator*

Bellingham
Dooley, Kathleen Ann *elementary school educator*
Morse, Karen Williams *academic administrator*

Benton City
Omel, June M. *elementary school educator*

Bothell
Constantino, Karen Marie *elementary school educator*

Camas
Kotsovos, Jerry Frank *retired secondary school educator*

Clinton
Powers, David Richard *educational administrator*

Ellensburg
McIntyre, Jerilyn Sue *academic administrator*

Federal Way
Rossi, Ruth Harris *special education educator*

Gig Harbor
Bernard, Lowell Francis *retired academic administrator, educator*

Granite Falls
Peterson, Andrea *elementary school educator*

Kelso
Janke, John Eric *secondary school educator*

Kenmore
Jennerich, Edward John *academic administrator, dean*

Kennewick
Merkel, Patricia Mae *retired school system administrator*

Kirkland
Argue, Don Harvey *college president, minister*
Rich, Clayton *retired academic administrator, educator*
Tyllia, Frank Michael *academic administrator, educator*

Lacey
Spangler, David Robert *academic administrator, engineer, educator*

Lakewood
Gilchrist, Debra L. *college librarian*
McEwen, Doris Ann *education educator*

Longview
Altman, Bernie *retired secondary school educator, editor*

Lynnwood
Tebbs, Carol Ann *secondary school educator, academic administrator*

Mount Vernon
Langworthy, William Clayton *retired college official*

Olympia
Bergeson, Teresa *school system administrator*
Esbeck, Edward S. *retired education educator*
Jackson, Thelma Harrison *educational consultant, researcher*
Markham, J. David *secondary school educator, writer, historical consultant*

Pullman
Bates, Robert C. *academic administrator*
Elstad, Catherine Ann *dean*
Floyd, Elson Sylvester *academic administrator*
Lewis, Norman G. *academic administrator, researcher, consultant*
Paznokas, Lynda Sylvia *elementary school educator*

Richland
Brashear, Karen Kathleen *elementary school educator*
Glennen, Robert Eugene, Jr. *retired academic administrator*
Miller, James Vince *university president*

Seattle
Banks, James Albert *research director, educator*
Bruce, Harry *dean, library and information science educator*
Carlson, Dale Arvid *retired dean*
Cox, Frederick Moreland *retired dean, social worker*
Denny, Brewster Castberg *retired university dean*
Eaton, Philip W. *academic administrator*
Emmert, Mark Allen *academic administrator, educator*
Gerberding, William Passavant *retired university president*
Goodlad, John Inkster *education educator, writer*
Hampton, Shelley Lynn *hearing impaired educator*
Jiambalvo, James *dean*
Murdock, Tullisse Antoinette (Toni Murdock) *academic administrator*
Ostrom, Katherine (Kate) Elma *retired secondary school educator*
Ramsey, Paul Glenn *dean, internist*
Ray, Charles Kendall *retired dean*
Silver, Michael *education educator*
Somerman, Martha J. *dean, dental educator*
Stringer, William Jeremy *university official*
Sundborg, Stephen V. *academic administrator*
Tschernisch, Sergei P. *academic administrator*
Wilson, Lizabeth Anne (Betsy) *dean, library director*
Woods, Nancy Fugate *dean, women's health nurse, educator*

Shelton
Barnard, Susan *literature and language educator*
Milander, Henry Martin *educational consultant*

Shoreline
Bailey, Sandra *secondary school educator, department chairman*

Spanaway
Parker, Lynda Christine Rylander *secondary school educator*

Spokane
Baker, Danial Edwin *pharmacist, educator*
Danke, Virginia *educational administrator, travel consultant*
Linn, Diana Patricia *retired elementary school educator*
McCulloh, Thayne Martin *university administrator, consultant*
Novak, Terry Lee *dean, educator*
Robinson, William P. *academic administrator, consultant, speaker*
Spitzer, Robert J. *academic administrator*

Stanwood
Birkestol, Annabelle Mollie Elsie *retired elementary school educator*

Tacoma
Leitz, Paula Helen *education educator*
Magden, Ronald Earnest *education educator*

Toppenish
Ross, Kathleen Anne *academic administrator*

University Place
Henterly, Mary B. *biology educator*

Vancouver
Vossler, Deborah J. *mathematics and science educator*

Walla Walla
Bridges, George S. *academic administrator, sociology educator*

Washougal
Semke-Fox, Suzanne Marie *retired middle school educator*

Yakima
Beehler, Tobi Lorraine *elementary school educator, education educator*

WEST VIRGINIA

Athens
Marsh, Joseph Franklin, Jr. *retired academic administrator*

Berkeley Springs
Morris, Sarah *literature and language educator*

Bethany
Smith, G(odfrey) T(aylor) *college president*

Bluefield
Chryssikos, Alexandra Gianelos *secondary school educator*

Chapmanville
Wilson, Terilyn Barrett *elementary school educator*

Charleston
Arrington, Carolyn Ruth *school system administrator, consultant*
Cook, Debra Jo *counseling administrator, elementary school educator*
Davis, Billie Johnston *school counselor*
Paine, Steven L. *school system administrator*
Richardson, Sally Keadle *academic administrator*

Clarksburg
Leuliette, Connie Jane *secondary school educator*

Dunbar
Russell, James Alvin, Jr. *college administrator*

Fairmont
Hardway, Wendell Gary *retired academic administrator*

Harrisville
White, Kathleen Ann *elementary school educator*

Huntington
Gould, Alan Brant *academic administrator*
Hayes, Robert Bruce *former college president, educator*
Joyce-Norris, Elaine Rozelle *elementary school educator*
Kent, Calvin Albert *academic administrator*
Kopp, Stephen James *academic administrator*
McKown, Charles Henry *dean*

Hurricane
Chaney, Robin White *secondary school educator, consultant*

Martinsburg
Dugger, Debra Martin *school counselor*
Hayes, Carol Sue *elementary school educator*

Matewan
Call, Bridget Kay *literature and language educator*

Morgantown
Alkadry, Mohamad G. *public administration educator*
Allamong, Betty Davis *retired academic administrator, biology professor*
Bajura, Richard Albert *academic administrator, mechanical engineer, educator*
Bucklew, Neil S. *former academic administrator, educator*
D'Alessandri, Robert M. *academic administrator, retired dean*
Garrison, Michael S. *academic administrator, lawyer, educator*
Koelbl, James J. *dean*
Moxley, Roy Anthony *early childhood educator*

Parkersburg
Dennis, James L. *history educator*
Francis, Lynne Ann *elementary school and music educator*

Philippi
Markwood, Stephen Ernest *academic administrator, educator*

Saint Albans
Smith, Robert Carlisle *department administrator, welding educator*

South Charleston
Fishkin, Anne Sonya *retired special education educator*

Spencer
Parker, Theresa Ann Boggs *retired special education educator, retired music educator*

Wheeling
Hickcox, Leslie Kay *education educator, consultant*

WISCONSIN

Appleton
Beck, Jill *academic administrator, dancer, educator*

Baraboo
Umhoefer, Aural M. *retired dean, educational consultant*

Barneveld
Kolb, Victoria L. *retired mathematics educator*

Barron
Kienbaum, Janice Mae *reading specialist*

Beloit
Burris, John Edward *academic administrator, biologist, educator*
Wheeler, Karla *education educator*

Clintonville
Johnson, Edward C. *literature and language educator, social sciences educator*

De Forest
O'Neil, J. Peter (James Peter O'Neil) *elementary school educator, computer scientist*

Delafield
Haugner, Carolyn M. *elementary school educator*

Dousman
Petersen, Jonathan Christian *elementary school educator, music educator*

Eagle
Kalnes, Donna M. Simondet *retired principal, alcohol and drug abuse education program director*

Eau Claire
Field, Barbara Kay *elementary school educator*

Elkhorn
Reinke, Doris Marie *retired elementary school educator*

Fish Creek
Abegg, Martin Gerald *retired academic administrator*

Fond Du Lac
Boelhower, Patricia Lee *history educator*

Genesee Depot
Kaldhusdal, Terry Lee *elementary school educator*

Germantown
Rudebeck, Carol A. *school system administrator*

Glendale
Schenker, Eric *university dean, economist*

Green Bay
Hardy, Deborah Lewis *dean, educator, dental hygienist*
Oshefsky, Carol Ann *retired elementary school educator*
Thill, Linda Susan *secondary school educator*

Hartford
Falkenstein, Sara André *retired elementary school educator*

Holmen
Meyer, Karl William *retired university president*

Hortonville
Forton, Gregory A. *secondary school educator*

Hudson
Dahle, Carol Jo *secondary school educator, director*
Dahle, Johannes Upton *retired academic administrator*

Jackson
Goede, Michael Jon *secondary school educator*

Janesville
Kubina, June M. *elementary school educator, music educator*

Kenosha
Campbell, F(enton) Gregory *academic administrator, historian*
Iaquinta, Leonard Phillip *academic administrator, writer, consultant, not-for-profit fundraiser*

La Crosse
Gow, Joe *academic administrator*
Medland, William James *university chancellor*

Madison
Burmaster, Elizabeth *school system administrator*
Busby, Edward Oliver *retired dean*
Davis, Kenneth Boone, Jr. *dean, law educator*
Farrell, Patrick V. *academic administrator*
Frazier, Kenneth L. *university librarian*
Grobschmidt, Richard A. *school system administrator*
Hamers, Robert J. *chemistry educator, researcher*
Johnson, Richard Arnold *statistics educator, consultant*
Knetter, Michael Mark *dean*
Ladson-Billings, Gloria J. *education educator*
Ma, Zhenqiang *education educator*
Mash, Donald J. *college president*
Odden, Allan Robert *education educator*
Reilly, Kevin P. *academic administrator*
Sapiro, Virginia *academic administrator, political science professor*
Skochelak, Susan E. *dean*
Spencer, Cheryl L. *literature and language educator*
Turng, Lih-Sheng *education educator*
Uttal, Lynet *education educator*
Wiley, John D. *academic administrator*

Manitowoc
Nelson, Robert Louis *education educator, consultant*

Markesan
Kastenschmidt, Betty M. *elementary school educator, director*

Menomonee Falls
Hinrichs-Dahms, Holly Beth *elementary school educator*
Woger, John Allen *band director, department chairman*

Mequon
Ellis, William Grenville *academic administrator, management consultant*
Sisney, Ned *education educator*

Milwaukee
Aman, Mohammed Mohammed *dean, library and information science professor*
Barth, Karl Luther *retired seminary president*
Coffman, Terrence J. *retired academic administrator*
Dunn, Michael J. *dean*
Feinsilver, Donald Lee *psychiatry professor*
Kearney, Joseph D. *dean, law educator*
Keshvala, Seelpa H *secondary school educator*
Lobb, William K. *dean, dental educator*
Matusiak, Krystyna K. *school librarian, translator*
Peng, Zhong-Ren *education educator*
Rheams, Annie Elizabeth *education educator*
Sankovitz, James Leo *retired development director, lobbyist*
Schroeder, John H. *university chancellor*
Simmons-Welburn, Janice *dean, library director*
Velez, William *education educator*
Wake, Madeline Musante *academic administrator, nursing educator*
Waller, Mary Bellis *educational consultant, researcher*
Weiner, Wendy L(ou) *elementary school educator, writer*
Wild, Robert Anthony *academic administrator*

Monroe
Figi, Matthew L. *secondary school educator*

New Richmond
Zuberbier, Jo Ann *elementary school educator*

Oak Creek
Gagliani, William Dennis *school librarian*

Oshkosh
Earns, Lane Robert *academic administrator, historian, educator*
Olejniczak, Bernard Charles *education educator*
Rainwater, Terry I. *counseling administrator*
Ristow, Thelma Frances *retired elementary school educator*

Pulaski
Stangel, Philip David *secondary school educator, band instructor*

Racine
Rodrigues-Pavao, Antonio *vocal music teacher*

Ripon
Jeffries, Paul Franklin *philosophy professor*

River Falls
Fry, Blake Edward *academic administrator*
Krey, DeAn Marie *retired education educator*
Thibodeau, Gary A. *academic administrator*

Sheboygan
Fritz, Kristine Rae *retired secondary school educator*

Shorewood
Lietz, Jeremy Jon *educational administrator, writer*

Superior
Erlenbach, Julius E. *academic administrator, musician*
Jacobs, Laura Elizabeth *school librarian, educator, archivist*
Morden, Annette Sonja Knudson *retired education educator*
Vance, Mary Lee *academic administrator*

Three Lakes
Bauknecht, Barbara Belle *retired pre-school educator*

Tomah
Neurohr, Shirley Ann *retired special education educator*

Union Grove
Dawson, Rose Dorothy *retired elementary school educator*

Washburn
Nutt, Sandra Kay *elementary school educator*

Waterford
Hanson, Jody Elizabeth *special education educator*

Waukesha
Gustafson, Mardel Emma *secondary school educator, writer*
Hastad, Douglas Noel *academic administrator, physical education educator*
Lightfoot, Alfred J. *retired education educator*

Waupaca
Feldt, Mary *elementary school educator*

Wausau
Rusch, Denise Marie *school system administrator*

Whitewater
Busse, Eileen Elaine *special education educator*
Chapman, Stephanie Lynn *education educator*
Connor, James Richard *retired academic administrator*
Kolb, Sharon Marie *education educator, director, consultant*

Wisconsin Rapids
Olson-Hellerud, Linda Kathryn *elementary school educator*

WYOMING

Afton
Nethercott, Mark A. *physics educator*

Casper
Eskew, Sandra Caye *elementary school educator*
Foster, Vicki Anne *secondary school educator*
Kilts, Laurie Dawn *elementary school educator*
Rickabaugh, René Lane *principal*

Cheyenne
McBride, James M. *school system administrator*
Weigner, Brent James *secondary school educator*

Green River
Albers, Dolores M. *secondary school educator*

Jackson
Massy, William Francis *education educator, consultant*

Laramie
Buchanan, Tom *academic administrator*
Farrell, Mary M(aggie) *Dean of Libraries*
Kirkwood, Carol *literature and language educator*
Yamamoto, Masahiro *adult education educator*

Powell
LaRowe, Miles *academic administrator*

Torrington
Lewis, Mary Jane *retired elementary school educator*

TERRITORIES OF THE UNITED STATES

AMERICAN SAMOA

Pago Pago
Jyothibhavan, Joserose S. *chemistry educator*
Poumele, Claire Tuia *school system administrator*

GUAM

Barrigada
McDonald Terlaje, Patricia *counselor*

Hagatna
Artero, Margaret T. *academic administrator, military officer*

Mangilao
Inoue, Yukiko *educational research educator*

NORTHERN MARIANA ISLANDS

Saipan
Borja, David M. *school system administrator*
Camacho, Charlotte DLG *principal, elementary school educator*
Dela Cruz, Acelia Castro *elementary school educator*

PUERTO RICO

Cabo Rojo
Rivera-Martinez, Socorro *retired elementary school educator, assistant principal*

Caguas
Ortiz, Víctor Raúl *parochial school educator*

Mayaguez
Coriano, Irmarie *mathematics educator, department chairman*

San Juan
Carreras, Francisco José *retired academic and foundation administrator*
Joglar, Francisco *academic administrator*
Matheu, Federico Manuel *university chancellor*
Rey-Hernandez, Cesar A. *school system administrator*

Trujillo Alto
Crespo de Sanabia, María Milagros *retired education educator*

VIRGIN ISLANDS

Frederiksted
Birbahadur, Dindial *secondary school educator*

St Croix
Charles, Sharon Patricia *elementary school educator*

St Thomas
Larsen, Lauren *school system administrator*
Michael, Noreen *academic administrator*

MILITARY ADDRESSES OF THE UNITED STATES

EUROPE

APO
Bowker, Rayanne Sones *elementary school educator*
Salerno, Patricia J. *elementary school educator*

CANADA

ALBERTA

Calgary
Neale, Ernest Richard Ward *retired university official, consultant*
Smith, Rowland James *educational administrator*
Watanabe, Mamoru *internist, researcher*
White, Terrence Harold *academic administrator, sociologist*

Edmonton
Ingles, Ernie Boyce *academic administrator, library director*
Kratochvil, Byron George *chemistry educator, researcher*
Tyrrell, D. Lorne J. *university dean*

BRITISH COLUMBIA

Cobble Hill
Cox, Albert Reginald *retired dean, retired cardiologist*

Fernie
McFarlin-Kosiec, Barbara Ann *secondary school educator, literature and language professor, small business owner*

Surrey
Lee, Jeong-Kyu *education educator, researcher, academic administrator*

Vancouver
Finnegan, Cyril Vincent *retired dean, zoology educator*
Singer, Sue *academic administrator*

MANITOBA

Winnipeg
Poettcker, Henry *retired academic administrator*

NEWFOUNDLAND AND LABRADOR

Saint John's
May, Arthur W. *retired academic administrator, educator*

NOVA SCOTIA

Halifax
Jaeger, Leslie Gordon *academic administrator*

Wolfville
Ogilvie, Kelvin Kenneth *academic administrator, chemist, educator*

ONTARIO

Gloucester
Malouin, Jean-Louis *adult education educator*

Kingston
Spencer, John Hedley *biochemistry educator*

Ottawa
Philogene, Bernard J. R. *academic administrator, science educator*

Peterborough
Theall, Donald Francis *retired university president*

Saint Catharines
Ayanso, Anteneh Wondimu *information systems educator*

Toronto
Evans, John Robert *academic administrator, cardiologist*
Hayhurst, James Frederick Palmer *career and business consultant, inspirational speaker, writer*
Knowlton, Thomas A. *retired dean, food products executive*
Kushner, Eva *academic administrator, educator, author*
Naylor, C. David *academic administrator*
Ostry, Sylvia *academic administrator, economist*
Sessle, Barry John *adult education educator, researcher*

Waterloo
Berczi, Andrew Stephen *academic administrator, educator*

QUEBEC

Montreal
Freedman, Samuel Orkin *university official*

Quebec City
Habashi, Fathi *retired metallurgy professor, consultant*

SASKATCHEWAN

Regina
Barber, Lloyd Ingram *retired university president*

Saskatoon
Knott, Douglas Ronald *dean, agricultural sciences educator, researcher*

Montreal
Lowy, Frederick Hans *academic administrator, psychiatrist*

Saint Catharines
Bordonaro, Karen Elizabeth *school librarian, educator*

Toronto
Scardamalia, Marlene *education educator, researcher*

MEXICO

Ciudad Juarez
Tabuenca-Cordoba, Maria-Socorro *education educator, researcher*

Mexico City
de la Fuente Ramirez, Juan Ramon *academic administrator*

ARGENTINA

District Capital
Frasch, Alberto Carlos C. *molecular genetics educator*

AUSTRALIA

Melbourne
Searby, Richard Henry *academic administrator, lawyer*

BRITISH VIRGIN ISLANDS

Tortola
Chalwell-Brewley, Lavon Patricia *biology educator*

CHILE

Valdivia
Teitelboim, Claudio *academic administrator*

ENGLAND

Leeds
Pillay, Anand *education educator, researcher*

London
May, Robert McCredie (Lord May of Oxford) *biology educator*

Oxford
Thomas, Sarah E. *university librarian*
Varese, Federico *sociology professor*

Richmond-upon-Thames
Smith, Norman Raymond *academic administrator*

FRANCE

Fontainebleau
Demers, Elizabeth Anne *education educator*

GERMANY

Obbornhofen
Edwards, Grey Holt, Jr. *academic administrator, adult education educator*

Ottilienstr
Clarke, Ingrid Gadway *retired academic ombudsman, consultant*

Starnberg
Huber, Franz *retired research director*

GUANA ISLAND

Barrigada
Perez, Annie Rivera *elementary school educator*

HONG KONG

Hong Kong
Tsui, Lap-Chee *academic administrator, molecular genetics educator*

New Territories
Lau, Lawrence Juen-Yee *academic administrator, economics professor, consultant*

IRELAND

Cork
Lyons, Nona Mary *adult education educator*

JAMAICA

Mona
Harris, Eon Nigel *dean, rheumatologist, internist*

JAPAN

Okayama
Nii, Shiro *director, virologist, educator*

Tokyo
Nakajima, Hiroshi *education educator*

Tsukuba
Shimizu, Kazuhiko *education educator*

LEBANON

Waterbury, John *academic administrator, political science professor, writer*

POLAND

Gdansk
Mokrzecki, Lech Marian *history of education educator*

REPUBLIC OF KOREA

Seoul
Lee, Sungho H. *education educator, consultant, academic administrator*
Sohn, Jungyul *education educator*
Song, Mi-Yeon *education educator, physician*

SCOTLAND

Saint Andrews
Dover, Sir Kenneth James *chancellor, retired classicist*

SINGAPORE

Hunter, Howard Owen *academic administrator, law educator*

SWEDEN

Uppsala
Champion, Margrét Gunnarsdóttir *literature and language educator*

TAIWAN

Kaohsiung
Lambert, Marianne T. *retired elementary school educator*

ADDRESS UNPUBLISHED

Adams, Leocadia Donat *secondary school educator, writer*
Aiken, Michael Thomas *former academic administrator*
Aldrow-Liput, Priscilla Reese *retired elementary school educator*
Alfonso-Bica, Kristy Lynn *elementary school educator*
Allen, Betty Noldon *education educator, consultant*
Allen, Carol E. *retired elementary school educator*
Allen, Charles Eugene *university administrator, agriculturist, educator*
Allen, Charlotte *secondary school educator*
Allen, Ralph Carnell *retired assistant principal*
Allred, Dawn Peterman *adult education educator*
Almore-Randle, Allie Louise *special education educator, academic administrator*
Alutto, Joseph Anthony *academic administrator, former dean, management educator*
Ament, Kyle Tyler *director*
Amos, Linda K. *academic administrator*
Anderson, Gregory Thomas *secondary school educator, researcher, historian*
Anderson, Joan R. *secondary school educator*
Anderson, Paul Wayne *assistant principal*
Anderson, Shawn Renee *director*
Angeles, Rodolfo B. *elementary school educator*
Appleton, Kevin *academic administrator*
Archer, Lillian Patricia *academic administrator, dean*
Armacost, Mary-Linda Sorber Merriam *educational consultant*
Armstrong, Jacque *pre-school educator*
Armstrong-Law, Margaret *school administrator*
Arndt, Laura Denise Lyons Bodeen *mathematics educator*
Arnett, Edward McCollin *chemistry educator, researcher*
Arp, Arlene *elementary school educator*
Ashcraft, David John *secondary school music educator*
Atherton, Barbara Klein *elementary school educator*
Auston, David Henry *former academic administrator, electrical engineer, educator*
Babbitt, Samuel Fisher *retired university official*
Baker, Eva Lee *education educator, researcher*
Baker, Katherine June *elementary school educator, minister, artist*
Balaji, Rengarajan V. *grant specialist*
Ballard, David M. *elementary school educator*
Banks, Carolyn Duty *retired history educator*
Baptiste, La Verne Johnson *retired secondary school educator*
Barr, Adam *biology educator*
Barretto, Anjali *education educator*
Barry, Phillip Owen *college president*
Bartel, Arthur Gabriel *retired principal, alderman, culinary arts instructor*
Bartosiak, Stan Theodore *secondary school educator*
Bastin, Thoma *educational consultant*
Baumgartner, Andrew C. *retired elementary school educator*
Baxter, Cecil William, Jr. *retired academic administrator*
Beadle, Elizabeth Ahrens *retired elementary school educator*
Beaver, Barbara Leann *elementary school educator, writer*
Becht, Lawrence John *elementary school educator*
Beck, Barbara Nell *elementary school educator*
Becker, Allienne R. *education educator, writer*
Bekavac, Nancy Yavor *retired academic administrator, lawyer*
Belanger, Cherry Churchill *elementary school educator*
Belvis, Renee Magdalena *elementary school educator*
Bennet, Douglas Joseph, Jr. *former academic administrator*
Bentley, Charmaine Clark O'Fallon *secondary school educator*
Berger, Barbara *special education educator, consultant*
Berger, Deborah Kornbluth *educator, consultant, real estate agent*
Bergeron, Patricia Ann *education educator, consultant*
Bergman, Hermas John (Jack) *retired college administrator*
Berkhoudt, Thomas Walter *director*
Bernstein, I. Melvin *dean, materials scientist*
Bert, Clara Virginia *retired secondary school educator, administrator*
Beuthien, Gayle Dawn *special education educator, swim coach*
Beyeler, Julia *retired academic administrator*
Bhatnagar, Abha *school system administrator, department chairman*
Bigelow, Sharon Lee *elementary school educator*
Bigelow, Vivian Lou *elementary school educator, secondary school educator*
Bilancia-Vittum, Denise *secondary school educator*
Bishop, Charles Edwin *academic administrator, economist, educator*
Bishop, Ina Sue Marquis (Ina Sue Marquis Bishop) *retired dean*
Blackledge, David William *retired academic administrator*
Blake, Simone Elaise *retired school librarian*
Block, Gene David *academic administrator, biologist, educator*
Bloes, Richard K. *audio-visual specialist, artist*
Bloodworth, Gladys Leon *elementary school educator*
Boesch, Diane Harriet *retired elementary school educator*
Bogren, Carol Ferrer *secondary school educator*
Boiler, Elizabeth Anne *literature and language educator*
Boise, Audrey Lorraine *retired special education educator*
Bondi, Joseph Charles, Jr. *education educator, consultant*
Boothe, Leon Estel *academic administrator emeritus, consultant*
Booton, Carolyn Ann *mathematics educator*
Bottolfson, Wahnita Joan *parochial school educator*
Bourque, Boyd D. *secondary school educator*
Bowen, Richard Lee *retired academic administrator, political scientist, educator*
Bowling, John C. *academic administrator*
Box, Thadis Wayne *university dean emeritus, educator*
Bradford, Marlene Kay *history educator, writer*
Branch, Felecia Ann-Seldon *elementary school educator*
Brewer, Angela Sue *middle school educator*
Brewer, Carey *retired academic administrator*
Brick, Arline Roth *education educator*
Broman, Per Fredrik *education educator*
Bromund, Alice A. *retired elementary school educator*
Brooke, Francis John III *retired academic administrator*
Brown, David Richard *school system administrator, minister*
Brown, Denise Marie *elementary school educator*
Brown, Pearlie Murray *retired school librarian*
Brownell, Blanche Parisi *retired secondary school educator*
Brownlee, Paula Pimlott *higher education consultant*
Bryan, Lawrence Dow *college president*
Bryant, Jennifer Campbell *mathematics educator*
Bryant, Melissa Lee *elementary school educator*
Buchanan, Carolee Horstman *special education educator, consultant*
Buckler, Marilyn Lebow *school psychologist, educational consultant*
Buckley, Eleanor Jane *retired elementary school educator*
Bullock, Mary Brown *adult education educator*
Bullock, Molly *retired elementary school educator*
Burch-Martinez, Berkeley Alison *primary school educator*
Burke, Joseph C. *former university official*
Burkhart, Catherine Ray *retired secondary school educator*
Burns, Kathleen Adley *educational consultant*
Burton, Bruce Arthur *education educator*
Butler, Debra Yvonne *special education educator, small business owner*
Butler, Denise Elizabeth *primary school educator*
Butler, Donna Marcia *retired mathematics educator*
Byerly, Steven Lee *educational consultant*
Byrd, Janice Adele *elementary school educator*
Cabcabin, Diana M. *elementary school educator, consultant*
Cahill, Charles L. *retired academic administrator, chemistry professor*
Cain, William Howard *secondary school educator*
Cakir, Hasan *research analyst*
Caldera, Louis Edward *former academic administrator, former federal official*
Caldwell, Ann Wickins *academic administrator*
Calfano, Brian Robert *education educator*
Camara, David John *school librarian*
Cameron, Lucille Wilson *retired dean*
Canelli, Jeanne *early childhood educator*
Cardona, Julio Jose *student affairs director, educational researcher*
Carlin, John William *educator, retired governor*
Carlin, Marian P. *secondary school educator*
Carrigan, David Owen *history educator*
Carson, Alice Hines *secondary school educator*
Carson, Denise Wilkinson *retired gifted and talented educator*
Cash, Joseph Carl *history educator, government educator*
Castiglia, Patricia Anne Thorson *dean, nursing educator*
Castronova, John *special education educator*
Caucia, Louisa B. *retired elementary school educator*
Cerny, William *retired education educator, musician*
Chafel, Judith Ann *education educator*
Chandler, Alice *retired academic administrator, educational consultant*
Chansley, Deborah Lynn *education educator*
Chappell, Annette M. *educational consultant, minister*
Charles, Marilyn Kay *secondary school educato*
Charleton, Margaret Ann *child care administrator, consultant*
Chase, Barbara Landis *headmaster*
Chase, Francis Marvin, Sr. *education educator, consultant*
Chase, James Richard *retired college president*
Chasteen, Beverly Joan *parochial school educator, retired secondary school educator*
Chen, Feng *adult education educator, researche*
Chevalier, Denise Ann *director*
Chiaramonte, Christine Loren *elementary schoo educator*
Christine, Chan B. *educational consultant, researcher*
Christopherson, Myrvin Frederick *college president*
Cibes, William Joseph, Jr. *retired academic administrator*

Claiborne, Kenya Wynette *secondary school educator*
Clark, Edward Eugene *academic administrator, educator, lawyer*
Clark, James Milford *retired college president*
Clarke, Ciana Bernadine Bennett *education educator, researcher*
Clayton, Julia B. *academic administrator, musician*
Clifford, Brother Peter *academic administrator, religious studies educator*
Cochrane, Walter E. *academic administrator, conductor, music supervisor, clarinet soloist*
Cockram, Suzanne M. *elementary school educator*
Cody, Frank Joseph *education educator, consultant*
Coffee, Joseph Denis, Jr. *retired college chancellor*
Cohen, Gloria Ernestine *elementary school educator*
Colburn, David R. *academic administrator*
Cole, Nancy Stooksberry *educational research executive*
Coleman, Gary William *retired elementary school educator*
Coleman, Mary Sue *academic administrator*
Collens, Lewis Morton *retired academic administrator, law educator*
Collier, Herman Edward, Jr. *retired college president*
Compton, Norma Haynes *retired dean, artist*
Connell, George Edward *retired academic administrator, research scientist*
Conquest, Claire M. *secondary school counselor*
Cook, Edward Joseph *college president*
Cook, Sister Mary Mercedes *school system administrator, director*
Cook, Myrtle *special education and elementary school educator*
Cooper, James Michael *education educator*
Cooper, Kathleen Bell *dean, former federal agency administrator*
Cooperman, Barry S. *academic administrator, chemist, educator*
Copeland, Bonnie S. *former school system administrator*
Copeland, Henry Jefferson, Jr. *former college president*
Copeland, Phillips Jerome *retired academic administrator, military officer*
Corbin, Veronica L. *secondary school educator, information scientist, consultant*
Corey, Judith Ann *retired elementary school educator*
Corkins, Bob *school system administrator*
Corts, Thomas Edward *academic administrator*
Cothran, Anne Jennette *academic administrator*
Crabtree, Jacquelynn Kay *elementary school educator*
Craiglow, James Hawkins *academic administrator*
Cramer, Robert Vern *retired college administrator, consultant*
Crawford, Kenneth Charles *retired academic administrator*
Crawley, Cheryl K. *school system administrator*
Cross, Kathryn Patricia *education educator*
Crotts, Carolyn Pearl *school librarian*
Crutchfield, Marjorie Alice *retired elementary school educator, director*
Cruz-Connerton, Mayra *elementary school educator*
Cunard, Derek *academic administrator*
Cupp, Lucy Paschall *retired elementary school educator, minister*
Curry, Goldie *elementary school educator*
Curry Scott, Shirley Goodman *retired director*
Dable, Carol M. *primary school educator*
Daniels, Edgar Roth *educator*
Daniels, Mary P. *academic administrator, technologist*
Darden, Lauretta *elementary school educator*
Davenport, Lawrence Franklin *academic administrator*
Davis, Anna Jane Ripley *elementary school educator*
Davis, Elizabeth Eileen *education educator*
Davis, Hiram Joe *public school administrator*
Davis, Joseph Lloyd *academic administrator, consultant*
Davis, Lanita Irene *secondary school educator*
Davison, Helen Irene *secondary school educator, counseling administrator*
DeAndrade, Kristy A. *elementary school educator*
DeCastro, Cristina L. *secondary school educator*
DeJarnatt, Kitty M. *special education educator*
Delahanty, Rebecca Ann *school system administrator*
DeMary, Jo Lynne *retired school system administrator, former elementary school educator*
DeNisi, Angelo *dean*
Dent, Julie *executive director*
Derrick, Kathryn Thill *secondary school educator*
Diamond, Richard *retired educator*
Diamond, Robert Mach *higher education administrator*
DiCello, Carmen Charles *health educator*
Dirks, Roger L. *mathematics educator*
Dispenza, Mary Catherine *director, educator, photographer*
DiStefano, Philip *academic administrator*
Diviney, Nancy Lynn *elementary school educator*
Dixon, Jane Frazier *elementary school educator, consultant*
Dobson, Dorothy Lynn Watts *retired elementary school educator*
Dockery, J. Lee *retired medical school administrator*
Dohmen, Mary Holgate *retired primary school educator*
Doligosa, Annie Lumampao *elementary school educator, researcher*
Donaldson, Wilma Crankshaw *elementary school educator*
Donberger, Karen Shepard *special education and elementary school educator*
Donoff, R. Bruce *dean, oral surgeon, dental educator*
Donovan, Gerald Alton *retired academic administrator, dean*
Doss, Delia L. *mathematics educator*
Doud, Guy R. *motivational speaker, former secondary education educator*
Dowtin, Amanda Elizabeth *elementary school educator*
Drake, Evelyn Downie *retired secondary school educator*
Drake, George Albert *retired academic administrator, historian, educator*
Dressler, Christy Anna *elementary school educator*
Dreyer, Jeffrey S. *parochial school educator*
Drum, Alice *academic administrator, educator*
Drummond, Dixie Dale *retired adult education educator*
Duderstadt, James Johnson *academic administrator, engineering educator*
Duffy, Ann Patricia *retired elementary school educator*
Duffy, John Joseph *retired academic administrator, historian, educator*
Duminuco, Vincent Joseph *academic administrator, educator*
Dunbar, Diana (Diane) L. *educator, dancer, artist, writer, storyteller*
Duncan, Robert Bannerman *dean, strategy and organizations educator*
Dunn, Helen Elizabeth *retired secondary school educator*
Duplessis, Audrey Joseph *school system administrator*
Dutson, Thayne R. *dean*
Dycus, Elizabeth Rasmussen *academic administrator*
Earenfight, Theresa Marie *education educator*
Ebbs, George Heberling, Jr. *university executive*
Eddy, Kelly J. *history educator*
Edelman, Norman Herman *dean, medical educator, academic administrator*
Edwards, Ardis Lavonne Quam *retired elementary education educator*
Edwards, Mark U., Jr. *academic administrator, history professor, writer*
Edwards, Robert Hazard *retired college president*
Einoder, Camille Elizabeth *retired secondary school educator*
Eliot, Charles William John *former university president*
Ellis, Sophia (Lugene) Holley *retired secondary school educator*
Elrod, Deborah Lee *special education educator*
Elzay, Richard Paul *retired dean, dental educator, department chairman*
Epp, Dianne Naomi *secondary school educator*
Eppolito, Mary *assistant principal, educator*
Erb, Thomas Owen *education educator*
Espiricueta, Sylvia *counseling administrator*
Estes, Leslie Karen *educator*
Evans, Geraldine Ann *former academic administrator*
Evans, James Handel *academic administrator, architect*
Evans, Richard Austin *education educator, consultant*
Ewald, Laura Anne *school librarian*
Fair, Jean Everhard *retired education educator*
Faria, Me'Shell Anita *special education educator*
Farquhar, Robin Hugh *educational consultant, former university president*
Farrington, Gregory C. *former academic administrator*
Fay, Miriam Soler *school counselor, educator*
Fearon, Charlene O'Brien *special education educator*
Feldstein, Joshua *educational administrator*
Felicetti, Daniel A. *academic administrator*
Felix, Arthur Martin *chemistry educator, researcher*
Fell, Elizabeth P. *education educator*
Felton, Helen Martin *retired adult education educator, writer*
Feng, Jianhua *education educator*
Fergusson, Frances Daly *former academic administrator*
Fernandes, Jane K. *former academic administrator, sign language professional*
Fernández-Velazquez, Juan Ramon *university chancellor*
Ferry, Joan Evans *school counselor*
Fetters, Doris Ann *retired secondary education educator*
Fife, Jonathan Donald *education educator*
Filchock, Ethel *education educator*
Finale, Frank L. *retired elementary school educator, writer*
Finckenauer, James O. *criminal justice educator, researcher*
Finn, Jane E. *education educator*
Fishburn, Janet Forsythe *dean*
Fisher, Charles Harold *chemistry educator, researcher*
Fleetwood, Mary Annis *education association executive*
Fleming, Horace Weldon, Jr. *academic administrator*
Fleury, Paul Aimé *dean, physicist*
Forbes, Mary Allison *psychology educator*
Ford, Loretta C. *retired dean, educator, consultant, nurse*
Ford, Ralph Lee *academic administrator*
Forget, Mark Alan *educational consultant, educator*
Foriest, JoAnn M. *education educator*
Forsyth, Ben Ralph *retired academic administrator, medical educator*
Foster, Martha Tyahla *pre-school administrator*
Foy, Betty Lou Jones *educational administrator*
Foyston, Frederick L. (Rick Foyston) *literature and language educator, coach*
Francis, Norman C. *academic administrator*
Francoeur, Christina *special education educator*
Freeland, Richard Middleton *former academic administrator, historian*
French, Roderick Stuart *university chancellor*
Frick, Ivan Eugene *retired academic administrator, educational consultant*
Fridley-Hereford, Vivian Suzanne *secondary school educator*
Frost, Rita Kenton *special education and education educator*
Fugett, Roberta Lynn *special education educator*
Fuller, Maxine Compton *retired secondary school educator*
Fulmer, Vincent Anthony *retired college president*
Gabel, Katherine *retired academic administrator*
Galagan, Carol Anne *special education educator*
Garcia, Julia Theresa *secondary school educator*
Garland, James C. *retired academic administrator*
Genesoni, Jacqueline *mathematics educator*
Gentilcore, Eileen Marie Belsito *principal*
Ghausi, Mohammed Shuaib *retired dean, electrical engineer, educator*
Gibson, Lisette L. *elementary school and music educator*
Gibson, Pamela Hemenway *elementary school educator*
Gilbert, Stanley Dean *history educator*
Gile, Carole S. *retired education educator*
Gilliar, Beate C. *educator*
Giusti, Joseph Paul *retired academic administrator, consultant*
Glantz, Lawrence G. *special education and social studies educator*
Glatter, Rebecca Jan *secondary school educator*
Glaze, Lynn Ferguson *pre-school administrator*
Glismann, Clementine *retired elementary school educator*
Glynn, Edward *retired academic administrator*
Goach, Kenneth Edmund *professional counselor*
Goff, Renee Rosenstock *gifted and talented educator*
Goforth, Jill Hastings *principal*
Golden, Sheila S. *retired special education educator*
Goldenberg, Kim *retired academic administrator, internist, consultant*
Gonzalez, Karen Eileen *middle school educator*
Gonzalez, Rose Marie Juarez *retired education educator*
Goodman, Robert Mark *dean, educator*
Goodrich, Kenneth Paul *retired dean*
Gordis, David Moses *academic administrator, rabbi*
Gordon, Sharon Ann *mathematics and pre-school educator*
Gorsuch, Edward Lee *former chancellor*
Gorton-Horan, Ann Hilbert *vice principal*
Goyol, Apollos Bitrus *education educator*
Graves, Wallace Billingsley *retired university executive*
Gray, Hazel Irene *retired special education educator, counselor, consultant*
Gray, Richard Moss *retired college president*
Grebstein, Sheldon Norman *academic administrator*
Green, Patricia Pataky *school system administrator, consultant*
Greene, Jo *school system administrator*
Greenway, Joan M. *dean*
Griffith, Rosita Denise *elementary school educator*
Griggs, Joyce L. *secondary school educator*
Grossman, Carolyn Sylvia Cort *retired elementary school educator*
Groves, Bernice Ann *retired elementary and secondary school coordinator, educator*
Gruetzmacher, Nancy Lynn *retired middle schoool educator*
Guinther, Christine Louise *special education educator*
Gumpert, Carolyn L. *secondary school educator*
Gunning, Carolyn Sue *dean, provost, nursing educator*
Gunsaulis, Linda C. *elementary school educator*
Gupta, Sanju *education educator, researcher*
Gupta, Yash *dean*
Guskin, Alan E. *university president*
Gustafson, Richard Alrick *retired university president*
Guyon, John Carl *retired university administrator*
Haaland, Gordon Arthur *retired academic administrator*
Haas, Suzanne Alberta *elementary and secondary school educator*
Habecker, Eugene Brubaker *academic administrator*
Haden, Clovis Roland *retired academic administrator, engineering educator*
Hadley, William Melvin *retired dean*
Hagan, Joseph Henry *educational consultant*
Hageman, Richard Philip, Jr. *educational administrator*
Hairfield-Marrs, Judy L. *elementary school educator*
Hait, Patrick David *elementary school music educator*
Hale, Nancy Annette Bills *kindergarten educator*
Hall, Charles Worth Leo *college administrator*
Hall, Christopher George Longden *academic administrator*
Hall, James William *university chancellor*
Hamecs, Francella Cheslock *elementary and secondary school educator*
Hammer, Joyce Mae *retired gifted and talented educator*
Hammond, Ann P. *retired elementary, high school and college educator, poet*
Hancock, Charles R. *education educator*
Hanna, Noreen Anelda *adult education educator, consultant*
Hardage, Page Taylor *elementary school educator*
Hare, Norma Q. *retired school system administrator*
Harman, Rebecca Howard *educator*
Harrington, Jean Patrice *academic administrator*
Harris, Dolores M. *retired academic administrator, adult education educator*
Harris, Margaret T. *school system administrator*
Harris, Merle Wiener *college administrator, educator*
Harris, Nancy Lee *special education educator, behavior analyst*
Harris-Barber, Daisy *elementary school educator*
Harrison, Andre L. *education educator, director*
Hartman, Rosemary Jane *retired special education educator*
Hartzell, Karl Drew *retired dean, historian*
Haskell, Anne *secondary school educator*
Hasselmo, Nils *retired academic administrator, linguist*
Hatfield, Stacey *elementary school educator*
Hatton, Barbara R. *academic administrator*
Haugland, Susan Warrell *education educator, consultant*
Hazel, Mary Belle *university administrator*
Heath, Joseph Nounnan *retired literature and language educator, writer*
Heck, James Baker *retired education educator*
Heidt-Dunwell, Debra Sue *vocational school educator*
Heinsohn Kropp, Holly Lynn *educational consultant, history professor, researcher*
Heinze, Mark William *elementary school educator*
Helman, Alfred Blair *retired academic administrator, educational consultant*
Hemby, James Benjamin, Jr. *college president*
Hendershott, Anna Lorraine *educational director*
Henikoff, Leo M., Jr. *academic administrator, medical educator*
Henley, Patricia Joan *consultant, former superintendent*
Henley, Robert Lee *school system administrator*
Henry, Martin Daniel *military academy vice president*
Hensley, Patricia Drake *principal*
Herbert, Adam William, Jr. *former academic administrator, educator*
Herbert, James Charles *academic administrator*
Herman, Ellen Rombs *retired literature and language educator, painter*
Herold, Rochelle Snyder *early childhood educator*
Herring, Joan Sanders *secondary school educator*
Herron, Orley R. *college president*
Hess, Wendi Elizabeth *secondary school educator*
Hesser, Elise L. *retired elementary school educator*
Hill, Antony J. deV. *headmaster, history educator*
Hill, Emita Brady *academic administrator, consultant*
Hill, Jerry Dean *secondary school educator*
Hill, Martha N. *dean, community health nurse*
Hill, Virgil Lusk, Jr. *academic administrator, military officer*
Hitchcock, Walter Anson *retired educational consultant*
Hodgson, Joseph *education educator*
Hoff, Peter Sloat *academic administrator, educator*
Hoffman, Edward Ted Charles III *director, educator*
Hoffman, Judy Greenblatt *preschool director*
Hoffman, Sharon Lynn *adult education educator*
Hoffschneider, Gertrude Delores *pre-school educator*
Hogan, William T. *retired academic administrator*
Holbrook, Karen Ann *retired academic administrator, biologist*
Holloway, Ernest Leon *retired university president*
Holly, Michael Ann *director*
Holston, Carla *elementary school educator*
Holtkamp, Susan Charlotte *elementary school educator*
Honsa, Thomas Patrick *secondary school educator, history professor*
Hooper, Henry Olcott *retired academic administrator, physicist*
Hopp, Phillip Edward *gifted and talented educator*
Hopping, Richard Lee *retired academic administrator*
Horner, Matina Souretis *retired academic administrator, corporate financial executive*
Horton, Christina Marie *literature and language educator*
Hosford, Kittybelle Adcock *retired education educator*
Hostert, Sharon Ann *elementary school educator, assistant principal*
Houghton, Karen Theresa *reading specialist educator, mathematics educator*
Houseman, Ann Elizabeth Lord *educational administrator*
Houston, Shannon D. *school system administrator, assistant principal*
Howard, James Kenton *academic administrator, journalist*
Howard, Marilyn *retired school system administrator*
Howell, Norman Glen *elementary school educator*
Hudson, Janice Whitaker *secondary school educator*
Huffman, Durward Roy *academic administrator, electrical engineer*
Hughes, Eugene Morgan *university president*
Hughes, Mary Alice *adult education educator, consultant*
Hull, McAllister Hobart, Jr. *retired university administrator*
Hunnicutt, Victoria Anne Wilson *educational consultant*

Hunt, Sarah Mincey *elementary school educator*
Huntsman, Lee L. *former academic administrator, director*
Hutchinson, Michael Philip *education educator*
Huttenback, Robert Arthur *academic administrator, educator*
Ibanez, Manuel Luis *academic administrator, biologist, educator*
Impellizeri, John C. (Jack) *mathematics educator*
Innis, Daniel Eugene *dean, consultant*
Inos, Rita Hocog *retired school system administrator*
Irvin, Loretta Regan *elementary school educator*
Ishitani, Terrence Takatsugu *education educator, researcher*
Ishmael, Antionette Rose *elementary school educator, writer*
Iverson, Thomas Edwin *retired academic administrator, mathematician, educator*
Ivra, Augustine LaFranchiniax *pre-school educator*
Jackson, Miles Merrill *retired university dean*
Jackson Wright, Adrienne A. *educational consultant*
Jakubauskas, Edward Benedict *college president*
James, Allix Bledsoe *retired university president*
Janeway, Richard *retired academic administrator*
Jarsma, Cynthia Lynn *secondary school educator*
Javernick, Amy Sue *special education educator*
Jean, Claudette R. *retired elementary school educator*
Jen, Joseph Jwu-Shan *academic administrator, former federal agency administrator*
Jenerette, Joyce Williams *elementary school educator, educational consultant*
Jenkins, Brenda Gwenetta *pre-school administrator, special education educator*
Jenkins, Lawanna *elementary school educator*
Jenkins, William L. *former academic administrator*
Jiang, Wei *adult education educator*
Johnson, Dorothy Jean *retired secondary school educator*
Johnson, Jerrilyn Jenkins *academic administrator*
Johnson, Maryann Elaine *educational administrator*
Johnson, Matilee Howard *retired headmistress*
Johnson, Sylvia Sue *university administrator, educator*
Johnson, Trina Lynn *special education educator*
Johnson, Yvonne Thomas *elementary school educator*
Johnston, Carolyn S. *elementary school educator, reading specialist*
Johnstone, D. Bruce *education educator, academic administrator*
Jones, Donya *elementary school educator*
Jones, Jack Bristol *education educator*
Jones, Joel Mackey *academic administrator*
Jones, Julie Ann *elementary school educator, choreographer*
Jones, Louis, Jr., (Bucky Jones) *academic administrator*
Jones, Roslyn Joyce *secondary school educator*
Jones, Ruth A. *secondary school educator*
Jordan, I(rving) King *former academic administrator*
Jurkiewicz, Carole Lynn *education educator*
Kahn, Victoria Elaine Hopkins *special education educator*
Kallewaard, Susan L. *elementary school educator*
Kambutu, John *adult education educator*
Kampe, Carolyn Jean *elementary school educator, special education educator, art educator*
Kane, Cynthia A. *special education educator*
Kappner, Augusta Souza *academic administrator*
Karben, Shelley Valerie *elementary and special education school educator*
Karns, Elizabeth (Libby) A. *retired daycare administrator*
Kartchner, Gayla L. *elementary school educator*
Kazanchyan, Gevork *public health educator*
Kean, Thomas Howard *former academic administrator, governor*
Keane, Jeffry Robert *secondary school educator*
Keehn, Robin *community program specialist*
Kelly, Beverly Ann *elementary school educator*
Kelly, Timothy Johnston *secondary school educator*
Kelso, Charlotte Elizabeth *elementary school educator, health and physical education specialist*
Kempner, Maximilian Walter *dean, lawyer*
Kendall, Dorothy Irene *secondary school educator*
Kerins, Francis Joseph *college president*
Kern, Charles William *retired academic administrator, chemist, educator*
Kern, Ronald Paul *dean, consultant*
Kertzer, David Israel *academic administrator, anthropology educator, writer*
Kesler, Theodore B. *educational consultant*
Keyes, Joan Ross Rafter *education educator, writer*
Kidney, William Leslie *retired secondary school educator*
Kierscht, Marcia Selland *academic administrator, psychologist*
Kim, Heather *director*
Kim, Soongun *educational consultant*
King, Gundar Julian *retired dean*
King, James Calvin *mathematics educator*
King, John Ethelbert, Jr. *retired academic administrator*
King, Sheryl Jayne *retired secondary school educator, counselor*
Kinter, Kerri Anne *elementary school educator*
Kirk, Rea Helene (Rea Helene Glazer) *special education educator*
Kisiel, Ida Marie *education educator, writer*
Klein, Mary Ann *special education educator*
Kliebard, Herbert Martin *education educator, writer*
Kliebhan, Sister M(ary) Camille *academic administrator*
Kliszus, Edward A., Jr. *school system administrator*
Kneller, John William *academic administrator, retired literature and language educator*
Knighten, Latrenda *elementary school educator, consultant*
Koch, Molly Brown *retired parent educator*
Koenig, Allen Edward *higher education consultant*
Kogan, Esther *education educator, director*
Kohler, Peter Ogden *retired academic administrator, internist, educator*
Kolb, Dorothy Gong *elementary school educator*
Kolenda, Joanne L. *elementary school educator, secondary school educator, volunteer*
Komisar, David Daniel *retired academic administrator*
Konner, Joan Weiner *academic administrator, writer, educator, television producer and retired executive*
Kopielski, Camille Ann *counseling administrator, volunteer*
Koren, Michael *elementary school educator*
Kormondy, Edward John *retired academic administrator, science educator*
Koszegi, Kathleen A. *elementary school educator*
Kovarik, Madeline *education educator*
Kowalchick, Edward M. *headmaster*
Kraemer, Alfred Robert *school librarian*
Krall, Lisa Kristina *education educator*
Krall, Todd *program manager*
Kravetz, Katharine *education educator*
Kreitlow, Burton William *retired adult education educator*
Kruck, Donna Jean *special education educator, consultant*
Kumar, Ramya *academic administrator*
Lackenmier, James Richard *academic administrator, priest*
Lacy, Bill *former academic administrator, architect*
Ladewig, Anita C. *elementary school educator, researcher*
Ladner, Benjamin *former academic administrator*
Lamb, Michael Donald *secondary school educator*
Lambert, Daniel Michael *retired academic administrator*
Lampert-Shepel, Elina *education educator*
Lancaster, Jeanette (Barbara Lancaster) *dean, nursing educator*
Land, Jennifer Rebekah *mathematics educator, science educator*
Langdale, Noah Noel, Jr. *retired education educator, academic administrator*
Langton (Tomasiewicz), Dawn Theresa *literature and language educator*
Lantz, Joanne Baldwin *retired academic administrator*
Larsen, Donald E. *education educator*
Larson, Robert William *education educator, consultant*
Larson, Vicki Lord *academic administrator, communication disorders educator*
Lashley, Felissa Rose *dean, nursing educator, researcher*
Lauer, Jeanette Carol *dean, history educator, writer*
Lawless, Robert William *retired academic administrator*
Lawrence, Sally Clark *retired academic administrator*
Lawson, John Joseph *vocational educator, consultant*
Lawton, Kelly Marie Lee *secondary school educator, performing arts director*
Leach, Brenda Lee *special education educator*
Leath, Cheryl Lynn *retired pre-school educator, poet, painter*
Leather, Victoria Potts *college librarian*
Lee, Vanilla R. *school system administrator, educational consultant*
Leeper, Kathleen Marie *elementary school educator*
Lehman, Jeffrey Sean *academic administrator*
Lehmann, Doris Elizabeth *retired elementary school educator*
Leistner, Mary Edna *retired secondary school educator*
Leitzel, Joan Ruth *retired academic administrator*
LeMaire, Elizabeth Griffin *parochial school educator*
Lennon, Joseph Luke *retired academic administrator, priest*
Leonard, Sister Anne C. *school system administrator*
Lerner, Laurence M. *college administrator*
Le Shana, David Charles *retired academic administrator*
Leslie, Maureen Heelan *university director*
Lester, Robin Dale *historian, educator, writer, former headmaster*
Lester, Virginia Laudano *academic administrator*
Levin, Richard I. *dean, cardiologist, researcher*
Levine, Arthur Elliott *former academic administrator, educator*
Lewis, Ned Lehmon *secondary school educator*
Likins, Peter William *retired academic administrator*
Limerick, Dianne A. *mathematics educator, athletic trainer*
Lin, Qiuyun *education educator*
Link, Phoebe Forrest *education educator, writer, social worker, poet*
Linster, Michelle Lynn *education educator, consultant*
Little Gurley Brady O'Little, Cassandra Oneda *education educator*
Liverman, Betty Jean *elementary school educator*
Lober, Irene Moss *educational consultant*
Lockwood, Theodore Davidge *retired academic administrator*
Looser, Donald William *academic administrator*
Lord, Jerome Edmund *education administrator, writer*
Loser, Joseph Carlton, Jr. *dean, retired judge*
Love, Robert Lyman *retired education educator, consultant*
Lovett, Clara Maria *retired academic administrator, historian*
Lubner, Mary F. *retired elementary school educator*
Lucas, Michele Angelyn *learning consultant, special education educator*
Lucas, Teri Kathleen *secondary school educator*
Luna, Pedro P. *academic administrator*
Lundgren, Colleen Bowling *elementary school educator, consultant*
Lusztig, Peter Alfred *dean, educator*
Lutz, Jeanne V. *elementary school educator*
Lyall, Katharine Culbert *former academic administrator, economist, educator*
Lyne, Dorothy-Arden *secondary school educator*
Lynn, Naomi B. *academic administrator*
Lyons, Charles M. *education educator, former academic administrator*
Lyons, Richard Kent *dean, finance educator*
MacArthur, Marcia *primary school educator*
MacCormack, Jean F. *academic administrator*
Maddox, Nadana *secondary school educator*
Magruder, Jack *retired academic administrator*
Mahaffey, Marcia Hixson *retired educational administrator*
Major, Patrick Webb III *principal*
Makki, S. Kami *education educator*
Mallory, Arthur Lee *dean, retired state official*
Mangino, Christine *academic administrator*
Manley, Judith L. *director*
Mantei, Lorraine E. *school system administrator*
Manuel, Ralph Nixon *retired private school executive*
Marceau, Judith Marie *retired elementary school educator, small business owner*
Marier, Robert L. *dean, hospital administrator*
Markham, Reed B. *education educator, consultant*
Markovich, Alexandria *assistant principal*
Marshak, Robert Reuben *retired dean, medical educator, veterinarian*
Marshall, Dale Rogers *former academic administrator, political scientist, educator*
Marshall, Kathleen Ann *elementary school educator*
Martin, Bruce J. *elementary school educator*
Martin, John F. *academic administrator*
Martin, Martha Ann *secondary school educator*
Masi, Julia A. *elementary school educator*
Mason, Deirdre Dianne *secondary school educator*
Massey, Thomas Benjamin *retired university president*
Mastro, Christopher P. *secondary school educator*
Matasar, Ann B. *retired dean, finance educator*
Matera, Frances Lorine *retired elementary school educator*
Matsen, John Martin *academic administrator, pathologist*
Matsuda, Fujio *retired academic administrator*
Mattice, Howard LeRoy *education educator*
Mattoon, Scott Alexander *private school educator*
May, Ingrid Barbara *elementary school educator*
Mayer, Robert Anthony *retired college president*
Mayfield, Robert Charles *academic administrator, geographer, educator*
McAleese Dube, Eileen Marie *retired secondary school educator*
McBride, Mildred Maylea *retired elementary school educator*
McCabe, Linda Jean *elementary school educator*
McCann, Diana Rae *secondary school educator*
McCleary, William E(rnest) *retired school librarian, historian*
McCloy, Shirley *physical education educator*
McCormick, Heather N. *mathematics educator*
McCoy, Mary Jane *retired principal*
McDaniel, Sara Sherwood (Sally McDaniel) *trainer, consultant*
McGee, Harold Johnston *former academic administrator*
McGee, Jane Marie *retired elementary school educator*
McGowan, Susan *gifted and talented educator*
McHale, George T. *mathematics and computer science educator*
McIntyre, Virgie M. *retired elementary school educator*
McKendrick, John *director*
McKenna, Margaret Anne *former academic administrator*
McNamara, Brenda Norma *retired secondary school educator*
McSorley, Rita Elizabeth *adult education educator*
McTeer, Robert D., Jr. *former academic administrator, bank executive*
Mecham, Steven Ray *school system administrator*
Megna, Steve Allan *retired secondary school educator*
Melton, Emma Alexander *educational consultant, retired elementary school educator*
Mendoza, Karen Lynn *special education educator*
Menges, Martha *special education educator*
Mermelstein, Hope Leah *educational consultant*
Merriweather, Freda E. *education educator*
Metzler, Ruth Horton *genealogical educator*
Meyer, Frances Margaret Anthony *educational consultant*
Miller, Arjay *retired university dean*
Miller, Jerry Huber *retired university chancellor*
Miller, Linda Karen *retired secondary school educator, social studies educator, law educator*
Miller, Roberta Doris *elementary school educator*
Mills, Eugene Sumner *academic administrator*
Mills, Helene Audrey *retired education educator*
Mirk, Judy Ann *retired elementary school educator*
Mitchell, Lucille Anne *retired elementary school educator*
Moll, Maryann Elizabeth *education educator*
Monson, David Carl *school system administrator, state legislator, farmer*
Monteith, Larry King *chancellor emeritus*
Mooney, Michael Joseph *university professor*
Mooney, Thomas T. *history educator, geography educator*
Moore, Donald Walter *retired academic administrator*
Moore, Juel Ann *retired elementary school educator*
Moore, Thomas David *academic administrator*
Moore-Wleklinski, Patricia Marie *secondary school educator*
Moran, Thomas Harry *retired academic administrator*
Moran, Wendi K *biology educator*
Morgan, Arlene Notoro *university administrator*
Morgan, Mary Lou *retired education educator, volunteer*
Morgan, Ruth Prouse *academic administrator, educator*
Morley, James Everitt, Jr., (Jay Morley Jr.) *retired academic and educational association administrator*
Morrison, Rey Eileen *history educator, writer*
Mortensen-Say, Marlys *retired school system administrator*
Moulthrop, Rebecca Lee Stilphen *retired elementary school educator*
Mullen, Terri Ann *retired special education educator*
Musa, Samuel Albert *university executive*
Myers, Alison Kay *assistant principal*
Myers, Michele Tolela *former academic administrator*
Nadelman, Martin Hershel *college president*
Nagy, Donna M. *dean, law educator*
Nahmias, Maria Lynn *education educator*
Nance, Mary Joe *retired secondary school educator*
Ndura, Elavie *literature and language educator*
Neal, Dennis Melton *elementary school educator*
Nelsen, William Cameron *educational consultant*
Nelson, Carol Evelyn *retired pre-school educator*
Neunzig, Carolyn Miller *elementary, middle and high school educator*
New, Rosetta Holbrock *retired secondary school educator, retired department chairman, retired nutrition consultant*
Nguyen, Tuan *physics educator*
Nichols, Dennis Witt *rector*
Nielsen, Sue M. *elementary school educator*
Nixon, Sandra L. *retired registrar*
Noddings, Nel *education educator, writer*
Norris, Meredith Somerville *educator*
Nye, Linda Purcell *secondary school educator*
Oates, Thomas R. *former university executive*
O'Connell, William Raymond, Jr. *educational consultant, retired academic administrator*
O'Connor, Patrick John *education educator*
Offen, Ronald Charles *retired school librarian*
Ofstad, Evelyn Larsen Boyl *retired primary school educator, radio personality, film producer*
Oglesby, Elaine Sue *elementary school educator*
Ohberg, Pamela Anderson *retired high school drama educator*
Omtvedt, Irvin Thomas *academic administrator, educator*
O'Rangers, Eleanor Ann *medical education company executive*
Orr, Kenneth Bradley *academic administrator*
Outt, Helen May *retired elementary school educator, psychologist*
Outten, Kristina Marie *secondary school educator*
Pacheco, Manuel Trinidad *retired academic administrator*
Page, Amanda Lee *secondary school educator*
Page, Barbara Rose *primary school educator*
Palmer, Irene Sabelberg *retired dean, retired nursing educator, genealogist*
Paris-De Monte, Ileana M. *assistant principal*
Parisi, Valerie Marie *former dean, medical educator*
Park, John Thornton *retired academic administrator*
Parmenter, Kelli Denise *middle school educator, small business owner*
Parsons, Alexandra Clare *literature and language educator*
Pasupathy, Kalyan Sunder *education educator, consultant*
Patrick, Brenda Jean *educational consultant*
Patrick, Pauline Margaret *secondary school educator*
Pattillo, Manning Mason Calvert *academic administrator*
Patton, Kassie (Kathleen Moroney Patton) *former principal, director*
Paulsen, Frank Robert *college dean emeritus*
Paxton, J. Willene *retired academic administrator*
Payne, Ladell *retired academic administrator*
Pearce, Jody Ann *mathematics educator*
Pease-Pretty On Top, Janine B. *community college administrator*
Peck, Ernest James, Jr. *academic administrator*
Peduzzi, Claudia Claire *elementary school educator*
Pelikan, Donna Mae *retired secondary school educator*
Pencola, Annamaria Regina *elementary school educator*
Peoples, John Arthur, Jr. *former university president, consultant*
Peper, Charlotte Ann *educational consultant*
Perger, Donna Spagnoli *retired secondary school mathematics educator*
Perkins, Edward A., Jr. *secondary school educator*
Perkins, Samuel Swenson *education educator*

Perkner, Stanislav academic administrator, educator
Pescatore-Shirey, Hope Jean middle school reading educator
Peterson, Walter Fritiof retired academic administrator
Petit-Phare, Vanessa secondary school educator
Pettigrew, L. Eudora retired academic administrator
Pewitt, James Dudley retired academic administrator
Pfeifer, Edward C. secondary school educator
Pfennig, Dennis Joseph secondary school educator
Phelps, Bonnie Noreen retired secondary school educator
Phillips, Richard A. retired literature and language educator
Phillips, Tikera Monique elementary school educator
Philson, Richard Michael academic administrator
Phipard, Nancy Midwood retired special education educator, poet
Pierce, Susan Resneck academic administrator, literature educator, consultant
Pifer, Scott Thomas mathematics educator
Pinto, Rosalind retired secondary school educator, volunteer
Pitts, Allie Faye retired elementary school educator
Plants, Walter Dale retired elementary school educator, minister
Platis, James George secondary school educator
Polimeni, Rebecca H. special education educator
Pollack, Marsha secondary school educator
Ponitz, David H. former academic administrator
Power Anderson, Vanessa L. dean
Preer, Joan C. retired assistant principal, retired science educator
Price, Jason Todd director
Pritchard, Claudius Hornby, Jr. retired university president
Prokasy, William Frederick academic administrator
Propst, Harold Dean retired academic administrator
Pruitt, Anne Loring academic administrator, education educator
Pryor, Harold S. retired college president
Pulhamus, Marlene Louise retired elementary school educator
Puryear, James Burton college administrator
Query, Lois A. elementary school educator
Quinn Trank, Christine education educator
Quinonez, Tasha Marie elementary school educator
Quist, Roxanne Genevieve middle school teacher
Rabideau, Marilyn Ann elementary school educator
Rago, Dorothy Ashton retired elementary school educator
Ragone, David Vincent former university president
Ragsdale, Sandra Russell special education educator
Ramirez, Evangeline Rose elementary school educator
Ratterree, John Eric academic administrator
Ray, Susan Elaine principal
Reams, Patricia Lynn retired elementary school educator
Redmont, Bernard Sidney dean, communications educator
Reed, Leon Samuel secondary school educator, photographer
Reed, Susan J. elementary school educator
Reeves, Lucy Mary retired elementary school educator
Regel, Teresa Diamond elementary school educator
Rehnke, Mary Ann academic administrator
Reid, Helen Veronica provost
Reinke, Ralph Louis retired academic administrator
Remes, Robin Eva secondary school educator, cartographer
Rempt, Rodney P. retired academic administrator, career military officer
Rent, Clyda Stokes academic administrator
Reynolds, Karen Ann retired elementary school educator
Rice, Gary Russell retired special education educator
Rice, Patricia Oppenheim Levin retired special education educator, consultant
Richardson, Edward R. former academic administrator
Ricketson, Mary E. former dean, lawyer
Ridge, Davy-Jo Stribling retired school librarian
Ridout, Susan Ramp education educator
Rief, Michelle M. cultural studies educator
Rigg, Lyle D. headmaster
Riggio, Kerry Kerstin elementary school worker, researcher
Roaden, Arliss Lloyd retired academic administrator
Roberts, Kathleen Mary retired school system administrator
Roberts, Patricia Lee education educator
Robertson, Wyndham Gay university official, journalist
Robinson, James Alfred middle school educator
Robles, Rosalie Miranda elementary school educator
Rochelle, Lugenia academic administrator
Rodgers, Lois Eve secondary school educator
Rogers, Dorothea May education educator
Rojas, Victor Hugo Macedo retired vocational education educator
Roller, Pamela Jo elementary school educator
Roman, Alfred Victor science education educator
Romano, Louis George education educator
Romer, Roy R. retired school system administrator, former governor
Rosenberg, Raymond David special education educator, consultant
Rosenblum, Estelle H. retired dean, nursing educator
Rosenthal, Michael Ross academic administrator, consultant
Ross, Leonard Lester retired academic administrator
Roth, Paul Barry dean, educator, emergency medicine physician
Rottenstein, Jessica Brooke biology educator, earth science educator, researcher
Rowe, Ernest Ras education educator, academic administrator
Rowell, Barbara Caballero retired academic administrator
Rowley, Maxine Lewis education educator, retired academic administrator
Rubin, Ellen education/access consultant
Rubino, Stephen John secondary school educator
Russell, Florence L. elementary school educator
Rutgard, Lorraine Levin hearing impaired educator
Ryan, Daniel John university administrator
Saenz, Cecilia Sonia education educator
Saenz, Silvia Patricia special education educator
Salapatek, John (John Franklin) literature and language educator, writer
Salisbury, Micheal Wayne education educator
Samblis, Kelley C. educator, researcher
Samec, Diane Patricia retired elementary school educator
Sampson, Donna Rene mathematics educator
Sanchez, Alita Cassandra physical education educator, personal trainer
Sandwell, Kristin Ann special education educator
Santora, Ellen Durrigan education educator
Santos, Nicole Marie elementary school educator
Saul, Mark E. secondary school educator, consultant
Saunders, James Allen secondary school educator
Sava, Vasyl education educator
Savage, Kim I. academic administrator
Savercool, Susan Elisabeth elementary school educator
Sayre, Donna elementary school educator
Scandary, E. Jane special education educator, consultant
Scarborough, Ann Barlow secondary school educator
Schiller, Robert E. former school system administrator
Schmidly, David J. academic administrator, biology professor
Schmidt, Hans R. retired history educator
Schmidt, L. Lee, Jr. retired university official
Schmidt, Ruth Ann retired academic administrator
Schneider, Carolyn Alice Brauch elementary school educator
Schneider, Mary Louise retired elementary school educator
Schowalter, William Raymond college dean, educator
Schrage, Rose retired academic administrator
Schumacher, Cynthia Jo retired elementary and secondary education educator
Schumann, Nicholas M. elementary school educator
Schuster, Carol Joyce special education educator, consultant
Schwartz, Eleanor Brantley academic administrator
Scott, Gloria Randle former college president
Seligman, Joel academic administrator
Sell, LeeLou retired elementary school educator
Semple, Susan early childhood educator
Shah, Y. T. academic administrator
Shavender, Marilyn Faye retired elementary school educator
Shaw, David Robert secondary school educator, theater director
Shearer, Charles Livingston academic administrator
Shellman-Lucas, Elizabeth C. special education educator, researcher
Shepard, Christy J. special education educator
Shepard, Sara Lynette elementary school educator
Sherpa, Donna M. history educator
Sherrer, Charles David dean, clergyman
Shields, Cynthia Rose college administrator
Shields, Portia Holmes former academic administrator
Shore, Eleanor Gossard retired medical school dean
Shoun, Ellen Llewellyn retired secondary school educator
Shultz, Stephen A. secondary school educator
Shutler, Mary Elizabeth retired academic administrator
Sibo, Elsa Lynette secondary school educator
Siddeeq, Baiyinah Nawal Rubye secondary school educator
Silianoff, David secondary school educator, educator, mathematics educator
Simmonds, Robert Maurer education educator
Simmons, Lynda Merrill Mills retired principal
Simon, John Douglas academic administrator
Simons, Lynn Osborn educational consultant
Singleton, Robert Culton academic administrator, theology studies educator
Skaggs, Bebe Rebecca Patten college dean, clergywoman
Smith, Michelle Rene elementary school educator
Smith, Patricia (Pat) Ann elementary school educator
Solmssen, Peter retired academic administrator
Solomon, Elizabeth Ann mathematics educator
Sonnenschein, Hugo Freund academic administrator, writer, economist, educator
Sorber, Charles Arthur academic administrator
Sottile, Joseph James elementary school educator, poet
Sparks, Barbara Ann adult education educator, educational consultant, researcher
Spear, Peter D. retired academic administrator
Spencer, Lisa Ann special education educator
Spencer, Rex LeRoy retired secondary school educator
Spencer, Stephanie mathematics educator, director
Springer, Marlene retired academic administrator
Stafford, Rebecca retired academic administrator, sociologist, consultant
Stalker, Jacqueline D'Aoust academic administrator, educator
Stalnaker, Judith Ann education educator
Stamoolis, James John academic administrator, educator
Stanton, William F. retired elementary school educator, retail executive
Stark, Joan Scism education educator
Stasek, Lorraine Anne elementary school educator
Steinmiller, Janet L. literature and language educator
Stellar, Arthur Wayne school system administrator
Stephens, Norris Lynn school librarian
Stevens, Lori Ann LaBeau school librarian, educator
Stewart, John Wray Black college dean
Stewart, Lucille Marie retired special education coordinator, educator
Stiller, Stephen Joseph mathematics educator
Stomfay-Stitz, Aline Maria education educator
Suders, Joan Mary elementary school educator
Sullivan, Charles dean, educator, author
Sutro, Edmund J. secondary school educator, consultant
Sutton-Creech, Donna Lynn gifted and talented educator
Swager, Cleo Marie secondary school educator
Swailes, William E. counseling administrator
Swoap, Thomas Frank, Jr. history educator
Syverud, Kent Douglas dean, law educator
Szelenyi, Ivan adult education educator
Tackett, Stephen Douglas retired education services specialist
Talis, Esther R. educator, writer
Tanner, Laurel Nan education educator
Tarbi, William Rheinlander secondary education curriculum consultant, researcher
Tatum, Valorie elementary school educator, pharmacist
Tavalin, Fern educational consultant
Taylor Claud, Andrea retired educational consultant
Templeman, Lydia retired assistant principal
Tenenbaum, Inez Moore former school system administrator
TenHoeve, Thomas academic administrator
Terrell, Hellenna L. education educator
Terry, Edwin Wellington college librarian
Thomas, Beverly Irene special education educator, counseling administrator, educational diagnostician
Thomas, Brooke C. assistant principal
Thoreen, Mary Louise elementary school educator, consultant
Thornell, Patricia L. elementary school educator
Thueme, William Harold secondary school educator, counselor, travel coordinator
Tidmore, Bryce William retired secondary school educator
Timmons, Sharon L. retired elementary school educator
Tlou, Josiah S. education educator
Tompkins, Ellen Beth retired elementary school educator, consultant
Tonjes, Marian Jeannette Benton education educator
Tottori, Daichi academic and trade association administrator, accountant, lawyer
Touhill, Blanche Marie retired academic administrator, historian, educator
Towler, Evelyn Wheeler retired elementary school educator
Trachsel, Richard Keith principal, educator
Tramonte, Michael Robert education educator
Trebon, Thomas academic administrator
Treible, Kirk retired academic and foundation administrator
Trolliet, Donna Jean retired elementary school educator
Trusdell, Mary Louise Cantrell retired academic administrator
Tuitele, Lui retired school system administrator
Tunheim, Jerald Arden academic administrator, physicist, educator
Turnau, Vivian Williamson retired literature and language educator
Turnbull, Vernona Harmsen retired education educator, counseling administrator
Tzekova, Krassimira Krusteva resident director
Uehling, Barbara Staner academic administrator
Utter, Robert French dean, retired judge
Vagt, Robert F. former academic administrator
Vail, Nancy L. Scott retired elementary school educator, artist
Valentine, Phyllis Louise counseling administrator
VanBuren, Carolyn Jean special education educator
Van Patten, James Jeffers education educator
Verma, Surjit Kumar retired school system administrator
Voitier, Doris school system administrator
Volpe, Edmond L(oris) retired college president
Vonderhaar, Steven Paul counseling administrator
Wade, June Booth secondary school educator
Wagner, Anthony E. academic administrator, former state official
Wagner, Cheryl Jean elementary school educator
Wahl, Donald J. counseling administrator
Waldrep, B. Dwain education educator
Walker, Annette retired counseling administrator
Walker, Carolyn Mae retired secondary school educator
Walker, Donald Barclay retired criminal justice educator, consultant, researcher, writer
Walker, Pamela mathematics educator
Wallace, Ardelia Leslene elementary school educator
Wallace, Arthur, Jr. retired college dean
Waller, Eunice McLean retired elementary school educator
Walsh, Diana Chapman former academic administrator, sociologist, educator
Walsh, Russell W. director tutorial services
Wan, Guofang education professor
Wang, Fen adult education educator, researcher
Wang, Xiubin transportation educator
Warcken, Nancy B. elementary school educator
Warder, Richard Currey, Jr. dean, mechanical aerospace engineering educator
Ware, Gwendolyn C. retired counseling administrator
Warian, Christine Barbara elementary school educator
Warman, Linda K. retired secondary school educator
Warshaw, Carole Klein retired education educator
Washington, Michele educational consultant
Watrous, Robert Thomas academic director
Watson, Patricia Pullums school system administrator
Watts, Mary Ann retired elementary school educator
Weeks, Lori D. elementary school educator
Wehn, Karen Swaney education educator, consultant
Weinshall, Iris academic administrator
Wenger, James L. education educator
Wentworth, LaVerne Wellborn curriculum consultant
Westergard, Sue Benzel elementary education educator
Wetherell, Albert A. secondary school educator
Wheeler, David Laurie university dean
Whitaker, Bruce Ezell college president
White, Dawn Marie elementary school educator
White, Florence May retired special education educator
White, John Wesley, Jr. retired academic administrator
White, Lonnie Joe retired history educator
White, Pamela Jo elementary school educator
Whittington-Brown, Vanessa Elizabeth secondary school educator
Wiggins, Samuel Paul education educator
Wilkening, Laurel Lynn academic administrator, aerospace scientist
Williams, Lisa A. special education educator
Williams, Patricia Badia retired counseling administrator
Williams, Robert Sanders (Sandy Williams) dean, academic administrator, educator, researcher
Williams, Thelma B. retired principal
Willis, Solomon Lee mathematics educator
Willison, Bruce Gray dean
Wills, J. Robert retired academic administrator, theater educator, writer
Wilson, Carolyn Ross retired school system administrator
Wilson, Cheryl Yvonne elementary and secondary school educator
Wilson, Robin Scott retired academic administrator, writer
Wilson, Wendy Marie elementary school educator, consultant
Wimmer, Kathryn retired elementary school educator
Winter, Jeffrey B. elementary school educator
Winter-Neighbors, Gwen Carole special education and art educator, consultant
Winterstein, James Fredrick academic administrator
Wiseman, Douglas Carl education educator, department chairman, dean
Wittich, John Jacob retired academic administrator, finance company executive
Wood, Janis Louise retired assistant principal
Woodsworth, Anne retired academic administrator, librarian
Woolworth, Susan Valk primary school educator
Wright, Douglas Tyndall former university administrator
Wright, Frances Mary principal
Xia, Yusen education educator
Yandle, Stephen Thomas dean
Yohe, Harry Edward, Jr. special education educator
York, Herbert Frank university official
Young, Charles Edward former academic administrator
Young, Gail Diane secondary school educator
Young, Ruth Brooks retired elementary school educator
Young, Teresa Gail Hilger retired adult education educator
Youngblood, Sandra Lea retired secondary school educator
Youngs, Diane Campfield learning disabilities specialist, educator
Zacharias, Donald Wayne retired academic administrator
Zachary, Je'Quita Yvette elementary school educator, singer
Zahner Kraeft, Dorothy Simkin retired elementary school educator, school librarian
Zatsiorsky, Vladimir Moiseevich (Michailovich) biomechanics educator, researcher
Zdanis, Richard Albert academic administrator
Zilbert, Allen Bruce education educator, computer scientist, consultant
Zinser, Elisabeth Ann former academic administrator

Zufryden, Fred S. *academic administrator, finance educator, researcher*

ENGINEERING

UNITED STATES

ALABAMA

Auburn
Agrawal, Prathima *engineering educator*
Cochran, John Euell, Jr. *aerospace engineer, educator, lawyer*
Hanley, Thomas Richard *engineering educator*
Irwin, John David *electrical engineering educator*
Jaeger, Richard Charles *electrical engineer, educator, science association director*
Sforzini, Richard Henry *aerospace engineer, educator*
Srivastava, Puneet *engineering educator, researcher*

Auburn University
Eden, Mario Richard *engineering educator*
Jackson, Robert Lee *mechanical engineer, educator*

Birmingham
Ayasoufi, Anahita *engineer, researcher*
Goldman, Jay *industrial engineer, educator, dean emeritus*
Goodrich, Thomas Michael *engineering and construction executive, lawyer*
Jo, Young Gyun *nuclear engineer*
Nash, David J. *engineering and construction company executive, retired military officer*
Potter, John Leith *retired mechanical and aerospace engineer, retired educator, consultant*
Sisiopiku, Virginia P. *civil engineer*

Daphne
Jeffreys, Elystan Geoffrey *petroleum consultant*

Decatur
Smith, Troy Alvin *aerospace research engineer*

Florence
Badger, Phillip Charles *agricultural engineer*

Huntsville
Bendickson, Marcus J. *engineering company executive*
Daussman, Grover Frederick *electrical engineer, consultant*
Hunter, Herbert Erwin *aerospace engineer*
King, David A. *aerospace engineer*
Morgan, John Derald, Sr. *electrical engineer, educator, writer, researcher*
Ooi, Teng Keong *aerospace and mechanical engineer, educator*
Pittman, William Claude *electrical engineer*
Sackheim, Robert Lewis *aerospace engineer, educator*
Watson, Raymond Coke, Jr. *engineering executive, consultant, academic administrator*
Wieland, Paul Otto *environmental control systems engineer*

Loachapoka
Schafer, Robert Louis *agricultural engineer, researcher*

Madison
Dannenberg, Konrad K. *aeronautical engineer*
Emerson, William Kary *engineering company executive*

Mobile
Clarke, Charles Kendall *metallurgical engineer, consultant*
Hamid, Michael *electrical engineering educator, consultant*
Islam, Samantha *civil engineer, researcher*

Salem
Gibbons, Dona Alden Coe *electrical engineer, director*

Somerville
Johnson, Loyd *agricultural engineer, researcher*

Spanish Fort
van Aken, John Henry *retired marine engineer*

Thomasville
Davis, Gene *retired civil engineer*

Tuscaloosa
Barfield, Robert F. *mechanical engineer, educator, retired dean*
Moynihan, Gary Peter *industrial engineering educator*
Ray, Paul Sukhamay *engineering educator, researcher*

Tuskegee
Abu-elenin, Sherif Mohamed *electrical engineer, educator*
Egiebor, Nosa O. *engineering educator, consultant*

ALASKA

Chugiak
Mandell, Gordon Keith *aerospace engineer*

Fairbanks
Lin, Chuen-Sen *mechanical engineer, educator*

ARIZONA

Cave Creek
Collins, Jack Adam *mechanical engineer*

Chandler
Bailey, Gregory Emmett *systems engineer*
Braunisch, Henning *electronics engineer, researcher*
Chang, Je-Young *electronics engineer*
Fordemwalt, James Newton *microelectronics engineering educator, consultant*
Janakiram, Mani *manufacturing engineer*
Wang, Jinlin *chemical engineer*

Glendale
Bai, Haowei *aerospace engineer, aerospace scientist*

Hereford
Hirth, John Price *metallurgical engineering educator*

Lake Havasu City
Hurt, Nathan Hampton, Jr. *mechanical engineer*

Mesa
Rummel, Robert Wiland *aeronautical engineer, writer*
Singhal, Avinash Chandra *engineering administrator, educator*

Paradise Valley
Russell, Paul Edgar *electrical engineering educator*

Phoenix
Aksoy, Hakan *mechanical engineer*
Freyermuth, Clifford L. *structural engineering consultant*
Fullmer, Steven Mark *engineering executive*
Lindeman, Richard Russell *electronics engineer*
Miller, Michael Jon *survey engineer*
Sochacki, Andrzej *mechanical engineer, researcher, tourism educator*

Prescott
Bieniawski, Zdzislaw Tadeusz Richard *engineering educator, writer, consultant*
Chesson, Eugene *retired civil engineering educator, consultant, volunteer*
Kahne, Stephen James *systems engineering educator, engineering company executive, academic administrator*

Scottsdale
Ballinger, Charles William *sanitary engineer, consultant*
Gookin, Thomas Allen Jaudon *civil engineer*

Sonoita
Coates, Wayne Evan *agricultural engineer*

Sun City
Davies, Percy (Pete) Charles *mechanical engineer*

Sun City West
Brown, Ruth Geisler *retired electronics engineer*

Tempe
Balanis, Constantine Apostle *electrical engineering educator*
Berman, Neil Sheldon *retired chemical engineering professor*
Carpenter, Ray Warren *engineering educator, materials engineer*
Chiriac, Victor Adrian *aerospace engineer, researcher*
Crouch, Peter E. *engineering educator*
Farmer, Richard G. *engineering educator*
Ferry, David Keane *electrical engineering educator*
Harris, Warren Lynn *computer engineer*
Jang, Jin-Wook *electronics engineer*
Karády, George György *electrical engineering educator, consultant*
Mahajan, Subhash *electronic materials educator*
Si, Jennie *engineering educator*
Tsakalis, Konstantinos *electrical engineer, educator*
Vittal, Vijay *electrical engineer, educator*

Tucson
Arnell, Walter James William *engineering educator, consultant*
Brunton, Daniel William *mechanical engineer*
Gaither, William Samuel *civil engineering executive, consultant*
Harrington, Roger Fuller *electrical engineering educator, consultant*
Kececioglu, Dimitri Basil *reliability engineering educator, consultant*
Kerwin, William James *electrical engineering educator, consultant*
Kohloss, Frederick Henry *retired engineer*
Mense, Allan Tate *research and development engineering executive*
Ogilvie, T(homas) Francis *marine engineering educator*
Peterson, Thomas W. *engineering educator*
Riley, Mark Richard *biochemical engineer, educator*
Slack, Donald Carl *agricultural engineer, educator*
Smerdon, Ernest Thomas *engineering educator*
Venkata, Subrahmanyam Saraswati *engineering educator, researcher*
Wyant, James Clair *engineering company executive, educator*
Yoon, Jeong-Yeol *biological engineer, educator*

ARKANSAS

Fayetteville
Bajwa, Sreekala G. *agricultural engineer, educator*

Gaddy, James Leoma *chemical engineer, educator*
Karim, Khursheed *engineering educator, researcher*

CALIFORNIA

Aliso Viejo
Steuert, Douglas Michael *engineering and construction management company executive*

Alpine
Roberts, Dwight Loren *engineering consultant, writer*

Altadena
Coles, Donald Earl *retired engineering educator*

Anaheim
McNulty, James Francis *engineering executive*
Watson, Oliver Lee III *aerospace engineer, manufacturing executive*

Arroyo Grande
Wobrock, Jesse Lucas *biomechanical engineer*

Atherton
Lowry, Larry *engineering company executive*

Berkeley
Bea, Robert G. *civil engineering educator*
Bell, Alexis T. *chemical engineer, educator*
Berger, Stanley Allan *mechanical and biomechanical engineering educator*
Birdsall, Charles Kennedy *electrical engineer*
Blanch, Harvey Warren *chemical engineering educator*
Bogy, David B(eauregard) *mechanical engineering educator*
Cairns, Elton James *chemical engineering professor*
Casey, James *engineering educator*
Derenzo, Stephen E. *electrical engineering and computer science educator, researcher*
Dharan, Hari *mechanical engineer, educator*
Dornfeld, David Alan *engineering educator*
Fenves, Gregory L. *engineering educator*
Frisch, Joseph *mechanical engineer, educator, consultant*
Fuerstenau, Douglas Winston *mineral engineering educator*
Garrison, William Louis *civil engineering educator*
Govindjee, Sanjay *engineering educator*
Hsu, Chieh Su *applied mechanics engineering educator, researcher*
Hu, Chenming *engineering educator*
Kastenberg, William Edward *engineering professor, former academic administrator*
King, Cary Judson III *chemical engineer, educator, academic administrator*
Kuh, Ernest Shiu-Jen *electrical engineering educator*
Leitmann, George *mechanical engineer, educator*
Lewis, Edwin Reynolds *biomedical engineering educator, academic administrator*
Liepmann, Dorian *engineering educator*
Ma, Fai *mechanical engineering educator*
Majumdar, Arunava *mechanical engineer, educator*
Monismith, Carl Leroy *civil engineering educator*
Muller, Richard Stephen *electrical engineer, educator*
Ott, David Michael *engineering company executive*
Pagni, Patrick John *mechanical engineering science educator, safety engineer, researcher*
Penzien, Joseph *structural engineering educator*
Pigford, Thomas Harrington *nuclear engineering educator*
Pister, Karl Stark *engineering educator*
Polak, Elijah *engineering educator, computer scientist*
Prausnitz, John Michael *chemical engineer, educator*
Sastry, Sosale Shankara *electrical engineer, computer scientist, educator*
Schultz, E. Eugene, Jr. *computer engineer, director*
Varaiya, Pravin P. *electrical engineer*
Wiegel, Robert Louis *consulting engineering executive*
Wright, Paul Kenneth *mechanical engineer, educator*
Yeung, Ronald Wai-Chun *engineering educator, researcher*

Berry Creek
Miller, Joseph Arthur *manufacturing engineer, consultant, educator*

Boonville
Hanes, John Ward *civil engineer, sculptor, rancher, director*

Brea
Brown, Ronald Malcolm *engineering corporation executive*

Buellton
Hashimoto, Tadao *engineering company executive*
Porter, Bruce Jackman *computer engineer, application developer, portfolio manager, civil engineer*

Campbell
Levy, Salomon *mechanical engineer*
Ross, Hugh Courtney *electrical engineer*

Carlsbad
Wilson, Donald Grey *engineering management consultant*

Carmel
Youngdahl, Paul Frederick *mechanical engineer*

Carmichael
Throner, Guy Charles, Jr. *aerospace engineering executive, scientist, inventor, consultant*

Carson
Mende, Howard Shigeharu *mechanical engineer*
Siegel, Neil Gilbert *computer engineer, consultant*

Chico
Allen, Charles William *mechanical engineer, educator*
Roth, Ronald Lee *engineering educator*

Claremont
Dym, Clive Lionel *engineering educator*
Molinder, John Irving *engineering educator, consultant*
Monson, James Edward *electrical engineer, educator*
Tanenbaum, Basil Samuel *engineering educator*

Clovis
Brahma, Chandra Sekhar *civil engineering educator*

Concord
Crandall, Ira Carlton *electrical engineer, consultant*
Hooper, Mark Scheller *electrical engineer, educator*

Costa Mesa
Brady, John Patrick, Jr. *electronics educator, consultant*
Sharpe, Constantine *engineer, consultant, mathematics professor*

Coto De Caza
Sheehy, Jerome Joseph *electrical engineer*

Covina
Paulson, Raymond Arnold *science engineering executive*

Culver City
Mann, Michael Martin *engineering executive*

Cupertino
Haskell, Barry Geoffry *computer engineer, researcher*

Davis
Al-Asaad, Hussain *electrical engineer, educator*
Bombardelli, Fabián Alejandro *hydraulic engineer, researcher*
Chancellor, William Joseph *agricultural engineering educator*
Cheney, James Addison *civil engineering educator*
Gates, Bruce Clark *chemical engineer, educator*
Lavernia, Enrique Jose *materials science and engineering educator*
Marino, Miguel Angel *engineering educator*
Tchobanoglous, George *civil engineering educator*
Wang, Shih-Ho *electrical engineer, educator*

Del Mar
Wilkinson, Eugene Parks *nuclear engineer, director*

El Segundo
Hsia, Irene Yee *electrical engineer*
Webb, Darryl Willard *systems engineer*

Emeryville
Chung, Caleb *inventor, toymaker, toy company executive*
Zwoyer, Eugene Milton *retired consulting engineering executive*

Encinitas
Deets, Dwain Aaron *retired aerospace technology executive*
Kim, Kyehee *environmental engineer, consultant*

Encino
Friedman, George Jerry *aerospace engineering executive*
Knuth, Eldon Luverne *engineering educator*

Fairfield
Edson, William Alden *retired electrical engineer, researcher*

Fallbrook
Harsha, Philip Thomas *retired aerospace engineer*

Folsom
Chowdhury, Ali Asraf *electrical engineer, researcher, director*
Ettlich, William F. *electrical engineer*

Fontana
Rainsberry, Patrick Ryan *engineer*

Fremont
Chao, Kwang-Chu *chemical engineer, educator*
Chen, Wai-Kai *electrical engineering and computer science educator, consultant*
Le, Thuy Trong *nuclear engineer, educator*
Monajemi, Pezhman *electrical engineer*
Pelton, Alan Roy *engineer, researcher, engineering educator*
Wu, James Chen-Yuan *aerospace engineering educator*

Fullerton
Rubin, Arthur Leonard *systems engineer, mathematician*

Glendale
Dallas, Saterios (Sam Dallas) *aerospace engineer, researcher, consultant*

Goleta
Sensiper, Samuel *electrical engineer*

Hacienda Heights
Love, Daniel Joseph *consulting engineer*

Huntington Beach
Leveton, Ian Sinclair *civil engineer*
Nguyen, Han Van *mechanical engineer*

Indian Wells
Jorgensen, Gordon David *retired engineering company executive*

Irvine
Alexopoulos, Nicolaos George *electrical engineering educator, dean*
Ang, Alfredo Hua-Sing *civil engineering educator*
Chelapati, Chunduri Venkata *civil engineering educator*
Mohraz, Ali *engineering educator*
Samueli, Henry *electrical engineer, educator, entrepreneur*
Schoendorfer, Donald W. *engineer*
Sirignano, William Alfonso *aerospace and mechanical engineer, educator*
Sklansky, Jack *electrical and computer engineering educator, researcher*
Stubberud, Allen Roger *electrical engineering educator*
Ting, Albert Chia *biomedical engineer, researcher*
Wickramasinghe, Hemantha Kumar *electrical engineer, physicist*

Kensington
Oppenheim, Antoni Kazimierz *mechanical engineer*

La Canada Flintridge
Macmillan, Robert Smith *electronics engineer*

La Jolla
Asbeck, Peter Michael *engineering educator*
Chang, William Shen Chie *electrical engineering educator*
Chien, Shu *physiology and bioengineering educator*
Fung, Yuan-Cheng Bertram *bioengineering educator, writer*
Gandhi, Tarak *computer engineer*
Karbhari, Vistasp M. *engineering educator, researcher*
Levy, Ralph *engineering executive, consultant*
Linden, Paul Fredrick *environmental engineer, educator*
Milstein, Laurence Bennett *electrical engineering educator, researcher*
Nahavandi, Amir Nezameddin *retired engineering firm executive*
Nemat-Nasser, Sia *engineering educator, researcher*
Palsson, Bernhard O. *engineering educator*
Penner, Stanford Sol *engineering educator*
Rudee, Mervyn Lea *engineering educator, researcher*
Schmid-Schoenbein, Geert Wilfried *biomedical engineer, educator*
Telengator, Alexander M. *engineer*

La Verne
Lou, Yiming *chemical engineer*

Lafayette
Krueger, Robert Edward *mechanical engineer, manufacturing executive*

Laguna Hills
Hammond, R. Philip *chemical engineer*

Lake Forest
Fahim, Amr *electrical engineer*
Schroeder, John A. *systems engineering consultant, educator*

Lancaster
Hodges, Vernon Wray *mechanical engineer*

Livermore
Goodwin, Bruce T. *engineer*
Hallquist, John O. *engineering company executive*
Johnson, Roy Ragnar *electrical engineer, researcher*
King, Ray John *electrical engineering educator, engineering company executive*

Lomita
Balcom, Orville *engineer*

Lompoc
Means, James Andrew *retired engineer*

Long Beach
Dillon, Michael Earl *mechanical engineering executive, educator*
Kumar, Rajendra *electrical engineering educator*
Sidhwa, Frank N. *engineering executive*
Wagdy, Mahmoud F. *engineering educator*

Los Alamitos
Eckelman, Richard Joel *engineering specialist*

Los Altos
Peterson, Victor Lowell *aerospace engineer, consultant*
Sharpe, Roland Leonard *structural engineer, consultant*

Los Altos Hills
Fondahl, John Walker *civil engineering educator*

Los Angeles
Abidi, Asad Ali *electrical engineer, educator*
Bendiksen, Oddvar Olav *aerospace engineer, educator*
Buffington, Gary Lee Roy *safety engineer, construction executive*
Chang, Jane P. *chemical engineering educator*
Cheng, Tsen-Chung *electrical engineering educator*
Chobotov, Vladimir Alexander *aerospace engineer, educator*
Chui, Chi On *electrical engineer, educator*
Crombie, Douglass Darnill *aerospace communications system engineer*
Danziger, Bruce Edward *structural engineer*
Dapkus, Paul D. *engineering educator*
Dhir, Vijay K. *mechanical engineering educator*
Didkovsky, Leonid V. *engineer*
Dorman, Albert A. *engineering executive, consultant, architect*
Estrin, Deborah Lynn *computer engineer, educator*
Fathpour, Sasan *optical engineer, researcher*
Garcia, Andrew Bernard *chemical engineer*
Hollander, Sidney *computer systems engineer*
Hovanessian, Shahen Alexander *electrical engineer, educator, consultant*
Itoh, Tatsuo *engineering educator*
Ju, Jiann-Wen (Woody Ju) *mechanics educator, researcher*
Ken, Susanto Suwarno *engineer*
Kim, Jeongbin John *mechanical engineering educator*
King-Ning, Tu *materials science and engineering educator*
Kuehl, Hans Henry *electrical engineering educator*
Madni, Asad Mohamed *engineering executive*
Marmarelis, Vasilis Zissis *engineering educator, writer, consultant*
Mataric, Maja J. *engineering educator*
Maxworthy, Tony *mechanical and aerospace engineering educator*
Mendel, Jerry Marc *electrical engineering educator*
Muntz, Eric Phillip *aerospace and mechanical engineering educator, consultant*
Newman, Richard G. *engineering company executive*
Nikias, Chrysostomos L. (Max Nikias) *engineering educator*
Nobe, Ken *chemical engineering professor*
Okrent, David *engineering educator*
O'Neill, Russell Richard *engineering educator*
Ozcan, Aydogan *electrical engineer, educator*
Parente, Robert Bruce *electrical engineer, consultant*
Perrine, Richard Leroy *environmental engineer, educator*
Ramo, Simon *retired engineering executive*
Reed, Irving Stoy *electrical engineer*
Robson, Glenn R. *engineering and design company executive*
Rubinstein, Moshe Fajwel *engineering educator*
Sadraie, Hamid Reza *civil engineer, researcher*
Safadi, M. Oussama *engineering educator*
Safonov, Michael George *electrical engineering educator, consultant*
Sahimi, Muhammad *engineering educator*
Scholtz, Robert Arno *electrical engineering educator*
Settles, F. Stan, Jr. *engineering educator, manufacturing executive*
Sewell, William George III *electronics engineer, writer*
Speyer, Jason Lee *aeronautical engineer, educator*
Swamikannu, Xavier *environmental engineer, state official*
Synolakis, Costas E. *engineering educator*
Udwadia, Firdaus Erach *engineering educator, consultant*
Wagner, Christian Nikolaus Johann *materials engineering educator*
Welch, Lloyd Richard *electrical and communications engineer, educator, consultant*
Willner, Alan Eli *electrical engineer, educator*
Wilson, Gary Thomas *engineering executive*
Yablonovitch, Eli *electrical engineering educator*
Yang, Bingen *mechanical engineering educator*
Yen, Teh Fu *civil and environmental engineering educator*

Los Gatos
Rosenheim, Donald Edwin *electrical engineer*
Saha, Samar Kanti *electronics engineer, educator*

Malibu
Bedrosian, Edward *retired electrical engineer*
Dominguez, Sylvia Margarita *electrical engineer, researcher*

Menlo Park
Cohen, Danny *computer engineer*
George, Dileep *electrical engineer*
Honey, Richard Churchill *retired electrical engineer*
Labiosa, William Bruce *civil engineer, researcher*
Levenson, Milton *chemical engineer, consultant*
McCarthy, Roger Lee *mechanical engineer*

Moffett Field
Sharma, Surendra Prasad *aerospace engineer, scientist*
Statler, Irving Carl *aerospace engineer*

Monarch Beach
Dougherty, Elmer Lloyd, Jr. *retired chemical engineering professor, consultant*

Monrovia
Edwards, Kenneth Neil *chemical engineering executive*
Pray, Ralph Emerson *metallurgical engineer*

Monterey
Butler, Jon Terry *computer engineering educator, researcher*

Mountain View
Chu, Wai C. *engineer, researcher*
Hoagland, Albert Smiley *electrical engineer, researcher*
Johnson, Conor Deane *mechanical engineer*

Murrieta
Geffe, Philip Reinhold *electrical engineer, consultant*

Newark
Shah, Haresh Chandulal *civil engineering educator*

Norco
Lu, Guiyang *electrical engineer, executive*

North Hollywood
de la Houssaye, Brette Angelo-Pepe *electrical engineer, researcher, educator*

Northridge
Bradshaw, Richard Rotherwood *engineering executive*
Kiddoo, Robert James *engineering service company executive*
Ro, Won Woo *engineering educator, researcher*
Torgow, Eugene N. *electrical engineer*

Oakland
Jaramillo, Carlos Alberto *civil engineer*
Lee, Low Kee *electronics engineer, consultant*
Schell, Farrel Loy *transportation engineer*

Occidental
Rumsey, Victor Henry *electrical engineering educator emeritus*

Oceanside
McLean, Arthur Frederick *mechanical engineer*
Yurist, Svetlan Joseph *mechanical engineer*

Palm Desert
Osborne, Bartley Porter, Jr. *aeronautical engineer*

Palmdale
Bevilaqua, Paul M. *aeronautical engineer*
Farr, Donald Eugene *engineering scientist*

Palo Alto
Brown, David Randolph *electrical engineer*
Diffie, Whitfield (Whit) *computer and communications engineer*
Hodge, Philip Gibson, Jr. *mechanical and aerospace engineering educator*
Kapoor, Ashok Kumar *engineer*
Keshavarzian, Abtin *electrical engineer, researcher*
Kim, Wan Hee *engineering educator*
Moll, John Lewis *retired electronics engineer*
Quate, Calvin Forrest *engineering educator*
Schafer, Ronald William *electrical engineering educator*
Taylor, John Joseph *nuclear engineer, researcher*

Palos Verdes Estates
Abbott, A. Dwight *retired astronautical engineer*
Raue, Jorg Emil *electrical engineer*
Seide, Paul *civil engineering educator*
Yarbrough, Allyson Debra *electrical engineer*

Palos Verdes Peninsula
Denke, Paul Herman *retired aircraft engineer*
Mirels, Harold *aerospace engineer*

Pasadena
Breckinridge, James Bernard *optical engineer*
Bridges, William Bruce *electrical engineer, educator, researcher*
Culick, Fred Ellsworth Clow *engineering and physics professor*
Davis, Mark E. *chemical engineering educator*
Elachi, Charles *aerospace engineer*
Flagan, Richard Charles *chemical engineering educator*
Gould, Roy Walter *engineering educator*
Hilbert, Robert S(aul) *optical engineer*
Hornung, Hans Georg *aeronautical engineering educator, science administrator*
Jennings, Paul Christian *civil engineering educator, academic administrator*
List, Ericson John *environmental engineering science educator, consultant*
Martin, Craig Lee *engineering company executive*
Muñoz Fernández, Michela *electrical engineer, researcher*
Murray, Richard M. *engineering educator*
Ortiz, Michael *engineering educator*
Phillips, Robert *engineering educator, researcher*
Poon, Peter Tin-Yau *engineer, physicist*
Roshko, Anatol *aeronautical engineer*
Sabersky, Rolf Heinrich *mechanical engineer*
Seinfeld, John Hersh *chemical engineering professor*
Sharif, Masoud *electrical engineer, researcher*
Shimada, Katsunori *retired electrical engineer*
Sidick, Erkin *optical engineer*
Smith, Michael Robert *electro-optical engineer, physicist*
Stroupe, Ashley W. *engineer*
Wood, Lincoln Jackson *aerospace engineer*
Yariv, Amnon *electrical engineering educator, research scientist*

Pauma Valley
Fitzgerald, Shane Michael *engineer*

Pinole
Emmanuel, Jorge Agustin *chemical engineer, environmental consultant*

Playa Del Rey
Raymer, Daniel P. *aeronautical engineering company executive, aeronautical engineer*
Weir, Alexander, Jr. *chemical engineer, consultant*

Pleasanton
Novak, Randi Ruth *systems engineer, computer scientist*
Shaw, Charles Alden *engineering executive*
Van Dreser, Merton Lawrence *ceramics engineer*

Pomona
Teague, Lavette Cox, Jr. *systems educator, consultant*
Tomiyasu, Kiyo *retired consulting engineer*

Rancho Cucamonga
Alvarez, Tirso Reyes, Jr. *engineer*

Rancho Mirage
Kramer, Gordon *mechanical engineer*

Rancho Palos Verdes
Frassinelli, Guido Joseph *retired aerospace engineer*

Redondo Beach
Brodsky, Robert Fox *aerospace engineer, educator, author*

Richmond
O'Rear, Dennis John *chemical engineer, consultant*

Riverside
Balandin, Alexander A. *electrical engineer, educator*
Beni, Gerardo *electrical engineer, educator*

Rolling Hills Estates
Wong, Sun Yet *engineer, consultant*

Running Springs
Liddle, Sidney George *retired mechanical engineer, researcher*

Sacramento
Crimmins, Philip Patrick *retired metallurgical engineer, lawyer*
Duan, Lian *civil engineer*
Forsyth, Raymond Arthur *civil engineer, consultant*
Ghuzlan, Khalid A. *civil engineer*
Lathi, Bhagawandas Pannalal *retired electrical engineering educator*
Unde, Madhavji Anant (Mark Unde) *engineering executive*

Salinas
Newberry, Conrad Floyde *aerospace engineering educator*

San Carlos
Symons, Robert Spencer *electronics engineer*

San Diego
Anderson, Karl Richard *aerospace engineer, consultant*
Anderson, Paul Maurice *electrical engineering educator, researcher, consultant*
Auld, Robert Henry, Jr. *biomedical engineer, educator, consultant, writer*
Conly, John Franklin *retired engineering educator*
Dahlberg, Kenneth C. *engineering executive*
Dean, Richard Anthony *mechanical engineering executive*
De Angelis, Flavio *electrical engineer, researcher*
Forster, Geoffrey Peter *engineering executive*
Friedman, Arthur Daniel *electrical engineer, computer scientist, investment company executive, educator*
Gupta, Madhu Sudan *electrical engineering educator*
Inoue, Michael Shigeru *industrial and electrical engineer*
Jing, Zhigang *electrical engineer*
Larson, Arvid Gunnar *electrical engineer*
Lieber, Richard Louis *biomedical engineering scientist, educator*
Plotkin, Allen *aerospace engineer, educator*
Rowson, Sebastian *engineering executive*
Ruane, James Edward, Jr. *engineering executive*
Schmidt, Thomas Charles *biomedical engineer, researcher*
Sell, Robert Emerson *electrical engineer*
Slate, John Butler *biomedical engineer*
Tricoles, Gus Peter *electrical engineer, physicist, consultant*
Ward, Charles Raymond *systems engineer*

San Francisco
Abramson, Norman *retired engineering educator, electronics executive*
Bechtel, Riley Peart *engineering company executive*
Bechtel, Stephen Davison, Jr. *retired engineering company executive*
Dolby, Ray Milton *electrical engineer, company executive*
Granik, Vladimir *mechanic engineering educator, researcher*
Koffel, Martin M. *engineering company executive*
Koutsoftas, Demetrious Charles *geotechnical engineering consultant*
Lee, Samuel Sangwon *civil engineer, environmental engineer, agricultural engineer*
Merrick, Fred Harold *retired marine engineer*
Shushkewich, Kenneth Wayne *structural engineer*
Tang, Man-Chung *civil engineer, company executive*
Uyehara, Otto Arthur *mechanical engineering educator emeritus, consultant*

San Gabriel
Shao, Zhenhua *electrical engineer, consultant*

San Jose
Dennison, Ronald Walton *engineer*
Gill, Hardayal Singh *electrical engineer*
Hung, Donald Lu-Cheng *electrical engineer, computer engineer, educator*
Kim, Young-Hoon *systems engineer, researcher*
Markle, David A. *optical engineer*
Ngo, Chiu Y. *electrical engineer*
Pham, Christopher Hoang *electrical engineer, educator*
Rosenblum, Frank Michael *civil engineer, consultant, surveyor*
Tretz, Christophe Robert *electrical engineer*
Zheng, Min *engineer*

San Luis Obispo
Anderson, Warren Ronald *electrical engineering educator*
Lo, ChienKuo *engineering educator*

San Luis Rey
Melbourne, Robert Ernest *civil engineer*

San Marcos
Purdy, Alan Harris *biomedical engineer*

San Pedro
Ellis, George Edwin, Jr. *chemical engineer*
McCarty, Frederick Briggs *electrical engineer, consultant*
Simmons, William *retired aerospace engineer, research and development company executive*

San Rafael
Douglas, James *construction engineering educator*

Sand City
Coile, Russell Cleven *electrical engineer, consultant*

Santa Ana
Amoroso, Frank *retired communication system engineer, consultant*
Dean, William Evans *aerospace engineer, engineering company executive, consultant*
Kelly, James Patrick, Jr. *retired engineering executive*

Santa Barbara
Bowers, John Edwards *engineering educator*
Coldren, Larry Allen *electrical engineering educator, consultant*
Crispin, James Hewes *engineering and construction company executive*
Fredrickson, Glenn Harold *chemical engineering and materials educator*
Homsy, George *mechanical and chemical engineer, educator*
Hong, Dongwoo *electrical engineer*
Kokotovic, Petar V. *electrical and computer engineering educator*
Kramer, Edward John *materials engineering educator*
Kroemer, Herbert *electrical engineering educator*
Lawrance, Charles Holway *retired civil and sanitary engineer*
Lick, Wilbert James *mechanical engineering educator*
McMeeking, Robert Maxwell *mechanical engineer, educator*
Mitra, Sanjit Kumar *electrical and computer engineering educator*
Nakamura, Shuji *engineering educator*
Tirrell, Matthew V. *engineering educator*
Wade, Glen *electrical engineer, educator*

Santa Clara
Chan, Shu-Park *electrical engineering educator*
Congistre, John Huber *electronics engineer, retired military officer*
Dobberphul, Daniel *engineering company executive*
Kamal, Abu Hena M. *electrical engineer, researcher*
Medepalli, Kamesh *engineer, researcher, educator*
Mukherjee, Sayandev *electrical engineer, researcher*
Parden, Robert James *engineering educator, management consultant*
Roknaldin, Farzam *mechanical engineer, educator*
Roy, Abhra *plasma engineer, researcher*
Wang, Min *electronics engineer*

Santa Cruz
Kang, Sung-Mo (Steve Kang) *electrical engineering educator*
Rabus, Dominik Gerhard *electrical engineer, researcher*
Sadjadpour, Hamid Reza *engineering educator*
Varma, Anujan *computer engineer, educator*
Wiberg, Donald Martin *electrical engineering educator, consultant*

Santa Monica
Gritton, Eugene Charles *nuclear engineer, director*
Kayton, Myron *engineering company executive*
Sherman, Zachary *civil engineer, aerospace engineer, consultant*
Tito, Dennis Anthony *former aerospace engineer, financial advisor*

Santa Rosa
Grundy, Richard David *engineer*

Seal Beach
Matz, Sean Cormick *electrical engineer*
Whelan, David A. *engineering executive*

Sebastopol
Norman, Arnold McCallum, Jr. *engineer*

Sonoma
Muchmore, Robert Boyer *engineering executive, consultant*
Sasaki, Y(asunaga) Tito *engineering executive*

South Pasadena
Kopp, Eugene Howard *communications and electrical engineer, consultant*

South San Francisco
Hull, Cordell William *engineering, construction, and project management executive, investor*
Tananbaum, James *medical engineering company executive*

Stanford
Aziz, Khalid *petroleum engineering educator*
Boahen, Kwabena *bioengineering educator*
Boudart, Michel *chemical engineer, consultant, chemist, educator*
Cannon, Robert Hamilton, Jr. *aerospace engineering educator*
Cantwell, Brian *aeronautical engineer, educator*
Cox, Donald Clyde *electrical engineering educator*
Enge, Per Kristian *engineering educator*
Eshleman, Von Russel *electrical engineering educator, aerospace scientist*
Fan, Shanhui *engineering educator*
Franklin, Gene Farthing *engineering educator, consultant*
Fuller, Gerald G. *engineering educator*
Goodman, Joseph Wilfred *electrical engineering educator*
Gray, Robert Molten *electrical engineering educator*
Hesselink, Lambertus *electrical engineering and physics educator*
Horowitz, Mark A. *electrical engineering and computer science educator*
Howard, Ronald A. *systems engineer, educator*
Kailath, Thomas *electrical engineer, educator*
Khosla, Chaitan S. *chemical engineer*
Kino, Gordon Stanley *electrical engineering educator*
Krawinkler, Helmut *engineering educator, consultant*
Kroo, Ilan M. *aeronautical engineer, educator*
Kwon, Young-Nam *environmental engineer*
Leckie, James Oliver *engineering educator*
Linehan, John H. *engineering educator, biomedical engineer*
Linvill, John Grimes *engineering educator*
Macovski, Albert *electrical engineer, educator*
McCarty, Perry Lee *civil and environmental engineering educator*
Meng, Teresa H. *electrical engineer, educator*
Mitchell, Reginald Eugene *mechanical engineering educator*
Orr, Franklin Mattes, Jr. *petroleum engineering educator*
Ott, Wayne Robert *environmental engineer*
Parkinson, Bradford Wells *astronautical engineer, educator*
Paulraj, Arogyaswami Joseph *engineering educator, consultant*
Perry, William James *engineering educator, former secretary of defense*
Plummer, James D. *electrical engineering educator*
Springer, George Stephen *mechanical engineering educator*
Street, Robert Lynnwood *civil, mechanical and environmental engineer*
Swartz, James R. *chemical engineer, educator*
Sweeney, James Lee *engineering educator*
Tomlin, Claire J. *aeronautical engineer, educator*
Van Dyke, Milton Denman *aeronautical engineering educator*
Vincenti, Walter Guido *aeronautical engineer, emeritus educator*
White, Robert Lee *electrical engineer, educator*

Studio City
Delnik, Alexander *engineering executive, consultant*

Sunnyvale
Chen, Xiao *process engineer*
Choi, Hoon *electrical engineer*
Ensminger, Dale *retired mechanical and electrical engineer*
Goo, Jung-Suk *semiconductor company research engineer*
Guan, Xiang *electrical engineer*
Jayanarayanan, Sankaran Kartik *electrical engineer*
Leong, Chia Ken *mechanical engineer*
Oei, Lok S. *digital communications systems and DSP engineer, researcher*
Weinberg, William Henry *chemical engineer, physicist, educator*

Tarzana
Hansen, Robert Clinton *electrical engineer, consultant*
Lindley, Charles Alexander *aerospace engineer, consultant*

Temecula
Minogue, Robert Brophy *retired nuclear engineer*

Thousand Oaks
Marshall, David B. *structural ceramics professional*
Zhou, Sophia Huai *biomedical engineering scientist*

Torrance
Muley, Arun *aerospace engineer*
Paulson, Robert Lawrence *aerospace engineer, consultant*
Sorstokke, Susan Eileen *systems engineer*

Ukiah
Scheffey, David Harold *civil engineer, musician*

Ventura
Gaynor, Joseph *chemical engineer, management consultant*

Victorville
Sedeño, Eugene Raymond *electronics engineer, consultant*

Walnut Creek
Carlin, Herbert J. *electrical engineering educator, researcher*
Hanson, Robert Duane *engineering educator*
Parker, Denny S. *engineering company executive*

Watsonville
Brown, Alan Charlton *retired aeronautical engineer*

Westlake Village
Caligiuri, Joseph Frank *retired engineering executive*

Whittier
Stahl, James F. *engineer*

Woodland Hills
Piersol, Allan Gerald *mechanical engineer*

Yorba Linda
Lynch, Frank Thomas *aeronautical engineer, consultant*
Porcello, Leonard Joseph *engineering research and development executive*

COLORADO

Bayfield
Collins, William Leroy *retired telecommunications engineer*

Boulder
Anseth, Kristi S. *tissue engineer, educator*
Arslan, Haydar *civil engineer, researcher*
Barnes, Frank Stephenson *electrical engineer, educator*
Born, George Henry *aerospace engineer, educator*
Cathey, Wade Thomas *electrical engineering educator*
Corotis, Ross Barry *civil engineer, educator, academic administrator*
Davis, Robert Heater *chemical engineering educator*
Hanna, William Johnson *electrical engineering educator*
Hauser, Ray Louis *engineer, researcher, entrepreneur*
Hill, David Allan *electrical engineer*
Jin, Xiaoying *electrical engineer, computer engineer, researcher*
Joy, Edward Bennett *electrical engineer, educator, consultant*
McGuire, Robin K. *engineering company executive*
Mulhern, Martin Robert *engineer*
Murnane, Margaret Mary *engineering and physics educator*
Nordgren, Ronald Paul *retired engineering educator, researcher*
Reitsema, Harold James *aerospace engineer*
Sani, Robert LeRoy *chemical engineering professor*
Smith, Ernest Ketcham *electrical engineer*
Sodal, Ingvar Edmund *electrical engineer, science administrator*
Timmerhaus, Klaus Dieter *chemical engineering professor*
Uberoi, Mahinder Singh *aerospace engineer, researcher*
Willam, Kaspar J. *civil engineer, educator*
Zable, Jack Louis *mechanical engineer, educator*

Broomfield
Boulos, Paul Fares *civil and environmental engineer*

Centennial
Goughnour, Roy Robert *civil engineer, educator, director*
Grant, Paul *chemical engineer, real estate broker, lawyer*

Colorado Springs
Adnet, Jacques Jim Pierre *astronautical and electrical engineer, consultant*
Harvey, William Tarver *biomedical engineer, chronic disease physician*
Heilman, John Edward *engineering consultant*
Morris, Steven Lynn *engineering consultant, retired military officer*
Watts, Oliver Edward *engineering company executive*
Ziemer, Rodger Edmund *electrical engineering educator, consultant*

Columbine Valley
Gagin, Lawrence Vincent *ceramics engineer, consultant*

Denver
Bialasiewicz, Jan Tadeusz *electrical engineering educator*
Chamberlain, Adrian Ramond *transportation engineer*
Fay, Richard James *mechanical engineer, engineering executive, educator*
Harris, James Robert *structural engineer*
Jones, Irvin R. *engineering educator*
McCandless, Bruce, II, *aerospace engineer, retired astronaut*
Reshotko, Eli *aerospace engineer, educator*

Englewood
Ervin, Patrick Franklin *nuclear engineer*
Olcer, Nuri Yelman *engineering researcher, educator*
Peterson, Ralph Randall *engineering executive*

Estes Park
Ojalvo, Morris *civil engineer, educator*
Webb, Richard C. *engineering company executive*

Fort Collins
Abt, Steven R. *civil engineer, educator*
Barbezat, Eugene LaVar *computer engineer, retired military officer*
Kaufman, Harold Richard *mechanical engineer and physics educator*
Matthies, Frederick John *civil and environmental engineer*
Notaros, Branislav M. *electrical engineer, educator*
Richardson, Everett Vern *hydraulic engineer, educator, administrator, consultant*
Roesner, Larry August *civil engineer*

Golden
Siegrist, Robert L. *engineering educator, consultant*
Sloan, Earle Dendy, Jr. *chemical engineering educator*
Zhang, Ruichong *civil and mechanical engineer, educator*

Greenwood Village
Arvizu, Dan Eliab *mechanical engineer*
Haliw, Jerome Michael *civil engineer*

Lakewood
Barrett, Michael Henry *civil engineer*

Littleton
Colvis, John Paris *aerospace engineer, mathematician, research scientist*
Kielmeyer, William Henry *ceramics engineer, researcher*

Longmont
Doyle, James Thomas *electronics engineer*

Louisville
Syed, Yasser Fouad Khaderi *electrical engineer*

Loveland
Fleischer, Gerald Albert *industrial engineer, educator*

Superior
Middlebrooks, Eddie Joe *environmental engineer*

U S A F Academy
Musselman, Randall L. *electrical engineer, educator*

Wheat Ridge
Scherich, Erwin Thomas *civil engineer, consultant*

CONNECTICUT

Bloomfield
Cornell, Robert Witherspoon *retired mechanical engineer*
De Maria, Anthony John *electrical engineer*
Kissa, Karl Martin *electrical engineer*

Branford
Sipprell, George Sidney *aerospace engineer, consultant*

Darien
Forman, J(oseph) Charles *chemical engineer, consultant, writer*

East Hartford
Jacobson, Clas A. *engineering educator, director*
Staroselsky, Alexander *mechanical engineer, materials scientist*

Enfield
Oliver, Bruce Lawrence *retired information systems educator*

Groton
Firebaugh, Millard S. *naval engineer*

Hartford
Bronzino, Joseph Daniel *electrical engineer*

Jewett City
Pucel, Robert Albin *electronics engineer, researcher*

Milford
Bubencik, John William, II, *civil engineer, consultant, transportation engineer*

Mystic
Thompson, Robert Allan *aerospace engineer*

New Haven
Elimelech, Menachem *environmental and chemical engineering educator*
Narendra, Kumpati Subrahmanya *electrical engineer, educator*

Newington
Peterson, Mary Elizabeth Dreisbach *mechanical engineer*

North Branford
Mead, Lawrence Myers, Jr. *retired engineering executive*

Norwalk
Bays, John Theophanis *consulting engineer*

ld Lyme
ersam, Charles Henry, Jr. *engineer, educator, entrepreneur, writer*

range
bay, Ivan *mechanical engineering educator*

idgefield
cConnell, John Edward *retired electrical engineering company executive*

outh Windsor
obbs, David Ellis *mechanical engineer*

tamford
ngel, Gerald L. *engineering educator*
agaraj, Devaraysamudram R. *engineer, researcher*

torrs Mansfield
zymek, Zbigniew Marian *engineering educator*
tkin, Edward Thaddeus *aerospace engineer, consultant*
haw, Montgomery Throop *chemical engineering professor*
ephens, Jack Edward *civil engineer, consultant*

tratford
'air, Sylvia H. *aerospace engineer*

Vest Hartford
hou, Hong *engineering educator*

ELAWARE

ear
nnul, Edward *chemical engineer, writer*

ewes
eaufait, Frederick W(illiam) *retired engineering educator*

ewark
llen, Herbert Ellis *environmental chemistry educator*
ttoh-Okine, Nii Otokunor Nii *civil and environmental engineering educator*
arteau, Mark Alan *chemical engineering and chemistry educator*
eris, Antony Nicolas *chemical engineer, educator*
yrne, John Michael *energy and environmental educator*
i Toro, Dominic M. *engineering educator*
rasad, Ajay Krishna *mechanical engineering educator*
ussell, Thomas William Fraser *chemical engineer, educator*
andler, Stanley Irving *chemical engineering educator*
Vagner, Norman Joseph III *chemical engineering educator, researcher*
Vei, Bingqing *engineering educator*

ISTRICT OF COLUMBIA

Vashington
nthony, Donald Barrett *engineering executive*
rkilic, Galip Mehmet *mechanical engineer, educator*
ainum, Peter Montgomery *aerospace engineer, consultant*
lanchard, Bruce *civil engineer, consultant*
urton, William Joseph *engineering executive*
eason, Jonathan Pierce *environmental engineer, federal agency administrator*
ella Torre, Edward *electrical engineer, educator*
isner, Howard *engineering executive, educator*
arris, Charles Alexander *mechanical engineer, educator*
iallorenzi, Thomas Gaetano *optical engineer*
ershey, Robert Lewis *mechanical engineer, management consultant*
hozeimeh, Issa *electrical engineer, educator*
oester, Frederick. H. *aviation systems engineer*
orman, Can E *engineering educator, department chairman*
arventano, David *engineering and construction management company executive*
ickholtz, Raymond Lee *electrical engineering educator, consultant*
ust, William David, Jr. *retired structural engineer*
kinner, Robert Earle, Jr. *civil engineer, engineering executive*
olnik, Merrill I. *electrical engineer*
ownsend, Marjorie Rhodes *aerospace engineer, engineering executive*
Vang, John Cheng Hwai *communications engineer, researcher*
Vhitesides, John Lindsey, Jr. *aerospace engineering educator, researcher*
Vhitworth, Horace Algernon *mechanical engineer*

LORIDA

melia Island
illy, Wesley Cooper *marine engineer*

ventura
Volfenson, Azi U. *electrical, mechanical and industrial engineer, consultant*

Boca Raton
in, Yukweng M. *engineer, educator*
Aussenden, Georg Antonio *electronics engineer*

Bonita Springs
ustrulid, William A. *mining engineer, consultant*
atzen, Raphael *consulting chemical engineer*

Bradenton
Garvick, Kenneth Ryan *broadcast engineer, announcer, educator*

Brandon
Stephens, Robert David *environmental engineering executive*

Coral Gables
Saffir, Herbert Seymour *structural engineer, consultant*
Sumanth, David Jonnakoty *industrial engineer, educator*

Dania Beach
Messer, Allen Person *mechanical engineer, construction executive*

Davie
Upadhiaya, Umesh Chandra *engineer, consultant*

Daytona Beach
Helfrick, Albert Darlington *electronics engineering educator, consultant, department chairman*
Pang, Shuo *engineering educator*

Deland
Freeman, Ronald Eugene *environmental engineer*
Rattman, William John *electronics and electro-optic engineer*

Fort Lauderdale
Li, Min-Tang *systems engineer*

Fort Myers
Scott, Kenneth Elsner *mechanical engineering educator*

Gainesville
Anderson, Timothy J. *chemical engineering professor*
Balabanian, Norman *electrical engineering educator*
Blanch, Paul Bradford *biomedical engineer, researcher*
Capehart, Barney Lee *industrial and systems engineer, educator*
Cristescu, Nicolaie Dan *engineering educator*
Delfino, Joseph John *environmental engineering sciences educator*
Fossum, Jerry George *electrical engineering educator*
Fregly, B. J. *engineering educator*
Hollien, Harry Francis *communications engineer*
Isaacs, Gerald William *retired agricultural engineering educator, consultant*
Khargonekar, Pramod Prabhakar *engineering educator*
Kurzweg, Ulrich Hermann *engineering science educator*
Law, Mark Edward *electrical engineer, educator*
Lee, Won Suk *engineering educator*
O, Kenneth Kyongyop *engineering educator*
Sah, Chih-Tang *electrical and computer engineering educator*
Schmertmann, John Henry *civil engineer, educator, consultant*
Sherif, S. A. *engineering educator*
Slavickas, Rimas Anthony *electrical engineer, educator, researcher*
Tuleko, James Stanley *engineering educator, nuclear engineer*
Verink, Ellis Daniel, Jr. *metallurgical engineering educator, consultant*
Xie, Huikai *engineering educator*

Gulf Breeze
Bothfeld, Robert *retired industrial engineer, director, retired mechanical engineer, director*

Jacksonville
Arbogast, Gordon Wade *systems engineer, educator, consultant, retired military officer*
Mueller, Edward Albert *retired transportation engineer*
Vasana, Susan (Chun-Ye) *engineering educator*

Jupiter
Migliaro, Marco William *electrical engineer*
Wolff, Edward Alvin *electronics engineer*

Kennedy Space Center
Amador, José Jorge *computer engineer, researcher*

Keystone Heights
Ohanian, Mihran Jacob *nuclear engineer, educator, dean, researcher*

Lady Lake
Granger, Robert Alan *mechanical and aerospace engineering educator*

Lake Placid
Walter, William Paul *retired bioengineer*

Lauderhill
Swisher, Charles Francis *electrical engineer, consultant*

Longboat Key
Gollobin, Leonard Paul *chemical engineer*
Workman, George Henry *structural engineering consultant*

Lutz
Anderson, Karl Franklin *systems engineer, researcher*

Melbourne
Arrasmith, William W. *engineering educator*
Bostater, Charles R., Jr. *marine engineer, educator*
Burton, Dale Edward *aerospace engineering exectuve*
Maloratsky, Leo G. *electrical engineer*

Miami
Ajamil, Luis *civil engineer*
Dede, Mehmet Ismet Can *robotics researcher, educator*
Jones, William Kinzy *materials engineering educator*
Levy, Cesar *mechanical engineer, educator*
Makki, Shamila *project manager engineer, researcher*
Melesse, Assefa Mekonnen *engineering educator, researcher*
Veziroglu, Turhan Nejat *mechanical engineering educator, researcher*

Naples
Lynn, Larry (Verne Lauriston Lynn) *engineering executive*
Sowman, Harold Gene *ceramics engineer, researcher*
Suziedelis, Vytautas A. *retired engineering corporation executive*
Thampi, Mohan Varghese *environmental health and civil engineer*

Nokomis
Beck, George William *retired industrial engineer*
Novak, Robert Louis *civil engineer, pavement management consultant*

Orlando
Bhutta, Adeel Aslam *computer engineer, educator*
Delfyett, Peter *engineering educator*
DeMara, Ronald Francis *computer engineer, educator*
Qahwash, Murad *engineer, educator*
Yu, Chuanzhao *electrical engineer, researcher*

Osprey
Jones, George Yovicic *civil engineer*

Palm Beach
Callahan, Edward William *chemical engineer, retired manufacturing executive*

Palm Beach Gardens
Gillette, Frank C., Jr. *retired mechanical engineer*

Panama City
D'Arcy, Gerald Paul *engineering executive, consultant*

Pensacola
Mazzeo, Daniel Patrick *aerospace engineer, consultant*

Plantation
Alisetti, Edwin Luis *engineer, corporate financial executive*
Hsu, Jiun-Jia *engineering educator, transportation engineer*

Port Charlotte
Kok, Hans Gebhard *consulting engineer*

Port Orange
Millar, Gordon Halstead *mechanical engineer, agricultural products executive*

Saint Augustine
Lund, Frederick Henry *aerospace and electrical engineer*

Saint Cloud
Everett, Woodrow Wilson *electrical engineer, educator*

Saint Petersburg
Cardenas-Valencia, Andres Manuel *chemical engineer, researcher*
Collins, Carl Russell, Jr. *industrial engineer*

Sarasota
Derr, Frederick Mueller *civil engineer*
Deutsch, Sid *biomedical engineer, educator*
Long, Robert Radcliffe *fluid mechanics engineer, educator*
Metzger, Sidney *retired communications engineer*
Mitchell, John Noyes, Jr. *retired electrical engineer*

Satellite Beach
Clark, John F. *space systems engineering educator*
Van Arsdall, Robert Armes *engineer, retired military officer*

Sun City Center
Edwards, Paul Beverly *retired science and engineering educator*
Jeffries, Robert Joseph *retired engineer, information technology executive, educator*

Sunrise
Goldenberg, Felix *retired electrical engineer, researcher*

Tallahassee
Coloney, Wayne Herndon *civil engineer*
Dea, David Young Fong *electrical engineer, consultant*
De Forest, Sherwood Searle *agricultural engineer, agricultural products executive*
Gor'kov, Peter (Lev Petrovich) *biomedical engineer*
Hall, Houghton Alexander *electrical engineer, municipal official*
Lee, Peter John *research engineer*
Srivastava, Sanjeev Kumar *electrical engineer, researcher*
Weissman-Berman, Deborah *biostatistics and composites engineer, researcher*
Yu, Ming *engineering educator, researcher*

Tampa
Carnahan, Robert Paul *civil engineer, educator, researcher, consultant*
Ghiu, Silvana Melania Stefania *process and development engineer*
Hunter, Larry Lee *retired electrical engineer*
Macferran, Ernest Leslie *mechanical engineer*

Tavares
Kaiser, Robert Lee *retired engineering executive*

The Villages
Dupies, Donald Albert *retired civil engineer*

Venice
Przemieniecki, Janusz Stanislaw *engineering executive, former government senior executive and college dean*
Slate, Floyd Owen *retired engineering educator*

West Palm Beach
Aaron, M. Robert *electrical engineer*
Davis, Paul B. *retired mechanical and civil engineer*

Winter Haven
Johnson, Gordon Selby *consulting electrical engineer*

Winter Park
Granberry, Edwin Phillips, Jr. *safety engineer, consultant*

GEORGIA

Albany
Marbury, Ritchey McGuire III *engineering executive, surveyor*

Alpharetta
Sierra Mejia, Mauricio Andres *communications engineer*
Yeatman, Henry Clay *mechanical engineer*

Athens
McCutcheon, Steven Clifton *civil and environmental engineer, hydrologist*
Mohamoud, Yusuf Mohamed *agricultural engineer*
Nelson, Stuart Owen *agricultural engineer, researcher, educator*

Atlanta
Abdel-Khalik, Said Ibrahim *nuclear and mechanical engineering educator*
Bao, Gang *biomedical engineer, educator*
Bellanca, Joseph Paul *engineering construction executive*
Berryman, Robert Mogabgab *systems engineer*
Braun, Robert David *aerospace engineer, educator*
Crawford, Kyle A. *industrial engineer*
Cressler, John David *electrical engineering educator*
Eckert, Charles Alan *chemical engineering educator*
Ellingwood, Bruce Russell *structural engineer, educator*
Faber, Olaf Ulrich *structural engineer*
Forney, Larry J. *chemical engineer, educator*
Giddens, Don Peyton *engineering educator, researcher*
Guerra, Larry Cacao *engineer, researcher*
Harrison, George Brooks *engineer, researcher, retired military officer*
Hess, Dennis William *chemical engineering educator*
Hodges, Dewey Harper *aerospace engineer, educator*
Jett-Parmer, Jonathan Jackson *mechanical engineer*
Juang, Fred (Biing-Hwang Juang) *engineering educator*
Landen, Ashley Renee *mechanical engineer*
Loven, Andrew Witherspoon *environmental engineering company executive*
McDowell, David Lynn *mechanical engineering educator*
McIntire, Larry Vern *biomedical engineering educator*
Meindl, James Donald *electrical engineering educator, academic administrator*
Nerem, Robert Michael *engineering educator, consultant*
Pritchett, Amy R. *aerospace engineer, educator*
Rahnema, Farzad *engineering educator, department chairman*
Rouhani, Shahrokh *civil engineering environmental educator, consultant*
Salant, Richard Frank *mechanical engineer, educator*
Stacey, Weston Monroe, Jr. *nuclear engineer, physicist, educator*
Tentzeris, Emmanouil Manos *engineering educator, researcher*
Thuesen, Gerald Jorgen *industrial engineer, educator*
Vachon, Reginald Irenee *mechanical engineer*
Vito, Raymond P. *engineering educator, researcher*
Winer, Ward Otis *mechanical engineer, educator*
Wu, Jeff (Chien-Fu Wu) *engineering educator*
Yavari, Arash *engineering educator*
Yoganathan, Ajit Prithiviraj *biomedical engineer, educator*

Avondale Estates
Bastin, Clinton *retired chemical engineer, nuclear scientist*

Big Canoe
Bendelius, Arthur George *engineering firm executive*

Blairsville
Kerr, Walter Belnap *retired electrical engineer, language researcher, consultant*

Columbus
Haneman, Vincent Siering, Jr. *consulting engineer, educator, dean*
Sweeney, Robert David *retired communications engineer*

Doraville
Wempner, Gerald Arthur *engineering educator*

Duluth
Colwell, Gene Thomas *engineering educator*

Flowery Branch
Reynolds, George Anthony, Jr. *engineering executive*

Gainesville
Jones, William Benjamin, Jr. *retired electrical engineering educator*

Hinesville
Thomas, James, Jr. *retired engineering executive, retired military officer*

Jasper
Wiltse, James Cornelius *retired electrical engineer*

Kennesaw
Bonaparte, Rudolph *engineering company executive*

Macon
Aldridge, Melvin Dayne *engineering educator*
Hails, Robert Emmet *retired aerospace engineer, manufacturing executive, retired military officer*
Leonard, Michael Steven *industrial engineering educator*

Marietta
Choi, Sukhwan *engineer*
Garrett, Joseph Edward *aerospace engineer*
Miles, Thomas Caswell *aerospace engineer*

Norcross
Ockwell, Gary *electrical engineer, marketing professional*

Savannah
Henne, Preston A. *engineering executive*
Hsu, Ming-Yu *engineering educator*

Sky Valley
Geer, Ronald Lamar *mechanical engineer, consultant, retired oil industry executive*

Smyrna
Tripp, Victor K. *electrical engineer, researcher*

Statesboro
Molina, Gustavo *engineering educator, researcher*

Stone Mountain
Bacon, Louis Albert *retired consulting civil engineer*

Toccoa
Cross, Kim L. *engineer, sales executive*

Townsend
Hicks, Harold Eugene *chemical engineer*

Warner Robins
DePriest, C(harles) David *engineering executive, retired military officer*

HAWAII

Honolulu
Ako, Harry *engineering educator, researcher*
Chen, Wai-Fah *civil engineering educator*
Cox, Richard Horton *civil engineering executive*
Franz, Charles Norman *engineer*
Ghasemi Nejhad, Mehrdad N. *mechanical engineering educator*
Koide, Frank Takayuki *electrical engineering educator*
Ogburn, Hugh Bell *chemical engineer, consultant*
Wang, Jaw-Kai *bioengineering educator*
White, Gary Richard *electrical engineer*

Kapaau
McFee, Richard *electrical engineer, physicist*

Mililani
Camery, John William *computer engineer*

IDAHO

Boise
Cory, Wallace Newell *retired civil engineer*
Zarges, Thomas H. *engineering executive*

Idaho Falls
Miller, Gregory Kent *structural engineer*
Riemke, Richard Allan *nuclear engineer*

Inkom
Ambrose, Tommy W. *chemical engineer, engineering executive*

Moscow
DeShazer, James Arthur *biological engineer, educator, research administrator*

Pocatello
Jacobsen, Richard T. *mechanical engineering educator*
Valentine, Ralph Schuyler *chemical engineer, director*

ILLINOIS

Abbott Park
Krivoshik, Andrew Peter *engineer, physician*

Argonne
Ahmed, Shabbir *chemical engineer*
Chang, Yoon Il *nuclear engineer*
Kumar, Romesh *chemical engineer*
Myles, Kevin Michael *metallurgical engineer*

Aurora
Koopman, Richard Nelson *engineer, consultant*

Belleville
Thien-Stasko, Vicki Lynn *civil engineer*

Bloomington
Pannell, Thierry Edgard *engineer, information technology manager*

Champaign
Katehi, Linda P.B. *engineering educator*
Korst, Helmut Hans *mechanical engineer, educator*
Rose, Walter Deane *retired engineering educator*

Chicago
Babcock, Lyndon Ross, Jr. *environmental engineer, educator*
Banerjee, Prashant *industrial engineer, computer scientist, educator*
Chung, Paul Myungha *mechanical engineer, educator*
Dix, Rollin C(umming) *mechanical engineering educator, consultant*
Dutta, Mitra *engineer, educator*
Epstein, Raymond *engineering and architectural executive*
Fahnestock, Jean Howe *retired civil engineer*
Fowler, Martin *software engineer, consultant*
Garg, Vijay Kumar *telecommunications engineer*
Gerstner, Robert William *structural engineering educator, consultant*
Gupta, Krishna Chandra *mechanical engineering educator*
Guralnick, Sidney Aaron *engineering educator*
Hartnett, James Patrick *engineering educator*
Ivanov, Kamen Petkov *engineering educator*
Lee, Gyungho *engineering educator*
Lin, James Chih-I *biomedical and electrical engineer, educator*
Linden, Henry Robert *chemical engineer, researcher*
Liu, Derong *electrical and computer engineer, educator*
Mahani, Mohammad Shadbakht *engineering educator*
McCaul, Joseph Patrick *chemical engineer*
Miller, Irving Franklin *chemical, biomedical engineer, academic administrator, educator*
Miller, Verne William *computer engineer, consultant*
Minkowycz, W. J. *mechanical engineering educator*
Murata, Tadao *engineering and computer science educator*
Nair, R. Shankar *structural engineer*
Rikoski, Richard Anthony *electrical engineering executive*
Sawyer, Deborah *environmental engineering company executive*
Warner, Carrie *architectural engineer*
Wimmer, Markus Anton *biomedical engineer, educator*
Wong, Thomas Tang Yum *engineering educator*

Chicago Heights
Kavis, George *engineer, photographer*

Clarendon Hills
Moritz, Donald Brooks *mechanical engineer, consultant*

Crystal Lake
Gosalia, Keyoor Chetan *electrical engineer*
Janes, Brian D. *electronics specialist*

Darien
Hanson, Martin Philip *mechanical engineer, farmer*

Decatur
Koucky, John Richard *metallurgical engineer, manufacturing executive*

Deerfield
Saida, Toyoyasu *chemical and biochemical engineer*

Dekalb
Gau, Jenn-Terng *engineering educator*

Des Plaines
Relwani, Nirmal Murlidhar (Nick Relwani) *mechanical engineer*

Elmhurst
Parker, James John *engineer, marketing professional*

Evanston
Achenbach, Jan Drewes *engineering scientist*
Backman, Vadim *biomedical engineer, educator*
Bazant, Zdenek Pavel *engineering educator*
Belytschko, Ted *engineering educator*
Bobco, William David, Jr. *consulting engineering company executive*
Brazelton, William Thomas *chemical engineer, educator, dean*
Carr, Stephen Howard *materials engineer, educator*
Colgate, J. Edward *mechanical engineering educator*
Daskin, Mark Stephen *engineering educator*
Fessler, Raymond R. *metallurgical engineering consultant*
Fine, Morris Eugene *materials engineer, educator*
Frey, Donald Nelson *industrial engineer, educator, retired manufacturing executive*
Goldstick, Thomas Karl *biomedical engineering educator*
Keer, Leon Morris *engineering educator*
Krizek, Raymond John *engineering educator, consultant*
Murphy, Gordon John *electrical engineer, educator*
Ottino, Julio Mario *engineering company executive, educator*
Rittmann, Bruce Edward *environmental engineering educator, researcher*
Schofer, Joseph Landy *civil engineer, educator*
Shah, Surendra Poonamchand *engineering educator*
Smith, Spencer Bailey *engineering and business educator*
Taflove, Allen *electrical engineer, educator, researcher, consultant*
Van Ness, James Edward *electrical engineering educator*
Weertman, Julia Randall *materials engineering educator*

Forsyth
Graf, Karl Rockwell *nuclear engineer*

Gilman
Ireland, Herbert Orin *retired engineering educator*

Glencoe
Dean, H. Clark *retired civil engineer, genealogist*

Glenview
Brady, Sharon *engineering executive*
Brunner, Robert E. *engineering executive*
Flaum, Russell M. *engineering executive*
Gresh, Philip M. *engineering executive*
Hansen, Thomas J. *engineering executive*
Hindman, Craig A. *engineering executive*
Kropp, Ronald D. *engineering executive*
Martel, Roland M. *engineering executive*
Panarese, William C. *civil engineer*
Parry, David C. *engineering executive*
Santi, E. Scott *engineering executive*
Speer, David Blakeney
Sutherland, Allan C. *engineering executive*
Van Zelst, Theodore William *civil engineer, engineering company executive*
Zentmyer, Hugh J. *engineering executive*

Gurnee
Sommerlad, Robert Edward *environmental research engineer*

La Grange
Hoisington, Steven H. *industrial engineer*
Mehlenbacher, Dohn Harlow *civil engineer, consultant*

Lake Forest
Lambert, John Boyd *chemical engineer, consultant*

Libertyville
Szini, Istvan Janos *electronics engineer*

Lindenhurst
Theis, Peter Frank *engineering executive*

Lisle
Hayes, Richard J., Jr. *engineering company executive*

Lombard
Hambley, Douglas Frederick *geological and environmental engineer*

Moline
Taylor, Byron Keith *industrial engineer*

Naperville
Joyce, William H. *engineering company executive, chemical engineer*
Kotynek, George Roy *mechanical engineer, educator, marketing executive*
Vora, Manu Kishandas *chemical engineer, consultant*

Norridge
Petrakis, Myron Titos *retired mechanical engineer*

Northbrook
Boettcher, Robert Walter *civil engineer*

Oak Forest
Kogut, Kenneth Joseph *engineer, consultant*

Oak Park
Clark, John Peter III *engineer, consultant*

Palatine
Kieft, Gerald Nelson *mechanical engineer*

Park Forest
Williams, Jack Raymond *civil engineer*

Park Ridge
Taillon, Armand Philip *mechanical engineer*

Peoria
Hindi, Riyadh *engineering educator, researcher*
Xia, Kaiming *mechanical engineer*

Plainfield
Chakrabarti, Subrata Kumar *marine research engineer*

Quincy
Centanni, Ross J. *engineering executive*

Rockford
Eliason, Jon Tate *electrical engineer*
Gieras, Jacek Franciszek *engineering educator, research scientist*
Roberts, James Brian *engineer*

Rolling Meadows
Bohlin, Dawn Lenore *electrical engineer*

Schaumburg
Aryanfar, Farshid *electrical and electronics engineer*
Kornowski, Robert Richard *engineer, science educator*

Skokie
Corley, William Gene *engineering research executive*

Sycamore
Ballee, Shawn Alexander *engineering educato*

Urbana
Adesida, Ilesanmi *engineering educator, researcher, dean*
Amenu, Geremew Gurmessa *engineering educator, researcher*
Barenberg, Ernest John *engineering educator, consultant*
Bergeron, Clifton George *engineer, educator*
Blahut, Richard Edward *electrical and comput engineering educator*
Braatz, Richard Dean *chemical engineer*
Buckius, Richard O. *mechanical engineer, educator*
Chao, Bei Tse *mechanical engineering educato*
Chato, John Clark *mechanical and bioengineering educator*
Coleman, Paul Dare *physics and electrical engineering educator*
Conry, Thomas Francis *mechanical engineerin educator*
Eden, James Gary *electrical engineer, physicis educator, researcher*
Garcia, Marcelo Horacio *engineering educator, consultant*
Hall, William Joel *retired civil engineer, educator*
Hannon, Bruce Michael *engineering educator*
Hess, Karl *engineering educator, science educator*
Holonyak, Nick, Jr. *electrical engineering educator*
Huang, Thomas Shi-Tao *electrical engineering educator, researcher*
Jacobson, Sheldon Howard *engineering educat*
Jiang, Shengxiang *electrical engineer, research*
Jones, Benjamin Angus, Jr. *retired agricultural engineering educator, science administrator*
Krein, Philip T. *electrical engineer, educator, electronics executive*
Kumar, Panganamala Ramana *electrical and computer engineering educator*
Leon, Arturo Segundo *civil engineer, researche*
Loui, Michael Conrad *engineering educator*
Makela, Jonathan James *engineering educator*
Maxwell, William Hall Christie *civil, environmental engineer, educator*
Meng, Ling-Jian *engineering educator*
Miley, George H. *nuclear and electrical engineering educator, plasma engineer, ener conversion scientist*
Rao, Nannapaneni Narayana *electrical enginee*
Seebauer, Edmund Gerard *chemical engineer, educator*
Snoeyink, Vernon L. *civil engineer, educator*
Solomon, Wayne C. *aerospace engineer, educator*
Stewart, D. Scott *engineering educator, consultant*
Wah, Benjamin Wan-Sang *electrical and computer engineering educator*
Zukoski, Charles Frederick, IV, *chemical engineering educator, academic administrato*

Wilmette
Wadden, Richard Albert *environmental enginee educator, science administrator, consultant*

Wood Dale
Bullen, Daniel Bernard *mechanical engineerin educator*

INDIANA

Carmel
Fisher, Mark Leighton *software engineer*

Crown Point
Litko, Kenneth R. *aerospace engineer, researcher*

Elkhart
Bloom, Terry Raymond *chemical engineer*

Fort Wayne
Hippensteele, David Simon *engineer*
Lyons, Jerry Lee *mechanical engineer*
Ogle, James Workman *aerospace engineer*
Streeter, Robert Davenport *electrical engineer, consultant*

Hammond
Pierson, Edward Samuel *engineering educator, consultant*

Indianapolis
Anwar, Sohel *engineering educator*
Griffith, Roy Lloyd *design engineer*
Kalwara, Joseph John *engineer*
Poinsette, Donald Eugene *engineering executive management consultant*

Kokomo
Miller, Robert Frank *retired electronics engineering educator*

.afayette
'tzel, James Edward *environmental engineering educator*
'ox, Robert William *mechanical engineering educator*
ieddes, Leslie Alexander *engineering educator, forensic engineer, physiologist*
.iley, Peter Edward *retired engineering educator*
)sborn, John Robert *retired engineering educator*
'ipes, Robert Byron *mechanical engineer, educator*

/Iuncie
eymour, Richard Deming *technology educator*

Jotre Dame
iray, William Guerin *engineering educator*
ıcropera, Frank Paul *mechanical engineering educator*
Ierz, James Logan *electrical and materials engineering educator, researcher*
Iichel, Anthony Nikolaus *electrical engineering educator, researcher*
)vaert, Timothy Christopher *mechanical engineering educator*
chmitz, Roger Anthony *chemical engineer, educator, academic administrator*
mith, James Ormal *engineering educator*
tadtherr, Mark A. *chemical engineer, educator*

outh Bend
ɔrgensen, Robert William *aerospace engineer*

'erre Haute
adar, M. Affan *engineering educator*

Varsaw
Iroczkowski, Matthew *biomedical engineer*

Vest Lafayette
.dams, Robin Sue *engineering educator*
.lbright, Lyle Frederick *chemical engineering educator*
arany, James Walter *industrial engineering educator*
uckmaster, Dennis Rene *agricultural engineer, educator*
'ohen, Raymond *retired mechanical engineer, educator*
'ooper, James Albert, Jr. *electrical engineering educator*
elleur, Jacques William *retired engineering educator*
rnevich, Vincent Paul *engineering educator*
rankenberger, Jane Rossing *agricultural engineer*
race, Richard Edward *engineering educator*
ambrusch, Susanne *computer engineering educator*
ıckson, Mark James *engineering educator*
ımieson, Leah H. *engineering educator*
adisch, Michael R. *engineering educator*
andgrebe, David Allen *electrical engineer*
in, Pen-Min *electrical engineer, educator*
u, Chang *engineering professor*
Iarshall, Francis Joseph *aerospace engineer*
aik, Sameer Vijaykumar *mechanical engineer, educator*
ng, Chee-Mun *engineering educator*
eroulis, Dimitrios *engineering educator, consultant*
amkrishna, Doraiswami *chemical engineering educator, researcher*
eklaitis, Gintaras Victor *chemical engineer, educator*
alvendy, Gavriel *industrial engineer, educator*
chwartz, Richard John *electrical engineering educator, researcher*
aber, Margaret Ruth *retired engineering technology educator*
homas, Marlin Uluess *industrial engineer, educator, academic administrator*
arma, Arvind *chemical engineering educator, researcher*
iskanta, Raymond *mechanical engineering educator*
'ankat, Phillip Charles *chemical engineering educator*
'illiams, Theodore Joseph *engineering educator*
'on, You-Yeon *engineering educator*
ao, Bin *mechanical engineering educator*

OWA

.mes
nderson, Robert Morris, Jr. *electrical engineer*
aumann, Edward Robert *environmental engineering educator*
lack, James Robert *industrial engineer*
owler, Nicola *engineering educator*
rown, Robert C. *engineering educator*
uchele, Wesley Fisher *retired agricultural engineering educator*
himenti, Dale E. *engineering educator*
ogandzic, Aleksandar *electrical engineer, educator*
oziel, Jacek *agricultural engineer, educator*
ushner, Mark Jay *engineering and physics educator*
arsen, William Lawrence *engineering educator*
kiishi, Theodore Hisao *mechanical engineering educator*
ınders, Wallace Wolfred, Jr. *civil engineer*
'ickert, Jonathan Adam *engineering educator*
'ilder, David Randolph *retired materials engineer*

ettendorf
eyderman, Arthur Jerome *engineer, civilian military employee*

ambridge
olvin, Thomas Stuart *agricultural engineer, farmer*

Cedar Rapids
Smith, Bruce Vaughn *electrical engineer*

Clear Lake
Brown, Robert Grover *engineering educator*

Emmetsburg
Farnsworth, Steven Robert *safety engineer*

Iowa City
Abdel-Malek, Karim A. *biomedical engineer, educator*
Park, Joon Bu *biomedical engineer, researcher, educator*
Patel, Virendra Chaturbhai *mechanical engineer, educator*

Madrid
Handy, Richard Lincoln *civil engineer, educator*

Muscatine
Stanley, Richard Holt *consulting engineer*
Thomopulos, Gregs G. *consulting engineering company executive*

Ottumwa
Tuller, Joey David *manufacturing engineer*

West Des Moines
Conner, William Bruce *facilty engineer*

KANSAS

Colby
Lamm, Freddie Ray *research agricultural engineer*

Emporia
Alshare, Khaled A. *information systems educator*

Garden City
Alam, A.N.M. Mahbub Ul *engineer, educator*

Lawrence
Benjamin, Bezaleel Solomon *structural engineer, educator*
Darwin, David *engineering educator, consultant*
Green, Don Wesley *chemical and petroleum engineering educator*
Grzymala-Busse, Jerzy Witold *engineering educator*
Lan, Chuan-Tau Edward *aerospace engineering educator*
Moore, Richard Kerr *electrical engineering educator*
Muirhead, Vincent Uriel *retired aerospace engineer*
Roskam, Jan *aerospace engineer*
Rowland, James Richard *electrical engineering educator*
Willhite, G. Paul *chemical engineer, petroleum engineer, educator*

Leawood
Karmeier, Delbert Fred *engineer, consultant, realtor*

Manhattan
Argoti, Andres *chemical engineer, researcher*
Gorton, Robert L. *retired mechanical engineer*
Johnson, William Howard *retired agricultural engineer, educator*
Lee, E(ugene) Stanley *engineering educator*
Simons, Gale Gene *nuclear and electrical engineer, educator*
Singh, Devinder *chemical engineer*

Overland Park
Lucas, James Raymond *company executive, writer, consultant, speaker*
Rodman, Leonard C. *engineering and construction executive*

Wichita
Holland, Phillip Kent *aerospace engineer*
McKee, George Moffitt, Jr. *civil engineer, consultant*
Wilhelm, William Jean *civil engineering educator*

KENTUCKY

Bowling Green
Collett, Walter Lee *electrical engineer, educator*

Georgetown
Caroland, William Bourne *structural engineer*

Lexington
Baker, Merl *engineering educator*
Brock, Louis Milton, Jr. *engineering educator, researcher*
Drake, Vaughn Paris, Jr. *electrical engineer*
Holsapple, Clyde Warren *decision and information systems educator*
Male, Alan Thomas *engineering educator, foundation administrator*

Louisville
Cornelius, Wayne Anderson *electrical and computer engineering consultant*
Garcia, Rafael Jorge *retired chemical engineer*
Gregory, James Francis *electrical engineer*
Kantardzic, Mehmed M. *engineering educator*
Tran, Long Trieu *industrial engineer*

Morehead
Mason, Patrick Samual *manufacturing engineer*
Mohammed, Jaby *engineering educator*

Murray
Ferreyra, Rafael Andres *agricultural and biological engineer, consultant, researcher*

Winchester
Studebaker, John Milton *utilities engineer, consultant, educator*

LOUISIANA

Baker
Cross, James Edward *electrical engineering educator*

Baton Rouge
Bernhard, James M., Jr. *engineering executive*
Chen, Peter Pin-Shan *engineering, computer science and Internet/web educator, data processing executive*
Corripio, Armando Benito *retired chemical engineering professor*
Gammon, Malcolm Ernest, Sr. *surveying and engineering executive*
Khonsari, Michael M. *mechanical engineering educator*
Moody, Gene Byron *engineering executive, small business owner, minister*
Pike, Ralph Webster *chemical engineer, educator, academic administrator*
Sinclair, Glenn Bruce *mechanical engineering educator, researcher*
Tumay, Mehmet Taner *geotechnical engineering educator, researcher, consultant*

Dubach
Straughan, William Thomas *structural engineering consultant, educator*

Hammond
Parish, Richard Lee *engineer, consultant*

Harvey
Simon, Keith R. *safety engineer, petroleum engineer, radio personality*

Kenner
Hallila, Bruce Allan *welding engineer*

Lafayette
Marshak, Alan Howard *electrical engineer, educator*

Lake Charles
Levingston, Ernest Lee *engineering company executive*

Metairie
Nicoladis, Michael F. *engineering company executive*

Napoleonville
Blanchard, Donald Pierre, Jr. *engineer*

New Orleans
Lannes, William Joseph III *electrical engineer*
Wang, Ting *mechanical engineering educator*

Ruston
Sterling, Raymond Leslie *civil engineering educator, researcher, consultant*

Shreveport
Foreman, John Patrick *electrical engineer*

Slidell
Stuart, Charles Edward *electrical engineer, oceanographer*
Tewell, Joseph Robert, Jr. *retired electrical engineer*
Winsor, William John III *engineer, consultant*

Vivian
Collier, Samuel Melvin *aerospace engineer*

MAINE

Falmouth
Rohsenow, Warren Max *retired mechanical engineer, educator*

Orono
Landis, Eric N. *civil engineer, educator*

Scarborough
Raisbeck, Gordon *systems engineer, consultant*

Waterville
Laurence, Robert Lionel *chemical engineering professor*

MARYLAND

Aberdeen Proving Ground
Clayton, John Daniel *mechanical engineer, researcher*
Cozby, Richard Scott *electronics engineer, military officer*
VanLandingham, Mark Reed *materials engineer*

Adelphi
Nguyen, Lam Huy *electronics engineer*

Annapolis
Cooper, Robert Alfred *electrical engineer*
Criscimagna, Ned Henry *engineer*
Johnson, Bruce *engineering educator*
Rogers, David Freeman *aerospace engineering educator*
Salem, Thomas Eric *electrical engineer, educator*
Trescott, Sara Lou *water resources engineer*
Weese, John Augustus *retired mechanical engineer*

Baltimore
Alarcon, Cesar L *electrical engineer*
Apsel, Alyssa *electrical and computer engineer*
Bardhan, Tridip K. *engineering educator, researcher*
Dalrymple, Robert Anthony III *civil engineering educator*
Jelinek, Frederick *electrical engineer, educator*
Jones, Nicholas Patrick *civil engineering educator*
Katz, Joseph Louis *chemical engineer, educator*
Klimantov, Alexius George *engineering executive*
Lemer, Andrew Charles *engineer, economist*
Nathanson, Harvey Charles *electrical engineer*
Thakor, Nitish Vyomesh *biomedical engineering educator*
West, James Edward (James Edward Maceo West) *acoustical engineer, educator*
Yue, Wusi *mechanical engineer, researcher*

Bethesda
Burdeshaw, William Brooksbank *engineering executive*
Kemelhor, Robert E(lias) *mechanical engineer*
Kinsey, John Allen *systems engineer, technical director*
Kutemeyer, Peter Martin *industrial engineering executive*
Larsen-Basse, Jorn *mechanical and materials engineering educator, researcher, consultant*
Saville, Thorndike, Jr. *coastal engineer*

Chevy Chase
Cheng, David Keun *engineering educator*
Lebow, Irwin Leon *communications engineering consultant*
Rockwell, Theodore *nuclear engineer*

College Park
Anderson, John David, Jr. *aerospace engineer*
Ayyub, Bilal M. *engineer, company executive, educator, researcher*
Baecher, Gregory B. *civil and environmental engineer, educator*
Barbe, David Franklin *electrical engineer, educator*
Chopra, Nikhil *systems engineer, researcher*
Deshmukh, Om Dadaji *electrical engineer, researcher*
Farvardin, Nariman *engineering educator*
Galloway, Gerald Edward, Jr. *civil engineer, educator*
Granatstein, Victor Lawrence *electrical engineer, educator*
Gupta, Ashwani Kumar *mechanical engineering educator*
Kang, Kyeongpyo *transportation engineer, researcher*
Lathan, Corinna Elisabeth *aerospace engineer*
Levine, William Silver *electrical engineer, educator*
Marcus, Steven Irl *electrical engineering educator*
Newcomb, Robert Wayne *electrical engineer, educator*
Smidts, Carol *mechanical engineer, educator*
Sreenivasan, Katepalli Raju *mechanical engineer, educator*
Taylor, Leonard Stuart *engineering educator, consultant*
Tilley, David Rogers *engineering educator, researcher*

Columbia
Saini, Simarjeet Singh *electronics engineer*
Straja, Sorin Radu *chemical engineer, mathematician, computer programmer*
Valencia Lavao, Jesus M. *electrical engineer, consultant*

Crofton
Laurenson, Robert Mark *mechanical engineer*
Vranish, John Michael *electrical engineer, researcher*

Easton
Brodt, Burton Pardee *retired chemical engineer, writer, researcher*
Kerr, James Wilson *engineer*

Elkridge
Morgan, Gary Lorin *systems engineer, director, researcher*

Fort Washington
Caveny, Leonard Hugh *mechanical engineer, aerospace scientist, consultant*

Gaithersburg
Cookson, Alan Howard *electrical engineer, researcher*
Ferrell, Charles Madison *nuclear engineer, physicist*
Levine, Robert Sidney *chemical engineer, consultant*
Wang, Francis Wei-Yu *biomedical materials scientist, researcher*
Wiederhorn, Sheldon Martin *materials scientist engineer*
Wright, Richard Newport III *retired engineering executive, engineering educator*

Germantown
Sorensen, John Noble *retired mechanical and nuclear engineer*

Greenbelt
Amato, Deborah Douglass *aerospace engineer*
Ericsson, Aprille Joy *aerospace engineer*
U-yen, Kongpop *electrical engineer*

Hagerstown
Ksienski, Aharon Arthur *retired electrical engineer*

Hunt Valley
Kinstlinger, Jack *engineering executive, consultant*

Kensington
Freeman, Ernest Robert *retired engineering executive*

La Plata
Zinn, Michael Wallace *aerospace engineer*

Lanham
Cheng, Jian-Yu *mechanical engineer, researcher, application developer*

Laurel
Damarla, Thyagaraju *electronics engineer*
Eaton, Alvin Ralph, Jr. *aeronautical engineer, applied physics executive, systems engineer*
Land, H. Bruce III *electronics engineer, aerospace engineer*
Land, Henry Bruce III *electronics engineer, researcher*
Levitt, Gerald Steven *engineering executive*
Weerackody, Vijitha *electrical engineer, researcher*

Linthicum Heights
Skillman, William Alfred *consulting engineering executive*

Lutherville
Parekh, Dhirajlal Gokaldas *electrical engineer*

Parkville
Jensen, Arthur Seigfried *retired engineer, physicist, consultant*

Patuxent River
Stroup, Darryl Ray *systems engineer*

Potomac
Williams, Peter MacLellan *nuclear engineer*

Queenstown
Corn, Morton *environmental engineer, educator*

Reisterstown
Broadbent, J. Street *engineering executive*

Rockville
Abron, Lilia A. *chemical engineer*
Ashar, Hansraj G. *structural engineer, nuclear regulator*
Burdick, William MacDonald *biomedical engineer*
Davies-Venn, Christian *environmental engineer*
Geem, Zong Woo *engineer*
McDonald, Capers Walter *biomedical engineer, manufacturing executive, entrepreneur, educator*
Reddy, Thikkavarapu Ramachandra *electrical engineer*
Seagle, Edgar Franklin *environmental engineer, consultant*

Silver Spring
Koltnow, Peter Gregory *engineer, consultant*
Mok, Carson Kwok-Chi *structural engineer*
Scipio, L. Albert, II, (Louis Albert Scipio II) *retired aerospace science engineering educator, historian*
Shalowitz, Erwin Emmanuel *civil engineer*
White, Edmund William *chemical engineer*

Suitland
Brooks, Richard C. *electrical engineer, federal official*
Reupke, William Albert *engineer*

Towson
Huang, Joseph Chen-Huan *civil engineer*

West Bethesda
Jessup, Stuart Dodge *marine engineer*
Sevik, Maurice *acoustical engineer, researcher*

MASSACHUSETTS

Acton
An, Hong *engineer*
Hicks, Walter Joseph *electrical engineer*

Amherst
Franks, Lewis E. *electrical and computer engineering educator, researcher*
Nash, William Arthur *civil engineer, educator*
Swift, Calvin Thomas *electrical and computer engineering educator*
Vogl, Otto *polymer science and engineering educator*
Winter, Horst Henning *chemical engineer, educator*

Andover
Agassounon, William B. G. *engineer, researcher, scientist*
Jakes, William Chester *electrical engineer*

Auburndale
Drake, Elisabeth Mertz *chemical engineer, consultant*

Bedford
Jelalian, Albert V. *electrical engineer*
Winter, David Louis *retired systems engineer, human factors scientist*

Belmont
Merrill, Edward Wilson *chemical engineering professor*

Billerica
Kinsman, Robert Preston *biomedical plastics engineer*
Srinivasan, Purushothaman *electrical engineer, researcher*

Boston
Baillieul, John Brouard *aerospace engineering and applied mathematics educator*
Basagni, Stefano *computer engineer, educator*
De Luca, Carlo John *biomedical engineer, educator*
Desai, Tejal Ashwin *biomedical engineer, educator*
Doherty, Robert Francis, Jr. *aerospace engineer*
Frank-Kamenetskii, Maxim D. *biomedical engineer*
Fraser, Donald C. *engineering executive, educator*
Jain, Rakesh K. *chemical engineering and tumor biology educator*
Langer, Robert Martin *retired chemical engineering company executive, consultant*
Livingston, Frederic Holleyman *mechanical engineer*
Miaoulis, Ioannis Nikolaos *mechanical engineer, educator*
Moore, Richard Lawrence *structural engineer, consultant*
Pierce, Allan Dale *engineering educator, researcher, editor*
Teich, Malvin Carl *electrical engineering educator*

Burlington
Angle, Colin *electrical engineer, robotic company executive*
Greiner, Helen *mechanical engineer*
Rhee, Sokwoo *mechanical engineer*

Cambridge
Abernathy, Frederick Henry *mechanical engineering educator*
Antoniadis, Dimitri Alexander *electrical engineering educator*
Apostolakis, George E. *engineering educator, researcher*
Argon, Ali Suphi *mechanical engineering educator*
Barnhart, Cynthia *engineering educator, researcher*
Battin, Richard Horace *aeronautical engineer*
Beér, János Miklós *engineering educator*
Belcher, Angela *engineering educator*
Beranek, Leo Leroy *acoustical engineer, consultant*
Bhatia, Sangeeta N. *biomedical engineer, educator*
Bras, Rafael Luis *engineering educator*
Brenner, Howard *chemical engineering educator*
Bulovic, Vladimir *engineering educator*
Caplice, Christopher *engineering educator*
Chakraborty, Arup K. *chemical engineering educator*
Chen, Chau-Chyun *chemical engineer*
Chen, Sow-Hsin *nuclear science and engineering educator, researcher*
Chung, Soon-Jo *engineer, researcher*
Clifford, Gari David *engineering educator, biomedical engineer*
Cohen, Robert Edward *chemical engineering professor, consultant*
Colton, Clark Kenneth *chemical engineering professor*
Covert, Eugene Edzards *aerospace engineer, aeronautics professor*
Crandall, Stephen Harry *engineering educator*
Crawley, Edward Francis *aerospace engineering educator*
de Neufville, Richard Lawrence *engineering educator*
de Weck, Oliver *engineering educator, researcher*
Dewey, Clarence Forbes, Jr. *engineering educator*
Drela, Mark *aeronautical engineer, educator*
Duffy, Robert Aloysius *aeronautical engineer*
Dugundji, John *aeronautical engineer*
Eagleson, Peter Sturges *civil and environmental engineer, educator*
Fay, James Alan *mechanical engineering educator*
Flemings, Merton Corson *engineering educator, materials scientist*
Frey, Daniel D. *engineering educator, researcher*
Fujimoto, James G. *electrical engineering educator*
Gallager, Robert Gray *electrical engineering educator*
Griffith, Linda G. (Linda Griffith-Cima) *biomedical engineer, chemical engineer, educator*
Gyftopoulos, Elias Panayiotis *mechanical and nuclear engineering educator*
Hansen, Kent Forrest *nuclear engineering educator*
Harris, Wesley L. *aeronautical engineer, educator*
Hastings, Daniel *aeronautical engineer, educator*
Heywood, John Benjamin *mechanical engineering educator*
Hunter, Ian W. *engineering educator, researcher*
Ippen, Erich Peter *electrical engineer, educator, physicist*
Kaashoek, M. Frans *computer science and engineering educator*
Kadak, Andrew C. *engineering educator, former company executive*
Kazimi, Mujid Suliman *nuclear engineer, educator*
Kirtley, James L., Jr. *electrical engineer, educator*
Kong, Jin Au *electrical engineering educator*
Ladd, Charles Cushing III *civil engineer, educator*
Lagace, Paul Alfred *aeronautical engineering educator*
Langer, Robert Samuel, Jr. *chemical and biomedical engineering educator*
Lee, Se-Hee *electrical engineer, researcher*
Leveson, Nancy G. *aeronautical engineer*
Magee, Christopher L. *systems engineer*
Marini, Robert Charles *environmental engineering executive*
Markey, Winston Roscoe *aeronautical engineering educator*
Marks, David Hunter *civil engineering educator*
McGarry, Frederick Jerome *civil engineering educator*
Mei, Chiang Chung *civil engineer, educator*
Mikaelian, Tsoline *aerospace engineer*
Milgram, Jerome H. *marine and ocean engineer, educator*
Mindell, David A. *engineering educator*
Moavenzadeh, Fred *engineering educator*
Munguia Tapia, Emmanuel *electrical engineer, researcher, computer scientist*
Narayanamurti, Venkatesh *engineering educator, physics professor*
Newman, Dava Jean *aerospace engineering educator, director*
Penfield, Paul Livingstone, Jr. *electrical engineering educator*
Probstein, Ronald Filmore *mechanical engineering educator*
Rivest, Ronald L. *engineer*
Rogers, Peter Phillips *environmental engineer, educator, urban planner*
Roos, Daniel *engineering educator*
Rose, Robert Michael *materials engineering educator*
Ruina, Jack Philip *electrical engineer, educator*
Russell, Kenneth Calvin *metallurgical engineering educator*
Samson, Leona D. *biological engineering educator, research center director*
Schiller, Peter Harkai *biomedical engineering and physics educator*
Sheffi, Yossi *engineering educator, researcher*
Smith, Kenneth Alan *chemical engineer, educator*
Staelin, David Hudson *electrical engineering educator, consultant*
Stevens, Kenneth Noble *electrical engineer, educator*
Suresh, Subra *materials engineer, educator*
Sussman, Joseph *engineering educator, researcher*
Tarokh, Vahid *engineering educator*
Todreas, Neil Emmanuel *nuclear engineering educator*
Tomita, Masaru *engineering educator, researcher*
Triantafyllou, Michael Stefanos *engineering educator*
Trilling, Leon *aeronautical engineering educator*
Tsitsiklis, John N. *electrical engineering and computer science educator*
Ungar, Eric Edward *mechanical engineer*
Vander Velde, Wallace Earl *aeronautical and astronautical engineering educator*
White, David Calvin *electrical engineer, educator, energy executive, consultant*
Whitman, Robert Van Duyne *civil engineer, educator*
Williams, James Henry, Jr. *mechanical engineer, educator, consultant*
Wilson, David Gordon *mechanical engineering educator*
Wuensch, Bernhardt John *ceramic engineering educator*
Young, Laurence Retman *biomedical engineer, educator*
Zhang, Shuguang *biomedical engineer*
Zhukovsky, Alexander *mechanical engineer*
Zue, Victor W. *engineering educator*

Carlisle
Drew, Philip Garfield *retired engineering company executive, consultant*

Charlestown
Ntziachristos, Vasilis *radiology, bioengineering educator*

Concord
Davidson, Frank Paul *retired macroengineer, lawyer*
Fowler, Charles Albert *electronics engineer*
Villers, Philippe *mechanical engineer*

Dartmouth
Michel, Howard E. *electrical engineer, director*

Framingham
Crossley, Frank Alphonso *retired metallurgical engineer*

Franklin
LaRowe, Richard Philip *systems engineer*

Hampden
Joubert, Raymond Ernest *retired electrical engineer*

Holbrook
Crandlemere, Robert Wayne *engineering executive*

Lexington
Bailey, Fred Coolidge *retired engineering consulting company executive*
Beusch, John Ulrich *engineer, researcher*
Brookner, Eli *electrical engineer*
Bussgang, Julian Jakub *electronics engineer, consultant*
Dinneen, Gerald Paul *electrical engineer, retired federal official*
Freed, Charles *engineering consultant, researcher*
Garrelick, Joel Marc *acoustical scientist, consultant*
Gelb, Arthur *electrical and systems engineering executive*
Keicher, William Eugene *electrical engineer*
Morrow, Walter Edwin, Jr. *electrical engineer, lab administrator*
Stonebraker, Michael R. *electrical engineering, computer science educator*
Zayhowski, John J. *electrical engineer, researcher*

Longmeadow
Lemnios, Andrew Zachery *aerospace engineer, educator, researcher*

Lynn
Chow, Humphrey Wai *mechanical engineer*

Lynnfield
Meyer, Piotr Jan *electronics engineer*

Marlborough
Bennett, C. Leonard *electrical engineer*
Knight, Douglas A. *mechanical engineer*

Medford
Abriola, Linda Marie *civil and environmental engineer*
Astill, Kenneth Norman *mechanical engineerin educator*
Greif, Robert *mechanical engineering educator*
Uhlir, Arthur, Jr. *electrical engineer, academic administrator*

Medway
Hoag, David Garratt *retired aerospace enginee*

Nantucket
Kales, Paul Albert *engineering educator, cartoonist*
Saperstein, Lee Waldo *mining engineering educator*

Natick
Berglund, Larry Glenn *mechanical engineer, educator*
Latanision, Ronald Michael *materials science and engineering consultant*
Pokorny, Joseph Wenceslaus III *engineer*

Needham
Powell, Adam Clayton *engineering educator, consultant*

Newton
Marrone, Philip A. *chemical engineer*
Sheridan, Thomas Brown *mechanical engineering and applied psychology educato researcher, consultant*

Northborough
Wang, Jun *process engineer, materials scientist*

Norwood
Memishian, Jack *electronics engineer*
Sheingold, Daniel H. *electrical engineer*

Paxton
Clarke, Edward Nielsen *engineering science educator*

Peabody
Peters, Leo Francis *environmental engineer*

Pittsfield
Feigenbaum, Armand Vallin *systems engineer, information technology executive*
Shammas, Nazih Kheirallah *environmental engineer, consultant, engineering educator*

Shutesbury
Abbott, Douglas Eugene *engineering educator*

Swampscott
Kaufman, William Morris *electrical engineer, consultant*

Tewksbury
Faccini, Ernest Carlo *mechanical engineer*

Waban
Mark, Melvin *mechanical engineering educato consultant*

Waltham
Gumpertz, Werner Herbert *structural engineeri company executive*

Wellesley
Weil, Thomas Alexander *retired electronics engineer*

Westborough
Gionfriddo, Maurice Paul *aeronautical enginee research and development company executiv*

Weston
Katz, William Emanuel *retired chemical engineer*

Winchester
Hansen, Robert Joseph *civil engineer*

Woburn
Serfaty, Daniel *human systems engineer*

Worcester
Katz, Robert Nathan *ceramics engineer, educat*

Wrentham
Bittenbender, Brad James *safety engineer*

Yarmouth Port
Stott, Thomas Edward, Jr. *retired engineering executive*

MICHIGAN

Ann Arbor
Adriaens, Peter *environmental engineer, consultant*
Awtar, Shorya *engineering educator, consultan*
Becher, William Don *retired electrical enginee educator, writer*
Bielello, John Charles *engineering educator, director*

Chaffin, Don Brian *industrial engineering educator, research director*
England, Anthony Wayne *engineering and science educator, dean*
Friedmann, Peretz Peter *aerospace engineer, educator*
Gibala, Ronald *metallurgical engineering educator*
Gilbert, Elmer Grant *engineering educator, control theorist*
Hayes, John Patrick *electrical engineering and computer science educator, consultant*
Koren, Yoram *mechanical engineering educator*
Kozma, Adam *electrical engineer*
Lee, John Chaeseung *nuclear engineering educator*
Martin, William Russell *nuclear engineering educator*
Merte, Herman, Jr. *mechanical engineering educator*
Meyer, John Frederick *engineering educator*
Petrick, Ernest Nicholas *mechanical engineer, researcher*
Pollock, Tresa M. *engineering educator*
Powell, Kenneth Grant *aerospace engineering educator*
Saitou, Kazuhiro *engineering educator*
Savari, Serap Ayse *engineering educator, researcher*
Schwank, Johannes Walter *chemical engineering educator*
Scott, Norman Ross *electrical engineering educator*
Senior, Thomas Bryan A. *electrical engineering educator, researcher, consultant*
Sobel, Alan *electrical engineer, physicist*
Steel, Duncan Gregory *engineering educator*
Sylvester, Dennis Michael *electrical engineer, educator*
Ulaby, Fawwaz Tayssir *engineering educator, director, science administrator*
Ulsoy, Ali Galip *engineering educator*
Wang, Lumin *nuclear engineer*
Wilson, Richard Christian *engineering firm executive*
Yang, Ralph Tzu-Bow *chemical engineer, educator*
Young, Edwin Harold *chemical and metallurgical engineering educator*

Auburn Hills
Boyle, Olabisi Ariyo *manufacturing engineer*
Liu, C. Q. *engineer*

Battle Creek
Risukhin, Vladimir Nikolayevich *aeronautical engineer, educator*

Bingham Farms
Gratch, Serge *retired mechanical engineering educator*

Charlotte
Burpee, Lyle Frederick *retired industrial engineer*

Dearborn
Cairns, James Robert *mechanical engineering educator*
Gandhi, Haren S. *chemical engineer*
Hrovat, Davorin D. *engineer*
Kang, Hong Tae *engineering educator*
Little, Robert Eugene *engineering educator*
Mi, Chunting Chris *engineering educator*
Prasad, Priya *engineer, researcher*
Yang, Guangbin *engineer*

Detroit
Battah, Hammam Jamil *civil engineer, utilities executive*
Chou, Clifford Chi Fong *research engineering executive*
Curtis, Robert O. *mechanical engineer*
Kummler, Ralph H. *chemical engineer, educator, dean*
McWhorter, Sharon Louise *engineering executive, inventor, consultant*
Rathod, Mulchand *mechanical engineering educator*
Rivin, Eugeny (Eugene) I. *engineering educator, researcher, consultant*
Yang, Kai *engineering educator*

East Lansing
Andersland, Orlando Baldwin *retired engineering educator*
Chen, Kun-Mu *electrical engineering educator*
Cutts, Charles Eugene *retired engineering educator*
Foss, John Frank *mechanical engineering educator*
Goodman, Erik David *engineering educator*
Lloyd, John Raymond *mechanical engineering educator*
Pierre, Percy Anthony *engineering educator*
Ross, Anthony Dewayne *engineering educator*
Saul, William Edward *engineering educator*
von Bernuth, Robert Dean *agricultural engineering educator, consultant*

Eastport
Tomlinson, James Lawrence *mechanical engineer*

Farmington
Meyer, Jerome Charles *consulting civil engineer*

Farmington Hills
Hurd, Mary K. *civil engineer, writer*

Flushing
Cain, William David *electronics engineer, writer*

Grand Rapids
Anyalebechi, Prince N. *engineering educator, consultant*
Ljungren, Wendy *engineering executive*

Vranish, Kenneth *electrical engineer, consultant*

Greenbush
Paulson, James Marvin *retired engineering educator*

Grosse Pointe Shores
Burke, Thomas Joseph *civil engineer*
Holness, Gordon Victor Rix *engineering executive, mechanical engineer*

Holland
Stynes, Stanley Kenneth *retired chemical engineer, educator*

Houghton
Crittenden, John Charles *engineering educator*
Heckel, Richard Wayne *metallurgical engineering educator*
Huang, Eugene Yuching *civil engineer, educator*
Mukherjee, Abhijit *mechanical engineer, educator*
Narain, Amitabh *aerospace and mechanical engineering educator*

Kalamazoo
Litynski, Daniel Mitchell *optical engineer, educator, physicist, retired military officer*

Lansing
Shirtum, Earl Edward *retired civil engineer*

Leland
Soutas-Little, Robert William *mechanical engineer, educator*

Livonia
Uicker, Joseph Bernard *retired engineering company executive*

Madison Heights
Peaslee, Robert Leon *metallurgical engineer, consultant*
Xia, Jiding *chemical engineering educator*

Mattawan
Greene, Timothy James *industrial engineering educator*

Midland
Meister, Bernard John *retired chemical engineer*
Robbins, Lanny Arnold *chemical engineer*

Niles
Marshall, Gerald Francis *optical engineer, consultant, physicist*

North Branch
Stevenson, James Laraway *engineering company executive, electronics engineer, computer engineer, communications engineer, engineering educator*

Pittsford
Shaffer, Richard Stanley *mechanical engineer, researcher*

Pontiac
Hampton, Philip Michael *consulting engineering company executive*
Wang, Yucong *engineering executive*

Portage
Underdal, Olav M. *engineering executive*

Rochester
Loh, Robert N. K. *engineering educator*
Polis, Michael Philip *engineering educator*

Rochester Hills
DiCosmo, Nino *engineering company executive*

Royal Oak
Fragomeni, James Mark *mechanical engineer, educator*

Shelby Township
Nagy, Louis Leonard *engineering executive, researcher*
Osuch, Debra K. *materials engineer*

Southfield
Hettiarachchi, Chamil Hiroshan *civil engineer, educator*
McKeen, Alexander C. *retired engineering executive, foundation administrator*
Song, Xubin *mechanical engineer, researcher*

Troy
Nefske, Donald Joseph *engineer*

University Center
Tuttle, Robert Bruce *mechanical engineer, educator*

Warren
Cai, Mei *materials engineer, researcher*

Wixom
Huff, Alvin Edward *retired engineer*

MINNESOTA

Brooklyn Park
DeBusk, Charles Richard *engineer, consultant*

Eden Prairie
Higgins, Robert Arthur *electrical engineer, educator, consultant*

Lakeville
Setterholm, Jeffrey Miles *systems engineer*

Madison
Husby, Donald Evans *engineering company executive*

Minneapolis
Abi-Ghanem, Georges Victor *civil engineer, environmental engineer*
Anderson, John Edward *mechanical engineering educator*
Ariyur, Kartik Balasubramanian *control systems engineer, researcher*
Cussler, Edward Lansing, Jr. *chemical engineer, educator*
Davis, Howard Ted *engineering educator*
Galambos, Theodore Victor *civil engineer, educator*
Garrard, William L. *aerospace engineer, educator*
Gulliver, John Stephen *civil engineering educator*
Hillstrom, Thomas Peter *engineering executive*
Johnson, Walter Kline *civil engineer*
Joseph, Daniel Donald *aeronautical engineer, educator*
Kvalseth, Tarald Oddvar *mechanical engineer, educator*
Lambert, Robert Frank *electrical engineer, educator, consultant*
Levinson, David Matthew *engineering educator, civil engineer*
Oriani, Richard Anthony *metallurgical engineer, educator*
Parhi, Keshab Kumar *electrical and computer engineering educator*
Persson, Erland Karl *electrical engineer, executive*
Pfender, Emil *mechanical engineering educator*
Scriven, L. E(dward) *engineering educator*
Sidebottom, Charles Benton *engineering executive*
Sparrow, Ephraim Maurice *mechanical engineering scientist, educator*
Srirangarajan, Seshan *electrical engineer, researcher*
Takyar, Mir Shahrouz *electrical engineer, researcher*
Wollenberg, Bruce Frederick *electrical engineering educator, consultant*

Oak Park Heights
Jones, Edwin Channing, Jr. *retired electrical and computer engineering educator*

Plymouth
Kodali, Dharma Rao *engineering educator*

Saint Paul
Abraham, John Patrick *mechanical engineer, educator*
Greenwood, Stephen John *environmental engineer*
Mooney, Matthew Thomas *engineering executive*
Stibbe, Craig Jule *engineer*

Shoreview
O'Dea, Thomas Joseph *clinical engineer, medical physicist*

Woodbury
Beck, Warren Randall *retired glass technologist*

MISSISSIPPI

Biloxi
Brinsmade, Akbar Fairchild *chemical engineering consultant*

Jackson
Caviness, Kimberly Sweat *environmental engineer*
Grossi, Jason *mechanical engineer, consultant*

Mississippi State
Babski-Reeves, Kari *industrial and systems engineering educator*
Eksioglu, Burak *engineering educator*
Thompson, Joe Floyd *aerospace engineer, researcher*
Truax, Dennis Dale *civil engineer, educator, consultant*

Starkville
Eksioglu, Sandra Duni *industrial engineering educator*
Jacob, Paul Bernard, Jr. *electrical engineering educator*
Liu, Qingyun *thermal and mechanical research engineer*
Riekels, Lynda Marie *materials engineer*

University
Cheng, Alexander Hung-Darh *engineering educator, consultant*
Smith, Allie Maitland *engineering educator*

MISSOURI

Ballwin
Cornell, William Daniel *mechanical engineer*

Columbia
Creighton, Donald Louis *mechanical engineer, consultant*
Day, Cecil LeRoy *agricultural engineering educator*
Edgington, Bobbie George *communications engineer, consultant*
Frisby, James Curtis *retired agricultural engineering educator*
Keyvan, Shahla *nuclear engineer, educator*
Kirawanich, Phumin *electrical engineer*
O'Connor, John Thomas *civil engineering educator*
Pringle, Oran Allan *mechanical and aerospace engineering educator*
Zhang, Yuwen *mechanical engineer, researcher, educator*

Florissant
Stevens, Robert Edward *engineering company executive*
Tomazi, George Donald *retired electrical engineer*

Four Seasons
Bivins, Susan Steinbach *systems engineer*

Fulton
Hinchie, William Jules *nuclear engineer, director*

Kansas City
Acheson, Allen Morrow *retired engineering executive*
Green, Frank Earl *retired civil engineer*

Kirkwood
Holsen, James Noble, Jr. *retired chemical engineer*

Rolla
Cudney, Elizabeth A.F. *industrial engineer*
Day, Delbert Edwin *ceramic engineering educator*
Galati, Nestore *materials engineer, researcher*
Isaac, Kakkattukuzhy M. *engineering educator, researcher*
Rao, Vittal Srirangam *electrical engineering educator*
Sauer, Harry John, Jr. *mechanical engineer, educator, academic administrator*
Venayagamoorthy, Ganesh Kumar *electrical engineer, computer engineer, educator*
Yu, Wei-Wen *retired engineering educator*

Saint Charles
Martin, Edward Brian *electrical engineer*

Saint Louis
Antonacci, Anthony Eugene *retired engineer*
Bradley, Edward Joseph, Jr. *electrical engineer*
Briggs, William Benajah *retired aerospace engineer*
Byrnes, Christopher Ian *engineering educator*
Dreifke, Gerald Edmond *electrical engineering educator*
Dudukovic, Milorad P. *chemical engineering educator, consultant*
Goldstein, Julius Lester *biomedical engineer, consultant*
Gould, Phillip Louis *engineering educator*
Haas, Daniel Louis *structural engineer*
Husar, Rudolf Bertalan *mechanical engineering educator*
Izuchukwu, John Ifeanyichukwu *industrial engineer, mechanical engineer*
McKelvey, James Morgan *chemical engineering educator, retired dean*
Peters, David Allen *mechanical engineering educator, consultant*
Ross, Monte *electrical engineer, researcher*
Rudy, Yoram *biomedical engineer, biophysicist, educator*
Shrauner, Barbara Wayne Abraham *electrical engineer, educator*
Sutera, Salvatore Philip *mechanical engineer, educator*
Szabo, Barna Aladar *engineering educator*
Zurheide, Charles Henry *consulting electrical engineer*

University City
McVey, Francis Daniel *mechanical engineer, software developer, educator*
Winter, David Ferdinand *electrical engineering educator, consultant*

MONTANA

Bozeman
Cokelet, Giles Roy *biomedical engineering educator*
Nehrir, M. Hashem *electrical engineer, educator*
Sanks, Robert Leland *environmental engineer, retired educator*
Stanislao, Joseph *engineering educator, consultant*

Great Falls
Walker, Leland Jasper *civil engineer*

Harlem
Brekke, Alan Lee *industrial engineer*

Kalispell
Freiberg, Robert Jerry *engineering executive*

Pony
Anderson, Richard Ernest *agricultural engineer, consultant, rancher*

NEBRASKA

Clay Center
Hahn, George LeRoy *agricultural engineer, biometeorologist*

Kimball
Kinnison, Daniel E. *manufacturing engineer*

Lincoln
Bahar, Ezekiel *electrical engineering educator*
Edison, Allen Ray *electrical engineer, educator*
Edwards, Donald Mervin *systems engineer, educator, dean*
Sicking, Dean L. *civil engineer, educator*
Splinter, William Eldon *agricultural engineering educator*
Woollam, John Arthur *electrical engineering educator, physics professor*

Omaha
Houser, Kevin *engineering educator*

Tunnicliff, David George *retired civil engineer*

NEVADA

Boulder City
Wyman, Richard Vaughn *engineering educator, company executive*

Henderson
Wennerstrom, Arthur John *aeronautical engineer*

Incline Village
Merdinger, Charles John *civil engineer, educator, military officer, academic administrator*
Thompson, David Alfred *industrial engineer*

Las Vegas
Culp, Gordon Louis *consulting engineer, management consultant*
Das, Biswajit *electrical engineer, educator*
French, Richard Harry *hydrologic and hydraulic engineer, consultant*
Haas, Robert John *aerospace engineer*
Herzlich, Harold J. *chemical engineer*
Massier, Paul Ferdinand *mechanical engineer*
Mc Elroy, John Harley *electrical and industrial engineering educator*
Messenger, George Clement *engineering executive, consultant*
Neumann, Edward Schreiber *transportation engineering educator*
Palmieri, Frederick William *structural engineer*
Ramos, Albert A. *electrical engineer*
Rolff, James Robert *retired locomotive engineer, writer*
Sanders, Charlotta Elisabeth *nuclear engineer, educator*

Reno
Carr, James Russell *engineering educator*
Danko, George *engineering educator*
Fuerstenau, M(aurice) C(lark) *metallurgical engineer*
Kleppe, John Arthur *electrical engineer, educator, company executive*
Mandl, William John *electronics engineer, researcher*

NEW HAMPSHIRE

Farmington
Panek, William Dominick *systems engineer executive*

Hanover
Lotko, William *engineering educator*
Queneau, Paul Etienne *retired metallurgical engineering educator*

Laconia
Parthasarathy, Vinod *manufacturing engineer, consultant*

Manchester
Hower, Philip Leland *semiconductor device engineer*

Nashua
Woodruff, Thomas Ellis *electronics consulting executive*
Yannone, Ronald Matthew *systems engineer, researcher*

New Castle
Klotz, Louis Herman *structural engineer, educator, engineering executive, consultant*

New London
Crane, Robert Kendall *engineering educator, researcher, consultant*

Portsmouth
Baumann, Hans D. *engineering executive*

Warner
Hunt, Everett Clair *engineering educator, researcher, consultant*

NEW JERSEY

Absecon
Cartlidge, Edward Sutterley *mechanical engineer*

Atlantic City
Felder, Wilson Norfleet, II, *engineering executive*

Basking Ridge
Drewry, Don Neal *fire protection engineer*

Bedminster
David, Edward Emil, Jr. *electrical engineer, executive, management consultant*

Bridgewater
Fung, Shun Chong *retired chemical engineer*

Cherry Hill
Batterman, Steven Charles *engineering mechanics and bioengineering professor, consultant*

Colts Neck
Candelora, Deborah Michael *engineer, sculptor*

Cranbury
Zurick, Jack *electrical engineer, consultant*

Cranford
Hrycak, Peter *retired engineering educator*

East Brunswick
Daniel, Charles Timothy *transportation engineer, consultant*
Liebowitz, Larry Arnold *electroceramics materials engineer*

Englewood
Deresiewicz, Herbert *retired mechanical engineering educator, consultant*

Ewing
Brunda, Daniel Donald *retired aerospace engineer, consultant, inventor, writer*

Fort Monmouth
Perlman, Barry Stuart *electrical engineer, researcher, director*

Freehold
Christ, Duane Marland *retired computer systems engineer*

Glassboro
Slater, C. Stewart *chemical engineering educator*

Helmetta
Gabay, Eleonora V. *mechanical engineer, educator*

Hewitt
Selwyn, Donald *engineering administrator, researcher, inventor, educator*

Highland Park
Spencer, Herbert Harry *structural engineer, researcher, computer analyst*

Hillsborough
Sun, Wei *electrical engineer*

Hoboken
Boesch, Francis Theodore *electrical engineer, educator*
Griskey, Richard George *chemical engineering professor*
Lawrence, Victor B. *computer and systems engineer*
Savitsky, Daniel *retired structural engineer, educator*
Sisto, Fernando *mechanical engineering educator*
Xing, Yiping *electrical engineer, researcher*

Holmdel
Lang, Howard Lawrence *electrical engineer*

Jackson
Tague, Charles Francis *retired engineering company executive, real estate company executive, construction executive*

Kinnelon
Haller, Charles Edward *engineer, consultant*

Lakewood
Fanuele, Michael Anthony *retired electronics engineer, research engineer*

Livingston
Daman, Ernest Ludwig *mechanical engineer*
Stevens, William Dollard *mechanical engineer, consultant*

Manasquan
Abate, John E. *electrical engineer, consultant*

Manchester
Madan, Deepak S. *engineering executive*

Middletown
Tomicki, Stephen G. *engineer*

Montclair
Eager, George Sidney, Jr. *electrical engineer, engineering executive*

Morris Plains
Bennett, John Charles *former engineering and construction executive*

Morristown
Johnson, David Blackwell *safety engineer*
Kittelberger, Larry E. *engineering executive*
Lieberman, Lester Zane *engineering company executive*
Rainal, Attilio Joseph *retired electronics engineer*
Raziq, Yaqub *telecommunications engineer*

New Brunswick
Jaluria, Yogesh *mechanical engineering educator, department chairman*
Weng, George Jueng-Cious *engineering educator*

New Providence
Chen, Young-Kai *electronics engineer, researcher*

Newark
Bar-Ness, Yeheskel *electrical engineer, educator*
Dhawan, Atam Prakash *engineering educator, dean*
Friedland, Bernard *electrical engineer, educator*
Hanesian, Deran *chemical engineer, educator, environmental scientist, consultant*
Meegoda, Jay Namunu *engineering educator, professional engineer*
Pfeffer, Robert *chemical engineer, academic administrator, educator*
Rosato, Anthony Dominick *mechanical engineer, educator*
Spillers, William Russell *civil engineering educator*

Newfoundland
Van Winkle, Edgar Walling *retired electrical engineer*

North Brunswick
Frenkiel, Richard Henry *retired systems engineer, consultant*

North Caldwell
Meserlian, Donald C. *mechanical engineer, consultant*

Ocean
Reich, Bernard *communications engineer*

Paramus
Michalek, Romuald *environmental engineer, engineering company executive*

Parsippany
Theiss, Richard Edward *electrical engineer, applications engineer*

Passaic
Lindholm, Clifford Falstrom, II, *engineering executive, mayor*

Pennington
Zhang, Hong (Rick) *design engineer, researcher*

Pennsauken
Alday, Paul Stackhouse, Jr. *retired mechanical engineer*

Piscataway
Balaguru, Perumalsamy *civil engineering educator*
Linke, Richard A. *optical engineer*
Poses, Frederic M. *engineering company executive*
Salkind, Alvin J. *engineering educator, dean, consultant*
Vieth, Wolf Randolph *chemical engineering educator*
Welkowitz, Walter *biomedical engineer, educator*
Zhang, Dajun *biomedical engineering educator*

Princeton
Bartolini, Robert Alfred *electrical engineer, researcher*
Billington, David Perkins *civil engineering educator*
Calderbank, Robert *engineering educator, researcher*
Chou, Stephen Y. *electrical engineer, educator*
Curtiss, Howard Crosby, Jr. *mechanical engineer, educator*
Debenedetti, Pablo Gaston *chemical engineering professor*
Gillham, John Kinsey *chemical engineering professor*
Gmachl, Claire *electrical engineer, educator*
Lam, Sau-Hai (Harvey) *aeronautical engineering educator*
Lechner, Bernard Joseph *consulting electrical engineer*
Leonard, Naomi Ehrich *aerospace engineer, educator*
Liu, Bede *electrical engineering educator*
Miles, Richard Bryant *mechanical and aerospace engineering educator*
Poor, Harold Vincent *electrical engineering educator*
Russel, William Bailey *engineering educator*
Song, Zhen *electrical engineer, researcher*
Stengel, Robert Frank *engineering and applied science educator*
Tsui, Daniel C. *electrical engineer, physicist*
VanMarcke, Erik Hector *civil engineer, educator*
Verdu, Sergio *engineering educator*
Wei, James *chemical engineering professor, academic dean*

Princeton Junction
Bair, William Alois *engineer*
Denlinger, Edgar Jacob *retired electronics engineering executive, researcher*
Haddad, James Henry *chemical engineer, consultant*
Lull, William Paul *engineering consultant*
Vahaviolos, Sotirios John *electrical engineer, researcher, engineering executive*

Ridgewood
Farrell, Gregory Alan *biomedical engineer*

Rumson
Rowe, Harrison Edward *electrical engineer*

Scotch Plains
Quackenbush, Schuyler *engineer, consultant*

Sea Bright
Plummer, Dirk Arnold *chemical, electrical, and electronics engineer*

Short Hills
Wharton, Lennard *engineering company executive*

Skillman
Brill, Yvonne Claeys *engineer, consultant*

Somerville
Sivanesan, Sivaruban *mechanical engineer*

South Plainfield
Kennedy, John William *engineering company executive*

Summit
Fukui, Hatsuaki *retired electrical engineer, art historian*
Rosensweig, Ronald Ellis *chemical engineer, consultant*

Swedesboro
Lovell, Theodore *electrical engineer, consultant*

Teaneck
Ehrlich, Ira Robert *mechanical engineering consultant*
Reinish, Gloria Brooks *electrical engineer, educator*

Titusville
Cooper, Paul *retired mechanical engineer, director, researcher*

Upper Saddle River
Wallace, William III *engineering executive*

Voorhees
Litman, Bernard *electrical engineer, consultant*
Siskin, Edward Joseph *engineering and construction company executive*

Watchung
Michaelis, Paul Charles *engineering physicist executive*
Tornqvist, Erik Gustav Markus *chemical engineer, research scientist, consultant*

Wayne
Geiger, David E. *engineer*
Schmidt, Barnet Michael *communications and electronic engineer*

West New York
Gruenberg, Elliot Lewis *electronics engineer and company executive*

Westfield
Bhagat, Phiroz Maneck *mechanical engineer*

NEW MEXICO

Alamogordo
Ernst, James Allan *safety engineer, consultant*

Albuquerque
Anderson, Lawrence Keith *electrical engineer, consultant*
Ardelean, Emil Valentin *mechanical engineer, researcher*
Baum, Carl Edward *electrical engineer, researcher*
Brinker, Charles Jeffrey *chemistry and chemical engineering educator*
Dorato, Peter *electrical and computer engineering educator*
Finch, Robert Jonathan *communications engineer, consultant*
Hall, Jerome William *research engineering educator*
Mansell, Justin Dennis *optical engineer, consultant*
Peck, Ralph Brazelton *civil engineering educator, consultant*
Tolendino, Lawrence Francis *electrical engineer*

Belen
Toliver, Lee *mechanical engineer*

Carlsbad
Piper, Lloyd Llewellyn, II, *engineer, government and service industry executive*

Cerrillos
Lutz, Raymond Price *retired industrial engineer, educator*

Elephant Butte
Lederer, John Martin *retired aeronautical engineer*

Embudo
Rogers, Benjamin Talbot *mechanical engineer, consultant*

Las Cruces
Ford, Clarence Quentin *mechanical engineer, educator*
Hansuk, Sohn *industrial engineer, educator*

Los Alamos
Andrews, Malcolm John *engineering educator*
Dudziak, Donald John *nuclear engineer, educator*
Ramirez, Juan *mechanical engineer, researcher*
Stoddard, Stephen Davidson *ceramics engineer, retired state senator*
Wohlberg, Brendt *electrical engineer, researcher*
Wooten, H. Omar *systems engineer, researcher*

Placitas
Hidy, George Martel *chemical engineer, engineering executive*

Roswell
Sun, Hui *industrial engineer, operations research analyst*

Santa Fe
Goorley, John Timothy *nuclear engineer*
Kaman, Helen S. *retired aerospace engineer, artist*
Morrison, Malcolm Cameron *engineering management professional*

NEW YORK

Albany
Fanuele, Frank John *engineering executive, electrical engineer*
Happ, Harvey Heinz *electrical engineer, educator*
Roy, Rob J. *biomedical engineer, anesthesiologist, educator*

Astoria
Unsal-Tunay, Nuran *geological engineer, researcher*

Bethpage
Conti, James Joseph *retired chemical engineer, educator*

Big Flats
Orsillo, James Edward *computer engineer, information technology executive*

Binghamton
Khasawneh, Mohammad Turki *industrial engineer, educator*

Brewster
Nadel, Norman Allen *civil engineer*

Briarcliff Manor
Cavalcanti, Dave Alberto Tavares *electrical engineer*

Bronxville
Brunale, Vito John *aerospace engineer*

Brooklyn
Armenakas, Anthony Emmanuel *aerospace engineering educator*
Birenbaum, Leo *retired engineering educator*
Goodman, David Joel *electrical engineering educator, science facility director*
Haralick, Robert Martin *electrical engineering educator*
Liu, Yong *engineering educator*
McLean, William Ronald *retired electrical engineer, consultant*
Palmer, Marc *engineer, lawyer*
Parlamis, Michael Frank *civil engineer, construction executive*
Reznikov, Lev *process engineer, researcher*
Shaw, Leonard Glazer *retired electrical engineering educator, consultant*
Wei, Xinzhou *engineering educator*

Buffalo
Alexandridis, Paschalis *chemical engineer, educator*
Chang, Ching Ming (Carl) *engineering executive, mechanical engineer, educator, writer*
Karwan, Mark Henry *engineering educator*
Meredith, Dale Dean *civil engineering educator*
Pados, Dimitris A. *electrical engineer, educator*
Reismann, Herbert *engineer, educator*
Ruckenstein, Eli *chemical engineering professor*
Sarjeant, Walter James *electrical and computer engineering educator*
Shaw, David Tai-Ko *electrical and computer engineering educator, academic administrator*
Xu, Jinhui *engineering educator*
Zirnheld, Jennifer L. *engineering educator, researcher*

Chappaqua
Pomerene, James Herbert *retired computer engineer*

Clarence
Greatbatch, Wilson *biomedical engineer*

Clinton
Pagani, Albert Louis *aerospace system engineer*

Cold Spring
Pugh, Emerson William *electrical engineer*

Dix Hills
Braun, Ludwig *retired engineering educator*

East Norwich
Rosen, Meyer Robert *chemical engineer*

Farmingdale
Bandyopadhyay, Amitabha *engineering educator*

Flushing
Birnstiel, Charles *consulting engineer*
Stahl, Frank Ludwig *civil engineer*

Franklin Square
Cantilli, Edmund Joseph *safety engineer, educator, translator, writer, consultant*

Garden City Park
Radu, Bogdan *aerospace engineer*

Greenlawn
Sachman, Henry Lee *electrical engineer, company executive*

Hauppauge
Buckley, Robert Matthew *electrical engineer*

Hempstead
Goldstein, Stanley Philip *engineering educator*

Horseheads
Shabanowitz, Harry *electronics engineer, educator*

Huntington
Christiansen, Donald David *electrical engineer, editor, publishing executive, consultant*
LaTourrette, James Thomas *retired electrophysics, electrical engineering and computer science educator*

Huntington Station
Agosta, Vito *mechanical and aerospace engineering educator*

Inwood
Chernov, Yuriy D. *engineering executive*

Ithaca
de Boer, Pieter Cornelis Tobias *mechanical and aerospace engineering educator*
Fick, Richard Irwin *environmental engineer, educator*
Eastman, Lester Fuess *electrical engineer, educator*
Fuchs, W. Kent *engineering educator*
George, Albert Richard *mechanical and aerospace engineer, educator*
Haith, Douglas A. *engineering educator, researcher*
Leibovich, Sidney *engineering educator*
Loucks, Daniel Peter *environmental systems engineer*
Maxwell, William Laughlin *retired industrial engineering educator*
McGuire, William *civil engineer, educator*
Meyburg, Arnim Hans *transportation engineer, educator, consultant*
Olbricht, William Lee *engineering educator*
O'Rourke, Thomas Denis *civil engineer, educator*
Parlange, Jean-Yves *environmental engineer, educator*
Pope, Stephen Bailey *mechanical engineer, educator*
Rodríguez, Ferdinand *chemical engineer, educator*
Smith, Julian Cleveland, Jr. *chemical engineering professor*
Tiwari, Sandip *electrical and computer engineering educator*
Williamson, Charles Harvey Kaye *mechanical and aerospace engineering educator*
Yavuz, A. Kadir *aerospace engineer, researcher*

Jamestown
Leising, David Michael *industrial engineer*

Jericho
Shinners, Stanley Marvin *electrical engineer*

Katonah
Bashkow, Theodore Robert *electrical engineering consultant, former educator*

Kew Gardens
Chipkin, Frederick *textile designer, consultant, artist, writer*

Lansing
Emelett, Stephen John *electrical engineer, researcher*

Melville
Bongiorno, Joseph John, Jr. *electrical engineering educator*
Bultan, Aykut *communications systems engineer*
Olesen, Robert Lind Ole *electrical engineer*
Schmid, Charles Ernest *acoustical engineer, academic administrator*
Taub, Jesse J. *electrical engineering researcher*

Mineola
Newman, Malcolm *mechanical and civil engineering consultant*

Montrose
Reber, Raymond Andrew *chemical engineer*

Mount Sinai
Kopp, Richard Edgar *electrical engineer*

New Hyde Park
Hyman, Abraham *electrical engineer*

New York
Acrivos, Andreas *chemical engineering professor*
Ahmad, Jameel *civil engineer, researcher, educator*
Boley, Bruno Adrian *engineering educator*
Bove, John Louis *chemistry and environmental engineering educator, researcher*
Brazinsky, Irv(ing) *chemical engineering educator, department chairman*
Briskman, Robert David *engineering executive*
Caplow, Ted *environmental engineer*
Chen, Tak-Ming *retired civil engineer, consultant*
Chevray, Rene *engineering educator*
Chowdhury, Md Shoaib *engineer*
Chung, Jung Git *retired aerospace engineer*
Cowin, Stephen Corteen *biomedical engineering educator, consultant*
DiMaggio, Frank Louis *civil engineering educator*
Fawcett, Christopher Babcock *civil engineer, construction and water resources company executive*
Fogel, Irving Martin *consulting engineer*
Gan, Yong Xue *materials engineer, educator*
Goldfarb, Donald *industrial engineering educator*
Grunes, Robert Lewis *engineering executive, consultant*
Habib, Ibrahim Wahby *computer engineer, educator*
Hielscher, Andreas Helmut *biomedical engineer*
Jarvik, Robert Koffler *biomedical research scientist*
Lai, W(ei) Michael *retired engineering educator*
Lammie, James Louis *engineering executive, retired military officer*
Laufer, Mark Vladimir *retired engineering educator*
Manassah, Jamal Tewfek *electrical engineer, educator, management consultant*
Masri, Safwan Malek *industrial engineer, educator*
Ng, David *electrical engineer*
O'Neill, Thomas J. (Tom O' Neill) *engineering company executive*
Osgood, Richard Magee, Jr. *electrical engineering professor, researcher*
Paaswell, Robert Emil *civil engineer, educator*
Rubenstein, Leonard *engineering company executive*
Sadegh, Ali M. *mechanical engineering educator, researcher, consultant*
Schoenfeld, Robert Louis *biomedical engineer*
Schwartz, Mischa *electrical engineering educator*
See, SawTeen *structural engineer*
Seinuk, Ysrael A. *architectural engineer*
Shinnar, Reuel *engineering educator, consultant*
Smith, Gordon H. *civil and forensic engineer, consultant*
Subak-Sharpe, Gerald Emil *electrical engineer, educator*
Sullivan, Kenneth Wayne *engineer*
Tamboli, Akbar Rasul *consulting engineer*
Tomasetti, Richard L. *structural engineer*
Tsividis, Yannis P. *electrical engineering educator*
Tudor, Helen E. A. *materials engineer, consultant*
Vogelman, Joseph Herbert *scientific engineering company executive*
Watkins, Charles Booker, Jr. *mechanical engineering educator*
Weinstein, Herbert *chemical engineer, educator*
Yao, David Da-Wei *engineering educator*
Yapijakis, Constantine *environmental engineer, educator, consultant*
Yegulalp, Tuncel M. *mining engineer, educator*

Niskayuna
Fatić, Vuk Marko *electrical engineer, educator, researcher*
Rasheed, Adam *aerospace engineer, researcher*

Northport
Weber, Ray Everett *engineering executive, consultant*

Norwood
Church, Richard Dwight *electrical engineer, scientist*

Olean
Ross, Anthony Robert *retired drafting engineer*

Owego
Zendle, Howard Mark *systems engineer, researcher*

Oxford
Ryan, Kenneth Eugene *engineer*

Phoenix
Ackerman, Roger G. *ceramics engineer*

Pittsford
Joos, Felipe Miguel *mechanical engineer, researcher*

Plainview
Sangesland, Odd Einar *mechanical engineer, consultant*

Plattsburgh
Treacy, William Joseph *electrical and environmental engineer*

Pleasantville
Pike, John Nazarian *optical engineering consultant*
Urban, Joseph Jaroslav *engineer, consultant*

Potsdam
Chin, Der-Tau *chemical engineer, educator*

Poughkeepsie
Chu, Richard Chao-Fan *mechanical engineer*
Logue, Joseph Carl *electronics engineer, consultant*
Padegs, Andris *electrical engineer, company executive*
Schmidt, Roger R. *engineer*

Rego Park
Nakanishi, Yuko Julie *engineering educator, consultant*

Rochester
Anthamatten, Mitchell Lewis *chemical engineer, educator*
Begishev, Ildar *electronics engineer*
Carstensen, Edwin Lorenz *retired biomedical engineer, biophysicist*
Coumou, David J. *electrical engineer, consultant*
Drummond, Malcolm McAllister *electronics engineer*
Kurdziel, Michael Thomas *engineering executive*
Parker, Kevin James *electrical engineer, educator*
Stratton, John Alfred *electrical engineer, educator*

Rye
Lehman, Lawrence Herbert *consulting engineering executive*

Scarsdale
Borg, Robert Frederic *civil engineer*

Schenectady
Davis, Lewis Berkley *mechanical engineer*
Mikata, Yozo *mechanical engineer, application developer*
Ringlee, Robert James *retired consulting engineering executive*
Weber, Charles S. *mechanical engineer*

Smithtown
Rockensies, John William *mechanical engineer*

Stony Brook
Chiang, Fu-Pen *mechanical engineering educator, researcher*
Gambino, Richard Joseph *materials engineer, educator*
White, Henry J. *engineering educator, consultant*
Zemanian, Armen Humpartsoum *electrical engineer, mathematician*

Suffern
Coronel, Victor Felipe *engineering educator*

Syracuse
Braiman, Mark Stephen *biomedical educator, researcher*
Driscoll, Charles Thurston, Jr. *civil and environmental engineering educator*
Kim, Yong-Woo *engineer, educator, consultant*
Sargent, Robert George *engineering educator*

Tappan
Cardenas, Raul Rodolfo, Jr. *engineering executive, educator, consultant*
Dell, Robert Christopher *environmental engineer, educator, artist*

Tonawanda
Drozdziel, Marion John *aeronautical engineer*

Troy
Belfort, Georges *chemical engineering educator, consultant*
Bergles, Arthur Edward *mechanical engineering educator*
Block, Robert Charles *nuclear engineering educator*
Dobry, Ricardo *engineering educator*
Dvorak, George J. *mechanics and materials engineering educator*
Freyssinier Nova, Jean Paul *engineering research professor*
Gerhardt, Lester A. *engineering educator, dean*
Gill, William Nelson *chemical engineering professor*
Glicksman, Martin Eden *materials engineering educator*
Gutmann, Ronald J. *retired electrical engineering educator*
Haddock, Jorge *industrial engineering educator, consultant*
Hsu, Cheng *decision sciences and engineering systems educator*
Lahey, Richard Thomas, Jr. *nuclear and fluid mechanics engineer*
Littman, Howard *chemical engineer, educator*
McDonald, John Francis Patrick *electrical engineering educator*
Sanderson, Arthur Clark *engineering educator*
Shephard, Mark Scott *civil and mechanical engineering educator*
Shur, Michael *electrical engineer, educator, consultant*
Woods, John William *electrical, computer and systems engineering educator, consultant*
Zimmie, Thomas Frank *civil engineer, educator*

Upton
Fthenakis, Vasilis *chemical engineer, consultant, educator*
Steinberg, Meyer *chemical engineer*

Watervliet
Elrahman, O. Abd *environmental and transportation engineer, educator*
Troiano, Edward *mechanical engineer, researcher*

Webster
McWilliams, C. Paul, Jr. *engineering executive*

White Plains
Foster, John Horace *consulting environmental engineer*
Haines, Daniel Webster *engineering consultant, engineering educator*
Huang, Han *systems engineer*
Mitchell, Robert Dale *engineer, consultant*

Williamsville
Metzger, Ernest Hugh *aerospace engineer, research scientist*

Yorktown Heights
Das, Koushik K. *industrial researcher*
Dennard, Robert Heath *engineering executive, scientist*
Kim, Keunwoo *electrical engineer, researcher*
Terman, Lewis Madison *retired electrical engineer, researcher, director*

NORTH CAROLINA

Cary
Conrad, Hans *materials science and engineering educator*
Hauser, John Reid *electrical engineering educator*
Vick, Columbus Edwin, Jr. *retired civil engineering design firm executive*

Chapel Hill
Green, Paul Eliot, Jr. *retired optical engineer*
Hobgood, W. Sands *systems engineer*
Marchionini, Gary Joseph *information science educator*
McKinney, Ross Erwin, Sr. *civil engineering educator*
Okun, Daniel Alexander *environmental engineering educator*

Charlotte
Cooke, Steven John *chemical engineer, consultant, scientist*
Elanayar, Sunil K. *research and development engineer*
Fitzpatrick, James Ward, Jr. *retired engineering educator*
Jordan, Robert Sands *electrical engineer*
Valasquez, Joseph Louis *industrial engineer*

Columbus
Brooks, Jerry Claude *safety engineer, educator*

Durham
Bejan, Adrian *mechanical engineering educator*
Carter, Calvin H., Jr. *materials engineer*
Casey, H(orace) Craig, Jr. *electrical engineering educator*

Edmond, John *engineering company executive*
Ekici, Kivanc *aerospace engineer, researcher*
Goodwin, Frank Erik *materials engineer*
Petroski, Henry *engineering educator, writer*
Plonsey, Robert *electrical and biomedical engineer*
Stiff-Roberts, Adrienne D. *electrical engineer, educator*
Utku, Senol *civil engineer, computer science educator*

Granite Falls
Humphreys, Kenneth King *engineer, educator, professional society administrator*

Greensboro
Bolick, Ronnie Lee *mechanical engineer*
Eromon, David Ighogboya *electronics engineer, educator*
Fujino, Michimasa *aeronautical engineer*
Lou, Jianzhong *chemical engineer, educator*
Oliver, Terry James *retired electronics engineer, communications engineer*
Seong, Younho *engineering educator*

Morrisville
Baumann, Karsten *engineer, researcher*

New Bern
Moeller, Dade William *environmental engineer, educator*
Painter, Jack Timberlake *civil engineer*
Whitehurst, Brooks Morris *chemical engineer*

Raleigh
Barrett, Rolin Farrar, Jr. *mechanical engineer, consultant*
Beatty, Kenneth Orion, Jr. *chemical engineer, educator*
Bitzer, Donald Lester *electrical engineer, educator, retired lab administrator*
Gardner, Robin Pierce *engineering educator*
Hall, Carol K. *chemical engineering educator, researcher*
Holton, William Coffeen *electrical engineering executive*
Kolbas, Robert Michael *electrical engineering educator*
Larsen, Ralph Irving *retired environmental engineer*
Loboa, Elizabeth Grace *biomedical engineer, educator*
Masnari, Nino Antonio *electrical engineer, educator*
Murray, Raymond Le Roy *nuclear engineering educator*
Odum, Jeffery Neal *mechanical engineer*
Ozturk, Mehmet Cevdet *engineering educator*
Phillips, Oliverio Michelsen *retired chemical engineer*
Sneed, Ronald Ernest *retired project engineer, engineering educator*
Turinsky, Paul Josef *nuclear engineer, educator*
Wehring, Bernard William *nuclear engineering educator*
Williams, Hugh Alexander, Jr. *retired mechanical engineer, consultant*
Yim, Man-Sung *engineering educator, consultant*
Zorowski, Carl Frank *engineering educator, academic administrator*

Research Triangle Park
Bottomley, Gregory E. *electrical engineer, researcher*
Everett, LaTonya Michelle *computer engineer*
Isler, Raymond Earl *engineer*

Thomasville
Hinkle, William Paul *mechanical and electrical engineer, consultant*

Whispering Pines
Kuhn, Matthew *retired engineering company executive*

Wilmington
Ao, Qi *nuclear engineer, research scientist*

Winston Salem
Bourne, Henry Clark, Jr. *electrical engineer, educator, retired academic administrator*

NORTH DAKOTA

Fargo
Reitan, Daniel Kinseth *electric and computer engineering educator*
Yadav, Om Prakash *reliability engineer, educator*

OHIO

Ada
Estell, John K. *computer science and engineering educator, department chair*

Akron
Ahn, Dae Up *polymer engineer, researcher*
Brown, David Rupert *engineering executive*
Daniels, Christopher *mechanical engineer, educator*
Isayev, Avraam Isayevich *polymer engineer, educator*
Jana, Sadhan C. *engineering educator, researcher*
Phares, James Kenneth *retired electronics engineer*

Athens
Irwin, Richard Dennis *electrical engineering educator*

Aurora
Kirchner, James William *retired electrical engineer*

Barberton
Kitto, John Buck, Jr. *mechanical engineer*

Cincinnati
Agrawal, Dharma Prakash *engineering educator*
Bahr, Donald Walter *retired chemical engineer*
Cabezas, Heriberto *chemical engineer, researcher*
Ghia, Kirti N. *fluid mechanics engineer, aerospace educator*
Greenberg, David Bernard *chemical engineering educator*
Hodge, Bobby Lynn *mechanical engineer, manufacturing executive*
Kowel, Stephen Thomas *electrical engineer, educator*
Martin, John Bruce *chemical engineer*
Morgan, William Richard *mechanical engineer*
Ratliff, Thomas Asbury, Jr. *retired engineer*
Sinha, Sunil K. *aerospace engineer, consultant*
Smith, Leroy Harrington, Jr. *mechanical engineer, consultant*
Wei, Heng *engineering educator*
Weisman, Joel *retired engineering educator*
Wisler, David Charles *aerospace engineer*

Cleveland
Abramson, Alexis R. *mechanical engineering educator*
Angus, John Cotton *chemical engineering educator*
Bhadra, Narendra *biomedical engineer, researcher*
Burghart, James Henry *electrical engineer, educator*
Deissler, Robert George *fluid dynamics researcher*
Hardy, Richard Allen *mechanical engineer, engineering executive*
Kirsch, James F. *materials executive*
Ko, Wen-Hsiung *electrical engineering educator*
Madden, James D. *forensic engineer*
Prahl, Joseph Markel *mechanical engineering educator*
Saada, Adel Selim *civil engineer, educator*
Savinell, Robert Francis *engineering educator*
Slobozhanin, Lev Arkadievich *fluid mechanics engineer, researcher*
T'ien, James Shaw-Tzuu *engineering educator*
Wilson, Jack *aeronautical engineer*

Columbus
Adeli, Hojjat *engineer, educator, computer scientist*
Alexander, Carl Albert *materials engineer, engineering educator*
Altan, Taylan *engineering educator, director*
Bhushan, Bharat *mechanical engineer*
Brodkey, Robert Stanley *chemical engineering educator*
Brust, Frederick William, Jr. *structural and mechanical engineer*
Cruz, Jose Bejar, Jr. *engineering educator*
Fan, Liang-Shih *chemical engineering educator*
Fenton, Robert Earl *electrical engineering educator*
Harris, Ronald David *chemical engineer*
Houser, Donald Russell *mechanical engineering educator, consultant*
Kennedy, Lawrence Allan *mechanical engineering educator*
Miller, Don Wilson *nuclear engineering educator*
Moulton, Edward Quentin *civil engineer, educator*
Ozkan, Umit Sivrioglu *chemical engineering professor*
Peters, Leon, Jr. *retired engineering educator*
Rapp, Robert Anthony *metallurgical engineering educator*
Sebo, Stephen Andrew *electrical engineer, educator, researcher, consultant*
Singh, Rajendra *mechanical engineering educator, director*
Stefanescu, Doru Michael *metallurgical engineer, educator*
Zakin, Jacques Louis *chemical engineering educator*

Dayton
Ballal, Dilip Ramchandra *mechanical engineering educator*
Coutu, Ronald Armand, Jr. *electrical engineer, program manger*
Houpis, Constantine Harry *retired electrical engineering educator*
Kazimierczuk, Marian Kazimierczuk *electrical engineer, educator*
Kumar, Binod *materials engineer, educator*
Mukhopadhyay, Sharmila Mitra *materials engineer, educator*
Phillips, Chandler Allen *biomedical engineer, human factors engineer*
Schmitt, George Frederick, Jr. *materials engineer*
Vukelich, Sharon Irene *aerospace engineer, consultant*

Gahanna
Majtenyi, Steven Istvan *retired civil engineer, consultant*

Gates Mills
Enyedy, Gustav, Jr. *chemical engineer*

Lakeside Marblehead
Haering, Edwin Raymond *chemical engineering educator, consultant*

Mansfield
Sheridan, Mark William *mechanical engineer, financial planner*

Mayfield Heights
Grants, Valdis *engineering manager*

Medina
Rog, Joseph W. *engineering company executive*

Middletown
Newby, John Robert *metallurgical engineer*

North Olmsted
Bluford, Guion Stewart, Jr. *engineering company executive*

Orrville
Daniel, Deckler *engineering educator*

Oxford
Ward, Roscoe Fredrick *engineering educator*

Shaker Heights
Siegel, Robert *heat transfer engineer*

Springboro
Saxer, Richard Karl *metallurgical engineer, retired military officer*

Tipp City
Glassmeyer, James Milton *aerospace, computer, and electronics engineer*

Toledo
Dukkipati, Rao Venkateswara *engineering educator, researcher, scientist*
Koo, Benjamin Hai Chang *structural engineer, educator*
Wolff, Edwin Ray *retired construction engineer, consultant*

Valley View
Petroski, James *thermal engineer*

West Chester
Arasakesari, Subramaniam *chemical engineer, researcher, consultant*
Tanov, Romil R. *mechanical engineer, researcher*

Wilberforce
Habash, Khalil M. *computer engineer, educator*

Worthington
Compton, Ralph Theodore, Jr. *electrical engineering educator*
Wu, Tien Hsing *civil engineering educator, consultant*

Wright Patterson Afb
Mall, Shankar *engineering mechanics educator, researcher*
Rizzetta, Donald P. *aerospace engineer*

Yellow Springs
Trolander, Hardy Wilcox *engineering executive, consultant*

Youngstown
Cernica, John N. *engineering educator, civil engineer, consultant*
Fok, Thomas Dso Yun *civil engineer*

OKLAHOMA

Bartlesville
Hankinson, Risdon William *retired chemical engineer*

Norman
Altan, M(ustafa) Cengiz *mechanical engineering educator*
Bert, Charles Wesley *mechanical and aerospace engineer, educator*
Campbell, John Morgan *retired chemical engineer*
Gollahalli, Subramanyam Ramappa *engineering educator*
Khoury, Naji *engineering educator*
Lai, Feng Chyuan *engineering educator*
Lamb, Peter James *meteorology educator, researcher, consultant*
MacFarland, Miriam Katherine (Mimi) *computer engineer, consultant, writer, educator*
Oliver, Dean S. *petroleum engineer, educator*
Zelby, Leon Wolf *electrical engineer, educator, consultant*

Oklahoma City
Miller, Herbert Dell *petroleum engineer*

Sperry
Dunn, Albert Edgar *electrical engineer*

Stillwater
Case, Kenneth Eugene *industrial engineering educator*
Maddox, Robert Nott *chemical engineer, educator*
Mize, Joe Henry *industrial engineer, educator*
Thompson, David Russell *engineering educator, dean*

Tulsa
Ahmed, Ramadan *engineering educator, educator*
Azar, J. J. *engineering educator*
Hong, Jianhui *chemical engineer*
Liu, Xiaofan Sophie *engineering educator*
Williams, John Horter *civil engineer, energy industry executive*

OREGON

Beaverton
Campbell, Richard Lynn *research engineer*
Chartier, Vernon Lee *electrical engineer*

Bend
Knitowski, David Alan *civil engineer, urban planner*

Corvallis
Byers, William D. *engineering executive*
Engelbrecht, Rudolf *electrical engineering educator*
Temes, Gabor Charles *electrical engineering educator*
Zhang, Eugene *engineering educator*

Eugene
Langfeldt, Andrew *engineer*

Florence
Ericksen, Jerald Laverne *retired science engineering educator*

Hillsboro
Berger, Otto *engineer*
Bohr, Mark T. *architectural engineer*
Heath, Matthew W. *engineer*
Hiranandani, Manish Ashok *electrical engineer*

John Day
Tuttle, Kenneth Lewis *retired engineering educator, consultant, researcher*

Klamath Falls
Woodall, David Monroe *engineer, researcher, dean*

Lake Oswego
Gehrig, Edward Harry *electrical engineer, consultant*

Myrtle Point
Walsh, Don *engineer, consultant*

Portland
Al-Rabadi, Anas Naser Essa *electrical and computer engineer*
Hall, Howard Pickering *engineering and mathematics educator*
Kennedy, R(obert) Evan *engineering executive, consultant, retired structural engineer*
Kocaoglu, Dundar F. *engineering management educator, industrial engineer, civil engineer*
Pham, Kinh Dinh *electrical engineer, executive, educator*

PENNSYLVANIA

Allentown
Foster, Edward Paul (Ted Foster) *process industries executive*
Gewartowski, James Walter *retired electrical engineer*
Valero-Lopez, Ari Yakov *electrical engineer*

Apollo
Musselman, Larry L. *chemical engineer*

Ashland
Polyakov, Yuriy Sergeyevich *engineer, researcher*

Bala Cynwyd
Aziz, Adnan *manufacturing engineer, marketing products engineer*
Staley, Kenneth Bernard *civil engineer*

Bethel Park
Korchynsky, Michael *metallurgical engineer*

Bethlehem
El-Aasser, Mohamed S. *engineering educator, academic administrator*
Gardiner, Keith Mattinson *engineering executive educator*
Koch, Thomas L *engineering educator*
Pense, Alan Wiggins *metallurgical engineer, academic administrator*
Sengupta, Arup Kumar *engineering educator, researcher*
Sircar, Shivaji *chemical engineer, researcher*
Tuzla, Kemal *mechanical engineer, researcher*

Blue Bell
Sun, Hun H. *retired electrical and biomedical engineering educator*

Boalsburg
Gettig, Martin Winthrop *retired mechanical engineer*

Bryn Mawr
Hegedus, L. Louis *chemical engineer, consultan retired research and development company executive*

Camp Hill
Ellis, Stephen A. *engineering executive, consultant*

Chadds Ford
Isakoff, Sheldon Erwin *chemical engineer*

Cheltenham
Weinstock, Walter Wolfe *systems engineer*

Chester
Huang, Zhongping *engineering educator*

Coopersburg
Bolle, Donald Martin *retired engineering educator*
Peserik, James E. *electrical engineer, consultan safety engineer, computer engineer*
Siess, Alfred Albert, Jr. *engineering executive, management consultant*

Coraopolis
Kay, George Paul *environmental engineer*

Cranberry Township
McNamara, Michael Lee Perry *automation engineer*

Downingtown
Deb, Arun Kumar *environmental engineer*

Erie
Dockstader, Emmett Stanley *civil engineer, construction executive*

Exton
Berry, Matthew M. *aerospace engineer*

Glen Mills
Churchill, Stuart Winston *chemical engineering educator*

Greensburg
Ference, Edward W. *engineering executive, structural engineer*
Langer, Alois *biomedical engineer*
Spaeder, Francis Xavier *forensic electrical engineer*

Harrisburg
Kulicki, John M. *structural engineer*

Hershey
Lim, Jung Yul *biomedical engineer*

Homestead
Mandel, Herbert Maurice *civil engineer*

Huntingdon Valley
Verrant, John Alan *engineering executive*
West, A(rnold) Sumner *chemical engineer*

Irwin
Kuhn, Howard Arthur *engineering executive, educator*

Jamison
Touhill, C. Joseph *environmental engineer*

Lancaster
Ebersole, J. Glenn, Jr. *engineering, marketing, management, public relations and strategic planning executive*
Graffis, Leister F. *retired engineering executive*

Lansdale
Hargens, Charles William III *electrical engineer, consultant*

Lewisburg
Aldrich, Robert Adams *agricultural engineer, consultant*

Lititz
Lehman, Richard William *electrical engineer*

Moon Township
Rabosky, Joseph George *engineering consulting company executive*

Mount Pleasant
Roadman, Joseph Peter *engineering consultant*

Murrysville
Yang, Wen-Ching *chemical engineer*

Nanticoke
Eddy, Carl F. *engineering educator*

New Holland
Wagner, Bradley Jeremiah *agricultural engineer*

Newtown
Rao, Sudhakar *aerospace engineer, researcher*

Newtown Square
Perrone, Nicholas *engineering company executive*

Philadelphia
Bilgutay, Nihat Mustafa *engineering educator, associate dean*
Bordogna, Joseph *engineering educator, former science foundation executive*
Cohen, Ira Myron *retired aeronautical and mechanical engineering educator*
Crocker, John C. *chemical and biomolecular engineer, educator*
Director, Stephen William *electrical and computer engineering educator, academic administrator*
Falkie, Thomas Victor *mining engineer, engineering executive*
Fegley, Kenneth Allen *systems engineering educator*
Fromm, Eli *engineering educator*
Glandt, Eduardo Daniel *chemical engineering educator*
Guron, Dov *biomedical engineer, educator*
Khanna, Nitin *engineering executive*
Lawley, Alan *materials engineer, educator*
Lewin, Peter Andrew *electrical engineer, educator*
Litt, Mitchell *chemical engineer, bioengineer, educator*
Mao, Weidong *communications engineer, technology executive*
Morlok, Edward Karl *engineering educator, consultant*
Mulford, Richard Albert *mechanical engineer, professional society administrator*
Nikolov, Zhorro *engineering educator, director*
Popovics, Sandor *civil engineer, educator, researcher*
Quinn, John Albert *chemical engineering professor*
Walker, Allen Lyon *engineer*
Walker, Danielle *engineering executive*
Winston, Flaura K. *engineering researcher*

Pittsburgh
Amon, Cristina Hortensia *mechanical engineering educator, researcher*
Biegler, Lorenz Theodor *chemical engineering educator*
Bloom, William Millard *furnace design engineer*
Carelli, Mario Domenico *nuclear engineer*
Casasent, David Paul *electrical engineer, educator, data processing executive*
Charap, Stanley Harvey *electrical engineering educator*
Choset, Howie *engineering educator, researcher*
Demetri, Kathryn J. *civil engineer*
Dutt, Varun *systems and software engineer*
Dzombak, David Adam *environmental engineering educator*
Fu, Weinong *electrical engineer*
Grossmann, Ignacio Emilio *chemical engineering educator*
Hendrickson, Chris Thompson *civil and environmental engineering educator, researcher*
Higgs, C. Fred III *mechanical engineer, educator*
Hoburg, James Frederick *electrical engineering educator*
Jordan, Angel Goni *electrical and computer engineering educator*
Khosla, Pradeep Kumar *engineering educator*
Kryder, Mark Howard *computer and electrical engineering executive, educator, consultant*
Leney, George Willard *retired consulting engineer*
Li, Ching-Chung *electrical engineering educator*
Maly, Wojciech P. *engineering educator, researcher*
McAvoy, Bruce Ronald *engineer, consultant*
Mehalik, Matthew M. *industrial engineer, educator*
Mickle, Marlin Homer *electrical engineer, educator*
Milnes, Arthur George *electrical engineer, educator*
Morgan, M(illett) Granger *electrical engineering educator, researcher*
Neufeld, Ronald David *environmental engineer, educator*
Neuman, Charles P. *electrical and computer engineering educator*
Nielsen, Paul Douglas *engineering executive, retired military officer*
O'Donnell, William James *engineering executive*
Peterson, Robert Scott *electrical engineer*
Pettit, Frederick Sidney *metallurgical engineering educator, department chairman*
Ruh, Edwin *ceramic engineer, consultant, researcher*
Savvides, Marios *electrical and computer engineer, research professor*
Shea, John Joseph *electrical engineer*
Simaan, Marwan *electrical engineering educator*
Stahl, Laddie L. *engineering company executive*
Westerberg, Arthur William *retired chemical engineering professor*
Whittaker, William L. (Red Whittaker) *engineering educator, research scientist*
Woo, Savio Lau-Yuen *bioengineering educator*
Xia, Yunkai *engineer*

Reading
Moriarty, John Klinge *electrical engineer, consultant*

Schnecksville
Hansel, James Gordon *retired engineer, educator*

Sewickley
Fells, Charles Dayton *civil engineer, educator*

State College
Albright, Gifford Harry *retired architectural engineering educator, consultant*
Barnoff, Robert Mark *civil engineering educator*
Brown, John Lawrence, Jr. *electrical engineering educator*
Foderaro, Anthony Harolde *nuclear engineering educator*
Grimes, Dale Mills *physics and electrical engineering educator*
Hettche, L. Raymond *engineering educator, retired research scientist*
Olson, Donald Richard *mechanical engineering educator*
Sibul, Leon Henry *electrical engineer*

Swarthmore
Krendel, Ezra Simon *systems and human factors engineering consultant*

University Park
Bose, Nirmal Kumar *electrical engineer, mathematics educator*
Cross, Leslie Eric *electrical engineering educator*
Davids, Norman *engineering educator, researcher*
Holl, John William *engineering educator*
Irwin, Mary Jane *engineering educator*
Kabel, Robert Lynn *chemical engineering professor*
Knott, Kenneth *industrial engineering educator, consultant*
Liu, Zi-Kui *materials engineer, educator*
Manbeck, Harvey B. *agricultural and biological engineer, educator*
McCormick, Barnes Warnock *aerospace engineering educator*
Osseo-Asare, Kwadwo *engineering educator*
Ramani, Raja Venkat *engineering educator*
Scanlon, Andrew *structural engineering educator*
Tittmann, Bernhard Rainer *engineering science and mechanics educator*
Todd Copley, Judith A. *engineering educator*
Vannice, M. Albert *chemical engineering professor, researcher*
Vrentas, James Spiro *chemical engineering professor*
Wormley, David Neal *engineering educator*
Wysk, Richard A. *engineering educator, researcher*
Zhang, Qiming *engineering educator, researcher*

Villanova
McLaughlin, Philip VanDoren, Jr. *mechanical engineering educator, researcher, consultant*
Tomlinson, J. Richard *retired engineering services company executive*

Waynesboro
Martin, Harold G. *engineering consultant*

West Mifflin
Ardash, Garin *mechanical engineer*

West Point
Buckland, Barry Christopher *chemical engineer*

Yardley
Hochreiter, Joseph Christian, Jr. *engineering company executive*

York
Horn, Russell Eugene *engineering executive, consultant*
Horn, Russell Eugene, Jr. *engineering executive*
Kennedy, Christopher Robin *ceramics engineer, director*

RHODE ISLAND

Bristol
Danzberger, Alexander Harris *retired chemical engineer, consultant*

Middletown
Ellison, William Theodore *marine engineer*

Newport
Cray, Benjamin A. *mechanical engineer*
Ruffa, Anthony Armand *mechanical engineer*

Providence
Freund, Lambert Ben *engineering educator, researcher, consultant*
Glicksman, Maurice *engineering educator, retired dean, provost*
Hazeltine, Barrett *electrical engineer, educator*
Lawal, Taiwo Munir *civil engineer*
Needleman, Alan *mechanical engineering educator*
Nurmikko, Arto Veikko *engineering educator*
Richman, Marc Herbert *engineer, forensic specialist, educator*
Suuberg, Eric Michael *chemical engineering educator*
Weiner, Jerome Harris *mechanical engineering educator*

Wakefield
Boothroyd, Geoffrey *industrial and manufacturing engineering educator*

SOUTH CAROLINA

Beaufort
Pinkerton, Robert Bruce *mechanical engineer*

Bluffton
Jerger, Edward William *engineering educator, dean*

Charleston
Fei, James Robert *engineering executive, consultant*
Haemmerich, Dieter *biomedical engineer*
Wen, Xuejun *biomedical engineer, educator*

Clemson
Greenstein, Joel Sandor *industrial engineering educator*
Jalili, Nader *mechanical engineer, educator*
Luo, Jian *engineering educator, researcher*
Pursley, Michael Bader *engineering educator, communications systems researcher, consultant*
Zumbrunnen, David Arnold *engineering educator*

Columbia
Baskin, C. R. *civil engineer*
Gibbons, Joseph Harrison *engineering educator, farmer*
Graulty, Robert Thomas *engineer, consultant*
Ladmer, William Edward *food product engineering executive*

Greer
Hu, Yiping *metallurgical engineer*

Hartsville
Menius, Espie Flynn, Jr. *electrical engineer*

Hilton Head Island
Huckins, Harold Aaron *chemical engineer*
Windman, Arnold Lewis *retired mechanical engineer*

Johns Island
Silveston, Peter Lewis *engineering educator, consultant*

Myrtle Beach
Feck, Asmus Wilhelm *retired mechanical engineer*

Orangeburg
Hong, Jae-Dong *industrial engineering educator*

SOUTH DAKOTA

Brookings
Qian, Li *engineering educator*

Pierre
Larsen, Wallace Lawrence *retired transportation engineer, county official*

Rapid City
Bang, Sangchul *engineering educator*
Gowen, Richard Joseph *electrical engineer, educator, retired academic administrator*
Pillay, Gautam *chemical engineer, chemist, academic administrator*
Ramakrishnan, Venkataswamy *civil engineer, educator*
Scofield, Gordon Lloyd *mechanical engineer, educator*

Spearfish
Addy, Alva Leroy *mechanical engineer*

TENNESSEE

Brentwood
Clevenger, William Thomas *electrical engineer*

Chattanooga
Duckworth, Jerrell James *electrical engineer*

Cookeville
Chowdhuri, Pritindra *retired electrical engineer, educator*
Hossain, Faisal *engineering educator*
Mohr, Benjamin John *engineering educator*
Sissom, Leighton Esten *engineering educator, dean, consultant*
Ting, Kwun-Lon *engineer, educator, consultant*

Crossville
Bell, Charles Eugene, Jr. *retired industrial engineer*

Greenbrier
Newell, Paul Haynes, Jr. *engineering educator*

Jackson
Cole, John Frankland *electrical engineer, educator*

Johnson City
Rahmani, Ramin Khosravi *mechanical engineer, researcher*

Kingsport
Siirola, Jeffrey John *chemical engineer*
Tant, Martin Ray *chemical engineer, biomedical engineer*

Knoxville
Alexeff, Igor *retired electrical engineering educator*
Beavers, James Earl *engineer, director, consultant*
Bose, Bimal Kumar *electrical engineering educator*
Fu, Joshua S. *environmental engineer, educator, research scientist*
Irick, David Kim *engineering educator, consultant*
Mc Dow, John Jett *biosystems engineering educator*
Mise, Jesse Sherden *structural engineer, consultant*
Naoumov, Viatcheslav I. *mechanical engineer, educator*
Oakes, Thomas Wyatt *environmental engineer, computer engineer*
Prados, John William *retired engineering educator*
Richards, Stephen Harold *engineering educator*
Roth, John Reece *electrical engineer, educator, researcher, inventor*
Schuler, Theodore Anthony *retired civil engineer*
Uhrig, Robert Eugene *nuclear engineer, educator*
Wu, Jie *electronics engineer, educator*

Martin
Wheeler, Edward *engineering educator*

Maryville
Oakes, Lester Cornelius *retired electrical engineer, consultant*

Memphis
Born, Robert Heywood *consulting civil engineer*
Daugherty, James Albert *retired aeronautical engineer*
Rue, Douglas Michael *solutions engineer*

Nashville
Galloway, Kenneth Franklin *engineering educator*
Hahn, George Thomas *materials engineering educator, researcher*
Jiang, Xiaomo *engineering researcher*
LeVan, Martin Douglas *chemical engineering professor*
Schnelle, Karl Benjamin, Jr. *chemical engineering professor, consultant, researcher*
Speece, Richard Eugene *civil engineer, educator*

Oak Ridge
Pannala, Sreekanth *aerospace engineer*
Zinkle, Steven John *engineer, researcher*

Winchester
Whetsel, Roger Girton *retired aerospace engineer*

TEXAS

Allen
Biard, James Robert *retired electrical engineer, consultant*

Alpine
Kittlitz, Rudolf Gottlieb, Jr. *chemical engineer, researcher*

Amarillo
Von Eschen, Robert Leroy *electrical engineer, consultant*

Arlington
Lewis, Frank Leroy *electrical engineer, educator, researcher*
Liu, Hanli *biomedical engineer, educator*
Rollins, Albert Williamson *civil engineer, consultant*
Stevens, Gladstone Taylor, Jr. *retired industrial engineer, retired educator*

Austin
Abraham, Jacob A. *computer engineering educator, consultant*
Akins, Vaughn Edward *retired engineering company executive*
Bae, Sungkoo *aeronautical engineer, aerospace engineer, researcher*
Baker, Lee Edward *biomedical engineering educator*
Bishop, Robert Harold *aerospace engineering educator*
Brannon-Peppas, Lisa *chemical engineer, researcher*
Breen, John Edward *civil engineer, educator*
Brock, James Rush *chemical engineering professor*
Bronaugh, Edwin Lee *retired electrical engineer*
Burns, Ned Hamilton *civil engineering educator*
Carlton, Donald Morrill *retired research, development and engineering executive*
Cywar, Adam Walter *engineering executive*
Dougal, Arwin Adelbert *electrical engineer, educator*
Fair, James Rutherford, Jr. *engineering educator, consultant*
Fowler, David Wayne *architectural engineering educator*
Georgiou, George *chemical engineer, educator*
Goodenough, John Bannister *engineering educator, physicist, researcher*
Harris, Richard Lee *engineering executive, retired military officer*
Hassibi, Arjang *engineering educator, director*
Himmelblau, David Mautner *chemical engineer*
Hixson, Elmer L. *retired engineering educator*
Holmquist, Darrel Vernon *geotechnical engineer, arbitrator, mediator*
Howell, John Reid *mechanical engineering educator, director*
Hughes, Thomas Joseph Robert *mechanical engineering educator, consultant*
Hull, David George *aerospace engineering educator, researcher*
Jensen, Paul Allen *mechanical engineer*
Johnson, Sandra K. *electrical engineer*
Koen, Billy Vaughn *mechanical engineering educator*
Kyriakides, Stelios K. *aerospace engineer, educator*
Lamb, Jamie Parker, Jr. *retired mechanical engineer*
Lindsay, Leslie *packaging engineer*
Loo, Lynn (Yueh-Lin) *chemical engineer*
Mc Ketta, John J., Jr. *chemical engineering professor*
Nichols, Steven Parks *mechanical engineer, educator, academic administrator, lawyer*
Oden, John Tinsley *engineering educator, mathematician, consultant*
Peppas, Nicholas Athanassiou *chemical and biomedical engineering educator, consultant*
Reese, Lymon Clifton *civil engineering educator*
Reible, Danny David *environmental chemical engineer, educator*
Reiter, David S. *engineering company executive, lawyer*
Richards-Kortum, Rebecca Rae *biomedical engineering educator*
Rylander, Henry Grady, Jr. *mechanical engineering educator*
Sandberg, Irwin Walter *retired electrical and computer engineering educator*
Schechter, Robert Samuel *chemical engineer, educator*
Sciance, Carroll Thomas *chemical engineer, educator*
Steinfink, Hugo *chemical engineering professor*
Stokoe, Kenneth H., II, *civil engineer, educator*
Streetman, Ben Garland *electrical engineering educator*
Swartzlander, Earl Eugene, Jr. *engineering educator, former electronics company executive*
Thurston, George Butte *mechanical and biomedical engineering educator*
Truchard, James J. *engineering executive*
Tucker, Richard Lee *civil engineer, educator*
Walton, Charles Michael *civil engineering educator*
Welch, Ashley James *engineering educator*
Willson, C. Grant *chemical engineering and chemistry professor*
Wise, Gary Lamar *electrical engineer, educator, mathematician, researcher*

Bacliff
Bacani, Nicanor-Guglielmo Vila *civil and structural engineer, consultant*

Baird
Rodenberger, Charles Alvard *aerospace engineer, consultant*

Beaumont
Hopper, Jack Rudd *chemical engineering professor*
Koehn, Enno *engineering educator, researcher*

Beeville
Littlejohn, John Joseph *petroleum engineer*

Big Spring
Fryrear, Donald William *agricultural engineer, researcher*

Bryan
Bigham, Robert Eric *engineer*
Samson, Charles Harold, Jr., (Car Samson) *retired engineering educator, consultant*

Burleson
Hunter, Louis G. *retired aerospace engineer*

Bushland
Howell, Terry Allen *agricultural engineer*

Cat Spring
Ramsey, Mary Catherine *mechanical engineer, consultant*

Channelview
Dunn, Donald Glenn *electrical engineer, consultant*

College Station
Akin, Bilal *electrical engineer*
Bennett, G(eorge) Kemble *engineering educator*
Buchanan, Walter Woolwine *electrical engineer, educator, academic administrator*
Butenko, Sergiy *engineering educator*
Butler-Purry, Karen L. *electrical engineer, educator*
Ehsani, Mehrdad (Mark) *electrical engineering educator, consultant*
Ewing, Richard Edward *mathematics, chemical and petroleum engineering educator*
Fletcher, Leroy Stevenson *mechanical engineer, educator*
Hall, Kenneth Richard *chemical engineering professor, consultant*
Hann, Roy William, Jr. *civil engineer, educator*
Kuhn, Beverly Thompson *transportation engineer*
Lee, William John *petroleum engineering educator, consultant*
Lu, Mi *computer engineer, educator*
Lytton, Robert Leonard *civil engineer, educator*
Mathewson, Christopher Colville *engineer, geologist, educator*
Ntaimo, Lewis *engineering educator, researcher*
Page, Robert Henry *retired engineering educator, researcher*
Painter, John Hoyt *engineer*
Patton, Alton DeWitt *electrical engineering consultant*
Radovic, Miladin *engineering educator, researcher*
Reddy, J. N. *mechanical engineering educator*
Reinschmidt, Kenneth Frank *engineering and construction executive, educator*
Richardson, Herbert Heath *retired mechanical engineer, educator, dean, academic administrator*
Riskowski, Gerald Lee *engineering educator*
Saric, William Samuel *aerospace engineering educator*
Ullman, Gerald Lee *transportation engineer*

Dallas
Berry, James F. (Jim Berry) *engineering executive*
Doty, Elmer *aeronautical engineer*
Eberhart, Robert Clyde *biomedical engineering educator, researcher*
Fontana, Robert Edward *electrical engineer, educator, retired military officer*
Francisco, Glen Leif *engineer, engineering executive*
Huang, Yen Ti *civil engineer*
Kovacevic, Radovan *mechanical engineering educator*
Malouf, Mark E. *structural engineer, consultant*
McLane, William Delano *mechanical engineer*
Medlin, Homer Lewis *engineering executive*
Rainwater, R. Steven *systems engineer*
Ray, Hillol Kumar *environmental engineer, poet*
Schulze, Richard Hans *environmental engineering executive*
Sengupta, Chaitali *computer engineer*
Szygenda, Stephen A. *electrical and computer engineering educator, researcher*
Xiu, Liming *electrical engineer*
Zhou, Desheng *petroleum engineer*

Denton
Kougianos, Elias *engineering educator, consultant*

Edinburg
Lozano, Karen *engineering educator*
Vasquez, Horacio *mechanical engineer, educator*

El Paso
Heide, John Wesley *engineering executive*

Fort Worth
Astrup, Jens Leo *retired civil engineer*
Cunningham, Atlee Marion, Jr. *aeronautical engineer*
Maldonado, Francisco Javier *electrical research engineer*
Mayyas, Mohammad A. *mechanical engineer, researcher*
Nichols, James Richard *civil engineer, consultant*
Wise, Charla Kamm *aeronautics company executive*

Frisco
Mihm, John Clifford *chemical engineer*

Galveston
Ingole, Sudeep Prabhakar *engineering educator, researcher*
Otis, John James *civil engineer*

Garland
Christensen, Allan Robert *electrical engineer, financial consultant, social services counselor*

Georgetown
Hartman, Thomas Bennett *mechanical engineer*
Moore, Pat Howard *engineering and construction executive, educator*

Houston
Ahmad, Farrukh *environmental engineer, chemist*
Akers, William Walter *chemical engineering educator*
Arnold, Ken E. *engineering company executive*
Athanasiou, Kyriacos A. *biomedical engineer*
Bai, Yong *engineering executive, educator*
Bomba, John Gilbert *civil engineer, consultant*
Bovay, Harry Elmo, Jr. *retired engineering company executive*
Burrus, (Charles) Sidney *electrical engineering educator*
Chapman, Alan Jesse *engineering educator*
Cheatham, John Bane, Jr. *retired mechanical engineering educator*
Duerr, David *civil engineer*
Focht, John Arnold, Jr. *engineer*
Frank, Karen Denise *aerospace engineer*
Hasen, Michael *engineering company executive, civil engineer*
Henley, Ernest Justus *retired chemical engineering professor*
Horton, Thomas Edward, Jr. *mechanical engineering educator*
Hsu, Thomas Tseng-Chuang *civil engineer, educator*
Huang, Beiqing *mechanical engineer, educator*
Huang, Hsien-Lu *electrical engineer*
Huang, Shawn Shaoping *engineer*
Jackson, Michael Lynn *civil and structural engineer, sales executive*
Kavandi, Janet Lynn *aerospace power engineer, chemist*
Kobayashi, Riki *retired chemical engineer, educator*
Krause, William Austin *engineering executive*
Krishen, Kumar *research technologist*
Larin, Kirill V. *biomedical engineer, educator*
Lienhard, John Henry, IV, *mechanical engineer, educator*
Luss, Dan *chemical engineering professor*
Mangieri, Mark Louis *computer engineer*
Matthews, Charles Sedwick *petroleum engineer, consultant*
Mawhood, Aristide Roscoe *mechanical engineer*
McLeod, Harry O'Neal, Jr. *retired petroleum engineer, consultant*
Miele, Angelo *engineering educator, researcher, consultant, author*
Millican, Elliot Stephen *mechanical engineer*
Morris, Owen Glenn *engineering corporation executive*
O'Geary, Dennis Traylor *retired engineering company executive*
Peng, Liang-Chuan *mechanical engineer*
Powell, Alan *engineering educator, research scientist*
Prats, Michael *petroleum engineer, educator*
Qiao, Fengxiang *transportation engineer, educator*
Tomson, Mason B. *environmental engineer, educator*
Tsai, Tom Chunghu *chemical engineer*
Warren, Tommy Melvin *petroleum engineer*
Wren, Robert James *aerospace engineering manager*

Irving
Barnard, Ray F. *engineering and construction management company executive*
Boeckmann, Alan L. *engineering and construction management company executive*
Flowers, Garry W. *engineering and construction management company executive*
Gilbert, H. Steven *engineering and construction management company executive*
Pascal, Tracey Michele *software engineer, director*
Walley, James Marvin, Jr. *engineering executive, management consultant, real estate company executive*

League City
Kanuth, James Gordan *chemical engineer*

Leander
Ramirez, Ciro *mechanical engineer, consultant*

Lubbock
Archer, James Elson *engineering educator*
Dudek, Richard Albert *engineering educator*
Kiesling, Ernst Willie *civil engineering educator, dean*
Kristiansen, Magne *electrical engineer, educator*
Martin, Clyde F. *engineering educator*
Mehta, Kishor Chandulal *civil engineering educator*

Mc Kinney
Gill, David bRIAN *electrical engineer, educator*

Mineral Wells
Mei, Anhua *mechanical engineer, researcher*

Pasadena
Martinez, Fernando V. *civil engineer*

Port Aransas
Lehmann, William Leonardo *electrical engineer, educator*

Richardson
Al-Dhahir, Naofal *engineering educator*

Rockport
Minor, Joseph Edward *civil engineer, educator*

Rosharon
Marya, Manuel Paul Claude *metallurgical and materials engineer*

Round Rock
O'Connor, Clint Haynie *electrical engineer*

Sachse
Rogers, Mal David, Jr. *chemical engineer*

San Antonio
Abramson, Hyman Norman *engineering and science research executive*

San Marcos
Fischer, Joyce Faye *engineering educator*

Spring
Szymczak, Edward Joseph *mechanical engineer*
Woodward, Clifford Edward *chemical engineer*

Stafford
Le, Duy-Loan *electrical engineer*

The Woodlands
Evans, Walter Reed *retired engineering executive, consultant*
Griffith, James William *systems engineer, consultant*

Tyler
Layton, Robert E., Jr. *retired aeronautical engineer*
Sathyamoorthy, Muthukrishnan *engineering educator, associate provost*

Uvalde
Barrett, James Bruce *systems engineer*

Waco
Farison, James Blair *electrical engineer, biomedical engineer, educator*

Webster
Kobayashi, Herbert Shin *electrical engineer*

Weslaco
Yang, Chenghai *agricultural engineer, researcher*

UTAH

Dugway
Benson, Morgan *energy engineer, retired military officer*

Holladay
Silver, Barnard Joseph Stewart *mechanical and chemical engineer, consultant, inventor*

Ivins
Theurer, Byron W. *aerospace engineer, business owner*

Logan
Bowles, David Stanley *engineering educator, consultant*
Hargreaves, George Henry *civil and agricultural engineer, researcher*
Keller, Jack *agricultural engineering educator, consultant*
Qi, Xiaojun *engineering educator*
Ren, Wei *control systems educator*

Manti
Funk, William Henry *retired environmental engineering educator*

Murray
Volberg, Herman William *electronics engineer, consultant*

Ogden
Davidson, Thomas Ferguson *retired chemical engineer*

Provo
Jackson, James F. *nuclear engineer, educator*
Jensen, Michael Allen *engineering educator*
Youd, T. Leslie *retired civil engineer*

Salt Lake City
Anderson, Charles Ross *civil engineer*
Barney, Kline Porter, Jr. *engineering company executive, consultant*
Call, Charles H., Jr. *civil engineer*
DeVries, Kenneth Lawrence *mechanical engineer, educator*
Gandhi, Om Parkash *electrical engineer*
Ghosh, Sambhunath (Sam) *environmental engineer, educator*
Sandquist, Gary Marlin *engineering educator, researcher, consultant, writer, military officer*
Sohn, Hong Yong *chemical and metallurgical engineer, educator*
Stringfellow, Gerald B. *engineering educator*
Virkar, Anil V. *materials engineer, educator*

VERMONT

Burlington
Marshall, Jeffrey Scott *mechanical engineer, educator*
Outwater, John Ogden *mechanical engineering educator*
Pinder, George Francis *engineering educator, research scientist*

Essex Junction
Jin, Zhenrong *electrical engineer, researcher*

Shelburne
Anderson, Richard Louis *electrical engineer*

White River Junction
Xie, Chi *transportation engineer, researcher*

VIRGINIA

Afton
Stefanovic, Victor R. *electrical engineer, consultant*

Alexandria
Cook, Charles William *aerospace engineer, consultant, educator*
Gould, Phillip *engineer*
Harris, Dale William *systems engineer*
Hesterberg, Larry Allen *aerospace engineer*
Ikossi, Kiki *electrical and computer engineer*
Lasser, Howard Gilbert *chemical engineer, consultant*
MacLaren, William George, Jr. *engineering executive*
Murray, Russell, II, *aeronautical engineer, security consultant*
Poehlein, Gary Wayne *retired chemical engineering professor*
Weisberg, Leonard R. *retired engineering executive, researcher*
Wilcox, David Eric *electrical engineering, educator, consultant, business owner*

Annandale
Nelson, Harold E. (Bud Nelson) *fire protection engineer*
Ochs, Walter J. *civil engineer, consultant*

Arlington
Allen, David *systems engineer*
Bement, Arden Lee, Jr. *engineering educator, government agency administrator*
Brighton, John A. *mechanical engineer, academic administrator*
Cox, Henry *engineer, researcher*
Hall, Carl William *agricultural and mechanical engineer*
Hazelrigg, George Arthur, Jr. *systems engineer, educator*
Heineken, Frederick George *biochemical engineer*
Lala, Jaynarayan Hotchand *computer engineer*
Oliver, Robert M. *engineer*
Rahman, Muhammad Abdur *mechanical engineer*
Reagan, Lawrence Paul, Jr. *engineering executive, consultant*
Salmon, William Cooper *mechanical engineer, company executive*
Stevens, Donald King *retired aeronautical engineer, consultant*
Surko, Stephen William *systems engineer*

Ashburn
Hershey, Paul Christian *engineer*
Nickle, Dennis Edwin *electronics engineer, consultant, deacon*

Bedford
Ramsey, Forrest Gladstone, Jr. *retired engineering company executive*

Blacksburg
Agah, Masoud *electrical engineer, educator*
Aref, Hassan *fluid mechanics engineer, educator*
Batra, Romesh Chander *engineering educator, researcher*
Brown, Gary Sandy *electrical engineering educator*
Disney, Ralph L(ynde) *retired industrial engineering educator*
Gray, Festus Gail *electrical engineer, educator, researcher*
Hanowski, Richard Joseph *transportation engineer, director*
Lee, Fred C. *electrical engineering educator*
McCue, Leigh Shaw *aerospace engineer, educator*
Mitchell, James Kenneth *civil engineer, educator*
Perez, Miguel A. *industrial engineer, researcher*
Phadke, Arun G. *engineering educator*
Price, Dennis Lee *industrial engineer, educator*
Randall, Clifford Wendell *civil engineer, educator*
Schetz, Joseph Alfred *aerospace engineer, educator*
Squires, Arthur Morton *chemical engineer, educator*

Blue Ridge
Elmore, Walter A. *electrical engineer, consultant*

Burke
Lynch, Charles Theodore, Sr. *materials science engineering researcher, consultant, educator*

Chantilly
Austin, Wanda Murry *systems engineer*

Charlottesville
Aylor, James Hiram *engineering educator*
Berger, Toby *electrical engineer, educator*
Dorning, John Joseph *nuclear engineering, physics, and applied mathematics educator*
Fink, Lester Harold *retired engineering company executive, educator*
Gaden, Elmer Lewis *retired engineering educator*
Garber, Nicholas Jack *civil engineer, educator*
Haj-Hariri, Hossein *engineering educator, department chairman*
Hoel, Lester A. *civil engineering educator, department chairman*
Hudson, John Lester *chemical engineering professor*
Inigo, Rafael Madrigal *retired electrical engineering educator*
Krzysztofowicz, Roman *systems engineering and statistical science educator, consultant*
Laurencin, Cato Thomas *biomedical engineer, orthopaedic surgeon*
Pierce, Shayn *biomedical engineer, educator*
Reynolds, Albert Barnett *nuclear engineer, educator*
Theodoridis, George Constantin *biomedical engineering educator, researcher*
Townsend, Miles Averill *aerospace and mechanical engineering educator*

Chesapeake
Bockwoldt, Todd Shane *nuclear engineer*

Drakes Branch
Locke, Thomas Edward, Jr. *retired industrial engineer*

Dulles
Dodson, Carl Edward *nuclear engineer, real estate agent, minister, assistant superintendent*

Edinburg
Trindal, Wesley Steele *mechanical engineer*

Fairfax
Boone, James Virgil *retired engineering executive, researcher*
Chen, Chun-Hung *engineering educator*
Cook, Gerald *electrical engineering educator*
Felsburg, David F. *engineering executive, educator*
Gertler, Janos John *electrical engineer, educator*
Harrison, Robert Allen *retired operations research analyst*
Houck, Mark Hedrich *engineering educator*
Palmer, James Daniel *information technology educator*
Sage, Andrew Patrick *systems engineering and management educator*
Selk, Stephen Jeffrey *chemical engineer*
Villarreal, Carlos Castañeda *engineering executive*

Fairfax Station
Duff, William Grierson *electrical engineer, educator*

Falls Church
Jones, Russel Cameron *civil engineer, educator*
Klopfenstein, Rex Carter *electrical engineer*
Lorenzo, Michael *engineer, real estate broker, government official*
May, Carol Lee *mechanical engineer*
Sveinsson, Linda Rodgers *engineering company executive*
Tether, Anthony John *aerospace executive*

Fredericksburg
Hasenfus, Harold Joseph *retired mechanical engineer, naval technical director*
Medding, Walter Sherman *retired environmental engineer*

Hampton
Bartels, Robert Edwin *aerospace engineer*
Joshi, Suresh Meghashyam *engineer, researcher*
McAdaragh, Raymon Michael *aerospace engineer, researcher*
Refaat, Tamer F. *electrical engineer, researcher*
Sobieski, Jaroslaw *aerospace engineer*
Sun, Rensheng *electrical engineer, educator*

Lynch Station
Skeen, David Ray *systems engineer, consultant, engineering executive, educator*

Lynchburg
Wang, Kaihong *mechanical engineer, researcher*

Manassas
Haddad, Nadim Fawzi *engineer, researcher*

Mc Lean
Carnicero, Jorge Emilio *aeronautical engineer, transportation executive*
Dobson, Donald Alfred *retired electrical engineer*
Kappaz, Michael H. *engineering executive, energy executive*
Rosenbaum, David Mark *engineering executive, consultant, educator*
Schauer, Franz Peter *civil and nuclear engineer, educator*
Shortal, Terence Michael *systems company executive*
Stine, John Andrew *communications engineer, researcher*

Middleburg
Langley, Rolland Ament, Jr. *engineering and management consultant*

Montross
Fountain, Robert Roy, Jr. *retired engineering company executive, farmer, military officer*

Newport News
Donaldson, Coleman duPont *retired aeronautical engineer, aerospace engineer, consultant*
Hubbard, Harvey Hart *aeroacoustician, noise control engineer, consultant*
Inman, Jonathan Russell *mechanical engineer*

Norfolk
Donohue, David Patrick *engineering executive, retired military officer*
Karim, Mohammad Ataul *electrical engineering educator, researcher*
Poyner, Kenneth G. *systems engineer, writer*
Wiltse, James Clark *civil engineer*

Reston
Choi, Michael Kamwah *aerospace and mechanical engineer, researcher*
Harvey, Aubrey Eaton III *industrial engineer*
Kahn, Robert E. *electrical engineer*

Richmond
Aiken, Peter Haynes *systems engineer, educator, architect, consultant, data engineer*
Compton, Olin Randall *consulting electrical engineer, researcher*
Gad-el-Hak, Mohamed *aerospace and mechanical engineering educator, researcher*
Gu, Xing *semiconductor engineer, researcher*
Mattauch, Robert Joseph *retired electrical engineering educator, retired dean*
McCune, John Brian *broadcast engineer*
Morkoç, Hadis *electrical engineer, educator*

Sprinkle, William Melvin *acoustical engineer, engineering executive*

Roanoke
Landis, John William *retired engineering executive, consultant, government advisor*

Salem
Shaffner, Patrick Noel *retired architectural engineering executive*

Springfield
Casazza, John Andrew *electrical engineer, energy executive*
Ferrante, Jon Visconti *leadership and technology transfer executive, consultant*
Meikle, Philip G. *engineer, retired government agency executive*
Sonnemann, Harry *electrical engineer, consultant*

Suffolk
Noblitt, Nancy Anne *aerospace engineer*

Vienna
Keiser, Bernhard Edward *engineering executive, communications engineer, consultant*
Mujumdar, Vilas Sitaram *structural engineer, researcher*
Salah, Sagid *retired nuclear engineer*
Woodward, Kenneth Emerson *retired mechanical engineer*

Virginia Beach
Bradshaw, Denis James *engineer, graphic designer*

Wallops Island
Krause, David John *aerospace engineer*

Warrenton
Gullace, Marlene Frances *systems engineer, consultant*

Waynesboro
Lane, Lawrence Jubin *retired electrical engineer, consultant*

Williamsburg
Aaron, Bertram Donald *engineering executive, management consultant*
Coakley, Richard Walker *retired chemical engineer*

Woodbridge
Kreipke, Merrill Vincent *civil engineer, consultant*

WASHINGTON

Auburn
Whitmore, Donald Clark *retired engineer*

Bellevue
Gope, Dipanjan *computer engineer*
Grosvenor, Allan Dace *engineer*
Parks, Donald Lee *mechanical engineer, human factors engineer*

Bellingham
Jansen, Robert Bruce *consulting civil engineer*

Brush Prairie
Edlich, Richard French *biomedical engineer, educator*

Dupont
Pettit, Ghery St. John *electronics engineer*

Edmonds
Peckol, James Kenneth *consulting engineer*
Schmit, Lucien André, Jr. *retired structural engineer*

Issaquah
Evans, Ersel Arthur *engineering executive, consultant*
Reid, John Mitchell (Jack Reid) *biomedical engineer, researcher, consultant*
Wright, Theodore Otis *forensic engineer*

Kenmore
Guy, Arthur William *electrical engineering educator, researcher*

Lummi Island
Ewing, Benjamin Baugh *environmental engineer, educator, consultant*

Mercer Island
Bridgforth, Robert Moore, Jr. *aerospace engineer*

Mountlake Terrace
Schweyen, Stephen Gregory *engineering company executive*

Mukilteo
Bohn, Dennis Allen *engineering executive*

Olympia
Sesonske, Alexander *nuclear and chemical engineer*

Pullman
Katona, Michael George *civil engineer, educator*
Stock, David Earl *mechanical engineering educator*

Redmond
Willard, H(arrison) Robert *electrical engineer*

Renton
Sun, Zuo *aerospace engineer, researcher*

Richland
Blumenkranz, David Benjamin *chemical engineer, consultant*
Singhal, Subhash C. *engineer*
Stenner, Robert David *environmental and health research engineer, toxicologist*
Trent, Donald Stephen *thermo fluids engineer*
Westergard, Billie *project engineer*

Sammamish
Yocam, Eric Wayne *engineer*

Seattle
Bowen, Jewell Ray *chemical engineering professor*
Cogan, Tom (Thomas J. Cogan) *aerospace engineer*
Davis, Earl James *chemical engineering professor emeritus*
Finlayson, Bruce Alan *retired chemical engineering professor*
Galloway, Patricia Denese *civil engineer*
Gilbert, Paul H. *engineering executive, consultant*
Hoffman, Allan Sachs *chemical engineer, educator*
Ishimaru, Akira *electrical engineering educator*
Jorgensen, Jens Erik *mechanical engineer, educator*
Kapur, Kailash Chander *industrial engineering educator*
Kevorkian, Jirair *aeronautics and astronautics engineering educator*
Kim, Yongmin *electrical engineer, educator, biomedical engineer*
Kobayashi, Albert Satoshi *mechanical engineering educator*
Lee, Cheegwan *environmental engineer, consultant*
Lidstrom, Mary E. *chemical engineering and microbiology professor*
Mc Feron, Dean Earl *mechanical engineer, educator*
Oman, Henry *retired electrical engineer, engineering executive*
Raese, David Senna *aerospace and mass properties engineer, consultant*
Rojas, Eddy M. *engineering educator*
Schmidt, Peter Gustav *marine engineer*
Spindel, Robert Charles *electrical engineering educator*
Sutter, Joseph F. *aeronautical engineer, consultant, retired air transportation executive*
Wenk, Edward, Jr. *civil engineer, educator, writer, policy analyst*

Vashon
Moser, Sarah Gunning *manufacturing engineer, small business owner*

WEST VIRGINIA

Charleston
Lewis, Charles Raymond, II, *traffic engineer, consultant*

Morgantown
De Vore, Paul Warren *technology educator*
Halabe, Udaya Bhatta *civil engineering educator, researcher*
Peng, Syd S. *mining engineer, educator*

WISCONSIN

Brookfield
Curfman, Floyd Edwin *retired engineering educator*
Thomas, John *mechanical engineer, artist*

Genoa
Parkyn, John Duwane *nuclear engineer*

Green Bay
LaRue, Lillian Jayne *electrical engineer, educator*

Hartford
Aubuchon, Richard E. *engineering executive*

La Crosse
Davy, Michael Francis *civil engineer, consultant*

Madison
Beachley, Norman Henry *mechanical engineer, educator*
Bird, Robert Byron *chemical engineering educator, author*
Boyle, William Charles *engineering educator*
Choi, Hongseok *mechanical engineer, researcher*
Dietmeyer, Donald Leo *retired electrical engineering educator*
Emmert, Gilbert Arthur *retired engineering educator*
Gustafson, David Harold *industrial engineering and preventive medicine educator*
Hill, Charles Graham, Jr. *chemical engineering educator*
Lakes, Roderic Stephen *biomedical engineering educator*
Lasseter, Robert Haygood *electrical engineering educator, consultant*
Lightfoot, Edwin Niblock, Jr. *retired chemical engineering educator*
Lillesand, Thomas Martin *engineer, educator*
Lovell, Edward George *mechanical engineering educator*
Novotny, Donald Wayne *electrical engineer, educator*
Peercy, Paul Stuart *engineering educator*
Perepezko, John H. *engineering educator*
Rusi, Eduard *engineering educator*
Russell, Jeffrey Scott *engineering educator*
Shohet, Juda Leon *electrical and computer engineering educator, researcher, information technology executive*

Skiles, James Jean *electrical and computer engineer, educator*
Smith, Michael James *industrial engineering educator*
Webster, John Goodwin *biomedical engineering educator, researcher*

Menomonie
Asthana, Rajiv *engineering educator, researcher*

Milwaukee
Chandler, Edward William *communication systems engineer, electrical engineer, electrical engineering educator*
Chen, Qinghua *engineering educator*
Cutler, Verne Clifton *engineering educator, consultant*
Demerdash, Nabeel Aly Omar *electrical engineer*
Fournelle, Raymond Albert *engineering educator*
Gaggioli, Richard Arnold *mechanical engineering educator*
Graef, Luther William *civil engineer*
Heinen, James Albin *electrical engineering educator*
Reyer, Steven E. *engineering educator*
Stemper, Brian D. *biomedical engineer, educator*
Widera, Georg Ernst Otto *mechanical engineering educator, consultant*
Yeh, Chia-Chou *electrical engineer, researcher*

Racine
Stephens, James Linton *mechanical engineer*

Richland Center
Heinen, John Timothy *environmental engineer*

Soldiers Grove
Ewing, Brian Kim *retired engineering executive, writer*

Spooner
Frey, Paul Howard *chemical engineer, engineering consultants company executive*

Stevens Point
Drew, Richard Allen *retired electrical engineer*

Waukesha
Bonnett, James W. *engineer*

Woodruff
Polasek, Edward John *retired electrical engineer, consultant*

WYOMING

Lander
Field, Francis Edward *electrical engineer, educator*

Laramie
Mingle, John Orville *engineer, educator, lawyer, consultant*
Rechard, Paul Albert *retired civil engineering company executive, consultant*
Towler, Brian Francis *petroleum engineer, educator*

TERRITORIES OF THE UNITED STATES

PUERTO RICO

Mayaguez
Suarez, Luis Edgardo *civil engineering educator*

VIRGIN ISLANDS

St Croix
Lee, Sidney Phillip *chemical engineer, state senator*

CANADA

ALBERTA

Calgary
Glockner, Peter G. *civil and mechanical engineering educator*
Hovdestad, Wayne Roy *petroleum engineer*
Lam, Galen Ka-Ron *electrical engineer*
Malik, Om Parkash *electrical engineering educator, researcher*
McDaniel, Roderick Rogers *petroleum engineer, consultant*

Edmonton
Beaulieu, Norman C. *engineering educator, writer*
Lock, Gerald Seymour Hunter *retired mechanical engineering educator*
Offenberger, Allan Anthony *retired electrical engineering educator*
Otto, Fred Douglas *chemical engineering professor*

BRITISH COLUMBIA

Lake Country
Muggeridge, Derek Brian *engineering executive, consultant*

Langley
Thomas, Howard Paul *civil engineer, consultant*

Vancouver
Salcudean, Martha Eva *mechanical engineer, educator*
Young, Lawrence *electrical engineering educator*

Victoria
Antoniou, Andreas *electrical engineering educator*
Rathore, Akshay Kumar *electrical engineer, researcher*

Westbank
Wedepohl, Leonhard Martin *electrical engineering educator*

MANITOBA

Winnipeg
Kuffel, Edmund *electrical engineering educator*
Mufti, Aftab A. *civil engineering educator*

NEW BRUNSWICK

Fredericton
Bray, Dale Irving *civil engineering educator*

NEWFOUNDLAND AND LABRADOR

Saint John's
Clark, Jack Ivor *civil engineer, researcher*

ONTARIO

Burlington
Harris, Philip John *retired engineering educator*

Hamilton
Bandler, John William *electrical engineering educator, consultant*
Campbell, Colin Kydd *electrical and computer engineering educator, researcher*
Crowe, Cameron Macmillan *chemical engineering professor*
Garland, William James *nuclear engineer, educator*
Wong, Kon Max *electrical engineer educator*

Kingston
Batchelor, Barrington de Vere *civil engineer, educator*
Lewis, William John *aerospace engineer*

London
Davenport, Alan Garnett *civil engineer, educator*
Inculet, Ion I. *electrical engineer, educator, science association director, consultant*

Mississauga
Foda, Rabiz Nasir *industrial and electrical engineer*
Gupta, Rajesh *engineer, consultant*

North York
Buzacott, John Alan *engineering educator*
Tse, Philip Kui *airport engineering maintenance consultant*

Oshawa
Zhang, Dan *engineering educator, researcher*

Ottawa
Ahmadi, Mojtaba *engineering educator, consultant*
Altman, Samuel Pinover *mechanical engineer, research consultant*
Bozozuk, Michael *civil engineer*
Georganas, Nicolas D. *electrical engineering educator, academic administrator*
Shiari, Behrouz *mechanical engineer, researcher*

Toronto
Davison, Edward Joseph *electrical engineering educator*
Endrenyi, Janos *research engineer, educator*
Janischewskyj, Wasyl *electrical engineering educator*
Meagher, George Vincent *mechanical engineer*
Salama, C. Andre Tewfik *electrical engineering educator*
Slemon, Gordon Richard *electrical engineering educator*
Smith, Peter William Ebblewhite *electrical engineer, educator, research scientist, physicist*
Venetsanopoulos, Anastasios Nicolaos *electrical engineer, educator*
Wonham, Walter Murray *electrical engineer, educator*
Zeng, Hong *audio system architect, researcher*

Waterloo
Penlidis, Alexander *chemical engineering professor*
Sedra, Adel Shafeek *engineering educator, academic administrator*
Vlach, Jiri *electrical engineering educator, researcher*

Windsor
Hackam, Reuben *electrical engineering educator*

QUEBEC

Montreal
Dealy, John Michael *chemical engineer, educator*
Haccoun, David *electrical engineering educator*
Ladanyi, Branko *civil engineer, educator*
Lamarre, Bernard *engineering executive*
Paidoussis, Michael Pandeli *mechanical engineering educator*
Ramachandran, Venkatanarayana Deekshit *electrical engineering educator*
Saint-Pierre, Guy *engineering executive*
Selvadurai, Antony Patrick Sinnappa *civil engineer, mathematician, educator, consultant*

Varennes
Bartnikas, Raymond *electrical engineer, educator*

SASKATCHEWAN

Regina
Mollard, John Douglas *engineering and geology executive*

Saskatoon
Smith, C. D. *civil engineering educator*

Montreal
Pierre, Samuel J. *engineering educator*

MEXICO

Caolniatizapan
Ramirez-Mireles, Fernando *electrical engineer*

AUSTRALIA

Cammeray
Besley, Morrish Alexander (Tim Besley) *civil engineer*

BRAZIL

Santa Catarina Florianopolis
da Costa, Newton Carneiro Affonso, Jr. *engineering educator, researcher*

CHINA

Beijing
Yao, Andrew Chi-Chih *engineering educator*

Chengdu
Ma, Shijun *engineering educator*

Shanghai
Yun, Liang *marine engineer, educator*

CYPRUS

Nicosia
Elias, Kyriakides *electrical engineer, educator, researcher*

DENMARK

Horsholm
Svensson, Sven Eilif *civil engineer, consultant*

EGYPT

Assiut
Abdel-Hakim M. Aly, Alaa El-Din *engineer, researcher*

ENGLAND

Beaconsfield
Lindley, David *mechanical engineer*

Cambridge
Hawthorne, Sir William Rede *aerospace and mechanical engineer, educator*

Coulsdon
Vijayaratnam, Kanapathipillai *civil and environmental engineer, consultant, director, educator*

Reading
Thacker, Charles P. *computer engineer, engineering executive*

Southampton
Brebbia, Carlos Alberto *engineering educator, consultant*

Westminster
Broers, Lord Alec Nigel *engineering educator*

FRANCE

Le Vesinet
Fourt, Bernard-Francois P. *retired engineer*

GERMANY

Aachen
Pischinger, Franz Felix *engineer, researcher, engineering educator*

Freiberg
Zabecki, David Tadeusz *engineer, educator, military historian, military officer*

Munich
Schmidt, Stefan *mechanical engineer, economist*

GREECE

Athens
Zevgolis, Ioannis *geotechnical engineer, researcher*

HONG KONG

Hong Kong
Kao, Charles Kuen *electrical engineer, educator*
Leung, Ka-Cheong *engineering educator*

HUNGARY

Sopron
Sitkei, György *engineer, educator*

INDIA

Calcutta
Kothari, Hemraj *mechanical engineer, management consultant*

New Delhi
Mashelkar, Raghunath Anant *chemical engineer*

Noida
Jain, Prem Chand *mechanical engineer*

Tiruchirappalli
Ramesh, Srikrishnaperumal Thanga *engineering educator*

IRELAND

Dublin
Dooge, James Clement Ignatius *civil engineer, hydrologist*

ISRAEL

Be'er Sheva
Brosilow, Coleman Bernard *chemical engineering educator*

Haifa
Ziv, Jacob *communications engineer*

ITALY

Bologna
Keller, Kenneth Harrison *engineering educator*

Como
Casati, Fabio *engineer*

JAPAN

Fukuoka
Ishibashi, Akira *mechanical engineer, educator*

Hirosaki
Sato, Hiroyuki *materials engineer, researcher*

Kinokawa-shi
Yamawaki, Nobuyuki *engineering educator, biomedical engineer, researcher*

Nagoya
Sakai, Toshihiko *engineer*
Sendo, Takeshi *mechanical engineering educato researcher, writer*

Shizuoka
Anma, So *engineer, consultant*

Tokushima
Kinno, Hitoshi *mechanical engineer, educator*

Tokyo
Hori, Yukio *engineering educator, scientific association administrator*
Ono, Eiichi *engineering educator, researcher*

JORDAN

Zarka
Abu-Khader, Nabil *electrical engineer, educator*

Zarqa
Al-Bataineh, Osama Mohammad *biomedical engineer*

MALAYSIA

Skudai
Ruzairi, Abdul Rahim *engineer, educator, director*

PHILIPPINES

Mondaluyong City
Abiera, Roberto *mechanical engineer*

POLAND

Szczecin
Wierzcholski, Wunschik Christoph *mechanical engineer, mathematician, information scientist*

Warsaw
Klemens, Rudolf Henryk *mechanical engineer*

Wroclaw
Golinski, Joseph Antoni *mechanical engineer*

PORTUGAL

Algés
Horta, José Carlos de Oliveira Sousa *civil engineering consultant*

Lisbon
Portela, Antonio Gouvea *retired mechanical engineer, researcher*

REPUBLIC OF KOREA

Busan
Ha, Chang Sik *polymer science educator*
Lee, Heesoo *engineering educator*

Cheonan
Shin, Hyun Joon *industrial engineering professor*

Chuncheon
Lee, Won Gyu *chemical engineer, educator*

Daejeon
Choi, Yong-Seok *communications engineer, researcher*
Jeong, Seong-Il *aerospace engineer, researcher*

Gyeonggi Yongin
d'Auriol, Brian J. *engineering educator, researcher*

Gyeonggi-do Suwon
Lee, Byoung-Kuk *engineering educator*

Incheon
Cho, Chongdu *mechanical engineer, educator*
Hwang, Beongbok *engineering educator*

Seoul
Cha, Suk Won *engineering educator, researcher*
Hong, Seungkwan *engineering educator*
Zi, Goangseup *engineering educator*

Wonju
Jeon, Byong-Hun *environmental engineer, educator*

Yuseung
Lee, Kwangil *electrical engineer, researcher*

RUSSIA

Moscow
Kirpilenko, Grigory Grigor'evich *engineer, researcher*
Krikalev, Sergei Konstantinovich *flight engineer, cosmonaut, researcher*

SAUDI ARABIA

Dhahran
Muqaibel, Ali Hussein *engineer, educator*

SINGAPORE

Singapore
Kong, Adams Wai Kin *electrical engineer, researcher*
oon, Boon Yi *engineer*

SWITZERLAND

Lausanne
wartz, Melody A. *biomedical engineer, educator*

Zurich
Morari, Manfred *chemical engineer, educator*

TAIWAN

Kaohsiung
iang, Tyng-Yeu *engineering educator*

Taichung
iang, Chenju *engineering educator*

Tainan
Hsiao, Shih Wen *mechanical engineer, educator*
uang, Ting-Chia *chemical engineering professor, researcher*
in, Jiin-Huey Chern *engineering educator*

VENEZUELA

Caracas
hang-Mota, Roberto *electrical engineer*

ADDRESS UNPUBLISHED

Abetti, Pier Antonio *electrical engineer, management consultant, educator*
Aguinsky, Richard Daniel *electrical engineer, engineering executive*
Ahmed, Walid Khairy Mohamed *electrical engineer*
Alfriend, Kyle Terry *aerospace engineer*
Allen, Richard S. *engineering company executive*
Altschaeffl, Adolph George *retired civil engineering educator*
Amann, Charles Albert *mechanical engineer, researcher*
Amundson, John Kay *electrical engineer*
Anderson, John Gaston *electrical engineer, consultant*
Arimilli, Ravi K. *computer engineer*
Armaingaud, Franck *engineer*
Armanios, Daniel Erian *mechanical engineer, political science scholar*
Asadorian, Diana C. *electrical engineer, educator*
Asiabanpour, Bahram *engineering educator*
Atilgan, Timur Faik *retired structural engineer*
Axford, Roy Arthur *nuclear engineering educator*
Aydin, Levent *electrical engineer*
Bai, Zongwu *polymer engineer*
Bakht, Baidar *civil engineer, researcher, educator*
Baktir, Selcuk *electrical and computer engineer, researcher*
Baltazzi, Evan Serge *retired engineering research consulting company executive*
Bar-Cohen, Avram *mechanical engineering educator*
Baron, Stanley N. *retired electrical engineer*
Barsun, Hans Frederick *engineer*
Bartlett, Desmond William *engineering company executive*
Basova, Yulia *chemical engineer, researcher*
Bauer, Richard Carlton *nuclear engineer*
Bauhan, Hobart Baker *retired mining engineer, retired farmer*
Beach, Harry Lee, Jr. *mechanical engineer, aerospace engineer*
Beard, Leo Roy *retired civil engineer*
Bechtel, Stephen E. *mechanical engineer, educator*
Beckjord, Eric Stephen *nuclear engineer, researcher*
Bergeron, Elmo P. *chemical engineer, consultant*
Bergstrom, Sheryl Lindsey *jet propulsion administrator*
Bernath, John Charles, Jr. *electronics engineer*
Bers, Abraham *electrical engineering and physics educator*
Bershad, Neil Jeremy *electrical engineering educator*
Bertin, John Joseph *aeronautical engineer, educator, researcher*
Beumer, Richard Eugene *retired engineering executive*
Beyene, Nahom Minassie *aerospace engineer*
Bhada, Rohinton Khurshed *chemical engineering educator*
Bhangale, Tushar *biomedical engineer, researcher*
Bhatia, Rajan *engineer, physicist, researcher*
Bier, Karla *manufacturing engineer, chemical engineer, educator*
Binkley, David Martin *electrical engineer, educator, musician*
Blagojevic, Goran *electrical engineer, consultant*
Blakesley, Wayne Lavere, Jr. *retired production engineer*
Bloch, Erich *retired electrical engineer, science foundation director*
Boch, David Paul *engineering technical specialist*
Boriboonsomsin, Kanok *transportation engineer*
Bornhorst, Kenneth Frank *electromagnetics and systems engineer*
Bose, Anjan *electrical engineering educator, academic administrator*
Bowman, Bruce Alan *civil engineer*
Brennan, Lawrence Edward *retired electronics engineer*
Brickell, Charles Hennessey, Jr. *marine engineer, retired military officer*
Bridger, Baldwin, Jr. *electrical engineer*
Brown, Steven Harry *engineering executive*
Brozowski, Laura Adrienne *mechanical engineer*
Brubaker, James Edward *mechanical engineer*
Brungraber, Robert J. *civil engineer, educator*
Buckman, Raymond William, Jr. *engineering educator*
Bunch, Jennings Bryan, Jr. *retired electrical engineer*
Burchard, John Kenneth *retired chemical engineer*
Buritz, Robert Samson *retired electrical engineer*
Butler, Donald Philip *electrical engineer, educator*
Byrd, Lloyd Garland *retired civil engineer*
Cai, Zhijun *mechanical engineer*
Carey, Stephanie L. *systems engineer, educator*
Carlson, Robert Codner *industrial engineering educator*
Carnahan, Brice *chemical engineer, educator*
Carnesale, Albert *engineering educator, former academic administrator*
Cerny, Louis Thomas *civil and transportation engineer, consultant*
Cha, Soyoung Stephen *mechanical engineer, educator*
Chan, KitYu Evan *civil engineer*
Chandra, Abhijit *engineering educator*
Chang, Chong Hyuck *engineer*
Chang, Runzi *electrical engineer*
Chang, Ying Chih *engineering educator, researcher*
Chang-Yong, Nam *engineer, researcher*
Charwat, Andrew Franciszek *engineering educator*
Cheddie, Denver Faron *engineering educator, researcher*
Chen, Ho-Hong H.H. *industrial engineering executive, educator*
Chen, Qiang *engineer*
Chen, Qiming *engineer*
Chen, Shoei-Sheng *retired mechanical engineer*
Cheng, Wan-Lee *mechanical engineer, educator*
Chiang, I-Ting *engineering educator*
Chiang, Mung *engineering educator, consultant*
Cho, Alfred Yi *electrical engineer*
Chou, Chung-Kwang *bio-engineer*
Chouery, Farid Alexandre *electrical and structural engineer, consultant*
Chouteau, Kristin N. *engineer*
Chow, Winston *engineering executive, researcher*
Chryssakis, Christos *mechanical engineer*
Chu, Jack J. (Jack J. Zhu) *electrical engineer*
Chung, Woo Cheol *electrical engineer*
Clancy, Mathew P. *chemical engineer*
Claridge, Elmond Lowell *retired engineering educator*
Clarno, Kevin Taylor *nuclear engineer*
Cleave, Mary L. *environmental engineer, former astronaut*
Clewett, Raymond Winfred *mechanical design engineer*
Clough, Ray William, Jr. *civil engineering educator*
Coar, Richard John *mechanical engineer, aerospace transportation executive, consultant*
Cohen, Murray *aerospace engineer, consultant*
Collins, James Duffield *marine engineer, editor*
Collins, Michael *aerospace consultant, astronaut*
Cromer, Donald L. *aerospace and electrical engineer*
Crowl, Steven Craig *aerospace engineer*
Cruikshank, Thomas Henry *energy services and engineering executive*
Cui, Hongliang *engineering company executive, researcher*
Cummins, Nancyellen Heckeroth *electronics engineer*
Cutting, Sean Eugene *aeronautical engineer*
Czop, Andrew Paul *electrical engineer*
Dally, James William *mechanical engineering educator, consultant*
Daly, Donald F. *retired engineering company executive*
Dargan, Pamela Ann *systems engineer, consultant*
Day, Donald Lee *retired engineering educator*
Der Torossian, Papken *engineering executive*
Diakunchak, Ihor S. *retired mechanical engineer*
Diaz, Nina Isabel *industrial engineer*
Dickerson, John Robert *retired automotive engineer*
Donohue, George L. *mechanical engineer, educator*
Donohue, Marc David *chemical engineering professor*
Douglas, Karin Nadja *engineer*
Drucker, Alan Steven *mechanical engineer*
Dull, William Martin *retired engineering executive*
Dupuis, Russell Dean *electrical engineer, researcher*
Durrani, Sajjad Haidar *retired aerospace and communications engineer*
Dyer, Ira *ocean engineering educator, consultant*
Eaglet, Robert Danton *electrical engineer, aerospace scientist, consultant, retired military officer*
Eberstein, Arthur *former biomedical engineering educator, researcher*
Ebrahim, Arbin *electrical engineer, researcher*
Edgar, Thomas Flynn *chemical engineering professor*
Edwards, Victor Henry *chemical engineer*
Elam, Matthew *industrial engineer, educator*
El-Moursy, Magdy *electronics engineer*
Ernst, Edward Willis *retired electrical engineering educator*
Ettinger, Harry Joseph *retired industrial hygiene engineer, consultant*
Evans, Gerald William *engineering educator, consultant*
Eyman, Earl Duane *electrical science educator, consultant*
Farrell, Jeffrey Michael *electrical engineer, consultant*
Fay, Craig Alan *engineering executive*
Feeser, Larry James *retired civil engineering educator, researcher*
Ferguson, Lloyd Elbert *retired manufacturing engineer*
Fernandez, Fernando Lawrence *aeronautical engineer, research and development company executive*
Fetkovich, Michael J. *retired petroleum engineer*
Fingerson, Leroy Malvin *engineering executive, mechanical engineer*
Fischer, Maxim *electronics engineer*
Fishman, Bernard *mechanical engineer*
Fisk, Edward Ray *retired civil and structural engineer, author, educator*
Fitzroy, Nancy deLoye *engineering executive, mechanical engineer*
Flanagan, James Loton *electrical engineer, educator, researcher*
Flick, Carl *electrical engineer, consultant*
Foley, Gary J. *chemical engineer, researcher, computer scientist, federal agency administrator*
Folsom, Tyler Cleveland *computer engineer, educator*
Fontana, Mario H. *nuclear engineer*
Forman, Edgar Ross *mechanical engineer*
Fox, Joan Phyllis *environmental engineer, engineering executive*
Frank, Michael Victor *risk assessment engineer*
Freedman, Joseph *retired sanitary and public health engineering consultant*
Freeman, Herbert *retired computer engineering educator*
Freiman, Charles Visvald *retired engineering foundation administrator*
Frowner, Byron *retired electrical engineer, researcher*
Geary, Stephen R. *engineer, educator, engineering executive*
Gens, Ralph Samuel *electrical engineering consultant*
Gentry, Donald William *engineering executive, mining engineer*
George, Kiranraj *electrical engineer, researcher*
Gere, James Monroe *civil engineering educator*
Gerges, Rafik Refaat Wessa *structural engineer*
Ghovanloo, Maysam *engineer, educator*
Glaser, Peter Edward *retired mechanical engineer, consultant, educator*
Glenn, Chance Michael *engineering educator, researcher, singer, writer*
Glenn, Roland Douglas *chemical engineer*
Gopalakrishnan, Kasthurirangan *civil engineer, research scientist*
Gottlieb, Lynn *engineer*
Gougar, Hans David *nuclear engineer, director*
Gouse, S. William, Jr. *mechanical engineering executive, researcher*
Graber, Samuel David *environmental and water resources engineer, consultant*
Grandi, Attilio *engineering consultant*
Grew, Raymond Edward *mechanical engineer*
Grooms, Henry Randall *retired civil engineer*
Gross, Geoffrey Fries *systems architect*
Gubbins, Keith Edmund *chemical engineering educator*
Gupta, Kuldip Chand (KC) *retired electrical and computer engineering educator, researcher*
Guymon, Gary LeRoy *civil engineering educator*
Haberman, Charles Morris *mechanical engineer, educator*
Hackney, James Acra III *industrial engineer, consultant, retired manufacturing executive*
Halasz, Stephen Joseph *retired electro-optical systems engineer*
Halpin, Daniel William *engineering educator, consultant*
Halverstadt, Robert Dale *mechanical engineer, metal products executive*
Hammam, M. Shawky *electrical engineer, educator*
Hands, Eric William *civil engineer, researcher*
Hanneman, Rodney Elton *metallurgical engineer*
Hanson, John M. *civil engineering and construction educator*
Haque, Rezaul *design engineer*
Hardy, Chester Alfred *engineer*
Harrison, Gordon Ray *engineering executive, consultant, research scientist*
Hartman, George M. *retired engineering contracts manager*
Hastings, Lindsay Marie *industrial engineer*
He, Pingan *systems engineer*
He, Shouling *engineering educator*
Hecker, Michael Hanns Louis *retired electrical engineer, speech scientist*
Heilmeier, George Harry *electrical engineer, researcher*
Heirman, Donald Nestor *training engineering company executive, consultant, educator, director, research scientist*
Hendricks, David Wesley *engineering executive*
Herman, William Arthur *engineering and physics laboratory director*
Herrmann, Jeffrey William *engineering educator*
Hiler, Edward Allan *agricultural and engineering educator*
Hinderliter, Richard Glenn *electrical engineer*
Hjerpe, Carl William *retired mechanical engineer, banker*
Hockeimer, Henry Eric *engineering executive*
Hoeppner, David William *mechanical engineering educator*
Hofmann, Andreas G. *engineer, researcher*
Hogan, Neville John *mechanical engineering educator, consultant*
Holeman, Russell Kent *civil engineer, director, construction executive*
Hood, James Brian *systems engineer*
Hopkins, Daniel Nelson *materials engineer*
Horowitz, Barry Martin *engineering company executive*
Hounkpevi, Franck O. *electrical engineer, researcher*
Howard, Dean Denton *electrical engineer, researcher, consultant*
Howe, Roger T. *engineering educator*
Huang, Shouhua *electronics engineer*
Hung, James Chen *engineering educator, consultant*
Hunter, William Michael *electrical engineer, civil engineer technician*
Israelachvili, Jacob Nissim *chemical engineer*
Jacobs, Richard Alberto *mechanical engineer*
James, Charles Franklin, Jr. *retired engineering educator*
Jasper, Norman Hans *engineer*
Jensen, Marvin Eli *retired agricultural engineer, science administrator*
Johnson, David Wilfred, Jr. *ceramics engineer, researcher*
Johnson, Lennart Ingemar *materials engineering consultant*
Johnson, Noel Lars *biomedical engineer*
Johnson, Stewart Willard *civil engineer*
Jordan, Howard Emerson *retired engineering executive, consultant*
Jugulum, Rajesh *engineer, researcher*
Juricic, Davor *engineering educator*
Kaler, Eric William *chemical engineer, educator*
Kamalasadan, Sukumar *electrical and computer engineering educator, researcher*
Katona, Peter Geza *biomedical engineer, educator*
Kazemitabar Amirkolaie, Seyed Javad *engineer, researcher*
Kemper, John Dustin *mechanical engineering educator*
Kenderian, Shant *engineer, consultant*
Kennedy, Leo Raymond *engineering executive*
Kercher, David Max *retired mechanical engineer*
Kesselring, Debbie Anne *systems engineer*

Kice, John Edward *engineer, educator, consultant*
Kilinc-Balci, Fatma Selcen *textile engineer, researcher*
Kim, Wonsuk *mechanical engineer, researcher*
Kiraz, Bahri *plastics and mechanical engineer, consultant*
Kirk, Donald Evan *electrical engineering educator, dean*
Kirkland, Virgil Wayne *retired electrical engineer*
Kirshenbaum, Ari P. *engineering educator*
Klein, Martin *ocean engineering consultant*
Kleinsorge, William Peter *metallurgical engineer*
Klippert, Richard Hobdell, Jr. *engineering executive*
Klohn, Earle Jardine *retired engineering company executive, consultant*
Knight, Patricia Marie *biomedical engineer, consultant*
Knott, Wiley Eugene *retired electronics engineer*
Koglin, Terry Lee *mechanical engineer, consultant*
Kogut, Lior *mechanical engineer, researcher*
Konchitsky, Alon *electronics engineer, communications executive*
Kong, Xuan *electrical engineer, educator*
Koros, William John *chemical engineering educator*
Korotkov, Roman Y. *engineer, research scientist*
Kozak, Alexander L. *engineer*
Koziara, Eugene Harry *retired aerospace engineer*
Kreith, Frank *research engineer, consultant*
Kretschmer, Frank Frederick, Jr. *electrical engineer, researcher, consultant*
Kucij, Timothy Michael *engineer, minister, musician*
Kung, Douglas C. *systems engineer*
Kunze, Otto Robert *retired agricultural engineering educator*
Kwon, O-Mun *electrical engineer, researcher*
Kyriakides, Elias *electrical engineer, educator*
Laborde, Enrique *retired communications engineer*
Lai-Yuen, Susana *engineering educator*
Langston, James Leland *electronics engineer*
Lao, Debang *electrical engineer, researcher*
Lecat, Robert J. *retired aeronautical engineer*
Lee, Burton Hoyt *aerospace engineer*
Leifert, Terence *engineer*
Lemlich, Robert *chemical engineer, educator*
Levinson, Herbert Sherman *civil and transportation engineer*
Levinson, Stephen Eliot *electrical engineer, educator*
Lewis, Homer Dick *retired nuclear engineer*
Lewitt, Miles Martin *computer engineering company executive*
Li, Jianliang *engineer*
Li, Tingye *electrical engineer*
Liang, Junxiang *retired aeronautics and astronautics engineer, educator*
Liang, Qingqing *electronics engineer*
Lin, Edward C. *engineering educator*
Lind, Niels Christian *civil engineering educator*
Loizos, Dimitrios *electrical engineer, researcher*
Longobardo, Anna Kazanjian *engineering executive*
Loper, Carl Richard, Jr. *metallurgical engineer, educator*
Lowe, John III *consulting civil engineer*
Loy, Richard Franklin *civil engineer*
Lucht, Orren Jesse *retired mechanical engineer*
Luger, Donald R. *engineering company executive*
Lund, Rita Pollard *aerospace engineer, consultant*
Luthy, Richard Godfrey *environmental engineering educator*
Lyon, Martha Sue *research engineer, retired military officer*
MacDonough, Robert Howard *consulting engineer, tax specialist, consultant*
Madix, Robert James *chemical engineer, educator*
Mahle, Christoph Erhard *electrical engineer*
Mahmoodi, Hamid *engineer*
Maikish, Charles John *engineer, lawyer*
Mandyam, Giridhar Dhati *electronics engineer*
Maring, Donald George, Jr. *electrical engineer*
Marks, John *engineer, consultant*
Marshall, John Paul *broadcast engineer*
Mason, John Latimer *engineering executive*
Masters, George Windsor, Jr. *electrical engineer, educator*
Mates, Robert Edward *mechanical engineering educator*
May, Gary Stephen *electrical engineer*
Mayaram, Kartikeya *electrical engineer, educator*
Mazumder, Sandip *engineer, researcher*
McAlonis, Christopher M. *engineer*
McCambridge, John James *retired civil engineer*
McCauley, Harold Homer *retired mechanical engineer*
McDonald, Mark Douglas *electrical engineer*
McFadden, Peter William *retired mechanical engineering educator*
McGuire, Michael John *environmental engineer*
McLaughlin, William Irving *space technical manager, writer*
McLellon, Richard Steven *aerospace engineer, consultant*
McNair, John William, Jr. *civil engineer*
Meadors, Howard Clarence, Jr. *electrical engineer*
Mehta, Jatin Vinodrai *biomedical engineer*
Meiksin, Zvi H. *electrical engineering educator*
Memik, Gokhan *engineering educator*
Merriam, Robert W. *engineering executive, educator*
Michlik, John F. *engineer*
Miele, Joel Arthur, Sr. *civil engineer*
Miller, Donald Kenneth *engineering consultant*
Milligan, Victor *consulting engineer*
Mirza, Zakir Hussain *aerospace company consultant*
Miskus, Michael Anthony *electrical engineer*
Mitzner, Kenneth Martin *electrical engineer, consultant*
Moazed, Khosrow L. *retired engineering educator*
Mohieldin, Ahmed Nader *electrical engineer*
Mohler, Ronald Rutt *electrical engineering educator*
Moll, David Carter *civil engineer*
Mooney, John Joseph *chemical engineer*
Moore, Fay Linda *systems engineer*
Morfopoulos, V. *metallurgical engineer, materials engineer*
Morgan, James John *environmental engineering educator*
Morgan, Ronald Brian *retired aerospace engineer, advocate, writer, lecturer*
Morley, Lloyd Albert *electrical engineering educator*
Morris, Donald George *engineering company executive*
Morris, John Woodland, II, *retired engineering consultant, military officer*
Mortimer, Richard Walter *mechanical engineer, educator*
Mow, Van C. *engineering educator, researcher*
Mramor, Marti *engineer, linguist*
Munger, Paul R. *engineering educator*
Munoz, Mario Alejandro *civil engineer, retired consultant*
Munzner, Robert Frederick *biomedical engineer*
Nahman, Norris Stanley *electrical engineer*
Nakayama, Wataru *engineering educator, consultant*
Nassau, David L. *engineer*
Nativi Nicolau, Juan Jose *industrial engineer*
Nelson, Thomas Adams *electrical engineer, consultant*
Nguyen, Charles Cuong *engineering educator, researcher, dean*
Nguyen, Clifford Ham-Thiem *telecommunications engineer*
Nichols, Robert Leighton *civil engineer*
Nielsen, Jakob *computer interface engineer*
Nkansah, Franklin Daniel *electrical engineer, educator*
Noe, John *validation engineer*
Nusim, Stanley Herbert *chemical engineer, consultant*
Ocal, Tarkan *computer engineer*
Ogata, Katsuhiko *engineering educator*
Oh, Jung Hun *computer engineer*
Oppenheim, Alan Victor *electrical engineering educator*
Ortolano, Ralph J. *engineering consultant*
Ott, Karl Otto *nuclear engineer, consultant*
Ottavi, Marco *computer engineer, researcher*
Özalp, Nesrin *mechanical engineer, research scientist*
Paik, John Kee *structural engineer*
Paikowsky, Samuel G. *civil engineering educator*
Panagiotopoulos, Athanassios Zois *chemical engineering educator*
Parker, Michael Seth *technical development manager*
Parrish, Edward Alton, Jr. *electrical and computer engineering educator, academic administrator*
Patience, Gregory Scott *chemical engineer, educator*
Pedersen, Karen Sue *electrical engineer*
Peebles, Peyton Zimmermann, Jr. *electrical engineer, educator*
Pence, Ira Wilson, Jr. *engineering executive, researcher*
Pniakowski, Andrew Frank *structural engineer*
Porter, Philip Thomas *retired electrical engineer*
Potvin, Alfred Raoul *engineering executive*
Prevatt, David O. *civil engineer, researcher*
Pruden, Ann Lorette *chemical engineer, researcher, management consultant*
Pruehsner, William Robert *biomedical engineer*
Qi, Xiaoning *electrical engineer, electronics engineer, researcher*
Qiu, Xiangjun *mining engineer*
Quan, Gang *engineering educator*
Raghavan, Rajagopal S. *retired petroleum engineer*
Rainer, Rex Kelly *civil engineer, educator*
Ramakrishnan, Kannan *mechanical engineer*
Ramer, James LeRoy *civil engineer*
Ramirez, Martin Ruben *engineering educator*
Ramirez Nafarrate, Adrian *industrial engineer*
Ranjan, Rahul *engineer, researcher*
Ratner, Buddy Dennis *biomedical engineer, educator*
Raven, Francis Harvey *mechanical engineer, educator*
Reaves, Ray Donald *civil engineer*
Reid, Robert Lelon *engineering educator, dean*
Reza, Shahed *electrical engineer*
Riden, Michael David *nuclear engineer*
Robe, Thurlow Richard *retired engineering educator, dean*
Rodriguez, Angel Luis *electrical engineer*
Rose, James Turner *aerospace engineer, consultant*
Ross, Gerald Fred *electrical engineering executive, researcher*
Rubbert, Paul Edward *retired engineering executive*
Rudd, D(ale) F(rederick) *chemical engineering professor*
Rumschitzki, David Sheldon *chemical engineering educator*
Russo, Roy Lawrence *retired electronics engineer*
Ruud, Clayton Olaf *engineering educator*
Saeks, Richard Ephraim *engineering executive*
Schell, Allan Carter *retired electrical engineer*
Schmidt, Robert *retired mechanics and civil engineering educator*
Schoen, Allen Harry *retired aerospace engineering executive*
Schultz, Albert Barry *engineering educator*
Scott, Benjamin *retired electrical engineer*
Scott, Charles David *chemical engineer, consultant*
Seaden, George *civil engineer*
Seader, Junior DeVere (Bob Seader) *retired chemical engineering professor*
Secchiutti, Ronald *electrical engineering designer*
Sechrist, Chalmers Franklin, Jr. *electrical engineering educator*
Seible, Frieder *structural engineer, educator*
Seldner, Betty Jane *environmental engineer, consultant, aerospace transportation executive*
Shaffer, Bernard William *mechanical and aerospace engineering educator*
Shank, Maurice Edwin *aerospace engineer, consultant*
Shapiro, Amir *mechanical engineer, researcher*
Shartle, Stanley Musgrave *engineering executive, consultant, surveyor*
Sheaffer, Richard Allen *electrical engineer*
Shulman, Yechiel *engineering educator*
Siegal, Rita Goran *engineering company executive*
Siljak, Dragoslav D. *engineering educator, researcher*
Simpson, Murray *electrical engineer, consultant*
Skov, Arlie Mason *petroleum engineer, consultant*
Skromme, Lawrence H. *consulting agricultural engineer*
Smally, Donald Jay *consulting engineering executive*
Smeallie, Kevin Wayne *engineering company executive, consultant*
Smith, Amy B. *mechanical engineer, educator*
Smith, Wayne Calvin *chemical engineer, consultant*
Socolow, Robert Harry *engineering educator, physicist*
Somasundaran, Ponisseril *surface and colloid engineering educator*
Spanos, Pol Dimitrios *engineering educator*
Spanovich, Milan *retired civil engineer*
Spiegel, Herman D.J. *architecture and structural engineering educator*
Spriggs, Richard Moore *ceramics engineer, science administrator, researcher*
Srinivasagupta, Deepak *chemical engineer, researcher*
Stancell, Arnold Francis *chemical engineering educator, retired oil industry executive*
Starkweather, Gary Keith *optical engineer, computer company executive*
Stella, Marie Vita *retired engineer, consultant, homeland and information security*
Sterner, Chris Stephen *nuclear engineer, educator*
Stiffler, Jack Justin *electrical engineer*
Storm, Hunter Alexandra (Eugenia Lynn Morris) *information security engineer*
Su, Fei *electrical engineer, researcher*
Su, Kendall Ling-Chiao *engineering educator*
Sudan, Ravindra Nath *electrical engineer, physicist, educator*
Sui, Haichang *electrical engineer, researcher*
Sun, Ruidong *petroleum engineer*
Taber, Geoffrey Alexander *industrial engineer, quality assurance professional*
Tadepalli, Srikanth *mechanical engineer, researcher*
Taiebat, Mahdi *civil engineer*
Taiganides, E. Paul *agricultural and environmental engineer, consultant*
Tamaro, George John *retired consulting engineer*
Taylor, Anthony Baldwin *civil engineer*
Taylor, Carson William *retired electrical engineer*
Thackston, Edward Lee *civil engineering educator*
Thie, Joseph Anthony *nuclear engineer*
Thornhill, Harlen Webster *retired aircraft engineer*
Tontiruttananon, Channarong *electrical engineer, researcher*
Trauger, Donald Byron *nuclear engineer, lab administrator*
Tsoukalas, Lefteri H. *engineering educator, department chairman*
Tsygan, Leonid Iosifovich *civil engineer, writer*
Tucker, Duane Ernest *engineer, military officer*
Tung, Ye *engineering educator*
Turner, Ginger L. *management science and engineering scholar*
Upatnieks, Juris *retired optical engineer*
Urbanik, Thomas, II, *civil engineering educator, researcher*
Vaidyanathan, Vijay V. *engineering educator*
Valbonesi, Lucia *systems engineer*
van Schilfgaarde, Jan *retired agricultural engineer, federal agency administrator*
Velev, Miroslav N. *electrical and computer engineer, educator*
Velzy, Charles O. *mechanical engineer*
Vér, István László *acoustical engineer, consultant*
Verbov, Lev Falkovich *metallurgical engineer, freelance/self-employed translator, writer*
Vest, Charles Marstiller *engineering educator, former academic administrator*
Viest, Ivan Miroslav *structural engineer, consultant*
Villforth, John Carl *engineer, health physicist*
Voigt, Karl Albert *electrical engineer, military officer*
Wackernagel, Mathis *engineering company executive, director*
Waller, Steven R. *engineer*
Walsh, Michael P. *mechanical engineer*
Waxman, Ronald *computer engineer*
Weber, Thomas William *chemical engineering professor*
Weil, Randolph Allen *engineering executive*
Weinberger, Arnold *retired electrical engineer*
Weinbrenner, George Ryan *aeronautical engineer*
Weingarten, Joseph Leonard *aerospace engineer*
Weiss, Alvin Harvey *chemical engineer, educator, research scientist, consultant*
Weldon, William Forrest *electrical and mechanical engineer, educator*
Weller, Sol William *chemical engineering professor*
Wentz, William Henry, Jr. *aerospace engineer, educator*
Wheeler, George Charles, Jr. *materials engineer, process engineer*
Whitcomb, Richard Travis *aeronautical consultant*
White, Charles Olds *aeronautical engineer*
White, Stanley Archibald *electrical engineer, researcher*
White, William Dudley *safety engineer*
Wigand, Robert Charles, Jr. *retired civil engineer, retired aerospace engineer*
Wilde, Daniel Underwood *computer engineering educator*
Williams, Charles Wesley *retired engineering executive, consultant, researcher*
Williams, Howard Walter *aerospace engineer, engineering executive*
Williams, Thomas W. *electrical engineer*
Willis, Selene Lowe *electrical engineer, application developer, consultant, information technology manager*
Wilson, Melvin Edmond *retired civil engineer*
Wolfe, Charles Morgan *electrical engineering educator*
Woll, Harry J. *electrical engineer*
Woo, Derek *electrical and computer engineer*
Woodland, N. Joseph *retired optical engineer, retired mechanical engineer*
Wozencraft, John McReynolds *retired communications engineer*
Wu, Min *computer and electrical engineer*
Wu, Xin *electrical engineer, researcher, educator*
Xoubi, Ned *nuclear engineer*
Xu, Dongming *engineer, researcher*
Yang, Bing-Shiang *engineering educator*
Yong, Raymond Nen-Yiu *civil engineering educator*
Young, Jeremy Edward *systems engineer*
Young, Tzay Y. *electrical and computer engineering educator*
Yue, Alfred Shui-Choh *metallurgical engineer, consultant*
Yuen, Stanley Manfung *engineering company executive, electrical engineer*
Yun, James Kyoon *electrical engineer*
Zahran, Mohamed Mostafa *electrical engineer, educator*
Zanjacomo, Paulo Regis *engineering executive*
Zelinski, Joseph John *engineering educator, consultant*
Zellers, Robert Charles *materials engineer, consultant, speaker*
Zhang, Li *engineer, researcher, educator*
Zhang, Shibao *electrical engineer*
Zhao, Hong *biomedical engineer, educator*
Zhao, Kezhong *electrical engineer*
Zimmerman, Marlin U., Jr. *chemical engineer*

FINANCE: BANKING SERVICES

See also **FINANCE: INVESTMENT SERVICES**

UNITED STATES

ALABAMA

Birmingham
Banton, Julian Watts *banker*
Dick, John R. *bank executive*
Horsley, Richard David *banker*
Jones, D. Paul, Jr. *bank executive, lawyer*
Marks, Charles Caldwell *retired banker, manufacturing executive*
Moore, Jackson Watts *bank executive*
Morgan, Hugh Jackson, Jr. *retired bank and energy executive*
Northen, Charles Swift III *retired bank executiv*
Powell, William Arnold, Jr. *retired bank executive*
Weatherly, Robert Stone, Jr. *banker*

Dothan
Peterson, Roger *community bank executive, retired international investment banker, manufacturing executive, air force officer*

Montgomery
Hoffman, Richard William *retired banker*
Lowder, Robert E. *bank executive*

ALASKA

Anchorage
Cuddy, Daniel Hon *bank executive*
Rasmuson, Edward Bernard *banker*
Reed, Frank Metcalf *bank executive, director*

ARIZONA

Paradise Valley
Unruh, James Arlen *bank executive*

Phoenix
Ralston, Barbara Jo *bank executive*
Richardson, Judy McEwen *investment banker, consultant, cartoonist*

Scottsdale
Garfield, Ernest *bank executive, consultant*
Leonard, George Edmund *bank executive, credi manager, marketing professional*

Surprise
Koessel, Donald Ray *retired bank executive*

Tucson
Abelt, Ralph William *bank executive*
Sampsel, Hunter *mortgage company executive*

ARKANSAS

Bentonville
Walton, Jim Carr *bank executive*

Little Rock
Green, Johnnie D. *loan officer*
Gulley, Wilbur Paul, Jr. *retired savings and loan association executive*

CALIFORNIA

Arcadia
Ulrich, Peter Henry *banker*

Bakersfield
Sawyer, Nelson Baldwin, Jr. *credit union executive*

Berkeley
Chirurg, James Thomas *holding company executive*

Beverly Hills
Balash, Jeffrey Linke *investment banker*
Goldsmith, Bram *banker*
Israel, Richard Stanley *investment banker*
Walker, William Tidd, Jr. *investment banker*

Burbank
Miller, Clifford Albert *merchant banker*

Carmel
Barton, Hugh Perry *bank executive*
Dobey, James Kenneth *banker*

City Of Industry
Contreras-Sweet, Maria *bank executive*

Costa Mesa
Giannini, Valerio Louis *investment banker*
Harley, Halvor Larson *bank executive, lawyer*

Encinitas
Ford, William Francis *retired bank holding company executive*

Escondido
Newman, Barry Ingalls *retired bank executive*

Fresno
Smith, Richard Howard *banker*

Glendale
Cross, Richard John *bank executive*

Goleta
Nahra, Lynda J. *bank executive*

Irvine
Jamshidipour, Yousef *bank executive, economist, financial advisor*

La Mesa
Schmidt, James Craig *retired bank, savings and loan association executive*

Lafayette
Dethero, J. Hambright *banker*

Lake Arrowhead
Fitzgerald, John Charles, Jr. *investment banker*

Long Beach
Hancock, John Walker III *banker*

Los Angeles
Barren De Serres, Bruce Willard (H.R.H. The Duke Bruce Willard Barren de Serres) *merchant banker*
Cho, Eung-Rae (Brian) *bank executive*
Cohee, Kevin *bank executive*
Kang, Alvin *bank executive*
Kim, Min Jung *bank executive*
Mahmoodzadegan, Navid A. *investment banker*
Min, Soo Bong *bank executive*
Riegler, Alan Martin *bank technology consultant*
Riordan, George Nickerson *investment banker*
Sohn, Sung Won *bank executive*

Malibu
DeMieri, Joseph L. *retired bank executive*

Menlo Park
Hazen, Paul Mandeville *banker*
Quinn, Kevin Anthomy *investment banker*
Roberts, George R. *investment banker*
chmidt, Chauncey Everett *banker, director*

Newport Beach
asey, Thomas Clark *retired trust company executive, investment advisor*
Matzdorff, James Arthur *investment banker, internet marketing professional*
rince, Thomas E. *bank executive*

Ontario
Myers, Christopher D. *bank executive*

Orinda
rowbridge, Thomas, Jr. *mortgage company executive*

asadena
reeman, Ralph Carter *investment banker, management consultant*
eys, Scott *bank executive*

Ng, Dominic *bank executive*
Patton, Richard Weston *retired mortgage company executive*
Perry, Michael W. *bank executive*

Rancho Cordova
Ling, Robert Malcolm *banker, publishing executive*

Riverside
Case, Janice Chang *trust officer, property manager, naturopathic physician, psychologist, lawyer*

San Diego
Rady, Ernest S. *thrift and loan association executive*
Reinhard, Christopher John *merchant banker, venture capitalist, biotechnologist, director*
Wiesler, James Ballard *retired banker*
Yacovone, Ellen Elaine *banker*

San Francisco
Atkins, Howard Ian *bank executive*
August-deWilde, Katherine *banker*
Bee, Robert Norman *banker*
Boutros, George F. *investment banker*
Callahan, Patricia R. *bank executive*
Dellas, Robert Dennis *investment banker*
Demarest, David Franklin, Jr. *banker, retired government official*
Gillette, Frankie Jacobs *retired savings and loan association executive, federal agency administrator, social worker*
Hoyt, David A. *bank executive*
Ji, Tingting *mortgage company executive, consultant*
Kovacevich, Richard M. *bank executive*
Lee, Pamela Anne *bank executive, accountant, financial analyst*
Liu, Peter *bank executive*
Loughlin, Michael J. *bank executive*
Matthews, Gilbert Elliott *investment banker*
McGettigan, Charles Carroll, Jr. *investment banker*
McGrath, Don John *bank executive*
Modjtabai, Avid *bank executive*
Ostler, Clyde W. *banker*
Safreno, Casey *investment banker*
Stumpf, John G. *bank executive*
Tolstedt, Carrie L. *bank executive*
Warner, Harold Clay, Jr. *banker, investment company executive*
Woo Ho, Doreen *investment banker*
Yellen, Janet Louise *bank executive*

San Jose
Hall, Robert Emmett, Jr. *investment banker, realtor*

San Rafael
Djordjevich, Miroslav-Michael *bank executive*
Payne, David L. *bank executive*

Santa Barbara
Anderson, Donald Meredith *bank executive*
Tilton, David Lloyd *savings and loan association executive*

Santa Monica
Davis, Stephen Edward Folwell *banker*
Heimbuch, Babette E. *bank executive*

Santa Rosa
Meekins, Deborah *bank executive*

Tarzana
Weil, Leonard *banker*

Walnut Creek
Rhody, Ronald Edward *bank, communications executive*
Saavedra, Charles James *banker*

COLORADO

Denver
Grant, William West III *banker*
Imhoff, Walter Francis *investment banker*
Kemper, J. Mariner *bank executive*
Nicholson, Will Faust, Jr. *bank executive*
Orullian, B. LaRae *retired bank executive*

Englewood
Rosser, Edwin Michael *mortgage company executive*

Estes Park
Piper, Mark Harry *retired banker*

Greeley
Smith, Jack Lee *bank executive*

Greenwood Village
Corboy, James McNally *investment banker*
Davidson, John Robert (Jay) *bank executive*
Sims, Douglas D. *bank executive*

CONNECTICUT

Cos Cob
Kane, Jay Brassler *banker*

Essex
Miller, Elliott Cairns *retired bank executive, lawyer*

Fairfield
Brett, Arthur Cushman, Jr. *banker*
Cooper, L.E., Jr. *bank executive, lawyer, writer*

Greenwich
Bedrosian, Gregory Ronald *investment banker*
Nevin, Crocker *investment banker*

Stockman, David Alan *investment banker, former congressman*

Hartford
Fiszel, Geoffrey Lynn *investment banker, investment advisor*

New Canaan
MacEwan, Nigel Savage *retired merchant banker*

New Haven
Patterson, Peyton R. *bank executive*

Norwalk
Baylis, Robert Montague *investment banker*
Piper, Thomas Laurence III *banker*

Ridgefield
Mesznik, Joel R. *investment banker*

Waterbury
Smith, James Copenhaver *bank executive*

Weston
Zimmerman, Bernard *investment banker*

Westport
Donaldson, James Neill *banker*
Kelly, Paul Knox *investment banker*

DELAWARE

Wilmington
Cecala, Ted Thomas, Jr. *banker, accountant*
Cohen, Betsy Z. *bank executive*
Krulak, Charles Chandler *bank executive*
Porter, John Francis III *banker*

DISTRICT OF COLUMBIA

Washington
Carson, Thomas Bode *bank executive, consultant*
Conlin, Linda Mysliwy *bank executive, former federal agency administrator*
Decker, Brett M. *bank executive*
Douglas, Leslie *investment banker*
Guenther, Jack Donald *banker*
Holbrooke, Richard Charles Albert *investment banker, former ambassador*
Lambright, James H. *bank executive*
Mathias, Edward Joseph *merchant banker*
McNamara, Robert Strange *former world bank president, secretary of defense*
Morales, Hector E., Jr. *bank executive, lawyer*
Moreno, Luis Alberto *bank executive*
Pollock, Alexander John *banker*
Rotberg, Eugene Harvey *investment banker, lawyer*
St. John, Julie *mortgage company executive*
Swad, Stephen M. *mortgage company executive*
Tomlinson, Alexander Cooper *investment banker, consultant*
Weatherstone, Sir Dennis *retired bank executive*
Wolfowitz, Paul Dundes *former President of the World Bank, former federal agency administrator*
Zoellick, Robert Bruce *President of the World Bank, former federal agency administrator*

FLORIDA

Boca Grande
de Saint Phalle, Thibaut *investment banker, financial consultant*

Boca Raton
Goldberger, Melvin Tobias *bank executive*

Coral Gables
Brownell, Edwin Rowland *banker, civil engineer, land surveyor*

Dunedin
Rosa, Raymond Ulric *retired banker*

Englewood
Simis, Theodore Luckey *investment banker, information technology executive*

Fort Lauderdale
Leach, Ralph F. *banker*
Thayer, Charles James *investment banker*

Highland Beach
Lane, James McConkey *retired investment banker*

Key Biscayne
Wilson, Robert Gordon *investment banker*

Lantana
Barrett, Robert James III *investment banker*

Marco Island
Cooper, Thomas Astley *bank executive*

Miami
Aguirre-Sacasa, Francisco Xavier *international banker, diplomat*

Miramar
Navarro, Richard *banker*

Naples
Kley, John Arthur *banker*
Kvetko, Colleen M. *bank executive*
Martinuzzi, Leo Sergio, Jr. *banker*

Nokomis
Hawley, Phillip Eugene *investment banker*

North Miami Beach
Kropp, James Herbert, Sr. *investment manager*

North Palm Beach
Lynch, William Walker *banker*

Ocala
Harris, Charles Edison *banker, lawyer*

Orlando
Hoepner, Theodore John *banker*
Shirek, John Richard *retired savings and loan executive*

Palm Beach
Coleman, Denis Patrick, Jr. *investment banker*
Frankel, Charles James III *banker*

Palm Beach Gardens
Andrews, Holdt *investment banker*

Pensacola
Stuart, Walter Bynum III *retired banker*

Pompano Beach
Kester, Stewart Randolph *banker*

Ponte Vedra Beach
de Selding, Edward Bertrand *retired bank executive*
O'Brien, Raymond Vincent, Jr. *banker*

Punta Gorda
Haswell, Carleton Radley *banker*

Saint Petersburg
Godbold, Francis Stanley *investment banker, security firm executive*

Sarasota
Phillips, Howard William *investment banker*

Tampa
Michaels, John Patrick, Jr. *investment banker, media broker*

Temple Terrace
Rink, Wesley Winfred *retired bank executive*

Tequesta
Turrell, Richard Horton, Sr. *banker*

Tierra Verde
Stewart, John Murray *bank executive*

Vero Beach
Crosby, John Griffith *investment banker*
Sheehan, Charles Vincent *investment banker*

West Palm Beach
Addison, Ferguson Lofton Lightbourne *retired bank executive*
Kiely, Dan Ray *fund manager, consultant, real estate company executive*

GEORGIA

Atlanta
Abbott, Gay O. *bank executive*
Barron, Patrick Kenneth *bank executive*
Biggins, J. Veronica *bank executive*
Breeden, Mimi *bank executive*
Chancy, Mark A. *bank executive*
Chapman, Hugh McMaster *banker*
Chau, Pin Pin *bank executive*
Dierker, David F. *bank executive*
Dorfman, Richard *bank executive*
Dowling, Roderick Anthony *investment banker*
Freeman, Thomas E. *bank executive*
Hollis, Timothy Martin *bank executive*
Humann, L. Phillip *bank executive*
Kelly, Craig James *bank executive*
Kirby, C. Eugene, Jr. *bank executive*
Lockhart, Dennis P. *bank executive*
Long, Robert Richard *banker*
McNabb, Dianne Leigh *investment banker, accountant*
Patterson, Dennis M. *bank executive*
Reed, William R., Jr. *bank executive*
Rogers, William H., Jr. *bank executive*
Shufeldt, Robert Charles *bank executive*
Sullivan, Timothy E. *bank executive*
Wells, James M. III *bank executive*
Williams, James Bryan *banker*

Columbus
Anthony, Richard E. *bank executive*
Carr, Leila S. *bank executive*
Green, Fred L. III *bank executive*
James, Elizabeth R. (Lee Lee James) *bank executive*

Hinesville
Smith, Barbara *bank executive*

Kennesaw
Whittingham, Harry Edward, Jr. *retired banker*

Savannah
Clemmons, John B. *bank executive, director, retired mathematics educator*

Stockbridge
Grimes, Richard Allen *banker, educator*

HAWAII

Honolulu
Johnson, Lawrence M. *retired bank executive*
Midkiff, Robert Richards *trust company, finance company executive, consultant*
Tanoue, Donna A. *bank executive, former federal agency administrator*
Wolff, Herbert Eric *banker, former army officer*

IDAHO

Ketchum
McElhinny, Wilson Dunbar *banker*

Twin Falls
Eaton, Curtis Howarth *banker, lawyer*

ILLINOIS

Burr Ridge
McCormack, Robert Cornelius *investment banker*

Chicago
Adams, Austin A. *bank executive*
Bartter, Brit Jeffrey *investment banker*
Bobins, Norman R. *banker*
Bobrinskoy, Charles Kellogg *investment banker*
Canmann, Michael *investment banker*
Citera, Peter M. *mortgage company executive*
Costello, Ellen M. *bank executive*
Dancewicz, John Edward *investment banker*
Evans, Charles L. *bank executive*
Fenton, Clifton Lucien *investment banker*
Freund, Kristen P. *bank executive*
Glickman, Robert Jeffrey *bank executive*
Hasten, Joseph Erwin *bank executive*
Lorenz, Katherine Mary *bank executive*
Lyon, Charles Herbert Randolph *investment banker*
Mitchell, Lee Mark *private equity investor, executive*
Montgomery, Charles Howard *retired bank executive*
Reilly, Robert Frederick *investment banker*
Rizzi, Joseph Vito *banker*
Schulte, David Michael *investment banker*
Scully, John Edward, Jr. *banker*
Stirling, James Paulman *investment banker*
Tescher, Jennifer *bank executive*
Ward, Jonathan P. *investment banker*
Weston, Roger Lance *banker*

Des Plaines
Vancastle, Robin *bank executive*

Dundee
Weck Farrag, Kristin W. *bank executive*

Evanston
Scholten, Menno Nico *banking consultant*

Fox River Grove
Abboud, Alfred Robert *banker, investor, consultant, director*

Highwood
Brown, Lawrence Haas *retired banker*

Kenilworth
Corrigan, John Edward, Jr. *retired banker, lawyer*

Lake Forest
Ross, Robert Evan *bank executive*
Seaman, Irving, Jr. *banker*
Swift, Edward Foster III *investment banker*

Mattoon
Horsley, Jack Everett *retired bank executive, writer, lawyer*

Melrose Park
Giancola, James J. *bank executive*

Northbrook
Gratalo, John, Jr. *banker, small business owner*
Keehn, Silas *retired bank executive*
Sewright, Charles William, Jr. *mortgage banking advisory services company executive*

Oak Brook
Iles, Eileen Marie *bank executive, risk management consultant, accountant*

Palatine
Hershenhorn, Robert Gene *bank executive*

Skokie
Griffiths, Robert Pennell *banker*

Winnetka
Klapperich, Frank Lawrence, Jr. *investment banker*

INDIANA

Columbus
Abts, Henry William *retired banker*

Greenwood
Broscoe, Peter A. *mortgage company executive, consultant*

Indianapolis
Stitle, Stephen A. *bank executive*

La Porte
Bakwin, Edward Morris *banker*

Muncie
Anderson, Stefan Stolen *retired banker*

South Bend
Jones, Wellington Downing III *banker*

IOWA

Cedar Rapids
Wax, Nadine Virginia *retired bank executive*

Clinton
Kearney, Michael John *banker*

Des Moines
Heiden, Cara *mortgage company executive*

Maquoketa
Tubbs, Edward Lane *banker*

KANSAS

Coldwater
Adams, Elizabeth Herrington *banker*

Leawood
Gregory, Lewis Dean *trust company executive*

Liberal
Richard, Loren Dru *bank executive*

Olathe
Roby, Brian L. *bank executive*

Pratt
Loomis, Howard Krey *banker, director*

Shawnee Mission
McEachen, Richard Edward *banker, lawyer*

Topeka
Bunten, William Daniel *retired banker*

KENTUCKY

Louisville
Griffith, Mary H. *bank executive*
Guillaume, Raymond Kendrick *banker*

LOUISIANA

Baton Rouge
McDonald, Alden J., Jr. *bank executive*

Covington
Blossman, Alfred Rhody, Jr. *banker*

Lafayette
Hail, Karen L. *bank executive*

New Orleans
Milling, R(oswell) King *bank executive, lawyer*

MAINE

Camden
Daly, Sean G. *bank executive*

Cape Elizabeth
Cotter, Joseph Francis *retired bank executive, hotel executive*

Portland
Masrani, Bharat B. *bank executive*
Ryan, William J. *bank executive*
Suehrstedt, Wendy P. *bank executive*

MARYLAND

Annapolis
Schleicher, Nora Elizabeth *bank executive, treasurer, accountant*

Baltimore
Baldwin, Henry Furlong *banker*
Barnhill, Gregory Hurd *investment banker*
Hopkins, Samuel *retired investment banker*
Kent, Edgar Robert, Jr. *investment banker*
Liberto, Joseph Salvatore *retired bank executive*
Schaefer, Robert Wayne *banker*

Bethesda
Rosenbaum, Greg Alan *merchant banker, consultant*
Saul, B. Francis, II, *bank executive, director*

Centreville
Griffith, Alan Richard *retired banker*

Owings Mills
Sanner, George Bradley *bank executive*

MASSACHUSETTS

Boston
Aquilino, Daniel *banker*
Brown, William L. *retired banker*
Campanelli, Joseph P. *bank executive*
Finnegan, Neal Francis *retired banker*
Gifford, Charles K. *banker*
Hill, Richard Devereux *retired banker*
Pline, Jennifer Alice *trust company executive*
Rosengren, Eric S. *bank executive*
Vermilye, Peter Hoagland *banker*

Cambridge
Edgerly, William Skelton *banker*

Dover
Aldrich, Frank Nathan *banker*

Longmeadow
Lo Bello, Joseph David *bank executive*

Newton
Teig, Marlowe Gilman *investment banker*

Reading
Burbank, Nelson Stone *investment banker*

West Wareham
Worrell, Cynthia Lee *bank executive*

Westport
Nichols, C. Walter III *retired trust company executive*

Westwood
Riley, Henry Charles *banker*

Winchester
Brennan, Francis Patrick *banker*

MICHIGAN

Detroit
Babb, Ralph W., Jr. *bank executive*
Beran, John R. *banker*
Buttigieg, Joseph J. *bank executive*
Jeffs, Thomas Hamilton, II, *retired bank executive*
Piper, William Howard *bank executive*

Farmington Hills
Heiss, Richard Walter *retired bank executive, consultant, lawyer*

Frankfort
Foster, Robert Carmichael *banker*

Grosse Pointe
Mengden, Joseph Michael *retired investment banker*

Grosse Pointe Farms
Surdam, Robert McClellan *retired banker*

Lansing
Cunningham, Paula Diane *bank executive, former academic administrator*
Reid English, Cristen *bank executive*

Saginaw
Evans, Harold Edward *retired banker*

Southfield
Shields, Robert Emmet *merchant banker, lawyer*

Waterford
Houston, E(rnest) James, Jr. *banker, consultant*

MINNESOTA

Chanhassen
Severson, Roger Allan *bank executive*

Eden Prairie
Hanson, Dale S. *retired bank executive*

Edina
Campbell, James Robert *retired bank executive*

Minneapolis
Carlson, Jennie Peaslack *bank executive*
Cecere, Andrew *bank executive*
Cooper, William Allen *bank executive*
Davis, Richard K. *bank executive*
Griffith, Sima Lynn *investment banker, consultant*
Grundhofer, Jerry A. *bank executive*
Grundhofer, John F. *bank executive*
Pohlad, Carl R. *bank executive, professional sports team executive*
Stern, Gary Hilton *bank executive*
Thormodsgard, Diane L. *bank executive*

Wayzata
Brown, Neil W. *bank executive*
Nagorske, Lynn A. *bank executive*
Rich, Willis Frank, Jr. *banker*

MISSISSIPPI

Gulfport
Thatcher, George Robert *banker, writer, journalist, columnist*

Tupelo
Ramage, Martis Donald, Jr. *banker*

MISSOURI

Bridgeton
Brunngraber, Eric Henry *banker*

Clayton
Kemper, David Woods, II, *banker*

Independence
Barker, Keith Rene *investment banker*

Kansas City
Hoenig, Thomas M. *bank executive*
Kemper, Rufus Crosby, Jr. *retired bank executive*

Saint Louis
Barksdale, Clarence Caulfield *retired banker*
Bealke, Linn Hemingway *banker*
Blake, Allen H. *bank executive*
Bryant, Ruth Alyne *banker*
Costigan, Edward John *retired investment banker*
Dierberg, James F. *bank executive*
Joyner, Dee Ann *bank executive*
Kling, S(tephen) Lee *banker*
Maurer, Frederic George III *bank executive*
Poole, William *bank executive*
Rasche, Robert Harold *banker, retired economics educator*
Stoecker, David Thomas *retired banker*

Saint Peters
Beckmann, Bill *mortgage company executive*

Springfield
Budzinsky, Armin Alexander *investment banker*

Walker
Martin, Phillip Dwight *bank consulting company executive, mayor*

NEBRASKA

Lincoln
Lundstrom, Gilbert Gene *bank executive, lawyer*

Sutton
Johnson, Michael Randy *bank executive*

NEVADA

Logandale
Smiley, Robert William, Jr. *investment banker*

Reno
Binns, James Edward *retired banker*

NEW HAMPSHIRE

New Castle
Mapel, William Marlen Raines *retired bank executive*

Sanbornville
Berg, Warren Stanley *retired bank executive*

Silver Lake
Tregenza, Norman Hughson *investment banker*

NEW JERSEY

Bay Head
O'Brien, Robert Brownell, Jr. *banker, consultant, yacht broker, opera company executive*

Bridgewater
DeMaio, Donnalee A. *bank executive*

Chatham
Leonett, Anthony Arthur *banker*

Cherry Hill
Falese, Robert D., Jr. *bank executive*

Cliffside Park
Goldstein, Howard Bernard *investment banker*

Jersey City
Goldberg, Arthur *merchant banker, financial consultant, educator*

Liberty Corner
Feeks, J. Michael *bank executive*

Little Falls
Casey, Karen Anne *banker*

Madison
Armstrong, Richard William *bank executive, management consultant*

Morristown
Kearns, William Michael, Jr. *investment banker*
Moore, Milo Anderson *banker*

Paramus
Hermance, Ronald E., Jr. *bank executive*

Princeton
Ganoe, Charles Stratford *banker, consultant*
Mills, Bradford *merchant banker*
Winder, Bayly Philip *bank executive*

Short Hills
Bartels, Stanley Leonard *investment banker*

Shrewsbury
Feeney, John Robert *banker*

Spring Lake
D'Luhy, John James *investment banker*

Summit
Lewis, Donald Emerson *banker*
Mueller, Paul Henry *retired bank executive*

Tenafly
Bernstein, William Robert *banker*

West New York
Koo, Yonghoi *investment banker*

NEW MEXICO

Santa Fe
Clyde, Larry Forbes *banker*
Dreisbach, John Gustave *investment banker*
Morrissey, Michael Joseph *investment banker*

NEW YORK

Albany
Dushensky, Jacqueline Amelia *banker, educator*
Zou, Linda *bank executive*

Bedford
Philip, Peter Van Ness *former trust company executive*

Briarcliff Manor
Oakley, Richard Putney *investment banker*

Brooklyn
Bottiglia, Frank Robert *bank executive*
Cohen, Alan *investment banker*
Coleman, Maurice L. *bank executive*
Singer, Eric T. *investment banker*

Buffalo
Sadler, Robert E., Jr. *bank executive*
Wilmers, Robert George *bank executive*

Cherry Valley
Humes, Graham *investment banker*

East Hampton
Good, Allen Hovey *investment banker, real estate broker*

Elmont
Cusack, Thomas Joseph *retired banker*

Great Neck
Katz, Edward Morris *banker*

Greenwich
Smethurst, E(dward) William, Jr. *investment banker*

Hartsdale
Katz, John *investment banker*

Larchmont
Kaufmann, Henry Mark *mortgage banker*

Locust Valley
Comfort, William Twyman, Jr. *banker*

Long Island City
Markus, Maura *bank executive*

Melville
Strauss, Michael *mortgage company executive*

New York
Adams, John Brett *investment banker, pharmaceutical executive*
Agostinelli, Robert Francesco *investment banker*
Alemany, Ellen R. *bank executive*
Allen, Claxton Edmonds III *investment banker*
Armine, Cindy A. *bank executive*
Bains, Leslie Elizabeth *banker*
Ballard, Charles Alan *investment banker*
Barbeosch, William Peter *bank executive, lawyer*
Barry, Nancy Marie *bank executive*
Beim, David Odell *investment banker, educator*
Bellanger, Serge René *bank executive*
Biglari, Hamid *investment banker*
Black, Steven D. *bank executive*
Boardman, D(ennie) Dixon *investment banker*
Braunstein, Douglas *bank executive*
Bravo, Luis Fernando *investment banker*
Brody, Kenneth David *investment banker*
Brown, G(lenn) William, Jr. *bank executive*
Burke, James Joseph, Jr. *investment banker*
Carey, William Polk *investment banker*
Castle, John Krob *merchant banker*
Cavanagh, Michael J. *bank executive*
Cephas, Derrick D. *bank executive, lawyer*
Chalsty, John Steele *investment banker*
Chammah, Walid A. *investment banker*
Childs, John Farnsworth *retired bank executive*
Christodoulou, Marilena *investment banker, finance company executive*
Clifford, Stewart Burnett *banker, director*
Cohen, Jonathan Little *investment banker*
Coulter, David A. *investment banker*
Crockett, Andrew Duncan *bank executive*
Cromwell, Oliver Dean *investment banker*
Darst, David Martin *investment banker, writer, educator*
David-Weill, Michel Alexandre *retired investment banker*
Davis, George Linn *banker*
Deans, Patricia Herrmann *investment banker*
Debs, Richard A. *investment banker*
DelliBovi, Alfred A. *bank executive, former federal agency administrator*
DeNunzio, David Ames *investment banker*
Deutsch, David Neil *investment banker*
Dooley, Douglas John *bank executive*
Drew, Ina R. *bank executive*
Duke, Ellen (Bebe Duke) *bank executive*
Dwek, Cyril S. *bank executive*
Elliott, Steven G. *bank executive*
Epstein, Stuart Joel *investment banker*
Erdoes, Mary Callahan *bank executive*
Farley, Terrence Michael *banker*
Feder, Harry Simon *bank executive*
Fishman, Alan H. *mortgage company and former bank executive*
FitzPatrick, Daniel M. *trust company executive, lawyer*
Flaherty, Pamela Potter *bank executive*
Flowers, J. Christopher *investment banker*
Forbes, Jim (James D. Forbes) *investment banker*
Frank, Frederick *investment banker*
Fredericks, Ivy Lindstrom *investment banker*
Friedberg, Barry Sewell *investment banker*
Fruitman, Frederick Howard *investment banker*
Furman, Roy Lance *investment banker, theater producer*
Gamble, Theodore Robert, Jr. *investment banker*
Gant, Donald Ross *investment banker*
Garner, Albert Headden *investment banker*
Garrett, Robert *investment banker, director*
Geithner, Timothy F. *bank executive*
Gellert, Michael Erwin *investment banker*
Godridge, Leslie V. *bank executive*
Gold, Jeffrey Mark *investment banker*
Goldberg, Laurence *investment banker*
Goldmark, Peter Francis *banker*
Gossett, Robert Francis, Jr. *merchant banker*
Greenhill, Robert Foster *investment banker*
Greenstein, Abraham Jacob *mortgage company executive, accountant*
Greenthal, Jill A. *investment banker*
Haddon, James Francis *banker*
Hakala, Thomas John *private banker, financial planner, accountant*
Halpern, Merril Mark *retired investment banker*
Hamdan, Lawrence Anise *investment banker, lawyer*
Hance, James Henry, Jr. *former bank executive*
Harlan, Leonard Morton *merchant banker*
Hartman, Alan *investment banker*
Hassell, Gerald L. *bank executive*
Heaton, Eric *investment banker*
Heimann, John Gaines *investment banker*
Henry, Lawrence C. (Lonny Henry) *investment banker*
Herregat, Guy-Georges Jacques *retired banker*
Hersch, Dennis Steven *bank executive, lawyer*
Hill, J(ames) Tomilson *investment banker*
Horowitz, Gedale Bob *investment banker*
Howard, Bonnie *bank executive*
Hricik, Lorraine E. *bank executive*
Hurley, Dean C. *bank executive, lawyer*
Ingrassia, Timothy J. *investment banker*
Iskenderian, Mary Ellen *bank executive*
Janiak, Anthony Richard, Jr. *investment banker*
Johansson, Jerker Mats *investment banker*
Johnson, Scott Stuart *merchant banker*
Johnson, Thomas Stephen *banker*
Kaden, Lewis B. *bank executive, lawyer, educator*
Kaufmann, Mark Steiner *banker, director*
Kelly, Robert P. *bank executive*
Kindler, Robert Alan *investment banker*
Kirdar, Nemir Amin *banker*
Kravis, Henry R. *investment banker*
Lawrence, Christopher Rueckert *investment banker*
Layton, Donald Harvey *retired banker*
Lazio, Rick Anthony (Enrico Anthony Lazio) *bank executive, former congressman*
LeBlond, Richard Knight, II, *banker*
Lee, James Bainbridge, Jr. *bank executive*
Leighton, Lawrence Ward *investment banker*
Leung, Firman *investment bank executive*
Levy, Jack *investment banker*
Lieb, Richard Jay *investment banker*
Lincoln, Edmond Lynch *investment banker*
Lipper, Kenneth *investment banker, film producer, writer*
Lowman, David *mortgage company executive*
MacLellan, Steve *bank executive*
Manges, James Horace *investment banker*
Maurer, Jeffrey Stuart *trust company executive*
Maxwell, Anders John *investment banker*
McFarland, Alan Roberts *investment banker*
Mc Gillicuddy, John Francis *retired banker*
McGuire, Raymond J. *investment banker*
McMullan, William Patrick III *investment banker*
Meachin, David James Percy *investment banker*
Mendoza, Roberto G., Jr. *banker*
Menschel, Robert Benjamin *investment banker*
Merriss, Philip Ramsay, Jr. *banker*
Miller, Garfield Lankard III *investment banker*
Milstein, Howard P. *bank executive*
Mintz, Norman Nelson *investment banker, educator, retired academic administrator*
Mnuchin, Alan Geoffrey *investment banker*
Myerberg, Marcia *investment banker*
Nasser, Jacques *banker, former automotive company executive*
Needham, George Austin *investment banker*
Nemazee, Hassan *investment banker*
Newbold, John Lowe *retired banker, financial consultant*
Nolan, William Joseph III *banker*
Obolensky, Ivan *investment banker, foundation administrator, writer*
Ostrander, Thomas William *investment banker*
Pandit, Vikram S. *investment banker*
Peetz, Karen B. *bank executive*
Perella, Joseph Robert *investment banker*
Peretsman, Nancy B. *investment banker*
Perlmutter, Louis *investment banker, lawyer*
Petrie, Donald Joseph *banker*
Poll, Robert Eugene, Jr. *bank executive*
Porter, Grant A. *investment banker*
Potter, William James *investment banker*
Powell, Scott C. *bank executive*
Price, Michael J. *investment banker*
Prizzi, Jack Anthony *investment banking executive*
Purse, Charles Roe *investment banker*
Rainis, Eugene Charles *bank executive*
Rattner, Steven Lawrence *investment banker*
Repko, William Clarke *banker*
Rhodes, William Reginald *banker*
Roberts, Donald Munier *retired banker, trust company executive*
Rockefeller, David *banker*
Roosevelt, Theodore, IV, *investment banker*
Rose, Robert Neal *investment banker*
Ross, Wilbur Louis, Jr. *investment banker*
Rubin, Robert Samuel *investment banker*
Sadiq, Aamir *investment banker, engineer*
Safra, Joseph *bank executive*
Salmans, Charles Gardiner *banker*
Sandelman, Jonathan E. (Jon) *investment banker*
Sarkozy, Olivier (Pierre Olivier Sarkozy) *investment banker*
Scaturro, Philip David *investment banker, academic administrator*
Scharf, Charles W. *bank executive*
Schiff, David Tevele *investment banker*
Schumacher, Robert Denison *banker*
Schwarzman, Stephen Allen (Steve Schwarzman) *investment banker*
Scott, Margaret Simon *retired mortgage broker*
Senior, Enrique Francisco *investment banker*
Sevilla-Sacasa, Frances Aldrich *bank executive*
Shanks, Eugene Baylis, Jr. *banker*
Shedlin, Gary Stephen *investment banker*
Shipley, Walter Vincent *retired bank executive*
Slacik, Claudia *bank executive*
Slusser, William Peter *investment banker*
Smith, Gordon A. *bank executive*
Smith, Hilary Cranwell Bowen *investment banker*
Smith, Phillips Guy *banker*
Smith, Raymond W. *investment banking executive*
Spielvogel, Sidney Meyer *investment banker*
Staley, James E. *bank executive*
Stein, Howard S. *retired banker*
Stern, James Andrew *investment banker*
Straton, John Charles, Jr. *investment banker*
Svenson, Charles Oscar *investment banker*
Swarz, Jeffrey Robert *investment banker, biotechnologist, neuroscientist*
Tagliaferri, Lee Gene *investment banker*
Tang, C. Mark *investment banker, venture capitalist*
Tanner, Harold *investment banker*
Taubman, Paul J. *investment banker*
Taussig, Andrew Richard *investment banker*
Taylor, Richard William *investment banker, portfolio manager*
Towbin, A(braham) Robert *investment banker*
Tysoe, Ronald W. *investment banker, former retail executive*
Van Dine, Vance *investment banker*
Van Saun, Bruce W. *bank executive*
von Fraunhofer-Kosinski, Katherina *bank and advertising executive*
Wadsworth, John (Jack) Spencer, Jr. *investment banker*
Walters, Milton James *investment banker*
Warner, Miner Hill *investment banker*
Wasserstein, Bruce *investment banker*
Weil, Frank A. *investment banker, lawyer*
Weinberg, John Sidney *investment banker*
Weinberg, Peter Amory *investment banker*
Weiner, Walter Herman *bank executive, lawyer*
Weintz, Jacob Frederick, Jr. *retired investment banker*
Wellin, Keith Sears *investment banker*
Weymouth, Elizabeth K. *bank executive*
Wheeler, Jane *investment banker*
Whitcomb, James Howard, Jr. *investment banker*
Whiting, Gordon James *investment banker*
Whittemore, Laurence Frederick *bank executive*
Winkelried, Jon A. *investment banker*
Winters, William Thomas *bank executive*
Wit, Harold Maurice *retired investment banker, lawyer*
Woetzel, Kurt D. *banking executive*
Wolff, William F. III *investment banker*
Wolitzer, Steven Barry *investment banker*
Wright, Deborah C. *bank executive*
Yancey, Richard Charles *investment banker*
Young, Robert Craig *banker*

Orchard Park
Kwiatkowski, Timothy D. *bank executive*

Oyster Bay
Schwab, Hermann Caspar *banker*
Walsh, Charles Richard *retired banker*

Purchase
Roach, John Hendee, Jr. *bank and financial services executive, investment banker*
Tokarz, Michael Theodore *merchant banker*

Quogue
Hines, William Eugene *banker*

Rochester
Hanson, Karen Noble *financial holding company executive*
Rulison, Joseph Richard *investment banker*
Wayland-Smith, Robert Dean *retired banker*

Rye
Gambee, Robert Rankin *investment banker*

Saratoga Springs
Wait, Charles Valentine *banker*

Scarsdale
Abbe, Colman *investment banker*

Shelter Island
Dowd, David Joseph *banker, construction executive*

Southampton
Brokaw, Clifford Vail III *investment banker*

Stamford
Bergleitner, George Charles, Jr. *investment banker*

Syracuse
Gray, Charles Augustus *banker*

Tonawanda
Haller, Calvin John *banker*

West Harrison
Verano, Anthony Frank *retired banker*

White Plains
Bober, Lawrence Harold *retired banker*
Bushkin, Merle Jerome *investment banker*

Wyandanch
Newman, Samuel *retired trust company executive*

Yonkers
Philipps, Edward William *former banker, real estate appraiser*
Singer, Cecile Doris *bank executive, former state legislator*

NORTH CAROLINA

Charlotte
Alphin, J. Steele *bank executive*
Baird, Douglas James *investment banker*
Bessant, Cathy (Catherine Pombier) *bank executive, marketing professional*
Brinkley, Amy Woods *bank executive*
Brown, Edward J III *bank executive*
Clark, Ranjana B. *bank executive*
Cochran, John R. III *bank executive*
Desoer, Barbara J. *bank executive*
Fox, William J. *bank executive, former federal official*
Hammonds, Bruce L. *bank executive*
Jenkins, Benjamin P. III *bank executive*
Jones, Milton H., Jr. *bank executive*
Kelly, Stanhope A. *bank executive*
Lewis, Kenneth D. *bank executive*
McFayden, Shannon W. *bank holding company executive*
McGee, Liam E. *bank executive*
Migoya, Carlos *bank executive*
Oken, Marc D. *retired bank executive*
Price, Joe L. *bank executive*
Smith, Wilburn Jackson, Jr. *retired bank executive*
Sutton, Cecilia (Cece Sutton) *bank executive*
Taylor, Gene *bank executive*
Taylor, R. Eugene *bank executive*
Thompson, G. Kennedy (Ken Thompson) *bank executive*
Truslow, Donald K. *bank executive*
Wilson, Paul Lowell *mortgage company executive, lawyer*
Wurtz, Thomas J. *bank executive*

Fairmont
Byrne, James Frederick *banker*

Gastonia
Teem, Paul Lloyd, Jr. *bank executive*

Greenville
Wilkerson, William Holton *banker*

Hampstead
Snyder, Clair Allison *banker*

Matthews
Veyera, Jeffrey Alan *bank executive*

Raleigh
Hardin, Eugene Brooks, Jr. *bank executive*

Wilson
Stewart, Burton Gloyden, Jr. *retired banker*

Winston Salem
Allison, John Andrew, IV, *bank executive*
Medlin, John Grimes, Jr. *banker, director*
Wanders, Hans Walter *banker*

NORTH DAKOTA

Cando
Jorde, Terry J. *bank executive*

OHIO

Cincinnati
Carmichael, Greg D. *bank executive*
Kabat, Kevin Thomas *bank executive*
Marshall, Christopher G. *bank executive*
Schaefer, George A., Jr. *bank executive*

Cleveland
Bell, James R. III *bank executive*
Bibb, Paul E. (Buck Bibb) *bank executive*
Carter, E. Kennedy, Jr. *bank executive*
Clark, Paul G. *bank executive*
Couture, Jon N. *bank executive*
Crowl, Robert B. *bank executive*
Daberko, David A. *bank executive*
DeKaser, Richard J. *bank executive*
Dunham, J. Andrew *bank executive*
Frate, Daniel J. *bank executive*
Geraghty, Paul D. *bank executive*
Gillespie, Robert Wayne *banker*
Glickman, Carl David *banker*
Goetz, Kenneth M. *bank executive*
Gorney, Jon L. *bank executive*
Grebenc, Jane *bank executive*
Gulick, James P. *bank executive*
Jelinek, Gregory M. *bank executive*
Kelly, Jeffrey D. *bank executive*
Khayat, Clark *bank executive*
Lathe, Timothy J. *bank executive*
Lyons, Janis E. *bank executive*
Manning, W. Robert, Jr. *bank executive*
McCartin, Joseph T. *bank executive*
McCrodden, Bruce A. *bank executive*
Mooney, Beth *bank executive*
Naraine, Chameli *bank executive*
Pianalto, Sandra *bank executive*
Price, T. Michael *bank executive*
Raskind, Peter E. *bank executive*
Rice, Philip L. *bank executive*
Richlovsky, Thomas Andrew *bank executive*
Rowe, Robert C. *bank executive*
Schecter, William H. *bank executive*
Seifert, Shelley Jane *bank executive*
Stone, Karin L. *bank executive*
Tengel, Jeffrey J. *bank executive*
Warren, Russell James *investment banker, consultant*
Weeden, Jeffrey Blane *bank executive*
Yanoti, Timothy *bank executive*

Columbus
Arvia, Anne L. *bank executive*
Hoaglin, Thomas E. *savings and loan association executive*
McCoy, John Bonnet *retired bank executive*

New Albany
Page, Linda Kay *bank executive*

Newark
McConnell, William Thompson *bank executive*

Pepper Pike
Mc Call, Julien Lachicotte *banker*

Rocky River
O'Brien, John Feighan *investment banker*

Toledo
Carson, Samuel Goodman *retired bank executive*
Koppus, Betty Jane *retired savings and loan association executive*

Kunze, Ralph Carl *retired savings and loan association executive*

OKLAHOMA

Bartlesville
Doty, Donald D. *retired bank executive*

Nichols Hills
Trost, Louis Frederick, Jr. *banker, financial planner*

Oklahoma City
Mildren, Jack *bank executive, retired state official*
Reich, Richard Allen *bank executive*

Wewoka
Rains, Mary Jo *banker*

OREGON

Bend
Moss, Patricia L. *bank executive*

Lake Oswego
McKay, Laura L. *bank executive, consultant*

Portland
Davis, Raymond P. *bank executive*
Hayward, Lani *bank executive*

Sandy
Rosier, David Lewis *retired investment banker*

PENNSYLVANIA

Ambler
Carey, Francis James *investment banker*

Devon
Boehne, Edward George *banker*
Wilson, Malcolm Campbell *investment trust management executive*

Gladwyne
Geisel, Cameron Meade, Jr. *retired bank executive*

Lancaster
Ashby, Richard James, Jr. *bank executive, lawyer*

Lansdale
Fawley, John Jones *retired banker*

Meadowbrook
Johnson, Victor Lawrence *banker, director*

New Holland
Roesch, Clarence Henry *banker*

New Hope
Hover, John Calvin, II, *banker*

Philadelphia
Dugan, Brendan J. *bank executive*
Murdoch, Lawrence Corlies, Jr. *retired banker, economist*
Plosser, Charles Irving *bank executive, economics professor*
Powlen, David Michael *investment banker, consultant*
Reintzel, Warren Andrew *trust company executive*

Pittsburgh
Demchak, William S. *bank executive*
Gulley, Joan Long *banker*
Hansen, Stephen Christian *banker*
Jefferson, Joseph Murray *banker*
Johnson, Richard J. *bank executive*
Milsom, Robert Cortlandt *banker, director*
Oeler, Robert P. *bank executive*

Radnor
Eagleson, William Boal, Jr. *banker*

Saint Davids
Sheftel, Roger Terry *merchant banker*

Sinking Spring
Bausher, Verne C(harles) *retired bank executive*

Souderton
Hoeflich, Charles Hitschler *banker*

West Conshohocken
Boenning, Henry Dorr, Jr. *investment banker*

RHODE ISLAND

Little Compton
Middendorf, J. William, II, *investment banker*

Newport
Sands, Harold Winthrop *banker, financial planner*

Providence
Fish, Lawrence Kingsbaker *bank executive*
McCleary, Benjamin Ward *investment banker*

SOUTH CAROLINA

Columbia
Boggs, Jack Aaron *banker, mayor, publisher, municipal government official*
Johnson, William Woodward (Hootie Johnson) *bank executive, retired sports association executive*

SOUTH DAKOTA

Sioux Falls
Sanford, T. Denny (Thomas Denny Sanford) *bank executive*

TENNESSEE

Knoxville
Blake, Gerald Rutherford *retired banker*
Joseph, Pamela A. *bank executive*
Lawson, Fred Raulston *banker*

Memphis
Baker, Gerald L. *bank executive*

Murfreesboro
Ford, William F. *banker*

Nashville
Bottorff, Dennis C. *banker*
Burch, John Christopher, Jr. *investment banker*
Daane, James Dewey *banker*
Harrison, Clifford Joy, Jr. *banker*
Heard, Edwin Anthony *banker*
Shell, Owen G., Jr. *retired bank executive*

TEXAS

Abilene
Bentley, Clarence Edward *savings and loan association executive*

Austin
Lemens, William Vernon, Jr. *banker, finance company executive, lawyer*
Schneider, James M. *bank executive, former computer company executive*

Dallas
Fisher, Richard Welton *bank executive*
Fritz, Terrence Lee *investment banker, strategic consultant*
Gumbiner, Anthony Joseph *investment banker, lawyer*
Reid, Langhorne III *merchant banker*

Houston
Anderson, D(arryl) Kent *bank executive*
Ball, George L. *investment banker*
Currie, John Thornton (Jack Currie) *retired investment banker*
Innes, Deborah *bank executive*
Knapp, David Hebard *retired banker*
Neuhaus, Philip Ross *investment banker*
Trauber, Stephen M. (Steve Tauber) *investment banker*

Irving
Olson, Gary Robert *banker*

New Braunfels
Pharis, Ruth McCalister *retired bank executive*

Pasadena
Moon, John Henry, Sr. *banker*

San Antonio
Condos, J. Alexander *mortgage company executive*
Daley, William M. *bank executive, former federal government official*
Duncan, A. Baker *investment banker*
Evans, Richard W., Jr., (Dick) *bank executive*

UTAH

Park City
Montgomery, James Fischer *savings and loan association executive*

Saint George
Beesley, H(orace) Brent *bank executive*

Salt Lake City
Chillingworth, Lori *bank executive*
Simmons, Harris H. *bank executive*
Speer, Susan H. *bank executive*
Urie, Alan T. *bank executive*

VERMONT

Charlotte
Sim, Craig Stephen *retired investment banker*

Lyndon Center
Dame, William Page III *bank executive, educational administrator*

Manchester
Carey, James Henry *banker*

Rutland
Haley, John Charles *retired bank executive*

VIRGINIA

Alexandria
Birely, William Cramer *investment banker*
Tucker, Howard McKeldin *investment banker, consultant*

Arlington
Leland, Marc Ernest *trust company executive, consultant, lawyer*
Ochoa-Brillembourg, Hilda Margarita *investment banker*
Rogers, James Frederick *banker, management consultant*

Ashburn
Pavsek, Daniel Allan *banker, educator*

Charlottesville
Bull, George Albert *retired banker*

Falls Church
Gonzalez, Eugene Robert *investment banker*

Mc Lean
Kanas, John Adam *bank executive*

Philomont
Kok, Frans Johan *investment banker*

Portsmouth
Duke, Betsy (Elizabeth A.) *bank executive*

Reston
Pocalyko, Michael Nicholas *investment banker, venture capitalist*

Richmond
Black, Robert Perry *bank executive*
Lacker, Jeffrey Malcolm *bank executive, economist*
Moore, Andrew Taylor, Jr. *banker*
Talley, Charles Richmond *retired bank executive*

Roanoke
Kinzer, Donald Marshall *banker*
Sweaton, Cheryl Anne *bank customer service specialist*

WASHINGTON

Coupeville
Piercy, Gordon Clayton *bank executive, educator*

Everett
Nelson, Carol Kobuke *bank executive*

Lakewood
Owen, Thomas Walker *banker, portfolio manager*

Seattle
Arnold, Robert Morris *banker*
Bley, John L. *financial executive*
Brooks, Alfred R. *bank executive*
Campbell, Robert Hedgcock *investment banker, lawyer*
Casey, Tom (Thomas W. Casey) *bank executive*
Corcoran, James B. *bank executive*
Horvath, Debora *bank executive*
Killinger, Kerry Kent *bank executive*
Longbrake, William Arthur *bank executive*
Riccobono, Richard M. *bank executive, former federal administrator*
Rice, Norman B. *bank executive, former mayor*
Rotella, Stephen J. *bank executive*
Schneider, David C. *bank executive*

Sequim
Laube, Roger Gustav *retired banker*

Spokane
Horton, Susan Pittman *bank executive*
McWilliams, Edwin Joseph *banker*
Stanley, Heidi *bank executive*

Tacoma
Dressel, Melanie J. *bank executive*

WISCONSIN

Brookfield
Bauer, Chris Michael *banker*
Walters, Ronald Ogden *mortgage banker*

Green Bay
Beideman, Paul S. *bank executive*

Milwaukee
Attanasio, Mark L. *investment banker, professional sports team executive*
Murphy, Judith Chisholm *trust company executive*

Racine
Baumgardt, George Francis *bank executive, musician, director*

WYOMING

Cheyenne
Knight, Robert Edward *bank executive, educator*

Wilson
Sage, Andrew Gregg Curtin, II, *former investment banking house executive*

TERRITORIES OF THE UNITED STATES

PUERTO RICO

Hato Rey
Carrion, Richard L. *bank executive*

CANADA

ONTARIO

Toronto
Augustine, Jerome Samuel *merchant banker*
Cleghorn, John Edward *bank executive*
Fullerton, R. Donald *banker*
Godsoe, Peter Cowperthwaite *retired banker*
Gordon, Harold Sonny *bank executive*
Lawson, Jane Elizabeth *retired bank executive*
MacDougall, Hartland Molson *retired bank executive*
Maidment, Karen E. *bank executive*
Mulholland, William David, Jr. *retired bank executive*
Palozzi, Dina *bank executive*
Storey, Susan *investment banker*
Taylor, Allan Richard *retired banker*
Techar, Frank J. *bank executive*
Thomson, Richard Murray *retired bank executive*
Webb, Anthony Allan *banker, director*

QUEBEC

Montreal
Torrey, David Leonard *investment banker*

Mount Royal
Elie, Jean André *investment banker*

MEXICO

Mexico City
Ortiz, Guillermo *banker*

ENGLAND

London
Binney, Robert Harry *bank executive*
Collins, Paul John *banker*
Duke, Lawrence Kenneth *banker*
Mosselmans, Carel Maurits *investment banker*
Quint, David Paul *investment banking executive*
Studzinski, John Joseph Paul *investment banking executive*
Warner, Scott Dennis *investment banker*

GERMANY

Frankfurt
Papademos, Lucas *bank executive*

Munich
Viermetz, Kurt F. *banker*

NETHERLANDS

Amsterdam
Martinez, Arthur C. *bank executive, retired retail executive*

SPAIN

Madrid
Botín, Ana Patricia *bank executive*

ADDRESS UNPUBLISHED

Ackerman, Jack Rossin *investment banker*
Alper, Andrew Michael *former investment banker*
Andreas, David Lowell *retired banker*
Ashton, Thomas Walsh *investment banker*
Atkins, Victor Kennicott, Jr. *private investor*
Baker, Henry S., Jr. *retired bank executive*
Bansak, Stephen A., Jr. *investment banker, financial consultant*
Baramova, Irina Antonova *investment banker*
Barnewall, Marilyn MacGruder *retired banker*
Barrow, Charles Herbert *investment banker*
Baxter, Nevins Dennis *bank consultant*
Becker, John Alphonsis *retired bank executive*
Bibby, Douglas Martin *mortgage association executive*
Birky, John Edward *banker, financial consultant*
Bitner, John William *banker*
Boykin, Robert Heath *retired banker*
Boyles, James Kenneth *retired banker*
Britt, John Roy *banker*
Brosda von Kupferberg, Baron Alexander Christian *investment banker*
Buckels, Marvin Wayne *savings and loan association executive*
Burden, Ordway Partridge *investment banker*
Busse, Leonard Wayne *banker, financial consultant*
Christenson, Gregg Andrew *bank executive*
Clark, Thomas Carlyle *retired banker*
Clifton, Russell B. *retired mortgage company executive, consultant*
Cockrum, William Monroe III *investment banker, educator*
Cook, Charles Wilkerson, Jr. *bank executive, retired municipal official*
Cooney, John Thomas *retired banker*
Cottrell, Mary-Patricia Tross *bank executive*
Crawford, Stephen S. *investment banker*
Curry, John Michael *investment banker*
Czarnecki, Gerald Milton *investment banker, venture capitalist*
Dean, John Wesley III *investment banker, former federal official*
DeMartini, Richard Michael *retired bank executive*
de Molina, Alvaro G. *former bank executive*
Derickson, Sandy (Sandra L.) *bank executive*
deVeer, Robert Kipp, Jr. *investment banker*
Di Rita, Larry (Lawrence T.) *bank executive, former federal agency administrator*
Dittenhafer, Brian Douglas *banker, economist*

Dodson, Samuel Robinette III *retired investment banker*
Donaldson, William Henry *investment banker, former federal agency administrator*
Doyle, L. F. Boker *retired trust company executive*
Dublon, Dina *former bank executive*
Duteil, Hervé Pierre *bank executive*
Fahringer, Catherine Hewson *retired savings and loan association executive*
Fetters, Norman Craig, II, *retired banker*
Finocchiaro, Alfonso G. *bank executive*
Fitzgerald, William Allingham *savings and loan association executive, director*
Fix, John Neilson *banker*
Ford, Gregory Ray *investment banker*
Gaffney, Thomas *retired banker*
Gainor, Thomas Edward *bank executive*
Geithner, Paul Herman, Jr. *retired banker*
Giblin, Patrick David *retired bank executive*
Goldberg, David Alan *investment banker, lawyer*
Gonzales, Ernesto Luis B. *bank executive*
Gouw, Julia Suryapranata *bank executive*
Graham, Vicary M. *trust company executive*
Greer, K. Gordon *banker*
Grim, Patricia Ann *retired banker*
Grosland, Emery Layton *retired banker*
Guillama-Alvarez, Noel Jesus *merchant banker, healthcare executive*
Guynn, Jack (George C. Guynn) *retired bank executive*
Helfer, Ricki Tigert *banking consultant*
Hetland, James Lyman, Jr. *banker, lawyer, educator*
Hickey, Joseph Michael *investment banker*
Hoff, Charles Worthington III *retired banker*
Hogan, Robert Henry *trust company executive*
Holcomb, Gene Ann *federal loan officer*
Howard, Donald Searcy *banker*
Hower, Frank Beard, Jr. *retired banker*
Huntington, Lawrence Smith *investment banker*
Ingersoll, Paul Mills *banker*
Istock, Verne George *retired bank executive*
Jennings, Joseph Ashby *banker*
Jepson, Robert Scott, Jr. *bank executive*
Johnson, Randall Clyde *mortgage company executive*
Jones, Charles Hill, Jr. *banker*
Jones, Harold Antony *retired banker*
Jones, Richard Melvin *bank executive, director, former retail executive*
Jungbluth, Connie Carlson *private banker*
Kaiser, Suzanne Billo *investment banker, writer*
Kane Hittner, Marcia Susan *bank executive*
Kapnick, Stewart *investment banker*
Keevil, Philip Clement *investment banker*
Keir, Gerald Janes *banker*
Keith, Robert William *banker*
Kilts, James M. *investment banker, former consumer products company executive*
Klett, Gordon A. *retired savings and loan association executive*
Kooken, John Frederick *retired bank holding company executive*
Kotler, Steven *investment banker*
Kulenovic, Dzafer Jeff *bank executive, advocate*
Kulesha, Kevin John *investment banker*
Larr, Peter *retired bank executive*
Lawer, Betsy *banker, small business owner, vintner, director*
Lee, Steve Chi Kong *bank executive*
Lewis, Perry Joshua *investment banker*
Lucander, Henry *investment banker*
MacWilliams, Kenneth Edward *investment banker*
Masa, George John *retired bank executive*
Maxwell, Robert William *investment banker, financial analyst*
McCutchan, William M. *banker*
McGough, Brian Edward *investment banker, lawyer*
McGuinn, Martin Gregory *retired bank executive, lawyer*
McGuirk, Ronald Charles *retired bank executive, economic advisor*
McMennamin, Michael J. *savings and loan executive, investment banker*
Meeker, Guy Bentley *banker*
Mehta, Shailesh J. *banker*
Menaker, Ronald Herbert *retired bank executive*
Meyer, Henry Lewis III *bank executive*
Minehan, Cathy Elizabeth *retired bank executive*
Mistry, Percy Shiavak *investment banker*
Moll, Lloyd Henry *retired bank executive*
Moriarty, Donald William, Jr. *bank executive*
Morris, Tammy Kay *bank executive*
Morrison, John M. *bank executive*
Moskow, Michael H. *retired bank executive*
Moyse, Hermann III *banker*
Muñoz, Carlos Ramón *retired bank executive*
Nuzzo, Anthony Gerald *bank executive*
O'Callaghan, Barry *investment banker*
Oman, Mark C. *bank executive*
Osborn, William George *savings and loan association executive*
Paris, Gordon A. *investment banker*
Pefley, Norman Gordon *bank executive*
Perrotta, Antonio *trust company executive*
Pett, John Lyman *banker*
Poehner, Raymond Glenn *retired bank executive*
Pontius, Stanley N. *bank holding company executive*
Pool, Philip Bemis, Jr. *investment banker*
Porter, Walter Thomas, Jr. *retired bank executive*
Price, William James, IV, *investment banker*
Renyi, Thomas A. *bank executive*
Reuber, Grant Louis *banking insurance company executive*
Rice, Joseph Albert *retired bank executive*
Rishel, Richard Clinton *retired bank executive*
Robards, Thomas Frederick *banker*
Rogers, Alice Louise *retired bank executive, writer, researcher*
St. Clair, Jesse Walton, Jr. *retired savings and loan association executive*
Santomero, Anthony M. *financial consultant, former bank executive, public policymaker*
Schaut, Joseph William *retired bank executive*
Schless, Phyllis Ross *investment banker*
Searle, Philip Ford *banker*
Seeds, Sharon Lynn *bank processor*
Semrod, T. Joseph *banker*
Shah, Bipin Chandra *banker*
Shelton, James Douglas *banker*
Shinn, George Latimer *investment banker, consultant, finance educator*
Shuman, Stanley S. *investment banker*
Sidhu, Jay S. *former bank executive*
Siefers, Robert George *banker*
Slater, Jeffrey Keith *banker*
Smith, Catherine H. *bank executive*
Solomon, Jack David *investment banker*
Sorgenfrei, Robert L. *retired trust company executive*
Stansell, Ronald Bruce *retired investment banker*
Stegenga, James Jay *bank examiner*
Stephenson, Herman Howard *retired banker*
Stewart, Carleton M. *retired bank executive, director*
Stone, Edmund Crispen III *banker*
Stotter, Harry Shelton *banker, lawyer*
Surface, James Louis, Sr. *trust officer, lawyer*
Swope, Donald Downey *retired banker*
Tarnopol, Michael Lazar *bank executive*
Tatlock, Anne M. *retired trust company executive*
Taylor, David George *retired banker*
Thaler, Richard Winston, Jr. *investment banker*
Thompson, J. Andy *bank executive*
Thurmond, John Peter, II, *bank executive, rancher, archaeologist*
Tily, Stephen Bromley III *retired bank executive*
Tyrrell, Gerald Gettys *banker*
Tyson, H. Michael *retired bank executive*
Urkowitz, Michael *banker*
Vennat, Michel *former bank executive, lawyer*
Walters, Glen Robert *retired banker*
Walton, Alice Louise *bank executive*
Watts, Anthony Lee *bank executive*
Webb, Carl B. *banker*
West, Rexford Leon *retired bank executive*
Whitehead, John Cunningham *former bank executive*
Whitney, Edward Bonner *retired investment banker*
Wilson, Don Matthew III *corporate banking executive*
Winnowski, Thaddeus Richard (Ted Winnowski) *investment banker, consultant*
Young, George Haywood III *investment banker*
Zauder, Gail S. *investment banker*
Zilkha, Ezra Khedouri *banker*

FINANCE: FINANCIAL SERVICES

UNITED STATES

ALABAMA

Birmingham
Coyne, Edward James, Sr. *international business educator*
Hendley, Dan Lunsford *retired finance company executive*
Newton, Don Allen *economic development consultant*
Ritter, C. Dowd *diversified financial services company executive*

Decatur
Michelini, Sylvia Hamilton *auditor*
Talley, Richard Woodrow *accountant*

Dothan
Lord, Jacqueline Ward *retired accountant, photographer, artist*

Huntsville
Graves, Benjamin Barnes *business administration educator*
Stewart, Verlindsey Laquetta *accounting educator*

Mobile
Ellzey, Wayne Ewell *retired accountant*

Montgomery
Smith, Larry Steven *financial analyst, accountant, farmer*

Tuscaloosa
Axel, Bernard *finance executive*
Gup, Benton Eugene *banking educator*
Mayer, Morris Lehman *marketing educator*
Ray, Nelda Howton *financial consultant*

ALASKA

Anchorage
Riendl, Robin Wendy *wealth advisory specialist, financial advisor*
Rylander, Robert Allan *financial service executive*

Elmendorf Afb
Fassler, Kerin Irene *accountant*

ARIZONA

Carefree
Smoot, David Paul *finance company executive*

Chino Valley
Norton, Douglas Ray *former auditor general*

Flagstaff
Everett, Judith *merchandising educator*

Goodyear
Eppen, Gary Dean *business educator*

Mesa
Linxwiler, Louis Major, Jr. *retired finance company executive*

Phoenix
Hathaway, Peter S. *corporate financial executive*
Kunkel, Joe Carroll *finance company executive*
Lemon, Leslie Gene *retired diversified financial services company executive, lawyer*
Mullen, Daniel Robert *finance company executive*
Sanchez, Steven M. *financial executive*
Upson, Donald V. *retired corporate financial executive*
Van Fleet, David Dominic *management educator*

Scottsdale
Shower, Robert Wesley *corporate financial executive*
Washburn, Jerry Martin *accountant, corporate executive*

Sun City West
Schrag, Adele Frisbie *business education educator*

Surprise
Miller, James Rumrill III *finance educator*

Tempe
Kaufman, Herbert Mark *finance educator*
Pany, Kurt Joseph *finance educator, consultant*
Reckers, Philip Merle *accountant, educator*

Tucson
Cain, Vernon *retired diversified financial services company executive*
Carleton, Willard Tracy *retired finance educator*
Cope, Thom K. *account executive, lawyer*
Hellon, Michael Thomas *tax specialist, political organization worker*
Horne, William McHenry *finance educator*
Márquez-Peterson, Lea *business broker*
Smith, Kenneth Rodger *finance educator*
Villica-a, Taunya *corporate financial executive*

Wickenburg
Daniel, James Richard *accountant, corporate financial executive*

ARKANSAS

Arkadelphia
Webster, Robert Lee *accounting educator, researcher*

Conway
Horton, Joseph Julian, Jr. *economics and finance educator*
McNew, Bennie Banks *retired finance educator*

Fayetteville
Rosenberg, Leon Joseph *marketing educator*
White, Donald D. *finance educator, consultant*

Little Rock
Britt, Billy Jean *retired elementary school educator, economic education specialist*
Goodner, Norman Wesley *governmental relations specialist*
Waters, Zenobia Pettus *retired finance educator*

Mena
Wiles, Betty Jane *accountant*

Sherwood
George, James Edward *accountant*

CALIFORNIA

Anaheim
Lano, Charles Jack *retired financial executive*

Bakersfield
Bacon, Leonard Anthony *accounting educator*

Bell Canyon
Labbett, John Edgar *financial analyst*

Berkeley
Berk, Jonathan Bryan *finance educator*
Bucklin, Louis Pierre *business educator, consultant*
Staubus, George Joseph *finance educator*

Beverly Hills
Griffith, Clark Dexter *corporate financial executive*

Brea
Oh, Tai Keun *business educator, consultant*

Burbank
Thornton, Cameron Mitchell *financial planner*

Calabasas
Goldfield, Emily Dawson *finance company executive, artist*
Mozilo, Angelo R. *diversified financial services company executive*
Sambol, David E. *diversified financial services company executive*
Sieracki, Eric P. *diversified financial services company executive*

Camarillo
Smith, David Michael *financial planner*

Campbell
Vincent, David Ridgely *financial consultant*

Carmel
de Vos, Paula Francesca *finance company executive, investment advisor, consultant*

Claremont
Christian, Suzanne Hall *financial planner*
Jones, Nancy Langdon *financial planner, writer*

Coronado
Baumer, Edward Ferdinand *finance company executive*

Costa Mesa
Metzger, Vernon Arthur *management educator, consultant*

Crestline
Douglas, Cindy Holloway *financial consultant*

Culver City
Eckel, James Robert, Jr. *financial planner*

Encino
Luna, Barbara Carole *financial analyst, accountant*

Fairfield
Schunke, Hildegard Heidel *accountant*

Fallbrook
Freeman, Harry Lynwood *retired accountant*

Foster City
Burke, Kevin *finance company executive*
Coghlan, John Philip *corporate financial executive*
Fry, Derek A. *finance company executive*
Milholland, Terence V. *finance company executive*
Saunders, Joseph W. *finance company executive*
Sommer, Kenneth *finance company executive*

Fresno
Harris, Breck Anthony *business educator, writer, researcher*
Tellier, Richard Davis *management educator*

Fullerton
Foote, Paul Sheldon *business educator, administrator, consultant*

Glendale
Levy, Murray *business educator*

Granada Hills
Lehtihalme, Larry K. (Lauri Lehtihalme) *financial planner*

Hayward
Kohl, John Preston *finance educator, consultant*
McKenzie, Brian Bruce *finance educator*

Indio
Hamilton, Allen Philip *financial advisor*

Irvine
Alch, Mark Lee *finance educator, researcher, real estate investor*
Callé, Craig R.L. *finance company executive*
Cole, Robert K. *diversified financial services company executive*
Farrar, Donald Keith *retired finance company executive*
Feldstein, Paul Joseph *management educator*
Gibson, Patrick Daniel *accountant, historian*
Madden, Thomas A. *finance educator*
Morton, Roger Larkin *finance educator*
Parnes, Andrew H. *financial executive*
Premchand, Arigapudi *retired financial consultant*
Rankin, James *finance company executive*

La Quinta
Rothrock, Roger Lee *corporate financial executive, retired military officer*

Lakewood
Bogdan, Carolyn Louetta *financial specialist, retired small business owner*

Larkspur
Hanna, Nessim *marketing educator*

Lincoln
Dorn, Mary Ann *retired auditor*
Patten, Thomas Henry, Jr. *retired finance educator, personnel director*

Los Altos
Scifres, Donald Ray *finance company executive*

Los Angeles
Allen, Sharon *accounting firm executive*
Allen, Suzanne *financial planning executive, insurance agent, writer, educator*
Anderson, John Edward *diversified holding company executive, lawyer*
Bennis, Warren Gameliel *business administration educator*
Berman, Geoffrey Louis *diversified financial services company executive*
Beyer, Robert D. *corporate financial executive*
Borsting, Jack Raymond *business administration educator*
Brown, Kathleen *diversified financial services company executive*
Chan, David Ronald *tax specialist, lawyer*
Day, Robert Addison, Jr. *investment management company executive*
Goedde, Alan George *financial company executive*
Kim, Iksuk *marketing educator*
Leach, Anthony Raymond *financial executive*
Lowy, Peter *corporate financial executive*

McGagh, William Gilbert *financial consultant*
Mock, Theodore Jaye *finance educator*
More, Philip Harvey Birnbaum *business administration educator*
Morrow, Winston Vaughan *financial executive*
Mosich, Anelis Nick *accountant, writer, educator, consultant*
Ramer, Lawrence Jerome *corporation executive*
Resnick, Lynda *corporate financial executive*
Rowen, Howard *financial consultant*
Stancill, James McNeill *finance educator, consultant*
Tang, Christopher S. *finance educator*
Taylor, Peter J. *diversified financial services company executive*
Udvar-Hazy, Steven F. *leasing company financial executive*
Walendowski, George Jerry *accounting and business educator*
Westerfield, Randolph W. *finance educator, former dean*
Weston, John Frederick *business educator, consultant*

Malibu
Baskin, Otis Wayne *business educator*

Manhattan Beach
Allmon, Michael Bryan *accountant, financial consultant*
Pettersen, Thomas Morgan *accountant, corporate financial executive*

Menlo Park
McDonald, Warren George *accountant, mortage company, savings and loan association executive, consultant*
Messmer, Harold Maximilian, Jr., (Max Messmer) *financial services executive*
Scholes, Myron S. *financier, former law and finance educator*
Vaughan, Gregory V. *financial planner*
Zollinger, Cynthia *financial consultant*

Mill Valley
Mumford, Christopher Greene *corporate financial executive*

Milpitas
Ligan, Warren J. *corporate financial executive*

Monrovia
Lim, SallyJane *financial planner, diversified insurance and financial advisor, realtor*

Moraga
Tom, Randolph L. *corporate financial executive, lawyer*

Napa
Hess, Donald Marc *diversified financial services company executive*

Newport Beach
Bron, Guillermo (Bill Bron) *lending company executive*
Bruggeman, Terrance John *corporate financial executive*
Gross, William H. (Bill Gross) *financial analyst, investment company executive*
Leets, Peter J. *consulting firm executive*
Shackleton, Robert James *finance company executive*

Newport Coast
Pavony, William H. *financial consultant, management consultant*

Novato
Bibeault, Donald Bertrand *corporate executive, investor*

Oakland
Lee, Jong Hyuk *accountant*

Oceanside
Garfin, Louis *retired actuary*

Orange
Uslay, Can *finance educator*

Pacific Palisades
Hagenbuch, Rodney Dale *financial consultant*

Palo Alto
Curtis, Mark T. *financial planner*
Dillon, Adrian T. *financial executive*
Herrick, Tracy Grant *fiduciary*
Horngren, Charles Thomas *finance educator*
Morrison, William Fosdick *business educator, retired electrical company executive*

Palos Verdes Peninsula
Manning, Christopher Ashley *finance educator, consultant*

Pasadena
Axelson, Charles Frederic *retired accounting educator, food products executive*
Gillis, Christine Diest-Lorgion *financial planner, stockbroker*
Hirschmann, James William III *diversified financial services company executive*
Hunt, Hazel Analue Stanfield *retired accountant*

Pittsburg
Williams-Thomas, Elizabeth A. *financial planner, consultant*

Pleasanton
Edwards, Robert L. *corporate financial executive*

Pomona
Lin, Lianlian *management educator*

Poway
Mueller, Gerhard Gottlob *retired financial accounting executive, educator*

Rancho Mirage
Steele, Charles Glen *retired accountant*

Rancho Santa Fe
Kessler, A. D. *business and financial consultant, investment advisor, real estate consultant, educator, writer*

Redlands
Pick, James Block *business professor, writer*

Riverside
Stewart, David Wayne *marketing educator, psychologist, consultant, dean*

Rocklin
Dwyer, Darrell James *finance company executive*

Sacramento
Betts, Bert A. *retired treasurer, accountant*
Gardner, Jerry Lee *financial consultant*
Wiens, Robert Niessen *retired financial analyst*

Salinas
Stevens, Wilbur Hunt *accountant*

San Clemente
Petruzzi, Christopher Robert *business educator, consultant*
Taylor, James Walter *business and management educator*

San Diego
Behrens, Henry William *international business educator, investment company executive*
Buska, Sheila Mary *chief financial officer, columnist, writer*
Gengor, Virginia Anderson *financial planning executive, educator*
Jeub, Michael Leonard *financial consultant*
Markowitz, Harry Max *finance and economics educator*
Riedy, Mark Joseph *finance educator*
Sopp, Mark W. *corporate financial executive*
Stambaugh, Larry G. *financial consultant*
West, James Harold *finance company executive*

San Francisco
Barlow, William Pusey, Jr. *accountant*
Bauch, Thomas Jay *financial consultant, retired lawyer, apparel executive*
Buse, Elizabeth L. *finance company executive*
Cuggino, Michael Joseph *financial executive*
Dawson, Peter A. *corporate financial executive*
Floum, Joshua R. *finance company executive, lawyer*
Fuller, James William *financial planner*
Herringer, Frank Casper *diversified financial services company executive*
Im, Subin *marketing educator*
James, George Barker, II, *financial executive*
MacNaughton, Angus Athole *finance company executive*
McElhinney, Bruce *finance company executive*
Michelman, Douglas *finance company executive*
Palmer, William Joseph *accountant*
Paterson, Richard Denis *corporate financial executive*
Sasaki, Robert J. *financial services executive*
Sheedy, William M. *finance company executive*
Simini, Joseph Peter *accountant, financial consultant, writer, former educator*
Uri, George Wolfsohn *accountant*
Weihrich, Heinz *management educator*
Williams, R. Neil *finance company executive*

San Jose
Ceran, Jennifer Ellen *treasurer*
Clark, Michael Steven *accountant*
Effren, Gary Ross *financial executive*
Holland, David K. *treasurer*
Jiang, William Yuying *business educator, consultant, researcher*
Landis, Kevin *diversified financial services company executive*
Mathur, Shishir *finance educator, researcher*
Smith, David Eugene *business administration educator*

San Luis Obispo
Blakeslee, Diane Pusey *financial planner*
Thatcher, Janet Solverson *financial advisor, writer*

San Marcos
Kagan, Stephen Bruce (Sandy Kagan) *corporate financial executive*

San Marino
Grantham, Richard Robert *financial consultant*

San Mateo
Johnson, Charles Bartlett *corporate financial executive*
Johnson, Gregory E. *diversified financial services company executive*
Johnson, Rupert Harris, Jr. *diversified financial services company executive*

San Ramon
Crowe, Stephen J. *comptroller*
Vaughn, John Rolland *auditor*

Santa Ana
Kennedy, Parker S. *finance company executive*

Santa Barbara
Egan, Susan Chan *securities analyst, writer*

Santa Clara
McGowan, Stephen T. *corporate financial executive*

Santa Monica
Markoff, Steven C. *finance company executive*
Moses, Samuel B. *accountant, consultant*

Santa Rosa
Biderman, Charles Israel *diversified financial services company executive*

Sherman Oaks
Ferguson, Lisa Beryl *accountant*
Hein, Todd Jonathan *accountant*

Stanford
Beaver, William Henry *accounting educator*
Duffie, Darrell *finance educator*
Holloway, Charles Arthur *public and private management educator*
McDonald, John Gregory *financial investment educator*
Montgomery, David Bruce *marketing educator*
Paté-Cornell, Marie-Elisabeth Lucienne *finance, engineering educator*
Pfeffer, Jeffrey *business educator*

Stockton
Plovnick, Mark Stephen *business educator*
Taylor, Francis Michael *auditor, municipal official*
Weick, Cynthia Wagner *business educator*

Tarzana
Goldberg, Harvey *corporate financial executive*

The Sea Ranch
Carter, Richard Duane *management educator*

Upland
Sheridan, Christopher Frederick *financial consultant, human resources executive*

Valley Springs
Vitrac, Jean-Jacques Charles *international business consultant*

Van Nuys
Harutyunyan, Armine *billing company executive*

Visalia
O'Leary, Deanna Kay *benefits compensation analyst, consultant*

Vista
Ferguson, Margaret Ann *tax specialist, consultant*

Walnut
Budzak, Stephen Howard *tax specialist, consultant*

Walnut Creek
McCauley, Bruce Gordon *financial consultant*
Scott, Phillip W. *financial consultant*

West Sacramento
Anderson, William Wallace *financial executive*

Westlake Village
Detterman, Robert Linwood *financial planner*
Erdelyi, Eileen Edith *financial planner and advisor*

Woodland Hills
Babayans, Emil *financial planner*
Tuthill, Walter Warren *accountant, management consultant*

COLORADO

Boulder
Bangs, F(rank) Kendrick *former business educator*
Melicher, Ronald William *finance educator*
Stanton, William John, Jr. *marketing educator, author*

Broomfield
Seabrook, Raymond J. *corporate financial executive*

Castle Rock
Barnard, Rollin Dwight *retired financial executive*

Centennial
Milliken, Douglas Gordon *financial consultant, municipal official*

Clifton
Konola, Claudette June *finance company executive, consultant*

Colorado Springs
Spicer, Ronald L. *financial services educator*

Conifer
Boese, Michelle Lynne *accountant, consultant*

Denver
Clark, Suzanne *accountant*
Cook, Albert Thomas Thornton, Jr. *financial advisor*
Hall, Richard Murray, Jr. *finance executive, consultant*
Hayter, Anthony *finance educator, department chairman*
Hughes, Bradley Richard *finance company executive*
Levinson, Shauna T. *financial services executive*
Lincoln, Alexander III *financial analyst, lawyer, private investor*
O'Toole, James Joseph *business educator*
Search-Winters, Michelle Dawn *corporate financial executive, consultant*

Englewood
Flowers, David J. *corporate financial executive*

Fort Collins
Ewing, Jack Robert *accountant*
Kinnison, Robert Wheelock *retired accountant*

Henderson
Reibold, Dorothy Ann *accountant, researcher*

Highlands Ranch
Townsend, James Douglas *controller, accountant*
Wittbrodt, Edwin Stanley *financial planner, consultant, retired military officer*

Lakewood
Axley, Hartman *retired estate planner, underwriter*
Hadley, Marlin LeRoy *financial planner, consultant*
Nichols, Vicki Anne *financial consultant, librarian*

Longmont
Sandler, Thomas R. *accountant, director*

Monte Vista
Rausch, Paul Matthew *financial executive*

Monument
McIver, Deborah Kay *tax specialist, entrepreneur, small business owner*

Nederland
Thomas, Daniel Foley *retired diversified financial services company executive*

Steamboat Springs
Potter, William Bartlett *diversified financial services company executive*

Twin Lakes
Homan, Ralph William *finance company executive*

CONNECTICUT

Avon
Mazur, Edward John, Jr. *financial planner*

Bethel
Tomasko, Edward A. *financial planner*

Danbury
Moskowitz, Stanley Adam *finance company executive*
Proctor, Richard Jerome, Jr. *business educator, expert witness, accountant*

Darien
Lim, Ralph Wei Hsiong *finance educator*
Schell, James Munson *finance company executive*

East Hartford
Barredo, Rita M. *auditor*

Fairfield
Booth, George Keefer *corporate financial executive*
Janki, Daniel C. *corporate financial executive*
Neal, Michael A. *corporate financial executive*
Sherin, Keith S. *corporate financial executive*

Farmington
Centofanti, Joseph *accountant*

Greenwich
Hewitt, Dennis Edwin *financial executive*
Horton, Jared Churchill *retired diversified financial services company metal products executive*
Macaulay, William Edward *financial executive*
Smith, Rodger Field *financial executive*
Tarantino, Dominic A. *retired professional services firm executive*
von Braun, Peter Carl Moore Stewart *finance company executive*

Hamden
He, Xiaohong *finance educator*
Ibbotson, Roger G. *financial educator*
Sheikh, Aamer *accounting educator*

Hartford
Geisler, James E. *corporate financial executive*
Hayes, Gregory J. *corporate financial executive*

Litchfield
Kenagy, Robert Coffman *planning consulting company executive*
Martin, R. Keith *business and information systems educator, consultant*

Madison
James, John Whitaker, Sr. *finance company executive*

Mystic
Nolf, David M. *financial consultant*

New Canaan
Kamerschen, Robert Jerome *retired business executive, private investor, consultant*

New Haven
Abdelsayed, Wafeek Hakim *accounting educator*
Garten, Jeffrey E. *finance educator*
Sonnenfeld, Jeffrey Alan *management educator*

Old Lyme
Fairfield-Sonn, James Willed *management educator, consultant*

Prospect
Powell, Raymond William *financial planner, school administrator*

Rocky Hill
Wilson, Karen Lynn *esthetician*

Stamford
Gonnelli, Patrick M. *finance company executive*
Jason, J. Julie *portfolio manager, writer, lawyer*
Loh, Arthur Tsung Yuan *finance company executive*
Mactas, Mark V. *diversified financial services company executive*
Nissen, David R. *corporate financial executive*
Pansini, Michael Samuel *financial analyst, tax specialist*
Reardon, Michael J. *finance company executive*
Ressel, Teresa Mullett *diversified financial services company executive, former federal agency administrator*
Williams, Reba White *corporate financial executive, writer, researcher*
Wilson, Mark *corporate financial executive*

Trumbull
Ewing, Anna M. *stock exchange executive*

Waterford
Hinkle, Janet *financial analyst*

West Hartford
Detmar-Pines, Gina Louise *business strategy and policy educator*

West Haven
Boronico, Jess Stephen *management science educator, dean*
Haley, George Thomas *marketing educator*

Westport
Birinyi, Laszlo *financial analyst, investment advisor*
DeFeo, Philip D. *private equity firm executive*
McKane, David Bennett *business executive*
Ready, Robert James *finance company executive*
Scheinman, Stanley Bruce *corporate financial executive*

Wilton
Hersh, Ira Paul *tax specialist, financial consultant*

Windsor
Ferraro, John Francis *corporate financial executive*

DELAWARE

Dover
Kim, Dae Ryong *management information systems educator*

Newark
Gehrlein, William Vincent *business professor*
Velury, Uma *finance educator, researcher*

Wilmington
Copeland, Tatiana Brandt *accountant*
Fredrick, Susan Walker *tax company manager*
Griffin, Jo Ann Thomas *retired financial planner, tax specialist*
Mand, Martin Gary *financial executive*
Rogoski, Patricia Diana *corporate financial executive*
Vecchione, Kenneth A. *corporate financial executive*

DISTRICT OF COLUMBIA

Washington
Armstrong, Alexandra *financial planner*
Belt, Bradley Deck *financial services executive*
Blakely, Robert T. *financial executive*
Chambers, Letitia Pearl Caroline *consulting firm executive*
Collamore, Thomas Jones *corporate financial executive*
Dacey, Robert Frank *accountant*
DiGanci, Todd T. *financial regulatory service executive*
Droms, William George *finance educator, investment advisor*
Ellis, Katheryn *finance company executive*
Finneran, John Patrick, Jr. *finance company executive, educator*
Florida, Richard Louis *finance educator, writer*
Flügelman, Máximo Enrique *financier, composer*
Hale, Janet S. *accounting firm executive, former federal agency administrator*
Johnson, James A. *finance company executive*
Kilby, Theodore Morgan, Jr. *auditor, educator*
Larsen, Richard Gary *finance company executive*
Levin, Robert J. *finance company executive*
Levy, Michael B. *business educator*
Ludwig, Eugene Allan *financial consultant, lawyer, former US Comptroller of the Currency*
Malek, Frederic Vincent *finance company executive*
Mayo, John W. *finance educator*
McIntyre, Marvin H., II, *financial consultant*
Merrifield, Dudley Bruce *finance educator, federal official*
Merrill, Susan L. *financial regulatory service executive, lawyer*
Mosso, Lyle David *finance company executive*
Mudd, Daniel H. *finance company executive*
Niemeier, Charles D. *accountant*
Olbeter, Erik R. *financial analyst, investment advisor*
Pollard, Daniel L. *financial analyst*
Rieser, Joseph A., Jr. *tax specialist*
Schapiro, Mary L. *financial regulatory service executive*
Schloss, Howard Monroe *financial regulatory service executive*
Sweeney, Richard James *finance professor*
Szamosfalvi, Jozsef *corporate financial executive, consultant*
Taylor, David Kerr *international business educator, consultant*
Walker, David Alan *finance educator*
Zoeller, Jack Carl *diversified financial services company executive*
Zwiener, David K. *financial consultant, former insurance company executive*

FLORIDA

Aventura
Fishel, Peter Livingston *finance company executive*
Kliger, Milton Richard *diversified financial services company executive*

Belleair Bluffs
Sexton, Donald Lee *retired business administration educator*

Boca Raton
Miles, Jesse Mc Lane *retired accounting company executive*
Miller, Eugene *business educator, consultant*
Rosenberg, Lee Evan *financial planner*
Sigel, Marshall Elliot *financial consultant*

Boynton Beach
Bartholomew, Arthur Peck, Jr. *accountant*
Mittel, John J. *diversified financial services company executive, economist*

Bradenton
Hashmi, Sajjad Ahmad *finance educator, dean*

Clearwater
Campolettano, Thomas Alfred *international contract manager*
Crites, Richard Ray *financial planner, finance company executive, investment advisor*
Feldman, Marvin Herschel *financial consultant*

Coral Gables
Banks, Russell *financial planner, consultant*

Coral Springs
Sommerer, John *accountant, former mayor*

Crestview
Scott, George Gallmann *accountant*

Deerfield Beach
Siegel, Steven L. *finance company executive, consultant*

Deland
Plane, Donald Ray *retired management science educator*

Fort Lauderdale
Bamberg, Louis Mark *wealth planning and business insurance specialist*
Cobb, David Keith *accountant*
Shoemaker, William Edward *corporate financial executive*
Vasquez, William Leroy *business educator, consultant*

Gainesville
Shugan, Steven Mark *finance educator*

Hobe Sound
Caspersen, Finn Michael Westby *diversified financial services company executive*

Jacksonville
Edwards, Marvin Raymond *investment counselor, economical consultant*
Kalas, Frank Joseph, Jr. *financial, information systems consultant*
Munoz, Oscar *corporate financial executive*
Tomlinson, William Holmes *management educator, retired military officer*
Vane, Terence G., Jr. *finance company executive, lawyer*

Juno Beach
Frevert, James Wilmot *retired financial planner, investment advisor*

Jupiter
De George, Lawrence Joseph *diversified financial services company executive*

Lady Lake
Di Benedetto, Ann Louise *retired accounting administrator*

Lake Mary
Cosler, Steven Douglas *diversified financial services company executive*

Lake Wales
Connor, John Thomas, Jr. *portfolio manager*
Luing, Gary Alan *financial management educator*

Largo
Shillinglaw, Gordon *retired finance educator*

Miami
Birns, Ira Michael *corporate financial executive*
Capraro, Franz *accountant*
Dimitrijevic, Marko *finance company executive*
Freeman, Lewis Bernard *forensic accountant, lawyer*
Goel, Steve *treasurer*
Jamieson, Mark T. *corporate financial executive*
Natoli, Joseph T. *financial administrator, former publishing executive*
Nunez-Lawton, Miguel G. *financial analyst*
Pomeranz, Felix *accounting educator*

Miami Beach
Cohen, Philip Herman *accountant*
Howard, Melvin *financial executive*

Miami Shores
Diener, Betty Jane *business educator*

Naples
Hansen, Claire V. *financial executive*
Madigan, Joseph Edward *financial executive, director, consultant*
Ordway, John Danton *retired pension fund administrator, lawyer, accountant*

New Port Richey
Assini, Vincent Paul *financial executive*
Mills, Edward Warren *corporation executive*

Niceville
Litke, Donald Paul *acquisition executive, retired military officer*

North Palm Beach
Higgins, Jay F. *diversified financial services company executive*

Orlando
Kellison, Stephen George *actuarial consultant*

Oviedo
Drummer, Donald Raymond *diversified financial services company executive, educator*

Palatka
Ginn, John Arthur, Jr. *financial consultant*

Palm Beach
Harper, Mary Sadler *wealth advisor and relationship manager*

Pensacola
Apap, Antonio *finance educator, portfolio manager*

Port Saint Lucie
Harris, Eric *accountant, auditor*

Saint Petersburg
Bryant, Timothy Clark *investment brokerage executive*
Freeman, Corinne *financial analyst, retired mayor*
Meyer, Robert Allen *finance educator*
Naimoli, Vincent Joseph *diversified financial services company executive*
Shuck, Robert F. *financial executive*
Wasserman, Susan Valesky *accountant, artist, small business owner*

Sarasota
Bailey, Robert Elliott *financial executive*
Drake, Diana Ashley *retired financial planner*
Dryce, H. David *accountant, consultant*
Morris, Gordon James *financial company executive, consultant*
Schmalzried, Marvin Eugene *financial consultant*

Sun City Center
Malkin, Moses Montefiore *retired employee benefits administration company, diversified financial services company executive*

Tallahassee
Bowen, Paul L. *information systems and accounting educator*
Cronin, Jerome Joseph, Jr. *marketing educator, consultant*

Tampa
Alexander, William Olin *retired finance company executive*
Henard, Elizabeth Ann *controller*
Hernandez, Gilberto Juan *accountant, auditor, management consultant*
Hlavay, Jay Alan *financial analyst*
Lebouitz, Martin Frederick *diversified financial services company executive, consultant*
Nord, Walter Robert *business administration educator, researcher, consultant*
Plumeri, Joseph James, II, *financial executive*

Venice
Meyerhoff, Jack Fulton *corporate financial executive*

Vero Beach
Conway, Earl Cranston *business educator, retired manufacturing company executive, educator*
Koontz, Alfred Joseph, Jr. *financial analyst, consultant*
Riefler, Donald Brown *financial consultant*
Satuloff, Barth *accountant, dispute resolution professional, investment strategist, publishing executive, rancher*

Wesley Chapel
Mendelsohn, Louis Benjamin *financial analyst*

West Palm Beach
Herrick, John Dennis *financial planner, consultant, retired food products executive*
Livingstone, John Leslie *accountant, economist, management consultant, educator*
Sims, Ashley Jane *accountant*

Weston
Holtzman, Gary Yale *retired diversified financial services company executive*

Windermere
Powell, Thomas Ervin *financial consultant, small business owner*

Winter Haven
Goodman, Karen Lacerte *financial services executive*

Winter Park
Gray, Anthony Rollin *retired finance company executive*
Starr, Martin Kenneth *management educator*
Therrien, Francois Xavier, Jr. *business and tax consultant*

GEORGIA

Alpharetta
Corby, Francis Michael, Jr. *business executive*
Kurtz, Robert Arthur *finance company executive*
Myers, Michael Todd *accountant, telecommunications industry executive, director*

Athens
Miller, Herbert Elmer *accountant*
Zinkhan, George Martin III *marketing educator*

Atlanta
Benston, George James *accountant, economist*
Cooper, Marc-Antonie *finance educator*
Hanna, Frank Joseph, Jr. *credit company executive*
Hays, William Grady, Jr. *corporate financial and banking consultant*
Lobb, William Atkinson *financial services executive*
Malhotra, Naresh Kumar *marketing educator*
Parsons, Leonard Jon *marketing educator, consultant*
Reece, Richard Kent *finance executive*
Smith, Richard F. *financial services company executive*
Winchester, Jesse Gregory *finance company executive*

Carrollton
Cochran, J. Guyton, Jr. *corporate financial executive*

Columbus
Blanchard, James Hubert *finance company executive*

Conyers
Spearman, Maxie Ann *financial analyst, administrator*

Dalton
Turner, Jackson Parks *financial company executive*

Decatur
Jones, Debbie Jo *finance educator*

Kennesaw
Robinson, Kenneth Charles *management educator*

Lawrenceville
Ahn, Steven *finance company executive, educator*

Macon
Kitchens, William Charlie *accountant*

Marietta
Aronoff, Craig Ellis *business educator, consultant*
Edwards, Charles Mundy III *financial consultant*

Milledgeville
Engerrand, Doris Dieskow *retired business educator*

Savannah
Smith, Elizabeth Mackey *retired financial consultant*

Statesboro
Murkison, Eugene Cox *finance educator*

West Point
Andrews, Gerald Bruce, Sr. *business executive*

Woodstock
Austin, John David *retired financial executive*

HAWAII

Hilo
Kojima, Sheri S. *high school business educator*

Honolulu
Betts, James William, Jr. *financial analyst, consultant*
Hirai, Craig Kazuo *accountant*
Hook, Ralph Clifford, Jr. *business educator*
Kawamura, Georgina K. *finance company executive, state official*
Ng, Wing Chiu *accountant, educator, application developer, lawyer, advocate*
Palia, Aspy Phiroze *marketing educator, researcher, consultant*
Pilar, L. Prudencio R. *financial services executive*
Rhee, Mooweon *business educator*
Solidum, James *finance and insurance executive*
Sterrett, James Melville *accountant, consultant*

ILLINOIS

Batavia
Morefield, Michael Thomas *financial executive*

Belleville
Fietsam, Robert Charles *accountant*

Bellwood
Miller, Denyce Karlina *tax specialist*

Bloomington
Curry, Alan Chester *actuary*

Buffalo Grove
Johnson, Craig Theodore *portfolio manager*

Carbondale
Baker, Clora Mae *business educator*
Mathur, Ike *finance educator*

Champaign
Brighton, Gerald David *retired finance educator*
Perry, Kenneth Wilbur *finance educator*
Schoenfeld, Hanns-Martin Walter *finance educator*
Spice, Dennis Dean *financial consultant*

Chicago
Barré, Laura *finance company executive*
Bell, Angela Marie *accountant*
Blake, Aileen B. *finance company executive*
Chapman, Alger Baldwin *financial services company executive, lawyer*
Christianson, Stanley David *finance company executive*
Chromizky, William Rudolph *accountant*
Fitzgerald, Robert Maurice *financial and retired bank executive*
Fleming, Richard H. *finance executive*
Forbes, John Edward *retired financial consultant*
Goss, Howard S(imon) *financial executive*
Heineman, Ben Walter *corporation executive*
Kalt, David *diversified financial services company executive*
Kamerick, Eileen Ann *corporate financial executive, lawyer*
Kudish, David J. *financial executive*
Kullberg, Duane Reuben *accounting firm executive*
Lorch, Robert K. *corporate financial executive*
Mallory, Robert Mark *controller, finance company executive*
Mayer, Raymond Richard *business administration educator*
McDonnell, David Croft *diversified financial services company executive*
Mitchell, J. Barry *corporate financial executive*
Nusbaum, Edward E. *accounting company executive*
Pavelich, Daniel L. *retired account and tax management consulting executive*
Pritzker, Nicholas J. *diversified financial services company executive*
Rasin, Rudolph Stephen *corporate financial executive*
Reed, M. Scott *accounting company executive*
Ryan, Patrick G. *diversified financial services company executive, director*
Schornack, John James *accountant*
Schueppert, George Louis *financial executive*
Schumann, William Henry III *corporate financial executive*
Spanjol, Jelena *finance educator*
Sullivan, Bernard James *accountant*
Tyler, W(illiam) Ed *finance company executive*

Deerfield
Boyd, Joseph Don *diversified financial services company executive*
Heiman, Marvin Stewart *finance company executive*

Edwardsville
Douglas, Thomas John *finance educator*

Elgin
FitzGerald, Timothy J. *corporate financial executive*

Elmhurst
Choyke, Phyllis May Ford (Mrs. Arthur Davis Choyke Jr.) *management executive, editor, poet*

Evanston
Corey, Gordon Richard *financial advisor, former utilities executive*
Dranove, David Stuart *business educator, consultant, economist*
Jacobs, Donald P. *finance educator*
Kotler, Philip *marketing educator, writer*
Prince, Thomas Richard *accountant, educator*
Sawhney, Mohanbir S. *finance educator*
Scott, Walter Dill *management educator*
Stern, Louis William *marketing educator, consultant*

Geneva
Young, Jack Allison *financial executive*

Glen Ellyn
Holman, James Lewis *financial consultant, management consultant*

Glencoe
Silver, Ralph David *financial planner*

Glendale Heights
Cook, Doris Marie *retired accountant, educator*

Glenview
Levin, Donald Robert *business and finance executive, motion picture producer, professional sports team owner*

Greenville
Filby, Ivan Leonard *management educator*

Gurnee
Hall, Terry *accountant*

Highland Park
Afterman, Allan B. *accountant, educator, financial consultant, researcher*

Hinsdale
Urbik, Jerome Anthony *financial consultant*

Itasca
Civgin, Don *corporate financial executive*

Kenilworth
Bott, Harold Sheldon *accountant, management consultant*

La Grange Park
Perkins, William H., Jr. *retired finance company executive*

Lisle
Ruyle-Hullinger, Elizabeth Smith (Beth Ruyle) *municipal financial advisor, consultant*

Lombard
Garrett, Paul James *financial planner*

Macomb
Bauerly, Ronald John *marketing educator*

Mount Prospect
Epstein, Stephen Roger *financial executive*

Naperville
Tan, Li-Su Lin *accountant, insurance company executive, consultant*

Northbrook
Feibel, Frederick Arthur *financial consultant*

Northfield
Shillestad, John Gardner *diversified financial services company executive*

Oak Brook
Ciccarone, Richard Anthony *financial executive*
Grimes, Steven P. *corporate financial executive*

Oakbrook Terrace
Keller, Dennis James *management educator*

Palatine
Spinner, Lee Louis *accountant*

Park Ridge
Russell, William Steven *treasurer*

Peoria
Vaughan, David John *corporate financial executive*

Prospect Heights
Aldinger, William F. III *diversified financial services company executive*

Quincy
Mallory, Troy L. *accountant*

Riverwoods
Georgiadis, Margaret H. (Margo) *finance company executive*
Guthrie, Roy A. *financial company executive*
Hochschild, Roger C. *finance company executive*
Mandel, Karyl Lynn *accountant*
Nelms, David W. *finance company executive*
Offereins, Diane M. *finance company executive*

Rosemont
Doheny, Daniel P. *corporate financial executive*

Springfield
Hynes, Daniel W. *comptroller*
Morris, Donald *tax specialist*
Travis, Lawrence Allan *accountant*

Wilmette
Wishner, Maynard Ira *retired finance company executive, lawyer*

INDIANA

Bloomington
Belth, Joseph Morton *retired business educator*
Bonser, Charles Franklin *public administration educator*
Dalton, Dan R. *finance educator, former dean*
DeHayes, Daniel Wesley *business educator*
Gordon, Paul John *management educator*
Hustad, Thomas Pegg *marketing educator, association executive*
Wentworth, Jack Roberts *business educator, consultant*

Carmel
Pickens, Robert Bruce *retired accountant*

Columbus
Miller, William Irwin *finance company executive*

Evansville
Gaither, John Francis *accountant, consultant*

Fort Wayne
Gutreuter, Jill Stallings *financial consultant, planner*

Hobart
Arand, Frederick Francis *accountant, finance company executive*

Indianapolis
Fisher, Gene Lawrence *controller, accountant*
Furlow, Mack Vernon, Jr. *retired chief financial officer, treasurer, financial analyst*
Goodwin, William Maxwell *financial executive*
Kaufman, Barton Lowell *financial services company executive*
Onochie, Florence N. *accountant*

Logansport
Bland, Leonard A. *auditor, consultant*

Notre Dame
Reilly, Frank Kelly *business educator*
Shannon, William Norman III *finance educator, food service executive*
Vecchio, Robert Peter *business management educator*

Portage
Schroeder, Marvis Lynn *accountant, artist*

South Bend
Cohen, Ronald S. *accountant*

Terre Haute
Steinbaugh, Robert P. *management and finance educator*

West Lafayette
Bisi, Arnab *management educator*
Cooper, Arnold Cook *management educator, researcher*
Lewellen, Wilbur Garrett *management educator, consultant*
Moskowitz, Herbert *management educator*
Vroom, Govert *finance educator*

IOWA

Ames
Kaufmann, Jeffrey Baer *finance educator*

Cedar Falls
Rajendran, Kadiampatti Natarajan *marketing educator*

Des Moines
Poppe, Pamela J. *accountant*
Scholten, Gary P. *finance company executive*
Smith, Diana Marie *business educator*
Vaughan, Therese Michele *insurance educator*
Zimpleman, Larry Donald *actuary*

Iowa City
Collins, Daniel W. *accountant, educator*
Lie, Erik *finance educator*
Riesz, Peter Charles *marketing educator, consultant*

Ottumwa
Lang, Janelle J. *accountant*

West Des Moines
Gleason, Robert Lyle *financial analyst, realtor*
Henderson, Jason Craig *financial advisor*

KANSAS

Lawrence
Beedles, William LeRoy *finance educator, consultant*
Conard, John Joseph *finance company executive*
Hirschey, Mark *finance educator, investment advisor*

Leawood
Dykes, Archie Reece *finance company executive*

Lindsborg
Fisk, Irwin Wesley *financial investigator*

Logan
Manion, Kay Daureen *financial and office manager*

Mission
Churchill, James Garton *retired finance company executive*

Overland Park
Guckenheimer, Daniel Paul *financial advisor*
Stem, Carl Herbert *business educator*

Shawnee Mission
Johnson, Bradford McClure *financial consultant, investor*

Topeka
Mc Candless, Barbara J. *financial consultant*

Wichita
Feilmeier, Steve *corporate financial executive*

KENTUCKY

Louisville
Landan, Henry Sinclair *financial and business consultant*
Linen, Jonathan S. *diversified financial services company executive*
McKim, Ruth Ann *financial planner*
Taylor, Robert Lewis *management educator*

Madisonville
Kington, Barry Clark *investor, consultant*

Masonic Home
Coryell, Glynn Heath *financial services executive*

LOUISIANA

Baton Rouge
Bedeian, Arthur George *business educator*
Crumbley, Donald Larry *accounting educator, writer*
DeVille, Donald Charles *accountant*
Thomas, Jeffrey Cone *financial executive, consultant*

Covington
Doody, Louis Clarence, Jr. *retired accountant*

Kenner
McShan, Clyde Griffin, II, *diversified financial services company executive*

Metairie
Gereighty, Andrea Saunders *diversified financial services company executive, poet*

New Orleans
Barach, Jeffrey Alvan *management educator*
Cook, Victor Joseph, Jr. *business educator, consultant*

Ruston
Mesak, Hani Ibrahim *marketing educator*
Phillips, Thomas J., Jr. *accountant, educator*

Shreveport
Burton, George Aubrey, Jr. *accountant*
Goodman, Sylvia Klumok *film center executive*

MAINE

Camden
Dyer, Barbara F. *retired accountant, writer*

Cumberland Foreside
Martin, Joseph Robert *retired corporate financial executive*

Friendship
MacIlvaine, Chalmers Acheson *retired financial executive, former association executive*

Hampden
Scroggins, M. Suzanne Paonessa *budget analyst*

MARYLAND

Adelphi
Sutherland, Alan Roy *business educator*

Annapolis
Ames, Steven Reede *financial planner*
Gavian, Peter Wood *securities analyst*
Seznec, Jean-Francois *international trade and investment manager*

Baltimore
Langmead, Joseph Michael *accountant, consultant, educator*
Legum, Jeffrey Alfred *holding company executive*
Mason, Raymond Adams (Chip) *diversified financial services company executive*
Rogers, Brian Charles *portfolio manager, investment company executive*
Roupe, James Paul *accountant*

Bethesda
Castelli, Alexander Gerard *accountant*
Gould, W. Scott *financial administrator*
Palumbo, James Fredrick *finance company executive*
Schwarz, Louis Jay *financial advisor*

Chevy Chase
Linowes, David Francis *finance educator, corporate financial executive*

College Park
Fu, Michael C. *management science educator*
Sims, Henry P., Jr. *management educator*

Columbia
Kurlander, Neale *accountant, law educator*

Gaithersburg
Johnson, George H. *finance company executive*
Ruth, James Perry *financial planner*

Greenbelt
Jenkins, Norman *accountant*

Hyattsville
Lovick, Norman *accountant*

Kensington
Murray, Thomas James *financial planner, publisher*

Potomac
Rhode, Alfred Shimon *finance educator*

Princess Anne
Sharma, Dinesh Kumar *management science educator*

Rockville
Burt, Marvin Roger *financial advisor, investment manager*
Edwards, Bert Tvedt *accountant*

Silver Spring
Yasher, Michael *retired accountant*

Stevenson
Hilgenberg, John Christian *corporate financial executive, consultant*

Takoma Park
Urciolo, John Raphael, II, *finance and real estate educator, developer*

Towson
Kues, Irvin William *financial planner*
Mangan, Michael D. *corporate financial executive*

Trappe
Blades, G(ene) Granville *accountant*

Upper Marlboro
Seibel, Charles Burgess *accountant, educator*
Symlar, Jesse Lee *finance executive*

West River
Atkinson, Dorothy Scott *retired accountant*

Wye Mills
Schnaitman, William Kenneth *retired finance company executive*

MASSACHUSETTS

Allston
Mills, Daniel Quinn *business educator, consultant, author*

Amherst
Manz, Charles Craig *management educator*
Roberts, Chris *strategy and finance educator, researcher*

Ashfield
Gabriel, Peter Paul *business educator*

Ashland
Pettinella, Nicholas Anthony *corporate financial executive*

Barnstable
Temkin, Robert Harvey *accountant*

Belmont
Rich, Sharon Lee *financial planner*

Boston
Aber, John William (Jack) *finance educator, consultant*
Akin, Steven Paul *finance company executive*
Baker, Charles Duane *business administration educator*
Black, Scott M. *diversified financial services company executive*
Bower, Joseph Lyon *business administration educator*
Boyd, David Preston *business educator*
Brooke, Peter A. *corporate financial executive*
Bruns, William John, Jr. *business administration educator*
Carmany, George Walter III *finance company executive, consultant*
Cash, James Ireland, Jr. *retired business educator*
Christenson, Charles John *retired business educator*
Deshpandé, Rohit *business educator*
Domini, Amy Lee *portfolio manager*
Eddleston, Kimberly Ann *management educator*
Elfner, Albert Henry III *retired portfolio manager*
Esper, Susan *diversified financial services company executive*
France, Joseph David *financial analyst*
Gifford, Nelson Sage *finance company executive*
Hardy, Victoria Elizabeth *finance educator*
Hayes, Robert Herrick *technology management educator*
Hayes, Samuel Linton III *business educator*
Ives, J. Atwood *financial executive*
Kaplan, Robert S. *business educator, former investment banker*
Kaufmann, Patrick J. *business educator*
Lawson, Rodger A. *diversified financial services company executive*
Lin, Lihui *business educator*
Lodge, George C(abot) *business administration educator*
Marshall, Martin Vivan *business administration educator, consultant*
Maxwell, J. B. *financial, marketing professional, consultant*
McArthur, John Hector *business educator*
McCraw, Thomas Kincaid *business history educator emeritus, editor, writer*
McFarlan, Franklin Warren *business administration educator*
Miller, Bill (William H. Miller III) *diversified financial services company executive*
Park, William H(erron) *finance company executive*
Pitts, James Atwater *finance company executive*
Sharma, Raj *financial consultant*
Shemin, Barry L. *actuary*
Sloane, Carl Stuart *corporate executive, educator, management consultant*
Stevenson, Howard Higginbotham *business educator*
Swain, Scott D. *finance educator, researcher*
Young, David William *retired management educator*

Boxboro
Parmese, Gabriel J. *corporate financial executive*

Brookline
Reedy, Harry Lee *financial services executive*

Cambridge
Allen, Thomas John *business educator*
Brynjolfsson, Erik *finance educator, researcher*
Chatterjee, Sharmila *marketing educator*
Cutler, David M. *finance educator*
Ellison, Glenn *finance educator*
Hauser, John Richard *marketing and management science educator*
Leonard, Herman Beukema (Dutch) *public finance, management, and leadership educator*
Magnanti, Thomas L. *management and engineering educator*
Malone, Thomas W. *business educator, researcher*
Mora, Elizabeth *comptroller, academic administrator*
Pounds, William Frank *management educator*
von Hippel, Eric Arthur *innovation educator*
Watts, Ross Leslie *finance educator*

Chestnut Hill
Safizadeh, M. Hossein *finance educator*

Concord
Weiss, James Michael *financial analyst, portfolio manager*

Foxboro
Bush, Raymond T. *accountant, architectural firm executive*
Karelitz, Richard Alan *treasurer, lawyer*

Framingham
Komola, Christine T. *corporate financial executive*

Hopkinton
Teuber, William J., Jr. *corporate financial executive*

Leominster
Ford, John Stephen *treasurer*

Lexington
Farb, Thomas Forest *financial executive*
Klein, Lawrence Allen *finance educator*

Lowell
Teague, Bernice Rita *accountant*

Natick
Leno, Sam R. *corporate financial executive*

Needham
Safran, Edward Myron *financial consultant, bank executive*

Plainville
Zani, Frederick Caesar *retired financial consultant*

Randolph
Cammarata, Richard John *financial advisor*

South Hadley
Fisher, William Thomas *business administration educator*

Sudbury
Meltzer, Donald Richard *retired treasurer*

Tewksbury
Black, Richard Bruce *corporate executive, consultant*

Waltham
Ackerman, Robert Wallace *private equity manager*
O'Connell, Jeanne *financial planner, insurance broker*

Wellesley
Tofias, Allan *retired accountant*

Weston
Valente, Louis Patrick (Dan Valente) *financial planner, director*

Worcester
Banks, McRae Cave, II, *management educator, consultant*
Greenberg, Nathan *accountant*

MICHIGAN

Ann Arbor
Elger, William Robert, Jr. *accountant*
Lyon, Thomas Peyton *finance educator, consultant*
Prahalad, C.K. *finance educator, corporate strategist*
Seyhun, Hasan Nejat *finance educator, department chairman*
Wilhelm, Edward W. *corporate financial executive*

Auburn Hills
Knight, Jeffrey Alan *corporate financial executive*

Battle Creek
Fisher, David Russel *business educator*

Berrien Springs
Maguad, Ben Abrico *management educator*

Bloomfield Hills
Poth, Stefan Michael *retired diversified financial services company executive*

Clarkston
Kruzan, James Brendan *financial planner*

Detroit
Datta, Sudip *finance educator*
Locniskar, Dana Michael *financial consultant*

East Lansing
Kang, Jun-Koo *finance educator*
Luccock, Thomas Nelson *auditor, director*
Miracle, Gordon Eldon *advertising educator*
Wilson, R. Dale *marketing educator*

Farmington Hills
Kern, Michael L. III *corporate financial executive*
Smith, Isabel Francis *financial planner*

Grosse Pointe Farms
Fromm, Joseph L. *financial consultant*

Lansing
Feight, Theodore J. *financial planner*

Livonia
McHard, James Lorin *corporate financial executive, freelance/self-employed composer, writer*
Valerio, Michael Anthony *diversified financial services company executive*

Maple City
Duff, James George *retired finance company and automotive executive*

Marquette
Camerius, James Walter *marketing educator, corporate researcher*
Carnahan, George Richard *retired finance educator*

Midland
Merszei, Geoffrey E. *corporate financial executive*

Plymouth
Longhofer, Ronald Stephen *financial consultant*

Portage
Zhang, Charles C. *financial planner*

Southfield
Boyce, Daniel Hobbs *finance company executive*

Troy
Dellinger, Robert J. *corporate financial executive*
Donlon, James D. III *controller, corporate financial executive*
Weingart, Robert Paul *financial consultant*

University Center
Hall, David McKenzie *business and management educator*

Utica
Egan, Ron *corporate financial executive*

Waterford
Gulda, Edward James *diversified financial services company executive*

West Bloomfield
Rauwerdink, William Jay *accountant*

MINNESOTA

Bloomington
Kuntz, Lila Elaine *business educator*

Crookston
Shol, Kim Durand *accountant, computer scientist*

Eden Prairie
Johnson, Howard Arthur, Jr. *corporate executive, operations analyst, financial officer*

Kasson
Brown, Patrick Joseph *corporate financial executive, consultant*

Minneapolis
Avella, Joseph Ralph *university professor*
Berman, Walter S. *treasurer*
Berry, David J. *former financial services company executive*
Berryman, Robert Glen *accounting educator, consultant*
Cracchiolo, James M. *diversified financial services company executive*
Geiger, Mark Watson *management educator*
Goldberg, Luella Gross *diversified financial services company executive*
Hoffmann, Thomas Russell *business management educator*
Kinney, Earl Robert *mutual funds company executive*
Montgomery, Henry Irving *financial planner*
Reha, Rose Krivisky *retired finance educator*
Rudelius, William *marketing educator*
Schwartz, Howard Wyn *business and marketing educator, consultant*

Minnetonka
Morisato, Susan Cay *actuary*

Nevis
Stibbe, Austin Jule *retired accountant*

Saint Cloud
Supanvanij, Janikan *finance educator*

Saint Paul
Fishman, Jay Steven *diversified financial services company executive*
Heyman, William Herbert *financial services executive*

MISSISSIPPI

Hattiesburg
Doty, Duane Harold *business educator*

Jackson
Flowers, Kriste K. *financial analyst*

Mississippi State
Chrisman, James Joseph *management educator*
Vance, David A. *information systems educator*

Ocean Springs
Furlow, William Lawrence *retired financial consultant*

Starkville
Thomas, Garnett Jett *accountant*

Tupelo
Nash, Henry Warren *marketing educator*

MISSOURI

Columbia
Cunningham, Billie M. *accounting educator*
Lansford, Raymond William *retired finance educator*
Nikolai, Loren Alfred *accounting educator*

Farmington
Lees, William Glenwood *retired finance and retail executive*

Kansas City
Bloch, Henry Wollman *diversified financial services company executive*
Brandmaier, Jeff *diversified financial services company executive*
Ernst, Mark A. *diversified financial services company executive*
Graebner, Carol F. *diversified financial services company executive, lawyer*
Jones, Charles Calhoun *estate and business planning consultant*
Mustard, Mary Carolyn *financial executive*
Pruitt, Stephen Wallace *finance educator*
Rowland, Landon Hill *diversified holding company executive*
Stevens, James Hervey, Jr. *retired financial planner*

Lees Summit
Foudree, Charles M. *financial consultant*

Maryland Heights
Stiften, Edward J. *corporate financial executive*

Maryville
Wanorie, Tekle O. *finance educator*

O Fallon
McElhatton, Jerry *credit card company executive*

Saint Louis
Armstrong, Theodore Morelock *corporate financial executive*
Brockhaus, Robert Herold, Sr. *business educator, consultant*
Chayet, Sergio *finance educator*
Crider, Robert Agustine *international financier, protective services official*
Deng, Ping *finance educator*
Fitch, Rachel Farr *health policy analyst*
Folz, Carol Ann *benefits compensation analyst*
Frank, Terrence Dooley *diversified financial services company executive, director*
James, William W. *financial consultant*
Liggett, Hiram Shaw, Jr. *retired diversified financial services company executive*
Lock, Albert Larry, Jr. *finance company executive*
Rich, Harry Earl *corporate financial executive*
Setser, Christie Elaine *auditor*
Shepperd, Thomas Eugene *accountant*
Snyder, William W. *corporate financial executive*
Wiggins, Dewayne Lee *financial executive*
Winter, Richard Lawrence *diversified financial services company executive*

Springfield
Denton, D. Keith *management educator*

MONTANA

Billings
Stapleton, Corey *financial planner*

Bozeman
Davis, Nicholas Homans Clark *finance company executive*

Havre
Freeman, Neil *accounting and computer consulting firm executive, owner*

Helena
Toole, Joan Trimble *financial consultant*

Rollins
Greer, Willis Roswell, Jr. *finance educator*

NEBRASKA

Boys Town
DiBacco, T. Jay *financial services executive, retired military officer*

Fremont
Dunklau, Rupert Louis *financial planner, consultant*

Lincoln
Digman, Lester Aloysius *management educator*
Lee, Sang M. *management educator*
Lienemann, Delmar Arthur, Sr. *accountant, real estate developer*

Omaha
Fairfield, Bill L. *finance company executive*
Jaksich, Daniel J. *controller*
Munger, Charles T. *diversified company executive*

NEVADA

Las Vegas
Duva-Mikhail, Donna Marie *financial executive*
Hobbs, Guy Stephen *financial executive*
Mellor, Eli *diversified financial services company executive, writer*
Merrill, Wendy Jane *financial services company executive*
Parry, Clint *business coaching executive*
Williams, Mary Irene *business education educator*

NEW HAMPSHIRE

Amherst
Atwater, Verne Stafford *finance educator*

Bedford
Steadman, David Rosslyn Ayton *corporate financial executive, director*

Goffstown
Martel, Eva Leona *accountant*

Hanover
French, Kenneth Ronald *finance educator*
Govindarajan, Vijay *finance educator*
Logue, Dennis Emhardt *finance educator, writer, banker, consultant*

Manchester
Merideth, Susan Carol *business administration educator*

Nashua
Hemming, Walter William *retired financial consultant*
Matarazzo, Maria C. *finance educator, department chairman*

New Castle
Levin, Harvey Jay *financial institution design and construction specialist, developer, auctioneer*

Peterborough
Day, John Sidney *management sciences educator*

NEW JERSEY

Avon By The Sea
Bruno, Grace Angelia *accountant, retired educator*

Bernardsville
Flynn, Marie Cosgrove *retired portfolio manager, corporate financial executive*

Bloomfield
Conta, Richard Vincent *actuary*

Camden
Baveja, Alok *finance educator*

Chatham
Earle, Jean Buist *finance executive*

Cherry Hill
Gorenberg, Charles Lloyd *finance company executive*

Cranbury
Kemmerer, Peter Ream *financial executive*

Edison
Pedescleaux-Muckle, Gail *retired business analyst, writer, artist, consultant*

Ewing
McCarty, John Albert *management educator*

Florham Park
Bossen, Wendell John *retired financial planner*
Cangemi, Michael Paul *accountant, author, consultant*

Fort Lee
Armellino, Michael Ralph *retired portfolio manager*
Soejima, Daisuke *diversified financial services company executive, economist*
Underwood, Steven Clark *finance company executive*
Weinstock, George David *financial services company executive*

Franklin Lakes
Reed, JoAnn A. *corporate financial executive*

Galloway
Newell, Eric James *financial planner, retired insurance company executive*

Hightstown
Darr, Walter Robert *financial analyst*

Ho Ho Kus
Deupree, Marvin Mattox *financial consultant*

Iselin
Accardi, Joseph Ronald *accountant*

Jackson
Cohen, Walter Stanley *financial consultant*
Hagberg, Carl Thomas *financial executive*

Jersey City
Laski, John N. *finance educator*

Lawrenceville
Nygren, Lan Ma *finance educator*

Livingston
Leone, Joseph M. *finance company executive*
Peek, Jeffrey M. *finance company executive*

Lyndhurst
Herndon, John Laird *accounting firm executive*

Mahwah
Birnberg, Jack *financial executive*

Medford
Micko, Alexander S. *corporate financial executive, educator, treasurer*

Middletown
Meyler, William Anthony *financial analyst*

Monmouth Beach
Herbert, LeRoy James *retired accounting firm executive*

Montclair
Luftglass, Murray Arnold *corporate financial executive*
Mukherjee, Avinandan *business educator*

Morristown
Anderson, David J. *corporate financial executive*
Cregan, Frank Robert *financial executive, consultant*
Kirby, Fred Morgan, II, *finance company executive*
Ross, Thomas J., Jr. *personal financial adviser*

Mount Laurel
Mann, Louis Eugene *financial planner*

New Brunswick
Foley, Eugene Arthur *accountant, consultant*
Mills, George Marshall *financial consultant*

Newark
Arabie, Phipps *marketing educator, researcher*
Chaplin, C. Edward (Chuck) *diversified financial services company executive*
Clymer, Brian William *diversified financial services company executive, retired state official*
Contractor, Farok *business and management educator*
Grier, Mark B. *diversified financial services company executive*
Odenath, David R., Jr. *diversified financial services company executive*
Ryan, Arthur Frederick *diversified financial services company executive*
Strangfeld, John R., Jr. *diversified financial services company executive*

Parsippany
Langrana, Anita *financial analyst, personal trainer*
Wechter, Ira Martin *tax specialist, financial planner*

Plainsboro
Schreyer, William Allen *retired finance company executive*

Princeton
Ait-Sahalia, Yacine *finance educator*
Goldfarb, Irene Dale *retired financial planner*
Harvey, Norman Ronald *retired finance company executive*

Princeton Junction
Cohen, Florence Emery *retired financial services executive*

Ramsey
Balter, Leslie Marvin *business communications educator*

Red Bank
Daidone, Lewis Eugene *finance company executive*
Oberst, Robert John *financial analyst*
Walker, Ira Allen *financial consultant*
Watson, Charles M. *financial consultant*

Ridgefield Park
Denning, Karen Craft *finance educator*

River Edge
Gass, Manus M. *accountant, construction executive*

Rivervale
Becker, Murray Leonard *corporate financial consultant, actuary*

Rochelle Park
Gaer, Michael Ira *financial planner*

Roseland
Byer, Theodore Scott *accountant*
Golden, Robert Charles *finance company executive*

Short Hills
Alesio, Steven W. *financial services company executive*
Gibson, William Lee *financial consultant*
Mebane, William Black *controller, financial consultant*
Price, Michael F. *money management executive*

Skillman
Liro, Joseph R. *diversified financial services company executive*

Spring Lake
O'Connor, Francis X. *financial executive*

Springfield
Devitt, H. William III *treasurer, corporate financial executive*

NEW MEXICO

Albuquerque
Kaehele, Bettie Louise *accountant*
Leach, Richard Maxwell, Jr., (Max Leach Jr.) *corporate professional, consultant*
Tchoumak, Adelina *corporate financial executive*

Las Cruces
Bell, M. Joy Miller *financial planner, real estate agent*
Constantini, Louis O. *financial consultant, stockbroker*
Peterson, Robin Tucker *marketing educator*

Portales
Musonera, Etienne *finance educator, consultant*

Santa Fe
Thornburg, Garrett, Jr. *finance company executive*
Watkins, Stephen Edward *accountant, publishing executive*

Taos
Brown, David Warfield *management educator, lawyer, academic administrator*

NEW YORK

Albany
Blount, Stanley Freeman *marketing educator*
Hancox, David R(obert) *audit administrator, educator*

Amherst
Jen, Frank Chifeng *finance and management educator*

Baldwinsville
Wilson, Harold Batting *treasurer*

Bayside
Gerus, John Patrick *portfolio manager, retired educator*

Binghamton
Zhou, Nan *finance educator*

Briarcliff Manor
Goldschmidt, Robert Alphonse *financial executive*

Bronx
Lee, Dong Hwan *business administration educator*

Brooklyn
Fischman, Myrna Leah *accountant, educator*
Hechtman, Howard *financial analyst*
Richardson, Alfonso Austin *accountant, financial services executive*

Buffalo
Carlson, Bruce William *diversified holding company executive*
Gruen, David Henry *financial analyst*
Jacobs, Jeremy Maurice, Sr. *diversified financial services company and professional sports team executive*
Shick, Richard Arlon *finance educator*

Chittenango
Cassell, William Walter *retired accounting operations consultant*

Clifton Park
Van Slyke, Rosemary *tax specialist*

Commack
Kurtz, Joel Barry *finance executive*

Coram
Saunders, Audrey J. *tax specialist, writer*

East Greenbush
Mucci, Patrick John *financial consultant, realtor, commercial loan broker*

East Hampton
Salzman, Robert Jay *accountant*

East Meadow
Cymbler, Murray Joel *corporate financial executive*

East Rochester
Murray, James Doyle *accountant, educator*

Eden
Thomas, Jimmy Lynn *retired treasurer*

Flushing
Sanborn, Anna Lucille *pension fund administrator, consultant*

Fredonia
Aghazadeh, Seyed-Mahmoud *finance educator*

Geneseo
Lim, Seong Bae *business educator*

Great Neck
Brill, Steven Charles *financial planner, lawyer*

Hempstead
Aaron, Merik Roy *financial executive, lawyer, judge, educator*
Lazarus, Harold *management educator*

Hicksville
Stein, Melvin A. *accountant*

Hopewell Junction
Donovan, Andrew Joseph *financial consultant*

Huntington
Slutsky, Leonard Alan *finance executive, consultant*

Ithaca
Daouk, Hazem *finance educator*
Dyckman, Thomas Richard *accountant, educator*
Kimes, Sheryl Elaine *business educator*
Lesser, William Henri *marketing educator*

Jericho
Shapiro, Marjorie *accountant*

Lakewood
Deppas, Louis Anthony *financial adviser*

Lewiston
LoTempio, Julia Matild *retired accountant*

Lockport
Koelmel, John R. *finance company executive*

Massena
Pollard, Fred Don *finance company executive, director*

Medford
Snyder, Mark Jeffrey *financial planner, actuary*

Melville
Feller, Benjamin E. *actuary*

Merrick
Cherry, Harold *actuary, consultant*

Monroe
Fontana, John Arthur *employee benefits specialist*

New City
Borelli, Francis J(oseph) (Frank Borelli) *diversified financial services company executive*

New York
Albano, David Warren *financial executive, business analyst*
Altfest, Lewis Jay *financial planner*
Anderson, Theodore Wellington *portfolio strategist*
Assael, Henry *marketing educator*
Audet, Paul L. *diversified financial services company executive*
Banga, Ajay *diversified financial services company executive*
Bateman, Paul *diversified financial services company executive*
Bennett, Paul B. *stock exchange executive*
Berger, Stephen *finance company executive*
Berkowitz, Brad Alan *portfolio manager*
Bernstein, Richard *financial analyst, investment advisor*
Bibliowicz, Jessica M. *financial analyst*
Blankfein, Lloyd C. *diversified financial services company executive*
Bleser, Philip F. *diversified financial services company executive*
Bovin, Denis Alan *diversified financial services company executive*
Bradley, John Francis *financial services company executive*
Brand, Jason *diversified financial services company executive*
Bromberg, Debra *financial analyst, investment advisor*
Brustein, Lawrence *finance company executive*
Buller, Steven E. *diversified financial services company executive*
Buttner, Jean Bernhard *diversified financial services company executive*
Caffrey, Patricia *diversified financial services company executive*
Calello, Paul *diversified financial services company executive*
Calio, Nicholas E. *diversified financial services company executive*
Caputo, Lisa M. *finance company executive*
Carter, Peyton Franklin III *accountant*
Cashin, Richard M., Jr. *diversified financial services company executive*
Cayne, James E. (Jimmy) *diversified financial services company executive*
Chang-Robbins, Joyce *diversified financial services company executive*
Chenault, Kenneth Irvine *finance company executive*
Claire, Thomas Andrew *financial executive, consultant, educator, writer*
Clark, Howard Longstreth, Jr. *finance company executive, director*
Clark, Michael K. *diversified financial services company executive*
Clark, Robert Henry, Jr. *finance company executive*
Clinton, Chelsea Victoria *financial consultant, former first daughter*
Cockrell, Sanford Alonza III *accountant*
Cohn, Bertram Josiah *portfolio manager*
Cohn, Gary D. *diversified financial services company executive*
Conway, E. Virgil *financial consultant, lawyer*
Corrigan, E(dward) Gerald *diversified financial services company executive*
Coughlin, Christopher J. *financial executive*
Craig, Charles Samuel *marketing educator*
Cramer, Jim (James J. Cramer) *financial information executive*
Crane, Charles Grant *financial analyst*
Crittenden, Gary Lewis *diversified financial services company executive*
Cruz, Zoe *diversified financial services company executive*
Cumming, Ian M. *holding company executive*
Cummings, John W. *diversified financial services company executive*
De Lisi, Nancy *corporate financial executive*
Demirtas, K. Ozgur *finance educator*
Devlin, Robert Manning *diversified financial services company executive*
Dimon, Jamie (James L. Dimon) *diversified financial services company executive*
DiPiazza, Samuel A., Jr. *finance company executive*
Domowitz, Ian *finance company executive*
Donahue, Lisa J. *corporate financial executive, consultant*
Druskin, Robert A. *diversified financial services company executive*
Duch, Stephen *corporate financial executive*
Edelson, David Bick *diversified holding company executive*
Edsparr, Patrik L. *diversified financial services company executive*

Edward, Jeffrey N. *diversified financial services company executive*
Elmer, Russell S. *diversified financial services company executive, lawyer*
Engel, Amy J. *corporate financial executive*
Englander, Israel A. *financier*
Engle, Robert F. *finance educator*
Evans, Mary Johnston *corporate director*
Farber, Jeffrey Mark *diversified financial services company executive*
Farley, Thomas W. *stock exchange executive*
Fink, Laurence D. *diversified financial services company executive*
Finn, Brian D. *financial services executive*
Flynn, Timothy P. *finance company executive*
Fowler, John M. *finance executive*
Freiberg, Steven J. *diversified financial services company executive*
Fridson, Martin Steven *finance company executive*
Frye, Clayton Wesley, Jr. *finance company executive*
Gallo, Martha J. *diversified financial services company executive*
Gardner, H. McIntrye (Mac Gardner) *diversified financial services company executive*
Gilligan, Edward P. *diversified financial services company executive*
Glauber, Robert R. *former financial regulatory service executive*
Golden, William Theodore *trustee, corporate director*
Goldstein, Jeffrey Alan *corporate financial executive*
Goodman, Kim C. *credit card and former computer company executive*
Goodman, Roy Matz *corporate financial executive, former state senator*
Gorman, James P. *finance company executive*
Gottlieb, Paul Mitchel *corporate financial executive*
Graf, John A. *finance company executive*
Graf, Peter Gustav *accountant, lawyer*
Grebow, Edward *finance company executive*
Greenberg, Alan Courtney (Ace Lev Petrovich) *diversified financial services company executive*
Gries, Michael F. *diversified financial services company executive*
Griffin, Michael Daniel *investment counselor*
Groves, Ray John *accountant*
Harris, Ethan S. *diversified financial services company executive*
Hayes, John D. *diversified financial services company executive*
Hecht, William David *accountant*
Heleniak, David William *diversified financial services company executive, lawyer*
Henderson, Edward Drewry, Jr. *finance company executive*
Henry, Daniel T. *diversified financial services company executive*
Henry, Emil William, Jr. *diversified financial services company executive, former federal agency administrator*
Hensel, Katherine Ruth *portfolio manager, investment advisor*
Hines, Walter James *stock exchange executive*
Horan, Anthony J. *diversified financial services company executive*
Hornstein, Mark *financial executive*
Hyman, Edward *financial analyst, economist*
Jackson, Mike *finance company executive*
James, Hamilton Evans (Tony James) *private equity executive*
Jarvis, Rebecca *financial reporter*
Jing, Bing *business educator*
Johnson, Clarke Courtney *financial consultant, educator*
Johnson, J. Chester *corporate financial executive, consultant, writer*
Joseph, Michael Sarkies *accountant*
Joynt, Stephen W. *financial services company executive*
Kaplan, Todd P. *diversified financial services company executive*
Kaufman, Henry *diversified financial services company executive*
Keegan, Peter W. *diversified holding company executive*
Kelleher, Colm *diversified financial services company executive*
Kelly, Alfred F., Jr. *diversified financial services company executive*
Kenneally, Michael E. *diversified financial services company executive*
Kennedy, Kevin W. *finance company executive*
Kennedy, Thomas Patrick *financial executive*
Kessinger, Kevin M. *diversified financial services company executive*
Kessler, Stuart *accountant, financial planner*
Kirsch, Donald *financial consultant*
Kirsh, Michael Alan *financial estate planner*
Klein, Michael S. *diversified financial services company executive*
Knerr, Anthony David *financial consultant*
Koeppel, Noel Immanuel *financial planner, securities broker, real estate broker*
Kohut, John Walter *corporate executive*
Kopelman, Richard Eric *management educator*
Kozlowski, Cheryl M. *fixed income analyst*
Kraus, Peter Steven *diversified financial services company executive*
Krawcheck, Sallie L. *diversified financial services company executive*
Krell, David *stock exchange executive*
Ladjevardi, Hamid *portfolio manager*
Lamb, Robert Boyden *finance and management educator*
Lane, Jeffrey Bruce *diversified financial services company executive*
Langford, Laura Sue *corporate financial executive*
Laue, Bruce Antonio *financial consultant, writer*
Leibowitz, Martin L. *financial services company executive*
Lerner, Frederic Howard *finance executive, educator*
Lessing, Brian Reid *actuary*
Lessing, Stephen M. *finance company executive*
Leven, Ann Ruth *financial consultant*
Levkovich, Tobias M. *financial analyst, investment advisor*
Lewis, W. Walker *strategic and financial advisory company executive*
Lewis, William M. *diversified financial services company executive*
MacDonald, Alan S. *diversified financial services company executive*
Mack, John J. *diversified financial services company executive*
Maclin, Samuel Todd *diversified financial services company executive*
Madden, Michael Daniel *finance company executive*
Maher, Jonathan Bannon *finance executive*
Maheras, Thomas G. *diversified financial services company executive*
Malernee, James Kent, Jr. *financial consultant*
Mandelbaum, Harold Neil *accountant*
Mandelbaum, Jay *diversified financial services company executive*
Marano, Thomas *diversified financial services company executive*
Marlas, James Constantine *diversified financial services company executive*
Masterson, Ellen Hornberger *accountant*
McCall, H. Carl *financial services executive, former state comptroller*
McCormack, Richard Thomas Fox *diversified financial services company executive, former ambassador*
McCree, Donald Hanna III *diversified financial services company executive*
McDaniel, Raymond W., Jr. *financial information company executive*
Meehan, Sandra Gotham *corporate financial executive, consultant, writer*
Mergenthaler, Frank *corporate financial executive*
Meyer, Fred Josef *finance company executive*
Meyer, Pearl *compensation executive consultant*
Miller, Heidi G. *diversified financial company executive*
Molinaro, Samuel L., Jr. *diversified financial services company executive*
Morgan, Frank Edward, II, *corporate financial executive*
Morse, Edward Lewis *energy economist, director*
Mosse, Peter John Charles *financial services executive*
Moyles, Philip Vincent, Jr. *financial services company executive*
Mulligan, John J. *corporate financial executive*
Murphy, John B. *portfolio manager*
Nally, Dennis Mathew *finance company executive*
Nides, Thomas Richard *diversified financial services company executive*
Norman, Stephen Peckham *finance company executive*
Ostling, Paul James *corporate financial executive*
Paddock, Anthony Conaway *financial consultant*
Palion, Peter Thaddeus *financial planner*
Papps, Bruce William *financial analyst, investment company executive*
Parrett, William G. *accounting company executive*
Peppet, Russell Frederick *accountant*
Perry, Richard C. *financier*
Petach, Ann Marie *diversified financial services company executive*
Pfeifler, Brian C. *financial planner*
Pincus, Lionel I. *financial executive, entrepreneur*
Presby, J. Thomas *financial advisor, director, arbitrator*
Prince, Charles O., III, (Chuck Prince) *diversified financial services company executive*
Puth, David W. *diversified financial services company executive*
Quigley, James B. *diversified financial services company executive*
Quigley, James H. *accounting firm executive*
Radin, Amy Janine *financial services company executive*
Ramirez, Maria Fiorini *financial consultant*
Randich, Steven J. *financial services company executive*
Rebell, Arthur Leslie *diversified holding company executive*
Reiss, Dale Anne *corporate financial executive*
Rielly, J(ohn) P. *corporate financial executive*
Ritch, Kathleen *diversified financial services company executive*
Roethenmund, Otto Emil *finance company and bank executive*
Rohatyn, Felix George *diversified financial services company executive, former ambassador*
Rosenberg, Alan David *accountant*
Rowe, David Lee *financial advisor*
Rubin, Robert Edward *diversified financial services company executive, former secretary of the treasury*
Rutherfurd, John *financial information company executive*
Ryan, T. Timothy (Thomas Timothy Ryan Jr.) *diversified financial services company executive, former federal agency administrator*
Saint-Donat, Bernard Jacques *finance company executive*
Salzberg, Barry *accounting firm executive*
Sangiuliano, Barbara Ann *tax consultant*
Saperstein, Richard S. *financial consultant*
Savas, Emanuel S. *finance educator, public official*
Schaefer, John H. *finance company and security firm executive*
Schick, Thomas *diversified financial services company executive*
Schlein, Michael Edward *diversified financial services company executive*
Schoenhut, Frederick W. *stock exchange executive*
Schueneman, Diane L. *diversified financial services company executive*
Schwartz, Alan David *diversified financial services company executive*
Schwartz, Robert *finance educator*
Sclafani, Joseph L. *diversified financial services company executive*
Scully, Robert William (Bob Scully) *diversified financial services company executive*
Segal, Martin Eli *retired actuarial and consulting company executive*
Shafir, Robert S. *finance company executive*
Sharma, Deven *financial information company executive*
Sharp, J(ames) Franklin *finance educator, portfolio manager*
Shaw, David Elliot *financial executive*
Shenkman, Mark Ronald *investment and finance executive*
Showalter, David Scott *accounting executive*
Sidwell, David H. *diversified financial services company executive*
Siegel, Arthur Herbert *finance company executive*
Siguler, George William *diversified financial services company executive*
Simmons, John Derek *retired financial consultant*
Slotkin, Todd *diversified financial services company executive*
Snell, Audrey *financial analyst, investment advisor*
Sobbott, Susan *diversified financial services company executive*
Soros, George *pension fund administrator*
Speziale, Richard Salvatore *financial executive*
Sprayregen, James H.M. *diversified financial services company executive, lawyer*
Squeri, Stephen *diversified financial services company executive*
Stein, Elliot, Jr. *business executive*
Steinhardt, Michael H. *diversified financial services company executive*
Stross, Randall E. *business history professor, columnist*
Tabassum, Shakil Mahmud *financial executive*
Tavel, Mark Kivey *finance company executive, economist*
Taylor, John Read, Jr. *financial management company executive*
Thoman, G. Richard *corporate financial executive*
Tiesi, Joseph A. *corporate financial executive*
Tillman, Vickie A. *financial information company executive*
Tisch, Andrew Herbert *diversified holding company executive*
Tisch, James Solomon *diversified holding company executive*
Toy, Stephen J. *corporate financial executive*
Trachtenberg, Matthew J. *financial services executive, philanthropist*
Trinkaus, John William *management educator*
Turley, James S. *corporate financial executive*
Turner, Patrick Noel Waddington *portfolio manager*
Updike, Helen Hill *financial advisor*
Volk, Stephen Richard *diversified financial services company executive, investment banker, lawyer*
Volpe, Thomas J. *corporate financial executive*
Voss, Linda I. *finance company executive*
Warren, David P. *stock exchange executive*
Weill, Sandy (Sanford I. Weill) *former diversified financial services company executive*
Weinberger, Mark Alan *corporate financial executive, former federal agency administrator*
Weingrow, Howard Louis *finance company executive*
Whiting, Anthony *executive search consultant*
Whitman, Martin J. *portfolio manager*
Wright, Joseph Robert, Jr. *corporate executive*
Wyss, David Alen *diversified financial services company executive*
Yeung, Bernard Yin *finance educator*
Zand, Dale Ezra *business management educator*
Zinman, Richard Scott *financial planner*

Niagara Falls
Askins, Arthur James *accountant, auditor*

Nyack
Brecht, Warren Frederick *retired business executive*

Orchard Park
Keenan, John Paul *leadership and management educator, consultant, director, psychologist*

Pearl River
Bryant, Karen Worstell *financial advisor, investment company executive*

Pine Plains
Trapp, Peter Jarl Rudolf *portfolio manager, farmer*

Pittsford
Snyder, Donald Edward *finance company executive*

Pleasant Valley
Odescalchi, Edmond Péry *international financial consultant, author*

Pomona
Landau, Lauri Beth *accountant, consultant*

Poughkeepsie
Hansen, Karen Thornley *accountant*
Klingenberg, Beate *management educator, director*

Pound Ridge
Darcy, Keith Thomas *finance company executive, educator, not-for-profit developer*

Purchase
Dunbar, W. Roy *finance company executive*
Flanagan, Lawrence *finance company executive*
Heuer, Alan J. *finance company executive*
Macnee, Walter M. *finance company executive*
McWilton, Chris A. *finance company executive*
Michl, Michael W. *finance company executive*
Newell, Lionel L. III *treasurer*
Selander, Robert W. *finance company executive*

Rochester
Ashley, Stephen B. *finance company executive*
DuBrin, Andrew John *management educator, writer, behavioral sciences educator, writer*
Golisano, B. Thomas *financial services company and professional sports team executive*
Goyer, Virginia L. *accountant*
Judge, Jonathan J. *financial services company executive*
Marriott, Marcia Ann *business, economics professor, health facility administrator*
Schwert, G(eorge) William III *finance educator*

Rye
Gabelli, Mario J. *diversified financial services company executive*

Rye Brook
Berk, Alan S. *accountant*

Scarsdale
Gladstone, William Louis *accountant*
Gollin, Stuart Allen *accountant*
O'Brien, Edward Ignatius *corporate financial executive, director, investor, lawyer*

Shelter Island
Shaw, Alan Roger *finance educator, retired company executive*

Staten Island
Clark, Sylvia Dolores *business educator*
Gelbein, Jay Joel *accountant*

Syracuse
Marcoccia, Louis Gary *accountant, academic administrator*

Tarrytown
Ferrari, Robert Joseph *finance educator, retired bank executive*
Hyman, Leonard Stephen *financial consultant, economist, writer*

Troy
Phan, Phillip Hin Choi *business educator, consultant*

Uniondale
Guerrera, Lisa E. *financial planner*
Reddy, Gerard Anthony *financial consultant*

Valhalla
Christesen, John D. *business educator*
De Nicola, Peter Francis *tax executive*

Valley Stream
Ellis, Bernice *financial planner, investment advisor*

Waccabuc
Tognino, John Nicholas *diversified financial services company executive*

Wappingers Falls
Hogan, Edward Robert *financial services executive*

Water Mill
Kreimer, Michael Walter *financial planner, investment company executive*

Webster
Nicholson, Douglas Robert *accountant*

Westbury
Mondello, John Paul *financial consultant*

White Plains
Gillingham, Stephen Thomas *financial planner*
Kroner, Arnold Friedrich *financial consultant, economist*
Lightstone, John B. *finance company executive*
Prabhu, Vasant M. *corporate financial executive*
Ramos, Denise L. *corporate financial executive*
Sacco, John Michael *accountant*
Zuckerman, Marc Abraham *finance educator*

Windsor
Warner, Roberta Arlene *retired accountant, financial services executive*

Woodside
Hofmann, Herbert C. *diversified holding company executive*

Yonkers
Johansen, Robert Joseph *consulting actuary*

NORTH CAROLINA

Asheville
Horwitz, Bertrand Nathan *finance educator*
Letzig, Betty Jean *financial consultant*

Chapel Hill
Perreault, William Daniel, Jr. *business administration educator*
Rosen, Benson *business administration educator*
Ross, Coleman DeVane *accountant, insurance company executive*

Whybark, David Clay *business educator, researcher*

Charlotte
Anderson, Gerald Leslie *finance company executive*
Goodwin, William H., Jr. *diversified financial services company executive*
Halas, Paul Anthony, Jr. *business appraisal and valuation specialist, consultant*
Mancuso, Michael John *retired corporate financial executive*
Moynihan, Brian T. *finance company executive*
Schulz, Walter Kurt *accountant, information technology consultant*
Stepp, James Michael *finance company executive*

Durham
Bettman, James Ross *management educator*
Breeden, Douglas Tower *finance educator, consultant, former dean*
Keller, Thomas Franklin *business administration educator*
Rondinelli, Dennis A(ugust) *business administration educator, researcher*
Staelin, Richard *business administration educator*

Greensboro
Englar, John David *finance educator, textiles executive, lawyer*
Jones, Thomas Owen, Jr. *finance educator, military officer*

Raleigh
Jessen, David Wayne *accountant*
Lenard, Mary Jane *finance educator*

Salisbury
Tseng, Howard Shih Chang *business educator, investment company executive, economics professor*

Tryon
Flynn, Kirtland, Jr. *accountant*

Winston Salem
Mecimore, Charles Douglas *retired accounting educator*

NORTH DAKOTA

Grand Forks
Haskins, James P. *finance educator, consultant*
Patton, Gregory Kenneth *management educator*

OHIO

Ada
Cooper, Ken Errol *retired management educator*

Amelia
Hayden, Joseph Page, Jr. *finance company executive*

Bowling Green
Lunde, Harold Irving *retired management educator*

Cincinnati
Anderson, Jerry William, Jr. *diversified financial services company executive, educator*
Bell, Sandra Elizabeth *corporate financial executive*
Conaton, Michael Joseph *diversified financial services company executive*
Dougherty, Charlotte Anne *financial planner, insurance and securities representative*
Gates, Katherine A. *accountant, writer*
Goodwin, John P. *treasurer*
Huenefeld, Thomas Ernst *financial consultant, retired banker*
Lawson, Randall Clayton, II, *finance company executive*
Mantel, Samuel Joseph, Jr. *management educator, consultant*
McMullen, W. Rodney *financial officer*
Miles, John Bill *retired accountant, tax specialist*
Schiff, John Jefferson, Jr. *finance company executive*
Siekmann, Donald Charles *accountant*
Westbrook, Lynda A. *financial consultant*
Wulker, Laurence Joseph *portfolio manager, educator, financial planner*

Cleveland
Boyle, Kammer *financial planner, investment advisor, research analyst, options trader*
Hennessy, Sean P. *corporate financial executive*
Koch, Charles John *credit agency executive*
Lerner, Randolph D. *finance company executive*
Mayne, Lucille Stringer *finance educator*
Stratton-Crooke, Thomas Edward *financial consultant*
Weiss, Zev *corporate financial executive*

Columbus
Adams, Marty E. *diversified financial services company executive*
Anand, Jaideep *management educator, consultant*
Berry, William Lee *business administration educator*
Collier, David Alan *management educator*
Kidder, C. Robert *finance company executive*
LaLonde, Bernard Joseph *finance educator*
Raabe, William Alan *tax writer, business educator*
Rosholt, Robert A. *diversified financial services company executive, insurance company executive*
Schneider, Cindy E. Gower (Lones) *financial advisor*

Cuyahoga Falls
Moses, Abe Joseph *financial planner, consultant*

Dayton
Hoge, Franz Joseph *accounting firm executive*
Singhvi, Surendra Singh *financial consultant*

Dublin
Heneman, Robert Lloyd *management educator*

Fairfield
Stecher, Kenneth W. *financial corporation executive*

Harrison
Kocher, Juanita Fay *retired auditor*

Holland
Sacksteder, Thomas Michael *corporate financial executive, entrepreneur, writer*

Kent
Ryans, John Kelley, Jr. *marketing educator*

Mansfield
Shah, James M. *actuary*

Strongsville
Pinkerton, Richard LaDoyt *retired management educator*

Toledo
Geisler, Nathan David *financial consultant*
Hartmann, Ann Wilson *financial planner*
Hiltz, Kenneth A. *corporate financial executive*

University Heights
Murphy, Paul Regis, Jr. *business educator*

Youngstown
Edirisooriya, Gunapala *finance educator*

OKLAHOMA

Lawton
Davis, Ellen Marie *business educator*

Moore
Lee, Myung Woo *accountant, financial secretary*

Oklahoma City
Crites, Carl D. *auditor*
Harrington, Gary Burnes *retired controller*

Okmulgee
Mitcham, Julius Jerome *accountant*

Stillwater
Chakraborty, Goutam *marketing educator*

Tulsa
Kaiser, George B. *corporate financial executive*

OREGON

Eugene
Lindholm, Richard Theodore *economics and finance educator*
Miner, John Burnham *industrial relations educator, writer*

Grants Pass
Smith, Barnard Elliot *management educator*

Newport
Sonnier, Patricia Bennett *business management educator*

Portland
Epperson, Eric Robert *finance executive, film producer*
Finley, Lewis Merren *financial consultant*
McMahon, Paul Francis *finance company executive*
Stewart, Marlene Metzger *financial planning practitioner, insurance agent*
Watne, Donald Arthur *retired accountant, educator*
Weber, George Richard *financial and internet marketing executive, writer*
White, Roberta Lee *financial analyst*

West Linn
Luchterhand, Ralph Edward *financial advisor*

PENNSYLVANIA

Allentown
Abel, James E. *treasurer*
Heitmann, George Joseph *business educator, consultant*

Allison Park
LaDow, C. Stuart *financial consultant*

Ardmore
Waetzman, Larry Samuel *diversified financial services company executive*

Bala Cynwyd
Cohen, Rachel Rutstein *financial planner*
McGill, Dan Mays *insurance business educator*
Miller, L. Martin *accountant, financial planner*

Bethlehem
Barsness, Richard Webster *management educator, academic administrator*
Hobbs, James Beverly *business administration educator, writer, academic administrator*
Stella, John Anthony *financial executive*

Blue Bell
Haugen, Janet B. *corporate financial executive*

Braddock
Slack, Edward Dorsey III *financial systems professional, consultant*

Bristol
McClain, John T. *corporate financial executive*

Bryn Mawr
Giese, William Herbert *tax accountant*
Moyer, F. Stanton *financial executive*

Carlisle
Robinson, Ronald Michael *financial executive, consultant*

Chesterbrook
DiCandilo, Michael D. *corporate financial executive, accountant*

Du Bois
Forsythe, Velma Brown *accountant, consultant, literature educator*

Elizabethtown
Dickel, David I. III *financial analyst*

Flourtown
Christy, John Gilray *diversified financial services company executive*

Gladwyne
Stearns, Milton Sprague, Jr. *financial executive*

Glenside
Ralston, Steven Philip *portfolio manager, financial analyst*

Harrisburg
Willow, Judith Ann Loye *tax preparer*

Havertown
Brinker, Thomas Michael *finance company executive*

Hermitage
Gurgovits, Stephen J. *financial executive*

Horsham
Rassmann, Joel H. H. *corporate financial executive*

Indiana
Falcone, Thomas William *finance educator*

Kennett Square
Bell, Philip Wilkes *accountant, economist, educator*

King Of Prussia
Burda, Steven *financial analyst and manager*
Yeo, Mark Andrews *diversified financial services company executive*

Kutztown
Ogden, James Russell *marketing educator, consultant, lecturer, writer*

Lebanon
McMindes, Roy James *aggregate company executive*

Lemoyne
Custer, John Charles *portfolio manager*

Macungie
Moore, Joyce Kristina *financial planner, director*

Newtown Square
Mestre, Oscar Luis *financial consultant*
Reiley, T(homas) Phillip *consultant*

Oaks
West, Alfred Paul, Jr. *financial services executive*

Philadelphia
Alexander, William Herbert *business educator, former construction executive*
Anderson, Rolph Ely *finance educator*
Babbel, David Frederick *finance and insurance educator*
Blume, Marshall Edward *finance educator*
Booth, Anna Belle *accountant*
Di Benedetto, C. Anthony *marketing educator*
Donaldson, Thomas *business educator*
Eaker, Seth A. *financial consultant*
Hindelang, Thomas Joseph *finance educator, dean*
Kamp, R. Stephen *finance educator*
Keim, Donald Bruce *finance educator*
Kimberly, John Robert *management educator, consultant*
Kotabe, Masaaki *business educator*
Ksansnak, James Edward *diversified financial services company executive, accountant*
Lodish, Leonard Melvin *marketing educator, entrepreneur*
Michel-Kerjan, Erwann O. *finance educator*
Ramani, Girish *marketing educator, researcher*
Rose, Jane A. *financial planner*
Rosenbloom, Bert *marketing educator, consultant, writer*
Rowan, Richard Lamar *business management educator*
Selles, Robert Hendrikus *retired actuary*
Siegel, Jeremy James *financial analyst, educator*
Summers, Anita Arrow *finance educator*
Wachter, Susan Melinda *finance educator*
Webber, Ross Arkell *management educator*
Young, John Paul *accountant*
Ziegler, Donald Robert *accountant*

Pittsburgh
Guyaux, Joseph C. *corporate financial executive*
Haley, Roy W. *finance company executive*
Ijiri, Yuji *finance educator*
Johnson, Michael Pennington *finance educator, consultant*
Kelly, Edward J. III *diversified financial services company executive*
King, William Richard *business educator, writer, consultant*
Kriebel, Charles Hosey *management sciences educator*
McGuire, Timothy William *economics and management educator, dean*
Means, Dwight Bardeen, Jr. *financial consultant, educator*
Rohr, James Edward *diversified financial services company executive*
Saykiewicz-Sajkiewicz, Jan Napoleon *marketing educator*
Stevens, William Talbert *financial services executive*
Thorne, John Reinecke *finance educator, venture capitalist*
Zoffer, H. Jerome *business educator, dean*

Portland
Groff, Arthur M. *controller*

Reading
McCullough, Eileen (Eileen McCullough LePage, Elli McCullough) *financial consultant, writer, editor, educator*

Richboro
Higginbotham, Kenneth James *finance company executive*

Sayre
Dinich, Michael Andrew *financial planner*

Sewickley
Bly, James Charles, Jr. *finance company executive*
Jehle, Michael Edward *financial advisor, lawyer*

Slippery Rock
Iossifova, Albena Roumenova *business educator, researcher*

University Park
McKeown, James Charles *finance educator, consultant*

Valley Forge
Phelizon, Jean Francois *finance company executive*

Villanova
Nawrocki, David Norman *finance educator*

Wayne
Sims, Robert John *financial planner*

West Chester
Blasiotti, Robert Vincent *accountant, consultant*
Cox, Karen Michelle *finance educator, computer company executive*
Handzel, Steven Jeffrey *accountant*

West Conshohocken
Saul, Ralph Southey *diversified financial services company executive*
Schneider, John K. *financial advisor*

Wilkes Barre
McHale, Maureen Bernadette Kenny *controller*

Wynnewood
Robinson, Robert L. *retired diversified financial services company executive, lawyer*
Sanyour, Michael Louis, Jr. *diversified financial services company executive*

Wyomissing
Gebbia, Robert James *tax executive*

Yardley
Gilmour, D(avid) James *financial and systems analyst*

York
Day, Ronald Richard *retired financial executive*
Wise, Charles William III *financial advisor*

RHODE ISLAND

Barrington
Hjerpe, Edward Alfred III *finance and banking executive*

Cranston
Langlois, Michael A. *financial consultant*

East Providence
Tripp, Michael Windsor *accountant*

Greenville
Carter, Wilfred Wilson *retired finance company executive, controller*

Kingston
Mazze, Edward Mark *marketing educator, consultant*

Providence
Nelson, Jonathan M. *finance capital executive*

Warwick
McNeil, Paul Joseph, Jr. *financial analyst*

SOUTH CAROLINA

Charleston
Donnem, Sarah Lund *financial analyst, non-profit and political organization consultant*
Lader, Philip *corporate financial executive, lawyer, academic administrator, diplomat*
Prewitt, William Chandler *finance company executive*

Columbia
Cuervo-Cazurra, Alvaro *finance educator*
Edwards, James Benjamin *accountant, educator*
Hollis, Charles Eugene, Jr. *finance company executive*
Monahan, Thomas Paul *accountant*
Pritchett, Samuel Travis *finance and insurance educator, researcher, consultant*

Greenville
Oxner, Glenn Ruckman *financial executive*
Porter, Charles Michael (Mike Porter) *diversified financial services company executive*

Johnsonville
Davis, Aquilla *diversified financial services company executive*

Rock Hill
Cornick, Michael F(rederick) *accounting educator*

Seneca
Hodges, Marlane Fairleigh *retired management educator*

Sumter
Blakely, Delores Phinella *financial consultant, business advisor, evangelist*
Van Bulck, Hendrikus Eugenius *accountant*

West Columbia
Byars, Merlene Hutto *accountant, artist, writer*

SOUTH DAKOTA

Aberdeen
Hollingsworth, John Arthur *business educator*

Platte
Pennington, Beverly Melcher *financial services company executive*

Rapid City
Hefling, Debra L. *financial representative*

Sioux Falls
Rogers, David Hughes *banking and financial service professor, dean, real estate company executive*

TENNESSEE

Alamo
Finch, Evelyn Vorise *financial planner*

Cleveland
Rhodes, Arthur Delano *benefits administrator*

Crossville
Lansford, Edwin Gaines *accountant*

Jellico
Walden, James William *accountant, educator*

Knoxville
Naoumova, Irina Yevgenievna *business educator, consultant*

Lebanon
White, Lawrence Edward *finance executive*

Madison
Hadley, John Livingston, V, *management executive, writer*

Memphis
Brandon, Elvis Denby, Jr. *financial planner*
Brandon, Elvis Denby III *financial planner*
Brandon, Raymond Wilson *financial planner, securities principal*
Iles, Roger Dean *business educator*
Umholtz, Clyde Allan *financial analyst*

Nashville
Brophy, Jeremiah Joseph *retired finance company executive, military officer*
Burnett, Michael Bruce *benefits compensation analyst*
Christie, William Gary *finance educator*
Clemens, Peter J., IV, *corporate financial executive*
Ford, Gerald J. (Jerry) *finance company executive*
Gore, Steven Lowell *accountant*
Ullestad, Merwin Allan *tax specialist, director*
Weingartner, H(ans) Martin *finance educator*

Rockford
Nesbit, Sandi Michelle *corporate financial executive*

Soddy Daisy
Randall, Kay Temple *accountant, retired real estate agent*

TEXAS

Addison
Rinehart, Neil *financial consultant*

Aledo
Reilly, Michael Atlee *finance company executive, venture capital investor*

Amarillo
Robinson, Ola Mae *accountant*

Argyle
Pettit, John Douglas, Jr. *management educator*

Arlington
de Jong, Pieter Johannes *finance educator, physical therapist*
Massah, Cherilyn *retired auditor*
Moore, Herff Leo, Jr. *management educator*
Swanson, Peggy Eubanks *finance educator*

Austin
Alpert, Mark Ira *marketing educator*
Anderson, Urton Liggett *accounting educator*
Cundiff, Edward William *retired marketing educator*
Granof, Michael H. *finance educator, department chairman*
Kimberlin, Sam Owen, Jr. *financial consultant*
Larson, Kermit Dean *finance educator*

Boerne
Tom, James Robert *accountant*

Brownwood
Bell, Mary E. Beniteau *accountant*
DeHay, Jerry Marvin *business educator, small business owner*

Burton
Knauss, Robert Lynn *corporate financial executive*

College Station
Boyd, Lorraine Alison *finance educator*
Mahajan, Arvind *finance educator*
Wichern, Dean William *business educator*

Corsicana
Smerge, Raymond G. *finance company executive*

Dallas
Bishop, Gene Herbert *corporate financial executive*
Eads, John A. *accountant*
Grant, Joseph Moorman *finance company executive*
Guthrie, M. Philip *corporate financial executive*
Harris, Curtis Dean *financial consultant*
Hay, Jess Thomas *retired finance company executive*
Howland, Grafton Dulany *financial counselor*
Jobe, Larry Alton *finance company executive*
Moore, Thomas Joseph *finance company executive*
Morgan, Gregory Paul *financial investment advisor*
Porter, Biggs C. *corporate financial executive*
Pullen, Timothy L. *corporate financial executive*
Shimer, Daniel Lewis *finance company executive*
Smith, Patsy Juanita *financial executive*
Vanderveld, John, Jr. *diversified financial services company executive*
Walker, Gordon Beverley Moore, Jr. *business educator*

Denton
Brock, Horace Rhea *finance educator*
Newell, Charldean *public administration educator*

El Paso
Cadena, Frederico Eduardo *finance company executive*
Kelley, Sylvia Johnson *financial services firm executive*

Fort Sam Houston
Blueitt, Odis R. *financial analyst, military officer*

Fort Worth
Bass, Robert Muse *financier*
Berce, Daniel Eugene *financial services company executive, accountant*
Clark, Emory Eugene *diversified financial services company executive*
Dominiak, Geraldine Florence *retired accounting educator*
Rainwater, Richard Edward *financial consultant, investor*
Rogers, Dale Craig *finance company executive*
Warren, Peter Gigstad *financial planner*

Frisco
Bloskas, John D. *retired finance company executive*

Garland
McGill, Maurice Leon *corporate financial executive*

Georgetown
Sellers, Fred Evans *accounting educator*

Grand Prairie
Ebozue, Benson Obian *financial analyst*

Hitchcock
Shaffer, Richard Paul *financial planner, real estate company executive, military officer*

Hockley
Williams, James Lee *finance company executive*

Houston
Barnett, Donald Blake *corporate financial executive*
Crispin, Andre Arthur *diversified financial services company executive*
D'Agostino, James Samuel, Jr. *corporate financial executive*
Dorman, Margaret K. *corporate financial executive*
Elkins, James Anderson III *financial consultant*
Getz, Lowell Vernon *financial advisor*
Harris, Venita Van Caspel *retired financial planner*
Horvitz, Paul Michael *finance educator*
Janssens, Joe Lee *accountant*
Karnes, John Herbert, Jr. *corporate financial executive, lawyer*
Larkin, William Vincent, Jr. *corporate financial executive*
Mahadeva, Manoranjan *financial executive, accountant*
McEachern, Stephen Mathew *accountant*
Rawson, Jim Charles *finance company executive*
Sarofim, Fayez Shalaby *finance company executive*

Huntsville
Sower, Victor Edmund *management educator*

Irving
Brown, Linda Harper *bookkeeping company executive*

Laredo
Cai, Gangshu *finance educator*
Ortiz, Jaime *business educator*

Lubbock
Riley, Jennifer Bell *finance educator*
Wolfe, Verda Nell *pension consultant, financial planner*

Mc Kinney
Kessler, John Paul, Jr. *financial planner*

Midland
Groce, James Freelan *financial adviser*

Normangee
Cox, Jack Ronald, Jr. *finance educator*

Pasadena
Scott, William Floyd *accountant*

Plano
Bravard, Jean-Louis *diversified financial services company executive*
Day, Kevin Thomas *retired business executive, investment banker, foundation administrator*
Wayne, Jeanette Marie *auditor*

Richardson
Burke, Thomas William *benefits compensation analyst*
Oliff, Michael D. *finance educator*

Richland Hills
Haynes, Ruth Elaine *accountant*

Rosharon
Jenkins, Judith Alexander *bank consultant*

Round Rock
Puri, Rajendra Kumar *business and tax specialist, consultant*

San Antonio
Darling, John Rothburn *business educator*
Forgione, Dana Anthony *accounting educator*
Fuhrmann, Charles J., II, *financial consultant, educator*
Jones, James Richard *business administration educator*
Lalwani, Ashok K. *marketing educator*
Stevens, Dennis Max *auditor*
Weber, William Wesley *accountant*

San Marcos
Palmer, Roger Raymond *finance educator*
Taylor, Ruth Arleen Lesher *marketing educator*

Spring
Kehoe, John Kimball *finance educator, consultant*

Sugar Land
Keefe, Carolyn Joan *retired tax accountant*

Waco
Rose, John Thomas *finance educator*

Wimberley
Skaggs, Wayne Gerard *retired diversified financial services company executive*

UTAH

Orem
Hunt, H(arold) Keith *retired business management educator, marketing consultant*

Salt Lake City
Alter, Edward T. *treasurer*
Brady, Rodney Howard *diversified financial services and broadcast company executive, retired academic administrator, federal official*
Elkins, Glen Ray *retired diversified management services company executive*
Johnson, Auston Gilbert III *auditor*
Nelson, Roger Hugh *corporate financial executive, educator, consultant*

VERMONT

Brandon
Konwin, Thor Warner *financial executive*

Quechee
Vitty, Roderic Bemis *retired financial planner, publishing executive*

Rutland
Norris, Richard Anthony *accountant*

VIRGINIA

Abingdon
Jones, Mary Trent *endowment fund trustee*

Alexandria
Brickhill, William Lee *international finance consultant*
Hammad, Alam E. *international business consultant, educator*

Annandale
Hulbert, Mark J. *financial analyst, columnist*

Arlington
Caplan, Mitchell H. *diversified financial services company executive*
Page, Harry Robert *business administration educator*

Blacksburg
Chatfield, Dean Charles *business professor*
Moore, Laurence John *business educator*
Patterson, Douglas MacLennan *finance educator*

Bristol
Creger, David Lee *financial planner, insurance executive*

Chantilly
Carlson, Robert Charles *financial planner, writer*

Charlottesville
Davis, Edward Wilson *business administration educator*
DeMong, Richard Francis *finance and investments educator*
Ellett, John Spears, II, *retired taxation educator, accountant, lawyer*
Harris, Robert Shields *finance educator*
Minehart, Jean Besse *retired tax accountant*
Sahr, Morris Gallup *financial planner*
Shenkir, William Gary *business educator*
Sihler, William Wooding *finance educator*

Chester
Roane, David James, Jr. *information technology auditor*

Chesterfield
Garnett, Douglas Acree *financial analyst, researcher*

Fairfax
Meamber, Laurie Ann *marketing educator*

Falls Church
Nason, Charles Tuckey *retired diversified financial services company executive*
Rosenberg, Theodore Roy *finance company executive*

Glen Allen
Rajkowski, E. Mark *corporate financial executive*

Harrisonburg
Fritz, Diane F. *controller*
Harper, Steven R. *finance educator*
Ramsey, Jackson Eugene *management educator*

Keswick
Pochick, Francis Edward *financial consultant*

Lexington
Cline, Philip Lee *business and economics educator*
DeVogt, John Frederick *management science and business ethics educator, consultant*

Mc Lean
Bailar, Gregor S. *finance company executive*
Bitsberger, Timothy S. *finance company executive, former federal agency administrator*
Boyd, Ralph F., Jr. *finance company executive, former federal agency administrator*
Cook, Patricia L. *finance company executive*
Fairbank, Richard D. *diversified financial services company executive*
Fritz, Thomas Vincent *business executive*
George, Paul G. *finance company executive*
Goktepe, Janet Rose *retired financial analyst*
Kautt, Glenn Gregory *financial planner, consultant*
McQuade, Eugene M. *finance and former bank executive*
Perlin, Gary Laurence *diversified financial services company executive*
Piszel, Anthony S. (Buddy Piszel) *finance company executive*
Smialowski, Joseph A. *finance company executive*
Stowe, Alexis Mariani *accountant, consultant*
Syron, Richard F. (Richard Francis Syron) *finance company executive, economist*

Mineral
Mayo, Louis Allen *diversified financial services company executive*

Newport News
Le Mons, Kathleen Ann *securities company executive, portfolio manager, investment officer*

Norfolk
McKee, Timothy Carlton *taxation educator*

Reston
Andrews, C(harles) E(lliot), (Jr.) *finance company executive*
Autor, Robert S. *finance company executive*
Lord, Albert L. *finance company executive*
Polemitou, Olga Andrea *accountant*

Richmond
Austin, John D. *corporate financial executive*
King, Robert Leroy *business administration educator*
Phillips, Thomas Edworth, Jr. *financial advisor, investment management consultant*

Plack, Vernon C. *financial analyst, investment advisor*
Ritter, Robert T. *diversified financial services company executive*
Scott, Sidney Buford *finance company executive*
Wagner, Jody M. *treasurer*

Vienna
Kumar, Verinder *accountant, financial executive*
Townsend, Irene Fogleman *accountant, tax specialist*

Weems
Martin, William Raymond *retired financial manager*

Williamsburg
Gottfried, Mark Ellis *accountant, consultant*
Holstein, William Kurt *business administration educator*
Kottas, John Frederick *business administration educator*
McLennan, Barbara Nancy *tax specialist*
Montgomery, Joseph William *financial consultant*
O'Connell, William Edward, Jr. *retired finance educator*
Paige, Hilliard Wegner *corporate financial executive, consultant*
Pearson, Roy Laing *business administration educator*

WASHINGTON

Bellevue
Armstrong, Ronald E. *corporate financial executive*
Graham, John Robert, Jr. *financial executive*
Mylnechuk, Larry Herbert *financial executive*

Edmonds
Monroe, James Walter *retired corporate financial executive*

Issaquah
von Speyer, Jacques *financier*

Medical Lake
Grub, Phillip Donald *business educator*

Mukilteo
Brown, Bruce Baden *accountant*

Olympia
Myers, Sharon Diane *auditor*

Seattle
Baker, Roland Jerald *finance educator*
Bocian, Peter *corporate financial executive*
Klein, Jonathan D. *finance company executive*
MacLachlan, Douglas Lee *marketing educator*
Sandstrom, Alice Wilhelmina *accountant*
Szkutak, Tom *corporate financial executive*
Vuoto, Anthony F. *corporate financial executive*
Zhou, Yong-Pin *finance educator*

Shelton
McNabb, David E. *business educator, writer*

Shoreline
Hanson, Kermit Osmond *business administration educator, retired dean*

Spokane
Burton, Robert Lyle *accounting firm executive*
Cameron, Alex Brian *accountant, educator*
Teets, Walter Ralph *accounting educator*

Tacoma
Feroz, Ehsan Habib *accounting educator, researcher, writer*

WEST VIRGINIA

Charleston
Lamb, Patrick John *retired financial consultant, state official*

Elkins
Payne, Gloria Marquette *business educator*

Harpers Ferry
Boucher, Wayne Irving *policy analyst*

Huntington
Wenzel, Loren Alvin *finance educator*

Morgantown
Griffith, Charles T. *accountant, consultant*

WISCONSIN

Appleton
Stellmacher, Jon Michael *corporate financial executive*

Cashton
Haas, James Wayne *accountant*

Eau Claire
Rusch, Gerald Allen *financial representative*
Weil, D(onald) Wallace *business administration educator*

Franklin
Schutte, Richard David *diversified financial services company executive*

Madison
Aldag, Ramon John *management and organization educator*
Nevin, John Robert *business educator, consultant*

Milwaukee
Bergmann, Thomas E. *corporate financial executive*
Culver, Curt S. *diversified financial services company executive*
Furlong, Mark Francis *diversified financial services company executive, bank executive*
Grabowski, Michael Joseph *financial executive*
Kuester, Dennis J. *diversified financial services company and bank executive*
McDonald, R. Bruce *corporate financial executive*
Poliner, Gary A. *corporate financial executive*
Schnoll, Howard Manuel *financial consultant, investment company executive*
Schwister, Jay Edward *portfolio manager*
Yue, Xiaohang *finance educator*
Zore, Edward John *financial services executive*

New Berlin
Gebhard, LaVerne Elizabeth *retired accounting educator*

Oconomowoc
Kneiser, Richard John *accountant*

Superior
Robek, Mary Frances *business education educator*

Waupun
Wendt, Thomas *finance company executive*

WYOMING

Laramie
Spiegelberg, Emma Jo *business education educator, academic administrator*

Sheridan
Ryan, Michael Louis *controller*

TERRITORIES OF THE UNITED STATES

GUAM

Talofofo
Taylor, James John *finance educator*

PUERTO RICO

Hatillo
Santos, Isabel Rodriguez *high school marketing educator*

Mayaguez
Ruiz-Vargas, Yolanda *finance educator*

VIRGIN ISLANDS

St John
Campbell, Thomas Douglas *business executive*

CANADA

ALBERTA

Calgary
Serletis, Apostolos *finance educator*

BRITISH COLUMBIA

Vancouver
Mattessich, Richard Victor (Alvarus) *business administration researcher*

NOVA SCOTIA

Bedford
Hennigar, David John *portfolio manager, director*

ONTARIO

London
Osbaldeston, Gordon Francis *finance educator, retired federal agency administrator*

Markham
Are, Ayokunnu Olanrewaju *financial advisor, investment banker*

Ottawa
Beatty, Perrin *business association executive*

Toronto
Baxendale, Sonia A. *diversified financial services company executive*
Cockwell, Jack Lynn *finance company executive*
Cook-Bennett, Gail *pension fund administrator*
Cunningham, Gordon Ross *finance company executive*
Hore, John Edward *retired commodity futures educator*
Kerr, David Wylie *corporate financial executive, director*
Mann, George Stanley *diversified financial services company executive, real estate company officer*
Mercier, Eileen Ann *pension fund chairman*
Morneau, William *pension and benefits company executive*
Poprawa, Andrew *diversified financial services company executive, accountant*
Price, Timothy R. *accountant*
Schwartz, Gerald Wilfred *business executive*
Silk, Frederick C.Z. *financial consultant*
Stymiest, Barbara *stock exchange executive*
Weston, W. Galen, Sr., (Galen Weston) *diversified financial services company executive*

Willowdale
Sze, Michael Ming-Chih *actuary, consultant*

QUEBEC

Montreal
Desmarais, Paul *diversified management and holding company executive*
Gratton, Robert *diversified financial services company executive*
Laurin, Pierre *finance company executive*
Ngo, Van Tan (Tan Van) *financial planner, poet*
Speirs, Derek James *diversified financial services company executive*
Thompson, John Douglas *corporate financial executive*

Verdun
Lessard, Michel M. *finance company executive*

Windsor
Van Den Brande, Rene Albert *retired accountant*

AUSTRALIA

Melbourne
Batrouney, Clive M. *finance company executive*

BELGIUM

Diegen
Dörken, Uwe R. *finance company executive*

BERMUDA

Pembroke
Freimark, Jeffrey Philip *corporate financial executive*

CHINA

Beijing
Christianson, Wei Sun *diversified financial services company executive*
Thornton, John L. *former diversified financial services company executive*

Hong Kong
Pacter, Paul Allan *accounting standards researcher*

Tianjin
Leyden, Michael Joseph, II, (Lei Jie Ming) *finance educator, entrepreneur, writer*

CYPRUS

Nicosia
Aloneftis, Andreas *business executive*

DENMARK

Horsholm
Sørensen, Erik *retired diversified financial services company executive*

ENGLAND

Coventry
Thomas, Howard *business educator*

Henley on Thames
Bullock, Peter Bradley *company director, consultant*

Leicester
Valente, Giorgio *finance educator*

London
Eustace, Dudley Graham *diversified financial services company executive*
Ioannou, Constantinos Elia *accountant*
Sarkis, Ziad Joseph *private equity executive*

FRANCE

Paris
Ricol, Rene Jean *accountant*
Vandame, Jean-Marie Richard *diversified financial services company executive*

GREECE

Athens
Kenourgios, Dimitris *finance educator*
Papadakis, Panagiotis Agamemnon *corporate financial executive*

ICELAND

Reykjavik
Leitner, James *finance company executive*

JAPAN

Kyoto
Kashida, Jeffrey Shinji *diversified financial services company executive*

Tokyo
Kobayashi, Noritake *business educator*

MALAYSIA

Cyberjaya
Lai, Ming-Ming *finance educator*

MOROCCO

Tangier
Ashler, Philip Frederic *international trade and development advisor*

SAUDI ARABIA

Riyadh
Olayan, Lubna S. *finance company executive*

SCOTLAND

St Andrews
Lee, Thomas Alexander *accountant, educator*

SPAIN

Zaragoza
Yadav, Prashant *economics educator*

SWITZERLAND

Geneva
Gueudet, Edouard Philippe *financial consultant*

Zurich
Dougan, Brady W. *diversified financial services company executive*

TAIWAN

Hsinchu
Wang, David *finance educator*

TURKEY

Konya
Unusan, Cagatay *finance educator*

ADDRESS UNPUBLISHED

Abbott, Edward Leroy *finance executive*
Abdelrahman, Talaat Ahmad Mohammad *financial executive*
Adler, Jack Saul *retired accountant*
Alaimo, Terry M. *financial consultant*
Albano, Pasquale Charles *finance educator, management consultant*
Aldrich, David Alan *accountant, consultant*
Aldridge, Adrienne Yingling *accountant, financial analyst, writer*
Alexander, Barbara Toll *financial consultant*
Almeida, Richard Joseph *finance company administrator*
Alper, Merlin Lionel *corporate financial executive*
Alvare, Charles Daguerre *financial advisor, educator*
Anaya, Richard Alfred, Jr. *financial consultant*
Arenberg, Julius Theodore, Jr. *retired accounting company executive*
Ashby, Franklin Charles, Jr. *corporate financial executive, educator*
Ashworth, Bessie *benefits compensation analyst, writer*
Atcheson, Sue Hart *business educator*
Atwood, Donna Elaine *retired financial manager*
Awazu, Yukika *corporate executive, researcher, consultant, writer*
Bagwill, John Williams *retired pension fund administrator*
Bains, Harrison MacKellar, Jr. *retired corporate financial executive*
Bákér, J. A., II, *executive management advisor and consultant, monetary architect, financial engineer emeritus*
Balakrishnan, P. V. (Sundar) *marketing educator*
Banker, Rajiv D. *finance educator, consultant*
Bartlett, Richard Allan *finance company executive*
Bartlett, Shirley Anne *accountant*
Batt, James Murray *retired financial consultant*
Baumann, Martin F. *former finance company executive*
Bechkoff, Jennifer "Kat" *business educator*
Beller, Luanne Evelyn *retired accountant*
Bellon, Venetia Rochelle *retired financial consultant*

Bellows, Howard Arthur, Jr. *corporate financial executive*
Belluomini, Frank Stephen *accountant*
Bennett, Peter Dunne *retired marketing educator*
Benson, Donald Erick *finance company executive*
Bertucelli, Robert Edward *accountant, educator*
Biklen, Stephen Clinton *retired diversified financial services company executive*
Bilecki, Ronald Allan *financial planner*
Bishop, Mark D. *finance company executive, director*
Bisignano, Frank *diversified financial services company executive*
Bolt, Dawn Maria *financial planner*
Borum, Rodney Lee *corporate financial executive*
Bowne, Shirlee Pearson *credit manager*
Boyer, Robert Allan *finance company executive*
Bradley, Elizabeth Clay *financial planner, educator*
Brainard, Melissa *accountant*
Branson, Harley Kenneth *finance company executive*
Broome, Oscar Whitfield, Jr. *finance educator*
Brown, James Nelson, Jr. *retired accountant*
Burns, James William *financial executive*
Burton, John Campbell *accounting educator, former dean*
Buscaglia, Robert M. *financial analyst*
Bussan, James A. *tax specialist*
Butler, John Musgrave *financial consultant*
Cain, David Lee *retired corporate executive*
Caldwell, Benjamin Dale *corporate financial executive, consultant*
Campbell, Joseph John *technology and financial company executive*
Carner, Dorothy Ann *financial advisor*
Carpenter, Michael A. *diversified financial services company executive*
Casey, Micheal William *portfolio manager*
Cavill, Ronald William *financial planner*
Charlton, Jesse Melvin, Jr. *retired management educator, lawyer*
Cheesman, John Michael *corporate financial executive*
Chen, Eric Yen-Po *accountant, consultant*
Chiang, Wen-Chyuan *operations management educator*
Chong, James Tzeh-min *finance educator, researcher*
Clayton, Richard Reese *retired diversified financial services company executive*
Coe, Emma A. *finance educator*
Colburn, Kenneth Hersey *retired financial executive*
Compton, R. Brian *finance company executive*
Conner, William J. III *diversified financial services company executive*
Connor, William Edwin, II, *finance company executive*
Conti, Indalicio Palomar *finance educator*
Cooper, John Arnold *financial analyst*
Cope, Laurence Brian *financial, energy and strategic consulting executive*
Corbet, Kathleen A. *former financial information company executive*
Cotsakos, Christos Michael *retired internet financial services company executive*
Coulter, Jack Benson, Jr. *financial planner*
Crisci, Mathew G. *financial consultant, writer*
Crook, Robert Wayne *retired portfolio manager*
Culp, Mildred Louise *corporate financial executive*
Curran, Michael J. *finance company executive*
Danforth, Arthur Edwards *finance executive*
D'Angelo, Vincent A. *diversified financial services company executive, consultant*
Dean, Thompson *diversified financial services company executive, investment banker*
Denn, Cyril Joseph *retired financial advisor*
Dorsey, Dolores Florence *retired corporate treasurer, finance company executive*
Doss, Jessica Yarina *financial analyst*
Dossin, Ernest Joseph III *credit manager*
Doto, Paul Jerome *retired accountant*
Dow, Mary Alexis *auditor*
Easton, Charles Clement, Jr. *corporate financial executive*
Edwards, James D. *accounting company executive*
Ellis, Lynn Webster *retired finance educator, telecommunications consultant*
Eng, Adrienne Rose *corporate financial executive*
Estrin, Herbert Alvin *financial consultant, film company executive*
Falcon, Armando, Jr. *financial consultant, lawyer*
Farrall, Harold John *retired accountant*
Farrar, John Edson, II, *finance company executive, consultant, investment advisor*
Faucette, Gloria Marie *accountant, educator*
Fletcher, Denise Koen *strategic and financial consultant*
Forman, Sydney *finance company executive*
Foster, Roseanne H. *business educator*
Fox, Edward Alan *retired finance company executive*
Frank, Charles Raphael, Jr. *financial consultant, director*
Frank, Edgar Gerald *retired finance company executive*
Frank, Ronald Edward *marketing educator*
Frankenstein, John *international management educator, consultant*
Friedman, Joan M. *retired accountant, educator*
Friedman, Tully Michael *finance company executive*
Furst, E. Kenneth *accountant*
Gaiber, Lawrence Jay *financial company executive*
Gaines, Brenda J. *retired financial services company executive*
Galda, Dwight William *finance company executive*
Galvin, Anthony J. *auditor*
Gambrell, Luck Flanders *corporate financial executive*
Ganguly, Ananda Roop *business management educator*
Garcia-Granados, Sergio Eduardo *portfolio manager, writer, historian*
Geissinger, Frederick Wallace *finance company executive*
Genét, Barbara Ann *accountant, travel company executive*
George, Jennifer M. *management professor, psychology professor*
Gitelson, Susan Aurelia *corporate executive, philanthropist*
Gleijeses, Mario *holding company executive*
Goeltz, Richard Karl *finance company executive*
Goldberger, George Stefan *finance company executive*
Goodsell, Charles True *public administration educator, researcher*
Gorman, Charlotte A. *business executive*
Graham, Howard Lee, Sr. *finance company executive*
Granik, Russ (Russell T. Granik) *financial advisory firm executive, former sports association executive*
Griffin, Carleton Hadlock *accountant, educator*
Grimaldi, David *financial advisor*
Gruver, William Rolfe (Bill Gruver) *finance educator, retired investment banker*
Gyemant, Robert Ernest *diversified financial services company executive, merchant banker*
Haeske, Ron A. *financial analyst, singer*
Hamilton, Jean *financial services executive, e-commerce and software executive*
Hamlin, Dan William *accountant, management consultant*
Hand, Herbert Hensley *finance educator, writer, entrepreneur*
Handy, Edward Otis, Jr. *retired diversified financial services company executive*
Hanvy, Phillip Wayne *benefits compensation analyst*
Harper, James Weldon III *finance consultant*
Harrison, William Burwell, Jr. *retired diversified financial services company executive*
Hartman, David G. *actuary*
Hasija, Sameer *finance educator, consultant*
Hayek, Carolyn Jean *financial consultant, retired judge*
Healy, Steven Michael *accountant, city official*
Heller, Robert *financial executive, economist*
Hendrix, Stephen C. *financial executive, consultant*
Henry, William Ray *business administration educator*
Hensley, Ralph Henry III *federal management analyst*
Hickson, Ernest Charles *financial executive*
Hill, Lowell Dean *agricultural marketing educator*
Holland, Joseph John *retired financial executive*
Holloran, Thomas Edward *business educator*
Holton, Grace Holland *accountant*
Homann, Bruce Kendall *financial analyst*
Hovendick, James V. *business law educator, retired aerospace engineer*
Howard, J. Timothy *former finance company executive*
Hubbe, Henry Ernest *financial forecaster, trading manager*
Huber, Wesley David *accountant, educator*
Hudak, Thomas F(rancis) *finance company executive*
Hume, Susan Rachel *finance educator*
Hunger, J(ohn) David *business educator*
Iapalucci, Samuel H. *financial executive*
Jamison, John Callison *business educator, investment banker*
Johnson, Freda S. *financial analyst, consultant*
Johnson, Suzanne Nora *former diversified financial services company executive, lawyer*
Kaplan, Leonard Eugene *accountant*
Kass, David Norman *accountant, lawyer*
Kercheval, John William III *finance professor, aerospace and defense executive, vulture capitalist, former investment banker*
Kessler, Roslyn Marie *financial analyst*
Khuong, Loc Huu *finance educator*
Kilmann, Ralph Herman *business educator*
King, Alfred Meehan *financial executive*
King, Algin Braddy *retired marketing educator*
King, Ronald Lee *retired accountant, government agency administrator*
Kingsbery, Walton Waits, Jr. *retired accounting firm executive*
Kissinger, Henry Alfred *international consulting company executive, former secretary of state*
Kohan, Dennis Lynn *finance educator*
Kolarik, William Joel, II, *accountant*
Kornblatt, M. David *corporate financial executive*
Kotter, John Paul *organizational behavior educator, management consultant*
Kozlowski, Damian Mark *diversified financial services company executive*
Krulitz, Leo Morrion *financial planner, publishing executive, director*
Kulesza, Chester Stephen (Bud Kulesza) *financial executive*
Landeck, Carl *corporate financial executive*
Laskawy, Philip Alan *retired accounting and management consulting firm executive*
Lee, Jonathan Owen *financial services company executive, lawyer*
Leff, Ilene J(afnel) *corporate executive, federal official*
Lehman, John F., Jr. *private equity executive*
Leibler, Kenneth Robert *finance company executive*
Leiby, Arthur Daniel *accountant*
Leong, Stephanie Mei *financial planner*
Lerner, Herbert J. *tax consultant*
Lesher, John Lee, Jr. *consulting services company executive*
Lester, Alicia Louise *financial analyst*
Leventhal, Ellen Iris *portfolio manager*
Levy, Louis Edward *retired accounting firm executive*
Lewins, Steven *financial analyst, investment company executive, legislative staff member, retired military officer*
Lewis, James Lee, Jr. *actuary*
Lieberman, Anne Marie *retired financial executive*
Lieberman, Gail Forman *financial consultant*
Lindeman, Barry James *internal auditor, nurse, minister*
Lister, Harry Joseph *financial company consultant*
Loken, Barbara *marketing educator, social psychologist*
Loren, Allan Z. *former financial services company executive*
Lucca, David Alan *money manager*
Lyons, Susanne D. *former finance company executive*
MacDonald, Ronald Francis *diversified financial services company executive*
Magnano, Salvatore Paul *retired finance company executive, treasurer*
Malter-Hoffman, Kelly A. *finance company executive, consultant*
Mankin, Robert Stephen *diversified financial services company executive*
Mapes, William W. *auditor*
Martin, Johnny Benjamin *accountant*
Maruyama, Magoroh *business educator, researcher, consultant*
Mason, George Henry *retired business educator*
May, Phyllis Jean *financial executive*
Mayoras, Donald Eugene *corporate executive, writer, consultant, educator*
McClinton, Donald George *retired diversified holding company executive*
McColgan, Ellyn A. *diversified financial services company executive*
McCutchen, William Walter, Jr. *retired management educator*
McDonough, William J. *diversified financial services company executive*
McFarlane, Donovan Anthony *finance educator, poet, researcher*
McKinney, Mark A. *finance educator*
Means, Elizabeth-Rose Thayer *financial planner, lawyer, writer*
Mednick, Robert *accountant*
Menachem, Andrew *financial advisor*
Messmer, Donald Joseph *business management educator, marketing consultant*
Millard, Donald Rex *financial executive*
Miller, Alan J. *retired financial company executive*
Miller, Donald Muxlow *accountant*
Minna, Anthony Joseph *financial planner, lawyer*
Miselson, Alex J. (Jacob Miselson) *portfolio manager, securities analyst, investment theorist*
Moore, Cornell Leverette *financial services executive, lawyer*
Morgan, William J. *retired accounting company executive*
Morman, Dean Smith *accountant, consultant*
Mosner, Lawrence J. *retired financial administration company executive*
Moyer, R. Charles *finance company executive, educator, retired dean*
Mudry, Michael *pension and benefit consultant*
Mullet, Robin M. *retired accountant*
Munoz, Cheryl Ann *portfolio manager*
Murphy, Alexis D. *auditor*
Myers, Phillip Fenton *corporate financial, information technology executive*
Neff, John Brown *financial portfolio manager*
Newill, James Wagner *accounting executive*
Nguyen, Van Thuan *finance educator*
Niehoff, Karl Richard Besuden *finance company executive*
Nold, Aurora Ramirez *finance company executive*
Noonan, Patrick Sutton *management educator*
North, John Adna, Jr. *accountant, real estate appraiser*
Norton, Karen Ann *accountant*
Ortiz-Walters, Rowena *management educator*
Osborn, Kenneth Louis *financial executive*
Paige, Vivian Jo-Ann *accountant*
Palmer, Jessica A. *former diversified financial services company executive*
Pan, Yue *finance educator*
Pappas-Speairs, Nina *financial planner, educator*
Parameswaran, Raju *accountant*
Payton, Thomas William *finance company executive*
Perkins, Jon Douglas *accountant, educator*
Perry, Nancy Bland *accountant*
Peruzzo, Albert Louis *actuary, accountant*
Petru, Suzanne Mitton *retired health care finance executive*
Pfeister, Raymond Lynn *diversified financial services company executive*
Philippon, Thomas *finance educator*
Pino, Richard Edmund *corporate financial executive*
Pitts, Gregory Scott *corporate financial executive*
Purcell, Philip James *retired diversified financial services company executive*
Purdy, Kevin Moore *estate planner*
Pyle, Robert Milner, Jr. *financial consultant*
Quant, Harold Edward *retired financial services company executive, rancher*
Quirk, Kenneth Paul *accountant*
Raffegeau, Jean Michel *audit and consulting company executive*
Raines, Franklin Delano *former finance company executive*
Rajani, Prem Rajaram *transportation company financial executive*
Rakes, Ganas Kaye *retired finance and banking educator*
Rauh, Joshua D. *finance educator*
Ray, Marjorie *retired financial planner*
Reidy, Thomas Michael *financial executive*
Renouf, Anne *corporate financial executive, consultant*
Richardson-Bowman, Lequetta Devera *finance company executive, consultant*
Richey, Ellen *credit card company executive*
Ridenhour, Marilyn Housel *retired accountant*
Rizzo, Jeffrey F. *corporate financial executive*
Robertson, A. Haeworth *actuary, foundation executive, benefits consultant*
Robertson, Jack Clark *accounting educator*
Roble, Carole Marcia *accountant*
Rockwell, Elizabeth Dennis *retirement specialist, financial planner*
Rodriguez, Elena Garcia *retired pension fund administrator*
Rogan, Robert *management educator, consultant, osteopath, psychiatrist, lawyer*
Roller, David Isaac *financial services company executive*
Rose, Arthur Royal *financial planner, tax consultant*
Rosenberg, Sheli Zysman *retired finance company executive*
Rowe, William Davis *finance company executive*
Ruben, Jeffrey M. *finance company executive, lawyer*
Rush, Richard Henry *finance company executive, educator, writer*
Rushing, John Alan *business educator*
Russell, Walter Dallas, Jr. *diversified financial services company executive*
Ryan, Leo Vincent *business educator*
Rytkonen, Juha Kalevi *corporate financial executive*
Saks, Stephen Howard *accountant, health organization executive*
Salom, Roberto *retired finance company executive*
Saucier, Guylaine *corporate financial executive*
Sayles, Leonard Robert *management educator, consultant*
Scanlon, Peter Redmond *retired accountant*
Scheel, Nels Earl *corporate financial executive, accountant*
Schein, Edgar Henry *management educator*
Schellenberger, Robert Earl *retired management educator, department chairman*
Schnitzer, Iris Taymore *diversified financial services company executive, lawyer, arbitrator, mediator*
Schoen, William Jack *finance company executive*
Seiple, John W., Jr. *corporate financial executive*
Seligson, Carl Harold *corporate financial executive*
Serrie, Hendrick *retired anthropology and international business educator*
Servien, Louis-Marc (Comte De Boisdauphin, Lord of Quendon) *finance company, import/export company executive*
Severino, Elizabeth Forrest *consulting company executive, animal communicator, spiritual healer*
Sexton, Carol Burke *finance company executive, consultant*
Sharkey, Vincent Joseph *finance company executive*
Sheridan, Patrick Michael *retired finance company executive*
Sherman, Howard D. *financial consultant*
Shoop, Glenn Powell *investment consultant*
Shuchart, Eugene Joseph *retired accountant*
Shultis, Robert Lynn *finance educator, consultant, retired professional society administrator*
Silberstein, Alan Mark *financial services executive*
Simon, Donald John *financial planner, small business owner*
Simon, Ronald Isaac *financial executive*
Smart, Jill Bellavia *financial consultant*
Smith, Harold Charles *pension fund administrator*
Snare, Carl Lawrence, Jr. *retired accountant, financial planner*
Snortland, Howard Jerome *financial consultant*
Snyder, Alan Carhart *finance company executive*
Somide, Adegboyega Adesina *financial analyst, state official, educator, writer*
Souveroff, Vernon William, Jr. *corporate financial executive*
Spector, Warren J. *former investment company executive*
Srinivasan, Venkataraman *marketing and management educator*
Staloff, Arnold Fred *financial services executive*
Stanfill, Dennis Carothers *corporate financial executive*
Stawnychy, Zoriana Maria *financial executive*
Stockholm, Charles M. *diversified financial services company executive*
Stofferson, Terry Lee *financial analyst*
Strong, John Scott *finance educator*
Tan, Soo Chuen *financial analyst, researcher*
Tang, Yue *financial analyst*
Tew, E. James, Jr. *management services company executive*
Thomson, Todd Stuart *former diversified financial services company executive*
Tongue, Paul Graham *financial executive*
Trail, Margaret Ann *retired employee benefits company executive*
Trent, Robert Harold *retired business educator*
Tripoli, Masumi Hiroyasu *financial consultant*
Tu, Yufeng *business educator*
Turner, Henry Brown *finance company executive, director*
Tyler, Richard James *personal and professional development educator*
Vreeland, Russell Glenn *tax manager, accountant, consultant*
Vu, Joseph Duong *financial educator*
Wagner, John Edward *equity specialist*
Wall, M. Danny *finance company executive*
Waltermire, Thomas Allen *finance company executive*
Webster, Ronald D. *diversified financial services company executive*
Wesselink, David Duwayne *finance company executive*

Wheatland, Richard, II, *fiduciary services executive, museum executive*
White, Margit Triska *financial advisor*
White, Ronald Leon *retired business executive*
Whitney, Ralph Royal, Jr. *financial executive*
Widner, Roberta Ann *accountant, artist*
Wilhelmsen, Harold John *accountant*
Wilkinson, Harry Edward *management educator, consultant*
Williams, Alfred B. *retired management educator*
Williams, Doyle Z. *finance educator*
Wilson, Robert M. *diversified financial services company executive*
Workman, John P., Jr. *marketing professor*
Worley, Richard B. *financial consultant*
Yastine, Barbara A. *former diversified financial services company executive*
Zhang, Jiawei *finance educator*
Zimmerman, Helene Loretta *retired business educator*
Zuck, Alfred Miller *public administration educator*

FINANCE: INSURANCE

UNITED STATES

ALABAMA

Albertville
Chandler, Terry Winford *insurance company executive, real estate developer, small business owner*

Birmingham
Hudson, C. B., Jr. *insurance company executive*
Johns, John D. *insurance company executive, lawyer*

Lexington
Freeman, Sandra Dianne *insurance agent, educator*

ALASKA

Anchorage
Trevithick, Ronald James *underwriter*

ARIZONA

Paradise Valley
Tyner, Neal Edward *retired insurance company executive*

Rio Verde
Harding, John Hibbard *retired insurance company executive*

Scottsdale
Vairo, Robert John *insurance company executive*

Sun City
Reynolds, John Francis *insurance company executive*

Tucson
Haney, Robert Locke *retired insurance company executive*
Ziehler, Tony Joseph *insurance agent*

ARKANSAS

Little Rock
Bradford, Jay Turner *insurance company executive, state legislator*

CALIFORNIA

Auburn
Jeske, Howard Leigh *retired insurance company executive, lawyer*

Cupertino
Knapp, George Griff Prather *retired insurance executive*

Encino
Parrott, Dennis Beecher *retired insurance industry executive*

Garden Grove
Williams, J(ohn) Tilman *insurance company executive, real estate agent, municipal official*

Hermosa Beach
Winthrop, Kenneth Ray *insurance executive*

Irvine
Matros, Richard K. *insurance company executive*

Los Angeles
Houston, Ivan James *insurance company executive*
Inman, James Russell *claims consultant*
Jones, Denecia *insurance agent*
Joseph, George *insurance company executive*
Ross, Ami L. *insurance company executive, finance company executive*
Tirador, Gabriel *insurance company executive*

Marina Del Rey
Dexheimer, Henry Phillip, II, *insurance agency executive*

Newark
Gupta, Anju *risk management consultant*

Newport Beach
Marcoux, Carl Henry *insurance company executive, writer, historian*
Morris, James T. *insurance company executive*
Tran, Khanh T. *insurance company executive*

Oakland
Halvorson, George Charles *healthcare insurance company executive*

Palm Desert
Karson, Lillian P. *risk management consultant*

Paso Robles
Webster, David Arthur *retired life insurance company executive*

Rancho Mirage
Fromm, Erwin Frederick *retired insurance company executive*

Richmond
Ziesenhenne, John William *insurance agent*

San Diego
Baxter, Robert Hampton *insurance company executive*
Rotter, Paul Talbott *retired insurance executive*
Vasudevan, Sriram *risk management consultant, energy executive*

San Francisco
Enfield, Donald Michael *insurance company executive*
Lamberson, John Roger *insurance company executive*
Martinez, Belinda *health insurance company executive*
Stewart, Richard Edwin *insurance consulting company executive*

San Juan Capistrano
Gardner, Carol Ann *insurance company executive*

San Rafael
Keegan, Jane Ann *insurance executive, consultant*

Santa Ana
DeRoy, Craig I. *title insurance company executive, lawyer*
Gilmore, Dennis J. *insurance company executive*
McMahon, Frank V. *insurance company executive*

Santa Monica
Schaeffer, Leonard David *health insurance company executive*

Sherman Oaks
Milgrim, Darrow A. *insurance company executive*

Thousand Oaks
Herman, Joan Elizabeth *health insurance company executive*
Valdez, Josh *health insurance company executive*

Woodland Hills
Clarey, Patricia T. *health insurance company executive, former state official*
Helwig, David S. *healthcare insurance company executive*

Woodside
Freitas, Antoinette Juni *insurance company executive*

COLORADO

Aurora
Nelson, Marvin Ray *retired life insurance company executive*

Englewood
Hardy, Wayne Russell *insurance and investment broker*
Manley, Richard Walter *insurance company executive*

Littleton
Volpe, Richard Gerard *insurance accounts executive, consultant*

Superior
Forshee, Gladys Marie *insurance agent, writer*

CONNECTICUT

Bloomfield
Cordani, David M. *insurance company executive*
Storrer, Scott A. *insurance company executive*

East Hartford
Lautzenheiser, Barbara Jean *insurance company executive*

Essex
Miller, Walter Neal *insurance company consultant*

Greenwich
Berkley, William Robert *insurance holding company executive*
Clements, Robert *insurance executive*
Fuller, Theodore *retired insurance executive*
Lederman, Ira Seth *insurance company executive, lawyer*

Hartford
Ayer, Ramani *insurance company executive*
Bertolini, Mark T. *insurance company executive*
Bombara, Beth Ann *insurance company executive*
Brennan, Troyen A. *insurance company executive, physician, educator, lawyer*
Campbell, Timothy R. *insurance company executive*
Casazza, William James *insurance company executive, lawyer*
deRaismes, Ann M. *insurance company executive, human resources specialist*
Geyer, James A *insurance company executive*
Johnson, David M. *insurance company executive*
Mullane, Denis Francis *insurance company executive*
Price, Robert J. *insurance company executive*
Sargent, Joseph Denny *insurance executive*
Scully, John Carroll *life insurance marketing research company executive*
Wilde, Wilson *insurance company executive*
Williams, Ronald A. *health insurance company executive*
Wright, Elease *insurance company executive*
Znamierowski, David M *insurance company executive*
Zubretsky, Joseph M. *insurance company executive*

Middletown
Bohan, Lawrence Stewart *retired insurance company executive*

New Canaan
Burns, John Joseph, Jr. *financial and insurance holding company executive*
Cohen, Richard Norman *insurance executive*
Ylvisaker, James William *insurance executive*

Stamford
Chickering, Howard Allen *insurance company executive, lawyer*
Hudson, Harold Jordon, Jr. *retired insurance executive*
Schiff, Jayne Nemerow *underwriter*

Trumbull
Berg, Charles G. *insurance company executive*

Vernon Rockville
Wolff, Gregory Steven *insurance company executive*

West Hartford
Wilder, Michael Stephen *former insurance company executive*

Weston
Thompson, N(orman) David *insurance company executive*

DELAWARE

Wilmington
Nottingham, Robinson Kendall *insurance company executive*

DISTRICT OF COLUMBIA

Washington
Martin, Julie A. *retired insurance company executive*
Pitt, Harvey Lloyd *risk management consultant, former federal agency administrator*
Simpson, Louis A. *insurance company executive*

FLORIDA

Atlantic Beach
Preble, Robert Curtis, Jr. *insurance executive*

Boca Raton
Kaye, Barry *insurance company executive*
Richardson, R(oss) Fred(erick) *insurance company executive, consultant*

Bonita Springs
Rainey, Barbara White *insurance company executive*

Boynton Beach
Bryant, Donald Loyd *insurance company executive*

Fort Lauderdale
Lilley, Mili Della *insurance company executive, entertainment management consultant*

Fort Myers
Mc Queen, Robert Charles *retired insurance executive*

Gainesville
Boothroyd, Herbert J. *insurance company executive*

Holiday
Peterson, George Folke *retired insurance company executive, writer*

Jacksonville
Bickett, Brent B. *insurance company executive*
Foley, William Patrick, II, *insurance company executive*
Lyon, Wilford Charles, Jr. *insurance executive*
Quirk, Raymond R. (Randy Quirk) *insurance company executive*
Stinson, Alan Lynn *insurance company executive*

Key Largo
Daenzer, Bernard John *insurance company executive, consultant*

Lake Mary
Swonger, Thomas K. H., Jr. *insurance company executive*

Miami
Heggen, Arthur William *insurance company executive*
Shusterman, Nathan *underwriter, financial consultant*
Van Wyck, George Richard *insurance company executive*

New Port Richey
Hanahan, James Lake *retired insurance executive*

Oldsmar
Caronis, George John *insurance executive*

Ormond Beach
Burt, Wallace Joseph, Jr. *insurance company executive*

Ponte Vedra Beach
MacKowski, John Joseph *retired insurance company executive*

Redington Beach
Alpert, Barry Mark *insurance company and banking executive*

Saint Petersburg
Fraser, John Wayne *insurance executive, consultant, underwriter*

Sarasota
Bushey, Alan Scott *retired insurance holding company executive*

Spring Hill
Vanderburg, Paul Stacey *insurance executive, consultant*

Tallahassee
Hunt, John Edwin *insurance company executive, consultant*

Tampa
Bishopric, Karl *insurance company executive, retired investment banker, real estate company executive, retired advertising executive*
Sullivan, Joseph Peter *risk and insurance management consultant*

Winter Park
Kraft, Kenneth Houston, Jr. *insurance agency executive*

GEORGIA

Alpharetta
Fowler, Vivian Delores *insurance company executive*

Atlanta
Black, Kenneth, Jr. *retired insurance company executive*
Gregory, Mel Hyatt, Jr. *retired insurance company executive*
Hilliard, Robert Glenn *insurance company executive, lawyer*
Hubbell, Fred Shelton *insurance company executive*

Columbus
Amos, Daniel Paul *insurance company executive*
Amos, Paul Shelby, II, *insurance company executive*
Baker, Janet *insurance company executive*
Blanck, Susan *insurance company executive*
Cloninger, Kriss III *insurance company executive*
Cox, Kermitt L. *insurance company executive*
Davis, Rebecca C. *insurance company executive*
Friou, Phillip J. (Jack Friou) *insurance company executive*
Hart, Angela *insurance company executive*
Herbert, Jeff *insurance company executive*
Janke, Kenneth S., Jr. *insurance company executive*
Jeffery, William Jeremy *insurance company executive*
Kirkland, Ronald E. *insurance company executive*
Lester, James D. III *insurance company executive*
Ottman, Bob *insurance company executive*
Pringle, David L. *insurance company executive*
Rogers, Ralph A., Jr. *insurance company executive*
Shields, Gerald W. *insurance company executive*
Tillman, Audrey Boone *insurance company executive*
White, Teresa Lynne *insurance company executive*

Lagrange
Hudson, Charles Daugherty *insurance executive*

Savannah
Dodge, William Douglas *risk management consultant*

HAWAII

Honolulu
Kanehiro, Kenneth Kenji *risk management consultant, educator*
Noguchi, Hideo *insurance company executive*

ILLINOIS

Bloomington
Blackburn, John D. *insurance company executi*

nner, Kim M. *insurance company executive, lawyer*
t, Edward Barry, Jr. *insurance company executive, lawyer*
sord, Michael L. *insurance company executive*
d, Jon David *retired insurance company executive*

icago
ams, John S. *insurance company executive*
tholomay, William C. *insurance brokerage company and professional sports team executive*
ger, David P. *insurance company executive*
dley, Thomas A. *insurance company executive*
se, Gregory C. *insurance company executive*
Moss, Jon W. *insurance company executive, lawyer*
nandez, Geno *insurance company executive*
kelman, Ruth Amidon *insurance company executive*
ome, Jerrold V. *retired insurance company executive*
ner, Alexander Robert *insurance company executive*
enz, Hugo Albert *retired insurance executive, consultant*
nning, Frederick James *insurance company executive*
Caskey, Raymond F. *insurance company executive*
cells, Frederick R. *underwriter*
oonis, Harold Arthur *insurance agent, portfolio manager*
dgers, James Foster *insurance research executive, economist*
thwell, Donald G. *insurance company executive*
ee, James C. *insurance company executive*
, Richard Carl *insurance company executive*
aro, Aldo Charles *insurance company executive*

alena
andall, John Lynn *retired insurance company executive, consultant*

asca
llagher, J. Patrick, Jr. *insurance company executive*

oline
ddleton, Marc Stephen *corporate insurance risk manager*

aperville
awford, Raymond Maxwell, Jr. *management consultant*
sch, Theodore Edward *retired insurance company executive, lawyer*
mbeck, Harold Arthur *insurance company executive*

orthbrook
ane, Catherine S. *insurance company executive*
ipe, Frederick F. *insurance company executive*
ockett, Joan M. *insurance company executive*
uikshank, John W. III *insurance agent*
le, Danny Lyman *insurance company executive*
ohmann, James E. *insurance company executive*
ddy, Edward M. *insurance company executive*
cCabe, Michael J. (Mick) *insurance executive, lawyer*
ke, Robert William *insurance company executive, lawyer*
che, Michael J. *insurance company executive*
ebenson, George E. *insurance company executive*
monson, Eric A. *insurance company executive*
renson, Steven P. *insurance company executive*
lla, Casey J. *insurance company executive*
alker, Joan H. *insurance company executive*
ilson, Thomas Joseph *insurance company executive*

ark Ridge
vald, Robert Frederick *insurance company executive, consultant*

ock Island
ardner, Henry Petersen (Peter Lardner) *insurance company executive*

pringfield
odge, Edward John *retired insurance company executive*
mpson, William Arthur *insurance company executive*

Vheeling
eemster, Joseph Robert *risk management consultant*

NDIANA

armel
usman, Catherine Bigot *retired insurance company executive, consultant*
ieur, C. James *insurance company executive*

olumbus
sborn, DeVerle Ross *insurance company executive*

ort Wayne
unsire, P(eter) Kenneth *insurance company executive*
einer, Paul Andrew *retired insurance executive*

Greenwood
Gaunce, Michael Paul *insurance company executive*

Indianapolis
Boxer, Mark L. *healthcare insurance company executive*
Braly, Angela Fick *health insurance company executive, lawyer*
DeVeydt, Wayne S. *health insurance company executive*
Dorr, Marjorie W. *healthcare insurance company executive*
Glasscock, Larry Claborn *health insurance company executive*
Lewis, Randall J. *healthcare insurance company executive*
Lytle, L(arry) Ben *insurance company executive, lawyer*
McKinney, E. Kirk, Jr. *retired insurance company executive*
Nussbaum, Samuel R. *healthcare insurance company executive, medical educator*
Rosenblatt, Alice F. *healthcare insurance company executive*
Watts, John S., Jr. *insurance company executive*

Pendleton
Kischuk, Richard Karl *insurance company executive*

Schererville
Jarrett, Alexis *insurance agent, lawyer*

IOWA

Des Moines
Brooks, Roger Kay *insurance company executive*
Gersie, Michael H. *insurance company executive*
Godlasky, Thomas C. *insurance company executive*
Griswell, J. Barry *insurance company executive*
Kalainov, Sam Charles *insurance company executive*
Kelley, Bruce Gunn *insurance company executive, lawyer*
Williams, Carl Chanson *insurance company executive*

KANSAS

De Soto
Strubbe, Thomas R. *insurance industry executive*

Eudora
Miller, David Groff *insurance agent*

Newton
Morford, Marie Arlene *insurance company executive*

KENTUCKY

Louisville
Hickey, Bobby Ray *underwriting assistant*
Jones, David A., Jr. *insurance company executive*
McCallister, Michael B. *insurance company executive*
McCormick, Steven Thomas *insurance company executive*
Rosky, Theodore Samuel *insurance company executive*

Owensboro
Webb, Otis D. *retired underwriter*

LOUISIANA

Kenner
Kuebler, David Wayne *insurance company executive, private investigator*

New Orleans
Marks, Charles Dennery *insurance consultant*

MAINE

Portland
Buckley, Paul Richard, Sr. *insurance executive*
Reid, Rosemary Anne *insurance agent*

MARYLAND

Baltimore
Goodman, William Richard *insurance adjusting company executive*
Hecht, Alan Dannenberg *insurance executive*
Morris, David Michael *insurance executive, lawyer*

Brandywine
Jaffe, Morris Edward *insurance company executive, financial analyst*

Elkton
Jasinski-Caldwell, Mary L. *insurance company executive*

Reisterstown
Tirone, Barbara Jean *retired health insurance administrator*

MASSACHUSETTS

Boston
Aborn, Foster Litchfield *insurance company executive*
Brown, Stephen Lee *retired insurance company executive*
Bunker, Beryl H. *retired insurance company executive, volunteer*
Condrin, J. Paul *insurance company executive*
Fontanes, A. Alexander *insurance company executive*
Kelly, Edmund Francis *insurance company executive*
Langwell, Dennis J. *insurance company executive*
Morton, Edward James *insurance company executive*
Van Faasen, William C. *health insurance company executive*

Duxbury
Wangler, William Clarence *retired insurance company executive*

East Falmouth
Forte, Wesley Elbert *former insurance company executive, lawyer*

Needham
Rodman, Sumner *insurance company executive*

North Attleboro
Koussa, Harold Alan *insurance account executive*

North Chatham
O'Brien, Robert Emmet *insurance company executive*

North Dighton
Silvia, David Alan *insurance broker*

Quincy
Moran, James Joseph, Jr. *insurance company executive*

South Orleans
Hale, Margaret Smith *insurance company executive, educator*

Springfield
Castellani, Frederick C. *insurance company executive*
Crandall, Roger W. *insurance company executive*
Glavin, William Francis, Jr. *insurance company executive*
Gunton, Howard E. *insurance company executive*
Johnson, Robert Allison *life insurance company executive*
Reese, Stuart Harry *insurance company executive*
Rollings, Michael Thomas *insurance company executive*
Sarsynski, Elaine A. *insurance company executive*

Tewksbury
Shea, William J. *former insurance company executive*

Waltham
Roosevelt, James, Jr. *insurance company executive, lawyer*

Webster
Fels, Gerald *insurance company executive*

Wellesley
Baker, Charles D. *health insurance company executive*

West Hyannisport
Gingold, George Norman *insurance company executive, lawyer*

Worcester
Angelini, Michael P. *insurance company executive*
Eppinger, Frederick H., Jr. *insurance company executive*

MICHIGAN

Alma
Merwin, Gregory Alan *insurance agent, retired special education educator*

Detroit
Whitmer, Richard E. *insurance company executive*

Kalamazoo
Curry, John Patrick *insurance company executive, management consultant*

Lansing
Arends, Herman Joseph *former insurance company executive*
Fisher, John W. *insurance company executive*
Looyenga, Roger L. *insurance company executive*

MINNESOTA

Bemidji
Bridston, Paul Joseph *strategic management consultant*

Coon Rapids
Bordner, Patricia Anne *insurance agent, writer*

Hibbing
Calligan, William Dennis *retired life insurance company executive*

Minneapolis
Boushek, Randy L. *insurance company executive*
Crosmer, Janie Lynn *insurance company executive*
Feldman, Nancy Jane *insurance company executive*
Keets, John David, Jr. *insurance company executive*
Mikan, G. Mike *healthcare services company executive*
Munsell, William A. *healthcare insurance company executive*
Nicholson, Bruce J. *insurance company executive*
Quam, Lois *insurance company executive*
Tuckson, Reed V. *physician, health insurance company executive*
Turner, John Gosney *insurance company executive, director*
Wichmann, David S. *health care services company executive*

Minnetonka
Rivet, Jeannine M. *health insurance company executive*
Robbins, Orem Olford *insurance company executive*
Sheehy, Robert J. *insurance company executive*

Owatonna
Annexstad, Albert T. *insurance company executive*

Saint Paul
Benet, Jay S. *insurance company executive*
Clarke, Charles J. *insurance company executive*
Ettinger, Irwin R. *insurance company executive*
Johnson, James Erling *insurance executive*
Lipp, Robert I. *insurance company executive*
MacLean, Brian W. *insurance company executive*
Senkler, Robert L. *insurance company executive*

MISSISSIPPI

Clinton
Montgomery, Keith Norris, Sr. *insurance agent, military officer*

MISSOURI

Maryland Heights
Buselmeier, Bernard Joseph *insurance company executive*

Saint Louis
Bryant, Donald L., Jr. *insurance and benefits company executive*
Mullens, William Reese *retired insurance company executive*

NEBRASKA

Holdrege
Hendrickson, Bruce Carl *life insurance company executive*

Omaha
Haney, J. Terrence *retired insurance consultant*
Jetter, Arthur Carl, Jr. *insurance company executive*
Neary, Daniel P. *insurance company executive*

NEVADA

Henderson
Johnson, Joan Bray *insurance company consultant*

NEW HAMPSHIRE

Hanover
Kemp, Karl Thomas *insurance company executive*

Manchester
Ehrlich, Charles Gordon *insurance company executive, lawyer*

Rochester
Dworkin, Gary Steven *insurance company executive*

NEW JERSEY

Augusta
Martin, Richard L. *retired insurance executive*

Branchville
Murphy, Gregory E. *insurance company executive*

Glen Rock
Mc Elrath, Richard Elsworth *retired insurance company executive*

Madison
Parker, Henry Griffith III *insurance executive*

New Vernon
McCormack, John Joseph, Jr. *insurance company executive*

Newark
Blount, Susan L. *insurance company executive, lawyer*
Carbone, Richard J. *insurance company executive*
Koster, Barbara *insurance company executive*
Marino, William J. *insurance executive*
Myers, Priscilla A. *insurance company executive*

Winters, Robert Cushing *insurance company executive*

Paramus
Crow, Lynne Campbell Smith *insurance company representative*

Plainfield
Schram, Henry B. *insurance company executive*

Princeton
Sandman, Peter M. *risk management consultant*

Ridgewood
O'Leary, Paul Gerard *retired insurance company executive*

Short Hills
MacKinnon, Malcolm D(avid) *retired insurance company executive*

Spring Lake
Bonhag, Thomas Edward *insurance company executive, financial planner, consultant*

Summit
Gerathy, E. Carroll *retired insurance company executive, real estate developer*

Warren
Cox, Robert C. *insurance company executive*
Degnan, John J. *insurance company executive, lawyer*
Finnegan, John D. *insurance company executive*
Krump, Paul J. *insurance company executive*
McElwee, Andrew Allison, Jr. *insurance company executive*
Motamed, Thomas Firouz *insurance company executive*
O'Reilly, Michael *insurance company executive*
Robusto, Dino E. *insurance company executive*

Whitehouse Station
Fiscus, Philip Wayne *underwriter*

Wyckoff
Munson, William Leslie *insurance company executive*

NEW MEXICO

Albuquerque
Wainio, Mark Ernest *insurance company consultant*

NEW YORK

Albany
Cole, John Adam *insurance executive*

Amityville
Imbert, Richard Conrad *insurance company executive, real estate developer*

Armonk
Brown, Joseph W., Jr., (Jay Brown) *insurance company executive*
Dunton, Gary C. *insurance company executive*
Ferguson, Roger Walter, Jr. *reinsurance company executive, former federal official*

Bemus Point
Ross, Roderic Henry *retired insurance company executive*

Binghamton
Best, Robert Mulvane *insurance company executive*

Bronx
Elkins, Alfred David *insurance company executive*

Brooklyn
Faison, Seth Shepard *retired insurance broker*

Cobleskill
Wilson, Lewis Lansing *insurance executive*

Cohocton
Sarfaty, Wayne Allen *insurance agent, financial planner*

Dryden
Baxter, Robert Banning *insurance company executive*

Geneva
Vecchiotti, Tony V. *insurance agent*

Great Neck
Lipsky, Jack Bender *insurance company executive*

Lindenhurst
Hungerford, Gary A. *insurance executive, columnist, writer, editor*

Long Island City
Henrikson, C. Robert *insurance company executive*
Rein, Catherine Amelia *insurance company executive, lawyer*

Mineola
Miller, Loring Erik *insurance agent, broker*

New Rochelle
Leaf, Robert Jay *dental insurance consultant*

New York
Bartley, Matthew B. *insurance company executive*
Bensinger, Steven J. *insurance company executive*
Biggs, John Herron *retired insurance company executive*
Broatch, Robert E. *insurance company executive*
Cabiallavetta, Mathis *insurance company executive*
Callahan, Dennis S. *insurance company executive*
Camacho, Philip Bruce *insurance company executive*
Campbell, Judith E. *retired insurance company executive*
Cherkasky, Michael G. *insurance company executive*
Clayton, Jon Kerry *insurance company executive*
Crystal, James William *insurance company executive*
Davis, Karen *insurance company executive, educator*
Dolan, Raymond Bernard *insurance company executive, director*
Flynn, William Joseph *insurance company executive*
Frenkel, Jacob Aharon *insurance company executive*
Gilmour, Joseph A. *insurance company executive*
Harris, David Henry *retired life insurance company executive*
Hildebrand, Phillip J. *insurance company executive*
Hohn, Harry George *retired insurance company executive, lawyer*
Hutchings, Peter Lounsbery *retired insurance company executive, director*
Kandarian, Steven A. *insurance company executive*
Kaplan, Theodore Norman *insurance company executive*
Launer, Leland C., Jr. *insurance company executive*
Manning, Dennis J. *insurance company executive*
Mathas, Theodore A. *insurance company executive, lawyer*
Mathieson, Garrett Alfred *insurance brokerage executive*
Melone, Joseph James *retired insurance company executive*
Moran, Thomas J. *insurance company executive*
Mullaney, William J. *insurance company executive*
Murray, Richard Maximilian *insurance company executive*
Nadler, David A. *insurance company executive*
Peninger, Michael J. *insurance company executive*
Platusich, Christian Michael *underwriter*
Pollock, Robert B. *insurance company executive*
Procope, Ernesta Gertrude *insurance company executive*
Sandler, Robert Michael *insurance company executive*
Schwartz, Robert George *retired insurance company executive*
Somers, John Arthur *insurance company executive*
Sproule, Michael E. *insurance company executive*
Sternberg, Seymour *insurance company executive*
Sullivan, Martin J. *insurance company executive*
Toppeta, William John *insurance company executive, lawyer*
Vidal, David Jonathan *insurance company executive, journalist*
Weber, Lisa M. *insurance company executive*
Wendlandt, Gary E. *insurance company executive*
Wheeler, William J. *insurance company executive*
Willumstad, Robert B. *insurance company executive, retired diversified financial services company executive*
Wintrob, Jay S. *insurance company executive*
Wisner, Frank George *insurance company executive, former ambassador*
Yalen, Gary N. *retired insurance company executive*

Northport
Miller, Philip John *insurance agent, consultant*

Saratoga Springs
Ford, Dexter *retired insurance company executive*

Scarsdale
Decaminada, Joseph Pio *retired insurance company executive*

Schenectady
Murray, Edward Rock *insurance broker*

Staten Island
Gavrity, John Decker *retired insurance company executive*

Syosset
Kniffin, Paula Sichel *insurance sales executive*

NORTH CAROLINA

Camden
Hammond, Roy Joseph *reinsurance company executive*

Chapel Hill
Clark, Arthur Watts *insurance company executive*
Fine, J(ames) Allen *insurance company executive*

Winston Salem
Beardsley, Charles Mitchell *retired insurance company executive*

NORTH DAKOTA

Grand Forks
Wogaman, George Elsworth *insurance company executive, financial consultant*

OHIO

Canton
Schauer, Thomas Alfred *insurance company executive*

Cincinnati
Barrett, John F. *insurance company executive*
Hardy, Thomas Cresson *insurance company executive*
Horrell, Karen Holley *insurance company executive, lawyer*
Klein, Jerry Emanuel *insurance planning and financial planning executive*
Lindner, Carl H. III *insurance company executive*
Lindner, Carl Henry, Jr. *insurance company executive, professional sports team owner*
Lindner, S(tephen) Craig *insurance company executive*
Runk, Fred J. *retired insurance company executive*
Scheineson, Irwin Bruce *insurance and investment company executive*

Cleveland
Clapp, Kent W. *insurance company executive*
Domeck, Brian C. *insurance company executive*
Lewis, Peter Benjamin *insurance company executive*
Renwick, Glenn M. *insurance company executive*

Columbus
Duryee, Harold Taylor *insurance consultant*
Jurgensen, William G. *insurance company executive*
Rasmussen, Stephen S. *insurance company executive*
Sharma, Manu *risk management consultant, researcher*
Shisler, Arden L. *insurance and transportation company executive*
Thresher, Mark R. *insurance company executive*

Fairfield
Benoski, James E. *insurance company executive*
Carmichael, Dan R. *insurance company executive*

Powell
Emanuelson, James Robert *retired insurance company executive*

OKLAHOMA

Oklahoma City
Ille, Bernard Glenn *insurance company executive, director*
Watson, Brenda Bennett *insurance company executive*

Tulsa
Hoe, Richard March *insurance and securities consultant, writer*

OREGON

Portland
Parsons, Eric E. *insurance company executive*

Waldport
Ginter, Carolyn Augusta Romtvedt *retired underwriter*

PENNSYLVANIA

Bala Cynwyd
Shepard, Geoffrey Carroll *insurance company executive*

Bushkill
Garretto, Leonard Anthony, Jr. *insurance company executive*

Camp Hill
Mead, James Matthew *insurance company executive*

Elkins Park
Hart, William C. *underwriter, educator, writer*

Erie
Garcia, Philip A. *insurance company executive*
Hirt, F. William *insurance company executive*
Ludrof, Jeffrey A. *insurance company executive*

Harleysville
Browne, Michael L. *insurance company executive*

Hatboro
Quigley, Robert Charles *insurance industry consultant*

King Of Prussia
Katz, Arnold Martin *insurance brokerage firm executive*
Volpe, Ralph Pasquale *retired insurance company executive*

Newtown Square
Staats, Dean Roy *retired reinsurance executive*

Philadelphia
Bell, Michael W. *insurance company executive*
Glass, Dennis Robert *insurance company executive*
Hanway, H. Edward *insurance company executive*
Hartley, Paul E. *insurance company executive*
Kaplan, Keith Eugene *insurance company executive, lawyer*
Murabito, John M. *insurance company executive*
Rohan, Karen S. *insurance company executive*
Stonecipher, David A. *insurance company executive*

Pittsburgh
Melani, Kenneth R. *insurance company executive*

Ridgway
Aiello, Gennaro C. *insurance company executive*

Wayne
Yoskin, Jon William, II, *insurance company executive*

RHODE ISLAND

Johnston
Subramaniam, Shivan Sivaswamy *insurance company executive*

Lincoln
DiMuccio, Robert A. *insurance company executive*

SOUTH CAROLINA

Columbia
Averyt, Gayle Owen *retired insurance executive*

Georgetown
Schumaker, William Thomas *retired insurance company executive*

SOUTH DAKOTA

Aberdeen
Stoia, Viorel G. *life underwriter*

TENNESSEE

Athens
Trent, Henry Gibson, Jr. *insurance company executive, educator*

Chattanooga
Copeland, Floyd Dean *insurance company executive, lawyer*
Greving, Robert C. *insurance company executive*
Watjen, Thomas Ros *insurance company executive*

Nashville
Howell, John Floyd *insurance company executive*

Seymour
Steele, Ernest Clyde *retired insurance company executive*

TEXAS

Alvin
Lyons, Phillip Michael, Sr. *insurance accounting and real estate executive*

Austin
Mullen, Ron *insurance company executive*
Payne, Tyson Elliott, Jr. *retired insurance executive*

Dallas
Cline, Bobby James *insurance company executive*
Madden, Teresa Darleen *insurance agency owne*
Weakley, Clare George, Jr. *insurance company executive, theologian, entrepreneur*

El Paso
Goldfarb, William D. *underwriter, investor*

Fort Worth
Blackburn, Wyatt Douglas *insurance executive*

Galveston
Moody, Robert Lee *insurance company executiv*

Hillsboro
Haddaway, James David *retired insurance company official*

Houston
Bramanti, Frank J. *insurance company executive*
Couch, Jesse Wadsworth *retired insurance company executive*
Dean, Robert Franklin *insurance company executive*
Hook, Harold Swanson *former management consulting executive*
Lindsey, John H. *former insurance agency executive*
Morris, Stewart, Jr. *title insurance company executive*
Skalka, Michael B. *insurance company executive, lawyer*

Livingston
Stovall, Jerry Coleman *insurance company executive*

Mc Kinney
McAndrew, Mark S. *insurance company executive*

North Richland Hills
Gedwed, William J. *insurance company executive*

San Antonio
Claus, Christopher W. *insurance company executive*
Colyer, Kirk Klein *insurance and real estate investment executive*
Conklyn, Elizabeth D. *insurance company executive*
Davis, Robert G. *insurance company executive*
Garrison, David H. *insurance company executive*
Luby, Michael A. *insurance company executive*
Matus, Kristi Ann *insurance company executive*
Parker, Stuart Blain *insurance company executive*
Peacock, S. Wayne *insurance company executive*
Robles, Josue, Jr. *insurance company executive*
Strong, Wendi Ellen *insurance company executive*
Wellberg, Edward Louis, Jr. *insurance company executive*

UTAH

Bountiful
Clay, Orson C. *insurance company executive, director*

Ogden
Buckner, Elmer La Mar *retired insurance company executive*

VERMONT

Montpelier
MacLeay, Thomas H. *insurance company executive*

VIRGINIA

Charlottesville
Long, Charles Farrell *insurance company executive*

Chesterfield
Tate, Wendy K. *insurance company executive, risk management consultant*

Glen Allen
Kirshner, Alan I. *insurance company executive*
Rogal, Andrew L. *insurance company executive*

Lynchburg
McRorie, William Edward *retired insurance company executive*

Norfolk
Dungan, William Joseph, Jr. *insurance agent, educator, economist*

Norton
Wells, Charles Rayburn *retired insurance company executive*

Penhook
Hahn, John William *retired insurance company executive*

Richmond
Fraizer, Michael D. *insurance company executive*
Kelleher, Patrick B. *insurance company executive*

Williamsburg
Herrmann, Benjamin Edward *former insurance executive*

WASHINGTON

Federal Way
Pitts, Melissa Dawn *underwriter*

Kirkland
McDonald, Joseph Lee *insurance broker*

Seattle
Eigsti, Roger Harry *retired insurance company executive*
Lari, Ross *insurance company executive*

Vancouver
Bettman, Donald Reese *loss control inspector*

Walla Walla
Perry, Louis Barnes *retired insurance company executive*

Woodland
Jansen, Walter Eugene *insurance executive*

WISCONSIN

Hudson
Anderson, Gregory Shane *insurance executive*

Madison
Anderson, David R. *insurance company executive*
DuRose, Stanley Charles, Jr. *retired insurance company executive*
Larson, John David *insurance company executive, lawyer*
Post, Jeffrey H. *insurance company executive*
Salzwedel, Jack C. *insurance company executive*
Schultz, Daniel R. *insurance company executive*
Waldo, Robert Leland *retired insurance company executive*

Milwaukee
Janavitz, Kurt L. *insurance company executive*
Johannes, Kay L. *insurance company executive*
Trytek, David Douglas *insurance company executive*

Nashotah
Vincent, Norman L. *retired insurance company executive*

Stevens Point
Schuh, Dale R. *insurance company executive*

WYOMING

Teton Village
Conrad, Donald Glover *insurance executive*

TERRITORIES OF THE UNITED STATES

PUERTO RICO

Caguas
Aviles Miranda, Maximo *insurance company executive*

CANADA

NOVA SCOTIA

North Sydney
Nickerson, Jerry Edgar Alan *business executive*

BERMUDA

Pembroke
Stempel, Ernest Edward *insurance executive*

HONG KONG

Hong Kong
Tse, Edmund Sze-Wing *insurance company executive*

ISRAEL

Givat Brener
Tritter, Richard Paul *strategic consultant*

SOUTH AFRICA

Cape Town
Cleary, Sean Michael *risk management executive*

ADDRESS UNPUBLISHED

Adam, John, Jr. *insurance company executive emeritus*
Adams, John Carter, Jr. *retired insurance executive*
Armstrong, F(redric) Michael *retired insurance company executive, consultant*
Becker, JoAnn Elizabeth *retired insurance company executive*
Bellamy, James Carl *retired insurance company executive*
Bergquist, Sandra Lee *claims consultant*
Bertrand, Frederic Howard *retired insurance company executive*
Bolnick, Howard Jeffrey *insurance company executive, educator, investor*
Borda, Richard Joseph *retired insurance company executive*
Boscia, Jon Andrew *insurance company executive*
Briggs, Philip *insurance company executive*
Browne, Ray *insurance agent, retired congressman*
Burkett, Lawrence V. *retired insurance company executive, lawyer*
Carey, Edward John *insurance company executive*
Carver, Kendall Lynn *insurance company executive*
Chilvers, Derek *insurance company executive*
Clark, Edgar Sanderford *insurance broker, consultant*
Coleman, Ronald Lee *insurance claims executive*
Conroy, Thomas Francis *insurance company consultant*
Cooper, Charles Gordon *retired insurance company executive*
Countryman, Gary Lee *retired insurance company executive*
D'Alessandro, David Francis *insurance company executive*
Davis, Rex Lloyd *insurance company executive*
Diakos, Stephen Samuel *billing and insurance specialist*
DiPiazza, Michael Charles *insurance company executive*
Duckworth, Tara Ann *insurance company executive*
Emek, Sharon Helene *risk management consultant*
Faller, Keith *healthcare insurance company executive*
Fey, John Theodore *retired insurance company executive*
Fibiger, John Andrew *life insurance company executive*
Goulet, Charles Ryan *retired insurance company executive*
Greenberg, Maurice Raymond (Hank) *retired insurance company executive*
Hartwig, Robert Paul *insurance institute executive, economist*
Hincks, Marcia Lockwood *retired insurance company executive*
Hinds, Edward Dee *insurance and investment professional, financial planner*
Holden, William Willard *insurance executive*
Howe, James Tarsicius *retired insurance company executive*
Impellizzeri, Anne Elmendorf *insurance company executive, non-profit executive*
Jacobson, James Bassett *retired insurance and financial services company executive*
Johnson, Glendon E. *retired insurance company executive*
Jones, Lupe Sirena *insurance agent*
Khan, Ahmed Mohiuddin *insurance company executive*
Lacey, Cloyd Eugene *retired insurance company executive*
Ladd, Joseph Carroll *retired insurance company executive*
Langer, Ray Fritz *retired insurance executive*
Leatherdale, Douglas West *insurance company executive*
Lee, Katrina LaShawn *health insurance business consultant*
Maatman, Gerald Leonard *insurance company executive*
Maginn, John Leo *retired insurance company executive*
Maloney, Therese Adele *retired insurance company executive*
McCarthy, Harold Charles *retired insurance company executive*
McKenna, Terence Patrick *retired insurance company executive*
McLaughlin, Michael John *retired insurance company executive*
Metcalf, Wayne C. III *retired insurance company executive*
Moses, Michael James *insurance company executive, small business owner*
Moynahan, John Daniel, Jr. *retired insurance company executive*
Nagler, Stewart Gordon *retired insurance company executive*
Nelson, Walter Gerald *retired insurance company executive*
Newman, Steven Harvey *insurance company executive, director*
Norris, Darell Forest *retired insurance company executive*
O'Hare, Dean Raymond *retired insurance company executive, director*
Olsen, David Alexander *insurance executive*
Papa, Vincent T. *insurance company executive*
Pearson, Paul Holding *insurance company executive*
Peters, Douglas Alan *risk management and compliance consultant*
Porter, Dixie Lee *retired insurance company executive, consultant*
Resnick, Myron Jay *retired insurance company executive, lawyer*
Rockwood, Frederick Whitney *insurance company executive*
Rodino, Vincent Louis *insurance company executive*
Roenigk, Martin Allen *insurance company executive*
Rondepierre, Edmond Francois *insurance executive, lawyer*
Rowe, John Wallis (Jack Rowe) *retired insurance company executive, education educator*
Rowell, Lester John, Jr. *retired insurance company executive*
Ryan, James *insurance company executive*
Sanders, Franklin D. *retired insurance company executive*
Smith, Floyd Leslie *insurance company executive*
Snyder, William Burton *insurance company executive*
Stabler, Russel W. *insurance agent*
Stewart, Gordon Curran *retired insurance institute executive*
Strong, John David *insurance company executive*
Tresnowski, Bernard Richard *retired health insurance company executive*
Tringale, Anthony Rosario *insurance executive*
Underhill, Jacob Berry III *retired insurance company executive*
Van Houten, James Forester *former insurance company chief executive, educator, consultant*
Vasholz, Lothar Alfred *retired insurance company executive*
Viscardi, Peter G. *risk management and environmental affairs executive*
Volk, Austin N. *retired insurance company executive*
Wahweah, Linda McNeil *insurance agent, writer*
Weber, John Walter *insurance company executive*
Wentz, Sidney Frederick *insurance company executive, foundation administrator*
Whiteley, Benjamin Robert *retired insurance company executive*
Wills, William Ridley, II, *retired insurance company executive, historian*
Young, Dona Davis Gagliano *insurance company executive, lawyer*
Zebroski, Edwin Leopold *risk management consultant*
Zupsic, Matthew Michael *insurance company executive*

FINANCE: INVESTMENT SERVICES

UNITED STATES

ALABAMA

Birmingham
Comer, Donald III *investment company executive*
Tucker, Thomas James *retired investment company executive*

Montgomery
Blount, Winton Malcolm III *investment executive*

ALASKA

Anchorage
Hickel, Walter Joseph *investment company executive, government agency administrator*
Jay, Christopher Edward *stockbroker*

ARIZONA

Phoenix
Binns, James Hazlett, Jr. *entrepreneur*
Franke, William Augustus *investor*
Stern, Richard David *investment company executive*
Taylor, Elizabeth Jane *investment advisor, real estate company executive, marketing executive*

Scottsdale
Doede, John Henry *investment company executive*
Gentry, Warren Miller *investment company executive*
Getz, Bert Atwater *investment company executive*
Parsons, Bob (Robert R. Parsons) *entrepreneur, domain register and web host company executive*
Wu, Eric *entrepreneur*

Tucson
Lomicka, William Henry *investor*
Schannep, John Dwight *brokerage house executive*

ARKANSAS

Little Rock
Good, Mary Lowe *investment company executive, educator*
Light, Jo Knight *stockbroker*
Whiteside, Charles B. III *investment company executive*

CALIFORNIA

Antioch
Archuleta, Keith Anthony *entrepreneur, business and management consultant*

Atherton
Sollman, George Henry *venture capitalist*

Belvedere Tiburon
Rayner, Arno Alfred *investment company executive, consultant*

Berkeley
Blume, James Beryl *investment advisor*

Beverly Hills
Covitz, Carl D. *investment company executive, federal and state official*
Eisner, Michael Dammann *investment and former entertainment company executive*
Evans, Louise *investor, retired psychologist*
Gordy, Berry *entrepreneur, film producer, recording industry executive*
Gores, Tom T. *investment company executive*
Kerkorian, Kirk *investor, former motion picture company executive, consultant*
Matise, John J. *investment company executive*
Seidel, Joan Broude *securities dealer, investment advisor*
Sigler, Mary Ann *investment company executive, accountant*

Camarillo
Sullivan, Michael Evan *investment company executive*

Carmel
Hamilton, Beverly Lannquist *investment executive*

Chino Hills
Ofner, William Bernard *investor, lawyer*

Coronado
Smith, Albert Cromwell, Jr. *investment company executive, writer*

Costa Mesa
Kiang, Assumpta (Amy Kiang) *brokerage house executive*

Fremont
Grant, Alan J. *business executive, educator*

Fresno
Dauer, Donald Dean *investment company executive*

Gardena
Kelly, Sean *entrepreneur*

Irvine
Jones, Joie Pierce *entrepreneur, acoustician, writer, educator*
Le Bon, Douglas Kent *investment manager*

La Jolla
Stone, Donald Diamond *investment and sales executive*

Los Altos
Carsten, Jack Craig *venture capitalist*

Los Angeles
Angeloff, Dann Valentino *brokerage house executive*
Barrack, Thomas J., Jr. *real estate investor, lawyer*
Bernstein, Arthur Harold *venture capital executive*
Binder, Gordon M. *venture capitalist*
Brown, Jim *investment company executive*
Gores, Alec E. *venture capitalist*
Holly, Krisztina J. *entrepreneur, academic administrator*
Johnson, Jeffrey M. *private equity company executive, former publishing executive*
Larkin, Thomas Ernest, Jr. *investment management company executive*
Nogales, Luis Guerrero *investment company executive*
Saban, Haim *investment company executive, television producer*
Trumbull, Stephen Michael *entrepreneur, musician*

Menlo Park
Davies, Paul Lewis III *venture capitalist*
Doerr, (L.) John *venture capitalist*
Fenton, Noel John *venture capitalist*
Goldstein, Jon *investment advisor*
Joy, Bill (William Nelson Joy) *venture capitalist, former computer software company executive*
Khosla, Vinod *investment company executive*
Kramlich, C(harles) Richard (Dick) *venture capitalist*
Lucas, Donald Leo *investor*
Lynch, Charles Allen *investment company executive, director*
Marquardt, David F. *venture capitalist*
Moritz, Michael J. *venture capitalist*
Perkins, Tom (Thomas James Perkins) *venture capital company executive*
Wolfson, Mark Alan *investor, educator, dean*

Mount Hamilton
Guggenheim, Alan Andre Albert Paul Edouard *international consultant*

Newport Beach
Thorp, Edward Oakley *investment management company executive*

North Hills
Iacocca, Lee (Lido Anthony) *venture capitalist, retired automotive executive*

Oakland
Al Malik, Amir Isa *entrepreneur, consultant, musician*

Orange
Tuggle, Francis Douglas *entrepreneur, consultant, management educator, scientist*

Palo Alto
Breyer, James William *venture capitalist*
Kawasaki, Guy *venture capitalist, investment banker, evangelist, entrepreneur, blog writer, writer*

Palos Verdes Estates
Mennis, Edmund Addi *investment management consultant*

Pasadena
Arnott, Robert Douglas *investment company executive*
Fredericks, Ward Arthur *venture capitalist*

Pinedale
Falcone, Patricia Jeanne Lalim *investor, foundation administrator*

Roseville
Grant, Barbara *venture capitalist*

Sacramento
Ailman, Christopher J. *investment company executive*

San Diego
Batchelder, David H. *investment advisory firm executive*
Brandes, Charles H. *investment company executive*
Dunn, David Joseph *investment company executive*
Wadlington, W. M. *retired commodity futures trader, financial engineer*

San Francisco
Bettinger, Walter W., II, *investment company executive*
Buckner, John Knowles *investor*
Casnocha, Benedict T. *entrepreneur*
Dachs, Alan Mark *investment company executive*
Draper, William Henry III *venture capitalist*
Hagenbuch, John Jacob *investor*
Halliday, John Meech *investment company executive*
Hellman, F(rederick) Warren *investor*
Levine, Alison *entrepreneur, leadership development consultant, adventurer*
Mahoney, Michael James *investment company executive*
Marduel, Alix *venture capitalist*
Martinetto, Joseph R. *investment company executive*
McDonald, Mary Ann Melody *investment management executive*
Pfau, George Harold, Jr. *investment advisor*
Philipp, Peter Eric *investment company executive, educator*
Pottruck, David Steven *venture capitalist*
Redo, David Lucien *investment company executive*
Rock, Arthur *venture capitalist*
Rosenstein, Barry *investment company executive*
Rowen, Harvey Allen *investment company executive*
Schioldager, Amy Lee *investment company executive*
Schwab, Charles R. *investment company executive*
Shansby, John Gary *investor*
Steyer, Thomas Fahr *investment company executive*
Thiel, Peter A. *investment company executive*
Weisel, Thomas W. *investment company executive*
Winblad, Ann *investment company executive*

San Mateo
Jamieson, Edward B. *investment company executive*
Krikorian, Blake *entrepreneur, consumer electronics company executive*

Santa Ana
Martinez, Rueben *entrepreneur*

Santa Barbara
Bartlett, James Lowell III *investment company executive*
Emmeluth, Bruce Palmer *investment company executive, venture capitalist*
Lovelace, Jon (Jonathan Bell Lovelace) *investment management company executive*
Vos, Hubert Daniel *investor*

Santa Clara
Dave, Tushar A. *Indo-US venture capital company executive*
Dham, Vinod K. *Indo-US venture capitalist company executive*

Santa Monica
Calacanis, Jason McCabe *internet entrepreneur, blogger*
Lederman, Bruce Randolph *investment company executive, retired lawyer*
Shahani, Sudhin *entrepreneur, Internet company executive*
Tennenbaum, Michael Ernest *investor*
Unterman, Thomas *venture capitalist, lawyer*

Sausalito
Apatoff, Michael John *entrepreneur*

Simi Valley
Sproles, Kevin *entrepreneur, Internet company executive*

Solana Beach
Ellsworth, Robert Fred *investment executive, former government official*

Studio City
Setlin, Alan John *entrepreneur*

Sunnyvale
Rubin, Gary Andrew *entrepreneur, computer engineer*

Tarzana
Lauter, James Donald *retired stockbroker*
Neece, Olivia Helene Ernst *investment company executive, consultant*

Thousand Oaks
Gregory, Calvin *real estate investor*

Torrance
Enright, Stephanie Veselich *investment company executive, financial consultant*

Walnut Creek
Swaney, Thomas Robbins *venture capitalist*

Woodland Hills
Feiman, Thomas E. *investment company executive*

Woodside
Fisher, Kenneth Lawrence *investment management firm executive*

COLORADO

Arvada
Weitzel, Ginger M. *entrepreneur, critical care nurse*

Aurora
Ton, Paul *investor, educator*

Boulder
Mehalchin, John Joseph *entrepreneur, finance company executive*

Cherry Hills Village
Van Loucks, Mark Louis *venture capitalist, financial planner*

Denver
Black, Gary D. *investment company executive*
Case, Steve (Stephen M.) *healthcare investment company executive, former media and entertainment company executive*
Eppler, Jerome Cannon *investment advisor*
Gampel, Elaine Susan *investment company executive, consultant*
Scheid, Steven L. *investment company executive*
Wagner, Judith Buck *investment firm executive*

Evergreen
Jackson, William Richard *entrepreneur*

Grand Junction
Skogen, Haven Sherman *investment company executive*

Greenwood Village
Jaegers, Donna Marie *securities analyst*

Littleton
Lode, Trygve Tennyson *entrepreneur, actor*

CONNECTICUT

Darien
Koontz, Carl Lennis, II, *retired investment counselor*

Essex
Galiette, Brad W. *entrepreneur*

Fairfield
Gad, Lance Stewart *investment advisor, lawyer, private investor*

Greenwich
Applegarth, Paul Vollmer *investment and development executive*
Asness, Clifford S. *investment company executive*
Duff, Philip *investment company executive*
Ford, William E. *investment company executive*
Ganek, David Kent *investor*
Hanson, Janet Tiebout *investment company executive*
Jones, Paul Tudor, II, *investment executive*
Lampert, Edward S. (Eddie Lampert) *investment company executive*
Mandel, Stephen, Jr. *investment company executive*
Owens, Bill (William Forrester Owens) *investment company executive, former governor*
Schneider, John Arnold *investor*
Tournillon, Nicholas Brady *investment company executive*
Winkler, Charles Howard *investment company executive*

Hartford
Marra, Thomas M. *investment company executive*

Litchfield
Booth, John Thomas *private investor*
Sherva, Dennis G. *retired investment company executive*

New Canaan
Bisbee, Gerald Elftman, Jr. *investment company executive*
Grace, Julianne Alice *retired investment company executive*
Pike, William Edward *retired investment company executive*
Stadther, Michael Jon *entrepreneur, writer, publisher*

Norwalk
Hathaway, Carl Emil *investment company executive*

Sharon
Learsy, Raymond J. *private investor*

Simsbury
Borges, Francisco Lopes *venture capitalist*

South Kent
Keehner, Michael Arthur Miller *investment banking executive*

Southport
Wilbur, E. Packer *investment company executive*

Stamford
Cohen, Steven A. *investment company executive*
Hawley, Frank Jordan, Jr. *venture capital executive*
La Penta, Robert Vincent *venture capitalist*

Westport
Dalio, Raymond T. *investment company executive*
Lust, Herbert Cohnfeldt III *securities trader*
O'Keefe, John David *brokerage house executive*
Rudd, Nicholas *investor, consultant*
Samberg, Arthur J. (Art Samberg) *investment company executive*
Stewart, Martha Kostyra *entrepreneur, lecturer, author*
Walton, Alan George *venture capitalist*

DELAWARE

Millsboro
Lasher, Hiram Nelson *entrepreneur, consultant*

Wilmington
Kalil, James, Sr. *investment executive*
Lee, James Harold *investment company executive*

DISTRICT OF COLUMBIA

Washington
Ansary, Cyrus A. *investment company executive, lawyer*
Burris, Howard L. *investment company executive*
Coreth, Joseph Herman *investment advisor*
D'Aniello, Daniel A. *investment company executive*
Darman, Richard *investor, former federal official*
Fisher, Robert Dale *stockbroker, retired naval officer*
Furash, Edward Elliott *investment company executive, banker, educator, writer, theater producer*
Gilburne, Miles R. *venture capitalist*
Hartwell, Stephen *investment company executive*
Johnson, Sheila Crump *entrepreneur*
Kent, Jill Elspeth *entrepreneur, art appraiser, lawyer*
Klein, Michael Roger *investor, foundation administrator*
McCaul, Elizabeth *investment advisor, former state agency administrator*
Mosbacher, Robert A. *investment company executive*
Nordlinger, Gerson *investor*
Powell, Michael Kevin *investment company executive, former federal official*
Rubenstein, David M. *investment company executive*
Selin, Ivan *entrepreneur*
Shrier, Adam Louis *investment company executive, consultant*
Simon, John A. *investment company executive*
Tanous, Peter Joseph *investment advisor*
Wheeler, Thomas Edgar *private equity executive*

FLORIDA

Alva
Darlow, George Anthony Gratton *investor*

Boca Raton
Barbarosh, Milton Harvey *merchant banking executive*
Hampton, Benjamin Bertram *brokerage house executive*
Young, David L. *entrepreneur, retail executive*

Boynton Beach
Allison, Dwight Leonard, Jr. *investor*

Coral Gables
Nunez-Portuondo, Ricardo *investment company executive*
Steinberg, Alan Wolfe *investment company executive*

Fort Lauderdale
Berrard, Steven R. *investment company and former automotive retail company executive*
Huizenga, H. Wayne *entrepreneur, professional sports team executive*
Vladem, Paul Jay *investment advisor*

Fort Myers
Pouliot, Assunta Gallucci *retired business school owner, director, consultant*

Gainesville
Oliver, Robert Bruce *retired investment company executive*

Hobe Sound
Parker, H. Lawrence *retired investor, rancher, investment banker*

Jacksonville
Monsky, John Bertrand *investment company executive*
Schultz, Frederick Henry *investor, former government official*
Videla, Fabian *investment company executive, consultant*

Lake Placid
Viater, John Ronald *investment company executive*

Marco Island
Pettersen, Kjell Will *securities trader, consultant*
Truesdell, Timothy L. *private investor*

Miami
Arison, Shari *investment company executive*
Batcheller, Joe Ann *entrepreneur*
Dorion, Robert Charles *entrepreneur, investor*

Naples
Frantzen, Henry Arthur *retired investment company executive*

North Palm Beach
Dreyfoos, Alexander W., Jr. *investor, research scientist*

Palm Beach
Bagby, Joseph Rigsby *financial investor*
Johnson, Theodore Mebane *brokerage house executive*
McCarter, Thomas Nesbitt III *investment company executive, consultant*

Palm Beach Gardens
Kleinberg, Lawrence H. *investor, consultant*
Mergler, H. Kent *investment counselor*

Palm Harbor
Schultz, Barbara Marie *investment advisor*

Pompano Beach
Grossman, Daniel V *investor*
Rifenburgh, Richard Philip *investment company executive*

Port Saint Lucie
Olson, Edward Charles *entrepreneur, conservationist, foundation administrator, consultant, ecologist, writer*

Punta Gorda
Presley, Brian *investment company executive*

Saint Petersburg
Emerson, William Allen *retired investment company executive*
James, Thomas A. *investment company executive*
Nichols, Katie *investment company executive*
Short, James F. *investment company executive*

Sarasota
Balliett, John William *entrepreneur, real estate company executive*

Tampa
Hanford, Agnes Rutledge *retired investment advisor*
Sigety, Charles Birge *investment company executive*

Tierra Verde
Gaffney, Thomas Francis *private investor*

Vero Beach
Bewkes, Eugene Garrett, Jr. *investment company executive, consultant*
Bigler, Harold Edwin, Jr. *retired investment company executive*

Village Of Golf
Birle, James Robb *investor*

West Palm Beach
Kulok, William Allan *entrepreneur, venture capitalist*

GEORGIA

Atlanta
Bowen, Harold J. (Jay) III *investment company executive*
Green, Holcombe Tucker, Jr. *investment company executive*
Jackson, Geraldine *entrepreneur*
Keough, Donald Raymond *investment and former beverage company executive*
McMahon, Donald Aylward *investor, corporate director*
Merkel-Moran, Christa Ilse *investor, linguist, educator*
Mitchell, Stephen Milton *investment company executive*
Sprecher, Jeffrey C. *commodities exchange executive*
Wheeler, Chris D. *investment company executive*

Austell
Orr, Zellie *entrepreneur, educator, writer, researcher*

Cumming
Drew, Paul S. *entrepreneur*

Lagrange
Callaway, Mark Clayton *investment company executive*

Saint Simons Island
Turbidy, John Berry *investor, management consultant*

HAWAII

Hilo
Dinges, Richard Allen *entrepreneur*

Honolulu
Haight, Warren Gazzam *investor*
Lee, Lorrin L. *internet marketing entrepreneur, architect, writer*

ILLINOIS

Chicago
Amboian, John Peter, Jr. *investment company executive*
Baldwin, Shawn D. *investment company executive*
Bergonia, Raymond David *venture capitalist*
Block, Philip Dee III *retired investment company executive*
Brodsky, William J. *investment company executive*
Carey, Charles P. *mercantile exchange executive*
Case, Donni Marie *investment company executive*
Chaleff, Carl Thomas *investment company executive*
Claeys, Jerome Joseph III *investment company executive*
Cloonan, James Brian *investment company executive*
Cressey, Bryan Charles *venture capitalist*
Crown, James Schine *investment company executive*
Dan, Bernard W. *former commodities exchange executive*
Desmond, Bevin *investment research company executive*
Donohue, Craig S. *mercantile exchange executive*
Duffy, Terrence A. *mercantile exchange executive*
Fagan, Shawn Francis *investment company executive*
Fossett, Steven (J. Steven Fossett) *retired investor, adventurer*
Gardner, Chris(topher) *securities trader, entrepreneur*
Gill, Phupinder *mercantile exchange executive*
Goldstein, William A. *investment counsel*
Gorchow, Bruce D. *investment company executive*
Gordon, James A. *investment company executive*
Griffin, Kenneth C. *investment company executive*
Herron, David A. *stock exchange executive*
Hickey, Jerome Edward *investment company executive*
Hobson, Mellody *investment company executive*
Kelly, Arthur Lloyd *investment company executive*
Kerr, Michael H. *stock exchange executive, lawyer*
Krause, James R. *mercantile exchange executive*
Leszinske, William O. *investment company executive*
Manske, Susan E. *investment advisor*
Marcovici, Michael *investment company executive*
Miner, Thomas Hawley *entrepreneur*
Oliver, Harry Maynard, Jr. *retired brokerage house executive*
Osborn, William A. *investment company executive*
Pritzker, Penny *investor*
Rizzello, Joseph Samuel *stock exchange executive*
Rogers, John W., Jr. *investment company executive*
Ross, Robin S. *investment company executive*
Schwertfeger, Timothy R. *investment company executive*
Slansky, Jerry William *investment company executive*
Stearns, Neele Edward, Jr. *investment company executive*
Underwood, Robert Leigh *venture capitalist*
Vroman, Kendal *investment company executive*
Wasendorf, Russell R., Sr. *brokerage house executive*
Weinberg, David B. *investor*
Weiner, Gerald Arne *stockbroker*
Whitney, Kent R.E. *securities trader*
Wilhelm, David C. *investment company executive*
Williams, Frederick Tyrone *entrepreneur, pastor*
Wilmouth, Robert K. *commodities trader*

Deerfield
Howell, George Bedell *investment company executive*

Highland Park
Uhlmann, Frederick Godfrey *securities trader*

Itasca
Balasa, Mark Edward *investment consultant*

Lake Forest
Young, Ronald Faris *commodities trader*

Naperville
Calamos, John Peter, Sr. *brokerage house executive*
Penisten, Gary Dean *entrepreneur*
Vanagas, Rimantas (Ray) Andrius (Ray Vanagas) *entrepreneur, real estate developer, real estate company executive*

Northbrook
Colburn, David Dunton *investment advisor*
Edelson, Ira J. *venture capitalist*

Oak Brook
Peckenpaugh, Robert Earl *investment advisor*
Spohr, Earl Clyde *retired investment advisor, military officer*

Oakbrook Terrace
Tang, George Chickchee *investment company executive*

Park Ridge
Albert, Elizabeth Franz (Mrs. Henry B. Albert) *investor, artist, conservationist*

River Forest
Wirsching, Charles Philipp, Jr. *retired brokerage house executive, securities trader*

Vernon Hills
Krasny, Michael P. *investment company executive*

Westmont
Warner, H. Ty *entrepreneur, manufacturing executive*

Willow Springs
Jashel, Larry Steven (L. Steven Rose) *entrepreneur, media consultant*

Wilmette
Albright, Townsend Shaul *brokerage house executive, consultant*

INDIANA

Bloomington
Kuratko, Donald F. *entrepreneurial educator, consultant*

Carmel
Walsh, John Charles *investment company executive, director*

Evansville
Brill, Alan Richard *entrepreneur*

Indianapolis
Sheehan, Kevin Edward *venture capitalist*

IOWA

Bettendorf
Rathje, James Lee *broker*

Des Moines
Pappajohn, John G. *venture capitalist*

KANSAS

Sharon Springs
Picknick, Kevin M. *commodities trader*

Shawnee Mission
Braude, Michael *commodities trader, researcher*

Topeka
Hedrick, Lois Jean *investment company executive, state official*

KENTUCKY

Louisville
Saunders, Robert Samuel *venture capitalist*

Murray
Boston, Betty Lee *investment company executive, financial planner, consultant*

LOUISIANA

Monroe
Hawley, Jeffrey Lance *investments executive, accountant*

New Orleans
Dahlberg, Carl Fredrick, Jr. *entrepreneur*
Doley, Harold Emanuel, Jr. *securities company executive*

MAINE

Bryant Pond
Conary, David Arlan *investment company executive*

MARYLAND

Ashton
Zehner, Lee Randall *entrepreneur, chemist*

Baltimore
Bowman, Donald Eugene *investment advisor*
Brown, Eddie C. *investment company executive*
Collins, Marquis Tyrone *investment company executive*
Curley, John Francis, Jr. *mutual fund executive*
Egan, Cynthia L. *investment company executive*
Himelfarb, Richard Jay *investment company executive*
Hopkins, Henry Holt *mutual fund attorney*
Kennedy, James Aloysius Charles *investment company executive*

Bethesda
Allmon, Charles W. *investment advisor*
Koonce, Calvin Scott *brokerage firm executive, physicist*
Meakem, Carolyn Soliday *investment executive, financial planner, money manager, consultant*

Bowie
Gourdine-Tyson, Natachia *investment company executive, writer*

Chevy Chase
Goldsmith, Stephen *investment company executive, former mayor*

Lutherville
Aitken, Christopher Charles *investment consultant*

Lutherville Timonium
Cappiello, Frank Anthony, Jr. *investment advisor*

Rockville
Jacques, Joseph William *investment advisor*

MASSACHUSETTS

Acton
Boghani, Ashok Balvantrai *entrepreneur, management consultant*

Ashland
Morrison, Gordon Mackay, Jr. *retired investment company executive*

Belmont
Lloyd, Boardman *investment company executive*

Boston
Antonellis, Joseph C. *investment company executive*
Bekenstein, Joshua *venture capital company executive*
Bennett, George Frederick *retired investment company executive*
Berstein, Robert L. *investment company executive*
Bressler, Richard J. *investment company and former entertainment company executive*
Carey, John Andrew *investment company executive*
Curran, Michael J. *stock exchange executive*
de Burlo, Comegys Russell, Jr. *investment company executive, educator, retired treasurer*
Eckstein, Jens W. *venture capitalist, biotechnologist*
El-Erian, Mohamed A. *investment manager*
Estin, Hans Howard *retired investment company executive*
Gozonsky, Edwin O. O. *investment broker*
Haldeman, Ed (Charles Edgar Haldeman Jr.) *investment company executive*
Hobbs, Gerald S. (Jerry) *private equity firm executive*
Hooley, Joseph (Jay) L. *investment company executive*
Hunt, William W. *investment company executive*
Johnson, Abigail Pierrepont *investment company executive*
Johnson, Edward Crosby, III, (Ned Johnson) *investment company executive*
Lange, Harry W. *investment company executive*
Lee, David Stoddart *retired investment company executive*
Logue, Ronald E. *investment company executive*
Nunnelly, Mark Edward *investor*
Oates, William Armstrong, Jr. *investment company executive*
Peckham, John Munroe III *investment executive, author, lecturer*
Pozen, Robert Charles *investment company executive*
Price, Steven *venture capitalist, communications executive, lawyer*
Resch, Edward J. *investment company executive*
Voss, Peter S. *investment company executive*
Waite, Charles Prescott *entrepreneur*
Watkins, Leroy J. III *entrepreneur*

Cambridge
Alexander, Seth *investment company executive*
Anquetil, Patrick Armand *investment company executive, researcher*
Goldberg, Marc Evan *healthcare venture capitalist*
Leiden, Jeffrey Marc *venture capitalist, molecular biologist, cardiologist*
Sahagun, Aaron *entrepreneur, Internet company executive*
Sahagun, Allan *entrepreneur, Internet company executive*

Carlisle
Fohl, Timothy *investment company executive*

Concord
Schiller, Pieter Jon *retired venture capital executive*
Wickfield, Eric Nelson *investment company executive*

Lincoln
Holberton, Philip Vaughan *entrepreneur, educator*

Manchester
Porter, Henry Homes, Jr. *investor*

Medford
Goldberg, Pamela Winer *entrepreneur, educator*

Newton
Saffran, Kalman *entrepreneur, venture capitalist*

Orleans
Baird, Julian Thompson, Jr. *entrepreneur*

Pepperell
Holmes, Jean Louise *real estate investor, humanities educator*

Siasconset
Albani, Thomas J. *investor*

Southborough
Chryssis, George Christopher *entrepreneur*

Stockbridge
Fitzpatrick, Jane *entrepreneur*

Taunton
Ricciardi, Louis Michael *brokerage house executive*

Waltham
Cox, Howard Ellis, Jr. *venture capitalist*
Hooper, Marcia Jacobs *venture capitalist, former communications executive*
Metcalfe, Robert M. *venture capitalist, former science engineer, publishing executive, writer*

Wellesley
Tierney, Thomas J. *social entrepreneur*

West Roxbury
Lovell, Francis Joseph *retired investment company executive*

Weston
Alcock, George Lewis, Jr., (Peter) *investor, business strategist*

MICHIGAN

Ann Arbor
Weiser, Marc *venture capitalist*

Birmingham
Kothari, Rajesh Ujamlal *investment company executive*

Detroit
Blaszkiewicz, David *investment company executive*

Farmington Hills
Ellmann, Sheila Frenkel *investment company executive*

Flint
Acuff, A. Marshall, Jr. *retired investment company executive*

Livonia
Katzman, David *investment company and professional sports team executive*

Madison Heights
Janke, Kenneth *investment consultant*

Northville
Dempsey, Donald Chandler *stockbroker, financial planner*

Southfield
Prokop, Kevin *investment company executive*

Trenton
Tang, Cyrus *investment company executive*

West Bloomfield
Mamut, Mary Catherine *retired entrepreneur*

MINNESOTA

Excelsior
Fazio, Anthony Lee *investment company executive*

Minneapolis
Bagan, Mark G. *grain exchange executive*
Dale, John Sorensen *investment company executive, portfolio manager*
Fauth, John J. *venture capitalist*
Gallagher, Gerald Raphael *venture capitalist*
Piper, Addison Lewis *securities executive*

Minnetonka
Anderson, David Wayne *entrepreneur, former federal agency administrator*
Bean, Glen Atherton *entrepreneur*
Pillsbury, George Sturgis *retired investment advisor*

Saint Paul
Rodriguez, Roberto Miguel *investment company executive*
Rothmeier, Steven George *investment company executive*

Stillwater
Horsch, Lawrence Leonard *venture capitalist, corporate financial executive*

Waubun
Christensen, Marvin Nelson *venture capitalist*

Wayzata
Wyard, Vicki Shaw *investment and insurance company executive*

MISSOURI

Kansas City
Morgison, F. Edward *investment broker*
Stowers, James Evans, Jr. *investment company executive*

Lees Summit
Korschot, Benjamin Calvin *retired investment company executive*

Saint Louis
Anagnostopoulos, Constantine Emmanuel *venture capitalist, former company executive*
Bagby, Robert L. *investment company executive*
Bickel, Floyd Gilbert III *investment counselor*
Keffler, Karl Joseph *investment company executive, lawyer*
Sigmund, Greg S. *investment company executive*
Skrainka, Alan Frederick *securities analyst*

MONTANA

Polson
Marchi, Jon *retired brokerage house executive, rancher, venture capitalist*

NEBRASKA

Omaha
Buffett, Warren Edward *entrepreneur, investment company executive*
Carson, Ron *investment company executive*
Cross, Walter Thomas *investment company executive*
De Santiago, Dena Kalene *investment company executive, writer*
Hamburg, Marc D. *investment company executive*
Moglia, Joseph H. *brokerage house executive*
Ricketts, John Joe *securities company executive*
Tomczyk, Fredric J. *brokerage house executive*
Winter, Jimmy *entrepreneur, systems administrator*

NEVADA

Boulder City
Stephenson, Arthur Emmet, Jr. *investment company executive*

Carson City
Alexander, Judy Lynne *investor*

Las Vegas
Kasama, Hideto Peter *international business and investment advisor*

Reno
Harsh, Antoinette Mollett *investor*

Sparks
Holder, Harold Douglas, Sr. *investor, hotel executive*

NEW HAMPSHIRE

Derry
Sapareto, Frank Vincent, II, *investment advisor, state legislator*

Dover
Parks, Joe Benjamin *entrepreneur, retired state legislator*

NEW JERSEY

Avenel
Berg, Louis Leslie *investment executive*

Basking Ridge
Tamarelli, Alan Wayne *venture capitalist*

Brookside
Fairchild, Samuel Wilson *investor, retired federal agency administrator, financial services executive*

Chatham
Tepper, David Alan *hedge fund manager*

Clinton
Isaacman, Jared *entrepreneur*

Cresskill
Uehling, Gordon Alexander, Jr. *investment company executive*

East Brunswick
Hurst, Gregory Squire *investment company executive, theater director and producer*

Englewood
Kramer, Orin Stuart *investment services company executive*

Fair Lawn
Melen, Alex *entrepreneur, Internet company executive*

Fort Lee
Lippman, William Jennings *investment company executive*

Hackensack
Feldman, Vitaly *entrepreneur*
Heilborn, George Heinz *investor*
Koretsky, Alexander *entrepreneur*

Lincoln Park
Sichuk, George *entrepreneur, writer, biochemist, physiologist*

Little Falls
Shern, Stephanie Marie *investment company executive, accountant*

Mendham
Kirby, Allan Price, Jr. *investment company executive*
Pierson, Robert David *investor*

Montclair
Jones, Sylvia Calpurnia *investment company executive*

Morristown
Kirby, Jefferson W. *investment company executive*

New Brunswick
Mills, Dorothy Allen *investor*

Newark
Pinkett, Randal D. *entrepreneur*

Park Ridge
Giovannoli, Joseph Louis *entrepreneur, lawyer*

Pennington
Madison, T. Jerome *business executive*

Princeton
Chamberlin, John Stephen *investor, consumer products company executive*
Doll, Robert C. *investment company executive*
Fernholz, Erhard Robert *investment executive*
Gund, Gordon *venture capitalist, investment company executive*
Johnston, Robert Fowler *venture capitalist*
Treu, Jesse Isaiah *venture capitalist*

Red Bank
Hertz, Daniel Leroy, Jr. *entrepreneur*

Rumson
Strong, George Hotham *private investor, consultant*

Short Hills
Howe, James Everett *investment company executive*

Skillman
Tenenbaum, Bernard Hirsh *entrepreneur, educator*

Totowa
Tuthill, Jay Dean, II, *investment executive*

Upper Saddle River
Oolie, Sam *manufacturing and investment company executive*

Watchung
Cox, Archibald, Jr. *investor*

NEW MEXICO

Albuquerque
Green, Francis William *investment consultant, former missile scientist*

NEW YORK

Armonk
Gerstner, Louis Vincent, Jr. *investment company and retired information technology executive*

Babylon
Brackett, Ronald E. *investment company executive, lawyer*

Bay Shore
Williams, Tonda *entrepreneur, consultant*

Bedford Corners
Singer, Craig *entrepreneur, inventor, executive, investor, consultant*

Binghamton
Taylor, Kenneth Douglas *stockbroker, finance and computer consultant, educator*

Blue Point
Owen, Thomas Llewellyn *investment company executive*

Brooklyn
Ross, Randolph Ernest *investor*
Slack, Ryan *entrepreneur*

Buffalo
Irwin, Robert James Armstrong *investment company executive*
Littlewood, Douglas Burden *brokerage house executive*

Glens Falls
Pearsall, Glenn Lincoln *brokerage house executive*

Great Neck
Appel, Gerald *investment advisor*

Harrison
Crawford, R. George *investment company executive, educator, filmmaker*

Hempstead
Sodano, Salvatore F. *former stock exchange executive*

Ithaca
Hojnowski, Jules Austin *entrepreneur*
Merle, H. Etienne *broker, director, restaurateur*

Lynbrook
Wong, Edward Vincent *investment company executive*

Manhasset
Calvin, Donald Lee *stock exchange official*
Gardner, Robert *financial services executive*

Maspeth
Blitz, Nelson, Jr. *entrepreneur*

Massapequa
Pettersen, Kevin Will *investment company executive*

Mount Kisco
Kohlberg, James A. *venture capitalist*
Kohlberg, Jerome, Jr., (Jerry Kohlberg) *venture capitalist, lawyer*

New Hyde Park
Richards, Bernard *investment company executive*

New York
Acampora, Ralph Joseph *brokerage firm executive*
Ackman, William Albert *investment company executive*
Allen, Herbert Anthony, Jr. *investment company executive*
Allison, Herbert Monroe, Jr. *investment company executive*
Alliton, Vaughn *brokerage executive*
Andersen, K(ent) Tucker *investment executive*
Anderson, Fred D. *investment company executive, retired computer company executive*
Applegate, Jeffrey M. *investment company executive*
Aronson, Edgar David *venture capitalist*
Attwood, James Albert, Jr. *investment company executive*
Baha, Christian J. *investment company executive*
Bailey, Jerome H. (Jerry Bailey) *mercantile exchange executive*
Barr, John W. *investment company executive, foundation administrator*
Barry, Thomas Corcoran *investment advisor*
Beinecke, Frederick William *investment company executive*
Bell, Martin Allen *investment company executive*
Bellas, Albert Constantine *investment executive*
Bendelac, Roger E. *investment executive, financial consultant*
Benton, Daniel C. *investment company executive*
Berezovsky, Boris Abramovich (Platon Elenin) *entrepreneur*
Birkelund, John Peter *investment company executive*
Blalock, Sherrill *investment advisor*
Blavatnik, Leonard *investment company executive*
Boyd, Michael Alan *investment company executive, lawyer*
Britz Lotti, Diane Edward *investment company executive*
Brody, Alan Jeffrey *investment company executive*
Brown, Ronald *retired stockbroker*
Browning, Candace *investment company executive*
Bruce, Duncan Archibald *investor, writer*
Brunie, Charles Henry *investment manager*
Buckles, Robert Howard *retired investment company executive*
Butte, Amy S. *brokerage house executive*
Cai-Lee, Wendy *entrepreneur*
Carhart, Mark Monroe *investment company executive*
Carter, Marshall Nichols *stock exchange executive*
Castellano, Michael John *investment company executive*
Cecil, Donald *retired investment company executive*
Chai, Nelson J. *stock exchange executive*
Chanos, James S. *investment company executive*
Chapin, Samuel R. *investment company executive*
Chapman, Max C., Jr. *investment company executive*
Chunilal, Damian *investment company executive*
Cohen, Abby Joseph *investment company executive*
Cole, Carolyn Jo *brokerage house executive*
Concannon, Christopher R. *stock exchange executive*
Condron, Christopher M. (Kip) *investment company executive*
Conigliaro, Laura Claire *securities analyst*
Considine, Jill M. *securities trader*
Conway, Richard Francis *investment company executive*
Cooperman, Leon G. *investment company executive*
Cortez, Ricardo Lee *investment management executive*
Curry, Boykin (Ravenel Boykin Curry IV) *investment manager*
Dallen, Russell Morris, Jr. *investment company and publishing company executive, lawyer*
Daniels, Randy A. *investment company executive, former state official*
Darlington, Henry, Jr. *retired investment broker*
Davis, J. Morton *investment company executive, venture capitalist, economist*
Davis, Jordan S. *venture capitalist*
Dehn, James Keith *investment company executive*
Dias Griffin, Anne *investment advisor*
Diker, Charles M. *investment advisor*
Di Palma, Joseph Alphonse *investment company executive, lawyer*
Dorsett, Burt *investment company executive*
Drapkin, Donald G. *venture capitalist*
D'Souza, Rohit *investment company executive*
Edwards, Jeffrey N. *investment company executive*
Effron, Blair Wayne *investment advisor*
Einiger, Carol Blum *investment company executive*
Elliman, Christopher J. (Kim Elliman) *investment company executive*
Ercklentz, Alexander Tonio *investment company executive*
Errico, R. Christopher *investment advisor*
Evnin, Anthony Basil *venture capital investor*
Fahey, James Edward *brokerage house executive*
Fakahany, Ahmass L. *investment company executive*
Feldberg, Meyer *investment advisor, university dean emeritus*
Filimonov, Mikhail Anatolyevitch *investment company executive*
Findakly, Hani K. *investment company executive*
Fiorilla di Santa Croce, John Leopoldo *investment company executive, lawyer*
Fisher, Peter R. *investment company executive, former federal agency administrator*
Fleming, Gregory James *investment company executive*
Flinn, Michael de Vlaming *investment company executive*
Freidheim, Scott J. *investment company executive*
Friedenberg, Daniel Meyer *investor, writer*
Friedman, Robert Laurence *investment company executive*
Fuld, Richard Severin, Jr., (Dick Fuld) *investment banking executive*
Genader, Robert J. *investment company executive*
Gero, Anthony George *securities and commodities trader*
Goelet, Robert G. *investment company executive*
Goldfarb, David *investment banking executive*
Goldman, Neal *entrepreneur, information technology executive*
Golub, Steven J. *investment company executive*
Gottesman, David Sanford *investment company executive*
Gray, Farrah *entrepreneur, writer*
Gray, James L. *investment company executive*
Gregory, Joseph M. *investment company executive*
Greifeld, Robert *stock exchange executive*
Gruss, Martin David *investor*
Gubert, Walter Alexander *investment company executive*
Gutfreund, John Halle *investment company executive, consultant*
Hanau, Kenneth John III *venture capitalist*
Handler, Richard B. *investment company executive*
Hansmann, Ralph Emil *investment executive, director*
Hart, Gurnee Fellows *investment counselor*
Haskell, John Henry Farrell, Jr. *investment company executive*

Hennessee, E. Lee *securities trade executive, financial consultant*
Herman, Darren *entrepreneur, marketing executive*
Herrmann, Lacy Bunnell *investment company executive, entrepreneur, venture capitalist*
Hochman, Richard H. *investment company executive*
Holland, Michael Francis *investment company executive*
Horn, Karen Nicholson *investment company executive, former bank executive*
Hyman, Morton Peter *private equity investment company executive*
Ilacqua, Rosario Salvatore *securities analyst*
James, Marc Stephen *brokerage house executive*
Jamison, Douglas W. *venture capitalist*
Janney, Stuart Symington III *investment company executive*
Janulis, Theodore P. *investment company executive*
Jenrette, Richard Hampton *investment and insurance company executive*
Jepson, Hans Godfrey *investment company executive, director*
Jones, Abbott C. *investment company executive*
Jones, Alan Kent *investment company executive*
Jones, Frank Joseph *securities exchange executive*
Kehoe, John P. *investor relations executive*
Kelly, William Michael *investment company executive*
Kerschner, Edward *brokerage house executive*
Ketchum, Richard G. *stock exchange executive, lawyer*
Kim, Dow *investment company executive*
Kinney, Catherine R. *stock exchange executive*
Kinney, Gilbert Hart *investor*
Klein, Jeffrey Peter *investor*
Kovner, Bruce S. *investment company executive*
Kraemer, Harry M. Jansen, Jr. *investment and former medical products executive*
Kressel, Henry *venture capitalist*
Lackritz, Marc E. *securities industry association executive*
Lamle, Hugh Roy *investment advisor, consultant*
Lamport, Anthony Matthew *venture capitalist*
Lang, Everett Francis, Jr. *brokerage house executive*
Langone, Kenneth G. *investment company executive*
Lasser, Joseph Robert *investment company executive*
Lauder, Ronald Stephen *investor*
Lawrence, Bryan Hunt *investment company executive*
Lawson-Johnston, Peter, II, *investment company executive*
Lebenthal, Alexandra *investment firm executive*
Levitt, Arthur, Jr. *investment company executive, former federal agency administrator*
Lichtenstein, Warren G. *investment company executive*
Lieber, Robert C. *investment company executive*
Lindahl, Sheena *entrepreneur*
Loeb, Daniel Seth *investment company executive*
Loeb, John Langeloth, Jr. *investment counselor, consultant*
Lowitt, Ian T. *investment company executive*
Luke, Douglas Sigler *investment company executive*
Lutnick, Howard William *brokerage house executive*
Lynch, Gary G. *investment company executive, lawyer*
MacAllaster, Archie *investment company executive*
Mager, Ezra Pascal *investment company executive*
Marron, Donald Baird *venture capitalist*
Mayer, William Emilio *investor*
McCann, Robert J. *investment company executive*
McCooey, Robert H., Jr. *brokerage house executive*
McDade, Herbert H. III *investment company executive*
McDonald, James S. *investment company executive*
McGee, Hugh E. III *investment company executive*
McNulty, James J. *former mercantile exchange executive*
Meeker, Mary G. *brokerage house executive*
Metz, Emmanuel Michael *investment company executive, lawyer*
Millard, Robert B. *investment company executive*
Miller, Corbin Russell *investment company executive*
Millet, T. Kelley *securities trader*
Mindich, Eric *investment company executive*
Mnuchin, Steven T. *investment company executive*
Moltz, James Edward *brokerage house executive*
Morris, William Charles *investor*
Morse, Robert Parker *investment company executive*
Murphy, John Vincent *investment company executive*
Murray, Eileen K. *investment company executive*
Nabi, Stanley Andrew *brokerage house executive*
Nazem, Fereydoun F. *venture capitalist, entrepreneur*
Newsome, James E. *mercantile exchange executive*
Niederauer, Duncan L. *stock exchange executive*
Niemiec, David Wallace *investment company executive*
Noris, Peter Dana *investment company executive*
Novogratz, Michael E. *investment company executive*
Offit, Morris Wolf *investment company executive*
Olinger, Chauncey Greene, Jr. *investment company executive, editorial consultant*
O'Meara, Christopher M. *investment company executive*
O'Neal, E. Stanley (Stanley O'Neal) *investment company executive*
Pappas, Milton J. *venture capitalist*
Patricof, Alan Joel *investment company executive*
Paul, Andrew Mitchell *investment advisor*
Peltz, Nelson A. *investment company executive*
Peterson, Peter George *investment company executive*
Petno, Douglas B. *investment company executive*
Pittman, Robert Warren *investor*
Pollack, Stephen J. *investment company executive, stockbroker*
Pouschine, John Laurence *private equity investment executive*
Proctor, Georganne C. *investment company executive*
Putnam, Jerry (Gerald D. Putnam) *stock exchange executive*
Quick, Peter *stock exchange executive*
Quirk, John James *investment company executive*
Rand, Lawrence Anthony *investor, finance company executive*
Richardson, Frank Elmer III *investor*
Robbins, Rachel F. *stock exchange executive, lawyer*
Robinson, James D. III *venture capitalist*
Rogers, James Beeland, Jr., (Jim Rogers) *retired investment company executive*
Rogers, Theodore Courtney *investment company executive*
Rosenblatt, Lief D. *investment company executive*
Rosenbloom, Daniel *investment advisor, lawyer*
Rosenfeld, Gerald *investment company executive, financial analyst*
Rothschild, Nathaniel Philip (Victor James) *investment company executive*
Salomon, Richard E. *investment company executive*
Sapir, Tamir *entrepreneur*
Saul, Andrew M. *investment company executive*
Schaeffer, Richard *mercantile exchange executive*
Schafer, Oscar S. *investment company executive*
Schick, Harry Leon *investment company executive*
Schiff, Frank *investment company executive*
Scott, William Clement III *investor*
Sender, Adam D. *investment company executive, art collector*
Shapiro, Robert Frank *investment company executive*
Siebert, Muriel (Mickie) *brokerage house executive, retired bank executive*
Simmons, Michael *entrepreneur, publishing executive*
Simpkins, Neil P. *investment and automotive company executive*
Smith, Malcolm Bernard *investment company executive*
Snow, Jack (John William Snow) *investment company executive, former secretary of the treasury*
Solotar, Joan S. *securities analyst*
Sorte, John Follett *investment firm executive*
Stein, David Fred *investment company executive*
Sterling, Robert Lee, Jr. *investment company executive*
Stern, Walter Phillips *investment company executive*
Stewart, E(dward) Nicholson *investment management executive*
Suhler, John Stuart *investor*
Summers, Larry (Lawrence Henry) *investment company executive, political science professor, former academic administrator, former secretary of the treasury*
Tam, Alice Oi-Lai *entrepreneur, director*
Tamke, George William *venture capitalist*
Tananbaum, Steven Andrew *investment consultant*
Tendler, David *investment company executive*
Thain, John A. *stock exchange executive, former diversified financial services company executive*
Thorne, Nathan C. *investment company executive*
Tizzio, Thomas Ralph *brokerage house executive*
Tozer, W. James, Jr. *investment company executive*
Train, John *investment advisor, federal official*
Ule, Guy Maxwell, Jr. *stockbroker*
Viniar, David A. *investment company executive*
von Mueffling, William *investment company executive*
Walker, George H. *investment company executive*
Walker, George Herbert, IV, *investment company executive*
Wareham, Raymond Noble *brokerage house executive*
Wijnberg, Sandra S. *investment company executive*
Williams, Christopher *investment company executive*
Williams, Dave Harrell *investment company executive*
Wolf, Peter Michael *investment manager, consultant, writer*
Wolkoff, Neal L. *stock exchange executive*
Yetman, Gary *investment company executive*
Zeitlin, Jide James *investor*
Zeuschner, Erwin Arnold *brokerage house executive*
Zwickler, Allen *investment advisor, educator*

Purchase
Black, Leon David *private investment company executive*
Wachenheim, Edgar III *investment company executive*

Riverhead
Orben, Jack Richard *investment company executive, director*

Ronkonkoma
Leventhal, Norman B. *entrepreneur*

Roslyn
Landsman, Richard *investment company executive, finance educator*

Rye
Bostock, Roy Jackson *investment company executive*

Sag Harbor
Brody, Eugene David *investment company executive*

Southampton
Culp, Michael Bronston *investor, writer, publisher*

Tuxedo Park
Davis, Shelby Moore Cullom *investment company executive, consultant*

Westbury
Lorber, Howard Mark *investments executive*

White Plains
Gottlieb, Lester M. *entrepreneur*

Woodstock
Ober, Stuart Alan *investment advisor, writer*

NORTH CAROLINA

Chapel Hill
Drutz, David Jules *venture capitalist*

Charlotte
Cameron, Donald John *retired commodities trader*
Cummings, Stephen Emery *investment banking executive*
May, Benjamin Tallman *securities specialist, administrator*
Ragan, Robert Allison *private investment executive, financial consultant*

Greensboro
Johnson, Marshall Hardy *investment company executive*

Murphy
Pezzella, Jerry James, Jr. *investment and real estate company executive*

West End
Krallinger, Joseph Charles *entrepreneur, consultant, writer*

NORTH DAKOTA

Grand Forks
Gjovig, Bruce Quentin *entrepreneur, consultant*

OHIO

Alpha
James, Francis Edward, Jr. *investment advisor*

Bay Village
Hook, John Burney *investment company executive*

Brookfield
Manos, Thomas G. *investment company executive*

Bryan
Oberlin, Earl Clifford III *securities brokerage company executive*

Cincinnati
Anning, Robert Doan Hopkins *brokerage company executive*
Klein, Sophia H. *entrepreneur*
Lucke, Robert Vito *investment company executive*

Cleveland
Brentlinger, Paul Smith *venture capital executive*
Charnas, Michael (Mannie) *investment company executive*
Morgenthaler, David Turner *venture capitalist*
Summers, William B., Jr. *brokerage house executive*

Columbus
Barthelmas, Ned Kelton *brokerage house executive*
Cenname, August *investment advisor*
Shinkel, Bernie (Bernard Albert Shinkel) *investment advisor*

Strongsville
Cameron, David Ronald *entrepreneur, historian, researcher*

Westerville
Barr, John Michael *investor, management consultant*

OKLAHOMA

Bethany
McGowan, Bernard Wayne (Bernie) *venture capitalist, writer*

Lawton
Carraher, Shawn Michael *investment company executive, management educator*

Muskogee
Kang, Heesam *investment analyst, educator*

Stillwater
Fried, Vance Hoyt *entrepreneur, educator*

Tulsa
Neas, John Theodore *investment company executive*

Woodward
Riffel, Loren Darrel *retired entrepreneur*

OREGON

Chiloquin
Reed, David George *entrepreneur*

Medford
Hennion, Carolyn Laird (Lyn) *investment executive*

Portland
Arthur, Michael Elbert *financial advisor, lawyer*
Cohen, Stuart F. *investment company executive*
Coleman, Debi (Deborah Ann) *investment and former computer company executive*
Milton, Catherine Higgs *entrepreneur*
Rutherford, William Drake *investment executive*
Stott, Peter Walter *investment company executive*

PENNSYLVANIA

Berwyn
Hambrecht, William R. *investment banking firm executive*

Blue Bell
Giordano, Nicholas Anthony *brokerage house executive*

Clarks Summit
Janoski, Henry Valentine *investment advisor, former banker*

Lafayette Hill
King, Leon *investment advisor*

Lancaster
Carlisle, James Patton *entrepreneur*

Ligonier
Mellon, Seward Prosser *brokerage house executive*

New Hope
Sergey, John Michael, Jr. *investment company executive, consultant*

Newtown Square
Lewis, James Earl *investor*

Paoli
Denny, William Murdoch, Jr. *investment management executive*

Philadelphia
Frucher, Meyer S. (Sandy Frucher) *stock exchange executive*
Gowa, Andrew *investor, lawyer*
Neff, P(aul) Sherrill *venture capitalist*
Palmer, Russell Eugene *investment company executive, retired dean*
Savitz, Samuel J. *actuarial consulting firm executive*
Spector, Adam B. *investment company executive*
Wilde, Norman Taylor, Jr. *investment banking company executive*
Woosnam, Richard Edward *venture capitalist, lawyer*

Pittsburgh
Bernt, Benno Anthony *entrepreneur, investor*
Donahue, John Francis *investment company executive*
Druckenmiller, Stanley F. *investment company executive*
Hillman, Henry Lea *investment company executive*
Walton, James Mellon *investment company executive*

Radnor
Buck, James Mahlon, Jr. *venture capitalist*
Hemphill, James S. *investment management executive, financial advisor*

Sewickley
Maurer, Richard Michael *investment company executive*

Valley Forge
Bogle, John Clifton *investment company executive*
Brennan, John Joseph *mutual fund company executive*
Combs, Ann Laine *investment company executive, former federal agency administrator*

Villanova
Lewis, Wayne H. *investment company executive*

Wexford
Stover, Richard L. *investor*

Wilkes Barre
Yarmey, Richard Andrew *investment manager*

Williamsport
McDonald, Peyton Dean *brokerage house executive*

York
White, Timothy Paul *brokerage house executive*

RHODE ISLAND

Narragansett
Stark, Dennis Edwin *private investor, retired bank executive*

Providence
Joukowsky, Artemis A. W. *private investor*

Wakefield
Mason, Scott MacGregor *entrepreneur, inventor, consultant*

SOUTH CAROLINA

Columbia
Brockelsby, Jeffrey Lind *investment executive*

Johns Island
Cameron, Thomas William Lane *investment company executive*

Orangeburg
Dalton, Cheryl Renee *entrepreneur*

Sullivans Island
Romaine, Henry Simmons *retired investment company executive, consultant*

TENNESSEE

Nashville
Bradford, James C., Jr. *brokerage house executive*
Byrd, Andrew Wayne *investment company executive*
Hanselman, Richard Wilson *entrepreneur*
Kuhn, Paul Hubert, Jr. *investment advisor*
Nelson, Edward Gage *brokerage house and bank executive, consultant*
Roberts, Kenneth Lewis *investor, lawyer, foundation administrator*

TEXAS

Austin
Baumgartner, Robert *investment company executive, consultant*

Corpus Christi
Hepner, Jon R. *investment company executive*

Corsicana
Dyer, James Mason, Jr. *investment company executive*

Dallas
Bayne, James Elwood *investor*
Brown, Benjamin A. *investment advisor*
Buchholz, Donald Alden *stock brokerage company executive*
Carrozza, Vincent A. *investment company executive*
Crockett, Dodee Frost *brokerage house executive*
Durham, Michael Jonathan *investment professional*
Edmondson, James Howard *investor, former insurance executive*
Lynch, William Wright, Jr. *investment company executive, engineer*
Meyerson, Morton Herbert *investor, real estate company executive*
Muse, John R. *investment company executive*
Owen, Daniel Thomas *entrepreneur, venture capitalist*
Rachofsky, Howard *retired investor, art collector, patron*
Simmons, Harold C. *investment company executive, sugar company executive*
Stoffel, Paul T. *investment company executive*
Tucker, Keith A. *investment company executive*
Watson, Steven L. *investment company executive*
Wyly, Charles Joseph, Jr. *entrepreneur*

Fort Worth
Bass, Sid Richardson *investment company executive*
Bonderman, David *investment company executive, lawyer*

Horseshoe Bay
Anderson, Kenneth Ward *investor, consultant*

Houston
Barrere, Clem Adolph *business brokerage company executive*
Duncan, Charles William, Jr. *investor, retired federal official*
Glassell, Alfred Curry, Jr. *investor*
O'Connor, Ralph Sturges *investment company executive*
Parsons, Edmund Morris *investment company executive*
Richards, Leonard Martin *investment executive, consultant*
Vaughan, Eugene H. *investment company executive*
Wells, Damon *investment company executive*
Williams, Edward Earl, Jr. *entrepreneur, educator*

San Antonio
Terracina, Roy David *entrepreneur*

VERMONT

Middlebury
Pardee, Scott Edward *securities dealer*

Montpelier
Thwaites, Christian William *investment company executive*

Quechee
DeRouchey, Beverly Jean *investment company executive*

VIRGINIA

Alexandria
Boisi, Geoffrey T. *investment company executive*
Rahming, John Christopher *investment company executive, consultant*
Richards, Darrie Hewitt *investment company executive*

Arlington
Choksi, Mary Claire *investment company executive*
Drayton, Bill (William Drayton) *social entrepreneur, lawyer, management consultant*
Muñoz, George *investment company executive, former federal agency administrator*
Scarborough, Robert Henry, Jr. *entrepreneur*

Charlottesville
Gunter, Bradley Hunt *capital management executive*

Dutton
Washburn, John Rosser *entrepreneur*

Fairfax
Edelman, Ric *investment advisor*

Herndon
Burns, Patrick Owen *venture capital company executive*

Middleburg
Parkinson, James Thomas III *investment consultant*

Orange
Thompson, Louis Milton, Jr. *investment company executive, consultant*

Reston
Icahn, Carl Celian *investor*

Richmond
Scott, George Cole III *investment advisor*

Stanardsville
Anns, Philip Harold *brokerage house and pharmaceutical executive*

Suffolk
Holloway, Christopher Matthew *brokerage house executive*

Vienna
Holland, Joel Kent III *entrepreneur*
Isaac, William Michael *brokerage house executive, retired government agency administrator*

Virginia Beach
Melsheimer, Mel P(owell) *venture capitalist*

Williamsburg
Gordon, Baron Jack *stockbroker*
Roberson, Robert S. *investment company executive*

WASHINGTON

Bellevue
Wells-Henderson, Ronald John *investment counselor*

Kirkland
Ryles, Gerald Fay *investor, finance company executive*

Port Townsend
Jones, John Wesley *entrepreneur*

Renton
Reitz, Jennifer Lee *financial company managing partner*

Seattle
Alberg, Tom Austin *investment company executive, lawyer*
Heath, Richard Raymond *retired investment company executive*
Nelson, Allen F. *proxy solicitation company executive*
Ruckelshaus, William Doyle *investment company executive, former federal agency administrator*
Wright, Bagley *venture capitalist, entrepreneur, art collector*

Sequim
Kretschmer, Keith Hughes *investor*

WISCONSIN

Madison
Burish, Andrew D. *investment advisor*
Zinder, Newton Donald *investment advisor, consultant*

Mequon
Bloom, James Edward *commodity trading and financial executive*

WYOMING

Cheyenne
Myers, Rolland Graham *investment counselor*

Jackson
Hirschfield, Alan James *entrepreneur*

Wilson
Chrystie, Thomas Ludlow *investor*

TERRITORIES OF THE UNITED STATES

PUERTO RICO

Hato Rey
Ferrer, Miguel Antonio *brokerage house executive*

CANADA

ALBERTA

Calgary
Cumming, Thomas Alexander *brokerage house executive*

BRITISH COLUMBIA

Vancouver
McCaw, John E., Jr. *investment company, professional sports team executive*
Saunders, Peter Paul *investor*

ONTARIO

Toronto
Dale, Robert Gordon *investment company executive*
Fox, Wayne C. *stock exchange and corporate financial executive*
Leech, James William *investment company executive*
Lindsay, Roger Alexander (Baron of Craighall) *investment executive*
Nesbitt, Richard *stock exchange executive*

QUEBEC

Montreal
Cedraschi, Tullio *investment company executive*
Gillespie, Thomas Stuart *investment company executive*
Bertrand, Luc *stock exchange executive*

MEXICO

Mexico City
Trevino, Guillermo Prieto *stock exchange executive*

AUSTRALIA

Melbourne
Fahour, Ahmed *investment company executive*

THE BAHAMAS

Nassau
Templeton, John Marks *investment counsel, financial analyst*

BERMUDA

Tuckers Town
Heizer, Edgar Francis, Jr. *venture capitalist*

CHINA

Hong Kong
Li, Ka-Shing *international entrepreneur*

ENGLAND

London
Flint, Douglas J. *investment company executive*
Forst, Edward C. *investment company executive*
Forsyth, Stephen A. *venture capitalist, department chairman*
Jourdren, Marc Henri *investment banking company executive*
Minnick, Mary E. *investment company executive, former beverage company executive*

GERMANY

Frankfurt
von Rosen, Rüdiger *stock exchange executive*

MONGOLIA

Ulaanbaatar
Mandel, Leslie Ann *investment advisor, writer*

SAUDI ARABIA

Riyadh
Alsaud, Prince Alwaleed Bin Talal Bin AbdulAziz *investment company executive, investor, entrepreneur*

SPAIN

Betlem
Cecchini, Leo *entrepreneur*

SWITZERLAND

Baar
Rich, Marc David *commodities trader*

Geneva
Farman-Farmaian, Ghaffar *investment company executive*

Lausanne
Bloemsma, Marco Paul *investor*

Zurich
Wassmer, Rudolf Andreas *entrepreneurial engineer*

ADDRESS UNPUBLISHED

Aall, Christian Bergengren *entrepreneur*
Ackerman, Melvin *investment company executive*
Albanese, Thomas *entrepreneur*
Albers, Charles Edgar *retired investment company executive*
Allen, Donald Vail *investment company executive, pianist*
Amos, Wally (Famous Amos) *entrepreneur*
Antezano, Antonio *investment company executive*
Arbuckle, John Finley, Jr. *retired investment advisor*
Aurin, Robert James *entrepreneur*
Bacharach, Melvin Lewis *venture capitalist*
Bacon, Caroline Sharfman *investor, consultant*
Bahbah, Bishara Assad *investment company executive, consultant*
Bailey, Rita Maria *investment advisor, psychologist*
Bantry, Bryan *entrepreneur, air transportation executive*
Batt, Nick *property and investment executive*
Beitler, Stephen *investment company executive, venture capitalist*
Beldock, Donald Travis *investor*
Bennett, Matthew Damon *entrepreneur, researcher*
Benson, James M. *investment company executive*
Berkley, Stephen M. *entrepreneur, investor*
Berlin, Howard Richard *investment company executive, retired portfolio manager*
Beyman, Jonathan Eric *investment company executive*
Blum, Barbara Davis *investor*
Bowles, Barbara Landers *investment company executive*
Brady, Nicholas Frederick *investment company executive, former secretary of the treasury*
Bratt, Nicholas *investment and research and development company executive*
Breeden, Richard C. *investment company executive, former federal agency administrato*
Brown, Herbert Graham *entrepreneur*
Burkle, Ronald W. *entrepreneur, retired food service executive*
Callard, David Jacobus *investment company executive*
Carr, Harold Noflet *investment company executive*
Chandler, Jeffrey *family trust and agricultural products executive*
Chapman, Geneva Joyce *entrepreneur, educator, writer*
Clark, Jim (James H.) *entrepreneur, real estate company and former computer software company executive*
Clawson, John Addison *investment company an retired chemicals executive*
Clemmensen, Larry P. *investment company executive*
Codo, Christina *securities executive*
Cohen, Claire Gorham *investment company executive*
Colker, David A. *former stock exchange executive*
Corbett, Alice Catherine *investor*
Cormie, Donald Mercer *investment company executive*
Crawford, Richard Eben, Jr. *retired investment advisor*
Cunningham, Ronnie Walter *venture capitalist*
Czinger, Kevin Robert *entrepreneur, venture capitalist*
Dean, Edwin Becton *entrepreneur*
De Lutis, Donald Conse *investment advisor, consultant*
de Neufville, Pierre *retired brokerage house executive*
Diaz-Verson, Salvador, Jr. *investment advisor*
Dietz, Arthur Townsend *investment counseling company executive*
Doherty, Charles Vincent *investment advisor*
Downing, Hudson Uroquhart *retired securities trader, bank executive*
Drake, Rodman Leland *investment company executive, consultant*
Drakeman, Donald Lee *venture capitalist*
Duarte, Prospero Villacin *retired entrepreneur*
Dunn, John Raymond, Jr. *stockbroker*
Dunn, Richard Joseph *retired investment adviso*
Elliott, Edward *investment executive, financial planner*
Ellis, Laurel Glynn *retired entrepreneur*
Engelbreit, Mary *art licensing entrepreneur*
Enomoto, Daisuke (Dice-K) *entrepreneur, investor*
Erwin, Mary R. *investment advisor*

stes, Jack Charles *entrepreneur, oil industry executive, research scientist*
arrar, David Holleman *investor*
ernandez, Antonio S. *investment company executive*
itts, Catherine Austin *investment advisor*
iumefreddo, Charles A. *brokerage house executive*
orstmann, Theodore J. *investment firm executive*
rankenberger, Bertram, Jr. *investor, consultant*
ranklin, Edward Ward *international investment consultant, lawyer, actor*
reed, Eva Praeger *investment advisor*
lasberg, Laurence Brian *investment company executive*
lass, Noah N. *entrepreneur*
ilick, J. Leslie *entrepreneur*
iodwin, Pamela June *financial services executive*
ioel, Karan *entrepreneur*
ioldman, Alan Ira *brokerage house executive*
iood, Walter Raymond *investment company executive*
ioodman, Bennett J. *hedge fund executive*
rasso, Dick (Richard A. Grasso) *former stock exchange executive*
reene, Frank Sullivan, Jr. *investment company executive*
riego, Linda *entrepreneur*
lapner, Mary Lou *securities trader, writer*
larris, Carla Ann *investment company executive*
lilton, Andrew Carson *investment company and retired manufacturing executive, management consultant*
linshaw, Ernest Theodore, Jr. *private investor, retired Olympic team official, retired finance company executive*
lintz, Scott Raymond *investor, financial consultant*
lochheimer, Frank Leo *brokerage and financial industry executive*
olte, Debra Leah *investment company executive, financial analyst*
oward, James Webb *brokerage house executive, engineer, lawyer*
udson, Donald J. *stock exchange executive*
urt, William Holman *investment management company executive*
ester, M(elvin) Douglas *investment company executive, retired beverage company executive*
errytone, Samuel Joseph *financial property broker*
ohnson, Michael Warren *international relations specialist*
ahn, Herta Hess (Mrs. Howard Kahn) *retired investment company executive*
azi, Sumaya *entrepreneur*
eegan, James Joseph *entrepreneur*
ellogg, Peter R. *securities dealer*
nox, Lance Lethbridge *venture capitalist*
reitzer, Lois Helen *investor*
agomasino, Maria Elena *investment company and retired bank executive*
ally, John Patrick *investment company executive*
asser, Lawrence J. *former investment company executive*
eahy, T. Liam *business development and technology investor*
ee, Thomas H. *investment company executive*
evel, Leon Jules *investor, director*
evins, John Raymond *investment advisor, educator, management consultant*
ew, Ginger Ehn *investment company executive, lawyer*
ewis, Brock *investment company executive*
ewis, Hunter *investment advisor, writer*
nde, Ronald Keith *investor*
ttle, Arthur Dehon *investor*
ogan, Kent *retired securities industry executive*
ynch, Thomas Peter *retired investment company executive*
agner, Marjorie J. (Marge Magner) *investment company executive*
alik, Om *former venture capitalist, blog website company executive, journalist*
alin, Robert Abernethy *retired investment company executive*
andile, Michael Angelo *investment advisor*
arshall, Conrad Joseph *entrepreneur*
ayer, Anthony John *investment company executive*
cCausland, Thomas James, Jr. *retired brokerage house executive*
cClane, Robert Sanford *entrepreneur, bank executive*
cGreevey, Lisa S. *investment company executive*
cNeill, Robert Patrick *investment advisor*
ehiel, Dennis *investment company executive*
ehta, Ravi Ravinder Singh *commodities trader, consultant*
ikitka, Gerald Peter *brokerage house executive, consultant*
olitor, Michael A. *entrepreneur, consultant*
organ, Owain David *investment company executive*
orgenroth, Earl Eugene *entrepreneur*
adel, Elliott *investment company executive*
cholas, Lawrence Bruce *company executive*
mbach, Lawrence Thomas *securities trader, researcher*
ordley, Gerald David *investor, writer*
le, Edward Proctor, Jr. *investment advisor*
alde, Jose Angel *entrepreneur, consultant*
ven, Tony Quinn *investment company executive, horse trainer*
cholski, Richard Francis *securities trader, financial consultant*
adino, Albert Edward *venture capitalist*
lumbo, Michael *investment company executive*
rdue, Dwight Edward *venture capitalist*
rker, Towana D. *entrepreneur, director*
uken, Thomas Weir *venture capital executive, mediator*
up, Martin Arnold *securities investor, real estate investor*
Petersen, Dorothy Virginia *investment company executive*
Peterson, Dawn Michelle *entrepreneur, writer*
Pinkney, D. Timothy *investment company executive*
Pope, Dale Allen *investment company executive*
Poppel, Seth Raphael *entrepreneur*
Rahe, Maribeth Sembach *investment management executive*
Rappaport, Irving S. *entrepreneur, lawyer, consultant*
Reed, John Shepard *former stock exchange executive*
Reeves, Michael Spencer *investment company executive*
Ridgway, Rozanne LeJeanne *corporate director, retired ambassador*
Roberts, David Glen *prospector, investor*
Rothstein, Gerald Alan *investment consultant*
Ryan, Timothy Patrick *investment company executive*
Rydén, Bengt Gunnar *retired stock exchange executive*
Santry, Barbara Lea *venture capitalist*
Sells, Boake Anthony *private investor*
Shuler, Jon Emmett *securities industry professional*
Shuman, Ann *investment company executive*
Smith, Thomas Eugene *investment company executive, financial consultant*
Snyder, Nathan *entrepreneur, investor*
Solberg, Ronald Louis *investment adviser, portfolio manager*
Stephens, Donald R(ichards) *investor*
Stiles, Thomas Beveridge, II, *retired investment company executive*
Stone, Edward Luke *investor, realtor*
Stuart, Gerard William, Jr. *investment company executive, alderman, city official*
Swensen, David Frederick *investment advisor*
Tarr, Kenneth J. *retired investment company executive*
Taylor, Diana Lancaster *investment company executive, former state official*
Thomas, James Edward, Jr. *brokerage house executive*
Tilson, Whitney R. *investment company executive*
Trongale, Nicholas Albert *entrepreneur, researcher*
Urciuoli, J. Arthur *brokerage house executive*
Uys, Jurgen Peter Brinker *securities analyst*
Valentine, Gene C. *securities dealer*
Vallee, Jacques Fabrice *venture capitalist*
Volkay, Chris John *investment company executive*
Waite, Dennis Vernon *brokerage house executive, consultant*
Waitt, Theodore W. (Ted Waitt) *venture capitalist, former computer company executive*
Walsh, William Desmond *investor*
Welch, Martin E. III *investor, retail executive*
Whelan, James Robert *investor, mining company executive*
Wruble, Brian Frederick *investor*
York, Jerome B. *investment company executive, former computer retail executive*
Zarb, Frank Gustave *investment company executive*
Zwerling, Gary Leslie *retired investment company executive*

GOVERNMENT: AGENCY ADMINISTRATION

UNITED STATES

ALABAMA

Birmingham
Wheeler, Cathy Jo *federal agency administrator*

Clanton
Baughman, Bruce Prentiss *state agency administrator*

Huntsville
Schumann, J. Paul *retired federal agency administrator*

Mobile
Bostwick, Robert Otis *government agency administrator*

Montgomery
Baker, Jimmy H. *former state finance administrator*
Harrison, John D. *state agency administrator*
Wall, William Herbert *state coordinator student loan programs*

ALASKA

Anchorage
Burke, Marianne King *state agency administrator, finance company executive, consultant*

Juneau
Usera, Vincent L. *state agency administrator*

ARIZONA

Goodyear
Carlson, Norman A. *retired federal agency administrator*

Phoenix
Chavez, Nelba R. *state and former federal agency administrator*
Cocking, Jill Hager *protective services official*
Eyring, Michael Borth *forensic specialist*
Harris, Jack F. *police chief*
Rotellini, Felecia A. *state agency administrator*
Wilson, Stephen Rip *public policy consultant*

Scottsdale
Jarman, Beth S. *former state agency administrator, consultant*

Tucson
Walker, Franklin Curtis *federal agency administrator*

ARKANSAS

Little Rock
Adcock, Robert H., Jr., (Bunny) *state agency administrator*

CALIFORNIA

Alpine
Oliverio, Ponzio *protective services official, educator*

Arroyo Grande
Willis, Ralph Walker *retired firefighter*

Bakersfield
Bernard, Alexander *protective services official*

Beverly Hills
Snowden, David L. *protective services official*

Canyon Country
Catalani, Richard William *forensic specialist, writer*

City Of Industry
Cavanaugh, Janis Lynn *protective services official, educator*

Escondido
Brown, Brian Ellis *protective services official*

Fowler
Bowman, Joseph Paul *protective services official, writer, retired military officer*

Irvine
Rogan, James Edward *former federal agency administrator, former congressman*

La Jolla
Whaley, Storm Hammond *retired federal agency administrator*

Los Angeles
Bratton, William J. *police chief, former commissioner*
Itabashi, Hideo Henry *coroner, pathologist, educator, consultant*

Norco
McNeal, Phyllis Paulette *parole agent*

Pasadena
Parker, Robert Allan Ridley *federal agency administrator, astronaut*
Rinaldi, James J. *federal agency administrator*

Richmond
Shaw, Angelynn Renee *protective services official*

Sacramento
Bersin, Alan Douglas *state agency administrator, lawyer*
Campbell, Tom *state agency administrator, dean, former congressman*
Kelley, Michael A. *state agency administrator*
Marin, Rosario *state agency administrator, former federal agency administrator*
Patino, Douglas Xavier *government agency administrator, academic administrator*
Roberts, Paul Dale *state agency administrator, writer*

San Diego
Lansdowne, William M. *police chief*

San Francisco
Tarnoff, Peter *federal agency administrator, consultant*

Santa Barbara
Aylesworth, Owen Roy *retired firefighter, genealogist, philanthropist*

Santa Monica
Timmer, Barbara *state agency administrator*

Stanford
Krasner, Stephen David *federal agency administrator, political science educator*

Susanville
Rogers, Winton (Larry) Lawrence *public information officer*

Westlake Village
Seymour, Jeffrey Alan *governmental relations consultant*

COLORADO

Brighton
Wagner, Samuel Albin Mar *state agency administrator*

Centennial
Wilks, Dana Lyn *protective services official, writer*

Colorado Springs
Howard, Larry Bruce *forensic specialist, consultant*

Denver
Adkins, Jeanne M. *state agency administrator*
Fulkerson, Richard J. *state agency administrator*
Mencer, Sue (Constance Suzanne Mencer) *former federal agency administrator*

Eldorado Springs
Lovins, L. Hunter *public policy institute executive, consultant, educator*

Englewood
McGraw, Jack Wilson *federal agency administrator*

Pueblo
Deasy, Irene M. *retired protective services official*

Vail
McGee, Michael Jay *protective services official, educator*

CONNECTICUT

Hartford
Pitkin, Howard F. *state agency administrator*

Southbury
Foxworth, Johnnie Hunter *retired state agency administrator*

Suffield
Hanzalek, Astrid Teicher *public information officer, consultant*

DELAWARE

Dover
Danberg, Carl Christian *state agency administrator, former state attorney general*
Glen, Robert Alexander *state agency administrator*

Newark
Le Min, Thomas Francis *law enforcement official, educator*

Ocean View
Taylor, Stan *retired state agency administrator*

Wilmington
Wasson, Robert E. *state agency administrator*

DISTRICT OF COLUMBIA

Washington
Adams, A. John Bertrand *public affairs consultant, director*
Allred, C. Stephen *federal agency administrator*
Almquist, Katherine J. *federal agency administrator*
Andersen, Margo K. *federal agency administrator*
Andrew, James M. *federal agency administrator*
Andrews, Terrence Michael *senior policy advisor*
Aoki, Steven *federal agency administrator*
Apple, Daina Dravnieks *federal agency administrator*
Artman, Carl Joseph *federal agency administrator*
Bair, Sheila Colleen *federal agency administrator*
Baker, Stewart Abercrombie *federal agency administrator, lawyer*
Barnett, Thomas O. *federal agency administrator*
Barrett, Thomas J. *federal agency administrator, retired military officer*
Bartuska, Ann *government official, biologist*
Baruah, Sandy K. (Santanu Kumar Baruah) *federal agency administrator*
Bateman, Paul William *federal agency administrator*
Battista, Robert James *federal agency administrator, lawyer*
Baxter, Sandra L. *government agency administrator*
Beato, Cristina V. *government agency administrator*
Bergner, Jeffrey Thomas *federal agency administrator*
Bernardi, Roy A. (Romolo Albert Bernardi) *federal agency administrator*
Bernhardt, David Longly *federal agency administrator*
Blackwill, Robert D. *former federal agency administrator*
Blakey, Marion Clifton *federal agency administrator*
Blazy, Louis Joseph III *federal agency administrator*
Boardman, Joseph H. *federal agency administrator*
Bodine, Susan P. *federal agency administrator*
Bohigian, David Steele *federal agency administrator*
Bomar, Mary Amelia *federal agency administrator*
Bonicelli, Paul J. *federal agency administrator*
Boucher, Richard A. *federal agency administrator*
Boyer, Jan E. *federal agency administrator*
Boykin, William G. (Jerry Boykin) *federal agency administrator, career military officer*
Bradley Gardner, Janice *federal agency administrator*

Brailer, David J. *federal agency administrator*
Brand, Rachel L. *federal agency administrator, lawyer*
Brenner, Joel F. *federal agency administrator*
Briggs, Ethel DeLoria *federal agency administrator*
Briggs, Kerri Layne *federal agency administrator*
Brouillette, Dan R. *former federal agency administrator*
Brown, Dana A. *federal agency administrator*
Brown, Harold *former secretary of defense*
Brown, Morgan *federal agency administrator*
Buchanan, Gale Arlon *federal agency administrator, former dean*
Burgess, Ronald L., Jr. *federal agency administrator, career military officer*
Burns, R(obert) Nicholas *federal agency administrator, former ambassador*
Cabrera, Orlando J. *federal agency administrator*
Campanelli, Richard M. *federal agency administrator*
Campbell, Benton J. *federal agency administrator*
Campbell, Bradford P. *government agency administrator*
Capka, J. Richard (Joseph Richard Capka) *federal agency administrator, retired military officer*
Carbonell, Josefina G. *federal agency administrator*
Carfine, Kenneth E. *government agency administrator*
Carranza, Jovita *federal agency administrator, retired delivery service executive*
Cartwright, Brian Grant *federal agency administrator, lawyer*
Casscells, Samuel Ward III *federal agency administrator, cardiologist, educator*
Caswell, James L. *government agency administrator*
Cavett, Deborah J. *federal agency administrator*
Chavarria, Adam *federal agency administrator*
Chealander, Steven Russell *federal agency administrator*
Chellaraj, Rajkumar *federal agency administrator*
Cherry, Schroeder *federal agency administrator*
Christopherson, Charles Richard, Jr., (Chuck Christopherson) *federal agency administrator*
Chu, David S.C. *federal agency administrator, economist*
Chun, Shinae *federal agency administrator*
Ciccoella, Charles S. (Chick) *federal agency administrator*
Clapper, James R., Jr. *federal agency administrator, retired military officer*
Clark, Michell C. *federal agency administrator*
Clement, Paul Drew *federal agency administrator, lawyer*
Clerihue, Randolph James *federal agency administrator*
Cole, Bruce Milan *federal agency administrator, art historian*
Connaughton, Sean Thomas *federal agency administrator*
Conner, Charles F. *federal agency administrator*
Conway, John Thomas *federal agency administrator, lawyer, engineer*
Cooper, Daniel L. *federal agency administrator*
Cox, (Charles) Christopher *federal agency administrator, former congressman*
Cox, John W. *federal agency administrator*
Crawford, Lester Mills, Jr. *former federal agency administrator*
Creel, Harold Jennings, Jr. *federal commission administrator, lawyer*
Cresanti, Robert Charles *federal agency administrator*
Curry, Thomas J. *federal and former state agency administrator*
Curtis, Charles B. *former federal agency administrator*
Cushing, Michael *federal agency administrator*
D'Agostino, Thomas Paul *federal agency administrator*
Dailey, Dell Lee *federal agency administrator, military officer*
Dale, Shana L. *federal agency administrator*
Daniels, Stephen M. *government official*
Davies, J. Clarence (Terry Davies) *public information officer, consultant*
Davis, Michele A. *federal agency administrator, former mortgage company executive*
Dempsey, Joan *federal agency administrator*
de Rato y Figaredo, Rodrigo *international banking official*
DeSutter, Paula A. *federal agency administrator*
DeTrani, Joseph *federal agency administrator*
Devaney, Earl E. *federal agency administrator*
Dhillon, Uttam *federal agency administrator*
Diaz, Alphonso Vincent *federal agency administrator*
Diaz, Nils Juan *federal agency administrator*
Doan, Lurita Alexis *federal agency administrator*
Dobriansky, Paula Jon *federal agency administrator, ambassador*
Domenech, Edgar A. *federal agency administrator*
Donnelly, Shaun Edward *government agency administrator*
Dorfman, Cynthia Hearn *government agency administrator*
Dorr, Thomas C. *federal agency administrator*
Downie, Richard Duncan *government agency administrator, retired military officer*
Dreeben, Michael R. *federal agency administrator*
Dugan, John Cunningham *federal agency administrator, lawyer*
Dunn, David *federal agency administrator*
Dunne, Patrick W. *federal agency administrator, retired military officer*
Duvall, Tyler Davis *federal agency administrator*
Edelman, Eric Steven *federal agency administrator, former ambassador*
Eggenberger, Andrew Jon *federal agency administrator*
Ellis, Joe W. *federal agency administrator*
England, Gordon Richard *federal agency administrator*
Ervin, Clark Kent *former federal agency administrator*
Feith, Douglas Jay *former federal agency administrator*
Felix, Larry R. *federal agency administrator*
Figueroa, Orlando *federal agency executive*
Fine, Glenn A. *federal agency administrator*
Finley, James I. *federal agency administrator*
Fisher, Alice S. *federal agency administrator, lawyer*
Fong, Phyllis Kamoi *federal agency administrator, lawyer*
Ford, Cecilia Sparks *federal agency administrator*
Fore, Henrietta Holsman *federal agency administrator*
Foresman, George W. *federal agency administrator*
Fort, Randall Martin *federal agency administrator*
Foulke, Edwin Gerhart, Jr. *federal agency administrator, lawyer*
Franco, Omar *government agency administrator*
Frazer, Jendayi Elizabeth *federal agency administrator, former ambassador*
Freeman, Chas W., Jr. *federal agency administrator, writer, ambassador*
Freeman, Sharee M. *federal agency administrator*
Fried, Daniel *federal agency administrator, former ambassador*
Fromer, Kevin *federal agency administrator*
Gambatesa, Donald Anthony *federal agency administrator*
Garnette, Cheryl Petty *government agency administrator*
Garre, Gregory *federal agency administrator*
Garza, Deborah A. *federal agency administrator, lawyer*
Gerstenmaier, William H. *federal agency administrator, aerospace engineer*
Gillis, John W. *federal agency administrator*
Glasbrenner, Karl Christian *federal agency administrator*
Glassman, Cynthia Aaron *federal agency administrator, former commissioner*
Godwin, Kimberly Ann *federal agency administrator, lawyer*
Goldway, Ruth Y. *postal regulatory commissioner*
Gonzalez, Emilio T. *federal agency administrator*
Gorn, Janet Marie *government official*
Grandmaison, J. Joseph *federal agency administrator*
Gray, George M. *federal agency administrator*
Gray, Lyons *federal agency administrator*
Greaux, Cheryl Prejean *federal agency administrator*
Greene, Charles M. *federal agency administrator*
Griffin, Michael D. *federal agency administrator, aerospace scientist*
Griffin, Richard J. *federal agency administrator*
Grimes, John Grayson *federal agency administrator*
Grossman, Marc Issaiah *former federal agency administrator*
Gruenberg, Martin J. *federal agency administrator, lawyer*
Gulliford, James B. *federal agency administrator*
Halaska, Terrell L. *federal agency administrator*
Hall, H. Dale *federal agency administrator*
Hampton, Thomas E. *state agency administrator*
Hanley, Allison Anne *federal agency administrator*
Harvey, Thomas Edward *federal agency administrator*
Hayden, Michael Vincent *CIA Director, career military officer*
Heddell, Gordon S. *federal agency administrator*
Helgerson, John Leonard *federal agency administrator*
Herbst, John Edward *federal agency administrator, former ambassador*
Hernandez, Israel *federal agency administrator*
Hersman, Deborah A. P. *federal agency administrator*
Hess, Michael Edward *federal agency administrator*
Hevel, Gary Francis *public information officer, consultant*
Higgins, Bradford R. *federal agency administrator*
Higgins, John P., Jr., (Jack) *federal agency administrator*
Higgins, Kathryn O'Leary (Kitty) *federal agency administrator, former consulting firm executive*
Hill, Christopher R. *federal agency administrator, former ambassador*
Hill, David R. *federal agency administrator, lawyer*
Hill, John H. *federal agency administrator*
Hill, Kent Richmond *federal agency administrator*
Hopkins, Charles L. *government agency administrator*
Horn, Sharon K. *government agency administrator*
Horner, Constance Joan *federal agency administrator*
Howard, John *federal agency administrator*
Howard, Robert T. *federal agency administrator*
Hughes, Karen Parfitt *federal agency administrator*
Hulon, Willie T. *federal agency administrator*
Hungar, Thomas G. *federal agency administrator, lawyer*
Hunt, Earl Stephen *federal agency administrator*
Hutchison, Claude B., Jr. *federal agency administrator*
Iklé, Fred Charles *former federal agency administrator, policy advisor, defense expert*
Isakowitz, Steven Jeffrey *federal agency administrator, aeronautical engineer*
Iverson, Kristine Ann *federal agency administrator*
Jackson, Darryl W. *federal agency administrator*
Jackson, Michael P. *federal agency administrator, former engineering company executive*
Jacobs, Alonzo *federal agency contracting officer*
Jeffery, Reuben III *federal agency administrator*
Jenson, William G. *federal agency administrator*
Johnson, Charles E. *federal agency administrator*
Johnson, Robert Wayne *federal agency administrator*
Jonas, Tina Westby *federal agency administrator*
Jordan, Mosina H. *federal agency administrator*
Justesen, Troy Ralph *federal agency administrator*
Kappes, Stephen R. *federal agency administrator*
Karsner, Andy (Alexander Armand Karsner) *federal agency administrator*
Kearney, Stephen Michael *federal agency administrator*
Keenum, Mark Everett *federal agency administrator, former legislative staff member*
Keisler, Peter Douglas *federal agency administrator, lawyer*
Kendrick, Kim *federal agency administrator*
Kennedy, Patrick F. *federal agency administrator, former ambassador*
Kesselman, Marc L. *federal agency administrator*
Kilgore, Edwin Carroll *retired federal agency administrator*
Kimbell, Abigail R. *federal agency administrator*
Kimmitt, Robert Michael *federal agency and former business executive*
Kincannon, Charles Louis (Louis Kincannon) *federal agency administrator*
Kirsanow, Peter N. *federal agency administrator*
Klepner, Jerry D. *federal agency administrator*
Kneedler, Edwin S. *federal agency administrator*
Kneuer, John M.R. *federal agency administrator*
Knight, Bruce Irving *federal agency administrator*
Kolevar, Kevin M. *federal agency administrator*
Kolodner, Robert M. *federal agency administrator, health information technology executive*
Korb, Donald L. *federal agency administrator, lawyer*
Kringen, John A. *federal agency administrator*
Krongard, Howard J. *federal agency administrator, lawyer*
Kunder, James R. *federal agency administrator*
Kussman, Michael James *federal agency administrator*
La Force, Hudson III *federal agency administrator*
Lagon, Mark P. *federal agency administrator*
Lampl, Peggy Ann *public information officer*
Langfeld, Stanley Chaitt *government executive*
Lanier, Cathy L. *police chief*
Lappin, Harley G. *federal agency administrator*
Larson, Alan Philip *former federal agency administrator*
LaSpada, Carmella *government agency administrator*
Lastowka, James Anthony *former federal agency administrator, lawyer*
Lautenbacher, Conrad Charles, Jr. *federal agency administrator, retired naval officer*
Lavin, Franklin Leo *federal agency administrator, former ambassador*
Lebryk, David A. *federal agency administrator*
Ledbetter, Kenneth W. *federal agency administrator*
Leonard, Bill (J. William Leonard) *federal agency administrator*
Leos, Kathleen *federal agency administrator*
Levett, Todd A. *government agency administrator*
Levey, Stuart A. *federal agency administrator*
Levinson, Daniel Ronald *federal agency administrator, lawyer*
Lewis, Dennis M. *federal agency administrator, former hospital administrator*
Lewis, Lorraine *former federal agency administrator*
Liebman, Wilma B. *federal agency administrator*
Lipsky, John Phillip *international banking official*
Livingood, Wilson S. *protective services official*
Lloyd, James D. *federal agency administrator*
Lockhart, James Bicknell III *federal agency administrator*
Lofthus, Lee J. *federal agency administrator*
Lowenkron, Barry Frederick *federal agency administrator*
Lowery, Clay *federal agency administrator*
Loy, James Milton *former federal agency administrator, retired coast guard officer*
Luthi, Randall B. *federal agency administrator, former state legislator*
Maddox, Lauren M. *federal agency administrator*
Magner, Timothy J. *federal agency administrator, educator*
Mancuso, Mario *federal agency administrator*
Manfreda, John J. *federal agency administrator*
Mangano, Philip F. *federal agency administrator*
Mansfield, Gordon Hall *federal agency administrator*
Maples, Michael D. *federal agency administrator, military officer*
Martella, Roger Romulus, Jr. *federal agency administrator, lawyer*
Martin, Kevin J. *federal agency administrator*
Martinez Tucker, Sara (Sara Alicia Tucker) *federal agency and former educational association administrator*
Maxwell, David Ogden *federal agency administrator, mortgage company executive*
Mc Afee, William *government official*
McCarthy, Peter B. *federal agency administrator*
McClellan, Mark B. *former federal agency administrator*
McCormack, Sean Ian *federal agency administrator*
McCormick, David Harold *federal agency administrator*
McDonald, Frances D. *government official, editor, lawyer*
McGee, James M. *federal agency administrator*
McKay, Margo Marquita *federal agency administrator, lawyer*
McKee, Margaret Jean *federal agency administrator*
McMurray, Claudia Anne *federal agency administrator, lawyer*
McQueary, Charles E. (Chuck McQueary) *federal agency administrator*
Medish, Mark *federal government official*
Meisburg, Ronald Edward *federal agency administrator, lawyer*
Menarchik, Douglas (Edward Douglas Menarchik) *federal agency administrator*
Merritt, Carolyn *government agency administrator*
Mesecar, Doug *federal agency administrator*
Miller, John *federal agency administrator, former news correspondent*
Miller, John Ripin *former federal agency administrator, former congressman*
Moe, Ronald Chesney *public administration researcher*
Mok, Samuel Tinsing *federal agency administrator*
Mondello, Lisette McSoud *federal agency administrator*
Monroe, Jane D. *federal agency administrator*
Monroe, Stephanie Johnson *federal agency administrator*
Montanez-Johner, Nancy *federal agency administrator*
Moore, Powell Allen *former federal agency administrator*
Morford, Craig S. *federal agency administrator, prosecutor*
Morgan, Linda Joan *former federal agency administrator, lawyer*
Morrissey, Patricia A. *federal agency administrator*
Moschella, William Emil *federal agency administrator*
Moten, Sarah Elizabeth *federal agency administrator*
Moy, Edmund C. *federal agency administrator*
Mueller, Robert Swan III *FBI director*
Mull, Stephen D. *federal agency administrator, former ambassador*
Munson, Richard Jay *government agency administrator*
Muris, Timothy Joseph *former federal agency administrator, lawyer, educator*
Murphy, Edward Joseph *government agency administrator*
Murphy, Frances M. *federal agency administrator*
Nakayama, Granta Y. *federal agency administrator, lawyer*
Nason, David George *federal agency administrator*
Nason, Nicole R. *federal agency administrator*
Neal, Darwina Lee *federal agency administrato*
Negroponte, John Dimitri *federal agency administrator, former national intelligence director, ambassador*
Nelson, Keith A. *federal agency administrator*
Nethery, John Jay *government official, military officer*
Nitze, William Albert *government official, lawyer, not-for-profit developer, energy executive*
Norquist, David L. *federal agency administrat*
Norwalk, Leslie V. *federal agency administrat*
Obering, Trey (Henry A. Obering II) *federal agency administrator, career military officer*
O'Brien, Patrick Michael *federal agency administrator*
Ohl, Joan Eschenbach *federal agency administrator*
Oldham, Cheryl *federal agency administrator*
Oliver, LeAnn Michelle *government official*
Olsen, Jody (Josephine K. Olsen) *federal agen administrator*
Omass, George A. *federal agency administrat*
Opfer, George J. *federal agency administrator*
Orbach, Raymond Lee *federal agency administrator, physicist, researcher*
Ostendorff, William Charles *federal agency administrator, career military officer*
O'Sullivan, Stephanie L. *federal agency administrator*
Owsley, Douglas W. *forensic osteologist, researcher, anthropologist*
Oxford, Vayl *federal agency administrator*
Padilla, Christopher Alan *federal agency administrator*
Patenaude, Pamela Hughes *federal agency administrator*
Patron, June Eileen *retired government agency administrator*
Paulison, R(obert) David *federal agency administrator*
Peacock, Marcus C. *federal agency administrator*
Perle, Richard Norman *former federal agency administrator*
Peters, Marybeth *copyrights register*
Pistole, John S. *federal agency administrator*
Pittman, R. Allen *federal agency administrato*
Ports, James Franklin *federal agency administrator, former state legislator*
Potter, Jack (John E. Potter) *federal agency administrator*
Powell, Benjamin Albond *federal agency administrator, lawyer*
Powell, Dina Habib *federal agency administra*
Powell, Donald E. *federal agency administrat*
Preston, Steven C. *federal agency administrat former service company executive*

Price, Deborah A. *federal agency administrator*
Quello, James Henry *government official*
Radzely, Howard M. *federal agency administrator, lawyer*
Reich, John M. *federal agency administrator*
Renkiewicz, Martin *federal agency administrator*
Reynolds, Jerry (Gerald A.) *federal agency administrator*
Richlen, Scott Lane *federal government program administrator*
Riggs, Barbara *federal agency administrator*
Rodley, Carol A. *federal agency administrator*
Rood, John C. *federal agency administrator*
Rosenfeld, Ronald Allen *federal agency administrator*
Rosenker, Mark Victor *federal agency administrator*
Rudman, Mara E. *government official*
Rutherford, Boyd Kevin *federal agency administrator*
Ryan, Anthony William *federal agency administrator*
Sauerbrey, Ellen Elaine Richmond *federal agency administrator, former ambassador*
Scarlett, (Patricia) Lynn *federal agency administrator*
Schafer, Jacqueline Ellen *federal agency administrator*
Schaitberger, Harold *protective services official, labor union administrator*
Schaumber, Peter Carey *federal agency administrator*
Schmitt, Glenn Ralph *federal agency administrator*
Schneider, Ann Imlah *federal agency administrator, education consultant*
Schneider, Paul Allan *federal agency administrator*
Schoettle, Enid C.B. *federal agency administrator*
Schofield, Regina Brown *federal agency administrator*
Schornagel, Karl William *government agency administrator*
Scolese, Christopher *federal agency administrator*
covel, Calvin L. III *federal agency administrator*
edgwick, Jeffrey Leigh *federal agency administrator, political science professor*
ell, Clay (Jeffrey Clay Sell) *federal agency administrator*
equeira, Leon R. *federal agency administrator*
hane, Jeffrey Neil *federal agency administrator, lawyer*
hannon, Thomas A., Jr. *federal agency administrator*
hearer, Paul Scott *federal agency and trade association administrator*
imon, Raymond Joseph *federal agency and former school system administrator*
imonson, Stewart Gerard *retired federal agency administrator*
'mpson, James S. *federal agency administrator*
rri, Erik R. *federal agency administrator, economist*
kinner, Richard L. *federal agency administrator*
kinner, Thomas V. *federal agency administrator*
mith, (J.) Dorrance *federal agency administrator*
olomon, Eric *federal agency administrator*
ontag, Ed *former federal agency administrator*
proat, Edward F., III, (Ward Sproat) *federal agency administrator*
purgeon, Dennis Ray *federal agency administrator, former manufacturing executive*
anley, Daniel Raymond, Sr. *federal agency administrator*
aples, George McDade *federal agency administrator, former ambassador*
eel, Robert K. *federal agency administrator, former diversified financial services company executive*
eele, Ana Mercedes *retired federal agency administrator*
einberg, Andrew B. *federal agency administrator, lawyer*
oner, John Richard *federal agency administrator*
rasser, Richard Joseph, Jr. *federal agency administrator*
uboleski, Stanley C. *federal agency administrator, mining engineer*
ullivan, Daniel S. *federal agency administrator*
ullivan, Mark J. *federal agency administrator*
umwalt, Robert Llewellyn III *federal agency administrator, pilot*
vagel, Phillip L. *federal agency administrator*
albert, Kent Dean *federal agency administrator, lawyer*
margo, Mauricio J. *federal agency administrator*
enpas, Ronald Jay *federal agency administrator, former prosecutor*
omas, Harry K., Jr. *federal agency administrator, former ambassador*
ompson, Lawrence Hyde *retired federal agency official*
omsen, Linda Chatman *federal agency administrator*
orson, Eric M. *federal agency administrator*
nsley, Nikki Lee Rush *federal agency administrator*
bey, William Hayward *federal agency administrator, former investment banker*
wey, Carroll Francis *senior education specialist*
oy, Tevi D. *federal agency administrator*
uscott, Carl Joseph *security firm executive, former federal agency administrator*
chetter, Ronald Allen *federal agency administrator*
ierk, William F. *federal agency administrator, lawyer*
goff, Kathleen Platt *federal agency administrator*
Vanderwagen, W. Craig (William Craig Vanderwagen) *federal agency administrator, physician*
Vaughn, Gladys Gary *federal agency administrator, researcher, not-for-profit executive*
Venkayya, Rajeev V. *federal agency administrator, biomedical researcher, educator*
Ventimiglia, Vincent J., Jr. *federal agency administrator*
Vickers, Michael G. *federal agency administrator*
Wahlquist, Brent T. *federal agency administrator*
Wainstein, Kenneth L. *federal agency administrator, former prosecutor*
Walsh, Dennis P. *federal agency administrator*
Warder, Lawrence A. *federal agency administrator*
Washington, Linda Jacobs *federal agency administrator*
Watson, Harlan L(eroy) *federal agency administrator, physicist, economist*
Watson, Peter S. *former federal agency administrator*
Watson, Rebecca Wunder *federal agency administrator, lawyer*
Weems, Kerry N. *federal agency administrator*
Weimer, Thomas R. (R. Thomas Weimer) *federal agency administrator*
Weiner, Robert Stephen *federal agency administrator*
Weinstein, Kenneth N. *federal government administrator*
Welch, C. David *assistant secretary of state, former ambassador*
Wells, Linton, II, *federal agency administrator*
Werner, Robert William *federal agency administrator*
Whitaker, Scott *former federal agency administrator, lobbyist*
White, John W. *federal agency administrator, lawyer*
Whitehurst, Grover Jay *federal agency administrator, psychologist, educator*
Wienecke, Nathaniel Frederick *federal agency administrator*
Wilkie, Robert Leon, Jr. *federal agency administrator*
Williams, Darlene F. *federal agency administrator*
Williams, Julie Lloyd *federal agency administrator, lawyer*
Wolanin, Thomas Richard *federal agency administrator, educator*
Wolff, Otto J. *federal agency administrator*
Worden, Robert L. *government agency administrator, researcher*
Young, Donald Alan *federal agency administrator*
Young, John Jacob, Jr. *federal agency administrator*

FLORIDA

Bonita Springs
Dunning, Herbert Neal *government agency administrator, chemist*

Delray Beach
Schenkel, Suzanne Chance *retired natural resource specialist*

Fort Lauderdale
Carter Pereira, Claudine Renee *forensic specialist*

Fort Myers
Lounsbury, David Arthur *protective services official, educator*
Zeldes, Ilya M. *forensic scientist, lawyer*

Fort Pierce
Belcher, Dorothy S. *state correctional department administrator*

Gulf Stream
Nalen, Craig Anthony *federal agency administrator*

Indian Rocks Beach
DeLucia, Gene Anthony *government administrator, computer company executive*

Jensen Beach
Peterson, David Frederick *retired government agency administrator*

Lake City
Gay, John Marion *retired federal agency administrator, financial analyst*

Lithia
Richmond, Nancy Mason *retired state agency administrator*

Niceville
Crawford, Jackie R. *retired federal agency administrator*

North Miami
Plotkin-Spotts, Sharon Lee *protective services official, educator*

Polk City
Carr, Richard William *federal program manager*

Ponte Vedra Beach
Soderberg, Nancy *former government official, writer*

Sebring
Wright, Leonard Douglas *protective services official, retired military officer*

Tallahassee
Braswell, Jackie Boyd *state agency administrator*
Saxon, Don B. *state agency administrator*
Thomas, James Bert, Jr. *retired federal agency administrator*

Tampa
Yeshion, Theodore Elliot *crime laboratory director*

GEORGIA

Atlanta
Aiken, Vernoy Fred *government agency administrator*
Braswell, Robert M. *state agency administrator*
Gerberding, Julie Louise *federal agency administrator*
Jaffe, Harold W. *federal agency administrator*
McGowan, Angela Kay *government agency administrator, researcher*
Mecke, William Moyn *public information officer*
Pennington, Richard J. *police chief*

Brunswick
Moran, John Bernard *retired government official*

Grovetown
Jones, Jerry W. *protective services official, investor*

Kennesaw
Paterson, Paul Charles *retired private investigator, security consultant*

Morrow
Culver, Dan Louis *federal agency administrator*

Peachtree City
Ebneter, Stewart Dwight *utility industry management consultant*

HAWAII

Honolulu
Chapman, Duane Lee (Dog) *bail enforcement agent, television personality*
Griffin, Dominic B. III *state agency administrator*
Keogh, Richard John *firearms and explosives consultant*
Saiki, Patricia *federal agency administrator, congressman*

Mililani
Hunkele, Lester Martin III *retired federal agency administrator*

IDAHO

Boise
Gee, Gavin M. *state agency administrator*
Smith, Marsha H. *state agency administrator, lawyer*

Idaho Falls
Rydalch, Ann *federal agency administrator*

ILLINOIS

Chicago
Cline, Philip J. *police superintendent*
Coyle, Dorothy *government agency administrator*
Dickman, Martin J. *federal agency administrator*
Kuczwara, Thomas Paul *federal agency administrator, lawyer*
Nash, Donald Gene *federal investigator, economist*
Padron, D. Lorenzo *state agency administrator*
Ruder, David Sturtevant *government official, lawyer, educator*
Thomas, Cherryl T. *former federal agency administrator*
Van Pelt, Robert Irving *retired firefighter*

Flora
Shrum, John *equal rights officer*

Northlake
Haack, Richard Wilson *retired police officer*

Springfield
Phelps, David Dwain *state agency administrator, former congressman*
Schroeder, Joyce Katherine *state agency administrator, research analyst*

INDIANA

Indianapolis
Engleman Connors, Ellen Gayle *former federal agency administrator*
Gerdes, Ralph Donald *fire safety consultant*
Holden, James R. *state agency administrator*
Ripley, Judith G. *state agency administrator*

North Vernon
Hicks, Gregory Steven *government agency administrator*

Schererville
Opacich, Milan *protective services official, musician*

South Bend
Hellyer, Timothy Michael *protective services officer*

Sweetser
Hueston, Travis Earl *protective services official*

IOWA

Des Moines
Brickman, Kenneth Alan *state agency administrator*
Gronstal, Thomas B. *state agency administrator*
Martens, Harvey Arthur *retired government worker, academic administrator*
Nelson, Charlotte Bowers *public administrator*

Kellogg
Anderson, Dale C. *state agency professional, travel consultant*

KANSAS

Overland Park
McCann, Vonya B. *federal agency administrator, telecommunications industry executive*

Topeka
Thull, Tom (John Thomas Thull) *state agency administrator*

KENTUCKY

Frankfort
Lawrence, Cordell G. *state agency administrator*

Lexington
Calvert, C. Emmett *former state agency administrator*

Louisville
Adams, Robert Waugh *state agency administrator, economist, educator*

LOUISIANA

Alexandria
Phillips, Virginia *retired federal employee*

Baton Rouge
Ducrest, John P. *state agency administrator*
Parks, James William, II, *public facilities executive, lawyer*

New Orleans
Collins, Harry David *forensic, mechanical and nuclear engineer, claims consultant*

Shreveport
Raley, Kelli B. *forensic specialist*

MAINE

Augusta
LaFountain, Lloyd P. III *state agency administrator*

MARYLAND

Baltimore
Abrams, Rosalie Silber *retired state agency official*
Barnhart, Jo Anne B. *federal agency administrator*
Corley, Rose Ann McAfee *government official*
Derwart, Gregory M. *state agency administrator*
Koch, Edgar Frank *protective services official*
Rzepkowski, James Edward *state agency administrator*
Steensgaard, Anthony Harvey *federal agency administrator*
Turnbaugh, Charles W. *state agency administrator*

Bel Air
O'Bryon, James Fredrick *defense consultant*

Beltsville
Tso, Tien Chioh *federal agency administrator, researcher, agronomist*

Bethesda
Abrams, David B. *federal agency administrator*
Aldridge, Edward Cleveland, Jr., (Pete Aldridge) *former federal agency administrator*
Alexander, Duane Frederick *federal agency administrator, pediatrician, researcher*
Alving, Barbara *federal agency administrator, hematologist*
Battey, James F., Jr. *federal agency administrator, neurologist*
Berg, Jeremy Mark *federal agency administrator, biochemist, researcher*
Buetow, Kenneth H. *federal agency administrator*
Collins, Francis S. *federal agency administrator, geneticist, physician*
Doroshow, James Halpern *federal agency administrator, oncologist*
Fauci, Anthony Stephen *federal agency administrator, allergist, immunologist*
Fefferman, Hilbert *government official, lawyer*
Grady, Patricia A. *federal agency administrator*
Harford, Joe B. *federal agency administrator*
Hodes, Richard J. *federal agency administrator, immunologist, researcher*
Hrynkow, Sharon Hemond *federal agency administrator, neuroscientist, researcher*
Insel, Thomas R. *federal agency administrator, psychiatrist*
Jones, John Franklin, Jr., (Jack F. Jones) *federal agency administrator*
Joyce, Bernita Anne *retired federal agency administrator*
Katz, Stephen Ira *federal agency administrator*
Landis, Story Cleland *federal agency administrator, neurobiologist*

Larrabee, Barbara Princelau *retired intelligence officer*
Morgan, John Davis *government agency administrator, consultant*
Murrett, Robert B. *federal agency administrator, career military officer*
Niederhuber, John Edward *federal agency administrator, oncologist, surgeon, immunologist*
O'Callaghan, Jerry Alexander *federal agency administrator*
Ostrander, Elaine A. *federal agency administrator, geneticist*
Pettigrew, Roderic I. *federal agency administrator, radiologist, researcher*
Pinn, Vivian W. *federal agency administrator, pathologist*
Rabson, Alan Saul *federal agency administrator, pathologist, educator*
Richardson, John *retired international relations executive*
Ruffin, John *federal agency administrator, researcher*
Ruiz-Bravo, Norka *federal agency administrator*
Sieving, Paul A. *federal agency administrator, ophthalmologist, educator*
Singer, Dinah S. *federal agency administrator, immunologist, researcher*
Springfield, Sanya A. *federal agency administrator*
Stanfield, Brent B. *federal agency administrator*
Tabak, Lawrence A. *federal agency administrator, dentist*
Wellems, Thomas E. *federal agency administrator*
White, Jeffrey D. *federal agency administrator*
Zerhouni, Elias Adam *federal agency administrator*

Chevy Chase
Broide, Mace Irwin *public information officer*
Reilly, Edward Francis, Jr. *federal agency administrator, former state senator*

Clinton
Sander, Clarence Ellis, Jr. *retired protective services official*

Easton
Colton, Elizabeth Wishart *government agency administrator*

Emmitsburg
Cade, Gregory Brian *federal agency administrator, fireman*

Fort George G Meade
Alexander, Keith B. *federal agency administrator, career military officer*
Black, William B., Jr. *federal agency administrator*

Frederick
Baker, Joanne Evelyn *retired government agency administrator*
Wiltrout, Robert H. *federal agency administrator*

Gaithersburg
Hertz, Harry Steven *government official*
Jeffrey, William Alan *federal agency administrator, physicist*
Semerjian, Hratch Gregory *federal agency administrator*

Kensington
Rosenthal, Alan Sayre *government official, lawyer*
Suraci, Charles Xavier, Jr. *retired federal agency administrator, air transportation executive, consultant*

Laurel
Chrismer, Ronald Michael *federal agency administrator*

Madison
Hoffman, Alicia Coro *retired federal executive*

Rockville
Adelsperger, Jennifer *forensic scientist*
Clark, Harry Westley *federal agency administrator*
Cline, Terry L. *federal agency administrator*
Croyle, Robert T. *federal agency administrator, psychologist, educator*
Dal Pan, Gerald J. *federal agency administrator*
Davis, Beverly Watts *federal agency administrator*
Duke, Elizabeth M. *federal agency administrator*
Epstein, Jay Stuart *federal agency administrator*
Gray, Paulette Styles *federal agency administrator, biologist*
Grim, Charles W. *federal agency administrator*
Hawk, Ernest T. *federal agency administrator*
Klein, Dale Edward *federal agency administrator, engineering educator*
Lumpkin, Murray M. *federal agency administrator*
Manderscheid, Ronald William *program administrator*
Power, A. Kathryn *federal agency administrator*
Rutstein, David C. *United States public health service administrator*
Shekar, Sam S. *federal agency administrator*
Strausberg, Robert L. *federal agency administrator*
Telesetsky, Walter *federal agency administrator*
Throckmorton, Douglas Carl *federal agency administrator*
Uhl, Kathleen *federal agency administrator*
van Dyck, Peter Cuyler *federal agency administrator*
von Eschenbach, Andrew C. *federal agency administrator, oncologist, urologic surgeon*
Whitescarver, Jack Edward *federal agency administrator*

Silver Spring
de Zafra Atwell, Dorothea Elizabeth *retired government agency administrator*
Dunnigan, John H. *federal agency administrator*
Ganley, Charles James *federal agency administrator, internist*
Johnson, David L. *federal agency administrator, retired military officer*
Kline, Jerry Robert *retired administrative judge, ecologist*
Maas, Joe (Melvin Joseph Maas) *retired federal agency administrator*
Mahoney, James R. *federal agency administrator*
Mlay, Marian *retired government official*
Spinrad, Richard William *federal agency administrator, oceanographer*
Ware, Thaddeus Van *retired government official*
Williams, Paul *retired federal agency administrator*

Upper Marlboro
Bune, Karen Louise *state agency administrator, legal assistant*

Woodbine
Uhl, Scott Mark *state agency administrator*

MASSACHUSETTS

Boston
Antonakes, Steven L. *state agency administrator*
Crimlisk, Jane Therese *probation officer*
Reitnauer, Andrew Richard *forensic specialist*

Cambridge
Carter, Ashton Baldwin *former federal agency administrator*
Donahue, John David *federal agency administrator, educator*
Hunt, Swanee G. *public policy educator, former ambassador*

Chatham
O'Connell, Brian *community organizer, educator, writer*

Lexington
Thernstrom, Abigail *federal agency administrator, writer*

Waltham
Stuntz, Linda Gillespie *government official, lawyer*

Watertown
Tompkins, Curtis Johnston *government agency administrator*

Westborough
Horwitz, Eleanor Catherine *public information officer*

MICHIGAN

Ann Arbor
Bierbaum, Rosina M. *federal agency administrator*

Detroit
Bully-Cummings, Ella M. *police chief*
Moss, Leslie Otha *homeland security specialist*
Thomas, Craig Damon *protective services official*

Gaylord
Jones, John Paul *probation officer, psychologist*

Houghton
Fink, William Orman *retired federal agency administrator, management consultant*

Lansing
Couto, C. Douglass *state agency administrator*
Watters, Linda A. *state agency administrator*

Lenox
Shaw, Charles Rusanda *retired government investigator*

Midland
Adams, Thomas Walton *corrections official*

Southfield
Gleichman, John Alan *protective services official*

MINNESOTA

Brainerd
Peterson, Donn Neal *forensic engineer, engineering company executive*

Elk River
Richardson, Mark P. *protective services official, educator*

Saint Paul
Murphy, Kevin M. *state agency administrator*

MISSISSIPPI

Jackson
Allison, John S. *state agency administrator*

Pearl
Latham, Robert Richard, Jr. *retired emergency services administrator*

Vicksburg
Houston, James R. *government agency administrator*

MISSOURI

Brighton
Copus, Phyllis Lee *retired federal agency administrator*

Fort Leonard Wood
Collins, Pamela Marie *forensic specialist, educator*
Meyer, Ronald G. *forensic specialist*

Jefferson City
Bailes, Shawn Michael *criminalist*
McClure, D. Eric *state agency administrator*

Kansas City
Parker, Dennis Gene *former sheriff, martial arts instructor*
Warlen, Stephen Clarence *forensic specialist, consultant*

Saint Louis
King, Joseph, Jr. *federal agency administrator*

MONTANA

Helena
Goodwin, Annie M. *state agency administrator*

Miles City
Coffman, Richard C. *retired protective services official*

NEBRASKA

Lincoln
Munn, John *state agency administrator*

Omaha
Bang, Michele Alene *protective services official*
Hansen, James Allen *state agency administrator*
Mactier, Ann Dickinson *state agency administrator*

NEVADA

Fallon
Jones, Gilbert Leed *retired law enforcement officer, coroner, author, educator*

Henderson
Wieting, Gary Lee *federal agency executive*

Las Vegas
Kondrup, Steven W. *state agency administrator*
Lally, Norma Ross *retired federal agency administrator*

Reno
Svahn, John Alfred *federal agency administrator*

NEW HAMPSHIRE

Concord
Hildreth, Peter C. *state agency administrator*
Mevers, Frank Clement *state agency administrator, archivist*

Goffstown
Day, Russell Clover *state agency administrator*

Hanover
Koop, C. Everett (Charles Everett Koop) *former Surgeon General of the United States, educator*

NEW JERSEY

Adelphia
Carter, Harry Robert *fire protection consultant*

Camden
Venegas, Arturo, Jr. *protective services official*

East Orange
Ilogienboh, Caroline O. *protective services official, publishing executive*

Fort Monmouth
Poulos, Andrew, Jr. *protective services official, director*

Hamilton
Allen, Stacey R. *forensic specialist*

Kenilworth
Gen, Martin *protective services executive*

New Brunswick
Coscia, Anthony R. *state agency administrator, lawyer*

Princeton
Whipple, William, Jr. *government policy consultant, writer*

Tabernacle
DiBella, Russell Thomas *federal investigator*

Toms River
Moran, Jeffrey W., Jr. *county surrogate*

Trenton
Caspersen, Sidney J. *state agency administrator*
Goldman, Steven M. *state agency administrator*
Socolow, David Jacob *state agency administrator*

NEW MEXICO

Albuquerque
Gutierrez, Sidney M. *federal agency administrator*
Jaramillo, Mari-Luci *retired federal agency administrator*
Varela, Alan Mark *state agency administrator, lawyer*

Kirtland Afb
Tritten, James John *federal agency administrato educator*

Santa Fe
Johnson, Eric B. *police chief*
Verant, William J. *state agency administrator*

NEW YORK

Albany
Bradley, Edward James *state official, computer programmer and analyst*
Eristoff, Andrew S. *state agency administrator*

Central Islip
Viera, Robert, Sr. *protective services official*

Chappaqua
Laun, Louis Frederick *government official*

Garden City
Laureano, Mari *government agency administrator, writer*

Huntington
Kirwin, Barbara Rosa *forensic specialist*

New York
Beausoleil, Doris Mae *retired federal agency housing specialist*
Falkenrath, Richard A. *protective services offici*
Hirsch, Charles S. *city health department administrator*
Kelly, Raymond Walter *police commissioner*
Lat, David B. *former assistant US attorney, online-journalist, editor, blogger*
Levin, Susan Bass *state agency administrator, lawyer*
Neiman, Richard H. *state agency administrator*
Noble, Ronald Kenneth *secretary general of Interpol*
Pack, Sandy (Sandra Lee Pack) *former federal agency administrator*
Piovezahn, Alessandro R. *public information officer, marketing professional, consultant*
Sheehan, Michael Andrew *former protective services official, former federal agency administrator*
Shorris, Anthony Ernest *state agency administrator*
Sorensen, Gillian Martin *United Nations officia*
Stewart, Ruth Ann *public policy educator*
Talbot, Phillips *retired Asian affairs specialist*
Turso, Vito Anthony *government agency administrator, public information officer*

Romulus
Ostrander, Robert Edwin *retired United Nation interregional advisor, petroleum company executive*

Valhalla
Czarnecki, Anthony J. *correction administrator educator*

NORTH CAROLINA

Canton
Roberts, Bill Glen *retired protective services official*

Chapel Hill
Umminger, Bruce Lynn *government agency administrator, research scientist, educator, consultant*

Charlotte
Swecker, Chris (Christophe E. Swecker) *protective services official, former federal agency administrator*

Elizabeth City
Williams, Rita Carroll *protective services offici language educator, poet, librarian*

Greensboro
Ward, Charles A. *federal agency administrator*

Raleigh
Freeman, Franklin Edward, Jr. *government agency administrator*
Sanford, Jo Anne *state agency administrator*
Smith, Joseph A., Jr. *state agency administrato*

Research Triangle Park
Schwartz, David A. *federal agency administra*

Shelby
Oliver, Jeffrey Michael *protective services official*

NORTH DAKOTA

Bismarck
Karsky, Timothy J. *state agency administrator*

OHIO

Cleveland
Grabow, Raymond John *mayor, lawyer*

Columbus
Gillmor, Karen Lako *state agency administrator*
McInturff, Floyd M. *retired state agency administrator*
Moncrief, Jacqueline C. *retired state agency administrator*
Reardon, John B. III *state agency administrator*
Taylor, Joel Sanford *government agency administrator, retired lawyer*

Delaware
Ciochetty, John Bryan *protective services official*

Euclid
Ramsey, Charles *retired government agency administrator*

Fairfield
McHenry, Kathryn *forensic specialist*

Hiram
Chema, Thomas V. *government official, consultant, academic administrator, lawyer*

Montpelier
Deckrosh, Hazen Douglas *retired state agency educator and administrator*

North Canton
Dishong, Morris William *forensic specialist, nurse*

Pomeroy
Brockert, Joseph Paul *government executive, writer, editor, designer*

Zanesville
stok, Christine Markward *retired executive director social service agency, consultant*

)KLAHOMA

)klahoma City
'hompson, Mick *state agency administrator*
Wheeler, Jane Frances *protective services official*

Tulsa
)eihl, Michael Allen *federal agency administrator*

Wagoner
Iadley, Charline A. *protective services official*

)REGON

Gresham
azenby, Justin Wyatt *forensic scientist*

Portland
aylor, James Gilbert *protective services official*

alem
atman, David C. *state agency administrator*

'ENNSYLVANIA

llentown
ill, John Andrew *protective services official*

angor
chiavone, John *state agency administrator*

ettysburg
oach, James Clark *federal agency administrator*

Iarrisburg
eider, Victoria A. *state agency administrator*
'entzel, Paul H., Jr. *state agency administrator*

hiladelphia
kiyama, Cliff *forensic science educator, criminologist, researcher, consultant*
ohnson, Sylvester *police commissioner*

nionville
e Marino, Donald Nicholson *federal agency administrator, diversified financial services company executive*

'allingford
ook, Harvey Carlisle *law enforcement official*

'est Chester
arter, Shawn David *protective services official*

HODE ISLAND

rovidence
edlund, Ellen Louise *state agency administrator, educator*
roli, Dennis F. *state agency administrator*

aunderstown
nauss, John Atkinson *retired federal agency administrator, oceanographer, educator, retired dean*

)UTH CAROLINA

olumbia
cobs, Louie A. *state agency administrator*

orth Charleston
avidson, Margaret A. *federal agency administrator, lawyer*

wansea
abinet, George Walker, Jr. *retired state agency administrator*

SOUTH DAKOTA

Pierre
Novotny, Roger *state agency administrator*

Rapid City
Duhamel, Judith Reedy Olson *public information officer, former state senator*

TENNESSEE

Johnson City
Freeman, Michael Byron *protective services official, consultant*

Knoxville
Paul, Jerald S. *former federal agency administrator, state legislator*

Memphis
Knight, H. Stuart *law enforcement official, consultant*

Mount Juliet
Chester, Thomas Wayne *state agency administrator*

Nashville
Davis, Kelvisha Lashae *forensic specialist*
Gonzales, Greg *state agency administrator*
Smith, Donnie Kay *state agency administrator, retired military officer*

TEXAS

Amarillo
Fisher, Timothy Roy *protective services official*

Austin
Ashworth, Kenneth Hayden *public information administrator*
Combs, Susan *state agency administrator*
James, Randall S. *state agency administrator*

Baytown
Leiper, Robert Duncan *local government official*

Bryan
Owens, Harold B. *former state agency consultant*

Cedar Hill
Jackson, Jewel *retired state agency administrator*

Dallas
King, Clifford Thomas *protective services official, martial arts instructor, educator*
Kunkle, David M. *police chief*
Mathis-Thorton, Dianna Dawn *protective services official, writer, publishing executive, not-for-profit developer*

Duncanville
Fewel, John Gerrard *government agency administrator, director*

Garland
Sparks, Raymond Fredrick *protective services official*

Pharr
Medina, Jesse James *protective services official, educator*

San Antonio
Welch, Billy E. *retired government agency administrator, retired management consultant*

Wharton
Maxfield, Rose Mary *retired government official*

UTAH

Salt Lake City
Leary, G. Edward *state agency administrator*
Sparks, Mildred Thomas *state agency administrator, educator*

Tooele
Jansen, Lambertus *retired state agency administrator, judge, criminal justice educator*

VERMONT

Montpelier
Thabault, Paulette J. *state agency administrator*

Springfield
Putnam, Paul Adin *federal agency administrator*

VIRGINIA

Alexandria
Hale, Robert Fargo *federal association executive*
Hark, William Henry *retired federal agency administrator, aerospace physician*
Harting, Harry Lloyd, Jr. *government agency administrator, retired military officer*
Hughes, Grace-Flores *federal agency administrator*
Johnson, JoAnn Mardelle *federal agency administrator*
Knowlton, William Allen *federal agency administrator, educator*
Leestma, Robert *retired federal agency administrator, educational association administrator*
Leonhart, Michele Marie *federal agency administrator*
Tandy, Karen P. *federal agency administrator*

Annandale
Christianson, Geryld B. *government agency administrator, consultant*
Gioconda, Thomas F. *program manager, retired military flag officer*

Arlington
Askey, Thelma J. *federal agency administrator*
Baginski, Maureen A. *former federal agency administrator*
Chatfield, William Austin *federal agency administrator*
Covington, James Edwin *government agency administrator, psychologist*
Dudas, Jonathan W. *federal agency administrator*
Hawley, Edmund S. (Kip) *federal agency administrator*
Hinton, Thomas Allen *government agency administrator*
Kicklighter, Claude Milton (Mick Kicklighter) *federal agency administrator*
McDonald, Bernard Robert *retired federal agency administrator*
Meadows, Vickers B. *federal agency administrator*
Moore, Guy Will *retired public information officer, historian, writer*
Rymer, Jon T. *federal agency administrator*
Spaulding, Wallace Holmes *retired federal agency professional*
Stickler, Richard E. *federal agency administrator*
Walcher, Greg E. *government agency administrator, small business owner*

Chantilly
Fitzgerald, Dennis D. *federal agency administrator*
Kerr, Donald MacLean, Jr. *federal agency administrator, physicist*

Charlottesville
Roseberry, Edwin Southall *retired state agency administrator*

Fairfax
Jones, George Fleming *international consultant*

Fairfax Station
Kaminski, Paul Garrett *former federal agency administrator, investment banker*

Falls Church
Rooney, Kevin Davitt *federal agency administrator*

Flint Hill
Williamson, Richard Hall *federal agency administrator*

Fort Belvoir
Tegnelia, James A. *federal agency administrator*

Fredericksburg
Kusserow, Richard Phillip *federal agency administrator, corporate financial executive*

Great Falls
Turner, Stansfield *former CIA director, retired military officer*

Hampton
Roe, Lesa B. *federal agency administrator*

Herndon
Bridges, Roy Dubard, Jr. *former federal agency administrator*

Leesburg
Ink, Dwight A. *government agency administrator*

Lorton
Fulmer, Ashlee Susan *forensic specialist*

Mc Lean
Burke, Sheila P. *federal agency administrator*
Cannon, Mark Wilcox *retired government official*
Chase, Ernest Frank, Jr. *retired federal agency administrator*
Doyle, Frederick Joseph *retired government research scientist*
Leiter, Michael E. *government agency administrator*
Lion, Linda N. *retired federal agency administrator*
Mahan, Clarence *federal agency administrator, writer*
Yancik, Joseph John *retired government official*

Mineral
Donald, James Robert *federal agency administrator, writer, economist*

Oakton
Entzminger, John Nelson, Jr. *federal agency administrator, electrical engineer*

Quantico
Dones, Darvis Darell *government agency administrator*
Mangan, Terence Joseph *retired federal agency administrator*

Reston
Rosendhal, Jeffrey David *federal agency administrator, educator, astronomer, consultant*

Richmond
Blake, Peter A. *state agency administrator*
Face, E. Joseph, Jr. *state agency administrator*
Sutherland, Page Hamilton *retired government relations executive*

Spotsylvania
Hill, Jimmie Dale *retired federal agency administrator*

Upperville
Johnson, Manuel Holman, Jr. *government official, economics educator, business executive*

Waynesboro
Edwards, William Bennett *firearms industry consultant, gun dealer*

Williamsburg
Flanders, Raymond Alan *dentist, governmental health agency administrator, author*
Gentry, James William *retired state agency administrator*

WASHINGTON

Bothell
Anders, Harley Dillon, Sr. *retired federal agency administrator*

Olympia
Jarvis, Scott *state agency administrator*

Poulsbo
Romaine, Grant Hirsch *protective services official*

Seattle
Krochalis, Richard F. *federal agency administrator*
Stamper, Norman H. *protective services official*

Sequim
Huntley, James Robert *government official, international affairs scholar*
Meacham, Charles Harding *federal agency administrator*

Shelton
Leverich, Denis *protective services official, educator*

Vancouver
Ogden, Daniel Miller, Jr. *public official, educator*

WEST VIRGINIA

Charleston
Stark, Larry A. *state agency administrator*

Cottageville
Clark, Paul M. *retired protective services official*

Parkersburg
Zeck, Van *federal agency administrator*

WISCONSIN

Madison
Keating Heinemann, Lorrie T. *state agency administrator*

WYOMING

Cheyenne
Vogel, Jeffrey C. *state agency administrator*

TERRITORIES OF THE UNITED STATES

GUAM

Barrigada
Ilagan, Artemio B. *territorial agency administrator*

PUERTO RICO

San Juan
Padilla, Alfredo *state agency administrator*

CANADA

BRITISH COLUMBIA

Kelowna
Basdeo, Sahadeo *government official, educator, politician*

ONTARIO

Ottawa
MacFarlane, John Alexander *retired federal agency administrator*

Toronto
Fraser, William Neil *retired government agency administrator*
Macdonald, Donald Stovel *public policy advisor*
Tsubouchi, David H. *Canadian provincial official*

EGYPT

Cairo
Sallam, Ismail Awad-Allah *government agency administrator, educator*

ENGLAND

London
Clark, Cynthia Zang Facer *federal agency administrator*

HONG KONG

Wanchai
Paulus, Michael John *government official, economist, bank executive*

MALAWI

Lilongwe
Eastham, Alan Walter, Jr. *foreign service officer, lawyer*

PORTUGAL

Lisbon
Hansen-Nord, Jørgen *Danish agency administrator*

SUDAN

Malakal
Wieu, Andrew W. Riang *government agency administrator*

UNITED STATES

APO
Carner, George *foreign service executive, economic strategist*

ADDRESS UNPUBLISHED

Aamodt, Roger Louis *retired federal agency administrator*
Adams, Timothy D. *former federal agency administrator*
Allen, Charles E. *federal agency administrator*
Alvarez, Aida M. *former federal agency administrator*
Amorello, Matthew John *former state agency administrator, state senator*
Anderson, Wayne Carl *public information officer, retired corporate financial executive*
Armitage, Richard Lee *former federal agency administrator*
Azar, Alex Michael, II, *former federal agency administrator, lawyer*
Baker, Robert (Robbie) Michael *protective services official*
Baquet, Charles R. III *former federal agency administrator, international studies educator*
Barnett, Patricia Ann *development professional*
Barram, David J. *federal agency administrator*
Barros, Colleen *federal agency administrator*
Basham, W. Ralph *federal agency administrator*
Bashaw, Daniel James *investigator*
Bauer, Virginia Samaras *state agency administrator*
Bayer, Robert Edward *retired federal agency administrator*
Bell, Phillip Jackson *federal agency administrator*
Bishop, C. Diane *state agency administrator, educator*
Bosworth, Dale N. *former federal agency administrator*
Bradbury, Steven G. *federal agency administrator*
Brooks, Linton Forrestall *former federal agency administrator*
Brown, Dale Susan *retired federal agency and academic administrator, consultant, writer, learning disabilities website manager*
Brown, Michael DeWayne *former federal agency administrator, lawyer*
Brubaker, Crawford Francis, Jr. *federal agency administrator, aerospace scientist, consultant*
Brubaker, William W., Jr. *federal agency administrator, civil engineer*
Bush, Frederick Morris *former federal agency administrator*
Cambone, Stephen Anthony *former federal agency administrator*
Campbell, Arthur Andrews *retired federal agency administrator*
Carmona, Richard Henry *former Surgeon General of the United States*
Cheek, William Shields, Jr. *protective services official*
Clark, John F. *federal agency administrator*
Clarke, Victoria C. (Torie Clarke) *former federal agency administrator*
Claytor, Richard Anderson *retired federal agency administrator*
Cohen, Jay M. *federal agency administrator, retired military officer*
Cox, Courtland *minority business administrator*
Crane, Barry D. *former federal agency administrator*
Cremer, Leon E. *retired federal agency administrator, lawyer*
Crossley, Nancy Ruth *retired federal agency administrator*
Crowell, Craven H., Jr. *retired federal agency administrator*
Crumpton, Henry A. (Hank Crumpton) *former federal agency administrator*
Curie, Charles G. *former federal agency administrator*
Delaney, John *protective services official*
Dewey, Arthur Eugene *former federal agency administrator*
Dingle, Carol A. *state agency administrator, writer*
Dominguez, Michael L. *federal agency administrator, former civilian military employee*
Doret, Peter *state agency administrator, lawyer*
Fackner, Robert E. *protective services official, consultant*
Farris, Ronald M. *retired intelligence officer*
Faulkner, Frances Mayhew *retired federal agency administrator*
Feiner, Ava Sophia *public affairs consultant, management consultant, economist*
Felt, Mark (Deep Throat, William Mark Felt Sr.) *former federal agency administrator*
Fiene, Brian D. *protective services official, retired military officer*
Fisher, Linda J. *former federal agency administrator*
Flory, Peter Cyril Wyche *federal agency administrator*
Forbes-Richardson, Helen Hilda *state agency administrator*
Franco, Adolfo Alberto *former federal agency administrator*
Frazier, Henry Bowen III *retired federal agency administrator*
Friday, Elbert Walter, Jr. *federal agency administrator, meteorologist*
Gaddy, Sidney Warren *government agency administrator*
Gall, Mary Sheila *former federal agency administrator*
Garman, David Kline *former federal agency administrator*
Gauss, John A. *former federal agency administrator, retired naval officer*
Golding, Carolyn May *former government senior executive, consultant*
Gonzalez, Richard *maritime safety officer*
Goss, Porter Johnston *former CIA director, former congressman*
Green, Grant S., Jr. *former federal agency administrator*
Gregory, Frederick Drew *federal agency administrator*
Guttau, Michael K. *state agency administrator, banker*
Hayes, Paula Freda *federal agency administrator*
Helms, J. Lynn *retired federal agency administrator*
Henke, Robert Joseph *federal agency administrator*
Heyman, Ira Michael *federal agency administrator, law educator, museum executive*
Hickok, Eugene Welch *former federal agency administrator*
Hodsoll, Francis Samuel Monaise *government official*
Horinko, Marianne Lamont *former federal agency administrator*
House, George R. *protective services official, farmer*
Huhtala, Marie Therese *federal agency administrator, former ambassador*
James, Kay Coles *former federal agency administrator*
Jameson, Patricia Marian *government agency administrator*
Jennings, Jeffrey Scott *government agency administrator*
Johnson, Henry Louis *former federal agency and school system administrator*
Johnstone, Stowell *former state agency administrator*
Joseph, Robert G. *former federal agency administrator*
Karnas, Fred G., Jr. *poverty and homeless specialist*
Kaveeshwar, Ashok G. *former federal agency administrator*
Kawamoto, Keith Hitoshi *protective services official*
Kearns, Merle Grace *state agency administrator*
Keene, Mary Ellen *federal agency executive*
Kelly, James Andrew *former federal agency administrator, policy research executive*
Kelso, John Hodgson *retired federal agency administrator*
Keys, John W. III *former federal agency administrator*
Kim, Wan J. *former federal agency administrator, lawyer*
Krantz, Michael Scott *protective services official, educator*
Krieg, Kenneth Joseph *former federal agency administrator*
Kutscher, Ronald Earl *retired federal agency administrator*
LaBarre, Carl Anthony *retired federal agency administrator*
Lee, Tonia Reneé *entertainer, former government agent, educator*
Lewis, Samuel Winfield *retired federal agency administrator, diplomat*
Likins, Rose Marie *former federal agency administrator, ambassador*
Lokmer, Stephanie Ann *international business development consultant*
Lovelace, Rose Marie Sniegon *federal space agency administrator*
Lovell, Malcolm Read, Jr. *public information officer, educator, retired trade association administrator, federal official*
Loy, Frank Ernest *retired federal agency administrator*
Lu, Natalie *federal agency administrator*
Luce, Thomas Warren III *former federal agency administrator*
MacFarlane, Cathy M. *federal agency administrator*
Magaw, John W. *former federal agency administrator*
Mainella, Fran (Frances P. Mainella) *educator, former federal agency administrator*
Malley, Raymond Charles *retired foreign service official, industrial executive*
Manson, Harold Craig *former federal agency administrator, former judge*
McCaleb, Neal A. *former federal agency administrator*
McClain, Lena Alexandria *protective services official*
McCormick, Robert Junior *former federal agency administrator*
McDowell, Elaine *retired federal government executive, educator*
McHale, Paul F., Jr. *federal agency administrator, former congressman*
McLaughlin, John Edward *former federal agency administrator*
McLean, Walter Franklin *government agency administrator, business consultant, legislator, minister*
McManus, William Paul *police chief*
McPherson, Ted R. (Edward Russell McPherson) *former federal agency administrator*
McTaggart, Timothy Robert *state agency administrator, lawyer*
Mehan, George Tracey III *former federal agency administrator*
Meyer, Donald Robert *state agency administrator, lawyer*
Minners, Howard Alyn *federal agency administrator, researcher, preventive medicine physician*
Molholm, Kurt Nelson *retired federal agency administrator*
Molz, Redmond Kathleen *public affairs educator*
Morales, Diane K. *former federal agency administrator*
Moseley, James R. *former federal agency administrator, farmer*
Murr, James Coleman *retired federal agency administrator*
Myers, Julie L. *federal agency administrator*
Newman, Constance Berry *federal agency administrator*
Nolan, Jeanada H. *retired state agency administrator, social worker, educator*
Nyquist, Maurice Otto *retired federal agency administrator, scientist*
O'Brien, Odessa Louise *protective services official*
Oleson, John Roy *retired US foreign services officer, consultant*
Oliver, Jerry Alton *former police chief*
O'Neill, Molly Ann *federal agency administrator*
Padden, Anthony Aloysius, Jr. *retired federal government official*
Parker, Susan Brooks *government agency administrator*
Pasternack, Robert Harry *former federal agency administrator*
Pearson, Jennie Sue *retired government administrator*
Pearson, W(illiam) Robert *former federal agency administrator, former ambassador*
Perkins, Raymond Lamont *retired government official*
Pitofsky, Robert *federal agency administrator, law educator*
Prosper, Pierre-Richard *former federal agency administrator*
Provitt, Linda K. *forensic specialist, mental health services professional, consultant*
Quarles, Randal Keith *former federal agency administrator, lawyer*
Quintana-Allenson, Ana M. *government agency executive*
Rabon, Anthony Perez *protective services official*
Raley, Bennett William *former federal agency administrator*
Ramsey, Charles H. *former police chief*
Rascon, Alfred V. *former federal agency administrator*
Reynolds, Frank Miller *retired government agency administrator*
Ridgway, James Mastin *retired government agency administrator*
Ringler, Kenneth J., Jr. *former state agency administrator*
Rodgers, Bruce Alan *government agency administrator, psychologist*
Roe, Mary Ann *retired postmaster*
Rosenberg, Alison P. *public policy officer*
Runge, Jeffrey William *former federal agency administrator*
Scheinberg, Phyllis F. *federal agency administrator*
Schoenberg, Mark George *government agency administrator*
Schoenberger, James Edwin *retired federal agency administrator*
Schur Kaufman, Susan *retired public affairs consultant*
Schwartz, Carol Levitt *government official*
Scoppetta, Nicholas *fire commissioner*
Shasteen, Donald Eugene *retired government official, small business consultant*
Shute, Richard Emil *federal agency administrator, engineer*
Skaff, Joseph John *state agency administrator, retired military officer*
Slater, Eve E. *former federal agency administrator*
Smith, Nancy Angelynn *federal agency administrator*
Sorter, Bruce Wilbur *federal program administrator, educator, consultant*
Spooner, David M. *federal agency administrator, lawyer*
Steffy, Marion Nancy *state agency administrator*
Stenbit, John Paul *former federal agency administrator*
Swinburn, Carol Ditzler *retired state and municipal agency administrator*
Swoap, David Bruce *government and state agency administrator, consultant, art director*
Taylor, Francis X. *former federal agency administrator, retired military officer*
Ter Horst, Jerald Franklin *public affairs counselor*
Tobias, Randall Lee *former federal agency administrator, retired pharmaceutical company executive*
Towle, Leland Hill *retired federal agency administrator*
Trachtenberg, Eric Bertram *foreign service officer, economist*
Trent, Richard H. *protective services official, educator, paramedic*
Truesdale, John Cushman *federal agency administrator, lawyer*
Turner, John Freeland *former federal agency administrator, retired state legislator*
Tweed, Lorna Barbara *protective services official, paramedic*
Uhler, Walter Charles *government official, writer*
Vandiver, Sara Elizabeth Sharp Rankin *retired postmaster*
Walz, Edward George *protective services official*
Wendt, E. Allan *international affairs consultant*
Whitman, Christine Todd *former federal agency administrator, governor*
Widner, Ralph Randolph *retired public administrator*
Williams, B. John, Jr. *retired federal agency administrator, lawyer*
Williams, Michael Richard *protective services official*
Williams, Sue M. *federal agency administrator, writer*
Winkenwerder, William, Jr. *former federal agency administrator*
Winn, Morris X. *former federal agency administrator*
Winter, Roger Paul *former federal agency administrator*
Withrow, Mary Ellen *federal agency administrator*
Wooldridge, Sue Ellen *former federal agency administrator, lawyer*
Wright, Sylvia *government agency administrator*
Wu, Benjamin H. *federal agency administrator, lawyer*
Young, Edwin S. W. *federal agency official*
Young, Frank Edward *retired federal agency and religious organization administrator*
Yurechko, John Joseph *federal agency administrator, director*
Zaltman, Mark Allen *federal agency administrator*

GOVERNMENT: EXECUTIVE ADMINISTRATION

UNITED STATES

ALABAMA

Birmingham
Boomershine, Donald Eugene *bureau executive development official*

Montgomery
Chapman, Beth Killough *state official*
Folsom, Jim (James Elisha Folsom Jr.) *lieutenant governor, former governor*
Ivey, Kay Ellen *state official*
King, Troy *state attorney general*
Riley, Bob (Robert Renfroe Riley) *governor*

Semmes
Phelps, James Franklin *retired county official*

ALASKA

Anchorage
Knowles, Tony *former governor*
Parnell, Sean *lieutenant governor, former state legislator, lawyer*

Fairbanks
Murkowski, Frank Hughes *former governor, former senator*

Juneau
Colberg, Talis J. *state attorney general*
Galvin, Patrick *state official*
Palin, Sarah Heath *governor*

Kodiak
Selby, Jerome M. *mayor*

ARIZONA

Marana
Davidson, Gilbert *city manager*

Mesa
Hawker, Keno *mayor, trucking company executive*

Phoenix
Brewer, Janice Kay *state official*
Goddard, Terry *state attorney general*
Gordon, Phillip Bruce *mayor*
Meeks, Jacquelynn *city health department administrator*
Mofford, Rose *former governor of Arizona*
Napolitano, Janet Ann *governor*

Quartzsite
Michel, Verlyn Lyle *mayor, consultant*

Scottsdale
Quayle, Dan (James Danforth Quayle) *former Vice President of the United States*

Quayle, Marilyn Tucker *wife of former United States Vice President, lawyer*

Sun Lakes
Sharpless, Joseph Benjamin *retired county official*

Tucson
Walkup, Robert E. *mayor*

ARKANSAS

Bella Vista
Medin, Myron James, Jr. *city manager*

Heber Springs
Rawlings, Paul C. *retired government official*

Little Rock
Beebe, Mike (Michael Dale Beebe) *governor, former state attorney general, lawyer*
Cheek, James Richard *ambassador*
Daniels, Charlie L. *state official*
Halter, Bill (William A. Halter) *lieutenant governor*
McDaniel, Dustin *state attorney general*
Priest, Sharon Devlin *retired state official, not-for-profit developer*
Shoffner, Martha Ann *state official*
Stodola, Mark Allen *mayor, former prosecutor*
Weiss, Richard A. *state official*

CALIFORNIA

Arroyo Grande
Benedict, Lawrence Neal *foreign service officer*

Benicia
von Studnitz, Gilbert Alfred *state official*

Berkeley
Taylor, John Lockhart *retired municipal official*

Carlsbad
Wollam, Jean Farr *retired diplomat*

Carson
Dropeza, Jenny *state official*

Claremont
Pedersen, Richard Foote *diplomat, academic administrator*

Coronado
Hostler, Charles Warren *retired ambassador, international affairs consultant*

Felicity
Istel, Jacques Andre *mayor*

Grass Valley
Cassella, Dennis Gene *retired county official*

Hollister
Monaco, Reb Leon *county official*

La Jolla
Shakespeare, Frank *ambassador*

Laguna Woods
Hussey, William Bertrand *retired diplomat*

Long Beach
Foster, Robert G. (Bob Foster) *mayor*
Sato, Eunice Noda *former mayor, consultant*

Los Angeles
Bustamante, Cruz M. *former lieutenant governor*
Fielding, Jonathan Evan *city health department administrator, pediatrician*
Molina, Gloria *municipal official*
Roman, Mary Ann *federal official*
Villaraigosa, Antonio Ramon *mayor*

Marina
Mettee-McCutchon, Ila *municipal official, retired military officer*

Menlo Park
Lane, Laurence William, Jr. *retired ambassador, publisher*

Montebello
Calderon, Ronald *state official*

Monterey Park
Smith, Betty Denny *county official, administrator, fashion executive*

Moreno Valley
White, Charles R. *former mayor*

Napa
Battisti, Paul Oreste *retired municipal official*

Oakland
Dellums, Ronald Vernie *mayor, retired congressman*

Oceanside
Lyon, Richard *retired mayor, military officer*

Ontario
Mastrup-Hamill, Faye Myers *city official*

Palo Alto
Schnabel, Rockwell Anthony *former ambassador*

Pasadena
Bogaard, William Joseph *mayor, lawyer, educator*

Redlands
Hanson, Gerald Warner *retired county official*

Richmond
Corbin, Rosemary MacGowan *former mayor*

Sacramento
Bowen, Debra Lynn *state official, former state legislator*
Brown, Jerry, Jr., (Edmund Gerald Brown Jr.) *state attorney general, former mayor, governor*
Dunnett, Dennis George *retired state official*
Fargo, Heather *mayor*
Garamendi, John R. *lieutenant governor, former state legislator*
Hunter, Patricia Rae (Tricia Hunter) *state official*
Lockyer, Bill (William Lockyer) *state official, former state attorney general*
Schwarzenegger, Arnold Alois *governor*
Wyland, Mark *state official*

San Diego
Bliesner, James Douglas *municipal/county official, consultant*
Golding, Susan G. *former mayor*
Rahmani, Reza Mossaver *writer, retired Iranian Air Force officer, banker, tour operator*
Sanders, Jerry *mayor, former social services executive*
Shepard, Jean M. *city health department administrator*

San Francisco
Gore, Al (Albert Arnold Gore Jr.) *former Vice President of the United States*
Hewitt, Conrad W. *former commissioner, accountant*
Katz, Mitchell H. *city health department administrator*
Newsom, Gavin *mayor*
Reilly, William Kane *former government official, educator, lawyer, conservationist*

San Jose
Reed, Charles Rufus (Chuck Reed) *mayor, lawyer*

San Luis Obispo
Shlaudeman, Harry Walter *retired diplomat*

Santa Monica
Aaron, David L. *diplomat, author*

Seaside
Panetta, Leon Edward *former White House chief of staff, former congressman*

Stanford
Abraham, (Edward) Spencer *former Secretary of Energy*

Stockton
Meissner, Katherine Gong *municipal official*

Tracy
Waziri, Ghaus Ghulam *diplomat*

Walnut Creek
Walston, Roderick Eugene *federal official*

Yuba City
Kemmerly, Jack Dale *retired state official*

COLORADO

Aurora
Nicholas, Thomas Peter *municipal official*
Sheffield, Nancy *city agency administrator*

Boulder
Minger, Terrell John *public administration and natural resource institute executive*

Buena Vista
Scott, Gerald Wesley *retired American diplomat*

Colorado Springs
Abbott, Gina *municipal government executive*
Rivera, Lionel *mayor*
Swihart, James W., Jr. *diplomat*

Commerce City
Hogan, Aden Ellsworth, Jr. *city government administrator*

Denver
Brown, Keith Lapham *retired ambassador*
Coffman, Mike (Michael H. Coffman) *state official, former state legislator*
Cohen-Vader, Cheryl Denise *municipal official*
Cuba, Stanley L. *government official*
Hickenlooper, John W. *mayor*
Kennedy, Cary *state official*
O'Brien, Barbara *lieutenant governor*
Ritter, Bill (August William Ritter Jr.) *governor, former prosecutor*
Suthers, John William *state attorney general*

Pueblo
Occhiato, Michael Anthony *municipal official*

CONNECTICUT

Canton Center
Humphrey, Samuel Stockwell *town official, physicist*

Easton
Meyer, Alice Virginia *state official*

Hartford
Blumenthal, Richard *state attorney general*
Bysiewicz, Susan *state official*
Fedele, Michael Christian *lieutenant governor, computer company executive*
Margulies, Beth Zeldes *state attorney general*
Nappier, Denise L. *state official*
Rell, M. Jodi *governor*

New Haven
Zedillo Ponce de León, Ernesto *former president of Mexico*

Northford
James, William Hall *former state official, educator*

Stamford
Dennies, Sandra Lee *city official*
Malloy, Dannel Patrick *mayor*

DELAWARE

Dover
Carney, John C., Jr. *lieutenant governor*
Markell, Jack A. *state official*
Minner, Ruth Ann *governor*
Windsor, Harriet Smith *state official*

Newark
Woo, S. B. (Shien-Biau Woo) *retired state official, physicist, educator*

Wilmington
Biden, Beau (Joseph Robinette Biden III) *state attorney general, lawyer*

DISTRICT OF COLUMBIA

Washington
Abdenur, Roberto Mameri Pinto *ambassador*
Abell, Charles S. *federal official*
Abell, Richard Bender *federal judicial officer, lawyer*
Abrams, Elliott *federal official*
Abshire, David Manker *former ambassador, research executive*
Adams, Roger C. *federal official, lawyer*
Addington, David S. *federal official, lawyer*
Adelstein, Jonathan Steven *commissioner*
Aguirre, Eduardo, Jr. *ambassador, former federal agency administrator*
Albright, Madeleine Korbel *former secretary of state*
Allgeier, Peter Frederick *ambassador*
Almaguer, Frank *ambassador*
Andersen, Robert Allen *retired federal official*
Aranoff, Shara L. *federal official*
Arietti, Michael Ray *ambassador*
Arnall, Roland E. *ambassador*
Atherton, Charles Henry *federal commission administrator*
Atkins, Paul S. *commissioner*
Ayres, Mary Ellen *federal official*
Azcuenaga, Mary Laurie *government official*
Bachula, Gary R. *federal official*
Baicker, Katherine (Kate) *federal official, economics professor*
Baker, Douglas B. *federal official*
Bandler, Donald Keith *international consultant, former ambassador*
Barbosa, Rubens Antonio *former ambassador*
Berger, Sandy (Samuel R. Berger) *former national security advisor*
Bernanke, Ben Shalom *chairman board of governors of the Federal Reserve System*
Beyrle, John R. *ambassador*
Bhatia, Karan K. *ambassador*
Blahous, Charles P. *federal official*
Blanchard, James Johnston *ambassador, retired governor*
Bodman, Samuel Wright III *secretary of energy, former specialty chemicals and materials company executive*
Bolten, Joshua Brewster *White House chief of staff*
Bost, Eric M. *ambassador, former federal agency administrator*
Boswell, Eric J. *federal official*
Boyce, Ralph L. (Skip Boyce) *ambassador*
Bradtke, Robert A. *ambassador*
Brazeal, Aurelia Erskine *former ambassador*
Breathitt, Linda K. *energy advisor, former federal energy commissioner*
Brewster, Robert Charles *diplomat, consultant*
Broome, David *federal official*
Browning, Steven Alan *ambassador*
Burns, William Joseph *ambassador, former federal agency administrator*
Bush, George Walker *43rd President of the United States*
Bush, Laura Welch *First Lady of United States*
Butchart, Mark Steven *diplomat*
Cabral, Anna Escobedo *federal official*
Cain, James P. *ambassador, lawyer*
Campbell-Smith, Patricia *federal official*
Carson, Johnnie *former ambassador, academic administrator*
Casey, Kathleen L. *commissioner*
Chao, Elaine Lan (Hsiao) *secretary of labor*
Cheney, Dick (Richard Bruce Cheney) *Vice President of the United States*
Chertoff, Michael *secretary of homeland security, former federal judge*
Chien, Nguyen Tam *ambassador*
Chilton, Bart (Bartholomew Hamilton Chilton) *commissioner*
Clark-Bourne, Kathryn Orpha *retired consul*
Cleland, Joseph Maxwell (Max Cleland) *federal official, former senator*
Cloud, John Albert, Jr. *ambassador*
Collins, James Franklin *retired ambassador*
Combs, Linda Morrison *federal official*
Coneway, Peter Richard *ambassador, retired diversified financial services company executive*
Connaughton, James L. *federal official*
Cook, Michael Blanchard *government executive*
Copps, Michael Joseph *commissioner*
Corbin, Michael *diplomat*
Crocker, Chester Arthur *diplomat, federal agency administrator*
Crowder, Richard Thomas *ambassador*
Cusick, Robert Irwin *federal official, lawyer*
Cutler, Walter Leon *diplomat, foundation executive*
Danilovich, John J. *federal official, former ambassador*
Davidson, Donetta Lea *federal official, former state official*
Debevoise, Eli Whitney, II, *federal official, lawyer*
Denett, Paul Alfred *federal official*
Duemling, Robert Werner *diplomat, museum director*
Duffy, Michael F. *commissioner*
Dunn, David B. *ambassador*
Dunn, Michael V. *commissioner*
Dybul, Mark Richard *ambassador*
Eagleburger, Lawrence Sidney *former secretary of state*
Earp, Naomi Churchill *federal official, lawyer*
Eaton, William A. *ambassador, former federal agency administrator*
Edwards, John Frederick *federal official*
Elwood, Patricia Cowan *city official, political scientist, consultant*
Ely-Raphel, Nancy *diplomat*
Ensenat, Donald Burnham *ambassador, lawyer*
Fahmy, Nabil *ambassador*
Farr, George Frank, Jr. *retired federal official*
Fenty, Adrian M. *mayor*
Fielding, Fred Fisher *federal official, lawyer*
Fingar, Thomas *federal official*
Fleisher, Eric Wilfrid *retired foreign service officer*
Foley, April H. *ambassador*
Foley, Tom (Thomas Stephen Foley) *former ambassador, former congressman*
Ford, Charles A. *ambassador*
Francke, Rend Rahim *former ambassador*
Franklin, Barbara Hackman *former government official*
Fratto, Tony (Salvatore Antonio) *federal official*
Fritsche, Claudia *diplomat, ambassador*
Gaa, Willy C. *ambassador*
Galbraith, Peter Woodard *former ambassador*
Gandhi, Natwar M. *city manager*
Garthoff, Raymond Leonard *retired diplomat, diplomatic historian*
Gates, Robert Michael *secretary of defense, former academic administrator*
Gati, Toby T. *international advisor*
Gessaman, Donald Eugene *retired government executive*
Giffin, Gordon D. *former ambassador, lawyer*
Gillespie, Ed (Edward Walter Gillespie) *federal official, former political organization administrator*
Gilliom, Judith Carr *federal official*
Ginsberg, Marc Charles *former diplomat, investment company executive*
Glazer, Charles Louis *ambassador*
Glendening, Parris Nelson *former governor, political science educator*
Gnehm, Edward W., Jr. *ambassador*
Golkiewicz, Gary J. *federal official*
Graber, Richard William *ambassador, lawyer*
Gribbin, Robert E. III *diplomat*
Griffin, Christine M. *commissioner*
Grove, Brandon Hambright, Jr. *diplomat*
Guhin, Michael Alan *ambassador*
Gutierrez, Carlos Miguel *secretary of commerce, former grocery manufacturing company executive*
Hadley, Stephen John *national security advisor*
Hagin, Joseph Whitehouse, II, *federal official*
Hale, David M. *ambassador*
Hannah, John P. *federal official*
Harbour, Pamela Jones *commissioner, lawyer*
Harrop, William Caldwell *retired ambassador*
Hastings, George L. *federal official*
Hatfield, Fred (Frederick William Hattfield) *former commissioner*
Hays, Sharon Lynn *federal official*
Hein, Jay F. *federal official*
Hillman, Jennifer Anne *federal official*
Hoffman, Alfred, Jr. *ambassador, real estate developer*
Hooks, Aubrey *ambassador*
Horowitz, Herbert Eugene *retired diplomat*
Hubbard, Allan Brooks *federal official, former chemical company executive*
Hume, Cameron R. *ambassador*
Ishimaru, Stuart Jon *commissioner, lawyer*
Iskandar, Harris *attache*
Jackson, Alphonso Roy *secretary of housing and urban development*
Jackson, Jeanine E. *ambassador*
Jacobson, Tracey Ann *ambassador*
Jarque, Carlos M. *former federal official*
Jawad, Said Tayeb (Said Tayeb Djawad) *ambassador, commentator, writer*
Johanns, Michael Owen *secretary of agriculture, former governor*
Johnson, Clay III *federal official*
Johnson, Collister, Jr., (Terry Johnson Jr.) *federal official*
Johnson, David Timothy *diplomat*
Johnson, Donald Crandall
Johnson, Esther R. *federal official*
Johnson, Jennifer J. *federal official*
Johnson, Stephen L. *federal official*
Jones, James Robert *ambassador, retired congressman, lawyer*
Jones, Richard Henry *ambassador*
Kaplan, Joel David *federal official*
Kato, Ryozo *ambassador*
Kattouf, Theodore E. *former ambassador*
Kauzlarich, Richard Dale *retired ambassador, political scientist, consultant*
Keating, Francis Anthony, II, *retired governor, lawyer*
Kelliher, Joseph Timothy *commissioner*
Kelly, John Joseph, Jr. *federal official*
Kelly, Suedeen G. *commissioner*

Kempthorne, Dirk Arthur *secretary of the interior, former governor*
Kenney, Kristie Anne *ambassador*
Killgore, Andrew Ivy *former ambassador*
Kohn, Donald L. *federal official, economist*
Kolb, Charles Edward Mealey *federal government official, lawyer*
Koskinen, John Andrew *foundation executive*
Kostelnik, Michael Charles *commissioner, retired military officer*
Kovacic, William Evan *commissioner, law educator*
Kroszner, Randall Scott *federal official, economics professor*
LaFleur, Christopher J. *ambassador*
Lake, (W.) Anthony *former national security advisor*
Lane, Charlotte R. *federal official, lawyer*
Langdale, Mark *ambassador, former hotel executive*
Lazear, Edward Paul *federal official, economics professor*
Leavitt, Michael Okerlund *secretary of health and human services*
Leibowitz, Jon *commissioner*
Levitte, Jean-David *ambassador*
Lewis, Ann Frank *former government official*
Lowe, Mary Frances *federal official*
Lowenstein, James Gordon *former diplomat, international consultant*
Lucas, James Walter *federal official*
Lukken, Walter L. *commissioner*
Lundsager, Margrethe (Meg Lundsager) *federal official*
Lute, Douglas E. *federal official, career military officer*
Madras, Bertha Kalifon *federal official, neuroscientist, researcher*
Magee, Charles Thomas *international consultant, retired diplomat*
Majoras, Deborah Platt *commissioner*
Manning, David Geoffrey *ambassador*
Manzanares, J. Robert *ambassador*
Marburger, John Harmen III *federal official*
Marcoullis, Erato Kozakou *ambassador*
Marcus, Kenneth L. *federal official*
Marine, Michael W. *ambassador*
Martinez, Carmen Maria *ambassador*
Masekela, Barbara Joyce Mosima *ambassador*
McCallum, Robert Davis, Jr. *ambassador, former federal agency administrator*
McCaw, Susan Rasinski *ambassador*
McConnell, Mike (John Michael McConnell) *Director of National Intelligence, retired military officer*
McCormick, William Paul *ambassador*
McDowell, Robert M. *commissioner*
McEldowney, Nancy *diplomat*
McLarty, Thomas F., III, (Mack McLarty) *former White House Chief of Staff*
McMillin, Stephen S. *federal official*
McPhie, Neil Anthony Gordon *federal official*
Meece, Roger A. *ambassador*
Meridor, Sallai *ambassador*
Meyerrose, Dale William *federal official, retired military officer*
Milam, William Bryant *former ambassador, senior policy scholar*
Miller, William Green *former ambassador*
Millman, Laura Diane *federal official*
Mishkin, Frederic Stanley *federal official, economics educator*
Moeller, Philip D. *commissioner*
Mombouli, Serge *ambassador*
Moran, Christian J. *federal official*
Moritsugu, Kenneth Paul *federal official, career military officer*
Mulford, David Campbell *ambassador, former finance company executive*
Natsios, Andrew Stephen *diplomat, former federal agency administrator*
Nazareth, Annette LaPorte *commissioner, lawyer*
Newman, Sherryl Hobbs *former district secretary*
Nicholson, Jim (Robert James Nicholson) *secretary of veterans affairs, former ambassador*
Norland, Donald Richard *retired foreign service officer*
Obiozor, George Achulike *ambassador*
Okun, Deanna Tanner *federal official*
Orr, Bobette Kay *diplomat*
Owen, Henry *former ambassador, consultant*
Parris, Mark Robert *former ambassador, policy advisor*
Pasi, Geeta *diplomat*
Patterson, Anne Woods *ambassador, former federal agency administrator*
Paulson, Hank (Henry Merritt Paulson Jr.) *secretary of the treasury, former diversified financial services company executive*
Pearce, Drue *federal official, former state legislator*
Pearson, Daniel R. *federal official*
Pendleton, Miles Stevens, Jr. *diplomat*
Perino, Dana Marie *White House press secretary*
Peters, Mary Elizabeth *secretary of transportation*
Phillips, James D. *retired diplomat*
Phillips, Stanley Davis *ambassador*
Phommahaxay, Phanthong *ambassador*
Pionk, Jerome Lee *federal official*
Placke, James Anthony *retired diplomat*
Polt, Michael C. *ambassador*
Powell, Nancy Jo *federal official, former ambassador*
Quainton, Anthony Cecil Eden *diplomat*
Railton, W(illiam) Scott *retired commissioner*
Randt, Clark Thorp, Jr. *ambassador, lawyer*
Ranneberger, Michael E. *ambassador*
Ray, Charles Aaron *ambassador*
Reed, John Hathaway *former ambassador*
Ricciardone, Francis Joseph, Jr. *ambassador*
Rice, Condoleezza *secretary of state, former national security advisor*
Richardson, Scott *federal official, researcher, writer*
Roberts, Walter Ronald *retired diplomat*
Rogers, Thomasina Venese *commissioner*
Rogowsky, Robert Arthur *federal official, educator*
Rooney, Francis *ambassador*
Rosch, John Thomas (Tom) *commissioner, lawyer*
Rose, Mary McNally *federal official*
Rosenfeld, Arthur F. *federal official, lawyer*
Ross, Dennis B. *former diplomat*
Russell, Richard Mather *federal official*
Sanders, Robin Renee *former ambassador*
Sanderson, Janet A. *former ambassador*
Sarukhan, Arturo *ambassador*
Sayre, Robert Marion *ambassador*
Schieffer, J. Thomas (John Thomas Schieffer, Tom Schieffer) *ambassador, former professional baseball team executive*
Schlicher, Ronald Lewis *ambassador*
Schneider, Cynthia Perrin *former ambassador, political science professor*
Schneider, Mark Lewis *foreign policy executive, retired government agency administrator*
Schulte, Gregory L. *ambassador*
Schwab, Susan Carroll *ambassador, former academic administrator*
Scott, Stephanie D. *city official*
Scowcroft, Brent *former national security advisor, retired military officer*
Seck, Mamadou Mansour *ambassador, military officer*
Sellin, Theodore *diplomat, consultant*
Shinn, David Hamilton *former diplomat, educator, writer*
Shirzad, Faryar *federal official*
Silverman, Leslie E. *commissioner*
Simmons, Anne L. *federal official*
Singer, Linda J. *attorney general*
Smalley, Robert Manning *diplomat*
Smith, Elaine Diana *foreign service officer*
Smith, Patricia Grace *federal official*
Sobel, Clifford M. *ambassador*
Solberg, Mary Ann *federal official*
Sommers, Jill E. *commissioner*
Sonnenfeldt, Helmut *former government official, educator, consultant, writer*
Spector, Melbourne Louis *retired foreign service officer*
Spellings, Margaret LaMontagne *secretary of education*
Spitzer, Marc Lee *commissioner, former state legislator*
Springer, Linda M. *federal official*
Stadtler, Walter Edward *diplomat*
Stapleton, Craig Roberts *ambassador*
Stern, Todd D. *government official, lawyer*
Stock, Ann *federal official*
Sullivan, Kevin F. *federal official*
Suro-Bredie, Carmen Cecilia *federal official*
Sutter, Eleanor Bly *retired diplomat*
Swimmer, Ross Owen *federal official*
Tate, Deborah Taylor *commissioner*
Taubman, Nicholas F. *ambassador*
Taylor, William B., Jr. *ambassador*
Teare, Richard Wallace *retired foreign service officer*
Thawley, Michael *diplomat*
Thompson, Horace A., III, (Topper Thompson) *commissioner, lawyer*
Timken, William Robert, Jr. *ambassador, former manufacturing executive*
Townsend, Fran (Frances Fragos Townsend) *federal official*
Ushakov, Yury Viktorovich *ambassador*
Van de Water, Read *federal official*
van Voorst, Carol *ambassador*
Varney, Christine A. *federal official*
Vento, Sergio *ambassador*
Veroneau, John K. *ambassador*
Vershbow, Alexander R. *ambassador*
Verville, Elizabeth Giavani *federal official*
Villarosa, Shari *ambassador*
Vowell, Denise K. *federal official*
Walker, David Michael *federal official*
Walters, John P. *federal official*
Wang, Kim *commissioner, librarian*
Ware, Marilyn *ambassador, former utilities company executive*
Warsh, Kevin Maxwell *federal official*
Watson, Arthur Dennis *federal official*
Wayne, Earl Anthony *ambassador, former federal agency administrator*
Wayne, Stephen J. *government educator, writer*
Weisberg, Robert *ambassador*
Weizmann, Howard Charles *federal official*
Wellinghoff, Jon *commissioner*
Wells, Barry L. *federal official*
Wexler, Anne *government relations and public affairs consultant*
Whitney, Benson K. *ambassador*
Wilkins, David Horton *ambassador, former state legislator*
Williamson, Clint (John Clint Williamson) *ambassador*
Wilson, Michael Holcombe *ambassador, investment banker, former Canadian government official*
Wilson, Ross *ambassador*
Wise, Bob (Robert Ellsworth Wise Jr.) *former governor, former congressman*
Wolf, John S. *ambassador, federal agency administrator*
Wolff, Candida (Candi) *federal official*
Wolters, Curt Cornelis Frederik *foreign service officer*
Wood, Michael M. *ambassador*
Yamamoto, Donald Yukio *ambassador*
Zarate, Juan Carlos *federal official*
Ziman, Barry Russell *government relations executive*
Zinmeister, Karl *federal official*

FLORIDA

Aventura
Garcia, Marc Anthony *diplomat*

Bal Harbour
Horton, Jeanette *municipal government official*

Boynton Beach
Polinsky, Janet Naboicheck *retired state official, retired state legislator*
Warshaw, Stanley Irving *federal official, consultant*

Brooksville
Anderson, Richard Edmund *city manager, management consultant*

Fernandina Beach
Smeeton, Thomas Rooney *government affairs consultant*

Fort Lauderdale
Burleigh, A. Peter *ambassador*
Gunzburger, Suzanne Nathan *municipal official, social worker*
Johnson, Mary Margaret Dickens *governmental and commercial researcher, consultant*

Fort Myers
Lamach, Bernard D. *professional engineer, county commissioner*

Gainesville
Heflin, Martin Ganier *diplomat, political scientist*

Hollywood
Giulianti, Mara Selena *mayor*

Jacksonville
Goldhagen, Jeffrey Lee *city health department administrator*

Malabar
de Vos, Peter Jon *ambassador*

Mexico Beach
Mullen, John P. *retired government executive*

Miami
Diaz, Manuel A. *mayor*
Magrath, Kathleen Barry *retired municipal official*

Oakland Park
Atkinson, Christopher Lee *county official*

Sarasota
Morrow, William Earl *retired government official, retired law educator*

Tallahassee
Browning, Kurt S. *state official*
Crist, Charlie (Charles Joseph Crist Jr.) *governor, former state attorney general*
McCollum, Bill (Ira William McCollum Jr.) *state attorney general, former congressman*
Mortham, Sandra Barringer *former state official, medical association administrator*
Sink, Adelaide Alexander *state official*

Tampa
Freedman, Sandra Warshaw *former mayor*
Martinez, Bob *former federal official, governor*
Platt, Jan Kaminis *former county official*

GEORGIA

Atlanta
Baker, Thurbert E. *state attorney general*
Cagle, Casey *lieutenant governor*
Carter, Jimmy (James Earl Carter Jr.) *39th President of the United States*
Dean, James Edward *retired state official*
Ebersole, W. Daniel *state official*
Franklin, Shirley Clarke *mayor*
Handel, Karen *state official*
Laney, James Thomas *former ambassador, educator*
Perdue, George (Sonny Perdue) *governor, former state legislator*
Scott, Donald Lavern *city manager, librarian, former army officer*
Taylor, Mark *former lieutenant governor*

Brunswick
Patrick, Connie L. *federal official*

Canton
Angulo, Charles Bonin *foreign service officer, lawyer*

Conyers
Kelly, John Hubert *diplomat*

Saint Simons Island
Douglas, William Ernest *retired commissioner*

Tucker
Streeb, Gordon Lee *diplomat, economist*

HAWAII

Honolulu
Aiona, James R., Jr. *lieutenant governor*
Bennett, Mark J. *state attorney general*
Bronster, Margery S. *retired state attorney general, lawyer*
Hannemann, Mufi *mayor*
Lingle, Linda *governor*

Mililani
Olsen, Harris Leland *diplomat, writer, real estate company executive, educator*

IDAHO

Boise
Benham, James H. *state official*
Crane, Ron G. *state official*
Kustra, Robert W. (Bob Kustra) *former state official, academic administrator*
Otter, Butch (C. L. Otter, Clement Leroy Otter) *governor, former congressman*
Risch, Jim (James E.) *lieutenant governor, former governor, state legislator*
Terteling-Payne, Carolyn Ann *city official*
Wasden, Lawrence *state attorney general*
Wilson, Jack Fredrick *retired federal government official*
Ysursa, Ben T. *state official*

ILLINOIS

Carbondale
Cole, Brad *mayor*

Champaign
Semonin, Richard Gerard *retired state official*

Chicago
Balanoff, Clem *county election director*
Craig, John Bruce *former ambassador, air transportation executive*
Daley, Richard Michael *mayor*
Dempsey, Mary A. *library commissioner, lawyer*
Enenbach, Mark Henry *community action agency executive, educator*
Hoffman, David H. *city manager*
Hubberman, Ron *state official*
Lee, Yoon Mo *state official*
Lufrano, Michael Richard *lawyer*
Madigan, Lisa *state attorney general*
Mason, Terry *city health department administrator, urologist*
Natarus, Burton F. *land use consultant, lawyer*
Olk, Frederick James *county official, legal assistant*
Quinn, Patrick *lieutenant governor*
Robbins, Audrey *county employee*
Topinka, Judy Baar *state official, political organization worker*
Trotter, Cortez *city official, former fire commissioner*
Walker, Thomas Ray *city aviation commissioner*
Wood, Patrick Henry III *former federal official*

Glenview
Olson, Roy Arthur *retired government official*

Hinsdale
Mehuron, William Otto *retired federal official*

Machesney Park
Vaughn, Linda Marie *municipal official*

Springfield
Blagojevich, Rod R. *governor, former congressman*
Giannoulias, Alexi *state official*
White, Jesse *state official*

Urbana
Edgar, Jim *former governor*
Prussing, Laurel Lunt *mayor, economist*

INDIANA

Fort Wayne
Lee, Timothy Earl *international agency executive, paralegal*

Indianapolis
Caine, Virginia A. *city health department administrator*
Carter, Steve *state attorney general*
Daniels, Mitchell Elias, Jr. *governor, former federal official*
Mourdock, Richard E. *state official*
Peterson, Bart *mayor*
Rokita, Todd *state official*
Skillman, Becky Sue *lieutenant governor, former state legislator*

La Porte
Morris, Leigh Edward *mayor, retired health facility administrator*

IOWA

Creston
Nurnberg, Roger C. *county official*

Des Moines
Bergman, Bruce E. *municipal official*
Corning, Joy Cole *retired state official*
Culver, Chet (Chester John Culver) *governor*
Deluhery, Patrick John *retired state official*
Fitzgerald, Michael Lee *state official*
Jacobs, Libby Swanson *state official*
Judge, Patty Jean *lieutenant governor, nurse*
Mauro, Michael Anthony *state official*
Miller, Thomas J. *state attorney general*

Marion
Pate, Paul Danny *mayor*

Oelwein
McFarlane, Beth Lucetta Troester *retired mayor*

KANSAS

Coffeyville
Garner, Jim D. *state official, lawyer*

Garden Plain
Stovall, Carla Jo *former state attorney general*

Hutchinson
Kerr, Dave *state official, marketing professional*

Pittsburg
Trent, Darrell M. *ambassador, academic administrator, transportation executive*

Pratt
Hayden, (John) Michael *state official, former governor*

Topeka
Jenkins, Lynn M. *state official, former state legislator*
Morrison, Paul J. *state attorney general, former prosecutor*
Parkinson, Mark Vincent *lieutenant governor, former state legislator*
Sebelius, Kathleen Gilligan *governor*
Thornburgh, Ron E. *state official*

Wichita
Knight, Robert G. *mayor, investment banker*

KENTUCKY

Frankfort
Fletcher, Ernie (Ernest Lee Fletcher) *governor, former congressman*
Grayson, Trey (C.M. Grayson) *state official*
Miller, Jonathan S. *state official*
ence, Stephen Beville *lieutenant governor*
onego, Ian G. *assistant attorney general*
tumbo, Gregory D. *state attorney general*

Lexington
Miller, Pamela Gundersen *retired mayor*

Versailles
Parish, William S. *former ambassador, horse breeder*

LOUISIANA

Baton Rouge
Blanco, Kathleen Babineaux *governor*
Dardenne, Jay (John Leigh Dardenne Jr.) *state official, former state legislator, lawyer*
oti, Charles C., Jr. *state attorney general*
Kennedy, John Neely *state official*
andrieu, Mitchell Joseph *lieutenant governor*
Mc Call, Jerry Chalmers *retired federal official*

La Place
Blair, Ruth Reba *retired government official, notary public*

New Orleans
Blakely, Edward James *city manager, economics professor*
agin, Ray (Clarence Ray Nagin Jr.) *mayor*

MAINE

Augusta
aldacci, John Elias *governor, former congressman*
unlap, Matthew Gordon *state official, former state legislator*
emoine, David G. *state official*
McCormick, Dale *state official*
owe, G. Steven *state attorney general*

Brunswick
ing, Angus S., Jr. *former governor*

Lincolnville
enaco, Parker Alden *state official, lawyer, arbitrator*

MARYLAND

Annapolis
ndrews, Archie Moulton *retired federal official*
lagett, Virginia Parker *state official*
opp, Nancy Kornblith *state official*
'Malley, Martin Joseph *governor, former mayor, lawyer*

Baltimore
umann, R. Karl *commissioner, former state official*
rown, Anthony Gregory *lieutenant governor, lawyer*
urran, J. Joseph, Jr. *former state attorney general*
ixon, Sheila *mayor*
ansler, Douglas F. *state attorney general, former prosecutor*
iser, Ann *retired government researcher*
arfstein, Joshua M. *city health department administrator, pediatrician*
illis, John T. *former secretary of state*

Bethesda
owsher, Charles Arthur *retired government official, financial executive*
ennin, Joseph Francis *former government official, lawyer*
awazoe, Robin Inada *federal official*
rby, Harmon Elwood *retired ambassador*
aingen, Lowell Bruce *diplomat*
alloy, Edward Michael *diplomat, educator*
orrison, Bruce Andrew *federal official, public information officer*
orth, William Haven *foreign service officer*
owell, Edward Morgan *retired foreign service officer, educator*
oddard, Philip Hendrick *foreign affairs analyst, consultant, writer*
st, George Southall *retired diplomat*

Chevy Chase
Albright, Raymond Jacob *federal official*

Cockeysville
Barnes, Peter *federal official*

College Park
Benedick, Richard Elliot *diplomat*
Gansler, Jacques Singleton *public policy educator*

Columbia
Scates, Alice Yeomans *retired federal official*

Easton
Shepard, William Seth *diplomat, writer*

Fort Washington
Smoot, Burgess Howard *federal official*

Gaithersburg
French, Judson Cull *federal official*

Hollywood
Newhouse, Alan Russell *retired federal official*

North Bethesda
Szabo, Daniel *federal official*

Potomac
Roesser, Jean Wolberg *state official*

Rockville
Chiogioji, Melvin Hiroaki *retired federal official, entrepreneur*
Jaczko, Gregory Bela *commissioner, physicist*
Lyons, Peter B. *commissioner*
Merrifield, Jeffrey S. *commissioner*
Woodcock, Janet *federal official*

Severna Park
Meima, Ralph Chester, Jr. *retired diplomat, real estate company executive*

Silver Spring
Bassett, William, Jr. *geospatial intelligence officer*
Ewing, Blair Gordon *federal official*

West Bethesda
Vogelgesang, Sandra Louise *former ambassador, writer, consultant*

MASSACHUSETTS

Boston
Auerbach, John M. *city health department administrator*
Cahill, Timothy P. *state official*
Coakley, Martha *state attorney general, former prosecutor*
Galvin, William Francis *state official*
Menino, Thomas M. *mayor*
Patrick, Deval Laurdine *governor, lawyer*
Romney, (Willard) Mitt *former governor*
Shattuck, John *diplomat, civil rights lawyer, educator*

Bridgewater
Heffernan, Peter John *state official*

Cambridge
Fraker, Ford M. *ambassador*
Gergen, David Richmond *federal official, magazine editor*
Porter, Roger Blaine *federal official, educator*
Ramcharan, Bertrand *former international organization official*

Canton
Fuchs, Lawrence Howard *federal official, educator*

Dartmouth
Connors, Robert Leo *city official*

Roslindale
Sullivan, Dorothy Rona *state official*

Sherborn
Kennedy, Chester Ralph, Jr. *retired state official, art director*

South Yarmouth
Nichols, Robert Lyman *retired foreign service officer, lecturer*

Watertown
Reilly, Thomas F. *former state attorney general*

MICHIGAN

Ann Arbor
Davis, Robert Leach *retired federal official*
Ford, Betty Ann (Elizabeth Ann Ford) *former First Lady of the United States, health facility executive*
Levitsky, Melvyn *former ambassador*
Sheldon, Ingrid Kristina *retired mayor, controller*

Battle Creek
Baldwin, Susan Olin *commissioner, management consultant*

Cadillac
Walker, Dale Maxwell *city official*

Detroit
Kilpatrick, Kwame Malik *mayor*
Maseru, Noble A.W. *city health department administrator*

Dowagiac
Ott, C(larence) H(enry) *ambassador, retired accounting professor*

Fennville
Kamman, Curtis Warren *retired ambassador*

Grand Rapids
Logie, John Hoult *former mayor, lawyer*

Lansing
Cherry, John D., Jr. *lieutenant governor, former state senator*
Cox, Mike (Michael A. Cox) *state attorney general*
Granholm, Jennifer Mulhern *governor*
Kleine, Robert J. *state official*
Land, Terri Lynn *state official*

Muskegon
Roy, Paul Emile, Jr. *county official*

Pontiac
Pardee, Jeffrey Clark *county government official*

Warren
Kolakowski, Diana Jean *county commissioner*

MINNESOTA

Burnsville
Hatch, Mike *former state attorney general*

Chisholm
Peterson, Marjorie *former mayor*

Golden Valley
Leppik, Margaret White *municipal official*

Minneapolis
Carlson, Arne Helge *former governor*
Mondale, Joan Adams *wife of former Vice President of United States*
Rybak, R. T. *mayor*

Northfield
Levin, Burton *diplomat*

Saint Paul
Hanson, Tom *state official*
Molnau, Carol L. *lieutenant governor, former state legislator*
Pawlenty, Timothy James *governor*
Ritchie, Mark *state official*
Swanson, Lori A. *state attorney general, lawyer*

MISSISSIPPI

Jackson
Barbour, Haley Reeves *governor*
Clark, Eric C. *state official*
Hood, Jim *state attorney general*
Reeves, Tate *state official*
Tuck, Amy *lieutenant governor*
Winter, William Forrest *retired governor, lawyer*

MISSOURI

Columbia
Lubensky, Earl Henry *diplomat, anthropologist*

Jefferson City
Blunt, Matt (Matthew Roy Blunt) *governor, former state official*
Carnahan, Robin *state official*
Kinder, Peter D. *lieutenant governor, former state senator*
Nixon, Jeremiah W. (Jay) *state attorney general*

Kansas City
Barnes, Kay *former mayor*
Danner, Kathleen Frances Steele *federal official*
Davis, Richard Francis *city government official*
Funkouser, Mark *mayor*
Price, Charles H., II, *former ambassador*

Saint Charles
Gross, Charles Robert *county official, former state senator, former bank executive*

Saint Louis
Brauer, Stephen Franklin *diplomat, manufacturing company executive*

MONTANA

Billings
Larsen, Richard Lee *city manager, consultant, retired mayor, arbitrator*

Clancy
Ekanger, Laurie *retired state official, consultant*

Helena
Bohlinger, John C. *lieutenant governor, former state legislator*
Cooney, Mike *former secretary of state*
Johnson, Brad *state official*
McGrath, Mike *state attorney general*
Schweitzer, Brian *governor*

Missoula
Brown, Bob (Robert Joseph Brown) *former state official*

NEBRASKA

Benkelman
Whiteley, Rose Marie *city clerk, treasurer*

Lincoln
Beermann, Allen J. *former state official*
Bruning, Jon Cumberland *state attorney general*
Gale, John A. *state official*
Heineman, David Eugene *governor*
Osborn, Shane *state official*
Seng, Coleen Joy *mayor*
Sheehy, Rick *lieutenant governor, former mayor*

Omaha
Fahey, Mike *mayor*

NEVADA

Carson City
Gibbons, Jim (James Arthur Gibbons) *governor, former congressman*
Krolicki, Brian Keith *lieutenant governor, former state official*
Marshall, Kate *state official*
Masto, Catherine Marie Cortez *state attorney general, former county official*
Miller, Ross James *state official, prosecutor*

Henderson
McKinney, Sally Vitkus *state official*

Las Vegas
Goodman, Oscar Baylin *mayor, lawyer*

NEW HAMPSHIRE

Antrim
Scales, John Thomas *state official*

Auburn
Herman, William George *municipal official*

Concord
Ayotte, Kelly A. *state attorney general*
Gardner, William Michael *state official*
Hill, Donald S. *state commissioner*
Lynch, John H. *governor*
Provencher, Catherine A. *state official*

Goffstown
Holden, Carol Helen *county official*

Nashua
Bergeron, Paul Robert *city clerk*
Pignatelli, Debora Becker *state official*

NEW JERSEY

Cape May Point
Fraser, Malcolm Cavanagh *mayor*

Egg Harbor Township
Polillo, Ronald R. *federal official*

Fort Lee
Mack, Earle Irving *former ambassador, real estate company executive*

Irvington
Paden, Harry *municipal official*

Jersey City
Healy, Jerramiah *mayor*

Kearny
John, Ricky *state official*

Mays Landing
Mooney, Lori *county official*

Morristown
Healey, Thomas J. *former government official, brokerage house executive*

Newark
Booker, Cory Anthony *mayor, lawyer*
Pryor, Stefan I. *city manager, real estate developer*

Princeton
Keevey, Richard Francis *federal official, state official, educator*
Kurtzer, Daniel Charles *former ambassador*
Matlock, Jack Foust, Jr. *diplomat*
Oxman, Stephen A. *federal official*

Sea Isle City
Tull, Theresa Anne *retired diplomat*

Somerset
Soaries, DeForest B., Jr. *former state official*

Trenton
Abelow, Bradley *state official*
Corzine, Jon Stevens *governor, former senator*
Martin, James Hanley *state attorney general*
Milgram, Anne M. *state attorney general*
Palmer, Douglas Harold *mayor*
Wells, Nina Mitchell *state official*

NEW MEXICO

Albuquerque
Chavez, Martin Joseph *mayor, lawyer*
Giller, Edward Bonfoy *retired government official, military officer*
Madrid, Patricia A. *former state attorney general*

Clovis
Bradley, Walter D. *lieutenant governor, real estate broker*

Placitas
Reade, Lewis P. *diplomat, engineer, consultant*

Santa Fe
Coss, David *mayor*

Dasenbrock, Reed Way *state official, former academic administrator, literature educator*
Denish, Diane D. *lieutenant governor*
Herrera, Mary E. *state official*
King, Gary K. *state attorney general*
Lewis, James Beliven *state official*
Richardson, Bill (William Blaine Richardson III) *governor*

NEW YORK

Albany
Brewer, Aida M. *state official*
Cortés-Vázquez, Lorraine *state official*
Cuomo, Andrew Mark *state attorney general, former secretary of housing and urban development*
Daines, Richard F. *state health commissioner, former health services executive*
DiNapoli, Thomas Peter *state official, former state legislator*
Grannis, Pete (Alexander Banks Grannis) *state official, former state legislator*
Jennings, Gerald D. (Jerry Jennings) *mayor*
Maloney, Sean Patrick *state official, lawyer*
O'Donnell, Denise Ellen *state official, former prosecutor*
Ortloff, George Christian, Sr., (Chris Ortloff) *commissioner, journalist*
Paterson, David Alexander *lieutenant governor, former state legislator*
Spitzer, Eliot Laurence *governor, former state attorney general*

Armonk
Wago, Mildred Hogan *retired municipal official*

Brooklyn
Markowitz, Marty (Martin Markowitz) *city manager*

Buffalo
Brown, Byron W., Jr. *mayor, former state legislator*
Giambra, Joel Anthony *municipal official*

Canandaigua
Barden, George V. *county official, watershed specialist*

Hauppauge
Levy, Steve A. *county official, former state legislator*

Kew Gardens
Marshall, Helen M. *county official*

Lawrence
Berman, Carol *retired commissioner*

Mineola
O'Connell, Maureen C. *county official, former state legislator*

Nedrow
Lyons, Oren *Native American chieftain, conservationist*

New York
al-Nasser, Nassir Abdulaziz *ambassador*
Arias, Ricardo Alberto *ambassador, lawyer*
Aswady, Adiyatwidi Adiwoso *diplomat*
Ataeva, Aksoltan *diplomat*
Ayafor, Martin Chungong *ambassador*
Baja, Lauro Liboon, Jr. *diplomat*
Berruga-Filloy, Enrique *ambassador*
Blinken, Donald *ambassador, investment banker*
Bloomberg, Mike (Michael Rubens) *mayor*
Bowles, Newton Rowell *United Nations executive*
Boykin, Keith O. *former government official, writer*
Brown, Carroll *retired diplomat, association executive, consultant*
Buissonnière, Marine *international organization administrator; physician*
Burian, Peter *ambassador*
Chaves, Jose Maria *diplomat, lawyer, foundation administrator, educator*
Christian, Leslie Kojo *ambassador*
Clinton, Bill (William Jefferson Clinton) *42nd President of the United States*
Cosgrave, Paul J. *commissioner*
Curiel, Carolyn *former ambassador*
Curley, Walter Joseph Patrick *diplomat, investment banker*
Davis, Richard Joel *former government official, lawyer*
Doctoroff, Daniel L. *municipal official*
Doyle, Michael W. *international official, educator*
Durrant, M. Patricia *diplomat*
Eisenstadt, G. Michael *diplomat, writer, educator, researcher*
Feldman, Daniel Lee *former state official*
Ferguson, Sarah *The Duchess of York*
Frieden, Thomas R. *city health department administrator, epidemiologist*
Friedman, Stephen *federal official, former diversified financial services executive*
Gardner, Richard Newton *diplomat, lawyer, educator*
Gaspar-Martins, Ismael *Angolian diplomat, former government minister, business executive*
Gotbaum, Betsy *municipal official*
Guillot, Cyril Etienne *international organization administrator*
Haass, Richard Nathan *federal official*
Ikouebe, Basile *ambassador*
Ilkin, Baki *diplomat, Turkish government official*
Kallstrom, James K. *state official*
Katz, Abraham *retired foreign service officer*
Khalilzad, Zalmay Mamozy *ambassador*
Kumalo, Dumisani Shadrack *ambassador*
Levin, Herbert *retired diplomat, foundation administrator*
Løj, Ellen Margrethe *ambassador*
Mbanefo, Arthur Christopher Izuegbunan *diplomat*
McFarland, Kathleen Troia (KT McFarland) *government defense consultant*
McInerney, Mark A. *county official*
Muñoz, Heraldo (Heraldo Muñoz Valenzuela) *diplomat*
Murphy, Richard William *retired diplomat*
Ney, Edward N. *ambassador, advertising and public relations executive*
Nussbaum, Bernard W. *federal official, lawyer*
Okun, Herbert Stuart *diplomat, educator*
Omotoso, Edward *diplomat, journalist*
Platt, Nicholas *retired ambassador*
Prendergast, Sir Kieran *former international organization official*
Qazi, Ashraf Jehangir *ambassador*
Raab, Jennifer J. *city commissioner*
Rabiu, Badru I.O. *federal official*
Rapoport, Miles S. *former state official*
Ripert, Jean-Maurice *ambassador*
Rock, Allan Michael *ambassador, former Canadian government official*
Sadik, Nafis *United Nations administrator*
Sadik-Khan, Janette I. *city manager, former federal agency administrator*
Saleh, Mohammed *diplomat*
Sawers, Sir John *ambassador*
Spatafora, Marcello *ambassador*
Streator, Edward *retired diplomat, management consultant*
Stringer, Scott M. *city manager, former state legislator*
Swing, William Lacy *ambassador*
Verbeke, Johan C. *ambassador*
Voto-Bernales, Jorge *ambassador*
Wang, Guangya *ambassador, international organization official*
Wolff, Alejandro Daniel *ambassador*
Wyzner, Eugeniusz *diplomat*
Zackheos, H.E. Sotirios *ambassador*

Ovid
Dresser, David Leland *municipal official*

Syracuse
Ortiz, Fernando, Jr. *commissioner*

Troy
McDermott, Robert J. *commissioner*
Toren, Mark *state official, statistician*

Watertown
Coe, Benjamin Plaisted *retired state official*

NORTH CAROLINA

Cary
Trebing, David Martin *public policy executive*

Chapel Hill
Schoonover, Brenda B. *ambassador*

Charlotte
Brynn, Edward Paul *former ambassador*
McCrory, Patrick *mayor*

High Point
Pate, William Patrick *city manager*
Phillips, Earl Norfleet, Jr. *diplomat, financial services executive*

Mill Spring
Saunders, Barry Wayne *state official*

New Bern
Linkonis, Suzanne Newbold *retired probation officer, retired counselor*

Pittsboro
Cotter, Michael William *retired ambassador*

Raleigh
Cooper, Roy Asberry III *state attorney general*
Easley, Michael F. *governor*
Marshall, Elaine Folk *state official*
Perdue, Beverly Eaves *lieutenant governor, geriatric consultant*

Southern Pines
Toon, Malcolm *former ambassador*

Wilson
Wyatt, Edward Avery, V, *city manager*

NORTH DAKOTA

Bismarck
Dalrymple, Jack *lieutenant governor, former state legislator*
Hoeven, John *governor*
Jaeger, Al (Alvin A. Jaeger) *state official*
Schmidt, Kelly *state official*
Stenehjem, Wayne Kevin *state attorney general, lawyer*

Minot
Watne, Darlene Claire *county official*

OHIO

Akron
Plusquellic, Donald L. *mayor*

Cincinnati
Mallory, Mark L. *mayor, former state legislator*

Cleveland
Campbell, Jane Louise *former mayor*
Jackson, Frank G. *mayor*

Columbus
Brunner, Jennifer Lee *state official, lawyer*
Coleman, Michael Bennett *mayor*
Dann, Marc *state attorney general, former state senator*
Fisher, Lee I. *lieutenant governor, former state attorney general*
Lashutka, Gregory S. *mayor, lawyer*
Long, Teresa C. *city health department administrator*
Strickland, Ted *governor, former congressman*

Dayton
Lashley, William Bartholomew *county official*
McLin, Rhine Lana *mayor, former state legislator*

Mansfield
Converse, Sandra *city finance director, financial planner*

Medina
Ballard, John Stuart *retired mayor, lawyer, educator*

Toledo
Carroll, William J. *municipal official*

Worthington
Speck, Samuel Wallace, Jr. *state official*

OKLAHOMA

Ada
Anoatubby, Bill *governor of Chickasaw Nation*

Norman
Corr, Edwin Gharst *ambassador*

Oklahoma City
Askins, Jari *lieutenant governor, former state representative*
Cornett, Mick *mayor*
Edmondson, Drew (William Andrew Edmondson) *state attorney general*
Henry, Brad (C. Brad Henry) *governor*
Meacham, Scott *state official*
Savage, Susan M. *state official, former mayor*

Tulsa
Butkin, Robert A. *former state treasurer, law educator*
Madison, Eddie Lawrence, Jr. *public relations consultant, editor, writer*
Rooney, Laurence Francis III *ambassador to the Vatican, construction executive*
Taylor, Kathy *mayor*

OREGON

Eugene
Bascom, Ruth F. *retired mayor*

Lake Oswego
Campbell, Colin Herald *former mayor*

Portland
Katz, Vera *former mayor, college administrator, state legislator*
Potter, Tom *mayor*

Salem
Bradbury, Bill (William Chapman Bradbury III) *state official*
Edwards, Randall *state official*
Kulongoski, Ted (Theodore Ralph Kulongoski) *governor, former state supreme court justice*
Myers, Hardy *state attorney general*

PENNSYLVANIA

Easton
Murphy, Bruce Allen *government educator, law educator, writer*

Girardville
Dempsey, Thomas Joseph *retired postmaster*

Harrisburg
Baker Knoll, Catherine *lieutenant governor*
Corbett, Thomas Wingett, Jr. *state attorney general, lawyer*
Cortés, Pedro A. *state official*
Hafer, Barbara *state official*
Pizzingrilli, Kim *state official*
Rendell, Edward Gene *governor, retired mayor, lawyer*
Wolfe, Gary Donald *commissioner, retired librarian*

Newtown
Brennan, Thomas John *city and state official, consultant, educator*

Philadelphia
Godley, Joanne *city health department administrator*
Harris, Raymond Jesse *retired federal official*
Schweiker, Mark S. *former governor*
Street, John F. *mayor*

Pittsburgh
Kerber, Frank John *retired diplomat*
Mitchell, George Charles *diplomat, international consultant, mediator, educator, writer*
O'Neill, Paul Henry *former secretary of the treasury*
Ravenstahl, Luke R. *mayor*
Simpson, Daniel H. *ambassador*

State College
Lamb, Robert Edward *retired diplomat, professional society administrator*

York
Wiles, William Wharton *retired federal government official*

RHODE ISLAND

Harmony
Fogarty, Charles Joseph *former lieutenant governor*

Kingston
Sundlun, Bruce *former governor*

Providence
Caprio, Frank Thomas *state official, lawyer*
Carcieri, Donald L. *governor*
Lynch, Patrick C. *state attorney general*
Mollis, Ralph (A. Ralph Mollis) *state official, former mayor*
Roberts, Elizabeth H. *lieutenant governor, former state legislator*

SOUTH CAROLINA

Columbia
Bauer, R. Andre *lieutenant governor*
Hammond, Mark *state official*
McMaster, Henry Dargan *state attorney general*
Page, Randall *state official*
Sanford, Marshall (Mark Sanford) *governor, former congressman*

SOUTH DAKOTA

Gettysburg
Burge, Steven Donald *city administrator*

Pierre
Daugaard, Dennis M. *lieutenant governor, former state senator*
Larson, Vern L. *state official*
Long, Larry *state attorney general*
Nelson, Chris A. *state official*
Rounds, Mike (Marion Michael Rounds) *governor*

TENNESSEE

Brownsville
Banks, Webb Follin *mayor*

Memphis
Herenton, Willie W. *mayor*
Madlock, Yvonne *city health department administrator*

Nashville
Bailey, Stephanie B.C. *city health department administrator*
Bredesen, Philip Norman *governor*
Cooper, Robert Elbert, Jr. *state attorney genera*
Darnell, Riley Carlisle *state official, lawyer*
Gore, Tipper (Mary Elizabeth Gore) *wife of the former Vice President of the United States*
Ramsey, Ronald L. *lieutenant governor, state senator, realtor*
Sims, Dale *state official*
Thomas, Hazel Beatrice *state official*

Oak Ridge
Holloway, Jacqueline *county commissioner*

Townsend
Sundquist, Don *retired governor, retired congressman, sales executive*

TEXAS

Austin
Abbott, Greg *state attorney general, former sta supreme court justice*
Connor, Geoffrey Scott *former state official, lawyer*
Cooke, Carlton Lee, Jr. *mayor*
Dewhurst, David *lieutenant governor*
Perry, Rick *governor*
Wilson, Phil (Samuel Philip Wilson) *state offic*
Wynn, Will *mayor*

Beaumont
Lord, Evelyn Marlin *mayor*

Brenham
Pipes, Paul Ray *county commissioner*

Dallas
Lake, Joseph Edward *ambassador*
Leppert, Thomas C. *mayor, former constructio executive*
Thompson, Zachary *city health department administrator*

El Paso
Cook, John *mayor*
Wardy, Joe *former mayor*

Fort Worth
Moncrief, Michael Joseph *mayor, former state legislator*

Giddings
Dismukes, Carol Jaehne *county official*

Harlingen
Matz, James Richard *municipal official*

Houston
Bush, George Herbert Walker *41st President o the United States*
Dinkins, Carol Eggert *federal official, lawyer*
Marcotte, Michael Steven *municipal official*

White, Bill (William Howard White) *mayor*

Lubbock
Stuart, Frank Adell *county official*

Mineola
Stevenson, David Wayne *municipal official*

New Braunfels
Krueger, Robert Charles *former ambassador, congressman, senator*

Plano
Evans, Pat *mayor*

San Antonio
Catto, Henry Edward *former government official, retired ambassador*
Garza, Ed *former mayor*
Hardberger, Phillip Duane *mayor, judge, lawyer, journalist*
Henderson, Connie Chorlton *retired city planner, artist, writer*

UTAH

North Salt Lake
Johnson, Frank *educator, retired state official*

Salt Lake City
Allen, Ronald Carl *commissioner, artist, consultant, former state senator, computer company executive*
Anderson, Ross Carl *mayor, lawyer*
Herbert, Gary Richard *lieutenant governor*
Huntsman, Jon Meade, Jr. *governor, former federal agency administrator*
Shurtleff, Mark L. *state attorney general*

VERMONT

Burlington
Kunin, Madeleine May *former ambassador to Switzerland, former governor*

Montpelier
Douglas, Jim (James Holley) *governor*
Dubie, Brian E. *lieutenant governor*
Markowitz, Deborah Lynn *state official*
Sorrell, William H. *state attorney general*
Spaulding, George B. *state official*

Peacham
Engle, James Bruce *ambassador*

South Londonderry
Spiers, Ronald Ian *diplomat*

VIRGINIA

Alexandria
Byrne, John Edward (JEB Byrne) *retired federal official*
Connell, Mary Ellen *diplomat*
Costagliola, Francesco *retired government official*
itton, Harvey Nelson, Jr. *former government official*
Gwadosky, Dan A. *former state official, federal agency administrator*
Havens, Harry Stewart *retired federal official, management consultant*
Helman, Gerald Bernard *diplomat*
Kaplan, Richard Alan *government official*
oren, Donald Patrick *federal official, retired military officer*
McNicol, David Leon *retired federal official, researcher*
Powell, Colin Luther *former secretary of state, former Chairman of the Joint Chiefs of Staff*
Pringle, Robert Maxwell *diplomat*
ucker, Alvin Leroy *retired government official*

Annandale
Rogers, Stephen Hitchcock *retired ambassador*

Arlington
ggrey, Orison Rudolph *former ambassador, consultant, academic administrator*
olster, Archie Milburn *retired foreign service officer*
ddy, John Joseph *diplomat*
dmondson, William Brockway *retired foreign service officer*
Galloway, William Jefferson *retired foreign service officer*
Haig, Alexander Meigs, Jr. *former secretary of state, retired military officer*
eivilin, Donna Mae *retired government executive*
atzen, Jay Kenneth *retired diplomat, state legislator, government agency administrator*
rys, Sheldon Jack *retired diplomat*
Mc Donald, John Warlick *diplomat*
chmanek, David Alan *defense analyst*
Pendleton, Mary Catherine *retired foreign service officer*
yatt, Everett Arno *federal official*
undquist, M. Alexandra (Alix Sundquist) *diplomat, consultant*

Charlottesville
ewsom, David Dunlop *ambassador, educator*

Chesapeake
Myrick, Bismarck *diplomat, history professor*

Crozet
eswick, James Bigelow *former government official, biomedical engineer*

Dulles
acobs, Janice Lee *ambassador*

Perry, June Carter *ambassador*
Skodon, Emil Mark *ambassador*
Wood, William Braucher *ambassador*

Fairfax
Haskett, Dianne Louise *retired mayor, lawyer, consultant*

Falls Church
Bingman, Charles Franklin *government executive, educator*
Ward, George Frank, Jr. *international programs executive, ambassador*

Fredericksburg
Jones, Harry Edward *diplomat, writer*

Gainesville
Ferrara, Peter Joseph *federal official, lawyer, author, educator*

Great Falls
Minikes, Stephan Michael *ambassador, lawyer, banker*

Haymarket
Doolittle, Warren T. *retired federal official*

King George
Newhall, David III *retired federal official*

Lake Ridge
Stottlemyer, David Lee *federal official*

Lynchburg
Stephens, Bart Nelson *former foreign service officer*

Manassas
Storing, Paul Edward *retired foreign service officer*

Mc Lean
Cahill, Harry Amory *diplomat, educator*
Healy, Theresa Ann *retired ambassador*
Russell, Theodore Emery *diplomat*
Smith, Russell Jack *diplomat, consultant*
Trout, Maurice Elmore *diplomat*

Reston
Myers, Mark D. *federal official, geologist*

Richmond
Bolling, Bill (William T. Bolling) *lieutenant governor, former state senator*
Hanley, Katherine Keith *state official*
Jagdmann, Judy (Judith Williams Jagdmann) *commissioner, former state attorney general*
Kaine, Timothy Michael *governor*
McDonnell, Bob (Robert Francis) *state attorney general, former state legislator*
Powell, J. Braxton *state official*
Wilder, L(awrence) Douglas *mayor, former governor*

Spotsylvania
Hardy, Dorcas Ruth *business and government relations executive*

Stafford
Williams, Carlisle M., Jr. *municipal official, insurance company executive*

Stanardsville
Keel, Alton Gold, Jr. *ambassador*

Susan
Ambach, Dwight Russell *retired foreign service officer*

The Plains
Gibbons, John Howard (Jack Gibbons) *federal official, physicist*

Vienna
DeWitt, Charles Barbour *federal official*

Virginia Beach
Fraser, Ruth Hodges *city clerk*
Friedman, Andrew Mitchell *director housing and neighborhood preservation*
Oberndorf, Meyera E. *mayor*

Winchester
Ojeda Eiseley, Jaime de *former Spanish ambassador, educator*

WASHINGTON

Battle Ground
Ezelle, Robert Eugene *diplomat*

Edmonds
Thyden, James Eskel *diplomat, educator, lecturer*

Everett
O'Keefe, Kathleen Mary *state official*

Olympia
Gregoire, Christine O. *governor, former state attorney general*
McKenna, Rob *state attorney general, former councilman*
Murphy, Michael Joseph *state official*
Owen, Bradley Scott *lieutenant governor*
Reed, Sam *state official*

Seattle
Gouldthorpe, Kenneth Alfred Percival *state official, editor*
Johnson, Darryl Norman *former ambassador*
Kennedy, Mary Virginia *retired diplomat*
Nickels, Greg *mayor*
Plough, Alonzo L. *city health department administrator*

Sumas
Hemry, Larry Harold *former federal agency official, writer, inventor*

WEST VIRGINIA

Charleston
Hechler, Ken *retired state official, retired congressman, writer, political science professor*
Ireland, Betty *state official*
Manchin, Joe, III, (Joseph Manchin III) *governor, former state official*
Mc Graw, Darrell Vivian, Jr. *state attorney general*
Perdue, John D. *state official*

WISCONSIN

Ashland
Smith, Jane Schneberger *retired city administrator*

Eau Claire
Frank, John LeRoy *commissioner, lawyer, educator*

Franklin
Wheaton, Douglas B. *city manager, lawyer*

Madison
Bauman, Susan Joan Mayer *mayor, lawyer, commissioner*
Doyle, Jim (James Edward) *governor, former state attorney general*
Earl, Anthony Scully *retired governor, lawyer*
La Follette, Douglas J. *state official*
Lautenschlager, Peggy A. *former state attorney general*
Lawton, Barbara *lieutenant governor*
Sass, Dawn Marie *state official*
Thompson, Barbara Storck *state official*
Van Hollen, J(ohn) B(yron) *state attorney general, former prosecutor*
Voight, Jack C. *state official*

Milwaukee
Barrett, Thomas M. *mayor, former congressman*

Pewaukee
Farrow, Margaret Ann *former lieutenant governor*

WYOMING

Cheyenne
Crank, Patrick J. (Pat Crank) *state attorney general*
Freudenthal, Dave (David D. Freudenthal) *governor*
Lummis, Cynthia Marie *former state official, lawyer*
Maxfield, Max R. *state official*
Thomson, Thyra Godfrey *former state official*
Woodhouse, Gay Vanderpoel *former state attorney general, lawyer*

Evanston
Harris, Mark W. *mayor, lawyer*

Laramie
Dickman, Francois Moussiegt *former foreign service officer, educator*

TERRITORIES OF THE UNITED STATES

AMERICAN SAMOA

Pago Pago
Ripley, Afa, Jr. *attorney general*
Sunia, Aitofele Toese F. *lieutenant governor*
Tulafono, Togiola T.A. *governor*

GUAM

Hagatna
Camacho, Felix Perez *governor*
Cruz, Michael W. *lieutenant governor, surgeon*
Gutierrez, Carl T. C. *former governor*
Limtiaco, Alicia Garrido *attorney general, former prosecutor*

NORTHERN MARIANA ISLANDS

Saipan
Fitial, Benigno Repeki *governor*
Gregory, Matthew T. *attorney general*
Villagomez, Timothy P. *lieutenant governor*

PUERTO RICO

San Juan
Acevedo-Vilá, Aníbal *governor, former congressional representative*
Bonilla, Fernando J. *Puerto Rican government official*
Sanchez-Ramos, Roberto J. *attorney general*
Santini, Jorge *mayor*

VIRGIN ISLANDS

Charlotte Amalie
Stapleton, Marylyn Alecia *diplomat*

Christiansted
Francis, Gregory R. *lieutenant governor*

St Thomas
de Jongh, John P., Jr. *governor, real estate company executive*
Frazer, Vincent F. *attorney general*
Turnbull, Charles Wesley *former governor*

MILITARY ADDRESSES OF THE UNITED STATES

EUROPE

APO
Cejas, Paul L. *diplomat, executive*
Crocker, Ryan Clark *ambassador*
Marshall, Brian Laurence *federal official*
Morella, Constance Albanese *ambassador, former congresswoman*
Untermeyer, Charles Graves (Chase Untermeyer) *ambassador, diplomat*
Yates, John Melvin *ambassador*

FPO
Tuttle, Robert Holmes *ambassador, former federal official*

PACIFIC

APO
Stanton, William Anthony *diplomat*

CANADA

MANITOBA

Winnipeg
Curtis, Charles Edward *Canadian government official*

ONTARIO

Aurora
Cellucci, (Argeo) Paul *former ambassador, governor*

Brampton
Malhi, Gurbax Singh *Canadian government official*

Nobleton
Embleton, Tony Frederick Wallace *retired Canadian government official*

Ohawa
Day, Stockwell Burt *government official*

Ottawa
Armstrong, Henry Conner *former Canadian government official, consultant*
Austin, Jacob (Jack Austin) *Canadian government official*
Bélisle, Paul Charles *Canadian government official*
Bevilacqua, Maurizio *member of Canadian parliament*
Buchanan, John MacLennan *Canadian provincial official*
Copps, Sheila *former Canadian government official, political journalist, commentator*
Fairbairn, Joyce *Canadian government official*
Fitzpatrick, Brian *Canadian legislator*
Gold, Lorne W. *Canadian government official*
Guarnieri, Albina *Canadian legislator*
Harb, Mac *Canadian senator*
Hervieux-Payette, Céline *Canadian senator*
Kilgour, David *Canadian member parliament*
Kingsley, Jean-Pierre *federal official*
MacDonald, Flora Isabel *Canadian government official*
Mills, Bob *member of Canadian parliament*
Penner, Keith *former Canadian government official*
Peterson, James Scott (Jim Peterson) *Canadian government official*
Roland, Anne *registrar Supreme Court of Canada*
Southam, G(ordon) Hamilton *former Canadian government official*
Stanford, Joseph Stephen *diplomat, lawyer, educator*
Volpe, Joseph *Canadian government official*
Yalden, Maxwell Freeman *Canadian diplomat*
Yeomans, Donald Ralph *Canadian government official, consultant*

Toronto
Bartleman, James K. *lieutenant governor*
Clarkson, Adrienne *former Governor General of Canada*
Gotlieb, Allan E. *former ambassador*
Holyday, Douglas Charles *city councillor*
MacLaren, Roy *retired Canadian government official*
Mohler, Brian Jeffery *diplomat*

QUEBEC

Montreal
Gabbour, Iskandar *city and regional planning educator*
Mulroney, Brian (Martin Brian Mulroney) *former Prime Minister of Canada*

Quebec City
Thibault, Lise *Canadian lieutenant governor*

SASKATCHEWAN

Saskatoon
Blakeney, Allan Emrys *Canadian government official, lawyer, educator*

Ontario
Warren, Jack Hamilton *retired diplomat, banker, trade policy advisor*

MEXICO

Colonia Cuauhtemoc
Garza, Antonio O., Jr. *ambassador*
Carabias Lillo, Julia *government official*
Téllez Kuenzler, Luis *former government official, investment banker*

AUSTRALIA

Camberwell
Peterson, Douglas Pete (Pete Peterson) *former ambassador, retired congressman*

Double Bay
Peacock, Penne Korth *ambassador*

BELGIUM

Brussels
Gray, C. Boyden (Clayland Boyden Gray) *ambassador, lawyer*
Nuland, Victoria *ambassador*

BOSNIA-HERZEGOVINA

Sarajevo
Lozančić, Niko *President of Federation of Bosnia and Herzegovina*

CHILE

Santiago
Wilkey, Malcolm Richard *retired ambassador, retired judge*

CHINA

Beijing
Jiabao, Wen *Chinese government official*

ENGLAND

London
Elizabeth, , II, (Elizabeth Alexandra Mary) *By the Grace of God of the United Kingdom of Great Britain and Northern Ireland and of Her Other Realms and Territories Queen, Head of the Commonwealth, Defender of the Faith*
Ischinger, Wolfgang *ambassador, diplomat*
Meyer, Sir Christopher J.R. *former ambassador*

Surrey
Weston, Sir John (Sir Philip John Weston) *retired diplomat*

FRANCE

Paris
Dean, John Gunther *diplomat*
Lagarde, Christine *French government official, lawyer*
Myerson, Jacob Myer *retired diplomat*
Oliver, Louise V. *ambassador*

Port-Fréjus
Crapon de Caprona, Count Noël François Marie *retired senior United Nations official*

GEORGIA

Tbilisi
Noghaideli, Zurab *Prime Minister of Georgia*

GERMANY

Berlin
Köhler, Horst *President of Federal Republic of Germany*

INDIA

New Delhi
Malone, David Michael *diplomat, educator*

IRELAND

Dublin
Foley, Thomas Coleman *ambassador, investor*

ITALY

Spogli, Ronald P. *ambassador*

MALAYSIA

Perak
Yussuf Izzuddim, Shah Ghafraullah Sultan *Sultan of Perak*

NETHERLANDS

The Hague
Mocumbi, Pascoal Manuel *former prime minister of Mozambique*
Tomka, Peter *diplomat, arbitrator, judge, lawyer*

PARAGUAY

Asuncion
Cason, James Caldwell *ambassador*

PERU

Lima
Kuczynski, Pedro-Pablo *Prime Minister of Peru*
Struble, James Curtis *ambassador*

PHILIPPINES

Makati
Mabilangan, Felipe Hugo, Jr. *diplomat*

SINGAPORE

Singapore
Herbold, Patricia Louise *ambassador*

SPAIN

Canary Islands
Wells, Melissa Foelsch *retired ambassador*

SWEDEN

Stockholm
Wachtmeister, Count Wilhelm H.F. *diplomat*

SWITZERLAND

Bern
Abe, Nobuyasu *ambassador*

Geneva
Brown, Kent Newville *ambassador*

THAILAND

Bangkok
McMillion, Margaret Kim *foreign service officer*

ADDRESS UNPUBLISHED

Abramowitz, Morton I. *former ambassador*
Adams, Edwin Melville *retired diplomat, actor, writer*
Adams, Weston *former diplomat, military officer, lawyer*
Allen, Claude Alexander *former federal official*
Amato Chiaramonte Bordonaro, Baron Carlo Camillo *ambassador, consultant*
Anderson, Carlen Joseph *city agency administrator*
Andjaba, Martin *ambassador*
Angula, Helmut Kangulohi *Prime Minister of Namibia*
Arcos, Cresencio S. *ambassador*
Armstrong, Anne Legendre *retired ambassador*
Arnett, David Leslie *former diplomat, speaker, writer*
Ash, Roy Lawrence *former federal official*
Ater, Al *former state official*
Atwater, Phyllis Y. *municipal official*
Babauta, Juan Nekai *former governor, congressional representative*
Baca, Jim *mayor*
Baker, James Edward *city planner*
Baldyga, Leonard J. *retired diplomat, consultant*
Bandar, Prince bin Sultan bin Abd al-Aziz Al Saud *former ambassador*
Baptista, Robert Charles, Jr. *federal official, lawyer*
Bartlett, Dan (Daniel Joseph Bartlett) *former federal official*
Bassin, Jules *foreign service officer*
Bates, Barbara J. Neuner *retired municipal official*
Battle, Vincent M. *former ambassador*
Baxley, Lucy *former lieutenant governor*
Beard, Ann Southard *diplomat, oil industry executive*
Beasley, David Muldrow *former governor, consultant*
Benson, Craig Robert *former governor*
Benson, Joanne E. *retired lieutenant governor*
Bernstein, Stuart A. *former ambassador*
Betti, John Anso *federal official, retired automotive executive*
Bies, Susan Schmidt *former federal official*
Binsfeld, Connie Berube *former state official*
Bishop, Oliver Richard *retired state official*
Black, Shirley Temple (Mrs. Charles A. Black) *retired ambassador, retired actress*
Blackwell, Ken (John Kenneth Blackwell) *former state official, former mayor*
Blankenship, J. Richard *former ambassador*
Bliss, Donald Tiffany, Jr. *ambassador*
Bolen, David Benjamin *former ambassador*
Bolton, John Robert *former ambassador, federal agency administrator*
Botelho, Bruce Manuel *mayor, retired state attorney general*
Bowen, Otis Ray *former secretary of health and human services, former governor*
Boyatt, Thomas David *retired ambassador*
Bradley, Jennette B. *former state official, lieutenant governor*
Bremer, (L.) Paul (Lewis Paul Bremer III) *former diplomat*
Bremer Martino, Juan Jose *former ambassador*
Brill, Kenneth C. *federal official, former ambassador*
Broadrick-Allen, Sandra Carol *retired city manager, civic worker, consultant*
Brock, William Emerson *former secretary of labor*
Brook, Scott Jonathan Bradley *mayor, lawyer*
Brown, June Gibbs *retired government official*
Brown, Kay (Mary Kathryn Brown) *retired state official, consultant, political organization worker*
Brown, Lee Patrick *retired mayor, federal official, protective services official, educator*
Brown, Pamela S. *former attorney general*
Brownell, Nora Mead *former commissioner*
Brownfield, William R. *former ambassador*
Burchman, Leonard *federal official, journalist*
Bush, Barbara Pierce *former First Lady of the United States, volunteer*
Bush, Jeb (John Ellis Bush) *former governor*
Butenis, Patricia A. *ambassador*
Calderón, Sila Maria *former governor*
Campbell, John *former ambassador*
Card, Andy (Andrew Hill Card Jr.) *former White House Chief of Staff*
Carlucci, Frank Charles III *former secretary of defense*
Carney, Timothy Michael *ambassador*
Carpenter, David Erwin *retired county official, land use planner*
Carter, Rosalynn Smith (Eleanor Rosalynn Carter) *former First Lady of the United States*
Chanos, George J. *former state attorney general*
Chem, Widhya *ambassador*
Cherry, Robert Steven III *municipal official*
Chrétien, Raymond A.J. *retired ambassador*
Clark, William, Jr. *diplomat*
Clarke, Henry Lee *foreign service officer, ambassador*
Clarke, Richard Alan *former federal official*
Clayton, Raymond Edward *municipal official*
Condayan, John *foreign service officer*
Coop, Frederick Robert *retired city manager*
Coppie, Comer Swift *retired state official*
Corkery, James Caldwell *retired Canadian government executive, mechanical engineer*
Cornell, Robert Arthur *federal official*
Cosman, Francene Jen *former government official*
Crouch, J.D. (Jack Dyer Crouch II) *former federal official, former ambassador*
Cunningham, James Blair *ambassador*
Daglis, Lisa Genine *deputy attorney general*
Dailey, Jim *former mayor*
Daly, Paul Sylvester *former mayor, retired academic administrator, management consultant*
Danni, F. Robert *town official*
Deming, Rust M. *ambassador*
Dennis, Gigi (Ginette E. Dennis) *former state official*
DeThomas, Joseph Michael *former ambassador*
Dillon, Robert Sherwood *retired diplomat*
Dominguez, Cari M. *former federal official*
Dornbush, K. Terry *former ambassador, consulting company executive, educator*
Dozier, Therese Knecht *department of education advisor, former education association administrator*
Drue, Kerry Erica *former attorney general*
Egan, Wesley William *former ambassador*
Eisenhower, John Sheldon Doud *former ambassador, writer*
Eliot, Theodore Lyman, Jr. *former ambassador, consultant*
Elson, Edward Elliott *diplomat*
Emmons, Robert Duncan *diplomat*
Ewing, Raymond Charles *retired ambassador*
Fiddick, Paul William *public official, broadcast executive*
Fields, C(lara) Virginia *former city manager*
Fischer, David J. *retired mayor*
Fleischer, Ari (Lawrence Ari Fleischer) *former White House press secretary*
Ford, Christopher Ashley *federal official, lawyer*
Ford, Ford Barney *retired federal official*
Franke, Wayne Thomas *retired government affairs director, consultant*
Fraser, Donald MacKay *retired mayor, congressman*
Gadsden, James Irvin *ambassador*
Gardom, Garde Basil *former lieutenant governor of British Columbia*
Geisel, Harold Walter *diplomat*
Gilmore, Kathi *former state treasurer*
Golden, Olivia Ann *state official, human services administrator*
Goldthwait, Christopher E. *ambassador*
Gonzales, Alberto R. *former United States attorney general, former state supreme court justice*
Gonzales, Ron *mayor, former county supervisor*
Goodling, Monica Maria *former federal official*
Grady, Wayne Joseph *retired government official*
Graves, William Preston *former governor*
Greenspan, Alan *former Chairman of the Board of Governors of the Federal Reserve System, economist*
Guinn, Kenny C. (Kenneth Carroll Guinn) *former governor*
Hall, Tony P. *former ambassador, retired congressman*
Hanmer, Stephen Read, Jr. *retired federal official*
Hao, Lawrence Kaholo *state official, clinical hypnotherapist*
Harder, Robert Clarence *state official*
Harris, Jeremy *former mayor*
Harris, Joe Frank *former governor*
Hawke, John Daniel, Jr. *former federal official*
Hays, Dennis K. *former ambassador*
Hazeltine, Joyce *former state official*
Healey, Kerry Murphy *former lieutenant governor*
Heed, Peter W. *former state attorney general*
Heimbold, Charles Andreas, Jr. *former ambassador*
Henke, Tracy Ann *federal official*
Henry, Sherrye P. *political advisor, radio personality*
Henry, Stephen Lewis *retired lieutenant governor, orthopedic surgeon, educator*
Hester, Nancy Elizabeth *county government official*
Hodges, Heather M. *ambassador*
Holiday, Edith Elizabeth *former presidential adviser, cabinet secretary*
Holmes, Henry Allen *diplomat, educator*
Hood, Glenda E. *former state official, former mayor*
Householder, Larry *state official, small business owner*
Howard, Robert Elliott *former federal official, consultant, educator*
Huckabee, Mike (Michael Dale) *former governo*
Huddle, Franklin Pierce, Jr. *diplomat*
Huddleston, Vicki Jean *ambassador*
Hull, Edmund J. *former ambassador*
Hull, Jane Dee *former governor, state legislator*
Hunt, Lorraine T. *former lieutenant governor*
Isaac, Teresa Ann *former mayor, lawyer*
Jacobsen, Diane DeMell *foreign policy specialis*
Javits, Eric Moses *ambassador, lawyer*
Jennings, Toni (Antoinette Lee Jennings) *former lieutenant governor, former state senator*
Johnson, Brenda LaGrange *ambassador*
Johnson, Bruce E. *former lieutenant governor, state legislator*
Kane, Mary Deely *former state official*
Katzenbach, Nicholas deBelleville *former Unite States attorney general*
Keegan, John Charles *former mayor, retired military officer, former state legislator*
Kendig, William Lamar *retired federal official, accountant*
Kenny, James Casey *former ambassador, construction company executive*
Kernan, Barbara Desind *federal official*
Kernan, Joseph Eugene III *former governor*
Kiffmeyer, Mary *former state official*
Koken, M. Diane *former state official, insuranc company executive*
Koldenhoven, Dean *former mayor*
Koplan, Stephen *former federal official*
Korologos, Tom Chris *former ambassador*
Kottkamp, Jeffrey Dean *lieutenant governor, lawyer*
Kramer, Mary Elizabeth *ambassador, former state legislator*
Kulstad, Guy Charles *public works official*
Leach, Howard H. *former ambassador, former health care products company executive*
LeBlanc, Daniel G. *state official*
Ledogar, Stephen J. *retired diplomat*
Leman, Loren Dwight *former lieutenant governor, civil engineer*
Levy, Leah Garrigan *federal official*
Loiello, John Peter *diplomat, international consultant*
Luti, Bill (William Joseph Luti) *federal official, retired military officer*
Mabus, Raymond Edwin, Jr. *former ambassado governor*
MacAulay, Lawrence A. *former Canadian government official, member of Parliament*
Macedo de la Concha, Rafael *former Mexican government official*
Maestrone, Frank Eusebio *diplomat*
Maisto, John F. *former ambassador*
Marchi, Sergio Sisto *Canadian government official*
Martin, Paul *former Prime Minister of Canada*
Mathews, Mary Kathryn *retired government official*
Mathieu, Gail Dennise *ambassador*
Mattingly, Mack Francis *former ambassador, senator, entrepreneur*
Mazankowski, Donald Frank *Canadian government official*
McClellan, Scott K. *former White House press secretary*
McClennen, Miriam J. *former state official*
McClinton, James Leroy *city administrator*
Mc Coy, Tidal Windham *former government official*
McDougall, Donald Blake *retired provincial official, librarian*
McGreevey, Jim (James Edward McGreevey) *former governor*
McKeachnie, Gayle F. *former lieutenant governor*
McNamara, Ted (Thomas Edmund McNamara) *federal official, former ambassador*
McPherson, Bruce A. *former state official, former state legislator*
Meyer, Joseph B. *state official*
Millane, Lynn *retired municipal official*
Miller, Laura M. *former mayor, journalist*
Miller, Thomas J. *former ambassador*
Moe, Lonn Andre *state revenue official*
Montgomery, Betty Dee *former state attorney general, retired state legislator*
Moore, John Eddy *former lieutenant governor*
Morris, Robert Gemmill *retired foreign service officer*
Murphy, Gerald *retired federal official*

Murray, Timothy Patrick *lieutenant governor, former mayor*
Navarrete, Jorge Eduardo *ambassador*
Nelson, Norman Daniel *government official*
Nemfakos, Charles Panagiotis *defense industry executive, strategic consultant*
Newsom, Kevin *federal official, lawyer*
Norquist, John Olaf *former mayor*
Norton, Jane Ellen Bergman (Jane Bergman) *former lieutenant governor*
Obermann, Richard Michael *governmental technology and policy analyst*
O'Neill, Beverly Lewis *former mayor, former college president*
Ong, John Doyle *former ambassador, retired manufacturing executive*
O'Sullivan, Meghan L. *former federal official*
Pearl, Laurence Dickson *retired federal government executive*
Pederson, Sally J. *former lieutenant governor*
Petrequin, Harry Joseph, Jr. *foreign service officer*
Petro, Jim (James Michael) *former state attorney general*
Peyton, John *mayor*
Pirsch, Carol McBride *retired county official, state senator, community relations manager*
Plame, Valerie Elise *former intelligence agent*
Pleuger, Guenter *diplomat*
Pont Marchese, Marisara *former Puerto Rican government official*
Portman, Robert Jones *former federal official, former ambassador*
Powers, John T., Jr. *former mayor*
Pridmore, Roy Davis *retired federal official*
Purcell, Bill *mayor*
Qualls, Roxanne *mayor*
Quinn, Eugene Frederick *diplomat, minister*
Rahman, Abu Tayeb Rafiqur *former United Nations official*
Ralston, Susan Bonzon *former federal official*
Randolph, Virgella *retired federal official*
Ratliff, William *former state senator, lieutenant governor, civil engineer*
Reagan, Nancy Davis (Anne Francis Robbins) *former First Lady of the United States, volunteer*
Redd, Scott (John Scott Redd) *federal official, retired military officer*
Reinhardt, John Edward *former international affairs specialist*
Renkes, Gregg D. *former state attorney general*
Reno, Janet *former United States attorney general*
Rickert, Jonathan Bradley *retired foreign service officer*
Ricks, Mark G. *former lieutenant governor, former state senator*
Ridge, Tom (Thomas Joseph) *former secretary of homeland security, governor*
Ries, Charles P. *ambassador*
Rimler, Anita A. *former state official*
Rimsza, Skip *former mayor*
Riordan, Richard J. *former state official, former mayor*
Rivers, Beverly D. *former district secretary*
Rocca, Christina B. *ambassador, former federal agency administrator*
Rosenthal, James D. *retired federal official, retired ambassador*
Ross, Christopher Wade Stelyan *diplomat*
Rossin, Lawrence George *ambassador*
Rove, Karl Christian *former federal official*
Rudin, Anne *retired mayor, nursing educator*
Rumsfeld, Donald Henry *former secretary of defense*
ussack, John A. *federal official*
anders, Jackie Wolcott *ambassador*
atterfield, David Michael *ambassador*
choettler, Gail Sinton *former ambassador*
embler, Melvin F. *former ambassador, real estate developer*
entenne, Justine *corporate ombudsman consultant*
helley, Kevin Francis *former state official*
hivers, Mitchell Everett *diplomat*
lutz, Pamela Jo Howell *ambassador*
mith, Jean Kennedy *former ambassador*
mith, Pamela Hyde *ambassador*
mith, Robert Powell *former ambassador, retired foundation administrator*
nider, L. Britt *federal official*
now, Tony *former White House press secretary, political commentator, analyst*
pencer, John Daniel *former mayor*
teele, Michael S. *former lieutenant governor*
tevens, Kenneth Allen *retired defense department worker*
itziel, Judd *foreign affairs officer*
ridiron, Iver Allison *former attorney general*
roup, Kala Mays *former education commissioner, educational alliance administrator*
umpe, Warren Robert *county official, retired engineering executive*
ullivan, Kevin B. *former lieutenant governor, state legislator*
wett, Richard Nelson (Dick Swett) *diplomat, former congressman*
aft, Bob (Robert Alphonso Taft II) *former governor*
ambs, Lewis Arthur *diplomat, historian, educator*
aylor, Sara Marie *former federal official*
eater, Dorothy Seath *retired county official*
erpeluk, Peter G., Jr. *former ambassador*
homas, Ralph Charles III *federal official*
homas, Regena L. *former state official*
enken, Arthur T. *retired foreign service officer*
ownsend, Kathleen Kennedy *former lieutenant governor*
nderwood, Cecil Harland *retired governor, diversified financial services company executive*
aleri, Tony *Canadian government official, small business owner*
an Cleave, Michelle Kim *former federal official*
Vasquez, Gaddi H. *ambassador, former federal agency administrator*
Ventura, Jesse (James Janos) *former governor*
Vigil-Giron, Rebecca *former state official*
Vilsack, Tom (Thomas James) *former governor*
Walker, George Herbert III *former ambassador, retired investment banking company executive*
Walker, Gordon Davies *government official, writer, lecturer, consultant*
Walker, Olene S. *former governor*
Wallace, Nicolle (Nicolle Devenish) *former federal official*
Watkins, James David *federal official, military officer*
Webster, Christopher White *foreign service officer*
Williams, Anthony Allan (Tony) *former mayor*
Williams, Roger (J. Roger Williams) *former state official*
Williamson, Richard Salisbury *ambassador*
Wilson, Joseph Charles, IV, *former ambassador*
Winter, Harvey John *retired government official*
Wolf, Dale Edward *state official*
Wood, Corinne Gieseke *former lieutenant governor*
Zischke, Douglas Arthur *foreign service officer*

GOVERNMENT: LEGISLATIVE ADMINISTRATION

UNITED STATES

ALABAMA

Birmingham
Allen, Maryon Pittman *former senator, clothing designer, journalist*
Hilliard, Earl Frederick *congressman, lawyer*

Mobile
Edwards, Jack *congressman, lawyer*

Montgomery
Dixon, Larry Dean *state legislator*

ALASKA

Anchorage
Sturgulewski, Arliss *state legislator, director*

Juneau
Kohring, Victor H. *state legislator*
Stevens, Gary Lee *state senator*

North Pole
James, Jeannette Adeline *state legislator, accountant, small business owner*

ARIZONA

Phoenix
Brown, Jack A. *state representative, rancher, real estate broker*
Kyl, Jon Llewellyn *senator*
Salmon, Matt *former congressman, communications company executive*
Steffey, Lela *state legislator, banker*

Tucson
Bartlett, David Carson *state legislator*

Waddell
Turner, Warren Austin *state legislator*

ARKANSAS

Greenwood
Walters, Bill *retired state senator*

Little Rock
Pryor, David Hampton *former senator*

CALIFORNIA

Bakersfield
Ashburn, Roy *state senator*

Compton
Dymally, Mervyn Malcolm *retired congressman*

Fountain Valley
Armstrong, Jeffrey Lee *representative, oceanographer*

Long Beach
Karentte, Betty *state legislator*

Monterey
Browder, John Glen *former congressman, educator*

Sacramento
Chu, Judy May *assemblywoman*
Kuehl, Sheila James *state legislator*
Pavley, Fran J. *state representative*
Strickland, Anthony *state representative*
Tran, Van Thai *state legislator*
Yee, Leland Y. *state senator*

San Mateo
Mullin, Gene *state legislator*

Santa Ana
Seymour, John *former senator*

Stockton
Singleton, Marvin Ayers *state legislator, otolaryngologist*

West Covina
Torres, Esteban Edward *former congressman, trade association administrator*

COLORADO

Colorado Springs
Lamborn, Douglas L. *congressman*
Sinclair, William Donald *state legislator, retired church official*

Denver
Anderson, Norma V. *retired state legislator*
Faatz, Jeanne Ryan *councilman*
Meiklejohn, Alvin J., Jr. *state legislator, lawyer, accountant*
Takis, Stephanie *retired state senator*
Williams, Suzanne *state senator*

Fort Collins
Schaffer, Robert (Bob Schaffer) *former congressman*

Grand Junction
Bishop, Tilman Malcolm *retired state legislator*

CONNECTICUT

Branford
Gejdenson, Sam *former congressman*

Glastonbury
Googins, Sonya Forbes *state legislator, retired banker*

Hartford
Carter, Annette Wheeler *state legislator*
Fahrbach, Ruth C. *state legislator*
Jepsen, George C. *state legislator, lawyer*
Mushinsky, Mary M. *state legislator*

Ledyard
McGrattan, Mary K. *state legislator*

New Britain
Murphy, Christopher S. *congressman, former state senator*

New Haven
Dyson, William R. *state legislator, educator*

Riverside
Powers, Claudia McKenna *state legislator*

Stonington
Simmons, Robert Ruhl *former congressman*

Vernon Rockville
Courtney, Joe (Joseph D. Courtney) *congressman*

DELAWARE

Dover
Amick, Steven Hammond *state legislator, lawyer*

Newark
Neal, James Preston *state senator, project engineer*

DISTRICT OF COLUMBIA

Washington
Abercrombie, Neil *congressman*
Ackerman, Gary Leonard *congressman*
Aderholt, Robert B. *congressman, lawyer*
Akaka, Daniel Kahikina *senator*
Akin, Todd (William Todd Akin) *congressman, former state legislator*
Alexander, (Andrew) Lamar *senator, former secretary of education, governor*
Alexander, Rodney M. *congressman*
Allard, (Alan) Wayne *senator, veterinarian*
Allen, Thomas H. *congressman, lawyer*
Altmire, Jason *congressman*
Andrews, Robert Ernest *congressman, lawyer*
Armey, Dick (Richard Keith Armey) *state representative*
Baca, Joe *congressman*
Bachmann, Michele *congresswoman, former state legislator*
Bachus, Spencer T. III *congressman, lawyer*
Backlin, Jim *legislative staff member*
Baird, Brian N. *congressman*
Baker, Richard Hugh *congressman*
Baldwin, Tammy *congresswoman, lawyer*
Barrasso, John Anthony *senator, orthopedic surgeon*
Barrow, John Jenkins *congressman, lawyer*
Bartlett, Roscoe G. *congressman*
Barton, Joe Linus *congressman*
Bates, James T. *chief of staff*
Baucus, Max Sieben *senator*
Bayh, Evan (Birch Evan Bayh III) *senator, former governor*
Bean, Melissa *congresswoman*
Becerra, Xavier *congressman, lawyer*
Bennett, Robert F. *senator*
Berkley, Shelley (Rochelle Levine Berkley) *congresswoman, lawyer*
Berman, Howard Lawrence *congressman, lawyer*
Berry, Marion *congressman*
Biden, Joseph Robinette, Jr. *senator*
Biggert, Judith Borg *congresswoman, lawyer*
Bilbray, Brian Patrick *congressman*
Bilirakis, Gus Michael *congressman, former state representative*
Bingaman, Jeff, Jr., (Jesse Francis Bingaman) *senator*
Bishop, Rob *congressman*
Bishop, Sanford Dixon, Jr. *congressman, lawyer*
Bishop, Timothy H. *congressman*
Blackburn, Marsha *congresswoman*
Bliley, Thomas Jerome, Jr. *former congressman*
Blunt, Roy D. *congressman*
Boehner, John Andrew *congressman*
Bond, Christopher Samuel (Kit Bond) *senator, lawyer*
Bonner, Josiah Robins, Jr., (Jo Bonner) *congressman*
Bono, Mary Whitaker *congresswoman*
Boozman, John *congressman*
Bordallo, Madeleine Zeien (Mrs. Ricardo Jerome Bordallo) *congresswoman*
Boren, Daniel David *congressman*
Boswell, Leonard L. *congressman*
Boucher, Rick (Frederick C. Boucher) *congressman, lawyer*
Boustany, Charles W., Jr. *congressman, surgeon*
Boxer, Barbara *senator*
Boyd, F. Allen, Jr. *congressman, farmer*
Boyda, Nancy *congresswoman*
Brady, Kevin Patrick *congressman*
Brady, Robert A. *congressman*
Braley, Bruce *congressman*
Broun, Paul C., Jr. *congressman, physician*
Brown, Corrine *congresswoman*
Brown, Henry E., Jr. *congressman*
Brown, Michael D. *shadow senator*
Brown, Sherrod Campbell *senator, former congressman, former state official*
Brownback, Sam Dale *senator, lawyer*
Buchanan, Vern (Vernon G. Buchanan) *congressman*
Bunning, Jim (James Paul David Bunning) *senator, former professional baseball player*
Burgess, Michael C. *congressman*
Burns, Conrad Ray *former senator*
Burr, Richard M. *senator, former congressman*
Burton, Dan L. *congressman*
Butterfield, George Kenneth, Jr. *congressman, former state supreme court justice*
Buyer, Steven Earle *congressman, lawyer*
Byrd, Robert Carlyle *senator*
Calvert, Ken *congressman*
Camp, David Lee *congressman, lawyer*
Campbell, John B. T. III *congressman, former state senator*
Cannon, Christopher Black *congressman, lawyer*
Cantor, Eric I. *congressman, lawyer*
Cantwell, Maria E. *senator*
Capito, Shelley Moore *congresswoman*
Capps, Lois Ragnhild Grimsrud *congresswoman, former school nurse*
Capuano, Michael Everett *congressman, lawyer*
Cardin, Benjamin Louis *senator, former congressman*
Cardoza, Dennis *congressman*
Carnahan, Russ (John Russell Carnahan) *congressman, lawyer*
Carney, Christopher Paul *congressman, political science educator*
Carper, Thomas Richard *senator, former governor*
Carr, Bob *congressman, lawyer*
Carson, Julia M. *congresswoman*
Carter, John Rice *congressman, lawyer*
Casey, Robert Patrick, Jr., (Bob Casey) *senator*
Castle, Michael N. *congressman, lawyer*
Chabot, Steven Joseph *congressman, lawyer*
Chambliss, Saxby (C. Saxby Chambliss) *senator*
Chandler, Ben (Albert Benjamin Chandler III) *congressman, former state attorney general*
Christian-Christensen, Donna Marie *congresswoman*
Clarke, Yvette Diane *congresswoman*
Clay, William Lacy, Jr. *congressman*
Cleaver, Emanuel, II, *congressman, former mayor, minister*
Clinton, Hillary (Hillary Diane Rodham Clinton) *senator, lawyer, former First Lady of United States*
Clyburn, James Enos (Jim Clyburn) *congressman*
Coble, (John) Howard *congressman, lawyer*
Coburn, Tom (Thomas Allen Coburn) *senator*
Cochran, Thad (William Thad Cochran) *senator*
Cohen, Steve (Stephen Ira Cohen) *congressman, former state legislator*
Cole, Tom *congressman*
Coleman, Norman, Jr. *senator, former mayor*
Collins, Susan Margaret *senator*
Conaway, Mike *congressman*
Conrad, Kent (Gaylord Kent Conrad) *senator*
Conyers, John, Jr. *congressman*
Cooper, James Hayes Shofner (Jim Cooper) *congressman, lawyer*
Corker, Bob (Robert Phillips Corker Jr.) *senator*
Cornyn, John *senator*
Costa, Jim *congressman*
Costello, Jerry F., Jr. *congressman, former county official*
Cramer, Robert E., Jr., (Bud Cramer) *congressman, lawyer*
Crapo, Michael Dean *senator, former congressman, lawyer*
Crenshaw, Ander *congressman, lawyer*
Crowley, Joseph *congressman*
Cubin, Barbara Lynn *congresswoman*
Cuellar, Henry *congressman, lawyer*
Culberson, John Abney *congressman, lawyer*
Cummings, Elijah E. *congressman*
Davis, Artur *congressman, lawyer*
Davis, Danny K. *congressman*
Davis, David Lee *congressman*
Davis, Geoff *congressman*
Davis, Jo Ann S. *congresswoman*
Davis, Lincoln *congressman*
Davis, Susan A. *congresswoman*
Davis, Thomas M. III *congressman*
Deal, Nathan J. *congressman, lawyer*
DeFazio, Peter Anthony *congressman*
Delahunt, William D. *congressman*
DeLauro, Rosa L. *congresswoman*
Diaz-Balart, Lincoln *congressman, lawyer*
Diaz-Balart, Mario *congressman*

Dicks, Norman De Valois *congressman*
Dingell, John David *congressman*
Dodd, Christopher John *senator*
Doggett, Lloyd Alton, II, *congressman, retired judge*
Dole, Elizabeth Hanford (Liddy) *senator, former federal agency administrator*
Domenici, (Pete) Vichi *senator*
Donnelly, Joseph *congressman, lawyer*
Dooley, Calvin Millard *former congressman*
Doolittle, John Taylor *congressman*
Dorgan, Byron Leslie *senator*
Doyle, Michael F. (Mike) *congressman*
Drake, Thelma Day *congresswoman*
Dreier, David Timothy *congressman*
Duncan, John J., Jr. *congressman*
Durbin, Dick (Richard Joseph Durbin) *senator*
Edwards, Chet (Thomas Chester Edwards) *congressman*
Ehlers, Vernon James *congressman*
Ellsworth, Brad (Bradley Ellsworth) *congressman, former police officer*
Emanuel, Rahm *congressman*
Emerson, Jo Ann H. *congresswoman*
Engel, Eliot Lanze *congressman*
Ensign, John Eric *senator, former congressman*
Enzi, Michael Bradley *senator, accountant*
Eshoo, Anna Georges *congresswoman*
Etheridge, Bob (Bobby Ray Etheridge) *congressman*
Everett, Terry *congressman*
Faleomavaega, Eni Fa'auaa Hunkin *congressman*
Farr, Sam *congressman*
Fattah, Chaka *congressman, former state legislator*
Feeney, Tom *congressman*
Feingold, Russell Dana *senator, lawyer*
Feinstein, Dianne *senator*
Ferguson, Michael A. (Mike) *congressman*
Filner, Bob *congressman*
Flake, Jeff *congressman*
Forbes, James Randy *congressman*
Fortenberry, Jeffrey Lane *congressman*
Fortuño, Luis *congressman*
Frank, Barney *congressman*
Franks, Trent *congressman*
Frelinghuysen, Rodney P. *congressman*
Gallegly, Elton William *congressman*
Garrett, Scott (E. Scott Garrett) *congressman, lawyer*
Gerlach, Jim (James William Gerlach) *congressman*
Giffords, Gabrielle *congresswoman, former state senator*
Gilchrest, Wayne Thomas *congressman, secondary school educator*
Gillibrand, Kirsten Rutnick *congresswoman, lawyer*
Gillmor, Paul Eugene *congressman, lawyer*
Gilman, Benjamin Arthur *former congressman, lawyer*
Gingrey, Phil (John Phillip Gingrey) *congressman*
Gingrich, Newt (Newton Leroy Gingrich) *former congressman*
Gohmert, Louis Buller, Jr., (Louie Gohmert) *congressman, former judge, lawyer*
Gonzalez, Charles A. *congressman*
Goode, Virgil H., Jr. *congressman*
Goodlatte, Bob (Robert William) *congressman, lawyer*
Gordon, Barton Jennings (Bart Gordon) *congressman, lawyer*
Gradison, Bill (Willis David Gradison Jr.) *former congressman*
Graham, Lindsey Olin *senator*
Granger, Kay *congresswoman*
Grassley, Chuck (Charles Ernest Grassley) *senator*
Graves, Samuel B., Jr. *congressman, retired state legislator*
Green, Al *congressman*
Green, Gene (Raymond Eugene Green) *congressman*
Gregg, Judd Alan *senator, former governor*
Grijalva, Raul *congressman*
Gutierrez, Luis V. *congressman, elementary education educator*
Hagel, Chuck (Charles Timothy Hagel) *senator*
Hall, John J. *congressman, musician*
Hall, Ralph Moody *congressman*
Hare, Phil (Philip G. Hare) *congressman*
Harkin, Thomas Richard *senator*
Harman, Jane *congresswoman*
Hastert, Dennis (John Dennis Hastert) *congressman*
Hastings, Alcee Lamar *congressman, retired judge*
Hastings, Doc (Richard Norman Hastings) *congressman*
Hatch, Orrin Grant *senator*
Hayes, Robin (Robert Cannon Hayes) *congressman*
Hensarling, Jeb *congressman*
Herger, Walter William *congressman*
Higgins, Brian *congressman*
Hill, Baron Paul *congressman*
Hilleary, Van (William Vanderpool Hilleary) *former congressman, lawyer*
Hinchey, Maurice D. *congressman*
Hinojosa, Rubén *congressman*
Hiscock, Richard Carson *legislative staff member*
Hodes, Paul William, II, *congressman, lawyer*
Hoekstra, Peter *congressman, manufacturing executive*
Holden, Tim (Thomas Timothy) *congressman, protective official*
Holt, Rush D. *congressman, physics educator, researcher, consultant*
Honda, Michael M. *congressman*
Hooley, Darlene *congresswoman*
Hoyer, Steny Hamilton *congressman*
Hulshof, Kenny Charles *congressman*
Hunter, Duncan Lee *congressman*
Hutchinson, Tim *former senator*
Hutchison, Kay Bailey *senator*
Inglis, Bob (Robert Durden) *congressman*
Inhofe, James M. *senator*
Inouye, Daniel Ken *senator*
Inslee, Jay Robert *congressman*
Isakson, Johnny (John Hardy Isakson) *senator, former congressman*
Israel, Steven Jay *congressman*
Issa, Darrell E. *congressman*
Jackson, Jesse Louis, Jr. *congressman*
Jackson Lee, Sheila *congresswoman*
Jefferson, William Jennings (Jeff Jefferson) *congressman*
Jindal, Bobby Piyush *congressman*
Johnson, Eddie Bernice *congresswoman*
Johnson, Nancy Lee *former congresswoman*
Johnson, Samuel (Sam Johnson) *congressman*
Johnson, Timothy Peter *senator*
Johnson, Timothy Vincent *congressman, lawyer*
Jones, Stephanie Tubbs *congresswoman, lawyer, prosecutor*
Jordan, Jim (James D. Jordan) *congressman, former state legislator*
Kagen, Steven L. *congressman, physician*
Kanjorski, Paul Edmund *congressman, lawyer*
Kasten, Robert W., Jr. *former senator*
Keller, Ric *congressman, lawyer*
Kemp, Jack French *former congressman*
Kennedy, Patrick Joseph *congressman*
Kennedy, Ted (Edward Moore Kennedy) *senator*
Kennelly, Barbara B. *retired congressman, federal agency administrator*
Kerry, John Forbes *senator*
Kildee, Dale Edward *congressman*
Kilpatrick, Carolyn Cheeks *congresswoman*
Kind, Ronald James *congressman, lawyer*
King, Steve *congressman*
Kingston, Jack *congressman*
Kirk, Mark Steven *congressman*
Klein, Ronald Jay *congressman, former state legislator, lawyer*
Kline, John *congressman*
Klobuchar, Amy Jean *senator, lawyer*
Knollenberg, Joseph Castl (Joe Knollenberg) *congressman*
Kohl, Herbert H. *senator, professional sports team owner*
Kuhl, Randy (John R. Kuhl Jr.) *congressman, lawyer*
LaHood, Ray H. *congressman*
Lampson, Nick (Nicholas Valentino Lampson) *congressman*
Landrieu, Mary Lorretta *senator*
Langevin, James R. (Jim Langevin) *congressman, former state official*
Lantos, Thomas Peter *congressman*
Larsen, Richard Ray (Rick Larsen) *congressman*
Larson, John Barry *congressman, insurance executive*
Latham, Tom *congressman*
Leahy, Patrick Joseph *senator*
Lee, Barbara *congresswoman*
Lent, Norman Frederick, Jr. *former congressman*
Levin, Carl Milton *senator*
Levin, Sander Martin *congressman, lawyer*
Lewis, Charles Jeremy (Jerry Lewis) *congressman*
Lewis, John Robert *congressman*
Lewis, Ron *congressman*
Lieberman, Joe (Joseph Isadore Lieberman) *senator*
Lincoln, Blanche Lambert *senator*
Linder, John E. *congressman, dentist*
Lipinski, Daniel *congressman*
Loebsack, Dave *congressman, former political science professor*
Lofgren, Zoe *congresswoman*
Lott, (Chester) Trent *senator*
Lugar, Dick (Richard Green Lugar) *senator*
Lungren, Daniel Edward *congressman, former state attorney general*
Lynch, Stephen F. *congressman*
Mack, Connie *congressman*
Mack, Connie, III, (Cornelius McGillicuddy III) *former senator*
Mahoney, Tim (Timothy Edward Mahoney) *congressman*
Maloney, Carolyn Bosher *congresswoman*
Manzullo, Donald A. *congressman, lawyer*
Marchant, Kenny *congressman*
Markey, Edward John *congressman*
Marshall, Jim (James Creel Marshall) *congressman*
Martinez, Mel(quiades) (Rafael) *senator, political organization administrator, former secretary of housing and urban development*
Matheson, James David (Jim) *congressman*
Matsui, Doris Okada *congresswoman*
McCain, John (John Sidney McCain III) *senator*
McCarthy, Carolyn *congresswoman*
McCarthy, Kevin *congressman, former state legislator*
McCaskill, Claire C. *senator, former auditor*
McCaul, Michael T. *congressman*
McCollum, Betty *congresswoman*
McConnell, (Addison) Mitchell, Jr. *senator, lawyer*
McCrery, James (Jim McCrery) *congressman*
McDermott, James A. *congressman, psychiatrist*
McGovern, James P. *congressman*
McHenry, Patrick Timothy *congressman*
McIntosh, David M. *former congressman*
McIntyre, Mike (Douglas Carmichael McIntyre II) *congressman*
McKeon, Howard Phillip (Buck McKeon) *congressman, former mayor*
McMorris Rodgers, Cathy *congresswoman*
McNerney, Jerry (Gerald M. McNerney) *congressman, engineer*
McNulty, Michael Robert *congressman*
Meek, Kendrick B. *congressman*
Megginson, Elizabeth R. *legislative staff member, director, lawyer*
Melancon, Charles *congressman*
Menendez, Robert (Bob Menendez) *senator, former congressman*
Mica, John L. *congressman*
Michaud, Michael Herman *congressman*
Mikulski, Barbara Ann *senator*
Miller, Brad (Ralph Bradley Miller) *congressman*
Miller, Candice S. *congresswoman*
Miller, Gary G. *congressman*
Miller, George *congressman*
Miller, Jeff *congressman*
Mitchell, Harry E. *congressman, former state legislator*
Molinari, Susan *former congresswoman*
Mollohan, Alan Bowlby *congressman*
Moore, Dennis *congressman*
Moore, Gwendolynne S. (Gwen Moore) *congresswoman*
Moran, Jerry *congressman*
Moran, Jim (James Patrick Moran Jr.) *congressman, stock broker*
Murkowski, Lisa Ann *senator*
Murphy, Timothy F. *congressman*
Murray, Patty (Patricia J. Murray) *senator*
Murtha, John Patrick, Jr. *congressman*
Musgrave, Marilyn N. *congresswoman*
Myrick, Sue Wilkins *congresswoman, former mayor*
Nadler, Jerrold Lewis *congressman, lawyer*
Napolitano, Grace F. *congresswoman*
Neal, Richard Edmund *congressman, former mayor*
Nelson, (Earl) Ben(jamin) *senator, former governor, lawyer*
Nelson, Bill (Clarence William Nelson) *senator, former state treasurer*
Neugebauer, Randy (Robert R. Neugebauer) *congressman*
Norton, Eleanor Holmes *congresswoman, lawyer, educator*
Nunes, Devin *congressman*
Nunn, Sam (Samuel Augustus Nunn) *former senator, lawyer*
Obama, Barack Hussein, Jr. *senator, former state legislator*
Oberstar, James L. *congressman*
Obey, David Ross *congressman*
Olver, John Walter *congressman*
Ortiz, Solomon Porfirio *congressman*
Pallone, Frank, Jr. *congressman, lawyer*
Panetta, Michael *shadow representative*
Pascrell, William J., Jr. *congressman*
Pastor, Edward *congressman*
Paxon, L. William *former congressman*
Payne, Donald Milford *congressman*
Pearce, Steve (Stevan E. Pearce) *congressman*
Pelosi, Nancy Patricia *congresswoman*
Pence, Michael Richard *congressman*
Perlmutter, Ed (Edwin George Perlmutter) *congressman, former state legislator*
Peterson, Collin C. *congressman*
Peterson, John E. *congressman*
Petri, Thomas Evert *congressman*
Pickering, Chip (Charles Willis Pickering Jr.) *congressman*
Platts, Todd Russell *congressman, state legislator*
Poe, Ted *congressman, former judge*
Pomeroy, Earl Ralph *congressman, retired commissioner*
Porter, John Edward *former congressman*
Porter, Jon Christopher, Sr. *congressman*
Price, David Eugene *congressman, education educator*
Price, Thomas E. *congressman*
Pryor, Mark Lunsford *senator*
Putnam, Adam Hughes *congressman, farmer, rancher*
Quinn, Jack (John Francis Quinn) *former congressman, English language educator*
Radanovich, George P. *congressman*
Rademaker, Stephen Geoffrey *legislative staff member, former federal agency administrator*
Rahall, Nick Joe, II, (Nick Rahall) *congressman*
Ramstad, James *congressman, lawyer*
Rangel, Charlie (Charles Bernard Rangel) *congressman*
Reed, John Francis (Jack) *senator*
Regula, Ralph Straus *congressman, lawyer*
Rehberg, Dennis R. *congressman*
Reichert, David G. (Dave Reichert) *congressman*
Reid, Harry Mason *senator*
Renzi, Rick (Richard George Renzi) *congressman*
Reyes, Silvestre *congressman*
Reynolds, Thomas M. *congressman*
Richardson, Laura A. *congresswoman*
Roberts, Charles Patrick (Pat Roberts) *senator*
Rockefeller, John Davison, IV, (Jay Rockefeller) *senator, retired governor*
Rodriguez, Ciro Davis *congressman*
Rogers, Harold Dallas (Hal) *congressman*
Rogers, Mike *congressman*
Rogers, Mike (Michael J. Rogers) *congressman*
Rohrabacher, Dana *congressman*
Ros-Lehtinen, Ileana Carmen *congresswoman*
Ross, Mike *congressman*
Rothman, Steven R. *congressman*
Roybal-Allard, Lucille *congresswoman*
Royce, Ed (Edward Randall Royce) *congressman*
Ruppersberger, Charles Albert, III, (Dutch) *congressman*
Rush, Bobby L. *congressman*
Ryan, Paul *congressman*
Salazar, John T. *congressman*
Salazar, Ken(neth) Lee *senator, former state attorney general*
Sali, Bill (William Thomas Sali) *congressman, former state legislator*
Sanchez, Linda T. *congresswoman*
Sanchez, Loretta *congresswoman*
Sanders, Bernard (Bernie Sanders) *senator, former congressman*
Sandlin, Max Allen, Jr. *former congressman*
Sandlin, Stephanie Herseth *congresswoman, lawyer*
Sarbanes, John Peter Spyros *congressman, lawyer*
Saxton, Jim (Hugh James Saxton) *congressman*
Schakowsky, Janice *congresswoman*
Schiff, Adam Bennett *congressman, lawyer*
Schmidt, Jean *congresswoman*
Schumer, Chuck (Charles Ellis) *senator*
Schwartz, Allyson Y. *congresswoman*
Scott, David Albert *congressman*
Scott, Robert Cortez *congressman, lawyer*
Sensenbrenner, F(rank) James, Jr. *congressman*
Serrano, José Enrique *congressman*
Sessions, Jeff (Jefferson Beauregard Sessions III) *senator, former state attorney general*
Sessions, Pete *congressman*
Shadegg, John Barden *congressman*
Shays, Christopher *congressman*
Shea-Porter, Carol *congresswoman, social worker*
Shelby, Richard Craig *senator, former congressman*
Sherman, Bradley James *congressman*
Shimkus, John Mondy *congressman*
Sikorski, Gerry *congressman*
Simpson, Michael K. *congressman*
Sires, Albio *congressman, former state legislator*
Skelton, Ike (Isaac Newton Skelton IV) *congressman*
Slaughter, Louise McIntosh *congresswoman*
Smith, Adam *congressman*
Smith, Adrian M. *congressman, real estate agen[t]*
Smith, Christopher Henry *congressman*
Smith, Gordon Harold *senator*
Smith, Lamar Seeligson *congressman*
Snowbarger, Vince *former congressman*
Snowe, Olympia J. *senator*
Snyder, Vic *congressman, physician*
Solis, Hilda Lucia *congresswoman, educational administrator*
Souder, Mark Edward *congressman*
Space, Zack (Zachary T. Space) *congressman*
Specter, Arlen *senator*
Spratt, John McKee, Jr. *congressman, lawyer*
Stabenow, Deborah Ann *senator, former congresswoman*
Stark, Fortney Hillman (Pete Stark) *congressma[n]*
Stearns, Clifford Bundy *congressman, diversified financial services company executive*
Stevens, Ted (Theodore Fulton) *senator*
Strauss, Paul *shadow senator*
Stupak, Bart T. *congressman, lawyer*
Sullivan, John A. *congressman*
Sununu, John Edward *senator*
Sutton, Betty *congresswoman, lawyer*
Tancredo, Thomas G. *congressman*
Tanner, John S. *congressman, lawyer*
Taylor, Gene (Gary Eugene Taylor) *congressma[n]*
Tenorio, Pedro A. *resident representative*
Terry, Lee Raymond *congressman, lawyer*
Tester, Jon(athan) *senator, former state legislato[r], farmer*
Thomas, Bill (William Marshall Thomas) *retire[d] congressman*
Thompson, Bennie G. *congressman*
Thompson, Mike (C. Michael Thompson) *congressman*
Thornberry, Mac (William McClellan Thornberry) *congressman*
Thune, John Randolph *senator*
Tiahrt, Todd (W. Todd Tiahrt) *congressman, former state senator*
Tierney, John F. *congressman, lawyer*
Towns, Edolphus *congressman*
Turner, Michael R. *congressman*
Udall, Mark *congressman*
Udall, Thomas S. (Tom) *congressman*
Upton, Frederick Stephen *congressman*
Van Hollen, Christopher, Jr. *congressman*
Visclosky, Peter John *congressman, lawyer*
Vitter, David Bruce *senator, former congressma[n]*
Voinovich, George Victor *senator, former governor*
Walden, Greg *congressman*
Walker, Robert Smith *former congressman*
Walz, Tim (Timothy J. Walz) *congressman, social science educator*
Wamp, Zachary Paul *congressman*
Warner, John William *senator*
Wasserman-Schultz, Debbie *congresswoman*
Waters, Maxine *congresswoman*
Watson, Diane Edith *congresswoman*
Watt, Melvin Luther *congressman, lawyer*
Watts, J. C., Jr. *former congressman, retired professional football player*
Waxman, Henry Arnold *congressman*
Webb, Jim (James Henry Webb Jr.) *senator, former civilian military employee*
Weiner, Anthony David *congressman*
Welch, Peter F. *congressman, former state legislator*
Weldon, David Joseph, Jr. *congressman, physician*
Weller, Gerald C. *congressman*
Westmoreland, Lynn A. *congressman*
Wexler, Robert *congressman*
Whitehouse, Sheldon *senator, former state attorney general*
Whitfield, Edward (Wayne) *congressman*
Wicker, Roger F. *congressman, lawyer*
Wilson, Charles A., Jr. *congressman, funeral director*
Wilson, Joe (Addison Graves) *congressman, former senator, lawyer*
Wofford, Harris *senator, lawyer*
Wolf, Frank Rudolph *congressman, lawyer*
Woolsey, Lynn C. *congresswoman*
Wortley, George Cornelius *congressman, consultant*
Wyden, Ron(ald) (Lee) *senator*
Wynn, Albert Russell *congressman*
Yarmuth, John Allan *congressman*
Young, Bill (Charles William Young) *congressman*
Young, Donald E. *congressman*

FLORIDA

Bradenton

Woodson-Howard, Marlene Erdley *former state legislator*

Dade City
Brown-Waite, Virginia (Ginny Brown-Waite) *congresswoman*

Ormond Beach
Lynn, Evelyn Joan *state senator, consultant*

Tallahassee
Blanton, Faye Wester *legislative official*

Tampa
Castor, Kathy *congresswoman*
Davis, Helen Gordon *retired state senator*

GEORGIA

Americus
Hooks, George Bardin *state legislator, insurance and real estate company executive*

Athens
McBee, Mary Louise *retired state legislator, academic administrator*

Atlanta
Butler, Gloria Singleton *state legislator*
Coleman, Terry Lewis *state legislator*
Darden, George Washington, III, (Buddy Darden) *former congressman, lawyer*
Miller, Zell Bryan *former senator, governor*

Columbus
Harbison, Ed *state legislator, broadcast journalist, motivational speaker*

Decatur
Majette, Denise *former congresswoman*
McKinney, Cynthia Ann *former congresswoman*

Donalsonville
Ponder, Dan E., Jr. *former state legislator, food service executive*

Lawrenceville
Wall, Clarence Vinson *state legislator*

Lithonia
ohnson, Henry C. (Hank Johnson) *congressman, lawyer*

Rincon
Purcell, Ann Rushing *state legislator, human services manager*

Savannah
ohnson, Eric B. *state legislator*

Smyrna
Atkins, William Austin, Sr., (Bill Atkins) *former state legislator*

HAWAII

Honolulu
Baker, Rosalyn Hester *state senator*
Case, Edward E. *former congressman, lawyer*
Hirono, Mazie Keiko *congresswoman, former lieutenant governor*
Magaoay, Michael Y. *state representative*
Sakamoto, Norman Lloyd *state legislator, civil engineer*
akumi, Roy Mitsuo *state legislator*

DAHO

oise
lack, Pete *retired state legislator, educator*
eough, Shawn *state legislator*
aRocco, Larry *former congressman*
odge, Patti Anne *state senator*

erome
ell, Maxine Toolson *state legislator, librarian*

LLINOIS

loomingdale
oskam, Peter James *congressman, former state legislator, lawyer*

hicago
erman, Arthur Leonard *retired state legislator*
oherty, Brian Gerard *alderman*
arris, Gregory Scott *state representative*
ones, Emil, Jr. *state legislator*

acksonville
indley, Paul *former congressman, author, educator*

ontiac
wing, Thomas William *congressman, lawyer*

pringfield
ollins, Annazette R. *state representative*
urrie, Barbara Flynn *state legislator*
aniels, Lee Albert *state legislator*
annig, Gary L. *state representative*
efferson, Charles E. *state representative*
lingler, Gwendolyn Walbolt *state representative*
osel, Renée *state representative*
adigan, Michael Joseph *state legislator*
artinez, Iris *state senator*
ankau, Carole *state senator*
arke, Terry Richard *state legislator*

ycamore
urzynski, James Bradley *state legislator*

estchester
ightford, Kimberly A. *state legislator*

INDIANA

Columbus
Garton, Robert Dean *state legislator*

Indianapolis
Kenley, Howard *state legislator*
Wilson, Richard Harry, Jr. *congressional chief of staff*

Shoals
Boyd, Earl E., Jr. *councilman*

West Lafayette
Scholer, Sue Wyant *retired state legislator*

IOWA

Des Moines
Boettger, Nancy J. *state legislator*
Jochum, Pam *state representative*
Ragan, Amanda *state senator*

Sioux City
Andersen, Leonard Christian *former state legislator, real estate investor*
Doyle, Donald Vincent *retired state legislator, lawyer*

KANSAS

Clay Center
Braden, James Dale *former state legislator*

Hutchinson
O'Neal, Michael Ralph *state legislator, lawyer*

Overland Park
Vratil, John Logan *state legislator, lawyer*

Salina
Horst, Deena Louise *state legislator*

Shawnee Mission
Sader, Carol Hope *former state legislator*

Topeka
Carlin, Sydney *state representative*
Gordon, Lana G. *state representative*
Kirk, Nancy A. *state legislator, nursing home administrator*
Petty, Marge D. *state senator*
Saville, Pat *state senate official*
Schmidt, Derek *state legislator*

Wichita
Pottorff, Jo Ann *state legislator*

KENTUCKY

Frankfort
Palumbo, Ruth Ann *state legislator*
Richards, Jody *state legislator, communications educator, small business owner*
Stine, Katie Kratz *state legislator*

Shelbyville
Miller, Mary Helen *retired state government administrator*

LOUISIANA

Lake Charles
Mount, Willie Landry *state legislator*

New Orleans
Irons, Paulette Riley *state legislator, lawyer*

MAINE

Augusta
Edmonds, Beth *state legislator*
Martin, John Lewis *state legislator*

Belgrade Lakes
Kany, Judy C(asperson) *retired state senator*

Brunswick
Pfeiffer, Sophia Douglass *retired state legislator, lawyer*

MARYLAND

Annapolis
Barve, Kumar P. *state legislator*
Busch, Michael *state legislator*
Doory, Ann Marie *legislator*
Hollinger, Paula Colodny *state legislator*
Kelley, Delores Goodwin *state legislator*
Love, Mary Ann E. *state legislator*
Madden, Martin Gerard *former state legislator*
Ruben, Ida Gass *state senator*

Bethesda
Reed, Miriam Bell *legislative staff member*

Frederick
Byron, Beverly Butcher *retired congresswoman*

MASSACHUSETTS

Boston
Canavan, Christine Estelle *state legislator*
Chandler, Harriette Levy *state legislator, management consultant, educator*
Creedon, Geraldine *state legislator*
Creem, Cynthia Stone *state legislator, lawyer*
Jehlen, Patricia D. *state legislator*
Nielsen, Mark D. *former state legislator*
Rogeness, Mary Speer *state legislator*
Walrath, Patricia A. *state legislator*
Wolf, Alice Koerner *state legislator, former mayor*

Chelmsford
Cleven, Carol Chapman *retired state legislator*

Newton Highlands
Hummel, Margaret P. *state representative*

Springfield
Melconian, Linda Jean *state senator, lawyer, educator*

MICHIGAN

Jackson
Walberg, Tim (Timothy Lee Walberg) *congressman, former state legislator*

Lansing
Hoffman, Philip Edward *legislative consultant*
Hopgood, Hoon-Yung *state representative*

Livonia
McCotter, Thaddeus George *congressman*

MINNESOTA

Brainerd
Samuelson, Donald B. *former state legislator*

Eden Prairie
Luther, William P. *former congressman*

Excelsior
Oliver, Edward Carl *retired state legislator, insurance company executive, small business owner*

Minneapolis
Greenfield, Lee *state legislator*
Reichgott Junge, Ember Darlene *retired senator, lawyer, writer, broadcast commentator, radio personality, communications executive*
Spear, Allan Henry *state legislator, historian, educator*

Saint Paul
Abrams, Ronald Lawrence *state legislator*
Chaudhary, Satveer *state senator*
Ellison, Keith *Congressman-elect, lawyer*
Pappas, Sandra Lee *state senator*

MISSISSIPPI

Jackson
Coleman, Mary H. *state legislator*

MONTANA

Butte
Harrington, Dan William *state senator*

Cut Bank
Roush, Glenn A. *state senator*

Dillon
Tash, Bill *state senator*

Helena
Hill, Richard (Rick) Allan *former congressman*
Mahlum, Dale Duane *state legislator, small business owner*

Medicine Lake
Nelson, Linda J. *state legislator*

Winifred
Butcher, Edward Bernie *state senator*

NEBRASKA

Lincoln
Kristensen, Douglas Allan *former state legislator*
Preister, Donald George *state legislator, greeting card manufacturer*
Schimek, DiAnna Ruth Rebman *state legislator*

NEVADA

Elko
Heller, Dean *congressman, former state official*

Las Vegas
Wiener, Valerie *state senator, writer, communications executive*

Reno
Raggio, William John *state legislator*

NEW HAMPSHIRE

Concord
Bradley, Paula E. *former state legislator*
Clemons, Jane Andrea *state legislator*
Cote, David Edward *state legislator*
Eaton, Thomas R. *state legislator*
Ferland, Brenda L. *state representative*
Flora, Kathleen M. *retired state representative*
Foster, Linda Timberlake *state legislator*
Francoeur, Sheila T. *state representative*
Gatsas, Ted (Theodore L. Gatsas) *state legislator*
Ginsburg, Ruth *state representative*
Hager, Elizabeth Sears *state legislator, social services administrator*
Kaen, Naida *state representative*
Larsen, Sylvia B. *state legislator*
Norelli, Terie Thompson *state legislator*
Nowe, Ronald John *state legislator, small business owner*
Pilliod, James P. *state legislator, physician*
Stickney, Nancy Carver *state legislator*

Derry
Katsakiores, George Nicholas *state legislator, retired food service executive*

Dover
Pelletier, Arthur Joseph *state legislator, educator*

Durham
Wheeler, Katherine Wells *retired state legislator*

Hanover
Copenhaver, Marion Lamson *retired state legislator*
Crory, Elizabeth Lupien *retired state legislator*

Manchester
Arnold, Barbara Eileen *state legislator*

Moultonborough
Patten, Betsey Leland *state legislator*

Windham
Arndt, Janet S. *former state legislator, educator*

NEW JERSEY

Flemington
Lance, Leonard *state legislator*

Matawan
Thompson, Samuel Donald *assemblyman*

Mays Landing
LoBiondo, Frank A. *congressman*

Newark
Lautenberg, Frank Raleigh *senator*

Ocean City
Hughes, William John *former congressman, diplomat*

Paterson
Pou, Nellie *assemblywoman*

Plainfield
Green, Gerald B. *state legislator*

Short Hills
Ogden, Maureen Black *retired state legislator*

Teaneck
Weinberg, Loretta *state legislator*

Trenton
Baroni, Bill (William E. Baroni Jr.) *state legislator*
Codey, Richard James (Dick Codey) *state senator, former acting governor*

Westfield
Kean, Tom, Jr., (Thomas Howard Kean Jr.) *state senator*

Woodbridge
Vitale, Joseph F. *state legislator*

NEW MEXICO

Albuquerque
Rutherford, Thomas Truxtun, II, *state legislator, municipal official*
Sanchez, Raymond G. *former state legislator*
Schmitt, Harrison Hagan *former senator, geologist, astronaut, consultant*
Wilson, Heather Ann *congresswoman*

Corrales
Eisenstadt, Pauline Doreen Bauman *state legislator*

Hobbs
Reagan, Gary Don *state legislator, lawyer*

Sandia Park
Beffort, Sue Wilson *state legislator*

NEW YORK

Albany
Bruno, Joseph L. *state legislator*
Jacobs, Rhoda S. *state legislator*
Smith, Ada LaVerne *state legislator*
Stavisky, Toby Ann *state legislator*
Volker, Dale Martin *state legislator, lawyer*

Auburn
Arcuri, Michael A. *congressman*

Brooklyn
Velázquez, Nydia Margarita *congresswoman*

Derby
Pordum, Francis J. *former state legislator, educator, marketing professional*

Jamaica
Flake, Floyd Harold *former congressman*
Meeks, Gregory Weldon *congressman*

Massapequa Park
King, Peter Thomas *congressman, lawyer*

New York
Abate, Catherine M. *retired state legislator*
Bradley, Bill (William Warren Bradley) *former senator*

Farrell, Herman D., Jr., (Denny Farrell) *state legislator, former political organization administrator*
Nussle, Jim (James Allen Nussle) *former congressman*
Quinn, Christine Callaghan *councilwoman*
Silver, Sheldon *state legislator, lawyer*

Ossining
Galef, Sandra Risk *state legislator, educator*

Rego Park
Lowey, Nita Melnikoff *congresswoman*

Rochester
John, Susan V. *state representative*

Staten Island
Fossella, Vito John, Jr. *congressman*

Syracuse
Meier, Raymond A. *former state legislator, lawyer*
Walsh, James Thomas (Jim Walsh) *congressman*

Watertown
McHugh, John Michael *congressman*

NORTH CAROLINA

Advance
Cochrane, Betsy Lane *former state senator*

Asheville
Shuler, (Joseph) Heath *congressman, real estate company executive, retired professional football player*

Burlington
Holt, Bertha Merrill *state legislator*

Chapel Hill
Kinnaird, Eleanor Gates *state legislator, lawyer*

Charlotte
Clodfelter, Daniel Gray *state legislator, lawyer*

Clemmons
Foxx, Virginia Ann *congresswoman, small business owner*

Greensboro
Shaw, Robert Gilbert *retired state legislator, food service executive*

Greenville
Jones, Walter Beaman, Jr. *congressman*

Hickory
Ballenger, Cass (Thomas Cass Ballenger) *former congressman, retired plastics company executive*

Raleigh
Lancaster, H(arold) Martin *congressman, academic administrator*
Stevens, Richard Yates *state senator*
Sutton, Ronnie Neal *state legislator, lawyer*
Tally, Lura Self *state legislator*

Southern Pines
Funderburk, David Britton *retired congressman, ambassador, consultant*

NORTH DAKOTA

Ashley
Kretschmar, William Edward *state legislator, lawyer*

Bismarck
Nelson, Carolyn *state legislator*

Edgeley
Schimke, Dennis J. *former state legislator*

Minot
Tollefson, Ben C. *state legislator, retired utilities executive*

OHIO

Akron
Seiberling, John Frederick *retired congressman, lawyer, educator*

Beachwood
Budish, Armond David *state legislator, lawyer, journalist*

Cincinnati
McEwen, Bob *former congressman*

Cleveland
Jerse, Edward *state representative*
Oakar, Mary Rose *congresswoman*

Columbus
Buehrer, Stephen *state senator*
Cordray, Richard A. *state legislator*
Glenn, John Herschel, Jr. *former senator, astronaut*
Pryce, Deborah Denine *congresswoman*
Setzer, Arlene J. *state representative, retired secondary school educator*
Smith, Shirley A. *state legislator, state representative*
Tiberi, Patrick Joseph *congressman, former state legislator*
Wachtmann, Lynn R. *state legislator*

Lakewood
Kucinich, Dennis John *congressman*

Painesville
LaTourette, Steven C. *congressman*

Springfield
Hobson, David Lee *congressman, lawyer*

Toledo
Kaptur, Marcia Carolyn (Marcy Kaptur) *congresswoman*
Perz, Sally *former state legislator, former academic administrator*

Warren
Ryan, Timothy J. *congressman*

OKLAHOMA

Oklahoma City
Fallin, Mary Copeland *congresswoman, former lieutenant governor*
Jones, Tad *state representative*
Mass, Michael Don *state legislator*
Riley, Nancy C. *state legislator*

Stillwater
Lucas, Frank D. *congressman*

OREGON

Albany
Oakley, Carolyn Le *state legislator, city manager, director*

Marylhurst
Hatfield, Mark Odom *former senator*

Mcminnville
Nelson, Donna Gayle *state representative*

Portland
Blumenauer, Earl *congressman*
Furse, Elizabeth *retired congressman, small business owner*
Gordly, Avel Louise *state legislator, political organization worker*
Lang, Philip David *retired state legislator, insurance company executive*
Wu, David *congressman*

Salem
Burdick, Ginny Marie *state senator*
Carter, Margaret L. *legislator*
Tomei, Carolyn *state representative*
Yih, Mae Dunn *state legislator*

PENNSYLVANIA

Bethlehem
Dent, Charles Wieder (Charlie Dent) *congressman*

Bristol
Murphy, Patrick J. *congressman*

Chalfont
Wilson, Jean Louise *retired state legislator*

Harrisburg
O'Brien, Dennis M. *state legislator*
Perzel, John Michael (Jay Perzel) *state legislator*
Pileggi, Dominic F. *state senator*
Scarnati, Joseph B. III *state senator*
Vance, Patricia H. *state senator*
Williams, Constance *state senator*

Hermitage
English, Philip Sheridan *congressman*

Hollidaysburg
Shuster, William (Bill Shuster) *congressman*

Langhorne
Fitzpatrick, Michael G. *former congressman, lawyer*

Media
Sestak, Joe (Joseph A. Sestak Jr.) *congressman, retired military officer*

Philadelphia
Jacobs, Jonathan Mark *parliamentary consultant*
Josephs, Babette *legislator*
Roebuck, James Randolph, Jr. *state legislator*

Tunkhannock
Sherwood, Donald Lewis *former congressman*

Unionville
Pitts, Joseph R. (Joe Pitts) *congressman*

Wayne
Rubley, Carole A. *state legislator*

RHODE ISLAND

Providence
Algiere, Dennis Lee *state legislator*
Gibbs, June Nesbitt *state senator*

Warwick
Revens, John Cosgrove, Jr. *state legislator, lawyer*

SOUTH CAROLINA

Anderson
Barrett, James Gresham *congressman*

Columbia
Courson, John Edward *state legislator, insurance company executive*

Leatherman, Hugh Kenneth, Sr. *state legislator, engineering executive*

Greenville
DeMint, Jim (James Warren DeMint) *senator, former congressman*
Manly, Sarah Letitia *retired state legislator, ophthalmic photographer, angiographer*
Mann, James Robert *former congressman*

SOUTH DAKOTA

Miller
Morford, JoAnn (JoAnn Morford-Burg) *state senator, investment company executive*

Mud Butte
Ingalls, Marie Cecelie *former state legislator, retail executive*

Pierre
Pederson, Gordon Roy *state legislator, retired military officer*

TENNESSEE

Mason
Wilder, John Shelton *state senator, former lieutenant governor*

Memphis
Ford, Harold Eugene *retired congressman*

TEXAS

Aubrey
Denny, Mary Craver *retired state legislator, business owner*

Austin
Giddings, Helen *state representative, personnel management director*
Shapiro, Florence *state legislator, advertising and public relations executive*

Beaumont
Brooks, Jack Bascom *former congressman*

Garland
Driver, Joe Luther *state legislator, consultant, insurance agent*

Laredo
Zaffirini, Judith *state legislator, small business owner*

UTAH

Corinne
Ferry, Miles Yeoman *state legislator*

Provo
Valentine, John Lester *state legislator, lawyer*

Salt Lake City
Black, Wilford Rex, Jr. *retired state legislator*
Carnahan, Orville Darrell *retired state legislator, academic administrator*
Shepherd, Karen *retired congresswoman*
Walker, Carlene Martin *state senator*

West Valley City
Peterson, Millie M. *state senator*

VERMONT

Middlebury
Nuovo, Betty A. *state representative*

Milton
Rivero, Marilyn Elaine Keith *state legislator*

Montpelier
Paquin, Edward H., Jr. *retired state legislator, not-for-profit developer*

Rutland
Ferraro, Betty Ann *retired state senator*

Saint Albans
Keenan, Kathleen *state legislator*

VIRGINIA

Alexandria
Collins, Cardiss *retired congresswoman*

Arlington
Gravel, Mike (Maurice Robert Gravel) *former senator*

Fairfax
Miller, Emilie F. *former state senator, consultant*

Mc Lean
Callahan, Vincent Francis, Jr. *state legislator, publishing executive*
Paul, Andrew Robert *defense and government consultant*

Newport News
Trible, Paul Seward, Jr. *former United States senator*

Vienna
Higginbotham, Wendy Jacobson *legislative staff member, writer*

WASHINGTON

Olympia
Haugen, Mary Margaret *state legislator*
Long, Jeanine Hundley *retired state legislator*
Roach, Pam *state legislator*
Spanel, Harriet *state legislator*

Vancouver
Smith, Linda A. *retired congresswoman*

WEST VIRGINIA

Charleston
Jenkins, Evan H. *state legislator, medical association administrator, lawyer*
McCabe, Brooks Fleming, Jr. *state legislator*
Tomblin, Earl Ray *state legislator, lieutenant governor*

Shinnston
Spears, Jae *state legislator*

WISCONSIN

Black Earth
Klug, Scott Leo *former congressman*

Fort Atkinson
Lorman, Barbara K. *retired state senator*

Madison
Albers, Sheryl Kay *state legislator*
Barish, Lawrence Stephen *nonpartisan legislative staff administrator*
Darling, Alberta Helen *state legislator, art gallery director, marketing professional*
Kastenmeier, Robert William *congressman*
Roessler, Carol Ann *state legislator*
Turner, Robert Lloyd *state legislator*
Young, Rebecca Mary Conrad *retired state legislator*

Nashotah
Neumann, Mark W. *former congressman, real estate developer*

WYOMING

Cheyenne
Kunz, April Brimmer *state legislator, lawyer*
Mockler, Esther Jayne *state senator*

Cody
Simpson, Alan Kooi *retired senator, lawyer*

Laramie
Hansen, Matilda *former state legislator*
Maxfield, Peter Charles *state legislator, lawyer, educator*

TERRITORIES OF THE UNITED STATES

PUERTO RICO

San Juan
Rossello, Pedro Juan *legislator, former governo*

VIRGIN ISLANDS

St Thomas
Berry, Lorraine Ledee *state senator*

CANADA

BRITISH COLUMBIA

Vancouver
McWhinney, Edward Watson *Canadian government legislator*

ONTARIO

Ottawa
Cools, Anne C. *Canadian senator*
Dryden, Ken *legislator, former sports team executive, retired professional hockey player*
Murray, Lowell *Canadian senator*
Telegdi, Andrew *member of parliament*
Vellacott, Maurice *legislator*
Yelich, Lynne *member of parliament*

ADDRESS UNPUBLISHED

Allen, George Felix, Jr. *former senator, govern*
Bass, Charles Foster *former congressman*
Bassano, C. Louis *state legislator, fuel oil company executive*
Beals, Nancy Farwell *former state legislator*
Beauprez, Bob (Robert L. Beauprez) *former congressman*
Bilbray, James Hubert *retired congressman, lawyer, consultant*
Bilirakis, Michael *former congressman, lawyer, corporate financial executive*
Binienda, John J. *state legislator*
Blanchard, MaryAnn N. *state legislator*
Boehlert, Sherwood Louis *former congressman*
Bonilla, Henry *former congressman, broadcast executive*
Bonsack, Rose Mary Hatem *state legislator, physician*

Bradley, Jeb (Joseph E. Bradley) *former congressman*
Broderick, B. Michael, Jr. *state legislator, banker*
Brown, Mary Ellen *former state legislator, accountant*
Burns, Max *former congressman*
Callahan, Sonny (H.L. Callahan) *former congressman*
Campbell, Ben Nighthorse *former senator*
Carpenter, Robert C. *state legislator, retired banker*
Carson, Brad Rogers *former congressman*
Carstairs, Sharon *legislator*
Chocola, Chris (Joseph Christopher Chocola) *former congressman, lawyer*
Churchill, Robert Wilson *state legislator, lawyer*
Cleland, Max (Joseph Maxwell Cleland) *former senator*
Coyne, William Joseph *former congressman*
Crahalla, Jacqueline R. *state representative*
Craig, Larry Edwin *former senator*
Danner, Patsy Ann *former congresswoman*
Daschle, Thomas Andrew *former senator*
Dayton, Mark Brandt *former senator*
De Gette, Diana Louise *congresswoman, lawyer*
DeLay, Tom (Thomas Dale DeLay) *former congressman*
DeWine, Mike (Richard Michael DeWine) *former senator, lawyer*
Duniphan, J. P. *state legislator, small business owner*
Dunlap, Patricia C. *state legislator*
Dunn, Jennifer Blackburn *former congresswoman*
Evans, Lane Allen *retired congressman*
Federing, Eric K. *legislative staff member, public information officer*
Finestone, Sheila *senator, retired legislator*
Fitzgerald, Peter Gosselin *former senator, lawyer*
Foley, Mark Adam *former congressman*
Forbes, Michael Patrick *former congressman*
Foust, Robert Schmertz *retired legislative staff member, educator*
Fox, Galen W. *state representative*
Franks, Robert D. (Bob Franks) *former congressman*
Frederick, Virginia Fiester *state legislator*
Frist, Bill (William Harrison Frist) *retired senator, thoracic surgeon*
Ganske, J. Greg *former congressman, plastic surgeon*
Gibbons, Sam Melville *retired congressman, government agency administrator*
Graham, Bob (Daniel Robert Graham) *former senator, former governor*
Green, Mark Andrew *former congressman*
Gutknecht, Gil (Gilbert William Gutknecht Jr) *former congressman, former state legislator*
Hammerschmidt, John Paul *retired congressman, lumber company executive*
Harris, Katherine H. *former congresswoman, former state official*
Hart, Gary W. *retired senator, lawyer*
Hart, Melissa Anne *former congresswoman*
Hawkins, Mary Ellen Higgins *retired state legislator, public relations executive*
Hayworth, J.D. (John David Jr.) *former congressman*
Hearn, Joyce Camp *retired state legislator, educator, consultant*
Hefley, Joel Maurice *former congressman*
Helms, Jesse *retired senator*
Herman, Lynn Briggs *state legislator*
Hickey, Win E(spy) *former state legislator, social worker*
Holliday, Robert Kelvin *retired state legislator, publishing executive*
Hollings, Fritz (Ernest Frederick) *former senator*
Horn, Stephen *retired congressman, political scientist*
Hostettler, John Nathan *former congressman*
Houghton, Amory, Jr. *former congressman*
Hyde, Henry John *retired congressman*
Ipsen, Grant Ruel *state legislator, insurance and investments professional*
Istook, Ernest James, Jr., (Jim) *former congressman, lawyer*
James, Sharpe *state senator, former mayor*
Jeffords, James Merrill *former senator*
Jenkins, Bill (William Lewis Jenkins) *former congressman*
Johnson, Jay Withington *former congressman*
Kasich, John R. *former congressman*
Kelly, Sue (Susan Weisenbarger Kelly) *former congresswoman*
Kennedy, Mark Raymond *former congressman*
Kolbe, Jim (James Thomas Kolbe) *retired congressman*
Konnyu, Ernest Leslie *former congressman*
Leach, Jim (James Albert Smith Leach) *former congressman*
Lebowitz, Catharine Koch *state legislator*
Lee, Conrad S. *councilman*
Lipinski, William Oliver *former congressman*
Mandel, Adrienne Abramson *state legislator*
Martinez, Matthew Gilbert *former congressman*
May, Edgar *former state legislator*
McCarthy, Karen P. *former congresswoman, former state legislator*
McGovern, George Stanley *former senator*
Meshel, Harry *former state senator, political party official*
Meyers, Jan *retired congresswoman*
Miller, Patricia Louise *state legislator, nurse*
Munt, Janet Staples *state senator*
Murat, William M. *legislative staff member*
Nickles, Don (Donald Lee Nickles) *former senator*
Nielsen, Linda Miller *councilman*
Northup, Anne Meagher *former congresswoman*
Ortiz, Felix W. *state legislator*
Osborne, Tom (Thomas William Osborne) *former congressman, former college football coach*
Ose, Douglas *former congressman*
Owens, Major Robert Odell *former congressman*
Pascoe, Patricia Hill *former state legislator*
Patterson, Elizabeth Johnston *retired congresswoman*
Paul, Ronald Ernest *congressman*
Pease, Edward A. *former congressman*
Pell, Claiborne *former senator*
Pendleton, Florence Howard *former shadow senator*
Pettis-Roberson, Shirley McCumber *retired congresswoman*
Petzold, Carol Stoker *state legislator*
Pevear, Roberta Charlotte *retired state legislator*
Pombo, Richard William *former congressman, rancher, farmer*
Pressler, Larry *former senator, lawyer*
Redfield, Pamela A. *state legislator*
Rossi, Dino J. *former state legislator*
Roukema, Margaret Scafati *congresswoman*
Russell, Carol Ann *city council member, retired company executive*
Ryun, Jim (James Ronald Ryun) *former congressman*
Sabo, Martin Olav *former congressman*
St. Germain, Fernand Joseph *retired congressman*
Sarbanes, Paul Spyros *former senator*
Satterthwaite, Helen Foster *retired state legislator*
Saucier, Gene Duane *retired state legislator, import/export company executive*
Schexnayder, Charlotte Tillar *state legislator*
Schwarz, Joe (John J.H. Schwarz) *former congressman, physician*
Searle, Rodney Newell *state legislator, farmer, insurance agent*
Sekula-Gibbs, Shelley *former congresswoman, dermatologist*
Shaw, (Eugene) Clay, (Jr.) *former congressman*
Shuster, Bud *business executive, former congressman*
Sinagra, Jack G. *former state senator*
Skinner, Patricia Morag *state legislator*
Smith, Nick H. *former congressman, archivist, farmer*
Snelling, Barbara W. *retired state legislator*
Sodrel, Michael Eugene *former congressman, small business owner*
Stickney, Jessica *former state legislator*
Stuhr, Elaine Ruth *state legislator*
Sweeney, John E. *former congressman*
Talent, James Matthes *former senator, congressman, lawyer*
Tauscher, Ellen O. *congresswoman*
Taylor, Charles Hart *former congressman*
Tebedo, MaryAnne *state legislator*
Toomey, Patrick Joseph *former congressman*
Treppler, Irene Esther *retired state senator*
Turner, Kathy Rae *councilman, former mayor, retired real estate agent*
Vellenga, Kathleen Osborne *retired state legislator*
Wallach, Patricia *councilman, retired mayor*
Watkins, Wesley Wade *retired congressman*
Weldon, Curt (Wayne Curtis Weldon) *former congressman*
Wirth, Kelley K. *state representative*
Young, Jacqueline Eurn Hai *former state legislator, consultant*
Zanetti, Teresa A. *state representative*
Zimmerman, Harold Samuel *retired state legislator, publishing executive, state agency administrator*

HEALTHCARE: DENTISTRY

UNITED STATES

ARIZONA

Phoenix
Manhold, John Henry *dental educator, consultant*

Scottsdale
Winkler, Sheldon *dentist, educator*

Tucson
Hawke, Robert Francis *dentist*

CALIFORNIA

Beverly Hills
Shlosberg, Stuart R. *prosthodontist*

Eureka
Hise, Mark Allen *dentist*

Fullerton
Choi, John U. *periodontist, educator*

Hollywood
Hoesli, Hanna *dentist*

Loma Linda
Lee, Sean S. *dentist, researcher*

Long Beach
Papazian, George Ara *dentist*

Los Angeles
Dorfman, William M. *dentist*
Dummett, Clifton Orrin *dentist, educator*
Etessami, Hirbod (Hiri Etessami) *endodontist, educator*

Manteca
Tonn, Elverne Meryl *pediatric dentist, dental benefits consultant, forensic odontologist*

Northridge
Logan, Lee Robert *orthodontist, department chairman*

Pasadena
Mc Carthy, Frank Martin *oral surgeon, educator*

San Francisco
Bensinger, David August *dentist, dean*
Gekelman, Diana *dentist, dental educator, researcher*
Greenspan, Deborah *dental educator*
Olsen, Steven Kent *dentist*
Wescott, William Burnham *oral maxillofacial pathologist, educator*

San Jose
Yoshizumi, Donald Tetsuro *dentist*

San Rafael
Greene, John Clifford *dentist, retired dean*
Gryson, Joseph Anthony *orthodontist*

COLORADO

Lakewood
Colaiannia, Louis Mario *dentist, composer, pianist*

CONNECTICUT

Brookfield
Cohen, Mark Steven *dentist*

Farmington
Hall, Robert Stevens *dentist*

Southbury
Hopf, Frank Rudolph *retired dentist*

DELAWARE

Hockessin
Ulmer, William H., Sr. *dentist*

Wilmington
Granite, Edwin L *oral surgeon*

DISTRICT OF COLUMBIA

Washington
Calhoun, Noah Robert *oral maxillofacial surgeon, educator*
Richeson, James Grady, Jr. *dentist*

FLORIDA

Bay Harbor Islands
Rosenbluth, Morton *periodontist, educator*

Bradenton
Engelman, Melvin Alkon *retired dentist, dental products executive*

Cortez
Levine, Harvey Davis *retired dentist*

Daytona Beach
Lawson, Scott D. *oral surgeon*

Fort Lauderdale
Siegel, Michael Alan *dental educator*

Fort Myers
Laboda, Gerald *oral and maxillofacial surgeon*

Gainesville
Catalanotto, Frank A. *dentist*
Javid, Nikzad Sabet *dentist, prosthodontist educator*

Jacksonville
Halil, Susan Terrell *dental hygienist*

Jupiter
Nessmith, H(erbert) Alva *dentist*

Miami
Higley, Bruce Wadsworth *orthodontist*
Iver, Robert Drew *dentist*

Naples
Rosen, Michel *retired prosthodontist*

Tampa
Pasetti, Louis Oscar *retired dentist*
Perret, Gerard Anthony, Jr. *orthodontist*

Winter Park
McKean, Thomas Wayne *retired dentist, retired military officer*

GEORGIA

Atlanta
Freedman, Louis Martin *dentist*

Augusta
Baker, Philip Steven *dentist, educator*
Lapp, Carol Anne *oral biology educator*
Rogers, Michael Bruce *orthodontist*

HAWAII

Honolulu
Nishimura, Pete Hideo *oral surgeon*

Pearl City
Sue, Alan Kwai Keong *dentist*

ILLINOIS

Chicago
Barr, Sanford Lee *dentist*
Bramson, James B. *dentist, dental association administrator*
Glenner, Richard Allen *dentist, dental historian*
Graber, Thomas M. *orthodontist, researcher*
Hardaway, Ernest, II, *oral and maxillofacial surgeon, public health service officer*
Hirsch, Martin *dentist*
Santangelo, Mario Vincent *retired dentist*
Yale, Seymour Hershel *dental radiologist, educator, gerontologist, dean*

Lake Forest
Jones, Gordon Kempton *dentist, retired military officer*

Lake In The Hills
Shirazi, Eman Ali *dentist*

Naperville
Grimley, Jeffrey Michael *dentist*

Park Ridge
Kenney, John Patrick *dentist*

Riverwoods
Douglas, Bruce Lee *oral and maxillofacial surgeon, occupational and geriatric health educator, consultant*

Westmont
Schefdore, Ronald L. *dentist*

INDIANA

Evansville
Fritz, Edward Lane *dentist*
Raibley, Parvin Rudolph *dentist*

Indianapolis
Christen, Arden Gale *dental educator, researcher, consultant*
Hartsfield, James Kennedy, Jr. *orthodontist, geneticist*
Martinez-Mier, Esperanza Angeles *dental educator, researcher*

Terre Haute
Roshel, John Albert, Jr. *orthodontist*

IOWA

Iowa City
Bishara, Samir Edward *orthodontist*
Olin, William Harold *orthodontist, educator*

KANSAS

Topeka
Fyler, Carl John *retired dentist*

KENTUCKY

Brandenburg
Bowen, Patricia Lederer *dental educator*

Danville
Morris, Alvin Leonard *retired dentist, academic administrator*

Louisville
Parkins, Frederick Milton *dental educator, dean*
Phillips, William Ault *pediatric dentist*

LOUISIANA

Metairie
Roussos, Christopher Wayne *dental association administrator*

MAINE

Kennebunkport
Mulvihill, James Edward *periodontist, educator*

MARYLAND

Bethesda
Kruger, Gustav Otto, Jr. *retired oral surgeon, educator, department chairman*

Columbia
Rovelstad, Gordon H. *dentist, researcher*

Potomac
Cotton, William Robert *retired dentist*

Simpsonville
Altschuler, Bruce Robert *research dentist*

Timonium
Zeren, Karl Joseph *dentist, educator*

MASSACHUSETTS

Boston
Johansen, Erling *retired dental educator, dean*
Kuo, Winston Patrick *pediatric and oral medicine dentist, biomedical researcher*
Sachdeo, Amit *dentist, researcher*
Woo, Sook-Bin *dentist, educator*

Fitchburg
Shemmeri, Thafur *pediatric dentist*

Hanover
Lonborg, James Reynold *dentist, former professional baseball player*

Newton Centre
Peck, Sheldon *orthodontist, educator, dental anthropologist, historian*

MICHIGAN

Ann Arbor
Brown, William Ernest *dentist*

East Lansing
Spagnuolo, Mark Mario *retired dentist*

MINNESOTA

Mankato
Dumke, Melvin Philip *dentist*

Minneapolis
Nixdorf, Donald *dentist, researcher*
Shapiro, Burton Leonard *dentist, geneticist, educator*

MISSISSIPPI

Flowood
Byrd, Joyce Marie *dentist*

MISSOURI

Chesterfield
Selfridge, George Dever *retired dentist, retired military officer*

Kansas City
Reed, Michael John *dentist, dean, oral biology educator*

MONTANA

Helena
Maes, Paul Joel *dentist*

NEBRASKA

Lincoln
Sullivan, Robert Emmett *pediatric dentist, educator*

Omaha
Hermsen, Kenneth Paul *dental educator, forensic odontologist*
Kimmes, Nicole S. *dentist, educator*
Lynch, Benjamin Leo *oral surgeon, educator*
Zaiman, K(oichi) Robert *dentist*

NEW HAMPSHIRE

Portsmouth
McArdle, Barry Francis *dentist*

NEW JERSEY

Cedar Grove
Mandel, Irwin Daniel *dentist*

Chatham
Hurley, Allyson Kingsley *dentist*

Freehold
Greenstein, Gary *periodontist, dental educator*

Hackettstown
Wiedemann, Charles Louis *dentist*

Ho Ho Kus
Van Slooten, Ronald Henry Joseph *dentist*

Lawrenceville
Kulak, Chester B. *dentist*

Voorhees
Lampert, S. Henry *retired dentist*
Piermatti, Jack *dentist*

Woodbridge
Galkin, Samuel Bernard *orthodontist*

NEW MEXICO

Farmington
Graham, Warren Kirkland *dentist*

NEW YORK

Bellmore
Lederman, Gary *dentist*

Brooklyn
Schweikert, Edgar Oskar *dentist*

New York
Arvystas, Michael Geciauskas *orthodontist, educator*
Denmark, Stanley Jay *orthodontist*
Glassman, Debra *dentist*
Glassman, Steven *dentist*
Kahn, Norman *dental educator, pharmacologist*
Lituchy, Gregg *dentist*
Lowenberg, Marc Gregory *dentist*
Marder, Michael Zachary *dental educator, researcher*
Mitchell, Dennis Anthony *dentist, educator*
Rosenthal, Larry W. *cosmetic dentist*
Rozenberg, Lana *cosmetic dentist*
Scarola, John Michael *dentist, educator*
Sendax, Victor Irven *dentist, educator, dental implant researcher*
Wank, Gerald Sidney *periodontist, educator*

Ossining
Maloney, William James *dentist, educator*

Rochester
Bowen, William Henry *dental researcher, educator*

Troy
Bryant, Kimberly Ziegler *dental hygienist, educator*
Medicus, Hildegard Julie *retired dentist, orthodontist, educator*

Yonkers
Torrese, Dante Michael *prosthodontist, educator*

NORTH CAROLINA

Chapel Hill
Proffit, William Robert *orthodontics educator*
Stamm, John William Randolph *dentist, educator*
White, Raymond Petrie, Jr. *dentist, educator, dean*

Charlotte
Hufanda, Joseph *dentist*
McClelland, Richard Lee *dentist*

Matthews
Twisdale, Harold Winfred *dentist*

OHIO

Beachwood
Robertson, Ned *dentist*

Columbus
Jolly, Daniel Ehs *dental educator*
Schricker, Scott Raymond *dental educator*

Cuyahoga Falls
Barsan, Robert Blake *dentist*

Milford
Creath, Curtis Janssen *pediatric dentist*

Sylvania
Kastner, Michael James *dentist*

OKLAHOMA

Oklahoma City
Shillingburg, Herbert Thompson, Jr. *dental educator*

PENNSYLVANIA

Clarion
Foreman, Thomas Alexander *dentist*

Collegeville
Sharifi, Azalea A. *orthodontist and general dentist*

Erdenheim
Schiff, Lawrence Alan *dentist*

Lansdale
Strohecker, Leon Harry, Jr. *orthodontist*

New Holland
West, Daniel Charles *dentist*

Newtown
Paghdiwala, Abid F *dentist*

Norristown
Steinberg, Arthur Irwin *periodontist, educator*

Philadelphia
Fielding, Allen Fred *oral and maxillofacial surgeon, educator*
Pappas, Charles Nicholas III *dentist, educator*
Stoopler, Eric T. *dentist, dental educator*
Vanarsdall, Robert Lee, Jr. *orthodontist, educator*

Pittsburgh
Collins, Bobby McManus, II, *dental educator*

Willow Grove
Ohama, Gary Louis *dental ceramist*

RHODE ISLAND

Warren
Mehlman, Edwin Stephen *endodontist*

SOUTH CAROLINA

Charleston
Cordova, Maria Asuncion *dentist*

West Columbia
Witherspoon, Walter Pennington, Jr. *orthodontist*

TENNESSEE

Memphis
Butts, Herbert Clell *retired dentist, educator*
Cannon, Joe Louis *retired orthodontist*

Nashville
Martin, James Larence *dentist, educator*
Medwedeff, Fred M. *retired dentist*

TEXAS

Dallas
Ajlouni, Raed Fakhry *dentist, educator*
McWhorter, Kathleen *orthodontist*

Flower Mound
Kolodny, Stanley Charles *oral surgeon, retired military officer*

Livingston
Davidson, John Robert *retired dentist*

Plano
Taylor, Paul Peak *pediatric dentist, educator*

San Antonio
Goksel, Tamer *oral surgeon, director*
Langland, Olaf Elmer *retired dental educator*

VERMONT

Rutland
Carroll, La Shun La Rue *dentist*

VIRGINIA

Richmond
Laskin, Daniel M. *oral and maxillofacial surgeon, educator*

Virginia Beach
Lowe, Cameron Anderson *dentist, endodontist, educator*

WASHINGTON

Bellevue
Carlson, Curtis Eugene *orthodontist, periodontist*
Page, Roy Christopher *periodontist, scientist, educator*

Everett
Oliver, William Donald *orthodontist*

Seattle
Baker-Johnson, Marcia J. *dental hygienist*
Beirne, Owen Ross *dental educator, researcher*
Hollender, Lars Gösta *dental educator*
Roberts, Frank Alan *periodontist, researcher, dental educator*
Spoor, Rhys *dentist*

Spokane
Bulan, Liana *dentist*

WISCONSIN

New Glarus
Sippy, David Dean *dentist*

Shawano
Swetlik, William Philip *orthodontist*

WYOMING

Casper
Keim, Michael Ray *dentist*

GERMANY

Witten
Gaengler, Peter Wolfgang *dentist, researcher*

ADDRESS UNPUBLISHED

Armstrong, Edward Bradford, Jr. *oral and maxillofacial surgeon, educator*
Barkmeier, Wayne W. *dentist, researcher, educator*
Beagrie, George Simpson *dentist, educator, retired dean*
Bentley, Kenneth Chessar *oral and maxillofacial surgeon, educator*
Braun, Stanley *orthodontist, educator*
Brooke, Ralph Ian *dental educator*
Christiansen, Richard Louis *orthodontist, educator, dean*
Collins, Frank, Jr. *dentist, educator*
Fletcher, Vernon Jerome *dental association administrator, director*
Geistfeld, Ronald Elwood *retired dental educator*
Gist, William Claude, Jr. *retired dentist*
Goldstein, Leonard Barry *dentist*
Hammer, Wade Burke *retired oral and maxillofacial surgeon, educator*
Herman, David Jay *orthodontist*
Hoffman, Jerry Irwin *retired dental educator*
Houk, Irene Miller *dentist*
Ismail, Yahia H. *dentist, prosthodontist*
Kaslick, Ralph Sidney *dentist, educator*
Khosla, Ved Mitter *oral and maxillofacial surgeon, educator*
Kolokythas, Antonia *oral surgeon, oncologist*
Lee, Seokwoo S. *periodontist, educator*
Lee, Winnie Sita *dentist*
Löe, Harald *retired dentist, educator, researcher*
Meffert, Roland Matthew *periodontist, educator*
Molinaro, Joseph Daniel *dentist, director*
Nabers, Claude Lowrey *retired periodontist, writer*
Newbrun, Ernest *oral biology and periodontology educator*
Panzer, Milton *retired orthodontist, volunteer*
Paris, David Andrew *dentist*
Patel, Snehal Raman *oral surgeon*
Rahimi, Hessam *dentist*
Rehak, James Richard *orthodontist*
Riley, Cheryl M. *prosthodontist, military officer*
Rippert, Eric Theodore *oral and maxillofacial surgeon, healthcare consultant*
Sabeti, Mike A. *endodontist, periodontist, educator*
Sinkford, Jeanne Craig *dental association administrator, retired dentist, dean, educator*
Slaughter, Freeman Cluff *retired dentist*
Taylor, John Calvin *dentist*

HEALTHCARE: HEALTH SERVICES

UNITED STATES

ALABAMA

Birmingham
Cates, Marshall E. *pharmacist, medical educator*
Cooper, Karen René *health facility administrator, nursing administrator*
Grinney, Jay *health facility company executive*
Hoidal, David *health facility administrator*
Lowman, John D., Jr. *physical therapist, researcher*
Mohon, Earlene Mann *counselor*
Owens, Sandra Nell *nurse*
Perry, Helen *medical/surgical nurse, secondary school educator*
Pickett, Stephen Alan *hospital administrator*
Roth, William Stanley *hospital foundation executive*
Stephens, Deborah Lynn *health company executive*

Daphne
Curreri, Peter William *health facility administrator, consultant*

Falkville
Dunn, Donna R. *public health service officer*

Florence
Foote, Dorothy Gargis *nursing educator*

Lafayette
Woody, Mary Florence *nursing educator, academic administrator*

Mobile
Clark, Jack *retired health facility administrator*
Wisner, Pamela L. *social worker*

Montgomery
Munson, Edward Harry, Jr. *medical investigator*
Williamson, Donald Ellis *public health service officer, state agency administrator*

Pelham
Lee, James A. *health facility finance executive*

Talladega
Swain, Mary Madgalene Dickerson *pediatrics nurse*

Theodore
Carbo, Tammera Melissa *counselor, counseling administrator*
Hollis, Julia Ann Roshto *critical care, medical, and surgical nurse*

Tuscaloosa
Farahat, Medhat S. *researcher*
Orcutt, Ben Avis *retired social work educator*

Tuskegee Institute
Paris, Deidre Eileen *artificial intelligence researcher, educator*

ALASKA

Anchorage
Kincaid, Karen Owers *nursing educator*

Bethel
Turner, Kathy Ann *special education services professional, director*

Big Lake
Gillette, Muriel Delphine *nurse*

Palmer
Young-Campbell, Laura L. *speech pathology/audiology services professional*

Soldotna
Moore, Hubert, Jr. *retired addictions counselor, consultant*

ARIZONA

Casa Grande
McGillicuddy, Joan Marie *psychotherapist, consultant*

Fort Huachuca
Sleeper, Nancy JoAnn *mental health services professional*

Glendale
Cacciatore, Joanne *social worker*

Patton, Lynn Radonic *pharmacist, educator*

Mesa
Ahearn, Geraldine *medical/surgical nurse, writer, poet*
David, Susan Holcombe *child and family therapist*

Payson
Lasys, Joan *medical/surgical nurse, educator*

Peoria
Nelson, Mary Kathryn *bilingual counselor, small business owner, real estate agent, artist, insurance agent*

Phoenix
Farmer, Kenneth Lloyd, Jr. *health facility administrator, retired military officer*
Garcia, Ernest G. *audiologist, technologist*
Hunt, Linda *hospital administrator*
Johnson, Elizabeth Misner *health services executive*
Meyer, Hermann Belton Perrin *retired neonatologist, health facility administrator, bioethicist*
Mitchell, Wayne Lee *retired health facility administrator*
Norris, John Steven *healthcare company executive*

Rio Verde
Ramsey, David Selmer *retired health facility administrator*

Scottsdale
Brown, Frederick Lee *health facility administrator*
Jayaraman, Ganapathi Subramaniam *healthcare industry executive*
Meyers, Marlene O. *retired hospital administrator*
Pelham, Judith *health system administrator*
Richardson, Mary L. *psychotherapist*
Summerhill, Ronald Raymond *psychotherapist, psychologist*
Timmons, Evelyn Deering *pharmacist*
Weaver, Linda Marie *pharmacist, education educator*

Tucson
Alo, Adeniyi *pharmacist, federal agency administrator*
Barrette-Mozes, Susan Jean *counselor, psychotherapist*
Diáz, Elena R. *community health nurse*
Dyer-Raffler, Joy Ann *retired special education diagnostician, educator*
Hanson, Thor *retired health agency executive, retired naval officer*
Neal, Alaine (Diann Neal) *nursing administrator*
Pierce, Roger Arnold, II, *pharmacist, director*
Shropshire, Donald Gray *hospital executive*
Tompkins, Emil *chiropractor*
Yuan, Nicole Patricia *healthcare educator*

Wickenburg
Brooks, Donna Jean *counselor, educator*

Yuma
Houggard, Santa Carol Hall *family nurse practitioner, consultant*
Kiley, Thomas *rehabilitation counselor*
Rush, Dorie Mae *nursing educator*

ARKANSAS

Eureka Springs
McCullough, V. Beth *pharmacist, educator*

Fayetteville
Banks, David Russell *former health care executive*

Fort Smith
Churchey, Randy L. *health facility administrator*

Jonesboro
Hanners, G(ary) Dale *retired psychological mental health professional*

Little Rock
Brown, Larry Douglass *research consultant, writer*
Elders, Joycelyn (Minnie Jocelyn Elders, Minnie Joycelyn Lee) *public health service officer, endocrinologist, former Surgeon General of the United States*

State University
Barredo, Ronald De Vera *physical therapist, educator*

CALIFORNIA

Agoura Hills
Canatsey, Ken *nurse*
Merchant, Roland Samuel, Sr. *health facility administrator, educator*

Aliso Viejo
Dunn, Dana-Lori *counselor*

Anaheim
Lee, Donna Jean *retired nurse*

Arleta
Kelley, Frances A. *occupational therapist, consultant*

Auburn
Olesen, Erik L. *psychotherapist, writer*

Berkeley
Bissell, Mina J. *lab administrator, biochemist*
Enoch, Jay Martin *optometrist, research scientist, educator*
Gilbert, Neil Robin *social work educator, writer, consultant*
Gumbs, Pam *pharmacist*
Harris, Michael Gene *optometrist, lawyer, educator*
Hill, Lorie Elizabeth *psychotherapist*
Lashof, Joyce Cohen *public health service officer, educator*
Tutashinda, Kweli (Brian P. Altheimer) *chiropractic physician, educator*
Westheimer, Gerald *optometrist, educator*

Beverly Hills
Rinsch, Maryann Elizabeth *occupational therapist*

Carlsbad
Benjamin, Theresa Mary *retired psychotherapist*
Craig, Jenny *human services manager*

Cathedral City
Berry, Ester Lorée *vocational nurse*

Cerritos
Woodson-Glenn, Yolanda *social worker*

Chico
Akimoto, Martin Wayne *mental health services professional*

Chula Vista
McKenzie, Scott Arthur *public health service officer, consultant*

Claremont
Martin, Jay Herbert *psychoanalyst, language professor, political science professor*

Clovis
Von Prince, Kilulu Magdalene *retired occupational therapist, sculptor*

Cypress
Scott, Gregory W. *health care company executive*

Davis
Schneeman, Barbara Olds *nutritionist, educator*
Stern, Judith Schneider *nutritionist, researcher, educator*
Stroeve, Pieter *chemical engineering researcher, educator*

Desert Hot Springs
Zarres, Sharon L. *marriage and family therapist, health facility administrator*

Duarte
Riggs, Arthur D. *health facility administrator, research scientist*

El Monte
White-Whitfield, Lisa Denise *social worker*

Emeryville
Chang, Ying-Lan *technologist*

Encinitas
Mazak, Arlene Patricia *marriage and family therapist*

Fontana
Ferreri, Michael Victor *optometrist*

Frazier Park
Edwards, Sarah Anne *social worker, psychologist*

Fresno
Corless, Dorothy Alice *nursing educator*
De La Cruz-Reyes, Pilar L. *nursing administrator*

Fullerton
Montgomery, Thom Mathew *health program administrator, counselor*

Glendale
Shou, Sharon Louise Wikoff *vocational rehabilitation counselor*

Glendora
Lasko, Allen Howard *pharmacist*

Hawthorne
Fila, John Charles *psychoanalyst*

Highland
Tacal, Jose Vega, Jr. *retired public health official, veterinarian*

Inglewood
Epstein, Marsha Ann *public health service officer, physician*

La Jolla
Johnson, Gayle Ann *cardiology nurse*
Morello, Candis Marguerite *pharmacist, educator*

Laguna Beach
Arnold, John David *management counselor*

Laguna Niguel
Carr, Bernard Francis *hospital administrator*

Lake Elsinore
Young, Patricia Janean *speech pathology/audiology services professional*

Lake View Terrace
McCraven, Eva Stewart Mapes *health service administrator*

Lincoln
Helzer, James Dennis *retired health facility administrator*

Lodi
Bernhoft, Franklin Otto *psychotherapist, psychologist*

Loma Linda
Llerandi Phipps, Carmen Guillermina *nutritionist and dietitian*
Molnar, Violet *mental health nurse*

Lompoc
Wagner, Geraldine Marie *nursing educator, consultant*

Long Beach
Brown, Lester B. *social worker, educator*
Janssen, Maridith Annette *recreational therapist, educator*
Mathieu, Susan Leifer *recreational therapist, educator*
Mullins Berg, Ruth Gladys *nurse*

Los Angeles
Andersen, Ronald Max *health services researcher, educator*
Baron, Melvin Farrell *pharmacy educator*
Boswell, James Douglas *medical research executive*
Breslow, Lester *public health physician, educator*
Cordova, Richard D. *hospital administrator*
de la Rocha, Castulo *health services executive*
Fongwa, Marie Ngetiko *nurse midwife*
Harrison, Gail G. *public health educator*
Looney, Claudia Arlene *health facility administrator*
McCabe, Edward R. B. *hospital administrator, educator, physician*
Noce, Walter William, Jr. *hospital administrator*
Priselac, Thomas M. *health facility executive, educator*
Rice, Thomas Howard *healthcare educator*
Roberts, Robert Winston *social worker, educator, dean*
Rosenthal, J. Thomas *hospital administrator, medical educator*
Sayed, M. Gary *healthcare administrator, educator, scientist*
Silverstein, Suzanne *art therapist*
Soohoo, Elena *strategic planning administrator*
Stoughton, W. Vickery *healthcare executive*
Territo, Mary C. *health facility administrator, hematologist, educator*
Thompson, Judith Kastrup *nursing researcher*
Utz, Sarah Winifred *nursing educator*
van Dam, Heiman *psychoanalyst*
Ver Steeg, Donna Lorraine Frank *nurse, sociologist, educator*

Lower Lake
Garcia, Beatrice Maude *social worker, director*

Marysville
Myers, Elmer *psychiatric social worker*

Menlo Park
Holmquest, Donald Lee *health organization director, nuclear medicine physician, lawyer, retired aerospace engineer*

Mill Valley
Castleman, Breaux Ballard *health management company executive*

Modesto
Smith, Heather Lynn *psychotherapist, recreational therapist*

Monterey
Robinson, Marla Holbrook *community care nurse*

Moorpark
Young, Victoria E. *occupational health nurse, lawyer*

Moraga
Allen, Richard Garrett *healthcare educator*

Murrieta
Rose, Norma Louise *retired human services manager*

Newport Beach
Smeal, Kemp Leslie *psychotherapist, musician*

North Hollywood
Elliott, John Foster *psychotherapist, writer*

Oakland
Crane, Robert Meredith *health facility administrator*
Hafey, Joseph Michael *health association executive*
Miller, Barry *researcher, psychologist*

Oakley
Hirning, Fredric Carl *pharmacist*

Ontario
Chavez, Virginia *counselor*
Fangerow, Kay Elizabeth *nurse*

Orange
Williams, Benjamin R. *health facility administrator*

Palos Verdes Peninsula
Ahmady, Ali *lab administrator, director*

Panorama City
Lugg, Marlene Martha *immunization coordinator, health information systems specialist, health planner*

Pasadena
Brotman, Richard Dennis *counselor*
Chu, Benjamin K. *hospital administrator*
Holmes, Louis Ira *physician assistant, educator, photojournalist*
Nackel, John George *health facility administrator*

Perris
Zimmer, Paul Gerald, II, *retired community care licensing professional*

Pittsburg
Gustafson, Sally Ann *counselor, cosmetologist, educator*

Pomona
Gupta, Eric K. *pharmacist, educator*

Redlands
Coleman, Arlene Florence *retired pediatrics nurse*

Redwood City
LeVoir, Lurese Cherene *dietetic technician*

Reseda
Hoover, Pearl Rollings *nurse*

Riverside
Chang, Sylvia Tan *health facility administrator, educator*

Roseville
Netto, Paul V. *critical care nurse*

Sacramento
Burks, Rocky Alan *disability access manager and consultant*
Drachnik, Catherine Meldyn *recreational therapist, artist, counselor*
Kasch, Mary Courteol *occupational therapist*

San Andreas
Cretan, Donna *neonatal nurse, lactation consultant*

San Bruno
Leung, Prudence Marguerite *pharmacist*

San Diego
Astroth, Margo Foltz *mental health nurse, nurse psychotherapist*
Jenkins, Adrienne *women's health nurse*
Schmidt, Terry L. *healthcare executive*

San Francisco
Gardner, Annette Lenore *health policy researcher, political scientist*
Harlan, Neil Eugene *retired health facility administrator*
Holzemer, William L. *nursing educator*
Laret, Mark R. *health facility executive*
Mahley, Robert W. *health facility administrator*
Murphy, Richard A. *health science association administrator*
Rosales, Suzanne Marie *hospital coordinator*
Speidel, John Joseph *public health professional, educator*
Young, Lowell Sung-yi *health facility administrator, medical educator*
Zieff, Susan Gail *healthcare educator*

San Jose
Ha, Kiet Tuan *hospital administrator*
Quadros, Orpha May *retired social worker, educator*

San Mateo
Morris, Richard Gilbert *retired medical transcriber*

San Rafael
Amada, Gerald *retired psychotherapist*
Friesecke, Raymond Francis *health company executive, director*
Malifrando, Frank *healthcare executive, theater producer, consultant, film producer, international real estate investor, publisher*

Santa Barbara
Salotti, Kathryn E. *marriage and family therapist*

Santa Clara
Poyadue, Florene Stewart *nurse, foundation administrator*

Santa Monica
Archambault, Nicole Marie *speech pathology/audiology services professional, consultant*
Brook, Robert Henry *public health service officer, internist, educator*
McGlynn, Elizabeth A. *health policy analyst*
Rice, Pamela Ann *marriage and family therapist*

Santa Paula
Broughton, Margaret Martha *mental health nurse*

Santa Rosa
Jann, Gregg *counselor, sales executive, consultant*

Santee
Schenk, Susan Kirkpatrick *nursing educator, consultant, small business owner*

Saratoga
Greenleaf, John Edward *human research consultant*

Sherman Oaks
Krueger, Kenneth John *nutritionist, educator*

Simi Valley
Erzinger, Kathy McClam *nursing educator*

Sonoma
Markey, William Alan *health facility administrator, consultant*

South San Francisco
Lee, Leonard S. *health facility administrator*

Spring Valley
Siddiqui, Razia Sultana *retired psychotherapisst, educator*

Stanford
Henriksen, Thomas Hollinger *researcher*
Marsh, Martha H. *hospital administrator*
Mc Namara, Joseph Donald *researcher, retired protective services official*

Studio City
Childs, Erin Therese *psychotherapist*
Weiner, Sandra Samuel *critical care nurse, consultant*

Sunol
Rebello, Marlene Munson *speech pathologist, consultant*

Thousand Oaks
Allan, Brent Russotto *public health service officer*

Torrance
Ebeling, Vicki *marriage and family therapist, writer*

Truckee
Todd, Linda Marie *nutrition researcher, circulation manager, financial consultant, pilot*

Tustin
Kim, Han Pyong *researcher*

Vallejo
Toms, Kathleen Moore *nurse*

Van Nuys
Dea, Fay Suey *counselor, educator*
Greene, Albert Lawrence *healthcare executive*

Ventura
Bircher, Andrea Ursula *retired psychiatric mental health clinical nurse specialist*

Visalia
Gray, Kris Diane *nursing consultant, forensic specialist*

Walnut Creek
Nolan, Janiece Simmons *health facility administrator*

Westlake Village
Dimitriadis, Andre C. *health care executive*

Woodland
Bauer, Cynthia Renae *nurse*

Woodland Hills
Brandewie, Richard Anthony *laser and optics consultant*
Pettit, John W. *health facility administrator*
Rich, Marvin P. *health association executive*
Yates, Gary L. *marriage and family therapist*

Yuba City
Price, Ardythe Bernadeane *nurse*

COLORADO

Aurora
Morrow, Caroline Donovan *retired social worker*

Boulder
Holdsworth, Janet Nott *women's health nurse*
Middleton-Downing, Laura *psychiatric social worker, artist, small business owner*
Princeton, Joy Carol *retired nursing educator*

Centennial
Frame, Roger Everett *school psychologist*

Colorado Springs
Baldvins, Lynn Ann *medical/surgical nurse, army officer*
Cameron, Paul Drummond *health facility administrator*
Strickland, Sylvia Raye *social worker*
Weslin, Anna Therese *clinical nurse specialist, dance consultant*

Denver
Edelman, Joel *health facility administrator*
McCollum, Marianne *pharmacist, educator, medical researcher*
Plummer, Ora Beatrice *nursing educator, consultant*
Rael, Henry Sylvester, Sr. *retired health administrator, financial and management consultant*
Taussig, Lynn Max *healthcare administrator, pulmonologist, pediatrician, educator*
Witt, Catherine Lewis *neonatal nurse practitioner, writer*

Fort Collins
Savage, Eldon Paul *retired environmental health educator*

Fort Garland
Taylor-Dunn, Corliss Leslie *marriage and family therapist*

Grand Junction
Hoagland, Christina Gail *occupational therapist, industrial drafter*

Greeley
Linde, Lucille Mae (Lucille Jacobson) *motor-perceptual specialist*

Longmont
Jones, Beverly Ann Miller *nursing administrator, retired patient services administrator*

Meeker
Omer, Robert Wendell *hospital administrator*

CONNECTICUT

Avon
Shulman, Steven J. *health services company executive*

Bloomfield
Thorpe, James *retired researcher*

Bridgeport
King, Sister Eleace *special education services professional*
Macdonald, Karen Crane *occupational therapist, geriatrics services professional*
Trefry, Robert J. *health facility administrator*

East Haven
Vermette, Raymond Edward *retired health facility administrator*

Ellington
Evarts, Brian *social worker, educator*

Glastonbury
Cassotto, Mary Lou Grace *counselor, educator, lawyer*

Greenwich
Krauser, Robert Stanley *healthcare executive*

Guilford
Pâquin, Trudy *gerontological nurse*

Hartford
Moore-Beckham, Rosalind Elizabeth *retired social worker*

Milford
Muth, Eric Peter *optician, consultant*

New Haven
Armbruster, Paula *social worker, director, child mental health educator*
Benfer, David William *hospital administrator*
De Rose, Sandra Michele *psychotherapist, educator, administrator*
Grey, Margaret *nursing educator*
Kirshbaum, Daniel Joseph *researcher*
Krauss, Judith Belliveau *nursing educator*
Lord, Ruth *retired researcher, philanthropist, writer*
McCorkle, Ruth *oncological nurse, educator, researcher*
Stiber, Julie Anne *social worker*

New London
Tassinari, Melissa Sherman *teratologist, developmental toxicologist*

Niantic
Roman, José Luis *nursing administrator*

Putnam
Desaulniers, Rene Gerard Lesieur *retired optometrist*

Redding
Benyei, Candace Reed *psychotherapist*

Southbury
Bowen, Christopher Edward *researcher, director*

Stamford
Bostin, Marvin Jay *hospital and health services consultant*

Storrs Mansfield
Petrovic, Kimberly Ann *nursing researcher, nursing educator*
Wang, Fei *pharmacist, educator*

Suffield
Bianchi, Maria *critical care specialist, acute care nurse practitioner*

Waterbury
Zasada, Mary Eileen *nursing administrator*

DELAWARE

Hockessin
Croyle, Barbara Ann *health facility administrative executive*

Lewes
Fried, Jeffrey Michael *health care administrator*

Rehoboth Beach
Penrose, Cynthia C. *retired health care consultant*

Wilmington
Baker, John David *health facility administrator, not-for-profit fundraiser, real estate agent*
Fidance, Christina Marie *human services administrator*
McDonough, Kenneth Lee *pharmaceutical company medical administrator*
Schmerling, Erwin Robert *counselor, retired physicist*
Wallace, Jesse Wyatt *pharmaceutical scientist*

DISTRICT OF COLUMBIA

Washington
Alleyne, Sir George A.O. *public health administrator, educator*
Alward, Ruth Rosendall *nursing consultant*
Arling, Donna Dickson *social worker*
Baigis, Judith Ann *nursing educator, academic administrator*
Bailar, John Christian III *retired public health educator, physician, statistician*
Baird, Donna Selma *counselor, educator*
Beale, Susan Yates *social worker*
Behney, Clyde Joseph *health policy researcher*
Brown, Lawrence George *medical director*
Burris, James Frederick *federal healthcare administrator, educator*
Chalk, Rosemary Anne *health science association administrator*
Corrigan, Janet M. *health science association administrator*
Delgado, Jane *health policy executive, writer, psychologist*
DeParle, Nancy-Ann Min *former federal agency administrator, lawyer*
Dodgen, Daniel W. *health policy advisor, psychologist*
Eckenhoff, Edward Alvin *health facility administrator, educator*
Fineberg, Harvey Vernon *medical institute administrator*
Gaynor, Suzanne Marie *healthcare executive, researcher*
Ginsburg, Paul B. *health facility administrator*
Grob, George Frederick *health science association administrator*
Harling, Barbara Jean *social worker*
Hartmann, Robert Sankey *health facility administrator, not-for-profit fundraiser*
Higgins, Paul John *medical director, career military officer*
Jones, Stanley Boyd *retired researcher*
Kelley, Patrick W. *health science association administrator, preventive medicine physician*
Lewis, Benjamin Pershing, Jr. *pharmacist, retired public health service officer*
Lewis, Prudence Fox *Christian science practitioner*
Lightfoot, James Ellison *researcher, director*
Lombardo, Fredric Alan *pharmacist, educator*
Martinez, Rose Marie *health science association administrator*
Michnich, Marie E. *health policy analyst, consultant, educator*
Mitchell, Ruthie Yvette *human services administrator, director*
Nightingale, Stuart Lester *public health service officer*
Pierce, John Randall *medical inspector, pediatrician*
Pollack, Ronald Frank *healthcare organization executive, lawyer*
Pope, Andrew *health science association administrator*
Porter, John Weston *counselor, consultant, administrator*
Rios, Elena *health association administrator*
Rowland, Diane *health facility administrator, researcher*
Salisbury, Dallas L. *researcher, director*
Sanchez-Way, Ruth Dolores *public health administrator*
Satcher, David *public health service officer, former Surgeon General of the United States*
Spencer, Harrison Clark, Jr. *public health administrator, educator*
Stoiber, Susanne A. *health science organization administrator*
Tipre, Dnyanesh Nishikant *pharmacist, researcher*
Walker, Audrey Thayer *social worker, psychotherapist*
Wells, Samuel Fogle, Jr. *research center administrator*
Wuzor, Geoffrey Onyema *psychotherapist*
Wysocki, Susan *women's health nurse practitioner*
Yarwood, Bruce *health science association administrator*

FLORIDA

Altamonte Springs
LeBlanc, Janet M. *addictions and relationship counselor*

Avon Park
Cranfill, Virginia May *retired nursing administrator*

Boca Raton
Foreman, Barbara Blatt *healthcare facility administrator*
Richman, Joseph Herbert *retired public health service officer*
Rothberg-Blackman, June Simmonds *retired nursing educator, psychotherapist*

Chattahoochee
Carrasco, José Aníbal *recreational therapist*

Clearwater
Barry, Joyce Alice *dietician, consultant*
Halsey, Jean Michele *nursing educator*

Daytona Beach
Cardwell, Harold Douglas, Sr. *retired rehabilitation services professional*

Deerfield Beach
Gambino, S(alvatore) Raymond *lab administrator, educator*
Solomon, Barry Jason *human services administrator, consultant*

Delray Beach
Ellsweig, Phyllis Leah *retired psychotherapist*

Deltona
Bondinell, Stephanie *counselor, academic administrator*

Doral
Brioso-Mesa, Maureen Diane *mental health services professional*

Ellenton
Edson, Herbert Robbins *retired foundation and hospital executive, military officer*

Fernandina Beach
Kurtz, Myers Richard *retired hospital administrator*

Fort Lauderdale
Adams, Nancy R. *nurse, retired military officer*
Alpert, Martin Jeffrey *chiropractic physician*
Kornblau, Barbara L. *physical therapist, educator*
Maniscalco-Feichtl, Maria *pharmacist, educator*
Rentoumis, Ann Mastroianni *psychotherapist*

Fort Myers
Thurman, Cynthia Denise *human services administrator*

Gainesville
Acholonu, Wilfred W., Jr. *clinical pharmacy specialist, educator*
Balaban, Murat Omer *food science educator*
Bzoch, Kenneth Rudolph *speech and language educator, department chairman*
Carter, Christopher Scott *health facility administrator*
Graham-Hutchinson, Joanna *counselor, minister*
Kersey, Talana S. *mental health counselor*
Puckett, Ruby Parker *nutritionist, food service executive, writer*
Small, Natalie Settimelli *retired pediatric mental health counselor*

Hillsboro Beach
Marshall, Jo Taylor *social worker*

Jacksonville
Cherry, Barbara Waterman *speech and language pathologist, physical therapist*
Davis, Linda Lennon McConnell *critical care nurse*
Mack, Jeannette Ana *medical technician*
O'Connor, R. D. *retired healthcare executive*
Sanders, Marion Yvonne *retired geriatrics nurse*
ScarborougH, Marion Nichols *nutritionist, recreational facility executive*

Jensen Beach
Gamble, Raymond Wesley *retired marriage and family therapist, clergyman*

Kissimmee
Goode, Betty Ruth *retired social worker*

Largo
Bush, Debra W. *occupational health nurse*
Hamlin, Robert Henry *public health service officer, educator, management consultant*
Moscato, Joseph Louis, Jr. *health facility administrator, military officer*

Melbourne
Hughes, A. N. *psychotherapist*

Miami
Dann, Oliver Townsend *psychoanalyst, psychiatrist, educator*
Himburg, Susan Phillips *dietician, educator*
Newton, Terry Fernando *health facility specialist, writer*
Osinski, Martin Henry *healthcare consultant*
Saland, Deborah *psychotherapist, educator*
Schafer, Marie *nurse, educator*
Schor, Olga Seemann *mental health counselor, real estate broker*

Miami Springs
Neasman, Annie Ruth *health facility administrator*

Miramar
Asika-Enahoro, Chidi Maureen *rehabilitation services professional, consultant, writer*

Mount Dora
Crone, Eugene N. *addictions specialist, retired educator*

Naples
Cotrone, Janice Lynne *nursing consultant*
Mavrides, Elaine *retired mental health services professional, retired social worker*
Seavey, Christopher Gordon *psychotherapist, alcohol/drug abuse services professional*
Vumbacco, Joseph V. *health services executive*
Whitman, Burke William *health services executive*

New Port Richey
Charters, Karen Ann Elliott *critical care nurse, health facility administrator*

New Smyrna Beach
Faherty, Sandra Lee *social worker, psychotherapist*

Ocala
Kilmark, Robert Martin *retired lab administrato*

Orange Park
Rice, Ronald James *hospital administrator*

Orlando
Eastmond-Robinson, June Patricia *nursing educator*
Sharp, Christina Krieger *retired nursing educat*

Palm Beach Gardens
Holloway, Edward Olin *human services manager*
Sonnier, Joseph A. *lab administrator, physician*

Panama City Beach
Nelson, Edith Ellen *dietician*

Parkland
Harris, Jacqueline Myers *speech/language pathology services professional*

Pembroke Pines
Alber, Oro Linda *healthcare educator, consultant*

Pensacola
Appleyard, Diane Paige *human service administrator*
Ewing, Charles William, Jr. *healthcare educator*
Maygarden, Jerry Louis *healthcare foundation executive*
Shimmin, Margaret Ann *retired women's health nurse*

Plant City
Henry, J. Myrle *pharmacist*

Plantation
Gonshak, Isabelle Lee *nurse, volunteer*

Poinciana
Spero, Barry Melvin *retired health facility administrator*

Port Charlotte
Kidd, A. Paul *health facility and government agency administrator*

Port Saint Lucie
Beatrice, Ruth Hadfield *hypnotherapist, retired elementary school educator, financial administrator*
Priore, Louis Vincent *pharmacist*

Rockledge
Means, Michael David *hospital administrator*

Saint Petersburg
Jordan, William Reynier, Sr. *retired therapist, poet*
McCluskey, Charles James, Jr. *physician assistant*
McNeill, Felita Gale *nurse, military officer*

Sanford
Mena, Michele M. *counselor, educator*

Sarasota
Carr, Patricia Ann *community health nurse*
Harris, Judith Ann White *occupational health nurse, educator*
Lieberman, Carol *healthcare marketing communications consultant*
Middleton, Norman Graham *social worker, psychotherapist*

Sebring
Westberry, Paula I. *nursing administrator*

Stuart
Cocoves, Anita Petzold *psychotherapist*

Tallahassee
Blair, Maudine *psychotherapist, communications executive, management consultant*
Ilich, Jasminka Z. *dietician, educator*
Ross, Levi Andre *public health educator*

Tamarac
Krause, John L. *retired optometrist*

Tampa
Boutros, Linda Nelene Wiley *medical/surgical nurse*
Castellano, Josephine Massaro *medical records specialist*
Galwankar, Sagar Chandramohan *public health service officer*
Goldman, Mark S. *alcohol/drug abuse services professional, educator, reseracher*
Reiske, Steven Robert Warren *human services manager*
Russell, Diane Elizabeth Henrikson *career counselor*

Venice
Barritt, Evelyn Ruth Berryman *nurse, educator, dean*

West Palm Beach
Bernhardt, Marcia Brenda *mental health counselor*
Koslow, Stephen Hugh *health science association administrator, pharmacologist, neuroscientist*

Weston
Gordon, Lori Heyman *psychotherapist, author, educator*

Winter Park
Desmarais, Paul Leo *critical care nurse*
Douglas, Kathleen Mary Harrigan *retired psychotherapist, educator*
Haendiges, Anne R. *marriage and family therapist*

Winter Springs
San Miguel, Sandra Bonilla *social worker*

Zephyrhills
Walton, Shirley Dawn *retired medical technician*

GEORGIA

Albany
Wernick, Joel *health facility administrator*

Alpharetta
Bunker, Kimberly LeAnn *critical care nurse, emergency nurse practitioner*

Atlanta
Baird, Marianne Saunorus *critical care clinical nurse specialist, administrator*
Bales, Virginia Shankle *health science association administrator*
Barker, William Daniel *hospital administrator*
Chandler, Robert Charles *healthcare consultant*
Foege, William Herbert *public health administrator, educator*
Gray, Charnelda L. *pharmacist*
Honaman, J. Craig *health facility administrator*
Hopkins, Donald Roswell *public health physician*
Johnson, Carl Frederick *marriage and family therapist*
Martin, David Edward *health sciences educator*
Polhamus, Barbara *nutritionist, educator*
Salmon, Marla E. *nursing educator, dean*
Schuchat, Anne *health facility administrator*
Seffrin, John Reese *health science association administrator, educator*
Sherbinski, Linda Anne *nurse anesthetist, nursing educator*
Walton, Carole Lorraine *clinical social worker*
Weed, Roger Oren *rehabilitation services professional, educator*

Augusta
Gillespie, Edward Malcolm *hospital administrator*
Phillips, Marjorie Shaw *pharmacist, educator*

Brunswick
Herndon, Alice Patterson Latham *public health nurse*

Columbus
Bryant, Mollie Annette *rehabilitation services professional, director*
Purol, R.M. Scott *psychiatric nurse*
Simmons, Lynda Teel *nurse, healthcare executive*

Decatur
Hinman, Alan Richard *public health physician, epidemiologist*
Rosenberg, Mark L. *health facility administrator*

Evans
Feldman, Elaine Bossak *medical nutritionist, educator*

Fayetteville
Cokuslu, Lynda Elizabeth McCord *medical assistant*

Jasper
Ledford, Shirley Louise *practical nurse*

Kennesaw
Smith, Carol L. *human services administrator, consultant*

Kingsland
Barlow, Paula C. *nurse*

Lawrenceville
Swanson, Lynnette Sue *special olympics coordinator, special education educator*

Lithonia
Sigh, Robert Virgil *public health physician*

Macon
Faircloth, Laurie Ricketson *critical care nurse*
Patterson, Kenneth *nurse*

Marietta
McEntire, Betty *health facility administrator*
O'Neil, Kelly Lynn *pharmacist*

Roswell
Herron, Harriette A. *retired occupational health nurse*

Savannah
Eaves, George Newton *health facility administrator, educator*

Statesboro
Bartels, Jean Ellen *nursing educator*

HAWAII

Haleiwa
Shigemasa, Teresa *mental health services professional, educator*

Honolulu
Cadman, Edwin Clarence *health facility administrator, retired educator*
Fischer, Joel *social work educator*
Kennedy, Faye *retired social worker, author*
Lum, Jean Loui Jin *nursing educator*
Wilson, William James *healthcare executive*

Kamuela
Chen, Chien-hsing *Chinese traditional health practices educator*

Kapolei
Stewart, Bobby Gene *laboratory director*

IDAHO

Boise
Brownson, Mary Louise *counselor, educator, artist*

Ketchum
Parry, Janet *retired health facility administrator*

Pocatello
Eichman, Charles Melvin *counselor*

ILLINOIS

Alton
Kessler, William Eugene *healthcare executive*

Arlington Heights
Baptist, Allwyn J. *healthcare consultant*

Belleville
Shim, Sang Koo *mental health services professional*

Berwyn
Hudik, Martin Francis *hospital administrator, educator, consultant, writer*

Bolingbrook
Day, Mary Ann *medical/surgical nurse*
Price, Theodora Hadzisteliou *individual, child and family therapist*

Bourbonnais
Sayson, Joselito *physical therapist, educator*

Carbondale
Kawewe, Saliwe Moyo *social work educator, researcher*
Malkin, Marjorie J. *recreational therapist, educator*
M'Cormack, Fredanna Antoinette Durosimi *dietician, educator*

Centralia
Whitten, Mary Lou *nursing educator*

Champaign
May, Linda Karen Cardiff *occupational health nurse, safety engineer, consultant*
Strauser, David Ross *healthcare educator, director*

Chatham
Chew, Keith Elvin *health facility administrator*

Chicago
Andreoli, Kathleen Gainor *nurse, educator, dean*
Berman, Laura *sex therapist*
Dawson, Caron *medical and legal consultant*
Goodman, Larry J. *health facility administrator*
Gulati, Martha *health facility administrator, cardiologist*
Hacker, Eileen Danaher *nursing educator, researcher*
Heltne, Paul Gregory *researcher, museum director*
Hill, Barbara Benton *healthcare executive*
Johanson, Gregory John *psychotherapist, minister*
Komiske, Bruce King *hospital administrator*
Lal, Anil *health facility administrator*
Lerner, Wayne M. *healthcare executive*
Logemann, Jerilyn Ann *speech pathologist, educator*
Lundquist, Dana Richard *health facility administrator*
Meccia, Francis (Frank) Anthony *physician assistant*
Messner, Leonard Vincent *optometrist, educator*
Reed, Vastina Kathryn (Tina Reed) *child and adolescent psychotherapist*
Shannon, Iris Reed *health facility administrator, consultant*
Spergel, Irving Abraham *social worker, researcher*
Szerlag, Chester Theodore *health care executive*
Thomas, Leona Marlene *healthcare educator*
Wilhelm, John L. *health facility administrator*
Wittbrodt, Elizabeth S. *occupational therapist, educator*
Zimmerman, D. Patrick *psychotherapist, health facility administrator*

Decatur
Mayfield, Peggy Lee *counselor*

Deerfield
Nitzki-George, Diane M. *pharmacist, medical writer*
Ramirez, Ralph Henry *nurse, corporate executive*
Shakno, Robert Julian *hospital and social services administrator*

Dekalb
Crosser, Carmen Lynn *marriage and family therapist, social worker, consultant*

Des Plaines
D'Anca, John Arthur *psychotherapist, educator*

East Saint Louis
Lane-Trent, Patricia Jean *social worker*

Edwardsville
Gupchup, Gireesh Vijay *pharmacist, educator*
Madison, Grace Lenore *retired medical/surgical nurse, psychologist, educator*
Wiley, Lakesha M. *pharmacist, educator*

Elgin
Beyer, Karen Haynes *social worker*

Evanston
Hughes, Edward F. X. *healthcare educator, preventive medicine physician*
Neaman, Mark Robert *hospital administrator*

Freeport
Weaver, Michael Glenn *pharmacist*

Galena
Alexander, Barbara Leah Shapiro *clinical social worker*

Glen Ellyn
Cummings, Joan E. *health facility administrator, educator*

Glenview
Coulson, Elizabeth Anne *physical therapist, educator, state representative*

Harrisburg
Rushing, Philip Dale *retired social worker*

Hillside
Savic, Jelena *technologist, educator*

Hinsdale
Kim, Micaela *speech pathology/audiology services professional*

Ingleside
D'Andrea, Dana M. *medical/surgical nurse, lawyer*

Lake Bluff
Fletcher, Dorothy Jean *hospital administrator, educator*

Lemont
Hayes, Randy Alan *family therapist, process improvement specialist*

Lincolnshire
Fradin, Russell P. *human resources company executive, former computer company executive*

Macomb
Hopper, Stephen Rodger *hospital administrator*

Matteson
van der Hoek, Sherry A. *counselor*

Maywood
Barbato, Anthony L. *hospital administrator, medical educator*
Hummel, Patricia *pediatric nurse practitioner, researcher*

Mokena
Hunter, Steven L. *medical center administrator*

Moline
Gleich, Carol S. *health professions education executive*

Niles
Roepenack, Dwight Elmer *public health service officer*

Northbrook
Kahn, Sandra S. *psychotherapist*

Northfield
Lubawski, James Lawrence *healthcare consultant*

Oak Park
Varchmin, Thomas Edward *public health service officer*

Park Ridge
Campbell, Bruce Crichton *hospital administrator*
Pippen, Jennifer Lynn *therapist, consultant*

Peoria
Perrilles, Angela Terese *physical therapist*
Walker, Philip Chamberlain, II, *health facility administrator*

Plainfield
Schinderle, Robert Frank *retired hospital administrator*

Quincy
Reynolds, Judith Amy *nutritionist, consultant, animal scientist, educator*

Rockton
Pennell, Danny Joe *social worker*

Savoy
Bednar, Susan Gail *social worker, mediator, consultant, social sciences educator*

Skokie
Langguth, Margaret Witty *health facility administrator*
McCarthy, Michael Shawn *health care company executive, lawyer*

Springfield
McCown, Linda Jean *medical technology educator*

Tinley Park
Daniels, Kurt R. *speech and language pathologist*

Urbana
Baker, David Hiram *nutritionist, educator*
Eddy-Johnson, Deanna M. *home health care advocate*
Erdman, John W. *nutritionist, educator*
Visek, Willard James *nutritionist, animal scientist, physician, educator*

Watseka
Freed, Susan Dianne *health facility administrator*

Westchester
Clarke, Richard Lewis *health science association administrator*

Westmont
Tieken, Robert W. *relocation services company executive, retired tire manufacturing company executive*

Wheaton
Lawrence-Water, Bette Ann *community health leader*
Pape, Patricia Ann *social worker, consultant*

Wilmette
Ellis, Helene Rita *social worker*

INDIANA

Anderson
Bracken, Linda Darlene *medical/surgical nurse*

Bloomington
Wigley, Diana Gail *respiratory therapist*

Bluffton
Brockmann, William Frank *retired health facility administrator*

Fort Wayne
Egly, Sharon Kay *speech pathology/audiology services professional, director*
Kennedy, Elizabeth *health facility administrator*
Wooten, Marc *hospital administrator, medical educator*

Indianapolis
Buhner, Byron Bevis *health science facility administrator*
Corley, William Edward *hospital administrator*
Davis, Edgar Glenn *healthcare executive, educator*
Gilroy, Sue Anne *hospital administrator, former state official*
Handel, David Jonathan *health facility administrator*
Harden, Anita Joyce *nurse*
Hitchens, William Randolph (Randy) *healthcare executive*
Kitterman, Laura Ann *occupational therapist*
Malloy, William Xavier *pharmacist*
Moelhman, Amy Jo *social worker*
Pishchalnikov, Yuri A. *researcher*
Riegsecker, Marvin Dean *pharmacist, state senator*
Roscoe, Michael Shannon *physician assistant, educator*
Schroyer, Michael Kevin *healthcare consultant, hospital executive*

Kokomo
Coppock, Janet Elaine *mental health nurse*

Lafayette
McBride, Angela Barron *nursing educator*
Novak, Julie Cowan *nursing educator, researcher, clinician*

Logansport
Walter, Patricia L. *psychotherapist, consultant*

Michigan City
Zolvinski, Susan Kaye *medical director*

Mishawaka
Haley, David Alan *healthcare executive*

Muncie
Hoffman, Mary Catherine *retired nurse, anesthetist*

New Albany
Rhodes, Betty Fleming *rehabilitation services professional, nurse*

San Pierre
Begley, Heidi Marie *nurse, entrepreneur*

Tell City
Thrasher, Mary Ahlf Marcroft *educator, social worker*

West Lafayette
Belcastro, Patrick Frank *pharmacist, researcher*
Christian, John Edward *health science association administrator, educator*
Kirksey, Avanelle *nutrition educator*
Peck, Garnet Edward *pharmacist, educator*
Shaw, Stanley Miner *pharmacist, educator*

IOWA

Altoona
Berkenes, Joyce Marie Poore *social worker, director*

Burlington
Gerdner, Linda Ann *nursing researcher, educator*

Cedar Rapids
Stephens, Ralph Renne *massage therapy educator*
Ziese, Nancylee Hanson *social worker*

Council Bluffs
Alley, Mary Lou Vande Woude *retired medical/surgical nurse*
Montgomery Linman, Sina Jo *pediatric nurse practitioner*

Davenport
Beckman, Robert W. *pharmacist*

Des Moines
Ramsden, Mary Catherine *substance abuse specialist*
Wallace, Samuel Taylor *health system administrator*
Walters, Clayton William *health facility administrator, rehabilitation services professional, consultant*

Glenwood
Campbell, William Edward *mental hospital administrator*

Iowa City
Anderson, Rachel L. *healthcare educator, researcher*
Densen, Paul Maximillian *retired health facility administrator*
Katen-Bahensky, Donna *health facility administrator*
Muir, Ruth Brooks *alcohol/drug abuse services professional, consultant*
Wurster, Dale Erwin *pharmacist, educator, retired dean*

Osage
Christensen, Pamela Karen *pediatric nurse*

Spirit Lake
Quaday-Gray, Ailene Diann *retired speech pathology/audiology services professional*

Walford
Brooks, Debra L. *healthcare executive, neuromuscular therapist*

Waverly
Eick-Gamm, Kimberly Marie *social worker*

West Des Moines
Matthews, Alexander *health facility administrator*
Owens, Fredric Newell *animal nutritionist, educator*

KANSAS

Colby
Morrison, James Frank *optometrist, state legislator*

Hays
Caprez, Judith V. *social worker, director*

Humboldt
Finney, Paul *acupuncturist, Chinese herbologist, entrepreneur*

Hutchinson
Davis, Mary Elizabeth *speech pathologist, educator, counselor*

Kansas City
Godwin, Harold Norman *pharmacist, educator*
Jerome, Norge Winifred *nutritionist, anthropologist, educator*

Larned
Rehorn, Lois M(arie) (Lois Marie Smith) *nursing administrator*

Lawrence
Mc Coin, John Mack *social worker*

Manhattan
Shanklin, Carol W. *dietician, educator*

North Newton
Goering, Jacob D. *retired psychoanalyst*

Shawnee Mission
Breen, Katherine Anne *speech and language pathologist*

Topeka
Varner, Charleen LaVerne McClanahan *nutritionist, educator, dietician*

Wichita
Da'Luz Vieira-Jones, Lorraine Christine C. *acupuncturist, researcher*
Dorr, Stephanie Tilden *psychotherapist*
Guthrie, Diana Fern *nursing educator*

KENTUCKY

Brooksville
Dorton, Truda Lou *medical/surgical and geriatrics nurse*

Lexington
Bennett, Victoria Elizabeth *rehabilitation nurse, dialysis nurse and technician*
DeLuca, Patrick Phillip *pharmacist, educator, medical association administrator*
Garman, Ray Fillmore *occupational physician, director*
Huberfeld, Nicole Lauren *healthcare educator*
Nau, David Paul *pharmacist, educator*

Louisville
Bloem, James H. *managed health care executive*
Carlisle, Douglas R. *health facility administrator*
Grevious, Inez Cobble *health facility administrator*
Hanson, Dennis Michael *retired health facility administrator*
Hathcock, Bonita Catherine (Bonnie Hathcock) *managed health care company executive*
Kehrt, Bettie F. *medical transcriptionist*
Kuntz, Edward Lawrence *healthcare executive*
Lunsford, W. Bruce *health facility administrator and products executive*
Mather, Elizabeth Vivian *healthcare executive*
Mountz, Wade *retired healthcare executive*
Noland, Thomas Turley, Jr. *managed healthcare company executive*

Murray
Keller, Randal Joseph *toxicology educator*

Radcliff
Cole, Jessie Mae *nursing assistant, freelance/self-employed writer*

Richmond
Hall, Kathy *health facility administrator*

Russellville
Harper, Shirley Fay *nutritionist, educator, consultant, lecturer*

LOUISIANA

Alexandria
Mathews, Peggy Anne *nurse*

Baton Rouge
Broussard, Malcolm Joseph *pharmacist, consultant*

Houma
Hukins-Rodrigue, Dana Ann *nurse*

Leesville
Gutman, Lucy Toni *social worker, educator*

Mandeville
Treuting, Edna Gannon *retired nursing administrator, educator*

Metairie
Evans, Carol Rockwell *nursing administrator*
O'Neill, James H. *psychotherapist, educator*

Natchitoches
Egan, Shirley Anne *retired nursing educator*

New Orleans
Allen, Rondall E. *pharmacist, educator*
Carlson, Robert Marshall *health facility administrator*
Culbertson, Richard Allen *healthcare educator, health facility administrator*
Howard, Richard Ralston, II, *medical health advisor, researcher, financial consultant*
Meekers, Dominique Armand *public health professor, demographer*
Melcher, Joe A. *audiologist, educator*
Schexnayder, Randall V. *pharmacist, dean*

Pearl River
Thiel, David Brian *physician assistant*

Shreveport
Heacock, Donald Dee *social worker*

Ville Platte
Patsicostas, Susan Joanna *mental health services professional, psychotherapist*

MAINE

Bangor
Ballesteros, Paula Mitchell *nurse*

Brewer
Dauphinee, Jo Anne Louise *retired nurse*

Brooklin
Schmidt, Lynda Wheelwright *psychotherapist*

Dresden
Iserbyt, Charlotte Thomson *researcher, writer, educational consultant*

East Boothbay
Eldred, Kenneth McKechnie *acoustician, consultant*

Ellsworth
Young, Lucia Patat *psychotherapist*

Fort Fairfield
Shapiro, Joan Isabelle *lab administrator, medical/surgical nurse*

Freeport
Cushman, Margaret Jane *herbalist, nurse*

Portland
Wipfler, William John *health facility administrator*

MARYLAND

Adamstown
Munson, John Christian *acoustician*

Annapolis
Goldwater, Marilyn R(ubin) *medical/surgical nurse, state legislator*
Klejnot, Getha Jean *school nurse practitioner, music educator*

Arnold
Gagné, Doreen Frances *nurse practitioner, educator*

Baltimore
Abeloff, Martin David *medical administrator, educator, researcher*
Beilenson, Peter Lowell *former public health official*
Bridges, John Francis Patrick *healthcare educator, researcher*
Buccino, Daniel L. *psychotherapist, consultant*
Campbell, Jacquelyn C. *community health nurse*
Englar, Nancy Ellen *nurse, consultant, nursing educator*
Henderson, Donald Ainslie *public health service officer*
Kumin, Libby Barbara *speech language pathologist, educator*
Larch, Sara Margaret *healthcare executive*
Lawson, Edward Earle *neonatal/perinatal nurse practitioner*
Meltzer, Arthur Adam *researcher*
Peterson, Ronald R. *health service administrator*
Pickett, Eugenia V. *social worker*
Ray, Carol Reneé *researcher*

Bethesda
Gaarder, Marie *speech pathologist*
Graeff, Alan S. *health association executive*
Greenwald, Peter *health facility administrator, director, epidemiologist, researcher*
Hausman, Steven Jack *health science association*
Hsu, S. Dana *technologist*
Jonas, Gary Fred *healthcare executive*
McDonough, Thomas P. *health care company executive*
Obrams, Gunta Iris *clinical research administrator*
Oddis, Joseph Anthony *health associations executive*
Polsby, Gail K. *psychotherapist*
Pospisil, George Curtis *health science administrator*
Robinson, Sharon Beth *health science association administrator*
Stover, Ellen L. *health scientist, psychologist*
Taylor, Lindsay David, Jr. *healthcare executive, bank executive, federal agency administrator*
Tracy, Thomas Miles *international health organization official*
Wise, Allen F. *health care company executive*
Wolf, Dale B. *health care company executive*

Bowie
Speller-Brown, Barbara Jean *pediatric nurse practitioner*

Capitol Heights
Johnson, Louise Street *medical/surgical nurse*

Chevy Chase
Pedersen, Wesley Niels M. *public relations and public affairs counselor*

Clarksville
Hung, Mei-Jong Chow *social worker*

Columbia
Pacifico, Joseph Carl *counselor*
Piou-Brewer, Magalie *psychotherapist, educator, small business owner*

Damascus
Styer, Joanne Louise *retired dietician*

Elkton
Mayer, Margaret Ellen *medical coding specialist*

Ellicott City
Cooke, Catherine E. *pharmacist, consultant*

Gaithersburg
Dowd, Carolyn Lay *social worker*
Gloyd, Rita A. *retired social worker*
Quraishi, Mohammed Sayeed *retired health facility administrator, research scientist*

Germantown
Kilani, Ahmed Fathy *lab administrator, director*

Hagerstown
Harrison, Lois Smith *hospital executive, educator*

Lothian
Flowers, Murhl Lynn *retired pharmacist*

Lutherville
Goodman, Valerie Dawson *psychiatric social worker*

Marriottsville
Strange, Donald Ernest *healthcare company executive*

Mitchellville
Kendall, Katherine Anne *social worker*

Owings Mills
Ryan, Judith W. *geriatrics nurse, educator*

Potomac
Wolman, Eric *health care consultant*

Rockville
Groban, Mark D. *health care company executive*
Long, Cedric William *health facility administrator*
Lushniak, Boris D. *public health service officer*
O'Donnell, James Francis *retired health scientist administrator*
Parham-Hopson, Deborah *health programs administrator*
Scully, Martha Seebach *speech and language pathologist*
Weinel, Pamela Jean *nurse administrator*

Severna Park
Rheinstein, Peter Howard *healthcare company executive, physician, lawyer*

Silver Spring
Arvin, Linda Lee *counselor*
Blakeney, Barbara A. *public health service officer*
Daniel, J. Christopher *health facility executive, family medicine physician, military officer*
Young, Jay Alfred *chemical safety and health consultant, editor, writer*

Takoma Park
Stephenson, Patricia Ann *public health researcher, educator*

Westminster
Lippy, Karen Dorothy Fethe *nurse psychotherapist*

MASSACHUSETTS

Andover
Govern, Frank Stanley *health facility and research administrator, healthcare educator, writer*

Arlington
Junger, Miguel Chapero *retired acoustics researcher*

Attleboro
Bischoff, Marilyn Brett *clinical social worker, personal life coach, psychotherapist*

Auburndale
Kibrick, Anne *retired nursing educator, dean*

Belmont
Kargman, Marie Witkin *marriage and family therapist*

Boston
Baker, Annette L. *pediatric nurse practitioner*
Berkman, Lisa F. *public health educator*
Blumenthal, David *health policy expert*
Cohen, Alan Barry *researcher, educator*
Dwyer, Johanna Todd *nutritionist, educator*
Felix-Getzik, Erika Michele *pharmacist*
Fowler, Floyd Jackson, Jr. *researcher*
Frank, Richard G. *healthcare educator*
Gura, Kathleen Marie *pediatric pharmacist, educator*
Hudd, Timothy R. *pharmacist, educator*
Kee, Chea-su *optometrist, educator*
Lowenstein, Arlene Jane *nursing educator, health facility administrator*
Mandell, James *health facility executive, urologist, educator*
Miller, Candace Marie *healthcare educator*
Mongan, James John *healthcare system administrator*
Quick, Jonathan Dickinson *health organization executive*
Reinherz, Helen Zarsky *social worker, researcher*
Sahney, Vinod K. *health care executive*
Shin, Sunny Hyucksun *social worker, educator*
Slavin, Peter L. *hospital administrator*
Sullivan, Patricia Eileen *physical therapist, educator*
Tammaro, Kelly Ann *pharmacist, researcher*
Watanabe, Mark David *pharmacist, educator*
Wirth, Dyann Fergus *public health educator, microbiologist*
Zaleznik, Abraham *psychoanalyst, management specialist, educator*

Boxford
Siegert, Barbara (Barbara Marie Siegert) *health care administrator*

Boylston
Larson, Roland Elmer *health facility administrator*

Brockton
Moore, Mary Johnson *retired community health nurse*

Cambridge
Botkin, James W. *leadership and executive coach*
Chodorow, Nancy Julia *psychotherapist, educator*
Cushman, Ellen *counselor*
Gassend, Blaise Laurent Patrick *technologist, researcher*
Narayanamurti, Venkatesh *health science association administrator*
Orfield, Antonia Marie *optometrist, researcher*
Sabeti, Pardis Christine *researcher*
Sapirie, Stephen Alan *public health administrator*
Severin, Christina *public health service officer*

Canton
Bihldorff, John Pearson *hospital director*
Sawtelle, Carl S. *psychiatric social worker*

Centerville
Condon, Ann Blunt *psychotherapist*

Chestnut Hill
Burgess, Ann Wolbert *nursing educator*
Mahoney, Kevin J. *social worker, educator*
Munro, Barbara Hazard *nursing educator, dean, researcher*

Chicopee
Dame, Catherine Elaine *acupuncturist*

Danvers
Kocur, Sean Edward *lab administrator*

Framingham
Austin, Sandra Ikenberry *nursing educator, consultant*

Great Barrington
Frye-Moquin, Marsha Marie *social worker*

Holyoke
Dearborn, Maureen Markt *speech and language clinician*

Hyannis
Nicholson, Ellen Ellis *clinical social worker*

Lexington
Fullerton, Derek Paul *public health service officer*

Ludlow
Budnick, Thomas Peter *social worker*

Natick
Wallace-Taylor, Elizabeth *medical/surgical nurse*

Needham
Ryan, Una Scully *health science association administrator, medical educator*

Newton
Mullen, Maureen Ann *social worker*
Winder, Alvin Eliot *public health educator, clinical psychologist*

Oxford
Holbrook, Howard George *pharmacist*

Rockland
Dunne, Myra Schley *nurse, consultant*

Sharon
Berzon, Faye Clark *retired nursing educator*

Southbridge
Mangion, Richard Michael *health facility administrator*

Sudbury
Ames, Lois Winslow Sisson *social worker, educator, writer*
Henderson, Ernest III *healthcare executive*

Tewksbury
Herlihy-Chevalier, Barbara Doyle *retired mental health nurse*
Tabea, Emile Victor *health facility administrator*

Waltham
Schneider, Craig David *health policy analyst*

Watertown
Pellegrom, Daniel Earl *health and development executive*

Wellesley Hills
Carroll, Deirdre Holden *psychiatric nurse practitioner, educator, medical researcher*

Woods Hole
Speck, William T. *former physician, health facility administrator*

Worcester
Harper, Doreen C. *nursing educator*

Yarmouth Port
Phelps, Judson Hewett *health facility administrator, marketing professional*

MICHIGAN

Allen Park
Kirby, Dorothy Manville *social worker*

Ann Arbor
Allen-Meares, Paula G. *social work educator, dean*
Bashshur, Rashid L. *health facility administrator, educator*
Beeton, Alfred Merle *lab administrator, director, biologist, educator, environmentalist*
Griffith, John Randall *health facility administrator, educator*
Hinshaw, Ada Sue *nursing educator, former dean*
Israel, Barbara A. *healthcare educator*
Ketefian, Shaké *nursing educator*
Oakley, Deborah Jane *public health service officer, nursing educator*
Romani, John Henry *health science association administrator, educator*
Rupp, Ralph Russell *retired audiologist, educator, author*
Sung, Kyu-Taik *social worker, educator, gerontologist, researcher*

Bay City
Lore, John S. *health facility administrator*

Dearborn
Bowersox, Patricia Anne *social worker*

Detroit
Fussell, Karen Marie *social worker, protective services official*
Hanks, Robin *rehabilitation nurse*
Jackson, Linda Shorter *nutritionist, educator*
Moses, Gregory H., Jr. *health services administrator*
Redman, Barbara Klug *nursing educator*
Ruckdeschel, John Charles *health facility administrator*
Schlichting, Nancy Margaret *hospital administrator*
Warden, Gail Lee *healthcare executive*
Washington, Olivia Grace Mary *psychotherapist, educator, counselor, researcher*

Dexter
Hanamey, Rosemary T. *nursing educator*

East Lansing
Noel, Mary Margaret *nutritionist, educator*

Farmington
Aubertin, Madeline Katherine *retired nursing educator, medical/surgical nurse, mental health services professional*

Farmington Hills
Friedman, Rozanne Golston *psychotherapist*

Ferndale
Forkan, Eveleen *counselor, educator, researcher*

Flint
Palinsky, Constance Genevieve *hypnotherapist, educator*
Williams, Veronica Myres *psychotherapist, social worker*

Franklin
Sax, Mary Randolph *speech and language pathologist*

Grand Ledge
Evert, Sandra Florence (Sandra Wheeler) *medical/surgical nurse, consultant*

Grosse Pointe
Marshall, Douglas William *health research administrator, educator*

Grosse Pointe Park
Knapp, Mildred Florence *retired social worker*

Grosse Pointe Woods
Barnhart, Mary C. *health facility administrator*

Holly
Evans Snowden, Audra Lynn *counselor*

Ionia
Ulmer, Evonne Gail *health science association administrator*

Jonesville
Corwin, Danny Willard *rehabilitation services professional, director*

Kalamazoo
Bennett, Arlie Joyce *clinical social worker*
Bernknopf, Allison Cori *pharmacist, educator*
Lander, Joyce Ann *retired nursing educator, retired medical/surgical nurse*
Ortiz-Button, Olga *social worker*

Livonia
Gepford, Barbara Beebe *retired nutrition educator*

Mears
Loomis, Norma Irene *marriage and family therapist*

Oak Park
Coleman, Dorothy Charmayne *nurse*

Owosso
McKean, Sherry Lynn *medical technician*

Saginaw
Moyer, Genevieve J. *counselor*

Southfield
Martin, Marcella Edric *retired community health nurse*
Sedler, Rozanne Friedlander *social worker, educator*
Torraco, Pamela Louise *psychotherapist*

Traverse City
Anderson, Carol Lynn *social worker, educator*

Warren
Bell, Julie Marie *health facility administrator, consultant*

Watervliet
Watkins, M(artha) Anne *family practice nurse practitioner*

Wixom
Becker, John Raymond *pharmacist*
Welch, Cherie Lynn *healthcare educator*

Ypsilanti
Fox, Diane Porretta *nursing educator*

MINNESOTA

Arden Hills
Ciske, Karen Lysbeth *retired medical/surgical nurse*

Bemidji
Martinson, Ida Marie *retired medical/surgical nurse, physiologist*

Bloomington
Nichols, Donna Mardell *nurse anesthetist*

Burnsville
Foss, Emma Thoren *retired social worker*

Duluth
Harlander, Ronald Stanley, Jr. *pharmacist*

Elysian
Thayer, Edna Louise *health facility administrator*

Granite Falls
Alness, Mae Christine *retired medical/surgical nurse*

Minneapolis
Drake, Dallas Sumner *researcher*
Hackman, Anna *pharmacist*
Hemsley, Stephen J. *healthcare company executive*
Kane, Robert Lewis *public health service officer, educator*
Kilbourne, Barbara Jean *health and housing executive*
Larson, Sheryl Ann *social worker, researcher, writer*
Sprenger, Gordon M. *hospital administrator*
Steen-Hinderlie, Diane Evelyn *social worker, musician*
Suryanarayanan, Raj Gopalan *pharmacist, researcher, consultant, educator*
Welters, Anthony *health services executive*

Minnetonka
Penshorn, John S. *health facility administrator*

New Brighton
Appel, William Frank *pharmacist*

Robbinsdale
Anderson, Scott Robbins *hospital administrator*

Rochester
Cortese, Denis A. *healthcare executive, medical educator*
Gervais, Sister Generose *hospital consultant*
Mrazek, David Allen *child and adolescent psychiatrist*
Robbins, Thomas Landau *researcher, editor*

Saint Paul
Barry, Anne M. *public health officer*
Shepherd, Terry L. *health facility administrator*
Wiersma, Kevin *lab administrator*

White Bear Lake
Bruhn, JoAnn Marie *radiologic technologist, writer, speaker*

MISSISSIPPI

Brandon
Hall, Breda Faye Kimbrough Inman *counselor, educator*

Columbus
Jones, Carol A. *nutritionist, artist*

Jackson
Rawson, John Elton *neonatologist, medical educator*
Tchounwou, Paul Bernard *environmental health specialist, toxicologist, educator*
Uzodinma, Minta LaVerne Smith *retired nursing administrator, nurse midwife*
Young, Brianne Lamonica *rehabilitation services professional*

Mississippi State
Hosie, Thomas Walsh *counselor, educator*

Moss Point
Bolton, Betty J. *medical/surgical nurse, poet*

Mound Bayou
Robinson, Oliver Dale *counselor, pastor*

Ocean Springs
Lee, Kathleen Mary *health facility administrator, nursing executive*

Pass Christian
Henrion, Rosemary Provenza *psychotherapist, educator*

Shaw
Garner, Mable Tecola *health facility administrator*

University
McCurdy, Christopher Robert *pharmacist, educator*

MISSOURI

Arcadia
Davis, Jo *nurse, writer, professional speaker, small business owner, photographer*

Cape Girardeau
Langenfeld, Mark E. *healthcare educator*

Chesterfield
Ashworth, Ronald Broughton *health facility executive, accountant*

Columbia
Gysbers, Norman Charles *counselor, educator*
Hensley, Elizabeth Catherine *nutritionist, educator*

Creve Coeur
Burch, Kelly Joan *pharmacist, consultant*

Jefferson City
Bussabarger, Mary Louise *mental health services professional*

Joplin
Miller, Toni M. Andrews *critical care nurse*

Kansas City
Eddy, Charles Alan *chiropractor*
Fetsch, Susan Hackler *nursing administrator, educator*
Krieg, Nancy Kay *social worker, poet, musician*
Oliver, Thornal Goodloe *retired health facility administrator*

Lees Summit
Brown, Doris Jane *medical technician*

Liberty
Foskett, Cynthia *nurse, analyst*
Samuel, Robert Thompson *optometrist*

O Fallon
Gross, Stanley Merhl *chiropractor*

Saint Charles
Tabaka, Sandra Lee *retired medical/surgical nurse*

Saint Louis
Baum, M(ary) Carolyn *occupational therapist*
Diekman, Connie *nutritionist*
Ezenwa, Josephine Nwabuoku *social worker*
Foy, Betsy D. *health facility administrator, educator*
LaBruyere, Thomas Edward *health facility administrator*
Molloff, Florence Jeanine *speech and language therapist*
Pryor, David Bram *health science association administrator*
Schoenhard, William Charles, Jr. *health system executive*
Stacy, Zachary Aaron *pharmacist*
Stretch, John Joseph *social worker, educator, management consultant*
Wilbanks, Donnie Jo *healthcare educator*

Springfield
Amtower, Debra Lynn *nursing consultant*

Walnut Shade
McCall, Charles Barnard *health facility administrator, educator*

MONTANA

Missoula
Hulme, Janet A. *physical therapist, writer, small business owner*

Victor
Davenport, Anne Marilyn *dietitian*

NEBRASKA

Lincoln
Anderson, Sonya L. *physical therapist, educator*
Steffan, Judy Mae *medical/surgical nurse*

Omaha
Hachten, Richard Arthur, II, *healthcare system executive*
Hoie, Eric B. *pharmacist, educator*

Scottsbluff
Shoemaker, Troy *hazardous materials response team coordinator, fire captain*

NEVADA

Henderson
Oesterman, Paul Joseph *pharmacist, educator*
Van Noy, Terry Willard *health care executive*

Las Vegas
Duke, Edward Marion, III, (Mickey Duke) *health facility administrator, consultant*
Duncombe, Patricia Warburton *retired social worker*
Francis, Timothy Duane *chiropractor*
Gilchrist, Ann Roundey *medical/surgical nurse*
Marlon, Anthony M. *healthcare company executive, cardiologist*
Meiner, Sue Ellen Thompson *adult nurse practitioner, consultant, gerontologist*
Michel, Mary Ann Kedzuf *retired nursing educator*
Wakefield, Marie A. *counselor, educational association administrator*

Reno
Bonaldi-Moore, Lorraine Kay *nursing educator*
Middlebrooks, Deloris Jeanette *retired nursing educator*
Pinson, Larry Lee *pharmacist, state agency administrator*

NEW HAMPSHIRE

Concord
White, Jeffrey George *healthcare consultant*

Littleton
Lucas, Kurt John *health facility director*

Meriden
Brent, Patricia Lee *health facility administrator, writer*

Plymouth
Gorin, Stephen H. *social worker, educator*

Salem
Stone, Patricia A. *special education services professional, consultant*

NEW JERSEY

Belle Mead
Sarle, Charles Richard *health facility executive*

Belvidere
Walsh, John Alfred *retired social worker*

Browns Mills
Henderson, Kathleen Denise Ross *medical/surgical nurse, educator*

Burlington
Rowlette, Henry Allen, Jr. *social worker, counseling psychologist*

Chatham
Murphy, Joseph James *chiropractic physician*

Cherry Hill
Blakney, Juanita Mosley *psychotherapist*

Deptford
Johns, Michael Douglas *healthcare executive, medical device executive, former federal government official*

East Orange
Hudson-Zonn, Eliza *nurse, psychologist*

East Rutherford
Cathey, Gertrude Brown *retired medical/surgical nurse*

Edgewater Park
Mednick, Sheldon Ira *pharmacist*

Edison
Blumengold, Jeffrey Gene *health facility administrator*
Winter, Robin Okner *health facility administrator*

Elizabeth
Horan, Gary S. *healthcare executive*
Rauh, Linda Ann *rehabilitation services professional, counselor*

Englewood
Gulko, Edward *healthcare executive, consultant*

Freehold
Ehling, Elizabeth Sullivan *psychotherapist, marriage and family therapist*

Green Brook
Spoeri, Randall Keith *healthcare company executive*

Hackensack
Alvarez, Manuel *hospital executive, medical educator, medical news correspondent*
Ferguson, John Patrick *health facility administrator*
Imus, Deirdre (Coleman) *health facility administrator, writer*

Highland Park
Blum, Lisa Carrie *social worker, researcher*
Grady, Joyce (Marian Joyce Grady) *psychotherapist, consultant*

Hillsdale
Kohan, Lois Rae *community health nurse*

Jersey City
Mahood, Marie I. *counselor, educator*

Kinnelon
Preston, Andrew Joseph *pharmacist, drug company executive*

Livingston
Adelsberg, Harvey *hospital administrator*

Lodi
Pitocco, Barbara Mary *psychotherapist, social worker*

Madison
Ellenbogen, Leon *nutritionist, biochemist, retired pharmaceutical executive*

Mahwah
Hailparn, Diana Finnegan *psychotherapist, writer*

Manasquan
Kelman, Marybeth *retired health care consultant, health policy analyst*

Matawan
Nolan, Sharon Theresa *nurse, educator*

Metuchen
Macarin-Mara, Lynn *psychotherapist, consultant*

Millville
Caldwell, Linda E. *critical care nurse*

Monmouth Junction
Kaminker, Marcia Kahn *physical therapist*

Monroe Township
Stein, Florence Taub *retired social worker*

Moorestown
McDaniel, Joanava B. *nurse*

Morristown
Prince, Leah Fanchon *lab administrator, executive secretary*

New Brunswick
Brilliant, Eleanor Luria *retired social work educator*
Huhmann, Maureen Brigitte *dietitian, researcher*

New Providence
Ring, Timothy Michael *human services administrator, pharmaceutical executive*

Newfield
Dreher, Frank H., Jr. *retired optician*

Paterson
Daniels, Cheryl Lynn *pediatrics nurse*
Thomas, Alyce M. *nutritionist, consultant*

Perth Amboy
Cruz, Nelson Xavier *healthcare executive*

Princeton
Agrawal, Shruti *researcher*
Kelly, Paul J. *lab administrator, physician, researcher*
Logue, Judith Felton *psychoanalyst, educator*
Marks, James S. *public health service administrator*

Red Bank
Brown, Valerie Anne *psychotherapist, social worker, educator*
Carmody, Margaret Jean *retired social worker*
Gutentag, Patricia Richmand *social worker, family counselor, occupational therapist*

Ridgewood
Clements, Lynne Fleming *marriage and family therapist, application developer*

Roseland
Malafronte, Donald *health facility administrator, consultant*

Rutherford
Suarez, Sally Ann Tevis *health facility administrator, nurse, consultant*

Sicklerville
Browna, Jo McIntyre *nurse*

South Orange
Budin, Wendy C. *nursing educator, researcher*
Hansell, Phyllis Shanley *nursing educator, administrator, researcher, consultant*
Hecht, Marion B. *counselor*

Teaneck
Alperin, Richard Martin *social worker, psychoanalyst*

Teterboro
Hagemann, Robert A. *health care company executive*
Mohapatra, Surya N. *laboratory executive*

Titusville
Reema, Jain *pharmacist, pharmaceutical executive*

Vauxhall
Jacobs-Smith, Ruby Eudora *retired medical/surgical nurse, public health service officer*

Warren
Kozberg, Donna Walters *rehabilitation services professional*
Yang, Tsong-Toh (T.T.) *pharmacist, researcher*

West Caldwell
Schiff, Robert *healthcare consulting company executive*

West New York
Schmidt, Nancy Anne *psychotherapist*

West Orange
Bornstein, Lester Milton *retired health facility administrator*
De Lisa, Joel Alan *rehabilitation physician, research executive*

Willingboro
Bevels, Esther Marie *medical technician, director*
Green, Riva Lee *social worker, minister*

NEW MEXICO

Alamogordo
Patch, Lisa E. *health services director, nurse*

Albuquerque
Erickson, Sue Alice *health educator, consultant, nurse*

Dulce
Polczynski, Eric James *pharmacist*

Farmington
Thompson, Joseph T., Jr. *health facility administrator*

Las Cruces
Little, Karen J. *counselor*

Santa Fe
Pulitzer, Roslyn Kitty *social worker, psychotherapist*

Truth Or Consequences
Rush, Domenica Marie *health facilities administrator*

NEW YORK

Albany
DeNuzzo, Rinaldo Vincent *pharmacy educator*
Evans, Jennifer G. *pharmacist*
Gellis, Zvi Dan *healthcare educator*
Marciniak, Macary Weck *pharmacist, educator*

Amherst
Brogan, Michael Spencer *physical therapist, educator*

Apalachin
Linder, Fannie Ruth *psychotherapist, concert soprano*

Astoria
Matheson, Linda *retired social worker*

Bayside
Kennedy, Mary Theresa *mental health services professional*

Beacon
Kanzer, Lynn Karen *medical record technician*

Binghamton
Bronstein, Laura *social worker, educator*

Bronx
Hilliard, Carol *nurse, educator, consultant, researcher*
Mazabel, Hector Antonio *psychotherapist, guidance counselor, researcher, journalist, announcer*
Megalli, Maguid Ramzi *health facility administrator*
Richards, Shana Natalie *physical therapist*

Brooklyn
Ebesu, Duane Ken *human services administrator*
Eliasi, Jennifer Rebecca *dietician, consultant*
Gonsalves, Patricia E. *surgical nurse*
Gross, Stephen Mark *pharmacist, dean*
Gustin, Mark Douglas *healthcare executive*
Hawkins, Vivian Agatha *mental health nurse, educator*
Landau, Joel *health services administrator*
Lockey, James Peter *public health service officer*
Murillo-Rohde, Ildaura Maria *marriage and family therapist, consultant, educator, retired dean*
Najib, Jadwiga S. *pharmacist, educator*
Peters, Mercedes *psychotherapist*
Samuel, Carren C. *hospital administrator*
Toranzo, Nilsa Caridad *special education services professional*
Wilkow, Brian Richard *hospital administrator and clinician*
Wrotten, Marylean *medical coordinator, counselor*

Buffalo
Blane, Howard Thomas *alcohol/drug abuse services professional, researcher*
Duchan, Judith Felson *retired speech pathology/audiology services professional*
Germain, Pamela *health facility administrator, educator*
Hoffman, Faith Louise *social worker*
Nielsen, Nancy H. *health organization executive*

Camillus
Thompson, Mary Cecilia *nurse midwife*

Canandaigua
Ditmars, James Everett *social worker, actor*

Chappaqua
Boal, Lyndall Elizabeth *social worker*

Cortland
Brush, Florence Clapham *kinesiologist, exercise physiologist, physical education educator*

East Aurora
Dohn, Julianne *child protective services specialist*

Eastchester
Giuliano, Robert Paul *pharmacist*

Flushing
Kim, Sun-Hae *retired medical/surgical nurse, writer, retired nurse midwife, retired physical therapist*

Forest Hills
Alves, Flavio P. *researcher, director*

Garden City
Scollard, Patrick John *hospital executive*

Glenmont
Coye, Mary P. *counselor*
Haizlip, Viola *medical/surgical nurse*

Glens Falls
Vitvitsky, Jack *physician assistant*

Great Neck
Feldman, Gary Marc *nutritionist, consultant*

Greenfield Center
Templin, John Leon, Jr. *healthcare consulting executive*

Hartsdale
Schweitzer, Caren S. *social worker*

Hastings On Hudson
Stillman, Jeanne Betsock *public health administrator, consultant*

Haverstraw
Eidelman, Sharon (Sherry) R. *marriage and family therapist*

Holley
Ruck, Rosemarie Ulissa *retired social worker, freelance/self-employed writer*

Huntington Station
Williams, Una Joyce *psychiatric social worker*

Hurley
Petruski, Jennifer Andrea *speech and language pathologist*

Hyde Park
Rider, Kathleen Mary *dietician*

Ithaca
Habicht, Jean Pierre *public health educator*
Stephens, John Charles *audiologist, educator*
Wills, Michael Stephen *nutritionist, quality assurance professional*
Winter, Travis Ford *social worker*

Jackson Heights
Chang, Lydia Liang-Hwa *social worker, educator*

Jamaica
Ambizas, Emily Marguerite *pharmacist, educator*

Geffner, Donna Sue *speech pathology/audiology services professional, audiologist, educator*

Johnstown
Swanker-Gibson, Jahnn Hansen *mental health nurse*

Loudonville
Ribley-Borck, Joan Grace *medical/surgical rehabiliation nurse*

Manhasset
Croce, Anne Lally *nurse, commissioner*

Manlius
Gibson, Judith W. *psychotherapist*

Marcellus
Pirozzi, Mildred Jean *retired nursing administrator*

Medford
Brower, Robert Charles *rehabilitation counselor, small business owner*

Middletown
Ojeda, Joseph A. *psychotherapist*
Radeboldt-Daly, Karen Elaine *retired medical/surgical nurse*

Millbrook
Turndorf, Jamie *psychotherapist*

Mount Vernon
NelsonWilliams, Cecelia Elaine *dietician, nutritionist*

New York
Bailey, Darlyne *social worker, educator*
Barrett, Elizabeth Ann Manhart *psychotherapist, consultant, nursing educator*
Batavia, Mitchell *physical therapist, educator*
Boufford, Jo Ivey *health facility administrator, educator*
Brodie-Baldwin, Helen Sylvia *retired college and human services administrator*
Buehler, Thomas *psychotherapist, expressive therapist, artist*
Burns, M. Michele *human resources company executive*
Cagliuso, Nicholas Vincent, Sr. *public health service officer*
Camp, Sharon L. *reproductive health organization administrator*
Cardinale, Kathleen Carmel *retired health facility administrator*
Clemens, Rosemary A. *health facility administrator, foundation administrator*
Coleman, Jo-Ann S.E. *social worker*
Croft, Kathryn Delaine *social worker, consultant*
Daniel, Samuel J. *hospital administrator, medical educator*
Dehn, Cathleen Patterson *health facility administrator*
Dinerman, Miriam *social work educator*
Donald, Arnold W. *health science association administrator, former food products executive*
Drayer, Burton Paul *hospital administrator, neuroradiologist*
Ethan, Carol Baehr *psychotherapist, psychoanalyst*
Fagin, Claire Mintzer *nursing administrator, educator*
Fink, Matthew E. *health facility executive, educator*
Forbes, Sally *researcher, editor, curator*
Forese, Laura Lee *hospital administrator, orthopedist*
Franciosa, Joseph Anthony *healthcare consultant*
Gangwisch, James Edward *social worker, researcher*
Giordano, Bill A. *psychotherapist*
Glickman, Robert Morris *health facility administrator, dean*
Gold, William Elliott *health care management consultant, educator*
Goodwin, Beatrice *nursing educator, consultant*
Gure, Anna Valerie *retired social worker, consulting psychotherapist*
Hoyt, Pamela *nurse*
Kamerman, Sheila Brody *social work educator*
Kapoor, Neera *optometrist, research scientist*
Kassel, Catherine M. *community, maternal, and women's health nurse, consultant*
Kove, Miriam *psychotherapist*
Kuttler, Judith Esther *retired psychotherapist*
Lawrence, Lauren *psychotherapist, writer*
Levitt, Harry *speech and hearing scientist*
Malone, Beverly Louise *nursing administrator, former dean*
Mattson, Marlin Roy Albin *health facility administrator, psychiatry educator*
Mayeux, Richard *hospital administrator, neurologist*
McGonagle, Duncan Francis *mental health nurse, substance abuse counselor*
Mitchell, Mary Jenkins *public health service officer*
Moskowitz, Randi Zucker *nurse*
Mundinger, Mary O'Neil *nursing educator*
Murphy, Stacia *health service association executive*
Nasser, Jennifer Ann *nutritionist, researcher, healthcare educator*
Neubauer, Peter Bela *psychoanalyst*
Novick, Richard Paul *research scientist, public health institute administrator*
O'Shea, Elizabeth Therese *counselor*
Packer, Linda S. *psychotherapist*
Pakter, Jean *maternal and child health consultant*
Pandolfi, Frances *health facility administrator*
Pardes, Herbert *health facility executive, psychiatrist, educator*
Paulson, Loretta Nancy *psychoanalyst*
Pennisi, Liz *women's health nurse*
Pickering, Laurel *public health service officer*
Piombino, Nicholas *psychotherapist*
Rackow, Eric C. *hospital administrator*
Radwin, Jerome J. *public health service officer*
Redlener, Irwin Elliot *health facility administrator, educator*
Resnick, Rhoda Brodowsky *psychotherapist*
Reynolds, John R. *hospital executive*
Richards, Cecile *healthcare network executive*
Rothenberg, Eleanore *psychotherapist*
Roye, Carol *nursing educator*
Saffar, Jean-Marc *healthcare consultant*
Scott, Mimi Koblenz *psychotherapist, actress, journalist, playwright*
Sharoff, Leighsa *nursing educator, researcher*
Sochet, Mary Allen *psychotherapist, educator, writer*
Solomon, Libertina *retired pharmacist, educator*
Spriggs, David Randall *healthcare administrator, educator*
Turo, Joann K. *psychoanalyst, psychotherapist, consultant*
Varmus, Harold Eliot *health science administrator, educator, science researcher*
Watson, Anthony L. *health facility executive*
Whyatt, Robin M. *healthcare educator*
York, Janet Brewster *nurse, family and sex therapist, artist*
Yoshiuchi, Ellen Haven *healthcare educator, clinical counselor*
Zagoren, Joy Carroll *health facility director, researcher*
Zolla-Pazner, Susan *hospital administrator, biologist, biomedical researcher*

Niskayuna
Laskaris, E(vangelos) Trifon *technologist, researcher*

Orchard Park
Askew, Gloria Yarbrough *dietician*

Orient
Cochran, Judy Anne *psychiatric nurse practitioner*

Ossining
Beard, Janet Marie *health facility administrator*
Robinson, Karen Vajda *dietician*

Patchogue
McPherson, Sherry Lynn *social worker*

Pittsford
Huston, Samuel Richard *health facility executive*
Maxey, Joseph T. *marriage and family therapist, educator, hospital administrator*

Port Chester
Gregory, Lisa *marriage and family therapist*

Poughkeepsie
Deiters, Sister Joan Adele *psychoanalyst, nun, chemistry professor*
Heller, Mary Bernita *psychotherapist*

Rochester
Aydelotte, Myrtle Kitchell *retired nursing administrator*
Braley, Oleta Pearl *community health nurse, writer*
Hurlbut, Robert Harold *health care services executive*
Jain, Manish *researcher*
Nace, Morton Oliver, Jr. *human services manager*
Sammler, Anne Michelle *healthcare educator*
Tantillo, Mary Darlene *nurse*

Roslyn
Aptekar, Doris Mae Weinberg *psychotherapist, school psychologist, hypnotherapist*

Rye
Newburger, Howard Martin *psychoanalyst*
Wilmot, Irvin Gorsage *former hospital administrator, educator, consultant*

Saranac Lake
Caguiat, Carlos Jose *health facility administrator, priest*

Scarsdale
Glickenhaus, Sarah Brody *speech therapist*

Schenectady
Oliker, David William *healthcare management administrator*

Shelter Island
Nicklin, George Leslie, Jr. *psychoanalyst, educator, physician, writer*

Sleepy Hollow
Resnick, Adrienne Jo *clinical social worker, psychotherapist*

Staten Island
De Luca, Andrea (Helen Siglain) *psychoanalyst*
Gaeta, Rosemarie *psychotherapist*
Lazzara, Margo Valentine *counselor, writer*

Suffern
Raven, Luisa Antonia *psychotherapist, nurse*

Syracuse
Fitzgerald, Harold Kenneth *social work educator, consultant*
Swartz, Michael Frederick *physician assistant*

Tarrytown
Gutheil, Irene A. *social work educator, researcher*
Safian, Keith Franklin *hospital administrator*

Troy
Thompson, Barbara Ellen *occupational therapist, educator*

Tuckahoe
Thornton, Elaine Seretha *oncology clinical nurse specialist*

Valhalla
Iatropoulos, Michael John *health research executive, pathology educator*

White Plains
Fowlkes, Nancy Lanetta Pinkard *social worker*

Whitestone
Prisco, Frank J. *psychotherapist*

Williamsville
Perry, J. Warren *health facility administrator, educator*

NORTH CAROLINA

Burlington
King, David Paul *health services executive, lawyer*
MacMahon, Thomas P. *healthcare company executive*
Powell, James Bobbitt *health facility administrator, pathologist*

Chapel Hill
Azar, Henry Amin *retired medical historian, educator*
Baker, Edward L., Jr. *public health physician*
Gordon-Larsen, Penny *nutritionist, educator, researcher*
Murray, Michael Dennis *pharmacist*
Popkin, Barry Michael *nutrition educator*
Rimer, Barbara K. *health facility administrator, educator, dean*
Winstanly, Derek Miles *medical practitioner, company executive*
Zeisel, Steven H. *nutritionist, scientist, educator*

Cherry Point
Knoell, Michael David *health facility administrator, military officer*

Dunn
Hill, Susan Beasley *recreational therapist*

Durham
Brantley, Jeffrey Garland *health science association administrator*
Fulkerson, William *hospital administrator, pulmonologist*
McBane, Sarah Elizabeth *pharmacist, educator*
Yu, Bing *researcher*

Elizabeth City
Griffin, Gladys Bogues *critical care nurse, educator*

Fairmont
Spencer, Melissa Johanna *psychotherapist, special education educator*

Fayetteville
Jansen, Michael John *health facility administrator*
MacRae, Elizabeth (Elizabeth MacRae Halsey) *counselor, actor*

Greensboro
Allen, Jesse Owen III *organizational behavior specialist*
Evans, Jonathan Christopher *social worker*
Harris-Offutt, Rosalyn Marie *counselor, consultant, mental health nurse, writer*
Knesel, Ernest Arthur, Jr. *health facility administrator, chemicals executive*
McDaniel, James Mark, Jr. *health care executive*
Mozell, Herbert Lee *mental health services professional*
Penley, Virginia Long *social worker*
Schwenn, Lee William *retired health facility administrator*

Hendersonville
Jefferson, Letitia Gibson *rehabilitation counselor*

High Point
Scearse, Patricia Dotson *nursing educator, dean*

Newland
Lustig, Susan Gardner *occupational therapist*

Pembroke
Meadors, Allen Coats *health facility and academic administrator, educator*

Raleigh
Johnson, Mary Pauline (Polly Johnson) *nursing administrator*

Rutherfordton
Crummie, Ann Vaughn *mental health services professional*

Weaverville
Hauschild, Douglas Carey *optometrist*

Wilmington
Askew, Jennifer P. *pharmacist*
Maness, Eleanor Palmer *researcher*

Winston Salem
Cook, Sharon Warren *social worker, educator*
Preslar, Len Broughton, Jr. *hospital administrator*

NORTH DAKOTA

Dickinson
Kessel, Lloyd R. *nursing administrator, educator*

Grand Forks
Nielsen, Forrest Harold *research nutritionist*

Valley City
Stillings, Dennis Otto *research association administrator, consultant*

OHIO

Ada
Allison, Jeffery Clay *pharmacist, educator*

Akron
West, Michael Alan *retired hospital administrator*

Ashland
Gearhart, Randall F. *healthcare educator*

Bucyrus
Cooper, April Helen *family practice nurse practitioner*

Canton
Covert, Susan Jane *rehabilitation services professional, director*

Cincinnati
Besier, James Louis *pharmacist, educator*
Chapman, Jamie L. *pharmacist*
Curtis-Francis, Kelley Ann *pharmacist*
Derstadt, Ronald Theodore *health facility administrator*
De Witt, Jeanette Marie *physical therapist*
Goldstein, Sidney *pharmacist*
Henney, Jane Ellen *health facility administrator, educator, oncologist*
Hensgen, Herbert Thomas *medical technologist*
Schubert, William Kuenneth *hospital medical center executive*
Stinson, Mary Florence *retired nursing educator*
Trokhan, Paul Dennis *technologist, researcher*

Cleveland
Blum, Arthur *social worker, educator*
Cosgrove, Delos M. (Toby Cosgrove) *health facility administrator, surgeon*
Freire, Gloria Medonis *social worker*
Kohn, Mary Louise Beatrice *nurse*
Rothstein, Fred C. *health facility administrator*
Siedlecki, Sandra Lee *nursing educator, researcher*

Columbus
Duckworth, Winston Howard *researcher*
Fawcett, Sherwood Luther *lab administrator*
Guglielmi, Rhonda E. *nursing administrator*
Meezan, William Alan *social work educator, consultant*
Schuller, David Edward *cancer center administrator, otolaryngologist*
Sims, Richard Lee *retired hospital administrator*
Stevenson, Joanne Sabol *nursing educator, consultant, retired dean*

Coshocton
McGinnis, Tammy Marie *health services manager*

Dayton
Gladden, Robert Wiley *healthcare executive*
Nixon, Charles William *retired acoustician*

Dover
Haggis, Mary Ripley *nurse, genealogist*

Dublin
Ford, Brendan A. *health facility administrator*
Labrum, Ronald K. *health facility administrator*

Eaton
Kisling, Fanny *counselor, educator*

Elyria
Myers, John T. *physical therapist, educator*

Fairfield
Zierolf, Mary Louise *nurse anesthetist*

Findlay
Stephani, Nancy Jean *social worker, journalist*

Independence
Van Kirk, Robert John *nursing case manager, educator*

Kettering
Peres, Frank J. *healthcare administrator*

Lancaster
Varney, Richard Alan *health facility administrator*

Mason
Clements, Michael Craig *health services consulting executive, retired renal dialysis technician*

Middletown
Gordon, Sandy Gale Combs *medical/surgical nurse*

North Olmsted
Semple, Jane Frances *health facility director*

Owensville
Seifert, Caroline Hamilton *community health nurse*

Ravenna
Turcotte, Margaret Jane *retired nurse*

Reynoldsburg
Odor, Richard Lane *mental health administrator, psychologist*

Sandusky
Runner, Jack Charles *health facility executive*

Sebring
Kelley-Hall, Maryon Hoyle *retired social worker*

Shaker Heights
Miller, Holly Dara *hospital administrator, physician*

Sidney
Leffler, Carole Elizabeth *retired women's and mental health nurse*
Menz, Robert L. *psychotherapist, minister*

Sylvania
Camp, Alice Ann *medical transcriptionist*

Tallmadge
Kaul, Mohan Lal *retired social worker, educator, writer*

Toledo
Ayoub, Judith Lorene *retired nursing educator*
Cavanaugh, Steven M. *healthcare company executive*
Francis, Barbara Joan *nurse, paralegal*
Lessick, Mira Lee *nursing educator*
Ormond, Paul A. *healthcare company executive*

Worthington
Bernhagen, Lillian Flickinger *retired school health consultant*
Lentz, Edward Allen *consultant, retired health administrator*

Wright Patterson Afb
Meccia, Neil Rocco *health facility administrator, physician*

Youngstown
Itts, Elizabeth Ann Dunham *retired psychotherapist, consultant*
Miller, Kenneth Lee *counselor, educator*

OKLAHOMA

Bethany
Alexander, Patrick Byron *hospital administrator*
Arbuckle, Averil Dorothy (Cookie Arbuckle) *healthcare facility administrator*

Broken Arrow
Muller, Patricia Ann *nursing administrator, educator*

Edmond
Laughlin, Monique Myrtle Weant *mental health counselor*

Frederick
Stone, Voye Lynne *women's health nurse practitioner*

Lamont
Covalt, Edna Irene *retired medical/surgical nurse*

Muskogee
Heck, Jennifer Leigh *neonatal clinical nurse specialist, educator*

Oklahoma City
Forni, Patricia Rose *nursing educator*
Jones, Renee Kauerauf *health facility administrator*
McClellan, Mary Ann *pediatric nurse practitioner*
McEwen, Irene Ruble *physical therapy educator*
Mustion, Alan Lee *pharmacist*
Nakagawara, Van B. *optometrist, researcher*
Resman-Targoff, Beth Holly *pharmacist, educator*
Spencer, Melvin Joe *retired health facility administrator, retired lawyer, retired consultant*

Tulsa
Bransford-Young, Angharad Ann *counselor, educator*
Carpenter, Nancy J. *health science association administrator*
Cherry, Andrew Lawrence, Jr. *social work educator, researcher*

Wilburton
Carey, Levenia Marie *counselor*

OREGON

Ashland
Masters, Robert Edward Lee *psychotherapist, sexologist*

Central Point
Brown, Christopher Patrick *health care administrator, educator*

Corvallis
Oldfield, James Edmund *retired nutrition educator*

Eugene
Acker, Martin Herbert *psychotherapist, educator*
Camp, Delpha Jeanne *counselor*
Peterson, Donna Rae *health facility administrator, gerontologist, director*
Weiss, Marianna Shrenger *psychotherapist*
Wilhite, Tamara Sue *public health service officer*

Florence
Van Horn, O. Frank *retired counselor, consultant*

Klamath Falls
Klepper, Carol Herdman *mental health therapist*

Milwaukie
Orloff, Barbara-Lee Marguerite Hewitt *retired social worker*

Pendleton
Smiley, Richard Wayne *researcher*

Portland
Korb, Christine Ann *music therapist, researcher, educator*
Loveless, Peggy Ann *social work administrator*
Shireman, Joan Foster *social work educator*

Redmond
Dey, Charlotte Jane *retired community health nurse*

Salem
Edge, James Edward *health care administrator*
Zumwalt, Roger Carl *hospital administrator, consultant*

Sandy
Jensen, Judy Dianne *psychotherapist, consultant*

PENNSYLVANIA

Acme
Babcock, Marguerite Lockwood *addictions treatment therapist, educator, writer*

Bala Cynwyd
Peret, Karen Krzyminski *health facility administrator*

Camp Hill
Crider, Rudyard Lee *psychotherapist*

East Stroudsburg
Henley, Richard James *health facility administrator*

Hamburg
Schappell, Abigail Susan *retired speech, language and hearing specialist, massage therapist, Reiki master*

Harrisburg
Bailey, Diandrea Michelle *rehabilitation services professional*
Cadieux, Roger Joseph *geriatrics services professional*

Hershey
Moskowitz, Jay *health science association administrator, educator, dean*
Paz, Harold Louis *hospital administrator, internist, educator*

Hulmeville
Jackson, Mary L. *health services executive*

Huntingdon Valley
Cohen, Michael R. *health facility administrator, pharmacist*

Kennett Square
Hager, George V., Jr. *health services executive*

King Of Prussia
Goldsmith, Eleanor Jean *retired hospital administrator*
Miller, Alan B. *hospital management executive*

Lancaster
Brunner, Lillian Sholtis *nurse, writer*

Lansdale
Bierman, Arnold *optometrist*
Nithoo, Rovindranath *pharmacist*

Lincoln University
Norris, Jo Anne Wareham *school counselor*

Mc Kees Rocks
Wardell, Tamara Lynn *critical care nurse*

Mc Keesport
Lodor, Marci Ann *dietitian*

Meadville
Steen, John *health policy company executive, consultant*

Mechanicsburg
Ortenzio, Rocco Anthony *health facility administrator*

Mount Pleasant
Morgan, Joyce Kaye *social worker*

Newtown Square
Garthwaite, Thomas Leonard *medical officer*

Northern Cambria
Fisher, Connie Marie *physical therapist*

Orwigsburg
Mason, Joan Ellen *nurse*

Philadelphia
Altschuler, Steven M. *health facility executive, pediatrician, gastroenterologist*
Borislow, Alan Jerome *hospital dental department chairman*
Butler, Marie Gladys *nursing educator*
Charney, Natalie J. *mental health services professional, educator, researcher*
Clarkin, John Francis *health care management executive*
Cooper, Richard Alan *health policy consultant*
DeVoe, Andrew *healthcare system executive*
Freeman, Ellen Wood *research professor*
Hynes, Virtner Gilmore *rehabilitation services professional*
Kumanyika, Shiriki K. *nutrition epidemiology researcher, educator*
Luz, Virginia Olivar *dietician*
McFadden, Cori Erin *psychotherapist, educator*
Muller, Ralph W. *hospital administrator*
Potter, Alice Catherine *medical technician*
Rogers, Joseph A. *mental health association administrator*
Shapiro, Paula *retired maternal/women's health nurse*
Solomon, Phyllis Linda *social work educator, researcher*
Williams, Sankey Vaughan *health services researcher, internist*

Pittsburgh
Bruno, Audrei Ann *nurse educator, administrator*
Fetterolf, Donald Edward *physician executive, consultant*
Fowler, Fred Joseph *human services manager*
George, John Anthony *health corporation executive*
Goldstein, Bernard David *public health service officer, educator*
Granati, Diane Alane *retired ophthalmic nurse*
Kuehm, Julie K. *nurse, educator*
Lenhart, Cheryl Hayes *nursing administrator, consultant*
Moore, Pearl B. *retired nursing educator*
Omiros, George James *medical foundation executive*
Pennell, Daniel Mark *researcher*
Romoff, Jeffrey Alan *healthcare executive*
Rudy, Ellen Beam *nursing educator*
Shin, Sungjae *nutritionist*
Wilson, Frances Helen *retired occupational therapist*
Zanardelli, John Joseph *healthcare organization executive*

Port Matilda
Holt, Frieda M. *nursing educator, retired academic administrator*

Pottstown
Coulter, Kathleen Marie *psychotherapist, consultant*

Reading
Bell, Frances Louise *medical technologist*
Sauer, Elissa Swisher *nursing educator*
Shultz, Lois Frances Casho *nursing supervisor*

Richboro
Maholic, Nancy L. *nurse*

Scranton
McKenna, Ann K. *nutritionist, educator*
West, Daniel Jones, Jr. *health care consultant, educator*

Spring House
van Steenwyk, John Joseph *healthcare plan consultant*

Swarthmore
Devin, Lee (Phillip) *researcher, consultant, dramaturg, author*

University Park
Mayers, Stanley Penrose, Jr. *public health service officer, educator*

Villanova
Haynor, Patricia Manzi *nursing educator, consultant*

Washington Boro
Snyder, John Jacob *researcher*

West Mifflin
Rosko, Maryann A. *nurse*

West Point
Grabenstein, John Douglas *pharmacist, military officer*

Willow Street
Keiser, Paul Harold *retired hospital administrator*
Wesbury, Stuart Arnold, Jr. *health science association administrator, educator*

Wynnewood
Anyanwu, Chukwuma Uchenna *clinical pharmacist, biomedical researcher*

Wyomissing
Gordon, Mildred Harriet Gross *hospital executive*

York
Alcon, Sonja L. *retired medical social worker*
Bartels, Bruce Michael *health facility administrator*
Rosen, Raymond *health facility executive*
Thomas, Tracey Williams *researcher*

RHODE ISLAND

Kingston
LaPlante, Kerry L. *pharmacist, educator*

Newport
Cicilline, J. Clement *mental health services professional, state legislator*
Woods, Donald E. *healthcare executive*

Pawtucket
Cheever, James Jefferson *counselor*

Providence
Kenna, George Anthony *pharmacist, researcher*
Mello, Kerry L. *pharmacist*
Price, William Walley, Jr. *counselor, artist*

Warwick
Horn, Donna M. *pharmacist, medical association administrator*
Richards, Priscilla Ann *medical/surgical nurse*

SOUTH CAROLINA

Aiken
Jefferson, Helen Butler *public health service officer*
Wright, G. Todd *lab administrator, director*

Bishopville
Miller, Blondell Stephenson *social worker, minister*

Columbia
Amidon, Roger Lyman *public health service officer, educator*
Houston, Kevin Todd *speech and language pathologist*
McLendon, Brian Andrew *lab administrator, educator*
Nagi, Samuel Njuguna *psychotherapist, director*
Seigler, Ruth Queen *college nursing administrator, educator, consultant, nurse*

Easley
Howe, Linda Arlene *nursing educator, writer*

Florence
Waddill, Cynthia Kay *orthopaedic nurse practitioner*

Gaffney
Griffin, Penni Oncken *social worker, educator*

Hilton Head Island
Wesselmann, Glenn Allen *retired health facility administrator*

Hopkins
Garrett, Robin Scott *health facility administrator*

Spartanburg
Jones, William Osborne, II, *physician assistant, nephrologist*

Summerville
Burke, Rhonda Williams *counselor*
Deavers, James Frederick *optometrist, clinical nutritionist*

SOUTH DAKOTA

Rapid City
Brookes, Leslie Joan *retired maternal/surgical nurse*
Corwin, Bert Clark *optometrist*

Sioux Falls
VanDemark, Michelle Volin *critical care, neuroscience nurse*

Vermillion
Sevening, Diane Kay *alcohol/drug abuse studies educator, researcher*

TENNESSEE

Antioch
Brown, Katherine Yvonne *occupational therapist, educator*

Bartlett
Huffman, D. C., Jr. *pharmacist, educator, health science association administrator*

Brentwood
Carpenter, William F. III *hospital management company executive, lawyer*
Chapdelaine, Perry Anthony, Jr. *public health service officer, preventive medicine physician, educator*
Smith, Wayne Thomas *healthcare company executive*

Camden
Jasper, Doris J. Berry *nurse*

Clarksville
Staivisky, Jeanne Louise *counselor, alcohol/drug abuse services professional*

Cleveland
Preston, Forrest L. *healthcare executive*

Cookeville
Reynolds, Barbara C. *retired mental health educator, dean*

Franklin
Fink, Robert Michael *pharmacist*
Miller, Dennis Edward *health medical executive*

Jackson
Seaton, Robert Lamar *pharmacist*

Jellico
Hausman, Keith Lynn *health facility administrator, physical therapist*

Knoxville
Adams, Gerald Dwayne *medical technician*
Brown, Patricia Ann *child health nurse*
Matteson, Karla J. *health science association administrator*
McGuire, Sandra Lynn *nursing educator*
Mc Hargue, Carl Jack *lab administrator*
Trout, Monroe Eugene *health facility administrator*

La Follette
Watson, S. Michele *school nurse*

Linden
Mitchell, Elizabeth Marelle *family practice nurse practitioner, medical/surgical nurse, nursing educator*

Memphis
Bargagliotti, Lillian Antoinette *nursing educator*
Carter, Michael Allen *nursing educator*
Diggs, Walter Whitley *health science facility administrator*
Shulkin, Barry *health facility administrator*

Nashville
Bolian, George Clement *healthcare executive, psychiatrist*
Brigham, Nicolette Bainbridge *special education services professional*
Brown, Tommie Florence *social work educator*
Brukardt, Gary A. *health facility administrator*
Buerhaus, Peter I. *nursing administrator*
Dalton, James Edgar, Jr. *health facility administrator*
Frist, Thomas Fearn, Jr. *hospital management company executive*
Johnson, R. Milton *healthcare executive*
Johnston, William P. *health facility administrator*
Kaiser, Allen Bernard *health facility administrator*
McNutt, Mona Belle *social worker*
Perlin, Jonathan Brian *health services company executive, former federal agency administrator*
Urmy, Norman B. *hospital administrator*

Oak Ridge
Jones, Virginia McClurkin *retired social worker*

Somerville
Macdonald, Sally Polk Bowers *retired addictions therapist*

TEXAS

Abilene
Kirby, D'Lyla *speech pathology/audiology services professional, educator*

Addison
Goldmann, James Allen *healthcare consultant*

Amarillo
Arnold, Winnie Jo *retired mental health nurse*
Meloro, Peggy Arm-Bosley *retired rehabilitation nurse, small business owner*

Arlington
McCuistion, Robert Wiley *hospital administrator, management consultant, lawyer*
Oehler, Judith Jane Moody *retired counselor*

Austin
Barrera, Elvira Puig *retired counselor, academic administrator*
Davis, Donald Robert *nutritionist, researcher, consultant*
Durbin, Richard Louis, Sr. *health facility administrator, consultant*
Fleming, Francine Faye *legal nurse consultant*
Golden, Kimberly Kay *critical care nurse*
Hayes, Patricia Ann *health facility administrator*
Kirk, Lynda Pounds *biofeedback therapist, neurotherapist, counselor*
Lansford, James Lowell *technologist*
Larkam, Beverley McCosham *social worker, marriage and family therapist*
Strassels, Scott A. *pharmacist, researcher*

Brenham
Dalrymple, Christopher Guy *chiropractor*

Bryan
Buckley, John Joseph, Jr. *healthcare executive*

Carrollton
Withrow, Lucille Monnot *nursing home administrator*

Cedar Hill
Findley, Milla Jean *nutritionist*

Chillicothe
Brock, Helen Rachel McCoy *retired mental health and community health nurse*

Colleyville
Donnelly, Barbara Schettler *retired medical technologist*

Copperas Cove
Hardin, Ann *marriage and family therapist*

Corpus Christi
Benepe, Virginia Lynn *medical/surgical nurse, oncological nurse, educator*
Wilkinson, Malcolm Doyle *retired pharmacist*

Dallas
Blair, Gary Wesley *pharmacist*
Bradley, John Andrew *health facility administrator*
Brown, Stephen F. *health facility administrator*
etter, Trevor *healthcare industry executive*
France, Newell Edwin *retired health facility administrator*
Harris, Hazel Lynn *medical/surgical nurse*
Hitt, David Hamilton, Sr. *retired health facility administrator*
Johnson, Murray H. *optometrist, researcher, consultant, lecturer*
Kangas, Edward A. *healthcare company and former diversified financial services company executive*
Madzik, Elizabeth May *hospital administrator*
Miller, Jo Carolyn Dendy *family and marriage counselor, educator*
Newman, Steven L. *health care executive*
Quinones, Marissa Escobar *pharmacist*
Schecter, Arnold Joel *public health physician, researcher*
Schochet, Barry P. *health care executive*
Solomon, Risa Greenberg *clinical social worker, child and family therapist, former entertainment industry executive*
Timpa, Vicki Ann *government health program administrator*
Wassenich, Linda Pilcher *retired health policy analyst, social worker*
Watson, Claude Armstead *counselor*
Wheeler, M. Cass *health science association administrator*

Denton
Brewer, Louie George, Jr. *blood bank specialist*
Surprise, Juanee *chiropractor, nutrition consultant*

Early
Ross-Parsons, Donna Michelle *counselor, small business owner*

Edinburg
Wilson, Bruce Keith *men's health nurse*

El Paso
Edmonds, Velma McInnis *nursing educator*
Flores, Yolanda *speech pathology/audiology services professional, consultant*
Hedrick, Wyatt Smith *pharmacist*
Jordan, Shannon Collen *medical/surgical nurse*
Juarez, Antonio *psychotherapist, consultant, counselor, educator*
Mitchell, Paula Rae *nursing educator, dean*
Moya, Eva M. *health services executive*

Fort Worth
Adams, Lavonne Marilyn Beck *critical care nurse, educator*
Robinson, Nell Bryant *nutrition educator*

Galveston
Munsell, Debra S. *physician assistant, educator*
Protas, Elizabeth J. *physical therapist, academic administrator*

Garland
Kemp, Pamela Jean *marriage and family therapist*

Georgetown
Smitheram, Margaret Etheridge *health facility administrator, director*

Grand Prairie
Solomon, Arthur Charles *pharmacist*

Helotes
Rojo, Ruth M. *nutritionist, consultant, director*

Hewitt
Wilson, Thomas W. *pharmacist*

Houston
Altman, William Carl *health facility administrator, industrial relations specialist, investment company executive, consultant*
Arcilla, Juanita R. *physical therapist*
Bahl, Saroj Mehta *nutritionist, educator*
Bates, Gwen Lee *health facility administrator, consultant*
Battin, R. Ray (Rosabell Harriet Ray) *audiologist, neuropsychologist*
Callender, Norma Anne *counselor, public relations executive*
Caskey, Caroline T. *lab administrator*
Davis-Lewis, Bettye *nursing educator*
Demory-Luce, Debby Kay *dietician, consultant*
Golinkin, Webster Fowler *healthcare executive, media consultant*
Gunn, Joan Marie *health facility administrator*
Hanrahan, Lawrence Martin *healthcare consultant*
Hawkins, Barbara Reed *mental health nurse*
Hempfling, Linda Lee *nurse*
Holmes, Harry Dadisman *health care administrator*
Johnson, Sandra Ann *counselor, educator*
Mallow Corbett, Stephanie *pharmacist, educator*
Montgomery, Denise Karen *nurse*
Moore, Lois Jean *health science facility administrator*
Peabody, Arlene L. Howland Bayar *retired enterostomal therapy nurse*
Potluri, Venkateswara Rao *medical facility administrator*
Reed, Kathlyn Louise *occupational therapist, educator*
Robbins, Susan Paula *social work educator*
Sawh, Ravi-Persad *lab administrator, researcher*
Shaffer, Anita Mohrland *counselor, educator*
Sherer, Jeffrey Todd *pharmacist, educator*
Shiao, Shyang-Yun Pamela K. *nursing educator, researcher*
Spikes, Patricia White *medical technologist*
Tervalon, Josephine M. *psychotherapist, social worker*
Tsui, Stephen Alan *researcher*
Vassilopoulou-Sellin, Rena *researcher*
Wagener, Christine Elizabeth *psychotherapist, educator*
Wallace, Mark Allen *hospital administrator*
Williams, Ella *healthcare educator*
Wilson, Gerald Everette *funeral services company executive*

Keene
Taroy-Valdez, Lolita B. *nursing educator, nurse*

Kingsville
Bleidt, Barry Anthony *pharmacy educator*

La Porte
Fotsch, George Bernard III *chemical addiction counselor*

Laredo
Chavez, Mary Rose *counselor, educator*

Livingston
Rauscher, Richard Conrad *psychotherapist, writer*

Lockney
Williams, Jamie Gaye *medical transcriptionist*

Lubbock
Brimée, Jean-Michel *physical therapist, educator*
Broselow, Linda Latt *medical office technician, aviculturist*
Feola, Mario *researcher*
Yoder-Wise, Patricia Snyder *nursing educator*

Mcallen
Arredondo, Jenna Dolores *speech pathology/audiology services professional*
Conrad, Philip Jefferson *social worker*
Ramirez, Linda Manning *counselor*
Tupper, Ron *public health service officer, finance educator*

Midland
Syed, Elizabeth Chance *health facility administrator, critical care nurse*

Panhandle
Sherrod, Lloyd Bruce *retired nutritionist*

Pasadena
Azuonye, Felix O. *pharmacist*
Kenagy, Cheri Lynn *nurse*

Plano
Becker, Doreen Doris *medical/surgical nurse*
Shelton, James D. (Denny Shelton) *hospital management company executive*

Port Arthur
Vinecour, Oneida Agnes *nurse*

Red Oak
Jones, Genia Kay *critical care nurse, consultant*

Richardson
Krauss, Henry Frederick, Jr. *optometrist*

Roanoke
Kleinkort, Joseph Alexius *physical therapist, ergonomist, consultant*

Rockwall
Johnston, Nicklett Rose *research nurse, clinical perfusionist*

San Antonio
Avant, Patricia Kay *nursing educator*
Blokzyl, Matthew Augustus *respiratory therapist*
Crabtree, Ben C. *neuromuscular therapy clinic director*
DeNice, Marcella Louise *counselor*
Downing, Jane Katherine *psychiatric nurse, lawyer*
Gonzalez, Hector Hugo *nursing educator*
Greenbaum, Yvonne Lee *medical/surgical nurse*
Robertson, Samuel Luther, Jr. *psychotherapist, educator*
Swansburg, Russell Chester *retired nursing educator, writer, consultant*
Vadlamudi, Ratna K. *healthcare educator*
Walsh, Nicolas Eugene *rehabilitation services professional, educator*

Smithville
Dearmin, Christopher Carl *medical technician*

Spur
Warren, Jennifer Elizabeth *family nurse practitioner*

Sugar Land
Heitzenrater, James F *hospital administrator*
Ritzen, Horst Reinhold *retired pharmacist*
Wagner, Donald Bert *health facility administrator*

Taylor Lake Village
Jenicek, Alicia Joanne *nursing consultant*

Temple
Hoffer, John Lee *health facility administrator, medical educator*

Texarkana
Bertrand, Betty Harleen *nurse*

Texas City
Mitchell, Susan Elaine *pharmacist*

Tyler
Mastern, Dean Scott *personal growth and development consultant*

Waller
Evans, Nancy Peltier *behavioral specialist, educator*

Woodway
Packard, Joyce Hornaday *retired counselor*

Zephyr
Lancaster, Carroll Townes, Jr. *health services executive*

UTAH

Centerfield
Parkin, Fern Agnes Marvel *medical/surgical nurse, nursing educator*

Ogden
Seager, Dauna Gayle Olson-Stokes *speech therapist*

Orem
Takke, Karyn Coppock *social worker, educator*

Provo
Luthy, Karlen E. *adult nurse practitioner, educator*

Salt Lake City
James, Brent Carl *health care executive, biomedical sciences educator*
Melton, Arthur Richard *public health administrator*
Wirthlin, Richard Bitner *researcher*

VERMONT

Burlington
Drizo, Aleksandra *researcher, educator*

Castleton
Leenman, Willem P. *mental health services professional, director*

East Thetford
Cummings Rockwell, Patricia Guilbault *psychiatric nurse*

Putney
Gill, Jane Roberts *retired psychotherapist, clinical social worker*

Shelburne
Mead, Philip Bartlett *healthcare administrator, educator, retired obstetrician*

Vergennes
Eric, Bechhoefer Robert *technologist*

VIRGINIA

Alexandria
Barnes, John D. *health science association administrator*
Gormley, Dennis Michael *research scholar*
Grachek, Marianna Kern *healthcare administrator*
Pastin, Mark Joseph *health science association administrator, educator*
Shern, David Len *mental health services professional, former dean*

Annandale
Abdellah, Faye Glenn *retired public health service officer*

Arlington
Hickman, Elizabeth Podesta *retired counselor*
Kerns, Wilmer Lee *researcher*

Blacksburg
Glasser, Wolfgang Gerhard *science researcher, educator*

Centreville
Malouff, Frank Joseph *health care association executive*

Charlottesville
Howell, Robert Edward *hospital administrator*
Wiggins, Barbara Sue *pharmacist, educator*

Chesapeake
Hudgins, Paul Granville *health facility administrator*

Clifton Forge
Miller, Catherine H. *nursing administrator, property manager*

Colonial Heights
Morgan, Barbara M. *psychotherapist, educator*

Crozet
Detmer, Don Eugene *health informatics, management and policy researcher*

Fairfax
Fitzgerald, Helen Teresa *social worker, writer*
Knee, Ruth Irelan *social worker, health care consultant*
Zhou, Qiuping *nursing educator, director*

Fairfax Station
Barringer, Joan Marie *counselor, educator, artist, writer*

Falls Church
Klingman, Charles David *health services researcher*

Farmville
Terry, Wayne Gilbert *healthcare educator, hospital administrator*

Hampton
Barrow, Irene Marie *speech pathology educator*

Lorton
Hunter, Cherye Renee *counselor*

Lynchburg
Pursley, Frank James *retired personal development specialist*

Mc Lean
Walsh, Marie Leclerc *nurse*

Newport News
Warren, Daniel Churchman *health facility administrator*

Norfolk
Davis, Russell Haden *psychotherapist, consultant*
Hartman, Deanna Mears *retired family counselor, addiction counselor*
Myers, Richard Brad *pharmacist, director*

Richmond
Ballentine, Ron *pharmacist, educator*
Balster, Robert Louis *alcohol/drug abuse services professional, researcher*
Barker, Thomas Carl *retired health facility administrator*
Bovender, Jack Oliver, Jr. *hospital management company executive*
Freund, Emma Frances *technologist*
Gandy, Gerald Larmon *rehabilitation counseling educator, psychologist, writer*
Griffith, William Herbert *retired psychotherapist, minister*
Johnson, Katherine Anne *health facility administrator, lawyer*
Neal, Gail Fallon *physical therapist, educator*

Roanoke
Kinzie, Brenda Asburry *counselor*
Klein, Deborah Rae *nurse*
Werner, Mark J. *healthcare executive, pediatrician*

Springfield
Dake, Marcia Allene *retired nursing educator, dean*
Williams, Cecilia Lee Pursel *optometrist*

Vienna
Kader, Nancy Stowe *nursing consultant, bioethicist, philosopher*

Virginia Beach
Carlson, James G. *healthcare services executive*
McDonald, Linda L. *massage therapist*
McWaters, Jeffrey L. *healthcare executive*

Williamsburg
Farrar, John Thruston *health facility administrator*
Ringlesbach, Dorothy Louise *retired nurse, writer*

Woodbridge
Flori, Anna Marie DiBlasi *health facility administrator, nurse, anesthesiologist*
Monaco, Anthony John *retired health facility administrator, writer*

WASHINGTON

Camano Island
Hartley, Celia Love *retired nursing educator, administrator, consultant, writer*

Centralia
Gimbel, Hervey Willis *public health physician, medical administrator*

Chehalis
Burrows, Robert Paul *optometrist*

Ellensburg
Carrothers, Carol Ann *special education services professional, educator*

Federal Way
Blywise, Barbara *mental health services professional*

Fort Lewis
Lubbers, Alice Dianne *operating room nurse*

Lynnwood
Lynch, Juneann M. *medical/surgical nurse, nursing educator*

Mukilteo
Atal, Bishnu Saroop *retired speech research executive, educator*

Oak Harbor
Miller, Robert Scott *clinical social worker, psychiatric hospital surveyor*

Port Angeles
Muller, Carolyn Bue *physical therapist, volunteer*

Seattle
Berni, Rosemarian Rauch *rehabilitation and oncology nurse*
Dear, Ronald Bruce *retired social work educator*
de Tornyay, Rheba *nursing educator, retired dean*
Hansen, Thomas Nanastad *hospital administrator, pediatrician*
Kates, Carolyn Louise *physical therapist*
Katz, Treuman P. *health facility administrator*
Loyer Nelson, Edith Merilynn *retired social worker*
Miller, Crystal Ann *respiratory therapist*
Monsen, Elaine Ranker *nutritionist, educator, editor*
Sellick, Kathleen A. *hospital administrator*
Thomassen, Pauline Frances *medical and surgical nurse*

Seaview
McNeil, Helen Jo Connolly *nursing educator, public health administrator*

Spokane
Baugh, Bradford Hamilton *occupational and environmental health advisor*
Cope, Kathleen Adelaide *critical care nurse, parish nurse, educator*
Iltz, Jason L. *pharmacist, educator*
Moon, Loretta Marie *recreational therapist*
Robinson, Herbert Henry III *psychotherapist, educator*

Tacoma
Maloney, Patsy Loretta *nursing educator*

Yakima
Simonson, Susan Kay *hospital clinical care coordinator*

WEST VIRGINIA

Charles Town
Starks, Doris N. *retired nursing educator, administrator*

Hedgesville
Boland, Gerald Lee *health facility administrator*

Morgantown
Collins, James William *health science association administrator, director, epidemiologist, mechanical engineer*

Parkersburg
Wilson, Roberta Bush *retired psychotherapist, accountant*

Ranson
Rudacille, Sharon Victoria *medical technician*

Wheeling
Good, Laurance Frederic *hospital administrator*

WISCONSIN

Columbus
Brinkman, Michael Owen *health care consultant, educator*

Eau Claire
Brill, Donald Maxim *researcher, educator*
Kirkhorn, Lee-Ellen Charlotte *community health nurse, educator*

Fond Du Lac
Christie, Jacqueline Ann *nurse*

Franklin
Stenzel, Mary Francis *social worker*

Green Bay
McIntosh, Elaine Virginia *nutrition educator*

Hudson
Sanders, Travis Allen *health facility administrator, director*

Lake Geneva
Lemke, Sherry Ellen *therapist*

Madison
Berven, Norman Lee *counselor, psychologist, educator*
Derzon, Gordon M. *hospital administrator*
Jacobsen, Kendra *health facility administrator*
Johnson, Jean Elaine *nursing educator*
Marlett, Judith Ann *nutritional sciences educator, researcher*

Milwaukee
Eshetu, Gwendelbert Lewis *retired social worker*
Neumann, Donald A. *physical therapist, educator*
Winters, Jill Mary *nursing educator, director*

Wauwatosa
Mancuso, Joseph Edward *medical psychotherapist*

WYOMING

Cheyenne
Laycock, Anita Simon *psychotherapist*

Jackson Hole
Farkas, Carol Garner *nurse, administrator*

Rock Springs
Thompson, Josie *nurse*

TERRITORIES OF THE UNITED STATES

GUAM

Mangilao
Duenas, Laurent Flores *health and nursing consultant*

PUERTO RICO

San Juan
Almodovar, Edna *pharmacist, educator*
Quinones-Burgos, Dayna *pharmacist, educator*

Santa Isabel
Lugo-Paoli, Luz Minerva *counselor, educator*

VIRGIN ISLANDS

Charlotte Amalie
Garfield, Winifred L. *nursing administrator*

Christiansted
Christian, Cora L.E *health facility administrator, physician*

CANADA

ALBERTA

Edmonton
Fields, Anthony Lindsay Austin *health facility administrator, oncologist, educator*

NOVA SCOTIA

Harbourville
Forsyth, George Lionel *psychotherapist, author*

ONTARIO

Etobicoke
Scholefield, Peter Gordon *health facility administrator*

Mississauga
Shivji, Khushnooda Amin *hospital administrator*

Toronto
Turnbull, John Cameron *retired pharmacist, consultant*

MEXICO

Alvaro Obregon
Sepúlveda Amor, Jaime *public health service officer*

BRAZIL

São Paulo
Riecken, Claudia *researcher, director*

ECUADOR

Quito
Wesberry, James Pickett, Jr. *retired anti-corruption specialist, management consultant, speaker, author*

ENGLAND

London
de Savorgnani, Adriane Aldrich *healthcare administrator, nurse*

JAPAN

Kyoto
Tsuji, Toshizo *hospital administrator, educator*

LATVIA

Riga
Lācis, Aris *health facility administrator, cardiac surgeon*

REPUBLIC OF KOREA

Seoul
Yoo, Vak Yeong *health facility administrator*

SWITZERLAND

Geneva
Heymann, David L. *public health service officer*
Kim, Jim Yong *public health service officer, preventive medicine physician*
Maglacas, A. Mangay *nursing researcher, educator*

ADDRESS UNPUBLISHED

Abbott, Regina A. *neurodiagnostic technologist, consultant, business owner*
Abu-Khalaf, Murad *researcher*
Achi, May Ifeoma *pharmacist, consultant*
Ackermann, Barbara Bogel *counselor*
Adair, Irmalee Traylor *social worker*
Aehlert, Barbara June *health facility administrator*
Agarwal, Sanjiv *nutritionist, researcher*
Alberts, Renée Miller *counselor, alcohol/drug abuse services professional*
Alford, Renee Marie *speech pathology/audiology services professional, educator*
Amabile, Celene *pharmacist*
Ambersound, Rochelle Lillian *retired social worker*
Anderson, Allamay Eudoris *retired health educator, home economist*
Anderson, Jack Roy *healthcare company executive*
Anderson, Linda Jean *critical care nurse, psychiatric nurse practitioner*
Aon, Frank Joseph Garcia *lab administrator, materials scientist*
Arcus, Sam George *social worker, educator, writer*
Arehole, Shalini *audiologist, educator*
Arking, Lucille Musser *nurse, epidemiologist, consultant*
Arnold, Janet Nina *health facility administrator, consultant*
Austan, Frank Acosta *clinician, educator*
Austin, John H. *health care administrator*
Babao, Donna Marie *retired community health and psychiatric nurse, educator*
Babitzke, Theresa Angeline *health facility administrator*
Baier, Edward John *retired public health service officer, industrial hygiene engineer, consultant*
Bailey, Jami Lea *pharmacist*
Baldwin, William Russell *optometrist, foundation administrator*
Ball, John Robert *healthcare executive*
Barahona, Francisco *researcher*
Barker, Virginia Lee *nursing educator*
Barud, Stephanie *pharmacist, educator*
Bass, Lynda D. *retired medical/surgical nurse, nursing educator*
Bast, Kenneth George *healthcare executive*
Baymiller, Lynda Doern *social worker*
Bear, Geraldine M. *nursing assistant, poet*
Becker, Nancy May *nursing educator*
Beckford, Omar Marien *researcher*
Belco, Karen Marie *cardiology nurse*
Bell, Susan Jane *nurse*
Benefield, Emily Anne *nurse, human services manager*
Berger, Miriam Roskin *dance therapist, educator*
Berman, Richard Angel *health facility administrator*
Berry, Sharon *medical/surgical nurse, legal nurse consultant*
Biegel, David Eli *social worker, educator*
Blake, Kimberly Bosworth *pharmacist*
Blomstrand, Doreen Kathryn *retired physician assistant*
Blonz, Edward Robert *nutritionist, biochemist*
Blumberg, Mark Stuart *health service researcher, scientist, director*
Bockius, Ruth Bear *nursing educator*
Bohanon, Kathleen Sue *neonatologist*
Boone, Donna Clausen *physical therapist, statistician, researcher*
Boresi, Joy Suzanne *pharmacist*
Borg, Ruth I. *home nursing care provider*
Bottone, JoAnn *health services executive*
Boyd, Mary Frances *retired school nurse, pastor*
Braun, Mary Lucile Dekle (Lucy Braun) *psychotherapist, consultant, counseling administrator, educator*
Brewer, Barbara Bagdasarian *nursing administrator*
Brodie, Alice Velma *health and ethics advocate*
Brosz, Margaret Headley *pediatrics nurse*
Brown, Barbara June *hospital and nursing administrator*
Brown, Billye Jean *retired nursing educator*
Brown, Geraldine *nurse, freelance writer*
Brown, Laima Adomaitis *art therapist, artist, writer*
Brown, Michael Robert *healthcare corporation executive*
Browne, Thomas Jeffrey *healthcare executive*
Bryant, Bertha Estelle *retired medical/surgical nurse*
Budnicki, Michael J. *nurse*
Burgess, Donna Angele *researcher*
Burke, Karen A. *medical/surgical nurse*
Butz, Jami Lipan *psychiatric pharmacy specialis*
Buzard, James Albert *healthcare management consultant*
Calabrese, Kirk Robert *medical transcriptionist*
Cameron, Joseph Alfred III *pharmacist*
Campbell, Edward Wallace *nutritionist*
Carpentieri, Sarah C. *neuropsychologist, researcher, clinical psychologist*
Carrera, Jaganath *acupuncturist, yoga educator*
Carson, Regina E. *healthcare administrator, pharmacist, educator, geriatric specialist*
Carter, Melva Jean *retired medical technician*
Cauthorne-Burnette, Tamera Dianne *family practice nurse practitioner, consultant*
Ceasor, Augusta Casey *medical technician, microbiologist, clinical laboratory scientist*
Centafont, Lucy Ann Alexander *occupational therapist, consultant*
Chalikian, Alice Beatrice *chiropractor*
Chang, Debbie I-Ju *health programs and research executive, director*
Chapman, Thomas William *hospital executive*
Charles, Luenda E. *public health service officer, researcher*
Chojnowski, Donna Applegate *cardiac nursing administrator, heart failure nurse practitioner*
Cholewka, Patricia Anne *nursing educator*
Chow, Rita Kathleen *nursing consultant*
Clark, David Joseph *pharmacist*
Cohen, Carolyn A. *healthcare educator*
Cohen, Lawrence Alan *health facility administrator*
Compton, Diane Groat *professional counselor, researcher*
Condry, Robert Stewart *retired hospital administrator*
Conte, Julie Villa *nurse, administrator*
Cooper, Eugene Bruce *speech pathology/audiology services professional, educator*
Couch, Daniel Michael *healthcare executive*
Cox, John Curtis *health facility administrator*
Cromwell, Florence Stevens *occupational therapist*
Culton, Paul Melvin *retired counselor, educational administrator, professor, interpreter*
Cunningham, Terence Thomas III *hospital administrator*
Dagenais, Simon *chiropractor, epidemiologist*
Daniel, Jonathan Alexander *chiropractor, educator*
Daniels, Lydia M. *health care administrator*
Davenport, Ann Adele Mayfield *retired home care agency administrator*
Davis, June Fiksdal *medical facility owner, flor designer*

Davis, Margaret Thacker *retired critical care, medical and surgical nurse*
Davis, Samuel *hospital administrator, educator, consultant*
Dean, Rosemarie Denise *medical transcription supervisor*
De Antoni, Edward Paul *lab administrator*
DeBrincat, Susan Jeanne *nutritionist*
Deiro, Judith Anne *chemical dependency educator*
DeLapp, Tina Davis *retired nursing educator*
Desilets, Alicia R. *pharmacist, educator*
Dickens, Joyce Rebecca *addictions therapist, educator*
Dillon Rydman, Linda Gay *nurse, consultant*
Dimaira, Ann B. *medical/surgical nurse*
Dincecco, Jennie Elizabeth Williams Swanson *healthcare administrator, mentor, educator, volunteer*
Diorio, Eileen Patricia *retired medical technologist, philosophy educator*
Doberenz, Alexander R. *retired nutrition educator, chemist*
Douglas, Janice Green *physician, educator*
Drews, Jürgen *pharmaceutical researcher*
Dudley, Thora Louise *rehabilitation services professional*
Duel, Ward Calvin *retired healthcare consultant*
Duerksen, George Louis *music therapist, educator*
Dumas, Sandra Lee *medical technician, microbiologist*
Dyer, Wayne Walter *psychologist, writer, radio and television personality*
Dy-Liacco, Gabriel S. *psychotherapist, social sciences educator*
Eaton, Shirley M. *medical/surgical nurse*
Edelsberg, Sally Comins *retired physical therapist, educator*
Edelstein, Rosemarie (Hublou) *medical, surgical and geriatric nurse, educator*
Ehret, Megan J. *pharmacist, educator*
Eimers, Jeri Anne *retired counselor*
Eltayeb, Emil *pharmacist, researcher*
English, Patricia Dorzell *women's health nurse practitioner*
Erenstein, Alan *emergency nurse practitioner, nursing consultant*
Fernandez, Margaret J. *pharmacist*
Fields, Velma Archie *medical/surgical nurse*
Fierman, Ella Yensen *retired psychotherapist*
Finley, Sarah Maude Merritt *retired social worker*
Fischer, Carl Robert *retired health facility administrator*
Flanagan, Nancy A. *nursing educator, researcher*
Fleksher, Cassandra C. *psychology and research rehabilitation professional*
Floyd, William R. *former health facility administrator*
Fogelman, Ann Florence *nutrition consultant, educator, researcher*
Fondiller, Shirley Hope Alperin *nursing educator, journalist, historian*
Foran, Jessica Lea *veterinary technician, educator*
Ford-Reed, Lillie Mae *geriatrics services professional*
Forson, Heather Leah *physician assistant*
Fountain, Linda Kathleen *health science association executive*
Fralix Gold, Carolyn M. *medical/surgical nurse, educator, consultant*
Frank, Dennis *psychotherapist, educator*
Frederick-Mairs, T(hyra) Julie *administrative health services official*
Frenzel, Frances Johnson *nurse, educator, real estate broker, poet*
Friedman, Kenni *health facility administrator, councilman*
Fristoe, Macalyne *speech pathology/audiology services professional, psychologist, educator, writer*
Fuke, Dawn C. *clinical pharmacy specialist*
Fulton, Conchetta White *pharmacist, educator*
Gable, Karen Elaine *retired healthcare educator*
Gabriel, Judith A. *bodywork therapist, educator, writer*
Gallaher, Frederick Blake *emergency mgmt. specialist*
Gandhi, Sandip R. *pharmacist*
Garcia y Carrillo, Martha Xochitl *pharmacist*
Garland, Elsie M. *counselor*
Garner, Algean, II, *healthcare company administrator, consultant*
Garza, Cutberto *nutrition educator*
Gaudio, Maxine Diane *biofeedback therapist, stress management consultant*
Gavin, Mary Jane *retired medical/surgical nurse*
Geraghty, James D. *health science association administrator*
Gerry, Debra Prue *psychotherapist, recording artist, writer*
Gerstner, Mary Jane *nurse*
Giberson, Joan Alyne *retired school nurse practitioner*
Gimenes, Sonia Regina Rosendo *family therapist, psychologist*
Gladden, Vivianne Cervantes *healthcare consultant, writer*
Godager, Jane Ann *retired social worker*
Goldberg, Edwin *rehabilitation specialist, interfaith clergyman*
Goldberg, Lois D. *health facility administrator, disability analyst*
Gonzales, Richard Robert *counselor*
Gottlieb, Gary L. *hospital administrator*
Govan, Gladys Vernita Mosley *retired critical care nurse, medical/surgical nurse*
Graham, Garth N. *public health service officer, medical educator*
Graham, Jewel Freeman *social worker, lawyer, educator*
Graham, Olive Jane *retired medical/surgical nurse*
Grant, Richard Earl *retired medical and legal consultant*
Greenfield, Linda Sue *nursing educator*
Greggs, Elanora *social worker*
Grenier, Laura Margiotta *medical/surgical nurse*
Griffiths, Yolanda W. *occupational therapist, educator*
Grolli, Frank Thomas *retired pharmacist*
Gromacki, Susan Jean *optometrist*
Hall, Zach Winter *former health science association administrator*
Hammond, Robie Lee *health science association administrator*
Harbaugh, Janice M. *counselor, consultant*
Hardin, Bridgette Everhart *educational research analyst*
Haren, Elizabeth Gaye *counselor*
Harms, Nancy Ann *nursing educator*
Harrell, Richard Godwin *alcohol/drug abuse services professional*
Harris, Erica Renee *researcher*
Harwell, Denise *researcher*
Hayden, Paul Allan *speech pathology educator, consultant, researcher*
Hays, Patrick Gregory *healthcare executive*
Healy, Patricia Colleen *social worker*
Heatherley, James Lawrence *psychotherapist, educator*
Hegar, Rebecca L. *social worker, educator, consultant*
Henneman, Richard Bruce *counselor, pastor*
Henneman, Stephen Charles *psychotherapist*
Henry, Sue *retired social worker, educator*
Hertz, Kenneth Theodore *healthcare executive*
Hickman, Lucille *physical therapist*
Hicks, Allen Morley *retired hospital administrator*
Hines, Colleen M. *clinical nurse specialist*
Hodge, Shawna Marie *nutritionist, consultant, researcher*
Hoeben, Barbara J. *pharmacist*
Hofmann, Paul Bernard *healthcare consultant*
Holland, Rosemary Sheridan *program evaluation consultant*
Hollinger, Peggy Louise *elementary school counselor*
Holmes, Suzanne McRae *medical/surgical nurse*
Horsley, Heidi *psychotherapist, educator, radio personality*
Horvath, Annette *home care administrator*
Houtz, Duane Talbott *hospital administrator*
Howard, John W.S. *mental health services professional, alcohol/drug abuse services professional, theology studies educator*
Howe, John Prentice III *health facility administrator, physician*
Hsu, Donald I. *pharmacist, educator*
Huey, Constance Anne Berner *mental health counselor*
Hurley, Kathy Lee *mental health services professional, director*
Hutchinson, Edna M. *home care nurse*
Imeokparia, Remi *healthcare educator, department chairman*
Inscho, Jean Anderson *retired social worker, landscape artist*
Isong, Enó *public health service officer*
Jackson-Tkac, Stephanie Ann *nurse*
Jacobs, Arthur Dietrich *health services executive, educator, researcher*
Jacoby, Erika *social worker*
Janke, Norma E. *legal nursing consultant*
Jenai, Marilyn *psychotherapist*
Jenkins, Melanie Shun *dietician, counselor*
Jensen, Eva Marie *medical/surgical nurse*
Johnson, Doris Jean *social worker*
Johnson, Hazel Winifred *nurse, retired army officer*
Johnson, June Alexis *counselor, social worker*
Johnson, Nichole Sharese *school nurse practitioner, basketball coach*
Johnson, Sally A. *nurse, educator*
Johnson-Moran, Kelly Kathleen *health facility administrator, writer*
Jones, David Allen *retired health benefits company executive*
Jones, Jolene Rebecca *medical transcriptionist, educator*
Jones, Lisa Maria Draper *counselor*
Jones, Wayne Allen *psychotherapist, publisher*
Jones Tergeoglou, Beverly Gloria *special education services professional*
Jordan, Deovina Nasis *nursing administrator*
Joseph, Eleanor Ann *retired health science association administrator, consultant*
Kaemper, Laura Jean *medical transcriptionist*
Kahol, Kanav *researcher*
Kaiser, Nina Irene *healthcare consultant*
Kane, Jennifer Lynn *pharmacist, medical/surgical nurse*
Karp, Rosanne *oncology and women's health nurse*
Kelly, Lucie Stirm Young *retired nursing educator*
Kerr, Frederick Hohmann *retired health facility and academic administrator*
Kezlarian, Nancy Kay *marriage and family therapist*
King, Imogene M. *retired nursing educator*
King, Sheldon Selig *health facility administrator, educator*
Kohn, Jean Gatewood *retired health facility administrator, pediatrician*
Korshunov, Vyacheslav Slava A. *pharmacist, educator*
Kretchmar, Leslie *medical/surgical nurse*
Krishnamurthy, Kathiravan *research associate*
Kuhler, Deborah Gail *grief therapist, retired state legislator*
Kuo, Chun-Fang Frank *counselor, educator*
Lachapelle, Cleo Edward *retired social worker, real estate broker*
Laird, Cheryl F. *mental health services professional, paralegal*
Lamberton, Jacquelyn Edmunds *retired psychotherapist*
Landis, Donna Marie *nursing administrator, women's health nurse*
Laney, Marti Olsen *psychoanalyst, researcher*
Langenkamp, Sandra Carroll *retired human services administrator*
Lanterman, Jennifer L. *researcher, educator*
Lass, Diane *marriage and family therapist*
Latiolais, Minnie Fitzgerald *retired nurse, health facility administrator*
La Torre, Carissa Danitza *counselor*
Latta, George Haworth III *neonatal/perinatal nurse practitioner*
Law, Marcia Elizabeth *rehabilitation services professional*
Lee, Chava Cherta *psychotherapist, consultant*
Leigh, Vincenta M. *health administrator*
Leon, Nellie *health educator*
L'Eplattenier, Nora Sweeny Hickey *nursing educator*
Levin, Gilbert Victor *biotechnology company executive*
Lilly-Hersley, Jane Anne Feeley *nursing researcher*
Lindstrom, Rosetta Arline *retired medical technician*
Livingston, Vernon *retired health facility administrator*
Loarie, Thomas Merritt *healthcare executive*
Lofton, Kevin Eugene *medical facility administrator*
Logan, David Bruce *health facility administrator, nurse*
Lubic, Ruth Watson *health facility administrator, nurse midwife*
Luce, Donald Sanders *social worker*
Lutz, Tamara Jean *nursing consultant*
Lyngbye, Jørgen *hospital advisor, researcher*
Lysne, Allen Bruce *laboratory director*
Macera, Michelle Heffner *marriage and family therapist*
Mackay, Leo Sidney, Jr. *healthcare company executive, former federal agency administrator*
MacKenzie, Donald Murray *health facility administrator*
Madrid, Cirilo L. *health facility administrator*
Maiolini, Gloria J. *nursing case manager, poet, writer*
Majors, Nelda Faye *physical therapist*
Malks, Betty F. *social worker*
Maplesden, Carol Harper *marriage and family therapist, music educator*
Marcoux, Julia A. *midwife*
Mare, Jennifer Le *medical technician*
Martin, Karen Siebenthal *community health nurse*
Martin, Sarah Michael *pharmacist, educator*
Martin, William Collier *hospital administrator*
Materia, Kathleen Patricia Ayling *nurse*
Mates, Lawrence A., II, *medical company executive, consultant*
Matterson, Joan McDevitt *physical therapist*
McCall-Rodriguez, Leonor *healthcare services company executive, entrepreneur*
McCarthy, Rhoda Ann *retired nursing administrator, retired medical/surgical nurse*
McClintock, William Thomas *healthcare consultant*
McCuistion, Peg Orem *retired health facility administrator*
McEvoy, Lorraine Katherine *oncology nurse*
McKay, Michael Kevin *nurse, priest*
McKay, Paul Patrick *healthcare educator*
McNulty, Kathleen Anne *social worker, consultant, psychotherapist*
Mecklenburg, Gary Alan *hospital executive*
Melendez, Sonia Ivette *counselor*
Meng, Anne L. *pediatric nurse practitioner*
Mewani, Rajshree R.(amchand) *researcher*
Michael, Jerrold Mark *public health service officer, educator, retired dean*
Milewski, Barbara Anne *pediatrics nurse, neonatal/perinatal nurse practitioner, critical care nurse*
Milnor, Hazel *nurse*
Milunas, J. Robert *health care organization executive*
Miracle, Doris Jean *retired medical/surgical nurse*
Mitchell, Carol Ann *nursing educator*
Molaison, Elaine Fontenot *dietician, nutritionist, educator*
Momah, Ethel Chukwuekwe *retired women's health nurse*
Monck, Maureen F. *psychoanalyst*
Moore, Jean E. *social worker, academic administrator, educator, radio personality*
Morgan, Elizabeth K. *retired critical care nurse*
Morrison, Richard Drury *health policy consultant, medical educator*
Muñoz Dones De Carrascal, Eloisa (Eloise Munoz Dones) *hospital administrator, pediatrician, educator*
Murillo, Jose R., Jr. *pharmacist*
Murphy, Margaret A. *nursing educator, adult nurse practitioner*
Murray, Julia Kaoru (Mrs. Joseph E. Murray) *occupational therapist*
Myers, Charles Edwin *child therapist, educator*
Nadelson, Sandra G. *nursing educator*
Nardozzi, Peter Michael *pharmacist, clinical educator, lecturer, entrepreneur*
Nelson, Alice Carlstedt *retired nursing educator*
Nesbitt, John Arthur *recreational therapist, writer, educator, researcher*
Neumann, Forrest Karl *retired health facility administrator*
Nichols, Elizabeth Grace *nursing educator, dean*
Nickel, Janet Marlene Milton *retired geriatrics nurse*
Nidetz, Myron Philip *health care delivery systems consultant*
Nisbet, Toma A. *nursing administrator*
Nolly, Robert J. *pharmacist, educator, health facility administrator*
Norbeck, Jane S. *retired nursing educator*
Norkin, Cynthia Clair *retired physical therapist*
Norris, Mackie Lyvonne Harper *registered nurse, health care consultant*
O'Baire-Kark, Marika *nurse, educator, poet, writer*
Obot, Isidore Silas *public health service officer*
Oerter, Cynthia Lynn *medical technologist*
Olmsted, Jennifer *medical transcriptionist*
Onufrock, Richard Shade *retired pharmacist*
Paavola, Fred G. *pharmacist*
Paparella, Leon Ralph *psychotherapist, consultant*
Paps, Betty Lou *nursing educator*
Parham, Ellen Speiden *nutrition educator*
Parker, Joel Louise *nursing administrator*
Parks, Jean Anne *retired acute care nurse*
Patel, Tillian K. *critical care nurse*
Patton, Susan Oertel *clinical social worker, educator*
Penrod, Marian Penuel *wellness consultant, retired school librarian*
Peringian, Lynda Ann *dietician, writer*
Peters, Carol Ann Dudycha *counselor*
Phillips, Caroline L. *lab administrator*
Phillips, Shay E. *pharmacist, educator*
Pierce, John Thomas *physician, industrial hygienist, clinical toxicologist*
Pilous, Betty Scheibel *medical/surgical nurse*
Pipchick, Margaret Hopkins *advance practice psychiatric nurse, marriage and family therapist*
Plauche, Nancy Caroline *retired counselor*
Poe, Laura *nursing educator, administrator*
Prema, Nitya *marriage and family therapist, artist*
Quiala, Maribel *psychotherapist, consultant*
Raguckas, Sarah *pharmacist, educator*
Rahming, Etta Lorraine *social worker, consultant, psychotherapist, school psychologist*
Raju, Minnie M. *application analyst, critical care nurse*
Rajupalepu, Rahi K. *technologist, consultant*
Rand, Joella Mae *retired nursing educator, counselor*
Raphael, Carol *health care administrator*
Ray, Marilyn Anne *nursing educator, researcher*
Reck, Elizabeth Torre *social worker, educator*
Rehth, Ann *counselor*
Reilly, Robert Joseph *counselor*
Remkus, Connie Elaine *nutritional consultant*
Ribonson-Smith, Sonia Anthonette *counselor, mental health services professional*
Rice, Claretha Mayes *medical/surgical nurse, educator*
Richburg, Billy Keith *healthcare manager, consultant, entrepreneur*
Ridolfi, Dorothy Porter Boulden *nurse, real estate broker*
Rindone, Joseph Patrick *clinical pharmacist, educator*
Ritman, Barbara Ellen *counselor*
Ritter, Elise Dawn *therapist, clinical social worker, writer, artist, photographer*
Robinson, Gail Patricia *retired mental health counselor*
Rogalski, Lois Ann *speech and language pathologist*
Rogers, Elizabeth London *retired geriatrics services professional*
Rollins, Diann Elizabeth *occupational health nurse, educator, primary school educator*
Romano, Joseph Anthony *healthcare education and marketing consultant*
Roper, Sally Ann *health facility administrator*
Rowe, Melinda Grace *public health service officer*
Royce, Paul Chadwick *healthcare administrator*
Rubin, Phyllis Getz *health association executive*
Sabatini, Nelson John *healthcare executive*
Sabundayo, Beulah Perdue *pharmacist, researcher*
Sadow, Harvey S. *healthcare company executive*
Sahl, Jacob *retired technologist, secondary school educator, researcher*
Salerno, Sister Maria *advanced practice nurse, educator*
Saluko, Ayodelo V. *hospital administrator*
Samolyk, Keith Andrew *cardiovascular perfusionist, director*
Samples, Phil Lovin *pharmacist, military officer*
Sandorsen, Cassiopeia *public health service officer*
Santina, Dalia *nutritionist, writer, skin care specialist*
Savoy, Suzanne Marie *nursing educator*
Scala, James *health facility administrator, consultant, writer*
Scherer, Ronald Callaway *voice scientist, educator*
Schmidtke, Suzanne de Fine *retired social worker*
Schneider, Catherine Chemin *occupational therapist, consultant*
Schroeder, LaVerne *medical/surgical nurse*
Schutzer, Karen Ann *nurse*
Sciuva, Margaret W. *counselor*
Sears, Sandra Jones *medical/surgical nurse, consultant*
Seib, Billie McGhee Rushing *nursing administrator, consultant*
Shannon, Mary Lou *adult health nursing educator*
Shaughnessy, Allen F. *pharmacist, educator*
Shepherd, Douglas *hospital administrator*
Sikes, Michelle M. *health sciences scholar*
Silver, Audrey Wilma *nurse, educator, writer*
Simms, Maria Ester *health facility administrator*
Simon, Bernece Kern *retired social worker*
Simpson, Jack Benjamin *medical technologist, business executive*
Simpson, John Noel *health facility administrator*
Sims, Elizabeth LaNeal *retired healthcare association executive*
Skrocki, Edmund Stanley, II, *health fair promoter, executive*
Slaughter, Djuanique Naté *healthcare analyst, project manager, consultant*
Smaragdis, Paris *audiologist, researcher*
Smith, Connie *hospital administrator*
Smith, Kelly M. *pharmacist, educator, researcher*

Sneider, Joyce Pappachristou *dietician, educator*
Snyder (Mackley), Louise Marie *speech pathology/audiology services professional, consultant*
Somes, Joan Marie *emergency nurse practitioner*
Spalding, Diana Joelle *social worker*
Speer, Nancy Girouard *health facility administrator*
Spivey, Christina Alease *social worker, researcher*
Spottswood, Lydia Carol *nurse, health facility administrator*
Stadler, Selise McNeill *laboratory and x-ray technician*
Stash, Susan Michele *critical care nurse*
Stein, Sandra Therese *pharmacist*
Storm, J. Reni *nurse, consultant*
Stratton, Mariann *retired military nursing executive*
Suber, Robin Hall *former medical and surgical nurse*
Sugintas, Nora Maria *healthcare executive*
Svoboda, Janice June *nurse*
Swann, Charena Rai *psychotherapist, social worker*
Tack, Theresa Rose *women's health nurse*
Tanguay, Jeanne Marie *social worker*
Taylor, Edna Jane *retired employment program counselor*
Taylor, Nathalee Britton *retired nutritionist, freelance/self-employed writer*
Tepper, Morris *retired health science association administrator, mathematics professor*
Terry, Frances Jefferson *retired psychiatric nurse practitioner*
Thompson, Claire Louisa *nurse, educator, consultant, human services manager*
Thrasher, Rose Marie *critical care and community health nurse*
Tompkins, Christopher Paul *researcher*
Trager, D. David *retired pharmacist, consultant*
Trejos, Franklin Anthony *retired physician assistant*
Udrys, Almis Gerardas *health policy consultant*
Van de Bogart, Debra Scherwerts *medical/surgical nurse, researcher*
Vladeck, Bruce Charney *healthcare educator, former academic administrator*
Vogel, H. Victoria *psychotherapist, educator, writer, stress disorder and addiction recovery counselor*
Vogel, Susan Carol *nursing administrator*
Vohs, James Arthur *health plan administrator*
Waggoner, Kathleen Alice *psychotherapist*
Walker, Henry Gilbert *health care executive, consultant*
Wallskog, Joyce Marie *nursing educator, retired psychologist*
Walters, Farah M. *health services company administrator, former hospital administrator*
Warfel, M(artha) Kay *speech pathology/audiology services professional*
Watson, Easter Jean *psychotherapist, financial program consultant*
Watson, Robert Joe *retired health facility administrator, retired career officer*
Weickert, Wanda Opal *child welfare and attendance counselor, psychotherapist, educator*
Weil, Susan Ellen *dietician, consultant*
Weil, Thomas P. *retired health services consultant*
Weiner, Anne Lee *social worker*
Wetherbe, Herbert John *pharmacist*
White, Eugene Vaden *retired pharmacist*
Wieland, William Dean *healthcare consulting executive*
Williams, Elizabeth *human services administrator*
Williams, Freda Videll *speech pathology/audiology services professional*
Williams, Jatika *social worker, educator*
Williams, Shannon Renee *mental health services professional*
Wilson, Troy Lynn *technologist*
Wish, LeslieBeth Berger *psychotherapist, writer, management consultant*
Wissel-Littmann, Jeffrey G. *health facility executive*
Wolfberg, Melvin Donald *optometrist, educational association administrator, consultant*
Woteki, Catherine Ellen *nutritionist*
Wright, Dell *residential care and treatment facility executive*
Wu, Li-Tzy *alcohol/drug abuse services professional, researcher*
Yadeka, Theophilus Adeniyi *hospital administrator*
Yadrick, Robert Martin *occupational analyst*
Yale (Yeleyenide-Yale), Melpomene Fotine *researcher, anthropologist, archaeologist, art historian, conservator*
Yarbrough, Kathryn Davis *public health nurse*
Youngblood, Sylvia T. *counselor*
Zimmerman, Jo Ann *retired health science association administrator, educator, retired lieutenant governor*

HEALTHCARE: MEDICINE

UNITED STATES

ALABAMA

Alabaster
Counce, Diane Ryder *neurologist, researcher*

Auburn
Parsons, Daniel Lankester *pharmaceutics educator*

Birmingham
Adkison, David Paul *orthopedic surgeon*
Andrews, James R. *orthopedic surgeon*
Bittner, Vera *cardiologist*
Bloomer, Joseph Robert *physician, educator*
Bonatz, Ekkehard *hand surgeon*
Briggs, Dick Dowling, Jr. *physician, educator*
Bueschen, Anton Joslyn *physician, educator*
Caulfield, James Benjamin *pathologist, educator*
Childs, Alex Joseph *gynecologist*
Clayton, Orville Woolford *surgeon*
Cooper, Max Dale *pediatrician, researcher*
Curtis, John J. *medical educator*
Dhall, Rohit *neurologist*
Diethelm, Arnold Gillespie *surgeon*
Elewski, Boni Elizabeth *dermatologist, educator*
Finley, Wayne House *medical educator*
Fisher, Winfield Stitt III *medical educator*
Fleming, William Cary *retired physician, consultant*
Hedden, William James *plastic surgeon*
Hirschowitz, Basil Isaac *physician*
Johnston, Carden *emergency physician, pediatrician, educator*
Kimberly, Robert Parker *medical educator*
Kirby, Russell Stephen *epidemiologist, researcher, geographer*
Kirchner, John Shirk *orthopedic surgeon*
Klein, Michael J. *pathologist, surgeon*
Koopman, William James *medical educator, internist, immunologist*
Meezan, Elias *pharmacologist, educator*
Moturi, Sricharan *psychiatrist*
Nielsen, Vance Girard *anesthesiologist, researcher*
Oakes, Walter Jerry *pediatric neurosurgeon*
Omura, George Adolf *medical oncologist*
Oparil, Suzanne *cardiologist, educator, researcher*
Persaud, Tarek O. *ophthalmologist*
Pittman, Constance Shen *endocrinologist, educator*
Pittman, James Allen, Jr. *endocrinologist, educator*
Rich, Robert Regier *physician, medical educator, immunologist*
Russell, Richard Olney, Jr. *retired cardiologist*
Sibley, David Hurley *cardiologist*
Siegel, Herrick Jove *orthopedic surgeon*
Stevenson, Edward Ward *retired otolaryngologist, surgeon*
Trigg, Jack Walden, Jr. *retired physician*
Vasconez, Luis Oswaldo *plastic surgeon, educator*
Volanakis, John Emmanuel *immunologist, rheumatologist*
Winstead, Nathaniel Scott *gastroenterologist*

Cullman
Morris, Sylvia June Burbank *retired physician*

Fairhope
Mozley, Paul David *retired obstetrics and gynecology educator*

Florence
Eich, Wilbur Foster III *retired pediatrician*

Huntsville
Huber, Donald Simon *physician*
Laughlin, Edward Humes *surgeon, educator*
Nuessle, William Raymond *surgeon*

Mobile
Barik, Sailen *biomedical scientist, educator*
Brogdon, Byron Gilliam *radiologist, educator*
Guarino, Anthony Michael *pharmacologist, educator, consultant, counselor*
Hariadi, John Wesley *otolaryngologist, surgeon*
Littleton, Jesse Talbot III *radiology educator*
Pitcock, James Kent *otolaryngologist*
Rodning, Charles Bernard *surgeon*
Scantlebury, Velma Patricia *surgeon*
Shuayto, Marwan Ibrahim *neurologist*
Smith, Jesse Graham, Jr. *dermatologist, educator*

Montgomery
Myers, Ira Lee *physician*

Orange Beach
Conrad, Marcel Edward *hematologist, oncologist, educator*

Tuscaloosa
Keeton, J. E. *retired psychiatrist*
Pieroni, Robert Edward *internist, educator, military officer*
Sinclair, Robert Ewald *retired physician*

Tuskegee Institute
Casimire-Etzioni, Athema Louise *veterinary pathologist*

Vestavia
Nuckols, Frank Joseph *psychiatrist*

ALASKA

Anchorage
Christensen, Ronald E. *physician*
Etzel, Ruth Ann *pediatrician, epidemiologist, educator*
Mills, William James, Jr. *orthopedist, surgeon, researcher*

ARIZONA

Gilbert
Eitner, James William *physician, medical consultant, administrator*

Green Valley
Bachman, David Christian *orthopedic surgeon*
Forsyth, Garyfallia Lillian *nurse educator*
Moser, Robert Harlan *internist, educator, writer*
Reichlin, Seymour *endocrinologist, educator*

Lake Havasu City
Livingstone, E. Franklin *rehabilitation physician, director*

Mesa
Cooley, Jack Crain *cadriovascular surgeon*
Cox, Heidi Pinkerton *pediatric surgeon*
Hagen, Nicholas Stewart *medical educator, consultant*

Oro Valley
Abbassian, Assad *urologist*

Paradise Valley
Burkholder, Peter Miller *retired physician, educator*
Cohen, Robert *plastic surgeon*
Lorenzen, Robert Frederick *ophthalmologist*
Targovnik, Selma E. Kaplan *dermatologist*

Phoenix
Ammon, John Richard *anesthesiologist*
Charlton, John Kipp *pediatrician*
Dib, Nabil *cardiologist, researcher*
Diethrich, Edward Bronson *heart institute executive, cardiovascular surgeon*
Friedman, Shelly Arnold *cosmetic surgeon*
Guerra, Aldo Benjamin *plastic and cosmetic surgeon*
Heppell, Jacques Philippe *surgeon, educator*
Jacobsen, William M. *plastic surgeon*
Johnson, Mystie L. *obstetrician, gynecologist, department chairman*
Khan, Mohammed Yousuf *physician, consultant*
Laufer, Nathan *cardiologist*
Lovett, William Lee *surgeon*
Patel, Naresh Pratap *medical educator, physician, consultant*
Pershad, Ashish *cardiologist*
Reed, Wallace Allison *anesthesiologist*
Sage, Webster LeGene, Jr. *ophthalmologist*
Shortliffe, Edward Hance *internist, medical educator, computer scientist*
Singer, Jeffrey Alan *surgeon*
Teague, Robert Cole *physician*
Zerella, Joseph T. *retired pediatric surgeon*

Prescott
Garcia-Buñuel, Luis *neurologist*

Rio Verde
Culligan, John Austin *thoracic surgeon*

Scottsdale
Bradway, John Kent *orthopedist*
Dahl, Mark Victor *dermatologist, educator*
Dean, Bruce Linton *radiologist*
Evans, Tommy Nicholas *obstetrician, gynecologist, educator*
Gregory, Robert Erb *surgeon*
Harrison, Nedra Joyce *surgeon*
Kathuria, Rajeev S. *cardiovascular surgeon, thoracic surgeon*
Kinney, Carolyn *physician*
Lewis, John Christopher *allergist*
Orford, Robert Raymond *physician, consultant*
Parish, James Michael *medical educator*
Parson, Shaun D. *plastic surgeon*
Reznick, Richard Howard *pediatrician*
Roarke, Michael Charles *medical educator, nuclear medicine physician*
Sanderson, David R. *physician*
Sheridan, Donald Charles *orthopedist, hand surgeon*
Shors, Clayton Marion *retired cardiologist*
Tazelaar, Henry Dale *physician, educator*
Underwood, Paul Lester *cardiologist*
Watkins, Eugene Leonard *surgeon, educator*

Sedona
Briney, Allan King *retired radiologist*
Hawkins, David Ramon *psychiatrist, writer, researcher, spiritual teacher*

Sells
Ostrum, Robert F. *orthopaedic surgeon*

Sun City
Nicchi, Vincent, Jr. *cardiologist*

Tempe
Anand, Suresh Chandra *physician*
Schneller, Eugene Stewart *health administration and policy educator*

Tubac
Pardue, A. Michael *retired plastic and reconstructive surgeon*

Tucson
Ablin, Richard Joel *immunologist, educator*
Addis, Ilana Beth *obstetrician*
Ahern, Geoffrey Lawrence *behavioral neurologist*
Alberts, David Samuel *physician, pharmacologist, educator*
Alpert, Joseph Stephen *cardiologist, educator*
Anderson, Dayna *medical researcher*
Capp, Michael Paul *pediatrician, educator*
Corrigan, James John, Jr. *pediatrician, educator, dean*
Dalen, James Eugene *cardiologist, educator*
DeLuca, Dominick *medical educator, researcher*
Demeure, Michael J. *surgeon, researcher*
Ewy, Gordon Allen *cardiologist, researcher, educator*
Favre, Kelly Ann *surgeon*
Fishkind, William J. *ophthalmologist*
Foley, Louise *medical educator, retired military officer*
Galloway, James Malcolm *cardiologist*
Goldfarb, Robert Paul *neurological surgeon*
Graham, Anna Regina *pathologist, educator*
Grana, William A. *orthopedist, surgeon*
Harris, David Thomas *immunology educator*
Hattery, Robert Ralph *radiologist, educator*
Houser, Harold Byron *epidemiologist*
Katakkar, Suresh Balaji *hematologist, oncologist*
King, Joseph Willet *child psychiatrist*
Kischer, Clayton Ward *human embryologist, educator*
Larson, Jon M. *physiatrist*
Levenson, Alan Ira *psychiatrist, physician, educator*
Levine, Norman *physician*
Marcus, Frank Isadore *cardiologist, educator*
Martin, Loren Winston *allergist*
Meislin, Harvey Warren *emergency healthcare physician, professional society administrator*
Perry, Lewis Charles *emergency medicine physician, osteopath*
Quan, Stuart Fun *internist, educator*
Rietschel, Robert Louis *dermatologist*
Rogers, Lee Frank *radiologist*
Russell, Findlay Ewing *physician*
Ryan, Kenneth J. *immunologist, educator*
Shahidullah, Mohammad *medical researcher, medical educator*
Weil, Andrew Thomas *physician, educator*
Woolfenden, James Manning *nuclear medicine physician, educator*
Yurkanin, J. Paul *surgeon, educator*
Zheng, Wenxin *gynecologist, pathologist*

Yuma
Anderson, John Albert *physician*

ARKANSAS

El Dorado
Tommey, Charles Eldon *retired surgeon*

Fayetteville
Fink, William James *retired surgeon*
Hightower, Randall Dee *oncologist*
Nowlin, William B. *surgeon*
Parker, Lee Bryan *retired physician*

Fort Smith
Howell, James Tennyson *allergist, immunologist, pediatrician*
Snider, James Rhodes *radiologist*

Holiday Island
Pischke, Frank John *retired otolaryngologist*

Hot Springs
Kamel, Hosam Kamal *medical educator, researcher, geriatrician*

Jonesboro
Jones, Kenneth Bruce *surgeon*

Little Rock
Bissada, Nabil Kaddis *urologist, educator, researcher, author*
Brosnahan, Godela *nephrologist, medical educator*
Bruce, Thomas Allen *physician, educator*
Campbell, Gilbert Sadler *surgeon, educator*
Chahoud, Georges *medical educator, preventive medicine physician*
Frazier, Elizabeth Ann *pediatric cardiologist*
Hart, Ronald Wilson *radiobiologist, educator, toxicologist, business adviser*
Hough, Aubrey Johnston, Jr. *pathologist, physician, educator*
Hutchins, Laura Fulper *physician, medical educator*
Imamura, Michiaki *cardiac surgeon, pediatric and congenital cardiothoracic surgery*
Jansen, G. Thomas *dermatologist*
Jaquiss, Robert Douglas Benjamin *pediatric cardiac surgeon*
Lang, Nicholas Paul *surgeon*
Lucy, Dennis Durwood, Jr. *neurologist, educator*
Mehta, Jawahar Lal *cardiologist*
Metzer, Walter Steven *neurologist, educator*
O'Brien, Mark Stephen *pediatric neurosurgeon*
Olden, Kevin William *medical researcher*
Raza, Asim *psychiatrist*
Sotomora-von Ahn, Ricardo Federico *pediatrician, educator*
Ward, Harry Pfeffer *hematologist, retired academic administrator*

Scranton
Uzman, Betty Ben Geren *retired pathologist*

CALIFORNIA

Agoura Hills
deCiutiis, Alfred Charles Maria *oncologist, television producer*

Alameda
Whorton, M. Donald *physician, epidemiologist*

Aliso Viejo
Kizer, Kenneth Wayne *emergency physician, executive, educator*

Anaheim
Glazer, Sidney *physician, director*
Litvak, David A. *surgeon*
Yocum, Lewis Albert *orthopedist, surgeon*

Aptos
Miura, Masako Kusayanagi *retired dermatologist*

Arcadia
Baerg, Richard Henry *podiatrist, surgeon*

Arroyo Grande
Grisez, James Louis *physician, plastic surgeon*

Auburn
Henrikson, Donald Merle *forensic pathologist*

akersfield
wkins, Brandon James *podiatrist, surgeon*
ınes, Fernando *plastic surgeon, educator*
arma, Sanjiv *cardiologist*
), Jimmy Ong *embryologist*
inello, Irene M. *internist*

aldwin Park
ng, Mark I. *urologist, surgeon*

elmont
'is, Eldon Eugene *retired surgeon*

elvedere
allerstein, Robert Solomon *retired psychiatrist*

elvedere Tiburon
shman, Robert Allen *retired neurologist, educator, department chair*
offman, Julien Ivor Ellis *pediatrician, cardiologist, educator*

erkeley
bel, Carlos Alberto *immunologist*
ıffler, Patricia Ann *epidemiologist, educator, dean*
offin, Grange Simons *pediatrician*
rossman, Elmer Roy *pediatrician*
eingold, Arthur Lawrence *epidemiologist, educator*
mpelis, Constantine Harry *immunologist, educator*
inkelstein, Warren, Jr. *physician, educator*

everly Hills
boolian, Andre *plastic surgeon*
lessi, David Michael *surgeon*
llen, Howard Norman *cardiologist, educator*
lter, Gary *plastic and reconstructive surgeon, urologist*
rieff, Allen Ives *physician*
ao, Katherine Sung *pediatric cardiologist*
erger, Andre *plastic surgeon*
aster, Andrew Ian *ophthalmologist*
atz, Boris *endocrinologist, educator*
orbin, Frederic H. *plastic surgeon*
ein, William *ophthalmologist*
isher, (Donald) Garth *plastic surgeon*
olshani, S. Daniel *plastic surgeon*
riffin, Anthony *plastic surgeon*
aworth, Randal Digby *plastic surgeon*
adz, Bruce B. *plastic surgeon*
arpman, Harold Lew *cardiologist, educator, writer*
im, David Edwin *plastic surgeon*
lein, Arnold William *dermatologist*
otler, Robert *cosmetic surgeon*
i, Linda (Linda Jian-Yuh Li) *plastic surgeon*
Iarshak, Harry *plastic surgeon*
Ienkes, John Hans *pediatric neurologist*
Ioelleken, Brent Roderick Wilfred *surgeon*
'assif, Paul S. *facial plastic and reconstructive surgeon*
almer, Francis Roger III *plastic surgeon*
erlman, Jon Arthur *plastic surgeon*
ohost, Gerald Michael *cardiologist, medical educator*
ey, Robert M. *plastic surgeon*
osenthal, Richard Jay *psychiatrist*
udkin, George Henry *plastic surgeon*
yan, Frank Harry *plastic surgeon*
emel, George Herbert *plastic surgeon*
abak, Steven William *cardiologist*
uan, Robin Tsu-Wang *plastic surgeon*

orrego Springs
trong, John Oliver *plastic surgeon, educator*

urbank
enner, Andrew Ihor *surgeon*
chlaerth, John Burr *oncologist, gynecologist*
hao, Chonghao *neurologist, educator*

amarillo
aiman, Sarah *retired physician*

anyon Country
ivero, Luis Raul *aerospace physician, military officer*

anyon Lake
parks, Dale Boyd *allergist, health facility administrator*

arlsbad
hopra, Deepak *preventive medicine physician, writer*

armel
elch, William Campbell *internist, editor*

armel Valley
hapman, Robert Galbraith *retired hematologist, administrator*

erritos
ee, Jhemon Hom *physician*

hico
itter, Dale William *obstetrician, gynecologist*

hino
ee, Sung Ho *psychiatrist*

hula Vista
Albala, A. Ari *medical educator, director, psychiatrist*
Allen, Henry Wesley *biomedical researcher, consultant*
ohen, Elaine Helena *pediatrician, cardiologist, educator*

Claremont
ohnson, Jerome Linné *cardiologist, educator*
ang, Yao Liang *medical educator, researcher, surgeon*

Corona Del Mar
Tobis, Jerome Sanford *physician*

Coronado
Mock, David Clinton, Jr. *internist*

Culver City
Muller, Jenny Helen *physician, psychiatrist*

Dana Point
Fisher, Delbert Arthur *pediatric endocrinologist, educator, retired health facility administrator*

Davis
Cardiff, Robert Darrell *pathology educator*
Gardner, Murray Briggs *pathologist, educator*
Jensen, Hanne Margrete *pathologist, educator*
Kass, Philip Howard *epidemiology educator*
Palmer, Philip Edward Stephen *radiologist*
Rhode, Edward Albert *veterinary medicine educator, veterinary cardiologist*
Richman, David Paul *neurologist, educator, researcher*
Schaefer, Saul *cardiologist*

Delano
Salmassi, Sadegh *physician*

Downey
Hackney, Jack Dean *physician*
Perry, Jacquelin *orthopedist, surgeon*
Shapiro, Richard Stanley *physician*

Duarte
Margolin, Kim Allyson *internist, hematologist, oncologist*

East Palo Alto
Hantash, Basil M. *dermatologist, educator*

El Dorado Hills
Sparks, Robert Dean *medical administrator, gastroenterologist*

El Macero
Stowell, Robert Eugene *pathologist, retired educator*

Elk Grove
Forbes, Kenneth Albert Faucher *retired urological surgeon*

Emeryville
Fields, Howard Lincoln *neurologist, physiologist, educator*
Pao, Bing Shih *emergency physician*

Encino
Elkins, Brad S. *ophthalmologist*
Lesavoy, Malcolm Alan *plastic surgeon*
Rosner, Louis Joseph *medical educator*
Teplinsky, Joel Jack *plastic surgeon*

Escondido
McCarberg, Bill Harold *physician*

Folsom
Anderson, Jeffrey Lee *physician, anesthesiologist, consultant*
Ewing, Russell Charles, II, *physician*

Fountain Valley
Kieu, Quynh Dinh *pediatrician, not-for-profit developer*
Nguyen, Thanh-Van *otolaryngologist*

Fremont
Khalsa, Prabhjot Singh *neurologist*
Zandi, Iraj *plastic surgeon*

Fresno
Cunningham, Mark Alan *surgeon*
Joishy, Suresh K. *oncologist*
Leigh, Hoyle *psychiatrist, educator, writer*
Patton, Jack Thomas *family practice physician*

Fullerton
Sugarman, Michael *physician, rheumatologist*

Goleta
Zuk, Carmen Veiga *psychiatrist*

Grass Valley
Ely, Parry Haines *dermatologist, educator*

Greenbrae
Parnell, Francis William, Jr. *otolaryngologist*

Gualala
Ring, Alice Ruth Bishop *retired preventive medicine physician*

Half Moon Bay
Robertson, Abel L., Jr. *pathologist*

Hayward
Bachicha, Joseph Alfred *physician, educator*

Hemet
Mata, David Joseph *physician*

Hillsborough
Kraft, Robert Arnold *retired medical educator, physician*
Packard, Peter *retired internal medical educator*

Huntington Beach
Pineda, Anselmo *neurosurgery educator*
Welsh, William Daniel *geriatric medicine family practice physician*

Indian Wells
Hrabal, Antonin *physician, educator*

Inglewood
Dorr, Lawrence D. *orthopedic surgeon*
Zarif, Farid *internist, nutritionist*

Irvine
Chernock, Michelle Leigh *medical researcher*
Friedenberg, Richard Myron *radiologist, physician, educator*
Kohli, Gurmander Singh *plastic surgeon*
Miledi, Ricardo *neurobiologist*
Nalcioglu, Orhan *radiologist, educator*
Pal, Sukumar *immunologist, researcher*
Qin, Yufen *immunologist, researcher*
Quilligan, Edward James *retired obstetrician, gynecologist, educator*
Smith, Andrew Donald *plastic surgeon*
Werlin, Lawrence B. *obstetrician, gynecologist, endocrinologist*
Wong, Nathan Donald *medicine and epidemiology researcher, educator*

Kentfield
German, Donald Frederick *physician*
Schmid, Rudi (Rudolf Schmid) *retired internist, educator, academic administrator*

La Canada Flintridge
Byrne, George Melvin *physician*

La Crescenta
Riccardi, Vincent Michael *pediatrician, educator, entrepreneur*

La Habra
Estrada, Isabel Victoria *obstetrician, gynecologist*

La Jolla
Akiskal, Hagop Souren *psychiatric researcher, educator*
Atai, Manucher *retired surgeon*
Bailey, David Nelson *pathology educator, dean, academic administrator*
Blanchard, Daniel G. *cardiologist*
Blantz, Roland C. *nephrologist, educator*
Carmichael, David Burton *physician*
Chao, Edward C. *internist*
Chisari, Francis V. *pathologist*
Cleveland, Don W. *biomedical researcher*
Coden, Daniel Jay *ophthalmologist*
Covell, Ruth Marie *medical educator, academic administrator*
Dalessio, Donald John *internist, neurologist, educator*
Dillin, Andrew *medical researcher, educator*
Dimsdale, Joel Edward *psychiatry educator*
Dixon, Frank James *pathologist, educator*
Edgington, Thomas S. *pathologist, molecular and vascular biologist, educator*
Edwards, Charles Cornell *surgeon, medical association administrator*
Garland, Cedric Frank *epidemiologist, educator*
Gill, Gordon N. *medical educator*
Goldman, Mitchel Paul *dermatologist*
Hamburger, Robert N. *pediatrician, educator, consultant*
Han, Jiahuai *medical researcher*
Hofmann, Alan Frederick *biomedical researcher, educator*
Horner, Anthony Adam *pediatrician, educator*
Kaback, Michael *medical educator*
Katzman, Robert *neurologist, educator*
Klonoff-Cohen, Hillary Sandra *epidemiologist*
McKay, Dianne Brenda *nephrologist*
Mendoza, Stanley Atran *pediatric nephrologist, educator*
Miller, Scott R. *plastic surgeon*
Moossa, A. R. *surgeon, educator*
Nakamura, Robert Motoharu *pathologist*
Nyhan, William Leo *pediatrician, educator*
Rearden, Carole Ann *clinical pathologist, educator*
Reed, John C. *physician, researcher*
Rubenstein, Howard S. *physician, writer*
Rubin, Lewis J. *physician, researcher*
Schneider, Gerald L. *plastic surgeon*
Seagren, Stephen Linner *oncologist*
Silver, Dee Edward *physician, neurologist*
Singer, Robert *plastic surgeon*
Steinberg, Daniel *preventive medicine physician, educator*
Swain, Judith Lea *cardiologist, educator*
Tan, Eng Meng *immunologist, biomedical researcher*
Taupenot, Laurent *medical educator, researcher*
Taylor, Palmer W. *pharmacology educator*
Thompson, Charlotte Ellis *pediatrician, educator, writer*
Tsuang, Ming Tso *psychiatrist, educator*
Vogt, Peter K. *oncologist*
Walker, Richard Hugh *orthopaedic surgeon*
Wong, Wade Hwu *radiologist, educator*

La Quinta
Calvin, James Willard *thoracic and vascular surgeon*
Pitkin, Roy Macbeth *retired obstetrician, educator*

La Verne
McDonough-Treichler, Judith Dianne *medical educator, consultant*

Lafayette
Kang, Isamu Yong *retired nuclear medicine physician*

Laguna Hills
Lagrew, David Crutcher *obstetrician, gynecologist, medical association administrator, director*
Widyolar, Sheila Gayle *dermatologist*

Laguna Woods
Berk, Jack Edward *gastroenterologist, educator*
Ross, Mathew *medical educator*

Lancaster
Campano, Ruwanthi *surgeon*

Lemoore
Gerhard, H. John *orthopaedic surgeon, military officer*

Lincoln
Chong, Vernon *retired surgeon, military officer*

Livermore
Hah, Sang Soo *biomedical researcher*

Loma Linda
Bailey, Leonard Lee *surgeon*
Behrens, Berel Lyn *physician, academic and health facility administrator*
Bull, Brian Stanley *pathologist, educator*
Chan, Philip J. *medical educator*
Coggin, Charlotte Joan *cardiologist, educator*
Condon, Stanley Charles *gastroenterologist*
Herrmann, Paul C. *physician, chemist*
Llaurado, Josep G. *nuclear medicine physician, researcher*
Slater, James Munro *radiation oncologist*
Strother, Allen *biochemical pharmacologist, researcher*
Wareham, Ellsworth Edwin *cardiothoracic surgeon, educator*
Wood, Virchel Edgar *orthopedist, surgeon, educator*

Long Beach
Chiou, Shiun-Kwei *medical researcher*
Kwaan, Jack Hau Ming *retired physician*
Macer, George Armen, Jr. *orthopedic hand surgeon*
Molina, Joseph Mario (Mario Molina) *medical administrator*
Worcester, Howard Lester *internist*
Wu, Sing-Yung *physician, researcher*

Los Alamitos
Wu, Henry H. *urologist, surgeon*

Los Altos
Orman, Nanette Hector *psychiatrist*

Los Angeles
Alkalay, Arie L. *pediatrician*
Alkon, Ellen Skillen *physician*
Apt, Leonard *physician*
Apuzzo, Michael Lawrence John *neurological surgeon*
Aronowitz, Joel Alan *plastic and reconstructive surgeon*
Avidan, Alon Y. *physician*
Beart, Robert W., Jr. *colon and rectal surgeon, educator*
Bernstein, Sol *cardiologist, educator*
Bessman, Samuel Paul *pediatrician, educator, biochemist*
Black, Keith Lanier *neurosurgeon, educator*
Blahd, William Henry *nuclear medicine physician, director*
Bodey, Bela *immunologist, pathologist, oncologist*
Bondareff, William *psychiatrist, educator*
Borenstein, Daniel Bernard *psychiatrist, educator*
Brackmann, Derald E. *otolaryngologist*
Braunstein, Glenn David *physician, educator*
Catlin, Don H. *molecular pharmacologist, educator*
Chandor, Stebbins Bryant *pathologist*
Cherry, James Donald *pediatrician*
Chopra, Inder Jit *endocrinologist*
Chu, Robert Lance *physician*
Chuong, Cheng-Ming *pathologist, educator*
Clemente, Carmine Domenic *anatomist, educator*
Coates, Thomas J. *medical association administrator*
Cook, Ian Ainsworth *psychiatrist, researcher, educator*
Cote, Richard James *pathologist, researcher*
Danoff, Dudley Seth *surgeon, urologist*
Davidson, Ezra C., Jr. *obstetrician, gynecologist, academic administrator, educator*
Detels, Roger *epidemiologist, retired dean*
Diamond, Jason Brett *facial plastic surgeon, otolaryngologist*
Don, Manuel *medical researcher*
Edgerton, Bradford Wheatly *plastic surgeon*
Edween, Julie *plastic surgeon*
Ellenbogen, Richard *plastic surgeon*
Engel, Jerome, Jr. *neurologist, neuroscientist, psychiatry professor*
Engel, William King *neurologist, educator*
Enstrom, James Eugene *epidemiologist*
Eo, SuRak *plastic surgeon, educator*
Ettenger, Robert Bruce *physician, pediatric nephrologist*
Farias-Eisner, Robin P. *gynecologic oncologist, educator*
Feig, Stephen Arthur *pediatrician, preventive medicine physician, hematologist, oncologist, educator*
Feng, Lei *medical researcher*
Figlin, Robert Alan *hematologist, oncologist*
Fincher, Edgar Franklin *dermatologic surgeon*
Fodor, Peter Bela *plastic surgeon, educator*
Fonkalsrud, Eric Walter *pediatric surgeon, educator*
Forrester, James Stuart *cardiologist, medical educator*
Francis, Charles K. *medical educator*
Gabriel, Ronald Samuel *child neurologist*
Ganz, Patricia Anne *medical educator, physician*
Gatti, Richard A. *medical educator, medical geneticist*
Geller, Kenneth Allen *otolaryngologist*
Geller, Stephen Arthur *pathologist, educator*
Gewertz, Bruce Labe *surgeon, educator*
Goin, Marcia Kraft *physician*
Gonick, Harvey Craig *nephrologist, educator*
Goodwin, Scott Craig *interventional radiologist*
Gorney, Roderic *psychiatrist, educator*
Grody, Wayne William *physician, educator*
Haywood, L. Julian *cardiologist, educator*
Hecht, Joel Randolph *oncologist*
Henriksen, Eva Hansine *retired anesthesiology educator*
Hirai, Denitsu *surgeon*

Hirsch, Anthony Terry *physician*
Hoang, Duc Van *pathologist, educator*
Hodis, Howard Neil *medical educator*
Hohn, Arno R. *pediatric cardiologist*
Hollander, Daniel *gastroenterologist, educator*
Horwitz, David A. *rheumatologist, educator*
House, John William *otolaryngologist*
Hubbell, Wayne Lester *ophthalmologist, educator, chemist, educator*
Hyde, Manly Richard *thoracic surgeon*
Ignarro, Louis J. *pharmacology educator*
IsHak, Waguih William *psychiatrist*
Jacobson, Edwin James *medical educator*
Jadvar, Hossein *nuclear medicine physician, biomedical engineer*
Jalali, Behnaz *psychiatrist, educator*
Jobe, Frank Wilson *orthopedic surgeon*
Johnson, Cage Saul *hematologist, educator*
Kahn, Fredrick Henry *retired internist*
Kamil, Elaine Scheiner *pediatric nephrologist, educator*
Kapoor, Vishal *plastic surgeon*
Kaufman, Francine R. *pediatric endocrinologist*
Kaunitz, Jonathan Davidson *physician*
Kelly, Arthur Paul *physician*
Kent, Dolores *obstetrician, gynecologist, plastic surgeon*
Kim, Kwang-Jin *medical educator*
Kleeman, Charles Richard *nephrologist, educator, researcher*
Kobashigawa, Jon Akira *internist, cardiologist, researcher, educator*
Kramer, Barry Alan *psychiatrist, educator*
Lawrence, Sanford Hull *physician, immunochemist, author*
Lazareff, Jorge Antonio *neurosurgeon, researcher*
Liberman, Robert Paul *psychiatry educator, researcher, writer*
Macavinta-Tenazas, Gemorsita *physician*
Maloney, Robert Keller *ophthalmologist, medical educator*
Mani, Marc *plastic surgeon*
Marjoram, Paul *medical educator, researcher*
Martinez, Miguel Acevedo *urologist, consultant, lecturer*
McFadden, P. Michael *physician, surgeon*
Mellinkoff, Sherman Mussoff *medical educator*
Mihan, Richard *retired dermatologist*
Miller, Timothy Alden *plastic and reconstructive surgeon*
Miranda, M. Jeanne *psychiatrist*
Mondino, Bartly J. *ophthalmologist*
Morgan, Elizabeth *plastic surgeon*
Morgan, Marshall T. *emergency physician*
Motykie, Gary *plastic surgeon*
Moxley, John Howard III *internist*
MoY, Ronald Leonard *dermasurgeon*
Murphree, A. Linn *ophthalmologist*
Nakra, Tanuj *plastic surgeon*
Natale, Ronald Bruno *oncologist*
Nelson, Marvin Dale, Jr. *radiologist, educator*
Nissenson, Allen Richard *physician, educator*
Noble, Ernest Pascal *pharmacologist, biochemist, educator, psychiatrist*
Oyeyipo, Bolanle T. *geriatrician*
Parmelee, Arthur Hawley, Jr. *pediatric medical educator*
Pi, Edmond Hsin-Tung *psychiatry educator*
Poa, Li *cardiac surgeon*
Qiao, Jian-Hua *pathologist, researcher*
Ramanathan, Rangasamy *pediatrician*
Rao, Narsing A. *ophthalmologist, pathologist, educator*
Reinisch, John Ferdinand *plastic surgeon, educator*
Reynolds, Charles Patrick *pediatric oncologist, researcher*
Rimoin, David Lawrence *medical geneticist*
Rodriguez, Ensor *physician, scientist, writer*
Roven, Alfred Nathan *surgeon*
Rubin, Robert Terry *psychiatrist, researcher, educator*
Ryan, Stephen Joseph, Jr. *ophthalmologist, educator*
Sarnat, Bernard George *plastic surgeon, educator, researcher*
Scheibel, Arnold Bernard *psychiatrist, educator, research director*
Schelbert, Heinrich Ruediger *nuclear medicine physician*
Schwarz, Ernst Ruediger *cardiologist, researcher*
Shen, Wei-Chiang *medical educator*
Sherman, Randolph *plastic and reconstructive surgeon, educator*
Shields, William Donald *physician, educator*
Siegel, Michael Elliot *nuclear medicine physician, educator*
Siegel, Sheldon C. *pediatrician, immunologist, allergist*
Siegel, Stuart Elliott *pediatric oncologist, educator*
Skaggs, David L. *orthopedist, educator*
Smith, Chadwick Fitzhugh *orthopaedic surgeon, educator*
Solomon, David Harris *geriatrician, educator*
Stein, James Eric *pediatric surgeon*
Stern, Mariana Carla *epidemiologist, educator*
Stiehm, E. Richard *pediatrician, educator*
Straatsma, Bradley Ralph *ophthalmologist, educator*
Streeter, Oscar Edward, Jr. *radiation oncologist*
Sullivan, Stuart Francis *anesthesiologist, educator*
Sutterby, Larry Quentin *internist*
Tabachnick, Norman Donald *psychiatrist, educator*
Takahashi, Masato *pediatric cardiologist, educator*
Tolo, Vernon Thorpe *orthopedist, educator*
Vari, Sandor George *physician, research scientist*
Vescio, Robert Allen *oncologist, educator*
Wallach, Howard Frederic *psychiatrist*
Wasterlain, Claude Guy *neurologist*
Weiner, Leslie Philip *neurology educator, researcher*
Weiss, Martin Harvey *neurosurgeon, educator*
Wells, Kenneth Brooks *medical educator, researcher*
Whybrow, Peter Charles *psychiatrist, educator, director, author*
Wilkinson, Alan Herbert *nephrologist, educator*
Wilson, Miriam Geisendorfer *retired physician, educator*
Wincor, Michael Z. *psychopharmacology educator, clinician, researcher, director*
Withers, Hubert Rodney *radiotherapist, radiobiologist, educator*
Wong, Wing-Yen *hematologist, educator*
Woodley, David Timothy *dermatology educator*
Wu, Shi-Qi (Samuel Wu) *medical geneticist*
Yamaguchi, Dean Takao *medical educator, researcher*
Yersiz, Hasan *medical educator*
Zalavras, Charalampos *orthopedic surgeon*
Zisman, David Abram *medical educator, health facility administrator*

Madera
Pollack, Henry Clinton III *pediatric emergency physician*

Malibu
Morgenstern, Leon *surgeon*

Manhattan Beach
Grollman, Julius Harry, Jr. *cardiovascular and interventional radiologist*

Marina Del Rey
Khurana, Sanjay Kumar *spine surgeon, director*
Stevens, William Grant (Grant Stevens) *plastic surgeon*
Stoker, David Allen *plastic surgeon*

Menlo Park
Harris, Edward Day, Jr. *physician*
Hoffman, Thomas Edward *dermatologist*
Kovachy, Edward Miklos, Jr. *psychiatrist, consultant*

Mill Valley
Harris, Jeffrey Saul *physician, consultant, health facility administrator*
Kolb, Felix Oscar *physician*

Milpitas
Chiu, Peter Yee-Chew *physician*

Mission Hills
Niku, Soheil Daniel *urologist*

Modesto
Khanna, Kanwal *rheumatologist*
Suntra, Charles Ratapol *surgeon, educator*

Montara
Calman, Sandra Gogins *physician, researcher*

Monterey
Black, Robert Lincoln *pediatrician, educator*
Lehr, Jeffrey Marvin *immunologist, allergist*

Monterey Park
Maronde, Robert Francis *internist, pharmacologist*

Morgan Hill
Nchekwube, Emeka J. *neurologist, surgeon*

Mountain View
Abel, Elizabeth Ann *dermatologist*
Brilliant, Larry (Lawrence Brilliant) *preventive medicine physician, epidemiologist, technology pioneer, writer, educator, entrepreneur, social venture capitalist*
Warren, Richard Wayne *obstetrician, gynecologist*

Napa
Pickett, Justus Cunningham *medical association administrator*

Newbury Park
Bleiberg, Leon William *surgeon, podiatrist*

Newhall
Stein, Karl N. *plastic and reconstructive surgeon*

Newport Beach
Batniji, Rami K. *facial plastic surgeon*
Chiu, John Tang *physician*
Connolly, John Earle *surgeon, educator*
Domanskis, Edward *plastic surgeon*
Grover, Sanjay *plastic surgeon*
Ip, T. Y. Steven *plastic surgeon*
Shamoun, John Milam *plastic surgeon*
Solmer, Richard *surgeon*
Viehe, Richard B. *podiatrist*

Novato
Kassel, Arthur David *retired orthopaedic surgeon*

Oakland
Der, David F. *family practice physician, retired general surgeon*
Epstein, Ervin Harold, Jr. *dermatologist, educator, researcher*
Hoffinger, Scott A. *pediatric orthopaedic surgeon*
Killebrew, Ellen Jane (Mrs. Edward S. Graves) *cardiologist, educator*
Klatsky, Arthur Louis *cardiologist, epidemiologist*
Ng, Lawrence Ming-Loy *pediatrician*
Pang, Dachling *neurosurgeon, educator*
Rosen, Frederick Semenov *otolaryngologist*
Sharpton, Thomas *physician*
Wang, Michael Lee *ophthalmologist*

Oceanside
Curtin, Thomas Lee *ophthalmologist*

Orange
Abolhoda, Amir *surgeon*
Alkire, Michael T. *anesthesiologist, researcher*
Amin, Alpesh N. *internist*
Armstrong, David Ligon *psychiatrist*
Barr, Ronald Jeffrey *dermatologist, pathologist*
Borghei, Peyman *medical researcher*
Chang, Jae Chan *hematologist, oncologist, educator*
Cramer, Steven Craig *neurologist, educator*
Crumley, Roger Lee *surgeon, educator, otolaryngologist*
DiSaia, Philip John *obstetrician, gynecologist, radiology educator*
Dorne, Howard Leslie *radiologist*
Fisher, Mark Jay *neurologist, neuroscientist, educator*
Haydon, Michael *obstetrician, gynecologist*
Hubbell, Floyd Allan *internist, educator*
Lott, Ira Totz *pediatric neurologist*
Matallana, Lynne *medical association administrator*
Meier, Steven W. *orthopedist, surgeon, consultant*
Morgan, Beverly Carver *pediatrician, educator*
Palafox, Brian A. *surgeon*
Rowen, Marshall *radiologist*
Simjee, Aisha *ophthalmologist, educator*
Smith, Ronald Edward *ophthalmologist*
Vaziri, Nosratola Dabir *internist, nephrologist, educator*
Wong, Brian Jet-Fei *surgeon*
Yu, Jen *medical educator*

Orinda
Schneider, Peter A. *urologist, surgeon*

Pacific Palisades
Beck, John Christian *physician, educator*
Claes, Daniel John *physician*
Daniels, John R. *oncologist, educator*
Love, Susan Margaret *surgeon, educator, writer*
Rachelefsky, Gary Stuart *medical educator*

Palm Desert
Widran, Jerrold Joseph *urologist*

Palm Springs
Gaede, James Ernest *physician, educator*

Palo Alto
Adamson, Geoffrey David *endocrinologist, surgeon*
Ashford, John Wesson, Jr. *psychiatrist, researcher*
Bensch, Klaus George *pathology educator*
Blessing-Moore, Joann Catherine *allergist, pulmonologist*
Britton, M(elvin) C(reed), Jr. *rheumatologist*
Chen, Stephen Shi-hua *pathologist, biochemist*
Dement, William Charles *medical researcher, educator*
Druker, David *medical association administrator*
Dubin, Anne *medical educator*
Fries, James Franklin *internal medicine educator*
Galel, Susan Alpert *transfusion medicine physician*
Haddad, Francois *cardiologist, researcher*
Hays, Marguerite Thompson *nuclear medicine physician, educator*
Holman, Halsted Reid *physician, educator*
Keeffe, Emmet Britton *medical educator*
Michie, Sara H. *pathologist, educator*
Moss, Richard B. *pediatrician*
Needleman, Philip *cardiologist, pharmacologist*
Ning, Shoucheng *cancer biologist, head and neck surgeon*
Peng, Stanford Lee-Yu *physician*
Perlroth, Mark Guido *medical educator*
Pizzo, Philip A. *pediatrician, educator, dean*
Raffin, Thomas A. *physician*
Salvatierra, Oscar, Jr. *transplant surgeon, urologist, educator*
Schendel, Stephen Alfred *surgeon, educator*
Schurman, David Jay *orthopedic surgeon, educator*
Shuer, Lawrence Mendel *neurosurgery educator*
Silverman, Norman Henry *cardiologist, educator*
Strober, Samuel *immunologist, educator*
Tune, Bruce Malcolm *pediatrics educator, renal toxicologist*
Urquhart, John *medical researcher, educator*
Yuan, Nanci *pediatrician, pulmonologist, educator*

Palos Verdes Estates
Myhre, Byron Arnold *pathologist, educator*

Palos Verdes Peninsula
Narasimhan, Padma Mandyam *physician*
Thomas, Claudewell Sidney *psychiatrist, educator*
Van Der Meulen, Joseph Pierre *neurologist*

Panorama City
Bass, Harold Neal *pediatrician, medical geneticist*
Sue, Michael Alvin *allergist*

Pasadena
Buchwald, Jed Zachary *environmental health researcher, science history educator*
Glovsky, Myron Michael *medical educator*
Goldweber, Robert *emergency physician*
Harvey, Joseph Paul, Jr. *orthopedist, educator*
Lake, Kevin Bruce *medical association administrator*
Opel, William *medical research administrator*
Shaw, Anthony *pediatric surgeon, retired educator*
Short, Elizabeth M. *internist, educator, retired federal agency administrator*
Wong, Raymond Shiu-Loong *radiologist*

Perris
Cohen, Joseph I. *forensic pathologist*

Piedmont
Montgomery, Theodore Ashton *physician*
Reich, Stanley Benjamin *radiologist, medical educator*

Pinole
Naughton, James Lee *internist*

Placerville
Vandenberg, Byron F. *cardiologist*

Pleasant Hill
Hollister, Arthur Clair, Jr. *epidemiologist, consultant, retired public health service officer*

Pomona
Gambone, Joseph Charles *medical educator, consultant*
Rao, Yallapragada S. *oncologist*
Vo, Huu Dinh *pediatrician, educator*

Portola Valley
Fogarty, Thomas James *surgery educator*
Hafkenschiel, Joseph Henry, Jr. *cardiologist, educator*

Rancho Mirage
Atiba, Joshua Olajide Oluwabunmi *internist, philanthropist, oncologist, educator, pharmacologist*
Chuang, Tsu-Yi *dermatologist, epidemiologist, educator*
Cohn, M. James *radiologist*
Cone, Lawrence Arthur *medical educator*
Leydorf, Mary Malcolm *physician, writer*
Shen, Alfred C. *neurosurgeon*
Stone, Richard Alan *medical educator*
Weil, Max Harry *internist, cardiologist, educator, researcher*

Rancho Palos Verdes
Kwan, Benjamin Ching Kee *ophthalmologist*
Neilan, Aidan Joseph *radiologist*

Rancho Santa Fe
Affeldt, John Ellsworth *retired physician*
Carr, David Turner *physician*
Nadler, Henry Louis *pediatrician, educator, geneticist*
Rockoff, S. David *radiologist, physician, educator*

Rancho Santa Margarita
Bunkis, Juris *plastic surgeon*

Redding
Nwangburuka, Okechukwu Nkem *psychiatrist*
Renard, Ronald Lee *allergist*

Redlands
Skoog, William Arthur *retired oncologist*

Redwood City
Sweet, Victoria *medical educator, physician*

Rialto
Alav, Faramarz *cardiologist, internist*

Richmond
Arnon, Stephen Soulé *physician, research scientist*

Ridgecrest
Ferguson, Earl Wilson *cardiologist, medical executive, telemedicine consultant*

Riverside
Bricker, Neal S. *physician, educator*
Evangelista, Allan *surgeon, medical researcher*
Green, Dolores L. *medical association administrator*
Jung, Timothy Tae Kun *otolaryngologist*
Linaweaver, Walter Ellsworth, Jr. *physician*

Rolling Hills
Ehrlich, Michelle *dermatologist*

Rolling Hills Estates
Bellis, Carroll Joseph *surgeon, educator*

Sacramento
Barasch, Eugene Franklin *radiologist, physicist, researcher*
Bogren, Hugo Gunnar *radiology educator*
Chapman, Michael William *orthopedist, educator*
Cunningham, Mary Elizabeth (Mary Cunningham-Lusby) *physician*
Davies, Angela *oncologist, educator*
Fitzgerald, Faith Thayer *internist*
Flamm, Melvin Daniel, Jr. *cardiologist*
Fung, Maxwell Alexander *medical educator*
Gandara, David Raymond *internist, oncologist, educator*
Hales, Robert Ernest *psychiatrist, educator*
Howell, Lydia Pleotis *pathologist, educator*
Jackson, Richard Joseph *epidemiologist, educator, pediatrician, preventive medicine physician*
Kennedy, Harold Lee *physician*
Lamb, Philina May Ann *dermatologist, educator*
Laslett, Lawrence J. *physician, educator*
Lee, Edmond *internist, cardiologist*
Leong, Albin B. *pediatric pulmonologist, allergist, educator*
Lim, Alan Young *plastic surgeon*
Lippold, Roland Will *retired surgeon*
Lynch, Peter John *retired dermatologist*
Makker, Sudesh Paul *physician*
Nagy, Stephen Mears, Jr. *physician, allergist*
Parsapour, Kourosh *medical educator*
Rab, George T. *pediatric orthopedic surgeon*
Robinson, Muriel Cox *psychiatrist*
Rossiter, Stephen J. *surgeon*
Schott, Robert James *internist, cardiologist*
Sharma, Arjun Dutta *cardiologist*
Stevenson, Thomas Ray *plastic surgeon*

Styne, Dennis Michael *physician, educator*
Tong, John *plastic surgeon, educator, ophthalmic surgeon*
Tung, Prabhas *plastic surgeon*
Wolfman, Earl Frank, Jr. *surgeon, educator*
Wolkov, Harvey Brian *oncologist, researcher*
Yen, Andrew W. *internal medicine physician*

Saint Helena
Darter, Robert Wells *surgeon, physician*

Salinas
Helmer, James John, Jr. *physician, educator*

San Bernardino
De Haas, David Dana *emergency physician*
Wilkin, Linda D. *sports medicine physician, educator*

San Bruno
Bradley, Charles William *podiatrist, educator*

San Diego
Austad, Eric David *plastic and reconstructive surgeon*
Ball, Edward David *hematologist, oncologist*
Beeson, Stephen Charles *physician*
Benirschke, Kurt *retired pathologist, educator*
Bloom, Floyd Elliott *internist, neuroscientist*
Chambers, Henry George *orthopedic surgeon*
DeMaria, Anthony Nicholas *cardiologist, educator*
Friedlander, Sheila Fallon *dermatologist, educator*
Friedman, Paul Jay *retired radiologist*
Goltz, Robert William *dermatologist, educator*
Greenberg, Barry *physician*
Jacoby, Irving *physician*
Jamieson, Stuart William *surgeon, educator*
Kaplan, George Willard *urologist*
Kaushansky, Kenneth *medical educator*
Kellogg, Huston Glenn *pediatrician, medical educator*
Koka, Prasad S. *biomedical researcher*
Krous, Henry Franklin *pathologist, educator*
Langenberg, Bret James *surgeon*
Levy, Jerome *dermatologist, retired military officer*
Mahm, Walter K. *dermatologist, researcher*
Marthemore, Jacqueline Gail *internist, educator, hospital administrator*
Pitt, William Alexander *cardiologist*
Ross, William Bradley *physician*
Ray, Albert *physician, educator*
Resnik, Robert *medical educator*
Roizen, Michael F. *anesthesiologist, medical educator, writer*
Ross, John, Jr. *cardiologist, educator*
Schmidt, Joseph David *urologist*
Singer, Richard Jonathan *medical educator, anesthesiologist*
Wasserman, Stephen Ira *allergist, immunologist, educator*
Whittington, Anne Elizabeth *diabetes educator*
Widder, Kenneth Jon *pathologist, educator*

San Francisco
Alvarado, Jorge A. *ophthalmologist, researcher*
Amend, William John Conrad, Jr. *physician, educator*
Anooshian, Robert Vahan *plastic surgeon*
Bainton, Dorothy Ford *pathologist, educator*
Barondes, Samuel Herbert *psychiatrist, educator*
Basbaum, Allan I. *medical educator, researcher*
Behrens, M. Kathleen *medical researcher*
Benet, Leslie Zachary *pharmacologist, educator*
Bikle, Daniel David *research physician*
Boles, Roger *otolaryngologist*
Botvinick, Elias H. *nuclear medicine physician, researcher, medical educator*
Bourne, Henry R. *pharmacology professor, department chairman, researcher*
Bradford, David S. *surgeon*
Brotman, Martin *gastroenterologist*
Brown, Eric Joel *biomedical researcher*
Capaldini, Lisa Claire *physician, educator*
Ciccarone, Daniel *medical educator, researcher, physician*
Clever, Linda Hawes *physician*
Cobbs, Price Mashaw *social psychiatrist*
Cooper, Allen David *medical researcher, educator*
Cornett, Patricia Anne *oncologist, educator*
Crawford, J. Brooks *ophthalmologist, educator*
Crawford, Michael Howard *cardiologist, educator, researcher*
Croughan, Mary *medical educator*
Cuns, Michael Jay *dermatologist, educator*
Darney, Philip Dempsey *gynecologist, educator*
David, George *psychiatrist, economic theory lecturer*
Dawson, Chandler Robert *ophthalmologist, educator*
Eicken, Raymond Friedrich *neuropsychiatrist, neuroscientist*
Egan, Kristin *otolaryngologist*
El-Sayed, Ivan Homer *otolaryngologist, researcher*
Engleman, Ephraim Philip *rheumatologist*
Epstein, Charles Joseph *pediatrician, geneticist, biochemist, educator*
Epstein, John Howard *dermatologist*
Ferriero, Donna M. *pediatric neurologist*
Fessel, Walford Jeffrey *rheumatologist*
Frnberg, Laurence *pediatrician, educator, dean*
Frick, Oscar Lionel *pediatrician, educator*
Friedman, Gary *plastic surgeon*
Ganem, Donald E. *immunologist*
Gellin, Gerald Alan *dermatologist*
Gibbs, Patricia Hellman *physician*
Glantz, Stanton A. *medical researcher*
Glogau, Richard G. *dermatologist*
Goode, Erica Tucker *internist*
Gooding, Charles Arthur *radiologist, physician, educator*
Gooding, Gretchen Ann Wagner *physician, educator*

Greenspan, Francis S. *physician*
Greenspan, John S. *dental and medical educator, researcher, academic administrator*
Grossman, William *medical researcher, educator*
Grumbach, Melvin Malcolm *pediatrician, educator*
Havel, Richard Joseph *physician, educator*
Henderson, Isaac Craig *oncologist, researcher*
Heyman, Melvin Bernard *pediatric gastroenterologist*
Higashida, Randall Takeo *radiologist, neurosurgeon, medical educator*
Hoffman, William Yanes *plastic surgeon*
Hoskins, H. Dunbar *ophthalmologist, medical association administrator*
Hoyt, Creig Simmons *ophthalmologist, educator*
Hsu, Chi-yuan *nephrologist, researcher*
Ikeda, Clyde Junichi *plastic and reconstructive surgeon*
Jonsen, Albert R(upert) *retired medical ethics educator*
Kan, Yuet Wai *hematologist, educator*
Katzung, Bertram George *pharmacologist*
Kegeles, Susan M. *medical educator, researcher*
Kenyon, Cynthia J. *medical researcher*
King, Talmadge E. *physician*
Kline, Howard Jay *cardiologist, educator*
Koo, John Ying Ming *psychiatrist, dermatologist*
Lo, Bernard *medical educator*
Low, Randall *internist, cardiologist*
Lucia, Marilyn Reed *physician*
Maas, Corey *plastic surgeon*
Mason, Dean Towle *cardiologist*
Mathes, Stephen John *plastic and reconstructive surgeon, educator*
McAninch, Jack Weldon *urological surgeon, educator*
McCulley, Timothy J. *ophthalmologist, surgeon, educator*
Miller, Ronald D. *medical educator, researcher*
Miller, Walter Luther *pediatrician, educator*
Mustacchi, Piero *preventive medicine physician, educator*
Norris, Philip John *medical educator, researcher*
O'Connor, G(eorge) Richard *ophthalmologist*
Ousterhout, Douglas Kenneth *plastic surgeon*
Petrakis, Nicholas Louis *epidemiologist, medical researcher, educator*
Phillips, Theodore Locke *radiologist, educator*
Rajagopal, Usha *plastic surgeon*
Roe, Benson Bertheau *surgeon, educator*
Rosinski, Edwin Francis *medical educator*
Rudolph, Abraham Morris *pediatrician, educator*
Rutherford, George Williams III *preventive medicine physician*
Sarkar, Rajabrata *surgeon*
Schechter, Naomi R. *oncologist*
Schmidt, Robert Milton *preventive medicine physician, educator, medical association administrator*
Schrock, Theodore R. *surgeon*
Schroeder, Steven Alfred *medical educator*
Seebach, Lydia Marie *physician*
Shaw, Richard Eugene *cardiovascular researcher*
Sheppard, Dean *medical educator*
Sherr, Elliott Harold *neurologist, researcher*
Shinefield, Henry Robert *pediatrician*
Shinohara, Katsuto *medical educator*
Smith, David Elvin *physician*
Smith, Lloyd Hollingsworth *physician*
Spivey, Bruce E. *ophthalmologist, educator, health facility administrator*
Stamper, Robert Lewis *ophthalmologist, educator*
Steinsmith, William *internist, research scientist*
Su, Hua *medical educator*
Suess, Fred *plastic surgeon*
Vail, Thomas Parker *orthopaedic surgeon*
Van Dyke, Craig *psychiatrist, director*
Volpe, Peter Anthony *surgeon*
Way, E(dward) Leong *pharmacologist, toxicologist, educator*
Wintroub, Bruce Urich *dermatologist, educator, researcher*
Yao, John Sen *physician*
Ying, Weihai *biomedical researcher, educator*
Zippin, Calvin *epidemiologist, educator*

San Gabriel
Chen, John Calvin *retired psychiatrist, educator*

San Jose
Avakoff, Joseph Carnegie *medical and law consultant*
Johnson, Allen Halbert *surgeon*
Lippe, Philipp Maria *neurosurgeon, educator, academic administrator*
Nelson, Lionel M. *otolaryngologist*
Press, Barry Harris Jay *plastic surgeon*
Stevens, David Alec *medical educator*
Weinmann, Robert Lewis *neurologist*

San Juan Capistrano
Zalta, Edward *otolaryngologist, physician*

San Leandro
Zeller, Scott L. *psychiatrist*

San Luis Obispo
Pinkel, Donald Paul *pediatrician*
Weaver, Karl E. *psychiatrist*

San Marino
Terry, Roger *retired pathologist, consultant*

San Mateo
Chabra, Anand *public health physician, epidemiologist*
Sutherland, Vanna Rae *psychiatrist*
Van Kirk, John Ellsworth *retired cardiologist*
Wong, Otto *epidemiologist*

San Pablo
Woodruff, Kay Herrin *pathologist, educator*

San Pedro
Kline, Frank Menefee *psychiatrist*

San Rafael
Hoffman, Charles Louis *physician*

San Ramon
Litman, Robert Barry *physician, writer, television and radio commentator*

Santa Ana
Afifi, Alaa Youssef *cardiothoracic surgeon*
Lappin, Michael Bruce *ophthalmologist, surgeon, medical educator*
Myers, Marilyn Gladys *pediatric hematologist, oncologist*
Sporty, Lawrence Douglas *psychiatrist*
Vaccaro, Jerome Vincent *psychiatrist, educator, healthcare executive*

Santa Barbara
Avery, Robert Logan *ophthalmologist*
Behrman, Richard Elliot *pediatrician, dean*
Bischel, Margaret DeMeritt *physician, consultant*
Ellis, Eugene Joseph *cardiologist*
Fisher, Steven Kay *neurobiology educator*
Handel, Neal *plastic surgeon, researcher*
Jovanovic, Lois *medical researcher*
Kohn, Roger Alan *surgeon*
Liebhaber, Myron I. *allergist*
Mathews, Barbara Edith *gynecologist*
Ray, Charles Dean *neurosurgeon, spine surgeon, bioengineer, inventor*

Santa Clara
Castellino, Ronald Augustus Dietrich *radiologist, educator*
Chin, Albert Kae *research physician*

Santa Cruz
Pletsch, Marie Eleanor *plastic surgeon*
Shorenstein, Rosalind Greenberg *internist*

Santa Monica
Buxton, William Glenton *neurologist, director*
Carr, Ruth Margaret *plastic surgeon*
Gupta, Rishab Kumar *medical association administrator, educator, researcher*
Hoefflin, Steven M. *plastic surgeon*
Jain, John Kumar *medical educator, health facility administrator*
Katz, Roger *pediatrician, allergist, immunologist, educator*
Kawamoto, Henry K. *plastic surgeon*
Lincoln, Thomas L. *pathologist, educator*
McGuire, Michael Francis *plastic surgeon*
O'Connor, Edward Joseph *neurologist*
Rand, Robert Wheeler *neurosurgeon, educator*
Resnick, Jeffrey I. *plastic surgeon*
Schultz, Victor M. *physician*
Shim, Elisabeth K. *dermatologist*
Singer, Frederick Raphael *medical researcher*
Stern, Walter Eugene *neurosurgeon, educator*
Teitelbaum, Steven *plastic surgeon*
Thompson, Dennis Peters *plastic surgeon*
Tompkins, Ronald K. *retired surgeon, educator*
Zarem, Harvey Alan *plastic surgeon*

Santa Paula
Edwards, Samuel Roger *retired internist*

Santa Rosa
Bozdech, Marek Jiri *physician, educator*
Cohn, Joseph David *surgeon*
Kopes-Kerr, Colin P. *physician, publishing executive*
McAvoy, John Martin *plastic surgeon*
Mir-Sepasi, M. Hossein *cardiac thoracic surgeon*
Smith, Thomas Kent *retired radiologist*

Sausalito
Ornish, Dean *medical association administrator, medical educator*

Sepulveda
Yano, Elizabeth Martin *epidemiologist, researcher*

Sherman Oaks
Grossman, Peter H. *plastic surgeon*
Stein, Kira D. *psychiatrist*

Sierra Madre
Nation, Earl F. *retired urologist, educator*

Sonoma
Emery, John Edward *plastic surgeon, vintner*

South Pasadena
Whang, Sukoo Jack *pathologist, microbiologist*

South San Francisco
Caro, Ivor *dermatologist*
Ferrara, Napoleone M.A. *molecular oncologist*
Humphrey, Patrick Paul *pharmacologist*
Hurst, Deborah *pediatric hematologist*
Tessier-Lavigne, Marc Trevor *neurobiologist, researcher*

Stanford
Abrams, Herbert LeRoy *radiologist, educator*
Arber, Daniel Alan *hematologist, pathologist*
Bauer, Eugene Andrew *dermatologist, educator*
Blau, Helen Margaret *pharmacology educator*
Brown, J. Martin *oncologist, educator*
Chase, Robert Arthur *surgeon, educator*
Cohen, Harvey Joel *pediatric hematology and oncology educator*
Curet, Myriam Jeanette *surgeon, educator*
Donaldson, Sarah Susan *radiologist*
Egbert, Peter Roy *ophthalmologist, educator*
Farquhar, John William *physician, educator*
Fee, Willard Edward, Jr. *otolaryngologist*
Fire, Andrew Z. *pathologist, educator, geneticist*
Friedman, Gary David *epidemiologist*
Fuller, Margaret Tatnall *biomedical researcher*
Garber, Alan Michael *internist, educator, economist*
Glover, Gary H. *radiologist, educator*

Henderson, Victor Warren *behavioral and geriatric neurologist, epidemiologist, researcher, educator*
Hlatky, Mark Andrew *cardiologist, researcher*
Horwitz, Ralph Irving *internist, epidemiologist, educator, dean*
Hunt, Sharon Ann *cardiologist*
Jacobs, Charlotte De Croes *oncologist, educator*
Jardetzky, Oleg *retired medical educator, researcher*
Klima, Roger Radim *physiatrist*
Koza, John R. *medical educator, writer*
Kraemer, Helena Antoinette Chmura *psychiatry educator*
Leibel, Steven Arnold *radiologist*
Levy, Ronald *medical educator, researcher*
Malenka, Robert C. *psychiatrist, educator*
Mansour, Tag Eldin *pharmacologist, educator*
Mark, James B. D. *surgeon, educator*
Marmor, Michael Franklin *ophthalmologist, educator*
McDevitt, Hugh O'Neill *immunologist, educator*
McDougall, Iain Ross *nuclear medicine educator*
McQuillen, Michael Paul *neurologist, educator*
Mignot, Emmanuel *medical researcher*
Mitchell, Beverly Shriver *hematologist, oncologist, educator*
Oberhelman, Harry Alvin, Jr. *surgeon, educator*
Olcott, Cornelius, IV, *surgeon*
Owens, Douglas K. *physician, researcher*
Polan, Mary Lake *obstetrics and gynecology educator*
Reddy, Vadiyala Mohan *cardiothoracic surgeon*
Reitz, Bruce Arnold *cardiac surgeon, educator*
Robbins, Robert Clayton *surgeon*
Rosenberg, Saul Allen *oncologist, educator*
Rubenstein, Edward *physician, educator*
Schatzberg, Alan Frederic *psychiatrist, researcher*
So, Yuen T. *neurologist, educator*
Stamey, Thomas Alexander *urologist, educator*
Stefanick, Marcia Lynn *medical educator, researcher*
Weissman, Irving L. *medical researcher*
Zarins, Christopher Kristaps *surgeon, educator*

Stockton
Nakanishi, Alan *ophthalmologist, state representative*

Sylmar
Corry, Dalila Boudjellal *internist, educator*
Kamangar, Nader *physician, director, researcher, pulmonologist, educator*

Tarzana
Teitell, Michael Alan *immunologist*

Templeton
Abernathy, Shields B. *allergist, immunologist, internist*

Thousand Oaks
Eisenberg, Paul Richard *cardiologist, consultant, educator*
Farshidi, Ardeshir B. *cardiologist, educator*
Pakula, Anita Susan *dermatologist*

Torrance
Black, James Jens *plastic surgeon*
Brasel, Jo Anne *pediatrician, educator*
Brass, Eric Paul *internal medicine and pharmacology educator, academic administrator*
Budoff, Matthew Jay *cardiologist*
Daar, Eric Steven *medical educator*
Emmanouilides, George Christos *physician, educator*
Hammer, Terence Michael *physician*
Hansen, James Edward *medical educator, researcher*
Katz, Ronald Lewis *physician, educator*
Kopple, Joel D. *medical educator*
Mehringer, Charles Mark *medical educator*
Omari, Bassam O. *cardiothoracic surgeon*
Oudiz, Ronald *cardiologist*
Stabile, Bruce Edward *surgeon*
Sun, Nora Chi-Jun *pathologist*
Swerdloff, Ronald S. *physician, educator, researcher*
Tanaka, Kouichi Robert *hematologist, educator*

Tustin
Herdeg, Howard Brian *retired physician*

Twain Harte
Schneider, James Richard *orthopedist*

Ukiah
McClintock, Richard Polson *dermatologist*

Vacaville
Che, Maggie *endocrinologist, researcher*

Valencia
Samadi, Albert A. *urologist*

Vallejo
Towne, Sarah Patton *physician*

Ventura
Abul-Haj, Suleiman Kahil *pathologist*
Villaveces, James Walter *allergist, immunologist, consultant*

Visalia
Riegel, Byron William *ophthalmologist*

Walnut Creek
Bakshi, Nandini *neurologist*
Cannon, Grace Bert *retired immunologist*
Carson, Jay Wilmer *pathologist, educator*
Collen, Morris Frank *retired medical association administrator, physician, consultant, researcher*
Man, Pang Ling *retired psychiatrist*
Rihn, Richard John *retired physician*

West Hills
Monosson, Ira Howard *physician*

Westminster
Luong, Khanh Vinh Quoc *nephrologist, researcher*
Nguyen, Lan Thi Hoang *physician, educator*

Whittier
Arenowitz, Albert Harold *psychiatrist*
Kirsch, Scott Douglas *family practice physician, director*
Prickett, David Clinton *physician*

COLORADO

Alamosa
Taylor, Wallace Edmondson, Jr. *otolaryngologist*

Aspen
Oden, Robert Rudolph *surgeon*

Aurora
Alvero, Ruben J. *medical educator*
Battaglia, Frederick Camillo *physician*
Bunn, Paul A., Jr. *oncologist, educator*
Churchill, Mair Elisa Annabelle *medical educator*
Haas, Robert Lance *surgeon, consultant*
Nora, Audrey Hart *physician*
Shore, James H(enry) *psychiatrist*

Boulder
McFarland, Robert Bruce *physician*
Pneuman, Linda Jackson *retired physician*

Colorado Springs
Anderson, Paul Nathaniel *oncologist, educator*
Barber, Michael J. *cardiologist, educator*
Gifford, Marilyn Joyce *emergency physician, consultant*
Hegarty, Joseph Lee *neurotologist*
Kleiner, John Philip *cardiologist*
Liebscher, Gregory J. *plastic surgeon*
Metz, Brian K. *cardiologist*
Mou, Thomas William *retired physician, medical educator, consultant*

Denver
Adler, Charles Spencer *psychiatrist*
Barber, Patricia Louise *clinical specialist*
Brega, Kerry Elizabeth *physician, researcher*
Dobersen, Michael Joseph *pathologist, researcher*
Eickhoff, Theodore Carl *infectious disease physician, epidemiologist*
Fennessey, Paul Vincent *pediatrics and pharmacology educator, researcher*
Freedman, Robert *psychiatrist*
Gabow, Patricia Anne *internist, health facility executive*
Ghiselli, Gary *spine surgeon*
Golitz, Loren Eugene *dermatologist, pathologist, medical association administrator*
Gravlee, Glenn P(age) *anesthesiologist, educator, director*
Greyson, Clifford Russell *internist*
Guber, Myles Stuert *surgeon*
Huang, Linda Chen *plastic surgeon*
Iseman, Michael Dee *medical educator*
Jafek, Bruce William *otolaryngologist, educator*
Johnson, Candice Elaine Brown *pediatrician, educator*
Johnston, Richard Boles, Jr. *pediatrician, educator, biomedical researcher*
Jones, M. Douglas, Jr. *pediatrician, educator*
Kappy, Michael Steven *pediatrics educator*
Kassan, Stuart S. *rheumatologist*
Keep, Marcus Floyd *neurosurgeon*
Kendig, Lynne E. *physician*
Koul, Hari Krishen *surgery professor, scientist*
Krikos, George Alexander *pathologist, educator*
Krugman, Richard David *pediatrician, academic administrator, educator*
Langsley, Pauline Royal *psychiatrist*
Larsen, Gary Loy *physician, researcher*
Lee, Lela A. *dermatology educator, researcher*
Lewis, Evan Larson *urologist*
Lindenfeld, JoAnn *physician, educator*
Lipkin, Alan F. *otolaryngologist*
Lubeck, Marvin Jay *ophthalmologist*
Marrack, Philippa Charlotte *immunologist, researcher*
Martin, Richard Jay *medical educator*
Mehler, Philip S. *internist*
Meyers, Arlen *physician*
Moore, Ernest Eugene, Jr. *surgeon, educator*
Morin, Christopher Joseph *vascular surgeon*
Mueller, Kathryn Lucile *medical educator*
Petty, Thomas Lee *internist, educator*
Pomerantz, Marvin *thoracic surgeon*
Rainer, William Gerald *cardiac surgeon*
Repine, John Edward *internist, educator*
Sakai, Joseph Thomas *psychiatrist, educator*
Schiff, Donald Wilfred *pediatrician, educator*
Schrier, Robert William *physician, educator*
Shlay, Judith Carol *physician*
Sokol, Ronald Jay *pediatric gastroenterologist, researcher*
Song, John I. *otolaryngologist, surgeon*
Stamm, Carol Ann *obstetrician, gynecologist*
Sujansky, Eva Borska *pediatrician, geneticist, educator*
Szefler, Stanley James *pediatrics and pharmacology educator*
Taylor, Edward Stewart *obstetrician, educator*
Toll, Henry Wolcott, Jr. *pathologist*

Durango
Wigton, Chester Mahlon *physician*

Englewood
Bloch, Clifford Alan *pediatric endocrinologist*
Knize, David Maurice *plastic surgeon*

Fort Collins
Phemister, Robert David *veterinary medical educator*
Wang, Tian *immunologist, educator*

Glenwood Springs
Jaffrey, Ira *oncologist, educator*

Grand Junction
Janson, Richard Anthony *plastic surgeon*

Greeley
Cook, Donald Evan *pediatrician, educator*
Jaouen, Richard Matthie *plastic surgeon*

Greenwood Village
Grainger, John R. *medical association administrator*
Holloman, Kenneth Raymond *pathologist, educator*

Highlands Ranch
Bublitz, Deborah Keirstead *pediatrician*

Lafayette
Mehl, Albert L. *pediatrician, poet, composer*
Thornbury, John Rousseau *radiologist, physician*

Lakewood
Eikleberry, Lois Schillie *physician*
Shenoi, Ranee Melanie *physiatrist*

Littleton
Forstot, Stephan Lance *ophthalmologist*

Lone Tree
Miller, Allan Marquess *hematologist*
Washington, Reginald Louis *pediatric cardiologist*

Longmont
Yost, Byron A. *retired physician*

Loveland
King, Joan Caluda *medical educator, neuroscientist*

Sterling
Mitchell, Stacy Marie *medical transcriptionist*

Thornton
Shih, Franklin *physician*

Vail
Bevan, William Arnold, Jr. *emergency physician*
Philippon, Marc Joseph *orthopaedic surgeon*

Wheat Ridge
Brown, Steven Brien *radiologist*
Fleischaker, Gordon Henry, Jr. *pediatrician*

Wolcott
Flacke, Joan Wareham *physician, anesthesiologist, educator*

CONNECTICUT

Avon
Hinz, Carl Frederick, Jr. *immunologist, educator*

Bethany
Niederman, James Corson *retired internist, educator*

Branford
Petrie, Stewart Judson *retired obstetrician, gynecologist*

Bridgeport
Aleali, Seyed Hossain *internist*
Kosinski, Edward John *cardiologist, educator*
Lobdell, David Hill *pathologist*
Maiocco, Kenneth Joseph *dermatologist*
Mcpherson, Craig A. *cardiologist, educator*
Salam, Adil *pulmonary critical care physician*
Wilchinsky, Mark E. *orthopaedic surgeon*

Danbury
Leebens, Patricia Kay *psychiatrist*

Derby
Katz, David Lawrence *preventive medicine physician, researcher*

East Hartford
McLarney, Thomas Joseph *physician*

Essex
Lorenze, Mark David *orthopedist, surgeon*

Fairfield
Burd, Robert Meyer *hematologist, oncologist, educator*
Morrison, Murray Allan *orthopaedic surgeon*
Stanton, Robert Alan *orthopaedic surgeon*

Farmington
Donaldson, James Oswell III *neurologist, educator*
Grunnet, Margaret Louise *retired pathologist, educator*
Liebowitz, Neil Robert *psychiatrist*
McCawley, Austin *psychiatrist, educator*
Owens, Guy *retired neurosurgeon*
Rothfield, Naomi Fox *physician*
Runowicz, Carolyn Dilworth *physician*
Schenkman, John Boris *pharmacologist, educator*
Shanley, John David *epidemiologist*
Silverman, David Irving *cardiologist*

Glastonbury
Singer, Paul Richard *ophthalmologist*

Greenwich
Blumberg, Joel Myron *cardiologist*
Bonheim, Nelson Alfred *gastroenterologist, educator*
Grant, Ronald Alfred *psychiatrist, pastoral counselor, psychoanalyst*

Hamden
Nuland, Sherwin *surgeon, writer*
Reiser, Morton Francis *psychiatrist, educator*

Hartford
Ahman, Arnold J. *pediatrician*
Cole, Solon Robert *pathologist, educator*
Delgado, Joao *emergency physician, toxicologist*
Dworkin, Paul Howard *pediatrician*
Gould, Bruce Elliott *physician, medical educator, academic administrator*
Jahiel, Rene Ino *physician*
Jung, Betty Chin *epidemiologist, educator, nurse*
Klimek, Joseph John *physician, educator*
Knox, Thomas Isaac *cardiologist*
Painter, Robert Lowell *surgeon, educator*
Ramanan, Sundaram V. *internist, hematologist, oncologist*

Kensington
Harwin, S. Martin *pediatrician*

Lakeville
Lipton, Lester *ophthalmologist, entrepreneur*

Madison
Snell, Richard Saxon *anatomist*

Meriden
Horton, Paul Chester *psychiatrist*
Shapiro, Philip Edwin *dermatologist, dermatopathologist, educator*

Milford
Scaniffe, Joseph Albert *anesthesiologist, consultant*

Mystic
Burrow, Gerard Noel *internist, educator*

New Britain
Petit, William Arthur, Jr. *endocrinologist*

New Canaan
Ackerman, Sigurd Howard *psychiatrist*
Coughlin, Francis Raymond, Jr. *surgeon, educator, lawyer*

New Haven
Ariyan, Stephan *plastic surgeon*
Askenase, Philip William *medicine and pathology educator*
Bakhos, Charles Tanos *surgeon*
Baltimore, Robert Samuel *pediatrician, epidemiologist*
Barash, Paul George *anesthesiologist, educator*
Bartoshuk, Linda M. *otolaryngologist, educator*
Behrman, Harold Richard *endocrinologist, physiologist, educator*
Berland, Gretchen K. *medical educator, filmmaker*
Bloomgarden, Gary Michael *neurosurgeon*
Boyer, James Lorenzen *internist, educator*
Braverman, Irwin Merton *dermatologist, educator*
Cha, Charles *surgical oncologist, hepatobiliary surgeon*
Cleary, Paul David *sociomedical educator*
Cohen, Lawrence Sorel *internist, educator*
Collins, William F., Jr. *neurosurgery educator*
Comer, James Pierpont *psychiatrist, educator*
Cullen, Mark Richard *medical educator*
Davey, Lycurgus Michael *neurosurgeon*
Ehrenkranz, Richard Allan *pediatrician*
Ferholt, J. Deborah Lott *pediatrician*
Fikrig, Erol *rheumatologist, medical educator*
Forget, Bernard G. *hematologist, educator*
Foster, Roger Sherman, Jr. *surgeon, educator, health facility administrator*
Friedlaender, Gary Elliott *orthopedist, educator*
Genel, Myron *pediatrician, educator*
Goldstein, Daniel Robert *cardiologist*
Gonzalez, Caleb *ophthalmologist, educator*
Goodrich, Isaac *neurosurgeon, educator*
Gross, Ian *academic pediatrician, neonatologist*
Hebert, Steven C. *medical educator*
Horwich, Arthur L. *medical educator*
Hostetter, Margaret K. *pediatrician, medical educator*
Jatlow, Peter I. *pathologist, medical educator, researcher*
Kalyanpur, Arjun *radiologist*
Kashgarian, Michael *pathologist, educator*
Khoshnood, Kaveh *epidemiologist, educator*
King, Robert Alan *psychiatrist, educator*
Krumholz, Harlen Marc *cardiologist, internist, educator*
Kushlan, Samuel Daniel *internist, educator, hospital administrator*
Leckman, James Frederick *psychiatry and pediatrics educator*
Leffell, David Joel *dermatologist, surgeon, writer, photographer, medical school administrator, educator*
Lentz, Thomas Lawrence *biomedical educator, dean, researcher*
Lesser, Robert Lewis *ophthalmologist*
Levine, Robert John *internist, medical educator, ethicist*
Lifton, Richard P. *medical educator, researcher*
Longo, Walter E. *colon and rectal surgeon, educator, director*
Lopez, Javier *psychiatrist*
Lytton, Bernard *urology educator*
McClain, Brenda C. *pain management physician*
Miller, I. George *physician, educator, researcher*
Mukherjee, Sandip Kumar *cardiologist*
Musto, David Franklin *medical researcher, educator, historian, consultant*
Norbeck, Timothy Burns *medical association executive*
Persing, John Arthur *surgeon*
Powsner, Seth M. *psychiatrist, educator*
Rose, Aron D. *ophthalmologist, educator*
Sartorelli, Alan Clayton *pharmacologist, educator*
Sasaki, Clarence Takashi *surgeon, educator*
Schlessinger, Joseph *pharmacology educator*
Schottenfeld, Richard Steven *psychiatrist*
Seashore, Margretta Reed *physician, educator*
Shapiro, Eugene David *pediatrician, epidemiologist, educator*
Shaywitz, Bennett Arthur *medical educator*
Shulman, Gerald I. *physician, scientist, endocrinologist, educator*
Smith, Brian Richard *hematologist, oncologist, pathologist*
Spencer, Dennis Dee *medical educator, director*
Stahl, Richard Sheldon *surgeon*
Stern, Robert *psychiatrist*
Tsai, James C. *ophthalmologist, researcher*
Volkmar, Fred Robert *psychiatrist, educator, director*
Waxman, Stephen George *neurologist, neuroscientist*
Weidhaas, Joanne Barnes *medical educator*
Weiss, Robert M. *urologist, educator*
Zaret, Barry Lewis *cardiologist, medical educator*
Zhang, Yawei *epidemiologist*

New London
Schoenberger, Steven Harris *physician, research consultant*
Urbanetti, John Sutherland *internist, consultant*

New Milford
Mullen, John E. *orthopedist, surgeon*

Niantic
Douglas, Robert Gordon, Jr. *physician*

Norfolk
Mermann, Alan Cameron *retired pediatric educator, chaplain*

Norwalk
Carius, Michael Lee *emergency medicine physician*
Falsone, Jack Joseph *physician*

Old Greenwich
Lorefice, Laurence Santo *psychiatrist*

Putnam
Day, John Anthony, Jr. *pulmonologist*

Ridgefield
Egan, Kenneth J. *dermatologist*

Southington
Byeff, Peter David *hematologist, oncologist*

Stamford
Cook, Colin Burford *psychiatrist*
Cutler, Kenneth B., Jr. *dermatologist, educator*
Erichson, Robert B. *hematologist, oncologist*
Goodhue, Peter Ames *obstetrician, gynecologis educator*
Horowitz, Steven F. *cardiologist*
Klein, Neil Charles *physician*
Rosenstock, Arthur Richard *plastic surgeon, educator*
Walsh, Thomas Joseph *ophthalmologist*

Stratford
Feinberg, Dennis Lowell *dermatologist*
Mahoney, Maurice Jeremiah *medical educator*

Vernon Rockville
Marmer, Ellen Lucille *pediatrician, cardiologis*

Wallingford
Lelas, Snjezana *pharmacologist, researcher*

Waterbury
Chabria, Shiven B. *physician, educator*
Dudrick, Stanley John *surgeon, research scientist, educator*
Fischbein, Charles Alan *pediatrician*
Garsten, Joel Jay *gastroenterologist*

West Hartford
Silver, Herbert *physician*

Westport
Clausman, Gilbert Joseph *retired medical librarian*
Sacks, Herbert Simeon *psychiatrist, educator, consultant*

Woodbridge
Mason, John Wayne *psychoneuroendocrinologi retired medical educator*

DELAWARE

Bethany Beach
Klein, Gershon A. *pediatrician*

Dover
Wilson, Samuel Mayhew *surgeon*

Lewes
Saliba, Anis Khalil *surgeon*

Milton
Provost, Thomas Taylor *dermatology educator, researcher*

Newark
Gardner, Timothy Joseph *surgeon, educator*
Lemole, Gerald Michael *surgeon*

Rockland
Levinson, John Milton *obstetrician, gynecolog*

Wilmington
Abdel-Misih, Raafat Z. *surgeon, educator*
Alexander, Michael Allen *pediatrician, educator*
Barthold, Julia Spencer *urologist, researcher*
Benes, Solomon *retired biomedical scientist, physician*
Frelick, Robert Westcott *physician, consultant*
Goldberg, Morton Edward *pharmacologist*
Gonzalez, Ricardo *surgeon, educator*
Pell, Sidney *epidemiologist*
Reeves, Grafton Dulany *pediatric endocrinologist*
Shah, Udayan Kanaiyalal *surgeon*
Smith, S(tewart) Gregory *ophthalmologist, inventor, product developer, consultant, author*
Vinocur, Charles David *pediatric surgeon*

DISTRICT OF COLUMBIA

Washington
Adamson, Richard Henry *pharmacologist*
Ahlgren, James David *oncologist*
Ahmed, Atif Ali *pathologist*
Aisen, Paul S. *neurologist, researcher, educator*
Akukwe, Chinua *public health physician, health service executive*
Allen, Beverly E. *medical librarian*
Anthony, Virginia Quinn Bausch *medical association executive*
Arling, Bryan Jeremy *internist*
Attinger, Christopher Ernst *medical educator*
Avery, Gordon Bennett *medical educator, neonatologist*
Banta, James Elmer *epidemiologist, educator, dean*
Barnet, Robert Joseph *cardiologist, philosopher*
Batshaw, Mark Levitt *pediatrician*
Beers, Nathaniel Brittingham Savio *pediatrician*
Benjamin, Georges Curtis *emergency physician, consultant*
Benoit, Marilyn B. *psychiatrist, consultant*
Blumenthal, Susan Jane *physician, psychiatrist, educator*
Borenstein, David Gilbert *internist, writer, rheumatologist*
Bourne, Peter Geoffrey *physician, educator, writer*
Bruce, Derek Andrew *neurosurgeon, educator*
Burris, Boyd Lee *psychiatrist, psychoanalyst, physician, educator*
Callaway, Clifford Wayne *physician*
Callender, Clive Orville *surgeon*
Catoe, Bette Lorrina *pediatrician, educator*
Chamberlain, John Loomis III *retired pediatrician, educator*
Chase, Thomas Newell *neurologist, researcher, educator*
Cheng, Tsung O. *cardiologist, educator*
Chesanow, Charles *psychiatrist*
Chester, Alexander Campbell III *physician*
Collins, Robert Ellwood *surgeon*
Colon, Jose Ernesto *pathologist*
Cooper, Byron Stanley *internist, educator*
Davis, David Oliver *radiologist, educator*
Delahay, John N. *orthopedist, surgeon*
Dennis, Gary C. *neurosurgeon, educator*
de Quadros, Ciro A. *epidemiologist, educator*
Deutsch, Stanley *retired anesthesiologist, educator*
Dey, Radheshyam Chandra *cytologist*
Dimberg, Lennart Axel *medical researcher, physician*
Earll, Jerry Miller *internist, educator, endocrinologist*
Ein, Daniel *allergist*
Engler, Renata Johanna Martha *allergist, immunologist, internist, educator*
Epps, Roselyn Elizabeth Payne *pediatrician, educator*
Erdtmann, Frederick J. *physician, retired military officer*
Escolar, Diana M. *neurologist, researcher*
Finkelstein, James David *physician, educator*
Fishbein, Thomas Marlon *general surgeon, transplant surgeon*
Fowler, Paul Raymond *physician, lawyer*
Gardner, William Albert, Jr. *pathologist, medical products executive*
Gehrig, Leo Joseph *retired surgeon*
Gordon, James Samuel *psychiatrist*
Gray, Sheila Hafter *psychiatrist, researcher*
Grealy, Mary R. *medical association administrator*
Hamburg, Margaret Ann (Peggy Hamburg) *public health administrator*
Harter, Donald Harry *neurologist, medical educator*
Hicks, Jocelyn Muriel *laboratory medicine specialist*
Hsia, Judith Ann *physician*
Hussain, Syed Taseer *biomedical researcher, educator*
Hwang, Jimmy John *internist, oncologist*
Isaacs, Joseph C. *medical association administrator*
Jonas, Richard Andrew *medical educator*
Jose, Pedro A. *physician*
Kahn, Charles N., III, (Chip Kahn) *medical association administrator*
Kirch, Darrell Gene *medical association and former academic administrator, dean*
Korn, David *pathologist, educator*
Latham, Patricia S. *physician*
Lauerman, William *medical educator*
Lefemine, Armand Angelo *thoracic surgeon, educator*
Lessin, Lawrence Stephen *hematologist, oncologist, educator*
Lewin, John Calvert *medical association administrator*
Little, John William *plastic surgeon, educator*
Liu, Minetta Chung-sui *oncologist, educator*
Longnecker, David Eugene *anesthesiologist, educator*
Macht, Steven *plastic surgeon, consultant*
Mandel, Harold George *pharmacologist, educator*
Manderson, Easton L. *orthopedist, surgeon*
Maniscalco-Theberge, Mary Elizabeth *surgeon, medical educator*
Mann, Marion *pathologist, educator*
Mann, Oscar *retired physician, internist, educator*
Mattsson, Ake *psychiatrist, physician*
McGinnis, James Michael *physician*
Miller, Richard N. *former medical association administrator*
Monteiro, Maristela Goldnadel *physician, researcher*
Mullick, Florabel Garcia *pathologist, director*
Murray, Robert Fulton, Jr. *physician*
Myers, Ernest M. *otolaryngologist, head and neck surgeon*
Natarajan, Aruna *physician, educator, researcher*
Neviaser, Robert Jon *orthopaedic surgeon, educator*
Novitch, Mark *physician, retired pharmaceutical executive*
Oertel, Yolanda Castillo *pathologist, educator*
Olding, Michael *plastic and reconstructive surgeon*
Paulson, Jerome Avrom *pediatrician*
Payne, Fred J. *epidemiologist, educator*
Pellegrino, Edmund Daniel *internist, educator, retired academic administrator*
Pelton, Jeffrey J. *surgeon*
Potter, John Francis *oncologist, surgeon*
Puchalski, Christina M. *physician, medical educator*
Rankin, Edward Anthony *orthopedist, surgeon*
Rayner, Victoria Leigh *medical educator, consultant*
Reaman, Gregory Harold *pediatric hematologist, oncologist*
Redman, Robert Shelton *pathologist, dentist*
Reich, Walter *psychiatrist, medical educator, political science professor, writer, museum director*
Robinowitz, Carolyn Bauer *psychiatrist, educator, director*
Ruckman, Roger Norris *pediatric cardiologist*
Ruehle, Charles Joseph *pathologist, military officer*
Ruetter, Gunter H. *surgeon*
Shah, Rahul K. *surgeon, researcher*
Shanahan, Sheila Ann *pediatrician, educator*
Siegel, Robert Steven *internist, oncologist, educator*
Simon, Gary Leonard *internist, educator*
Sly, Ridge Michael *pediatrician, allergist, immunologist, educator*
Smith, Lee Elton *surgery educator, retired military officer*
Spagnolo, Samuel Vincent *internist, pulmonary specialist, educator*
Spear, Scott Lawrence *plastic surgeon*
Spies, James B. *radiologist, educator*
Sugarbaker, Paul H. *oncologist, surgeon*
Valachovic, Richard W. *medical association administrator*
Verghese, Mohan *urologist, surgeon*
Vezina, Gilbert *pediatric neuroradiologist*
Wartman, Steven A. *medical association administrator*
Werkman, Sidney Lee *psychiatrist, educator*
Witorsch, Philip *internist, educator*
Wolfe, Sidney Manuel *physician*

FLORIDA

Altamonte Springs
Nazari, Kourosh *ophthalmologist*

Amelia Island
Schiebler, Gerold Ludwig *pediatrician, educator*

Atlantic Beach
Walker, Richard Harold *pathologist, educator*

Atlantis
Daniel, George K. *cardiologist*

Bay Pines
Jewell, Vanessa yoder *surgical physician's assistant*
Law, David Hillis *physician*
Okano, Takeshi *thoracic surgeon*

Boca Raton
Buchbinder, Ligaya H. *dermatologist*
Friend, Harold Charles *neurologist*
Haugen, Christine *plastic surgeon*
Kramer, Cecile Edith *retired medical librarian*
Lemanski, Larry Fredrick *medical educator, academic administrator*
Man, Daniel *plastic surgeon*
Parra-Davila, Eduardo *surgeon, educator*
Pasternack, Stefan Alan *psychiatrist, psychoanalyst*
Sperry, Len Thomas *psychiatrist and preventive medicine educator*
Weiner, Howard Marc *physician*

Bonita Springs
Boothby, Richard Alfred *gynecologist, educator*
Dougherty, James *retired orthopedist*
Kopf, George Michael *retired ophthalmologist*

Boynton Beach
Glickman, Franklin Sheldon *dermatologist, educator*
Pataky, Paul Eric *ophthalmologist*
Wick, Mitchell A. *physician*

Bradenton
Grace, David *physician*
Peterson, Richard J. *surgeon*
Vereb, Teresa B. *psychiatrist*

Cape Coral
(Pickett) Harrison Flint, Nancy Elizabeth *retired medical administrator*
Martin, Benjamin Gaufman *ophthalmologist*

Clearwater
Bailey, Robin Keith *medical educator*
Blumencranz, Peter William *surgeon*

Coral Gables
Brandt, Frederic Sheldon *dermatologist*
Giuffrida, Theodore John *dermatologist*
Perez, Josephine *psychiatrist, educator*
Quillian, Warren Wilson, II, *pediatrician, educator*
Wolf, Aizik Loft *neurosurgeon*
Zvijac, John E. *orthopedist, surgeon*

Davie
Penhollow, Tina Marie *health science researcher, educator*

Daytona Beach
Bower, Roger Harrison *endocrinologist, director*
Duma, Richard Joseph *epidemiologist, microbiologist, educator, pathologist, researcher, physician*
Solomon, George *physician, military officer*

Deland
Goldberg, Paul Bernard *gastroenterologist, clinical researcher*

Delray Beach
Rosenfeld, Steven Ira *ophthalmologist*

Duck Key
Prout, George Russell, Jr. *medical educator, urologist*

Englewood
Sanders, W(illiam) Eugene, Jr. *retired internist*

Fernandina Beach
Barlow, Anne Louise *pediatrician, medical researcher*

Fort Lauderdale
Chernow, Bart *critical care physician*
Cox, Linda Susan *allergist, immunologist*
Droege, Marcus *medical educator, researcher*
Glick, Richard Stephen *internist, rheumatologist*
Lichtinger, Moises *obstetrician, gynecologist*
Lodwick, Gwilym Savage *radiologist, educator*
Parker, Sasha Smilka *medical educator, nurse, consultant*
Potparic, Zoran *plastic surgeon*
Revis, Don Ray, Jr. *plastic surgeon*
Rubinson, Howard Alan *physician*
Shen, Michael Yue-Hua *cardiologist*
Spector, Israel *oncologist*
Tristano, Antonio Gino *medical researcher*
Velez, Ines *oral pathologist, educator*
Whitmore, Douglas Michael *physician*

Fort Myers
Mandelkorn, Robert Marc *ophthalmologist*
Meng, Gunter Richard *surgeon*

Fort Pierce
Channon, Christopher T. *ophthalmologist*
Starner, Don Edward *radiologist, educator*

Gainesville
Baz, Maher Afif *internist, educator, medical director lung transplant program*
Behnke, Marylou *pediatrician, educator*
Berns, Kenneth Ira *physician*
Burns, Theodore Weber *gastroenterologist*
Conti, Charles Richard *medicine and cardiology educator*
Copeland, Edward Meadors III *surgeon, educator*
Drago, Valeria *neurologist, researcher*
Drummond, Willa Hendricks *neonatologist, educator, information technology executive*
Flotte, Terence Robin *pediatrician, pulmonologist*
Greer, Melvin *medical educator*
Hardt, Nancy Sisson *pathology and laboratory medicine educator*
Herzog, Roland W. *medical educator*
LeVeen, Robert Frederick *radiologist*
Mazzaferri, Ernest Louis *endocrinologist, educator*
Modell, Jerome Herbert *anesthesiologist, educator*
Mubarak, Kamal K. *pulmonologist, intensivist*
Neiberger, Richard Eugene *pediatrician, nephrologist, educator*
Neims, Allen Howard *pediatrician, educator, dean, researcher*
Pepine, Carl John *physician, educator*
Pfaff, William Wallace *medical educator*
Ramos-Caro, Francisco A. *dermatologist, educator*
Rhoton, Albert Loren, Jr. *neurosurgeon, educator*
Rubin, Melvin Lynne *ophthalmologist, educator*
Small, Parker Adams, Jr. *pediatrician, educator*
Suzuki, Howard Kazuro *retired anatomist, educator*
Tisher, Charles Craig *nephrologist, educator, dean*
Toskes, Phillip Paul *gastroenterologist, educator, researcher*
Uthman, Basim Mohammad *neurologist, epileptologist, consultant*
Weinstein, David A. *endocrinologist, director*
Wingard, John Reid *medical educator*
Yuan, Zhen *biomedical researcher*

Hallandale
Braverman, Stanley Deems *ophthalmologist*

Hialeah
Roman, Eloy *oncologist*
Sosa, Jorge Luis *surgeon*

Hollywood
Duffner, Lee R. *ophthalmologist*
Sandberg, Joel S. *ophthalmologist*
Sofman, Michael S. *dermatologist*

Inverness
Esquibel, Edward V. *psychiatrist, health facility administrator*

Jacksonville
Aldana, Philipp Roque *neurosurgeon*
Bartley, George B. *ophthalmologist, surgeon*
Bosworth, William Posey *physician, physical education educator*
Boylan, Kevin Bernard *neurologist*
Buckner, Jan Craig *oncologist, educator*
Camacho, George *internist*
Goodwin, Jane Ayers *pediatric anesthesiologist*
Johnson, Douglas William *radiologist*
Laucks, Richard Conrad *otolaryngologist*
Mass, M. F. *allergist, immunologist*
Mercer, Erica Schalow *urologist, educator*
Mills, David Michael *ophthalmologist, plastic surgeon*
Mizrahi, Edward Alan *allergist*
Mooradian, Arshag Dertad *internist, educator*
Moreno-Aspitia, Alvaro *physician, researcher*
Perdikis, Galen *plastic surgeon*
Raynor, Eileen Margolies *otolaryngologist, educator*
Stein, Keith Lance *health system administrator*
Thorsteinsson, Gudni *physiatrist*
Van Cleve, Robert Baldwin *cardiologist*

Jupiter
Ernst, Calvin Bradley *retired vascular surgery educator*
Farner, Gordon Noble *retired orthopedist, surgeon*
Zelnick, Ronald Stuart *surgeon*

Kennedy Space Center
Darwood, John Joseph *physician*

Key West
Wisniewski, P. Michelle *retired obstetrician, gynecologist*

Lady Lake
Pflum, William John *physician*

Lakeland
Jurbala, Brian Michael *orthopedic surgeon*
Pepine, Mary *dermatologist*

Largo
Grove, Jeffrey Scott *family practice physician*
Krolick, Merrill A. *cardiologist*
Wheat, Myron William, Jr. *cardiothoracic surgeon*

Leesburg
Moore, Wistar *cardiovascular surgeon*

Longboat Key
McCollough, Newton Clark III *orthopaedic surgeon*

Loxahatchee
Wisnicki, Jeffrey Leonard *plastic surgeon*

Lutz
Cualing, Hernani Del Mundo *physician, researcher*

Maitland
Cicilioni, Orlando Joseph *plastic surgeon*
Rijken, Pieter *medical association administrator*

Marco Island
Krause, Charles Joseph *otolaryngologist*

Melbourne
Greenblatt, Hellen Chaya *immunologist, microbiologist*
Grenevicki, Lance Francis *surgeon*
Magee, Thomas Henry *radiologist, educator*
Pocoski, David John *cardiologist*

Miami
Anderson, Douglas Richard *ophthalmologist, educator, researcher*
Bandstra, Emmalee S. *physician, pediatrician, researcher, educator*
Benjamin, Latanya T. *dermatologist*
Bird, Vincent G. *urologist, researcher, educator*
Blechman, Wilbur Jordan *medical educator*
Block, Norman Louis *oncologist, educator*
Bolooki, Hooshang *cardiac surgeon*
Burke, Redmond Paul *pediatric cardiologist, surgeon*
Chiron, Harlan S. *orthopedic surgeon, educator*
Dominguez-Bendala, Juan *medical educator*
Duchesne, Carlos A. *epidemiologist, military officer*
Eftekhari, Nasser *physiatrist*
Eisdorfer, Carl *psychiatrist, health facility administrator*
Elsas, Louis Jacob, II, *medical educator*
Enriquez, Cristino Catud *radiologist, internist, cardiologist*
Eshraghi, Adrien A. *head and neck surgeon, medical educator, researcher*
Fernandez, Alberto De Dios *physician*
Freshwater, Michael Felix *hand surgeon, educator*
Furst, Alex Julian *thoracic and cardiovascular surgeon*
Ginsberg, Myron David *neurologist*
Green, Barth *neurosurgeon*
Harezi, Ilonka Jo *medical technology research executive*
Heros, Roberto Cosme C. *neurosurgeon*
Herz, Marvin Ira *psychiatrist, researcher*
Hochstein, Leonard Mark *plastic surgeon*
Howell, Ralph Rodney *pediatrician, geneticist, educator*
Irwin, Robert W. *medical educator*
Karp, Carol *ophthalmologist, educator*
King, Booker Terry, Jr. *surgeon*
Kitsos, Constantine Nicholas *plastic surgeon*
Lasseter, Kenneth Carlyle *pharmacologist*

Lemberg, Louis *cardiologist, educator*
Lippman, Marc Estes *oncologist, educator, medical researcher*
Llorente, Maria Dorta *psychiatrist, geriatrician, educator*
Lubarsky, David Alan *anesthesiologist, educator*
Maulion, Richard Peter *psychiatrist, physician, neurolinguist*
Olvey, Stephen Earl *internist*
Page, Larry Keith *neurosurgeon, educator*
Panthaki, Zubin Jal *medical educator, plastic surgeon*
Pericak-Vance, Margaret A. *medical geneticist, educator, health facility administrator*
Persoff, Myron Mayer *plastic surgeon*
Pham, Si Mai *cardiothoracic surgeon*
Porter, Wayne Randolph *dermatologist*
Puliafito, Carmen Anthony *ophthalmologist, healthcare executive*
Ricordi, Camillo *surgeon, researcher*
Robles, Carlos *hematologist, oncologist*
Rodriguez, René F. *orthopedic surgeon*
Rubell, Donald *gynecologist, hotel executive, art collector*
Rusconi, Paolo *pediatric cardiologist*
Schally, Andrew Victor *endocrine oncologist, researcher*
Scully, Sean Patrick *orthopaedic surgeon, educator*
Sherman, Andrew Lawrence *physiatrist, educator*
Simpson, Joe Leigh *obstetrics and gynecology educator*
Skyler, Jay S. *medical educator, consultant*
Smalling, William E. *pediatrician, neonatologist*
Tejada, Francisco *physician, educator*
Thaller, Seth Ray *plastic surgeon*
Wheeler, Steve Dereal *neurologist*
Wolff, Grace Susan *pediatric cardiologist*
Wolfson, Aaron Howard *radiation oncologist, educator*
Zaydon, Thomas John, Jr. *plastic surgeon*

Miami Beach
Justiniani, Federico Roberto *internist, educator*
Katz, Brian Jeffrey *dermatologist*
Mandy, Stephen Howard *dermatologist, educator*

Naples
Crandall, Blane Mitchell *obstetrician, gynecologist*
Gehring, David Austin *cardiologist, physician, health facility administrator*
Greene, David *surgeon, researcher*
Pfister, Raymond Lawrence *otolaryngologist*
Randall, Neil Warren *gastroenterologist*
Schwartz, Stephen Gregory *ophthalmologist*
Temple, Donald *retired allergist, dermatologist*
Thomas, John Melvin *retired surgeon*

North Palm Beach
Stein, Mark Rodger *allergist*

Ocala
Altenburger, Karl Marion *allergist*
Schwenk, Gordon Cameron *ophthalmologist*

Oldsmar
Gambone, Victor, Jr. *internist, geriatrician*

Orange City
Orgega, Gregory Luis *hematologist, oncologist*
Ortega, Gregory Luis *hematologist, oncologist*

Orange Park
Fetchero, John Anthony, Jr. *otolaryngologist*

Orlando
Bodager, Dean W. *epidemiologist*
Haas, Brian D. *surgeon*
Hornick, Richard Bernard *physician*
Kolattukudy, Pappachan Ettoop *medical center executive, biochemist, educator*
Kollas, Chad D. *medical educator*
Naser, Saleh A. *medical researcher, educator*
Okun, Neil Jeffrey *vitreoretinal surgeon*
Pollack, Robert William *psychiatrist, corporate financial executive*
Shub, Harvey Allen *surgeon*
Taitt, Earl Paul *psychiatrist, military officer*
Wallace, Mark Raymond *physician*

Osprey
Caradonna, Stephanie Ann *dermatologist*

Palm Beach
Simon, Harold *radiologist*

Palm Beach Gardens
Baynham, G. Clay *surgeon*
Kapnick, Samuel Jason *oncologist*

Palm Harbor
Harrell, Carl Randall *plastic surgeon*

Palm Springs
Abou-Sayed, Hatem *plastic surgeon*

Panama City Beach
Reading, Anthony John *retired psychiatrist, educator*

Pensacola
Canady, Alexa Irene *pediatric neurosurgeon, educator*
Gill, Becky Lorette *retired psychiatrist*
Kichler, Jack *dermatologist*
Vuksta, Michael Joseph *surgeon*

Placida
Prabhudesai, Mukund M. *pathology educator, health facility administrator, researcher, academic administrator*

Plantation
Gewirtzman, Garry Bruce *dermatologist*

Pompano Beach
Cherla, Gautam V. *physician, nephrologist, researcher*
Phillips, Floyd Leigh *plastic surgeon*

Ponte Vedra Beach
Harris, John Borgeson *plastic surgeon*
ReMine, William Hervey, Jr. *retired surgeon*

Port Charlotte
Hegleh, Joseph A. *ophthalmologist*

Saint Petersburg
Betzer, Susan Elizabeth Beers *physician, geriatrician*
Bolhofner, Brett Robinson *orthopedist*
Buckspan, Randy Jay *plastic surgeon*
Collins, Paul Steven *vascular surgeon*
Gilbert, Gordon Joel *neurologist, electroencelographer*
Hamilton, John McFarland *plastic surgeon, real estate developer*
Lanza, Donald Charles *otolaryngologist, rhinologist*
Linhart, Joseph Wayland *retired cardiologist, educational administrator*
Root, Allen William *pediatrician, educator*
Rosenblum, Martin Jerome *ophthalmologist*

Sanford
Drewry, Marcia Ann *physician*
Oostwouder, Peter Henry *physician*

Sarasota
Apfelbach, George Leonard, Jr. *urologist*
Aull, Susan *physician*
Bowers, Charles Richard *surgeon*
Cavanagh, Denis *gynecologist, obstetrician, educator, gynecological oncologist*
Cummings, Martin Marc *physician, educator, academic administrator*
El Shahawy, Mahfouz *internist, educator, cardiologist*
Iverson, Robert Louis, Jr. *retired internist, physician*
Jelks, Mary Larson *retired pediatrician*
Levy, Gerhard *pharmacologist*
Magenheim, Mark Joseph *physician, epidemiologist, educator*
Marks, Charles *surgeon, educator*
Milam, Cathy P. *dermatologist*
O'Malley, Thomas Anthony *gastroenterologist, internist*
Runge, Paul E. *ophthalmologist, educator*
Zavon, Mitchell Ralph *occupational medicine physician*

Spring Hill
Del Toro-Politowicz, Lillian *medical association administrator, geriatrics services professional, consultant*

Stuart
Patterson, Robert Arthur *physician, health care consultant, retired health care company executive, retired air force officer*
Sabol, Stuart J. *otolaryngologist*
Stark, Richard Boies *surgeon, artist*

Sun City Center
Crow, Harold Eugene *physician, educator*

Sunrise
Garramone, Charles *plastic surgeon*

Tallahassee
Deeb, Larry Charles *pediatric endocrinologist, epidemiologist*
Hernandez, Jose Yolando Balagtas *surgeon*
Hernandez, Minerva Cuadrante *physician, consultant*
Maguire, Charlotte Edwards *retired pediatrician*
Rahman, Saleh Mahmudir *medical educator*

Tampa
Afield, Walter Edward *psychiatrist, educator, health facility administrator*
Agazzi, Siviero *neurosurgeon*
Armstrong, Peter F. *surgeon, pediatrician, orthopedist*
Barness, Lewis Abraham *physician*
Branch, William Terrell *urologist, educator*
Bunker-Soler, Antonio Luis *physician*
Dalton, William Steven *oncologist, educator*
Dessureault, Sophie *oncologist, surgeon, educator*
Edwards, Charles M. *medical educator*
Eichberg, Rodolfo David *physiatrist, educator*
Gabrilovich, Dmitry I. *immunologist, educator*
Gallagher, Scott Farrell *surgeon, researcher*
Gilbert-Barness, Enid F. *pathologist, educator*
Greenfield, George B. *radiologist*
Guida, Wayne Charles *medical educator, research scientist*
Hulls, James Robert *emergency physician*
Humphrey, Deborah A. *medical educator, internist*
Jacobs, Timothy Andrew *epidemiologist, consultant*
Jacobson, Howard Newman *obstetrics and gynecology educator, researcher*
Knox, Michael Dennis *medical educator, research center administrator*
Kriz, Frank Kenneth, Jr. *surgeon*
Lockey, Richard Funk *allergist, immunologist, educator*
Malone, John I. *pediatrics educator, biomedical researcher*
McIlwain, Harris H. *physician, researcher*
Muroff, Lawrence Ross *nuclear medicine physician, educator*
Older, Jay Justin *ophthalmic plastic surgeon*
Olson, Robert Eugene *physician, biochemist, educator*
Pedowitz, Robert Alan *orthopaedic surgeon, researcher*

Pfeiffer, Eric Armin *psychiatrist, gerontologist, writer*
Powers, Pauline Smith *psychiatrist, educator, researcher*
Rowlands, David Thomas *pathology educator*
Sanberg, Paul Ronald *medical educator*
Sanchez-Ramos, Juan Ramon *physician, medical educator*
Shenefelt, Philip David *dermatologist*
Shephard, Bruce Dennis *obstetrician, educator, medical writer*
Silbiger, Martin L. *radiologist, educator, dean*
Smith, David John, Jr. *plastic surgeon*
Spellacy, William Nelson *obstetrician, gynecologist, educator*
Sullebarger, John Thompson *internist, educator, cardiologist*
Vila, Hector *anesthesiologist, department chairman*
Watkins, Joan Marie *retired osteopath, retired physician*

Titusville
Duffy, John Charles *psychiatrist, educator, consultant*

Trenton
Ivey, James Frederick, Jr. *physician*

Venice
Abernathy, George Thomas *cardiologist, consultant*
Hrachovina, Frederick Vincent *retired osteopathic physician*
Shamsham, Fadi Michel *cardiologist*

Vero Beach
Christopher, Robert Paul *retired physical medicine physician*
Schwarz, Berthold Eric *psychiatrist*

Weeki Wachee
Finney, Roy Pelham, Jr. *urologist, surgeon, inventor*

West Palm Beach
Brumback, Clarence Landen *physician*
Jacobson, Robert Julian *oncologist, director*
Levin, Ronald Mitchell *geriatrician*
Merey, John Howard *ophthalmologist*
Newmark, Emanuel *ophthalmologist*
Pottash, A. Carter *psychiatrist, hospital executive*
Whitfield, Graham Frank *orthopedic surgeon*

Weston
Lazar, Marioara *psychiatrist*
Messa, Charles Angelo III *plastic surgeon*
Nogueras, Juan Jose *surgeon*

Winter Haven
Susac, John Obren *neurologist, consultant*

Winter Park
Pineless, Hal Steven *neurologist*
Wilson, Cecil Bruce *internist*

GEORGIA

Acworth
Oloni, Anthony Olushegun *medical association administrator, director*

Albany
Erhardt, Walter L., Jr. *medical association administrator*
Peach, Paul E. *physician, health facility administrator*
Ratz, John Louis *dermatologist*

Americus
Tu, Chanh M. *ophthalmologist*

Athens
Cook, Joel *radiologist*

Atlanta
Arias, Ileana *psychiatrist, educator*
Berga, Sarah L. *obstetrician, gynecologist, educator*
Berger, Mitchell Zachary *oncologist*
Berkelhamer, Jay Ellis *pediatrician*
Berkelman, Ruth *medical educator*
Bernardino, Carlo Roberto *ophthalmologist, educator*
Bijol, Vanesa *nephrologist, educator, pathologist, researcher*
Boden, Scott David *orthopedic surgeon, spine surgeon, educator*
Brandenburg, David Saul *gastroenterologist, educator*
Bremner, James Douglas *psychiatrist, researcher, education educator*
Cates, Christopher Upton *cardiologist*
Clearo, Kellie Anne *internist, pharmacist, psychiatrist*
Cooper, Gerald Rice *clinical pathologist*
Cooper-Ruspoli, Annie Nataf *psychiatrist, director*
Correa, Adolfo *epidemiologist, educator*
Curran, James W. *epidemiologist, educator, dean*
Davis, Lawrence William *radiation oncologist*
Davis, Michael *medical educator*
DeLong, Mahlon R. *neurologist, educator*
De Rosa, Christopher Thomas *biomedical researcher*
Dietz, William Harry *pediatrician*
D'Orsi, Carl Joseph *medical educator, radiologist, researcher*
Dutt, Kamla *medical educator*
Fajardo, Geroncio Cagigas *epidemiologist*
Falk, Henry *pediatrician, epidemiologist, researcher*
Fischbach, Peter *pediatrician*
Frias, Jaime Luis *retired pediatrician, educator*
Galambos, John Thomas *internist, medical educator*

Ganaway, George Kenneth *psychiatrist, psychoanalyst, educator, researcher*
Gayle, Helene D. *pediatrician, public health service officer*
Goldman, John Abner *rheumatologist, immunologist, educator*
Gordon, Frank Jeffrey *medical educator*
Gupta, Sanjay *neurosurgeon, educator, medical correspondent, journalist*
Hall, Wilbur Dallas, Jr. *medical educator*
Hao, Chunhai *pathologist, researcher*
Hatcher, Charles Ross, Jr. *surgeon, health facility administrator*
Hester, Thomas Roderick, Jr. *plastic surgeon, educator*
Higginbotham, Eve Juliet *ophthalmologist, educator, dean*
Hudgins, Roger J. *pediatric neurosurgeon*
Hug, Carl Casimir, Jr. *pharmacology and anesthesiology educator, medical ethics educator*
Hughes, James Mitchell *epidemiologist, educator*
Igietseme, Joseph Ugbodaga *biomedical researcher, educator*
Israili, Zafar Hasan *pharmacologist, educator*
Johns, Michael Marieb Edward *otolaryngologist, academic administrator*
Jurkiewicz, Maurice John *surgeon, educator*
Kaelin, Darryl Louis *medical educator*
Karp, Herbert Rubin *neurologist, educator*
King, Spencer Bidwell III *cardiologist, educator, medical educator*
Klippel, John H. *physician, medical association administrator*
Lubin, Michael Frederick *physician, educator*
Mackay, Gregory James *plastic surgeon*
Mansour, Kamal A. *cardiothoracic surgeon*
Minneman, Kenneth Paul *pharmacology educator*
Nahai, Foad *plastic surgeon, educator*
Nunn, Donald Ray *plastic surgeon*
Oakley, Godfrey Porter, Jr. *medical educator*
Olansky, Sidney *retired dermatologist*
Osburne, Robert Carl *endocrinologist, educator*
Peacock, Lamar Batts *retired physician*
Reed, James Whitfield *internist, educator, endocrinologist*
Rohr-Kirchgraber, Theresa M.B. *adolescent medicine*
Sands, Jeff Michael *medical educator*
Saslow, Debbie L. *cancer control specialist, director*
Savera, Adnan Tabrez *surgical pathologist, director*
Sexson, William Robert *pediatrician, educator*
Singh, Narendra *cardiologist, researcher, medical educator*
Smith, Robert Boulware III *vascular surgeon, educator*
Spangler, Dennis Lee *physician*
Steinhaus, John Edward *retired anesthesiologist, educator*
Stillwagon, Gary Bouldin *radiation oncologist*
Tait, C. Downing, Jr., (Columbus Downing Tait Jr.) *physician, medical educator*
Taylor, Andrew T., Jr. *radiologist, educator*
Thacker, Stephen Brady *medical association administrator, epidemiologist*
Thattassery, Emil George *cardiologist*
Udoff, Eric Joel *diagnostic radiologist*
Vega, J. David *thoracic surgeon*
Wenger, Nanette Kass *cardiologist, researcher, educator*
Weyand, Cornelia Maritta *medical educator*
Wineski, Lawrence E. *medical educator, biomedical researcher*
Wood, William C. *surgeon, medical educator, academic chairman*
Yancey, Asa Greenwood, Sr. *physician, educator*

Auburn
Hutchinson, Leslie Julian *preventive medicine physician*

Augusta
Atteberry, Linda Rose *surgeon, retired military officer*
Bollag, Wendy Bollinger *medical educator, scientist*
Carroll, James Edwin *child neurologist, researcher*
Dolen, William Kennedy *allergist, immunologist, pediatrician, educator*
Ellison, Lois Taylor *internist, educator, medical association administrator*
Fincher, Ruth Marie Edla *medical educator, dean*
Given, Kenna Sidney *surgeon, educator*
Hooks, Vendie Hudson III *surgeon*
Horuzsko, Anatolij *medical researcher*
Hsu, Stephen De *medical educator*
Johnson, William Michael *physician*
Lee, Gregory Price *neuropsychology educator*
Luxenberg, Malcolm Neuwahl *ophthalmologist, educator*
Mansberger, Arlie Roland, Jr. *surgeon*
Ownby, Dennis Randall *pediatrician, allergist, educator, researcher*
Pryor, Carol Graham *obstetrician, gynecologist*
Ryan, James Walter *physician, researcher*
Wray, Betty Beasley *allergist, immunologist, pediatrician*

Austell
Halwig, J. Michael *allergist*

Brunswick
Perniciaro, Charles Vincent *dermatologist, educator, entrepreneur*

Buford
Byrd, Larry Donald *behavioral pharmacologist*

Columbus
Chan, Philip *retired dermatologist, retired military officer*

Decatur
Brown, William Virgil *internal medicine educator*
Farley, Monica M. *medical educator*
Gebhart, Ronald John *infectious disease specialist, administrator*
Henderson, Ralph Hale *physician*
Posey, Douglas Harris *pathologist*

Dublin
Giannini, A. James *psychiatrist, educator, researcher, author*

Duluth
Evans, Paul *osteopath*

Fort Stewart
Warner, Christopher Hugh *psychiatrist*

Lagrange
Copeland, Robert Bodine *internist, cardiologist*
West, John Thomas *retired surgeon*

Lawrenceville
Fetner, Robert Henry *radiobiologist*

Macon
Robinson, Joe Sam *neurosurgeon, educator*
Young, Henry E. *tissue engineering medical educator*

Marietta
Ranu, Harcharan Singh *biomedical scientist, administrator, orthopaedic biomechanics educator*

Martinez
Colborn, Gene Louis *anatomy educator, researcher*

Roswell
McCloud, Melody T. *obstetrician-gynecologist, surgeon*
Yune, Marc E. *surgeon*

Savannah
Fishburne, John Ingram, Jr. *retired obstetrician/gynecologist, educator*
Greco, Richard Jude *plastic and reconstructive surgeon*
Krahl, Enzo *retired surgeon*
Lindley, James Gunn, Jr. *neurosurgeon*
Skelton, William Douglas *physician*
Wirth, Fremont Philip, Jr. *neurosurgeon, educator*
Zoller, Michael *otolaryngologist, head and neck surgeon, educator*

Smyrna
Jeffords, Keith (Kelland Keith Jeffords Jr.) *plastic surgeon*

Stockbridge
Friedman, Robert Barry *neurosurgeon*

Stone Mountain
Gotlieb, Jaquelin Smith *pediatrician*

Tifton
Dorminey, Henry Clayton, Jr. *allergist*

Tucker
iali, Ye *medical researcher*

Valdosta
Beal, John M. *surgeon, medical educator*
Morgan, Joe Leland *physician, psychiatrist*

Warner Robins
Gayton, Johnny Lee *ophthalmologist, educator, recreational facility executive*

HAWAII

Honolulu
Ahmed, Iqbal *psychiatrist, consultant*
Brady, Stephen R. P. K. *physician*
Chesne, Edward Leonard *physician*
Curb, Jess David *medical educator, researcher*
Fong, Bernard W.D. *physician, educator*
Goldstein, Sir Norman *dermatologist*
Goodhue, William Walter, Jr. *pathologist, military officer, educator*
Guerrero, Reuben Castro *oncologist, internist*
Ho, Reginald Chi Shing *medical educator*
Issell, Brian F. *oncologist, internist*
Lane, Thomas Jay III *surgeon, educator*
Lim, S. Peter *psychiatrist, educator, health facility administrator, researcher*
Lau, H. Lorrin *obstetrician, gynecologist*
Lee, Yeu-Tsu Margaret *surgeon, educator*
Moreno-Cabral, Carlos Eduardo *cardiac surgeon*
Obana, William G. *neurosurgeon*
O'Shaughnessy, Edward Joseph *urologist, retired medical educator*
Parsa, Fereydoun Don *plastic surgeon*
Schatz, Irwin Jacob *cardiologist, educator*
Sugiki, Shigemi *ophthalmologist, educator*
Yew, David *physician, director*

Kailua
Kuratynski, Theresa Joan *physician*

Koloa
Donohugh, Donald Lee *physician*

Lahaina
Percy, Helen Sylvia *physician*

Lihue
Mulliney, John James *radiologist, educator*

Mililani
Gardner, Sheryl Paige *gynecologist*
Akita, George Torao *retired pharmacologist*

Waikoloa
Copman, Louis *radiologist*

IDAHO

Boise
Badke, Frederick Robert *cardiologist*
Eiriksson, Charles Einar *cardiologist*
Nelson, Kristin Schad *cosmetic surgeon*
Parent, Mark Gordon *cardiologist*
Priest, Marshall Franklin III *cardiologist*
Redshaw, James Douglas *neurologist*
Seale, Walter Louis *cardiologist*

Coeur D' Alene
McCormick, Chad Donald *otolaryngologist*

Fort Hall
Himmler, Bruno Jon *physician, military officer*

Idaho Falls
Lee, Glenn Richard *medical association administrator, educator*

Pocatello
Risinger, Fred Owen *pharmacologist*

Post Falls
Riggs, Jack Timothy *emergency physician, retired lieutenant governor*

ILLINOIS

Arlington Heights
Ehrenpreis, Eli Daniel *physician, educator, biomedical researcher*
Jensen, Lynn Edward *retired medical association administrator, economist*
Ruder, John Regan *physician*

Aurora
Cain, Thomas Robert *interventional radiologist*

Barrington
Young, Michael Phillip *orthopedist, surgeon*

Belleville
Stanford, Edward Joseph *gynecologist*

Berwyn
Galinsky, Dennis Lee *radiation oncologist, educator*
Misurec, Rudolf *physician, surgeon*

Bloomington
Trefzger, Richard Charles *surgeon*

Bolingbrook
Malicay, Manuel Alaban *physician*

Champaign
Freedman, Philip *internist, educator*
Gold, Paul Ernest *psychology and behavioral neuroscience educator*

Charleston
Ramsey, Charles Estel *retired physician, retired surgeon*

Chicago
Abcarian, Herand *surgeon, educator*
Abelson, Herbert Traub *pediatrician, educator*
Albrecht, Ronald Frank *anesthesiologist*
Andersen, Burton Robert *immunologist, educator, medical historian*
Arnold, Damon Theodore *physician*
Arruda, Jose *nephrologist*
Arvanitakis, Zoe *neurologist, researcher*
Bailey, Robert Converse *epidemiologist, anthropologist, educator*
Bakay, Roy Arpad Earle *neurosurgeon, educator*
Bakris, George L. *nephrologist, educator, clinical researcher*
Baldwin, DeWitt Clair, Jr. *pediatrician, educator*
Balk, Robert A. *medical educator*
Barker, Walter Lee *thoracic surgeon*
Baron, Joseph Mandel *hematologist*
Barton, John Joseph *obstetrician, gynecologist, administrator, educator, researcher*
Beck, Robert N. *nuclear medicine educator*
Becker, Michael Allen *internist, rheumatologist, educator*
Bell, Carl Compton *psychiatrist, researcher*
Benson, Al Bowen III *oncologist, educator*
Bezanilla, Francisco *biomedical researcher*
Boggs, Joseph Dodridge *pediatric pathologist, educator*
Bonomi, Philip David *physician*
Bonow, Robert Ogden *medical educator*
Bowman, James Edward *pathologist, educator*
Briones, Teresita Landicho *medical researcher, educator*
Burck, Joseph Russell *medical educator, consultant, minister*
Burt, Richard K. *physician, educator*
Cameron, Kenzie Alynn *medical researcher, educator*
Caro, William Allan *physician, educator*
Celesia, Gastone Guglielmo *neurologist*
Chambers, Donald Arthur *biochemistry and molecular medicine educator*
Chan, Lawrence Siu-Yung *dermatologist, educator*
Charles, Allan G. *obstetrician, educator*
Charrow, Joel *pediatrician, geneticist, educator, director*
Chatterton, Robert Treat, Jr. *reproductive endocrinology educator*
Chen, David *spinal cord injury physician*
Chmell, Samuel Jay *orthopedic surgeon*
Christoffel, Katherine Kaufer *pediatrician, epidemiologist, educator*
Chunprapaph, Boonmee *physician, educator*
Coe, Fredric L. *internist, educator, researcher*
Cohen, Melvin R. *physician, educator*
Cole, Brian Jared *orthopedist*
Colley, Karen J. *medical educator, researcher*
Conway, James Joseph *radiologist, educator*
Curry, Raymond Howard *physician*
Davidson, Michael H. *cardiologist, researcher*
Davison, Richard *internist, educator*
Dayal, Vijay Shanker *physician, educator*
Deamant, Catherine D. *internist*
Diamond, Seymour *physician*
Dunaif, Andrea Elizabeth *endocrinologist*
Dunea, George *nephrologist, educator*
Elias, Sherman *obstetrician, gynecologist, clinical geneticist, educator*
Evans, Thelma Jean Mathis *internist*
Farhadi, Ashkan *physician, researcher, writer*
Feingold, Daniel Leon *anesthesiologist, consultant*
Feldman, Ted *cardiologist*
Ferguson, Mark Kendric *surgeon, educator*
Flaherty, Timothy Thomas *radiologist*
Fraley, Andrea Lyn *physiatrist*
Franco, Carlo Diaz *surgeon, anatomist, anesthesiologist*
Freitag, Frederick Gerald *osteopathic physician*
Friedman, Michael *surgeon*
Galante, Jorge Osvaldo *orthopedic surgeon, educator*
Galatzer-Levy, Robert Milton *psychiatrist*
Gerbie, Albert Bernard *obstetrician, gynecologist, educator*
Gewurz, Anita Tartell *physician, medical educator*
Gittler, Michelle S. *physiatrist*
Givone, Donna Marie *pharmacologist*
Glass, Ronald Bernhard Jacob *radiologist*
Goldberg, Arnold Irving *psychoanalyst, educator*
Golomb, Harvey Morris *hematologist, oncologist, educator*
Gorbien, Martin John *medical educator, geriatrician*
Gordon, Leo I. *hematologist, oncologist, educator*
Greenberger, Paul Allen *allergist, immunologist, educator, medical researcher*
Gregory, Stephanie Ann *hematologist, educator*
Grevious, Mark Allen *plastic surgeon*
Griem, Katherine Leslie *radiation oncologist*
Hambrick, Ernestine *retired colon and rectal surgeon*
Harris, Gerald David *surgeon*
Hellman, Samuel *radiologist, educator*
Herbst, Arthur Lee *obstetrician, gynecologist*
Hibbard, Judith Usher *obstetrician*
Hill Rotman, Carlotta H. *physician*
Honig, George Raymond *pediatrician*
Hsieh, Patrick C. *neurosurgeon*
Hsueh, Wei *pathologist, educator*
Huckman, Michael Saul *neuroradiologist, educator*
Hughes, John Russell *neurologist, educator*
Inan, Zabrin *psychiatrist*
Ivankovich, Anthony D. *anesthesiologist, educator*
Iyer, Kishore *transplant surgeon*
Jameson, James Larry *medical educator, endocrinologist, internist*
Jampol, Lee Merrill *ophthalmologist, educator*
Jensen, Harold Leroy *medical liability insurance administrator, physician*
Jilhewar, Ashok *gastroenterologist*
Johnson, Timothy Patrick *health and social researcher*
Kahrilas, Peter James *medical educator, researcher*
Katz, Adrian Izhack *medical educator*
Kiani, Reza *endocrinology and internal medicine educator*
Kirschner, Barbara Starrels *gastroenterologist*
Kirsner, Joseph Barnett *physician, educator*
Kittle, Charles Frederick *surgeon*
Kloss, Linda L. *medical association administrator*
Kuiken, Todd Alan *medical researcher, rehabilitation services professional, educator*
Lavani, Romeen M. *physician*
Lease, John G. *plastic surgeon*
Lee, Raphael Carl *plastic surgeon, biomedical engineer*
Leff, Alan Richard *medical educator, researcher*
Leventhal, Bennett Lee *psychiatry and pediatrics educator, academic administrator*
Lindquist, Lee A. *geriatrician, educator*
Lopez, Carolyn Catherine *physician*
Luchins, Daniel Jonathan *psychiatrist*
Lurain, John Robert III *gynecologist*
Mahaffey, John Christopher *medical association executive*
Malkinson, Frederick David *dermatologist, educator*
Martin, Gary Joseph *medical educator*
McCarthy, Patrick M. *surgeon*
McGee, Edwin C., Jr. *surgeon*
Metz, Charles Edgar *radiology educator*
Millichap, Joseph Gordon *neurologist, educator*
Morgan, Elaine R. *hematologist, oncologist, medical educator*
Mukai, Ai *physiatrist*
Naclerio, Robert Michael *otolaryngologist, educator*
Nahrwold, David Lange *surgeon, educator*
Narahashi, Toshio *pharmacology educator*
Nyhus, Lloyd Milton *retired surgeon, educator*
Olson, Jack Conrad, Jr. *geriatrician*
Page, Ernest *retired medical educator*
Pappas, George Demetrios *anatomist, cell biologist, educator*
Pensler, Jay Michael *plastic surgeon, educator*
Poznanski, Andrew Karol *pediatric radiologist*
Prinz, Richard Allen *surgeon*
Pugh, Carla M. *surgeon, educator*
Rafeyan, Roueen *psychiatrist, educator*
Ramsey-Goldman, Rosalind *physician*
Replogle, Robert Lee *cardiovascular surgeon, thoracic surgeon*
Robertson, William Wright, Jr. *orthopedist, educator*
Robinson, June Kerswell *dermatologist, educator*
Rogers, Eugene Jack *retired medical educator*
Roizen, Nancy J. *physician, educator*
Roos, Raymond Philip *medical educator*
Rosen, Steven Terry *oncologist, hematologist*
Rosseau, Gail L. *neurosurgeon, educator*
Rowley, Janet Davison *physician*
Ruo, Bernice *physician, researcher*
Sabbagha, Rudy Elias *obstetrician, gynecologist, educator*
Sandler, Richard H. *pediatric gastroenterologist*
Sandlow, Leslie Jordan *gastroenterologist, educator*
Schafer, Michael Frederick *orthopedic surgeon*
Schenck, Robert Roy *hand surgeon*
Schilsky, Richard Lewis *oncologist, researcher*
Sciarra, John J. *obstetrician, gynecologist, educator*
Scommegna, Antonio *obstetrician, gynecologist, educator*
Seeler, Ruth Andrea *pediatrician, educator*
Serry, Cyrus *medical educator*
Shields, Thomas William *surgeon, educator*
Short, Marion Priscilla *neurogenetics educator*
Siegler, Mark *internist, educator*
Smith, Earl Charles *nephrologist, educator*
Smith, Joanne C. *physiatrist*
Smith, Lewis J. *medical educator, researcher*
Socol, Michael Lee *obstetrician, gynecologist, educator*
Song, David *plastic surgeon, medical educator*
Sorrentino, Matthew Joseph *internist, educator*
Sparberg, Marshall Stuart *gastroenterologist, educator*
Spring, Bonnie Joan *preventive medicine educator*
Stamler, Jeremiah *physician, educator*
Stanos, Steven Peter, Jr. *osteopath*
Steinhorn, Robin H. *neonatologist, educator*
Strassner, Howard Taft, Jr. *obstetrician, educator*
Stulberg, Samuel David *surgeon, physician*
Tanna, Angelo Peter *ophthalmologist, educator, researcher*
Tatar, Arnold Marshall *internist, educator*
Telfer, Margaret Clare *internist, hematologist, oncologist*
Tomar, Russell Herman *pathologist, educator, researcher*
Trafimow, Jordan Herman *orthopedist*
Umbdenstock, Richard J. *medical association administrator*
Valyi-Nagy, Tibor G. *neuropathologist, virologist*
Vigneswaran, Wickii Thambiah *cardiothoracic surgeon, educator*
Volgman, Annabelle Santos *cardiologist, educator*
Wagner, Annette M. *dermatologist, surgeon*
Walton, Robert Lee *plastic surgeon*
Webster, James Randolph, Jr. *physician*
Whitington, Peter Frank *pediatric hepatologist, educator*
Wied, George Ludwig *physician*
Williams, Kim Allan *cardiologist, educator*
Williams, Philip Copelain *obstetrician, gynecologist*
Williamson, Wayne C. *internist, geriatrician*
Willoughby, William Franklin, II, *retired physician, researcher*
Yao, Tito Go *pediatrician*
Yudkowsky, Rachel *medical educator*
Zee, Phyllis C. *physician, educator, researcher*
Zeine, Rana Ramsey *neuropathologist, research professor*
Zhu, Mingzhao *immunologist, microbiologist*

Chicago Heights
Yalavarthi, Ramaraja *physician*

Darien
Gardner, Howard Garry *pediatrician, educator*
Kulkarni, Bidy *reproductive endocrinologist, biomedical researcher, consultant*

Deerfield
Sanner, John Harper *retired pharmacologist*

Des Plaines
Quintanilla, Antonio Paulet *retired physician, educator*

Downers Grove
Cornell, Susan *medical educator*
Dahdal, Wafa Y. *pharmacologist, educator*

Elgin
Yarkony, Gary Michael *physician, researcher*

Elmhurst
Blain, Charlotte Marie *internist, educator*

Evanston
Bloomer, William David *radiologist, oncologist, educator*
Brendler, Charles Burgess *urologist, educator*
Crawford, James Weldon *psychiatrist, educator, administrator*
Gaiha, Vishnu Das *cardiologist*
Khandekar, Janardan Dinkar *oncologist, educator*
Miller, Stephen Herschel *surgeon, educator*
Mustoe, Thomas Anthony *physician, plastic surgeon*
Peterson, Lance Robert *physician*
Schwartz, Neena Betty *endocrinologist, educator*
Sener, Stephen Francis *oncologist, surgeon*
Sprang, Milton LeRoy *obstetrician, gynecologist, educator*
Stumpf, David Allen *pediatric neurologist*
Traisman, Howard Sevin *retired pediatrician*
Vick, Nicholas A. *neurologist*

Evergreen Park
Zumerchik, John *urologist*

Galena
Bezkorovainy, Anatoly *medical educator, retired biochemist*

Glen Ellyn
Dieter, Raymond Andrew, Jr. *physician, thoracic and vascular surgeon*

Glencoe
Milloy, Frank Joseph, Jr. *surgeon*

Glenview
Casas, Laurie Ann *plastic surgeon*
Graff, Jeffrey G. *emergency physician*
Haebich, Arthur T. *retired thoracic surgeon*

Godfrey
King, Ordie Herbert, Jr. *oral pathologist*

Harvey
Heilicser, Bernard Jay *emergency physician*

Herrin
Gauto, Nelson Fernando *plastic surgeon, consumer products company executive*

Hillsboro
Mulch, Robert F., Jr. *physician*

Hines
Best, William Robert *internist, educator, dean*
Zvetina, James Raymond *pulmonologist*

Hinsdale
Brueschke, Erich Edward *physician, researcher, educator*
Lonchyna, Vassyl A. *thoracic surgeon*

Jerseyville
Sharp, Elaine Cecile *obstetrician, gynecologist*

Joliet
Layman, Dale Pierre *retired medical educator, researcher, writer*
Ring, Alvin Manuel *pathologist, educator*

Lake Bluff
Kyncl, John Jaroslav *pharmacologist*

Lake Forest
Kelly, Daniel John *physician*
Levy, Nelson Louis *immunologist, educator, surgeon*
Pawl, Ronald Phillip *neurosurgery educator*
Salter, Edwin Carroll *retired pediatrician*
Weinberg, Milton, Jr. *retired cardiovascular and thoracic surgeon*
Wilbur, Richard Sloan *medical association administrator, physician*

Libertyville
Baraniewski, Henry M. *surgeon*
Bush, Eugene Nyle *retired pharmacologist, pharmacist*

Lisle
Colbert, Marvin Jay *retired internist, educator*

Lombard
Bachop, William Earl, Jr. *retired anatomist, zoologist*
Henkin, Robert Elliott *nuclear medicine physician*

Long Grove
Ausman, Robert K. *surgeon, research and development company executive*

Macomb
Dexter, Donald Harvey *surgeon, educator*

Marion
Munas, Falies A. *psychiatric physician*

Maywood
Akhavan-Heidari, Mehdi *cardiothoracic surgeon*
Albain, Kathy S. *oncologist*
Aranha, Gerard V. *surgeon*
Biller, Jose *neurologist, educator*
Dado, Diane Valentina *plastic and reconstructive surgeon*
Flanigan, Robert Charles *urologist, educator*
Gianopoulos, John George *obstetrician*
Hanin, Israel *pharmacologist, educator*
Light, Terry Richard *orthopedic hand surgeon*
Miele, Lucio *physician, medical researcher, pharmacologist*
Moran, John Francis *cardiologist*
Nand, Sucha *medical educator*
Newman, Barry Marc *pediatric surgeon*
Origitano, Thomas Charles *neurological surgeon*
Stankiewicz, James A. *otolaryngologist*
Warpeha, Raymond Leonard *surgeon, educator*
Wheeler, John S., Jr. *urologist*

Mc Gaw Park
Bernardo, Angelito Alday *nephrologist, medical products executive*

Melrose Park
Klein, Lloyd William *cardiologist, researcher*
Lai, Robert *urologist, surgeon*

Moline
Arnell, Richard Anthony *radiologist*

Naperville
Bufalino, Vincent John *cardiologist, medical administrator*
Folk, Frank Anton *surgeon, educator*
Miller, Charles E. *gynecologist*
Pollak, Raymond *general and transplant surgeon*
Zinger, Michael *reproductive endocrinologist*

Normal
Cooley, William Emory, Jr. *radiologist*

North Chicago
Barsano, Charles Paul *medical educator, dean*
Chedid, Antonio *pathologist, educator, researcher*
Gall, Eric Papineau *internist, educator*
Hawkins, Richard Albert *medical educator, administrator*
Kim, Yoon Berm *immunologist, educator*
Nair, Velayudhan *pharmacologist, educator, academic administrator*
Sierles, Frederick Stephen *psychiatrist, educator*

Northbrook
Byun, Michael *plastic surgeon*
Cucco, Ulisse P. *retired obstetrician, gynecologist*
Hindo, Walid Afram *radiology educator, researcher*

Oak Brook
Christian, Joseph Ralph *physician*
Ding, Jianchi *embryologist, researcher*
Imran, Ayesha *internist*

Oak Park
Matsuda, Takayoshi *surgeon, educator, biomedical researcher*

Oakbrook Terrace
Becker, Robert Jerome *allergist, consultant*

Orland Park
Drugas, Theodore George *retired surgeon*

Park Ridge
Bitran, Jacob David *internist*
Samuels, Brian Louis *oncologist, researcher*
White, John Vincent *surgeon, consultant*

Peoria
Frederick, Richard C. *emergency physician, educator*
Lanzino, Giuseppe *physician*
Lichtenstein, Steven Jay *ophthalmologist*
Meriden, Terry *physician*

Pinckneyville
Cawvey, Clarence Eugene *retired physician*

River Forest
Moore, Vernon John, Jr. *pediatrician, consultant, lawyer*
Tiesenga, Marvin Francis *surgeon*

Rock Island
Banas, John Stanley *obstetrician, gynecologist*

Rockford
Heerens, Robert Edward *physician*

Rushville
Dohner, Russel Rowland *physician*

Saint Charles
Ghaderi, Bahram *plastic surgeon*

Sandwich
Kola, Ramesh *oncologist*

Silvis
Kontos, George John, Jr. *surgeon*

Spring Valley
Gallagher, Donald *physician*

Springfield
Frank, Stuart *cardiologist*
Godwin, John E. *hematologist*
Holland, John Madison *retired family practice physician*
Mikell, Frank Leonard *cardiologist*
Myers, Phillip Ward *otolaryngologist*
Reddy, Ranga Vallela *anesthesiologist*
Woodson, Gayle Ellen *otolaryngologist*
Yaffe, Stuart Allen *physician*

Sterling
Tóth, Peter Paul *physician, researcher*

Sugar Grove
Debartolo, Hansel Marion, Jr. *otolaryngologist, plastic surgeon*

Urbana
Kaufman, Jerome Benzion *retired neurosurgeon*
Krock, Curtis Josselyn *pulmonologist*
Nelson, Ralph Alfred *physician*
Oliphant, Uretz John *physician, surgeon*
O'Morchoe, Charles Christopher Creagh *anatomist, surgeon, educator*
Weir, William Bradley *emergency physician*
Youngen, Gregory Keith *medical librarian*

Warrenville
Zhang, Li *neurologist*

Washington
Stine, Robert Howard *retired pediatrician, allergist*

West Chicago
Paulissen, James Peter *retired pediatrician, county official*

Wheeling
Levitin, Yelena *surgeon*

Wilmette
Day, Emerson *physician*
Hier, Daniel Barnet *neurologist*

Winnetka
Rossi, Ennio C. *internist, educator*
Rubnitz, Myron Ethan *pathologist, educator*

INDIANA

Alexandria
Irwin, Gerald Port *physician*

Anderson
King, Charles Ross *physician*

Bedford
Hunter, Harlen Charles *orthopedic surgeon*

Beech Grove
Hughes, Charles E. III *plastic surgeon*

Bloomington
Bishop, Michael D. *emergency physician*
Moore, Ward Wilfred *medical educator*
O'Loughlin, Valerie Dean *medical educator*

Carmel
Cohen, Marlene Lois *pharmacologist*
Winslow, Catherine P. *plastic surgeon*

Chesterton
Martino, Robert Salvatore *orthopedic surgeon*

Fishers
Thomas, John Arlen *pharmacologist, educator, science administrator*

Fort Wayne
Bacchus, Harold Mustapha *physician*
Lee, Shuishih Sage *pathologist*
Philpott, Jonathan M. *surgeon*
Richardson, Joseph Hill *physician, medical educator*

Highland
Steen, Lowell Harrison *retired physician*

Indianapolis
Allen, Stephen D. (Stephen Dean Allen) *pathologist, microbiologist*
Aprison, Morris Herman *retired experimental and theoretical neurobiology educator*
Bergstein, Jerry Michael *nephrologist*
Brandt, Ira Kive *pediatrician, geneticist*
Brickley, Richard Agar *retired surgeon*
Brown, Edwin Wilson, Jr. *preventive medicine physician, educator*
Broxmeyer, Hal Edward *medical educator*
Capello, William Naldo *surgeon*
Cheng, Liang *pathologist*
Cohen-Gadol, Aaron *neurosurgeon*
Coleman, John Joseph III *surgery educator*
Croffie, Joseph M. *gastroenterologist, educator*
Dalsing, Michael Cletus *surgeon, educator*
Daly, Walter Joseph *medical educator*
Dyken, Mark Lewis, Jr. *neurologist, educator*
Eigen, Howard *pediatrician, educator*
Einhorn, Lawrence Henry *oncologist, medical educator*
Fehrenbacher, John W. *surgeon*
Foley, Brian Scott *physiatrist, medical educator*
Foster, Richard S. *urologist, educator*
Fridell, Jonathan Aaron *transplant surgeon*
Ghetti, Bernardino Francesco *neuropathologist, educator*
Grosfeld, Jay Lazar *surgeon, educator*
Hansell, Richard Stanley *obstetrician, gynecologist, educator*
Hastings, Hill *surgeon*
Helper, Debra J. *gastroenterologist*
Holden, Robert Watson *radiologist, educator, dean*
Huler, Robert Jay *surgeon*
Inui, Thomas Spencer *physician, educator*
Irwin, Glenn Ward, Jr. *medical educator, physician, academic administrator*
Jackson, Valerie Pascuzzi *radiologist, educator*
Johnston, Cyrus Conrad, Jr. *medical educator*
Knoebel, Suzanne Buckner *cardiologist, educator*
Kunkler, Arnold William *retired surgeon, educator*
Lemberger, Louis *pharmacologist*
Lumeng, Lawrence *physician, educator*
MacDougall, John Duncan *thoracic surgeon*
Madura, James Anthony *surgeon, educator*
Malachowski, Robert Michael *retired pediatrician*
Manders, Karl Lee *neurosurgeon*
Mattar, Wissam Elias *physician*
McKeag, Douglas Bruce *physician, educator*
Miyamoto, Richard Takashi *otolaryngologist*
Molitoris, Bruce Albert *nephrologist, educator*
Norins, Arthur Leonard *dermatologist, educator*
Nurnberger, John I., Jr. *psychiatrist, educator*
Perkins, Stephen W. *plastic surgeon*
Pitt, Henry Anthony *surgeon, researcher, medical educator*
Richter, Judith Anne *pharmacologist, educator*
Rogers, Robert Ernest *medical educator*
Ross, Edward *cardiologist*
Roth, Lawrence Max *pathologist, educator*
Saxena, Romil *pathologist, educator*
Schmetzer, Alan David *psychiatrist*
Siderys, Harry *surgeon, educator*
Smith, James Warren *pathologist, educator, microbiologist, parasitologist*
Stehman, Frederick Bates *obstetrician, gynecologist, educator*
Stuhldreher, David Brosnan *urologist*
Sundaram, Chandru P. *urologist*
Sutton, Gregory Paul *obstetrician, gynecologist*
Van Natta, Bruce Wayne *plastic surgeon*
Watanabe, August Masaru *physician, educator, retired pharmaceutical executive*
Weber, George *oncology and pharmacology educator, researcher*
Wilson, Fred M., II, *ophthalmologist, educator*
Woolling, Kenneth Rau *vascular internist*
Yao, Yongxue *immunologist*
Yee, Robert Donald *ophthalmologist*
Yung, Chi-Wah Rudy *ophthalmologist, educator*
Zipes, Douglas Peter *cardiologist, researcher*

Lafayette
Hamdi, Hamid S. *neurologist, neurorehabilitation specialist, consultant, researcher*
Langston, Edward Lee *physician, pharmacist*

Logansport
Brewer, Robert Allen *physician*

Madison
Snodgrass, Robert Eugene *retired psychiatrist*

Marion
Fisher, Pierre James, Jr. *physician*

Merrillville
Han, Dennis Paul *physician*
Nguyen, Thach Ngoc *cardiologist*
Yu, Peter Legaspi *rehabilitation physician*

Michigan City
Mothkur, Sridhar Rao *radiologist*

Mishawaka
Sobol, Zbigniew W. *orthopedist, surgeon*

Muncie
Nanko, Raymond S. *physician*
Roch, Lewis Marshall, II, *ophthalmic surgeon, medical entrepreneur*

New Albany
Chowhan, Naveed Mahfooz *oncologist*

Newburgh
Slovachek, Donn Richard *obstetrician, gynecologist*

Notre Dame
Vakulenko, Sergei Borisovich *medical researcher, educator*

Richmond
Howanitz, E. Paul *thoracic surgeon*

Schererville
Galante, Gustavo E. *plastic surgeon*

Scottsburg
Kho, Eusebio *surgeon*

South Bend
Anderson, Kenneth Paul *nephrologist, administrator*
Davis, Glen Anthony *pediatrician*

Sullivan
Chavez, Mary Ann *osteopathic family physician*

Valparaiso
Canganelli, Vincent Guglielmo *retired psychiatrist*

Walton
Chu, Johnson Chin Sheng *retired physician*

West Lafayette
Borowitz, Joseph Leo *pharmacologist, educator*
Cramer, William Anthony *biochemistry and biophysics researcher, educator*
Frey, Harley Harrison, Jr. *retired anesthesiologis*
Poulos, James Thomas *endocrinologist, educato*
Rutledge, Charles Ozwin *pharmacologist, educator*
Stob, Martin *retired physiology educator*
Tacker, Willis Arnold, Jr. *medical educator, researcher*

IOWA

Cedar Rapids
Maikon, Marc Steven *podiatrist*
Norris, Albert Stanley *psychiatrist, educator*

Clinton
Woodman, Grey Musgrave *psychiatrist*

Clive
Neis, Arthur Veral *healthcare and development company executive*

Davenport
Shammas, Nicolas Wahib *internist, cardiologist*

Des Moines
Cherney, Eugene Joseph *plastic surgeon, directc*
Habib, Shahid *medical association administrato*
Olds, John Ward *internist*
Rosenberg, Steven Joel *urologist*
Song, Joseph *pathologist, educator*
Wattleworth, Roberta Ann *physician*

Iowa City
Abboud, Francois Mitry *physician, educator*
Andreasen, Nancy Coover *psychiatrist, educato neuroscientist*
Beaver, Hilary A. *medical educator, ophthalmologist*
Bedell, George Noble *internist, educator*
Buckwalter, Joseph Addison *orthopedic surgeor educator*
Burns, C(harles) Patrick *hematologist, oncologi*
Clifton, James Albert *physician, educator*
Cooper, Reginald Rudyard *orthopedic surgeon, educator*
Eckstein, John William *internist, educator, retired dean*
El-Shanti, Hatem Isam *pediatrician, geneticist*
Fellows, Robert Ellis *medical educator, researcher*
Fiegel, Jennifer *biomedical researcher, educator*
Galask, Rudolph Peter *obstetrician, gynecologis*
Gantz, Bruce Jay *otolaryngologist, educator*
Grose, Charles Frederick *pediatrician, epidemiologist*
Hammond, Harold Logan *oral and maxillofacia pathologist, retired educator*
Heistad, Donald Dean *cardiologist*
Kennedy, Colleen M. *medical educator*
Kerber, Richard E. *cardiologist*
Konety, Badrinath R. *surgeon, researcher*

Lamping, Kathryn G. *medical educator, medical researcher*
Lauer, Ronald Martin *pediatric cardiologist, researcher*
Magboul, Magboul M. *anesthesiologist, educator*
Mason, Edward Eaton *surgeon*
Medh, Jheem D. *medical educator, biochemist, researcher*
Morriss, Frank Howard, Jr. *pediatrics educator*
Mullan, Brian *medical educator*
Murray, Jeffrey C. *medical educator, pediatrician*
Nelson, Herbert Leroy *psychiatrist*
Niebyl, Jennifer Robinson *obstetrician, gynecologist, educator*
Perkins, Edward S. *ophthalmologist*
Ponseti, Ignacio Vives *orthopaedic surgery educator*
Richerson, Hal Bates *internist, allergist, immunologist, educator*
Russell, Stephen Richard *medical educator*
Sheffield, Val C. *medical geneticist*
Snyder, Peter M. *medical educator, medical researcher*
Strauss, John Steinert *dermatologist, educator*
Tsalikian, Eva *physician, educator*
Van Gilder, John Corley *neurosurgeon, educator*
Weintraub, Neal L. *medical educator, cardiologist*
Welsh, Michael James *medical educator, biophysicist, educator*
Williams, Richard Dwayne *physician, educator, urologist*
Ziegler, Ekhard Erich *pediatrics educator*

Marshalltown
Cassidy, Eugene Patrick *pathologist*
Thomas, David Llewellyn *physician*

Sioux City
Ayi, Bertha Serwa *infectious disease specialist, internist*

Waterloo
Kaaki, Bilal *obstetrician, gynecologist*

West Des Moines
Alberts, Marion Edward *retired physician*
Weresh, Matthew John *orthopedic surgeon*

KANSAS

Coffeyville
Hawley, Raymond Glen *pathologist*

Concordia
Fowler, Wayne Lewis, Sr. *internist*

Fort Leavenworth
Wilhelm, Gary Bretz *physician*

Hutchinson
Crater, Timothy Andrews *internist*

Kansas City
Anderson, Harrison Clarke *pathologist, educator, biomedical researcher*
Arakawa, Kasumi *physician, educator*
Damjanov, Ivan *pathologist, educator*
Dunn, Marvin Irvin *physician*
Grantham, Jared James *nephrologist, educator*
Hudson, Robert Paul *medical educator*
Huet, Raul *psychiatrist*
ohnson, Joy Ann *diagnostic radiologist*
Lawrence, Walter Thomas *plastic surgeon*
Lee, Kyo Rak *radiologist, educator*
McCallum, Richard Warwick *medical researcher, clinician, educator*
Meyers, David George *internist, cardiologist, educator*
Mohn, Melvin Paul *anatomist, educator*
Perez, Victor Manuel *physician, plastic surgeon*
Rawitch, Allen Barry *medical educator, academic administrator*
Schloerb, Paul Richard *surgeon, educator*
Sciolaro, Charles Michael *cardiothoracic and vascular surgeon*
Suzuki, Tsuneo *molecular immunologist*
Taylor, Sarah Ann *oncologist, educator*
Vacek, James *cardiologist*
Voogt, James Leonard *medical educator*
Xiao, Zhousheng *pharmacologist, bone biologist*
Ziegler, Dewey Kiper *neurologist, educator*

Lawrence
Buck, Henry William, Jr. *obstetrician, gynecologist*
Hajdu, Michael A. *cardiologist*
Miller, Don Robert *surgeon, educator*

Leawood
Barnthouse, Chris David *orthopedic surgeon*
Bortnick, Daniel Philip *plastic surgeon*
Gutek, E(dward) Philip *plastic and reconstructive surgeon, educator*
Hartzler, Geoffrey Oliver *retired cardiologist*
Nouhan, Regina Marie *plastic surgeon*

Louisville
abbar, Abdul *physician, educator, gastroenterologist*

Manhattan
Di Terlizzi, Roberta *pathologist, educator*
Durkee, William Robert *retired internist*
Leslie, John Franklin *pathologist, educator*
Oehme, Frederick Wolfgang *medical researcher, educator*

Olathe
Monzon, Carlos Manuel *physician*

Overland Park
ettinger, Michael Eugene *corneal surgeon*
andry, Mark Edward *podiatrist, researcher*

Pittsburg
Chubb, Richard Marshall *retired physician*
Morgan, Lyle Warner, II, *medical educator*
Sullivan, William John *osteopath*

Prairie Village
Fairchild, Robert Charles *pediatrician*

Pratt
Rehman, Qaiser *rheumatologist, researcher*

Shawnee Mission
Bell, Deloris Wiley *physician*
Fleming, Michael O. *physician*
Henley, Douglas E. *medical association administrator*
Price, James Gordon *physician, educator*
Thomas, Christopher Yancey III *surgeon, educator*

Topeka
Menninger, William Walter *psychiatrist*
Slaughter, Jerry *medical association administrator*

Wichita
Burket, George Edward, Jr. *retired family physician*
Cobb, Jill *pathologist*
Guthrie, Richard Alan *physician*
Rieger, James A. *plastic surgeon*
Rosenberg, Matthew William *plastic surgeon*

KENTUCKY

Berea
Lamb, Irene Hendricks *medical researcher*

Danville
Nickens, Harry Carl *medical association administrator*

Elizabethtown
Rahman, Rafiq Ur *oncologist, educator*

Elkton
Manthey, Frank Anthony *physician, director*

Highland Heights
Luse, Kimberly Ann *radiologist, educator*

Lexington
Anderson, James Wingo *physician*
Bricker, John Timothy *pediatric cardiologist*
Chance, Kenneth Bernard, Sr. *endodontist educator, academic administrator*
Clawson, David Kay *orthopedic surgeon*
Davey, Diane Davis *pathologist, educator*
Dhir, Anir *surgeon*
Espinosa, Patricio Sebastian *neurologist, researcher*
Hagen, Michael Dale *family physician educator*
Holsinger, James Wilson, Jr. *cardiologist, physician*
Iocono, Joseph Anthony *pediatric and trauma surgeon*
Kaplan, Martin P. *allergist, immunologist, pediatrician*
Kibler, William Benjamin *orthopedist, surgeon*
McRoberts, J. William *urologist, surgeon, researcher*
Means, Robert Taylor, Jr. *hematologist, educator, researcher*
Moliterno, David J. *cardiologist, educator*
Mukherjee, Debabrata *cardiologist, researcher*
Puffer, James C. *sports medicine physician, educator, medical association administrator*
Reynolds, Eric William *medical educator*
Steinhubl, Steven Rudolf *cardiologist, educator*
Tollison, Joseph W. *family practice physician*
Weitzel, William David *psychiatrist*
Whayne, Thomas French, Jr. *cardiologist, educator*
Woodring, John Howell *radiologist*
Young, Paul Ray *medical association administrator, physician*

Louisville
Amin, Mohammad *urology educator*
Andrews, Billy Franklin *pediatrician, educator*
Aronoff, George Rodger *medicine and pharmacology educator*
Ballew, Laurie K. *psychiatrist*
Bhola, Rahul *ophthalmologist*
Breidenbach, Warren Conrad *plastic surgeon, hand surgeon*
Callen, Jeffrey Phillip *dermatologist, educator*
Chagpar, Anees Bahadurali *surgeon*
Chien, Sufan *surgeon, educator*
Cohen, Burton Jack *otolaryngologist, educator*
Danzl, Daniel Frank *emergency physician*
DeMunbrun-Harmon, Donne O'Donnell *retired family physician*
Elin, Ronald John *pathologist, educator*
Farman, Allan George *radiologist, pathologist, educator*
Galandiuk, Susan *colon and rectal surgeon, educator*
Gall, Stanley Adolph *immunologist, researcher*
Garretson, Henry David *neurosurgeon*
Jones, Veronnie Faye *medical educator, dean*
Kaplan, Henry Jerrold *ophthalmologist, educator*
Parker, Joseph Corbin, Jr. *pathologist, educator, department chairman*
Pence, Hobert Lee *physician*
Richardson, James David *surgeon*
Schoo, Bernard John *surgeon*
Schwab, John Joseph *psychiatrist, educator*
Scott, Ralph Mason *retired radiologist, educator*
Shirwan, Haval *immunologist, educator*
Syed, Ibrahim Bijli *medical educator, physicist*
Tobin, Gordon Ross *surgery educator*
Waddell, William Joseph *pharmacologist, toxicologist*
Weisskopf, Bernard *pediatrician, child behavior, development and genetics specialist, educator*
Wright, Jesse Hartzell *psychiatrist, educator*

Madisonville
Stulc, Jaroslav Peter *surgeon, educator*

Waco
Hackman, Vicki Lou *physician*

LOUISIANA

Alexandria
Hanley, Henry Gorman *cardiologist*

Baton Rouge
Bray, George August *internist, researcher, educator*
Brooks, Burke Jay, Jr. *oncologist*
Cherry, William Ashley *surgeon, state health official, educator*
Dhurandhar, Nikhil V. *biomedical researcher, educator*
Gettys, Thomas Wigington *medical researcher*
Ishler, Harold LeRoy, Jr. *retired physician*
Kastin, Abba Jeremiah *endocrinologist, researcher*
Kidd, James Marion III *allergist, immunologist, educator*
Puyau, Francis Albert *retired radiology educator, physician*
Spell, Derrick W. *oncologist, educator*
Tarver, Dave L. *medical association administrator*

Belle Chasse
Arimura, Akira *biomedical researcher, educator*

Kenner
Farber, George Allan *dermatologist, educator*

Lafayette
Appley, Alan J. *neurosurgeon*
Domingue, James Neal *neurologist*
Marinkovic, Serge Peter *urologist, educator, surgeon*
Meza, Luis Alberto *internist, researcher*

Lake Charles
Clement, Richard Joseph *retired obstetrician, gynecologist*
Drez, David Jacob, Jr. *orthopedic surgeon, educator*
Gunderson, Clark Alan *orthopedic surgeon*
Lacoste, Alan Daniel *physician, educator, medical company executive*

Madisonville
Young, Lucy Cleaver *retired physician*

Mandeville
Cargille, Charles M. *internist, educator*
Lamid, Sofian *physician, educator*

Marrero
Kushner, Frederick Gary *cardiologist, medical educator*

Metairie
Edisen, Clayton Byron *physician*
Jacobs, Benjamin Franklin *cardiologist*
Lake, Wesley Wayne, Jr. *internist, allergist, medical educator*
Metzner, David Mark *plastic and reconstructive surgeon*
Snyder, David Warren *cardiologist*

Minden
Kemmerly, James Robert *obstetrician, gynecologist*

Monroe
Cooksey, John Charles *ophthalmologist, retired congressman*

New Orleans
Agrawal, Krishna Chandra *pharmacology educator*
Beck, David Edward *surgeon*
Berenson, Gerald Sanders *physician*
Cohn, Isidore, Jr. *surgeon, educator*
Culotta, Vincent Anthony, Jr. *obstetrician, gynecologist*
Duncan, Margaret Caroline *physician*
Easson, William McAlpine *psychiatrist, educator*
Espinoza, Luis Rolan *rheumatologist, researcher*
Ewin, Dabney Minor *surgeon*
Fisher, James William *pharmacologist, medical educator*
Frohlich, Edward David *medical educator*
Fuselier, Harold Anthony, Jr. *urologist, director, educator*
Giles, Thomas Davis *cardiologist, internist, educator*
Glancy, David Lucas *internist*
Gould, Harry J. III *neurology educator*
Griffin, Jeffrey Farrow *surgeon*
Hollier, Larry Harold *vascular surgeon, hospital administrator, dean*
Hyslop, Newton Everett, Jr. *infectious disease specialist*
Incaprera, Frank Philip *internist*
Jenkins, James Stephen *internist*
Kewalramani, Laxman Sunderdas *surgeon, consultant*
Kline, David Gellinger *neurosurgery educator*
Kolinsky, Michael Allen *emergency physician*
Locke, William *retired endocrinologist*
Lopez, Manuel *immunology and allergy educator*
Martin, David Hubert *internist, epidemiologist, educator*
Martin, Louis Frank *surgery and healthcare outcomes analyst*
McSwain, Norman Ellsworth, Jr. *surgeon, educator*
Millikan, Larry Edward *dermatologist*
Navar, Luis Gabriel *physiology educator, director, researcher*
Nicholl, Jeffrey Scott *neurologist, educator*
Nichols, Ronald Lee *surgeon, educator*
Ochsner, John Lockwood *thoracic-cardiovascular surgeon*
O'Quinn, April Gale *obstetrician, gynecologist, educator*
Pankey, George Atkinson *internist, educator, researcher*
Porter, George Homer III *physician, medical foundation executive*
Reyes, Raul Gregorio *surgeon*
Reza, Ali Hajmohammad *cardiologist*
Riddick, Frank Adams, Jr. *physician, healthcare administrator*
Threefoot, Sam Abraham *physician, educator*
Timmcke, Alan Edward *colon and rectal surgeon*
Ventura, Hector Osvaldo *cardiologist*
Waring, William Winburn *pediatric pulmonologist, educator*

Opelousas
Lafleur, Kenneth Charles *ophthalmologist*
Pinac, André Louis III *obstetrician, gynecologist*

Pineville
Webb, Watts Rankin *surgeon*

Shreveport
Brannon, Guy Emilio *psychiatrist*
Casey Wall, Holly *plastic surgeon*
Chu, Quyen Dinh *surgeon, educator, oncologist*
Conrad, Steven Allen *critical care and emergency physician, biomedical engineer, educator*
Fort, Arthur Tomlinson III *obstetrician, educator*
Jawahar, Ajay *neurosurgeon, educator*
Jones, Kenneth B., Jr. *surgeon*
McDonald, John Clifton *surgeon*
Misra, Raghunath Prasad *physician, educator*
Nathan, Cherie-Ann Olympia *surgeon, educator*
Shelby, James Stanford *surgeon, researcher*
Veeramachaneni, Ravindra *pathologist*
Wall, Simeon Heninger, Jr. *plastic surgeon*
Wolf, Robert Edward *physician, educator*

Slidell
McBurney, Elizabeth Innes *dermatologist, physician, educator*
Muller, Robert Joseph *gynecologist*

Sulphur
Toniette, Sallye Jean *physician*

MAINE

Augusta
Hussey, John Francis *physician, geriatrician*

Bar Harbor
Nass, Meryl J. *physician, writer, research scientist*

Belfast
DeSilvey, Dennis Lee *cardiologist, educator, academic administrator*

Biddeford
Daly, Frank *anatomist*
Ford, Charles Willard *medical educator*

Brunswick
Aranson, Robert *physician, director*

Ellsworth
Richards, (A)lbert Dewey *retired physician, medical educator, writer*

Falmouth
Schraft, Susan *radiologist*

Lubec
Hayes, Ernest M. *podiatrist*

Orono
Weiss, Robert Jerome *retired psychiatrist, educator*

Portland
Dyro, Frances Mary Agnes *medical educator,*

Scarborough
Clark, Gordon Hostetter, Jr. *physician*

South Portland
Wheeler, Hewitt Brownell *surgeon, educator*

Southport
Gibson, Edgar Thomas *retired surgeon, educator*

Topsham
Arnold, Charles Burle, Jr. *retired psychiatrist*

Yarmouth
Northrup, Christiane *obstetrician, gynecologist*

MARYLAND

Annapolis
Halpern, Joseph Alan *physician*
Kushner, Jack *retired physician*
Welch, Robert Bond *ophthalmologist, educator*

Arnold
Harris, Roger Clark *psychiatrist, consultant*
Lee, Yu-Jin *retired military physician*

Baltimore
Achuff, Stephen Charles *cardiologist*
Aneja, Alka *child psychiatrist*
Aronson, Neal Irwin *neurosurgeon, medical educator*
Aurelian, Laure *medical sciences educator*
Bahrami, Hossein *epidemiologist, physician*

Baker, R. Robinson *surgeon*
Baker, Timothy Danforth *physician, educator*
Baumgartner, William Anthony *cardiac surgeon*
Belzberg, Allan Joel *neurosurgery educator*
Bigelow, George E. *psychology and pharmacology scientist*
Billig, Donal Michael *surgeon*
Blattner, William Albert *physician, epidemiology researcher*
Blumenthal, Roger Scott *cardiologist*
Bochner, Bruce Scott *immunologist, educator*
Brem, Henry *neurosurgeon, educator, researcher*
Brieger, Gert Henry *medical educator*
Brodie, Angela M. *biomedical researcher, educator*
Brody, Eugene Bloor *psychiatrist, educator, editor*
Budimirovic, Dejan B. *academic child psychiatrist*
Busuttil, Steven James *surgeon*
Cameron, Duke Edward *cardiac surgeon, educator*
Cao, Dengfeng *pathologist*
Carrier, France *medical educator*
Carson, Benjamin Solomon *neurosurgeon*
Chen, Yu *acupuncturist, Chinese herbologist*
Cohen, Steven Paul *anesthesiologist, researcher*
Connaughton, James Patrick *psychiatrist*
Conway de Macario, Everly *immunologist, molecular biologist*
Cornwell, Edward E. III *surgeon*
Cummings, Charles William *otolaryngologist, educator*
Dang, Chi Van *hematology and oncology educator*
Dannenberg, Arthur Milton, Jr. *experimental pathologist, immunologist, educator*
DeAngelis, Catherine D. *pediatrics educator*
DeLateur, Barbara Jane *medical educator*
DePaulo, J. Raymond, Jr. *psychiatrist, researcher*
DeWeese, Theordore L. *radiation oncologist*
Diaz-Montes, Teresa P. *oncologist, obstetrician, gynecologist*
Dobs, Adrian Sandra *endocrinologist, educator*
Drachman, Daniel Bruce *neurologist, educator*
Eisenberg, Howard Michael *neurosurgeon*
Erozan, Yener Sahir *pathologist, educator*
Ettinger, David Seymour *oncologist*
Ferentz, Kevin Scott *physician*
Fox, Harold Edward *obstetrician, researcher, gynecologist, educator*
Gamaldo, Charlene Edie *medical educator*
Gimenez, Luis Fernando *physician, educator*
Godenne, Ghislaine Dudley *physician, psychotherapist, educator*
Goldberg, Morton Falk *ophthalmologist, educator*
Goldman, Lynn Rose *medical educator*
Goldman, Stuart Miles *podiatrist*
Gordis, Leon *physician*
Greenough, William Bates III *medical educator*
Griffin, Diane Edmund *research physician, virologist, educator*
Griffin, John W. *neurologist, medical educator*
Griffith, Lawrence Stacey Cameron *cardiologist, educator*
Haas, Mark *pathologist*
Harris, James Carol Overton, Jr. *psychiatrist, pediatrician*
Heldman, Alan Wohl, Jr. *medical educator*
Hellmann, David Bruce *medical educator*
Herpel, Laura Bogan *pulmonologist, researcher*
Hofkin, Gerald Alan *gastroenterologist*
Huang, Judy *neurosurgeon*
Hungerford, David Samuel *orthopedic surgeon, educator*
Hussain, Mehboob *medical educator*
Jaar, Bernard Georges *nephrologist, researcher*
Johns, Richard James *physician, educator*
Johnson, Kenneth Peter *neurologist, researcher*
Johnson, Richard Tidball *microbiology and neuroscience educator, virologist, researcher*
Kastor, John Alfred *cardiologist, educator*
Kavoussi, Louis Raphael *urologist*
Kelen, Gabor David *emergency physician*
Kerr, Douglas Anthony *neurologist, researcher*
Kessler, Irving Isar *epidemiologist, consultant*
Knapp, David Allan *pharmaceutical educator, researcher, dean*
Kwon, Chul Soo *psychiatrist*
Lawrence, Robert Swan *physician, educator*
Lazarus, Gerald Sylvan *dermatologist, educator, dean*
Levien, David Harold *surgeon*
Litrenta, Frances Marie *psychiatrist*
Liu, Jun O. *pharmacologist, educator*
Long, Donlin Martin *surgeon, educator*
Longo, Dan Louis *internist, researcher, oncologist*
Macario, Alberto Juan Lorenzo *physician*
Makarov, Danil Victor *urologist*
Matheson, Nina W. *medical researcher*
McHugh, Paul R. *psychiatrist, neurologist, educator*
McKhann, Guy Mead *neurologist, educator*
Miller, Edward Doring *anesthesiologist, hospital administrator, dean*
Miller, Michael *physician, educator*
Myslinski, Norbert Raymond *medical educator*
Nelkin, Barry David *oncology researcher and educator*
Nichols, David Gregory *anesthesiologist, pediatrician, educator*
Norman, Philip Sidney *physician*
O'Toole, Tara Jeanne *medical educator, former federal agency administrator*
Perler, Bruce Alan *vascular surgeon*
Powe, Neil Richard *physician, educator, epidemiologist, public health service officer*
Quinn, Thomas Charles *medical researcher, educator*
Rabb, Hamid *nephrologist, educator*
Rayson, Glendon Ennes *internist, preventive medicine specialist, writer*
Rose, Noel Richard *immunologist, microbiologist, educator*
Rumbaugh, Jeffrey Arlin *neurologist, neuroscientist*
Samet, Jonathan Michael *epidemiologist, educator*
Saudek, Christopher D. *medical educator*
Schoenrich, Edyth Hull *internist, preventive medicine physician*
Silbergeld, Ellen Kovner *epidemiologist, toxicologist, researcher*
Slezak, Sheri *plastic surgeon*
Snyder, Solomon Halbert *psychiatrist, pharmacologist*
Sommer, Alfred *ophthalmologist, medical educator, researcher*
Standiford, Harold C. *medical educator*
Starfield, Barbara Helen *pediatrician, educator*
Talalay, Paul *pharmacologist, educator*
Tamargo, Rafael J. *neurological surgeon, educator*
Taylor, Carl Ernest *preventive medicine physician, epidemiologist, educator*
Tchantchou, Flaubert *medical researcher*
Terry, Peter Browne *medical educator*
Velculescu, Victor E. *oncologist, educator*
Vogelstein, Bert *oncology educator*
Walsh, Patrick Craig *urologist*
Weisfeldt, Myron Lee *cardiologist, educator*
Weiss, James Lloyd *cardiology educator*
Welker, James Anthony *physician*
Wilson, Donald Edward *internist, educator, dean*
Wolfe, Nathan *epidemiologist*
Young, Barbara *psychiatrist, psychotherapist, educator, photographer*
Zhao, Xianfeng Frank *pathologist, educator*

Bethesda
Akhondi, Hossein *internist, researcher*
Alter, Harvey J. *hematologist, educator*
Anderson, George Kenneth *physician, retired military officer, foundation administrator*
Apud, Jose Antonio *psychiatrist, educator*
Arons, Bernard S. *psychiatrist, educator, health services administrator*
Austin, Christopher *neurologist, researcher*
Avila, Nilo Alonso *radiologist*
Berzofsky, Jay A. *medical researcher*
Brown, Dudley Earl, Jr. *psychiatrist, educator, health science association administrator, federal agency administrator, retired military officer*
Bukh, Jens *medical researcher*
Cai, Tao *biomedical researcher*
Candotti, Fabio *pediatrician*
Chanock, Robert Merritt *pediatrician*
Chen, Kevin Gang *oncologist, researcher, molecular pharmacologist*
Cohen, Robert Abraham *retired physician*
Cohen, Sheldon Gilbert *physician, historian, immunologist*
Crout, J(ohn) Richard *pharmacologist, researcher*
Cruz, Wilhelmina Mangahas *critical care physician, educator*
Danforth, David Newton, Jr. *surgeon, oncologist*
Datiles, Manuel Bernaldes III *ophthalmologist, researcher*
De Cherney, Alan Hersh *obstetrics and gynecology educator*
Dietrich, Robert Anthony *pathologist, consultant, medical association administrator*
Eaton, William A. *biomedical researcher*
Emanuel, Ezekiel J. *oncologist, bioethicist*
Farci, Patrizia *medical educator, researcher*
Fleisher, Thomas Arthur *physician*
Gabelnick, Henry Lewis *medical research administrator*
Gallin, John I. *medical researcher*
Gastwirth, Glenn Barry *medical association administrator*
Gershengorn, Marvin Carl *internist, researcher, educator*
Giedd, Jay Norman *psychiatrist*
Goldstein, Murray *medical epidemiologist and research administrator*
Goodwin, Frederick King *psychiatrist*
Gottesman, Michael Marc *biomedical researcher*
Guttmacher, Alan Edward *physician, medical educator*
Guttman, Helene Nathan *biomedical consultant, transpersonal counselor*
Hallett, Mark *neurologist, educator, medical researcher, director*
Harlan, Linda Carol *epidemiologist*
Harris, Curtis Craig *medical researcher*
Haseltine, Florence Pat *obstetrician, gynecologist, medical association administrator*
He, Liusheng *biomedical researcher*
Herman, Mary Margaret *neuropathologist*
Hingson, Ralph W. *medical educator*
Hutton, John Evans, Jr. *surgeon, educator, retired military officer*
Ito, Yoichiro *pathologist, researcher*
Jaffe, Elaine Sarkin *pathologist*
Johnson, Joyce Marie *psychiatrist, public health service officer, epidemiologist*
Joy, Robert John Thomas *medical educator*
Kapikian, Albert Zaven *physician, epidemiologist*
Kirschstein, Ruth Lillian *physician*
Klee, Claude Blenc *medical researcher*
Kramer, Barnett Sheldon *oncologist*
Krause, Richard Michael *medical scientist, government official, educator, researcher*
Kunos, George *pharmacologist*
Lane, H. Clifford *internist*
Levine, Zachary Thomas *neurosurgeon*
Li, Qingdi Quentin *physician, research scientist, medical educator*
Linehan, William Marston *urologic surgeon, cancer researcher*
Lipman, David J. *medical association administrator, researcher*
Lowy, Douglas Ronald *oncologist, researcher*
Mackall, Crystal L. *medical researcher*
Marini, Ann Marie *medical researcher, educator*
Masur, Henry *internist*
Mattison, Donald Roger *gynecologist, toxicologist, educator, medical association administrator, public health service officer*
McCurdy, Harry Ward *otolaryngologist*
Melenhorst, Jan Joseph *immunologist*
Mullan, Fitzhugh *public health physician*
Nabel, Elizabeth Guenthner *cardiologist, researcher*
Neumann, Ronald Daniel *nuclear medicine physician, educator*
North, A. Frederick *physician*
Nyirjesy, Istvan *obstetrician, gynecologist*
Ognibene, Frederick Peter *internist*
Ommaya, Ayub Khan *neurosurgeon, educator*
Pacher, Pál *pharmacologist, educator, researcher*
Paul, William Erwin *immunologist*
Perlin, Seymour *psychiatrist, educator*
Peterson, Charles Marquis *medical educator*
Pollard, Harvey B. *medical educator, neuroscientist*
Quinnan, Gerald Vincent, Jr. *medical educator*
Quon, Michael James *medical researcher, internist*
Rapoport, Judith *psychiatrist*
Rennert, Owen Murray *pediatrician, geneticist, educator*
Reynolds, Herbert Young *internist*
Rhim, Johng Sik *physician, medical researcher*
Rice, Charles Lane *surgeon, educator*
Robbins, John Bennett *medical researcher*
Rossouw, Jacques E. *preventive medicine physician, researcher*
Saffiotti, Umberto *pathologist*
Samelson, Lawrence Elliot *medical researcher*
Schrump, David Stuart *medical association administrator, researcher*
Shin, Eui-Cheol *medical researcher*
Shulman, Lawrence Edward *biomedical researcher, rheumatologist*
Smoller, Bruce Melvyn *psychiatrist*
Sobel, Mark Esar *pathologist, researcher*
Stetler-Stevenson, William George *pathologist*
Sturtz, Donald Lee *surgeon, educator, military officer*
Teimourian, Bahman *plastic surgeon*
Ursano, Robert Joseph *psychiatrist*
Vaitukaitis, Judith Louise *medical researcher*
Volkow, Nora Dolores *medical researcher, director*
Waldmann, Thomas Alexander *medical researcher, physician*
Webster, Thomas Glenn *psychiatrist, educator*
Weinberger, Daniel R. *psychiatrist, neurologist*
Western, Karl August *physician, epidemiologist*
Willenbring, Mark Leon *psychiatrist*
Wu, Carl *medical researcher*

Burtonsville
Penska, Keith Henry *psychiatrist*

Chevy Chase
Alpert, Seymour *anesthesiologist, educator*
Cech, Thomas Robert *medical association administrator, chemistry professor*
Croft, Joseph David *medical educator*
Dufresne, Craig Roger *plastic surgeon, educator*
Eng, Gloria D. *retired pediatrician*
Feldman, Bruce Allen *otolaryngologist*
Hani, Antoine George *psychiatrist, psychoanalyst*
Harlan, William Robert, Jr. *internist, educator, researcher*
Hersh, Stephen Peter *psychiatrist, psycho-oncologist, chronic pain expert, educator*
Kay, Stephen R. *surgeon*
Khairalla, Eric William *plastic surgeon*
Lynn, D. Joanne *physician, researcher*
Pogue, John Marshall *physician*
Posnick, Jeffrey Craig *plastic surgeon*
Resnik, Harvey Lewis Paul *psychiatrist*
Rose, John Charles *internist, educator*
Shannon, Stephen Curtis *medical association administrator, occupational health physician*
Wiesel, Sam W. *medical educator, academic administrator*
Williams, Charles Laval, Jr. *retired preventive medicine physician*

College Park
Katz, Ronald Alan *dermatologist*
Sacks, Charles Bernard *psychiatrist, educator*

Columbia
Campbell-Alston, Deirdre Adina *anatomist, physiologist, researcher*
Drexler, Milton *medical association administrator*
Hyman, Lawrence Robert *psychiatrist*
Strahlman, Richard Scott *pediatrician*

Darnestown
Cohen, Sanford Irwin *physician, educator*
Gottlieb, Julius Judah *retired podiatrist*

Easton
Rever, George Wright *psychiatrist, health facility administrator*

Frederick
Anderson, Arthur Osmund *pathologist, immunologist, bioethicist, military officer*
Copeland, Neal G. *medical researcher*
Keefer, Larry Kay *medical researcher*
Malin, Howard Gerald *podiatrist*
Marquez, Victor E. *medical researcher*
Sharifi, Nima *oncologist, researcher*

Gaithersburg
Brodine, Charles Edward *physician*
Dermody, William Christian *biomedical consultant*
Fratantoni, Joseph Charles *medical researcher, biotechnologist, hematologist*
Lenfant, Claude Jean-Marie *physician, director*
Schwartzberg, Allan Zelig *psychiatrist, educator*

Glen Burnie
Jamaris, Joseph Kastytis *neurosurgeon*

Greenbelt
Obamogie, Mercy A. *physician*

Kensington
Mirkin, Gabe Baron *physician, medical educator, writer, radio personality*
Szára, Stephen István *pharmacologist, consultant*

Lutherville
Elma, Bayani Borja *physician*

Lutherville Timonium
Auwaerter, Paul Gisbert *physician, educator*
Meyer, Jon Keith *psychiatrist, psychoanalyst, educator*
Park, Lee Crandall *psychiatrist*
Sternberger, Ludwig Amadeus *neurologist, educator*

Montgomery Village
Durning, Steven James *internist, educator*

North Bethesda
Flax, Herman Jacob *physiatrist*
Friedman, Roger Jay *plastic surgeon*

Olney
Uscinski, Ronald Henry *medical educator*

Owings Mills
Heck, Albert Frank *retired neurologist*
Vogel, James Edmond *plastic surgeon*

Patuxent River
Charlot, Joseph Leonce, Jr. *preventive medicine physician*

Potomac
Gaston, Marilyn Hughes *physician, administrator, public health expert, author*
Harvey, John Collins *internist, educator*
Korengold, George Matthew *physician*
Waugaman, Richard Merle *psychiatrist, educator*

Rockville
Birns, Mark Theodore *physician*
Bough, Kristopher *pharmacologist*
Clancy, Carolyn M. *internist, federal agency administrator*
DuPont, Robert Louis *psychiatrist, physician*
Gonzalez-Licea, Augustin *pathologist, public health service officer*
Goodman, Jesse *physician, director, public health facility administrator, research scientist*
Haffner, Marlene Elisabeth *internist, public health administrator*
Hoffman, Stephen Lev *physician*
Kowarski, Allen Avinoam *endocrinologist, educator*
Leach, Berton Joe *medical educator*
Leventhal, Carl M. *neurologist, consultant, retired government agency administrator*
Lloyd, Douglas Seward *physician, public health administrator*
Malik, Waheed Ahmad *cardiologist*
McMurry, James Finley, Jr. *endocrinologist, researcher*
Ralph, Robert Alan *ophthalmologist, educator*
Steinberg, William Mark *physician*
Sundlof, Stephen Frederick *veterinary administrator*
Tabor, Edward *medical researcher*
Temple, Robert *physician, federal agency administrator*
Toro, Jorge R. *dermatologist, researcher*
Vorosmarti, James *physician*
Watkins, Frederick Harvey *plastic surgeon*

Silver Spring
Beard, Lillian B. McLean *pediatrician, consultant*
Berger, Allan Sidney *psychiatrist, educator*
Freilich, Daniel Adam *epidemiologist*
Gaydos, Joel Carl *physician*
Gilbert, Charles Richard Alsop *obstetrician, gynecologist, surgeon, educator*
Heppner, Donald Gray, Jr. *immunology research physician, army officer*
Kriegel, Robin *medical association administrato*
Mosholder, Andrew Donald *psychiatrist*
Niebuhr, David William *epidemiologist, educato*
Supanich, Barbara Ann *physician*
Waldrop, Francis Neil *physician*

Stevenson
Hendler, Nelson Howard *physician, health facility administrator, director*

Timonium
Forrester, Alfred Whitfield *psychiatrist, educato*

Towson
Adams, Joseph Andrew *internist, health facility administrator, educator*
Meny, Robert George *former medical research administrator, physician*
Spodak, Michael Kenneth *forensic psychiatrist*
Wilkinson, Charles P. *ophthalmologist*

Upper Marlboro
Jones-Lukács, Elizabeth Lucille *physician*

Waldorf
Wiggins, Stephen Edward *physician*

Wheaton
White, Martha Vetter *allergist, immunologist*

Woodbine
Mc Indoe, Darrell Winfred *retired nuclear medicine physician*

Worton
Rienhoff, William Francis III *retired surgeon, thoracic surgeon*

MASSACHUSETTS

Acton
Benz, Edward John, Sr. *clinical pathologist*

Amesbury
Heyman, Joseph Martin *gynecologist*

Amherst
Fleischman, Paul Robert *psychiatrist, writer*
Palmer, John Derry *physiology educator*

Belmont
Cohen, Bruce Michael *psychiatrist, educator, scientist, health facility administrator*
Coyle, Joseph Thomas *psychiatrist*
de Marneffe, Francis *psychiatrist, hospital administrator*
Onesti, Silvio Joseph *psychiatrist*
Pope, Harrison Graham, Jr. *psychiatrist, educator*
Stoll, Andrew Lawrence *psychopharmacologist*
Zhang, Kehong *pharmacologist, educator*

Boston
Abrahm, Janet Lee *hematologist, oncologist, educator, palliative care specialist*
Abu-moustafa, Adel H. *medical educator, dean*
Adelstein, S(tanley) James *radiologist, educator*
Adler, Dale Steven *internist, cardiologist*
Akins, Cary Willard *surgeon, educator*
Albert, Martin Lawrence *behavioral neurologist, writer, educator, researcher*
Albright, Eric D. *medical librarian, director*
Alpert, Joel Jacobs *pediatrician, educator*
Anderson, Kenneth Carl *physician, educator*
Angelo, E. Joanne *child, adolescent and adult psychiatrist*
Antman, Elliot Marshall *cardiologist, educator*
Antman, Karen Hamm *oncologist, educator, dean*
Armstrong, Scott Allen *oncologist*
Ausiello, Dennis Arthur *nephrologist*
Austen, K(arl) Frank *internist, educator*
Austen, W(illiam) Gerald *surgeon, educator*
Azadzoi, Kazem M. *urologist, educator*
Bailin, Michael Traherne *physician*
Baldwin, John Charles *surgeon, researcher*
Banks, Henry H. *orthopedist, educator, dean*
Barnett, Guy Octo *physician, educator*
Barouch, Dan Hung *physician, scientist, educator*
Bates, David Westfall *internist, educator, medical researcher*
Baughman, Kenneth Lee *cardiologist, educator*
Becker, James Murdoch *surgeon, educator*
Benacerraf, Baruj *pathologist, educator*
Benoist, Christophe O. *immunologist, educator*
Benz, Edward John, Jr. *internist, hematologist, geneticist, educator, health facility administrator*
Bernhard, William Francis *thoracic and cardiovascular surgeon*
Berson, Eliot Lawrence *ophthalmologist, medical educator*
Bieber, Frederick Robert *medical geneticist*
Bistrian, Bruce Ryan *internist, educator*
Black, Paul Henry *medical educator, researcher*
Black, Peter *neurosurgeon, educator*
Blacklow, Robert Stanley *internist, educator*
Bloch, Kurt Julius *physician*
Borus, Jonathan Frederick *psychiatrist, educator*
Brain, Joseph David *biomedical researcher, educator*
Braunwald, Eugene *physician, educator*
Brazelton, Thomas Berry *pediatrician, educator*
Brenner, Barry Morton *physician*
Brenner, Michael Barry *rheumatologist, educator*
Briscoe, David Michael *physician, scientist, researcher*
Burstein, Harold John *oncologist*
Buxbaum, Robert C(ourtney) *internist*
Callow, Allan Dana *surgeon*
Canellos, George Peter *hematologist, oncologist, educator*
Cao, Xinhua *medical researcher*
Caplan, Louis Robert *neurologist, educator*
Carey, Martin Conrad *gastroenterologist, molecular biophysicist, educator, medical geneticist*
Cavazos, Lauro Fred *medical educator, former secretary of education*
Chabner, Bruce A. *oncologist, researcher*
Chobanian, Aram *medical educator, cardiologist, former academic administrator*
Choo, Sin H. *neurosurgeon*
Ciraulo, Domenic Anthony *psychiatrist, educator*
Clapham, David E. *pharmacology educator*
Coffin, John Miller *medical researcher, biology professor*
Cohen, Alan Seymour *internist*
Cohn, Lawrence H. *cardiothoracic surgeon*
Collins, Tucker *pathologist, molecular biologist*
Creevy, William R. *orthopedist, surgeon, educator*
Crowley, William Francis, Jr. *endocrinologist, educator*
Crum, Christopher Paul *pathologist, educator*
Daley, George Quentin *hematologist, biomedical research scientist*
Daly, Benedict Dudley Thomas, Jr. *cardiothoracic surgeon, educator*
D'Amico, Anthony Victor *radiation oncologist*
Demling, Robert Hugh *surgeon, researcher*
DeSanctis, Roman William *cardiologist, educator*
Devlin, Phillip M. *radiologist, medical educator*
Duhy, Robert George *physician*
Dolin, Raphael *medical educator*
Drazen, Jeffrey Mark *medical educator*
Dvorak, Harold Fisher *retired pathologist*
Eustathiou, Jason Alexander *oncologist, radiologist*
Egdahl, Richard Harrison *surgeon, educator, health science association administrator*
Eisenberg, Leon *psychiatrist, educator*
Ellis, Franklin Henry, Jr. *surgeon, educator*
Epler, Gary Robert *physician, author, educator*
Epstein, Arnold M. *medical educator*
Epstein, Franklin Harold *internist, educator*
Erban, John Kalil III *medicine educator, cancer specialist, researcher*
Estes, Nathan Anthony Mark III *cardiologist, medical educator*
Ferzoco, Stephen John *surgeon*
Folkman, Moses Judah *surgeon, educator*
Freedberg, A. Stone *physician*
Frei, Emil III *physician, educator, researcher*
Friedlander, Robert Max *neurosurgeon*
Friedman, Sandra L. *pediatrician*
Garber, Jeffrey Richard *endocrinologist*
Gates, Jonathan Dean *surgeon, educator*
Gawande, Atul A. *surgeon, writer*
Gelfand, Jeffrey Alan *physician, educator*
Gelman, Simon *anesthesiologist, educator*
Gipson, Ilene Kay *ophthalmologist, educator*
Glassroth, Jeffrey *internist, educator*
Glimcher, Melvin Jacob *orthopedic surgeon*
Goldberg, Irving Hyman *molecular pharmacology and biochemistry educator*
Goldie, Sue J. *health service researcher*
Gottlieb, Alice B. *dermatologist*
Greenblatt, David J. *pharmacologist*
Greenes, Robert A. *medical educator*
Gregory, Shawn Alen *cardiologist, physician, researcher*
Grillo, Hermes Conrad *surgeon*
Groopman, Jerome *medical educator*
Grundfast, Kenneth Martin *otolaryngologist*
Halamka, John D. *emergency physician, information technology executive*
Hamrah, Pedram *ophthalmologist, scientist*
Harmon, William E. *nephrologist*
Harper, Marvin Bruce *pediatrics educator, hospital administrator*
Harris, Mitchel Brion *orthopedist, surgeon*
Hartigan, Carol *orthopedist*
Hay, Elizabeth Dexter *embryologist, educator*
Healy, Gerald Burke *otolaryngologist*
Hedley-Whyte, John *anesthesiologist, educator*
Hendren, William Hardy III *surgeon*
Herndon, James Henry *orthopedic surgeon, educator*
Hiatt, Howard H. *internist, educator*
Hickey, Paul Robert *anesthesiologist, educator*
Hill, Nicholas S. *physician, researcher*
Howley, Peter Maxwell *pathology educator*
Ingwall, Joanne S. *medical educator*
Jones, Daniel Bougere *surgeon*
Joyce-Brady, Martin Francis *medical educator*
Kahn, Barbara B. *endocrinologist*
Kang, Jing X. *medical researcher, educator*
Kantoff, Philip W. *oncologist*
Kaplan, Marshall Myles *medical educator, researcher, gastroenterologist*
Karnovsky, Morris John *pathologist, biologist*
Kassirer, Jerome Paul *medical educator*
Kazemi, Homayoun *internist, educator*
Kesari, Santosh *neurologist, oncologist, neuroscientist*
Khalsa, Sat Bir Singh *biomedical researcher*
Kiang, Nelson Yuan-sheng *medical educator*
Kieff, Elliott Dan *medical educator*
Kim, David Hanwuk *surgeon, orthopedist, researcher*
Kim, Dong H. *neurosurgeon, medical geneticist, educator*
Kim, Ducksoo *radiologist, inventor, educator*
Kircher, Moritz Florian *radiologist, researcher*
Kitz, Richard John *anesthesiologist, educator*
Kocher, Mininder Singh *pediatric orthopaedic surgeon, epidemiologist*
Komaroff, Anthony Leader *physician*
Krane, Stephen Martin *rheumatologist, educator*
Kressel, Herbert Yehude *medical educator*
Lamont, John Thomas *gastroenterologist, educator*
Laufer, Marc R. *gynecologist*
Lazar, Harold Lee *cardiothoracic surgeon*
Lee, Charles *cytologist*
Lee, Thomas Henry *internist, cardiologist, healthcare executive*
Levine, Robert A. *cardiologist*
Liangos, Orfeas *nephrologist, researcher*
Ling, Pei-Ra *medical educator*
Lisbon, Alan *anesthesiologist, critical care physician*
Little, John Bertram *radiologist, educator, researcher*
Livingston, David Morse *internist, biomedical researcher*
Loscalzo, Joseph *cardiologist, biochemist*
Ludwig, David S. *endocrinologist*
Maisel, William Howard *cardiologist, internist*
Mannick, John Anthony *surgeon*
Manson, JoAnn Elisabeth *endocrinologist*
Marcus, Karen Jean *medical educator*
Martin, Joseph Boyd *neurologist, educator, retired dean*
Mathisen, Douglas J. *thoracic surgeon*
May, James Warren, Jr. *plastic surgeon, medical association executive*
McCormick, Marie Clare *pediatrician, educator*
McDougal, William Scott *urology educator*
McNeil, Barbara Joyce *radiologist, educator*
Merk, Frederick Bannister *biomedical educator, researcher*
Meyer, Jack Edward *radiologist, educator*
Meyerhardt, Jeffrey Abraham *internist, oncologist*
Mihm, Martin Charles, Jr. *pathologist, educator*
Moellering, Robert Charles, Jr. *internist, educator*
Moorman, Donald Wayne *surgeon, healthcare administrator*
Morgan, James Philip *pharmacology and cardiology educator*
Moss, Alan C. *physician, researcher*
Myers, Jeff L. *surgeon*
Nadelson, Carol Cooperman *psychiatrist, educator*
Naimi, Shapur *cardiologist, educator*
Nathan, David Gordon *pediatrician, educator*
O'Brien, J(ohn) Patrick *psychiatrist, educator*
Odze, Robert D. *pathologist*
Olubodun, Joel Oladapo *medical researcher, physician*
Pallotta, Johanna Antonia (Johanna Stephen) *endocrinologist, educator*
Parad, Richard Barry *pediatrician, researcher*
Paul, Oglesby *cardiologist, educator*
Pearce, Elizabeth Niewoehner *endocrinologist, researcher*
Pochi, Peter Ernest *physician*
Poussaint, Alvin Francis *psychiatrist, educator*
Rabkin, Mitchell Thornton *physician, educator, hospital administrator*
Rao, Anjana *immunologist, educator*
Rattner, David W. *surgeon*
Relman, Arnold Seymour *physician, editor, educator*
Reppert, Steven Marion *pediatrician, research scientist, educator*
Richie, Jerome Paul *surgeon, educator*
Ridker, Paul M. *cardiologist, medical educator*
Rockoff, Mark Alan *pediatric anesthesiologist*
Rogers, Gary Francis *plastic surgeon*
Rohrer, Richard Jeffrey *surgeon, educator*
Rosenblatt, Michael *internist, academic administrator, educator, researcher*
Roth, Sanford Irwin *pathologist, educator*
Rubin, Iris Kedar *dermatologist*
Russell, Paul Snowden *surgeon, educator*
Rutkove, Seward Brian *neurologist, educator, neuroscientist*
Ryan, Thomas John *cardiologist*
Sachs, David Howard *surgeon, immunologist, educator*
Sadeghi-Nejad, Abdollah *pediatrician, educator*
Sallan, Stephen E. *pediatrician*
Saper, Clifford Baird *neurology educator*
Scadden, David Thomas *hematologist, oncologist, research scientist*
Schaller, Jane Green *pediatrician*
Schlossman, Stuart Franklin *physician, educator, researcher*
Schneider, Eric C. *medical educator, physician*
Scott, James Arthur *radiologist, educator*
Seddon, Johanna Margaret *ophthalmologist, epidemiologist*
Seidman, Christine E. *medical educator*
Selkoe, Dennis Jesse *neurologist, researcher, educator*
Sellke, Frank William *cardiothoracic surgeon, researcher*
Seshadri, Sudha *neurologist, educator*
Shields, Lawrence Thornton *orthopaedic surgeon, educator*
Shore, Miles Frederick *psychiatrist, educator*
Singh, Reshmi L. *medical educator*
Slack, Warner Vincent *medical educator, researcher*
Sloan, Steven Richard *medical educator, director*
Snydman, David Richard *infectious diseases specialist, educator*
Sodroski, Joseph G. *medical educator*
Sparrow, Joshua D. *child psychiatrist*
Speizer, Frank E. *physician, researcher*
Spellman, Mitchell Wright *surgeon, academic administrator, educator*
Sperling, Reisa A. *neurologist, researcher*
Spiegel, Joan Elizabeth *anesthesiologist, educator*
Springer, Timothy Alan *health researcher, immunology educator*
Stair, Thomas Osborne *physician, educator*
Stampfer, Meir Jonathan *epidemiologist, nutritionist, educator*
Steere, Allen Caruthers, Jr. *physician, educator*
Stewart, Elizabeth AnNella *gynecologist, researcher*
Stossel, Thomas Peter *medical educator, researcher, director*
Suh, Wonsuk Warren *radiation oncologist*
Suit, Herman Day *radiation oncologist, medical educator*
Surman, Owen Stanley *psychiatrist*
Swartz, Morton Norman *medical educator*
Sykes, Megan *immunologist*
Taubman, Martin Arnold *immunologist, educator*
Tavakkolizadeh, Ali *surgeon*
Theoharides, Theoharis Constantin *pharmacologist, physician, educator*
Thibault, George Edwin *medical educator, non-profit healthcare organization administrator*
Tilly, Jonathan L. *obstetrician, gynecologist, reproductive biologist*
Tompkins, Ronald Gary *surgeon, educator, biomedical investigator*
Treves, S. Ted *nuclear medicine physician, educator, hospital administrator*
Trichopoulos, Dimitrios Vassilios *epidemiologist, educator*
Trier, Jerry Steven *gastroenterologist, educator*
Tromanhauser, Scott Glenn *orthopaedic surgeon*
Vacanti, Joseph Philip *pediatric and transplant surgeon*
Vollmer, Charles Mahlon, Jr. *surgeon*
Waldinger, Robert Jon *psychiatrist*
Wang, Zhi *biomedical researcher*
Warshaw, Andrew Louis *surgeon, researcher*
Weiss, Earle Burton *physician*
White, Augustus Aaron III *orthopaedic surgeon*
Whittemore, Anthony Dunster *vascular surgeon, chief medical officer*
Wu, Julian K. *neurosurgeon*
Wyszynski, Diego Federico *epidemiologist, educator*
Young, Anne B. *neurologist, educator*
Yuan, Junying *medical educator, researcher*
Zon, Leonard I. *pediatrics educator, researcher*

Boylston
Hanshaw, James Barry *pediatrician, educator*

Brockton
Carlson, Desiree Anice *pathologist*

Brookline
Alarcon, Rogelio Alfonso *retired internist, retired researcher*
Goldsmith, Gary Norman *psychiatrist, psychoanalyst*
Hyman, Albert Lewis *cardiologist, educator*
Jakab, Irene *psychiatrist*
Schwartz, Bernard *physician*
Tyler, H. Richard *physician*

Burlington
Berkoben, John Perri *physician*
Choi, In-Sup *radiologist*
Clerkin, Eugene Patrick *physician, educator*
Cosgrove, Garth Rees *neurosurgeon*
Freidberg, Stephen Roy *neurosurgeon*
Hurd, Joseph Kindall, Jr. *obstetrician, gynecologist*
Jones, Harvey Royden, Jr. *neurologist*
Moschella, Samuel L. *dermatology educator*
Oberfield, Richard Alan *oncologist*
Schoetz, David John, Jr. *colon and rectal surgeon, educator*
Seckel, Brooke Rutledge *plastic surgeon*

Cambridge
Barrett, J. Carl *medical researcher, molecular biologist*
Berwick, Donald Mark *medical institute administrator*
Brusch, John Lynch *physician, educator, hospital administrator*
Cansev, Mehmet *physician, researcher*
Carr, Daniel Barry *anesthesiologist, endocrinologist, researcher, pharmaceutical executive*
Chen, Lincoln Chin-ho *medical educator*
Eisen, Herman Nathaniel *immunology researcher, medical educator*
Ette, Ene Ikpong *clinical pharmacologist*
Ewing, Scott Edwin *physiatrist, educator*
Fishman, Mark Charles *biomedical researcher*
Friedman, Jeffrey Robert *psychiatrist, educator*
Grossman, Jerome Harvey *medical association administrator, educator*
Guarente, Leonard P. *medical geneticist, educator*
Havens, Leston Laycock *psychiatrist, educator*
Herr, Hugh Miller *biomechatronics researcher, educator*
Hirsch, Martin Stanley *internist, epidemiologist, researcher*
Liau, Gene *medical educator*
London, Irving Myer *physician, educator*
Mathews, Joan Helene *pediatrician*
McCunney, Robert Joseph *physician*
McMahon, Andrew Paul *embryologist, educator*
Mootha, Vamsi Krishna *biomedical researcher, educator*
Nathanson, Larry *medical educator*
O'Shea, Erin K. *biomedical researcher*
Reichle, Ralph L. *radiologist*
Tsai, Li-Huei *pathologist, researcher*
Wacker, Warren Ernest Clyde *internist, educator*

Charlestown
Ackerman, Jerome Leonard *biomedical researcher*
Cutrer, Fred Michael *neurologist*
Isselbacher, Kurt Julius *internist, educator*
Kazantsev, Aleksey Gregory *medical educator*
Leaf, Alexander *preventive medicine physician, epidemiologist*
Potts, John Thomas, Jr. *physician, educator*
Zamecnik, Paul Charles *oncologist, medical researcher*

Chelmsford
Edelstein, Robert A. *urologist*
Menitoff, Paul Alan *psychiatrist*

Chestnut Hill
Cohen, David Joel *medical educator*
Dahlben, Salin Abraham *neuropsychiatrist*
Flax, Martin Howard *pathologist, retired educator*
Gottlieb, Marise Suss *epidemiologist*
Kosasky, Harold Jack *fertility researcher*
Thier, Samuel Osiah *physician, educator*

Clinton
Lanza, Robert Paul *medical scientist*

Concord
Boger, William Pierce III *ophthalmologist*
Coles, Robert *child psychiatrist, educator, writer*

Dorchester
Loh, Shaun *radiologist*

Dover
Buyse, Marylou *pediatrician, geneticist, medical administrator*

East Boston
Patinkin, Terry Allan *physician*

Falmouth
Sato, Kazuyoshi *pathologist*

Foxboro
Thompson, Michael David *physician*

Framingham
Klapholz, Henry *obstetrician, gynecologist, educator*
Ramachandran, Vasan Srini *medical educator*
Zamvil, Linda Susan *psychiatrist, educator*

Gardner
Du Buske, Lawrence Michael *immunologist, rheumatologist*

Gloucester
White, Harold Jack *pathologist*

Harvard
Monath, Thomas Patrick *physician*

Hyannis
Cochrane, Paul Hollis *general practice physician*

Jamaica Plain
Pierce, Chester Middlebrook *retired psychiatrist, educator*

Lexington
Letts, Lindsay Gordon *pharmacologist, educator*
Waksman, Byron Halsted *immunologist, educator, medical association administrator*

Lincoln
Brandt, John Henry *physician*

Lowell
Dubner, Daniel William *pediatrician*

Lynn
Copeland, Paul Michael *endocrinologist*

Manchester
Prout, Curtis *internist, educator*

Marlborough
Johannes, Richard Scott *medical association administrator*

Mattapoisett
Mazer, Mike *cardiologist, retired nephrologist, artist*

Melrose
Desforges, Jane Fay *retired internist, hematologist, educator*

Milton
Zervas, Nicholas Themistocles *neurosurgeon*

Natick
Gottlieb, Michael Norman *internist, educator, health facility administrator*
Nirmel, Krishna *neurosurgeon*

Needham
Osser, David Neal *psychiatrist, educator*

Newton
Bassuk, Ellen Linda *psychiatrist*
Bernier, George Matthew, Jr. *oncologist, educator, dean*
Davidson, Barry A. *plastic surgeon*
Garcia, Eduardo *neurologist, consultant*
Jellinek, Michael Steven *psychiatrist, pediatrician*
May, Harold Louis *retired surgeon, not-for-profit developer*
Sasahara, Arthur Asao *cardiologist, educator, researcher*

Newton Center
Eichler, Marc *neurosurgeon*

North Dighton
Cserr, Robert *psychiatrist, physician, hospital administrator*

Northborough
Fulmer, Hugh Scott *physician, educator*

Norwood
Berliner, Allen Irwin *dermatologist*
Pence, Robert Dudley *biomedical researcher, consultant, hospital administrator*

Oxford
Schur, Walter Robert *physician*

Peabody
Birdsall, Melinda R. *gynecologist*
Lipman, Richard Paul *pediatrician*
Perryman, Jonathan Richard *orthopedist, surgeon*

Petersham
Chivian, Eric Seth *psychiatrist, environmental scientist, educator*

Rockland
Blethen, Sandra Lee *pediatric endocrinologist*

Somerville
Klass, Perri Elizabeth *pediatrician, writer*

South Wellfleet
Blau, Monte *retired radiology educator*

South Weymouth
Coombs, Alice A. Tolbert *anesthesiologist, internist*
Young, Michael Chung-En *allergist, immunologist, pediatrician*

Springfield
Farkas, Paul Stephen *gastroenterologist*
Friedmann, Paul *surgeon, educator, research and development company executive*
Ganai, Sabha *surgeon, researcher*
Kirkwood, John Robert *neuroradiologist*
Kottamasu, Mohan Rao (K.V.R. Mohan Rao) *physician, health facility administrator*
Liptzin, Benjamin *psychiatrist*
McGee, William Tobin *internist*
Romero, Ricardo Vicente *gastroenterologist*

Stockbridge
Shapiro, Edward Robert *psychiatrist, educator, health facility administrator, psychotherapist*

Stoughton
Joseph, Anthony Barnett *psychiatrist*

Sudbury
Lamont-Havers, Ronald William *retired physician, medical association administrator*

Waban
Rogoff, Jerome Howard *psychiatrist, psychoanalyst, forensic expert*
Shklar, Gerald *pathologist, periodontist, educator*

Waltham
Lackner, James Robert *aerospace medicine educator*
Landaw, Stephen Arthur *physician, educator*
Leach, Robert Ellis *orthopedist, surgeon, educator*

Wayland
Edelman, Stuart Edward *psychiatrist*
Moncure, Ashby Carter *surgeon, educator*

Wellesley
Craven, Donald Edward *epidemiologist, researcher*
Falchuk, Kenneth R. *gastroenterologist*
Murray, Joseph Edward *retired plastic surgeon*
Sexton, John Joseph *oral and maxillofacial surgeon, educator*

Wellesley Hills
Spierings, Egilius Leonardus Hendricus *pharmacologist, neurologist, headache specialist, clinical trialist*

West Falmouth
Bass, Norman Herbert *neurologist, educator, research scientist, hospital administrator, academic administrator*

West Springfield
Desai, Veena Balvantrai *obstetrician, gynecologist, educator*

Weston
Jayasankar, Subramanyan *orthopaedic surgeon*

Westwood
Bloomingdale, Lewis Morgan *retired psychiatrist*

Williamstown
Stuebner, Erwin August, Jr. *internist*
Wilkins, Earle Wayne, Jr. *retired surgery educator*

Woods Hole
Laster, Leonard *internist, gastroenterologist, academic administrator, educator, writer, researcher*
Prendergast, Robert Anthony *pathologist educator*

Worcester
Alkassab, Firas *rheumatologist*
Balaji, Kethandapatti C. *urologist, oncologist, researcher*
Bernhard, Jeffrey David *dermatologist, educator, editor*
Byatt, Nancy *psychiatrist*
Chern, Shyh-Shi Richard *radiologist*
Cosar, Ediz Fergün *pathologist, researcher*
Drachman, David Alexander *neurologist*
Haas, Richard Allen *physician*
Hunter, Richard Edward *retired physician*
Illanes, Diego Sebastian *obstetrician, gynecologist*
Madison, John Mark *pulmonologist, educator*
Mello, Craig C. *molecular medicine educator, researcher*
Morse, Leonard J. *epidemiologist, public health service officer*
Selin, Lisa K. *physician*
Tonkonogy, Joseph Moses *physician, neuropsychiatrist, researcher*
Townes, Philip Leonard *pediatrician, educator*
Uschuplich, Vedran *pathologist*
Young, Stephen Bernard *urogynecologist, surgeon*
Zurier, Robert Burton *rheumatology educator*

Yarmouth Port
Gordon, Benjamin Dichter *pediatrician, educator, health facility administrator*

MICHIGAN

Ada
Mason, James Hamilton *surgeon*

Ann Arbor
Abrams, Gerald David *pathologist, educator*
Akin, Cem *internist, allergist, medical researcher*
Ansbacher, Rudi *physician*
Bacon, George Edgar *pediatrician*
Baler, Blanche Kimoto *retired child psychiatrist*
Barsan, William George *emergency physician*
Bartlett, Robert Hawes *surgeon*
Bloom, Jane Maginnis *emergency physician*
Bolling, Steven Fredric *cardiac surgeon, educator*
Bowdler, Anthony John *internist, educator*
Boxer, Laurence Alan *physician, research educator*
Brophy, Patrick David *pediatrician, researcher*
Burdi, Alphonse Rocco *anatomist*
Burke, Robert Harry *surgeon, educator*
Carlson, Bruce Martin *anatomist*
Casey, Kenneth Lyman *neurologist*
Cerny, Joseph Charles *urologist, educator*
Chey, William D *physician, researcher*
Chiodo, Anthony *medical educator*
Coran, Arnold Gerald *pediatrician, surgeon*
Del Monte, Monte Anthony *medical educator*
Donabedian, Avedis *physician, educator*
Doyle, Constance Talcott Johnston *physician, educator, medical association administrator*
Fajans, Stefan Stanislaus *retired internist*
Farmer, Cheryl Christine *internist, industrial hygienist*
Fox, David Alan *rheumatologist, immunologist*
Frohna, John G. *pediatrician*
Galea, Sandro *epidemiologist*
Gelehrter, Thomas David *medical educator, geneticist*
Gikas, Paul William *medical educator*
Gilman, Sid *neurologist*
Goldstein, Steven Alan *medical and engineering educator*
Greden, John Francis *psychiatrist, educator*
Greenfield, Lazar John *surgeon, educator*
Gurm, Hitinder S. *cardiologist, educator*
Hoff, Julian Theodore *neurosurgeon, educator*
Hollenberg, Paul Frederick *pharmacology educator*
Horowitz, Samuel Boris *biomedical researcher, educational consultant*
Humes, Harvey David *nephrologist, educator, director*
Johnson, Timothy R. B. *obstetrician, gynecologist, educator*
Klinkman, Michael Scott *medical educator*
Kuhl, David Edmund *nuclear medicine physician, educator*
Lichter, Allen S. *oncologist, educator, dean*
Lichter, Paul Richard *ophthalmology educator*
Lozoff, Betsy *pediatrician, educator*
Mancuso, Peter *medical educator*
Margolis, Philip Marcus *psychiatrist, educator*
Markel, Howard *physician, educator*
Miller, Josef M. *otolaryngologist, educator*
Modell, Stephen Mark *medical researcher, educator*
Monto, Arnold Simon *epidemiology educator*
Mulholland, Michael William *surgeon, researcher*
Oliver, William John *pediatrician, educator*
Orringer, Jeffrey S. *dermatologist, educator*
Pearlman, Mark *medical educator, researcher*
Pitt, Bertram *cardiologist, educator, consultant*
Powsner, Edward Raphael *physician*
Rao, Panduranga S. *nephrologist, educator*
Reddy, Venkat Narsimha *ophthalmologist, researcher*
Rosenthal, Amnon *pediatric cardiologist*
Saper, Joel R. *neurologist, educator*
Sarkar, Subrata *medical educator*
Schottenfeld, David *retired epidemiologist, educator*
Schteingart, David Eduardo *internist*
Seibold, James Richard *physician, educator*
Sloan, Herbert Elias *physician, surgeon*
Smith, Donald Cameron *retired preventive medicine physician*
Srinivasan, Ashok *radiologist*
Strang, Ruth Hancock *pediatrician, educator, cardiologist, priest*
Stross, Jeoffrey Knight *internist, educator*
Swaroop, Anand *medical educator*
Teener, James W. *neurologist, medical educator*
Thompson, Norman Winslow *surgeon, educator*
Todd, Robert Franklin III *oncologist, educator*
Ward, Peter Allan *pathologist, educator*
Weder, Alan B(rian) *internist, medical educator*
Weg, John Gerard *physician*

Au Gres
Dhawan, Vikas *plastic surgeon*

Beverly Hills
Castle, Maurice Emmett *orthopedist, surgeon*

Bingham Farms
Giles, Conrad Leslie *ophthalmic surgeon*

Bloomfield Hills
Ball, Patricia Ann *physician*
Brent, Robert Lewis *urologist*
Coburn, Ronald Murray *ophthalmologist, surgeon*
Gagliardi, Raymond Alfred *physician*
Mathog, Robert Henry *otolaryngologist, educator*
O'Hara, John Paul III *orthopedic surgeon*
Stunz, John Henry, Jr. *retired physician, consultant*

Brighton
Clark, Robert Thomas *ophthalmologist*

Clarkston
Wydra, Frank Thomas *healthcare executive*

Clinton Township
Ho, Robert En Ming *neurosurgeon, educator*

Dearborn
Fordyce, James George *physician*

Detroit
Abramson, Hanley Norman *pharmacy educator*
Bahl, Gautam *radiologist*
Balon, Richard *psychiatrist, educator*
Bhandari, Akshay *urologist*
Bock, Brooks Frederick *emergency physician*
Cohen, Sanford Ned *pediatrician, educator, academic administrator*
Dombrowski, Mitchell Paul *obstetrician, researcher*
Elder, Jack S. *urologist, educator*
Enam, Syed Ather *neurosurgeon, researcher*
Gardin, Julius Markus *cardiologist, educator*
Gilmer-Hill, Holly *medical educator*
Haddad, Ramsi *medical geneticist, educator*
Hashimoto, Ken *dermatologist, educator*
Hawley, Robert C., Jr. *pathologist*
Kelley, Mark Albert *physician, educator, health products executive*
Kim, Do Gyoon *biomedical researcher*
Lim, Henry Wan-Peng *dermatologist*
Lisak, Robert Philip *neurologist, researcher, educator*
Losanoff, Julian Emil *surgeon, educator*
Lupulescu, Aurel Peter *medical educator, researcher, physician*
Maiese, Kenneth *neurologist, neuroscientist*
Mani, Nandita S. *medical librarian*
Miller, Orlando Jack *obstetrician, gynecologist, educator, geneticist*
Nathanson, Saul David *oncologist, surgeon, educator*
Ostrea, Enrique Mapua, Jr. *pediatrician, medical educator*
Ouellette, Daniel Ronald *pulmonary and critical care medicine specialist*
Prasad, Ananda Shiva *medical educator*
Rajpurkar, Atul Dattatraya *urologist*
Reddy, Daniel Joseph *vascular surgeon*
Rivers, Emanuel P. *emergency physician, medical educator*
Rosman, Howard S. *cardiologist, educator*
Schiffer, Charles Alan *oncologist, educator*
Schweitzer, Vanessa Gayl *otorhinolaryngologist*
Shade, George Henry, Jr. *obstetrician, gynecologist, educator*
Shah, Aashit K. *neurologist*
Silverman, Norman Alan *cardiac surgeon*
Sima, Anders Adolph Fredrik *pathologist*
Skundric, Dusanka S. *medical educator, researcher*
Smith, Wilbur Lazar *radiologist, educator*
Sokol, Robert James *obstetrician, gynecologist, educator*
Tyburski, James Gerard *surgeon*
Voudoukis, Ignatios John *internist, cardiologist*
Whitehouse, Fred Waite *endocrinologist, researcher*
Wiener, Joseph *pathologist, educator*

East Lansing
Beckmeyer, Henry Ernest *anesthesiologist, pain management specialist, educator*
Gottschalk, Alexander *radiologist, educator*
Monson, Carol Lynn *osteopath, psychotherapist*
Pervaiz, Mohammad Hassan *cardiologist*
Pysh, Joseph John *neurologist*
Ristow, George Edward *neurologist, educator*
Rosenman, Kenneth D. *medical educator*
Watson, Ralph Edward *internist, educator*

Farmington Hills
Aboulafia, Elie David *vascular surgeon*
Gordon, Craig Jeffrey *oncologist, educator*

Fife Lake
Knecht, Richard Arden *family practitioner*

Flint
Wheeler, Michael Thomas *pain medicine specialist, director*

Frankenmuth
Shetlar, James Francis *physician*

Freeland
Lutes, Byron B. *retired surgeon*

Grand Rapids
Daniels, Joseph *neuropsychiatrist*
Harrison, Robert Ward *retired surgeon*
Robson, Larry J. *physician*
Swanson, Alfred Bertil *orthopaedic and hand surgeon, educator*
Taber, Rodman Eastman *thoracic surgeon*
Verdier, David D'Ooge *ophthalmologist, educator*
Watkins, James Kelley *retired urologist*
Wendt, Vernon Earl *internist, cardiologist*
Wilt, Jeffrey Lynn *pulmonary and critical care physician, educator*

Grosse Ile
Stryker, Joan Copeland *retired obstetrician, retired gynecologist, educator*

Grosse Pointe Shores
Sphire, Raymond Daniel *anesthesiologist, educator*

Grosse Pointe Woods
Sul, Yi Chul *neurologist*

Holland
Zuidema, George Dale *surgeon, educator*

Kalamazoo
Campbell, William Bernard *cardiologist*
Fischell, Tim Alexander *cardiologist*
Saber, Alan A. *surgeon*
Sridharan, Sugandhi *neurologist*

Lake Angelus
Kresge, Bruce Anderson *retired physician*

Lansing
Vincent, Frederick Michael, Sr. *neurologist, educator*

Livonia
Baskin, Victoria *child and adolescent psychiatrist*
Nahra, Khalil Salim *colon and rectal surgeon*

Marine City
Brown, Ronald Delano *endocrinologist*

Marquette
Lincke, Eric Theodore *retired surgeon*
Mahmood, Tallat *oncologist, hematologist*

Milford
Oliveri, Eugene Alfred *gastroenterologist*

Niles
Gibbs, Denis Laurel *radiologist*

Northport
Schultz, Richard Carlton *plastic surgeon*

Petoskey
Kleppe, Lars W. *retired pathologist*
Meengs, William Lloyd *cardiologist*

Pontiac
Bautista, Marieta Pascual *psychiatrist*

Richland
Atkinson, Arthur John, Jr. *pharmacologist, educator, consultant*

Rochester
Youn, Anthony Sungjin *plastic surgeon*

Rochester Hills
Badalament, Robert Anthony *urologist, oncologist*

Royal Oak
Britt, Stephen Thomas *medical educator*
Doty, Angela Joy *emergency physician, military officer*
Dworkin, Howard Jerry *retired nuclear medicine physician, educator*
LaBan, Myron Miles *physician, hospital administrator*
O'Neill, William Walter *physician, educator*
Proctor, Conrad Arnold *physician*
Schaffner, Adam David *plastic surgeon*
Seidman, Joel C. *pulmonary physician*

Saginaw
Ferlinz, Jack *cardiologist, educator*
Hammel, Iriana Simona *geriatrician*

Saint Joseph
Wood, Dirk Gregory *surgeon, physician, forensic consultant*

Southfield
Perez-Cruet, Mick Jorge (Miguelangelo Jorge Perez-Cruet) *neurosurgeon, educator*
Sobel, Robert A. *retired orthopedic surgeon*
Zubroff, Leonard Saul *surgeon*

Sterling Heights
Rizk, Maged *cardiologist, researcher*

Troy
Golusin, Millard R. *obstetrician, gynecologist*
Schafer, Sharon Marie *anesthesiologist*

Waterford
Zielinski, Michael Edmund *osteopath*

West Bloomfield
Jones, Lewis Arnold, Jr. *physician, radiologist, consultant*
Sarwer-Foner, Gerald Jacob *psychiatrist, educator*
Sawyer, Howard Jerome *physician*

Westland
Geiringer, Steve R. *medical educator*

Ypsilanti
Gillard, Montgomery *dermatologist*

MINNESOTA

Austin
Rioux, Pierre August *psychiatrist*

Burnsville
Lakin, James Dennis *allergist, immunologist, director*

Duluth
Aufderheide, Arthur Carl *pathologist*
McKee, David Charles *neurologist*

East Grand Forks
Crow, Judson Lewis *plastic surgeon*

East Gull Lake
Simons, John Nelson *surgeon, consultant*

Edina
Tagatz, George Elmo *retired obstetrician, gynecologist, educator*

Excelsior
Bilka, Paul Joseph *retired physician*
Martinson, Elmer James *retired surgeon*

Golden Valley
Altafullah, Irfan M. *neurologist*

Hastings
Orr, Jennie Marie (Jennie Thomas) *family physician*

Lauderdale
Resch, Joseph Anthony *neurologist*

Minneapolis
Aamoth, Gordon M. *medical association administrator*
Bache, Robert James *physician, educator*
Buchwald, Henry *surgeon, educator, researcher*
Burchell, Howard Bertram *retired internist*
Chavers, Blanche Marie *pediatrician, educator, researcher*
Church, Timothy Robert *medical educator, researcher*
Craig, James Lynn *physician, health services administrator*
Dykstra, Dennis Dale *physiatrist*
Fisch, Robert Otto *medical educator*
Freese, Andrew *neurosurgeon, educator*
Goldberg, Stanley Morton *surgeon, educator*
Haines, Stephen John *neurosurgeon*
Hanson, Arthur Stuart *physician, consultant*
Hays, Thomas S. *medical educator, researcher*
Hom, David Brian *surgeon*
Ingbar, David H. *physician, researcher*
Joseph, Marilyn Susan *gynecologist*
Judson, Patricia Lynn *obstetrician, gynecologist, oncologist*
Keane, William Francis *nephrology educator, research foundation executive*
Kim, Suck-Won *psychiatrist, educator*
Leon, Arthur Sol *research cardiologist, exercise physiologist*
Leppik, Ilo E. *neurologist, educator*
Loh, Horace H. *pharmacology educator*
Luepker, Russell Vincent *epidemiology educator*
Malmquist, Carl Phillip *psychiatrist*
Mandel, Sheldon Lloyd *dermatologist, educator*
Miner, James Ross *emergency physician, educator*
Moller, James Herman *pediatrician, educator*
Monga, Manoj *medical educator*
Najarian, John Sarkis *surgeon, educator*
Osterholm, Michael T. *epidemiologist, public health service officer*
Phibbs, Clifford Matthew *surgeon, educator*
Powell, Deborah Elizabeth *pathologist, dean*
Pyles, Lee Allan *cardiologist, biomedical researcher*
Quie, Paul Gerhardt *pediatrician, educator*
Slocum, Rosemarie *physician services consultant, recruiter*
Stenwick, Michael William *retired internist, geriatrician, consultant*
Swiontkowski, Marc Francis *orthopedist*
Thompson, Roby Calvin, Jr. *orthopedic surgeon, educator, department chairman*
Thompson, Theodore Robert *pediatric educator*
Toscano, James Vincent *medical foundation administrator*
Ulstrom, Robert A. *retired pediatrician*
Wang, Yang *cardiologist, educator, medical researcher*
Wild, John Julian *surgeon, researcher, medical educator*
Zaleske, David Joseph *surgeon, research scientist, health facility administrator*

Minnetonka
Bahl, Tracy L. *healthcare executive*
Sandy, Lewis Gordon *physician, healthcare executive*

Olivia
Cosgriff, James Arthur *physician*

Rochester
Bakkum-Gamez, Jamie Nadine *obstetrician, gynecologist*
Bartholomew, Lloyd Gibson *physician*
Bowie, E(dward) J(ohn) Walter *hematologist, researcher*
Brown, Arnold Lanehart, Jr. *pathologist, educator, dean*
Cofield, Robert Hahn *orthopedic surgeon, educator*
Currier, Bradford Leonard *spine and orthopedic surgeon*
Danielson, Gordon Kenneth, Jr. *cardiovascular surgeon, educator*
Dearani, Joseph Albert *medical educator*
DeRemee, Richard Arthur *retired internist, educator, researcher*
Douglass, Bruce E. *physician*
Engel, Andrew George *neurologist*
Fervenza, Fernando C. *nephrologist, educator*
Forstrom, Lee Arthur *physician*
Fye, W. Bruce III *cardiologist*
Garcia Franco, Carlos Enrique *thoracic surgeon*
Gersh, Bernard J. *cardiologist, researcher, educator*
Gibbons, Raymond John *cardiologist*
Gorman, Colum Alphonsus *retired endocrinologist*
Gracey, Douglas Robert *internist, educator, physiologist*
Haddy, Francis John *internist, educator*
Hunder, Gene Gerald *rheumatologist, educator*
Kantarci, Kejal *radiologist, researcher*
Knopman, David S. *neurologist*
Kyle, Robert Arthur *medical educator, oncologist*
LaRusso, Nicholas F. *gastroenterologist, educator, scientist*
Lee, Hon-Chi *medical educator*
Lucas, Alexander Ralph *child psychiatrist, educator, writer*
Mackenzie, Ronald Alexander *anesthesiologist*
Malkasian, George Durand, Jr. *obstetrician, educator*
McAlpine, Donald Eugene *physician*
Moir, Christopher Robert *surgeon*
Neel, Harry Bryan III *surgeon, scientist, educator*
Nelson, Audrey May *physician*
Ngaage, Dumbor Laateh *cardiothoracic surgeon*
Pairolero, Peter Charles *surgeon, educator*
Perry, Harold Otto *dermatologist*
Phillips, Sidney Frederick *gastroenterologist, educator*
Piepgras, David G. *neurosurgeon, educator*
Pittelkow, Mark Robert *physician, dermatologist, educator, medical researcher*
Platt, Jeffrey Louis *surgeon, director, immunologist, educator, pediatric nephrologist*
Podratz, Karl C. *gynecologic surgeon, oncologist, educator*
Pulido, Jose S. *physician*
Rasimas, Joseph James *psychiatrist*
Rogers, Roy Steele III *dermatologist, educator, dean*
Rosenow, Edward Carl III *medical educator*
Scott, John Paul *medical educator*
Seferian, Edward G. *medical educator*
Siekert, Robert George *retired neurologist, retired educator*
Silber, Michael H. *neurologist*
Sim, Franklin H. *orthopedic surgery educator*
Stegall, Mark D. *surgeon, medical educator*
Stickler, Gunnar Brynolf *pediatrician*
Tak, Tahir *cardiologist, researcher*
Talley, Nicholas Joseph *medical educator, research scientist, physician*
Ward, Louis Emmerson *retired physician*
Whisnant, Jack Page *neurologist*
Wiebers, David Owen *physician*
Wood, Douglas Lynn *medical educator*
Woods, John Elmer *plastic surgeon*
Wylam, Mark Edward *medical educator, researcher*

Saint Cloud
Olson, Barbara Ford *physician*
Rice, Steven William *ophthalmologist*

Saint Louis Park
Beecher, Lee Hewitt *psychiatrist*
Saliterman, Steven S. *internist, educator*

Saint Paul
Broccard, Alain Fransois *pulmonologist*
Burton, Charles Victor *neurosurgeon*
Cavert, Henry Mead *retired physician, educator*
Comer, Beth Megan-Simkins *forensic scientist*
Crabb, Kenneth Wayne *obstetrician, gynecologist*
Edwards, Jesse Efrem *pathologist, educator*
Holter, Arlen Rolf *cardiothoracic surgeon*
Michael, Alfred Frederick, Jr. *physician, medical educator*
Smith, George Floyd *medical educator*
Swaiman, Kenneth Fred *pediatric neurologist, educator*
Westermeyer, Joseph John *psychiatrist*
Wilson, Leonard Gilchrist *medical educator*

Stillwater
Asch, Susan McClellan *pediatrician*

Virginia
Knabe, George William, Jr. *pathologist, educator*

Wayzata
Muschenheim, Frederick *retired pathologist*

MISSISSIPPI

Flowood
Das, Suman Kumar *plastic surgeon, researcher*
Zoog, Eric James *emergency physician*

Houston
Griffin, T. David *family physician, pharmacist*

Iuka
Segars, Kelly Scott, Sr. *physician, banker*

Jackson
Bloom, Sherman *retired pathology educator, photographer*
Boronow, Richard Carlton *gynecologist, educator*
Cowan, Bryan D. *medical educator, department chairman*
Cruse, Julius Major, Jr. *pathologist, educator*
de-Shazo, Richard Denson *medical educator, academic administrator*
Hall, John E. *medical educator*
Herndon, Robert McCulloch *neurologist, researcher*
Houston, Gerry Ann *oncologist*
Hughson, Michael Donald *pathologist, researcher, medical educator*
Iliescu, Radu *medical educator*
Izevbigie, Ernest B. *biomedical researcher*
Marshall, Gailen Daugherty, Jr. *allergist, educator*
Moll, George William *pediatrician, educator*
Munera, Pedro Antonio *child and adolescent psychiatrist*
Nix, J. Elmer *retired orthopedist, surgeon*
O'Mara, Charles Snow *surgeon*
Phillips, Joshua *pediatrician*
Roy, Sitesh Ranen *pediatrician, allergist, immunologist, educator*
Thigpen, James Tate *oncologist, educator*

Laurel
Lacey, Peeler Grayson *diagnostic radiologist*
Lindstrom, Eric Everett *ophthalmologist*

Ocean Springs
Austin, Claude Lidell *retired surgeon*

Tupelo
Hill, J. Edward *physician, educator*

University
Doerksen, Robert John *pharmacy educator*

Whitfield
Montgomery, John Harold *psychiatrist*

MISSOURI

Belton
Blim, Richard Don *retired pediatrician, health facility administrator*

Cape Girardeau
Sacha, Robert Frank *osteopath, educator*

Chesterfield
Omell, Gary H. *radiologist*
Salem, Bakr Ibramim *cardiologist*

Columbia
Anderson, Ralph Robert *endocrinologist, educator*
Colwill, Jack Marshall *physician, educator*
Cunningham, Milamari Antoinella *retired anesthesiologist*
Eggers, George William Nordholtz, Jr. *anesthesiologist, educator*
Giblin, Michael F. *medical researcher, educator*
Hardin, Christopher Demarest *medical educator*
James, Elizabeth Joan Plogsted *pediatrician, educator*
König, Peter *pediatrician, educator*
LeMaster, Joseph William *physician, epidemiologist*
Lewis, Michael Robert *medical researcher, educator*
Perry, Michael Clinton *internist, educator, academic administrator*
Puckett, Charles Linwood *plastic surgeon, educator*
Stephenson, Hugh Edward, Jr. *retired surgeon*
Tarnove, Lorraine *medical association executive*
Tobias, Joseph Drew *pediatric anesthesiologist*
Witten, David Melvin *retired radiology educator*

Florissant
Owen, Robert Frederick *internist, rheumatologist*
Tanphaichitr, Kongsak *rheumatologist, allergist, immunologist, internist*

Jefferson City
Swarens, Cork (C.C. Swarens) *medical association administrator*

Joplin
Daus, Arthur Steven *neurological surgeon*
Dodson, Robert Wayne *surgeon*
Habermann, James Herbert *retired pathologist*

Kansas City
Angoff, Gerald Harvey *cardiologist*
Berenbom, Loren David *cardiologist*
Bernhardt, Mark *orthopedic surgeon, educator*
Butler, Merlin Gene *physician, medical geneticist, educator*
Dimond, Edmunds Grey *medical educator*
Forker, Alan Duane *medical educator*
Friedlander, Edward Robert *pathologist*
Hagan, John Charles III *ophthalmologist*
Hall, Robert T. *pediatrician, medical educator, researcher*
Huston, Kent Allen *rheumatologist*
Kindred, Lynn Herbert *cardiologist*
Lofland, Gary Kenneth *cardiac surgeon*
Long, Edwin Tutt *surgeon*
McCallister, Ben D. *internist, cardiologist, educator*
McGregor, Douglas Hugh *pathologist, educator*
McPhee, Mark Steven *gastroenterologist, educator*
Molteni, Agostino *pathology educator*
O'Brien, James Edward *surgeon*
Piepho, Robert Walter *pharmacy educator, researcher*
Poston, Walker Seward, II, *medical educator, researcher*
Rada, David Charles *dermatologist*
Rutherford, Barry D. *cardiologist*
Seligson, Frederic Lee *physician, cardiothoracic surgeon*
Truog, William Edward III *pediatrician, educator, researcher*
Young, Thomas William *medical examiner*

Kirksville
French, Michael Francis *medical educator*
Holman, Charles Raymond *osteopathic physician*

Maryland Heights
Miller, Steven *medical administrator*
Motchan, Dennis Glenn *physician*

North Kansas City
Hellman, Richard *endocrinologist*

Oak Grove
Davis, Jo *naturopathic physician*

Saint Joseph
Gupta, Chakshu *pathologist*
Malani, Ashok K. *physician*

Saint Louis
Agarwal, Banke *gastroenterologist, educator*
Alpers, David Hershel *gastroenterologist, educator*
Bach, Richard Gordon *internist, cardiologist, educator*
Bacon, Bruce Raymond *physician*
Balci, Cem N *radiologist*
Ballinger, Walter Francis *surgeon, educator*
Banerjee, Bhaskar *gastroenterologist, medical educator*
Berland, David I. *psychiatrist, educator*
Bhalla, Sanjeev *radiologist*
Bjerregaard, Preben *cardiologist, educator*
Brandt, Keith E. *plastic surgeon, educator*
Branham, Gregory Harris *facial plastic surgeon*
Braverman, Alan Charles *cardiologist, educator*
Bridwell, Keith Happ *orthopedic surgeon*
Burke, William *neurologist*
Chambliss, Linda R. *obstetrician, consultant*
Chaplin, David Dunbar *medical research specialist, educator*
Chaplin, Hugh, Jr. *preventive medicine physician, educator*
Chole, Richard Arthur *otolaryngologist, department chairman*
Cloninger, Claude Robert *psychiatrist, epidemiologist, educator, researcher*
Constantino, John Nicholas *medical educator, researcher*
Correa-Perez, Juan Ramon *andrologist, embryologist, researcher*
Cryer, Philip Eugene *endocrinologist*
Damiano, Ralph James, Jr. *cardiovascular and thoracic surgeon*
Dewald, Paul Adolph *psychiatrist, educator*
DiPersio, John F. *oncologist*
Dodge, Philip Rogers *neurologist, educator*
Dougherty, Charles Hamilton *pediatrician*
Dykewicz, Mark Steven *physician*
Eberlein, Timothy J. *surgeon*
Evens, Ronald Gene *radiologist, educator, health facility administrator*
Evers, Alex Steven *anesthesiologist, internist, educator*
Farria, Dione Marie *radiologist, educator*
Felthous, Alan Robert *psychiatrist*
Fitch, Coy Dean *internist, educator*

Fleshman, James W. *medical association administrator*
Flye, M. Wayne *surgeon, immunologist, educator, writer*
Frey, Sharon Elizabeth *internist, adult infectious disease physician*
Garrett, Ted Eugene *surgeon*
Gay, William Arthur, Jr. *thoracic surgeon*
Gelberman, Richard H. *orthopedist, surgeon*
Goldberg, Anne Carol *physician, educator*
Gordon, Jeffrey Ivan *gastroenterologist, educator, molecular biologist, researcher*
Grossberg, George Thomas *psychiatrist, educator*
Grubb, Robert L., Jr. *neurosurgeon*
Hammerman, Marc Randall *nephrologist, educator*
Hanley, Thomas Patrick *obstetrician, gynecologist*
Heiken, Jay Paul *physician*
Holmes, Nancy Elizabeth *pediatrician*
Holtzman, David Michael *neurologist*
Hsueh, Eddy C. *surgeon, oncologist*
Hyers, Thomas Morgan *internist, biomedical researcher*
Jacobs, Donald Louis *medical educator*
Johnson, Robert Graham *surgeon, educator, researcher*
Jones, Timothy R. *plastic surgeon, director*
Kaminski, Donald Leon *surgeon, gastroenterologist, educator*
Kipnis, David Morris *physician, educator*
Knutsen, Alan Paul *pediatrician, immunologist, allergist*
Kolker, Allan Erwin *ophthalmologist*
Koo, Michele *plastic surgeon*
Kornfeld, Stuart A. *hematology educator*
Kouchoukos, Nicholas Thomas *surgeon*
Lenke, Lawrence Gerald *orthopedic surgeon, educator*
Lewis, Lawrence M. *emergency physician, researcher*
Lewis, Robert David *ophthalmologist, educator*
Ley, Timothy James *hematologist, molecular biologist*
Ludmerer, Kenneth Marc *medical educator*
Mackinnon, Susan *plastic surgeon*
Majerus, Philip Warren *physician*
Manske, Paul Robert *orthopedic hand surgeon, educator*
Mantovani, John F. *pediatric neurologist*
Martin, Kevin John *nephrologist, educator*
McDonald, Douglas Joel *orthopedic surgeon, educator*
McMahon, Robert M. *physician, lawyer*
Middelkamp, John Neal *pediatrician, educator*
Moon, Marc R. *cardiac surgeon*
Moran, Christopher John *radiologist, educator*
Morley, John Edward *physician*
Myerson, Robert J. *radiologist, educator*
Nayak, Laxmeesh Mike *plastic surgeon*
Neely, John Gail *otolaryngologist*
Neidorff, Michael F. *health care executive*
Owens, William Don *anesthesiology educator*
Payne, Meredith Jorstad *physician*
Peck, William Arno *internist, educator, dean, academic administrator*
Prensky, Arthur Lawrence *pediatric neurologist, educator*
Purkerson, Mabel Louise *physician, educator, physiologist*
Rao, Dabeeru C. (D.C. Rao) *epidemiologist, educator*
Rednam, Krishna Rao Venkata *ophthalmologist*
Reiss, Craig Keith *cardiologist, educator*
Rich, Keith M. *neurosurgeon*
Riew, K. Daniel *cervical spine surgeon*
Robins, Lee Nelken *medical educator*
Rosenbaum, Herbert Edwin *neurology educator*
Royal, Henry Duval *nuclear medicine physician, educator, director*
Ryall, Jo-Ellyn M. *psychiatrist*
Saltman, Robert Jon *physician, medical educator*
Schonfeld, Gustav *medical educator, researcher, administrator*
Schwartz, Alan Leigh *pediatrician, educator*
Shapiro, Larry J. *pediatrician, educator, scientist, dean*
Siegel, Barry Alan *radiologist*
Slatopolsky, Eduardo *nephrologist, educator*
Slavin, Raymond Granam *allergist, immunologist*
Smith, Morton Edward *ophthalmology educator, dean*
Spector, Gershon Jerry *otolaryngologist, educator, researcher*
Strunk, Robert Charles *physician*
Teitelbaum, Steven Lazarus *pathology educator*
Ternberg, Jessie Lamoin *pediatric surgeon, educator*
Thach, William Thomas, Jr. *neurologist, educator*
Tiefenbrunn, Alan James *medical educator*
Virgo, Katherine Sue *medical researcher*
Walsh, David Joseph *pediatric neurologist, educator*
Wells, Samuel Alonzo, Jr. *surgeon, educator*
Whyte, Michael P. *genetics educator, researcher, director*
Wilson, Margaret Mary Georgiana *geriatrician, researcher, physician*
Yamaguchi, Ken *surgeon, educator*
Yarasheski, Kevin Edward *medical educator*
Yi, Xiaobin *anesthesiologist, pain management specialist*
Yokoyama, Wayne Makoto *medical educator, researcher, internist*
Young, Paul Andrew *anatomist*
Young, Vernon Leroy *plastic surgeon, researcher*
Zazulia, Allyson Robyn *neurologist, educator*
Ziskind, Andrew A. *cardiologist, medical educator, health facility administrator*

Saint Peters
Wang, William Weiqi *physician*

Sedalia
Chaar, Bassem T. *hematologist, oncologist*

Springfield
Clothiaux, Pierre Laurent *orthopedic surgeon*
Geter, Rodney Keith *plastic surgeon*
Hackett, Earl Randolph *neurologist*
Kienstra, Matthew Allen *plastic surgeon*
Verret, Daniel Joseph *otolaryngologist*

Town And Country
Levin, Marvin Edgar *physician*

MONTANA

Big Sky
Strickler, Jeffrey Harold *pediatrician*

Billings
Glenn, Guy Charles *pathologist*
Habein, Harold Clinton *retired surgeon*
Knapp, Howard Raymond *internist, clinical pharmacologist*

Harlem
Andrews, Robert Bruce, Jr. *physician, military officer*

Missoula
Fawcett, Don Wayne *retired anatomist*

Whitefish
Miller, Ronald Alfred *family physician*

NEBRASKA

Bennington
Burgher, Louis William *physician, educator, academic administrator*

Elkhorn
Walk, Louis Bernard *physician*

Fort Calhoun
Ware, Frederick *internist, educator, nephrologist*

Hastings
Dungan, John Russell, Jr., (12th Viscount Dungan of Clane, Hereditary Prince of Fermoy and Arra) *anesthesiologist, health facility administrator*

Lincoln
Koger, Michael Pigott *physician, writer*
Michels, Dale E. *physician*
Wilson, Charles Stephen *cardiologist, educator*

Omaha
Armitage, James O. *medical educator*
Baltaro, Richard J. *pathologist, medical educator*
Benson, John Alexander, Jr. *internist, educator*
Casale, Thomas Bruce *medical educator*
Fusaro, Ramon Michael *dermatologist, preventive medicine physician, researcher*
Hodgson, Paul Edmund *surgeon, department chairman*
Howard, Thomas Clement *surgeon*
Huurman, Walter William *pediatric orthopaedic surgeon, educator*
Imray, Thomas John *radiologist, educator*
Khoynezhad, Ali *cardiothoracic surgeon, researcher*
Korbitz, Bernard Carl *hematologist, consultant*
Madariaga, Miguel G. *epidemiologist*
Mardis, Hal Kennedy *urological surgeon, educator, researcher*
Maurer, Harold Maurice *pediatrician*
Mohiuddin, Syed Maqdoom *cardiologist, educator*
O'Brien, Richard L(ee) *physician, educator, academic administrator*
Plotkin, Horacio *pediatric endocrinologist, orthopedic surgeon, educator*
Rogan, Eleanor Groeniger *oncologist, educator*
Sankaranarayanan, Jayashri *medical educator*
Sasson, Aaron R. *surgeon*
Schlessinger, Joel *dermatologist, researcher, entrepreneur*
Shilling, Kay Marlene *psychiatrist*
Skoog, Donald Paul *retired pathologist, educator*
Sooriyaarachchi, Gamini Sarathchandra *oncologist, hematologist, educator*
Swindells, Susan *HIV specialist*
Thorson, Alan Glen *surgeon*
Tinker, John Heath *anesthesiologist, educator*
Treves, John *neurosurgeon*
Ward, Vernon Graves *retired internist*

Papillion
Dvorak, Allen Dale *radiologist*

Scottsbluff
Kabalin, John Nicholas *urologist*

NEVADA

Glenbrook
Goldsmith, Harry Sawyer *surgeon, educator*

Henderson
Cambeiro, Arthur Michael *plastic surgeon*
Lang, Sheldon *pathologist*
Wax, Arnold *physician*

Las Vegas
Ahmad, Shamoon *hematologist, oncologist, consultant*
Boman, Keith Gregory *cardiologist*
Buzard, Kurt Andre *ophthalmologist*
Goodenberger, Daniel Marvin *medical educator*
Hoepfner, Mark Thomas *surgeon*
Kurlinski, John Parker *physician*
Merkin, Albert Charles *pediatrician, allergist*
Moritz, Timothy Bovie *psychiatrist*
Noback, Richardson Kilbourne *medical educator*
Schaffer, Martin David *cardiologist*
Shires, George Thomas *surgeon, educator*
Speck, Eugene Lewis *internist*
Vogelzang, Nicholas John *medical oncologist*
Zamboni, William Arnold *plastic and reconstructive surgeon, lab director*

Reno
Akiyama, Toshio *cardiologist, educator, researcher, director*
Crognale, Michael Anthony *medical educator, neuroscientist, consultant*
Cunningham, Steve *orthopedic surgeon*
Guneyi, Umit Ahmet *physician, consultant*
MacKintosh, Frederick Roy *oncologist*
Small, Elisabeth Chan *psychiatrist, educator*
Welcome, Richard Mark *radiologist*
Zager, Bernard Solomon *physician, consultant*
Zanjani, Esmail D. *medical educator, research scientist*

NEW HAMPSHIRE

Bow
Emery, Paul Emile *psychiatrist*

Campton
Scrimshaw, Nevin Stewart *physician, nutritionist, educator*

Concord
Bagan, Merwyn *neurological surgeon*
Stadelmann, Wayne Karl *plastic surgeon*
Vidaver, Robert Maxwell *medical educator*

Grantham
Figley, Melvin Morgan *radiologist, physician, educator*

Hanover
Chapman, Robert James *psychiatrist, educator*
Dmitrovsky, Ethan *oncologist, medical educator, researcher*
Petitto, Laura-Ann *cognitive neuroscience educator*
Rolett, Ellis Lawrence *cardiologist, educator*
Zubkoff, Michael *medical educator*

Lebanon
Bernat, James Lawrence *neurologist, educator*
Carr, Charles F. *orthopedist*
Collins, E. Dale *surgeon, educator*
Cronenwett, Jack LeMoyne *vascular surgeon educator*
DeMars, Leslie R. *oncologist, obstetrician, gynecologist, educator*
Ferrell, Richard Bradley *neuropsychiatrist*
Fillinger, Mark F. *vascular surgeon, researcher*
Glass, Donald David *anesthesiologist*
Kelley, Maurice Leslie, Jr. *gastroenterologist, educator*
Koval, Kenneth Joseph *orthopedist, surgeon*
McCollum, Robert Wayne *epidemiologist, educator*
Oxman, Thomas Elliot *psychiatrist*
Phillips, Joseph Michael *neurosurgeon*
Rao, Sreeramoju Gautami *oncologist*
Sedlacek, Martin *nephrologist*
Silberfarb, Peter Michael *psychiatrist, educator*
Torkelson, Andrew Thomas *cardiologist*
van Leeuwen, Dirk Jacob *hepatology educator*
Waugh, Theodore Rogers *orthopedic surgeon*
Whitley, Rob *medical educator, sociologist, researcher*

Lee
Young, James Morningstar *internist, military officer*

Littleton
Kelly, Dorothy Helen *pediatrician, educator*

Lyme
Cornwell, Gibbons Gray III *retired internist, educator*
McIntyre, Oswald Ross *physician*

Manchester
Lavery, Robert Michael *internist, cardiologist*

Mirror Lake
Culleton, James Frederick *neurologist*

Nashua
Hermansen, Marcus C. *pediatrics professor, director*
Knights, Edwin Munroe *pathologist*
Siroty, William Charles *physician*

Rye
Wilson, Ralph Sloan *retinal surgeon*

Stoddard
Cahill, George Francis, Jr. *physician, educator*

NEW JERSEY

Bayonne
Pelosi, Marco Antonio *obstetrician and gynecologist, plastic surgeon*

Belle Mead
Goodnick, Paul Joel *psychiatrist*

Berkeley Heights
Momeni, Reza *plastic surgeon*

Bernardsville
Dixon, Rosina Berry *physician, pharmaceutical executive, consultant*

Bridgewater
Bernson, Marcella S. *psychiatrist*
Hirsch, Paul J. *orthopedist, surgeon, health facility administrator, medical educator*
Scully, John Thomas *obstetrician, gynecologist, educator*
Taylor, Duncan Paul *pharmacologist, researcher*

Browns Mills
Cha, Se Do *internist*
McGrath, Lynn Bernard *surgeon*
Moore, Roger Addison *pediatrician, anesthesiologist*

Camden
Ances, I. G(eorge) *obstetrician, gynecologist*
Hollenberg, Steven Michael *physician, researcher*
Parra, Raul O. *urologist, educator*
Parrillo, Joseph Edison, Jr. *allergist, immunologist, cardiologist*
Pratter, Melvin Richard *medical educator*
Rajaram, Sri-Sujanthy *internist, medical educator*
Ross, Steven Elliot *surgeon*

Cape May Court House
Altman, Brian David *pediatric ophthalmologist*

Cedar Knolls
Hariri, Robert Joseph *neurosurgeon, research scientist*

Cherry Hill
Goldberg, Jack *hematologist*
Kahn, Marc Leslie *orthopedic surgeon*
Margolis, Gerald Joseph *psychiatrist, psychoanalyst*
Olearchyk, Andrew *cardiothoracic surgeon, educator*
Swibinski, Edward Thomas *internist, endocrinologist, educator*
Werbitt, Warren *gastroenterologist, educator*

Cranford
Mendelson, Joel Stuart *allergist, immunologist*

Demarest
Dornfest, Burton Saul *anatomy educator*

East Brunswick
Kaufman, Matthew *otolaryngologist, plastic surgeon*

East Hanover
Nemecek, Georgina Marie *molecular pharmacologist*
Verma, Anila *epidemiologist*

East Orange
Agarwal, Shashi Kant *cardiologist*
Chiang, Tom *medical educator, researcher*
Khanna, Yash Kumar *family practice physician, pediatrician*
McCampbell, Edwin Lee *physician*

Eatontown
Danikas, Dimitrios *plastic surgeon*

Edison
Gizzi, Martin Sherman *neurologist, neurophysiologist*
Sinma, Binod K. *urologist, consultant*
Walters, Arthur Scott *neurologist, educator, clinical research scientist*

Elizabeth
Berger, Harold Richard *physician*
Rosenstein, Neil *surgeon, genealogist, researcher*
Sananman, Michael Lawrence *neurologist*

Elmwood Park
Weisberger, James David *hematopathologist*

Englewood
Abramson, David Lawrence *plastic surgeon, educator*
Dardik, Herbert *vascular surgeon, general surgeon*
Elias, Steven *surgeon*
Frieden, Faith Joy *obstetrician*
Goldweit, Richard Scott *cardiologist*
Harish, Ziv *allergist, immunologist*
Tobias, Geoffrey *otolaryngologist, plastic surgeon*
Wuhl, Charles Michael *psychiatrist*

Englewood Cliffs
Yu, Fei *internist*

Fair Lawn
Namerow, David Mark *pediatrician*

Flemington
Rubin, Arkady *biostatistics and data management researcher, executive*
Rushton, Alan R. *physician, medical researcher, historian*

Forked River
Novak, Dennis E. *physician*

Fort Lee
Chessler, Richard Kenneth *gastroenterologist, endocrinologist*
Goldfarb, Joel Peter *internist, gastroenterologist*
Huang, Jianzhong *biomedical researcher*
Li, Tien-Shun *obstetrician, gynecologist, educator*

Freehold
Dinrstein, Charles Robert *vascular surgeon*

Glen Ridge
Rubin, Roberta Gail *retired pathologist*
Vaccaro, John J. *neurologist*
Zbar, Lloyd Irwin Stanley *otolaryngologist, educator*

Glen Rock
Goldstone, Robert Allen *orthopaedic surgeon*

Green Brook
Hertzberg, Henry *retired radiologist*

Guttenberg
Wright, Jane Cooke *oncologist, educator, consultant*

Hackensack
Agress, Harry, Jr. *radiologist, nuclear medicine physician*
Haines, Kathleen Ann *pediatrician, educator*
Masullo, Alfredo Salvatore *dermatologist*
Pecora, Andrew Louis *hematologist, oncologist*
Rauscher, Gregory Edwin *plastic surgeon*
Smith, Daniel *oncologist, gynecologist*

Hackettstown
Singh, Harjit *medical educator, artist*

Haddonfield
Capelli, John Placido *nephrologist, educator*
Fisher, George Ross III *physician, educator*
Gatti, Eugene Anthony *immunologist, pediatrician*
Jensh, Ronald Paul *retired anatomist*

Hamilton
Sporn, Aaron Adolph *physician, educator*

Hillsborough
Herman, David J. *infectious diseases physician*

Hillsdale
Copeland, Lois Jacqueline *physician*

Holmdel
Kane, Michael Joel *physician*

Jersey City
Demos, Nicholas John *physician, surgeon, researcher*
Gordon, Robert Dana *transplant surgeon*

Kendall Park
Kesarwala, Hemant *pediatrician, educator*

Lawrenceville
Antonacci, Mark Darryl *orthopedist, surgeon*
Pouleur, Hubert Gustave *cardiologist, consultant*
Rosenthal, Albert Lester *dermatologist, educator*
Witte, Arnold Stewart *neurologist*

Linden
Bukosky, Richard J. *allergist*

Little Silver
Marcus, Abir A. *psychiatrist*

Livingston
Fodero, Joseph Peter *plastic surgeon*
Gordon, Frederick James *orthopedist, surgeon*
Jaffe, Leonard *orthopedist, surgeon, educator*
Samojlik, Eugeniusz *medical educator, health facility administrator*
Santoro, Elissa Jeanne *breast oncology surgeon*
Segal, Jeffrey L. *gynecologist, obstetrician, researcher*

Long Branch
Luria, Martin Jay *endocrinologist*

Lumberton
Campagnolo, Mary Frances *physician*

Maplewood
Haggerty, Mary Ann *medical educator*
Shuttleworth, Anne Margaret *psychiatrist*

Margate City
Trocki-Videll, Cyla *psychiatrist, medical association administrator*
Videll, Jared Steven *cardiologist*

Marlton
Kahn, Sigmund Benham *retired internist, dean*

Medford
Lawson-Ndu, Ovunda A. *emergency physician, surgeon*

Midland Park
Baum, Richard David *urologist*

Monmouth Junction
Brolin, Robert Edward *physician, surgeon*
Chau, Wai Yip *surgeon*

Monroe Township
Spierer, Robert *family practice physician*

Montclair
Holmes, Nathaniel J. *surgeon*
Rosen, Allen David *plastic surgeon*

Morris Plains
Goldenberg, David Milton *experimental pathologist, oncologist*

Morristown
Adler, Kenneth R. *oncologist*
Fiel, Stanley Bruce *internist, pulmonologist, educator, researcher*
Finkel, Marion Judith *internist, pharmaceutical administrator*
Giacchi, Renato *physician*
Lazar, Eric Loren *pediatric surgeon, director*
Moritz, Mark William *vascular surgeon*
Parr, Grant Van Siclen *surgeon*
Rogachefsky, Arlene Sandra *dermatologist*
Sachs, Richard Gregory *cardiologist*
Scott, Richard Thomas, Jr. *reproductive endocrinologist*
Smart, Frank Wilson *physician*
Zaubler, Thomas Scot *psychiatrist, educator*

Neptune
Laraya-Cuasay, Lourdes Redublo *pediatrician, pulmonologist, educator*
Rice, Stephen Gary *pediatrician, sports medicine physician, educator*

New Brunswick
Aisner, Joseph *oncologist, medical educator*
August, David Allen *surgeon*
Bertino, Joseph Rocco *oncologist, educator*
Borah, Gregory *surgeon, educator*
Boyarsky, Andrew Harold *surgeon, educator*
Carson, Jeffrey L. *internist*
Chandler, James John *surgeon, educator*
Corbett, Siobhan Aiden *surgeon*
Day-Salvatore, Debra Lynn *medical geneticist*
Dhib-Jalbut, Suhayl S. *physician*
DiPaola, Robert *internist*
Drachtman, Richard Allan *pediatrician, educator*
Ettinger, Lawrence Jay *pediatric hematologist, oncologist, educator*
Goldberg, Michael Ira *obstetrician, gynecologist*
Goldrich, Michael Seth *otolaryngologist*
Graham, Alan Morrison *surgeon*
Greenwald, Alfred Emanuel *retired cosmetic surgeon*
Kaufman, Kenneth Roland *psychiatrist, educator*
Khachadurian, Avedis *physician*
Kostis, John Basil *cardiologist*
Lepore, Frederick Everett *neurologist, educator*
Leventhal, Elaine A. *internist*
Makhija, Mohan *nuclear medicine physician*
Mann, Richard Alan *physician, educator*
Moreyra, Abel E. *medical educator*
Nosko, Michael Gerrik *neurosurgeon, educator*
Notterman, Daniel A. *pediatrician, educator*
Olson, Robert Martin *plastic surgeon*
Pitchumoni, Capecomorin Sankar *gastroenterologist, educator*
Raska, Karel Frantisek Julian, Jr. *pathologist, virologist, educator*
Rubin, Eric Howard *oncologist, researcher*
Saidi, Parvin *hematologist, medical educator*
Salas, Max *pediatrician, educator*
Schneider, Stephen Harley *medical educator*
Scholz, Peter M. *surgeon, director*
Shindler, Daniel *cardiologist*
Snyder, Barbara K. *pediatrician, educator*
Spotnitz, Alan Jeffrey *cardiothoracic surgeon*
Todd, Mary Beth *oncologist, researcher*
Trooskin, Stanley Z. *surgeon*
Upton, Arthur Canfield *experimental pathologist, educator*
Weinstein, Melvin Phillip *physician educator*
Weiss, Lynne S. *pediatrician, educator*
Weiss, Robert Edward *urologist, educator*

Newark
Baker, Herman *medical educator, writer*
Bielory, Leonard *allergist, immunologist, medical school administrator*
Cherniack, Neil Stanley *pulmonologist, educator*
Cohen, Stanley *pathologist, educator*
Cook, Stuart Donald *neurologist, educator*
Depre, Christophe *medical educator*
Ellner, Jerrold Jay *infectious diseases specialist*
Evans, Hugh E. *pediatrician, educator*
Goldstein, Ira Morris *neurosurgeon*
Granick, Mark S. *medical educator*
Haycock, Christine Elizabeth *retired medical educator*
Iffy, Leslie *medical educator*
Kou, Victoria *medical educator*
Little, Alan Brian *gynecologist, educator*
Louria, Donald Bruce *medical educator*
Maqsood, Ahsan *cardiologist, researcher*
Ming, Xue *pediatrician, pediatric neurologist, neuroscientist, pharmacologist*
Mitchell, Jason Wayne *radiologist*
Reichman, Lee Brodersohn *physician*
Ryan, Lisa Kathleen *environmental and medical science educator*
Schleifer, Steven J. *psychiatrist, educator*
Weiss, Gerson *endocrinologist, educator*

Newton
Colizza, Wayne Anthony *orthopaedic surgeon*

North Brunswick
Jones, Frank A., Jr. *psychiatrist, educator*

Northfield
Margolis, Thomas Ira *vitreoretinal ophthalmologist*

Northvale
Urgas, Sandra S. *emergency physician*

Nutley
Bridge, Thomas Peter *psychiatrist, researcher*
Mostillo, Ralph *medical association administrator*

Oradell
Merliss, Harry *orthopedist, surgeon*

Paramus
Gartner, Michael Constantin *plastic surgeon*
Liva, Edward Louis *eye surgeon*

Paterson
Fink, David Leonard *surgeon*

Peapack
Eddey, Gary Erwin *physician, administrator, educator*

Pennington
Fong, Donald P. *psychiatrist*

Phillipsburg
Drago, Joseph Rosario *urologist, educator*

Piscataway
Colaizzi, John Louis *medical educator*
Conney, Allan Howard *pharmacologist, researcher*
Escobar, Javier Ignacio *psychiatrist*
Flick, Ferdinand Herman *surgeon, preventive medicine physician*
Menza, Matthew A. *psychiatrist*
Sahota, Amrik *medical researcher, educator, lab administrator*
Swee, David Ethan *physician*
Volfson-Doubova, Elena *psychiatrist, researcher*
Young, Wise *neurosurgeon, educator, medical researcher*

Point Pleasant Beach
Massey, Dorothy Williams *ophthalmologist, writer*

Princeton
Carr, Marcus Eugene, Jr. *internist*
Carver, David Harold *retired pediatrician*
Hait, William Neil *oncologist, educator*
Lavizzo-Mourey, Risa Juanita *medical foundation and academic administrator*
Lumpkin, John Robert *public health physician, state official*
Manyak, Michael John *urologist, educator, researcher*
Meade, Dale Michael *experimental physicist*
Mehlman, Myron A. *medical educator, toxicologist*
Mueller, Peter Sterling *psychiatrist, educator*
Murphy, Coleen T. *biomedical researcher, educator*
Sierocki, John Stanley *oncologist*
Sigal, Leonard H. *physician*
Sugerman, Abraham Arthur *psychiatrist, educator*
von der Schmidt, Edward III *neurosurgeon, veterinarian*

Princeton Junction
Amenta, Peter Sebastian *pathologist*

Red Bank
Braddom, Randall Lee *physiatrist, educator*
Clever, Marcia Sue *psychiatrist*
Scaccia, Frank John *plastic surgeon, otolaryngologist*

Ridgewood
Baddoura, Rashid Joseph *emergency physician*
Bronstein, Eric H. *surgeon*
Carbone, Tracy *pediatrician, educator*
Kopeloff, Iris Hope *dermatologist*
Sumers, Anne Ricks *ophthalmologist, museum director*

Rockaway
Husar, Walter Gene *neurologist, neuroscientist, educator*

Roseland
Clemente, Celestino *physician, surgeon*
Panagides, John *pharmacologist*

Saddle Brook
Salerno, William Douglas *cardiologist*

Saddle River
Goodman, Jerome David *psychiatrist*
Weissmann, Heidi Seitelblum *radiologist, educator*

Short Hills
Chaiken, Bernard Henry *internist, gastroenterologist*
Duberstein, Joel Lawrence *internist, pulmonologist, educator*

Shrewsbury
Elkwood, Andrew Ira *plastic surgeon*
Norwitz, Steven Barry *plastic and reconstructive surgeon, health facility administrator*
Rose, Michael Ian *plastic surgeon*
Rosenblum, Bruce Robert *neurosurgeon*

Somerset
De Salva, Salvatore Joseph *retired pharmacologist, toxicologist*
Pappert, Amy S. *dermatologist, educator*

South Plainfield
Kwon, Ik Hyun *internist*

South River
Kirshner, Jacob *physician*

Spring Lake
Harrigan, John Thomas, Jr. *physician, obstetrician, gynecologist*

Springfield
Kwartler, Jed Aryeh *otolaryngologist*

Stratford
Levitas, Andrew Stephen *child psychiatrist, educator*

Summit
Carniol, Paul J. *plastic and reconstructive surgeon, otolaryngologist*
Gaudino, Mario *physician, pharmaceutical company executive, scientist*
Greenberg, Rosalie *child psychiatrist*
Halperin, John Jacob *neurology educator, researcher*
Hodosh, Richard M. *neurosurgeon*

Teaneck
Ladenheim, Jules Calvin *neurosurgeon*

Tenafly
Gerst, Paul Howard *physician*
Golomb, Frederick Martin *surgeon, educator*

Tinton Falls
Macdonald, Donald Arthur, Jr. *physician, surgeon*

Toms River
Fox, Daniel Emery *orthopedic surgeon*
Marchese, Michael James, Jr. *radiation oncologist*

Totowa
Giliberti, Orazio Lucia *ophthalmologist*

Trenton
Gomez, William *orthopedist*
Gupta, Rajendra Prasad *physician*

Turnersville
DePace, Nicholas Louis *physician*

Verona
Cirello, Richard *physician, director*
Malanga, Gerard Anthony *sports medicine physician, director*

Vineland
Clinton, Lawrence Paul *psychiatrist*
Sinakin, Herbert Morris *dermatologist*

Voorhees
Glasofer, Eric David *allergist, immunologist, pediatrician, educator*
Schwartz, Bennett K. *dermatologist*

Waldwick
Sorabella, Philip A. *radiologist*

Wall
Monaco, Robert Anthony *radiologist*
Motley, John Paul *retired psychiatrist*
O'Neill, James Paul *psychiatrist*

Watchung
Eisenberg, Richard R. *dermatologist*
Rubin, Robert Jay *colon and rectal surgeon*

Wayne
Gollance, Robert Barnett *ophthalmologist*
Rosenthal, Herbert Seymour *orthopedist, surgeon*

West Caldwell
Brundage, Gertrude Barnes *pediatrician*

West Orange
Asaadi, Mokhtar *plastic surgeon*
Bennett, Alan Hugh *retired medical educator*
Brodkin, Roger Harrison *dermatologist, educator*
Casella, Anthony John *cardiologist*
Decter, Edward M. *orthopedist, surgeon*
Gans, Bruce Merrill *physiatrist, educator, health facility administrator*
Ghali, Anwar Youssef *psychiatrist, educator*
Hill, George James *physician, educator*
Langsner, Alan Michael *pediatric cardiologist*
Linsenmeyer, Todd Alan *urologist, physician, educator*
Martin, Boston Faust *neurosurgeon*
Rogal, Gary Jeffrey *cardiologist*
Rosa, Richard Angelo *orthopedist, surgeon, educator*
Tutela, Rocco *plastic surgeon*
Whang, Matthew Ihn Seong *urologist*

Westfield
Vijayakumar, Asha *ophthalmologist*

Westwood
Landzberg, Joel Serge *cardiologist*
Possick, Paul Aaron *dermatologist*

Woodbury
Stambaugh, John Edgar *oncologist, hematologist, educator, pharmacologist*

Wyckoff
Gartner, Joseph John, II, *obstetrician, gynecologist*
Ginsberg, Barry Howard *endocrinologist, educator*
Marcus, Linda Susan *dermatologist*

NEW MEXICO

Alamogordo
Ashdown, Franklin Donald *physician, composer*

Albuquerque
Allen, Richard Cutler *surgeon, researcher*
Berman, Stanley Zissman *allergist, immunologist, educator, internist*
Brown, Lee Kelvin *pulmonary, critical care and sleep medicine physician, researcher*
Chang, Barbara Karen *medical educator, director*
Chilton, Lance Alix *pediatrician*
Clarke, Gray B. *psychiatrist*
Cobb, John Candler *medical educator*
Eldredge, Jonathan DeForest *medical librarian, educator, social informaticist*
Gordon, Larry Jean *sanitarian, environmental health consultant*
Heffron, Warren A. *physician, educator*
King, Lowell Restell *pediatric urologist*
Knospe, William Herbert *medical educator*
Mapel, Douglas Wayne *epidemiologist, educator, pulmonologist, critical care specialist*
Omer, George Elbert, Jr. *orthopaedic surgeon, educator*
Reichard, Robert Ross *pathologist*
Rivero, Dennis P. *orthopedist*
Rosenberg, Robert D. *radiologist, researcher*
Strasburger, Victor C. *pediatrician*
Summers, William Koopmans *psychiatrist, internist, researcher*
Uhlenhuth, Eberhard Henry *psychiatrist, educator*
Worrell, Audrey Martiny *geriatric psychiatrist*

Clovis
Paladugu, Ramesh *surgeon*

Farmington
Neidhart, James Allen *oncologist, educator*

Los Alamos
Smith, Fredrica Emrich *rheumatologist, internist*

Portales
Goodwin, Martin Brune *retired radiologist*

Roswell
Choudhary, Adil Mushtaq *gastroenterologist*

Santa Fe
Alfidi, Ralph Joseph *retired radiologist, educator, researcher*
Hoffmann, Louis Gerhard *immunologist, educator*
Kiefer, Helen Chilton *emergency and trauma physician, neurologist*
Kingsmore, Stephen Francis *physician, research scientist*
Schiller, William Richard *surgeon*
Williams, Ralph Chester, Jr. *physician, educator*

Silver City
Remillard, Jean D. *medical association administrator*

NEW YORK

Albany
Arseneau, James Charles *physician*
Carl, Allen Laurence *surgery educator*
Catalano, Robert Anthony *ophthalmologist, hospital administrator, writer*
Cromie, William J. *urologist*
Davis, Paul Joseph *endocrinologist*
Howard, Lyn Jennifer *medical educator*
Lepow, Martha Lipson *pediatric educator, consultant*
Noonan, John Daniel *plastic surgeon*
Saifi, Javid *surgeon*
Snitkoff, Gail Goodman *immunologist, educator*
Swartz, Donald Percy *physician*
Tepper, Clifford *allergist, immunologist, educator*
Veille, Jean-Claude *obstetrician, educator*
Zimmerman, Earl Abram *neurologist, educator*

Amityville
Upadhyay, Yogendra Nath *physician, educator*

Ardsley
Swift, Michael Ronald *internist, educator*

Armonk
Mellors, Robert Charles *physician, scientist, educator*

Babylon
Schwartz, Benjamin Michael *gynecologist, oncologist*

Bedford
Tischler, Gary Lowell *psychiatrist, educator*

Bellerose
Miller, Paul J. *orthopedist, surgeon*

Bethpage
Marcus, Craig Harlan *ophthalmologist*

Brewster
Perez, Louis Anthony *radiologist*

Briarcliff Manor
Erkamp, Ramon Quido *medical researcher, consultant*
Pousada, Lidia *physician*

Bronx
Abbott, Rick *pediatric neurosurgeon, educator*
Alderman, Elizabeth *pediatrician, educator*
Bark, Nigel Martyn *psychiatrist*
Bella, Jonathan N. *cardiologist*
Blaufox, Morton Donald *hypertension specialist, nuclear medicine physician, educator*
Brandt, Lawrence Jay *internist, gastroenterologist, educator*
Burgio, Michael *medical researcher*
Cohen, Herbert Jesse *pediatrician, educator*
Coupey, Susan McGuire *pediatrician, educator*
Das, Ashoke Kumar *internist, consultant*
Diaz-Fuentes, Gilda *pulmonologist*
Dolich, Barry H. *plastic surgeon, educator*
Drepaul, Loris Omesh *internist, infectious diseases physician*
Dutcher, Janice Jean Phillips *oncologist*
Fleischer, Norman Samuel *endocrinology administrator, medical educator*
Frater, Robert William Mayo *surgeon, educator*
Freeman, Leonard Murray *radiologist, nuclear medicine physician, educator*
Greenstein, Stuart Mark *surgical educator*
Hait, Gershon *pediatric cardiologist*
Heagarty, Margaret Caroline *retired pediatrician*
Hirano, Asao *neuropathologist, educator*
Hodgson, W(alter) John (Barry Hodgson) *surgeon*
Horwitz, Susan Band *pharmacologist*
Kahn, Thomas *medical educator*
Kalnicki, Shalom *radiologist, educator*
Kalpana, Ganjam V. *biomedical researcher*
Koss, Leopold G. *pathologist, educator*
Lieber, Charles Saul *internist, educator*
Michler, Robert E. *heart surgeon*
Min, Sang Hee *internist, researcher*
Mullangi, Sivaprasad *surgeon*
Nitowsky, Harold Martin *physician, educator*
Oertel, Michael *researcher, medical educator*
Oktay, Maja Hrzenjak *medical educator*
Radel, Eva *pediatrician, hematologist*
Reichgott, Michael Joel *medical educator, dean, physician*
Reinus, John F. *hepatologist, medical educator*
Rosenstreich, David Leon *medical educator, immunologist, allergist*
Ruben, Robert Joel *pediatric otorhinolaryngologist, educator*
Sable, Robert Allen *gastroenterologist*
Safyer, Steven Michael *medical association administrator, educator*
Satir, Birgit H. *medical educator, researcher*
Scharff, Matthew Daniel *immunologist, cell biologist, educator*
Schaumburg, Herbert Howard *neurology educator*
Schlussel, Seymour *obstetrician, gynecologist*
Shafritz, David Andrew *physician, research scientist*
Shapiro, Nella Irene *surgeon, educator*
Sonnenblick, Edmund Hiram *medical educator, cardiologist*
Spitzer, Adrian *pediatrician, educator*
Stanley, E. Richard *biomedical researcher*
Stein, Ruth Elizabeth Klein *physician*
Strauch, Berish *plastic surgeon, hand and cosmetic surgeon*
Tellis, Vivian Anthony *transplant surgeon, administrator*
Veith, Frank J. *vascular surgeon, researcher, educator*
Walsh, Christine Ann *cardiologist*
Wiernik, Peter Harris *oncologist, educator*

Bronxville
Bertles, John Francis *physician, educator*

Brooklyn
Abott, Michael Larry *physician*
Ackerman, Jacob Lewis *ophthalmologist*
Aizman, Alexander *ophthalmologist*
Alfonso, Antonio Escolar *surgeon*
Bandler, Martin *physician*
Behm, Dutsi *physician*
Bernstein, Larry Howard *clinical pathologist*
Berry, Richard S. *physician*
Biro, Laszlo *dermatologist*
Borgen, Patrick Ivan *surgeon*
Chao, Tsai Chung *physician, medical association administrator*
Clark, Luther Theopolis *physician, educator, researcher*
Collins, Ronald Leslie Leopold *neurosurgeon*
Cottrell, James E. *anesthesiologist, medical educator*
Erber, William Franklin *gastroenterologist*
Fleischer, Marian *surgeon*
Friedman, Eli A. *nephrologist, educator*
Furchgott, Robert Francis *pharmacologist, educator*
Garrow, Eugene *pediatric surgeon*
Gotta, Alexander Walter *anesthesiologist, educator*
Hollander, Gerald Martin *physician*
Jacobowitz, Israel Jacob *cardiothoracic surgeon*
Kilanko, Oyenike Eunice *obstetrician, gynecologist*
Kirshenbaum, Richard Irving *retired public health physician*
Li, John K.H. *pathologist, department chairman*
Lichstein, Edgar *cardiologist*
Lichter, Stephen Marc *oncologist*
Lowery, Robert Chesley *thoracic surgeon, educator*
Luka, Bishoy *pharmacologist, educator*
Mayer, Ira Edward *gastroenterologist*
Menezes, Nelson *surgeon*
Merlin, Lisa Ruth *neurologist, researcher*
Mirra, Suzanne Samuels *pathologist*
Nemazie, Siamack *nephrologist, consultant*
Orugunta, Raveendra Babu *pediatrician*
Plotz, Charles Mindell *physician, educator*
Price, Ely *dermatologist*
Purvin, Jack Mitchell *physician*
Rafiq, Muhammad Amir *nephrologist*
Rezkalla, Laurence *internist*
Sacchi, Terrence J. *cardiologist*
Sadr, Ali *neurosurgeon*
Savits, Barry Sorrel *surgeon*
Schwarz, Richard Howard *obstetrician, gynecologist, educator*
Shalita, Alan Remi *dermatologist*
Shelov, Steven Patrick *pediatrician, educator*
Shulman, Abraham *otolaryngology educator, hospital administrator*
Song, Mark *surgeon, educator*
Tessler, Sidney *pulmonologist*
Weber, Michael A. *physician, researcher*
Wolintz, Arthur Harry *neurologist, ophthalmologist*

Buffalo
Ambrus, Clara Maria *physician*
Ambrus, Julian L. *physician, educator*
Ballow, Mark *immunologist, educator*
Batt, Ronald Elmer *gynecologist, historian, biomedical research scientist*
Boden, William Edward *cardiologist, educator*
Brody, Harold *neuroanatomist, gerontologist, educator*
Cao, Shousong *medical researcher, educator*
Chu, Tsann Ming *immunochemist, educator*
Creaven, Patrick Joseph *pharmacologist*
Cullen, Paul *medical educator*
Czyrny, James Joseph *physiatrist*
Dosluoglu, Hasan Haldun *surgeon*
Genco, Robert Joseph *immunologist, periodontist, educator, scientist*
Halbreich, Uriel Morav *psychiatrist, educator*
Hohn, David *physician*
Kurlan, Marvin Zeft *retired surgeon*
Lele, Amol Shashikant *obstetrician, gynecologist*
Mihich, Enrico *medical researcher*
Milgrom, Felix *immunologist, educator*
Mindell, Eugene Robert *surgeon, educator*
Mutton, Holly Beth *psychiatrist*
Naughton, John Patrick *cardiologist, educator*
Nolan, James Paul *internist, educator, researcher*
Piver, M. Steven *gynecologic oncologist*
Popat, Saurin Rajnikant *otologist, surgeon*
Seller, Robert Herman *cardiologist, physician*
Shedd, Donald Pomroy *surgeon*
Stoll, Howard Lester, Jr. *dermatologist*
Trevisan, Maurizio *epidemiologist*
Vladutiu, Adrian O. *physician, educator*
Wright, John Robert *retired pathologist, educator*

Canandaigua
Beal, Myron Clarence *osteopath*
Wormer, Thomas Andrew *surgeon*

Carmel
Foster, Lawrence G. *orthopedist, surgeon*

Castle Point
Mehta, Rakesh Kumar *physician, educator*

Cedarhurst
Cohen, Harris L. *diagnostic radiologist, consultant*

Chester
Amelar, Richard Daniel *urologist*

Chestnut Ridge
Day, Stacey Biswas *physician, educator*

Cooperstown
Bordley, James, IV, *surgeon*
Franck, Walter Alfred *rheumatologist, medical educator, health facility administrator*
Leonardo, James M. *hematologist, educator, oncologist, director*
Veenema, Ralph James *retired urologist*

Cortland
Rohr, Richard Edward *physician, administrator*

East Setauket
Coccaro, Stephen F. *plastic surgeon*
Dervan, John Patrick *cardiologist*
Malbon, Craig Curtis *pharmacology educator, dean*

East Syracuse
Nivarthi, Raju Naga *anesthesiology educator*

Elmhurst
Masci, Joseph Richard *medical educator*
Prypchan, Lida D. *psychiatrist*

Elmira
Graham, David Richard *orthopedic surgeon*
Nast, Edward Paul *cardiothoracic surgeon, vascular surgeon*

Elmsford
Demopoulos, Harry Byron *retired pathologist, pharmaceutical researcher*
Panitz, Lawrence *physician*

Fayetteville
Chevli, Renate Naren *gynecologist, obstetrician*

Fishers Island
Baue, Arthur Edward *retired surgeon, educator, health facility administrator*

Fishkill
Brocks, Eric *ophthalmologist, surgeon*

Flushing
Galdamez, Ricardo *internist*
Hon, John Wingsun *physician*
Nussbaum, Michel Ernest *physician*
Wang, Zeng-Yu *neurologist, immunologist*

Forest Hills
Eden, Alvin Noam *pediatrician, writer*
Seldes, Richard M. *orthopedist, consultant*
Tvildiani, Dimitry *cardiologist*

Fresh Meadows
Godfrey, Philip M. *plastic surgeon*

Garden City
Brewer, Bruce William *plastic surgeon*
Deane, Leland Marc *plastic surgeon, director*
Douglas, Barry K. *plastic surgeon*
Good, Larry Irwin *gastroenterologist, educator*
Spinowitz, Alan Lee *dermatologist*

Garnerville
Zugibe, Frederick Thomas *retired pathologist, forensic specialist*

Garrison
Callahan, Daniel John *biomedical researcher*

Geneva
Crumlish, Jane C. *pediatrician*
Lieberg, Olaf U. *orthopaedic surgeon*

Gouverneur
Kuehl, Alexander Edward *physician, health facility administrator, educator, writer*

Great Neck
Dines, David Michael *surgeon, educator*
Fisher, Barry G. *orthopedist, surgeon*
Gold, Alan H. *plastic surgeon*
Goldman, Ira Steven *gastroenterologist*
Jacono, Andrew A. *Plastic Surgeon*
Kechijian, Paul *dermatologist, educator*
Rosenberg, Richard F. *physician, radiologist*
Samuel, Paul *retired cardiologist*
Scherr, Lawrence *internist, healthcare educator, historian*
Schlesinger, Irwin D. *neurologist*
Shons, Alan Rance *plastic surgeon, surgical oncologist, educator*
Wolff, Edward *physician*

Great River
Hayman, Martin Arthur *psychiatrist, educator*

Hamburg
Calkins, Evan *physician, educator*

Hampton Bays
Jacobs, George Braun *neurosurgeon*

Hartsdale
Bomback, Fred M. *pediatrician*
Chait, Maxwell Mani *physician*

Hastings On Hudson
Green, Nancy Sue *pediatrician, health science association administrator*
Rosch, Paul John *internist, educator*

Hawthorne
Nandedkar, Sanjeev Dattatraya *medical researcher, educator*
Pianka, George *orthopedic surgeon*

Hewlett
Cohen, David Leon *physician*
Steinfeld, Philip Sheldon *pediatrician*

Hicksville
Polatsch, Bernard *obstetrician, gynecologist*

Huntington
Engstrand, Beatrice C. *neurologist, educator*
Winick, Martin *pediatric surgeon*
Zingale, Robert G. *surgeon*

Ithaca
Dietert, Rodney Reynolds *immunology and toxicology educator*
Foote, Robert Hutchinson *medical educator*
Kallfelz, Francis A. *veterinary medicine educator*
Nikitin, Alexander Yu. *pathologist*
Whitaker, Susanne Kanis *veterinary medical librarian*

Jamaica
Cantor, Jerome Owen *surgical pathologist, educator, researcher*
Garner, Steven C. *radiologist, emergency physician*
Kemeny, M. Margaret *oncologist, surgeon, hospital administrator, educator*
Lam, Sum *medical educator*

Jamestown
DJang, Arthur H.K. *pathologist, preventive medicine physician*

Johnson City
Coddington, Arthur Michael, Jr. *pediatrician, dermatologist*
Goddard, Bryan Lance *physician, director*

Katonah
Bauman, Jonathan Hugh *psychiatrist*
Stillman, Michael Allen *dermatologist*

Kenmore
Elibol, Tarik *gastroenterologist, educator*

Kingston
Johnson, Marie-Louise Tully *dermatologist, educator*

La Fayette
Cady, Duane Maynard *surgeon*

Larchmont
Rockland, Lawrence Howard *psychiatrist, educator*
Sklarew, Robert Jay *biomedical research educator, consultant*
Stahl, William Martin *retired surgeon*

Lewiston
Cooper, David R. *neurosurgeon*

Lloyd Harbor
Sheard, Charles III *dermatologist*

Lockport
Carr, Edward Albert, Jr. *pharmacologist, educator, physician*

Long Beach
Harris, Steven M. *urologist*

Malverne
Van Bosse, Harold J.P. *orthopedic surgeon*

Mamaroneck
Coleman, Marshall Donald *psychiatrist, psychoanalyst*
Halpern, Abraham Leon *psychiatrist*
McLarnon, Mary Frances *neurologist*

Manhasset
Arnofsky, Adam Garett *cardiothoracic surgeon*
Bernstein, David *gastroenterologist*
Boal, Bernard Harvey *cardiologist, educator, author*
Bosworth, Jay L. *radiation oncologist*
Budman, Cathy Linda *psychiatrist, physician*
D'Olimpio, James Thomas *oncologist*
Esposito, Rick Anthony *thoracic surgeon*
Hall, Michael Howard *thoracic surgeon*
Hartman, Alan Roy *surgeon, educator*
Kalimi, Robert *cardiovascular surgeon*
Milhorat, Thomas Herrick *neurosurgeon*
Pogo, Gustave Javier *cardiothoracic surgeon, educator*
Rochelson, Burton L. *obstetrician*
Shelat, Amit Mahesh *neurologist*
Vatsia, Sheel Kumar *cardiothoracic surgeon*

Manlius
Prior, John Thompson *pathology educator*

Massapequa
Labow, Theodore Allan *dermatologist, educator*

Zwanger, Jerome *physician*

Melville
Copperman, Stuart Morton *pediatrician, educator*

Mineola
Brand, Donald Albert *medical researcher, educator*
Kokotos, William J. *cardiothoracic surgeon*
Niederman, Michael Steven *physician, educator*
Schubach, Scott Leslie *cardiac physician*
Vintzileos, Anthony Mark *obstetrician, gynecologist*

Mount Kisco
Hayworth, Scott David *physician*
Powell, Jeffrey Scott *endocrinologist*
Schneider, Robert Jay *oncologist*

Mount Sinai
Feinberg, Sheldon Norman *pediatrician, educator*

New City
O'Dowd, Charles Edwyn *physician*
Sayegh, Nabil *urologist*

New Hyde Park
Bonagura, Vincent R. *pediatrician, educator, researcher*
Fried, Wendy B. *obstetrician, gynecologist*
Gecelter, Gary Raymond *gastrointestinal surgeon, researcher*
Hainline, Brian *neurologist*
Handelsman, John Ellis *pediatric orthopedist, surgeon*
Jacobson, Marc Stephen *pediatrician, educator*
Kamler, Kenneth Mark *microsurgeon*
Kolitz, Jonathan Elianhu *hematologist, oncologist*
Mealie, Carl A. *emergency physician, educator*
Medarov, Boris I. *pulmonologist, researcher, critical care physician*
Mehrotra, Bhoomi *hematologist, oncologist*
Palestro, Christopher J. *physician*
Punwaney, Juanita *dermatologist*
Rini, Josephine Nancy *nuclear medicine physician*
Schneider, Steven Jack *neurosurgeon*
Seltzer, Vicki Lynn *obstetrician, gynecologist*
Smith, Robin Errol *pediatrician, neurologist, educator*
Wolf-Klein, Gisele Patricia *geriatrician*

New Rochelle
Eaton, Richard Gillette *retired surgeon, educator*
Gitler, Bernard *cardiologist, critical care specialist*
Perry-Böttinger, Lynne Valencia *interventional cardiologist*
Rovinsky, Joseph Judah *obstetrician, gynecologist*

New Windsor
Mandel, Joel Emanuel *orthopedist*

New York
Abdel Dayem, Hussein Mahmoud *nuclear medicine physician, radiology educator*
Adlersberg, Jay Ben *internist*
Ahn, Jung Hwan *physiatrist, educator*
Alderson, Philip Otis *radiologist, educator*
Alexis, Andrew F. *dermatologist*
Alikhani, Zoubin *internist, molecular biologist, researcher*
Alizadeh, Kaveh *plastic surgeon, educator*
Altchek, David Wilson *orthopedist, surgeon*
Altman, Lawrence Kimball *physician, journalist*
Altman, Roy Peter *pediatric surgeon*
Ames, Richard Pollard *physician, educator, lecturer*
Antell, Darrick Eugene *plastic surgeon, educator*
Appelbaum, Paul Stuart *psychiatrist, medical educator, department chairman*
Armenakas, Noel Anthony *medical educator*
Aron, Alan Milford *pediatric neurology educator*
Ascherman, Jeffrey Alan *plastic and reconstructive surgeon*
Aston, Sherrell Jerone *plastic surgeon, educator*
Aufses, Arthur Harold, Jr. *surgeon, educator*
Austin, John H.M. *radiologist*
Axel, Richard *pathology and biochemistry educator*
Axelrod, Deborah Mona *surgeon*
Baden, Michael M. *pathologist, educator*
Bakal, Ron Sharone *urologist*
Baker, Daniel Clifton III *plastic surgeon, educator*
Balamaceda, Casilda *neurologist, oncologist*
Baldwin, David Shepard *physician*
Balinberg, Edmond B. *physician*
Barakat, Richard *oncologist, gynecological surgeon*
Barchas, Jack David *psychiatrist, medical researcher, educator, behavioral molecular neurobiologist*
Barker, Barbara Ann *ophthalmologist*
Barlow, Barbara Ann *surgeon*
Barondess, Jeremiah Abraham *physician*
Bartholomew, Lincoln Edwin *physician*
Bauer, Joel J. *surgeon, educator*
Beal, M. Flint *neurologist*
Belgorod, Barry Miles *surgeon, educator*
Ben-Avi, Simon Stephen *biomedical researcher, educator*
Beraka, George Joseph *plastic surgeon*
Berger, Frank Milan *biomedical researcher, retired pharmaceutical executive*
Berger, Marvin *medical educator*
Bergman, Donald Arthur *endocrinologist, educator*
Berk, Paul David *internist, research scientist, educator*
Berkowitz, Richard Lee *obstetrician, gynecologist, director*
Berman, Carol Wendy *psychiatrist*
Bernstein, Robert M. *dermatologic surgeon*
Bessey, Palmer Quintard *surgeon*
Bessler, Marc *surgeon, educator*
Beverley, Cordia Luvonne *gastroenterologist*
Bickers, David Rinsey *dermatologist, educator, department chairman, health facility administrator*
Biel, Leonard, Jr. *urologist*
Bilsky, Mark Harvey *neurosurgeon*
Bird, Hector Ramón *child psychiatrist, psychoanalyst, educator*
Black, Henry Richard *physician*
Blaser, Martin Jack *medical educator, researcher*
Blitzer, Andrew *otolaryngologist, educator, research scientist, writer*
Boachie-Adjei, Oheneba *orthopedic surgeon*
Bochner, Bernard H. *urologic surgical oncologist*
Bogdonoff, Morton David *internist, educator*
Boolbol, Susan K. *surgeon*
Borer, Jeffrey Stephen *cardiologist*
Bosl, George Joseph *physician, oncologist*
Brauner, Gary Jules *dermatologist, cosmetic laser surgeon*
Breinin, Goodwin M. *physician*
Brennan, Murray Frederick *surgeon, oncologist*
Bristow, Cynthia Lynn *immunologist*
Brodman, Michael Lewis *gynecologist, educator*
Broumand, Stafford R. *Plastic Surgeon*
Brown, Arthur Edward *physician*
Brown, Carol Leslie *gynecological oncologist*
Brown, Jason Walter *neurologist, educator, researcher*
Brust, John Calvin Morrison *neurologist, educator*
Buch, Jan *medical research administrator, director*
Buchbinder, Ellen Maud *allergist*
Buschke, Herman *neurologist*
Bussel, James *pediatrician, obstetrician, gynecologist, educator*
Butler, Vincent Paul, Jr. *internist, educator*
Butts, Hugh Florenz *physician, psychiatrist, psychoanalyst*
Buxton, Douglas Francisco *ophthalmologist, educator*
Bystryn, Jean-Claude *dermatologist, educator*
Caddick, Sarah J. *medical association administrator, biomedical researcher*
Cahill, John Donald *emergency medicine physician, educator*
Cammarata, Angelo *surgical oncologist*
Cammisa, Frank P., Jr. *surgeon, educator*
Campbell, Magda *retired child psychiatrist, researcher, educator*
Cancro, Robert *psychiatrist, educator*
Cantor, Richard Ira *physician, corporate health executive*
Casden, Andrew Michael *orthopedist*
Case, David Bartlett *internist, educator*
Case, Robert Brown *physician*
Cerfolio, Nina Estelle *psychiatrist, educator*
Chahinian, A(ram) Philippe *oncologist*
Chandler, Michael Jonathan *allergist, physician*
Chandrasekhar, Sujana S. *otologist, educator, neurotologist*
Chang, Stanley *ophthalmologist*
Chapman, Paul B. *oncologist*
Charash, Bruce D. *cardiologist, educator*
Charon, Rita *internist, medical educator, writer*
Cheema, Faisal Habib *surgeon, researcher*
Chen, Jonathan *pediatric surgeon*
Chiu, David Tak Wai *surgeon*
Chutorian, Abe M. *pediatrician, educator*
Close, Lanny Garth *otolaryngologist, educator*
Cohen, Howard A. *cardiologist*
Cohen, Noel Lee *otolaryngologist, educator*
Cohen, Seymour Martin *oncologist, hematologist, educator*
Cohen, Sidney Maximilian *neurologist*
Coleman, Donald Jackson *ophthalmologist, educator*
Coleman, Morton *oncologist, hematologist, educator*
Colen, Helen Sass *plastic surgeon*
Colen, Stephen R. *plastic and reconstructive surgeon*
Colibazzi, Tiziano *psychiatrist*
Coller, Barry Spencer *internist, pathologist, hematologist, educator, department chairman*
Compte, Maria Emilia *physician, educator, administrator*
Constantinides, Minas Spiros *otolaryngologist, plastic surgeon*
Copeland, Michelle *plastic surgeon*
Cordeiro, Peter Gabriel *surgeon, plastic surgeon*
Craig, Edward Vincent *orthopedic surgeon, educator*
Crane, Stephen Charles *medical association executive*
Cucin, Robert Louis *plastic surgeon, lawyer*
Cunningham-Rundles, Charlotte *physician, educator*
Davis, Kenneth Leon *psychiatrist, pharmacologist, medical educator*
Davis, Owen Kidder *physician, endocrinologist*
Debiec, Jacek *psychiatrist, research scientist, educator*
Defendi, Vittorio *medical association administrator, pathologist*
Desloge, Rosemary Byrne *otolaryngologist, educator*
De Vivo, Darryl Claude *pediatrician, neurologist*
Diaz, Angela *pediatrician, educator*
DiResta, Gene Robert *biomedical researcher, director*
Disa, Joseph James *plastic surgeon*
Divon, Michael Y. *obstetrician and gynecologist*
Dohrenwend, Bruce Philip *epidemiologist, social sciences educator*
Dorfman, Howard David *pathologist, educator*
Downey, John Alexander *physician, educator*
Doyle, Eugenie Fleri *pediatrician, cardiologist, educator*
Dranovsky, Alex *psychiatrist, researcher*
Dubois, Michel *anesthesiologist*
Du Mont, Nicolas *psychiatrist, educator*
Dworetzky, Murray *retired physician, educator*
Edelstein, Barbara A. *radiologist*
Edelstein, David Robert *medical educator*
Ennis, Ronald Dov *radiation oncologist*
Erlenmeyer-Kimling, L. *psychiatrist, researcher*
Estabrook, Alison *surgeon, educator*
Evans, Mark Ira *obstetrician, geneticist*
Fahn, Stanley *neurologist, educator*
Farhi, Jane-Iris *cardiologist, internist*
Field, Steven Philip *medical educator*
Fins, Joseph Jack *internist, medical ethicist*
First, Michael Bruce *psychiatrist, educator*
Fisher, Laura Lani *physician, medical educator*
Flax, Herschel *surgeon*
Forrest, David Vickers *psychiatrist, educator*
Fortner, Joseph Gerald *surgeon, educator*
Foster, Craig Allen *plastic surgeon*
Fowler, Dennis L. *surgeon, director*
Fox, Arthur Charles *cardiologist, educator*
Frances, Richard Joseph *psychiatrist*
Frantz, Andrew Gibson *endocrinologist, educator, dean*
Freedman, Alfred Mordecai *psychiatrist, educator*
Freedman, Michael Leonard *geriatrician, educator*
Freeman, Harold Paul *oncologist, educator, medical center director*
Friedman, Ira Hugh *surgeon*
Friedman, Jeffrey M. *medical researcher, educator*
Fukata, Masayuki *gastroenterologist, hematologist*
Fuster, Valentin *cardiologist, educator*
Gabrilove, Jacques Lester *physician*
Galanter, Marc *psychiatrist, educator*
Galland, Leo *internist, researcher*
Gandy, Sam *neurologist, neuroscientist, educator*
Gebbie, Kristine Moore *medical educator*
Gellhorn, Alfred *physician, educator*
Gelmann, Edward Paul *oncologist, educator*
Gendler, Ellen *dermatologist*
Gersony, Welton Mark *pediatrician, cardiologist, educator*
Gertler, Menard M. *physician, educator*
Ghossaini, Soha Nadim *medical educator*
Giardina, Elsa Grace Vonna *cardiologist, educator*
Ginsberg, Henry *medical educator, researcher*
Glasberg, H(erbert) Mark *psychiatrist, educator*
Glasberg, Scot Bradley *plastic surgeon*
Glassman, Alexander Howard *psychiatrist, researcher*
Glesby, Marshall Jay *physician, educator*
Gliklich, Jerry *physician, educator*
Gold, Arnold P. *neurologist*
Goldberg, Nieca *cardiologist, educator*
Goldfarb, C. Richard *radiologist, educator*
Goldfrank, Lewis Robert *physician*
Goldsmith, Michael Allen *oncologist, educator*
Goldsmith, Stanley Joseph *nuclear medicine physician, educator*
Goldstein, Marc *surgeon, urologist, educator, health facility administrator*
Goldstein, Martin S. *obstetrician, gynecologist, educator*
Gordon, Alan Lee *psychiatrist*
Gordon, Marsha L. *dermatologist*
Gotschlich, Emil Claus *physician*
Gottlieb, Geoffrey Jon *dermatologist*
Gotto, Antonio Marion, Jr. *internist, educator*
Grafstein, Bernice *physiology and neuroscience educator, researcher*
Green, Maurice Richard *neuropsychiatrist*
Green, Wayne Hugo *psychiatrist, psychoanalyst*
Greenberg, Benjamin *physician*
Griffiths, Sylvia Preston *physician, educator*
Gruen, Alison Brett *dermatologist*
Guth, Amber Azniv *surgeon, educator*
Guthrie, Randolph Hobson, Jr. *plastic surgeon, consultant*
Haas, Steven B. *orthopedist, surgeon, educator*
Haddad, Heskel Marshall *ophthalmologist, educator*
Haddad, Jamil Raouf *retired physician*
Hadden, John Winthrop *immunopharmacology educator*
Hadjiangelis, Nicos Pavlos *medical educator, consultant*
Haight, David Hulen *ophthalmologist*
Hajjar, Katherine Amberson *physician, pediatrician*
Hambrick, George Walter, Jr. *dermatologist, educator*
Hamburg, David A. *psychiatrist, foundation administrator*
Hammer, Scott M. *medical researcher, educator*
Hann, Lucy E. *radiologist, educator*
Harris, Henry William *physician*
Hartl, Roger *physician, researcher*
Hawkins, Katherine Ann *hematologist, educator, lawyer*
Herr, Harry Wallace *medical researcher, educator, surgeon, urologist*
Hershman, Elliott B. *orthopedist, surgeon*
Hertzig, Margaret E. *psychiatrist*
Herzog, Thomas *obstetrician, gynecologist, gynecological oncologist and surgeon, educator*
Hidalgo, David Arthur *plastic surgeon*
Hirsch, Harvey Stuart *psychiatrist*
Hirsch, Jules *physician, researcher*
Hirschhorn, Kurt *pediatrics educator*
Ho, David D. (Da-i Ho) *research physician, virologist, scientific organization director*
Hochlerin, Diane *pediatrician, educator*
Hochman, Judith Sheryl *cardiologist, researcher*
Hoffman, Lloyd Alan *plastic surgeon*
Holcomb, Kevin Michael *obstetrician, gynecologist, gynecologic oncologist*
Holland, Jimmie C. *psychiatrist, educator*
Holt, Peter Rolf *gastroenterologist, educator*
Hoskins, Donald W. *retired medical association administrator*
Hoskins, William John *obstetrician, educator, gynecologist*
Hudis, Clifford Alan *internist, oncologist*
Hugo, Norman Eliot *retired plastic surgeon, educator*
Hyman, Bruce Malcolm *ophthalmologist*
Imber, Gerald *plastic surgeon*
Imparato, Anthony Michael *vascular surgeon, educator, researcher*
Isaacson, Steven Robert *surgeon*
Isom, O(ttis) Wayne *thoracic surgeon, educator*
Ivanov, Iliyan *psychiatrist, researcher, artist*
Jacobson, Julius H., II, *vascular surgeon, writer*
Jaffe, Fredrick F. *surgeon*
Jan, Dominique Michel *surgeon, educator*
Jarecki, Henry George *physician, financial planner*
Javitt, Norman B. *medical educator, researcher*
Jelks, Glenn William *plastic surgeon*
Jessell, Thomas M. *medical educator*
Johnson, Horton Anton *pathologist*
Johnson, Warren Douglas *infectious diseases physician, researcher*
Jonas, Saran *neurologist, educator*
Jones, Jacqueline Eleanor *otolaryngologist*
Josephson, Jordan Stuart *otolaryngologist*
Jurka, Edith Mila *psychiatrist, researcher*
Kalsner, Stanley *pharmacologist, physiologist, educator*
Kane, Michael Arthur Christopher *plastic surgeon*
Kanick, Virginia *retired radiologist*
Kanof, Norman B. *dermatologist*
Kapelman, Barbara Ann *internist, hepatologist, gastroenterologist, educator*
Kaplitt, Michael Gordon *neurosurgeon, medical educator*
Kappas, Attallah *physician*
Karasu, T(oksoz) Byram *psychiatrist, educator, writer*
Karp, Nolan S. *plastic surgeon*
Katz, Bruce Elliot *dermatologist*
Katz, Jose *cardiologist, theoretical physicist, educator*
Katz, Lois Anne *internist, nephrologist*
Kaufman, David Marc *pediatric neurologist*
Kelly, Patrick Joseph *neurosurgeon, educator*
Khatamee, Masood Ahmad *obstetrician, gynecologist*
Killip, Thomas *cardiologist*
Kim, Ana H. *otolaryngologist, educator*
Kinne, David Weir *retired surgeon*
Kirschenbaum, Alexander *medical educator*
Kizer, Jorge Ruben *cardiologist, epidemiologist*
Klapholz, Marc *cardiologist*
Klapper, Andrew Mark *plastic surgeon*
Kleber, Herbert David *psychiatrist, educator*
Klein, Harvey *medical educator*
Klimstra, David S. *pathologist*
Knapp, Albert Bruce *gastroenterologist*
Knapp, Robert Charles *retired obstetrics and gynecology educator*
Kolker, Adam Ross *plastic surgeon, educator*
Kolodny, Edwin Hillel *neurologist, geneticist, director*
Komisar, Arnold *otolaryngologist, educator*
Kopenhaver, Patricia Ellsworth *podiatrist*
Koplewicz, Harold Samuel *child and adolescent psychiatrist*
Kourides, Ione Anne *endocrinologist, researcher, educator*
Kreek, Mary Jeanne *physician*
Krueger, Richard Bohn *psychiatrist*
Kumra, Vandana *otolaryngologist*
Ky, Alex Jenny *surgeon, educator*
Lachman, Leigh Jay *plastic surgeon, educator*
Lachmann, Elisabeth Amanda *physician*
Lalwani, Anil Kumar *otolaryngologist*
Landrigan, Philip John *epidemiologist*
Landry, Donald William *physician, educator, director, scientist*
Langer, David J. *neurological surgeon*
LaQuaglia, Michael Patrick *pediatric surgeon, neuroblastoma researcher*
Laragh, John Henry *cardiologist, surgeon, educator*
Larson, Steven Mark *physician*
Laskin, Richard Sheldon *orthopedic surgeon*
Laufman, Harold *surgeon, consultant*
Laurence, Jeffrey Conrad *immunologist, educator*
Lawson, William *otolaryngologist, educator*
Ledger, William Joe *obstetrician, educator*
Lee, Vivian S. *radiologist*
Leeds, Norman E. *medical educator, radiologist*
Leeman, Eve *psychiatrist*
Leifer, Edgar *physician, retired medical educator*
Leon, Martin Bert *cardiologist, educator*
Lessnau, Klaus-Dieter Karl *pulmonologist, director, medical educator*
Levin, Frances R. *psychiatrist, educator*
Levine, Robert H. *medical educator, psychiatrist*
Levitan, Max Fishel *anatomist, geneticist, educator*
Levy, Albert *physician*
Lewis, Jonathan Joseph *surgical oncologist, molecular biologist, educator, entrepreneur*
Lewy, Robert Max *physician*
Libby, Daniel M. *pulmonologist*
Lichtman, Adam David *anesthesiologist, educator*
Lieberman, James Sanford *physiatrist, neurologist*
Ligh, Jonathan Kennard *ophthalmologist*
Lipkin, Martin *medical educator, researcher*
Liu, Kai-Lih *epidemiologist*
Lobo, Rogerio Arnaldo *obstetrician, gynecologist*
Lockshin, Michael Dan *rheumatologist*
Lodge, Henry Sears *physician*
Loeb, John Nichols *physician, educator*
Loeb, Thomas Wolf *plastic surgeon*
Loft, Lloyd Mark *otolaryngologist*
Loo, Marcus Hsieu-Hong *urologist, physician, educator*
Lopez, Ralph Ivan *pediatrics educator*
Lunemann, Jan D. *neurologist, researcher*
Luntz, Maurice Harold *ophthalmologist*
Lyden, David Charles *oncologist, cell biologist*
Macken, Daniel Loos *cardiologist, educator*
Malitz, Sidney *psychiatrist, educator*
Malkin, Stanley Lee *neurologist*

Manger, William Muir *internist, educator, writer, research scientist*
Marangoz, Salih *orthopedist*
Marcus, Eric Robert *psychiatrist*
Margulis, Alexander Rafailo *physician, educator*
Marin, Deborah B. *psychiatrist, educator*
Markowitz, John C. *psychiatrist*
Markowitz, Martin H. *biomedical researcher*
Marks, Paul Alan *oncologist, cell biologist, educator*
Masterson, James Francis *psychiatrist*
Matarasso, Alan *plastic and reconstructive surgeon*
Mayo-Johnston, Julia A. *psychiatry professor, psychotherapist*
McClelland, Shearwood Junior *orthopaedic surgeon*
McDowell, David Michael *psychiatrist, educator, researcher*
Meisner, Jay *plastic surgeon*
Mellins, Robert B. *pediatrician, educator*
Mesnikoff, Alvin Murray *psychiatrist, educator*
Michelis, Michael Frank *nephrologist*
Michels, Robert *psychiatrist, educator*
Michelsen, Christopher Bruce Hermann *surgeon*
Mildvan, Donna *infectious diseases physician*
Miller, Philip Jay *plastic surgeon*
Miller, Theodore T. *radiologist*
Mohr, Jay Preston *neurologist, educator*
Moore, Anne *physician*
Moss-Salentijn, Letty (Aleida) *anatomist, educator*
Muchnick, Richard Stuart *ophthalmologist, educator*
Murphy, Ramon Jeremiah Castroviejo *physician, pediatrician*
Naftolin, Frederick *gynecologist, educator*
Naidich, Thomas Paul *neuroradiologist, educator*
Naka, Yoshifumi *surgeon, researcher*
Nash, Thomas *physician*
Nass, Ruth *pediatric neurologist*
Neuberg, Hans W. *internist, educator*
Neuwirth, Michael G. *orthopedist, surgeon, educator*
Neuwirth, Robert Samuel *obstetrician, gynecologist, educator*
New, Maria Iandolo *pediatrician, educator*
Newhouse, Jeffrey H. *radiologist, educator*
Newman, Robert Gabriel *physician*
Newsome, Frederick V. *medical educator*
Nicholas, Stephen J. *orthopedic surgeon, sports medicine physician*
Nimkarn, Saroj *endocrinologist, researcher*
Norton, Larry *oncologist, researcher*
Novick, Nelson Lee *dermatologist, internist, consultant, cosmetic dermasurgeon, writer*
Nussenzweig, Michel Claudio *immunologist, educator*
Oberfield, Sharon Elefant *pediatric endocrinologist*
Ocean, Allyson Joy *oncologist, educator*
Ochoa, Manuel, Jr. *oncologist*
Oettgen, Herbert Friedrich *physician*
Ofri, Danielle *internist*
Olsson, Carl Alfred *urologist, department chairman*
Omura, Yoshiaki *medical educator*
Oratz, Ruth *physician*
Ordorica, Steven Anthony *obstetrician, gynecologist, educator*
O'Reilly, Richard John *pediatrician*
Orkin, Louis Richard *physician, educator*
Osborn, June Elaine *pediatrician, microbiologist, educator, foundation administrator*
Oz, Mehmet Cengiz *cardiac surgeon, writer*
Packer, Stuart Howard *medical educator*
Padgett, Douglas Edmund *orthopedist, surgeon, educator*
Panicek, David *radiologist*
Pappagallo, Marco *neurologist, pain medicine specialist*
Pastores, Gregory McCarthy *pediatrician, medical geneticist, researcher*
Pastores, Stephen M. *internist*
Pearlman, Steven Jay *otolaryngologist, surgeon, educator*
Pedley, Timothy Asbury, IV, *neurologist, educator, researcher*
Perin, Noel I. *neurosurgeon*
Pfeifer, Tracy M. *plastic surgeon*
Phillips, Gerald Baer *internal medicine scientist, educator*
Pierson, Richard Norris, Jr. *medical educator*
Pile-Spellman, John Martin *radiology and neurosurgery educator*
Pitman, Gerald H. *plastic surgeon*
Plum, Fred *neurologist*
Pogue, Velvie Anne *nephrologist, educator*
Polenz, Joanna Magda *psychiatrist*
Polydorides, Alexandros Demetrios *pathologist*
Pomp, Alfons *surgeon*
Posner, Jerome Beebe *neurologist, educator*
Potter, Hollis Gromisch *radiologist*
Prager, Kenneth Michael *pulmonologist, educator*
Quackenbush, Margery Clouser *psychoanalyst, researcher*
Rabinowitz, Jack Grant *radiologist, educator*
Radecki, Jeffrey *sports medicine physician*
Rainess, Alan Edward *psychiatrist, neurologist, educator*
Ramsay, David Leslie *physician, dermatologist, educator*
Ranz, Jules M. *psychiatrist, director*
Rausen, Aaron Reuben *pediatric hematologist, oncologist*
Raviv, Tal *ophthalmologist*
Rayfield, Elliot James *medical educator*
Raynor, Richard Benjamin *neurosurgeon, educator*
Redo, S(averio) Frank *retired surgeon*
Reidenberg, Marcus Milton *physician, educator*
Reisberg, Barry *geriatric psychiatrist, neuropsychopharmacologist*
Ren, Christine *surgeon*
Rhodes, Rosamond *medical educator, philosophy educator*
Richert, John Rolin *neuroimmunologist, educator*
Rifkind, Arleen B. *pharmacologist, researcher, educator*
Ristich, Miodrag *psychiatrist*
Ritch, Robert Harry *ophthalmologist, educator*
Rivlin, Richard Saul *internist*
Rodriguez, Alcibiades J. *neurologist, educator*
Romano, John Francis *dermatologist*
Romita, Mauro Charles *plastic surgeon*
Romo, Thomas III *plastic surgeon*
Rosenberg, Harold Nmi *preventive medicine physician, consultant*
Rosenblum, Jay Alan *neurologist*
Rosenfeld, Isadore *cardiologist, educator*
Rosenfield, Allan *medical educator, dean, obstetrician, gynecologist*
Roubin, Gary Sidney Samuel *interventional cardiologist, educator, researcher*
Rovit, Richard Lee *neurosurgeon*
Rowland, Lewis Phillip *neurology educator, editor, clinical investigator*
Rozbruch, S. Robert *orthopedist, researcher*
Rubin, Albert Louis *internist, nephrologist, educator*
Rubin, Theodore Isaac *psychiatrist, writer*
Rudloff, Udo *surgeon, researcher*
Rusch, Valerie Williams *thoracic surgeon*
Sachar, David Bernard *gastroenterologist, educator*
Sacks, Oliver Wolf *neurologist, writer*
Sadick, Neil Scott *dermatologist*
Sadock, Benjamin James *psychiatrist, educator*
Salans, Lester Barry *physician, research scientist, educator*
Salgo, Peter Lloyd *internist, writer, anesthesiologist, journalist, commentator*
Salky, Barry A. *surgeon*
Salvati, Edwardo A. *surgeon*
Sampson, Hugh Albert, Jr. *medical educator*
Sandhu, Harvinder Singh *spinal surgeon, educator*
Saphir, Richard Louis *pediatrician*
Saxena, Brij B. *endocrinologist, biochemist, educator*
Sceusa, Nicholas A. *pharmacologist*
Schaffner, Bertram Henry *psychiatrist*
Schechter, Daniel Scott *child and adolescent psychiatrist, researcher*
Schiff, Howard Irwin *urologist*
Schlegel, Peter Niles *urologist, educator*
Schley, William Shain *otolaryngologist*
Schneck, Jerome M. *psychiatrist, historian, medical educator*
Schuster, Carlotta Lief *psychiatrist*
Schwartz, Theodore H. *neurosurgeon*
Sclafani, Anthony Paul *plastic surgeon, educator, biomedical researcher*
Scott, Norman (W. Norman Scott) *orthopedist, sports medicine physician, surgeon*
Scott, Susan Craig *plastic surgeon*
Sculco, Thomas Peter *surgeon*
Sedlin, Elias David *orthopedist, educator*
Seely, Robert Daniel *cardiologist, medical association administrator*
Selby, Ronald M. *orthopedic surgeon*
Seltzer, Terry F. *endocrinologist, medical educator*
Sessions, Roy Brumby *otolaryngologist, educator*
Shabto, Uri *vitreo-retinal surgeon*
Shah, Jatin Premanand *head and neck surgeon, educator*
Shapiro, Theodore *psychiatrist, educator*
Shatkin, Jess Parker *psychiatrist*
Shepherd, Gillian Mary *physician*
Sherman, John Eric *plastic surgeon*
Sherman, Spencer E. *ophthalmologist*
Siebert, John Weston *surgeon, plastic surgeon*
Silver, Richard Tobias *oncologist, educator*
Sitarz, Anneliese Lotte *pediatrician, educator, physician*
Skolnik, Richard Alan *plastic surgeon*
Smith, Craig Richey *thoracic surgeon*
Snyderman, Nancy *surgeon, medical journalist*
Soave, Rosemary *internist*
Sobel, Howard D. *dermatologist*
Solomon, Gail Ellen *physician*
Sonett, Joshua Robert *medical educator, surgeon*
Spencer, Frank Cole *medical educator*
Speyer, James L. *oncologist*
Spiegel, Herbert *psychiatrist, educator*
Stein, Marvin *psychiatrist, historian*
Stein, Zena A. *retired epidemiologist, educator*
Steinberg, Jonathan S. *cardiologist, educator*
Steinglass, Peter Joseph *psychiatrist, educator*
Stelwagon, Jennifer Cooper *psychiatrist*
Stimmel, Barry *cardiologist, educator, internist, dean*
Stone, Michael Howard *psychiatry educator*
Stoopler, Mark Benjamin *physician*
Strauchen, James Arthur *medical educator, pathologist*
Stübgen, Joerg-Patrick *neurologist*
Sullivan, Alison Elizabeth *pediatrician, child psychiatrist*
Sullivan, Stephen Gene *psychiatrist, pharmacologist, health facility administrator*
Sultan, Mark R. *plastic surgeon*
Susser, Mervyn Wilfred *epidemiologist, educator*
Swift, Ronnie Gorman *psychiatrist, educator*
Swistel, Daniel George *surgeon*
Tabbal, Nicolas G. *plastic surgeon*
Taha, Assad M. *surgeon*
Tancredi, Laurence Richard *medical educator, psychiatrist*
Temple, Donald Edward *medical association administrator*
Tenenbaum, Joseph *cardiologist*
Tepler, Jeffrey *oncologist*
Thomas, Stephen Jay *anesthesiologist*
Thomson, Gerald Edmund *physician, educator*
Thorne, Charles Hedges McKinstry *plastic surgeon*
Tilson, M(artin) David III *surgeon, scientist, educator*
Tolchin, Joan Gubin *psychiatrist, educator*
Tortolani, Anthony John *surgeon, educator*
Tourlitsas, John Constantine *radiologist*
Turino, Gerard Michael *internist, educator*
Turtil, Lawrence Charles *psychiatrist*
Tzimas, Nicholas Achilles *orthopedic surgeon, educator*
Ulin, Richard Irwin *pediatric orthopedist, educator*
Vaughan, Edwin Darracott, Jr. *urologist, surgeon*
Veronneau-Troutman, Suzanne *retired ophthalmologist*
Vilcek, Jan Tomas *immunologist, medical educator*
Vlahov, David *epidemiologist*
Walden, Jennifer Lee *plastic surgeon*
Wang, Frederick Mark *pediatrician, ophthalmologist, educator*
Wang, Lu-Hai *medical educator, biochemist*
Warren, Michelle Palmieri *internist, endocrinologist*
Warren, Russell Frederick *orthopedist*
Weinstein, I. Bernard *oncologist, geneticist, director, educator*
Weiss, Carol Juliet *psychiatrist*
Weiss, Paul Richard *plastic surgeon*
Weissmann, Gerald *internist, researcher, educator, editor, writer*
Welch, Martha Grace *physician, researcher*
Werman, David Sanford *psychiatrist, psychoanalyst*
Westrich, Geoffrey Howard *orthopaedic surgery*
Wexler, Leonard Howard *pediatric oncologist*
Wexler, Patricia Susan *dermatologist, surgeon*
Wharton, Ralph Nathaniel *psychiatrist, educator*
Winawer, Sidney J. *physician, educator*
Winick, Myron *nutrition professor, physician*
Winn, H. Richard *surgeon*
Wittes, Robert E. *physician, science foundation director*
Wolden, Suzanne Leesa *pediatric radiation oncologist*
Wolfe, Scott W. *orthopedic hand surgeon*
Wolff, William I. *surgeon, educator*
Wood-Smith, Donald *plastic surgeon*
Worman, Howard Jay *internist, educator*
Wunsch, Hannah *anesthesiologist, researcher*
Young, Bruce Kenneth *obstetrician, gynecologist, educator*
Young, Estelle Irene *dermatologist, educator*
Yu, Yi-Hao *endocrinologist, educator, physician, research scientist*
Yurt, Roger William *surgeon, educator*
Zevon, Scott J. *plastic surgeon*
Zhen, Juan *medical researcher*
Zimmerman, Sol Shea *pediatrician*
Zinn, Keith Marshall *ophthalmologist, educator*
Zitrin, Arthur *physician*

Niagara Falls
DeFelice, Eugene Anthony *internist, educator, magician*

Northport
Graber, Mark L. *internist*

Orangeburg
Greenberg, William Michael *psychiatrist*
Levine, Jerome *psychiatrist, educator*

Orchard Park
Lee, Richard Vaille *internist, educator*

Ossining
Wolfe, Mary Joan *physician*

Pawling
Caplan, Ronald Mervyn *obstetrician, gynecologist*

Pittsford
Faloon, William Wassell *physician, educator*

Plainview
Layne, Jeffrey Todd *urologist*

Plattsburgh
Bedworth, David Albert *health educator*

Port Jefferson
Ahmad, Arif *surgeon*
Dranitzke, Richard J. *surgeon*

Port Washington
Rogatz, Peter *retired physician*

Poughkeepsie
Abraham, Manoj Timothy *plastic surgeon, educator*
Carino, Aurora Lao *psychiatrist, health facility administrator*
Wolfersteig, Jean Lois *medical association administrator, educator*

Purchase
Frost, Elizabeth Ann McArthur *physician*

Rego Park
Davidov, Ludmila G. *psychiatrist*
Solowey, Carl *dermatologist, educator*

Rhinebeck
Crum, Albert B. *psychiatrist, consultant*

Richmond Hill
Gintautas, Jonas *physician, scientist, administrator*
Malhotra, Madhu Bala *psychiatrist*

Rochester
Anderson, Porter Warren, Jr. *retired pediatrics educator*
Baum, John *physician*
Bidlack, Jean Marie *pharmacologist, educator, researcher*
Blumberg, Neil *hematologist, educator*
Bonfiglio, Thomas Albert *pathologist, educator*
Brody, Bernard B. *internist, educator*
Brooks, Walter S. *dermatologist*
Burton, Richard Irving *orthopedist, educator*
Chess, Patricia R. *pediatrician, medical educator, researcher*
Chey, William Yoon *physician*
Ciccone, J. Richard *psychiatrist, educator*
Cohen, Nicholas *immunologist, educator*
D'Angio, Carl T. *pediatrician, educator*
DeWeese, James Arville *surgeon, educator*
Dimopoulos, Vassilios Georgios *physician, researcher*
Dreyfuss, Eric Martin *allergist*
Farmer, Richard Gilbert *academic physician, foundation administrator*
Golden, Reynold Stephen *geriatrician, educator*
Khorana, Alok Anand *oncologist, medical researcher*
Kieburtz, Karl David *physician, educator, researcher*
Kurlan, Roger *neurologist, educator*
Lichtman, Marshall Albert *hematologist, educator, researcher*
Lyman, Gary Herbert *epidemiologist, cancer researcher, educator*
Lyness, Jeffrey Marc *psychiatrist, educator*
Maquat, Lynne E. *biomedical researcher*
McAnarney, Elizabeth R. *pediatrician, educator*
McDonald, Joseph Valentine *neurosurgeon*
McMeekin, Thomas Owen *dermatologist*
Moss, Arthur Jay *physician*
Nazarian, Lawrence Fred *pediatrician*
O'Brien, Jeanne H. *medical educator*
Pilcher, Webster Hotchkiss *neurosurgeon*
Powers, James Matthew *neuropathologist, educator, researcher*
Ren, Clement L. *immunologist, researcher*
Rizk, Toufic Assaad *vascular surgeon*
Rothberg, Paul G. *medical geneticist, educator*
Schaefer, Katherine L. *medical researcher, educator*
Smith, Julia Ladd *oncologist, physician*
Sparks, Charles Edward *pathologist, educator*
Sparks, Janet Lindsay Dehoff *pathologist, educator*
White, Ann Marie *medical educator*
Wiley, Jason LaRue, Jr. *neurosurgeon*
Williams, Thomas Franklin *physician, educator*

Rockville Centre
Teyan, Frederick Gene *pediatrician*

Rome
Min, Balshik *pathologist*

Roslyn
Greenberg, Steven M. *physician*
Mazlen, Roger Geoffrey *ophthalmologist, pharmacologist*

Rye
Barker, Harold Grant *surgeon, educator*
Curtin, Brian Joseph *retired ophthalmologist*
Waltz, Joseph McKendree *neurosurgeon, educator*

Sands Point
Lear, Erwin *anesthesiologist, educator*

Scarsdale
Edis, Gloria Toby *pediatrician*
Lipman, Marvin Matthew *physician, medical educator, medical editor, writer*
Mercando, Anthony Dominic *cardiologist*
Moser, Marvin *physician, educator, author*
Soley, Robert Lawrence *plastic surgeon*

Schenectady
Depan, Harry John *cardiothoracic surgeon*
Ritterband, Arnold B. *internist*
Schenck, John Frederic *physician*

Scotia
de la Rocha, Carlos A. *retired physician*

Sleepy Hollow
Chia, David Thien-Shing *internist, gastroenterologist*

Slingerlands
Beer, Paul Marius *ophthalmologist, educator*
Ipsen, Carol Anne *psychiatrist, educator*

Smithtown
Koss, Tamara *dermatologist, educator*
Tuzel, Suzanne L. *psychiatrist*

Somers
Bauman, William Allen *pediatrician, educator, health systems consultant*
Reznick, Steven Michael *orthopedic surgeon, educator*
Rubin, Samuel Harold *internist, consultant*

Staten Island
Bruckstein, Alex Harry *internist, gastroenterologist, geriatrician*
Ferzli, George Salem *surgeon*
Maiman, Mitchell *oncologist, gynecologist*
Popler, Kenneth *behavioral health services administrator, psychologist*
Stathopoulos, Peter *internist*

Stony Brook
Andriola, Mary Repole *neurologist, pediatrician*
Baker, David A. *obstetrician, gynecologist, educator*
Cole, Steven *psychiatrist, educator*
Corman, Marvin Leonard *surgeon, educator*
Dagum, Alexander B. *plastic surgeon*
Fine, Richard Nisan *pediatrician, educator, dean*
Fritts, Harry Washington, Jr. *internist, educator*
Hurst, Lawrence *orthopedic surgeon*
Jaber, Rajaa *physician, educator*
Jonas, Steven *preventive medicine physician, author*
Kuchner, Eugene Frederick *neurosurgeon, educator, neuroscientist*

, Dorothy Spiegel *preventive medicine ysician*
e, M. Cristina *medical researcher, educator*
g, Jerome Zhengrong *radiology educator*
c, Michael Lynn *medical educator, ostetrician*
ers, Morton Allen *radiologist, educator*
heit, Alan Goodman *obstetrician, ynecologist*
be, Cedric Joseph, Jr. *retired pediatric rgeon*
engart, Todd Kenneth *cardiothoracic rgeon, researcher, neurosurgeon, consultant*
ert, Frank C. *thoracic surgeon*
gbigel, Roy Theodore *epidemiologist, lucator, research scientist*
iopoulos, Apostolos K. *vascular surgeon*
, Stephen Charles *cardiologist, ectrophysiologist*
sbrot, Deborah Marcia *psychiatrist*
son, Thomas Allen *pediatrician, ndocrinologist*

fern
ispoti, Andre John *allergist, immunologist*

acuse
er, Bruce Edward *orthopedic surgeon, onsultant*
ker, Lorne Arthur *family physician*
dicott, Catherine V. *medical educator, esearcher*
une, John B. *medical educator*
drickson, Bruce E. *orthopedist*
d, Joseph *medical researcher*
lan, Eugene Alken *psychiatry professor, epartment chairman*
uzzi, Daniel D. *medical association dministrator*
gers, Sherry Anne *physician*
eten, Barbara Wiard *ophthalmologist, nedical educator*
sz, Thomas Stephen *psychiatrist, educator, riter*
liams, William Joseph *retired hematologist, ducator*
ff, L. Thomas *physician, educator*

rrytown
chiarella, Antonio *physician, educator*
d, Barry Elliot *internist, gastroenterologist*
Murtry, James Gilmer III *neurosurgeon*

xedo Park
gan, Ellen Frances (Mrs. Walston Shepard Brown) *ophthalmologist, educator*
netz, Bernard George, Jr. *endocrinologist*

ton
nilton, Leonard Derwent *physician, nolecular biologist*

lhalla
onow, Wilbert Solomon *physician, educator*
nen, Martin Bruce *physician*
Guercio, Louis Richard Maurice *surgeon, ducator*
shman, William Howard *cardiologist, ducator, department chairman, ardiovascular pharmacologist, gerontologist*
odman, Alvin Irwin *internist, nephrologist, ducator*
hiosa, Mario Anthony, Jr. *pharmacologist*
ne, Susan Anderson *medical educator, nternist*
dden, Robert Edward *surgeon, educator*
rks, Stephen J. *neurologist, educator*
guidula, Faustino Nazario *surgeon, educator*
erson, Stephen Joseph *internist*
ai, Bijan *physician, investigator*
eger, Nadav *pediatrician, pulmonologist*
lliams, Gary Murray *pathologist, educator*

lley Stream
tta, Rajiv V. *oncologist, surgeon, department chairman*

stal
nberg, Raul *internist*

antagh
chs, Jodi Ian *ophthalmologist*

ater Mill
gstrom, Jack Walter Carl Kling *retired pathology educator*

est Islip
fkin, Matthew D. *radiologist*

hite Plains
ran, Xiaolei Yu *physician, psychiatry professor*
rnard, Robert William *plastic surgeon*
ers, Martin Henry *physician*
ass, John Paul *physician, biochemist*
tz, Michael *pediatrician, educator*
tscher, Martin L. *pediatrician, neurologist*
arano, Anthony Joseph *cardiologist*
lson, Mario *physiatrist*
effer, Cynthia Roberta *psychiatrist, educator*
verman, Amy Jocelyn *psychiatrist*
aus, Marc Joshua *internist, poet*
eisand, Robert L. *thoracic surgeon*
eisburger, John Hans *medical researcher*

illiamsville
iman, Joseph Bruce *dermatologist, educator*
gra, Pearay L. *pediatrician, educator*
isman, Robert E. *allergist, educator*
kate, Albert C. *physician*

oodbury
eenberg, Stephen Todd *plastic surgeon*

nkers
ennin, Gerald Stanley *ophthalmologist*

Novick, Stephen Alan *cardiologist*
Spagnuolo, Mario *physician*

Yorktown Heights
Berk, George Ellis *cardiologist*
Mayer, Gerard J. *physician*

NORTH CAROLINA

Advance
Guth, Caryl Joy *retired anesthesiologist*

Asheville
Turcot, Marguerite Hogan *medical researcher*
White, Terry Edward *physician*

Banner Elk
Hutcheson, James Sterling *retired physician, allergist*

Black Mountain
Blackwell, Anna Nelle *medical educator, medical technician*

Burlington
Wilson, William Preston *psychiatrist, educator*

Carrboro
Prather, Donna Lynn *psychiatrist*

Cary
Kimbrell, Odell Culp, Jr. *internist*

Chapel Hill
Andreoni, Kenneth A. *surgeon*
Atashili, Julius *epidemiologist*
Ballard, David Eugene *anesthesiologist*
Bernard, Stephen Alan *oncologist*
Bondurant, Stuart *physician, educational association administrator*
Boyarsky, Saul *urologist, educator*
Callahan, Leigh Fleming *medical educator, researcher*
Carey, Lisa Anne *oncologist, educator*
Carson, Culley Clyde III *urologist, educator*
Coeytaux, Remy Rene *physician, researcher*
Coles, William Henry *ophthalmologist, educator*
Collier, Albert M. *pediatrician, educator, director*
Cromartie, William James *medical educator, researcher*
De Friese, Gordon H. *health services researcher*
De Rosa, Guy Paul *orthopedic surgery educator*
Dirschl, Douglas Ray *surgeon, educator*
Drossman, Douglas Arnold *medical investigator, educator, gastroenterologist*
Erdem, Nurum Filiz *geriatrician*
Finkel, Alan Glen *neurologist, educator*
Fletcher, Suzanne Wright *epidemiologist, medical educator, editor*
Fowler, Wesley Caswell, Jr. *obstetrician, gynecologist*
Goldsmith, Lowell Alan *medical educator*
Goyer, Robert Andrew *pathology educator*
Greganti, Mac Andrew *physician, educator*
Hawkins, David Rollo, Sr. *psychiatrist, educator*
Henson, O'Dell Williams, Jr. *retired anatomy educator*
Houpt, Jeffrey Lyle *psychiatrist, educator, former dean*
Hulka, Jaroslav Fabian *obstetrician, gynecologist*
James, Alton Everette, Jr. *radiologist*
Kremer, Michael *surgeon*
Lachiewicz, Paul Francis *orthopedist, surgeon, educator*
Lavelle, John Paul *urologist*
Lohr, Jacob Andrew *pediatrician, educator*
Martikainen, A(une) Helen *retired health specialist educator*
McMillan, Campbell White *pediatrician, educator, hematologist*
Miller, C. Arden *physician, educator*
Pagano, Joseph Stephen *internist, educator, researcher*
Peacock, Erle Ewart, Jr. *surgeon, lawyer, educator*
Pillsbury, Harold Crockett III *otolaryngologist*
Shea, Thomas Charles *physician, educator*
Sheldon, George Frank *medical educator*
Spencer, Roger Felix *psychiatrist, educator*
Stockman, James Anthony III *pediatrician*
Taft, Timothy Ned *orthopedist, surgeon, sports medicine physician*
Tolley, Aubrey Granville *psychiatrist, health facility administrator*
Trejo, JoAnn *medical researcher*
West, Alisha Nicole *otolaryngologist, surgeon*
Wilcox, Benson Reid *cardiothoracic surgeon, educator*
Wilfert, Catherine M. *medical association administrator, pediatrician, epidemiologist, educator*
Winfield, John Buckner *rheumatologist, educator*
Yeatts, Karin Beatrice *epidemiologist*

Charlotte
Hall, James Bryan *gynecologist, oncologist*
Jacobs, Gordon Waldemar *surgeon, educator*
Kennelly, Michael J. *neurologist, surgeon*
Perry, Glenn *orthopedic surgeon*
Plunkett, Steven R. *radiologist*
Schafermeyer, Robert William *emergency physician, educator, health policy consultant*
Shulstad, Andrew Robert *pediatrician*
Thompson, John Albert, Jr. *dermatologist*

Cornelius
Riou, Jean-Pierre Alain *plastic surgeon*
Schneider, Lori Beth *neurologist*

Durham
Afshari, Natalie Adel *ophthalmologist, surgeon, educator*
Agre, Peter Courtland *medical educator*
Albala, David Mois *urologist, educator*
Anderson, William Banks, Jr. *ophthalmology educator*
Anlyan, William George *surgeon, educator, academic administrator*
Armstrong, Brenda Estelle *pediatrician, cardiologist*
Bennett, Peter Brian *medical researcher, educator*
Blazer, Dan German, II, *psychiatrist, epidemiologist*
Blazing, Michael August *internist*
Bollinger, Ralph Randal *surgeon, researcher*
Borges-Neto, Salvador *radiologist, cardiologist, educator*
Bradford, William Dalton *pathologist, educator*
Brodie, Harlow Keith Hammond *psychiatrist, educator*
Buckley, Rebecca Hatcher *allergist, immunologist, pediatrician, educator*
Burks, A. Wesley *pediatrics educator*
Cai, Xinjiang *cardiologist, researcher*
Carter, James Harvey *psychiatrist, educator*
Cohen, Harvey Jay *geriatrician, hematologist, oncologist, educator*
Colvin, O. Michael *medical association administrator, medical educator*
Cook-Deegan, Robert Mullan *physician, educator*
Crawford, Jeffrey C. *oncologist, educator*
Dzau, Victor Joseph *cardiologist, director, researcher*
Edwards, Christopher Levon *medical association administrator*
Falletta, John Matthew *pediatrician, educator*
Foreman, John William *pediatrician, educator*
Frank, Michael M. *physician*
Freemark, Michael Scott *pediatric endocrinologist, educator*
Frothingham, Thomas Eliot *pediatrician*
Gainetdinov, Raul Radikovich *pharmacologist, researcher*
Georgiade, Gregory Stephen *plastic surgeon, educator*
Giannopoulos, Athina *physician, surgeon*
Greenfield, Joseph Cholmondeley, Jr. *physician, educator*
Hammond, Charles Bessellieu *obstetrician, gynecologist, educator*
Haynes, Barton Ford *medical educator*
James, Sherman Athonia *epidemiologist, educator*
Jennings, Robert Burgess *experimental pathologist, medical educator*
Jirtle, Randy *medical educator, geneticist*
Katz, Samuel Lawrence *pediatrician, researcher*
Kemper, Alex R. *pediatrician, educator*
Kirkpatrick, John Paxton *oncologist, educator*
Kishnani, Priya Sunil *medical geneticist*
Klitzman, Bruce *physiologist, plastic surgery educator, researcher*
Koepke, John Arthur *hematologist, clinical pathologist*
Krishnan, Krishnaswamy Ranga Rama R. *psychiatry educator*
Krucoff, Mitchell Wolfe *cardiologist*
Lagoo, Anand Shreeram *pathologist, educator*
Lefkowitz, Robert Joseph *biomedical researcher, educator*
Leppert, Phyllis Carolyn *obstetrician, gynecologist*
Levin, Lawrence Scott *plastic surgeon*
MacIntyre, Neil Ross, Jr. *medical educator*
Mark, Daniel Benjamin *cardiologist*
Masand, Prakash S. *psychiatrist, researcher*
Matchar, David B. *physician, researcher*
McNamara, James O. *physician, scientist*
Michener, James Lloyd *medical educator*
Miller, David Edmond *physician*
Ohman, E. Magnus *cardiologist, educator*
Olsen, Elise *dermatologist, researcher*
Ortel, Thomas Lee *oncologist, hematologist, educator*
Ostbye, Truls *medical researcher, educator*
Pinnell, Sheldon Richard *dermatologist, researcher, retired educator*
Pizzo, Salvatore Vincent *pathologist*
Rabinovich, Egla Consuelo *pediatrician, rheumatologist*
Robboy, Stanley J. *pathologist, educator*
Sabiston, David Coston, Jr. *surgeon, educator*
Seewaldt, Victoria L. *medical educator, researcher*
Shelburne, John Daniel *pathologist*
Tedder, Thomas Fletcher *immunology educator, researcher*
Thompson, William Moreau *radiologist, educator*
Toloza, Eric M. *thoracic surgeon*
Voynow, Judith Ann *pediatric pulmonologist, educator*
Weiner, Richard David *psychiatrist, researcher*
Wilcox, Allen James *epidemiologist*
Wilkins, Robert Henry *neurosurgeon, educator, editor*
Williams, Redford Brown *medical educator*
Young, Terri L. *ophthalmologist*
Zenn, Michael Robert *plastic and reconstructive surgeon*

Ellerbe
Rankin, Pressley Robinson, Jr. *physician*

Fayetteville
Lowe, James Edward, Jr. *plastic and reconstructive surgeon*

Flat Rock
Weill, Hans *medical educator*

Fletcher
Hill, Ronald Charles *surgeon, educator*

Four Oaks
Jordan, Lyndon Kirkman *physician*

Greensboro
Houston, Frank Matt *dermatologist*

Greenville
Babb, Joseph Dolby *physician*
Habal, Nizar *oncologist, surgeon, educator*
James, James Franklin *psychiatrist, educator, academic administrator*
Johnson, Cynda Ann *physician, educator*
Lee, Kenneth Stuart *neurosurgeon, educator*
Pories, Walter Julius *surgeon, educator*
Tingelstad, Jon Bunde *retired pediatrician, educator*
Waugh, William Howard *physician, research scientist*

Henderson
Serafin, Donald *plastic surgeon, educator*

Hendersonville
Reinhart, John Belvin *retired child and adolescent psychiatrist, educator*
Roberts, James Allen *retired urologist, educator*

Hickory
Lefler, Wade Hampton, Jr. *ophthalmologist*

High Point
Bardelas, Jose Antonio *allergist*
Draelos, Zoe Diana *dermatologist, consultant*
Kandt, Raymond S. *neurologist*

Hillsborough
Johnston, William Webb *pathologist, educator*

Huntersville
Atrak, Taisser M. *pediatrician, director*

Kure Beach
Wiebe, Richard Herbert *reproductive endocrinologist, educator*

Maiden
Peeler, Forrest Edwards *retired physician*

Mebane
Langley, Ricky Lee *occupational medicine physician*

Monroe
Taylor, Jimmy Lynn *retired family practice physician, administrator*

Morganton
Baden, Thomas James *dermatologist*

Mount Airy
Thoppil, Cecil Koshey *pediatrician, consultant, educator*

New Bern
McKee, Francis John *medical association consultant, lawyer*
Sinning, Mark Alan *thoracic and vascular surgeon*

Pine Knoll Shores
Graham, Gloria Flippin *dermatologist*

Pinehurst
Heim, Lori Joan *physician*

Raleigh
Barish, Charles Franklin *internist, gastroenterologist, researcher*
Bateman, Angela Anderson *anesthetist*
Baynes, Ronald Edward *pharmacologist, educator*
Doyle, Kevin Michael *otolaryngologist*
Gordon, Morris Aaron *medical mycologist*
Hardison, Cynthia Ann Stoltze *retired hematologist, oncologist*
Hawkins, Eleanor Carroll *veterinary educator*
Hughes, Francis P. *medical association administrator*
Parsons, William Jonathan *cardiologist*
Riviere, Jim Edmond, Jr. *pharmacologist, toxicologist, educator*
Speer, Kevin Paul *surgeon*

Research Triangle Park
Roses, Allen David *neurologist, educator*

Southern Pines
Warren, Donald William *medical and dental educator*

Southport
Kahai, Jugta *pediatrician*

Thomasville
Sprinkle, Robert Lee, Jr. *podiatrist*

Tryon
Mellberg, James Richard *retired dental research chemist*

Waxhaw
Edwards, Irene Elizabeth (Libby) *dermatologist, educator, medical researcher*

Waynesville
McKinney, Alexander Stuart *retired neurologist*

Wilmington
De Maria, Alfred Anthony *neurologist*
Richey, Luke Merritt *otolaryngologist, researcher*
Stratas, Byron Aristotle *ophthalmologist*
Wilkins, Lucien Sanders *gastroenterologist*

Wilson
Kushner, Michael James *neurologist, consultant, educator*
Ladwig, Harold Allen *neurologist*

Winston Salem
Atala, Anthony John *surgeon*
Donofrio, Peter Daniel *neurology educator*

Dyer, Raymond B. *diagnostic radiology physician*
Eldridge, J. Charles *endocrinologist, educator, researcher*
Ferree, Carolyn Ruth *retired radiation oncologist, educator*
Fleischer, Alan Bernard, Jr. *dermatologist, educator*
Griffin, Andrew Steven *urologist*
Hammon, John William, Jr. *medical educator, thoracic surgeon*
Harle, Thomas Stanley *radiologist*
Herrington, David McLeod *cardiologist, educator*
Howell, Charles Maitland *dermatologist*
James, Francis Marshall III *anesthesiologist*
Kaur, Mandeep *dermatologist, educator*
Kohut, Robert Irwin *otolaryngologist, educator*
Lipscomb, Lewis D. *obstetrician, gynecologist*
Maynard, Charles Douglas *radiologist*
Mclorie, Gordon Arthur *urologist, educator*
Meis, Paul Jean *retired obstetrics and gynecology educator*
Moody, Dixon McGuire *radiologist*
O'Donovan, Cormac A. *neurologist, educator*
O'Steen, Wendall Keith *anatomist, neurologist, educator*
Podgorny, George *emergency physician*
Powell, Bayard Lowery *oncologist, educator*
Simon, Jimmy Louis *pediatrician, educator*
Sink, Kaycee M. *geriatrician, medical educator*
Stein, Barry Edward *medical educator*
Tannu, Nilesh Suresh *medical researcher*
Toole, James Francis *medical educator*
Torti, Frank Michael *internist, health facility administrator*
Weller, Robert Stephen *anesthesiologist*

NORTH DAKOTA

Bismarck
Leidenix, Monte John *ophthalmologist, researcher*
Spagnolia, Thomas Nickolas *neurosurgeon, consultant*

Fargo
Mitchell, James Edward *physician, educator*

Grand Forks
Gaul, Gerald *ophthalmologist*
Jackson, Jon *medical educator, consultant*
Sharma, Sushil K. *medical educator*
Wakefield, Mary Katherine *medical association administrator, medical educator*
Yoshida, Glen Yoshio *otolaryngologist*

Williston
Adducci, Joseph Edward *obstetrician, gynecologist*

OHIO

Akron
Allen, Marc Kevin *emergency physician, educator*
Emmett, John Colin *retired inventor, consultant*
Evans, Douglas McCullough *surgeon, educator*
Henry, Jed William *urologist*
Milsted, Amy *biomedical educator*
Schoenfeld, Andrew Jason *orthopedist, surgeon*
Timmons, Gerald Dean *pediatric neurologist*

Athens
Bacal, Kira *emergency physician, educator*

Avon Lake
Poblete, J. Vicente *medical director*

Batavia
Siddiqi, Munawar *anesthesiologist, consultant*

Beachwood
Friedman, Arnold Bernard *retired pediatrician*
Moskowitz, Roland Wallace *internist*
Varner, Arthur E. *allergist, researcher*

Bexley
Yashon, David *neurosurgeon, educator*

Bratenahl
Jones, Trevor Owen *biomedical industry executive, management consultant*

Brunswick
Kuchynski, Marie *physician*

Bryan
Carrico, Virgil Norman *physician*

Canton
Howland, Willard J. *radiologist, educator*
Nadas, John Adalbert *psychiatrist, educator*

Chagrin Falls
Lingl, Friedrich Albert *psychiatrist*

Chardon
Dobyns, Brown McIlvaine *retired surgeon, educator*
Kellis, Michael John *osteopathic physician*

Cincinnati
Alexander, James Wesley *surgeon, educator*
Bellet, Paul Sanders *pediatrician, educator*
Biro, Frank M. *pediatrics educator*
Bissler, John Joseph *nephrologist, educator*
Boat, Thomas Frederick *pediatrician, pulmonologist, researcher, educator*
Boyd, Deborah Ann *pediatrician*
Buncher, Charles Ralph *epidemiologist, educator, biostatistician*
Ching, Ho *surgeon*
Coberly, LeAnn *internist*
de Courten-Myers, Gabrielle Marguerite *retired neuropathologist*
Dick, Barry Lee *surgeon*
Diwan, Abhinav *medical educator, researcher*
Do, Twee T. *orthopedist*
Dunsker, Stewart B. *neurosurgeon*
Goebel, Jens *physician*
Harding, Warren Gamaliel III *surgeon*
Heaton, Charles Lloyd *dermatologist, educator*
Heimlich, Henry J. *physician, surgeon, educator*
Hess, Evelyn Victorine *medical educator*
Hillard, James Randolph *psychiatry educator*
Howington, John *thoracic surgeon, educator*
Joffe, Stephen Neal *surgeon, medical educator*
Keck, Paul E., Jr. *psychiatrist*
Kereiakes, Dean James *cardiologist*
Kircher, Christopher *neurologist, consultant*
Kleindorfer, Dawn Olson *medical educator, neurologist*
Kuntz, Charles, IV, *neurosurgeon*
Lehmann, Corinne E. *medical educator*
Levinson, Joseph E. *retired internist, rheumatologist, educator*
Lichtin, Leon (Judah Leon Lichtin) *retired pharmaceutical educator*
Loftus, Jean M. *plastic surgeon*
Loggie, Jennifer Mary Hildreth *retired physician, educator*
Long, Don Scott *physiatrist*
Lower, Elyse E. *physician, educator*
Maeder, Michael C. *endocrinologist*
Maltz, Robert *surgeon*
Mehta, Parinda Apurva *pediatrician, medical educator, hematologist, oncologist*
Munir, Muhammad *pain medicine physician, director*
Nakata, Akinori *epidemiologist, psychologist, researcher*
Nussbaum, Michael Scot *physician, medical educator*
O'Hara, Sara Marie *radiologist*
Pathak, Sanjeev *psychiatrist, researcher*
Pomerantz, Wendy Jane *pediatrician, educator*
Reddy, Likith V. *maxillofacial surgeon, director*
Sarembock, Ian Joseph *internist, cardiologist*
Schreiner, Albert William *internist, educator*
Simpson, Lisa Ann *physician, educator*
Sundberg, Ruth Dorothy *hematologist, educator*
Visscher, Marty Orrico *biomedical researcher*
Welsh, George Franklin *plastic surgeon, educator*
West, Clark Darwin *pediatric nephrologist, educator*
Whitsett, Jeffrey Allen *pediatric educator*
Wiot, Jerome Francis *radiologist*
Wood, Robert Emerson *pediatrics educator*
Yi, Michael *internist, pediatrician*

Cleveland
Agani, Faton Hilmi *anatomist, educator*
Anderson, James M. *pathologist*
Awais, George Musa *obstetrician, gynecologist*
Baker, Saul Phillip *geriatrician, cardiologist, internist*
Barnett, Gene Henry *neurosurgeon*
Berger, Melvin *allergist, immunologist*
Berger, Nathan Allen *medical educator, academic administrator*
Bethoux, François Andre *physiatrist, researcher*
Bodner, Donald Roger *urologist, medical educator*
Bowerfind, Edgar Sihler, Jr. *internist, educator, retired medical association administrator*
Boyd, Arthur Bernette, Jr. *surgeon, clergyman, beverage company executive*
Brody, Robert *dermatologist, educator*
Bruner, William Evans, II, *ophthalmologist, educator, researcher*
Castele, Theodore John *radiologist*
Cerqueira, Manuel DeCastro *nuclear medicine physician*
Chak, Amitabh *gastroenterologist, researcher*
Connors, Alfred Francis *internist, researcher*
Cooper, Gregory Scott *epidemiologist, gastroenterologist, educator*
Copelan, Edward A. *medical educator*
Cowan, Dale Harvey *internist, lawyer*
Creasey, Graham Harold *surgeon, researcher*
Daroff, Robert Barry *neurologist, educator*
Davis, Pamela Bowes *pediatric pulmonologist*
Deschenes, Isabelle *medical educator, researcher*
Dreicer, Robert *oncologist, director, medical educator*
Eiben, Robert Michael *pediatric neurologist, educator*
Ellis, Lloyd H., Jr. *emergency physician, art historian*
Elston, Robert C. *medical educator*
Eng, Charis Eu Li *oncologist, geneticist*
Falcone, Tommaso *reproductive endocrinologist*
Fazio, Victor Warren *physician, colon and rectal surgeon*
Fu, Zhenghong Alex *medical educator*
Fung, John Julian *transplant surgeon, immunologist*
Gildea, Thomas Robert *pulmonologist*
Goldman, Steven Andrew *plastic surgeon, educator*
Hajj-Ali, Rula Adel *rheumatologist, researcher*
Heresi, Gustavo A. *physician*
Hermann, Robert Ewald *retired surgeon*
Holzbach, Raymond Thomas *gastroenterologist, educator, writer*
Iannotti, Joseph Patrick *orthopedic surgeon*
Jeyakumar, Anita *pediatrician, otolaryngologist*
Kaouk, Jihad *urologist*
Kass, Lawrence *hematologist, oncologist, educator*
Kinsella, Timothy J. *radiation oncologist*
Kraay, Matthew Joseph *orthopedist, educator*
Krasuski, Richard *cardiologist*
Lamm, Michael Emanuel *pathologist, immunologist, educator*
Lefferts, William Geoffrey *internist, educator*
LeGrand, Susan Buchanan *palliative medicine physician, educator*
Lenkoski, Leo Douglas *retired psychiatrist, educator*
Levitan, Nathan *internist, hematologist, medical oncologist*
Lowe, John Burton *medical association administrator, molecular biologist, educator, pathologist*
Lytle, Bruce Whitney *cardiovascular surgeon*
Macklis, Roger Milton *physician, educator, researcher*
Malangoni, Mark Alan *surgeon, educator*
McHenry, Martin Christopher *physician, educator*
Montague, Drogo K. *urologist*
Mood, Girish Rudra Naik *physician*
Neuhauser, Duncan vonBriesen *medical educator*
Nissen, Steven E. *cardiologist, researcher*
Novick, Andrew Carl *urologist*
Olness, Karen Norma *medical educator*
Ornt, Daniel B. *physician*
Raaf, John Hart *surgeon, educator, health facility administrator*
Raghavan, Derek *oncologist, medical researcher, educator*
Rakita, Louis *retired cardiologist*
Ransohoff, Richard Milton *neurologist, researcher*
Rao, Shaoqi *medical educator*
Remick, Scot Clifton *oncologist, clinical investigator, educator*
Resnick, Martin I. *urologist, educator*
Rome, Ellen S. *physician*
Ruff, Robert Louis *neurologist, physiologist, researcher*
Shatila, Ahmad Hussain *surgeon, oncologist*
Stanton-Hicks, Michael D'Arcy *anesthesiologist, pain medicine specialist*
Stavitsky, Abram Benjamin *immunologist, educator*
Stern, Robert C. *pediatrician, medical educator*
Stewart, William James *cardiologist*
Sweetenham, John W. *medical educator*
Taylor, Harris C. *endocrinologist, consultant*
Ubogu, Eroboghene Ekamereno *physician*
Waldo, Albert Leon *internist, educator*
Walters, Mark Douglas *obstetrician, gynecologist, director*
Webster, Leslie Tillotson, Jr. *pharmacologist, educator*
Wish, Jay Barry *nephrologist, specialist*
Wolinsky, Emanuel *internist, educator*
Yetman, Randall John *plastic surgeon*
Young, Jess Ray *retired internist*

Columbus
Balcerzak, Stanley Paul *retired hematologist, oncologist, director, medical educator*
Barth, Rolf Frederick *pathologist, educator*
Berntson, Gary Glen *psychiatry, psychology and pediatrics educator*
Beversdorf, David Quentin *neurologist, researcher*
Billings, Charles Edgar *physician*
Bloomfield, Clara Derber *oncologist, educator, medical institute administrator*
Blum, William George *hematologist, clinical researcher educator*
Boué, Daniel Robert *pediatric pathologist, neuropathologist, educator*
Bullock, Joseph Daniel *pediatrician, educator*
Caniano, Donna Anne *surgeon, educator*
Capen, Charles Chabert *veterinary pathology educator*
Caragine, Louis Philip, Jr. *neurosurgeon*
Christoforidis, A. John *radiologist, educator*
Doolittle, Kenneth Herbert *retired urologist*
Ellison, Edwin Christopher *surgeon, educator*
Elsharydah, Ahmad *anesthesiologist*
Galantowicz, Mark Edward *cardiothoracic surgeon*
Ghafourifar, Pedram *pharmacologist, director*
Haque, Malika Hakim *pediatrician*
Huheey, Marilyn Jane *ophthalmologist, educator*
Kresty, Laura Ann *medical researcher, educator*
Lander, Ruth A. *medical association administrator*
Leier, Carl Victor *internist, cardiologist*
Lewis, Richard Phelps *cardiologist, educator*
Long, Sarah Elizabeth Brackney *physician*
Morrow, Grant III *medical research director, pediatrician*
Mueller, Charles Frederick *radiologist, educator*
Needham, Glen Ray *entomology and acarology educator, researcher*
Newton, William Allen, Jr. *pediatrician, pathologist*
Nwomeh, Benedict C. *pediatric surgeon*
Otterson, Gregory Alan *oncologist, educator*
Pease, William Stoess *physiatrist, educator*
Ruberg, Robert Lionel *surgery educator*
Rund, Douglas Andrew *emergency physician*
Ryan, James M. *cardiologist, educator*
Sayers, Martin Peter *pediatric neurosurgeon*
Smead, William Lewis *surgeon, educator*
Stoner, Gary David *cancer researcher*
Tomczak, Rodney Louis *retired surgeon, medical educator*
Valdivia Arenas, Martin A. *pulmonary and critical care physician*
Vogel, Thomas Timothy *surgeon, educator, lay worker*
Wise, William Edward, Jr. *colon and rectal surgeon, oncologist*
Yu, Chack Yung *pediatrics educator, molecular biologist*

Dayton
Ambalavanan, Siva *nephrologist, educator*
Chin, Hong Woo *oncologist, educator, researcher*
Gillig, Paulette Marie *psychiatry educator, researcher*
Mohler, Stanley Ross *preventive medicine physician, educator*
Monk, Susan Marie *pediatrician, educator*
Mosier, William Arthur *psychiatrist, psychotherapist, director, medical educator, researcher*
Nanagas, Maria Teresita Cruz *pediatrician, educator*
Prayson, Michael J. *orthopedic surgeon, medical educator, director*
Ruegsegger, Donald Ray, Jr. *radiological physicist, educator*
Weinberg, Sylvan Lee *cardiologist, educator, editor, writer*
Wilson, William Campbell McFarland *gastroenterologist*

Fairfield
Wilson, James Miller, IV, *cardiovascular surgeon, educator*

Galena
Berggren, Ronald Bernard *surgeon, retired educator*

Gallipolis
Senthil Nathan, Selvaraj *internist, geriatrician*

Grove City
Kilman, James William *surgeon, educator*

Jackson
Dallura, Sal Anthony *physician*

Kettering
Cline, Allen Lee *endocrinologist, medical educator*
De Guzman, Ricardo D. *retired physician*

Madison
Stafford, Arthur Charles *medical association administrator*

Mansfield
Capaldo, Guy *obstetrician, gynecologist*
Houston, William Robert Montgomery *ophthalmologist, surgeon*

Mason
Beary, John Francis III *rheumatologist, pharmaceutical executive, medical researcher*

North Canton
Di Simone, Robert Nicholas *radiologist, educator*

Norwalk
Gutowicz, Matthew Francis, Jr. *radiologist*

Norwood
Wright, Creighton Bolter *cardiovascular surgeon, educator*

Port Clinton
Woodson, Riley Donald *thoracic and cardiovascular surgeon, lawyer*

Rootstown
Nora, Lois Margaret *neurologist, educator, academic administrator, dean*

Shaker Heights
Smith, Jonathan David *medical educator*

Solon
Kratche, Richard P. *physician*

Springfield
Kurian, Pius *nephrologist, educator*

Steubenville
Reddy, Vardhan Jonnala *surgeon*

Sylvania
Burkhart, Craig Garrett *dermatologist, research*

Toledo
Barrett, Michael John *anesthesiologist*
Comerota, Anthony James *vascular surgeon, biomedical researcher*
Ebraheim, Nabil Anwar *orthopedist, surgeon*
Elmer, Lawrence William *neurologist, research*
Jacobs, Lloyd A. *vascular surgeon*
Kanjwal, Mohammed Y. *cardiologist*
Maiwald, Diane Cecile *dermatologist*
Mrak, Robert Emil *neuropathologist, educator*
Mulrow, Patrick Joseph *medical educator*
Rejent, Marian Magdalen *retired pediatrician*
Shaikh, Bahu Sultan *physician, educator*
Shelley, Walter Brown *dermatologist, educator*
Talmage, Lance Allen *obstetrician, gynecologi military officer*

Uniontown
Krabill, Robert Elmer *osteopathic physician*

Westerville
St. Pierre, Ronald Leslie *public health and medical educator, academic administrator*

Willoughby
Carter, John Robert *retired physician*

Wooster
Zink, Harry A. *ophthalmologist*

Worthington
Winter, Chester Caldwell *surgeon, educator, historian, writer*

Yellow Springs
Von Gierke, Henning Edgar *biomedical scienc educator, former government official, researcher*

Zanesville
Ray, John Walker *otolaryngologist, educator, broadcast commentator*

OKLAHOMA

Claremore
Whinery, Michael Albert *physician*
Wittenberg, Henry Taylor, Jr. *physician, surge*

nond
ns, Donald E. *physiatrist*

gfisher
vell, Arthur Wilcox *physician, surgeon*

vton
o, Orville Lynn *retired physician,*
armacologist, educator

skogee
, Bartis Milton *retired physician*

man
, John Robert *retired physician*

ahoma City
ews, Mitchell Dewayne *internist, educator,*
an
gbola, Oluwatoyin Fatai *pediatric renal*
ysician, researcher
ardus, Carl Robert, Jr. *radiologist, educator*
alis, John Russell *physician*
in, James Robert *pediatrician, allergist*
ns, William Edward, Jr. *aeromedical*
ministrator, researcher, psychologist
p, Philip Cinnamon *medical researcher*
in, Daniel Joseph *urologist, educator,*
partment chairman
y, Warren Vernon *allergist*
ster, David William *plastic surgeon*
ntelli, James William *ophthalmic plastic*
rgeon
erstadt, Donald Bruce *urologist, educator*
npton, James Wilburn *hematologist,*
icologist
olds, Jay Alan *radiologist, nuclear medicine*
ysician
lonee, Sue *epidemiologist, researcher*
r, Bakr M. *surgeon, health facility*
lministrator
e, David Wilkin, II, *ophthalmologist,*
lucator, health facility administrator
z-Cruet, Jorge *geriatric psychiatrist,*
searcher
ferbaum, Betty Jane *psychiatrist, educator*
ades, Everett Ronald *medical educator*
savik, Ivar Kristian *obstetrician, gynecologist*
in, Richard A. *orthopedic surgeon*
lani, Udho *physician, cardiologist*
sh, Jack Daryl *retired medical educator,*
riter
dom, Peggy Jean *neurologist*
raich, Mark Lee *pediatrician, educator*
di, Nazih *retired surgeon*

asso
l, Walter George, Jr. *retired osteopath*

lwater
fer, Anthony Wayne *veterinary pathologist,*
lucator
per, Donald Lee *physician*
ng, Sidney Alton *veterinary medical*
lucator, parasitologist
ng, Guolong *immunologist, educator*

sa
ofleisch, John McDowell *cardiologist,*
lucator
autti, Ronald Stephan *orthopedist*
Cullough, Robert Dale, II, *osteopath*
les, John Barnwell *obstetrics and gynecology*
lucator
nket, Daniel Clark *pediatrician, educator*
, Burhan *retired physician*

ita
r, Charles Sumner, II, *orthopedic surgeon,*
lucator

REGON

nd
gletary, DeJuan Theresa *child and adolescent*
sychiatrist

rvallis
rd, William McKenzie *chemical*
arcinogenesis researcher, biochemistry
rofessor

gene
lis, Dennis K. *orthopedic surgeon*
vell, Mark Laurence *plastic surgeon*
nball, Reid Roberts *psychiatrist*
escher, Richard Alvin *retired*
astroenterologist
e, Thomas Leroy Willis *retired pediatrician*

esham
ok, John Edwin *surgeon*

ke Oswego
chens, Tyra Thornton *pathologist, educator*
en, Robert Michael *anesthesiologist, writer*

edford
ll, Roger V. *cardiac surgeon*
ekhar, Stephen S. *obstetrician, gynecologist*

ilwaukie
lovsky, Robert Joel *naturopathic physician,*
pharmacist, educator

rth Plains
ood, James Anderson *cardiac surgeon*

egon City
rke, William Romney *urologist*

rtland
ker, Diane R.H. *dermatologist*
ll, Melvyn *medical educator*
rry, John Maynard *urologist*
er, Tomasz M. *physician*

Bennett, William Michael *internist, educator, nephrologist*
Blank, Eugene *pediatrician, radiologist, educator*
Blanke, Charles D. *medical educator*
Bloom, Joseph D. *psychiatrist, medical educator*
Campbell, John Richard *pediatric surgeon*
Carter, Charles Conrad *medical educator*
Casey, Daniel E. *psychiatrist, educator*
Conlin, Michael Joseph *physician*
Crawshaw, Ralph *psychiatrist*
Druker, Brian Jay *medical educator, researcher*
Fraunfelder, Frederick Theodore *ophthalmologist, educator*
Goodman, Richard H. *biomedical researcher*
Greer, Monte Arnold *endocrinologist, educator*
Hamilton, Bronwyn Elizabeth *radiologist*
Hedges, Jerris *medical educator, health services researcher*
Jacob, Stanley Wallace *surgeon, educator*
Kendall, John Walker, Jr. *internist, researcher, dean*
Liem, Timothy K. *surgeon*
Mandel, Gail *immunologist*
Ng, John Daniel *ophthalmologist, educator*
Patterson, James Randolph *physician*
Prendergast, William John *ophthalmologist*
Rushanaedy, Agustinus *urologist*
Schmidt, Waldemar Adrian *pathologist, educator*
Scott, John D. *pharmacologist*
Shangraw, Robert Edward *medical educator, researcher*
Sutherland, Donald Wood *retired cardiologist*
Swanstrom, Lee Leray *surgeon*
Taylor, Robert Brown *physician, educator, writer*
Wilson, William Harwell *psychiatrist, educator*
Zerbe, Kathryn Jane *psychiatrist*

Roseburg
Oliphant, Charles Romig *retired physician*

PENNSYLVANIA

Allentown
Barraco, Robert Don *surgeon*
Chang, Chris C.N. *pediatric surgeon*
Chowdary, Raj P. *plastic surgeon*
Gaylor, Donald Hughes *surgeon, educator*
Maffeo, Alphonse A. *anesthesiologist*
Palumbo, Robert Craig *sports medicine physician, director, not-for-profit developer*
Szwerc, Michael Francis *thoracic surgeon*

Allison Park
Dodani, Sunita *physician, educator*
Hollerman, Charles Edward *retired pediatrician*

Altoona
Gurman, Andrew William *orthopedist, educator*
McKibbin, Ralph David *gastroenterologist, consultant*

Bakerstown
Beachley, Michael Charles *radiologist*

Bala Cynwyd
Glat, Paul Mitchell *plastic surgeon*
Masket, Samuel *medical association administrator*
Mezrow, Craig *plastic surgeon*
Shore, Eric Eugene *internist, consultant, lawyer*

Bethel Park
Tranovich, Michael A. *orthopedist*

Bethlehem
Cole, Jack Eli *physician*

Bradford
Laroche, Roger Renan *psychiatrist*

Bryn Mawr
Brunt, Manly Yates, Jr. *psychiatrist*
Godinez, Marye H. *anesthesiologist*
Huth, Edward Janavel *internist, educator, editor*
Levitt, Robert E. *gastroenterologist*
Liu, Hans Hamilton *infectious disease physician, educator*
Noone, R. Barrett *plastic surgeon*
Price, Trevor Robert Pryce *psychiatrist, educator*

Camp Hill
Tokuhata, George K. *retired medical educator, epidemiologist, consultant*
Yates, James Arthur *plastic surgeon*

Carlisle
Vickery, Jon Livingstone *neurologist*

Center Valley
Risher, William Henry *cardiothoracic surgeon, educator*

Clairton
Brodland, David G. *dermatologist, surgeon*

Coatesville
Ainslie, George William *psychiatrist*
Bell, Robert Lloyd *retired neurosurgeon*
Lee, Daniel *retired physician, public health service officer*
Makous, Norman *retired internist, cardiologist, educator*

Collegeville
Stiles, Gary Lester *cardiologist, molecular pharmacologist, educator*

Cranberry Township
Walsh, Arthur Campbell *retired psychiatrist*

Danville
Blankenship, James Colegrove *cardiologist*
Pierce, James Clarence *surgeon, educator*
Ramdas, Jagadeesh *physician*

Darby
Eiser, Arnold Robert *physician executive, bioethicist, nephrologist, internist*

Devon
Earley, Laurence Elliott *retired medical educator*

Dillsburg
Jackson, George Lyman *retired nuclear medicine physician*

Dunmore
Sebastianelli, Mario Joseph *internist, nephrologist, health facility administrator*

Easton
Grunberg, Robert Leon Willy *nephrologist, educator*
Trigiano, Lucien Lewis *physician*

Erie
Mason, Gregg Claude *orthopedic surgeon, researcher*
Michaelides, Doros Nikita *internist, medical educator*

Exton
Smith, Joseph Lorenzo, II, *otolaryngologist*

Fort Washington
Pappas, Charles Engelos *plastic surgeon*

Fountainville
Brown, Madeline Morgan *internist*

Gaines
Beller, Martin Leonard *retired orthopaedic surgeon*

Gap
Klinefelter, Hylda Catharine *retired obstetrician, gynecologist*

Gibsonia
Krause, Helen Fox *retired otolaryngologist*

Gladwyne
Katz, Julian *gastroenterologist, educator*
Kaye, Donald *internist, educator*
Morrison, Gail *internist, nephrologist, educator*
Pendergrass, Henry Pancoast *radiologist, nuclear medicine physician*
Webber, John Bentley *orthopedic surgeon*

Glenside
Reiss, George Russell, Jr. *physician*

Greensburg
Gebrosky, Norman Paul *urologist*

Harrisburg
Frankel, Carl Abbott *ophthalmologist*
Logue, James Nicholas *epidemiologist*
Rudy, Frank R. *pathologist*

Haverford
Aronson, Carl Edward *pharmacology and toxicology educator*
Goppelt, John Walter *physician, psychiatrist*

Hershey
Caputo, Gregory Michael *internist, educator*
Cherry, Robert A. *surgeon*
Davis, Dwight *cardiologist, educator*
Eyster, Mary Elaine *hematologist, educator*
Kauffman, Gordon Lee, Jr. *surgeon, educator*
Madewell, John Edward *radiologist*
Marks, James Garfield, Jr. *dermatologist*
Naeye, Richard L. *pathologist, educator*
Pierce, William Schuler *cardiac surgeon*
Quraishi, Sadeq Ali *anesthesiologist, educator*
Reese, Carl Thomas *urologist*
Rohner, Thomas John, Jr. *urologist*
Severs, Walter Bruce *pharmacology educator, researcher*
Tan, Tjiauw-Ling *psychiatrist, educator*
Thomas, Patrick Robert Maxwell *oncologist, educator, academic administrator*
Uhde, Thomas Whitley *psychopharmacology, psychiatrist*
Vender, Robert Louis *medical educator*
Vesell, Elliot Saul *pharmacologist, educator*
Waldhausen, John Anton *retired surgeon, editor*
Wassner, Steven Joel *pediatric nephrologist, educator*
Zelis, Robert Felix *cardiologist, educator*

Horsham
DeHoratius, Raphael Joseph *rheumatologist*

Hummelstown
Biebuyck, Julien Francois *anesthesiologist, medical administrator, educator*

Huntingdon Valley
DiBello, Joseph Nicholas *plastic surgeon*

Jenkintown
Greenspan-Margolis, June E. *psychiatrist*
Sadoff, Robert Leslie *psychiatrist, educator*

Kennett Square
Brooks, Joae Graham *psychiatrist*
Richardson, Dean Wheeler *equine surgeon, veterinary educator*

Lancaster
Burlingame, Mark Wayne *cardiothoracic surgeon*
Kendall, Leigh Wakefield *surgeon, hospital administrator*

Lansdale
Schwartz, Louis Winn *ophthalmologist*
Sensenig, David Martin *retired surgeon*

Lower Gwynedd
Pendleton, Robert Grubb *pharmacologist*

Malvern
Saruk, Michael *dermatologist, educator*
Zaleski, John R. *medical researcher*

Media
Li, Weiye *ophthalmologist, educator, biochemist*

Middletown
Walters, Marian R. *research administrator*

Monongahela
Yovanof, Silvana *physician*

Mount Gretna
Agudo, Mercedes Engracia *psychiatrist*

Narberth
Strom, Brian Leslie *internist, educator*

New Castle
Panella, Michael Joseph *pathologist, lawyer*

New Hope
Ecker, Sidney Wolf *urologist, consultant*
Raabe, Gerhard Karl *epidemiologist*

New Tripoli
Hess, Darla Bakersmith *cardiologist, educator*

Newtown
Somers, Anne Ramsay *retired medical educator*

Newtown Square
Cordes, Eugene Harold *retired pharmacy and chemistry educator*
de Rivas, Carmela Foderaro *retired psychiatrist, health facility administrator*

North Wales
Calder, Robert Austin *preventive medicine physician, administrator*
Gorby-Schmidt, Martha Louise *pharmacologist, researcher*

Paoli
Burget, Dean Edwin, Jr. *plastic surgeon*

Pennsburg
Shuhler, Phyllis Marie *physician*

Philadelphia
Acker, Michael A. *thoracic surgeon, educator*
Adetunji, Babatunde Abayomi *forensic psychiatrist*
Allen, Julian Lewis *medical educator, researcher*
Ances, Beau M. *neurologist*
Arce, A. Anthony *psychiatrist, educator*
Asbury, Arthur Knight *neurologist, educator*
Baltuch, Gordon Hirsh *neurosurgeon*
Barchi, Robert Lawrence *clinical neurologist*
Barker, Clyde Frederick *surgeon, educator*
Bartlett, Scott Paul *plastic surgeon*
Baserga, Renato Luigi *pathology educator*
Baum, Stanley *radiologist, educator*
Baxt, William Gordon *medical educator*
Beck, Aaron Temkin *psychiatrist, educator*
Beck, John Robert *pathologist, information scientist*
Becker, Lance B. *medical educator*
Bibbo, Marluce *physician, educator*
Bilaniuk, Larissa Tetiana *neuroradiologist, educator*
Boden, Guenther *endocrinologist*
Bove, Alfred Anthony *medical educator*
Bowman, Marjorie Ann *physician, educator*
Brady, Luther W., Jr. *radiologist, educator*
Brooks, John Samuel Joseph *pathologist, researcher*
Brozena, Susan C. *cardiologist*
Brunk, Samuel Frederick *oncologist*
Callahan, James Michael *physician, educator*
Cassel, Christine Karen *physician*
Chen, Lan X. *physician, educator*
Chiu, Alexander G. *otolaryngologist, educator*
Clearfield, Harris Reynold *physician*
Colman, Robert Wolf *hematologist, educator*
Conn, Rex Boland, Jr. *pathologist, educator*
Cooper, Edward Sawyer *cardiologist, internist, educator*
Corbin, Theodore J., Jr. *emergency physician*
Cotsarelis, George *dermatologist, educator*
Dalinka, Murray Kenneth *radiologist, educator*
Daly, John M. *surgeon, educator*
D'Angio, Giulio John *radiologist, educator*
Dasgupta, Indranil *physician, educator*
Davis, Glenn Craig *psychiatrist*
Dichter, Marc Allen *physician*
DiPalma, Joseph Rupert *pharmacology educator, dean*
Djerassi, Isaac *medical researcher*
Doty, Richard L. *medical researcher*
Douglas, Steven Daniel *immunologist, educator, director*
Ehrlich, George Edward *rheumatologist, consultant*
Eisen, Howard Joel *internist, researcher*
Eisenberg, Ted Steven *plastic and reconstructive surgeon*
Feldman, Arthur M. *cardiologist*
Feldman, Jeffrey Mark *anesthesiologist*
Finck, Christine M. *pediatric surgeon, educator*
Fisher, Robert *gastroenterologist, health facility administrator*
Fishman, Alfred Paul *physician*
Foti, Margaret *medical association administrator, editor, consultant*
Frank, Barbara Balis *gastroenterologist, educator*
Friedman, Harvey Michael *infectious diseases educator*
Gaiser, Robert Raymond *obstetric anesthesiologist, educator*
Gartland, John Joseph *physician, writer*
Gausas, Roberta Elisabeth *oculoplastic and orbital surgeon*

Gavrin, Jonathan Robert *medical educator, internist*
Gerner, Edward William *medical educator*
Glick, Jane Mills *biomedical researcher, educator*
Glick, John H. *oncologist, medical educator*
Goldfarb, Stanley *internist, educator*
Gonzalez-Scarano, Francisco Antonio *neurologist, virologist*
Greenstein, Jeffrey Ian *neurologist*
Gueson, Emerita Torres *obstetrician, gynecologist*
Hadjiliadis, Denis *physician*
Hansen-Flaschen, John Hyman *medical educator, researcher*
Herling, Irving Marc *internal medicine educator, cardiologist*
Horwitz, Eric M. *radiation oncologist*
Hou, J. Steve *pathologist*
Jessup, Mariell *physician, director*
Jimenez, Sergio A. *internist, educator, rheumatologist*
Johnson, Joseph Eggleston III *physician, educator*
Jordan, V. Craig *endocrine pharmacologist, educator*
Kaiser, Larry Robert *thoracic surgeon*
Kang, Ju-Seop *medical educator, consultant, medical researcher*
Kang, Yoogoo *anesthesiologist, educator*
Kaufman, Russel Eugene *hematologist, oncologist*
Kazazian, Haig Hagop, Jr. *pediatrician, researcher, educator*
Kefalides, Nicholas Alexander *physician, educator*
Kelley, William Nimmons *physician, educator, science administrator, dean*
Kennedy, David William *otolaryngologist, medical administrator, educator*
Klein, Michael Elihu *physician*
Knudson, Alfred George, Jr. *medical geneticist*
Kresh, J. Yasha *cardiovascular researcher, educator*
Kurtz, Alfred Bernard *radiologist*
Lee, David Inkoo *urologist*
Lee, Virginia M. -Y. *medical educator, health science association administrator*
Leventhal, Lawrence Jay *rheumatologist, educator*
Levinson, Arnold Irving *allergist, immunologist*
Levitt, Jerry David *medical educator*
Lewis, Frank Russell, Jr. *surgeon*
Limoges, Richard Frederick *psychiatrist*
Lippa, Carol Frances *neurologist*
Lipshutz, Laurel Sprung *psychiatrist*
Long, Sarah Sundborg *pediatrician, educator*
Lubiniecki, Gregory Michael *physician*
Luger, Selina *medical educator*
Ma, Xin-Liang *biomedical researcher, educator*
Madow, Leo *psychiatrist, educator*
Malkowicz, Stanley Bruce *urologist*
Mancall, Elliott Lee *retired neurologist, educator*
Marcotte, Paul John *neurosurgeon, educator*
Margo, Katherine Lane *family physician, educator*
Marino, Ignazio Roberto *transplant surgeon, educator, researcher*
Mastroianni, Luigi, Jr. *physician, educator*
McGuire, Kandace Peterson *surgeon*
Meropol, Neal J. *oncologist, researcher*
Ming, Si-Chun *pathologist, educator*
Morrow, Monica *medical educator*
Mullin, Daniel Karl *emergency physician, educator*
Nash, David Bret *physician*
Naylor, Mary D. *medical professor, director*
Nimoityn, Philip *cardiologist*
Nowell, Peter Carey *pathologist, educator*
O'Malley, Bert William, Jr. *head and neck surgeon, educator, researcher*
Panitch, Howard Barry *pediatric pulmonologist*
Pfeifer, Samantha M. *obstetrician, gynecologist*
Pien, Grace *medical educator*
Potsic, William Paul *otolaryngologist, educator*
Rickels, Karl *psychiatrist, educator*
Ritchie, Wallace Parks, Jr. *retired surgeon, educator*
Rogers, Fred Baker *medical educator*
Rorke-Adams, Lucy Balian *pathologist, educator*
Rosen, Arye *microwave, optoelectronics and medical researcher*
Rubin, Stephen Curtis *gynecologic oncologist, educator*
Russo, Irma Haydee Alvarez de *pathologist*
Savage, Michael Paul *cardiologist, educator*
Schotland, Donald Lewis *retired medical educator, neurologist*
Schumacher, H(arry) Ralph *internist, rheumatologist, medical educator, researcher*
Schwartz, Gordon Francis *surgeon, educator*
Schwartz, Marshall Zane *pediatric surgeon*
Segal, Bernard Louis *cardiologist, educator*
Shapiro, Sandor Solomon *hematologist*
Shuman, Charles R. *medical educator, internist*
Silberberg, Donald H. *neurologist*
Smith, David Stuart *anesthesiology educator, physician*
Son, Young-Jin *medical educator*
Sox, Harold Carleton, Jr. *physician, educator, editor*
Spaeth, George Link *ophthalmologist, educator, writer*
Spergel, Jonathan Michael *pediatrician, allergist, immunologist, researcher*
Stallings, Virginia A. *pediatric gastroenterologist*
Stuart, Marie Jean *physician, hematologist, researcher*
Stunkard, Albert James *psychiatrist, educator*
Suh, Byungse *medical educator*
Suzuki, Jon Byron *medical educator, periodontist, microbiologist*
Tannen, Richard Laurence *nephrology educator*
Thompson, Craig B. *physician*
Tooker, John Phillip *internist, educator, medical association administrator*
Torg, Joseph Steven *orthopaedic surgeon, educator*
Tourtellotte, Charles Dee *internist, rheumatologist, educator*
Tran, Judith Thuha *psychiatrist*
Trojanowski, John Q. *medical educator, health facility administrator*
Van Arsdalen, Keith Norman *urologist*
vanBemmelen, Paul S. *surgeon, educator*
Velazquez, Omaida Caridad *vascular surgeon, researcher*
Volgin, Denys V. *medical researcher*
Wein, Alan Jerome *urologist, educator, researcher*
Weitz, Howard Hy *cardiologist, educator*
Weller, Elizabeth Boghossian *child and adolescent psychiatrist*
Whitaker, Linton Andin *plastic surgeon*
Willi, Steven Matthew *physician, educator, researcher*
Wolfe, John Hall *medical researcher, educator, consultant*
Woody, George Edward *psychiatrist, educator*
Wu, Hong *pathologist*
Yanoff, Myron *ophthalmologist*
Young, Donald Stirling *clinical pathology educator*
Young, Robert Crabill *medical researcher, science administrator, internist*
Zderic, Stephen Anthony *urologist, surgeon*
Zweiman, Burton *allergist, immunologist, educator*

Pittsburgh
Adelson, P. David *pediatric neurosurgeon*
Aggarwal, Shushma *anesthesiologist, educator*
Allen, Thomas E. *obstetrician, gynecologist*
Aneja, Rajesh *medical educator, pediatrician*
Bodnar, Lisa M. *medical educator*
Bradley, James P. *orthopedist*
Brent, David A. *psychiatrist, medical educator*
Carrau, Ricardo L. *otolaryngologist, educator*
Chelly, Jacques E. *anesthesiologist*
Chi, David H. *otolaryngologist*
Cohen, Bernard Irvin *plastic surgeon*
DeGroat, William Chesney *pharmacology educator*
DeKosky, Steven Trent *neurologist*
Dixit, Balwant Narayan *pharmacology and toxicology educator*
Doft, Bernard Harvey *ophthalmologist*
Einhorn, Jerzy *internist, endocrinologist, consultant*
Fernstrom, John Dickson *pharmacology and nutrition researcher, educator*
Fiaschi-Taesch, Nathalie Madeleine *medical educator*
Fireman, Philip *pediatrician, allergist, immunologist*
Fisher, Bernard *surgeon, educator*
Fontes, Paulo A. *surgeon, educator*
Friday, Gilbert Anthony, Jr. *pediatrician*
Geskin, Larisa *dermatologist, researcher*
Good, Candace R. *psychiatrist, educator*
Greenamyre, John Timothy *medical educator*
Hardesty, Robert Lynch *surgeon, educator*
Heckler, Frederick Roger *plastic surgeon*
Herberman, Ronald Bruce *medical association administrator, immunologist*
Jannetta, Peter Joseph *neurosurgeon, educator*
Jarrett, Fredric *surgeon, educator*
Joyce, Judith Marie *radiologist*
Kassam, Amin B. *neurosurgeon, educator*
Kochanek, Patrick Michael *pediatrician, educator*
Levine, Arthur Samuel *pediatric hematologist, dean, educator, oncologist, researcher*
Levine, Macy Irving *physician*
Levine, T. Barry *cardiologist, educator*
Lunsford, Lawrence Dade *medical educator*
Lyjak Chorazy, Anna Julia *pediatrician, educator, retired health facility administrator*
Magovern, James Anthony *thoracic surgeon*
McCafferty, Leo Raymond *plastic surgeon*
Mello-Thoms, Claudia *medical educator, researcher*
Mosesso, Vincent Nicholas, Jr. *emergency physician, health facility administrator*
Muder, Robert Richard *physician, epidemiologist*
Mulsant, Benoit Henri *psychiatrist, educator, medical researcher*
Muluk, Satish Chandra *vascular surgeon*
Myers, Eugene Nicholas *otolaryngologist, educator*
Needleman, Herbert Leroy *psychiatrist, pediatrician*
Noeckert, Robert J. *ophthalmologist, educator*
Orenstein, David M. *medical educator*
Palevsky, Paul Marc *nephrologist, educator*
Pollack, Ian Fredric *physician, researcher*
Quigley, Matthew Richard *neurosurgeon*
Rogers, Robert Mark *physician*
Roth, Loren H. *psychiatrist*
Russo, Linda M. *pediatric cardiologist*
Sanfilippo, Joseph Salvatore *gynecologic endocrinologist, educator*
Sherman, Frederick Scott *pediatric cardiologist*
Siker, Ephraim S. *anesthesiologist*
Simmons, Richard L. *surgeon*
Snyderman, Carl Henry *otolaryngologist*
Solano, Francis X., Jr. *internist*
Soran, Z. Ozlem *medical educator*
Stein, Bradley Daniel *child and adolescent psychiatrist, researcher*
Vogel, Victor Gerald *medical educator, researcher*
Wald, Niel *public health educator*
Wedhsler, Lawrence Richard *neurologist, educator*
Winter, Peter Michael *anesthesiologist, educator*
Yellon, Robert Forrest *surgeon, medical educator*
Zafonte, Ross D. *physiatrist*

Plymouth Meeting
Nobel, Joel J. *biomedical researcher*

Radnor
Liang, Bailin *immunologist*
Silvestry, Frank E. *cardiologist*

Reading
Lusch, Charles Jack *oncologist, director*
Pumariega, Andres Julio *medical administrator, educator, researcher*

Rydal
Johnson, Waine Cecil *dermatologist, educator*

Sayre
Ali, Arshad *medical researcher*
Moody, Robert Adams *neurosurgeon*

Sellersville
Rilling, David Carl *surgeon*

Somerset
Nair, Velupillai Krishnan *cardiologist*

Springfield
Sing, Robert Fong *physician*

Strasburg
Morton, D. Holmes *physician*

Sugarloaf
Waldron, Theodore Charles *physician*

Swarthmore
Carey, William Bacon *pediatrician, educator*

Swiftwater
Bybel, Michael John *medical researcher*

Temple
Denaro, Anthony Thomas *psychiatrist*

Thorndale
Hodess, Arthur Bart *cardiologist*

University Park
Stern, Robert Morris *gastroenterologist, psychologist, researcher*

Upper Saint Clair
Raymond, Bruce Allen *retired surgeon, medical association administrator*

Waynesboro
Cryer, Theodore Hudson *ophthalmologist, educator*

West Conshohocken
Templeton, John Marks, Jr. *retired pediatric surgeon, foundation administrator*

West Grove
Snow, James Byron, Jr. *otolaryngologist, research administrator, educator*

West Reading
Sutherland, Robert D. *orthopedist, surgeon*

Wilkes Barre
Casale, Alfred Stanley *thoracic and cardiovascular surgeon*

Williamsport
Martin, Thomas John *pediatrician, sports medicine physician*

Wyndmoor
Brown, Gary Christian *ophthalmologist, director*

Wynnewood
Alter, Milton *retired neurologist*
Frankl, William Stewart *cardiologist, educator*
Marks, Gerald *surgeon, educator*
Rosefsky, Jonathan Benensohn *pediatrician*

Wyomissing
Hildreth, Eugene A. *physician, educator*

Yardley
Fraser, David William *epidemiologist*
Newsom, John Harlan *physician*

York
Rhoads, Jonathan Evans, Jr. *surgeon, medical educator*

RHODE ISLAND

Barrington
Carpenter, Charles Colcock Jones *internist, educator*

Kingston
Blissmer, Bryan *medical researcher, educator*

Newport
Rous, Stephen Norman *urologist, educator*

North Kingstown
Jarvis, William David *pharmacologist, researcher*

Pawtucket
Chopra, Pradeep *physician, educator*
Crowley, James Patrick *hematologist, medical educator, immunologist*
Glicksman, Arvin S(igmund) *radiation oncologist*

Providence
Amaral, Joseph Ferreira *surgeon*
Aronson, Stanley Maynard *physician, educator*
Besdine, Richard William *medical educator, researcher*
Biron, Christine Anne *medical science educator, researcher*
Blazar, Andrew S. *reproductive endocrinologist*
Block, Stanley Hoyt *pediatrician, allergist*
Brown, Larry K. *psychiatrist, researcher*
Cady, Blake *surgical oncologist*
Degroot, Leslie Jacob *medical educator*
Donahue, John Edward *physician*
Easton, J(ohn) Donald *neurologist, educator*
Gass, Jennifer S. *oncologist, surgeon*
Gilmore, Judith Marie *physician*
Gohh, Reginald Yuchengco *nephrologist*
Guggenheim, Frederick Gibson *psychiatrist, educator*
Helfand, Stephen L. *biomedical researcher, educator*
Jenny, Carole *physician, researcher*
Kane, Agnes Brezak *pathologist, educator*
Knopf, Paul Mark *immunologist*
Kramer, Peter David *psychiatrist, psychology professor*
LaFrance, William Curt Phillip, Jr. *neuropsychiatrist, educator, medical researcher*
Lewis, David Carleton *medical educator, academic administrator*
Mayer, Kenneth Hugh *physician*
Mc Donald, Charles J. *dermatologist, educator*
Oh, William *physician*
Pueschel, Siegfried M. *pediatrician, educator*
Rhodes, Ramona Lagiers *medical educator, researcher*
Treaba, Diana Olguta *physician*
Tucci, Joseph Ralph *endocrinologist, educator*
Vezeridis, Michael Panagiotis *surgeon, educator*
Weitberg, Alan Barry *physician, researcher*
Yap, George S. *immunologist, educator*

Riverside
Lekas, Mary Despina *retired otolaryngologist*

Wakefield
Reed, LoriJean Kinsey *anesthesiologist*

Westerly
Moore, Edwin J.T. *retired obstetrician, gynecologist*

Woonsocket
Coady, Michael Anthony *surgeon, department chairman*
Wanebo, Harold J. *surgeon, educator*

SOUTH CAROLINA

Aiken
Bransome, Edwin Dagobert, Jr. *internal medicin educator*

Anderson
Chipman, Dennis Clarence, Jr. *forensic psychiatrist, consultant*

Charleston
Allen, Robert Johnson *plastic surgeon*
Austin, Linda S. *psychiatrist*
Bell, Norman Howard *retired endocrinologist, educator*
Bowman, C. Michael *physician*
Chiaramida, Salvatore *cardiologist, educator, health facility administrator*
Crawford, Fred Allen, Jr. *cardiothoracic surgeo educator*
Daniell, Herman Burch *pharmacologist*
Dobson, Richard Lawrence *dermatologist, educator*
Finn, Albert Frank, Jr. *physician*
Garr, David Ross *physician, educator*
Glassman, Armand Barry *physician, educator, scientist, administrator, pathologist*
Gupta, Monika *nephrologist, researcher*
Hartsock, Langdon All *medical educator, department chairman, physician*
Hoffman, Brenda Joyce *gastroenterology educator*
Jaffa, Ayad A. *medical educator, researcher*
Jaffe, Murray Sherwood *retired surgeon*
Khan, Mushfiquddin *neuropharmacologist, researcher*
Kraveka, Jacqueline Maria *pediatrician, oncologist, researcher, scientist*
Lazarchick, John *hematologist, educator*
Margolius, Harry Stephen *pharmacologist, physician*
Maria, Bernard L. *pediatric neurologist*
McConnell, Bright III *orthopaedic surgeon*
McCurdy, Layton *medical educator*
Mohr, Lawrence Charles *physician*
Nixon, Daniel Walker *oncologist, researcher*
Osguthorpe, John David *otolaryngologist, educator*
Othersen, Henry Biemann, Jr. *surgeon, physician, educator*
Reves, Joseph Gerald (Jerry Reves) *anesthesiology educator, dean*
Saifan, Chadi *physician*
Simpson, William M., Jr. *family medicine educator*
Stuart, Robert Kenneth *internist, hematologist, oncologist, educator*
Underwood, Paul Benjamin *gynecologist, oncologist, educator*
Waller, John Louis *anesthesiologist, educator*
Wilson, Frederick Allen *gastroenterologist, health facility administrator, educator*

Columbia
Almond, Carl Herman *surgeon, physician, educator*
Brooker, Jeff Zeigler *retired cardiologist*
Bryan, Charles Stone *internist, educator*
da Silva, Ercio Mario *physician*
Donald, Alexander Grant *psychiatrist, educato*
Flanagan, Clyde Harvey, Jr. *psychiatrist, psychoanalyst, educator*
Gaffney, Thomas Edward *physician*
Humphries, John O'Neal *cardiologist, educato dean*
Sheppe, Joseph Andrew *surgeon*
Shmunes, Edward *dermatologist*
Still, Charles Neal *retired neurologist, medica educator, consultant*

ht, Harry Hercules *psychiatrist*

way
lillan, Michael Reid *retired orthopedic rgeon*

rence
ichele, Domenic John *neurologist, uroradiologist*
eau, Stephen Alan *allergist*

rgetown
arn, Arthur Mason *orthopedist, surgeon, nsultant*

enville
ner, Jack Wilbur III *psychiatrist, educator, lministrator*
loom II, James Robert *surgeon*
augh, Corey Andrew *bioengineering searcher*
ore, Donald Gibson, Jr. *pathologist*

ton Head Island
, Robert Eugene *retired internist*
all, Charles Patton *internist, retired ncologist*
elman, Karl *physician*
l, James Bernard *internist, educator*
es, Robert Charles *radiologist*
s, William Robert *epidemiologist, educator*
imer, Gary Lee *physician*
hrig, C(harles) Burns *internist, consultant*

ian
arty, Charles Michael *pulmonologist, searcher*

Of Palms
ott, Larry Paul *radiologist, educator*
ger, Edgar Olin III *retired obstetrics and necology educator*
ltmann, Hulda Justine *pediatrician, docrinologist*

unt Pleasant
verton, Timothy David *psychiatrist*
ze, John Christopher *dermatologist, educator*

rtle Beach
wartz, Steve Wendelin *physician*

angeburg
ak, Randolph Duncan, Jr. *surgeon*

brook
ver, Philip Jeffrey *cardiologist*

artanburg
lge, Gameel Byron *retired surgeon*
nley, Richard Turner *pediatric hematologist, ncologist*

llivans Island
y, John Bayne, Sr. *retired radiologist, edical educator*

nter
vell, Elizabeth Boykin *retired pediatrician*

rfside Beach
aro, Mary Kaye Asperheim *pediatrician, riter*

st Columbia
tzow, Friedrich Wilhelm *neuropathologist*
llips, Karen Diane *surgeon*

UTH DAKOTA

t Springs
ok, William Franklin *radiologist*

ux Falls
penter, Paul Lynn *cardiologist*
as-Melley, Adela Teresa *pediatrician, surgeon*
ton, Lawrence Jules *medical educator*
ua, Richard Allen *pathologist*
hards, George Alvarez *psychiatrist, educator*
vada, Edward Thaddeus, Jr. *physician, ducator*

nkton
ney, Brooks *gynecologist, educator*

NNESSEE

attanooga
npbell, William O'Neal *retired physician*
rshall, Willis Henry *psychiatrist*
nsey, Stephanie Denise *medical ranscriptionist*
ck, Edwin Haywood III *surgeon*

okeville
olenski, Lisabeth Ann *physician*

rmantown
wry, Robert Wilbur *pathologist, educator*

ay
nbs, Stephen Paul *pediatrician, health facility dministrator*

ndersonville
t, Alvin Miller III *anatomist, educator, cell biologist, writer*

xson
gler, Christopher Paige *surgeon, researcher*

ckson
aim, Mark Wendell *physician, molecular biologist, gastroenterologist, photographer*

Jefferson City
Muncy, Estle Pershing *physician*

Johnson City
Coogan, Philip Shields *pathologist*
Giorgadze, Tamar Alfred *pathologist, physician*
Hamdy, Ronald Charles *geriatrician*
Olsen, Martin E. *obstetrician, educator*
Pandian, Shantha G. *psychiatrist*
Rush, Daniel Scott *vascular surgeon, educator*
Taylor, Grant David *urologist*

Kingsport
Solomon, Joseph Alphous *physician*

Knoxville
Filston, Howard Church *pediatric surgeon*
Kennedy, Alfred Parker, Jr. *pediatrician, surgeon*
Kliefoth, A. Bernhard III *neurosurgeon*
Reath, David Brooke *plastic surgeon*
Wallace, Lorraine Silver *medical educator, researcher*

Maryville
Howard, Cecil Byron *retired pediatrician*

Memphis
Allen, David Mark *psychiatrist, educator, director*
Amonette, Rex. A. *physician*
Anghelescu, Doralina Lucia *anesthesiologist*
Beranova-Giorgianni, Sarka *biomedical researcher, educator*
Bhattacharya, Syamal Kanti *biomedical scientist, educator*
Chesney, Russell Wallace *pediatrician*
Cox, Clair Edward, II, *urologist, medical educator*
Currey, Thomas Arthur *ophthalmologist*
Gerald, Barry *retired radiology educator, neuroscientist*
Heimberg, Murray *pharmacologist, biochemist, physician*
Helton, Kathleen Jacobson *neuroradiologist*
Herrod, Henry Grady III *pediatrics professor, allergist, immunologist*
Hughes, Walter Thompson *pediatrician, educator*
Hunt, James Calvin *physician, academic administrator*
Korones, Sheldon Bernarr *pediatrician, educator*
Lazar, Rande Harris *otolaryngologist*
Morreim, E. Haavi *medical ethics educator*
Nienhuis, Arthur Wesley *physician, researcher*
Razzouk, Bassem Ibrahim *hematologist, oncologist*
Riely, Caroline Armistead *gastroenterologist, educator*
Robertson, James Thomas *neurosurgeon*
Sherr, Charles J. *immunologist, researcher*
Shochat, Stephen Jay *pediatrician, surgeon*
Thompson, Jerome Walter *otolaryngologist*
Tonkin, Ina Lynn Dyer *physician, cardiovascular radiologist, educator*
Van Middlesworth, Lester *physiology, biophysics and medicine educator, internist*
Waller, Robert Rex *ophthalmologist, educator, foundation administrator*
Wheless, James Warren *neurologist*
Wilcox, Harry Hammond *retired anatomist*

Murfreesboro
Coleman, Jack Andrew, Jr. *otolaryngologist*

Nashville
Allen, George Sewell *neurosurgery educator*
Allison, Fred, Jr. *internist, retired medical educator*
Arteaga, Carlos Luis *medical researcher, director*
Baldwin, Harold Scott *pediatrician, educator*
Bates, George William *obstetrician, gynecologist, educator*
Bennett, Marc Logan *otolaryngologist*
Bernard, Louis Joseph *surgeon, educator*
Brill, Aaron Bertrand *nuclear medicine educator*
Brown, Wendy Weinstock *nephrologist, educator*
Burnett, Lonnie Sheldon *obstetrics and gynecology educator*
Capdevila, Jorge H. *medical educator, biochemistry educator*
Carroll, Frank Edward, Jr. *radiologist, researcher*
Chang, Sam S. *urologist, surgeon, educator*
Chari, Ravi S. *surgeon*
Davis, Stephen N. *endocrinologist*
Diaz, José J. *surgeon*
Dmochowski, Roger *urologist, educator*
DuBois, Raymond N. *medical educator, researcher*
Epps, Anna Cherrie *immunologist, educator, dean*
Etherington, Carol A. *medical association administrator*
Fields, James Perry *dermatologist, dermatopathologist, allergist, pharmacologist, pharmacist*
Fleischer, Arthur C. *medical educator, radiologist*
Gallagher, Martin Joseph *neurologist, neuroscientist*
Hagan, Kevin F. *plastic surgeon, educator*
Harris, Raymond Clement *nephrologist, educator*
Hays, Stephen Robert *pediatrician*
Hueneke, Michael *plastic surgeon*
Jarquin Valdivia, Adrian Alberto *internist, neurologist, researcher*
Jennings, Henry Smith III *cardiologist*
Johnson, David Horton *oncologist*
Lee, Donald Han *surgeon, orthopedist*
Lynch, John Brown *plastic surgeon, educator*
Marney, Samuel Rowe, Jr. *allergist, immunologist, educator*
Maron, David Joel *cardiologist, educator*
Martin, Peter Robert *psychiatrist, pharmacologist*
Masys, Daniel Richard *medical educator, department chairman*
Maxwell, George Patrick *plastic surgeon*
May, James M. *medical educator, researcher*
McAndrew, Mark Philip *orthopaedic surgeon, educator, clinical researcher*
Morrow, Jason Drew *pharmacologist, medical researcher*
Moses, Harold L. *oncologist*
Neilson, Eric Grant *physician, educator, health facility administrator*
Oates, John Alexander III *medical educator*
O'Neill, James Anthony, Jr. *pediatric surgeon, educator*
Ossoff, Robert Henry *otolaryngologist, surgeon*
Pagnani, Michael Joseph *orthopaedic surgeon*
Partain, Clarence Leon *radiologist, nuclear medicine physician, educator, health facility administrator*
Passman, Marc A. *vascular surgeon*
Petrie, William Marshall *psychiatrist*
Pinson, Charles Wright *surgeon, educator, academic administrator*
Polk, David Brent *pediatrician, educator*
Raj, Satish Ramnarayan *cardiologist, researcher*
Roberts, John Robert *cardiothoracic surgeon, consultant*
Robertson, David *neurologist, educator*
Robinson, Nathaniel David, Jr. *physician, consultant*
Ross, Joseph Comer *pulmonologist, educator, academic administrator*
Rothenberg, Mace L(awrence) *physician, medical educator*
Schaffner, William *medical educator*
Sergent, John Stanley *rheumatologist, educator*
Shack, R. (Robert) Bruce *plastic surgeon, department chairman*
Smith, Bradley E. *anesthesiologist*
Spengler, Dan Michael *orthopedic surgery educator, surgeon*
Stahlman, Mildred Thornton *pediatrician, pathologist, educator, researcher*
Starkey, Thomas D. *surgeon*
Stead, William Wallace *medical educator, researcher, department chairman*
Sternberg, Paul *ophthalmologist, researcher*
Takahashi, Takamune *medical researcher, educator*
Weinger, Matthew B. *anesthesiologist, educator*
Zhang, Mingzhi *nephrologist, educator*

Oak Ridge
Spray, Paul Ellsworth *retired surgeon*

Ooltewah
Birch, Lorna May *geriatrician*

Signal Mountain
Swann, Nat Henderson, Jr. *physician*

Williamsport
Dysinger, Paul William *preventive medicine physician, educator*

Winchester
Miller, Monte Baldwin *retired internist*

TEXAS

Abilene
Morgan, Clyde Nathaniel *dermatologist*

Amarillo
Laur, William Edward *retired dermatologist*
Marupudi, Sambasiva Rao *surgeon, educator*
Parker, Gerald M. *osteopath, researcher*
Parker, Lynda Michele *psychiatrist*
Pratt, Donald George *physician*
Saadeh, Constantine Khalil *internist, educator, health facility administrator*
Siddiqui, Afzal A. *medical educator*

Arlington
Tingley, Floyd Warren *retired internist*

Austin
Elequin, Cleto, Jr. *retired physician*
Ersek, Robert Allen *plastic surgeon*
Fleeger, David Clark *colon and rectal surgeon*
Foley, Neal T. *cardiovascular surgeon*
Fyfe, Steven Trey *otolaryngologist*
George, Timothy Merrill *neurosurgeon, educator*
Ivy, John L. *medical educator, researcher*
Leeman, Daniel J. *otolaryngologist*
Neavel, Celia Beth *medical association administrator*
Painter, Theophilus Shickel, Jr. *internist, allergist*
Sawyer, William Dale *internist, educator, dean, foundation administrator*
Schleuse, William *retired psychiatrist, psychoanalyst*
Sutton, Beverly Jewell *psychiatrist*
Winegar, Bradford Charles *otolaryngologist, surgeon, researcher*

Bastrop
Johanning, Gary Lee *medical educator*

Baytown
Williams, Drew Davis *surgeon*

Beaumont
Lozano, Jose *nephrologist*
Sooudi, Matthew M. *retired surgeon*

Bellaire
Haywood, Theodore Joseph *physician, educator*

Boerne
Wittmer, James Frederick *preventive medicine physician, educator*

Brownsville
Imperial, Henry L. *internist*

Bryan
Dirks, Kenneth Ray *medical educator, army officer*

College Station
Carlton, Paul Kendall, Jr. *physician*
Kier, Ann B. Burnette *pathology educator*
Wenger, Scott Andrew *orthopedist, surgeon*

Corpus Christi
Al-Akash, Samhar I. *pediatrician, nephrologist*
Ayar, Divyang *radiologist*
Blankenship, Billy Jim *surgeon*
Cook, Kenneth Ray *radiologist*
Lim, Alexander Rufasta *neurologist, clinical investigator, clinical neurophysiologist, educator, writer*
Rotta, Alexandre Tellechea *pediatrician, educator*
Sisley, Nina Mae *physician, public health service officer*

Dallas
Antich, Peter *radiologist, educator*
Ashfaq, Raheela *pathologist, educator*
Auchus, Richard J. *internist, endocrinologist*
Barnes, Madge Lou *physician*
Beard, Bruce H. *retired psychiatrist*
Bergstresser, Paul Richard *dermatologist, educator*
Bick, Rodger Lee *hematologist, researcher, oncologist, educator*
Bonte, Frederick James *radiologist, educator, physician*
Boswell, George Marion, Jr. *orthopedist, health facility administrator*
Burns, Alton Jay *plastic surgeon*
Byrd, Henry Stephenson (Steve) *plastic surgeon, educator*
Caetano, Raul *psychiatrist, educator*
Cavanagh, Harrison Dwight *ophthalmologist, educator*
Charlton, Michael Thomas *surgeon*
Cheatum, Don Elwood *rheumatologist*
Cloud, Robert Royce *surgeon*
Cobb, Melanie H. *biomedical researcher*
Cooper, Daniel E. *orthopedic surgeon*
Cowling, Terianne *medical researcher*
Cox, Rody P(owell) *internist, educator*
Daley, Jennifer *internist, educator*
Dao, Kathryn H. *rheumatologist*
de Lemos, James Andrew *cardiologist, researcher*
Dossett, Andrew Bienvenu *orthopedic and spine surgeon*
Einspruch, Burton Cyril *psychiatrist*
Ellenbogen, Paul H. *radiologist*
Flatt, Adrian Ede *surgeon*
Forbess, Joseph Matthew *thoracic surgeon, educator*
Fordtran, John Satterfield *physician*
Foster, Daniel Willett *medical educator*
Frenkel, Eugene Phillip *physician*
Friedberg, Errol Clive *pathology educator, researcher*
Fyfe, Alistair Ian *cardiologist, scientist, educator*
Gant, Norman Ferrell, Jr. *obstetrician, gynecologist, educator*
Gibby, Diane Louise *physician, plastic surgeon*
Gilman, Alfred Goodman *pharmacologist, educator*
Glick, Gina Phillips Moran *retired physician*
Griffeth, Landis King *nuclear medicine physician*
Gross, Gary Neil *allergist, physician*
Hamas, Robert Steven *plastic surgeon*
Hobbs, Helen Haskell *medical geneticist*
Holman, James *allergist*
Houpt, Karen Rae *dermatologist*
Johnson, Robert Lee, Jr. *physician, educator, researcher*
Kaiser, Fran Elizabeth *endocrinologist, gerontologist*
Kaplan, E. Paul *urologist*
Lakhanpal, Sharad *physician*
Layton, Kennith F. *neuroradiologist*
Lerman, Mark Jeffrey *nephrologist, medical administrator*
Lewis, Jerry M. *psychiatrist, educator*
Lichliter, Warren Eugene *surgeon, educator*
Lister, George *pediatrician*
Lotan, Yair *urologist*
Maddrey, Willis Crocker *medical educator, internist, academic administrator, consultant, researcher*
Martin, Jack *physician*
Mc Clelland, Robert Nelson *surgeon, educator*
McConnell, John Dowling *urologist, educator*
Menter, M(artin) Alan *dermatologist*
Mitchell, Teddy Lee *physician*
Nemunaitis, John J. *oncologist, medical association administrator*
Newman, Keith David *surgeon*
Nikaidoh, Hisashi *pediatric cardiac surgeon, professor*
Odom, Floyd Clark *surgeon*
Parameswara, Vinay Kumar *medical educator*
Richmond, John Revere *physician, educator*
Roberts, William Clifford *medical association administrator*
Robertson, Rose Marie *cardiologist, educator*
Rodriguez, Raul Pedro *plastic surgeon*
Rohrich, Rod(ney) James *plastic surgeon, educator*
Rosenberg, Roger Newman *neurologist, educator, department chair*
Rosenblatt, Randall Lee *internist*
Rush, Augustus John *psychiatrist*
Sagalowsky, Arthur I. *urologist, educator*
Salyer, Kenneth E. *surgeon*
Schaffer, Joseph Ira *physician, educator*
Schiller, Joan Hoff *oncologist, educator*
Stone, Marvin Jules *hematologist, oncologist, educator*
Sucato, Daniel J. *orthopaedic surgeon*
Suter, Robert Eduard *emergency physician, educator*
Thiele, Dwain Louis *medical educator, department vice chairman*
Thompson, James Nicholas *medical association administrator*

Tran, Quoc-Hung *psychiatrist*
Vandermeer, Robert D. *orthopedic surgeon*
Waddell, Douglas Howard *family physician*
Wang, Xiaodong *biomedical researcher, educator*
Whitman, Jeffrey *ophthalmologist*
Wildenthal, C(laud) Kern *physician, educator*
Wilson, Jean Donald *endocrinologist, educator*
Wolford, Larry M. *surgeon*

El Paso

Hanbali, Fadi *neurosurgeon, educator*
Harlass, Frederick E. *obstetrician, gynecologist*
Taber, David O. *urological surgeon*
Williams, Darryl Marlowe *medical educator*
Zaloznik, Arlene Joyce *retired oncologist, military officer*

Fort Sam Houston

Hewitson, William Craig *physician, career officer*
Hutton, Robert Lee *pathologist*
McNeil, Christopher Ryan *emergency physician, military officer*

Fort Worth

Bailey, Susan Rudd *physician*
Cox, James Sidney *physician*
Gillette, Paul Crawford *pediatric cardiologist*
Hahn, Marc B. *physician, dean*
Kowalski, Debra Atkisson *physician*
Lichtman, David Michael *orthopedist, health facility administrator, educator, retired military officer*
Nazarian, Manucher *surgeon*
Schussler, Irwin *psychiatrist, educator*
Tobey, Martin Alan *cardiologist*
Willard, Ralph Lawrence *retired surgeon, physician, academic administrator, educator*
Yanni, John Michael *pharmacologist*

Frisco

Culpepper, Guy Lee *physician*
Gajraj, Noor *anesthesiologist, educator*

Galveston

Burns, Chester Ray *retired medical educator*
Chonmaitree, Tasnee *pediatrician, educator, epidemiologist*
Dawson, Earl Bliss *medical educator*
Gonzalez, Emilio Bustamante *rheumatologist, educator*
Goodwin, Jean McClung *psychiatrist*
Hawkins, Hal K(enneth) *pathologist*
James, Thomas Naum *cardiologist, educator*
Keeney, Susan E. *pediatrician, educator*
Klein, Gordon Leslie *pediatrician, educator*
Kumar, Santosh *medical educator, research scientist*
Powell, Don Watson *gastroenterologist, educator*
Riall, Taylor Sohn *surgeon, researcher*
Rosanio, Salvatore *cardiologist, educator*
Sandstead, Harold Hilton *physician, researcher, educator, director*
Simmons, Anthony *virology educator, physician, researcher*
Smith, David English *pathologist, educator*
Snyder, Ned *gastroenterologist, medical educator*
Szauter, Karen *gastroenterologist*
Townsend, Courtney M. *surgeon*
Tyson, Kenneth Robert Thomas *surgeon, educator*
Vedernikov, Yuri P. *pharmacologist, educator*
White, Robert Brown *medical educator*

Georgetown

Manning, Robert Thomas *internist, educator*

Grapevine

Ansohn, John Hugo *emergency physician, educator*

Harlingen

Klein, Garner Franklin *cardiologist, internist*
Salcedo-Dovi, Hector Eduardo *anatomist, educator, surgeon*

Houston

Adrogue, Horacio Esteban *nephrologist, educator*
Alexanian, Raymond *hematologist*
Alford, Bobby Ray *otolaryngologist, educator, academic administrator*
Allen, Steven Jeffrey *anesthesiologist, educator*
Appel, Stanley Hersh *neurologist, educator*
Ayus, Juan Carlos *nephrologist*
Bailey, Harold Randolph *surgeon, educator*
Ballo, Matthew T. *radiation oncologist, educator*
Barrett, Bernard Morris, Jr. *plastic and reconstructive surgeon*
Batsakis, John George *pathology educator*
Beaudet, Arthur L. *medical genetics researcher*
Bethea, Louise Huffman *allergist*
Bevers, Therese Bartholomew *physician, educator*
Bikram, Malavosklish *medical educator*
Bodey, Gerald Paul *retired medical educator*
Boutros, Sean *plastic surgeon*
Bowden, M. Gabriela *biomedical researcher, educator*
Brody, Baruch Alter *medical educator, academic administrator*
Brown, David M. *surgeon, researcher*
Brown, Jacqueline Elaine *obstetrician, gynecologist*
Buja, L. Maximilian *pathologist, academic administrator, educator*
Bungo, Michael William *cardiologist, educator, science administrator*
Burzynski, Stanislaw Rajmund *internist*
Buster, John Edmond *obstetrician, medical researcher*
Catlin, Francis Irving *physician*
Chang, Chung-Che *hematopatholgist, medical researcher, medical educator*
Cheung, Min Rex *medical educator*
Chevray, Pierre M. *medical educator*
Chiou-Tan, Faye *physician, educator*
Cleeland, Charles S. *medical educator, researcher*
Clifton, Guy L. *neurosurgeon, educator*
Cohn, William Ettlinger *cardiologist, thoracic surgeon, product designer*
Cooley, Denton Arthur *surgeon, educator*
Couch, Robert Barnard *physician, medical researcher, microbiologist, immunologist, educator*
Coverdale, John Howard *psychiatrist*
Cox, James D. *radiologist*
Deter, Russell Lee, II, *obstetrical ultrasonographer*
Dodd, Gerald Dewey, Jr. *radiologist, educator*
Doubleday, Charles William *dermatologist, educator*
Drutz, Jan Edwin *pediatrics educator*
DuPont, Herbert Lancashire *medical educator, researcher*
Eisner, Diana *pediatrician*
Eng, Cathy *oncologist, educator*
Engelhardt, Hugo Tristram, Jr. *physician, educator*
Esteva, Francisco Javier *physician, researcher*
Evans, Harry Launius *pathology educator*
Feigon, Judith Tova *ophthalmologist, educator, surgeon*
Fishman, Marvin Allen *pediatric neurologist, educator*
Fornage, Bruno Denis *radiologist, educator*
Freireich, Emil J. *hematologist, educator*
Friedman, Paul M. *dermatologist*
Gabbard, Glen Owens *psychiatrist, psychotherapist*
Gale, Stephen C. *surgeon, educator*
Gertzbein, Stanley David *orthopedic surgeon*
Gigli, Irma *dermatologist, educator, academic administrator*
Goldman, Stanford Milton *medical educator*
Gould, Kenneth Lance *cardiologist, researcher, educator*
Graham, David Yates *gastroenterologist*
Graves, Daniel Edward *medical association administrator, researcher*
Green, Linda Kathleen *pathologist, educator*
Grigore, Alina M. *anesthesiologist*
Grossman, Herbert Barton *urologist, researcher*
Grossman, Robert George *neurosurgeon, department chairman*
Gunn, Albert Edward, Jr. *internist, health facility administrator, lawyer, educator*
Gupta, Monesha *pediatrician, educator*
Gupta, Shefali *internist, nephrologist*
Guynn, Robert William *psychiatrist, educator*
Haden-Pinneri, Kathryn *pathologist*
Hall, Robert Joseph *internist, educator*
Hamid, Basem *neurologist, consultant*
Hamill, Marshall Bowes *medical educator*
Hamilton, Carlos Robert, Jr. *endocrinologist, consultant, academic administrator*
Handy, Beverly C. *medical educator*
Haynie, Thomas Powell III *physician*
Hebert, Adelaide *dermatologist, pediatrician*
Hellerstein, Lewis Jan *hematologist, oncologist, consultant*
Hong, Waun Ki *oncologist, researcher*
Hsu, Sylvia *dermatologist, educator*
Hutchens, Jerome Enos *psychiatrist*
Jankovic, Joseph *neurologist, educator*
Johnson, Marilyn *retired obstetrician, gynecologist*
Jones, Edith Irby *internist*
Jordon, Robert Earl *physician*
Justino, Henri *pediatric cardiologist*
Kahan, Barry Donald *surgeon, educator*
Katrana, David John *plastic and reconstructive surgeon*
Katta, Rajani *dermatologist*
Kaufman, Raymond Henry *retired physician, retired educator*
Key, James Everett *ophthalmologist*
Kimyai-Asadi, Arash *surgeon*
Klein, Nora J. *pediatrician*
Kline, Mark Wendel *pediatric medicine educator*
Komaki Cox, Ritsuko U. *medical educator*
Komanduri, Krishna V. *physician, research scientist*
Kosten, Thomas R. *psychiatrist, educator*
Kraft, Irvin Alan *psychiatrist*
Kraus, Gary Edward *neurosurgeon*
Kridel, Russell William Hayes *plastic surgeon, educator*
Krishnan, Sunil *radiologist, educator, oncologist, researcher*
Lakkis, Nasser *cardiologist, educator*
Levin, Bernard *physician*
Liu, Jing *pathologist, educator*
Liu, Jinsong *pathologist*
LoMonaco, John Joseph, Jr. *plastic surgeon*
Max, Ernest *surgeon*
McPherson, Alice Ruth *ophthalmologist, educator*
Medeiros, L. Jeffrey *hematologist, educator*
Mendelsohn, John *oncologist, hematologist, educator, health facility executive*
Mentz, Henry A. III *plastic surgeon*
Milam, John Daniel *pathologist, educator*
Miller, Gary Evan *psychiatrist, mental health services professional*
Miller, Robert Harold *otolaryngologist, educator*
Mintz-Hittner, Helen Ann *physician, researcher*
Mitch, William Evans *nephrologist*
Murad, Ferid *physician*
Murphy, William Alexander, Jr. *diagnostic radiologist, educator*
Nosé, Yukihiko *surgeon, educator*
Oldham, John Michael *physician, psychiatrist, educator*
Onn, Amir *medical educator, researcher*
Orengo-Nania, Silvia *ophthalmologist*
Phung, Nguyen Dinh *medical educator*
Powers, William Edward *emergency physician, medical educator, flight surgeon*
Quiros-Tejeira, Ruben Eloy *pediatrician, educator, researcher*
Raijman, Isaac *gastroenterologist, educator*
Rakel, Robert Edwin *physician, educator*
Rapini, Ronald Peter *dermatology educator*
Rappaport, Norman Harvey *plastic surgeon*
Rayala, Suresh Kumar *medical educator*
Reece, Gregory Paul *plastic surgeon, educator*
Ribble, John Charles *medical educator*
Riley, William John *neurologist*
Risin, Semyon Aaron *pathologist, educator*
Robb, Geoffrey Lawrence *plastic surgeon*
Ross, Michael Wallis *public health educator*
Ross, Patti Jayne *obstetrics and gynecology educator*
Rudolph, Andrew Henry *dermatologist, educator*
Ruiz, Pedro *psychiatrist*
Sanderson, Mary Louise *medical association administrator*
Sargent, John *psychiatrist*
Scharold, Mary Louise *psychoanalyst, psychiatrist, educator*
Schoolar, Joseph Clayton *psychiatrist, pharmacologist, educator*
Schusterman, Mark A. *surgeon, plastic surgeon*
Shan, Kesavan *cardiologist, researcher*
Shearer, William Thomas *pediatrician, educator*
Shulman, Robert Jay *pediatrician, nutritionist, gastroenterologist, educator*
Smythe, Cheves McCord *internist, geriatrician, educator, dean*
Sostman, Dirk *physician, clinical researcher, medical educator*
Spira, Melvin *plastic surgeon*
Stewart, David James *oncologist, educator*
Sutton, Jeffrey Paul *physician, scientist*
Swick, Todd J. *medical association administrator*
Swisher, Stephen G. *thoracic surgeon*
Tanous, Helene Mary *radiologist, educator*
Tweardy, David John *physician, educator*
Vallbona, Carlos *physician*
Vanderploeg, James M. *preventive medicine physician*
Varma, Datla G.K. *radiologist, researcher*
Walker, William Easton *surgeon, educator, lawyer*
Weiner, Bradley Kenneth *surgeon, researcher*
White, Ronald Joseph *biomedical researcher, physiologist, educator*
Willis, Arthur William *ophthalmologist*
Winston, Leland A. *orthopedic surgeon, educator*
Woo, Stanley Y. *medical educator, director, optometrist*
Worthing, Louie Fabian III *plastic surgeon*
Yeh, Edward Tu-Hsing *cardiologist, educator, medical researcher*
Yeoman, Lynn Chalmers *medical educator*
Young, David *anesthesiologist, educator*
Zacharias, Nikolaos Marios *obstetrician, gynecologist, perinatologist*
Zoghbi, Huda Y. *neurologist, geneticist, educator*

Humble

Trowbridge, John Parks *physician*

Huntsville

Conwell, Halford Roger *physician*

Irving

Ali, Ashraf *psychiatrist*

Kemp

Melton, Kathy A. *medical transcription educator*

Kingsville

Nutan, Mohammad Tawhidul Haque *pharmacy educator, researcher*
Sethi, Rajat *cardiologist, educator*

Lackland Afb

Fadare, Oluwole *pathologist, researcher, director*
Perry, William Brian *colorectal surgeon*

Laredo

Hudson, Robert Donald *dermatologist*

Laughlin A F B

Files, Douglas Scott *surgeon, military officer*

Lubbock

Beck, George Preston *anesthesiologist, educator*
Chiriva Internati, Maurizio *immunologist, researcher*
Frezza, Eldo E. *surgeon, educator*
Gill, Gurdev S. *orthopaedic surgeon*
Illner-Canizaro, Hana *physician, researcher, oral surgeon*
May, Donald Robert Lee *ophthalmologist, educator, academic administrator, farmer*
Mittemeyer, Bernhard Theodore *urology and surgery educator*
Sabatini, Sandra *physician*

Lufkin

Thames, William Dennis, Jr. *physician*

Magnolia

Girard, Louis Joseph *retired ophthalmologist, educator*

Marshall

Sudhivoraseth, Niphon *pediatrician, immunologist, allergist*

Mc Kinney

Sundaram, Shankar M. *surgeon*

Mcallen

Casso, Ramiro Raul *physician, academic administrator*
Ramirez, Mario Efrain *physician*

Meadowlakes

Nussbaum, Paul Stowell *retired urologist*

Mineral Wells

Braun, Gustav Milan *otolaryngologist, surgeon*

Pasadena

Mullins, Jack Allen *cardiologist, educator*
Shapiro, Edward Muray *dermatologist*

Pearland

Hammond, Raymond William *pharmacothe[illegible] specialist*

Plano

Emerson, Roger Hill, Jr. *orthopeadist*
Hu, Mei Melvin *interventional physiatrist*
Miller, Waenard Livingston *cardiologist*
Suleman, Amer *internist, cardiologist*

Red Oak

Shaw, Sue Ann *medical transcriptionist*

Richardson

Acosta, Eduardo G. *physiatrist, director*

Rockwall

Kotas, Robert Vincent *pediatrician, educato[illegible]*

San Angelo

Fischer, Duncan Kinnear *neurosurgeon*

San Antonio

Angel, Luis F. *pulmonologist, director*
Aust, Joe Bradley *surgeon, educator*
Baker, Floyd Wilmer *surgeon, retired milita[illegible] officer*
Becker, Quinn Henderson *orthopedic surgeo[illegible] military officer*
Beckmann, Charles Henry *cardiologist, educ[illegible]*
Campbell, Robert Murray, Jr. *surgeon, researcher*
Corrigan, Helen González *retired cytologist*
Croft, Harry Allen *psychiatrist*
Cura, Marco Antonio *interventional radiolog[illegible] educator*
Danney, Mark Maxwell *pediatrician*
Digicaylioglu, Murat Haydar *medical educat[illegible]*
Dumitru, Daniel *physiatrist*
Farrell, Michael Lynn *medical educator*
Gonzalez-Marrero, Virnalisis M. *dermatolog[illegible]*
Hare, Henry Phillip, Jr. *psychiatrist*
Hermann, Robert Charles, Jr. *neurologist, educator*
Hughes, Philip S. H. *dermatologist*
Jackson, Carlayne E. *neurologist, educator*
Kasinath, Balakuntalam S. *medical researche[illegible]*
Lefeber, Edward James, Jr. *internist, educato[illegible]*
LeMaistre, Charles Aubrey *retired internist, epidemiologist, educator*
Leon, Robert Leonard *psychiatrist, educator*
Martin, James Charles *physician*
McFadden, Robert Stetson *hepatologist*
McFee, Arthur Storer *physician*
McGill, Henry Coleman, Jr. *pathologist, educator, researcher*
Meffert, Jeffrey John *dermatologist*
Ognibene, Andre John *internist, educator, re[illegible] military officer*
O'Rourke, Robert A. *cardiologist, educator*
Patterson, Jan Evans *epidemiologist, educato[illegible]*
Persellin, Robert Harold *physician*
Pestana, Carlos *surgeon, retired dean, educat[illegible]*
Pruitt, Basil Arthur, Jr. *surgeon, retired milit[illegible] officer*
Restrepo, Ruben Dario *physician, educator*
Reuter, Stewart Ralston *retired radiologist*
Schenker, Steven *internist, educator*
Shanklin, Kenneth Dale *plastic surgeon*
Smith, Reginald Brian Furness *retired anesthesiologist, educator*
Williams, Thomas Eugene *pediatric hematologist, pediatric oncologist, pharmaceutical executive*
Wilson, Martha C. *physician*
Zilveti, Carlos Benjamin *preventive medicine physician, pediatrician*

Seabrook

Fischer, Craig Leland *physician*
Patten, Bernard Michael *neurologist, writer, educator*

Southlake

Bogdan, Michael Andrew *plastic surgeon*

Temple

Dehmer, Gregory Joseph *cardiologist*
Donner, Ludvik Rafael *pathologist, educator*
Feldtman, Robert *surgeon*
Hayward, Ronald Hamilton *surgeon*
Holleman, Vernon Daughty *internist, educato[illegible]*
Lynch, Dennis James *plastic surgeon*
Rohack, John James *cardiologist*

The Woodlands

Desjardins, Raoul *medical association administrator, financial consultant*
Graham, James Michael *orthopedic spine surgeon, educator*
Shannon, Thomas O. *plastic surgeon*

Tyler

Harrison, Preston Ershel, Jr. *neurologist*
Kronenberg, Richard Samuel *physician, educ[illegible]*
Neuenschwander, Pierre Fernand *medical educator*
Wrenn, Christopher Jay *physician*

Waco

Richie, Rodney Charles *critical care and pulmonary medicine physician*

Webster

Farnam, Jafar *allergist, immunologist, pediatrician*

West Lake Hills

Burns, Thomas Patrick *orthopedic surgeon*

Willis

Rappaport, Martin Paul *internist, nephrologist educator*

Thomas, Orville C. *retired allergist*

UTAH

Bountiful
Ross, Gerald Harvey *family practice and environmental medicine physician*

Hurricane
Green, Peter Carlyle *retired physician, farmer*

Layton
Yates, York J. *plastic surgeon*

Logan
Roberts, Donald Wilson *pathologist, consultant*

Mapleton
Hillyard, Ira William *retired pharmacologist, educator*

Provo
Bott, Jay Cordell *oncologist, hematologist*

Salt Lake City
Bauer, A. Robert, Jr., (August Robert Bauer Jr.) *surgeon*
Betz, A. Lorris *pediatrician, educator*
Burke, John Patrick *internist, educator*
Capecchi, Mario Renato *genetics educator*
Carey, John Clayton *pediatrician, educator, medical geneticist*
Fujinami, Robert Shin *neurology educator*
Gifford, Thomas Owen *physician*
Gleich, Gerald Joseph *immunologist, researcher, educator*
Gray, Douglas D. *child and adolescent psychiatrist*
Grosser, Bernard Irving *psychiatrist, educator*
Horne, Benjamin Davies *epidemiologist*
Hutchinson, Douglas Truman *surgeon*
Meyers, Rebecka Louise *pediatric general surgeon*
Moser, Royce, Jr. *preventive medicine physician, educator*
Nelson, John C. *obstetrician, gynecologist*
Nelson, Russell Marion *surgeon, educator*
Palmer, David Keith *otolaryngologist*
Parkinson, Justin Paul *urologist*
Pysher, Theodore James *pathologist, medical educator*
Rosenberg, Thomas D. *orthopedic surgeon*
Sorensen, John B. *surgeon*
Tani, Lloyd Yasuo *pediatrician, educator*
Thomas, David Snow *plastic surgeon*
Wolf, Harold Herbert *pharmacy educator*
Wright, Larry Jan *epidemiologist*

West Valley City
Shah, Saurabh B. *surgeon*

VERMONT

Brattleboro
agallianos, Dennis Dionysios *psychiatrist*

Burlington
Cooper, Sheldon Mark *immunologist, rheumatologist, educator, researcher*
Donahoo, William Troy *medical educator*
Gennari, F(rank) John *medical educator*
Grunberg, Steven Marc *medical educator*
Lucey, Jerold Francis *pediatrician*
Taylor, Magdalena Raczkowska *psychiatrist, educator*
Riddick, Daniel Howison *obstetrician, gynecologist, priest*
ampas, John P. *radiologist*
hao, Feng-Qi *endocrinologist, educator*

Colchester
obel, Burton Elias *cardiologist, educator*

Dorset
amford, Joseph Charles, Jr. *gynecologist, obstetrician, educator, medical missionary, author*

Jacksonville
ell, Ralph Bishop *retired pediatrician, researcher*
ein, Karen Kramer *pediatrician, epidemiologist*

Norwich
atz, Arnold Martin *medical educator*

Randolph
insinger, William Elliott *orthopedist, surgeon*

Randolph Center
ax, Daniel Saul *neurologist, educator*

South Burlington
hinozaki, Tamotsu *retired physician, retired anesthesiologist*

Underhill
anforth, Elliot, Jr. *medical educator*

West Danville
ollack, Irwin William *psychiatrist, educator*

White River Junction
erman, Stephen Alan *neurologist*
yers, Warren Powers Laird *internist, educator*

Woodstock
llian, Edward James *retired pediatrician*

VIRGINIA

Alexandria
lch, Charles M. *surgeon, educator*
hapman, Anthony Bradley *psychiatrist*
Fisher, Donald Wayne *medical association administrator*
Hurtado, Rodrigo Claudio *allergist*
Nicholas, Lynn B. *medical association administrator*
Rayman, Russell Barry *physician*
Wilhide, Stephen D. *medical association administrator*
Wilson, Tyler J. *medical association administrator*

Annandale
Shamburek, Roland Howard *physician*

Arlington
Adams, Hunter (Patch Adams) *internist, health facility administrator*
Feerick, John Paul *neurologist, researcher, military officer*
Ferraz, Francisco Marconi *neurological surgeon*
Nguyen-Dinh, Thanh *internist, geriatrician, acupuncturist*
Nirschl, Robert Phillip *orthopedic surgeon*
Sanz, Luis E. *gynecologist, educator*
Thompson, Geraldine Kelleher Richter *retired orthopedist*
Yates, Allison A. *medical association administrator*

Blacksburg
Salinas, Orlando Franco *physician*

Charlottesville
Adams, Reid *physician*
Balogun, Rasheed Abiodun *medical educator*
Beller, George A. *cardiologist, educator*
Cantrell, Robert Wendell *otolaryngologist, head and neck surgeon, educator*
Carey, Robert Munson *physician, educator*
Cherry, Kenneth Jerome, Jr. *surgeon*
Epstein, Robert Marvin *anesthesiologist, educator*
Flickinger, Charles John *anatomist, educator*
Grosh, William W. *internist*
Guerrant, Richard Littleton *medical educator*
Hunt, William B. *pulmonologist*
Jevtovic-Todorovic, Vesna *physician, researcher*
Jones, Rayford Scott *surgeon, educator*
Kalantarinia, Kambiz *medical educator*
Kassell, Neal Frederic *neurosurgery educator*
Kattwinkel, John *pediatrician, educator*
Keats, Theodore Eliot *radiologist, educator*
Kelly, Thaddeus Elliott *medical geneticist*
Laws, Edward Raymond, Jr. *neurological surgery educator*
Lin, Kant *plastic surgeon, educator*
Marshall, John Crook *internal medicine educator, researcher*
Morgan, Raymond F. *plastic surgeon*
Muller, William Henry, Jr. *retired surgeon, educator*
Nolan, Stanton Peelle *surgeon, educator*
Owen, John Atkinson, Jr. *internist, educator*
Peterson, Kent Wright *physician*
Peura, David *medical educator*
Platts-Mills, Thomas Alexander E. *immunologist, educator, researcher*
Powers, Robert David *physician*
Rehm, Patrice Koch *radiologist, educator*
Reynolds, Robert Edgar *academic administrator*
Rich, Tyvin Andrew *radiation therapist*
Rowlingson, John Clyde *anesthesiologist, physician, educator*
Scheld, William Michael *internist, educator*
Schneider, Edward Martin *retired internist, medical educator*
Sheehan, Jason *neurosurgeon*
Thorner, Michael Oliver *medical educator*
Weary, Peyton Edwin *retired medical educator*
Winston, David Charles *pathologist*

Chesapeake
Jackson, Cynthia Ann *medical association administrator, health consultant*

Chester
Walton, G. Clifford *physician*

Christiansburg
Hawley, Rollin James *neurologist*

Fairfax
Baghi, Heibatollah *medical educator*
Colvin, Donald Bernard *surgeon*
Schulman, Joseph Daniel *physician, health facility administrator, medical geneticist, educator*
Stage, Thomas Benton *psychiatrist*

Falls Church
Elliott, Virginia F. Harrison *retired anatomist, publisher, educator, investment advisor, kinesiologist, philanthropist*
Evans, Peter Yoshio *ophthalmologist, educator*
Kurtzke, John Francis, Sr. *neurologist, epidemiologist*
Lefrak, Edward Arthur *cardiovascular and thoracic surgeon*
Mukherjee, Dipankar *surgeon*
Nathan, Steven D. *pulmonologist*
Scott, Hugh Patrick *former surgeon, military officer, medical advisor*

Gainesville
Lee, Won Jay *radiologist*
Lukowsky, Gerhard Hans *internist*

Hampton
Enriquez, Manuel Hipolito *physician*

Irvington
Ritchie, George G., Jr. *retired psychiatrist*

Keswick
Rowe, William Joseph *internist*

Locust Grove
Gulya, Aina Julianna *retired medical association administrator*

Lynchburg
Solyom, Antal Endre *retired psychiatrist*

Manassas
Cooper, James Nelson *medical educator*

Manquin
Osgood, Nancy Jean *medical educator, writer*

Marion
Armbrister, Douglas Kenley *surgeon*

Mc Lean
Filerman, Gary Lewis *medical educator*
Laning, Robert Comegys *retired physician, retired military officer*
Wallace, Robert Bruce *retired surgeon*
Wright, William Evan *physician, consultant*

Midlothian
Friedel, Robert Oliver *physician*

Monterey
Tabatznik, Bernard *retired cardiologist*

Newport News
Behlmar, Cindy Lee *medical association administrator, management consultant*
Forbes, Sarah Elizabeth *gynecologist, real estate company officer*

Norfolk
Farmer, Evan R. *dermatologist, researcher*
Faulconer, Robert Jamieson *pathologist, educator*
Hood, Antoinette Foote *dermatologist*
Javaheri, Ashkan *physician*
Karakla, Daniel W. *otolaryngologist, surgeon*
Kreger, David Lawrence *gastroenterologist*
Lester, Richard Garrison *radiologist, educator*
Lowe, Eric Jeffrey *hematologist, oncologist, director*
Magee, William Preston, Jr. *plastic surgeon*
Panneton, Jean M. *vascular surgeon*
Platsoucas, Chris Dimitrios *immunologist*
Qureshi, Faiqa *pediatric emergency physician*
Rohn, Reuben David *medical educator, director*
Wolcott, Hugh Dixon *obstetrics and gynecology educator*

North Garden
Moses, Hamilton III *neurologist, hospital administrator, author*

Norton
Vest, Steven Lee *gastroenterologist, hepatologist, internist*

Oakton
Levin, Warren Mayer *family practice physician*

Portsmouth
DeMaio, Marlene *orthopedist, surgeon*
Wolf, Jeffrey Stephen *physician*
Yarbrough, Terry Pinckney *physician*

Reston
Harrison, William Henry *retired medical educator*

Richmond
Arango-Lasprilla, Juan Carlos *medical educator*
Atkinson, Richard Lee, Jr. *internal medicine educator*
Blumberg, Michael Zangwill *allergist*
Buttery, Christopher Malcolm Gedda *medical educator*
Christie, Laurence Glenn, Jr. *surgeon, educator*
Dhindsa, Harinder Singh *emergency physician, educator*
Dunn, Leo James *obstetrician, gynecologist, educator*
Fairman, Ralph Paul *physician, medical educator*
Fierro, Marcella Farinelli *forensic pathologist, educator*
Hardy, Richard Earl *rehabilitation counseling educator*
Hutcher, Neil Edward *surgeon*
Kaplowitz, Lisa Glauser *physician, educator*
Kendler, Kenneth S. *medical educator*
Kornstein, Susan G. *medical educator*
Kum-Nji, Philip *pediatrician, educator*
Lawrence, Walter, Jr. *surgeon, educator*
Leshner, Robert Theodore *neurologist*
Manjili, Masoud H. *immunologist, educator*
Merrell, Ronald Clifton *surgeon, educator*
Mollen, Edward Leigh *pediatrician, allergist, clinical immunologist*
Moskowitz, William B. *cardiologist*
Mullinax, Perry Franklin *rheumatologist, immunologist, allergist*
Neal, Marcus Pinson, Jr. *radiologist, educator*
Nestler, John Edwin *endocrinology educator*
Owen, Duncan Shaw, Jr. *internist, retired educator*
Richardson, David Walthall *cardiologist, educator, consultant*
Shipman, Jean Pugh *medical librarian*
Sirica, Alphonse Eugene *pathology educator*
Strauss, Jerome Frank III *reproductive endocrinologist, educator*
Torres Filho, Ivo *medical educator*
Turner, Elaine S. *allergist, immunologist*
Weaver, Michael F. *internist, researcher*
Wilkinson, David Stanley *pathologist, consultant, researcher, educator*
Xi, Lei *medical educator*

Roanoke
Hutcheson, Jack Robert *hematologist, medical oncologist*

Roseland
Stemmler, Edward Joseph *physician, retired health facility administrator, dean*

Spotsylvania
Singleton, Tanya *nursing educator*

Springfield
Furst, Eric Jonathan *physician, surgeon*

Sterling
Jaffe, Russell Merritt *pathologist, research director*

Suffolk
Carroll, George Joseph *pathologist, educator*

Vienna
Schwartz, Richard Harvey *pediatrician*

Virginia Beach
Carlston, John A. *allergist*
Choe, Kyle Seung *facial plastic surgeon*
Schreiber, Mark Traudt *psychiatrist*

Ware Neck
Tabb, Waller Crockett *retired allergist, immunologist*

White Stone
Kingsbury, Ellen Ann Dagon *anesthesiologist, general practitioner*

Williamsburg
Connell, Alastair McCrae *physician*
Davis, Richard Bradley *pathologist, educator, internist*
Jacoby, William Jerome, Jr. *internist, retired military officer*
Maloney, Milford Charles *retired internal medicine educator*

Winchester
Bechamps, Gerald Joseph *surgeon*
Helentjaris, Diane *physician*
Moore, Richard Carroll, Jr. *physician*

WASHINGTON

Auburn
Nazaire, Michel Harry *physician*

Bainbridge Island
Hubbard, Stephen *cardiologist, consultant*

Bellevue
Hackett, Carol Ann Hedden *physician*
Hackett, John Peter *dermatologist*
Marosan, George *plastic surgeon*
Phillips, Zaiga Alksnis *pediatrician*
Rand, Richard P. *plastic surgeon*
Shifrin, Donald Lee *pediatrician*
Smith, Bruce Cameron *physician*

Bellingham
Davis, Brantley Pierce *physician, researcher*
Howe, Warren Billings *physician*

Blaine
Steward, David John *retired anesthesiologist, educator, researcher*

Bothell
Grewal, Iqbal S. *immunologist, biotechnology company executive*

Burien
McClean, Patrick H. *otolaryngologist*
Risse, Guenter Bernhard *physician, historian, educator*

Clyde Hill
Condon, Robert Edward *surgeon, educator, consultant*

Coupeville
Mayhew, Eric George *medical researcher, educator, consultant*

Edmonds
Yoon, Jay Myoung *oncologist, hematologist, internist*

Everett
Valentine, Mark Conrad *dermatologist*

Fort Lewis
Beekley, Alec C. *surgeon, researcher*

Friday Harbor
Geyman, John Payne *physician, educator*

Issaquah
Barchet, Stephen *obstetrician, gynecologist, retired military officer*

Kirkland
Aikawa, Jerry Kazuo *internist, educator*
Barto, Deborah Ann *physician*
Dunn, Jeffrey Edward *neurologist*

Lynden
Hibbs, Clair M. *retired pathologist*

Mercer Island
Dunner, David Louis *medical educator*
Elgee, Neil Johnson *retired internist, endocrinologist, educator*
Levenson, Robert Montie *retired physician*

Mukilteo
White, Lowell Elmond, Jr. *retired medical educator*

Olympia
Fisher, Nancy Louise *pediatrician, geneticist, retired nurse*

Port Orchard
Thoman, Mark Edward *pediatrician*

Puyallup
Hwang, Chan S. *physiatrist, consultant*
Saxey, Roderick *radiologist, writer*

Richland
Bair, William J. *retired radiobiologist*

Sammamish
Gaboriau, Henri P. *plastic surgeon*

Seattle
Abu-Raddad, Laith Jamal *mathematical epidemiologist, educator*
Allison, Kimberly Heller *pathologist, educator*
Ansell, Julian S. *urologist, educator*
Appelbaum, Frederick Ray *oncologist*
Blake-Inada, Louis Michael *cardiologist, researcher*
Bornstein, Paul *medical educator, biochemist*
Bowden, Douglas McHose *neuropsychiatric scientist, foundation director*
Buck, Linda B. *medical educator*
Catterall, William A. *pharmacology, neurobiology educator*
Cha, Junho *medical researcher*
Chatard, Peter Ralph Noel, Jr. *aesthetic plastic surgeon*
Chin, Simon H. *plastic surgeon*
Corey, Lawrence *medical educator*
Dale, David C. *physician, educator*
Dawson, Patricia Lucille *surgeon*
Day, Robert Winsor *preventive medicine physician, researcher*
Distad, B. Jane *neurologist*
Ellis, Georgiana Kehr *internist, oncologist*
Eschbach, Joseph Wetherill *nephrology educator*
Fine, James Stephen *physician*
Gartman, David Miner *cardiothoracic surgeon*
Giblett, Eloise Rosalie *retired hematologist*
Goff, Barbara Ann *obstetrician, gynecologist, gynecologic oncology*
Goodkin, Robert *neurosurgeon, educator*
Gottlieb, Jourdan *plastic surgeon*
Groudine, Mark Terry *oncologist*
Guntheroth, Warren Gaden *pediatrician, educator*
Hazzard, William Russell *geriatrician, educator*
Hellström, Ingegerd *medical researcher*
Henderson, Maureen McGrath *medical educator*
Holmes, King Kennard *medical educator*
Hornbein, Thomas Frederic *anesthesiologist*
Isik, Frank *plastic surgeon*
Kahn, Steven Emanuel *medical educator*
Katon, Wayne J. *psychiatrist, researcher*
Kaufman, Joel Daniel *medical educator, medical researcher*
Kimball, Harry Raymond *medical association administrator, educator*
Klebanoff, Seymour Joseph *medical educator*
Knight, Christopher L. *medical educator*
Kraft, George Howard *physician, educator*
Krohn, Kenneth Albert *radiologist, educator*
Larrabee, Wayne Fox, Jr. *facial plastic surgeon*
Larson, Eric B. *medical educator, director, internist*
Lemire, Ronald John *pediatrician, educator*
Lendvay, Thomas Sean *pediatric urologist, medical educator*
Maier, Ronald Vitt *surgeon, educator*
Matsen, Frederick Albert III *orthopedic educator*
McClure, R. Dale *physician*
Moore, Daniel Charles *retired anesthesiologist*
Motulsky, Arno Gunther *internist, geneticist, educator*
Nelson, James Alonzo *radiologist, educator*
O'Brien, Kevin D. *medical educator*
Oelschlager, Brant Kurt *surgeon, researcher*
Ojemann, Jeffrey G. *neurosurgeon*
Ostrow, Jay Donald *gastroenterology educator, researcher*
Pagon, Roberta Anderson *pediatrician, educator*
Pauwels, Judith *physician, medical educator*
Perrin, Edward Burton *biomedical researcher, public health educator*
Phillips, William Robert *physician*
Pierson, David John *medical educator*
Rabak, David William *retired family practice physician, educator, consultant*
Raghu, Ganesh *physician, educator*
Ravenholt, Reimert Thorolf *epidemiologist, researcher*
Rivara, Frederick Peter *pediatrician, educator*
Robertson, William Osborne *physician*
Robinson, Lawrence R. *medical educator, vice-dean, director*
Sale, George Edgar *pathologist*
Saneto, Russell Patrick *pediatric neurologist, epileptologist, neurobiologist*
Schimmelbusch, Werner Helmut *psychiatrist*
Sinanan, Mika Narad *surgeon, educator*
Steiner, Robert Alan *neuroendocrinologist, educator*
Stenchever, Morton Albert *obstetrician, gynecologist*
Stolov, Walter Charles *medicine physiatrist, educator*
Storey, Mitchel D. *sports medicine physician*
Thirlby, Richard Coller *surgeon*
Thomas, Edward Donnall *internist, hematologist, retired medical educator*
Todaro, George Joseph *pathologist, researcher*
Vallières, Eric *thoracic surgeon*
Vater, Youri L. *medical educator*
Walker, William O., Jr. *pediatrician*
Weaver, Lois Jean *physician, educator*
Welk, Richard Andrew *plastic surgeon*
Yarington, Charles Thomas, Jr. *surgeon, educator, health facility administrator*
Yue, Agnes Kau-Wah *otolaryngologist*

Shoreline
Merendino, K. Alvin *surgeon, educator*

Spokane
Cohen, Arnold Norman *gastroenterologist*
Garrison, Mark W. *medical educator*
Gibson, Melvin Roy *retired pharmacology educator*
Hakan, Kaya *oncologist, hematologist*
Lee, Hi Young *physician, acupuncturist*
Lollis, Blake David *physician, military officer*
MacKay, Alexander Russell *neurosurgeon*
Mielke, Clarence Harold, Jr. *hematologist*

University Place
Pliskow, Vita Sari *anesthesiologist*

Walla Walla
Chaidarun, Sushela Songtanin *endocrinologist, researcher*
Krizan, Kelly Joe *physician, leather craftsman*
McIlvaine, Patricia Morrow *physician*

Wenatchee
Gotthold, William Eugene *emergency physician*
Primm, Richard Kirby *physician*

Woodinville
Couser, William Griffith *nephrologist, academic administrator, educator*

WEST VIRGINIA

Charleston
Boland, James Pius *surgeon, educator*
Cunningham, Kimberly Ellen *medical transcriptionist*
Goins, Michael Roy *otolaryngologist*
Horswell, Bruce Brian *facial surgeon*

Clarksburg
Sarino, Edgardo Formantes *radiologist, physician*

Fayetteville
Cook, Lewis Anderson *physician, anthropologist*

Frankford
Mazzio-Moore, Joan L. *retired radiology educator, physician*

Huntington
Cocke, William Marvin, Jr. *plastic surgeon, educator*
Foster, Earl James *orthopedist*
Locascio, Joseph A. *surgeon, educator*
Molina, Rafael Evencio *retired urologist*
Mufson, Maurice Albert *infectious diseases physician, educator*
Oakley, Gerard Joseph *gynecologist*

Hurricane
Blair, Paul Alex *otolaryngologist, plastic surgeon*

Kingwood
Moyers, Sylvia Dean *retired medical librarian*

Morgantown
Albrink, Margaret Joralemon *medical educator*
Chisholm, Lionel Donald John *ophthalmologist*
Ducatman, Alan Marc *physician*
Fleming, William Wright, Jr. *pharmacology educator, department chairman*
Glover, Douglas Dennis *obstetrics, gynecology and pharmacology educator*
Gustafson, Robert Allen *pediatric cardiothoracic surgeon*
Pinheiro, Germania Araujo *physician, researcher*

Point Pleasant
Rerych, Stephen Karl *surgeon*

Ronceverte
Hooper, Anne Dodge *pathologist, educator*

WISCONSIN

Appleton
Boren, Clark Henry, Jr. *general and vascular surgeon*
Luther, Thomas William *retired dermatologist*
Warrick, Paul David *otolaryngologist*

Baileys Harbor
Schultz, Richard Otto *ophthalmologist, educator*

Brookfield
Olson, David Carl *physician*

Eagle River
Agre, James Courtland *physiatrist*

Fitchburg
Zolot, Marvin Mitchell *internist*

Fond Du Lac
Treffert, Darold Allen *psychiatrist, writer, hospital administrator*

Green Bay
Milson, Bertram Irving *surgeon*
Pukel, Clifford Stuart *physician*
Reinke, Mark Kevin *otolaryngologist*

Greenfield
Mayr, James Francis *physician*

Hales Corners
Kuwayama, S. Paul *physician, immunologist, allergist*

Hartland
Atlee, John Light *retired physician, consultant*

Janesville
Gianitsos, Anestis Nicholas *surgeon*

La Crosse
Bouri, Anil K. *neurologist, director*
Rademacher, Dana Ellis *urologist*
Smith, Martin Jay *physician, biomedical research scientist*
Webster, Stephen Burtis *dermatologist, educator*

Madison
Albert, Daniel Myron *ophthalmologist, educator*
Arndt, George Arthur *anesthesiologist, consultant*
Bridges, Alan J. *physician*
Burgess, Richard Ray *oncologist, molecular biologist, biotechnologist, educator, researcher, consultant*
Cohen, Marcus *allergist, immunologist*
Connors, Kenneth Antonio *retired pharmacy educator*
Cripps, Derek J. *dermatologist, educator*
Crow, James Franklin *retired genetics educator*
DeMets, David L. *medical educator, biomedical researcher*
Fahien, Leonard August *physician, educator*
Farrell, Philip M. *physician, dean, educator, researcher*
Fleming, Michael F. *medical educator*
Ford, Charles Nathaniel *otolaryngologist, educator*
Graziano, Frank Michael *medical educator, researcher*
Greer, Frank Roland *pediatrician, neonatologist*
Hansen, Sherri M. *psychiatrist*
Heatley, Gregg Alan *ophthalmologist*
Javid, Manucher J. *retired neurosurgeon, educator*
Jefferson, James Walter *psychiatrist, educator*
Johnson, Maryl Rae *cardiologist*
Laessig, Ronald Harold *preventive medicine and pathology educator, state official*
Lemanske, Robert F., Jr. *allergist, immunologist*
Linzer, Mark *medical educator, internist*
MacKinney, Archie Allen *physician*
Maki, Dennis G. *epidemiology educator*
Malter, James Samuel *pathologist, educator*
Mehta, Minesh P. *oncologist, educator*
Nordby, Eugene Jorgen *orthopedic surgeon*
Pitot, Henry Clement III *pathologist, educator*
Rakel, David Paul *sports medicine physician, director*
Reynolds, Ernest West *retired internist, educator*
Rikkers, Layton Frederick *surgeon*
Roberts, Leigh Milton *psychiatrist*
Schutta, Henry Szczesny *neurologist, educator*
Sondel, Paul Mark *pediatric oncologist, educator*
Stein, James Howard *medical educator, researcher*
Wald, Arnold *gastroenterologist*
Walker, Duard Lee *medical educator*
Westman, Jack Conrad *child psychiatrist, educator*
Whiffen, James Douglass *surgeon, educator*
Yevzlin, Alexander Sasha *nephrologist, medical products executive*

Manitowoc
Trader, Joseph Edgar *orthopedic surgeon*

Marshfield
Kuehner, Marvin Ernest *surgeon*
Vidaillet, Humberto J., Jr. *physician, administrator, researcher*

Mequon
Braun, Michael Andrew *radiologist*
Terry, Leon Cass *neurologist, educator*

Milton
Enlow, Donald Hugh *retired anatomist, dean*

Milwaukee
Baumgardner, Dennis J. *physician, researcher, educator*
Chan, Carlyle Hung-lun *psychiatrist, educator*
Chitambar, Christopher Rajiv *internist, oncologist, hematologist*
Fink, Jordan Norman *allergist, educator*
Foldy, Seth Leonard *physician, educator*
Gershan, William M. *pediatrician, educator*
Hackbarth, Donald A., Jr. *medical educator, orthopedist*
Hur, Su-Ryong *physician, anesthesiologist*
Jordan, Ruth Ann *retired physician*
Kopell, Brian Harris *neurosurgeon, director*
Kroft, Steven Howard *hematopathologist, medical educator*
Larson, David Lee *surgeon*
Levy, Stuart Arthur *pulmonologist, consultant*
Namdari, Bahram *surgeon*
Pagel, Paul Stanley *anesthesiologist*
Sato, Thomas T. *surgeon, educator*
Shetty, Kaup Rajmohan *endocrinologist, educator*
Simpson, Deborah *medical educator*
Soergel, Konrad Hermann *physician*
Stokes, Kathleen Sarah *dermatologist, educator*
Towne, Jonathan Baker *vascular surgeon*
Yancey, Kim Bruce *dermatology researcher*
Youker, James Edward *radiologist*

Monroe
Frantz, John A. *physician, writer*
Rogerson, Anthony Richard *otolaryngologist*

Nashotah
Hollister, Winston Ned *pathologist*

Oconto Falls
Dolibois, John Michael *surgeon*

Onalaska
Waite, Lawrence Wesley *osteopathic physician, educator*

Oshkosh
Cheng, Theresa *neurosurgeon*
Cooper, Janelle Lunette *neurologist, educator*

Plover
Loteyro, Corazon Bigata *physician*

Racine
Stewart, Richard Donald *internist, educator, writer*

Stoughton
Mason, Craig Alan *clinician*

Wauwatosa
Kalogjera, Ikar Jaksa *psychiatrist, educator*

Weyauwega
Maasch, Lloyd Palmer *physician*

WYOMING

Casper
Bennion, Scott Desmond *physician*
Scaling, Sam T. *obstetrician, gynecologist*
Wieder, Brian H. *neurosurgeon*

Cheyenne
Lanier, Robert Lewis *oncologist*

Laramie
Kelley, Robert Otis *anatomist, educator*
Cohen, David John *cardiothoracic surgeon*

TERRITORIES OF THE UNITED STATES

NORTHERN MARIANA ISLANDS

Saipan
Lamkin, Celia Belocora *physician*

PUERTO RICO

Bayamon
Cabrera-Otero, Sylvia *physician*
Carro, Eric F. *neurosurgeon*

Humacao
MacDonald, Gordon Rhodes *retired urologist, military officer*

Mayaguez
Sahai, Hardeo *medical statistics educator*

San Juan
Cordero, Jose Fernando *pediatrician, dean*
Del Toro Soto, Jaime *psychiatrist*
Oms, Luis J. *physician*
Santos Pico, Jose V. *neurosurgeon*

MILITARY ADDRESSES OF THE UNITED STATES

EUROPE

APO
Leibrecht, Murl Edwin *preventive medicine physician, consultant, retired military officer*
Walsh, Douglas Shawn *medical association administrator, dermatologist, director, military officer*

PACIFIC

FPO
Ecker, Robert Doniger *neurosurgeon*

CANADA

ALBERTA

Calgary
Smith, Eldon *cardiologist, physiologist, educator*

Edmonton
Gyenes, Gábor *physician, educator*
Halloran, Philip Francis *nephrologist, immunologist*
Oberg, Lyle *physician, academic administrator*

BRITISH COLUMBIA

Parksville
Weir, Bryce Keith Alexander *neurosurgeon, neurologist, educator*

Vancouver
Baird, Patricia Ann *physician, educator*
Clarren, Sterling Keith *pediatrician*
Doyle, Patrick John *otolaryngologist, department chairman*
Eaves, Allen Charles Edward *hematologist, health facility administrator*
Friedman, Sydney M. *anatomist, educator, medical researcher*
Hardwick, David Francis *pathologist*
Ling, Victor *oncologist, educator*
McGeer, Edith Graef *retired neurological science educator*
Mizgala, Henry F. *physician, consultant, retired medical educator*

MANITOBA

Winnipeg
Haworth, James Chilton *pediatrics educator*
Schacter, Brent Allan *oncologist, health facility administrator*

NOVA SCOTIA

Halifax
Chowdhury, Dhiman *physician, consultant*
Langley, George Ross *medical educator*
Murray, Thomas John (Jock Murray) *physician, neurologist, educator*
Tonks, Robert Stanley *pharmacologist, educator, retired dean*

Mahone Bay
Collins, John Alfred *retired obstetrician, gynecologist, educator*

ONTARIO

Hamilton
Bienenstock, John *pathologist, educator, health facility administrator*
Hirsh, Jack *medical researcher*
Roland, Charles Gordon *physician, medical educator, historian*

Kingston
Kaufman, Nathan *retired pathologist, educator*
Low, James A. *physician*

London
Marotta, Joseph Thomas *medical educator*
Rudnick, Abraham *psychiatrist, philosopher*

Manotick
Osmond, Dennis Gordon *anatomist, researcher, medical educator*

Ottawa
de Bold, Adolfo J. *pathologist, educator, physiologist, researcher*
Hagen, Paul Beo *pharmacologist*
Hurteau, Gilles David *retired obstetrician, gynecologist, educator, dean*
Lavoie, Lionel A. *physician, health science association administrator*
Vassilyadi, Michael *pediatric neurosurgeon*

Toronto
Karkas, Leslie Gabriel *plastic surgeon*
Lindsay, William Kerr *surgeon*
Mc Culloch, Ernest Armstrong *internist, educator*
Nguyen, San Duy *psychiatrist, educator*
Ogilvie, Richard Ian *clinical pharmacologist*
Ole, Michael Joseph *cardiologist*
Ill, James Edgar *medical educator, researcher*

Windsor
Ferguson, John Duncan *medical research educator*

QUEBEC

Montpellier
Poirier, Louis Joseph *neurology educator*

Montreal
Burgess, John Herbert *cardiologist, educator*
Guess, Richard Leigh *orthopedic surgeon, dean*
Ducharme, Francine Carole *nursing educator, researcher*
Freeman, Carolyn Ruth *oncologist*
Genest, Jacques *nephrologist, clinical scientist, science administrator*
Gold, Phil *immunologist, educator, researcher*
Goldbloom, Victor Charles *pediatrician*
Goltzman, David *endocrinologist, educator, researcher*
Jones, Barbara Ellen *neurologist, educator*
Kramer, Michael Stuart *pediatric epidemiologist*
Macaulay, Ann C. *physician*
Mac Lean, Lloyd Douglas *surgeon*
Mulder, David S. *cardiovascular surgeon*
Nattel, Stanley *cardiologist, research scientist*
Pasternac, André *cardiologist, educator*
Scriver, Charles Robert *medical researcher, human geneticist, retired medical educator*
Snell, Linda S. *internist, educator*

Saint Lambert
Bermont, Yves Wilfrid *anatomy educator, researcher*

SASKATCHEWAN

Saskatoon
Houston, C(larence) Stuart *radiologist, educator*
Olsson, Alan Graham *thoracic surgeon, researcher*

Toronto
Kogel, Aubie *endocrinologist, academic administrator*
Bullock, Bruce Godfrey *psychiatrist, educator*

MEXICO

Tijuana
Gayet, Arturo S. *ophthalmologist, surgeon, consultant*

ARGENTINA

Buenos Aires
Gondolesi, Gabriel Eduardo *transplant surgeon*
Montes, Leopoldo Feliciano *dermatologist, educator*

ARMENIA

Yerevan
Adamyan, Tsovinar *medical educator*

AUSTRALIA

Camperdown
Zobras, Helen *gynecologist, director*

Nedlands
Marshall, Barry James *gastroenterologist*
Oxnard, Charles Ernest *anatomist, anthropologist, biologist, educator*

Parkville
Denton, Derek Ashworth *medical researcher, foundation administrator*
Metcalf, Donald *biomedical researcher*

Queensland
Ho, Yik Hong *colon and rectal surgeon*

AUSTRIA

Grossgmain
Mueller, Christa *radiologist*

BANGLADESH

Dhaka
Brooks, W. Abdullah *pediatrician, researcher*

BELGIUM

Brussels
Boon, Thierry *biomedical researcher*
Ciarka, Agnieszka *internist, researcher*

BULGARIA

Sofia
Alexiev, Borislav Alexandrov *pathologist*

COLOMBIA

Bogotá
Reina, Carrillo José Gabriel *physician, surgery educator*

CZECH REPUBLIC

Prague
Tuma, Stanislav Josef *radiologist*

ENGLAND

Headington
Bell, John Irving *medical researcher, educator*

London
Butler, Peter E. *plastic surgeon*
Muir-Taylor, Douglas James *ophthalmologist*
Murray, Robin MacGregor *psychiatrist, educator, consultant*
Rutter, Michael Llewellyn *child psychology educator*

Oxford
Peto, Sir Richard *medical researcher*

Redhill
Donaldson, David *pathologist*

FINLAND

Helsinki
Liewendahl, Bo Kristian *retired pathologist, nuclear medicine physician*

FRANCE

Paris
Gontier, Jean Roger *medicine and physiology educator*

GERMANY

Bavaria Murnau
Trapp, Oliver Marcus *surgeon, consultant*

Berlin
Jahnke, Kristoph *internist, hematologist, oncologist, researcher*

Bremen
Fahle, Manfred *ophthalmology researcher*

Cologne
Korenkov, Michael *surgeon*

Dresden
Wartenberg, Katja Eltriede *neurologist*

Furth
Rau, Magda *ophthalmologist*

Halle
Schmoll, Hans Joachim *hematology and oncology educator*

Mannheim
Solz, Hermann *plastic surgeon*

Munich
Heywang-Koebrunner, Sylvia H. *radiologist, educator*

Regensburg
Eisenmann-Klein, Marita *plastic surgeon*

Seeheim-Jugenheim
Halama, Niels *physician, researcher*

Tübingen
Nüsslein-Volhard, Christiane *medical researcher*

Wuppertal
Schubert, Guenther Erich *pathologist*

GREECE

Athens
Boudoulas, Harisios *cardiologist, researcher, medical educator*

Larisa
Zacharoulis, Dimitris *surgeon, researcher*

GUATEMALA

Guatemala City
Herrera-Llerandi, Rodolfo Eduardo *surgeon, educator*
Mishaan, Emilio *transplant surgeon, educator*

HAITI

Port-au-Prince
Pape, Jean William *physician, researcher*

INDIA

Gurgaon Haryana
Katariya, Kushagra *cardiothoracic surgeon, educator*

Haryana Rohtak
Chauhan, Ashok Kumar *medical educator*

Hyderabad
Gummaraju, Srinivas Chakravarthy *oncologist, hematologist*

Karnataka
Ravish, I. R. *urologist, surgeon*

Lucknow
Kumar, Raj *medical educator*

New Delhi
Reddy, K. Srinath *cardiologist*

ISRAEL

Jerusalem
Abramsky, Oded *neurologist*
Hazboun, Viveca *psychiatrist*

ITALY

Padua
Pozzan, Tullio *medical educator*

Palermo
Fiumara, Ettore *neurosurgeon*

Rome
Balducci, Alessandro *nephrologist, educator*

Siena
Rappuoli, Rino *immunologist*

JAPAN

Gunma
Okada, Ryozo *medical educator, researcher*

Hamamatsu
Kaneko, Masao *radiology educator, researcher, specialist*

Hirakata
Shigemitsu, Toshiro *ophthalmologist, researcher*

Kushimoto
Akura, Junsuke *ophthalmologist, researcher*

Okayama
Morooka, Hiroshi *neurosurgeon*
Okada, Shigeru *medical educator*

Saitama
Hozumi, Motoo *medical educator, researcher*

Sapporo
Nakagawa, Koji *retired endocrinologist, educator*
Sakai, Yu *pathologist*

Tochigi
Honma, Koichi *pathologist, researcher*
Hyodo, Haruo *radiologist, educator*

Tokorozawa
Nakamura, Hiroshi *urology educator*

Tokyo
Sakuta, Manabu *neurologist, educator*

Toyama
Sumiyoshi, Tomiki *psychiatrist, researcher*

JORDAN

Amman
Saadeh, Sherif Nabil *gastroenterologist, hepatologist, researcher*

KENYA

Mombasa
Harrell, Jerry DeWitt *ophthalmologist, director*

LEBANON

Beirut
Khatib, Rustom Atfat *gynecologist, researcher, endocrinologist, consultant, economist*

MALAYSIA

Selangor
Azer, Samy Aziz *gastroenterologist, educator*

MOROCCO

Rabat
Rafi, Mostafa *ophthalmologist*

NETHERLANDS

Maastricht
Van Praag, Herman Meir *psychiatrist, educator, researcher*

Vlaardingen
Smith, Arlan Robert *plastic and reconstructive surgeon*

NEW ZEALAND

Auckland
Gluckman, Peter *endocrinologist, fetal physiologist*

NIGERIA

Enugu
Ozumba, Benjamin Chukwuma *obstetrician, gynecologist, educator*

PERU

Trujillo
Ungaro, Mario *pathologist, educator*

PHILIPPINES

Quezon City
Padlan, Eduardo Agustin *retired immunologist*

REPUBLIC OF KOREA

Busan
Lee, Young Woo *neurosurgery educator*
Sung, Gyung Tak *urologist, department chairman*

Daegu
Yim, Man Bin *neurosurgeon, educator*

Gwangju
Kim, Kwang Seog *medical educator*

Seoul
Chi, Je Geun *retired pathologist*
Jee, Won-Hee *radiologist, educator*
Kwon, Yang *neurosurgeon, medical educator*
Lee, Il-Ok *anesthesiologist, education educator*

RUSSIA

Moscow
Zubritsky, Alexander Nickolaevich *pathologist*

SAUDI ARABIA

Riyadh
Wagoner, Michael D. *ophthalmologist*

SLOVENIA

Maribor
Strojnik, Tadej *neurosurgeon, researcher*

SOUTH AFRICA

Bloemfontein
Stulting, Andries Andriessen *ophthalmologist*

SPAIN

Pamplona
Masdeu, Jose Cruz *neurologist, health facility administrator*

SWEDEN

Göteborg
Norrby, Klas Carl Vilhelm *pathology educator*

SWITZERLAND

Aargau
Bodis, Stephan B. *radiologist, oncologist, educator*

Basel
Eriksen, Erik Fink *endocrinologist, internist, researcher*
Nidecker, Andreas Cornelis *radiologist, educator*

Geneva
Ross, Eleanor *retired medical association administrator*

Versoix
Mahler, Halfdan Theodor *physician, health organization executive*

Zurich
Domingue, Gerald James *medical researcher, microbiologist, immunologist, educator, clinical bacteriologist*
Zinkernagel, Rolf Martin *immunology educator*

TAIWAN

Kaohsiung
Wang, Gwo Jaw *orthopedic surgery educator*

Taipei
Chen, Ding-Shinn *gastroenterologist, educator*

TANZANIA

Moshi
Pomfret, David B. *medical educator, internist*

TURKEY

Adana
Diler, Rasim Somer *psychiatrist, researcher*

ADDRESS UNPUBLISHED

Ablow, Keith Russell *writer*
Aboufakher, Rabeea *cardiologist*
Abrams, Arthur Jay *retired physician*
Abrams, Fredrick Ralph *physician, clinical ethicist*
Achauer, Bruce Michael *plastic surgeon*
Achord, James Lee *retired gastroenterologist*
Adair, Stefan Rene *plastic surgeon*
Adams, Forrest H. *retired pediatrician*
Adams, James Thomas *surgeon*
Aduen, Javier Francisco *physician, researcher*
Adzick, Nick Scott *surgeon, educator*
Aguilar-Bryan, Lydia *medical educator, researcher*
Ahmad, Syeda Sultana *physician*
Aldrich, Franklin Dalton *medical researcher, consultant*
Alexander, Jessica Aronow *anesthesiologist*
Alexander, Jonathan *cardiologist, consultant*
Alexiades-Armenakas, Macrene Renee *dermatologist, scientist, researcher, educator, consultant*
Al-Shawwa, Bahauddin A. *pediatrician, medical educator*
Altekruse, Joan Morrissey *retired preventive medicine physician*
Altshuler, Kenneth Z. *psychiatrist, educator*
Amacher, Arthur Loren *neurosurgeon*
Amiel, Howard *ophthalmologist, corneal surgeon*
Amis, Edward Stephen, Jr. *radiologist, retired military officer*
Anderson, Geraldine Louise *medical researcher*
Anderson, Richard McLemore *internist*
Andreoli, Thomas Eugene *physician*
Andrews, William Cooke *physician*
Andrus, Jennifer Gail *otolaryngologist, surgeon, educator, educational consultant*
Angel, Carlos Alberto *pediatric surgeon, urologist*
Antoun, Mikhail *medicinal chemistry and pharmacognosy educator*
Anversa, Piero *medical educator*
Appenzeller, Otto *neurologist, researcher*
Applebaum, Edward Leon *otolaryngologist, educator*
Arenberg, Irving Kaufman Karchmer *otolaryngologist*
Argiris, Athanassios *oncologist, researcher*
Arora, Sandeep *cardiologist*
Asma, Evren *medical researcher*
Atkinson, Holly Gail *physician, journalist, educator, human rights activist, writer*
Aurora, Sheena Kaur *neurologist*
Avant, Robert Frank *retired physician*
Avery, Mary Ellen *pediatrician, educator*
Azad, Nilofer Saba *oncologist*
Aziz, Faisal *surgeon*
Babar, Sardar Ijlal *pulmonologist*
Badger, William John *urologist, surgeon*
Badgley, Theodore McBride *retired psychiatrist, neurologist*
Bajaj, Mandeep *medical researcher, educator*
Baker, Deborah *medical educator*
Baker, Richard *physician, consultant*
Baliga, Radhakrishna *pediatrician, educator, nephrologist, director*
Baliga, Ragavendra Ramakrishna *cardiologist, researcher*
Ball, Carroll Raybourne *anatomist, researcher, medical educator*
Baney, Richard Neil *retired physician, internist*
Bar, Robert S. *endocrinologist, educator*
Barbo, Dorothy Marie *obstetrician, gynecologist, educator*
Bardin, Clyde Wayne *biomedical researcher*
Barnett, Benjamin Lewis, Jr. *retired physician, educator*
Baron, Jeffrey *retired pharmacologist*
Basmajian, John Varoujan *medical researcher, educator*
Batalden, Paul Bennett *pediatrician, educator*
Baum, Jules Leonard *ophthalmologist, educator*
Baxter, John Darling *internist, endocrinologist, educator, health facility administrator*
Bayes, Beverley Joan *retired pediatrician*
Beattie, George Chapin *retired orthopedist, surgeon*
Beckett, Victoria Ling *physician*
Beckson, Mace *psychiatrist*
Bejanishvili, Saba *neurologist*
Bellows, Charles Frederick III *surgeon, educator*
Bencardino, Jenny Teresa *musculoskeletal radiologist*
Benfield, John Richard *surgeon, educator*
Bennett, Edward Virdell, Jr. *surgeon*
Bercu, Barry Bernard *pediatric endocrinologist*
Berenson, Abbey Belina *gynecologist, educator*
Berglund, Robin G. *psychiatrist, management consultant*
Berman, Russell Scott *oncologist, educator*
Berry, Gail W. *psychiatrist, educator*
Berry, Phil Hunter, Jr. *orthopedic surgeon*
Beutler, Ernest *physician, research scientist*
Bhaloo, Salim *otolaryngologist*
Bhavsar, Dhaval *medical researcher*
Biagiotti, Guy A. *urologist, medical association administrator, director*
Bianchi, Matt *neurologist, researcher*
Bigby, JudyAnn *medical educator*
Billion, John Joseph *surgeon, retired state representative*
Bin, Joo Won *physician*
Blacker, Deborah *epidemiologist, educator, psychiatrist*
Blankfein, Robert Jerome *retired neurologist*
Blazina, Janice Fay *pathologist*
Bleicher, Sheldon Joseph *endocrinologist, medical educator*
Blount, Benroe Wayne *physician, department chairman*
Boddie, Arthur Walker, Jr. *surgeon, cancer researcher*
Bodner, Bruce Ira *ophthalmologist*
Bogle, Jane E. *medical transcriptionist*
Bolliger, Eugene Frederick *former surgeon*
Bonanno, Bruce Brian *emergency physician*
Bone, Henry Grady III *physician, clinical researcher*
Boone, Charles W. *physician, pathologist*
Boone, Stephen Christopher *retired neurosurgeon*
Borden, Ernest Carleton *oncologist, educator*
Bormann, Marie L. *medical transcriptionist, small business owner*
Borschel, Debaroti Mullick *internal medicine physician*
Botsford, Mary Henrich *retired ophthalmologist*
Bougas, James Andrew *physician, surgeon, educator*
Boynes, Sean G. *dental anesthesiologist, researcher*
Braasch, John William *retired surgeon, consultant*
Braude, Robert Michael *retired medical librarian*
Breda, John Alexander *physician, musician*
Brenes, Jeremy *homeopath, researcher*
Brent, Robert Leonard *medical educator*
Brett-Major, David Michael *physician, military officer*
Brewer, Timothy Francis III *retired cardiologist*
Briccetti, Albert B. *physician, consultant*
Brin, Foster Blake *psychiatrist*
Brinn, Louis Bernard *radiologist*
Bristow, William Harvey, Jr. *psychiatrist*
Brizio-Molteni, Loredana *surgeon, educator*
Broome, Claire Veronica *epidemiologist, researcher*
Brott, Walter Howard *retired cardiac surgeon, educator, military officer*
Brown, Bruce P. *radiologist*
Brown, George W. *social psychiatrist*
Brown, Seth M. *otolaryngologist*
Brownlee, Robert Calvin *pediatrician, educator*
Bruce, David Lionel *retired anesthesiologist, educator*
Bruns, David Eugene *medical educator, researcher*
Bubrick, Melvin Phillip *surgeon*
Buchanan, J(ohn) Robert *physician, educator*
Bucove, Arnold David *psychiatrist*
Buhain, Wilfrido Javier *medical educator*
Buist, Neil Robertson MacKenzie *pediatric educator, medical association administrator*
Burk, Raymond Franklin, Jr. *internist, educator, medical researcher*
Burke, Michael Desmond *pathologist, educator*
Burket, John McVey *retired dermatologist*
Burman, Kenneth Dale *physician*
Bursten, Stuart Lowell *physician, biochemist*
Bustreo, Flavia *epidemiologist*
Butchko, Harriett Hays *physician*
Butler, Douglas John *physician*
Bynes, Frank Howard, Jr. *physician*
Cagle, Roger E. *physician*
Cain, Russell M. *psychiatrist, educator, administrator*
Calvert, William Preston *radiologist*
Campbell, Andrew William *immunotoxicology physician*
Caplin, Olga Yeryomina *psychiatrist*
Carroll, Karen Colleen *pathologist, epidemiologist*
Carswell, Jane Triplett *retired family physician*
Casele, Holly *obstetrician*
Cassell, Eric Jonathan *physician*
Caston, J(esse) Douglas *retired medical educator*
Castro, Maria Graciela *medical educator, geneticist, researcher*
Catalano, Louis William, Jr. *neurologist*
Cefalo, Robert Charles *obstetrician, gynecologist*
Censullo, Michael *radiologist*
Cha, Stephen S. *emergency physician*
Chafkin, Rita M. *retired dermatologist*
Chalif, Ronnie *medical association administrator, artist*
Chang, David Z. *oncologist*
Chang, Hernan Robert *infectious disease consultant*
Chang, Victor Tsu-Shih *oncologist, researcher, educator*
Chassin, Jameson Lewis *retired surgeon*
Chaves-Carballo, Enrique *neuropediatrician*
Chen, Kuen Hai *physician*
Cherry, Sabrina *psychiatrist*
Chiang, Michael Fred *physician*
Chirinos, Julio Alonso *physician, researcher*
Chiu, Dorothy *retired pediatrician*
Chock, Clifford Yet-Chong *family practice physician*
Chretien, Jane Henkel *internist*
Chretien, Paul Bernard *oncologist, medical researcher*
Christenson, William Newcome *retired occupational and internal medicine physician*
Christy, Nicholas Pierson *physician*
Chung, Benjamin Inbeh *urologist*
Cibull, Michael Lee *pathologist, educator*
Clausen, Jerry Lee *psychiatrist*
Cleaver, James Edward *radiologist, educator*
Clemendor, Anthony Arnold *obstetrician, educator, gynecologist, educator*
Cobabe, Alvin Fred *retired surgeon, small business owner*
Cobbs, Charles Glenn *retired medical educator*
Coe, Rodney Michael *medical educator*
Cohen, Michael *urologist*
Cohen, William Nathan *radiologist*
Cohen-Schwartz, Dawn Sheri *radiologist*
Collins, Allen Howard *psychiatrist*
Colman, Jenny Meyer *psychiatrist*
Colonnier, Marc Leopold *retired anatomist*
Connor, Roger Arthur *retired dermatologist*
Conomy, John Paul *neurologist, educator, lawyer*
Conrad, Harold Theodore *psychiatrist*
Conrad-England, Roberta Lee *pathologist*
Contiguglia, Joseph Justin *preventive medicine physician, internist*
Cordes, Brett McCormack *otolaryngologist*
Correa-de-Araujo, Rosaly Lia *medical researcher, medical educator*
Courtnay, Wiliam Gerard *osteopathic physician*
Coutifaris, Christos *gynecologist, research scientist*
Cox, James Elmer *medical educator, department chairman*
Cox, William Andrew *cardiovascular thoracic surgeon*
Craighead, John Edward *pathology educator*
Cremeens, Joanne *medical researcher*
Crino, Marjanne Helen *anesthesiologist*
Cronce, Paul Calvin *retired dermatologist*
Cuetter, Albert Cayetano *neurologist*
Cullen, Shawn Paul *emergency physician, military officer*
Culligan, Patrick John *obstetrician, urogynecologist, surgeon, researcher*
Daher, Edouard *cardiologist*
Daly, Miriam Shamer *retired family physician*
Dana, Edward Runkle *retired physician*
Daniel, William Walter, Jr. *retired radiologist*
Danse, Ilene Homnick Raisfeld *physician, educator, toxicologist, sculptor*
Daram, Sumanth Reddy *medical educator*
Date, Elaine Satomi *physiatrist, educator*
Davidson, Mayer B. *endocrinologist, educator, researcher*
Davidson, Richard J. *retired medical association administrator*
Davis, Mary Helen *psychiatrist, educator*
Davis, Mellar Pilgrim *oncologist*
Dawson, Geraldine *medical educator, social worker*
DeBakey, Michael Ellis *surgeon, educator*
Decker, Mark Jonathan *radiologist*
DeDio, Robert *otolaryngologist*
Delaney, Wayne Edward *retired surgeon*
Delgado, Roger Rodriguez *surgeon, educator*
Delgado Guay, Marvin Omar *internist, geriatrician*
DellaVecchia, Michael Anthony *ophthalmologist, pathologist, educator*
DeMartino, Anthony Gabriel *cardiologist, internist*
DePalma, Ralph George *surgeon, educator*
DeStafeno, John J. *ophthalmologist*
Detweiler, David Kenneth *veterinary physiologist, educator*
DeVita, Vincent Theodore, Jr. *oncologist*
Dews, P(eter) B(ooth) *retired pharmacology educator, physician*
Dhara, Venkata Ramana *physician, educator*
Diaz, Fernando Gustavo *neurosurgeon*
Dicksheet, Sharadkumar *plastic surgeon*
Dickson, James Francis III *surgeon*
Diehl, Louis F. *hematologist*
Diener, Erwin *immunologist*
Dimancescu, Mihai D. *neurosurgeon, researcher, educator*
Ding, Jinwen *biomedical researcher*
DiPietro, Joseph A. *dermatologist*
Divakaran, Vijay Ganesh *medical researcher*
Djang, David S.W. *physician*
Dodge, R(alph) Edward, Jr. *physician*
Doherty, Peter Charles *immunologist*
Dolev, Jacqueline *physician, researcher*
Donahue-Mathov, Sara Heather *radiologist, educator*
D'Ooge, Benjamin Wayne *emergency physician*
Dow, David Sontag *retired ophthalmologist*
Drance, Stephen Michael *ophthalmologist, educator*
Draper, Edgar *psychiatrist*
Dreskin, Stephen Charles *immunologist, allergis*
Drucker, Mitchell David *physician, educator*
Dryman, Amy *epidemiologist*
Dubin, Howard Victor *dermatologist*
Dugan, Charles Clark *retired physician, surgeon*
Dumont, Allan Eliot *retired physician, educator*
Dunagin, William G. *dermatologist*
Dunaway, Frank Rosser III *emergency physicia*
Dunn, Jack Newton *urologist*
Dunn, Linda Kay *retired physician*
Durant, John Ridgeway *retired oncologist, heal facility administrator, consultant*
Durell, Jack *psychiatrist*
Dutta, Sanjeev *surgeon*
Dyar, Kathryn Wilkin *pediatrician*
Dybner, Ruben *urologist*
Dyck, Walter Peter *gastroenterologist, educator, academic administrator*
Dziewanowska, Zofia Elizabeth *pharmaceutical executive*
Eachempati, Soumitra R. *surgeon*
Echols, Robert L. *emergency physician*
Edwards, John Allen *physician, director*
Edwards, Larry David *internist, educator, dean*
Ehigie, Benjamin Odion *radiographer, technologist*
Ehlers, Kathryn Hawes (Mrs. James D. Gabler) *physician*
Eichenwald, Heinz Felix *physician*
Eisenberg, Carola *psychiatrist, educator*
Eisenstat, Theodore Ellis *colon and rectal surgeon, educator*
Eisold, John Francis *physician*
Elgart, Mervyn L. *retired dermatologist, educator*
Elledge, Stephen Joseph *medical educator*
Ellis, Lawrence Dobson *internist, educator*
Enger, Shelley McClelland *epidemiologist, researcher*
Engle, Howard A. *retired pediatrician*
Engle, Mary Allen English *retired physician*
Enhorning, Goran *obstetrician, gynecologist*
Epps, Charles Harry, Jr. *retired orthopaedic surgery educator, dean*
Erbay, Nazli *radiologist*
Erkonen, William Edward *radiologist, medical educator*
Esterly, Nancy Burton *retired physician*
Euwer, Rebecca L. *dermatologist*
Evans, Daniel A. *pediatrician, educator*
Evans, Wayne *obstetrician, perinatologist*
Everett, Mark Allen *dermatologist, educator*
Eviatar, Lydia *pediatrician, neurologist*
Fabunan, Ruben G. *physician, research scienti inventor*
Fanos, Kathleen Hilaire *osteopathic physician, podiatrist*
Faris, James Vannoy *cardiologist, educator, health facility administrator*
Fariss, Bruce Lindsay *endocrinologist, consultant*
Farr, Barry Miller *physician, epidemiologist*
Feinstein, Robert P. *dermatologist*
Feldman, Eva Lucille *neurology educator*
Feldman, Marc David *psychiatrist*
Felgar, Raymond Eugene *pathologist, educato*
Ferencz, Charlotte *pediatrician, epidemiologist, preventive medicine physician, educator*
Ferguson, Emmet Fewell, Jr. *retired surgeon*
Ferguson, John D. *cardiovascular surgeon, researcher, retired military officer*
Fernandes, Verônica Rolim S. *cardiologist, researcher*
Fietsam, Robert, Jr. *physician*
Filley, Christopher Mark *neurologist, research*
Fink, Mitchell Phillip *surgeon, researcher*
Fink, Raymond *medical educator*
Finkelstein, Daniel *ophthalmologist*
Fitch, Frank Wesley *pathologist, immunologis dean, educator*
Fitzpatrick, Raymond John *retired urologist*
Fleishman, Philip Robert *internist*
Fluth, John Adam *medical educator*
Fogel, Esther Marian (Esther Marian Roseig) *veterinary researcher*
Fomon, Samuel Joseph *pediatrician, educator*
Fontane, Emily *physician, educator*
Fontes, Manuel Lopes *medical educator, researcher*
Foreman, Spencer (Spike Foreman) *pulmonologist, retired hospital administrato*
Fornari, Victor M. *psychiatrist*
Fortmann, Stephen Paul *medical educator, researcher, epidemiologist*

Fountain, Karen Schueler *retired physician*
Fournier, Dudley John *surgeon*
Foyouzi-Youssefi, Reyhaneh *pharmacologist*
Fragen, Andrew J. *surgeon*
Francis, Warren William *retired surgeon, educator*
Frangos, Spiros G. *medical educator*
Freedman, Aaron David *retired medicine and biochemistry educator, dean*
Freeman, Theodore Monroe *physician*
Frey, Charles Frederick *surgeon, educator*
Friedensohn, Henry *retired physician*
Friedman, Kent Parks *nuclear medicine physician, educator*
Friedmann, Theodore *physician*
Fukuda, Keiji *epidemiologist*
Furnas, David William *plastic surgeon, educator*
Gahagan, Thomas Gail *obstetrician, gynecologist*
Gajl-Peczalska, Kazimiera J. *retired surgeon, pathologist, educator*
Galbraith, William Bruce *internist, educator*
Gale, Stanley William *psychiatrist*
Galvin, Matthew Reppert *psychiatry educator*
Gardner, John Howland III *neurologist*
Garrett, Marshall Lee *anesthesiologist, educator*
Gartner, Lawrence Mitchell *pediatrician, medical educator*
Gathright, John Byron, Jr. *colon and rectal surgeon, educator*
Gaylin, Willard *physician, educator*
Geha, Alexander Salim *cardiothoracic surgeon, educator*
Gelberg, Lillian *family medicine physician, educator*
Genieser, Nancy Branom *radiologist*
Genkins, Gabriel *physician*
George, Alfred L., Jr. *medical educator, researcher*
Gerald, Michael Charles *pharmacy educator, dean*
Gerard, Gary *neurologist*
Gerber, Milo Phil *urologist*
Gewitz, Michael Harold *pediatric cardiologist*
Gharabawi Garibaldi, George Milad *psychiatrist, neuroscientist*
Ghavamian, Taghi *orthopedist, surgeon*
Gherardi, Gherardo Joseph *pathologist*
Ghogawala, Zoher *neurosurgeon*
Gibb, Ginari Rene *psychiatrist*
Gibson, Milton Eugene *cardiologist*
Gilchrist, Gerald Seymour *pediatric hematologist, oncologist, educator*
Gill, Thomas James III *pathologist, educator*
Gillespie, Gary Don *physician*
Gilmartin, Geoffrey Scott *physician, researcher*
Ginley, Thomas H., Jr. *urologist*
Girgis, Michael M. *physician*
Glaser, Robert Joy *retired internist, foundation administrator*
Glass, Dorothea Daniels *physiatrist, educator*
Glassheim, Jeffrey Wayne *allergist, immunologist, pediatrician*
Glenn, James Francis *urologist, educator*
Glenn, Morton Bernard *retired internist*
Glynn, Kevin Peltier *pulmonologist*
Godfrey, Norman V. *plastic surgeon*
Goffman, Thomas Edward *radiation oncologist*
Gogbashian, Andrew *surgeon, researcher*
Gold, Judith Hammerling *psychiatrist*
Goldberg, Lee Dresden *endocrinologist, educator*
Goldberg, Mark Arthur *neurologist*
Goldberg, Martin *internist, educator*
Goldberg, Michael Ellis *neurologist, neuroscientist*
Golden, Gerald Samuel *retired national medical board executive*
Goldmann, Morton Aaron *cardiologist, educator*
Goldstein, Avram *pharmacology educator*
Goldstein, Burton Jack *psychiatrist*
Goldstein, Dora Benedict *pharmacologist, educator*
Gonnering, Russell Stephen *ophthalmic plastic surgeon*
Goodfellow, Robin Irene *surgeon*
Goodman, Cynthia Diane *public health physician*
Goodwin, Andrew Wirt, II, *radiologist*
Gorden, David Lee *surgeon, educator*
Gosavi, Sucheta *internist*
Gottfried, Eugene Leslie *physician, educator*
Gould, Howard Richard *retired physician*
Grabstald, Harry *urologist, oncologist*
Graham, David G. *preventive medicine physician, psychiatrist*
Graham, James Herbert *retired dermatologist*
Graham, Michael Haw *orthopedist*
Gray, Mary Jane *retired obstetrician, gynecologist*
Graziani, Leonard Joseph *pediatric neurologist, researcher*
Green, David *hematologist*
Green, Morris *retired pediatrician, educator*
Greenberg, Carolyn Phyllis *retired anesthesiologist*
Greene, Donald Richard *dermatologist, educator*
Greene, Jerry George *retired physician*
Greene, Warner Craig *medical educator, administrator*
Greenfield, Val Shea *ophthalmologist*
Greer, Robert Bruce III *orthopedist, educator*
Gregory, David Steven *physician*
Grendell, James Henry *medical educator*
Greuner, David A. *surgeon*
Griffith, B(ezaleel) Herold *retired plastic surgeon, retired educator*
Griner, Paul Francis *physician*
Grossman, Joyce Renee *pediatrician, internist*
Grosso, Sue Jane Rivas *radiologist*
Grunt, Jerome Alvin *retired pediatric endocrinologist*
Gulay, Robert Roman *epidemiologist, educator*
Gulbrandsen, Patricia Hughes *physician*
Gulotta, Stephen J. *cardiologist*
Gundian, Julio Cesar *urologist*
Gundu, Suryakanth R. *gastroenterologist, educator*
Gutbeck, Christian Georg *medical educator*
Haddady, Shirin *medical educator*
Haddy, Theresa Brey *pediatrician, educator, hematologist, oncologist*
Hafez, Mahmoud A. *orthopedic surgeon*
Haft, Gail Klein *pediatrician*
Haga, Kazunori *medical researcher*
Haggerty, Robert Johns *pediatrician, educator*
Hakim-Elahi, Enayat *obstetrician, gynecologist, educator*
Haller, Jordan D. *cardiovascular surgeon*
Halliday, William Ross *retired physician, speleologist, writer*
Hallman, Linda D. *medical association administrator*
Hammar, Sherrel Leyton *medical educator*
Hammond, Graeme Lord *surgeon, educator*
Hand, Roger *physician, educator*
Handford, H. Allen *retired psychiatrist, medical educator*
Hanna, Duke Ellsworth *retired neurological surgeon*
Hanna, Michael George, Jr. *immunologist, pharmaceutical executive*
Hansell, John Royer *retired pathologist*
Hardaway, Robert Morris III *retired surgeon*
Harford, Robert R. *dermatologist*
Harmatuk, Frances A. *retired psychiatrist, anesthesiologist*
Harmel, Merel Hilber *anesthesiologist, educator*
Harrigan, Rosanne Carol *medical educator*
Harrington, John Tolan *medical educator, internist, nephrologist, retired dean*
Harris, Elaine K. *medical consultant*
Harrop, Daniel Smith III *psychiatrist*
Harrow, Jeffrey John *spinal cord injury physician*
Hart, Cecil William Joseph *otolaryngologist, surgeon*
Hart, Paul Vincent, Jr. *emergency and acute care physician, inventor*
Harvey, Birt *retired pediatrician, educator*
Hasselmeyer, Eileen Grace *medical researcher*
H'Doubler, Francis Todd, Jr. *surgeon*
Healy, Bernadine P. *physician, educator, former federal official*
Heckadon, Robert Gordon *plastic surgeon*
Hedley-Whyte, Elizabeth Tessa *neuropathologist*
Hel, Zdenek *immunologist, educator*
Helfand, Arthur Erwin *podiatrist*
Hellerstein, David Joel *psychiatrist, researcher, writer*
Henderson, Cynthia *medical librarian*
Henderson, Melford J. *epidemiologist, molecular biologist, chemist*
Hendry, Jean Sharon *psychopharmacologist*
Hennessey, William Joseph *physician*
Henney, Christopher Scot *immunologist*
Heptinstall, Robert Hodgson *physician*
Herman, Martin Neal *neurologist, educator*
Herrera, Guillermo Antonio *pathologist, educator, researcher*
Hicks, Paul B. *psychiatrist, director*
Higginbotham, Edith Arleane *radiologist, researcher*
Hill, John Sylvester *allergist*
Himes, John Harter *medical researcher, educator*
Hinz, William Max *retired pediatrician, military officer*
Hirose, Teruo Terry *surgeon, educator*
Hirsch, Lawrence Leonard *physician, retired educator*
Hogg, Virginia Lee *retired medical educator*
Holifield-Kennedy, Linda R. *physician*
Hollowell, John W. *retired urologist*
Holmes, David Richard, Jr. *cardiologist*
Holtzman, Robert Neil Nehemiah *neurosurgeon, neurologist*
Holz, George G., IV, *medical educator, research scientist*
Hood, William Boyd, Jr. *cardiologist, educator*
Horswill, C. Weir *retired obstetrician-gynecologist, photographer*
Hoshiwara, Isao *ophthalmologist, consultant*
Hoskins, John Howard *retired urologist, educator*
Howard, Terry Thomas *obstetrician, gynecologist*
Howards, Stuart S. *urologist, educator*
Howell, Joel DuBose *internist, educator*
Howell, Julius Ammons *retired plastic surgeon*
Hricak, Hedvig *radiologist*
Humayun, Mark S. *ophthalmologist, educator*
Hutcheon, Duncan Elliot *physician educator*
Hutter, Adolph Matthew, Jr. *cardiologist, educator*
Huvos, Andrew *internist, cardiologist, educator*
Iannuzzi Sucich, Michele F. *physician*
Irwin, Peter John *orthopaedic surgeon*
Iserson, Kenneth Victor *bioethicist, writer, medical educator*
Islam, Saleem *pediatric surgeon, researcher*
Izenstark, Joseph Louis *retired radiologist, physician, educator*
Jaakkola, Maritta Sylvia *respiratory medicine consultant, researcher*
Jacobs, Gretchen Huntley *psychiatrist*
Jacobson, Eugene Donald *medical educator, academic administrator, researcher*
Jaffe, Charles J. *allergist*
Jaffé, Ernst Richard *medical educator, dean*
Jain, Archana *medical educator*
Jalba, Mihai Sergiu *epidemiologist, pulmonologist, physician, researcher*
Janicak, Philip Gregory *psychiatrist, educator*
Jaquith, George Oakes *ophthalmologist*
Javitt, Daniel C. *psychiatrist, researcher*
Javitt, Jonathan C. *ophthalmologist*
Johnson, Frank Edward *surgeon educator*
Johnson, Leonard Morris *retired pediatric surgeon*
Johnson, Pam Clarene *radiographer, bone densitometrist, consultant*
Johnson, William G. *neurologist, educator*
Johnston, Paul Warren *retired surgeon*
Jolly, Meenakshi *rheumatologist*
Jones, Ervin E. *physician, educator*
Jones, Walton Linton *internist, retired government agency administrator*
Jorapur, Vinod *physician, researcher*
Jorda, Merce Maria *pathologist*
Joseph, Ramon Rafael *internist, educator*
Judge, Nancy Elizabeth *obstetrician, gynecologist*
Judge, Rajinder *psychiatrist*
Kaback, Keith Ross *emergency physician, educator*
Kahwash, Eiad B. *medical educator, poet*
Kaim, Samuel C. *retired psychiatrist*
Kalof, Alexandra N. *pathologist, educator*
Kang, Bann C. *immunologist*
Kantor, Harvey Sherwin *medical educator*
Kaplan, Gabriela Diana *radiologist*
Kaplan, Gerson Nathaniel *retired radiologist*
Kaplan, Paul Elias *physiatrist, writer, educator*
Kaplowitz, Neil *gastroenterologist, educator*
Kapur, Vishesh *medical educator, epidemiologist*
Katz, Andres U. *surgeon*
Kaufman, Stephen Lawrence *radiologist, educator*
Kaushik, Prashant *rheumatologist, educator*
Kaye, Gordon Israel *pathologist, anatomist, educator*
Keating, Mark Taylor *physician, medical educator*
Kebert, Kent Lerdy *ophthalmologist*
Keeney, Virginia T. *retired child psychiatrist*
Keill, Stuart Langdon *psychiatrist*
Kell, Michael Jon *physician, researcher*
Keller, Roberta Lynn *physician, researcher*
Kelley, Patrick Alan *neurologist, educator*
Kent, Georgia L. *obstetrician, gynecologist, healthcare executive, educator*
Kenton, Edgar Jackson III *neurologist*
Kettelkamp, Donald Benjamin *retired orthopedist*
Khan, Arfa *radiologist, educator*
Khan, Junaid H. *surgeon*
Khuri, Fadlo Raja *oncologist, educator*
Kieback, Dirk Guenter *gynecologist, researcher*
Kile, Robert Merlin *emergency physician*
Kim, Deok-Ho *biomedical researcher*
Kim, Robert J. *cardiologist*
Kim-Farley, Robert James *epidemiologist, educator*
Kindberg, Shirley Jane *pediatrician*
King, Hueston Clark *retired otolaryngologist, educator*
Kinzie, Jeannie Jones *radiation oncologist, nuclear medicine physician*
Kirchner, Peter Thomas *nuclear medicine physician, educator, consultant*
Kirkland, Rebecca Trent *endocrinologist*
Kirkpatrick, Charles Harvey *immunologist, researcher*
Kirkpatrick, Garland Penn *retired pediatrician*
Kisker, Carl Thomas *pediatrician, educator*
Kivikoski, Asko Ilmari *retired obstetrician, gynecologist*
Kizilisik, Aydin Tarik *surgeon, researcher*
Kline, Richard C. *oncologist*
Knable, Michael *medical researcher*
Knecht, Ben Harrold *retired surgeon*
Knobloch, Ferdinand J. *psychiatrist, educator*
Kobak, Alfred Julian, Jr. *obstetrician, gynecologist*
Koch, John Michael *psychiatrist*
Koenig, Kristi L. *emergency physician*
Kohrman, Arthur Fisher *pediatrics educator*
Kolesnikov, Evgeni *surgeon, scientist, consultant*
Kolff, Willem Johan *retired internist, medical educator*
Koller, Loren D. *veterinary medicine educator*
Konstantinova, Irina Vital'evna *immunologist, researcher*
Koreman, Dorothy Goldstein *physician, dermatologist*
Kornel, Ludwig *medical educator, physician, scientist*
Kotin, Paul *pathologist*
Kovacs, William Joseph *physician, educator*
Kramer, Richard Jay *gastroenterologist, educator*
Kreider, Clement Horst, Jr. *neurosurgeon*
Krim, Mathilde *medical educator*
Kudo, Toshifumi *surgeon, researcher*
Kumar, Vikas *neuropharmacologist, researcher*
Kundel, Harold Louis *radiologist, educator*
Kupersmith, Joel *internist, medical school dean*
Kurnick, Nathaniel Bertrand *retired oncologist, hematologist*
Kurth, Donald James, Jr. *medical educator, mayor*
Kwik, Christine Irene *physician, retired military officer, retired foreign service officer*
Kylstra, Johannes Arnold *physician*
Lago, Rodrigo M. *internist*
Lake, Carol Lee *anesthesiologist, physician, educator*
Lambert, George H. *physician, director*
Lane, Richard Allan *preventive medicine physician, educator*
Lang, Richard Gordon *physician*
Langell, John Thomas *surgeon, researcher*
Lanham, Richard J. *oncologist, educator*
Lapuz-De La Pena, Erlinda Laron *retired pathology professor*
Larkin, John Edward, Jr. *orthopedic surgeon*
Larson, Richard Smith *pathologist, researcher*
Larson, Roger Keith *physician, writer*
Lasher, Lara Elaine *epidemiologist, researcher*
Lauderdale, Vance, Jr. *anesthesiologist*
Lauterbach, Edward Charles *psychiatric educator*
Lauterstein, Joseph *cardiologist*
Lawless, Michael Rhodes *pediatrics educator*
Lawrence, David Long *radiologist*
Layton, Robert Glenn *radiologist*
Leazer, William *retired biomedical consultant*
Lee, Cathy *emergency physician*
Lee, Charles Sung Chull *otolaryngologist*
Lee, Paul P. *ophthalmologist, educator, lawyer*
Lee, Thomas E. *emergency physician*
Lee, Thomas Tehwen *neurosurgeon*
Lesch, Michael *cardiologist*
Lester, Mark Charles *neurosurgeon*
Levin, Alan Scott *pathologist, allergist, immunologist, lawyer*
Levin, Ian *radiologist*
Levin, Jack *physician, biomedical investigator, educator*
Levin, Steven Jonathan *physician*
Levitt, Seymour Herbert *radiologist, educator*
Levy, Norman B. *psychiatrist, educator*
Li, Maria *neurosurgeon*
Lichtman, Emily Ann *radiologist*
Liebowitz, Daniel S.F. *retired medical educator*
Liess, Benjamin D. *otolaryngologist*
Lillehoff, Piper *psychiatrist*
Lin, Henry C. *physician, researcher*
Lincicome, David Richard *biomedical scientist, animal scientist*
Linz, Anthony James *osteopathic physician, consultant, educator*
Liotta, Lance Allen *pathologist*
Lipkin, David Lawrence *physician*
Lipman, Hannah Ilene *medical educator*
Lipton, Glenn E. *orthopaedic surgeon*
Liu, Songtao *medical researcher*
Lobrano, Mary Elizabeth *radiologist, director*
Lobue, Ange *psychiatrist, author*
Loddenkemper, Tobias *neurologist*
Lohmann, Christoph Hubertus *orthopaedic surgeon, researcher*
Lohmann, George Young, Jr. *neurosurgeon, health facility administrator, artist*
Lollis, Stuart Scott *neurosurgeon*
Loomis, Salora Dale *psychiatrist*
Looney, Gerald Lee *medical educator, administrator*
Lopera, Gustavo Adolfo *cardiologist, electrophysiologist*
Loschen, Earl Lee *psychiatrist, educator*
Low, Eugene Jensen *pathologist*
Lowe, John C. *medical researcher, director*
Lucas, Katherine E. *epidemiologist*
Luce, Edward Andrew *plastic surgeon*
Ludwig, Stephen *pediatrics and emergency medicine educator*
Luedeman, Gerald Warren *radiologist*
Luke, Robert George *nephrologist, medical educator*
Luviano, Damien M. *ophthalmologist*
Maben, Hayward Clinton, Jr. *cardiothoracic surgeon*
Macleod, Angus *retired internist*
Maffei, Frank Anthony *pediatrician, educator*
Mage, Rose Goldman *immunologist, educator*
Magnes, Harry Alan *physician*
Magro, Cynthia Maria *pathologist*
Maguire, James Harvey *physician*
Mahesh, Virendra Bhushan *endocrinologist*
Mahmood, Nafeesa F. *physician, consultant*
Maioriello, Richard Patrick *retired otolaryngologist*
Mak, Linda L. *dermatologist*
Mala, Theodore Anthony *physician, consultant*
Malach, Monte *physician*
Malluche, Hartmut Horst *nephrologist, medical educator*
Malone, Robert Wallace *surgeon*
Mandell, Gerald Lee *internist, educator*
Mangelsdorf, Thomas Kelly *psychiatrist, consultant*
Mangla, Sundeep *radiologist, research scientist*
Mankin, Henry Jay *orthopedist, educator, health facility administrator*
Mankoff, David Abraham *nuclear medicine physician*
Mannelli, Paolo *psychiatrist, educator*
Manning, John Warren III *retired surgeon, medical educator*
Manyam, Bala Venkatesha *medical researcher, neurology educator*
Mao, Aiwu *physician, radiologist*
Marcdante, Karen Jean *medical educator*
Marco, Cura A. *medical educator*
Mariano, Ana Virginia *retired pathologist*
Marino, Giovanni *surgeon*
Markham, Charles Henry *neurologist*
Marrin, Charles Ainsworth Staveley *cardiovascular and thoracic surgeon, educator*
Marshall, Deborah Jill *immunologist*
Marshall, Wayne Keith *anesthesiology educator*
Martin, Clyde Verne *psychiatrist*
Martin, Daniel C. *surgeon, gynecologist, educator*
Martin, George Monroe *pathologist, gerontologist, educator*
Massey, Robert Unruh *internist, educator, dean*
Materson, Richard Stephen *physician, educator*
Mathew, Trini Ann *internist*
Mauger, Thomas F. *ophthalmologist, department chairman*
Maul, Ronald Allen *surgeon*
Mavilio, Domenico *medical researcher, physician*
Mayuga, Kenneth A. *physician*
Mazza, David S. *pediatrician*
McAbee, Gary *neurologist, lawyer*
McBride, Brian F. *biomedical researcher, consultant*
McCarthy-Allen, Mary Frances *medical foundation administrator, not-for-profit fundraiser, consultant*
McCullough, David Legarde *urologist*
McCullough, Laurence Bernard *medical educator, consultant*
Mc Dermott, John Francis *psychiatrist, physician*
McGlashan, Thomas Hamel *psychiatrist, educator*
McGrath, Mary Helena *plastic surgeon, educator*
McKinney, William T. *psychiatrist, educator*
McLawhon, Ronald William *pathology educator, biochemist*
Mclendon, Roger Edwin *neuropathologist, educator*
McLeskey, Charles Hamilton *anesthesiologist, educator, pharmaceutical executive*
Meerschaert, Joseph Richard *retired physician*
Mehta, Ariz Ruyintan *physiatrist, researcher*
Meilman, Edward *physician*
Mellette, Julian Ramsey, Jr. *dermatologist, dermatologic surgeon*
Mellins, Harry Zachary *radiologist, educator*
Mellon, Matthew J. *urologist*

Menachery, Elizabeth P. *physician*
Mendels, Joseph *psychiatrist, educator*
Mengel, Charles Edmund *internist, educator*
Messerle, Judith Rose *retired medical librarian, public relations executive*
Meyer, Carol Frances *retired pediatrician, allergist*
Meyer, Roger Jess Christian *pediatrics educator*
Michaels, Andrew David *medical educator, cardiologist*
Micozzi, Marc Stephen *medical educator, writer*
Millar, John Donald *physician, environmental services administrator, essayist, consultant, musician*
Miller, Anthony Bernard *physician, researcher*
Miller, Charles Leland *pediatrician*
Miller, Conrad S. *emergency physician, writer*
Miller, Geoffrey *child neurologist*
Miller, Jack David R. *radiologist, physician, educator*
Miller, Ross Hays *retired neurosurgeon*
Millikan, Clark Harold *physician*
Milnor, William Robert *physician*
Miskimen, Theresa Marie *psychiatrist, educator*
Modny, Cynthia Jean *dermatologist*
Montgomery, Hubert Theron, Jr. *physician, health care administrator*
Moore, William Henry *radiologist*
Moossy, John *neurologist, consultant, pathologist*
Morehead, Richard Scott *medical educator*
Morrissey, Thomas Paul *medical educator, physician*
Moser, Robert Lawrence *pathologist, health facility administrator*
Moses, Jeffrey Warren *cardiologist, educator*
Motto, Jerome Arthur *psychiatrist, educator*
Mruthinti, Shyamala *pharmacologist, educator*
Mueller-Heubach, Eberhard *medical educator*
Mulcahy, Gabriel M. *pathologist*
Mullins, Charles Brown *physician, academic administrator*
Murat, Yusef J. *plastic surgeon*
Murphey, Sheila Ann *infectious diseases physician, educator, researcher*
Murugan, Thirumagal Anandhi *medical researcher*
Mushlin, Alvin I. *medical educator, researcher*
Myerowitz, P(aul) David *cardiac surgeon, educator, writer*
Myers, Allen Richard *rheumatologist*
Nackhla, G. Habib *retired physician*
Naqvi, Tasneem Zehra *cardiologist, researcher, consultant*
Naraev, Boris G. *physician*
Nardell, Edward Anthony *pulmonologist, researcher*
Nelp, Wil B. *physician, medical educator*
Nelson, Christopher Grant *dermatologist*
Nelson, John Woolard *neurology educator, physician*
Nguyen, Khanh Gia *medical educator*
Nicholls, Richard Aurelius *retired obstetrician, gynecologist*
Nicholson, Henry Hale, Jr. *retired surgeon*
Nieto, Juan Manuel *emergency medicine physician*
Nilakantan, Vani *medical educator, consultant, research scientist*
Nkoy, Flory Lumu *medical educator*
Noji, Eric K. *epidemiologist*
Noonan, Jacqueline Anne *pediatrician, educator*
Nora, James Jackson *physician, writer, educator*
Norbeck, George *psychiatrist, consultant*
Norrid, Henry Gail *osteopathic physician and surgeon, researcher, educator, healthcare facility administrator*
Novack, Alvin John *physician*
Novello, Antonia Coello *pediatric nephrologist, former state health commissioner, United States Surgeon General*
Nusbaum, Margaret Rebecca Harvey *physician, educator, military officer*
Oh, Robert *physician*
Oktem, Ozgur *medical doctor, researcher*
Olds, Jacqueline *psychiatrist, educator*
O'Leary, Dennis Sophian *accrediting body executive*
Omura, Emily Fowler *retired dermatologist*
Orbison, James Archer, Jr. *cardiologist, surgeon*
Orlando, Lori Ann *medical researcher, educator*
Orlowska, Rey Elaine *plastic surgeon*
Orth, David Nelson *endocrinologist, educator, sculptor, potter*
Orton, Sharyn *epidemiologist, government agency administrator*
Ory, Steven Jay *physician, educator*
Pachter, Lee M. *pediatrician*
Pacifico, Albert Dominick *cardiovascular surgeon*
Packard, John Mallory *physician, researcher*
Padian, Nancy *medical educator, epidemiologist*
Palacio, Carlos *physician, medical educator*
Pallin, Samuel Lear *ophthalmologist, educator, medical director*
Park, Myung Kun *medical educator*
Parker, Brent Mershon *retired medical educator, internist, cardiologist*
Parkin, James Lamar *retired otolaryngologist, educator*
Parrish, Matthew Denwood *psychiatrist*
Patchin, Rebecca J. *anesthesiologist, educator, administrator*
Patel, Nima P. *surgeon*
Patel, Uptal Dinesh *nephrologist, researcher*
Pathak, Anant Madhav *retired anesthesiologist*
Patki, Kiran C. *pharmacologist, researcher*
Paul, Norman Leo *psychiatrist, educator*
Pauly, John Edward *retired anatomist*
Payne, Anita Hart *reproductive endocrinologist, researcher*
Pecha, Brian S. *physician*
Pecora, David Victor *retired surgeon*
Pederson, William Christopher *plastic surgeon*
Pedini, Egle Damijonaitis *radiologist*
Pedini, Kenneth *radiologist*
Peixoto Neto, Jose Ulysses *internist, researcher*
Pellegrino, Peter *retired surgeon*
Pelletier, Louis Conrad *surgeon, educator, health facility administrator*
Perl, Harold *neonatologist, pediatrician*
Perlmutter, David H. *physician, educator*
Pesola, Gene Raymond *physician*
Peszke, Michael Alfred *psychiatrist, writer*
Peterson, Ann Sullivan *physician, consultant*
Petkovska, Iva *medical researcher*
Petriashvili, Marina *physician*
Petz, Thomas Joseph *internist*
Pflum, Barbara Ann *retired allergist*
Phillips, John P(aul) *retired neurosurgeon*
Pierangeli, Silvia Susana *medical educator, consultant*
Pierce, Donald Shelton *retired orthopedic surgeon, educator*
Pierce, Michael Norman *internist*
Pindyck, Frank *surgeon*
Pinter, Gabriel George *retired physiology educator*
Pirodsky, Donald Max *psychiatrist, educator*
Pirro, Alfred Anthony, Jr. *emergency physician*
Pittman, Roy Clinton, Jr. *neurosurgeon, theologian, lawyer, philosopher*
Podichetty, Vinod Kumar *medical researcher*
Poehling, Katherine *pediatrician*
Polascik, Mary Ann *ophthalmologist*
Polfliet, Sarah Jean *physician*
Poppers, Paul Jules *anesthesiologist, educator*
Prange, Hilmar Walter *neurology educator*
Prasad, Navin *ophthalmologist*
Prince, George Edward *retired pediatrician*
Propst, Anthony Mark *obstetrician, gynecologist*
Prusiner, Stanley Ben *neurologist, biochemist, virologist, educator*
Purvez, Akhtar *interventional pain management specialist, writer, speaker, advocate*
Pust, Ronald E. *physician, educator*
Quencer, Robert Moore *neuroradiologist, researcher*
Quick, Adam D. *neurologist*
Quintero, Elias Matthew *biomedical researcher*
Qutub, Amina Ann *biomedical researcher, entrepreneur*
Race, George Justice *pathology educator*
Ragheb, Samia *immunologist, educator*
Raichle, Marcus Edward *radiology, neurology educator*
Raines, Jeff *biomedical scientist, medical research director*
Rako, Susan *psychiatrist, writer*
Ram, Chitta Venkata *physician*
Ramirez-Rivera, Jose *physician*
Randall, Peter *retired plastic surgeon*
Randolph, Judson Graves *pediatric surgeon*
Ranney, Helen Margaret *retired internist, hematologist, educator*
Ranney, Richard Raymond *periodontist educator, researcher, dean*
Rausher, David Benjamin *internist, gastroenterologist*
Rawnsley, Howard Melody *pathologist, educator*
Reader, George G. *retired internal-public health medicine educator*
Rebhun, Joseph *allergist, immunologist, medical educator*
Reddy, Ravinder *medical educator, director*
Redman, John Fletcher *urologist, educator*
Regan, Peter Francis III *physician, medical educator*
Reiss, Robert Francis *physician*
Ren, Xing Jian *physician*
Reno, Joseph Harry *retired orthopedist*
Renshaw, Charles Lucius *retired surgeon*
Rewcastle, Neill Barry *neuropathologist*
Rhodes, Linda Jane *psychiatrist*
Rich, Norman Minner *surgeon*
Richardson, Willie Forrest, Jr. *physician, consultant*
Richmond, Julius Benjamin *retired pediatrician, former Surgeon General of the United States, health policy educator*
Rifkin, Stephen *nephrologist*
Rigby, Perry Gardner *medical association administrator, internist, medical educator*
Rigg, Charles Andrew *pediatrician*
Ritter, Ann Marie *pediatric neurosurgeon*
Rivadeneira, David Edward *colon and rectal surgeon, researcher*
Rivet, Dennis James *neurosurgeon*
Roach, James W. *orthopedist, surgeon*
Roberts, Alan Silverman *orthopedic surgeon*
Roberts, Albert Dee *internist*
Roberts, Melville Parker *neurosurgeon*
Roberts, Stanley Dwayne *physician, educator, academic administrator*
Robinson, Rebecca Lynne *medical researcher*
Rock, John Aubrey *gynecologist, obstetrician, educator, administrator, retired chancellor*
Rodgers, Lawrence Rodney *internist, educator*
Rodriguez, William Julio *physician*
Roe, Thomas F. *retired endocrinologist*
Rogers, Mark Charles *physician, entrepreneur, anesthesiologist, pediatrician, educator*
Rollins, Faye Lorraine *medical transcriptionist*
Roman, Stanford Augustus, Jr. *medical educator, dean*
Roncal, Rogelio *psychiatrist*
Rosati, Diane Claire *epidemiologist, educator, artist*
Rosen, Paul Peter *pathologist*
Rosenblum, Mindy Fleischer *pediatrician*
Rosenfeld, Nachman *plastic surgeon*
Roshan, Daniel *obstetrician, gynecologist*
Rothenberg, Albert *psychiatrist, educator*
Rotunda, Adam Michael *dermatologist*
Rouman, James Christ *anesthesiologist*
Rubin, Michael P. *surgeon, researcher*
Rubin, Robert Joseph *internist, nephrologist, consultant*
Ruiz-Deya, Gilberto *urologist*
Russo, Jose *pathologist*
Russo, Vincent Joseph *surgeon*
Ryan, John Joseph *physician*
Salazar, Omar Mauricio *radiation oncologist, educator*
Salmen, Charles R. *medical research scholar*
Salpeter, Shelley *medical educator*
Sandhu, Sukhminder Kaur *epidemiologist, researcher*
Sandler, Harold *retired cardiologist, research scientist, consultant*
Sangster, Paul Edward *radiologist*
Santos, Arthur Magno *thoracic cardiovascular surgeon*
Saravolatz, Louis Donald *epidemiologist, medical educator*
Sargent, William Winston *retired anesthesiologist*
Sawczuk, Ihor S. *urologist*
Scardino, Peter T. *urologic oncologic surgeon*
Schauf, Victoria *pediatrician, educator*
Scheiber, Stephen Carl *psychiatrist, director*
Schenker, Marc Benet *preventive medicine physician, medical educator, department chairman*
Scher, Jordan Mayer *pharmacologist, psychiatrist, alcohol/drug abuse services professional*
Scherger, Joseph Edward *family physician, educator*
Scheuerman, Walter George *retired neurologist, retired surgeon*
Schiff, Martin *physician, surgeon*
Schneck, Stuart Austin *retired neurologist, educator*
Schneider, Calvin *physician*
Schneider, Jan *retired obstetrics and gynecology educator*
Schneider, Thomas Aquinas *surgeon, educator, retired surgeon*
Schulman, Harold *obstetrician, gynecologist*
Schulman, Sidney *neurologist, educator*
Schultz, Robert Jordan *orthopaedic surgeon, educator*
Schwartz, Judy Ellen *thoracic surgeon*
Schwarz, M. Roy *physician, administrator*
Scott, Bradford *surgeon*
Seiff, Stephen S. *ophthalmologist*
Seldin, David C. *internist, medical educator*
Seli, Emre Utku *reproductive endocrinology and infertility specialist, physician researcher*
Seltser, Raymond *epidemiologist, educator, oncologist*
Semler, William Ludwig *retired obstetrician, retired gynecologist*
Sena, Charalena *dental office executive*
Sever, John Louis *medical researcher, educator*
Shabot, Myron Michael *critical care educator*
Shader, Richard Irwin *psychiatrist, pharmacologist, educator*
Shafipour, Pouya *physician, dermatologist*
Shah, Nandlal Chimanlal *retired physiatrist*
Shane, John Marder *endocrinologist*
Shapiro, Donald P. *retired otolaryngologist*
Sharma, Avanti *physician*
Sharma, Padmanee *immunologist, oncologist*
Sharp, Dan Steven *epidemiologist*
Shaw, Ronald Ahrend *physician, educator*
Shayman, James Alan *nephrologist, educator*
Sheldon, Stephen *pediatric sleep medicine educator, researcher*
Shemonsky, Natalie Kaplin *physician, lawyer*
Shenderov, Kevin *immunologist*
Shepard, Richard Blount *surgeon, educator*
Sher, Leo *psychiatrist*
Sherman, John Foord *biomedical consultant*
Sherman, Joseph Owen *pediatric surgeon*
Sherman, Roger Talbot *surgeon, educator*
Sherris, David Allan *surgeon, researcher, educator*
Shetty, Mulki Radhakrishna *retired oncologist*
Shi, Jiaqi *medical educator*
Shifrin, Harris David *physician*
Shils, Maurice Edward *physician, educator, research scientist*
Shohet, Stephen Byron *medical educator*
Short, William Frederick *gynecologist*
Shorter, Nicholas Andrew *pediatric surgeon*
Shumacker, Harris B., Jr. *retired surgeon, educator, author*
Shuster, Frederick *retired internist, gastroenterologist*
Siffert, Robert Spencer *orthopedic surgeon*
Sigmon, J. Lewis, Jr. *medical educator*
Silver, Malcolm David *pathologist, educator*
Simmons, Richmond Hogle *retired obstetrician, gynecologist*
Simonian, Simon John *surgeon, scientist, educator, health science association administrator*
Singer-Chang, Gail Leslie *medical and social sciences educator, consultant*
Singer-Granick, Carol J. *pediatric endocrinologist, educator*
Singh, Meenakshi *pathologist, educator*
Sivak-Callcott, Jennifer A. *ophthalmologist*
Sklar, Eric B. *neurologist*
Skolnick, Lawrence *neonatal physician, medical association administrator*
Skotzko, Christine *psychiatrist, department chairman*
Slavit, David Hal *otolaryngologist*
Slim, Michel S. *surgeon, educator, health facility administrator*
Sloan, Michael Allan *neurologist*
Small, Melvin D. *physician, educator*
Smith, Martin Henry *retired pediatrician*
Smith, Raymond Leigh *retired plastic surgeon*
Smith, Stuart Lyon *psychiatrist, corporate financial executive*
Smits, Helen Lida *medical association administrator, educator*
Snyderman, Ralph *medical educator, physician*
Sobkowicz, Hanna Maria *retired neurologist*
Sola, Augusto *pediatrician, educator*
Soliemanzadeh, Peyman *plastic surgeon, otolaryngologist*
Soltero-Harrington, Luis Rubén *retired surgeon, educator*
Somers, Emmanuel *retired pathologist*
Sontag, James Mitchell *oncologist, researcher*
Spackman, Thomas James *radiologist*
Speicher, Carl Eugene *pathologist*
Speir, William Arthur, Jr. *critical care physician*
Sperber, Alan B. *urologist*
Spitzer, Daniel E. *neurosurgeon*
Stallone, George R. *neurophysiologist*
Stanbury, John Bruton *retired pharmacologist, educator*
Starling, James Ralph *surgeon, educator*
Stein, Paul David *cardiologist*
Stein, Robert Benjamin *biomedical researcher, physician*
Steinbach, Lynne Susan *radiologist, educator*
Steinberg, Jeffrey Mark *obstetrician, gynecologist, medical researcher*
Steinberg, Russell Max *behavioral pediatrician, educator*
Stemerman, David H. *radiologist*
Stepanek, John *emergency physician*
Stevens, Qualls E. *neurosurgeon*
Stewart, Michael Glenn *otolaryngologist, educator*
Stollerman, Gene Howard *internist, educator*
Stolley, Paul David *medical educator, researcher*
Stone, James Robert *surgeon*
Stonnington, Henry Herbert *physician, association administrator, educator*
Strain, James Ellsworth *pediatrician, educator, retired medical association administrator*
Strongin, Jonathan David *physician*
Summers, David Stewart *neurologist, consultant*
Sunde, Douglas *plastic surgeon*
Supino, Phyllis Gail *medical researcher, educator*
Surawicz, Borys *physician, educator*
Sutnick, Alton Ivan *internist, educator, researcher, consultant, dean*
Suzuki, Kunihiko *biomedical educator, researcher*
Svensson, Lars Georg *cardiovascular and thoracic surgeon*
Swerdlow, Martin Abraham *pathologist, educator*
Sykiotis, Gerasimos *biomedical researcher*
Szakal, Andras Kalman *immunologist, anatomis educator*
Tagiuri, Consuelo Keller *child psychiatrist, educator*
Talamo, Jonathan Haskell *ophthalmologist, educator*
Tamborlane, William V., Jr. *pediatrician, educator*
Tandon, Rajiv *psychiatrist, educator*
Taqueti, Viviany R. *immunologist*
Taranta, Angelo (Visca Taranta) *physician, educator*
Taren, James Arthur *neurosurgeon, educator*
Taylor, Peyton Troy, Jr. *oncologist, educator*
Taylor, William Colton *physician, educator*
Tepper, Lloyd Barton *preventive medicine physician, educator*
Terr, Lenore Cagen *psychiatrist, writer*
Terris, Susan *physician, cardiologist, researche*
Theodorescu, Dan *urologic oncologist, molecul biologist*
Thornton, Yvonne Shirley *obstetrician, writer, musician*
Thorsen, Marie Kristin *radiologist, educator*
Tidswell, Mark *medical researcher*
Tiefenbrun, Jonathan *surgeon*
Toledo, Frederico Granchi Steidel *physician, scientist*
Tolia, Vasundhara K. *pediatric gastroenterologist, educator*
Tong, Tommy R. *surgeon, pathologist*
Tourtellotte, Wallace William *neurologist, educator*
Tranquada, Robert Ernest *retired internist, educator*
Troost, Bradley Todd *neurologist, educator*
Tropez-Sims, Susanne *pediatrician, educator*
Tsoukas, Maria Magdalene *dermatologist, educator*
Tucker, Gary Jay *psychiatrist, educator*
Turk, Richard Errington *retired psychiatrist*
Turndorf, Herman *anesthesiologist, educator*
Turner, Harry Spencer *preventive medicine physician, educator*
Turner, John Sidney, Jr. *retired otolaryngologis educator*
Unger, Gere Nathan *emergency physician, lawyer*
Unger, Roger Harold *physician, research scientist*
Uppot, Raul N. *radiologist, researcher*
Utas, Cengiz *nephrologist*
Vakili, Bahman Fakhimi *urologist*
Valentine, William Newton *retired physician, educator*
Valinsky, Mark Steven *podiatrist*
Vallabhan, Girish C. *urologist*
Van Brunt, Edmund Ewing *physician*
Van Heertum, Ronald Lanny *physician*
van Nagell, John Rensselaer *oncologist, gynecologist*
Van Stone, William Webb *psychiatrist*
Varnholt, Heike *pathologist*
Vasudev, Brahm Sarup *nephrologist*
Vest, Gayle Southworth *obstetrician, gynecologist*
Vilenchik, Michael Marc *radiobiologist, biophysicist, bio-oncologist*
Villanueva, Benito *physician, educator*
Vinkey, Rachel Burdick *psychiatrist*
Vittetoe, Marie Clare *retired clinical laborator science educator*
Vlahos, Efstratios G. *retired cardiologist*
Volkman, Alvin *retired physician, research scientist, educator*
Vyas, Nisha Anne *physician*
Walker, Lorenzo Giles *surgeon, educator*
Wang, Nancy *pathologist, educator*
Ward, Chester Lawrence *physician, consultant*
Wasmuth, Carl Erwin *retired physician, lawye*
Waterhouse, Keith *urologist, educator, retired surgeon*
Waters, William Carter III *retired internist, educator*

Waterston, Robert Hugh *medical educator, researcher, medical geneticist, department chairman*
Watson, Donald Charles, Jr. *cardiothoracic surgeon, educator*
Watters, Raymond Wendell *family medicine physician*
Way, Barbara Haight *retired dermatologist*
Weiner, H. Richard *internist*
Weinreb, Herbert L. *physician*
Weinshenker, Naomi Joyce *clinical psychiatrist, educator, researcher*
Weiss, Lyn Denise *physician*
Weiss, Stefan Craig *dermatologist, director*
Weiss, Steven Gary *physician*
Weller, Thomas Huckle *physician, retired medical educator*
Welsh, Louis Ward *otolaryngologist*
Wen, Leana S. *epidemiologist*
Wessel, Morris Arthur *retired pediatrician*
Westernoff, Trent H. *surgeon*
Whelan, Joseph L. *neurologist*
White, Kerr Lachlan *retired physician, foundation administrator*
White, Richard Thomas *radiologist*
Whitehead, Edgar Douglas *urology educator*
Whitehorn, Clark Allan *retired urologist*
Whitman, Gregory Theodore *neurologist*
Whitsell, John Crawford, II, *general surgeon*
Wieland, Gilbert Darryl *medical researcher, anthropologist, gerontologist*
Wilk, Ronald *physician*
Wilkins, Fred Clayton *physician, educator, engineer*
Williams, James Buchanan *retired surgeon*
Williams, Robert Leon *retired psychiatrist, neurologist, educator*
Williams, Steven D. *plastic surgeon*
Willock, Marcelle Monica *retired medical educator*
Wilmore, Douglas Wayne *surgeon, educator*
Wilson, Mary Elizabeth *epidemiologist, physician, educator*
Wilson, Myron Robert, Jr. *retired psychiatrist*
Wingate, Robert Lee, Jr. *internist*
Winslow, Walter William *psychiatrist, educator*
Wishnick, Marcia Margolis *pediatrician, geneticist, educator*
Wivel, Nelson Auburn *physician, medical researcher, educator, biotechnology consultant*
Woldman, Sherman *pediatrician*
Wolf, Jacqueline L. *gastroenterologist*
Woo, Benjamin Kai Pan *psychiatrist*
Woo, Kenneth Roger *urologist*
Wood, Maurice *medical educator*
Woolston-Catlin, Marian *retired psychiatrist*
Worner, Theresa Marie *internist, educator*
Wright, Kevin Dale *medical researcher*
Wyngaarden, James Barnes *retired physician*
ia, Guohua *scientist, psychiatrist, psychologist*
affe, Sumner Jason *pediatrician, educator, science administrator*
alam, Arnold Robert *allergist, immunologist, consultant*
amamoto, Joe *retired psychiatrist, educator*
archoan, Robert *clinical immunologist, researcher*
ee, Henry Chan Myint *cardiologist*
ielding, K. Lemone *physician*
odaiken, Ralph E. *pathologist, occupational health physician, educator*
ollick, Bernard Lawrence *otolaryngologist, surgeon*
oshizumi, Marc O. *ophthalmologist, educator*
oumans, Julian Ray *neurosurgeon, educator*
oung, Alfred Byron *neurosurgeon*
abetakis, Paul Michael *nephrologist, educator*
acarías, Fernando R. K. *physician*
arins, Bertram *orthopedic surgeon*
awacki, Bruce Edwin *surgeon, educator, ethicist*
elazny, Gary A. *dermatologist*
hou, Pengbo *medical educator*
umwalt, Ross Eugene *forensic pathologist, educator*

HUMANITIES: LIBERAL STUDIES

UNITED STATES

LABAMA

thens
usick, Sean R. *history professor, writer*

uburn
nacher, Richard Earl *retired literature educator*
ewis, Walter David *historian, educator*
ttleton, Taylor Dowe *humanities educator*

ay Minette
mon, Janice Crowder *language educator, consultant*

irmingham
len, Lee Norcross *historian, educator*
rden, Cedric Jerome, Sr. *language professor*
ntley, Horace *history professor*
rd, Liesl Hope *language educator*

amp Hill
elzer, John T.S. *translator, editor*

cksonville
ector, Daniel Earl *historian, educator*

llian
rnette, Ollen Lawrence, Jr. *historian*

Loachapoka
Schafer, Elizabeth Diane *historian, writer*

Mobile
Kargleder, Charles Leonard *language educator*

Montgomery
Cornett, Lloyd Harvey, Jr. *retired historian*
Napier, Cameron Mayson Freeman *historic preservationist*
Rose, Shirley Kelly *retired language educator*
Westhauser, Karl E. *historian*
Witkosky, David V. *language educator*

Ramer
Napier, John Hawkins III *historian*

Talladega
Jeffers, Trellie Lee James *language educator, dean*

Troy
Blum, Elizabeth Dian *history professor*

Tuscaloosa
Crowley, John William *literature and language professor*
Freyer, Tony Allan *historian, educator*
Hendrix, Mary Elizabeth *language educator, researcher*
Hocutt, Max Oliver *retired philosophy educator*
Janiga-Perkins, Constance Gabrielle *language educator*
Pass, Charlotte Louise *literature educator, consultant*

ALASKA

Anchorage
Norris, Frank B. *historian*

Soldotna
Stuart, Jodi Marie *language educator*

ARIZONA

Apache Junction
Bracken, Harry McFarland *philosophy educator*
Maher, John *literature educator, writer*

Casa Grande
Landers, Patricia Glover *language educator*

Chandler
D'Angelo, Frank Joseph *literature and language professor*

Davis Monthan Afb
Miller, Charles Wallace *historian, environmental geologist, educator*

Fountain Hills
Mousseux, Renate *language educator*

Glendale
Wise, John Macgregor *speech educator*

Green Valley
Brewington, Arthur William *retired English language educator*

Parker
Cravath, Jay Lewis *cultural educator*

Phoenix
Rister, Gene Arnold *humanities educator*
Schiffner, Adrienne Anita *art historian, educator*

Safford
Kaliher, Michael Dennis *historian, librarian*

Scottsdale
Gwinn, Mary Dolores *organization administrator, writer, lecturer*
Land, George Ainsworth *philosopher, consultant, writer*

Sun City
Oppenheimer, Max, Jr. *foreign language educator, consultant*

Surprise
Clark, Lloyd *historian, writer, educator*

Tempe
Brack, O. M., Jr. *language educator*
Green, Monica H. *history professor*
Iverson, Peter James *historian, educator*
MacKinnon, Stephen R. *Asian studies administrator, educator*
Wetsel, William David *literature educator*
Wong, Timothy C. *language and literature educator*

Tucson
Adjarian, Maude Madeleine *literature educator, researcher*
Beezley, William H. *history professor*
Birkinbine, John, II, *philatelist*
Boyle, Christopher George *language educator, counseling administrator*
Dinnerstein, Leonard *historian, educator*
Gelfand, Howard Michael *history professor*
Herrnstadt, Richard Lawrence *American literature educator*
Schulz, Renate Adele *German studies and second language acquisition educator*
Shaul, David Leedom *linguist, archivist*

ARKANSAS

Arkadelphia
Graves, John William *historian*

Batesville
Bordeau, Catherine *French Professor*

Conway
Stiritz, Marette McCauley *English language educator, consultant*
Wu, Hui *language educator*
Ziegler, John Alan *historian, political scientist, educator*

Fayetteville
Levine, Daniel Blank *classical studies educator*
Woods, Randall Bennett *history professor*

Fort Smith
Colbert, Alice Taylor *history professor*

Gravette
Duncan, Jean Marie *language educator*

Jonesboro
Elkins, Francis Clark *historian, educator, director*

Little Rock
Lewis, Johanna Miller *historian, educator*
Vinikas, Vincent *historian, educator*

Mena
Eddleman, Floyd Eugene *retired language educator*

Monticello
Babin, Claude Hunter *history professor*

State University
Milner, Clyde A., II, *historian*

West Fork
Higgins, Sarah Jean *literature and language professor*

Wickes
Riley, Faith Lynch *retired historian, writer*

CALIFORNIA

Aliso Viejo
La Marca, Jeffry Peter *language educator, consultant*

Arcadia
Yen, Wen-Hsiung *language and music professional, educator*

Bakersfield
Flachmann, Michael Charles *English language educator*
Kegley, Jacquelyn Ann *philosophy educator*
Meyers, Christopher *humanities educator, consultant*
Peterson, Pamela Carmelle *language educator*

Berkeley
Alter, Robert Bernard *literature educator, critic*
Anderson, William Scovil *classics educator*
Campbell, John *philosopher, educator*
Chihara, Charles Seiyo *philosophy educator*
Costa, Gustavo *Italian studies scholar*
Crews, Frederick Campbell *humanities educator, writer*
Donghi, Tulio Halperin *history professor*
Gallagher, M. Catherine *English literature educator*
Herr, Richard *history professor*
Kay, Paul de Young *linguist*
Litwack, Leon Frank *historian, educator*
Lloyd, Elisabeth Anne *philosophy educator*
Long, Anthony Arthur *classics educator*
Mavroudi, Maria *philologist, educator*
Middlekauff, Robert Lawrence *historian, educator, academic administrator*
Muscatine, Charles *language educator, writer*
Partridge, Loren Wayne *art historian, educator*
Rauch, Irmengard *linguist, educator*
Scheffler, Samuel *philosophy educator*
Selz, Peter Howard *art historian, educator*
Shannon, Thomas Frederic *German language educator*
Slezkine, Yuri *history professor*
Taruskin, Richard Filler *musicologist, educator*
Zwerdling, Alex *language educator*

Carmel
Chung, Kyung Cho *Korean history specialist, writer, educator*
Wright, Constance Storey *retired humanities educator*

Carson
Ivers, Louise H. *art history professor*

Chula Vista
Capehart, Bonnie *language educator*

Claremont
Ackerman, Gerald Martin *art historian, consultant*
Atlas, Jay David *philosopher, consultant, linguist, educator*
Barron, Hal S. *historian, history professor*
Burns, Richard Dean *historian, educator, writer*
Davis, Nathaniel *humanities educator*
Deese, E(thel) Helen *retired literature and language professor*
Lofgren, Charles Augustin *historian, educator*
McKirahan, Richard Duncan *classics and philosophy educator*
Moss, Myra Ellen (Myra Moss Rolle) *philosophy educator*
Pinney, Thomas Clive *retired English language educator*
Silverman, Victor *history professor, writer, filmmaker*
Sontag, Frederick Earl *philosophy educator*
Wakefield, Andre *history professor*
Wheeler, Geraldine Hartshorn *historian, writer*
Woodress, James Leslie, Jr. *language educator*

Danville
Frerk-Demaria, Deborah *language educator*

Davis
Altisent, Marta *humanities educator*
Druzhnikov, Yuri Ilya *literature educator, writer*
Hayden, John Olin *English literature educator, writer*
Hoffman, Michael Jerome *humanities educator*
Waddington, Raymond Bruce, Jr. *language educator*
Williamson, Alan Bacher *literature educator, poet, writer*
Willis, Frank Roy *historian, educator*

Dinuba
Surabian, Carol Anne *language educator, consultant*

Fountain Valley
Crecelius, Daniel Neil *history professor*

Fresno
Bundy-DeSoto, Teresa Mari *language educator, vocalist*
Kouymjian, Dickran *art historian, educator*

Fullerton
Bjorklund, Nancy Basler *history professor*
Carrithers, Joseph Edward *English composition and literature educator*

Garden Grove
Cochrum, Ellen Joan *language educator*

Glendale
de Grassi, Leonard *art historian, educator*

Hacienda Heights
Dodson, Arleen Cecilia *language educator*

Hayward
Hammond, Marian Corleene *retired literature educator*

Hemet
Culverwell, Albert Henry *historian*

Huntington Beach
Winterowd, Walter Ross *language educator*

Irvine
Boyd, Carolyn Patricia *history professor*
Bruce-Novoa, Juan David *literature and language professor, writer*
Gilbert, Margaret P. *philosophy professor, researcher*
Hine, Robert Van Norden, Jr. *historian, educator*
Lillyman, William John *language educator, academic administrator*
Pomeranz, Kenneth L. *history professor*

La Jolla
Langacker, Ronald Wayne *linguistics educator*
McDonald, Marianne *classicist*
Olafson, Frederick Arlan *philosophy educator*
Oreskes, Naomi *science historian*
Wesling, Donald Truman *English literature educator*
Wright, Andrew *English literature educator*

La Verne
O'Brien, James D. *language educator, communications executive*

Lafayette
Lichterman, Martin *history professor*

Livermore
Hiskes, Dolores G. *language educator*

Lomita
Welch, Lynne G. *language and music educator*

Long Beach
Alkana, Linda Kelly *history professor*
DelGaudio, Julian Joseph *history professor*
Nguyen, Huong Tran *former elementary and secondary language educator, former district office administrator*

Los Altos
Nivison, David Shepherd *language educator, philosopher*

Los Angeles
Allen, Michael John Bridgman *language educator*
Alpers, Edward Alter *history professor*
Bahr, Ehrhard *Germanic languages and literature educator*
Baker, Donald *literature educator*
Boime, Albert Isaac *art historian, educator*
Bradshaw, Murray Charles *musicologist, educator*
Caram, Eve La Salle *language educator, writer*
Clark, Irene L. *literature and language professor*
Cohen, S(tephen) Marshall *philosophy educator*
Dumitrescu, Domnita *Spanish language educator, researcher*
Frank, Peter Solomon *art historian, curator, critic*
Hines, Thomas Spight *historian, educator, architecture critic*
Hundley, Norris Cecil, Jr. *historian, educator*
Kelley, Robin Davis Gibran *history professor, writer*
Kelly, Henry Ansgar *language educator*
Kolve, V. A. *English literature educator*
Laird, David *humanities educator emeritus*
Lauerhass, Ludwig, Jr. *history professor*
Levine, Philip *classics educator*
Mellor, Ronald John *history professor*
Minkova, Donka *language educator*

Morrell, Ernest Davis *literature and language professor*
Parsons, Terence Dwight *linguist, educator*
Rouse, Richard Hunter *historian, educator*
Schaefer, William David *language educator*
See, Carolyn *English language educator, writer, book critic*
Shuger, Debora Kuller *humanities educator*
Stockwell, Robert Paul *linguist, educator*
Trenton, Patricia Jean *art historian*
Tritle, Lawrence Alan *history professor*
Troy, Nancy J. *art history educator*
Wortham, Thomas Richard *literature and language professor*

Malibu
Larson, Edward John *history and law professor*
Marshall, Donald Glenn *English language and literature educator*

Marina Del Rey
Rimer, John Thomas *language educator, academic administrator, writer*

Menlo Park
Bales, Royal Eugene *retired philosophy educator*

Merced
Hallman, Max O. *humanities professor, philosophy professor, director*

Modesto
Nicholson, Coy Lee *English educator, writer*

Monterey
Franke, Jack Emil *foreign language educator*
Peet, Phyllis Irene *women's studies educator*

Newport Beach
Brown, Giles Tyler *history professor, lecturer*
Mc Culloch, Samuel Clyde *history professor*

Northridge
Omatsu, Glenn *Asian American studies professor*
Orenstein, Michael (Ian Orenstein) *philatelic dealer, columnist*

Norwalk
Ernest, Roger Craig *language educator*

Oakland
Berry, Kathleen A. *English language educator*
Joseph, Marc Alter *philosopher, educator*

Orange
Williams, Danna Beth *reading specialist, educator*

Oxnard
Hill, Alice Lorraine *historian, researcher, genealogist*

Pacific Grove
Lim, Byung-Joon Lucas *language educator, department chairman*

Pacific Palisades
Perloff, Marjorie Gabrielle *literature educator*

Palmdale
Kilanowski, Dana Marcotte *historian, writer, filmmaker, archaeologist*

Palo Alto
Cherno, Melvin *humanities educator*
Knoles, George Harmon *history educator*
Mommsen, Katharina *retired literature and language professor, foundation administrator*

Palos Verdes Peninsula
Alkon, Paul Kent *language educator*

Pasadena
Gregory, Timothy Peter *historian, consultant*
Kousser, J(oseph) Morgan *historian, educator*
Williams, Bradley Bennett *historian*

Paso Robles
Gerstung, Estella Rose *literature and language professor*

Pebble Beach
Dallmann, William Charles *speech educator, writer*

Piedmont
Putter, Irving *retired French language educator*

Placerville
Nesbitt, Paul Edward *historian, author, educator*

Pleasant Hill
Fischer, Laurence Eliot *literature educator, consultant*

Pomona
Cranston, John Welch *historian, educator*

Portola Valley
Carnochan, Walter Bliss *retired humanities educator*

Rancho Cucamonga
Quinn, D. Michael *history professor*

Rancho Santa Fe
Ruiz, Ramón Eduardo *history professor*

Rialto
Hunley, John Dillard *retired historian, ombudsman*

Riverside
Barkin, Kenneth David *history professor*
Elliott, Emory Bernard *language educator, school system administrator*
Salzman, Michele Renee *historian, educator*
Schwitzgebel, Eric *philosopher, educator*
Snyder, Henry Leonard *historian, educator, writer*
Yount, Gwendolyn Audrey *humanities educator*

Rocklin
Blank, Lenore Kim *literature and language professor, consultant*
Bowen, Brenda Denise *literature and language professor*

Sacramento
Carr, Gerald Francis *language educator*
Guisepi, Robert Anthony *historian, writer*
Meindl, Robert James *language educator, poet*

San Diego
Brandes, Raymond Stewart *historian, educator, dean*
Dunlop, Marianne *retired language educator*
Stein, Franklin Joseph *language educator*
Vanderbilt, Kermit *language educator*
Wawrytko, Sandra Ann *humanities educator*
Withee, Diana Keeran *art historian, art dealer, educator*

San Francisco
Arnold, Lauren *art historian, writer*
Bardsley, Kay *historian, archivist, dance professional*
Cherny, Robert Wallace *historian, educator*
Costa-Zalessow, Natalia *foreign language educator*
Dennehy, Raymond Leo *philosopher, educator*
Felstiner, Mary Lowenthal *retired history professor*
Hansen, Carol Louise *literature and language professor*
Kelley, Michael Garhart Roosevelt *historian, educator, writer*
McGuire, William Albert *humanities educator*
Needleman, Jacob *philosophy educator, writer*
Satin, Joseph *language educator, retired dean*
Stahr, Celia Suzanne *art historian, educator*
Stump, David James *philosopher, educator*

San Juan Capistrano
Carlson, Lawrence Arvid *retired English language educator, real estate agent*

San Marcos
Rolle-Rissetto, Silvia *foreign languages educator, writer, artist*

San Marino
Rolle, Andrew *historian, writer*
Zall, Paul Maxwell *language educator, consultant*

San Pablo
Cromartie, J. Vern *humanities educator*

Santa Barbara
Abbott, Horace Porter *English literature educator*
Chafe, Wallace LeSeur *linguist, educator*
Crawford, Donald Wesley *philosophy educator, university official*
Curland, David Joseph *retired language educator*
Del Chiaro, Mario Aldo *art historian, archaeologist, etruscologist, educator*
Fingarette, Herbert *philosopher, educator*
Göllner, Marie Louise *musicologist, retired educator*
Gunn, Giles Buckingham *language, religios studies and global and international studies educator*
Gutierrez-Jones, Carl Scott *English educator*
Helgerson, Richard *English literature educator*
Humphreys, Richard Stephen *history professor, researcher*
Kalman, Laura *history professor*
Mahlendorf, Ursula Renate *literature educator*
McGee, James Sears *historian, educator*
Rose, Mark Allen *humanities educator*
Russell, Jeffrey Burton *historian, educator*
Wilkins, Burleigh Taylor *philosophy educator*

Santa Cruz
Stevens, Stanley David *historian, researcher, retired librarian, archivist*

Santa Maria
Lewis, Mark Kevin *history professor, minister*

Santa Paula
Lattimore, Steven *classicist, educator*

Santa Rosa
Aman, Reinhold Albert *philologist, writer*

Santee
Peters, Raymond Eugene *historian, writer*

Sherman Oaks
Howe, Daniel Walker *historian, educator*

Stanford
Baker, Keith Michael *history professor*
Bell, Susan Groag *historian, researcher*
Brooks, Helen Bousky *literature and language professor, performing arts educator*
Dekker, George Gilbert *literature professor, writer, former academic administrator*
Duus, Peter *retired historian*
Eitner, Lorenz Edwin Alfred *art historian, educator*
Felstiner, John *literature educator, translator*
Findlen, Paula Elizabeth *history educator*
Fredrickson, George Marsh *history professor*
Gelpi, Albert Joseph *language educator, department chairman, critic*
Gumbrecht, Hans Ulrich *literary criticism philosophy educator*
Harrison, Robert Pogue *literature educator*
Jollimore, Troy *philosophy professor, poet*
Jurafsky, Daniel *linguist*
Kennedy, David Michael *historian, educator*
Loftis, John (Clyde), Jr. *language educator*
Marrinan, Michael Joseph *art historian, educator*
Martin, Richard Peter *classics educator, consultant*
Moretti, Franco *professor of comparative literature*
Pentcheva, Bissera V. *art history educator*
Robinson, Paul Arnold *historian, educator, writer*
Sag, Ivan A. *linguist, educator*
Saller, Richard Paul *classics educator*
Sheehan, James John *historian, educator*
Stansky, Peter David Lyman *historian, writer, retired professor*
Traugott, Elizabeth Closs *linguist, educator, researcher*

Stockton
Fung, Rosaline Lee *language educator*
Limbaugh, Ronald Hadley *retired historian, cultural organization administrator*

Torrance
Imbarus, Aura *language educator, consultant*

Vallejo
Brown, Earl Kent *historian, minister*

Van Nuys
Ewing, Guin Porter *historian, art collector*
Zucker, Alfred John *English and history educator, academic administrator, historian*

Venice
Padilla, Mario René *literature educator, writer*

Ventura
Armstrong, Dianne Owens *language educator*

Whittier
Paddy, David *literature and language professor*

COLORADO

Boulder
Engel, Barbara Alpern *history professor*
Hall, Joan Lord *literature and language educator*
Limerick, Patricia Nelson *history professor*
Rood, David S. *linguistics educator*

Cherry Hills Village
Conroy, Mary Elizabeth *history professor*

Colorado Springs
Cramer, Owen Carver *classics educator, department chairman*
Dassanowsky, Robert von *language and film professor, writer, producer*
Stavig, Mark Luther *language educator*
Tucker, Frank Hammond *history professor*
Yaney, George *retired history professor*

Denver
Frederick, Robert Allen *history professor*
Hughes, J(ohnson) Donald *history professor, editor*
Owen, Elizabeth Marie *art historian, educator*
Storey, Brit Allan *historian*

Fort Collins
McComb, David Glendinning *history professor*

Golden
Dickinson, Carol Rittgers *art historian, writer*
Eckley, Wilton Earl, Jr. *humanities educator*
Pegis, Anton George *retired language educator*

Greeley
Downey, Matthew T. *history professor, writer*
Worley, Lloyd Douglas *language educator*

Greenwood Village
Chico, Beverly Ann *history professor, humanities educator*

Palisade
Fay, Abbott Eastman *history professor*

Trinidad
Marshall, Sandra Lee *historian, writer*

CONNECTICUT

Branford
Whitaker, Thomas Russell *English literature educator*

Bridgeport
Psarras, Mary Auten *language educator, tax specialist*

Colebrook
McNeill, William Hardy *retired historian, writer*

East Granby
Scanlon, Lawrence Eugene *language educator*

Essex
Hieatt, Allen Kent *retired language educator*
Hieatt, Constance Bartlett *English language educator*

Fairfield
Miller, Frederick Edwin, Jr. *history professor, government agency administrator*
Newton, Lisa Haenlein *philosopher, educator*

Farmington
Reeves, John Drummond *retired English language professional, writer*

Greenwich
Wiener, Malcolm Hewitt *historian, writer*

Guilford
Colish, Marcia Lillian *history professor*
Hare, Peter Hewitt *philosophy educator*

Hamden
Kagan, Donald *historian, educator*
McClellan, Edwin *literature educator*

Ivoryton
Osborne, John Walter *historian, educator, author*

Middletown
Buel, Richard Van Wyck, Jr. *retired history professor, editor, writer*
Gillmor, Charles Stewart *historian, researcher, educator*
Meyer, Priscilla Ann *literature and language professor*
Pomper, Philip *historian, educator*
Reed, Joseph Wayne *American studies educator, artist*
Schwarcz, Vera *historian, educator, poet*
Shapiro, Norman Richard *literature and language professor*
Slotkin, Richard Sidney *literature educator*
Turco, Alfred, Jr. *language educator*
Wensinger, Arthur Stevens *literature and language professor, writer, translator*

Milford
Foster, Patrick R. *historian, writer*

New Britain
Biskupski, Mieczyslaw Boleslaw *historian, writer*
Emeagwali, Gloria Thomas *humanities educator*
Leeds, Barry Howard *literature and language professor*

New Haven
Abramson, Arthur Seymour *linguistics educator, researcher*
Bloom, Harold *humanities educator, writer*
Blum, John Morton *historian, educator*
Borroff, Marie *English language educator*
Brooks, Peter (Preston) *literature educator, department chairman, writer*
Bynum, Terrell Ward *humanities educator, consultant*
Falco, Thomas Gilbert *historian, researcher*
Frank, Roberta *literature educator*
Gilbert, Creighton Eddy *art historian*
Goffart, Walter André *history professor*
Hallo, William Wolfgang *literature and languag professor, writer*
Harries, Karsten *philosophy educator, researche*
Hersey, George Leonard *retired art historian*
Hollander, John *humanities educator, poet*
Hyman, Paula E(llen) *history professor*
Insler, Stanley *philologist, educator*
Kevles, Daniel Jerome *historian, educator, writ*
Manley, Lawrence G. *literature educator*
Marcus, Ruth Barcan *philosopher, educator, writer, lecturer*
Mazzotta, Giuseppe Francesco *literature and language professor*
Peterson, Linda H. *English language educator*
Pollitt, Jerome Jordan *art historian, educator*
Prochaska, Alice *historian, librarian*
Prown, Jules David *art historian, educator*
Rawson, Claude Julien *literature and language professor*
Robinson, Fred Colson *language educator*
Scully, Vincent Joseph, Jr. *architectural historian, educator, writer*
Shore, Marci *historian*
Smith, John Edwin *philosophy educator*
Snowden, III, Frank Martin *history professor*
Spence, Jonathan Dermot *historian, educator*
Turner, Frank Miller *historian, educator*
Underdown, David Edward *historian, educator*
Venclova, Tomas A. *literature and language professor, writer*
Wandycz, Piotr Stefan *historian, educator*
Winroth, Anders *historian, educator*
Wolterstorff, Nicholas Paul *philosophical theology educator*
Yeazell, Ruth Bernard *English language educator*

New London
Ringel, Faye Joyce *literature educator*

Newington
Chiarenza, Frank John *language educator*

Old Lyme
Willauer, George Jacob *English literature educator*

Orange
Davis, David Brion *historian, educator*

Pleasant Valley
Decker, Robert Owen *history professor, clergyman*

Pomfret
Chase, Thomas Stanhope *language educator, department chairman*

Quaker Hill
Hasse, Wilma Hahn *retired English professor*

Salisbury
Kilner, Ursula Blanche *genealogist, educator, writer*

Storrs Mansfield
Beall, J. C. *philosopher, educator*
Cazel, Fred A., Jr. *history professor*
Charters, Ann *literature educator*
Coons, Ronald Edward *historian, educator*
Dennis, Kelly *art history professor*
Gross, Robert Alan *history professor*

umbull
len, Richard Stanley (Dick Allen) *literature and language professor, writer*

ashington
ab, Daniel Joseph *history professor*

est Hartford
llins, Alma Jones *language educator, writer*

illimantic
cock, Emil *history professor*

oodbridge
pré, Louis *retired philosopher, educator*
einer, Diana Elizabeth Edelman *art historian, educator, academic administrator*

ELAWARE

over
egory, Frank R. *history professor*

ockessin
lbuena-Briones, Angel Julian *retired language educator, author*

ewark
y, Robert Androus *literature and language professor, retired library director, editor, publisher*
x, Alan *philosophy educator*
oson, Ann Eden *art historian, educator*
throp, Thomas Albert *language educator, publisher*
mmel, Stuart *history professor*
einer, Roger Jacob *linguistics educator, writer, researcher*
eintraub, Stanley *arts and humanities educator, writer*
olters, Raymond *historian, educator*

ilmington
rley, Elisabeth Anne *art historian, educator, writer*
eavel, Ann Callanan *humanities educator, communications consultant*
lles, Bryant Franklin, Jr. *retired history and art professor*

STRICT OF COLUMBIA

rt McNair
ines, Edgar Frank, Jr. *historian*

ashington
oston, Gábor *history professor*
brecht, Kathe Hicks *art historian, visual resources manager*
rdahl, Robert Max *history professor, association and former academic administrator*
esenbach-Lucas, Sigrun *language educator, consultant*
oun, Elizabeth *art historian, curator*
eney, Lynne Vincent *humanities educator, writer*
ugherty, Jude Patrick *philosopher, educator, dean*
r, Judith Banzer *retired literature educator, writer, lecturer*
ss, Clive Frank Wilson *history professor*
ench, Valerie *history professor*
mmond, William Michael *historian, educator*
elan, Patrick Aidan *philosophy educator*
ss, Leon Richard *humanities educator*
zin, Michael *historian, writer*
lley, David Christopher *philosopher*
nnedy, Robert Emmet, Jr. *historian, educator*
eidler, Charles W(illiam) *linguist, educator*
einheder, Hazel Fuller *retired genealogist, historian*
winger, Matthew B. *historian*
chtman, Allan Jay *historian, educator, consultant*
vingston, Robert Gerald *historian, journalist*
arr, Phebe Ann *retired historian, educator*
ller, Jeanne-Marie Anderson (Mrs. Nathan J. Miller) *language educator, academic administrator*
ori, Yoshiko *language educator*
ujica, Barbara Louise *language educator, writer*
os, Lawrence Raymond *history educator*
bb, James Willis *romance languages educator*
berts, Jeanne Addison *retired literature educator*
senblatt, Jason Philip *literature and language professor*
shwald, Aviel Isaiah *history professor*
char, Howard Morley *history educator*
amon, Linda Bradley *English literature educator*
ott, Gary Thomas *historian*
verino, Roberto *language educator, academic administration executive*
nko, Jan *English, foreign language and literature educator*
iner, Ruth *musicologist, educator*
ne, Jeffrey Kim *environmental historian, curator*
oboda, Patricia Helen *art historian*
ylor, Estelle Wormley *language educator, dean*
sco, Robert Frederick *church historian, educator*
atch, Robert Marlin *philosopher, researcher*
ll, John Obert *history professor*
tek, John W. *history professor*

ORIDA

lleair Bluffs
exander, Christina Anamaria *translator, performing company executive*

Big Pine Key
Fleischer, Roland Edward *art history professor*

Boca Raton
Dickenson, Katharine Horn *historic preservationist*
Goo, Jahyun *humanities educator*
McFarland, Thomas *English literature educator*

Coconut Creek
Diffine, Suzanne Michele *language educator*

Cooper City
Maugere, Dennis Paul *historian, educator*

Coral Gables
Sabat-Rivers, Georgina *Latin American literature educator*
Spivey, Donald *history professor*

Davie
Wang, Xiao *language educator*

Daytona Beach
Duval, Cynthia *art historian, museum administrator, consultant, curator*
Kruse, Marylin Lynn *retired language educator*
Zenkovsky, Betty Jean *modern languages educator*

Fort Lauderdale
Austin, John Norman *classics educator*

Fort Myers
Curtin, Constance O'Hara *language educator, writer*

Fort Walton Beach
Register, Annette Rowan *literature educator*

Gainesville
Davis, Richard Hunt, Jr. *historian*
Freifeld, Alice *history professor*
Hartigan, Karelisa Voelker *classics educator*
Link, William Allen *history educator*
Pleasants, Julian McIver *history educator, summer school director*

Gulfport
Miller, Rosiland *retired art history educator, writer*

Hillsboro Beach
O'Connell, Richard (James) *English literature educator, poet*

Jacksonville
Carpenter, JoAnn Deakin *history professor*
Roberts, Ricky Elias *linguist, educator*

Key Biscayne
Ross, Marilyn J. *language and communications educator*

Lake Worth
Wilson, William J. *language educator*

Leesburg
Duffy, John Lewis *retired Latin, English and reading educator*

Lutz
Currey, Cecil Barr *retired history professor*

Marathon
Wiecha, Joseph Augustine *language educator*

Melbourne
Jones, Elaine Hancock *humanities educator*

Miami
Camner, Howard *writing educator, writer, poet*
Falco-Leshin, JoAnna M. *literature and language professor*
Klass, Roni *literature and language professor*
Leeder, Ellen Lismore *literature and language professor, literary critic*
Neu, Charles Eric *historian, educator*
Parks, Arva Moore *historian*
Schwartz, Kessel *modern language educator*
Zayas-Bazan, Eduardo *foreign language educator*

Miami Shores
Gonzalez, Pedro Blas *philosopher, educator*

Mulberry
Bowman, Hazel Lois *retired English language educator*

Oldsmar
Thompson, Mack Eugene *historian, educator*

Orlando
Krise, Thomas Warren *academic administrator, literature and language professor, retired military officer*
Murphrey, Elizabeth Hobgood *history professor, librarian*

Osprey
Goffard, Lucien H. *language educator*

Palm Beach
Gaudieri, Alexander V.J. *art historian, educator, museum director*

Pensacola
Brown, Susan Louise *philosopher, educator*
Maddock, Lawrence Hill *retired language educator, writer*

Port Charlotte
Winters, Stanley B. *history professor, consultant, writer*

Port Richey
Long, Michael Eldon *government and history educator*

Saint Augustine
Puma, Vincent Douglas *literature and language professor*

Sarasota
Benowitz, June Melby *historian, educator*
Brown, Stephen Ira *philosophy professor*
Dungy, Kathryn R. *humanities educator*
Platt, Franklin Dewitt *retired history professor*
Taplin, Winn Lowell *historian, retired federal agency administrator*

Stuart
Gilbert, Glenn Gordon *retired linguistics educator*

Tallahassee
Bartlett, Richard Adams *historian, writer, retired history professor*
Golden, Leon *classicist, educator*
Halpern, Paul G. *retired history professor*
Hunt, Mary Alice *retired humanities educator*
Kaelin, Eugene Francis *retired philosophy educator*
Laird, Doris Anne Marley *retired humanities educator, musician*
Mele, Alfred R. *philosophy educator*
Rogers, William Warren *historian, educator, publishing executive, writer*

Tampa
Anton, John Peter *philosopher, educator*
Hegarty, Thomas Joseph *retired history professor*
Mitchell, Mozella Gordon *language educator, minister*
Perry, James Frederic *philosophy educator, writer*
Seiler, Christine Kay *history professor*
Tillson, Albert Holmes, Jr. *history educator*
Tunstall, Graydon Allen *history professor, professional society administrator*
Turner, Stephen Park *philosopher, sociologist, educator*
Williams, Kimberly Elizabeth *history professor*

Temple Terrace
Crispell, Brian Lewis *history professor*

West Palm Beach
Chapman, Roger Eugene *historian, educator*

Winter Park
Benedict, Dorothy Jones *genealogist, researcher*
Mason, Aimee Hunnicutt Romberger *retired philosophy and humanities educator*
Seymour, Thaddeus *language educator*
Wilson, Robley Conant, Jr. *language educator, editor, writer*

GEORGIA

Alpharetta
Whitley, Lena Frances *French educator*

Americus
Isaacs, Harold *history professor*

Andersonville
Boyles, Frederick Holdren *historian*

Athens
Kibler, James Everett *English language educator, writer*
Kretzschmar, William Addison, Jr. *language educator*
Miller, Ronald Baxter *language educator, writer*
Moran, Mary (Molly) Hurley *English language educator*
Winfield, Richard Dien *humanities educator*

Atlanta
Allitt, Patrick Nicholas *history professor, writer*
Benario, Herbert William *classicist, educator*
Brown, Lorene B(yron) *retired library educator*
Burns, Thomas Samuel *history professor*
Chafee, Ingrid Roberta Hoover Coleman *retired language educator*
Goldstein, Eric L. *historian, educator*
Hallen, Barry *philosopher, educator*
Hartle, Robert Wyman *retired literature and language professor*
Kuntz, Marion Lucile Leathers *classicist, historian, educator*
Lu, Hanchao *humanities educator, writer*
Luce, Willard Ray *historian, director*
Meyer, James Sampson *art historian, educator*
Oliver-Warren, Mary Elizabeth *retired library science educator, library and information scientist*
Pindle, Arthur Jackson, Jr. *philosopher, researcher*
Stewart, Michael McFadden *speech professional*

Augusta
Dyer, James Harold, Jr. *language educator*
Mixon, Kenneth Wayne *history professor, department chairman*

Bainbridge
Kirkland, William Michael *history professor*

Byron
Morton, Eric *liberal arts educator*

Carrollton
Morton, Elizabeth Gron *art historian, educator*

Cochran
Ricks, John Addison III *history professor*

Dahlonega
Williams, Linda Stallworth *literature and language professor*

Dalton
Nielsen, Mary Tanzy *literature and language professor, department chairman*

Decatur
Dillingham, William Byron *literature educator, author*
Manley, Frank *language educator, writer*
Showers Johnson, Violet Mary-Ann Iyabo *history professor*

Gainesville
Nichols, Dana *language educator*

Hinesville
Etheridge, James Ralph *history professor*

Hoschton
Sneed, Larry Allan *history professor*

Macon
Huffman, Joan Brewer *history professor*
Papagan, Harry Gregory *literature and language professor*

Morrow
Gooden, Randall Scott *historian, archivist*

Saint Simons Island
Schneider, Duane Bernard *English literature educator*
Spivey, Ted Ray *language educator*

Savannah
Swartz, Anne *art historian*
Yagami, Kazuo *historian*

Valdosta
Cronin, Kevin Stewart *historian, educator*

Villa Rica
Blevins, Ernest Everett *genealogist, researcher, historian*

Waleska
Ast, Thesesa Lynn *history professor*

HAWAII

Honolulu
Bender, Byron Wilbur *linguistics educator*
Dyen, Isidore *linguistic scientist, educator*
Hoffmann, Kathryn Ann *humanities educator*
Jordan, Amos Azariah, Jr. *foreign affairs educator, retired military officer*
Niyekawa, Agnes Mitsue *foreign language professor*
Rehg, Kenneth Lee *linguistics educator*
Stephan, John Jason *historian, educator*
Varley, Herbert Paul *Japanese language and cultural history educator*

Pearl City
Fujita, James Hiroshi *history educator*

IDAHO

Jerome
Ricketts, Virginia Lee *historian, researcher*

Moscow
Greever, Janet Groff *history professor*
Harris, Robert Dalton *retired history professor, researcher, writer*

Rexburg
Ivers, John Joseph *language educator, dean*

ILLINOIS

Anna
Pleinta, Tod Algiers *philosopher, educator*

Arlington Heights
Ehrmann, Susanna *language educator, photographer, writer*

Barrington
Graham, Berta *humanities educator, researcher*

Belvidere
Wells, April *language educator*

Bloomington
Bridges, Roger Dean *historian*
Laurenti, Joseph Luciano *language educator, writer*

Carbondale
Hahn, Robert Alan *philosophy educator*
Lanigan, Richard Leo, Jr. *humanities educator, writer, editor*
Weeks, Theodore R. *history professor*

Champaign
Douglas, George Halsey *language educator, writer*
McGlathery, James Melville *retired foreign language educator*
Smith, Ralph Alexander *cultural and educational policy educator*
Watts, Emily Stipes *retired English language educator*

Chicago
Bevington, David Martin *English literature educator*
Biggs, Robert Dale *Near Eastern studies educator*

Boyer, John William *history professor, dean*
Brinkman, John Anthony *historian, educator*
Chang, Peter M.J. *musicologist, educator*
Cohen, Charles Emil *art historian, educator*
Cohen, Ted *philosopher, educator*
Crone, Anna Lisa *Russian literature educator*
Cullen, Charles Thomas *historian, librarian*
Danzer, Gerald Arlin *history professor*
De Armas, Frederick Alfred *foreign language educator*
Debus, Allen George *historian, educator*
Dembowski, Peter Florian *foreign language educator*
D'Emilio, John *humanities educator, writer*
Eze, Emmanuel Chukwudi *philosophy professor*
Frantzen, Allen John *English language educator*
Geyer, Michael *history professor*
Goldsmith, John Anton *linguist, educator*
Gossett, Philip *musicologist*
Grant, Robert McQueen *humanities educator*
Gray, Hanna Holborn *historian, educator*
Haley, George *Romance languages educator*
Harris, Neil *historian, educator*
Hast, Adele *historian, editor, writer*
Hellie, Richard *historian, educator*
Hilbert, David R. *philosopher, educator*
Hillocks, George, Jr. *language educator, researcher*
Hung, Wu *art historian, educator*
Johnson, Janet Helen *literature educator*
Kaegi, Walter Emil *history professor*
Karanikas, Alexander *language educator*
Katz, Friedrich *history educator*
Keenan, James George *classics educator*
Knight, Cranston S. *history professor*
Lawler, James Ronald *French language educator*
Manning, Sylvia *language educator*
McCloskey, Deirdre Nansen *economics and history educator*
Michaels, Walter Benn *English professor, writer*
Murrin, Michael J. *literature educator, writer*
Najita, Tetsuo *history professor*
Nashat, Guity *historian, education educator, researcher*
Opitz, Donald L. *science historian*
Pippin, Robert B. *philosopher, educator*
Remini, Robert Vincent *historian*
Rosales, Veronica *language educator*
Roy, David Tod *literature educator*
Schroeder, Christopher *literature and language professor, writer*
Sewell, William Hamilton, Jr. *historian*
Shaughnessy, Edward Louis *language educator*
Sljivic-Simsic, Biljana B. *Slavic and Baltic languages educator*
Sochen, June *history professor*
Thaden, Edward Carl *history professor*

Dekalb
Stahl, Norman A. *literature and language professor, department chairman*

Des Plaines
Page, Helen (Lyn) Bard Ward *literature educator*
Valdes, Annmarie *history professor, researcher*

Edwardsville
Petry, Alice Hall *scholar, educator, writer*

Elmhurst
Scurlock, Jo Ann *history professor, researcher*
Stanger, John Goodman *literature and language professor, archivist*

Evanston
Reiss, Lenore Ann *language educator, retired secondary school educator*
Sheridan, James Edward *history professor*
Van Zanten, David Theodore *humanities educator*
Weil, Irwin *literature and language professor*
Wills, Garry *historian*
Wright, John *classics educator*

Forest Park
Creighton, Robert Emmett *retired language educator, retired chaplain*

Freeport
Giaimo, Paul Sebastian *English and philosophy educator*

Galesburg
Hellenga, Robert Riner *language educator, writer*

Hoffman Estates
Kahn, Elizabeth *language educator, department chairman*

Homewood
Schillings, Denny Lynn *retired history professor, educational and grants consultant*

Mount Vernon
Hall, Sharon Gay *retired language educator, artist*

Normal
Olsen, Patrice Elizabeth *history professor, photographer*
Shields, John Charles *literature educator*
Trouille, Mary Seidman *foreign language educator*

Palos Hills
Mc Intyre, James R. *history professor, researcher*

River Forest
Jackson, William Vernon *Latin American studies and library science educator*

Riverside
Dunn, Barbara Ann *language educator*

Robinson
Wolven, Ann Reed *literature and language professor, journalist*

Rock Island
Symons, Van Jay *humanities educator*

Rockford
Hoshaw, Lloyd *retired historian, educator*

Romeoville
Hoppe, Elizabeth Anne *philosopher, educator*

Seymour
Carringer, Robert *language educator*

Springfield
Jackson, Jacqueline Dougan *literature educator, writer*
Neginsky, Rosina *literature educator, writer, poet*
Temple, Wayne Calhoun *historian, writer*

Sycamore
Whisenhunt, Donald Wayne *historian, educator, dean*

Urbana
Antonsen, Elmer Harold *Germanic languages and linguistics educator*
Arnstein, Walter Leonard *retired historian*
Haile, H. G. *German language and literature educator*
Hendrick, George *retired English language educator*
Hoxie, Frederick Eugene *history professor*
Kaufmann, Urlin Milo *English literature educator*
Kim, Chin-Woo *linguist, educator*
Koenker, Diane P. *history professor*
Love, Joseph LeRoy *history professor, former cultural studies center administrator*
McColley, Robert McNair *historian, educator*
Neal, Larry Dwight *retired economic historian, educator*
Nelson, Cary Robert *language educator*
Rodgers, Daryl Mark *language educator*
Solberg, Winton Udell *historian, educator*
Talbot, Emile Joseph *French language educator*

Westchester
Masterson, John Patrick *retired language educator*

Wilmette
Monter, E. William *retired history professor*

INDIANA

Bloomington
Anderson, Judith Helena *English language educator*
Asai, Rika *musicologist, educator*
Choksy, Jamsheed Kairshasp *historian, religious scholar, humanities educator, language educator*
Dunn, Jon Michael *logician, dean*
Engber, Cheryl Ann *retired language educator, linguist*
Gros Louis, Kenneth Richard Russell *humanities educator*
Hanson, Karen *philosopher, educator*
Johnson, Owen Verne *historian, educator*
Juergens, George Ivar *history professor*
Lebano, Edoardo Antonio *foreign language educator*
Martins, Heitor Miranda *foreign language educator*
Mickel, Emanuel John *foreign language educator*
Peterson, M. Jeanne *historian, educator*
Ransel, David Lorimer *history professor*
Rosenberg, Samuel Nathan *French and Italian language educator*
Sinor, Denis *history professor, linguist*
Stoeltje, Beverly June *liberal studies educator*
Wilson, George Macklin *history educator, cultural studies center administrator*

Carmel
Sukapdjo, Wilma Irene *language educator*

Cedar Lake
Bocock, Scott Gregory *historian*

Crawfordsville
Barnes, James John *historian, educator*

Fort Wayne
Miller, Dawn L. *composition literature educator*

Gary
Osan, Ana M. *language educator*

Goshen
Nolt, Steven M. *historian*

Greencastle
Dittmer, John Avery *history professor*
Spicer, Harold Otis *retired English language educator, communications educator*
Weiss, Robert Orr *speech educator*

Greenwood
Knapp, Sylvia Clare *retired language educator*

Indianapolis
Baetzhold, Howard George *retired language educator*
Bodenhamer, David Jackson *historian, educator*
Boling, Joseph Edward *numismatist, retired military officer*
Connor, Ulla M. *linguistics educator*
Davis, Kenneth Wayne *language educator, business communication consultant*
Fox, Stephen Lee *language educator*
Krasean, Thomas Karl *historian*
Lindseth, Erik Lars *humanities educator*
Mason, Thomas Alexander *historian, educator, author*
Odell, James Calvin *history professor, theology studies educator*
Plater, William Marmaduke *literature and language professor, academic administrator*

Middlebury
Mulholland, Janet Lynn Healy *retired language educator, writer*

Muncie
Martínez, Iván David *language educator, translator*
Zhuk, Sergei Ivanovich *history professor, researcher*

Notre Dame
Appleby, R(obert) Scott *history educator*
Jemielity, Thomas John *language educator*
Lanzinger, Klaus *language educator*
Matthias, John Edward *English literature educator*
McInerny, Ralph Matthew *philosopher, educator, writer*
Noll, Mark A. *history professor*
O'Rourke, William Andrew *literature and language professor, writer*
Raymer, John David *literature and language professor*

South Bend
Cook, Pamela Margaret *French educator*
van Inwagen, Peter Jan *philosophy educator*

Terre Haute
Baker, Ronald Lee *folklore educator*
De Marr, Mary Jean *English language educator*
Gennaro, Rocco Joseph *philosopher, educator*
McCarter, David Harold *historian, volunteer*

Valparaiso
Peters, Howard Nevin *foreign language educator*

West Lafayette
Bertolet, Rodney Jay *philosophy educator*
Blakesley, David Edward *language educator, small business owner*
Broden, Thomas Francis III *French language educator*
Contreni, John Joseph, Jr. *humanities educator*
Mc Bride, William Leon *philosopher, educator*
Mork, Gordon Robert *historian, educator*
Roberts, Randy W. *history professor*
Williams, David Jon *historian, artist*
Woodman, Harold David *historian, educator*

Westfield
Hayashi, Tetsumaro *retired literature educator, writer, editor*

IOWA

Ames
Avalos, Hector Ignacio *language educator*
Courteau, Joanna *foreign language educator*
Maxwell Dial, Eleanore *foreign language educator*
Nostwich, Theodore Daniel *literature educator, researcher*

Cedar Falls
Broadie, Richard R. *history professor*
Clohesy, William Warren *philosopher, educator*
Schnucker, Robert Victor *historian, educator*

Cedar Rapids
Fitzpatrick, John Charles *humanities educator, curator*

Centerville
Moritz, Dana Dee *language educator*

Davenport
Holleran, Karen Elaine *literature and language professor*
Patterson, Nicholas Noel *language educator, journalism educator*

Des Moines
Webb, Mary Christine *reading recovery and in-class educator*

Fairfield
Rogers, Benjamin Franklin *retired history professor*

Forest City
Biggs, Douglas Lee *historian, educator*

Grinnell
Kintner, Philip L. *history professor*
Michaels, Jennifer Tonks *foreign language educator*

Iowa City
Addis, Laird Clark, Jr. *philosopher, educator, musician*
Aspel, Paulene Violette *retired language educator*
Ertl, Wolfgang *German language and literature educator, artist*
Folsom, Lowell Edwin *language educator*
Gelfand, Lawrence Emerson *historian, educator*
Green, Peter Morris *classics educator, writer, translator*
Hawley, Ellis Wayne *historian, educator*
Kerber, Linda Kaufman *historian, educator*
McKee, Christopher Fulton *historian, educator*
Mills, Margaret H. *linguist*
Raeburn, John Hay *language educator*
Solbrig, Ingeborg Hildegard *retired literature educator, writer*

Mount Pleasant
Brereton, Todd Richard *history professor*

Oskaloosa
Porter, David Lindsey *history and political science professor, writer*
Robbins, Janet Linda *language educator*

Pella
Den Adel, Raymond Lee *classics educator*

KANSAS

Atchison
Lane, Elizabeth Ann *genealogist, researcher*

Chanute
Dillard, Dean Innes *English language educato academic administrator*

Dighton
Stanley, Ellen May *historian, consultant*

Emporia
Lovett, Christopher C. *history professor, consultant*

Fort Leavenworth
King, Curtis Steeble *history professor*

Hiawatha
Searight, Karen S. *language educator*

Lawrence
Alexander, John Thorndike *historian, educator*
Cienciala, Anna Maria *history professor*
Clowes, Edith W. *language educator, consulta literature educator, consultant*
Earle, Jonathan Halperin *history professor*
Eldredge, Charles Child III *art history educat*
Gunn, James Edwin *language educator*
Li, Chu-Tsing *art historian, educator*
Rath, Eric Clemence *history professor*
Saul, Norman Eugene *historian, educator*
Schoeck, Richard J. *English and humanities scholar, poet*
Tuttle, William McCullough, Jr. *history profes*
Woelfel, James Warren *philosophy and humanities educator*
Worth, George John *retired English literature educator*

Leawood
Ivey, Donald James *historian, archivist*

Manhattan
Higham, Robin *historian, editor, publisher*

North Newton
Sprunger, Keith L. *historian, educator*

Olathe
Anderson, Joshua M. *speech educator*

Onaga
Dillinger, Susan Alice *reading specialist*

Overland Park
Burger, Henry G. *linguist, anthropologist, writ*
Paulsen, Ruth Ann *French and Spanish langu educator*

Topeka
Sheldon, Roy Albert *literature and language professor*

Wichita
Spurgeon, Kenneth R. *history professor*
Waters, Mary A. *literature and language professor*

KENTUCKY

Berea
Drake, Richard Bryant *retired history professo*

Bowling Green
Jackson, Carlton Luther *history professor, writ*

Crestwood
Perry, Norah D. *language educator*

Danville
Levin, William Robert *art historian*

Georgetown
Klotter, James C. *historian, educator*

Glasgow
Coomer, Merle Joan *retired language educato*

Highland Heights
Ramage, James Alfred *history professor*

Lexington
Coffman, Edward McKenzie *retired history professor*
Thelin, John Robert *historian, educator, researcher*
Warth, Robert Douglas *history professor*

Louisville
Mackey, Thomas Clyde *historian*

Richmond
Dunston-Coleman, Aingred Ghislayne *history professor*
Huch, Ronald Kind *historian, educator*

Southgate
Glenn, Jerry Hosmer, Jr. *retired language educator*

LOUISIANA

Amite
Duncan, Johnny Lee *historian*

Baton Rouge
Arceneaux, William *historian, educator, association administrator*
Cooper, William James, Jr. *history professor*
Culbert, David Holbrook *historian, educator, editor, writer*
Doty, Gresdna Ann *theatre historian, educator*
Hardy, John Edward *language educator, writer*
Ricapito, Joseph Virgil (Giuseppe Ricapito) *literature educator*
Sabliov, Cristina Mirela *humanities educator*
Shindo, Charles J. *historian, director*
Wheeler, Otis Bullard *retired language educator, retired director*

Bogalusa
Villarrubia, Glenda Boone *reading specialist, reading coordinator, educational consultant, educator*

Lafayette
Brasseaux, Carl Anthony *historian, educator, academic administrator, curator*
Carstens, Jane Ellen *retired library science educator*
Damico, Jack Samual *speech educator*
Raffel, Burton Nathan *literature educator, poet, translator*

Monroe
Chardkoff, Joan Corb *language educator*
Galle, Jeffrey Wayne *literature and language professor, department chairman*

Natchitoches
LeBreton, Marietta M. *history professor*
Wells, Carol McConnell *genealogist, retired archivist*

New Orleans
rumfield, William Craft *Slavic studies educator, photographer, writer*
rost, Dan R. *history professor, department chairman*
Iall, Gwendolyn Midlo *historian, educator*
Iasselbach, Karlheinz *retired literature educator*
uza, Radomir Vaclav *historian, educator*
Iichney, Todd Michael *history professor*
'aolini, Gilberto *literature educator*
'oesch, Jessie Jean *art historian*
Reck, Andrew Joseph *philosopher*
Roberts, Louise Nisbet *philosopher, educator*
chalow, Frank Hickey *philosopher, educator*

Ruston
Dodge Robbins, Dorothy Ellin *language educator*
Roach, Susan *literature educator*

MAINE

Bar Harbor
'arpenter, William Morton *language educator, writer*

Brunswick
Iodge, James Lee *German language educator*
evine, Daniel *historian, educator*

Bucksport
'es, Edward Dawson *folklore educator*

Castine
erleant, Arnold *philosopher*

Dresden
urco, Lewis Putnam *language educator*

Portland
essler, Carol Farley *retired English language educator*
chwanauer, Francis *philosopher, educator*

Rockport
oodwin, Doris Helen Kearns *historian, writer*

anford
llan, Jonathan David *autograph dealer, pop culture historian*

Scarborough
adik, Marvin Sherwood *art historian, consultant, retired museum director*
uch, Leah D.T. *language educator*

Waterville
assett, Charles Walker *literature and language professor*
mon, David L. *art historian*

West Boothbay Harbor
arshall, Howard Lowen *musicologist, retired music educator*

MARYLAND

Annapolis
rann, Eva Toni Helene *philosophy educator*
amoie, Laura Croghan *history professor*
ucas, George Ramsdell, Jr. *philosophy educator*

Baltimore
chinstein, Peter Jacob *philosopher, educator*
aldwin, John Wesley *history professor*
hapelle, Suzanne Ellery Greene *history professor*
ohen, Warren I. *history professor*
ooper, Jerrold Stephen *historian, educator*
aeri, Niloofar M. *linguist, educator*
vin, John Thomas *humanities educator*
ohnson, Michael Paul *historian, educator*
dson, Horace Freeland *history professor, writer*
essler, Herbert Leon *art historian, educator, academic administrator*
Kimbrough, Natalie *history professor*
Knight, Franklin W. *historian, educator*
Kurth, Lieselotte *foreign language educator*
Lidtke, Vernon LeRoy *history professor*
McCarthy, Patricia Anne *reading educator*
Nichols, Stephen George *Romance languages educator*
Paulson, Ronald Howard *language educator, humanities educator*
Ranum, Orest Allen *historian, educator*
Williams, Michael J. *philosopher, educator*
Ziff, Larzer *literature and language professor*

Bel Air
Lu, David John *historian, writer*

Bethesda
Child-Olmsted, Gisèle Alexandra *retired language educator*
Fee, Elizabeth *medical historian, administrator*
Highfill, Philip Henry, Jr. *retired language educator*
van der Linden, Frank Morris *historian*

Betterton
Kohl, Benjamin Gibbs *historian, educator*

Bowie
Cook, Hardy Merrill III *literature and language professor*
LeCounte, Lola Houston *literature and language professor, educational consultant*
Sterling, Richard Leroy *English and foreign language educator*

Capitol Heights
Gerstl, Cynthia Koren *foreign and English language educator*

Catonsville
Oden, Gloria *language educator, poet*

Chevy Chase
Cline, Ruth Eleanor Harwood *translator*
Fern, Alan Maxwell *art historian, retired museum director*

College Park
Bedos-Rezak, Brigitte Miriam *historian, educator*
Brush, Stephen George *historian, educator*
Hallett, Judith Peller *classical studies educator*
Olson, Keith Waldemar *historian, educator*
Oster, Rose Marie Gunhild *foreign language professional, educator*
Panichas, George Andrew *language educator, critic, editor*
Pasch, Alan *philosopher, educator*
Weart, Spencer Richard *historian*

Columbia
Marshall, Linda Murphy *linguist, government official*

Cumberland
Riggs, Robert Meldrum *French educator*

Ellicott City
Loerke, William Carl *art historian, educator*

Germantown
Naake, Joan Murray *English professor*

Glen Burnie
Sanchez-Barnett, Susan Lynn *historian, educator*

Harwood
Dudley, William Sheldon *historian*

Hyattsville
Golden, Marita *literature educator, writer, foundation administrator*
Rodgers, Mary Columbro *literature educator, writer, academic administrator*
Supanick, Beverly Jane *language educator*

La Plata
Stephanic, Barbara Jean *art historian, writer, curator, researcher*

Largo
Haines, Corrie Gerald *history professor*

Lusby
Eshelman, Ralph Ellsworth *historian, consultant, paleontologist*

Mitchellville
Embree, Ainslie Thomas *history professor*
Griffen, Clyde Chesterman *retired historian*
Heald, Morrell *humanities educator*

North Potomac
Kapsch, Robert James *engineering and architectural historian*

Pasadena
De Pauw, Linda Grant *historian, educator, writer*

Rockville
Cantelon, Philip Louis *historian*
Clarke, Nina Honemond *historian, writer, retired principal*
Fein, Stephanie Lynne *language educator*
Hewlett, Richard Greening *historian*
LeCompte, Andrew C. *freelance/self-employed interpreter*

Severna Park
Schick, Edgar Brehob *language educator*

Silver Spring
Borkovec, Vera Z. *literature and language professor*
Calinger, Ronald Steve *historian*
Cole, Wayne Stanley *historian, educator*
Doherty, William Thomas, Jr. *historian, retired educator*
Johnson, Richard August *literature and language professor*
Papas, Irene Kalandros *English language educator, poet, writer*
Rothberg, Morey David *historian, editor*

Towson
Ali, Omar H. *history professor*
Baker, Jean Harvey *history professor*
Propst, M. Teresa Carson *historian*

MASSACHUSETTS

Amherst
Baker, Lynne Rudder *philosophy educator*
Brooks, A. Taeko *historian*
Gibson, Walker *retired language educator, poet, writer*
Kinney, Arthur Frederick *humanities educator, writer*
Oates, Stephen Baery *retired historian*
Pritchard, William H. *literature educator, writer*
Rosbottom, Ronald Carlisle *language and humanities educator*
Taubman, Jane Andelman *literature and language professor*
Wolff, Robert Paul *philosophy educator*
Wyman, David Sword *retired historian, educator*

Auburndale
Lindgren, Charlotte Holt *language educator*

Bedford
Cady, Dona M. *humanities educator*

Belmont
Cavarnos, Constantine Peter *philosopher, writer*
Dohanian, Diran Kavork *art historian, educator*

Beverly
Pierard, Richard Victor *history educator*

Boston
Bardaglio, Peter Winthrop *humanities educator, former academic administrator*
Blakely, Allison *history professor*
Cardona, Rodolfo *Spanish language and literature educator*
Daniels, Norman *philosopher, educator*
Diamandopoulos, Peter *philosophy professor*
Golder, Herbert Alan *classics educator*
Henry, DeWitt Pawling, II, *literature educator, art association administrator, writer*
Hintikka, Jaakko *philosopher, educator*
Jin, Xuefei (Ha Jin) *literature educator, writer*
Kleiner, Fred Scott *art historian, archaeologist, educator, editor*
Lyons, David Barry *philosophy and law educator*
Mc Carthy, Joseph Michael *historian, educator*
Properzio, Paul J. *classicist, educator*
Rosen, Stanley Howard *humanities educator*
Scanlon, Dorothy Therese *history professor*
Wermuth, Paul Charles *retired language educator*

Brookline
Michopoulos, Aristotle V. *humanities educator, researcher*
Moon, John Ellis van Courtland *retired historian*

Cambridge
Armitage, David Richard *historian*
Asani, Ali S. *foreign language and religious studies educator*
Bailyn, Bernard *historian, educator*
Bhabha, Homi K. *humanities educator, writer*
Billings, Joshua *literature scholar*
Blair, Ann *historian*
Bolster, Arthur Stanley, Jr. *history professor*
Brustein, Robert Sanford *literature and language professor, theater director, writer*
Chomsky, (Avram) Noam *linguistics and philosophy educator*
Conley, Tom Clark *literature educator*
Craig, Albert M. *history professor, researcher*
Damrosch, Leopold, Jr. *English educator*
Elkins, Caroline M. *history professor, writer*
Engell, James Theodore *language educator, department chairman*
Fanger, Donald Lee *Slavic language and literature educator*
Ferguson, Niall Campbell Douglas *history professor, writer*
Fisher, Philip J. *English language and literature educator*
Fisher, Stephen Carey *musicologist, editor*
Flier, Michael Stephen *Slavic languages educator*
Ford, Patrick Kildea *Celtic studies educator*
Gates, Henry Louis, Jr. *literature and language professor, historian*
Graham, Loren Raymond *historian, educator*
Greenblatt, Stephen Jay *literature and language professor, writer*
Guthke, Karl Siegfried *language educator*
Hanan, Patrick Dewes *foreign language professional, educator*
Iriye, Akira *historian, educator*
Jones, Christopher Prestige *classicist, educator, historian, consultant*
Keller, Evelyn Fox *philosophy of science professor*
Kelly, Sean Dorrance *philosophy educator*
Keyser, Samuel Jay *linguist, educator*
Kirby, William C. *history professor, former dean*
Koester, Helmut Heinrich *history professor*
Lagemann, Ellen Condliffe *history and education professor, dean*
Laiou, Angeliki Evangelos *history professor*
Lee, Lester P., Jr. *historian*
MacMaster, Robert Ellsworth *historian, educator*
Maier, Charles Steven *history professor*
Maier, Pauline *historian, educator*
Malmstad, John Earl *literature and language professor*
Mazlish, Bruce *historian, educator*
McDonald, Christie Anne *literature and language professor, writer*
Menand, Louis *literature educator, writer*
Nykrog, Per *French literature educator*
O'Neil, Wayne *linguist, educator*
Owen, Edward Roger John (E. Roger Owen) *Middle Eastern studies professor, writer*
Perdue, Peter C. *history professor*
Reyes-Cubides, William *language educator, researcher, writer, actor*
Ritvo, Harriet *historian*
Rosenberg, Charles Ernest *historian, educator*
Rosenkrantz, Barbara Gutmann *science and medicine historian*
Rotberg, Robert Irwin *historian, political scientist, educator, academic administrator*
Sevcenko, Ihor *history and literature professor*
Simon, Eckehard (Peter) *foreign language educator*
Smith, Merritt Roe *history professor*
Stauffer, John William *cultural historian*
Tarrant, Richard J(ohn) *classicist, educator*
Thernstrom, Stephan *historian, educator*
Thorburn, David *literature educator*
Trumpbour, John *historian, researcher, director*
Vanger, Milton Isadore *historian, educator*
Vendler, Helen Hennessy *literature educator, poetry critic*
Ware, Susan W. *historian*
Weitzman, Arthur Joshua *language educator*
Wolff, Christoph Johannes *music historian, educator*
Ziolkowski, Jan Michael *medievalist educator*

Canton
Parker, Virginia Marie *language educator*

Chelmsford
DiPillo, Patricia Anne *language educator, researcher*

Chestnut Hill
Blanchette, Oliva *philosophy educator*
Hachey, Thomas Eugene *British and Irish history educator*
O'Toole, James Michael *history educator*
Pendas, Devin Owen *history professor*
Reed, James Eldin *historian, consultant, educator*
Valette, Rebecca Marianne *Romance languages educator*

Framingham
Casper, Leonard Ralph *American literature educator*

Granby
Ingham, Norman William *literature educator, genealogist*

Great Barrington
Rodgers, Bernard Francis, Jr. *literature and language professor*

Holland
McGrory, Mary Kathleen *humanities educator, retired academic administrator*

Lenox
Berofsky, Bernard *philosopher, educator*

Leverett
Margolis, Nadia *language educator, translator, medievalist*

Lowell
Carlsmith, Christopher *history professor*
McAfee, Noelle Claire *philosopher, educator*

Medford
Bedau, Hugo Adam *philosophy educator*
Caviness, Madeline Harrison *art history educator, researcher*
Dennett, Daniel Clement *philosopher, writer, educator*
Fyler, John Morgan *language educator*
Jackendoff, Ray Saul *linguistics educator*
Sherwin, Martin J. *history professor*
Ueda, Reed Takashi *historian, educator*
Wilson, Jonathan Michael *literature educator, writer*

Milton
Frazier, Marie Dunn *speech professional, public relations executive, personnel director*

Needham
Kenslea, Timothy Joseph *historian, educator*

Newton
Marshall, Robert Lewis *musicologist, educator*

North Andover
Herstein, Gary L. *philosophy professor, researcher*

North Dartmouth
Yoken, Mel B(arton) *language educator, writer, radio personality*

North Easton
Varella, Hazel L. *historian, educator*

Northampton
Elkins, Stanley Maurice *historian, educator*
Smith, Malcolm Barry Estes *philosopher, educator, lawyer*
von Klemperer, Klemens *historian, educator*

Randolph
Morrissey, Edmond Joseph *philologist*

Revere
Paananen, Victor Niles *language educator*

Sherborn
Cushing, Steven *linguist, educator, writer, researcher, consultant*

Shutesbury
Creed, Robert Payson, Sr. *retired literature educator*

Somerville
Imende-Cooney, Elizabeth F. *literature educator, consultant*

South Hadley
Berek, Peter *literature and language professor*
Brownlow, Frank Walsh *literature and language professor*
Farnham, Anthony Edward *language educator, department chairman*
Horsnell, Margaret Eileen *retired historian*

Springfield
Habermehl, Lawrence LeRoy *philosophy educator*
Miller, Leroy Paul, Jr. *language educator*

Stoughton
Hall, Roger Lee *musicologist, educator, composer*

Sunderland
Baritz, Loren *history professor*

Waltham
Fischer, David Hackett *historian, educator*
Sachs, Murray *French language and literature educator, researcher*
Scheffler, Israel *philosopher, educator*
Schrecker, John *historian, educator*
Staves, Susan *humanities educator*

Watertown
Rivers, Wilga Marie *language educator*

Wellesley
Bidart, Frank *English educator, poet*
Martin, Tony *humanities educator*
Mistacco, Vicki E. *foreign language educator*

Wellfleet
Mc Feely, William Shield *historian, writer*

Wenham
Wang, Dong *history professor, director*

Weston
Higgins, Sister Therese *literature educator, former college president*
Oates, Mary Josephine *historian, educator*

Williamstown
Bell, Robert *literature educator*
Dalzell, Robert Fenton, Jr. *historian, educator*
Dew, Charles Burgess *historian, educator*
Fuqua, Charles John *retired classicist*
Graver, Lawrence Stanley *language educator*
Graver, Suzanne Levy *English literature educator*
Norton, Glyn Peter *literature educator*
Oakley, Francis Christopher *historian, educator*
Pistorius, George *language educator, educator*
Rudolph, Frederick *history professor*

Worcester
Billias, George Athan *historian, educator*
Dwork, Debórah *history professor*
Vaughan, Alden True *history professor*
Zeugner, John Finn *historian, educator, writer*

Yarmouth Port
Weiner, Charles *historian, educator*

MICHIGAN

Albion
Cocks, Geoffrey Campbell *history professor*

Allendale
Parker, Kelly Andrew *philosopher, educator*

Ann Arbor
Alexander, Buzz (William) *literature and language professor*
Blouin, Francis Xavier, Jr. *history professor*
Bornstein, George Jay *literary educator*
Chang, Chun-Shu *historian, educator, writer*
Chang, Hsueh-lun Shelley *historian, researcher, writer*
Cowen, Roy Chadwell, Jr. *language educator*
Curley, Edwin Munson *philosophy educator*
Delbanco, Nicholas Franklin *language educator, writer*
Dunnigan, Brian Leigh *historian, curator*
Eisenstein, Elizabeth Lewisohn *historian, educator*
Ferrell, Robert Hugh *historian, educator*
Feuerwerker, Albert *historian, educator*
Forsyth, Ilene Haering *art historian*
Hackett, Roger Fleming *historian, educator*
Hannoosh, Michele Ann *language educator*
Izzo, Herbert John *language and linguistics educator, researcher*
Janko, Richard Charles Murray *humanities educator*
Knott, John Ray, Jr. *language educator*
MacCormack, Sabine Gabriele *history educator*
McCarus, Ernest Nasseph *retired language educator*
Mizruchi, Mark Sheldon *sociology professor, business administration professor*
Munro, Donald Jacques *philosopher, educator*
Nelson, Roy Jay *retired French educator*
Perkins, Bradford *historian, educator*
Pernick, Martin Steven *history professor*
Potter, David Stone *Greek and Latin educator*
Railton, Peter Albert *philosophy educator*
Stolz, Benjamin Armond *foreign language educator*
Trautmann, Thomas Roger *history professor, anthropology educator*
Turits, Richard Lee *history professor*

Belmont
Wooster, Stephanie Lynne *art historian, artist*

Beulah
Tanner, Helen Hornbeck *historian, consultant*

Dearborn
Little, Daniel Eastman *philosopher, educator, director*
Papazian, Dennis Richard *retired historian, educator, commentator*

Detroit
Brill, Lesley *literature and film studies educator*
Brunk, Thomas Walter *art historian*
Chauderlot, Fabienne-Sophie *foreign language educator*
Covensky, Edith *language educator, poet*
Schwartz, Matthew Barahal *historian*
Small, Melvin *historian, educator*

Dewitt
Hutting, Lori A. *language educator*

East Lansing
Anderson, David Daniel *retired humanities educator, writer, editor*
Fisher, Alan Washburn *historian, educator*
Hine, Darlene Clark *history educator, administrator*
Natoli, Joseph *language educator*
Schoenl, William James *history professor*
Seaton, James Everett *humanities educator*
Tzitsikas, Helene *retired literature educator*

Escanaba
Wood, D. Ann *language and music educator*

Farmington
Ellens, J(ay) Harold *philosopher, educator, psychotherapist, minister*

Grand Rapids
Collier, Brian *history professor*
Luttikhuizen, Henry Martin *art historian, curator*
Schmidt, Gary David *language educator*
Vande Kopple, William John *literature and language professor*

Grosse Pointe
Hendrie, Janice Ellen *language educator*

Howell
Rohrabacher, Janet Hammond *genealogist, archivist*

Jackson
Feldmann, Judith Gail *language professional, educator*

Jerome
Dillon, Merton Lynn *historian, educator*

Kalamazoo
Breisach, Ernst A. *historian, educator*
Coss, Barbara Sue *humanities educator*
Dybek, Stuart *language educator, writer*
Julien, Catherine *history professor*
Miazga, Ronald C. *language educator*
Stavig, Richard Thorson *retired literature educator*

Livonia
Holtzman, Roberta Lee *French and Spanish language educator*

Rochester
Estes, Todd A. *historian*

Sault Sainte Marie
Money, Robert McGuffey *history professor*

Southfield
Stern, Marvin *history professor*

University Center
Clark, Basil Alfred *language educator*
Dadlez, Anna Romana *language educator*

West Bloomfield
Williamson, Marilyn Lammert *literature educator, academic administrator*

Ypsilanti
Cere, Ronald Carl *languages educator, consultant, researcher*
Wegner, John Mark *historian*

MINNESOTA

Duluth
Schroeder, Fred Erich Harald *humanities educator*

Mankato
Janc, John J. *language educator*
Preska, Margaret Louise Robinson *historian, educational association administrator*

Marshall
Pichaske, David Richard *language educator*

Minneapolis
Bales, Kent Roslyn *language educator*
Bashiri, Iraj *Central Asian studies educator*
Erickson, Gerald Meyer *classical studies educator*
Farah, Caesar Elie *language educator, historian*
Fergus, Patricia Marguerita *language educator, writer, editor*
Firchow, Evelyn Scherabon *German language and literature educator, writer*
Firchow, Peter Edgerly *language professional, educator, writer*
Garner, Shirley Nelson *language educator*
Hellman, Geoffrey P. *philosopher, educator*
Karras, Ruth Mazo *history professor*
Kohlstedt, Sally Gregory *historian, educator*
Ross, Donald, Jr. *language educator, academic administrator*
Seidel, Robert Wayne *science historian, educator*
Tracy, James Donald *historian, educator*
Weiss, Gerhard Hans *German language educator*

Moorhead
Buckley, Joan N. *retired literature and language professor*
Shoptaugh, Terry Lee *historian, archivist*

Northfield
Clark, Clifford Edward, Jr. *history professor*
Iseminger, Gary Hudson *philosophy educator*
Paas, John Roger *language educator*
Soule, George Alan *literature educator*
Yandell, Cathy Marleen *language educator*

Saint Cloud
Hofsommer, Donovan Lowell *history professor*

Saint Paul
Huzar, Eleanor Goltz *historian, educator*
Mather, Richard Burroughs *retired Chinese language and literature educator*
Monson, Dianne Lynn *literacy educator*
Weiner, Carl Dorian *retired historian*

Vadnais Heights
Polakiewicz, Leonard Anthony *foreign language and literature educator*

Waseca
Strand, Melvin LeRoy *English educator*

MISSISSIPPI

Cleveland
Boschert, Thomas Neville *historian, educator*

Clinton
Bigelow, Martha Mitchell *retired historian*

Gulfport
Swetman, Glenn Robert *literature and language professor, poet*

Hattiesburg
Scarborough, William Kauffman *historian, educator*
Wiest, Andrew Allen *history professor, writer*
Zelner, Kyle Forbes *historian, educator*

Jackson
Daniels, Patsy Jean *literature professor*

Mayhew
Marsh, Patricia Guyton *humanities educator*

Mississippi State
Cook, Susan Deborah *language educator, writer*
Lowery, Charles Douglas *historian, dean, educator*

Oxford
Landon, Michael de Laval *retired history professor*

Raymond
Simpson, William M. *history professor*

Senatobia
Banham, Sandra Rodgers *language educator*

MISSOURI

Ballwin
Robbert, Louise Buenger *retired historian*

Belton
Bryant, Tammi D. *history professor*

Bolivar
Goss, Curtis Dale *language educator*
Smith, James O. *history professor, writer*

Cape Girardeau
Smallwood, David Andrew *language educator, education educator*

Columbia
Bien, Joseph Julius *philosophy educator*
Fulweiler, Howard Wells *language professional*
Gupta, Bina *philosopher, educator*
Horner, Winifred Bryan *humanities educator, researcher, consultant, writer*
Keown, Linda Jane *language educator*
Looser, Devoney Kay *English literature educator*
Mullen, Edward John, Jr. *Spanish language educator*
Overby, Osmund Rudolf *art historian, educator*
Schwartz, Richard Brenton *English language educator, dean, writer*
Strickland, Arvarh Eunice *history professor*
Timberlake, Charles Edward *historian, educator*

Gainesville
Sayles, Wayne Gerald *numismatist, writer*

Joplin
Fang, Qiang *history professor*

Kansas City
Bitner, Teddy Dwight *history professor, military officer*
Hoffmann, Donald *architectural historian*

Kirksville
Hanley, Mark Young *historian, educator, researcher*
Ling, Huping *history professor*
Maldonado-Class, Joaquin *language educator*
Rose, Lynn (M. Lynn Rose) *history professor*

Marshall
Zank, Virginia *literature and language professor*

Parkville
Brackett, Mary Virginia *language educator, writer*

Poplar Bluff
Samuell, Tiechera Dawn *language educator*

Saint Louis
Barmann, Lawrence Francis *historian, educator*
Berg, Darrell Matthews *musicologist*
Herbert, Kevin Barry John *classics educator*
O'Gorman, Gerald Joseph *language educator*
Rowan, Steven William *history professor*
Ruland, Richard Eugene *literature educator, critic, historian*
Sale, Merritt *classicist, educator, comparatist*
Schwarz, Egon *language educator, writer, critic*
van den Berg, Sara Jane *language educator*
Weixlmann, Joseph Norman, Jr. *language educator, academic administrator*
Wellman, Carl Pierce *philosophy educator*

Saint Peters
Long, Lydia Ann *literature and composition professor*

Salem
Wood, Thomas Wesley *humanities educator, editor*

Sarcoxie
Elliott, Diane Reid *history professor*

Springfield
Bartee, Wayne C. *retired history professor*
Burgess, Ruth Lenora Vassar *speech and language educator*
Easley, June Ellen Price *genealogist*
Moran, Jon S. *humanities educator*

Warrensburg
Leonard, Raymond W. *historian, educator*

Windyville
Condron, Barbara O'Guinn *philosopher, educator, academic administrator, writer*

MONTANA

Billings
DeRosier, Arthur Henry, Jr. *historian*

Bozeman
Hufstetler, Mark Allan *historian*
Warrick, Kimberley Kaye *language and social studies educator*

Missoula
Kittredge, William Alfred *humanities educator*

NEBRASKA

Lincoln
Leinieks, Valdis *classicist, educator*
Mach, Jan Ellen Walkenhorst *literature educator, editor*
Sawyer, Robert McLaran *historian, educator*

Omaha
Kuhlman, Thomas Ashford *retired American studies educator, writer*
Rainey, Deana Lee Parks *language educator*

Wayne
Weixelman, Joseph Owen *history professor*

York
McNeese, Beverly Diane *language educator*

NEVADA

Henderson
Tierno, Joel Thomas *philosopher, educator*

Las Vegas
Donaghy, Henry James *literature educator, academic administrator*
Gafford, Mary May Grimes *retired humanities educator*
Jarvis, Renee Marie *language educator*

Reno
Glotfelty, Cheryll *literature and language professor*

Winnemucca
Westmoreland, Jessie Allred *literature educator*

NEW HAMPSHIRE

Derry
Holmes, Richard Dale *history consultant*

Durham
Gold, Janet Nowakowski *Spanish language educator*
Hapgood, Robert Derry *language educator*

Harris, John William *historian, educator*
Simic, Charles *language educator, poet*

Exeter
Rimkunas, Barbara *historian, educator*

Hanover
Bien, Peter Adolph *language educator, writer*
Christesen, Paul C. *classical studies educator*
Daniell, Jere Rogers, II, *retired historian*
Garthwaite, Gene Ralph *historian, educator*
Gert, Bernard *philosopher, educator*
Luxon, Thomas Hyatt *language educator, director*
Mansell, Darrel Lee, Jr. *language educator*
Oxenhandler, Neal *literature educator, writer*
Russell, Robert Hilton *Romance languages and literature educator*
Scherr, Barry Paul *foreign language educator*
Shewmaker, Kenneth Earl *history professor*

Keene
Higgins, Roland Louis *history professor*

Kingston
Walen, Harry Leonard *historian, lecturer, author*

Lyndeborough
Roper, Stephanie Abbot *history professor, writer*

Meredith
Heald, Bruce Day *English and music educator, historian*

Plymouth
Hunnewell, Richard *art historian, educator*

Portsmouth
Harter, Hugh Anthony *foreign language educator*

NEW JERSEY

Atlantic Highlands
Levine, George Lewis *literature and language professor, critic*

Avon By The Sea
Potter, Emma Josephine Hill *language educator*

Bedminster
DeCostanzo, Marybeth *language educator*

Blackwood
Perkins, Rita Wade *historian, educator*

Bordentown
Spitzer, Lois Nancy *language educator*

Bradley Beach
Unger, Irwin *historian, educator*

Cape May
Savage, Maureen Walls *retired history professor*
Turner, Almon Richard *retired art historian, educator*

Chester
Lynch, Beverly Love *language educator*

Cranford
Russell, John Joseph *English educator*

Dumont
Radock, Geoffrey Johnston *English professor*

Glassboro
Donahue, Mary Lee *literature and language professor, editor*
Korieh, Chima J. *history professor*

Hewitt
Mollenkott, Virginia Ramey *English literature and language educator, writer, guest lecturer*

Hightstown
Schorske, Carl Emil *historian, educator*

Hillsdale
Sageao, Carolynn Finnen *language educator*

Jersey City
Jennings, Sister Vivien *literature and language professor*
Codeiro, José M. *art historian, educator*

Lawrenceville
Maxwell, Max Anthony *retired language educator*

Lincroft
Lago, Paul Edward *historian, educator*

Lodi
McParland, Robert Patrick *literature educator, writer*

Madison
Rosales Herrera, Raúl Joaquin *language educator*
Skaggs, Merrill Maguire *humanities educator*

Montclair
Sardarkar, Aditya *humanities educator*

Morristown
Fredericks, Robert Joseph *language company executive*

New Brunswick
Chambers, John Whiteclay, II, *history professor*
Gillette, William *historian, educator*
Grob, Gerald N. *historian, educator*
Hartman, Mary Susan *historian, educator*
Jenkins, Reese V. *historian, educator*
O'Neill, William Lawrence *retired history professor*

Qualls, Barry V. *literature professor*
Reed, James Wesley *social historian, educator*
Stich, Stephen Peter *philosophy educator*

Newark
Morales, Grisel *language educator*
Schweizer, Karl Wolfgang *historian, educator, author*
Varzegar, Minoo *literature educator, reading specialist*

North Brunswick
Moon, Kathleen K. *language arts educator*

Nutley
Marée, Kathleen Nancy *retired language educator*

Princeton
Aarsleff, Hans *linguistics educator*
Bowersock, Glen Warren *retired historian, educator*
Brombert, Victor Henri *literature educator, author*
Brown, Leon Carl *historian, educator*
Bynum, Caroline Walker *history professor, writer*
Cooper, John Madison *philosophy educator*
Corngold, Stanley Alan *language educator, writer*
Ermolaev, Herman Sergei *Slavic languages educator*
Frankfurt, Harry Gordon *philosophy professor*
Frey, Julia Bloch *language and art educator, historian*
Goheen, Robert Francis *classicist, educator, former ambassador*
Grafton, Anthony Thomas *history professor*
Habicht, Christian Herbert *history professor*
Harman, Gilbert Helms *philosophy educator*
Hollander, Robert B., Jr. *retired romance languages educator*
Howarth, William (Louis) *literature and language professor, writer*
Howell, David Luke *history professor*
Hynes, Samuel *language educator, writer*
Jordan, William Chester *historian, educator*
Keeley, Edmund LeRoy *literature educator, writer, translator*
Knoepflmacher, Ulrich Camillus *literature educator*
Mc Pherson, James Munro *history professor*
Moote, A. Lloyd *history professor*
Moynahan, Julian Lane *retired literature educator, writer*
Nehamas, Alexander *philosophy educator*
Painter, Nell Irvin *historian, educator, writer*
Paret, Peter *historian*
Rabb, Theodore K. *historian*
Rodgers, Daniel Tracy *historian, educator*
Shimizu, Yoshiaki *art historian, department chairman*
Singer, Peter Albert David *philosophy educator, writer*
Walter, Hugo Günther *humanities educator, poet*
West, Cornel Ronald *humanities educator, writer*
White, Morton Gabriel *philosopher, writer, historian, retired educator*
Wilentz, Sean *historian, educator, writer*
Wilmerding, John *art historian, educator, curator*
Yu, Ying-Shih *retired history professor, writer*
Ziolkowski, Theodore Joseph *literature educator, writer*

Stewartsville
Busch, Beverly Gail *English language educator, literature educator, instructional resource center administrator*

Teaneck
Fjordbotten, Alf Lee *language educator*
Gordon, Lois G. *language educator*
Wiener, Joel Howard *historian, educator*

Toms River
Bosley, Karen Lee Foley *language educator, communications educator*

Trenton
George, Emery Edward *foreign language and studies educator, writer*

Wall
Applegate, Donald Edward *history professor*
Mudd, Mary *historian*

Wayne
Rogoff, Paula Drimmer *English and foreign language educator*

West Long Branch
DeRosa, Christopher Samuel *history professor*

NEW MEXICO

Albuquerque
Davies, Thomas Mockett, Jr. *history professor*
Davis, Jon L. *logistics consultant*
Fuller, Anne Elizabeth Havens *English language and literature educator, consultant*
Hutton, Paul Andrew *historian, educator, writer*
Lange, Dale Lowell *language educator, researcher*
Peña, Juan José *retired interpreter*
Richter, Harvena *retired literature educator, poet*
Thomson, Iain Donald *philosopher, educator*

Farmington
Peterson Gerstner, Janet *English professor*

Las Vegas
Simpson, Dorothy Audrey *retired speech educator*

Roswell
Kitchen, Richard *history professor, researcher*

Santa Fe
Lehmberg, Stanford Eugene *historian, educator*
Long, Timothy Edward *philosopher, research scientist*
Maehl, William Henry *historian, academic administrator, consultant*
Peters, Margaret Annette *English language educator*

Taos
Bolls, Imogene Lamb *English language educator, poet*

NEW YORK

Albany
Colombí-Monguió, Alicia de *language and humanities educator*
Donovan, Robert Alan *language educator*
Reese, William Lewis *philosophy educator*
Wittner, Lawrence Stephen *history professor*

Amherst
Kurtz, Paul *philosopher, educator, writer, publisher*
Shook, John Robert *philosopher*

Annandale On Hudson
Ashbery, John Lawrence *language educator, poet, playwright, art critic*

Bayside
Clingan, Edmund *history professor*

Binghamton
Bix, Herbert Philip *historian, educator*
Cho, Sungdai *linguist, educator*
Gaddis Rose, Marilyn *literature educator, translator*
Guay, Robert E. *philosopher, educator*
Sklar, Kathryn Kish *historian, educator*
Stein, George Henry *historian, educator, administrator*

Brockport
Blake, Robert William *retired literature and language professor, writer*
Dabbagh, Mahmoud *language educator, linguist, researcher*
Leslie, William Bruce *history professor*
White, Christopher Todd *language educator, anthropologist*

Bronx
Bullaro, Grace Russo *literature, film and foreign language educator, critic*
Dean, Nancy *literature educator, retired playwright*
Hallett, Charles Arthur, Jr. *language educator, humanities educator*
Spatt, Hartley Steven *humanities educator*
Stertz, Stephen Allen *historian, educator*
Ultan, Lloyd *historian, educator*
Valgemae, Mardi *language educator*

Bronxville
Peters, Sarah Whitaker *art historian, writer*
Pollin, Burton Ralph *language educator*

Brooklyn
Barran, Thomas Paul *language educator*
Blasi, Alberto *Romance languages educator, writer*
Buttaro, Lucia *language educator, consultant*
Crawford, Clinton *art historian, educator*
Curtis-Tweed, Phyllis Marie *humanities educator*
Flam, Jack Donald *art historian, educator*
Forsberg, Suzanne *humanities educator*
King, Margaret Leah *history professor*
Kriftcher, Noel N. *humanities educator, director*
Lobron, Barbara L. *speech educator, editor, photographer, writer*
Lopate, Phillip *language educator, writer*
Spector, Robert Donald *language educator*

Buffalo
Iggers, Georg Gerson *history professor*
Merini, Rafika *humanities educator, writer, language educator*
Milligan, John Drane *historian, educator*
Peradotto, John Joseph *retired classics educator, editor*
Ross, Gary Earl *writing educator*
Siedlecki, Peter Anthony *English language and literature educator*
Twagilimana, Aimable *language educator, writer*
Williams, Lillian Serece *historian, social studies educator*
Woolverton, Diane Marie *literature and language professor*

Canton
Goldberg, Rita Maria *foreign language educator*

Charlton
Kekes, John *philosopher, educator*

Churchville
Clarke, Stephan Paul *retired language educator, writer*

Clinton
Kodat, Catherine Gunther *literature and language professor*

Cobleskill
Rivera, Salvador, Jr. *history and sociology educator, researcher*

Corning
Asonevich, Walter Jozef *English educator*

Cortland
Anderson, Donna Kay *musicologist, educator*

Dobbs Ferry
Poian, Edward Licio *historian*

East Hampton
Bromley, Bruce Ditmas *language educator, writer*

Elmira
Leveen, Pauline *retired history professor, government professor*

Flushing
Bird, Thomas Edward *foreign language and literature educator*
Rabassa, Gregory *language educator, translator, poet*
Tytell, John *literature educator, writer*

Forest Hills
Kra, Pauline Skornicki *French language educator*
Nero, Shondel J. *language educator*

Garden City
Bouchard, Wendy Ann Borstel *language educator*
Jenkins, Kenneth Vincent *literature educator, writer*
McNair, Marcia L. *language educator, writer, editor*
Okoampa-Ahoofe, Kwame *language educator, historian*

Gardiner
Mabee, Carleton *historian, educator*

Great Neck
Druks, Herbert Michael *history educator*

Hamilton
Rotter, Andrew Jon *history educator*
Soderberg, Dale LeRoy *language educator, drama director, producer*
Staley, Lynn *literature educator*

Hancock
Senia, Grace Melanie *language and music educator*

Hillsdale
Parmet, Herbert Samuel *historian, writer*

Holley
Lepkowski, Suzanne Joy *language educator*

Ithaca
Abrams, Meyer Howard *language educator*
Bathrick, David *foreign language educator, academic administrator*
Brazell, Karen Woodard *literature educator*
Colby-Hall, Alice Mary *language educator*
Eddy, Donald Davis *language educator*
Groos, Arthur Bernhard, Jr. *German studies and music educator*
Harris, Robert Lee, Jr. *history professor*
Hohendahl, Peter Uwe *German language and literature educator*
Hull, Isabel Virginia *history professor*
LaCapra, Dominick Charles *historian, educator*
LaFeber, Walter Frederick *historian, educator, writer*
Laquatra, Joseph *humanities educator*
Lewenstein, Bruce Voss *science historian*
McDougal, Stuart Yeatman *comparative literature educator, author*
Porte, Joel Miles *language educator*
Radzinowicz, Mary Ann *language educator*
Rawlings, Hunter Ripley III *classicist, former academic administrator*
Silbey, Joel Henry *history professor*
Sosna, Morton Philip *historian, academic administrator*
Zaslaw, Neal *musicologist*

Jamaica
Beliavsky, Ninah *linguistics professor*
Coppa, Frank John *historian, educator*
Ekbatani, Glayol *language educator, director, writer*
Jefferson, Wayne *language educator*
Parmet, Robert David *historian, educator*

Jericho
Astuto, Philip Louis *retired language educator*

Keuka Park
Armstrong, James Francis III *retired language educator, writer*

Kings Park
Fay, Thomas A. *philosopher, educator*

Larchmont
Folter, Roland *historian, rare book dealer, writer*

Monsey
Erickson, Barbara Martha *historian, writer*

New Hyde Park
Low, Frederick Emerson *language educator*

New Paltz
Brown, Peter David Gilson *German language educator*

New Rochelle
Fitch, Nancy Elizabeth *historian, educator*

New York
Bagnall, Roger Shaler *history professor, director*
Baker, Paul Raymond *historian, educator*
Belknap, Robert Lamont *literature educator*
Bender, Thomas *historian, educator*
Berghahn, Volker Rolf *history professor*
Birns, Nicholas Boe *literature educator, editor*
Block, Ned *philosopher, educator*
Bonfante, Larissa *classics educator*

Brown, Jonathan *art historian, educator*
Bulliet, Richard Williams *historian, educator, writer*
Cahn, Steven Mark *philosopher, educator*
Caro, Robert Allan *historian, writer*
Cavallo, Jo Ann *language educator*
Caws, Mary Ann *literature and language professor*
Coatsworth, John Henry *history professor, writer, dean*
Compagnon, Antoine Marcel *French language educator*
Cook, Blanche Wiesen *historian, educator, journalist*
de Menil, Lois Pattison *historian, philanthropist*
Donoghue, Denis *language professional, educator*
Driver, Martha Westcott *literature educator, researcher, writer*
Elderfield, John *art historian, museum curator*
Estraikh, Gennady *humanities educator*
Ferrante, Joan Marguerite *language and literature educator, writer*
Fine, Kit *philosophy educator*
Flescher, Sharon *art historian, educator*
Foner, Eric *historian, educator*
Force, Pierre Marie *French language and literature educator*
Freedberg, David Adrian *art historian, educator*
Gasman, Daniel E. *retired history professor, writer*
Gay, Peter *historian, educator, writer*
Ginter, Valerian Alexius *urban historian, educator*
Gleason, Barbara Jo *literature and language professor*
Gluck, Carol *history professor*
Gordon, Linda *history educator*
Gromada, Thaddeus V. *historian, academic administrator*
Grunfeld, A. Tom *history professor*
Harris, Frederick John *foreign language and literature educator*
Harris, Katherine Safford *speech and hearing educator*
Harris, William Vernon *history professor*
Hartman, Joan Edna *retired literature educator, dean, provost*
Harvey, David W. *humanities educator*
Heffner, Richard Douglas *historian, educator, communications consultant, television producer*
Hendin, Josephine Gattuso *language educator, writer*
Herzog, John E. *numismatist*
Hirsch, Edward Mark *language educator, poet*
Hirschhorn, Bernard *educator, historian, researcher, writer*
Hoeflin, Ronald Kent *philosopher, writer*
Holquist, James Michael *literature educator, department chairman*
Hovde, Carl Frederick *language professional, educator*
Howe, Florence *literature educator, writer, publisher*
Hu, Danian *history professor*
Hulsebosch, Daniel Joseph *historian, educator*
Jackson, Kenneth Terry *historian, academic administrator*
Kaiser, Walter *language educator*
Karsen, Sonja Petra *retired literature educator*
Kastan, David Scott *literature educator, writer*
Katz, Esther *historian, educator*
Kerz, Louise (Louise Hirschfeld) *historian*
Kimber, Karen Beecher *ESL educator*
Kitcher, Philip Stuart *philosophy educator*
Krinsky, Carol Herselle *art historian, educator*
Kroeber, Karl *language educator*
Kruger, Steven F. *literature educator*
Lao, Joseph R. *humanities educator, researcher*
Leibowitz, Herbert Akiba *literature and language professor, writer*
Lewyn, Ann Salfeld *retired English as a second language educator*
Lippman, Sharon Rochelle *art historian and therapist, filmmaker*
London, Herbert Ira *humanities educator, academic administrator*
Malin, Irving *language educator, critic*
Markowitz, Gerald E. *historian, educator*
May, Gita *literature educator*
Mayerson, Philip *classics educator*
Maynard, John Rogers *language educator*
Maysilles, Elizabeth *speech communication professional, educator*
Mehta, Linn Cary *literature educator*
Mendelson, Edward James *English literature educator*
Middendorf, John Harlan *English literature educator*
Middlebrook, Diane Wood *English language educator, writer*
Miller, Nancy K. *literature educator*
Miller, Peter N. *historian, educator*
Mintz, Samuel Isaiah *language educator, writer*
Mitterand, Henri C. *literature educator, writer*
Moreno, Barry *historian, writer*
Myers, Gerald Eugene *humanities educator*
Odenweller, Robert Paul *philatelist, trade association administrator, retired pilot*
Oppenheimer, Paul *literature educator, poet*
Papalia, Diane Ellen *humanities educator*
Paxton, Robert Owen *historian, educator*
Plottel, Jeanine Parisier *foreign language educator*
Prettyman, Alfred Emerson *language and behavioral science educator, publishing executive*
Quiñones Keber, Eloise *art historian, educator*
Randall, Francis Ballard *retired historian, educator, writer*
Ravitch, Diane Silvers *historian, educator, writer, government official*
Raymond, Dorothy Sarnoff *communications consultant, former actress, former singer*
Reynolds, David Spencer *humanities educator, writer*
Rheins, Carl Jeffrey *historian, director*
Richtman, Jack *French language educator*
Rosand, David *art historian, educator*
Rosenberg, John David *language educator, critic*
Rosengarten, Frank *retired language educator, retired literature educator, writer*
Rothman, David J. *historian, educator*
Rowen, Ruth Halle *musicologist, educator*
Rubenstein, Sanford Marvin *English professor, poet*
Salvesen, Magda Abercromby *art and garden historian*
Schama, Simon *historian, educator, author*
Scheindlin, Raymond Paul *literature educator, religious organization administrator*
Schiffer, Stephen *philosopher, educator*
Schirokauer, Conrad *history professor*
Scribner, Charles III *art historian, writer*
Seigel, Jerrold Edward *historian, writer*
Selig, Karl-Ludwig *literature and language professor*
Shapiro, James Stephen *English professor*
Shneidman, J. Lee *historian, educator*
Solomon, Maynard Elliott *musicologist, retired recording industry executive*
Spector, Johanna Lichtenberg *ethnomusicologist, former educator*
Stade, George Gustav *humanities educator*
Stein, Judith *history professor*
Steinberg, Leo *art historian, educator*
Stern, Fritz Richard *historian, educator*
Stevens, Rosemary Anne *medicine and public health historian, artist*
Stimpson, Catharine Rosalind *literature educator, writer*
Tanselle, George Thomas *language educator, foundation administrator*
Taran, Leonardo *classicist, educator*
Tusiani, Joseph *foreign language educator, author*
Unger, Peter Kenneth *philosophy educator*
Walker, Robert Harris *historian, writer, editor*
Warren, Arete Bernice *art historian*
Wasser, Henry *retired American literature and sociology educator*
Weil-Garris Brandt, Kathleen (Kathleen Brandt) *art historian*
Weinberg, H. Barbara *art historian, educator, curator*
Wixom, William David *art historian, museum administrator, educator*
Wolff, Larry *history professor*
Wortman, Marlene Stein *historian*
Wortman, Richard S. *historian, educator*
Wyschogrod, Edith *philosophy educator*
Yerushalmi, Yosef Hayim *historian, educator*
Yurchenco, Henrietta Weiss *musicologist, writer*

Newburgh
Adams, Barbara *language educator, poet, writer*

Northport
Russo, Christine Fiorella *language educator*

Oakland Gardens
Polak, Emil Joseph *history professor, researcher*

Oswego
Smiley, Marilynn Jean *musicologist*

Pittsford
French, Henry Pierson, Jr. *retired historian, educator*

Pleasantville
Benton, Janetta Rebold *art historian, professor, writer*
Meisel, Martin *retired English and comparative literature educator*
Mirakian-Escobar, Rachel Ann *language educator*

Port Washington
Williams, George Leo *historian, retired secondary school educator, landmark director*

Potsdam
Lunt, Lora G. *language educator, director*

Poughkeepsie
Bartlett, Lynn Conant *English literature educator*
Daniels, Elizabeth Adams *English language educator*
Hathaway, Richard Dean *retired language educator*
Hytier, Adrienne Doris *French language educator*
Peck, H. Daniel *literature educator*
Sharp, Ronald Alan *language educator, writer, dean*

Purchase
Waller, Gary Fredric *language educator, poet*

Rochester
Black, Candace Regan *language educator*
Caton, Scott Brenon *history professor*
Chiarenza, Carl *art historian, critic, artist, educator*
Fausold, Martin Luther *history professor*
Gordon, Dane Rex *philosophy educator, minister*
Hauser, William Barry *historian, educator*
Herminghouse, Patricia Anne *foreign language educator*
Hollis, Susan Tower *history professor*
Johnson, Bruce Marvin *language educator*
Lansky, Lewis *history professor*
Meconi, Honey *musicologist, writer*
Young, Mary Elizabeth *history professor*
Zagorin, Perez *historian, educator*

Rockville Centre
Fitzgerald, Janet Anne *philosophy educator, academic administrator*

Saint Bonaventure
Mazon, Margaret Fausold *language educator*

Saratoga Springs
Boyers, Robert *literature and language professor*
Caruso, Adrienne Iorio *retired language educator*

Scarsdale
Brilliant, Richard *art historian, educator*
Graff, Henry Franklin *historian, educator*

Schenectady
Morris, John Selwyn *philosopher, educator, retired academic administrator*

Selden
Howard, Douglas L. *literature and language professor*

Slingerlands
Zacek, Joseph Frederick *historian, educator*

Snyder
Levine, George Richard *language educator*

Southampton
Brophy, James David, Jr. *humanities educator*

Staten Island
Holder, Calvin Beresford *history professor*
Stearns, Stephen Jerold *history professor, writer*

Stony Brook
Goldberg, Homer Beryl *language educator*
Grim, Patrick Neal *philosopher, educator, logician*
Harris, Alice *linguist, educator*
Ihde, Don *philosopher, educator*
Kuspit, Donald Burton *art historian, critic, educator*
Levin, Richard Louis *retired language educator*
Mignone, Mario B. *language educator*
Moskowitz, Anita Fiderer *art historian, educator*
Semmel, Bernard *historian, educator*
Silverman, Hugh J. *philosophy educator*
Simpson, Louis Aston Marantz *language educator, writer*

Syracuse
Alston, William Payne *philosophy educator*
Powell, James Matthew *history professor*
Prettyman, John A. *English language educator*
Ray, Romita *art historian, educator*
Sternlicht, Sanford *literature educator, writer*
Tatham, David Frederic *art historian, educator*
Waddy, Patricia A. *historian, retired architecture educator*

Troy
Ahlers, Rolf Willi *philosopher, theologian*

Utica
Wagner, Frederick Reese *retired language educator*

Valhalla
Leone, Stephen Joseph *language educator, computer technician, consultant*
Sclafani, Charles Carlo *language educator, department chairman*

Vestal
Quataert, Donald *historian, educator*

Wantagh
Smits, Edward John *historian, consultant*

Williamsville
Drew, Fraser Bragg Robert *language educator*
Saveth, Edward Norman *historian, educator*

Wyandanch
Fonseca, Alejandra *language educator*

NORTH CAROLINA

Andrews
Fonda, Ronald Alan *epistemologist*

Asheville
Voigt, Ellen *literature educator*

Buies Creek
Platt, Rorin Morse *history professor, historian*

Cary
Mata, Elizabeth Adams *language educator, land investor*

Chapel Hill
Baron, Samuel Haskell *historian*
Browning, Christopher R. *historian, educator*
Davis, Sarah Irwin *retired language educator*
Debreczeny, Paul *retired language educator, writer*
Feinberg, Lawrence Edward *language educator, researcher*
Flora, Joseph M(artin) *language educator*
Grendler, Paul Frederick *historian, educator*
Gritter, Elizabeth *historian, researcher*
Gura, Philip Francis *English and American literature educator*
Heninger, Simeon Kahn, Jr. *language educator*
Kohn, Richard H. *historian, educator*
Nelson, Philip Francis *musicologist, consultant, conductor*
Rabil, Albert, Jr. *humanities educator*
Schier, Donald Stephen *language educator*
Smith, Sidney Rufus, Jr. *linguist, educator*
Strauss, Albrecht Benno *retired language educator, editor*
Williamson, Joel Rudolph *humanities educator, writer*
Yow, Valerie Raleigh *historian, writer, counselor*

Charlotte
Castro, Mary McDermott *language educator*
Myers, Robert Manson *language educator, writer*

Davidson
Cole, Richard Cargill *language educator*

Durham
Budd, Louis John *language educator*
Butters, Ronald Richard *language educator*
Chafe, William Henry *history professor*
Colton, Joel *historian, educator*
Davis, Calvin De Armond *historian, educator*
Lerner, Warren *historian, educator*
Scott, Anne Byrd Firor *history professor*
Smith, Grover C(leveland) *language educator*
Thompson, James Howard *historian, librarian*
Williams, George Walton *language educator*

Efland
Weinberg, Gerhard Ludwig *history professor*

Fayetteville
Curry, Virginia Frances *retired language educator*

Fearrington Village
Cell, Gillian Townsend *retired historian, educator*

Franklin
Johnson, Herbert Alan *historian, lawyer*

Greensboro
Cushman, Keith *English professor*
Penninger, Frieda Elaine *retired literature educator*

Greenville
Beers, Burton Floyd *historian, educator*

Hendersonville
Harris, James Braxton *retired humanities educator, freelance/self-employed writer*

High Point
Chavis, Glenn Romero *retired historian, writer*

Jacksonville
Kimball, Lynn Jerome *historian*

Mount Olive
Marbais, Peter Christian *language educator*

Pinehurst
Linville, Ray Pate *English educator, retired military officer, editor, writer*
Nordloh, David Joseph *literature and language professor, dean*

Raleigh
Moore, Nancey Fay *history educator*
Rhodes, Donald Robert *musicologist, educator, retired electrical engineer*

Vilas
Stolberg, Mary Margaret *historian*

Winston Salem
Barnett, Richard Chambers *historian, educator*
Borwick, Susan Harden *musicologist, educator*
Hendricks, J(ames) Edwin *historian, educator, consultant, author*
Miller, Richard Harry *philosopher, educator*
Shapere, Dudley *philosophy educator*

NORTH DAKOTA

Bismarck
Newborg, Gerald Gordon *state archives administrator*
Rettig, Pam *literature educator*

Grand Forks
Huang, Xiaozhao *language educator*

Mayville
McMahon, Dalton Edward *history professor, social sciences educator, department chairm*

Wahpeton
Reubish, Gary Richard *English language educator*

OHIO

Akron
Knepper, George W. *historian, educator*
Williams, William Proctor *literature educator*

Athens
Borchert, Donald Marvin *philosopher, educato*
Brobst, Peter John *history professor*
Ehrlich, Philip *philosophy educator*
Matthews, Jack (John Harold Matthews) *language educator, writer*
Torres, Daniel *literature educator*
Whealey, Lois Deimel *humanities scholar*

Berea
Kennelly, Laura Ballard *literature educator, writer*

Bowling Green
Browne, Ray Broadus *popular culture educato*
Middleton, Charles Ronald *history educator*

Brecksville
Pappas, Effie Vamis *language educator, financ educator, writer, poet, artist*

Cincinnati
Alexander, John Kurt *history professor*
Bleznick, Donald William *Romance language educator*
Ciani, Alfred Joseph *dean*

Harmon, Patrick *historian, retired editor, commentator*
Paulson, Eric J. *literacy education educator*
Schrier, Arnold *historian, educator*

Cleveland
Baskind, Samantha *art historian*
Ciccia, Angela Hein *speech educator, speech pathology/audiology services professional*
Dancyger, Ruth *art historian*
Friedman, Barton Robert *language educator*
Greppin, John Aird Coutts *philologist, editor, educator*
Miller, Genevieve *retired medical historian*
Nelson, Sue Grodsky *humanities educator, consultant*
Salomon, Roger Blaine *retired language educator*
Taylor, Margaret Wischmeyer *retired language educator*

Columbus
Babcock, Charles Luther *classics educator*
Battersby, James Lyons, Jr. *language educator*
Beja, Morris *English literature educator*
Boyle, Kevin Gerard *historian, educator, writer*
Brooke, John L. *history professor*
Findley, Carter Vaughn *historian, educator*
Hare, Robert Yates *musicologist, educator*
Jarvis, Gilbert Andrew *humanities educator, writer*
Jebsen, Harry Alfred Arthur, Jr. *history professor*
Kasulis, Thomas Patrick *humanities educator*
Kuhn, Albert Joseph *language educator*
Peterson, Gale Eugene *historian*
Scanlan, James Patrick *philosophy and Slavic studies educator*
Stephan, Alexander Friedrich *German language and literature educator*
Williams, Susan Shidal *language educator*

Concord
Ulsenheimer, Dean *language educator*

Dayton
Dorn, Jacob Henry *history professor*
Harden, Oleta Elizabeth *literature educator, academic administrator*
McWhorter, Stanley Bruce *retired language educator*
Seon, Yvonne *cultural educator, minister*
Vice, Roy Lee *history professor*

Granville
Knobel, Dale Thomas *historian, educator, university president*
Lisska, Anthony Joseph *humanities educator, philosopher*
Santoni, Ronald Ernest *philosophy educator*

Kent
Beer, Barrett Lynn *historian*
Hassler, Donald Mackey, II. *English language educator, writer*
Marovitz, Sanford Earl *English language and literature educator*
Reid, S.W. *language educator*

Kirtland
Asnien, Phyllis Arline *humanities educator, writer*

Lyndhurst
Harper, Williard Flemmett *language educator*

Marietta
Wilbanks, Jan Joseph *retired philosopher*

North Canton
Yazzano, Frank Paul *historian, educator*

Oxford
Pratt, William Crouch, Jr. *literature and language professor, writer*
Yamauchi, Edwin Masao *history professor*

Painesville
McQuaid, Kim *historian, educator, writer*

Shaker Heights
de Coningh, Lise N. *language educator*

Solon
Gallo, Donald Robert *retired literature educator*

Springfield
Davis, Robert Leigh *language educator*

Stow
Siber, Carol Shattuck *language educator*

Toledo
Brown, Nancy J. *literature educator*
Campbell, James *philosopher, educator*
Glaab, Charles Nelson *historian, educator*
Herring, Katherine L. *historian*
Smith, Robert Freeman *history professor*

Urbana
Phillips, Julieanne Appleson *history professor*

West Farmington
Smith, Agnes Monroe *history professor*

Wooster
Schilling, W. A. Hayden *history professor*

Yellow Springs
Fogarty, Robert Stephen *historian, educator, editor*

Youngstown
Bowers, Bege Kaye *literature and communications educator, academic administrator*
Brown, Steven Ray *language professional*

Zanesville
Holdren, Susan *literature and language professor, foundation administrator*

OKLAHOMA

Ada
Daniel, Arlie V. *speech education educator*

Edmond
Hayes, Kevin J. *literature educator*

Lawton
Thomlinson, Vivian Aytes *literature and language professor*

Norman
Brown, Sidney DeVere *history professor*
Fears, Jesse Rufus *historian, educator, academic dean*
Harjo, Pattipeg Snyder *language educator*
Levy, David William *history educator*
Lowitt, Richard *history professor*
Savage, William Woodrow, Jr. *historian, consultant, social sciences educator*

Oklahoma City
Bowlby, Leymond Ambrose *linguist, translator*
Harding, Susan M. *language educator*
Holt, Karen Anita Young *language educator*
Maddux, Vernon Ray *retired history professor*

Stillwater
Fischer, LeRoy Henry *historian, educator*
Luebke, Neil Robert *philosophy educator*
Max, Elizabeth *retired language educator*

Tulsa
Buckley, Thomas Hugh *historian, educator*
Henneke, Ben Graf *retired humanities educator*
Randle, Rodger A. *human relations professor, political science professor*

OREGON

Eugene
Pascal, C(ecil) Bennett *classics educator*
Wickes, George *English literature educator, writer*

Madras
Ramsey, Jarold William *literature and language professor, writer*

Mcminnville
Ramsay, Violeta *language educator, consultant*

Medford
Frost, Orcutt William *historian, educator*

Newport
Pavlish, Catherine Ann *language educator, writer*

Port Orford
Drinnon, Richard *retired historian*

Portland
Brashier, Kenneth E. *humanities educator*
Eifler, Karen Elizabeth *language educator*
Englert, Walter George *classics and humanities educator*
Horowitz, David A. *history professor, writer*
Orloff, Chet *historian*
Schmidt, Stanley Eugene *retired speech educator*
Steinman, Lisa Malinowski *English literature educator, writer*
Vaughan, Thomas James Gregory *historian, writer*

Redmond
Blue, Frederick Judd *retired history professor, writer*

Salem
Dmytryshyn, Basil *historian, educator*

Spray
Fussner, F. Smith *history professor, retired rancher*

PENNSYLVANIA

Aaronsburg
Teeple, Bruce Jeffery *historian, writer*

Ambler
Hilty, James Walter *historian, educator, media consultant*

Annville
Foley, Brian Joseph *philosophy educator*
Tezanos-Pinto, Rosa *Hispanic American literature educator*

Ardmore
Speakman, Joseph M. *retired history professor*

Atglen
Curiel, Judith Rea *language educator*

Bala Cynwyd
Dorwart, Bonnie Brice *historian, retired rheumatologist*
Murphey, Murray Griffin *history professor*

Berwyn
Bluestone, Ellen Hope *literature, writing, and women's studies professor, writer*

Bethlehem
Beidler, Peter Grant *retired language educator*
Parmet, Harriet Abbey L. *literature educator*
Saeger, James Schofield *history professor, writer*
Smolansky, Oles M. *retired humanities educator*

Boyertown
Fortes, Brenda Joyce *language educator*

Bryn Mawr
Dudden, Arthur Power *historian, educator*
Gaisser, Julia Haig *classics educator*
Krausz, Michael *philosopher, educator*
Lane, Barbara Miller (Barbara Miller-Lane) *humanities educator*
Lang, Mabel Louise *classics educator*
McCabe, Louise Beachboard *language educator*

Butler
Walsh, Joy Irene *literature educator, language educator*

California
Crawford, Paul Fleming *historian*

Canonsburg
Southern, David *history professor*

Carlisle
Bergeron, Arthur William, Jr. *historian, writer*
Crane, Conrad C. *history professor*
Fox, Arturo Angel *Spanish language educator*
Shrader, Charles Reginald *historian*

Chambersburg
O'Connor, John Morris III *retired humanities educator*

Chester
Buck, Lawrence Paul *history professor, former academic administrator*

Clarks Green
Bourcier, Richard Joseph *retired French language and literature educator*

Clarks Summit
Cagley, Susan A. *history professor*

Claysville
Stewart, Pamela Widdup *language educator, musician*

East Petersburg
Pedrow, Brenda M. *retired language educator*

East Stroudsburg
Smith, Elizabeth Leigh *literature and language professor*
Switzer, Sharon Cecile *language educator, researcher*

Easton
Lamb-Faffelberger, Margarete Barbara *foreign language educator*
Schlueter, June Mayer *literature educator, writer*

Ebensburg
Wojcik, Jason Paul *history professor*

Elizabethtown
Bartoli, Jill Sunday *reading and language arts educator*
Kenley, David Lynn *history professor*

Elkins Park
Davidson, Abraham Aba *art historian, educator, photographer*

Fairfield
Freund, John Richard *former English educator*

Freeport
Smits, Ronald Francis *language educator, poet*

Greensburg
Lu, Shu Jiang *literature and language professor*

Harrisburg
Dinniman, Andrew Eric *international studies and history professor, state senator*
Khanzhina, Helen P. *language and literature educator, translator*
Smith, Eric Ledell *historian*

Haverford
Brand, Charles Macy *history professor*
Gutwirth, Marcel Marc *literature educator*
Jorden, Eleanor Harz *linguist, educator*

Lancaster
Binkley, Luther John *philosophy educator*
Steiner, Robert Lisle *retired language educator*

Lansdowne
Purcell, Mary Hamilton *speech educator*

Leesport
Jackson, Eric Allen *philatelist*

Lewisburg
Payne, Michael David *English language educator*

Ligonier
Vogelsang, Eric R. *language educator, basketball and soccer coach*

Lock Haven
Kerszberg, Annik Doquire *language educator*
Story, Julie Ann *language educator*

Loretto
Jareb, Jerome *history professor, researcher*

Lykens
Sultzbaugh, John Stephan *historian, educator*

Merion Station
Littell, Marcia Sachs *Holocaust and genocide studies professor*

Mifflinburg
Messimer, Donald McKee, Jr. *language educator*

Millersville
Farkas, Kerrie R.H. *literature and language professor*
Miller, Steven Max *humanities educator*

Nanticoke
Pajka, R. Bonnie *language educator*

New Freedom
Sedlak, Valerie Frances *retired English language and literature educator, academic administrator*

Newtown Square
DeLuca, Jennie M. *English educator*

Philadelphia
Beeman, Richard Roy *historian, educator*
Berry, Mary Frances *history professor, former federal agency administrator*
Betancourt, Philip P. *art historian, archaeologist, educator*
Daemmrich, Horst Sigmund *German language and literature educator*
Davis, Allen Freeman *history professor, writer*
Fusco, Richard *English literature educator*
Gelles, Richard James *sociology and psychology professor, academic administrator*
Hackney, (Francis) Sheldon *history professor, former academic administrator*
Hahn, Steven *history professor, writer*
Knauer, Georg Nicolaus *philologist*
Morello, Celeste Anne *historian, criminologist*
Moss, Roger William *historian, writer, administrator*
Peters, Edward Murray *history professor*
Regan, Robert Charles *English language educator*
Ridley, Harrison, Jr. *history professor*
Sachs, Katherine Stein *art historian*
Schiffman, Harold Fosdick *Asian language educator*
Sebold, Russell Perry III *Romance languages educator, writer*
Sugrue, Thomas J. *history professor, social sciences educator*
Winkler, Gail Caskey *historian, writer*
Woodside, Lisa Nicole *humanities educator*

Phoenixville
Lukacs, John Adalbert *historian, retired educator*

Pittsburgh
Anthony, Edward Mason *linguistics educator*
Arac, Jonathan *literature and language professor*
Balas, Edith *art historian, educator*
Clack, Jerry *classics educator*
Drescher, Seymour *historian, educator, writer*
Gale, Robert Lee *retired literature educator, critic*
Goldstein, Donald Maurice *historian, educator*
Gupta, Anil K. *philosophy professor*
Harris, Ann Birgitta Sutherland *art historian*
Hicks, Wendell *history professor, political scientist, publishing executive*
McClendon, Michele Rosalind *literature educator*
McDuffie, Keith A. *literature educator*
Miller, David William *historian, educator*
Paulston, Christina Bratt *linguistics educator*
Rawski, Evelyn Sakakida *history professor*
Rescher, Nicholas *philosopher, author, educator*
Sheon, Aaron *art historian, educator*
Sieg, Wilfried *philosophy educator*
Tarr, Joel Arthur *historian, educator*
Trotter, Joe William, Jr. *history professor, writer*
Udler, Rubin Yakovlevich *linguist*
Weingartner, Rudolph Herbert *philosophy educator*
Wilson, Mark Lowell *philosopher, educator*

Pottstown
Nestler, Patricia C. *English professor*

Schnecksville
Molano, Charles Hernando *Spanish professor, consultant*

Scranton
Lawhon, Patricia Patton *literature and language professor, writer educator*
Zaydon, Jemille Ann *language educator, communications educator*

Slippery Rock
McIlvaine, Robert Morton *literature educator*

Somerset
Rose-Deal, Mary Frances *language educator*

State College
Brault, Gerard Joseph *French language educator*
Goldschmidt, Arthur Eduard, Jr. *historian, educator, writer*
Redford, Donald Bruce *historian, archaeologist*
Robinett, Betty Wallace *linguist, educator*
Schmalstieg, William Riegel *retired Slavic languages educator*

Swarthmore
North, Helen Florence *classicist, educator*
Oswald, Martin *retired classicist*

University Park
Ebitz, David MacKinnon *art historian, educator, museum director*
Halsey, Martha Taliaferro *Spanish language educator*
Kadir, Djelal *literature educator*
Lima, Robert *language educator*

Naydan, Michael M. *foreign language educator*

Villanova
Bergquist, James Manning *history professor*
Helmetag, Charles Hugh *foreign language educator*
Hunt, John Mortimer, Jr. *classical studies educator*

Wapwallopen
Cardimona, Kimberly Marie *language educator*

West Chester
Gougher, Ronald Lee *language educator*
Heston, Thomas J. *historian, educator*
Hipple, Walter John *language educator*

Whitehall
Tcherviakova, Olga A. *language educator*

Wilkes Barre
Hepp, John Henry, IV, *historian, lawyer*

York
Gyenes, Scott Matthew *history professor*

RHODE ISLAND

Cumberland
Clemente, Alice Rodrigues *language educator*

East Greenwich
Greene, Jack Phillip *historian, educator*

Jamestown
Wright, Harrison Morris *historian, educator*

Kingston
Kim, Yong Choon *philosopher, theologian, educator*

Middletown
Carroll, Rosemary Frances *historian, educator, lawyer*

Newport
Haas, William Paul *humanities educator, retired academic administrator*

North Kingstown
Mellor, Kathy *English as a second language educator*

Providence
Ackerman, Felicia Nimue *philosophy educator, writer*
Bensmaia, Reda *French studies educator, researcher*
Blasing, Mutlu Konuk *English language educator*
Campbell, James T. *history professor*
Donovan, Bruce Elliot *literature educator, dean*
Enteman, Willard Finley *retired philosopher*
Fornara, Charles William *historian, classicist, educator*
Gleason, Abbott *history professor*
Grace, Richard John *history professor*
Green, Angel Yvonne *literature educator*
Harleman, Ann *literature educator, writer*
Kim, Jaegwon *philosophy educator*
Konstan, David *classics and comparative literature professor, researcher*
Lenox, William F. *literature and language professor*
Lesko, Leonard Henry *historian, educator, writer*
Monteiro, George *language educator, writer*
Olson, Jeannine Evelyn *history professor*
Putnam, Michael Courtney Jenkins *classics educator*
Raaflaub, Kurt Arnold *classics educator*
Ribbans, Geoffrey Wilfrid *language educator*
Rohr, Donald Gerard *history professor*
Saint-Amand, Pierre Nemours *humanities educator*
Schulz, Juergen *art historian, educator*
Sosa, Ernest *philosopher, educator*
Walker, Corey David Bazemore *humanities educator*
Wideman, John Edgar *English literature educator, novelist*
Wood, Gordon Stewart *historian, educator, writer*
Wright, Carolyn D. *language educator, poet*

Saunderstown
Waters, Chris Harold *literature and language professor, poet*

Smithfield
Litoff, Judy Barrett *history professor*

SOUTH CAROLINA

Aiken
Hootman, Harry Edward *English professor, retired nuclear engineer*
Sykes, Richard Nesbit *retired history professor, department chairman*

Charleston
Barrett, Michael Baker *historian, educator*
Mowry, Maxwell Reed *language educator*

Clemson
Bailey, Beatrice Naff *language educator, researcher*
Bartley, Abel Alphonso *history professor*
Lander, Ernest McPherson, Jr. *history and economics professor*
Riley, Helene Maria Kastinger *Germanist*
Underwood, Richard Allan *English language educator*

Columbia
Briggs, Ward Wright *classics educator*
Edgar, Walter Bellingrath *historian, educator*
Geckle, George Leo III *language educator*
Long, Eugene Thomas III *philosophy educator, academic administrator*
Synnott, Marcia Graham *history professor*

Conway
Bachman, Maria K. *English professor*

Due West
Carlock, John Bruce, Jr. *language educator*

Nesmith
Pressley, Deloris N. *literacy educator*

Orangeburg
McIver, Barbara Basore *language educator*

Pageland
Simon, Kindra Lee *language educator, translator*

Rembert
Woodward, Margaret Newbern *language educator*

Travelers Rest
Bailey, Helen McShane *historian, consultant*

Winnsboro
Meyer, Jack Allen *historian, consultant*

SOUTH DAKOTA

Brookings
Evans, David Allan *language educator*

Sioux Falls
Carlson Aronson, Marilyn A. *language educator*
Huseboe, Arthur Robert *American literature educator*
Staggers, Kermit LeMoyne, II, *history and political science professor, state legislator, municipal official*

Spearfish
Reznikov, Andrey *linguist, educator*

TENNESSEE

Big Sandy
Chastain, Kenneth Duane *retired foreign language educator, writer*

Chattanooga
Gartman, Max Dillon *language educator*
Resnick, Irven Michael *philosophy educator*

Dayton
Cornelius, Richard Meredith *literature and language professor*
Ketchersid, William Lester *history professor*

Gallatin
Durham, Walter Thomas *historian, researcher*

Jefferson City
Baumgardner, James Lewis *history professor*

Knoxville
Cutler, Everette Wayne *history professor*
Davis, John Kerr *philosopher, educator, lawyer*
Kulikowski, Michael *history professor*

Martin
Howard, Nathan Dale *history professor*
Parker, Henry Herbin *humanities educator*

Memphis
Bhagat, Shaum P. *speech educator*
Stagg, Louis Charles *English language and literature educator*

Murfreesboro
Corlew, Robert Ewing *history professor, academic administrator*
Phillips, Philip Edward *English professor*

Nashville
Beach, Margaret Smith *retired language educator*
Boorman, Howard Lyon *history professor*
Compton, John Joseph *philosophy educator*
Conkin, Paul Keith *history professor*
Cook, Ann Jennalie *literature educator, cultural organization administrator*
Dickerson, Dennis Clark, Sr. *historian, educator*
Girgus, Sam B. *English literature educator*
Halperin, John William *English literature educator*
Jarman, Mark Foster *language educator*
Lee, Douglas A. *musicologist*
Pfanner, Helmut Franz *German language educator*
Risko, Victoria J. *language educator*
Sevin, Dieter Hermann *literature and language professor*
Voegeli, Victor Jacque *historian, educator, dean*

Sewanee
Poe, George Wilkinson *literature and language professor*
Williamson, Samuel Ruthven, Jr. *historian, educator*
Winton, Calhoun *literature educator*

Shiloh
Allen, Stacy Dale *historian, parks director*

TEXAS

Arlington
Adam, Thomas *humanities educator*
Hoefer, Richard A. *social work educator, non-profit management consultant*

Austin
Baltzer, Rebecca A. *musicologist, researcher, consultant*
Brown, Norman Donald *history professor*
Causey, Robert Louis *philosopher, educator, consultant*
Dulles, John Watson Foster *history professor*
Farrell, Edmund James *retired English language educator, writer*
Freeman, Robert Schofield *musicologist, educator, pianist*
Friedman, Alan Warren *humanities educator*
Galinsky, Gotthard Karl *classicist, educator*
Harms, Robert Thomas *linguist, educator*
Hinojosa-Smith, Roland *language educator, writer*
Hopkins, Antony Gerald *history professor*
Louis, William Roger *historian*
Middleton, Christopher *Germanic languages and literature educator*
Moag, Rodney Frank *language educator, country and bluegrass singer, musician, record producer*
Oshinsky, David M. *history professor, writer*
Rich, John Martin *humanities educator, researcher*
Seung, Thomas Kaehao *philosophy educator*
Sutherland, William Owen Sheppard *retired language educator, consultant*
Velz, John William *retired literature educator*
Whitbread, Thomas Bacon *language educator, writer*

Bastrop
Phillips, Joseph Michael *historian, writer*

Baytown
Lee, Gordon Kay *humanities educator*

Beaumont
Bradley, Jerry Wayne *language educator, department chairman*
Needham, Keith Alan *language educator*

Bertram
Albert, Susan Wittig *writer*

Brownsville
Britten, Thomas Anthony *history professor*

Bryan
Bryant, Keith Lynn, Jr. *history professor*

Canyon
Stuntz, Jean Allison *history professor*

College Station
Cannon, Garland *linguist, educator*
Dethloff, Henry Clay *historian, educator*
Ezell, Margaret M. *language educator*
Harner, James Lowell *language educator*

Commerce
Linck, Charles Edward, Jr. *English language educator*

Corpus Christi
Snouffer, Nancy Kendall *literature and language educator*
Wooster, Robert *history professor*

Dallas
Chavez, John Richard *historian, educator*
Chawner, Lucia Martha *language educator*
Comini, Alessandra *art historian, educator*
Countryman, Edward Francis *historian, educator*
Crain, John Walter *historian, educator*
Fagin, Stephen Andrew *historian*
Hunter, Robert Grams *retired language educator*
Nabors, Marion Carroll *retired English educator*
Terry, Marshall Northway, Jr. *language educator, writer*
Weber, David J. *history educator*

Denton
Golden, Richard M. *history professor*
Hurley, Alfred Francis *historian, academic administrator emeritus, retired air force officer*
Kesterson, David Bert *language educator, dean, academic administrator*
Lawhon, Tommie Collins Montgomery *humanities educator*
Mihalcea, Rada Flavia *language educator*
Snapp, Harry Franklin *historian, educator*

Devine
Passty, Jeanette Nyda *literature and language professor, writer*

Edinburg
Ayala, Kara J. *speech educator, researcher*

El Paso
Cuartas, Beatriz H. *humanities educator*
Lujan, Rosa Emma *bilingual specialist, trainer, consultant, assistant principal*
Müller, Gene Alan *historian, consultant*

Fort Worth
Bernard, Robert William *language educator, theology studies educator, humanities educator*
DeLotto, Jeffrey Daniel *language educator, writer*
Gilderhus, Mark Theodore *historian, educator*
Reuter, Frank Theodore *historian, educator*
Robin, Clara Nell (Claire Robin) *English language educator*
Shehan, Geraldean Harrison *ESL educator*

Galveston
Bloomfield, Maxwell Herron III *retired history and law professor*

Grapevine
Stack, George Joseph *philosopher, writer*

Harlingen
Martin, Leland Morris (Pappy) *historian, educator*

Houston
Achenbaum, W(ilbert) Andrew *historian, gerontologist*
Belk, Joan Pardue *language and literature educator*
Brinkley, Douglas G. *historian, writer, educator*
Castañeda, James Agustín *language educator, golf coach*
Chance, Jane *English literature educator*
Drew, Katherine Fischer *history professor*
Espree, Mildred Michelle *language educator, writer*
Hattaway, Karen Ann *literature and language professor*
Kanellos, Nicolás *language and liberal studies educator*
Lamb, Sydney MacDonald *linguistics educator*
Leguillon, Rolande Lucienne *French educator*
Lowry, Montecue Judson *military historian*
Martin, James Kirby *historian, educator*
Minter, David Lee *English literature educator*
Patten, Robert Lowry *language educator*
Pospisil, JoAnn *historian, archivist*
Pryor, William Daniel Lee *humanities educator*
Schnoebelen, Anne Mary *musicologist, educator*
Scoggins, Brenda Carol *language educator, department chairman*
Shafiei-Sarardi, Majoud *language educator*
Sher, George Allen *philosophy educator*
Steiner, Uwe *language educator*
Urbina, Manuel, II, *legal research historian, history professor*
Vallbona, Rima-Gretel Rothe *retired foreign language educator, writer*

Huntsville
Raymond, Kay E(ngelmann) *Spanish language educator, consultant*

Irving
Sommerfeldt, John Robert *historian, educator*
Wood, Robert E. *philosopher, educator*

Kingsville
Hunter, Leslie Gene *history educator*

Lake Jackson
Tarrant, Sasha Ranae Adams *history professor*

Lewisville
Wrenn, Susan Stroud *language educator*

Longview
Williams, Willie Alvin *retired literature educato*

Lubbock
Bullock, James Jefferson, II, *literature and language professor, director*
Ketner, Kenneth Laine *philosopher, educator*

Mesquite
Budd, Rose Antoinette *language educator*

Missouri City
de Kanter, Ellen Ann *retired English and forei language educator*

Montgomery
Kelsey, Clyde Eastman, Jr. *philosophy educator psychology professor*

Mount Pleasant
Vaughn, William Preston *retired historian, educator*

Richardson
Redman, Timothy Paul *language educator, writer*

San Antonio
Flores, Belinda Bustos *bilingual educator, administrator*
Graff, Harvey J. *history and humanities educat*
Grimshaw, James Albert, Jr. *retired language educator*
Kellman, Steven G. *literature educator, author*
Leighton, Albert Chester *history professor*
Myers, Ellen Howell *historian, educator*
Rollin, Michael Fredrick *history professor*
Salvucci, Linda *history professor*
Smith, Rebecca Lynn *language educator*
Tallon, Michael *language educator*
Villavazo, Kristen Lee *language educator*
von Raffler-Engel, Walburga (Walburga Engel) *retired language educator*

San Marcos
Ronan, Clifford John *literature and language professor*

Stephenville
Schmelzer, Janet L. *history professor, research*

Texas City
Hammett, Beth A. *language educator*

Tyler
McGoff, William Stanley *speech educator, consultant*

Waco
Hunt, Maurice Arthur *language educator, researcher*
Jeffrey, David Lyle *literature and language professor, writer*
Kvanvig, Jonathan Lee *philosophy educator*
Murray, Kathleen Sarah-Jane *literature and language professor*

AH

an
er, Milton Lawrence *historian, educator*
ier, C. Brock *humanities educator, writer*

m
, Bruce Budge *humanities educator*

vo
er, Roni Jo *literature and language ofessor*
, James Karl *German language educator*
phy, John Joseph *literature educator, critic, itor*
es, Jeffery D. *history professor*
Larry Howard *literature educator*
, Neil Longley *history professor*
ng, Bruce Wilson *language educator*

it George
lanella, Peter *literature and language ofessor, writer*

Lake City
, Janice Gail Arnold *literacy educator*
sen, Brigham Dwaine *history professor*

monton
e, Arlene Haslam *genealogist*

RMONT

lington
iels, Robert Vincent *history professor, former ate senator*
tz, Susan Marie *language educator*
, Robert William *philosophy religious udies educator*

tleton
by, Judith Marie *humanities educator*

t Calais
, Anthony *language educator*

ddlebury
ers, Jan Maria *historian, museum director*
bs, Travis Beal *historian, educator*
z, Michael Ray *Slavic languages educator*
od, Paul Kleber *history professor*
, Van Horn *German language educator*

rwich
nelman, Richard Howard *French and umanities educator*

elburne
ger, John George *foreign language educator*

lliston
karzewski, Debra Sue *language educator*

RGINIA

nandale
tton, Joyce Dupras *English language ducator*
cheon, Wallace Schoonmaker *historian, ducator*
citelli, Emile James *philosopher, educator*
thern, Kimberly Elaine *art historian, ducator*

lington
ard, Dean Conrad *historian, retired historical enter director*
gley, Harold David *historian, educator*
se, Mary Mundy *literature and language rofessor*
th, Louis John *historian*
mpson, Wayne Wray *historian*
cox, Shirley Jean Langdon *genealogist*

hland
e, Milton Thomas *American literature and ulture educator, author*

acksburg
swald, Herman Kenneth *language educator, etired academic administrator*

ntreville
Gennaro, Eida Mendoza *interpreter, real state agent*

arlottesville
oot, William Wright *history professor*
nold, Albert James *foreign language educator*
testin, Martin Carey *retired literature and anguage professor*
langer, Terry *historian, educator*
ck, Patricia C. *historian, educator*
ackel, Theodore Joseph *historian*
vidson, Hugh MacCullough *French language and literature educator*
bes, John Douglas *architectural and economic historian*
rrett, George Palmer, Jr. *language educator, writer*
aebner, Norman Arthur *historian, educator*
rsch, Eric Donald, Jr. *language educator*
mphreys, Paul William *philosophy educator, consultant*
anson, Deborah G. *philosopher, educator*
anson, Richard Marc *civics educator*
aehe, Enno Edward *history professor*
ne, Ann Judith *history and women's studies educator, director*
ngbaum, Robert Woodrow *language educator*
ffler, Melvyn P. *history professor*
venson, Jacob Clavner *language educator*
tle, Wm. A. (William Alfred Little) *language educator, researcher, musicologist*

McGann, Jerome John *language educator*
Megill, Allan *historian*
Midelfort, Hans Christian Erik *history professor*
Mikalson, Jon Dennis *classics educator*
Nelson, Raymond John *language educator, dean*
Nohrnberg, James Carson *language educator*
Perkowski, Jan Louis *language, literature and folklore educator*
Pertzoff, Margaret Henderson *history professor*
Peterson, Merrill Daniel *historian, educator*
Rini, Joel *language educator, linguist*
Rubin, David Lee *humanities educator, critic, editor*
Schuker, Stephen Alan *historian, educator*
Sedgwick, Alexander *retired historian, educator*
Shaw, Donald Leslie *Spanish language educator*
Spearing, Anthony Colin *English literature educator*
Stocker, Arthur Frederick *classics educator*
Wagoner, Jennings Lee, Jr. *historian, educator*
Zunz, Olivier Jean *history professor*

Covesville
Williams, Patricia Anne *philosopher, writer*

Danville
Hayes, Jack Irby *historian, educator*

Fairfax
Horton, Lois Elaine *history professor*
King, James Cecil *retired language and literature educator, medievalist*
Lavine, Thelma Zeno *philosophy educator*
Stearns, Peter Nathaniel *history professor, academic administrator*

Fort Lee
Sterling, Keir Brooks *historian, educator*

Fredericksburg
Dorman, John Frederick *genealogist*
Eslinger-Brown, Vanessa Pauline *humanities educator*
Mezo, Richard Eugene *literature and language professor, writer*
Somma, Thomas P. *art historian, museum director*

Great Falls
Castro-Klaren, Sara *Latin American literature professor*

Hampden Sydney
Arieti, James Alexander *classics educator, writer*

Hardyville
White, Gordon Eliot *historian, writer*

Harrisonburg
Frazier, Chapman Hood *literature and language professor*

Lexington
Barrett, John Gilchrist *retired historian*
Koeniger, Alfred Cash *history professor*
Koons, Kenneth Edward *historian, educator, historian, consultant*
Ryan, Halford Ross *speech educator*
Stephens, Laurence David, Jr. *linguist, investor, oil industry executive*

Lovettsville
Foard, Douglas W. *historian*

Lynchburg
Coates, Ardith Williams *language educator*
Henderson, Horace Edward *World War II historian, peace advocate*
Melton, Brian Christopher *history professor, writer*
Partie, David John *language educator*

Newport News
Duskin, J. Eric *history professor*
Santoro, Anthony Richard *history professor*

Norfolk
Byrne, William Andrew *historian, educator*
Hirrel, Leo P. *historian, retired military officer*
Newby-Alexander, Cassandra Lynn *history professor*
Wilson, Harold Stacy *history professor, writer*

Oakton
MacCracken, Thomas Gregg *musicologist*

Petersburg
Garrott, Carl Lee *foreign language educator*

Portsmouth
Paquette, William Arthur *historian, educator*

Quinton
Hinkle, Douglas Paddock *retired languages educator*

Richlands
Surles, Harold Brady *history professor*

Richmond
Hall, James H(errick), Jr. *philosophy educator, writer*
Levit, Héloïse B. (Ginger Levit) *art historian, journalist, art dealer, consultant*
Rilling, John Robert *history professor*
Terry, Robert Meredith *foreign language educator*
Ward, Harry Merrill *history professor*

Sumerduck
McCamy, Sharon Grove *English educator*

Sweet Briar
Piepho, Lee (Edward Lee Piepho) *humanities educator*

Vienna
Drumheller, Linda Blocher *language educator*
Farrace, Melissa Anne *language educator, secondary school educator*

Virginia Beach
Reece-Porter, Sharon Ann *international human rights educator*

Williamsburg
Axtell, James Lewis *history professor*
Ball, Donald L. *retired language educator*
Chappell, Miles Linwood, Jr. *art historian, educator*
Crapol, Edward P. *history professor*
Hoffman, Ronald *historian, educator*
Landen, Robert Geran *retired historian, academic administrator*
McGiffert, Michael *retired historian*
Nettels, Elsa *English language educator*
Sherman, Richard Beatty *historian, educator*
Wallach, Alan *art historian, educator*

Winchester
Meschutt, David Randolph *historian*
Tisinger, Catherine Anne *retired history professor*

Woodbridge
Hood, Ronald Chalmers III *historian, writer*

Yorktown
Romjue, John Lawson *historian, writer*

WASHINGTON

Auburn
Sims, Marcie Lynne *language educator, writer*

Bainbridge Island
Berg, Walter Louis *retired history professor*

Bothell
Watts, Linda Susan *humanities educator*

Burien
Burgess, Charles Orville *history professor*

Cheney
Smith, Grant William *language educator, volunteer*

Des Moines
McMannon, Timothy J. *history professor*

Kirkland
Pope, Deborah Renaye *literature and language professor*

Lake Forest Park
Adams, Hazard Simeon *retired language educator, writer*

Olympia
Bruce, Robert Vance *historian, educator*
Coontz, Stephanie Jean *history professor, writer*

Pullman
Condon, William Francis, Jr. *literacy educator*
Streamas, John *ethnic and American studies professor*
Swan, Susan Linda *history professor*

Seattle
Barlow, Tani E. *history and women's studies professor*
Coburn, Robert Craig *philosopher, educator*
Coldewey, John Christopher *English literature educator*
Ellison, Herbert Jay *historian, educator*
Estes, Kenneth William *history professor, military officer*
Fine, Arthur I. *philosopher, educator*
Harmon, Daniel Patrick *classics educator*
Heer, Nicholas Lawson *language educator*
Himma, Kenneth Einar *philosophy educator*
Keyt, David *philosophy and classics educator*
Korg, Jacob *English literature educator*
Matchett, William H(enry) *English literature educator*
Nutting, Maureen Murphy *historian, educator*
Pressly, Thomas James *history professor*
Snow-Smith, Joanne Inloes *art history educator*
Sun, Yilin *language educator*
Whorton, James Clifton *history professor*

Spokane
Carriker, Robert Charles *history professor*
Migliazzo, Arlin C. *history professor*
Stackelberg, John Roderick *history professor*

Tacoma
Thomas, Ronald Robert *English literature educator, writer*

Vancouver
Donovan, Thomas John *retired humanities educator*

Walla Walla
Carlsen, James Caldwell *retired musicologist*

Yakima
Meshke, George Lewis *retired drama and humanities educator*

WEST VIRGINIA

Charles Town
Na, Tsung Shun (Terry Na) *Chinese studies educator, writer*

Morgantown
Blaydes, Sophia Boyatzies *English language educator*
Bush, Carletta Ann *historian, educator*

Reedsville
Williford, Drury Fisher, Jr. *retired historical researcher, writer, editor*

WISCONSIN

Appleton
Chaney, William Albert *retired history professor*
Goldgar, Bertrand Alvin *historian, educator*

De Pere
Kersten, Frederick Irving *retired philosopher, educator*
Patterson, Wayne K. *historian, educator*

Ferryville
Tedeschi, John Alfred *historian, educator, librarian*

Hales Corners
McNally, Vincent Joseph *historian, educator*

Kenosha
Kummings, Donald Dale *language educator*

Madison
Berg, William James *language educator, writer, translator*
Berghahn, Klaus Leo *German and Jewish studies educator*
Bogue, Allan George *historian, educator*
Ciplijauskaite, Birute *humanities educator*
Cronon, William *history professor*
Drewal, Henry John *art historian, educator*
Dubrow, Heather *literature educator*
Frykenberg, Robert Eric *historian, educator*
Hamerow, Theodore Stephen *historian, educator*
Kingdon, Robert McCune *historian, educator*
Kleinhenz, Christopher *foreign language educator, researcher, director*
Knowles, Richard Alan John *language educator*
Kutler, Stanley Ira *historian, lawyer, educator*
Powell, Barry Bruce *classicist, educator*
Scarano, Francisco A. *humanities educator*
Sewell, Richard Herbert *retired historian, retired educator*
Sonnedecker, Glenn Allen *pharmaceutical historian, educator*
Vowles, Richard Beckman *literature educator*
Weinbrot, Howard David *language educator*
Wink, Andre *history professor*
Zell, Josephine May *retired language educator*

Middleton
O'Brien, James Aloysius *foreign language educator*

Milwaukee
Alred, Gerald James *literature and language professor*
Friedman, Paula Sopkin *literature educator*
Gallop, Jane (Jane Anne Gallop) *women's studies educator, writer*
Noonan, Timothy Paul *musicologist, educator*
Sherman, Daniel James *history professor, director*
Siegel, Kristi Ellen *language educator*
Siegel, Robert Harold *English literature educator, writer*
Swanson, Roy Arthur *classicist, educator*
Theis, Peter George *retired classicist*
Ullman, Pierre Lioni *retired Spanish educator*
Yu, Hong *humanities educator*

River Falls
Smith, Clyde Curry *historian, educator*

Stevens Point
Mertz, Paul Eric *retired history professor, writer*

Sturgeon Bay
Maher, Virginia Jones *art historian, educator*

Wausau
Veninga, James Frank *humanities educator, editor, writer*

WYOMING

Cody
Garry, James B. *historian, naturalist, storyteller, writer*
Price, B. Byron *historian*

Laramie
Chisum, Emmett Dewain *historian, researcher, archaeologist*
Nye, Eric W. *English language and literature educator*
Williams, Roger Lawrence *historian, educator*

Powell
Myers, Rex Charles *historian, educator, retired dean*

Sheridan
Aguirre Batty, Mercedes *Spanish, English and literature educator*

TERRITORIES OF THE UNITED STATES

GUAM

Barrigada
French, Jennifer Suzanne *language educator*

PUERTO RICO

Ponce
Hernandez, Carlos I. *historian, educator*

San Juan
Lockwood-Benet, Mildred M. *language educator*
Ocasio-Melendez, Marcial Enrique *history professor*

CANADA

BRITISH COLUMBIA

Burnaby
Kitchen, John Martin *historian, educator*

North Saanich
Saddlemyer, Ann (Eleanor Saddlemyer) *humanities educator, critic, theater historian*

Richmond
Durrant, Geoffrey Hugh *retired language educator*

Vancouver
Batts, Michael Stanley *retired language educator*
Bentley, Thomas Roy *retired language educator, writer*
Conway, John S. *history professor*
Newmeyer, Frederick Jaret *linguist, educator*
Nosco, Peter Erling *humanities educator, consultant*
Overmyer, Daniel Lee *humanities educator*
Pacheco-Ransanz, Arsenio *language educator, historian, educator*
Unger, Richard Watson *history professor*

MANITOBA

Winnipeg
Rozumnyj, Jaroslav *literature educator*

NEW BRUNSWICK

Saint John
Condon, Thomas Joseph *university historian*

NOVA SCOTIA

Halifax
Gray, James *English literature educator*

ONTARIO

Brampton
Paikeday, Thomas M. *lexicographer, linguistic consultant*

Flamborough
Lee, Alvin A. *literary educator, scholar, author*

Hamilton
McKay, Alexander Gordon *classics educator*

Kingston
Akenson, Donald Harman *historian, educator*

London
Gerber, Douglas Earl *classics educator*

Nepean
Kallmann, Helmut Max *musicologist, retired librarian*

North York
Adelman, Howard *philosophy educator*
Thomas, Clara McCandless *retired literature educator*

Ottawa
Dray, William Herbert *philosophy educator*
Labarge, Margaret Wade *medieval history professor, historian, writer*
Squire, Anne Marguerite *retired humanities educator*
Staines, David McKenzie *language educator*

Saint Catharines
Sivell, John Norman *language educator*

Toronto
Blewett, David Lambert *English literature educator*
Granatstein, Jack Lawrence *historian*
Millgate, Michael (Michael Henry Millgate) *retired literature educator*
Morey, Carl Reginald *musicologist*
Skvorecky, Josef Vaclav *literature educator, writer*
Wevers, John William *retired Semitic languages educator*

Waterloo
Haworth, Lawrence Lindley *philosophy educator*
Suits, Bernard Herbert *philosophy educator*

PRINCE EDWARD ISLAND

Charlottetown
Sanborn, George Freeman, Jr. *genealogist*

QUEBEC

Montreal
Beugnot, Bernard Andre Henri *literature educator*
Kinsley, William Benton *literature educator*

North Hatley
Jones, Douglas Gordon *retired literature educator*

MEXICO

Guadalajara
Yashima, Mutsuo *language educator*

Mexico City
Leon-Portilla, Miguel *historian, educator*

AUSTRIA

Graz
Weisstein, Ulrich Werner *English literature educator*

BRAZIL

Rio deJaneiro
Sluberski, Thomas Richard *international educator, journalist, theologian*

DENMARK

Farum
Larsen, Poul Steen *retired information science educator*

ENGLAND

Cambridge
Garrow, David Jeffries *historian, author*

London
Abu-Deeb, Kamal Mikha'il *humanities educator*
Boucher, Bruce Ambler *art historian, art critic*
Graubard, Stephen Richards *historian, educator, editor*
Lowenthal, David *historian, geographer*

Oxford
Carey, John *language educator, critic*

FRANCE

Vence
Polk, William Roe *historian*

Villeneuve d'Ascq
Allain, Louis *literature educator*

GERMANY

Berlin
Piper, Adrian Margaret Smith *philosopher, artist, educator*

Münster
Spevack, Marvin *language educator*

Nuremberg
Doerries, Reinhard René *historian, educator*

Sonnenberg-Wiesbaden
Lynch, Lucia *language educator*

ITALY

Bologna
Eco, Umberto *semiotics educator, author*

Padua
Shea, William Rene *historian, history and philosophy professor*

Verona
Pozzo, Riccardo *philosophy educator*

JAPAN

Kanagawa
Fukatsu, Tanefusa *retired classicist, educator*

Kashiwara
Hori, Keiko *English literature educator*

Mitaka
Kazama, Toshio *retired humanities educator*

Osaka
Akase, Masako *humanities educator*

NEPAL

Kathmandu
Baker, Ian Archbald *explorer, educator, writer, photographer*

NETHERLANDS

Amsterdam
Kolko, Gabriel *historian, educator*

SCOTLAND

Cellardyke Fife
Roff, William Robert *historian, educator, writer*

Stirling
Lenman, Bruce Philip *historian, educator*

SPAIN

Madrid
Abellan, José Luis *humanities educator*

SWEDEN

Lerum
Borei, Sven Hans Emil *translator, writer, educator*

SWITZERLAND

Geneva
Bader, William Banks *historian, former corporate executive, foundation executive*

TAIWAN

Taipei
Lai, Shu-Fen *language educator*

THAILAND

Northaburi
Austermann, Christopher Brent *language educator*

ADDRESS UNPUBLISHED

Abbott, Rebecca Phillips *art historian, consultant, photographer, director*
Adams, David Parrish *historian, epidemiologist, educator*
Adams, Phyllis Yewell *foreign language educator*
Adler, Raphael *retired humanities educator, speech pathology/audiology services professional*
Amin, Iran Arbabi *language educator*
Amussen, Susan Dwyer *history professor*
Anderson, Jeffrey Elton *history professor*
Anderson, Jerry Maynard *retired speech educator*
Andrews, Karen Leigh *language educator*
Ansbro, John Joseph *philosopher, educator*
Araujo, Ilka Vasconcelos *musicologist, pianist*
Arnold, Marygwen Suella *language educator, medical/surgical nurse*
Arnquist, Carol Anne *humanities educator*
Attebery, Louie Wayne *language educator*
Azadpur, Mohammad *philosopher, educator*
Bailey, Charles-James Nice *linguistics educator*
Baker, Ronald James *language educator, academic administrator*
Bannister, Robert Corwin, Jr. *historian, educator*
Bartelt, William E. *historian, educator*
Bateman, John Jay *classics educator*
Bates, Margaret P. *historian*
Baxter, Stephen Bartow *retired historian*
Baym (Stillinger), Nina *literature educator, researcher, writer*
Belk, Leotis S. *language educator*
Bell, Albert Atwood, Jr. *history professor, writer*
Benor, Sarah Bunin *language educator, religious studies educator*
Benseler, David P. *foreign language educator*
Benson, Lucy Wilson *historian, consultant*
Bercovitch, Sacvan *English language professional, educator*
Berlin, Robert Harry *historian, educator*
Beschloss, Michael *historian, writer, lecturer, commentator*
Biles, Gloria C. *historian, educator*
Binns, Jane Camille *humanities educator*
Blackbourn, David Gordon *history professor*
Blackmun, Barbara Winston *art historian, educator, academic administrator*
Blake, King Charles *humanities educator, writer*
Blissett, William Frank *English literature educator*
Blumin, Stuart M. *history professor*
Bolsterli, Margaret Jones *English professor, farmer*
Bordelon, Suzanne Mackie *writing and rhetoric educator*
Bosmajian, Haig Aram *speech communication educator*
Boyle, Richard John *art historian, author*
Bremer, Ronald Allan *genealogist, editor*
Brewster, Elizabeth Winifred *literature educator, poet, writer*
Bridges, Leonard Hal *retired history educator, writer*
Brunner, Kathleen Marie *humanities educator*
Bucholz, Robert Orland *history professor, writer*
Buell, Lawrence Ingalls *language educator*
Burchell, Kenneth Wayne *historian, appraiser*
Burns, William Earl *historian*
Bush, Sarah Lillian *historian*
Caldwell, Louise Phinney *historical researcher, community volunteer*
Calleo, David Patrick *history professor, political scientist*
Campbell, Joyce S. *language educator, department chairman*
Carls, Alice Catherine *history professor*
Carter, Kathy Deonne *language educator*
Cawley, Joseph Douglas *retired reading professor*
Chappell, Fred Davis *language educator, poet*
Cher-Killigm, Beatrice M. *history professor, art educator*
Chesson, Michael Bedout *history professor, writer*
Ciraolo, Debra *sign language interpreter, consultant*
Clark, Eve Vivienne *linguist, educator*
Clogan, Paul Maurice *English language and literature educator*
Collins, Jean Katherine *language educator*
Collins, Martha *English language educator, writer*
Collmer, Robert George *retired language educator*
Conway, Jill Kathryn Ker *historian, writer, former academic administrator*
Cordova, Ruben Charles *art historian, curator, photographer*
Corrigan, Brian Jay *literature educator, writer*
Courtenay, William James *historian, educator*
Courtés, Joseph Jean-Marie *humanities educator, writer*
Courtney, Edward *retired classics educator*
Crandall, Elizabeth Walbert *retired home economics professor*
Craver, Earlene *historian, educator*
Cunningham, William Francis, Jr. *literature and language professor, academic administrator*
Dallek, Robert *historian, professor, writer*
Dechene, Arthur C., Jr. *philosopher, religious studies educator*
De Cou-Landberg, Michelle V. *retired language educator*
Delaty, Simone *retired language educator*
Delli, Bertrun H. *art historian*
De Lorenzo, William E. *retired foreign language educator*
Del Rio, Kathleen O. *language educator*
Der-Houssikian, Haig *linguist, educator*
Di Carlo, Armando *Italian language educator*
Dickstein, Morris *language educator, writer*
Djordjevic, Dimitrije *historian, educator*
Doebler, Bettie Anne *language educator, researcher, poet*
Donnelley, Strachan *philosopher*
Downs, Dorothy Rieder *art historian, consultant, writer*
Dragushanskaya, Lyudmila *language educator, department chairman*
Dudden, Alexis *history professor*
Duhl, Olga Anna *literature educator, researcher*
Dunbar, Maurice Victor *language educator*
Durek, Dorothy Mary *retired language educator*
Dye, Nancy Schrom *historian, educator, former academic administrator*
Eadie, John William *historian, educator*
Ebert, Robert Peter *German language professor*
Eckstein, Jerome *philosopher, retired educator*
Edens, Betty Joyce *reading recovery educator*
Edmonds, Crystal D. *language educator, distance learning coordinator*
Edwards, Annmarie Monica *language educator, career coach, entrepreneur*
Eire, Carlos *historian, educator, writer*
Ellis, John Hubert *retired history professor*
Ellis, Joseph John Michael III *historian, professor*
Elrick, Donald *retired literature educator*
Emmett, Rita *professional speaker*
Erickson, Carol Jean *literature and language professor*
Espenlaub, Margo Linn *women's studies educator, writer, artist*
Evans, Frank Bernard *retired historian*
Evans, Tony *language educator*
Fagan, Drew Stephen *language educator*
Fagles, Robert *classicist, educator, translator*
Fatemi, Faramarz Saifpour *history and political science professor, consultant*
Feather, Gloria Anne *language educator*
Feeney, Matthew Edward *linguist, educator*
Flint, John E. *retired historian*
Forster, Merlin Henry *foreign languages educator, writer, researcher*
Franklin, John Hope *historian, writer*
Froberg, Brent Malcolm *classics educator*
Fuentes, Beatriz Pastor *language educator, department chairman*
Gaddis, John Lewis *history professor*
Galiardo, Christopher James Francis *language educator, political organization worker*
Gamble, Vanessa Northington *historian, healthcare educator, bioethicist*
Gatewood, Willard Badgett, Jr. *retired historian, writer*
Gaustad, Edwin Scott *historian, educator*
Gerlach, Jeanne Elaine *English language educator*
Gettleman, Marvin E. *retired history professor*
Giesey, Ralph Edwin *retired historian*
Gillespie, Gerald Ernest Paul *comparative literature educator, writer*
Gillett, Mary Caperton *military historian*
Glass, William Robert *history professor*
Glick, Ruth Burtnick *literature educator, writer*
Goldman, Alvin Ira *philosopher, educator*
Gonzalez, Gabriela *history professor*
Gonzalez-del-Valle, Luis Tomas *Spanish language educator*
Gordon, Leonard H(erman) D(avid) *history educator*
Grabitske, David M. *historian*
Graham, Lanier *art historian, curator*
Graham, Susette Ryan *retired English educator*
Greene, John Colton *retired historian*
Grinnell, Helen Dunn *musicologist, arts administrator*
Gruber, Ira Dempsey *historian, educator*
Hadda, Janet Ruth *language educator, lay psychoanalyst*
Hain, Pamela Chase *historian, writer*
Halliburton, Lloyd *retired Romance philology educator*
Hamblin, Terry Robert, Jr. *historian, educator*

elin, Marcel *historian, educator*
ilton, Virginia Van der Veer *historian, ducator*
dy, Rollo Leroy *philosopher, researcher*
lin, James Neal *language educator, writer*
dy, Michele *literature and language ofessor*
ng, Ellen Stone *philosophy educator*
, Arthur Alvin *historian, author*
ernan, James Anthony Walsh *language and erature educator*
ernan, Thomas Carroll *English literature and nerican studies educator*
drix, Scott Norton *history professor*
ost, Jurgen *historian, educator*
rman, Laura Gardner *art historian, educator*
lgen, Maurice Denzil *retired history ofessor, writer*
rder, Dirk *history educator*
fman, Daniel (Gerard) *literature educator, oet*
i, Melvin George *retired history professor*
aker, Bonnie *language educator*
shiar, Bobbie Kay *retired language arts ducator*
vard, Michael Eliot *historian, educator*
bard, Holly Annon *language arts educator*
gel, Donna Marie *historian, writer, artist, rchivist*
ghes, Amy Stoddart *literature and language rofessor*
ghes, Thomas Parke *history professor*
nter, J(ames) Paul *literature and language rofessor, literary critic*
cheon, Linda Ann *English language educator*
sias, Maria Estrella *language educator, riter*
ac, Susan Victoria *literature and language rofessor, department chairman*
, Alfred Lyon *philosophy educator, historian*
obson, Matthew Frye *historian, educator*
ness, Muriel Whitlock *reading specialist*
nson, Hiroko *art history educator*
nson, Janet Hovey *English language educator*
nson, John Prescott *retired philosophy ducator*
nsrud, Brian C. *literature educator, scholar*
es, Peter d'Alroy *historian, writer, retired ducator*
donsky, Christine Elaine *historian, educator*
ninsky, Alice Richkin *retired literature ducator*
plan, Robert B. *linguistics educator, onsultant, researcher*
cz, Andrzej *literature educator*
i, Daven Michael *English and religious tudies professor*
linsky, Simon *language educator, writer*
stor, Frank Sullivan *language educator*
uffman, B. Suzanne *historian, genealogist*
ufman, Luna Amalia *musicologist*
lman, Ari *history professor, educator*
nnett, Lee Boone, Jr. *historian, educator*
nworthy, Scott *humanities educator*
oler, William Westcott *French language and iterature educator*
nder, Suzanne Fonay Wemple *retired istorian, retired educator*
rby, Lisa Anne *literature educator*
nghoffer, Judith Apter *historian, consultant*
lb, Harold Hutchinson, Jr. *language educator*
lbert, Jack *language educator*
szarski, Richard *art historian, curator*
akaur, Linda E. *language educator*
amer, Dale Vernon *retired language educator*
avitz, Ellen King *musicologist, educator*
ltermann, Udo *architectural and art historian, educator, writer*
bor, Earle Gene *literature and language professor*
djevardi, Habib *historian*
Hood, Marvin John *retired language educator*
queur, Walter *history professor, writer*
urent, Pierre-Henri *retired history professor*
wlor, LynnAnn Jennifer *reading educator*
wson, Carolina Donadio *language educator, translator*
vinsky, Frieda Libby *language educator*
wis, Douglas *retired art historian*
wis, Emanuel Raymond *historian, psychologist, retired librarian*
sio, Donald John *historian, educator*
ngsworth, Robert Morrow *language educator*
tchin, Roger Williams *history professor, writer*
wenthal, Constance *art historian, consultant*
cas, Janet Marie *language educator*
ons, John David *literature and language professor*
acDonald, Priscilla Ann *history professor*
aehl, William Harvey *retired historian*
ahoney, John L. *English literature educator*
ahoney, Michael Robert Taylor *art historian, educator*
akimura, Yasuhiro *history professor*
app, Edward Charles *speech educator*
arcopoulos, George John *history professor*
arion, Marjorie Anne *English language educator, educational consultant*
artin, Trisa *education and human development educator*
arx, Michael William *language educator, writer*
aryks, Robert A. *history professor*
atsuda, Paul Kei *literature and language professor*
aurer, Trent W. *humanities educator*
auskopf, Seymour Harold *history professor*
cCardell, John Malcolm, Jr. *history professor, academic administrator*
cCormick, John Owen *retired comparative literature educator*
IcDermott, Agnes Charlene Senape *philosophy educator*
IcDiarmid, Lucy *literature educator, writer*
IcDonough, Richard Michael *philosophy educator*
c Fadden, Joseph Michael *historian, educator*
McGann, Lisa B. Napoli *language educator*
McGinnis, Jon David *philosopher, educator*
McKee, Betty Davis *English language educator*
McMaster, Juliet Sylvia *English language educator*
McMinn, J. B. *retired philosophy educator, composer*
Miller, Ilana Deborah *history professor*
Miller, Walter James *retired literature educator, writer*
Mindlin, Paula Rosalie *retired reading educator*
Miscella, Maria Diana *humanities educator*
Molloy, Sylvia *language educator*
Morgan, Edmund Sears *retired history professor*
Morrill, Penny Chittim *art historian*
Morrison, Margaret Anne *literature educator*
Muegge, Uwe *terminology professor*
Muñiz, Olga M. *language educator, consultant*
Murnion, William Edward *philosopher*
Murphy, Francis *language educator*
Murphy, Robert James *language educator, consultant, pianist, pipe organ performer*
Nagel, Thomas *philosopher, lawyer, educator*
Naumer, Carola *art historian, educator*
Nelson, Geralda *language educator*
Nephew, Julia Anne *language educator*
Newmark, Leonard Daniel *linguistics educator*
Nicholas, Lynn Holman *historian, researcher, writer*
Nitzarim, Yoel David *language educator*
Nochman, Lois Wood Kivi (Mrs. Marvin Nochman) *retired literature educator*
Noor, Ronny *language educator, writer*
Norberg, Arthur Lawrence, Jr. *historian, physicist, educator*
Novak, Michelle Anne *history professor*
Noyalas, Jonathan Alex *history professor, consultant*
Nugent, Helen Jean *history professor*
Nugent, Walter Terry King *historian*
Odenigbo, Innocent Chukwunwike *linguist, writer, consultant*
Palmer, John Anthony III *language professor, secondary school educator, music educator*
Palmer, Marilyn Joan *English composition educator*
Palmieri, Dora Ann *retired language educator*
Palter, Robert Monroe *humanities educator*
Panzer, Mary Caroline *historian, museum curator*
Pauley, Bruce Frederick *retired history professor*
Pease, Neal *history professor*
Peralta, Luis Francisco *language educator*
Perdigó, Luisa Marina *foreign language and literature educator*
Perkins, Leeman Lloyd *musicologist, educator*
Perlingieri, Ilya Sandra *art historian, writer*
Persico, Joseph Edward *historian, biographer*
Peterson, Betty W. *language educator, writer*
Pflanze, Otto Paul *history professor*
Pham, Lee *literature and language professor, consultant*
Pickrel, Paul *language educator*
Podbilski, Lisa Lyn *Mandarin Chinese educator*
Polzonetti, Pierpaolo *musicologist, music educator*
Post, Gaines, Jr. *retired history professor, dean, academic administrator*
Preston, Thomas Ronald *language educator, researcher*
Proctor, Robert Neel *history educator*
Pugliese, Stanislao *history educator, researcher*
Pulitzer, Emily Rauh (Mrs. Joseph Pulitzer Jr.) *art historian, consultant*
Rainville, Allison M. *language educator*
Rebay, Luciano *language educator, literary critic*
Reed, Betty Jamerson *historian, educator*
Reeves, Kathleen Walker *English language educator*
Reid, Ivonne Figueroa *language educator*
Reiman, Donald Henry *language educator*
Resnick, Kirsten Fay Markuson *history professor*
Reynolds, Donald Martin *art historian, foundation administrator, educator*
Reznikov, Vladimir Lvovich *historian, playwright*
Riasanovsky, Nicholas Valentine *retired historian, educator*
Richards, David Gleyre *German language educator*
Richardson, Margaret Ann *art historian, educator*
Richardson, Robert Dale, Jr. *language educator*
Rickard, Ruth David *retired history and political science professor*
Ricks, Thomas Miller *historian, academic administrator*
Righter, Kathleen Anne *language educator*
Roberts, Philip John *history professor, editor*
Robinson, Harlow Loomis *language educator, historian, writer*
Robinson, Mary Elizabeth Goff *retired historian, researcher*
Rodriguez, Timothy Allen *language educator*
Rogers, Katharine Munzer *English literature educator*
Rollins, Alfred Brooks, Jr. *historian, educator*
Rose, Sarah Elizabeth *genealogist, writer, counselor, web site designer*
Rosenberg, David Alan *military historian, strategic analyst*
Rouman, John Christ *classics educator*
Ruan, Jiening *literature and language professor, director, director, writer*
Rubin, Louis Decimus, Jr. *retired language educator, writer, publishing executive*
Ruffin, Herbert George, II, *history professor*
Runner, Jeffrey Thomas *linguist*
Ruoff, A. LaVonne Brown *language educator*
Russell, Andrew Benjamin *historian, educator*
Ryan, Marleigh Grayer *language educator*
Sahner, Christian C. *historian*
Saiah, Sue Lynn *linguist, educator*
Saint-Jacques, Bernard *linguistics educator*
Samuels, Maurice Anthony *French literature educator*
Sapienza, Madeline *historian, researcher*
Sardegna, Verónica Gabriela *language educator*
Sawai, Dahleen Emi *language educator*
Saxon, Burton Roy *humanities educator*
Sayre, Robert Freeman *language educator*
Scaringello, Nina Maria *literature and language professor*
Schadow, Karen E. *public speaking trainer, educator*
Schlagel, Richard H. *retired philosophy educator*
Schmidt, Albert John *retired history professor*
Schmitz, Dennis Mathew *retired language educator*
Schneider, Valerie Lois *retired speech educator*
Schofield, Robert E. (Robert Edwin Schofield) *historian, educator, academic administrator*
Schor, Laura Struminger *historian*
Schroeder, Brian S. *philosopher, educator*
Schwantes, Carlos Arnaldo *history professor, consultant*
Schwartz, Brian Michael *philosopher, think-tank executive*
Schwartz, Leon *foreign language educator*
Seaman, Natasha *art historian, educator*
Searl, Stanford Jay, Jr. *language educator*
Seidenman, Neil Arnold *interpreter*
Seniors, Paula Marie *history professor, researcher*
Shaeffer, John Nees *historian, educator*
Shaw, Joseph Thomas *Slavic languages educator*
Sheffey, Ruthe T. *language educator*
Sheppard, Jennifer Modlin *retired genealogist*
Shillingsburg, Miriam Jones *literature educator, academic administrator*
Shindle, William Richard *retired musicologist, educator*
Sieburth, Richard *literature educator, interpreter*
Silverman, Kenneth Eugene *language educator, writer*
Skinner, Daniel Thomas *language educator*
Smither, Howard Elbert *musicologist, educator*
Smock, Raymond William *historian*
Spadafora, David Charles *historian, educator*
Srinivasan, Amia P. *Philosophy scholar*
Staley, Thomas Fabian *language professional, academic administrator*
Stanford, Charlotte A. *humanities educator*
Stanton, Robert John, Jr. *retired language educator, writer*
Steiner, Elizabeth *philosopher, psychologist, educator*
Stendahl, Brita Kristina *humanities and social studies educator*
Stephenson, Clarence David *historian, educator, writer, researcher*
Stocker, Christine Marie *language educator*
Stoesen, Alexander Rudolph *retired history educator*
Stolarik, M. Mark *history professor*
Stoudt, Ralph Joseph, Jr. *language educator*
Street, John Charles *linguistics educator*
Strotman, Linda Ann *language educator*
Sullivan, Mary Rose *retired English language educator*
Sundstrom, Aileen Lois *speech educator*
Sutton, Julia *musicologist, dance historian*
Swerdlow, Amy *historian, educator, writer*
Tallet, Jorge Antonio *philosopher, writer*
Taw, James S. *history professor*
Tayler, Irene *retired English literature educator*
Taylor, Henry Splawn *retired literature educator, poet*
Taylor-Anderson, Jill *reading specialist*
Tedesco, Paul Herbert *humanities educator*
Teel, Patricia Jo *English language educator*
Teuscher, Simon Hans *history professor, researcher*
Thompson, Ewa M. *foreign language educator*
Thomson, Virginia Winbourn *humanities educator, writer*
Thoreson, Ryan R. *social anthropology scholar*
Thorson, Connie Capers *library educator*
Tice, Bradley Scott *humanities educator*
Tise, Larry Edward *historian, cultural organization administrator*
Titcomb, Caldwell *music and theatre historian*
Tollison, Courtney L. *history professor*
Tong, Rosemarie *humanities educator, philosopher*
Toplin, Robert Brent *history professor, television producer*
Trejos, Charlotte Marie *humanities educator, consultant*
Trelease, Allen William *historian, educator*
Tyrrell, Joseph Morten *retired history professor*
Unterberger, Betty Miller *retired history professor*
Valencia, Margarita *Spanish language educator*
VanArsdel, Rosemary Thorstenson *retired English studies educator*
van der Marck, Jan *art historian*
Verhoff, Glen Charles *reading educator, choir director*
Verhoff, Julie *international relations scholar*
Walker, Philip Doolittle *retired literature and language professor, composer*
Walker, Ruth Charlotta *language educator, real estate broker*
Walsh, Michael Thomas *historian, musician*
Weatherburn, Stephen James *humanities educator*
Weber, Bruce Edward *art historian*
Weintraub, Sam *retired reading educator*
Wheeler, Burton M. *language educator, dean*
Whitburn, Merrill Duane *English literature educator*
White, Charles Sidney John *retired humanities educator*
Wiebenson, Dora Louise *architectural historian, editor, writer*
Wiener, Jon *history professor*
Williams, Robert Chadwell *history professor*
Wills, John Elliot, Jr. *retired historian, writer*
Wiswall, Dorothy Roller *language educator*
Wizda, Christine Anne *history professor*
Wolfe, Margaret Ripley *historian, educator, consultant*
Woodbridge, John Dunning *history professor*
Woodward, Ralph Lee, Jr. *retired historian, educator*
Wright, Josephine Rosa Beatrice *musicologist, educator*
Wruck, Erich-Oskar *retired foreign language educator, administrator*
Yannella, Donald *literature and language professor*
Yoon, Bogum *literacy educator*
Zaferson, William S. *philosophy educator, publisher*
Zakim, Tom Edward *history professor*
Zelizer, Julian E. *historian, educator*
Zhou, Yiqun *humanities educator*
Zimmermann, Thomas Callander Price *retired historian, educator*
Zinn, Howard *historian, educator, playwright*

HUMANITIES: LIBRARIES

UNITED STATES

ALABAMA

Athens
Kemp, Ann *retired librarian*

Auburn University
MacEwan, Bonnie *librarian, dean*

Birmingham
Beard, Craig Wyeth *librarian*
Sirmans, Barbara C. *library director*
Spence, Paul Herbert *librarian*
Stephens, Jerry Wayne *librarian, director*

Gardendale
McKay, Marie Conyers *librarian, writer*

Huntsville
Abram, Stephen *librarian, writer*

Jacksonville
Hubbard, William James *library director*
McAbee, Sonja Louise *library administrator*

Montgomery
Mitchell, Rebecca *library director*
Owes, Jaunita *library director*
Shepard, Judith Bethea *librarian*

Spanish Fort
Economos, Cora Matheny *librarian*

Tuscaloosa
Grogg, Jill Elaine *library and information scientist*
Osburn, Charles Benjamin *retired librarian, dean*
Pitschmann, Louis A. *librarian, dean, educator*

ALASKA

Anchorage
Braund-Allen, Julianna Elise *librarian*
Keller, Karen A. *library director*

Juneau
Schorr, Alan Edward *librarian, publishing executive*
Shelton, Kathryn H. *librarian*

ARIZONA

Chandler
Brown, Brenda *library director*

Glendale
Honsa, Vlasta *retired librarian*

Mesa
Wolf, Heather *library director*

Phoenix
Anderson, Vicki *retired librarian*
Finch, Carol *librarian*
Garvey, Toni *library director*
Hanley, Fred William *librarian, educator*
Mason, Michael Lamott *librarian, researcher, writer*
Roof, Sally Jean-Marie *library and information scientist, educator*
Wells, GladysAnn *library director*
Willocks, Robert Max *retired librarian*

Scottsdale
Hamilton, Rita *library director*

Sun City
Crisman, Mary Frances Borden *librarian*
Williams, William Harrison *retired librarian*

Surprise
Telban, Ethel *retired librarian*

Tempe
Duvernay, Jennifer *librarian*
Maynard, Michael *librarian*
O'Clair, Katherine Clemens *library and information scientist*
Schmidt, Sherrie *library director, dean*

Tucson
Coleman, Anita S. *professor of library science*
Ledeboer, Nancy *library director*
White, Herbert Spencer *library and information scientist, educator, dean*

ARKANSAS

Bella Vista
Medin, Alice Louise *librarian*

Fayetteville
Jones, Phillip John *librarian*
Schaper, Louise Levy *library director*
Thorup, Shawna Saavedra *librarian*

Greers Ferry
Martindale, Carla Joy *retired librarian*

Little Rock
Alsobrook, David Ernest *library director, archivist, historian*
Ashcraft, Carolyn *state librarian*
Mulkey, Jack Clarendon *retired library director*

Lonoke
Ross, Philip Rowland *retired library director*

Springdale
Hogensen, Margaret Hiner *retired librarian*

CALIFORNIA

Altadena
Dutton, Pauline Mae *fine arts and reference librarian*

Aptos
Heron, David Winston *librarian*

Auburn
Sanborn, Dorothy Chappell *retired librarian*

Bakersfield
Duquette, Diane Rhea *library director*
Hersberger, Rodney M. *library association executive, school librarian*

Belmont
Musmann, Klaus *librarian*

Berkeley
Buckland, Michael Keeble *librarian, educator*
Harlan, Robert Dale *library and information scientist, educator, academic administrator*
Leonard, Thomas C. *librarian, dean*
Minudri, Regina Ursula *librarian, consultant*

Carson
Anuakan, Robyn Iset *archivist, educator, film producer*

Chula Vista
Palmer, David J. *library director, municipal official*

Cupertino
Fletcher, Homer Lee *librarian*

Davis
Sharrow, Marilyn Jane *library administrator*

Downey
Todd, Margaret Donnellan *library director*

El Cerrito
Alldredge, Noreen S. *librarian*
Kao, Yasuko Watanabe *retired library director*

Fremont
Bray, Richard Daniel *librarian*
Hofacket, Jean *library director*
Wood, Linda May *librarian*

Fresno
Bosch Cobb, Karen *library director*
Tyckoson, Dave *library director, library association executive*

Fullerton
Ayala, John L. *retired librarian, dean*
Johnson, Carolyn Elizabeth *librarian*

Glendale
Hunt-Coffey, Nancy *library director*
Michelson, Lillian *librarian, researcher*
Woolls, Esther Blanche *library science educator*

Gustine
Ramirez, Nola Marie *librarian*

Irvine
Gylseth, Doris Hanson (Doris Lillian Gylseth) *retired librarian*

Lafayette
Morehouse, Valerie Jeanne *librarian*

Loma Linda
Cimpoeru, Petre *archivist, educator*

Long Beach
Proust, Joycelyn Ann *retired librarian*
Schmidt, Eleanore *library director*

Los Angeles
Bates, Marcia Jeanne *information scientist educator*
Bergman, Emily Anne *librarian*
Chang, Henry C. *library administrator*
Cheng, Hong *library and information scientist*
Crampon, Jean Elaine *librarian*
Cuadra, Carlos Albert *library and information scientist, consultant*
Holmes, Fontayne *library director*
McGarry, Dorothy *librarian*
Patron, Susan Hall *librarian, writer*
Richardson, John Vinson, Jr. *library and information science professor*
Shank, Russell *librarian, educator*
Shoaf, R. Wayne *librarian*
Song, Yongyi *librarian*
Starr, Kevin *librarian, educator*
Whiteman, David Bruce *librarian, poet*
Wooler, John William *multi-media specialist*

Marina
Paget, Ruth Pennington *librarian, educator, writer*

Menlo Park
White, Cecil Ray *librarian, consultant*

Modesto
Czopek, Vanessa *library director*

Monterey
Reneker, Maxine Hohman *librarian*

Monterey Park
Wilson, Linda *librarian*

Mountain View
Di Muccio, Mary-Jo *retired librarian*
Healy, Jodi *library services manager*

Northridge
Duran, Karin Jeanine *librarian*
Lampert, Lynn Denise *librarian, educator*

Oakland
Green, David Edward *retired librarian, priest, translator*
Lee, Ella Louise *librarian, educator*
Martinez, Carmen Lorena *library director*
Price, Gary *librarian*
Rubin, Rhea Joyce *library consultant*
Woodbury, Marda Liggett *librarian, writer*

Oceanside
Lange, Clifford Elmer *retired librarian*

Palo Alto
Sack, John R. *library and information scientist*

Pasadena
Sanders, Jan W. *librarian, Library Association Executive*

Pollock Pines
Rickard, Margaret Lynn *library director, consultant*

Pomona
Jackson, Mary Ellen *librarian, consultant*

Redlands
Burgess, Larry Eugene *library director, historian, educator*
Hanks, Richard Alan *archivist*

Riverside
Custen, Barbara S. *library director*

Sacramento
Gold, Anne Marie *library director*
Gray, Walter P. III *historian, archivist, consultant*
Hildreth, Susan *state librarian*
Killian, Richard M. *library director*

San Bernardino
Burgess, Michael (Robert Reginald Burgess) *librarian, writer*
Roop, Ophelia Georgiev *library director*

San Diego
Dyer, Charles Richard *law library director, educator*
Sauer, David Andrew *librarian, writer*
Tatár, Anna *library director*

San Francisco
Aldrich, Michael Ray *library curator, health educator*
Bocobo-Balunsat, Dalisay *librarian, journalist*
Brechka, Frank Tilson *retired librarian, historian*
Herrera, Luis *library director*
Thacker-Estrada, Elizabeth Lorelei *librarian, historian*

San Jose
Light, Jane Ellen *library director*
Schmidt, Cyril James *librarian*
Yiotis, Kristin *librarian, educator*

San Juan Capistrano
Peterson, Fred McCrae *retired librarian*

San Luis Obispo
Dowell, David Ray *library administrator*

San Mateo
Johnson, Victoria L. *library director*

Santa Ana
Adams, John M. *library director*
Richard, Robert John *library director*

Santa Barbara
Gartrell, David Christian *archivist*
Larsgaard, Mary Lynette *librarian, writer*

Santa Clara
Hopkinson, Shirley Lois *library and information scientist, educator*
Ostwald, Venice Eloise Varner *librarian, educator, minister, writer*

Santa Cruz
Ripma, Mary *librarian*

Santa Rosa
Hoskins, Anthony Glenn *librarian*
Pearson, Roger Lee *library director*
Rosaschi, Jim *librarian*

Sebastopol
Sabsay, David *library director, consultant*

Simi Valley
Blackwood, (R.) Duke *library director*

Stanford
Danielson, Elena Schafer *retired archivist*
Derksen, Charlotte Ruth Meynink *librarian*
Keller, Michael Alan *librarian, musicologist*

Stockton
Gertler, Fred *librarian, dean*
Rencher, Natalie R. *library director*
Wong, Patricia M.Y. *library director*
Yamashita, Kenneth Akira *library administrator, librarian*

Thousand Oaks
Brogden, Stephen Richard *library director*

Turlock
Parker, John Carlyle *retired librarian and archivist, editor*

Woodland Hills
Zeitlin, Eugenia Pawlik *librarian, educator, writer*

Yorba Linda
Naftali, Timothy J. *library director, historian, educator, writer*

COLORADO

Boulder
Bintliff, Barbara Ann *library director, law educator*
Hill, Janet Swan *library and information scientist, educator*
O'Brien, Elmer John *librarian, educator*
Wertheimer, Marilyn Lou *librarian, educator*

Canon City
Cochran, Susan Mills *research librarian*

Colorado Springs
Budington, William Stone *retired librarian*
Miller, Paula J. *library director*

Denver
Amore, Shirley C. *library director*
Ashton, Rick James *retired librarian*
Garcia, June Marie *librarian*
Hainer, Eugene *state librarian*
Smith, Sallye Wrye *librarian*
Switzer, Teri Reynolds *library association executive*
White, Joyce Louise *librarian*

Edwards
Chambers, Joan Louise *retired librarian, dean*

Fort Collins
Mc Clellan, William Monson *retired library director*

Grand Junction
Bragdon, Lynn Lyon *library administrator*

Lakewood
Knott, William Alan *library director*

Louisville
Maddock, Jerome Torrence *library and information scientist*

Thornton
Fritze, Sheila Kay *librarian*

CONNECTICUT

Coventry
Aho, Sandra Christine *textile conservator*

Fairfield
Bryan, Barbara Day *retired librarian*

Glastonbury
Bailey, Barbara *library director*

Greenwich
Gonzalez, Mario M. *librarian*

Hartford
Kaimowitz, Jeffrey Hugh *librarian*
Wiggin, Kendall French *state librarian*

New Britain
Chasse, Emily Schuder *librarian, educator*

New Haven
Okerson, Ann Shumelda Lillian *librarian*
Stahl, Nanette *librarian, biblicist*
Stuehrenberg, Paul Frederick *librarian*

Niantic
Deakyne, William John *library director, musician*

North Canton
Swibold, Gretchen Ann *librarian, writer*

Old Greenwich
McClelland, Kate *librarian*

Plainville
Chase, Peter *library director*

Portland
Nocek, Janet *library director*

Simsbury
Berberich, Patricia Louise *librarian*
Roberts, Celia Ann *librarian*

Southbury
Rorick, William Calvin *retired librarian, portrait artist*

Storrs Mansfield
Franklin, Brinley *library director*
Kline, Nancy Mattoon *librarian*
Wilsted, Thomas P. *archivist, director*

Wilton
Poundstone, Sally Hill *library director*

Windsor
Christian, George *library organization administrator*

DELAWARE

Dover
Norman, Anne E. C. *state librarian*
Wetherall, Robert Shaw *librarian*

Newark
Brynteson, Susan *library director*

Wilmington
Williams, Richmond Dean *library consultant and appraiser*

DISTRICT OF COLUMBIA

Washington
Adamson, Jeremy E. *library director*
Baum, Ingeborg Ruth *librarian*
Beall, Julianne *librarian*
Billington, James Hadley *librarian, historian*
Campbell, Laura Elizabeth *library administrator*
Chute, Mary L. *library director*
Cooper, Ginnie *library director*
Cylke, Frank Kurt *librarian*
Dorn, Georgette Magassy *library official*
Doumato, Lamia *librarian, historian*
Fitzsimmons, Beth Duston (Carolyn Beth Fitzsimmons) *library and information scientist*
Galloway, Hoyt Wilson *library director*
Graham, David E. *librarian*
Haley, Roger Kendall *librarian*
Harlem, Susan Lynn *librarian*
Hedges, Kamla King *library director*
Heiss, Harry Glen *archivist*
Henry, Charles Jay *library and information scientist*
Johnson, Bruce Chr. *librarian*
Kalfatovic, Martin Robert *librarian, writer*
Lamont, Bridget Later *librarian, consultant*
Lee, Hwa-Wei *librarian, educator, consultant*
Lippincott, Joan K. *library director*
Lynch, Clifford A. *library and information scientist*
Mann, Thomas *reference librarian*
Marcum, Deanna Bowling *library administrator*
Mekkawi, Mohamed *library director*
Meyer, Margaret Vaughan *librarian, educator*
Missar, Charles Donald *retired librarian*
Mulhollan, Daniel Patrick *research director*
Player, Thelma B. *librarian*
Ray, Joyce Marie *archivist, historian*
Rovelstad, Mathilde V(erner) *retired library and information scientist, educator*
Smith, George Vinal *librarian*
Stevens, Roberta A. *librarian*
Tillett, Barbara Ann Barnett *librarian, director*
Turtell, Neal Timothy *librarian*
Wand, Patricia Ann *librarian*
Wattenmaker, Richard Joel *archivist, director*
Wertz, Virginia Loryma *retired librarian*

FLORIDA

Boynton Beach
DeVries, Janet Mary *archivist, curator*

Clearwater
Glymph, Dianne Tyler *librarian*

Coral Gables
Walker, William D. *library director*

Coral Springs
Hershenson, Miriam Hannah Ratner *librarian*

Daytona Beach
Sigerson, Marjorie Lorraine *librarian*

Deland
Bradford, Jane Turner *librarian*
Caccamise, Genevra Louise Ball (Mrs. Alfred E. Caccamise) *retired librarian*

Destin
Burns, Jurate *library director*
Deel, Frances Quinn *retired librarian*

Englewood
McCall, Gene William *conservator, sculptor, artist, furniture designer*

Fort Lauderdale
Beach, Cecil Prentice *librarian*
Cannon, Robert Eugene *library director*
Morris, Sharon *librarian*
Riggs, Donald Eugene *librarian, academic administrator*

Gainesville
Russell, Judith *librarian, dean*

Haines City
Kirk, Sherwood *retired librarian*

Hialeah
Diaz, Diane Linda *library director*
Medvinsky, Nathalia *library director*

Lakeland
Reich, David Lee *library director*

Lighthouse Point
Gauthier, Doreen Ann *librarian*

Madison
Hiss, Sheila Mary *librarian*

Miami
Comras, Rema *retired library director*
Rourke, Diane McLaughlin *librarian*
Santiago, Raymond *library director, educator*
Treyz, Joseph Henry *librarian*
Zaleski-Vegazo, Ilene *librarian*

Naples
Hall, Beverly Barton *librarian*

Oakland Park
Kilpatrick, Clifton Wayne *book dealer*

Ocala
Tesmer, Nancy Ann Stutler *retired librarian*

Orlando
Allison, Anne Marie *retired librarian*
Hodel, Mary Anne *library director*

Port Charlotte
Donovan, William Alan *retired librarian*

Saint Leo
Neuhofer, Mary Dorothy *archivist, librarian*

Saint Petersburg
Gaines, Mary S. *library director*
Kent, Allen *library and information sciences professor*

Sarasota
Brandhorst, Wesley Theodore *retired library and information scientist*
De Gennaro, Richard *retired library director*
Hummel, Dana D. Mallett *librarian*
Retzer, Mary Elizabeth Helm *retired librarian*
Scalera, Michelle *conservator*
Straight, Elsie Hosking *retired librarian, sculptor*

Tallahassee
Dresang, Eliza T. *library and information scientist*
Fiore, Carole Diane *library consultant*
Goldstein, Julia Sonia *librarian*
McClure, Charles Robert *library and information science educator, consultant*
Ring, Judith A. *state librarian*
Thompson, Jean Tanner *retired librarian*
Wiegand, Wayne August *library and information science educator*
Zachert, Martha Jane *retired librarian*

Tampa
Harkness, Mary Lou *librarian*
Leach, Michael Andrew *library and information scientist*
Luddington, Betty Walles *retired multi-media specialist*
McCook, Kathleen de la Peña *librarian, educator*
tines, Joe *library director, educator*

University Park
Compain, Rita *librarian*

Venice
sp, William George *librarian*

West Palm Beach
erwillegar, Jane Cusack *librarian, educator*

Winter Park
Bloodworth, Velda Jean *librarian, educator*
Rogers, Rutherford David *librarian*
hang, Wenxian *librarian*

GEORGIA

Athens
mes, Kathryn S. *library director*
Donovan, James M. *librarian, anthropologist*

Atlanta
lagg Davis, Vivian Annette *librarian, researcher, public information officer*
akes, Jay Edward *library director, former federal agency administrator*
Iathews, Brian Scott *librarian*
McDavid, Sara June *librarian*
Iosakhere, Akilah Shukura Montsho *librarian, consultant, editor, writer*
oberts, Edward Graham *librarian*
obison, Carolyn Love *retired librarian*
inger, Ross *library and information scientist*
zabo, John F. *library director*
eatch, Julian Lamar, Jr. *library director*
Vallace, Gladys Baldwin *librarian*
ates, Ella Gaines *librarian, consultant*

Bainbridge
anstone, Catherine *library and information scientist*

Barnesville
dams, Cynthia Ann *librarian, media specialist, language educator*
nderson, Nancy Dixon *librarian*

Cleveland
dwards, John Carver *retired archivist*

Columbus
rimsley, Reagan Louis *archivist, educator*

Fayetteville
Neal, Joan Burkes *librarian*

Marietta
Kendall, Susan Gardes *librarian*

Rome
Doyle, James Donald, Jr. *librarian*
Mosley, Mary Mac *retired librarian*

Statesboro
Mitchell, Wilfrid Bede *librarian, library association executive*

Thomasville
Tillinghast, Nancy *library director*

Warner Robins
Merk, P. Evelyn *retired librarian*

HAWAII

Honolulu
Mochida, Paula T. *library director*
Schindler, Jo Ann *librarian, director*
Yee, Florence *library director*

Kahului
Tolliver, Dorothy *librarian*

Kailua
Wright, John Cotton *archivist, consultant*

Lihue
Stevens, Robert David *librarian, educator*

IDAHO

Boise
Joslin, Ann *state librarian*

Moscow
Force, Ronald Wayne *retired librarian*

ILLINOIS

Calumet City
Muñoz, Romeo Solano *audio visual curator*

Carbondale
Bauner, Ruth Elizabeth *library director*
Carlson, David Harold *library director, dean*

Champaign
Rayward, Warden Boyd *librarian, educator*
Richardson, Selma Katherine *retired library and information scientist*
Ruan, Lian Jin *library director*
Urban, Richard J. *library and information scientist*

Channahon
Blomstedt, Erik Ragnar *library administrator*

Chicago
Bentley, Carol Ligon *retired library and information scientist*
Brown, Richard Holbrook *library director, historian, researcher*
Choldin, Marianna Tax *librarian, educator*
Fiels, Keith Michael *executive director American Library Association*
Funk, Carla Jean *library association director*
Gerdes, Neil Wayne *library director, educator*
Gómez, Martín *library association executive*
Hagan, Kate (Kathryn T. Hagan) *library director, editor*
Hanrath, Linda Carol *librarian, archivist*
Levine, Jenny *library and information scientist, writer*
Miletich, Ivo *library and information scientist, bibliographer, educator, linguist, literature research specialist*
Nadler, Judith *library director*
Parr, Virginia Helen *retired librarian*
Phillip, Cynthia A. *librarian*
Rishworth, Susan Knoke *archivist, researcher*
Seal, Robert A. *library director*
Sullivan, Peggy *librarian, consultant*
Szydlowski, Joseph Edward *music librarian*

Dekalb
Hamilton, David Arnold *retired librarian*

Downers Grove
Saricks, Joyce Goering *librarian*

East Peoria
Bell, Lori (Lorelei Junot) *library director, library and information scientist*
Pope, Kitty *library director*

Elgin
Medal, Carole Ann *library director*

Evanston
Beatty, Virginia Lewis *librarian, archivist, consultant*
Bethel, Kathleen Evonne *librarian*
Cates, Jo Ann *library director*
Crawford, Susan *library director, educator, editor, writer*
Pritchard, Sarah Margaret *library director*

Freeport
Vogt, Lorna Corrine *retired librarian, small business owner*

Galesburg
Coatney, Louis Robert *librarian, historian*

Glen Ellyn
Slusar, Linda *library and information scientist*

Indian Head Park
Bamberger, Mary Ann *archivist, consultant*

Jacksonville
Gallas, Martin Hans *librarian*

Joliet
Johnston, James Robert *library director*

Lake Forest
Miller, Arthur Hawks, Jr. *librarian, archivist*

Lincolnwood
Beck, Cynthia Marie *archivist, researcher*

Naperville
Holba Puacz, Jeanne *librarian, educator*

Quincy
Tyer, Travis Earl *librarian, consultant*

Richton Park
Nevins, Patrick Fredrick *librarian*

River Forest
Stephens, Michael *library and information scientist, educator*

Riverside
Van Cura, Joyce Bennett *librarian*

Schaumburg
Adrianopoli, Barbara Catherine *librarian*

Skokie
Anthony, Carolyn Additon *librarian*
Bush, Gail *librarian, educator, director, writer*

Springfield
Brown, Malcolm Charles *conservator*
Craig, Ann *library director*
Schroeder-Lein, Glenna Ruth *librarian, historian*

Urbana
Bennett, Scott Boyce *retired librarian, consultant*
Brichford, Maynard Jay *archivist*
O'Brien, Nancy Patricia *librarian, educator*
Searing, Susan Ellis *librarian*
Watson, Paula D. *retired librarian*

Wheaton
Shuster, Robert Douglas *archivist*
Thompson, Bert Allen *retired librarian*
Tucker, Beverly Sowers *library and information scientist*

Wheeling
Long, Sarah Ann *librarian*
Meehan, Tamiye Marcia *library director*
Roalkvam, Donald L. *library and information scientist*

Wilmette
Hansen, Andrew Marius *retired library director*

Zion
Hilyard, Nann Blaine *librarian*

INDIANA

Bloomington
Dalmau, Michelle *library and information scientist*
Meho, Lokman I. *library and information scientist, educator*
Pauwels, Colleen Kristl *library director, educator*
Rudolph, Lavere Christian *library director*
Steele, Patricia Ann *librarian, dean*
Studwell, William Emmett *librarian, writer*

Evansville
Scheer, John C. *librarian*

Fort Wayne
Krull, Jeffrey Robert *library director*

Indianapolis
Bramble, Laura *library director*
Brooker, Roberta L. *library director*
Gnat, Raymond Earl *librarian*
Irwin, Marilyn M. *librarian, educator*
Terry, Linda Faye *librarian*
Turner-Wright, Marie Annetta *retired librarian*
Young, Philip Howard *library director*

Lafayette
McKowen, Dorothy Keeton *librarian, educator*
Mobley, Emily Ruth *library director, educator, dean*

Liberty
Sowers, Marilyn Rae *librarian*

Muncie
Dolak, Fritz *librarian, information administrator*
Schaefer, Patricia *retired librarian*
Yeamans, George Thomas *librarian, educator*

Notre Dame
Hayes, Stephen Matthew *librarian*

Plainfield
Cullin, Rob *librarian*

Richmond
Farber, Evan Ira *librarian*
Kirk, Thomas Garrett, Jr. *librarian*

West Lafayette
Andrews, Theodora Anne *retired librarian, educator*
Markee, Katherine Madigan *librarian, educator*
Mullins, James Lee *librarian, dean*
Nixon, Judith May *librarian*

IOWA

Ames
Madison, Olivia *librarian, dean*
Shonrock, Diana Donner *science and technology librarian, consultant, Library Association Executive*

Carlisle
Berning, Robert William *librarian*

Cedar Rapids
Renter, Lois Irene Hutson *retired librarian*

Davenport
Runge, Kay Kretschmar *library consultant*

Des Moines
Wegner, Mary *state librarian*

Iowa City
Baker, Nancy L. *university librarian, educator*
Bentz, Dale Monroe *retired librarian*
Huttner, Sidney Frederick *librarian*
McCartney, David Farnham *archivist, educator*
Miller, Dwight Merrick *archivist, historian*

West Bend
Wuebker, Colleen Marie *retired librarian*

West Branch
Mather, Mildred Eunice *retired archivist*
Walch, Timothy George *library director*

KANSAS

Abilene
Holt, Dan *library director*

Enterprise
Wickman, John Edward *librarian, historian*

Fort Leavenworth
Barker, Ray Todd *archivist, writer*

Lawrence
Crowe, William Joseph *librarian*
Haricombe, Lorraine *library director, dean*

Mankato
Underwood, Deanna Kay *librarian*

Olathe
Morrison, Ray Leon *library director, education educator*

Pittsburg
Lee, Earl Wayne *library science educator*

Topeka
Brandau, Christie Pearson *librarian*
Millsap, Gina J. *library director*

Wichita
Berner-Harris, Cynthia Kay *library director*

KENTUCKY

Campbellsville
Burch, John Russell, Jr. *library director*

Danville
Pappas, Marjorie L. *library studies educator*

Frankfort
Gibbons, Judith A. *librarian*
Onkst, Wayne *state librarian*

La Grange
Morgan, Mary Dan *librarian*

Lexington
Diedrichs, Carol Pitts *library director, dean*
Imhoff, Kathleen Ruth Tostrud *library administrator*
Mason, Ellsworth Goodwin *retired librarian*
Sineath, Timothy Wayne *librarian, educator, dean*
Steensland, Ronald Paul *librarian*
Young, Sandra Cooper *retired librarian*

Louisville
Bell, Mary Margaret *archivist*
Buthod, Craig *library director*
Deering, Ronald Franklin *librarian, minister*
Shobe, David Soren *librarian, director*

Morehead
Besant, Larry Xon *retired librarian, administrator, consultant*
Pritchard, Elsie Tomlinson *librarian*

Paducah
Kirk, Terri G. *library media specialist*

Wilmore
Pohl, Gunther Erich *retired library administrator*

LOUISIANA

Baton Rouge
Acosta, Lydia M. *library director*
Cargill, Jennifer S. *library director, dean, educator*
Hamilton, Rebecca L. *state librarian*
Lusk, Glenna Rae Knight (Mrs. Edwin Bruce Lusk) *librarian*
Patterson, Charles Darold *librarian, educator*

Covington
Stahr, Beth A. *librarian*

Metairie
Dickerson, Lon Richard *library administrator*

Monroe
Smith, Donald Raymond *librarian*

New Orleans
Skinner, Robert Earle *librarian, writer*

New Roads
Hymel, Melissa K. *librarian*

Ponchatoula
Kuechmann, Christopher Robert *library director*

Schriever
Shaffer, Margaret Minor *retired library director*

Shreveport
Brazile, Orella Ramsey *library director*
McLemore, Laura Lyons *archivist, history educator*
Pelton, James Rodger *library director*
Wood, Julienne Louise *librarian, historian*

MAINE

Augusta
Nichols, J. Gary *state librarian*

Bangor
Rea, Ann W. *librarian*

Waterville
Muehlner, Suanne Wilson *library director*

MARYLAND

Annapolis
Papenfuse, Edward Carl, Jr. *archivist, state official*
Werking, Richard Hume *librarian, historian, academic administrator*

Baltimore
Bluh, Pamela M. *library director, library association executive*
Bradley, Wanda Louise *librarian*
Harris, Reginald Mervyn, Jr. *librarian, writer*
Hayden, Carla Diane *library director, educator*
Leonard, Angela Michele *librarian, educator*
Magnuson, Nancy *librarian*
McAdam, Paul Edward *retired library administrator*
Nasr, Nadia *library and information scientist*
Padilla, Irene *library director*
Sleeman, Bill *library and information scientist*
Tabb, Winston *library director*

Beltsville
Young, Peter Robert *library director*

Bethesda
Conger, Lucinda *retired librarian*
Knachel, Philip Atherton *librarian*
Lindberg, Donald Allan Bror *library director, pathologist, educator*
Yang, Key Paik *librarian, archivist*

Bowie
Wardrip, Elizabeth Jane *retired librarian*

Chestertown
Rather, Lucia Porcher Johnson *library administrator*

Chevy Chase
Basa, Enikö Molnár *retired librarian*

College Park
Bellardo, Lewis Joseph, Jr. *archivist*
Fawcett, Sharon Kay Atchison *archivist*
Kurtz, Michael Joseph *archivist, educator*
Lowell, Howard Parsons *archivist, federal agency administrator*
Lowry, Charles Bryan *librarian, dean*
Morphy, Martha A. *archivist*
Mosley, Raymond A. *archivist*
Wasserman, Paul *library and information science professor*
Weinstein, Allen *archivist*

Columbia
Gruhl, Andrea Morris *librarian*
Klein, Sami Weiner *librarian*

Crofton
Williams, J. Linda *librarian*

Gaithersburg
Broderick, John Caruthers *retired librarian*

Germantown
Lewis, Robert John Cornelius Koons *retired library director*

Glen Burnie
Mc Cabe, Gerard Benedict *retired library administrator*

Greenbelt
Moore, Virginia Bradley *librarian*

Hagerstown
Baykan, Mary Catherine *library administrator*

Laurel
Pikas, Christina Kirk *librarian, researcher*

Rockville
Hamilton, Parker *library director*
Lavoie, Daniel Joseph, II, *archivist, historian*
Renninger, Mary Karen *retired librarian*

Salisbury
Wolter, John Amadeus *librarian, federal official*

Silver Spring
Null, Elisabeth Higgins *librarian, editor*

Springdale
Keith, Patricia *multi-media specialist*

Towson
Fish, James Henry *library director*
Tull, Willis Clayton, Jr. *retired librarian*

MASSACHUSETTS

Amherst
Bridegam, Willis Edward, Jr. *retired librarian*
Schafer, Gerald Lewis (Jay Schafer) *library director*

Boston
Armstrong, Rodney *librarian*
Christopher, Irene *librarian, consultant*
Cloonan, Michele V. *library director*
Fulchino, Stephen A. *State Librarian*
Hebard, Barbara Adams *conservator*
Hudson, Robert E. *library director*
Margolis, Bernard Allen *library administrator*
Mifflin, Jeffrey Allen *archivist, consultant, historian, researcher*
Putnam, Thomas J. *library director*
Trinkaus-Randall, Gregor *librarian, archivist, preservation administrator*
Warro, Edward A. *library director, dean*
Wendorf, Richard Harold *library director, educator*

Brighton
Woodall, Bridgette A. *archivist*

Brookline
Brenner, Robin E. *librarian*

Cambridge
Cline, Nancy M. *librarian, department chairman*
Cole, Heather Ellen *librarian*
Darnton, Robert Choate *library director, historian, educator*
Flannery, Susan Marie *library administrator*
Koepp, Donna Pauline Petersen *librarian*
Schrock, Nancy Carlson *conservator, consultant*
Stoddard, Roger Eliot *scholar*
Whiteside, Ann Baird *library director*
Wolpert, Ann J. *library director*

Canton
Kelley, Irene W. *retired librarian, musician, artist*

Carver
Neubauer, Richard A. *library science educator, consultant*

Chestnut Hill
Yavarkovsky, Jerome Harold *library director*

Cohasset
Morse, Elizabeth *conservator*

Dover
Peirce, Bonnie *librarian*

East Orleans
Natale, Barbara Gustafson *retired librarian*

Heath
Howland, Margaret E.C. *retired librarian*

Lexington
Freitag, Wolfgang Martin *retired librarian*

Lincoln
Bracken, (Myra) Jeanne Munn *librarian, writer*

Lowell
Karr, Ronald Dale *librarian, historian*

Marstons Mills
Martin, Susan Katherine *librarian*

Medford
Michalak, Jo-Ann *library director*

Mill River
Jaffe, Katharine Weisman *retired librarian*

Natick
Rendell, Kenneth William *rare and historical documents dealer, consultant*

Newton
Glick-Weil, Kathy *library director*

North Easton
Bundy, Annalee Marshall *library director*

Northampton
Piccinino, Rocco Michael *librarian*

Sandwich
Parsons, Stuart W. *librarian*

Shirley Center
Holden, Harley Peirce *retired archivist*

Springfield
Stack, May Elizabeth *retired library director*
Utley, F. Knowlton *library director, educator*

Waltham
Hanson, Perry *library and information scientist*

Woburn
Preve, Roberta Jean *librarian, researcher*

Woods Hole
Gifford, Prosser *retired library administrator*

Worcester
Dunlap, Ellen S. *library administrator*
McCorison, Marcus Allen *librarian, cultural organization administrator*
Shuster, Helen M. *library director*

MICHIGAN

Adrian
Geyer, Richard Douglas *librarian, editor, poet*

Allendale
Murray, Diane Elizabeth *librarian*

Ann Arbor
Beaubien, Anne Kathleen *librarian*
Blumenthal, Jane Leonardi *library director*
Buckley, Francis J., Jr. *librarian*
Daub, Peggy Ellen *library administrator*
Didier, Elaine K. *library director, educator*
Dougherty, Richard Martin *library and information science professor*
Dunlap, Connie *librarian*
Gordon, Anitra *librarian*
Johnson, Brenda L. *university librarian*
Wilkins, John P. *university librarian*

Battle Creek
Lincoln, Margaret *library media specialist*

Bloomfield Hills
Papai, Beverly Daffern *retired library director*

Clinton Township
Neal, Larry P. *library director*

Dearborn
Adkins, Elizabeth W. *archivist*
Powell, Ronald Rowe *library science educator*

Detroit
Field, Judith Judy *librarian*
Godzak, Roman Paul *archivist*
Mika, Joseph John *library director, educator*
Skowronski, Nancy *library director*
Spyers-Duran, Peter *librarian, educator*
Yee, Sandra Gayle Brown *library director, dean*

East Lansing
Chapin, Richard Earl *retired librarian*
Haka, Clifford Hughey *library director*

Farmington Hills
Damron, Jayne *librarian*

Flint
White, David C. *archivist, historian*

Grosse Pointe
Casey, Genevieve M(ary) *librarian, educator*

Harsens Island
Woodford, Arthur MacKinnon *retired library director, historian*

Holt
Smith, Betty W. *librarian*

Kalamazoo
Grotzinger, Laurel Ann *librarian, educator*

Lansing
Roberston, Nancy R. *state librarian*

Midland
Potts, Sandra *library director*

Mount Pleasant
Messick, Frederic Morton *librarian*

Petoskey
Kukla, Edward Richard *rare books and special collections librarian*

Plymouth
Berry, Charlene Helen *librarian, musician*

Port Huron
Wu, Harry Pao-Tung *retired librarian*

Redford
Karpinski, Huberta *library trustee*

MINNESOTA

Blue Earth
Siem, Pauline M. *library director*

Breezy Point
Anderson, Gail Marie *retired librarian*

Duluth
Pearce, Donald Joslin *retired librarian*

Hopkins
Young, Margaret Labash *librarian, information consultant, editor*

Minneapolis
Hadley, Katherine G. (Kit) *library director*
Johnson, Donald Clay *librarian, curator*
Johnson, Margaret Ann (Peggy) *library administrator*
Shaughnessy, Thomas William *retired librarian*

Minnetonka
Bjerke, Dana *librarian*

Rochester
Key, Jack Dayton *librarian*

Roseville
Miller, Suzanne Marie *library director, educator*

Saint Cloud
Inkster, Christine Davis *librarian, educator*

Saint Paul
Granger, Steven Tandvig *archivist, consultant*
Huggins, Melanie *library director*
Wagner, Mary Margaret *library and information scientist, educator*

Saint Peter
Fister, Barbara Ruth *librarian, educator, writer*
Haeuser, Michael John *library administrator*

MISSISSIPPI

Columbus
Tousley, Rebecca Perkins *retired librarian*

Jackson
Smith, Sharman Bridges *state librarian*

Mississippi State
Ballard, Michael B. *archivist*

Natchez
McLemore, Joan Meadows *librarian, consultant*

MISSOURI

Blue Springs
Peters, Thomas Andrew *library and information scientist, writer*

Chesterfield
Landram, Christina Louella *librarian*

Columbia
Almony, Robert Allen, Jr. *librarian*
Cogswell, James A. *library director*
Cogswell, Jim *library director*

Greenwood
Zeller, Marilynn Kay *retired librarian*

Hermann
Wilson, C. Daniel, Jr. *library director*

Independence
Devine, Michael J. *library director, educator*
Wilding, Richard J. *library director*

Jefferson City
Conroy, Margaret M. *library director*

Joplin
Nodler, Charles Edward, Jr. *archivist, history professor*

Kansas City
Edwards, Cynthia G. *archivist*
Kemper, R(ufus) Crosby III *library director*
Nelson, Freda Nell Hein *librarian*
Thomas, Marcia Markowitz *library director, educator*

Parkville
Schultis, Gail Ann *library director*

Saint Louis
Brown, Bettye *librarian, educator*
Guenther, Charles John *librarian, writer*
Lauenstein, Ann Gail *librarian*
McGuire, Waller F. *library director*
Pace, Charles *library director*

Springfield
Busch, Annie *library director*
Horny, Karen Louise *library administrator*

MONTANA

Billings
Cochran, William Michael *librarian*

Forsyth
Heser, Cheryl J. *library director*

Helena
Fitzpatrick, Lois Ann *library administrator*
Newell, Bruce *library director*
Staffeldt, Darlene Maria Preble *library director*

NEBRASKA

Beatrice
Riedesel, Laureen Falk *library director*

Boys Town
DiBacco, Nadine Louise *retired library director photographer, writer*

Lincoln
Connor, Carol J. *library director*
Giesecke, Joan Ruth *librarian, dean*
Montag, John Joseph, II, *librarian*
Wagner, Rod *library director*

Omaha
Sass, Rivkah K. *library director*

NEVADA

Carson City
Jones, Sara Sue Fisher *librarian*
Rocha, Guy Louis *archivist, consultant, histori*

Hawthorne
Pierce, Mildred Louise *librarian*

nderson
Thomas F. *library director*

s Vegas
isey, Inez Linn *librarian, educator*
ters, Daniel L. *library director*

no
nmings, Nancy *library director*
s, Robert Donald *library director*

W HAMPSHIRE

rlin
erty, Katherine Mann *librarian, writer*

ncord
k, Michael Charest *librarian*

eter
omas, Jacquelyn May *librarian*

ffstown
enberg, Arnold Sherman *retired librarian, educator*

nover
rrell, Jeffrey Lanier *library director*

lton
lman, Hendrik *library and information science professor*

wmarket
chell, Sylvia Fitts *librarian*

ymouth
ona, David A. *library director, educator*
son, Casey *library and information scientist*

W JERSEY

mden
ck, Susan J. *academic librarian*

iffside Park
elariu, Ana Radu *library director*

gewater
liner, Barbara *retired librarian, consultant*

lison
ey, Barbara Polk *retired librarian*

anders
bert, Rita L. *librarian*

rt Lee
omara, Rita Ecke *library director, writer*

arfield
ckles, I. MacArthur *librarian*

lassboro
ight, William Cook *archivist, director*

len Rock
voie, Brietta Dolores Giger *retired librarian*

aledon
ugherty, June Eileen *librarian*

oboken
ddicombe, Richard Palmer *librarian*

opewell
oodward, Daniel Holt *librarian, researcher*

rsey City
laong, Grace F. *library director*
ng, Judy Horng *librarian*
eaver-Gardner, Priscilla *library director*

ambertville
isworth, Christyl J. *conservator, artist*

aurel Springs
eveland, Susan Elizabeth *library administrator, researcher*

inden
rves, Dennis Patrick *library director*

odi
aretzky, Joanne Louise *librarian*
aretzky, Stephen *library director, educator, researcher*

ong Branch
ichman, Frederic Charles *library director*

ladison
ibinstein, Ernest *librarian, educator*

Iontclair
IcConnell, Lorelei Catherine *retired library director*

Iorristown
aks, Robert Gilman *librarian*

lew Brunswick
enda, Kayo *librarian*
aunt, Marianne I. *university librarian*
esk, Michael E. *library and information science educator*
adford, Marie Louise *library science educator*
irock, Betty Jane *library and information science professor*

ewark
rey, Wilma J. *library director*

North Branch
Sittler, Ryan Lee *librarian*

Oakland
Reutty, Michele Marie *library director*

Piscataway
Etter, Zana Claire *library director*
Ranzan, David Aldrich *archivist*

Plainsboro
Baeckler, Virginia Van Wynen *librarian, writer*

Point Pleasant
Greene, Ellin *library service educator*

Princeton
Burger, Leslie B. *library director, library association executive*
Engard, Nicole C. *library and information scientist*
Fox, Mary Ann Williams *librarian*
Hermann, Janie *librarian*
Trainer, Karin A. *librarian*

Princeton Junction
Butorac, Frank George *librarian, educator*

Rockaway
Kelsey, Ann Lee *library administrator*

South Orange
Bao, Xue-Ming *librarian, educator*

Succasunna
Romance, Mary C. *library director*

Teaneck
Weiss, Mitchell Joseph *librarian*

Toms River
Matteo, Christine E. *librarian*

Trenton
Blake, Norma E. *library director*
Russell, Joyce Anne Rogers *retired librarian*

Union
Rogge, Rena Wolcott *librarian*

Vineland
Schmid, Patti A. *library director*

Voorhees
Brahms, William Bernard *librarian, publisher, writer*

West Milford
Hannon, Patricia Ann *library director*

Whiting
Randall, Lynn Ellen *librarian*

NEW MEXICO

Albuquerque
Clarke, Julia L. *library director*
Freeman, Patricia Elizabeth *multi-media specialist, educational consultant*
Lewis, Linda Kathryn *librarian*
Neville, Bruce David *librarian*
Snell, Patricia Poldervaart *librarian, consultant*
Wilkinson, Frances Catherine *librarian, educator*

Carlsbad
Regan Gossage, Muriel *librarian*

Los Alamos
Ramsey, Margie *librarian*

Rio Rancho
Harmon, Joanna Kimball (Ethel Jo Harmon) *retired archivist, writer*

Santa Fe
Akeroyd, Richard G., Jr. *library director*

NEW YORK

Albany
Aceto, Vincent John *librarian, educator*
Ebert, Loretta Caren *librarian*
Knee, Michael J. *science librarian, consultant*
Merbler, Candace Anne *librarian*
Shubert, Joseph Francis *librarian*
Welch, Janet Martin *librarian*
Wilber, Roger Alan *library supervisor, writer*

Alfred
Johnson, Carla Conrad *library dean*

Beechhurst
Wingate, Constance Blandy *retired librarian*

Bellmore
Andrews, Charles Rolland *library administrator*

Brentwood
McKeever, Edna *archivist, educator*

Brightwaters
Kavanagh, Eileen J. *librarian*

Bronx
Cohen, Selma *retired librarian*
James, Gesille *librarian*
Pomrenze, Colonel *archivist, consultant*

Brooklyn
Benz, Susan *library and information scientist*
Evans, Beth *library and information scientist*
Glassman, Paul *library administrator, architecture educator*
Hill, Victoria Ruth *librarian*
Loum, Anthony Webster *librarian*
Mack-Harvin, Dionne L. *library director*
Schneider, Adele Goldberg *librarian, educator*
Sharify, Nasser *librarian, educator, writer*
Thomas, Lucille Cole *librarian*

Buffalo
Bobinski, George Sylvan *librarian, educator*
Finnegan, Marchand Marie (Shonnie Finnegan) *archivist, consultant*
Mahaney, Michael C. *library director*
Roberts, Stephen M. *library director*
Stoss, Frederick Warren *librarian, educator*

Canaan
Lewis, Marjorie *librarian*

Centereach
Feinberg, Sandra Lee *library director*

Dansville
Dearing, Teresa Allison *librarian*

Dryden
Slocum, Robert Bigney *retired librarian*

Edmeston
Blackman, Dorothy J. *library director*

Goshen
Watson, Georgianna *retired librarian*

Hempstead
Freese, Melanie Louise *librarian, educator*

Honeoye Falls
Masterson-Smith, Julie *librarian*

Hyde Park
Koch, Cynthia M. *library director*

Ithaca
Perry, Margaret *librarian, writer*

Jamaica
Galante, Thomas W. *library director*
Garcia-Febo, Loida *librarian*

Kinderhook
McCreight, JoAnn Oakley *retired librarian*

Liverpool
Wightman, Sharon Leilani *librarian*

Mineola
Hammer, Deborah Marie *librarian, paralegal*

Nassau
Benamati, Dennis Charles *librarian, editor, consultant*

New Hartford
Anthony, Donald Charles *librarian, educator*

New Paltz
Nyquist, Corinne Elaine *librarian*

New York
Belliveau, Gerard Joseph, Jr. *librarian*
Berger, Pearl *librarian, dean*
Berner, Andrew Jay *library director, writer*
Boziwick, George E. *music librarian, composer*
Brody, Catherine Tyler *archivist, historian, writer*
Browar, Lisa Muriel *librarian*
Davis, Jacqueline Zurat *library director, arts administrator*
Dodson, Howard *research center administrator*
Ferriero, David S. *library director*
Fletcher, Harry George III *library director*
Freedman, Jenna *library and information scientist*
Hewitt, Vivian Ann Davidson (Mrs. John Hamilton Hewitt Jr.) *retired librarian*
Kagan, Ilse Echt *librarian, researcher, historian*
Kent, Susan *library director, consultant*
Khalil, Mounir A. *librarian, educator*
Klause, Annette Curtis *librarian, writer*
Kordish, Heike Christiane *library director*
LeClerc, Paul *library director*
Little, Robert David *library science professor*
LoSchiavo, Linda Bosco *library director*
Lubetski, Edith Esther *librarian*
Lundquist, John Milton *librarian, Egyptologist, author, travel writer, photographer*
Mackey, Patricia Elaine *university librarian*
Margalith, Helen Margaret *retired librarian*
McDonough, Kristin *library director*
McKeever, Kent *library director, law librarian*
Meyerhoff, Erich *librarian, director*
Miller, Barbara Kenton *retired librarian*
Miller, Philip Efrem *librarian*
Palmer, Robert Baylis *librarian*
Pierce, Charles Eliot, Jr. *library director, educator*
Rachow, Louis A(ugust) *librarian*
Record, William John *librarian*
Root, Nina J. *librarian, writer*
Roumani-Denn, Vivienne Rachel *library and information scientist, consultant*
Swan, Philip George *librarian, educator, director, artist*
Sweetman, Kimberly Burke *librarian, consultant*
Taranto, Barbara *library director*
Thomas, Dorothy *indexing consultant, writer*
Von Drasek, Lisa *librarian*
Whittingham, Charles Arthur *library director, publishing executive*

Oneonta
Johnson, Richard David *retired librarian*

Poughkeepsie
Van Zanten, Frank Veldhuyzen *library director*

Rexford
Nitecki, Joseph Zbigniew *librarian*

Rochester
Buff, Iva Moore *librarian, musicologist*
Cohen, Ann Ellen *librarian*
Cunningham, Robert Del *librarian*
Dow, Ronald F. *librarian, dean*
Smith, Paula V. *library director*
Swanton, Susan Irene *retired library director*

Roosevelt
Jackson, Andrew Preston *library director*

Rye
Harrington, Diane *librarian, writer*

Saint Bonaventure
Anderson, John Thomas *librarian, historian*
Tenglund, Ann M. *librarian*

Schenectady
Huth, Geoffrey Anthony *archivist, artist*
Mancuso, J(ohn) James *librarian*

Staten Island
Auh, Yang John *librarian, educational administrator*
Black, Lawrence *librarian*

Stony Brook
Filstrup, (E.) Christian *library director, dean*

Syracuse
Elkins, Elizabeth A. *library director*
Stam, David Harry *librarian*
Verheyen, Peter David *librarian, conservator*

Tarrytown
Osborne, Robin *library and information scientist*

Tonawanda
Loos, William H(enry) *librarian, consultant*

White Plains
Manville, Stewart Roebling *archivist*
Marino, Jane B. *library director*
Scott-Williams, Wendy Lee *library and information scientist*

Williamsville
Cloudsley, Donald Hugh *retired library administrator*

Woodside
Sfiroudis, Gloria Tides *library and information scientist, educator*

NORTH CAROLINA

Burlington
Ellington, Beth Elder *librarian*

Chapel Hill
Jones, Houston Gwynne *archivist, history professor*
Moran, Barbara Burns *librarian, educator*
Pruett, James Worrell *librarian, educator, musicologist*
Strauss, Diane Carol Wheeler *librarian, educator, writer*

Charlotte
Blowers, Helene *library and information scientist*
Brown, Charles M. *library director*
Czarnecki, Kelly *librarian*
Rhue, Monika Rivera *archivist*
Sintz, Edward Francis *librarian*

Columbus
Wetherby, Ivor Lois *retired librarian*

Cove City
Hawkins, Elinor Dixon (Mrs. Carroll Woodard Hawkins) *retired librarian*

Creedmoor
Muller, William Albert III *retired library director*

Davidson
Park, Leland Madison *librarian*

Durham
Auld, Skip (Hampton Auld) *library director*
Canada, Mary Whitfield *retired librarian*
Carrington, Bessie Meek *librarian*

Elon
Nash, Katie C. *archivist*

Gastonia
Burns, Judith O'Dell *library assistant, educator*

Greensboro
Neerman, Sandra M. *library director*

Greenville
White, Larry Nash *library and information scientist*

New Bern
Jones, Victor Thomas, Jr. *librarian*

Pittsboro
Boyce, Emily Stewart *retired library and information scientist, educator*

Raleigh
Boone, Mary L. *library director*
Littleton, Isaac Thomas III *retired library director*
Lynema, Emily *library and information scientist, university librarian*
Moore, Thomas Lloyd *library director*
Nutter, Susan K. *librarian, academic administrator*

Salisbury
McKinzie, James S. *librarian*

Winston Salem
Sutton, Lynn Sorensen *librarian*

Winton
Williams, Sue Darden *library director*

NORTH DAKOTA

Bismarck
Ott, Doris Ann *librarian*

Mayville
Karaim, Betty June *retired librarian*

OHIO

Akron
Jennings, David C. *library director, educator*
Rebenack, John Henry *retired librarian*

Bellaire
Kniesner, John Thomas *librarian*

Bluffton
Dudley, Durand Stowell *retired librarian*

Bowling Green
Singer, Carol Ann *librarian, researcher*

Cadiz
Thompson, Sandra Lee *library administrator*

Canton
Krider, Patricia Ann *library director*
Metzger, Janet *librarian*

Cincinnati
Abate, Anne Katherine *librarian, consultant, educator*
Brehm-Heeger, Paula *library director, library association executive*
Everson, Jean Watkins Dolores *librarian, media consultant, educator*
Fender, Kimber L. *library director, educator*
Jenkins, Paul Owen *library director, educator*
Kuhn, Keith C. *library director*
Montavon, Victoria A. *university librarian, dean*
Proffitt, Kevin *archivist*

Cleveland
Downey, Kay *librarian*
Gardner, Richard Kent *retired librarian, educator, editor*
Mates, Barbara T. *librarian, library association executive*
Neal, Carolyn V. *librarian*
Venable, Andrew A., Jr. *library director*

Columbus
Branin, Joseph J. *library director*
Brown, Rowland Chauncey Widrig *library and information scientist, consultant*
Budler, Joanne *library director*
Hengst, Linda Ruth *library director*
Losinski, Patrick A. *library director*
Olson, Ray Alan *librarian*
Sawyers, Elizabeth Joan *librarian, director*
Studer, William Joseph *library director*
Swarlis, Linda *library and information scientist*

Dayton
Klinck, Cynthia Anne *library director*
Wyllie, Stanley Clarke *retired librarian*

Delaware
Schlichting, Catherine Fletcher Nicholson *librarian, educator*

Dublin
Baker, Mary Evelyn *retired librarian*
Dempsey, Lorcan *library and information scientist*
Jordan, Robert (Jay) L. *computer library service and research organization executive*

East Palestine
Rohrbaugh, Lisa Anne *librarian*

Euclid
Linderman, Eric Graham *librarian*

Fremont
Hill, Becky (Rebecca Baker Hill) *librarian*

Hubbard
Trucksis, Theresa A. *retired library director*

Kent
Paschen, Stephen H. *archivist, historian*
Weber, Mark W. *library director, dean*

Middleburg Heights
Maciuszko, Kathleen Lynn *librarian, educator*

Middletown
Schaefer, Patricia Ann *retired librarian*

Mount Healthy
Scheffel, Kenneth Paul *retired archivist*

North Ridgeville
Cobbledick, Susie Diane *librarian*

Northfield
Stavole, Janet M. *librarian, director*

Oberlin
English, Ray *library administrator*
Greenberg, Eva Mueller *retired librarian*
Moore, Jane Ross *librarian, educator*

Parma
Feldman, Sari *library director*

Pemberville
King, Laura Jane *librarian, genealogist*

Saint Marys
Dicke, Candice Edwards *librarian, educator*

Tiffin
Hillmer, Margaret Patricia *library director*

Toledo
Kona, Martha Mistina *librarian*
Scoles, Clyde Sheldon *library director*

Wickliffe
Fisher, Nancy DeButts *library director*

OKLAHOMA

Edmond
Morris, Donna *library director*

Hodgen
Brower, Janice Kathleen *library and information scientist*

Lawton
Bonnell-Mihalis, Pamela Gay Scoggins *library director*
Kroll, Connie Rae *librarian, information services consultant*

Muskogee
Hilbern, Sandra J. *library director*

Norman
Lee, Sul Hi *library administrator, dean*
Lester, June *library and information scientist, educator*
Lura, Susan *librarian*
Masters, Anne *library director*
Sherman, Mary Angus *public library administrator*
Van Fleet, Connie Jean *library and information scientist, educator*
Wallace, Danny P. *library and information scientist, educator*
Yi, Myongho *library and information scientist*

Oklahoma City
McVey, Susan C. *library director*

Tulsa
Alexander, Adrian W. *library director, dean*
Clement, Evelyn Geer *librarian, educator*

OREGON

Astoria
LaMear, Arline Joan *librarian, writer*

Beaverton
Burson-Dyer, Lorraine *library executive*
Pond, Patricia Brown *library and information scientist, educator*

Corvallis
Main, Michael Dee *information developer*

Eugene
Briston, Heather Irene *archivist*
Edwards, Ralph M. *librarian*

Joseph
Coppin, Caryl Mary *retired librarian*

Portland
Browne, Joseph Peter *retired librarian*
Lum, Gregory *high school librarian*
Raphael, Molly (Mary E. Raphael) *library director*

Roseburg
Reenstjerna, Frederick Roberts *librarian, writer*

Salem
Scheppke, Jim *library director*

Wilsonville
Humphrey, Lois Ellen *librarian*

PENNSYLVANIA

Allentown
Flautz, Nancy A. *librarian*
Sacks, Patricia Ann *librarian, consultant*

Altoona
Kinney, Janis Marie *librarian, consultant*

Audubon
Tanis, James Robert *library director, history professor, clergyman*

Beaver Falls
Miller, Albert Jay *retired library director*

Bethlehem
Paustian, Paul Robert *librarian*
Taggart, Bruce M. *library administrator*

Coatesville
Sauer, James Leslie *librarian, educator*

Coplay
Norbeck, Jack Carl *library exhibitor*

Corsica
Elza, Betty Ann *retired librarian*

Cranberry Township
Lorenz, John George *librarian, consultant*

Du Bois
Emmer, Barbara Louise *librarian*

Easton
Schott, Michael J. *library director*

Gladwyne
Fletcher, Marjorie Amos *librarian*

Greensburg
Duck, Patricia Mary *librarian*

Harrisburg
Emerick, John L. *library director*
Zales, Mary Clare *library director*

Huntingdon
Stiffler, Stuart Alden *retired library director*

Kingsley
McNabb, Corrine Radtke *librarian*

Lancaster
Snelson, Pamela *librarian, association executive, researcher*
Zeager, Lloyd *librarian*

Lock Haven
Chang, Shirley Lin (Hsiu-Chu Chang) *librarian, educator*

Mansfield
Donahue, Martha *retired librarian*

Mc Murray
Celento, Florence M. *librarian*

New Holland
Fanus, Pauline Rife *librarian*

New Kensington
Gilley, Jennifer R. *librarian*

Philadelphia
Alford, Larry P. *university librarian*
Arnold, Lee *library director, archivist*
Azzolina, David Sean *librarian*
Davidoff, Joanne Malatesta *multi-media specialist*
Diaz, Magna M. *librarian*
Mancall, Jacqueline Cooper *library and information scientist, educator*
Rogers, Carton (H. Carton Rogers III) *library director*
Shelkrot, Elliot L. *library director*

Pittsburgh
Dabrishus, Michael John *librarian*
Jenkins, Georgann Klaus *librarian*
Josey, E(lonnie) J(Unius) *librarian, retired state agency administrator*
Miller, Rush Glenn, Jr. *library director*
Minnigh, Joel Douglas *library director*
Mistick, Barbara Knaus *library director*
Richey, Cynthia K. *library director*
St. Clair, Gloriana Strange *librarian, dean*
Willard, Louis Charles *librarian*
Wohleber, Lynne Farr *archivist, librarian*

Punxsutawney
Dinsmore, Roberta Joan Maier *library director*

Reading
Mack, Sara Rohrbach *librarian, educator*

Riegelsville
Banko, Ruth Caroline *retired library director*

Scranton
Brandreth, Elizabeth Anne *library director*

Somerset
Kline, Eva Jane *library services administrator, educator*

Strasburg
Bell, Kurt Robert *archivist*

University Park
Eaton, Nancy Ruth Linton *librarian, dean*
Joyce, William Leonard *librarian*
Stout, Leon James *archivist, librarian*

Warrington
Hostert, Leona Teressa *retired librarian, researcher*

Wayne
Garrison, Guy Grady *librarian, educator*

Wilkes Barre
Mech, Terrence Francis *library director*

Wyomissing
Doherty, Edmond John *retired librarian*

Yardley
Soultoukis, Donna Zoccola *library director*

RHODE ISLAND

Bristol
McMullen, Susan Taylor *librarian*

Coventry
Schweinsburg, Jane Duberg *librarian*

Kingston
Caldwell, Naomi Rachel *library and information scientist, educator, writer*

Providence
Boksenbaum, Howard *library director*
Hamerly, Michael T. *librarian, historian*

Riverside
Schwegler, Nancy Ann *librarian, writer*

Wakefield
Alexander, Jacqueline Peterson *retired librarian*

SOUTH CAROLINA

Bluffton
Cann, Sharon Lee *retired health science librarian*

Clemson
Wall, Kay *librarian, dean*

Columbia
Goble, David S. *library director*
Hastings, Samantha Kelly *library and information science professor, director*
Helsley, Alexia Jones *archivist*
Rawlinson, Helen Ann *librarian*
Toombs, Kenneth Eldridge *librarian*
Warren, Charles David *library administrator*
Zimmerman, Nancy Picciano *library and information scientist, educator*

Georgetown
Bazemore, Trudy McConnell *librarian*

Greenville
Scales, Pat R. *library association executive, library director*

Hardeeville
Kadar, Karin Patricia *librarian*

North Augusta
Rowland, Arthur Ray *librarian*

Orangeburg
Byers, Keith Thomas *librarian*
UmBayemake, Linda *library branch manager, rehabilitation services professional*

SOUTH DAKOTA

Pierre
Liegl, Dorothy M. *library director*

Sioux Falls
Thompson, Ronelle Kay Hildebrandt *library director*

TENNESSEE

Englewood
Brown, Helen Dodson *retired librarian*

Germantown
Loper, Linda Sue *librarian*

Greeneville
Smith, Myron John, Jr. *librarian, author*

Jackson
Hoyle, Shetina Yevette *librarian*

Kingsport
Smith, JoAnn Carroll *library and information scientist*

Knoxville
Cottrell, Jeannette Elizabeth *retired librarian*
Dewey, Barbara I. *librarian, dean*
Felder-Hoehne, Felicia Harris *librarian, researcher*
Lowe, Alan Conner *library director*
Purcell, Aaron D. *archivist, historian*

Lebanon
Burns, George Franklin *archivist, retired English language educator*

Maryville
Tabor, Curtis Harold, Jr. *retired librarian, minister*

Memphis
Crawford, Sheila Jane *librarian, reading specialist*
Drescher, Judith Altman *library director*
Pourciau, Lester John, Jr. *retired librarian*
Wallis, Carlton Lamar *librarian*

Nashville
Carmack, Catherine Elise *archives administrator*
Gmeiner, Timothy J. *music librarian, music director*
Hall, Taffey Rena *archivist*
Nicely, Donna D. *library director*
Radcliff, Joyce B. *librarian*
Shockley, Ann Allen *librarian, writer*
Stewart, David Marshall *librarian*
Sugg, Jeanne D. *library director*

Oak Ridge
McNeilly, Kathy Eden *librarian, library director*

TEXAS

Abilene
Tucker, John Mark *librarian, educator*

Arlington
Siegfried, Cary Ann *library director*

Austin
Billings, Harold Wayne *retired library director, editor, writer*
Branch, Brenda Sue *library director*

vers, Betty Sue *library director, educator*
:y, David Bergen, II, *archivist, information ience educator, writer*
:h, Fred Milton *library director, educator*
iroth, Barbara *library and information ientist*
ly, Stephanie *librarian*
n, Robert W. *library administrator*
ie, John Ross *archivist, educator, library and formation scientist, educator*
ett, Sandra *archivist, information scientist*
:oe, Paul Stephen *librarian, researcher*
Loriene *library association executive, brary and information scientist*
d, Peggy D. *library director*
th, Patricia H. *library association director*

wnwood
:ks, Patsy Ann Landry *librarian, educator*

nyon Lake
vden, Virginia Massey *librarian*

dar Hill
kman, Traphene Parramore *retired library irector, consultant*

dar Park
n, Pauline Poha *library director*

dspring
ich, Robert Craig *librarian*

llege Station
ok, C. Colleen *librarian, dean*
:h, Warren L., Jr. *library director, archivist*
zweiss, Robert F. *archivist, educator*
:itelli, Felicia Ann *librarian, musician, iusicologist*

rpus Christi
iales, Herbert Glenn *library director*

llas
:kstruck, Lloyd DeWitt *librarian*
ins, Laurie A. *library director*
bin, Duane *library and information science irector, theology educator*
ch, Robert Daniel, Jr. *library director*
Combs, Gillian M. *library director, dean*
ompson, B. Lolana *archivist*
ing, Julia Anne *librarian, elementary school educator*

nton
ars, Michelle Morgan *archivist*
ole, Eva Duraine *librarian*
ipson, Carol Mann *librarian, educator, editor*
ipp, Elizabeth *librarian, educator*
igger, Keith *library and information scientist, educator*

Paso
ibriz, Lorely *library and information scientist*
:y-Casiano, Carol A. *library director*
rdner, Kerry Ann *librarian*

rt Worth
d, Harold Jacob *library administrator*
Tonnancour, Paul Roger Godefroy *library administrator*
Richard T. *retired library director, secondary school educator*
binson, Gleniece Armstrong *library director*
kes, Mary Taggart *librarian*

alena Park
erro, Robert, Jr. *librarian*

arland
iusch, Claire *library director*

eorgetown
nith, John Brewster *library administrator*

ouston
gwood, David P. *librarian, writer*
oule, Michelle L. *librarian, writer*
enington, David Mead *retired library director*
wson, Rhea Brown *library director*
owman, Sara Allison *library director*
iller, Sabrina Wares *librarian*
idoff, Leonard Irving *librarian, consultant*
issell, John Francis *retired librarian*

aredo
eber, Janice Ann *library director, grant writer*

ubbock
lausen, Jane *library director*
ood, Richard Courtney *library director, educator*

larshall
lagrill, Rose Mary *library director*

lcallen
IcGee, William Howard John *library director*
odriguez, Maria Dolores *librarian*

alestine
Villiams, Franklin Cadmus, Jr. *bibliographer*

lano
aumbach, Joyce *library director*

ichardson
all, Larry David *library director*

ound Rock
icklefs, Dale Lynne *library director*

an Angelo
hatfield, Mary Van Abshoven *retired librarian*

an Antonio
rewster, Olive Nesbitt *retired librarian*
Jones, Daniel Hare *librarian, consultant*
Newton, Virginia *archivist, historian, librarian*
Salazar, Ramiro S. *library director*
Trent, Joyce Miller *librarian*

Sweetwater
Taylor, Martha Sue *librarian*

Tyler
Albertson, Christopher Adam *librarian*
Green, Douglas Alvin *retired library director*

Waco
Hair, William Bates III *librarian, dean*

Wichita Falls
Parker, Eva Annette *librarian*

UTAH

Moab
Tallman, Eve *library director*

Orem
Hall, Blaine Hill *retired librarian*

Provo
Jensen, Richard Dennis *librarian*
Olsen, Randy J. *university librarian*

Salt Lake City
Mogren, Paul Andrew *librarian*
Morris, Donna Jones *library director*
Ogburn, Joyce L. *library director*
Watt, Ronald G. *archivist*

VERMONT

Bethel
West, Jessamyn Charity *librarian, blogger*

Burlington
Saule, Mara *librarian, dean*

Corinth
Bellamy, John Stark, II, *librarian, historian, writer*

Montpelier
McShane, Sybil Brigham *library director*

Northfield
Farkas, Meredith G. *librarian*

VIRGINIA

Alexandria
Berger, Patricia Wilson *retired librarian*
Cross, Dorothy Abigail *retired librarian*
Gernand, Bradley Elton *archivist, librarian*
O'Brien, Patrick Michael *library administrator*
Plitt, Jeanne Given *librarian*

Arlington
Bromley, Marilyn Modlin *librarian*
Stone, Stuart Lee Morrison *librarian, language educator*

Blacksburg
Bailey, Annette F. *librarian*
Hitchingham, Eileen *librarian, dean*

Chesapeake
Stillman, Margaret (Peggy Stillman) *library director*

Fairfax
Clay, Edwin S. III *library director*

Falls Church
Yoshimura, Yoshiko *librarian*

Fredericksburg
Edmunds, Jeffrey Garth *librarian*

Harrisonburg
Gill, Gerald Lawson *librarian*

Isle Of Wight
Huber, Janet Barlow *librarian*

Langley Afb
Smail, Leslie Anne *librarian*

Lexington
Gaines, James Edwin, Jr. *retired librarian*
Krantz, Linda Law *librarian*
Leach, Maurice Derby, Jr. *librarian, educator*

Mc Lean
Murphy, Mary *retired librarian*

Norfolk
Maas, Norman Lewis *library director*

Poquoson
Tai, Elizabeth Shi-Jue Lee *library director*

Portsmouth
Monroe, Evelyn Jones *retired librarian*

Rapidan
Grimm, Ben Emmet *library director, consultant*

Reston
Bradley, Murray L(ee) *librarian*

Richmond
Coalter, Milton J., Jr. *library director, educator*
Henderson, Harriet *librarian, director*
Kozlowski, Ronald Stephan *retired librarian*
Lyons, Curtis A. *archivist*
Martin, Ann McCarthy *library-media specialist, library association executive*
McDaid, Jennifer Davis *archivist*
Sterling, Anne D. *library association executive*
Treadway, Sandra Gioia *library director*
Vann, John Daniel III *library consultant, historian*
Van Neste, Karen Lane *librarian, editor*
Yelich, Nolan T. *library director*

Salem
Cirasunda, Esther Bond *librarian*

Springfield
Doran, Doris Jeanne *librarian*

Staunton
Vettel, Eric J. *library director*

Suffolk
Bowman, Dorothy Marie *retired librarian*
Burd, Joyce Ann *librarian*

Verona
MacTavish, Susanne Hanna *retired library and information scientist*

Virginia Beach
Sims, Marcy (Martha J. Sims) *library director*

Washington
Arbelbide, C(indy) L(ea) *librarian, historian, author*

Williamsburg
Brooks, Philip Coolidge, Jr. *archivist, curator, historian*
Moorman, John A. *librarian*
Trott, Barry *librarian*

Wise
Benke, Robin Paul *librarian*

Woodbridge
Andrews, Michael William *library and information scientist*

WASHINGTON

Bainbridge Island
Harrison, Cynthia L. *librarian*

Everett
Simmons, Eileen *librarian*

Issaquah
Ptacek, William H. *library director*

Lummi Island
Hanson, Polly (Pauline) Mae Early *librarian*

Maple Valley
Willson, David Allen *retired reference librarian, writer*

Olympia
Hutchins, Diane Elizabeth Rider *librarian*
Walsh, Jan *library director*
Zussy, Nancy Louise *librarian*

Port Townsend
Hiatt, Peter *retired library and information scientist*

Seattle
Bishop, Virginia Wakeman *retired librarian, humanities educator*
Boylan, Merle Nelson *librarian, educator*
Eisenberg, Michael Bruce *library and information scientist, educator*
Hill, Chrystie R. *library and information scientist*
Jacobs, Deborah L. *library director*
Mason, Marilyn Gell *library administrator, writer, consultant*
McCracken, Peter H. *librarian*
Pearl, Nancy Linn *librarian*

Spokane
Bender, Betty Wion *librarian*
Bunker, Nancy A(nn) *librarian, researcher*
Bynagle, Hans Edward *library director, philosophy educator*
Murray, James Michael *librarian, lawyer*
Wirt, Michael James *library director*

Tacoma
Parikh, Neel *library director*

Vancouver
Bridgewater, Rachel *library and information scientist*

WEST VIRGINIA

Charleston
Waggoner, James D. (J.D. Waggoner) *library director*

Glenville
Tubesing, Richard Lee *library director*

Morgantown
Bender, Nathan Edward *librarian, archivist*
Pyles, Rodney Allen *archivist, county official*

Shepherdstown
Elliott, Jean Ann *retired library director*

WISCONSIN

Eau Claire
Tiefel, Virginia May *librarian*

Madison
Beatty, Mark A. *librarian*
Bunge, Charles Albert *library science educator*
Dimick, Barbara L. *library director*
Hawkinson, Lorraine A. *librarian*
Horning, Kathleen T. *library director*
Scherdin, Mary Jane Liskovec *retired librarian, researcher*

Menomonie
Lueder, Dianne Carol *library director*

Milwaukee
Hubbard, John M. *library and information scientist*
Kiely, Paula *city librarian*
Runkel, Phillip M. *archivist*
Valance, Marsha Jeanne *library director, storyteller*

Richland Center
Gollata, James Anthony *library director, educator*

Sheboygan Falls
Potter, Calvin J. *retired library director*

Thiensville
Roselle, William Charles *librarian*

WYOMING

Casper
Anderson, Kevin Stuart *archivist, librarian*

Cheyenne
Boughton, Lesley D. *library director*

TERRITORIES OF THE UNITED STATES

AMERICAN SAMOA

Pago Pago
Fung-Chen-Pen, Emma Talauna Solaita *librarian, director*

PUERTO RICO

San Juan
Muñoz-Solá, Haydeé Socorro *library administrator*

CANADA

ALBERTA

Lethbridge
Rand, Duncan Dawson *retired librarian*

BRITISH COLUMBIA

Coquitlam
Hainsworth, Melody May *library and information scientist, researcher*

Vancouver
Piternick, Anne Brearley *librarian, educator*
Rothstein, Samuel *librarian, educator*

Victoria
Richards, Vincent Philip Haslewood *librarian*

NOVA SCOTIA

Bedford
Birdsall, William Forest *retired librarian*

Dartmouth
Horrocks, Norman *librarian, educator, editor*

ONTARIO

Guelph
Land, Reginald Brian *library administrator*

Ottawa
Scott, Marianne Florence *retired librarian, educator*
Sylvestre, Jean Guy *former national librarian*
Wallot, Jean-Pierre *archivist, historian*

Toronto
Bryant, Josephine Harriet *library executive*
Moore, Carole Irene *librarian*

QUEBEC

Montreal
Large, John Andrew *library and information service professor*

Quebec City
Bonnelly, Claude *library director*

SASKATCHEWAN

Saskatoon
Kennedy, Marjorie Ellen *librarian*

Hamilton
Etches-Johnson, Amanda *library and information scientist*

ARMENIA

Yerevan
Sargsyan, David *library director*

BAHRAIN

Manama
Sarhan, Mansoor Mohamed *library director*

CZECH REPUBLIC

Prague
Kalkus, Stanley *librarian, administrator, consultant*
Turková, Helga *librarian*

ENGLAND

London
Mizumura, Megumi *conservator*

Oxford
Shaw, Dennis Frederick *former library director, chartered physicist, consultant*
Vaisey, David George *librarian, archivist*

FRANCE

Paris
Cagle, William Rea *retired librarian*

GERMANY

Cologne
Neisser, Horst *library director, writer*

Halle
Thamm, Jochen Walter *library director*

Lübeck
Fligge, Jörg *librarian, library director*

Stuttgart
Geh, Hans-Peter *retired library director, consultant*

GUATEMALA

Antigua
Rodgers, Frank *librarian*

HUNGARY

Budapest
Poprády, Géza *librarian*

IRELAND

County Kildare
Kabdebo, Thomas George *library director*

ISRAEL

Jerusalem
Rozett, Robert Bernard *library director, historian*

JAPAN

Osaka
Horii, Reiichi *library director, educator*

KAZAKHSTAN

Almaty
Sadykova, Vera Philippovna *librarian, educator*

SWEDEN

Stockholm
Lidman, Tomas Erik *national archivist*

SWITZERLAND

Geneva
Jacquesson, Alain L. *librarian*

ADDRESS UNPUBLISHED

Abbott, George Lindell *retired librarian*
Abid, Ann B. *art librarian*
Adkins, Thomas Samuel *library director*
Aho, Melissa Kay *librarian, educator, writer*
Allen, Norma Ann *librarian, educator*
Allen, Patricia J. *retired library director*
Anderson, Herschel Vincent *retired librarian*
Anderson, Rachael Keller (Rachael Keller) *retired library director*
Baker, Carolyn Simmons *library director, consultant, researcher*
Baker, Zachary Moshe *librarian*
Barkley, Terrell Wayne *archivist, curator, school librarian*
Battin, Patricia Meyer *librarian*
Beatty, Judy Iola Spencer *library director*
Berkley, Erma Van Meter *retired librarian*
Berman, Miriam Naomi *librarian*
Berman, Sanford *librarian*
Blackburn, Joy Martin *retired librarian*
Blalock, Louise *librarian, public administrator*
Bowen, Jean *retired librarian, consultant*
Brady, Jean Stein *retired librarian*
Brechtel, Unda Jurka *retired library director*
Bromwell, Linda Anne *librarian, writer*
Brooks Shoemaker, Virginia Lee *librarian*
Brown, Carol Ann *librarian, director*
Brown, Elizabeth Eleanor *retired librarian*
Bulow, Jack Faye *retired library director*
Burson, Betsy Lee *librarian*
Byrd, Joan Eda *retired librarian*
Campbell, Henry Cummings *librarian*
Canelas, Dale Brunelle *retired library director*
Carr, E. Barbara *librarian*
Carter, Yvonne Breaux *retired librarian*
Cassell, Kay Ann *librarian*
Chirico-Elkins, Ursula *retired librarian*
Chu, Ellin Resnick *librarian, consultant*
Clement, Hope Elizabeth Anna *retired librarian*
Clement, Yvonne Madeline *librarian*
Conaway, Margaret Grimes (Peggy Conaway) *library administrator*
Cooper, Jacquelyn Barber *librarian*
Costa, Kathy *retired librarian*
Cottam, Keith M. *librarian, educator, administrator*
Crahan, Elizabeth Schmidt *librarian*
Curley, Elmer Frank *librarian*
Daffron, MaryEllen *retired librarian*
deBear, Richard Stephen *library planning consultant*
Debraski, Sarah Cornish *librarian*
Desnoyers, Megan Floyd *retired archivist, educator*
Dickinson, Donald Charles *library science professor*
Dickinson, Gail Krepps *library science educator*
Domzella, Janet *retired library director*
Drake, Miriam Anna *retired librarian, educator, writer, consultant*
Dulin, Eric D. *archivist*
Dunham, Elizabeth Grace *librarian*
Dykstra Lynch, Mary Elizabeth *library and information scientist, educator*
Dyson, Allan Judge *retired librarian*
Eaton, Katherine Girton *retired library educator*
Edmonds, Anne Carey *librarian*
Efird, Frank Kimball, Jr. *archivist*
Elder, Mary Louise *retired librarian*
Ellington, Mildred L. *retired librarian*
Else, Carolyn Joan *retired library director*
Elwood-Akers, Virginia Edythe *librarian, retired archivist*
Erickson, Alan Eric *librarian*
Erwin, Linda McIntosh *retired librarian*
Estes, Elaine Rose Graham *retired librarian*
Euster, Joanne Reed *retired librarian*
Fasick, Adele Mongan *library and information scientist, educator*
Fawcett, John Thomas *archivist*
Felsted, Carla Martindell *librarian, writer, editor*
Ford, Barbara Jean *librarian, educator*
Frank, Larry James *library director*
Frankel, Mary Ann (Kate Frankel) *librarian, educator*
Frantz, Ray William, Jr. *retired librarian*
Fredeman, Betty Coley (Betty Coley) *retired librarian, editor*
Gainey, Lilah Leigh *librarian*
Gallant, Stephen Laurie *librarian*
Garypie, Rudolph Renwick *retired library director*
Gatch, Milton McCormick, Jr. *library director, clergyman, educator*
Gaulke, Mary Florence *retired library administrator*
Giebel, Miriam Catherine *librarian, genealogist*
Gold, Leonard Singer *librarian, translator, curator*
Gorman, Michael Joseph *retired library director, educator*
Gould, Martha Bernice *retired librarian*
Gray, Gloria Meador *librarian*
Greenberg, Hinda Feige *library director*
Gregor, Dorothy Deborah *retired librarian*
Gudmundsson, Finnbogi *library administrator*
Gundersheimer, Werner Leonard *library director*
Hangen, Terra *librarian, writer*
Hazekamp, Phyllis Wanda Alberts *retired library director*
Heanue, Anne Allen *retired librarian*
Herold, Jeffrey Roy Martin *retired library director*
Hewitt, Ruth Price *retired librarian, elementary school educator*
Hoffmann, Frances Porter *librarian*
Hoke, Sheila Wilder *retired librarian*
Holt, Helen *librarian, consultant, former government official*
Howard, Joseph Harvey *retired librarian*
Howder, Murray Louis *librarian, educator*
Hughes, Sue Margaret *retired librarian*
Jenkins, Darrell Lee *librarian*
Johnson, Clifton Herman *archivist, retired professional society administrator*
Johnson, Wayne Harold *librarian, retired municipal official*
Kadhim, Estelle Beverly *retired librarian*
Kallenberg, John Kenneth *retired librarian*
Kaser, David *retired librarian, educator, consultant*
Kear, Rebecca JoAnn *retired librarian*
Kendall, Charles Terry *librarian*
Kesseler, Matthew John *librarian*
Kiser, Nagiko Sato *retired librarian*
Klein, Susan Elaine *librarian*
Knechtmann, James Allen *archivist, researcher*
Korenic, Lynette Marie *librarian*
Kreitzburg, Marilyn June *academic librarian*
Lane, Laura Alice *retired librarian*
Larson, Larry *retired librarian*
Leary, Margaret A. *law library director*
Lee, Harrison Hon *librarian, consultant*
Lee, Pali Jae (Polly Jae Stead Lee) *retired librarian, writer*
Lehner-Quam, Alison Lynn *library administrator*
Leonhardt, Thomas Wilburn *librarian, library director*
Levenback, Karen L. *librarian, archivist, educator, writer, editor*
Lindgren, William Dale *librarian*
Lovelace, Julianne *former library director*
Lowell, Virginia Lee *retired librarian*
Lucker, Jay K. *library consultant*
MacDonald, Alan Hugh *academic administrator*
Mackey Catoe, Margaret Emmie *library media specialist*
Mahajan, Ashutosh *library and information scientist*
Maltby, Florence Helen *library science educator*
Margoshes, Miriam Kagan *information specialist*
Martin, Robert Sidney *librarian, educator*
Massey, Stephen Charles *rare book dealer, consultant*
McBurney, Margot B. *retired librarian*
McGlothlen, John M. *librarian*
McInnes, Robert A. *archivist*
Meany, Philip Augustus *retired library director*
Metz, T(heodore) John *librarian, educator*
Miller, Beverly A(nn) *reference librarian*
Miller, Jacqueline Winslow *library director*
Miller, Marilyn Lea *library and information scientist, educator*
Morgan, Jane Hale *retired library director*
Morton, Donald John *librarian*
Naulty, Susan Louise *archivist*
Noonan, Daniel W. *archivist*
Ortego, Gilda Baeza *library director, educator*
Owen, Amy *library director*
Pakala, James Cotton *library director, minister*
Parker, Sara Ann *librarian, consultant*
Pearce-Moses, Richard *librarian*
Peters, Connie Jane *librarian, media specialist*
Pitman, LaVern Frank *librarian*
Poad, Flora Virginia *retired librarian, retired elementary school educator*
Pruter, Robert Douglas *librarian*
Ramser, Wanda Tene *librarian, educator*
Renfro, Patricia Elise *library director, academic administrator*
Repinski, Sara *library director*
Rhoads, James Berton *archivist, consultant, federal official, educator*
Ricketts, Sondra Lou *librarian*
Roark, Barbara Ann *librarian*
Roberts, Judith Marie *librarian, educator*
Robinson, Verna Cotten *retired librarian, real estate manager*
Rosenthal, Susan Barbara *retired librarian*
Rouse, Roscoe, Jr. *retired librarian, educator*
Rump, Marjorie *library director*
Runkle, Martin Davey *library director*
Sager, Donald Jack *librarian, consultant, retired publishing executive*
Scheiberg, Susan L. *librarian*
Schlesinger, Deborah Lee *retired librarian*
Schlosser, Anne Griffin *librarian*
Scott, Carol Seeley *retired librarian, researcher*
Scott, Catherine Dorothy *librarian, library and information scientist, consultant*
Shaw, Kathleen M. Troutner *retired librarian*
Siefert-Kazanjian, Donna *corporate librarian*
Slavens, Thomas Paul *library science educator*
Smith, Barbara Jeanne *retired librarian*
Smith, Charles Hyde *librarian, historian, geographer*
Sparks, William Sheral *retired librarian*
Sprince, Leila Joy *retired librarian*
Stavely, Keith Williams Fitzgerald *librarian*
Stewart, Dorothy K. *librarian*
Strait, Viola Edwina Washington *librarian*
Stubbs, Kendon Lee *retired librarian*
Summers, Lorraine Dey Schaeffer *retired librarian*
Suput, Ray Radoslav *librarian*
Swartz, Renee Becker *library advocate, civic volunteer*
Sweetland, Loraine Fern *librarian, educator*
Tavella, Elise Shannon *librarian*
Trezza, Alphonse Fiore *librarian, educator*
Trujillo, Maive *library director*
Turner, Marguerite Rose Cowles *retired library director*
VanMeter, Vandelia L. *retired library director*
Van Orden, Phyllis Jeanne *librarian, educator*
Van Valkenburgh, Holly Viola *librarian, consultant*
Varner, Joyce Ehrhardt *retired librarian*
von Hake, Margaret Joan *librarian*
Wald, Ingeborg *librarian, translator*
Wang, Chen-ku *retired library director*
Wartluft, David Jonathan *retired librarian, minister*
Watts, Doris Earlene *retired librarian*
Weiherer, Patricia Dee *retired librarian*
Weingand, Darlene Erna *librarian, educator*
Wertsman, Vladimir Filip *librarian, writer, library and information scientist, translator*
Wilkins, Barratt (George Wilkins) *librarian*
Willis, Paul Allen *retired librarian, retired dean*
Wilson, Patricia Potter *library and information science educator*
Winn, Carolyn Pautke *librarian, consultant*
Wong Smith, Helen Mei Lin *librarian, archivist, consultant*
Woodrum, Patricia Ann *librarian*
Wright, Barbara Clare *business librarian*
Wynar, Bohdan Stephen *retired librarian, writer, editor*
Yiotis, Gayle *archivist, researcher, anthropologist, writer*
Zack, Daniel Gerard *library consultant*

HUMANITIES: MUSEUMS

UNITED STATES

ALABAMA

Huntsville
Baldaia, Peter *curator*

Mc Calla
Kes, Vicki *museum director*

Mobile
Richelson, Paul William *curator*

Montgomery
Johnson, Mark Matthew *museum administrator*

ALASKA

Skagway
Sanders, Debra Kay *curator*

ARIZONA

Glendale
Almstead, Sheila Louise *art gallery owner*

Green Valley
Lusk, Harlan Gilbert *national park superintendent, business executive*

Phoenix
Loscher, Tricia Diane *curator, director*

Portal
Zweifel, Richard George *curator*

Scottsdale
Krane, Susan *museum director, curator*

Tempe
Zeitlin, Marilyn Audrey *museum director*

Tucson
King, James Edward *retired museum director, consultant*

CALIFORNIA

Arcata
Bailey, Stephen Fairchild *retired museum director, ornithologist, birding tour guide*

Bakersfield
Enriquez, Carola Rupert *museum director*

Berkeley
Benedict, Burton *retired museum director, anthropologist*
Consey, Kevin Edward *museum administrator*
Day, Lucille Lang *museum administrator, educator, writer*
Grossman, Bonnie *art gallery director*

Carlsbad
Misiorowski, Elise Besson *museum director*
Nosanow, Barbara Shissler *museum director, curator*

Carmel Valley
Wolfe, Maurice Raymond *retired museum director, educator*

Carson
Zimmerer, Kathy Louise *museum director*

Del Mar
Smith, Geoffrey Arthur *museum staff member, surgeon*

Irvine
Stern, Jean *museum director*

La Jolla
Beebe, Mary Livingstone *curator*
Davies, Hugh Marlais *museum director*

Los Angeles
Barron, Stephanie *curator*
Brand, Michael *museum director*
Byrnes, James Bernard *museum director, consultant*
Govan, Michael *museum director*
Hirano, Irene Ann Yasutake *museum director*
Hopkins, Henry Tyler *museum director, art educator*
Martin, Joel W. *curator, biology professor*
Nottage, James H. *museum administrator, curator, historian*
Philbin, Ann *art facility director*
Rich, Andrea Louise *museum administrator*
Strick, Jeremy *curator*
Talley, Vernon Andrew *museum administrator*

Menlo Park
Mozley, Anita Ventura *retired curator, retired a[rt] historian*

Moraga
Silcox, Frances Eleanor *museum and exhibits planning consultant*

Oakland
Frye, L. Thomas *curator*

adena
ey, Edward Richmond *historical site administrator*

acho Palos Verdes
in, Robert Alan *museum director, curator*

erside
ren, Katherine Virginia *art gallery director*

ramento
tt, Kyle K. *curator, historian*

Carlos
macher, Henry Jerold *museum director, retired military officer*

Diego
er, Michael W. *museum director*
genecker, Martha W. *museum director*
rsen, Martin Eugene *curator*

Francisco
ezra, Neal *museum director, curator*
er, Molly M. *museum program director*
hanan, John Edward, Jr. *museum director*
gard, Timothy Anglin *curator*
ton, Alan Edward *curator*
eill, Brian *national recreation area administrator*
off, Ralph *curator*
, Emily Joy *museum director*
k, J. William *art conservator*

Jose
nandez, Jo Farb *museum director, consultant*

Marino
rdoch, John *museum director*

ta Barbara
peles, David *museum director*

nford
zierski, Maciej M. *curator*

e Sea Ranch
s, Jacquelynn *museum director, art historian*

lare
elick, Ellen Catherine *museum executive director, chief curator, artist, educator, civic volunteer*

semite National Park
gang, David M. *curator*

LORADO

fton
nard, Michael Joseph *museum director*

lorado Springs
Mieux, Linda Dailey *museum director*
ndall, Jessy *curator, writer*

nver
rp, Lewis Inman *museum director, curator*
lson, Steve *museum director*

eblo
rce, Jina *curator, artist*

NNECTICUT

naan
ner, Abram *museum director, artist*

w Haven
key, Leo Joseph *museum curator, educator*
yers, Amy *museum director*
kin, Jenni *curator, critic*
mble, Angus A. G. *curator, writer*

est Hartford
ade, Wilson Hinsdale *museum director, consultant*

eston
ver, Sandra *art dealer, painter*

ELAWARE

ilmington
ankenship, Roy *conservator, artist, writer*
uni, Stephen Thomas *museum director*

STRICT OF COLUMBIA

ashington
ll, Ford Watson *museum association administrator*
rtin, Margaret A.H *museum administrator*
oomfield, Sara J. *museum director*
etzfelder, Deborah May *retired museum staff member*
hler, Leslie Lynn *museum director*
nch, Lonnie III *museum director*
rr, Carolyn Kinder *art gallery director*
nwill, Kinshasha Holman *museum director*
wyer Southern, Kathy *museum administrator*
nd, John Oliver *museum curator*
arvey, Eleanor Jones *museum curator*
ennedy, Roger George *museum program and parks director*
etchum, James Roe *curator*
ornicker, Louis Sampson *museum curator*
arin, Richard *museum program director*
rson, Judy L. *museum director, curator*
gro, Patrice *museum director*
cKinney, David Duane *museum director, architectural historian*

McLean, Kathleen *exhibition consultant, museum director*
Neufeld, Michael John *curator, historian*
Pachter, Marc *museum director*
Patton, Sharon F. *museum director*
Raby, Julian *art gallery director*
Radice, Anne-Imelda Marino *museum director, former federal agency administrator*
Rifkin, Ned *museum director*
Sant, Victoria P. *museum administrator*
Solinger, Janet W. *museum executive*
Stevenson, Frances Kellogg *retired museum program director*
Stevenson, Nancy Nelson *museum director*
Sultan, Terrie Frances *curator*
Vaughan, James M. *historic trust administrator*
Viso, Olga *museum director*
Wolanin, Barbara Ann Boese *curator, art historian*

FLORIDA

Daytona Beach
Libby, Gary Russell *museum director emeritus, writer*

Fort Lauderdale
Cavendish, Kim L. Maher *museum administrator*
Santis, Jorge Hilker *curator*

Gainesville
Dickinson, Joshua Clifton, Jr. *museum director, educator*
Wing, Elizabeth Schwarz *museum curator, educator*

Jacksonville
Dundon, Margo Elaine *museum director*

Miami
Delehanty, Suzanne *museum director*

Miami Beach
Camber, Diane Woolfe *museum director*

Orlando
Morrisey, Marena Grant *art museum administrator*

Panama City
Hough, Douglas Ralph *museum director*

Saint Augustine
Harper, Robert Walter III *museum director*

Saint Petersburg
Connelly, David O'Brien *museum administrator, journalist*

Sarasota
Weber, Joanna *curator*
Wetenhall, John *museum director*
Zahn, Carl Frederick *museum program director, photographer, graphics designer*

Tallahassee
Palladino-Craig, Allys *museum director, educator*

Tampa
de Quesada, Alejandro Manuel *film and museum consultant, writer*

Vero Beach
Gedeon, Lucinda Heyel *museum director*

GEORGIA

Atlanta
Bibb, Daniel Roland *art restorer*
King, Linda Orr *museum director, consultant*
Shapiro, Michael Edward *museum director*
Taylor, David Randy *museum staff member, consultant*
Vigtel, Gudmund *retired museum director*
Waterhouse, Richard *museum administrator, artist*

Marietta
Barksdale, Daryl *historic preservationist*

Milledgeville
Davis, Matthew Scott *curator, history professor*

Robins Afb
Wolfe, Sarah Catharine *curator*

HAWAII

Kaneohe
Lagoria, Georgianna Marie *curator, writer, editor, visual art consultant*

Mililani
Magee, Donald Edward *retired national park service administrator*

IDAHO

Coeur D' Alene
Dahlgren, Dorothy *museum director*

Inkom
Jackson, Allen Keith *retired museum administrator*

Pocatello
Stucki, Margaret Elizabeth *art gallery director, writer, painter*

ILLINOIS

Carbondale
Whitlock, John Joseph *museum director*

Chicago
Alexander, Karen *museum staff member*
Balzekas, Stanley, Jr. *museum director*
Cuno, James *museum director*
Czestochowski, Joseph Stephen *administrator, publisher, investor*
Dittmer, Frances R. *curator*
Fitzpatrick, Robert John *museum director*
Knappenberger, Paul Henry, Jr. *science museum director*
Mc Carter, John Wilbur, Jr. *museum executive*
McCullagh, Suzanne *curator*
Mosena, David R. *museum administrator*
Nordland, Gerald *museum administrator, historian, consultant*
Pascale, Mark *curator, educator*
Rondeau, James Edward *curator*
Serrell, Beverly *museum consultant*
Smith, Elizabeth Angele Taft *curator*
Spock, Michael *museum administrator*
Whyte, Alison Anne *conservator*

Evanston
Danilov, Victor Joseph *museum administrator, educator, writer*
Robertson, David Alan *museum director, educator*

Libertyville
Pegg, Richard Anderson *curator*

Princeton
Collins, N. Dana *art gallery owner, consultant, retired art educator*

Rock Island
Leinicke, Kris Gayman *museum director, educator*

Springfield
Hallmark, Donald Parker *museum director, educator*

INDIANA

Bloomington
Calinescu, Adriana Gabriela *curator, art historian*

Evansville
Streetman, John William III *museum director*

Indianapolis
Anderson, Maxwell L. *museum director*
Warkel, Harriet G. *curator*

Muncie
Blume, Peter Frederick *museum director*

IOWA

Cedar Falls
Huber, Mary Therese *museum director, consultant*
Taylor, Darrell Richard *art gallery director, artist*

Davenport
Babbitt, Margaret Sargent *museum administrator*
Johansen Kastell, Christina Marie *curator*
Robinson, Michelle *curator*

Des Moines
Thompson, Jerome Lafayette *curator*

KANSAS

Pleasanton
Earnest, Ola May *curator*

Pratt
Shrack, Christopher George *curator, educator*

Salina
Toelle, Jennifer M. *museum staff member*

Wichita
Jones, Schuyler *museum director, anthropologist*

KENTUCKY

Lexington
Walsh-Piper, Kathleen A. *museum director*

Louisville
Becker, Gail Roselyn *museum director*
Morrin, Peter Patrick *museum director*

LOUISIANA

Baton Rouge
Livesay, Thomas Andrew *museum director, educator*

New Orleans
Bullard, Edgar John III *museum director*
Casellas, Joachim *art gallery executive*
Fagaly, William Arthur *curator*
Schehr, Kevin John *art gallery owner*

Slidell
Dearing, Reinhard Josef *curator, retired city official*

MAINE

Hancock
Silvestro, Clement Mario *museum director, historian*

Lamoine
Schmidt, Christine Alice *art gallery owner*

Rockland
Crosman, Christopher Byron *museum director*

MARYLAND

Annapolis
Mason-Chaney, Lisa *curator*

Baltimore
Bolger, Doreen *museum director*
Hofmann, Irene E. *art museum director*
Lee, Steven Xavier *museum director, artist and environmentalist*

Bethesda
Fraser, Catriona Trafford *art gallery director, photographer*

Clinton
Whittington, Ralph Edward *retired curator, librarian*

College Park
Quick, Edward Raymond *museum director, educator, curator*

Edgewater
Dierking, Lynn D. *educational administrator*

Friendship
Clagett, Diana Wharton Sinkler *museum docent*

Hyattsville
Shestack, Alan *museum administrator*

Landover
Grasselli, Margaret Morgan *curator*
Luchs, Alison *curator, art historian*
Penny, Nicholas Beaver *museum curator*
Powell, Earl Alexander III *art museum director*

Mitchellville
Marsh, Caryl Amsterdam *retired curator, psychologist*

Saint Marys City
Sullivan, Martin Edward *museum director*

Suitland
Johnson, Jessica Susan *conservator*

Thurmont
Schuettinger, Bruce Michael *conservator*

MASSACHUSETTS

Boston
Cronin, Bonnie Kathryn Lamb *museum director*
Curran, Emily Katherine *museum director*
Emerson, Anne Devereux *museum administrator*
Gaither, Edmund Barry *museum director, curator*
Hawley, Anne *museum director*
Hills, Patricia Gorton Schulze *curator, art historian*
Nold, Carl Richard *museum administrator*
Price, Michael Witwer *art gallery owner, lawyer*
Robinson, Jeri *museum program director*
Rogers, Malcolm Austin *museum director, art historian*
Vermeule, Cornelius Clarkson III *museum curator*
Wu, Tung *curator, artist, art historian, educator*
Zannieri, Nina *museum director*

Cambridge
Ellis, David Wertz *retired museum director, consultant, arbitrator*
Gaskell, Ivan George Alexander De Wend *art museum curator, educator*
Lentz, Thomas W. *museum director, curator*
Sigel, Anthony B. *art conservator*
Slive, Seymour *museum director, art educator*
Tucker, Louis Leonard *retired historical society administrator*
Watson, Rubie S. *museum director*

Chestnut Hill
Netzer, Nancy *museum director, art historian, educator*

Fitchburg
Jareckie, Stephen Barlow *museum curator*

Lexington
Ott, John Harlow *museum administrator*

Milton
Randall, Lilian Maria Charlotte *museum curator*

Northampton
Fabing, Suzannah *museum director*
Holbert, Kelly McKay *exhibition coordinator, art historian*

Provincetown
McCarthy, Christine M. *museum director*

Salem
Corrigan, Karina Helen Hiltje *museum administrator*

Springfield
Muhlberger, Richard Charles *museum director, writer, educator*

Waltham
Arena, Albert A. *museum director*

Wellesley
Mickenberg, David *museum director, art director, historian*

West Brookfield
Higgins, Brian Alton *art gallery owner, artist*

Williamstown
Conforti, Michael Peter *museum director, art historian*

Worcester
Welu, James A. *art museum director*

MICHIGAN

Ann Arbor
Bailey, Reeve Maclaren *museum curator*
Steward, James *museum director, art history educator*

Charlevoix
Miles, David Loren *museum director*

Detroit
Beal, Graham William John *museum director*
Darr, Alan Phipps *curator, historian*
Parrish, Maurice Drue *museum executive*
Peck, William Henry *curator, archaeologist, educator, art historian, writer*
Terry, Robin *museum director*

East Lansing
Bandes, Susan Jane *museum director, educator*
Dewhurst, Charles Kurt *museum director, curator, language educator*

Mackinaw City
Brisson, Steven Charles *curator*

Muskegon
Fitzgerald, Rebecca Anne *curator, historian*

MINNESOTA

Minneapolis
Crippen, John Raymond *museum director*
Griswold, William M. *museum director, curator*
Halbreich, Kathy *museum director*
King, Lyndel Irene Saunders *museum director*

Saint Paul
Archabal, Nina M(archetti) *historic site director*

MISSISSIPPI

Washington
Munyer, Cheryl *museum administrator*

MISSOURI

Columbia
Goodrich, James William *retired historian executive*

Florissant
Luebke, Martin Frederick *retired curator, retired private school educator*

Fredericktown
Sudmeyer, Alice Jean *art gallery owner*

Independence
Potts, Barbara Joyce *retired historic site director*

Kansas City
McKenna, George LaVerne *art museum curator*
Schall, Jan Joan *curator, educator*
Wilson, Marc Fraser *art museum director*

Osceola
Johnson, Thomas Moore, II, *curator, lawyer*

Saint Joseph
Chilcote, Gary M. *museum director, reporter*

Saint Louis
Eyerman, Charlotte *curator, art historian*

Washington
Houseman, Marc Alan *museum director*

MONTANA

Billings
Peterson, Robyn Gayle *museum director*

Missoula
Brown, Robert Munro *museum director*
Millin, Laura Jeanne *museum director*

NEBRASKA

Beatrice
Clawson, Rita Louise *curator*

Boys Town
Lynch, Thomas Joseph *museum director*

Omaha
Wilson, John Human III *curator, art historian*

NEVADA

Boulder City
McBride, Dennis Ray *curator, writer*

Las Vegas
Herridge, Elizabeth *museum director*

NEW HAMPSHIRE

Franconia
Leich, Jeffrey R. *museum director*

Mont Vernon
Buckley, Charles E. *retired museum director, curator*

Portsmouth
Nylander, Jane Louise *museum director, educator, writer*

NEW JERSEY

Budd Lake
Ocello, Claudia Barbara *museum program director*

Holmdel
Smith, Sibley Judson, Jr. *historic site administrator, educator*

Howell
Culver, Vicky *art gallery director, artist*

Montclair
Sims, Patterson *curator*

Morristown
Miller, Steven H. *museum director*

Newark
Buck, Rebecca A. *museum administrator, registrar*
Connor, Holly Pyne *curator, art historian*
Price, Mary Sue Sweeney *museum director*

Ramsey
Libin, Laurence Elliot *retired curator*

Ridgewood
Fox, Ingrid *curator*

NEW MEXICO

Albuquerque
Baker, Laura Kay *art gallery owner, writer*

Las Cruces
Reynolds, Terry Ray *curator, anthropologist, educator*

Placitas
Smith, Richard Bowen *retired national park superintendent*

Santa Fe
Mauldin, Barbara Barieau *curator*

Silver City
Bettison, Cynthia Ann *museum director, archaeologist*

Taos
Witt, David L. *curator, writer*

NEW YORK

Astoria
Schwartz, David Peter *curator*

Blue Mountain Lake
Bond, Hallie E. *curator, historian*
Welsh, Caroline Mastin *museum director, curator, art historian*

Bronx
Block, Holly *museum director*

Brooklyn
Desmarais, Charles Joseph *museum director, writer*
Lehman, Arnold Lester *museum official, art historian*

Buffalo
Bayles, Jennifer Lucene *museum program director, educator*
Dreishpoon, Douglas Scott *curator, art historian*

Corning
Spillman, Jane Shadel *curator, writer, researcher*
Whitehouse, David Bryn *museum director*

East Hampton
Strassfield, Christina Mossaides *curator*

Hamilton
Moynihan, William J. *museum executive*

Hyde Park
Hunt, Mark Alan *museum director*

Katonah
Simpson, William Kelly *curator, Egyptologist, educator*

Mumford
Conrad, Jacob B. *curator, historian*

New York
Adler, Tracy L. *curator*
Bailey, Colin Barry *curator*
Barlow, Anne Julia *curator*
Barnett, Vivian Endicott *curator*
Basquin, Mary Smyth (Kit Basquin) *museum administrator*
Beck, Martha Ann *curator, director*
Bergen, Jeffrey Bruce *art gallery owner*
Bothmer, Dietrich Felix von *curator, archaeologist*
Bull, David *fine art conservator*
Carneiro, Robert Leonard *curator, anthropologist*
Christiansen, Keith *curator*
Christoffers, Lynn Beryl *curator, artist*
Cohen, Mildred Thaler *art gallery director*
de Montebello, Philippe Lannes *museum director*
Draper, James David *art museum curator*
Eldredge, Niles *curator, paleontologist*
Ferber, Linda S. *museum director*
Flood, Richard Sidney *curator*
Flynn, John J. *museum curator*
Foster, Carter *curator*
Freed, Stanley Arthur *retired museum curator*
Futter, Ellen Victoria *museum administrator*
Glimcher, Arnold B. *art gallery executive*
Golden, Thelma *curator*
Gumpert, Lynn *gallery director*
Gund, Agnes *retired museum administrator*
Haskell, Barbara *curator*
Henry, Sarah M. *museum staff member, historian*
Hoffman, Nancy *art gallery director*
Hotchner, Holly *museum director, curator, conservator*
Hoving, Thomas *museum director, consultant, writer*
Howat, John Keith *retired museum executive*
Ilse-Neuman, Ursula *curator*
Kallir, Jane Katherine *art gallery director, author*
Kardon, Janet *museum director*
Kleeblatt, Norman L. *museum curator*
Kramer, Linda Konheim *curator, art historian*
Krueger, Sam Quan *museum administrator*
Kuchta, Ronald Andrew *museum director, editor, curator*
Kujawski, Elizabeth Szancer *art curator, consultant*
Lerner, Martin *museum curator*
Levai, Pierre Alexandre *art gallery executive*
Levine, Louis D. *museum administrator, archaeologist*
Littman, Brett *museum director, art critic*
Lowry, Glenn David *art museum director*
Martin, Mary-Anne *art gallery owner*
Mertens, Joan R. *museum curator, art historian*
Mitchell, Patricia Edenfield *broadcast museum administrator*
Momin, Shamim *curator*
Morris, Robert Lee *gallery administrator, jewelry designer*
Murdock, Robert Mead *curator*
Pesner, Carole Manishin *art gallery owner*
Picón, Carlos Arturo *curator*
Platnick, Norman I. *curator, entomologist*
Poulet, Anne Litle *museum director, art historian*
Rafferty, Emily Kernan *museum administrator*
Rosenbaum, Joan Hannah *museum director*
Rosevear, Cora *curator*
Shakespeare, Valerie Monroe *curator, director, art gallery owner*
Simon, Ronald Charles *curator, educator*
Sutton, Karen E. *museum director*
Tisch Sussman, Laurie *art gallery director*
Tobach, Ethel *retired curator*
Toll, Barbara Elizabeth *art gallery director*
Wardropper, Ian Bruce *museum curator, educator*
Weinberg, Adam D. *museum director*

Raquette Lake
Bridger, Beverly Maria *historic site director*

Rochester
Bannon, Anthony Leo *museum director*
Keeler, William Conrad III *curator, librarian, archivist*
Maples, Philip G. *museum director*

Sands Point
Olian, JoAnne Constance *curator, art historian*

Stuyvesant
Tripp, Susan Gerwe *museum director*

Syracuse
Trop, Sandra *museum director*

Tupper Lake
Welsh, Peter Corbett *museum director, historian*

Utica
Schweizer, Paul Douglas *museum director*

Waterford
Gold, James Paul *museum director*

West Point
Jensen, Leslie Dwight *curator*

NORTH CAROLINA

Chapel Hill
Bolas, Gerald Douglas *museum director, art historian, educator*
Riggs, Timothy Allan *museum curator*
Weakley, Alan Stuart *curator*

Raleigh
Kuhler, Renaldo Gillet *retired museum director, medical illustrator*

Wilmington
Seapker, Janet Kay *museum administrator, architectural historian, history consultant*

Winston Salem
Rauschenberg, Bradford Lee *museum program director*
Whittington, Stephen Lunn *museum director*

OHIO

Akron
Kahan, Mitchell Douglas *museum director*

Canton
Perry, Stephen A. *museum administrator, former federal agency administrator*

Cincinnati
Betsky, Aaron *art museum director*
Brown, Daniel *curator, executive secretary*
Crew, Spencer *museum administrator*
Lee, Eric McCauley *museum director, art historian*
Long, Phillip Clifford *retired museum director*
Storrs, Glenn William *museum administrator, paleontologist*
Sung, Hou-mei *curator, researcher*

Cleveland
Barrie, Dennis Ray *museum director*
Chung, Anita *curator*
Robinson, William H. *curator, art historian, educator*
Rub, Timothy F. *museum director*

Columbus
Vasseur, Dominique Henri *curator*

Dayton
Meister, Mark Jay *museum director, professiona society administrator*

Groveport
Motts, Warren Earl *museum director*

Kirtland
Johnston, Stanley Howard, Jr. *curator*

Toledo
Bacigalupi, Don *museum director*
Page, Jutta Annette *curator*

University Heights
Cook, Alexander Burns *curator, artist, educator*

OKLAHOMA

Oklahoma City
George, Hardy *curator*

Ripley
Chlouber, Dale Edward *curator*

Tulsa
Newell, David L. *curator*

OREGON

Milwaukie
Eichinger, Marilynne Katzen *museum administrator*

Portland
Taylor, J. Mary (Jocelyn Mary Taylor) *museum director, educator, zoologist*

PENNSYLVANIA

Altoona
Moffitt, Charles William *art gallery director*

Chadds Ford
Duff, James Henry *museum director, environmental services administrator*

Erie
Vanco, John L. *art museum director*

Fayetteville
Etchison, Bruce *retired museum director, conservator*

Galeton
Bull, Inez Stewart *retired curator, director, singer, writer, musician, educator*

Harrisburg
Buss, George Edward, Jr. *museum program director*
Mahey, John Andrew *retired museum director*

Merion Station
Gillman, Derek A. *museum director, academic administrator*

Monessen
Vivian, Cassandra *museum administrator, write photographer*

Philadelphia
Bantel, Linda Mae *former museum curator, consultant*
Bloom, Joel N. *science museum director*
Burke, Brother Daniel *museum director, educa*
McNamara, Kevin John *museum administrator*
Reimer, Charles Wilson *curator, consultant*
Shoemaker, Innis Howe *art museum curator*
van Rhyn, Jacqueline J. *curator*
Wint, Dennis Michael *museum director*

Pittsburgh
Bodine, William Beekman, Jr. *museum directo*
Dawson, Mary Ruth *curator, educator*
Hillenbrand, David M. *museum administrator*
King, Elaine A. *curator, art historian, critic*

Reading
DeEsch, Vasti F. *museum registrar*
Dietrich, Bruce Leinbach *museum administrat astronomer, educator*

Sewickley
Kornetchuk, Elena *curator, art dealer*

Strasburg
Lindsay, George Carroll *former museum direc*

University Park
Muhlert, Jan Keene *art museum director*

Wynnewood
Camp, Kimberly N. *museum administrator, artist*

RHODE ISLAND

Providence
Fishman, Bernard Philip *museum director*

Saunderstown
Leavitt, Thomas Whittlesey *retired museum director, educator*

SOUTH CAROLINA

Charleston
Long, J. Grahame *curator*
Richardson, Anne Worsham *art gallery owner, artist*
Sloan, Mark Hamilton *art gallery director, educator, author*

Greenville
Davis, Joan Carroll *retired museum director*

Mount Pleasant
Macdonald, Robert Rigg, Jr. *retired museum director*

Pawleys Island
Matelic, Candace Tangorra *museum director, educator*
Noble, Joseph Veach *retired museum director*

West Columbia
Harmon, Horace Elmer, Jr. *museum director, consultant*

TENNESSEE

Greeneville
Corey, Mark *historic site director*

Johnson City
Gerhardt, E. Alvin, Jr. *retired museum director*

Oak Ridge
Shapiro, Selma *retired museum director*

TEXAS

Canyon
ela, Richard Joseph *conservator, educator*

Corpus Christi
ocke, Michelle Ivy *curator*

Dallas
offman, Marguerite Steed *former art gallery director*
ane, John Rodger *museum director*
udolph, William Keyse *curator*
ucker, Kevin W. *curator*

El Paso
piora, Leonard Paul *retired museum director, art appraiser*

Fort Worth
uping, Michael G. *curator*
otts, Timothy F. *museum director*
ler, Ronnie Curtis *museum director, art historian*
arner, Malcolm John *curator*

Fredericksburg
anhart, Marcia Y(ockey) *art museum director*

Houston
owron, Edgar Peters *art museum curator, administrator*
reene, Alison de Lima *curator*
e, Janie C. *curator*
arzio, Peter Cort *museum director*
amirez, Mari Carmen *curator*
verance, Diana Lynn *curator*
rauss, Cindi *curator*
cker, Anne Wilkes *curator, historian, photographer, critic*

ost
eff, Marie Taylor *museum director, artist*

Round Top
rnon, Karen *art gallery owner, educator*

San Antonio
rilleaux, Rene Paul *curator*
iego, William J. *museum director*

UTAH

Logan
vis, Daniel M. *curator, librarian*

Provo
ay, Campbell *museum director*

Salt Lake City
orge, Sarah B. *museum director*

VERMONT

Bennington
anklin, Jamie *curator, consultant*
lliams, Robert Joseph *retired museum director, educator*

Manchester
Kouwenhoven, Gerrit Wolphertsen *retired museum director*

Montpelier
Dumville, John P. *historic site director*

Waitsfield
Dodds, Judy B. *curator, consultant, artist*

VIRGINIA

Alexandria
Lundeberg, Philip Karl Boraas *curator, historian*

Arlington
Demetrion, James Thomas *retired museum director, consultant*
Gurian, Elaine Heumann *museum consultant*

Charlottesville
Linden, Peppy G. *museum director*

Kilmarnock
Ibañez, Alvaro *museum director, patent design company executive, artist*

Lynchburg
Elson, James Martin *retired landmark director*

Mc Lean
Forman, Lee Lavinthal *museum administrator*

Richmond
Nyerges, Alexander Lee *museum director*
O'Leary, Elizabeth Lokey *curator*
Rasmussen, William Meade Stith *curator, historian*
Ravenal, John B. *curator*

Roanoke
Fitzgerald, Mary Eileen *museum program director*

Sterling
Friedheim, Jerry Warden *museum consultant*

Tazewell
Weeks, Ross Leonard, Jr. *museum executive*

Williamsburg
Christison, Muriel Branham *retired museum director, art history educator*
Sullivan, Timothy Jackson *museum and retired academic administrator, educator*

WASHINGTON

Bainbridge Island
Cosgrove, Theresa Margaret *museum director*

Bellevue
Warren, James Ronald *retired museum director, journalist*

Bellingham
Clark-Langager, Sarah Ann *curator, academic administrator*

Goldendale
Skillern, Michael Phillip *museum administrator*

Redmond
Sobey, Edwin J. C. *museum director, oceanographer, consultant*

Seattle
Andrews, Richard Otis *museum director*
Bufano, Ralph A. *retired museum executive*
Chew, Ron Alpha *museum director*
Gates, Mimi Gardner *museum director*

Tacoma
Callan, Josi Irene *museum director*

WISCONSIN

Madison
Garver, Thomas Haskell *curator, consultant, writer*
Garvre, Fanny P. *art gallery owner*

Milwaukee
Peltz, Cissie Jean *art gallery director, cartoonist*

Prairie Du Sac
Seltzner, Rachel *curator, science educator*

Racine
Taragin, Davira Spiro *curator*

WYOMING

Cody
Donoghue, Ann Marie *museum administrator, consultant*

Laramie
Guerin, Charles Allan *museum director, artist*
Moldenhauer, Susan *museum director, curator*

CANADA

ALBERTA

Canmore
Janes, Robert Roy *museum director, archaeologist, editor*

BRITISH COLUMBIA

Victoria
Finlay, James Campbell *retired museum director*

ONTARIO

London
Poole, Nancy Geddes *art gallery curator, writer*

Ottawa
McAvity, John Gillis *museum director, association executive, museologist*

FRANCE

Biarritz
Friedman, Richard Everett *curator, art appraiser*

HUNGARY

Budapest
Gotsch, John Warren *contemporary arts house director*

MADAGASCAR

Antananarivo
Rakotoarisoa, Jean Aimé *director museum*

ADDRESS UNPUBLISHED

Abram, Ruth Jacobeth *museum administrator and founder*
Adams, Margaret Bernice *retired museum official*
Ahrens, Kent *museum director, art historian*
Anderson, Dean William *museum consultant*
Bishop, Budd Harris *retired museum director*
Booker, Nana Laurel *art gallery owner, honorary consul*
Castile, Rand (Jesse Randolph III) *retired museum director*
Cikovsky, Nicolai, Jr. *retired curator, art historian, educator*
Cilella, Salvatore George, Jr. *museum director*
Collischan, Judy Kay *art gallery director, museum director, critic, artist*
Deutsch, James I. *curator*
Deutschman, Louise Tolliver *curator*
Douglas, Diane Miriam *museum director*
Doyle, Christine Ellen *museum researcher, educator*
Ebie, William D. *retired museum director*
Erwin, Douglas Hamilton *museum director, paleobiologist*
Faunce, Sarah Cushing *retired curator*
Frankel, Diane *former museum institute administrator*
Fri, Robert Wheeler *retired museum director*
Friedman, Martin *museum director, arts adviser*
Furlong, George Morgan, Jr. *museum program director, retired military officer*
Gabriel, Jeanette Hanisee *curator, art historian*
Glenn, Constance White *art museum director, educator, consultant*
Greenwald, Alice Marian *museum director*
Gribbon, Deborah *museum director*
Grinell, Sheila *museum director*
Grossman, Cissy *curator, art historian, appraiser*
Hall, Robert L. *curator, educator*
Hasse, John Edward *music curator*
Hayes, Charles Franklin III *retired museum director*
Hellmers, Norman Donald *retired historic site director*
Herwig, Nelson Gene *retired curator, retired counselor*
Hightower, John Brantley *retired museum administrator*
Hodson, Sara Suzanne *manuscripts curator*
Ives, Colta Feller *museum curator, educator*
Jacobowitz, Ellen Sue *curator, museum administrator*
Kahn, James Steven *retired museum director*
Kelm, Bonnie G. *art museum director, educator, art appraiser, consultant*
Klobe, Tom *retired art gallery director*
Knowles, Elizabeth Pringle *museum director*
Krakosky, Norah *historic site staff member*
Krens, Thomas *museum director*
Lutts, Ralph Herbert *scholar, educator, museum administrator*
Malaro, Marie C. *retired museum administrator, lawyer*
McKinnon, Karl Luther *museum director*
Melder, Keith E. *retired curator*
Mercuri, Joan B. *museum administrator*
Metcalf, William Edwards *museum curator, educator*
Millard, Charles Warren III *museum director, writer*
Morris, Jack Austin, Jr. *art gallery executive*
Naeve, Milo Merle *retired curator, director*
Nasgaard, Roald *museum curator*
Neidich-Ryder, Carole Louise *curator, educator*
Newman, Bruce Murray *retired art gallery owner*
Nickles, Shelley Kaplan *curator, educator*
Organ, Rita C. *museum administrator, consultant*
Pal, Pratapaditya *curator*
Perrot, Paul Norman *museum director*
Pitman-Gelles, Bonnie Louise *museum administrator, educator*
Prakapas, Eugene Joseph *art gallery director*
Reuther, Ronald Theodore *museum director*
Rigaud, Edwin Joseph *museum administrator*
Robertson, Charles James *museum director emeritus*
Rouse, Terrie Suzitte *museum director*
Ryskamp, Charles Andrew *museum director, educator*
Sadinsky, Rachael *curator, art appraiser*
Saunders, Richard Henry III *museum director*
Schlageter, Robert William *museum administrator*
Schneider, Janet M. *museum administrator, painter, curator*
Schoener, Allon *museum and organization consultant*
Sebolt-George, Alberta *retired museum administrator*
Segger, Martin Joseph *museum director, educator, art historian*
Selin, Nina Evvie *museum director, electric power industry executive, volunteer*
Sherrell-Leo, Cindy *retired museum administrator*
Shimoda, Jerry Yasutaka *retired national historic park manager*
Sill, Robert Michael *curator*
Sims, Lowery Stokes *museum curator and administrator, writer, educator*
Skramstad, Harold Kenneth, Jr. *museum consultant*
Small, Lawrence M. *former museum executive*
Starr, Maurice Kenneth (Kenneth Starr) *museum director*
Steadman, David Wilton *retired museum director, deacon*
Stearns, Robert Leland *curator*
Storr, Robert *curator, art educator, painter*
Stuart, Joseph Martin *museum administrator*
Subotnick, Ali *curator, writer*
Summerfield, John Robert *textile curator*
Trutor, Genevieve Williamson *museum director*
Virani, Shanil *data analyst*
Walker, Roslyn Adele *retired museum director*
Way, Jacob Edson III *museum director*
Weber, Jean Macphail *museum director*
West, W. Richard *museum director*
Williams, Patterson Bouic *museum program director*
Wilson, Karen Lee *museum staff member, researcher*
Yates, Steven A. *curator, artist*

INDUSTRY: MANUFACTURING
See also **FINANCE: FINANCIAL SERVICES**

UNITED STATES

ALABAMA

Albertville
Rice, Fuhrman D. (Runt Rice) *retired paper company executive*

Birmingham
Bennett, Joe Claude *pharmaceutical executive*
Cohen-DeMarco, Gale Maureen *pharmaceutical executive*
Gorrie, M. Miller *construction executive*
Hall, Robert Alan *construction company executive*
James, Donald M. *construction materials executive*
Neal, Phil Hudson, Jr. *retired manufacturing executive*
Sklenar, Herbert Anthony *industrial products manufacturing company executive*
Styslinger, Lee Joseph, Jr. *manufacturing executive*

Gadsden
Farr, Dwayne Louis *automotive executive*

Montgomery
Taylor, Watson Robbins *construction company executive*

Opelika
Jenkins, Richard Lee *manufacturing executive*

Valley
Ogle, D. Clark *textiles executive*

ALASKA

Haines
Kaufman, David Graham *construction executive*

ARIZONA

Carefree
Wearly, William Levi *retired manufacturing executive*

Chandler
Kim, James Joo-Jin *electronics company executive*

Mesa
DeRosa, Francis Dominic *chemical company executive*

Peoria
Cook, Mary Margaret *steamfitter, educator*

Phoenix
Carter, Ronald Martin, Sr. *pharmaceutical executive*
Church, Steve *electronics executive*
Dewane, John Richard *retired manufacturing executive, small business owner*
Giedt, Bruce Alan *paper company executive*

Giltner, Phil (F. Phillips Giltner III) *food distributing executive*
Hamada, Rick *electronics executive*
Kamins, Edward *electronics executive*
Klepinger, John William *trailer manufacturing company executive*
Mondry, Lawrence N. *automotive executive*
Phillips, Steve *electronics executive*
Sadowski, Raymond *electronics executive*
Stegmayer, Joseph Henry *housing industry executive*
Vallee, Roy A. *electronics executive*
White, Edward Allen *electronics executive*

Prescott
Forth, Kevin Bernard *beverage distributing industry consultant*
Parkhurst, Charles Lloyd *electronics executive*

Scottsdale
Farley, James Newton *retired manufacturing executive, electrical engineer*
Freedman, Stanley Marvin *manufacturing executive*
Gans, Eugene Howard *cosmetic and pharmaceutical company executive, consultant*
Grenell, James Henry *retired manufacturing company executive*
Howard, William Gates, Jr. *electronics company executive*
Jesky, T. J. *pharmaceutical products executive*
Kolander, David J. *retired chemicals executive*
Levine, Stanley Walter *chemical company executive*
Lloyd, Eugene Walter *retired construction company executive*
Rethore, Bernard Gabriel *manufacturing and mining company executive, consultant*
Van Brunt, Gary T. *tire dealer company executive*
Walsh, Edward Joseph *food products and cosmetics executive*

Surprise
Lazar, Max Seymour *retired pharmaceutical company executive*

Tempe
Fulton, Ira *construction executive*

Tucson
Acker, Loren Calvin *medical products executive*
Francesconi, Louise L. *defense equipment manufacturing company executive*
Leonard, Michael A. *retired automotive executive*
Repp, Page W., Jr. *construction executive*

ARKANSAS

Fort Smith
Flanders, Donald Hargis *manufacturing executive*

Little Rock
Bell, Richard Eugene *agricultural products executive, state official*
Givens, John Kenneth *automotive executive*
Shell, Robert J. *construction executive*

Springdale
Bond, Richard L. *food products executive*
Leatherby, Dennis *food products executive*
Miquelon, Wade D. *food products executive*
Schaffer, Archie III *food products executive*
Tyson, John H. *food products executive*

Tontitown
McMennamy, Roger Neal *automotive executive*

CALIFORNIA

Alameda
Caldwell, William Mackay, IV, *cloning and stem cell research company executive*

Alamo
Liggett, Lawrence Melvin *vacuum equipment manufacturing company executive*

Atherton
Goodman, Sam Richard *electronics executive*
Hogan, Clarence Lester *retired electronics executive*

Belmont
Endriz, John Guiry *retired electronics executive*

Berkeley
Coffman, Robert Lee *pharmaceutical executive*
Janney, Daniel S. *health products executive*
Mettinger, Karl Lennart *pharmaceutical executive*

Beverly Hills
Winthrop, John *wines and spirits company executive*

Brisbane
Mashouf, Manny *apparel executive*

Burbank
Joseff, Joan Castle *manufacturing executive*
Raulinaitis, Pranas Algis *electronics executive, consultant*

Burlingame
Azarnoff, Daniel Lester *pharmaceutical executive, consultant*

Calabasas
Dreier, R. Chad *construction and mortgage company executive*

Camarillo
Cleary, Thomas Charles *technology company executive*

Weiss, Carl *aerospace company executive*

Carlsbad
Baker, Donna M. *research and development company executive, lawyer*
Crooke, Stanley Thomas *pharmaceutical executive*

Carmel Valley
Kasson, James Matthews *electronics executive*

Carson
Bensussen, Gale K. *health products company executive*
Berenato, Joseph C. *manufacturing executive*
Heiser, James S. *manufacturing executive*

Chatsworth
Bhartia, Prakash *defense research management executive, educator*

Chino
Goodman, Lindsey Alan *furniture manufacturing executive, architect*

Claremont
Forti, William Bell *manufacturing executive*
Tollenaere, Lawrence Robert *retired industrial products company executive*

Colusa
Carter, Jane Foster *agricultural industry executive*

Corona
Chao, Allen Y. *pharmaceutical executive*

Coronado
Sack, Edgar Albert *electronics company executive*

Costa Mesa
Mohajer, Dineh *cosmetics company executive*

Cowan Heights
Ruttencutter, Brian Boyle *manufacturing company executive*

Crestline
Merrill, Steven William *research and development company executive*

Culver City
Leve, Alan Donald *electronics executive*

Cupertino
Mathias, Leslie Michael *electronic manufacturing company executive*
Sobrato, John A. *construction executive*

Dublin
Whetten, John D. *food products executive*

El Segundo
Thiry, Kent J. *health products executive*

Emeryville
Chiasson, William B. *electronic games executive*
Goldstein, Jack *biopharmaceutical executive, microbiologist*
Kalinske, Thomas J. *education, video game and toy company executive*
Katz, Jeffrey G. *electronic games executive*
Pien, Howard *pharmaceutical executive*
Renton, Hollings C. *health products executive*

Encino
Darvish, Daniel K. *research and development company executive, director*

Escalon
Barton, Gerald Lee *food products executive*

Escondido
Gerhardt, Emery William *food products executive*

Fair Oaks
Chernev, Melvin *retired beverage company executive*

Foster City
Denny, James M. *pharmaceutical and former retail executive*
Martin, John C. *pharmaceutical company executive*
Rabbat, Guy *electronics executive, consultant*
Rosen, Howard B. *biopharmaceutical company executive*

Fountain Valley
Hoffman, Richard W. *automotive executive*
Wilhite, Steve *automotive executive*

Fremont
Alsborg, Thomas C. *electronics executive*
Bagley, James W. *semiconductor equipment company executive*
Huang, Robert *electronics executive*
Korn, Laurence *health products executive*
Newberry, Stephen G. *semiconductor equipment company executive*
Polk, Dennis *electronics executive*
Rusch, Thomas William *manufacturing executive*
Zimmer, George A. *men's apparel executive*

Fullerton
Garrett, Scott T. *medical products executive*
Miller, Arnold *electronics executive*

Hillsborough
Keller, John Francis *retired food products executive, mayor*

Hollywood
Parks, Robert Myers *appliance manufacturing company executive*

Huntington Beach
McKnight, Robert B., Jr. *sporting goods manufacturing executive*

Irvine
Alspach, Philip Halliday *manufacturing executive*
McGregor, Scott A. *electronics company executive*
Pyott, David Edmund Ian *pharmaceutical executive*
Scarborough, Stephen J. *construction executive*
Wetterau, Mark S. *food products/distributor executive*

La Jolla
Elander, Richard Paul *microbiologist, consultant*
Geckler, Richard Delph *retired metal products executive*
Snyder, Evan *cloning and stem cell company administrator, neuroscientist, educator*

La Palma
McNamee, Lawrence Ross, Jr. *manufacturing executive*

La Puente
Hitchcock, Frederick E., Jr., (Fritz) *automotive company executive*

Lake Forest
Higby, Lawrence M. *medical products executive*

Lompoc
Bongiorno, James William *electronics executive*

Los Altos
Beer, Clara Louise Johnson *retired electronics executive*

Los Angeles
Adler, Fred Peter *retired electronics company executive*
Atchley, Raymond Deval *technology company executive*
Birren, James Emmett *research and development company executive*
Campion, Robert Thomas *manufacturing executive*
Charney, Dov *apparel executive*
dePaolis, Potito Umberto *food company executive*
Hannah, David H. *metal products executive*
Hutchins, Joan Morthland *manufacturing executive, farmer*
Mezger, Jeffrey T. *construction executive*
Murdock, David H. *food products executive*
Perkins, William Clinton *manufacturing executive*
Resnick, Stewart Allen *diversified company executive*
Tamkin, S. Jerome *manufacturing executive, consultant*

Lynwood
Nelson, Maurice Sandy, Jr. *metal products company executive*

Marina Del Rey
Bennett, Joel Herbert *construction executive*

Mckinleyville
Thueson, David Orel *pharmaceutical executive, researcher, writer, educator*

Menlo Park
Carlson, Curtis R. *electronics research industry executive*
Halperin, Robert Milton *retired electrical machinery company executive*
Jackson, Jeanne Pellegren *apparel executive*
Kamin, William Stephen *food products executive, photographer*
Marks, Michael E. *electronics executive*
Moos, Walter Hamilton *pharmaceutical company executive*
Saifer, Mark Gary Pierce *pharmaceutical executive*
Taft, David Dakin *chemicals executive*
Westcott, Brian John *manufacturing executive*

Milpitas
Hasler, William Albert *electronics executive*
Lin Chien, Chester *electronics executive*
London, Craig *electronics executive*
O'Connor, Kevin *electronics executive*
Patel, Kiran *manufacturing executive*
Wang, Susan S. *manufacturing executive*

Mission Viejo
Faley, Robert Lawrence *retired instruments company executive*

Montecito
Meghreblian, Robert Vartan *manufacturing executive, physicist*
Purl, O. Thomas *retired electronics company executive*

Monterey
Hanlon, James Allison *confectionery company executive*
Nesheim, Robert Olaf *retired food products executive*

Newport Beach
Bennett, Bruce W. *retired construction executive, civil engineer*
Johnson, William Stanley *metal distribution company executive*
Kaye, Michael S. *corporate executive*
Lyon, William, Sr. *construction executive*

Oakland
Heinrich, Daniel J. *chemicals executive*

Oakville
Mondavi, Robert Gerald *winery executive*

Oceanside
Montgomery, Michael Davis *research and development company executive, real estate investor*

Ojai
Parsons, Richard Walter *construction executive*

Orange
Kaempen, Charles Edward *manufacturing executive*

Palm Desert
Epstein, Marvin Morris *retired construction company executive*

Palo Alto
Balzhiser, Richard Earl *research and development company executive*
Bennett, Alan Jerome *electronics executive, physicist*
Guertin, Timothy E. *medical products executive*
Seethaler, William Charles *manufacturing executive*
Smith, Julie Ann *pharmaceutical executive*
Solomon, Darlene J.S. *electronics executive*
Staprans, Armand *electronics executive*
Sullivan, William P. *electronics executive*

Palos Verdes Peninsula
Grant, Robert Ulysses *retired manufacturing executive*
Leone, William Charles *retired manufacturing executive*
Thomas, Hayward *retired manufacturing executive*
Wilson, Theodore Henry *retired electronics executive, aerospace engineer*

Pasadena
Bishop, Robert Calvin *pharmaceutical compan executive*
Hunter, Milton *construction company executive retired career military officer*
Marlen, James S. *chemical, plastics and buildi materials manufacturing company executive*
McNulty, James F. *construction company executive*
Smith, Howard Russell *manufacturing executiv director*
Smith, Ora Everett *corporate executive, lawyer*
Wadden, Christopher David *food products executive*
Watson, Noel G. *construction executive*

Placerville
Sundgren, Donald E. *construction executive*

Playa Del Rey
Mishelevich, David Jacob *medical products executive*

Pleasanton
Ching, David T. *food products executive*
Gordon, Robert A. *food products executive, lawyer*

Portola Valley
Graham, William James *packaging company executive*

Rancho Dominguez
Janura, Jan Arol *apparel manufacturing executive*

Rancho Murieta
Irelan, Robert Withers *retired metal products executive*

Rancho Santa Fe
Derbes, Daniel William *manufacturing executi*
Jordan, Charles Morrell *retired automotive designer*
Root, Alan Charles *diversified manufacturing company executive*
Step, Eugene Lee *retired pharmaceutical executive*

Redding
Emmerson, Archie Aldis (Red Emmerson, A.A Emmerson) *sawmill owner*

Redondo Beach
Kagiwada, Reynold Shigeru *electronics execu*

Redwood City
Bremser, George, Jr. *electronics executive*
Nosler, Peter Cole *construction company executive*
Wang, Chen Chi *electronics executive, real estate company executive, diversified financ services company executive*

Rescue
Ackerly, Wendy Saunders *construction compa executive*

Richmond
Biddle, Michael *plastics company executive*

Riverside
Chamberlain, Willard Thomas *retired metal products executive*
Smith, Elden Leroy *recreational vehicle and manufactured housing company executive*

Rocklin
Tal, Jacob *electronics executive*

Sacramento
Aldrich, Thomas Albert *former brewing executive, consultant*
Baccigaluppi, Roger John *agricultural produc executive*

Anselmo
'erini, John Edward *construction company ecutive*

Carlos
ıard, Martin *automotive executive, ctronics engineer*

Clemente
:, Earnest Hubert, Jr. *tool company ecutive*
berg, Howard *chemical company executive, nsultant*

Diego
ne, Brian Kiernan *pet food and supplies npany executive*
am, Ginger L. *pharmaceutical executive*
s, Richard B. *pharmaceutical executive*
ı, Dean Leslie *research and development mpany executive, golf consultant, writer*
, Atsuo *pharmaceutical executive*
s, Alan James *pharmaceutical executive, armacologist*
Gene Wells *industrial executive*
Clare I. *electronics company executive*
, William R. *biotechnology company ecutive*
os, Alexander Gus *construction and ofessional sports team executive*
ıas, Robert McGuffey *automotive executive, ucator*

Francisco
rson, R. John *apparel executive*
obell, Jeffrey C. *health products executive*
, Robert Douglas *apparel executive*
mergren, John H. *health products executive*
kins, Trip *electronics executive*
tt, George Frederick, Jr. *forest products mpany executive*
ı, Paul C. *health products executive*
cic, Paul E. *health products executive*
, David William *research executive*
oney, David L. *former pharmaceutical olesale and healthcare management mpany executive*
auley, Matthew K. *apparel executive*
or, Robert E. *building materials company ecutive, lawyer*
n, Marc *health products executive*
, Pamela J. *health products executive*
enfreund, Alan *retired pharmaceutical mpany executive*
kley, Douglas John *fire alarm company ecutive*
ager, Henrik C. *building services company ecutive*
tt, Randall N. *health products executive*
, Herbert Bullard *chemical manufacturing ecutive*
k, Paul John III *construction executive*
'ord, Richard G. *food products executive*
erbach, William Joseph *retired paper mpany executive*

Jose
W. Donald *electronics executive*
John C. *electronics executive*
Richard S. *manufacturing executive*
Yido *electronics executive*
kawa, Koji Ogura *technology company 'ministrator*
a, Clements Edward *electronics company ecutive*
egos, George *electronics executive*
gers, T(hurman) J. *semiconductor company ecutive*
so, Paul M. *electronics executive*
oeder, Kenneth L. *electronics executive*
, Jure *electronics executive*
e, David L. *electronics executive*
, Brad A. *research and development mpany executive, biologist*

Luis Obispo
ivan, Thomas James *retired manufacturing mpany executive*

Mateo
nedy, W(ilbert) Keith, Jr. *retired electronics ecutive, transportation executive*

ıta Ana
ngartner, Anton Edward *automotive sales ofessional*

ıta Barbara
in, Dwight Clay *retired grain company ecutive*
ne, Joshua H. *medical products executive*
dle, William Roscoe *retired glass company ecutive*

ıta Clara
ett, Craig R. *electronics company executive*
ett, Ronald W. *biopharmaceutical executive*
dy, Kenneth Charles *pharmaceutical ecutive*
is, George S. *manufacturing executive*
s, Richard J., Jr. *electronics company ecutive*
gin, Federico *electronics executive*
ve, Andrew Steven *electronics executive*
a, Brian L. *electronics executive*
ng, Jen-Hsun *electronics executive*
ore, Gordon E. *electronics executive, searcher*
gan, James C. *manufacturing executive*
ray, Patricia *electronics company executive*
llini, Paul S. *electronics company executive*
o, Mark R. *manufacturing executive*
nter, Michael R. *manufacturing executive*

ıta Rosa
son, Jess S. *vintner*

Saratoga
Houston, Joseph Brantley, Jr. *optical instrument company executive*
Rollo, F. David *healthcare company executive, cardiologist*

Sherman Oaks
Reiner, Thomas Karl *manufacturing executive, engineering scientist*

Simi Valley
Lewis, Richard B. *manufacturing and logistics executive*

Soquel
Cureton, Glen *pharmaceutical executive*

South San Francisco
Brewer, Richard B. *biotechnology company executive*
Desmond-Hellmann, Susan *medical products manufacturing executive*
Lacey, David *biotechnology company executive*
Lipsky, Ian David *biochemical manufacturing executive, director*
Potter, Myrtle S. *research and development company executive*

Stanford
Elliott, David Duncan III *science company executive*
Miller, William Frederick *research and development company executive, educator, financial consultant*

Sunnyvale
Brachman, Ron *research and development company executive*
Burkett, Marvin D. *electronics executive*
Doluca, Tunc *electronics executive*
Gifford, John F. *retired electronics executive*
McCollam, Craig A. *manufacturing executive*

Sylmar
Tutor, Ronald N. *construction executive*

Thousand Oaks
Bonanni, Fabrizio *medical products executive*
Bradway, Robert *medical products executive*
Daly, Jim *medical products executive*
Dere, Willard Honglen *medical products executive*
Fenton, Dennis Michael *medical products executive*
Flanagan, Thomas James *medical products executive*
Harper, Sean *medical products executive*
McNamee, Brian *medical products executive*
Miletich, Joseph P. *medical products executive*
Morrow, George J. *medical products executive*
Perlmutter, Roger *medical products executive*
Sharer, Kevin W. *medical products executive*

Torrance
Amemiya, Koichi *motor vehicle company executive*

Tulare
Regan, Timothy James *grain company executive*

Tustin
Hester, Norman Eric *chemical company technical executive, chemist*

Ukiah
Newell, Barbara Ann *coatings company executive*

Upland
Goodman, John M. *construction executive*

Valencia
Mann, Alfred *pharmaceutical executive*

Vallejo
Womack, Thomas Houston *manufacturing executive*

Ventura
Barber, Jerry Randel *retired medical device company executive*
Chouinard, Yvon *sportswear outfitter executive*

Villa Park
Hawe, David Lee *manufacturing consultant, venture capitalist*

Walnut
Johnson, Keith Liddell *retired chemicals executive*

Watsonville
Dorey, William G. *construction executive*
Watts, David H. *construction company executive*

West Hollywood
Estevez, Luis de Galvez *designer, manufacturer*

Westlake Village
Colburn, Keith W. *electronics executive*
DeLorenzo, David A. *food products executive*

Wilmington
Hamai, James Yutaka *manufacturing executive*

Woodland Hills
Gellert, Jay M. *health and medical products executive*
Greaves, Roger F. *health and medical products executive*
Mayhew, Karin D. *health and medical products executive*
Olson, David W. *health and medical products executive*
Scheff, Jonathan H. *health and medical products executive*
Sivori, John P. *health and medical products executive*
Woys, James E. *health and medical products executive*

Woodside
Gates, Milo Sedgwick *retired construction company executive*

COLORADO

Arvada
Holden, George Fredric *food products executive, consultant, public information officer, writer*

Boulder
Clark, Melvin Eugene *chemical company executive*
Davies, David Huw *electronics executive, engineering company executive*
Mancino, John Gregory *software company executive*

Broomfield
Hoover, R. David *packaging company executive*

Colorado Springs
Stanley, David John *research and development company executive*

Denver
Barry, Henry Ford *chemicals executive*
Boyer, William Joseph *food products executive*
Hohner, Kenneth Dwayne *retired fodder company executive*
Leprino, James G. *food products executive*
Livingston, Johnston Redmond *manufacturing executive*
Mizel, Larry A. *housing construction company executive*
Oakes, Terry Louis *apparel executive*
Wolf, Timothy Van de Wint *food products executive*

Englewood
Gertz, David Lee *homebuilding company executive*

Fort Collins
Watz, Martin Charles *brewery consultant*

Golden
Coors, Peter Hanson *brewery company executive*
Kiely, W. Leo III *brewery company executive*

Greeley
Carrico, Stephen J. *construction company executive*
Cordell, Larry Kenneth (L. Kenny) *agricultural products executive*
Morgensen, Jerry Lynn *construction company executive*
Rovit, Sam Brian *food products executive*
Silcock, Raymond P. *food products executive*

Greenwood Village
Appel, Joel *household cleaner manufacturing executive*

Jefferson
Maatsch, Deborah Joan *manufacturing executive*

Lakewood
Heath, Gary Brian *manufacturing executive, engineer*

Littleton
Battilega, John A. *research and development company executive*
Dasgupta, Arijit (Bapi) *agricultural products executive*

Wellington
Grant, Lewis O. *agricultural products executive, meteorology educator*

CONNECTICUT

Bloomfield
Coburn, Richard Joseph *electronics executive, electrical engineer*
Hermann, Robert Jay *former manufacturing executive, consultant*

Branford
Chapman, Roger Stevens, Jr. *construction company executive*
Rothberg, Jonathan M. *medical products executive, researcher*

Bridgeport
Semple, Cecil Snowdon *retired manufacturing executive*

Bristol
Barnes, Carlyle Fuller *manufacturing executive*
Barnes, Wallace *manufacturing executive*

Broad Brook
Kement, Isabella Viniconis *retired construction company executive*

Cheshire
Keiser, David Wharton *pharmaceutical executive*

Danbury
Angel, Stephen F. *chemicals executive*
Good, Jennifer L. *pharmaceutical executive*
Sawyer, James S. *manufacturing executive*

Darien
Dordelman, William Forsyth *food company executive*
Sprole, Frank Arnott *retired pharmaceutical executive, lawyer*

Dayville
Funk, Michael S. *food products executive*

Fairfield
Beccalli-Falco, Ferdinando *manufacturing executive*
Daley, Pamela *diversified services, technology and manufacturing company executive*
Dineen, John C. *manufacturing executive*
Donnelly, Scott C. *manufacturing executive*
Johnsen, Walter Craig *manufacturing executive*
Reif, Deborah *manufacturing executive*
Trotter, Lloyd G. *manufacturing executive*

Greenwich
Cameron, Dort *electronics executive*
Dettmer, Robert Gerhart *retired beverage company executive*
Farbish, Alfred B. *waterproofing materials executive*
Mango, Wilfred Gilbert, Jr. *construction, real estate company executive*

Hartford
Bousbib, Ari *manufacturing executive*
Chênevert, Louis *manufacturing executive*
Darnis, Geraud *manufacturing executive*
David, George Alfred Lawrence *manufacturing executive*
Doucette, John J. *manufacturing executive*
Finger, Stephen N. *aircraft manufacturing executive*

Lyme
Bloom, Barry Malcolm *research and development company executive, consultant*

Madison
Golembeski, Jerome John *manufacturing executive*

Middlebury
Fickenscher, Gerald H. *chemicals company executive*

Milford
Palazzi, Joseph Lazarro *manufacturing executive*

Naugatuck
Flannery, Joseph Patrick *manufacturing executive, director*

New Canaan
Burns, Ivan Alfred *grocery products and industrial company executive*
Sachs, John Peter *carbon company executive*

New Haven
Jacob, Deirdre Ann Bradbury *manufacturing executive, finance educator, consultant*

North Branford
Ingram, George *manufacturing executive*

Norwalk
Guzzi, Anthony J. *construction executive*
Harris, Holton Edwin *plastics machinery manufacturing executive*
MacInnis, Frank T. *construction and holding company executive, securities trader*
White, Tony L. *health and medical products executive*

Old Lyme
Mangin, Charles-Henri *electronics company executive*

Plainville
Glassman, Gerald Seymour *metal products executive*

Ridgefield
Levine, Paul Michael *paper company executive, consultant*

Riverside
Deering, Allan Brooks *retired soft drink company executive*

Somers
Blake, Stewart Prestley *retired ice cream company executive*

South Kent
Samartini, James Rogers *retired appliance company executive*

Southport
Wheeler, Wilmot Fitch, Jr. *diversified manufacturing company executive*

Stafford
Klatell, Robert Edward *retired electronics executive, lawyer*

Stamford
Allott, Anthony J. *packaging industry executive*
Buzzard, James A. *paper, packaging and chemical company executive*
Caldwell, Philip *retired automobile manufacturing and finance company executive*
Critelli, Michael J. *manufacturing executive, lawyer*
Evans, Robert Sheldon *manufacturing executive, director*
Faraci, John Vincent, Jr. *paper company executive*
Fast, Eric Carson *manufacturing executive*
Friedman, Michael *pharmaceutical executive*
Gladstone, Herbert Jack *manufacturing executive*
Gross, Ronald Martin *forest products executive, consultant*
Horrigan, D. Gregory *packaging products executive*
Lesko, Newland A. *paper company executive*
Levitan, Gutman *research and development company executive, communications engineer*

Luke, John Anderson, Jr. *paper, packaging and chemical company executive*
Martin, Murray D. *manufacturing executive*
Munera, Gerard Emmanuel *manufacturing executive*
Nevans, Roy Norman *food products executive, producer*
Parrs, Marianne M. *paper and lumber company executive*
Silver, R. Philip *packaging products executive*
Thomas, Dennis *retired paper company executive, federal official*

Thomaston
Mühlanger, Erich *ski manufacturing company executive*

Wallingford
Cohen, Gordon S. *health products executive*
Loeffler, Martin H. *electronics executive*

Waterbury
Luedke, Frederick Lee *manufacturing executive*
Wood, Robert L. *chemicals executive*

West Hartford
Raffay, Stephen Joseph *manufacturing executive, director*

Westport
Baker, Leonard Morton *manufacturing executive*
Breitbarth, S. Robert *manufacturing executive*
Defeo, Ronald M. *machinery manufacturing executive*
Hedge, Arthur Joseph, Jr. *manufacturing executive*
Riordan, Thomas J. *manufacturing executive*

DELAWARE

Dagsboro
Mortenson, Thomas Theodore *health products executive, management consultant*

Greenville
Miller, Duane King *health and beauty care company executive*

Newark
Gantzer, Mary Lou *medical products executive*

Rockland
Rubin, Alan A. *pharmaceutical and biotechnology consultant*

Wilmington
Anton, David L. *research and development company executive, biotechnologist, researcher*
Borel, James Calvin *chemical company executive*
Connelly, Thomas M., Jr. *chemicals executive*
Davis, John Ripoll *manufacturing executive*
Goodmanson, Richard R. *chemicals executive*
Gulyas, Diane H. *manufacturing executive*
Holliday, Chad (Charles O. Holliday Jr.) *chemicals executive*
Holtzman, Arnold Harold *chemical company executive*
Keefer, Jeffrey L. *chemicals executive*
Kullman, Ellen Jamison *chemicals executive*
Lassen, John Kai *development company executive*
McLeer Free, Laureen Dorothy *drug development and pharmaceutical professional*
Rogerson, Craig Allan *manufacturing executive*
Rose, Selwyn H. *chemicals executive*
Sager, Philip Travis *pharmaceutical executive, cardiologist, researcher*
Uffner, Michael S. *automotive executive*
Vaddi, Krishna *pharmaceutical executive*

DISTRICT OF COLUMBIA

Washington
Andrews, Bruce *automotive executive, lawyer*
Becker, Brenda L. *medical products executive, former federal official*
Beier, David *medical products executive*
Brown, Lester Russell *research and development company executive*
Choudhury, Raj Deo *automotive executive*
Clark, Jeffrey Raphiel *research and development company executive*
Cole, Kenneth W. *automotive executive*
Comas, Daniel L. *manufacturing executive*
Culp, H. Lawrence *manufacturing executive*
Giuliano, Louis J. *former industrial manufacturing company executive*
Gottschalk, Thomas A. *automotive executive, lawyer*
Griffin, Robert Thomas *automotive company executive*
Harman, Sidney *audio and video company executive*
Herrett, Richard Allison *agricultural research institute administrator*
Mathews, Jessica Tuchman *research executive, federal official, newswriter*
Moore, Robert Madison *food products executive, lawyer*
Paliwal, Dinesh C. *electronics executive*
Persinger, Del Louis *pharmaceutical company executive*
Principi, Anthony Joseph *pharmaceutical company executive, former secretary of veterans affairs*
Rales, Mitchell P. *automotive parts company executive*
Rales, Steven M. *automotive parts company executive*
Riche, Robert S. *research and development company executive*
Schorsch, Louis L. *metal products executive*
Shepherd, Alan J. *construction executive, management consultant*

FLORIDA

Amelia Island
Adelman, Robert Paul *retired construction executive, lawyer*

Bartow
Kincart, Robert Owen *technological executive*

Boca Raton
Feld, Joseph *construction executive*
Oussani, James John *manufacturing executive*
Wyatt, James Luther *drapery hardware company executive*

Bonita Springs
Costley, Gary Edward *food company executive*
Sargent, Charles Lee *manufacturing executive*

Boynton Beach
Honeycutt, Kevin *construction executive, consultant*
Jensen, Reuben Rolland *former automotive company executive*

Bradenton
Bailey, Higgins D. *health products executive*
Carnes, James Edward *retired electronics executive*
Dudley, Perry, Jr. *retired electronics executive*
Howe, Carroll Victor *construction equipment company executive*
Price, Edgar Hilleary, Jr. *manufacturing executive, consultant*

Cape Coral
Stuart, Robert *container manufacturing executive*

Clearwater
Chisholm, William DeWayne *retired contractor*
Kiehl, E. Robert *manufacturing executive, consultant*
Smith, Marion Pafford *retired avionics company executive*

Coral Gables
Burini, Sonia Montes de Oca *apparel manufacturing executive, public relations executive*
Jackson, Yvonne Ruth *former pharmaceutical executive*

Daytona Beach
Scott, John Brooks *retired research and development company executive*

Deerfield Beach
Brown, Colin *automotive executive*

Delray Beach
Goldenberg, George *retired pharmaceutical executive*

Fernandina Beach
Ash, Frederick Melvin *retired manufacturing executive*

Fort Lauderdale
Carter, James Thomas *contractor, pilot*
Jackson, Michael J. *automotive retail company executive*
Levy, Michael *electronic manufacturing company executive*
Maroone, Michael E. *automotive executive*
Peltzer, Douglas Lea *manufacturing executive*
Rojas, Jesus Jon *health products executive, researcher*
Short, Michael J. *automotive executive*

Fort Myers
Edmonds, Scott A. *apparel executive*
Haug, Warren R. *research and development consultant*
Wendeborn, Richard Donald *retired manufacturing executive*

Fort Pierce
Steel, Philip S. *manufacturing executive*

Green Cove Springs
Slade, Tom *manufacturing executive, political organization worker*

Heathrow
Darbelnet, Robert Louis *automobile association executive*

Hialeah
Engler, Eva Kay *dental and veterinary products company executive*

Highland Beach
Frager, Albert S. *retired food products executive*

Hobe Sound
Casey, Edward Paul *manufacturing executive*

Hollywood
Isenberg, Abraham Charles *shoe manufacturing company executive*
Spencer, Richard Thomas III *health products executive*

Holmes Beach
Kaiser, Albert Farr *manufacturing executive*

Islamorada
Gates, Richard Daniel *retired manufacturing executive*

Jacksonville
Bodkin, Lawrence Edward *inventor, essayist, research and development company executive, consultant*
Nussbaum, Bennett *food products executive*
Smith, David A. *medical services executive*
Thomas, Lee Muller *forest products company executive, former government official*
Welch, Philip Burland *electronics and office products company executive*

Jupiter
Feinberg, Herbert *apparel executive, real estate company executive*
Garfinkel, Harmon Mark *retired specialty chemicals company executive*

Key Largo
Davidson, Thomas Noel *metal products executive*

Lady Lake
Akins, Zane Vernon *agricultural products executive*

Lake Mary
Bindley, William Edward *pharmaceutical executive*

Lakeland
Hatten, William Seward *manufacturing executive, consultant*
Mutz, Oscar Ulysses *manufacturing and distribution executive*

Longboat Key
Dalgleish, Stuart McNaught *retired manufacturing executive*

Marco Island
Guerrant, David Edward *retired food company executive*
Moore, Faye Halfacre *jewelry manufacturer*

Melbourne
Buchanan, Richard Kent *electronics company executive*

Melbourne Beach
Glaubinger, Lawrence David *retired manufacturing company executive*

Merritt Island
Roub, Bryan R(oger) *electronics executive*

Miami
Becker, Steven Richard *beverage corporation executive, consultant*
Beckwitt, Richard *construction executive*
Borkan, William Noah *electronics executive, biomedical engineer, entrepreneur, venture capitalist, real estate developer*
Braman, Norman *automotive and former sports team executive*
de Cespedes, Jorge L. *pharmaceutical executive*
Frigo, James Peter Paul *industrial hardware company executive*
Frost, Phillip *pharmaceutical executive, dermatologist*
Gross, Bruce E. *construction executive*
Jaffe, Jonathan M. *construction executive*
Medina Milgrom, Genie *pharmaceutical company executive*
Miller, Stuart A. *construction executive*
Nahmad, Albert H. *manufacturing executive*
Risi, Louis James, Jr. *manufacturing executive*
Robins, Craig *construction executive*
Zubieta, Alberto Aleman *construction executive*

Miami Beach
Lanzkron, Rolf Wolfgang *manufacturing executive*

Naples
Askins, Wallace Boyd *manufacturing executive*
Butler, Frederick George *retired drug company executive*
Gade, Marvin Francis *retired paper company executive*
LaRusso, Anthony Carl *company executive, lecturer, consultant*
Salentine, Thomas James *pharmaceutical executive*
Sampson, John Eugene *food products executive, consultant*
Sekowski, Cynthia Jean *health products executive, medical consultant, contact lens specialist*
Swanson, Donald Frederick *retired food company executive*
Vanderslice, Thomas Aquinas *electronics executive*
von Arx, Dolph William *food products executive*

New Port Richey
Lake, Victor Hugo *former manufacturing company executive*
Maysilles, Daniel Bruce *pharmaceutical services executive*
Sebring, Marjorie Marie Allison *former home furnishings company executive*
Vajk, Hugo *manufacturing executive*

Orlando
Brownlee, Thomas Marshall *manufacturing executive*
Cawthon, Frank H. *retired construction company executive*
Hughes, David Henry *manufacturing executive*
Morgan, Thomas I. *manufacturing executive*
Smyth, Joseph Vincent *manufacturing executive*

Ormond Beach
Connors, Michele Perrott *wholesale beverage company executive*

Ozona
Bennett, John Joseph *electronics executive*

Palm Beach
Karman, James Anthony *manufacturing executive*

Palm Beach Gardens
Fleisher, Seymour *manufacturing executive*
Jaffe, Jeff Hugh *retired food products executive*
Staub, W. Arthur *health care products executive*

Palm City
Conklin, George Melville *retired food products executive*
Wishart, Ronald Sinclair *retired chemical company executive*

Palm Coast
Lewis, William Headley, Jr. *manufacturing executive*

Palm Harbor
Grace, John Eugene *business company executiv*

Pensacola
Jones, Harry Gordon *electronics executive*

Saint Petersburg
Lewis, Chris A. *manufacturing executive*
Main, Timothy L. *electronics company executiv*
Mills, William Harold, Jr. *construction executiv*
Morean, William D. *manufacturing executive*

Sarasota
Berkoff, Charles Edward *pharmaceutical and biotech consultant*
Daoust, Donald Roger *pharmaceutical executiv microbiologist, cosmetics executive*
Doores, Stephen Curtis *manufacturing executiv*
Jellison, Brian D. *manufacturing executive*
Miranda, Carlos Sa *food products company executive*
Mullane, John Francis *pharmaceutical executiv*
Wadsworth, Dyer Seymour *minerals executive*
West, Bob *pharmaceutical executive*

Stuart
Derrickson, William Borden *manufacturing executive*

Summerfield
McNulty, Carrell Stewart, Jr. *retired manufacturing executive, architect*

Tamarac
Auletta, Joan Miglorisi *construction company executive, mortgage and insurance broker*

Tampa
Flom, Edward Leonard *retired metal products executive*
Genter, John Robert *grocery industry executive*
Johnson, Thomas S. *electronics executive*
Moszkowski, Neal *health products executive*

Tavares
Gross, Paul Allan *health products executive*

Venice
Lanford, Luke Dean *retired electronics compar executive*

Vero Beach
Bright, Willard Mead *retired manufacturing executive, director*
Janicki, Robert Stephen *retired pharmaceutica executive*
Reed, Sherman Kennedy *chemicals executive, consultant*
Standish, John Spencer *textile manufacturing company executive*
Wilcox, Harry Wilbur, Jr. *retired manufacturin executive*

Village Of Golf
Boer, F. Peter *chemical company executive*

Wesley Chapel
Revelle, Donald Gene *manufacturing and heal care company executive, consultant*

West Palm Beach
Brown, Paul A. *medical services executive*
Fanjul, Alfie, Jr., (Alfonso Fanjul) *food produc executive*
Fanjul, Pepe (Josè Fanjul) *food products executive*
Furlaud, Richard Mortimer *pharmaceutical executive*
Jenkins, Ruben Lee *chemicals executive*
Marini, Alex P. *manufacturing executive*
Vecellio, Leo Arthur, Jr. *construction company executive*

Windermere
Hahn, Dowon *pharmaceutical researcher, educator*

Winter Park
Kincaid, Rodney Lyle *construction company executive*
Merrill, Harvie Martin *manufacturing executiv director*
Whitworth, Hall Baker *forest products compa executive*

GEORGIA

Alpharetta
Adams, Kenneth Francis *automotive executive*
Brands, James Edwin *medical products execu*
Thomas, Robert L. *retired manufacturing company executive*

Atlanta
Allan, Alexander R.C. (Sandy Allan) *food products executive*
Anderson, Ray C. *carpet company executive*
Beazer, Brian C. *construction executive*
Bostic, James E., Jr. *paper company executive*
Brock, John F. *beverage company executive*
Cathy, S. Truett *food products executive*

Corr, James Vanis *furniture manufacturing executive, accountant*
Cummings, Alexander B., Jr. *food products executive*
Davis, Marvin Arnold *manufacturing executive*
Dobson, Rick *metals company executive*
Douglas, J. Alexander M. (Sandy) *beverage company executive*
Douglas, William W. *food products executive*
Fayard, Gary P. *beverage company executive*
Finan, Irial *beverage company executive*
Francis, Julie *beverage company executive*
Gallagher, Thomas C. *diversified manufacturing executive*
Hyland, Gregory E. *home building products executive*
Isdell, (Edward) Neville *beverage company executive*
Johnson, Carrie Clements *executive*
Johnson, (Frederick) Ross *international management advisory company executive*
Kelley, Brian P. *beverage and former relocation services company executive*
Kent, Muhtar *beverage company executive*
Kline, Lowry F. *beverage company executive, lawyer*
Liebmann, Seymour W. *construction executive, consultant*
Love, Gay McLawhorn *manufacturing executive*
Lund, Victor L. *healthcare company executive*
Marr, Daniel G. *food products executive*
McCarthy, Ian J. *construction executive*
Merrill, Allan P. *construction executive*
Mildenhall, Jonathan *beverage company executive*
Moeller, Joseph W. *forest products company executive*
Murphy, James Jeffrey *electronics executive*
Nagel, Vernon J. *chemicals and eletronics executive*
Nix, Jerry W. *automotive executive*
Palmer, Vicki R. *food products executive*
Prince, M. David (Morris David Prince) *retired electronics executive, computer graphics designer, educator*
Schmitt, Edward A. *manufacturing executive*
Smith, John Francis, Jr., (Jack Smith) *retired automotive executive*
Tripodi, Joseph V. *beverage company executive, former insurance company executive*

Ball Ground
Tucker, Robert Dennard *health care products executive*

Braselton
Hopper, James Robert *manufacturing executive*

Brunswick
Iannicelli, Joseph *chemical company executive, consultant*

Calhoun
Lorberbaum, Jeffrey S. *textiles executive*

Cartersville
Swanson, William Fredin III *manufacturing executive*

Conley
Marcus, James Elbert *manufacturing executive*

Dalton
Bouckaert, Carl M. *manufacturing executive*

Duluth
Brody, Aaron Leo *food and packaging consultant*
Eschenhagen, Martin H. *manufacturing executive*

Kennesaw
Martinez, Ricardo *emergency medicine company executive*

Lawrenceville
Pannick, Janice Carol *automotive dealerships executive*
McDonald, James Francis *electronics company executive*
Schoen, Marc Alan *pension and employee benefits executive*

Marietta
Blount, Daniel J. *lumber company executive*
Humphrey, Stephen M. *paperboard company executive*
Scheible, David W. *paper company executive*

Milledgeville
Williamson, John Thomas, Sr. *minerals company executive*

Moultrie
Green, William Jerome *uniform manufacturing company executive*

Norcross
Albright, James Alfred *paperboard and packaging company executive*

Roswell
Abernathy, Robert E. *health products executive*
Auer, Joanne B. *health products executive*
Baughman, Richard Bankston *retired manufacturing executive*
Bittung, Lizanne C. *health products executive*
Spencer, Jan B. *health products executive*

Savannah
Cartledge, Raymond Eugene *retired paper company executive*
Haib, Kenneth Bryden *research and development company executive, physicist, economist*
Langer, Harvey, Jr. *retired manufacturing executive*

Spitz, Seymour James, Jr. *retired fragrance company executive*

Thomasville
Avera, Stephen R. *food products company executive, lawyer*
Deese, George E. *food products company executive*
Flowers, Langdon Strong *food company executive*

West Point
Glover, Clifford Clarke *retired construction company executive*

HAWAII

Honolulu
Hughes, Robert Harrison *former agricultural products executive*
Lewis, Peter Cushman *electric company executive*
Usui, Leslie Raymond *apparel executive*

Kaneohe
Vincent, Thomas James *retired manufacturing executive*

IDAHO

Boise
Appleton, Steven R. *electronics executive*
Benson, Kenneth Victor *manufacturing executive, lawyer*
Cleary, Edward William *retired diversified forest products company executive*
Hanks, Stephen Grant *construction executive, lawyer*
Harad, George Jay *retired manufacturing executive*
Hlobik, Lawrence S. *agricultural products executive*
Lewis, Roderic W. *electronics executive, lawyer*
Simplot, Jack (John Richard Simplot) *diversified food products company executive*
Simplot, Scott R. *diversified food products company executive*
Stephens, William Thomas *forest products manufacturing company executive*
Van Helden, Pete *food products executive*
Washington, Dennis R. *contracting company executive*

ILLINOIS

Abbott Park
Ashley, Richard W. *pharmaceutical executive*
Dempsey, William G. *pharmaceutical executive*
Frazier, Douglas Byron *healthcare manufacturing manager*
Freyman, Thomas C. *pharmaceutical executive*
Gonzalez, Richard A. *pharmaceutical executive*
Liepmann, Holger A. *pharmaceutical executive*
Nemmers, Joseph M., Jr. *pharmaceutical executive*
White, Miles D. *pharmaceutical executive*

Arlington Heights
Li, Norman N. *chemicals executive*

Aurora
Noglows, William P. *electronics executive*

Barrington
Burrows, Brian William *retired research and development company executive*
Nadig, Gerald George *retired manufacturing executive*

Champaign
Clark, Nicholas Leland *contractor*
Stotler, Edith Ann *retired grain company executive*

Chester
Welge, Donald Edward *food manufacturing executive*

Chicago
Adelson, Lawrence Seth *electronics executive, lawyer*
Bacevicius, John Anthony, V, (John Bace) *research and development company executive*
Barnes, Brenda C. *food products executive*
Bernick, Howard Barry *manufacturing executive*
Borenstine, Alvin Jerome *search company executive*
Bosowski, Edward M. *manufacturing executive*
Brake, Cecil Clifford *retired diversified manufacturing executive*
Bryan, John Henry *food and consumer products company executive*
Cline, William Chambers *automotive executive*
Cooper, Charles Gilbert *cosmetics executive*
Covalt, Robert Byron *chemicals executive*
Crown, Lester *manufacturing executive*
deKool, L.M. (Theo DeKool) *food products executive*
Dienst, Daniel W. *metal products executive*
Edlis, Stefan T. *plastics company executive*
Ferguson, Diana S. *food products executive*
Garner, Margaret *construction executive*
Giesen, Richard Allyn *manufacturing executive*
Gordon, Ellen Rubin *candy company executive*
Gordon, Melvin Jay *food products executive*
Gratz, Jay M.
Haben, Mary Kay *candy company executive*
Heisley, Michael E., Sr. *manufacturing executive, professional sports team owner*
Hinrichs, Charles A. *paper company executive*
Jezuit, Leslie James *manufacturing executive*
Klinger, Steven J. *paper company executive*
Lazarus, Steven *technology company exective*

McKee, Keith Earl *manufacturing technology executive*
Metcalf, James S. *manufacturing executive*
Moore, Patrick J. *paper company executive*
Murphy, Michael Emmett *retired food company executive*
Nichols, John Doane *diversified manufacturing corporation executive*
Novak, John G. *construction executive*
Novich, Neil S. *metals distribution company executive*
Nühn, Adriaan *food products executive*
Osborne, Robert Stephen *automotive executive, lawyer*
Parrish, Overton Burgin, Jr. *pharmaceutical corporation executive*
Patel, Homi Burjor *apparel executive*
Pepper, J. David, II, (Dave Pepper) *construction executive*
Perez, William D. (Bill Perez) *candy company executive, former sports apparel company executive*
Ptak, Frank Stanley *manufacturing executive*
Reum, W. Robert *manufacturing executive*
Senior, Richard John Lane *linen and uniform services executive*
Stack, Stephen S. *manufacturing executive*
Steinfeld, Manfred *furniture manufacturing executive*
Stone, Alan *container company executive*
Umans, Alvin Robert *manufacturing executive*
Walsh, Matthew M. *construction executive*
Waters, Ronald V. III *candy company executive*
Williams, Richard Lucas III *electronics executive, director, lawyer*
Wrigley, William, Jr., (Bill Wrigley Jr.) *candy company executive*

Crystal Lake
Anderson, Lyle Arthur *retired manufacturing executive*
Pearson, Nels Kenneth *retired manufacturing executive*
Siebel, Carl A. *manufacturing executive*

Decatur
Camp, William H. *agricultural products executive*
Mulhollem, Paul B. *agricultural products executive*
Rice, John D. *agricultural products executive*
Schmalz, Douglas J. *agricultural company executive*
Staley, Henry Mueller *manufacturing executive*
Woertz, Patricia Ann *agricultural company executive, retired oil company executive*

Deerfield
Davis, Robert M. *medical products executive*
Parkinson, Robert L., Jr. *medical products executive, health facility administrator*
Reid-Anderson, James *diagnostic equipment company executive*

Dekalb
Troyer, Alvah Forrest *agricultural products executive, horticulturist*

Des Plaines
Frank, James S. *automotive executive*
Johnston, Kurt Malcolm *pharmaceutical company executive*
O'Dwyer, Mary Ann *automotive executive*

Downers Grove
Fraleigh, Christopher J. *food products executive*
Nolan, James W. *food products executive*
Porter, Chris *food products executive*

Elmhurst
Duchossois, Craig J. *manufacturing executive*

Evanston
Menke, Allen Carl *retired manufacturing executive*

Frankfort
Burhoe, Brian Walter *automotive executive*

Franklin Park
Simpson, Michael *retired metals service center executive*

Glen Ellyn
Cvengros, Joseph Michael *manufacturing company executive*

Glenview
Blase, Anthony Idomeneus *retired electronics executive, writer, poet*
Bruns, Nicolaus, Jr. *retired agricultural products executive, lawyer, educator*
Gillis, Marvin Bob *retired chemical executive, consultant*
Hickey, John Thomas *retired electronics company executive*
Smith, Harold B. *manufacturing executive*

Highland Park
Korzenski, Robert M. *manufacturing executive*
Rudo, Milton *retired manufacturing executive*

Hoffman Estates
Nicholas, Arthur Soterios *manufacturing executive*

Lake Forest
Begley, Christopher B. *pharmaceutical executive*
Carroll, Barry Joseph *manufacturing and real estate executive*
Dreimann, Leonhard *manufacturing executive*
Hamilton, Peter Bannerman *manufacturing executive, lawyer*
Hammar, Lester Everett *retired manufacturing executive*
Keyser, Richard Lee *distribution company executive*

Larson, Peter N. *manufacturing executive*
Leemputte, Peter G. *manufacturing executive*
McCoy, Dustan Elwood *manufacturing executive, lawyer*
O'Mara, Thomas Patrick *manufacturing executive*
Romans, Donald Bishop *manufacturing executive*
Sherrill, Gregg M. *automotive executive*

Lanark
Abbott, David Henry *manufacturing executive*

Lincolnshire
Anderson, David J. *manufacturing executive*
Simes, Stephen Mark *pharmaceutical executive*

Lisle
Krehbiel, Frederick August, II, *electronics executive*
Krehbiel, John H., Jr. *retired electronics company executive*
Slark, Martin P. *electronics executive*

Moline
Jones, Nathan Jerome *farm machinery manufacturing company executive*
Lane, Robert W. *farm equipment manufacturing executive*
Mack, Michael J., Jr. *manufacturing executive*

Mount Sterling
Tracy, Patrick F. *food products executive*

Naperville
Katai, Andrew Andras *chemical company executive*
Smetana, Mark *food products executive*
Wake, Richard W. *food products executive*
Wake, Thomas G. *food products executive*

Niles
Herb, Marvin J. *food products executive*
Schyvinck, Christine *electronics executive*

Northfield
Carlin, Donald Walter *retired food products executive, consultant*
Hadley, Stanton Thomas *manufacturing executive, director, lawyer*
Knight, James Atwood *manufacturing executive*
Lynch, Kirsten *food products executive*
McLevish, Timothy R. *food products executive*
Pratt, Murray Lester *manufacturing executive*
Rosenfeld, Irene B. *food products company executive*
Smeds, Edward William *retired food company executive*
Sneed, Paula Ann *food products executive*
Stepan, Frank Quinn *chemicals executive*
Stepan, Frank Quinn, Jr., (F. Quinn Stepan Jr.) *chemical company executive*

Oak Brook
Alvarez, Ralph *food products executive*
Dillon, Mary *food products executive*
Skinner, James A. (James A. Skinner) *food products executive*
Thompson, Don *food products executive*

Palos Hills
Skender, Joseph *construction executive*

Palos Park
Nelson, Lawrence Evan *manufacturing executive, consultant*

Peoria
Burritt, David B. *manufacturing executive*
Levenick, Stuart L. *manufacturing executive*
Oberhelman, Douglas R. *tractor company executive*
Owens, James W. *manufacturing executive*
Shaheen, Gerald L. *manufacturing executive*
Vittecoq, Gerard R. *manufacturing executive*
Wunning, Steven H. *manufacturing executive*

Prospect Heights
Byrne, Michael Joseph *manufacturing executive*

River Forest
Douglas, Kenneth Jay *food products executive*

Rockford
Bippus, David Paul *manufacturing executive*
O'Donnell, William David *retired construction firm executive*

Rosemont
Meinert, John Raymond *apparel executive, investment banker*
Reyes, J. Christopher *food products distribution executive*

Schaumburg
Delaney, Eugene A. *electronics executive*
Desai, Samir T. *electronics executive*
Galvin, Robert W. *electronics executive*
Karp, Jeff *construction executive*
Moloney, Daniel M. *electronics executive*
Nottenburg, Richard N. *electronics executive*
Reed, Stuart C. *electronics executive*
Soon-Shiong, Patrick *pharmaceutical executive*

Union
Perlick, Richard Allan *steel company executive*

Vernon Hills
Ling, Chung-Mei

Warrenville
Horne, John R. *farm equipment company executive*
Lannert, Robert Cornelius *manufacturing executive*

Westchester
Faison, Ralph E. *communications equipment manufacturing executive*
Scott, Samuel C. *food products executive*

Wheaton
Back, Robert Wyatt *investment company and pharmaceutical executive, consultant*

Wheeling
Keats, Glenn Arthur *manufacturing executive*

Wilmette
Coughlan, Gary Patrick *pharmaceutical executive*
Pearlman, Jerry Kent *electronics company executive*

Winnetka
Markey, Maurice *food products executive*
Puth, John Wells *manufacturing executive, consultant*

Wood Dale
Storch, David *manufacturing executive*

Woodridge
Stall, Alan David *packaging company executive*

INDIANA

Anderson
Carrell, Terry Eugene *manufacturing executive*

Batesville
Classon, Rolf Allan *pharmaceutical company executive*
Soderberg, Peter H. *health products executive*

Bloomington
Cook, William Alfred *medical products executive*
Webb, Lisa Michelle *regulatory affairs manager*

Brownstown
Robertson, Joseph Edmond *grain processing company executive*

Carmel
Shoup, Charles Samuel, Jr. *chemicals and materials executive*

Columbus
Blackwell, Jean Stuart *manufacturing executive*
Boll, Charles Raymond *engine company executive*
Loughrey, F. Joseph *manufacturing executive*
Solso, Theodore M. *manufacturing executive*
Wall, John *manufacturing executive*

East Chicago
Chukwulebe, Bernard Obioma *manufacturing executive, consultant*

Elkhart
Khilnani, Vinod M. *manufacturing executive*
Mathias, Margaret Grossman *manufacturing company executive, leasing company executive*
Mischke, Frederick Charles *retired manufacturing executive*

Evansville
Koch, Robert Louis, II, *manufacturing company executive, mechanical engineer*
Muehlbauer, James Herman *manufacturing and distribution executive*

Fort Wayne
Busse, Keith E. *manufacturing executive*
Rhoad, Richard E. *manufacturing executive*

Indianapolis
Andretti, Michael Mario *racing company executive, retired professional race car driver*
Connelly, Deirdre P. *pharmaceutical executive*
Hunt, Robert G. *construction company executive*
Kenney, Philip G. *construction executive*
Kirkham, James Alvin *manufacturing executive*
Lacy, Andre Balz *industrial executive*
Lechleiter, John C. *pharmaceutical executive*
Lorell, Beverly H. *medical products executive*
Lugar, Thomas R. *manufacturing executive*
Mays, William G. *chemical company executive*
McConnell, William F., Jr. *medical products executive*
Mc Farland, H. Richard *food products executive*
Murphy, Anthony J. *pharmaceutical executive*
Paul, Steven M. *pharmaceutical executive*
Peribere, Jerome A. *agricultural products executive*
Ralston, Ronald Lee *retired manufacturing tradesman*
Ramakrishnan, Divakar *pharmaceutical executive*
Rice, Derica W. *pharmaceutical executive*
Santini, Gino *pharmaceutical executive*
SerVaas, Beurt Richard *manufacturing executive*
Smith, K. Clay *machinery transport company executive*
Stewart, Paul Arthur *pharmaceutical company executive*
Taurel, Sidney *pharmaceutical executive*

Lafayette
Meyer, Brud Richard *retired pharmaceutical executive*

Middlebury
Corson, Thomas Harold *retired manufacturing executive*
Guequierre, John Phillip *manufacturing executive*

Mishawaka
Rubenstein, Pamela Silver *manufacturing executive*

Munster
Corsiglia, Robert Joseph *retired electrical construction company executive*

Plainfield
Laikin, Robert J. *electronics executive*

Portage
Popp, Joseph Bruce *manufacturing executive*

Warsaw
Binder, Jeffrey R. *medical products executive*
Dvorak, David C. *medical products executive, lawyer*
Elliott, J. Raymond *medical products executive*

Washington
Graham, David Bolden *food products executive*

IOWA

Ames
Abbott, David L. *agricultural products executive*

Cedar Rapids
Jones, Clayton M. *computer and electronics company executive*
Nyquist, John Davis *retired radio manufacturing company executive*

Davenport
Juckem, Wilfred Philip *manufacturing executive*

Des Moines
Damos, Craig *construction executive*

Dubuque
Crahan, Jack Bertsch *retired manufacturing executive*
Tully, Thomas Alois *building materials executive, consultant, educator*

Humboldt
Dodgen, John N. *manufacturing executive*

Muscatine
Askren, Stan A. *manufacturing executive*
Housh, E. William *manufacturing executive*

Okoboji
Pearson, Gerald Leon *food products executive*

Pella
Dout, Anne Jacqueline *manufacturing and sales company executive*

Sioux City
Bennett, Michael L. *agricultural products executive*

West Des Moines
Pomerantz, Marvin Alvin *manufacturing executive*

KANSAS

Derby
Helms, Neville Troy *manufacturing company administrator*

Hutchinson
Dick, Harold Latham *manufacturing executive*

Leawood
Terry, Robert Brooks *food products executive, lawyer*

Lenexa
Ascher, James John *pharmaceutical executive*
Jackson, Charles Wayne *food products and former telecommunications industry executive*

Mission
Bresky, Steven J. *agricultural products executive*

Olathe
Burrell, Gary *retired manufacturing executive*
Kao, Min H. *manufacturing executive*

Shawnee Mission
Gamet, Donald Max *appliance company executive*

Wichita
Schuster, James Edward *defense equipment manufacturing company executive*

KENTUCKY

Bellevue
Carpenter, Woodrow Wilson *manufacturing executive, ceramics engineer*

Bowling Green
Ahmed, S. Basheer *research and development company executive, educator*
Holland, John Ben *clothing manufacturing company executive*

Covington
Froesel, David W., Jr. *medical products executive*
Gemunder, Joel Frank *healthcare company executive*
O'Brien, James J. *manufacturing executive*
Quin, Joseph Marvin *manufacturing executive*

Erlanger
Cuneo, Dennis Clifford *automotive company executive*

Highland Heights
Kenny, Gregory B. *industrial equipment executive*

Louisville
Diaz, Paul J. *health products executive*
Goodman, Bruce *health products executive*
Heiden, Charles Kenneth *metal products executive, consultant, retired military officer*
Lechleiter, Richard A. *medical products executive*
Margulis, Heidi *health products executive*
Moya, Steve *health products executive*
Pottinger, Ronald Wayne *food products executive*
Shield, Gene *health products executive*
Street, William May *retired beverage company executive*
Varga, Paul C. *beverage products executive*
Vogel, Werner Paul *retired machine company executive*

Newport
Castellini, Robert H. (Bob Castellini) *food products executive, professional sports team executive*

LOUISIANA

Baton Rouge
Calabrese, Michael Raphael *manufacturing executive, lawyer, consultant*

Denham Springs
May, Kenneth Nathaniel *retired food industry consultant*

Mandeville
Donahue, Maura W. *construction executive*

New Orleans
Cospolich, James Donald *electronics executive, consultant*

MAINE

Andover
Kaltsos, Angelo John *electronics executive, educator, photographer*

Ellsworth
Whedon, Ralph Gibbs *manufacturing executive*

Falmouth
Cabot, Lewis Pickering *manufacturing company executive, art consultant*

Kennebunk
Damon, Edmund Holcombe *retired plastics company executive*

Kennebunkport
Featherman, Bernard *steel company executive*

New Vineyard
Smith, Frederick Orville, II, *agricultural products executive, retired military officer*

Scarborough
Shire, Donald Thomas *retired chemicals executive, lawyer*

South Bristol
Wells, Arthur Stanton *retired manufacturing executive*

South Portland
Thompson, Mark S. *electronics executive*

MARYLAND

Arnold
Constants, Dorothy Marie *manufacturing executive*

Baltimore
Baines, Henry T., Sr. *supermarkets executive*
Foster, Lester Anderson, Jr. *metal products executive*
Hackerman, Willard J. *construction executive*
Plank, Kevin A. *apparel executive*

Bethesda
Forster, Peter C. *construction executive*
Manasse, Henri Richard, Jr. *pharmaceutical executive*
Mellor, James Robb *retired electronics executive*
Spector, Eleanor Ruth *manufacturing executive*

Chevy Chase
Bissinger, Frederick Lewis *retired manufacturing executive*
Ewing, Frank Marion *paper company executive, real estate developer*

Columbia
Festa, (Al)Fred E. *chemicals executive*
Fishbune, Robert *food products executive*
Norris, Paul J. *chemicals executive*

Easton
Peterson, James Kenneth *manufacturing executive*

Frederick
Lin, George *research and development company executive, biomedical researcher*

Jessup
Spievack, Alan R. *research and development company executive, surgeon*

Ocean City
Corun, Ronald Lewis *asphalt refining executive*

Potomac
Epstein, Mark Robert *electronics executive*

Rockville
Landon, John Campbell *research and development company executive*
Miller, Kenneth Michael *electronics executive, director*
Watkins, H. Thomas *biopharmaceutical compan executive*
Yoshikawa, Hiromi *pharmaceutical executive*

Saint Michaels
Peck, Charles Edward *retired construction and mortgage executive*

Salisbury
Perdue, James A. (Jim Perdue) *food products executive*

Silver Spring
Coates, Robert Jay *retired electronics executive*

Sparks
Lawless, Robert J. *food products executive*

Temple Hills
Ourisman, Mandell Jack *automotive executive*

White Hall
Radigan, Frank Xavier *retired pharmaceutical executive*

MASSACHUSETTS

Andover
Keleher, David *electronics executive*

Attleboro
Hammerle, Fredric Joseph *metal products executive*
Wroe, Thomas, Jr. *semiconductor company executive*

Billerica
Kolb, Charles Eugene *research and developmer company executive*

Boston
Burnes, Kennett Farrar *chemicals executive*
Hoskins, William Keller *pharmaceutical executive, lawyer, mediator, arbitrator*
Leaman, J. Richard, Jr. *paper company executi*
Towers, John R. *manufacturing executive, lawy*

Burlington
Sproull, Robert Fletcher *research and development company executive*

Cambridge
Berger, Harvey James *pharmaceutical executiv physician, educator*
d'Arbeloff, Alexander V. *electronics executive*
Dunsire, Deborah *pharmaceutical executive*
Forney, G(eorge) David, Jr. *retired electronics executive*
Frosch, Robert Alan *retired automobile manufacturing executive, physicist*
Lewis, Henry Rafalsky *manufacturing executiv*
Matsui, Connie L. *pharmaceutical executive*
Schaub, Robert George *pharmaceutical execut*
Termeer, Henricus Adrianus *pharmaceutical executive*

Canton
Fireman, Paul Barry *footwear and apparel company executive*
Harrington, Paul *apparel executive*

Charlestown
English, Todd *food company executive, chef*

Cohasset
Dickstein, Harvey Leonard *pharmaceutical executive, researcher*

Dalton
Crane, Lansing E. *paper company executive*

Danvers
Dolan, John Ralph *retired electronics executiv*
Waite, Charles Morrison *food products execut*

Easthampton
Perkins, Homer Guy *manufacturing executive*

Falmouth
Litschgi, Richard John *computer manufacturin company executive*

Framingham
Bose, Amar Gopal *electronics executive, electrical engineering educator*
Lesser, Richard G. *retired apparel executive*
Ziomek, Carol Ann *medical products executiv*

Hanson
Norris, John Anthony *health products executiv lawyer, educator*

Haverhill
Bigelow, Peter *electronics executive*

Hingham
Llewellyn, John Schofield, Jr. *former food company executive*
Sullivan, Trudy F. *apparel executive*
Zetcher, Arnold B. *apparel executive*

Lexington
Baron, Sheldon *research and development company executive*
Goell, James Emanuel *electronics executive*
McGirr, David William John *pharmaceutical executive*
Smith, Robert Louis *construction company executive*

agmeadow
up, John Gardiner *retired paper company executive*

ick
e, John E. *medical products executive*
iolette, Paul A. *medical products executive*
iolas, Peter M. *medical products executive*
n, James Robert *biomedical device manufacturing company executive*

vton
ob, Stephen Darrow *health products executive*

rth Andover
, Harold Seymour *retired manufacturing executive, entrepreneur, consultant*
aini, Ralph Humbert III *electronics executive*

rth Chatham
son, E. B. *manufacturing executive, consultant, writer*

rwood
Chiang J. *pharmaceutical executive, physician scientist*

ange
ers, Robert Alfred *microwave company executive*

tsfield
ley, Charlene *manufacturing executive*

incy
in, Robert Joseph *food products executive*
ng, Richard William *chemicals executive*

xbury
third, Brandy K. *gym owner and fitness instructor*

elburne Falls
ras, Joseph Hill *pulp and paper company executive*

uthborough
in, Philip Todd *medical executive*

dbury
atsch, Marshall E(manuel) *medical products company executive, inventor*

altham
nstein, Stanley Joseph *manufacturing executive*
tarella, Paolo *former automotive executive*
ckers, Marijn E. *electronics executive*
yd, John Taylor *electronics executive*
nklin, Charles E. *manufacturing executive*
ister, Paul M. *medical products executive*
vu, Heidi *defense equipment manufacturing company executive, electrical engineer*
anson, William Henry *defense equipment manufacturing company executive*
jsgras, David C. *manufacturing executive*

ellesley
Camillo, Gary Thomas *manufacturing executive*
lius, Gilbert Keistutis *manufacturing executive*
rcus, Richard Greenwald *manufacturing executive*
nme, Gregory Louis *health products executive*
ayer, Gaylord Bertram, Jr. *retired electronics executive, private investor*

ellesley Hills
rkson, Cheryl Lee *healthcare executive*
rcus, William Michael *rubber and vinyl products manufacturing company executive*

eston
d, Theodore Shafick *retired microwave company executive*

estwood
shner, Jeffrey L. *manufacturing executive*

ilmington
khshoori, Daryoosh *chemicals executive*

inchester
kson, Francis Joseph *research and development company executive*

orcester
est, Michael D. *cloning and stem cell research company executive*

ICHIGAN

nn Arbor
le, David Edward *automotive executive, educator*
cker, Raymond Frank *chemicals and metal products executive*
Laat, Gilbert *automotive executive*
erbach, Steven John *retired electronics company executive*
rzig, David Jacob *retired pharmaceutical company executive, consultant*
cCormack, Terry R. *automotive executive*
otawi, Karim *textiles executive*
ounts, L. David *food products executive*

uburn Hills
avidson, William M. *manufacturing executive, professional sports team owner*
eid, Russell Joseph *glass manufacturing executive*
rrar, Stephen Prescott *glass products manufacturing executive*

Gerson, Ralph Joseph *manufacturing executive*
Kalina, John *auto parts company executive*
LaSorda, Thomas W. *automotive company executive*
Manganello, Timothy M. *auto parts company executive*
Meyer, Deborah Wahl *automotive executive*
Nardelli, Robert Louis *automotive executive, former consumer home products company executive*
Unger, Susan J. *automotive executive*

Battle Creek
Banks, Donna Jo *food products executive*
Bryant, John A. *food products executive*
Jenness, James M. *food products executive*
Mackay, David (A.D. David Mackay) *food products executive*
Montie, Jeffrey W. *food products executive*
Pilnick, Gary H. *food products executive, lawyer*

Belleville
Stebbins, Donald J. *car parts manufacturing company executive*

Benton Harbor
Brown, Mark E. *manufacturing executive*
Fettig, Jeff M. *manufacturing executive*
Swift, David L. *manufacturing executive*
Templin, Roy W. *manufacturing executive*
Thieneman, Michael D. *manufacturing executive*
Todman, Michael A. *manufacturing executive*
Yaggi, W. Timothy *manufacturing executive*

Beulah
Edwards, Wallace Winfield *retired automotive executive*

Birmingham
Foxen, Richard William *manufacturing executive*
Maxwell, Jack Erwin *manufacturing executive*
Sharf, Stephan *automotive executive*

Bloomfield Hills
Cregg, Roger A. *construction executive*
Dugas, Richard J., Jr. *construction executive*
Ellinghausen, James R. *construction executive*
Keane, Peter J. *construction executive*
O'Shaughnessy, Robert T. *automotive executive*
Petruska, Steven C. *construction executive*
Pulte, William J. *construction executive*

Brighton
Crabtree, John David *manufacturing company executive*

Cass City
Althaver, Lambert Ewing *manufacturing executive*

Dearborn
Bannister, Michael E. *automotive executive*
Cischke, Susan Mary *automotive executive*
Codina, Francisco *automotive executive*
Fields, Mark *automotive executive*
Ford, Bill (William Clay Ford Jr.) *automotive company executive*
Ford, William Clay *automotive and professional sports team executive*
Johnston, Michael Francis *auto parts company executive*
Kuzak, Derrick M. *automotive executive*
Leclair, Don (Donat R. Leclair Jr.) *automotive executive*
Leet, Kenneth H.M. *automotive executive*
Leitch, David G. *automotive executive, lawyer*
Lundy, J(oseph) Edward *retired automobile company executive*
Marcin, Robert H. *automotive executive*
Mays, J. C. *automotive executive*
Mulally, Alan R. *automotive company executive, former aerospace company executive*
Ojakli, Ziad S. *automotive executive*
Parry-Jones, Richard *automotive executive*
Pestillo, Peter John *auto parts company executive, lawyer*
Smither, Nick *automotive executive*
Zimmerman, Martin B. *automotive executive*

Detroit
Barclay, Kathleen S. *automotive executive*
Burns, Lawrence D. *automotive executive*
Clarke, Troy A. *automotive executive*
Cyprus, Nicholas Stanley *automotive executive, accountant*
Dauch, Richard E. *automotive executive*
Forster, Carl-Peter *automotive executive*
Gerosa, Peter R. *automotive executive*
Gillum, Roderick D. *automotive executive*
Henderson, Frederick A. (Fritz) *automotive executive*
Kalman, Andrew *manufacturing executive, director*
LaNeve, Mark R. *automotive executive*
Lutz, Robert Anthony *automotive company executive*
Nicholson, James M. *chemicals executive*
Soave, Anthony *manufacturing executive*
Szygenda, Ralph J. *automotive executive*
Wagoner, Rick (G. Richard Wagoner Jr.) *automotive executive*

Fraser
Winget, Larry J., Sr. *automotive industry executive*

Grand Rapids
Baker, Hollis MacLure *furniture manufacturing company executive*
Currie, William G. *forest products executive*
Glenn, Michael B. *forest products executive*
Hackett, James P. *manufacturing executive*
Maines, Charles John *electronics manager*
Murray, Mark Andrew *food products executive, former academic administrator, economist*
Sadler, David G(ary) *manufacturing executive*
Secchia, Peter F. *forest products executive, former United States ambassador to Italy*
Woodrick, Robert *food products executive*

Grosse Pointe
Manetta, Richard L. *chemicals executive, lawyer*
Wilkinson, Warren Scripps *manufacturing executive*

Grosse Pointe Farms
Obolensky, Marilyn Wall (Mrs. Serge Obolensky) *metals company executive*

Holland
Haworth, Richard G. (Dick Haworth) *office furniture manufacturer*

Houghton
Utt, Glenn S., Jr. *retired medical products executive*

Howell
Tupper, Leon F. *manufacturing executive*

Jackson
Kelly, Robert Vincent, Jr. *metal products executive*

Kalamazoo
Hudson, Roy Davage *retired pharmaceutical executive*
MacMillan, Stephen P. *health products executive*

Livonia
Cantie, Joseph S. *automotive executive*
Drouin, Joe *automotive executive*
Lake, Peter J. *automotive executive*
Lunn, Steven *automotive executive*
Marchuk, Neil *automotive executive*
Plant, John Charles *automotive executive*

Madison Heights
Kafarski, Mitchell I. *chemical processing company executive*

Midland
Banholzer, William F. *chemical company executive*
Burns, Stephanie A. *chemicals executive*
Carbone, Anthony J. *chemicals executive*
Cook, Phillip H. *chemicals executive*
Gambrell, Michael R. *chemicals executive*
Haller, Heinz *chemicals executive*
Hampton, Leroy *retired chemical company executive*
Holder, Julie Fasone *chemicals executive*
Kepler, David E., II, *chemicals executive*
Kreinberg, Romeo *chemicals executive*
Kresge, Charles T. *chemicals executive*
Liveris, Andrew N. *chemical company executive*
Schmidt, William C. *retired chemicals executive*
Veurink, Gary R. *chemicals executive*
Walthie, Theo H. *chemicals executive*

Milford
Bennur, Mallikarjuna *automotive executive*

Monroe
Darrow, Kurt L. *manufacturing executive*

Northville
Clawson, Curtis J. *manufacturing executive*

Novi
Jeffe, Sidney David *automotive executive, engineer*
Johnson, S.A. (Tony Johnson) *automotive executive*
Malcolm, Mark *automotive executive*
McElya, James S. *automotive executive*

Owosso
Acton, David L(awrence) *automobile company executive*

Plymouth
Leuliette, Timothy D. *automotive executive*
Vlcek, Donald Joseph, Jr. *food products executive, wholesale distribution executive, writer*

Portage
Brown, John Wilford *health products executive*

Reed City
Rautiola, Norman A. *manufacturing executive*

Rochester Hills
Akeel, Hadi Abu *robotics executive*
Denton, Lawrence A. *automotive executive*

Romeo
Stryker, James William *retired automotive executive, former military officer*

Royal Oak
Cook, Noel Robert *manufacturing executive*
DeMaria, Mark *construction executive*

Saint Joseph
King, George Raleigh *retired manufacturing executive*

Southfield
Alapont, José Maria *automotive executive*
Brackenbury, James M. *manufacturing executive*
DelGrosso, Douglas G. *manufacturing executive*
Gouldey, Glenn Charles *manufacturing executive*
Herrera-Lasso, Miguel *manufacturing executive*
Kamsickas, James *automotive executive*
Lynch, George Michael *auto parts manufacturing executive*
Maibach, Ben C. III *construction company executive*
Rossiter, Robert E. *manufacturing executive*
Salvatore, Louis R. *manufacturing executive*
Scott, Raymond E. *manufacturing executive*
Simoncini, Matthew J. *manufacturing executive*
Vandenberghe, James H. *manufacturing executive*
Zimmer, Paul Joseph *manufacturing executive*

Tecumseh
Buker, Edwin L. *manufacturing executive*
Herrick, Todd W. *manufacturing executive*

Traverse City
Clous, James M. *electrical equipment company executive, engineer*

Troy
Battenberg, J. T. III *automotive company executive*
Buschmann, Siegfried *retired manufacturing executive*
Butler, Kevin M. *electronics executive*
Mahone, Barbara Jean *automotive executive*
McClure, Charles G. *automotive executive*
Miller, Robert Stevens, Jr., (Steve Miller) *automotive company executive*
O'Neal, Rodney *automotive company executive*
Sloan, Hugh Walter, Jr. *automotive executive*
Walker, Bette *automotive executive*
Weber, Mark R. *automotive executive*

Whitehall
Squier, David Louis *manufacturing executive*

Wixom
Sugiyama, Toru Tom *automotive executive*

Zeeland
Volkema, Michael A. *office furniture manufacturer*
Walker, Brian C. *manufacturing executive*

MINNESOTA

Austin
Ettinger, Jeffrey M. *food products executive, lawyer*

Bayport
Garofalo, Donald R. *window manufacturing executive*

Eagan
Clemens, T. Pat *manufacturing executive*

Eden Prairie
Henningsen, Peter, Jr. *manufacturing executive*

Edina
Brown, Charles Eugene *retired electronics company executive*
Kunin, Myron *hair care company executive*

Golden Valley
Hogan, Randall J. *manufacturing and electronics executive*

La Crescent
Gelatt, Charles Daniel *manufacturing executive*

Lindstrom
Messin, Marlene Ann *plastics company executive*

Marshall
Burr, Tracy L. *food products executive*
Pippin, M. Lenny *food products executive*

Medina
Tiller, Thomas C. *manufacturing executive*

Mendota Heights
Cohen, Robert *medical device and pharmaceutical manufacturing and marketing executive*
Frechette, Peter Loren *dental products executive*

Minneapolis
Bader, Kathleen M. *chemicals executive*
Buhrmaster, Robert C. *manufacturing executive*
Collins, Arthur D., Jr. *medical products executive*
Cook, William M. *manufacturing executive*
Curler, Jeffrey H. *packaging manufacturing executive*
Dallas, H. James *medical products executive*
DeMane, Michael F. *medical products executive*
Durkin, G. Michael *food products executive*
Ellis, Gary *medical products executive*
Ferrari, Giannantonio *electronics executive*
George, William Wallace *former manufacturing executive*
Gockel, John Raymond *construction executive*
Hale, Roger Loucks *manufacturing executive, director*
Hawkins, William A. III *medical products executive*
Hoffman, Michael J. *manufacturing executive*
Jacobs, Irwin Lawrence *diversified corporate executive*
Lenehan, James T. *former pharmaceutical executive*
Lumpkins, Robert L. *food products executive*
Mansfield, William L. *manufacturing executive*
Melrose, Kendrick Bascom *manufacturing executive*
Murphy, Daniel J., Jr. *aerospace and defense manufacturing company executive, military officer*
Oesterle, Stephen N. *medical products executive, cardiologist, educator*
Page, Gregory R. *agricultural products and diversified services company executive*
Pletcher, Carol H. *chemicals executive*
Reyelts, Paul C. *chemical company executive*
Roe, John H. *manufacturing executive*
Rompala, Richard M. *chemical company executive*
Spoor, William Howard *food products executive*
Van Dyke, William Grant *manufacturing executive*

Wurtele, Christopher Angus *paint and coatings company executive*

Minnetonka
Erlandson, Patrick J. *health products executive*

Plymouth
Friswold, Fred Ravndal *manufacturing executive*
Kahler, Herbert Frederick *manufacturing executive*
Prokopanko, James T. *agricultural products executive*

Saint Paul
Buckley, George W. *manufacturing executive*
Campbell, Patrick D. *manufacturing executive*
Debertin, Jay D. *energy and food products executive*
Johnson, John D. *energy and food products executive*
Kluempke, Patrick M. *energy and food products executive*
Knutson, Dan *food products executive*
Larson, Thomas D. *energy and food products executive*
Palmquist, Mark L. *energy and food products executive*
Policinski, Chris *food products executive*
Schmitz, John *energy and food products executive*
Schram, Lee J. *manufacturing executive*
Schuman, Allan L. *chemicals executive*
Starks, Daniel J. *medical technology and services executive*
Volpi, Michele *chemicals executive*
Westbrock, Leon E. *energy and food products executive*
Wiltz, James W. *medical products executive*

Wayzata
Blodgett, Frank Caleb *retired food company executive*
Luthringshauser, Daniel Rene *manufacturing executive*
Staley, Warren R. *agricultural products and diversified services company executive*
Sullivan, Austin Padraic, Jr. *retired diversified food company executive*

Winona
Oberton, Willard D. *industrial supply company executive*

MISSISSIPPI

Hattiesburg
Chain, Bobby Lee *electrical contractor, former mayor*

Jackson
Julian, Michael *grocery company executive*

MISSOURI

Carthage
Haffner, David S. *manufacturing executive*
Jett, Ernest Carroll, Jr. *paper company executive, lawyer*
Wright, Felix E. *manufacturing executive*

Chesterfield
Carpenter, Will Dockery *chemicals executive*
Winter, William Earl *retired beverage company executive*

Clayton
Rupp, Joseph D. *metal products executive*

Fulton
Backer, William Earnest *food products executive*

Grain Valley
Olsson, Björn Eskil *railroad supply company executive*

Independence
Nordsieck, Karen Ann *custom apparel company executive*

Kansas City
Bass, Lee Marshall *food products company executive*
Berkley, Eugene Bertram (Bert) *envelope company executive*
Dees, Stephen Phillip *agricultural products executive, lawyer*
Dunn, Terrence P. *manufacturing executive*
Hebenstreit, James Bryant *agricultural products executive, venture capitalist*
Johnson, Richard Dean *pharmaceutical consultant, educator*
Jung, Craig D. *food products executive*
Kafoure, Michael D. *food products executive*

Lees Summit
Henley, Joseph Oliver *manufacturing executive*

Maryland Heights
Holmes, Michael *health products executive*
Ignaczak, Edward B. *health products executive*
Lowenberg, David A. *pharmaceutical executive*
McNamee, Patrick *health products executive*
Motheral, Brenda R. *health products executive*
Paz, George *health products executive*
Porter, Douglas W. *health products executive*
Rey-Giraud, Agnès *health products executive*
Steward, David L. *technology company executive*

Saint Charles
Pundmann, Ed John, Jr. *automotive company executive*

Saint Louis
Armstrong, J. Hord III *pharmaceutical company executive*
Baker, W. Randolph *brewery company executive*
Browde, Anatole *electronics company executive, consultant*
Brown, JoBeth Goode *food products executive, lawyer*
Busch, August Adolphus, IV, *brewery company executive*
Clark, Robert G. *construction executive*
Crews, Terrell K. *agricultural products executive*
Edison, Bernard Alan *retired apparel executive*
Farr, David N. *electronics executive*
Fromm, Ronald A. *apparel executive*
Galvin, Walter J. *electrical equipment manufacturing executive*
Grant, Hugh *agricultural products executive*
Gupta, Surendra Kumar *chemicals executive*
Harvey, David R. *chemical company executive*
Hirsch, Raymond Robert *chemicals executive, lawyer*
Holliman, W. G. (Mickey), Jr. *furniture manufacturing executive*
Hunt, Kevin J. *food products executive*
Hunter, John C. III *chemicals executive*
Keyes, Marion Alvah, IV, *manufacturing executive*
Lambright, Stephen Kirk *brewing company executive, lawyer*
McGinnis, W. Patrick *diversified company executive*
Monroe, Thomas Edward *business and financial executive*
Nagarkatti, Jai Prakash *chemical company executive*
Quinn, Jeffry N. *chemicals executive, lawyer*
Reynolds, Robert A., Jr. *electric distributor executive*
Shanahan, Michael Francis *retired manufacturing executive, former hockey team executive*
Skarie, David P. *food products executive*
Snively, David Frederick *agricultural products company executive, lawyer*
Stearley, Robert Jay *retired packaging company executive*
Stokes, Patrick T. *brewery company executive*
Swain, David O. *manufacturing executive*
Weldon, Virginia V. *retired food products executive, retired pediatrician*

Springfield
Henslee, Gregory L. *automotive executive*
O'Reilly, David E. *auto parts company executive*
Wooten, Rosalie (Rosalie O'Reilly Wooten) *automotive company executive*

Washington
Stelzner, Paul Burke *textile company executive*

Webster Groves
Conerly, Richard Pugh *retired manufacturing executive*

Wentzville
Cowger, Gary L. *automotive executive*

MONTANA

Big Sky
Ryan, Raymond D. *retired steel and insurance company executive*

NEBRASKA

Lincoln
Fisher, Calvin David *food products executive*

Lindsay
Parker, Gary Dean *manufacturing executive*

Omaha
Bolles, Al *food products executive*
Chow, Joan K. *food products executive*
Faith, Marshall E. *grain company executive*
Gehring, John F. *food products executive*
Goslee, Dwight J. *agricultural products executive*
Grewcock, Bruce E. *construction and mining executive*
Hardy, Jim, Jr. *food products executive*
Hawaux, André J. *food products executive*
Heckman, Gregory A. *food products executive*
Hollis, Dean *food products executive*
Johnson, Owen C. *food products executive*
Knudsen, Doug *food products executive*
McCook, Jacqueline K. Heslop *food products executive*
Perez, Peter Michael *food products executive*
Pouw, King T. *food products executive*
Rodkin, Gary M. *food products executive*
Stinson, Kenneth E. *construction and mining company executive*

NEVADA

Boulder City
Fisher, Paul Cary *writing supplies company executive*
Johnsen, Ken C. *steel products company executive*

Carson City
Burns, Dan W. *manufacturing executive*

Genoa
Goode, John Martin *manufacturing executive*

Incline Village
Strack, Harold Arthur *retired electronics executive, military officer, financial consultant, musician, writer*
Yount, George Stuart *paper company executive*

Las Vegas
Arell, Bobby Ray, Jr. *pharmaceutical executive, management consultant*
Derrick, William Dennis *retired physical plant administrator, consultant*
Jakopec, Carl Thomas *pharmaceutical executive*

Reno
Jacobson, Raymond Earl *electronics executive*
Tedford, Jack Nowlan III *construction executive, small business owner*

NEW HAMPSHIRE

Bedford
Cronin, Timothy Cornelius III *computer manufacturing executive*

Bennington
Verney, Richard Greville *paper company executive*

East Andover
Gould, Donald Everett *retired chemical company executive, consultant*

Keene
Cohen, Richard B. *grocery company executive*
Miller, Rita *die-casting company executive, personnel consultant*

Milton
Shean, Timothy Joseph *manufacturing executive*

Nashua
Egan, John Frederick *retired electronics executive*

New Castle
Baker, Robert I. *manufacturing executive*

North Hampton
Taylor, Donald *retired manufacturing executive*

Portsmouth
Breen, Edward Deveaux *manufacturing executive*

Stratham
Swartz, Jeffrey B. *apparel executive*

Winchester
MacKay, Neil Duncan *plastics company executive, consultant*

NEW JERSEY

Basking Ridge
Conklin, Donald Ransford *retired pharmaceutical executive*
Dorsa, Caroline *software company executive*

Bridgeton
Howell, James Burt III *retired agricultural products company sales consultant*

Bridgewater
Maynard, Kenneth Irwin *pharmaceutical executive, medical educator, researcher*

Camden
Conant, Douglas R. *food products executive*
Golub, Harvey *food products and former financial services company executive*
Reardon, Nancy Anne *food products executive*
Schiffner, Robert A. *food products executive*

Carteret
Vitrano, Frank G. *supermarket executive*

Cedar Knolls
Schectman, Stephen Barry *pharmaceutical executive*

Colts Neck
Schmalz, Elizabeth Moody *cosmetics company executive*

Cranford
Mazur, Leonard L. *pharmaceutical company executive*

Denville
Minter, Jerry Burnett *electronics executive*

East Brunswick
Wildnauer, Richard Harry *pharmaceutical executive*

East Hanover
Dodsworth, Roy W. *pharmaceutical company executive*

Edison
Alexander, John Charles *pharmaceutical executive, preventive medicine physician*
Samek, Edward Lasker *medical transcription executive*

Englewood
Rotondi, Nicholas John *automotive executive*

Englewood Cliffs
Lawrence, James A. *food products executive*
Neis, Arnold Hayward *pharmaceutical company executive*

Fair Haven
McKissock, David Lee *retired manufacturing company executive*

Farmingdale
Schluter, Peter Mueller *electronics executive*

Flemington
Huguenel, Jean M. *pharmaceutical executive, director, legal assistant*

Fort Monmouth
Schwering, Felix Karl *electronics executive, researcher*
Thornton, Clarence Gould *electronics executive, civilian military employee*

Franklin Lakes
Considine, John R. *pharmaceutical company executive*
Klepper, Kenneth O. *healthcare executive*
Ludwig, Edward J. *medical technology executive*
Snow, David B. *pharmaceutical executive*

Gibbstown
Krebs, Meiken *chemicals executive*

Hainesport
Sylk, Leonard Allen *manufacturing executive, real estate developer*

Highlands
Hansen, Christian Andreas, Jr. *plastics and chemical company executive*

Hillsborough
Kenyhercz, Thomas Michael *pharmaceutical company executive*

Holmdel
Kogelnik, Herwig Werner *electronics company executive*

Hope
McDonald, John Joseph *electronics executive*

Iselin
Perry, Barry W. *manufacturing executive*
Smith, Orin Robert *chemical company executive*

Jersey City
Perhach, James Lawrence *pharmaceutical executive*
Pietrini, Andrew Gabriel *automotive aftermarket executive*

Kendall Park
Hershenov, Bernard Zion *research and development company executive*

Kenilworth
Bertolini, Robert J. *pharmaceutical executive*
Cox, Carrie *pharmaceutical executive*
Hassan, Fred *pharmaceutical executive*

Little Falls
Varis, Agnes *pharmaceutical executive*

Little Silver
Brennan, William Joseph *manufacturing executive*

Madison
Essner, Robert Alan *pharmaceutical executive*
Mahady, Joseph M. *former pharmacy products company executive*
Poussot, Bernard Jean *pharmaceutical executive*

Mahwah
Gerstein, David Brown *manufacturing and professional sports team executive*

Mantoloking
Shane, Kevin *apparel executive, entrepreneur*

Medford
Springer, Douglas Hyde *retired food products executive, lawyer*

Morristown
Cameron, Nicholas Allen *manufacturing executive*
Cote, David M. *diversified technology and manufacturing company executive*
Fradin, Roger Brent *manufacturing executive*
Martelet, Francois R. *pharmaceutical executive*
Williams, Joseph Dalton *pharmaceutical executive*

Neptune
Riordan, John A. *retired food products executive*

New Brunswick
Darretta, Robert J. *pharmaceutical executive*
Deyo, Russell C. *health products executive, lawyer*
Foster-Cheek, Kaye I. *health products executive*
Goggins, Colleen A. *health products executive*
Haines, William Joseph *retired pharmaceutical executive*
Larsen, Ralph S(tanley) *retired pharmaceutical executive*
Mullinix, Kathleen Patricia *food products executive, biochemist*
Peterson, Per A. *health products executive*
Poon, Christine A. *pharmaceutical company executive*
Scodari, Joseph C. *health products executive*
Sosa, Joseph F. *pharmaceutical executive*
Valeriani, Nicholas J. *health products executive*
Weldon, William C. *pharmaceutical executive*

New Providence
Chatterji, Debajyoti *retired manufacturing executive*
McCaffrey, Robert Henry, Jr. *retired manufacturing company executive*

Newark
Emery, Charles Christian, Jr. *health care and information systems executive*
Gibson, Kathleen M. *computer and electronics executive*

Northvale
Di Mino, André Anthony *manufacturing executive, consultant*

ey
sh, Robert Joseph *electronics executive*

land
eimer, Heidi *cosmetics company executive*

. Ridge
ra, Mark P. *automobile rental and leasing mpany executive*
usa, Paul J. *automotive executive*

ippany
arini, William Nicholas *pharmaceutical ecutive*
man, Mark S. *electronics company executive*

pack
Peter *pharmaceutical company executive*

nsauken
ckman, Harold *food manufacturing mpany executive*

Brook
Dongwook *research and development mpany executive*

ataway
oia, G(iambattista) Peter *manufacturing ecutive*

npton Plains
n, Charles Joseph *metals corporation ecutive*

nceton
man, Richard Isaac *health information ecutive*
pbell, Robert Emmett *retired health oducts executive*
naugh, James Henry *health products ecutive, retired federal official*
semi, Seifi *chemicals executive*
blatt, Barry Lance *manufacturing executive*
ica, Joseph A. *pharmaceutical executive*
n, Gregory H. *fiber optic manufacturing ecutive, researcher*
, Bora M. *research and development mpany executive, electrical engineer*

nway
Coss, Malcolm *pharmaceutical executive, emist*

itan
k, Lori Lyn *medical products executive*

l Bank
by, James Larry *home building company ecutive*

gefield
s, Rory B. *pharmaceutical executive*

gewood
ey, Frank Henry *retired chemicals executive*

erton
rien, James Jerome *construction anagement consultant*

ddle Brook
key, William V. *manufacturing executive*
sey, David *manufacturing executive*

aucus
ah, Ezra *apparel executive*
, Paul Foo-Hung *electronics executive*

merset
nson, Louis Vincent, II, *manufacturing ecutive*

uth Hackensack
en, Brett I. *health products executive*

uth Plainfield
kken, William *construction executive*
bert, Paul W. *construction executive*

mmit
lars, Laurence Edward *retired health care roducts executive*
hary, Louis George *chemical company onsultant*

aneck
nberg, Robert S. *plastics company executive, arketing professional*

enton
ky, Tom *agricultural products executive*
comi, Frank Joseph *pharmaceutical executive*

ayne
edman, Martin Burton *retired chemicals xecutive*
yman, Samuel J. *chemical manufacturing ompany executive*
rey, Robert George, Jr. *manufacturing xecutive*

est Orange
enberg, R. Neal *restoration company xecutive*

est Paterson
ey, David *chemicals executive*
nady, Kathleen *pharmaceutical executive*

estfield
Lean, Vincent Ronald *former manufacturing ompany financial executive*

hitehouse Station
stice, David W. *pharmaceutical executive*

Bossidy, Larry (Lawrence Arthur) *pharmaceutical company and former industrial manufacturing executive*
Clark, Richard T. *pharmaceutical company executive*
Deese, Willie A. *pharmaceutical executive*
Frazier, Kenneth C. *pharmaceutical executive, lawyer*
Gilmartin, Raymond V. *pharmaceutical company executive*
Kellogg, Peter Newman *pharmaceutical executive*
McGlynn, Margaret G. *pharmaceutical executive*
McGuire, John Lawrence *pharmaceutical executive*
Scalet, J. Chris (James Christopher Scalet) *pharmaceutical executive*
Weber, Ann *pharmaceutical executive, researcher*
Yarno, Wendy *pharmaceutical executive*

Woodcliff Lake
Tarlowe, Jeffrey L. *health products executive*

NEW MEXICO

Albuquerque
Friberg, George Joseph *electronics company executive, entrepreneur*
Korman, Nathaniel Irving *research and development company executive*
Palmer, Sharon-Joy *agricultural research company executive*
Roberts, Dennis William *construction executive*

Los Alamos
Gregg, Charles Thornton *research and development company executive, molecular biologist, researcher*

Sandia Park
Wilczynski, Janusz S. *manufacturing executive, retired physicist*

NEW YORK

Albany
Heshmat, Hooshang *manufacturing executive*
Kuhla, Donald E. *chemicals executive*
Schulman, Ruth Meryl Aronson *research and development company executive*

Amityville
Soloway, Richard Lewis *electronics executive*

Bohemia
Rudolph, Scott *pharmaceutical executive*

Briarcliff Manor
Bingham, J. Peter *electronics research executive*

Brooklyn
Luterman, Gerald *electronics company executive*
Zisser, Martin Shepherd *fur apparel manufacturer, investor, securities trader*

Buffalo
Rich, Robert E., Jr. *frozen foods company executive*
Starks, Fred William *chemicals executive*

Cazenovia
Carlson, William Clifford *retired defense industry executive, military officer*

Clifton Park
Scher, Robert Sander *instrument design company executive*

Corning
Volanakis, Peter F. *manufacturing executive*

Cross River
Lang, Robert Mays, Jr. *manufacturing and not-for-profit executive*

Deer Park
Kanders, Warren Beatty *manufacturing executive, investment banker*

Derby
Goodell, Joseph Edward *manufacturing executive*

East Amherst
Watson, Stewart Charles *construction executive*

East Hampton
Karp, Harvey Lawrence *metal products executive*

East Northport
Kehoe, Thomas J. *food products executive*

Elma
Hawk, George Wayne *retired electronics company executive*

Fairport
Sands, Richard E. *food products executive*
Sands, Robert *food products executive*

Fayetteville
Pachter, Irwin Jacob *pharmaceutical consultant*

Glen Cove
Burnham, Harold Arthur *pharmaceutical executive, physician*

Great Neck
Arams, Frank Robert *electronics executive*

Greenvale
Krasnoff, Eric *health products executive*

Hartsdale
Martin, Daniel Richard *pharmaceutical executive*

Hauppauge
Hausman, Howard *electronics executive*

Hicksville
Tucci, Gerald Frank *manufacturing executive*

Hoosick Falls
Dodge, Cleveland Earl, Jr. *retired manufacturing executive, director*

Islandia
Artzt, Russell M. *electronics executive*

Ithaca
Cottrell, G. Walton *manufacturing executive*

Lakewood
Anderson, Raymond Quintus *diversified company executive*

Larchmont
Cavanna, Dino Francesco *chemicals executive*
Hinerfeld, Norman Martin *manufacturing executive*

Lockport
Schultz, Gerald Alfred (Jerry Schultz) *retired chemicals executive*
Steinagle, Martin Gene *contractor, paralegal, poet, writer*

Long Island City
Ackerman, Jason *food products executive*
DiGiovanni, Eleanor Elma *scaffold installation company executive*

Mamaroneck
Mizrahi, Abraham Mordechay *retired health products executive, pediatrician*

Melville
Bergman, Stanley M. *health products executive*
Breslawski, James P. *health products executive*
Duval, Daniel Webster *electronics executive*
Gilroy, Kevin *electronics executive*
Kissinger, Walter Bernhard *retired automotive executive*
Kornberg, Fred *electronics executive*
Long, Michael J. *electronics executive*
Mathur, Bhawnesh *electronics executive*
McMahon, John P. *electronics executive*
Mitchell, William Edmund *electronics executive*
Morris, M. Catherine *electronics executive*
Reilly, Paul J. *electronics executive*
Waddell, John Comer *electronics executive*

Monroe
Dierna, Joseph Biagio *construction company executive, land development consultant*

New Hyde Park
Vultaggio, Don J. (Dominick Vultaggio) *beverage company executive*

New Rochelle
Tassone, Gelsomina (Gessie Tassone) *metal products executive*

New York
Alford, Katherine *food products executive*
Amen, Robert M. *manufacturing and retired paper company executive*
Andreotti, Lamberto *pharmaceutical executive*
Armen, Garo H. *research and development company executive*
Attal, Laurent *cosmetics executive*
Axelrod, Norman N(athan) *technology and product development consultant*
Bagger, Richard Hartvig *pharmaceutical executive*
Barnes, Jhane Elizabeth *fashion design company executive, designer*
Barton, Lewis *food products executive, consultant*
Bear, Stephen E. *pharmaceutical executive*
Beattie, E. Scott *cosmetics executive*
Bernstein, Richard Allen *food products executive*
Bonfield, Andrew R.J. *pharmaceutical executive*
Boswell, Gina R. *cosmetics executive*
Bresani, Federico Fernando *manufacturing executive*
Brestle, Daniel J. *cosmetics executive*
Brown, Bobbi *cosmetics executive*
Call, Neil Judson *manufacturing executive*
Camilleri, Louis C. *consumer goods company executive*
Campbell, Robert David *manufacturing and metal products executive*
Carvette, Anthony M. *construction executive*
Casey, Gerard William *retired food products executive, lawyer*
Celentano, John E. *pharmaceutical executive*
Chirico, Emanuel *apparel executive*
Clarke, Kenneth Kingsley *retired electronics executive*
Cornelius, James Milton *pharmaceutical company executive*
Cramb, Charles W. *cosmetics executive*
D'Amelio, Frank Anthony *pharmaceutical executive, former telecommunications industry executive*
Davoren, Peter J. *construction executive*
Denmark, Bernhardt *manufacturing executive*
de Notaristefani, Carlo *pharmaceutical executive*
Dixon, Wendy L. *pharmaceutical executive*
Donaghy, James K. *construction executive, contractor*
Earl, Christopher D. *health products executive*
Ewing-Mulligan, Mary *food products executive*
Farber, John J. *chemical company executive*
Feczko, Joe *cosmetics executive*
Feczko, Joseph M. *pharmaceutical executive*
Fischer, Joseph L. *pharmaceutical executive*
Fribourg, Paul J. *grain company executive*
Geckle, Robert Alan *manufacturing executive*
Goodale, Toni Krissel *research and development company executive*
Gould, Harry Edward, Jr. *paper company executive*
Greeff, Douglas Haven *cosmetics executive*
Gromek, Joseph R. *apparel executive*
Gunn, Tim (Timothy M. Gunn) *apparel executive*
Hoffman, Ronald L. *manufacturing executive*
Hooper, Anthony C. *pharmaceutical executive*
Juliber, Lois D. *manufacturing executive*
Jung, Andrea *cosmetics company executive*
Kelson, Richard B. *metal products executive*
Kennedy, David L. *cosmetics company executive*
Kindler, Jeffrey B. *pharmaceutical company executive, lawyer*
Kleinfeld, Klaus *metal products executive, former electronics executive*
Koch, David Hamilton *chemical company executive*
Krill, Kay (Katherine Lawther Krill) *apparel executive*
Kuhbach, Robert Gerdes *manufacturing executive*
Kunes, Richard W. *cosmetics executive*
LaMattina, John L. *pharmaceutical executive*
Langhammer, Fred H. *cosmetics company executive*
Lauder, Aerin *cosmetics executive*
Lauder, Evelyn H. *cosmetics executive*
Lauder, Leonard Alan *cosmetic and fragrance company executive*
Lauder, William P. *cosmetics executive*
Leung, Sandra *pharmaceutical executive, lawyer*
Levinson, Robert Alan *textiles executive*
Lifton, Robert Kenneth *manufacturing executive*
Lord, Marvin *apparel executive*
May, Peter William *business executive*
May, William Frederick *manufacturing executive*
McFadden, Mary Josephine *fashion industry executive*
McKinnell, Hank (Henry A. McKinnell Jr.) *pharmaceutical executive*
McKinnon, Floyd Wingfield *textile executive*
McLane, Charles D., Jr. *metal products executive*
Mc Namara, Robert A. *construction company executive*
Mina, Richard T. *apparel executive*
Montero, Sylvia *pharmaceutical executive*
Moore, Charles Hewes, Jr. *manufacturing executive*
Mosbacher, Georgette Paulsin *cosmetics executive*
Mullen, Robert W. *construction executive*
Munroe, George Barber *retired mining and manufacturing company executive*
Muscari, Joseph Charles *manufacturing executive*
Natori, Josie Cruz (Josefina Almeda Cruz Natori) *apparel executive*
Oglesby, Charles R. *automotive executive*
Panagos, Steven Gregory *food products executive*
Pietruski, John Michael, Jr. *pharmaceutical executive*
Pollard, Veronica *automotive executive*
Press, Jim (James E. Press) *automotive executive*
Puschel, Philip P. *textiles executive*
Randall, Jessie *apparel executive*
Read, Ian C. *pharmaceutical executive*
Reece, Thomas L. *manufacturing executive*
Reed, W. Allen *automotive executive*
Reidy, Maureen J. *fashion industry executive*
Reitan, Bernt *metal products executive*
Rennert, Ira Leon *manufacturing executive*
Rosenberg, Robert Charles *housing corporation executive*
Rosenthal, Tamara *apparel executive*
Rubin, Joel Edward *manufacturing executive*
Scarpa, A. Michael *apparel and corporate financial executive*
Scarpa, Michael *apparel executive*
Schulhof, Michael Peter *electronics company executive*
Shedlarz, David L. *pharmaceutical executive*
Shineman, Edward William, Jr. *retired pharmaceutical executive*
Sigal, Elliott *pharmaceutical executive*
Smith, J. Gordon *automotive executive*
Solomon, Howard *pharmaceutical executive*
Spector, Jonathan *business research organization executive, former dean*
Steere, William Campbell, Jr. *pharmaceutical executive*
Steiner, Jeffrey Josef *manufacturing executive*
Stockton, Susan *food products executive*
Szymanczyk, Michael E. *tobacco products executive*
Takhar, Bonnie *apparel executive*
Targoff, Michael Bart *space and communications company executive*
Tishman, Daniel R. *construction executive*
Tse, Charles Yung Chang *pharmaceutical executive, lawyer*
von der Heyden, Karl Mueller *retired manufacturing executive*
Warren, Andrew C. *apparel executive*
Waxman, Allen *pharmaceutical executive*
Weber, Mark *apparel executive*
Whiting, Susan Dickinson *media research company executive*
Wieser, Helmut *metal products executive*
Wolgemuth, Richard Lee *pharmaceutical executive*
Woolard, Edgar S., Jr. *retired chemical company executive*
Yee, Bennie Sene *construction manager, electrical engineer*
Zito, Robert Thomas *pharmaceutical executive*

Pittsford
Dobbs, Herbert Hotaling *automotive executive, consultant, research scientist, retired military officer*
Green, Martin Lincoln *retired medical products executive*

Poughkeepsie
Sherman, Ethan *contractor, publisher*
Slade, Bernard Newton *electronics executive*

Purchase
Bryant, Daniel James *food and beverage company executive, former federal agency administrator*
Finnerty, Louise Hoppe *food products executive*
Goodman, Richard *food products executive*
Nooyi, Indra Krishnamurthy *food products executive*
Reinemund, Steven S. *retired food products executive*
Trudell, Cynthia M. *food products executive, former automotive executive*
Wallach, Kenneth L. *paper company executive*
White, Michael Dennis *food products executive*

Rhinecliff
Conklin, John Roger *retired electronics company executive*

Rochester
Bouyoucos, John Vinton *retired research and development company executive*
Collins, Christopher Carl *manufacturing executive*
Duke, Charles Bryan *electronics executive, physicist, educator*
Gustin, Carl E., Jr. *manufacturing executive*
Sieg, Albert Louis *photographic company executive*
Zarrella, Ronald L. *pharmaceutical executive*

Roslyn Heights
Guthart, Leo A. *electronics executive*

Rye Brook
Kuntzman, Ronald *research and development company executive*
Masson, Robert Henry *paper company executive*

Sands Point
Wurzel, Leonard *retired candy manufacturing company executive*

Scarsdale
Blitman, Howard Norton *construction executive*
Johnson, Boine Theodore *manufacturing executive, mayor*

Schenectady
Fell, Samuel Kennedy (Ken) *infosystems executive*
Sternlicht, Beno *research and development company executive*

Seaford
Setzler, William Edward *retired chemicals executive*

Sidney
Werner, David A. *paper company executive*

Somers
Beracha, Barry Harris *food products executive*

Spring Valley
Mittleberg, Eric Michael *pharmaceutical executive*

Syracuse
Steigerwald, Louis John III *corporate executive*

Tarrytown
Yancopoulos, George D. *pharmaceutical executive*

Turin
Klossner, Windy *food products executive*

Utica
Antzelevitch, Charles *research and development company executive*

Wantagh
Blum, Melvin *chemical company executive, researcher*

Webster
Curtis, Deana A. *electronics executive, small business owner*

West Harrison
Reichelderfer, Brenda L. *manufacturing executive*

West Seneca
Bidlack, Jerald Dean *manufacturing executive*

Westbury
Brooks, David H. *manufacturing executive*

White Plains
Abrams, Leigh Jeffrey *manufacturing executive*
Fisher, Jerome *apparel executive*
Loranger, Steven R. *industrial manufacturing company executive*

Whitestone
Bikoff, J. Darius *beverage company executive*
Oza, Rohan *beverage company executive*
Rahr, Stewart *health medical products executive*

Woodbury
Guttenplan, Harold Esau *retired food company executive*

Yonkers
Holtz, Gilbert Joseph *steel company executive*
Lukach, Arthur S., Jr. *manufacturing executive*

Youngstown
Alpert, Norman *chemical company executive*

NORTH CAROLINA

Asheville
Coli, Guido John *chemical company executive*

Beaufort
Cullman, Hugh *retired tobacco company executive*

Blowing Rock
Barnebey, Kenneth Alan *food products executive*

Chapel Hill
Cummings, Sandra Eileen *medical products executive*

Charlotte
Belk, Thomas Milburn, Jr., (Tim) *apparel executive*
Browning, Peter Crane *manufacturing executive*
Dickson, Thomas Walter *textile company executive*
DiMicco, Daniel R. *manufacturing executive*
Ferriola, John J. *manufacturing executive*
Kearney, Christopher J. *manufacturing executive, lawyer*
Kuechle, Scott E. *manufacturing executive*
Larsen, Marshall O. *manufacturing executive*
Lea, Scott Carter *retired packaging company executive*
Lisenby, Terry S. *manufacturing executive*
Lott, Hamilton, Jr. *manufacturing executive*
McKinnish, Richmond D. *manufacturing executive*
Nelson, Thomas C. *manufacturing executive*
Parrish, D. Michael *manufacturing executive*
Peacock, A(lvin) Ward *textile company executive*
Roberts, David A. *manufacturing executive*
Rutkowski, Joseph A. *manufacturing executive*
Seidel, James P. *manufacturing executive*
Siegel, Samuel *metals company executive*
Smith, B. Scott *automotive executive*
Smith, O. Bruton *automotive company executive*
Spangler, Clemmie Dixon, Jr. *construction company executive*
Squires, James Ralph *development company executive*
Sulg, Madis *manufacturing executive, entrepreneur*

Durham
Gillings, Dennis B. *medical products executive*
Ladd, Marcia Lee *medical products executive*
Maar, Rosina *medical products executive*
Sharma, Anand *manufacturing executive*

Fayetteville
Richardson, Emilie White *manufacturing, investment company executive, educator*

Gastonia
Kimbrell, Willard Duke *textiles executive*
Lawson, William David III *retired cotton company executive*

Greensboro
McDonald, Mackey J. *apparel executive*
Shearer, Robert K. *apparel executive*
Wiseman, Eric C. *apparel executive*

Hertford
Johnson, Donald Lee *retired agricultural materials processing company executive*

High Point
Fenn, Ormon William, Jr. *furniture company executive*

Kitty Hawk
Sjoerdsma, Albert *research and development company executive*

Morrisville
Harker, Brian J. *tobacco company executive*
Harrison, Pete (Robert E. Harrison) *tobacco company executive*

Mount Airy
Woltz, Howard Osler, Jr. *retired metal products executive*

Pinehurst
O'Neill, John Joseph, Jr. *retired chemicals executive*

Raleigh
Prior, William Allen *electronics company executive*
Risher, James A. *electronics executive*
Sloan, O. Temple, Jr. *automotive equipment executive*
Wilson, Donald Hurst III *biopharmaceutical industry executive*
Zelnak, Stephen P., Jr. *construction materials company executive*

Rocky Mount
Stubbs, Will, Jr. *pharmaceutical company manager*

Weldon
Barringer, Paul Brandon, II, *lumber company executive*

Wilmington
Buckland, Wendy *medical products executive*

Winston Salem
Brewster, Daryl G. *food products executive*
Chaden, Lee A. *apparel and former food products executive*
Hanes, Ralph Philip, Jr. *retired textiles executive, horse breeder*
Maselli, John Anthony *food products executive*
McKnight, Gregory Richard *research director*
Noll, Richard A. *apparel executive*

NORTH DAKOTA

West Fargo
Schneider, Dennis Eugene *manufacturing executive*

OHIO

Akron
Haines, Terry L. *plastics company executive*
Kaufman, Donald Leroy *building products executive*
Keegan, Robert J. *manufacturing executive*
Kramer, Richard J. *manufacturing executive*

Avon Lake
Newlin, Stephen Dore *chemicals executive*
Patient, William F. *chemicals executive*

Beachwood
Demetriou, Steven J. *metal products executive*

Bellville
Hooker, James Todd *manufacturing executive*

Boardman
Skinner, William Philip, Jr. *manufacturing executive*

Canton
Griffith, James W. *manufacturing executive*
Swidarski, Thomas W. *manufacturing executive*
Timken, Ward J., Jr. *manufacturing executive*

Chagrin Falls
Brophy, Jere Hall *manufacturing executive*
Heckman, Henry Trevennen Shick *retired steel executive*

Cincinnati
Aguirre, Fernando *food products executive*
Christensen, Paul Walter, Jr. *retired gear manufacturing company executive*
Farmer, Richard T. *uniform rental and sales executive*
Farmer, Scott D. *apparel executive*
Heschel, Michael Shane *retail food products executive*
Hutton, Edward Luke *medical products executive*
Jones, Daniel W. *construction executive*
Ruthman, Thomas Robert *manufacturing executive*
Sakkab, Nabil Yaqub *research and development company executive*
Schlotman, J. Michael *food products executive*
Stern, Joseph Smith, Jr. *former footwear manufacturing company executive*

Cleveland
Arnold, Craig *manufacturing executive*
Buente, Stephen M. *manufacturing executive*
Carson, Randy W. *manufacturing executive*
Christopher, William F. *metal products executive*
Collins, Duane E. *manufacturing executive*
Connor, Christopher M. *manufacturing executive*
Cutler, Alexander MacDonald *manufacturing executive*
Decker, John William *metal products executive*
Fearon, Richard H. *manufacturing executive*
Haeck, James F. *manufacturing executive*
Holmes, Arthur S. *manufacturing executive*
Ivy, Conway Gayle *paint company executive*
Jenson, Jon Eberdt *metal products executive*
Luke, Randall Dan *retired manufacturing executive, lawyer*
Mandel, Jack N. *manufacturing executive*
McFadden, John Volney *retired manufacturing company executive*
Morikis, John G. *manufacturing executive*
Pugh, David L. *manufacturing executive*
Sweetnam, James E. *manufacturing executive*
Thomas, Richard Stephen *construction executive*
Vande Steeg, Nickolas W. *manufacturing executive*
Washkewicz, Donald E. *manufacturing executive*
Weiss, Morry *greeting card company executive*

Columbus
Carter, William H. *chemicals executive*
Cottingham, Richard Sumner *paper company executive*
Daab-Krzykowski, Andre *pharmaceutical and nutritional manufacturing company administrator*
Evans, Daniel E. *manufacturing executive, restaurant chain company executive*
Knilans, Michael Jerome *retired food products executive*
Kohrt, Carl Fredrick *research and development company executive*
Lazar, Theodore Aaron *retired manufacturing executive, lawyer*
Margolis, Jay M. *clothing executive*
McConnell, John P. *metal products executive*
Milford, Frederick John *retired research and development company executive*
Morrison, Craig O. *chemicals executive*
Pfening, Frederic Denver III *manufacturing executive*
Spoerry, Robert F. *manufacturing executive*
Turney, Sharen Jester *apparel executive, cosmetics executive*
Wexner, Abigail *apparel executive*
Wigington, Ronald Lee *retired chemical information services executive*
Yenkin, Bernard Kalman *coatings and resins company executive*

Cuyahoga Falls
Butcher, Jack Robert (Jack Risin) *manufacturing executive, film producer, actor, artist*

Dayton
Harlan, Norman Ralph *construction executive*
Isaacson, Milton Stanley (Jim) *research and development company executive, engineer*
Mathile, Clayton Lee *pet food company executive*
McIlroy, Alan F. *manufacturing executive*
Suwyn, Mark A. *paper company executive*

Delaware
Eells, William Hastings *retired automobile company executive*
Huml, Donald Scott *manufacturing executive*

Dublin
Borror, Douglas G. *construction company executive*
Clark, R. Kerry (Kerry Clark) *health products executive*
Clement, Henry Joseph, Jr. *diversified building products executive*
Dolch, Gary D. *health products executive*
Fong, Ivan Kenneth *health products executive, lawyer*
Henderson, Jeffrey W. *health products executive*
Lamp, Benson J. *tractor company executive*
Lynch, Michael A. *health products executive*
Papa, Joseph C. *pharmaceutical executive*
Parrish, Mark *health products executive*
Rishel, James Burton *manufacturing executive, director*
Rosenbaum, Mark E. *health products executive*
Schlotterbeck, David L. *health products executive*
Slagle, Tom *medical products executive*
Troup, Gordon A. *health products executive*
Walsh, Daniel J. *health products executive*
Walter, Robert D. *health products executive*
Winstead, Dwight *medical products executive*

Elyria
Mixon, Aaron Malachi III *medical products executive*

Findlay
Armes, Roy V. *manufacturing executive*

Garrettsville
Diskin, Michael Edward *plastics company and food service executive*

Gates Mills
Veale, Tinkham, II, *retired chemicals executive, engineer*

Hamilton
Epp, Mary Elizabeth *retired technologies consultant*

Holland
D'Anniballe, Priscilla Lucille *contracting company executive*

Jackson Center
Thompson, Wade Francis Bruce *manufacturing executive*

Mansfield
Gorman, James Carvill *manufacturing executiv*

Mason
Kohlhepp, Robert J. *apparel executive*
Wilson, Frederic Sandford *pharmaceutical company executive*

Mayfield Heights
Rankin, Alfred Marshall, Jr. *manufacturing executive*

Medina
Matejka, Robert *chemicals executive*
Smith, Richey *manufacturing executive*
Sullivan, Frank C. *manufacturing executive*
Sullivan, Thomas Christopher *coatings compar executive*

Mentor
Callsen, Christian Edward *health products executive*

Middletown
Wainscott, James Lawrence *steel industry executive*

Milan
Henry, Joseph Patrick *chemicals executive*

New Albany
Jeffries, Michael S. (Mike Jeffries) *apparel executive*

New Bremen
Dicke, James Frederick, II, *manufacturing executive*

North Canton
Lynham, C(harles) Richard *manufacturing executive*

North Ridgeville
Stewart, Arden Ruth *retired automotive execu*

Orrville
Smucker, Richard K. *food products executive*
Smucker, Timothy P. *food products executive*

Perrysburg
King, John Joseph *manufacturing executive*

Randolph
Pecano, Donald Carl *automotive manufacturin executive*

Solon
Rosica, Gabriel Adam *retired manufacturing executive, electrical engineer*

Tipp City
Tighe-Moore, Barbara Jeanne *electronics executive*

Toledo
Brown, David T. *manufacturing executive*
Burns, Michael J. *automotive executive*
DeBacker, Michael Lee *automotive executive, lawyer*
Romanoff, Milford Martin *retired building contractor*

Thaman, Michael H. *building material systems executive*

West Chester
Mack, Mark Philip *chemical company executive*

Wickliffe
Cooley, Charles P. *chemicals executive*
Hambrick, James L. *chemicals executive*

Winchester
Koford, Stuart Keith *electronics executive*

Youngstown
Kessler, Ronald N. *plastics company executive*

OKLAHOMA

Norman
Roller, Chad B. *research and development company executive*

Oklahoma City
Turner, Eugene Andrew *manufacturing executive*

Tulsa
Thomas, Robert Eggleston *retired manufacturing executive*

OREGON

Beaverton
Bird, Lewis L. III *apparel executive*
Blair, Donald W. *apparel executive*
Clarke, Thomas E. *apparel executive*
Denson, Charles D. *apparel executive*
DeStefano, Gary M. *apparel executive*
Edwards, Trevor *apparel executive*
Knight, Philip Hampson *apparel executive*
Parker, Mark G. *apparel executive*

Eugene
Woolley, Donna Pearl *lumber company executive*

Hillsboro
Barnes, Keith Lee *electronics executive*

Klamath Falls
Wendt, Richard L. *manufacturing executive*

Medford
de Boer, Sidney B. *automotive executive*
Heimann, M.L. (Dick Heimann) *auto dealership executive*

Portland
Boyle, Gertrude *sportswear company executive*
Donegan, Mark *metal products executive*
Drinkward, Cecil *construction company executive*
Champlin, Robert Boisseau, Sr. *retired textile manufacturing executive*
Champlin, Robert Boisseau, Jr. *manufacturing company executive, minister, writer*

Tualatin
Javorsky, William D. *semiconductor company executive*

PENNSYLVANIA

Allentown
Baker, Dexter Farrington *manufacturing executive, director*
Emmer, Richard L. *electronics executive*
Hutton, William Michael *manufacturing executive*
Jones, John P. III *chemicals executive*
Jovett, John Robert *retired chemical company executive*
McGlade, John E. *chemicals executive*

Allison Park
Backus, John King *former chemical company research administrator*

Avondale
Bel, Daniel Denwood, Sr. *manufacturing executive*

Belle Vernon
Kapiennik, Carl Francis *manufacturing executive, planetarium and science institute administrator*

Bensalem
Born, Dorrit J. *apparel executive*

Berwyn
Birch, John Walter *mining equipment company executive*

Bethlehem
Barnette, Curtis Handley *steel company executive, lawyer*
Hartmann, Robert Elliott *retired manufacturing executive*
Lettinger, William Charles *electronics company executive*
Marsh, Robert Harry *chemicals executive*
St. John, Anthony Paul *retired manufacturing executive*

Blue Bell
Gregson, Nigel Christopher *pharmaceutical executive, consultant*
Adam, Will *electronics executive, consultant*

Bradford
Rice, Lester *electronics company executive*

Bristol
Card, Wesley Roy *apparel and footwear company executive*
Kimmel, Sidney *apparel company executive, film producer*

Camp Hill
Blouch, Timothy Craig *food company executive*

Canonsburg
Coury, Robert J. *pharmaceutical executive*
Puskar, Milan *pharmaceuticals executive*

Chadds Ford
Lee, David A.H. *pharmaceutical executive*

Chambersburg
Rumler, Robert Hoke *agricultural products executive, consultant, retired trade association administrator*

Chesterbrook
Hilzinger, Kurt John *health products executive*

Conshohocken
Lotman, Herbert *food processing executive*
Naples, Ronald James *manufacturing executive*
Spaeth, Karl Henry *retired chemicals executive, lawyer*

Denver
Milner, Charles Fremont, Jr. *manufacturing executive*

Devon
Porter, Roger John *research and development company executive, neurologist, pharmacologist*

Easton
Sun, Robert Zu Jei *manufacturing company executive, inventor, educator*

Eighty Four
Magerko, Margaret Hardy (Maggie) *lumber company executive*

Emmaus
Bowers, Klaus D(ieter) *electronics executive, researcher*

Erie
Renkis, Alan Ilmars *plastics formulating company executive*

Frazer
Baldino, Frank, Jr. *biopharmaceutical executive*

Gap
Beiler, Anne F. *food company executive*

Greentown
Forcheskie, Carl S. *former apparel company executive*

Hanover
Kline, Donald *food company executive*

Hershey
Buck, Michele *food products executive*
Lenny, Richard Herbert *food products executive, marketing professional*
Thomas, Andrea B. *food products executive*

Hollidaysburg
Bloom, Lawrence Stephen *retired clothing company executive*

Horsham
Christian, Mildred Stoehr *health products executive*
Luby, Michael J. *research and development company executive*
Sachs, Keith L. *manufacturing executive*
Toll, Robert Irwin *home construction company executive*

King Of Prussia
Webb, Richard Stephen *manufacturing executive*

Lancaster
High, S. Dale *construction executive*
Liddell, W. Kirk *specialty contracting company executive*
Lockhart, Michael D. *manufacturing executive*

Latrobe
Cardoso, Carlos M. *metal products executive*
Daughenbaugh, Terry L. *metal products executive*
Tambakeras, Markos I. *machine tool manufacturer*

Levittown
Henshaw, Jonathan Cook *retired manufacturing executive*

Ligonier
Pilz, Alfred Norman *manufacturing executive*

Lyon Station
Breidegam, DeLight Edgar, Jr. *battery company executive*

Malvern
Espe, Matthew J. *manufacturing executive*
Paul, Gerald D. *electronics executive*
Stetson, John Batterson, IV, *construction executive*
Zandman, Felix *electronics executive*

Marion Center
Purdy, David Lawrence *medical products executive*

Mc Murray
Langenberg, Frederick Charles *manufacturing executive*

Mechanicsburg
Ortenzio, Robert A. *health and medical products executive*

New Freedom
Eikenberg, John Robert *retired electronics executive*

New Kensington
Zaidi, Mohammad A. *metal products executive*

Newtown
Ross, Edwin William *rubber company executive*

Newtown Square
Benenson, James, Jr. *manufacturer*
Grubb, Gary S. *pharmaceutical executive*

North Wales
Kim, Peter Sungbai *pharmaceutical and research and development company executive, educator*

Paoli
Hermance, Frank S. *electronics executive*

Philadelphia
Barrett, J. Patrick *manufacturing executive*
Conway, John W. *manufacturing executive*
Croisetiere, Jacques M. *chemicals executive*
Garnier, Jean-Pierre *pharmaceutical executive*
Gupta, Rajiv Lochan *chemicals executive*
Katherine, Robert Andrew *chemicals executive*
Leonard, William *automotive supplies and retired food services company executive*
Neubauer, Joseph *food services company executive*
Payne, Deborah Anne *retired medical company officer*
Potamkin, Robert *automotive executive*
Rachor, Jeffrey C. *automotive supplies company executive*
Rutherford, Alan W. *manufacturing executive*
Sutherland, L(ewis) Frederick *food products executive*

Pipersville
McNutt, Richard Hunt *manufacturing executive*

Pittsburgh
Barkus, Bruce E. *health products executive*
Belda, Alain J. P. *metal products executive*
Berkman, Louis *steel company executive*
Bunch, Charles E. *manufacturing executive*
Connelly, John J. *metal products executive*
Frank, Alan I W *manufacturing executive*
Goodish, John H. *metal products executive*
Haggerty, Gretchen R. *metal products executive*
Harrell, Edward Harding *wine festival executive*
Hassey, L. Patrick *metal products executive*
Heilman, Marlin Stephen *medical products executive*
Hernandez, William H. *chemical company executive*
Huntington, James Cantine, Jr. *retired equipment manufacturing company executive*
Jeremiah, Barbara S. *metal products executive*
Kutka, J. James, Jr. *metal products executive*
Lego, Paul Edward *retired manufacturing executive*
Minnaugh, Mark J *food products/retail grocery executive*
Navetta, Christopher J. *metal products executive*
Nollen, Meg (Margaret Roach Nollen) *food products executive*
Paul, Robert Arthur *steel company executive*
Ruskin, Ryan Scott *packaging company executive*
Sterling, Thomas W. *metal products executive*
Straub, Terrence D. *metal products executive*
Surma, John P., Jr. *metal products executive*
Thomas, Paul D. *metal products executive, human resources specialist*
Winkleblack, Arthur B. *food products executive*

Royersford
Black, Jeffrey P. *manufacturing executive*

Rydal
Reese, Francis Edward *retired chemical company executive, consultant*

Saint Marys
Johnson, J. M. Hamlin *manufacturing executive*

Sewickley
Bouchard, James Paul *metal products executive*

State College
Byrom, Fletcher Lauman *chemical manufacturing company executive*
Huck, John Lloyd *pharmaceutical executive*

Valley Forge
Dachowski, Peter Richard *manufacturing executive*

Warminster
Hull, Lewis Woodruff *manufacturing executive*
Kan, Kevin S. *automotive executive*

Warrendale
O'Donnell, James V. *apparel executive*

Wayne
Salinas, Eliseo *research and development company executive, psychiatrist, researcher*
Wilson, James Lawrence *retired chemical company executive*
Yost, R. David (David Yost) *pharmaceutical executive*

West Chester
Gadsby, Robin Edward *chemicals executive*

Heaps, Marvin Dale *retired food services company executive*

West Point
Choi, Dennis W. *pharmaceutical executive, neurologist, educator*

Willow Street
Coleman, Ernest Albert *plastics and materials consultant*
Jones, Joseph Louis *retired manufacturing executive*
Reese, Harry Edwin, Jr. *electronics executive*

York
Wise, Bret W. *chemical company executive*

Zelienople
Efaw, Cary Ross *manufacturing executive*

RHODE ISLAND

North Kingstown
Novich, Bruce Eric *chemicals executive*

Pawtucket
Trueb, Martin R. *toy company executive*

Providence
Bready, Richard Lawrence *manufacturing executive*
Choquette, Paul Joseph, Jr. *construction company executive*
Gilbane, Thomas F., Jr. *construction executive*
Papitto, Ralph Raymond *manufacturing executive*

West Kingston
Dowdell, Rodger B., Jr. *electronics executive*

Woonsocket
Crawford, (Edwin) Mac *pharmaceutical company executive*
McLure, Howard A. *pharmaceutical executive*
Ryan, Thomas M. *pharmaceutical company executive*
Sgarro, Douglas A. *pharmaceutical executive, lawyer*

SOUTH CAROLINA

Aiken
Seabrook, John Martin *retired food products executive, chemical engineer*

Camden
Daniels, John Hancock *agricultural products company executive*

Charleston
Leonard, Guy Meyers, Jr. *international holding company executive*
Martin, Roblee Boettcher *retired cement manufacturing executive*

Clinton
Cornelson, George Henry, IV, *retired textile company executive*

Fort Mill
Bowles, Crandall Close *textiles executive*

Greenville
Bauknight, Clarence Brock *construction and retail executive, consultant*
Newman, R. Donald *paper company executive*
Paterson, David J. *paper company executive*
Varin, Roger Robert *textile executive*

Hartsville
DeLoach, Harris E.(Eugene), Jr. *manufacturing executive, lawyer*

Hilton Head Island
Cunningham, William Henry *retired food products executive*
Harty, James D. *former manufacturing company executive*
Lewis, Gene Evans *retired medical equipment company executive*
Mersereau, Hiram Stipe *wood products company consultant*
Pritchard, Dalton Harold *retired electronics executive*
Rulis, Raymond Joseph *manufacturing executive, consultant*
Russell, Allen Stevenson *retired metal products executive*
Wright, Marshall *manufacturing executive, diplomat*

Kiawah Island
Korb, William Brown, Jr. *retired manufacturing executive*

Murrells Inlet
Kelly, Gerald Wayne *chemical coatings company executive*

North Charleston
Zucker, Jerry *chemical manufacturing executive*

Spartanburg
Dent, Frederick Baily *retired textiles executive, ambassador*
Milliken, Roger *textile/chemical company executive*

Townville
Wright, George Cullen *retired electronics company executive*

SOUTH DAKOTA

Dakota Dunes
Leman, Eugene D. *meat industry executive*

Rapid City
Daughenbaugh, Randall Jay *retired chemical company executive, consultant*
Voyles, C. Robert *electronics executive*

Sioux Falls
Christensen, David Allen *retired manufacturing executive*
Rosenthal, Joel *manufacturing executive*
Stowers, Mark David *chemicals executive*

TENNESSEE

Bartlett
Huffman, Delton Cleon, Jr. *pharmacy association executive*

Brentwood
Wright, James F. *agricultural products executive*

Bristol
Markison, Brian A. *pharmaceutical executive*

Collegedale
McKee, Ellsworth R. *food products executive*

Cookeville
Wilson, Terrence Raymond *manufacturing executive*

Franklin
Andrews, William Frederick *manufacturing executive*
White, David R. *healthcare company executive*

Kingsport
Coover, Harry Wesley *manufacturing executive*
Ferguson, J. Brian *chemicals executive*
Findley, Don Aaron *manufacturing executive*
Head, William Iverson, Sr. *retired chemical company executive*

Knoxville
Martin, James Robert *identification company executive*

Lebanon
Evins, Dan W. *food products executive*

Memphis
Dunnigan, T. Kevin *retired electrical and electronics manufacturing company executive*
Mantey, Elmer Martin *food company executive*
O'Hagan, William D. *metal products manufacturing executive*
Pileggi, Dominic J. *electronics executive*
Rhodes, William C. III *automotive executive*

Nashville
Bracken, Richard M. *healthcare company executive*
Cook, E. Gary *manufacturing executive*
Fitzgerald, Edmund Bacon *electronics executive*
Frost, Richard W. *manufacturing executive*
Frost, Rick *manufacturing executive*
Harris, J. George (Jacob George Harris) *health products executive*
Juszkiewicz, Henry Edward *musical instrument company executive*
Martin, Charles Neil, Jr. *health care management company executive*
Wire, William Shidaker, II, *retired apparel and footwear manufacturing company executive*

Oak Ridge
Poutsma, Marvin L. *retired chemical research administrator*

Tullahoma
Jackson, William David *research and development company executive*

Union City
Graham, R(ichard) Newell *soft drink bottling company executive*

TEXAS

Addison
Holl, David B. *cosmetics company executive*
Rogers, Richard Raymond *cosmetics company executive*

Amarillo
Attebury, William Hugh *construction company executive*

Angleton
Fu, Cary T. *electronics executive*
Nigbor, Donald E. *electronics executive*

Arlington
Mc Keen, Chester M., Jr. *retired manufacturing executive*

Austin
Culp, Joe C(arl) *electronics executive*
Duke, Carol Michiels *health products executive*
Inman, Bobby Ray *retired electronics executive*
Jastrow, Kenneth M. *forest products, real estate and financial company executive*
Lang, Roberta Lynn *food products company executive, lawyer*
Mackey, John P. *food products executive*
Thornton, Joseph Scott *research and development company executive, materials scientist*
Vykukal, Eugene Lawrence *pharmaceutical executive, director*

Boerne
Richmond, James Ellis *retired restaurant company executive*

Carrollton
Illes, George Maximilian *retired food products executive*

Conroe
Steed, Theresa Jean *manufacturing executive*

Coppell
McCally, Charles Richard *construction company executive, consultant, mathematician, educator*

Corpus Christi
Kane, Sam *meat company executive*

Crowley
Kemp, Thomas Joseph *retired electronics executive*

Dallas
Albright, Michael *construction executive*
Angelilli, Lawrence *construction executive*
Barnes, Robert Vertreese, Jr. *construction executive*
Black, Robert W. *health products executive*
Bosch, Joseph A. *construction executive*
Bradford, William Edward *oil field equipment manufacturing company executive*
Brekhus, Melvin G. *construction executive*
Buthman, Mark A. *health products executive*
Callahan, Jack F., Jr. *food products executive*
Delagi, Greg *electronics executive*
Eller, Timothy R. *construction and real estate company executive*
Engibous, Thomas James *electronics executive*
Engles, Gregg L. *food products executive*
Ethridge, Joseph Alfred *manufacturing executive*
Falk, Thomas J. *health products executive*
Gafford, Ronald J. *construction executive*
George, Arthur L. *electronics executive*
Guerin, Dean Patrick *metal products executive*
Hames, Michael J. *electronics executive*
Heacock, David *electronics executive*
Hirsch, Laurence Eliot *construction executive, investment banker*
Hunter, Robert Charles *entertainment executive*
Kemp, Mark D. *construction executive*
Keown, Michael H. *food products executive*
Leedom, John Nesbett *manufacturing executive, state legislator*
Lovett, Melendy *electronics executive*
Lowe, Gregg A. *electronics executive*
March, Kevin P. *electronics executive*
McElvain, David Plowman *retired manufacturing, finance company executive*
Murphy, John Joseph *manufacturing executive*
Palmer, Anthony J. *health products executive*
Pearce, Ronald *retired cosmetic company executive*
Ritchie, Kevin *electronics executive*
Roach, John D. *building products company executive*
Robertson, Beverly Carruth *retired steel company executive*
Rosson, Glenn Richard *building products and furniture company executive*
Roth, James Frank *chemicals executive, chemist*
Sherman, Floyd F. *construction executive*
Smith, Catherine R. *construction executive*
Solomon, William Tarver *general construction company executive*
Sterin, Steven M. *chemicals executive*
Stewart, Robert S. *construction executive*
Templeton, Richard K. *electronics executive*
Tucker, J. Walter, Jr. *manufacturing executive*
Van Scoter, John C. *electronics executive*
Wallace, Timothy R. *manufacturing executive*
Weidman, David N. *chemicals executive*
West, Teresa L. (Terri West) *electronics executive*
Whitaker, Darla *electronics executive*
Wyant, Clyde W., Jr. *manufacturing executive*
Zumwalt, Richard Dowling *flour mill executive*

Diboll
Harbordt, Charles Michael *forest products executive*

Flower Mound
Kumar, Surinder *food products executive*

Fort Worth
Corbusier, Drue *apparel and home furnishings executive*
Curts, Harold Layne *construction executive*
Dwyer, Stacey H. *construction executive*
Fuller, Samuel R. *construction executive*
Horton, Donald R. *construction executive*
Roland, Billy Ray *electronics company executive*
Thornton, Charles Victor *metals executive*
Tomnitz, Donald J. *construction executive*
Wheat, Bill W. *construction executive*

Georgetown
Gerding, Thomas Graham *medical products executive*

Granbury
Adams, Christopher Steve, Jr. *retired electronics executive, military officer*

Hempstead
Propst, Catherine Lamb *biotechnology and pharmaceutical company executive*

Houston
Blickwede, Donald Johnson *retired metal products executive*
Boren, William Meredith *manufacturing executive*
Carrig, Kenneth J. *food products executive*
Carroll, Charles A. *manufacturing executive*
Chambers, Norman C. *manufacturing executive*
Chang, Nancy T. *pharmaceutical executive*
Chao, Albert *chemicals executive*
Chavez, Brenda G. *construction executive, real estate agent*
DeNicola, T. Kevin *chemicals executive*
De Wree, Eugene Ernest *manufacturing executive*
Friedkin, Thomas H. *automotive executive*
Gelb, Morris *chemicals executive*
Goff, Robert Burnside *retired food company executive*
Gonçalves, C. Lourenço *metal products executive*
Goodman, John B. *heating/air conditioning manufacturing executive*
Hafner, Joseph A., Jr. *food products executive*
Helland, George Archibald, Jr. *manufacturing executive, federal official*
Hesterberg, Earl J. *automotive executive*
Huff, Danny W. *paper products executive*
Huffington, Roy Michael *business executive, former ambassador*
Hynes, Thomas N. (Toby) *automotive company executive*
Jean, Raymond A. *manufacturing executive*
Katopodis, Louis *supermarket chain executive*
Klausmeyer, David Michael *scientific instruments manufacturing company executive*
Lukens, Max L. *manufacturing executive*
Macdonald, Sheila L. *manufacturing executive*
McShane, Michael *manufacturing executive*
Menscher, Barnet Gary *steel company executive*
Munisteri, Joseph George *construction executive*
Netherland, Joseph H. *manufacturing executive*
Nichols, Michael Cooper *food products executive, lawyer*
Riedel, Alan Ellis *manufacturing executive, lawyer*
Rock, Douglas Lawrence *manufacturing executive*
Ross, R. Dale *medical products executive*
Rudolph, Richard L. *medical products executive, physician*
Schneiders, Richard J. *food service company executive*
Schnieders, Richard J. *food products executive*
Schumacher, Diane Kosmach *manufacturing executive, lawyer*
Scott, Danny Eugene *metal products executive, metallurgical engineer*
Smith, Dan F. *chemicals executive*
Stubblefield, John K., Jr. *food products executive*
Thompson-Draper, Cheryl L. *electronics and real estate company executive*
Usher, Thomas James *metal products executive*
Utt, William P. (Bill Utt) *construction executive*
Wiater, Richard M. *manufacturing executive*
Wilkinson, Bruce W. *construction executive*
Wilson, Carl Weldon, Jr. *construction company executive, civil engineer*

Irving
Kling, Lewis M. *multi-industry executive*
McClean, Murray R. *metal products executive*
Rabin, Stanley Arthur *metal products manufacturer*

Longview
Mann, Jack Matthewson *bottling company executive*

Pasadena
Gross, Cynthia Sue *petrochemicals manufacturing executive*

Pittsburg
Cogdill, Richard A. *food products executive*
Goolsby, O. B., Jr. *food products executive*
Pilgrim, Lonnie (Bo Pilgrim) *food products executive*

Plano
Bain, Travis Whitsett, II, *manufacturing and retail executive*
Naor, Daniel *food products executive*
Papalia, Rocco Dominic *food products executive*

Richardson
Bluedorn, Todd M. *manufacturing executive*
Goodspeed, Linda A. *manufacturing executive*
Holmen, Orrie Jeffrey *electronics company executive*
Schjerven, Robert E. *manufacturing executive*

Rockwall
Fisher, Gene Jordan *retired chemical company executive*

San Antonio
Burzik, Catherine M. *health products executive*
Cisneros, Henry G. *homebuilding and broadcast executive, retired federal official*
de la Garza, Luis Adolfo *automotive executive, lawyer*
Gates, Mahlon Eugene *retired research and development company executive, retired military officer*
Kotecki, Kevin *beer company executive*
McGuire, William Dennis *healthcare consultant*
Zachry, Henry Bartell, Jr. *construction executive*

Seguin
Robinson, Ronald Alan *manufacturing executive*

Temple
McLane, Robert Drayton, Jr. *food products company executive*

The Woodlands
Stolle, Russell Robert *chemicals executive*

Tyler
Smith, Howard Thompson *manufacturing executive*

Valley Spring
Bonner, Herbert Dwight *construction management educator*

UTAH

Hinckley
Riding, Randy Lynn *welder*

Orem
Segelman, Alvin Burton *pharmaceutical executive, educator, research scientist*

Salt Lake City
Esplin, J. Kimo *chemicals executive*
Frank, Thomas *construction executive, management and design executive*
Hankins, Anthony P. *chemicals executive*
Hembree, James D. *retired chemical company executive*
Hulme, Paul G. *chemicals executive*
Huntsman, Jon Meade *chemicals executive*
Huntsman, Peter R. *chemicals executive*
Keenan, Thomas J. *chemicals executive*
Kern, Michael J. *chemicals executive*
Ninow, Kevin J. *chemicals executive*
Ridd, Brian V. *chemicals executive*
Sorenson, James LeVoy *research and development company executive*
Stanutz, Donald J. *chemicals executive*
Stitley, James Walter, Jr. *food manufacturing executive*

VERMONT

Brownsville
Olderman, Gerald *retired medical device company executive*

Burlington
Burton, Jake (Jake Burton Carpenter) *sports apparel executive*

Quechee
Dorsey, Jeremiah Edmund *pharmaceutical company executive*

South Burlington
Pizzagalli, James *construction executive*

VIRGINIA

Alexandria
Crundwell, Duncan James *electronics executive*
Wynn, Robert E. *electronics executive, retired military officer*

Arlington
Culligan, Thomas M. *electronics executive*
Franklin, Jude Eric *electronics executive*
Gracey, James Steele *manufacturing executive, director, management consultant*
Howlett, Clifford Theodore, Jr., (Kip Howlett) *chemicals executive*
Junker, Bobby Ray *research and development company executive, physicist*

Bassett
Spilman, Robert Henkel *furniture company executive*

Bedford
Brooks, Robin C. *food products executive*

Charlottesville
Jolly, Bruce Dwight *manufacturing executive*
Wolcott, John Winthrop III *retired manufacturing executive*

Courtland
Minor, Edward Colquitt *paper company executive, lawyer*

Deltaville
Koedel, John Gilbert, Jr. *retired metal product executive*

Earlysville
Bartoes, Richard Alan *agricultural products executive*

Edinburg
Rhodes, Stephen Michael *poultry company executive*

Fairfax
Umbel, Tammie *cosmetics executive*

Falls Church
Chabraja, Nicholas D. *equipment manufacturi executive, lawyer*
Hall, Charles M. *manufacturing executive*
Lanese, Herbert J. *multi-industry executive*
Redd, L. Hugh *manufacturing executive*

Forest
Ehrhorn, Richard William *electronics executi*

Hampton
DeCuir, Bryan Jude *automotive technician, computer engineer*

Manassas
Parrish, Frank Jennings *retired food products executive*

Mc Lean
Dempsey, James Raymon *manufacturing executive*
Mars, Forrest E., Jr. *candy company executive*
Mars, Jacqueline Badger *food products execu*
Mars, John Franklyn *candy company executiv*
Persavich, Warren Dale *diversified manufacturing company executive*

Mechanicsville
Bierman, James L. *health products executive*

Higday, Paul T. *medical products distribution company executive*
Hinkle, Barton Leslie *retired electronics company executive*
Minor, George Gilmer III *drug and hospital supply company executive*
Smith, Craig R. *health products executive*

Powhatan
Eberle, Charles Edward *paper and consumer products executive*

Radford
Taylor, William Irving *retired chemicals executive*

Reston
Rastogi, Anil Kumar *health products executive*
Saville, Paul C. *construction executive*
Schar, Dwight C. *construction executive*

Richmond
Browning, Keith D. *automotive executive*
Bunzl, Rudolph Hans *retired manufacturing executive*
Folliard, Thomas J. *automotive executive*
Gottwald, Floyd Dewey, Jr. *chemicals executive, director*
Gottwald, William M. *chemicals executive*
Helwig, Arthur Woods *retired chemical company executive*
Murphey, Robert Stafford *pharmaceutical executive*
Rohr, Mark C. *chemicals executive*
Sledd, Robert C. *food products executive*
Spinner, Steven L. *food products executive*
Watts, Robert Glenn *retired pharmaceutical executive*

Roanoke
Brouillard, John Charles (Jack) *automotive parts and former grocery company executive*
Waldron, Karen *development, construction and management company executive*

Round Hill
Jannes, Martin Roy *telecommunications company executive*

Smithfield
Cole, Michael H. *food products executive*
Luter, Joseph Williamson III *meat packing and processing company executive*
Manly, Robert W., IV, *food products executive*
Pope, C. Larry *food products executive*
Zadeh, Mansour T. *food products executive*

Suffolk
Birdsong, George Yancy *manufacturing executive*

Winchester
Holland, James Tulley *retired plastics company executive*

Yorktown
Cross, Leroy *retired sugar company executive*

WASHINGTON

Anacortes
Randolph, Carl Lowell *chemicals executive*

Bellevue
Bardillo, James G. *automotive executive*
Hangl, Kenneth R. *automotive executive*
Pigott, Charles McGee *transportation equipment manufacturing executive*
Pigott, Mark C. *automotive executive*
Simpton, Thomas E. *automotive executive*
Umbreull, Michael A. *automotive executive*

Bothell
Boynton, Alton L. *pharmaceutical executive*

Camano Island
Howes, Garth Anthony *electronics executive, consultant*

Clinton
Boltby, Kenneth Fraser *retired manufacturing executive*

Coupeville
Bloom, Richard David *retired electronics executive*

Federal Way
Ballard, Ernesta *lumber company executive*
Corbin, William R. *wood products executive*
Hanson, Richard E. *paper company executive*
Hogans, Mack L. *paper company executive*
Rogel, Steven R. *forest products company executive*
Taggart, Richard J. *forest products company executive*
Weyerhaeuser, George H., Jr. *paper manufacturing company executive*

Friday Harbor
Baum, David Ernest *machinery manufacturing company executive*

Issaquah
Wainwright, Paul Edward Blech *construction company executive*

Kent
Ho, Abraham Meu Sen *retired manufacturing executive*
Hebeler, Henry Koester *retired electronics executive, aerospace engineer*

Lake Stevens
Garden, Rome L. *aircraft manufacturing company executive*

Manson
Stager, Donald K. *retired construction company executive*

Maple Valley
Brown, Thomas Andrew *retired aircraft/weaponry manufacturing executive*

Medina
Schlotterbeck, Walter Albert *manufacturing executive, lawyer*

Mercer Island
Gould, Alvin R. *manufacturing executive*

Naches
Assink, Nellie Grace *agricultural executive*

Oak Harbor
Daugherty, Kenneth Earl *research company executive, educator*

Seattle
Friend, Stephen H. *biotechnology company executive*
Holley, Rick R. *lumber company executive*
Kilpatrick, John Aaron *construction and development company executive*
Lincoln, Howard *manufacturing company and sports team executive*
Lombard, Kenneth T. *beverage and music company executive*
Schoenfeld, Walter Edwin *manufacturing executive*
Smith, Orin C. *retired food products executive*

Spokane
Siegel, Louis Pendleton *retired forest products executive*

Tacoma
Hudson, Edward Voyle *retired apparel executive*
Hutchings, George Henry *food company executive*

WISCONSIN

Appleton
Boldt, Oscar Charles *construction executive, director*
Grayson, David S. *paper company executive*
Seifert, Kathi P. *manufacturing executive*
Spiegelberg, Harry Lester *retired paper company executive*

Beloit
Knueppel, Henry W. *manufacturing executive*

Clintonville
Simpson, Vinson Raleigh *manufacturing executive, director*

Fort Atkinson
Jones, Alan Porter, Jr. *food manufacturing executive*

Glendale
Feitler, Robert *shoe company executive*

Green Bay
Kress, William F. *manufacturing executive*

Hartland
Burrus, Daniel Allen *research and development company executive, consultant*

Kenosha
Pinchuk, Nicholas Thomas *manufacturing executive*

Kohler
Kohler, Herbert Vollrath, Jr. *diversified manufacturing company executive*
Wells, Richard A. *manufacturing executive*

Madison
Macfarlane, Alastair Iain Robert *manufacturing executive, consultant*
Shain, Irving *retired chemicals executive, academic administrator*

Manitowoc
Growcock, Terry D. *manufacturing executive*
Tellock, Glen E. *manufacturing executive*

Markesan
Chamberlain, Robert Glenn *retired tool manufacturing executive*

Middleton
Bass, Bill *apparel executive*

Milwaukee
Adami, Norman J. *brewery executive*
Barth, John M. *manufacturing executive*
Beals, Vaughn Le Roy, Jr. *retired motorcycle manufacturing executive*
Bleustein, Jeffrey L. *motorcycle company executive*
Colbert, Virgis W. *food products executive*
Davis, Don H., Jr. *multi-industry high-technology company executive*
Grade, Jeffery T. *manufacturing executive*
Hanson, John Nils *industrial high technology manufacturing company executive*
Jones, Paul W. *manufacturing executive*
Keyes, James Henry *manufacturing executive*
Long, Tom *brewery executive*
Manning, Kenneth Paul *specialty chemical company executive*
Myers, C. David *manufacturing executive*
Nosbusch, Keith D. *multi-industry high-technology company executive*
O'Toole, Robert Joseph *retired manufacturing executive*
Roell, Stephen A. *manufacturing executive*

Shiely, John Stephen *manufacturing executive, lawyer*
Sterner, Frank Maurice *manufacturing executive*
Sutherlin, Michael W. *paper company executive*
Wandell, Keith E. *manufacturing executive*
Ziemer, James L. *motorcycle company executive*

Neenah
Kalmanson, Steven R. *health products executive*

Oconomowoc
Peebles, Allene Kay *manufactured housing company executive*

Oshkosh
Siepmann, James Patrick *research and development company executive, retired physician*

Pleasant Prairie
Cherry, Peter Ballard *electrical products corporation executive*
Morrone, Frank *electronics executive*

Racine
Campbell, Edward Joseph *retired machinery company executive*
Johnson, H(erbert) Fisk *manufacturing executive*
Konz, Gerald Keith *retired manufacturing executive*
McCollum, W. Lee *chemical company executive*
Rayburn, David B. *manufacturing executive*
Rosso, Jean-Pierre *electronics executive*
Wambold, Richard Lawrence *manufacturing executive*

Sheboygan
Yurk, Todd Michael *retired health products executive*

South Milwaukee
Kitzke, Eugene David *research and development company executive*

Sturtevant
Johnson, S. Curtis *chemicals executive*
Lonergan, Edward F. *manufacturing executive*

Sussex
Losee, John Frederick, Jr. *manufacturing executive*
Stromberg, Gregory *printing ink company executive*

Waukesha
Hogan, Joseph M. *health products executive*
Maas, Duane Harris *distilling company executive*

West Bend
Gehl, William D. *manufacturing executive*
Schaefer, Gordon Emory *food products executive*

Wisconsin Rapids
Engelhardt, LeRoy A. *retired paper company executive*

WYOMING

Wilson
Gordon, Stephen Maurice *manufacturing company executive, rancher*
Harrell, Samuel Macy *agribusiness executive*

TERRITORIES OF THE UNITED STATES

PUERTO RICO

Dorado
Spector, Michael Joseph *agribusiness executive*

CANADA

ALBERTA

Calgary
Holman, J(ohn) Leonard *retired manufacturing corporation executive*

BRITISH COLUMBIA

Victoria
Fuller, James Chester Eedy *retired chemical company executive*

MANITOBA

Winnipeg
MacKenzie, George Allan *medical products executive*

NEW BRUNSWICK

Fredericton
Grotterod, Knut *retired paper company executive*

NOVA SCOTIA

Stellarton
Sobey, David Frank *food company executive*

ONTARIO

Aurora
Lanthier, Ronald Ross *retired manufacturing executive*

Brampton
Kraemer, Philipp *manufacturing company executive, inventor*

Cambridge
White, Joseph Charles *manufacturing and retailing company executive*

Greely
Lister, Earle Edward *retired research executive*

Hamilton
Mott, Rodney B. *metal products executive*

Nepean
Chudobiak, Walter James *electronics executive*

Ottawa
Beare-Rogers, Joyce Louise *retired research and development executive*

Peterborough
Burwick, David *beverage company executive*

Toronto
Connell, Philip Francis *food industry executive*
Wleugel, John Peter *manufacturing executive*

QUEBEC

Montreal
Beaudoin, Laurent *train manufacturing company executive*
Molson, Eric H. *brewery company executive*
Rolland, Lucien Gilbert *paper company executive, director*

SASKATCHEWAN

Regina
Phillips, Roger *retired steel company executive*

MEXICO

Mexico City
Aramburúzabála, Maria Asunción *food products executive*
Vargas Legaspi, Juan *manufacturing executive*

AUSTRALIA

Milsons Point
Foster, Milo George *manufacturing executive*

BELGIUM

Brussels
Buysse, Paul Henri Maria *manufacturing executive*

CHINA

Beijing
Dingman, Michael David *manufacturing executive, investor*

EGYPT

Giza
Digham, Fadel *research and development company executive, director*

ENGLAND

Beckenham
Lader, Malcolm Harold *pharmaceutical consultant*

Brentford
Bondy, Rupert *pharmaceutical executive, lawyer*

Cheshunt Hertfordshire
Leahy, Sir Terry *food products executive, marketing professional*

London
Baird, Dugald Euan *automotive executive*
Barnevik, Percy Nils *electrical company executive*
Bravo, Rose Marie *apparel executive*
Brennan, David R. *pharmaceutical executive*
Mellon, Tamara *apparel executive*
Walsh, Paul S. *beverage executive*

Milton Keynes
Throdahl, Mark Crandall *medical products executive*

Wiltshire
Dyson, Sir James *manufacturing executive, inventor*
Ahrendts, Angela J. *apparel executive*

FINLAND

Tampere
Andriano, Kirk Patrick *pharmaceutical executive*

FRANCE

Paris
Burke, Michael *apparel executive*
Choay, Patrick Henri *pharmaceutical executive*
Payri, Joel *pharmaceutical marketing executive*

GERMANY

Bad Homburg
Klatten, Susanne Quandt *pharmaceutical executive*

Düsseldorf
Schulz, Ekkehard *metal products executive*

Munich
Bangle, Christopher Edward (Chris Bangle) *automotive company car designer*
Loescher, Peter Hans *electronics executive*

Schleusingen-Gethles
Frank, Dieter *retired chemicals executive*

Stuttgart
Zetsche, Dieter *automotive executive*

GREECE

Athens
Larounis, George Philip *manufacturing executive, director*

HONG KONG

Cheung Sha Wan
Dyer, David F. *apparel company executive*

JAPAN

Tokyo
Hirai, Kazuo (Kaz) *electronics executive*
Ohga, Norio *retired electronics executive*
Saba, Shoichi *electronics executive, director*
Wakumoto, Yoshihiko *electronics company executive, grants executive*

Toyota
Toyoda, Shoichiro *automotive executive*

REPUBLIC OF KOREA

Incheon
Gerson, Donald Franklin *pharmaceutical executive*

SINGAPORE

Singapore
McNamara, Michael *electronics executive*

SPAIN

Madrid
Feltenstein, Harry David, Jr. *chemicals executive*

SWEDEN

Stockholm
Johnson, Antonia Axson *food products executive*
Stewart, S. Jay *automotive executive*

TAIWAN

Taipei
Chuang, Yii-Der *retired manufacturing executive, diplomat*

ADDRESS UNPUBLISHED

Abbas Borhan, Richat *research and development company executive*
Acerra, Michele (Mike Acerra) *engineering and construction company executive*
Adams, Jennifer *medical products executive*
Adkinson, Brian Lee *manufacturing executive*
Alden, Ingemar Bengt *pharmaceuticals executive*
Alexander, Jon M. *contractor, consultant*
Alexander, Judd Harris *retired paper company executive*
Allemang, Arnold A. *chemicals executive*
Alm, John Richard *beverage company executive*
Amstutz, Daniel Gordon *agricultural products executive, consultant, retired federal agency administrator, grain company executive*
Anderegg, Karen Klok *business executive*
Anderer, Joseph Henry *textile company executive*
Anderson, Joseph Norman *retired food products executive, academic administrator*
Andersson, Bo I. *automotive executive*
Andersson, Craig Remington *retired chemical company executive*
Andreas, Dwayne Orville *agricultural products executive*
Archibald, Nolan D. *household and industrial products company executive*
Arlotta, John J. *pharmaceutical executive*
Aschauer, Charles Joseph, Jr. *retired health products executive*
Atchison, Joseph Edward *pulp and paper industry consultant*
Autrey, Wesley *Construction Worker*
Bainton, Donald J. *diversified manufacturing company executive*
Baldwin, Ralph Belknap *retired manufacturing executive, astronomer*
Barca, George Gino *international winery executive, financial investor, consultant*
Barfield, Tim *manufacturing executive*
Barrow, Robert Earl *retired agricultural fraternal executive*
Barton, Robert H. III *automotive executive*
Batts, Warren Leighton *retired manufacturing executive*
Beck, Albert *manufacturing executive*
Beighey, Lawrence Jerome *packaging company executive*
Bekkers, John *former food products executive*
Bergmann, Donald Gerald *pharmaceutical company executive*
Bernthal, Harold George *health products executive, director*
Berry, Robert Vaughan *retired electrical manufacturing company executive*
Best, Lawrence C. *retired medical products executive*
Beutler, Arthur Julius *manufacturing executive*
Bevington, Edmund Milton *electrical machinery manufacturing company executive*
Biggs, Arthur Edward *retired chemicals executive, social services administrator*
Bishop, Charles Joseph *retired manufacturing executive*
Bishop, Kim Irene *pharmaceutical consultant, psychopharmacologist*
Blanchard, Richard Frederick *construction executive*
Blumenthal, W. Michael (Werner Michael Blumenthal) *retired manufacturing company executive, former secretary of the treasury*
Boothe, Nancy Nancy *construction executive*
Bowers, Richard Philip *manufacturing executive*
Boyle, Tim *apparel executive*
Brancato, Leo John *manufacturing executive*
Brandeis, Barry *retired apparel executive*
Bratton, William Edward *electronics executive, management consultant*
Brennan, Gerald D. (Jerry) *biotechnology company executive*
Britt, Ronald Leroy *retired manufacturing company executive*
Bronfman, Edgar Miles, Sr. *retired liquor company executive*
Brooker, Robert Elton, Jr. *retired manufacturing company executive*
Brown, Jerry Milford *health products executive*
Bru, Abelardo E. *retired food products executive*
Bucy, J. Fred, Jr. *retired electronics company executive*
Bull, Bergen Ira *retired equipment manufacturing company executive*
Burkart, Walter Mark *retired manufacturing company executive*
Burson, Charles W. *retired agricultural products executive, former federal official, state attorney general*
Busch, August Adolphus III *retired brewery company executive*
Busch, J. Herbert *electrical contractor, writer*
Bush, Norman *research and development company executive*
Caine, Arnold *pharmaceutical executive*
Calarco, Vincent Anthony *specialty chemicals company executive*
Campbell, James P. *manufacturing executive*
Candlish, Malcolm *manufacturing executive*
Cash, W. Larry *health products executive*
Caskey, Charles Thomas *biotechnology executive, biology and genetics educator*
Cassidy, James Mark *construction company executive*
Castaldi, David Lawrence *health products executive*
Castor, Jon Stuart *electronics executive*
Chalupsky, Mary Etta Griffith *health products executive*
Changeri, Michael Dennis *contractor, protective services official*
Chaykin, Robert Leroy *manufacturing and marketing executive*
Chen, Di *electronics executive, optical engineer, consultant*
Chihorek, John Paul *electronics company executive*
Chmielinski, Edward Alexander *retired electronics company executive*
Chopra, Samir *pharmaceutical and real estate company executive*
Chu, James *electronics executive*
Cicolani, Angelo George *research and development company executive, operating engineer*
Clark, Wesley M. *manufacturing executive*
Clear, Albert F., Jr. *retired hardware manufacturing company executive*
Cloud, Bruce Benjamin, Sr. *retired construction executive*
Clouston, Ross Neal *retired food and related products company executive*
Comer, Evan Philip *manufacturing executive*
Cooley, James William *retired executive researcher*
Cooper, Norton J. (Sky) *liquor, wine and food company executive*
Coors, Jeffrey H. *technology manufacturing executive*
Coppola, Michael N. *former automotive parts executive*
Corace, Joseph Russell *automotive executive*
Correll, Alston Dayton, Jr., (Pete) *forest products company executive*
Cotting, James Charles *manufacturing executive, director*
Cox, John Francis *retired cosmetic company executive*
Cox, Wilford Donald *retired food company executive*
Coyne, Brian J(oseph) *pharmaceutical researcher*
Craft, Edmund Coleman *retired manufacturing executive*
Crawford, James Dee *chemical distribution executive*
Culwell, Charles Louis *retired manufacturing executive*
Curtis, Arnold Bennett *retired lumber company executive*
Dailey, Franklyn Edward, Jr. *electronic image technology company executive, analyst, consultant*
Danziger, Glenn Norman *retired chemicals executive*
Darrow, William Richard *retired pharmaceutical company executive, consultant*
Dattilo, Thomas A. *retired manufacturing executive*
Davis, Darrell L. *retired automotive executive*
Deromedi, Roger K. *food products executive*
Diener, Royce *retired health products executive*
DiGregorio, Amanda Elizabeth *medical products executive*
Dinkel, John George *automotive executive, consultant*
Dohrmann, Russell William *retired manufacturing executive*
Dolezal, Dale Francis *truck manufacturing company executive*
Dollens, Ronald W. *pharmaceutical executive*
Dragon, William, Jr. *footwear and apparel company executive*
Drew, Walter Harlow *retired paper company executive*
Drexler, Richard Allan *manufacturing executive*
Drohan, David F. *medical products company executive*
Dur, Philip Alphonse *retired shipbuilding executive, military officer*
Durr, Robert Joseph *construction executive, mechanical engineer*
Dye, Robert Harris *retired manufacturing company executive*
Elverum, Gerard William, Jr. *retired electronics and aerospace transportation executive*
Encarnación, Jose M. Izquierdo *construction executive, former Puerto Rico secretary of state*
Engels, Lawrence Arthur *retired metal products executive*
Engle, Steven B. *biotechnology company executive*
Esher, Brian Richard *manufacturing executive*
Evans, Barton, Jr. *retired analytical instrument company executive*
Fan, Jiang *manufacturing executive*
Farha, Todd S. *health products executive*
Farrell, W. James *metal products manufacturing company executive*
Fein, Seymour Howard *pharmaceutical executive*
Finlay, Robert Derek *food products executive*
Fitch, Robert McLellan *research and development company executive, consultant*
Flaherty, William E. *chemicals executive, metal products executive*
Flaster, Donald J. *retired pharmaceutical executive*
Flitcraft, Richard Kirby, II, *former chemical company executive*
Fluharty, David Arthur *automotive executive, statistician, consultant*
Fogg, Richard Lloyd *food products executive*
Foote, William Chapin *manufacturing executive*
Forese, James John *business machine company executive*
Fowler, James D., Jr. *leadership executive*
French, Clarence Levi, Jr. *retired shipbuilding company executive*
Frieling, Gerald Harvey, Jr. *specialty steel company executive*
Frisco, Louis Joseph *retired electronics executive, electrical engineer*
Fritz, Rene Eugene, Jr. *manufacturing executive*
Garruto, John Anthony *cosmetics executive*
Geraghty, Elizabeth *food products executive*
Gifford, John Irving *retired agricultural equipment company executive*
Glover, James Todd *manufacturing executive*
Goldberg, Lee Winicki *furniture company executive*
Golden, Charles Edward *retired pharmaceutical company executive*
Graber, William Raymond *former pharmaceutical executive*
Graham, Stuart Edward *construction company executive*
Graham, Wallace Karl *chemicals executive*
Gray, Richard Alexander, Jr. *retired chemical company executive*
Greenberg, Jack M. *former food products executive*
Greetham, Elizabeth M. *former health products executive*
Grove, Richard Charles *retired power tool company executive*
Haas, Frederick Carl *retired paper company executive, retired chemicals executive*
Haas, Howard Green *retired bedding manufacturing company executive*
Habicht, Frank Henry *retired manufacturing executive*
Hagenlocker, Edward E. *retired automobile company executive*
Hake, Ralph F. *former appliance manufacturing executive*
Hakimoglu, Ayhan *electronics executive*
Halperin, Jerome Arthur *retired pharmaceutical executive*
Hammann, Gregg C. *fitness equipment executive*
Hardis, Stephen Roger *retired manufacturing company executive*
Harper, Charles Michel *food products executive, director*
Harrell, Henry Howze *tobacco company executive*
Hartmann, George Herman *retired manufacturing executive*
Hausman, Arthur Herbert *electronics company executive*
Hawkins, Ellis Delano *manufacturing, insurance company, gaming executive*
Hayes, John Patrick *retired manufacturing company executive*
Heilmann, Christian Flemming *manufacturing executive*
Heimbinder, Isaac *lawyer*
Henderson, Charles Brooke *research and development company executive*
Hennessey, Robert John *pharmaceutical company executive*
Henning, George Thomas, Jr. *retired steel company executive*
Herbert, Gavin Shearer *health care products company executive*
Herman, Rayna S. *pharmaceutical consultant*
Herman, Robert Lewis *cork company executive*
Herzfeld, Siegfried *manufacturing executive, consultant*
Hiatt, Arnold *apparel and retail executive*
Hind, Harry William *pharmaceutical company executive*
Hirsch, Horst Eberhard *metal products executiv consultant*
Hirsh, Bernard *supply company executive, consultant*
Hixson, Harry F., Jr. *health products executive*
Holden, Betsy D. *former food products compan executive*
Hood, Edward Exum, Jr. *retired electronics executive*
Hook, Jerry B. *pharmaceutical consultant*
Hornak, Thomas *retired electronics company executive*
Houghton, James Richardson *retired manufacturing executive*
Hsiao, Richard *research and development company executive*
Hudson, Franklin Donald *manufacturing executive, consultant*
Hudson, Katherine Mary *manufacturing executive*
Hume, Frederick Raymond *electronics executiv*
Hurd, Richard Nelson *pharmaceutical executiv*
Hushen, John Wallace *manufacturing executive*
Hyde, Lawrence Henry, Jr. *manufacturing executive*
Iacono, James Michael *research and development company executive, nutrition educator*
Ivanchenko, Lauren Margaret Dowd *pharmaceutical executive*
Ix, Robert Edward *food products executive*
Jackson, Hunter *health products executive*
Jackson, John Wyant *biotechnology company executive*
Jackson, Robert Howard *food company executive, scientist*
Jackson, William Elmer, Jr. *retired packaging company administrator*
Janak, Peter Harold *retired automotive compan executive*
Jimenez, Joseph *management executive*
Johnson, Irving Stanley *pharmaceutical executive, research scientist*
Johnson, William R. *food products executive*
Johnston, Lawrence R. *former food products executive*
Johnstone, John William, Jr. *retired chemical company executive*
Jolowsky, Christene Marie *pharmaceutical executive, director*
Jones, Christine Massey *retired furniture company executive*
Jones, Eugene Gordon *pharmaceutical compar executive*
Jones, Robert Henry *automotive distribution executive*
Joyce, William Robert *textile machinery company executive*
Kallay, Michael Frank, II, *medical products executive*
Kampouris, Emmanuel Andrew *retired corpor executive*
Kaplan, Edward L. *retired electronics executiv*
Katen, Karen L. *retired pharmaceutical comp executive*
Kavli, Fred *retired manufacturing and engineering executive*
Keeler, James Leonard *food products executiv*
Keen, Constantine *retired manufacturing executive*
Keith, Brian Thomas *automotive executive*
Kelly, Anthony Odrian *textiles executive*
Kerber, Ronald Lee *industrial corporation executive*
Kern, Irving John *retired food company executive*
Khan, Jamil Akber *chemical company executi*
Killian, William Paul *manufacturing executive*
King, Susan Bennett *retired glass company executive*
Kiselik, Paul Howard *manufacturing executive*
Klaehne, Eberhard O.W. *pharmaceutical executive, chemist*
Kogan, Richard J. *former pharmaceutical company executive*
Kolb, Gloria Ro *medical products executive*
Krenicki, John, Jr. *manufacturing executive*
Krominga, Lynn *cosmetics executive, lawyer*
Kulik, Rosalyn Franta *food company executiv consultant*
Kurnick, Robert H., Jr. *automotive executive, lawyer*
Labrecque, Richard Joseph *retired industrial executive*
Lala, Dominick Joseph *manufacturing executi*
Landon, Robert Gray *retired manufacturing company executive*

ane, William W. *electronics executive*
aney, Michael L. *manufacturing executive*
angbo, Arnold Gordon *former food company executive*
anger, Dennis Henry *pharmaceutical company executive*
apinsky, Joseph F. *manufacturing executive*
asky, William M. *manufacturing executive*
avin, Bernice E. *cosmetics executive*
eBlanc, Leonard Joseph *retired electronics company executive*
eff, Joseph Norman *yarn manufacturing company executive*
ennox, Donald D(uane) *retired automotive and housing components company executive*
eveille, Gilbert Antonio *food products executive*
evin, Michael Stuart *steel company executive*
ew, Roger Alan *manufacturing executive*
ewis, Martin R. *paper company executive, consultant*
ewis, Rita Hoffman *plastic products manufacturing company executive*
iberati, Maria Theresa *lifestyle company executive, cooking expert, writer*
nton, Michael Alan *food products executive*
nville, Randal L. *agricultural company executive*
ppincott, Philip Edward *retired paper company executive*
vengood, Scott A. *former food products executive*
ohman, Gordon Russell *retired manufacturing executive*
ongfield, William Herman *health products executive*
owden, John L. *retired manufacturing executive*
oye, Estelle C. *contractor, travel consultant*
ike, David Lincoln III *retired paper company executive*
ynch, Charles Andrew *chemicals executive*
aarbjerg, Mary Penzold *retired office equipment company executive*
acAvoy, Thomas Coleman *manufacturing executive, educator*
acMillan, Whitney *retired food products and import/export company executive*
adden, Richard Blaine *forest products executive*
agee, John Francis *research and development company executive*
ahoney, Robert William *electronic and security systems manufacturing executive*
anchester, Kenneth Edward *electronics executive, consultant*
angold, John Frederic *manufacturing executive, retired military officer*
annelly, Patrick J. *former beverage company executive*
anning, William Dudley, Jr. *retired specialty chemical company executive*
artin, Albert Charles *manufacturing executive, lawyer*
ason, Frank Henry III *automotive and rental company executive*
atsushima, Akira Paul *manufacturing executive*
axwell, Jerome Eugene *corporate executive*
cCracken, Edward R. *electronics executive*
cCurdy, Larry Wayne *automotive parts company executive*
cDonald, William Henry *manufacturing executive*
cDonell, Horace George, Jr. *instrument company executive*
cGuinn, Edwin J. *chemicals executive*
cKenna, William John *retired textile products executive*
cKennon, Keith Robert *chemical company executive*
cKinley, James Frank, Jr. *retired manufacturing executive*
cManus, Joanna Quilala *medical device sales manager, physician assistant*
cNitt, Willard Charles *food products executive*
eilan, Celia *food products executive*
ichaels, Jack D. *manufacturing executive*
ilberg, Joachim *retired automotive executive*
iller, Harold Edward *retired manufacturing conglomerate executive, consultant*
ills, Charles N. *healthcare supplies and products company executive*
ontrone, Paul Michael *former scientific instruments company executive*
oore, John Ronald *manufacturing executive*
oore, Malcolm Frederick *manufacturing executive*
oretti, August Joseph *pharmaceutical executive, lawyer*
orgenstein, William *shoe company executive*
orris, G. Ronald *automotive executive*
orrison, Robert Scheck *former manufacturing, food marketing processing company executive*
orton, James Carnes, Jr. *automotive executive*
osemann, Lloyd Kenneth, II, *retired research and development company executive*
otsenbocker, Rex Alan *construction company executive*
ott, Stewart Rawlings *food products executive, political organization worker*
eller, Robert Louis *manufacturing executive*
kamal, David Samier *sign manufacturing company executive*
urray, Roderick Charles *manufacturing executive*
ula, Richard D. *former heath products company executive*
lson, Glen David *health products executive, physician*
cholas, Henry Thompson III *former electronics company executive*
ckerson, Guy Robert *lumber company executive*
e, Elnora (Ellie Noe) *retired chemicals executive*
vak, Alan Lee *retired pharmaceutical company executive*
Brien, George Aloysius, Jr. *paper company executive*
O'Connor, Kevin *construction materials manufacturing executive*
O'Donnell, Kevin *retired metal products executive*
O'Neill, Harry William *retired research market and opinion company executive*
Ordal, Caspar Reuben *retired executive*
Oster, Lewis Henry *manufacturing executive, industrial engineer, consultant*
Owens, Charles Vincent, Jr. *pharmaceutical executive, consultant*
Owens, Gail Frances *pharmaceutical executive*
Padilla, James Jerome (Jim Padilla) *retired automotive executive*
Palmer, Grant *medical products executive*
Pasek, Mark Edward *manufacturing executive*
Peapples, George Alan *retired automotive executive*
Pearce, Paul Francis *retired electronics executive, aerospace engineer*
Peck, Arthur John, Jr. *retired manufacturing executive, lawyer*
Perkins, Cheryl A. *paper company executive*
Petersen-Frey, Roland *manufacturing executive*
Peterson, Carl Eric *metal products executive, banker*
Peterson, Robert Austin *retired manufacturing executive*
Pfeiffer, Gary M. *chemicals executive*
Philips, Laura Alma *former pharmaceutical executive*
Pickett, Cecil B. *pharmaceutical executive*
Pond, Byron O., Jr. *retired manufacturing executive*
Potts, Gerald Neal *manufacturing executive*
Powell, Thomas Edward III *biological supply company executive, physician*
Preston, Seymour Stotler III *chemicals executive*
Pruis, John J. *manufacturing executive*
Pyatt, Kedar Davis, Jr. *research and development company executive*
Pylipow, Stanley Ross *retired manufacturing company executive*
Qualls, Robert L. *manufacturing and bank executive, educator, retired state official*
Rao, Rama Krishna R. *pharmaceutical company executive*
Ray, Jane Zimrude *retired machine shop executive*
Reavis, Hubert Gray, Jr. *retired metal products executive*
Regan, Paul Jerome, Jr. *manufacturing company executive, consultant*
Regelbrugge, Roger Rafael *steel company executive*
Reilley, Dennis H. *retired chemicals executive*
Reilly, David N. (Nick Reilly) *automotive executive*
Reinhard, Joao Pedro *chemicals company executive*
Renne, Paul F. *retired food products executive*
Rheney, Susan O. *paper company executive*
Rhodes, Peter Edward *label company executive*
Richard, Edward H. *manufacturing executive, retired municipal official*
Richardson, Thomas Andrew *business executive, educator*
Richman, Peter *electronics executive*
Richter, Robert C. *retired automotive executive*
Risdon, Michael Paul *manufacturing executive*
Rivera, Richard Edwin *former restaurant chain executive*
Robbins, Ray C. *retired manufacturing executive*
Roesner, Peter Lowell *manufacturing executive*
Roorda, John Francis, Jr. *manufacturing executive, consultant*
Rosenberg, Rudy *chemical company executive*
Ross, Dennis E. *retired automotive executive, lawyer*
Ross, Ivy E. *apparel executive, artist*
Rothwell, Timothy *pharmaceutical executive*
Rudy, Raymond Bruce, Jr. *retired food company executive*
Rukeyser, Robert James *manufacturing executive*
Ryan, George William *manufacturing executive*
Rymar, Julian W. *manufacturing executive, director*
Salathe, John, Jr. *retired manufacturing executive*
Sapoff, Meyer *retired electronics executive*
Savin, Ronald Richard *chemicals executive*
Schor, Joseph Martin *pharmaceutical executive, biochemist*
Schwartz, Bernard Leon *retired space and communications company executive*
Serenbetz, Robert *manufacturing executive, financial planner*
Shapira, David S. *food products and retail grocery executive*
Sharkey, Leonard Arthur *automobile company executive*
Shea, Bernard Charles *retired pharmaceutical executive*
Shepherd, Mark, Jr. *retired electronics company executive*
Sherman, George M. *former food products executive*
Sherman, Patsy O'Connell *retired manufacturing executive, chemist*
Shuster, Robert G. *electronics executive, consultant*
Siefert, David Michael *research and development company executive*
Siegel, Jack Morton *retired pharmaceutical executive*
Silver, George *metal trading and processing company executive*
Silverman, Stanley Wayne *chemical company executive*
Sim, Jai-hoon *electronics researcher*
Simeral, William Goodrich *retired chemical company executive*
Sissel, George Allen *manufacturing executive, lawyer, engineer*
Slusser, Eugene Alvin *electronics executive, consultant*
Smith, Frederick Coe *retired manufacturing executive*
Smith, Goff *industrial equipment manufacturing executive*
Smith, Robert Hugh *retired engineering construction company executive*
Snider, George Runyon, Jr. *retired franchising company executive*
Soderberg, Leif G. *electronics company executive*
Somers, Louis Robert *retired food company executive*
Sopranos, Orpheus Javaras *manufacturing executive*
Southerland, S. Duane *manufacturing executive*
Stadelman, William Ralph *chemicals executive*
Staginnus, Ulf *pharmaceutical executive, health economist*
Stavropoulos, William S. *retired chemical company executive*
Stein, Robert Alan *electronics executive*
Stephens, Thomas G. *automotive executive*
Stern, Arthur Paul *electronics executive*
Stevens, Anne L. *metal products executive, retired automotive executive*
Stewart, Joseph Turner, Jr. *retired pharmaceutical executive*
Stiritz, William P. *food products executive*
Stone, Alan John *manufacturing company executive, real estate company executive*
Stott, Don S. *precious metals products executive*
Stratton, Robert *retired electronics executive*
Sullivan, Eugene John Joseph *manufacturing executive, director*
Sullivan, G. Craig *household products executive*
Tallett, Elizabeth Edith *biopharmaceutical company executive*
Tane, Susan Jaffe *retired manufacturing company executive*
Tannenberg, Dieter E.A. *retired manufacturing executive*
Tarrance, Vernon Lance, Jr. *research and development company executive*
Taub, Alan I. *automotive executive, researcher*
Taylor, Robert Morgan *electronics executive*
Templin, Kenneth Elwood *paper company executive*
Teplow, Theodore Herzl *retired valve company executive*
Thomas, Tom *retired plastics company executive*
Thompson, Ralph Newell *former chemical corporation executive*
Thompson, Richard Leon *pharmaceutical executive, lawyer*
Thorp, Benjamin A. III *retired paper company executive*
Toan, Barrett A. *former health products executive*
Tombros, Peter George *pharmaceutical executive*
Torbica, Zeljko Marko *construction executive, educator*
Toupin, Harold Ovid *retired chemical company executive*
Uffelman, Malcolm Rucj *electronics executive*
Ulsh, Gordon A. *battery manufacturing company executive*
Van Houten, G. David, Jr. *beverage company executive*
Van Tassel, James Henry *retired electronics executive*
Vanzura, Liz (Elizabeth K. Vanzura) *automotive executive*
Vitt, David Aaron *health products executive*
Volkhardt, John Malcolm *retired food products executive*
Watkins, Dean Allen *electronics executive, educator*
Wavle, James Edward, Jr. *pharmaceutical company executive, lawyer*
Weaver, William Charles *manufacturing executive*
Wechsler, Sergio *automotive executive, consultant*
Weiswasser, Stephen *electronics executive*
Welburn, Edward T. *automotive executive*
Welch, Oliver Wendell *retired pharmaceutical executive*
White, Bertram Milton *chemicals executive*
White, Ralph Paul *automotive executive, consultant*
Wiesen, Donald Guy *retired diversified manufacturing company executive*
Wilds, Daniel O. *health products executive*
Wiley, Carl Ross *timber company executive*
Willauer, Whiting Russell *retired manufacturing executive, systems engineer*
Williams, Dorothy Standridge *retired food products manager, civic worker*
Wilson, Martin D. *pharmaceutical executive*
Winkler, Joseph Conrad *former recreational products manufacturing executive*
Winn, Joseph Lampher *retired electronics executive*
Witt, Hugh Ernest *manufacturing executive, consultant*
Wold-Olsen, Per *pharmaceutical executive*
Wolff, Brian Richard *metal products executive*
Wollert, Gerald Dale *retired food products executive, securities trader*
Wright, David L. *food and beverage company executive*
Wuensche, Vernon Edgar *construction company executive*
Yarymovych, Michael Ihor *retired manufacturing company executive*
Yeager, Kurt Eric *research and development company executive*
Ying, John L. *manufacturing executive*
Yontz, Kenneth Fredric *medical and chemical company executive*
Young, Jay Maitland *health products executive, consultant*
Zaidi, Asad R. *medical products executive, biomedical engineer*
Zajac, John *semiconductor equipment company executive*
Zeffren, Eugene *cosmetics executive*

INDUSTRY: SERVICE

UNITED STATES

ALABAMA

Athens
Lafevor, Kimberly Ann *human resources specialist, educator*

Birmingham
Etterer, Sepp *industrial relations specialist, consultant, application developer*
Harris, Aaron *management consultant*
Stitt, Frank *food service executive*

Gadsden
Grimm, James R. (Ronald) *management consultant*

Huntsville
McIntyre-Ivy, Joan Carol *data processing executive*

Hurtsboro
Bouilliant-Linet, Francis Jacques *global management consultant*

Mobile
Hart, Eric Mullins *consumer products company executive*
Rummel, Harold Edwin *travel company, retail executive*

Montgomery
Luna, Patricia Adele *marketing executive*
Murkett, Philip Tillotson *human resource executive*

ALASKA

Anchorage
Porcaro, Michael Francis *advertising executive*

Fairbanks
Helfferich, Merritt Randolph *industry and education consultant*
Thompson, Daniel Emerson *vending machine service company executive*

ARIZONA

Chandler
Brunello-McCay, Rosanne *sales executive*
Williams, James Eugene *management consultant*

Flagstaff
Bolin, Richard Luddington *industrial development specialist, consultant*
Stewart, Roger Charles *consumer products executive*

Glendale
Yazzie, Aaron Franklin *events laborer*

Green Valley
Ragan, James Thomas *communications executive*

Mesa
Johnson, Doug *advertising and public relations executive*
Luth, William Clair *geochemist, retired research manager*
Murphy, Edward Francis *sales executive*

Paradise Valley
Day, Richard Putnam *marketing professional, arbitrator, employee benefits consultant*

Peoria
Gould, Dorothy Mae *executive secretary, soprano*
Murgatroyd, Eric Neal *data processing executive*
Schindler, William Stanley *retired public relations executive*
Willis, Edward Oliver *management consultant, state agency administrator*

Phoenix
Armstrong, Nelson William, Jr. *gaming company executive*
Chadwick, Simon *management consultant*
Curcio, Christopher Frank *deputy director*
Drain, Albert Sterling *business management consultant*
Genrich, Mark L. *corporate communications director*
Smith, George *marketing professional*
Tarbell, Mark *chef*
Wright, Margaret Taylor *marketing consultant, publisher*

Rio Verde
Scott, Louis Edward *advertising executive*

Saddlebrooke
Taviss, Patricia Ann *management consultant, library association executive*

Scottsdale
Allen, A. William, III, (Bill) *food service executive*
Blinder, Martin S. *management consultant, art dealer*
Doglione, Arthur George *data processing executive*

Fukuda, Nobuo *chef*
Grier, James Edward *hotel executive, lawyer*
Kilburn, Penelope White *retired data processing executive*
Kumar, Kv *management consultant*
Lavenson, Susan Barker *hotel corporate executive, consultant*
Rodriguez, Douglas *chef*
Schleifer, Thomas C. *management consultant, author, lecturer*
Schmitz, Shirley Gertrude *marketing professional, sales executive*
Slager, Donald W. *waste management executive*
Strock, James Martin *communications executive, writer, entrepreneur*
Thompson, Bradford *chef*
Woods, Duane C. *waste management executive*
Zillmer, John J. *waste management administrator*

Sun City West
Berkenkamp, Fred Julius *management consultant*
Forti, Lenore Steimle *business consultant*
Stevens, George Richard *business consultant, public information officer*

Tempe
Cortright, Barbara Jean *public relations executive, writer*
Laybourne, Stanley *computer technology company executive*
Meehan, Robert Henry *human resources, business educator, electronics executive*

Tucson
Barton, Stanley Faulkner *retired management consultant*
Click, Carrie *public relations executive*
Cooper, Corinne *communications consultant, lawyer*
Jones, Frank Wyman *management consultant, director, mechanical engineer*
Kennedy, Lydia *human resources specialist*
Lewis, Wilbur H. *educational management consultant*
Pedersen, Arlene *web design company executive*
Reinius, Michele Reed *executive recruiter*
Rose, Hugh *management consultant*
Scholly, Edwin *chef*
Walker, Ronald Hugh *retired management consultant*
Wilder, Janos *chef*
Williams, Alan Keiser *management consultant*
Zuckerman, Mel (Melvin Zuckerman) *hotel executive*

ARKANSAS

Conway
Hatcher, Joe Branch *management consultant*

Jonesboro
Tims, Robert Austin *data processing official, pilot*

Little Rock
McCaleb, Annette Watts *executive secretary*

Pine Bluff
Long, Edward Arlo *management consultant, retired manufacturing executive*

West Memphis
Howell, Kathy Aileen *advertising executive*

CALIFORNIA

Agoura Hills
Gressak, Anthony Raymond, Jr. *sales executive*
Schmidt, Frank Broaker *executive recruiter*

Alameda
Janowitz, Jeffrey Mark *management consultant*
Potash, Jeremy Warner *public relations executive*

Alamo
Whalen, John Sydney *management consultant*

Aliso Viejo
Blum, Scott Allen *Internet company executive*
Dutile, Robert Arthur *executive management consultant*
Grover, Neel *Internet company executive*
Harder, Wendy Wetzel *communications executive*

Altadena
Eisen, Glenn Philip *management consultant, educator*

Alviso
Ramsay, Michael *communications company executive*
Rogers, Thomas Sydney *communications company executive*
Sordello, Steve *communications executive*

Anaheim
Miller, Mark A. *information technology training executive*
Warring, Jerome Thomas *management consultant*

Aptos
Trounstine, Philip John *communications consultant, academic administrator*

Atherton
Anderson, Harry W. (Hunk) *retired food service executive*
Baran, Paul *computer executive*

Belmont
Vieux, Alex Serge *computer company executive, educator, journalist, entrepreneur*

Berkeley
Waters, Alice *executive chef, restaurant owner, writer*

Beverly Hills
Bollenbach, Stephen Frasier *hotel executive*
Cantor, Alan Bruce *management consultant, application developer*
Hardy, Sean *chef*
Hart, Matthew J. *hotel and recreation executive*
Hefter, Lee *chef*
Hilton, (William) Barron *hotel executive*
La Forgia, Robert M. *hotel executive*
McKenzie-Swarts, Molly *human resources specialist, hotel executive*
Richman, Keith *communications executive*
Riess, Gordon Sanderson *management consultant*
Zarem, Abe Mordecai *management consulting executive*

Brentwood
Hansen, B. J. (Bobby J. Hansen) *management consultant, real estate investor and developer*

Burbank
Caouette, David Paul *public relations executive*
Cheng, Albert *communications executive*
Garner, Scott *communications executive*

Calabasas
Stark, Martin J. *management consultant*

Camarillo
Cobb, Shirley Ann Dodson *public relations consultant, journalist*

Cambria
Morse, Richard Jay *human resources specialist, consultant*

Campbell
Battista, Richard *chef, educator*

Carlsbad
Gibson, Terry Grant *security firm executive*
Ritchie, Doris Lee *executive secretary*

Carmel
Pippi, Mike *entertainment management*
Skidmore, Howard Franklyn *public relations counsel*
Smith, Gordon Paul *management consultant*

Carpinteria
Adizes, Ichak *management consultant, writer*
Morgan, Alfred Vance *management consulting company executive*
Puzder, Andrew F. *food service executive, lawyer*

Chatsworth
Weisbrod, Ken (Joseph Louis Weisbrod) *marketing professional*

Chico
Curry, William Sims *management consultant*

Citrus Heights
Leisey, Donald Eugene *learning materials executive*

Claremont
Hawkins, Gregory J. *consumer products company executive*

Concord
Braunesreither, Lori Jean *environmental services administrator*

Corona
White, Joy Mieko *retired communications executive*

Corona Del Mar
O'Brien, John William, Jr. *management consultant*

Corte Madera
Tate, John William *consumer products company executive, former food products executive*

Costa Mesa
Hopkins, Denise S. *marketing executive*

Culver City
Boonshaft, Hope Judith *public relations executive*
Van Galder, Valerie *marketing executive*

Cupertino
Cook, Timothy D. *computer company executive*
Draper, Paul *winemaker*
Fadell, Anthony M. (Tony) *computer company executive*
Jobs, Steve(n) (Paul) *computer company executive*
Oppenheimer, Peter *computer company executive*

Daly City
Hargrave, Sarah Quesenberry *consulting company and public relations executive*

Dublin
Chen, John S. *computer company executive*

El Cajon
Yoshizu, Jeri *public relations executive*

El Dorado Hills
Briggs, Rex *marketing executive, writer*

El Segundo
Eckert, Robert A. *consumer products company executive*
Keane, Michael E. *computer services company executive*
Kilpatrick, Frank Stanton *marketing executive*

Laphen, Michael W. *computer services company executive*
Shanks, Eric *communications executive*
Vollrath, Frederick E. *human resources specialist, career officer*

Encino
Greenberg, Allan *advertising and marketing research consultant*

Eureka
Hannaford, Peter Dor *public relations executive, writer*

Foster City
Liu, Leonard *software services company executive*
Lutvak, Mark Allen *computer company executive*
Miller, Jon Philip *marketing professional, pharmaceutical executive*
Yan, Martin *celebrity chef*

Fountain Valley
Berman, Steven Richard *computer company executive*

Fremont
Sanchez, Marla Rena *communications executive*

Fresno
Ganulin, Judy *public relations professional*

Glendale
Hughes, Bradley Wayne *storage company executive*
Misa, Kenneth Franklin *management consultant*
Stewart, Julia A. *food service executive*
White, Jennifer Elizabeth Belk *corporate training specialist*

Granite Bay
Holtz, Sara *marketing consultant*

Half Moon Bay
Fennell, Diane Marie *marketing professional, process engineer*

Healdsburg
Keane, Douglas *chef*

Hillsborough
Westerfield, Putney *management consulting executive*

Huntington Beach
Dostourian, Dick *computer systems executive*

Indian Wells
Jennings, Richard Milburn *resort developer*
Kelley, John Paul *communications consultant*

Indio
Garra, Raymond Hamilton, II, *marketing executive*

Irvine
Coleman, J. Edward *computer company executive*
Pocock, J. Michael *communications executive*
Seller, Gregory Erol *marketing executive, consultant, writer*
Sherwood, Rod(erick) III *computer company executive*
Snyder, Rick (Richard D. Snyder) *computer company executive*

Joshua Tree
Hope, Harry Joe (Joeseph) *retired corporate communications specialist, writer*

Kentfield
Edgar, James Macmillan, Jr. *management consultant*

La Habra
Chase, Cochrane *advertising agency executive*

La Jolla
Bardwick, Judith Marcia *management consultant*
Katinsky, Steven B. *communications company executive*

La Quinta
Eversole, Barbara Louise *administrative assistant*

La Verne
Jalbert, Janelle Jennifer *executive recruiter, secondary school educator*

Laguna Niguel
Greenberg, Lenore *public relations professional*

Lake Forest
Coyne, John F. *computer company executive*
Massengill, Matthew H. *computer company executive*
Shakeel, Arif *computer company executive*

Lincoln
Maupin, Michael Dennis *quality assurance professional*

Livermore
Bollinger, William Anthony *security specialist, educator*
Tripodes, James G. *nuclear safety and environmental regulatory affairs professional*
Zalk, David Mark *industrial hygienist, occupational health researcher*

Long Beach
Brown, Roxanne (Jerene Roxanne Brown) *sales executive*
Halili, Antonio Marquez *facilities maintenance mechanic*
Sosoka, John Richard *consulting firm executive, engineer*

Los Altos
Michael, Harold Kaye (Bud Michael) *sales, marketing and operations executive*

Los Angeles
Belkind, Elizabeth *chef*
Beltramo, Michael Norman *management consultant*
Bloch, Paul *public relations executive*
Bohle, Sue *public relations executive*
Brandt, William Arthur, Jr. *consulting executive*
Cecere, Domenico *homebuilding company executive*
Chernin, Peter F. *multimedia company executiv*
Clow, Lee *advertising agency executive*
Coleman Smith, Salaam *communications executive*
Cora, Cat *chef*
Crosby, Peter Alan *management consultant*
Dayton, Sky *telecommunications company executive*
Doll, Lynne Marie *public relations agency executive*
Faber, George Donald *retired communications executive*
Feldman, Robert C. (Bob) *public relations executive*
Geoffrion, Arthur Minot *management scientist*
Giffin, Margaret Ethel (Peggy Giffin) *management consultant*
Gottfried, Ira Sidney *management consulting executive*
Gross, Lee *chef*
Hansen, Alexander E. *advertising agency executive*
Harris, Godfrey *public policy consultant*
Hartsough, Gayla Anne Kraetsch *management consultant*
Hatamiya, Lon Shoso *consultant, former state official*
Hateley, J. Michael *human resources executive*
Hopkins, Michael *communications executive*
Hull, LeAnne von Neumeyer *public relations and communications executive, research consultant, writer*
Islam, Mohammad *chef*
Jensen, David Gram *management consultant*
Kalis, Murray *advertising agency executive, writer*
Kline, Richard Stephen *communications and public affairs executive*
Kozberg, Joanne Corday *public affairs consultant*
Krieger, Ellie *chef, dietitian, TV personality*
Lagasse, Emeril *chef, restaurant owner, television show host, writer*
LeFevre, David *chef*
Lentz, David *chef*
Levine, Michael *public relations executive, author, television and radio personality*
Mamer, John William *business educator*
Marianella, Vincenzo *bartender*
Mathias, Alice Irene *business management consultant*
Mendoza, Ron *chef*
Murray, Alice Pearl *data processing company executive*
Nadler, Gerald *management consultant, educa*
Palevsky, Max *industrialist, director*
Peel, Mark *chef, restaurant owner*
Rice, Regina Kelly *marketing executive*
Richardson, James *chef*
Sitrick, Michael Steven *communications executive*
Spindler, Paul *communications executive, consultant*
Spivak, Kenin Mathew *personal care industry executive*
Stern, Susan Toy *human resources specialist*
Tardio, Thomas A. *public relations executive*
Torres, Cynthia Ann *marketing professional*
Wasserman, Casey *management consultant*

Los Gatos
Janvier, Pascal Paul *chef, educator*

Malibu
Dankanyin, Robert John *management consult*
Smith, Yvonne Smart *advertising executive*

Manhattan Beach
McQuillin, Richard Ross *management consul*

Manteca
Talmage, Kenneth Kellogg *consumer product company executive*

Marina Del Rey
Gold, Carol Sapin *international management consultant, speaker, writer*
Jeffrey, John Orval *Internet company executi lawyer*

Menlo Park
Kvamme, Mark D. *marketing professional*
Waddell, M. Keith *human resources specialis*

Milpitas
Corrigan, Wilfred J. *computer company executive*
Levy, Kenneth *computer company executive*
Simson, Claudine *computer company executi*
Talwalkar, Abhi Y. (Abhijit Y. Talwalkar) *computer company executive*
Tufano, Paul J. *computer company executive*

Monrovia
Jemelian, John Nazar *management consultant*

Montecito
Hanley, Kevin Lance *maintenance company executive*

Moreno Valley
Calley, Tranquil Hudson *retired travel consultant, educator*
Guerrero, Donna Marie *sales executive*

Beach
nier, T. J. *management consultant*

ntain View
ett, Stephen M. *computer software company cutive*
p, Robert R. *computer company executive*
bell, William V. *computer company cutive*
Scott David *computer software company cutive*
eus, Aart J. *computer software company cutive*
John *computer company executive*
am, Paul *Internet company executive, writer*
nan, Reid *Internet company executive*
George Ping Shan *business consultant*
Dan *Internet company executive*
shi, A. Salam *computer company executive*
, William Alford, Jr. *Internet company cutive*
eton, James John *marketing executive, iter*

a
ello, Michael *chef*
nann, Walter James *consulting company ecutive*

port Beach
i, Daniel A. *Internet company executive*
ock, Ellen Marie *communications executive*
ue, Dennis Michael *management consultant*
k, Albert Davenport, Jr. *advertising ecutive*
rroth, Lindsey *hotel executive*
, Michael Robert Alexander *marketing ecialist*

port Coast
off, George C. *retired consumer products npany executive*
ns, James O. *service company executive*

View
ant, John Randall *management consultant*

land
, Jacqueline *human resources specialist*
ss, Donald R. *consumer products company ecutive*
one, Jim *Internet company executive*
a, Douglas R. *Internet company executive*
er, Melissa Bernice *advertising executive*
er, Russell Dearnley, Jr. *investigator*

anside
s, Nicholas Paul *management consultant*
ham, Donald *computer company executive*

n, David Ratcliff *management consultant, iter*

ific Palisades
eland, John Howard *communications ecutive, television producer*

n Desert
er, Donald Ross *management consultant*

m Springs
old, Stanley Norman *management consultant, ucator*
, Walter, Jr. *business consultant*

mdale
, Joseph N. *communications executive*

o Alto
erjee, Prith *computer company executive, mputer engineering professor*
chini, Gina *Internet company executive*
chard, Gilles *computer company executive*
lley, (R.) Todd *communications and mputer company executive*
n, Debra L. *computer company executive*
in, Judith *computer company executive*
man, Jon E. *computer company executive*
hterman, James Robert, Jr. *computer mpany executive, not-for-profit executive*
loran, Jean M. *human resources specialist*
d, Mark V. *computer company executive*
i, Vyomesh I. *computer company executive*
ak, Catherine A. *computer company ecutive*
ns, Cathy *computer company executive*
t, Randy (Randall D. Mott) *computer mpany executive*
le-May, Donovan *marketing executive*
ez de Alonso, Marcela *human resources pecialist, information technology executive*
fro, John M. *human resources specialist*
ison, Shane V. *computer company executive*
hn, Nor Rae *computer company executive*
knor, Carolyn M. *computer company xecutive*
ler, Peter William *public relations executive*
ob, Maynard G., Jr. *Internet company xecutive*
kler, Michael *computer company executive*

radise
nstein, Elizabeth Ann *retired executive ecretary*

sadena
ne, Stephen Howard *data processing xecutive*
nandez, Enrique, Jr., (Rick Hernandez) *ecurity firm executive*
olan, Gary *executive recruiter*
Bryant, Daniel R. *consumer products company xecutive*
vens, Roy W. *sales and marketing executive*
tkins, John Francis *management consultant*

Paso Robles
Boxer, Jerome Harvey *data processing executive, accountant, management consultant, vintager*
Pasky, Gary Jerome *consumer products company executive*

Petaluma
Meyer, Julie Cathleen *marketing executive, director*
Purcell, Steven Richard *international management consultant, engineer, economist*

Pleasanton
Burd, Steven A. *food service executive*

Rancho Cucamonga
Gavin, Mary Ellen *marketing professional, consultant*

Rancho Mirage
Abel, Michael L. *marketing executive*
Nelson-Walker, Roberta *management software company executive*

Rancho Palos Verdes
Curtis, Carole Ortale *executive recruiter, consultant*
Douglass, Craig Bruce *computer technology executive*

Rancho Santa Fe
Best, Jacob Hilmer, Jr. *retired hotel chain executive*
Matthews, Leonard Sarver *advertising and marketing executive*

Rancho Santa Margarita
Parth, Frank R. *consulting company executive, educator*

Redlands
Rankin, Alex C. *management executive*

Redwood City
Johnson, James Harding *advertising executive*
Penner, Susanne Mary *communications executive*
Trobough, John *communications executive*

Rutherford
Staglin, Garen Kent *computer company executive, venture capitalist*

Sacramento
Franz, Jennifer Danton *public opinion and marketing researcher*
Swatt, Stephen Benton *communications executive, consultant*
Wilson, Donald Eugene *management consultant*

Salinas
Jeffries, Russell Morden *communications company official*

San Bernardino
Martinez, Benjamin Ray *security officer, retired military non-commissioned officer*
Roberts, Katharine Adair *retired bookkeeper*

San Bruno
Reider, Suzie *Internet company executive, marketing professional*

San Carlos
Eby, Michael John *marketing research and technology consultant*
Vanderryn, Jack *environmental services administrator*

San Clemente
Konney, Paul Edward *health products executive, lawyer*

San Diego
Adams, Loretta *marketing executive*
Altman, Steven *financial consulting company executive, academic administrator*
Bryan, John Rodney *management consultant*
DiRuscio, Lawrence William *advertising executive*
Harris, James Michael *sales executive*
Jacobs, Irwin Mark *communications executive*
Jacobs, Paul E. *communications company executive*
Jagoda, Barry Lionel *communications executive, writer*
Kameir, Christian *marketing executive*
Kaysen, Gavin N. *chef*
Lam, Carol Chien-Hua *communications executive, former prosecutor, lawyer*
Lang, Linda A. *food service executive*
Larson, Mark Devin *communications executive*
Myers, James M. *pet products executive*
Nelson, Craig Alan *management consultant*
Neumann, Linda Kay *marketing professional*
North, Robert L. *computer software executive*
Nugent, Robert J., Jr. *fast food company executive*
Obright, Neil Allen *data processing executive*
Padovani, Roberto *communications executive*
Payack, Paul J.J. *marketing professional, writer*
Rautenstrauch, Gary M. *marketing executive*
Robertson, Michael *Internet company executive*
Warner, John Hilliard, Jr. *technical services company executive*
Wertheim, Robert Halley *national security consultant*

San Francisco
Adelson, Jay *Internet company executive*
Appleman, Nate *chef*
Bajwa, Hashem *advertising executive*
Bancel, Marilyn *fund raising management consultant*
Benioff, Marc *Internet company executive*
Bernstein, Gerald William *management consultant, researcher*
Bierly, Shirley Adelaide *communications executive*
Biesty, Jennifer *chef*
Blanc, Maureen *public relations executive*
Butenhoff, Susan Grace *public relations executive*
Colton, Roy Charles *management consultant*
Conway, Craig A. *retired computer company executive*
Danko, Gary J. *chef*
Des Jardins, Traci *chef, restaurant owner*
Dommen, Mark *chef*
Doumani, Lissa *chef*
Falkner, Elizabeth *chef*
Garcia, Michael *Sommelier*
Jones, J. Gilbert *private investigator*
Jones, Stanton William *management consultant*
Jossel, Laurence *chef*
Kantor, Gail *Internet company executive, concert producer*
Kertzman, Mitchell E. *former software company executive, venture capitalist*
Kielarowski, Henry Edward *marketing executive*
Klammer, Joseph Francis *retired management consultant*
Krasinski, Nicole *chef*
Kunz, Heidi *healthcare company executive*
Lahlou, Mourad *chef*
LeFurgy, Rich *advertising executive*
Leong, Belinda *chef*
Mendlin, Ronald C. *employment specialist, writer*
Murphy, Kathleen Anne Foley *marketing communications executive*
O'Brien, Sean *chef*
Parker, Diana Lynne *restaurant manager, special events director*
Phan, Charles *chef*
Pollack, Jeffrey Lee *restaurateur*
Pritzker, John A. *leisure services executive*
Raglin, Jonny *Bar Chef*
Rieger, Julie *marketing executive*
Rodgers, Judy *chef*
Ross, Elizabeth *marketing executive*
Rudolph, Peter *chef*
Saeger, Rebecca *advertising executive*
Shorenstein, Douglas W. *corporate executive*
Simmons, Russel *Internet company executive, entrepreneur*
Smith, Quincy *Internet company executive*
Stoppelman, Jeremy *Internet company executive, entrepreneur*
Syhabout, James *chef*
Torme, Margaret Anne *public relations executive, management consultant*
Wakabayashi, Seiji *chef*
Wernick, Sandra Margot *advertising and public relations executive*
Williams, Evan *Internet company executive*

San Jose
Bannick, Matthew *Internet company executive*
Bostrom, Susan L. *marketing executive*
Chizen, Bruce R. *computer company executive*
Cobb, William C. *Internet company executive*
Compton, Charles (Kip) *communications executive*
Connors, Mary Jean *communications executive*
DCamp, Kathryn Acker *human resources executive*
Dutta, Rajiv *Internet company executive*
Fister, Michael J. *computer company executive*
Jordan, Jeff *Internet company executive*
Narayen, Shantanu *computer software company executive*
Omidyar, Pierre M. *Internet company executive*
Roelandts, Willem P. *data processing executive*
Scott, Edward William, Jr. *computer company executive*
Swan, Robert H. *Internet company executive*
Wallace, Richard P. *computer company executive*
Warnock, John Edward *computer company executive*
Whitman, Meg (Margaret C. Whitman) *Internet company executive*
Zwern, Arthur Louis *computer company executive*

San Marcos
Barnes, Howard G. *communications executive, film producer*

San Mateo
Gordon, William Bingham (Bing Gordon) *software marketing executive*
Hamoui, Omar *advertising executive*
Helfert, Erich Anton *management consultant, writer, educator*
Krikorian, Jason *consumer electronics company executive*
Land, Karl-Heinz *corporate communications specialist*
Shah, Bhupen *consumer electronics company executive*

San Rafael
Bartz, Carol A. *computer software company executive*
Bass, Carl *computer software company executive*
Finkelstein, James Arthur *management consultant*
Wilson, Ian Holroyde *management consultant, futurist*

San Ysidro
Ortiz, Antonio Ignacio *public relations executive*

Santa Ana
Barnett, Daniel A. *sales executive, consultant*
Carter, Curtis William *communications executive*
Tanaka, Richard I. *computer company executive*

Santa Barbara
Emmons, Robert John *corporate executive, poet*
McKee, Kathryn Dian Grant *human resources consultant*
Scheinfeld, James David *retired travel company executive*
Schultz, Arthur Warren *retired communications executive*

Santa Clara
Bray, Tim (Timothy William Bray) *computer company executive, software developer*
Bryant, Andy D. *computer company executive*
Culbertson, Leslie S. *computer company executive*
Gelsinger, Patrick P. *computer company executive*
Hutcheson, Jerry Dee *manufacturing company executive*
Maloney, Sean M. *computer company executive*
Morris, Sandra K. *computer company executive*
Pollace, Pamela L. *public relations executive*
Rudolph, Ronald Alvin *human resources specialist*
Shavers, Cheryl L. *technology and business consultant*
Sodhani, Arvind *computer company executive*

Santa Monica
Bachrach, Charles Lewis *advertising agency executive*
Calcanis, Jason McCabe *Internet company executive*
Davie, Jill *chef*
Feniger, Susan *chef, television personality, writer*
Griffith, Huw *advertising executive*
Lempert, Philip *advertising executive, writer, news correspondent*
McCreary, Lori L. *entertainment business executive*
Milliken, Mary Sue *chef, television personality, writer*
Ovitz, Michael S. *communications executive*
Patel, Chandra Kumar Naranbhai *communications executive, educator, entrepreneur, researcher*
Postaer, Larry *advertising executive*
Rice, Donald Blessing *corporate executive, former federal official*
Rubin, Gerrold Robert *advertising executive*
Ryan, Jane Frances *corporate communications executive*
Wangard, Gregg *chef*

Santa Rosa
Ash, John *chef*

Saratoga
Syvertson, Clarence Alfred *management consultant, engineer*

Scotts Valley
Crandell, Kenneth James *management consultant, entrepreneur*
Luczo, Stephen J. *computer equipment company executive*
Park, Chong S. *computer company executive*
Pope, Charles C. *computer hardware company executive*
Watkins, William D. *computer hardware company executive*
Wingert, Michael J. *computer company executive*

Seal Beach
Burge, Willard, Jr. *software company executive*

Sebastopol
McCarthy, Thomas Edward *retired telecommunications executive*

Sherman Oaks
Cook, Paul Maxwell *technology company executive*
Merritt, Jean *consulting firm executive, psychotherapist*
Yasnyi, Allan David *communications company executive*

Simi Valley
Ritacco, Patsy Richard *sales executive*

Soquel
Tomash, Erwin *retired computer company executive*

South Lake Tahoe
Nason, Rochelle *conservation organization administrator*

South San Francisco
Lewis, Jason Alvert, Jr. *communications executive*

Stockton
Hackley, Carol Ann *public relations educator, consultant*
Jacobs, Marian *advertising executive*

Studio City
Laba, Marvin *management consultant*
La Cava, Donald Leon *communications executive*
Mc Donald, Meg *public relations executive*
Moseley, Chris Rosser *marketing executive*
Silverman, Bruce Gary *advertising executive, consultant*

Sun Valley
Miller, Flemon Marshall *public works manager*

Sunnyvale
Butterfield, Stewart *Internet company executive*
Colligan, Edward T. *computer company and communications executive*
Decker, Sue (Susan Lynne Decker) *Internet company executive*
Dunaway, Cammie *marketing executive*
Ewald, Robert Hansen (Bo Ewald) *computer software company executive*
Filo, David *Internet company executive*
Jorgensen, Blake J. *Internet company executive*
Karnstedt, David *marketing executive*
Koogle, Timothy K. *communications executive*

Lin, Frank C. *computer company executive*
Nash, Jill *communications executive*
Parnafes, Itzik *Internet company executive*
Ratchev, Boris A *management consultant*
Rosensweig, Daniel L. *Internet company executive*
Sartain, Libby *human resources specialist*
Schneider, Hilary A. *Internet company executive*
Semel, Terry S. *Internet company executive*
Yang, Jerry *Internet company executive*

Tehachapi
Smith-Thompson, Patricia Ann *public relations consultant, educator*

Temple City
Lau, Bobby Wai-Man *marketing professional, investment advisor*

Thousand Oaks
Bustillos, Timothy D. *management consultant*
Fulton, Michael L. *optical company executive, researcher*

Tracy
Kiggins, Mildred L. *marketing professional*

Twentynine Palms
Fultz, Philip Nathaniel *management analyst*

Universal City
Press, Terry *marketing executive*

Valencia
Pocrass, Richard Dale *management consultant*

Vallejo
Davis, William Albert *parks director*

Venice
Choo, Kristy *chef*

Villa Park
Britton, Thomas Warren, Jr. *retired management consultant*

Vista
Mitchell, Thomas Edward, Jr. *communications cabling executive*

Walnut Creek
Henshaw, Guy Runals *management consultant*
Novotny, Glenn W. *consumer products company executive*

West Covina
Musich, Robert Lorin *motivational speaker*

West Hollywood
Antin, Jonathan *hairstylist, entrepreneur*
DeWolfe, Chris T. *Internet company executive*
Einstein, Clifford Jay *advertising executive*
Lefebvre, Ludovic *chef*
Morris, Brian *advertising executive*
Mulholland, Julie A. *marketing executive*

Westlake Village
Power, J.D., III, (James David Power III) *marketing executive*
Troxell, Lucy Davis *management consultant*

Windsor
Fieri, Guy *chef*

Woodland Hills
Ennis, Thomas Michael *management consultant*
Kern, Russell Marc *marketing executive*
Morishita, Akihiko *trading company executive*

Woodside
Arthur, Greer Martin *leasing firm executive*

Yountville
Keller, Thomas A. *chef*
Lee, Corey *chef*

COLORADO

Aurora
Ritchie, Coy Doyle *management consultant*

Black Hawk
Jones, Linda May *tour guide, writer*

Boulder
Burns, Daniel Hobart *management consultant*
Hibbs, John David *computer company executive, electrical engineer, small business owner*
Koren, Norman Lee *computer company executive*

Broomfield
Crowe, James Quell (Jim) *communications executive*

Castle Rock
Yamnik, Dale Arthur *quality assurance professional, food products executive*

Centennial
Chandramouli, Srinivasan (Chandra Chandramouli) *management and systems consultant*

Colorado Springs
Partridge, Garold Clyde *marketing executive*
Yanney, Patrick Steven *human resources specialist*

Denver
Blatter, Frank Edward *travel company executive*
Case, Paul Watson, Jr. *communications executive*
Dunham, Joan Roberts *administrative assistant*
Greenberg, David Ethan *communications consultant*
Karsh, Philip Howard *retired advertising executive*
LaMendola, Walter Franklin *technology business executive, educator*
Lazarus, Steven S. *management and marketing consultant*
Myhren, Trygve Edward *communications company executive*

Durango
Foster, James Henry *advertising and public relations executive*

Englewood
Fries, Michael T. *communications executive*
Han, Bernard L. *communications executive*
Maffei, Gregory B. *media company executive, former computer software company executive*
Malone, John C. *media company executive*
Vogel, Carl E. *communications executive*

Evergreen
Evans, David Lynn *management consultant*

Fort Collins
Neil, Stuart *management consultant, real estate broker*

Frederick
Emlen, Warren Metz *retired computer company executive*

Golden
Olson, Marian Katherine *management consultant*

Greeley
Miller, Diane Wilmarth *retired human resources director*

Greenwood Village
Benson, Robert Craig III *business consultant*
Gold, Christina A. *data processing company executive*
Wittman, Vanessa Ames *communications executive*

Lakewood
Martinen, John A. *travel company executive*

Littleton
Aigner-Clark, Julie *consumer products company executive*
Ergen, Charles W. *communications professional*
Hopping, William Russell *hospitality industry consultant, appraiser*
Kullas, Albert John *management consultant, systems engineer*

Longmont
Newman, Dean Gordon *business consultant*

Louisville
Adams, Eula L. *data storage executive*

Monument
De Francesco, John Blaze, Jr. *public relations consultant, writer*

Niwot
Farrington, Helen Agnes *personnel director*

Parker
Parker, Juston Scott *travel company executive*

Sedalia
Cooley, Andrew Lyman *computer company executive*

Snowmass Village
Strand, Curt Robert *hotel executive*

CONNECTICUT

Beacon Falls
Vignola, Andrew Michael, Sr. *computer company executive*

Bristol
Jha, Manish *communications executive*

Colebrook
Burrows, John Edward *communications company executive, writer*

Cos Cob
Murphy, R. Blair *management consulting company executive*

Danbury
Mann, Richard O. *public relations consulting company executive*

Darien
Cronk, Leonard *management consultant*
McKim, Paul Arthur *management consultant, retired gas industry executive*

East Haddam
Clarke, Cordelia Kay Knight Mazuy *management consultant, artist*
Clarke, Logan, Jr. *management consultant*

Fairfield
Henson, Daniel S. *marketing executive*
Luther, David Byron *management consultant*
Lynch, John F. *human resources specialist*
Peters, Susan P. *human resources specialist*

Farmington
Trani, John M. *former consumer products company executive*

Greenwich
Ball, John Fleming *advertising and film company executive*
Bara, Jean Marc *finance and communications executive, artist*
Carmichael, William Daniel *management consultant, educator*
Donley, James Walton *management consultant*
Genachowski, Julius *communications executive*
Gierer, Vincent A., Jr. *tobacco and wine holding company executive*
Goergen, Robert B. *consumer products company executive*
Kessler, Murray S. *consumer products company executive*
Kneeland, Michael J. *rental company executive*
Paulson, Paul Joseph *advertising executive*
Perless, Ellen *advertising executive*
Scott, Mariette A. *marketing executive*
Srere, Benson M(ortimer) *communications executive, consultant*
Wyman, Ralph Mark *multifamily office firm executive*

Guilford
Britt, David Van Buren *retired educational communications executive*

Hartford
Bucknall, William L., Jr. *human resources professional*
Vincensi, Avis A. *sales executive, medical educator*

Kent
Friedman, Frances *public relations executive*

Milford
DeLuca, Fred *food service executive*

New Britain
Loree, James M. *consumer products company executive*
Lundgren, John F. *consumer products company executive*

New Canaan
Crossman, William Whittard *retired wire cable and communications executive*
Means, David Hammond *retired advertising executive*
Ward, Richard Vance, Jr. *management consultant*

New Haven
Huwiler, Joan P. *public relations executive, consultant*

Newtown
Cole, Richard John *marketing executive*
Goodwick, David Lee *retired advertising executive*
Johnstone, Gregg Martin *communications executive*

Norwalk
Boyd, Jeffery Hawthorne *travel company executive, lawyer*
Gold, Richard N. *management consultant*
Nightingale, William Joslyn *management consultant*
Yeosock, Michael Michael *funeral director, civil engineer*

Old Saybrook
Norcia, Stephen William *advertising executive*
Phillips, William E. *advertising agency executive*

Redding
Kobak, James Benedict *management consultant*
Welsh, John Francis *retired advertising executive*

Ridgefield
Lodewick, Philip Hughes *equipment leasing company executive*

Riverside
Geismar, Richard Lee *communications executive*
McSpadden, Peter Ford *retired advertising agency executive*
Schur, Jeffrey *advertising executive*

Salisbury
Block, Zenas *retired management consultant, educator*
Dresser, James van Benschoten *retired management consultant*

Sandy Hook
Rosenblatt, Stephen Paul *marketing and sales promotion company executive*

South Windsor
Famiglietti, Nancy Zima *computer company executive*

Southbury
Caravatt, Paul Joseph, Jr. *communications executive*
Welton, Sharon Marie *food service executive*

Southport
Ambrosino, Ralph Thomas, Jr. *retired telecommunications executive*

Stamford
Burns, Ursula M. *printing company executive*
Burston, Richard Mervin *marketing executive*
Burton, Robert Gene *printing company executive*
Carter, Jerome N. *human resources specialist, paper company executive*
Dell, Warren Frank, II, *management consultant*
Dolan, Thomas J. *printing company executive*
Firestone, James A. *printing company executive*
Hicks, Wayland R. *rental company executive*
Kucic, Joseph *management consultant, industrial engineer, network engineer, information security specialist*
Mac Donald, Michael C. *printing company executive*
Martin, John K. *communications executive*
Miller, Wilbur Hobart *retired management consultant*
Motroni, Hector John *printing company executive*
Mulcahy, Anne Marie *printing company executive*
Nazemetz, Patricia *human resources specialist*
Pappas, Alceste Thetis *consulting company executive, educator*
Shassian, Donald R. *telecommunications company executive*
Silver, Charles Morton *communications compa[ny] executive*
Stern, Brian E. *printing company executive*
Vandebroek, Sophie Verdonckt *printing compa[ny] executive*
Zimmerman, Lawrence A. *printing company executive*

Wallingford
Karotkin, Rose A. *marketing professional*

Waterford
Walsh, Peter Joseph *marketing professional*

West Hartford
Glasser, Joseph *management consultant, educator*
Mackey, William Arthur Godfrey *analytical testing company executive*

Weston
Falber, Harold Julius *marketing professional*
Murray, Thomas J. *advertising executive*

Westport
Blau, Barry *marketing professional, financial consultant*
Feskoe, Gaffney Jon *management consultant*
Kurz, Mitchell Howard *marketing communications executive*
Lewis, Margaret Mary *marketing professional*
Schriever, Fred Martin *management consultant financial investor*

Wilton
Bishop, William Wade *advertising executive*
Mitchell, Richard Boyle *security firm executive*
Nickel, Albert George *advertising agency executive*

Winsted
Stawicki, Joseph John, Jr. *marketing executive*

Woodbridge
Alvine, Robert *industrialist, entrepreneur, wor[ld] business leader, philanthropist, business ow[ner]*

DELAWARE

Camden Wyoming
Bailey, Kay Wood *management consultant*

Greenville
DeWees, Donald Charles *security firm executi[ve]*

Wilmington
Axente, Liviu Mircea *management consultant*
Bloom, David Andrew *communications operations director*
Peterson, Russell Wilbur *environmental servic[es] administrator, retired governor*
Shipley, Samuel Lynn *advertising and public relations executive*
Turover, Benjamin Philip *account executive*

DISTRICT OF COLUMBIA

Washington
Aikens, Martha Brunette *park service administrator*
Amarelo, Monica A. *public relations executive writer*
Andres, Jose *chef*
Augustine, Hilton H., Jr. *computer company executive*
Berman, Ellen Sue *energy and telecommunications executive, theatre producer*
Briggum, Sue Marie *corporate executive*
Brown, Nadine *sommelier*
Brown, Warren *chef*
Browner, Carol M. *management consultant, former federal agency administrator*
Buben, Jeffrey Alan *restaurant owner, chef*
Cafritz, Peggy Cooper *communications execu[tive]*
Citronelle, Michel Richard *chef*
Clifton, James K. *market research company executive*
Cogman, Don V. *public relations executive*
Cohen, Herman Nathan *private investigator*
Cohen, William Sebastian *consultant, former Secretary of Defense*
Coltman, Edward Jeremiah *communication executive*
Comerford, Cristeta *chef*
Conte, Tony *chef*
Cook, Frances D. *management consultant*
Corso, John Anthony *management consultant, educator*
Dach, Leslie Alan *public relations company executive*
Davis, Rex Darwin *business consultant*
Dawson, Mimi Weyforth *public policy consultant*
Denysyk, Bohdan *marketing professional, consultant*
Dezenhall, Eric B. *management consultant, writer*
Drapeau, Mark David *defense contractor*
Duberstein, Kenneth Marc *management consultant, former White House chief of st[aff]*
Eisenhower, Susan *business and political consultant*
Esposo, Arnel *chef*

Fanning, Fred Eldridge *public administrator*
Fields, Stuart Howard *labor relations specialist*
Fishel, Andrew S. *managing director*
Ford, Carl W., Jr. *consulting firm executive, former federal agency administrator*
Fukushima, Katsuya *chef*
Fuller, Edwin Daniel *hotel executive*
Gest, Kathryn Waters *public relations executive*
Grant, Carl N. *communications executive, sales executive*
Griffin, Kelly Ann *public relations executive, consultant*
Grigsby, Sharlyn Ann *human resources specialist*
Hagen, Wendy W. *public relations executive*
Hager, Susan Kulka *public relations executive*
Harrington, Kathleen M. *public relations company executive, former federal agency administrator*
Hasselmo, Ann Hayes Die *executive recruiter, consultant, psychologist, educator, retired academic administrator*
Havlicek, Franklin J. *communications executive*
Higgins, James Henry III *marketing executive*
Hightower, Dennis Fowler *retired entertainment company executive, educator*
Howard, Jack *industrial relations specialist, consultant*
Howe, Fisher *management consultant, retired foreign service officer*
Huberman, Benjamin *technology consultant*
ones, A. Elizabeth *corporate communications specialist, former federal agency administrator*
Kaludis, George *management consultant, publishing executive, educator*
Kotler, Milton *marketing company executive*
Kraus, Margery *management consultant, communications company executive*
rump, Gary Joseph *marketing executive, lawyer, judge*
ahreche, Hichem *chef*
asko, Joel *marketing executive*
awson, Kelli *communications executive*
indemann, Adam *communications executive*
isboa-Farrow, Elizabeth Oliver *public and government relations consultant*
ovelace, Gail T. *human resources specialist*
ubic, Benita Joan Alk *travel company executive*
uchok, Joseph Alan *communications executive, consultant*
Mansfield, Edward Patrick, Jr. *advertising executive*
Marriott, John W. III *hotel executive*
Marriott, John Willard, Jr. *lodging and senior living executive*
McBride, Jonathan Evans *management consultant, director*
McQuillan, Laurence Joseph *communications consultant, educator*
Mederos, Carolina Luisa *public policy consultant*
Melton, Carol A. *communications executive*
Mineta, Norman Yoshio *management consultant, former secretary of transportation*
Monis, Johnny *chef*
Moore, Bob Stahly *communications executive*
Morgan, Bruce Ray *management consultant*
'Connor, Tom *corporate executive, management consultant*
alumbo, Benjamin Lewis *public relations executive, consultant*
feiffer, Leonard, IV, *executive recruiter, consultant*
ines, Wayne Lloyd *public relations executive*
yle, Robert Noble *public relations executive*
ainey, Jean Osgood *public relations executive*
eed, Travis Dean *public relations executive*
ice, Lois Dickson *retired computer company executive*
odman, Peter Warren *foreign policy specialist*
osebush, James Scott *growth strategy executive, former government official*
otunda, Donald Theodore *public relations consultant*
uta, Frank A. *chef*
eats, Peggy Chisolm *public affairs executive*
eaver, Barton *chef*
aw, William J. *hotel facility executive*
ear, Natalie Pickus *conference and event management executive*
ol, Michael *counter-money laundering consultant*
mith, Dean *communications advisor, arbitrator*
orenson, Arne M. *hotel executive*
wain, Susan Marie *communications executive*
te, Sheila Burke *public relations executive*
rzian, Grace Paine *communications executive*
mmons, William Evan *consulting firm executive*
er, Robin *hotel executive*
ndaele, Bart *chef*
ckery, Raymond Ezekiel, Jr. *international business consultant, lawyer*
llarreal, June Patricia *retired sales executive*
se, Kathryn Kahler *marketing and communications executive*
alcott, John L. *communications executive*
hittlesey, Judith Holloway *public relations executive*
illiams, Steven A., Jr. *environmental services administrator, former federal agency administrator*
itt, James Lee *management consultant, former federal agency administrator*
sutake, Noriaki *chef*
llish, Charles Barry *retired public relations executive*
ebold, Eric *chef*

LORIDA

popka
slie, John William *public relations and advertising executive*

rcadia
angler, Colleen Ann *marketing professional*
hite, Will Walter III *public relations consultant, writer*

Aventura
Schwartz, Gerald *public relations and fundraising agency executive*

Bascom
Hart, James Whitfield, Jr. *retired public relations executive, lawyer*

Boca Raton
Dorfman, Allen Bernard *international management consultant*
Dunhill, Robert *advertising executive*
Langbort, Polly *retired advertising executive*
Rhein, Arthur *computer company executive*
Vissicchio, Andrew John, Jr. *linen service company executive*
Yoder, Patricia Doherty *public relations executive*

Bonita Springs
Gillis, James R. *consumer products company executive*
Hauserman, Jacquita Knight *management consultant*
Tuchman, Alan *consumer products company executive*

Boynton Beach
Charles, Joel *forensic audio and video recording analyst, voice identification consultant*
Sondak, Arthur *retired management consultant*
Turner, Lisa Phillips *human resources executive*

Bradenton
Green, Raymond Ferguson St. John *marketing and advertising executive*
Houston, Stanley Dunsmore *retired public relations executive*

Cape Coral
Milaski, John Joseph *management consultant*
Nightingale, Suzanne M. *management consultant*

Casselberry
Pantuso, Vincent Joseph *food service consultant*

Celebration
Renard, Meredith Anne *marketing and advertising professional*

Clearwater
Aragones, Tesa *advertising executive*
Dutkowsky, Robert M. *computer company executive*
Howells, Jeffrey P. *computer company executive*
Mitchell, Scott Patrick *advertising executive, Internet company executive*
Raymund, Steven A. *computer company executive*

Coconut Grove
Softness, John *public relations executive*

Coral Gables
Buchsbaum, Karen Fuson *public relations executive, consultant*
Cole, Todd Godwin *management consultant transportation*
Gould, Taffy *Internet company executive, real estate executive*
Hertz, Arthur Herman *communications executive*
Lomonosoff, James Marc *marketing professional*

Delray Beach
Autelitano, Philip M. *marketing professional, consultant, writer*
Brewer, Robert H. *consumer products company executive*
Brown, Charles E. *consumer products company executive*
Campbell, Cynthia *consumer products company executive*
Charyk, Joseph Vincent *retired satellite telecommunications executive*
Ehrlich, Geraldine Elizabeth *management consultant*
Hardiman, Joseph Raymond *security firm executive*
Luechtefeld, Monica *consumer products company executive*
McKay, Patricia A. *consumer products company executive*
Moline, Jennifer M. *consumer products company executive*
Odland, Steve *consumer products company executive*
Rubin, Chuck (Carl Rubin) *consumer products company executive*
Vanderlinde, Daisy *consumer products company executive*

Destin
Davis, Christopher Kevin, Sr. *sales executive*

Dunedin
Metcalf, Robert John Elmer *industrial consultant*
Ruff, Kenneth *management consultant, information technology manager*

Eustis
King, Robert Howard *marketing professional*

Fort Lauderdale
Ambrose, Judith Ann *retired wedding and floral designer*
Cantwell, John Walsh *advertising executive*
Fine, Howard Alan *management consultant*
Jotcham, Thomas Denis *marketing communications consultant*
Kjellmark, Eric William, Jr. *management consultant, performing company executive*
Krause, Roy G. *office staffing firm executive*
O'Connor, James E. *waste management executive*
Scotti, Diego *marketing executive*
Smith, Mark W. *management consultant*
Wojcik, Cass *decorative supply company executive, retired municipal official*
Zimmerman, Jordan *advertising and marketing executive*

Fort Myers
Antonic, James Paul *international marketing consultant*
Blanchard, Richard Emile, Sr. *retired management services executive, consultant*
Fulker, Edmund Norman *management consultant*
Goyak, Elizabeth Fairbairn *retired public relations executive*

Fort Pierce
Thoma, Richard William *chemical safety and waste management consultant*

Grand Island
Johnson, Tesla Francis *data processing executive, educator*

Hallandale Beach
Duffy, Earl Gavin *hotel executive*

Havana
Beare, Muriel Anita Nikki *public relations executive, author*

Highland Beach
Upbin, Hal J. *consumer products company executive*

Hollywood
Angstrom, Wayne Raymond *communications executive*
Sundel, Martin *management consultant, psychologist, educator*

Jacksonville
Fahner, Harold Thomas *marketing executive*
Matta, Mark W. *human resources specialist, manufacturing executive*
Maxwell, W(ilbur) Richard *retired management consultant*
Motsett, Charles Bourke *retired sales, marketing and leadership executive*
Prussin, Jeffrey A. *management consultant*
Sederbaum, William *marketing professional*

Jacksonville Beach
Saltzman, Irene Cameron *consumer products company executive*

Juno Beach
Woltz, Kenneth Allen *retired management consultant*

Jupiter
Baum, Herbert Merrill *consumer products company executive*
Gerson, Irwin Conrad *advertising executive*

Key Biscayne
Cardozo, Richard Nunez *marketing professional, educator, entrepreneur*
Evans, Peter Kenneth *advertising executive*

Key Largo
Schmetterer, Robert Allen *advertising executive*

Lake Buena Vista
Rasulo, James A. *theme park executive*
Schmudde, Lee Gene *resort executive, corporate lawyer*

Lake Placid
Adams, Herbert Ryan *management consultant, retired minister, mediator*

Lake Worth
Saffir, Leonard *public relations executive*

Lakeland
Hrabusa, John T. *human resources specialist, food products executive*
Jenkins, Howard M. *supermarket executive*
Meads, Walter Frederick *communications executive, consultant, writer*
Phillips, David P. *grocery company executive*
Siedle, Robert Douglas *management consultant*

Longwood
Bernabei, Raymond *management consultant*
Faller, Donald E. *marketing and operations executive*

Lutz
Miller, Bonnie Sewell *marketing professional, writer*

Marco Island
Kelly, Robert Donald *management consultant*

Melbourne
Koenig, Harold Paul *management consultant, ecologist, evangelist, writer*
Lance, Howard L. *communications executive, industrial engineer*

Miami
Amos, Betty Giles *food service executive, accountant*
Arison, Micky *cruise line company executive, professional sports team owner*
Bogusky, Alex *advertising executive*
Chidsey, John W. *food service executive*
Dasburg, John Harold *restaurant executive*
Ehrlich, Morton *marketing executive, management consultant*
Ellek, Antonio *management consultant*
Gómez Martinez, Juan Carlos *advertising executive*
Gonzalez, Eddie *advertising executive*
Henderson, Diego M. *marketing professional*
Hicks, Jeff J. *advertising executive*
Nadeau, Joseph Eugene *health care management, information systems consultant*
Ponzi Kay, Marylou *human resources specialist*
Sherman, Beatrice Ettinger *hotel executive*
Stewart, Adam Mark *hotel executive*
Warren, Mark Edward *cruise line executive, lawyer*
Weiser, Sherwood Manuel *hotel and corporation executive, lawyer*

Miami Beach
Popper, Joanna *marketing executive, filmmaker*
Sharlach, Jeffrey *public relations executive*
Todd, Christopher Michael *marketing executive, consultant*

Naples
Berman, Robert S. *marketing consultant*
Bileydi, Sumer *advertising agency executive*
Kozitka, Richard Eugene *retired consumer products company executive*
Marshall, Charles *communications company executive*
Mehaffey, John Allen *marketing executive, publishing executive*
Moore, Mechlin Dongan *communications executive, management consultant*

New Port Richey
Rhodes, Eric Foster *employee relations consultant, writer*

Niceville
DeLucca, Michael C. *business executive*

North Fort Myers
Bayuk, Thomas M., Sr. *restaurant owner, writer*
Gray, Carlos Gibson *restaurant manager, agricultural products supplier, entertainer, television producer*

Ocala
Sostilio, Robert Francis *office equipment marketing consultant*

Oldsmar
Brunner, George Matthew *management consultant, retired manufacturing executive*

Opa Locka
Wright, Jeanne Elizabeth Jason *advertising executive*

Orlando
Brouillard, Robert Paul *maintenance planning manager*
Goings, Everett Vernon (Rick) *consumer products company executive*
Madsen, Andrew H. *food service executive*
Otis, Clarence, Jr. *restaurant executive*
Smetheram, Herbert Edwin *management consultant*
Yesawich, Peter Charles *advertising executive*

Ormond Beach
Keller, Steven Ray *security consultant*

Osprey
Dyche, David Bennett, Jr. *management consultant*

Palm Beach
Fisher, Fenimore *business development consultant*
Flanagan, Joseph Patrick *advertising executive*
Karp, Richard M. *advertising and communications executive*
Moloney, Thomas Walter *management consultant*
Rumbough, Stanley Maddox, Jr. *industrialist*
Tiefel, William Reginald *hotel company executive*

Palm Beach Gardens
Mendelson, Richard Donald *former communications company executive*
Van Allen, Veronica Elaine *marketing and public relations professional*

Plantation
Schink, Robert Kelly *sales executive*

Pompano Beach
Hinson, Robert William *advertising executive, consultant*

Ponte Vedra Beach
Leek, Jay Wilbur *management consultant*

Port Charlotte
Reynolds, Helen Elizabeth *management consultant*

Saint Augustine
Preysz, Louis Robert Fonss III *management consultant, educator*

Saint Petersburg
Wales, Jimmy Donal (Jimbo Wales) *Internet company executive*

Santa Rosa Beach
Rees, Lane Charles *industrial relations consultant*

Sarasota
Beck, Robert Alfred *hotel executive, educator*
Fendrick, Alan Burton *retired advertising executive*
Landis, Edgar David *business consultant*
Lautner, Jane E. *development associate*
Lee, Nancy Ranck *management consultant*
Mattran, Donald Albert *management consultant, educator*
Poppel, Harvey Lee *management consultant, investment banker*
Schlegel, John Frederick *management consultant, personal trainer*

Shulman, Arthur *communications executive*
Stolley, Alexander *advertising executive*

Seffner
Seaman, Jeffrey *consumer products company executive*

Seminole
Evans, Thomas Passmore *management consultant*

Singer Island
Dixson, J. B. *communications executive*

Sunny Isles Beach
Edelcup, Norman Scott *management and financial consultant*

Sunrise
Sorensen, Allan Chresten *service company executive*

Tallahassee
Morgante, John-Paul *human resources specialist*
Nasser, Joseph Yousef *public safety administrator, consultant*
Steele, Richard J. *management consultant*

Tampa
Barrow, Lionel Ceon, Jr. *communications and marketing consultant*
Mangiapane, Joseph Arthur *retired consulting company executive, physicist*
Studer, William Allen *security consultant, retired military officer*
Willett, Nikki *computer company executive*

Tarpon Springs
Crismond, Linda Fry *public relations executive*

Titusville
Stewart, David Witherington *business consultant*

Venice
Bluhm, Barbara Jean *communications agency executive*

Vero Beach
Fisher, Andrew *management consultant*
Grimes, Howard Ray *management consultant*
Kamman, Alan Bertram *communications consulting company executive*
Leonsis, Ted *media and professional sports team executive*
McNamara, John J(oseph) *advertising executive, writer*
Nichols, Carl Wheeler *retired advertising agency executive*
Spivak, Alvin A. *retired public relations executive*

West Palm Beach
Burgess, R(oy) Brandon *communications executive*
Chen, Ming *quality assurance professional*
Ronan, William John *management consultant*
Stauderman, Bruce Ford *advertising executive, writer*

Weston
Barnes, William Douglas *advertising executive*

Winter Park
Halladay, Laurie Ann *public relations consultant, food products executive*
Powers, Ronald George *management consultant*

GEORGIA

Alpharetta
Frankel, Andrew Joel *management consultant, information scientist*
Goetz, Richard J. *communications executive*
Reed, Wendy *management consultant company executive, information technology executive*
Winegar, Albert Lee *computer company executive*

Atlanta
Anderson, Al H., Jr. *communications executive*
Arani, Ardy A. *marketing professional, sports association administrator*
Barros, Paulino R., Jr. *communications executive*
Bayne, Katie J. (Katherine) *marketing executive*
Blake, Frank (Francis Stanton) *consumer products company executive, lawyer*
Bradshaw, Rod Eric *personnel consultant*
Bremer, Karen Ingrid *food service executive*
Brooks, Martha Finn *consumer products company executive*
Brown-Olmstead, Amanda *public relations executive*
Burge, William Lee *retired credit manager*
Chasen, Sylvan Herbert *data processing executive, financial planner*
Cooper, Simon F. *hotel executive*
Costello, John H. III *business and marketing executive*
Crow, Tim *consumer products company executive*
Crump-Caine, Lynn *food service executive*
Curtis, Philip Kerry *executive recruiter, lawyer*
Danielson, Gilbert Lawrence *consumer products company executive*
Darden, Claibourne Henry, Jr. *marketing research professional*
DeAngelo, Joseph J. *consumer products company executive*
Deason, Stephen Earl *computer company executive*
DeRodes, Robert P. *consumer products company executive*
Dramis, Francis (Fran) A., Jr. *communications executive*
Esser, Patrick J. *communications executive*
Faulkner, Kristine *communications executive*
Fenton, Jeffrey J. *management consultant, wholesale distribution executive*
Gephardt, Dick (Richard Andrew Gephardt) *consulting compay executive, lawyer, former congressman*
Goodwin, George Evans *public relations executive*
Gorman, Steve M. *communications executive*
Hoffman, Fred L. *human resources specialist*
Holly, Timothy Arnold *security firm executive*
Huff, Rolla P. *Internet company executive*
Hussey, Kent J. *consumer products company executive*
Ketchum, Mark D. *consumer products company executive*
Liebman, Gregg *communications executive*
Lunsford, Mike (Michael Cameron Lunsford) *Internet company executive*
Marohn, William D. *consumer products company executive*
McChesney, Michael C. *computer company executive*
Osgood, Christopher Mykel *radio sales manager*
Osorio, Claudio E. *computer company executive*
Ouweleen, Michael *communications executive*
Perez, Beatriz R. *marketing executive*
Raper, Charles Albert *retired management consultant*
Robinson, J. Patrick *consumer products company executive*
Ryan, J. Bruce *healthcare management consulting executive*
Seeger, Guenter Otto *chef*
Shaw, Brad *communications executive*
Shepherd, Craig Allen *environmental services administrator*
Smith, Joanne *marketing executive*
Soupata, Lea N. *human resources specialist*
Stokes, James Sewell *environmental services administrator, not-for-profit developer*
Stormont, Richard Mansfield *hotel executive*
Taylor, Tom *marketing executive*
Tomaszewski, Richard Paul *market representation executive*
Tome, Carol B. *consumer home products company executive*
Trevathan, James E. *waste management executive*
Verrill, F. Glenn *advertising executive*
Wald, Michael Leonard *public relations executive*
Weidman, Sheila *marketing professional*
Wentworth, Lynn A. *housing products company executive, former telecommunications industry executive*
Williams, Ralph Watson, Jr. *retired security firm executive*
Winckler, Alicia Jean *human resources director*
Winograd, Audrey Lesser *retired advertising executive*
Yaccarino, Linda *marketing executive*

Carrollton
Thorn, Stuart Wallace *marketing and financial executive*

Cartersville
Morgan, Derek *chef*

Cedartown
Garner, Robby Glen *software research executive, roboticist*

Clarkesville
Dowden, Thomas Clark *telecommunication executive*

Columbus
Jinright, Noah Franklin *security firm executive, retired vocational school educator*

Decatur
Peacock, Scott *chef*

Duluth
Laubscher, Robert James *consumer products company executive*
Reed, Ralph Eugene, Jr. *political consultant, former political organization administrator*

Glennville
Craft, Mary Faye *public relations executive, consultant, television producer, poet*

Kennesaw
Roebuck, Deborah Mae Britt *management consultant, educator*

Lawrenceville
Davies, David B. *communications executive*

Lilburn
Magnan, Sarah E. *court reporter*

Marietta
Smith, Baker Armstrong *management executive, lawyer*
Spann, George William *management consultant*
Wenk, Michael Scott *environmental services administrator*

Norcross
Cramer, James Perry *management strategist, architectural author, educator*
Emery, William David *consulting company executive*
Herron, Bonnie L. *management consulting company executive*
Metz, Robert C. *media company executive*

Oakwood
Jondahl, Terri Elise *importing and distribution company executive*

Pine Mountain
Callaway, Howard Hollis *resort executive*

Roswell
Hill, Donald Dee *management consultant, educator, writer*
Moseley, Marc Robards *sales executive*
Rogers, Richard Hilton *hotel executive*

Saint Simons Island
Keenan, William W. (Kip) III *public relations executive*

Savannah
Lindqvist, Gunnar Jan *management consultant, international trade consultant*
Otter, John Martin III *retired television advertising consultant*

Smyrna
Lnenicka, Wade Sheridan *purchasing agent, councilman*

HAWAII

Honolulu
Devenot, David Charles *human resources specialist, artist*
Kelley, Richard Roy *hotel executive*
O'Neill, Charles Kelly *marketing professional, retired advertising executive*

Kailua Kona
Leonardo, Ann Adamson *marketing and sales consultant*
Pratt, Alan John *business and marketing consultant*

Kapaau
Ralston, Joanne Smoot *public relations executive*

Kihei
McGuire, Michael William *communications executive*

IDAHO

Boise
Sullivan, James Kirk *management consultant*

Idaho Falls
Barbe, Betty Catherine *marketing professional, retired financial analyst*
Planchon, Harry Peter, Jr. *research development manager*

Ketchum
Ziebarth, Robert Charles *management consultant*

Sandpoint
Benbrook, Charles Mallard *executive consulting company*

Sun Valley
Tillinghast, Charles Carpenter III *retired marketing company executive*

ILLINOIS

Addison
McDonald, David Eugene *transportation operator*

Arlington Heights
Fields, Sara A. *travel company executive*

Aurora
Lee, Robert Hugh *management executive*

Barrington
Murphy, Robert *executive search consultant*
Ross, Frank Howard III *management consultant*
Scanlon Hobbs, Laurie Ann *public relations professional*
Stephens, Norval Blair, Jr. *marketing consultant*

Belleville
Hedges, Patrick Armand *security firm executive*

Bloomingdale
Flaherty, John Joseph *quality assurance company executive*
Wolande, Charles Sanford *former computer company executive*

Bloomington
Dietz, William Ronald *corporate management professional*

Bolingbrook
Alvarado, Serafin *wine connoisseur*
Sheehan, James Patrick *printing company executive, former media company executive*

Broadview
Lazar, Jill Sue *home healthcare company executive*

Burr Ridge
Bottom, Dale Coyle *marketing executive, director, management consultant*
Zaccone, Suzanne Maria *sales executive*

Carol Stream
Gale, Neil Jan *Internet company executive, computer scientist, consultant*

Champaign
Mies, John Charles *Internet company executive*
Moore, Jerry Jay *sales executive, retired archaeologist*

Chicago
Achatz, Grant *chef*
Allen, Belle *management consulting firm and communications executive*
Amberg, Thomas L. *public relations executive*
Bailey, Robert, Jr. *advertising executive*
Barnhard, Steve *travel company executive*
Bayless, Rick *chef*
Bensinger, Peter Benjamin *consulting firm executive*
Bernardin, Thomas L. *advertising executive*
Bernatowicz, Frank Allen *management consultant*
Bess, Ronald W. *advertising executive*
Beugen, Joan Beth *communications executive*
Brown, Jeremy Earle *advertising executive*
Campbell, Alex *mobile marketing executive*
Carlson, Michael *chef*
Castorino, Sue *communications executive*
Cesario, Robert Charles *marketing executive*
Cordero, Vincent C. *television network executive*
Cox, Allan James *management consultant*
DeHart, Jacob *Internet company executive*
Doetsch, Virginia Lamb *former advertising executive, writer*
Donnelley, James Russell *printing company executive*
Draft, Howard Craig *advertising executive*
Dragonette, Rita Hoey *public relations executive*
Edelman, Daniel Joseph *public relations executive*
Fisher, Eugene *marketing professional, community leader*
Foster, James Reuben *travel company executive*
Friedman, Marla Lee *human resources specialist, marketing professional*
Furcon, John Edward *management and organizational consultant*
Furth, Yvonne *advertising executive*
Gamba, Sandro *chef*
Gand, Gale *chef, restaurateur*
Gardner, Howard Alan *travel company executive, writer, editor*
Geller, Laurence S. *hotel executive*
Goldring, Norman Max *marketing professional*
Gordon, Howard Lyon *advertising and marketing executive*
Green, Judson C. *marketing agency executive*
Green, RuthAnn *marketing and management consultant*
Haffner, Charles Christian III *retired printing company executive*
Hansen, Carl R. *management consultant*
Hayden, Harrold Harrison *communications executive*
Hayley, Kathryn *consulting company executive*
Healy, Sondra Anita *consumer products company executive*
Hofrichter, David Alan *management consultant*
Hollis, Donald Roger *management consultant*
Hoplamazian, Mark Samuel *hotel executive*
Huggins, Lois M. *human resources specialist, consumer products company executive*
Husting, Peter Marden *advertising consultant*
Kobs, James Fred *direct marketing consultant*
Koernig, Stephen K. *marketing professional, educator*
Kokonas, Nick J. *restaurant owner*
Kraus, Herbert Myron *public relations executive*
Krivkovich, Peter George *advertising executive*
Krupnick, Elizabeth Rachel *human resources consulting firm and former insurance company executive*
Kunda, Dolores *marketing executive*
Leadbetter, Tiffany *hotel executive*
Levy, Deborah *security company executive*
Lotti, Michael *marketing professional*
Lowry, James Hamilton *management consultant*
Mantuano, Tony *chef*
Matuano, Tony *chef*
McCallister, Richard Anthony *business consulting company executive*
McCann, Renetta *advertising executive*
McClain, Shawn *chef*
McConnell, E. Hoy, II, *advertising and public policy executive*
McCullough, Richard Lawrence *advertising executive*
McDonagh, Steve *chef*
Melamed, Leo *global consulting firm executive*
Melman, Richard *restaurateur*
Menchin, Robert Stanley *marketing executive*
Mityas, Sherif *management consultant*
Moster, Mary Clare *public relations executive*
Noonan, Jack *analytics software and solutions company executive*
Novack, Julie Ruth *internet marketing executive*
Paul, Ronald Neale *management consultant*
Philbin, Jack *communications executive*
Pincus, Theodore Henry *public relations executive*
Plotkin, Manuel D. *management consultant, educator, former corporate executive, former government official*
Posner, Kathy Robin *retired communications executive*
Prather, Susan Lynn *public relations executive*
Pritzker, Thomas Jay *hotel executive*
Quinlan, Thomas J. III *printing company executive*
Rabin, Joseph Harry *marketing research company executive*
Radomski, Robyn L. *marketing executive*
Raphaelson, Joel *retired advertising agency executive*
Redmond, Andrea *executive recruiter*
Reitman, Jerry Irving *advertising agency executive*
Rich, S. Judith *public relations executive*
Rooney, Phillip Bernard *service company executive*
Rosenthal, Albert Jay *advertising executive*
Ryan, J. Brendan *advertising executive*
Samuelson, Peter A. *management consultant*
Schindler, Judi(th) (Judith Kay Schindler) *public relations executive, marketing professional, consultant*
Schneider, Wesley Clair *marketing communications company executive*
Segal, Mindy *chef*
Sive, Rebecca Anne *public relations executive*

mall, Richard Donald *travel company executive*
mith, Art *chef*
tead, James Joseph, Jr. *security firm executive*
tern, Carl William, Jr. *management consultant*
trubel, Ella Doyle *advertising executive, public relations executive*
trubel, Richard Perry *Internet company executive*
winand, Andrew *advertising executive*
albot, Pamela *public relations executive*
eichner, Lester *general management executive*
hompson, Jayne Carr *public relations and communications executive, lawyer*
oback, Paul A. *recreational facility executive*
ribbett, Charles *executive recruiter*
rotter, Charlie *chef*
yson, Kirk W. M. *management consultant*
an Den Hende, Fred J(oseph) *human resources executive*
Vagner, Randy Susan *travel company executive*
Veinfurter, Daniel Joseph *business services executive*
Veinstein, Lisa *marketing executive*
Villiams, Marsha C. *travel company executive*
Vooldridge, Patrice Marie *marketing professional, personal trainer*

rete
anger, Steven *human resources specialist, consultant, psychologist*

rystal Lake
ruper, John Gerald (Jack Kruper) *sales and marketing executive*

eerfield
arbonari, Bruce A. *consumer products company executive*
ezak, Carol Spielman *communications executive, editor, writer, design consultant, medical librarian*
ntvedt, Craig P. *consumer products executive*
ete, Gayle Compton *advertising and marketing executive*
eich, Victoria J. *consumer products company executive*

es Plaines
ake, Ann M. *consumer products company executive*
aczor, Diane L. *marketing professional, researcher*
ntisteban, Joseph Henry *human resources specialist*

owners Grove
mes, Sandra Patience *sales executive*
ement, Paul Platts, Jr. *performance technologist, educator*
ozek, Ernest J. *customer service administrator*
hwemm, John Butler *printing company executive, lawyer*
enen, Michael J. *consumer products company executive*
ainhour, J. Patrick (James Patrick Spainhour) *outsourcing company executive, former apparel executive*
luchamy, Pethinaidu *marketing executive*

undee
rlini, James *management consultant*

burn
ansen, H. Jack *management consultant*
Allier, James Joseph *training services executive, educator*

gin
ogers, Carleton Carson, Jr. *trade show and convention executive*

wood
gon, Demond L., Sr. *sales executive*

vanston
lkins, Tim *marketing professor*
rson, Paul William *public relations executive*
bbins, Henry Zane *public relations and marketing executive*
rnabene, Russell C. *communications executive*

eneva
ontgomery, Joel Robert *communications executive, consultant*

len Ellyn
nti, Paul Louis *management consulting company executive*

lencoe
acs, Roger David *public relations executive*

lenview
anklin, Lynne *corporate communications specialist, writer*
ubbs, Robert W. *computer services company executive*
akoyama, James Hidefumi, Jr. *security firm executive*

ghland Park
kalar, John Stephen *printing company and publishing executive*
hen, Burton David *food service executive, lawyer*
rris, Thomas L. *public relations executive*

nsdale
hitney, William Elliot, Jr. *advertising agency executive*

offman Estates
, Gregory A. *human resources specialist*
oney, John Edward *communications company executive*

Joliet
McMiller, Anita Williams *leasing company executive*

Kenilworth
Weaver, Donna Rae *winery executive*

La Grange Park
Hixon, Carl Kilmer *retired advertising executive, writer*

Lake Bluff
Fryburger, Vernon Ray, Jr. *advertising executive, finance educator*
Griem, John Michael *management consultant*

Lake Forest
Bramhall, Robert Richard *management consultant*
Brewer, Paul Huie *advertising executive, artist, portrait painter*
Carter, Donald Patton *retired advertising executive*
Chieger, Kathryn Jean *consumer products company executive*
Crawford, Robert W., Jr. *furniture rental company executive*
Johnson, Richard Darrell *management consultant*
Mohr, Roger John *retired advertising agency executive*
Rand, Kathy Sue *public relations executive, consultant*
Stecko, Paul T. *packaging company executive*

Libertyville
Maczulski, Margaret Louise *event marketing professional, meeting manager*
Ritson, Scott Campbell *management consultant*
Tullman, Glen *management consultant*

Lincolnshire
Campbell, David D. *consumer products company executive*

Lincolnwood
Lebedow, Aaron Louis *consulting company executive*

Litchfield
Talley, Hayward Leroy *communications executive*

Lombard
Harris, Jeff M. *waste management executive*

Melrose Park
Bernick, Carol Lavin *consumer products company executive*
Cernugel, William John *consumer products company executive, distributor*
Marino, V. James *consumer products company executive*

Morton Grove
Smolyansky, Julie *consumer products company executive*

Mount Prospect
Sayers, Gale *computer company executive, retired professional football player*

Naperville
Bell, Bradley J. *water treatment company executive*
Fritz, Roger Jay *management consultant*
Modery, Richard Gillman *retired marketing and sales executive*
Shanine, George *sales executive, information technology executive*

Nashville
Barber, Donald Gene, Jr. *purchasing agent*

Niles
Beton, John Allen *communications company executive*

Normal
Devinatz, Victor Gary *industrial relations specialist, educator*

Northbrook
Clarey, John Robert *executive recruiter, consultant*
Pulsifer, Edgar Darling *retired leasing and sales company executive*
Ross, Debra Benita *marketing executive, jewelry designer*
Sprieser, Judith A. *former software company executive*
Sudbrink, Jane Marie *sales and marketing executive*
Wajer, Ronald Edward *management consultant*

Northfield
Grimes, Sally *marketing professional*
Irgang, Carole A. *marketing executive*
Vilim, Nancy Catherine *advertising executive*

Oak Brook
DeLorey, John Alfred *printing company executive*
Fenton, Tim *food service executive*
Fields, Janice L. *food service executive*
Floersch, Richard *human resources specialist*
Nelson, Robert Eddinger *retired management consultant*
Paull, Matthew H. *food service executive*

Oak Park
Cannon, Patrick Francis *public relations executive*
Devereux, Timothy Edward *advertising executive*
Fisher, Lawrence Edgar *market research executive, anthropologist*

Oakbrook Terrace
Hegenderfer, Jonita Susan *public relations executive*

Park Ridge
Matthews, Roy S. *management consultant*

Peoria
Banwart, Sidney C. *human resources executive*

Prospect Heights
Lynch, William Thomas, Jr. *advertising executive*

Riverside
Dengler, Robert Anthony *management consultant*

Rockford
Albert, Janyce Louise *human resources specialist, retired business educator, banker, consultant*
Wilson, L. C. *superintendent*

Rosemont
Leggett, Scott *chef, consultant*
Le Menager, Lois M. *incentive merchandise and travel company executive*

Saint Charles
Nellemann, Lynne O'Shea *management consultant*

Schaumburg
Brown, Gregory Q. *communications executive*
Fattori, Ruth A. *human resources specialist, electronics executive*
Fox, Thomas J. *communications executive*
Hill, Raymond Joseph *packaging company executive*
Keller, Casey (Kenneth Charles Keller Jr.) *communications executive*
Meredith, Thomas J. *communications, investment company executive*
Roman, Ray *communications executive*
Warrior, Padmasree *communications executive*
Zander, Edward J. *communications executive*

Skokie
Brennan, William P. (Bill Brennan) *computer company executive*
Sperzel, George E., Jr. *former personal care industry executive*

Springfield
Stroh, Raymond Eugene *retired personnel executive*

Vernon Hills
Claassen, W(alter) Marshall *employment company executive*
Powers, Anthony Richard, Jr. *educational sales professional*

Warrenville
Hand, Ann Sparenberg *marketing executive*

Wauconda
Meehan, Jean Marie Ross *human resources, occupational health and safety management consultant*

Westchester
Faulkner, Robert Lloyd *advertising executive, graphics designer*

Western Springs
Virant, Paul *chef*

Wheaton
Long, Charles Franklin *retired corporate communications executive*

Willowbrook
Foley, Joseph Lawrence *sales executive*

Winnetka
Cole, Kathleen Ann *advertising executive, social worker*
Thomas, John Thieme *management consultant*
Weldon, Theodore Tefft, Jr. *marketing executive*

Woodridge
O'Connor, William Michael *search company executive*

INDIANA

Carmel
Mahoney, Margaret Ellis *advertising executive*
Rati, Robert Dean *retired data processing executive*

Crown Point
Hendricks, Stanley Marshall, II, *executive recruiter, consultant*

Evansville
Morgan, George Henry *patent agent, consultant*
Zion, Roger Herschel *retired management consultant, retired congressman*

Fort Wayne
Balint, David Lee *communications executive*
Raby, Arend Christopher *sales executive*

Hammond
Boggs, William Norman *marketing professional, educator*

Indianapolis
Ayars, Patti *human resources specialist, health products executive*
Brown, Randy *human resources specialist, health insurance company executive*
Buranello, Raymond Terrence *quality assurance executive, chemist*
Burnett, Judith Jane *public relations executive*

Gilman, Alan B. *restaurant company executive*
Harden, Annette C. *recreation director*
Kirkpatrick, Robert Hugh *communications executive*
Muncie, Ronald James *environmental services administrator, minister*
Ruben, Gary A. *marketing and communications consultant*
Schenk, William Earl III *senior special agent, criminal investigator*
Spanogle, Robert William *marketing and advertising company executive, association administrator*

Jeffersonville
Chilton, Ronald Hanley *broadcasting executive, actor*

Liberty
Pringle, Lewis Gordon *marketing professional, educator*

Merrillville
Willadsen, Michael Chris *marketing professional, sales executive*

Muncie
Barber, Earl Eugene *management consultant*
Norris, Tracy Hopkins *retired public relations executive*

Munster
Neff, Bonita Dostal *communication development facilitator*

Santa Claus
Edwards, James Dallas III *management consultant*

Valparaiso
Blaschke, Lawrence Raymond *electronic security services professional*

Wabash
Scales, Richard Lewis *retired sales executive*

West Lafayette
Schendel, Dan Eldon *management consultant, finance educator*

IOWA

Ames
Bonomi, Ferne Gater *public relations executive*
Davis, Wayne Pitman *public relations executive*

Cedar Rapids
Baldwin, Cynthia Ann *industrial hygienist*
Stolte, Larry Gene *marketing executive, retired computer and publishing company executive*
Wiese, Daniel Edward *marketing and communications researcher*

Des Moines
O'Keefe, Mary A. *marketing executive*

West Des Moines
Marshall, Russell Frank *consulting company executive*

KANSAS

Junction City
Werts, Merrill Harmon *retired management consultant*

Lawrence
Knorr, Patrick *communications executive*

Leawood
King, Barbara Sackheim *travel company executive*
Mooney, Justin David *motel executive, consultant*

Overland Park
Fuller, Michael B. *communications executive*
Green, John Lafayette, Jr. *strategic planning executive, former educational association administrator*
Hill, Lloyd Lester *food service executive*

Ozawkie
Blodig, Allison Marie *environmental services administrator*

Shawnee Mission
Mealman, Glenn *corporate marketing executive*
Putman, Dale Cornelius *management consultant, lawyer*

Topeka
Sipes, Karen Kay *communications executive*

Wichita
Herr, Peter Helmut Friederich *sales executive*
Koch, Charles de Ganahl *industrial company executive*
Lerman, Kenneth Barry *marketing professional, consultant*
Menefee, Frederick Lewis *advertising executive*

KENTUCKY

Benton
Glass, Mary Jean *management executive*

Bowling Green
Garrison, Geneva *retired administrative assistant*

Covington
Surber, David Francis *public relations executive, consultant, television producer, journalist*

Hopkinsville
Neville, Thomas Lee *food service company executive*

Lexington
Millard, James Kemper *marketing executive*

Louisville
Beck, Peter *marketing executive, minister*
Byerlein, Anne P. *human resources specialist, food products executive*
Clayton, M. Courtland *management consultant*
Cook, Terrance *business executive*
French, Michael Bruce *business executive*
Hearl, Peter R. *food service executive*
Novak, David C. *restaurant company executive*
Travis, Nigel *food service executive*
Wagner, James Miller *funeral director*

Paducah
Justice, Phillip Howard *marketing professional*

Versailles
Troutt, Kenny *communications executive*

LOUISIANA

Lafayette
Cormier, Joseph Bowman *private investigator, consultant*
Sides, Larry Eugene *advertising executive*

Many
Dutton, Frank Elroy *data processing executive, writer*

Metairie
Grimm, John Lloyd *marketing professional*

New Orleans
Bacot, Marie *management consultant, researcher*
Link, Donald *chef*
Prudhomme, Paul *chef, restaurant owner*
Schnoebelen, Ian *chef*

Ruston
Hudnall, Jarrett, Jr. *management consultant, educator, marketing professional*

MAINE

Brooklin
Schmidt, Klaus Dieter *marketing professional, management consultant, educator*

Falmouth
Winton, Linda *international trainer, consultant*

Hollis Center
Kaake, Norman Bradford *quality assurance professional*

Portland
Corry, Steve *chef*
Hayward, Sam *chef*

Sumner
Rudd, David William *management consultant, chemical engineer, consultant*

Whitefield
Marden, Kenneth Allen *advertising executive*

York
Freeman, Neal Blackwell *communications corporation executive*

MARYLAND

Annapolis
Branand, Claire Diane *advertising executive, writer*
Crosby, Ralph Wolf *communications executive*
Tosé, Maurice B. *communications executive*

Baltimore
Brotman, Phyllis Block *advertising and public relations executive*
Clarizio, Lynda M. *advertising executive, lawyer*
Dickinson, Jane W. *retired executive secretary, volunteer*
Durbin, Dean D. *marketing executive*
Goldman, Duff (Jeffrey Adam Goldman) *chef*
Howes, James Guerdon *communication and transportation executive*
Talbot, Donald Roy *management consultant*

Beltsville
Miller, Ted Robert *management consultant*
Quirk, Frank Joseph *management consulting company executive*
Ritz, David M. *photographic retail company executive*

Bethesda
Allnutt, Robert Frederick *management consultant, lawyer*
Cody, Thomas Gerald *management consultant, writer*
Durek, Thomas Andrew *computer company executive*
Johnson, Eugene Clare *data processing company executive*
Marriott, Richard Edwin *hotel and contract services executive*
McClure, Brooks *management consultant*
Mc Gurn, Barrett *communications executive, writer*
Miller, Judith Wolfe Cohen *management consultant*
Nassetta, Christopher J. *hotel facility executive*
Neill, Denis Michael *management consultant*
Walter, W. Edward *hotel and corporate financial executive*

Bozman
Wyatt, Wilson Watkins, Jr. *communications executive, writer*

Cambridge
Digges, Edward S(imms) *business management consultant*
Spahr, Elizabeth *environmental research administrator*

Chestertown
Docksteader, Karen Kemp *marketing professional*

Chevy Chase
Baruch, Jordan Jay *retired management consultant*
Bisconti, Ann Stouffer *public opinion research company executive*
Michaelis, Michael *management and technical consultant*

Cockeysville Hunt Valley
Elkin, Lois Shanman *business systems company executive*
Whitehurst, William Wilfred, Jr. *management consultant*

College Park
Dorn, Norman Philip *management consulting firm executive*

Davidsonville
Montague, Brian John *consulting company executive*

Dayton
Ferrera, Arthur Rocco *food distribution company executive*

Ellicott City
Estin-Klein, Libbyada *advertising executive, writer*

Fort Washington
Satterthwaite, George, II, *security firm executive*

Gaithersburg
Carey, John Edward *communications executive*
Landel, Michel *food service and management company executive*

Germantown
Kaul, Pradman *communications executive*

Gibson Island
Forster, William Hull *management consultant*

Greenbelt
Fontaine, Kathleen Sturey *policy analyst*

Hagerstown
Higgins, M. Eileen *management consultant, educator*
Shaper, Christopher Thorne *sales executive*

Hanover
Bisciotti, Stephen J. *staffing company executive, professional sports team executive*

Kensington
Hum, Vance York *technology consulting executive*

Kingsville
Akehurst, Wallace Edward *marketing professional, consultant*

Lanham Seabrook
Liggins, Alfred C. III *broadcasting company executive*

Lutherville Timonium
Brustein, Abram Isaac *sales executive, insurance company executive*

Owings Mills
McNiesh, Celeste Angela *sales executive*

Potomac
Foley, Joseph Patrick *public relations executive*
Medin, A. Louis *computer company executive*
Shirvinski, Adam John *management consultant*

Rockville
Klosson, Michael *public policy director*

Silver Spring
Altschul, B. J. *public relations counselor*
Burke, Margaret Ann *computer company and communications executive*
Carter-Johnson, Jean Evelyn *management consultant*
Montalvo, Eileen *communications executive*
Moreno, Donna Marie *communications executive*
Rice, Michelle *communications executive*
Shih-Carducci, Joan Chia-mo *food service executive, educator, medical technologist, writer, biochemist*

Solomons
Harrington, John Vincent *retired communications executive, engineer, educator*

Sparks
Rallo, James Gilbert *management company executive*

Stevensville
Barrett, John Anthony *publishing and printing company financial executive*

Taneytown
Anderson, Mary Ann Grasso *business executive*

Towson
Chase, Jacquelyn Veronica *marketing professional*
Passano, E. Magruder, Jr. *management consultant*

University Park
Holder, Sallie Lou *training and meeting management consultant, coach*

MASSACHUSETTS

Bedford
Daltas, Arthur John *management consultant, software services manager*

Belchertown
Burstein, Michael Clifford *enterprise integration consultant*

Belmont
Bingham, George Walter Chandler *retired sales executive*
Klein, Martin Samuel *management consultant*

Beverly
Barger, Richard Wilson *hotel executive*

Boston
Berger, Jerome Morris *communications executive*
Billings, Rick *chef*
Buchin, Stanley Ira *management consultant, finance educator*
Burnham, David Henderson *management consultant*
Connors, Jack, Jr. *advertising executive*
Cornwall, Deborah Joyce *management consultant, consulting firm executive*
Dowd, Peter Jerome *public relations executive*
Eskandarian, Edward *advertising executive*
Farrar, Constance Mosher *marketing executive*
Finucane, Anne M. *communications executive, marketing executive*
Gardner, Geoff *chef*
Hayes, Andrew Wallace, II, *consumer products company executive*
Hickey, Elizabeth Louise *advertising agency executive*
Hunter, Durant Adams *executive search company executive*
husbands, andy *chef*
Kelly, Francis J. III *global marketing company executive*
Lang, Laura W. *marketing executive*
Leahy, John L. *software development company executive*
Levy, Stephen Raymond *retired data processing executive*
Luongo, C. Paul *public relations executive*
Lynch, Barbara *chef, restaurant owner*
Maffeo, Pino *chef*
Maister, David Hilton *consultant*
McClelland, Frank *chef, restaurant owner*
McGovern, Lore Harp *communications executive, philanthropist*
McGovern, Patrick J. *communications executive*
Merrill, John *chef*
Oringer, Kenneth *chef, restaurant owner*
Porter, Michael E. *competitive strategy educator*
Pytka, Stephen Milton *office equipment executive*
Reese, C. Richard *data processing executive*
Rimpel, Auguste Eugene, Jr. *management and technical consulting executive*
Sander, Alison Bishop *international consultant*
Saunders, Donald Leslie *hotel executive, real estate developer*
Schlow, Michael *food service executive*
Shapiro, Eli *business consultant, educator, economist*
Taylor, Jeff *Internet company executive*
Trafidlo, James Francis *marketing communications executive, commercial photographer*

Braintree
Driscoll, Megan *executive recruiter*

Cambridge
Adams, Jody *chef, restaurant owner*
Allaire, Jeremy *Internet company executive*
Bloom, Kathryn Ruth *public relations executive*
Bremer, Gabriel *chef*
de Monteiro, Nadsa *chef*
Knickrehm, Glenn Allen *management executive*
Little, John Dutton Conant *management scientist, educator*
Lydon, Amanda *chef*
Maws, Tony *chef*
McBride, Robert Albert *training services executive*
Poe, Mya *communications executive, director*
Rowley, Geoffrey Herbert *management consultant*
Sapienza, Tony *public relations executive*
Shaw, Anthony Raymond, Jr. *research executive*
Zollar, Alfred *computer company executive*

Canton
Allen, Frances L. (Britchford) *marketing executive*
Judson, Arnold Sidney *management consultant*
Kaigler, Denise *communications executive*
Luther, Jon L. *food service executive*

Chatham
Escalante, Judson Robert *business consultant*
Rhinesmith, Stephen Headley *management consultant*

Chelmsford
Fulks, Robert Grady *computer company executive*

Chelsea
Jenkins, Alexander III *consumer products company executive, consultant*

Chestnut Hill
O'Block, Robert Paul *management consultant*

Cohasset
Rabstejnek, George John *healthcare executive*

Concord
Eberle, William Denman *international management consultant*
Parrish, Thomas Kirkpatrick III *marketing consultant*

Dartmouth
Washburn, Stewart Putnam *management consultant*

Dover
Bonis, Laszlo Joseph *marketing executive, healthcare professional, chemist*
Mehta, Narinder Kumar *marketing executive*

Duxbury
Erickson, Phyllis Traver *marketing executive*

Fall River
Cabral, Gloria Maria *food service executive, educator*

Foxboro
Ferron, Jennifer *marketing executive*

Framingham
DeWerth, Gordon Henry *management consulta*
Margolis, Bruce Lewis *human resources executive*
Meador, Charles Lawrence *management and systems consultant, educator*

Gloucester
Hausman, William Ray *fund raising and management consultant*
Littlefield, Paul Damon *retired management consultant*
White, Horace Council *business manager*

Lexington
Brick, Donald Bernard *software company executive*
Dougherty, Richard Hamlen *management and healthcare consultant*

Marlborough
Murray, R. Scott *computer software company executive*

Needham
Grasso, James Anthony *public relations executive, educator*
Kanojia, Chet *communications executive*

Newton
Benner, Mary Wright *freelance/self-employed conference director*

Newton Center
Copithorne, David A. *public relations executi*

North Quincy
Rutherford, Scott *marketing professional, consultant*

Norwell
Case, David Knowlton *management consultan*

Norwood
Fishman, Jerald G. *semiconductor executive*

Osterville
Sommers, William Paul *management consulta research and development company executi*

Palmer
Dupuis, Robert Simeon *sales executive*

Peabody
Gordon, Bernard M. *computer company executive*
Southwick, Paul *retired public relations executive*

Pittsfield
Hochfelder, Scott Z. *toy company executive, lawyer*

Quincy
Hall, John Raymond, Jr. *fire protection execut*

Randolph
Huntington, Robert Howard *business management executive*

Rockport
Wiberg, Lars-Erik *occupational compatibility consultant*

Sherborn
Hancock, William Frank, Jr. *management consultant*

South Hamilton
Ryan, Heather Vickers *marketing professional*

Southbridge
Anderson, Ross Barrett *healthcare environme services manager*

Waban
Rossolimo, Alexander Nicholas *management consultant, corporate director*

Wakefield
Coletta, Gerard Charles *management consulta*

Waltham
Buchholz, William James *communications executive, educator*

iaskin, Steven Paul *marketing executive, consultant*
Lasputys, Joseph Edward *corporate executive, economist*

Vatertown
Gerritson, A. J. *advertising executive*

Vellesley
leisler, Elwood Douglas *hotel executive*
'sai, Ming *chef*

Vellesley Hills
Doorley, Thomas Lawrence III *management consultant*
nbrescia, Marcia *landscape company executive*

Veston
tambaugh, Armstrong A., Jr. *restaurant and hotel executive*

Villiamstown
Robinson, Hobart Krum *management consulting company executive*
prague, John Louis *management consultant*

Vinchester
aggart, Ganson Powers *management consultant*

Vorcester
amougis, George *health, safety and environmental consultant*

IICHIGAN

da
yall, Lynn *consumer products company executive*
an Andel, Steve Alan *consumer products company executive*
'eiss, Joseph Joel *consulting company executive*

nn Arbor
gno, John G. *management consultant*
elcher, Louis David *marketing professional, retired mayor*
randon, David A. *food service executive*
oley, Daniel Ronald *personnel director, lawyer*
lartin, Claude Raymond, Jr. *marketing consultant, educator*
'koui, Hossein Reza *quality assurance professional*

uburn Hills
ae, Nancy A. *human resources specialist, automotive executive*

enton Harbor
inkley, David A. *human resources specialist*

eulah
uch, Walter Edward *security firm executive*

irmingham
nith, Todd P. *marketing executive*

loomfield Hills
dams, Charles Francis *advertising and real estate company executive*
erline, James H. *advertising and public relations executive*
okhari, Raza Ali Babar *former marketing strategist*
ankel, Richard William *retired vending company executive*
ndy, William Haskell *training and communication systems executive*

harlotte
oung, Everett J. *management consultant, agricultural economist*

linton Township
oubareff, Kathy Olga *administrative assistant*

earborn
hmed, Saleem *management consultant, educator*
ymon, Joe W. *human resources specialist, automotive executive*

etroit
ssett, Tina *communications executive*
ake, Willie Edward *computer company executive, educator*
owell, Scott *restaurant manager, real estate developer*
ovak, Raymond Francis *environmental services administrator, pharmacology educator*
rcher, Robert *restaurant manager, retired professional football player*
ece, Terry Allen *travel company executive, Internet company executive*
hweitzer, Peter *advertising agency executive*
ern, Todd *restaurant manager*
pacio, Angela *marketing executive*

ast Lansing
dd, Ewen Cameron David *food safety director*

armington
erba, Gabriel *public relations consultant*

armington Hills
anna, Martin *public relations executive, marketing executive*

erndale
vaere, Jason *production company executive*

len Arbor
agner, Bruce Stanley *marketing professional*

rand Rapids
kstra, William Dwight *management executive, consultant*
Gordon, Dan A. *food service executive*
Messner, James W. *advertising executive*
Purchase-Owens, Francena *marketing professional, consultant, educator*
Roberts-Brown, Arlene Maria *executive assistant*
Spaulding, Dan *public relations executive*
Williams, Janice H. *business executive*

Grosse Pointe
Caldwell, John Thomas, Jr. *communications executive*

Grosse Pointe Park
Krebs, William Hoyt *industrial hygienist, health science association administrator*

Hastings
Jones, Kensinger *advertising executive, educator*

Holland
Garlough, William Glenn *marketing executive*

Lansing
Lobenherz, William Ernest *consumer products company executive, trade association administrator, lawyer*

Livonia
Barfield, Jon E. *employment company executive*
Chowdhury, Subir *management consultant*
Maibach, Ben C., Jr. *consumer products company executive*

Madison Heights
Scott, George Alfred *advertising executive, writer*

Marquette
Pesola, William Ernest *restaurant management executive*

Mount Clemens
Robinson, Earl, Jr. *marketing, transportation executive, educator, retired air force officer*

Novi
Flinchbaugh, Jamie *training services executive*
Kinsey, Charles John *industrial auctioneer, consultant, farmer, cattle breeder*

Portage
Seely, Robert Eugene *management consultant*

Rockford
Loux, Jonathan Dale *business development consultant, director*

Royal Oak
Stanalajczo, Greg Charles *computer company executive*

Southfield
Barnett, Marilyn *advertising executive*
Caponigro, Jeffrey Ralph *public relations counselor*
Jackson, Roger A. *human resources specialist, automotive executive*
Kalter, Alan *advertising agency executive*
Wood, Terry David *broadcasting executive*

Taylor
Barry, Alan H. *consumer products company executive*
Manoogian, Richard Alexander *consumer products company executive*
Wadhams, Timothy *consumer products company executive*

Tecumseh
Johnson, Kelly *chef*

Traverse City
Ginsberg, David Baron *retired management consultant*

Troy
Adderley, Terence Edward *human resources executive*
Camden, Carl T. *human resources company executive*
Chalil, Joseph Mathew *sales executive, consultant, liver disease specialist, medical products executive*
Williams, Leonard Todd, Jr. *hotel sales and marketing executive*

Walled Lake
Gillespie, J. Martin *sales and distribution company executive*

Warren
Hopp, Anthony James *advertising agency executive*

West Bloomfield
Lit, Mark Alan *recreational facility executive*
Smith, Nancy Hohendorf *sales executive, marketing professional*

MINNESOTA

Austin
Budd, Jim *communications manager*

Bloomington
Knotek, Robert Frank *retired management consultant, educator*

Chaska
Cohen, Cheryl Diane Durda *communications executive*

Farmington
Wurdeman, Lew Edward *Internet company executive, consultant*

Hastings
Avent, Sharon L. Hoffman *manufacturing company executive*

Hopkins
Dunlap, William DeWayne, Jr. *advertising agency executive*

Lake Crystal
Pawlitschek, Donald Paul *management consultant*

Mahtomedi
Brainerd, Richard Charles *human resources executive, consultant, educator*

Mankato
Schreier, Bradley *management executive*

Minneapolis
Blackwell, Todd V. *human resources specialist*
Burdick, Lou Brum *public relations executive*
deBruin Sample, Anne *human resources specialist*
Fallon, Patrick R. *advertising executive*
Finkelstein, Paul D. *personal care industry executive*
Forsythe, Thomas M. *communications executive*
Gage, Edwin C., III, (Skip Gage) *travel and marketing services executive*
Johnson, Lola Norine *retired advertising and public relations executive, educator*
Kelly, Charles Harold *advertising executive*
Koutsky, Dean Roger *advertising executive*
McKee, Tim *chef*
Mouser, Les (Lyman Mouser) *advertising executive*
Mulligan, Donal L. *consumer products company executive*
Pohlad, Robert C. *consumer products company executive*
Powell, Kendall J. *consumer products company executive*
Sanger, Stephen W. *consumer products company executive*
Scoville, James Griffin *industrial relations professor*
Tandon, Rajiv *training company executive*
Turner, Ronald L. *information services executive*
Veblen, Thomas Clayton *management consultant*
Viault, Raymond G. *food company executive*
Watson, Lucia *chef*
Wickesberg, Albert Klumb *retired management consultant*
Wikman, Michael Raymond *advertising executive*
Woodman, Stewart *chef*
Yourzak, Robert Joseph *management consultant, educator, engineer*
Zimmermann, Robert Laurence *marketing professional*

Minnetonka
Gillies, Donald Richard *marketing and advertising consultant, educator*
Kostka, Ronald Wayne *marketing consultant*
Nelson, Marilyn Carlson *hotel executive, travel company executive*
Porter, Jim *human resources specialist*
Schmidt, Russel Alan, II, *sales executive*

North Mankato
Taylor, Glen A. *printing, direct mail and technology executive, professional sports team owner*

Ottertail
Blaha, Verle Dennis *consumer products company executive, electrical engineer*

Pequot Lakes
Gray, Allen (Ernest Bungaard) *communications executive*

Rochester
Coleman, Mary Ellen *quality assurance professional*
Nevling, Harry Reed *human resources consultant*

Saint Paul
Axelrod, Leonard *management consultant*
Baker, Douglas M., Jr. *service industry executive*
Brooks, Phillip *advertising executive*
Courtney, Eugene Whitmal *computer company executive*
Fritze, Steven L. *service industry executive*

Wayzata
Schoen, Charles Judd *service executive*
Waldera, Wayne Eugene *crisis management executive*

MISSISSIPPI

Biloxi
Love, James Sanford III *communications executive*

Columbus
Labensky, Sarah Ross *culinary educator*

Ocean Springs
Culberson, Gary Michael *hotel manager*

MISSOURI

Blue Springs
Page, Leslie Andrew *retired consumer products company executive*

Branson
Lanning, James Wilford *sales executive, retired music educator*

Cape Girardeau
Smallwood, Glenn Walter, Jr. *utility marketing management executive*

Chesterfield
Stork, Donald Arthur *advertising executive*
Welshans, Merle Talmadge *retired management consultant*

Clayton
Vecchiotti, Robert Anthony *management and organizational consultant*

Columbia
Helvey, William Charles, Jr. *communications specialist*
Hoffsette, Leon Merle *security specialist, retired military officer*

Creve Coeur
Wasserman, Stephen Miles *communications director*

Farmington
Ashkin, Ronald Evan *international executive*

Fenton
Lipovsky, Robert P. *marketing executive*
Maritz, W. Stephen *marketing professional, service executive*

Independence
Burnett, Crystal Blythe *marketing professional*
Evans, Margaret Ann *human resources administrator, business owner*

Kansas City
Baker, Ronald Phillip *service company executive*
Benedict, Stephanie Michelle *purchasing agent, sales consultant*
Benner, Richard Edward, Jr. *marketing consultant, volunteer, investor*
Brown, Peter C. *movie theater company executive*
Courson, Marna B.P. *public relations executive*
Dillingham, John Allen *marketing professional*
Dwyer, William Michael *health care company advisor*
Garrelts, Colby *chef*
Hall, Donald Joyce, Sr. *greeting card company executive*
Robertson, Leon H. *management consultant, educator*
Solberg, Elizabeth Transou *public relations executive*
Tio, Celina *chef*
Warakomski, Alphonse Walter Joseph, Jr. *sales executive, marketing professional*

Lake Saint Louis
Dommermuth, William Peter *marketing consultant, educator*

O Fallon
Ractliffe, Robert Edward George *management executive*

Richmond Heights
Shaich, Ronald M. *food service executive*

Saint Charles
Wagner, Mary Ann *human resources executive*

Saint Louis
Bachmann, John William *security firm executive*
Bradley, Marilynne Gail *advertising executive, educator*
Brandt, Kimberly Glanz *recreational facility executive, director*
Bultas, William Fitzgerald *Internet company executive*
Burgess, William Patrick *management consultant*
Curran, Michael Walter *management scientist*
Davis, Irvin *advertising, public relations and broadcast executive*
Drury, Charles Louis, Jr. *hotel executive*
Ferguson, Gary Warren *retired public relations executive*
Johnson, Donn S. *communications executive*
Khoury, George Gilbert *printing company executive, sports association executive*
Klein, Ward M. *consumer products company executive*
Kornblet, Donald Ross *communications company executive*
Lents, Peggy Iglauer *marketing professional*
Newman, Andrew Edison *restaurant manager*
Pillai, Pragash *communications executive*
Raven, Peter Hamilton *botanical garden director, botany educator*
Sibbald, John Ristow *management consultant*
Siemer, Paul Jennings *public relations executive*
Taylor, Andrew C. *rental and leasing company executive*
Taylor, Jack Crawford *rental and leasing company executive*
Tyler, William Howard, Jr. *advertising executive, educator*

Warrenton
Dapron, Elmer Joseph, Jr. *communications executive*

MONTANA

Helena
Manuel, Vivian *public relations executive*

NEBRASKA

Lincoln
Hawley, Kimra *computer company executive*

Omaha
Caggiano, Joseph *advertising executive*

Eggers, James Wesley *executive search consultant*
Mew, Calvin Marshall *advertising executive*
Roskens, Ronald William *management consultant, retired academic administrator*
Ryan, Shelli Ann *public relations executive*

Oneill
Hedren, Paul Leslie *parks director, historian*

NEVADA

Carson City
Welch, Richard LeRoy *personal improvement company executive*

Henderson
Bruno, Cathy Eileen *management consultant, former state official, social sciences educator*
Cohan, George Sheldon *advertising and public relations executive*
Goldstein, Morris *retired consumer products company executive*

Incline Village
Mitton, Michael Anthony *environmental technology company executive*

Las Vegas
Adelson, Sheldon Gary *hotel and gaming company executive*
Arce, Phillip William *hotel and casino executive*
Atwood, Charles L. *recreational facility executive*
Boyd, William S. *hotel and gaming company executive*
Brock, Holly Melinda *marketing professional*
Ensign, Michael S. *resort company executive*
Griesche, Robert Price *hospital purchasing executive*
Hardie, George Graham *casino executive*
Henderson, Jeff *chef*
Huff, Dennis Lyle *marketing professional*
Jackson, Phillip Ellis *marketing executive, writer*
Lanni, Terry (Joseph Terrence Lanni) *hotel corporation executive*
Loveman, Gary W. *gaming company executive*
MacPherson, Grant *chef*
Mataseje, Veronica Julia *sales executive*
Murren, James Joseph *hotel executive*
Neilsen, Craig H. *hotel executive*
Satre, Philip Glen *casino entertainment executive, lawyer*
Schaeffer, Glenn William *casino corporate financial executive*
Shively, Judith Carolyn (Judy Shively) *administrative assistant*
Sillerman, Robert F. X. *communications executive, banker*
Smith, Keith E. *hotel and gaming company executive*
Sorrell, Michael E. *consulting company executive, hospitality executive*
Stark, S. Daniel, Jr. *casino and gaming resort company executive*
Welter, William Michael *marketing and advertising executive*
Wynn, Steve Alan (Stephen A. Wynn) *hotel and gaming company executive*

Reno
Ford, Victoria *retired public relations executive, writer, oral historian*
Frank, Lillian Gorman *human resources executive, management consultant*
Howard, Christopher Philip *management consultant, investor*

NEW HAMPSHIRE

Amherst
Soneira, Raymond Mario *computer company executive, scientist*

Bedford
Hall, Pamela S. *environmental services administrator*

Center Harbor
Shaw, Robert William, Jr. *management consultant, venture capitalist*

Concord
Roberts, George Bernard, Jr. *management and government relations consultant, former state legislator*

Deering
Spitzer, Morton Edward *management consultant*

Enfield
Gamache, R. Donald *retired business development executive*

Exeter
Harmon, Richard Wingate *management consultant*

Fitzwilliam
Schott, John Robert *international consultant, educator*

Grantham
Hansen, Herbert W. *management consultant*

Hampstead
Hargreaves, David William *retired communications company executive*

Hanover
Burnham, Patricia White *consultant, advocate, writer, business executive*

Jackson
Synnott, William Raymond *retired management consultant*

Litchfield
Darlington, David William *management consultant*

Merrimack
Gallup, Patricia *computer company executive*

Portsmouth
Dumont, Mary *chef*

Somersworth
Gow, Linda Yvonne Carignan Cherwin *travel executive*

Waterville Valley
Saenger, Bruce Walter *consulting firm executive*

West Lebanon
Lawton, Jacqueline Agnes *retired communications executive, management consultant*

NEW JERSEY

Allendale
Bisanzo, Mark Thomas *retired sales executive*
DeFeo, Neil P. *consumer products company executive*

Atlantic City
Irvine, Robert *chef*
Juliano, Mark J. *hotel and gaming company executive*

Basking Ridge
Buist, Richardson *retired corporate executive, retired banker*
Moden, Joleen *communications executive*
Perez, Glad M. *marketing professional*
Schmidt, William Max *management consultant, marketing and business development executive*

Bedminster
Eslambolchi, Hossein *communications executive*
Gardner, David John *communications executive, sound recording engineer*
Hart, Terry Jonathan *communications executive*
Laroia, Rajiv *communications executive*

Bernardsville
Dixon, Richard Wayne *retired communications company executive*
Teiger, David *management consultant*

Boonton
Bona, Frederick Emil *public relations executive*
Ward, Solveig Maria *marketing professional*

Brick
Roache, Patrick Michael, Jr. *management consultant*
Shortess, Edwin Steevin *marketing consultant*

Bridgewater
Sethi, Shyam Sunder *management consultant*
Skidmore, James Albert, Jr. *management, computer technology and engineering services company executive*

Butler
Ward, Robert Allen, Jr. *advertising executive*

Camden
Fricks, Ernest Eugene *management consultant*

Cedar Grove
Carlozzi, Catherine L. *corporate communications consultant, writer*

Clifton
Bronkesh, Annette Cylia *public relations executive*
DiNicola, Robert J. *consumer products company executive*

East Hanover
Nelson, Barbara Kasztan *marketing professional*

East Rutherford
Kempner, Michael W. *public relations executive*

Edison
Currie, Robert *communications executive*

Englewood
Fay, Toni Georgette *communications executive*

Englewood Cliffs
Klauberg, Laura *marketing executive*
Lagnado, Silvia *marketing executive*

Fair Haven
Wyndrum, Ralph William, Jr. *communications consultant*

Far Hills
Alexandre, Kristin Kuhns *public relations executive, writer*

Florham Park
Javaid, Hassan Bilal *management consultant*
Naimark, George Modell *marketing and management consultant*
Negi, Devendra S. *communications services company administrator*

Fort Lee
Seitel, Fraser Paul *public relations executive*

Franklin Lakes
Williams, Edward David *information technology management consultant*

Freehold
D'Andrea, Patricia Carlisle *marketing professional, communications executive*

Gladstone
Close, Donald Pembroke *management consultant*

Glen Ridge
Agnew, Peter Tomlin *employee benefit consultant*

Green Brook
Bohanan, David John *management consultant*

Green Village
Swift, John Francis *retired health care advertising company executive*

Hackettstown
Van Campen, Stephen Bernard *executive recruiter, consultant*
Walker, Carole A. *advertising executive*

Haddonfield
Baltake, Susan *marketing and communications professional*
Bauer, Raymond Gale *sales professional*

Hoboken
Bostwick, Randell Armour *retired food service executive*
Fassoulis, Satiris Galahad *communications executive, director*

Jackson
Woodman, G. Roger *management consultant*

Lawrenceville
Bishop, James Francis *personnel director, consultant*
Coleman, Wade Hampton III *management consultant, mechanical engineer, retired banker*
Weaver, Charles Lyndell, Jr. *marketing executive, educational consultant*

Livingston
Brody, Martin *hotel executive*

Madison
Byrd, Stephen Fred *human resource consultant*
O'Brien, Mary Devon *communications executive, consultant*

Mahwah
Gibbons, Robert Philip *management consultant, director*

Maple Shade
Mahon, Katherine A. (Kit Mahon) *public relations executive, writer*

Maplewood
Safian, Gail Robyn *public relations executive*

Marlton
Farwell, Nancy Larraine *public relations executive*
Klein, Gerhart Leopold *public relations executive*

Matawan
Amato, Vincent Vito *marketing and business consultant*

Mendham
Hambleton, George Blow Elliott *retired management consultant*

Millburn
Bablin, Mark Edward *security administrator, mortgage consultant*

Monmouth Junction
Lancaster, Barbara Mae *management consulting company executive*

Monroe Township
Cushman, Helen Merle Baker *retired management consultant*
Meshowski, Frank Robert *business consultant*

Montclair
Dubrow, Marsha Ann *management consultant, musicologist*
Greenwald, Robert *public relations executive*

Montvale
Avedon, Marcia J. *diversified industrial products company and former pharmaceutical executive*
Henkel, Herbert Ludwig *diversified industrial products company executive*

Moorestown
Bennington, William Jay *management consultant*
Carson, William Charles *sales and marketing executive*
Schwerin, Horace S. *marketing research consultant*

Morristown
Haselmann, John Philip *management consultant*
McConnell, John Howard *personnel management consultant, writer*
Weidenkopf, Thomas W. *human resources specialist*

Mountainside
Bertsch, Patricia Ann *nature center director*
Lipton, Bronna Jane *marketing communications executive*

Neptune City
Axelrod, Glen Scott *publishing and pet product company executive*

New Brunswick
Bradley, Dondeena G. *consumer products company executive*
Caldwell, Dale Gilbert *management consultant*

New Providence
Del Tiempo, Sandra Kay *sales executive*

Newark
Courter, James A. (Jim) *communications executive, retired congressman*
Jonas, Howard S. *communications executive*
Passantino, Benjamin Arthur *marketing executi*

North Bergen
Archbold, Michael G. *consumer products company executive, former retail executive*

North Brunswick
Bern, Ronald Lawrence *management consultan writer*

Oak Ridge
Kieren, Thomas Henry *management consultant*

Paramus
Grinberg, Efraim *watch manufacturing compan executive*
Grinberg, Gedalio *watch manufacturing compa executive*

Park Ridge
Kennedy, Brian James *marketing executive*
Koch, Craig R. *automobile rental company executive, automobile leasing company executive*

Parlin
Mogensen, Charles Ray, Jr. *retired food service executive*

Parsippany
Belmonte, Steven Joseph *hotel chain executive*
Ferguson, Thomas George *retired healthcare advertising agency executive*
Holmes, Stephen P. *hotel executive*
Nelson, Ronald L. *travel services company executive, former film company executive*
Salerno, F. Robert *travel company executive*
Weller, Robert N(orman) *hotel executive*

Pennington
Czach, Gabriela Bozena *personal care industry executive*

Pilesgrove
Mohrfeld, Richard Gentel *marketing professior*

Piscataway
Colcord, Herbert Nathaniel, III, (Skip) *corpora communications executive*

Plainsboro
Devine, Hugh James, Jr. *marketing executive*
Khan, Sajid A. *management consultant, entrepreneur*
Spiegel, Phyllis *public relations consultant, journalist*

Princeton
Cox, Douglas Lynn *management consultant, researcher*
Craigie, James R. *consumer products and forn sports equipment apparel company executive*
Davies, Robert Abel III *consumer products company executive*
Kelleher, Kathleen *marketing professional*
Kenny, Jane M. *government relations consulti executive*
Leetmaa, Ants *environmental services administrator, educator*
Morris, Mac Glenn *advertising executive*
Pfister, Marc *consumer products company executive, physician, researcher*
Siegel, Laurie *human resources specialist*

Princeton Junction
Hirschman, Barry H. *human resources special*

Randolph
Chen, Kevin S. *management executive, consultant, educator*

Red Bank
Pezzutti, Santo Costante *advertising executive, art director*

Ridgewood
Warner, John Edward *advertising executive*

Roseland
Butler, Gary C. *computer company executive*
Weinbach, Arthur Frederic *computer company executive*

Scotch Plains
Johnsen, Karen Kennedy *marketing profession*

Secaucus
Marcus, Alan C. *public relations consultant*

Short Hills
Harwood, Jerry *market research executive*
Schaefer, Charles James III *advertising executive, consultant*

Shrewsbury
Baker, Gerald David *marketing executive, consultant*

Somerset
Brophy, Joseph Thomas *computer company executive*
Karas, James *public relations executive, engineering executive*
Wallfesh, Henry Maurice *communications executive, writer*

Summit
Fuess, Billings Sibley, Jr. *advertising executive*
Weinstein, Stephen Brant *communications executive, researcher, writer*

Teaneck
Connola, Donald Pascal, Jr. *management consultant*
afer, Fred Seymour *data processing executive*

Three Bridges
awrence, Gerald Graham *management consultant*

Toms River
Kanarkowski, Edward Joseph *data processing company executive*

Trenton
Fischer, Pamela Shadel *public relations executive*
Holt, Jonathan Turner *public relations executive*

Upper Montclair
intle, Carmel Joseph *public relations executive*

Ventnor City
olton, Kenneth Albert *management consultant*

Warren
lass, Walter Paul *management consultant, educator*
DiPietro, Ralph Anthony *management and marketing consultant, educator*
Kozberg, Ronald Paul *health and human services administrator*

West Caldwell
ixon, Jo-Ann Conte *management consultant*
age, Frederick West *business consultant*

West Orange
yle, Corinne Silverman *management consultant*

Westfield
avoren, Steven Michael *marketing professional, psychologist*

Westwood
adakovich, Daniel I. *communications executive, consultant*

Whitehouse
nelton, Craig *food service executive*

Whitehouse Station
raddick-Weir, Mirian *human resources specialist*

Wyckoff
avery, Daniel P. *management consultant*

EW MEXICO

lbuquerque
arker, Lynn M. *management consultant*
chenberg, Peter Thompson *retired criminal investigator*
ayo, George Edward *management consultant*
orner, Harry Charles, Jr. *sales executive*
oyce, Stanton *motivational speaker, consultant, marketing professional, sales executive*
evenson, Bradford Allen *management consultant*
estwood, Albert Ronald Clifton *management consultant, researcher*

os Alamos
oepper, David Alan *retired management consultant*

Moriarty
aver, Jurgen F. *marketing consultant*

andia Park
eenwell, Ronald Everett *communications executive*

anta Fe
andt, Richard Paul *communications and entertainment company executive*
ercer, James Lee *management consultant*
errin, Seymour *computer company executive*
iller, Dwight Richard *professional hair care industry executive, cosmetologist, consultant*
elch, Jasper Arthur, Jr. *security company executive, consultant*

EW YORK

lbany
enges, Susan Debra Favreau *management consultant, retired protective services official*
halit, Robert Edward *advertising executive*

lbion
nier, Lee N. *funeral director*

mherst
ckell, Joe *paranormal expert*

nnandale On Hudson
arrow, Emily M. *public relations executive, writer*

rmonk
olduc, Ernest Joseph *management consultant, not-for-profit developer*
ata, Jon C. *computer company executive*
ohnstamm, Abby E. *marketing executive*
ughridge, Mark *computer company executive*
nchez, Adalio T. *data processing executive*

Baldwin
Chopra, Parveen Chander *management consultant, educator, researcher, community activist*

Beacon
Metz, Ferdinand *chef, educator, academic administrator*

Bedford
Husted, William Armstrong *sales executive*

Bedford Corners
Greene, Jesse J., Jr. *former computer company executive*

Bellerose
Paramekanthi, Srinivasan Mandayam *software services executive*

Bethpage
Dolan, James L. *communications executive, professional sports team owner*
Gottesman, Patricia Ann *marketing executive*
Janczak, Andrew Anthony *marketing professional*
Mahony, Sheila Anne *retired communications executive*
McCormack, Dermot *communications executive*

Brewster
Mahoney, Joëlle Katherine *astrological consultant, communications educator*
Shepard, Lance Hastings *marketing professional, consultant, newscaster*

Bridgehampton
Stuart, Greg *marketing professional, writer*

Bronx
Golden, Gail (Gail Golden Icahn) *travel company executive*
Hudson, Frederick Bernard *management consultant*

Bronxville
Ellinghaus, William Maurice *communications executive*
Parsons, Andrew John *management consultant, corporate administrator*

Brooklyn
Allison, Mary Ann *consulting company executive, writer, speaker*
Carswell, Lois Malakoff *botanical garden executive, consultant*
Galatianos, Gus A. *computer company executive, consultant, real estate developer, educator*
Hendra, Barbara Jane *public relations executive*
Heron, Earl D. *communications executive*
Laverty, Marilyn T. *public relations executive, media consultant*
Middleton, John Edison *management consultant*
Ogunkoya, Andrea *marketing executive*
Reichel, Walter Emil *advertising executive*
Reisler, Helen Barbara *public relations executive*

Buffalo
Daley, Ruth Margaret *advertising agency administrator*
Fryer, Appleton *sales executive, diplomat*
Goralski, Donald John *public relations executive, counselor*
Murphy, Dennis Patrick *hotel business entrepreneur*
Pegels, C. Carl *management consultant, educator*

Canaan
Hooper, Ian (John Derek Glass) *retired marketing communications executive*

Cheektowaga
Mruk, Eugene Robert *retired marketing professional, urban planner*

Chester
Mackerodt, Fred *public relations specialist*

Claverack
Barrett, William Gary *advertising and marketing executive*

Croton On Hudson
Plotch, Walter *management consultant, fund raising counselor*

Delmar
Button, Rena Pritsker *public relations executive*

East Hampton
Garten, Ina *chef*
Mencher, Stuart Alan *sales and marketing executive*

East Meadow
Fuchs, Jerome Herbert *management consultant*

Elmont
Butera, Ann Michele *consulting company executive*

Far Rockaway
Epstein, Samuel Abraham *sales executive*

Floral Park
Dudek, Henry Thomas *management consultant*

Forest Hills
Spiegel, Andrea *marketing executive*

Garden City
Conlon, Brian Thomas *promotion executive*
Conlon, Thomas James *marketing executive*
Doucette, Mary-Alyce *computer company executive*

Glen Head
Conway, David Antony *marketing professional*

Great Neck
Goldberg, Melvin Arthur *communications executive*
Helstein, Ivy Rae *communications executive, psychotherapist, writer*

Hancock
DeLuca, Ronald *former advertising agency executive, consultant*

Hartsdale
Greenawalt, Peggy Freed Tomarkin *advertising executive*
Pell, Arthur Robert *human resources specialist, consultant, writer*

Hastings On Hudson
Considine, Russel A. *executive recruiter, photographer*

Haverstraw
Alpert, Revell Judith *retired data processing executive*

Hawthorne
Wen, Sheree *computer company executive*

Hempstead
Connolly, Melissa Kane *public relations executive*

Honeoye Falls
Hillabrandt, Larry Lee *service industry executive*

Hurley
Smith, Lewis Motter, Jr. *retired advertising and direct marketing executive*

Hyde Park
Ryan, L. Timothy *chef, educator, academic administrator*

Inwood
Kofman, Leonid *consumer products company executive*

Irvington
Sherman, Norman Mark *advertising agency executive*

Islandia
Cooper, Nancy E. *computer software company executive*
Gupta, Yogesh *software company executive*
Handal, Kenneth V. *computer software company executive, lawyer*
Robinson, Douglas *computer company executive*
Swainson, John A. *software company executive*

Ithaca
Park, Roy Hampton, Jr. *advertising executive*
Seadle, Michael Steven *data processing executive, writer*

Jericho
Edson, Andrew Stephen *public relations executive*
Rosen, Robert Arnold *management consultant, real estate owner, manager, developer, investor, farmer*

Lake Luzerne
Goldstein, Manfred *retired management consultant*

Lancaster
Neumaier, Gerhard John *environmental services administrator, consultant*

Larchmont
Greenwald, Carol Schiro *professional services marketing research executive*
Plumez, Jean Paul *advertising executive, consultant*

Latham
Schwartz, Robert William *management consultant*
Wilkes, Brent Ames *management consultant*

Locust Valley
Fletcher, Mary Lee *retired marketing professional*

Loudonville
Burstein, Sharon Ann *corporate communications specialist, apparel designer*

Middle Island
Andrews, Gaylen *public relations executive*
Linick, Andrew S. *direct marketing expert*

Mount Kisco
Novak, Gregory *marketing professional*

New York
Abernathy, James Logan *public relations executive*
Achenbaum, Alvin Allen *marketing and management consultant*
Agisim, Philip *advertising and marketing executive*
Alexander, Roy *public relations executive, writer*
Allen, Alice *communications and marketing executive*
Alschuler, Steven *public relations executive, writer, consultant*
Andelbradt, Mark *chef*
Anderson, Arthur Allan *management consultant*
Andolsen, Alan Anthony *management consultant*
Andree, Tim *advertising executive*
Anthony, Michael *chef*
Antonuccio, Joseph Albert *management consultant*
Appel, Marsha Ceil *advertising executive*
Applebaum, Stuart S. *public relations executive*
Aronson, Donald Eric *management and tax consultant*
Axthelm, Nancy *advertising executive*
Bachrach, Nancy *retired advertising executive*
Baglivo, Mary L. *advertising executive*
Baird, Lisa P. *marketing executive*
Baird, Richard *human resources specialist*
Balazs, André T. *hotel executive*
Barksdale, James Love *communications executive*
Baron, Sheri *advertising agency executive*
Barton, Richard N. *computer company executive*
Bartow, Diane Grace *marketing professional, sales executive*
Baruch, Ralph M. *communications executive*
Bastianich, Lidia Matticchio (Lidia Motika) *chef, food service executive*
Batali, Mario Francis *chef*
Baumgarten, Barbara *human resources specialist*
Becker, Franklin *chef*
Becker, Susan Kaplan *management and marketing communication consultant, educator*
Beecher, William Manuel *management consultant*
Beinecke, William Sperry *retired consumer products company executive*
Bell, David Arthur *retired advertising agency executive*
Benno, Jonathan *chef*
Bergen, John Donald *public relations and communications executive*
Berlin, Andrew Mark (Andy Berlin) *advertising agency executive*
Bernard, David George *retired management consultant*
Bernbach, John Lincoln *marketing professional*
Biederman, Barron Zachary (Barry) *advertising agency executive*
Bishop, Susan Katharine *executive search company executive*
Bloomfield, April *chef*
Bloomgarden, Kathy Finn *public relations executive*
Boice, Craig Kendall *management consultant*
Bolton, Roger *public relations executive*
Bottomley, Michelle J. *advertising executive*
Boulud, Daniel *chef, restaurant owner*
Bowman, Robert A. *Internet company executive*
Brady, Adelaide Burks *public relations agency executive, giftware catalog executive*
Braverman, Robert Jay *management consultant, educator*
Brooke, Linda Hundley *retired human resources specialist*
Brooks, Gary *crisis management and family business consultant*
Bruno, Antoinette *food service executive*
Brunson, Curtis *communications systems company executive*
Brymer, Charles Edward (Chuck Brymer) *advertising executive*
Burson, Harold *public relations executive, director*
Burton, Peggy *advertising and marketing executive*
Buryk, Alexis *advertising executive*
Butler, David T. III *communications systems company executive*
Byrd, Eva Wilson *communications executive*
Calabrese, Rosalie Sue *management consultant, writer*
Capozzi, Lou *public relations executive*
Carmellini, Andrew *chef*
Caserta, Jennifer *communications executive*
Chajet, Clive *brand and corporate image consultant*
Chang, David *chef*
Chell, Beverly C. *retired media company executive, lawyer*
Cheney, Richard Eugene *public relations executive, psychoanalyst*
Chesney, Robert Henry *management consultant, director*
Chicco, Gianfranco *healthcare communications executive*
Chodorow, Jeffrey *restaurant owner*
Clarke, Frank William *communications executive*
Clayman, Greg *communications executive*
Colicchio, Tom *chef, food service executive*
Collier, Charlie *communications executive*
Comstock, Beth (Elizabeth J.) *marketing executive*
Conley, Terence P. *human resources specialist*
Cook, Ian M. *consumer products company executive*
Cooper, Stephen F. *management consultant, corporate recovery executive*
Corbin, Herbert Leonard *public relations executive, director*
Cortese, Edward *marketing and public relations executive*
Cox, L. Kevin *human resources specialist*
Craig, Elizabeth Coyne *marketing executive*
Craig, Pamela J. *management consulting firm executive*
Cruz, Juan-Carlos *chef*
Daly, Cheryl *communications and broadcast executive*
D'Ambrosio, Ralph G. *communications systems company executive*
Daniel, David Ronald *management consultant*
David, Miles *marketing executive*
Davidson, Donald William *advertising executive*
DeBow, Jay Howard Camden *public relations executive*
Deering, Suzy *advertising executive*
Desmond, Laura *advertising executive*
Deutsch, Donny *advertising executive*
DeVard, Jerri *marketing professional*
Devitre, Dinyar S. *consumer products company and corporate financial executive*
Dhondt, Steven Thomas *development officer*
Diamond, Heidi Janice *marketing professional*
Diamond, Matthew C. *media and marketing company executive*

Dietl, Bo (Richard A. Dietl) *private investigator, former police officer*
Diller, Barry *Internet company executive*
Dimling, John Arthur *marketing executive*
Donaldson, John Cecil, Jr. *consumer products company executive*
Dooner, John Joseph, Jr. *advertising executive*
Drewes, Robert W. *communications systems company executive*
Driscoll, Karen *communications executive*
Droga, David *advertising executive*
Dru, Jean-Marie Paul *advertising executive*
Drzik, John P. *management consulting firm executive*
Dubuc, Nancy *communications executive*
Ducasse, Alain *chef*
Duda, Michael *advertising executive*
Duff, Gill *advertising executive*
Dunn, James W. *communications systems company executive*
Dunne, Diane C. *marketing professional*
Dunst, Laurence David *advertising executive*
Duran, George *chef*
Edlow, Kenneth Lewis *security firm executive*
Eisler, Susan Krawetz *advertising executive*
Elkes, Terrence Allen *communications executive*
Engel, Alison Lange *marketing executive*
Ernst, John Louis *management consultant*
Esnault, Tony *chef*
Evans, Alfred Lee, Jr. *advertising executive*
Faber, Neil *advertising executive*
Fajors, Nique *interactive entertainment executive*
Falai, Tacopo *chef*
Falk, Edgar Alan *public relations consulting executive, writer*
Farinelli, Jean L. *management consultant*
Faris, George N. *management consultant*
Feder, Benjamin *computer game company executive*
Feintuch, Henry Philip *public relations executive*
Feldman, Allan Roy *corporate development and marketing executive*
Felsher, Steven G. *advertising executive, lawyer*
Fernandes, Jeanne Mary *retired human resources specialist*
Fernandez de Cordova, Sergio Alonso *advertising executive, publishing executive*
Fertitta, George A. *marketing executive*
Fili-Krushel, Patricia *media company executive*
Fine, Jo Renée *management consultant*
Finley, Skip *communications executive*
Finn, Peter *public relations executive*
Finzi, Benjamin *communications executive*
Flaherty, Clementina Santi *corporate communications specialist, writer*
Flanders, Karen *consumer products company executive*
Flaum, Sander Allen *advertising and marketing executive*
Flay, Bobby *chef, restaurateur*
Fleischman, Barbara Greenberg *public relations consultant*
Florence, Tyler *chef*
Fluhr, Howard *consulting firm executive*
Fogge, Len *advertising executive*
Folta, Carl D. *communications executive*
Frank, William Fielding *computer company executive, consultant*
Frankfort, Lew *consumer products company executive*
Friedman, Caitlin *public relations executive*
Furman, Anthony Michael *public relations executive*
Garfinkel, Lee *advertising agency executive*
Garner, Mark *communications executive*
Garvin, Andrew Paul *computer company executive, writer*
Gatfield, Stephen J. *advertising executive*
Geier, Philip Henry, Jr. *advertising executive*
Geller, Robert James *advertising executive*
Gerard-Sharp, Monica Fleur *communications executive*
Gianinno, Susan McManama *advertising executive*
Giblin, Jennifer *chef*
Gill, Linda A. *advertising executive*
Ginsburg, Sigmund G. *management and executive search consultant*
Glatt, Mitchell Steven *consumer products company executive*
Gold, Mari S. *public relations executive*
Goldfarb, Will *chef*
Goldschmidt, Charles *advertising agency executive*
Goldsmith, Clifford Henry *retired consumer products company executive*
Goldstein, Gary Sanford *executive recruiter*
Goldstone, Steven F. *former consumer products company executive*
Gosper, Brett *advertising agency executive*
Gottlieb, Jerrold Howard *advertising executive*
Green, William D. *management consulting firm executive*
Greenberg, David I. *consumer products company executive*
Greenland, Leo *advertising executive*
Greitzer, Matt *marketing professional*
Griffy, Timothy T. *human resources specialist, finance company executive*
Grossman, Lawrence Kugelmass *former communications and advertising executive*
Gumbinner, Paul S. *advertising and executive recruitment agency executive*
Gupta, Rajat Kumar *retired management consultant, electronics executive*
Haberman, Seth *advertising executive*
Hammond, Lou Rena Charlotte *public relations executive*
Hanson, Stephen *food service executive*
Hara, Eric *chef*
Hart, Karen Ann *advertising executive*
Hatcher, Kendra *advertising executive*
Hatheway, John Harris *advertising agency executive*
Heekin, Jim (James Robson Heekin III) *advertising executive*
Hegarty, John F., Jr. *advertising executive*
Heiferman, Scott *Internet company executive*
Heinzerling, Larry Edward *communications executive*
Herbert, Marilynne *public relations executive, freelance photographer*
Hernandez-Fallous, Jacqueline *marketing executive*
Hochhauser, Richard Michael *marketing professional*
Hoffmann, Ingrid *chef, television personality*
Holzer, Harold *museum and marketing executive, historian, writer*
Hong, Michael *communications executive*
Hopson, craig *chef*
Horowitz, Eliot *Internet company executive*
Hudes, Nana Brenda *marketing professional*
Hurst, Robert Jay *security firm executive*
Hynes, Aedhmar *public relations executive*
Ilson, Bernard *public relations executive*
Isogai, Masaharu *international corporate strategist, retired apparel executive*
Iuzzini, Johnny *chef*
Jacoby, Robert Harold *management consulting executive*
James, Robert Leo *advertising executive, director*
Jeffrey, Robert (Bob Jeffrey) *advertising executive*
Johnnes, Daniel *chef*
Johnson, Harold Earl *human resources specialist*
Johnson, John William, Jr. *executive recruiter*
Johnson, Verdia E. *marketing professional*
Jones, David *advertising executive*
Josell, Jessica (Wechsler) *public relations executive*
Just, Gemma Rivoli *retired advertising executive*
Karalekas, George Steven *advertising agency executive, political consultant*
Karp, Martin Everett *management consultant*
Kassel, Terry *human resources specialist*
Keane, Patrick *marketing executive*
Keenan, Michael Edgar *marketing professional*
Kelmenson, Leo-Arthur *advertising executive*
Kerik, Bernard Bailey *security firm executive, former police commissioner*
Kinsolving, Charles McIlvaine, Jr. *marketing executive*
Koplik, Michael R. *sales representation company executive*
Kotuk, Andrea Mikotajuk *public relations executive, writer*
Kraushar, Jonathan Pollack *communications and media consultant*
Kreisberg, Neil Ivan *advertising executive*
Kreuther, Gabriel *chef*
Krinsky, Robert Daniel *consulting firm executive*
Krukowski, Jan *communications executive*
Kuehn, Coleen P. *advertising executive*
Kuperman, Robert Ian *retired advertising agency executive*
Kyriakou, Linda Grace *communications executive*
Lackner, Bernard *hotel executive*
Lang, George *restaurateur*
Langton, Cleve Swanson *advertising executive*
Lannamann, Richard Stuart *executive search consultant*
Lao, Kenny *restaurant manager*
Laumont, Philippe Emile *communications executive*
Lazarus, Shelly (Rochelle Braff Lazarus) *advertising executive*
Lee, Christopher *chef*
Lee, Sandra *food service executive, product designer, chef*
Leslie, Seymour Marvin *communications executive, director*
Leubert, Alfred Otto Paul *management consultant*
Levine, Michael J. *sports products company executive*
Lieberman, Dave *chef*
Lipman, Ira Ackerman *security service company executive*
Lipton, Charles *public relations executive*
Lipton, Joan Elaine *advertising executive*
Liu, Tony *chef*
Lo, Anita *chef*
Loeb, Larry Morris *communications company executive*
Lorber, Barbara Heyman *communications executive, event producer*
Lubars, David *advertising executive*
Lucht, John Charles *management consultant, writer*
Maas, Jane Brown *advertising executive*
MacKay, Malcolm *executive search consultant*
Makovsky, Kenneth Dale *public relations executive*
Malgieri, Nick *food service executive, educator, chef, writer*
Manoff, Richard Kalman *advertising executive, writer, public health service officer, consultant*
Mansi, Joseph Anneillo *public relations company executive*
Marcosson, Thomas I. *management consultant, advertising executive*
Mark, Reuben *consumer products company executive*
Marone, Anthony F., Jr. *quality assurance professional*
Martínez-Lópes, Carmen Leonor *management consultant, educator*
Masi, Jane Virginia *marketing and sales consultant*
Masters, Jon Joseph *corporate governance specialist, management consultant*
Matsuhisa, Nobuyuki *chef, restaurant owner*
McAveney, Mary Susan *marketing executive*
McCabe, Mary F. *marketing professional*
McCaslin, Teresa Eve *human resources specialist*
McCumber, Chris *communications executive*
McGinnis, Arthur Joseph, Jr. *public relations executive*
McGrath, Michael G. *management consulting firm executive*
McInerney, Thomas J. *Internet company executive*
McKenna, William Michael *advertising executive*
McLennan, Hamish *advertising executive*
McManus, Paul M. *hotel executive*
Merkin, Ari *advertising executive*
Messner, Thomas G. *advertising executive, copywriter*
Meyer, Scott *communications executive*
Miller, Alan *computer company executive, management consultant*
Miller, Ernest Charles *management consultant*
Miller, Neil Stuart *advertising executive*
Miller, Robert *advertising executive*
Morris, Stephen Burritt *marketing information company executive*
Moulton, Sara *chef, magazine editor*
Moyer, David S. *executive search consultant*
Murphy, James Edward *public relations and marketing executive*
Murphy, Kenneth F. *human resources specialist*
Murphy, Mark Joseph *enterprise sales executive*
Nadler-Hurvich, Hedda Carol *public relations executive*
Nash, Edward L. *advertising executive*
Nawab, Akhtar *chef*
Neff, Thomas Joseph *search firm executive*
Nelson, Dean B. *media company executive*
Nelson, Merlin Edward *retired management consultant, lawyer*
Nieporent, Drew *restaurant group executive*
Nisenholtz, Martin Abram *telecommunications executive, educator*
Nish, Wayne Paul *chef, restaurant owner*
Nyweide, Jeffrey O. *management and business executive*
Okuwa, Makoto *chef*
Olafsson, Olaf *communications executive*
Olinger, Carla D(ragan) *medical advertising executive*
Oppenheim, Robert *beauty industry executive*
Osnos, Gilbert Charles *management consultant*
O'Sullivan, Eugene Henry *retired advertising executive, management consultant*
Pace, Wayne H. *communications executive*
Palmer, Charlie *chef, restaurant manager*
Parrette, Jean-Briac *communications executive*
Parrish, Steven C. *consumer products company executive*
Parsons, Richard Dean *communications executive*
Pasierb, Stephen John *advertising executive, marketing professional*
Paster, Howard G. *public relations and public affairs company executive*
Patrick, Stephen C. *consumer products company executive*
Payard, Francois *food service executive*
Pearlstine, Norman *communications consultant, former editor*
Pearson, Clarence Edward *management consultant, educator*
Pearson, Margit Linnea *management consultant*
Pelaccio, Zakary *chef*
Perelman, Ronald Owen *consumer products company executive*
Perlgut, Mark Ralph *public relations executive*
Perry, Brooke Elizabeth *public relations executive*
Planitzer, Russell E. *computer company executive*
Poe, Randall Ellsworth *public relations executive, author*
Pollock-O'Brien, Louise Mary *public relations executive*
Pompadur, I. Martin *communications executive*
Portale, Alfred *chef, restaurant owner*
Price, Robert *media and communications executive, investment banker, lawyer*
Primi, Don Alexis *advertising, public relations, rail transportation executive*
Quinlan, Mary Lou *former advertising executive, consultant*
Quintero, Ronald Gary *management consultant*
Radice, Frank J. *communications executive*
Raghavan, Sudheer *hotel executive*
Rauch, Arthur Irving *management consultant*
Ray, Rachael Domenica *chef, television personality*
Reals Ellig, Janice *marketing professional, human resources specialist*
Reda, James Francis *business consultant*
Redding, Markus Carl *management consultant, educator*
Reges, Marianna Alice *marketing executive*
Reilly, Edward T., Jr. *advertising executive*
Reinhard, Keith Leon *advertising executive*
Reynolds, James *management consultant*
Richardson, Grace Elizabeth *consumer products company executive*
Ritchie, Richard Lee *media company executive*
Robbins, John Clapp *management consultant*
Roberts, Francis Stone *advertising executive*
Roberts, Kevin *advertising executive*
Robertson, Andrew J. *advertising executive*
Robinson, Peter M. *business association executive*
Roche, Gerard Raymond *management consultant*
Roldan, Kenneth Arroyo *executive recruiter, lawyer*
Romano, Fernanda (Fefa Romano) *advertising executive*
Rose, Joanne W. *rating service executive*
Rosenshine, Allen Gilbert *retired advertising agency executive*
Roskin, William A. *communications executive*
Ross, Jo Ann *media buyer*
Roth, Michael I. *communications executive, lawyer*
Rothenberg, Randall *advertising executive*
Rothenberg, Robert Philip *public relations counselor*
Rubenstein, Howard Joseph *public relations executive*
Ruder, William *public relations executive*
Russo, Anthony Joseph *public relations professional*
Sacco, Amy *restaurant and nightclub owner*
Samuelsson, Marcus (Kasshun Tsegie) *food service executive*
Saxton, Catherine Patricia *public relations executive*
Scalamandre, Jill E. *marketing executive*
Scarpelli, Bob *advertising executive*
Schaedelin, Pierre *chef*
Schafer, Charles J. *communications systems company executive*
Schaffer, Kenneth B. *communications executive, mechanical engineer, consultant*
Schatz, Gary Stewart *marketing professional*
Schiller, Vivian *Internet company executive*
Schrager, Ian *hotel executive*
Schupak, Leslie Allen *public relations company executive*
Schuster, Reid S. *advertising executive*
Schwab, Frank, Jr. *management consultant*
Schwartz, Alan Victor *advertising executive*
Seaman, Alfred Jarvis *retired advertising agenc executive*
Secunda, Eugene *marketing professional, educator*
Seiden, Henry (Hank Seiden) *advertising executive*
Seiden, Steven Arnold *executive search consultant*
Serra, Matthew D. *consumer products company executive*
Shanahan, William Stephen *consumer products company executive*
Shapiro, Marvin Lincoln *communications company executive*
Sheehan, Mike *advertising executive*
Sherman, Eric *communications executive*
Sherman, Eugene Jay *retired marketing professional, economist*
Sherwood, Andrew *management consultant*
Shimizu, Masato *chef*
Shinder, Marcella Marie *marketing executive*
Shuler, Laura *marketing executive*
Siegel, Herbert Jay *communications executive, director*
Siegel, Lucy Boswell *public relations executive*
Sinclair, Daisy *communications executive*
Smith, Martin Jay *advertising and marketing executive*
Softness, Donald Gabriel *marketing professiona manufacturing executive*
Solomons, Seth *marketing executive*
Sorell, Kitty Julia *public relations executive*
Soter, George Nicholas *advertising executive*
Souham, Gérard *communications executive*
Speros, James Demitrios *advertising executive*
Spiegel, Elwyn *advertising executive, art director*
Sprague, Peter Julian *software company executive, lecturer*
Stanton, Amy *marketing executive*
Starr Kins, Gloria *public relations executive, writer, photojournalist, writer, editor*
Stern, Peter *communications executive*
Steves, Gale C. *marketing professional, writer, editor-in-chief, publishing executive*
Stotsky, Adam *communications executive*
Stoute, Steve *advertising executive, former recording industry executive*
Stratigos, William Narge *computer company executive*
Strear, Joseph D. *public relations executive*
Strianese, Michael T. *communications systems company executive*
Strickland, Shawn *communications executive*
Stringer, Sir Howard *entertainment company executive*
Stringham, Peter E. *advertising executive*
Stroock, Mark Edwin, II, *public relations company executive*
Sussman, Jeffrey Bruce *public relations and marketing executive*
Swid, Stephen Claar *communications executive director*
Sykes, John *communications company executi*
Tanaka, Patrice Aiko *public relations executive*
Tangney, Michael J. *consumer products compa executive*
Tarter, Fred Barry *advertising executive*
Taylor, Barbara Alden *public relations executi*
Thaler, Linda Kaplan *advertising executive*
Tilson, Dorothy Ruth *word processing executi*
Tisch, Jonathan Mark *hotel company executive*
Torrenzano, Richard *public relations executive*
Tortorello, Nicholas John *public opinion and market research company executive*
Truwit, Mitchell *Internet company executive*
Ubinas, Luis A. *management consultant*
Upson, Stuart Barnard *advertising agency executive*
Ureña, Alex *chef*
Vermeer, Maureen Dorothy *sales executive*
Vick, Edward Hoge, Jr. *advertising executive*
Viebranz, Curtis Gray *advertising executive*
Volk, Kristin *advertising agency executive*
von Baillou, Astrid *executive search consultan*
Vongerichten, Jean-Georges *food service executive, chef*
Waltuck, David *chef, restaurant owner*
Wanek, William Charles *public relations executive*
Wasow, Omar *Internet company executive*
Waters, Donald Joseph *data processing execut*
Weisenburger, Randall J. *advertising executive*
Weiss, Myrna Grace *management consultant*
Wenig, Devin Norse *communications executive*
Werfelman, William Herman, Jr. *public relatic executive*
Whaley, Charles Henry, IV, *communications company executive*
White, Benjamin *communications executive*
Whited, Mary Elizabeth *marketing professiona*
Willett, Roslyn Leonore *public relations executive, food service consultant, writer, editor*
Wise, Damon *chef*
Wolff, Richard Joseph *public relations executi consultant, historian*
Wren, John D. *advertising executive*

ht, Jason Howard Sebastian *communications executive*
ht, Tony *advertising executive*
Patricia *chef*
, Kimberly *public relations executive*
g, Brian *chef*
rra, Galen *chef*
ck, Strauss *entertainment company executive*

burgh
Bryan Allyn *postal maintenance worker, tist*

thport
enfeld, Kenneth Jay *management consultant*

ck
, Peter Simon *marketing executive*

anside
r, Arlene *advertising executive*

ining
natch, Theodore Bieley *management nsultant*

isades
on, Roberto Leonardo *environmental rvices administrator*

rl River
g, John Xiaowu *computer company ecutive*

ham
rle, Douglas Geoffrey *public relations nsultant*

asantville
weiler, Peter Quintus *planning consultant*

t Chester
oni-Charas, Dan *marketing executive*
enberg, William Mark *chef, restaurant owner*

t Washington
kett, John Byron *advertising executive, wyer*
son, Tod Stuart *market research company xecutive*
ds, Richard *computer marketing executive*

ughkeepsie
Buren, Denise Doring *corporate ommunications executive*

und Ridge
ino, John Anthony *management and human esources consultant*

rchase
elio, Bill (William J.) *computer company xecutive*
lson, Dawn Emily *food service company xecutive*
nston, Hugh Francis *corporate development anager*
rdock, Wendy Jean *management consultant*
rd, Stephen M., Jr. *computer company xecutive*

ogue
khardt, Ronald Robert *advertising executive, vriter, artist, filmmaker*

go Park
omayor, Alexander *management consultant*

nsselaer
ll, Raymond Whitford *public relations executive*

chester
rman, Robert L. *imaging company executive*
raci, Philip J. *imaging company executive*
ldberg-Schaible, Jocelyn Hope Schnier *market research professional*
rris, Diane Carol *merger and acquisition consulting firm executive*
llyar, Mary Jane *imaging company executive*
ngley, James T. *imaging company executive*
yd, William J. *imaging company executive*
mirez, Stevan G. *consumer products company executive*
larsky, Frank S. *imaging company executive*
gman, Colleen *food service executive*
gman, Daniel R. *food service executive*

ockville Centre
yer, Suzanne *advertising agency executive*
mpan, Jack Maurice *management consultant*

oscoe
rres, Jacques *food service executive, pastry chef*

oslyn
anoff, Stanley M. *communications executive*

ye
anklin, Martin E. *consumer products company executive*
aulakis, Arnold Francis *management consultant*
arson, Nathan Williams *communications, investment executive*

ye Brook
ariam, Thomas Fred *public relations executive, radio producer*

aint Huberts
eilson, Winthrop Cunningham III *retired communications executive, financial consultant, photographer*

Scarsdale
Clark, Merrell Mays *management consultant*
Kaufman, Robert Jules *communications consultant, lawyer*
Laufer, Leonard Justin *management consultant*
Schultz, Harley *consulting company executive*

Schenectady
Golub, Lewis *supermarket company executive*
Golub, Neil M. *supermarket chain executive*

Seaford
Spencer, Jean *retired business executive*

Setauket
Robinson, Richard M. *communications executive*

Sleepy Hollow
Marshall, Michael Borden *marketing executive*
Schmidt, Klaus Franz *advertising executive*

Somers
Azua, Maria *computer company executive, computer engineer*
Berisford, John L. *consumer products company executive*
Bronzo, Neal A. *consumer products company executive*
Crawford, Victor L. *consumer products company executive*
Drewes, Alfred H. *consumer products company executive*
Foss, Eric J. *consumer products company executive*
Franks, Brent J. *consumer products company executive*
Wladawsky-Berger, Irving *communications executive*

South Salem
Bongiorno, William J. *public relations executive*

Southampton
Bolster, Jacqueline Neben (Mrs. John A. Bolster) *communications consultant*

Staatsburg
Wentworth, Dennis Ladd *historic sites and parks administrator*

Staten Island
Fafian, Joseph, Jr. *management consultant*

Stony Brook
Ohannessian, Harry Haroutune *travel agency executive*

Syosset
Ruthchild, Geraldine Quietlake *training and development consultant, writer, poet*

Syracuse
Cooper, John Ambrose *management consultant, marketing professional*
Favalo, John Frank *marketing executive*

Tappan
Fox, Muriel *retired public relations executive*

Tarrytown
Kirsch, Abigail *culinary productions executive*

Thornwood
Bassett, Lawrence C. *management consultant*

Tuckahoe
Brecher, Bernd *management consultant*

Watervliet
Alber, Richard Lawrence *quality assurance professional*

White Plains
Adkins, Rodney *computer company executive*
Brown, Ronald C. *hotel executive*
Colwell, Howard Otis *advertising executive*
Duncan, Bruce W. *hotel and retired real estate company executive*
Fouse, Jacqualyn A. *consumer products company executive*
Lukaszewski, James Edmund *communications executive*
Sternlicht, Barry Stuart *hotel executive*
Sussberg, Milton Joel *marketing professional*

Whitestone
Kahn, Matt *marketing executive*

Wilton
Concemi, Alfred P. *marketing professional*

Woodmere
Schlissel, Fred *management consultant, educator*

Yonkers
Capodilupo, Elizabeth Jeanne Hatton *public relations executive*
Ortega, Maria A. *security firm executive, educator*

NORTH CAROLINA

Arden
Baker, Kerry Allen *management consultant*

Asheboro
Sanders, William Eugene *marketing executive*

Asheville
Mundt, Barry Maynard *management consultant*

Canton
Dixon, Shirley Juanita *retired restaurant owner*

Cary
Craig, Harold Kent *mechanical contracting executive, systems analyst*

Chapel Hill
Lochridge, Julie Deane *retired communications executive*

Charlotte
Bass-Hollis, Cynthia Gibson *environmental services administrator*
Eppes, Thomas Evans *advertising and public relations executive*
Lyerly, Elaine Myrick *advertising executive*
Van Alstyne, Vance Brownell *management consultant*
Wood, Donald Craig *retired marketing professional*

Concord
Burkard, Heather C. *prosecutorial investigator*

Denver
McIntosh, Anita Jane *retired administrative assistant*

Durham
Barker, Ben *chef, restaurant owner*
Barker, Karen *restaurant owner, chef*
Gunter, Emily Diane *communications executive, marketing professional, educator, real estate developer, writer*
Koepke, Tracey Lynn *marketing professional, writer*
Otterbourg, Robert Kenneth *public relations consultant, writer*
Taylor, James Francis *marketing professional*

Elon
Powell, William Council, Sr. *service company executive*

Flat Rock
Childress, Richard Thomas *international business consultant*

Greensboro
Staab, Thomas Robert *consumer product company financial executive*

Hampstead
Walters, Sherwood George *management consultant, educator*

Hendersonville
Carney, Robert Arthur *restaurant executive*

Hertford
McClung, Kenneth Austin, Jr. *training executive, performance consultant*

Hickory
George, Boyd Lee *consumer products company executive*

Huntersville
Stamey, Derrick *management consultant*

Lake Toxaway
Raynolds, Elaine Spalding *sales executive, photojournalist*

Mooresville
Johnston, James Wesley *retired consumer products company executive*
Mabry, Joseph M.(Mike), Jr. *consumer products company executive*
Niblock, Robert A. *consumer home products company executive*

North Wilkesboro
Parsons, Irene Adelaide *management consultant*
Stone, Larry Dean *consumer products company executive*

Pinehurst
McDannald, Clyde Elliott, Jr. *management consultation company executive*
Rees, Clifford Harcourt, Jr., (Ted Rees) *consulting company executive, retired trade association administrator, military officer*

Pittsboro
Griffith, Katherine Scott *retired communications executive, librarian, reporter*
Squire, Alexander *management consultant*

Raleigh
Doherty, Robert Cunningham *retired advertising executive*
Eberly, Harry Landis *retired communications company executive*
Karmanos, Peter, Jr. *computer company executive, professional sports team executive*
Leak, Robert Edwards *economic development consultant*
Mitchell, Memory Farmer *retired communications executive*

Research Triangle Park
Advani, Deepak *computer company executive*

Sanford
Brown, Eva Everlean *business executive*
Sodini, Peter J. *food service executive*

Southern Pines
Owings, Malcolm William *retired management consultant*

Trinity
McIlquham, David J. *consumer products company executive*

Vass
Glassman, Edward *public relations executive, educator, journalist*

Wake Forest
Gamble, Michael F. *human resources generalist*

Wilkesboro
Bridgeford, Gregory M. *consumer products company executive*
Hull, Robert F., Jr., (Bob) *consumer products company executive*

Winston Salem
Gunzenhauser, Gerard Ralph, Jr. *management consultant, investor*
Ivey, Susan M. *tobacco company executive*
Johnson, Frank William *marketing professional*
Lambeth, Judy (E. Julia Lambeth) *tobacco company executive, lawyer*
Marino, Nancy A. *marketing professional*
Muir, Douglas R. *food service executive*
Neal, Dianne M. *consumer products company executive*

NORTH DAKOTA

Fargo
Tharaldson, Gary Dean *hotel developer, owner*

Mandan
Heick, Leon Joseph *data processing executive*

OHIO

Akron
Crawford, Robert John *credit company executive*
Geier, Kathleen T. *human resources specialist*
Sonnecken, Edwin Herbert *management consultant*

Avon Lake
Morton, David Ray *sales and marketing executive*

Batavia
Meek, David Jason *recreational facility executive, real estate developer*

Cincinnati
Antoine, Richard L. *human resources specialist, consumer products company executive*
Arnold, Susan E. *consumer products company executive*
Artzt, Edwin Lewis *consumer products company executive*
Bateman, Sharon Louise *public relations executive*
Brown, Dale Patrick *retired advertising executive*
Byrnes, Bruce L. *consumer products company executive*
Coffey, Lela *advertising executive*
Daley, Clayton Carl, Jr. *consumer products company executive*
Dillon, David Brian *retail grocery executive*
Dougherty, David Francis *business process outsourcing executive*
Hawkins, Lawrence Charles *management consultant, educator*
Joffe, Craig P.R. *personal care industry executive*
Kernan, Jerome Bernard *retired marketing educator, researcher*
Kotchka, Claudia B. *consumer products company executive, accountant*
Lafley, Alan G. *consumer products company executive*
McDonald, Robert Alan (Bob McDonald) *consumer products company executive*
Orr, James Francis *business process outsourcing executive*
Pepper, John Ennis, Jr. *former consumer products company, historical museum executive*
Shipley, Tony L(ee) *software company executive*
Wall, Della *human resources specialist, manufacturing executive*
Yalamanchili, Surya *advertising executive*
Zaring, Allen G. *homebuilding company executive*

Cleveland
Danco, Léon Antoine *management consultant, educator*
DeGroote, Michael G. *management consulting company executive*
Dunbar, Mary Asmundson *communications executive, public information officer, consultant, investor*
Fountain, Ronald Glenn *management consultant, corporate financial executive, entrepreneur, educator*
Gallagher, Patrick Francis Xavier *public relations executive*
Henry, Edward Frank *retired data processing executive*
Perkovic, Robert Branko *retired international management consultant*
Roop, James John *public relations executive*
Simmons, Clinton Craig *human resources executive*
Stauffer, Thomas George *retired hotel executive*
Taw, Dudley Joseph *sales executive, director*
Woods, Jacqueline F. *public relations executive*

Columbus
Burke, Kenneth Andrew *advertising executive*
Davis, Steven A. *restaurant company executive*
Iammartino, Nicholas R. *corporate communications executive*
Mahoney, Kimberly Lynne *event and facility executive*
McClain, Thomas Emerson *retired communications executive*
Ress, Charles William *management consultant*
Tipton, Clyde Raymond, Jr. *communications and resources development consultant*

Dayton
Daoud, George Jamil *hotel and motel consultant*

Geswein, Gregory T. *software company executive*
Nuti, William R. *computer services company executive*
Riley, David Richard *retired management consultant, military officer*
Ringler, James M. (James M. Ringler) *computer services company executive*
Tatar, Jerome F. *business products executive*

Dublin
Anderson, Kerrii B. *food service executive*
Bird, Shelley *communications executive*
Fitzsimmons, Jay (Joseph J. Fitzsimmons) *food service executive*
Kinman, Gary W. *landscape company executive*
Pickett, James V. *food service executive*
Smith, K(ermit) Wayne *computer company executive*
Wang, Andrew Hsing-Jen *marketing professional, information technology executive, journalist, librarian*
Watkins, Carole S. *human resources specialist, medical products executive*
Wilkins, Jeffrey M. *computer company executive*

Elyria
Patton, Thomas James *marketing executive, sales executive*

Fostoria
Howard, Kathleen *computer company executive*

Galion
Cobey, Ralph *industrialist*

Gates Mills
Abbott, James Samuel III *marketing executive*
Reitman, Robert Stanley *management consultant, not-for-profit advisor*

Jackson
Benson, Steven Clark *management and engineering executive*

Kent
Bissler, Richard Thomas *mortician*

Lancaster
Katlic, John Edward *management consultant*
Phillips, Edward John *consulting firm executive*

Marysville
Hagedorn, James *landscape company executive*

Maumee
Konopinski, Virgil James *retired industrial hygienist, safety consultant*

Mayfield Heights
Newman, Joseph Herzl *advertising executive, consultant*

New Albany
Duggan, Thomas Patrick *management consultant*

Oberlin
Cartier, Brian Evans *consumer products company executive*

Olmsted Falls
Faller, Dorothy Anderson *training services executive, consultant*

Salem
Fehr, Kenneth Manbeck *retired computer company executive*

Sylvania
Block, Allan James *communications executive*
Ring, Herbert Everett *retired management executive*

Toledo
Paquette, Jack Kenneth *management consultant, writer, historian*
Stroucken, Albert P. L. *consumer products company executive, former chemical company executive*

West Chester
End, William Thomas *marketing executive*

Westlake
Doane, Tim *travel company executive*
Kuhn, Edwin P. *travel company executive*

Wooster
Schmitt, Wolf Rudolf *consumer products executive*

Xenia
Nutter, Zoe Dell Lantis *retired public relations executive*

Youngstown
Estrin, Melvyn J. *computer products company executive*

OKLAHOMA

Cleveland
Henry, Kathleen Marie *marketing executive*

Enid
Marquardt, Shirley Marie *retired management consultant*
Taveggia, Thomas Charles *management consultant*

Monkey Island
Vanatta, Chester B. *management consultant, educator*

Mustang
Laurent, Jerry Suzanna *communications executive*

Oklahoma City
Blackwell, John Adrian, Jr. *computer company executive*
Carballo, Bernard A. *computer company executive*
Dezhnyuk, Sergey Fedorovich *business executive, minister*
Greiner, Kenneth Donald, Jr. *retired management consultant, health facility administrator*
Grupe, Robert Charles *corporate communications specialist*
LaMotte, Janet Allison *retired management consultant*

Tulsa
Abbott, William Thomas *private investigator*
Frasier, Nikki *sales executive*
Gentry, Bern Leon, Sr. *management consultant*
Paxton, Gary L. *auto rental company executive*

OREGON

Beaverton
Nathanson, David *communications executive*
Temple, Mike *software company executive*

Bend
Denton, Jody *chef*

Clackamas
George, Oakie Lee *mechanic*

Eugene
Bennett, Robert Royce *engineering and management consultant*
Cawood, Elizabeth Jean *public relations executive*

Forest Grove
Carson, William Morris *manpower planning and development advisor*

Gleneden Beach
Parker, Edwin Burke *communications executive*

Jacksonville
Hennion, Reeve Lawrence *communications executive*

Lake Oswego
Parrick, Gerald Hathaway *communications and marketing executive*

Medford
Entorf, Richard Carl *retired management consultant*

Portland
Barbeau, Monique Andrée *chef*
Boulot, Philippe *chef*
Carter, John D. *recycling company executive*
Conkling, Roger Linton *management consultant, business administration educator, retired utilities executive*
Hinckley, Gregory Keith *software industry executive*
Kirk, Jill *management consultant*
Linstone, Harold Adrian *management consultant, educator*
Paley, Vitaly *chef, food service executive*
Rucker, Gabriel *chef*
Stanton, John W. *communications executive*
Urbanowski, John Richard *lighting systems company official*
Wieden, Dan G. *advertising executive*

Salem
Benson, Steven Donald *marketing professional, mechanical engineer, writer*

Tualatin
Hick, Kenneth William *marketing executive*

PENNSYLVANIA

Bala Cynwyd
Wheatley, William Arthur *consulting firm executive*

Beach Lake
Chatlos, William Edward *management consultant*

Bethel Park
Willard, John Gerard *communications executive, consultant, writer, educator*

Blue Bell
Carrow, John C. *computer company executive*
Kalinsky, Michael *management consultant*
Maddox, David M. *management consultant, career military officer*
McGrath, Joseph W. *computer services company executive*

Bryn Mawr
Peters, Douglas Scott *health care executive*

Camp Hill
Crist, Christine Myers *consulting executive*

Chambersburg
Furr, Quint Eugene *marketing executive*

Conshohocken
Thompson, Pamela Padwick *public relations executive*

Cranberry Township
Patten, Charles Anthony *management consultant, retired manufacturing company executive, writer, publisher*

Delmont
Thompson, Paul A. *business consultant, performance improvement expert*

Doylestown
McCafferty, Barbara Jean (BJ McCafferty) *sales executive*

Fairless Hills
Frazier, Brett W. *waste management executive*

Gettysburg
Hallberg, Budd Jaye *management consulting firm executive*

Harrisburg
Moritz, Milton Edward *security consultant*

Huntingdon Valley
Vollum, Robert Boone *management consultant*

Kennett Square
Hennes, Robert Taft *former management consultant, investment executive*

King Of Prussia
Clauson, Sharyn Ferne *consulting company executive, educator*
Fardone, Guy *communications executive*

Lafayette Hill
Edwards, JoAnn Louise *human resources executive*

Lancaster
Dodge, Arthur Byron, Jr.
Kelly, Robert Lynn *advertising executive*
Veitch, Boyer Lewis *printing company executive*

Lebanon
Deysher, Paul Evans *retired management consultant*

Lewisburg
Rote, Nelle Fairchild Hefty *management consultant*

Linwood
Johnson, John George, Jr. *industrial services executive*

Manns Choice
Braendel, Douglas Arthur *hotel executive*

Media
Barnett, Samuel Treutlen *consultant*
Garvin, Florence Ward *management consultant*

Mountainhome
Buttz, Charles William *outdoor advertising executive*

Narberth
Newhall, John Harrison *retired business executive, management consultant*

Nottingham
White, Richard Edmund *human resources specialist*

Oaks
Marland, Alkis Joseph *leasing company executive, computer scientist, educator, financial planner*

Philadelphia
Alchin, John Reginald *cable tv company executive*
Angelakis, Michael J. *communications executive*
Armstrong, C. Michael *retired communications executive*
Backstrom, C. Stephen *communications executive*
Banse, Amy L. *communications executive, lawyer*
Block, Arthur R. *communications executive, lawyer*
Breslow, Tina *public relations executive*
Burke, Stephen B. (Steve Burke) *communications company executive*
Cartmell, Elizabeth Bayley (Liza) *hospitality and food services executive*
Cohen, David Louis *communications executive*
Coulson, Zoe Elizabeth *retired consumer marketing executive*
Dooner, Marlene S. *communications executive*
Dougherty Buchholz, Karen *communications executive*
Feninger, Claude *retired hotel executive*
Finney, Graham Stanley *management consultant*
Foo, Susanna *chef*
Hemphill, John Lindsay III *administrative assistant*
Jennings, Richard *communications executive*
Logue-Kinder, Joan *public relations consultant*
Madden, Peter J. *advertising executive*
McDade, Sean *market research company executive*
McKee, Lynn B. *human resources specialist*
Mitchell, Brenda King *training services executive*
Morimoto, Masaharu *chef, television personality*
Roberts, Brian L. *communications executive*
Scott-Williams, Mildred P. *food service specialist*
Starr, Stephen *restaurant owner*
Tuan, Kailin *management consultant, educator*
Walter, William G. *consumer products company executive*
Yoh, William C. *outsourcing company executive*

Phoenixville
Brundage, Russell Archibald *retired data processing executive*

Pittsburgh
Bender, Charles Christian *retail home center executive*

Burger, Herbert Francis *retired advertising agency executive*
Cicero, J. Deborah *management consultant*
Dempsey, Jerry Edward *retired service company executive*
Ferrara, Albert E. *corporate executive*
Fine, Milton *hotel company executive, lawyer*
Franklin, Kenneth Ronald *management consultant*
Giel, James Arthur, Jr. *employee benefits management*
Kilkeary, Kevin P. *hospitality executive*
Neel, John Dodd *cemetery executive*
Peterman, Donna Cole *communications executiv*
Rathke, Sheila Wells *strategic planning and marketing executive*
Reichblum, Audrey Rosenthal *public relations and publishing executive*
Richardson, J. William *hotel executive*
Spector, Alfred Zalmon *computer specialist, educator, consultant*
Wabby, James Patrick *quality assurance professional, educator*

Plymouth Meeting
Siegal, Jacob J. *management and financial consultant*
Spiers-Lopez, Pernille (Pernille Lopez) *consume products company executive*

Port Royal
Wert, Jonathan Maxwell, II, *management consultant*

Radnor
Paier, Adolf Arthur *management consultant*

Reading
Ayala, Joe Serrano *marketing professional, personal trainer*
Carlino, Peter M. *gaming company executive*
Kraras, Gust C. *hotel executive*

Ridley Park
Walls, William Walton, Jr. *management consultant*

Royersford
Rhoads, Michael Dennis *sales executive*

Rydal
Boreen, Henry Isaac *computer company executive*

Sadsburyville
Gellman, Gloria Gae Seeburger Schick *marketing professional*

Southeastern
Amichetti, Dennis Joseph *advertising and marketing executive*
Rassbach, Herbert David *marketing executive*

State College
Subler, Edward Pierre *advertising executive*

Sunbury
Rich, Norman S. *food service executive*
Weis, Robert Freeman *supermarket company executive*

Swarthmore
Krizek, Edwin John *marketing professional*

Temple
Stump, Richard Carl *environmental services administrator, consultant*

Valley Forge
LaBoon, Lawrence Joseph *human resources specialist, consultant*

Wallingford
Adamiec, Jean Kraus *retired advertising executive*

Warminster
Thorne, John Watson III *advertising and marketing executive*

Warrendale
Savitt, Kathy *marketing, apparel executive*

Wayne
Carroll, Robert W. *retired management consultant*
Conde, Cristobal I. *computer company executiv*

West Chester
Dunlop, Edward Arthur *computer company executive*
Hanna, Colin Arthur *management consultant, political organization worker, consultant*
Meystel, Michael A. *Internet company executiv*
Murray, Lawrence *management consultant*

West Conshohocken
Mullen, Eileen Anne *human resources executiv*

Williamsport
Trometter, Mary Gionta *chef, educator*

Willow Grove
Asplundh, Christopher B. *tree service company executive*
Schiffman, Louis F. *management consultant*

Willow Street
Blevins, William Edward *management consulta*

Wyncote
Wolfson, Ivan Richard *management consultant*

Wynnewood
Belinger, Harry Robert *retired business executi*

Yardley
Huret, Barry S. *marketing professional, consultant*
Makadok, Stanley *management consultant*
Minter, Philip Clayton *retired communications company executive*
Newsom, Carolyn Cardall *management consultant*
Weaver, William Clair, Jr., (Mike Weaver) *human resources development executive*

York
Livingston, Pamela A. *corporate image and marketing management consultant*

RHODE ISLAND

Barrington
Mihaly, Eugene Bramer *management consultant*

Middletown
Leighton, Charles Milton *retired specialty consumer products executive*

North Kingstown
Kullberg, Gary Walter *advertising agency executive*

Pawtucket
Hassenfeld, Alan Geoffrey *consumer products company executive*
Ferrecchia, Alfred Joseph *toy company executive*

Providence
Schoenfeld, Barbara Braun *executive recruiter, lawyer, consultant*

Woonsocket
Trappier, Pearl Peters *retired bookkeeper*

SOUTH CAROLINA

Bluffton
Reuben, Alvin Bernard *communications and entertainment executive*

Charleston
Chardon, Marc d'Estournelles *software company executive*
de Wolff, Louis *management consultant*
Martin, Thomas Rhodes *communications executive, writer, educator*
Winter-Switz, Cheryl Donna *travel company executive*

Columbia
Farnum, Mary Ann Mook *information management manager*
Farnum, William Douglas *retired communications executive*
Silver, Rick *marketing professional*

Greenville
Axelson, Linda Rae *business director, event planning specialist*
Forman, D. Douglas *human resources specialist, hospital administrator*
Fitzgerald, Eugene Francis *management consultant*
Townes, Bobby Joe *travel agency executive*

Greer
Moore, Gareth *human resources specialist*
Lindstrom, Harold Walter *public relations executive*

Hartsville
Cecil, Allan *corporate communications executive*

Hilton Head Island
Donn, Margaret Elbow *human resources specialist*
McKeldin, William Evans *management consultant*
Patton, Joseph Donald, Jr. *management consultant*
Woodrum, Robert Lee *executive search consultant*

Lake Wylie
Ruggie, Frederick Denman *management consultant*
Sanford, James Kenneth *public relations executive*

Mauldin
Wood, Myra Linden Frank *consultant*

Pawleys Island
Grubb, William Francis Xavier *consumer products company executive, marketing professional*

Roebuck
McShane, Bernard *purchasing agent*

Seneca
Strong-Tidman, Virginia Adele *marketing professional*

Spartanburg
Guillade, Jean-Paul Eric *management consultant*
Reinhart-Oglesby, Debra Lynn *food service executive*

Summerville
Brooks, Jeffrey Martin *marketing and sales executive*

Sunset
Rodbeck, William Jan *marketing professional*

TENNESSEE

Brentwood
Lee, Robert Erich *Internet company executive, information technology consultant, biomedical imaging researcher*

Crossville
Frazier, June Marie *retired public relations executive*

Gallatin
Bradley, Nolen Eugene, Jr. *retired personnel executive, educator*
Brett, John Brendan, Jr. *retired advertising and public relations executive*

Gatlinburg
Cave, Kent R. *parks director*

Knoxville
Brown, Deanna G. *marketing executive*
Campbell, Michael L. *recreational facility executive*
Cox, Anna Lee *retired administrative assistant*
Mayfield, T. Brient, IV, *media and computer executive*
Sansom, William B. *consumer products executive*

La Vergne
Ingram, David B. *entertainment company executive*

Lebanon
Woodhouse, Michael A. *restaurant holdings company executive*

Lenoir City
Edwards, C. Karen *consultant company executive*

Memphis
Abston, Dunbar, Jr. *management consultant*
Brown, R. Larry *human resources specialist, transportation executive*
Krieger, Robert Lee, Jr. *human resource/management consultant, educator, writer, travel/meeting planner, political analyst, internet marketing consultant*

Nashville
Allbritton, Cliff *personal and organizational consultant*
Hartley, Michael J. *travel company executive*
Hillenmeyer, Henry Reiling, Jr. *restaurant company executive*
Lynn, C(harles) Stephen *franchising company executive*
Moore, William Grover, Jr. *management consultant, retired military officer*
Van Mol, Louis John, Jr. *public relations executive*

TEXAS

Addison
Grote, Dick (Richard Charles) *management consultant, educator, writer, radio commentator*

Arlington
English, Marlene Cabral *management consultant*
Sawyer, Dolores *motel chain executive*
Wiig, Karl Martin *knowledge management expert and consultant*

Austin
Curle, Robin Lea *computer company executive*
Decaro, Angelo Anthony, Jr. *data processing executive*
Gillespie, Danny, Jr. *management consultant, music foundation administrator*
Gilliand, Tom *chef, Restaurant Owner*
Green, Shirley Moore *retired communications executive, public information officer*
Gurasich, Stephen William, Jr. *advertising executive*
Hayden, Tim *marketing executive*
Martin, Thomas Brooks, Jr. *computer company executive*
Mathias, Reuben Victor (Vic Mathias) *organization executive, real estate investor*
Mathis, Marsha Debra *customer service administrator*
Mayer, Michel *computer company executive*
Mulconrey, Brian George *management consultant, futurist*
Pearson, Jim Berry, Jr. *human resources specialist*
Ravago, Miguel *chef, Restaurant Owner*
Spence, Roy Milam, Jr. *advertising executive*
Trabulsi, Judy *advertising and marketing executive*
Wahl, William Bryan *marketing professional, real estate company officer*
York, Candace A. *marketing professional, writer*
Young, Harrison, II, *software development and marketing executive*

College Station
Gunn, Clare Alward *travel consultant, writer, retired educator*
Hise, Richard Todd *marketing professional, educator, consultant*
Solymosy, Edmond Sigmond Albert *marketing professional, retired military officer*

Coppell
Owen, Cynthia Carol *sales executive*

Dallas
Beam, Justin *chef*
Becker, Nancy Woolverton *public relations executive, event planner*
Bombaci, Anthony *chef*
Bondy, Joanne *chef*
Brinker, Norman E. *restaurant company executive*
Brooks, Douglas H. *food service executive*
Campbell, Raymond III *publication director*
Carl, Robert E. *retired marketing company executive*
Cassel, Marc *chef*
Clapner, Katherine *chef*
Collins, Philip A. *management consultant*
Dalton, Harry Jirou, Jr., (Jerry Dalton) *public relations executive*
Dawson, Edward Joseph *merger and acquisition executive*
Dinkins, Jane Poling *management consultant, application developer*
Dozier, David Charles, Jr. *advertising and public relations executive*
Dykeman, Alice Marie *public relations executive*
England, Julie Spicer *computer company executive*
Evangelist, Shane *advertising executive*
Fairbairn, Ursula Farrell *human resources executive*
Fleming, Tom *chef*
Gilbert, David *chef*
Gottlich, Scott *chef*
Gray, James Larry *international business executive*
Grimes, David Lynn *communications executive*
Hage, Sharon *chef*
Heydrick, Linda Carol *consulting company executive, editor*
Holben, David *chef*
Horchow, S(amuel) Roger *marketing consultant*
Koeppel, Peter Stafford *advertising executive*
Levenson, Stanley Richard *public relations and advertising executive*
Lilyhorn, Gregory Dean *security firm executive*
Liskow, Frederic Cullen (Ric) *printing company executive*
Maxey, Kevin *chef*
May, Kenneth Austin *consumer products company executive*
Migdol, Marvin Jacob *public relations and marketing executive, consultant*
Mukherjee, Ann (Anindita Mukherjee) *advertising executive*
Niccol, Brian *marketing executive*
Pace, Carolina Jolliff *communications executive, investor*
Parks, J. Michael *data processing executive*
Pearson, Robert Lawrence *executive recruiter*
Pyles, Stephen *chef*
Rathburn, Kent *chef*
Richards, Stanford Harvey *advertising agency and design studio executive*
Sonsteby, Charles M. *food service executive*
Spiegel, Lawrence Howard *advertising executive*
Stern, Andrew Milton *public relations executive*
Swindle, Shannon *chef*
Wagner, Todd *Internet company executive*
Wilcox, Tre *chef*
Wilson, Morgan *chef*
Zeitlin, Laurie *printing company and information technology executive*

Del Rio
Prather, Gerald Luther *management consultant, retired judge, military officer*

El Paso
Cardwell, James A., Sr. *service company executive*
Roberts, Ernst Edward *marketing consultant*

Euless
Self, Mark Edward *communications consultant*

Flower Mound
Ross, Lesa Moore *quality assurance professional*

Fort Worth
Appel, Bernard Sidney *marketing professional, consultant, retired electronics executive*
Brundage, Jeffrey J. *human resources specialist, air transportation executive*
Lancarte, Lanny P., II, *chef*
Rollins, Kevin B. *former computer company executive*

Fredericksburg
Arnold, George Lawrence *retired advertising company executive*

Frisco
Hawk, Phillip Michael *service corporation executive*

Grapevine
Fontaine, R. Richard *computer game company executive*

Highland Village
Richardson, K. Scott *sales executive*

Houston
Aardsma, David A. *waste management executive*
Adams, C. Lee *marketing executive*
Anderson, William (Albion), Jr. *management consultant*
Bradley, Melvin LeRoy *communications executive*
Burnett, Susan Walk *personnel service company owner*
Caddell, Lynn M. *waste management executive*
Caldwell, Barry H. *waste management executive*
Cupp, B. Garland *computer company executive*
Curtiss, Jeff *consumer products company executive, lawyer*
Day, Twila M. *food service executive*
Ellis, Raymond Clinton, Jr. *retired hotel executive*
Flato, William Roeder, Jr. *software development company executive*
Gilbert, Jill Barson *management consultant*
Kors, R. Paul *search company executive*
Lapsley, Andrea Ricards *marketing and development professional, librarian*
Mampre, Virginia Elizabeth *communications executive*
Mays, Randall T. *communications company executive*
McCollam, Marion Andrus *consulting firm executive, educator*
Myers, James Clark *advertising and public relations executive*
Noland, Mary Richerson *retired management consultant*
O'Donnell, Lawrence III *waste management executive*
Romans, Jay *waste management executive*
Ryan, Thomas L. *funeral company executive*
Saizan, Paula Theresa *business consultant*
Saunders, William Arthur *management consultant*
Simpson, Robert G. *waste management executive*
Steiner, David P. *waste management executive*
Stephens, Sidney Dee *human resources specialist, retired chemical manufacturing company executive*
Wiglesworth, Michael Bland *advertising executive*

Huntsville
Stowe, Charles Robinson Beecher *management consultant, educator, lawyer*

Hurst
Bishara, Amin Tawadros *management and consulting firm executive*

Irving
Cornell, Brian C. *food service executive, retail executive*
Hawkins, William David *marketing executive*
Nugent, John Hilliard *communications executive*
Potter, Robert Joseph *technical and business executive*
Tidwell, James *Sommelier*
Wicks, William Withington *retired public relations executive*

Jacksboro
Patterson, Ronald R(oy) *management consultant*

Junction
Evans, Jo Burt *communications executive, rancher*

Lubbock
Dennison, Daniel Thomas *environmental compliance and lab administrator*
Fontenot, Andrea Dean *communications executive*
Jugenheimer, Donald Wayne *advertising executive, communications educator, academic administrator*

Memphis
Gerkey, Stephen J. *management consultant, writer, speech educator*

New Caney
Hayes, Ann Carson *computer company executive*

Plano
Dillon, Donald Ward *management consultant*
Dougherty, F(rancis) Kelly *data processing executive*
Heller, Jeffrey M. *data processing executive*
Scott, Terry Lee *communications executive*
Sivinski, Tina M. *human resources specialist*
Speese, Mark E. *rental company executive*
Theilmann, Michael T. *human resources specialist*

Port Arthur
Munoz, Andrea Lee *human resources specialist*

Round Rock
Bell, Paul D. *computer company executive*
Cannon, Michael R. *computer company executive, former electronics executive*
Carty, Donald J. *computer company and former air transportation executive*
Dell, Michael Seth *computer company executive*
Garriques, Ron G. *computer company executive*
Hudson, Michel Colette *management consultant*
Schuckenbrock, Steve (Stephen Francis Schuckenbrock) *computer company executive, former information technology executive*
Sheskey, Susan E. *computer company executive*

San Antonio
Butt, Charles Clarence *food service executive*
Clark, Wendy *advertising executive*
Garcia, Henry Frank *supply and project management consultant*
Mays, Mark Pitman *communication company executive*
Montemayor, Carlos Rene *advertising agency executive*
Orr, Joseph Newton *recreational guide, outdoor educator*
Whitesell, Stephen Ernest *parks director*

San Marcos
Moore, Patsy Sites *food service consultant*

Southlake
Gilliland, Michael S. (Sam Gilliland) *travel company executive*
Glueck, Jeffrey *travel company executive*
Peluso, Michelle *Internet company executive, travel company executive*
Sorge, Karen Lee *printing company executive, consultant*

Spring
Ciancimino, Joseph Andrew *data processing executive*

Spring Branch
Barban, Arnold Melvin *advertising executive, educator, writer*

Texas City
Hodges, Richard Dean *instrument and electrical technician*

The Woodlands
Brenneman, Gregory D. *food service executive*
Glenn, Gerald Marvin *marketing, engineering and construction executive*
Morrison, Scott David *management consultant, small business owner*

Trophy Club
Holley, Cyrus Helmer *management consulting service executive*

Waco
Voight, Carolyn Jean *administrative assistant*

Willis
Snider, Robert Larry *management consultant*

UTAH

Draper
Escobar, Anthony *marketing professional, consultant*

Midway
Zenger, John Hancock *training company executive*

Orem
Sawyer, Thomas Edgar *management consultant*

Park City
Milner, Harold William *hotel executive*

Salt Lake City
Atkinson, Geoff *marketing executive*
Covey, Stephen Merrill Richards *business consultant, speaker, author*
Davis, Gene *public relations executive, state legislator*
Davis, Loyd Evan *defense industry marketing professional*
Howell, Scott Newell *computer company executive, state legislator*
Robbins, Sherri Lynn *quality assurance professional*

VERMONT

Burlington
Post, Peter L. *marketing executive, writer*

East Dummerston
Bertone, Thomas Lee *management consultant*

Norwich
Stevenson, Josiah, IV, *management consultant*

Putney
Keil, John Mullan *advertising executive, artist*

Waitsfield
Esty, David Cameron *marketing and communications executive*

Wilmington
Little, Thomas M. *public relations executive*

Woodstock
Hoyt, Coleman Williams *postal consultant*
Matlins, Stuart M. *management consultant, publisher*

VIRGINIA

Abingdon
Ramos-Cano, Hazel Balatero *caterer, chef, innkeeper, restaurateur, entrepreneur*

Alexandria
Anderson, Maynard Carlyle *security firm executive*
Armstrong, Cathal *chef*
Bozell, Brent (L. Brent Bozell III) *communications executive*
Coons, Barbara Lynn *public relations executive, librarian*
Fosdick (Beebe), Cora Prifold *management consultant*
Foster, Robert Francis *communications executive*
Frommer, Lawrence Julian *retired travel company executive*
Gallagher, Anne Porter *communications executive*
Geary, Patrick Joseph *security and emergency planning administrator, writer*
Goolrick, Robert Mason *management consultant*
Harris, David Ford *management consultant, retired federal official*
Hilferty, Bryan Carey *public relations specialist*
Lantz, Phillip Edward *security firm executive, consultant*
Laurent, Lawrence Bell *communications executive, retired journalist*
McMillan, Charles William *consulting company executive*
Meisinger, Susan *human resources specialist*
Nelson, David Leonard *data processing executive*
Paulson, Gwen O. Gampel *government relations consultant, life and leadership coach*
Signorovitch, Dennis J. *communications executive, educator*
Simmons, Richard De Lacey *mass media executive*
Stone, Ann Elizabeth *marketing agency executive, consultant, entrepreneur, volunteer*
Thrasher, Todd *bar chef*
Verburg, Edwin Arnold *management consultant*
Walker, Edward Keith, Jr. *retired management consultant, retired military officer*

Annandale
Greinke, Everett Donald *management consultant*
Jarvis, Elbert, II, (Jay Jarvis) *employee benefits specialist*

Arlington
Adams, Jimmie Vick *communications systems company executive, retired military officer*
Alcalde, Hector *public relations executive*
Bennett, Christopher Lawrence *hotel executive, lawyer*
Claussen, Eileen Barbara *environmental services administrator, former federal agency administrator*
DeFeo, Charles Joesph *Internet company executive*
Erwin, Frank William *human resources consultant*
Fay, Kevin J. *public relations executive*
Harrison, Emmett Bruce, Jr. *public relations counselor*
Hewitt, Thomas Francis *hotel executive*
Newburger, Beth Weinstein *communications executive*
Rabaut, Thomas W. *defense industry executive*
RisCassi, Robert W. *communications systems company executive, retired military officer*
Samburg, A. Gene *security company executive*
Vuono, Carl E. *communications systems company executive, retired military officer*
Warshawsky, Mark Joel *human resources specialist, former federal agency administrator*
Whetsell, Paul W. *hotel executive*
Zorthian, Barry *communications executive*

Burgess
Burch, Michael Ira *public relations executive, retired federal agency administrator*

Charlottesville
Brown, Holmes *public relations executive*

Cobbs Creek
Crum, John Kistler *management consultant*

Dulles
Balis, Janet *Internet company executive*
Falco, Randy (Randel A.) *Internet company executive, former broadcast executive*
Grant, Ronald E. *Internet company executive*
Kumar, Nisha *Internet company executive*
Parker, Ira H. *Internet company executive, lawyer*

Dumfries
Locigno, Paul Robert *public relations executive*

Fairfax
Baker, Daniel Richard *computer company executive*
Bohan, Gloria *travel company executive*
Chalasani, Venkat *management consultant*
Hale, Thomas Morgan *professional services executive*
Witek, James Eugene *retired public relations executive*

Falls Church
Courtney, William Harrison *security firm executive*
Dao, Thuy Dinh *personal care industry executive*
Jones, Linda R. Wolf *consulting company executive*
Oliver, Walter M. *human resources specialist*

Glen Allen
Gulling, Mark V. *consumer products company executive*

Great Falls
Bachner, John Philip *business consultant*

Herndon
Huntoon, Nancy *security manager*

Keswick
Woods, Reginald Foster *management consulting executive*

Lake Ridge
Ingrassia, Anthony Frank *human resource specialist*

Leesburg
Lobanov-Rostovsky, Oleg *management consultant*

Lorton
Jackson, Gary Lee *security consultant*

Mc Lean
Estren, Mark James *communications executive, television producer, writer*
Ethell, Judy A. *consulting company executive*
Frostic, Frederick Lee *strategic planning and defense policy consultant*
Jayne, Edward Randolph, II, *executive search consultant*
Klaassen, Paul J. *personal care industry executive*
O'Brien, Morgan Edward *communications executive, lawyer*
Olson, Walter Justus, Jr. *management consultant*
Orkand, Donald Saul *management consultant*
Paschall, Lee McQuerter *retired communications executive*
Pilling, Donald L. *management consultant, retired military officer*
Rose, Susan Porter *management and governmental affairs consultant*
Shrader, Ralph W. *management consultant*
Smith, Esther Thomas *communications executive*
Watson, Jerry Carroll *advertising executive*
Webber, Diana L. *management consultant executive, engineering educator*
Wellings, Tom *chef*
Wilton, Elisabeth Starr *management consultant*

Middleburg
McNichols, Gerald Robert *consulting company executive*

Midlothian
Wadsworth, Robert David *advertising executive*

Norfolk
Blount, Robert Haddock *management consultant, retired military officer*

Oak Hill
Okay, John Louis *management consultant*

Palmyra
Levy, Bern *communications executive, optical applications consultant*

Portsmouth
Buxton, Margaret Rose *human resources specialist, director*

Reston
Abraham, Magid M. *Internet company executive*
Easton, Glenn Hanson, Jr. *management consultant, federal official, military officer*
Fernandez, Raul J. *data processing executive*
Fulgoni, Gian Marc *Internet company executive*
Kelly, Timothy E. *communications executive*
Maher, David Willard *Internet company executive*
Montoni, Richard A. *management consultant*
Pendergraft, David *management consultant*
Sarreals, Sonia *data processing executive, consultant*
Schick, Michael William *public relations executive*
Witt, Ruth Hutt *management consultant*

Richmond
Bohannon, Sarah Virginia *personnel professional*
Dan, Michael T. *security firm executive*
Fox, Sandra Gail *insurance marketing executive*
Freeman, George C. III *tobacco company executive, lawyer*
Hughes, Mike *advertising executive*
Jacobs, Harry Milburn, Jr. *advertising executive*
Joynes, Barbara Cole *marketing executive*
King, Allen B. *tobacco company executive*
Trott, Sabert Scott, II, *marketing professional, consultant*

Round Hill
Schleede, Glenn Roy *marketing professional, consultant*

Seaford
Jenkins, Margaret Bunting *human resources executive*

Springfield
Bruen, John Dermot *management consultant*

Suffolk
Hall, Wayne Michael *management consultant*

Vienna
Monroe, Robert Rawson *national security consultant*
Walker, William Woodard, Jr. *management consultant, telecommunications technology executive*

Virginia Beach
Alexander, William Powell *business advisor*
Hilgers, John Jack William *management and transportation consultant*
Wick, Robert Thomas *retired supermarket executive*

Williamsburg
Ackerman, Lennis Campbell *retired management consultant*
Finn, A. Michael *corporate communications specialist*
Hoving, John Hannes Forester *consulting firm executive*
McGarvie, Blythe J. *management consultant*
Morris, Robert Louis *management consultant*

Winchester
Bonometti, Robert John *technology management and strategy executive*
Engelage, James Roland *management consultant*
Gaither, George Manney *marketing consultant*

WASHINGTON

Anacortes
Cook, Don W. *human resources specialist, retired military officer, risk management consultant*
Hoffmann, Manfred Walter *consulting company executive*

Arlington
Gerwick-Brodeur, Madeline Carol *marketing and timing professional*

Bellevue
Connors, John G. *former computer software company executive*
Hall, Eleanor Williams *public relations executive*
Khosrowshahi, Dara *travel company executive*
McReynolds, Neil Lawrence *management consultant*
Myhrvold, Nathan P. *technology executive*

Everett
Jewell, Judy Ann *funeral director, counselor*

Federal Way
Muzyka-McGuire, Amy *marketing professional, nutritionist, consultant*

Gig Harbor
Stover, Miles Ronald *management consultant*

Hunts Point
Ebsworth, Barney A. *retired travel company executive*

Issaquah
Hilst, Glenn Rudolph *environmental sciences administrator, researcher*
Matthews, John *human resources specialist, wholesale distribution executive*

Kennewick
Brewton, Wesley Hopkins (Wes Brewton) *retir chef, retired real estate manager*

Kirkland
McCaw, Craig O. *communications executive*

Lacey
Breytspraak, John, Jr. *management consultant*

Medina
Dagnon, James Bernard *human resources executive*

Mercer Island
Dykstra, David Charles *management executive, consultant, accountant, author, educator*

Parkland
Johnson, LuAn K. *disaster management consultant*

Port Ludlow
Krugman, Stanley Lee *international manageme consultant*

Redmond
Balakrishnan, Radhesh *marketing professional*
Ballmer, Steven Anthony *computer software company executive*
Bradford, Joanne K. *computer software compa executive*
Brod, Frank H. *computer company executive, accountant*
Flake, Gary William *computer software compa executive*
Gates, Bill (William Henry Gates III) *compute software company executive*
Leblond, Antoine *computer company executive*
Liddell, Christopher P. *computer software company executive*
Martinez, Maria *computer software company executive*
Mathews, Mich *computer company executive*
Mundie, Craig James *computers software company executive*
Nelson, Kimberly Terese *computer software company executive, former federal agency administrator*
Ozzie, Ray (Raymond E. Ozzie) *computer software company executive*
Shirley, Jon Anthony *software company executive*
Troberman, Gayle Deborah *marketing executiv*

Seattle
Bates, Charles Walter *human resources executive, lawyer*
Bezos, Jeffrey Preston *multimedia company executive*
Bianco, James A. *research and development executive*
Burke, Jane *software company executive*
Carsberg, Scott *chef*
Coles, Martin *beverage company executive*
Dillon, Matthew *chef*
Donald, James L. *food service executive*
Duryee, David Anthony *management consulta*
Eastham, John D. *marketing executive*
Eggers, Susan J. *computer science educator*
Elgin, Ron Alan *advertising executive*
Eller, Marlin *security firm executive*
Gass, Michelle Petkers *advertising executive*
Glaser, Robert *communications executive*
Halvarsson, Misha *business development strategist, entrepreneur*
Hutton, Winfield Travis *management consulta educator*
Kelman, Glenn *Internet company executive, entrepreneur*
McAndrews, Brian *digital marketing executiv*
Pace, David A. *human resources specialist, re executive*
Patton, Jody *management company executive*
Sasenick, Joseph Anthony *consumer products company executive*
Schultz, Howard *beverage service executive*
Sundstrom, Johnathan *chef*
Taucher, Fred Horace *data procesing company executive*
Wilson, Jason *chef*

Spokane
Chamberlain, Barbara Kaye *communications executive*
Storey, Francis Harold *business consultant, retired bank executive*

Tacoma
Bartlett, Norma Thyra *retired administrative assistant*
Lind, Eric Hawthorn *sales executive*
Taylor, Peter van Voorhees *advertising and public relations consultant*

Vancouver
Ogden, Valeria Munson *management consulta state representative*

Walla Walla
Potts, Charles Aaron *management, publishing executive, writer*

Woodinville
Love, Keith Sinclair *communications executive*

WEST VIRGINIA

Charleston
Mc Gee, John Frampton *communications company executive*

Huntington
Reynolds, Marshall Truman *printing company executive*

Triadelphia
McCullough, John Phillip *management consultant, educator*

WISCONSIN

Algoma
Golomski, William Arthur Joseph *consulting company executive*

Appleton
Geller, Scott A. *management consultant*

Brookfield
Dillon, Donald F. *data processing executive*
Rettmann, Robert D. *corporate communications specialist*
ullivan, Owen *employment services executive*
Tabuki, Jeffrey W. *data processing company executive, former accounting company executive*

Darien
Miller, Malcolm Henry *manufacturing sales executive, real estate developer*

Janesville
Butters, John Patrick *travel company executive, educator*

Kohler
ohler, Laura E. *human resources executive*

Madison
Kempe, A. Henry *labor relations specialist, labor arbitrator, lawyer*

Mequon
lias, Paul S. *retired marketing executive*

Middleton
ee, Leslie Warren *marketing executive, educator*

Milwaukee
rbit, Bruce *direct marketing executive, consultant*
rkless, David *employment services executive*
eck, Barbara J. *employment services executive*
'Amato, Sandy *chef*
avidson, Rick *employment services executive*
avis, Susan F. *human resources specialist*
agerman, Douglas M. *consumer products company executive, lawyer*
unter, Victor Lee *marketing executive, consultant*
erres, Jeffrey A. *employment services executive*
hns, Tammy *employment services executive*
aughlin, Steven L. *advertising executive*
issen, Varina *employment services executive*
ising, Jonas *employment services executive*
ansom, Randy *marketing executive*
cher, Marc-Hans *marketing executive*
vera-Velazquez, Maria *marketing professional*
am, Robert Harry *human resources specialist, consultant*
choenfeld, Howard Allen *management consultant, lawyer*
wan, Mara E. *employment services executive*
an Handel, Michael J. *employment services executive*

ew Berlin
tten, Charles Arthur *sales executive*

lymouth
entine, Lee Michael *marketing professional*

acine
hnson-Leipold, Helen P. *outdoor recreation company executive*
hnson-Marquart, Winnie *consumer products company executive*
ein, Gabriella Sonja *retired communications executive*
acNair, David Cameron *marketing executive*

heboygan
ró, Marcel *chef*

outh Milwaukee
hwantes, Brianne Catherine *marketing professional*

aterford
arraker, Louis Rendleman *retired corporate executive*

ausau
adzinski, Mary Beth *administrative assistant*

YOMING

ackson
errick, Gregory Evans *computer company executive*

Yellowstone National Park
Lewis, Suzanne *parks director*
Patterson, Sally Jane *communications executive, consultant*

TERRITORIES OF THE UNITED STATES

PUERTO RICO

Manati
Martinez, Heriberto *human resources professional*

VIRGIN ISLANDS

St Thomas
O'Bryan, James A. *communications specialist, political organization administrator*

CANADA

ALBERTA

Calgary
Phillips, Robert Alexander Bell *management consultant*

BRITISH COLUMBIA

Vancouver
Campbell, Bruce Alan *corporate coach*

Victoria
Nuttall, Richard Norris *management consultant, physician*

NOVA SCOTIA

Halifax
Gratwick, John *management consulting executive, writer, consultant*

ONTARIO

Chatham
McKeough, William Darcy *supply company executive*

Freelton
Sonnenberg, Hardy *data processing executive, researcher, electrical engineer*

Mississauga
Tully, Mary Jean *travel company executive*

Niagara-on-the-Lake
Nielsen-Jones, Ian Richard *lottery and gaming executive, consultant*

Ottawa
Courtois, Bernard Andre *communications executive*
Griller, David *management consultant*
McLure, John Douglas *management consultant, former Canadian government official*
Silverman, Ozzie *consulting strategist*

Saint Catharines
Bergevin, V. Réal *customer relationship management executive*

Toronto
Ames, Steven *management consultant*
Bandeen, Robert Angus *management consultant*
Bandrowczak, Steven J. *communications executive*
Curlook, Walter *management consultant*
Dooher, Donna *chef*
Fatt, William Robert *hotel executive*
Fierheller, George Alfred *communications executive*
Gregor, Tibor Philip *retired management consultant*
Rogers, Edward Samuel *communications company executive*
Seiersen, Nicholas Steen *management consultant*
Taylor, Kathleen P. *hotel executive*

Willowdale
MacDonald, Brian Scott *management consultant*

QUEBEC

Leclercville
Morin, Pierre Jean *retired management consultant, social services administrator*

Montreal
Beauregard, Luc *public relations executive*
Sirois, Charles *communications executive*

Rosemere
Hopper, Carol *incentive program and trade association administrator*

Whistler
Rae, Barbara Joyce *employee placement company executive*

AUSTRALIA

Brighton
Bellin, Howard *management consultant*

North Sydney
Scott, Brian Walter *management consultant*

CHINA

Beijing
Akeley, Kurt Barton *computer graphics company executive, engineer*
Lin, James K. *communications executive, educator*
Ma (Xuezheng), Mary *retired computer company executive*

Shanghai
Jiang, Jason Nanchun *advertising executive*

CZECH REPUBLIC

Pribram
Kuba, John Albert *mortician*

EGYPT

Cairo
Fahmy, Ibrahim Mounir *hotel executive*

ENGLAND

Berkshire
Everitt-Newton, Katherine Evelyn *international management consultant*

Brentford
Gersappe, Sunil *marketing executive*

Canterbury
Holwell, Peter *management consultant*

London
Dyson, Tim *public relations executive*
Hallissey, Michael *retired management consultant*
Leaf, Robert Stephen *public relations executive*
Oliver, Jamie *chef, television personality*
Verwaayen, Ben J.M. *communications company executive*

Old Windsor
Marsh, Donna M. *sales executive, consultant*

Stroud
Robinson, John Beckwith *development management consultant*

FRANCE

Issy Les Moulineaux
Pouzilhac, Alain Duplessis de *advertising executive*

Marseille
Boutterin, Emmanuel *public relations executive*

Paris
Courtaud, Bernard Jean-Jacques *human resource consulting executive*
Marcus, Claude *advertising executive*
Robuchon, Joël *restaurateur*

GERMANY

Dresden
Gluch, Steffen *company executive*

Fulda
Beckman, James Wallace Bim *management consultant, educator*

Neu Isenburg
Hoare-Temple, Piers Howard *building maintenance executive*

GIBRALTAR

DeLeon, Russ *Internet company founder*

GREECE

Marousi
Joannou, Dakis *businessman*

HONG KONG

Kowloon
Fung, Victor K. (Victor Fung Kwok King) *consumer products trading company executive*

JAPAN

Mito
Kobayashi, Susumu *retired computer company executive*

Tokyo
Chiba, Machiko *cooking advisor*

SINGAPORE

Henretta, Deborah A. *consumer products company executive*

SOUTH AFRICA

Lesotho
Davis, Sarah Frances *management consultant, bishop*

Pretoria
Stocks, Rundell Kingsley *management, construction, education and general consultant*

SWEDEN

Saltsjö-Duvnäs
Gyll, John Sören *marketing executive*

Solna
Fleisher, Frederic Elliott *communications executive*

ADDRESS UNPUBLISHED

Abraham, Nathan Samuel *advertising agency and public relations executive, marketing and management consultant*
Ackerman, Raymond Basil *advertising executive*
Ahrens, Thomas H. *communications executive*
Alderfer, Clayton Paul *organizational consultant, writer*
Alderson, Vanessa *administrative assistant*
Alexander, Faith Dorothy *retired training services executive*
Allen, Bennie Carnel *employee relations specialist*
Allen, Louis Alexander *management consultant*
Allen, Richard Vincent *international business consultant, former national security advisor*
Amparado, Keith D. *communications company executive*
Anand, Sanjay *training services executive, consultant, entrepreneur, educator*
Anderson, Marcie *communications executive*
Anderson, Mark Robert *data processing executive, biochemist*
Anderson, Paul Irving *management executive*
Anderson, Tom *Internet company executive*
Ando, Kunitake *consumer products company executive*
Anschutz, Philip F. *communications and professional sports team executive*
Anthony, Wilma Tylinda *retired customer service administrator*
Antonishek, Joseph John *chef*
Appelbaum, Yonatan Asher *administrative assistant, city manager*
Appell, Louise Sophia *retired consulting company executive*
Arscott, R. Lyndon (Raymond Lyndon Arscott) *management consultant*
Asensi, Gustavo *advertising executive, cinematographer*
Ashkin, Rajasperi Maliapen *marketing executive*
Askins, Nancy Ellen Paulsen *training services executive*
Auden, Bruce James *chef, restauranteur, consultant*
Auerbach, Andrew Daniel Tretter *consulting executive*
Bacas, Andrew R. *data processing executive*
Bachelder, Cheryl Anne *former food service company executive*
Baker, Daniel Paul *advertising executive, entrepreneur*
Baldwin, Donovan A. *marketing professional, writer*
Balick, Kenneth D. *international business development consultant*
Bamberger, Gerald Francis *plastics marketing consultant*
Barca, Kathleen *marketing executive*
Barger, William James *management consultant, educator*
Barnett, Elizabeth Hale *organizational consultant*
Barr, Michael Charles *research director, lawyer*
Barrett, Beverly Frances *public relations specialist*
Bartlett, David *management consultant*
Bauer, Barbara Ann *marketing consultant*
Beasley, Barbara Starin *sales executive, marketing professional*
Beck, Timothy Daniel *human resources specialist, consultant*
Becker, Robert A. *advertising executive*
Behnava, Shahriyar *management consultant*
Beider, Marlys Anna *hotel executive, writer*
Benney, Douglas Mabley *direct marketing executive, consultant*
Benoit, Philip Grosvenor *communications executive, educator, writer*
Berger, Frank Stanley *management consultant*
Bernard, Cathy S. *management corporation executive*
Binder, Amy Finn *public relations company executive*
Birk, John Richard *management consultant*
Bishop, William Peter *management consultant, rancher, musician*
Black, Kris Susan Lynn *marketing company executive, speaker, author, poet*
Blaine, Davis Robert *valuation consultant, investment banker*
Blamer, Steven W. *former advertising executive*
Blanchard, Townsend Eugene *retired service companies executive*
Blatz, Linda Jeanne *sales manager*
Bloom, Gary L. *data processing executive*
Blum, Bradley D. *former food service executive*
Boatwright, Charlotte Jeanne *marketing professional, public relations executive*

Boehnen, David Leo *food service executive, lawyer*
Bonnie, Shelby W. *Internet company executive*
Booth, Margaret A(nn) *communications company executive*
Borges, William III *management consultant*
Botkin, Monty Lane *computer company executive*
Boudreaux, John *marketing and public relations executive*
Bourdain, Anthony *chef, writer*
Bouth, Michael T. *marketing executive*
Bow, Stephen Tyler, Jr. *business executive*
Bowes, Henry Edward *retired communications executive*
Bowick, Susan D. *retired computer company executive*
Boysen, Jonea Gene *marketing executive, copywriter*
Braddock, Richard S. *Internet company executive*
Bradford, Susan Anne *management consultant, writer*
Bradshaw, John Robert Covington III *Internet company executive*
Brady, Donna Elizabeth *sales, marketing and performing company executive*
Braun, Lloyd *Internet company executive*
Brazile, Francisco LaRue *management consultant*
Brennan, Donna Lesley *public relations company executive*
Brennen, Stephen Alfred *management consultant*
Broderson, Thelma Sylvia *retired marketing professional*
Brooks, Jeffrey James *environmental services administrator, educator*
Brotman, Stuart Neil *management consultant, law educator, communications executive*
Buck, Earl Wayne *private investigator, motel owner*
Burgdoerfer, Jerry J. *marketing and distribution executive*
Burge, John Wesley, Jr. *management consultant*
Burnett, Iris Jacobson *corporate communications specialist*
Burnham, J. V. *retired sales executive*
Burns, Michael Joseph *operations and sales-marketing executive*
Burroughs, Augusten Xon *advertising executive*
Busquet, Anne M. *Internet company executive*
Butler, Robert Leonard *retired sales executive*
Butler, Robert Thomas *retired advertising executive*
Butterfield, Bruce Scott *executive, editor, author, educator, consultant*
Butz, Earl Lauer *former secretary of agriculture, consultant*
Cage, Jack Hays *executive search consultant*
Caine, Raymond William, Jr. *retired public relations executive*
Carder, Paul Charles *retired advertising executive*
Carp, Daniel A. *former consumer products company executive*
Carpenter-Mason, Beverly Nadine *quality assurance professional, medical/surgical nurse, pediatric nurse practitioner, consultant, writer*
Carter, Dennis Lee *marketing professional*
Carter, Jaine M(arie) *human resources specialist, director*
Cartwright, Talula Elizabeth *leadership consultant, educator*
Casadesus, Penelope Ann *advertising executive, film producer*
Cavanagh, Richard Edward *corporate executive director*
Cecil, Alex Thomson *travel executive*
Chamberlain, William Edwin, Jr. *management consultant*
Chandler, Robert Leslie *public relations executive*
Chapman, Linda Lee *computer company executive, consultant*
Chaput, Eugene Michael *advertising executive*
Chaseman, Joel *communications consultant*
Chen, Kenichi *chef*
Chen, Philip Minkang *strategic consultant*
Chen, Steve Shih *Internet company executive*
Cheney, Mary Claire *Internet company executive*
Chevins, Anthony Charles *retired advertising agency executive*
Childs, John David *retired computer company executive*
Chitre, Subodh Subhash *computer company executive*
Chittum, Anthony *chef*
Chittum, Heather *chef*
Chou, Sunlin *retired computer company executive*
Chrisanthopoulos, Peter *advertising executive*
Chung, Caroline *marketing professional*
Citron, Richard Ira *management consultant*
Claflin, Bruce L. *software company executive*
Clark, Wesley Kanne *emergency management executive, educator, retired military officer*
Clarke, Janet Morrison *marketing executive*
Clarke, Terence Michael *public relations and advertising executive*
Cochetti, Roger James *international communications and internet company executive*
Coleman, Claire Kohn *public relations executive*
Coleman, Claudia L. *marketing executive*
Collins, Richard Stratton (Dick Collins) *retired public relations executive*
Connell, Carol Matheson *corporate communications specialist, consultant*
Connell, Shirley Hudgins *public relations professional*
Cordes, Jill *chef*
Cordova, Barbara Joy *activities director*
Cornish, Jay, Jr., (Thelbert Bernard) *Internet company executive*
Cortese, Richard Anthony *computer company executive*
Corwell, Ann Elizabeth *public relations executive*
Cotter, Robert F. *hotel executive*
Cowper, Stephen Cambreleng *international business consultant, former governor*
Cox, Robert *retired landscape company executive*
Crandall, John Alfred *corporation official*
Crawford, Bruce Edgar *advertising executive*
Crawford, William Walsh *retired consumer products company executive*
Cruver, Suzanne Lee *communications executive, writer*
Cuddihy, Robert Vincent, Jr. *finance and marketing executive*
Cunningham, Andrea Lee *public relations executive*
Curatola, Daniel L. *retired sales executive*
Dangoor, David Ezra Ramsi *consumer goods company executive*
Danzig, Voleen H. *marketing professional, educator*
Darien, Steven Martin *management consulting company executive*
DaVerne, Steven Richard *advertising director, artist, illustrator, behavior analyst, marketing professional, consultant*
David, Clive *events executive*
Davis, Robert W. *computer company executive*
Deacon, David Emmerson *advertising executive*
Dean, Leslie Alan (Cap Dean) *international economic, social and political development consultant, interagency and defense analyst*
De Laurentiis, Giada *chef*
de Margitay, Gedeon *acquisitions and management consultant*
Dennick, Lori Ann (L. Anne) *publicist, actress, journalist*
DePinto, David J. *public relations executive*
Dergarabedian, Paul *environmental services administrator, consultant*
deWilde, David Michael *management consultant, lawyer, finance company executive, retired recruiter*
Diamond, Susan Zee *management consultant*
DiDomenico, Mauro, Jr. *communications executive*
Diederichs, Janet Wood *public relations executive*
Diehl, Stephen Anthony *human resources consultant*
Dillon, Francis Patrick *retired human resources specialist*
Di Massa, Ernani Vincenzo, Jr. *communications executive, television producer, writer*
Dirvin, Gerald Vincent *retired consumer products company executive*
DiSpirito, Rocco *restaurant owner, chef*
Dixner, Arne Wilfred *environmental services administrator*
Doan, Mary Frances *advertising executive*
Dobler, Donald William *retired procurement and materials executive, dean*
Doherty, Evelyn Marie *data processing consultant*
Dolman, John Phillips, Jr., (Tim Dolman) *communications company executive*
Donahue, John Joseph *parks director*
Donovan, James Robert *business equipment company executive*
Douglas, Victoria Jean *marketing professional, communications executive, educator*
Dow, Peter Anthony *advertising executive*
Drake, Patti Linn *retired consumer products company executive*
Duffy, Dan *computer company executive*
Duffy, Martin Edward *management consultant, economist*
Duke, Robin Chandler Tippett *retired public relations executive, former ambassador*
Duke, William Edward *public affairs executive*
Dzhandzhulyan, Lev *business analyst, consultant*
Echols, Mary Evelyn *training services executive, writer*
Ecton, Donna R. *business executive*
Eddy, David Maxon *health policy and management advisor*
Edwards, Adrien *business executive*
Eibeler, Paul G. *former computer game company executive*
Eisenberg, Jay Lynn *marketing research professional*
Elix, Douglas Thorne *computer company executive*
Elkind, Mort William *management consultant*
Ellig, Bruce Robert *retired personnel director*
Elliot, Jared *financial management consultant*
Ellis, Steven George *public relations/corporate communications executive*
Emerling, Carol G. *management consultant*
Emerson, Daniel Everett *retired communications company executive*
Erb, Richard Louis Lundin *resort and hotel executive*
Estrin, Deborah Perry *human resources executive*
Fake, Caterina *Internet company executive*
Farrell, William Edgar *sales executive, management consultant*
Fay, Conner Martindale *retired marketing executive*
Feigin, Barbara Sommer *marketing consultant*
Feld, Carole Leslie *marketing executive*
Feller, Robert William Andrew *public relations executive, retired professional baseball player*
Fenimore, George Wiley *management consultant*
Ferguson, Gary Lee *public relations and security management executive*
Ferreira, Jo Ann Jeanette Chanoux *management consultant, delivery service executive*
Fine, Frederick L. *computer company and health products executive*
Finger, Jason Roy *food service executive, internet entrepreneur*
Fink, Daniel Julien *management consultant*
Fiorina, Carly (Cara Carleton Sneed Fiorina) *former computer company executive*
Fischer, Russell Leonard *public relations executive*
Fleming, Thomas A. *retired administrative assistant*
Flickinger, Harry Harner *management consultant*
Fluhr, Jeff *Internet company executive*
Forrester, Jay Wright *management consultant, educator*
Francis, Philip Hamilton *management consultant*
Franke, John Charles *retired human resources executive*
Frankowiak, James Raymond *public relations executive*
Frasca, Gabriel *chef*
Fudge, Ann Marie *former advertising executive*
Fuller, Kathryn Scott *former environmental services administrator*
Gadiesh, Orit *management consulting executive*
Gadomski, Robert Eugene *consulting and retired gas industry executive*
Gallagher, Michael Robert *retired consumer products company executive*
Garrison, William Lloyd *retired cemetery executive, social worker*
Gasser, Michael J. *consumer products company executive*
Gebauer, Kurt Manfred *management executive*
Geltzer, Sheila Simon *public relations executive*
Gendell, Gerald Stanleigh *retired public relations executive*
Geschke, Charles M. *computer company executive*
Gianturco, Delio Emanuele *management consultant, educator, author*
Gillice, Sondra Jupin *sales and marketing executive*
Glacel, Barbara Pate *management consultant*
Glass, Kenneth Edward *management consultant*
Gleaves, Leon Rogers *marketing and sales executive*
Gluys, Charles Byron *retired marketing management consultant*
Goldberg, Victor Joel *retired data processing company executive*
Golden, Bryan *management consultant, writer*
Goldfarb, Muriel Bernice *marketing and advertising consultant*
Goldsmith, Jeff Charles *management consultant*
Goldstein, Alfred George *consumer products company executive*
Gore, Tushar *marketing professional*
Gorsline, Stephen Paul *security specialist*
Gottlieb, Alan Merril *advertising, fundraising and broadcasting executive, writer*
Grace, Marcia Bell *advertising executive*
Greaser, Constance Udean *communications executive, researcher*
Greene, Alvin *management consultant*
Gregerson, Daniel P. *retired computer company executive*
Gregory, Nelson Bruce *retired motel owner, naval officer*
Grey, Ruthann E. *corporate communications specialist, director*
Gross, Laura Ann *marketing and communications professional, herbalist, acupuncturist*
Grosso, Doreen Elliott *management consultant*
Growick, Philip *advertising executive*
Grubb, Donald Hartman *paper industry company executive*
Grunder, Fred Irwin *retired industrial hygienist, consultant*
Grupe, Scott M. *management consultant*
Guarascio, Philip *advertising executive*
Gugel, Craig Thomas *advertising executive*
Gunderson, Ted Lee *security consultant*
Gurwitch, Arnold Andrew *communications executive*
Guskov, Sergey *security firm executive*
Gutheinz, Jean *public relations executive*
Haas, Aaron C. *sales executive*
Haas, Edward Lee *management consultant*
Haas, Mark Richard *management consultant researcher*
Haddad, Edmonde Alex *public affairs executive*
Hadl, John *marketing executive*
Hafemeister, Beverly Rae *consumer products company executive*
Hagel, John III *management consultant*
Haines, David Harry *consulting executive*
Hall, Adrienne A. *international marketing communications executive*
Hall, Donald Joyce, Jr. *consumer products company executive*
Hall, Hansel Crimiel *communications executive*
Hamilton, Thomas Michael *marketing executive*
Hamlin, Sonya B. *communications specialist*
Harari, Eli *computer company executive*
Harden, Mary Louise *human resources consultant, real estate broker, real estate appraiser*
Hargadon, Bernard Joseph, Jr. *retired consumer goods company executive*
Harlan, Raymond Carter *special investigator, writer, retired communication executive, educator, and military officer*
Harr, Lucy Loraine *public relations executive*
Harrington, Robert Dudley, Jr. *retired printing company executive*
Harris, Paul Smith *human resources professional*
Harris, Robert Norman *advertising executive, educator*
Hartger, Barbara J. *marketing professional*
Hartsock, Linda Sue *retired management consultant*
Harvey, Douglass Coate *retired photographic company executive*
Harvey, Glenn Francis *management consultant*
Harvey, Richard Dudley *marketing consultant*
Haupt, Roger A. *advertising executive*
Hausdorfer, Gary Lee *management consultant*
Hauser, Joyce Roberta *marketing professional*
Hausman, Harriet Seceley *administrator*
Hausmann, Charles Stewart *retired funeral director*
Haver-Allen, Ann *communications director*
Hayes, Janet Gray *retired management consultant, mayor*
Hazard, Christopher Wedvik *international business executive*
Hazard, Robert Culver, Jr. *hotel executive*
Heath, Ross Bradley *consulting company executive*
Heckmann, Richard J. *sporting goods company executive*
Heller, Arthur *advertising executive*
Helm, Lewis Marshall *communications executive*
Henry, Philip Lawrence *marketing professional*
Henselmeier, Sandra Nadine *retired training services executive*
Herz, Irene Laurel *web site design company executive, librarian*
Heuer, Martin *retired human resources specialis*
Heyer, Steven J. *former hotel and beverage company executive*
Hickerson, Glenn Lindsey *leasing company executive*
Hickey, Kevin Francis *software company executive*
Higbee, Beth *communications executive*
Hildebrandt, Frederick Dean, Jr. *management consultant*
Hindery, Leo Joseph, Jr. *communications executive*
Hirahara, Patti *public relations executive*
Hochhalter, Gordon Ray *advertising communications executive*
Hoffman, Darnay Robert *management consultar*
Holdaway, Phillip Wayman *retired environmente planner*
Hollander, Lawrence Jay *retired marketing executive*
Holzer, Edwin *advertising executive*
Holzman, D. Keith *management consultant, record company executive*
Hooper, Josh *advertising executive, writer, director*
Hopkins, Jan *communications executive, consultant, journalist, newscaster*
Hosokawa, David *advertising executive*
Houghtaling, Pamela Ann *communications professional, writer*
Howard, Gary Scott *communications executive*
Hrubec, Jane M. *advertising executive*
Hudson, Stanton Harold, Jr. *public relations executive, educator, academic administrator*
Hundt, Reed Eric *management consultant, former federal agency administrator*
Huppe, Alex *public relations executive*
Hurley, Chad Meredith *Internet company executive*
Immel, Barbara Kay Kephart *management consultant*
Inouye, Wayne Ryo *computer company executi*
Irvine, William Burriss *management consultant*
Irving, Janell NaKia *management consultant*
Irving, Jeffrey Alan *management consultant, educator, lawyer*
Isaac, Steven Richard *business executive, academic administrator, educator, owner*
Jackson, Eric Michael *marketing executive, writer, media specialist*
Jacobs, Bradley S. *former rental company executive*
Jelinek, John Joseph *public relations executive*
Jenkyn, Adrian John *computer company executive*
Jetley, Karun *software company executive, consultant*
Jiang, Tianyi *computer company executive*
Joanou, Phillip *advertising executive*
Johnson, Craig N. *management consultant*
Johnson, Elizabeth *communications executive, interpreter*
Johnson, Herbert Frederick *sales executive, retired academic administrator, librarian*
Johnson, Kevin *computer software company executive*
Johnson, Laymon, Jr. *management analyst*
Johnson, Norman Terry *public relations executive, writer*
Jones, David A. *former consumer products company executive*
Jones, Thomas Owen *computer company executive*
Kampmeier, Curt *management consultant*
Kane, Karen Marie *public affairs consultant*
Kanuk, Leslie Lazar *management consultant, educator*
Kaplan, David L. *retired communications educator, actor, artist, sculptor*
Kaprielian, Walter *advertising executive*
Karalis, John Peter *computer company executi lawyer*
Kassewitz, Ruth Eileen Blower *retired public relations executive*
Keala, Francis Ahloy *security executive*
Kegerreis, Robert James *management consulta marketing professional, educator*
Keller, Paul *advertising executive, researcher*
Kendrick, Peter Murray *communications executive, investor*
Kendzior, Robert Joseph *marketing executive*
Kennedy, Jerrie Ann Preston *public relations executive*
Kennedy, Karen Synce *advertising agency executive*
Kenny, Deborah *marketing professional, finan educator*
Kincaid, Steven Randall *marketing professiona*
King, Royce Arthur *retired farm equipment executive*
Kirk, Carmen Zetler *data processing executive*
Kirschenmann, Henry George, Jr. *managemen consultant, retired government official, accountant*
Klein, Charlotte Conrad *public relations executive*
Klein, Chuck *retired private investigator, write*
Kloepfer, William, Jr. *retired public relations executive*
Koelmel, Lorna Lee *data processing executive*

Komisarjevsky, Christopher P.A. retired public relations executive
Korologos, Ann McLaughlin communications executive, former secretary of labor
Kovach, Andrew Louis human resources specialist, consultant
Krakower, Bernard Hyman management consultant
Kramer, Peter Robin computer company executive
Kraus, Jill Gansman former jewelry industry marketing executive
Krupp, James Arthur Gustave management consultant
Kuhn, James Paul management consultant
Kull, Bryan Paul business consulting executive
Kushner, Harvey David management consultant
Kusterer, Thomas program director
Kwan, David Chung Man business executive
Kwon, Taek Internet company executive
aiskonis, Michael chef
aMantia, Charles Robert management consulting company executive
ambert, Kirsten Schnoor public relations executive, writer
ampert, Eleanor Verna retired human resources specialist
ampman, Richard H. (Dick Lampman) former computer company executive
arson, Charles Fred management consultant
avidge, Robert James marketing research executive
awrence, Margery H. (Margery Hulings Lawrence) marketing consultant
ayton, William George consultant, retired human resources and import/export company executive
azarus, Bruce I. restaurant and hotel management educator
eboeuf, Edmond Arthur human resources specialist
ee, Joseph William sales executive
ee, Richard Kenneth software company executive
ee, Soo-Hoon human resources specialist
eeds, Douglas Brecker advertising executive, theater producer
eMarbe, Edward S. marketing and engineering executive
enz, Henry Paul management consultant
epley, Rick Allen consumer products company executive
evchin, Max Internet company executive
even, Stephen H. retired human resources specialist
evick, Richard Scott communications executive, lawyer, consultant, educator
evien, Roger Eli strategy and innovation consultant
evitt, Brian Michael consumer products company executive, lawyer
vy, Arthur James public relations executive, writer
vy, Robert Edward retired management consultant
wis, George Ralph consumer goods company executive
ebrandt, Paul chef
ghtman, Harold Allen marketing executive
lley, William III business executive, consultant
nda, Gerald advertising and marketing executive
ndberg, Francis Laurence, Jr. management consultant
tman, Earl advertising and public relations executive
vermore, Ann Martinelli computer company executive
vingstone, Susan Morrisey management consultant, former federal agency administrator
chner, Philip Raymond retired communications executive, former commissioner
cke, Norton hotel and construction executive
ckwood, Robert W. management consultant
negan, Thomas Lee retired restaurant corporation executive
ngaberger, Tami home decor accessories company executive
relli, Michael Kevin consumer products company executive
si, Maxim John medical communications executive
tas, Judith Patton advertising executive
ce, Priscilla Mark public relations executive
nch, Charlotte Andrews retired communications executive, consultant
c Alister, Robert James executive recruiter
cNeill, James William environmental energy and management consultant
dison, Anne Conway marketing, public relations professional
eda, J. A. data processing executive, consultant
karov, Iouri advertising executive
llison, Howard Danford retired corporate communications specialist
lone, Claudine Berkeley management consultant
lphurs, Roger Edward biomedical marketing executive
neker, Roberta S(ue) public relations executive
nley, John Hugo computer company executive, educator
rano, Thomas J. marketing professional
rkey, Randolph David marketing professional
rsh, Don Ermal supermarket executive
rshall, Robert Charles computer company executive
rtin, Edwin Wilson corporate director, columnist, educational consultant, webmaster
rtin, James Kay management consultant
scheroni, Eleanor Earle marketing communications executive
ssey, William Walter, Jr. sales executive
Massoudi, Bahram Barry management consultant
Matlock, Kent advertising and public relations executive
Matschullat, Robert W. former consumer products company executive
Matthew, Lyn sales executive, consultant, marketing professional
Maxfield, Louise Fonda Gribble executive secretary
Mayer, Allan communications consultant, writer
McBride, Thomas Dwayne management consultant
McCandless, Carolyn Keller retired human resources specialist
McCann, Jim (James F. McCann) consumer products company executive
McCarthy, Daniel William management consultant
McCaslin, David E. hotel executive
McCloskey, J(ohn) Michael retired environmental services administrator
McDade, James Russell management consultant
McElwreath, Sally Chin corporate communications executive
McGuire, John W., Sr. advertising executive, marketing professional, writer
McKay, Melinda hotel executive
McKelvey, Andrew J. former advertising executive
McKeown, Lorraine Laredo travel company executive, writer
Mc Kinney, David E(wing) retired information processing products company executive, museum administrator
McNamara, Tom scientific consulting corporation executive
McPherson, Donald Scott labor and employment arbitrator/mediator
McVeigh-Pettigrew, Sharon Christine communications consultant
Meads, Donald Edward management services company executive
Meigher, S. Christopher III communications and media executive, publisher
Merrill, Frank Harrison data processing executive, consultant
Meyer, Edward Henry retired advertising executive
Meyers, Christine Laine marketing and media executive, consultant
Mikiewicz, Anna Daniella marketing and international business export manager
Miles, Laveda Ann advertising executive
Miles, Mary Ellen retired human resources specialist
Miles, Michael Arnold consumer products executive
Miller, Bernard Joseph, Jr. advertising executive
Miller, Ellen S. marketing executive
Minarik, Stephen Joseph III communications executive, former political organization administrator
Mitchell, John Charles marketing professional
Mobley, William Hodges management consultant, educator, writer, researcher
Moffat, MaryBeth consulting company executive
Molland, Maria U. Internet company executive
Monroe, William Lewis human resources executive
Montelongo, Michael D. marketing executive, former civilian military employee
Moog, Matthew Internet company executive
Moradi, Ahmad F. software company executive
Moran, Charles A. security firm executive, educator
Morano, Gerard John marketing executive
Morden, John Reid security-business intelligence consultant
Morgan, James Durward retired computer company executive
Morgan, Marianne corporate professional
Morrison, Denise M. sales executive
Mracky, Ronald Sydney marketing executive, tourism consultant, media specialist
Mulcahy, Robert Edward management consultant
Mulligan, David Keith consulting company executive, securities arbitrator
Murdock, Pamela Ervilla travel and advertising company executive
Mustard, Lewis Williams management consultant, educator
Myrie, Leslie Rolce, Jr. marketing executive
Nagler, Leon Gregory retired management consultant
Nason, Dolores Irene computer company executive, social welfare administrator, minister
Naughton, Eileen T. Internet company executive
Neel, Judy Murphy management consultant
Nelson, Bruce (Murray Bruce Nelson) former consumer products company executive
Netravali, Arun N. communications executive
Nevin, Robert Charles information systems executive
Niles, Thomas Michael Tolliver former business association executive
Novotny, Deborah A. management consultant, director
O'Brien, Cathy media company executive
O'Brien, David Peter corporate director
O'Brien, Robert John, Jr. public relations executive, former government official, air force officer
O'Byrne, Michael retired management consultant
Olins, Robert Abbot communications research executive
Olson, Dale C. public relations executive
Oppedahl, Phillip Edward computer company executive
O'Reilly, James marketing executive
O'Shea, Catherine Large marketing and public relations consultant
Ostberg, Henry Dean marketing executive
O'Sullivan, Paul Kevin management and instructional systems consultant
Palola, Harry Joel retired international affairs executive, consultant
Palumbo, Matthew Aloysius marketing executive
Parks, Judith Tyler business executive, consultant
Parra, Ro (Rosendo G. Parra) former computer company executive
Parsons, Vinson Adair retired computer company executive
Passaro, Paul Charles strategic planning consultant
Patterson, Dennis Joseph retired management consultant
Peden, Keith J. human resources specialist
Penny, Roger Pratt retired management consultant
Pépin, Jacques G. chef
Perez, Antonio M. imaging company executive
Perlmutter, Barbara S. retired public relations executive
Perlmutter, Diane F. marketing executive
Perry, Chris Nicholas retired advertising executive
Perry, James Benn former casino and hotel executive
Perry, James E. marketing executive, consultant
Peters, LeRoy Richard materials management consulting company executive
Phillips, Joyce Martha human resources executive
Pierog, Margaux Marie food service executive, restaurant manager
Piontkowski, Stephen Robert environmental services administrator
Pitman, Angelia Dee web site design company executive
Plottel, Gloria Susanne Stone marketing professional
Polen-Dorn, Linda Frances communications executive
Posner, Sidney advertising executive
Post, Richard Bennett retired human resources executive
Potash, Stephen Jon public relations executive
Potter, Bill R. business executive
Potter, James Earl retired international hotel management company executive
Price, Bruce Deitrick advertising executive, author
Pride, Benjamin David sales executive
Propp, Steven H. personnel director
Puck, Wolfgang chef
Pulley, Brett A. communications executive
Radkowsky, Karen advertising research specialist
Railsback, Sherrie Lee management consultant, educator
Rairdin, Craig Allen software company executive, software developer
Ransom, Margaret Palmquist public relations executive
Redstone, Shari Ellin amusement company executive
Reed, Anne F. Thomson management consultant
Reggio, Vito Anthony retired management consultant
Reilly, Charles Edmund, Jr. communications executive
Reisman, Judith Ann Gelernter media communications executive, educator
Rhea, Jerry Dwaine consumer lending director
Richards, Carmeleete A. computer company executive, network administrator, consultant
Richardson, Jeffrey Carl public relations executive
Ripert, Eric food service executive
Roberts, Carter S. environmental services administrator
Robins, Norman Alan management consultant, retired metal products executive
Robinson, Hugh Granville consulting management company executive
Robinson, Linda Gosden communications executive
Roehm, Julie A. marketing executive
Roemer, James Paul data processing executive, writer
Roland, Donald Edward advertising executive
Rook, Vicki Lynn safety specialist
Roseman, Jack computer services company executive
Rosen, Arthur Marvin advertising executive
Rosenfield, James Harold, Sr. communications executive
Rosensaft, Lester Jay management consultant, lawyer
Rubin, Martin N. meeting planner, consultant
Rubinstein, Jonathan J. computer company executive
Ruggles, Rudy Lamont, Jr. international security advisor
Russ, Edmond Vincent, Jr. marketing professional
Ryan, Melbagene T. retired food service and nutrition director
Rydholm, Ralph Williams advertising executive
Sacks, Temi J. public relations executive
Safford, Florence Viray Sunga travel agent, consultant
Safian, Shelley Carole advertising executive
Saligman, Harvey retired consumer products and services company executive
Sanchez, Fausto H. advertising executive
Sandage-Mussey, Elizabeth Anthea retired market research executive
Sanders, Walter Jeremiah, III, (Jerry Sanders) retired computer company executive
Satterwhite, R. Scott computer company executive
Sauerhaft, Stan retired public relations executive, consultant
Saywell, William George Gabriel business development and management consultant
Scerno, Joseph Benedict management consultant executive, arbitrator
Schadt, James Phillip investment and software executive
Schlafly, Hubert Joseph, Jr. communications executive
Schlensker, Gary Chris landscape company executive
Schonberg, Alan Robert personnel director
Schrader, William L. communications executive
Schramm, Bernard Charles, Jr. retired advertising agency executive
Schreckinger, Sy Edward advertising executive, consultant
Schubert, Helen Celia public relations executive
Schuessler, John T. (Jack Schuessler) retired food service executive
Schultz, Eileen Hedy creative director
Schulz, Raymond Alexander medical marketing professional, consultant
Schwartz, Michael Robinson management consultant
Sease, Gene Elwood communications executive
Seelig, Gerard Leo management consultant
Seidman, Glenn Elliott sales executive, marketing professional, consultant
Selkowitz, Arthur retired advertising executive
Shain, Kenneth Stephen management consultant, executive, writer
Shaker, William Haygood marketing professional, public policy reformer
Sharick, Merle Dayton, Jr. sales executive
Sharples, Ruth Lissak communications executive
Shaw, Cecelia retired chef
Shaw, Jack Allen communications company executive
Sheehan, Robert James, II, management and market research consultant
Shelton, Robert Warren marketing professional
Shevitz, Mark H. sales promotion and marketing executive
Shikuma, Eugene Yujin travel company executive
Shultz, Delray Franklin (Lucky Shultz) business coach, consultant
Sidebottom, William George communications executive
Sidnam, Alan Northcote retired advertising executive, venture capitalist
Siegel, George Henry management consultant
Silberman, H. Lee public relations executive, consultant
Simecka, Betty Jean marketing executive
Simon, Trevor management consultant, educator, human resources specialist
Simpson, Andrea Lynn communications executive
Sincoff, Michael Z. human resources and marketing executive, educator
Singer, David Michael marketing and public relations executive
Skala, Gary Dennis management consultant
Slosberg, Mike advertising executive
Smith, Dan chef
Smith, John W(esley), Jr. data processing executive, consultant
Snyder, John Millard travel company executive, educator
Sollender, Joel David management consultant, financial executive, accountant
Solomon, Neal Edward management consultant, executive recruiter, social theorist, entrepreneur, author
Sorger, Stephan Gunther marketing professional, educator
Sorstokke, Ellen Kathleen marketing executive, educator
Speer, Richard John security consultant
Spellman, Douglas Toby advertising executive
Spivak, Joan Carol communications executive
Stark, Diana public relations executive
Starkweather, Frederick Thomas retired data processing executive
Stebel, Michael David marketing professional, consultant
Stengel, Ronald Francis management consultant
Stenitzer, George Ignatius corporate communications specialist
Stepanski, Anthony Francis, Jr. computer company executive
Stevens, Art public relations executive
Stevens, Berton Louis, Jr. data processing executive
Stewart, Arthur Irving, III, (Art Stewart) management consultant
Stiles, Virginia Ford data processing executive, poet
Stone, Curtis celebrity chef
Stone, James Howard management consultant
Stone, Linda former computer company executive, consultant, speaker, writer
Strasser, Gabor management consultant
Streeter, Stephanie Anne former printing company executive
Strother, Patrick Joseph public relations executive
Stuart, Spencer Raymond management consultant
Stults, Walter Black management consultant, trade association administrator
Sudarsky, Jerry M. industrialist
Suh, Jung Sook Ky personnel consultant
Suissa, David advertising executive
Tarbutton, Lloyd T. hotel executive, consultant
Tarr, Curtis W. management consultant, educator
Temerlin, Liener advertising executive
Tenney, Frank Putnam marketing executive
Tesarek, Dennis George retired business consultant, writer, educator
Thomas, Joe Carroll retired human resources director
Thomas-Robinson, Gregory Leon sales executive
Thompson, Craig Snover corporate communications executive
Thompson, Dean M., II, marketing executive
Thompson, Jonathan Sims business executive
Thompson, Richard Stephen management consultant
Thornton, Felicia D. food service company executive
Tian, Li computer company executive, educator

Tomlin-Houston, Lisa *management consultant*
Tramonto, Rick *chef*
Tribus, Myron *management consultant, educator*
Troop, Paul Melvin *public relations executive, journalist*
Tuft, Mary Ann *executive search firm executive*
Turkel, Stanley *hotel executive, management consultant*
Unwin, Stephen Forman *advertising executive, educator*
Uvena, Frank John *retired printing company executive, lawyer*
Vallerand, Philippe Georges *sales executive*
Van Aken, Norman *chef*
Van der Horst, Brian Christopher *communications consultant, author, educator*
Van Dine, Alan Charles *advertising agency executive, writer*
Villines, Bobby T. *environmental services administrator, information technology manager*
Volpi, Mike (Michelangelo A. Volpi) *internet television service company executive*
Wadley, M. Richard *consumer products executive*
Walk, Barbra Denise *customer service administrator, tutor*
Walker, Gloria Lee *training services executive*
Walker, Ronald Tracy *retired personnel director*
Walmsley, Priscilla Helen *computer company executive*
Walsh, William Albert *management consultant, retired military officer*
Walter, J. Jackson *management consultant, foundation administrator*
Wangsness, Genna Stead *retired hotel executive, innkeeper*
Wardlow, Benjamin Franklin III *sales executive*
Weathersby, George Byron *management company executive*
Webb, William Timothy *mobile communications professional*
Weber, Donald B. *advertising executive, marketing professional*
Weber, Kenneth J. *hotel executive*
Weil, Lynne Amy *communications executive, writer*
Weiner, Richard *public relations executive*
Weinstein, Marta *packaging services company executive*
Weismantel, Gregory Nelson *management consultant, computer company executive*
Weiss, Jerry Kenneth *sales executive, consultant, marketing professional*
Wells, Peter Scoville *retired marketing professional*
Wendlinger, Robert Matthew *communications and memory consultant*
Wentz, Jeffrey Lee *information systems executive*
Werner, Stuart Lloyd *computer services company executive*
Wesley, Norman H. *consumer products company executive*
Wheaton, M. Gene *investigator, consultant*
Whiting, Brian Christopher *hospitality consultant*
Wicks, David O., Jr. *communications executive*
Williams, Louis Clair, Jr. *public relations executive*
Williams, Paul Stratton *executive recruiter*
Williams, Terrie Michelle *public relations executive*
Willig, Karl Victor *computer company executive*
Wimpress, Gordon Duncan, Jr. *management consultant, foundation administrator*
Winkler, Agnieszka M. *marketing executive*
Winkler, Lee B. *business consultant*
Witcher, Michael H. *homeland and national security expert*
Wolf, Stephen M. *consumer products company executive, former airline executive*
Wolf, William Martin *computer company executive, consultant*
Wood, Frances Diane *medical secretary, artist*
Worboys, Roger Dick *retired communications executive*
Worth, Gary James *communications executive*
Yocam, Delbert Wayne *retired software products company executive*
Yopconka, Natalie Ann Catherine *secretary officer, computer specialist, educator, entrepreneur, small business owner*
Youst, David Bennett *career development educator*
Zaghloul, Dina Amal *quality assurance professional, consultant*
Zeller, Joseph Paul *advertising executive*
Zhang, Ming *business and management consultant*
Ziegler, James L. *marketing executive*
Zinnen, Robert Oliver *management consultant, consultant*
Zipf, Jennifer E. *marketing professional*
Zuckerberg, Mark Elliot *Internet company executive, entrepreneur, programmer*

INDUSTRY: TRADE

UNITED STATES

ALABAMA

Birmingham
George, Frank Wade *small business owner, antiquarian book dealer*
Pizitz, Richard Alan *retail executive, real estate company officer*

Dothan
Malugen, J.T. (Joe Thomas) *retail executive*

Mobile
Jones, Joseph Seymour *small business owner, poet*

Tuscaloosa
Blackburn, John Leslie *small business owner*

ALASKA

Anchorage
Schnell, Roger Thomas *small business owner, retired state official*

Wrangell
Smith, Kimmie Christine *small business owner*

ARIZONA

Chandler
Basha, Edward N., Jr. *grocery chain owner*

Lakeside
McBride, Janet Marie *small business owner*

Phoenix
Francis, Philip L. *retail executive*
Pasholk, Paul Douglas *retail executive, government official*

Scottsdale
Williams-De Silva, Lisa Annette *small business owner, adult nurse practitioner*

Sun City
Thompson, Betty Jane *retired small business owner*

Tucson
Betteridge, Frances Carpenter *small business owner, retired lawyer, mediator*
Fay, Mary Anne *retail executive*

ARKANSAS

Bentonville
Castro-Wright, Eduardo *retail executive*
Chambers, Susan (M. Susan Chambers) *retail executive*
Curran, Patricia A. *retail executive*
Dillman, Linda M. *retail executive*
Dobbs, Johnnie *retail executive*
Duke, Michael T. *retail executive*
Fleming, John E. *retail executive*
Ford, Rollin *retail executive*
Glass, David D. *retail and professional sports team executive*
Hefner, Linda P. *retail executive*
Herkert, Craig R. *retail executive*
Holley, Charles Murphy, Jr. *retail company executive*
McMillon, Doug *retail executive*
Menzer, John Bruce *retail executive*
Mora, Alberto J. *retail executive, lawyer*
Schoewe, Thomas M. *retail executive*
Scott, H(arold) Lee, Jr., (Lee Scott) *retail executive*
Simon, William *retail executive*
Walton, (Samuel) Rob(son) *discount department store chain executive*
Zorn, Eric Stuart *retail executive*

Little Rock
Dillard, William, II, *department store chain executive*

CALIFORNIA

Camarillo
Van House, Robert Arthur *small business owner, contractor*

Carmel
Aurner, Robert Ray, II, *retail development executive*

Cathedral City
Jackman, Robert Alan *retail executive*

City Of Commerce
Martin, Richard J. *food wholesale executive*
Plamann, Alfred A. *wholesale distribution executive*

Colton
Brown, Jack H. *supermarket company executive*

Corona Del Mar
Freeman, Richard Dean *new business start-up service company executive*

Foster City
Pollitt, Byron H., Jr. *retail executive*

Fresno
Winslow, Norman Eldon *small business owner*

Laguna Beach
Pelton, Virginia Lue *small business owner*

Los Angeles
Hawley, Philip Metschan *retired retail executive, management consultant*
Roeder, Richard Kenneth *business owner, lawyer*
Sinay, Joseph *retail executive*

Menlo Park
VanHook, Tracie Lynnette *small business owner*

Modesto
Piccinini, Robert M. (Bob Piccinini) *grocery store chain executive*

Orange
Busby, Nita June *small business owner*

Pacific Palisades
Diehl, Richard Kurth *retail executive, consultant*

Palm Springs
Wiesner, John Joseph *retail chain store executive*

Palos Verdes Peninsula
Slayden, James Bragdon *retired retail executive*

Petaluma
Gervais, Cherie Nadine *small business owner*

Pleasanton
Balmuth, Michael A. *retail executive*
Everette, Bruce L. *retail executive*
Ferber, Norman Alan *retail executive*
Renda, Larree M. *retail executive*

Riverside
White, Clara Jo *small business owner, consultant*

San Diego
Saito, Frank Kiyoji *import and export firm executive*
Shields, Patricia Allene *retail executive*

San Francisco
Calhoun, John Joseph (Jack) *retail executive*
Fisher, Donald G. *retail executive*
Fisher, Doris *retail executive*
Fisher, Robert J. *retail executive*
Folkman, David H. *retail, wholesale and consumer products consultant*
Hansen, Marka *retail executive*
Harriss, Cynthia Therese (Cynthia Therese Clarke) *retail executive*
Lenk, Edward C. (Toby) *retail executive*
Lester, W. Howard *retail executive*
Murphy, Glenn T. *retail executive*
Peck, Art *retail executive*
Robertson, Dawn H. *retail executive*
Sage-Gavin, Eva Marie *retail executive*
Tasooji, Michael B. *retail executive*
Ullman, Myron Edward, III, (Mike Ullman) *retail executive*

San Jose
Davido, Scott *retail executive*

Santa Rosa
Monk, Diana Charla *small business owner*

South San Francisco
Walsh, J. Michael *wholesale distribution executive*

Stockton
Blodgett, Elsie Grace *small business owner, property manager*

Valencia
Joy, Alexa *small business owner, artist, educator*

Walnut Creek
Bryant, Warren F. *retail executive*

West Sacramento
Coyne, William J. *retail executive, former member house representatives*
Teel, Joyce Raley *retail executive*

Yountville
Bedell, Jay Dee *small business owner, writer*

COLORADO

Boulder
Johnson, Maryanna Morse *business owner*

Colorado Springs
Noyes, Richard Hall *bookseller*

Denver
Cashman, Michael Richard *small business owner*
Clinch, Nicholas Bayard III *small business owner*
Schwartz, Jeffrey H. *distribution facilities executive*

Englewood
Morton, John Douglas *retail executive*

CONNECTICUT

Avon
Kling, Phradie (Phradie Kling Gold) *small business owner, educator*

Enfield
Squires, William Allen *distribution company executive*

Essex
Thompson, George Lee *retail executive, consultant*

Fairfield
Wexler, Herbert Ira *retail company executive*

Greenwich
Rudy, Kathleen Vermeulen *small business owner*

Madison
Drought, James Henry *healthcare business owner, exercise physiologist*

Mansfield Center
Petrus, Robert Thomas *internet business owner, investor*

Stamford
Bennett, Carl *retired discount department store executive*
Hollinger, Morton *small business owner, artist*

DELAWARE

Odessa
Butler, Janet C. *shop owner*

DISTRICT OF COLUMBIA

Washington
Chalkley, Jacqueline Ann *retail company executive*
Smith, Jack Carl *import/export company executive*
Stern, Paula *international trade consultant*

FLORIDA

Boca Raton
Ricciardi, Salvatore *wholesale distribution executive*

Bradenton
Beall, Robert Matthews, II, *retail executive*
Rutstein, Stanley Harold *apparel retailing company executive*

Casselberry
Renee, Lisabeth Mary *small business owner, glass artist*

Clearwater
Maxwell, Richard Anthony *retail executive*
Turley, Stewart *retired retail company executiv*

Delray Beach
Holifield, Mark *retail executive*

Fort Lauderdale
Chung, Chia Mou (Charles Chung) *former Oriental art business owner*
Dwors, Robert F. *retail executive*
Loos, John Thompson *business owner*

Gainesville
McClellan, Richard Augustus *retired small business owner*

Jacksonville
Fisher, Michael D. *retail executive*
Lynch, Peter L. *retail executive*
McCook, Richard Paul *grocery chain financial executive*

Key Biscayne
de la Cruz, Carlos *wholesale distribution executive*

Lady Lake
McCully, Joanna Patricia *small business owne*

Lakeland
Barnett, Hoyt R. (Barney) *supermarket compa executive*

Merritt Island
Smith, David Edward *small business owner, aerospace engineer, aerospace scientist*

Miami
Chaplin, Harvey R. *wine and liquor wholesale executive*
Rawl, Arthur Julian (Lord of Cursons) *corpor director, retail executive, consultant, accountant, writer*
Richards-Vital, Claudia *small business owner, recreational facility executive*

Miramar
Catalano, Carl Philip *small business owner*

Naples
Ludwig, Richard Joseph *small business owner*

Orlando
Smetanka, Sally S. *small business owner*

Palm Beach Gardens
Runge, Donald Edward *food wholesale comp executive*

Palm Coast
Slatner, Thomas Allen *bookseller*

Pembroke Pines
Feldman, Jacqueline *retired small business owner*
Schaefer, Bonnie (E. Bonnie Schaefer) *retail executive*
Schaefer, Marla L. *retail executive*

Saint Augustine
Bishop, Claire DeArment *small business own retired librarian*

Saint Petersburg
Erman, Aila *small business owner*

San Antonio
Beverland, Jack Edwin *retired retail executive folk artist*

Sanford
Belanger, Devon Taylor *small business owner*

Sarasota
Meyer, B. Fred *small business executive, buil home and product designer*

Tampa
Davis, Blondell Gilliam *business manager, evangelist, artist, author, poet*
Keller, Shari Ann *small business owner*

University Park
Walker, Jane Stewart *small business owner, publishing executive, educator*

Winter Park
Alfond, Theodore B. *retired shoe company executive*
Kindlund, Newton Carlton *retail executive*

GEORGIA

Atlanta
Dayhoff, Diane *retail executive*
Judd, George R. *wholesale distribution executive*
Kalafut, George Wendell *retired distribution company executive, retired naval officer*
Macadam, Stephen E. *wholesale distribution executive*
Menear, Craig *retail executive*
Ridley, Clarence Haverty *retail executive*
Seegers, Harvey *retail executive*

Dunwoody
Maddox, Jerry Aven *retired catalog executive, writer*

Marietta
Short-Mayfield, Patricia Ahlene *business owner*

Norcross
Galfas, Timothy, II, *wholesale distribution executive*

Social Circle
Penland, John Thomas *retired import/export and development company executive*

Union City
Malcolm, Gloria J. *small business owner*

Valdosta
Halter, Henry James, Jr., (Diamond Jim Halter) *retail executive*

IDAHO

Boise
Herbert, Kathy J. *retail executive*
ong, William D. *grocery store executive*

ILLINOIS

Chicago
eli, Anne Tynion *retail executive*
ield, Marshall *retail executive*
oltz, Jay *small business owner*
eidemann, Lyle G. *retail executive*
ickell, Jake *internet retail executive, apparel designer, web site designer*
obins, Joel *import/export company executive*
omaino, Joseph Carmine *former retail executive, former postal inspector*
rablik, Edward Robert *import/export company executive*

Deerfield
ein, Jeffrey A. *retail executive*
iedl, George J. *retail executive*
udolphsen, William M. *retail executive*
aylor, Trent E. *retail executive*
agner, Mark A. *retail executive*
asson, Gregory D. *retail executive*

Des Plaines
ochnauer, Richard Wallis *wholesale distribution executive*

Glen Ellyn
aloun, John Charles *retired wholesale distribution executive*

Glencoe
ebenzahl, Kenneth *rare book and map dealer, author*

Hoffman Estates
rowley, William C. *retail executive*
ood, Mark *retail executive*
ewis, Aylwin B. *retail executive, former food service company executive*

Hoopeston
cks, Carol Ann *small business owner, educator*

Itasca
uncan, Sam K. *retail executive*

Lake Forest
oux, P. Ogden *distribution company executive*
yan, James T. *wholesale distribution executive*
asi-Diaz, Gloria *wholesale distribution executive*

Lombard
arnholt, Brandon K. *retail executive*

Melrose Park
oster, Carol Good *wholesale distribution executive*

Morton Grove
cKenna, Andrew James *wholesale distribution, printing company, sports association executive*

Northbrook
archol, Judith Marie *small business owner*

Oak Brook
odnik, David F. *retail company executive*

River Grove
tzsinger, Richard Mark *retail executive*
anton, Kathryn *retail executive*

Rock Island
Kirklin-Darif, Dianna Lynn *small business owner*

Saint Charles
LaHood, Julie Ann *small business owner*

Schaumburg
Richter, Glenn *retail executive*

INDIANA

Bicknell
Risley, Gregory Byron *retail executive, interior designer*

Columbus
MacAvery, Tristan Alexander (Tristan Black Bear) *small business owner, writer, actor*

Elkhart
Drexler, Rudy Matthew, Jr. *professional law enforcement dog trainer*

Fort Wayne
Cast, Anita Hursh *retired small business owner*
Curtis, Douglas Homer *small business owner*

Indianapolis
Cohen, Alan H. *retail executive*
Lazaran, Frank *former retail executive*

Jasper
Newman, Leonard Jay *retail jewel merchant, gemologist*

IOWA

Ankeny
Myers, Robert J. *retail executive*

Cedar Rapids
Baldwin, George Koehler *retired retail executive*

Des Moines
Barnhart, Dorothy May (Kohrs) *retired small business owner*

West Des Moines
Pearson, Ronald Dale *retail food stores corporation executive*

KANSAS

Kansas City
Baska, James Louis *wholesale grocery company executive*

Shawnee Mission
Moeller, Laura Lee *retired retail executive, library and information consultant*

Topeka
Cantrell, Duane L. *retail executive*
Porzig, Ullrich E. *retail executive*
Rubel, Matthew Evan *retail executive*

KENTUCKY

Eubank
Karriker, Danny Allen *small business owner, protective services official*

Louisville
Smith, Donald Ray *magazine dealer*

Owensboro
Thomas-Löwe, Christine L. *small business owner*

Winchester
Book, John Kenneth (Kenny) *retail store owner*

LOUISIANA

Baker
Baker, Otis McDowell *small business owner*

Coushatta
Wiggins, Mary Ann Wise *small business owner, educator*

Covington
Perez de la Mesa, Manuel Jose *swimming pool company executive*

Lafayette
Menutis, Ruth Ann *small business owner*

MAINE

Portland
Stanley, Eliot Hungerford *small business owner, writer, lawyer*

Sedgwick
Donnell, William Ray *small business owner, communications executive*

MARYLAND

Baltimore
Carper, Gertrude Esther *small business owner, real estate developer*
Erdman, Marie Mimmie *small business owner*
Hug, Richard Ernest *small business owner*
Schilling, Franklin Charles, Jr. *retail management professional*

Brandywine
Johnson, Madge Richards *business owner, fundraiser, consultant, recruiter*

Catonsville
Toomey, Sister Stephana *liturgical consultant, designer*

Germantown
Carper, Fern Gayle *small business owner, writer*

Kensington
Fasusi, Jimmy Adebayo *small business owner*

Laurel
Buffkins, LeRachel Harombe *small business owner*

Pikesville
Stein, Bernard Alvin *retail executive, consultant*

Potomac
Shapiro, Richard Gerald *retail executive, consultant*

Silver Spring
Miller, Kendra Danette *art services business owner*

MASSACHUSETTS

Auburn
Baker, David Arthur *retired small business owner, manufacturing executive*

Auburndale
Fowler, Frederick Victor, Jr. *import company executive*

Canton
Bentas, Lily Haseotes *retail executive*

Dudley
Van de Workeen, Priscilla Townsend *small business owner and executive*

Framingham
Barron, Arnold S. *retail executive*
Butka, Paul C. *retail executive*
Cammarata, Bernard *retail executive*
Campbell, Donald G. *retail executive*
Doody, Joseph G. *retail executive*
Feldberg, Sumner Lee *retired retail executive*
Flores, Greg *retail executive*
Gilbert, John F. *retail executive*
Herrman, Ernie *retail executive*
Lindenmeyer, Peter W. *retail executive*
Mahoney, John J. *office supply company executive*
Meyrowitz, Carol M. *retail executive*
Miles, Michael A., Jr. *retail executive*
Naylor, Jeffrey Gordon *retail executive*
Parneros, Demos *retail executive*
Rossi, Jerome R. *retail executive*
Sargent, Ronald L. *retail office and business products executive*
Sherr, Richard *retail executive*
Sweetenham, Paul *retail executive*
Tripathy, Nirmal K. *retail executive*
Vassalluzzo, Joseph S. *retail company executive*

Georgetown
deNapoli, Dyan *small business owner, educational consultant*

Holyoke
Radner, Sidney Hollis *retired retail executive*

Lexington
Chamberlain, David M. *retail executive*

Medfield
McQuillen, Jeremiah Joseph *distribution executive*

Natick
Zarkin, Herbert J. *wholesale distribution executive*

Pittsfield
Staley, Greg *retail executive*

Worcester
Candib, Murray A. *retail executive, consultant*

MICHIGAN

Ann Arbor
Jones, George L. *retail executive*
Pollock, Lawrence I. *retail executive, investment company executive*

Bad Axe
Sullivan, James Gerald *small business owner*

Bloomfield Hills
Robinson, Jack Albert *retail executive*

Grand Rapids
DeLapa, Judith Anne *business owner*
Meijer, Hank *retail company executive*
Sturken, Craig C. *retail executive*
Walsh, James *retail supermarket executive*

Harbor Beach
Falkenberg, Mary Elaine *small business owner*

Muskegon
McKitrick, James Thomas *retired retail executive*

Naubinway
Beaudoin, Robert Lawrence *small business owner*

Rothbury
Fischer, Dorothy Virginia *retired small business owner*

Royal Oak
Cain, Lawrence Edward *small business owner, language educator, researcher*

Southfield
Primo, Joan Erwina *retail and real estate consulting business owner*

Troy
Elder, Irma *retail executive*
Strome, Stephen *distribution company executive*

MINNESOTA

Eden Prairie
Jackson, Darren Richard *retail executive*
Jackson, Michael L. *wholesale distribution executive*
Knous, Pamela K. *wholesale distribution executive*
Noddle, Jeffrey *retail and food distribution executive*

Edina
Covington, Alec C. *retail executive*
Finkelstein, Phil *retail executive*
Froemming, Herbert Dean *retired retail executive*

Minneapolis
Ahlers, Linda L. *retail executive*
Dunn, Brian J. *retail executive*
Francis, Michael R. *retail executive*
Hale, James Thomas *retail executive, lawyer*
Paulu, Frances Brown *retired international center administrator*
Schulze, Richard M. *retail executive*
Scovanner, Douglas A. *retail executive*
Steinhafel, Gregg W. *retail executive*
Stephenson, Vivian M. *former retail executive*
Trestman, Frank D. *distribution company executive, director*
Ulrich, Robert J. *retail executive*
Walden, John *retail executive*

Richfield
Anderson, Bradbury H. *retail executive*
Ballard, Shari L. *retail executive*

Saint Paul
Nash, Nicholas David *retail executive*

Walker
Collins, Thomas William *caterer, consultant*

MISSOURI

Blue Springs
Lundy, Sadie Allen *small business owner*

Columbia
Drummond, William Kenneth *small business owner, mechanical engineer, consultant*

Cuba
Work, Bruce Van Syoc *small business owner, consultant*

Independence
Francis, Mary Frances Van Dyke *small business owner, real estate company executive, retired editor*

Kingsville
Stimac, John Anthony *small business owner, poet, cartoonist, inventor*

Saint Louis
Bridgewater, Bernard Adolphus, Jr. *retired retail executive*
Fingleton, Thomas D. *retail executive*
Schnuck, Craig D. *grocery store company executive*

NEBRASKA

Omaha
Cappellano, Rosemarie Zaccone *small business owner*

Sidney
Cabela, Richard N. *retail executive*
Highby, Dennis *retail executive*

NEVADA

Henderson
Fehr, Gregory Paris *marketing and distribution company executive*
Marcovitz, Leonard Edward *retail executive*

NEW HAMPSHIRE

Campton
Benton, Geraldine Ann *preschool owner, director*

Keene
Harris, Reuben *wholesale distribution executive*
Lichtenstein, Sally (Ali) Tucker *small business owner, writer, English and women's studies educator*

New Castle
Friese, George Ralph *retail executive*

Rochester
Coviello, Robert Frank *retail executive*

NEW JERSEY

Belle Mead
Dyer, Hugh Nelson III *management company owner*

Carteret
Standley, John T. *food market executive*

Edison
Kijowski, Rosemary Joan *small business owner, retired music educator*

Elizabeth
Gellert, George Geza *food importing company executive*

Freehold
Foster, Eric Harold, Jr. *retail executive*

Monroe Township
Zelin, Jerome *retired retail executive*

New Milford
Walsh, Joseph Michael *magazine distribution executive*

Park Ridge
Ciannella, Joeen Moore *small business owner*

Pennington
Donnelly, Gerard Kevin *marketing and retail executive*

Princeton
Bergman, Victoria Besterman *small business owner, consultant*
Campbell, Mildred Corum *business owner, nurse*
Hochschwender, Karl Albert *international trade and government relations consultant*

Union
Eisenberg, Warren *retail executive*
Feinstein, Leonard *retail executive*
Temares, Steven H. *retail executive*

Wayne
Arthur, Ray *retail executive*
Arthur, Raymond L. *retail toy and game company executive*
Babrowski, Claire Harbeck *retail executive*
Barbour, John *retail executive*
Brockett, Francesca L. *retail executive*
Creasey, F. Clay *retail executive*
Derby, Deborah *retail executive*
Kay, Christopher K. *retail executive, lawyer*
Markee, Richard L. *retail executive*
Storch, Gerald L. (Jerry Storch) *retail executive*

NEW YORK

Bellport
Regalmuto, Nancy Marie *small business owner, consultant*

Bronx
Lyons, Maxine Evadney *small business owner, poet*

Brooklyn
Moehring, Fred Adolf *wholesale distribution executive*

Ghent
Rao, Natti Sreerama *small business owner, consultant*

New York
Blum, Paul *retail executive*
Brizel, Michael Alan *retail executive, lawyer*
Brown, Andreas Le *retail executive, art gallery owner*
Catsimatidis, John Andreas *retail executive*
Dreiling, Richard W. *retail executive*
Drexler, Mickey (Millard Steven) *retail executive*
Farah, Roger N. *retail company executive*
Fernandez, James *retail products executive*
Frasch, Ronald L. *retail executive*
Holtz, Diane *retail executive*
Karp, Roberta Schuhalter *retail executive, lawyer*
Kowalski, Michael J. *retail products executive*
Laurie, Nancy Walton *retail executive*
Lazarus, Adrienne *retail executive*
Lombardi, Joseph J. *retail executive*
McComb, William L. *retail and former pharmaceutical executive*
Meads, Mindy *retail executive*
Mello, Dawn *retail executive*
Michelson, Gertrude Geraldine *retired retail executive*
Noce, Donna *retail executive*
Quint, Ira *retail executive*
Riggio, Leonard *book store company executive*
Riggio, Stephen *book store company executive*
Sadove, Stephen Irving *retail executive*
Schiller, Justin Galland *antiquarian bookseller, researcher, editor*
Schlussel, Joseph Lazar *business executive*
Sherman, Jeffrey Barry *retail executive*
Skinner, Robert C., Jr. *retail executive*
Spector, Anita Frohmann *retired buyer*
Stanton, Ronald P. *export company executive*
Toulantis, Marie J. *retail executive*
Washburn, Joan Thomas *small business owner*

Purchase
Johnson-Wolff, Christina Marie *retail executive*

Riverhead
Carpenter, Angie M. *former small business owner, editor, county legislator*

Schenectady
Myers, Darlene Marie *dance studio owner, choreographer*

NORTH CAROLINA

Black Mountain
Ingle, Robert P. *retail executive*

Charlotte
Gambrell, Sarah Belk *retail executive*
Kelly, R. James *retail executive*
Levine, Howard R. *retail executive*
Smith, Kenneth T. *retail executive*

Durham
Lieberman, Rochelle Phyllis *small business owner*

Fayetteville
Shaffer, Denny Richard *small business owner*

Greensboro
Goulder, Gerald Polster *retail executive, management consultant, lawyer*

Highlands
Shaffner, Randolph Preston *shop owner, educator, writer, publisher*

Mooresville
Black, Kenneth W., Jr. *retail executive*

Rocky Mount
Wordsworth, Jerry L. *wholesale distribution executive*

Salisbury
Candler, Faxon David *small business owner*

Wilkesboro
Brown, Michael K. *retail executive*
Canter, Charles W. (Nick) *retail executive*

Winston Salem
Strickland, Robert Louis *retired retail executive*

OHIO

Avon Lake
Parke, M(argaret) Jean *retired business owner, editor*

Beachwood
Fufuka, Natika Njeri Yaa *retail executive*

Bellevue
Davenport, Thomas Herbert *small business owner*

Chesterland
Aster, Ruth Marie Rhydderch *business owner*
Wood, Kenneth Anderson *small business owner, display designer*

Cincinnati
Cody, Thomas Gerald *retail executive, lawyer*
Cole, Thomas L. *retail executive*
Grove, Janet E. *retail executive*
Hodge, Robert Joseph *retail executive*
Hoguet, Karen M. *retail executive*
Kronick, Susan D. *retail executive*
Lundgren, Terry J. *retail company executive*
McGeorge, Don W. *retail executive*
Zimmerman, James M. *retail company executive*

Cleveland
Crosby, Fred McClellan *retail executive*

Columbus
Burgdoerfer, Stuart *retail executive*
Fishman, Steven S. *retail executive*
Potter, Michael J. *retail stores executive*
Redgrave, Martyn Robert *retail executive*
Schottenstein, Jay L. *retail executive*
Turney, Sharon Jester *retail executive*
Wexner, Leslie Herbert *retail executive*
Wilansky, Heywood *retail executive*

Dayton
Petrick, Joseph Anthony *small business owner, management consultant, educator*

Grove City
Rudy, Monica Elaine *small business owner, music educator*

Hudson
Webb, Darrell D. *retail executive*

New Albany
Schlesinger, Leonard Arthur *retail executive*
Stevens, Kenneth T. *retail executive*

Newark
Black, Boyd Carson *small business owner*

Pickerington
Callander, Kay Eileen Paisley *business owner, retired education educator, writer*

Reynoldsburg
Neal, Diane L. *retail executive*

Shandon
Wilson, James Ray *small business owner*

Toledo
Grundish, Lee Anne *small business owner, writer*

Youngstown
Catoline-Ackerman, Pauline Dessie *small business owner*

OKLAHOMA

Oklahoma City
Peace, H. W., II, *small business owner, retired oil industry executive*

Tulsa
Cadieux, Chester *retail executive*
Carter, Terry *retail executive*

OREGON

Beaverton
Shimojima, Chris *retail executive*

Forest Grove
Fuiten, Helen Lorraine *small business owner*

Salem
Robertson, Marian Ella (Marian Ella Hall) *small business owner, handwriting analyst*

Tualatin
Peters, Robert Wayne *small business owner*

PENNSYLVANIA

Altoona
Sheetz, Stanton R. *grocery retail executive*

Berwyn
Fry, Clarence Herbert *retired retail executive*

Camp Hill
Beasley, Ed *retail executive*
Cardinale, Gerald P. *retail executive*
Davis, Don P. *retail executive*
de Bruin, Jerry Mark *retail executive*
Donley, Douglas E. *retail executive*
Easley, Robert J. *retail executive*
Hall, Christopher S. *retail executive*
Keough, Philip J., IV, *retail executive*
Learish, John *retail executive*
Lester, Wilson A., Jr. *retail executive*
Lovett, Keith W. *retail executive*
Mastrian, James P. *retail executive*
McCarty, Todd *retail executive*
Miller, Robert G. *drug store chain company executive*
Panzer, Mark *retail executive*
Rugen, Karen *retail executive, corporate communications specialist*
Sammons, Mary F. *retail executive*
Shirtliff, Bryan *retail executive*
Tansky, Murray *retail executive*
Todd, Murray *retail executive*
Twomey, Kevin *retail executive*

Eighty Four
Hardy, Joseph A., Sr. *wholesale distribution executive*

Erie
Hagen, Thomas Bailey *business owner, former state official, retired insurance company executive*

Johnstown
Borkow, Mary P. *small business owner, consultant*

Mercer
DaCosta, Caroline Lee *small business owner*

Philadelphia
Galván, Gary *small business owner, educator*

Pittsburgh
Stack, Edward W. *retail executive*

Shiremanstown
Nesbit, William Terry *small business owner, consultant*

Silverdale
Carney, Shannon Maureen *small business owner, educator*

Washington
Erdner, Jon W. *small business owner, securities trader*

Wayne
Ward, Keca B. *small business owner, consultant*

West Chester
Ballbach, John M. *wholesale distribution executive*

Williamsport
Largen, Joseph *retail executive, purchasing agent*

Wormleysburg
Grass, Alexander *retail executive*

York
Bergren, Byron L. *retail executive*

RHODE ISLAND

Woonsocket
Bodine, Chris W. *retail executive*
Ferdinandi, V. Michael *retail executive*
Merlo, Larry J. *retail executive*
Rickard, David B. *retail executive*

SOUTH CAROLINA

Hilton Head Island
Davis, Mary Martha (Marty Davis) *small business owner, consultant*

Yemassee
Olendorf, William Carr, Jr. *small business owner*

TENNESSEE

Gallatin
Ellis, Joseph Newlin *retired wholesale distribution executive*

Goodlettsville
Beré, David L. *retail executive*
Perdue, David A., Jr. *retail executive*

Memphis
Giles, William (Bill) T. *retail executive*
Hayes, Michael J. *retail executive*
Wright Carrier, J. T. *business owner*

Nashville
Zibart, Michael Alan *wholesale book company executive*

Old Hickory
Reid, Donna Joyce *small business owner*

TEXAS

Athens
Geddie, Thomas Edwin *retired small business owner*

Austin
Wilson, Margaret Scarbrough *retail executive*

Bastrop
Reaves, Melvin Junior *retired small business owner*

Beaumont
Alter, Nelson Tobias *retail executive, wholesale distribution executive*

Corpus Christi
Finley, George Alvin III *wholesale executive, o[il] industry executive*

Dallas
Augur, Marilyn Hussman *distribution executive*
Haggar, J. M. III *retail executive*
Hegi, Frederick B., Jr. *wholesale distribution executive*
Katz, Karen W. *retail executive*
Moneypenny, Edward William *retail executive*
Tansky, Burton M. *department store executive*
Zine, Larry Joseph *film rental company executi[ve]*

El Paso
Saul, Charlie *small business owner, investor*

Fort Worth
Day, Julian C. *retail executive*
Roach, John Vinson, II, *retail company executi[ve]*
Smith, Alexander W. *retail executive*
West, Sylvia Wandell *small business owner, director, educator, researcher*

Gainesville
Brooks, Jerry Robert *small business owner*

Horseshoe Bay
Simpson, H. Richard (Dick Simpson) *retail buyer*

Houston
Levit, Max *wholesale distribution and food service executive*
Nesbitt, DeEtte DuPree *small business owner, investor*
Woodhouse, John Frederick *retired wholesale distribution executive*

Irving
Burton, Betsy (Mary Elizabeth) *retail executive*
Rouleau, R. Michael *retail executive*
Wyly, Samuel E. *retail executive*

Kingwood
Spartz, Alice Anne Lenore *retired retail executive*

Longview
McKinley, Jimmie Joe *small business owner*

Plano
Cavanaugh, Robert B. *department store executive*
Neppl, Walter Joseph *retired retail executive*

San Antonio
Condrill, Jo Ellaresa *freelance/self-employed small business owner, writer, consultant*
Jary, Mary Canales *business owner*
Williams, Docia Schultz *small business owner*

Seabrook
Spears, James Grady *small business owner*

Snyder
Gray, Donna Lea *small business owner*

Tyler
Brookshire, Bruce G. *retail grocery store executive*
Edwards, D. M. *retail, wholesale distribution and real estate company executive*

Waxahachie
Johnson, Ronald Kay *retail company executive*

UTAH

Salt Lake City
Fields, Debbi (Debra Fields Rose) *cookie franchise executive*

RMONT

chester
ton, Lorilee Ann *small business owner, countant*

by
, Harris *retired small business owner*

gennes
t, Edwin Randolph *retail executive, anufacturing executive*

RGINIA

stow
ock, Simon *retail executive*

arlottesville
chfield, William Gayle, Jr. *retail executive*

esapeake
ck, Macon F., Sr. *retail company executive*
ck, Macon F., Jr. *retail company executive*
er, Robert *retail executive*

eburn
kins, Alisa Dawn *small business owner*

rfax
h, Arthur James (Jay Pugh) *retired retail xecutive*

rfax Station
zublewski, Wendy Sue *small business owner, usician, freelance/self-employed writer*

ls Church
rison, H. Robert *small business owner, hotographer, retired municipal official*

Lean
demark, Robert Goodyear *retired retail xecutive*

rfolk
Venny, Lillian Nickell *trophy company xecutive*

coquan
necek, Albert Duncan, Jr. *retail executive, nvestment banker, management consultant*

rcellville
arples, Winston Singleton *automobile importer nd distributor*

chmond
ini, Jane Sloan *wholesale distribution xecutive*
s, Fiona P. *retail executive*
in, Philip J. *retail executive*
Corey, William E., Jr. *retail executive*
oonover, Philip J. *retail executive*
edfald, Peter C. *retail executive*

lem
nd, Edward Cabell *retail executive*

enna
wards, Phillip Milton *retired import/export ompany executive*

lliamsburg
athen, Charles Edward, Jr. *retired retail executive, management consultant*

ASHINGTON

aquah
atman, Jeffrey H. *wholesale distribution executive*
Cerchio, Richard D. *wholesale distribution executive*
lanti, Richard A. *wholesale business executive*
egal, James D. *wholesale distribution executive*

dmond
ke, Neil S. *retail executive*

attle
dge, Herbert Marvin *retail executive*
rmèzano, Keith *small business advisor, arbitrator, writer, web site designer*
ppel, Michael G. *retail executive*
ale, Olivia Mason *small business owner, import marketing executive*
oya, Cynthia Ann *small business owner, librarian*
rdstrom, Blake W. *retail executive*

verdale
lcomb, Mary Nelson *small business owner*

okane
ighton, Jack Richard *retired small business owner, education educator*
nes, Randy Dwain *retail executive*

coma
antz, Dale Nelson *automobile import processing company executive*

ncouver
ott, Gary LeRoy *small business owner, photographer*

kima
wland, Ruth Laura *small business owner*

WEST VIRGINIA

Martinsburg
Ayers, Anne Louise *small business owner, consultant, counselor*

WISCONSIN

Beloit
Hendricks, Kenneth *wholesale distribution executive*

Bowler
Bartholomaus, Brett William *small business owner*

Eau Claire
Menard, John R., Jr. *home improvement retail executive*

Menomonee Falls
Bonning, Kenneth *retail executive*
Boyle, Jack H. *retail executive*
Brennan, Donald A. *retail executive*
Eskenasi, Peggy *retail executive*
Gardner, Julie *retail executive*
Jeffries, Telvin *retail executive*
Kingsbury, Tom (Thomas A. Kingsbury) *retail executive*
Lesko, John J. *retail executive*
Mansell, Kevin B. *retail executive*
McDonald, Wesley S. *retail executive*
Montgomery, Larry (R. Lawrence Montgomery) *retail executive*
Nordeen, Jon K. *retail executive*
Worthington, John M. *retail executive*

Milwaukee
Mariano, Robert A. *retail executive*

WYOMING

Jackson
Law, Clarene Alta *small business owner, retired state legislator*

CANADA

MANITOBA

Winnipeg
Cohen, Albert Diamond *retail executive*

ONTARIO

Toronto
Verschuren, Annette *retail executive*

CHINA

Shanghai
Chueh, Chun Fei *import/export company executive*

ENGLAND

London
Habgood, Anthony John *wholesale distribution executive*

SWEDEN

Stockholm
van den Bosch, Margareta *apparel company executive*

ADDRESS UNPUBLISHED

Baker, Edward Kevin *retail executive*
Banks, Charles Augustus III *distribution executive*
Barth, David Keck *retired wholesale distribution executive, consultant*
Beavers, Karen Marjorie *small business owner*
Blum, Gerald Henry *retired retail executive*
Busch, Joyce Ida *small business owner*
Carlson-Rukavina, Patricia Ann *small business owner*
Carter-Miller, Jocelyn *former retail executive*
Castagna, Vanessa J. *retail executive*
Castro, Teresa Jacira *small business owner*
Charron, Paul Richard *retail executive*
Chevalier, Paul Edward *retired retail executive, lawyer*
Colgate, Stephen *small business owner*
Connolly, Violette M. *small business owner*
Cope, Kenneth Wayne *retail executive*
Crandall, Albert Earl *retail executive, accountant, entrepreneur*
Day, John Denton *small business owner, animal breeder*
DeBerry, Donna *retail executive*
Degn, Douglas J. *retired retail executive*
DeVivo, Ange *retired small business owner*
Donley, Russell Lee III *small business owner, former state legislator*
Dufour, Jack Edward *small business owner, retired special education educator*
Dusenbury, Ruth Ellen Cole *business owner*
Edwards, Patrick Ross *retail executive, lawyer, management consultant*
Edwards, Priscilla Ann *small business owner*
Ettore, Joseph R. *retired discount department store chain executive*
Eyler, John H., Jr. *retail toy and game company executive*
Farr, Ivanne Estelle *small business owner, consultant, artist, sculptor*
Fields, Douglas Philip, Sr. *building supply wholesale company executive*
Finnigan, Robert Emmet *retired small business owner*
Follit, Evelyn V. *former retail executive*
Gamroth, Arthur Paul *small business owner*
Girouard, Marvin J. *retired retail executive*
Goldner, Sheldon Herbert *retired import/export company executive*
Goldstein, Norman Ray *international trading company executive, consultant*
Gozon, Richard C. *retired paper distribution executive*
Grantham, Joyce Carol *small business owner, music educator*
Greenstein, Merle Edward *import/export company executive*
Hamed, Martha Ellen *retired small business owner*
Hirsch, Larry Joseph *retired retail executive, lawyer*
Holben, Sharie Cecilia *small business owner*
Houston, Brian Christopher Michael *small business owner*
Jenkins, Charles H., Jr. *retail company executive*
Jin, Byoungho *retail executive, educator*
Jourdan, Toni Christina *small business owner, actress, writer*
Keck, Leonhard *retired small business owner*
Kipper, Barbara Levy *wholesale distribution executive*
Kirby, Odell *retired small business owner, newswriter, writer*
Kogut, John Anthony *wholesale distribution executive*
Kuehni, Norman Arnold *small business owner*
Lang, William Charles *retail executive*
Lifson, Kalman Alan *retired retail and bank executive, portfolio manager*
Lipsey, Joseph, Jr. *wholesale distribution executive*
Masten, Jacqueline Gwendolyn *small business owner*
Matthews, Norman Stuart *retail executive*
McConnell, Jack Baylor *retired corporate executive, physician*
McDougall, Ronald Alexander *restaurant executive*
Meek, Forrest Burns *retired trading company executive*
Mench, John William *retail executive, electrical engineer*
Metz, Steven William *small business owner*
Miller, Jack Conway *small business owner, landscape company executive*
Milstein, Monroe Gary *retail executive*
Ming, Jenny J. *former retail executive*
Monaghan, Craig Thomas *former retail and automotive executive*
Nemiroff, Maxine Celia *small business owner, art historian*
Nicolas, Kenneth Lee *import/export company executive*
Nishimura, Joseph Yo *retired retail executive, accountant*
Orenstein, Fran M. *small business owner, writer*
Oxnam, Philip Linton *small business owner*
Paterson, Robert E. *retail executive*
Peach, Robert Westly *retired small business owner, engineer*
Phillips, Kathleen Gay *small business owner*
Raskin, Michael A. *retail executive, director*
Raymond, Ural Wayne *retired retail executive*
Reece, Karyn Lynn *business owner, consultant*
Ritchey, Samuel Donley, Jr. *retired retail executive*
Roberts, Patricia Lee *small business owner, consultant*
Rodbell, Clyde Armand *retired distribution executive*
Rodman, Sue A. *wholesale company executive, artist, writer*
Rogaczewski, Sherrie Reece *small business owner, singer*
Ross, Molly Owings *small business owner, sculptor*
Rowland, Allen R. *former retail executive*
Ruland, Mildred Ardelia *retired retail executive, retail buyer*
Shapiro, Marc Robert *retail executive*
Spitzer, Matthew Lawrence *retired retail store executive*
Stettner, Jerald Walter *retired retail executive*
Stronach, Belinda *former retail executive*
Taylor, Carolyn Roberts *small business owner, chef*
Terry, Carole Cosgrove *retired small business owner, historian, researcher*
Thompson, Mary Koleta *small business owner, not-for-profit developer*
Turner, Natalie A. *retired consultant*
Vernon, Carl Atlee, Jr. *retired wholesale food distributor executive*
Wagner, Cheri J. *business owner*
Wallpher, Luis Antonio *small business owner, painter, writer*
Weiss, Michael Allen *retired retail executive*
Wessling, Gregory Jay *retail executive*
West, Catherine G. *former retail executive*
Willingham, Mary Maxine *fashion retailer*
Zaktsman, Yona R. *business owner*

INDUSTRY: TRANSPORTATION

UNITED STATES

ALABAMA

Birmingham
Campbell, Charles Alton *transportation executive*
Haworth, Michael Elliott, Jr. *aerospace company executive*

Gulf Shores
Wallace, John Loys *retired aviation services executive*

ALASKA

Anchorage
Shively, John Terry *cruise line executive*
Sullivan, George Murray *transportation executive, consultant, retired mayor*
Williams, Eleanor Joyce *retired government air traffic control specialist*

ARIZONA

Goodyear
Borton, George Robert *retired airline captain*

Grand Canyon
Bryant, Leland Marshal *business and nonprofit executive*

Phoenix
Gillette, Robert J. *aerospace transportation executive*
Moyes, Jerry C. *transportation executive*

Prescott
Waldock, William David *aerospace transportation executive, educator*

Tempe
Crellin, Alan W. *air transportation executive*
Kerr, Derek J. *transportation executive*
Kirby, J. Scott *air transportation executive*
Parker, Doug (William Douglas Parker, W. Douglas Parker) *air transportation executive*

Tucson
Carroll, Dennis Jerome *aerospace transportation executive*
Mercker, Mary Alice *aviation school administrator*

ARKANSAS

Bella Vista
Pogue, William Reid *retired astronaut, foundation administrator, aerospace scientist, consultant*

Fort Smith
Davidson, Robert A. *trucking executive*
Young, Robert A. III *freight systems executive*

Lowell
Garrison, Wayne *transportation executive*
Thompson, Kirk *transportation executive*

CALIFORNIA

Concord
Uremovich, Michael Elliot *transportation company executive*

Dana Point
Wolf, Karl Everett *aerospace transportation executive, communications executive*

Edwards
Brand, Vance Devoe *astronaut, director*

El Segundo
Freeland, Pete *aerospace transportation executive, consultant*
McCarty, Shirley Carolyn *retired aerospace executive*
Musk, Elon *aerospace transportation executive*

Fremont
Smith, Bernald Stephen *retired pilot*

Hermosa Beach
Kokalj, James Edward *retired aerospace administrator*

Huntington Beach
Burson, Thomas Daniel *retired aerospace executive*

Irvine
Crowley, Daniel Francis, Jr. *transportation and logistics executive*

La Jolla
Drake, Hudson Billings *aerospace and electronics executive*

La Mesa
Hansen, Grant Lewis *retired air transportation executive*

La Palma
Knowles, Marie L. *transportation executive*

Long Beach
Myers, John Wescott *air transportation executive*

Los Altos
Bergrun, Norman Riley *aerospace executive*

Los Angeles
Bruce, William A. *airport executive*
Bush, Wesley G. *aerospace transportation executive*
Gasich, Welko Elton *retired aerospace defense executive, management consultant*
Ingram, Theodore Francis *transportation executive*
Lovett, Wayne J. *air transportation executive, lawyer*
Mager, Artur *retired aerospace executive*
Mall, William John, Jr. *aerospace transportation executive, retired military officer*
Michel, Gregg L. *cruise line executive*
Myers, Albert F. *aerospace executive*
Palmer, James F. *aerospace transportation executive*
Sugar, Ronald D. *aerospace transportation company executive*

Malibu
Ensign, Richard Papworth *transportation executive*

Marina Del Rey
Gregg, Lucius Perry, Jr. *aerospace executive*

Mckinleyville
Stuart, Henry Lee *retired rail transportation executive*

Mojave
Binnie, Brian *pilot, transportation executive*
Melvill, Michael W. *aircraft company executive, experimental test pilot*

Newbury Park
Lindsey, Joanne M. *flight attendant, poet*

Oakland
Andrasick, James Stephen *transportation executive*
Haskell, Arthur Jacob *retired water transportation executive*

Oceanside
Miller, Donald Eugene *retired air traffic controller*

Palm Desert
Unterman, Eugene Rex *aviation sales and consulting company executive*

Palos Verdes Peninsula
Slusser, Robert Wyman *aerospace transportation executive*

Ramona
Hoffman, Wayne Melvin *retired airline official*

Redlands
Skomal, Edward Nelson *retired aerospace transportation executive, electromagnetic environments consultant*

Redwood City
Mullooly, Michael Sean *pilot*

Richmond
Shladover, Steven Elliot *transportation research professional*

Sacramento
Acree, G. Hardy *airport executive*

San Diego
Butterfield, Alexander Porter *air transportation executive, former federal official*
Mc Kinnon, Clinton Dan *aerospace transportation executive*
Reading, James Edward *transportation executive*

San Francisco
Brice, Charles Steven *airline executive*
Foret, Mickey Phillip *retired air transportation executive*
Royer, Kathleen Rose *pilot*

San Jose
Stapleton, Beverly Cooper *aerospace executive*

San Luis Obispo
Williams, David Alexander *retired chief pilot*

San Mateo
Pileggi, Jennifer Wendy *transportation services executive*
Stotlar, Douglas W. *transportation executive*

Santa Monica
Roney, Robert Kenneth *retired aerospace transportation executive*

Saratoga
Reagan, Joseph Bernard *retired aerospace executive, management consultant*

Simi Valley
Eberhard-Neveaux, Christine *aviation executive, dispute resolution executive*

Stockton
Biddle, Donald Ray *aerospace transportation executive*

Torrance
Brown, Adriane M. *aerospace transportation executive*
Esmond, Donald V. *transportation executive*

Ventura
Downs, Floella McIntyre *retired ferry pilot, instructor, flight examiner*

COLORADO

Colorado Springs
White, Gayle Clay *aerospace company executive*

Denver
McMorris, Jerry *transportation company, sports team executive*
Menke, Sean E. *air transportation executive*

Littleton
Kleinknecht, Kenneth Samuel *retired air transportation executive*

CONNECTICUT

Groton
Leeds, Robin Leigh *transportation executive*

Hartford
Page, Stephen Franklin *aerospace transportation executive*

Norwalk
Smith, Gordon Eugene *pilot*

Stamford
Barker, James Rex *water transportation executive, director*

DISTRICT OF COLUMBIA

Washington
Altschul, Alfred Samuel *airline executive*
Campbell, William Henry, Jr. *rail transportation executive, former federal agency administrator*
Carmody, Carol Jones *transportation executive, former federal agency administrator*
Chapman, Thomas B. *air transportation executive*
Cox, Rebecca Gernhardt *air transportation executive*
Donovan, George Joseph *transportation executive, consultant*
Downs, Thomas Michael (Tom Downs) *transportation executive*
Howell, Mary L. *multi-industry company executive*
Kummant, Alexander K. *rail transportation executive*
Peck, Suzanne J. *transit authority administrator*
Willis, Kevin *airport administrator*

FLORIDA

Boca Raton
Garelick, Martin *retired transportation executive*
Iacobucci, Edward E. *air transportation and former software company executive*

Jacksonville
Gerkens, Henry H. *trucking executive*
Kneller, Michael K. *transportation services executive*
Ward, Michael J. *rail transportation executive*

Miami
Cento, Juan N. *delivery service executive*
Fain, Richard David *cruise line executive*
Goldstein, Adam M. *cruise line executive*
Swienton, Gregory T. *transportation company executive*

Naples
Myers, Robert Jay *retired aerospace transportation executive*

Orlando
Kennedy, James W. *aerospace transportation executive*
Leonard, Joseph B. *airline company executive*

Plantation
Fellows, John *delivery service executive*

Ponte Vedra Beach
Hamilton, William Berry, Jr. *retired transportation executive*

Sanibel
Hasselman, Richard B. *retired rail transportation executive*

Satellite Beach
Loney, Mary Rose *former airport administrator, aviation industry consultant*

Vero Beach
Ingwersen, Martin Lewis *water transportation executive*

Weeki Wachee
Luffsey, Walter Stith *air transportation executive, consultant*

GEORGIA

Atlanta
Abney, David P. *delivery service executive*
Anderson, Richard H. *air transportation executive*
Barnes, David A. *delivery service executive*
Bastian, Edward H. *air transportation executive*
Beystehner, John J. *transportation executive*
Bridges, Shirley Walton *air transportation executive*
Campbell, Michael H. *air transportation executive*
Davis, D. Scott *delivery service executive*
DeCosta, Benjamin R. *airport executive*
Eskew, Michael L. *package distribution company executive*
Gangwal, Rakesh *air transportation executive*
Gershenhorn, Alan *delivery service executive*
Hauenstein, Glen W. *air transportation executive*
Hill, Allen Edward *delivery service executive*
Kolshak, Joseph C. *air transportation executive*
Kuehn, Kurt P. *delivery service executive*
Loewy, Robert Gustav *aerospace executive, engineering educator*
Macenczak, Lee Andrew *air transportation executive*
McDevitt, John *delivery service executive*
Owens, Christine M. *delivery service executive*
Stent, Terry *pilot, art collector*
Stoffel, Robert E. *delivery service executive*
Thoms, Jannet *rapid transit executive*
Winestock, James F. *delivery service executive*

Decatur
Duffy, Thomas M. *transportation services executive, lawyer*

Marietta
Clarkson, Lawrence William *air transportation executive*

Roswell
Dolan, Dennis Joseph *pilot, lawyer*

Savannah
Lombardo, Joseph T. *aerospace transportation executive*

HAWAII

Honolulu
Doane, W. Allen *water transportation executive*

Mountain View
Peterson, Gerald Joseph *aerospace executive, consultant*

IDAHO

Boise
Ilett, Frank, Jr. *trucking executive, educator*

ILLINOIS

Argonne
Saricks, Christopher Lee *retired transportation analyst*

Arlington Heights
Hudson, Ronald Morgan *aviation planner*

Chicago
al-Chalabi, Suhail Abdul-Jabbar *transport economist, consultant*
Andolino, Rosemarie S. *airport terminal executive*
Apelbaum, Phyllis L. *delivery messenger service executive*
Bell, James A. *aerospace transportation executive*
Brown, Carole L. *transportation executive*
Burkhardt, Edward Arnold *rail transportation executive*
Doris, Carole R. *rail transportation executive*
Fischbach, Charles Peter *rail transportation executive, consultant, lawyer, arbitrator, mediator*
Foland, Jeffrey T. *air transportation sales executive*
Hill, Shepard W. *air transportation executive*
Koellner, Laurette *aerospace transportation executive*
Lower, Joseph *air transportation executive*
Luttig, J(ohn) Michael (John Michael Luttig) *aerospace transportation executive, former federal judge*
McNerney, James, Jr., (W. James McNerney) *aerospace transportation executive, former manufacturing executive*
Nord, Henry J. *transportation executive*
Stephens, Richard *aerospace transportation executive*
Tilton, Glenn F. *air transportation executive*

Downers Grove
Yeager, David P. *transportation executive*

Elk Grove Village
Brace, Frederic F. (Jake Brace) *air transportation executive*
Szadokierski, Cindy *air transportation executive*

Lake Forest
Krasnewich, Kathryn *water transportation executive*

Marion
Crane, Hugh Wingate *railroad executive*

Naperville
Benson, Kevin E. *transportation executive*
Stangl, Peter E. *transportation executive*

Oak Brook
Duerinck, Louis T. *retired rail transportation executive, lawyer*

Park Ridge
Carr, Gilbert Randle *retired railroad executive*

Warrenville
Ustian, Daniel C. *trucking executive*

Wood Dale
Goodwin, James E. *retired air transportation executive*

INDIANA

Fort Wayne
Sperone, Kenneth J. *transportation executive*

Indianapolis
Welch, Cody M. *transportation and warehousin[g] executive*
Wensits, David L. *aerospace transportation executive*

Noblesville
Morrison, Joseph Young *transportation executive, consultant*

KANSAS

Overland Park
Barger, Donald Gordon, Jr. *freight company executive*
Zollars, William D. *freight company executive*

Wichita
Meyer, Russell William, Jr. *air transportation executive*

KENTUCKY

Louisville
Hayes, William Meredith *pilot, retired military officer*

LOUISIANA

New Orleans
Johnson, Peter Forbes *transportation executive, business owner*

MARYLAND

Baltimore
Glassman, Jon David *aerospace executive*

Bethesda
Coutts, Robert B. *aerospace transportation executive*
Heath, Ralph D. *aerospace transportation executive*
Kubasik, Christopher E. *aerospace transportation executive*
Maguire, Joanne M. *aerospace transportation executive*
O'Neill, Malcolm R. *aerospace executive*
Tanner, Bruce L. *aerospace transportation executive*
Tourino, Ralph Gene *aerospace transportation executive*
Webber, Derek *aerospace executive, space tourism entrepreneur*

Owings Mills
Colussy, Dan Alfred *aviation executive*

Potomac
Fthenakis, Emanuel John *aerospace transportation and communications executiv[e]*

MASSACHUSETTS

Boston
Klotz, Charles Rodger *water transportation an[d] investment company executive*

Brookline
Frankel, Ernst Gabriel *shipping and aviation business executive, educator*

Cambridge
John, Richard Rodda *transportation executive*

Cotuit
Ballou, Kenneth Walter *retired business executive, dean*

East Boston
Coy, Craig P. *airport terminal executive*

Falmouth
McInnes, Donald Gordon *rail transportation executive*

Waltham
Caine, Franklyn A. *aerospace transportation executive*

MICHIGAN

Ann Arbor
Bagian, James Philip *former astronaut, public health service officer, medical educator*
Drake, John Warren *aviation consultant*
Yamashina, Tadashi (George) *transportation executive*

Detroit
Newman, Andrea Fischer *air transportation executive*

Grand Rapids
Auwers, Stanley John *motor carrier executive*

lling Heights
l, Melvin L. *retired railroad conductor, all business owner*

erford
Hall, Karl W. *air transportation executive, wyer*

NNESOTA

an
r, Kris *air transportation executive*
er, Michael J. *air transportation executive*
en, Neal S. *air transportation executive*
s, David M. *air transportation executive*
del, Jim *air transportation executive*
in, J. Timothy *air transportation executive*
n, Philip C. *air transportation executive*
ek, Crystal *air transportation executive*
er, Mary Carroll *air transportation executive*
hews, Daniel B. *air transportation executive*
ey, Timothy J. *air transportation executive*
erts, Andrew C. *air transportation executive*
nland, Douglas M. *air transportation ecutive*
e, Theresa *air transportation executive*

en Prairie
bloom, Chad M. *transportation executive*
noff, John P. *trucking executive*

nneapolis
ber, Donald Victor *retired transportation and gistics educator, consultant*
op, Donald William *air transportation xecutive*
on, James Richard *retired transportation xecutive*

rth Oaks
le, Donald Edward *retired rail transportation xecutive, lawyer*

SSOURI

nton
er, Scott *transportation services executive*
ler, Gerald P. *transportation executive*

nsas City
sden, Eleanor Marguerite *retired airline ompensation executive, consultant*
erty, Michael R. *rail transportation executive*

nt Louis
augh, James F. *aerospace transportation xecutive*
ff, George Stephen *aerospace transportation xecutive*
ggs, Leonard LeRoy, Jr. *air transportation xecutive, consultant*
Donnell, Sanford Noyes *air transportation xecutive*

BRASKA

naha
fy, Dennis J. *rail transportation executive*
ele, Charles R. *rail transportation executive*
ght, Robert M., Jr. *rail transportation xecutive*
aleski, John J. *rail transportation executive*
aefer, Barbara W. *rail transportation xecutive*
they, Donald Leon *airport authority director*
nison, Lynden *rail transportation executive*
ner, Robert W. *rail transportation executive*
rner, Clarence L. *transportation executive*
rner, Gregory L. *transportation executive*
ng, James R. *rail transportation executive*

EVADA

s Vegas
lker, Randall H. *air transportation executive*

llis Afb
lachowski, Nicole *pilot*

no
oen, Edward Joseph *transportation and nsurance companies executive*

arks
bitz, Eugene Leonard *aerospace company executive*

EW JERSEY

erry Hill
oden, Linda R. *aerospace transportation executive*
sor, Randolph Richardson *transportation consultant*

lgewater
nan, Armand *transportation executive, professional hockey club executive, lawyer*

emington
ttler, Carl Frederick *airline executive*

oonachie
ltschi, Albert Lee *air transportation executive*

orristown
cott, John Whiting *air transportation executive*

ount Laurel
tory, Ronald Louis *rail transportation executive*

Mullica Hill
Rose, Carol Ann *retired air transportation executive*

Newark
Baer, Susan M. *airport executive*
Sarles, Richard R. *rail transportation executive*

Pennington
Kelly, Quentin Thorn *water and power company executive, writer*

Roseland
Sugahara, Byron Masahiko *transportation executive*

Union
White, Robert Leslie Gordon, Jr. *aerospace transportation executive*

Wharton
Krosser, Howard S. *aerospace transportation executive*

Woodbridge
Santulli, Richard T. *air transportation executive*

NEW MEXICO

Albuquerque
Figueroa, Francisco Armando *aerospace transportation executive, accountant*
Raburn, Vern L. *air transportation executive, former internet company executive*
Weh, Allen Edward *aviation executive*

NEW YORK

Albany
Joyce, William George, Jr. *transportation executive*

Bethpage
Baglio, Vincent Paul *aerospace transportation executive*

Centerport
Trotta, Ric Charles *aerospace transportation executive, consultant*

Cooperstown
Rich, Walter George *railroad transportation executive*

Flushing
Kroeppel, Warren *airport terminal executive*

Forest Hills
Barger, David J. *air transportation executive*
Battaglia, Alex *air transportation executive*
Chew, Russell G. (Russ) *air transportation executive*
Neeleman, David G. *air transportation executive*

Greenport
Jackson, Richard Montgomery *air transportation executive*

Jamestown
Walker, Timothy Craig *transportation executive*

New York
Apostolakis, James John *shipping company and pharmaceutical executive*
Armstrong, Neil A. *former astronaut*
Chao, James Si-Cheng *maritime executive*
Fugazy, William Denis *transportation company executive*
Roberts, Howard H., Jr. *transportation executive*
Sander, Elliot Gene (Lee Sander) *transportation executive*
Sitomer, Richard *air transportation executive*
Spinetta, Jean-Cyril *airline executive*
Thayer, Russell III *air transportation executive*
Treitel, David Henry *aviation executive*
Weinstein, Martin *aerospace transportation executive, manufacturing executive, materials scientist*
Williams, Helena E. *rail transportation executive*

Northport
Reinertsen, Norman *retired air transportation executive*

Oyster Bay
Smith, Pamela Rosevear *air transportation executive*

Peekskill
Harte, Andrew Dennis *transportation company executive, travel agent*

White Plains
Aron, Adam M. *air transportation executive*

NORTH CAROLINA

Chapel Hill
Moellering, John Henry *aviation maintenance company executive*

Charlotte
Handy, John W. *shipping company executive, retired military officer*

Cherryville
Mayhew, Kenneth Edwin, Jr. *retired transportation executive*

Kannapolis
Thigpen, Alton Hill *transportation executive*

Spindale
Howard, Elizabeth Ann Blanton *transportation executive*

OHIO

Akron
Moriarty, John Timothy *transportation consultant, writer*

Bedford
Klukan, Joseph Frank *aerospace transportation executive, manufacturing executive*

Cleveland
Dannemiller, John C. *transportation company executive*

Columbus
Mason, Raymond E., Jr. *distributing company executive*

Rocky River
Shively, Daniel Jerome *retired transportation executive*

Wilmington
Hete, Joseph C. *air transportation executive*

Xenia
Bigelow, Daniel James *aerospace executive*

OKLAHOMA

Grove
Trippensee, Gary Alan *retired aerospace executive*

OREGON

Eugene
Toolson, Kay *transportation executive*

Medford
Rogers, Gardner Spencer *railroad company executive*

PENNSYLVANIA

Allentown
Doughty, George Franklin *airport administrator*

Clarion
Canaday, Doris Charlene *retired traffic representative*

Philadelphia
Camardo, Michael F. *retired aerospace transportation executive*
Terry, John Joseph *transportation investor*
Wiener, Morris Jay *air transportation executive*

Radnor
Cunningham, James Gerald, Jr. *transportation company executive*

Red Lion
Hartman, Charles Henry *transportation and not-for-profit executive, educator*

Washington
Kastelic, Robert Frank *aerospace transportation executive*

York
Grossman, Robert Allen *transportation executive*

RHODE ISLAND

Providence
Adu-Gyamfi, R. Siisi *multi-industry company executive*
Bohlen, Kenneth C. *multi-industry company executive*
Butler, John D. *multi-industry company executive*
Campbell, Lewis B. *multi-industry company executive*
French, Ted R. *multi-industry company executive*
Yates, Richard L. *multi-industry company executive*

SOUTH CAROLINA

Columbia
Conrad, Paul Ernest *transportation consultant*

TENNESSEE

Chattanooga
Pate, Lisa M. *transportation services executive, lawyer*
Quinn, Patrick *transportation executive*

Memphis
Carter, Robert B. *delivery service executive*
Glenn, T. Michael *delivery/messenger service executive*
Graf, Alan B., Jr. *delivery service executive*
Harris, Terrell Lee (Terry Harris) *delivery services company executive, former prosecutor*
Reid, Karen Denise *aerospace transportation executive, writer*
Richards, Christine P. *delivery service executive, lawyer*
Smith, Frederick Wallace *delivery service executive*

Morristown
Johnson, Evelyn Bryan *airport terminal executive*

Nashville
Ingram, Orrin Henry, II, *transportation executive*

TEXAS

Austin
Aadnesen, Christopher *rail transportation executive, consultant*

Dallas
Adams, John Lewis *transportation executive*
Arpey, Gerard J. *air transportation executive*
Barrett, Colleen Crotty *air transportation executive*
Fegan, Jeffrey P. *airport executive*
Kelleher, Herbert David *air transportation executive, lawyer*
Kelly, Gary C. *air transportation executive*
Laney, David M. *railroad industry executive, lawyer*
Wright, Laura L. *air transportation executive*

Denton
Alatzas, George *delivery service company executive*

El Paso
Sisney, Philip Lynn *retired pilot*

Fort Worth
Brennan, Edward A. *air transportation and former retail executive*
Endres, Arthur P. (Skip Endres) *rail transportation executive*
Horton, Thomas W. *air transportation and former telecommunications company executive*
Hund, Thomas N. *rail transportation executive*
Ice, Carl R. *rail transportation executive*
Kennedy, Gary F. *air transportation executive, lawyer*
Lanigan, John P., Jr. *rail transportation executive*
Nober, Roger *rail transportation executive*
Rose, Matthew K. *rail transportation executive*

Houston
Anderson, Clayton C. *astronaut*
Anderson-Lehman, Ron *air transportation executive*
Archambault, Lee Joseph *astronaut*
Ashby, Jeffrey S. *astronaut*
Baker, Ellen Shulman *astronaut, physician*
Bergsrud, Mark *air transportation executive*
Bonds, Michael P. *air transportation executive*
Brandenstein, Daniel Charles *astronaut, retired military officer*
Burbank, Daniel C. *astronaut*
Cabana, Robert D. *aerospace transportation executive, astronaut*
Cagle, Yvonne Darlene *astronaut*
Camarda, Charles J. *astronaut*
Chiao, Leroy *astronaut*
Cockrell, Kenneth Dale *astronaut*
Coleman, Catherine G. *astronaut*
Compton, James E. *air transportation executive*
Covey, Richard Oswalt (Dick Covey) *aerospace transportation executive, former astronaut*
Crane, James R. *delivery service executive*
Curbeam, Robert L., Jr. *astronaut*
Currie, Nancy Jane *astronaut*
Drew, Benjamin Alvin, Jr. *astronaut*
Erwin, Mark A. *air transportation executive*
Ferguson, Christopher J. *astronaut*
Fincke, Edward Michael (Mike) *astronaut*
Foreman, Michael J. *astronaut*
Forrester, Patrick G. *astronaut*
Fossum, Michael E. *astronaut*
Fuglesang, Christer *astronaut*
Grizzle, J. David *air transportation executive*
Higginbotham, Joan E. *astronaut*
Hilfman, David L. *air transportation executive*
Hobaugh, Charles O. *astronaut*
Horowitz, Scott Jay *astronaut, military officer*
Howell, Jefferson Davis, Jr. *aerospace transportation executive, retired military officer*
Jett, Brent W., Jr. *astronaut, military officer*
Kellner, Lawrence W. (Larry Kellner) *air transportation executive*
Kelly, James M. *astronaut, military officer*
Kelly, Mark E. *astronaut*
Kelly, Scott J. *astronaut, military officer*
Kilrain, Susan *astronaut*
Kotov, Oleg Valerievich *cosmonaut*
Kregel, Kevin R. *astronaut*
Laderman, Gerald *air transportation executive*
Lawrence, Wendy B. *astronaut*
Leonard, Charles H. (Chuck Leonard) *air transportation executive*
Lindsey, Steven W. *astronaut, military officer*
Lopez-Alegria, Michael Eladio *astronaut*
Lu, Edward Tsang *astronaut*
MacLean, Steve(n) G. *astronaut*
Marzetta, Dante R., II, *air transportation executive*
Mastracchio, Richard A. (Rick) *astronaut*
McArthur, William Surles, Jr. *astronaut, retired military officer*
Meehan, William A. *air transportation executive*
Melroy, Pamela Ann *astronaut*
Misner, Jeffrey J. *air transportation executive*
Moran, Mark J. *air transportation executive*
Morgan, Barbara R. *astronaut*
Nespoli, Paolo Angelo *astronaut*
Noguchi, Soichi *astronaut*
Ochoa, Ellen *astronaut*
Oefelein, William A. *astronaut, military officer*
Olivas, John D. (Danny) *astronaut*
Parazynski, Scott E. *astronaut*
Patrick, Nicholas J.M. *astronaut*
Pettit, Donald R. *astronaut, flight engineer, researcher*
Polansky, Mark L. *astronaut*

Ream, James B. (Jim Ream) *air transportation executive*
Ross, Jerry L. *astronaut*
Rowe, Zane Conrad *air transportation executive*
Runco, Mario, Jr. *astronaut, meteorologist, researcher*
Sellers, Piers J. *astronaut*
Shannon, Holden E. *air transportation executive*
Shapirov, Salizhan Shakirovich *cosmonaut*
Smisek, Jeffery A. *air transportation executive*
Stefanyshyn-Piper, Heidemarie M. *astronaut*
Stone, Robert G., Jr. *water transportation executive*
Sturckow, Frederick W. (Rick) *astronaut*
Swanson, Steven R. *astronaut*
Tanner, Joseph Richard *astronaut*
Thirsk, Robert Brent *astronaut*
Thomas, Andrew S.W. *astronaut*
Vittori, Roberto *astronaut*
Vladimirovich, Vinogradov Pavel *cosmonaut*
Walker, Charles D. *astronaut*
Walker, John E. (Ned Walker) *air transportation executive*
Wheelock, Douglas H. *astronaut, military officer*
Williams, David R. (Dafydd Rhys Williams) *astronaut*
Williams, Sunita L. *astronaut*
Wilson, Stephanie D. *astronaut*
Yuen, Benson Bolden *air transportation and software executive, consultant*
Zamka, George D. *astronaut*

Irving
Plaskett, Thomas George *transportation executive, director*

Lindale
Carter, Thomas Smith, Jr. *retired rail transportation executive*

New Braunfels
Rush, W.M. (Rusty) *trucking executive*

San Antonio
Rush, W. Marvin *trucking executive*

Zavalla
Devlin, Cynthia M. *air transportation executive, consultant*

UTAH

North Salt Lake
Bouley, Joseph Richard *pilot*

Orem
Snow, Marlon O. *trucking executive, state agency administrator*

Saint George
Atkin, Jerry C. *air transportation executive*

VERMONT

Manchester Center
Carr, Gerald Paul *retired astronaut, engineer, marketing professional, military officer*

Middlebury
Bergesen, Robert Nelson *transportation consultant*

VIRGINIA

Alexandria
Stempler, Jack Leon *aerospace executive*

Arlington
Gifford, Jonathan Lewis *transportation policy researcher, educator*
Harrington, George Fred *retired air transportation executive*
Hullin, Tod Robert *aerospace transportation executive*
Lakefield, Bruce R. *air transportation executive*
Mainwaring, Thomas Lloyd *transportation executive, director*
Stokes, B. R. *transportation executive, consultant*
Wahlquist, Andrew Folkman *government affairs executive*

Burgess
Harris, Paul Lynwood *retired aerospace transportation executive*

Catlett
Broderick, Anthony James *air transportation executive*

Chesterfield
Congdon, John Rhodes *transportation executive*

Dulles
Elias, Antonio L. *aerospace transportation executive*

Falls Church
Poza, Hugo Bernardo *aerospace company executive*

Gainesville
Levell, Edward, Jr. *retired airport director, aviation consultant*

Mc Lean
Checchi, Alfred A. *air transportation executive, financial consultant*

Norfolk
McKinnon, Arnold Borden *retired transportation company executive*
Moorman, Charles W. *transportation executive*
Squires, James A. *rail transportation executive*
Tobias, Stephen C. *rail transportation executive*

Poquoson
Holloway, Paul Fayette *retired aerospace transportation executive*

Reston
Kreyling, Edward George, Jr. *retired railroad executive*

Richmond
Watkins, Hays Thomas *retired railroad executive*

Sterling
Thompson, David Walker *astronautics company executive*

Vienna
Anderson, Eric C. *aerospace transportation executive*
Beyer, Barbara Lynn *transportation executive, consultant*
Rogers, Raymond Jesse *retired federal railroad associate administrator*

Williamsburg
Barausky, Kenneth P. *aerospace company executive*
Spitzer, Cary Redford *avionics consultant, electrical engineer*
Starry, Donn Albert *retired aerospace corporate executive, retired military officer*

WASHINGTON

Belfair
Hager, Robert Worth *retired aerospace executive*

Ellensburg
Hoover, Amy Lynn *pilot, educator*

Seattle
Ayer, William S. *air transportation executive*
Beighle, Douglas Paul *aerospace transportation executive*
Carson, Scott E. *aerospace transportation executive*
Dickenson, Larry *aerospace transportation executive*
Hirschmann, Franz Gottfried *aerospace executive*
Kruse, Stein *cruise line executive*
Rose, Peter J. *delivery service executive*
Tilden, Bradley Douglas *air transportation executive*

Spanaway
Loete, Steven Donald *pilot*

Vancouver
Robertson, Joel Thomas *railroad executive*

WISCONSIN

Appleton
Petinga, Charles Michael *transportation executive*

Green Bay
Lofgren, Christopher B. *trucking executive*
Schneider, Donald J. *trucking company executive*

Oshkosh
Bohn, Robert G. *transportation company executive*

WYOMING

Worland
Woods, Lawrence Milton *airline company executive*

CANADA

NOVA SCOTIA

Halifax
Renouf, Harold Augustus *retired transportation executive*

Lower Sackville
Ortlepp, Bruno *marine navigation educator, master mariner*

QUEBEC

Montreal
Rochette, Louis *water transportation executive*

Saint-Sauveur
Hanigan, Lawrence *retired rail transportation executive*

AUSTRALIA

Springfield
Spalvins, Janis Gunars *steamship company executive*

ENGLAND

London
Kallakis, His Excellency Achilleas Michalis S. (His Excellency Ambassador Achilleas M. Kallakis of the Republi *transportation executive, real estate company executive*

JAPAN

Tokyo
Kaneko, Isao *air transportation executive*
Matsuda, Masatake *rail transportation executive*

NETHERLANDS

Schiphol Rijk
Enders, Thomas *air transportation executive*

RUSSIA

Moscow
Padalka, Gennady Ivanovich *cosmonaut*

SWITZERLAND

Geneva
Aaronson, Robert Jay *air transportation executive*
Ballin, William Christopher *international shipping and investment advisor*

ADDRESS UNPUBLISHED

Adolph, Kathryn Ann *passenger service employee*
Aldrin, Buzz *retired astronaut*
Baddour, Anne Bridge *pilot*
Bain, Douglas G. *retired aerospace transportation executive, lawyer*
Barefoot, Tommy Dean *retired boat captain*
Benson, James *aerospace transportation executive*
Briggs, Hazen Spencer Pingree III *air traffic controller, educator*
Brown, Donald Douglas *transportation executive, consultant, retired military officer*
Brown, Robert E. *transportation executive*
Collins, Eileen Marie *astronaut*
Compton, William F. *retired air transportation executive*
Cook, Richard Kelsey *aerospace transportation executive*
Cook, Stephen Champlin *retired shipping company executive*
Cromar, Michael Earl *information and finance executive, distribution and transportation, oil and gas exploration and production executive*
Crowder, Richard Morgan *pilot*
Dely, Steven *retired aerospace company executive*
Dewar, James McEwen *marketing, aerospace and defense executive, developing nations consultant*
Dressler, David Charles *retired aerospace transportation executive*
Driskill, Thomas K. *transportation executive*
Duelfer, Charles Alfred *aerospace transportation executive, weapons inspector, director*
Evans, James Hurlburt *retired transportation and natural resources executive*
Felix, Cheryl A. *air transportation executive*
Fish, Howard Math *aerospace transportation executive*
Garriott, Owen Kay *astronaut, scientist*
Gibson, Robert Lee *astronaut*
Gitner, Gerald L. *air transportation executive, investment banker*
Goldstein, Bernard *transportation and hotel executive*
Graebner, James Herbert *transportation executive*
Gray, Richard Arden *retired transportation executive*
Gulcher, Robert Harry *aerospace transportation executive*
Heckel, John Louis (Jack Heckel) *aerospace management executive*
Higginbottom, Samuel Logan *retired air transportation executive*
Huybrechts, Steven Marc *space system technologist*
Johnson, Robert D. *aerospace transportation executive*
Jordan, Rickey Woodrow *retired automobile manufacturer technician*
Keenan, Anthony Lee *trucking executive*
Kennard, Lydia H. *former airport terminal executive*
Khidiatova, Alia *transportation executive*
Knight, Eric A. *aerospace executive, entrepreneur, inventor*
Kondas, Nicholas Frank *retired shipping company executive*
Kruesi, Frank Eugene *transportation executive, former federal agency administrator*
Lerner-Lam, Eva I-Hwa *transportation executive*
Lewis, Andrew Lindsay, Jr., (Drew Lewis) *former transportation and natural resources executive*
Lewis, Martin Edward *transportation executive, oil trader, foreign government concessionary*
Malishenko, Timothy Peter *aerospace company executive*
Marshall, Charles Noble *rail transportation executive*
Masiello, Rocco Joseph *air transportation executive, consultant*
McCarthy, Paul Fenton *aerospace transportation executive, retired military officer*
McDonald, Peter D. *air transportation executive*
Merrick, George Boesch *aerospace transportation executive*
Miller, Paul David *aerospace transportation executive, retired admiral*
Mullin, Leo Francis *airline executive*
O'Brien, Raymond Francis *transportation executive*
Pickering, Thomas Reeve *retired aerospace transportation executive, diplomat*
Pope, John Charles *former airline company executive*
Pospelov, Dmitriy *transportation executive*
Raskin, Fred Charles *retired transportation and utility holding company executive, educator*
Reed, John Shedd *former railway executive*
Ruegg, Donald George *retired rail transportation executive*
Saleh, Brian Behrooz *aerospace transportation executive*
Savitz, Maxine Lazarus *retired aerospace transportation executive*
Scannell, William Edward *aerospace transportation executive, consultant, psychologist*
Schaefer, C. Barry *rail transportation executive, investment company executive*
Schaupp, Joan Pomprowitz *trucking executive, writer*
Shockley, Edward Julian *retired air transportation executive*
Snowden, Lawrence Fontaine *retired air transportation executive, retired military officer*
Stevens, Robert J. *aerospace transportation executive*
Studeman, Bill (William Oliver Studeman) *aerospace transportation executive, former federal agency administrator, retired naval officer*
Swinburn, Charles *retired rail transportation executive*
Tague, John Patrick *air transportation executive*
Tregurtha, Paul Richard *water transportation executive*
Trubeck, William Lewis *air transportation company executive*
Tyurin, Mikhail *cosmonaut*
van Hoften, James Dougal Adrianus *retired astronaut, retired transportation executive*
Wallace, F. Blake *retired aerospace transportation executive, retired mechanical engineer*
Warrington, George D. *former transportation executive*
Washburn, Donald Arthur *retired transportation executive, investor*
Whitehurst, Jim (James M. Whitehurst) *former air transportation executive*
Yeager, Phillip Charles *transportation company executive*
Young, John Watts *retired astronaut*

INDUSTRY: UTILITIES, ENERGY, RESOURCES

UNITED STATES

ALABAMA

Birmingham
Beasley, James Barnie, Jr. *utilities executive*
Johnson, Wylie Pierson *electric utility executiv*

Foley
St. John, Henry Sewell, Jr. *utility company executive*

ALASKA

Fairbanks
Beistline, Earl Hoover *mining consultant*

ARIZONA

Phoenix
Adkerson, Richard C. *mining executive*
Huffman, Edgar Joseph *oil industry executive*
Post, William Joseph *utility executive*
Snider, Timothy R. *mining executive*

Scottsdale
Birkelbach, Albert Ottmar *retired oil industry executive*
Trimble, Thomas James *retired utilities executive, lawyer*

Sedona
Dansby, John Walter *retired oil industry executive*

Show Low
Pershing, Robert George *retired telecommunications industry executive*

Tempe
Hickson, Robin Julian *mining company execu*

Tucson
Heller, Frederick *retired mining executive*
Jamison, Harrison Clyde *retired oil company executive*
Maxon, Don Carlton *mining and construction executive, consultant*
Peeler, Stuart Thorne *gas industry executive, consultant*
Peters, Charles William *nuclear energy indust executive*

Youngtown
Black, Robert Frederick *retired gas industry executive*

KANSAS

orado
ig, Claiborne Payne *oil industry executive*
Harvey *oil industry executive*
rald, Kevin Gerard *oil industry executive*
, William C., Jr. *oil industry executive*
ns, Jerry West *retired oil company*
cutive, lawyer
, David M. *oil industry executive*

e Rock
s, Michael B. *utility company executive*
Joe Thomas *telephone company executive,*
mer state senator
Scott T. *telecommunications industry*
cutive
vay, Sharilyn *telecommunications industry*
cutive

IFORNIA

neda
long Liang *telecommunications industry*
cutive

no
er, James David *retired utilities executive*

keley
k, Lawrence James *energy executive, history*
fessor

arillo
Alister, Robert Stuart *retired oil industry*
cutive

mel
ilton, Lyman Critchfield, Jr.
ecommunications industry executive

om
n, William Joseph, Jr. *energy company*
ecutive

eta
agnon, Olivier L. *telecommunications*
lustry executive

ne
lau, Mark Steven *utilities executive*

Jolla
ker, Samuel Mayo, Jr. *retired utilities*
ecutive

Angeles
en, Stephen I. *oil industry executive*
. Kline R. *oil, gas and chemical company*
ecutive
ert, James M. *oil industry executive*
dles, Martinn Heroe *facility services*
mpany executive
on, Larry Dean *telecommunications and*
mputer systems company executive,
nsultant

rtinez
er, Jarold Alan *oil company research*
ecutive

nlo Park
egar, Claude Stout *retired oil industry*
ecutive

l Valley
no, Paul Mark *oil industry executive*

vport Coast
n, Peer Alden *public utility executive*

ific Palisades
yan, Henry Trist *mining executive,*
nsultant

o Alto
en, Karl Paley *nuclear energy consultant*
wenstein, Walter Bernard *nuclear energy*
dustry executive

os Verdes Peninsula
stie, Hans Frederick *retired utilities*
ecutive

adena
ss, Bill *energy executive*
ite-Thomson, Ian leonard *retired mining*
ecutive

aluma
lerickson, Arman Frederick *mining executive,*
etroleum engineer

semead
son, John E. *utilities executive*
herstone, Diane L. *utilities executive*
rer, Alan J. *utilities company executive*
lt, Polly L. *utilities executive*
se, Cecil R. *utilities executive*
Daniel, Thomas R. *utilities executive*
sky, Barbara J. *utilities executive*
enblum, Richard Mark *utilities executive*
di, Mahvash *utilities executive*

n Diego
man, Steven R. *telecommunications executive*
singer, Donald E. *utilities corporation*
xecutive
kell, Robert E. *electric power industry*
xecutive
kar, Sandip *telecommunications industry*
xecutive, researcher
male, Neal E. *utilities company executive*
ll, Mark A. *utilities executive*

San Francisco
Darbee, Peter A. *utilities executive*
Dickinson, Wade *oil industry executive, educator*
Flittie, Clifford Gilliland *retired petroleum company executive*
Goldstein, David Baird *energy executive, physicist*
Harvey, Kent M. *utilities executive*
Johns, Christopher P. *utilities executive*
McFadden, Nancy Elizabeth *utilities executive*
Rosenberg, Rand L. *utilities executive*
Simon, John R. *utilities executive*
Sproul, John Allan *retired utilities executive*
Zaccaria, Adrian *utilities executive*

San Jose
Capellas, Michael D. *telecommunications industry executive*
Derr, Kenneth T. *energy executive*
Mason, Thomas R. *utilities executive*
May, Robert P. *energy executive*
Prasad, Neil A. *telecommunications industry, computer company executive*

San Mateo
Ginn, Sam L. *telephone company executive*

San Ramon
Bethancourt, John E. *oil industry executive*
Gass, John D. *oil industry executive*
Kirkland, George L. *oil industry executive*
O'Reilly, David J. *oil industry executive*
Robertson, Peter James *oil industry executive*
Watson, John S. *oil company executive*
Wirth, Michael K. (Mike Wirth) *oil company executive*
Yarrington, Patricia E. *oil industry executive*
Zygocki, Rhonda I. *oil industry executive*

Santa Barbara
Mc Duffie, Malcolm *oil industry executive*

Santa Clara
Burke, Conrad *energy executive*

Santa Cruz
Kahn, Philippe *telecommunications industry executive, entrepreneur*

Santa Rosa
Wagner, Harold A. *retired gas industry executive*

South Pasadena
Finnell, Michael Hartman *mining executive*

Sunnyvale
Lundberg, Carl-Erik Wilhelm *telecommunications executive, researcher*
Olson, James (Jim Olson) *telecommunications industry executive*

Templeton
Gandsey, Louis John *petroleum and environmental consultant*

Thousand Oaks
Klein, Joseph Mark *retired mining executive*

Yountville
Savage, Michael John Kirkness *oil industry executive, performing arts company executive*

COLORADO

Boulder
Hill, Melvin James *retired oil industry executive*

Centennial
Owens, Marvin Franklin, Jr. *oil industry executive, director*

Denver
Anderson, Donald H. *energy executive*
Danos, Robert McClure *retired oil company executive*
Dyer, Edward James *public utilities commissioner*
Hall, Larry Dean *utilities executive, lawyer*
Kruger, Paula *telecommunications industry executive*
Larson, Randall J. *energy executive*
Lassonde, Pierre *mining executive*
Macey, William Blackmore *oil industry executive*
Mayer, Frederick Rickard *oil industry executive*
Mogg, Jimmy W. *gas industry executive*
Mueller, Edward A. *telecommunications industry executive*
Murdy, Wayne William *mining company executive, financial officer*
Notebaert, Richard C. *telecommunications industry executive*
O'Brien, Richard T. *mining executive*
Richards, Thomas E. *telecommunications industry executive*
Richardson, John W. *telecommunications industry executive*
Taylor, Teresa *telecommunications industry executive*
Thompson, Lohren Matthew *oil company executive*
Thornton, Roland *telecommunications industry executive*
Tregemba, Robert D. *telecommunications industry executive*
Trueblood, Harry Albert, Jr. *oil industry executive*
Yost, Dan *telecommunications industry executive*

Englewood
Bennett, Robert R. *telecommunications company executive*
Schleyer, William T. *cable company executive*

Golden
von Roedern, Bolko Graf *energy executive, researcher*

Littleton
Fryt, Monte Stanislaus *petroleum company executive, speaker, advisor*

Loveland
Bierbaum, J. Armin *petroleum company executive, consultant*

CONNECTICUT

Darien
Smith, Elwin Earl *mining and oil company executive*

Greenwich
Alonzo, Martin Vincent *mining and aluminum company executive, investor, financial consultant*
Davidson, Thomas Maxwell *oil industry executive*
DeCrane, Alfred Charles, Jr. *petroleum company executive*

Guilford
Morgan, Leon Alford *retired utilities executive*

Hartford
McHale, David R. *utilities executive*
Olivier, Leon J. *utilities executive*
Shivery, Charles W. *utilities executive*

Madison
Kay, Herbert *retired energy executive*

New Haven
Randell, Linda L. *utilities executive, lawyer*

Old Greenwich
Allen, Jefferson F. *oil industry executive*

Orange
Powers, Timothy H. *electric power industry executive*

South Windsor
van Dokkum, Jan *electric power industry executive*

Southport
Damson, Barrie Morton *oil and gas exploration company executive*

Stamford
Mc Kinley, John Key *retired oil company executive*
Neal, A. Michael *utilities executive*
Walsh, Kevin P. *energy executive, financial services executive*

DELAWARE

Rockland
Cosgrove, Howard Edward, Jr. *utilities executive*

DISTRICT OF COLUMBIA

Washington
Barry, Paul H. *utilities executive*
Bradshaw, Richard Eugene *science and technology government relations consultant*
Buchan, Douglas Charles *gas industry executive, government agency administrator*
DeGraffenreidt, James H., Jr. *gas company executive*
Fraulino, Philip Samuel *telecommunications industry executive*
Friedman, Gregory H. *energy administrator*
Hezir, Joseph S. *energy and environmental executive*
King, Gwendolyn S. *retired utility company executive, federal official*
Lytle, Gary R. *telecommunications industry executive*
McCollam, William, Jr. *utilities executive*
McGee, Robert Merrill *oil industry executive*
McSlarrow, Kyle E. *telecommunications association executive, former federal agency administrator*
Moler, Elizabeth Anne *utilities executive*
Raymond, Lee R. *retired oil company executive*
Rigby, Joseph M. *utilities executive*
Sant, Roger W. *retired energy executive*
Wraase, Dennis Richard *utilities executive, accountant*

FLORIDA

Belleair Beach
Ayers, Richard Wayne *electric power industry executive, writer, journalist*

Boca Raton
Gralla, Eugene *natural gas company executive*

Bradenton
Watkins, William, Jr. *electric power industry executive*

Deerfield Beach
Laser, Charles, Jr. *oil company executive*

Gainesville
Milbrath, Robert Henry *retired petroleum industry executive*

Indian River Shores
Wiegner, Edward Alex *financial and energy executive*

Jacksonville
Francis, James Delbert *oil industry executive*

Juno Beach
Dewhurst, Moray P. *utilities executive*
Hay, Lewis III *utilities executive*
Robo, James L. *utilities executive*

Largo
Dolan, John E. *retired utilities executive, consultant*

Longwood
Cirello, John *utility and engineering company executive*

Miami
Kasbar, Michael J. *energy executive*
Stebbins, Paul H. *energy executive*
Weiser, Ralph Raphael *oil industry executive*

Miami Beach
Taylor, Leslie George *mining and finance company executive*

Naples
Gelfand, Neal *oil industry executive*
Marienthal, George *telecommunications industry executive*
Marino, William Francis *telecommunications industry executive, consultant*

Palm Beach Gardens
Harnett, Joseph Durham *oil industry executive*

Pensacola
Story, Susan N. *utilities executive*

Ponte Vedra Beach
Wood, Quentin Eugene *oil industry executive*

Saint Petersburg
Fleming, William Sloan *energy and computer company executive*

Saint Petersburg Beach
Garnett, Stanley Iredale, II, *utilities executive, lawyer*

Sarasota
Torrey, Richard Frank *utilities executive*

Stuart
Kirkpatrick, Harold (Kirk) Wayne *telecommunications industry executive*

Tallahassee
Laughlin, William Eugene *retired electric power industry executive*

Tampa
Brown, Troy Anderson, Jr. *retired electric power industry executive*
Hudson, Sherrill W. *energy executive*

Vero Beach
Bennett, Jack Franklin *oil industry executive*

West Palm Beach
Koch, William I. *energy company executive*

GEORGIA

Atlanta
Arroyo, F. Thaddeus *telecommunications industry executive*
Bolch, Carl Edward, Jr. *oil industry executive, lawyer*
Bowers, W. Paul *utilities executive*
Carbonell, Joaquin R. III *telecommunications industry executive, lawyer*
Carter, Stephen M. *telecommunications manufacturing industry executive*
Dawson, Robert G. *telecommunications industry executive*
Dearman, Andrew J. III *utilities executive*
Dykes, Ronald Mitchell *retired telecommunications industry executive*
Evans, Dwight H. *utilities executive*
Fanning, Thomas Andrew *utilities executive*
Garrett, Michael D. *utilities executive*
James, Anthony R. *utilities executive*
McCrary, Charles D. *utilities executive*
Muller, Edward Robert *energy executive, lawyer*
Ramsey, Ira Clayton *retired petroleum industry executive*
Ratcliffe, David M. *utilities executive*
Sigman, Stanley T. *telecommunications industry executive*
Somerhalder, John W., II, *energy executive*

Duluth
McCracken, William Henry *retired mining executive*

Gainesville
Leet, Richard Hale *oil industry executive*

Roswell
Burgess, John Frank *retired utilities executive*

HAWAII

Honolulu
Lau, Constance H. (Connie Lau) *electric power industry executive*

Waikoloa
Calvert, Delbert William *retired energy executive*

IDAHO

Hayden
Griffith, William Alexander *former mining company executive*

ILLINOIS

Argonne
Ban, Stephen Dennis *gas industry executive*

Barrington
Perry, I. Chet *petroleum company executive*

Bloomington
Beeler, Charlotte Jean *oil and supply company executive, interior design business executive*

Chicago
Brooker, Thomas Kimball *oil industry executive*
Carlson, LeRoy Theodore, Jr. *telecommunications industry executive*
Clark, Frank M. *utilities executive*
Crane, Christopher M. *utilities executive*
Gillis, Ruth Ann M. *utilities executive*
McLean, Ian P. *utilities executive*
Meyers, Kenneth Raymond *telecommunications industry executive*
Morrow, Richard Martin *retired oil company executive*
Perez, David *utilities executive*
Rogers, Desiree Glapion *utilities executive*
Rowe, John William *utilities executive*
Skolds, John L. (Jack Skolds) *utilities executive*
Snodgrass, S. Gary *utilities executive*
Strobel, Pamela B. *energy executive*
Young, John F. *utilities executive*

Deerfield
Zywicki, Robert Albert *retired electric power industry executive*

Flossmoor
Pierce, Shelby Crawford *oil industry executive, consultant*

Joliet
Easton, Kenneth Glenn *retired utilities executive*

Naperville
Prabhu, Krish Anant *telecommunications industry executive, educator*
Strobel, Russ M. *gas industry executive, lawyer*

Pekin
Miller, Ronald H. *energy executive*

River Forest
Batlivala, Robert Bomi D. *oil industry executive, economics professor*

Riverwoods
Smith, E. Follin *retired energy executive*

Schaumburg
Borth, David E. *telecommunications industry executive, researcher*
Mark, Kelly S. *telecommunications industry executive, investment advisor*
O'Connor, James, Jr., (Jim O'Connor) *telecommunications industry executive*

INDIANA

Columbus
Able, Warren Walter *natural resource company executive, physician*

Evansville
Ellerbrook, Niel Cochran *gas industry executive*

Frankfort
Stonehill, Lloyd Herschel *gas industry executive, mechanical engineer*

Indianapolis
Grube, F. William *refining company executive*

Lawrenceburg
Dautel, Charles Shreve *retired mining company executive*

Merrillville
Skaggs, Robert C., Jr. *utilities executive, lawyer*

IOWA

Des Moines
Abel, Gregory E. *utility company executive*
Sokol, David L. *energy services provider company executive*

KANSAS

Eskridge
Taylor, Russell Benton *mining executive*

Overland Park
Betts, Gene M. *telecommunications industry executive*
Ferrell, James Edwin *nuclear energy industry executive*
Gerke, Thomas A. *telecommunications industry executive, lawyer*
Horen, Jeffrey Harry *telecommunications industry executive*
Strandjord, M. Jeannine *telecommunications industry executive*

Pittsburg
Nettels, George Edward, Jr. *retired mining executive*

Shawnee Mission
Pressman, Ronald R. *utilities executive*

Topeka
Moore, William B. *energy executive*
Spencer, William Edwin *retired telecommunications industry executive, engineer*

Wichita
Cadman, Wilson Kennedy *retired utilities executive*

KENTUCKY

Ashland
Hatfield, Bennett K. *mining executive*

Crescent Springs
Chellgren, Paul Wilbur *energy industry executive*

Lexington
Boyd, James Robert *energy executive*

Louisville
Ronald, Peter *utilities executive*
Staffieri, Victor A. *energy executive*

LOUISIANA

Monroe
Fouts, James Fremont *mining company executive*
Post, Glen Fleming III *telecommunications industry executive*

New Orleans
Denault, Leo P. *energy executive*
Leonard, J. Wayne *energy executive*
Lind, Thomas Otto *barge transportation company executive*
Moffett, James Robert *mining executive*
Sloan, Robert D. *energy executive, lawyer*
Smith, Richard J. *energy executive*
Taylor, Phyllis Miller *energy executive*
Williams, Ronald David *telecommunications industry executive*

MAINE

Casco
Brown, Ronald Osborne *telecommunications and computer systems consultant*

New Gloucester
Jasinski, Kenneth M. *energy executive*

Portland
von Schack, Wesley W. *utilities executive*

Yarmouth
Haynes, Peter Lancaster *utilities executive*

MARYLAND

Baltimore
Brooks, Thomas V. *energy executive*
Collins, John R. *energy executive*
Ihrie, Robert *oil, gas and real estate company executive*
Rosenberg, Henry A., Jr. *petroleum executive*
Shattuck, Mayo Adams III *utilities executive*

Bethesda
Chebaane, Mohamed *water management specialist, consultant*
McMurphy, Michael Allen *energy company executive, lawyer*
Olmsted, Jerauld Lockwood *telephone company executive*
Starkey, Russell Bruce, Jr. *energy executive*
Welch, John Kirtland *nuclear energy industry executive*

Glen Arm
Jackson, Theodore Marshall *retired oil industry executive*

Rockville
Griffith, Jerry Dice *energy executive, management consultant*

Silver Spring
Jacobs, George *broadcast engineering consulting company executive*

MASSACHUSETTS

Acton
Kalavade, Asa *telecommunications industry executive*

Boston
Kennedy, Joseph Patrick, II, *utilities executive, former congressman*
May, Thomas J. *electric company executive*
Stobaugh, Robert Blair *oil industry executive*

Cambridge
Olschwang, Dan *telecommunications industry executive, entrepreneur*

Centerville
Anderson, Gerald Edwin *retired utilities executive*
Scherer, Harold Nicholas, Jr. *electric power industry executive*

Chelsea
Kaneb, John A. *oil industry executive*

Needham
Cogswell, John Heyland *retired telecommunications industry executive, financial consultant*
Rafferty, James Paul *telecommunications executive*

Newton
Petrowski, Joseph H. *oil industry executive*

Plymouth
Staszesky, Francis Myron *electric power industry executive, consultant*

Waltham
Malis, Andrew Gary *telecommunications industry executive*
Slifka, Eric *oil industry executive*

Westborough
Bok, Joan Toland *utilities executive*

Weston
Goldstein, Arthur Louis *retired utilities executive*

MICHIGAN

Detroit
Anderson, Gerard M. *energy executive*
Earley, Anthony Francis, Jr. *utilities company executive, lawyer*
Ellyn, Lynne *energy executive*

Jackson
Joos, David W. *energy executive*
Webb, Thomas J. *utilities executive*
Whipple, Kenneth *utilities executive*

Troy
Opie, John D. *retired electric power industry executive*

MINNESOTA

Burnsville
O'Brien, Gerald James *utilities executive*

Eden Prairie
Switz, Robert E. *telecommunications executive*

Minneapolis
Bonavia, Paul J. *energy executive*
Gogel, Raymond E. *energy executive*
Kelly, Richard C. *energy executive*
Wilks, David M. *energy executive*

MISSISSIPPI

Gulfport
Topazi, Anthony J. *utilities executive*

Jackson
Lampton, Leslie B., Sr. *oil industry executive*
Waites, Robert Guinn *utilities executive*

MISSOURI

Chesterfield
Bunch, C. Robert *oil industry executive, lawyer*

Clayton
Novelly, Paul Anthony *petrochemical and refining company executive*

Kansas City
Baker, John Russell *utilities executive*
Chesser, Michael J. *gas and electric power industry executive*
Green, Richard Calvin, Jr. *electric power and gas industry executive*
Mackenzie, Nanci *gas company executive*
Potter, George William, Jr. *mining executive*
Riggins, William G. *electric power industry executive*

Saint Louis
Baxter, Warner L. *electric power industry executive*
Boyce, Gregory H. *energy executive*
Engelhardt, Irl F. *coal company executive*
Leer, Steven F. *mining executive*
Rainwater, Gary L. *electric power industry executive*
Smit, Neil *telecommunications industry executive*
Voss, Thomas R. *electric power industry executive*
Yaeger, Douglas Harrison *gas industry executive*

Springfield
Jura, James J. *electric utility executive*

MONTANA

Billings
Nance, Robert Lewis *oil industry executive*

Missoula
Brumit, Lawrence Edward III *oil industry executive*

NEBRASKA

Omaha
Crouse, Jerry K. *energy company executive*
Hawks, Howard L. *energy executive*
Scott, Walter, Jr. *telecommunications industry executive*

NEVADA

Las Vegas
Hartley, Thomas Y. *gas industry executive*
Higgins, Walter M. III *electric power industry executive*
Laub, William Murray, Sr. *retired utilities executive*
Shaw, Jeffrey William *gas industry executive*
Yackira, Michael William *electric power indust executive*

Reno
Gundersen, Wayne Campbell *energy executive, consultant*

Winnemucca
Hesse, Martha O. *gas industry executive*

NEW HAMPSHIRE

Portsmouth
Powers, Henry Martin, Jr. *oil industry executive*

NEW JERSEY

Basking Ridge
Collis, Sidney Robert *retired telephone compan executive*
D'Ambrosio, Louis J. *telecommunications industry executive*
Matthews, Craig Gerard *retired energy executiv*
McAdam, Lowell C. *telecommunications industry executive*
Schenker, Leo *retired utilities executive*

Bedminster
Flaherty, Kathleen Ruth *telecommunications industry executive*
Strigl, Dennis F. *telecommunications industry executive*

Belmar
Downes, Laurence M. *gas industry executive*

Eatontown
Nissov, Morten *telecommunications industry executive*

Florham Park
Kouroupas, Paul *telecommunications industry executive, lawyer*

Holmdel
Smith, Timothy G. *telecommunications industr executive*

Maplewood
Joel, Amos Edward, Jr. *telecommunications consultant*

Middletown
Sullivan, Timothy Patrick *telecommunications company executive*

Mount Laurel
Rabbe, David Ellsworth *oil industry executive*

New Providence
Carapezzi, William R., Jr. *telecommunications industry executive, lawyer*
Kim, Jeong H. *telecommunications industry executive, communications engineer*
Kritzmacher, John A. *telecommunications industry executive*
Mejia, Jose A. *telecommunications industry executive*
Russo, Patricia F. *telecommunications compan executive*

Newark
Byrd, Stephen C. *utilities executive*
Izzo, Ralph *utilities executive*
LaRossa, Ralph *utilities executive*
Levis, William *utilities executive*
Lopriore, Richard P. *utilities executive*
Moran, Eileen A. *utilities executive*
O'Flynn, Thomas M. *utilities executive*
Pego, Margaret M. *utilities executive*
Quinn, Kevin J. *utilities executive*
Simpson, Elbert C. *utilities executive*

Nutley
Mallard, Stephen Anthony *retired utilities executive*

Peapack
Walsh, Philip Cornelius *retired mining execut*

Piscataway
Chynoweth, Alan Gerald *retired telecommunications industry executive*

Princeton
Crane, David W. *energy executive*

Roseland
Fuller, S(heri) Marce *energy executive*

South Plainfield
Lewandowski, Andrew Anthony *utilities executive, consultant*

Voorhees
Correll, Donald L. *water services company executive*

Watchung
Cohen, Melvin Irwin *retired communications systems and technology executive*

Whippany
Alexander, Mark A. *energy executive*

NEW MEXICO

Albuquerque
Long, Robert Leroy *retired utilities executive consultant*
Ofte, Donald *retired nuclear energy industry executive*

Robinson, Charles Paul *nuclear energy industry executive, diplomat*
Sterba, Jeffry E. *energy executive*

High Rolls Mountain Park
Ellison, Luther Frederick *oil industry executive*

Hobbs
Garey, Donald Lee *oil industry executive*

Roswell
Anderson, Donald Bernard *oil industry executive*
Robinson, Mark Leighton *gas industry executive, petroleum engineer, farmer*

Santa Fe
Duhaime, Nina Lee *energy and research and development company executive*

NEW YORK

Brooklyn
Bishar, John Joseph, Jr. *utilities executive, lawyer*
Catell, Robert Barry *gas industry executive*
ani, Robert J. *gas industry executive*

Greenvale
Cordaro, Matthew Charles *energy and utility executive, educator*

rvington
Carey, Edward John *utilities executive*

New York
arr, William Pelham *telecommunications industry executive, lawyer, former United States attorney general*
artlett, Thomas A. *telecommunications industry executive*
elfer, Robert Alexander *oil and gas company executive*
erkett, Neil *telecommunications industry executive*
rown, Edward James, Sr. *utilities executive*
urke, Kevin *utilities executive*
asey, Thomas Jefferson *clean energy industry executive and entrepreneur, environmental activist*
orrea, Daniel *energy executive, physics engineer*
ahan, Andre *telecommunications industry executive*
'Alessio, Frederick D. *telecommunications company executive*
elaney, Robert Vincent *former gas company executive, economic development consultant*
enson, Terry *telecommunications industry executive*
iercksen, John W. *telecommunications industry executive*
ould, Andrew *oil industry executive*
ess, John B. *oil industry executive*
oglund, Robert N. *utilities executive*
llian, John F. *telecommunications industry executive*
ataille, Ronald H. *telecommunications industry executive*
ice, Charles Franklin *retired utilities executive, lawyer*
ynch, Dick *telecommunications industry executive*
yons, John Matthew *telecommunications industry, broadcast executive*
oam, Eli Michael *telecommunications industry executive, educator*
oski, Charles H. *telecommunications executive*
Connor, John Joseph *oil industry executive*
sborne, Richard de Jongh *mining and metals company executive*
eed, Marc C. *telecommunications industry executive, human resources specialist*
iesterholz, Virginia P. *telecommunications industry executive*
yan, Robert Leslie *oil company executive*
idenberg, Ivan G. *telecommunications industry executive*
ratton, John G. *telecommunications industry executive*
uke, Thomas Joseph *telecommunications company executive, former congressman*
ben, Doreen A. *telecommunications industry executive*
alker, F(rank) Borden *oil industry executive*
ebster, Catherine T. *telecommunications industry executive*
ffer, Rachelle *telecommunications industry executive*

skayuna
angan, John Leo *retired electric power industry executive, international trade specialist*

ochester
nderLinden, Camilla Denice Dunn *telecommunications industry executive*

ye
wi, David Steven *utilities executive, merchant banker*

racuse
rr, Darlene Dixon *electric power company executive*

hite Plains
derweiser, Irwin Philip *mining executive, lawyer*

illiamsville
kerman, Philip Charles *utilities executive, lawyer*

NORTH CAROLINA

Asheville
Haynes, John Mabin *retired utilities executive*

Charlotte
Barron, Henry B., Jr., (Brew) *energy executive*
Good, Lynn J. *energy executive*
Hauser, David L. *energy executive*
Janson, Julia S. *energy executive*
O'Connor, Thomas C. *energy executive*
Roche, Cathy *energy executive*
Rogers, James Eugene *energy executive*
Rolfe, Christopher C. *energy executive*
Shaw, Ruth G. *energy company executive*
Skains, Thomas E. *gas industry executive*
Turner, James Lee *energy executive*

Raleigh
Clapp, Allen Linville *electric supply and communications utility consultant, mediator/arbitrator*
Johnson, William Dean *power company executive*
McArthur, John R. *utilities executive, lawyer*
McGehee, Robert B. *energy executive*
Scott, Peter M. III *utility company executive*
Smith, Sherwood Hubbard, Jr. *retired electric utilities executive*

Southern Shores
Kegel, William George *mining company executive*

Statesville
Grogan, David R. *work saver company executive*

NORTH DAKOTA

Bismarck
Hildestad, Terry D. *energy executive*

OHIO

Akron
Alexander, Anthony J. *electric power industry executive*
Grigg, Richard R. *energy executive*
Marsh, Richard H. *energy executive*
Smart, George M. *energy executive, former packaging company executive*

Bannock
Gentile, Anthony *coal company executive*

Chagrin Falls
Miller, John Robert *oil industry executive*

Cincinnati
Ehrnschwender, Arthur Robert *former utility company executive*
Esamann, Douglas F. *utilities executive*
Ficke, Gregory C. *utilities executive*
Foley, Cheryl M. *electric power industry executive*
Murphy, Theodore R., II, *utilities executive*

Cleveland
Carrabba, Joseph A. *mining executive*
Kuehn, Richard Arthur *telecommunications consultant*
Stropki, John M., Jr. *electric power industry executive*

Columbus
Akins, Nicholas K. *electric power industry executive*
Baker, J. Craig *electric power industry executive*
English, Carl L. *electric power industry executive*
Hagan, Thomas M. *electric power industry executive*
Koeppel, Holly Keller *electric power industry executive*
Morris, Michael G. *electric power industry executive*
Powers, Robert P. *electric power industry executive*
Tomasky, Susan *electric power industry executive*
Welch, Dennis E. *electric power industry executive*

Dublin
Vassell, Gregory S. *electric utility consultant*

Findlay
Yammine, Riad Nassif *retired oil industry executive*

Lima
Pranses, Anthony Louis *retired electric power industry executive*

Marysville
Kelly, Thomas N., Jr. *telecommunications industry executive*

Perrysburg
Williamson, John Pritchard *retired utilities executive*

OKLAHOMA

Bartlesville
Price, Joe D. *pipeline developer*
Silas, Cecil Jesse *retired petroleum company executive*

Enid
Ward, Llewellyn Orcutt III *oil industry executive*

Jennings
Nixon, Arlie James *gas and oil company executive*

Oklahoma City
Campbell, David Gwynne *petroleum executive, geologist*
Hefner, William Johnson, Jr., (W. John Hefner Jr.) *oil and gas industry executive*
Houpt, Jeff *energy management executive*
Langton, Jackson Maurice *mining executive, geologist*
McClendon, Aubrey K. *energy executive*
Moore, Steven E. *energy executive*
Richels, John *energy executive, lawyer*
Ward, Tom L. *energy executive*

Tulsa
Berlin, Steven Ritt *oil industry executive*
Braumiller, Allen Spooner *gas industry executive, geologist*
Chappel, Donald R. *petroleum pipeline company executive*
Dinan, Curtis L. *gas industry executive*
Dotson, George Stephen *retired oil industry executive*
Gibson, John W. *gas industry executive*
Horkey, William Richard *retired oil industry executive*
Ingram, Charles Clark, Jr. *energy executive*
Kneale, James C. *gas company executive*
Kronfeld, Edwin *natural gas company executive*
Kyle, David L. *gas industry executive*
Lawhorn, Caron A. *gas industry executive*
Malcolm, Steven J. *petroleum pipeline company executive*
Nedom, H. Arthur *petroleum consultant*
Singer, George Alan *oil and gas company executive, arts association administrator*

OREGON

Lincoln City
Morrow, James Thomas *energy executive*

Portland
Bacon, Vicky Lee *lighting services executive*

Tualatin
West, Michael G. *electric power industry executive*

PENNSYLVANIA

Allentown
Farr, Paul A. *electric power industry executive*
Miller, James H. *electric power industry executive*
Spence, William H. *electric power industry executive*

Allison Park
Sullivan, Neil Maxwell *oil and gas company executive*

Bryn Mawr
Braha, Thomas I. *oil industry executive*

Camp Hill
Fazzolari, Salvatore D. *mining products executive*
Hathaway, Derek C. *mining products executive*

Coraopolis
Koepfinger, Joseph Leo *retired utilities executive*

Gladwyne
Patten, Lanny Ray *gas industry executive*

Greensburg
Evanson, Paul John *utilities executive*
Goulding, Philip L. *energy executive*

King Of Prussia
Greenberg, Lon Richard *energy executive, lawyer*
Walsh, John L. *energy executive*

Philadelphia
Adawi, Nadia Sharon *energy executive*
Calman, Robert Frederick *mining executive*
Delaney, Terence (Terry) P. *gas industry executive*
Drosdick, John Girard *oil industry executive*
Fischer, Bruce G. *gas industry executive*
Hofmann, Thomas W. *oil industry executive*
Krott, Joseph P. *gas industry executive, comptroller*
Kuritzkes, Michael S. *oil industry executive, lawyer*
McNeill, Corbin Asahel, Jr. *utilities executive*
Mulé, Ann C. *oil industry executive*
Mulholland, Paul A. *gas industry executive*
Naku, Rolf D. *gas industry executive*
O'Brien, Denis P. *utilities executive*
Owens, Robert W. *gas industry executive*
Roberts, Ralph Joel *telecommunications industry and cable broadcast executive*

Pittsburgh
Bartley, Burnett Graham, Jr. *oil industry executive*
Harvey, J. Brett *energy executive*
Schwass, Gary L. *utilities executive*
Stirewalt, John Newman *coal company executive*

Presto
Moeller, Audrey Carolyn *retired energy company executive, corporate secretary*

Valley Forge
Kelly, Peter *energy executive*

Wayne
Lefevre, Thomas Vernon *retired utilities executive*

Wilkes Barre
Lindemann, George L. *gas industry executive*

SOUTH CAROLINA

Columbia
Timmerman, William B. *utilities executive, accountant*

Jackson
Smith, Mark Eugene *nuclear engineering service company executive*

Murrells Inlet
Justice, Franklin Pierce, Jr. *oil industry executive*

TENNESSEE

Knoxville
McCullough, Glenn L., Jr. *electric power industry executive*
Moore, Richard Wayne *electric power industry executive, former prosecutor*

Nashville
Adams, Kenneth Stanley, Jr., (Bud) *energy executive, professional sports team executive*

TEXAS

Austin
Deisler, Paul Frederick, Jr. *retired oil company executive*
Gibson, Jerry Leigh *oil industry executive*
Groten, Barnet *energy executive*
Haas, Joseph Marshall *retired petroleum consultant*

Channelview
Nyberg, Donald Arvid *oil industry executive*

Corpus Christi
Benner, Richard Walter *oil industry executive, petroleum engineer, geologist*
Haas, Paul Raymond *petroleum company executive*
Norman, Wyatt Thomas III *landman, consultant*
Paulson, Bernard Arthur *oil industry executive, consultant*
Susser, Sam L. *oil industry executive, consumer products company executive*

Dallas
Baker, Tom *utilities executive*
Best, Robert Wayne *gas transmission company executive, lawyer*
Biegler, David W. *energy executive*
Blessing, Edward Warfield *petroleum company executive*
Campbell, Kevin P. *oil industry executive*
Clifton, Matthew P. *petroleum refining company executive*
Davis, Barry E. *energy executive*
Farell, Dan *utilities executive*
Fielder, Charles Robert *retired oil industry executive*
Gratton, Patrick John Francis *oil industry executive*
Harless, Katherine J. *telecommunications industry executive*
Hoglund, Forrest Eugene *retired petroleum company executive*
Hunt, Ray Lee *petroleum company executive*
Jennings, James Burnett *oil industry executive*
Jones, Everett Riley, Jr. *oil industry executive*
Nevins, William J. *oil and gas brokerage executive, consultant*
Nye, Erle Allen *electric power industry executive, lawyer*
Perry, George Wilson *oil and gas company executive*
Pickens, Boone (T. Boone Pickens, Thomas Boone Pickens Jr.) *oil industry executive*
Rabun, Daniel W. *oil and gas industry executive*
Reddy, J. Patrick *gas industry executive*
Rees-Jones, Trevor D. *oil industry executive*
Sizer, Phillip Spelman *gas industry executive, retired oil industry executive*
Slawter, John David, Jr. *oil industry executive*
Thorne, Carl F. *gas industry executive*
Warren, Kelcy L. *energy executive*
Wilder, C. John (John Wilder) *energy executive*
Wilson, Richard A. *oil and gas industry support services executive*

El Paso
Foster, Paul L. *oil industry executive*

Fort Worth
Boschetti, Philip J. *oil industry executive*
Brumley, Jon S. *oil industry executive*
Culbertson, Richard Donnell *oil industry executive, lawyer*
Hyde, Clarence Brodie, II, *oil industry executive*
Moncrief, William Alvin, Jr. *oil and gas producer*
Simpson, Bob R. *energy executive*

Frisco
Mackenzie, John *retired oil industry executive*

Gainesville
McCormack, Lowell Ray *oil industry executive, corporate financial executive, consultant*

Horseshoe Bay
Jorden, James Roy *oil industry executive, consultant*

Houston
Anderson, Paul Milton *energy executive*
Armstrong, Greg L. *oil industry executive*
Barracano, Henry Ralph *retired oil company executive, management consultant*
Berry, William B. *oil industry executive*
Blanton, Jack Sawtelle *oil industry executive*
Bonneville, Richard Briggs *retired gas industry executive*
Bookout, John Frank, Jr. *oil industry executive*
Bowen, William Jackson *retired gas industry executive*
Campbell, Eileen M. *oil industry executive*
Carrig, John A. *oil industry executive*
Carroll, Milton *oil industry executive*
Caruso, Nick J. *energy executive*
Cazalot, Clarence P., Jr. *oil industry executive*
Chalmers, David B. *petroleum executive*
Clark, James R. *oil industry executive*
Clark, Janet F. *oil industry executive*
Colson, John R. *electric power industry executive*
Creel, Michael Allen *energy executive*
DaCunha, Jeffrey J. *oil industry executive, researcher*
Dang, Kimberly Allen *energy executive*
Dasari, Ganeswara R. *oil industry executive*
Davidson, Charles D. *energy executive*
Davis, Leon *oil industry executive*
Deaton, Chad C. *oil and gas industry executive*
DeVault, John Lee *oil industry executive, geophysicist*
Dice, Bruce Burton *gas industry executive*
Dreyer, Alec Gilbert *electric power industry executive*
Drury, Leonard Leroy *retired oil company executive*
Duncan, Dan L. *energy executive*
Dunham, Archie Wallace *petroleum company and chemicals executive*
Erikson, Sheldon R. *oil industry executive*
Farris, G. Steven *energy executive*
Foshee, Douglas L. *gas industry executive*
Fowler, Fred J. *energy executive*
Fowler, W. Randall *energy executive*
Frederickson, Philip L. *oil industry executive*
Frost, John Elliott *minerals company executive*
Fulwiler, Robert Neal *oil industry executive*
Furbacher, Stephen A. *energy executive*
Gallogly, James Lawrence *oil industry executive, lawyer*
Gaut, C. Christopher *oil industry executive*
Gibbs, James R. *oil industry executive*
Goodman, Herbert Irwin *petroleum company executive*
Heminger, Gary R. *oil industry executive*
Hemminghaus, Roger Roy *energy company executive, chemical engineer*
Hildebrand, Jeffrey D. *oil industry executive*
Irwin, John Robert *oil and gas industry executive*
Jackson, John E. *gas industry executive*
Jacobs, Mark M. *energy executive*
Jaffe, Amy Myers *energy executive, educator*
Johnson, Wayne D. *gas industry executive*
Kean, Steven J. *energy executive*
Kelly, Janet Langford *oil industry executive, lawyer*
Kerr, Baine Perkins *oil industry executive*
Kinder, Richard Dan *natural gas pipeline, oil and gas company executive*
Kinnear, Peter D. *energy executive*
Kirkland, John David *oil and gas company executive*
Knesek, Michael John *energy executive*
Knickel, Carin S. *oil industry executive*
Kramer, Phillip D. *oil industry executive*
Krohn, Tracy W. *oil industry executive, gas industry executive*
Kuehn, Ronald L., Jr. *natural resources company executive*
Kuntz, Hal Goggan *petroleum exploration company executive, rancher*
Landrum, Brian *energy executive*
Lane, Andrew *oil industry executive*
Lesar, David J. *oil industry executive*
Limbacher, Randy L. *energy executive*
Lowe, John E. *oil industry executive, accountant*
Manias, William G. *oil industry executive*
Matheny, Kenneth L. *oil industry executive*
Mathis, James Forrest *retired petroleum company executive*
McClanahan, David M. *energy executive*
Miller, Merrill Anthony, Jr. *energy executive*
Mire, Weldon J. *oil industry executive, human resources specialist*
Mulva, James Joseph *oil industry executive*
Neumann, Henry W., Jr. *energy executive*
Papa, Mark Gary *oil and gas industry executive*
Pefanis, Harry N. *oil industry executive*
Plank, Raymond *energy executive*
Plank, Roger B. *energy executive*
Ragauss, Peter A. *oil industry executive*
Raspino, Louis A. *energy executive*
Reynolds, John Terrence *oil industry executive*
Roberts, David E., Jr. *oil industry executive*
Rodríguez, Félix M. *oil industry executive*
Roff, J(ohn) Hugh, Jr. *energy executive*
Segner, Edmund Peter III *natural gas company executive*
Shackouls, Bobby S. *oil and gas industry executive*
Shaper, C. Park *energy executive*
Smith, David Kingman *retired oil company executive, consultant*
Staff, Joel V. *energy executive*
Stewart, J.W. *energy executive, lawyer*
Taylor, Cindy B. *oil industry executive*
Thompson, Jerry E. *oil industry executive*
Thompson, Jon L. *retired oil industry executive*
Trice, David A. *oil industry executive*
Van Dyke, Gene *oil industry executive*
Van Eeckhoudt, Marc Victor Celestin *oil industry executive*
Van Wagenen, Paul G. *gas industry executive*
Whitlock, Gary L. *energy executive*
Wiley, Michael E. *oil industry executive*
Williams, Clay C. *energy executive*
Williams, Robert Henry *oil industry executive*
Williamson, Bruce A. *gas industry executive*
Wilson, Edward Converse, Jr. *oil and natural gas production company executive*
Wilson, Floyd C. *oil industry executive*
Wuori, Stephen J. *energy executive*
Wyatt, Oscar Sherman, Jr. *energy company executive*

Ingram
Hughes, David Michael *oil industry executive, rancher*

Irving
Albers, Mark W. *oil industry executive*
Cavanaugh, Lucille J. *oil industry executive*
Dingle, Philip *retired oil industry executive*
Humphreys, Donald D. *oil industry executive*
Longwell, Harry J. *retired oil industry executive*
Matthews, Charles W., Jr. *oil industry executive, lawyer*
Mulva, Patrick T. *oil industry executive*
Sheffield, Scott D. *oil industry executive*
Simon, J. Stephen *oil industry executive*
Tillerson, Rex W. *oil company executive*

Midland
Grover, Rosalind Redfern *oil and gas company executive*

Plano
Chopra, Anil *oil industry executive*
Schuh, Frank Joseph *oil industry executive, consultant*

Pottsboro
Hanning, Gary William *utilities executive, consultant, water transportation executive*

Richardson
Cox, David Leon *telecommunications industry executive*

Salado
Parks, Lloyd Lee *oil industry executive*

San Antonio
Arthur, Gary L., Jr. *energy executive*
Blank, Steven A. *energy executive*
Brown, Mary Rose *energy executive*
Browning, Jay D. *energy executive*
Burden, W. Eugene *oil industry executive*
Callaway, James W. (Jim) *telecommunications industry executive*
Ciskowski, Michael S. *energy executive*
Coughlin, Cathy M. *telecommunications industry executive*
Crownover, Mike *energy executive*
Dorman, David W. *former telecommunications industry executive*
Edwards, Gene *energy executive*
Edwards, S. Eugene *energy executive*
Ellis, James D. *telecommunications industry executive, lawyer*
Finnerty, William J. *oil industry executive*
Flagg, C.A. (Chuck Flagg) *oil industry executive*
Gorder, Joseph W. *energy executive*
Haywood, J. William *oil industry executive*
Jennings, Karen *telecommunications industry executive*
Kahan, James S. *telecommunications industry executive*
Killinger, Clayton *energy executive*
Klaerner, Curtis Maurice *gas industry executive*
Lewis, Everett D. *oil industry executive*
Lindner, Richard G. *telecommunications industry executive*
Marcogliese, Richard J. *energy executive*
McCoy, Reagan Scott *oil industry executive, lawyer*
Miller, Forrest E. *telecommunications industry executive*
Monroe, Joseph M. *oil industry executive*
Pawel, Nancy Emma Ray *oil industry executive, educator, artist*
Porter, Daniel J. *oil industry executive*
Renfro, Norm *energy executive*
Schwethelm, Otto C. *oil industry executive*
Smith, Bruce Alfred *oil industry executive*
Stephenson, Randall L. *telecommunications industry executive*
Upton, Wade *energy executive*
Westfall, Lynn D. *oil industry executive*
Whitacre, Edward E., Jr. *retired telecommunications industry executive*
Wilkins, Rayford, Jr. *telecommunications industry executive*
Wiskocil, Angiolina *telecommunications industry executive*
Wright, Gregory A. *oil industry executive*
Zesch, Hal *energy executive*

Snyder
Siegel, Mark S. *energy executive*
Talbott, Cloyce A. *energy executive*

Spring
Corbett, Luke R. *former energy company executive*

The Woodlands
Hackett, James T. *oil industry executive*
Kurz, Karl F. *oil industry executive*
Sharman, Richard Lee *telecommunications executive, consultant*
Walker, R. A. *oil industry executive*
Wilcox, Raymond I. *oil industry executive*

Tyler
Hughes, Arthur Hyde *accountant, energy industry executive, accountant*

Whitewright
Burg, John Parker *electric power industry executive*

Wichita Falls
Fowler, Robert Martin *oil industry executive, consultant*

UTAH

Ogden
Adams, J. Phillip *oil industry executive*

Park City
Edwards, Howard Lee *retired oil and gas industry executive, lawyer*

Salt Lake City
Cash, Roy Don *retired gas and petroleum company executive*
Holding, R(obert) Earl *oil industry executive*
Rattie, Keith O. *gas industry executive*
Sigal, Jill Lea *nuclear energy industry executive, former federal agency administrator*

VERMONT

Barnard
Larson, John Hyde *retired utilities executive*

Dorset
Hittle, Richard Howard *gas and oil industry executive, consultant*

North Clarendon
Freed, Walter Everett *petroleum company executive, state representative*

Springfield
Guité, J. C. Michel *telephone company owner*

VIRGINIA

Abingdon
Quillen, Michael J. *energy executive*

Alexandria
Copulos, Milton Russell *energy executive*
Hirsch, Robert Louis *energy analyst, consultant*

Arlington
Bakke, Dennis W. *energy company executive*
Hanrahan, Paul Thaddeus *utilities executive*
Harker, Victoria D. *electric power industry executive*
Luraschi, William R. *utilities executive, lawyer*

Chesterfield
Love, Dana Francis Ignatius *telecommunications industry executive*

Herndon
Gilbert, Douglas Brainerd *telecommunications industry executive*

Lynchburg
Womack, Edgar Allen, Jr. *energy executive, nuclear technology consultant*

Mc Lean
Singh, K. Paul *telecommunications industry executive*

Reston
Angelino, Mark E. *telecommunications industry executive*
Conway, William E., Jr. *telecommunications industry executive, venture capitalist*
Cowan, Keith O. *telecommunications industry executive*
Dziak, Jack *telecommunications industry executive*
Foosaner, Robert Stephen *telecommunications industry executive, lawyer*
Forsee, Gary D. *telecommunications industry executive*
Grivner, Carl J. *telecommunications industry executive*
Gude, Atish *telecommunications industry executive*
Kennedy, Leonard Jervey *telecommunications industry executive, lawyer*
LeFave, Richard T.C. *telecommunications industry executive*
Saleh, Paul N. *telecommunications industry executive*
Shindler, Steven M. *telecommunications industry executive*
West, Barry J. *telecommunications industry executive*

Richmond
Alewine, Betty *retired telecommunications executive*
Blankenship, Don L. *energy executive*
Capps, Thomas Edward *utilities company executive, lawyer*
Chewning, Thomas N. *energy executive*
Christian, David A. *energy executive*
Doswell, Mary Cummings *energy executive*
Farrell, Thomas Francis, II, *energy executive*
Hardy, Eva Teig *energy executive*
Hetzer, G. Scott *energy executive*
Johnson, Jay L. *energy executive*
Koonce, Paul D. *energy executive*
McGettrick, Mark F. *energy executive*
Radtke, Duane C. *energy executive*
Rogers, Steven A. *energy executive*
Sanderlin, James L. *energy executive*

Sterling
Oller, William Maxwell *retired energy executive, retired military officer*

Suffolk
Hines, Angus Irving, Jr. *petroleum marketing executive*

WASHINGTON

Bellevue
Reynolds, Stephen Philip *utility company executive*
Williamson, Charles R. *retired energy company executive*

Kirkland
Chapple, John H. *telecommunications industry and former professional sports team executi*

Olympia
Oberbillig, Molly Castleman *utilities executive*

Seattle
Rosput Reynolds, Paula Gail (Paula Rosput Reynolds) *energy executive*

Spokane
Eliassen, Jon Eric *retired corporate financial a utilities executive*
Ely, Gary G. *utilities company executive*

WEST VIRGINIA

Bluefield
Reid, William James *mining executive*

WISCONSIN

Green Bay
Weyers, Larry Lee *energy executive*

La Crosse
Rude, Brian David *utilities executive*

Madison
Bisbee, Joyce Evelyn *retired utility company executive*
Harvey, William D. *utilities executive, lawyer*

Milwaukee
Klappa, Gale E. *energy executive*

WYOMING

Casper
Stroock, Thomas Frank *oil and gas company executive*

Riverton
Bebout, Eli Daniel *oil industry executive*

TERRITORIES OF THE UNITE STATES

VIRGIN ISLANDS

St Thomas
Prior, Cornelius Bernard, Jr. *utilities executive, financial consultant*

CANADA

ALBERTA

Calgary
Anderson, J.C. *oil and gas industry executive, rancher*
Arledge, David A. *energy executive*
Daniel, Patrick D. *energy executive*
Haskayne, Richard Francis *retired petroleum company executive*
Horton, William Russell *retired utilities executive*
McKinnon, F(rancis) A(rthur) Richard *utilities executive*
Pourbaix, Alexander *energy executive*
Seaman, Daryl Kenneth *oil industry executive*
Southern, Nancy C. *utilities executive*
Swartout, Hank B. *oil and gas industry execu*

Red Deer
Donald, Jack C. *gas industry executive*

BRITISH COLUMBIA

Vancouver
Friedland, Robert M. *mining executive*
Keevil, Norman B. *mining executive*
Lyons, Terrence Allan *mining executive*
Willson, John Michael *retired mining compan executive*

ONTARIO

Brockville
Spalding, James Stuart *retired telecommunications industry executive*

North York
Blundell, William Richard Charles *retired electric company executive*

Richmond Hill
Fong, Maryanne T.P. *telecommunications industry executive, researcher*

Toronto
Clark, Maura J. *oil and gas industry executive*
Martin, Robert William *retired utilities execut*
Munk, Peter *mining executive*
Osler, Gordon Peter *retired utilities executive*

Wilson, Lynton Ronald *retired telecommunications industry executive*

QUEBEC

Montreal
Cyr, J. V. Raymond *telecommunications industry executive*

Calgary
Maier, Gerald James *gas industry executive*

Niagara Falls
Watson, George W. *energy executive*

CHINA

Beijing
Wu, Ying *telecommunications industry executive*

ENGLAND

London
Carroll, Cynthia B. *mining executive*
Duffy, Simon P. *telecommunications industry executive*
Mooney, James F. *telecommunications industry executive*
olk, George Washington *telecommunications executive, entrepreneur*

JAPAN

Yokohama
o, Noboru *electric power industry executive*

NETHERLANDS

Amsterdam
ahan, Rene *retired oil industry executive*

Rotterdam
n Wachem, Lodewijk Christiaan *petroleum company executive*

The Hague
ook, Linda Z. *utilities executive*

SINGAPORE

ll, Gregory Paul *oil industry executive*

ADDRESS UNPUBLISHED

n, Chungming *telecommunications industry executive*
nderson, Robert Orville *oil and gas company executive*
rlidge, John Walter *retired utilities executive*
rthur, John Morrison *retired utilities executive*
rham, Charles Dewey, Jr. *electric power industry executive, lawyer*
rnes, Wesley Edward *energy and environmental executive*
rr, James III *telecommunications company executive*
rrow, Thomas Davies *retired oil and mining company executive, consultant*
umgartner, John H. *gas industry executive*
avers, Roy Lackey *retired utilities executive, volunteer, writer*
rry, William Willis *retired utilities executive*
jur, Peter I. *retired petroleum company executive*
densteiner, Lisa M. *former utilities executive, lawyer*
others, John Alfred *retired oil company executive, chemicals executive*
own, Stephen S. *telecommunications industry executive*
uce, James Edmund *retired utilities executive*
yan, J(ames) P(erry), Jr. *energy executive*
rrow, Harold *retired gas industry executive*
tler, Jack Fairchild *electric power industry executive*
elle, Robert Frederick *electric power industry executive, educator*
ilders, Charles Eugene *mining company executive*
ffin, Bertha Louise *retired telecommunications industry executive*
llins, Steve Anthony *oil industry executive*
mer, Clarence C. *gas industry executive*
nger, Harry Milton *mining company executive*
llen, James G. *telecommunications industry executive*
rtis, Edward Joseph, Jr. *gas industry executive, management consultant*
a, Peter Allen *gas industry executive, geologist*
mere, Robert Houstoun, Jr. *oil industry executive*
ckey, Joseph William *utilities executive, engineer*
Giovanni, Anthony *retired coal mining company executive*
agoumis, Paul *electric utility company executive*
aper, E(rnest) Linn, Jr. *retired electric utility executive*
kmann, Rory Albert *telecommunications industry executive*
glish, Floyd Leroy *telecommunications industry executive*
skine, Rodney D. *oil industry executive*
Esrey, William Todd *telecommunications company executive*
Evans, John Derby *telecommunications industry executive*
Fagin, David Kyle *mining executive*
Feidler, Mark L. *telecommunications industry executive*
Feinberg, David M. *energy executive, lawyer*
Finger, Harold Ben *nuclear energy industry executive, consultant, government agency administrator*
Ford, Judith Ann Tudor *retired natural gas distribution company executive*
Fowke, Benjamin G.S. III *energy executive*
Frisbee, Don Calvin *retired utilities executive*
Fuller, Sandra Vivian *oil and gas industry executive*
Gabel, Ronald Glen *telecommunications executive*
Gardiner, Hobart Clive *petroleum company executive*
Gerard, Roy Dupuy *retired oil company executive*
Gerber, Murry S. *gas, oil and utilities executive*
Gottschalk, Charles M. *international energy consultant*
Greehey, William Eugene (Bill Greehey) *energy executive*
Greer, Carl Crawford *petroleum company executive*
Gurian, Mal *telecommunications executive*
Hall, Milton Reese *retired oil company executive, accountant, controller*
Heiney, John Weitzel *former utilities executive*
Herron, Edwin Hunter, Jr. *energy consultant*
Hines, Andrew Hampton, Jr. *utilities executive*
Huffman, James Thomas William *oil industry executive*
Hughes, Nicholas Melvin *mining company executive*
Hurst, Leland Lyle *natural gas company executive*
Hyland, Geoffrey Fyfe *retired energy executive*
Isaacs, Jonathan William *oil industry executive*
Jackson, Robert William *retired utilities executive*
Kaculi, Xhemal T. *oil industry analysis/design engineer*
Kaiser, Robert A. *telecommunications industry executive*
King, Gregory C. *energy executive*
King, William Collins *retired oil industry executive*
Kirkby, Maurice Anthony *oil industry executive*
Klesse, William R. (Bill Klesse) *energy executive*
Lamont, Edward Miner, Jr. *telecommunications industry executive*
Lauer, Len J. *former telecommunications executive*
Lefar, Marc P. *former telecommunications industry executive*
Lewis, Floyd Wallace *former electric utility executive*
Lilly, Edward Guerrant, Jr. *retired utilities executive*
Liu, Wei *telecommunications industry executive, researcher*
Loveland, Eugene Franklin *retired gas industry executive*
Lowrie, William G. *former oil company executive*
Lutz, Matthew Charles *oil industry executive, geologist*
MacFarlane, John Charles *utilities executive*
Mauch, Robert Carl *energy and financial services executive*
Mc Carthy, Walter John, Jr. *retired utilities executive*
McCready, Kenneth Frank *former electric utility executive*
McSweeny, William Francis *petroleum company executive, author*
Middleton, James Arthur *oil and gas company executive*
Mitchell, George Phydias *gas and petroleum company executive*
Montgomery, Roy Delbert *retired gas industry executive*
Morrell, Gene Paul *gas industry executive, consultant*
Munsey, Virdell Everard, Jr. *retired utilities executive*
Myers, Franklin *oil industry executive*
Nicholson, Leland Ross *retired utilities executive, energy consultant*
Nurenberg, David *retired oil company executive*
O'Connor, James John *retired utility company executive*
O'Hare, James Raymond *energy executive*
Ormasa, John *retired utilities executive*
Owens, William Arthur (Bill Owens) *telecommunications industry executive, retired military officer*
Peterson, Donald Kent *former telecommunications industry executive*
Pierce, Lisa Margaret *telecommunications industry executive, marketing professional, educator*
Portal, Gilbert Marcel Adrien *oil industry executive*
Priory, Richard Baldwin *former electric power industry executive*
Pryor, Richard Walter *telecommunications executive, retired air force officer*
Quillen, Lloyd Douglas *oil and gas executive*
Rawson, Richard J. *telecommunications industry executive, lawyer*
Rendu, Jean-Michel Marie *mining executive*
Richman, Paul *semiconductor industry executive, educator*
Roberts, Lawrence Gilman *telecommunications industry executive*
Roe, Thomas Coombe *former utility company executive*
Rogers, Justin Towner, Jr. *retired utility company executive*
Rose, Michael Elvin *oil and gas exploration company executive*
St. Clair, Thomas McBryar *mining and manufacturing company executive*
Salerno, Frederic V. *retired telecommunications company executive*
Sanders, Charles Franklin *energy executive, consultant*
Schenck, Jack Lee *retired electric utility executive*
Scott, Isadore Meyer *retired energy executive*
Senty, James A. *energy executive*
Serkes, Jeffrey D. *former energy executive*
Shannon, W. Patrick *telecommunications industry executive*
Shoup, Andrew James, Jr. *retired oil industry executive*
Sibbernsen, Richard *telecommunications industry executive*
Smith, Elmer *telecommunications industry executive*
Smith, Paul Vergon, Jr. *retired gas industry executive*
Snyder, Michael F. *telecommunications industry executive*
Soregaroli, A(rthur) E(arl) *mining executive, geologist*
Stratman, Joseph Lee *oil and gas industry executive, consultant, retired chemical engineer*
Thomas, Kenneth Glyndwr *mining executive*
Thompson, Jack Edward *mining company executive*
Thorn, Terence Hastings *energy executive, consultant, writer*
Tillinghast, John Avery *utilities executive*
Todd, Zane Grey *retired utilities executive*
Travis, Vance Kenneth *petroleum business executive*
Trutter, John Thomas *telecommunications industry executive, educator, writer*
Tucker, H. Richard *oil industry executive*
Vermylen, Paul Anthony, Jr. *oil industry executive*
Wannier, Mario Marc-Antoine *oil industry executive, multi-media specialist, director*
Weaver, William Schildecker *retired electric power industry executive*
Weeks, William Rawle, Jr. *oil industry executive*
Whisler, James Steven *retired mining executive, lawyer, rancher*
Wickstrom, Jon Alan *telecommunications executive, consultant*
Wilkerson, Matha Ann *retired oil company executive*
Williams, Neville *solar power company executive*
Wilson, Walter Clinton *retired oil and gas industry executive*
Wood, Willis Bowne, Jr. *retired utilities executive*
Wright, David John *telecommunications systems specialist, educator*
Wright, Randolph Earle *retired petroleum company executive*
Wrobel, Bruce J. *energy and utilities company executive*

INFORMATION TECHNOLOGY
See also SCIENCE: MATHEMATICS AND COMPUTER SCIENCE

UNITED STATES

ALABAMA

Florence
Foote, Avon Edward *web developer/producer, communications educator*

Huntsville
Sturges, Keith *information technology executive*

Mobile
McCleery, Winston Theodore *information technology executive*
Parman, Tracy Le *application developer*

Prattville
Hickman, Walter Dixon, II, *information technology manager*

ARIZONA

Scottsdale
Andermann, Mary Annette *application developer, consultant*
Friesen, Oris Dewayne *software engineer, historian*
Stott, Brian *software company executive, consultant*

Tempe
Crown, Eric J. *information systems executive*
Crown, Timothy A. *computer technology company executive*
Fennessy, Richard A. *information technology executive*
Pohlman, Craig Steven *application developer*

Tucson
Donoghue, John Charles *application developer, consultant*
Fredericksen, Dick Hartman *retired computer programmer*

CALIFORNIA

Antelope
Nenov, Ivo P. *mathematical and software researcher*

Berkeley
Karp, Richard Manning *computer science educator*
Séquin, Carlo H. *computer science educator*
Wieczorek, John Richard *application developer, systems analyst*

Calabasas
Jones, Richard K. *information technology executive*

Cupertino
Bregman, Mark *information technology executive*
Clyde, Robert Allan *computer software engineer*
Ive, Jonathan *information technology executive, product designer*
Johnson, Ron *information technology executive*
Nielsen, Tod *information technology executive*
Schiller, Philip W. *information technology executive*
Serlet, Bertrand *information technology executive*
Tamaddon, Sina *information technology executive*
Thompson, John W. *information technology executive*

Cypress
Romero, Tony *information technology executive*

Danville
Bergsten, James Robert *computer technology architect*

Del Mar
Fricke, Martin Paul *science company executive*

Folsom
Haga, Enoch John *computer educator, writer, editor*
Krishnaswamy, Dilip *computer architect*

Fremont
Tang, John *network technician, information scientist, educator*

Glen Ellen
Hurlbert, Roger William *information technology executive*

Glendale
Phipps, Robert Lee *information technology manager*

Hemet
Clark, Harold L. *technology company executive, consultant*

Irvine
Morhaime, Mike *video game company executive*
Pardo, Robert *game designer, video game software company executive*

Lafayette
Lewis, Sheldon Noah *technology consultant*

Los Alamitos
Weinberger, Frank *information management consultant*

Los Angeles
Boehm, Barry William *computer science educator*
Grouf, Nick *information technology, advertising executive*
Halloran, John Alan *information technology executive*

Martinez
Tong, Siu Wing *computer programmer*

Menlo Park
Cassidy, Mike *online game company executive*
Dubinsky, Donna L. *information technology executive*
Hewlett, Walter B. *application developer*
Scoble, Robert *podcast network company executive, blog writer*

Modesto
Kushar, Kent *information technology executive*

Mountain View
Armstrong, Tim *information technology executive*
Baker, Mitchell *computer software developer, foundation administrator*
Balogh, Aristotle N. *information technology executive*
Bloch, Joshua J. *software designer*
Brin, Sergey Mihailovich *information technology executive*
Brown, Shona L. *information technology executive*
Bunnell, Ben *information technology manager*
Cerf, Vinton Gray *information technology executive*
Coughran, William M., Jr. *information technology executive, researcher*
Drummond, David C. *information technology executive, lawyer*
Eschelbeck, Gerhard *information technology executive*
Eustace, Alan *information technology executive*
Gillis, Edwin *information technology executive*
Gitlin, Richard D. *telecommunications technology executive*
Halvorsen, Per-Kristian *software company executive, former educator, researcher*
Hughes, Gregory *information technology executive*

Kordestani, Omid *information technology executive*
Mayer, Marissa Ann *information technology executive*
Nucci, Antonio *information technology executive*
Page, Larry (Lawrence E. Page) *information technology executive*
Reyes, George *information technology executive*
Rosenberg, Jonathan *information technology executive*
Sarukkai, Sekhar *information technology executive*
Schmidt, Eric Emerson *information technology executive*
Singh, Sangita *information technology and marketing executive*
Wang, Sheldon *information technology executive, insurance company executive*

Newport Beach
Fielding, Roy Thomas *software scientist*

Oakland
Butterworth, Paul *information technology executive*
Smith, Christopher Allen *information technology executive, financial executive*

Orange
Ahlquist, John B. *application developer*

Palo Alto
Craparo, John S. *information technology executive*
Daniels, Russell *information technology executive*
Denzel, Nora *information technology executive*
Greene, Diane *information technology executive*
Lal, Dhananjay *information technology executive, researcher*

Redondo Beach
Sloan, Michael Dana *information systems specialist, management consultant*

Redwood City
Block, Keith *computer software company executive*
Burkhardt, Roger *information technology executive*
Catz, Safra A. *computer software company executive*
Ellison, Larry (Lawrence Joseph) *computer software company executive*
Henley, Jeffrey O. *computer software company executive*
Kurian, Thomas *computer software company executive*
Lee, V. Paul *entertainment software company executive*
Minton, Jennifer *computer software company executive*
Moore, Peter *interactive entertainment software company executive*
Phillips, Charles E., Jr. *computer software company executive*
Probst, Lawrence F. III *interactive software/gaming executive*
Riccitiello, John S. *interactive software/gaming executive, venture capitalist*
Rohde, James Vincent *software systems company executive*
Rottler, Juergen *computer software company executive*
Rozwat, Charles *computer software company executive*
Vrabeck, Kathy Patterson *video game company executive*
Wookey, John *computer software company executive*

Romoland
Nail, Phil *information technology executive*

Sacramento
Hummel, John *information technology executive*

San Bernardino
Baek, Eun-Ok *instructional technology educator*

San Diego
Goldstein, Mark Kingston Levin *information technology executive, researcher*
Rastetter, William H. *biotechnology company executive*
Short, Jay Milton *biotechnology company executive*
Simpson, William *information technology manager, consultant*
Suycott, Mark Leland *program manager, retired military officer*
Tom, Lawrence *technology executive*

San Francisco
Buckmaster, Jim *online community bulletin board company executive*
Cohen, Bram *web programmer*
Fanning, Shawn *information technology executive*
Hatt, David *application developer, composer*
Hirschmann, Peter *video game company executive*
Kapor, Mitchell David *application developer, foundation administrator*
Rosedale, Philip E. *computer software company executive*
Trott, Mena *application developer*

San Jose
Belluzzo, Rick E. (Richard) *information technology and former computer software company executive*
Chambers, John Thomas *computer systems network executive*
Chandler, Mark D. *computer systems network executive, lawyer*
Chuang, Alfred S. *information technology executive*
Coleman, William T. *information technology executive*
Emmett, Brian *software developer*
Fishback, Dennis *information technology executive*
Grandison, Tyrone Wilberforce André *systems administrator*
Helleboid, Olivier *information technology executive*
Ill, Charles III *information technology executive*
Judge, Paul *information technology executive*
Loiacono, John P. *information technology executive*
Morgridge, John P. *computer systems network executive*
Powell, Dennis D. *computer systems network executive*
Sauvageau, Yvon *application developer*

San Mateo
Farmer, Dan *computer security researcher, computer programmer*

San Ramon
Lyons, Robert *information technology executive*
Moore, Justin Edward *information technology executive*
Schofield, James Roy *computer programmer*

Santa Ana
Boyd, Larry C. *information technology executive*
Foster, Kent B. *information technology executive*
Humes, William D. *information technology executive*
Murai, Kevin M. *information technology executive*
Salem, Karen E. *information technology executive*
Spierkel, Gregory M. *information technology executive*

Santa Barbara
Boehm, Eric Hartzell *information technology executive*

Santa Clara
Bechtolsheim, Andy (Andreas) *information technology executive*
Benson, Jon H. *information technology executive*
Beveridge, Crawford W. *information technology executive*
Dai, Weili *information technology executive*
Denholm, Robyn *information technology executive*
Dessau, Nigel *information technology executive*
Fowler, John *information technology executive*
Fuller, Dale L. *software security company executive*
Gadre, Anil *information technology executive*
Grantham, Don *information technology executive*
Green, Rich *information technology executive*
Grossman, Jeremiah *information technology executive*
Harris, David M. *information technology executive*
Heel, Joe *information technology executive*
Howe, Bill *information technology executive*
Lehman, Michael Evans *information technology executive*
Lieto, Tim *information technology executive*
MacGowan, Bill *information technology executive*
McCabe, Eugene *information technology executive*
McNealy, Scott Glenn *information technology executive*
Miller, Dan *information technology executive*
Murdock, Ian *information technology executive*
Papadopoulos, Gregory Michael *information technology executive*
Schwartz, Jonathan Ian *information technology executive*
Stern, Hal *information technology executive*
Sutardja, Sehat *information technology executive*
Sutphin, Brian *information technology executive*
Tremblay, Marc *information technology executive*
Van Den Hoogen, Ingrid *information technology executive*
White, Ian *information technology executive*
Yen, David Wei-Luen *information technology executive*

Santa Monica
Sekularac, Nadezda *software architect, researcher*

Scotts Valley
Janssen, James Robert *consulting software engineer*

South Pasadena
Hsieh, Ming *information technology executive*

South San Francisco
Ryan, Tom *reporting applications platform company executive*

Stanford
Feigenbaum, Edward Albert *retired computer science educator*

Sunnyvale
Andreessen, Marc *software company executive, internet innovator*
Bazzi, Samer *software developer, consultant*
Calderoni, Robert M. *software company executive*
Cambou, Bertrand *information technology executive*
Hawkins, Jeff *information technology company executive*
Kriens, Scott G. *information technology executive*
McCoy, Thomas M. *information technology executive*
Payton, Paul Max *application developer*
Ruiz, Hector de Jesus *information technology executive*
Xie, Ken *software company executive*

West Sacramento
Wilson, Eric F.G. *information technology executive*

COLORADO

Aurora
Balle, James Christian *information technology manager*

Boulder
Kenney, Belinda Jill Forseman *information technology executive*

Broomfield
O'Hara, Kevin J. *information technology executive*

Colorado Springs
Gibson, John Robert *software engineer*
Heffron, Michael Edward *software engineer, computer scientist*

Denver
Rodriguez, Juan Alfonso *information technology executive*

Greenwood Village
Duques, Ric (Henry C. Duques) *information technology company executive*

Littleton
Marion, John Martin *instructional technology educator*

Louisville
Martin, Patrick J. *technology company executive*

CONNECTICUT

Danbury
Collar, Emilio, Jr. *information systems consultant*

Fairfield
Fash, Victoria R. *business executive*
Immelt, Jeffrey R. *diversified technology and services company executive*
Reiner, Gary M. *diversified technology and services company executive*
Rice, John G. *diversified technology and services executive*
Wright, Bob (Robert Charles Wright) *diversified technology and services company executive, former broadcast executive*

Mashantucket
Yale, John Paul *computer systems developer*

New Britain
Margiotta, Mary-Lou Ann *application developer*

New London
Carpenter, Bruce William *information technology manager, director*

Norwalk
Alvey, Brian *blogger*
Carlucci, David R. *information technology executive*

Norwich
Pudlo, Steven Edward *computer technician*

Stamford
Dammerman, Dennis Dean *diversified technology and services company executive*
Wilderotter, Maggie (Mary Agnes Wilderotter) *software company executive, former cable television executive*
Wilens, Michael Engber *information technology executive, biologist, microscopist*

Trumbull
Lang, James Richard *software designer, magician*

Westport
Frese, Edward Scheer, Jr., (Ted Frese) *information technology executive, consultant*

DELAWARE

Newark
Klevinsky, Thomas Jason *information technology executive*

DISTRICT OF COLUMBIA

Pentagon
Gourley, Robert *information technology executive*

Washington
Allen, Dwayne LeRoy *information systems specialist*
Belak, Michael James *information technology executive*
Dale, Adrianne Marie *information technology executive, consultant*
Day, Melvin Sherman *information and telecommunications company executive*
Gross, Patrick Walter *information technology executive*
Meyer, Paul *information technology executive*
Otto, Robert L. *information technology executive*
Rose, George Andrew *application developer, information systems specialist*
Shields, Christopher Andrew *website director*
Wertheim, Mitzi Mallina *information technology executive*
Wilson, Carl *information technology executive*

FLORIDA

Boca Raton
Breakstone, Robert Albert *information technology executive, consumer products company executive, consultant*

Celebration
Johnson, Derrick M. *information technology executive*

Deerfield Beach
Yerves, Ken *information technology executive*

Fort Lauderdale
Wood, James McKean *application developer*

Fort Pierce
Hurley, William Joseph *retired information technology executive*

Hollywood
Barish, Randall David *application developer*

Jacksonville
Chambers, Jack Allen *application developer, educator*
Payne, Timothy D. *information technology executive*
Portell, Keith S *application developer, consulta*

Miami
Clemence, Cheryl Lynn *systems administrator*
Watson, Doug *information technology executive*

Naples
Thomas, Gary Lynn *information technology executive*

Newberry
Thornton, J. Ronald *technology consultant*

Ocala
Strait, William Robert *computer technician*

Ormond Beach
Burke, Marguerite Jodi Larcombe *application developer, consultant*

Palm Beach Gardens
Ziglar, James W. *biometrics industry executive, lawyer, educator*

Plantation
Nair, Krishnakumar R. *application developer, researcher*

Punta Gorda
Ott, Walter Richard *information technology executive, writer*

Saint Petersburg
Frazier, A. D., Jr. *information technology executive, lawyer*

Sanibel
Trevor, Alexander Bruen *information technolo consultant*

Tampa
Bedgood, Alvin J. *information technology manager, director*
Moffett, Susan L. *information technology manager*

Winter Park
Johnson, Constance Ann Trillich *web site designer*
Steward, Sherry Ann *information technology executive, educator*

GEORGIA

Alpharetta
Herbig, Joan E. *information technology execu*

Atlanta
Blalock, Rebecca A. *information technology specialist*
Fleury, Marc *application developer*
Goldfarb, Eric Daniel *information technology executive*
Miller, Sue *information technology executive*
Norman, Elaine Mitchell *information technolo executive*
Powers, Susan J. *information technology executive*

Canton
Wilson, Brian Andrew *computing performance consultant, educator, writer, editor*

Norcross
Mangum, Mylle Bell *information technology executive*

Swainsboro
Watt, (Arthur) Dwight, Jr. *computer programming and microcomputer specialist*

IDAHO

Boise
Mahoney, James E. *information technology executive*

LINOIS

bbott Park
rke, Sandra E. *information technology executive*

urr Ridge
senberg, Robert Brinkmann *information technology executive*

hampaign
ang, Kathy Kuhl *computer programmer, analyst*

hicago
rgstein, Melvyn *information technology executive*
stin, Joseph Laurence, Jr. *information services executive*
yer, Dennis D. *information technology executive*
ed, Jason *software development company executive*
rzolini, Judith A. *information technology manager*
nsson, David Heinemeier *application developer*
, Chiang *information technology educator*
rson, Nancy Celeste *information technology manager*
nell-Stephens, June Alicia *information broker, consultant, librarian*
isman, Andrew Louis *information technology executive, lawyer*
ott, Nancy L. *information technology manager, health facility administrator, consultant*
iokla, John Julius *technology consultant*
cker, David F. *information technology executive*

ystal Lake
lperin, Richard George *information technology executive*

erfield
rshteyn, Yefim *application developer, researcher*

fingham
heree, Joseph G. *informaation technology educator*

anston
her, Andrew Taylor *computer software developer*

perville
der, Carl *information technology executive*

rk Ridge
son, George Malcolmson *application developer*

voy
Connell, William Stewart *application developer*

haumburg
rrison, Patricia B. *information technology executive*

ringfield
cock, Eric *application developer*

rnon Hills
vardson, John Albert *information technology executive*
in, Barbara A. *information technology executive*

arrenville
a, Art J. *information technology executive*

nnetka
, William Norman, Jr. *technology company executive*

odridge
henpurakal, Joseph Mathew *information technology executive*

DIANA

omington
nning, Jeremy David *application developer, dean, educator*
son, Jane Elizabeth *information management professional, adult education educator*
th, Janet Sue *systems process specialist*

rmel
tick, Russell M. *information technology executive*

ettsville
ng, Frederic Hisgen *information systems executive, data processing consultant*

rt Wayne
roll, Betty Jean *retired application developer*

rre Haute
, Susan M. *information specialist*

WA

ar Lake
a, Robert John *software engineer*

verly
nkhorst, Robert John *computer programmer, analyst*

KANSAS

Claflin
Lewis, Robert V., Jr. *computer programmer*

Kansas City
Olofson, Tom William *technology company executive*

Overland Park
Baldwin, William Allen *application developer*

KENTUCKY

Lexington
Canales, Denise Niles *software company executive*
Curlander, Paul Joseph *technology executive*

Louisville
Martin, David Allen *application developer, computer scientist*

LOUISIANA

Luling
Scherer, Donald James, II, *systems administrator, researcher*

MAINE

Yarmouth
Grover, Mark Donald *application developer, computer scientist*

MARYLAND

Baltimore
Park, Mary Woodfill *information consultant, librarian, writer*
Perlman, Beth S. *information technology executive*
Strull, Gene *technology consultant, retired manufacturing executive*

Beltsville
Basinger, William Daniel *computer programmer*

College Park
Miller, Raymond Edward *computer science educator*

Frederick
Merrill, Daniel A. *program manager*

Hyattsville
Asongu, Januarius Jingwa *business executive*

Rockville
Gibson, William M. *technology company executive*
Haber, Margaret Wilson *informatics specialist, director*
MacArthur, Diana Taylor *advanced technology executive*
Proffitt, John Richard *information technology executive, educator, public official*

Silver Spring
Rice, Rick Blackburn *application developer, systems analyst*
Tobe, Barbara Gaines *information technology executive*

MASSACHUSETTS

Beverly
Smith, Derek Armand *information technology executive*

Boston
Arnold, Kirk *information technology executive*
Ascenzo, Carl *information technology executive*
Kumar, Vikram Sheel *information technology executive*
Lane, Kathy S. *information technology executive, consumer products company executive*
Masi, Dale A. *project director, social sciences educator, research and development company executive*
Stallman, Richard Matthew *software developer*

Cambridge
Berners-Lee, Sir Timothy John *inventor of world wide web, research scientist, writer*
Brennan, Todd *information technology executive*
Brooks, Rodney Allen *information technology executive, educator*
Gagliardi, Ugo Oscar *systems software architect, educator*
Greenberg, Jerry A. *information technology executive*
Mandl, Robert *application developer*
Mullen, James C. *biotechnology company executive*
Roberts, Edward Baer *technology management educator*

Duxbury
Zachmann, William Francis *computer and communications industry market research company executive*

Foxboro
Martin, Peter Gerard *computer technician, consultant, secondary school educator*

Hopkinton
Goulden, David *information technology executive*
Tucci, Joseph M. *information technology executive*

Lexington
Ting, David *information technology executive*

Lynn
D'Entremont, Edward Joseph *application developer, educator*

Marlborough
Chong, James I. *information technology executive*
Willebeek-LeMair, Marc *information technology executive*

Mashpee
Kilmartin, Joseph Francis, Jr. *information technology executive*

Newton
Bagalay, John Earl *information technology executive, venture capitalist, consultant*

Newton Highlands
Bricklin, Daniel *software designer, consultant*

North Dartmouth
Xu, Haiping *application developer, educator*

Salem
McKenzie, Walter L. *information technology executive, consultant*

Sudbury
McCree, Paul William, Jr. *systems design and engineering company executive*

Waltham
Bleicher, Paul Alan *information technology executive, physician*
Heystee, Susan *information technology executive*
Hovsepian, Ronald W. *network management software company executive*
Messman, Jack L. *network management software company executive*

Woburn
Mehra, Raman Kumar *aerospace and defense technology executive, automotion and control engineering researcher*
Sharp, William Thomas *information technology executive*

MICHIGAN

Ann Arbor
Mendez, David *information systems and operations research educator*
Spence, David Wendel *application developer*
Vielmetti, Edward Marshall *webmaster*

Auburn Hills
Suravajjala, Mamatha *information technology manager*
Young, Stacy A. *information technology manager*

Bloomfield Hills
Weil, John William *technology management consultant*

Detroit
Kruse, Ronia *information technology executive*

Grand Rapids
Hoekstra, Mark Rains *information technology executive, consultant*

Southfield
Drebus, John Richard *computer consultant*

Troy
Walker, Bette M. *information technology executive*

West Bloomfield
Cox, Clifford Ernest *information systems consulting executive, former academic administrator*

Ypsilanti
Boone, Morell Douglas *information technology educator*

MINNESOTA

Buffalo
Moon, James Russell *retired technology education educator*

Eagan
Gouin, Warner Peter *information technology consultant*

Lino Lakes
Jezierski, Scott *wireless monitoring, security, and surveillance company executive*

Minneapolis
Beck, Joshua James *information technology executive*
Marinello, Kathryn V. *information technology executive*
Perlman, Lawrence *retired information technology executive*

Oakdale
Russomanno, Frank P. *information technology executive*

Roseville
El-Hilali, Oussama *application developer*

MISSOURI

Fenton
Hoffman, Gilbert L. *information technology executive*

Hazelwood
Burleski, Joseph Anthony, Jr. *information technology executive*

Kansas City
McDonnell, Thomas A. *information technology executive*
Patterson, Neal L. *information systems company executive*
Thompson, Mary Elizabeth *application developer*
West, Marc *information technology executive*

O Fallon
Raeuchle, John Steven *application developer*

Rolla
Datz, Israel Mortimer *information systems specialist*

Saint Louis
Elliott, Susan Spoehrer *information technology executive*
Hassell, Stephen C. *information technology executive*
Pollack, Seymour Victor *computer science educator*

Springfield
Rogers, Clayton Rush *application developer, small business owner, consultant*

NEBRASKA

Omaha
Barker, Thomas B. *information technology executive*

NEVADA

Incline Village
Duffield, David A. *application developer, former computer software company executive*

Las Vegas
Stanley, Tim *information technology executive*

North Las Vegas
Folden, Norman C. (Skip Folden) *information systems executive, consultant*
Kubilus, Norbert John *information technology executive*

Reno
Matthews, Thomas J. *game company executive*
Ragavan, Anpalaki Jeyabalasinkham *software developer, researcher*

NEW HAMPSHIRE

Franconia
Schaffer, David Edwin *retired systems administrator*

Nashua
Smith, Thomas Raymond III *software engineer*
Walz, Deborah Sue *application developer, musician*

Portsmouth
Boutin II, Bernie L. *information technology executive*

Weare
White, Karen Ruth Jones *information systems executive*

NEW JERSEY

Bedminster
Ripp, Joseph Allen *information technology executive*

Cherry Hill
Schelm, Roger Leonard *information systems specialist*

Clark
D'Onofrio, Justin Michael *information technology manager, consultant*

Englewood Cliffs
Vazacopoulos, Alkis *application developer, educator*
Wernick, Edward Raymond *information technology executive*

Hackensack
Mavrovic, Paul J. *information technology executive*

Harrison
Winkleblech, Eileen *computer technology educator, career planning administrator*

Hazlet
Uriarte, Chris J. *information technology executive*

Morristown
Musa, John Davis *information technology executive, writer*

New Brunswick
Griffin, Gary Arthur *technological products executive*

New Providence
Bruch, Ruth E. *information technology executive*
Hackenson, Elizabeth *information technology and telecommunications industry executive*

Newark
Edwards, Samuel Lawrence, II, *information technology executive, writer*
Nash, Alicia Lardé *application developer, physicist*

Somerset
Becker, Phyllis *information technology manager*

South Orange
Hoffert, Eric Michael *application developer, information technology executive*

Sparta
Bhattacharyya, Dev *information technology executive, consultant*

Union City
Portes, Fernando A. *project manager*

NEW MEXICO

Albuquerque
Alexis, Tracy L. *project manager, project specialist, information technology manager, small business owner*
Orona, Joseph Ryan *information technology executive*
Wellborn, Charles Ivey *strategic planning consultant*

Las Cruces
Kilmer, Neal Harold *application developer*

NEW YORK

Albany
Gaddy, Sheila Mae *application developer, geriatrics nurse, writer, volunteer*

Armonk
Daniels, Michael E. *information technology executive*
Donofrio, Nicholas M. *information technology executive*
Harreld, James Bruce *information technology executive*
Horn, Paul M. *information technology executive, crystallographer*
Kelly, John E. III *information technology executive*
Zeitler, William M. *information technology executive*

Brooklyn
Doucette, David Robert *information technology executive*
Gilmore, Jennifer A.W. *computer specialist, educator*

Corning
Flaws, James B. *technology executive*

East Setauket
Simons, James Harris *technology company executive*

Endicott
Markovich, Voya R. *information technology executive*

Greenwich
Edsforth, Maureen McGill *instructional technology specialist*

Hawthorne
Yoffa, Ellen J. *information technology executive*

Hicksville
Yen, Henry Chin-Yuan *computer systems programmer, software engineer, consulting company executive*

Islandia
Cron, Kenneth D. *information technology executive*

Larchmont
Wit, David Edmund *software company executive*

Maspeth
Heppa, Douglas Van *computer specialist*

Melville
Settle, Mark *information technology executive*

Mount Vernon
Chagula, Paul Machiya *information technology executive, consultant*

New York
Bahash, Robert J. *information technology executive*
Baron, Andrew Michael *blog website producer, educator, composer*
Bernardin, Jamie *information technology executive*
Bonnell, Bruno *information technology executive*
Boyer, Aurelia G. *information technology executive*
Bross, Matthew W. *information technology executive*
Calhoun, David L. *information and media company executive*
Caponnetto, Marianne *information technology executive*
Gorton, Mark Howard *information technology executive, entrepreneur*
Green-Dorsey, Jean Audrey *information technology executive*
Iannuzzi, Salvatore *information technology executive*
Iqbal, Syma U. *information technology executive*
Kavalerchik, Boris Yakovlevich *application developer, researcher*
Kheradpir, Shaygan *information technology executive*
McGarr, Keith *information technology executive*
McGraw, Harold W., III, (Terry McGraw) *information company executive*
Modruson, Frank B. *information technology executive*
Morgan, Suann Lee *information technology manager, consultant*
Obernauer, Marne, Jr. *technology industry executive*
O'Connor, Kevin *computer programming executive*
Padmanabhan, Anand *information technology executive*
Pierce, David *information technology executive*
Pincomb, Jessica *information technology executive*
Ramachandra, Goutham K. *software architect, software developer*
Rubin, Harry Meyer *software industry executive*
Salmi, Mika *information technology executive*
Shaw, Steven A. *information technology executive*
Shionoiri, Hideo *computer technologist*
Stein, Ellen Gail *information technology manager*
Stein, Jacob *computer programmer, analyst*
Widlund, Olof Bertil *computer science educator, mathematician*

Niskayuna
Huening, Walter Carl, Jr. *retired consulting application engineer*

Palisades
Andrews, Peter James *application developer, writer*

Pittsford
Herge, Henry Curtis, Jr. *information technology executive, consultant*
Saini, Vasant Durgadas *computer software company executive*

Rochester
Canzano, Daniel A. *information technology executive*
VanGelder, Kim E. *information technology executive*

Somers
Sanford, Linda S. *information technology executive*

Syracuse
Gartner, Joseph Charles *retired systems administrator*

Tarrytown
Kenney, Dion Patrick *information technology executive, entrepreneur*

Troy
Demertzoglou, Pindaro Epaminonda *systems administrator, educator*
Hendler, James Alexander *computer science educator, consultant*

Webster
Cusick, Patricia A. *information technology executive*

White Plains
Frase, Katharine *information technology executive*
MacDonald, J. Randall *information technology executive, human resources specialist*
Mills, Steven A. *information technology executive*
Moffat, Robert W., Jr. *information technology executive*
Palmisano, Samuel J. *information technology executive*
Rometty, Ginny (Virginia M. Rometty) *information technology executive*

Yorktown Heights
Winterton, Joseph Henry *computer software executive*

NORTH CAROLINA

Cary
Buckler, Sheldon A. *technology company executive*
Goodnight, James H. *software company executive*
Sall, John *information technology executive*
Sweeney, Tim *computer game developer, programmer*

Hendersonville
Blount, Cindy Karen *web site designer, web programmer*

Raleigh
Pace, Andrew K. *information technology library director*
Szulik, Matthew J. *information technology executive*

Research Triangle Park
Gentzsch, Wolfgang *grid computing and networking service company executive*

OHIO

Athens
Kurz, David Bryan *web site designer*

Beavercreek
Pasupuleti, Venumadhav *information technology executive*

Cincinnati
Cloyd, G. Gil *information technology executive*
Guard, Roger *information technology executive*
Laney, Sandra Eileen *information technology executive*

Columbus
Taylor, Celianna Isley *information systems specialist*

Dublin
Davids, Jody R. *information technology executive*

Upper Sandusky
Baker, Harrison Scott *application developer, consultant*

Westlake
Whitehouse, John Harlan, Jr. *systems software consultant, diagnostician*

OKLAHOMA

Ada
Baker, Judith Ann *retired computer technician*

Edmond
Smock, Donald Joe *real estate analyst, political scientist*

Tulsa
Davis, Lourie Irene Bell *retired computer education and information systems specialist*

OREGON

Beaverton
Torvalds, Linus Benedict *application developer*
Wedlake, Martine *application developer*

Hillsboro
Blackburn, Terry L. *systems administrator*

Portland
Baker, William I. *application developer*
Daim, Tugrul Unsal *technology management specialist, educator*

PENNSYLVANIA

Allentown
Beck, Glenn E. *information technology executive*
Dickson, John T. *information technology executive*

Blue Bell
Dillman, Frederick *information technology executive*

Carlisle
Wyn-Jones, Alun (William Wyn-Jones) *software developer, mathematician*

Coatesville
Albrecht, Thomas Charles III *computer technician*

Crum Lynne
Metzger, Scott *information technology executive*

Gap
Burton, Mary Louise Himes *information technology executive*

Glen Mills
Kaufman, Antoinette Dolores *information technology manager*

Levittown
Lombardi, Michael *application developer*

Malvern
Bhaskar, K.S. *information technology executive*

Palmyra
Singer, William Harry *retired artificial intelligence application developer, retired research scientist*

Pittsburgh
Drawbaugh, Daniel *information technology executive, biomedical engineer*
Humphrey, Watts Sherman *information technology executive, writer*
Woods, Allan P. *information technology executive*

Reading
Hart, LeRoy Banks *systems administrator, director*
Shin, Dong-Hee *communication technology educator*

Sharpsburg
Drango, Mark A. *mechanical services specialist*

Spring House
Payn, Clyde Francis *technology company executive*

Wayne
Patel, Niraj B. *information technology executive*

RHODE ISLAND

Providence
Authelet, Keith A. *information technology executive*
Breece, Elliott *network administrator, Internet entrepreneur*
Erikson, G(eorge) E(mil) (Erik Erikson) *information specialist, anatomist, archivist, science historian*
Savage, John Edmund *computer science educator, researcher*

SOUTH CAROLINA

Charleston
Pan, Bing *information technology educator, researcher*
Plichta, Thomas Edward *software engineering company executive*

Columbia
Duggan, Kevin *information technology professional*
Hudson, Carolyn Brauer *application develope educator*

Greenville
Baur, Michael L. *information technology executive*

SOUTH DAKOTA

Sioux Falls
Bjerkaas, Carlton Lee *information technology executive*

Spearfish
Ellis, Mary Louise Helgeson *retired healthca technology company executive*

TENNESSEE

Brentwood
Davis, James Richard *software engineer, consultant*

Fayetteville
Esslinger, Eric Jason *web site designer*

Kingsport
Hale, Jerry B. *information technology executi*

Memphis
Griffin, Clement M. *information technology executive*

Nashville
Williams, Noel Brown *information technolog executive*

Sparta
Lentini, Joseph Charles *retired webmaster, systems analyst*

TEXAS

Austin
Knowles, Harry Jay *internet personality, blog film critic*
Lam, Simon Shin-Sing *computer science educator*

Bandera
Bartley, Dee Gray *information technology executive*

Conroe
Johnson, Raymond K. *information technolog manager*

Dallas
Beer, James A. *information technology execu former air transportation executive*
Blodgett, Lynn R. *information technology company executive*
Cave, Ellis *information technology executive*
Deason, Darwin *information technology executive*
Kruse, Ann Gray *computer programmer*
Pickton, Robert (Bob) J. *information technol executive*
Rexford, John H. *information technology company executive*

Dell Computers
Jarvis, Mark *information technology executiv*

Denton
Garcia, Oscar Nicolas *computer science educ*

El Paso
Olisa, Nzedegwu Robert III *information technology executive, manufacturing execu*

Houston
Beauchamp, Robert E. *information technolog executive*
Kramm, Deborah Ann *information technolog executive*

Pearland
Liles, Clifton Roy *retired application develo*

Plano
Ansari, Amir *digital home and multimedia management technology company executiv*
Ansari, Anousheh *digital home and multimed management technology company executiv first female civilian space traveler*
Ansari, Hamid *digital home and multimedia management technology company executiv*

Michael Thames *information technology utive, consultant*
skey, Michael Keith *information iology executive*
neyer, Ronald Allen *information iology executive*
lanho *application developer*
Ronald Paul *information technology utive*
ı, Richard Thomas *information technology ager, researcher*

ırdson
Jim *information technology executive*

ıntonio
y, John T. *information technology utive*

ıenville
Alma Lynn *data research administrator*

H

ˌake City
nhall, Robert W. *information technology utive*

ı Jordan
en, Laren *retired programmer*

ĠINIA

ındria
n, Janey Price *information technology :utive*
ːld, Greg *media blogger*
ːld, Matthew *media blogger*

ındale
Jay Wook *information technology :utive*
ːlson, Douglas Alan *information ınology executive*

ıgton
d, Albert M. III *information technology :utive, former federal official, retired tary officer*
i, Paul Michael *information technology :utive*
y, Lowell Edwin (Jake Jacoby) *information ınology executive, retired military officer*
ın, J. Phillip (Jack London) *information ınology executive*
lls, Wesley Oliver, Sr. *retired electronics ineering technician*
ınor, Christopher John *information ınology manager, consultant*

rlottesville
ːrs, Robert Hawver *systems administrator*

es
nley, John *information technology cutive*

ı Church
ıro, Gerard J *information technology ːcutive*
ːll, Nanci Little *information technology ːcutive, nurse*
ıe, David J. *information systems specialist, repreneur*

ındon
ːn, John Joseph, Jr. *information technology ːcutive*
ıansen, John Christian *application veloper, linguist, consultant*

len
n, Joseph Bryan *application developer*

folk
, Kurt John *computer science educator*

ton
stian, Eliot Jordan *information technology ınager, consultant*
ory, John Forrest *information technology ecialist*

ımond
Gregory James *information technology ınager*
ıer, Jackie Rae *information technology ecutive*
ermid, Margaret E. (Lyn McDermid) *formation technology executive, engineer*

ingfield
r, Mark Francis *information technology ecutive*
k, Danny Richard *computer systems gineer*

rling
ːr, Mark D. *information technology ecutive*

SHINGTON

ınbridge Island
ıons, Franklin (Chip) Arthur *application veloper, systems analyst, writer*

levue
ınyi, Charles *software engineer*
, Hongqi *application developer, researcher*

Everett
Byrne, Patrick J. *information technology executive*

Federal Way
Mersereau, Susan *information systems company, data processing executive*

Kirkland
Gilleland, John Rogers *technology company executive*

Oak Harbor
Meaux, Alan Douglas *retired computer technician, artist*

Redmond
Ayala, Orlando *information technology executive*
Bach, Robert J. (Robbie Bach) *information technology executive*
DelBene, Kurt *information technology executive*
DeVaan, Jon S. *information technology executive*
Flessner, Paul *information technology executive*
Grebnev, Igor *application developer*
He, Xiaodong *application developer*
Markezich, Ron *information technology executive*
Mattrick, Donald A. *interactive entertainment software company executive*
Nadella, Satya *information technology executive*
Raikes, Jeff *information technology executive*
Smith, Bradford Lee *information technology executive, lawyer*
Turner, Kevin (B. Kevin Turner) *information technology executive*
Vaskevitch, David *information technology executive*

Seatac
Wells, Roger Stanley *software engineer*

Seattle
Crenshaw, Edward Lee, Sr. *aviation electronics technician*
Dalzell, Rick *information technology executive*
Desouza, Kevin Clyde *application developer, educator*
Lazowska, Edward Delano *computer science educator*
Mayo, Robert N. *computer science researcher*

Tacoma
Archangelsky, Dmitry A. *application developer, researcher*

WEST VIRGINIA

Charleston
Mills, Brad *computer technician*

Martinsburg
Day, Michael Gordon *information technology executive, educator*

WISCONSIN

Franksville
Palecek, Michael R. *information technology manager*

Green Bay
Lynch, Matthew J. *information technology executive, retail executive*

Milwaukee
Liu, Qingmin *software engineer, materials engineer*
Simoneau, Daniel Robert *application developer, accountant, educator, artist*

CANADA

ALBERTA

Edmonton
Davis, Wayne Alton *computer science educator*

ONTARIO

Waterloo
Balsillie, Jim *information technology executive*
Lazaridis, Mike *information technology executive, entrepreneur*

AUSTRALIA

Altona
Daniel-Dreyfus, Susan B. Russe *information technology executive*

Melbourne
Wolfram, David Anthony *information technology manager*

Sydney
Gomes, Ivan Joaquim *computer network designer*

ENGLAND

London
Assousa, George Elias *information technology executive, physicist, corporate executive*

FRANCE

Paris
Courtois, Jean-Philippe *information technology executive*

ITALY

Rome
Stigliano, Jose Maria *information technology executive, computer scientist*

JAPAN

Tokyo
Harada, Norio *software engineer, researcher, educator*

NEW ZEALAND

Gould, Wayne *application developer, retired judge*

ADDRESS UNPUBLISHED

Abu-Mostafa, Ayman Said *application developer, consultant*
Africa, Colby Tait *information technology executive, poet*
Alemneh, Daniel Gelaw *information technology manager, educator*
Alexander, Nancy A. *information technology manager, consultant*
Ali, Mohammed Zamshed *information technology executive, researcher*
Anderson, Christine Marlene *software engineer*
Anderson, Jacqueline Annette *information technology specialist*
Arsic, Antoinette *information specialist*
Bakke, Merlin Russell *application developer*
Bass, Steven Craig *computer science educator*
Belski, Keith Christopher *computer technician*
Bennett, Robert LeRoy *computer software development company executive*
Bergquist, Rick *software company executive*
Berry, Richard Lewis *information technology manager, writer, magazine editor, lecturer, programmer*
Blech, Ilan Asriel *retired technology company executive*
Bleszinski, Cliff (Clifford Michael Bleszinski) *game designer*
Buckley, Joseph Paul III *computer technician*
Castle, James Cameron *information technology executive*
Constantine, Larry L. *software designer, design and consultanting company executive*
Cooper, Roger Merlin *information technology executive, school system administrator, federal agency administrator*
Cosell, Bernard *retired computer systems architect*
Costandi, Wisam Emile *application developer, biomedical researcher, consultant*
Coullard, Chad *information systems specialist*
Creswell, Dorothy Anne *computer consultant*
Culy, Steven Wayne *application developer, physicist*
Dajnowicz, Jan *software and hardware designer, researcher*
Daniels, Daniel Baker *information technology manager, small business owner*
Davis, Ruth Margaret *information technology executive*
DiPentima, Renato Anthony *information technology executive*
Donohue, Susan K. *information technology executive, researcher*
Doud, Wallace C. *retired information technology executive*
Egan, Richard John *retired information technology executive, former ambassador*
Etheridge, Diana Carol *internet business executive*
Franklin, William Price *information technology manager*
Frei, Brent R. *computer software executive*
Gagnon, Robert *application developer*
Gareau, Jean L. *application technology executive*
Godhardt, Karen *information technology executive*
Goldberger, Arthur Earl, Jr. *information technology executive*
Grant, Daniel Gordon *information technology executive*
Guo, Dongbai *application developer*
Ha, Chong Wan *information technology executive*
Haddock, Robert Lynn *information services entrepreneur, writer*
Hamilton, Charles Edward *information technology consultant, military officer*
Hantman, Barry G. *software engineer*
Hariton, Lorraine Jill *information technology executive*
Heck, Debra Upchurch *information technology, procurement professional*
Hemann, Raymond Glenn *research company executive*
Herrmann, Thomas Francis *systems administrator*
Hill, Patricia Francine *information technology executive, educator*
Holt, George, Jr. *information technology executive*
Hooper, Michael Lee *application developer*
Horner, Grace Ann *application developer*
Hu, Weigang *software engineer*
Hughes-Tebo, Jacqueline Emma *regional coordinator*
Hurttgam, Mark Howard *information technology manager*
Jaw, Andrew Chung-Shiang *software analyst*
Jones, Carleton Shaw *information technology executive, lawyer*
Jordan, Michael Hugh *information technology executive*
Judd, Scott Randall *information technology manager*
Kadel, Lee A. *information technology manager, systems analyst*
Karim, Jawed *application developer*
Klauberg, William Joseph *information technology executive*
Kleinlein, Kathy Lynn *training and development executive*
Kramp, Suzan Marie *systems programmer*
La Blanc, Robert Edmund *information technology executive*
Land, Susan Kathleen *application developer*
Larson, Janice Talley *application developer*
Lee, Bryan *information technology executive*
Levy, Leslie Ann *application developer*
Litwin, Todd *software engineer*
Lyles, Mark Bradley *advanced technology company executive, military officer*
Manas, Gerald Bennett (Jerry Manas) *information technology manager*
Maruoka, Jo Ann Elizabeth *retired information systems manager*
Masagutov, Vakhid Erkinjonovich *application developer*
McCausland, Peter *technology company executive*
Menon, Jai M. *information technology manager*
Minshall, Greg *computer programmer*
Morgan, M. Jane *computer systems consultant*
Morrissey, Edward T., II, *conservative political blogger, nationally-syndicated radio co-host, columnist*
Mueller, Gary Alfred *software engineer*
Muntz, David S. *information technology executive*
Nam, Seung Yeob *network technician, researcher*
Nelson, Sandra E. *information technology executive*
Nicoll, Edward J. *information technology company executive*
Niederberger, Jane *information technology executive*
Nohr, Matthew Ryan *information technology analyst*
O'Connor, John Joseph *information technology manager*
Panko, George *application developer*
Papathomas, Georgia Nikolakopoulou *technology executive*
Paris, Steven Mark *application developer*
Persad, Chadee *information technology manager*
Piper, Ervin Leonard *retired information technology manager, consultant*
Raje, Sachin *information technology manager*
Reay, Stefanie *application developer, educator*
Reece, David Bryson *information systems administrator*
Rich, Jeffrey A. *former information technology company executive*
Rose, Paul Edward *systems administrator, educator*
Samenuk, George C. *former software security company executive*
Schatz, Wayne Ardale *district technology coordinator, educator*
Schneider, Sharon M. *systems administrator, information technologist*
Schwartz, Stephen Blair *retired information technology executive*
Sedighi, Artin *application developer, researcher*
Seitz, Henry W. *information technology manager*
Shaheen, George T. *software company executive*
Sheppard, Gayle Teresa *software executive*
Siebel, Thomas M. *software company executive*
Smith, Anne Marie Schoefer *application developer*
Smith, Theodore Glenn *technology educator, researcher*
Snow, Claude Henry, Jr. *information services executive, consultant*
Sodders, Michael Andrew *application developer*
Still, Homer Ibson *information technology executive*
Sweatman, Kelly *information technology executive*
Thompson, Kenneth *software engineer*
Thornton, Michael Albert *information technology manager*
Tolva, John *information technology manager*
Turner, Laura Louise *webmaster*
Valentine, Brian *information technology executive*
Visocki, Nancy Gayle *information services consultant*
Weber, Frederick D. *information technology executive*
White, Jan Tuttle *information technology executive*
Wilhelmi, Cynthia Joy *information technology manager, information scientist, consultant*
Woods, Dan *information technology manager, consultant*
Woods, Willie E. *information specialist*
Zhu, Yingwu *application developer, educator*
Zimmatore, John Joseph *information technology manager*
Zimmermann, Philip R. *software engineer, consultant*

Zimov, Bruce Steven *software engineer*

INTERNET *See* INFORMATION TECHNOLOGY

LAW: JUDICIAL ADMINISTRATION

UNITED STATES

ALABAMA

Ashland
Ingram, Kenneth Frank *retired state supreme court justice*

Birmingham
Bennett, Thomas B. *federal judge*
Houston, James Gorman, Jr. *retired state supreme court justice*
Pointer, Sam Clyde, Jr. *retired federal judge, lawyer*
Pryor, William Holcombe, Jr. *federal judge, former state attorney general, educator*

Mobile
Butler, Charles Randolph, Jr. *federal judge*
Cox, Emmett Ripley *federal judge*
Graddick, Charles Allen *judge*
Granade, Callie Virginia Smith *federal judge*
Howard, Alex T., Jr. *federal judge*
Milling, Bert William, Jr. *judge*
Pittman, Virgil *federal judge*

Montgomery
Black, Robert Coleman *judge, lawyer*
Bolin, Michael F. *state supreme court justice*
Brown, Jean Williams *former state supreme court justice*
Carnes, Edward E. *federal judge*
Cobb, Sue Bell *state supreme court justice*
Dubina, Joel Fredrick *federal judge*
Godbold, John Cooper *federal judge*
Hobbs, Truman McGill *federal judge*
Maddox, Alva Hugh *retired state supreme court justice*
McPherson, Vanzetta Penn *magistrate judge*
Murdock, Glenn *state supreme court justice*
Parker, Tom *state supreme court justice, lawyer*
Patterson, John Malcolm *judge*
See, Harold Frend *state supreme court justice*
Smith, Patricia M. (Patti) *state supreme court justice*
Steele, Rodney Redfearn *judge*
Stuart, Jacquelyn L. *state supreme court justice*
Watkins, W(illiam) Keith *federal judge*
Woodall, Thomas A. *state supreme court justice*

ALASKA

Anchorage
Bryner, Alexander O. *state supreme court justice*
Burgess, Timothy M. *federal judge, former prosecutor*
Eastaugh, Robert L. *state supreme court justice*
Fabe, Dana Anderson *state supreme court justice*
Matthews, Warren Wayne *state supreme court justice*
von der Heydt, James Arnold *federal judge*

Fairbanks
Kleinfeld, Andrew J. *federal judge*

Juneau
Carpeneti, Walter L. *state supreme court justice*

ARIZONA

Bisbee
Holland, Robert Dale *retired judge*

Phoenix
Anderson, Lawrence Ohaco *United States magistrate judge, lawyer*
Bales, W. Scott *state supreme court justice*
Berch, Rebecca White *state supreme court justice, lawyer*
Broomfield, Robert Cameron *federal judge*
Canby, William Cameron, Jr. *federal judge*
Carroll, Earl Hamblin *federal judge*
Gaines, Francis Pendleton III *judge*
Hawkins, Michael Daly *federal judge*
Hurwitz, Andrew D. *state supreme court justice*
Jones, Charles E. *retired state supreme court chief justice*
Martone, Frederick J. *judge*
McGregor, Ruth Van Roekel *state supreme court justice*
McNamee, Stephen M. *federal judge*
Ryan, Michael D. *state supreme court justice*
Schroeder, Mary Murphy *federal judge*
Silver, Roslyn Olson *federal judge*
Silverman, Barry G. *federal judge*
Strand, Roger Gordon *federal judge*
Weisenburger, Theodore Maurice *retired judge, poet, educator*
Winthrop, Lawrence Fredrick *judge*

Tempe
Arkfeld, Louraine C. *judge*

Tucson
Brammer, J. William, Jr. *judge, lawyer*
Cooper, Jean Saralee *retired judge*
Druke, William Erwin *judge, lawyer*
Marquez, Alfredo C. *federal judge*
Roll, John McCarthy *judge*

ARKANSAS

Batesville
Harkey, John Norman *judge*

El Dorado
Barnes, Harry Francis *federal judge*

Fayetteville
Smith, Lavenski R. (Vence) *federal judge*

Little Rock
Arnold, Morris Sheppard *federal judge*
Bird, Samuel N. *judge*
Corbin, Donald L. *state supreme court justice*
Danielson, Paul E. *state supreme court justice*
Glaze, Thomas A. *state supreme court justice*
Gunter, James Houston, Jr. *state supreme court justice*
Hannah, James *state supreme court justice*
Imber, Annabelle Clinton *state supreme court justice*
Roaf, Andree Layton *judge*
Wilson, William R., Jr. *federal judge*
Wright, Susan Webber *federal judge*

Texarkana
Stroud, John Fred, Jr. *judge*

CALIFORNIA

Alameda
Bartalini, C. Richard *judge*

Fort Bragg
Lehan, Jonathan Michael *judge*

Fresno
Coyle, Robert Everett *federal judge*
Ishii, Anthony W. *judge*
O'Neill, Lawrence Joseph *federal judge*

Glendale
Early, Alexander Rieman III *judge*

Los Angeles
Alarcón, Arthur Lawrence *federal judge*
Baker, Valerie L. *federal judge*
Bufford, Samuel Lawrence *federal judge*
Chavez, Victor Edwin *judge*
Collins, Audrey B. *judge*
Fleming, Macklin *retired judge*
Gutierrez, Philip S. *federal judge*
Johnson, Earl, Jr. *judge, author*
Kelleher, Robert Joseph *judge*
Manella, Nora Margaret *judge*
March, Kathleen Patricia *judge, lawyer*
Marshall, Consuelo Bland *federal judge*
Mohr, Anthony James *judge*
Mosk, Richard Mitchell *judge*
Rafeedie, Edward *federal judge*
Tevrizian, Dickran M., Jr. *judge*
Timlin, Robert J. *judge*
Wright, Otis Dalino, II, *judge*
Wu, George H. *federal judge*
Yager, Thomas C. *retired judge*
Zelon, Laurie Dee *judge*

Mendocino
Masterson, William A. *retired judge*

Oakland
Jensen, D. Lowell *federal judge*
Newsome, Randall Jackson *judge*
Tchaikovsky, Leslie J. *federal judge*

Pasadena
Boochever, Robert *judge*
Fernandez, Ferdinand Francis *federal judge*
Fisher, Raymond Corley *federal judge*
Goodwin, Alfred Theodore *federal judge*
Hall, Cynthia Holcomb *federal judge*
Johnson, Barbara Jean *retired judge, lawyer*
Kozinski, Alex *federal judge*
Nelson, Dorothy Wright *federal judge*
Paez, Richard A. *federal judge*
Rymer, Pamela Ann *federal judge*
Smith, Milan Dale, Jr. *federal judge*
Tashima, Atsushi Wallace *federal judge*
Wardlaw, Kim A. McLane *federal judge*

Pauma Valley
Lewis, Gerald Jorgensen *judge*

Redwood City
Grandsaert, John Leo *judge*

Riverside
Holmes, Dallas Scott *judge, educator*
Larson, Stephen G. *federal judge*

Sacramento
Callahan, Consuelo Maria *federal judge*
Karlton, Lawrence K. *federal judge*
Levi, David F. *federal judge*
Moulds, John F. *judge*
Van Camp, Brian Ralph *judge*

San Bernardino
Fortune, Lowell *judge*

San Diego
Bowie, Peter Wentworth *judge, educator*
Brewster, Rudi Milton *judge*
Gonzalez, Irma Elsa *federal judge*
Harutunian, Albert T(heodore) III *judge*
McKeown, Mary Margaret *federal judge*
Thompson, David Renwick *federal judge*
Thompson, Gordon, Jr. *federal judge*
Turrentine, Howard Boyd *federal judge*
Wallace, J. Clifford *federal judge*

San Francisco
Baxter, Marvin Ray *state supreme court justice*
Bea, Carlos Tiburcio *federal judge*
Berzon, Marsha S. *federal judge*
Browning, James Robert *federal judge*
Chin, Ming W. *state supreme court justice*
Corrigan, Carol A. *state supreme court justice*
Fletcher, William A. *federal judge, educator*
George, Ronald M. *state supreme court chief justice*
Haerle, Paul Raymond *judge*
Henderson, Thelton Eugene *federal judge*
Ikuta, Sandra Segal *federal judge*
Illston, Susan Y. *federal judge*
Jarvis, Donald Bertram *judge*
Kennard, Joyce L. *state supreme court justice*
Kolkey, Daniel Miles *former judge, lawyer*
Moreno, Carlos R. *state supreme court justice*
Noonan, John T., Jr. *federal judge, educator*
Patel, Marilyn Hall *judge*
Robertson, Armand James, II, *judge*
Schwarzer, William W. *federal judge*
Sneed, Joseph Tyree III *federal judge*
Walker, Vaughn R. *federal judge*
Werdegar, Kathryn Mickle *state supreme court justice*
Zimmerman, Bernard *judge*

San Jose
Whyte, Ronald M. *judge*

San Marino
Mortimer, Wendell Reed, Jr. *judge*

Santa Ana
Barr, James Norman *retired federal judge*
Ferguson, Warren John *federal judge*
Guilford, Andrew John *federal judge*
Stotler, Alicemarie Huber *federal judge*

Santa Barbara
Aldisert, Ruggero John *federal judge*

Studio City
Gold, Arnold Henry *judge*

Woodland Hills
Mund, Geraldine *judge*
Pregerson, Harry *federal judge*

COLORADO

Broomfield
Scott, Gregory Kellam *former state supreme court justice, lawyer*

Denver
Bender, Michael Lee *state supreme court justice*
Coan, Patricia A. *judge*
Coats, Nathan B. *state supreme court justice*
Ebel, David M. *federal judge*
Eid, Allison *state supreme court justice*
Felter, Edwin Lester, Jr. *judge*
Gorsuch, Neil McGill *federal judge, lawyer*
Hobbs, Gregory James, Jr. *state supreme court justice*
Kane, John Lawrence, Jr. *judge*
Keithley, Roger Lee *judge*
Kirshbaum, Howard M. *retired judge*
Krieger, Marcia Smith *federal judge*
Lucero, Carlos *federal judge*
Martinez, Alex J. *state supreme court justice*
McWilliams, Robert Hugh *federal judge*
Miller, Walker David *judge*
Mullarkey, Mary J. *state supreme court chief justice*
Nottingham, Edward Willis, Jr. *federal judge*
Porfilio, John Carbone *federal judge*
Rice, Nancy E. *state supreme court justice*
Rovira, Luis Dario *state supreme court justice*
Satter, Raymond Nathan *judge*
Tymkovich, Timothy Michael *federal judge*

Englewood
Erickson, William Hurt *retired state supreme court justice*

Fort Collins
Gandy, H. Conway *retired judge, state official*

Golden
Rodgers, Frederic Barker *judge*

Leadville
Watson, Jack Crozier *retired state supreme court justice*

CONNECTICUT

Bridgeport
Eginton, Warren William *federal judge*

Hartford
Bieluch, William Charles *judge*
Borden, David M. *state supreme court justice*
Bryant, Vanessa Lynne *federal judge, lawyer*
Droney, Christopher F. *judge*
Dupont, Antoinette Loiacono *judge*
Katz, Joette *state supreme court justice*
Killian, Robert Kenneth, Jr. *judge, lawyer*
Newman, Jon O. *federal judge*
Norcott, Flemming L., Jr. *state supreme court justice*
Palmer, Richard N. *state supreme court justice*
Peters, Ellen Ash *retired judge*
Rogers, Chase Theodora *state supreme court justice*
Schaller, Barry R. *judge*
Squatrito, Dominic J. *judge*
Sullivan, William J. *state supreme court justice*
Vertefeuille, Christine Siegrist *state supreme court justice*
Wright, Douglass Brownell *retired judge, lawyer*
Zarella, Peter T. *state supreme court justice*

New Britain
Meskill, Thomas J. *federal judge*

New Haven
Arterton, Janet Bond *federal judge*
Berdon, Robert Irwin *judge*
Cabranes, José Alberto *judge*
Calabresi, Guido *federal judge, educator*
Dorsey, Peter Collins *federal judge*
Walker, John Mercer, Jr. *federal judge*
Winter, Ralph Karl, Jr. *federal judge*

Oxford
Marano, Richard Michael *judge*

Vernon Rockville
Purnell, Oliver James III *judge*

Waterbury
McDonald, Francis Michael *judge trial refe retired state supreme court justice*
Upson, Thomas Fisher *judge, retired state senator, lawyer*

DELAWARE

Dover
Ridgely, Henry duPont *state supreme court justice*

Georgetown
Holland, Randy James *state supreme court justice*

Wilmington
Ambro, Thomas L. *federal judge*
Berger, Carolyn *state supreme court justice*
Jacobs, Jack Bernard *state supreme court ju*
Parsons, Donald Francis *judge*
Robinson, Sue L(ewis) *federal judge*
Roth, Jane Richards *federal judge*
Stapleton, Walter King *federal judge*
Steele, Myron Thomas *state supreme court c justice*

DISTRICT OF COLUMBIA

Washington
Alito, Samuel Anthony, Jr. *United States supreme court justice*
Allegra, Francis M. *federal judge, retired fe official*
Archer, Glenn LeRoy, Jr. *federal judge*
Armen, Robert K. (Kelly) III *federal judge*
Bacon, Sylvia *judge, educator*
Baker, James Edgar *federal judge, educator*
Bartnoff, Judith *judge*
Barton, Robert Leroy, Jr. *judge, educator*
Baskir, Lawrence M. *federal judge*
Bates, John D. *federal judge*
Bayly, John Henry, Jr. *judge*
Beghe, Renato *federal judge*
Belson, James Anthony *judge*
Blackburne-Rigsby, Anna *state supreme cour justice*
Block, Lawrence J. *federal judge*
Breyer, Stephen Gerald *United States supren court justice*
Brown, Janice Rogers *federal judge, former supreme court justice*
Bruggink, Eric G. *federal judge*
Bryson, William Curtis *federal judge*
Burnett, Arthur Louis, Sr. *judge*
Bush, Lynn Jeanne *federal judge*
Carluzzo, Lewis R. *federal judge*
Chabot, Herbert L. *federal judge*
Chiechi, Carolyn Phyllis *federal judge*
Clevenger, Raymond Charles III *federal judg*
Cohen, Mary Ann *federal judge*
Colvin, John O. *federal judge*
Couvillion, David Irvin *federal judge*
Crawford, Susan Jean *federal judge*
Damich, Edward John *federal judge*
Davis, Robert Nolan *federal judge, educator*
Dawson, Howard Athalone, Jr. *federal judge*
Dean, John F. *federal judge*
de Puget, Albert Borg Olivier *magistrate jud*
Dunlap, Charles J., Jr. *judge advocate, milit officer*
Dyk, Timothy Belcher *federal judge*
Edwards, Harry Thomas *federal judge*
Effron, Andrew S. *federal judge*
Erdmann, Charles Edgar (Chip Erdmann) *fe judge, former state supreme court justice*
Facciola, John Michael *judge*
Farrell, Michael W. *judge*
Ferren, John Maxwell *judge*
Firestone, Nancy B. *federal judge*
Fisher, John R. *district supreme court justice*
Foley, Maurice B. *federal judge*
Friedman, Daniel Mortimer *federal judge*
Futey, Bohdan A. *federal judge*
Gajarsa, Arthur J. *judge*
Gale, Joseph H. *federal judge*
Garland, Merrick Brian *federal judge*
Gerber, Joel *federal judge*
Gibson, Reginald Walker *federal judge*
Ginsburg, Douglas Howard *federal judge*
Ginsburg, (Joan) Ruth Bader *United States supreme court justice*
Glickman, Stephen H. *judge*
Goeke, Joseph Robert *federal judge, lawyer*
Goldberg, Stanley Joshua *federal judge*
Green, Joyce Hens *federal judge*
Greene, William P., Jr. *federal judge*
Griffith, Thomas Beall *federal judge*
Hagel, Lawrence B. *federal judge*
Haines, Harry Allen *federal judge*
Halpern, James S. *federal judge*
Henderson, Karen LeCraft *federal judge*
Hewitt, Emily Clark *federal judge, minister*
Hodges, Robert H., Jr. *federal judge*
Holmes, Mark V. *judge*
Horn, Marian Blank *federal judge*

Julian I. *federal judge*
, Bruce Edward *federal judge, lawyer*
augh, Brett Michael *federal judge*
ly, Anthony McLeod *United States eme court justice*
ohn Worth III *judge*
, Gladys *federal judge*
Warren R. *judge*
Kotelly, Colleen *federal judge*
r, Noël Anketell *judge*
a, Diane Lynn *federal judge*
Alan George *federal judge, former state rney general*
David *federal judge*
Richard J. *federal judge*
, Charles Frederick *federal judge*
, Arthur Andrew *judge*
Alan David *federal judge*
Thomas J. *federal judge*
Julia Cooper *retired judge*
and, Michael J. *judge, career military er*
lis, Lawrence Stanley *federal judge*
l, L. Paige *federal judge*
, Haldane Robert *federal judge*
nna, Juliet JoAnn *federal judge*
er, Bruce Stephan *judge*
, James F. *federal judge*
l, Paul Redmond *federal judge*
, Christine Odell Cook *federal judge*
George W. *federal judge, lawyer*
, Kimberly Ann *federal judge*
nan, William A. *federal judge, retired eer military officer*
er, Frank Quill *judge*
an, Pauline *federal judge*
Arthur Lee III *federal judge*
nos, Peter J. *federal judge*
Carolyn Miller *federal judge*
, S. Jay *federal judge*
Sharon *federal judge*
William C. *judge*
, Randall Ray *federal judge*
olph, A(rthur) Raymond *federal judge*
Jack L. *judge, career military officer*
ts, John Glover, Jr. *United States Supreme urt Chief Justice*
tson, James *federal judge*
s, Judith Ann Wilson *federal judge*
tein, Barbara Jacobs *federal judge*
Vanessa *judge*
, Robert Paul *federal judge*
Margaret A. *federal judge*
, Antonin Gregory *United States supreme urt justice*
, Alvin Anthony *federal judge*
len, Mary Jeanette *federal judge*
elb, Frank Ernest *judge*
lle, David Bryan *federal judge*
, Loren Allan *federal judge*
, Roy Philip *judge*
r, David Hackett *United States supreme urt justice*
man, John Montague *judge*
ns, John Paul *United States supreme court tice*
y, Scott Wallace *federal judge, lawyer*
an, Emmet G. *judge*
ney, Margaret Mary *federal judge*
, Stephen Jensen *federal judge*
David Stephen *federal judge*
, John Alfred *judge*
as, Clarence *United States supreme court tice*
npson, Phyllis D. *judge, lawyer*
nton, Michael B. *federal judge*
uez, Juan Flores *federal judge*
er, Annice McBryde *judge*
er, Curtis Lee, Jr. *judge*
, Patricia McGowan *retired federal judge*
ington, Eric T. *judge*
s, Thomas B. *federal judge*
en, Laurence J. *federal judge*
eler, Thomas Craig *federal judge*
ry, Robert Allen, Jr. *federal judge, lawyer*
e, John Paul *federal judge*
ams, Mary Ellen Coster *federal judge*
ams, Stephen Fain *federal judge*
ki, Victor J. *federal judge, lawyer*
, Robert John *federal judge*
r, Ronnie A. *judge*

ORIDA

nton Beach
stein, Edwin S. *judge*

arwater
s, Robert Timothy *judge*

and
se, Robert Kelly, Jr. *judge*

tin
nson, Wilkes Coleman *retired federal judge*

t Lauderdale
ch, Marcia Ellen *judge*
zalez, Jose Alejandro, Jr. *federal judge*
n, John Karl *judge*
Raymond B. *federal judge*
zer, Barry S. *federal judge*
w, Lurana S. *judge*
h, William J. *federal judge*

t Myers
oonover, Jack Ronald *senior judge*
fer, Robert Tinsley, Jr. *judge*

ksonville
er, Tyrie William *judge, law educator*
ding, David Michael *judge*
James Clinkscales *federal judge*
ward, Marcia Morales *federal judge*
son, Howell Webster, Sr. *federal judge*
esinger, Harvey Erwin *judge*

Tjoflat, Gerald Bard *federal judge*

Longboat Key
Morse, Marvin Henry *retired judge*

Miami
Barkett, Rosemary *federal judge*
Cristol, A. Jay *federal judge*
Davis, Edward Bertrand *retired federal judge, lawyer*
Freeman, Gill Sherryl *judge*
Highsmith, Shelby *federal judge*
King, James Lawrence *federal judge*
Marcus, Stanley *federal judge*
Miller Udell, Bronwyn *judge*
Rosinek, Jeffrey *judge*
Seitz, Patricia Ann *judge*
Siegel, Paul *judge*
Ungaro-Benages, Ursula Mancusi *federal judge*
Wilson, Thomas Strong, Jr., (Tam) *judge*

Ocala
Hodges, William Terrell *federal judge*

Orlando
Fawsett, Patricia Combs *federal judge*
Thorpe, Janet Claire *judge*
Young, George Cressler *federal judge*

Pensacola
Vinson, C. Roger *federal judge*

Safety Harbor
Dail, Joseph Garner, Jr. *retired judge*

Saint Petersburg
Grube, Karl Bertram *judge*

Seminole
Carrere, Charles Scott *judge, educator*

Tallahassee
Anstead, Harry Lee *state supreme court justice*
Bell, Kenneth B. *state supreme court justice*
Cantero, Raoul G. III *state supreme court justice*
Grimes, Stephen Henry *retired state supreme court justice*
Lewis, R. Fred *state supreme court justice*
McCord, Guyte Pierce, Jr. *retired judge*
Pariente, Barbara J. *state supreme court justice*
Quince, Peggy A. *state supreme court justice*
Strickland, Delphene Coverston *judge*
Webster, Peter David *judge*
Wells, Charles Talley *state supreme court justice*

Tampa
Jenkins, Elizabeth Ann *federal judge*
Wilson, Charles Reginald *federal judge*

West Palm Beach
Paine, James Carriger *federal judge*

GEORGIA

Atlanta
Benham, Robert *state supreme court justice*
Birch, Stanley Francis, Jr. *federal judge*
Carley, George H. *state supreme court justice*
Carnes, Julie Elizabeth *judge*
Deane, Richard Hunter, Jr. *former federal judge, lawyer*
Duffey, William Simon, Jr. *federal judge, former prosecutor*
Edmondson, J.L. (James Larry Edmondson) *federal judge*
Evans, Orinda D. *federal judge*
Hines, Preston Harris *state supreme court justice*
Hull, Frank Mays *federal judge*
Hunstein, Carol *state supreme court justice*
Melton, Harold D. *state supreme court justice*
O'Kelley, William Clark *federal judge*
Sears, Leah Ward *state supreme court justice*
Thompson, Hugh P. *state supreme court justice*
Ward, Horace Taliaferro *federal judge*

Augusta
Wood, Lisa Godbey *federal judge, former prosecutor*

Blairsville
Barrett, David Eugene *judge*

Columbus
Laney, John Thomas III *federal judge*

Macon
Anderson, Robert Lanier III *federal judge*
Brown, Stephen Phillip *judge*
Hershner, Robert Franklin, Jr. *judge*

Marietta
Smith, George Thornewell *retired state supreme court justice*

Newnan
Drake, W. Homer, Jr. *federal judge*

Rome
Murphy, Harold Loyd *federal judge*

Roswell
Feldman, Joel Martin *retired judge*

Savannah
Edenfield, Berry Avant *federal judge*
Moore, William Theodore, Jr. *federal judge*

HAWAII

Honolulu
Acoba, Simeon Rivera, Jr. *state supreme court justice, educator*
Clifton, Richard Randall *federal judge*
Duffy, James Earl, Jr. *state supreme court justice*
Gillmor, Helen *federal judge*
Levinson, Steven Henry *state supreme court justice*
Moon, Ronald T.Y. *state supreme court chief justice*
Nakayama, Paula Aiko *state supreme court justice*
Watanabe, Corinne Kaoru Amemiya *judge, state official*

IDAHO

Boise
Burdick, Roger S. *state supreme court justice*
Eismann, Daniel T. *state supreme court justice*
Jones, James Thomas *state supreme court justice, former state attorney general*
Jones, Warren Eugene *state supreme court justice*
McDevitt, Charles Francis *retired judge, lawyer*
Nelson, Thomas G. *federal judge*
Trott, Stephen Spangler *federal judge*
Trout, Linda Copple *state supreme court justice*
Winmill, B. Lynn *federal judge*

Pocatello
Smith, Norman Randy *federal judge*

Twin Falls
Hohnhorst, John Charles *judge*

ILLINOIS

Barrington
Wynn, Thomas Joseph *judge, educator*

Benton
Gilbert, J. Phil *federal judge*

Chicago
Bauer, William Joseph *federal judge*
Bower, Glen Landis *judge, lawyer*
Bucklo, Elaine Edwards *United States district court judge*
Burke, Anne M. *state supreme court justice*
Castillo, Ruben *federal judge*
Conlon, Suzanne B. *federal judge*
Cudahy, Richard D. *federal judge*
Easterbrook, Frank Hoover *federal judge*
Fitzgerald, Thomas Robert *state supreme court justice*
Flaum, Joel Martin *federal judge*
Funderburk, Raymond *judge*
Garman, Rita B. *state supreme court justice*
Gottschall, Joan B. *judge*
Hart, William Thomas *federal judge*
Johnson, Glenn Thompson *retired judge*
Kapala, Frederick J. *federal judge*
Kilbride, Thomas L. *state supreme court justice*
Lefkow, Joan Humphrey *federal judge*
Leighton, George Neves *retired judge*
Leinenweber, Harry D. *federal judge*
Miller, Benjamin K. *retired state supreme court justice*
Moran, James Byron *federal judge*
Norgle, Charles Ronald, Sr. *federal judge*
Pallmeyer, Rebecca Ruth *judge*
Posner, Richard Allen *federal judge*
Rovner, Ilana Kara Diamond *federal judge*
St. Eve, Amy J. *federal judge*
Shadur, Milton Irving *judge*
Sonderby, Susan Pierson *federal bankruptcy judge*
Thomas, Robert R. *state supreme court justice*
Williams, Ann Claire *federal judge*
Wood, Diane Pamela *federal judge*
Zagel, James Block *federal judge*

Downers Grove
McGarr, Frank James *retired federal judge, consultant*

Edwardsville
Crowder, Barbara Lynn *judge*

Hennepin
Bumgarner, James McNabb *judge*

Nashville
Karmeier, Lloyd A. *state supreme court justice*

Peoria
Heiple, James Dee *retired state supreme court justice*
Mihm, Michael Martin *federal judge*

Petersburg
Wood, Harlington, Jr. *federal judge*

Rockford
Reinhard, Philip Godfrey *federal judge*

Rolling Meadows
Roti, Thomas David *judge*

Skokie
Fein, Roger Gary *judge*

Springfield
Evans, Charles H. *federal judge*
Mills, Richard Henry *federal judge*

Taylorville
Spears, Ronald Dean *judge*

Wheaton
Leston, Patrick John *judge*

Wilmette
Bowman, George Arthur, Jr. *retired judge*

INDIANA

Boonville
Campbell, Edward Adolph *judge, electrical engineer*

Columbus
Sharpnack, John Trent *judge*

Crown Point
Dywan, Jeffery Joseph *judge*

Evansville
Capshaw, Tommie Dean *judge*

Fort Wayne
Lee, William Charles *judge*

Hammond
Lozano, Rudolpho *federal judge*
Van Bokkelen, Joseph Scott *federal judge, former prosecutor*

Indianapolis
Barker, Sarah Evans *judge*
Boehm, Theodore Reed *state supreme court justice*
Carlisle, Sheila A. *judge*
Dickson, Brent E. *state supreme court justice*
Foster, Kennard P. *magistrate judge*
McKinney, Larry J. *federal judge*
Rucker, Robert D. *state supreme court justice*
Shepard, Randall Terry *state supreme court chief justice*
Sullivan, Frank, Jr. *state supreme court justice*

Kokomo
Stein, Eleanor Bankoff *retired judge*

Lafayette
Kanne, Michael Stephen *federal judge*

Lagrange
Brown, George E. *judge, educator*

New Albany
Orth, Susan Lynn *judge*

South Bend
Brueseke, Harold Edward *judge*
Manion, Daniel Anthony *federal judge*
Miller, Robert L., Jr., (Bob Miller) *federal judge*
Ripple, Kenneth Francis *federal judge*
Sharp, Allen *federal judge*

IOWA

Cedar Rapids
Hansen, David Rasmussen *federal judge*
Mc Manus, Edward Joseph *federal judge*
Melloy, Michael J. *federal judge*

Chariton
Stuart, William Corwin *judge*

Council Bluffs
Peterson, Richard William *retired judge, lawyer*

Des Moines
Appel, Brent Robert *state supreme court justice, lawyer*
Bremer, Celeste F. *judge*
Cady, Mark S. *state supreme court justice*
Carter, James Harvey *retired state supreme court justice*
Colloton, Steven M. *federal judge*
Fagg, George Gardner *federal judge*
Harris, K. David *senior state supreme court justice*
Hecht, Daryl L. *state supreme court justice*
Jarvey, John Alfred *federal judge*
Larson, Jerry Leroy *state supreme court justice*
Lavorato, Louis A. *retired state supreme court justice*
Longstaff, Ronald Earl *federal judge*
McGiverin, Arthur A. *former state supreme court chief justice*
Streit, Michael J. *state supreme court justice*
Ternus, Marsha K. *state supreme court chief justice*
Vietor, Harold Duane *federal judge*
Walters, Ross A. *federal judge*
Wiggins, David Stewart *state supreme court justice*
Wolle, Charles Robert *judge*

Ida Grove
Snell, Bruce M., Jr. *judge*

Osceola
Reynoldson, Walter Ward *retired judge, lawyer*

KANSAS

Kansas City
Lungstrum, John W. *federal judge*
Vratil, Kathryn Hoefer *federal judge*
Waxse, David John *judge*

Lawrence
Briscoe, Mary Beck *federal judge*
Tacha, Deanell Reece *federal judge*

Topeka
Allegrucci, Donald Lee *state supreme court justice*
Beier, Carol Ann *state supreme court justice*
Crow, Sam Alfred *judge*
Davis, Robert Edward *state supreme court justice*
Johnson, Lee Alan *state supreme court justice*
Luckert, Marla Jo *state supreme court justice*
Marquardt, Christel Elisabeth *judge*

McFarland, Kay Eleanor *state supreme court chief justice*
Nuss, Lawton R. *state supreme court justice*
Rogers, Richard Dean *federal judge*
Rosen, Eric S. *state supreme court justice*

Wichita
Brown, Wesley Ernest *federal judge*

KENTUCKY

Bowling Green
Huddleston, Joseph Russell *retired judge, mediator, arbitrator*
Minton, John D., Jr. *state supreme court justice*

Frankfort
Cunningham, Bill *state supreme court justice*
Lambert, Joseph Earl *state supreme court chief justice*
Schroder, Wil *state supreme court justice*
Scott, Will T. *state supreme court justice*

Lexington
Coffman, Jennifer Burcham *judge*
Keller, James *retired state supreme court justice*
Noble, Mary C. *state supreme court justice*
Roach, John C. *state supreme court justice*
Varellas, Sandra Motte *judge*

London
Siler, Eugene Edward, Jr. *federal judge*

Louisville
Boggs, Danny Julian *federal judge*
Cowan, Frederic Joseph *judge*
Heyburn, John Gilpin, II, *federal judge*
Martin, Boyce Ficklen, Jr. *federal judge*
McAnulty, William E., Jr. *state supreme court justice*
Simpson, Charles R. III *judge*

Madisonville
Spain, Thomas B. *retired state supreme court justice*

Paducah
Foreman, James Louis *retired judge*

Pikeville
Van Tatenhove, Gregory F. *federal judge, former prosecutor*

Richmond
Chenault, James Stouffer *judge*

Wickliffe
Shadoan, William Lewis *retired judge*

LOUISIANA

Baton Rouge
Cole, Luther Francis *former state supreme court associate justice*
Noland, Christine A. *judge*
Parker, John Victor *judge*
Polozola, Frank Joseph *federal judge*
Riedlinger, Stephen C. *federal judge*

Lafayette
Davis, William Eugene *federal judge*
Duhe, John Malcolm, Jr. *federal judge*

New Orleans
Beer, Peter Hill *federal judge*
Berrigan, Helen Ginger *federal judge*
Brown, Jerry A. *federal bankruptcy judge*
Calogero, Pascal Frank, Jr. *state supreme court justice*
Clement, Edith Brown *federal judge*
Dennis, James Leon *federal judge*
Duval, Stanwood Richardson, Jr. *judge*
Johnson, Bernette Joshua *state supreme court justice*
Kimball, Catherine D. *state supreme court justice*
Knoll, Jeannette Theriot *state supreme court justice*
Livaudais, Marcel, Jr. *federal judge*
Porteous, G. Thomas, Jr. *judge*
Traylor, Chet D. *state supreme court justice*
Victory, Jeffrey Paul *state supreme court justice*
Weimer, John L. *state supreme court justice*
Wiener, Jacques Loeb, Jr. *federal judge*

Ponchatoula
Kuhn, James Edward *judge*

Shreveport
Shemwell, Robert H. *federal judge*
Stewart, Carl E. *federal judge*

MAINE

Auburn
Clifford, Robert William *state supreme court justice*

Bangor
Silver, Warren M. *state supreme court justice*

Portland
Alexander, Donald G. *state supreme court justice*
Bradford, Carl O. *judge*
Calkins, Susan W. *state supreme court justice*
Carter, Gene *judge*
Glassman, Caroline Duby *state supreme court justice*
Hornby, David Brock *federal judge*
Levy, Jon D. *state supreme court justice*
Lipez, Kermit V. *federal judge, former state supreme court justice*

McKusick, Vincent Lee *retired chief justice, arbitrator, lawyer, mediator*
Mead, Andrew M. *state supreme court justice*
Saufley, Leigh Ingalls *state supreme court chief justice*

Rockland
Collins, Samuel W., Jr. *judge*

MARYLAND

Accokeek
Beddow, Richard Harold *retired judge*

Annapolis
Battaglia, Lynne Ann *judge*
Greene, Clayton, Jr. *judge*
Nolan, Theresa A. *retired judge, mediator, arbitrator*

Baltimore
Bell, Robert M. *judge*
Blake, Catherine C. *judge*
Bredar, James Kelleher *judge*
Derby, Ernest Stephen *retired judge*
Garbis, Marvin Joseph *judge*
Gauvey, Susan Kathryn *judge*
Harvey, Alexander, II, *retired federal judge*
Legg, Benson Everett *federal judge*
Motz, Diana Gribbon *federal judge*
Motz, John Frederick *federal judge*
Niemeyer, Paul Victor *federal judge*
Rodowsky, Lawrence Francis *retired state judge*

Bethesda
Harris, Stanley S. *retired judge, arbitrator, mediator*
Nejelski, Paul Arthur *retired judge, freelance writer*

Greenbelt
Chasanow, Howard Stuart *retired judge, mediator*
Messitte, Peter Jo *judge*
Titus, Roger Warren *judge*

Rockville
Raker, Irma S. *judge*

Salisbury
Cathell, Dale Roberts *judge*

Upper Marlboro
Harrell, Glenn T., Jr. *judge*

MASSACHUSETTS

Boston
Boudin, Michael *federal judge*
Bowler, Marianne Bianca *federal judge*
Campbell, Levin Hicks *federal judge*
Collings, Robert Biddlecombe *judge*
Connolly, Thomas Edward *judge*
Cordy, Robert J. *state supreme court justice*
Cowin, Judith Arnold *state supreme court judge*
Feeney, Joan N. *judge*
Gorton, Nathaniel M. *federal judge*
Greaney, John M. *state supreme court justice*
Ireland, Roderick L. *state supreme court justice*
Katzmann, Gary Stephen *judge*
Lasker, Morris E. *judge*
Lindsay, Reginald Carl *judge*
Lynch, Sandra Lea *federal judge*
Marshall, Margaret Hilary *state supreme court chief justice*
O'Connor, Francis Patrick *former state supreme court justice*
O'Toole, George A., Jr. *judge*
Spina, Francis X. *state supreme court justice*
Stahl, Norman H. *judge*
Stearns, Richard Gaylore *judge*
Tauro, Joseph Louis *federal judge*
Torruella, Juan R. *federal judge*
Young, William Glover *federal judge*
Zobel, Rya Weickert *federal judge*

Cambridge
Kaplan, Benjamin *judge*

Harwich Port
Smith, Ralph Wesley, Jr. *retired federal judge*

Longmeadow
Keady, George Cregan, Jr. *judge*

Springfield
Neiman, Kenneth Paul *judge*

Worcester
Boroff, Henry Jack *federal judge, educator*

MICHIGAN

Ann Arbor
Guy, Ralph B., Jr. *federal judge*
O'Meara, John Corbett *federal judge*

Bay City
Ludington, Thomas Lamson *federal judge*

Detroit
Callahan, J(ohn) William (Bill Callahan) *judge*
Corrigan, Maura Denise *state supreme court justice*
Cox, Sean F. *federal judge*
Edmunds, Nancy Garlock *federal judge*
Feikens, John *federal judge*
Friedman, Bernard Alvin *federal judge*
Keith, Damon Jerome *federal judge*
Kelly, Marilyn *state supreme court justice*
Kennedy, Cornelia Groefsema *federal judge*
Levin, Charles Leonard *state supreme court justice*

Morgan, Virginia Mattison *judge*
Rosen, Gerald Ellis *federal judge*
Ryan, James Leo *federal judge*
Taylor, Anna Diggs *federal judge*

Grand Rapids
Bell, Robert Holmes *federal judge*
Brenneman, Hugh Warren, Jr. *judge*
Jonker, Robert James *federal judge*
Miles, Wendell A. *federal judge*
Quist, Gordon Jay *federal judge*

Kalamazoo
Enslen, Richard Alan *federal judge*

Lansing
Cavanagh, Michael Francis *state supreme court justice*
Harrison, Michael Gregory *judge*
Markman, Stephen J. *state supreme court justice*
McKeague, David William *judge*
Spence, Howard Tee Devon *retired judge, lawyer, consultant, arbitrator, government agency administrator*
Suhrheinrich, Richard Fred *federal judge*
Taylor, Clifford Woodworth *state supreme court justice*
Young, Robert P., Jr. *state supreme court justice*

Saginaw
McGraw, Patrick John *judge*

Saint Clair Shores
Hausner, John Herman *retired judge*

Southfield
Graves, Ray Reynolds *retired judge*

Traverse City
Weaver, Elizabeth A. *state supreme court justice*

MINNESOTA

Eden Prairie
Arthur, Lindsay Grier *retired judge, editor, writer*

Lake Elmo
Tomljanovich, Esther M. *retired judge*

Minneapolis
Alton, Ann Leslie *judge, lawyer, educator*
Davis, Michael J. *judge*
Doty, David Singleton *federal judge*
Kressel, Robert J. *federal judge*
Lebedoff, Jonathan Galanter *retired judge, mediator*
Loken, James Burton *federal judge*
Montgomery, Ann D. *federal judge, educator*
Murphy, Diana E. *federal judge*
Noel, Franklin Linwood *judge*
Rosenbaum, James Michael *federal judge*

Minnetonka
Rogers, James Devitt *judge*

Richfield
Amdahl, Douglas Kenneth *retired state supreme court justice*

Saint Paul
Alsop, Donald Douglas *federal judge*
Anderson, G. Barry *state supreme court justice*
Anderson, Paul Holden *state supreme court justice*
Anderson, Russell A. *state supreme court chief justice*
Gildea, Lorie Skjerven *state supreme court justice*
Hanson, Samuel Lee *state supreme court justice*
Kyle, Richard House *federal judge*
Lancaster, Joan Ericksen *judge*
Meyer, Helen M. *state supreme court justice*
Page, Alan C. *state supreme court justice*
Schiltz, Patrick Joseph *federal judge*
Willis, Bruce Donald *judge*

MISSISSIPPI

Aberdeen
Davidson, Glen Harris *federal judge*

Batesville
Carlson, George Clarence, Jr. *state supreme court justice*

Decatur
Gordon, Marcus *judge*

Gulfport
Senter, Lyonel Thomas, Jr. *federal judge*

Jackson
Banks, Fred Lee, Jr. *former state supreme court justice, lawyer*
Barksdale, Rhesa Hawkins *federal judge*
Cobb, Kay Beevers *state supreme court justice, retired state senator*
Diaz, Oliver E., Jr. *state supreme court justice*
Dickinson, Jess H. *state supreme court justice*
Easley, Charles D., Jr. *state supreme court justice*
Graves, James E. *state supreme court justice, educator*
Jolly, E. Grady *federal judge*
Lamar, Ann Hannaford *state supreme court justice*
Lee, Tom Stewart *judge*
Ozerden, Halil Suleyman (Sul) *federal judge*
Randolph, Michael K. *state supreme court justice*
Smith, James W., Jr. *state supreme court justice*
Sugg, Robert Perkins *retired judge*
Waller, William Lowe, Jr. *state supreme court justice*

Natchez
Bramlette, David C. III *retired federal judg*

Oxford
Mills, Michael Paul *judge*

MISSOURI

Cape Girardeau
Blanton, Lewis M. *federal judge*

Hannibal
Reinhard, James Richard *judge*

High Ridge
Karll, Jo Ann *retired judge, lawyer*

Jefferson City
Knox, William Arthur *judge*
Limbaugh, Stephen Nathaniel, Jr. *state supr court judge*
Price, William Ray, Jr. *state supreme court justice*
Russell, Mary Rhodes *state supreme court justice*
Stith, Laura Denvir *state supreme court just*
Teitelman, Richard B. *state supreme court j*
White, Ronnie L. *retired state supreme cou justice*
Wolff, Michael A. *state supreme court judge*

Kansas City
Benton, William Duane *federal judge*
Bowman, Pasco Middleton, II, *judge*
Gibson, John Robert *federal judge*
Laughrey, Nanette Kay *federal judge*
Whipple, Dean *federal judge*
Wright, Scott Olin *federal judge*

Saint Louis
Filippine, Edward Louis *federal judge*
Gruender, Raymond W. *federal judge, forme prosecutor*
Hamilton, Jean Constance *judge*
Jackson, Carol E. *federal judge*
Limbaugh, Stephen Nathaniel *federal judge*
Noce, David D. *judge*
Rendlen, Charles Earnest, III, (Sketch Rendl *federal judge, lawyer*
Seiler, James Elmer *judge*
Shaw, Charles Alexander *judge*
Stohr, Donald J. *federal judge*

MONTANA

Billings
Fagg, Russell *judge, lawyer*
Thomas, Sidney R. *federal judge*

Glendive
McDonough, Russell Charles *retired state supreme court justice*

Hamilton
Langton, Jeffrey H. *judge*

Helena
Cotter, Patricia O'Brien *state supreme court justice*
Gray, Karla Marie *state supreme court justice*
Harrison, John Conway *retired state supreme court justice*
Leaphart, W. William *state supreme court jus*
Morris, Brian *state supreme court justice*
Nelson, James C *state supreme court justice*
Rice, Jim *state supreme court justice*
Warner, John Arnan *state supreme court justi*

Missoula
Molloy, Donald William *federal judge, lawye*

Polson
Turnage, Jean Allen *retired state supreme co chief justice*

NEBRASKA

Lincoln
Beam, Clarence Arlen *federal judge*
Connolly, William M. *state supreme court ju*
Gerrard, John M. *state supreme court justice*
Hastings, William Charles *retired state supre court chief justice*
Heavican, Michael G. *state supreme court ju*
Hendry, John V. *retired state supreme court justice*
Kopf, Richard G. *federal judge*
McCormack, Michael *state supreme court ju*
Miller-Lerman, Lindsey *state supreme court justice*
Piester, David L(ee) *magistrate judge*
Stephan, Kenneth C. *state supreme court jus*
Urbom, Warren Keith *federal judge*
Wright, John F. *state supreme court justice*

Omaha
Riley, William Jay *federal judge*
Ross, Donald Roe *federal judge*
Shanahan, Thomas M. *judge*
Strom, Lyle Elmer *judge*

NEVADA

Carson City
Agosti, Deborah Ann *retired senior justice*
Cherry, Michael A. *state supreme court justi*
Gibbons, Mark *state supreme court justice*
Hardesty, James *state supreme court justice*
Maupin, A. William *state supreme court justi*
Parraguirre, Ronald David *state supreme cou justice*
Saitta, Nancy M. *state supreme court justice*

as Vegas
ecker, Nancy Anne *former state supreme court justice*
ybee, Jay Scott *federal judge, former federal agency administrator*
ouglas, Michael Lawrence *state supreme court justice*
ahan, James Cameron *judge*
o, Philip Martin *judge*
awlinson, Johnnie Blakeney *federal judge*

eno
unetti, Melvin T. *federal judge*
ng, Procter Ralph, Jr. *federal judge*
cKibben, Howard D. *federal judge*
eed, Edward Cornelius, Jr. *federal judge*
ndoval, Brian Edward *federal judge, former state attorney general*

EW HAMPSHIRE

oncord
rbadoro, Paul James *federal judge*
oderick, John T., Jr. *state supreme court chief justice*
alianis, Linda Stewart *state supreme court justice*
Clerico, Joseph Anthony, Jr. *federal judge*
iggan, James E., Jr. *state supreme court justice*
alway, Richard E., Jr. *state supreme court justice*
cks, Gary Ellis *state supreme court justice*
oward, Jeffrey R. *federal judge*
cAuliffe, Steven James *federal judge*

ochester
nes, Franklin Charles *judge*

EW JERSEY

tlantic City
ight, Edward R. *judge, psychologist, law educator*

amden
otman, Stanley Seymour *federal judge*
llman, Noel L. *federal judge, former prosecutor*
mas, Joseph Eron *judge*
skin, Lee B. *judge, state senator*
mandle, Jerome B. *federal judge*

g Harbor Township
shman, Shelley Bortin *retired judge*

emington
chsbaum, Peter A. *judge*

eehold
wman, James Michael *judge, lawyer*

ackensack
in, Gary S. *retired judge, lawyer*

illburn
ttner, Bernard A. *retired judge, lawyer*

orristown
nsbury, Stephan Charles *judge*

wark
rry, Maryanne Trump *federal judge*
mb, Renee Marie *federal judge*
bevoise, Dickinson Richards *federal judge*
entes, Julio M. *federal judge*
th, Leonard I. *judge*
eenaway, Joseph Anthony, Jr. *judge*
chberg, Faith S. *US district court judge*
genton, Susan Davis *federal judge*

merville
in, Barry Todd *state supreme court justice*

enton
oper, Mary Little *judge*
wen, Robert E. *federal judge*
enberg, Morton Ira *federal judge*
ens, Helen E. *state supreme court justice*
Vecchia, Jaynee *state supreme court justice*
ng, Virginia *state supreme court justice*
oner, Stuart Jeff *state supreme court justice, former state attorney general*
era-Soto, Roberto A. *state supreme court justice*
ridan, Peter Gerard *federal judge, lawyer*
llace, John E. *state supreme court justice*

W MEXICO

buquerque
nway, John E. *federal judge*
nsen, Curtis LeRoy *federal judge*
tz, Harris L *federal judge*
ker, James Aubrey *federal judge*

swell
dock, Bobby Ray *federal judge*

nta Fe
ck, Bruce D. *judge*
avez, Edward L. *state supreme court justice*
ly, Paul Joseph, Jr. *federal judge*
es, Petra Jimenez *state supreme court justice*
na, Patricio *state supreme court justice*
zquez, Martha Alicia *federal judge*
man, Ann *judge, lawyer*

W YORK

bany
ine, Eugene Peter *supreme court justice*
Donohue, Mary O. *judge, former lieutenant governor*
Graffeo, Victoria A. *state appeals court judge*
Jones, Theodore T., Jr. *judge*
Kaye, Judith Smith *state appeals court judge*
Levine, Howard Arnold *judge*
Meader, John Daniel *judge*
Miner, Roger Jeffrey *federal judge*
Pigott, Eugene F., Jr. *state appeals court judge*
Read, Susan Phillips *state appeals court judge*
Smith, Robert Sherlock *state appeals court judge*

Binghamton
Peckham, Eugene Eliot *judge, lawyer*
Regenbogen, Adam *judge*

Brooklyn
Amon, Carol Bagley *federal judge*
Bramwell, Henry *federal judge*
Cogan, Brian M. *federal judge*
Garaufis, Nicholas G. *federal judge*
Gershon, Nina *federal judge*
Glasser, Israel Leo *federal judge*
Irizarry, Dora L. *federal judge*
Korman, Edward R. *federal judge*
Mann, Roanne L. *federal judge*
Raggi, Reena *federal judge*
Ryan, Leonard Eames *judge*
Sifton, Charles Proctor *federal judge*
Townes, Sandra L. *federal judge*
Vitaliano, Eric Nicholas *federal judge*
Weinstein, Jack Bertrand *federal judge*

Buffalo
Bucki, Carl Leo *judge*
Skretny, William Marion *federal judge*

Central Islip
Bernstein, Stan *federal bankruptcy judge*
Boyle, E. Thomas *federal magistrate judge*
Cyganowski, Melanie L. *bankruptcy judge*
Eisenberg, Dorothy *federal judge*
Feuerstein, Sandra Jeanne *judge*
Hurley, Denis R. *federal judge*
Platt, Thomas Collier, Jr. *federal judge*
Seybert, Joanna *federal judge*
Spatt, Arthur Donald *federal judge*

Garden City
Harwood, Stanley *retired judge, lawyer, arbitrator, mediator*

Jamaica
Grayshaw, James Raymond *judge*

New York
Andrias, Richard T. *judge*
Aquilino, Thomas Joseph, Jr. *federal judge, educator*
Batts, Deborah A. *federal judge*
Berman, Richard Miles *judge*
Blinder, Albert Allan *judge*
Carman, Gregory Wright *federal judge*
Castel, P. Kevin *federal judge*
Cedarbaum, Miriam Goldman *federal judge*
Ciparick, Carmen Beauchamp *state appeals court judge*
Daniels, George Benjamin *federal judge*
Duffy, Kevin Thomas *federal judge*
Eaton, Richard Kenyon *federal judge*
Feinberg, Wilfred *federal judge*
Freedman, Helen E. *judge*
Gerber, Robert Evan *judge*
Goldberg, Richard W. *federal judge*
Gordon, Leo Maury *federal judge*
Griesa, Thomas Poole *federal judge*
Gropper, Allan Louis *judge*
Haight, Charles Sherman, Jr. *federal judge*
Hall, Peter W. *federal judge, former prosecutor*
Holwell, Richard J. *federal judge*
Jacobs, Dennis G. *federal judge*
Kaplan, Lewis A. *federal judge*
Katzmann, Robert Allen *federal judge*
Kearse, Amalya Lyle *federal judge*
Keenan, John Fontaine *federal judge*
Koeltl, John George *federal judge*
Kram, Shirley Wohl *federal judge*
Leisure, Peter Keeton *federal judge*
Leval, Pierre Nelson *federal judge*
Lippman, Jonathan *judge*
Livingston, Debra Ann *federal judge, educator*
Lynch, Gerard E. *federal judge*
Marrero, Victor *federal judge, lawyer*
McLaughlin, Joseph Michael *federal judge*
Meron, Theodor *judge, educator, researcher*
Musgrave, R. Kenton *federal judge*
Owen, Richard *federal judge*
Patterson, Robert Porter, Jr. *federal judge*
Peck, Andrew Jay *federal judge*
Pogue, Donald Carl *federal judge*
Preska, Loretta A. *federal judge*
Rakoff, Jed Saul *federal judge, author*
Restani, Jane A. *federal judge*
Ridgway, Delissa Anne *federal judge*
Sack, Robert David *federal judge, educator*
Sand, Leonard B. *federal judge*
Sotomayor, Sonia *federal judge*
Sprizzo, John Emilio *federal judge*
Stackhouse, John Ewell Harbour *judge*
Stanceu, Timothy Charles *federal judge*
Straub, Chester John *federal judge*
Swain, Laura Taylor *federal judge*
Tsoucalas, Nicholas *federal judge*
Wesley, Richard C. *federal judge*
Wood, Kimba M. *federal judge*

Penn Yan
Falvey, W(illiam) Patrick *judge*

Poughkeepsie
Dolan, Thomas Joseph *judge*
Rosenblatt, Albert Martin *retired state appeals court judge*

Rochester
Siragusa, Charles J. *judge*

Smallwood
Golden, Elliott *judge*

Syracuse
McCurn, Neal Peters *federal judge*
Munson, Howard G. *federal judge*
Pooler, Rosemary S. *federal judge*
Scullin, Frederick James, Jr. *federal judge*
Wells, Peter Nathaniel *judge, lawyer*

Utica
Cardamone, Richard J. *federal judge*

White Plains
Brieant, Charles La Monte *federal judge*
Carey, John *judge*
Conner, William Curtis *federal judge*
Hardin, Adlai Stevenson, Jr. *judge*
Nastasi, Aldo A. *judge*
Parker, Barrington D., Jr. *federal judge, lawyer*

NORTH CAROLINA

Asheville
Thornburg, Lacy Herman *federal judge*

Charlotte
Campbell, Hugh Brown, Jr. *judge*
Conrad, Robert J., Jr. *federal judge*
Horn, Carl III *federal judge*
Mullen, Graham C. *judge*
Voorhees, Richard Lesley *federal judge*
Whitney, Frank DeArmon *federal judge, former prosecutor*

Durham
Everett, Robinson Oscar *federal judge, educator*

Elizabeth City
Boyle, Terrence W. *federal judge*

Greensboro
Osteen, William L. *federal judge*
Stocks, William L. *federal judge*
Tilley, Norwood Carlton, Jr. *federal judge*

Greenville
Howard, Malcolm Jones *federal judge*

Hendersonville
Franks, Stephen Field *retired judge*

Morehead City
Wainwright, George L., Jr. *retired state supreme court justice*

Raleigh
Brady, Edward Thomas *state supreme court justice*
Eagles, Sidney Smith, Jr. *retired judge*
Edmunds, Robert Holt, Jr. *state supreme court justice*
Hudson, Robin E. *state supreme court justice*
Martin, John Charles *judge*
Martin, Mark D. *State Supreme Court Justice*
McGee, Linda Mace *judge, lawyer*
Parker, Sarah Elizabeth *state supreme court chief justice*
Timmons-Goodson, Patricia *state supreme court justice*

Randleman
Jordan, Lillian B. *judge*

Wilmington
Fox, James Carroll *federal judge*

Wilson
Leonard, J. Rich *federal judge, educator*

Winston Salem
Beaty, James Arthur, Jr. *federal judge*
Eliason, Russell Allen *judge*

NORTH DAKOTA

Bismarck
Crothers, Daniel J. *state supreme court justice*
Kapsner, Carol Ronning *state supreme court justice*
Maring, Mary Muehlen *state supreme court justice*
Neumann, William Allen *retired state supreme court justice*
Sandstrom, Dale Vernon *state supreme court justice*
VandeWalle, Gerald Wayne *chief justice*

Fargo
Bright, Myron H. *federal judge*
Bye, Kermit Edward *federal judge, lawyer*
Magill, Frank John *federal judge*

Minot
Kerian, Jon Robert *retired judge*

OHIO

Akron
Bell, Samuel H. *federal judge, educator*
Shea-Stonum, Marilyn *federal bankruptcy judge*

Bowling Green
Baird, James Abington *retired judge*

Cincinnati
Barrett, Michael Ryan *federal judge*
Beckwith, Sandra Shank *federal judge*
Clay, Eric L. *federal judge*
Cook, Deborah L. *federal judge, former state supreme court justice*
Dlott, Susan Judy *judge, lawyer*
Griffin, Richard Allen *federal judge*
Hopkins, Jeffery P. *federal judge*
Painter, Mark Philip *judge*
Panioto, Ronald Angelo *judge*
Perlman, Burton *judge*
Rogers, John Marshall *judge, educator*
Sutton, Jeffrey S. *federal judge*
Weber, Herman Jacob *senior district judge*

Cleveland
Aldrich, Ann *judge*
Boyko, Christopher Allan *federal judge*
Burke, Lillian Walker *retired judge*
Markus, Richard M. *judge, arbitrator*
Moore, Karen Nelson *judge*
Rhew, Perry James *federal judge*
Wells, Lesley *federal judge*

Columbus
Cole, Ransey Guy, Jr. *federal judge*
Cupp, Robert Richard *state supreme court justice, former state senator, attorney*
Frye, Richard Arthur *judge*
Holschuh, John David *federal judge*
Lanzinger, Judith Ann *state supreme court justice*
Mc Cormac, John Waverly *judge*
Moyer, Thomas J. *state supreme court chief justice*
Norris, Alan Eugene *federal judge*
O'Connor, Maureen *state supreme court justice*
O'Donnell, Terrence *state supreme court justice*
Pfeifer, Paul E. *state supreme court justice*
Smith, George Curtis *judge*
Stratton, Evelyn Lundberg *state supreme court justice*

Dayton
Knapp, James Ian Keith *judge*

Kettering
Porter, Walter Arthur *retired judge*

Lima
Rogers, Richard Michael *judge*

Lisbon
Dailey, Coleen Hall *magistrate*

Lucasville
Reno, Ottie Wayne *former judge*

Middletown
Powell, Stephen Walter *judge*

Sandusky
Stacey, James Allen *retired judge*

Toledo
Carr, James Gray *federal judge*
Zouhary, Jack *federal judge*

Warren
Nader, Robert Alexander *judge, lawyer*

Xenia
Wolaver, Stephen Arthur *judge*

OKLAHOMA

Guthrie
Brooks, Larry Roger *judge*

Lawton
Moore, Roy Dean *retired judge*

Norman
Trimble, Preston Albert *retired judge*

Oklahoma City
Cauthron, Robin J. *federal judge*
Colbert, Thomas *state supreme court justice*
Edmondson, James E. *state supreme court justice*
Hargrave, Rudolph *state supreme court justice*
Henry, Robert Harlan *federal judge, former attorney general*
Holloway, William Judson, Jr. *federal judge*
Kauger, Yvonne *state supreme court justice*
Lavender, Robert Eugene *state supreme court justice*
Leonard, Timothy Dwight *judge*
Opala, Marian Peter *state supreme court justice*
Russell, David L. *federal judge*
Taylor, Steven W. *state supreme court justice*
Thompson, Ralph Gordon *federal judge*
Walke, Geary Lynn *judge*
Watt, Joseph Michael *state supreme court justice*
West, Lee Roy *federal judge*
Winchester, James R. *state supreme court justice*

Tulsa
Eagan, Claire Veronica *chief district court judge*
Frizzell, Gregory Kent *federal judge*
Gabbard, Douglas, II, (James Gabbard) *judge*
Goodman, Jerry L(ynn) *judge*
Holmes, Jerome A *federal judge*
Kern, Terry C. *judge*
Seymour, Stephanie Kulp *federal judge*
Taylor, Joe Clinton *judge*

OREGON

Eugene
Walters, Martha Lee *state supreme court justice*

Medford
Panner, Owen M. *federal judge*

Portland
Beatty, John Cabeen, Jr. *judge*
Dunn, Randall Lawson *judge*
Graber, Susan P. *federal judge*
Jones, Robert Edward *federal judge*
King, Garr Michael *federal judge*
Leavy, Edward *federal judge*

Mosman, Michael W. *federal judge, former prosecutor*
O'Scannlain, Diarmuid Fionntain *federal judge*
Redden, James Anthony *federal judge*
Riggs, R. William *retired state supreme court justice*
Rosenblum, Ellen F. *judge*
Skopil, Otto Richard, Jr. *federal judge*
Van Hoomissen, George Albert *state supreme court justice*

Salem
Balmer, Thomas Ancil *state supreme court justice*
De Muniz, Paul J. *state supreme court chief justice*
Durham, Robert Donald, Jr. *state supreme court justice*
Gillette, W. Michael *state supreme court justice*
Kistler, Rives *state supreme court justice*
Linde, Hans Arthur *state supreme court justice*
Linder, Virginia Lynn *state supreme court justice*
Peterson, Edwin J. *retired judge, mediator, educator*

Troutdale
Unis, Richard L. *judge*

PENNSYLVANIA

Allentown
Platt, William Henry *judge*

Duncansville
Smith, D. Brooks *federal judge*

Easton
Van Antwerpen, Franklin Stuart *federal judge*

Harrisburg
Rambo, Sylvia H. *federal judge*
Saylor, Thomas G. *state supreme court justice*

Mechanicsburg
Eakin, J. Michael *state supreme court justice*

Philadelphia
Angell, Mary Faith *federal magistrate judge*
Baldwin, Cynthia Ackron *state supreme court justice*
Buckwalter, Ronald Lawrence *federal judge*
Castille, Ronald D. *state supreme court justice*
Chagares, Michael Arthur *federal judge*
Coleman, Gerald Charles *judge, educator*
Diamond, Paul Steven *federal judge, lawyer, educator*
Golden, Thomas M. *federal judge*
Hardiman, Thomas Michael *federal judge*
Jordan, Kent A. *federal judge*
Joyner, J(ames) Curtis *judge*
Kelly, Robert Francis *federal judge*
Ludwig, Edmund Vincent *federal judge*
McKee, Theodore A. *federal judge*
Nygaard, Richard Lowell *federal judge*
O'Neill, Thomas Newman, Jr. *federal judge*
Pollak, Louis Heilprin *judge, educator*
Reed, Lowell A., Jr. *federal judge*
Rendell, Marjorie O. *federal judge*
Scirica, Anthony Joseph *federal judge*
Shapiro, Norma Sondra Levy *federal judge*
Sigmund, Diane Weiss *judge*
Sloviter, Dolores Korman *federal judge*
Welsh, Diane M. *federal judge*
Yohn, William H(endricks), Jr. *federal judge*

Pittsburgh
Ambrose, Donetta W. *federal judge*
Baer, Max *state supreme court justice*
Brosky, John G. *retired judge*
Cappy, Ralph Joseph *state supreme court chief justice*
Cohill, Maurice Blanchard, Jr. *federal judge*
Conti, Joy Flowers *judge*
Diamond, Gustave *federal judge*
Fischer, Nora Barry *federal judge, lawyer*
Fisher, D. Michael *judge*
Fitzgerald, James J. III *state supreme court justice*
Fitzgerald, Judith Klaswick *federal judge*
Flaherty, John Paul, Jr. *chief justice emeritus*
Lally-Green, Maureen Ellen *judge, educator*
Ross, Eunice Latshaw *retired judge*
Skwaryk, Robert Francis *judge*
Standish, William Lloyd *judge*
Weis, Joseph Francis, Jr. *federal judge*
Zappala, Stephen A. *state supreme court justice*
Ziegler, Donald Emil *retired federal judge*

Scranton
Blewitt, Thomas Michael *chief US magistrate judge*
Conaboy, Richard Paul *federal judge*
Kosik, Edwin Michael *federal judge*
Nealon, William Joseph *federal judge*
O'Malley, Carlon Martin *judge*

West Chester
Griffith, Edward *judge*

Wilkes Barre
Schwartz, Roger Alan *judge*

Williamsport
Jones, John E. III *judge*
McClure, James Focht, Jr. *federal judge*
Muir, Malcolm *federal judge*

RHODE ISLAND

Providence
Flaherty, Francis Xavier *state supreme court justice*
Goldberg, Maureen McKenna *state supreme court justice*
Lagueux, Ronald Rene *federal judge*
Lisi, Mary M. *federal judge*
Robinson, William Philip III *state supreme court justice*
Selya, Bruce Marshall *federal judge*
Suttell, Paul Allyn *state supreme court justice*
Torres, Ernest C. *federal judge*
Weisberger, Joseph Robert *retired state supreme court justice*
Williams, Frank J. *state supreme court chief justice, historian, writer*

SOUTH CAROLINA

Anderson
Anderson, George Ross, Jr. *federal judge*

Camden
Jacobs, Rolly Warren *judge*

Columbia
Bristow, Walter James, Jr. *retired judge*
Burnett, E. C. III *state supreme court justice*
Currie, Cameron McGowan *federal judge*
Hamilton, Clyde Henry *federal judge*
Martin, John Randolph *judge*
Mason, Thomasine Grayson *judge*
Moore, James E. *state supreme court justice*
Pleicones, Costa M. *state supreme court justice*
Shedd, Dennis W. *federal judge*
Toal, Jean Hoefer *state supreme court chief justice*
Waller, John Henry, Jr. *state supreme court justice*

Greenville
Herlong, Henry Michael, Jr. *federal judge*
Simmons, Charles Bedford, Jr. *judge*
Traxler, William Byrd, Jr. *federal judge*
Wilkins, William Walter *federal judge*

Myrtle Beach
Harwell, David Walker *retired judge*

SOUTH DAKOTA

Pierre
Gilbertson, David *state supreme court justice*
Konenkamp, John K. *state supreme court justice*
Meierhenry, Judith Knittel *state supreme court justice*
Sabers, Richard Wayne *state supreme court justice*
Zinter, Steven L. *state supreme court justice*

Rapid City
Schreier, Karen Elizabeth *judge*

Sioux Falls
Piersol, Lawrence L. *federal judge*
Wollman, Roger Leland *federal judge*

TENNESSEE

Chattanooga
Edgar, R(obert) Allan *federal judge*
Franks, Herschel Pickens *judge*
Mattice, Harry Sandlin, Jr. *federal judge, former prosecutor*

Greeneville
Hull, Thomas Gray *federal judge*

Jackson
Boswell, G(eorge) Harvey *federal judge*
Todd, James Dale *federal judge*

Jonesborough
Kiener, John Leslie *retired judge*

Knoxville
Jarvis, James Howard, II, *judge*
Jordan, Robert Leon *judge*
Murrian, Robert Phillip *retired federal judge, educator*
Phillips, Thomas Wade *judge, lawyer*
Wade, Gary R. *state supreme court justice*

Memphis
Broffitt, Joyce Cassandra *judge*
Gibbons, Julia Smith *federal judge*
Gilman, Ronald Lee *federal judge*
Holder, Janice Marie *state supreme court justice*
Person, Curtis S., Jr. *judge, former state legislator, lawyer*

Nashville
Barker, William M. *state supreme court justice*
Brown, Joe Blackburn *judge*
Clark, Cornelia A. *state supreme court justice*
Daughtrey, Martha Craig *federal judge*
Echols, Robert L. *federal judge*
Koch, William C., Jr. *state supreme court justice*
Merritt, Gilbert Stroud *federal judge*
Trauger, Aleta Arthur *judge*
Wiseman, Thomas Anderton, Jr. *federal judge*

Newport
Porter, James Kenneth *retired judge*

Signal Mountain
Cooper, Robert Elbert *state supreme court justice*

TEXAS

Amarillo
Robinson, Mary Lou *federal judge*

Austin
Benavides, Fortunato Pedro (Pete Benavides) *federal judge*
Brister, Scott Andrew *state supreme court justice*
Garwood, William Lockhart *federal judge*
Green, Paul Warren *state supreme court justice*
Greenhill, Joe Robert *retired judge, lawyer*
Hecht, Nathan Lincoln *state supreme court justice*
Higginbotham, Patrick Errol *federal judge*
Jefferson, Wallace B. *state supreme court chief justice*
Johnson, Philip Wayne *state supreme court justice*
Justice, William Wayne *federal judge*
Keasler, Michael Edward *judge*
Medina, David *state supreme court justice*
Meyers, Lawrence Edward *state judge*
Nowlin, James Robertson *federal judge*
O'Neill, Harriet *state supreme court justice*
Owen, Priscilla Richman *federal judge, former state supreme court justice*
Pope, Andrew Jackson, Jr., (Jack) *retired judge*
Ray, Cread L., Jr. *retired judge*
Sparks, Sam *federal judge*
Wainwright, Dale V. *state supreme court justice*
Willett, Don R. *state supreme court justice*
Williams, Mary Pearl *judge*

Corpus Christi
Head, Hayden Wilson, Jr. *federal judge*
Hunter, Jack E. *retired judge*
Jack, Janis Graham *judge*

Dallas
Boyle, Jane J. *federal judge, lawyer*
Hankinson, Deborah G. *former state supreme court justice*
Lang, Douglas Stewart *judge*
Price, Robert Eben *judge*
Sanders, Harold Barefoot, Jr. *judge*

El Paso
Briones, David *judge*
Paxson, Sam M. *judge*

Fort Worth
King, Steve Mason *judge, lawyer*
McBryde, John Henry *federal judge*
Means, Terry Robert *federal judge*

Houston
Bue, Carl Olaf, Jr. *retired federal judge*
DeMoss, Harold Raymond, Jr. *federal judge*
Hanks, George Carol, Jr. *state judge*
Hittner, David *federal judge*
Hughes, Lynn Nettleton *federal judge*
King, Carolyn Dineen *federal judge*
Miller, Gray Hampton *federal judge, lawyer*
Reavley, Thomas Morrow *federal judge*
Rosenthal, Lee H. *federal judge*
Smith, Jerry Edwin *federal judge*
Sondock, Ruby Kless *retired judge*

Kaufman
Tygrett, Howard Volney, Jr. *judge, lawyer*

Laredo
Kazen, George Philip *federal judge*

Mcallen
Hinojosa, Federico Gustavo, Jr. *retired judge*
Hinojosa, Ricardo H. *federal judge*

Meadowlakes
Blackmon, Willie Edward Boney *judge, military officer*

Midland
Morrow, William Clarence *judge, lawyer, arbitrator*

New Braunfels
Zipp, Ronald Duane *judge, real estate broker, clergyman*

Richmond
Elliott, Brady Gifford *judge*

San Antonio
Furgeson, William Royal *federal judge*
Garza, Emilio Miller *federal judge*
Weiner, Marcia Myra *justice of the peace*

Sherman
Brown, Paul Neeley *federal judge*
Schell, Richard A. *federal judge*

Tyler
Guthrie, Judith K. *federal judge*

UTAH

Salt Lake City
Anderson, Stephen Hale *federal judge*
Benson, Dee Vance *federal judge*
Clark, Glen Edward *judge*
Durham, Christine Meaders *state supreme court chief justice*
Durrant, Matthew B. *state supreme court justice*
Greene, John Thomas *judge*
Jenkins, Bruce Sterling *federal judge*
McConnell, Michael W. *federal judge, law educator*
McKay, Monroe Gunn *federal judge*
Murphy, Michael R. *federal judge*
Nehring, Ronald E. *state supreme court justice*
Parrish, Jill Niederhauser *state supreme court justice*
Sam, David *federal judge*
Warner, Paul Michael *federal judge, former prosecutor*
Wilkins, Michael Jon *state supreme court justice*

VERMONT

Burlington
Sessions, William K. III *federal judge*

Montpelier
Burgess, Brian Louis *state supreme court justi*
Dooley, John Augustine III *state supreme cou justice*
Gibson, Ernest Willard III *retired state suprem court justice*
Johnson, Denise Reinka *state supreme court justice*
Reiber, Paul L. *state supreme court chief justi*
Skoglund, Marilyn *state supreme court justice*

Woodstock
Billings, Franklin Swift, Jr. *federal judge*

VIRGINIA

Abingdon
Jones, James Parker *federal judge*

Alexandria
Barry, Lance Leonard *judge*
Bostetter, Martin V. B., Jr. *bankruptcy court judge*
Brinkema, Leonie Milhomme *federal judge*
Hilton, Claude Meredith *federal judge*
Spencer, James R. *federal judge*

Annandale
Armstrong, Henry Jere *retired judge*

Arlington
Ablard, Charles David *administrative judge*

Charlottesville
Wilkinson, J(ames) Harvie III *federal judge*

Charlottesvle
Goodrich, George Herbert *retired judge*

Chesterfield
Davis, Bonnie Christell *judge*

Covington
Stephenson, Roscoe Bolar, Jr. *state supreme court justice*

Danville
Kiser, Jackson L. *federal judge*

Fairfax
Stitt, David Tillman *judge*
Williams, Marcus Doyle *judge*

King George
Revercomb, Horace Austin III *judge*

Lynchburg
Burnette, Ralph Edwin, Jr. *judge*
Moon, Norman K. *judge*

Norfolk
Adams, David Huntington *judge*
Bonney, Hal James, Jr. *federal judge*
Jackson, Raymond A. *federal judge*
Morgan, Henry Coke, Jr. *judge*

Richmond
Agee, G. Steven *state supreme court justice*
Carrico, Harry Lee *retired judge*
Dohnal, Dennis William *judge*
Gregory, Roger Lee *federal judge*
Hassell, Leroy Rountree, Sr. *state supreme co chief justice*
Keenan, Barbara Milano *state supreme court justice*
Kinser, Cynthia D. *state supreme court justic*
Koontz, Lawrence L., Jr. *state supreme court justice*
Lacy, Elizabeth Bermingham *state supreme c justice*
Lemons, Donald W. *state supreme court justi*
Tice, Douglas Oscar, Jr. *federal bankruptcy judge*
Williams, Karen Johnson *federal judge*
Williams, Richard Leroy *federal judge*

Roanoke
Turk, James Clinton *federal judge*

Staunton
Cochran, George Moffett *retired judge*

Stuart
Clark, Martin F(illmore), Jr. *judge*

WASHINGTON

Bellevue
Andersen, James A. *retired state supreme co*

Everett
Bowden, George Newton *judge*

Mercer Island
Noe, James Alva *retired judge*

Olympia
Alexander, Gerry L. *state supreme court justi*
Bridge, Bobbe Jean *state supreme court justi*
Chambers, Thomas Jefferson *state supreme c justice*
Fairhurst, Mary E. *state supreme court justic*
Johnson, Charles William *state supreme cour justice*
Johnson, James Martin *state supreme court justice, lawyer*
Madsen, Barbara A. *state supreme court just*
Owens, Susan *state supreme court justice*
Sanders, Richard Browning *state supreme co justice*
Smith, Charles Z. *retired state supreme cour justice*

eattle
laden, Edwin Mark *judge, lawyer*
oughenour, John Clare *federal judge*
immick, Carolyn Reaber *federal judge*
arris, Jerome *federal judge*
etcher, Betty Binns *federal judge*
ould, Ronald Murray *federal judge*
verstreet, Karen A. *federal bankruptcy judge*
allman, Richard C. *federal judge, lawyer*
einberg, John Lee *federal judge*
lly, Thomas Samuel *federal judge*

pokane
rant, William Joseph *retired judge*
ıbrogno, Cynthia *judge*
uackenbush, Justin Lowe *federal judge*
an Sickle, Frederick L. *federal judge*

acoma
ryan, Robert J. *federal judge*
ettle, Benjamin Hale *federal judge*
ang, Arthur Ching-li *judge, educator*

ukwila
almadge, Philip Albert *retired judge, state senator*

ancouver
arris, Robert L(ee) *judge*

akima
ıko, Lonny Ray *judge*

EST VIRGINIA

harleston
bright, Joseph P. *state supreme court justice*
enjamin, Brent D. *state supreme court justice, lawyer*
ewer, Lewis Gordon *judge, educator*
avis, Robin Jean *state supreme court chief justice*
ber, David Alan *federal judge*
oodwin, Joseph Robert *judge*
ing, Robert Bruce *federal judge*
arland, Melissa Kaye *judge*
aynard, Elliott E. *state supreme court justice*
cHugh, Thomas Edward *state supreme court justice*
ichael, M. Blane *federal judge*
archer, Larry Victor *state supreme court justice*

larksburg
eeley, Irene Patricia Murphy *federal judge*

lkins
iley, John Preston *federal judge, lawyer*
axwell, Robert Earl *federal judge*

heeling
nnston, Thomas E. *judge*
amp, Frederick Pfarr, Jr. *federal judge*

ISCONSIN

ppleton
oehlich, Harold Vernon *judge, retired congressman*

adison
rahamson, Shirley Schlanger *state supreme court chief justice*
rtell, Angela Gina Baldi *judge*
adley, Ann Walsh *state supreme court justice*
tler, Louis Bennett, Jr. *state supreme court justice*
abb, Barbara Brandriff *federal judge*
ooks, Neil Patrick *state supreme court justice*
artin, Robert David *judge, educator*
osser, David Thomas, Jr. *state supreme court justice and former legislator*
ggensack, Patience Drake *state supreme court justice*
abaz, John C. *judge*
lcox, Jon P. *state supreme court justice*
egler, Annette Kingsland *state supreme court justice*

ilwaukee
ans, Terence Thomas *federal judge*
odstein, Aaron E. *federal magistrate judge*
ssler, Joan F. *judge, lawyer*
apiro, James Edward *judge*
kes, Diane S. *federal judge, former state supreme court justice*

YOMING

asper
wnes, William F. *federal judge*

heyenne
immer, Clarence Addison *federal judge*
orby, Wade *federal judge*
lden, T. Michael *state supreme court justice*
l, William U. *state supreme court justice, former state attorney general*
e, Marilyn S. *state supreme court justice, lawyer*
Brien, Terrence Leo *federal judge*
gt, Barton R. *state supreme court chief justice*

well
rick, H. Hunter *retired judge, lawyer*

TERRITORIES OF THE UNITED STATES

AMERICAN SAMOA

Pago Pago
Kruse, F. Michael *judge*
Richmond, Lyle L. *judge*

GUAM

Hagatna
Carbullido, F. Philip *judge*
Manibusan, Joaquin V.E., Jr. *magistrate judge*
Maraman, Katherine Ann *judge*
Torres, Robert J., Jr. *judge*
Tydingco-Gatewood, Frances Marie *federal judge*
Unpingco, John Walter Sablan *federal judge*
Weeks, Janet Healy *retired supreme court justice*

NORTHERN MARIANA ISLANDS

Saipan
Castro, Alexandro C. *commonwealth supreme court justice*
Demapan, Miguel S. *commonwealth supreme court justice*
Manglona, John A. *commonwealth supreme court justice*
Munson, Alex Robert *judge*

PUERTO RICO

Hato Rey
Cerezo, Carmen Consuelo *judge*
Gelpi, Gustavo Antonio *federal judge*

San Juan
Acosta, Raymond Luis *federal judge*
Besosa, Francisco Augusto *federal judge*
Delgado-Colon, Aida M. *federal judge*
Dominguez, Daniel R. *judge*
Fiol Matta, Liana *judge*
Fusté, José Antonio *federal judge*
Fuster Berlingeri, Jaime B. *judge*
Hernández Denton, Federico *judge*
Rebollo López, Francisco *judge*
Rivera Pérez, Efraín E. *judge*
Rodriguez, Annabelle *judge, former attorney general*

Viejo San Juan
Casellas, Salvador E. *judge*

VIRGIN ISLANDS

Charlotte Amalie
Barnard, Geoffrey W. *judge*

Christiansted
Finch, Raymond Lawrence *judge*

St Croix
Cannon, George W., Jr. *judge*

St Thomas
Gomez, Curtis V. *judge*

CANADA

ALBERTA

Calgary
Major, John Charles *judge*

Edmonton
Stevenson, William Alexander *retired justice of Supreme Court of Canada*

NEW BRUNSWICK

Fredericton
Strange, Henry Hazen *judge*

NOVA SCOTIA

Halifax
Glube, Constance Rachelle *retired judge*

ONTARIO

Bracebridge
Evans, John David Daniel *judge*

Harrow
Kurtz, James P. *retired judge*

Ottawa
MacKay, William Andrew *judge*
Margeson, Theodore Earl *judge*
McLachlin, Beverley *Canadian supreme court chief justice*
Strayer, Barry Lee *retired judge*

Toronto
Boland, Janet Lang *judge*
McMurtry, R. Roy *federal judge*

QUEBEC

Montreal
Gonthier, Charles Doherty *retired judge*

Westmount
Rothman, Melvin L. *retired judge*

SASKATCHEWAN

Regina
Bayda, Edward Dmytro *retired chief justice*

BELIZE

Belize City
Brown, Sir George Noel *judge*

EGYPT

Cairo
Elaraby, Nabil A. *former judge, former diplomat*

GERMANY

Göttingen
Starck, Christian Walter *retired judge, law educator*

NETHERLANDS

The Hague
Aldrich, George Hoover *judge, arbitrator*
Allison, Richard Clark *judge*
Buergenthal, Thomas *judge*
Higgins, Dame Rosalyn *judge*
Jiuyong, Shi *judge*
Koroma, Abdul G. *judge*
Owada, Hisashi *judge*
Parra-Aranguren, Gonzalo *judge*

ADDRESS UNPUBLISHED

Aboussie, Marilyn *retired judge*
Albritton, William Harold III *federal judge*
Amestoy, Jeffrey Lee *former state supreme court chief justice, educator*
Anderson, Edward Riley *retired state supreme court justice*
Anthony, Joan Caton *administrative judge*
Askey, William Hartman *United States magistrate judge*
Austin, John DeLong *retired judge*
Baca, Joseph Francis *retired judge*
Baer, Harold, Jr. *senior federal judge*
Batchelder, Alice M. *federal judge*
Bedsworth, William W. *judge*
Beezer, Robert Renaut *federal judge*
Bertelsman, William Odis *federal judge*
Birch, Adolpho A., Jr. *retired state supreme court justice*
Black, Susan Harrell *federal judge*
Blatz, Kathleen Anne *former state supreme court justice*
Bosson, Richard Campbell *state supreme court justice*
Boudreau, Daniel J. *retired state supreme court justice*
Bowman, John J. *judge*
Brackett, Colquitt Prater, Jr. *judge, lawyer*
Brady, M(uriel) Jane *judge, former state attorney general*
Brett, Thomas Rutherford *federal judge*
Brown, Frank R. *judge*
Brown, Robert Laidlaw *state supreme court justice*
Buchwald, Naomi Reice *federal judge*
Buckingham, David Cowan *judge*
Callow, William Grant *retired judge*
Campbell, Vincent Bernard *judge, lawyer*
Carey, David P. *judge, career military officer*
Carson, Wallace Preston, Jr. *retired state supreme court justice*
Castagna, William John *federal judge*
Chapman, Robert Foster *federal judge*
Coffey, John Louis *federal judge*
Coffin, Frank Morey *retired federal judge*
Cohn, Avern Levin *district judge*
Colaianni, Joseph Vincent *judge*
Compton, Allen T. *retired state supreme court justice*
Cooper, William S. *retired state supreme court justice*
Cyr, Conrad Keefe *federal judge*
Dal Santo, Diane *retired judge, writer, arbitrator, mediator*
Davis, Marguerite Herr *judge*
Davis, William C., Jr. *judge*
Day, Roland Bernard *retired judge*
Dela Cruz, Jose Santos *retired commonwealth supreme court justice*
Dickey, Betty C. *former state supreme court justice*
Ditter, J. William, Jr. *federal judge*
Dixon, John Morris, Jr. *retired judge, lawyer*
Drowota, Frank F. III *retired state supreme court justice*
Duncan, Allyson K. *federal judge*
Dunn, Melvin Edward *retired judge*
Eaton, Joe Oscar *federal judge*
Enoch, Craig Trively *retired judge*
Fay, Peter Thorp *federal judge*
Figa, Phillip S. *judge*
Fiscus, Thomas J. *former judge, career military officer*
Fisher, Ann Lewis *judge*
Fletcher, Norman S. *retired state supreme court justice*
Freeman, Charles E. *state supreme court justice*
Gaynes, Thomas Edward, Jr. *retired judge, lawyer, educator, mediator*
Gebelein, Richard Stephen *judge, former state attorney general*
Glennon, Charles Edward *retired judge, lawyer*
Goldstein, Debra Holly *judge*
Gorence, Patricia Josetta *judge*
Grant, Isabella Horton *retired judge*
Graves, John William *state supreme court justice*
Habeck, James Roy *judge*
Hamblen, Lapsley Walker, Jr. *retired judge*
Hammond, Glenn Barry, Sr. *judge, electrical engineer*
Harding, Ray Murray, Jr. *retired judge*
Harris, Dale Hutter *retired judge*
Harwood, Robert Bernard, Jr. *former state supreme court justice*
Heaney, Gerald William *retired federal judge*
Hightower, Jack English *retired judge, former congressman*
Hodge, Verne Antonio *judge*
Hogan, Thomas Francis *federal judge*
Holdaway, Ronald M. *retired federal judge*
Howard, George, Jr. *federal judge*
Hyman, Michael Bruce *judge*
Ingram, George Conley *judge*
Ivers, Donald Louis *retired federal judge*
Jackson, Thomas Penfield *federal judge*
Jimenez, Dawn Marie *judge*
Johnstone, Douglas Inge *retired state supreme court justice, lawyer*
Johnstone, Martin E. *retired state supreme court justice*
Jones, Edith Hollan *federal judge*
Jones, Phyllis Gene *judge*
Jordan, Daniel Porter III *federal judge*
Jordan, Michelle Denise *judge*
Karr, Stephen William *retired judge*
Kehoe, L. Paul *state judge*
Kenworthy, William Eugene *judge*
Kline, Norman Douglas *retired judge*
Kooijmans, Pieter Hendrik *former judge*
Kramer, Kenneth Bentley *retired federal judge, former congressman*
Kravitch, Phyllis A. *federal judge*
Kunkle, William Joseph *judge, lawyer*
Lake, I. Beverly, Jr. *retired state supreme court justice*
Lee, Dan M. *retired state supreme court chief justice*
Legge, Charles Alexander *federal judge*
Linn, Richard *federal judge*
Lioi, Sara Elizabeth *judge*
Low, Harry William *judge*
Lyons, Champ, Jr. *state supreme court justice*
Manglona, Ramona V. *judge, former attorney general*
McClure, Ann Crawford *judge, lawyer*
McKee, Roger Curtis *retired federal judge*
McMorrow, Mary Ann Grohwin *retired state supreme court justice*
McPherson, James E. *judge*
Metzner, Charles Miller *federal judge*
Moore, Daniel Alton, Jr. *retired state supreme court justice*
Myers, Robert David *judge*
Nabers, Drayton, Jr. *retired state supreme court chief justice, insurance company executive*
Nadeau, Joseph P. *retired state supreme court justice*
Nangle, John Francis *federal judge*
Nelson, David Aldrich *former federal judge*
Nelson, Frederick Dickson *judge*
Neuman, Linda Kinney *retired state supreme court justice, lawyer*
Newbern, William David *retired state supreme court justice*
Newman, Theodore Roosevelt, Jr. *judge*
Nigro, Russell M. *former state supreme court justice*
Oakes, James L. *retired federal judge*
O'Connor, Sandra Day *retired United States Supreme Court Justice*
Ortique, Revius Oliver, Jr. *retired judge*
Payne, Mary Libby *retired judge*
Pearson, Henry Clyde *retired judge*
Phillips, James Dickson, Jr. *retired federal judge*
Pierce, Lawrence Warren *retired federal judge*
Pokras, Sheila Frances *retired judge*
Poritz, Deborah Tobias *former state supreme court justice and attorney general*
Porter, James Morris *retired judge*
Potter, Robert Daniel *federal judge*
Prado, Edward Charles *federal judge*
Prather, Lenore Loving *former state supreme court chief justice*
Quillen, William Tatem *retired judge, lawyer, educator*
Reinhardt, Stephen Roy *federal judge*
Resnick, Alice Robie *retired state supreme court justice*
Rezek, Francisco *former judge, former supreme court justice*
Richardson, Gerald B. *hearing officer, lawyer*
Robart, James Louis *federal judge, lawyer*
Romig, Thomas J. *judge, career military officer*
Rose, Robert Edgar *retired state supreme court justice*
Roszkowski, Stanley Julian *retired federal judge*
Schroeder, Gerald Frank *retired state supreme court justice*
Schultz, Louis William *retired judge*
Senechal, Alice R. *federal magistrate judge, lawyer*
Shearing, Miriam *retired state supreme court chief justice*
Shepherd, Bobby E. *federal judge*
Shubb, William Barnet *judge*
Silberman, Larry (Laurence Hirsch) *federal judge*
Smith, Fern M. *judge*
Smith, Jackson Barkley, Jr. *retired judge*
Southwick, Leslie Harburd *judge, lawyer*
Spector, Rose *former state supreme court justice*
Stafford, William Henry, Jr. *federal judge*
Stahl, Madonna *retired judge*
Staker, Robert Jackson *retired judge*
Stanton, Louis Lee *federal judge*
Stewart, Annette *judge*

Sullivan, Eugene Raymond *federal judge*
Sypolt, Diane Gilbert *retired judge*
Thurmond, George Murat *judge*
Vacchelli, Robert Francis *judge*
van Gestel, Allan *judge*
Waldon, Alton Ronald, Jr. *judge*
Walsh, Joseph Thomas *retired state supreme court justice*
White, Helene Nita *federal judge*
Wicker, Thomas Carey, Jr. *retired judge*
Widener, Hiram Emory, Jr. *judge*
Wilner, Alan M. *retired judge*
Wilson, Ronald A. *judge*
Wintersheimer, Donald Carl *retired state supreme court justice*
Wroble, Arthur Gerard *judge*
Yurasko, Frank Noel *judge*
Zazzali, James R. *retired state supreme court justice*

LAW: LAW PRACTICE AND ADMINISTRATION

UNITED STATES

ALABAMA

Andalusia
Fuller, William Sidney *lawyer*

Anniston
Klinefelter, James Louis *lawyer*
Woodrow, Randall Mark *lawyer*

Birmingham
Albritton, William Harold, IV, *lawyer*
Alexander, James Patrick *lawyer, educator*
Alford, Margie Searcy *lawyer, writer*
Baker, David Remember *lawyer*
Balch, Samuel Eason *lawyer*
Blan, Ollie Lionel, Jr. *retired lawyer*
Boardman, Mark Seymour *lawyer*
Bono, Alexander Dominic (Lex Bono) *lawyer*
Carmody, Richard Patrick *lawyer*
Carruthers, Thomas Neely *lawyer*
Chapman, Lavonya Kelley *lawyer, director*
Clark, William Northington *lawyer, retired military officer*
Cole, Charles DuBose, II, *law educator*
Coleman, Brittin Turner *lawyer*
Coleman, John James III *lawyer, educator*
Cooper, N. Lee *lawyer*
Corliss, Deane Kenworthy *lawyer*
Davis, Stacey Ann *lawyer*
Denson, William Frank III *lawyer*
Duke, J. Richard *lawyer*
Farley, Joseph McConnell *lawyer*
Friend, Edward Malcolm III *lawyer, educator*
Gale, Fournier Joseph III *lawyer*
Garner, Robert Edward Lee *lawyer*
Givhan, Robert Marcus *lawyer*
Haskell, Wyatt Rushton *lawyer*
Hinton, James Forrest, Jr. *lawyer*
Howell, William Ashley III *lawyer*
Hughey, James Fletcher, Jr. *lawyer*
Hutchison, Larry M. *lawyer*
Kracke, Robert Russell *lawyer*
Lacy, Alexander Shelton *retired lawyer*
Langum, David John *law educator, historian*
Long, Deborah Joyce *lawyer*
Long, Thad Gladden *lawyer*
Markstein, Daniel H. III *lawyer*
Mc Millan, George Duncan Hastie, Jr. *lawyer, former state official*
McWhorter, Hobart Amory, Jr. *lawyer*
Mendler, Joel A. *lawyer*
Mills, William Hayes *lawyer*
Molen, John Klauminzer *lawyer*
Nettles, Bert Sheffield *lawyer*
Newton, Alexander Worthy *lawyer*
Palmer, Robert Leslie *lawyer*
Piassick, Joel Bernard *lawyer*
Powell, Jerry W. *lawyer*
Quick, Frances King *lawyer*
Rogers, Ernest Mabry *lawyer*
Rotch, James E. *lawyer*
Rountree, Asa *lawyer*
Selfe, Edward Milton *lawyer*
Small, Clarence Merilton, Jr. *lawyer*
Spransy, Joseph William *corporate lawyer*
Stabler, Lewis Vastine, Jr. *lawyer*
Stelzenmuller, Cyril Vaughn *lawyer*
Stewart, Joseph Grier *lawyer*
Trimmier, Charles Stephen, Jr. *lawyer*
Vinson, Laurence Duncan, Jr. *lawyer*
Watkins, Donald V. *lawyer, entrepreneur*
Weeks, Arthur Andrew *lawyer, educator*
Wells, Huey Thomas, Jr. *lawyer*
Whatley, Joe Ramon, Jr. *lawyer*
Whittington, John P. *lawyer*
Wilson, James Charles, Jr. *lawyer*
Wrinkle, John Newton *lawyer*
Yoder, Stephen Alan *lawyer*

Clanton
Jackson, John Hollis, Jr. *lawyer*

Daphne
Crosby, Samuel Neil *lawyer*

Decatur
Mays, John E. *lawyer*

Demopolis
Dinning, Woodford Wyndham, Jr. *lawyer*
Lloyd, Hugh Adams *lawyer*

Dothan
Baxley, Wade H. *lawyer*
Huskey, Dow Thobern *lawyer*

Florala
Duplechin, D. James *lawyer*

Huntsville
Ryan, L. Thomas, Jr. *lawyer*
Watson, S.A. *lawyer, retired judge*

Jacksonville
Bundrum, Kenneth Owen *lawyer, writer*

Jasper
Thomas, Steven Allen *lawyer*

Lillian
Ray, Betty Jean G. *retired lawyer*

Mobile
Braswell, Louis Erskine *lawyer*
Harris, Benjamin Harte, Jr. *lawyer*
Helmsing, Frederick George *lawyer*
Holland, Lyman Faith, Jr. *lawyer*
Holmes, Broox Garrett *lawyer*
Johnston, Neil Chunn *lawyer*
Meigs, Walter Ralph *lawyer, dry dock and shipbuilding company executive*
Murchison, David Roderick *lawyer*
Peebles, E(mory) B(ush) III *lawyer*
Pierce, Donald Fay *lawyer*
Quina, Marion Albert, Jr. *lawyer*
Rhodes, Deborah Jean Johnson *prosecutor*
Roedder, William Chapman, Jr. *lawyer*

Montgomery
Byars, Walter Ryland, Jr. *lawyer*
Campbell, Maria Bouchelle *lawyer, consultant*
Canary, Leura Garrett *prosecutor*
Dees, Morris Seligman, Jr. *lawyer*
Ely, Robert Eugene *lawyer, author, educator*
Glassroth, Stephen R. *lawyer*
Gregory, William Stanley *lawyer*
Hamner, Reginald Turner *lawyer*
Hester, Douglas Benjamin *lawyer*
Kloess, Lawrence Herman, Jr. *retired lawyer*
Laurie, Robin Garrett *lawyer*
Lawson, Thomas Seay, Jr. *lawyer, actor*
Leslie, Henry Arthur *lawyer, retired bank executive*
McElvy, James Douglas *lawyer*
McFadden, Frank Hampton *lawyer, former judge*
Proctor, David Ray *lawyer*
Salmon, Joseph Thaddeus *lawyer*
Segall, Robert D. *lawyer*
Stevenson, Bryan Allen *lawyer*
Volz, Charles Harvie, Jr. *lawyer*
Wood, James Jerry *lawyer*

Moulton
Dutton, Mark Anthony *lawyer*

Mountain Brook
Southerland, Henry DeLeon, Jr. *retired lawyer, civil engineer*

Opelika
Samford, Yetta Glenn, Jr. *lawyer, director*

Point Clear
Holt, Thaddeus *lawyer*

Sheffield
Hamby, Gene Malcolm, Jr. *lawyer*

Tuscaloosa
Bassett, Debra Lyn *lawyer, educator*
Cook, Camille Wright *retired law educator*
Leonard, James *law librarian, educator*
Smalley, Donna Wesson *lawyer, educator*
Smith, Ralph Harrison *lawyer*
Williams, Roger Courtland *lawyer, arbitrator, mediator*

Tuskegee
Gray, Fred David *lawyer*

ALASKA

Anchorage
Bond, Marc Douglas *lawyer*
Brown, Keith E. *lawyer*
Butler, Rex Lamont *lawyer*
Cantor, James Elliot *lawyer*
Claman, Matthew W. *lawyer*
Cohen, Nelson P. *prosecutor*
De Lisio, Stephen Scott *lawyer, director, pastor*
Ealy, Jonathan Bruce *lawyer*
Fleischer, Hugh William *lawyer*
Grahame, Heather H. *lawyer*
Holl, Roger Elmo *lawyer*
Hughes, Mary Katherine *lawyer*
Katcher, Jonathon A. *lawyer*
Langworthy, Robert H. *law educator*
Linxwiler, James David *lawyer*
McClintock, Donald William III *lawyer*
Nosek, Francis John *lawyer, diplomat*
Oesting, David W. *lawyer*
Ostrovsky, Lawrence Zelig *lawyer*
Owens, Robert Patrick *lawyer*
Reeves, James N. *lawyer*
Roberts, John Derham *lawyer*
Ross, Wayne Anthony *lawyer*
Serdahely, Douglas J. *lawyer, former state judge*
Weinig, Richard Arthur *lawyer*
Wohlforth, Eric Evans *lawyer*

Bethel
Owen, Lauri J. *lawyer*

Fairbanks
Tiemessen, John J. *lawyer*

Juneau
Cole, Charles Edward *lawyer, state attorney general*
Rozell, William Barclay *lawyer*
Weyhrauch, Bruce Butler *lawyer, former state legislator*

Kodiak
Jamin, Matthew Daniel *lawyer, judge*
Ott, Andrew Eduard *lawyer*

Nondalton
Gay, Sarah Elizabeth *lawyer*

Salcha
Rice, Julian Casavant *lawyer*

Sitka
Graham, David Antony *lawyer*

ARIZONA

Bisbee
Moreno, Patricia Frazier *lawyer*

Carefree
Putney, Mark William *lawyer, utilities executive*
Whittington, Thomas Lee *lawyer*

Eloy
O'Leary, Thomas Michael *lawyer*

Flagstaff
Pickett, A. Dean *lawyer*
Stoops, Daniel J. *lawyer*

Kingman
Basinger, Richard Lee *lawyer*

Mesa
Gunderson, Brent Merrill *lawyer*
Hudkins, John W. *lawyer*

Paradise Valley
Howard, Lucia Fakonas *retired lawyer*
Tubman, William Charles *lawyer*

Phoenix
Allen, Robert Eugene Barton *lawyer*
Alsentzer, William James, Jr. *lawyer*
Atkinson, Joseph Matthew *lawyer*
Bain, C. Randall *lawyer*
Baker, William Dunlap *lawyer*
Bakker, Thomas Gordon *lawyer*
Begam, Robert George *lawyer*
Beggs, Harry Mark *lawyer*
Bellamy, Fredric *lawyer*
Birk, David R. *lawyer, electronics executive*
Blanchard, Charles Alan *lawyer, retired state senator*
Burke, Timothy John *lawyer*
Burnham, Rebecca Lynne *lawyer*
Case, David Leon *lawyer*
Coghill, William Thomas, Jr. *retired lawyer*
Cohen, Jon Stephan *lawyer*
Cole, George Thomas *lawyer*
Colton, Sterling David (David Colton) *lawyer*
Comus, Louis Francis, Jr. *lawyer*
Condo, James Robert *lawyer*
Cooledge, Richard Calvin *lawyer*
Cowley, Samuel C. *lawyer, transportation services executive*
Crozier, Scott A. *lawyer*
Davies, David George *lawyer, educator*
Dawson, John Joseph *lawyer*
Derdenger, Patrick *lawyer*
Derouin, James Gilbert *lawyer*
Donovan, Timothy R. *lawyer*
Dunipace, Ian Douglas *lawyer*
Ehmann, Anthony Valentine *lawyer*
Everett, James Joseph *lawyer*
Everroad, John David *lawyer*
Feinstein, Allen Lewis *lawyer*
Fellows, Gerald Lee *lawyer*
Fenzl, Terry Earle *lawyer*
Flickinger, Don Jacob *lawyer*
Gaffney, Donald Lee *lawyer*
Galbut, Martin Richard *lawyer*
Gallagher, Michael L. *lawyer*
Gilbert, Donald Roy *lawyer*
Goldstein, Stuart Wolf *lawyer*
Gomez, David Frederick *lawyer*
Grant, Merwin Darwin *lawyer*
Griller, Gordon Moore *legal association administrator, consultant*
Grimwood, Helen Perry *lawyer*
Halpern, Barry David *lawyer*
Hammond, Larry Austin *lawyer*
Hantel, Philip Edward *lawyer*
Hardwick, Catherine R. *lawyer*
Harrison, Mark Isaac *lawyer*
Hay, John Leonard *lawyer*
Hayden, William Robert *lawyer*
Hicks, William Albert III *lawyer*
Hochuli, Edward G. *lawyer*
Hoecker, Thomas Ralph *lawyer*
Howard, William Matthew *arbitrator, lawyer, writer*
Hoxie, Joel P. *lawyer*
Huntwork, James Roden *lawyer*
Jakubczyk, John Joseph *lawyer*
James, Charles E., Jr. *lawyer*
Jirauch, Charles W. *lawyer*
Johnson, Christopher D. *lawyer*
Johnston, Logan Truax III *lawyer*
Kant, Robert S. *lawyer*
Klahr, Gary Peter *retired lawyer*
Klausner, Jack Daniel *lawyer*
Knoller, Guy David *lawyer*
Kurn, Neal *lawyer*
Lee, Richard H(arlo) *lawyer*
Leshner, Stephen I. *lawyer*
Levetown, Robert Alexander *lawyer*
Loftin, Nancy Carol *lawyer, utilities executive*
Lubin, Stanley *lawyer*
Martori, Joseph Peter *lawyer*
Mast, Gregory Lewis *lawyer*
May, Bruce Barnett *lawyer*
McAuliffe, Daniel Joseph *lawyer*
McKellips, Gordon Wayne, Jr. *lawyer, land developer*
McRae, Hamilton Eugene III *lawyer*
Meschkow, Jordan M. *lawyer*
Miller, Robert J. *lawyer*
Olsen, Alfred Jon *lawyer*
O'Steen, Van *lawyer*
Perry, Lee Rowan *retired lawyer*
Pietzsch, Michael Edward *lawyer*
Placenti, Frank Michael *lawyer*
Platt, Warren E. *lawyer*
Plattner, Richard Serber *lawyer*
Price, Charles Steven *lawyer*
Refo, Patricia Lee *lawyer*
Rethore, Bernard M. *lawyer*
Rivera, Jose de Jesus *lawyer*
Rose, David L. *lawyer*
Rose, Scott A. *lawyer*
Rosenfeld, Lawrence J. (Larry) *lawyer*
Ross, Richard Frederick *lawyer*
Rudolph, Gilbert Lawrence *lawyer*
Sanders, Barry R. *lawyer*
Schneider, Elizabeth Kelley *law librarian, educator*
Sherk, Kenneth John *lawyer*
Short, Dean Chilton, II, *lawyer*
Silverman, Alan Henry *lawyer*
Smock, Timothy Robert *lawyer*
Storey, Norman C. *lawyer*
Sutton, Samuel J. *lawyer, educator, engineer*
Swartz, Melvin Jay *lawyer, writer*
Tennen, Leslie Irwin *lawyer, consultant*
Thompson, Joel Erik *lawyer*
Thompson, Terence William *lawyer*
Ulrich, Paul Graham *lawyer, writer, editor*
Verbin, Jeffrey Harold *lawyer*
Vryhof, John C. *lawyer*
Walker, Richard K. *lawyer*
Warner, Teddy Fleming *lawyer*
Williams, Quinn Patrick *lawyer*
Wirken, Charles William *lawyer*
Wolf, G. Van Velsor, Jr. *lawyer*
Yarnell, Michael Allan *mediator, arbitrator, la educator*

Prescott
Goodman, Mark N. *lawyer*
Madden, Paul Robert *lawyer, director*

Scottsdale
Bullerdick, Kim H. *lawyer, petroleum executiv*
Buri, Charles Edward *lawyer*
Calise, Nicholas James *lawyer*
Crawford, Robert F. *lawyer*
Hutchison, Stanley Philip *retired lawyer*
Inman, William Peter *lawyer*
Jorden, Douglas Allen *lawyer, municipal offici*
Krupp, Clarence William *lawyer, health facili administrator*
Leonard, Jeffrey S. *lawyer*
Lindgren, D(erbin) Kenneth, Jr. *retired lawyer*
Lowry, Edward Francis, Jr. *lawyer*
Lundeen, Bradley Curtis *lawyer*
Marks, Merton Eleazer *lawyer, international arbitrator, mediator, consultant*
Nielsen, Greg Ross *lawyer*
Overgaard, Cordell Jersild *lawyer, rancher, director*
Smith, David Burnell *lawyer, state legislator*
White, Jo Lynn *lawyer*

Sun City
Hauer, James Albert *lawyer*
Keesling, Karen Ruth *lawyer*
Treece, James Lyle *retired lawyer*

Surprise
Fennelly, Jane Corey *lawyer*

Tempe
Askland, Andrew *law educator, director*
Dhillon, Janet L. *lawyer, air transportation executive*
Fanning, Francis Gerard *lawyer*
Marchant, Gary Elvin *lawyer*
Matheson, Alan Adams *law educator*
Rogers, Mark Nicholl *lawyer*
Simes, Michael Louis *lawyer*
Spritzer, Ralph Simon *lawyer, educator*

Tucson
Amhowitz, Harris J. *lawyer, educator*
Blackman, Jeffrey William *lawyer*
Chiorazzi, Michael Gerard *law librarian, educator*
Cohen, Gary J. *lawyer*
Coker, Mich *lawyer*
D'Antonio, James Joseph *lawyer*
De Concini, Dennis *lawyer, retired senator, consultant*
Dobbs, Dan Byron *lawyer, educator*
Esposito, Joseph Louis *lawyer*
Farhang, Ali J. *lawyer*
Feldman, Stanley George *lawyer*
Froman, Sandra Sue *lawyer*
Gantz, David Alfred *lawyer, academic administrator*
Goldman, Gloria A. *lawyer*
Grand, Richard D. *lawyer*
Kozolchyk, Boris *law educator, consultant*
Kuklin, Susan Beverly *lawyer, librarian, educator*
Kuykendall, Gregory John *lawyer*
Mc Donald, John Richard *lawyer*
Meehan, Michael Joseph *lawyer*
Miller, Michael Douglas *lawyer*
Morrow, James Franklin *lawyer*
Noonan, James C. *lawyer, mediator, arbitrato*
Osborne, John Edwards *lawyer*
Pace, Thomas M. *lawyer*
Petersen, Frederick J. *lawyer*
Rose, Carol Marguerite *law educator*
Samet, Dee-Dee *lawyer*
Schorr, S. L. *lawyer*
Simmons, Sarah R. *lawyer*
Spaeth, Jan Mills *jury consultant*
Staubitz, Arthur Frederick *retired lawyer, hea products executive*
Strong, John William *lawyer, educator*
Tindall, Robert Emmett *lawyer, educator*
Treadwell-Rubin, Pamela A. *lawyer*

Natasha *lawyer*

r, David Joseph *lawyer, educator*
Jimmie Dee *lawyer*

ANSAS

own
John Cyrus III *lawyer, judge*

on
er, Marlo Bush *retired lawyer*

onville
Thomas C. *lawyer, former prosecutor*
Thomas D. *lawyer*

way
on, James Douglas (Jim Johnson) *lawyer*

sett
ll, Billy James *lawyer*

orado
Steven A. *lawyer, oil industry executive*

tteville
tt, Woodson William, Jr. *lawyer*
Lewis Everett, Jr. *retired lawyer*
, Charles Melvin *lawyer*
en, Douglas J. *lawyer, educator*
on, Charles Thomas, Jr. *lawyer, director*
an, Harrison M. *lawyer, educator*

Smith
Robert Cramer III *prosecutor*
er, Richard F. *lawyer*
Charles *lawyer*
ors, C. Brian *lawyer*

ison
, James D. *lawyer*

na
opf, Charles Buford *lawyer*

sboro
on, John C. *lawyer*

Village
artz, Robert P. *lawyer*

e Rock
, H(enry) William *lawyer*
rson, Philip Sidney *lawyer*
nnon, Charles Tad *lawyer*
, J. Bruce *lawyer*
ugh, Kathryn Corrothers *law librarian*
n, William Mell III *lawyer*
er, Russell Allen *lawyer*
John Wesley, Jr. *lawyer*
ht, William Dixon *lawyer, writer*
er, Paul Williams, Jr. *lawyer*
, Ronald Arthur *lawyer*
, Stephen Witsell *lawyer*
n, Jim Lee *lawyer*
e, Judith A. *lawyer*
hall, William Taylor *lawyer*
ey, Richard N. *lawyer, telecommunications ustry executive*
Ronald Alan *lawyer*
hey, Arthur Gage, Jr. *law educator*
on, Edward Sheffield *lawyer, retired utilities ecutive*
e, David Cannon *lawyer*
say, Richard L. *lawyer*
oeder, Paul J., Jr. *lawyer*
man, William Farrar *lawyer, former state gislator*
art, Amy Lee *lawyer*
kburger, Jean Dawson *lawyer*
, William Leake *lawyer*
, William Henry III *lawyer*
ry, Frederick Stanley *lawyer*
erspoon, Carolyn Brack *lawyer*

lvern
d, Jerry Lee *lawyer*

na
ilkill, Daniel B. *lawyer*

nticello
, William Kenneth *lawyer*

vport
kton, Marvin Dell *lawyer*

th Little Rock
, Claibourne Watkins, Jr. *lawyer*
er, (Clyde) Tab (Clyde Tab Turner) *lawyer*
ch, Morgan E. *lawyer*

e Bluff
s, John Harris *retired lawyer*
, David Lloyd *lawyer*
de, Joseph Arlin *lawyer*

scott
ser, Albert Glenn *lawyer*

gers
rs, Dane Jacob *lawyer, podiatrist*

rcy
hes, Thomas Morgan III *lawyer*

ingdale
zalez-Pita, J. Alberto *lawyer, food products ecutive*
son, R. Read *lawyer, food products executive*

st Memphis
leman, Julian Barton *lawyer*

CALIFORNIA

Alameda
Boltwood, Russell Lewis *lawyer, telecommunications industry executive*

Alamo
Madden, Palmer Brown *lawyer*
Schreiber, John T. *lawyer*

Alhambra
Determan, John David *lawyer*

Aliso Viejo
Fisher, Lawrence N. *lawyer, engineering and construction management company executive*

Alta Loma
Klein, Henry *lawyer*

Arcadia
Gelber, Louise C(arp) *lawyer*

Arroyo Grande
Saari, David John *retired law educator*

Atherton
Ferris, Robert Albert *lawyer, venture capitalist*

Bakersfield
Barmann, Bernard Charles, Sr. *lawyer*
Gong, Gloria Margaret *lawyer, pharmacist*
Tornstrom, Robert Ernest *lawyer, oil industry executive*

Belvedere Tiburon
Allan, Walter Robert *lawyer*
Stotter, Lawrence Henry *lawyer*

Berkeley
Arguedas, Cristina Claypoole *lawyer*
Barnes, Thomas G. *law educator*
Barr, Robert *lawyer, educator*
Berring, Robert Charles, Jr. *law educator, librarian, association administrator*
Blackburn, Robert Parker *lawyer*
Buxbaum, Richard M. *lawyer, educator*
Choper, Jesse Herbert *law educator, dean*
De Goff, Victoria Joan *lawyer*
Eisenberg, Melvin A. *law educator*
Ginger, Ann Fagan *lawyer*
Grubb, Erica B. *lawyer*
Halbach, Edward Christian, Jr. *law educator*
Haley, George Patrick *lawyer*
Jorde, Thomas *law educator*
Kadish, Sanford Harold *law educator*
Kagan, Robert Allen *law educator*
Kay, Herma Hill *law educator*
McNulty, John Kent *lawyer, educator*
Meador, Ross DeShong *lawyer*
Menell, Peter Seth *law educator*
Merges, Robert Patrick *law educator, writer*
Mishkin, Paul J. *lawyer, educator*
Moran, Rachel *law educator*
Pope, Alexander H. *retired lawyer*
Scheiber, Harry N. *law educator*
Seligman, Brad *lawyer*
Shapiro, Martin *law educator*
Vanden Heuvel, Kathleen *law librarian*
Wolfram, Charles William *law educator*
Woodhouse, Thomas Edwin *lawyer, trust company administrator*
Yoo, John Choon *law educator, former federal agency administrator*
Zimring, Franklin E. *lawyer, educator*

Beverly Hills
Alfonso, Frank A. *lawyer*
Amado, Honey Kessler *lawyer*
Anderson, Kenneth Allen *lawyer, hotel executive*
Bortman, David *lawyer*
Brockovich-Ellis, Erin *legal researcher*
Burns, Marvin Gerald *lawyer*
Clemens, Bruce Archer *lawyer*
Fagel, Bruce G. *lawyer, former emergency physician*
Fine, Richard Isaac *lawyer*
Glass, David J. *lawyer*
Grimwade, Richard Llewellyn *lawyer*
Hersh, Neal Raymond *lawyer*
Hogan, Steven L. *lawyer*
Isaacman, Alan L. *lawyer*
Jaffe, F. Filmore *lawyer, retired judge*
Johnson, Douglas L. *lawyer*
Joyner, Jeffrey K. *lawyer*
Kalawski, Eva *lawyer*
Karlin, Michael Jonathan Abraham *lawyer*
Kaufman, Robert *lawyer*
Kleiner, Madeleine A. *lawyer, hotel executive*
Lesowitz, Jessica R. *lawyer*
Ramer, Bruce M. *lawyer*
Rowles, Michael G. *lawyer*
Schiff, Gunther Hans *lawyer*
Sobelle, Richard E. *lawyer*
Thompson, Richard Dickson *lawyer*

Bodega Bay
Sorensen, Linda *lawyer*

Burbank
Brandis, Bernardine *lawyer*
Braverman, Alan N. *lawyer*

Burlingame
Cotchett, Joseph Winters *lawyer, writer*
Denten, Christopher Peter *lawyer*
Slabach, Stephen Hall *lawyer*

Calabasas
Geckle, Timothy J. *lawyer*
Samuels, Sandor Eli *lawyer, diversified financial services company executive*

Carlsbad
McCracken, Steven Carl *lawyer*
Mezzullo, Louis Albert *lawyer*

Carmel
Bengert, W. Raymond *lawyer, chemical engineer*

Century City
Clark, Shaun C. *lawyer*

Chatsworth
Klein, Jeffrey S. *lawyer, media executive*

Chino Hills
Pearson, April Virginia *lawyer*

Claremont
Ansell, Edward Orin *lawyer*
Ferguson, Cleve Robert *lawyer, educator*

Coachella
Trover, Ellen Lloyd *lawyer, rancher, art dealer*

Coalinga
Frame, Ted Ronald *lawyer*

Concord
Borson, Daniel Benjamin *lawyer, educator, physiologist, researcher*

Corona Del Mar
Allen, Russell G. *lawyer*

Coronado
Herring, Charles David *lawyer, educator*
Raushenbush, Walter Brandeis *retired law educator*

Costa Mesa
Afrasiabi, Peter R. *lawyer*
Aguilera, A. Eric *lawyer*
Andrassy, Kyra E. *lawyer*
Barbarosh, Craig A. *lawyer*
Caldwell, Courtney Lynn *lawyer, real estate consultant*
Daniels, James Walter *lawyer*
Daucher, Donald Alfred *lawyer*
Frieden, Clifford E. *lawyer*
Grogan, Virginia S. *lawyer*
Hay, Howard Clinton *lawyer*
Hurst, Charles Wilson *lawyer*
Jones, H(arold) Gilbert, Jr. *lawyer*
Marshall, Ellen Ruth *lawyer*
Matsen, Jeffrey Robert *lawyer*
Mooradian, George T. *lawyer*
Morrow, Donald L. *lawyer*
Rose, I. Nelson *lawyer, educator*
Ruben, Richard S. *lawyer*
Schaaf, Douglas Allan *lawyer*
Schaller, Gordon A. *lawyer*
Scheuneman, Christine A. *lawyer*
Shallenberger, Garvin F. *retired lawyer*
Tennyson, Peter Joseph *lawyer*

Culver City
Nicholas, Frederick M. *lawyer*

Cupertino
Courville, Arthur F. *lawyer*
Rosenberg, Donald Jay *lawyer, computer company executive*
Svalya, Phillip Gordon *lawyer*

Cypress
Olschwang, Alan Paul *lawyer, crossword and variety puzzle author*

Dana Point
Mallory, Frank Linus *lawyer*

Danville
Candland, D. Stuart *lawyer*
Jones, Orlo Dow *retired lawyer, retired pharmaceutical executive*

Darwin
Palazzo, Robert Paul *lawyer, accountant*

Davis
Bartosic, Florian *lawyer, educator*
Bruch, Carol Sophie *law educator*
Imwinkelried, Edward John *law educator*
Johnson, Kevin Raymond *law educator*
Oakley, John Bilyeu *law educator*
Wolk, Bruce Alan *law educator*
Wydick, Richard Crews *lawyer, educator*

Del Mar
Seitman, John Michael *arbitrator, mediator, lawyer*

Diablo
Burnison, Boyd Edward *lawyer*

East Palo Alto
Bates, William III *lawyer*
Frankle, Diane Holt *lawyer*
Lesser, Henry *lawyer*
Rinsky, Arthur C. *lawyer*
Schelling, Donald Lawrence *lawyer*

El Dorado Hills
Blasier, Robert Dalton, Jr. *lawyer*

El Segundo
Fisk, Hayward Dan *lawyer, computer services company executive*
Hunter, Larry Dean *lawyer, broadcast executive*
Muhlbach, Robert Arthur *lawyer*
Normile, Robert J. *lawyer*
Schohl, Joseph *lawyer*
Willis, Judy Ann *lawyer*

Emeryville
Howe, Drayton Ford, Jr. *lawyer*

Encinitas
Williams, Michael Edward *lawyer*

Encino
Genga, John Michael *lawyer*

Smith, Selma Moidel *lawyer, composer*
Sungaila, Mary-Christine (M.C. Sungaila) *lawyer*

Escondido
Guinn, Stanley Willis *retired lawyer*

Foster City
Alton, Gregg H. *lawyer*
Karnazes, Elizabeth Marie Barnson *lawyer, photojournalist*

Fremont
Chien-Hale, Elizabeth *lawyer*
Cummings, John Patrick *lawyer*
Gupta, Anu *lawyer*
Kitta, John Noah *lawyer*
Leung, Simon *lawyer, electronics executive*
Stinnett, Terrance LLoyd *lawyer*

Fresno
Berman, Richard P. *lawyer*
Ewell, A. Ben, Jr. *lawyer, small business owner*
Jenkins, David Ray *lawyer*
Lagle, John Franklin *lawyer*
Lambe, James Patrick *lawyer*
Little, Kevin Gerard *lawyer*
Palmer, Samuel Copeland III *lawyer*
Runyon, Brett L. *lawyer*

Fullerton
Ackerman, Richard Charles *lawyer, state legislator*
Bush, William Merritt *lawyer*
Frizell, Samuel *law educator*
Goldstein, Edward David *lawyer, former glass company executive*
Moerbeek, Stanley Leonard *lawyer*
Roberts, Mark Scott *lawyer*
Steinmeyer, Robert Jay *retired lawyer*

Glendale
Calabro, Alfred A. *lawyer*
Halaby, Noelle M. *lawyer*
Hoffman, Donald M. *lawyer*
Kazanjian, Phillip Carl *lawyer, educator*
Kendrick, Katherine *lawyer*
MacDonald, Kirk Stewart *lawyer*
Martinetti, Ronald Anthony *lawyer*
Scott, A. Timothy *lawyer*
Stack, Kevin J. *lawyer*

Gold River
Andrew, John Henry *lawyer, writer*

Grass Valley
Hawkins, Richard Michael *lawyer*

Greenbrae
Bonapart, Alan David *lawyer*

Half Moon Bay
Lambert, Frederick William *lawyer, educator*

Hayward
Beck, Edward William *lawyer*
Smith, John Kerwin *lawyer*

Healdsburg
Kemp, Alson Remington, Jr. *lawyer, retired educator*

Hercules
Richards, Gerald Thomas *lawyer, educator, writer*

Huntington Beach
Baroni, Michael L. *lawyer*
Garrels, Sherry Ann *lawyer*
Jensen, Dennis Lowell *lawyer*

Imperial Beach
Merkin, William Leslie *retired lawyer*

Indian Wells
Gassman, Andrea C. *paralegal, artist*
McDermott, Thomas John, Jr. *lawyer*

Indio
De Salva, Christopher Joseph *lawyer, consultant*

Irvine
Aitken, Ashleigh E. *lawyer*
Andersen, Erik M. *lawyer*
Basombrio, Juan C. *lawyer*
Bastiaanse, Gerard C. *lawyer*
Beard, Ronald Stratton *lawyer*
Christensen, Becky Vanderhoof *lawyer*
Crawford, Denise F. *lawyer*
DuBose, Guy Steven *lawyer*
Dull, David A. *lawyer*
Freeman, Douglas K. *lawyer*
Galuppo, Lynn T. *lawyer*
Grabowski, Richard Joseph *lawyer*
Halvorsen, Clay A. *lawyer, construction executive*
Hancock, S. Lee *lawyer, business executive*
Harpen, Shawn M. *lawyer*
Hensley, William Michael *lawyer*
Huang, Wendy Wan-Juoh *lawyer*
Ingram, Douglas Stephen *lawyer*
Keller, Jennifer L. *lawyer*
Knobbe, Louis Joseph *lawyer, educator*
Lowe, Kathlene Winn *lawyer*
Mattson, Robert Marvin, Jr. *lawyer*
Merken, Leo *lawyer*
Petrasich, John Moris *lawyer*
Re, Joseph R. *lawyer*
Rooklidge, William Charles *lawyer*
Scheithauer, Christopher C. *lawyer*
Seals, David W. *lawyer*
Specter, Richard Bruce *lawyer*
Stone, Samuel Beckner *lawyer*
Sunshine, Steven H. *lawyer*
Tachner, Leonard *lawyer*
Theologides, Stergios *lawyer, real estate company executive*
Tyler, Michael Robert *lawyer*

Umberg, Thomas John *lawyer*
Vines, Henry Ellsworth III *lawyer, accountant, financial planner*
Welsh, John Joseph (Jay) *lawyer*
Wintrode, Ralph Charles *lawyer*

La Canada Flintridge
Costello, Francis William *lawyer*

La Jolla
Buchholz, Debby *lawyer*
Karlen, Peter Hurd *lawyer, writer*
Kirchheimer, Arthur E(dward) *lawyer, business executive*
Mayer, James Hock *lawyer, mediator*
Morgens, Warren Kendall *retired lawyer*
Peterson, Paul Ames *lawyer, educator*
Shannahan, William Paul *lawyer*
Wilkins, Floyd, Jr. *retired lawyer*
Wilson, Bonnie Jean *lawyer, educator, investor*

Lafayette
Davies, Paul Lewis, Jr. *retired lawyer*
Freeman, Tom M. *lawyer*

Laguna Beach
Simons, Barry Thomas *lawyer*

Laguna Hills
DeGrave, Douglas Michael *lawyer*
Mathews, Stanton Terry *lawyer*
Reinglass, Michelle Annette *lawyer, mediator, arbitrator*

Laguna Niguel
McEvers, Duff Steven *lawyer*

Lake Forest
Bukaty, Raymond M. *lawyer*

Larkspur
Greenberg, Myron Silver *lawyer*
Ratner, David Louis *retired law educator*

Long Beach
Adkinson, Theodore H. *lawyer*
Bursley, Kathleen A. *lawyer*
Calhoun, John R. *lawyer*
Deukmejian, George *lawyer, retired governor*
Helwick, Christine *lawyer*
Levine, Arthur M. *law educator*
Sinclitico, Dennis J. *lawyer*
Stanton, Julia A. *lawyer*
Wise, George Edward *lawyer*

Los Altos
Yang, Roxana Hwu *lawyer, investor*

Los Angeles
Abbe, Alexander *lawyer*
Abell, Nancy L. *lawyer*
Abich, Yvette M. *lawyer*
Abrams, Norman *retired law educator, former academic administrator*
Abramson, Leslie Hope *lawyer*
Acain, Michael P. *lawyer*
Acosta, Maritoni A. *lawyer*
Adamek, Charles Andrew *lawyer*
Adams, Thomas Merritt *lawyer*
Adell, Hirsch *lawyer*
Adler, Erwin Ellery *lawyer*
Adler, Michael I. *lawyer*
Adler, Robert L. *lawyer*
Adler, Sara *arbitrator, mediator*
Aguilar, Valentin G., II, *lawyer*
Ahrens, Mary Elizabeth *lawyer*
Alden, John W. *lawyer*
Allred, Gloria Rachel *lawyer*
Altman, Scott *law educator, dean*
Aman, Kalley R. *lawyer*
Aminian Baghai, Arash *lawyer*
Amir, Michael M. *lawyer*
Anderson, Joshua E. *lawyer*
Angel, Arthur Ronald *lawyer, consultant*
Antin, Michael *lawyer*
Apfel, Gary *lawyer*
Aranas, Pauline *law librarian, educator*
Arbisser, Aton *lawyer*
Arbit, Beryl Ellen *legal assistant*
Arenella, Peter Lee *law educator*
Arnkra, Joe *legal administrator, writer*
Arnold, Dennis B. *lawyer*
Aronoff, Vera *law librarian*
Aronson, Seth *lawyer*
Aronzon, Paul S. *lawyer*
Asperger, James *lawyer*
Austen, Karl Ramsdell *lawyer*
Azad, Susan Stott *lawyer*
Bakaly, Charles George, Jr. *lawyer, mediator*
Barrett, Jane Hayes *lawyer*
Barth Menzies, Karen *lawyer*
Barton, Alan Joel *lawyer*
Barza, Harold A. *lawyer*
Basile, Paul Louis, Jr. *lawyer*
Baum, Michael Lin *lawyer*
Baumann, Richard Gordon *lawyer*
Baumgarten, Ronald Neal *lawyer*
Bender, Charles William *lawyer*
Bendix, Helen Irene *lawyer*
Berk, Blair *lawyer*
Berman, Myles Lee *lawyer*
Bernacchi, Richard Lloyd *lawyer*
Bibicoff, Hillary Sue *lawyer*
Biele, Hugh Irving *retired lawyer*
Bird, Terry W. *lawyer*
Bishop, Leah Margaret *lawyer*
Bitting, William M. *lawyer*
Blencowe, Paul Sherwood *lawyer, private investor*
Bloomberg, Coe Arthur *lawyer*
Blumberg, Grace Ganz *lawyer, educator*
Bobbitt, Leroy *lawyer*
Bodkin, Henry Grattan, Jr. *lawyer*
Bogen, Andrew E. *lawyer*
Bonesteel, Michael John *lawyer*
Bonner, Robert Cleve *lawyer*
Bordy, Michael Jeffrey *lawyer*
Bowers, Terree A. *lawyer*
Boxer, Lester *lawyer*
Boyce, David S. *lawyer*
Boyle, Kevin Richard *lawyer*
Bradley, Lawrence D., Jr. *lawyer*
Branca, John Gregory *lawyer, consultant*
Brandler, Jonathan M. *lawyer*
Braun, Harland W. *lawyer*
Bressan, Paul Louis *lawyer*
Brian, Brad D. *lawyer*
Brill, Laura W. *lawyer*
Bringardner, John Michael *lawyer, clergyman*
Brown, Michael K. *lawyer*
Bryan, Greyson *lawyer*
Bryan, Karen Smith *lawyer*
Bryant, Taimie L. *law educator*
Bugliosi, Vincent T. *lawyer*
Burch, Robert Dale *lawyer*
Burcham, David W. *law educator*
Burke, Robert Bertram *lawyer, political scientist, lobbyist*
Burke, Yvonne Watson Brathwaite (Mrs. William A. Burke) *lawyer*
Burten, Barry Lee *lawyer*
Buter, Irwin *lawyer*
Byrd, Christine Waterman Swent *lawyer*
Calabrese, Joseph A. *lawyer*
Capron, Alexander Morgan *lawyer, educator, bioethicist*
Carey, Stevens Anthony *lawyer*
Carlson, Robert Edwin *lawyer*
Carlton, John L. *lawyer*
Carr, Willard Zeller, Jr. *retired lawyer*
Carrey, Neil *lawyer, educator*
Casamassima, Christopher T. *lawyer*
Castro, Leonard Edward *lawyer*
Cate, Jan Harris *lawyer*
Cermak, John Frank, Jr. *lawyer*
Chan, Thomas Tak-Wah *lawyer*
Cheung, Sheri T. *lawyer*
Chiate, Kenneth Reed *lawyer*
Christol, Carl Quimby *lawyer, political science professor*
Christopher, Warren Minor *lawyer, former secretary of state*
Chu, Morgan *lawyer*
Chung, Tong Soo *lawyer*
Clair, John J., Jr. *lawyer*
Clark, R(ufus) Bradbury *lawyer, director*
Cleary, William Joseph, Jr. *lawyer*
Cochran, Steve *lawyer*
Cohen, Cynthia Marylyn *lawyer*
Cole, William Louis *lawyer*
Collier, Charles Arthur, Jr. *lawyer*
Concoff, Gary O. *lawyer*
Conley, Mark A. *lawyer*
Cook, Melanie K. *lawyer*
Cooley, Steve *prosecutor*
Cooper, Robert E. *lawyer*
Coupe, James Warnick *lawyer*
Crabtree-Ireland, Duncan *lawyer*
Curtiss, Thomas, Jr. *lawyer*
D'Angelo Melby, Donna Marie *lawyer*
Daniels, John Peter *lawyer*
Darby, G(eorge) Harrison *lawyer*
Darden, Christopher Allen *lawyer, actor, writer*
Dastin, Barry L. *lawyer*
Daum, John F. *lawyer*
Davis, Gray (Joseph Graham Davis) *lawyer, former governor*
De Brier, Donald Paul *lawyer, oil industry executive*
DeCarlo, John T. *lawyer*
de Castro, Hugo Daniel *lawyer*
Decker, Richard Jeffrey *lawyer*
Delgadillo, Rockard J. (Rocky Delgadillo) *lawyer*
Demoff, Marvin Alan *lawyer*
Denham, Robert Edwin *lawyer, investment company executive*
Diamond, Stanley Jay *lawyer*
Diaz, Maria G. *lawyer*
Dienes, Louis Robert *lawyer*
DiMeglio, David J. *lawyer*
Dinel, Richard Henry *lawyer*
Dixon, Patrick Richard *prosecutor*
Dodd, Jan Eve *lawyer*
Donaldson, Michael Cleaves *lawyer*
Donovan, John Arthur *lawyer*
Drooyan, Richard E. *lawyer*
Dudziak, Mary Louise *law educator*
Dunham, Scott H. *lawyer*
Eatman, Louis Perkins *lawyer*
Edelman, Scott Alan *lawyer*
Eley, Hunter R. *lawyer*
Ellingsen, Richard D. *lawyer*
Estrich, Susan Rachel *law educator*
Evans, Gregory Hinojosa *lawyer*
Ezer, Mitchel J. *lawyer*
Fairbank, Robert Harold *lawyer*
Farmer, Robert Lindsay *lawyer*
Feigen, Brenda S. *lawyer, film producer, writer*
Fein, Ronald Lawrence *lawyer*
Feldman, Larry Robert *lawyer*
Feldman, Lewis G. *lawyer*
Fenning, Lisa Hill *lawyer, mediator, retired judge*
Fields, Bertram Harris *lawyer*
Fields, Henry Michael *lawyer*
Finkel, Evan *lawyer*
Finnegan, Michael J. *lawyer*
Fisher, Barry Alan *lawyer*
Flagel, Mark Alan *lawyer*
Fleer, Keith George *lawyer, film company executive*
Foley, Martin James *lawyer*
Follick, Edwin Duane *law educator, dean, chiropractor*
Frackman, Russell Jay *lawyer*
Fragner, Matthew Charles *lawyer*
Franceschi, Ernest Joseph, Jr. *lawyer*
Fredman, Howard S. *lawyer*
Freier, Elliot G. *lawyer*
Frimmer, Paul Norman *lawyer*
Futami, Norman *lawyer*
Gallo, Jon Joseph *lawyer*
Galton, Stephen Harold *lawyer*
Garbacz, Gregory A. *lawyer*
Garrett, Elizabeth *law educator, academic administrator*
Gasparetti, Lorenzo E. *lawyer*
Geragos, Mark John *lawyer*
Gest, Howard David *lawyer*
Gilbertson, John T. *lawyer*
Girard, Robert David *lawyer*
Girardi, Thomas Vincent *lawyer*
Glazer, Michael *lawyer*
Glazier, Kenneth M. *lawyer*
Goldman, Allan Bailey *lawyer*
Goldman, Benjamin Edward *lawyer*
Goldman, Donald Aaron *lawyer*
Goldman, Joel A. *lawyer*
Goldsman, Melvin Saul *lawyer*
Goldstein, Robert David *law educator*
Goo, Valerie M. *lawyer*
Goodman, Max A. *lawyer, educator*
Gorman, Joseph Gregory, Jr. *lawyer*
Goss, Kent *lawyer*
Gould, David *lawyer*
Graves, Anna Marie *lawyer*
Gray, Jan Charles *lawyer, business owner*
Gray, Jeremy J.F. *lawyer*
Greaves, John Allen *lawyer*
Green, William Porter *lawyer*
Greenberg, Gordon Alan *lawyer*
Grobe, Charles Stephen *lawyer, accountant*
Grode, Susan A. *lawyer*
Gross, Allen Jeffrey *lawyer*
Grossman, Steven L. *lawyer*
Grush, Julius Sidney *lawyer*
Gurfein, Peter J. *lawyer*
Hahn, Elliott Julius *lawyer*
Halberstadter, David *lawyer*
Halkett, Alan Neilson *lawyer*
Handler, Carole Enid *lawyer, city planner*
Handler, Joel F. *law educator*
Handzlik, Jan Lawrence *lawyer*
Hansell, Dean *lawyer*
Hanson, John J. *retired lawyer*
Harkness, Nancy P. *lawyer*
Havel, Richard W. *lawyer*
Hayutin, David Lionel *lawyer*
Hedges, George Reynolds *lawyer, archaeologist*
Hedlund, Paul James *lawyer*
Heinke, Rex S. *lawyer*
Heitz, Kenneth R. *lawyer*
Heller, Philip *lawyer*
Henry, Carl Nolan *lawyer*
Herman, Stephen Charles *lawyer*
Heyler, Grover Ross *retired lawyer*
Hickman, Rose *lawyer*
Hieronymus, Edward Whittlesey *retired lawyer*
Hight, B. Boyd *retired lawyer*
Hobbs, Franklin Dean III *lawyer*
Hoffman, Valerie Jane *lawyer*
Holliday, Thomas Edgar *lawyer*
Holscher, Mark Charles *lawyer*
Holtzman, Robert Arthur *lawyer*
Huben, Brian David *lawyer*
Huebner, David *lawyer*
Hufstedler, Seth Martin *lawyer*
Hufstedler, Shirley Mount *lawyer, former secretary of education*
Husar, Linda S. *lawyer*
Hyman, Milton Bernard *lawyer*
Hyman, Ursula H. *lawyer*
Imre, Christina Joanne *lawyer*
Iredale, Nancy Louise *lawyer*
Irving, Paul Howard *lawyer*
Irwin, Philip Donnan *lawyer*
Jackson, Alan Jay *prosecutor*
Jeffrey, Sheri *lawyer*
Joaquin, Linton *lawyer*
Johnson, Jonathan Edwin, II, *lawyer*
Johnson, Philip Leslie *lawyer*
Jordan, Martha B. *lawyer*
Jordan, Robert Leon *lawyer, educator*
Juo, James *lawyer*
Kamine, Bernard S. *lawyer*
Kamm, Solomon M. *lawyer*
Kanoff, Mary Ellen *lawyer*
Kanter, Sandra May *lawyer*
Kaplan, Mark Vincent *lawyer*
Karst, Kenneth Leslie *law educator*
Katz, Jason Lawrence *lawyer, insurance company executive*
Katzenstein, Andrew M. *lawyer*
Kennerly, Nancy N. *lawyer*
Kesselman, David W. *lawyer*
Keville, Terri Donna *lawyer*
Khan, Amman A. *lawyer*
Kieffer, George David *lawyer*
Kim, Sabrina S. *lawyer*
Kirwan, Betty-Jane *lawyer*
Kirwan, R. DeWitt (Kyle) *lawyer*
Kitchens, Dean J. *lawyer*
Klein, Eric A. *lawyer*
Klinger, Marilyn Sydney *lawyer*
Kranwinkle, Conrad Douglas *lawyer, broadcast executive*
Krupka, Robert George *lawyer*
Kruse, Scott August *lawyer*
Kuechle, John Merrill *lawyer*
Kunowski, Herbert Peter *lawyer*
Kupietzky, Moshe Joseph *lawyer*
Kveton, Kyle *lawyer*
Kwoh, Stewart *lawyer, cultural organization administrator*
Langa, Brian D. *lawyer*
Langan, Kenneth J. *lawyer*
Langberg, Barry Benson *lawyer*
Lappen, Chester I. *lawyer*
Lauchengco, Jose Yujuico, Jr. *lawyer*
Lawler, Jean Marie *lawyer*
Layne, Jonathan K. *lawyer*
Leanse, Thomas J. *lawyer*
Leibow, Ronald Louis *lawyer*
Lesser, Joan L. *lawyer*
Letwin, Leon *law educator*
Leung, Frankie Fook-Lun *lawyer*
Levine, C. Bruce *lawyer*
Levine, Jerome L. *lawyer*
Levine, Marci Robyn *lawyer*
Levine, Meldon Edises *lawyer, retired congressman*
Lewis, Cynthia *law librarian*
Lewis, Marjorie Ehrich *lawyer*
Lindholm, Dwight Henry *lawyer*
Ling, Robert M., Jr. *lawyer, consumer prod company executive*
Lipsig, Ethan *lawyer*
Littleton, Christine A. *law educator*
Litvack, Mark D. *lawyer*
Logan, Ben H. III *lawyer*
Long, Gregory Alan *lawyer*
Longaker, Richard P., II, *lawyer*
Lui, Elwood *lawyer*
Lund, James Louis *lawyer*
Lurey, Michael S. *lawyer*
MacLaughlin, Francis Joseph *lawyer*
Mancino, Douglas Michael *lawyer*
Marcus, Stephen Howard *lawyer*
Marder, John Adam *lawyer*
Margo, Rod David *lawyer*
Marmorstein, Victoria E. *lawyer*
Marshall-Daniels, Meryl *mediator, executive coach*
Martinez, Vilma Socorro *lawyer*
May, Lawrence Edward *lawyer*
Mayorkas, Alejandro *lawyer, former prosecu*
McAniff, Edward John *lawyer*
McDermott, John E. *lawyer*
McKinzie, Carl Wayne *lawyer*
McKnight, Frederick L. *lawyer*
McLane, Frederick Berg *lawyer*
McLurkin, Thomas Cornelius, Jr. *lawyer*
McNevin, Christopher J. *lawyer*
Meaders, Donald W. *lawyer*
Meer, Jon Douglas *lawyer*
Meisinger, Louis M. *lawyer*
Melby, Donna D. *lawyer*
Mesereau, Thomas Arthur, Jr. *lawyer*
Meshki, Hamed *lawyer*
Metzger, Robert Streicher *lawyer*
Meyer, Bruce D. *lawyer*
Meyer, Catherine Dieffenbach *lawyer*
Meyer, Michael Edwin *lawyer*
Michaelson, Jon *lawyer*
Midler, Laurence H. (Larry) *lawyer*
Millard, Neal Steven *lawyer, educator*
Miller, Milton Allen *lawyer*
Mintz, Marshall Gary *lawyer*
Modabber, Zia F. *lawyer*
Moor, Carl H. *lawyer*
Morgenthaler-Lever, Alisa *lawyer*
Morrissey, J. Richard *lawyer*
Morrow, Margaret M. *lawyer, judge*
Moskowitz, Joel Steven *lawyer*
Murray, Anthony *lawyer*
Nachshin, Robert Jay *lawyer*
Neely, Sally Schultz *lawyer*
Neiter, Gerald Irving *lawyer*
Newman, David Wheeler *lawyer*
Newman, Michael Rodney *lawyer*
Nicholas, William Richard *lawyer*
Niles, John Gilbert *lawyer*
Nobumoto, Karen S. *prosecutor*
Nochimson, David *lawyer*
Norris, Edwin L. *lawyer*
Norris, William Albert *lawyer, mediator, retire judge*
Nugent, Gary W. *lawyer*
Oberstein, Norman S. *lawyer*
O'Brien, Robert Charles *lawyer*
Ochoa, Arthur J. *lawyer, hospital administrat*
O'Connell, Kevin *lawyer*
O'Donnell, Pierce Henry *lawyer*
Oh, Angela E. *lawyer*
O'Leary, Prentice Lee *retired lawyer*
Olivas, Daniel Anthony *lawyer*
Oliver, Dale Hugh *lawyer*
Olsen, Frances Elisabeth *law educator, theori*
Olson, Ronald Leroy *lawyer*
Oppenheim, Charles B. *lawyer*
Oppenheimer, Randy (Mark Randall Oppenheimer) *lawyer*
Ordin, Andrea Sheridan *lawyer*
Ostroff, Peter I. *lawyer*
Owen, Michael Lee *lawyer*
Pachino, Barton P. *lawyer*
Palmer, Charles Francis *lawyer*
Palmieri, Victor Henry *lawyer, director, investment advisor*
Panish, Brian Joseph *lawyer*
Parsky, Gerald Lawrence *lawyer*
Pascotto, Alvaro *lawyer*
Pasich, Kirk Alan *lawyer*
Perlis, Michael Fredrick *lawyer*
Perron, Edward Adrian *lawyer*
Perry, Ralph Barton III *lawyer*
Pesta, Ben W., II, *lawyer, writer*
Peterson, Kurt C. *lawyer*
Peterson, Linda S. *lawyer*
Petrocelli, Daniel M. *lawyer*
Petroff, Laura R. *lawyer*
Phillips, Stacy D. *lawyer*
Pircher, Leo Joseph *lawyer, director*
Piuze, Michael Joseph *lawyer*
Poindexter, William Mersereau *lawyer*
Pollock, John Phleger *lawyer*
Porter, John E. *lawyer*
Porter, Verna Louise *lawyer*
Power, John Bruce *lawyer*
Preonas, George Elias *lawyer*
Presant, Sanford Calvin *lawyer, educator, wri tax specialist*
Price, William Charlie *lawyer*
Pugsley, Robert Adrian *law educator*
Quicksilver, William Todd *lawyer*
Quinn, John B. *lawyer*
Quinn, John J. *lawyer*
Rabinovitz, Joel *lawyer, educator*
Racine, Scott H. *lawyer*
Raeder, Myrna Sharon *lawyer, educator*
Rakow, Jay *lawyer, film company executive*
Rappeport, Ira J. *lawyer*
Rath, Howard Grant, Jr. *lawyer*
Ray, Gilbert T. *lawyer*
Reddick, C.N. (Frank)lin III *lawyer*
Reeves, Barbara Ann *lawyer*

eisman, Ellen Kelly *lawyer*
enwick, Edward S. *lawyer*
euben, Don Harold *lawyer*
eyes Robbins, Ann Marie *lawyer, researcher, educator, former magistrate judge*
ichards, Eric Albert Stephan *lawyer*
ichland, Kent Lewis *lawyer*
ichter, Stuart M. *lawyer*
iff, Lawrence P. *lawyer*
ishwain, James Michael, Jr. *lawyer*
ising, Kevin D. *lawyer*
oberts, Virgil Patrick *lawyer, judge*
obertson, Hugh Duff *lawyer*
obison, William Robert *lawyer*
ogers, David Booth *lawyer*
osenthal, Sol *lawyer*
osett, Arthur Irwin *lawyer, educator*
oss, Bruce Shields *lawyer*
othenberg, Alan I. *lawyer, professional sports association executive*
ozanski, Stanley Howard *lawyer*
ust, Neil W. *lawyer*
ustand, Kay *lawyer*
uthberg, Miles N. *lawyer*
utter, Marshall Anthony *lawyer*
acks, Robert A. *lawyer*
ager, Kelli L. *lawyer*
alvaty, Benjamin Benedict *lawyer*
amet, Jack I. *lawyer*
amuels, Mark A. *lawyer*
axe, Deborah Crandall *lawyer*
hindler, David J. *lawyer*
hwartz, Robert M. *lawyer*
oular, Robert Frank *lawyer*
to, Theodore Paul *lawyer, educator*
acter, David Mervyn *lawyer*
anks, Patricia L. *lawyer*
apiro, Robert *lawyer*
eehan, Lawrence James *lawyer*
eller, John Willard *lawyer*
errell, John Bradford *lawyer*
erwood, Allen Joseph *retired lawyer*
ortz, Richard Alan *lawyer*
ostak, S. Richard *lawyer*
ultz, John David *lawyer*
egel, Robert (Bob) A. *lawyer*
bergeld, Arthur F. *lawyer*
va, Clarice F. (Clarice F. Chavira-Sliva) *lawyer*
mmons, Richard J. *lawyer*
nger, Martin Dori *lawyer*
oan, Sheldon Harold *lawyer*
nooke, Michael G. *lawyer*
ider, Darryl *lawyer*
lish, Jonathan Craig *lawyer*
itzer, Matthew Laurence *law educator*
ll, Richard J., Jr. *lawyer*
amm, Alan *lawyer*
arrett, Lucinda *lawyer*
ein, Laurence Jay *lawyer*
ein, Sheryl E. *lawyer*
nehart, William, Jr. *retired lawyer*
one, Gregory Paul *lawyer*
one, Lawrence Maurice *lawyer, educator*
out, Lynn Andrea *law educator*
rickland, Julia B. *lawyer*
rong, George Gordon, Jr. *lawyer, management consultant*
vanson, Daniel G. *lawyer, economist*
veeney, Paul W., Jr. *lawyer*
ggart, Jennifer T. *lawyer*
kesh, Fahi *lawyer*
r, Ralph William *lawyer, former federal government official*
ro, René P. *lawyer*
ylor, Minna *lawyer*
epper, R(obert) Bruce, Jr. *lawyer*
epstein, Daniel C. *lawyer*
rry, Timothy P. *lawyer*
rry, W. Burks *lawyer*
omas, Geoffrey L. *lawyer*
oren-Peden, Deborah Suzanne *lawyer*
orpe, Gegory B. *lawyer*
bisman, Stuart Paul *lawyer*
eister, George Marvin *lawyer*
ope, Sorrell *lawyer*
ygstad, Lawrence Benson *lawyer*
ropina, James R. *lawyer*
lenzuela, Manuel Anthony, Jr. *lawyer*
n de Kamp, John Kalar *lawyer*
nyo, Bruce Gordon *lawyer*
rat, Jonathan D. *law educator, dean*
rner, Carlton A. *lawyer*
ughn, William Weaver *retired lawyer*
ncent, Dirk L. *lawyer*
pert, Richard Sidney *lawyer*
n Kalinowski, Julian Onesime *lawyer*
lker, Paul R. *lawyer*
arren, Robert Stephen *lawyer*
sser, Dennis Matthew *lawyer*
sser, Laura Allison *lawyer*
sserman, Marcia Watson *legal administration consultant*
sserman, William Phillip *lawyer*
tson, Glenn Robert *lawyer*
yte, Alan (Paul) *lawyer*
atherup, Roy Garfield *lawyer*
iner, Perrie M. *lawyer*
iss, Walter Stanley *lawyer*
issman, Barry Leigh *lawyer*
streich, Benzion Joseph *lawyer*
ite, Robert Joel *lawyer*
lett, Robert E. *lawyer*
lliams, Bart H. *lawyer*
lliams, Harold Marvin *lawyer, retired foundation, academic and federal agency administrator*
lliams, Norma Jean *lawyer*
lliams, Richard Thomas *lawyer*
lliams, Robert E. *lawyer*
ne, Mark Philip *lawyer*
nterman, Craig L. *lawyer*
olfen, Werner F. *lawyer*
ood, Willard Mark *lawyer*
oods, Daniel James *lawyer*
oodsome, Edwin Valentine, Jr. *lawyer*
ight, Kenneth Brooks *lawyer*

Yang, Debra Wong *lawyer, former prosecutor*
York, Gary Alan *lawyer*
Zamos, Jerome *lawyer, real estate consultant*
Ziffren, Kenneth *lawyer*

Lynwood
Sterling, Arthur James *retired legal assistant*

Malibu
Davenport, David *lawyer, educator, academic administrator*
Factor, Max III *arbitrator, mediator*
Hanson, Gary A. *lawyer, educator, academic administrator*
Holmes, Henry W. *lawyer*
Naegele, Timothy Duncan *lawyer*
Nelson, Grant Steel *law educator*

Manhattan Beach
Mandel, Martin Louis *lawyer*
Pruetz, Adrian Mary *lawyer*
Rae, Matthew Sanderson, Jr. *lawyer*

Marina Del Rey
Donzis, Paul Bennett *lawyer, finance educator, ophthalmologist*
Schulman, Robert S. *lawyer*

Martinez
Williams, Charles Judson *lawyer, writer*

Menlo Park
Brest, Paul A. *law educator, foundation administrator*
Chao, Howard H. *lawyer*
Currie, Francis Sparre *lawyer*
Dyer, Charles Arnold *lawyer*
Edwards, John Wesley, II, *lawyer*
Fisher, Ora T. *lawyer*
Gunderson, Robert Vernon, Jr. *lawyer*
Haslam, Robert Thomas III *lawyer*
Hearst, William Randolph III *lawyer, former newspaper publisher*
Heuman, Donna *lawyer*
Karel, Steven *lawyer*
Kaufman, Christopher Lee *lawyer*
Kelly, Daniel Grady, Jr. *lawyer*
Kennelly, Dennis L. *lawyer*
Kerman, Peter F. *lawyer*
Kirk, Cassius Lamb, Jr. *retired lawyer, investor*
Madison, James Raymond *lawyer*
Medearis, Mark A. *lawyer*
Mendelson, Alan Charles *lawyer*
Mummery, Daniel R. *lawyer*
Stern, Julian Nathaniel *lawyer, pharmaceutical executive*
Yang, Joseph *lawyer*

Merced
Lashley, Lenore Clarisse *lawyer*

Mill Valley
Cole, Richard Charles *lawyer*
Nemir, Donald Philip *lawyer*
Schwartzbach, M. Gerald *lawyer*
Selvig, Jettie Pierce *lawyer*

Milpitas
DuChene, Todd Michael *lawyer*

Mission Viejo
Ruben, Robert Joseph *lawyer*
Tuohey, Conrad Gravier *lawyer*

Modesto
Murphy, John Thomas *lawyer*
Mussman, William Edward III *lawyer*

Montecito
Braun, David A(dlai) *lawyer*

Monterey
Bomberger, Russell Branson *lawyer, writer*
Gaver, Frances Rouse *lawyer*
Soskin, William H. *lawyer, accountant*

Monterey Park
Grasse, Wanda Gene *lawyer, writer*

Moraga
Kilbourne, George William *lawyer*

Mountain View
Davidson, Gordon Kirby *lawyer*
Fennell, Laura A. *lawyer*
Nash, Horace Lyons *lawyer*
Pasahow, Lynn Harold *lawyer*
Walker, John Kent, Jr. *lawyer*
Weiss, Rhett Louis *lawyer*
Wildman, Iris J. *retired law librarian*

Napa
Cahill, Richard Frederick *lawyer*
Kuntz, Charles Powers *lawyer*

Newport Beach
Allen, Terrence R. *lawyer*
Baskin, Scott David *lawyer*
Carmichael, David Richard *lawyer, insurance company executive*
Clark, Thomas P., Jr. *lawyer*
Currie, Robert Emil *retired lawyer*
Fehner, Michael Richard *lawyer*
Goldstein, Michael Gerald *lawyer, director*
Herron, J. Jay *lawyer*
Hueston, John Charles *lawyer*
Klink, Fredric J. *lawyer*
Krischer, Gordon Eugene *lawyer*
Livingston, Lori Winder *lawyer*
Millar, Richard William, Jr. *lawyer*
O'Donnell, Bernard Joseph, Jr. *lawyer*
Schiff, Laurie *lawyer*
Schnapp, Roger Herbert *lawyer, consultant*
Singer, Gary James *lawyer*
Tracy, James Jared, Jr. *retired legal association administrator*
Weissbard, Samuel Held *lawyer*

Wentworth, Theodore Sumner *lawyer*

North Fork
Flanagan, James Henry, Jr. *lawyer, finance educator*

North Hollywood
Ajalat, Sol Peter *lawyer*
Davis, Edmond Ray *lawyer*
Kreger, Melvin Joseph *lawyer*
Zimring, Stuart David *lawyer*

Northridge
Runquist, Lisa A. *lawyer*
Walcher, Alan Ernest *lawyer*

Oak Park
Vinson, William Theodore *lawyer*

Oakland
Allen, Jeffrey Michael *lawyer*
Banke, Kathy M. *lawyer*
Berry, Phillip Samuel *lawyer*
Bryant, Arthur H. *lawyer*
Davies, Colleen T. *lawyer*
Deming, Willis Riley *retired lawyer*
Drexel, Baron Jerome *lawyer*
Fleming, Jayne Elizabeth *lawyer*
Foust, Lawrence L. *lawyer*
Henel, Carolyn E. *lawyer*
Johnson, Kenneth F. *lawyer*
Kazan, Steven *lawyer*
Kohn, Steven M. *lawyer*
Leslie, Robert Lorne *lawyer*
Quinby, William Albert *lawyer, arbitrator, mediator*
Reese, Charles Woodrow, Jr. *lawyer*
Robinson, Charles Furlonge *lawyer*
Shapiro, David W. *prosecutor*
Stein, Laura *lawyer, consumer products company executive*
Trautman, William Ellsworth *lawyer*
Wallis, Eric G. *lawyer*
Weaver, Pauline Anne *lawyer*
Wood, James Michael *lawyer*

Occidental
Archer, Richard Joseph *lawyer*

Oceanside
Sullivan, Patrick James *lawyer*

Ontario
Dunn, Donald Jack *law librarian, educator, dean*

Orange
Batchelor, James Kent *lawyer*
Duncan, John Alexander *lawyer*
Duzey, Robert Lindsey *lawyer*

Orinda
Hartog, John A. *lawyer*
Hetland, John Robert *law educator*
Walsh, Joseph Richard *lawyer*

Oxnard
O'Hearn, Michael John *lawyer*
Sands, Velma Ahda *lawyer*

Pacific Palisades
Cale, Charles Griffin *lawyer, real estate and corporate financial company executive*
Flattery, Thomas Long *lawyer, administrator*
Kelley, Thomas Joseph *lawyer*
Sevilla, Stanley *lawyer*
Share, Richard Hudson *lawyer*
Verrone, Patric Miller *lawyer, writer*

Palm Desert
Bernhard, Herbert Ashley *lawyer*
Reinhardt, Benjamin Max *lawyer, arbitrator, mediator*
Wallace, Franklin Sherwood *lawyer, director*

Palm Springs
Diodosio, Charles Joseph *lawyer*
Kimberling, John Farrell *retired lawyer*

Palo Alto
Abrams, William F. *lawyer*
Baron, Frederick David *lawyer*
Baum, Brandon *lawyer, educator*
Beatus, Brian J. *lawyer*
Benton, Lee F. *lawyer*
Bradley, Donald Edward *lawyer*
Chang, Carmen *lawyer*
Charnas, Charles N. *lawyer, computer company executive*
Chinnis, C. Cabell, Jr. *lawyer*
Climan, Richard Elliot *lawyer*
del Calvo, Jorge A. *lawyer*
Dwyer, John Charles *lawyer*
Feldman, Boris *lawyer*
Flaum, Keith Avery *lawyer*
Fordis, Jean Burke *lawyer*
Fromm, Jeffery Bernard *lawyer*
Furbush, David Malcolm *lawyer*
Gaither, James C. *lawyer*
Gallo, Penny Howe *lawyer*
Gibson, Virginia Lee *lawyer*
Giza, David Alan *lawyer*
Gorman, Maureen J. *lawyer*
Greco, Joseph A. *lawyer*
Halluin, Albert Price *lawyer*
Hiscox, Frank S. *lawyer*
Hoak, Jonathan S., Sr. *lawyer*
Holston, Michael Joseph *lawyer, computer company executive*
Ivey, Thomas J. *lawyer*
Jackson, Cynthia L. *lawyer*
Katz, Ronald Stanley *lawyer*
King, Kenton J. *lawyer*
Korman, Martin *lawyer*
Lynch, Timothy Jeremiah-Mahoney *lawyer, educator, theologian, realtor, writer*
Masur, Joshua Michael *lawyer*
McCall, Jennifer Jordan *lawyer*

Michels, Dirk *lawyer*
Miller, Michael Patiky *lawyer*
Miller, Scott D. *lawyer*
Monroy, Gladys H. *lawyer*
Neal, Stephen Cassidy *lawyer*
Nopar, Alan Scott *lawyer*
Nuchi, Lior O. *lawyer*
Park, Marina H. *lawyer*
Patten, Valerie Lynn *lawyer*
Patterson, Robert Edward *lawyer*
Petkanics, Donna M. *lawyer*
Pooley, James Henry *lawyer*
Radcliffe, Mark Flohn *lawyer*
Randall, Jeffrey G. *lawyer*
Reback, Gary *lawyer*
Robinson, Walter J. III *lawyer*
Roos, John Victor *lawyer*
Salmon, Denis R. *lawyer*
Shi, Qin *lawyer, technologist*
Shulman, Ron E. *lawyer*
Smith, Gregory C. *lawyer*
Sonsini, Larry W. *lawyer*
Sullivan, Dennis C. *lawyer*
Tiffany, Joseph Raymond, II, *lawyer*
Unkovic, Nicholas C. *lawyer*
Vaughn, Issac J. *lawyer*
Voight, Jerry D. *lawyer*
Walker, Ann Yvonne *lawyer*
Waltzer, Garrett J. *lawyer*
Wheeler, Raymond Louis *lawyer*
White, Rick *lawyer, former congressman*

Palos Verdes Estates
Blackman, Lee L. *lawyer*
Brigden, Ann Schwartz *mediator, educator*
DeLuce, Richard David *lawyer*

Paramount
Hall, Howard Harry *lawyer*

Pasadena
Bunt Smith, Helen Marguerite *lawyer*
Call, Merlin Wendell *lawyer*
Calleton, Theodore Edward *lawyer, educator*
D'Angelo, Robert William *lawyer*
Haight, James Theron *lawyer*
Hunt, Gordon *lawyer*
Kleinpeter, Amy E. Clark *lawyer*
Leeson, Peter J., IV, *lawyer*
Logan, Francis Dummer *retired lawyer*
Markley, William C. *lawyer*
Miller, Susan Calabrese *lawyer, consumer products company executive*
Mosher, Sally Ekenberg *lawyer, musician*
Mueth, Joseph Edward *lawyer*
Myers, R(alph) Chandler *lawyer*
Silverstein, Robert P. *lawyer*
Solis, Carlos *lawyer*
Sullivan, William Francis *lawyer*
Tanner, Dee Boshard *retired lawyer*
Telleria, Anthony F. *lawyer*
van Schoonenberg, Robert G. *lawyer, consumer products company executive*
Wyatt, Joseph Lucian, Jr. *lawyer, writer*
Yohalem, Harry Morton *lawyer*
Zuetel, Kenneth Roy, Jr. *lawyer*

Penn Valley
Ingram, Jeffrey Charles *lawyer, educator*

Petaluma
Castagnola, George Joseph, Jr. *arbitrator, secondary school educator*

Piedmont
Seavey, William Arthur *lawyer, vintner*

Pittsburg
Williscroft-Barcus, Beverly Ruth *retired lawyer*

Pleasant Hill
Otis, Roy James *lawyer*

Pleasanton
Askanas, Mark S. *lawyer*
Fine, Marjorie Lynn *lawyer*
Opperwall, Stephen Gabriel *lawyer*
Scott, G. Judson, Jr. *lawyer*

Point Richmond
Edginton, John Arthur *lawyer*

Portola Valley
Nycum, Susan Hubbell *lawyer*
Olson, Walter Gilbert *lawyer*

Rancho Cordova
Hall-Barron, Deborah *lawyer*
Harrell, Gary Paul *lawyer*

Rancho Mirage
Leydorf, Frederick Leroy *lawyer*
Pierno, Anthony Robert *lawyer*

Rancho Palos Verdes
Schimmenti, John Joseph *lawyer*

Rancho Santa Fe
Peterson, Nad A. *retired lawyer*
Woolley, Roger Swire *lawyer*

Rancho Santa Margarita
Curtis, John Joseph *lawyer, writer*

Redlands
Nassar, William Michael *lawyer*

Redondo Beach
Neely, Alexis *lawyer*

Redwood City
Bell, Frank Ouray, Jr. *lawyer*
Bene, Steven G. *lawyer, game systems company executive*
Coddington, Clinton Hays *lawyer*
Cooperman, Daniel *lawyer, computer software company executive*

Fitzpatrick, Will *lawyer*
Linzner, Joel *lawyer*
Millard, Richard Steven *lawyer*
Pape, Glenn Michael *lawyer, financial planner*
Powers, Matthew Douglas *lawyer*
Sullivan, Kathleen Marie *lawyer, educator, former dean*
Verhoeven, Charles K. *lawyer*
Wilhelm, Robert Oscar *lawyer, civil engineer*

Richmond

Dolberg, David Spencer *lawyer*
Jenkins, Everett Wilbur, Jr. *lawyer, writer, historian*

Riverside

Akintimoye, Akindele D. *lawyer, consultant*
Darling, Scott Edward *lawyer*
Heiting, James Otto *lawyer*
Marlatt, Michael James *lawyer*
McGill, Leonard John *lawyer*
Schwartz, Bernard Julian *lawyer*
Sklar, Wilford Nathaniel *lawyer, real estate broker*

Rolling Hills

Rumbaugh, Charles Earl *arbitrator, mediator, educator, lawyer*

Rolling Hills Estates

Zerunyan, Frank Vram *lawyer, councilman*

Rosemead

Bouknight, Lon (J.A. Bouknight Jr.) *lawyer, utilities executive*

Running Springs

Marcus, John Richard *lawyer*

Sacramento

Bell, Wayne S. *lawyer, state agency official*
Blake, D. Steven *lawyer*
Bleckley, Jeanette A. *lawyer*
Burton, Randall James *lawyer*
Caso, Anthony T. *lawyer*
Costigan, Richard III *lawyer*
Day, James McAdam, Jr. *lawyer*
Fait, Glenn A. *lawyer, educator*
Felderstein, Steven Howard *lawyer*
Friedman, Morton Lee *retired lawyer*
Gray-Fuson, Joan Lorraine *lawyer*
Houpt, James Edward *lawyer*
Huh, Joan *lawyer*
Janigian, Bruce Jasper *lawyer, educator*
Keiner, Christian Mark *lawyer*
Malloy, Michael Patrick *law educator, consultant*
McGrath, William Arthur *arbitrator, mediator, lawyer, real estate broker*
Morgan-Prager, Karole *lawyer, publishing executive*
Root, Gerald Edward *legal administrator*
Scott, McGregor W. *prosecutor, lawyer*
Willis, Dawn Louise *legal assistant, small business owner*
Wishek, Michael Bradley *lawyer*

Salinas

Bolles, Donald Scott *lawyer*

San Anselmo

Murphy, Barry Ames *lawyer*
Truett, Harold Joseph, III, (Tim) *lawyer*

San Bernardino

Fullerton, Robert Victor *lawyer*

San Carlos

Foster, Mark Edward *lawyer, consultant, international lobbyist*
Lee, John Jin *lawyer*

San Diego

Aguirre, Michael Jules *lawyer*
Allen, P. Blake *lawyer*
Armstong, Robert G. *lawyer*
Bell, Robert Jeffrey *lawyer*
Bleiler, Charles Arthur *lawyer*
Boggs, William S. *lawyer*
Brierton, Cheryl Lynn *lawyer*
Brooks, John White *lawyer*
Brown, LaMar Bevan *lawyer*
Brownlie, Robert William *lawyer*
Celentino, Christopher *lawyer*
Chatroo, Arthur Jay *lawyer*
Chaudhri, Javade *lawyer, utilities executive*
Clark, Grant Lawrence *corporate lawyer*
Cohn, Marjorie F. *law educator, legal association administrator*
Copeland, Robert Glenn *lawyer*
Corbett, Luke Robinson *lawyer*
Dawe, James Robert *lawyer*
Dollarhide, Mary C. *lawyer*
Dorne, David J. *lawyer*
Eigner, William Whitling *lawyer*
Estep, Arthur Lee *lawyer*
Fisch, Sanford Michael *lawyer*
Forbes, Brian L. *lawyer*
Gerber, Robert Scott *lawyer*
Hagarty, Mark *lawyer*
Haile, Lisa A. *lawyer*
Heaton, Roger Laurence *lawyer*
Heidrich, Robert Wesley *lawyer*
Hewitt, Karen Peckham *prosecutor*
Hofflund, Paul *lawyer*
Insogna, Anthony M. *lawyer*
Kinsbruner Bush, Jennifer *lawyer*
Klinedinst, John David *lawyer*
Lathrop, Mitchell Lee *lawyer*
Lerach, William S. *lawyer*
Levine, Harvey Robert *lawyer*
McClellan, Craig Rene *lawyer*
McCoy, Lilys D. *lawyer*
McCurine, William, Jr. *lawyer*
McGinnis, Robert Earl *lawyer*
McMahon, Gerald Lawrence *lawyer*
Mebane, Julie S. *lawyer*
Mittermiller, James Joseph *lawyer*
Morris, Grant Harold *law educator*
Mullen, James Joseph III *lawyer*
Mulvaney, James Francis *lawyer*
Nicholas, Blair *lawyer*
O'Malley, James Terence (Terry) *lawyer*
Payne, Margaret Anne *lawyer*
Plourd, Christopher John *lawyer, consultant*
Pray, Ralph Marble III *lawyer*
Pugh, Richard Crawford *lawyer, educator*
Rains, Cameron Jay *lawyer*
Rehmus, Charles Martin *arbitrator*
Rice, Thomas Hilary (Speedy Rice) *lawyer*
Robbins, Darren J. *lawyer*
Roberts, William S. *lawyer*
Root, George Lincoln, Jr. *lawyer*
Roseman, Charles Sanford *lawyer*
Ross, Terry D. *lawyer*
Santee, Dale William *lawyer, air force officer*
Sceper, Duane Harold *lawyer*
Schoville, Dennis A(rnold) *lawyer*
Scott, Douglas Edward *lawyer*
Shapiro, Philip Alan *lawyer*
Shelton, Dorothy Diehl Rees *lawyer*
Shepherd, Bruce P. *lawyer*
Shippey, Sandra Lee *lawyer*
Smith, Steven Ray *law educator*
Snaid, Leon Jeffrey *lawyer*
Snyder, David Richard *lawyer*
Sullivan, Michelle Cornejo *lawyer*
Swinton, Stephen P. *lawyer*
Thorud, Jeffrey Scott *lawyer, legal studies director*
Valliant, James Stevens *lawyer*
Vitek, Reg(inald) A. *lawyer*
Wagner, Sandra M. *lawyer*
Weaver, Michael James *lawyer*
Wolfe, Deborah Ann *lawyer*

San Francisco

Abbott, Barry Alexander *lawyer*
Alderman, William Fields *lawyer*
Alexis, Geraldine M. *lawyer*
Alioto, Angela Mia *lawyer*
Allecta, Julie *lawyer*
Allen, Jose R. *lawyer*
Anderson, Edward Virgil *lawyer*
Arbuthnot, Robert Murray *lawyer*
Atkinson, Gordon C. *lawyer*
Auwers, Linda S. *lawyer*
Bailey-Wells, Deborah *lawyer*
Baker, Cameron *lawyer*
Barbagelata, Robert Dominic *lawyer*
Bauer, Steven M. *lawyer*
Baxter, Ralph H., Jr. *lawyer*
Baysinger, Kara *lawyer*
Benvenutti, Peter J. *lawyer*
Berning, Paul Wilson *lawyer*
Bleich, Jeffrey Laurence *lawyer, educator*
Blohm, Kenneth E. *lawyer*
Blum, Robert M. *lawyer*
Bomse, Stephen V. *lawyer*
Bondoc, Rommel *lawyer*
Borowsky, Philip *lawyer*
Bostwick, James Stephen *lawyer*
Bothwell, Anthony Peirson Xavier, Sr. *lawyer, educator*
Boven, Douglas George *lawyer*
Brandel, Roland Eric *lawyer*
Briscoe, John *lawyer*
Brosnahan, James Jerome *lawyer*
Brothers, Lynda Lee *lawyer*
Brown, Donald Wesley *lawyer*
Brown, Walter Francis, Jr. *lawyer*
Broyles, Deborah J. *lawyer*
Bruen, James A. *lawyer*
Burden, James Ewers *lawyer*
Burns, Brian Patrick *lawyer*
Bushnell, Roderick Paul *lawyer*
Byrne, Robert William *lawyer*
Cabraser, Elizabeth Joan *lawyer*
Callison, Russell James *lawyer*
Campbell, Scott Robert *lawyer, former food products executive*
Canady, Richard Warren *lawyer*
Cartmell, Nathaniel Madison III *lawyer*
Chambers, Guy Wayne *lawyer*
Chao, Cedric C. *lawyer*
Chapman, William B. *lawyer*
Clowes, John Howard *lawyer*
Cohn, Cindy A. *lawyer*
Coleman, Thomas Young *lawyer*
Collins, Mary Ann *lawyer*
Cominos, Dion Nicholas *lawyer*
Coombe, George William, Jr. *lawyer, retired bank executive*
Corash, Michèle B. *lawyer*
Cranston, Mary Bailey *lawyer*
Crawford, Roy Edgington III *lawyer*
Curran, Mary *lawyer*
Czachor, Bruce *lawyer, consultant*
Danoff, Eric Michael *lawyer*
Davis, Roger Lewis *lawyer*
Deamer, Bartley C. *lawyer*
Dell, Robert Michael *lawyer*
DeMuro, Paul Robert *lawyer*
Diekmann, Gilmore Frederick, Jr. *lawyer*
Dolinko, Robert A. *lawyer*
Donnelly, Thomas M. *lawyer*
Donovan, Charles Stephen *lawyer*
Dryden, Robert Eugene *lawyer*
Dubreuil, Francis W. *lawyer*
Dunne, Kevin Joseph *lawyer*
Durdik, Paul A. *lawyer*
Durie, Daralyn J. *lawyer*
Dworkin, Michael Leonard *lawyer*
Dwyer, Carrie Elizabeth *lawyer, investment company executive*
Edwards, Robin Morse *lawyer*
Effel, Laura *lawyer*
Eigner, Richard Martin *lawyer*
Elliott, Scott D. *lawyer*
Enscoe, Jon *lawyer*
Epsen, Robert A. *lawyer*
Ericson, Bruce Alan *lawyer*
Eth, Jordan David *lawyer*
Fairman, Marc P. *lawyer*
Falk, Jerome B., Jr. *lawyer*
Feng, Wendy Lai *lawyer*
Fergus, Gary Scott *lawyer*
Finberg, James Michael *lawyer*
Finck, Kevin William *lawyer*
Fink, Scott Alan *lawyer*
Fisher, Kathleen V. *lawyer*
Fogel, Paul David *lawyer*
Folberg, Harold Jay *lawyer, educator, dean*
Fong, Kevin Murray *lawyer*
Fontana, Gary Lynn *lawyer*
Foster, David Scott *lawyer*
Frank, Karen Susanna *lawyer*
Friedman, K. Bruce *lawyer*
Friese, Robert Charles *lawyer*
Furth, Frederick Paul *lawyer*
Garvey, Joanne Marie *lawyer*
Gibney, Robert L., Jr. *lawyer*
Gillette, Patricia K. *lawyer*
Glazer, Jack Henry *lawyer*
Golub, Howard Victor *lawyer*
Goodwin, David B. *lawyer*
Graff, Joan Messing *lawyer*
Gresham, Zane Oliver *lawyer*
Gross, David F. *lawyer*
Gruel, Steven Francis *lawyer*
Guggenhime, Richard Johnson *lawyer*
Gwire, William *lawyer*
Haas, Raymond P. *lawyer*
Haber, Scott R. *lawyer*
Harris, Kamala D. *prosecutor*
Harvey, D. Peter *lawyer, educator*
Hasson, Kirke Michael *lawyer*
Hecker, Peter S. *lawyer*
Heilbron, David Michael *lawyer, arbitrator, mediator*
Hendrick, James T. *lawyer*
Henson, Ray David *law educator, consultant*
Hernandez, Gary A. *lawyer*
Herrera, Dennis J. *lawyer*
Higgins, Daniel B. *lawyer*
Highman, Bruce James *lawyer*
Hilton, Stanley Goumas *lawyer, educator, writer*
Hinman, Harvey DeForest *lawyer*
Hirsch, (William) Reece *lawyer*
Hisert, George Arthur *lawyer*
Hofmann, John Richard, Jr. *retired lawyer*
Holden, Frederick Douglass, Jr. *lawyer*
Hosie, Spencer *lawyer*
Howard, Carl *retired lawyer*
Hubbell, Robert B. *lawyer*
Hudner, Philip *lawyer, rancher*
Huhs, John I. *lawyer*
Hunt, James L. *lawyer*
Hunter, William Dennis *lawyer*
Innes, Kenneth Frederick III *lawyer*
Jacobs, Michael Allen *lawyer*
Jaffe, Seth Roth *lawyer, retail executive*
James, David Lee *lawyer, writer, international advisor*
Johnson, Daniel, Jr. *lawyer*
Johnson, Michelle L. *lawyer*
Johnson, Stephen Patrick Howard *lawyer*
Jones, Frances Mary *law librarian*
Joseph, Allan Jay *lawyer*
Juster, Kenneth Ian *lawyer*
Kee, Terry Michael *lawyer*
Keenan, Richard *lawyer*
Keeshan, Lawrence W. *lawyer*
Keker, John Watkins *lawyer*
Kelly, J. Michael *lawyer*
Kennedy, Raoul Dion *lawyer*
Kern, Brad D. *lawyer*
Kern, John McDougall *lawyer*
Knapp, Charles Lincoln *law educator*
Knutzen, Martha Lorraine *lawyer*
Koeppel, John A. *lawyer*
Kozloff, Theodore J. *lawyer*
Krane, Hilary K. *lawyer, apparel executive*
Krevans, Rachel *lawyer*
Kuhl, Paul Beach *lawyer*
Lane, Fielding H. *lawyer*
Lane, Nathan III *lawyer*
Larrabee, Matthew L. *lawyer*
Larson, John William *lawyer*
Lee, Richard Diebold *lawyer, educator*
Leonard, Geoffrey Porter *lawyer*
Leshy, John David *lawyer, solicitor, educator*
Levie, Mark Robert *lawyer*
Levin, Barry Steven *lawyer*
Lieff, Robert Lawrence *lawyer*
Lindstrom, Gregory P. *lawyer*
Little, Jan Nielsen *lawyer*
Livermore, Robert Samuel Morgan *lawyer*
Livsey, Robert Callister *lawyer*
Londen, Jack W. *lawyer*
Lopes, James Louis *lawyer*
Lowell, Frederick K. *lawyer*
Lowenthal, Steven R. *lawyer*
Lyons, James Elliott *lawyer*
Malkin, Joseph M. *lawyer*
Maly, Michael Kip *lawyer*
Mann, Bruce Alan *lawyer, investment banking executive*
Manning, Jerome Alan *retired lawyer*
Marshall, Patrick C. *lawyer*
Marshall, Raymond Charles *lawyer*
Martel, John Sheldon *lawyer, writer*
Masters, Joseph *lawyer, construction executive*
Mattes, Martin Anthony *lawyer*
McDiarmid, Bruce W. *lawyer*
McElhinny, Harold John *lawyer*
McGinnis, James Landon *lawyer*
McGuckin, John Hugh, Jr. *lawyer*
McKenzie, John F. *lawyer*
Meadows, John Frederick *lawyer*
Miller, Ann G. *lawyer*
Miller, William Napier Cripps *lawyer*
Minnick, Malcolm David *lawyer*
Mitchell, Bruce Tyson *lawyer*
Monach, Andrew E. *lawyer*
Morrissey, John Carroll, Sr. *lawyer*
Moyle, Michael R. *lawyer*
Murray, Kathleen Anne *lawyer*
Musfelt, Duane Clark *lawyer*
Myers, Peter Scott *lawyer*
Odgers, Richard William *lawyer*
Offer, Stuart Jay *lawyer*
Okeke, Christian Nwachukwu *law educator*
Olson, Karl *lawyer*
Olson, Robert Howard *lawyer*
O'Neal, Stephen V. *lawyer*
Palmer, Venrice Romito *lawyer, educator*
Park, Hyun *lawyer, utilities executive*
Park, Roger Cook *law educator*
Parker, Harold Allen *lawyer, real estate compa officer*
Parrish, Jenni *law librarian, educator*
Paterson, Eva *legal association director, educator*
Paxton, Jay L. *lawyer*
Payne, Eugene C. III *lawyer*
Penskar, Mark Howard *lawyer*
Perry, E. Lynn *lawyer*
Petty, George Oliver *lawyer*
Philipsborn, John Timothy *lawyer, writer*
Pickett, Donn Philip *lawyer*
Plishner, Michael Jon *lawyer*
Pope, Marcia L. *lawyer*
Popofsky, Melvin Laurence *lawyer*
Potter, James G. *lawyer, food products executi*
Preovolos, Penelope Athene *lawyer*
Preuss, Charles Frederick *lawyer*
Pringle, Paul C. *lawyer*
Radlo, Edward John *lawyer, mathematician*
Ragan, Charles Ransom *lawyer*
Reding, John Anthony, Jr. *lawyer*
Reese, John Robert *lawyer*
Renfrew, Charles Byron *lawyer*
Renne, Paul A. *lawyer*
Rice, Denis Timlin *lawyer*
Richards, Norman Blanchard *lawyer*
Robinson, Ralph W. *lawyer*
Roethe, James Norton *lawyer*
Rogan, Richard A. *lawyer*
Roger, Kent M. *lawyer*
Rosen, Joshua Nathan *lawyer*
Rosen, Sanford Jay *lawyer*
Rosenfeld, Robert A. *lawyer*
Ross, Jeffrey S. *lawyer*
Rowland, John Arthur *lawyer*
Rubenstein, Donald P. *lawyer*
Rubin, Michael *lawyer*
Russoniello, Joseph Pascal *lawyer*
Ryan, Kevin Vincent *lawyer, former prosecuto*
Sanders, Joel Steven *lawyer*
Savage, Mark Randall *lawyer*
Sax, Paul J. *lawyer*
Schenkkan, Dirk McKenzie *lawyer*
Schools, Scott N. *prosecutor*
Seabolt, Richard L. *lawyer*
Seegal, John Franklin *lawyer*
Seeger, Laureen E. *lawyer, health products executive*
Seff, James M. *lawyer*
Seneker, Carl James, II, (Kim) *lawyer*
Shanahan, Lauri M. *lawyer, retail executive*
Shenk, George H. *lawyer*
Shiffman, Michael A. *lawyer*
Shostak, Linda E. *lawyer*
Silk, Thomas *lawyer*
Singer, Allen Morris *lawyer*
Siniscalco, Gary Richard *lawyer*
Smegal, Thomas Frank, Jr. *lawyer*
Smith, Brian D. *lawyer*
Smith, Kerry Clark *lawyer*
Snyder, Darin W. *lawyer*
Soberon, Presentacion Zablan *state bar administrator*
Sparks, Thomas E., Jr. *lawyer*
Speier, Jackie (Karen Jacqeline) *lawyer, forme state senator*
Staring, Graydon Shaw *lawyer*
Steel, Michael J. *lawyer*
Steer, Reginald David *lawyer*
Steskal, Christopher James *lawyer, former prosecutor*
Story, Joan H. *lawyer*
Street, Paul Shipley *lawyer*
Stromberg, Ross Ernest *lawyer*
Strother, James M. *lawyer*
Sugarman, Myron George *lawyer*
Sugarman, Paul William *lawyer*
Sullivan, Robert Edward *lawyer*
Sutton, John Paul *lawyer*
Tarun, Robert Walter *lawyer*
Taylor, William James (Zak Taylor) *lawyer*
Thomas, William Scott *lawyer*
Thompson, Patrick S. *lawyer*
Thompson, Robert Charles *lawyer*
Thornton, Charles Victor *lawyer*
Titelbaum, Daniel E. *lawyer*
Tobin, James Michael *lawyer*
Traynor, J. Michael *lawyer*
Uilkema, John K. *lawyer*
Van Buskirk, Ronald E. *lawyer*
Vazquez-Azpiri, A. James *lawyer*
Veaco, Kristina *lawyer*
Venning, Robert Stanley *lawyer*
Vesely, Jeffrey M. *lawyer*
Wald, Peter Allen *lawyer*
Walker, Walter Herbert III *lawyer, educator, writer*
Wang, William Kai-Sheng *law educator*
Warner, Paul L. *lawyer*
Weber, Arnold I. *lawyer*
Weber, Paula M. *lawyer*
Weitzel, Mark P. *lawyer*
Welborn, Caryl Bartelman *lawyer*
Whitehead, David Barry *lawyer*
Wild, Nelson Hopkins *lawyer*
Williams, Linda C. *lawyer*
Wingate, C. Keith *law educator*
Wirum, Andrea A. *lawyer*
Wolfe, Cameron Withgot, Jr. *lawyer*
Wong, Stanton D. *lawyer*
Wood, Robert Warren *lawyer*
Worthington, Bruce R. *lawyer, energy executi*
Wyle, Frederick S. *lawyer*
Yost, Nicholas Churchill *lawyer*
Young, Bryant Llewellyn *lawyer*
Young, Douglas Rea *lawyer*
Zeldin, Kim S. *lawyer*
Ziegler, R. W., Jr. *lawyer, consultant*
Ziering, William Mark *lawyer*

an Jose
lexander, Katharine Violet *lawyer*
ennion, David Jacobsen *lawyer*
ewley, Jeffrey Michael *lawyer*
ohn, Robert Herbert *lawyer*
enver, Thomas HR *lawyer*
oan, Gerald Xuyen Van *lawyer*
oody, Gregory L. *lawyer, energy executive*
awcett, Matthew Knowlton *lawyer*
allo, Joan Rosenberg *lawyer*
onzales, Daniel S. *lawyer*
ross, Lawrence Alan *lawyer*
annon, Timothy Patrick *lawyer, judge, educator*
ernández, Fernando Vargas *lawyer*
ckman, Steven H. *lawyer, electronics executive*
cobson, Michael R. *lawyer, Internet company executive*
atzman, Irwin *lawyer*
raw, George Martin *lawyer, writer*
IcManis, James *lawyer*
litchell, David Walker *lawyer*
lorgan, Robert Hall *lawyer*
arayan, Beverly Elaine *lawyer*
issly, Kenneth L. *lawyer*
ein, John C. *lawyer*
utzman, Thomas Chase, Sr. *lawyer*
owery, James E. *lawyer*

an Juan Capistrano
raves, Patrick Lee *lawyer*

an Marino
ranston, Howard Stephen *lawyer, management consultant*
albraith, James Marshall *lawyer, corporate executive*
omich, Lillian *lawyer*

an Mateo
rill, Lawrence J. *lawyer, accountant, bank executive*
ane, Steven Edward *mediator, arbitrator*
enney, William Fitzgerald *lawyer*
'Reilly, Terence John *lawyer*
mpson, Murray L. *lawyer*
yle, Craig S. *lawyer, investment company executive*

an Rafael
oomfield, Neil Jon *lawyer, real estate agent, educator*
hilvers, Robert Merritt *lawyer*
rexler, Kenneth *lawyer*
oth, Hadden Wing *lawyer, mediator, arbitrator*

an Ramon
arten, David Burton *lawyer*
mes, Charles Albert *lawyer, oil industry executive*

nta Ana
tken, Christopher R. *lawyer*
tken, Wylie A. *lawyer*
nesen, Mark R *lawyer*
rges, Fredrick Mario *lawyer*
llahan, Daniel J. *lawyer*
pizzi, Michael Robert *lawyer, former prosecutor*
Giorgio, Kenneth D. *lawyer, insurance company executive*
gorgio, Kenneth *lawyer*
llard, John Martin *lawyer, pilot*
arley, Robison Dooling, Jr. *lawyer, educator*
nowiecki, Joseph Samuel *lawyer, health facility administrator*
ei, Tom Y. K. *lawyer*
osich, Nicholas Joseph *lawyer*
tt, Herbert Jacob *lawyer*
orer, Maryruth *law librarian*
lentine-Sibert, Kimberly A. *lawyer*
agner, John Leo *lawyer, retired judge, mediator, arbitrator*

nta Barbara
-Tye, Kirk Thomas *lawyer*
ppello, A. Barry *lawyer*
enolf, Robert F. *lawyer*
lstrom, Kenneth Edward *lawyer*
etzinger, Timothy Edward *lawyer*
nger, Robert Marshall *lawyer*
eddon, Thomas William, Jr. *prosecutor*

nta Clara
ark, John M. III *lawyer*
llon, Michael A. (Mike) *lawyer, information technology executive*
ancy, Dorothy Jean *lawyer, educator*
ieh, Marina Cing *lawyer, educator*
mpert, Dennis Alan *lawyer*
rdlund, Donald Craig *lawyer, electronics executive*
well, D. Bruce (Bruce Sewell, Durward Bruce Sewell) *lawyer*
annon, David M. *lawyer*
non, James Lowell *lawyer*
eeney, Joseph J. *lawyer, manufacturing executive*

nta Clarita
tler, Richard Lee *lawyer*

nta Cruz
igmann, William Robert *lawyer, author*

nta Monica
nos, Reed C. *lawyer*
apman Holley, Shawn Snider *lawyer*
oper, Jay Leslie *lawyer*
ser, Thomas Christopher *lawyer, insurance company executive*
nego, William Joseph *lawyer*
ossman, Marshall Bruce *lawyer*
nerfeld, Robert Elliot *lawyer*
rsch, Richard Gary *lawyer*
rnstein, James E. *lawyer*
es, William Allen *lawyer*

Kinney, James Howard *lawyer, real estate company executive*
Kirkland, John C. *lawyer*
Levin, Marvin Eugene *lawyer*
McMillan, M. Sean *lawyer*
Modisett, Jeffrey A. *lawyer, former state attorney general*
Morgan, Kermit Johnson *lawyer*
Preble, Laurence George *lawyer*
Risman, Michael *lawyer, real estate developer, broker*
Rubenstein, Paul D. *lawyer*
Sherman, Victor *lawyer*
Shults, Roy L. *lawyer*
Soodik, Lynn *lawyer*
Tunney, John Varick *lawyer, former senator*
Weitzman, Howard L. *lawyer, former film company executive*
Wilson, Hugh Steven *lawyer*

Santa Rosa
Clement, Clayton Emerson *lawyer*
Courteau, Girard Robert *retired prosecutor*
Goldberg, Steven Murray *lawyer*
Handelman, Albert G. *lawyer*

Sausalito
Berkman, William Roger *lawyer, army reserve officer*
Gordon, Robert Eugene *lawyer*
O'Connor, Paul Daniel *lawyer*

Scotts Valley
Hudson, William L. *lawyer, electronics executive*

Seal Beach
Weitzman, Marc Herschel *lawyer*

Sebastopol
Rappaport, Stuart Ramon *lawyer*

Sherman Oaks
Ardalan, Pezhman Christopher *lawyer*
Crump, Gerald Franklin *retired lawyer*
Levin, Evanne Lynn *lawyer, educator*
Medearis, Miller *lawyer*
Mersel, Marjorie Kathryn Pedersen *lawyer*
Michelson, Louis Eli *lawyer*
Mikesell, Richard Lyon *lawyer, financial counselor*

Sonoma
Obninsky, Victor Peter *lawyer*

Stanford
Alexander, Janet Cooper *law educator*
Cohen, William *law educator*
Craswell, Richard *law educator*
Dickson, Lance E. *former law librarian, educator*
Ehrlich, Thomas *law educator*
Franklin, Marc Adam *law educator*
Friedman, Lawrence M. *law educator*
Goldstein, Paul *lawyer, educator*
Gould, William Benjamin, IV, *lawyer, federal agency administrator, educator*
Greely, Henry T. (Hank) *law educator*
Grundfest, Joseph Alexander *law and business educator*
Karlan, Pamela Susan *law educator*
Klausner, Michael David *law educator*
Lemley, Mark Alan *law educator*
Lessig, L. Lawrence III *lawyer, educator, writer*
Lomio, J. Paul *law librarian, researcher*
Marshall, Lawrence C. *law educator*
Martinez, Jenny S. *lawyer*
Rabin, Robert L. *law educator*
Rhode, Deborah Lynn *law educator*
Scott, Kenneth Eugene *lawyer, educator*
Sofaer, Abraham David *lawyer, judge, educator, consultant*
Thompson, Buzz (Barton H. Jr.) *law educator*
Weiner, Allen Sydney *law educator*
Williams, Howard Russell *law educator*

Stockton
Knapp, Christian Jakob *lawyer*
Parish, William Henry *lawyer*

Summerland
Bauer, Marvin Agather *retired lawyer*

Sunnyvale
Brigden, John *lawyer*
Callahan, Michael John *lawyer*
Doyle, Mary E. *lawyer*
McReynolds, Stephen Paul *lawyer*
Wehde, Albert Edward *lawyer*

Susanville
Gartner, Harold Henry III *lawyer*

The Sea Ranch
Robertson, David Govan *lawyer*

Thousand Oaks
Scott, David J. *lawyer, medical products executive*

Tiburon
Widman, Gary Lee *lawyer*

Torrance
Bryan, Sharon Ann *lawyer*
Carlson, Terrance L. *lawyer, aerospace transportation executive*
Moore, Christopher M. *lawyer*
Petillon, Lee Ritchey *lawyer*
Van Emburgh, Joanne *lawyer*

Tracy
Hay, Dennis Lee *lawyer*

Tustin
Madory, Richard Eugene *lawyer*

Ukiah
Sager, Madeline Dean *lawyer*

Universal City
Husband, Bertram Paul *lawyer*

Valencia
Lambirth, Timothy A. *mediator*

Van Nuys
Arabian, Armand *arbitrator, mediator, lawyer*

Victorville
Quadri, Fazle Rab *lawyer, government official*

Visalia
Crowe, John T. *lawyer*

Vista
Hennenhoefer, James A. *lawyer*

Walnut
McKee, Catherine Lynch *lawyer, educator*

Walnut Creek
Gill, Margaret Gaskins *lawyer*
Ginsburg, Gerald J. *lawyer, management consultant*
Hanschen, Peter Walter *lawyer*
Nord, Paul Elliott *lawyer, accountant*
Pagter, Carl Richard *lawyer*
Rainey, William Joel *lawyer*
Skaggs, Sanford Merle *lawyer*

Watsonville
Futch, Michael *lawyer, construction executive*

West Covina
Ebiner, Robert Maurice *lawyer*
Galen, Albert John *retired lawyer*
McHale, Edward Robertson *retired lawyer*

West Hollywood
Margolin, Bruce M. *lawyer*

Westlake Village
Carter, C. Michael *lawyer*
Hoefflin, Richard Michael *lawyer, judicial administrator*
Sindon, Geoffrey Stuart *lawyer*
Strote, Joel Richard *lawyer*
Weissman, Robert Allen *lawyer, real estate broker*

Woodland
Melton, Barry *lawyer, musician*

Woodland Hills
Adreani, Michael B. *lawyer*
Even, Randolph M. *lawyer*
Glick, Earl A. *lawyer*
Preston, John Elwood *lawyer*
Tiano, Linda V. *lawyer, insurance company executive*
Westen, Brodie Curtis, Jr., (Curt) *lawyer*

Yorba Linda
McCune, Brenda L. *lawyer*

Yuba City
Doughty, Mark Anthony *lawyer*

COLORADO

Arvada
Peck, Kenneth E. *lawyer*

Aspen
Peirce, Frederick Fairbanks *lawyer*

Aurora
Katz, Michael Jeffery *lawyer*
Nekritz, Edward Steven *lawyer*
Stauffer, Scott William *lawyer, accountant*

Basalt
Shipp, Dan Shackelford *lawyer*

Boulder
Bruff, Harold Hastings *law educator, former dean*
Deaktor, Darryl Barnett *lawyer*
Echohawk, John Ernest *lawyer*
Fenster, Herbert Lawrence *lawyer*
Fiflis, Ted James *lawyer, educator*
Flowers, William Harold, Jr. *lawyer*
Getches, David Harding *lawyer, educator, dean*
Gray, William R. *lawyer*
Nehls, Richard Charles *lawyer*
Peterson, Courtland Harry *law educator*
Porzak, Glenn E. *lawyer*
Purvis, John Anderson *lawyer, educator*
Smith, Paul E. *lawyer*
Steuben, Norton Leslie *lawyer, educator*
Stevens, Glenn H. *lawyer*
Wittemyer, John *lawyer*
Yee, Sienho *law educator*

Broomfield
Baker, Charles E. *lawyer*

Colorado Springs
Adams, Deborah Rowland *lawyer*
Deeny, Raymond M. *lawyer*
Evans, Paul Vernon *lawyer*
Everson, Steven Lee *lawyer, real estate company executive*
Kendall, Phillip Alan *retired lawyer*
Kubida, William Joseph *lawyer*
MacDougall, Malcolm Edward *lawyer*
Payne, Billy (William Porter Payne) *real estate lawyer, sports association executive*
Purvis, Randall W. B. *lawyer*
Sargent, Walter Harriman, II, *lawyer*
Slivka, Michael Andrew *lawyer*
Walker, Jonathan Lee *lawyer*

Commerce City
Trujillo, Lorenzo A. *lawyer, educator, consultant, director*

Denver
Aro, Edwin Packard *lawyer*
Austin, H(arry) Gregory *lawyer*
Bader, Gerald L., Jr. *lawyer*
Baer, Richard N. *lawyer, telecommunications industry executive*
Bain, Donald Knight *lawyer*
Banks, Britt D. *lawyer*
Bartlit, Fred Holcomb, Jr. *lawyer*
Beatty, Michael L. *lawyer*
Belitz, Paul Edward *lawyer*
Bell, Stephen D. *lawyer*
Benson, Robert Eugene *lawyer*
Benton, Auburn Edgar *lawyer*
Berry, Robert Worth *lawyer, retired military officer, educator*
Bess, Charles Wayne *lawyer*
Blair, Andrew Lane, Jr. *lawyer, educator*
Blitz, Stephen M. *lawyer*
Bluher, John H. *lawyer, diversified financial services company executive*
Blum, Gary Bernard *lawyer*
Breeskin, Michael Wayne *lawyer*
Brega, Charles Franklin *lawyer, director*
Briggs, Steve Clement *lawyer*
Butler, Daphne *lawyer*
Butler, David *lawyer*
Byrne, Thomas J. *lawyer*
Cain, Douglas Mylchreest *lawyer*
Calvin, Charles D. *lawyer*
Campbell, Leonard M. *lawyer*
Carlson, Erik B. *lawyer*
Carrigan, Jim R. *arbitrator, mediator, retired judge*
Cheroutes, Michael Louis *lawyer*
Clark, Phillip R. *lawyer*
Cooper, Billy J. *lawyer*
Cooper, Paul Douglas *lawyer*
Cope, Thomas Field *lawyer*
Copeland, Eugene Leroy *lawyer, writer*
Cox, William Vaughan *arbitrator, lawyer*
Crow, Nancy Rebecca *lawyer*
Dauer, Edward Arnold *law educator*
Davis, R. Steven *lawyer, telecommunications industry executive*
Dean, James Benwell *lawyer*
De Marino, Thomas John *lawyer*
Deutsch, Harvey Elliot *lawyer*
Dolan, Andrew Kevin *lawyer*
Dorr, Robert Charles *lawyer*
Dowdle, Patrick Dennis *lawyer*
Driver, Michael J. *lawyer*
Duffy, William J. *lawyer*
Dunn, Randy Edwin *lawyer*
DuVivier, Katharine Keyes *lawyer, educator*
Eid, Troy A. *prosecutor*
Elliff, J(ohn) Eric *lawyer*
Finegan, Cole *lawyer*
Fowler, Daniel McKay *lawyer*
Gehres, James *retired lawyer*
George, Russell Lloyd *lawyer, former state legislator*
Grant, Patrick Alexander *lawyer*
Green, Jersey Michael-Lee *lawyer*
Grissom, Garth Clyde *lawyer, director*
Haddon, Harold Alan *lawyer*
Hale, Allan L. *lawyer*
Hanna, Juliet Marie *lawyer*
Harris, Dale Ray *lawyer, arbitrator, mediator*
Hartley, James Edward *lawyer*
Hendrix, Lynn Parker *lawyer*
Hoagland, Donald Wright *lawyer*
Hodges, Joseph Gilluly, Jr. *lawyer*
Holme, Richard Phillips *lawyer*
Hopfenbeck, George Martin, Jr. *lawyer*
Houtsma, Peter C. *lawyer*
Imig, William Graff *lawyer, lobbyist*
Irwin, R. Robert *lawyer*
Jacobs, Paul Alan *lawyer*
Jones, Richard Michael *lawyer*
Judd, Joel Stanton *lawyer*
Kahn, Edwin Sam *lawyer*
Keller, Glen Elven, Jr. *lawyer*
Kelly, John Fleming *lawyer*
King, James M. *lawyer*
Kintzele, John Alfred *lawyer*
Krendl, Cathy Stricklin *lawyer*
Leone, William J. *lawyer, former prosecutor*
Levy, Mark Ray *lawyer*
Low, Andrew M. *lawyer*
Low, John Wayland *lawyer*
Lutz, John Shafroth *lawyer*
Lyons, James M. *lawyer*
Mackey, Pamela Robillard *lawyer*
Mahoney, Andrea Noel *lawyer*
Maldonado, Kirk Francis *lawyer*
Manzanares, Lawrence *city attorney*
Marquess, Lawrence Wade *lawyer*
Martz, Clyde Ollen *lawyer, educator*
Mathis, Karen J. *lawyer, legal association administrator*
McCabe, John L. *lawyer*
McConnell, Michael Theodore *lawyer*
McDowell, Karen Ann *lawyer*
McInnis, Scott Steve *lawyer, former congressman*
McIntosh, Carolyn Leigh *lawyer*
McLain, William Allen *lawyer*
McMichael, Donald Earl *lawyer*
Merker, Steven Joseph *lawyer*
Miller, Gale Timothy *lawyer*
Miller, Robert Nolen *lawyer*
Mitchem, Allen P. *lawyer*
Montgomery, C. Michael *lawyer*
Murane, William Edward *lawyer*
Newcom, Jennings Jay *lawyer, director*
Olsen, M. Kent *lawyer, educator*
Osman, Lee R. *lawyer*
Otten, Arthur Edward, Jr. *lawyer*
Palmer, David Gilbert *lawyer*
Peters, Stephen C. *lawyer*
Petros, Raymond Louis, Jr. *lawyer*
Phelps, Robert Frederick, Jr. *lawyer*

Phillips, Paul David, Jr. *lawyer*
Pozner, Larry S. *lawyer, educator*
Quiat, Gerald M. *lawyer*
Raine, Stanley M. *lawyer*
Raznick, Carol *lawyer*
Rich, Robert Stephen *lawyer*
Richardson, Thomas A. *lawyer*
Robertson, Jerry D. *lawyer*
Rockwood, Linda Lee *lawyer*
Roesler, John Bruce *lawyer*
Roth, Robert Charles *lawyer*
Samuels, Donald L. *lawyer*
Sayre, John Marshall *lawyer, former government official*
Schmidt, L(ail) William, Jr. *lawyer*
Seawell, Donald Ray *lawyer, performing company executive*
Shea, Kevin Michael *lawyer*
Shepherd, John Frederic *lawyer*
Shively, John D. *lawyer*
Snead, Kathleen Marie *lawyer*
Staelin, Earl Hudson *lawyer*
Starrs, Elizabeth Anne *lawyer*
Steefel, David Simon *lawyer*
Talley, Steven K. *lawyer*
Thomasch, Roger Paul *lawyer*
Timmins, Edward Patrick *lawyer*
Tisdale, Douglas Michael, Sr. *lawyer*
Touff, Michael *lawyer*
Ulrich, Theodore Albert *lawyer*
Villano, Stephen Paul *lawyer*
Walker, Samuel David *lawyer*
Weber, Matthew George *lawyer*
Wedgle, Richard Jay *lawyer*
Welton, Charles Ephraim *lawyer*
Wheeler, Malcolm Edward *lawyer, educator*
Williams, Michael Anthony *lawyer*
Wohlgenant, Richard Glen *lawyer, director*
Woodward, Lester Ray *lawyer*
Wunnicke, Brooke *lawyer*

Durango
Burnham, Bryson Paine *retired lawyer*

Englewood
DeMuth, Laurence Wheeler, Jr. *lawyer, utilities executive*
Markowski, Elizabeth M. *lawyer*
McCallie, Spencer Wyatt *lawyer*
Moskowitz, David K. *lawyer*
Spencer, Margaret Gilliam *lawyer*
Steinhauser, John William *retired lawyer*
Tanabe, Charles Y. *lawyer*

Evergreen
Prichard, Vincent Marvin *lawyer*

Fort Collins
Johnson, Donald Edward, Jr. *lawyer*
Murphy, Dennis Joseph *lawyer*
Rogers, Garth Winfield *lawyer*
Schwartz, Allen R. *lawyer*

Frisco
Helmer, David Alan *lawyer*

Golden
Carney, Deborah Leah Turner *lawyer*
Eiberger, Carl Frederick *lawyer*
Kopel, David Benjamin *lawyer*
Phillipson, Donald E. *lawyer*

Greeley
Wiseman, Donald F. *lawyer*

Greenwood Village
Aspinwall, David Charles *lawyer, insurance company executive*
Bain, James William *lawyer*
Dewald, Bruce Wayne *lawyer*
Dymond, Lewis Wandell *lawyer, educator*
Gallegos, Larry Duayne *lawyer*
Karr, David Dean *lawyer*
Lidstone, Herrick Kenley, Jr. *lawyer*
Money, David R. *lawyer, information technology executive*
Nixon, Scott Sherman *lawyer*
Poe, Robert Alan *lawyer*
Rairdon, James Lee *paralegal, educator*
Ramsey, John Arthur *lawyer*
Rothrock, Lindsey Nichole *lawyer*
Schlapbach, David *lawyer*

Highlands Ranch
Hagen, Glenn W. *lawyer*
Judson, Philip Livingston *retired lawyer, consultant*
Mierzwa, Joseph William *lawyer, consultant*

Hot Sulphur Springs
Edwards, Daniel Walden *prosecutor, lawyer*

Howard
Hopkins, Donald J. *retired lawyer*

Lakewood
Guyton, Samuel Percy *retired lawyer*
Humphrey, Charles Edward, Jr. *lawyer*
McElwee, Dennis John *lawyer, former pharmaceutical company executive*
Meyer, Lynn Nix *lawyer*
Thome, Dennis Wesley *lawyer*

Littleton
Meyer, Milton Edward, Jr. *retired lawyer, artist*

Lone Tree
Spelts, Richard John *lawyer*

Loveland
Clark, Roger Earl *lawyer*

Morrison
Bowen, Peter Geoffrey *arbitrator, business educator*

Norwood
Reagan, Harry Edwin III *lawyer*

Pagosa Springs
Kelly, Reid Browne *lawyer*

Pueblo
Farley, Thomas T. *lawyer*
Lytle, William David *lawyer*

Rocky Ford
Mendenhall, Harry Barton *lawyer*

Steamboat Springs
Moylan, James Joseph *lawyer*

Westminster
Sherk, George William *lawyer, educator*

Windsor
Downey, Arthur Harold, Jr. *lawyer, mediator*

CONNECTICUT

Avon
Godbout, Arthur Richard, Jr. *lawyer*
Harrison, Thomas Flatley *lawyer, environmental consultant*

Bethel
Medvecky, Thomas Edward *lawyer*

Bloomfield
Messemer, Glenn Matthew *lawyer*
Stravalle-Schmidt, Ann Roberta *lawyer*

Bridgeport
Bowen, Patrick Harvey *lawyer, consultant*

Cheshire
Twomey, Teresa Marie *lawyer*

Danbury
Bassett, Robert Andrews *lawyer*
Breedlove, James (Jim Breedlove) *lawyer*
Yamin, Robert Joseph *lawyer*

Darien
Beach, Stephen Holbrook *lawyer*
Dale, Erwin Randolph *retired lawyer, writer*
Himmelreich, David Baker *lawyer*
Prince, Kenneth Stephen *lawyer*

Derby
McEvoy, Sharlene Ann *law educator*

East Hartford
Dubin, Joseph William *federal mediator*

Enfield
Smith, Spencer Thomas *lawyer*

Essex
Pfarr, John S. *lawyer*

Fairfield
Backman, Gerald Stephen *retired lawyer*
Caruso, Daniel F. *lawyer, judge, former state legislator*
Denniston, Brackett Badger III *lawyer*
Huth, William Edward *lawyer*
Osis, Daiga Guntra *lawyer*
Ury, Frederic Stephen *lawyer*
Wales, Gwynne Huntington *retired lawyer*

Farmington
Grafstein, Joel M. *lawyer*
McCann, John Joseph *lawyer*
Wiechmann, Eric Watt *lawyer*

Greenwich
Atkins, Ronald Raymond *lawyer*
Brandrup, Douglas Warren *lawyer*
Coleman, Joel Clifford *lawyer*
Gelfman, Robert William *retired lawyer*
George, Cynthia Coulter *lawyer*
Kreiger, Bruce D. *lawyer*
Lanning, Christopher Glenn *lawyer*
Lynch, William Redington *retired lawyer*
More, Douglas McLochlan *lawyer*
Nemser, Earl Harold *lawyer*
Nimetz, Matthew *lawyer, investment company executive*
Pascarella, Henry William *lawyer*
Paul, Roland Arthur *lawyer*
Schoonmaker, Samuel Vail III *lawyer*
Schwed, Roger E. *lawyer, rental company executive*
Selby, Leland Clay *lawyer*
Sexton, David Farrington *lawyer, bank executive*
Storms, Clifford Beekman *lawyer*
Welt, Philip Stanley *lawyer, consultant*

Hamden
Margulies, Martin B. *lawyer, educator*
Peterson, George Emanuel, Jr. *retired lawyer*

Hartford
Alfano, Charles Thomas, Sr. *lawyer*
Anthony, Julian Danford, Jr. *lawyer*
Berall, Frank Stewart *lawyer*
Bergenn, James Walter *lawyer*
Blumberg, Phillip Irvin *law educator*
Bonee, John Leon III *lawyer*
Buck, Gurdon Hall *lawyer, urban planner, mediator*
Butler, Gregory B. *lawyer, utilities executive*
Cain, George Harvey *lawyer, association administrator*
Coyle, Michael Lee *lawyer*
Davis, Andrew Neil *lawyer, educator*
Del Negro, John Thomas *lawyer*
Gale, John Quentin *lawyer*
Godfrey, Robert Douglas *lawyer*
Herzog, Brigitte *lawyer*
Kennedy, Jack Stanners *lawyer*
Kirk, Darcy *law librarian, educator*
Kreczko, Alan James *lawyer, insurance company executive*
Leonhardt, Clifton Andrew *lawyer, public information officer*
Lloyd, Alex *lawyer*
Lotstein, James Irving *lawyer*
Louden, Wm. Bruce *lawyer*
Lyon, James Burroughs *lawyer*
Merriam, Dwight Haines *lawyer, land use planner*
Nolan, John Blanchard *lawyer*
O'Donnell, Edward Francis, Jr. *lawyer*
Orth, Paul William *retired lawyer*
Rich, Tracy Leon *lawyer, insurance company executive*
Richter, Donald Paul *lawyer*
Ryan, David Thomas *lawyer*
See, Edmund M. *lawyer*
Space, Theodore Maxwell *lawyer*
Strasser, Kurt Albert *law educator, researcher, author, dean*
Sussman, Mark Richard *lawyer*
Tancredi, James J. *lawyer*
Taylor, Allan Bert *lawyer*
Trachsel, William Henry *corporate lawyer*
Valentine, Debra A. *lawyer*
Voigt, Richard *lawyer*
Wolin, Neal Steven *lawyer*
Young, Roland Frederic III *lawyer*

Lakeville
Jerome, John James *lawyer*
Jones, Ronald David *retired lawyer*

Litchfield
Fiederowicz, Walter Michael *lawyer*
Fishman, Mitchell Steven *lawyer*

Madison
Clendenen, William Herbert, Jr. *lawyer*

Meriden
Lowry, Houston Putnam *lawyer*

Middletown
Janes, Norman K. *lawyer*

Milford
Berchem, Robert Lee, Sr. *lawyer*
Hogan, John W., Jr. *lawyer*

Monroe
Lindskog, David Richard *lawyer*
Oliver, Milton McKinnon *lawyer, translator*

New Britain
Beatt, Bruce H. *lawyer, metal products executive*

New Canaan
Ferro, Guy (Gaetano Ferro) *lawyer*
Resor, Stanley Rogers *retired lawyer*
Steinmetz, Richard Bird, Jr. *lawyer*
Wolff, Sanford Irving *lawyer*

New Haven
Ackerman, Bruce Arnold *law educator*
Behling, Paul Lawrence *lawyer, educator*
Brilmayer, R. Lea *lawyer, educator*
Burt, Robert Amsterdam *lawyer, educator*
Carty, Paul Vernon *lawyer*
Collier, David Beebe *lawyer, consultant*
Danaher, John Anthony III *prosecutor*
Days, Drew S. III *lawyer, educator*
Donohue, John Joseph *law educator*
Duke, Steven Barry *law educator*
Ellickson, Robert Chester *law educator*
Eskridge, William Nichol, Jr. *law educator*
Esty, Daniel Cushing *lawyer, educator*
Fishman, Mark I. *lawyer*
Fiss, Owen M. *law educator*
Freed, Daniel Josef *law educator*
Gallant, Brad (Keith Bradoc Gallant) *lawyer*
Gastwirth, Donald Edward *lawyer, literary agent*
Gewirtz, Paul D. *lawyer, educator*
Gildea, Brian Michael *lawyer*
Graetz, Michael J. *law educator*
Greenfield, James Robert *lawyer*
Hansmann, Henry Baethke *law educator*
Johnstone, Quintin *law educator*
Jolls, Christine Margaret *law educator*
Kauffman, Stephen Blair *law librarian, educator*
Langbein, John Harriss *lawyer, educator*
Macey, Jonathan R. *law educator*
Marcus, Edward Leonard *lawyer, political organization worker*
O'Connor, Kevin James *prosecutor, lawyer*
Post, Robert Charles *law educator*
Priest, George L. *law educator*
Prout, William H., Jr. *lawyer*
Reisman, William Michael *lawyer, educator*
Robinson, Dorothy K. *lawyer*
Romano, Roberta *law educator*
Rose-Ackerman, Susan *law and political economy educator*
Schloss, Irving Steven *lawyer*
Schneider, David Walter *lawyer*
Schuck, Peter Horner *lawyer, educator*
Stapleton, James Francis *lawyer*
Stith-Cabranes, Kate *law educator*
Sullivan, Shaun Stuart *lawyer*
Wagoner, Walter Dray, Jr. *lawyer*

New London
Asselin-Connolly, John Thomas *lawyer*
Johnstone, Philip MacLaren *lawyer*
Partnoy, Ronald Allen *lawyer*
Reardon, Robert Ignatius, Jr. *lawyer*

Norfolk
Jessup, Philip Caryl, Jr. *retired lawyer*

North Stonington
Svengalis, Kendall Frayne *law librarian, educator, publishing executive, writer*

Norwalk
Burton, David K. *lawyer*
Cammaker, Sheldon Ira *lawyer*
Jacobs, Mark Randolph *lawyer*
Knopp, Alex *lawyer, mayor*
Raikes, Charles FitzGerald *retired lawyer*
Walker, Kellye L. *lawyer*

Old Greenwich
Gayda, Michael D. *lawyer*

Orange
Davies, Richard Warren *lawyer*

Redding
Gooch, Anthony Cushing *retired lawyer*
Quinn, Andrew Peter, Jr. *lawyer, retired insurance company executive*

Ridgefield
Wiegley, Roger Douglas *lawyer*

Rocky Hill
Mandell, Joel *lawyer*

Roxbury
Friedman, John Maxwell, Jr. *lawyer*

Simsbury
Long, Michael Thomas *lawyer, manufacturing executive*

South Glastonbury
Schroth, Peter William *lawyer, management, educator*

Southbury
Russell, Allan David *lawyer*

Southport
Sanetti, Stephen Louis *lawyer*

Stamford
Bainton, J(ohn) Joseph *lawyer*
Barreca, Christopher Anthony *lawyer*
Cacace, Michael Joseph *lawyer*
Daniels, Daniel Lloyd *lawyer*
Della Rocco, Kenneth Anthony *lawyer*
duPont, Augustus Irénée *lawyer*
Glassman, Hilary E. *lawyer, communications executive*
Gold, Steven Michael *lawyer*
Griffith, Forrest Lee III *lawyer*
Hawkins, John Donald, Jr. *lawyer*
Hogan, Frank W. III *lawyer, manufacturing executive*
Hubschman, Henry A. *lawyer*
Lalli, Michael Anthony *lawyer*
Leader, Leonard *lawyer*
Liu, Don H. *lawyer, printing company executi*
Mayes, Michele Coleman *lawyer*
McGeeney, John Stephen *lawyer*
McGrath, Richard *lawyer*
Merritt, William Alfred, Jr. *retired lawyer, rea estate company executive*
Miller, Gregory James *lawyer*
Nichols, Ralph Arthur *lawyer*
Olschan, Jacqueline Nicola *lawyer*
Perle, Eugene Gabriel *lawyer*
Pickel, Alan Scott *lawyer*
Rose, Richard Loomis *lawyer*
Sarner, Richard Alan *lawyer*
Shanman, James Alan *lawyer*
Sherman, Mickey (Michael Sherman) *lawyer*
Skidd, Thomas Patrick, Jr. *lawyer*
Snediker, David E. *lawyer*
Staab, Diane D. *lawyer*
Teitell, Conrad Laurence *lawyer, writer*
Weitzel, William Conrad, Jr. *lawyer*
Willkie, Wendell Lewis, II, *lawyer*

Stonington
Brown, Meredith M. *lawyer*
Cole, Richard A. *retired lawyer*

Storrs Mansfield
Tucker, Edwin Wallace *law educator*

Torrington
Leard, David Carl *lawyer*
Lippincott, Walter Edward *law educator*
Wall, Robert Anthony, Jr. *lawyer*

Trumbull
Williams, Ronald Doherty *lawyer*

Waterbury
Dost, Mark W. *lawyer*
Schefsky, Lynn A. *lawyer, chemicals executive*
Wolfe, Harriet Munrett *lawyer*

West Hartford
Swerdloff, Ileen Pollock *lawyer*
Swerdloff, Mark Harris *lawyer*
Wolman, Martin *lawyer*

Weston
Aibel, Howard James *arbitrator, mediator*
Murray, Stephen James *lawyer*

Westport
Barberi, Robert Obed *lawyer*
Carr, Cynthia *lawyer*
Cohen, Eric I. *lawyer*
Cramer, Allan P. *lawyer*
Daw, Harold John *lawyer, director*
Dunham, Christopher Cooper *lawyer*
Fried, Burton Theodore *lawyer*
Heyman, Ronnie Feuerstein *lawyer*
Margolis, Emanuel *lawyer, educator*
Razzano, Pasquale Angelo *lawyer*
Saxl, Richard Hildreth *lawyer*
Sheiman, Ronald Lee *lawyer*

Wethersfield
Terk, Glenn Thomas *lawyer*

Wilton
Adams, Thomas Tilley *lawyer*

, Robert Dominick *lawyer*
e, Richard John *lawyer*
, James Casey *lawyer*
, Ralph Evan *lawyer*

dbridge
ng, Margaret Elaine *lawyer*

dbury
ano, Rosemary E. *lawyer*

AWARE

er
, Matthew P. *lawyer*
, Bruce Clifford *retired lawyer*

kessin
, F. L. Peter *lawyer*

on
w, Milton Michael *law educator*

ark
, Charles Myer *law educator*
gone, Gerard J. *international maritime law ucator*

oboth Beach
es, Richard Francis *lawyer*

mington
r, John Merwin *retired lawyer*
nann, Julian Henry, Jr. *lawyer*
enter, Edmund Nelson, II, *retired lawyer*
olly, Colm F. *prosecutor*
berto, Richard Anthony, Jr. *lawyer*
elstein, Jesse Adam *lawyer*
d, Israel J. *lawyer, chemicals executive*
n, James Samuel *lawyer*
sman, Jerome Kent *lawyer, accountant*
leg, John Andrew *lawyer*
man, James L(ouis) *lawyer*
ston, William David *lawyer*
s, Janet K. Pilling *lawyer*
, Richard Dillon *lawyer*
patrick, Andrew Booth, Jr. *lawyer*
man, Barry Martin *lawyer*
tol, Daniel Marvin *retired lawyer*
ee, Thomas Hugh *lawyer*
k, John Stephen *lawyer*
eever, Elizabeth M. *lawyer*
ner, Pamela *lawyer, educator*
ler, L. Arlen *lawyer, chemist*
ley, Stacey J. *lawyer, chemicals executive*
n, Samuel Augustus *lawyer*
hetto, John J. *lawyer*
d, Thomas James *law educator*
gers, Stephen John *lawyer, physician, nsultant*
nger, Frank Max *lawyer*
ple, James William *lawyer*
h, Craig Bennett *lawyer*
ks, W. Donald, II, *lawyer*
gatt, Bruce M. *lawyer*
van, Lawrence Matthew *lawyer*
as, Michael B. *lawyer*
sanen, Christine M. *lawyer, writer*
d, Rodman, Jr. *lawyer, director*
etzel, Robert William *lawyer*
, Richard Royal, Jr. *lawyer*
slow, Helen Littell *lawyer*

STRICT OF COLUMBIA

shington
onson, David Ernest *lawyer, educator*
ott, Alden Francis *lawyer, federal official*
eson, David Campion *retired lawyer, policy nalyst, writer*
ms, David G. *lawyer*
ms, Frances Grant, II, *lawyer*
mson, Terrence Burdett *lawyer*
ucci, Steven A. *lawyer*
er, Howard Bruce *lawyer*
er, Robert Martin *lawyer*
ast, Mark David *lawyer*
, Sanford King *lawyer*
en, Andrew C. *lawyer*
erg, James L. *lawyer*
recht, Ralph P. *lawyer*
ock, John Douglas *lawyer*
onas, Grant D. *lawyer, former federal agency dministrator*
xander, Clifford Joseph *lawyer*
xander, Donald Crichton *lawyer*
n, Richmond Frederick *lawyer*
rd, Nicholas W. *lawyer*
enburg, John D., Jr. *lawyer, retired military fficer*
arez, Scott G. *lawyer*
brose, Myles Joseph *lawyer*
es, Robert G. *lawyer*
ron, Cory M. *lawyer*
derson, Frederick Randolph, Jr. *lawyer, educator*
derson, James E. *lawyer*
derson, Stanton Dean *lawyer*
drew, Giaccia A. *lawyer*
drew, Joseph Jerald *lawyer*
drews, Mark Joseph *lawyer*
dril, David T. *lawyer*
thony, Stephen Pierce *lawyer*
atoff, David B. *lawyer*
ple, James Glenn *lawyer, educator*
ridge, Daniel F. *lawyer*
berger, Marcia A. *lawyer*
sbrook, J. Keith *lawyer*
l, Richard Daniel, Jr. *lawyer*
elrod, Jonathan Gans *lawyer*
er, Donald Belton *lawyer*
bayi, Robert S. *lawyer*
oby, Lon S. *lawyer*
chman, Kenneth Leroy, Jr. *lawyer*
der, W(illiam) Reece *lawyer*

Badillo, Alejandro *lawyer*
Baer, William J. *lawyer*
Baim, Eric M. *lawyer*
Bain, Scott E. *lawyer*
Baker, David Harris *lawyer*
Baker, Howard Henry, Jr. *lawyer, former ambassador, senator*
Baker, P. Jean *lawyer, mediator*
Baldridge, J. Douglas *lawyer*
Ball, Markham (Robert Ball) *lawyer, arbitrator, educator*
Ballard, Frederic Lyman, Jr. *lawyer*
Ballen, Robert Gerald *lawyer*
Bank, Rita M. *lawyer*
Banoun, Raymond *lawyer*
Banzhaf, John F. III *legal association administrator, educator*
Baran, Jan Witold *lawyer, educator*
Barbash, Barry P. *lawyer*
Barcella, Ernest Lawrence, Jr. *lawyer*
Barclay, George N. *lawyer*
Bardin, David Jonas *lawyer*
Barnes, Donald Michael *lawyer*
Barnes, Mark James *lawyer*
Barnett, Helaine M. *lawyer*
Barnett, Robert Bruce *lawyer*
Barnette, James D. *lawyer*
Barrett, Jane Frances *lawyer*
Barrie, John Paul *lawyer, educator*
Barron, Myra Hymovich *lawyer*
Barry, Dennis M. *lawyer*
Barshefsky, Charlene *lawyer, former federal official*
Barusch, Ronald Charles *lawyer*
Baskin, Maurice *lawyer*
Basseches, Robert Treinis *lawyer*
Battle, Michael A. *lawyer, former federal agency administrator, prosecutor*
Bauer, Richard P. *lawyer*
Bauer, Robert F. *lawyer*
Baumann, Linda Adriene *lawyer*
Baum-Villavicencio, Lynne Miriam *lawyer*
Bayh, Birch Evans, Jr. *lawyer, former senator*
Bea Roberts, Barbara Ann *legal secretary*
Becker, Brandon *lawyer*
Becker, Stephan E. *lawyer*
Beckwith, Edward Jay *lawyer*
Behan, Kathleen A. (Kitty Behan) *lawyer*
Beisner, John Herbert *lawyer*
Bell, Joseph Charles *lawyer*
Bell, Sheila Trice *lawyer*
Bell, Stephen Robert *lawyer*
Beller, Herbert N. *lawyer*
Bellinger, John B. III *lawyer, federal official*
Benner, C. Jonathan *lawyer*
Bennett, Alan R. *lawyer*
Bennett, Alexander Elliot *lawyer*
Bennett, Robert Stephen *lawyer*
Ben-Veniste, Richard *lawyer*
Berenson, Bradford A. *lawyer*
Beresford, Douglas Lincoln *lawyer*
Bergner, Jane Cohen *lawyer*
Berl, Joseph M. *lawyer*
Berlack, Evan Raden *lawyer*
Berlin, Kenneth *lawyer*
Berman, Joshua G. *lawyer*
Berman, Paul Justin *lawyer*
Bernabei, Lynne Ann *lawyer*
Bernard, Lawrence B. *lawyer*
Berner, Frederic George, Jr. *lawyer*
Bernhard, Berl *lawyer*
Bernstein, Mitchell Harris *lawyer*
Bernthal, Eric L. *lawyer*
Berrington, Craig Anthony *lawyer*
Berthelsen, Richard A. *lawyer*
Berz, David Richard *lawyer*
Besozzi, Paul Charles *lawyer*
Best, Judah *lawyer*
Bieber, Sander M. *lawyer*
Bierman, James Norman *lawyer*
Billauer, Barbara Pfeffer *lawyer, educator*
Bintz, Edward E. *lawyer*
Birnkrant, Henry Joseph *lawyer*
Bishop, James Dodson *lawyer, mediator*
Black, Stephen Franklin *lawyer, writer*
Blair, Robert Allen *lawyer*
Blake, Jonathan Dewey *lawyer*
Blalack, K. Lee *lawyer*
Blazek-White, Doris *lawyer*
Bleakley, Peter Kimberley *lawyer*
Bloch, Scott J. *lawyer*
Bloch, Susan Low *law educator*
Block, Joseph G. *lawyer*
Bloom, David I. *lawyer*
Bloomquist, Michael *lawyer*
Blumenfeld, Jeffrey *lawyer, educator*
Blumenthal, William *lawyer*
Bodansky, Robert Lee *lawyer*
Bodner, John, Jr. *lawyer*
Boehm, Steven Bruce *lawyer*
Bogard, Lawrence Joseph *lawyer*
Boggs, George Trenholm *lawyer*
Boggs, Judith Susan *lawyer, health policy analyst*
Boggs, Thomas Hale, Jr. *lawyer, director*
Boisture, Robert A. *lawyer*
Boland, Christopher Thomas, II, *lawyer*
Bolger, Robert J., Jr. *lawyer*
Bondareff, Joan M. *lawyer, retired government agency administrator*
Bonvillian, William Boone *lawyer*
Bookoff, Leslie *lawyer*
Bopp, Michael D. *lawyer*
Born, Brooksley Elizabeth *retired lawyer*
Borsari, George Robert, Jr. *lawyer, commentator*
Bosch, Michele C. *lawyer*
Bosco, Mary Beth *lawyer*
Boskey, Bennett *lawyer*
Boss, Lenard Barrett *lawyer*
Boyd, Benjamin S. *lawyer*
Boyd, Thomas Marshall *lawyer*
Braden, Gregory C. *lawyer*
Braga, Stephen Louis *lawyer*
Braker, Gregory S. *lawyer*
Brame, Joseph Robert III *lawyer*
Braswell, Mark K. *lawyer*

Breaux, John Berlinger *lawyer, communications professor, former senator*
Bregman, Arthur Randolph *lawyer, educator*
Brenner, Janet Maybin Walker *lawyer*
Bresnahan, Pamela Anne *lawyer, mediator, arbitrator*
Briggs, Alan Leonard *lawyer*
Brinkmann, Robert Joseph *lawyer*
Brody, Peter Martin *lawyer*
Brogan, Stephen (Steve) J. *lawyer*
Bromwich, Michael Ray *lawyer*
Bronstein, Alvin J. *lawyer*
Brower, Charles Nelson *lawyer, judge*
Brower, Gregory A. *lawyer*
Brown, Barbara Berish *lawyer*
Brown, David Nelson *lawyer*
Brown, Preston *lawyer*
Brown, Thomas Philip III *lawyer*
Browne, Richard Cullen *lawyer*
Brownell, F. William *lawyer*
Bruce, Carol Elder *lawyer*
Bruce, Estel Edward *lawyer*
Bruemmer, Russell John *lawyer*
Brunner, Thomas William *lawyer*
Bruno, Philippe M. *lawyer*
Brunsvold, Brian Garrett *lawyer, educator*
Buc, Nancy Lillian *lawyer*
Buckley, Jeremiah Stephen *lawyer*
Bucklin, Donald Thomas *lawyer*
Buechner, Jack W(illiam) *lawyer, consultant, educational association administrator*
Buffon, Charles Edward *lawyer*
Buffone, Samuel J. *lawyer*
Bulleit, Thomas Nelson, Jr. *lawyer*
Bumpus, Jeanne *lawyer*
Burchfield, Bobby Roy *lawyer*
Burdett, James R. *lawyer*
Burka, Robert Alan *lawyer*
Burke, Edmund W. *lawyer*
Burnley, James Horace, IV, *lawyer*
Burns, Stephen Gilbert *lawyer*
Burt, Jeffrey Amsterdam *lawyer*
Busby, David *lawyer*
Buscemi, Peter *lawyer*
Bush, Karen Lee *lawyer*
Butcher, Karen A. *lawyer*
Butler, Mary K. *prosecutor*
Butler, Michael Francis *lawyer*
Calamaro, Raymond Stuart *lawyer*
Callery, Grant *financial industry regulatory authority general cousel*
Callery, T. Grant *lawyer*
Calvani, Terry *lawyer*
Cameron, Donald B., Jr. *lawyer*
Campbell, Nancy Duff *lawyer*
Campos, Roel C. *lawyer, former commissioner*
Cantor, Herbert I. *lawyer*
Caplin, Mortimer Maxwell *lawyer, educator*
Caproni, Valerie E. *lawyer, federal agency administrator*
Carey, Sarah Collins *lawyer*
Carliner, David *lawyer*
Carlisle, Linda Elizabeth *lawyer*
Carneal, George Upshur *lawyer*
Carney, Robert Thomas *lawyer*
Carpenter, Russell H., Jr. *lawyer*
Carpenter, Sheila Jane *lawyer*
Carr, Lawrence Edward, Jr. *lawyer*
Carter, Barry Edward *law educator*
Carter, William Joseph *lawyer*
Cary, George S. *lawyer*
Casellas, Gilbert F. F. *lawyer*
Casserly, James Lund *lawyer*
Cassidy, Robert Charles, Jr. *lawyer*
Cavalier, Gina M. *lawyer*
Cavanaugh, James Michael *lawyer*
Chabot, Elliot Charles *lawyer*
Chandler, James Phillip III *law educator*
Chang, Sam Hsien-Cheng *lawyer*
Chanin, Michael Henry *lawyer*
Chapman, Paulette Elaine *lawyer*
Charytan, Lynn R. *lawyer*
Chatilovicz, Peter *lawyer*
Chavous, Kevin P. *lawyer*
Chorba, Timothy A. *lawyer, former ambassador*
Choukas-Bradley, James Richard *lawyer*
Christian, Betty Jo *lawyer*
Chused, Richard Harris *law educator*
Ciatto, Frank A. *lawyer*
Cirulnick, Arthur E. *lawyer*
Clagett, Brice McAdoo *lawyer, writer, genealogist*
Clark, LeRoy D. *law educator*
Clayman, Paul F. *lawyer*
Clayton, Carol A. *lawyer*
CLayton, Michael F. *lawyer*
Coan, Carl A.S., Jr. *lawyer*
Coats, Daniel Ray *lawyer, former ambassador, senator*
Cobb, Calvin Hayes, Jr. *lawyer*
Cobb, Ty *lawyer*
Cobbs, Nicholas Hamner *lawyer, judge*
Coffield, Shirley Ann *lawyer, educator*
Coffina, Scott A. *lawyer*
Cohen, Benedict S. *lawyer*
Cohen, David Blair *lawyer*
Cohen, Louis Richard *lawyer*
Cohen, Marc R. *lawyer*
Cohen, Sheldon Stanley *lawyer*
Cohen, Wayne R. *lawyer*
Cohn, Sherman Louis *lawyer, educator*
Colaizzi, Roger A. *lawyer*
Cole, John Pope, Jr. *lawyer*
Cole, Robert Theodore *lawyer*
Coleman, William Thaddeus, Jr. *lawyer, former secretary of transportation*
Colley, Mark Douglas *lawyer*
Collingsworth, Connie Renee *lawyer*
Collins, Daniel Francis *lawyer*
Collins, Wayne Dale *lawyer*
Collinson, Dale Stanley *lawyer*
Colson, Earl Morton *lawyer, educator*
Comstock, Robert Francis *lawyer*
Condrell, William Kenneth *lawyer*
Connelly, Warren E. *lawyer*
Conner, Frank M. (Rusty) III *lawyer*
Conron, Michael William *lawyer*

Cook, Harry Clayton, Jr. *lawyer*
Cook, Michael Harry *lawyer*
Cook, William E., Jr. *lawyer*
Cooke, Edmund *lawyer*
Cooney, John Fontana *lawyer*
Cooper, Alan Samuel *lawyer, educator*
Cooper, Charles Justin *lawyer, former federal agency administrator*
Cooper, J. Michael *lawyer*
Cooper, Richard Melvyn *lawyer*
Cooper, Ronald Stephen *lawyer*
Cooper, Thomas J. *lawyer*
Cope, John R(obert) *lawyer*
Corn-Revere, Robert *lawyer*
Cortese, Alfred William, Jr. *lawyer, consultant*
Corwin, Carolyn F. *lawyer*
Coston, William Dean *lawyer*
Couch, Robert M. *lawyer, federal agency administrator*
Covucci, George E. *lawyer*
Cowan, Eric Ward *lawyer*
Cowan, Joyce A. *lawyer*
Cox, M. Carolyn *lawyer*
Coyne, Patrick Joseph *lawyer*
Craft, Robert Homan, Jr. *lawyer*
Craig, Gregory Bestor *lawyer*
Crawford, Brett A. *lawyer*
Crocker, Thomas Edward *lawyer*
Crosby, William Duncan, Jr. *lawyer*
Cross, Meredith B. *lawyer*
Crowley, Juanita A. *lawyer*
Crown, Michele Fleurette *lawyer*
Cruden, John Charles *lawyer*
Crump, John *lawyer*
Cummings, Frank *lawyer*
Curtin, Peter J. *lawyer*
Cymrot, Mark Alan *lawyer*
Cynamon, David J. *lawyer*
Cys, Richard L. *lawyer*
Daley, Henry J. *lawyer*
Dalley, George Albert *lawyer, consultant*
Damelin, Harold D. *lawyer, former federal agency administrator*
Danas, Andrew Michael *lawyer*
Dane, Stephen Mark *lawyer*
Davidow, Charles E. *lawyer*
Davidson, Daniel Ira *lawyer*
Davidson, Daniel Morton *lawyer*
Davidson, Tom William *lawyer*
Davies, Charles R. *retired lawyer*
Davis, Smith Wormley *lawyer*
Davis, William E. *lawyer*
Davison, Calvin *retired lawyer*
Deal, Jill B. *lawyer*
Dean, Paul Regis *retired law educator*
Debolt, Paul A. *lawyer*
Dees, C. Stanley *lawyer*
Deese, Pamela McCarthy *lawyer*
deKieffer, Donald Eulette *lawyer*
de Leon, Sylvia A. *lawyer*
De Martino, Ralph Victor *lawyer*
Dembling, Paul Gerald *lawyer, former government official*
Denger, Michael Louis *lawyer*
Denison, Mary Boney *lawyer*
DeSchryver, David Alan *lawyer*
Deutsch, Peter R. *former congressman*
Dewey, Elizabeth R. *lawyer*
Dicello, Francis P. *lawyer*
Dienelt, John F. *lawyer*
Diercks, Walter Elmer *lawyer*
diGenova, Joseph E. *lawyer*
DiLenge, Thomas *lawyer*
Dinan, Donald Robert *lawyer*
Diner, Bryan C. *lawyer*
Dinh, Viet D. *law educator*
Disheroon, Fred Russell *lawyer*
Doebbler, Curtis F.J. *lawyer*
Dolan, Michael William *lawyer*
Dole, Bob (Robert Joseph Dole) *lawyer, retired senator*
Dolin, Mitchell F. *lawyer*
Donegan, Charles Edward *lawyer, educator*
Donilon, Thomas E. *lawyer, former federal agency administrator*
Doolittle, Jesse William, Jr. *lawyer*
Dorfman, Marc *lawyer*
Doria, Marilyn L. *lawyer*
Doty, James Robert *lawyer*
Dowd, John Maguire *lawyer*
Downs, Clark Evans *lawyer*
Doyle, A. Patrick *lawyer*
Duff, James C. *lawyer*
Duffy, John Fitzgerald *lawyer, educator*
Dunn, H. Stewart, Jr. *lawyer*
Dunner, Donald Robert *lawyer*
Durney, Michael Cavalier *lawyer*
Dwyer, Maureen Ellen *lawyer*
Dye, Stuart Selley *lawyer*
Eastment, Thomas James *lawyer*
Easton, John Jay, Jr. *lawyer*
Eckland, William S *lawyer*
Edelman, Alan Irwin *lawyer*
Edelman, Peter Benjamin *lawyer, educator*
Edge, Joe D. *lawyer*
Edlavitch, Susan T. *lawyer*
Edson, Charles Louis *lawyer*
Efrós, Ellen Ann *lawyer*
Eggleston, W. Neil *lawyer*
Ehrenhaft, Peter David *lawyer*
Ehrlich, Alan Marshall *lawyer, educator*
Eichen, Jeffrey L. *lawyer*
Eidleman, John C. *lawyer*
Eisenberg, Meyer *lawyer*
Eissenstat, Everett H. *lawyer*
Eizenstat, Stuart Elliot *lawyer, former federal agency administrator*
Elcano, Mary S. *lawyer*
El-Fishawy, Saad Samuel *lawyer*
Ellett, Ted (E. Tazewell Ellett) *lawyer*
Ellicott, John LeMoyne *lawyer*
Elliott, Edwin Donald, Jr. *lawyer, educator, federal agency administrator*
Ellis, Courtenay *lawyer*
Elmer, Brian Christian *lawyer*
Elrod, Eugene Richard *lawyer*
Emden, Craig A. *lawyer*

Engel, John *lawyer*
Epstein, Anthony Charles *lawyer*
Epstein, Gary Marvin *lawyer*
Epstien, Jay Alan *lawyer*
Evans, David C. *lawyer*
Ewing, Ky Pepper, Jr. *lawyer*
Fairbanks, Richard Monroe III *lawyer, educator, retired ambassador*
Fales, Lisa Jose *lawyer*
Faley, R(ichard) Scott *lawyer*
Fanone, Joseph Anthony *lawyer*
Farabow, Ford Franklin, Jr. *lawyer*
Faust, Emanuel, Jr. *lawyer*
Fedders, John Michael *lawyer*
Feder, Samuel L. *lawyer*
Feffer, Gerald Alan *lawyer*
Feinberg, Kenneth Roy *lawyer, educator*
Feinstein, Deborah *lawyer*
Feldman, Clarice Rochelle *lawyer*
Fels, Nicholas Wolff *lawyer*
Fennell, Stephen A. *lawyer*
Ferguson, Lewis Hamilton III *lawyer*
Ferrand, Louis George *lawyer*
Ferrara, Ralph C. *lawyer*
Ferrell, Elizabeth Ann *lawyer*
Ferrell, Michael J. *lawyer*
Ferris, Charles Daniel *lawyer, former government official*
Fiedler, Marc *lawyer, advocate*
Field, Andrea Bear *lawyer*
Finkel, Eugene Jay *lawyer*
Finn, Timothy John *lawyer*
Firestone, Charles Morton *lawyer, educator*
Fishburne, Benjamin Postell III *lawyer*
Fisher, Bart Steven *lawyer, educator, investment banker*
Fishman, Ira *lawyer*
Fitton, Tom (Thomas J. Fitton) *legal foundation administrator*
Fitzgerald, Kevin C. *lawyer*
Fitzpatrick, James Franklin *lawyer*
Flagg, Ronald Simon *lawyer*
Flannery, Ellen Joanne *lawyer*
Fleischaker, Marc L. *lawyer*
Fleischman, Aaron I. *lawyer*
Flowe, Benjamin Hugh, Jr. *lawyer*
Flowe, Carol Connor *lawyer*
Flyer, Michael R. *lawyer*
Ford, Ann K. *lawyer*
Ford, Harold Eugene, Jr. *law educator, former congressman*
Forester, John Gordon, Jr. *lawyer*
Forrest, Herbert Emerson *lawyer*
Fortuno, Victor M. *lawyer*
Foscarinis, Maria *lawyer*
Foster, C(harles) Allen *lawyer*
Foster, Hope S. *lawyer*
Fox, Hamilton Phillips, III, (Phil Fox) *lawyer*
Fox, Thomas C. *lawyer*
Frandsen, Richard A. *lawyer*
Frank, Richard Asher *lawyer, health products executive*
Frank, Robert J. *lawyer*
Frank, Theodore David *lawyer*
Franklin, Jonathan S. *lawyer*
Freed, Joel M. *lawyer*
Freedman, Jay Weil *lawyer*
Fried, Bruce Merlin *lawyer*
Friedrich, Dabney Langhorne *lawyer, commissioner*
Frost, Edmund Bowen *lawyer*
Frost, Martin, III, (Jonas Martin Frost III) *lawyer, former congressman*
Furey, Roger P. *lawyer*
Gage, Larry S. *lawyer*
Gallagher, Michael David *lawyer, former federal agency administrator*
Gallas, Philip S. *lawyer*
Gallo, Kenneth A. *lawyer*
Gardiner, Kent A. *lawyer*
Gardner, George Victor *lawyer*
Garland, Gloria Jean *lawyer*
Garr, Sally D. *lawyer*
Garrett, Theodore Louis *lawyer*
Garrish, Theodore John *lawyer*
Gaskell, Judith Ann *law librarian*
Gaynor, Kevin Allen *lawyer*
Gelb, Joseph Donald *lawyer*
Geller, Kenneth Steven *lawyer*
Geltman, Edward Alan *lawyer*
Genetski, Christian S. *lawyer*
Geniesse, Robert John *lawyer*
Gerber, Melanie K. *lawyer*
Gerson, Stuart Michael *lawyer*
Gesner, Lawrence H. *lawyer*
Gibbs, Lawrence Blair *lawyer*
Gideon, Kenneth Wayne *lawyer*
Gilbert, John Albert, Jr. *lawyer*
Gilfoyle, Nathalie Floyd Preston *lawyer*
Gillan, Kayla J. *lawyer*
Gillon, Peter M. *lawyer*
Gilmore, James Stuart III *lawyer, former governor*
Ginsburg, Martin David *lawyer, educator*
Gittleman, Richard M. *lawyer*
Glancz, Ronald Robert *lawyer*
Glasgow, Norman Milton *lawyer*
Gleklen, Jonathan Ian *lawyer*
Glick, Leslie Alan *lawyer*
Glynn, Edward F., Jr. *lawyer*
Goelzer, Daniel Lee *lawyer*
Goewey, David W. *lawyer*
Gold, Peter Frederick *lawyer*
Goldberg, Fred T., Jr. *lawyer*
Goldberg, Jolande Elisabeth *law librarian*
Goldberg, Seth A. *lawyer*
Goldblatt, Steven Harris *law educator*
Goldman, Steven Mark *lawyer*
Goldsmith, Barry Richard *lawyer, former federal agency administrator*
Goldstein, Frank Robert *lawyer*
Goldstein, Michael B. *lawyer*
Goldstein, Thomas C. *lawyer*
Gollin, Michael A. *lawyer*
Gonzalez, Cecilia H. *lawyer*
Goodman, Alfred Nelson *lawyer*
Gorelick, Jamie Shona *lawyer*
Gorrell, J. Warren, Jr. *lawyer*
Goshorn, Richard Henley *lawyer*
Gostin, Lawrence O. *lawyer, educator*
Gottfried, Keith Evan *lawyer*
Gottlieb, Robert Gene *lawyer*
Grady, Gregory *lawyer, banker*
Graham, Jonathan P. *lawyer*
Graham, Thomas Richard *lawyer*
Grainger, Amanda R. *lawyer*
Grant, Paula DiMeo *lawyer, mediator, nursing educator*
Green, Donald Hugh *lawyer*
Green, Douglas G. *lawyer*
Green, James Francis *lawyer, consultant*
Green, Thomas Charles *lawyer*
Greenberger, I. Michael *lawyer*
Greenberger, Marcia Devins *lawyer*
Grenier, Edward Joseph, Jr. *lawyer*
Gribbin, David James, IV, (D.J. Gribbin) *lawyer*
Griffis, Kirby T. *lawyer*
Griner, G. Christopher *lawyer*
Gross, Kenneth Andrew *lawyer*
Grunberg, Nancy R. *lawyer*
Gulland, Eugene D. *lawyer*
Gutierrez, Jay Matthew *lawyer*
Gutman, Harry Largman *lawyer, educator*
Guttman, Egon *law educator*
Haber, Jonathan H. *lawyer*
Hagner, John D. *lawyer*
Hailey, Gary D. *lawyer*
Haines, Martha Mahan *lawyer*
Haines, Terry L. *lawyer, consultant*
Halbert, Gary L. *lawyer*
Halloran, Michael James *lawyer*
Halprin, Albert *lawyer*
Halvorson, Newman Thorbus, Jr. *lawyer*
Hand, Lloyd N. *lawyer*
Hanlon, Stephen F. *lawyer*
Hanlon, William R. *lawyer*
Hansen, Kenneth *lawyer*
Hanzlik, Rayburn DeMara *lawyer*
Harman, William Boys, Jr. *lawyer*
Harper, Emery Walter *lawyer*
Harrington, Anthony Stephen *lawyer, diplomat, business executive*
Harrington, Clifford M. *lawyer*
Harris, Don Victor, Jr. *lawyer*
Harris, Jeffrey *lawyer*
Harris, Scott Blake *lawyer*
Harrison, Earl David *lawyer, real estate company officer*
Harrison, Marion Edwyn *lawyer*
Harrison, Mark B. *lawyer*
Harrison, Todd A. *lawyer*
Hart, Christopher Alvin *lawyer*
Harvey, Sheila McCafferty *lawyer*
Harwood, John H., II, *lawyer*
Hassett, Joseph Mark *lawyer*
Hastings, Douglas Alfred *lawyer*
Hauptman, Gregory B. *lawyer*
Hauser, Richard Alan *lawyer, foundation administrator*
Hausfeld, Michael D. *lawyer*
Hawkins, David G. *lawyer*
Hayes, David John *lawyer*
Hayes, John C., Jr. *lawyer*
Haynes, R. Michael *lawyer*
Haynes, William James, II, *lawyer*
Haythe, Winston McDonald *lawyer, real estate investor, educator*
Hebert, Jay Howell *lawyer*
Heckman, Jerome Harold *lawyer*
Heenan, Michael Terence *lawyer*
Heffernan, James Vincent *lawyer*
Hefferon, Thomas Michael *lawyer*
Hefter, Laurence Roy *lawyer*
Heideman, Richard D. *lawyer*
Heintz, John Edward *lawyer*
Heller, Jack Isaac *lawyer*
Heller, John Roderick III *lawyer, corporate financial executive*
Heller, Mark A. *lawyer*
Henderson, Douglas Boyd *lawyer*
Henderson, Frances J. *lawyer*
Henke, Michael John *lawyer, educator*
Hennessy, Ellen Anne *lawyer, financial consultant, educator*
Henry, Ronald Kenneth *lawyer*
Hensler, David J. *lawyer*
Herlihy, Scott C. *lawyer*
Heron, Julian Briscoe, Jr. *lawyer*
Herrling, Christopher J. *lawyer*
Herzstein, Robert Erwin *lawyer*
Hewitt, Paul Buck *lawyer*
Heyward, Peter E. *lawyer*
Hiatt, Jonathan Paul *lawyer, labor union administrator*
Hibbert, Robert George *lawyer, food company executive*
Hill, Stephen S. *lawyer*
Hills, Carla Anderson *lawyer, former secretary of housing and urban development*
Hills, Roderick M. *lawyer, former government official*
Hirschhorn, Eric Leonard *lawyer*
Hittner, George J. *lawyer*
Hobbs, Ann S. *lawyer*
Hoffinger, Adam Steven *lawyer*
Hoffman, E. Leslie *lawyer*
Hoffman, Joel Elihu *lawyer*
Hoffman, Kenneth R. *lawyer*
Hoffmann, Martin Richard *lawyer*
Holder, Eric H. *lawyer, former federal agency administrator*
Hollingsworth, Joe Gregory *lawyer*
Hollis, Sheila Slocum *lawyer*
Hollman, K. Hollyn *lawyer*
Horahan, Edward Bernard III *lawyer*
Horn, Charles M. *lawyer*
Horne, Michael Stewart *lawyer*
Hornyak, Joseph P. *lawyer*
Horowitz, Philip Martin *lawyer*
Horton, Philip W. *lawyer*
Horton, Roberta Lazarus *lawyer*
Horvitz, Steven Jay *lawyer*
House, W(illiam) Michael *lawyer*
Houseman, Alan William *lawyer*
Howard, Glen Scott *lawyer, consultant*
Howard, Jeffrey Hjalmar *lawyer*
Howard, Roscoe Conklin, Jr. *lawyer, former prosecutor*
Hoyt, Robert F. *lawyer*
Hranitzky, Rachel Robyn *lawyer*
Hubbard, Richard L. *lawyer*
Huberman, Richard Lee *lawyer*
Hudgins, Willie L., Jr. *lawyer*
Huge, Harry *lawyer*
Hughes, Elizabeth R. (Beth) *lawyer*
Hughes, Marija Matich *law librarian*
Hulkower, Mark J. *lawyer*
Hunnicutt, Charles Alvin *lawyer*
Hutchinson, (W.) Asa *lawyer, former federal agency administrator*
Hutchinson, James S. (Jamie) *lawyer*
Hutt, Peter Barton *lawyer*
Hutter, Paul J. *lawyer*
Huttler, Stephen B. *lawyer*
Hyman, Lester Samuel *lawyer*
Ireland, Oliver *lawyer*
Irving, Thomas L. *lawyer*
Isbell, David Bradford *lawyer, educator*
Iwry, J. Mark *lawyer*
Jackson, John Howard *lawyer, educator*
Jacobsen, Raymond Alfred, Jr. *lawyer*
Jacobson, David Edward *lawyer*
Jacobson, Richard Lee *lawyer, educator*
Jakes, J. Michael *lawyer*
Jamar, Steven Dwight *law educator*
Janney, Christopher G. *lawyer*
Jatras, James George *lawyer*
Jeffress, William Horace, Jr. *lawyer*
Jenkins, Thomas H. *lawyer*
Jennings, Deborah E. *lawyer*
Jensen, Mark A. *lawyer*
Jensen, Robert Neal *lawyer*
Jensen, Thomas C. *lawyer*
Jimenez, Frank R. *lawyer, civilian military employee*
Jochum, James J. *lawyer, former federal agency administrator*
Johnson, David Lee *lawyer*
Johnson, David Raymond *lawyer*
Johnson, Kelly A. *lawyer, former federal agency administrator*
Johnson, Philip McBride *lawyer*
Johnson, Richard A. *lawyer*
Jolly, Bruce O. *lawyer*
Jonas, John Francis *lawyer*
Jones, Aidan Drexel *lawyer*
Jones, George Washington, Jr. *lawyer*
Jones, Kelsey A. *law educator, law administrator*
Jones, Michael D. *lawyer*
Jordan, Robert Elijah III *lawyer*
Joyce, Frederick Mark (Rick) *lawyer*
Kabalkin, Barry E. *lawyer*
Kabel, Robert James *lawyer*
Kafka, Gerald Andrew *lawyer*
Kahan, Jonathan Seth *lawyer*
Kahin, Brian *lawyer, computer industry professional, consultant*
Kahn, Edwin Leonard *retired lawyer*
Kahn, Thomas S. *lawyer*
Kail, Floyd Michael *lawyer*
Kamnik, Joseph P. *lawyer*
Kantor, Mickey (Michael Kantor) *lawyer, former secretary of commerce*
Kaplan, Gilbert B. *lawyer*
Kaplan, Paul A. *lawyer*
Kaplan, Steven *lawyer*
Kaplun, Paul T. *lawyer*
Kapp, Robert Harris *lawyer*
Kappler, Ann M. *lawyer, finance company executive*
Kass, Benny Lee *lawyer*
Kassinger, Theodore William (Ted R. Kassinger) *lawyer, former federal agency administrator*
Katyal, Neal Kumar *law educator*
Katz, Hadrian Ronald *lawyer*
Katz, John W. *lawyer, state official*
Katz, Sherman E. *lawyer*
Katzen, Sally *lawyer, educator*
Kaufman, Billie Jo *law librarian, educator*
Kaufman, Joshua Jacob *lawyer*
Kaufman, Thomas Frederick *lawyer, educator*
Kautter, David John *lawyer*
Keeney, John Christopher *lawyer*
Keeney, John Christopher, Jr. *lawyer*
Keeney, Regina Markey *lawyer*
Keiner, R(obert) Bruce, Jr. *lawyer*
Kellner, Leon B. *lawyer*
Kelly, David M. *lawyer*
Kelly, Thomas J., Jr. *lawyer*
Kelly, William Charles, Jr. *retired lawyer*
Kendall, David E. *lawyer*
Kennard, Mary Elizabeth *lawyer*
Kennard, William Earl *former lawyer*
Kenney, Robert James, Jr. *lawyer*
Kent, M. Elizabeth *lawyer*
Kerr, Orin Samuel *law educator*
Kessler, Judd Lewis *lawyer*
Kies, Kenneth J. *lawyer*
Kiko, Colleen Duffy *lawyer*
Kiko, Philip George *lawyer*
Kilberg, William Jeffrey *lawyer, director*
Killefer, Campbell *lawyer*
Kim, Sukhan *lawyer*
Kinberg, Robert *lawyer*
King, Patricia Ann *law educator*
Kingham, Richard Frank *lawyer*
Kirk, Dennis Dean *lawyer*
Kirsch, Laurence Stephen *lawyer*
Kiser, Chérie R. *lawyer*
Kissel, Peter Charles *lawyer*
Kittrell, Steven Dan *lawyer*
Kittrie, Nicholas *international lawyer, writer*
Klain, Ronald Alan *lawyer*
Klarfeld, Peter James *lawyer*
Klawiter, Donald Casimir *lawyer*
Klee, Ann Renee *lawyer*
Klein, Roger A. *lawyer*
Kline, Thomas R. *lawyer*
Klingelhofer, Stephan E. *lawyer*
Knapp, Rosalind Ann *lawyer*
Knowles, Jeffrey D. *lawyer*
Kohn, Stephen Martin *lawyer*
Kolasky, William Joseph, Jr. *lawyer*
Korth, Fritz-Alan *lawyer*
Kovacs, William Lawrence *lawyer*
Kozusko, Donald D. *lawyer*
Kracov, Daniel A. *lawyer*
Kramer, Andrew Michael *lawyer*
Kramer, Franklin David *lawyer*
Kramer, William David *lawyer*
Krasnow, Erwin Gilbert *lawyer*
Kriesberg, Simeon M. *lawyer*
Kroener, William Frederick III *lawyer*
Kursh, Gail *lawyer*
Kurzweil, Jeffrey *lawyer*
Kushner, Gary Jay *lawyer*
Kutler, Alison L. *lawyer*
Kyhos, Thomas Flynn *lawyer*
Lackey, Michael E., Jr. *lawyer, educator*
Lake, William Truman *lawyer*
Lambert, Jeremiah Daniel *lawyer, educator*
Lambert, Steven Charles *lawyer*
Lamken, Jeffrey A. *lawyer*
Lamm, Carolyn Beth *lawyer*
Landry, Brock R. *lawyer*
Lane, Bruce Stuart *lawyer*
Lane, John Dennis *lawyer*
Langdon, James Calhoun, Jr. *lawyer*
Laporte, Gerald Joseph Sylvestre *lawyer*
Lardent, Esther Ferster *lawyer, consultant*
Larroca, Raymond G. *lawyer*
Larson, Philip C. *lawyer*
Latham, Patricia Horan *lawyer*
Latham, Peter Samuel *lawyer*
Latham, Weldon Hurd *lawyer*
Latimer, Allie B. *retired lawyer*
Latimer, Katharine Ruth *lawyer*
Laughlin, Felix B. *lawyer*
Laughlin, Gregory H. (Greg Laughlin) *law former congressman*
Laughlin, James Harold, Jr. *lawyer*
Lavelle, Joseph P. *lawyer*
Lavine, Henry Wolfe *lawyer*
Lawler, William E. III *lawyer*
Lazarus, Arthur, Jr. *lawyer*
Lazarus, Kenneth Anthony *lawyer*
Lederer, Max Donald, Jr. *lawyer*
Lee, Edward *lawyer*
Lee, Ronald Derek *lawyer*
Leibold, Arthur William, Jr. *lawyer*
Leipold, James G. *lawyer*
Lemov, Michael R. *lawyer*
Leo, Leonard A. *legal association adminis lawyer*
Lever, Jack Q., Jr. *lawyer*
Leveridge, Richard J. *lawyer*
Levin, Edward M. *lawyer*
Levine, Henry David *lawyer*
Levinson, Lawrence Edward *lawyer*
Levinstein, Mark Steven *lawyer, educator*
Levit, Lawrence A. *lawyer*
Levy, Gregg H. *lawyer*
Levy, Mark Irving *lawyer*
Lewis, Daniel Martin *lawyer*
Lewis, David John *lawyer*
Lewis, Eleanor Roberts *lawyer*
Lewis, Glenn C. *lawyer*
Lewis, Guy A. *prosecutor*
Lewis, Mark K. *lawyer*
Lewis, William Henry, Jr. *lawyer*
Lewris, Basil J. *lawyer*
Lichtenstein, Elissa Charlene *legal associat executive*
Liebeskind, Richard *lawyer*
Liebman, Ronald Stanley *lawyer*
Lifschitz, Judah *lawyer*
Lightfoot, William P., Jr. *lawyer*
Lighthizer, Robert E. *lawyer*
Lindsey, Seth Mark *lawyer*
Litt, Robert S. *lawyer*
Livingston, Bob (Robert Linlithgow Living Jr.) *lawyer, retired congressman*
Livingston, Donald Ray *lawyer*
Lobel, Martin *lawyer*
Locklear, Arlinda Faye *lawyer*
Loeb, G. Hamilton *lawyer*
Loepere, Carol Colborn *lawyer*
Loftus, Carroll Michael (Michael Loftus) *la*
Loots, James Mason *lawyer*
Lopatin, Alan G. *lawyer*
Lowe, Randall B. *lawyer*
Lowell, Abbe David *lawyer*
Lowther, Frederick M. *lawyer*
Lupo, Raphael V. *lawyer*
Luque, Nancy *lawyer*
Lurensky, Marcia Adele *lawyer*
Luskin, Robert David *lawyer*
Luxton, Jane Charlotte *lawyer*
Lybecker, Martin Earl *lawyer*
Lyons, Dennis Gerald *lawyer*
Lyons, Francis Xavier *lawyer*
Lyons, Mona *lawyer*
MacBeth, Angus *lawyer*
Macdonald, David Robert *lawyer, pension fu administrator*
MacDougall, Gordon Pier *lawyer*
Machen, Ronald C. *lawyer*
Macleod, John Amend *lawyer*
Madden, Jerome Anthony *lawyer*
Madden, Murdaugh Stuart *lawyer*
Madden, Thomas James *lawyer, educator*
Magielnicki, Robert L. *lawyer*
Magraw, Daniel Barstow, Jr. *lawyer, educato*
Mahar, Ellen Patricia *law librarian*
Mahinka, Stephen Paul *lawyer*
Mahoney, Maureen E. *lawyer*
Malinowski, Matthew J. *lawyer*
Mallory, Charles King III *lawyer*
Manatt, Charles Taylor *lawyer*
Manning, Michael J. *lawyer*
Manson, Joseph Lloyd III *lawyer*
Mapes, William Rodgers, Jr. *lawyer*
Marburg-Goodman, Jeffrey Emil *lawyer*
Marcuss, Stanley Joseph *lawyer*
Margeton, Stephen George *law librarian*
Markoski, Joseph Peter *lawyer*
Marks, Herbert Edward *lawyer*
Marks, Richard Daniel *lawyer*

Marlette, Cynthia *lawyer*
Marshall, Alison Buell *lawyer*
Martin, Billy (William R. Martin) *lawyer*
Martin, David Briton Hadden, Jr. *lawyer*
Martin, Guy *lawyer*
Martin, John Charles *lawyer*
Martin, Keith *lawyer*
Martin, Thomas Stephen *lawyer*
Marvin, Charles Rodney, Jr. *lawyer*
May, Timothy James *lawyer*
Mayer, Neal Michael *lawyer*
Mayers, Daniel Kriegsman *lawyer*
Mayo, George Washington, Jr. *lawyer*
Mays, Janice Ann *lawyer*
Mazo, Mark Elliott *lawyer*
McBride, Michael Flynn *lawyer*
McCaffrey, Judith Elizabeth *lawyer*
McCann, Clifton Everett *lawyer*
McClain, Tim S. *lawyer*
McClure, Frederick Donald *lawyer*
McClure, William Pendleton *lawyer*
McConnell, Nicholas Stillwell *lawyer*
McCoy, Jerry Jack *lawyer*
McCutchen, Tammy Dee *lawyer, former federal agency administrator*
McDaniels, William E. *lawyer*
McDavid, Janet Louise *lawyer*
McDiarmid, Robert Campbell *lawyer*
McDowell, Carter K. *lawyer*
McDowell, Heather L. *lawyer*
McElveen, Junius Carlisle, Jr. *lawyer*
McGovern, Michael *lawyer*
McGrath, Kathryn Bradley *lawyer*
McGuan, Kathleen H. *lawyer*
McGuirl, Marlene Dana Callis *law librarian, educator*
McHugh, James Lenahan, Jr. *lawyer*
McKeever, Joseph Francis III *lawyer*
McKinney, James DeVaine, Jr. *lawyer*
McLean, R. Bruce *lawyer*
McLucas, William Robert *lawyer, former federal agency administrator*
McNamara, Michael T. *lawyer*
McNulty, Paul J. *lawyer, former federal agency administrator*
Mc Phee, Henry Roemer *lawyer*
Mc Pherson, Harry Cummings, Jr. *lawyer*
McReynolds, Mary Armilda *lawyer*
McWilliams, Kenneth L. *lawyer*
ead, Christopher *lawyer*
ead, Kenneth Minor *lawyer, former federal agency administrator*
eans, Thomas Cornell *lawyer*
edina, Rubens *law librarian*
eese, Ed (Edwin Meese III) *law and public policy educator, former United States attorney general*
ehlman, Ken(neth) (Brian) *lawyer, former political organization administrator*
elamed, Arthur Douglas *lawyer*
eloy, Sybil Piskur *retired lawyer*
emmott, Scott A. *lawyer*
enaker, Frank H., Jr. *lawyer*
endelsohn, Martin *lawyer*
endoza, Julie C. *lawyer*
enkel-Meadow, Carrie Joan *law educator*
eshulam, Deborah R. *lawyer*
etz, Craig Huseman *lawyer*
eyer, Dennis Irwin *lawyer*
eyer, Katherine Anne *lawyer*
eyer, Lindsay Beardsworth *lawyer*
ichaels, Gary David *lawyer*
ichaelson, Martin *lawyer*
ickey, Paul F(ogle), Jr. *lawyer*
igliore, Marcus Charles *lawyer*
lch, Thomas H. *lawyer*
les, David Michael *lawyer*
les, John Jeffries *lawyer*
ller, Andrew Pickens *lawyer*
ller, Evan *lawyer*
ller, H. Todd *lawyer*
ller, James Forrest *lawyer*
ller, John T., Jr. *lawyer, educator*
ller, Laura Ariane *lawyer*
ller, Marshall Lee *lawyer*
llian, John C. *lawyer*
lls, Kevin Paul *lawyer*
lstein, Elliott Steven *lawyer, educator, academic administrator*
nardi, Ann Segura *lawyer, musician*
rengoff, Paul E. *lawyer, political blogger*
rkow, Frank J. *lawyer*
rvahabi, Farin *lawyer*
shkin, Barbara Friedman *lawyer*
xter, Christian John *lawyer*
oates, (G.) Paul *lawyer*
oe, Richard Palmer *lawyer*
offitt, William Benjamin *lawyer*
ogel, William Allen *lawyer*
onk, Carl Colburn *legal association and academic administrator, lawyer*
onroe, Carl Dean III *lawyer*
ontedonico, Joseph *lawyer*
ooney, Marilyn *lawyer*
oore, Amy Norwood *lawyer*
oore, Jerry A. III *lawyer*
oorehead, Donald V. *lawyer*
oot, John S. *lawyer*
oran, Anne E. *lawyer*
organ, Daniel Louis *lawyer, educator*
orillo, Juan P. *lawyer*
oring, John Frederick *lawyer*
orse, M. Howard *lawyer*
oses, Alfred Henry *lawyer, writer, diplomat*
ostoff, Allan Samuel *lawyer, consultant*
ckenfuss, Cantwell Faulkner III *lawyer*
ir, J. Dapray *lawyer*
leta, John B. *lawyer*
lloy, Patrick Aloysius *lawyer*
rphy, Betty Southard *lawyer*
rphy, Joseph Albert, Jr. *lawyer*
rry, Harold David, Jr. *lawyer*
venda, Kenneth Kaoma *legal association administrator, consultant*
ers, James R. *lawyer*
ce, Barry John *lawyer*
eve, Clifford Mike *lawyer*
Nagel, Trevor W. *lawyer*
Namrow, Eric S. *lawyer*
Nannes, Michael Edward *lawyer*
Nardi Riddle, Clarine *lawyer, federal official*
Nauheim, Stephen Alan *lawyer*
Navarro, Bruce Charles *lawyer*
Nemeroff, Michael Alan *lawyer*
Ness, Andrew David *lawyer*
Nethercutt, George Rector, Jr. *lawyer, consultant, former congressman*
Newberry, Edward J. *lawyer*
Newell, Mark E. *lawyer*
Newkirk, Thomas Charles *lawyer*
Nickel, Henry V. *lawyer*
Niehuss, John Marvin *lawyer*
Nirenberg, Darryl D. *lawyer*
Nolan, John Edward *lawyer*
Nordhaus, Robert Riggs *lawyer*
Norton, Floyd Ligon, IV, *lawyer*
Norwood, Deborah Anne *law librarian*
Novick, Robert T. *lawyer*
Nuland, Anthony C. J. *lawyer*
Oakley, Robert Louis *law librarian, educator*
Oberdorfer, John L. *lawyer*
O'Connor, Eileen J. *lawyer, former federal agency administrator*
Odle, Robert Charles, Jr. *lawyer*
O'Donnell, Patrick Emmett *lawyer*
Olchyk, Samuel *lawyer*
Olender, Jack Harvey *lawyer*
Oliphant, Charles Frederick III *lawyer*
Olmstead, Cecil Jay *lawyer*
Olson, Pamela Faith *lawyer, former federal agency administrator*
Olson, Theodore Bevry *lawyer, former federal agency administrator*
Oman, Ralph *lawyer*
O'Neil, Thomas Francis III *lawyer*
O'Neill, Brian Dennis *lawyer*
O'Neill, John H., Jr. *lawyer*
O'Neill, William Patrick *lawyer*
Onel, Suzan *lawyer*
Oosterhuis, Paul William *lawyer*
Oppenheimer, Franz Martin *lawyer*
Oshinsky, Jerold *lawyer*
Osnos, David Marvin *lawyer, director*
O'Toole, Francis J. *lawyer*
Outman, William Dell, II, *lawyer*
Overman, Dean Lee *lawyer, investor, writer*
Owen, Roberts Bishop *lawyer, arbitrator*
Owen, Stephen Lee *lawyer*
Oxley, Michael Garver *lawyer, former congressman*
Oyler, Gregory Kenneth *lawyer*
Pagel, Scott B. *law librarian, educator, dean*
Palmer, Christopher E. *lawyer*
Pantaleo, Peter S. *lawyer*
Paoletta, Mark R. A. *lawyer*
Pape, Stuart M. *lawyer*
Paper, Lewis J. *lawyer, educator*
Parker, Rich *lawyer*
Passaic, Joseph G. *lawyer*
Pate, Michael Lynn *lawyer*
Pate, R(obert) Hewitt (III) *lawyer, former federal agency administrator*
Patterson, Donna E. *lawyer*
Patton, Thomas Earl *lawyer*
Paul, John Charles *lawyer*
Paul, William McCann *lawyer*
Pavlick, John J., Jr. *lawyer*
Pearlman, Ronald Alan *lawyer, educator*
Pearson, Rebecca E. *lawyer*
Peck, Robert Stephen *lawyer, educator*
Pedersen, William Francis *lawyer*
Pemberton, Alan A. *lawyer*
Pensabene, Judith K. *lawyer*
Perkins, Nancy Leeds *lawyer*
Perkins, Samuel Thomas *lawyer*
Perlman, Matthew Saul *lawyer*
Perlstein, William James *lawyer*
Perry, Philip J. *lawyer, former federal agency administrator*
Peters, Frederick Whitten *lawyer*
Peterson, Charles Hayes *lawyer*
Petrash, Jeffrey Michael *lawyer*
Petruzzelli, Julie A. *lawyer*
Pfeiffer, Margaret Kolodny *lawyer*
Pfeiffer, Steven Bernard *lawyer*
Philbin, Patrick Francis *lawyer, former federal agency administrator*
Phillips, Carter Glasgow *lawyer*
Phillips, John R. *lawyer*
Picarello, Anthony, Jr. *lawyer*
Pickens, Scott C. *lawyer*
Pierce, Rudolph F. *lawyer*
Pierson, Stuart F. *lawyer*
Piorkowski, Joseph D., Jr. *lawyer, physician, educator, military officer*
Pitts, James T. *lawyer*
Plaine, Daniel J. *lawyer*
Plaine, Lloyd Leva *lawyer*
Platt, Leslie A. *lawyer*
Podberesky, Samuel *lawyer*
Podesta, John David *law educator, former White House chief of staff*
Poe, David Russell *lawyer*
Policy, Vincent Mark *lawyer*
Poneman, Daniel Bruce *lawyer*
Popofsky, Mark S. *lawyer*
Porges, Amelia *lawyer*
Posner, Ethan M. *lawyer*
Postol, Lawrence Philip *lawyer*
Potenza, Joseph Michael *lawyer*
Potter, Caryl A. III *lawyer*
Potts, Stephen Deaderick *lawyer*
Povich, David *lawyer*
Powers, Mary Ellen *lawyer*
Powers, Richard Edward, Jr. *lawyer*
Pozen, Sharis Arnold *lawyer*
Prater, Mark A. *lawyer, accountant*
Preston, Richard McKim *lawyer*
Preston, Stephen W. *lawyer*
Prettyman, Elijah Barrett, Jr. *lawyer*
Prezioso, Giovanni P. *lawyer*
Price, Daniel Martin *lawyer*
Price, Griffith Baley, Jr. *lawyer*
Price, Joseph Hubbard *lawyer*
Pritchard, Therese D. *lawyer*
Proger, Phillip A. *lawyer*
Przypyszny, John R. *lawyer*
Pulley, Lewis C. *lawyer*
Pupkin, Barry A. *lawyer*
Pusey, William Anderson *lawyer*
Quale, John Carter *lawyer*
Quarles, Steven Princeton *lawyer*
Quigley, Michael *lawyer*
Quinn, Thomas H. *lawyer*
Quint, Arnold Harris *lawyer*
Rabecs, Robert Nicholas *lawyer*
Rabekoff, Elise Jane *lawyer*
Rabinovitz, Bruce H. *lawyer*
Racine, Karl A. *lawyer*
Racine, Richard B. *lawyer*
Rahaim, Stephen *lawyer*
Raher, Patrick Michael *lawyer*
Raim, David Matthew *lawyer*
Raimo, Bernard (Bernie) *lawyer*
Ramey, Carl Robert *lawyer*
Ramirez, Ted L. *lawyer*
Rauh, Carl Stephen *lawyer*
Raul, Alan Charles *lawyer*
Razzano, Frank Charles *lawyer*
Reade, Claire Elizabeth *lawyer*
Reback, Joyce Ellen *lawyer*
Reeder, Joe Robert *lawyer, former federal official*
Rees, Grover Joseph III *lawyer, government official, diplomat*
Rehnquist, Janet *lawyer, former federal agency administrator*
Reichertz, Peter Stuart *lawyer*
Reid, Inez Smith *lawyer, educator, judge*
Rein, Bert Walter *lawyer*
Repper, George Robert *lawyer*
Rice, Paul Jackson *lawyer, educator*
Rich, John Townsend *lawyer*
Richards, Femi Soyinka *lawyer*
Richards, Suzanne V. *lawyer*
Richmond, Marilyn Susan *lawyer*
Rickard, Lisa Ann *lawyer*
Rickert, Anthony H. *lawyer*
Rissetto, Harry A. *lawyer*
Rizzo, John Anthony *lawyer*
Roberts, James Harold III *lawyer*
Roberts, Michael G. *lawyer*
Roberts, Michael T. *lawyer, educator*
Roberts, Michele A. *lawyer*
Rochon, Mark *lawyer*
Rockefeller, Edwin Shaffer *lawyer*
Rocque, Vincent Joseph *lawyer*
Rodemeyer, Michael Leonard, Jr. *lawyer*
Rogan, Michael P. *lawyer*
Rogers, William Dill *lawyer*
Rogovin, John A. *lawyer*
Rohner, Ralph John *lawyer, educator, dean*
Romeo, Peter John *lawyer*
Rose, Jonathan Chapman *lawyer*
Rosen, Jeffrey Adam *lawyer*
Rosen, Jeffrey Matthew *law educator, journalist*
Rosenblatt, Peter Ronald *lawyer, former ambassador*
Rosenbloom, David Harry *political science and law educator*
Rosenbloom, H(arry) David *lawyer*
Rosenhauer, James Joseph (Jim Rosenhauer) *lawyer*
Rosenkrantz, Steven Jay *lawyer*
Rosenthal, Douglas Eurico *lawyer*
Rosenthal, Seth A. *lawyer*
Rosenthal, Steven Siegmund *lawyer*
Rosman, Michael E. *lawyer*
Ross, Douglas *lawyer*
Ross, Stanford G. *lawyer, government official*
Ross, Terence P. *lawyer*
Rossides, Eugene Telemachus *lawyer, writer*
Rothenberg, Pamela V. *lawyer*
Rothstein, Paul Frederick *lawyer, educator*
Rouvelas, Emanuel Larry *lawyer*
Rowden, Marcus Aubrey *lawyer, retired government agency administrator*
Rowe, Richard Holmes *lawyer*
Roycroft, Howard Francis *lawyer*
Rubel, Eric A. *lawyer*
Rubenstein, Laurie R. *lawyer*
Rubin, Kenneth Allen *lawyer*
Ruddy, Frank *lawyer, retired ambassador*
Ruemmler, Kathryn H. *lawyer, former prosecutor*
Rule, Charles Frederick (Rick) *lawyer*
Rusch, Jonathan Jay *lawyer*
Russin, Jonathan *lawyer, consultant*
Russo, Roy R. *lawyer*
Ruthenberg, Kirk R. *lawyer*
Rutstein, David W. *lawyer, food products executive*
Ruttenberg, Charles Byron *lawyer*
Ruttinger, George David *lawyer*
Rutzen, Douglas *lawyer, educator*
Rutzick, Mark Charles *lawyer*
Ryan, Edward A. *lawyer, hotel executive*
Ryerson, Paul Sommer *lawyer*
Sacher, Steven Jay *lawyer*
Safir, Peter Oliver *lawyer*
St. Martin, Jo-Marie *lawyer*
Salaman, Alban *lawyer*
Salem, George Richard *lawyer*
Salsbury, Michael H. *lawyer*
Saltzburg, Stephen Allan *law educator, consultant*
Samuelson, Kenneth Lee *lawyer*
Sandman, James Joseph *lawyer*
Santorum, Rick (Richard John) *lawyer, former senator*
Santos, Leonard Ernest *lawyer*
Sartori, Michael A. *lawyer*
Satterthwaite, Janet F. *lawyer*
Saunders, Mary Jane *lawyer*
Sayler, Robert Nelson *lawyer, educator*
Saylor, David J. *lawyer*
Scalia, Eugene *lawyer*
Scanlon, Kerry Alan *lawyer*
Schafrick, Frederick Craig *lawyer*
Schellie, Peter D. *lawyer*
Schiffer, Lois Jane *lawyer*
Schill, Charles F. *lawyer*
Schiller, Jonathan David *lawyer*
Schlick, Austin C. *lawyer*
Schmidt, William Arthur, Jr. *lawyer*
Schneider, Lawrence Alan *lawyer*
Schneider, Matthew Roger *lawyer*
Schneider, Pauline A. *lawyer*
Schneller, Marina Velentgas *lawyer*
Schnitzer, Steven C. *lawyer*
Schor, Laurence *lawyer*
Schropp, James Howard *lawyer*
Schultz, William B. *lawyer*
Schwaab, Richard Lewis *lawyer*
Schwalb, Brian L. *lawyer*
Schwartz, Daniel C. *lawyer*
Schwartz, Victor Elliot *lawyer, educator*
Schwartzman, Andrew Jay *lawyer*
Schwebel, Stephen Myron *arbitrator, mediator, legal advisor*
Schwinger, David *lawyer*
Scott, Thomas Jefferson, Jr. *lawyer, electrical engineer*
Scriven, Wayne Marcus *lawyer*
Scully, Thomas A. *lawyer, former federal agency administrator*
Sega, A. Christopher *lawyer*
Segal, Theodore D. *lawyer*
Segall, Wynn H. *lawyer*
Sessions, William Steele *lawyer, former FBI director*
Shaffer, David James *lawyer*
Shapiro, Howard M. *lawyer, former prosecutor*
Sharma, Tina *lawyer*
Shay, Albert W. *lawyer*
Shelley, Herbert Carl *lawyer*
Shepard, Julian Leigh *lawyer, humanitarian*
Sherer, Samuel Ayers *lawyer, urban planner, consultant*
Sherman, Cary Howard *lawyer*
Sherman, Gerald Howard *lawyer, educator*
Sherman, Jonathan Henry *lawyer*
Sherman, Lawrence Jay *lawyer*
Sherzer, Harvey Gerald *lawyer*
Shrinsky, Jason Lee *lawyer*
Shull, Joe A. *lawyer*
Shulman, Stephen Neal *lawyer*
Siegel, David B. *lawyer*
Sikora, Clifford S. *lawyer*
Silberg, Jay Eliot *lawyer*
Silbert, Earl J. *lawyer*
Silver, Harry R. *lawyer*
Silverman, William A. *lawyer*
Silverstein, Martin J. *lawyer, former ambassador*
Simon, Barry S. *lawyer*
Simon, Gregory *lawyer*
Simon, Kenneth Mark *lawyer*
Simons, Barbara M. *lawyer*
Simons, Lawrence Brook *lawyer*
Simowitz, Lee H. *lawyer*
Simpson, John M. *lawyer*
Sims, Joe *lawyer*
Sinel, Norman Mark *lawyer*
Singer, Daniel Morris *lawyer*
Singer, Richard M. *lawyer*
Singleton, Harry Michael *lawyer*
Sinick, Marshall S. *lawyer*
Skall, Gregg P. *lawyer*
Skancke, Nancy J. *lawyer*
Slater, Rodney E. *lawyer, emergency management executive, former secretary of transportation*
Slater, Valerie A. *lawyer*
Slaughter, Kenneth S. *lawyer*
Sloan, Melanie Togman *lawyer, former prosecutor*
Slocombe, Walter Becker *lawyer, former federal official*
Smith, Brian William *lawyer, former government official*
Smith, Christopher (Kit Smith) *lawyer*
Smith, Daniel Clifford *lawyer*
Smith, Demaurice F. *lawyer*
Smith, Dwight Chichester III *lawyer*
Smith, Herbert G., II, *lawyer*
Smith, Jeffrey Hartman *lawyer*
Smith, Kingston Earl *lawyer*
Smith, Russell Louis *lawyer*
Smith, Tefft Weldon *lawyer*
Smith, Turner Taliaferro, Jr. *lawyer*
Smutny, Abby Cohen *lawyer*
Smyth, Paul Burton *lawyer*
Snyder, Allen Roger *lawyer*
Sohn, Michael N *lawyer*
Sokal, Allen Marcel *lawyer*
Sokler, Bruce Douglas *lawyer*
Sollers, Joseph Sedwick III *lawyer*
Solodky, Howard N. *lawyer*
Solomons, Mark Elliott *lawyer, art dealer, entrepreneur*
Sommers, Mark *lawyer*
Sonde, Theodore Irwin *lawyer*
Sorokowski, Andrew Dennis *lawyer, historian*
Sottile, James *lawyer*
Spaeder, Roger Campbell *lawyer*
Spagnoletti, Robert James *lawyer, former attorney general*
Spears, James M(it) *lawyer*
Spiegel, Daniel Leonard *lawyer*
Spiliotes, Nicholas James *lawyer*
Spivak, Mark R. *lawyer*
Splitt, David Alan *lawyer, writer*
Sprague, Mary Gabrielle *lawyer*
Squire, Daniel Harris *lawyer*
Stack, Robert B. *lawyer*
Starr, Judson Wilmarth *lawyer*
Staym, Randolph John *lawyer*
Steer, John Richard *lawyer*
Stein, Daniel Alan *lawyer*
Steiner, David Miller *lawyer*
Steinhardt, Ralph Gustav III *law educator*
Steinwurtzel, Richard A. *lawyer*
Stern, Elizabeth Espin *lawyer*
Stern, Gerald Mann *lawyer*
Stern, Samuel Alan *lawyer*
Stetson, Catherine E. *lawyer*
Stevens, Herbert Francis *lawyer, educator*
Stevens, Paul Schott *lawyer*
Stewart, David Pentland *lawyer, educator*
Stock, Stuart Chase *lawyer*

Stoll, Richard Giles *lawyer*
Stouck, Jerry *lawyer*
Strand, Margaret N. *lawyer*
Strauss, Stanley Robert *lawyer*
Strenio, Andrew John, Jr. *lawyer*
Stromberg, Clifford Douglas *lawyer*
Stroup, Richard L. *lawyer*
Stuart, Pamela Bruce *lawyer*
Sullivan, Brendan V., Jr. *lawyer*
Sullivan, Dwight H. *military lawyer*
Sullivan, John J. *lawyer*
Sullivan, Mary Anne *lawyer, government agency administrator*
Sullivan, Timothy *lawyer*
Summers, Edwin C. *lawyer, electronics executive*
Sundermeyer, Michael S. *lawyer*
Suneja, Vince H. *lawyer*
Sunshine, Steven C. *lawyer*
Sussman, Monica Hilton *lawyer*
Swankin, David Arnold *lawyer, consumer products company executive*
Swendiman, Alan Robert *lawyer*
Szymanski, Patrick Joseph *lawyer*
Taft, William Howard, IV, *lawyer*
Tallent, Stephen Edison *lawyer*
Tannenwald, Peter *lawyer*
Tannon, Jay Middleton *lawyer*
Taronji, Jaime, Jr. *lawyer*
Tars, Eric *lawyer, consultant*
Taurman, John David *lawyer*
Taylor, Jeffrey A. *prosecutor*
Taylor, Nancy Elizabeth *lawyer*
Taylor, Ralph Arthur, Jr. *lawyer*
Teague, Randal Cornell, Sr. *lawyer*
Temko, Stanley Leonard *lawyer*
Tendler, Paul Marc *lawyer*
Tenenbaum, Jeffrey S. *lawyer*
Terwilliger, George James III *lawyer*
Thaler, Paul Sanders *lawyer, arbitrator, mediator*
Theroux, Eugene *lawyer*
Thomas, Ritchie Tucker *lawyer*
Thomas, Scott E. *lawyer, former commissioner*
Thompson, Tommy (Thomas George) *lawyer, former secretary of health and human services*
Thornburgh, Dick (Richard L.) *lawyer, former United States attorney general*
Thornton, D. McCarty (Mac) *lawyer*
Tiedemann, Charles Welch (Chad) *lawyer*
Tigar, Michael Edward *law educator*
Tillman, Eugene *lawyer*
Todaro, Peter M. *lawyer*
Toensing, Victoria *lawyer*
Tom, Willard Ken *lawyer*
Tomlinson, Margaret Lynch *lawyer*
Tompert, James Emil *lawyer*
Tompkins, Joseph Buford, Jr. *lawyer*
Toner, Michael E. *lawyer, former commissioner*
Torgerson, William T. *lawyer, electric power industry executive*
Townsend, Brian Douglas *paralegal*
Townsend, John Michael *lawyer*
Trager, Michael David *lawyer*
Trilling, Helen Regina *lawyer*
Trinder, Rachel Bandele *lawyer*
Trooboff, Peter Dennis *lawyer*
Troyer, Thomas Alfred *lawyer*
Tsacoumis, Stephanie *lawyer*
Tucker, Marna S. *lawyer*
Tucker, Stefan Franklin *lawyer*
Tuohey, Mark Henry III *lawyer*
Turkus, Albert H. *lawyer*
Turnbull, Lowell D. *lawyer*
Turner, James Hilton, Jr. *lawyer*
Turner, Jim (James W.) *lawyer, former congressman*
Tyner, Lee Reichelderfer *lawyer*
Uehlein, Edward Carl, Jr. *lawyer*
Unger, Laura Simone *lawyer, commissioner*
Unger, Peter Van Buren *lawyer*
Urwitz, Jay P. *lawyer*
Vacketta, Carl Lee *lawyer, educator*
Vakerics, Thomas Vincent *lawyer*
Valentine, Steven Richards *lawyer*
Vanderver, Timothy Arthur, Jr. *lawyer*
Van Horn, Charles E. *lawyer*
van Horne, Jon W. *lawyer*
Van Tine, Kirk Kelso *lawyer, former federal agency administrator*
Vartanian, Thomas P. *lawyer*
Verner, James Melton *lawyer*
Verrill, Charles Owen, Jr. *lawyer*
Verveer, Philip L. *lawyer*
Vickery, Ann Morgan *lawyer*
Victory, Nancy J. *lawyer, former federal agency administrator*
Villa, John Kazar *lawyer*
Villacorta, Ybet *lawyer*
Vince, Clinton Andrew *lawyer*
Vines, Jim (James K.) *lawyer, former prosecutor*
Violante, Joseph Anthony *lawyer*
Vodra, William Wilson *lawyer*
Volner, Ian D. *lawyer*
Voorhees, Theodore, Jr. *lawyer*
Wadlow, R. Clark *lawyer*
Wagner, Martha Jo *lawyer*
Waite, Barbara L. (Pixie) *lawyer*
Wald, Douglas L. *lawyer*
Wald, Robert Lewis *lawyer*
Waldman, Daniel *lawyer*
Waldron, Gerard J. *lawyer*
Walgren, Doug *lawyer, former congressman*
Walker, Betty Stevens *lawyer*
Walker, Mary L. *lawyer*
Wall, Christopher Read *lawyer*
Wallace, Don, Jr. *law educator*
Walpin, Gerald *lawyer*
Walsh, Michael J. *lawyer*
Walter, Sheryl Lynn *lawyer*
Ward, Erica Anne *lawyer, educator*
Ward, Philip J. *lawyer*
Warin, Roger E. *lawyer*
Waters, Jennifer Nash *lawyer*
Watson, Thomas C. *lawyer*
Watters, Keith W. *lawyer*
Waxman, Seth Paul *lawyer*
Weadon, Donald Alford, Jr. *lawyer*
Webber, Richard John *lawyer*
Webster, William Hedgcock *lawyer, former CIA director*
Wegener, Mark Douglas *lawyer*
Weidenfeld, Edward Lee *lawyer*
Weigel, Kenneth George *lawyer*
Weiner, Robert Neil *lawyer*
Weingarten, Reid H. *lawyer*
Weinman, Howard Mark *lawyer*
Weinmann, Eric *retired lawyer*
Weinreich, Gadi *lawyer*
Weinstein, Harris *lawyer*
Weisbrod, Stephen Adam *lawyer*
Weisgall, Jonathan Michael *lawyer*
Weiss, Mark Anschel *lawyer*
Weiss, Stephen J. *lawyer*
Weissman, William R. *lawyer*
Wellen, Robert Howard *lawyer*
Wenner, Charles Roderick *lawyer*
West, Gail Berry *lawyer*
West, Togo Dennis, Jr. *lawyer, former secretary of veterans affairs*
Whalen, Thomas J. *lawyer*
Wharton, Leslie *lawyer*
Wheeler, Andrew R. *lawyer*
White, Melvin *lawyer*
White, Robert I. *lawyer*
White, Sharman Lynell *lawyer*
Whiting, Richard Albert *lawyer*
Whitley, Joseph D(ally) (Joseph Dally Whitley) *lawyer*
Wiacek, Raymond J. *lawyer*
Wieder, Bruce Terrill *lawyer, electrical engineer*
Wilder, Roland Percival, Jr. *lawyer*
Wiley, Richard Emerson *lawyer*
Wilkinson, Beth A. *lawyer, finance company executive*
Williams, Karen Hastie *lawyer*
Williamson, Edwin Dargan *lawyer, former federal official*
Wilson, D. Edward, Jr. *lawyer*
Wilson, Gary Dean *lawyer*
Wilson, Michael Moureau *lawyer, physician*
Wine, L. Mark *lawyer*
Winland, Thomas W. *lawyer*
Winnick, Steven Yale *lawyer*
Winston, Judith Ann *lawyer*
Winter, Douglas E. *lawyer, writer*
Wintrol, John Patrick *lawyer*
Wise, Joan S. *lawyer*
Wiseman, Alan M(itchell) *lawyer*
Wiseman, Thomas G. *lawyer*
Wiss, Marcia A. *lawyer*
Wixon, Henry N. *lawyer*
Wolf, William B., Jr. *lawyer*
Wolff, Elroy Harris *lawyer*
Wolff, Paul Martin *lawyer, sculptor*
Woodall, Samuel Roy, Jr. *lawyer*
Woodworth, Ramsey Lloyd *lawyer*
Work, Charles Robert *lawyer*
Worsley, James Randolph, Jr. *lawyer*
Worthy, K(enneth) Martin *retired lawyer*
Worthy, Patricia Morris *lawyer, educator*
Wrathall, James R. *lawyer*
Wray, Christopher Asher *lawyer, former federal agency administrator*
Wray, Robert *lawyer*
Wyss, John Benedict *lawyer*
Yablon, Jeffery Lee *lawyer*
Yambrusic, Edward Slavko *lawyer, consultant*
Yannucci, Thomas David *lawyer*
Yeutter, Clayton Keith *lawyer, former secretary of agriculture*
Yoches, Edward Robert *lawyer*
Young, Howard J. *lawyer*
Zagaris, Bruce *lawyer*
Zane, Phillip Craig *lawyer*
Zaucha, Jerome J. *lawyer*
Zax, Leonard A. *lawyer*
Zeidman, Philip Fisher *lawyer*
Zentay, John H. *lawyer*
Ziegler, Janice H. *lawyer*
Zimmer, Richard Alan *lawyer, retired congressman*
Zimmerman, Edwin Morton *lawyer*
Zolandz, Michael E., Jr. *lawyer*
Zotter, Bruce C. *lawyer*
Zwick, Kenneth Lowell *lawyer, director*
Zwillinger, Marc J. *lawyer*

FLORIDA

Alachua
Gaines, Weaver Henderson *lawyer*

Altamonte Springs
Chong, Stephen Chu Ling *lawyer*
Diefenbach, Dale Alan *retired law librarian*
Hoogland, Robert Frederics *lawyer*

Anna Maria
Hoffmann, Carl Konrad *lawyer*

Aventura
McKenna, Peter Dennis *lawyer*

Bartow
Cury, Bruce Paul *lawyer, judge, educator*

Bascom
Brooten, Kenneth Edward, Jr. *lawyer, writer, rancher*

Boca Raton
Anise, Nader *lawyer*
Beber, Robert H. *lawyer, diversified financial services company executive*
Buckstein, Mark Aaron *lawyer, educator, mediator*
Cowen, Edward S. *lawyer, consultant*
Fishman, Barry Stuart *lawyer*
Garlick, Michael *lawyer*
Godofsky, Stanley *lawyer*
Golis, Paul Robert *lawyer*
Gracin, Hank *lawyer*
Kartagener, Carol A. *lawyer*
Kassner, Herbert Seymore *lawyer*
Kitzes, William Fredric *lawyer, advocate, researcher*
Koch, Robert Charles *lawyer, community activist*
Marcus, Andrea Candace Sills *lawyer*
Martin, James Russell *lawyer*
Morris, Stuart R. *lawyer*
Pratt, David *lawyer*
Reinstein, Joel *lawyer*
Roselli, Richard Joseph *lawyer*
Silver, Barry Morris *lawyer*
Tescher, Donald R. *lawyer*
Wallach, Steven Ernst *lawyer, pilot*
Willis, John Alexander *lawyer*
Wolf, Jerome L. *lawyer*

Bonita Springs
Dignan, Thomas Gregory, Jr. *lawyer*
Hastings, Vivien N. *lawyer*

Boynton Beach
McNair, Russell Arthur, Jr. *lawyer*

Bradenton
Brenner, Frank *lawyer*
Groseclose, Lynn Hunter *lawyer*
Lopacki, Edward Joseph, Jr. *lawyer*
Padgett, Gail Blanchard *lawyer*
Shapiro, Richard Michael *lawyer*

Brandon
England, Lynne Lipton *lawyer, pathologist*

Brooksville
Cario, Jeffrey Peter *lawyer*

Bushnell
Hagin, T. Richard *lawyer*

Cape Coral
Parrett, Sherman O. *lawyer*
Vamos, Florence M. *lawyer*

Celebration
Schroeder, James White *retired lawyer*

Clearwater
Coleman, Jeffrey Peters *lawyer*
Dougall-Sides, Leslie K. *lawyer*
Falkner, William Carroll *lawyer*
Fine, A(rthur) Kenneth *lawyer*
Johnson, Timothy Augustin, Jr. *lawyer*
McCormack, John Robert *lawyer*
Sandefer, G(eorge) Larry *lawyer*
Tragos, George Euripedes *lawyer*
Vetter, David R. *lawyer*
Weidemeyer, Carleton Lloyd *lawyer*
Zschau, Julius James *lawyer*

Coconut Grove
Arboleya, Carlos Joaquin *lawyer, broker*

Coral Gables
Anthony, Andrew John *lawyer*
Cano, Mario Stephen *lawyer*
Coe, Jack Martin *lawyer, consultant*
Dady, Robert Edward *lawyer*
Friedman, Marvin Ross *lawyer*
Graham, H. Dillon III *lawyer*
Green, Stephanie *lawyer*
Haggard, William Andrew *lawyer*
Hirschhorn, Joel *lawyer*
Hoffman, Carl H. *lawyer*
Moss, Ambler Holmes, Jr. *lawyer, educator, former ambassador*
Murai, Rene Vicente *lawyer*
Sacasas, Rene *lawyer*
Stone, Bruce *lawyer*
Swan, Alan Charles *law educator*
Touby, Kathleen Anita *lawyer*

Coral Springs
Polin, Alan Jay *lawyer*

Dade City
Brennan, Thomas Emmett *lawyer*

Davie
Snyder, William Albert *lawyer*

Daytona Beach
Barker, Robert Osborne (Bob Barker) *mediator, educator*
Harris, Christy Franklin *lawyer*
Neitzke, Eric Karl *lawyer*

Deerfield Beach
Ward, L. Taylor III *lawyer*

Deland
James, Craig T. *former congressman*

Delray Beach
Fannin, David Cecil *lawyer, consumer products company executive*
Larry, R. Heath *lawyer, director*
Schechterman, Lawrence *lawyer, chef, business consultant*

Englewood
Van Leuven, Robert Joseph *lawyer*

Estero
Morgan, Dennis Richard *lawyer*

Eustis
Metz, Larry Edward *lawyer*

Fort Lauderdale
Adams, S.C. (Chase) *lawyer, writer, radio and television commentator, financial consultant*
Arneson, Margaret Susan *lawyer*
Barclay, David A. *lawyer*
Baskies, Jeffrey Alan *lawyer*
Benjamin, James Scott *lawyer*
Bogenschutz, J. David *lawyer*
Bunnell, George Eli *lawyer, director*
Bustamante, Nestor *lawyer*
Cane, Marilyn Blumberg *law educator*
Cole, Jonathan Edward *lawyer*
Coleman, Phyllis *law educator*
Dressler, Robert A. *lawyer*
Dutko, Michael Edward *lawyer*
Ferrando, Jonathan P. *lawyer, automotive executive*
Fleetwood, Clifford Gene ("The Father of Philosophical Art") *lawyer, publishing and recording industry executive, author*
Franz, William Mathew *lawyer*
Gardner, Russell Menese *lawyer*
Goldberg, Alan Joel *lawyer*
Golden, E(dward) Scott *lawyer*
Haliczer, James Solomon *lawyer*
Hargrove, John Russell *lawyer*
Hess, George Franklin, II, *lawyer*
Hirsch, Jeffrey Allan *lawyer*
Hoines, David Alan *lawyer*
Jarvis, Robert Mark *law educator*
Katz, Thomas Owen *lawyer*
Kelly, John Patrick *lawyer*
Kubler, Frank Lawrence *lawyer*
Lyons, Bruce Martin *lawyer*
Meeks, William Herman III *lawyer*
Mintz, Joel Alan *law educator*
Morris, Gerald Michael *lawyer, educator*
Moss, Stephen Bruce *lawyer*
Nyce, John Daniel *lawyer*
O'Brien, Patrick T. *lawyer*
Oltman, John Harold *patent lawyer*
Padula, Stephen Joseph *lawyer*
Polish, Sheldon S. *lawyer*
Richmond, Gail Levin *law educator*
Russell, Terrence Joseph *lawyer*
Sanders, Dale R. *lawyer*
Schneider, Laz Levkoff *lawyer*
Schreiber, Alan Hickman *lawyer*
Sherman, Richard Allen, Sr. *lawyer*
Sherr, Brian J. *lawyer*
Smith, Frank M. *lawyer*
Sullivan, Edward Delano *lawyer, investor*
Turner, Hugh Joseph, Jr. *lawyer*
Udolf, Bruce Lee *lawyer*
Wich, Donald Anthony, Jr. *lawyer*

Fort Myers
Colasurd, Richard Michael *lawyer*
Dalton, Anne *lawyer*
Medvecky, Robert Stephen *lawyer*

Fort Pierce
Conklin, Howard Lawrence *lawyer*
Sneed, Richard Durwood, Jr. *lawyer*

Gainesville
Boyes, Patrice Flinchbaugh *lawyer*
Criser, Marshall M. *lawyer, retired academic administrator*
Hiers, Richard Hyde *lawyer, educator, writer*
Israel, Jerold Harvey *law educator*
Kaimowitz, Gabe Hillel *lawyer*
Kurrus, Thomas William *lawyer*
Maurer, Virginia Gallaher *law educator*
Price, Mary Kathleen *law librarian, educator*
Smith, David Thornton *lawyer, educator*
Van Alstyne, W. Scott, Jr. *lawyer, educator*
Weyrauch, Walter Otto *law educator*

Gulfport
Podgor, Ellen Sue *law educator*

Haines City
Mc Dougall, Dugald Stewart *retired lawyer*

Hallandale
Lublinski, Michael *lawyer*

Hallandale Beach
Engel, Tala *lawyer*

Hobe Sound
Markoe, Frank, Jr. *lawyer, health facility administrator*

Hollywood
Korthals, Candace Durbin *lawyer*
Phillips, Gary Stephen *lawyer*
Rogovin, Lawrence H. *lawyer*

Homestead
Ireland, Patricia *lawyer*

Jacksonville
Ansbacher, Barry Barnett *lawyer*
Appel, Laurence Bruce *lawyer, retail executiv*
Beytagh, Francis X. *law educator*
Boyer, Tyrie Alvis *lawyer*
Braddock, Donald Layton *retired lawyer, accountant, real estate broker, investor*
Bradford, Dana Gibson, II, *lawyer*
Callender, John Francis *lawyer*
Cannon, L. Kinder III *lawyer*
Cavendish, Michael Robert *lawyer*
Christian, Gary Irvin *lawyer*
Cobb, James E. *lawyer*
Coker, Howard Coleman *lawyer*
Commander, Charles Edward *lawyer, real esta consultant*
Coxe, Henry M. III *lawyer*
Farmer, Guy Otto, II, *lawyer*
Fawbush, Andrew Jackson *lawyer*
Fitzsimmons, Ellen Marie *lawyer*
Gabel, George DeSaussure, Jr. *lawyer*
Hill, Debra S. *lawyer*
Ibold, Catherine Buhaly *lawyer, director*
Israel, Kimberly Held *lawyer*
Kelso, Linda Yayoi *lawyer*
Kent, John Bradford *lawyer*
Killea, Michael F. *lawyer*
Lee, Lewis Swift *retired lawyer*
Link, Robert James *lawyer, educator*
Main, James L. *lawyer*
Mantle, Raymond Allan *lawyer*
McBurney, Charles Walker, Jr. *lawyer*
Milton, Joseph Payne *lawyer*
Moseley, James Francis *lawyer*

eal, Michael Scott, Sr. *lawyer*
ips, John Michael *lawyer*
ns, Charles Palmer III *lawyer*
man, James Curtis, Jr. *lawyer*
owski, Peter T. *lawyer*
pard, William J. *lawyer*
el, Edward *lawyer*
ner, Halcyon E. *lawyer*
nas, Archibald Johns III *lawyer*
ver, Dianne Jay *lawyer*
e, Edward Alfred *lawyer*

ksonville Beach
orner, James G. *lawyer*
Villiams, John Lawrence III *lawyer*
narsh, Sara Elizabeth *lawyer*

per
Cormick, John Hoyle *lawyer*

sen Beach
Hale, Michael John *lawyer*

o Beach
pp, George M. *lawyer*
cer, Edward F. *lawyer, utilities executive*

iter
k, David Forrest *lawyer, investment advisor*
phrey, Gerald Robert *lawyer*

y Biscayne
hens, William Theodore *lawyer*

y Largo
tson, James Stewart *lawyer, environmental scientist, educator*

y West
Dougall, Peter *retired lawyer*

ke Mary
er, Elaine Terry *lawyer*

ke Placid
erts, William B. *lawyer*

ke Worth
e, Norman *retired lawyer, accountant*

keland
away, John A., Jr. *lawyer*
per, James Russell *retired law educator*
wlton, Kevin Charles *lawyer*

rgo
vena, John Harry *lawyer*

esburg
stin, Robert Eugene, Jr. *lawyer*
htel, Vincent John *legal administrator*

e Oak
ers, Lee Ira, Jr. *public defender*

ngboat Key
an, Thomas Lynn *lawyer, educator*

ngwood
nandez, H(ermes) Manuel *lawyer*
nasulo, Virginia Merrills *retired lawyer*

tz
ves, Timothy George *lawyer, consultant*

acclenny
wards, Gregory Lawrence *lawyer*

aitland
ley, Michael Keith *lawyer*
lder, Charles David *lawyer*

arco Island
rstetter, Wayne Arthur *law educator*

ary Esther
erf, John George, IV, *lawyer*

edley
Meara, Vicki A. *lawyer*

elbourne
lantyne, Richard Lee *lawyer*
own, Seymour R. *retired lawyer*
cciatore, S. Sammy *lawyer*
vallucci, Eugene S. (Gene Cavallucci) *lawyer*
kon, Richard Dean *lawyer, educator*
ment, Andrew Stanton *lawyer*
chtman, Jerry H. *lawyer*

elbourne Beach
rter, Mikele Stander *lawyer*

iami
osta, Alex (Rene Alexander Acosta) *prosecutor, former federal agency administrator*
varez, Cesar L. *lawyer*
nber, Laurie Kaufman *lawyer*
derson, Terence James *law educator*
gones, Frank R. (Francisco Angones) *lawyer*
sht, Adrienne *lawyer, broadcast executive, bank executive*
ker, Thomas Eugene *law educator*
umberger, Charles Henry *lawyer*
cerra, Robert John *lawyer*
rley, David Richard *lawyer*
rman, Bruce Judson *lawyer*
ack, Roy *lawyer*
oom, Mark David *lawyer*
umberg, Edward Robert *lawyer*
ochin, Robert M. *lawyer*
odsky, Richard Eugene *lawyer*
onis, Stephen Jay *lawyer*
own, Robert Donald *lawyer*
rnett, Henry *lawyer*
rr, Scott Allen *lawyer*
Casey, Daniel Arthur *lawyer*
Chabrow, Penn Benjamin *lawyer*
Chasen, Jerry Simon *lawyer*
Cohen, Jeffrey Michael *lawyer*
Connor, Terence Gregory *lawyer*
Cosgrove, John Francis *lawyer, mayor*
Critchlow, Richard H. *lawyer*
Curtis, Karen Haynes *lawyer*
David, Christopher Mark *lawyer*
Dunn, Richard M. *lawyer*
Eaton, Joel Douglas *lawyer*
England, Arthur Jay, Jr. *lawyer, former state justice*
Epstein, Gary M. *lawyer*
Essen, Richard Joel *lawyer*
Fatovic, Robert Dean *lawyer*
Fernandez, Jorge Luis *lawyer*
Ferrell, Milton Morgan, Jr. *lawyer*
Fishman, Lewis Warren *lawyer, educator*
Fleming, Joseph Z. *lawyer*
Gang, Robert C. *lawyer*
Garrett, Richard G. *lawyer*
Golden, John Dennis *lawyer*
Gong, Edmond Joseph *lawyer*
Gragg, Karl Lawrence *lawyer*
Green, Jonathan H. *lawyer*
Greer, Alan Graham *lawyer*
Gross, Leslie Jay *lawyer, real estate broker, mortgage company executive*
Grossman, Robert Louis *lawyer*
Gutiérrez, Nicolás, Jr. *lawyer*
Hall, Adam Stuart *lawyer*
Hall, Andrew Clifford *lawyer*
Halsey, Douglas Martin *lawyer*
Hartz, Steven Edward Marshall *lawyer, educator*
Helfand, Leonard T. *lawyer*
Hickey, John Heyward (Jack) *lawyer*
Hoffman, Kenneth Cary *lawyer*
Hoffman, Larry J. *lawyer*
Houlihan, Gerald John *lawyer*
Hudson, Robert Franklin, Jr. *lawyer*
Humphrey, Christine M. *lawyer*
Imperato, Joseph John *lawyer, composer*
Jacobson, Bernard *lawyer*
Jhabvala, Farrokh *lawyer*
Johnston, Philip Connelly *lawyer*
Kavoukjian, Michael Edward *lawyer*
Klock, Joseph Peter, Jr. *lawyer*
Korchin, Judith Miriam *lawyer*
Kravitz, Steven J. *lawyer*
Kreitzer, Michael N. *lawyer*
Krieger, Albert J. *lawyer*
Kurzban, Ira Jay *lawyer*
Lampen, Richard Jay *lawyer, investment banker*
Lancaster, Kenneth G. *lawyer*
Landy, Burton Aaron *lawyer*
Leibowitz, Mark Alan *lawyer*
Levine, Robert Jeffrey *lawyer*
Lipcon, Charles Roy *lawyer*
Long, Maxine Master *lawyer*
Louis, Paul Adolph *lawyer*
Martinez-Fraga, Pedro J. *lawyer*
Mehta, Eileen Rose *lawyer*
Mena, Daniel *lawyer, arbitrator*
Menendez Cambo, Patricia *lawyer*
Michaels, Todd Jordan *lawyer*
Miller, Raymond Vincent, Jr. *lawyer*
Milstein, Richard Craig *lawyer*
Murphy, Timothy James *lawyer*
Nostro, Louis *lawyer*
Nuernberg, William Richard *lawyer*
O'Connor, Kathleen Mary *lawyer*
Orlin, Karen J. *lawyer*
Osman, Edith Gabriella *lawyer*
Ovelmen, Richard J. *lawyer*
Papy, Charles C. III *lawyer*
Pastoriza, Julio *lawyer*
Podhurst, Aaron Samuel *lawyer*
Poston, Rebekah Jane *lawyer*
Pratt, John Patrick *lawyer*
Quentel, Albert Drew *lawyer*
Quirantes, Albert M. *lawyer*
Reilly, Kenneth James *lawyer*
Reiter, Luis *lawyer*
Roman, Ediberto *law educator*
Rossi, William Matthew *lawyer*
Rothman, David Bill *lawyer*
Rubin, Steven D. *lawyer*
Rubino, Frank A. *lawyer*
Saldana, Alfonso Manuel *lawyer*
Samole, Myron Michael *lawyer, management consultant*
Scheer, Mark Jeffrey *lawyer*
Schuette, Charles A. *lawyer*
Schulman, Clifford A. *lawyer*
Sears, John Patrick *lawyer*
Shore, H. Allan *lawyer*
Silber, Norman Jules *lawyer*
Simmons, Sherwin Palmer *lawyer*
Sirvén, José E. *lawyer*
Skolnick, S. Harold *lawyer*
Small, Daniel I. *lawyer*
Smith, Richard C. (Dick) *lawyer*
Solomon, Michael Bruce *lawyer*
Stanley, Sherry A. *lawyer*
Stansell, Leland Edwin, Jr. *lawyer, mediator, educator*
Stein, Allan Mark *lawyer*
Steinberg, Marty *lawyer*
Stokes, Paul Mason *lawyer*
Strafer, G. Richard *lawyer*
Sustana, Mark *lawyer, construction executive*
Thornburg, Frederick Fletcher *lawyer, educator*
Traurig, Robert Henry *lawyer*
Upshaw, Anthony N. *lawyer*
Vento, M. Thérèse *lawyer*
Walton, Rodney Earl *lawyer*
Weiner, Lawrence *lawyer*
Weinger, Steven Murray *lawyer*
Weinstein, Alan Edward *lawyer*
Weinstein, Andrew H. *lawyer*
Wing, James David *lawyer*
Wiseheart, Malcolm Boyd, Jr. *lawyer*
Zack, Stephen Neal *lawyer*

Miami Beach
Arbuz, Joseph Robert *lawyer*
McMahon, Joseph Einar *lawyer, consultant*

Miami Gardens
Ersek, Gregory Joseph Mark *lawyer*
Light, Alfred Robert *law educator*

Miami Lakes
Cohen, Ronald J. *lawyer*

Naples
Adams, John Marshall *lawyer*
Anderson, John Thomas *lawyer*
Blumenthal, Ronnie *lawyer*
Bruce, Jackson Martin, Jr. *lawyer*
Budd, David Glenn *lawyer*
Cimino, Richard Dennis *lawyer*
Cox, Joe Bruce *lawyer*
Crehan, Joseph Edward *lawyer*
Doub, William Offutt *lawyer*
Ericson, Roger Delwin *lawyer, forest resource company executive*
Faison, William Franklin, II, *lawyer, retired manufacturing corporation executive*
Goldman, Joel J. *retired lawyer*
Gopman, Jonathan E. *lawyer*
Lowery, William Herbert *lawyer*
McSwiney, Charles Ronald *lawyer*
Norton, Elizabeth Wychgel *retired lawyer*
Parry, Timothy R. *lawyer*
Peck, Bernard Sidney *lawyer*
Petersen, David L. *lawyer*
Rigor, Bradley Glenn *lawyer*
Smith, Numa Lamar, Jr. *lawyer*
Stevens, William Kenneth *lawyer*
Westman, Carl Edward *lawyer*

New Port Richey
Focht, Theodore Harold *lawyer, educator*

Niceville
Havens, Jason Edward *lawyer*

North Fort Myers
Miller, William Charles *lawyer*

North Miami Beach
Zipkin, Sheldon Lee *lawyer, educator*

North Palm Beach
Brophy, Gilbert Thomas *lawyer*

Orlando
Abbott, Charles Warren *retired lawyer*
Ahlers, Glen-Peter, Sr. *law library director, educator, consultant*
Arkin, J. Gordon *lawyer*
Blackwell, Bruce Beuford *lawyer*
Blaher, Neal Jonathan *lawyer*
Boyles, William Archer *lawyer*
Brumby, Andrew M. *lawyer*
Christiansen, Patrick T. *lawyer*
Clem, Alexander Murphree *lawyer*
Conti, Louis Thomas Moore *lawyer*
Doppelt, Ava K. *lawyer*
Eagan, William Leon *lawyer*
Edwards, James Alfred *lawyer*
Fildes, Richard James *lawyer*
Fleming-Brown, Julie A. *attorney, legal consultant*
Frey, Louis, Jr. *lawyer, federal official*
Gerber, Daniel J. *lawyer*
Gilbert, Suzanne E. *lawyer*
Gold, I. Randall *lawyer*
Gray, J. Charles *lawyer, cattle rancher*
Handley, Leon Hunter *lawyer*
Hoctor, James Joseph *lawyer*
Kelaher, James Peirce *lawyer*
Lefkowitz, Ivan Martin *lawyer*
Leonhardt, Frederick Wayne *lawyer*
Mason, J. Cheney *lawyer*
Mock, Frank Mackenzie *lawyer*
Murrell, Robert George *lawyer*
Nadeau, Robert Bertrand, Jr. *lawyer*
Nants, Bruce Arlington *lawyer*
Oneal-Coble, Leslie *lawyer*
Pierce, John Gerald (Jerry) *lawyer*
Ragland, Robert Allen *lawyer*
Rayle, Stephen Lane *criminal justice educator*
Reed, John Alton *lawyer*
Rounsaville, Keith Eugene *lawyer*
Russ, James Matthias *lawyer*
Salzman, Gary Scott *lawyer*
Shanahan, Rebecca M. *lawyer*
Shives, Paula J. *lawyer*
Sims, Roger W. *lawyer*
Skambis, Christopher Charles, Jr. *lawyer*
Spoonhour, James Michael *lawyer*
Stepter, Charles Raymond, Jr. *law librarian*
Stockton, Richard Lee *lawyer*
Weiss, Christopher John *lawyer*
Yates, Leighton Delevan, Jr. *lawyer*

Ormond Beach
Hayes, Larry B. *retired lawyer*
Logan, Sharon Brooks *lawyer*

Osprey
Partoyan, Garo Arakel *lawyer*

Palatka
Baldwin, Allen Adail *retired lawyer, writer*

Palm Beach
Adler, Frederick Richard *lawyer, corporate financial executive*
Alton, Howard Robert, Jr. *lawyer, food company executive, real estate executive*
Canary, Nancy Halliday *lawyer*
Crawford, Sandra Kay *lawyer*
Devins, Robert Sylvester *retired lawyer*
Parker, Ellis Jackson III *lawyer, broadcaster*

Palm Beach Gardens
Auerbach, Paul Ira *lawyer*
Farina, John *lawyer*
Freedman, Warren *lawyer, educator, judge*
Granat, Richard Stuart *lawyer, educator*
Kahn, David Miller *lawyer, educator*
Newman, Stephen Michael *lawyer*
O'Brien, Thomas George III *lawyer*
Tauber, Mark J. *retired lawyer*
Zane, Jeffrey P. *lawyer*

Palm Coast
Duncan, Donald William *lawyer*

Palm Harbor
Rezanka, Thomas W. *lawyer*
Richeson, Hugh Anthony, Jr. *lawyer*
Summers-Powell, Alan *lawyer*

Panama City
Barloga, Scott B. *lawyer*
Patterson, Christopher Nida *lawyer*

Patrick Afb
McAlwee, Martin Frederick *lawyer*

Pensacola
Bookman, Alan B. *lawyer*
Bozeman, Frank Carmack *lawyer*
Geeker, Nicholas Peter *lawyer, judge*
Levin, Fredric Gerson *lawyer*
McKenzie, James Franklin *lawyer*
Soloway, Daniel Mark *lawyer*
Windham, John Franklin *lawyer, educator*

Plant City
Buchman, Kenneth William *lawyer*
Sparkman, Steven Leonard *lawyer*

Pompano Beach
Gude, Nancy Carlson *lawyer*
Shulmister, M(orris) Ross *lawyer*

Ponte Vedra Beach
Davis, Wendell, Jr. *lawyer*

Port Charlotte
Levin, Allen Jay *lawyer*

Port Saint Lucie
Lambert, George Robert *lawyer, realtor*
Whitesell, William Mayberry III *legal association administrator*

Punta Gorda
Bailey, F. Lee (Francis Lee Bailey) *lawyer*

Saint Augustine
Brady, James Joseph *labor arbitrator*
Storey, Robert Davis *retired lawyer*
Yonkman, Fredrick Albers *lawyer, management consultant*

Saint Petersburg
Bairstow, Frances Kanevsky *arbitrator, mediator, educator*
Battaglia, Anthony Sylvester *lawyer*
Biasotti, Robert E. *lawyer*
Escarraz, Enrique III *lawyer*
Georges, Richard Martin *lawyer, educator, poet*
Glass, Roy Leonard *lawyer*
Jacob, Bruce Robert *law educator*
Janney, Oliver James *lawyer*
Lang, Joseph Hagedorn *lawyer*
Mann, Sam Henry, Jr. *retired lawyer*
Matecki, Paul L. *lawyer*
Paver, Robert L. *lawyer*
Ross, Howard Philip *lawyer*
Scott, Kathryn Fenderson *lawyer*
Steele, Alison *lawyer*

Sanford
Capps, James Leigh, II, *lawyer, military officer*
Heindl, Phares Matthews *lawyer*

Sanibel
Rothschild, Donald Phillip *retired lawyer, arbitrator*

Sarasota
Conetta, Tami Foley *lawyer*
Ehrlich, Bernard Herbert *lawyer, trade association administrator*
Fetterman, James Charles *lawyer*
Freeman, Richard Merrell *retired lawyer*
Garland, Richard Roger *lawyer*
Greenfield, Robert Kauffman *retired lawyer*
Heitler, George *lawyer*
Herb, Frank Steven *lawyer*
Hull, J(ames) Richard *retired lawyer*
Kimbrough, Robert Averyt *lawyer*
Knickerbocker, Robert Platt, Jr. *lawyer, consultant*
Phillips, Elvin Willis *lawyer*
Raimi, Burton Louis *lawyer*
Tachna, Ruth C. *retired lawyer*

Sea Ranch Lakes
Gore, George Henry *lawyer*

Sebring
McCollum, James Fountain *lawyer*
Trombley, Michael Jerome *lawyer*

Seminole
McKeown, H. Mary *lawyer, educator*

South Miami
Keedy, Christian David *lawyer*
Leinoff, Andrew Morris *lawyer*

Stuart
Bowdish, James L.S. *lawyer*
Gary, Willie E. *lawyer*
Viener, John D. *lawyer*

Tallahassee
Aurell, John Karl *lawyer*
Baggett, Fred W. *lawyer*
Barnett, Martha Walters *lawyer*

Buck, Thomas Randolph *retired lawyer, diversified financial services company executive*
Carson, Leonard Allen *lawyer*
Curtin, Lawrence N. *lawyer*
Dariotis, Terrence Theodore *lawyer*
Davis, William Howard *lawyer*
DeFoor, J. Allison, II, *lawyer, priest*
Ervin, Robert Marvin *lawyer*
Fonvielle, Charles David *lawyer*
France, Belinda Takach *lawyer, business owner*
Harper, Robert Augustus *lawyer*
Hatchett, Joseph Woodrow *lawyer, former federal judge*
Holcomb, Lyle Donald, Jr. *retired lawyer*
Johnson, Kelly Overstreet *lawyer*
Kerns, David Vincent *lawyer*
Kitchen, E.C. Deeno *lawyer*
Klick, Jonathan *law educator*
Levine, A. Kenneth *lawyer*
Mayhall, Clifford Wesley *lawyer*
Miller, Gregory R. *prosecutor*
Miller, Morris Henry *lawyer*
Minnick, Bruce Alexander *lawyer*
Norton, William Alan *lawyer*
Phipps, Benjamin Kimball, II, *lawyer*
Reid, Sue Titus *law educator*
Richard, Barry *lawyer*
Terry, Anne Curtis *lawyer, writer*
Thiele, Herbert William Albert *lawyer*
Waas, George Lee *lawyer*
Walker, Karen D. *lawyer*
Weems, Lori K. *lawyer*
Zaiser, Kent Ames *lawyer*

Tampa

Albritton, Arthur Dallas *lawyer*
Barbas, Stephen Michael *lawyer*
Barkin, Marvin E. *lawyer*
Barton, Bernard Alan, Jr. *lawyer*
Bedke, Michael A. *lawyer*
Bereday, Thaddeus Matthew Sigmund *lawyer*
Black, Caroline Kapusta *lawyer*
Buesing, Karen Meyer *lawyer*
Campbell, Richard Bruce *lawyer*
Christian, Terry Clifton *lawyer*
Corcoran, Clement Timothy III *lawyer, mediator, retired judge*
Cunningham, Anthony Willard *lawyer*
Davidson, Charles Thomas *lawyer*
Davis, Jim *lawyer, former congressman*
Davis, Richard Earl *lawyer*
Diehr, Beverly Hunt *lawyer*
Doliner, Nathaniel Lee *lawyer*
Ellwanger, Thomas John *lawyer*
Garrett, Howard Leon *lawyer*
Gilbert, Leonard Harold *lawyer*
Gonzalez, Joe Manuel *lawyer*
Grammig, Robert James (Bob Grammig) *lawyer*
Hamilton, William F. *lawyer*
Holliday, Ronald Sturgis *lawyer*
Huneycutt, Alice Ruth *lawyer*
Jones, John Arthur *lawyer*
Kadow, Joseph J. *lawyer*
Kelly, Thomas Paine, Jr. *retired lawyer*
Koch, Karl R. *policy advisor*
Koren, Edward Franz, Jr. *lawyer*
Lane, Robin R. *lawyer*
Lau, Mary Applegate *lawyer, arbitrator, mediator*
Levine, Jack Anton *lawyer*
Martin, Gary Wayne *lawyer*
McAdams, John Pope *lawyer*
McDevitt, Sheila Marie *retired lawyer, energy executive, business consultant*
O'Neill, Albert Clarence, Jr. *lawyer*
Pankau, Barbara Ropes *lawyer*
Pellett, Jon Michael *lawyer*
Preston, Brett Joseph *lawyer*
Roberson, Bruce Heerdt *lawyer*
Robinson, John William, IV, *lawyer*
Rydberg, Marsha Griffin *lawyer*
Sasso, Gary L. *lawyer*
Schwenke, Roger Dean *lawyer*
Smith, William Reece, Jr. *lawyer*
Somers, Clifford Louis *lawyer*
Spofford, George Edson, IV, *lawyer*
Stagg, Clyde Lawrence *lawyer*
Stallings, (Charles) Norman *lawyer*
Taub, Theodore Calvin *lawyer*
Thomas, Gregg Darrow *lawyer*
Thomas, Wayne Lee *lawyer*
Wagner, Frederick William (Bill) *lawyer*
Waller, Edward Martin, Jr. *lawyer*
Watson, Roberta Casper *lawyer*
Whatley, Jacqueline Beltram *lawyer*
Yang, Grace H. *lawyer*
Yerrid, C. Steven *lawyer*
Young, Gwynne A. *lawyer*
Zinober, Peter Wolfson *lawyer*

Venice

Clarke, Edward Owen, Jr. *lawyer*
Miller, Allan John *retired lawyer, oil industry executive*

Vero Beach

Ahrensfeld, Thomas Frederick *retired lawyer*
Case, Douglas Manning *lawyer*
Havens, Charles William III *retired lawyer*
Higgs, John H. *lawyer*
Ryce, Donald Theodore, Jr. *lawyer*

Village Of Golf

Sutter, William Paul *lawyer*

Wellington

Behren, Robert Alan *lawyer, accountant*

West Palm Beach

Ackerman, David P. *lawyer*
Barre, Steven Craig *lawyer*
Beall, Kenneth Sutter, Jr. *lawyer*
Beasley, James W., Jr. *lawyer*
Berner, Thomas Franklyn *lawyer*
Chopin, L. Frank *lawyer*
Chopin, Susan Gardiner *lawyer*
Clark, David William *lawyer, councilman*
Damsel, Charles H., Jr. *lawyer*
Djokic, Walter Henry *lawyer*
Gildan, Phillip Clarke *lawyer*
Henry, Thornton Montagu *lawyer*
Hill, Thomas William, Jr. *lawyer, educator*
Koffler, Warren William *lawyer*
Lamb, Kevin Thomas *lawyer*
Lampert, Michael Allen *lawyer*
Lane, Matthew Jay *lawyer*
Link, Scott J. *lawyer*
Loring, Arthur *lawyer, diversified financial services company executive*
McAfee, William James *lawyer*
Miller, Richard Jackson (Rick Miller) *lawyer*
Montgomery, Robert Morel, Jr. *lawyer*
Moore, George Crawford Jackson *lawyer*
Mrachek, Lorin Louis *lawyer*
Orlovsky, Donald Albert *lawyer*
Raab, Ira Jerry *lawyer, judge*
Schneider, Lisa A. *lawyer*
Spillias, Kenneth George *lawyer*
Strolla, Cory C. *lawyer*
Vilchez, Victoria Anne *lawyer*
Zeller, Ronald John *lawyer*

Windermere

McGuire, Edward David, Jr. *lawyer*

Winter Park

Ackert, T(errence) W(illiam) *lawyer*
Dempsey, Bernard Hayden, Jr. *lawyer*
Hadley, Ralph Vincent III *lawyer*
Heinle, Richard Alan *lawyer*
Helms, Roger D. *lawyer*
Johnson, Kraig Nelson *lawyer, arbitrator, mediator*
Jontz, Jeffry Robert *lawyer*
Kittleson, Henry Marshall *lawyer*
Morgan, Mary Ann *lawyer*
Swann, Richard Rockwell *lawyer, banker*
Troutman, Holmes Russell *lawyer*

GEORGIA

Acworth

Pope, Robert Daniel *lawyer*

Alpharetta

Hatcher, Barbara A. *lawyer*

Athens

Beaird, James Ralph *lawyer, educator, dean*
Carlson, Ronald Lee *law educator*
Cook, J. Vincent *lawyer*
Davis, Claude-Leonard *lawyer, academic administrator*
Ellington, Charles Ronald *lawyer, educator*
Hellerstein, Walter *lawyer*
Houser, Ronald Edward *lawyer, arbitrator, mediator*
Huszagh, Fredrick Wickett *lawyer, information technology executive, educator*
Kurtz, Paul Michael *law educator*
Puckett, Elizabeth Ann *law librarian, educator*
Shipley, David Elliott *lawyer, educator*
Tolley, Edward Donald *lawyer*

Atlanta

Abrams, Harold Eugene *lawyer*
Addison, James W. *lawyer*
Albert, Ross Alan *lawyer*
Aldridge, John *lawyer*
Alexander, Kent B. *lawyer*
Alexander, Miles Jordan *lawyer*
Allen, Pinney L. *lawyer*
Allen, Randall L. *lawyer*
Altman, Robert *lawyer*
Ames, Matthew B. *lawyer*
An, Dorothy *lawyer*
Anderson, Peter Joseph *lawyer*
Asbill, Richard M. *lawyer*
Attridge, Richard Byron *lawyer*
Austin, Jesse Hinnant III *lawyer*
Baker, Thomas William *lawyer*
Barkoff, Rupert Mitchell *lawyer*
Barnett, Preston B. *lawyer, communications executive*
Barr, Robert Laurence, Jr. *lawyer*
Barry, R. Michael *lawyer*
Batson, Richard Neal *lawyer*
Baum, Stanley M. *lawyer*
Beckham, Walter Hull III *lawyer*
Beerman, Joel I. *lawyer, chemical manufacturing company executive*
Bell, Griffin Boyette *lawyer, former United States attorney general*
Bennett, Jay D. *lawyer*
Bergeson, Donna Pottis *lawyer*
Billington, Barry E. *lawyer*
Bird, Wendell Raleigh *lawyer*
Blackburn, William Stanley *lawyer*
Blackford, Barbara L. *lawyer, manufacturing executive*
Blackstock, Jerry B. *lawyer*
Blank, A(ndrew) Russell *lawyer*
Block, Andrew *lawyer*
Bloodworth, Albert William Franklin *lawyer*
Boisseau, Richard Robert *lawyer*
Bonds, John Wilfred, Jr. *lawyer*
Bondurant, Emmet Jopling, II, *lawyer*
Boone, J. William *lawyer*
Booth, Gordon Dean, Jr. *lawyer*
Bowden, Henry Lumpkin, Jr. *lawyer*
Bowling, Daniel S. III *lawyer*
Boynton, Frederick George *lawyer*
Branch, Thomas Broughton III *lawyer*
Bratton, James Henry, Jr. *lawyer*
Brecher, Armin George *lawyer*
Brewster, William Howard *lawyer*
Brown, Janine *lawyer*
Buffenstein, Daryl R. *lawyer*
Butterworth, S. Kendall *lawyer*
Byrne, Granville Bland III *lawyer*
Cadenhead, Alfred Paul *lawyer*
Calhoun, Scott Douglas *lawyer*
Carpenter, David Allan *lawyer*
Carter, Dudley Rochelle *lawyer*
Chandler, Elizabeth B. *lawyer*
Cheatham, Sharif *lawyer*
Chilivis, Nickolas Peter *retired lawyer*
Clarke, Thomas Hal *lawyer*
Cobb, Charles Kenche, Jr. *lawyer, real estate broker*
Cohen, Ezra Harry *lawyer*
Cohen, George Leon *lawyer*
Cohen, Lori G. *lawyer*
Cohen, N. Jerold *lawyer*
Collins, Steven M. *lawyer*
Conboy, Kevin Patrick *lawyer*
Cook, Philip Carter *lawyer*
Croft, Terrence Lee *lawyer, mediator, arbitrator*
Culhane, John Joseph *lawyer, food products executive*
Curtis, J. Vaughan *lawyer*
Cutshaw, Kenneth Andrew *lawyer*
Dalton, John Joseph *lawyer*
David, Todd R. *lawyer*
Davis, Benjamin Alando *lawyer*
Davis, Frank Tradewell, Jr. *lawyer*
Deming, N. Karen *lawyer*
Denny, Richard Alden, Jr. *retired lawyer*
Dobbins, Benjamin Knox *lawyer*
Domby, Arthur H. *lawyer*
Dorris, William E. *lawyer*
Douglas, John Lewis *lawyer*
Doyle, Michael A. *lawyer*
Driver, Walter W., Jr. *lawyer*
Duffie, L. Traywick *lawyer*
Dunlevie, Steven S. *lawyer*
Durrett, James Frazer, Jr. *retired lawyer*
Dyson, James David *lawyer*
Eckl, William Wray *lawyer*
Edwards, Stephen Allen *lawyer*
Egan, Michael Joseph *retired lawyer, state legislator*
Eiselstein, William P. (Billy Eiselstein) *lawyer*
Elgison, Martin J. *lawyer*
Elliott, Mark Lee *lawyer*
Etheridge, Jack Paul *arbitrator, mediator, retired judge*
Fancher, Kristen L. *lawyer*
Farnham, Clayton Henson *lawyer*
Felton, Jule Wimberly, Jr. *lawyer*
Fleming, Julian Denver, Jr. *lawyer*
Forbes, Theodore McCoy, Jr. *arbitrator, mediator, retired lawyer*
Forry, Robert H. *lawyer*
Fortin, Raymond D. *lawyer, bank executive*
Fortuna, Julian Anthony *lawyer, accountant*
Foster, John Witherspoon *lawyer*
Frederick, Paula J. *lawyer*
Gambrell, David Henry *lawyer*
Garrett, E. Reid *lawyer*
Gary, Kenneth J. *lawyer*
Genberg, Ira *lawyer*
Gerakitis, Richard *lawyer*
Girth, Marjorie Louisa *lawyer, educator*
Glaser, Arthur Henry *lawyer, mediator*
Goldstein, Elliott *lawyer, director*
Grady, Kevin E. *lawyer*
Gramlich, Larry E. *lawyer*
Graves, Judson *lawyer*
Greene, Kevin C. *lawyer*
Greene, Mary Katherine *lawyer*
Grice, Richard W. *lawyer*
Groton, James Purnell *lawyer, arbitrator*
Grout, Robert W. *lawyer*
Hackett, Stanley Hailey *lawyer*
Harkey, Robert Shelton *retired lawyer*
Harris, Harold Stephen, Jr. *lawyer*
Harvey, James A. *lawyer*
Hasson, James Keith, Jr. *lawyer, educator*
Hatcher, James A. *lawyer*
Hawks, Barrett Kingsbury *lawyer*
Hay, Peter Heinrich *law educator*
Hays, Richard R. *lawyer*
Heady, Eugene Joseph *lawyer*
Healy, Bridget M. *lawyer*
Heberton, George H. *lawyer*
Heit, Marny *lawyer*
Heller, Dan L. *lawyer*
Herman, John C. *lawyer*
Hester, Francis Bartow, III, (Frank Hester) *lawyer*
Hinchey, John William *lawyer*
Hinkel, Daniel Farris *lawyer, writer, investment company executive*
Hinson, H. Douglas *lawyer*
Hobby, Scott M. *lawyer*
Hoff, Gerhardt Michael *lawyer, insurance company executive*
Hoffman, Michael William *lawyer, accountant*
Holland, George Edison, Jr., (Ed) *lawyer, utilities executive*
Hopkins, John David *lawyer*
Howard, Harry Clay *lawyer*
Howell, Arthur *lawyer*
Hunter, Forrest Walker *lawyer*
Ide, Roy William III *lawyer*
Isaf, Fred Thomas *lawyer*
Izard, John *lawyer*
Janney, Donald Wayne *lawyer*
Jenkins, Albert Felton, Jr. *lawyer*
Johnson, John H. *lawyer*
Johnson, Weyman Thompson, Jr. *lawyer*
Jones, Glower Whitehead *lawyer*
Jordak, John A., Jr. *lawyer*
Katz, Joel Abraham *lawyer*
Kaufman, Mark David *lawyer*
Kaufman, Mark Stuart *lawyer*
Kaywood, Sam K., Jr. *lawyer*
Kelly, Geoffrey J. *lawyer, beverage company executive*
Kelly, James Patrick *lawyer*
Kessler, Richard Paul, Jr. *lawyer*
Khoury, Kenneth F. *lawyer, air transportation executive*
Kilgore, Cada T. III *lawyer*
Killorin, Robert Ware *lawyer*
Kitchens, William H. *lawyer*
Kneisel, Edmund M. *lawyer*
Knowles, Marjorie Fine *law educator, dean*
Kontio, Peter *lawyer*
Kung, Lisa *lawyer*
Lackland, Theodore Howard *lawyer*
Lamberth, James A. *lawyer*
Lamon, Harry Vincent, Jr. *lawyer*
Landau, Michael B. *law educator*
Landon, James Henry *lawyer*
Latham, John L. *lawyer*
Leach, James Glover *lawyer*
Leonard, David Morse *lawyer*
Lester, Charles Turner, Jr. *lawyer*
Lewis, Stephen E. *lawyer*
Linder, Harvey Ronald *lawyer, arbitrator, mediator*
Linkous, William Joseph, Jr. *lawyer*
Lipshutz, Robert Jerome *lawyer, former government official*
Looby, Brian William *lawyer, lobbyist*
Loomis, Kenan Gregg *lawyer*
Loveland, L. Joseph, Jr. *lawyer*
Lowe, Jonathan Wayne *lawyer*
Lower, Robert Cassel *lawyer, educator*
Malone, Adam *lawyer*
Manley, David Bott III *lawyer*
Manning, George Taylor *lawyer*
Marshall, John Treutlen *lawyer, educator*
Marvin, Charles Arthur *law educator*
Mason, Karol V. *lawyer*
Mast, Kent E. *lawyer*
Matschullat, Dale Lewis *lawyer*
McAlpin, Kirk Martin *lawyer*
McClure, Teri Plummer *lawyer, delivery servi executive*
McDonald, Kristen *lawyer*
McGibbon, James R. *lawyer*
McNeill, Thomas Ray *lawyer*
Mercer, John T.W. *lawyer*
Miller, Douglas Linn *lawyer*
Mize, Gerald L., Jr. *lawyer*
Mobley, John Homer, II, *lawyer*
Moeling, Walter Goos, IV, *lawyer*
Morgan, Elizabeth Ann *lawyer*
Mowrey, Robert D. *lawyer*
Mull, Gale W. *lawyer*
Murphy, Kenyon W. *lawyer*
Nahmias, David E. *prosecutor*
Nelson, Allen W. *lawyer, insurance claims management company executive*
Newman, Stuart *lawyer*
Newton, Floyd Childs III *lawyer*
Noe, Elizabeth Hardy *lawyer*
Norman, Albert George, Jr. *lawyer*
Nurkin, Sidney J. *lawyer*
Oakley, Mary Ann Bryant *lawyer*
O'Day, Stephen Edward *lawyer*
Orr, A. Summey III *lawyer*
Owens, Laura Lewis *lawyer*
Palmer, Charles F. *lawyer*
Pelypenko, Elizabeth *lawyer*
Penn, Darren W. *lawyer*
Perry, Timothy Sewell *lawyer*
Persons, (W.) Ray (W. Ray Persons) *lawyer, legal association administrator*
Petrik, Michael Thomas *lawyer*
Pike, Larry Samuel *lawyer*
Pilcher, James Brownie *lawyer*
Pless, Laurance Davidson *lawyer*
Pottle, Steven L. *lawyer*
Price, Elizabeth Anne *lawyer*
Prucino, Diane L. *lawyer*
Quillian, J. Kirk *lawyer*
Quittmeyer, Peter Charles *lawyer*
Raby, Kenneth Alan *lawyer, retired military officer*
Rachel, David P. *lawyer*
Rafuse, Nancy E. *lawyer, director*
Ragland, William McKenzie, Jr. *lawyer, real estate developer*
Rawls, James C. *lawyer*
Reed, Glen Alfred *lawyer*
Reinhardt, Daniel Sargent *lawyer*
Remar, Robert Boyle *lawyer*
Rhodes, Thomas Willard *lawyer*
Riddell, Stephen W. *lawyer*
Riggs, Gregory Lynn *lawyer*
Riordan, Robert P. *lawyer*
Rogers, DeWitt Ralph *lawyer*
Rusche, Mark C. *lawyer*
Ryan, J. Brennan *lawyer*
Sanders, Carl E. *lawyer, former governor*
Sawyer, John C. *lawyer*
Schneider, Ryan A. *lawyer*
Schroder, Jack Spalding, Jr. *lawyer*
Schroeder, Eric Peter *lawyer*
Schulte, Jeffrey Lewis *lawyer*
Shapiro, George Howard *retired lawyer*
Shlanta, Paul R. *lawyer*
Sibley, James Malcolm *retired lawyer*
Silverstein, Leonard A. *lawyer*
Small, Gus H. *lawyer*
Smith, Alexander Wyly, Jr. *lawyer*
Smith, Edward Kendrick *lawyer*
Smith, Frank G. III *lawyer*
Smith, Jeffrey Michael *lawyer*
Smith, Scott C. *lawyer, legal association administrator*
Smith, Sidney Oslin, Jr. *lawyer*
Snyder, James C., Jr. *lawyer, consumer produ company executive*
Spangler, John I. III *lawyer*
Spikes, Jesse J. *lawyer*
Sprinkle, Shannon M. *lawyer*
Stallings, Ronald Denis *lawyer*
Stein, Grant T. *lawyer*
Stephenson, Mason Williams *lawyer*
Stockton, David A. *lawyer*
Strickland, Frank B. *lawyer*
Sweeney, Neal James *lawyer*
Swift, Frank Meador *lawyer*
Tanenbaum, Allan Jay *lawyer*
Taylor, George Kimbrough, Jr. *lawyer*
Tennant, Thomas Michael *lawyer*
Thomas, Lizanne *lawyer*
Thorpe, Jane Fugate *lawyer*
Thrower, Randolph William *lawyer*
Tinsley, Barbara V. *lawyer*
Travis, Robert M. *lawyer*

oerkom, Jack A. *lawyer, consumer ducts company executive*
r, Chilton Davis *lawyer*
Rex R. *lawyer*
tine, Richard J., Jr. *lawyer*
, Nicole Jennings *lawyer*
, W. Terence *lawyer*
, Robert W., Jr. *lawyer*
n, Robert G. *lawyer*
, Benjamin Taylor *lawyer*
ore, Steven P. *lawyer*
ams, David Howard *lawyer*
ams, Gary Randall *lawyer*
ams, Neil, Jr. *retired lawyer*
ams, Robert P., II, *lawyer*
ams, S. Linn *lawyer*
amson, R. Mark *lawyer*
n, Brent Lawrence *lawyer, mediator*
n, James Hargrove, Jr. *lawyer*
ler, Allen Warren *lawyer, educator*
berg, Harris Bryan *lawyer*
row, William N., Jr. *lawyer*
l, L. Lin, Jr. *lawyer*
ht, Frederick Lewis, II, *lawyer*
ht, Peter Meldrim *lawyer*
g, Michael Anthony *lawyer*
s, David M. *lawyer*
y, Sharon Janine *lawyer*

usta
ey, William J. *lawyer*
, Wyckliffe Austin, Jr. *lawyer*
r, Troy *lawyer*

houn
o, Salvatore J. *lawyer*

ege Park
rson, P(ickens) Andrew *lawyer*
es, Arch *lawyer, writer*

umbus
ch, Jason *lawyer*
kley, Jack Thomas *lawyer, retired ngressman*
ith, G. Sanders III *lawyer, finance company ecutive*
, John Anderson *lawyer*
son, Walter Frank, Jr. *lawyer*
lermilk, Joey M. *lawyer, insurance company ecutive*
lamry, Max Reginald *retired lawyer*
, William Marion *lawyer*
ck, James Duvall, Jr. *lawyer*
lasheff, Robert Stephen *lawyer*
ten, Joel Orba, Jr. *lawyer*

atur
Thomas A. *lawyer*
iams, Rita Tucker *lawyer*

glas
es, Dewey *lawyer*
s, Rebecca Littleton *lawyer*

uth
on, Stephen D. *lawyer*
tra, Larry John *lawyer*
n, Donnie Robert, Jr. *lawyer*
es, R. Scott *lawyer*

nwoody
ison, James W. *retired lawyer, air ansportation executive*

nesville
ider, Raymond Francis *lawyer*
vart, Jon Douglas *lawyer*

milton
d, Gary Ellis *lawyer*

per
ger, Edwin *lawyer*

wrenceville
idson, Brook A. *lawyer*

con
e, John Prince *lawyer, academic dministrator*
nford, James Michael *lawyer*
is, Edgar William, Jr. *lawyer*
es, Frank Cater *retired lawyer*
inson, W. Lee *lawyer*
od, Frank Maxwell *prosecutor, lawyer*

adison
Bose, Charles Wilson *lawyer*

rietta
strom, Michael Joseph *lawyer*
tley, Fred Douglas, Sr. *lawyer*
rung, Stephen Andrew *lawyer*
ram, Robert D. *lawyer*
vland, James Ferrell *lawyer*
uin, Jeffrey Dean *lawyer*

oultrie
lum, Rick Daniel *lawyer*

wnan
nklin, Bruce Walter *lawyer*

rcross
lonski, Zygmunt *lawyer*
, Jeff Zhengquan *lawyer*

rry
ger, James Norman *lawyer*

swell
ker, Anita Diane *lawyer*
mingham, Richard Gregory *lawyer*
ckner, William J. *lawyer*
gland, John Melvin *lawyer, clergyman*
mms, Thomas Bowman, Jr. *lawyer*

Nilsen, Arthur Christian *lawyer*
Roland, Raymond William *lawyer, mediator*

Saint Marys
Smith, Charles Courtland, Jr. *lawyer, state legislator*

Saint Simons Island
Edwards, Edith Martha *lawyer*
Taylor, Philip Raymond *lawyer*
Thau, William Albert *lawyer*

Sandy Springs
Owen, Robert Hubert *lawyer, real estate broker*

Savannah
Berry, Jack K. *lawyer*
Booth, Edmund A., Jr. *prosecutor*
Bowman, Catherine McKenzie *lawyer*
Conner, David Michael *lawyer*
Dennison, D. Brian *lawyer*
Dickey, David Herschel *lawyer, accountant*
Forbes, Morton Gerald *lawyer*
McCracken, Eugene Luke *lawyer*
Searcy, William Nelson *lawyer, director*
Stillwell, Walter Brooks III *lawyer*
Thompson, Richard S. *lawyer, former prosecutor*

Sea Island
Revoile, Charles Patrick *lawyer*

Sky Valley
Wilkinson, Albert Mims, Jr. *lawyer*

Smyrna
Seigler, Michael Edward *lawyer, librarian*

Statesboro
Brogdon, W.M. *lawyer*
Edenfield, Gerald M. *lawyer*
Franklin, James Burke *lawyer*
Wilson, LeVon Edward *lawyer, educator*

Tifton
Reinhardt, George Robert *lawyer*

Valdosta
Sinnott, John Patrick *lawyer, educator*

Watkinsville
Wight, Robert Joseph *lawyer*

HAWAII

Honolulu
Adams, Jo-Ann Marie *lawyer*
Akiba, Lorraine Hiroko *lawyer*
Akinaka, Asa Masayoshi *lawyer*
Bloede, Victor Carl *lawyer, consultant, director*
Boas, Frank *retired lawyer*
Callies, David Lee *lawyer, educator*
Case, James Hebard *lawyer*
Char, Vernon Fook Leong *lawyer*
Cowan, Stuart Marshall *lawyer*
Crumpton, Charles Whitmarsh *lawyer*
Dang, Marvin S.C. *lawyer*
Deaver, Phillip Lester *lawyer*
Devens, Paul *retired lawyer*
Dupont, Ralph Paul *lawyer, educator*
Erickson, Jackie Mahi *lawyer, electric power industry executive*
Fong, Peter C. K. *lawyer, judge*
Fried, L. Richard, Jr. *lawyer*
Fukumoto, Leslie Satsuki *lawyer*
Gay, E(mil) Laurence *lawyer*
Gelber, Don Jeffrey *lawyer*
Godbey, Robert Carson *lawyer*
Greeley, Burnham H. *lawyer*
Hart, Brook *lawyer*
Hazlett, Mark A. *lawyer*
Heller, Ronald Ian *lawyer*
Imanaka, Mitchell Akio *lawyer*
Ingersoll, Richard King *lawyer*
Iwai, Wilfred Kiyoshi *lawyer*
Katayama, Robert Nobuichi *retired lawyer*
Kawachika, James Akio *lawyer*
Kobayashi, Bert Takaaki, Jr. *lawyer*
Kupchak, Kenneth Roy *lawyer*
Lacy, John Robert *lawyer*
Lau, Eugene Wing Iu *lawyer*
Lee, Dale W. *lawyer*
Lilly, Michael Alexander *lawyer, writer*
Lombardi, Dennis M. *lawyer*
Longstreth, Robert Mayne *lawyer*
Louie, David Mark *lawyer*
Marks, Michael J. *lawyer*
Mau-Shimizu, Patricia Ann *lawyer*
Miller, Clifford Joel *lawyer*
Miller, Richard Sherwin *law educator*
Miyasaki, Shuichi *lawyer*
Moore, Ernest Carroll III *lawyer*
Morse, Jack Craig *lawyer, arbitrator*
Nakata, Gary Kenji *lawyer*
Nasky, H(arold) Gregory (Harold Gregory Nasky) *lawyer*
Okinaga, Lawrence Shoji *lawyer*
Oldenburg, Ronald Troy *lawyer*
Portnoy, Jeffrey Steven *lawyer*
Potts, Dennis Walker *lawyer*
Reber, David James *lawyer*
Reinke, Stefan Michael *lawyer*
Sakamoto, Ronald Rikio *lawyer, construction executive*
Sato, Glenn Kenji *lawyer*
Sia, Jeffrey H.K. *lawyer*
Starshak, James L. *lawyer*
Sumida, Kevin P.H. *lawyer*
Taylor, Carroll Stribling *lawyer*
Turbin, Richard *lawyer*
Umebayashi, Clyde Satoru *lawyer*
Weight, Michael Anthony *lawyer, former judge*
Woo, Vernon Ying-Tsai *lawyer, real estate developer*

Kailua Kona
Zola, Michael S. *lawyer*

Kapolei
Zabanal, Eduardo Olegario *lawyer*

Keaau
Alton, Lloyde Loren *retired defender*

Kihei
Burns, Richard Gordon *retired lawyer, writer, consultant*

Kula
Maloney, Michael Patrick *lawyer, mediator, arbitrator*
Richardson, Robert Allen *retired lawyer, educator*
Rohlfing, Frederick William *lawyer, retired judge, political scientist*

Paia
Richman, Joel Eser *lawyer, arbitrator, mediator*

IDAHO

Boise
Fawcett, Charles Winton *lawyer*
Geston, Mark Symington *lawyer*
Hoagland, Samuel Albert *lawyer, pharmacist*
Leroy, David Henry *lawyer*
McGown, John, Jr. *lawyer*
Meier, Joseph M. *lawyer*
Meyer, Christopher Hawkins *lawyer*
Minnich, Diane Kay *legal association administrator*
Moss, Thomas E. *prosecutor*
Myers, William Gerry III *lawyer*
Noack, Harold Quincy, Jr. *lawyer*
Park, William Anthony (Tony) *lawyer*
Parry, Richard D. *lawyer, construction executive*
Richardson, Betty H. *lawyer, former prosecutor*
Shurtliff, Marvin Karl *lawyer*
Silak, Cathy R. *lawyer, former state supreme court justice*

Caldwell
Kerrick, David Ellsworth *lawyer*

Hailey
Hogue, Terry Glynn *lawyer*

Lewiston
Tait, John Reid *lawyer*

Moscow
Vincenti, Sheldon Arnold *lawyer, educator*

Pocatello
Nye, W. Marcus W. *lawyer*

Twin Falls
Berry, L. Clyel *lawyer*

ILLINOIS

Abbott Park
Schumacher, Laura J. *lawyer, pharmaceutical executive*

Alton
Struif, L. James *lawyer*

Arlington Heights
Tucker, Bowen Hayward *lawyer*

Aurora
Camic, David Edward *lawyer*
Lowe, Ralph Edward *lawyer*

Barrington
Lee, William Marshall *lawyer*
Wyatt, James Frank, Jr. *lawyer*

Belleville
Bauman, John Duane *lawyer*
Boyle, Richard Edward *lawyer*
Hess, Frederick J. *lawyer*
Miller, Jan Paul *lawyer, former prosecutor*
Ripplinger, George Raymond, Jr. *lawyer*
Urban, Donald Wayne *lawyer*

Bloomington
Spears, Larry Jonell *lawyer*
Sullivan, Laura Patricia *lawyer, insurance company executive*

Bourbonnais
McClure, Thomas Edward *lawyer*

Buffalo Grove
Ward, Michael W. *lawyer*

Burr Ridge
Decker, Richard Knore *lawyer*

Calumet City
Scullion, Annette Murphy *lawyer, educator*

Carbondale
Clemons, John Robert *lawyer*
Duggan, James Edgar *law librarian*
Whittington, Rebecca Ann *lawyer*

Carrollton
Strickland, Hugh Alfred *lawyer*

Carthage
Glidden, John Redmond *lawyer*

Champaign
Boyle, Francis Anthony *law educator*
Johnston, Janis L. *law librarian, educator*
Kindt, John Warren *lawyer, educator*
Krause, Harry Dieter *law educator*
Maggs, Peter Blount *lawyer, educator*
Mamer, Stuart Mies *lawyer*

Miller, Harold Arthur *lawyer*
Nowak, John E. *law educator*
Rawles, Edward Hugh *lawyer*
Stone, Victor J. *retired law educator*

Chicago
Abrams, Lee Norman *lawyer*
Abt, Ralph Edwin *lawyer*
Acker, Ann E. *lawyer*
Acker, Frederick George *lawyer*
Adelman, Stanley Joseph *lawyer*
Adelman, Steven Herbert *lawyer*
Alberts, Barry S. *lawyer*
Allen, Henry Sermones, Jr. *lawyer*
Allen, Ronald Jay *law educator*
Allen, Thomas Draper *lawyer*
Anderson, Cathy C. *lawyer*
Anderson, David Boyd *lawyer, metal products executive*
Anderson, J. Trent *lawyer*
Anderson, Kimball Richard *lawyer*
Angst, Gerald L. *lawyer*
Anthony, Michael Francis *lawyer*
Antonio, Douglas John *lawyer*
Anvaripour, M. A. *lawyer*
Appel, Nina Schick *law educator, dean, academic administrator*
Aronson, Virginia L. *lawyer*
Athas, Gus James *lawyer*
Auerbach, Marshall Jay *lawyer*
Avery, Robert Dean *lawyer*
Axley, Frederick William *lawyer*
Babcock, Sandra L. *lawyer, educator*
Badel, Julie *lawyer*
Baer, John Richard Frederick *lawyer*
Baird, Douglas Gordon *law educator, dean*
Baird, James *lawyer*
Baker, Bruce Jay *lawyer*
Baker, Pamela *lawyer*
Baldwin, Shaun McParland *lawyer*
Bannon, John A. *lawyer*
Banoff, Sheldon Irwin *lawyer*
Barden, Larry A. *lawyer*
Barker, William Thomas *lawyer*
Barnes, James Garland, Jr. *lawyer*
Barr, John Robert *retired lawyer*
Barron, Harold Sheldon *lawyer*
Barron, Howard Robert *lawyer*
Bart, Susan Therese *lawyer*
Bashwiner, Steven Lacelle *lawyer*
Baugher, Peter V. *lawyer*
Baumgartner, William Hans, Jr. *lawyer*
Beck, Philip S. *lawyer*
Becker, Scott *lawyer*
Becker, Theodore Michaelson *lawyer*
Beem, Jack Darrel *retired lawyer*
Behnia, Roya *lawyer*
Bellows, Laurel Gordon *business lawyer*
Bennett, Edward James *lawyer*
Bennett, Robert William *law educator*
Bennington, Thomas Francis *lawyer, county official*
Benson, George W. *lawyer*
Berens, Mark Harry *lawyer*
Berenzweig, Jack Charles *lawyer*
Berger, Robert Michael *lawyer*
Berish, Brad A. *lawyer*
Berkoff, Adam T. *lawyer*
Berkoff, Mark Andrew *lawyer*
Berkowitz, Sean M. *lawyer*
Berman, Debbie L. *lawyer*
Bernick, David M. *lawyer*
Bernstein, Charles Bernard *lawyer*
Bernstein, H. Bruce *lawyer*
Berolzheimer, Karl *lawyer*
Bettman, Suzanne (Sue Bettman) *lawyer*
Biebel, Paul Philip, Jr. *lawyer*
Bitner, John Howard *lawyer*
Bixby, Frank Lyman *retired lawyer*
Bleiweiss, Shell J. *lawyer*
Block, Neal Jay *lawyer*
Blount, Michael Eugene *lawyer*
Blust, Larry D. *lawyer*
Bodenstein, Ira *lawyer*
Boehnen, Daniel A. *lawyer*
Bogaard, Jonathan Harvey *lawyer*
Boho, Dan L. *lawyer*
Boies, Wilber H. *lawyer*
Bosselman, Fred Paul *law educator*
Bostwick, Jarrett T. *lawyer*
Botica, Matthew J. *lawyer*
Bouma, Robert Edwin *lawyer*
Bowe, William J(ohn) *lawyer*
Bowen, Stephen Stewart *lawyer*
Boykin, Richard Renarda *lawyer, former legislative staff member*
Boykins, Michael L. *lawyer*
Bramnik, Robert Paul *lawyer*
Brennan, Joseph *lawyer*
Brennan, Noelle C. *lawyer*
Brice, Roger Thomas *lawyer*
Bridgman, Thomas Francis *retired lawyer*
Brizzolara, Charles Anthony *lawyer, director*
Bro, Ruth Hill *lawyer*
Bromley, Richard *lawyer*
Brown, Alan Crawford *lawyer*
Brown, Donald James, Jr. *lawyer*
Brown, Gregory K. *lawyer*
Brown, Matthew S. *lawyer*
Brown, Steven Spencer *lawyer*
Bryant, David J. *lawyer*
Bulger, Brian Wegg *lawyer*
Burgdoerfer, Jerry *lawyer*
Burke, John Michael *lawyer*
Burke, Michelle C. *lawyer*
Burke, Thomas Joseph, Jr. *lawyer*
Burns, Robert Patrick *law educator*
Busey, Roxane C. *lawyer*
Butler, John William, Jr. *lawyer*
Calabresi, Steven G. *law educator*
Callahan, Michael R. *lawyer*
Campbell, William J., Jr. *lawyer*
Canty, Dawn M. *lawyer*
Carlin, Dennis J. *lawyer*
Carlson, Walter Carl *lawyer*
Carpenter, David William *lawyer*
Carr, Jeffrey W. *lawyer, manufacturing executive*

Carr, Walter Stanley *lawyer*
Carren, Jeffrey P. *lawyer*
Carroll, William Kenneth *lawyer, educator, psychologist, theologian*
Cascino, Anthony Elmo, Jr. *lawyer, insurance company executive*
Ceko, Theresa C. *lawyer, educator*
Chafetz, Barry Richard *lawyer*
Chandler, Kent, Jr. *lawyer*
Cheely, Daniel Joseph *lawyer*
Chemers, Robert Marc *lawyer*
Cherry, Daniel Ronald *lawyer*
Chiles, Stephen Michael *lawyer*
Chizewer, David J. *lawyer*
Chomicz, Thomas E. *lawyer, consultant*
Cicero, Frank, Jr. *lawyer*
Clark, James Allen *lawyer, educator*
Clark, James E. *lawyer*
Clark, Michael A. *lawyer*
Clarke, Peter D. *lawyer*
Clemens, Richard Glenn *lawyer*
Clifford, Robert A. *lawyer*
Clinton, Edward Xavier *lawyer*
Cohen, Frederick H. *lawyer*
Cohen, Melanie Rovner *lawyer*
Cole, Thomas Amor *lawyer*
Collen, John *lawyer, educator*
Comiskey, Michael Peter *lawyer*
Congalton, Christopher William *lawyer*
Conklin, Thomas William *lawyer*
Conlon, William F. *lawyer*
Conway, Michael Maurice *lawyer*
Copeland, Edward Jerome *lawyer*
Corboy, Philip Harnett *lawyer*
Costello, John William *lawyer*
Coulson, William Roy *lawyer*
Crane, Charlotte *law educator*
Crane, Edward M. *lawyer*
Craven, George W. *lawyer*
Crisham, Thomas Michael *lawyer*
Crosby, John Bartlett *lawyer, health science association administrator*
Crossan, John Robert *lawyer*
Crull, Jan, Jr. *lawyer, investment banker, consultant*
Csar, Michael F. *lawyer*
Cummings, Andrea J. *lawyer*
Cunningham, Robert James *lawyer*
Cunningham, Thomas Justin *lawyer*
Currie, David Park *law educator*
Cusack, John Thomas *lawyer*
Custer, Charles Francis *lawyer*
Daley, Michael Joseph *lawyer*
Daley, Susan Jean *lawyer*
Dam, Kenneth W. *law educator, former federal agency administrator*
D'Amato, Anthony *law educator*
Dandridge, LeNor *paralegal*
Daniels, John Draper *lawyer*
Davis, Michael W. *lawyer*
Davis, Muller *lawyer*
Davis, Scott Jonathan *lawyer*
Dechene, James Charles *lawyer*
Dees, Richard Lee *lawyer*
de Hoyos, Debora M. *lawyer*
Deitrick, William Edgar *lawyer*
Delp, Wilbur Charles, Jr. *lawyer*
D'Esposito, Julian C., Jr. *lawyer*
Despres, Leon Mathis *lawyer, former city official*
Devine, Richard A. (Dick DeVine) *lawyer*
DeYoe, David P. *lawyer*
Diamond, Shari Seidman *law and psychology professor*
Ditelberg, Joshua L. *lawyer*
Dixon, Stewart Strawn *lawyer, consultant*
Dockterman, Michael *lawyer*
Domanskis, Alexander Rimas *lawyer*
Dondanville, Patricia *lawyer*
Donlevy, John Dearden *lawyer*
Donner, Ted A. *lawyer*
Douglas, Charles W. *lawyer*
Downs, Robert K. *lawyer*
Doyle, John Robert *lawyer*
Drake, Francis LeBaron *law librarian*
Drizin, Steven A. *lawyer, educator*
Dube, Monte I. *lawyer*
DuCanto, Joseph Nunzio *lawyer, educator*
Duhl, Michael Foster *lawyer*
Duncan, John Patrick Cavanaugh *lawyer*
Dunn, Edwin Rydell *lawyer*
Durchslag, Stephen P. *lawyer*
Durkin, Kevin P. *lawyer*
Dykstra, Paul Hopkins *lawyer*
Eaton, Maja Campbell *lawyer*
Edwards, Charles Lloyd *lawyer*
Edwards, Christine Annette *lawyer*
Egan, Kevin James *lawyer*
Eggert, Russell Raymond *lawyer*
Eimer, Nathan Philip *lawyer*
Ekdahl, Jon Nels *lawyer*
Elden, Gary Michael *lawyer*
Elson, Alex *lawyer, educator, arbitrator*
Elson, John S. *law educator*
Emerson, Carter Whitney *lawyer*
English, John Dwight *lawyer*
Epstein, Bennett L. (Buzz Epstein) *lawyer*
Erens, Jay Allan *lawyer*
Esrick, Jerald Paul *lawyer*
Etherton, Regina Picone *lawyer*
Evanich, Kevin Reese *lawyer*
Even, Francis Alphonse *lawyer*
Fahner, Tyrone C. *lawyer, former state attorney general*
Farber, Bernard John *lawyer*
Fazio, Peter Victor, Jr. *lawyer*
Feagley, Michael Rowe *lawyer*
Feinstein, Fred Ira *lawyer*
Feldman, Mark I. *lawyer*
Fellows, Jerry Kenneth *lawyer*
Felsenthal, Steven Altus *lawyer*
Ferber, Leonard *lawyer*
Ferguson, Stanley Lewis *lawyer*
Ferrini, James Thomas *lawyer*
Field, Robert Edward *lawyer*
Filpi, Robert Alan *lawyer*

Findlay, Donald Cameron *lawyer, former federal agency administrator, insurance company executive*
Finke, Robert Forge *lawyer*
Finnegan, Sheila *lawyer*
Fitzgerald, Patrick J., Jr. *prosecutor*
Fort, Jeffrey C. *lawyer*
Foudree, Bruce William *lawyer*
Fowler, Don Wall *lawyer*
Fox, Paul T. *lawyer*
Franch, Richard Thomas *lawyer*
Franklin, Richard Mark *lawyer*
Frano, Andrew Joseph *lawyer, civil engineer*
Fraumann, Willard George *lawyer*
Frazen, Mitchell Hale *lawyer*
Frederick, Thomas James *lawyer*
Freeborn, Michael D. *lawyer*
Freehling, Daniel Joseph *lawyer, consultant*
Freeman, Lee Allen, Jr. *lawyer*
Freeman, Louis S. *lawyer*
Friedman, Lawrence Milton *lawyer, finance company executive*
Friedman, Roselyn L. *lawyer, mediator*
Furlane, Mark Elliott *lawyer*
Futterman, Ronald L. *lawyer*
Gaggini, John Edmund *lawyer*
Galainena, M. David *lawyer*
Gallopoulos, Gregory Stratis *lawyer*
Gangemi, Columbus Rudolph, Jr. *lawyer, educator*
Garber, Samuel B. *lawyer, retail executive*
Garcia, Paul R. *lawyer*
Gavin, John Neal *lawyer*
Gearen, John Joseph *lawyer*
Gecker, James M. *lawyer*
Geiman, J. Robert *lawyer*
Gelman, Andrew Richard *lawyer*
Genson, Edward Marvin *lawyer*
George, John Martin, Jr. *lawyer*
Georges, Mara Stacy *lawyer*
Geraghty, Diane C. *law educator*
Geraldson, Raymond I., Jr. *lawyer*
Gerber, Dean N. *lawyer*
Geren, Gerald S. *lawyer*
Gern, Ronald L. *lawyer, real estate company executive*
Gertz, Theodore Gerson *lawyer*
Gianos, Diane E. *lawyer*
Gibbons, William John *lawyer*
Gilbert, Howard N(orman) *lawyer, director*
Gilford, Steven Ross *lawyer*
Gilson, Jerome *lawyer, writer*
Ginsburg, Allen J. *lawyer*
Gladden, James Walter, Jr. *lawyer*
Glieberman, Herbert Allen *lawyer*
Godfrey, Richard Cartier *lawyer*
Golan, Stephen Leonard *lawyer*
Goldblatt, Stanford Jay *lawyer*
Good, Steven Loren *real estate consultant*
Gordon, James S. *lawyer, director*
Gordon, Phillip *lawyer*
Goroff, David B. *lawyer*
Grant, Burton Fred *lawyer*
Grant, Robert Nathan *lawyer*
Greenbaum, Lewis *lawyer*
Greenberg, Richard T. *lawyer*
Greenspan, Jeffrey Dov *lawyer*
Grimm, Terry M. *lawyer*
Grossman, Robert Mayer *lawyer*
Guthman, Jack *lawyer*
Gutstein, Solomon *lawyer*
Hahn, Arthur W. *lawyer*
Hahn, Frederic Louis *lawyer*
Halperin, Errol R. *lawyer*
Halprin, Rick (Richard Allan Halprin) *lawyer*
Hamburger, Philip Andrew *law educator*
Hammond, Celeste M. *law educator*
Hannah, Wayne Robertson, Jr. *lawyer*
Hannay, William Mouat III *lawyer*
Hanson, Ronald William *lawyer*
Hardgrove, James Alan *lawyer*
Harmon, Teresa Wilton *lawyer*
Harrington, Carol A. *lawyer*
Harrington, James Timothy *lawyer*
Harris, Daniel Mark *lawyer*
Harris, Phillip H. *lawyer*
Harrison, Holly A. *lawyer*
Harrison, Louis S. *lawyer*
Harrold, Bernard *lawyer*
Hartz, Michael O. *lawyer*
Hatziavramidis, Katie *lawyer*
Hayes, David John Arthur, Jr. *legal association executive*
Hayward, Robert M. *lawyer*
Hayward, Thomas Zander, Jr. *lawyer*
Heatwole, Mark M. *lawyer, director*
Heinz, John Peter *lawyer, educator*
Heinz, William Denby *lawyer*
Heisler, Quentin George, Jr. *lawyer*
Helman, Robert Alan *lawyer*
Helmholz, R(ichard) H(enry) *law educator*
Henderson, Janet E. E. *lawyer*
Henning, Joel Frank *lawyer, writer*
Henry, Brian Thomas *lawyer*
Herald, J. Patrick *lawyer*
Herbert, William Carlisle *lawyer*
Herman, Sidney N. *lawyer*
Hess, Sidney J., Jr. *lawyer*
Hickey, John Thomas, Jr. *lawyer*
Hilliard, David Craig *lawyer, educator*
Hilliker, Donald Beckstett *lawyer*
Hodes, Scott *lawyer*
Hodgman, David Renwick *lawyer*
Hofer, Roy Ellis *lawyer*
Hoff, John Scott *lawyer*
Hoffman, Richard Bruce *lawyer*
Holleb, Marshall Maynard *lawyer*
Homburger, Thomas Charles *lawyer*
Horwich, Allan *lawyer*
Horwood, Richard M. *lawyer*
Hoskins, Richard Jerold *lawyer*
Howe, Jonathan Thomas *lawyer*
Howell, R(obert) Thomas, Jr. *lawyer, former food company executive*
Hummel, Gregory William *lawyer*
Hunt, Craig A. *lawyer, paper company executive*
Hunt, Lawrence Halley, Jr. *lawyer*

Hunter, James Galbraith, Jr. *lawyer*
Hynes, Brian *lawyer, lobbyist*
Isaacson, Samuel B. *lawyer*
Ismail, Tarek *lawyer*
Jachino, Daneen L. *legal administrator*
Jacobs, Caryn Leslie *lawyer, former prosecutor*
Jacobson, Marian Slutz *lawyer*
Jacobson, Richard Joseph *lawyer*
Jacoby, John Patrick *lawyer*
Jaconetty, Thomas Anthony *lawyer*
Jacover, Jerold Alan *lawyer*
Jager, Melvin Francis *lawyer*
Jahns, Jeffrey *lawyer*
Joern, Charles Edward, Jr. *lawyer*
John, Peter C. *lawyer*
Johnson, Elmer William *lawyer*
Johnson, Garrett Bruce *lawyer*
Johnson, Richard Fred *lawyer*
Jones, Sandra Yvonne *lawyer*
Jones, Sharon Elaine *lawyer*
Joseph, Robert Thomas *lawyer*
Joslin, Rodney Dean *lawyer*
Junewicz, James J. *lawyer*
Kallick, David A. *lawyer*
Kaminsky, Richard Alan *lawyer*
Kaplan, Howard Gordon *lawyer*
Kaplan, Jared *lawyer*
Kaplan, Joel H. *lawyer*
Kaplan, Wayne S. *lawyer*
Karlin, Edward J. *lawyer*
Katz, Avrum Sidney *lawyer*
Katz, Stuart Charles *lawyer, musician*
Kaufman, Andrew Michael *lawyer*
Kawitt, Alan *lawyer, arbitrator*
Kellman, Sandra Y. *lawyer*
Kelly, Charles Arthur *lawyer*
Kelly, Peter McClorey, II, *lawyer*
Kenney, Crane H. *lawyer*
Kenney, Frank Deming *lawyer*
Kikoler, Stephen Philip *lawyer*
Kim, Michael Charles *lawyer*
Kimbarovsky, Ross Edward *lawyer*
King, Sharon Louise *lawyer*
Kissel, Richard John *lawyer*
Kistenbroker, David H. *lawyer*
Kitch, Paul R. *lawyer*
Kite, Steven B. *lawyer*
Klenk, James Andrew *lawyer*
Klenk, Timothy Carver *lawyer*
Knight, Christopher Nichols *lawyer*
Knox, James Marshall *lawyer*
Knuepfer, Robert Claude, Jr. *lawyer*
Koch, Steven *lawyer, investment banker, finance company executive*
Kohn, Shalom L. *lawyer*
Kolek, Robert Edward *lawyer*
Kolmin, Kenneth Guy *lawyer*
Kopelman, Ian Stuart *lawyer*
Koppelman, Andrew Martin Mayer *law educator*
Kozak, John W. *lawyer*
Krakowski, Richard John *lawyer, public relations executive*
Kramer, Andrea S. *lawyer*
Kravitt, Jason Harris Paperno *lawyer*
Kriss, Robert J. *lawyer*
Kroll, Barry Lewis *retired lawyer*
Kurtz, David S. *lawyer*
Ladd, Jeffrey Raymond *lawyer*
Laidlaw, Andrew R. *lawyer*
Landes, William M. *law educator*
Landow-Esser, Janine Marise *lawyer*
Laner, Richard Warren *lawyer*
Lang, Gordon, Jr. *retired lawyer*
Lanznar, Howard S. *lawyer*
Latimer, Kenneth Alan *lawyer*
Learner, Howard Alan *lawyer*
LeDuc, John Andre *lawyer*
Lefco, Kathy Nan *law librarian*
Leonard, Laura L. *lawyer*
LeRoy, Spencer III *lawyer*
Levi, John G. *lawyer*
Levin, Charles Edward *lawyer*
Levin, Jack S. *lawyer*
Levin, Lawrence Daniel *lawyer*
Levine, Laurence Harvey *lawyer*
Levinson, Michael R. *lawyer*
Levy, Peter A. *lawyer*
Leyhane, Francis John III *lawyer*
Libowsky, Stephen David *lawyer*
Lien, John Donovan *lawyer*
Liggio, Carl Donald *lawyer*
Linklater, William J. *lawyer*
Lipton, Lois Jean *lawyer*
Listrom, Linda L. *lawyer*
Litwin, Burton Howard *lawyer*
Livingston, Bradford Lee *lawyer*
Lochbihler, Frederick Vincent *lawyer*
Lockwood, Gary Lee *lawyer*
Lona, Marie A. *lawyer*
Looman, James R. *lawyer*
Lorch, Kenneth F. *lawyer*
Lovejoy, Paul Robert *lawyer, air transportation executive*
Lowinger, Frederick Charles *lawyer*
Lubin, Donald G. *lawyer*
Luning, Thomas P. *lawyer*
Luscombe, George A., II, *lawyer*
Lutter, Paul Allen *lawyer*
Lyerla, Bradford Peter *lawyer*
Lynch, John James *lawyer*
Lynch, John Peter *lawyer*
Macaulay, Susan Jane *lawyer, educator*
MacCarthy, Terence Francis *lawyer*
Malinowski, Arthur Anthony *lawyer, arbitrator*
Malkin, Cary Jay *lawyer*
Malovany, Howard *lawyer*
Mancoff, Neal Alan *lawyer*
Mandell, Floyd A. *lawyer*
Mansfield, Karen Lee *lawyer*
Manzo, Edward David *lawyer*
Marick, Michael Miron *lawyer*
Martin, Arthur Mead *lawyer*
Martin, Laura Keidan *lawyer*
Marwedel, Warren John *lawyer*
Mascherin, Terri Lynn *lawyer*
Mason, Richard J. *lawyer*
Matis, Nina B. *lawyer*

Matsakis, Elias N. *lawyer*
McCaleb, Malcolm, Jr. *lawyer*
McChesney, Fred S. *law educator*
McClure, James Julius, Jr. *lawyer, former cit official*
McCormick, Steven D. *lawyer*
McCracken, Thomas James, Jr. *lawyer*
McCrohon, Craig *lawyer*
McCue, Judith W. *lawyer*
McDermott, John H. *lawyer*
McDonald, Sally J. *lawyer*
McDonald, Thomas Alexander *lawyer*
McDonough, John Michael *lawyer*
McGaan, Andrew Raymond *lawyer*
McGowan, Michael Jeremy *lawyer*
McGrath, William Joseph *lawyer*
McKenzie, Robert Ernest *lawyer*
McKinley, Anne C. *lawyer*
McLaren, Richard Wellington, Jr. *lawyer*
McLaughlin, T. Mark *lawyer*
McMasters, James *law librarian, educator*
McMenamin, John Robert *lawyer*
McVisk, William Kilburn *lawyer*
Mehlman, Mark Franklin *lawyer*
Mehrberg, Randall Eric *lawyer, utilities exec*
Melbinger, Michael S. *lawyer*
Melton, David Reuben *lawyer*
Meltzer, Robert Craig *lawyer, educator*
Menchetti, David Barry *lawyer*
Michaels, Richard Edward *lawyer*
Mikva, Abner Joseph *lawyer, retired judge*
Miller, Kenneth W. *lawyer*
Miller, Lee I. *lawyer*
Miller, Paul J. *lawyer*
Miller, Peter C. *lawyer*
Miller, Stephen Ralph *lawyer*
Minichello, Dennis *lawyer*
Minow, Newton Norman *lawyer, educator*
Montgomery, Charles Barry *lawyer*
Montgomery, Julie-April *lawyer*
Montgomery, William Adam *lawyer*
Morency, Paula J. *lawyer*
Morgan, Betsy Stelle *lawyer*
Morgan, Donna Evensen *lawyer*
Morrison, Portia Owen *lawyer*
Morrow, John E. *lawyer*
Morsch, Thomas Harvey *lawyer, educator*
Motherway, Nicholas J. *lawyer*
Mudd, Anne Chestney *mediator, law educator real estate broker*
Mullen, J. Thomas *lawyer*
Mullen, Michael T. *lawyer*
Muller, Kurt Alexander *lawyer*
Murdock, Charles William *lawyer, educator*
Murray, Daniel Charles *trial lawyer*
Murray, Daniel Richard *lawyer*
Murtaugh, Christopher David *lawyer*
Myers, Lonn William *lawyer*
Nahrstadt, Bradley Charles *lawyer*
Napleton, Robert Joseph *lawyer*
Neff, David M. *lawyer*
Neis, James Michael *lawyer*
Neumeier, Matthew Michael *lawyer, educator*
Newlin, Charles Fremont *lawyer*
Newman, Terry E. *lawyer*
Nicklin, Emily *lawyer*
Nicolaides, Mary *retired lawyer*
Niehaus, Mary C. *lawyer*
Niehoff, Philip John *lawyer*
Nijman, Jennifer T. *lawyer, department chairn*
Niro, Cheryl *lawyer*
Nitikman, Franklin W. *lawyer*
Nord, Robert Eamor *lawyer*
Notz, John Kranz, Jr. *arbitrator, mediator, ret lawyer*
Novak, Mark *lawyer*
Novak, Theodore J. *lawyer*
Novotny, David Joseph *lawyer*
Nowacki, James Nelson *lawyer*
Nugent, Lori S. *lawyer*
Nussbaum, Bernard J. *lawyer*
Nyhan, Lawrence J. (Larry) *lawyer*
O'Brien, James Phillip *lawyer*
Oesterle, Eric Adam *lawyer*
Offutt, Gerald M. *lawyer*
O'Hagan, James Joseph *lawyer*
O'Hare, John Mitchell *lawyer*
Olian, Robert Martin *lawyer*
Olson, Steven R. *lawyer*
O'Malley, John Daniel *lawyer, educator, bank*
O'Neil, Michael C. *lawyer*
Ostfeld, Gregory Edward *lawyer*
O'Toole, William George *lawyer*
Pallasch, B. Michael *lawyer, director*
Palmer, John Bernard III *lawyer*
Palmer, Robert Towne *lawyer, bank executive*
Panich, Danuta Bembenista *lawyer*
Parkhurst, Beverly Susler *lawyer, judge*
Parkhurst, Todd Sheldon *lawyer*
Partridge, Mark Van Buren *lawyer, educator, mediator, writer*
Pascal, Roger *lawyer*
Pavalon, Eugene Irving *lawyer*
Pedersen, Peer *lawyer*
Pelton, Russell Meredith *lawyer*
Pengra, R. Rene *lawyer*
Perzek, Philip John *lawyer*
Peter, Bernard George *lawyer*
Peters, Charles H.R. *lawyer*
Petersen, Donald Sondergaard *lawyer*
Peterson, Randall Theodore *law librarian, educator*
Peterson, Ronald Roger *lawyer*
Picker, Randal C. *law educator*
Piekarski, Victor J. *lawyer*
Pirok, Edward Warren *lawyer, consultant*
Pitt, George *lawyer, investment banker*
Pollock, Earl Edward *lawyer*
Pope, Michael Arthur *lawyer*
Portnoy, Elliott Ivan *lawyer*
Power, Joseph Aloysius, Jr. *lawyer*
Preece, Lynn Sylvia *lawyer*
Presser, Stephen Bruce *lawyer, educator*
Price, Paul L. *lawyer*
Prior, Gary L. *lawyer*
Pritikin, David T. *lawyer*
Pritikin, James B. *lawyer*

nnow, Douglas Lee *lawyer*
n, Imad Isa *lawyer*
ni, Duane C. *lawyer*
kin, James Winton *lawyer*
ey, George A., Jr. *lawyer*
paport, Richard J. *lawyer*
in, Richard D. *lawyer*
er, Gerald *lawyer*
al, Lazar Pol *lawyer*
sh, Martin Harris *law educator*
h, Allan J. *lawyer*
in, Ronald Ian *lawyer*
y, Daniel Edward *lawyer*
, Leslie Ann *lawyer, educator*
as, John Alexis *lawyer*
wick, Scott *lawyer*
ick, Donald Ira *lawyer*
n, James Michael *lawyer*
es, Victor H. *lawyer*
d, James Thomas *lawyer*
, Nancy Jean *lawyer*
ard, Howard M. *lawyer*
ards, Brian F. *lawyer*
man, John Marshall *lawyer, food products*
ecutive
man, Lawrence I. *lawyer*
mond, James Glidden *lawyer*
er, Mitchell Sheridan *lawyer*
y, James B., Jr. *lawyer*
y, Robert H. *lawyer*
hie, William Paul *lawyer*
, Stephen Mark *lawyer*
o, Ronald Stephen *lawyer*
bins, Ellen Sue *lawyer*
erts, John Charles *law educator*
ers, John L. III *lawyer*
rman, Douglass Frederick *lawyer*
ney, Matthew A. *lawyer*
er, Harry Joseph *lawyer*
ski, Gary Melchior *lawyer*
en, Barry S. *lawyer*
enblatt, Brian A. *lawyer*
enbloom, Lewis Stanley *lawyer*
enfeld, Howard H. *lawyer*
enfield, Andrew M. *lawyer, educator*
s, Curtis Bennett *lawyer*
siter, Peter L. *lawyer*
in, E(rwin) Leonard *lawyer*
nick, Lewis G. *lawyer*
nick, Paul David *lawyer*
stein, David Stewart *law educator*
dio, Louis Michael, Jr. *lawyer*
ning, Andrew Richard *lawyer*
ert, Donald William *lawyer*
koff, Alan Stuart *lawyer*
in, Paul Theodore *lawyer*
n, Edward F. *lawyer*
n, Thomas F. *lawyer*
l, John J. *lawyer*
off, Robert W. *lawyer*
eter, Alan N. *lawyer*
chez, Vincent A. *lawyer*
dberg, Craig M. *lawyer*
ders, Richard Henry *lawyer*
ay, Anup *lawyer*
nders, George Lawton, Jr. *lawyer*
wyier, Michael Tod *lawyer, director*
affer, Henry M. *lawyer*
affner, Howard Sheldon *lawyer*
arf, Stephanie A. *lawyer*
iller, Donald Charles *lawyer*
ink, James Harvey *lawyer*
midt, John R. *lawyer*
neider, Dan W. *lawyer, consultant*
neider, Robert Jerome *lawyer*
oenfield, Rick Merrill *lawyer*
oonhoven, Ray James *retired lawyer*
opf, William Grant *lawyer*
orer, Joseph U. *lawyer*
oumacher, Bruce Herbert *lawyer*
reck, Robert A., Jr. *lawyer*
river, John T. III *lawyer*
ulz, Keith Donald *corporate lawyer, writer*
upp, Anastasia Luka *retired lawyer*
wab, Stephen Wayne *lawyer*
wartz, Donald Lee *lawyer*
gland, William Lee *lawyer*
man, Russell Bertram *lawyer, department*
hairman
anet, Charles Joseph *lawyer*
anett, Michael *lawyer*
gi, Vincent A.F. *lawyer*
ritella, William David *lawyer*
wer, Alan Michael *lawyer*
kas, Peter Michael *lawyer, educator*
ank, Suzanne Adams *lawyer*
apiro, Keith J. *lawyer*
apiro, Stephen Michael *lawyer*
apiro, Steven A. *lawyer*
apo, Helene S. *law educator*
apo, Marshall Schambelan *lawyer, educator*
effield, Jeffrey T. *lawyer*
eppard, Berton Scott *lawyer*
epro, Richard W. *lawyer*
erman, Ian Matthew *lawyer*
erman, Jeremy P. *lawyer*
elds, Thomas Charles *lawyer*
ndler, Donald A. *lawyer*
aftan, Robert L. *lawyer*
ulruff, Stuart P. *lawyer*
gel, Howard Jerome *lawyer*
berman, Alan Harvey *lawyer*
verman, Gary R. *lawyer*
verman, Ross O. *lawyer*
non, Arthur Joseph *lawyer*
non, George T. *lawyer*
non, John Bern *lawyer*
illing, Raymond Inwood *lawyer*
nner, Mary Jacobs *lawyer*
larsky, Charles B. *lawyer*
wkowski, David John *lawyer*
art, Allen Rich, II, *retired lawyer*
edinghoff, Thomas J. *lawyer*
ith, Arthur B., Jr. *lawyer*
ith, Todd A. *lawyer*
olen, Lee M. *lawyer*
ovy, Jerold Sherwin *lawyer*

Solow, Michael Barry *lawyer*
Solow, Sheldon L. *lawyer*
Spector, David M. *lawyer*
Spellmire, George W. *lawyer*
Spiegler, Joseph Andrew *lawyer*
Spindler, George S. *lawyer, retired oil industry executive*
Sproger, Charles Edmund *retired lawyer*
Stack, Paul Francis *lawyer*
Stallworth, Stanley B. *lawyer*
Stanhaus, James Steven *lawyer*
Starkman, Gary Lee *lawyer*
Stassen, John Henry *lawyer*
Steinberg, Morton M. *lawyer*
Sternstein, Allan J. *lawyer*
Stetler, David J. *lawyer*
Stevens, Linda K. *lawyer*
Stevens, Stanley M. *lawyer*
Stevenson, Adlai Ewing III *lawyer, retired senator*
Stick, Michael Alan *lawyer*
Stiegel, Michael Allen *lawyer*
Stillman, Nina Gidden *lawyer*
Stoll, John Robert *lawyer, educator*
Stone, Geoffrey Richard *lawyer, educator*
Stone, Susan A. *lawyer*
Strohm, Bruce C. *lawyer, real estate company executive*
Such, Domingo P. III *lawyer*
Sullivan, Barry *lawyer*
Sullivan, Marcia Waite *lawyer*
Sullivan, Thomas Patrick *lawyer*
Swibel, Howard Jay *lawyer*
Swibel, Steven Warren *lawyer*
Swiger, Elinor Porter *lawyer*
Tabin, Julius *lawyer, physicist*
Tetzlaff, Theodore R. *lawyer*
Theobald, Edward Robert *lawyer*
Thomas, Dale E. *lawyer*
Thomas, Frederick Bradley *lawyer*
Thomas, Rhonda Churchill *lawyer*
Thomas, Stephen Paul *lawyer*
Thompson, James Robert, Jr. *lawyer, former governor*
Thompson, Michael *lawyer*
Toohey, James Kevin *lawyer*
Toth, Bruce A. *lawyer*
Treston, Sherry S. *lawyer*
Trio, Edward Alan *lawyer, accountant*
Trost, Eileen Bannon *lawyer*
Tryban, Esther Elizabeth *lawyer*
Turilli, M. Louise *lawyer*
Ungaretti, Richard Anthony *lawyer*
Utecht, Andrea E. *lawyer*
Valukas, Anton Ronald *lawyer, former prosecutor*
Van Demark, Ruth Elaine *lawyer*
Van Gorp, Jon D. *lawyer*
Van Tine, Matthew Eric *lawyer*
Ventrelli, Anita Marie *lawyer*
Vezeau, Timothy J. *lawyer*
Vishneski, John Stanley III *lawyer*
Vojcanin, Sava Alexander *lawyer*
Von Mandel, Michael Jacques *lawyer*
Vree, Roger Allen *lawyer*
Wahlen, Edwin Alfred *lawyer*
Wakschlag, Milton Samuel *lawyer*
Walsh, Michael S. *lawyer*
Wander, Herbert Stanton *lawyer*
Weaver, Timothy Allan *lawyer*
Webb, Dan K. *lawyer*
Webb, Robert W. *lawyer*
Weinberg, Walter S. *lawyer*
Weinkopf, Friedrich J. *lawyer*
Weinsheimer, William Cyrus *lawyer*
Weinstein, Margo *lawyer*
Weiss, John Robert *lawyer*
Weiss, Steven Allan *lawyer*
Weissman, Michael Lewis *lawyer*
Welch, Lyman W. *lawyer*
Welsh, Kelly Raymond *lawyer, investment company executive*
Werner, Raymond J. *lawyer*
Westerberg, Gary W. *lawyer*
Whalen, Wayne W. *lawyer*
White, Henry F., Jr. *legal association administrator, retired military officer*
White, Linda Diane *lawyer*
Whiting, Oran F. *lawyer*
Wieczorek, Dennis E. *lawyer*
Wildman, Max Edward *lawyer, director*
Wilson, Roger Goodwin *lawyer*
Wine-Banks, Jill Susan *lawyer*
Wise, William Jerrard *lawyer*
Witcoff, Sheldon William *lawyer*
Wolf, Charles Benno *lawyer*
Wolfe, David Louis *lawyer*
Wood, Mark D. *lawyer*
Woodford, Peter C. *lawyer*
Wright, Judith Margaret *law librarian, educator, dean*
Yeager, Mark Leonard *lawyer*
Zabel, Sheldon Alter *lawyer, educator*
Zagel, Margaret Maxwell *lawyer*
Zemm, Sandra Phyllis *lawyer*
Zenner, Sheldon Toby *lawyer*
Zolno, Mark S. *lawyer*

Chicago Heights
Cifelli, John Louis *lawyer*

Cicero
Paprocki, Thomas John *lawyer, priest*

Crystal Lake
Shank, William O. *lawyer*
Thoms, Jeannine Aumond *lawyer*
Wade, Edwin Lee *lawyer, writer*

Decatur
Dunn, John Francis *lawyer, state representative*
Reising, Richard P. *lawyer*
Smith, David James *lawyer*
Vigneri, Joseph William *lawyer*

Deerfield
Birmingham, William Joseph *retired lawyer*
Blanchard, Eric Alan *lawyer*
Green, Dana I. *lawyer, human resources specialist*
Lichtenstein, Susan R. *lawyer, medical products executive*
Persky, Marla Susan *lawyer*
Roche, Mark A. *lawyer, consumer products company executive*
Scott, John Joseph *lawyer*
Scott, Theodore R. *retired lawyer*
Vollen, Robert Jay *lawyer*

Des Plaines
Giampietro, Nicholas L. *lawyer*
Martan, Joseph Rudolf *lawyer*

Downers Grove
Kaput, Jim L. *lawyer*
Palmore, Rick (Roderick A.) *lawyer, food products executive*
Siedlecki, Nancy Therese *lawyer, funeral director*

East Alton
Clark, Mark Jeffrey *paralegal, researcher*

East Peoria
Kuehn, Brian Allen *lawyer*

Edwardsville
Carlson, Jon Gordon *lawyer*

Elgin
Roeser, Ronald O. *lawyer, consultant*

Elmwood Park
Spina, Anthony Ferdinand *lawyer*

Evanston
Creamer, Robert Allan *lawyer*
Morrison, John Horton *lawyer, arbitrator*
Nechin, Herbert Benjamin *lawyer*
Salem, Richard Allen *mediator*

Flossmoor
Garrison, Ray Harlan *lawyer*

Frankfort
Chin, Davis *lawyer*

Galesburg
Mustain, Douglas Dee *lawyer*

Galva
Everett, Reynolds Melville, Jr. *lawyer*

Geneva
Tyler, Lloyd John *retired lawyer*

Genoa
Cromley, Jon Lowell *lawyer*

Glen Ellyn
Hudson, Dennis Lee *lawyer, retired arbitrator, federal official*
O'Connell, Daniel James *lawyer*
Sandrok, Richard William *lawyer*

Glencoe
Perlberg, Jules Martin *lawyer*

Glenview
Berkman, Michael G. *lawyer*
Dul, John A. *lawyer, electronics executive*
Hagy, James C. *lawyer*
Knox, James Edwin *lawyer*
Marmet, Gottlieb John *lawyer*
Wooten, James H., Jr. *lawyer, engineering executive*

Granite City
Rarick, Philip Joseph *lawyer, retired state supreme court justice*

Hanover
Bleveans, John *lawyer*

Highland Park
Gash, Lauren Beth *lawyer, state legislator*
Hoseman, Daniel *lawyer*
Karol, Nathaniel H. *lawyer, consultant*
Nelson, Richard David *lawyer*
Reed, Jan Stern *lawyer*
Schindel, Donald Marvin *retired lawyer*

Hoffman Estates
Block, Janice L. *lawyer*
Dziezak, Judie D. *lawyer*
Harker, William R. *lawyer*
Zopp, Andrea Lynne *lawyer, retail executive*

Homewood
Olofsson, Daniel Joel *lawyer*

Jacksonville
Kuster, Larry Donald *lawyer*

Joliet
Lenard, George Dean *lawyer*
Teas, Richard Harper *lawyer*

Kenilworth
McKittrick, William Wood *lawyer*
Weaver, Clifford Lee *retired lawyer, winery owner*

La Grange
Kerr, Alexander Duncan, Jr. *lawyer*

Lake Forest
Covington, George Morse *lawyer*
Doyle, Joseph E. *lawyer, manufacturing executive*
Emerson, William Harry *retired lawyer*
Galatz, Henry Francis *lawyer*
Howard, John Lawrence *lawyer*
Palmer, Ann Therese Darin *lawyer*
Sikorovsky, Eugene Frank *retired lawyer*
Smith, Brian J. *lawyer*

Libertyville
DeSanto, James John *lawyer*
Rallo, Douglas *lawyer*

Lincolnshire
Michalik, John James *legal association administrator*
Para, Gerard Albert *lawyer, real estate broker, consultant*
Ryan, John *lawyer*
Ryan, John M. *lawyer, human resources company executive*

Lincolnwood
Carroll, Howard William *state legislator*
Kamensky, Marvin *lawyer*
Zaremski, Miles Jay *lawyer*

Lisle
Hecht, Louis Alan *lawyer*

Long Grove
Conway, John K. *lawyer*
Davis, Britton Anthony *retired lawyer*
Obert, Paul Richard *lawyer, manufacturing executive*

Marengo
Franks, Herbert Hoover *lawyer*

Matteson
Wigell, Raymond George *lawyer*

Melrose Park
Schmidt, Gary P. *lawyer, personal care industry executive*

Mokena
Sangmeister, George Edward *lawyer, consultant, congressman*

Moline
Cleaver, William Lehn *lawyer*
Jenkins, James Robert *lawyer, manufacturing executive*

Morris
Rooks, John Newton *lawyer*

Mount Vernon
Harvey, Morris Lane *lawyer*

Mundelein
Ackley, Robert O. *lawyer*

Murphysboro
McCann, Maurice Joseph *lawyer*

Naperville
Broad, Matthew *lawyer*
Corvino, Beth Byster *lawyer*
Everett, C(harles) Curtis *retired lawyer*
Gracey, Paul C., Jr. *lawyer, utilities executive*
Landsman, Stephen N. *lawyer*
Larson, Mark Edward, Jr. *lawyer, educator, financial planner*
Nortell, Bruce *lawyer*
Tibble, Douglas Clair *lawyer*

Niles
Ditkowsky, Kenneth K. *lawyer*

Normal
Bender, Paul Edward *lawyer*
Rochelle, Victor Cleanthus *retired lawyer*

Northbrook
Abbey, G(eorge) Marshall *lawyer, retired health facility administrator*
Bohlender, Hugh Darrow *lawyer*
Lapin, Harvey I. *lawyer*
Levenfeld, Milton Arthur *lawyer*
Rosemarin, Carey Stephen *lawyer*
Sernett, Richard Patrick *lawyer*
Wallace, Harry Leland *lawyer*

Oak Brook
Barnes, Karen Kay *lawyer*
Bennett, Margaret Airola *lawyer*
Congalton, Susan Tichenor *lawyer*
Mlsna, Kathryn Kimura *lawyer*
O'Brien, Walter Joseph, II, *lawyer*
Oldfield, E. Lawrence *lawyer*
Santona, Gloria *lawyer, food products executive*

Oak Park
Schubert, Blake H. *lawyer*
Sengpiehl, Paul Marvin *lawyer, retired state official*

Orland Park
Carroll, Michael F. *lawyer*

Palatine
Victor, Michael Gary *lawyer, physician*
Zamarin, Ronald George *lawyer*

Park Forest
Goodrich, John Bernard *lawyer, consultant*

Park Ridge
Hegarty, Mary Frances *lawyer*
LaRue, Paul Hubert *retired lawyer*
Wasko, Steven E. *lawyer*
Zimmermann, John Joseph *lawyer*

Peoria
Allen, Lyle Wallace *lawyer*
Bertschy, Timothy L. *lawyer*
Buda, James B. *lawyer, manufacturing executive*
Coletta, Ralph John *retired lawyer*
O'Brien, Daniel Robert *lawyer*
Parsons, Richard Hugo *lawyer*
Prusak, Maximilian Michael *lawyer*

Winget, Walter Winfield *retired lawyer*
Woods, Michael Lee *lawyer*

Pinckneyville
Johnson, Don Edwin *lawyer*

Prospect Heights
Cloney, Terence J. *lawyer*
Leopold, Mark F. *lawyer*

Riverwoods
Bartlett, Robert William *lawyer*
Gold, Deidra D. *lawyer*

Rockford
Cyrs, Michael Thomas *lawyer*
Johnson, Thomas Stuart *lawyer*
Reno, Roger *lawyer*
Tuite, Gerald Francis *lawyer, commercial real estate manager*

Rosemont
Tinaglia, Michael Lee *lawyer*

Saint Charles
Clancy, Wendell White *mediator, lawyer*

Schaumburg
Lawson, A. Peter *lawyer*
Marshall, John David *lawyer*
Nehs, (William) Scott *lawyer*

Shorewood
Heaphy, John Merrill *lawyer*

Skokie
Mierswa, David P. *lawyer, real estate investor*
Plotnick, Paul William *lawyer*

Springfield
Bergschneider, David Philip *legal administrator*
Darby, Karen Sue *law educator*
Heaton, Rodger A. *prosecutor*
Immke, Keith Henry *lawyer*
Kerr, Gary Enrico *lawyer, educator*
LeBlang, Theodore Raymond *law educator, lawyer*
Londrigan, Thomas Foster *lawyer*
Mathewson, Mark Stuart *lawyer, editor*
Morse, Saul Julian *lawyer*
Quinlan, William J. *lawyer*
Reed, Robert Phillip *lawyer*
Van Meter, Abram DeBois *lawyer, retired banker*

Sterling
Pace, Ole Bly III *lawyer*

Swansea
Tillery, Stephen M. *lawyer*

Taylorville
Austin, Daniel William *lawyer*

Tinley Park
Kenny, Mary Alice *lawyer*

Urbana
Balbach, Stanley Byron *lawyer*
Fitz-Gerald, Roger Miller *lawyer*
Frederick, Robert George *lawyer*
Grossman, Margaret Rosso *law educator*
Rich, Robert F. *law educator, political science professor*
Webber, Carl Maddra *lawyer*

Vernon Hills
Leahy, Christine A. *lawyer, information technology executive*
Richards, Alan Edward *lawyer*

Warrenville
Boardman, Robert A. *retired lawyer*
Covey, Steven K. *lawyer*
Johnson, Douglas Wells *lawyer*

Waukegan
Bairstow, Richard Raymond *retired lawyer*
Henrick, Michael Francis *lawyer*
Stone, Jed *lawyer*

Westchester
Hynes, Mary Ann *lawyer, food products executive*

Western Springs
Hanson, Heidi Elizabeth *lawyer*

Wheaton
Kincaid, John Bruce *lawyer*
Stein, Lawrence A. *lawyer*

Willowbrook
Walton, Stanley Anthony III *lawyer*

Wilmette
Baisley, James Mahoney *retired lawyer*
Bunge, Jonathan Gunn *lawyer*

Winnetka
Berner, Robert Lee, Jr. *lawyer*
Crowe, Robert William *lawyer, mediator*
Ellwood, Scott *lawyer*
Greenblatt, Ray Harris *lawyer*
Hales, Daniel B. *lawyer*
Hickman, Frederic W. *retired lawyer*
McWhirter, Bruce J. *retired lawyer*
Webster, David Macpherson *lawyer*

Woodridge
Farrug, Eugene Joseph, Sr. *retired lawyer*

INDIANA

Anderson
Woodruff, Randall Lee *lawyer*

Angola
Cain, Tim J. *lawyer*

Batesville
de Maynadier, Patrick D. *lawyer*

Bloomington
Aman, Alfred Charles, Jr. *law educator*
Baude, Patrick Louis *law educator*
Dilts, Jon Paul *law educator*
Nunn, Ken *lawyer*
Shreve, Gene Russell *law educator*

Carmel
Burkett, Robert E., Jr. *lawyer, insurance company executive*
Walseth, David G. *lawyer, insurance company executive*

Columbus
Crump, Francis Jefferson III *lawyer*
Eynon, Richard S. *lawyer*
Harrison, Patrick Woods *lawyer*
Rose, Marya Mernitz *lawyer*

Crown Point
Back, Michael Wayne *lawyer*

Danville
Baldwin, Jeffrey Kenton *lawyer, educator*
Baldwin, Patricia Ann *lawyer*

Elkhart
Gassere, Eugene Arthur *lawyer, investment company executive*
Treckelo, Richard M. *lawyer*

Evansville
Berger, Charles Lee *lawyer*
Clouse, John Daniel *lawyer*
Harrison, Joseph Heavrin *lawyer*
Hayes, Philip Harold *lawyer*
Miller, Daniel Raymond *prosecutor*
Reed, Helen Skuggedal *law librarian, musician*
Shoulders, Patrick Alan *lawyer, educator*
Wallace, Keith M. *lawyer*

Fort Wayne
Colvin, Sherrill William *lawyer*
Fink, Thomas Michael *lawyer*
Gehring, Ronald Kent *lawyer*
Helmke, Paul (Walter Paul Helmke Jr.) *lawyer, former mayor*
Lawson, Jack Wayne *lawyer*
Pope, Mark Andrew *lawyer, academic administrator*
Shoaff, Thomas Mitchell *lawyer*
Tourkow, Joshua Isaac *lawyer*

Franklin
Hamner, Lance Dalton *prosecutor*

Gary
Lewis, Robert Lee *lawyer*
Michelstetter, Stanley Hubert *lawyer*

Greenwood
Van Valer, Joe Ned *lawyer, real estate developer*

Hammond
Capp, David A. *prosecutor*
DeGuilio, Jon E. *lawyer*
Diamond, Eugene Christopher *lawyer, health facility administrator*
Ruman, Saul I. *lawyer*

Highland
Forsythe, Randall Newman *paralegal, educator*
Gladish, David Stephen *lawyer*

Indianapolis
Albright, Terrill D. *lawyer*
Allen, David James *lawyer*
Armitage, Robert Allen *lawyer, pharmaceutical executive*
Avery, Melissa J. *lawyer*
Badger, David Harry *lawyer*
Barkley, James M. *lawyer, real estate company executive*
Beckwith, Lewis Daniel *lawyer*
Blythe, James David, II, *lawyer*
Boldt, Michael Herbert *lawyer*
Born, Samuel Roydon, II, *retired lawyer, mediator*
Bowman, Frank O. *law educator*
Brooks, Susan W. *prosecutor*
Butt, P. Lawrence *lawyer*
Carney, Joseph Buckingham *lawyer*
Choplin, John M., II, *lawyer*
Cole, Roland Jay *lawyer*
Conour, William Frederick *lawyer*
Crews, Kenneth Donald *law educator, consultant, dean*
Daniels, Deborah Jean *lawyer, former federal agency administrator*
Dorocke, Lawrence Francis *lawyer*
Downs, Thomas K. *lawyer*
Drentlicher, David *lawyer, educator, physician*
Dutton, Stephen James *lawyer*
Elberger, Ronald Edward *lawyer*
Elzer, Robert W. *lawyer*
Ewbank, Thomas Peters *lawyer, retired banker*
Fels, James Alexander *lawyer, mediator*
FitzGibbon, Daniel Harvey *lawyer*
Fruehwald, Kristin Gail *lawyer*
Funk, David Albert *retired law educator*
Gilliland, John Campbell, II, *lawyer*
Hackman, Marvin Lawrence *lawyer*
Hiner, Leslie Davis *lawyer, consultant*
Horn, Brenda Sue *lawyer*
Hovde, F. Boyd *lawyer*
Jegen, Lawrence A. III *law educator*
Johnstone, Robert Philip *retired lawyer*
Kappes, Philip Spangler *lawyer*
Kautzman, John Fredrick *lawyer*
Kemper, James Dee *lawyer*
Kerr, William Andrew *lawyer, educator*
Kinney, Eleanor De Arman *law educator*
Kirk, Carol *lawyer*
Klaper, Martin Jay *lawyer*
Kleiman, Mary Margaret *lawyer*
Knebel, Donald Earl *lawyer*
Koch, Edna Mae *lawyer, nurse*
Koeller, Robert Marion *lawyer, director*
Kury, Bernard Edward *lawyer*
Lamkin, Martha Dampf *lawyer, foundation administrator*
Lee, Stephen W. *lawyer*
Lisher, John Leonard *lawyer*
Lobley, Alan Haigh *retired lawyer*
Lofton, Thomas Milton *lawyer*
Lowe, Louis Robert, Jr. *lawyer*
McCarthy, Kevin Bart *lawyer*
Merrill, William H., Jr. *lawyer, corporate financial executive*
Moffatt, Michael Alan *lawyer*
Neff, Robert Matthew *lawyer, finance company executive*
Newman, Norman Richard *lawyer*
Nolan, Alan Tucker *lawyer, writer, arbitrator*
Oldham, Steve Anthony *lawyer*
O'Neal, C. Duane *lawyer*
Padgett, Gregory Lee *lawyer*
Paul, Stephen Howard *lawyer*
Pence, Linda Lee *lawyer*
Pennamped, Bruce Michael *lawyer*
Petersen, James L. *lawyer*
Polak, Jonathan Garland *lawyer*
Reuben, Lawrence Mark *lawyer*
Reynolds, Robert Hugh *lawyer*
Roberts, William Everett *lawyer*
Russell, David Williams *lawyer*
Rusthoven, Peter James *lawyer*
Ryder, Henry Clay *lawyer*
Scaletta, Phillip Ralph III *lawyer*
Schlegel, Fred Eugene *lawyer*
Schreckengast, William Owen *retired lawyer*
Scism, Daniel Reed *lawyer*
Shula, Robert Joseph *lawyer*
Sommer, James Koch *lawyer*
Stayton, Thomas George *lawyer*
Strain, James Arthur *lawyer*
Swhier, Claudia Versfelt *lawyer*
Tabler, Bryan G. *lawyer*
Tabler, Norman Gardner, Jr. *lawyer*
Talesnick, Stanley *lawyer*
Townsend, Earl C., Jr. *lawyer, writer*
Vandivier, Blair Robert *lawyer*
Wellnitz, Craig Otto *lawyer, English language educator*
Whale, Arthur Richard *retired lawyer*
White, James Patrick *law educator*
Wishard, Gordon Davis *lawyer*
Yates, C. Daniel *lawyer*
Yeager, Joseph Heizer, Jr. *lawyer*

Jeffersonville
Hoehn, Elmer Louis *lawyer, state and federal agency administrator, educator, consultant*

La Porte
Kaminski, Leon R. *lawyer*

Lafayette
Hart, Russell Holiday *retired lawyer*
Layden, Charles Max *lawyer*
McCully, Thomas Richardson *lawyer*

Merrillville
Compton, Clyde D. *lawyer*
Miller, Richard Allen *lawyer*
Smith, Arthur Edward, Jr. *lawyer*

Muncie
Kelly, Eric Damian *lawyer, educator*

Munster
Amber, Douglas George *lawyer*

Noblesville
Church, Douglas D. *lawyer*

Notre Dame
Edmonds, Edmund P. *law librarian, educator, dean*
Gunn, Alan *retired law educator*
Robinson, John Hayes *law educator*

Plainfield
Fivel, Steven Edward *lawyer, communications executive*

Seymour
Pardieck, Roger L. *lawyer*

Shelbyville
Lisher, James Richard *lawyer*
McNeely, James Lee *lawyer*

South Bend
Carey, John Leo *lawyer*
Norton, Sally Pauline *lawyer*
Reinke, William John *lawyer*
Seall, Stephen Albert *lawyer*
Shaffer, Thomas Lindsay *lawyer, educator*
Vogel, Nelson J., Jr. *lawyer*

Terre Haute
Bopp, James, Jr. *lawyer*
Britton, Louis Franklin *lawyer*
Davis, Lant B. *lawyer*
Kesler, John A. *lawyer, real estate developer*

Vincennes
Emison, Ewing Rabb, Jr. *lawyer*
Smith, Bruce Arthur *lawyer*

Waterloo
McAlhany, Toni Anne *lawyer*

IOWA

Bettendorf
Skora, Susan Sundman *lawyer*

Burlington
Hoth, Steven Sergey *lawyer, educator*

Cedar Rapids
Chadick, Gary Robert *lawyer*
Collins, Kevin Heath *lawyer*
Nazette, Richard Follett *lawyer*
O'Brien, David A. *lawyer*
Pundt, Richard Arthur *lawyer*
Riley, Tom Joseph *lawyer*
Wilson, Robert Foster *lawyer*

Charles City
Mc Cartney, Ralph Farnham *lawyer*

Clear Lake
Enabnit, Ted *retired lawyer*

Clinton
Smith, Lauren Ashley *lawyer, clergyman, physicist, journalist*

Coralville
Coulter, Charles Roy *lawyer*
McAndrew, Paul Joseph, Jr. *lawyer*

Davenport
Bush, Michael Kevin *lawyer*
Dettmann, David Allen *lawyer*

Des Moines
Begleiter, Martin David *law educator, consulta*
Burns, Bernard John III *public defender*
Carroll, Frank James *lawyer, educator*
Claypool, David L. *lawyer*
Conlin, Roxanne Barton *lawyer*
Critelli, Nicholas *lawyer, barrister*
Crook, Charles Samuel III *lawyer*
Devine, Michael Buxton *attorney, barrister, educator*
Doyle, Richard Henry, IV, *lawyer*
Fisher, Thomas George *lawyer, retired media company executive*
Fisher, Thomas George, Jr. *lawyer*
Foxhoven, Jerry Ray *lawyer*
Frederici, C. Carleton *lawyer*
Graziano, Craig Frank *lawyer*
Hansell, Edgar Frank *lawyer*
Harris, Charles Elmer *retired lawyer*
Hill, Luther Lyons, Jr. *lawyer*
Jensen, Dick Leroy *lawyer*
Koehn, William James *lawyer*
Nickerson, Don C. *lawyer, retired prosecutor, judge*
Peddicord, Roland Dale *lawyer*
Shaff, Karen E. *lawyer, insurance company executive*
Shors, John Dennis *lawyer*
Simpson, Lyle Lee *lawyer*
Whitaker, Matthew George *prosecutor*

Dubuque
Hammer, David Lindley *lawyer, writer, investo*

Grundy Center
Kliebenstein, Don *retired lawyer*

Harlan
Salvo, J. C. *lawyer*

Indianola
Ouderkirk, Mason James *lawyer*

Iowa City
Bonfield, Arthur Earl *law educator*
Downer, Robert Nelson *lawyer*
Gittler, Josephine *law educator*
Hines, Norman William *law educator, retired dean*
Hobart, Thomas D. *lawyer*
Holland, Charles Joseph *lawyer*
Hovenkamp, Herbert *law educator*
Kurtz, Sheldon Francis *lawyer, educator*
Spies, Leon Fred *lawyer*
Wing, Adrien Katherine *law educator*

Jefferson
Pauley, James Leroy, Jr. *retired lawyer*

Keokuk
Hoffman, James Paul *lawyer*

Marshalltown
Brennecke, Allen Eugene *lawyer*

Mason City
Funkhouser, David Edward *lawyer*
Heiny, James Ray *lawyer*
Winston, Harold Ronald *lawyer*

Mount Pleasant
Vance, Michael C. *lawyer*

Muscatine
Nepple, James Anthony *lawyer*

Nevada
Countryman, Dayton Wendell *lawyer*

Ottumwa
Krafka, Mary Baird *lawyer*

Sioux City
Madsen, George Frank *lawyer*
Peterson, Delaine Charles *lawyer, bank execu*

West Des Moines
Hockenberg, Harlan David *lawyer*
Houser, Thomas J. *lawyer*
Johnson, John Paul *lawyer, judge*
Power, Joseph Edward *lawyer*
Tully, Robert Gerard *lawyer*

KANSAS

Arkansas City
Templar, Ted Mac *lawyer*

ge City
in, David James *lawyer*

Scott
on, Leigh Carleton *lawyer*

den City
l, Ward Eugene *lawyer*

chinson
es, John Francis *lawyer*
arer, William Brooks *lawyer*

vrence
d, Robert Clair *legal educator*
bull, H. Rutherford III *lawyer, educator*
er, Winton Allen, Jr. *lawyer, state legislator*

venworth
, Michael P. *lawyer*

coln
gle, Robert D. *lawyer, management*
nsultant, entrepreneur

sion
ker, H. Reed *lawyer*

the
holz, Mark Joseph (Mick) *lawyer*
kin, J. Michael *lawyer*
e, Phillip D. *prosecutor*
t, Robert Gene *lawyer*

erland Park
ahan, Michael Thomas *arbitrator, consultant,*
nstruction executive, writer
ray, Daniel J. *lawyer*
r, Norman Edward *lawyer, former state*
nator
ston, Jocelyn Stanwell *paralegal*
linger, Bruce (Donald Keplinger) *lawyer*
phy, Mark D. *lawyer, real estate developer*
ray, Thomas Veatch *lawyer*
ton, Roger D. *lawyer*
ds, Richard Dale *lawyer*

wnee Mission
gerow, John Nicholas *lawyer*
ker, David M. *lawyer*
d, Richard Lee *lawyer, state senator*
der, Jan Pleasant, Jr. *lawyer*
ton, William Clements *retired lawyer*
th, Edwin Dudley *lawyer*
der, Willard Breidenthal *lawyer*
ks, Billy Schley *lawyer*
rett, Frederick Kent *lawyer*
dever, William Dirk *lawyer*

peka
cannon, James M. *lawyer, educator, dean*
mitt, Lawrence Andrew *lawyer, educator*
od, Linda Diane Henry *lawyer, educator*
fin, Ronald Charles *law educator*
se, Richard Franklin *lawyer*
manek, Danton Charles *lawyer*
k, Larry D. *lawyer, energy executive*
ssey, Michael J. *lawyer, retail executive*
roer, Gene Eldon *lawyer*
ultz, Richard Allen *lawyer, farmer*

chita
el, Kevin J. *lawyer*
es, Ted D. *lawyer*
ger, Ronald Kay *lawyer*
cking, Thomas Robert *lawyer, former state*
eutenant governor
den, Mark V. *lawyer*
nson, Kevin Blaine *lawyer, educator*
lgren, Eric Franklin *prosecutor, lawyer*
ore, Tim J. *lawyer*
ks, Linda S. *lawyer*
ndels, Ed L. *lawyer*
art, Daniel Joseph *lawyer*
ensen, Harvey R. *lawyer*
phenson, Richard Ismert *lawyer*
ompson, Lee (Morris Thompson) *lawyer*
nkler, Dana John *lawyer*

NTUCKY

wling Green
cher, Larry K. *lawyer*

rlington
hlich, Anthony William *lawyer, judge*

tlettsburg
xon, Ronda Lynn *paralegal*

vington
usrath, David L. *lawyer*
r, Thomas Robert *lawyer*
basuk, Mark G. *lawyer, pharmaceutical*
executive
nd, Suzanne Prieur *lawyer*
binson, William T. III *lawyer*
haeffer, Andrew *lawyer*
an, David B. *lawyer*
ith, Pete A. *lawyer*
pner, Donald Leon *lawyer*
lnitzek, Stephen Dale *lawyer*

estwood
y, Ronald Dudley *lawyer*

rt Mitchell
ore, Donna *lawyer*

rt Thomas
halen, Paul Lewellin *lawyer, educator,*
mediator

ankfort
wling, Charles Bryan *legal association*
administrator
Carroll, Julian Morton *lawyer, retired governor, state senator*
Chadwick, Robert *lawyer, judge*
Hatchett, Edward Bryan, Jr. *lawyer*
Palmore, John Stanley, Jr. *retired lawyer*

Glasgow
Baker, Walter Arnold *lawyer*

Harrods Creek
Keeney, Steven Harris *lawyer*

Henderson
Sullivan, William Litsey *lawyer*

Independence
Brewer, Edward Cage III *law educator*

Lexington
Beshear, Steven Lynn *lawyer*
Cole, Vincent J. *lawyer*
Fryman, Virgil Thomas, Jr. *lawyer*
Goldman, Alvin Lee *lawyer, educator, arbitrator*
Hickey, John King *lawyer, career officer*
Lester, Roy David *lawyer*
McCoy, R. Burl *lawyer*
Michael, Douglas Charles *law educator*
Thapar, Amul R. *prosecutor*
Todd, James Marion *retired lawyer*
Turley, Robert Joe *lawyer*

London
Dyche, Jane Winkler *lawyer*
Keller, John Warren *lawyer*

Louisville
Ardery, Philip Pendleton *lawyer*
Ballantine, John Tilden *lawyer*
Barr, James Houston III *lawyer*
Brown, Bonnie Maryetta *lawyer*
Buckaway, William Allen, Jr. *lawyer*
Campbell, Christian Larsen *lawyer*
Conner, Stewart Edmund *lawyer*
Davidson, Gordon Byron *lawyer*
Dudley, George Ellsworth *lawyer*
Duffy, Martin Patrick *lawyer*
Ethridge, Larry Clayton *lawyer*
Ewald, Robert Charles *lawyer*
Fenton, Thomas Conner *lawyer*
Fuchs, Olivia Anne Morris *lawyer*
Gilman, Sheldon Glenn *lawyer*
Hallenberg, Robert Lewis *lawyer*
Herrington, E. Paul III *lawyer*
Hiestand, Sheila Patricia *lawyer*
Hipwell, Arthur P. *lawyer, managed health care company executive*
Hopson, Edwin Sharp *lawyer*
Huber, David L. *prosecutor*
Klotter, John Charles *retired law educator*
Lay, Norvie Lee *law educator*
Luber, Thomas J(ulian) *lawyer*
Lyndrup, Peggy B. *lawyer*
Maggiolo, Allison Joseph *lawyer*
Manly, Samuel *lawyer*
McCall, John Richard *lawyer*
Mellen, Francis Joseph, Jr. *lawyer*
Northern, Richard *lawyer*
Osborn, John Simcoe, Jr. *lawyer*
Pelfrey, D. Patton *lawyer*
Pettyjohn, Shirley Ellis *lawyer, real estate company executive*
Riedman, Mary Suzanne *lawyer*
Rose, Charles Alexander *lawyer*
Runyon, Keith Leslie *lawyer, editor*
Shaikun, Michael Gary *lawyer*
Silverthorn, Robert Sterner, Jr. *lawyer*
Skees, William Leonard, Jr. *lawyer*
Smith, R(obert) Michael *lawyer*
Spalding, Catherine *lawyer*
Talbott, Ben Johnson, Jr. *lawyer*
Vincenti, Michael Baxter *lawyer*
Vish, Donald H. *lawyer, writer, photographer*
Welsh, Sir Alfred John *lawyer, investment advisor*
Westberry, Robert Kent *lawyer*

Newport
Siverd, Robert Joseph *lawyer*

Owensboro
Miller, James Monroe *lawyer*

Prospect
Aberson, Leslie Donald *lawyer*
Willenbrink, Rose Ann *retired lawyer*

Somerset
Prather, John Gideon *lawyer*

LOUISIANA

Alexandria
Gist, Howard Battle, Jr. *lawyer*

Amite
Wedig, Regina Scotto *lawyer*

Baton Rouge
Blackman, John Calhoun, IV, *lawyer*
Boren, James Edgar *lawyer*
Brewer, Ralph Wright, Jr. *lawyer*
Casey, Robert Reisch *lawyer*
Combe, John Clifford, Jr. *lawyer*
Crawford, William Edward *law educator*
Dugas, David Roy *prosecutor, lawyer*
Fishman, Richard Glenn *lawyer, accountant*
Graphia, Gary P. *lawyer*
Green, Stuart Paul *law educator*
Hymel, L(ezin) J(oseph) *lawyer, former prosecutor*
Johnson, Joseph Clayton, Jr. *lawyer*
Litvinoff, Saul *lawyer, educator*
McKay, Michael Wendell *lawyer*
Moréteau, Olivier *law educator*
Pugh, George Willard *law educator*
Richards, Marta Alison *lawyer*
Riddick, Winston Wade, Sr. *lawyer*
Rubin, Michael Harry *lawyer, educator*
Stapp, Dan Ernest *retired lawyer, utilities executive*
Taylor, John McKowen *lawyer*
Unglesby, Lewis O. *lawyer*

Covington
Paddison, David Robert *lawyer*
Rice, Winston Edward *lawyer, priest*
Snyder, Charles Aubrey *lawyer*

Destrehan
Ates, J. Robert *lawyer*
Griffith, Steven Franklin, Sr. *lawyer, insurance agent*

Jefferson
Conino, Joseph Aloysius *lawyer*

Jennings
Marcantel, Bernard Norman *lawyer, judge*

La Place
Cicet, Donald James *lawyer*

Lafayette
Angers, Winston Thomas *lawyer, publishing executive*
Breaux, Paul Joseph *lawyer, pharmacist*
Broussard, Richard C. *lawyer*
Davidson, James Joseph III *lawyer*
Judice, Marc Wayne *lawyer*
Mansfield, James Norman III *lawyer*
Myers, Stephen Hawley *lawyer*
Neuner, Frank X., Jr. *lawyer*
Roy, James Parkerson *lawyer*
Skinner, Michael David *lawyer, lobbyist, consultant*

Lake Charles
Sanchez, Walter Marshall *lawyer*
Veron, J. Michael *lawyer, writer*

Mandeville
Deano, Edward Joseph, Jr. *lawyer, retired state legislator*
Ewen, Pamela Binnings *retired lawyer*

Marksville
Riddle, Charles Addison III *district attorney, former state legislator*

Metairie
Album, Jerald Lewis *lawyer*
Burns, William Glenn *lawyer*
deLaup, S. Guy *lawyer*
Fantaci, James Michael *lawyer*
Ford, Robert David *lawyer*
Hardy, Ashton Richard *lawyer*
Nehrbass, Seth Martin *lawyer*
Rosen, Charles, II, *retired lawyer*
Villarrubia, Todd M. *lawyer*

Monroe
Curry, Robert Lee III *lawyer*
Sartor, Daniel Ryan, Jr. *lawyer*

New Iberia
Hamilton, Roger Paul, Jr. *lawyer*

New Orleans
Abaunza, Donald Richard *lawyer*
Abbott, Hirschel Theron, Jr. *lawyer*
Acomb, Robert Bailey, Jr. *lawyer, educator*
Alsobrook, Henry Bernis, Jr. *lawyer*
Barry, Francis Julian, Jr. *lawyer*
Beahm, Franklin D. *lawyer*
Benjamin, Adelaide Wisdom *retired lawyer, community volunteer and activist*
Benjamin, Edward Bernard, Jr. *lawyer*
Bieck, Robert Barton, Jr. *lawyer*
Bronfin, Fred *lawyer*
Cheatwood, Roy Clifton *lawyer*
Claverie, Philip deVilliers *lawyer*
Coleman, James Julian *lawyer*
Coleman, James Julian, Jr. *lawyer, industrialist, real estate company executive*
Conroy, David Jerome *lawyer*
Crusto, Mitchell Ferdinand *lawyer, educator*
David, Robert Jefferson *lawyer*
Elkins, Gary J. *lawyer*
Eustis, Richmond Minor *lawyer*
Falgoust, Dean Thomas *lawyer, accountant*
Fierke, Thomas Garner *lawyer*
Force, Robert *law educator*
Gay, Esmond Phelps *lawyer*
Gertler, Meyer H. *lawyer*
Goins, Richard Anthony *lawyer, educator*
Grant, Arthur Gordon, Jr. *lawyer, educator*
Hardin, Harry S. III *lawyer*
Healy, George William III *lawyer, mediator*
Herman, Russ Michel *lawyer*
Hoffman, Donald Alfred *lawyer*
Hurley, Grady Schell *lawyer*
Jones, Philip Kirkpatrick, Jr. *lawyer*
Judell, Harold Benn *lawyer*
Landry, Sherry S. *lawyer*
Lemann, Thomas Berthelot *lawyer*
Letten, James B. *prosecutor*
Looney, Joseph W. *lawyer*
Lowe, Robert Charles *lawyer*
Marcus, Bernard *lawyer, arbitrator, mediator*
Masinter, Paul James *lawyer*
McGlone, Michael Anthony *lawyer*
McMillan, Lee Richards, II, *lawyer*
Mintz, Albert *lawyer*
Nuzum, Robert Weston *lawyer*
Osakwe, Christopher *lawyer, educator*
Palmer, Vernon Valentine *law educator*
Pearce, John Y. *lawyer*
Perlis, Sharon A. *lawyer*
Schnabel, Marta-Ann *lawyer*
Simon, H(uey) Paul *lawyer*
Smith, Juanita Bérard *lawyer, artist*
Steeg, Moise S., Jr. *lawyer*
Vance, Robert Patrick *lawyer*
Vaudry, J. William, Jr. *lawyer*
Wolfe, Richard Peel *lawyer*
Worley, Robert Bruce, Jr. *lawyer*

River Ridge
Didriksen, Caleb H. III *lawyer*

Shreveport
Bryant, J(ames) Bruce *lawyer*
Carmody, Arthur Roderick, Jr. *lawyer, director*
Cox, John Thomas, Jr. *lawyer*
Goodman, Robert Uhle *lawyer*
Hetherwick, Gilbert Lewis *lawyer*
Nelson, Ralph Stanley *lawyer*
Payne, Roy Steven *lawyer*
Perlman, Jerald Lee *lawyer*
Politz, Nyle Anthony *lawyer*
Washington, Donald W. *prosecutor*

Slidell
Shamis, Edward Anthony, Jr. *lawyer*
Singletary, Alvin D. *lawyer*

MAINE

Augusta
Cragin, Charles Langmaid *lawyer*
Johnson, Phillip Edward *lawyer*
LaFond, Peter B. *lawyer*

Bangor
Baber, Brett D. *lawyer*
Bickford, Meris J. *lawyer, bank executive*
Rudman, Paul Lewis *lawyer, former state supreme court justice*

Bass Harbor
Ervin, Spencer *lawyer*

Brunswick
Owen, H. Martyn *retired lawyer*

Castine
Wiswall, Frank Lawrence, Jr. *lawyer, educator*

Georgetown
Chapin, Richard *trustee, director*

New Gloucester
Connolly, Paul K., Jr. *lawyer, energy executive*

Orono
Tisher, Sharon S. *lawyer*

Orrs Island
Nelson, Robert Louis *lawyer*

Portland
Dana, Howard H., Jr. *lawyer, retired state supreme court justice*
Duff, John A. *law educator*
Graffam, Ward Irving *lawyer*
Hunt, David Evans *lawyer*
Jones, Blair Anthony *lawyer*
Kayatta, William J., Jr. *lawyer*
Khoury, Colleen A. *law educator, former dean*
Lancaster, Ralph Ivan, Jr. *lawyer*
LeBlanc, Richard Philip *lawyer*
O'Brien, Murrough Hall *lawyer*
Opperman, John R. *lawyer*
Rundlett, Ellsworth Turner III *lawyer*
Silsby, Paula D. *prosecutor*
Stauffer, Eric P. *lawyer*
Thompson, Peter L. *lawyer*
White, Jeffrey Munroe *lawyer*
Whiting, Stephen Clyde *lawyer*
Zarr, Melvyn *lawyer, educator*

Raymond
Coughlan, Patrick Campbell *lawyer, mediator*

Scarborough
Britton, Janet Lynn *lawyer*

South Paris
Eichorn, Daniel J. *lawyer*

South Portland
Delva, Paul D. *lawyer*
Webster, Peter Bridgman *lawyer*

Tenants Harbor
Bates, John Cecil, Jr. *lawyer*

Wells
Carleton, Joseph George, Jr. *lawyer, state legislator*

MARYLAND

Abingdon
Wolf, Martin Eugene *lawyer, educator*

Annapolis
Ferris, William Michael *lawyer*
Levitan, Laurence *lawyer, retired state senator*
Lillard, John Franklin III *lawyer*
Lucas, Steven Mitchell *lawyer*
Martino, Peter Dominic *lawyer, financial software company executive, real estate developer, real estate broker, federal agency administrator, consultant, management consultant*
Perkins, Roger Allan *lawyer*
Poe, Luke Harvey, Jr. *lawyer*
Shapiro, Susan Stobbart *lawyer*
Sheff, Ronald B. *lawyer*

Annapolis Junction
Koplow, Ellen *lawyer, brokerage house executive*

Ashton
Whelan, Roger Michael *lawyer, educator*

Baltimore
Archibald, James Kenway *lawyer*
Astrue, Michael James *lawyer*
Babb, Barbara A. *lawyer, educator*
Baker, Constance H. *lawyer*
Baker, William Parr *lawyer*
Bartlett, James Wilson III *lawyer*
Berlage, Jan Ingham *lawyer*
Berns, Peter Vernon *lawyer*
Blakeslee, Wesley Daniel *lawyer, consultant, director*
Blanton, Edward Lee, Jr. *lawyer*
Brockmeyer, Michael F. *lawyer*
Burch, Francis Boucher, Jr. *lawyer*
Burns, Scott Patrick *lawyer*
Calvert, Walter Randolph *lawyer*
Capute, Courtney G. *lawyer*
Carbine, James Edmond *lawyer*
Carlin, Paul Victor *legal association executive*
Carnell, Teresa Burt *lawyer*
Carney, Stephen Patrick *lawyer, retired insurance company executive*
Cason, Alan C. *lawyer*
Chagnon, Kathleen *lawyer*
Chalk, David *lawyer*
Chaplin, Peggy Louie *lawyer*
Chiu, Hungdah *law educator*
Ciccolo, Angela *lawyer*
Civiletti, Benjamin Richard *lawyer, former United States attorney general*
Cole, Emried Dargan, Jr. *lawyer*
Cook, Bryson Leitch *lawyer*
Coppel, Lawrence David *lawyer*
Crowe, Thomas Leonard *lawyer*
Curran, Robert Bruce *lawyer*
Deeley, C. Carey, Jr. *lawyer*
de Soto, Lisa *lawyer*
Devan, Deborah Hunt *lawyer*
DeVries, Donald Lawson, Jr. *lawyer*
Dewey, Joel Allen *lawyer*
DiBiagio, Thomas Michael *lawyer, former prosecutor*
Dougherty, John C. *lawyer*
Dubé, Lawrence Edward, Jr. *lawyer*
Dunn, Jeffrey A. *lawyer*
Eisner, Jonathan David *lawyer*
Ellin, Marvin *lawyer*
Erwin, H. Robert *lawyer*
Evans, Nolly Seymour *lawyer*
Eveleth, Janet Stidman *law association administrator*
Fergenson, Arthur Friend *lawyer*
Ferro, Elizabeth Krams *lawyer*
Finnerty, Joseph Gregory, Jr. *lawyer*
Finney, Jervis Spencer *lawyer, former prosecutor*
Fisher, Morton Poe, Jr. *lawyer*
Frerichs, Herbert Donald, Jr. *lawyer*
Friedman, Louis Frank *lawyer*
Gaither, John Francis, Jr. *lawyer, health products executive*
Garten, Morris L. *lawyer*
Gately, Mark Donohue *lawyer*
Gendron, Andrew *lawyer*
Gilbert, Blaine Louis *lawyer*
Gillece, James Patrick, Jr. *lawyer*
Goldman, Brian Arthur *lawyer, accountant*
Goldman, Meir *lawyer*
Gontrum, Barbara *law librarian, educator*
Gonya, Jeffrey Keenan *lawyer*
Gonzales, Louise Michaux *lawyer*
Gray, Frank Truan *lawyer*
Gray, Oscar Shalom *lawyer*
Guben, Jan K. *lawyer*
Hafets, Richard Jay *lawyer*
Hanks, James Judge, Jr. *lawyer*
Hecht, Donald D. *lawyer*
Honemann, Daniel Henry *lawyer*
Hopps, Raymond, Jr. *lawyer, film producer*
Howard, John Vincent, Jr. *lawyer*
Howell, Harley Thomas *lawyer*
Immelt, Stephen J. *lawyer*
Johnson, E. Scott *lawyer*
Johnson, Harry Sterling *lawyer*
Johnston, Edward Allan *lawyer*
Johnston, George W. *lawyer*
Jones, John Martin, Jr. *lawyer*
Kandel, Nelson Robert *lawyer*
Kenney, Brigid E. *lawyer*
Kolkin, Mitchell *lawyer*
Kremen, Richard M. *lawyer*
Kuryk, David Neal *lawyer*
Lemke, Thomas P. *lawyer, brokerage house executive*
Leppert, Cynthia L. *lawyer*
Levin, Edward Jesse *lawyer*
Levine, Richard E. *lawyer*
Liebmann, George W. *lawyer*
Loucks, Allen Frazier *prosecutor, lawyer*
Lundy, Audie Lee, Jr. *lawyer*
MacWilliams, Michael Broughton *lawyer*
Mathias, James D. *lawyer*
Mathias, Robert Joseph *lawyer*
McClung, A(lexander) Keith, Jr. *retired lawyer*
McPherson, Donald Paxton III *lawyer*
McWilliams, John Michael *lawyer*
Meagher, Anthony L. *lawyer*
Miller, Decatur Howard *lawyer*
Moser, M(artin) Peter *lawyer*
Murphy, Billy (William H. Murphy Jr.) *lawyer*
Myers, Eric B. *lawyer*
Nilson, George Albert *lawyer*
Noren, Marc B. *lawyer*
Nussbaum, Paul M. *lawyer*
Ohly, D. Christopher *lawyer*
Orman, Leonard Arnold *lawyer*
Pappas, George Frank *lawyer*
Parvis, Peter P. *lawyer*
Plant, Albin MacDonough *lawyer*
Pollak, Mark *lawyer*
Provorny, Frederick Alan *lawyer, educator*
Radding, Andrew *lawyer*
Radowich, Jeffrey J. *lawyer*
Ravenell, Kenneth W. *lawyer*
Reno, Russell Ronald, Jr. *lawyer*
Reynolds, William Leroy *lawyer, educator*
Robinson, Zelig *lawyer*
Rosenstein, Rod J. *prosecutor*
Rosenthal, William J. *lawyer*
Schlaff, Barbara E. *lawyer*
Schochor, Jonathan *lawyer, educator*
Schwartz, Howard S. *lawyer*
Scriggins, Larry Palmer *lawyer, director*
Shapiro, Harry Dean *lawyer*
Shea, James L. *lawyer*
Shelton, Robert Arthur *lawyer*
Shepherd, Kevin L. *lawyer*
Short, Alexander Campbell *lawyer*
Silver, Michael Joel *lawyer*
Sirota, Wilbert H. *lawyer*
Smith, Lisa J. *lawyer*
Smith, Robert G. *lawyer*
Smith, Robert W., Jr., (Jay) *lawyer*
Snell, Steven Layne *lawyer, consultant*
Somer-Greif, Penny Lynn *lawyer*
Suggs, Kenneth *lawyer*
Sykes, Melvin Julius *lawyer*
Thompson, Otho M. *lawyer, former solicitor*
Tiburzi, Paul A. *lawyer*
Tilghman, Richard Carmichael, Jr. *lawyer*
Tyler, Ralph Sargent III *lawyer*
Urban, Theodore W. *lawyer, brokerage house executive*
Walker, Irving Edward *lawyer*
Walter, Harold Mark *lawyer*
Warren, Melissa Allison *lawyer*
Wasserman, Richard Leo *lawyer*
Watkins, John B. *lawyer*
White, Pamela Janice *lawyer*
Whitman, Marland Hamilton, Jr. *lawyer*
Wilson, Thomas Matthew III *lawyer*
Winn, James Julius, Jr. *lawyer*
Wolf, Cyd Beth *lawyer, entrepreneur*
Wolf, Larry M. *lawyer*
Wright, James Dorsey *lawyer*
Yoskowitz, Irving Benjamin *lawyer, energy executive*
Zaccagnini, Anthony Jackson *lawyer*
Zinkham, W. Robert *lawyer*

Bel Air
Helfrich, Cornelius David *lawyer*
Miller, Max Dunham, Jr. *lawyer*

Bethesda
Abdoo, Elizabeth A. *lawyer*
Aisenberg, Irwin Morton *retired lawyer*
Baird, Bruce Allen *lawyer*
Bauersfeld, Carl Frederick *lawyer*
Bebchick, Leonard Norman *lawyer*
Berman, Marshall Fox *lawyer*
Comey, James B., Jr. *lawyer, aerospace company executive, former federal agency administrator*
Cox, Kenneth Allen *retired lawyer, communications executive, consultant*
Damico, Nicholas Peter *lawyer*
Daniels, Michael Paul *lawyer*
Deckelbaum, Nelson *lawyer*
DiPietro, Ralph John *lawyer*
Downey, Arthur Thomas III *lawyer*
English, William deShay *lawyer, director*
Feuerstein, Donald Martin *lawyer*
Frosh, Brian Esten *lawyer, state senator*
Gottlieb, Jonathan W. *lawyer*
Hagberg, Viola Wilgus *lawyer*
Hewes, Laurence Ilsley III *lawyer, management consultant*
Himelfarb, Stephen Roy *lawyer*
Hoffman, Ira Eliot *lawyer*
Murphy, James Paul *lawyer*
Nelson, William Eugene *lawyer*
Padgett, Nancy Weeks *retired law librarian, lawyer, consultant*
Pipkin, James Harold, Jr. *lawyer*
Rosenberg, Mark Louis *lawyer*
Schifter, Richard *lawyer*
Schoettler, James Anthony, Jr. *lawyer*
Silver, David *lawyer*
Strickler, Scott Michael *lawyer*
Weinberger, Alan David *lawyer, business executive*
Zielinski, Thomas C. *lawyer, insurance company executive*
Zipp, Joel Frederick *lawyer*

Bowie
McCarthy, Kevin John *lawyer*

Catonsville
Hubbard, Herbert Hendrix *lawyer*
Zumbrun, Alvin John Thomas *law and criminology educator*

Chestertown
Mowell, George Mitchell *lawyer*

Chevy Chase
Bruder, George Frederick *retired lawyer*
Coerper, Milo George *lawyer, priest*
Curzan, Myron Paul *lawyer*
Gildenhorn, Joseph Bernard *lawyer, real estate company executive, retired diplomat*
Meyerson, Christopher Cortlandt *lawyer*
Murphy, John Condron, Jr. *lawyer*
Nichols, Henry Eliot *lawyer, realtor, banker, columnist*
Pollard, Michael Ross *lawyer, health science association administrator*
Toy, Charles David *lawyer, business manager*
Weiss, Harlan Lee *lawyer*

College Park
Meagher, Joseph Patrick *law educator, consultant*
Neal, Edward Garrison *lawyer*
Petraitis, Karel Colette *lawyer*

Columbia
Bennett, P. Tyson *lawyer*
Closson, Walter Franklin *child support prosecutor*
Maseritz, Guy B. *lawyer*
Shaw, Donald Hardy *lawyer*

Crownsville
Irish, Leon Eugene *lawyer, non-profit organization executive, educator*

Dickerson
Duncan, Jack G. *lawyer*

Easton
Ikenberry, Henry Cephas, Jr. *lawyer*
Maffitt, James Strawbridge *lawyer*

Ellicott City
Lilly, John Richard, II, *lawyer*
Pairo, Preston Abercrombie, Jr. *lawyer*

Fort George G Meade
Deitz, Robert L. *lawyer*

Fort Meade
Potenza, Vito *lawyer*

Fort Washington
Alexander, Gary R. *lawyer, state legislator, lobbyist*
Vaughan, James Joseph Michael *lawyer*

Frederick
Borison, Scott Craig *lawyer*
Hogan, Ilona Modly *lawyer*

Friendship
Levy, David Lawrence *retired lawyer, legal association administrator*

Gaithersburg
Jestrab, Frank F. *retired lawyer*
McCann, Joseph Leo *lawyer, former government official*
McDowell, Donna Schultz *lawyer, educator*

Germantown
Fread, Joan P. *lawyer*

Glenwood
Hansen, Christopher Agnew *lawyer*

Glyndon
Renbaum, Barry Jeffrey *lawyer*

Greenbelt
Bonsib, Robert Charles *lawyer*
Fax, Charles Samuel *lawyer*
Greenwald, Andrew Eric *lawyer*

Hagerstown
Berkson, Jacob Benjamin *lawyer, writer*
Dunlap, John B. *lawyer, educator*

Hyattsville
Goodwin, Robert Cronin *lawyer*

Kensington
Dauster, William Gary *lawyer, economist*
Mathias, Joseph Marshall *lawyer, judge*

Laurel
Bartley, Shawn *lawyer*
Cecil, J. Robb *lawyer*

Linthicum
Ehrlich, Bob (Robert Leroy Ehrlich Jr.) *lawyer, former governor, congressman*

Lutherville
Freeland, Charles *lawyer, accountant*

Lutherville Timonium
Brown, Ellyn L. *lawyer, consultant*

North Potomac
Lehman, Leonard *retired lawyer, consultant*

Ocean City
Bright, Bruce Frederick *lawyer*
Phillips, J. Harrison III *lawyer*

Owings Mills
Chernow, Jeffrey Scott *lawyer, educator, writer*

Oxford
Bellinger, Edgar Thomson *lawyer*

Parkville
Hill, Milton King, Jr. *retired lawyer*

Pasadena
Asti, Alison Louise *lawyer*

Pikesville
Putzel, Constance Kellner *lawyer*

Point Of Rocks
Peppe, Ron *lawyer*

Potomac
Hall, William Darlington *lawyer*
Meyer, Lawrence George *lawyer*
Mullenbach, Linda Herman *lawyer*
Peter, Phillips Smith *lawyer*
Redding, Robert Ellsworth *lawyer*
Schmeltzer, Edward *lawyer*
Sherwood, Arthur Lawrence *lawyer*
Troffkin, Howard Julian *lawyer*

Randallstown
Holt, John J. *mediator, arbitrator, retired human resources specialist*

Reisterstown
Frank, Robert Louis *lawyer*

Rockville
Avery, Bruce Edward *lawyer*
Barkley, Brian Evan *lawyer, political consultant*
Berryman, Richard Byron *lawyer*
Bradshaw, Sheldon *lawyer*
Cheston, Sheila Carol *lawyer*
Conroy, J. Michael *lawyer, judge*
Cyr, Karen D. *lawyer*
De Jong, David Samuel *lawyer*
Donnally, Robert Andrew *lawyer*
Frye, Roland Mushat, Jr. *lawyer*
Hepfer, Cheryl Lynn *lawyer*
Kadish, Richard L. *lawyer*
Karson, Emile *lawyer*
Katz, Steven Martin *lawyer, accountant*
Kerxton, Alan Smith *lawyer*
Lessenco, Gilbert Barry *retired lawyer*
Pehrson, Gordon Oscar, Jr. *lawyer, venture capitalist*
Roth, Clifford Joel *lawyer, consultant*
Rothenberg, Alan David *lawyer*
Senger, Jeffrey M. *lawyer*
Tanenbaum, Richard Hugh *lawyer*
Thompson, James Lee *lawyer*
Tomar, Richard Thomas *lawyer*
Van Grack, Steven *lawyer*
Zaphiriou, George Aristotle *lawyer, educator*

Saint Michaels
Brown, Omer Forrest, II, *lawyer*

Silver Spring
Calvert, Gordon Lee *retired legal association executive*
Craig, Paul Max, Jr. *retired lawyer*
Lipstein, Robert A. *lawyer*
Rachanow, Gerald Marvin *lawyer, pharmacist*

Sparks
Skelton, Robert W. *lawyer, food products executive*

Towson
Ayres, Jeffrey Peabody *lawyer*
Bowen, Lowell Reed *lawyer*
Brennan, Michael J. *lawyer*
Carney, Bradford George Yost *lawyer, educator*
Comeau, Michael Gerard *lawyer*
Fenton, Charles E. *lawyer*
Gilliss, Edward Johnson *lawyer*
Koetter, Cornelia M. *lawyer*
Lutz, Randall Matthew *lawyer*
Miller, Herbert H. *lawyer*
Proctor, Kenneth Donald *lawyer*
Vettori, Paul Marion *lawyer*
Zink, John H. III *lawyer*

Trappe
Paul, James Caverly Newlin *law educator, retired dean*

West Bethesda
Scully, Roger Tehan, II, *lawyer*

Westminster
Dulany, William Bevard *lawyer*
Preston, Charles Michael *lawyer*
Staples, Lyle Newton *lawyer*

MASSACHUSETTS

Amherst
Howland, Richard Moulton *retired lawyer*

Arlington
Keshian, Richard *lawyer*

Barnstable
Mycock, Frederick Charles *lawyer*
Paquin, Thomas Christopher *lawyer*

Belmont
Greer, Gordon Bruce *retired lawyer, writer*
Zito, Frank R. *lawyer, accountant*

Boston
Abbott, William Saunders *lawyer*
Abrams, Roger Ian *lawyer, educator*
Adams, Lisa *lawyer*
Ajemian, Marianne *lawyer*
Alderman, Marlene H. *law librarian, educator*
Allen, Rosemary M. *lawyer*
Annas, George J. *health law educator*
Apjohn, Nelson George *lawyer*
Aresty, Jeffrey M. *lawyer*
Armistead, (Ivor) Cary III *lawyer*
Aronson, Neil H. *lawyer*
Auerbach, Joseph *former lawyer, educator*
Bachman, Katharine Elizabeth *lawyer*
Bae, Frank S.H. *law librarian, educator*
Baker, Hollie L. *lawyer*
Balliro, Joseph James, Sr. *lawyer*
Bapooji Ryan, Anita B. *lawyer*
Baram, Michael S. *lawyer, educator*
Barker, Christopher B. *lawyer*
Barnard, Deborah E. *lawyer*
Barron, Michael K. *lawyer*
Bass, Michael A. *lawyer*
Becker, Fred Ronald *lawyer*
Benjamin, William Chase *lawyer*
Bernhard, Alexander Alfred *lawyer*
Berube, Brian A. *lawyer, chemicals executive*
Bhatt, Manisha Hemendra *lawyer*
Bills, Jennifer Leah *lawyer*
Bines, Harvey Ernest *lawyer, educator, writer*
Birmingham, Thomas F. *lawyer, former state legislator*
Black, Edward G. *lawyer*
Bloch, Donald Martin *lawyer*
Bodner, Randall Wayne *lawyer*
Bodoff, Joseph Samuel Uberman *lawyer*
Bok, John Fairfield *retired lawyer*
Bonauto, Mary *lawyer*
Bonifaz, John Cristopher *lawyer*
Borden, Mark G. *lawyer*
Bornheimer, Allen Millard *lawyer*
Braceras, Roberto M. *lawyer*
Bragg, Lawrence D. III *lawyer*
Breakstone, Marc L. *lawyer*
Brodley, Joseph F. *lawyer, consultant, dean*
Brody, Richard Eric *lawyer*
Bromberg, Lee Carl *lawyer*

n, Michael Robert *lawyer*
anan, Robert McLeod *lawyer*
ess, John Allen *lawyer*
e, Matthew M. *lawyer*
eigh, Lewis Albert *lawyer*
ng, James C. *lawyer*
ett, Elizabeth B. *lawyer*
s, Thomas David *lawyer*
Frank Davies *lawyer, real estate company*
ecutive
on, Thomas Russell *lawyer*
l, Lawrence R. *lawyer*
eira, Charlene A. *lawyer*
arizzo, A. William *lawyer*
ey, J. W., Jr. *lawyer*
, Jeffrey N. *lawyer, investment company*
ecutive
oll, James Edward *lawyer*
er, T(homas) Barton *law educator*
er, Truman Snell *lawyer*
g, Hemmie *lawyer*
in, David Chester *lawyer*
ry, John Joseph (Jack) *lawyer*
nha, J. William *lawyer*
ey, James Francis *lawyer*
en, Kenneth A. *lawyer*
, Andrew Howard *lawyer*
man, Dennis M. *lawyer*
man, Virginia Flood *lawyer*
in, Philip Mark *lawyer*
ell, Howard Alan *lawyer*
ey, Robert Ambrose, Jr. *lawyer*
in, John Joseph, Jr. *lawyer*
ell, Charles C. III *lawyer*
y, Paul Patrick *lawyer*
s, James S. *lawyer*
nard, Richard Alan *law educator*
Amicis, Don S. *lawyer*
evoise, Charles Henry *lawyer*
ineas, Patricia Ann *lawyer*
aney, John White *lawyer*
Bono, Irene Lillian (Irene Stone Guild Del
ono) *lawyer*
nis, Kevin M. *lawyer*
ham, Casimir, Jr. *lawyer*
lin, Peter J. *lawyer*
kie, Robert Benjamin *lawyer, educator*
Cola, Joan Barbara *lawyer*
on, James Joseph *lawyer*
een, John K. *lawyer*
per, Thomas B. *lawyer*
fy, James Francis III *lawyer*
eski-Najjar, Debra *lawyer*
, Peter L. *lawyer*
ards, Richard Lansing *lawyer*
ert, Richard Michael *lawyer*
ante, Michael Barrett *lawyer*
i, Ivor R. *lawyer*
el, David Lewis *lawyer*
lander, John C. *lawyer*
ch, Richard Rex *lawyer*
rett, Jonathan Jubal *lawyer*
, Michael Leo *lawyer*
herry, Anthony M. *lawyer*
er, John Kenneth *lawyer*
, Terrence M. *lawyer*
her, Eric Robert *lawyer, educator*
her, Mark Alan *lawyer*
man, Robert A. *lawyer*
gerald, Warren Franklin *lawyer*
or, Richard Earl *lawyer*
tier, Albert Mark, Jr. *lawyer*
ier, James J(ohn) *lawyer*
, Francis Haney *lawyer*
ser, Robert Burchmore *lawyer*
edman, Joel F. *lawyer*
shtat, Harvey W. *lawyer*
f, Brian Michael *lawyer*
vin, Michele M. *lawyer*
dreau, Russell A., Jr. *lawyer, educator*
lt, Robert Mellor *lawyer*
aron, Paul R. *lawyer*
b, Richard Mark *lawyer*
bert, David A. *lawyer*
, Robert Tucker *lawyer*
er, A. Silvana *lawyer*
o, Frank III *lawyer*
zer, Martin A. *lawyer*
ason, Daniel J. *lawyer*
sband, Daniel Martin *lawyer*
dberg, Lena G. *lawyer, investment company*
executive
dman, Eric Scot *lawyer*
dman, Richard Harris *lawyer, director*
dstein, Jane D. *lawyer*
ason, S. Donald *lawyer*
odman, Louis Allan *lawyer*
ssels, Claus Peter Rolf *lawyer*
eco, Michael S. *lawyer*
een, Karen F. *lawyer*
eer, Allen Curtis, II, *lawyer, investment*
management executive
oss, Ira Kenneth *lawyer*
ddad, Ernest Mudarri *lawyer*
ddad, Mark E. *lawyer*
ey, Paul Richard *lawyer, state legislator*
l, David *law educator, dean, department*
chairman
l, Henry Lyon, Jr. *lawyer*
pert, David H. *lawyer*
lston, Daniel William *lawyer*
lström, Frederic Norman *lawyer*
ndly, Kevin John *lawyer, educator*
nlon, Francis X. *lawyer*
rrington, John Michael, Jr. *lawyer*
rvey, Christopher P. *lawyer*
rvey, Kenneth L. *lawyer*
wkey, G. Michael *lawyer, real estate*
developer
yes, Robert Francis *lawyer*
aly, Martin Russell *lawyer*
idt, Jeffrey L. *lawyer*
eken, Charles *lawyer*
ort, Steven Thomas *lawyer*
ran, Douglas S. *lawyer, utilities executive*
tchkiss, Andra Ruth *lawyer*
oward, Gregory Charles *lawyer*

Howard, Sheryl Andrea *lawyer*
Howe, Janice W. *lawyer*
Hrones, Stephen Baylis *lawyer, educator*
Hurley, Cornelius Keefe, Jr. *law educator*
Huston, Julia *lawyer*
Janos, Ellen L. *lawyer*
Johnston, Richard Alan *lawyer*
Johnston, Susan A. *lawyer*
Jones, Jeffrey Foster *lawyer*
Jones, Sheldon Atwell *retired lawyer*
Jordan, Alexander Joseph, Jr. *lawyer*
Kalkstein, Joshua Adam *lawyer*
Kanin, Dennis Roy *lawyer*
Karelitz, Robert N(elson) *lawyer*
Katz, Peter *lawyer*
Kearns, Ellen Cecelia *lawyer*
Keating, Michael Burns *lawyer, educator*
Kehoe, William Francis *lawyer*
Keller, Stanley *lawyer*
Kerry, Cameron F. *lawyer*
Khosla, Anil *lawyer*
Kidder, George Howell *lawyer*
Kindregan, Charles Peter *law educator*
Kirchick, William Dean *lawyer*
Kirsch, Robert L. *lawyer*
Klein, Bennett *lawyer*
Klem, Christopher A. *lawyer*
Klieman, Rikki Jo *lawyer, legal analyst*
Knag, Paul Everett *lawyer*
Kociubes, Joseph Leib *lawyer*
Kopelman, Leonard *lawyer*
Lampert, James B. *lawyer*
Last, Michael P. *lawyer*
LeBlanc, Marianne Camille *lawyer*
Lee, William F. *lawyer*
Lepore, Ralph Thomas III *lawyer*
Lettieri, Richard J. (Richard Joseph Lettieri)
lawyer
Levine, William Michael *lawyer*
Licata, Arthur Frank *lawyer*
Lieberman, Michael J. *lawyer*
Litwin, Paul Jeffrey *lawyer*
Loder, John Mark *lawyer*
Loeser, Hans Ferdinand *lawyer*
Loewenstein, Andrew B. *lawyer*
Looney, William Francis, Jr. *lawyer*
Loria, Martin A. *lawyer*
Lyons, Paul Vincent *lawyer*
Macauley, William Francis *lawyer*
Macdonald, Peter J. *lawyer*
MacLeish, Roderick, Jr. *lawyer*
Malt, Ronald Bradford *lawyer*
Mansfield, Christopher Charles *lawyer*
Marett, Louis J. *lawyer*
Markey, John K. *lawyer*
Martin, Gina Lynn *lawyer*
Martin, Stanley Allen *lawyer*
Matthews, Roger Hardin *lawyer*
Matuschak, Mark G. *lawyer*
Mayer, William P. *lawyer*
McAuliffe, Rosemary *lawyer*
McChesney, S. Elaine *lawyer*
McKenzie, Elizabeth McDaniel *law librarian*
McPhee, Joan *lawyer*
Meal, Douglas H. *lawyer*
Menna, Gilbert G. *lawyer*
Menoyo, Eric Felix *lawyer*
Merrill, Stephen *lawyer, consultant, retired*
governor
Meserve, William George *lawyer*
Meyer, Andrew C., Jr. *lawyer*
Mikels, Richard Eliot *lawyer*
Miller, Michelle D. *lawyer*
Miller, Peter M. *lawyer*
Milstein, Richard Sherman *lawyer*
Miner, Tracy A. *lawyer*
Minot, Winthrop Gardner *lawyer*
Mirabito, Anthony Jason *lawyer, educator*
Moffitt, Brenda A. *lawyer*
Moncreiff, Robert P. *lawyer*
Mone, Michael Edward *lawyer*
Montgomery, John T. *lawyer*
Montgomery, Susan Barbieri *lawyer*
Mooney, Michael Edward *lawyer*
Moore, Gregory E. *lawyer*
Moriarty, George Marshall *lawyer*
Motenko, Neil Philip *lawyer*
Muldoon, Robert Joseph, Jr. *lawyer*
Murley, Susan W. *lawyer*
Nagle, James W. *lawyer*
Nason, Leonard Yoshimoto *lawyer, writer*
Nelson, Patricia L. *lawyer*
Newberg, Joseph H. *lawyer*
Notopoulos, Alexander Anastasios, Jr. *lawyer*
Novack, Kenneth Joseph *lawyer*
Nunnally, Allen C. *lawyer*
Nutt, Robert L. *lawyer, educator*
O'Connell, Mary-Kathleen *lawyer*
O'Donnell, Thomas Lawrence Patrick *lawyer*
O'Leary, Joseph Evans *lawyer*
Olsen, Hans Peter *lawyer*
O'Neill, Philip Daniel, Jr. *lawyer, educator*
O'Reilly, William R., Jr. *lawyer*
Paine, William H. *lawyer*
Pappalardo, A. John *former prosecutor, lawyer*
Pappone, Michael J. *lawyer*
Park, William Wynnewood *law educator*
Partan, Daniel Gordon *lawyer, educator*
Patterson, John de la Roche, Jr. *lawyer*
Peckham, Thomas Elwood *lawyer*
Perera, Lawrence Thacher *lawyer*
Perkins, John Allen *lawyer*
Phelan, David C. *lawyer*
Pokross, David R., Jr. *lawyer*
Polebaum, Mark Neal *lawyer*
Pomeroy, Robert Corttis *lawyer*
Popeo, R. Robert *lawyer*
Porcelli, Frank Paul *lawyer*
Porter, Jeffrey R. *lawyer*
Poss, Stephen Daniel *lawyer*
Preston, Jerome, Jr. *retired lawyer*
Price, Robert F. *lawyer*
Quayle, Dwight W. *lawyer*
Quinan, Deborah Pechet *lawyer*
Raish, David Langdon *lawyer*
Reardon, Frank Emond *lawyer*
Redlich, Marc *lawyer*

Renehan, Richard William *lawyer*
Reppert, Sibley Putnam *lawyer*
Richmond, Alice Elenor *lawyer*
Rines, Robert Harvey *lawyer, educator, physicist,*
composer
Ritt, Roger Merrill *lawyer*
Robinson, Andrea J. *lawyer*
Rondeau, Patrick John *lawyer*
Ropple, Lisa M. *lawyer*
Rosenbaum, Jay D. *lawyer*
Rosenberg, Peter N. *lawyer*
Rosenblum, Peter M. *lawyer*
Rosenfeld, Jonathan D. *lawyer*
Ross, Nelson G. *lawyer*
Rossman, Stuart T. *lawyer*
Rothberg, Robert *lawyer*
Rowe, Larry Jordan *lawyer*
Rudavsky, Dahlia C. *lawyer*
Rudman, Jeffrey B. *lawyer*
Rudolph, James Leonard *lawyer*
Ryan, Allan Andrew, Jr. *lawyer, director,*
educator, writer
Ryan, Sean T. *lawyer*
Saloman, Syd Adam *lawyer*
Sargeant, Ernest James *lawyer, educator*
Sartory, Thomas J. *lawyer*
Sawyer, William C. *lawyer*
Scherkenbach, Frank Everett *lawyer*
Schwartz, Paul D. *lawyer*
Sears, John Winthrop *lawyer*
Shapiro, Robert N. *lawyer*
Shapiro, Sandra *lawyer*
Sheehan, Gregory D. *lawyer*
Sherman, Robert Alan *lawyer*
Shilepsky, Nancy Sue *lawyer*
Shulkin, Martin B. *lawyer*
Sigel, John D. *lawyer*
Singer, Steven D. *lawyer*
Sinnott, William F. *lawyer*
Sirkin, Joel H. *lawyer*
Smith, Craig R. *lawyer*
Smith, Edwin Eric *lawyer*
Smith, Philip Jones *lawyer*
Solet, Maxwell David *lawyer*
Soule, Robert Grove *lawyer*
Southard, William G. *lawyer*
Southgate, Richard W. *lawyer, director*
Speer, Brownlow Main *lawyer*
Steinberg, Donald R. *lawyer*
Steinberg, Laura *lawyer*
Stern, Donald Kenneth *lawyer*
Stewart, Craig E. *lawyer*
Stillwell, R. Newcomb *lawyer*
Stokes, James Christopher *lawyer*
Storey, James Moorfield *lawyer*
Sugarman, Paul Ronald *lawyer, educator,*
academic administrator
Sullivan, Michael J. *prosecutor*
Sunstein, Bruce David *lawyer*
Surkin, Elliot Mark *lawyer*
Swaim, C. Hall *lawyer*
Swope, Jeffrey Peyton *lawyer*
Tarantino, Louis Gerald *lawyer, management*
consultant
Taylor, Thomas William *lawyer*
Telegen, Arthur G. *lawyer*
Touster, Saul *law educator*
Trimmier, Roscoe, Jr. *lawyer*
Troupe, William Harold *lawyer*
Tse, Marian A. *lawyer*
Tuchmann, Robert *lawyer*
Vaughan, Herbert Wiley *retired lawyer*
Vigoda, Robert A. *lawyer*
Walek, David B. *lawyer*
Walsh, Joseph Hayes *lawyer*
Ware, Donald R. *lawyer*
Ware, Paul F., Jr. *lawyer*
Weinberg, Martin Gary *lawyer*
Weiner, Stephen Mark *lawyer*
Weitzel, John Patterson *lawyer*
Wellington, Carol Strong *law librarian*
Westcott, John McMahon, Jr. *lawyer*
Westra, James R. *lawyer*
White, Barry Bennett *lawyer*
White, Dennis J. *lawyer*
White-Lief, David Westcott *lawyer*
Whitlock, John L. *lawyer*
Whitters, James Payton III *lawyer, educator*
Wilcox, Steven Alan *lawyer*
Williams, John Taylor *lawyer*
Woodburn, Ralph Robert, Jr. *lawyer*
Young, Raymond Henry *lawyer*
Zack, Arnold Marshall *lawyer, mediator,*
arbitrator, judge

Braintree
Riccio, Frank Joseph *lawyer, educator*

Brighton
Garber, Paul William *lawyer*

Burlington
Cerveny, David John *lawyer*

Cambridge
Alexander, Susan H. *lawyer, pharmaceutical*
executive
Andrews, William Dorey *law educator*
Barron, David Jeremiah *law educator*
Bartholet, Elizabeth *law educator*
Bebchuk, Lucian Arye *law and finance educator*
Benkler, Yochai *law educator*
Bok, Derek Curtis *law educator, former*
academic administrator
Brewer, Scott *law educator*
Clark, Robert Charles *law educator, former dean*
Cogan, John Francis, Jr. *lawyer*
Connors, Frank Joseph *lawyer*
Dershowitz, Alan Morton *law educator*
Desan, Christine *law educator*
DesRosier, Thomas J. *lawyer*
Donahue, Charles, Jr. *law educator*
Elhauge, Einer Richard *law educator*
Fallon, Richard H., Jr. *law educator*
Field, Martha Amanda *law educator*
Fisher, Roger Dummer *negotiation expert, law*
educator

Frug, Gerald E. *law educator*
Glendon, Mary Ann *law educator*
Goldsmith, Jack Landman III *law educator,*
former federal agency administrator
Halley, Janet E. *law educator*
Halperin, Daniel I. *law educator*
Hanson, Jon D. *law educator*
Heineman, Benjamin Walter, Jr. *lawyer*
Hostage, John Brayne Arthur *law librarian*
Iuliano, Robert W. *lawyer*
Jackson, Howell E. *law educator*
Kaplow, Louis *law educator*
Kaufman, Andrew Lee *law educator*
Kayden, Jerold S. *lawyer, urban planner*
Kennedy, David William *law educator*
Kennedy, Duncan McLean *law educator*
Kennedy, Randall L. *law educator*
King, William Bruce *retired lawyer*
Lau, Vincent W. *lawyer*
Lewis, Scott P. *lawyer*
Mahoney, Kevin J. *lawyer*
Manning, John F. *law educator*
Martin, Harry Stratton III *law librarian,*
educator
McGurk, Michael R. *lawyer*
Meltzer, Daniel J. *law educator*
Miller, Steven E. *professor of international*
affairs
Moore, Mark Harrison *criminal justice and*
public policy educator
Ogletree, Charles J., Jr. *law educator*
Parker, Richard Davies *law educator*
Patton, Bruce M. *law educator, management*
consultant
Ramseyer, J. Mark *law educator*
Riley, Lynne F. *lawyer*
Sander, Frank Ernest Arnold *law educator*
Sapers, Carl Martin *lawyer, educator*
Schauer, Frederick Franklin *law educator*
Scott, Hal S. *law educator*
Shapiro, David Louis *law educator*
Shavell, Steven M. *law educator*
Steiker, Carol S. *law educator*
Steiner, Henry Jacob *law and human rights*
educator
Subramanian, Guhan *law educator*
Ta, Tai Van *lawyer, researcher*
Tribe, Laurence Henry *law educator*
Vagts, Detlev Frederick *law educator*
Warren, Alvin Clifford, Jr. *law educator*
Warren, Elizabeth A. *law educator*
Weinreb, Lloyd Lobell *law educator*
Wilkins, David Brian *law educator, director*
Wirth, Peter *lawyer*
Wolfman, Bernard *lawyer, educator*
Zittrain, Jonathan L. *law educator*

Canton
Masiello, Thomas Philip, Jr. *lawyer, risk*
management consultant

Chatham
Popkin, Alice Brandeis *lawyer*

Chelmsford
Dulchinos, Peter *retired lawyer*
Lerer, Neal M. *lawyer*

Chestnut Hill
Batchelder, Samuel Lawrence, Jr. *retired*
corporate lawyer
Qingwen, Xu *law educator, social worker,*
educator
Vance, Verne Widney, Jr. *retired lawyer*

Concord
Bander, Edward Julius *lawyer, librarian emeritus*
Glovsky, Susan G.L. *lawyer*

Danvers
Haber, Frederic *lawyer*

Dedham
Bolio, Jason S. *lawyer*

Dennis Port
Singer, Myer R(ichard) *lawyer*

Dover
Craver, James Bernard *lawyer*
Edwards, Carl Norman *lawyer*

Duxbury
Schwartz, Edward Arthur *lawyer*

East Boston
Crawford, Linda Sibery *lawyer, educator*

Edgartown
Gatting, Carlene J. *lawyer*

Framingham
Campbell, Kristin A. *lawyer, retail executive*
Heng, Gerald C.W. *lawyer*
McCauley, Ann *lawyer, retail executive*
Ryan, Dennis M. *lawyer, construction executive*

Gloucester
Birchfield, John Kermit, Jr. *lawyer*

Holden
Price, Robert DeMille *lawyer*

Holyoke
Resnic, Burton S. *lawyer*

Hopkinton
Dacier, Paul T. *lawyer, information technology*
executive

Hull
Medalie, Richard James *lawyer*
Medalie, Susan Diane *lawyer, management*
consultant

Hyannis
Segersten, Robert Hagy *lawyer, investment*
banker

Ipswich
Getchell, Charles Willard, Jr. *lawyer, publisher, foundation executive*

Lawrence
Wasserman, Stephen Alan *lawyer*

Leominster
Lambert, Lyn Dee *law librarian*

Lexington
Kent, Robert Brydon *law educator*

Lincoln
Gnichtel, William Van Orden *lawyer*

Lowell
Curtis, James Theodore *lawyer*
Martin, William Francis, Jr. *lawyer*
O'Donnell, Kathleen Marie *lawyer*

Lynnfield
McGivney, John Joseph *lawyer*

Marblehead
Page, George Alfred, Jr. *lawyer*

Medford
Berman, David *lawyer, poet*
Salacuse, Jeswald William *lawyer, educator*

Natick
Grassia, Thomas Charles *lawyer, educator, writer*
Marr, David E. *lawyer*
Sandman, Paul William *lawyer*

Needham
Bohnen, Michael J. *lawyer, foundation administrator*
Spelfogel, Scott David *lawyer*

New Bedford
Benoit, Richard Armand *lawyer, retired police chief*
Murray, Robert Fox *lawyer*

Newton
Baron, Charles Hillel *lawyer, educator*
Coquillette, Daniel Robert *lawyer, educator*
Frankenheim, Samuel *retired lawyer*
Glazer, Donald Wayne *lawyer, corporate financial executive, educator*
Huber, Richard Gregory *lawyer, educator*
Metzer, Patricia Ann *lawyer*
Peterson, Osler Leopold *lawyer*

Newton Center
Snyder, John Gorvers *lawyer*

Newton Centre
Anzalone, Filippa Marullo *law librarian, educator*

Northampton
Hastings, Wilmot Reed *lawyer, writer*

Norwood
Seif, Margaret K. *lawyer, electronics executive*
Singer, Paula Noyes *lawyer, computer company executive*

Pittsfield
Doyle, Anthony Peter *lawyer*

Plymouth
Della-Giustina, Jo-Ann *lawyer*

Prides Crossing
Garcia, Adolfo Ramon *lawyer, director*
Schlichtmann, Jan Richard *lawyer*

Quincy
Hayes, Mary Dianne Wixted *lawyer*
Motejunas, Gerald William *lawyer*

Randolph
Johnson, Laurence Michael *lawyer*

Salem
Moran, Philip David *lawyer*
Rabchenuk, Paul Thomas *lawyer*

Sandwich
Troy, Robert Sweeney, Sr. *lawyer*

Sherborn
Borgeson, Earl Charles *law librarian, educator*
Goglia, Charles A., Jr. *lawyer*

Siasconset
Rauch, George Washington *lawyer, director*

Southborough
Kriegsman, Edward Michael *lawyer*

Springfield
Burke, Michael Henry *lawyer*
Dibble, Francis Daniel, Jr. *lawyer*
Mason, Mark D. *lawyer*
McCarthy, Charles Francis, Jr. *lawyer*
Oldershaw, Louis Frederick *retired lawyer*
Parke, David Alan *lawyer*
Roellig, Mark D. *lawyer*
Santopietro, Albert Robert *lawyer*
Susse, Sandra Slone *lawyer*
Weiss, Ronald Phillip *lawyer*

Stoughton
Gabovitch, Steven Alan *lawyer, accountant*
George, Arthur Charles *lawyer*

Truro
Chaplin, Ansel Burt *lawyer*

Wakefield
Lucas, Robert Frank *lawyer*

Waltham
Barnes-Brown, Peter Newton *lawyer*
Chory, John H. *lawyer*
Faneuil, Edward J. *lawyer*
Hill, Anita Faye *law educator*
Hoogasian, Seth H. *lawyer*
Stephens, Jay B. *lawyer, defense equipment manufacturing company executive*

Watertown
Kaloosdian, Robert Aram *lawyer*

Wellesley
Burstein, Harvey *lawyer, educator*
Marx, Peter A. *lawyer*
Pike, Judith Robyn *lawyer*
Silberman, Robert A. S. *lawyer*
Wilchins, Stephen N. *lawyer*

Wellesley Hills
Carroll, Megan *lawyer, educator*

West Chatham
Rowley, Glenn Harry *lawyer*

West Falmouth
Carlson, David Bret *retired lawyer*

Weston
Bateman, Thomas Robert *lawyer*
Lashman, L. Edward *arbitrator, mediator, consultant*
Thomas, Roger Meriwether *lawyer*

Weymouth
Fitzsimmons, B. Joseph, Jr. *lawyer*

Winthrop
Brown, Patricia Irene *retired law librarian, lawyer*

Worcester
Balko, George Anthony III *lawyer, educator*
Cowan, Fairman Chaffee *lawyer*
Donnelly, James Corcoran, Jr. *lawyer*
Huber, J. Kendall *lawyer, insurance company executive*
Lougee, David Louis *lawyer*
Mirick, John O. *lawyer*
Moschos, Demitrios Mina *lawyer*
Uhl, Christopher Martin *lawyer*
Van Nostrand, Richard Charles *lawyer*

MICHIGAN

Ada
Mohr, Michael Arthur *lawyer*

Alpena
Hunter, Mark John *lawyer, photographer*

Ann Arbor
Allen, Layman Edward *law educator, research scientist*
Anderson, Austin Gothard *lawyer, consultant, academic administrator*
Buesser, Anthony Carpenter *lawyer*
Carney, Thomas Daly *lawyer*
Cooper, Edward Hayes *lawyer, educator*
Darlow, Julia Donovan *lawyer*
DeVine, Edmond Francis *retired lawyer*
Dew, Thomas Edward *lawyer*
Duquette, Donald Norman *law educator*
Ellmann, Douglas Stanley *lawyer*
Garris, Michael Jack *lawyer*
Gray, Whitmore *lawyer, educator*
Green, Thomas Andrew *lawyer, educator*
Hathaway, James C. *law educator*
Joscelyn, Kent Buckley *lawyer*
Kahn, Douglas Allen *law educator*
Kamisar, Yale *lawyer, educator*
Keppelman, Nancy *lawyer*
Krier, James Edward *law educator, writer*
Kuehn, George E. *lawyer*
Laycock, Harold Douglas *law educator, writer*
MacKinnon, Catharine Alice *lawyer, educator, writer*
Miller, William Ian *law educator*
Muraski, Anthony Augustus *lawyer*
Niehoff, Leonard Marvin *lawyer*
Payton, Sallyanne *law educator*
Reed, John Wesley *lawyer, educator*
Ryan, Marianne Elizabeth *lawyer*
St. Antoine, Theodore Joseph *retired law educator, arbitrator*
Sandalow, Terrance *law educator*
Scott, Rebecca J. *law and history educator*
Shaw, Sonia *retired lawyer*
Simpson, A.W. Brian *law educator*
Stein, Eric *retired law educator*
Sullivan, Teresa Ann *law and sociology educator, academic administrator*
Theut, C. Peter *lawyer*
Vining, (George) Joseph *law educator*
Waggoner, Lawrence William *law educator*
Walsh, James Joseph *lawyer*
White, James Boyd *law educator*

Auburn Hills
Gasparovic, John J. *lawyer*
Horiszny, Laurene Helen *lawyer*

Battle Creek
Steffel, Vern John, Jr. *lawyer*

Bay City
Greve, Guy Robert *lawyer*
Powers, David Louis *lawyer*

Benton Harbor
Hopp, Daniel Frederick *lawyer, manufacturing company executive*

Beverly Hills
Hertzberg, David Gordon *retired lawyer*

Bingham Farms
Baumkel, Mark S. *lawyer*
Berman, Leonard Keith *lawyer*
Goren, Steven Eliot *lawyer*

Birmingham
Demorest, Mark Stuart *lawyer*
Elsman, James Leonard, Jr. *lawyer*
Kienbaum, Thomas Gerd *lawyer*
Schaefer, John Frederick *lawyer*
Thorpe, Norman Ralph *lawyer, automotive executive, retired military officer*
Zacharski, Dennis Edward *lawyer*

Bloomfield
Kanter, Alan Michael *lawyer*
Reiter, Jesse Matthew *lawyer*

Bloomfield Hills
Adams, James Charles *lawyer*
Banas, C(hristine) Leslie *lawyer*
Burstein, Richard Joel *lawyer*
Charla, Leonard Francis *lawyer, publishing executive*
Clippert, Charles Frederick *lawyer*
Cook, Steven M. *lawyer, construction executive*
Cummings, Roger Holt *lawyer*
Dawson, Stephen Everette *lawyer*
Deron, Edward Michael *lawyer*
Devaney, Dennis Martin *lawyer, educator*
Gold, Edward David *lawyer*
Googasian, George Ara *lawyer*
Kasischke, Louis Walter *lawyer*
Kirk, John MacGregor *lawyer*
Ledwidge, Patrick Joseph *lawyer*
LoPrete, James Hugh *lawyer*
Martin, J(oseph) Patrick *lawyer, judge*
McCuen, John Francis, Jr. *lawyer*
McDonald, Patrick Allen *lawyer, educator, arbitrator*
Meyer, George Herbert *lawyer*
Nern, Christopher Carl *lawyer*
Norris, John Hart *lawyer, director*
Rader, Ralph Terrance *lawyer*
Simon, Evelyn *lawyer*
Smith, H(arold) Lawrence *lawyer*
Snyder, George Edward *lawyer*
Solomon, Mark Raymond *lawyer, educator*
Sommerfeld, David William *lawyer, educator*
Stewart, Michael B. *lawyer, mechanical and aerospace engineer*
Victor, Richard Steven *lawyer*
Williams, J. Bryan *lawyer*
Williams, Walter Joseph *lawyer*
Wise, John Augustus *lawyer, director*

Center Line
Cahill, Kimberly M. *lawyer*

Chesterfield
Danielson, Gary R. *lawyer*

Dearborn
Kahn, Mark Leo *arbitrator, educator*
Nelson, Alison R. *lawyer*

Decatur
Kinney, Gregory Hoppes *lawyer*

Detroit
Archer, Dennis Wayne *lawyer, former mayor*
Bilstrom, Jon Wayne *lawyer*
Boocock, Stephen William *lawyer*
Brand, George Edward, Jr. *retired lawyer*
Brustad, Orin Daniel *lawyer*
Calkins, Stephen *lawyer, educator*
Candler, James Nall, Jr. *lawyer*
Charfoos, Lawrence Selig *lawyer*
Cohan, Leon Sumner *lawyer, retired electric company executive*
Cohen, Norton Jacob *lawyer*
Cothorn, John Arthur *lawyer*
Cranmer, Thomas William *lawyer*
Deason, Herold McClure *lawyer*
Diehl, Nancy J. *lawyer*
Drutchas, Gregory G. *lawyer*
Dudley, Arthur, II, *lawyer*
Dudley, John Henry, Jr. *lawyer*
Dunn, William Bradley *lawyer*
Early, S. Allen III *lawyer*
Faison, W. Mack *lawyer*
Gershel, Alan M. *prosecutor*
Glotta, Ronald Delon *lawyer*
Hampton, Verne Churchill, II, *lawyer*
Hughes, Thomas A. *lawyer, utilities executive*
Kamins, John Mark *lawyer*
Kessler, Philip Joel *lawyer*
Krsul, John Aloysius, Jr. *lawyer*
Lawrence, John Kidder *lawyer*
Lewis, David Baker *lawyer*
Lockman, Stuart M. *lawyer*
Mamat, Frank Trustick *lawyer*
Maurer, David Leo *lawyer*
McIntyre, Michael John *lawyer, educator*
McKim, Samuel John III *lawyer*
Miller, Bruce Abraham *lawyer*
Mitseff, Carl *lawyer*
Murphy, Stephen Joseph III *prosecutor*
Myers, Rodman Nathaniel *lawyer*
Nemeth, Patricia Marie *lawyer*
Ortiz, Francis Robert *lawyer*
Peters, John Douglas *lawyer, artist*
Rassel, Richard Edward *lawyer*
Raymond, Richard Gerard, Jr. *lawyer*
Rogers, Paulleto *researcher, writer*
Rohr, Richard David *lawyer*
Rozof, Phyllis Claire *lawyer*
Rupley, Jerry T. *lawyer*
Saxton, William Marvin *lawyer*
Schwartz, Alan Earl *lawyer, director*
Scott, John Edward Smith *lawyer*
Sedler, Robert Allen *law educator*
Shannon, Margaret Anne *lawyer*
Sherrick, Daniel William *lawyer*
Smith, James Albert *lawyer*
Smith, S. Kinnie, Jr. *lawyer*
Sparrow, Herbert George III *lawyer, educator*

Tarnacki, Duane L. *lawyer*
Thelen, Bruce Cyril *lawyer*
Timm, Roger K. *lawyer*
Turner, Reginald Maurice, Jr. *lawyer*
Valade, Alan Michael *lawyer*
Volz, William Harry *lawyer, educator*
Whiteman, Richard Mark *lawyer*
Wittlinger, Timothy David *lawyer*
Wu, Frank H. *law educator, journalist*
Wyrick, Jermaine Albert *lawyer*
Zuckerman, Richard Engle *lawyer, educator*

East Lansing
Cascarilla, Richard A. *lawyer*
Lashbrooke, Elvin Carroll, Jr. *law educator, consultant*
Rasmusson, Thomas *lawyer*
White, James Alfred *lawyer*
Wilkinson, William Sherwood *lawyer*

Farmington
Shaevsky, Mark *lawyer*

Farmington Hills
Antone, Nahil Peter *lawyer, civil engineer*
Bernstein, Richard *lawyer*
Fenton, Robert Leonard *lawyer, writer, film producer*
Fershtman, Julie Ilene *lawyer*
Foley, Thomas John *lawyer*
Gordon, Arnold Mark *arbitrator, educator*
Mall, Sanford J. *lawyer*
Meyer, Philip Gilbert *lawyer*
Taravella, Christopher Anthony *lawyer*
Winzenreid, James Ernest *lawyer, entrepreneur*

Flint
Cooley, Richard Eugene *lawyer*
Hart, Clifford Harvey *lawyer*

Frankfort
Gerberding, Miles Carston *lawyer*

Franklin
Pappas, Edward Harvey *lawyer*

Grand Rapids
Barnes, Thomas John *lawyer*
Botsford, Jon Douglas *lawyer*
Bradshaw, Conrad Allan *retired lawyer*
Brinkmeyer, Scott S. *lawyer*
Bursch, John Joseph *lawyer*
Curtin, Timothy John *lawyer*
Davis, Henry Barnard, Jr. *lawyer*
DeYonker, Alex J. *lawyer, food products executive*
Harris, Richard W. *lawyer, educator, accountar*
Jennette, Noble Stevenson III *lawyer*
McCallum, Charles Edward *lawyer*
Mears, Patrick Edward *lawyer*
Noakes, William S., Jr. *lawyer*
Oetting, Roger H. *lawyer*
Rasmussen, Douglas John *lawyer*
Spies, Frank Stadler *lawyer*
Sytsma, Fredric A. *lawyer*
Van Haren, W(illiam) Michael *lawyer*

Greenville
Mullendore, James Myers *lawyer*

Grosse Pointe
Amsden, Ted Thomas *lawyer*
Goss, James William *lawyer*

Grosse Pointe Farms
Thurber, Peter Palms *lawyer*

Grosse Pointe Park
Centner, Charles William *lawyer, educator*
Mogk, John Edward *law educator, association executive, consultant*

Grosse Pointe Woods
Prather, Kenneth Earl *lawyer*

Harbor Springs
Smith, Wayne Richard *lawyer*
Turner, Lester Nathan *lawyer, international tra consultant*

Hickory Corners
Bristol, Norman *lawyer, arbitrator, retired foo products executive*

Highland
Bullard, Willis Clare, Jr. *lawyer*

Holland
Murphy, Max Ray *lawyer*

Inkster
Bullock, Steven Carl *lawyer*

Ishpeming
Steward, James Brian *lawyer, pharmacist*

Jackson
Brunner, James Edwin *lawyer*
Jacobs, Wendell Early, Jr. *lawyer*
Marcoux, William Joseph *lawyer*
Smith, Stanton Kinnie, Jr. *lawyer*

Jenison
Kruse, Pamela Jean *lawyer*

Kalamazoo
Enslen, Pamela Chapman *lawyer*
Gordon, Edgar George *retired lawyer*
Hall, Curtis E. *lawyer*
Lundquist, C. David *lawyer*
Marquardt, Michele C. *lawyer*
Van Slambrouck, John G. *lawyer*

Lake Orion
Robinson, Marietta S. *lawyer*

sing
:, Frederick Milton, Jr. *lawyer*
Stuart R. *lawyer*
er, Mark Courtland *lawyer*
ow, Daniel J. *lawyer*
Joseph Allen *lawyer*
r, Joe C., Jr. *lawyer*
gher, Byron Patrick, Jr. *lawyer*
Steven Charles *lawyer*
y, Frank Joseph *lawyer, former state orney general*
in, David Edward Shreve *lawyer*
ey, John Philip *law educator*
meyer, Norman Otto *law educator, nsultant*
er, Richard Earnest *legal foundation ninistrator, writer, consultant*

nia
sky, David L. *lawyer, automotive executive*
nan, Barry Paul *lawyer*

rquette
:, Ronald D. *lawyer*

land
:, Leonard Carroll *lawyer*
Charles James *lawyer, chemicals executive*

nroe
, Morton Ray *lawyer*
rd, Rocque Edward *lawyer*

skegon
gs, John Mancel III *lawyer*
, Eric Joseph *lawyer*
endry, John H., Jr. *lawyer*
a, Gerald Peter *lawyer*

thville
ey, Patrick C. *lawyer*
ri, V. M. *arbitrator, mediator, educator*
itt, Martin Jack *lawyer*

i
ta, David M. *lawyer, manufacturing ecutive*

ckney
on, Clarold Lawrence *lawyer, consultant*

mouth
tina, Carlo Jack *lawyer*
gan, Donald Crane *lawyer*
akowski, Nicholas J. *lawyer*
nson, Logan Gilmore *lawyer*

ntiac
son, William George *lawyer*

ckford
dy, Kenneth Alan *lawyer, corporate secretary*

yal Oak
gel, Christopher Emile *lawyer, educator*

inaw
ot, Craig Allen *lawyer*

nt Clair Shores
yn, Robert Bruce *lawyer*

ult Sainte Marie
ello, Steven John *lawyer*

uth Haven
man, Sheldon Robert *lawyer*

uthfield
dreoff, Christopher Andon *lawyer*
sey, Ronald D. *tax attorney*
oks, Ernie L. *lawyer*
ling, Robert Howard *lawyer*
vson, Dennis Ray *lawyer, manufacturing xecutive*
ong, Donald Alan *lawyer*
ger, Geoffrey Nels *lawyer*
, Stacy L. *lawyer*
d, Martin L. *lawyer*
odman, Barry Joel *lawyer*
don, Louis *retired lawyer*
obson, Michael F. *lawyer*
low, Robert David *lawyer*
z, Robert L. *lawyer*
chtman, Stephen Nathan *lawyer*
v, James William *lawyer*
Clow, Roger James *labor lawyer*
rganroth, Mayer *lawyer*
ivaggi, Daniel A. *lawyer, manufacturing xecutive*
itz, John Allan *lawyer*
ter, Thomas W.B. *lawyer*
chie, Alexander Buchan *lawyer*
chkind, Louis Philipp *lawyer*
rswell, Gerald Elliott *lawyer*
l, Sheldon Samuel *lawyer*
pey, Scott Raymond *lawyer*
ner, Lee Irwin *lawyer*

erling Heights
rkey, James Kevin *lawyer*
vak, Joseph Anthony *law librarian*

lvan Lake
rdarian, Christine Anne *lawyer*

ylor
sch, David L. *lawyer*
ckley, John Robert *lawyer, consumer products company executive*

averse City
andt, Joseph Edward *lawyer, educator*

oy
ber, Phillip George *lawyer*
erman, Irwin Michael *lawyer*

Baker, Vernon G., II, *lawyer, automotive executive*
Bishop, Michael *lawyer, state senator*
Cantor, Bernard Jack *lawyer*
Chapman, Conrad Daniel *lawyer*
Cunningham, Gary H. *lawyer*
Dillon, Joseph Francis *lawyer*
Gelder, John William *lawyer*
Haron, David Lawrence *lawyer*
Hilton, Michael E. *lawyer*
Kruse, John Alphonse *lawyer*
Lis, Daniel T. *lawyer*
May, Alan Alfred *lawyer*
Navarro, Monica *lawyer*
Paluda, Andrew Joseph *lawyer, consultant*
Pearce, Harry Jonathan *lawyer, manufacturing executive*
Peters, Thomas M. *lawyer*
Sherbin, David M. *lawyer*
Thoms, David Moore *lawyer*
Webster, Robert Byron *lawyer*

Van Buren Township
Donofrio, John *lawyer*

Walled Lake
Connelly, Thomas Joseph *lawyer*
Seglund, Bruce Richard *lawyer*

Warren
Bridenstine, Louis Henry, Jr. *lawyer*

Washington
Barrows, Ronald Thomas *lawyer*

West Bloomfield
Avery, Karin F. *lawyer*
Sullivan, Robert Emmet, Jr. *lawyer*
Tobin, Bruce Howard *lawyer*

Wyandotte
Pentiuk, Randall Alan *lawyer*

Ypsilanti
Barr, John Monte *lawyer*
Eggertsen, John Hale *lawyer*
McLain, Dennis O. *lawyer*

MINNESOTA

Anoka
Hicken, Jeffrey Price *lawyer*

Austin
Cavanaugh, James W. *lawyer*

Bayport
Bernick, Alan E. *lawyer, accountant*

Bemidji
Kief, Paul Allan *lawyer*

Bloomington
Broeker, John Milton *lawyer*
Dordell, Timothy Paul *lawyer*
Grinnell, Joseph Fox *lawyer*
Mooty, John William *lawyer*
Nelson, Eric John *lawyer*

Chatfield
Opat, Matthew John *lawyer*

Detroit Lakes
Stowman, David L. *lawyer*

Duluth
Burns, Richard Ramsey *lawyer*
Thibodeau, Thomas Raymond *lawyer*
Wirth, Erin Masson *lawyer*

Eagan
Dulas, DeAnne L. *lawyer*

Eden Prairie
Feuss, Linda Anne Upsall *lawyer*
Gernander, Barton Carl *lawyer*
Gilbert, James H. *lawyer, former state supreme court justice*
Hansen, Erik Frederick *lawyer*
Nilles, John Michael *lawyer*

Edina
Bakken, Eric Allen *lawyer*
Davidson, Ann D. *lawyer, aerospace transportation executive*
Drewes, Matthew A. *lawyer*
Neff, Fred Leonard *lawyer*
Renz, Christopher P. *lawyer*
Schaibley, Ann M. *lawyer*
Schulze, Chad William *lawyer*
Towey, Anne C. *lawyer*

Eitzen
Euller, Steven C. *lawyer*

Golden Valley
Ainsworth, Louis Lynde *lawyer, manufacturing executive*
Breimayer, Joseph Frederick *patent lawyer*
Schlichting, William Henry *lawyer, writer*

Grand Marais
Hennessy, William Joseph *prosecutor*

Hallock
Malm, Roger Charles *lawyer*

Hastings
May, Nicholas G.B. *lawyer*

Kenyon
Peterson, Franklin Delano *lawyer*

Lakeville
Pattee, Steven D. *lawyer*

Mankato
Kohlmeyer, Jason C. *lawyer*
Rosengren, Christopher Paul *lawyer*

Marshall
Paskach, David M. *lawyer, food products executive*
Sattler, Brian R. *lawyer*

Medina
McConnell, Mary Patricia *lawyer*

Mendota Heights
Cotter, Patrick Linnae *lawyer*

Minneapolis
Abramson, Norman M. *lawyer*
Ahern, Michael James *lawyer*
Ali, Jeffer *lawyer*
Anderson, Eric Scott *lawyer*
Anderson, Leslie J. *lawyer*
Baer, Timothy R. *lawyer, retail executive*
Baillie, James Leonard *lawyer*
Ballintine, Daniel John *lawyer*
Barden, Robert Christopher *lawyer, psychologist, educator, writer*
Beekman, Marvin Lee *lawyer*
Berens, William Joseph *lawyer*
Berg, Thomas Kenneth *lawyer*
Bergerson, David Raymond *lawyer*
Bland, J(ohn) Richard *lawyer*
Borger, John Philip *lawyer*
Brand, Steve Aaron *lawyer*
Branson, Timothy E. *lawyer*
Bress, Michael E. *retired lawyer*
Breyer, K. Jon *lawyer*
Brink, David Ryrie *lawyer*
Bruner, Philip Lane *lawyer*
Buckingham, Elizabeth C. *lawyer*
Buratti, Dennis P. *lawyer*
Burke, Forrest G. *lawyer*
Busdicker, Gordon Gene *retired lawyer*
Camarotto, David Earle *lawyer*
Caplan, Allan Hart *lawyer*
Cattanach, Robert Edward, Jr. *lawyer*
Chadwick, Eric Hugh *lawyer*
Champlin, Steven Kirk *lawyer*
Chosy, James Louis *lawyer, brokerage house executive*
Christiansen, Jay David *lawyer*
Cialkowski, David Michael *lawyer*
Ciresi, Michael Vincent *lawyer*
Clary, Bradley G. *lawyer, educator*
Connelly, Michael C. *lawyer, energy executive*
Constantine, Katherine A. *lawyer*
Corwin, Gregg Marlowe *lawyer*
Davis, Aaron W. *lawyer*
Deach, Jana Aune *lawyer*
Degnan, John Michael *lawyer*
DeVries Smith, Kate *lawyer*
Diviney, Craig David *lawyer*
Dorenkamp, Theodore III *lawyer*
Durocher, Vernle C. (Skip), Jr. *lawyer*
Eck, George Gregory *lawyer*
Eng, Holly S.A. *lawyer*
Engh, N. Rolf (Rolf Engh) *lawyer*
Fisher, Michele Renee *lawyer*
Flom, Gerald Trossen *lawyer*
Flynn Peterson, Kathleen A. *lawyer*
Forneris, Jeanne M. *lawyer*
Frase, Richard S. *law educator*
French, John Dwyer *retired lawyer*
Gagnon, Craig William *lawyer*
Gallagher, Patrick J. *lawyer*
Garon, Philip Stephen *lawyer*
Garton, Thomas William *lawyer*
Genereux, L. Joseph *lawyer*
Gill, Richard Lawrence *lawyer*
Goodman, Christopher Lawrence *lawyer*
Gordon, Corey Lee *lawyer*
Gottschalk, Stephen Elmer *retired lawyer*
Greener, Ralph Bertram *lawyer*
Gross, David J.F. *lawyer*
Hagglund, Clarance Edward *lawyer, publishing executive*
Hamel, Mark Edwin *lawyer*
Hansen, Robyn L. *lawyer*
Hanson, Kent Bryan *lawyer*
Hart, Buster Clarence *lawyer*
Haynsworth, Harry Jay, IV, *law educator*
Hayward, Edward Joseph *lawyer*
Heffelfinger, Thomas Backer *lawyer, former prosecutor*
Heiberg, Robert Alan *lawyer*
Helsene, Amy L. *lawyer*
Hendrixson, Peter S. *lawyer*
Herman, John Hughes *lawyer*
Herr, David Fulton *lawyer, educator*
Hinderaker, John Hadley *lawyer, political blogger*
Holden, Susan M. *lawyer*
Howland, Joan Sidney *law librarian, educator*
Hunt, Kay Nord *lawyer*
Hunter, Donald Forrest *lawyer*
Jackson, J. David *lawyer*
Jacobson, Carrie Isabelle *lawyer*
Jameson, Jennifer A. *lawyer*
Jarboe, Mark Alan *lawyer*
Johnson, Gary M. *lawyer*
Johnson, Larry Walter *lawyer*
Johnson, Richard J. *lawyer*
Jonason, William A. *lawyer*
Jones, Jeffrey A. *lawyer*
Joyce, Joseph M. *lawyer, retail executive*
Junek, John C. *lawyer, finance company executive*
Kalinsky, Robert A. *lawyer*
Kantor, David *lawyer*
Kaplan, Sheldon *lawyer, director*
Kelly, A. David *lawyer*
Keppel, William James *lawyer, educator, writer*
Keyes, Jeffrey J. *lawyer*
Kirtley, Jane Elizabeth *law educator*
Klaas, Paul Barry *lawyer*
Knopf, Matthew J. *lawyer*
Koneck, John Michael *lawyer*
Lancaster, Peter McCreery *lawyer*
Lavik, Bricker L. *lawyer*
Lavoie, James A. *lawyer*
Lazar, Raymond Michael *lawyer, educator*
Lebedoff, David Miller *lawyer, writer*
Lillehaug, David Lee *lawyer*
Lindsay, Michael Anthony *lawyer*
Loucks, Kathleen Margaret *lawyer*
Lucke, Stephen P. *lawyer*
Lueck, Martin R. *lawyer*
Magid, Creighton (Chip) Reid *lawyer*
Magnuson, Roger James *lawyer*
Mahoney, Kathleen Mary *lawyer*
Manthey, Thomas Richard *lawyer*
Marshall, Siri Swenson *lawyer, consumer products company executive*
Martin, Judith Moran *lawyer*
Martin, Phillip Hammond *lawyer*
Martinson, Bradley James *lawyer*
Matson, Timothy C. *lawyer*
Matthews, James Shadley *lawyer*
Maynard, Hugh M. *lawyer*
McDonald, John J., Jr. *lawyer*
McGunnigle, George Francis *lawyer, judge*
McIntyre, John Lawrence *lawyer*
McLaughlin, Patrick J. *lawyer*
McNamara, Michael John *lawyer*
Meier, Lisa M. *lawyer*
Melendez, Brian *lawyer*
Mellum, Gale Robert *lawyer*
Meshbesher, Ronald I. *lawyer*
Mitau, Lee R. *lawyer, bank executive*
Mondale, Walter Frederick *lawyer, former Vice President of United States*
Montpetit, Jeffrey M. *lawyer*
Moreno, Albert F. *lawyer, former apparel executive*
Morrison, Fred LaMont *law educator, dean*
Nelson, Julie Loftus *lawyer*
Nelson, Richard Arthur *lawyer*
Nemo, Anthony James *lawyer*
Ness, David Michael *lawyer*
Novak, Leslie Howard *lawyer*
Oh, Allen James *lawyer*
O'Neill, Brian Boru *lawyer*
O'Neill Moreland, Tamara *lawyer*
Ort, Shannon *lawyer*
Paar, Christopher R. *lawyer*
Parsons, Charles Allan, Jr. *lawyer*
Paulose, Rachel K. *prosecutor*
Payne, William Bruce *lawyer, director*
Pedersen, James F. *lawyer*
Peterson, David C. *lawyer*
Peterson, Neal N. *lawyer*
Pfau, James Michael *lawyer*
Platt, Nina *law librarian*
Potter, David B. *lawyer*
Pratte, Robert John *lawyer*
Price, Joseph Michael *lawyer*
Radmer, Michael John *lawyer, educator*
Raskind, Leo Joseph *law educator*
Rasmussen, Teresa J. *lawyer, insurance company executive*
Ratchye, Boyd Havens *lawyer*
Rein, Stanley Michael *lawyer*
Reinhart, Robert Rountree, Jr. *lawyer*
Reister, Raymond Alex *retired lawyer*
Remele, Lewis Albert, Jr. *lawyer*
Resnick, Phillip Stanley *lawyer*
Revnew, Thomas Richard *lawyer*
Rockenstein, Walter Harrison, II, *lawyer*
Rockwell, Winthrop Adams *lawyer*
Roe, Roger Rolland, Jr. *lawyer*
Rosenbaum, Robert A. *lawyer*
Rosenblatt, Cynthia Schaffer *lawyer*
Rothenberg, Elliot Calvin *lawyer, writer*
Saeks, Allen Irving *lawyer*
Safley, James Robert *lawyer*
Saksena, Marian E. *lawyer*
Santana, Lymari Jeanette *lawyer*
Satorius, John Arthur *lawyer*
Sawicki, Zbigniew Peter *lawyer*
Sawyer, Charles F. *lawyer*
Schermer, Judith Kahn *lawyer*
Schmaltz, David G. *lawyer*
Schneider, Elaine Carol *lawyer, researcher, writer*
Schnell, Robert Lee, Jr. *lawyer*
Schulkers, Joan M. *lawyer*
Scouton, David Earl *lawyer*
Seibert, Troy J. *lawyer*
Seifert, James J. *lawyer*
Shaheen, Christopher T. *lawyer*
Shnider, Bruce Jay *lawyer*
Short, Marianne Dolores *lawyer*
Sieben, Jeffrey Scott *lawyer*
Silver, Alan Irving *lawyer*
Simonson, James S. *lawyer*
Sipkins, Peter W. *lawyer*
Sippel, William Leroy *lawyer*
Sisk, Gregory Charles *lawyer, educator*
Skare, Robert Martin *lawyer, director*
Soland, Norman R. *corporate lawyer*
Sorenson, Christopher J. *lawyer*
Sortland, Paul Allan *lawyer*
Soule, George William *lawyer*
Stageberg, Roger V. *lawyer*
Stein, Robert Allen *lawyer, educator, former legal association administrator*
Stern, Leo G. *lawyer*
Stoeri, William R. *lawyer*
Strickland, Thomas L. *lawyer*
Struthers, Margo S. *lawyer*
Sullivan, E. Thomas *law educator*
Swanson, David P. *lawyer*
Tanick, Marshall Howard *lawyer, educator*
Thorson, Steven Greg *lawyer*
Tinkham, Thomas W. *lawyer*
Trucano, Michael *lawyer*
Van Brunt, William A. *lawyer*
Vedder, James J. *lawyer*
Veith, G. John *lawyer*
Voss, Barry Vaughan *lawyer*
Wahoske, Michael James *lawyer*
Wegerson, Edward J. *lawyer*
Weil, Cass Sargent *lawyer*
Weintraut, Steven James *lawyer*
Whelpley, Dennis Porter *lawyer*

Wicks, John R. *lawyer*
Wieneke, Darin Scott *lawyer*
Windhorst, John William, Jr. *lawyer*
Winer, Edward L. *lawyer*
Woods, Robert Edward *lawyer*
Yost, Gerald B. *lawyer*
Young, Christopher Aaron *lawyer*
Younger, Judith Tess *law educator*

Mound
Reske, Steven David *lawyer, writer*

New Ulm
Weinberg, Justin Peter *lawyer*

North Saint Paul
O'Brien, Daniel William *lawyer, lumber company executive*

Northfield
Lundergan, Barbara Keough *lawyer*

Osseo
Boyd, Kelly A. *lawyer, educator*

Plymouth
Mack, Richard L. *lawyer, software company executive*
Saville, Derric James *lawyer*

Rochester
Orwoll, Gregg S.K. *lawyer*
Schneider, Mahlon C. *lawyer*
Somsen, Henry Northrop *retired lawyer*
Stevens, Jeremy R. *lawyer*

Roseville
Fisher, Rebecca Rhoda *lawyer*
Fullerton, Denise S.S. *lawyer*

Saint Cloud
Hughes, Kevin John *lawyer*

Saint Paul
Allison, John Robert *lawyer*
Arnold, Valerie Downing *lawyer*
Bell, Lawrence T. *lawyer*
Cyr, Lisa Watson *lawyer*
Daly, Joseph Leo *law educator*
Fisk, Martin H. *lawyer*
Fitzgerald, Kelly Patrick *lawyer*
Galvin, Michael John, Jr. *lawyer*
Gehan, Mark William *lawyer*
Geis, Jerome Arthur *lawyer, educator*
Green, Gary Jule *lawyer*
Hintz, Chad Jason *lawyer*
Janzen, Peter S. *lawyer, food products executive*
Johnson, Paul Oren *lawyer*
Jones, C. Paul *lawyer, educator*
Kastelic, David Allen *lawyer, energy and food products executive*
Kelly, Patrick J. *lawyer*
Kirwin, Kenneth Francis *law educator*
Krop, Pamela S. *lawyer*
Lebedoff, Randy Miller *lawyer*
Leighton, Robert Joseph *lawyer*
Lillie, John Canfield III *lawyer*
Prohofsky, Dennis E. *lawyer, insurance company executive*
Schnitzer, Alan D. *lawyer*
Seymour, McNeil Vernam *lawyer*
Smith, Marschall Imboden *lawyer*
Spence, Kenneth F. III *lawyer, insurance company executive*
Thompson, Mark K. *lawyer*
Todd, John Joseph *lawyer*
Zibell, Donald Fredrick *lawyer*
Ziegler, Richard Ferdinand *lawyer*

South Saint Paul
Pugh, Thomas Wilfred *lawyer*

Waite Park
Pearson, Andrew R. *lawyer*

Waseca
Deike, Keith Lawrence *lawyer*

Wayzata
Heckt, Melvin Dean *lawyer*
Palmer, Brian Eugene *retired lawyer*
Reutiman, Robert William, Jr. *lawyer*
Schnobrich, Roger William *lawyer*

Winona
Brosnahan, Roger Paul *retired lawyer*

Woodbury
McCalip, David Ray *lawyer*

MISSISSIPPI

Batesville
Smith, Daniel Briggs, Jr. *lawyer*

Bay Saint Louis
Bernstein, Joseph *lawyer*

Brandon
Samsel, Maebell Scroggins (Midge Samsel) *paralegal*

Carthage
Moran, Mitch *lawyer*

Diamondhead
Reddien, Charles Henry, II, *lawyer, diversified financial services company executive, consultant*

Flowood
Wilson, William Roberts, Jr., (Bob Wilson) *lawyer, apparel executive*

Greenville
Martin, Andrew Ayers *lawyer, physician, educator*

Greenwood
Swayze, Charles J., Jr. *lawyer*

Gulfport
Harral, John Menteith *lawyer*
Phillips, Joy Lambert *lawyer, banker*

Hattiesburg
Adelman, Michael Schwartz *lawyer*

Hernando
Brown, William A. *lawyer, mediator, arbitrator*

Jackson
Adams, Charles P., Jr. *lawyer*
Chinn, Mark Allan *lawyer*
Clark, David Wright *lawyer*
Corlew, John Gordon *lawyer*
Currie, Edward Jones, Jr. *lawyer*
Drinkwater, William Wayne *lawyer*
Ellingburg, C. Michael *lawyer*
England, John F. *lawyer*
Hafter, Jerome Charles *lawyer*
Harkins, Patrick Nicholas III *lawyer*
Henegan, John C(lark) *lawyer*
Howell, Joel Walter III *lawyer*
Hughes, Byron William *oil industry executive*
Hutchison, Mark Stevenson *lawyer*
Lampton, Dunn O. *prosecutor*
Langford, James Jerry *lawyer*
McIntyre, James G. *lawyer*
Moize, Jerry Dee *lawyer, federal official*
Roberts, Richard Charlton III *lawyer*
Scanlon, Pat H. *lawyer*
Sweet, Dennis C. III *lawyer*
Travis, Jay A. III *lawyer*
Welch, W(alter) Scott III *lawyer*
West, Carol Catherine *law educator*
Wise, Robert Powell *lawyer*

Madison
Grant, Russell Porter, Jr. *lawyer, petroleum landsman*

Ocean Springs
Lawson-Jowett, Mary Juliet *lawyer*
Luckey, Alwyn Hall *lawyer*
O'Barr, Bobby Gene, Sr. *lawyer*

Olive Branch
Carnall, George Hursey, II, *lawyer*

Oxford
Greenlee, Jim Ming *prosecutor*
Howorth, David Bishop *retired lawyer*
Scruggs, Richard F. *lawyer*

Philadelphia
Duncan, Mark *prosecutor*

Southaven
Taylor, Ronald Louis *lawyer*

Tupelo
Clayton, Claude F., Jr. *lawyer*

Tylertown
Mord, Irving Conrad, II, *lawyer*

Vicksburg
Bailess, Robert R. *lawyer*
Mazzeo-Merkle, Linda Lou *legal administrator*

MISSOURI

Ballwin
Luberda, George Joseph *lawyer, educator*

Cape Girardeau
Lowes, Albert Charles *lawyer*
McManaman, Kenneth Charles *lawyer*

Carthage
Weissenberger, Harry George *lawyer*

Chesterfield
Gerard, Jules Bernard *law educator*
Hier, Marshall David *lawyer*
Pollihan, Thomas Henry *lawyer*

Clayton
Mohan, John J. *lawyer*
Mohrman, Henry Joe, Jr. *lawyer, investment manager*
Pain, George H. *lawyer*
Tremayne, Eric Flory *lawyer*

Columbia
Bunn, Ronald Freeze *retired lawyer, academic administrator, political scientist*
Easton, Stephen Douglas *lawyer, educator*
Fisch, William Bales *law educator*
Harter, Philip J. *lawyer, educator*
Mays, William Gay, II, *lawyer, real estate developer*
Moore, Mitchell Jay *lawyer, educator*
Parrigin, Elizabeth Ellington *lawyer*
Phillips, Walter Ray *law educator*
Turley, J. William *lawyer*
Welliver, Warren Dee *lawyer, retired judge*
Westbrook, James Edwin *law educator*
Whitman, Dale Alan *lawyer, educator*

Earth City
Wallace, Bob (Robert Eugene Wallace Jr.) *lawyer*

Farmington
Pratte, Geoffrey Lynn *lawyer, arbitrator*

Gainesville
Cline, Thomas William *prosecutor*

Hannibal
Terrell, James Daniel *lawyer*
Welch, Joseph Daniel *lawyer*

Hillsboro
Howald, John William *lawyer*

Hollister
Lowther, Gerald Halbert *lawyer*

Independence
Albano, Michael Santo John *lawyer*
Cady, Elwyn Loomis, Jr. *medicolegal consultant*
Minton, Kent W. *lawyer*
Smith, R(onald) Scott *lawyer*
Terry, Jack Chatterson *lawyer*

Jefferson City
Bartlett, Alex *lawyer*
Deutsch, James Bernard *lawyer*
Mitten, L. Russell *lawyer, former telecommunications industry executive*
Tettlebaum, Harvey M. *lawyer*

Joplin
Scott, Robert Haywood, Jr. *lawyer*

Kansas City
Anderson, Christopher James *lawyer*
Atkinson, David Neal *law educator*
Ayers, Jeffrey David *lawyer*
Balloun, Joseph Eugene *lawyer*
Bartunek, Robert R(ichard), Jr. *lawyer*
Bates, William Hubert *lawyer*
Beck, William G. *lawyer*
Beckett, Theodore Charles *lawyer*
Beihl, Frederick *retired lawyer*
Belzer, Irvin V. *lawyer*
Berkowitz, Lawrence M. *lawyer*
Bevan, Robert Lewis *lawyer*
Blanton, W. C. *lawyer*
Boggs, James Dotson *lawyer*
Bradshaw, Jean Paul, II, *lawyer*
Brandt, William Perry *lawyer*
Brous, Thomas Richard *lawyer*
Brown, Peter W. *lawyer*
Bryant, Richard Todd *lawyer*
Clarke, Milton Charles *lawyer*
Clegg, Karen Kohler *lawyer*
Connor, Kevin M. *lawyer*
Crawford, Randy M. *lawyer*
Cross, William Dennis *lawyer*
Davis, John Charles *lawyer*
Deacy, Thomas Edward, Jr. *lawyer*
Dicus, Stephen Howard *lawyer*
Dietrich, William Gale *lawyer, real estate developer, consultant*
Doan, Kirk Hugh *lawyer*
Egan, Charles Joseph, Jr. *lawyer, consumer products company executive*
Eldridge, Truman Kermit, Jr. *lawyer*
Fey, Laura Clark *lawyer*
Finch, Floyd Raymond, Jr. *lawyer*
Foster, Mark Stephen *lawyer*
Frantze, David Wayne *lawyer*
Freeman, Frederick Roe *lawyer*
Frisbie, Charles *lawyer*
Gardner, Brian E. *lawyer*
Geroe, Michael R. *lawyer*
Gorman, Gerald Warner *lawyer*
Graham, Harold Steven *lawyer*
Graves, Todd Peterson *lawyer, former prosecutor*
Handley, Gerald Matthew *lawyer, educator*
Harris, Charlie J., Jr. *lawyer*
Heeter, James A. *lawyer*
Hindman, Larrie C. *lawyer*
Howes, Brian Thomas *lawyer*
Johnson, Mark Eugene *lawyer*
Johnson, Mark P. *lawyer*
Johnston, John Steven *lawyer*
Joyce, Michael Patrick *lawyer*
Kaplan, Harvey L. *lawyer*
Kilroy, John Muir *lawyer*
Kilroy, William Terrence *lawyer*
Klamann, John Michael *lawyer*
Koelling, Thomas Winsor *lawyer*
Koerner, Wendell Edward, Jr. *lawyer, mediator*
Langworthy, Robert Burton *lawyer*
Lashley, Curtis Dale *lawyer*
Levings, Theresa Lawrence *lawyer*
Lindsey, David Hosford *lawyer*
Litan, Robert Eli *lawyer, economist*
Lotven, Howard Lee *lawyer*
Magariel, Dale L. *law librarian*
Magill, Kent B. *lawyer*
Marquette, I. Edward *lawyer*
Martucci, William Christopher *lawyer*
Matheny, Edward Taylor, Jr. *lawyer*
McLarney, Charles Patrick *lawyer*
McManus, James William *lawyer*
Milton, Chad Earl *lawyer*
Moore, Stephen James *lawyer*
Mordy, James Calvin *retired lawyer*
Murphy, John F. *lawyer*
Newsom, James Thomas *lawyer*
Northrip, Robert Earl *lawyer*
O'Dear, Craig Steven *lawyer*
Palmer, Dennis Dale *lawyer*
Pelofsky, Joel *lawyer*
Pemberton, Bradley Powell *lawyer*
Plax, Karen Ann *lawyer*
Price, James Tucker *lawyer*
Prugh, William Byron *lawyer*
Redfearn, Paul L. III *lawyer*
Reitz, Christopher M. *lawyer, gas industry executive*
Respeliers, Patrick J. *lawyer*
Robb, Gary Charles *lawyer*
Rogers, Charles Myers *lawyer*
Sampson, William Roth *lawyer*
Sands, Darry Gene *lawyer*
Schult, Thomas P. *lawyer*
Setzler, Edward Allan *lawyer*
Sexton, J. Stan *lawyer*
Shaw, John W. *lawyer*
Simpson, John W. *lawyer*
Slead, Roger W *lawyer*
Smithson, Lowell Lee *lawyer*
Spaeth, Nicholas John *lawyer, former state attorney general*
Spalty, Edward Robert *lawyer*
Tanner, Eric Benson *lawyer*
Todd, Stephen Max *retired lawyer*
Toll, Perry Mark *lawyer, educator*
Tyler, John Edward III *lawyer*
Van Dyke, Thomas Wesley *lawyer*
Vering, John Albert *lawyer*
Versfeld, Leon *lawyer*
Viani, James Laurence *retired lawyer*
Voran, Joel Bruce *lawyer*
Ward, R. Lawrence *lawyer*
Whisler, Joe B. *lawyer*
Whittaker, Judith Ann Cameron *lawyer*
Willy, Thomas Ralph *lawyer*
Wirken, James Charles *lawyer*
Wood, John F. *prosecutor*
Woody, Teresa Ann *lawyer*
Woolley, Brian N. *lawyer*
Wyrsch, James Robert *lawyer, educator, wr*

Lamar
Geddie, Rowland Hill III *lawyer*

Louisiana
Smith, Philip G. *lawyer*

Manchester
Forsman, Alpheus Edwin *retired lawyer*

Marshfield
Knust, Daniel Max *lawyer*

Maryland Heights
Boudreau, Thomas M. *lawyer, health produ executive*
Cooper, Richard Alan *lawyer*

Osage Beach
Peth, Howard Allen *law educator*
Troutwine, Gayle Leone *lawyer*

Saint Ann
Johnson, Harold Gene *lawyer*

Saint Charles
Ritter, Robert Thornton *lawyer*
Rollings, Dale Linn *lawyer*
Winning, J. Patrick *lawyer*

Saint Joseph
Kranitz, Theodore Mitchell *lawyer*

Saint Louis
Alber, John I. *lawyer*
Appleton, R. O., Jr. *lawyer*
Arnold, Fred English *lawyer*
Arnold, John Fox *lawyer*
Atwood, Hollye Stolz *lawyer*
Aylward, Ronald Lee *lawyer*
Baldwin, Edwin Steedman *lawyer*
Ball, Dan H. *lawyer*
Barken, Bernard Allen *lawyer*
Baum, Gordon Lee *lawyer, non-profit organization administrator*
Berwick, Philip *law librarian, director, dean*
Blanke, Richard Brian *lawyer*
Bobak, Mark T. *lawyer*
Boggs, Beth Clemens *lawyer*
Bonacorsi, Mary Catherine *lawyer*
Brickey, Kathleen Fitzgerald *law educator*
Brickler, John Weise *lawyer*
Brickson, Richard Alan *lawyer*
Brody, Lawrence *lawyer, educator*
Brownlee, Robert Hammel *lawyer*
Bryan, Henry C(lark), Jr. *retired lawyer*
Buckley, Kevin William *lawyer*
Burke, Thomas Michael *lawyer*
Burroughs, Harold R. *lawyer*
Carp, Larry *lawyer*
Carr, Gary Thomas *lawyer*
Clark, Stephen Robert *lawyer*
Clear, John Michael *lawyer*
Conran, Joseph Palmer *lawyer*
Copeland, Douglas Allen *lawyer*
Cornfeld, Dave Louis *lawyer*
Cornfeld, Richard Steven *lawyer*
Covington, Ann K. *lawyer, former state supr court justice*
Cullen, James D. *lawyer*
Cupples, Stephen Elliot *lawyer*
Danforth, John Claggett *lawyer, former ambassador, senator*
DeWoskin, Alan Ellis *lawyer*
Dorwart, Donald Bruce *lawyer*
Dowd, Edward L., Jr. *lawyer, former prosecu*
Dowd, Thomas F. *lawyer*
Downey, Michael Patrick *lawyer*
Duesenberg, Richard William *lawyer*
Ebert, Robert T. *lawyer*
Elliott, Howard, Jr. *lawyer, gas industry executive*
Ellis, Dorsey Daniel, Jr. *lawyer, educator*
Epstein, Robert Harry *lawyer*
Evans, Lawrence E. *lawyer, educator*
Falk, William James *lawyer*
Farnam, Thomas Campbell *lawyer, educator*
Fessenden, Ann T. *law librarian*
Floyd, Walter Leo *lawyer*
Fournie, Raymond Richard *lawyer*
Fox, G. Richard *lawyer*
Frank, Michael M. *lawyer*
Fredericks, Henry Jacob *lawyer*
Gianoulakis, John Louis *lawyer*
Gilhousen, Brent *lawyer*
Gillis, John Lamb, Jr. *lawyer*
Godiner, Donald Leonard *lawyer*
Goebel, John J. *lawyer*
Goldstein, Steven *lawyer*
Goran, Mark H. *lawyer*
Graham, Robert Clare III *lawyer*
Gray, Charles Elmer *lawyer, rancher, investo*
Greaney, Thomas L. *lawyer, educator*
Green, Dennis Joseph *retired lawyer*
Greenley, Beverly Jane *lawyer, educator*

arigila, Dale A. *lawyer*
erri, William Grant *lawyer*
haway, Catherine Lucille *prosecutor*
nsen, Charles *lawyer*
ris, Harvey Alan *lawyer*
ris, Whitney Robson *lawyer, educator, military officer, volunteer*
yman, Randy E. *lawyer*
llmuth, Theodore Henning *lawyer*
meling, Caroline L. *lawyer*
es, Bradley Stephen *lawyer*
ley, John James, Jr. *lawyer*
nson, E. Perry *lawyer*
nson, Sandra Hanneken *law educator*
ey, Lisa Annette *lawyer, brewery company executive*
es, Robert Gerard *lawyer*
ndel, Alan Harold *lawyer*
ler, Juan Dane *retired lawyer*
ly, Douglas Laird *lawyer, investment company executive*
in, Rosemary L. *lawyer*
basa, John Anthony *lawyer*
in, Alan Charles *lawyer*
hlmann, Fred Mark *lawyer*
se, Michael Francis *lawyer*
owitz, Albert *lawyer, writer*
its, Don Glaude *lawyer*
berman, Edward Jay *lawyer*
eles, Maxine Ina *lawyer, law educator*
ow, Mark I. *lawyer*
sberg, John V. *lawyer*
venhaupt, Charles Abraham *lawyer*
wther, Thomas Edward *lawyer*
chesi, Lionel Louis *lawyer*
arger, Jerry *lawyer*
ch, Robert Martin *lawyer, consultant*
dsen, Matthew J. *lawyer*
ndelstamm, Jerome Robert *lawyer*
rks, Murry Aaron *lawyer*
rtin, Lisa Demet *lawyer*
ssa, David J. *lawyer*
ssey, Raymond Lee *lawyer*
Carter, Charles Chase *lawyer*
Daniel, James Edwin *lawyer*
Kinnis, Michael Bayard *lawyer*
sel, George Vincent *lawyer*
rill, Charles Eugene *lawyer*
calfe, Walter Lee, Jr. *lawyer*
henfelder, Albert A. *lawyer*
ore, McPherson Dorsett *lawyer*
lligan, Michael Dennis *lawyer*
rray, George E. *lawyer*
ville, James Morton *retired lawyer, consumer products company executive*
wman, Charles Andrew *lawyer*
l, Edwin Lawrence *lawyer*
rlander, Michael I. *lawyer, consumer products company executive*
Keefe, Michael Daniel *lawyer*
on, Robert Grant *lawyer*
Malley, Kevin Francis *lawyer, educator, writer*
ns, Lloyd Alex *lawyer*
ner, Fredrick D. *lawyer, energy executive*
er, Christian Baird *lawyer*
tti, Rose Norma *lawyer*
enix, G. Keith *lawyer*
le, Robert Douglas *lawyer, apparel executive*
bitt, Daniel Thomas, Jr. *lawyer*
lin, Grier C. *lawyer*
dle, Veryl Lee *lawyer*
gkamp, Stephen H. *lawyer, educator*
erskamp, Douglas Dolvin *lawyer*
erts, Jeanne Delores *lawyer*
dman, David A. *lawyer*
e, Albert Schoenburg *lawyer, educator*
ak, Stephen H. *lawyer*
enstein, Jerome Max *lawyer*
ns, Alan Arthur *lawyer*
, Llewellyn III *lawyer*
neider, Amanda Jean *lawyer*
och, Alexander C. *lawyer, energy executive*
ramm, Paul Howard *lawyer*
baugh, William F. *lawyer*
ric, Anthony James *lawyer*
rby, Kathleen Reilly *lawyer*
stak, Burton H. *lawyer*
th, Arthur Lee *lawyer*
eman, Mark L. *lawyer*
tmann, Gayle G. *lawyer, consumer products company executive*
ivan, Edward Lawrence *lawyer*
ivan, Steven R. *lawyer*
zer, Frederick Michael III *lawyer, arbitrator, mediator*
dale, Kenneth Fulbright *lawyer*
y, Nicholas P. *law educator*
ler, Richard Norman *lawyer*
otte, John Arthur, Jr. *lawyer*
ey, Michael Roy *lawyer*
liver, Thomas K. *lawyer*
Fleet, Lisa A. *lawyer*
el, James John *lawyer*
k, Thomas E. *lawyer*
ner, Raymond Thomas, Jr. *lawyer, legal association administrator*
ker Tucker, Dana *lawyer*
sh, Joseph Leo III *lawyer*
sh, Thomas Charles *lawyer*
ters, Richard Donald *lawyer*
ss, Charles Andrew *lawyer*
ch, David William *lawyer*
iams, Theodore Joseph, Jr. *lawyer*
iamson, Keith Harvey *lawyer*
son, Margaret Bush *lawyer*
on, Michael E. *lawyer*
ers, W. Wayne *lawyer*
ff, Frank Pierce, Jr. *lawyer*
ght, Philip B. *lawyer*
ng, Marvin Oscar *lawyer*
nan, Allan H. *lawyer*

alia
, James Briggs, Jr. *lawyer*

ingfield
d, C. Ronald *lawyer*

Baxter-Smith, Gregory John *lawyer*
Christian, John Catlett, Jr. *lawyer*
FitzGerald, Kevin Michael *lawyer, mediator*
McDonald, William Henry *lawyer*
Schnake, Richard Lane *lawyer*

Stockton
Hammons, Brian Kent *lawyer*

Town And Country
Fagerberg, Roger Richard *lawyer*

Union
Schmelz, Brenda Lea *paralegal*

MONTANA

Billings
Aldrich, Richard Kingsley *lawyer*
Cromley, Brent Reed *lawyer, state senator*
Haughey, James McCrea *lawyer, artist*
Malee, Thomas *lawyer*
Mercer, William W. *prosecutor*
Sites, James Philip *lawyer*
Thompson, James William *lawyer*
Towe, Thomas Edward *lawyer*

Bozeman
Conover, Richard Corrill *lawyer*
Nelson, Steven Dwayne *lawyer*
Wylie, Paul Richter, Jr. *lawyer*

Butte
McCarthy, Bernard Francis *lawyer*

Great Falls
Doherty, Steve *lawyer, state legislator*
Hartelius, Channing Julius *lawyer*
Manning, John Willard *lawyer*

Havre
Maristuen, Keith A. *lawyer*
Moog, Mary Ann Pimley *lawyer*

Helena
Hunt, William Edward, Sr. *lawyer, retired state supreme court justice*
Meadows, Judith Adams *law librarian, educator*
Morrison, John Martin *lawyer*
Probasco, Peggy Lee *lawyer*

Missoula
Beal, Jon G. *lawyer*
Bowman, Jean Louise *lawyer, civic worker*
George, Alexander Andrew *lawyer*
Morales, Julio K. *lawyer*
Nygren, Christian Thomas *lawyer*
Schulte, John C. *lawyer*
Sullivan, Robert John *lawyer*
Willey, Charles Wayne *lawyer*

Whitehall
Bernard, Donald Ray *retired law educator*

Wilsall
Adams, Dirk Standley *lawyer*

NEBRASKA

Broken Bow
Sennett, John O. *lawyer*

Chadron
Bump, Bevin B. *lawyer*

Columbus
Schumacher, Paul Maynard *lawyer*

Kearney
Voigt, Steven Russell *lawyer*

Lincoln
Crump, Linda R. *lawyer*
Guthery, John M. *lawyer*
Leiter, Richard Allen *law librarian, educator*
Lichty, Warren Dewey, Jr. *lawyer*
Ogle, Robbin Sue *criminal justice educator*
Rembolt, James Earl *lawyer*
Robak, Kim M. *lawyer*
Rowe, David Winfield *lawyer*

Omaha
Achelpohl, Steven Edward *lawyer*
Barrett, Frank Joseph *lawyer, insurance company executive*
Brownrigg, John Clinton *lawyer*
Caporale, D. Nick *lawyer*
Creigh, James Carey *lawyer*
Dahlk, Thomas Harlan *lawyer*
Daub, Hal (Harold John Daub Jr.) *lawyer*
Dittrick, William G. *lawyer*
Fellman, Richard Mayer *retired lawyer*
Gleason, James Mullaney *lawyer, insurance company executive*
Hamann, Deryl Frederick *lawyer, bank executive*
Hemmer, J. Michael *lawyer, rail transportation executive*
Hupp, Michael M. *lawyer*
Huse, Frank Peter *lawyer*
Jansen, James Steven *lawyer*
Jenkins, Melvin Lemuel *lawyer*
Jensen, Sam *lawyer*
Krutter, Forrest Nathan *lawyer*
Lee, Dennis Patrick *lawyer, judge*
Lieben, Thomas Geoffrey *lawyer*
Mark, Wayne Joseph *lawyer*
McCusker, Thomas J. *lawyer, insurance company executive*
Reiser, Richard Scott *lawyer*
Rock, Harold L. *lawyer*
Schilken, Michael C. *lawyer*
Schropp, Tobin *lawyer*
Sharpe, Robert Francis, Jr. *lawyer, food products executive*
Stecher, Joe W. *prosecutor*

Stenberg, Donald B. *lawyer*
Vosburg, Bruce David *lawyer*
Wells, Roger W. *lawyer*

NEVADA

Carson City
McCarthy, Ann Price *lawyer*

Elko
Puccinelli, Andrew James *lawyer*
Vaughan, Robert Oren *lawyer*

Henderson
Berns, Philip Allan *lawyer*
Schwartz, Richard *retired lawyer*

Las Vegas
Arum, Robert *lawyer, sports events promoter*
Bernhard, Peter C. *lawyer, state agency administrator*
Bersi, Ann *lawyer*
Brammell, Stephen Harrison *lawyer*
Bridges, B. Ried *lawyer*
Bryan, Richard H. *lawyer, educator, former senator*
Buckley, Michael Edward *lawyer*
Chesnoff, David Zeltner *lawyer*
Collins, Frank Edwin *lawyer*
Consul, Vincent A. *lawyer*
Curran, William P. *lawyer*
Ecker, Howard *lawyer*
Eskin, Jeffrey Laurence *lawyer*
Faiss, Robert Dean *lawyer*
Gentile, Dominic P. *lawyer*
Goodwin, John Robert *lawyer, educator, writer*
Gostin, Irwin *retired lawyer*
Greene, Addison Kent *lawyer, accountant*
Gubler, John Gray *lawyer*
Hilbrecht, Norman Ty *lawyer*
Hill, Judith Deegan *retired lawyer*
Jacobs, Gary N. *lawyer, hotel executive*
James, Mark A. *lawyer, former state legislator*
James, Phyllis A. *lawyer*
Jost, Richard Frederic III *lawyer*
Kamer, Gregory Jay *lawyer*
Kardum, Karmen Ana *lawyer*
Kennedy, Margaret Alexis *law educator, researcher*
Kirsch, Lynn *lawyer*
Larson, Brian A. *lawyer*
Leleu, Jonathan Paul *lawyer*
Mansfield, Lorraine J. *lawyer*
McNulty, James Francis, Jr. *lawyer, consultant*
Moss, Gary Curtis *lawyer*
Norville, Craig Hubert *lawyer*
Oshins, Steven Jeffrey *lawyer*
Pitaro, Thomas F. *lawyer*
Rapoport, Nancy B. *law educator*
Rodefer, Jeffrey Robert *lawyer*
Sheets, Thomas R. *lawyer, gas industry executive*
Singer, Michael Howard *lawyer*
Sklar, Alan Curtis *lawyer*
Snyder, Arthur Kress *lawyer, restaurant owner*
Solomon, Jack Avrum, Jr. *lawyer, automotive executive, art dealer*
Stein, Stephen *lawyer*
Stoberski, Michael Edward *lawyer*
Terry, William B. (Bill) *lawyer*
Wilson, Joseph Morris III *lawyer*
Wright, Rick (Richard A. Wright) *lawyer*

Reno
Bell, Robert Cecil *lawyer*
Clontz, Donna *lawyer, writer, consultant*
Fletcher, Douglas Charles *lawyer*
Goodenow, Rew R. *lawyer*
Hibbs, Loyal Robert *lawyer*
Hill, Earl McColl *lawyer*
Hunterton, C. Stanley *lawyer*
Johnson, David D. *lawyer, game company executive*
Kaleta, Paul J. *lawyer, utilities executive*
Kent, Stephen Smiley *lawyer*
Pagni, Albert Frank *lawyer*
Santos, Herbert Joseph, Jr. *lawyer*
Walther, Steven T. *lawyer*
White, John, Jr. *lawyer*

NEW HAMPSHIRE

Concord
Colantuono, Thomas Paul *prosecutor, former state legislator*
Heard, Charles Wolfe *lawyer, consultant*
Potter, Fred Leon *lawyer, retired insurance company executive*
Rath, Thomas David *lawyer, retired prosecutor*
Uchida, Richard Y. *lawyer*

Dover
Beaupre, Timothy *lawyer*
Catalfo, Alfred, Jr., (Alfio Catalfo) *lawyer*
McManus, Anthony Aidan *judicial organization executive*

Hanover
Gardner, Peter Jaglom *lawyer, publishing executive*
Lundquist, Weyman Ivan *lawyer*
Mannix, Charles Raymond *law educator*

Keene
Bell, Ernest Lorne III *retired lawyer*
Gardner, Eric Raymond *lawyer*

Lancaster
Mekeel, Robert K. *lawyer*

Littleton
Merritt, Thomas Butler *lawyer*

Lyme
Carmichael, Donald Scott *retired lawyer, corporate financial executive*

Manchester
Dahar, Eleanor William *lawyer*
Dugan, Kevin F. *lawyer*
Haffer, Edward Anthony *lawyer*
Hood, James Calton *lawyer*
McNamara, Richard Bedle *lawyer*
Middleton, Jack Baer *lawyer*
Monson, John Rudolph *lawyer*
Shaheen, Bill (William Henry) *lawyer*
Stebbins, Henry Blanchard *lawyer*
Vogelman, Lawrence Allen *lawyer, educator*
Wells, Robert Alfred *lawyer*
Wright, Mark A. *lawyer*

Nashua
Jette, Ernest Arthur *lawyer*
Lumbard, Eliot Howland *lawyer, educator*

Newport
Stamatakis, Carol Marie *lawyer, former state legislator*

Orford
Martin, Allen *retired lawyer*

Peterborough
Bass, Perkins *retired lawyer, congressman*

Plainfield
Brown, Judith Olans *retired lawyer, educator*

Plymouth
Hopkins, William Hayes *lawyer, writer*

Portsmouth
Doleac, Charles Bartholomew *lawyer*
Lytton, William Bryan *lawyer*
Tober, Stephen Lloyd *lawyer*
Volk, Kenneth Hohne *lawyer*
Watson, Thomas Roger *lawyer*

Seabrook
Ganz, Mary Keohan *lawyer*

Warner
Coolidge, Daniel Scott *lawyer*

NEW JERSEY

Absecon
Byrne, Shaun Patrick *lawyer*

Allendale
Morris, Edward William, Jr. *lawyer*
Rosenblum, Edward G. *lawyer*

Atco
Goldstein, Benjamin *lawyer, educator*

Atlantic City
Zlotnick, Norman Lee *lawyer*

Basking Ridge
Craven, Pamela F. *lawyer*

Bayonne
Fitzpatrick, Harold Francis *lawyer*

Bloomfield
Lordi, Katherine Mary *lawyer*
Weisert, Kent Albert Frederick *lawyer*

Boonton
Walzer, James Harvey *lawyer, author*

Bridgewater
Steinhart, Jessica *lawyer*
Wood, J(oshua) Warren III *lawyer*

Budd Lake
Webb, John Gibbon III *lawyer*

Burlington
Tang, Paul C. *lawyer*

Camden
Kaden, Ellen Oran *lawyer, consumer products company executive*
Pomorski, Stanislaw *lawyer, educator*

Cape May Court House
Fineberg, Robert Alan *lawyer*

Carteret
Strassler, Marc A. *lawyer*

Chatham
Zegas, Alan Lee *lawyer*

Cherry Hill
D'Alfonso, Mario Joseph *lawyer*
Garrigle, William Aloysius *lawyer*
Kole, Janet Stephanie *lawyer, writer*
Myers, Daniel William, II, *lawyer*
Rose, Joel Alan *legal consultant*
Weinstein, Steven D. *lawyer*

Clark
Barr, Jon-Henry *lawyer*

Cliffside Park
Diktas, Christos James *lawyer*

Clifton
Feinstein, Miles Roger *lawyer*
Goldberger, Alan Steven *lawyer*
Lieb, L. Robert *lawyer*

Cranford
De Luca, Thomas George *lawyer*
McCreedy, Edwin James *lawyer*

East Brunswick
Applebaum, Charles *lawyer*

East Hanover
Zhang, Cynthia Hongbing *lawyer*

Edison
Behr, Omri M. *lawyer*
O'Brien, John Graham *lawyer*
Traub, Richard Kenneth *lawyer*
Vercammen, Kenneth Albert *lawyer, prosecutor*

Elmwood Park
Mangano, Louis *lawyer*
White, H. Katherine *lawyer*

Fairfield
Connell, William Terrence *lawyer, judge*

Far Hills
Corash, Richard *lawyer*

Flemington
Lenagh, Thomas Hugh *lawyer, financial advisor*
Miller, Louis H. *lawyer*
Nielsen, Lynn Carol *lawyer, educational consultant*

Florham Park
Altieri, James M. *lawyer*
Chase, Eric Lewis *lawyer*
Hardin, William Downer *retired lawyer*
Hull, Gerald W., Jr. *lawyer*
Kahn, Richard *lawyer*
Kandravy, John *lawyer*
Laulicht, Murray Jack *lawyer*
Lavey, Stewart Evan *lawyer*
Long, Stephen R. *lawyer*
Malone, Robert K. *lawyer*
Nittoly, Paul Gerard *lawyer*
O'Connell, Daniel Francis *lawyer*
Pantel, Glenn Steven *lawyer*
Reid, Charles Adams III *lawyer*
Ridley, John A. *lawyer*
Rosenberg, Paul I. *lawyer*
Rosenthal, Jeffrey M. *lawyer*
Smith, Theodore S. *lawyer*
Stryker, David Michael *lawyer*

Fort Lee
Goldberg, Harry Finck *lawyer, consultant*
Weiss, Simona *retired paralegal*

Franklin Lakes
Machlowitz, David Steven *lawyer*
Sherman, Jeffrey Scott *lawyer*

Garfield
Herpst, Robert Dix *lawyer, optical materials company executive*

Glen Ridge
Connolly, Joseph Thomas *retired lawyer, judge*

Glen Rock
Markey, Brian Michael *lawyer*

Hackensack
Abut, Charles C. *lawyer*
Bronson, Meridith J. *lawyer*
Caminiti, Donald Angelo *lawyer*
Croland, Barry I. *lawyer*
D'Alessandro, Dianne Marie *public defender*
Duus, Gordon Cochran *lawyer*
Forman, Michael H. *lawyer*
Greenberg, Steven Morey *lawyer*
Horowitz, Donald *lawyer*
Latimer, Stephen Mark *lawyer*
Mullin, Patrick Allen *lawyer*
Navatta, Anna Paula *lawyer*
Peterson, Linda Ellen *lawyer*
Pollinger, William Joshua *lawyer*
Spiegel, Linda F. *lawyer*
Steinbach, Harold I. *lawyer*
Vort, Robert A. *lawyer*
Weiner, Samuel *lawyer*

Hackettstown
Mulligan, Elinor Patterson *lawyer*

Haddonfield
Andres, Kenneth G., Jr. *lawyer*
Ewan, David E. *lawyer*
Fuoco, Philip Stephen *lawyer*
Heuisler, Charles William *lawyer*
Iavicoli, Mario Anthony *lawyer*
Spevak, Eric Scott *lawyer*

Hamilton
Ebert, Lawrence Burton *lawyer*

Hampton
Nevins, Arthur Gerard, Jr. *lawyer*

Hoboken
Sommers, George R. *lawyer*

Holmdel
Colmant, Andrew Robert *lawyer*

Hopewell
Lester, Pamela Robin *lawyer, consultant*

Iselin
Dornbusch, Arthur A., II, *lawyer*
Goodman, Barry S. *lawyer*

Jersey City
Amoruso, Leonard J. *lawyer*
D'Alessandro, Daniel *lawyer, educator, coach*
Merritt, Thomas M. *lawyer*
Ott, Gilbert Russell, Jr. *lawyer*
Signorile, Vincent A. *lawyer*
Yaworsky, Bohdan *criminal justice educator*

Kearny
Brady, Lawrence Peter *lawyer*
Dunne, Frederick R., Jr. *lawyer*

Kendall Park
Gupta, Rajat Kumar *lawyer, accountant*

Lawrenceville
Stark, Albert Maxwell *lawyer*

Liberty Corner
Apruzzese, Vincent John *lawyer*

Little Silver
Schmidt, Daniel Edward, IV, *lawyer, arbitrator*

Livingston
Ingato, Robert Joseph *lawyer*
Rinsky, Joel Charles *lawyer*
Sukoneck, Ira David *lawyer*

Lyndhurst
McNamara, Patrick James *lawyer*
Prevoznik, Michael E. *lawyer*
Scagnelli, John Mark *lawyer*

Madison
O'Connor, Charles P. *lawyer*
Stein, Lawrence V. *lawyer*

Mahwah
Bear, Larry Alan *retired lawyer, educator*

Manalapan
Stone, Fred Michael *lawyer*

Maplewood
Levine, Benjamin *lawyer*

Marlboro
Bass, David Steven *law educator, arbitrator, mediator*

Mc Afee
Fogel, Richard *lawyer, educator*

Millburn
Diamond, Richard S. *lawyer*

Milltown
Haws, Robert John *lawyer*

Montvale
Falcon, Raymond Jesus, Jr. *lawyer*
Nachtigal, Patricia *lawyer*

Montville
Buzak, Edward Joseph *lawyer*

Moorestown
Buckman, William H. *lawyer*
Hyland, William Francis *retired lawyer*
Slemmer, Carl Weber, Jr. *retired lawyer*

Morristown
Aspero, Benedict Vincent *lawyer*
Bartkus, Robert Edward *lawyer*
Bromberg, Myron James *lawyer*
Coleman, James H., Jr. *lawyer, former state supreme court justice*
Fontaine Newsome, Lynn *lawyer*
Gillen, James Robert *lawyer, insurance company executive*
Herzberg, Peter Jay *lawyer*
Humick, Thomas Charles Campbell *lawyer*
Jacobs, Andrew Robert *lawyer*
Korf, Gene Robert *lawyer*
Kreindler, Peter Michael *lawyer*
Nolan, J. Michael, Jr. *retired lawyer*
O'Grady, Dennis Joseph *lawyer*
Parker, Mary Lou *lawyer*
Pollock, Stewart Glasson *lawyer, state supreme court justice*
Rose, Robert Gordon *lawyer*
Rosenthal, Meyer Louis *lawyer*
Sherman, Sandra Brown *lawyer*
Stanton, Patrick Michael *lawyer*

Mount Holly
Mintz, Jeffry Alan *lawyer, mediator*

Mount Laurel
Koplin, Bernice J. *lawyer*

Mountain Lakes
Daniel, Royal Thomas III *lawyer, mechanical engineer, accountant*

Mountainside
Helander, Robert Charles *lawyer, arbitrator*

New Brunswick
Biribauer, Richard Frank *lawyer*
Miller, Arthur Harold *lawyer*
Miller, Lynn Fieldman *lawyer*
Yorke, Marianne *lawyer, real estate executive*

New Providence
McCarthy, G. Daniel *lawyer*
Reinsdorf, Judith A. *lawyer*

New Vernon
Kushen, Allan Stanford *retired lawyer, corporate executive*

Newark
Akin, Wanda M. *lawyer, literary and sports agent*
Alexander, Mark C. *law educator, policy advisor*
Aron, Lester *lawyer*
Askin, Frank *law educator*
Berry, Andrew T. *lawyer*
Bizub, Johanna Catherine *law librarian*
Blumrosen, Alfred William *law educator*
Brescher, John B., Jr. *lawyer*
Cahn, Jeffrey Barton *lawyer*
Christie, Christopher James *prosecutor, lawyer*
Christie, Scott S. *lawyer*
Cummis, Clive Sanford *lawyer*
Cunningham, LeeAnn *assistant prosecutor*
Day, Edward Francis, Jr. *lawyer*
Dee, Francis X. *lawyer*
Defeis, Elizabeth Frances *lawyer, educator*
Eittreim, Richard MacNutt *lawyer*
English, Nicholas Conover *lawyer*
Falck, David Phillip *lawyer, utilities executive*
Garde, John Charles *lawyer*
Gauster, Stephen Wilhelm *lawyer, corporate financial executive*
Gibbons, John Joseph *lawyer, retired federal judge*
Goldstein, Bruce I. *lawyer*
Goldstein, Marvin Mark *lawyer*
Haring, Eugene Miller *lawyer*
Karp, Donald Mathew *lawyer, banker*
Kott, David Russell *lawyer*
Krovatin, Gerald *lawyer*
La Rocco, Anthony P. *lawyer*
Levin, Simon *lawyer*
Lorell, Jeffrey W. *lawyer*
McGuire, William B(enedict) *lawyer*
McLean, David J. *lawyer*
Neuer, Philip David *lawyer, real estate consultant*
Phillips, John C. *lawyer*
Rak, Lorraine Karen *lawyer*
Reilly, William Thomas *lawyer*
Risinger, D. Michael *lawyer, educator*
Robertson, William Withers *lawyer*
Rothschild, Gita F. *lawyer*
Selover, R. Edwin *lawyer, utilities executive*
Siegal, Joel Davis *lawyer*
Simmons, Peter *law and urban planning educator*
Timoni, Stephen Anthony *lawyer, accountant*
Tischman, Michael Bernard *lawyer*
Vajtay, Stephen Michael, Jr. *lawyer*
Ward, Roger Coursen *lawyer*
Zuckerman, Herbert Lawrence *lawyer*

Newton
Cox, William Martin *lawyer, educator*
Morgenstern, Robert Terence *lawyer*

Oakland
Sosland, Karl Z. *lawyer*

Ocean
Brown, Sanford Donald *lawyer*

Ocean City
Kyriazis, Arthur John (Athanasios Ioannis Kyriazis) *lawyer, biotechnologist*

Old Bridge
Downs, Thomas Edward, IV, *lawyer*

Oradell
Blakeslee, Edward Eaton *lawyer, insurance company executive*
Mavroudis, John M. *lawyer*
Parish, J. Michael *lawyer, mutual fund executive, writer*

Paramus
Gilbert, Stephen Alan *lawyer, organization executive*
Levy, Joseph *lawyer*

Park Ridge
Rolfe, Harold E. *lawyer*

Parsippany
Buckman, James Edward *lawyer*
Cox, Melvin Monroe *lawyer*
Kallmann, Stanley Walter *lawyer*
McLester, Scott G. *lawyer, hospitality executive*
Sclafani, Karen C. *lawyer*
Wasser, Marilyn J. *lawyer, real estate company executive*

Paterson
Mussano, Theodore Anthony *retired court services supervisor*

Piscataway
Gustafsson, Mary E. *lawyer*
Lee, Barbara Anne *law educator*
Smith, Bob *lawyer, educator, state senator*

Pitman
Cloues, Edward Blanchard, II, *lawyer*

Plainfield
Ellington II, Michael L. *lawyer*

Pomona
Latourette, Audrey Wolfson *law educator*

Princeton
Ackourey, Peter Paul *lawyer*
Anderson, Ellis Bernard *retired lawyer, pharmaceutical executive*
Beidler, Marsha Wolf *lawyer*
Bergman, Edward Jonathan *lawyer, educator*
Burgess, Robert Kyle *lawyer*
Connor, Geoffrey Michael *lawyer*
Donohue, Andrew John *lawyer, securities executive*
Durst, Robert Joseph, II, *lawyer*
Frantz, Robert Wesley *lawyer*
Frenier, Diane M. *lawyer*
Greenman, Jane Friedlieb *lawyer, human resources executive*
Hall, Robert Turnbull III *lawyer*
Hill, James Scott *lawyer*
Kaplowitz, Karen (Jill) *lawyer, consultant*
Katz, Stanley Nider *law educator*
Keephart, Lydia Fabbro *lawyer, mediator*
Law, Stuart A., Jr. *lawyer*
Luchak, Frank Alexander *lawyer*
Murphy, J. Andrew (Drew) *lawyer*
O'Brien, Tim *lawyer*
Picco, Steven Joseph *lawyer*
Riordan, Thomas J. *lawyer, chemicals executive*
Schroeder, Glenn Carl *lawyer, educator*
Sullivan, Diane P. *lawyer*
Sutphin, William Taylor *lawyer*
Testa, James A. *lawyer*
Ufford, Charles Wilbur, Jr. *lawyer*
Vinicombe, Charles James *lawyer*
Warren, William L. *lawyer*

Randolph
Zelante, Thomas Andrew *lawyer*

Red Bank
Kenney-Baden, Linda *lawyer*
Reinhart, Peter Sargent *lawyer*

Ridgewood
Harris, Micalyn Shafer *lawyer, arbitrator, mediator, educator, consultant*
Seigel, Jan Kearney *lawyer*
Trocano, Russell Peter *lawyer*

Roseland
Benson, James Bracken *lawyer*
Brody, Jane L. *lawyer*
Eakeley, Douglas Scott *lawyer*
Eichler, Burton Lawrence *lawyer*
Farber, Zulima V. *lawyer, former state attorn general*
Hayden, Joseph A., Jr. *lawyer*
Kohl, Benedict M. *lawyer*
Leit, David Edward *lawyer*
McMahon, Edward Richard *lawyer*
Miceli, Marc Dominick *lawyer*
Positan, Wayne John *lawyer*
Post, John N. *lawyer*
Rosen, Charles Arthur *lawyer*
Slutsky, Kenneth Joel *lawyer*
Smith, Wendy Hope *lawyer*
Stern, Herbert Jay *lawyer*
Tarino, Gary Edward *lawyer*
Vanderbilt, Arthur T., II, *lawyer*
Vitiello, Anthony F. *lawyer*
Wovsaniker, Alan *lawyer, educator*

Saddle Brook
Cohn, Albert Linn *lawyer*
Herrmann, Jeffrey W. *lawyer*
Knopf, Barry Abraham *lawyer, educator*
Pearlman, Peter Steven *lawyer*

Salem
Petrin, Helen Fite *lawyer, consultant, mediat*

Scotch Plains
Klock, John Henry *lawyer*
Shaw, Alan *lawyer*

Sewell
Crouse, Farrell R. *lawyer*

Short Hills
Fast, Kenneth H. *lawyer*
Hazlehurst, Robert Purviance, Jr. *lawyer*
Kaye, Marc Mendell *lawyer*
Novack, Robert *lawyer*
Schirmeister, Charles F. *retired lawyer*
Siegfried, David Charles *retired lawyer*

Shrewsbury
Michaelson, Peter Lee *lawyer*

Somerset
Fink, Edward Murray *lawyer, educator*
Green, Jeffrey C. *lawyer*

Somerville
Fleischman, Joseph Jacob *lawyer*
Hutcheon, Peter David *lawyer*
Lieberman, Marvin Samuel *lawyer*
Ligorano, Michael Kenneth *lawyer*
Norris, Richard A. *lawyer, mediator*
Sponzilli, Edward George *lawyer*

South Plainfield
Santoro, Frank Anthony *lawyer*

Sparta
McMeen, Elmer Ellsworth III *lay minister, musician, retired lawyer*
McMeen, Sheila Taenzler *retired lawyer*

Spring Lake
Pandolfe, John Thomas, Jr. *lawyer*

Springfield
Javerbaum, Kenneth S. *lawyer*
Mytelka, Arnold Krieger *lawyer*
Wurgaft, Jack *lawyer*

Summit
Katz, Michael Albert *lawyer*
Kenyon, Edward Tipton *lawyer*
Lijoi, Peter Bruno *lawyer*
Macioce, Frank Michael *lawyer, financial services company executive*
Pfaltz, Hugo Menzel, Jr. *lawyer*
Woller, James Alan *lawyer*

Teaneck
Cowan, Wallace Edgar *retired lawyer*

Trenton
Bigham, William J. *lawyer*
Blackburn, Audrey Peyton *lawyer*
Caldwell, Wesley Stuart III *lawyer, lobbyist*
Doherty, Robert Christopher *lawyer*
Jones, Dale Edwin *public defender*
Metzger, John Mackay *lawyer*
Mojer-Torres, Lisa Nan *lawyer*
Sterns, Joel Henry *lawyer*

Turnersville
Rabil, Mitchell Joseph *lawyer*

Union
Bottitta, Joseph Anthony *lawyer*
Callahan, Michael J. *lawyer, retail executive*
Gorrin, Eugene *lawyer*
Greenstein, Richard Henry *lawyer*
Mark, Michael David *lawyer*

ıch, Allan N. *lawyer*

ion City
ıdon, Edania Cecilia *lawyer*

uxhall
ss, Mark Samuel *lawyer, educator, funeral director, writer*

ıeland
ck, Todd William *lawyer*

orhees
las, Steven William *lawyer*

all
gan, Mariellen *lawyer*
cciarone, A. Patrick *lawyer*

arren
nstein, Eric Martin *lawyer*
ndage, Maureen A. *lawyer, insurance company executive*
obson, Gary Steven *lawyer*
us, Steven Gary *lawyer*
a, Harminderpal Singh *lawyer*
tantonio, James Bartholomew *lawyer*

yne
rington, Kevin Paul *lawyer*
wartz, David Jay *lawyer*

st Orange
lan, Leo John *lawyer*
Kinney, John Adams, Jr. *lawyer*
hmond, Harold Nicholas *lawyer*
ıson, David *lawyer*
eeney, Gerald Bingham *lawyer*

st Paterson
th, Roy (R. Smith) *lawyer*

stfield
is, Daniel Harold *lawyer*
voshik, David Peter *lawyer*
hner, Alfred James, Jr., (Jim Lechner) *lawyer, ormer federal judge*

itehouse Station
lik, Bruce Neil *lawyer*

odbridge
can, Stephen Emanuel *lawyer*
wn, Morris *lawyer*
erman, Stuart A. *lawyer*
elstat, Martin L. *lawyer*

odbury
er, Lewis Gerard *lawyer*

W MEXICO

uquerque
dacke, Paul *lawyer*
ch, Arthur O'Neal *lawyer*
gman, Barbara E. *law educator*
erman, Paul Leonard *lawyer, educator*
a, Vincent Arthur, Jr. *lawyer, consultant, hotographer*
go, David Francis *lawyer, former governor*
ow, Kathleen M. *lawyer*
ıso, Mark John *lawyer*
ıpton, J. Douglas *lawyer*
oria, Philip S. (Sam) *lawyer*
ner, Terry D(wayne) *lawyer*
ise, R. Nelson *lawyer*
dberg, Catherine T. *lawyer*
ıez, Larry *prosecutor*
om, B(illy) Reid *lawyer*
, Frederick Michael *law educator*
ander, Nancy *lawyer*
z, Dennis Eugene *lawyer*
cher, Michael Lawrence *lawyer*
ater, W(illiam) Robert, Jr. *lawyer*
it, John Walter *lawyer*
ez, Martin III *lawyer*
Bride, Gerald Francis *lawyer*
re, Charles Loyd *lawyer*
ller, Diane Mayne *lawyer*
ıanson, Paul S. *lawyer, educator*
rien, Daniel J. *lawyer*
j, Craig Allen *lawyer*
z, Patrick T. *lawyer*
ıe, Lucy Ann Salsbury *law librarian, ducator, lawyer*
o, Edward Robert *lawyer*
ıl, Jerrald J. *lawyer*
zar, John Paul *lawyer*
ıler, Alison Kay *lawyer*
, Daniel Arthur *lawyer*
e, Lynn *lawyer*
nton, J. Duke *lawyer*
ockmorton, Rex Denton *lawyer*
l, Charles J. *lawyer*

vard
Thomas Paul *lawyer, retired state legislator, ınk executive*

rrales
n, Michael Barry *lawyer, arbitrator, writer*
pion, Kathleen Francis *lawyer, gifted and lented educator*

ning
man, Frederick Hood *lawyer*

mington
ller, Floyd Douglas *lawyer*
y, Mark Bradley *lawyer, minister*
s, Victor Allen *lawyer*

Cruces
mann, Rita Nunez *lawyer*

Los Alamos
Herr, Bruce *lawyer*

Placitas
Schoen, Stevan Jay *lawyer*

Roswell
Bassett, John Walden, Jr. *lawyer*
Haines, Thomas David, Jr. *lawyer*
Kraft, Richard Lee *lawyer*

Sandia Park
Rager, Rudolph Russell *retired lawyer*

Santa Fe
Aarons, Stephen D. *lawyer*
Adams, Mark Kildee *lawyer*
Bienvenu, John Charles *lawyer*
Brannen, Jeffrey Richard *lawyer*
Burton, John Paul (Jack Burton) *lawyer*
Carpenter, Richard Norris *retired lawyer, energy consultant*
Casey, Patrick Anthony *lawyer*
Connolly, Kevin Jude *lawyer*
Dodds, Robert James III *lawyer*
Farber, Steven Glenn *lawyer*
Hickey, John Miller *lawyer*
Johnson, Reverdy *lawyer*
Justice, Jack Burton *retired lawyer, writer*
McClaugherty, Joe L. *lawyer, educator*
Moll, Deborah Adelaide *lawyer*
Pound, John Bennett *lawyer*
Scheuer, Ralph H. *lawyer*
Schwarz, Michael *lawyer*
Wolkoff, Eugene Arnold *lawyer*
Zorie, Stephanie Marie *lawyer*

Seneca
Monroe, Kendyl Kurth *retired lawyer*

Taos
Boles, David LaVelle *lawyer*

NEW YORK

Albany
Alessi, Robert Joseph *lawyer, real estate developer, pharmacist*
Barsamian, John Albert *lawyer, arbitrator, criminologist, judge, educator*
Baum, Joseph Thomas *lawyer*
Bonventre, Vincent Martin *lawyer, educator*
Cogen, Richard M. *lawyer*
Dulin, Thomas N. *lawyer*
Everett, James W., Jr. *lawyer*
Kelly, Raymond Aloysius, Jr. *lawyer, educator*
Koff, Howard Michael *lawyer*
Laird, Edward DeHart, Jr. *lawyer*
Lefkowitz, Jerome *lawyer*
Picotte, Susan Carroll *lawyer*
Rostow, Charles Nicholas *lawyer, educator*
Ruggeri, Robert Edward *lawyer*
Sandhaas, Jill T. *lawyer*
Scott, William Proctor III *lawyer*
Tully, Mathew B. *lawyer*
Yanas, John Joseph *lawyer, director*
Zambri, Melissa Marie *lawyer, educator*

Albertson
Berlin, Mark A. *lawyer*

Alden
Pajak, David Joseph *lawyer, consultant*

Amagansett
Zychick, Joel David *lawyer*

Amherst
Jones, E. Thomas *lawyer*

Ardsley On Hudson
Stein, Milton Michael *retired lawyer*

Armonk
Boies, David *lawyer*
Rosenberg, Michael *lawyer*
Walsh, David James *lawyer*
Weber, Robert Carl *lawyer*
Wertheim, Ram D. *lawyer*

Ballston Spa
Brown, Ifigenia Theodore *retired lawyer*

Bath
BetzJitomir, Susan Marie *lawyer, educator, policy analysis researcher*

Bethpage
Schwartz, Jonathan D. *lawyer*

Binghamton
Beck, Stephanie G. *lawyer*
Gates, Gregory Ansel *lawyer*
Gerhart, Eugene Clifton *lawyer*
Gouldin, David Millen *lawyer*
Kramer, Philip Joseph *lawyer*
Madigan, Kathryn Grant *lawyer*

Bohemia
Breslin, Eileen Mary *lawyer*

Briarcliff Manor
Bernstein, Nadia Jacqueline *lawyer*
Bower, Thomas Michael *lawyer*

Bronx
Balka, Sigmund Ronell *lawyer*
Cornfield, Melvin *lawyer, director*
DuLaux, Russell Frederick *lawyer*
Kostelny, Albert Joseph, Jr. *lawyer*
O'Connor, William Riordan *lawyer, educator*
Richman, Murray *lawyer*
Weil, Gary Ronald *lawyer*

Bronxville
Cutler, Kenneth Burnett *lawyer, investment company executive*
Fuller, David Otis, Jr. *lawyer*
Garber, Robert Edward *lawyer, insurance company executive*
Hagendorn, William Hull *lawyer*

Brooklyn
Bloomfield, David Charles *lawyer, educator, not-for-profit public executive*
Golanski, Alani *lawyer*
Herzog, Lester Barry *lawyer*
Jacobson, Barry Stephen *lawyer, judge*
Josephson, William Howard *retired lawyer*
Kamins, Barry Michael *lawyer*
Karmel, Roberta Segal *lawyer, educator*
Kerwick, Colleen *lawyer, artist*
Leamer, Robert Eldon *lawyer, hospital administrator*
Marcus, Donald *lawyer*
Mauskopf, Roslynn R. *prosecutor*
Murphy, Kathleen Mary *former law firm executive, alternative healing professional*
Pearsall, Otis Pratt *retired lawyer*
Poser, Norman Stanley *law educator*
Rosenkranz, Richard Irwin *lawyer*
Roth, Robert *lawyer, journalist*
Solan, Lawrence Michael *lawyer*
Taylor, Shannon *lawyer, not-for-profit developer*

Buffalo
Bailey, Thomas Charles *lawyer*
Bean, Edwin Temple, Jr. *lawyer*
Brown, Lawrence Charles *lawyer*
Brydges, Thomas Eugene *lawyer*
Connors, Terrence M. *lawyer*
Day, Donald Sheldon *lawyer*
Doren, Robert Alan *lawyer*
Dubber, Markus Dirk *law educator*
Feroleto, John *lawyer*
Feuerstein, Alan Ricky *lawyer*
Fisher, Cheryl Smith *lawyer*
Flynn, Terrance Patrick *prosecutor, lawyer*
Gardner, Arnold Burton *lawyer*
Glanville, Robert Edward *lawyer*
Goldberg, Neil Alan *lawyer*
Goldblatt, Samuel *lawyer*
Grasser, George Robert *lawyer, real estate developer, consultant*
Greene, Robert Michael *lawyer*
Halpern, Ralph Lawrence *lawyer*
Headrick, Thomas Edward *lawyer, educator*
Heilman, Pamela Davis *lawyer*
Jasen, Matthew Joseph *lawyer, retired judge*
Joseph, Todd M. *lawyer*
Kristoff, Karl W. *lawyer*
Lippes, Gerald Sanford *lawyer*
Manning, Kenneth Alan *lawyer*
Mather, Lynn *law educator, political science professor*
Mattar, Lawrence Joseph *lawyer*
McElvein, Thomas Irving, Jr. *lawyer*
Merriman, Kevin Thomas *lawyer*
Monahan, John Michael *lawyer*
Mucci, Gary Louis *lawyer*
Murray, Glenn Edward *lawyer*
Odza, Randall M. *lawyer*
O'Loughlin, Sandra S. *lawyer*
Oppenheimer, Randolph Carl *lawyer*
Pearson, Paul David *lawyer, arbitrator, mediator*
Rachlin, Lauren David *lawyer*
Reich, William Zeev *lawyer*
Sahlem, James Robert *law librarian*
Salisbury, Eugene W. *lawyer, mediator*
Segalla, Thomas Francis *lawyer*
Wisbaum, Wayne David *lawyer*
Yonkman, Mark William *lawyer*

Camillus
Armani, Frank Henry *retired lawyer*

Canaan
Pennell, William Brooke *lawyer*

Carle Place
Mulhern, Edwin Joseph *lawyer*
Seiden, Steven Jay *lawyer*

Carmel
Laporte, Cloyd, Jr. *retired lawyer, manufacturing executive*
Lowe, Edwin Nobles *retired lawyer*

Cazenovia
Shattuck, George Clement *retired lawyer*

Cedarhurst
Klein, Irwin Grant *lawyer*
Taubenfeld, Harry S. *lawyer*

Central Islip
Morris, Jeffrey Brandon *law educator*

Chappaqua
Castrataro, Barbara Ann *lawyer*
Graham, Lawrence Otis *lawyer, writer, television commentator*
Pollet, Susan L. *lawyer*
Romney, Richard Bruce *lawyer*

Chatham
Weiner, Jack H. *lawyer*

Chautauqua
Schmidt, Edward Craig *lawyer*

Cheektowaga
Staehr, Jonathan Edward *lawyer*

Chestnut Ridge
Burns, Richard Owen *lawyer*

Chittenango
Baum, Peter Alan *lawyer*

Clifton Park
Hilts, Earl T. *lawyer, government official, educator*

Commack
Somer, Stanley Jerome *lawyer*
Steindler, Walter G. *retired lawyer*

Corning
Hatton, Vincent Paul *lawyer*
Hauselt, Denise Ann *lawyer*
Ughetta, William Casper *lawyer, manufacturing executive, director*

Cortland
Taylor, Leland Baridon *lawyer*

Croton Falls
Curtis, Frank R. *lawyer*

Croton On Hudson
Hoffman, Paul Shafer *lawyer*

Dansville
Vogel, John Walter *lawyer*

Depew
Saleh, David John *lawyer*

Dobbs Ferry
Maiocchi, Christine *lawyer*
Scudder, Charles Seelye Kellgren *lawyer*

Douglaston
Walsh, Sean M. *lawyer, computer scientist, criminologist*

East Greenbush
McConville, Edward Patrick *lawyer*

East Hampton
Ehren, Charles Alexander, Jr. *lawyer, educator*
Twomey, Thomas A., Jr. *lawyer, educator*
Wainwright, Carroll Livingston, Jr. *retired lawyer*

East Meadow
Adler, Ira Jay *lawyer*
Hyman, Montague Allan *lawyer, educator*

East Northport
Juliano, John Louis *lawyer*

East Norwich
Busner, Philip H. *retired lawyer, judge*

Eastchester
Katz, Kenneth Arthur *lawyer, accountant*

Elmira
Winner, George Henry *lawyer*

Fairport
Bartlett, Cody Blake *retired lawyer*
Mullin, Thomas J. *lawyer, food products executive*

Far Rockaway
Helfgott, Samson *lawyer*

Farmingdale
O'Brien, Joan Susan *lawyer, educator*

Floral Park
Chatoff, Michael Alan *lawyer*
Corbett, William John *lawyer, public relations executive, minister, consultant*
Giuffré, John Joseph *lawyer*

Flushing
Cohen, David *lawyer*
Farago, John Michael *law educator, consultant*
Kim, Hakyong *lawyer, accountant*
Schwartz, Estar Alma *lawyer*

Forest Hills
Kourides, Peter Theologos *lawyer*

Forestville
Adams, Lee Towne *lawyer*

Franklin Square
Vanora, Jerome Patrick *lawyer*

Freeport
Berg, Alan *lawyer, arbitrator*

Fresh Meadows
Greenberg, Robert Jay *law educator*

Garden City
Austin, Stuart *lawyer*
Balkan, Kenneth J. *lawyer*
Calamari, Joseph August *law librarian*
Caputo, Kathryn Mary *paralegal*
Cook, George Valentine *lawyer, consultant*
DiMascio, John Philip *lawyer*
Fishberg, Gerard *lawyer*
Freedman, Monroe Henry *law educator*
Ingber, Larry H. *lawyer*
Kaplan, Joel Stuart *lawyer*
Klein, Arnold Spencer *lawyer*
Kroll, Martin N. *lawyer*
Mastaglio, Peter James *lawyer*
Meng, M. Kathryn *lawyer*
Minicucci, Richard Francis *lawyer, former hospital administrator*
Nogee, Jeffrey Laurence *lawyer*
Ostrow, Michael Jay *lawyer*
Paterson, Basil Alexander *lawyer*
Persons, John Wade *lawyer*
Posch, Robert John, Jr. *lawyer*
Rosenberg, Lee *lawyer*
Schwarz, Carl A., Jr. *lawyer*

Geneva
Brind, David Hutchison *lawyer, judge*

Glen Cove
Lewis, Felice Flanery *retired lawyer, educator*
Rathkopf, Daren Anthony *lawyer*

Glens Falls
Bartlett, Richard James *lawyer*
McMillen, Robert Stewart *lawyer*

Gouverneur
Leader, Robert John *lawyer*

Great Neck
Kimm, Michael S. *lawyer*
Lupkin, Stanley Neil *lawyer*

Greenlawn
Robinson, Kenneth Patrick *lawyer, electronics executive*

Greenvale
Halper, Emanuel B(arry) *lawyer, real estate developer, consultant, writer*
Manzari, Laura Lynn *law educator*

Hamburg
Gaughan, Dennis Charles *lawyer*
Hargesheimer, Elbert III *lawyer*

Harrison
Kramer, Alan Sharfsin *lawyer*

Hastings On Hudson
Edelman, Paul Sterling *lawyer*
Thornlow, Carolyn *law firm administrator, consultant*

Hauppauge
Scheine, Edward Robert *lawyer*

Hempstead
Mahon, Malachy Thomas, Sr. *lawyer, educator*
Sharifov, Rovshan Chingiz *lawyer*

Herkimer
Kirk, Patrick Laine *lawyer*

Hewlett
Colfin, Bruce Elliott *lawyer, video producer*

Hicksville
Lieberman, Douglas Mark *lawyer*

Hillsdale
Lunde, Asbjorn Rudolph *lawyer*

Hollis
Singh, Harbachan *solicitor, barrister*

Hornell
Pulos, William Whitaker *lawyer*

Hudson
Agata, Burton C. *lawyer, educator*
Davis, Deborah Lynn *lawyer, art dealer*
Howard, Andrew Baker *lawyer*

Huntington
Brettschneider, Rita Roberta Fischman *retired lawyer*
German, June Resnick *lawyer*
Hochberg, Ronald Mark *lawyer*
Munson, Nancy K. *lawyer*
Selkirk, Alexander MacDonald, Jr. *lawyer*
Tucker, William P. *lawyer, writer*

Irvington
Jackson, Thomas Gene *lawyer*

Islandia
Buckley, Terrence Patrick *lawyer*
Fliegelman Olli, Amy *lawyer, computer company executive*
Pruzansky, Joshua Murdock *lawyer*

Ithaca
Alexander, Gregory Stewart *law educator*
Barcelo, John James III *law educator*
Clermont, Kevin Michael *law educator*
Cramton, Roger Conant *lawyer, educator*
Eisenberg, Theodore *law educator*
Germain, Claire Madeleine *law librarian, educator*
Gold, Michael Evan *law educator*
Hay, George Alan *law and economics educator*
Hillman, Robert Andrew *lawyer, educator*
Roberts, E. F. *law educator*
Schneiderman, Anne Mercedes *lawyer, neurobiologist*
Summers, Robert Samuel *lawyer, author, educator*

Jamaica
Angione, Howard Francis *lawyer, retired editor*
Brown, Kenneth Lloyd *lawyer*
Castro-Blanco, James *law educator*

Jamestown
Huston, Lana M. *lawyer*
Idzik, Martin Francis *lawyer*

Jamesville
DeCrow, Karen *lawyer, educator, writer*

Jericho
Blau, Harvey Ronald *lawyer, manufacturing executive*
Corso, Frank Mitchell *lawyer*

Katonah
Bandon, William Edward III *lawyer*

Keeseville
Turetsky, Aaron *lawyer*

Kew Gardens
Adler, David Neil *lawyer*

Larchmont
Berridge, George Bradford *retired lawyer*
Bloom, Lee Hurley *lawyer, consultant, retired consumer products company executive*
Burkett, Bradford Charles *lawyer*
McSherry, William John, Jr. *lawyer, consultant*
White, Thomas Edward *lawyer*

Latham
Catalano, Jane Donna *lawyer*

Lawrence
Bursky, Herman Aaron *lawyer*

Livingston Manor
Root, Stuart Dowling *lawyer, retired government agency administrator, banker*

Lockport
Penney, Charles Rand *lawyer, civic worker*

Long Beach
Levine, Samuel Milton *lawyer, retired judge, arbitrator, mediator*
Solomon, Robert H. *lawyer*

Long Island City
Wanderman, Susan Mae *lawyer*

Malverne
Benigno, Thomas Daniel *lawyer*

Manhasset
Kaminsky, Arthur Charles *lawyer*
Wachtler, Sol *lawyer, educator*

Melville
Brown, Peter Stewart *lawyer, electronics executive*
Cahn, Richard Caleb *lawyer*
Cummings, Anthony William *lawyer, educator, banker*
Ettinger, Michael Saul *lawyer*
Komaroff, Stanley *lawyer*
Lane, Arthur Alan *lawyer*
Millman, Bruce Russell *lawyer*
Reardon, George Martin *lawyer*
Schoenfeld, Michael P. *lawyer*
Starr, Jeffrey *lawyer, bank executive*

Middletown
Kossar, Ronald Steven *lawyer*

Mineola
Bartlett, Clifford Adams, Jr. *lawyer*
Bartol, Ernest Thomas *lawyer*
Block, Martin *lawyer*
Flanzig, Daniel *lawyer*
Halloran, Daniel James *lawyer*
Lynn, Robert Patrick, Jr. *lawyer*
Monaghan, Peter Gerard *lawyer*
Rubine, Robert Samuel *lawyer*
Schaffer, David Irving *lawyer*
Smolev, Terence Elliot *lawyer, educator*
Tannenbaum, Bernard *lawyer*
Will, Alfred Joseph *lawyer, engineer*

Montauk
Kahn, Richard Dreyfus *lawyer*

Mount Kisco
Curran, Maurice Francis *lawyer*
Kilbourn, Joseph A. *lawyer*

Mount Vernon
Madden, M. Stuart *lawyer*
Weisman, Richard Scott *lawyer*

New City
Fenster, Robert David *lawyer*

New Hartford
Chapin, Mary Q. *arbitrator, director, mediator, writer*

New Hyde Park
Jaffe, Richard S. *lawyer*
Lee, Brian Edward *lawyer*
Offner, Eric Delmonte *lawyer*
Pegalis, Steven E. *lawyer*

New Rochelle
Ferencz, Benjamin Berell *lawyer*
Gunning, Francis Patrick *lawyer, insurance company executive*
Hasson, Adam Isaac *lawyer*
Herman, William Charles *lawyer*

New York
Aaron, Roger S. *lawyer*
Aaron, Stewart D. *lawyer*
Abatemarco, Tracy J. *lawyer*
Abbott, James Edward *lawyer*
Abelman, Arthur F. *lawyer*
Abrahams, Robert M. *lawyer*
Abramowitz, Elkan *lawyer*
Abrams, Floyd *lawyer, educator*
Abrams, Robert *lawyer, state attorney general*
Abuhoff, Daniel Mark *lawyer*
Adams, George Bell *lawyer*
Adams, John Hamilton *lawyer*
Adams, Robert Brereton *lawyer*
Agranoff, Gerald Neal *lawyer*
Aguilar-Alvarez, Guillermo *lawyer*
Aidinoff, M(erton) Bernard *retired lawyer*
Ainbinder, Bruce *lawyer*
Aksen, Gerald *arbitrator, mediator, lawyer*
Albert, Garett J. *lawyer*
Alcott, Mark Howard *lawyer*
Alden, Steven Michael *lawyer*
Alfieri, Vincent *lawyer*
Allen, Leon Arthur, Jr. *lawyer*
Allen, William Thomas *law educator*
Allerhand, Joseph S. *lawyer*
Almon, Lorie *lawyer*
Aloe, Paul Hubschman *lawyer*
Alperin, Stuart N. *lawyer*
Alter, Eleanor Breitel *lawyer*
Alter, Paul R. *lawyer*
Alterman, Daniel L. *lawyer*
Altieri, Peter Louis *lawyer*
Amdur, Martin Bennett *lawyer*
Amsterdam, Anthony Guy *law educator*
Amsterdam, Mark Lemle *lawyer*
Anders, David Brian *prosecutor*
Andersen, Richard Esten *lawyer*
Andolina, Janet *lawyer*
Andrews, Gordon Clark *lawyer*
Andriola, Rocco F. *lawyer, diversified financial services company executive*
Andrus, Roger Douglas *lawyer*
Anesh, Mark K. *lawyer*
Angland, Joseph *lawyer*
Angus, Patricia Marie *lawyer*
Anthoine, Robert *lawyer, educator*
Appel, Albert M. *lawyer*
Appelbaum, Ann Harriet *lawyer*
Aquila, Francis Joseph *lawyer*
Arabatzis, Constance Elaine *lawyer*
Arditi, Ralph *lawyer*
Arenson, Gregory K. *lawyer*
Arffa, Allan J. *lawyer*
Arkin, Stanley S. *lawyer*
Arlen, Jennifer Hall *law educator*
Armbrust, Joseph W., Jr. *lawyer*
Aronson, Clifford Hank *lawyer*
Arouh, Jeffrey Alan *lawyer*
Arquit, Kevin James *lawyer*
Arrow, Allen H. *lawyer*
Ash, Karen Artz *lawyer*
Ashinoff, Reid L. *lawyer*
Atkins, Peter Allan *lawyer*
Auslander, Mitchell J. *lawyer*
Axelrod, Charles Paul *lawyer*
Axinn, Stephen Mark *lawyer*
Ayoub, Elsa *lawyer*
Bach, Thomas Handford *lawyer, investor*
Bachelder, Joseph Elmer III *lawyer*
Badertscher, David Glen *law librarian, consultant*
Bahler, Gary M. *lawyer*
Bahlke, Conrad George *lawyer*
Baio, Joseph T. *lawyer*
Baird, Zoë *lawyer*
Baity, John Cooley *lawyer*
Baker, Mark M. *lawyer, law educator*
Baker, Stuart David *lawyer*
Baker, William Harris *lawyer*
Bamberger, Michael Albert *lawyer, educator*
Bancroft, Margaret Armstrong *lawyer*
Bankston, Archie Moore *lawyer*
Bannigan, Eugene F. *lawyer*
Barandes, Robert *lawyer*
Barasch, Clarence Sylvan *lawyer*
Barasch, Mal Livingston *lawyer*
Barbur, Peter T. *lawyer*
Barist, Jeffrey *lawyer*
Barnard, Kevin Francis *lawyer*
Baron, Mitchell Neal *lawyer*
Baron, Robert Howard *lawyer*
Barrett, David A. *lawyer*
Barry, Desmond Thomas, Jr. *lawyer*
Barshay, Scott A. *lawyer*
Bartfeld, Daniel D. *lawyer*
Bartlett, Joseph Warren *lawyer*
Bason, George R., Jr. *lawyer*
Bass, Franklin F. *lawyer*
Bassen, Ned Henry *lawyer*
Bateman, Maureen Scannell *lawyer*
Bauer, Douglas F. *retired lawyer*
Baumgardner, John Ellwood, Jr. *lawyer*
Baumgarten, Sidney *lawyer*
Baumrin, Bernard Stefan Herbert *lawyer, educator*
Beattie, Richard Irwin *lawyer*
Beck, Andrew James *lawyer*
Becker, Steven H. *lawyer*
Beckman, Michael *lawyer*
Beeken, Timothy K. *lawyer*
Beekman, William Bedloe *lawyer*
Beerbower, Cynthia Gibson *lawyer*
Beerbower, John Edwin *lawyer*
Beeson, Ann *lawyer*
Beinecke, Candace Krugman *lawyer*
Bell, Jonathan Robert *lawyer*
Beller, Gary A. *lawyer, former insurance company executive*
Bellows, Carl D. *lawyer*
Ben-Ami, Leora *lawyer*
Bender, John Charles *lawyer*
Benenson, Mark Keith *lawyer*
Benjamin, Harvey E. *lawyer, sports association executive*
Benjamin, Jeff *lawyer, pharmaceutical executive*
Benkard, James W. B. *lawyer*
Bennett, Scott Lawrence *lawyer*
Berg, Madelaine R. *lawyer*
Berger, George *lawyer*
Berger, Max W. *lawyer*
Bergman, Arlene *lawyer*
Bergmann, Peter George *lawyer*
Bergtraum, Howard Michael *lawyer*
Berke, Barry H. *lawyer*
Berkery, Rosemary Theresa *lawyer, investment company executive*
Berman, Keith *solicitor, lawyer*
Bern, Marc Jay *lawyer*
Bernard, Richard Phillip *lawyer*
Bernstein, Daniel Lewis *lawyer*
Bernstein, David William *lawyer*
Bernstein, Donald Scott *lawyer*
Bernstein, Jay L. *lawyer*
Bernstein, Robert Jay *lawyer*
Bernstein, Warren J. *lawyer*
Berrien, Jacqueline A. *lawyer*
Berry, Dean C. *lawyer*
Beshar, Christine *lawyer*
Beshar, Peter Justus *lawyer, insurance company executive*
Beshar, Robert Peter *lawyer*
Beslow, William S. *lawyer*
Bevilacqua, Louis J. *lawyer*
Bezanson, Thomas Edward *lawyer*
Bezozo, Kenneth K. *lawyer*
Bialkin, Kenneth Jules *lawyer, director*
Bialo, Kenneth Marc *lawyer*
Bicks, Peter Andrews *lawyer*
Bienenstock, Martin J. *lawyer*
Bird, Paul S. *lawyer*
Birnbaum, Edward Lester *lawyer*
Birnbaum, Sheila L. *lawyer, educator*
Bjorklund, Victoria B. *lawyer*
Black, Barbara Aronstein *legal history educa*
Black, James Isaac (Jib) III *lawyer*
Black, Jerry Bernard *lawyer*
Black, Louis Engleman *lawyer*
Blackman, Kenneth Robert *lawyer*
Blair, Michael Walter *lawyer*
Blair, William McCormick, Jr. *lawyer*
Blanc, Roger David *lawyer*
Blanchard, Kimberly Staggers *lawyer*
Blasband, David *lawyer*
Blassberg, Franci J. *lawyer*
Blivaiss, David Harvey *lawyer, accountant*
Bliwise, Lester Martin *lawyer*
Block, Dennis Jeffrey *lawyer*
Bloom, Lisa Read *lawyer*
Blumkin, Linda Ruth *lawyer*
Boast, Molly Shryer *lawyer*
Bobrow, Richard S. *lawyer, former diversifie financial services executive*
Bockstein, Herbert *lawyer*
Boddie, Reginald Alonzo *lawyer*
Bodovitz, James Philip *lawyer*
Boehner, Leonard Bruce *lawyer*
Bogdanos, Matthew F. *lawyer, reserve militar officer, writer, boxer*
Bohm, Richard D. *lawyer*
Booth, Mitchell B. *lawyer*
Borchard, William Marshall *lawyer*
Borisoff, Richard Stuart *lawyer*
Bornstein, Gary A. *lawyer*
Bottari, Paul J. *lawyer*
Boulhosa, Michael L. *lawyer*
Bowers, William Charles *lawyer*
Boxer, Leonard *lawyer*
Boyle, Edward J. *lawyer*
Brach, Richard S. *lawyer*
Bradley, E. Michael *lawyer*
Brady, Bruce Morgan *lawyer*
Brafman, Benjamin *lawyer*
Braun, Jeffrey Louis *lawyer*
Breen, Kenneth Michael *lawyer, former prosecutor*
Breglio, John F. *lawyer*
Brennan, Patrick J. *lawyer*
Breslow, Stephanie R. *lawyer*
Brett, Barry J. *lawyer*
Brett, Harry P. *lawyer*
Brieger, George *lawyer*
Bring, Murray H. *retired lawyer*
Briskman, Louis Jacob *lawyer, broadcast executive*
Broadwater, Douglas Dwight *lawyer*
Brock, Charles Lawrence *lawyer, diversified financial services company executive, investment banker*
Broder, Douglas Fisher *lawyer*
Brodsky, David Michael *lawyer*
Brodsky, Samuel *lawyer*
Bromberger, Allen Richard *lawyer*
Brome, Thomas Reed *lawyer*
Bronstein, Peter E. *lawyer*
Brooks, Daniel Townley *lawyer*
Brooks, Roger G. *lawyer*
Broude, Richard Frederick *lawyer, educator*
Browdy, Joseph Eugene *lawyer*
Brown, Jennifer Kay *lawyer*
Brown, Loren H. *lawyer*
Brown, Paul M. *lawyer*
Brown, Ralph Sawyer, Jr. *retired lawyer*
Brownstein, Andrew Richard *lawyer*
Brownwood, David Owen *lawyer*
Brumm, James Earl *lawyer, import/export company executive*
Brundige, Robert William, Jr. *lawyer*
Bruner, Jerome S. *law educator*
Bryan, Barry Richard *lawyer*
Buchwald, Don David *lawyer*
Buckholz, Robert E., Jr. *lawyer*
Buckley, Susan *lawyer*
Budd, Thomas Witbeck *lawyer*
Burak, H(oward) Paul *lawyer*
Burdette, Brooks R. *lawyer*
Burgess, Lynne A. *lawyer*
Burgman, Dierdre Ann *lawyer*
Burgweger, Francis Joseph Dewes, Jr. *lawye*
Burns, Arnold Irwin *lawyer*
Burns, John MacDougal III *lawyer*
Burns, Stephen L. *lawyer*
Burrell, Lizabeth Lorie *lawyer*
Burrows, Kenneth David *lawyer*
Burrows, Michael Donald *lawyer*
Burstein, Judd *lawyer*
Burton, Eve Bradley *lawyer*
Bushnell, George Edward III *lawyer*
Bustin, George Leo *lawyer*
Butler, Samuel Coles *lawyer*
Buttenwieser, Lawrence Benjamin *lawyer*
Byowitz, Michael H. *lawyer*
Caginalp, Aydin S. *lawyer*
Cagney, Lawrence K. *lawyer*
Caiazzo, Nicholas R. *lawyer*
Calder, James J. *lawyer*
Caldwell, Leslie Ragon *lawyer, former prosecutor*
Califano, Joseph Anthony, Jr. *lawyer, former secretary of health education and welfare*
Callagy, John M. *lawyer*
Cambria, Christopher C. *lawyer, communica systems company executive*
Camera, Nicholas J. *lawyer*
Cameron, Timothy G. *lawyer*
Cami, Russell *lawyer*
Campise, James F. *lawyer*
Canellos, Peter C. *lawyer*
Cannell, John Redferne *lawyer*
Canoni, John David *lawyer*
Cantor, Melvyn Leon *retired lawyer*
Cappuccio, Paul T. *lawyer, communications executive*

Greene, Bernard Harold *lawyer*
Greene, Ira S. *lawyer*
Greene, Mark I. *lawyer*
Greenman, Frederick F., Jr. *lawyer*
Greenman, Paula S. *lawyer*
Greenspon, Robert Alan *lawyer*
Greenwald, David *lawyer*
Greenzang, Katherine *lawyer, insurance company executive*
Gregory, Robin N. *lawyer*
Grehan, Kevin J. *lawyer*
Greilsheimer, James Gans *lawyer*
Greiner, Stephen W. *lawyer*
Grew, Robert Ralph *retired lawyer*
Griffin, Michael F. *lawyer*
Griffith, William R. *lawyer*
Groh, Jennifer Calfa *law librarian*
Gross, John H. *lawyer*
Gross, Karen Charal *lawyer*
Gross, Steven Ross *lawyer*
Grossman, Dan Steven *lawyer*
Grossmann, Edward A. *lawyer*
Grubin, Sharon Ellen *lawyer, former federal judge*
Grubman, Allen J. *lawyer*
Gruenberger, Peter *lawyer*
Grunewald, Raymond Bernhard *lawyer*
Grushkin, Jay D. *lawyer*
Guedry, James Walter *lawyer, retired manufacturing executive*
Guggenheim, Martin Franklin *lawyer, educator*
Gulino, Frank *lawyer, educator*
Gupta, Paul R. *lawyer*
Gurfein, Richard Alan *lawyer*
Gutman, Henry B. *lawyer*
Gwathmey, Gaines *lawyer*
Haffner, F. Kinsey *lawyer*
Haig, Robert Leighton *lawyer*
Haimes, Burton Kenneth *lawyer*
Haims, Bruce David *lawyer*
Halberstam, Malvina *lawyer, educator*
Haley, James F., Jr. *lawyer*
Hall, Bryan H. *lawyer*
Hall, John Herbert *lawyer*
Hall, Richard *lawyer*
Hall, Thomas J. *lawyer*
Hallake, Marcello *lawyer*
Halliday, Joseph William *lawyer*
Halperin, Richard E. *lawyer, finance company executive*
Hamburg, Charles Bruce *lawyer*
Hamm, David Bernard *lawyer*
Handelsman, Lawrence Marc *lawyer*
Handler, Arthur M. *lawyer*
Handley, Siobhan A. *lawyer*
Hanft, James *lawyer*
Hanisch, Toula *legal assistant*
Hannon, Gerard V. *lawyer*
Hansen, Kristopher M. *lawyer*
Hanson, Jean Elizabeth *lawyer*
Haracz, Stephen M. *lawyer*
Harkrider, John David *lawyer*
Harlow, Ruth *lawyer*
Harms, David B. *lawyer*
Harper, Gerard Edward *lawyer*
Harris, Adam C. *lawyer*
Harris, Arlene *lawyer*
Harris, Joel B. (Joel Bruce Harris) *lawyer*
Harris, Theresa *lawyer*
Harrison, S. David *lawyer*
Hart, Mary T. *lawyer*
Hart, Robert M. *lawyer*
Hartmann, Carl Joseph *lawyer, consultant*
Hartnett, William M. *lawyer*
Hartzell, Andrew Cornelius, Jr. *retired lawyer*
Harvey, Peter C. *lawyer, former state attorney general*
Hasday, Robert Joel *lawyer*
Hass, Lawrence Joel *lawyer*
Hathaway, Gerald Thomas *lawyer*
Hauser, Rita Eleanore Abrams *lawyer*
Hawke, Roger Jewett *lawyer*
Hayes, Eddie (Edward W. Hayes) *lawyer*
Hayes, Gerald Joseph *lawyer*
Hazan, Scott L. *lawyer*
Headley, Mark J. *lawyer*
Healy, J. Kevin *lawyer*
Healy, Nicholas Joseph *retired lawyer*
Hearn, George Henry *lawyer, water transportation executive*
Hedden, Andrew S. *lawyer*
Hefter, Michael C *lawyer*
Heftler, Thomas E. *lawyer*
Heinzelman, Kris F. *lawyer*
Heisler, Stanley Dean *lawyer*
Heitner, Kenneth Howard *lawyer*
Held, Huyler Clark *lawyer*
Hellenbrand, Samuel Henry *lawyer*
Heller, Robert Martin *lawyer*
Hellerer, Mark R. *lawyer*
Henderson, Donald Bernard, Jr. *lawyer*
Hendry, Andrew Delaney *lawyer, consumer products company executive*
Henry, Sally McDonald *lawyer*
Henze, William F., II, *lawyer*
Herbst, Abbe Ilene *lawyer*
Herbst, Todd L. *lawyer*
Herlihy, Edward D. *lawyer*
Herman, Kenneth Beaumont *lawyer*
Herman, Peter Windley *lawyer*
Herold, Karl Guenter *lawyer*
Herschlein, James D. *lawyer*
Hershcopf, Gerald Thea *retired lawyer*
Hertz, Michael K. *lawyer*
Herz, Andrew Lee *lawyer*
Herzeca, Lois Friedman *lawyer*
Hess, Michael David *lawyer*
Hewitt, John R. *lawyer*
Hiden, Robert Battaile, Jr. *lawyer*
Hill, Alfred *law educator*
Hillman, Peter N. *lawyer*
Hirsch, Irving B. *lawyer*
Hirsch, Jerome S. *lawyer*
Hirschfeld, Michael *lawyer*
Hirschson, Linda Benjamin *lawyer*
Hirshfield, Stuart *lawyer*
Hirshon, Sheldon Ira *lawyer*
Hirshowitz, Melvin Stephen *lawyer*
Hoch, Benjamin *lawyer*
Hodes, Robert Bernard *lawyer*
Hoff, Jonathan M(orind) *lawyer*
Hoffman, Mathew *lawyer*
Hogan, Mary Beth *lawyer*
Holley, Steven Lyon *lawyer*
Hollyer, A(rthur) Rene *lawyer*
Holman, Bud George *lawyer*
Holsenbeck, George Penn *lawyer*
Holtzman, Elizabeth *lawyer*
Holtzmann, Howard Marshall *lawyer, judge*
Honigman, Steven *lawyer*
Hooker, Wade Stuart *lawyer*
Horowitz, Steven Gary *lawyer*
Houck, Rudolph S.(Rob) *lawyer*
Howe, Richard Rives *lawyer*
Howitt, John P. *lawyer*
Hritz, George F. *lawyer*
Hruska, Alan J. *lawyer, filmmaker*
Huck, L. Francis *lawyer*
Hudspeth, Stephen Mason *lawyer*
Huebner, Marshall Scott *lawyer*
Hulbert, Richard Woodward *lawyer*
Hull, Philip Glasgow *lawyer*
Hummel, Keith R. *lawyer*
Hunt, Franklin Griggs *lawyer*
Hupper, John Roscoe *retired lawyer*
Hurley, Lawrence Joseph *lawyer*
Hurlock, James Bickford *retired lawyer*
Huttner, Constance S. *lawyer*
Hutton, G. Thompson *lawyer*
Hyde, David Rowley *lawyer*
Hyman, Alan Barry *lawyer*
Hyman, Jerome Elliot *lawyer*
Hynes, Patricia M. *lawyer*
Iannuzzi, John Nicholas *lawyer, author, educator*
Ichel, David W. *lawyer*
Immergut, Mel M. *lawyer*
Indursky, Arthur *lawyer*
Insel, Michael S. *lawyer*
Intriligator, Marc Steven *lawyer*
Irvin, Patricia Louise *lawyer*
Isaacson, Allen Ira *lawyer*
Isquith, Fred Taylor *lawyer*
Issacharoff, Samuel *law educator*
Issler, Harry *lawyer*
Ivanhoe, Robert J. *lawyer*
Ivanick, Carol W. Trencher *lawyer*
Jackson, Jack P. *lawyer*
Jackson, Robert R. *lawyer*
Jacob, Edwin J. *lawyer*
Jacob, Marvin Eugene *lawyer*
Jacobs, Albert Lionel, Jr. *lawyer*
Jacobs, Arnold Stephen *lawyer*
Jacobs, Paul *lawyer*
Jacobs, Randall Scott David *lawyer*
Jacobs, Robert Alan *lawyer*
Jacobson, Gilbert H. *lawyer, director*
Jacobson, Jeffrey E. *lawyer, consultant, educator*
Jacobson, Jerold Dennis *lawyer*
Jaffe, Helene D. *lawyer*
Jaglom, Andre Richard *lawyer*
Jakes, Peter H. *lawyer*
Janklow, Morton Lloyd *lawyer, literary agent*
Janowitz, James Arnold *lawyer*
Jaroslawicz, David *lawyer*
Jassy, Everett Lewis *lawyer*
Jebejian, Sarkis *lawyer*
Jenner, Jesse Jacob *lawyer*
Jeydel, Richard K. *lawyer*
Jock, Paul F., II, *lawyer*
Joffe, Robert David *lawyer*
Johnson, David Harrover *lawyer, music company executive*
Johnson, David J., Jr. *lawyer*
Johnson, James D. *lawyer*
Johnson, Jeh Charles *lawyer*
Johnson, Peter James, Jr. *lawyer, legal analyst*
Jones, James A. III *lawyer*
Jordan, Vernon Eulion, Jr. *lawyer*
Joseph, Gregory Paul *lawyer*
Joseph, Leonard *lawyer*
Juceam, Robert E. *lawyer*
Kafin, Robert Joseph *lawyer*
Kahn, Alan Edwin *lawyer*
Kahn, Anthony F. *lawyer*
Kailas, Leo George *lawyer*
Kalik, Mildred *lawyer*
Kalish, Arthur *lawyer*
Kalish, Myron *lawyer*
Kalter, Albert *lawyer, educator*
Kambour, Annaliese Spofford *lawyer, media company executive*
Kamin, Sherwin *retired lawyer*
Kaminsky, Alan *lawyer*
Kamm, Linda Heller *lawyer*
Kandel, William Lloyd *lawyer, arbitrator, mediator, educator, writer*
Kane, Richard Joseph *lawyer*
Kane, Siegrun Dinklage *lawyer*
Kanner, Frederick W. *lawyer*
Kanter, Carl Irwin *retired lawyer*
Kanter, Stacy J. *lawyer*
Kanzer, Alan *lawyer*
Kaplan, Carl Eliot *lawyer*
Kaplan, Cathy M. *lawyer*
Kaplan, James I. *lawyer*
Kaplan, Joseph Solte *retired lawyer*
Kaplan, Madeline *legal administrator*
Kaplan, Mark Norman *lawyer*
Kaplan, Paul Michael *lawyer, educator*
Kaplan, Susan *lawyer*
Karan, Paul Richard *lawyer*
Karatz, William Warren *lawyer*
Karelis, Kathleen E. *lawyer, communications systems company executive*
Karmali, Rashida Alimahomed *lawyer*
Karp, Brad S. *lawyer*
Karp, David C. *lawyer*
Kartiganer, Joseph *retired lawyer*
Kasowitz, Marc Elliot *lawyer*
Katcher, Richard David *lawyer*
Katsh, Salem Michael *lawyer*
Katz, Avi *lawyer*
Katz, David A. *lawyer*
Katz, Jerome Charles *lawyer*
Katz, Robert James *lawyer*
Katz, Ronald Scott *lawyer*
Katz, Stuart Z. *lawyer*
Katzberg, Robert F. *lawyer*
Kaufman, Robert Max *lawyer, director*
Kaufman, Stephen Edward *lawyer*
Kavaler, Thomas J. *lawyer*
Kayle, Bruce E. *lawyer*
Kayser, Leo III *lawyer*
Kazanjian, John Harold *lawyer*
Kean, Hamilton Fish *lawyer*
Keany, Sutton *lawyer*
Keene, Lonnie *lawyer*
Keller, Bruce P. *lawyer*
Kelley, David N. *lawyer, former United States attorney*
Kelly, Anastasia Donovan (Stasia Kelly) *lawyer, insurance company executive*
Kelly, Christopher M. *lawyer*
Kelly, Thomas Michael *lawyer*
Kelman, Edward Michael *lawyer*
Keltner, Thomas Nethery, Jr. *lawyer*
Kende, Christopher Burgess *lawyer, educator*
Keneally, Kathryn Marie *lawyer*
Kennedy, Robert Francis, Jr. *lawyer, environmentalist*
Kenney, John Joseph *lawyer*
Kent, Steven *lawyer*
Keogh, Kevin *lawyer*
Kepke, Matthew Aaron *lawyer*
Kern, George Calvin, Jr. *lawyer*
Kerner, Gerald *lawyer*
Kernochan, John Marshall *lawyer, educator*
Kessel, Mark *lawyer*
Kessler, Jeffrey L. *lawyer*
Kezsbom, Allen *lawyer*
Kheel, Robert J. *lawyer*
Kiekhofer, William Henry *lawyer*
Kiernan, John S. *lawyer*
Kies, David M. *lawyer*
Kiessling, B. Robbins *lawyer*
Kilpatrick, Donald G. *lawyer*
Kimball, John Devereux *lawyer*
King, Henry Lawrence *lawyer*
King, Stephen C. *lawyer, commissioner, educator*
Kinney, Stephen Hoyt, Jr. *lawyer*
Kinzler, Thomas Benjamin *lawyer*
Kirby, John Joseph, Jr. *lawyer*
Kirkham, D. Collier *lawyer*
Kirman, Igor *lawyer*
Kirpalani, Susheel *lawyer*
Kirschbaum, Myron *lawyer*
Kirschner, Kenneth Harold *lawyer*
Klapper, Richard H. *lawyer*
Kleckner, Robert George, Jr. *retired lawyer*
Klein, Eleazer *lawyer*
Klein, Martin I. *lawyer*
Klein, Richard S. *lawyer*
Kleinbard, Edward D. *lawyer*
Kleinberg, Norman Charles *lawyer*
Kleinsinger, Stuart *retired lawyer, music producer*
Klemann, Gilbert Lacy, II, *lawyer*
Kline, Eugene Monroe *lawyer*
Klinger, Alan Mark *lawyer*
Klingsberg, David *lawyer*
Klipstein, Robert Alan *lawyer*
Klotz, Martin B. *lawyer*
Kobak, James Benedict, Jr. *lawyer, educator*
Kobi, Daniel Casey *lawyer*
Koblenz, Michael Robert *lawyer*
Kobrin, Lawrence Alan *lawyer*
Koch, Ed (Edward Irving Koch) *lawyer, former mayor*
Koch, Edward Richard *lawyer, accountant*
Koegel, William Fisher *lawyer*
Koen, Robert G. *lawyer*
Kohl, Robert L. *lawyer*
Kohlmann, Susan J. *lawyer*
Kohn, Immanuel *lawyer*
Kojevnikov, Boris Oleg *lawyer, consultant*
Koob, Charles Edward *lawyer*
Koopersmith, Kim *lawyer*
Koral, Alan Max *lawyer*
Kornberg, Alan William *lawyer*
Kornfeld, Neil S. *lawyer*
Kornreich, Edward Scott *lawyer*
Korotkin, Michael Paul *lawyer*
Kosakow, James Matthew *lawyer*
Koslow, Jonathan L. *lawyer*
Kraemer, Lillian Elizabeth *retired lawyer*
Kraines, Merrill M. *lawyer*
Kramer, Daniel Jonathan *lawyer*
Krane, Steven Charles *lawyer*
Krasner, Daniel Walter *lawyer*
Krasnow, Richard P. *lawyer*
Kreidman, Perry L. *lawyer*
Kreitzman, Ralph J. *lawyer*
Krieger, Sanford *lawyer*
Kroll, Sol *lawyer*
Krouse, George Raymond, Jr. *lawyer*
Krupman, William Allan *lawyer*
Krupp, Fred D. *lawyer, environmental services administrator*
Kubek, Gary W. *lawyer*
Kuby, Ronald Lawrence *lawyer*
Kuh, Richard Henry *lawyer*
Kuntz, Lee Allan *lawyer*
Kuntz, William Francis, II, *lawyer, educator*
Kurtz, Jerome *lawyer, educator*
Kurz, William Charles Frederick *lawyer*
Kurzweil, Harvey *lawyer*
LaBarre, Dennis W. *lawyer*
Lack, Robert Joel *lawyer*
Lacovara, Philip Allen *lawyer*
Lacy, Robinson Burrell *lawyer*
Lahey, John H. *lawyer*
Lamia, Thomas Roger *lawyer*
Lanchner, Bertrand Martin *lawyer, advertising executive*
Landau, David H. *lawyer*
Landon, Dain Charles *lawyer*
Langan, Richard F., Jr. *lawyer*
Lange, Marvin Robert *lawyer*
Langer, Bruce Alden *lawyer*
Lans, Deborah Eisner *lawyer*
Lansner, Ruth L. *lawyer*
Lapidus, Mitchell *lawyer*
Larose, Lawrence Alfred *lawyer*
Latza, William D. *lawyer*
Lauer, Eliot *lawyer*
Laufer, Jacob *lawyer*
Lavin, Howard S. *lawyer*
LeBlang, Skip Alan *lawyer*
Lebow, Mark Denis *lawyer*
Lederman, Lawrence *lawyer, writer, educato*
Lee, In-Young *lawyer*
Lee, Jerome G. *lawyer*
Lee, Paul Lawrence *lawyer*
Lefcourt, Gerald B. *lawyer*
LeFevre, David E. *lawyer, business executive*
Lefkowitz, David S. *lawyer*
Lefkowitz, Howard N. *lawyer*
Lehman, Mark E. *lawyer*
Leibert, Burton M. *lawyer*
Leichtling, Michael Alfred *lawyer*
Leland, Richard G(uy) *lawyer*
Lenobel, Jeffrey A. *lawyer*
Leonard, Edwin Deane *lawyer*
Lerner, Eric M. *lawyer*
Lerner, Jonathan J. *lawyer*
Lerner, Max Kasner *lawyer*
Lerner, Richard E. *lawyer*
Lesch, Michael Oscar *lawyer*
Lesk, Ann Berger *lawyer*
Lesman, Michael Steven *lawyer*
Levander, Andrew Joshua *lawyer*
Levie, Joseph Henry *lawyer, banker*
Levin, Ezra Gurion *lawyer*
Levin, Michael Joseph *lawyer*
Levin, Peter S.W. *lawyer*
Levine, Robert Jay *lawyer*
Levine, Ronald Jay *lawyer*
Levinson, Paul Howard *lawyer*
Levitan, David M(aurice) *lawyer, educator*
Levitan, Steve *lawyer*
Levy, Herbert Monte *lawyer*
Levy, Stanley Herbert *lawyer*
Lewin, Robert *lawyer*
Lewyn, Thomas Mark *lawyer*
Li, Tze-chung *lawyer, educator*
Liddle, Jeffrey L. *lawyer*
Liebenson, Jeffrey M. *lawyer*
Lieberman, Nancy Ann *lawyer*
Liebman, Lance Malcolm *law educator*
Liebmann, Jeff S. *lawyer*
Liftin, John Matthew *lawyer*
Liman, Lewis Jeffrey *lawyer*
Lindauer, Erik D. *lawyer*
Lindblom, Marjorie Press *lawyer*
Lindley, David Morrison *lawyer*
Lindo, Stephen T. *lawyer*
Lindsay, George Peter *lawyer*
Link, Robert O., Jr. *lawyer*
Linker, Arthur S. *lawyer*
Lippert, Nels T. *lawyer*
Lipscomb, James Louis *lawyer, insurance company executive*
Liptak, Adam *lawyer, reporter*
Lipton, Martin *lawyer*
Liss, Norman *lawyer*
Litman, Jack Theodore *lawyer*
Litvack, Sanford Martin *lawyer*
Litwin, Ethan *lawyer*
Lloyd, William Frederick *lawyer*
Loacker, Lynn J. *lawyer*
Lobenfeld, Eric Jay *lawyer*
Lobl, Herbert Max *lawyer, writer*
Lobrano, John D. *lawyer*
Loengard, Richard Otto, Jr. *lawyer*
Logan, Kenneth Richard *lawyer*
London, Martin *lawyer*
Longstreth, Bevis *lawyer*
Lord, Barbara Joanni *lawyer*
Loss, Margaret Ruth *lawyer*
Lotwin, Stanford Gerald *lawyer*
Loughlin, Walter P. *lawyer*
Loughran, Peter J. *lawyer*
Lowenfeld, Andreas Frank *law educator*
Lowenfels, Fred M. *lawyer*
Lowenfels, Lewis David *lawyer*
Lowenstein, Louis *law educator*
Lowy, George Theodore *lawyer*
Lum, Larry *lawyer*
Lunding, Christopher Hanna *lawyer*
Lupert, Leslie Allan *lawyer*
Luria, Mary Mercer *lawyer*
Lutzker, Elliot Howard *lawyer*
Lutzker, Joel E. *lawyer*
Luxenberg, Arthur Martin *lawyer*
Lyddane, John Lawrence Ashton *lawyer*
Lynch, Loretta E. *lawyer, former prosecutor*
Lynch, Luke Daniel, Jr. *lawyer*
Lynn, Theodore Stanley *lawyer*
Lyon, Carl Francis, Jr. *lawyer*
Macan, William Alexander, IV, *lawyer*
MacCrate, Robert *lawyer*
Mack, Dennis Wayne *lawyer*
MacLean, Babcock *lawyer*
MacRae, Cameron Farquhar III *lawyer*
Macris, Michael *lawyer*
Madden, John J. *lawyer*
Madden, John Patrick *lawyer*
Madison, George W. *lawyer, corporate financ executive*
Mahon, Arthur Joseph *lawyer*
Maidman, Richard Harvey Mortimer *lawyer*
Maitland, Guy Edison Clay *lawyer*
Malamud, Deborah C. *law educator*
Malfa, Frances *lawyer*
Malina, Michael *lawyer*
Malkin, Peter Laurence *lawyer, investor*
Mallin, Joel *lawyer*
Mallow, Matthew J. *lawyer*
Mandelker, Lawrence Arthur *lawyer*
Mandelstam, Charles Lawrence *lawyer*
Maneker, Morton M. *lawyer*
Maney, Michael Mason *lawyer*
Mann, James Brooks *lawyer*
Mantel, Allan David *lawyer*
Manuel, Charles B., Jr. *lawyer*
Marcus, Eric Peter *lawyer*
Marcus, Maria Lenhoff *lawyer, educator*
Marcusa, Fred Haye *lawyer*

Seifert, Thomas Lloyd *lawyer*
Seiff, Eric A. *lawyer*
Seigel, Stuart Evan *lawyer*
Seligman, Delice *lawyer*
Selver, Paul Darryl *lawyer*
Semlies, Lori R. *lawyer*
Senzel, Martin Lee *lawyer*
Serbaroli, Francis J. *lawyer, educator, writer*
Serchuk, Ivan *lawyer*
Serota, James Ian *lawyer*
Serota, Susan Perlstadt *lawyer, educator*
Setrakian, Berge *lawyer*
Seward, George Chester *lawyer*
Seymour, Everett Hedden, Jr. *lawyer*
Seymour, Karen Patton *lawyer, former prosecutor*
Seymour, Samuel Whitney *lawyer*
Shachar, Avishai *lawyer*
Shainwald, Sybil *lawyer*
Shakow, David Joseph *lawyer, educator*
Shane, Penny *lawyer*
Shannon, Careen Brett *lawyer, writer, law educator*
Shapiro, Isaac *lawyer*
Shapiro, Mark Jeffrey *lawyer*
Shapiro, Meryl *lawyer*
Shapiro, Michael *lawyer*
Shapiro, Steven R. *legal association administrator*
Sharfstein, Howard F. *lawyer*
Shargel, Gerald L. *lawyer*
Sharkey, Catherine Moira *law educator*
Sharma, Ravi Ivan *lawyer*
Shaw, Theodore Michael *legal association administrator*
Shea, Edward Emmett *lawyer, educator, writer*
Shea, James William *lawyer*
Shecter, Howard L. *lawyer*
Sheehan, Robert C. *lawyer*
Shen, Michael *lawyer*
Shenker, Joseph C. *lawyer*
Shepard, Robert M. *lawyer, investment banker, engineer*
Sheresky, Norman M. *lawyer*
Shields, Craig M. *lawyer*
Shientag, Florence Perlow *lawyer*
Shinkle, John Thomas *lawyer*
Shockey, George R., Jr. *lawyer*
Shorter, James Russell, Jr. *lawyer*
Shoss, Cynthia Renée *lawyer*
Shulman, Max Rees *lawyer*
Shutran, Richard *lawyer*
Shyer, John D. *lawyer*
Sidamon-Eristoff, Constantine *lawyer*
Siegel, Edward M. *lawyer*
Siegel, Jeffrey Norton *lawyer*
Siegel, Stanley *lawyer, educator*
Siffert, John Sand *lawyer, educator, writer*
Sigmond, Carol Ann *lawyer*
Silberberg, Richard Howard *lawyer*
Silberman, John Alan *lawyer*
Silkenat, James Robert *lawyer*
Siller, Stephen I. *lawyer*
Silver, Richard V. *lawyer, diversified financial services company executive*
Silverberg, Jay Lloyd *lawyer*
Silverberg, Michael Joel *lawyer*
Silverman, Arthur Charles *lawyer*
Silverman, Eric F. *lawyer*
Silverman, Laurence A. *lawyer*
Silverman, Moses *lawyer*
Silverstein, Paul N. *lawyer*
Simkin, Steven *lawyer*
Simmons, Peter Lawrence *lawyer*
Simms, Marsha E. *lawyer*
Simon, Bruce Harvey *lawyer*
Simone, Joseph R. *lawyer*
Simons, Albert III *lawyer*
Sinensky, Jeffrey *lawyer*
Sinsheimer, Warren Jack *lawyer*
Sirgado, Jo Anne E. *lawyer*
Sirkin, Michael S. *lawyer*
Siskind, Arthur Michael *lawyer*
Siskind, Donald Henry *lawyer*
Sjoblom, Thomas V. *lawyer*
Skaistis, Rachel G. *lawyer*
Skinner, Peter Graeme *retired lawyer*
Skirnick, Robert Andrew *lawyer*
Sklyar, Adelina M. *lawyer*
Sladkus, Harvey Ira *lawyer*
Slifkin, Daniel *lawyer*
Sloane, Howard G. *lawyer*
Slotnick, Barry Ivan *lawyer*
Small, Jeffrey *lawyer*
Small, Jonathan Andrew *lawyer, consultant*
Smart, Thomas A. *lawyer*
Smeall, Christopher *lawyer*
Smith, Bradley Youle *lawyer*
Smith, Edward Paul, Jr. *lawyer*
Smith, George Bundy *lawyer, retired state appeals court judge*
Smith, James Walker *lawyer*
Smith, Jason A. B. *lawyer*
Smith, Jeffrey Austen *lawyer*
Smith, Jeffrey G. *lawyer*
Smith, Karen A. *lawyer*
Smith, Robert Blakeman *lawyer*
Smith, Robert Everett *lawyer*
Smith, Stuart Alan *lawyer*
Smith, Thomas A. *lawyer, investment company executive*
Smith, Thomas Ramsaur, Jr. *lawyer*
Snider, Jerome Guy *lawyer*
Snow, Charles *lawyer*
Sobel, Gerald *lawyer*
Solano, Henry L. *lawyer*
Solarz, Alan H. *lawyer*
Solender, Michael Samuel *lawyer, diversified financial services company executive*
Solomon, Andrew P. *lawyer*
Solomon, Stephen L. *lawyer*
Solomon, Terri Marcia *lawyer*
Sorell Stehr, Deborah K. *lawyer*
Sorgi, Leonard *lawyer*
Sorkin, David James *lawyer*
Sorkin, Ira Lee *lawyer*
Sorkin, Laurence Truman *lawyer*
Sorter, George Hans *accounting and law educator, consultant*
Soussloff, Andrew D. *lawyer*
Sovern, Michael Ira *law educator*
Soyster, Margaret Blair *lawyer*
Spanbock, Maurice Samuel *lawyer*
Spatt, Robert Edward *lawyer*
Spear, Harvey M. *lawyer*
Spelfogel, Evan J. *lawyer, educator*
Spellman Sweet, Julie T. *lawyer*
Spencer, Michael C. *lawyer*
Sperling, Allan George *lawyer*
Spiegel, Jerrold Bruce *lawyer*
Spillane, Dennis Kevin *lawyer*
Spivak, Leonard A. *lawyer*
Squire, Walter Charles *lawyer*
Srulowitz, Marvin *lawyer*
Stadler, Brian M. *lawyer*
Standard, Kenneth G. *lawyer*
Starer, Brian Douglas *lawyer*
Starr, Michael *lawyer*
Stathis, Nicholas John *lawyer*
Stecher, Esta E. *lawyer, investment company executive*
Stein, Jane Wallison *lawyer*
Stein, Ronald J. *lawyer*
Stein, Stephen William *lawyer*
Steinberg, Arthur Jay *lawyer*
Steinberg, Howard Eli *lawyer, diversified financial services company executive*
Stephenson, Alan Clements *lawyer*
Stern, Donald Allan *lawyer*
Sternman, Joel W. *lawyer*
Sterns, William S. III *lawyer*
Steuer, Richard Marc *lawyer*
Stevens, Michael N. *lawyer*
Stever, Donald Winfred *lawyer*
Stewart, Geoffrey S. *lawyer*
Stewart, Lynne F. *lawyer*
Stewart, Richard Burleson *law educator*
Stillman, Charles Allen *lawyer*
Stoll, Neal Richard *lawyer*
Stone, David Philip *lawyer*
Stone, Merrill Brent *lawyer*
Stopnik, Scott H. *lawyer*
Strauss, Peter L(ester) *law educator*
Strickon, Harvey Alan *lawyer*
Strom, Milton Gary *lawyer*
Strossen, Nadine *legal association administrator, educator*
Strum, Jay Gerson *lawyer*
Struve, Guy Miller *lawyer*
Stuart, Alice Melissa *lawyer*
Stuart, Walter Bynum, IV, *lawyer*
Stumer, Mark Bradley *lawyer, consultant, restaurateur*
Sturman, Deborah Muscha *lawyer, columnist*
Sugarman, Irwin J. *lawyer*
Sulds, Jonathan L. *lawyer*
Sullivan, John W. *lawyer*
Sussman, Alexander Ralph *lawyer*
Sutin, Alan N. *lawyer*
Suydam, John J. *lawyer*
Sweeney, Thomas Joseph, Jr. *lawyer*
Synnott, Aidan John *lawyer*
Taber, Kenneth W. *lawyer*
Tacopina, Joseph *lawyer*
Tahbaz, Christopher K. *lawyer*
Tallackson, Jeffrey Stephen *lawyer*
Tanenbaum, Edward *lawyer*
Tanenbaum, Jeffrey L. *lawyer*
Tanenbaum, William Alan *lawyer*
Tanner, Douglas Alan *lawyer*
Tarnoff, Jerome *lawyer*
Tavss, John E. *lawyer*
Taylor, Edward A. *lawyer*
Taylor, Errol Bancroft *lawyer*
Taylor, John Chestnut III *lawyer*
Taylor, Willard B. *lawyer*
Teich, Howard Bernard *lawyer, volunteer, public information officer*
Teiman, Richard Barry *lawyer*
Teitelbaum, Herbert *lawyer*
Tenney, Dudley Bradstreet *retired lawyer*
Terrell, J. Anthony *lawyer*
Terry, Frederick Arthur, Jr. *lawyer*
Terry, James Joseph, Jr. *lawyer*
Testa, Michael Harold *lawyer*
Thackeray, Jonathan E. *lawyer*
Thal, Steven Henry *lawyer, consultant*
Thalacker, Arbie Robert *lawyer, director*
Thomas, Ann Freda *lawyer*
Thomas, Jeremiah Lindsay III *lawyer*
Thomas, Robert Morton, Jr. *lawyer, director*
Thomas, Roger Warren *lawyer*
Thompson, Katherine Genevieve *lawyer*
Thompson, Loran Tyson *lawyer*
Thompson, Timothy Lewis *lawyer*
Thoyer, Judith Reinhardt *lawyer*
Thurm, David Aaron *lawyer, publishing executive*
Thurston, Sally A. *lawyer*
Tierney, James Edward *law educator, former state attorney general*
Tilewick, Robert *lawyer*
Tillinghast, David Rollhaus *lawyer*
Tillinghast, Edward Hudson III *lawyer*
Todd, Ronald Gary *lawyer*
Tolley, B. Cary III *lawyer*
Toumey, Donald Joseph *lawyer*
Townsend, Robert I. III *lawyer*
Tracey, Dennis Henry III *lawyer*
Treadway, James Crispin Curran Corbett *lawyer, brokerage house executive, investor, federal official*
Trepper, Myron *lawyer*
Tricarico, Joseph Archangelo *lawyer*
Tuchmann, Eric P. *lawyer*
Tulchin, David Bruce *lawyer*
Tung, Ko-Yung *lawyer*
Turner, E. Deane *lawyer*
Turner, Roger D. *lawyer*
Tusk, Claude M. *lawyer*
Tween, Douglas M. *lawyer, former prosecutor*
Udell, Richard *lawyer*
Underberg, Mark Alan *lawyer*
Unger, Sydney Elliott *lawyer*
Uram, Gerald Robert *lawyer*
Urowsky, Richard J. *lawyer*
Valente, Peter Charles *lawyer*
Vardell, James C. III *lawyer*
Varet, Michael A. *lawyer*
Vassallo, Edward E. *lawyer*
Vassallo, John A. *lawyer*
Vassil, John Charles *lawyer*
Vega, Matias Alfonso *lawyer*
Verde, Michael I. *lawyer*
Vernon, Darryl Mitchell *lawyer*
Versfelt, David Scott *lawyer*
Victor, A. Paul *lawyer*
Vig, Vernon Edward *lawyer*
Vinegrad, Alan *prosecutor*
Vingoe, D. Grant *lawyer*
Vitale, Thomas M. *lawyer*
Vitkowsky, Vincent Joseph *lawyer*
Vittor, Kenneth Mark *lawyer*
Vollweiler, Cheryl P. *lawyer*
von Mehren, Robert Brandt *retired lawyer*
Vyskocil, Mary Kay *lawyer*
Wachsberger, Chaim *lawyer*
Wachtell, Herbert M. *lawyer*
Waddell, Mark E. *lawyer*
Wailand, George *lawyer*
Waks, Jay Warren *lawyer*
Wald, Bernard Joseph *lawyer*
Wald, Wayne A. *lawyer*
Waldenberg, Alan S. *lawyer*
Waldman, Seymour Morton *lawyer*
Waldron, Jeremy James *law educator*
Walker, John Lockwood *lawyer*
Walker, Kim A. *lawyer*
Walkovik, Donald C. *lawyer*
Wall, Charles R. *lawyer*
Wallace, Edward Corbett *lawyer*
Wallace, Nora Ann *lawyer*
Wallace, Walter C. *lawyer, government official*
Wallach, Eric Jean *lawyer*
Wang, Albert Huai-en *lawyer*
Wang, Xinsheng *lawyer*
Warden, John Lehman *lawyer*
Warnke, Gordon E. *lawyer*
Warren, Irwin Howard *lawyer*
Warren, James I. *lawyer*
Warren, William Bradford *lawyer*
Washburn, David Thacher *lawyer*
Watson, Solomon Brown, IV, *lawyer, publishing executive*
Waxenberg, Jay David *lawyer*
Waybourn, Kathleen Ann *lawyer, consultant*
Webster, Susan *lawyer*
Ween, Martin M. *lawyer*
Weiksner, Sandra S. *lawyer*
Weinberg, Jeffrey J. *lawyer*
Weinberger, Harold Paul *lawyer*
Weiner, Andrew Jay *lawyer*
Weiner, Earl David *lawyer*
Weiner, Stephen Arthur *lawyer*
Weingarten, Marc *lawyer*
Weinroth, Lois L. *lawyer*
Weinschel, Alan Jay *lawyer*
Weinstein, Herschel S. *lawyer, pharmaceutical executive*
Weinstock, Leonard *lawyer*
Weisbrod, Carl *lawyer, public official*
Weiser, Martin Jay *lawyer*
Weiss, Jack Meyar *lawyer*
Weiss, Jonathan Arthur *lawyer, writer*
Weiss, Lawrence N. *lawyer*
Weiss, Lisa Ann *lawyer*
Weiss, Melvyn I. *lawyer*
Weissman, David L. *lawyer*
Weissmann, Andrew *lawyer, former prosecutor*
Weithorn, Stanley Stephen *lawyer*
Weitz, Harvey *lawyer, educator*
Weitz, Perry *lawyer*
Weld, Jonathan Minot *lawyer*
Weld, William F. *former governor*
Welikson, Jeffrey Alan *lawyer*
Wellington, Harry Hillel *lawyer, educator*
Wells, Christopher M. *lawyer*
Wells, Theodore V., Jr., (Ted) *lawyer*
Welshimer, Mark J. *lawyer*
Weltman, Edward S. *lawyer*
Wender, Ira Tensard *lawyer*
Wenig, Cindy L. *lawyer*
Werder, Richard I., Jr. *lawyer*
Werner, Robert L. *lawyer, consultant*
Wesely, Edwin Joseph *lawyer*
Wesely, Marissa Celeste *lawyer*
West, Stephen Kingsbury *lawyer, director*
Westreich, Neil P. *lawyer*
Wetmore, Keith Chidester *lawyer*
Wexelbaum, Michael *lawyer*
Whelan, William J. III *lawyer*
Whitaker, G(eorge) Warren *lawyer*
White, Fred B. III *lawyer*
White, Harry Edward, Jr. *lawyer*
White, John Patrick *lawyer*
White, Katherine Patricia *lawyer*
White, Mary Jo *lawyer, former prosecutor*
White, Peter C. *lawyer*
White, W. Christopher *lawyer*
Whitmer, Frederick Lee *lawyer*
Whitney, Jonathan B. *lawyer*
Whitson, Jerry E. *lawyer*
Whoriskey, Robert Donald *lawyer*
Wickes, R(ichard) Paul *lawyer*
Wilcox, John Caven *lawyer, financial executive*
Wildermuth, Bruce R. *lawyer*
Wiles, Michael E. *lawyer*
Wilkinson, John Hart *lawyer*
Willett, John A. *lawyer*
Williams, Anthony *lawyer*
Williams, Patricia J. *law educator*
Williams, Vaughn Charles *lawyer*
Williams, William John, Jr. *lawyer*
Williamson, Douglas Franklin, Jr. *lawyer*
Willig, Kenneth C. H. *lawyer*
Willis, William Ervin *lawyer*
Willner, Barry A. *lawyer*
Wilson, Paul Holliday, Jr. *lawyer*
Wilson, Peter Scott *lawyer*
Wilson, Rowan D. *lawyer*
Wimpfheimer, Michael Clark *lawyer*
Windels, Paul, Jr. *lawyer*
Winfield, Richard Neill *lawyer*
Wing, John Russell *lawyer*
Winterer, Philip Steele *lawyer*
Wintner, Mark S. *lawyer*
Wise, Aaron Noah *lawyer*
Wise, Robert F., Jr. *lawyer*
Wiseman, Michael Martin *lawyer*
Witkin, Eric Douglas *lawyer*
Witmeyer, John Jacob III *lawyer*
Witten, Roger Michael *lawyer*
Wohl, Frank Harold *lawyer*
Wolf, Barry M. *lawyer*
Wolfe, James Ronald *retired lawyer*
Wolff, Jesse David *lawyer*
Wollan, Eugene *lawyer*
Woods, John Maynard *lawyer*
Woolery, James C. *lawyer*
Wray, Cecil, Jr. *lawyer*
Wynne, William Francis *lawyer*
Yablon, Heather D. *lawyer*
Yamin, Michael Geoffrey *lawyer*
Yankwitt, George B(ruce) *lawyer*
Yarett, Jordan Eliot *lawyer*
Yelenick, Mary Therese *lawyer*
Yerman, Fredric Warren *lawyer*
Yodowitz, Edward Jay *lawyer*
Young, Alice *lawyer*
Young, Jonathan *lawyer*
Youngwood, Alfred Donald *lawyer*
Zabel, William David *lawyer*
Zack, Robert G. *lawyer, investment company executive*
Zagorin, Janet Susan *legal firm administrato marketing professional*
Zaitzeff, Roger Michael *lawyer*
Zammit, Joseph Paul *lawyer*
Zaslowsky, David Paul *lawyer*
Zauderer, Mark Carl *lawyer*
Zedrosser, Joseph John *lawyer*
Zerin, Steven David *lawyer*
Ziegler, Henry Steinway *retired lawyer*
Zifchak, William C. *lawyer*
Zimand, Harvey Folks *lawyer*
Zimmerman, Diane Leenheer *law educator*
Zimmett, Mark Paul *lawyer, educator*
Zinberg, David J. *lawyer*
Zirinsky, Bruce R. *lawyer*
Zito, Robert John Amadeus *lawyer*
Zivin, Norman H. *lawyer*
Zochowski, T. Robert, Jr. *lawyer*
Zoogman, Nicholas Jay *lawyer*
Zornow, David Merrill *lawyer*
Zubkoff, Daniel J. *lawyer*
Zuckerman, Paul Herbert *lawyer*
Zukerman, Michael *lawyer*
Zweibel, Joel Burton *retired lawyer*
Zweifach, Lawrence J. *lawyer*

Newburgh
Liberth, Richard Francis *lawyer*
Milligram, Steven Irwin *lawyer*

Niagara Falls
Levine, David Ethan *lawyer*

Nyack
Tirana, Bardyl Rifat *lawyer*

Old Chatham
Severs, Charles A. III *lawyer*

Olean
Heyer, John Henry, II, *lawyer*

Orangeburg
Rivet, Diana Wittmer *lawyer, farmer*

Orchard Park
Sullivan, Mortimer Allen, Jr. *lawyer*

Ossining
Hall, H(erbert) Glen *lawyer*

Oswego
Greene, Stephen Craig *lawyer*

Oyster Bay
Coates, Winslow Shelby, Jr. *lawyer*
Wachsman, Harvey Frederick *lawyer, neurosurgeon*

Pearl River
Meyer, Irwin Stephan *lawyer, accountant*
Riley, James Kevin *lawyer*

Pelham
Gaffney, Mark William *lawyer*

Pittsford
Blyth, John E. *lawyer, educator*
Braunsdorf, Paul Raymond *lawyer*
Buzard, A. Vincent *lawyer*
Hampson, Thomas Meredith *lawyer*
Stonehill, Eric *lawyer*
Turri, Joseph A. *lawyer*
Willett, Thomas Edward *lawyer*

Pleasantville
DuPree, Clifford H. R. *lawyer*

Port Washington
Mayer, Renee G. *lawyer*
Rush, Curt Stefan *lawyer*
Ullman, Leo Solomon *lawyer*

Poughkeepsie
Dietz, Robert Barron *lawyer*
Kranis, Michael David *lawyer, judge*
Millman, Jode Susan *lawyer, writer*
Ostertag, Robert Louis *lawyer*
Shatz, Phillip *lawyer*
Taphorn, Joseph Bernard *lawyer*
Teal, Arabella W. *lawyer, former state attor general*

Ridge
Samuel William, Jr. *retired lawyer*

ase
, Bruno Joseph *lawyer*
Noah Jonathan *lawyer*
Edmund Joseph *lawyer, investment ing executive*
son, Larry Dean *lawyer, former federal cy administrator*
ı, James C. *lawyer*

elaerville
r, Raymond Russwald, Jr. *lawyer*

beck
, Steven Michael *lawyer*

head
pinto, V. Anthony *lawyer*

ester
Donald Robert *lawyer*
y, Michael Francis *lawyer*
l, Eugene Thomas *lawyer*
William Michael *lawyer*
Justin P. *lawyer*
ald, John T., Jr. *lawyer*
ith, Robert Lyell, Jr. *lawyer*
, Alexander *lawyer*
ck, Margery Fischbein *lawyer*
Joyce P. *lawyer, imaging company utive*
Ralph Millard Peter *lawyer, minister, cator*
, Stephen Michael *lawyer*
Sherry Stokes *lawyer*
ıd, Harold Arthur *lawyer*
Michael R. *lawyer*
ack, Staffan Bengt Gunnar *lawyer*
ory, John Brooks *retired lawyer*
, James Conklin *lawyer*
son, Patrice Burgert *lawyer*
no, Anthony Robert *lawyer*
Gerald Larry *lawyer*
Richard Edward *lawyer*
house, Michael Allan *lawyer, editor, sultant, columnist*
r, Leonard Allen *lawyer*
nacher, Jon Lee *lawyer*
rt, Sue S. *lawyer*
r, Scott MacNeely *lawyer*
neyer, Don Henry *lawyer*
r, Justin Leonard *lawyer*
Stephen Holden *lawyer*
Robert Warren *lawyer*
er, George Robert, Jr. *lawyer*

e
ns, Richard Duncan *lawyer, retired judge*

yn Heights
lo, Nelson A. *lawyer*

s, John Edward *lawyer, consumer products mpany executive*
stein, Peter Dobkin *lawyer*

s Point
es, Louis LeNoir, Jr. *lawyer*

sdale
l, Dennis *lawyer*
sco, Steven Ronald *lawyer*
dict, James Nelson *lawyer*
ert, Edward William *lawyer*
es, Stevan J. *mediator, arbitrator*
er, Roger Alan *lawyer, consultant*
nan, Richard M. *lawyer*
say, Sharon Winnett *lawyer, consultant*
chia, Vincent Michael *lawyer*
o, Kenneth Albert, Jr. *lawyer, art dealer*
Gundy, Gregory Frank *retired lawyer*

enectady
ne, Sanford Harold *lawyer*

oharie
combe, Raynor Bailey *lawyer*

roon Lake
son, Donald Raymond *lawyer*

tsville
ams, Henry Ward, Jr. *lawyer, writer*

ford
y, Raymond Joseph *lawyer*

kan
gman, Frederick *lawyer*

epy Hollow
, William Joseph *lawyer*

thtown
is, Lenore *lawyer*
dman, Richard Shalem *lawyer, orthopedic rgeon*
lman, Thomas Joseph, Jr. *lawyer*

ners
ffe, John Arthur *lawyer, director*
p, Steven M. *lawyer, consumer products ompany executive*

th Richmond Hill
eich, John F. *lawyer*

th Salem
vles, Frederick Oliver *lawyer*

thampton
ez, David *lawyer*
t, Jonathan James *lawyer*

Staten Island
Ferranti, Thomas, Jr. *lawyer*
Humphries, Edward Francis *lawyer*
Klingle, Philip Anthony *law librarian*

Stony Brook
Gulino, Lawrence Carl *mediator*

Syosset
Bermas, Stephen *lawyer*

Syracuse
Ackerman, Kenneth Edward *retired lawyer, educator*
Baldwin, Robert Frederick, Jr. *lawyer*
Barclay, H. Douglas (Hugh Douglas Barclay) *lawyer, legislator, diplomat*
Brickwedde, Richard James *lawyer*
Butler, John Edward *lawyer*
Cirando, John Anthony *lawyer*
Crane, David Michael *prosecutor, former judge advocate, educator*
Fitzpatrick, James David *lawyer*
Ford, Steven J. *lawyer, manufacturing executive*
Gaal, John *lawyer*
Hayes, David Michael *lawyer*
Hildebrandt, George Frederick *lawyer*
Hole, Richard Douglas *lawyer*
Lee, David Ames *lawyer, banker, editor, writer*
Luchsinger, John Francis, Jr. *lawyer*
O'Connor, Michael E. *lawyer*
Pinsky, Roy David *lawyer*
Richardson, M. Catherine *lawyer*
Rivette, Francis Robert *lawyer*
Suddaby, Glenn T. *prosecutor, lawyer*
Young, Douglas Howard *lawyer*
Zimmerman, Aaron Mark *lawyer*

Troy
Burch, Mary Seelye Quinn *law librarian, consultant*
Finkel, Sanford Norman *lawyer*
Jones, E. Stewart, Jr. *lawyer*

Tupper Lake
Johnson, David Wesley *lawyer*

Uniondale
Berzow, Harold Steven *lawyer*
Cassidy, David Michael *lawyer*
Duffy, James Raymond *lawyer*
Eilen, Howard Scott *lawyer, mediator*
Kotula, Michael Anthony *lawyer*
Lemle, Robert Spencer *lawyer*
Levy, Robert S. *lawyer*
Pratt, George Cheney *law educator, retired judge*

Utica
Brennan, John Joseph *lawyer, administrator*
Johnson, Mary Elizabeth *lawyer*

Valatie
Dorsey, Richard J. *lawyer*

Vestal
McGuire, John Thomas *lawyer, educator, writer*

Wantagh
Petris, Elli *paralegal*

Waterford
Glavin, A. Rita Chandellier (Mrs. James Henry Glavin III) *lawyer*
Novotny, F. Douglas *lawyer*

White Plains
Adams, Robert T. *lawyer*
Bender, Joel Charles *lawyer*
Berlin, Alan Daniel *lawyer, real estate company officer, consultant*
Bodnar, Peter O. *lawyer*
Carlisle, Jay Charles, II, *lawyer, educator*
Carlucci, Joseph P. *lawyer*
Culleton, James J. *lawyer, former prosecutor*
Doyle, Dennis T. *lawyer*
Feder, Robert *lawyer*
Gambardella, Thomas M. *lawyer*
Gjertsen, O. Gerard *lawyer*
Greenawalt, William Sloan *lawyer*
Greenspan, Leon Joseph *lawyer*
Greenspan, Michael Evan *lawyer*
Halpern, Philip Morgan *lawyer*
Hattar, Jacqueline *lawyer*
Kurzman, Robert Graham *lawyer, educator*
Landa, Howard Martin *lawyer, management consultant*
Levasseur, Guy J. *lawyer*
Longo, Ronald Anthony *lawyer*
Maffeo, Vincent Anthony *lawyer, director*
McNamara, Michael J. *law educator*
Milone, Lydia *lawyer*
Munneke, Gary Arthur *law educator, consultant*
Nesci, Vincent Peter *lawyer*
Newman, Marie Stefanini *law librarian, educator*
Null, William Seth *lawyer*
O'Brien, H. Michael *lawyer*
O'Brien, James F. *lawyer*
Payson, Martin F. *lawyer*
Pirro, Jeanine Ferris *prosecutor*
Quaranta, Philip *lawyer*
Robinson, Nicholas Adams *law educator, department chairman*
Ryan, Robert Davis *lawyer*
Sheehan, Timothy J. *lawyer*
Siegel, Kenneth S. *lawyer*
Silverberg, Steven Mark *lawyer*
Sloan, F(rank) Blaine *retired law educator*
Steccato, Carl L. *lawyer*
Topol, Robin April Levitt *lawyer*
Tumbarello, Phillip A. *lawyer*
Vignali, Rosario M. *lawyer*
Weiss, Terri Lynn *lawyer*
Worby, David E. *lawyer*
Young, Steven L. *lawyer*

Williamsville
Ciprich, Paula Marie *lawyer, gas industry executive*
Dobosiewicz, Elizabeth J. *lawyer*

Williston Park
Lilly, Thomas Joseph *lawyer*
Lynch, Kyle Thomas *lawyer*

Woodbury
Fischoff, Gary Charles *lawyer*
Mangia, Angelo James *lawyer*

Yonkers
Connors, James Patrick *lawyer*

NORTH CAROLINA

Asheville
Bissette, Winston Louis, Jr. *lawyer, mayor*
Chidnese, Patrick Nicholas *retired lawyer*
Davis, Roy Walton, Jr. *lawyer*
Elmore, Bruce Alexander, Jr. *lawyer*
Hamilton, Jackson Douglas *lawyer*
Lavelle, Brian Francis David *lawyer*
McDevitt, Larry S. *lawyer*
Wilson, Thomas Douglas, Jr. *lawyer*

Bryson City
Miller, Gary H. *lawyer*

Burlington
Slayton, John Howard *lawyer, corporate financial executive*
Smith, Bradford T. *lawyer*

Carthage
Gebhardt, Robert Charles *lawyer*

Cary
Montgomery, Charles Harvey *lawyer*
Taylor, Marvin Edward, Jr. *lawyer*

Chapel Hill
Boger, John Charles *law educator, dean*
Brower, David John *lawyer, urban planner, educator*
Crohn, Max Henry, Jr. *lawyer*
Gervais-Gruen, Elizabeth *lawyer*
Gressman, Eugene *lawyer*
Herman-Giddens, Gregory *lawyer*
Klinefelter, Anne *law librarian, educator*
Lawrence, David Michael *lawyer, educator*
Lilley, Albert Frederick *retired lawyer*
Loeb, Ben Fohl, Jr. *retired law educator*
Moore, Albert Cunningham *lawyer, insurance company executive*
Patz, Edward Frank *retired lawyer*
Southern, Robert Allen *lawyer*
Wegner, Judith Welch *lawyer, educator, dean*

Charlotte
Ayscue, Edwin Osborne, Jr. *lawyer*
Barber, Martha Gayle *lawyer*
Barber, Timothy G. *lawyer*
Barnhill, G. Michael *lawyer*
Bell, Kenneth Davis *lawyer*
Blanchfield, Francis J., Jr. *lawyer*
Brackett, Martin Luther, Jr. *lawyer*
Bragg, Ellis Meredith, Jr. *lawyer*
Buchan, Jonathan Edward, Jr. *lawyer*
Buckley, Charles Robinson III *lawyer*
Carroll, James P. *lawyer*
Chambers, Julius LeVonne *lawyer*
Connor, Michael S. *lawyer*
Cooper, Jason P. *lawyer*
Coss, Stephen K. *lawyer*
Cottingham, Tracy Thomas III *lawyer*
Culbreth, James Harold, Jr. *lawyer*
Durham, J(oseph) Porter, Jr. *lawyer, educator*
Erdman, David Williams *lawyer*
Fennebresque, John C. *lawyer*
Gage, Gaston Hemphill *lawyer*
Goldstein, Stuart N. *lawyer*
Gosnell, Guy R. *lawyer*
Gunson, Douglas R. *lawyer*
Hahn, Robert J. *lawyer*
Hankins, Irvin W. III *lawyer*
Hanna, George Verner III *lawyer*
Hinson, Bobby D. *lawyer*
Hord, Joy M. *lawyer*
Horoschak, Mark J. *lawyer*
Ives, H. Bryan III *lawyer*
Kelley, Janet Godsey *lawyer*
Lilly, James Edward *lawyer*
Lilly, Kevin L. *lawyer, manufacturing executive*
Linnert, Terrence Gregory *lawyer*
Loughridge, John Halsted, Jr. *lawyer*
Manly, Marc Edward *lawyer, energy executive*
Mayopoulos, Timothy J. *lawyer, bank executive*
McBryde, Neill Gregory *lawyer*
McCoy, Michael D. *lawyer*
McGill, John Knox *lawyer*
McMillan, William P. *lawyer*
Mehta, Kiran H. *lawyer*
Nedzbala, Michael *lawyer*
Newitt, John Garwood, Jr. *lawyer*
Pedigo, Paul F. *lawyer*
Rawlins, Donald Ray *lawyer*
Rikard, William L., Jr. *lawyer*
Shappert, Gretchen C(ecilia) F(rances) *prosecutor, lawyer*
Simmons, Charles B., Jr. *lawyer*
Sink, Robert C. *lawyer*
Thigpen, Richard Elton, Jr. *retired lawyer*
Thompson, Sydnor, Jr., (Charles William Sydnor Thompson Jr.) *lawyer, mediator, arbitrator*
Treanor, Mark C. *lawyer, diversified financial services company executive*
Trent, B. Keith *lawyer, energy executive*
Van Allen, William Kent *lawyer*
Van Hoy, Philip Marshall *lawyer*
Vinroot, Richard Allen *lawyer, mayor*
Wagner, Kenneth Lynn *lawyer*
Walker, Clarence Wesley *lawyer*
Wolson, Craig Alan *lawyer*
Wood, William McBrayer *lawyer*
Wyche, James Ramage *lawyer*
Yorke, John Bundy *lawyer*

Cherokee
Martin, Harry Corpening *lawyer, retired state supreme court justice*

Cherryville
Huffstetler, Palmer Eugene *lawyer*

Clinton
Davis, William Maxie, Jr. *lawyer*

Durham
Bernard, Pamela Jenks *lawyer*
Carpenter, Charles Francis *lawyer*
Carrington, Paul DeWitt *lawyer, educator*
Carroll, Kenneth G. *lawyer*
Chemerinsky, Erwin *law educator*
Christie, George Custis *lawyer, educator, writer*
Cox, James D. *law educator*
Dellinger, Walter Estes III *lawyer, educator*
Demott, Deborah Ann *law educator*
Dunshee, Melanie J. *law librarian, educator*
Fisher, Stewart Wayne *lawyer*
Fisk, Catherine Laura *lawyer, educator*
Haagen, Paul Hess *law educator*
Havighurst, Clark Canfield *law educator*
Holder, Angela Roddey *law educator*
Horowitz, Donald Leonard *lawyer, arbitrator, political scientist, educator*
Jenkins, Richard Erik *lawyer*
Marsh, William Andrew III *lawyer*
Maxwell, Richard Callender *retired lawyer, educator*
McMahon, John Alexander *law educator*
O'Neal, Cynthia Ann *lawyer*
Robertson, Horace Bascomb, Jr. *retired law educator*
Rowe, Thomas Dudley, Jr. *law educator*
Schwarcz, Steven Lance *lawyer, educator*
Sloan, Maceo Kennedy *lawyer, investment company executive*

Fayetteville
Mitchell, Ronnie Monroe *lawyer, educator*
Redding, Bobbie Newman *lawyer*
Ruppe, Arthur Maxwell *retired lawyer*
Townsend, William Jackson *lawyer*

Fletcher
Seagle, J. Harold *lawyer*

Gastonia
Stott, Grady Bernell *lawyer*

Goldsboro
Strickland, Donald Bennett *lawyer*

Greensboro
Brotherton, Joseph Faler *lawyer*
Bullock, Frank William, Jr. *lawyer, retired federal judge*
Clark, David McKenzie *lawyer*
Cummings, Candace S. *lawyer, apparel company executive*
Davis, Ferd Leary, Jr. *law educator, consultant*
Davis, Herbert Owen *lawyer*
Floyd, Jack William *lawyer*
Hanson, Randall A. *lawyer*
Hunter, Bynum Merritt *retired lawyer*
Koonce, Neil Wright *lawyer*
Lloyd, Robert Blackwell, Jr. *lawyer*
Medford, James A. *lawyer*
Melvin, Charles Edward, Jr. *lawyer*
Reed, Robert Alan *lawyer*
Schell, Braxton *lawyer*
Semmler, Carl D. *lawyer*
Slaughter, James H. *lawyer*
Smith, Lanty L(loyd) *lawyer, corporate financial executive*
Swan, George Steven *law educator*
Tucker, Robert Rand *lawyer*
Wagoner, Anna Mills S. *prosecutor*
Ward Black, Janet *lawyer*

Greenville
Colombo, Michael Allen *lawyer*
Dixon, Phillip Ray, Sr. *lawyer*
Stevens, David Boyette *law educator*

Hickory
Smith, Young Merritt, Jr. *lawyer*

High Point
McAllister, Kenneth Wayne *lawyer*
Sheahan, Robert Emmett *lawyer, consultant*

Jamestown
Schmitt, William Allen *lawyer*

Kannapolis
Brown, Bachman Storch, Jr. *lawyer*

Kitty Hawk
Tucker, Don Eugene *retired lawyer*

Lexington
Snyder, James Eugene, Jr. *lawyer*

Marion
Burgin, Charles Edward *lawyer*

Mooresville
Badr, Gamal Moursi *legal consultant*
McCanless, Ross William *lawyer, retail executive*

Murphy
Bata, Rudolph Andrew, Jr. *lawyer*

New Bern
Davis, James Lee *lawyer*
Overholt, Hugh Robert *lawyer, retired military officer*

North Wilkesboro
Keener, Gaither McDonald, Jr. *corporate lawyer*

Raleigh
Bar, Roselyn R. *legal association administrator, lawyer, executive secretary*
Blackburn, James B. III *lawyer*
Boyette, Richard T. *lawyer*
Carlton, Alfred Pershing, Jr. *lawyer*
Carter, Jean Gordon *lawyer*
Case, Charles Dixon *lawyer*
Cunningham, Michael *lawyer*
Davis, Egbert Lawrence III *lawyer*
Donadio, Donald A. *lawyer*
Dorsett, James K. III *lawyer*
Edwards, (Mary) Elizabeth *lawyer, writer*
Ellis, Lester Neal, Jr. *lawyer*
Ellis, Richard W. *lawyer*
Gale, James L. *lawyer*
Glass, Fred Stephen *lawyer*
Graham, William Edgar, Jr. *lawyer, utilities executive*
Harrison, Cecil W., Jr. *lawyer*
Huggard, John Parker *lawyer*
Hunt, James Baxter, Jr. *lawyer, former governor*
Hunter, Richard Samford, Jr. *lawyer*
Joyner, Walton Kitchin *lawyer*
Kapp, Michael Keith *lawyer*
Kirk-Duggan, Michael Allan *retired law, economics and computer sciences educator*
Lilliston, Andrew Wilson, Jr. *lawyer*
Long, David W. *lawyer*
Loper, Johnny M. *lawyer*
Lynch, John Christopher *lawyer*
Markoff, Brad Steven *lawyer*
McNish, Susan Kirk *retired lawyer*
Millberg, John C. *lawyer*
Mitchell, Burley Bayard, Jr. *lawyer*
Moore, Richard Hancock *lawyer, state official*
Neely, Charles B., Jr. *lawyer*
Newby, Paul Martin *state supreme court justice*
Parker, John Hill *lawyer*
Patterson, William S. *lawyer*
Powell, Durwood Royce *lawyer*
Roach, Wesley Linville *lawyer, insurance executive*
Rusher, Mary Nash Kelly *lawyer*
Simpson, Steven Drexell *lawyer*
Spearman, Robert Worthington *lawyer*
Spruill, W. Murray *lawyer*
Suhr, Paul Augustine *lawyer*
Timmons, Sean Abbott *lawyer*
Valois, Robert Arthur *lawyer*
Weisel, Michael Lloyd *lawyer, educator*
Wetsch, Laura Johnson *lawyer*

Research Triangle Park
Bolen, M. Christopher *lawyer*
Welborn, Reich Lee *lawyer*
Whichard, Willis Padgett *lawyer, retired educator, judge*

Rocky Mount
Ellis, J(ames) Nicholas *lawyer*
Zipf, Robert Eugene, Jr. *legal medicine consultant, pathologist*

Sanford
Raisig, Paul Jones, Jr. *lawyer*

Tabor City
Jorgensen, Ralph Gubler *lawyer, accountant*

Tarboro
Hopkins, Grover Prevatte *lawyer*

Trinity
Walker, Kenneth Lynn *lawyer*

Warsaw
Thompson, Eugene Cebron III *lawyer*

Washington
Rader, Steven Palmer *lawyer*

Willow Spring
Valvo, Barbara-Ann *lawyer, surgeon*

Wilmington
Jones, Lucian Cox *lawyer*
McCauley, Cleyburn Lycurgus *lawyer*
Medlock, Donald Larson *lawyer*
Wall, James J. *lawyer*

Winston Salem
Adams, Alfred Gray *lawyer*
Adams, Reid C., Jr. *lawyer*
Barnhill, Henry Grady, Jr. *lawyer*
Blynn, Guy Marc *lawyer*
Chilson, John A. *lawyer, military officer*
Clinard, Keith A. *lawyer*
Copenhaver, W. Andrew *lawyer*
Early, James H., Jr. *lawyer*
Edwards, Charles Archibald *lawyer*
Foy, Herbert Miles III *lawyer, educator*
Gitter, Allan Reinhold *lawyer*
Graham, William Thomas *lawyer*
Greason, Murray Crossley, Jr. *lawyer*
Gregg, Ellen M. *lawyer*
Gunter, Michael Donwell *lawyer*
Holton, Walter Clinton, Jr. *lawyer*
Humphrey, Dudley *lawyer*
King, Roberta B. *lawyer*
Leonard, R. Michael *lawyer*
Little, George L. *lawyer*
Michel, Sandra K. *lawyer, food products executive*
Moser, Kenneth Allen *lawyer*
Oldaker, Guy Brooklyn III *lawyer*
Oliver, Patricia *lawyer*
Osborn, Malcolm Everett *lawyer*
Parker, Marian F. *law librarian, educator*
Poovey, Mark Nixon *lawyer*
Quick, Elizabeth L. *lawyer*
Ragland, George A. *lawyer*
Robinson, Edward Norwood *lawyer*
Sandridge, William Pendleton, Jr. *lawyer*
Schollander, Wendell III *lawyer*
Schollander, Wendell Leslie, Jr. *lawyer*
Schroeder, Thomas D. *lawyer*
Sharpe, Keith Yount *retired lawyer, writer*
Smith, David Coventry *lawyer*
Sullivan, William Beaumont *lawyer*
Taylor, Daniel Russell, Jr. *lawyer*
Vaughan, Keith W. *lawyer*
Vaughn, Robert Candler, Jr. *lawyer*
Walker, George Kontz *law educator*
Wiley, C. Mark *lawyer, department chairman*
Wilson, Grover Gray *lawyer*
Womble, William Fletcher *lawyer*

NORTH DAKOTA

Bismarck
Gilbertson, Joel Warren *lawyer*
King, Lawrence Edmund *lawyer*
Klemin, Lawrence R. *lawyer*
Moore, Sherry Mills *lawyer*
Murry, Charles Emerson *lawyer, federal official*
Sandness, Paul K. *lawyer, energy executive*

Fargo
Herman, Sarah Andrews *lawyer*
Unhjem, Michael Bruce *lawyer*
Williams, Michael James *lawyer*
Wrigley, Drew H. *prosecutor, lawyer*

Grand Forks
Davis, W. Jeremy *retired lawyer, dean*
Maddock, Patrick Jerome *lawyer*
Widdel, John Earl, Jr. *lawyer*

Mandan
Bair, Bruce Blythe *lawyer*

OHIO

Ada
Fenton, Howard Nathan III *lawyer, educator*

Akron
Bartlo, Sam D. *lawyer*
Bishop, Christy B. *lawyer, researcher*
Cherpas, Christopher Theodore *lawyer*
Cody, Daniel Schaffner *lawyer*
Fisher, James Lee *lawyer*
Glinsek, Gerald John *lawyer*
Harvie, Crawford Thomas *lawyer*
Holloway, Donald Phillip *lawyer*
Lee, Brant Thomas *lawyer, educator, federal official*
Lombardi, Frederick McKean *lawyer*
Reilly, Elizabeth Ann *law educator, dean*
Richert, Paul *law educator*
Schrader, Alfred Eugene *lawyer*
Taylor, E. Jane *lawyer*
Tipping, Harry A. *lawyer*
Trotter, Thomas Robert *lawyer*
Vespoli, Leila L. *lawyer, energy executive*
Wolfe, John Leslie *lawyer*
Wright, Bradley Abbott *lawyer*

Athens
Hedges, Richard Houston *lawyer, epidemiologist*
Lavelle, William Ambrose *lawyer, judge*

Aurora
Berry, Dean Lester *lawyer*

Austintown
Hill, Thomas Allen *lawyer*

Avon Lake
Shiba, Wendy C. *lawyer*

Bay Village
Kapp, C. Terrence *lawyer*

Beachwood
Clegg, Christopher R. *lawyer*
Sullivan, John E. III *lawyer*

Beavercreek
Stadnicar, Joseph William *lawyer*

Bellevue
Aigler, William Frank *lawyer*

Bryan
Shaffer, Wayne Eugene *lawyer*

Canton
Bennington, Ronald Kent *lawyer*
Burkhart, William R. *lawyer*
Tyburski, Charles J. *lawyer*

Centerville
Giffen, Daniel Harris *lawyer, educator*

Chagrin Falls
Smith, Barbara Jean *lawyer*

Cincinnati
Adams, Edmund John *lawyer*
Albainy-Jenei, Stephen R. *lawyer*
Allison, Jon B. *lawyer*
Anderson, James Milton *lawyer, hospital administrator*
Anderson, William Hopple *lawyer*
Anstaett, Jennifer Griffin *lawyer*
Anthony, Thomas Dale *lawyer*
Auttonberry, Sheri E. *lawyer*
Bahlman, William Thorne, Jr. *retired lawyer*
Baldwin, William D.G. *lawyer*
Bell, Ronald A. *lawyer*
Bergeron, Pierre H. *lawyer*
Bishop, Jerome C. *lawyer*
Bissinger, Mark Christian *lawyer*
Black, Stephen L. *lawyer*
Blandford, Colleen M. *lawyer*
Blaske, Nathan H. *lawyer*
Blickensderfer, Matthew C. *lawyer*
Braun, Joseph J. *lawyer*
Bride, Nancy J. *lawyer*
Britt, Kent A. *lawyer*
Broderick, Dennis John *lawyer, retail executive*
Bronson, Michael J. *lawyer*
Burdette, Robert Bruce *retired lawyer*
Burke, Rachel E. *lawyer*
Cappel, Harry W. *lawyer*
Cathey, Christopher D. *lawyer*
Cawood, James M. III *lawyer*
Chesley, Stanley Morris *lawyer*
Childs, Erin C. *lawyer*
Christenson, Gordon A. *law educator*
Christopher, John E. *lawyer*
Cioffi, Michael Lawrence *lawyer*
Cissell, James Charles *lawyer*
Cobey, John Geoffrey *lawyer, consultant*
Coffaro, Steven C. *lawyer*
Combs, Eric K. *lawyer*
Cooney, Kevin L. *lawyer*
Cors, Jeanne Marie *lawyer*
Craig, L. Clifford *lawyer*
Cunningham, Pierce Edward *lawyer, city planner*
Davis, Robert Lawrence *lawyer*
Dehner, Joseph Julnes *lawyer*
Denton, D. Brock *lawyer*
Desai, Deepak K. *lawyer*
Diller, Edward Dietrich *lawyer*
Dornette, W(illiam) Stuart *lawyer, educator*
Eckner, Shannon F. *lawyer*
Ellerman, Paige L. *lawyer*
Erhart, Sue A. *lawyer*
Evans, James E. *lawyer*
Faller, Susan Grogan *lawyer*
Faulkner, Laura R. *lawyer*
Feichtner, Douglas J. *lawyer*
Fink, Jerold Albert *lawyer*
Fitzsimmons, Becky Barlow *lawyer*
Flamm, Justin D. *lawyer*
Friedman, Penny *lawyer, not-for-profit developer*
Fronduti, John S. *lawyer*
Frooman, Thomas E. *lawyer*
Garfinkel, Jane E. *lawyer*
Garretson, Matthew Lee *lawyer*
Gaunt, Karen Kreider *lawyer*
Gehrig, Michael Ford *lawyer*
Geoppinger, Jeffrey D. *lawyer*
Gettler, Benjamin *lawyer, manufacturing company executive*
Ghassomian, Kevin R. *lawyer*
Giannella, Andrew R. *lawyer*
Giles, Brian T. *lawyer*
Glass, Joanne Wissman *lawyer*
Goodman, Stanley *lawyer*
Habel, Christopher S. *lawyer*
Hardy, William Robinson *lawyer*
Harris, Irving *lawyer*
Hastings, Kerry P. *lawyer*
Hawkins, William H., II, *lawyer*
Hayden, Jeremy A. *lawyer*
Heldman, James Gardner *lawyer*
Heldman, Paul W. *lawyer, food service executive*
Hermanies, John Hans *retired lawyer*
Hess, Ashley W. *lawyer*
Hicks, Drew M. *lawyer*
Hicks, Sarah Ellington *lawyer*
Hinegardner, Laura A. *lawyer*
Hinners, Stacy Chubak *lawyer*
Hoefle, H. Frederick *lawyer*
Hoffheimer, Daniel Joseph *lawyer*
Hoffman, Bridget C. *lawyer*
Holschuh, John David, Jr. *lawyer*
Hust, Bruce Kevin *lawyer*
Hylander, Jessica S. *lawyer*
Jackson, Kory A. *lawyer*
Johnson, James J. *lawyer*
Jurs, Peter B. *lawyer*
Kallas, Hani R. *lawyer*
Kane, Scott A. *lawyer*
Katz, Reuven J. *lawyer*
Kelley, John Joseph, Jr. *lawyer*
Kern, David Graham *lawyer*
Kiel, Frederick Orin *lawyer*
Kindt, Monica V. *lawyer*
Kordons, Uldis *lawyer*
Langston, Malinda L. *lawyer*
Lauer, Richard T. *lawyer*
Lawrence, James Kaufman Lebensburger *lawyer*
Lawrence, Jennifer L. *lawyer*
Lindberg, Charles David *lawyer*
Liss, William J. *lawyer*
Lockwood, Bert Berkley, Jr. *law educator*
Longenecker, Mark Hershey, Jr. *lawyer*
Lorentz, Joshua A. *lawyer*
Love, Lisa A. *lawyer*
Lundrigan, Nicole M. *lawyer*
Lutz, James Gurney *lawyer*
Mahon, Stephen C. *lawyer*
Malof, Kevin K. *lawyer*
Mann, David Scott *lawyer*
Mason, Jeremy R. *lawyer*
Mason, Rachel J. *lawyer*
Maxwell, Robert Wallace, II, *lawyer*
McClain, William Andrew *lawyer*
McCluskey, Laurie A. *lawyer*
McGavran, Frederick Jaeger *lawyer*
McHenry, Powell *lawyer*
McKay, Bernard L. *lawyer*
McPeek, Bradley *lawyer*
Meister, Julia B. *lawyer*
Meyers, Karen Diane *lawyer, educator*
Meyers, Pamela Sue *lawyer*
Miller, W. Timothy *lawyer*
Moeddel, Michael J. *lawyer*
Mordino, Joseph T. *lawyer*
Nalbandian, John B. *lawyer*
Nechemias, Stephen Murray *lawyer*
Newman, Danny Merril *lawyer*
Oberhaus, Geoffrey Luther *lawyer*
O'Grady, Michael J. *lawyer*
O'Guinn, M. Dave III *lawyer*
O'Reilly, James Thomas *lawyer, educator, writer*
Pacheco, Bryan E. *lawyer*
Parker, R. Joseph *lawyer*
Petrie, Bruce Inglis *lawyer*
Porotsky, Richard D., Jr. *lawyer*
Porter, Robert Carl, Jr. *lawyer*
Rammes, Lisa M. *lawyer*
Ramsey, Jamie M. *lawyer*
Ramundo, Kimberly E. *lawyer*
Reichert, David *lawyer*
Reuter, Mark F. *lawyer*
Reynolds, Paul L. *lawyer, bank executive*
Rich, Robert Edward *lawyer*
Richardson, Eric W. *lawyer*
Roach, Adrienne J. *lawyer*
Rogers, Brie S. *lawyer*
Rohner, Nicholas K. *lawyer*
Rose, Donald McGregor *retired lawyer*
Ross, Lori A. *lawyer*
Rowe, Rachael A. *lawyer*
Rucker, Fanon A. *lawyer*
Ruh, Michael A., Jr. *lawyer*
Rumberg, Orly Robin *lawyer*
Ruwe, Bradley N. *lawyer*
Ryan, James Joseph *retired lawyer*
Schatz, Brett A. *lawyer*
Schuck, Thomas Robert *lawyer, farmer*
Shaffer, Robert M.M. *lawyer*
Shearer, David A., Jr. *lawyer*
Shore, Thomas Spencer, Jr. *retired lawyer*
Silbersack, Mark Louis *lawyer*
Smith, Sheila Marie *lawyer*
Smyth, Robery M. *lawyer*
Sprecher, Christina M. *lawyer*
Sprecher, Kevin S. *lawyer*
Stern, Noah J. *lawyer*
Swigert, James Mack *lawyer*
Teeters, Jeffrey R. *lawyer*
Tepe, Thomas M., Jr. *lawyer*
Thompson, James E. *lawyer*
Tobias, Paul Henry *lawyer*
Tomain, Joseph Patrick *law educator, retired dean*
Uhl, Judd R. *lawyer*
Valentine, Lona J. *lawyer*
Vander Laan, Mark Alan *lawyer*
Vogel, Cedric Wakelee *lawyer*
Wales, Ross Elliot *lawyer*
Weber, H. Patrick *lawyer*
Weeks, Steven Wiley *lawyer*
Weisenberger, Andrew *lawyer*
Wesloh, Steven M. *lawyer*
Wheatley, Christine S. *lawyer*
Wilkowski, E. Todd *lawyer*
Wilson, Christopher J. *lawyer*
Woodside, Frank C. III *lawyer, educator, physician*
Wuebbling, Donald J. *lawyer, insurance company executive*
Zahneis, Leona Beth *lawyer*
Zahniser, Rachel S. *lawyer*
Zamary, Kimberly Kyle *lawyer*
Zavatsky, Michael Joseph *lawyer*
Zimmerman, James M. *lawyer*

Cleveland
Adamo, Kenneth Robert *lawyer*
Adams, Albert T. *lawyer*
Andorka, Frank Henry *lawyer*
Andrews, Oakley V. *lawyer*
Ashmus, Keith Allen *lawyer*
Austin, Arthur Donald, II, *lawyer, educator*
Bacon, Brett Kermit *lawyer*
Bays, James C. *lawyer*
Berick, James Herschel *lawyer*
Binford, Gregory Glenn *lawyer*
Braverman, Herbert Leslie *lawyer*
Bravo, Kenneth Allan *lawyer*
Brennan, Maureen *lawyer*
Brucken, Robert Matthew *lawyer*
Burge, David Alan *lawyer, writer*
Burke, Kathleen B. *lawyer*
Cahn, James *lawyer, educator*
Cairns, James Donald *lawyer*
Calkins, Benjamin *lawyer*
Callahan, Thomas James *lawyer*
Carfagna, Peter A. *lawyer*
Carlson, James R. *lawyer*
Carson, Van *lawyer*
Cavanagh, Matthew John *lawyer*
Clarke, Charles Fenton *lawyer*
Coffey, Thomas William *lawyer*
Coleman, Deborah Ann *lawyer*
Collin, Thomas James *lawyer*
Conner, William Herbert *lawyer*
Coquillette, William Hollis *lawyer*
Crist, Paul Grant *lawyer*
Cudak, Gail Linda *lawyer*
Currivan, John Daniel *lawyer*
DeMetz, Kathleen Susan *lawyer*
Demitrack, Thomas *lawyer*
DiSilvio, Marilena *lawyer*
DiVenere, Anthony Joseph *lawyer*
Domiano, Joseph Charles *lawyer*
Doris, Alan S(anford) *lawyer*
Drinko, John Deaver *lawyer*
Dugan, Patrick J. *lawyer*
Duncan, Ed Eugene *lawyer*
Duvin, Robert Phillip *lawyer*
Emrick, Charles Robert, Jr. *lawyer*
Fabens, Andrew Lawrie III *lawyer*
Falsgraf, William Wendell *retired lawyer*
Fay, Regan Joseph *lawyer*
Feinberg, Paul H. *retired lawyer*
Felty, Kriss Delbert *lawyer*
Fischer, Michelle K. *lawyer*
Fletcher, Robert *retired lawyer*
Friedman, Harold Edward *lawyer*
Friedman, James Moss *lawyer*
Gentile Sachs, Valerie Ann *lawyer*
Glaser, Robert Edward *lawyer*
Goins, Frances Floriano *lawyer*
Gold, Gerald Seymour *lawyer*
Goldfarb, Bernard Sanford *lawyer*
Goler, Michael David *lawyer*
Goodman, David S. *lawyer*
Groedel, Caryn G. *lawyer*
Grossman, Theodore Martin *lawyer*
Haiman, Irwin Sanford *lawyer*
Harris, Paul N. *lawyer*
Hastings, Susan C. *lawyer*
Henes, Samuel Ernst *lawyer*
Hochman, Kenneth George *lawyer*

erner, Robert Jack *lawyer*
ffman, Sharona *law educator*
gg, James Stuart *lawyer*
llington, Richard Rings, Jr. *lawyer*
rst, J. Robert *lawyer*
rvitz, Michael John *lawyer*
obs, Leslie William *lawyer*
ke, Ronald Robert *lawyer*
genson, Mary Ann *lawyer*
hrl, Robert Conley *lawyer*
rp, Marvin Louis *lawyer*
tcher, Richard *lawyer*
tz, Lewis Robert *law educator*
lly, Dennis Michael *lawyer*
stner, Robert Steven *lawyer*
bane, Thomas Stanton *lawyer*
erly, Stephen John, Jr. *lawyer*
hn, William Irwin *lawyer*
rngold, Gerald *law educator, former dean*
amer, Edward George *lawyer*
amer, Eugene Leo *lawyer*
rit, Neil *lawyer*
wniczak, James Michael *lawyer*
ise, Robert K. *lawyer*
ivitt, Jeffrey Stuart *lawyer*
ken, Earl Murray *lawyer*
nnox, Heather *lawyer*
wis, John Bruce *lawyer*
wis, John Francis *lawyer*
we, James Allison *lawyer, educator*
rting, Michael G. *lawyer*
son, Thomas Albert *retired lawyer*
tia, Paul Ramon *lawyer*
Cartan, Patrick Francis *lawyer*
Carthy, Mark Francis *lawyer*
Guire, Mark M. *lawyer, manufacturing executive*
Kee, Thomas Frederick *lawyer*
Laughlin, Patrick Michael *lawyer*
hlman, Maxwell Jonathan *law educator*
issner, Michael G. *lawyer*
ssinger, Donald Hathaway *lawyer*
yer, G. Christopher *lawyer*
lisor, Kenneth Ray *lawyer*
lstone, David Jeffrey *lawyer*
ore, Kenneth Cameron *lawyer*
rrical, Glenn Edwin *lawyer*
sallam, Samer Makram *lawyer*
nce, Frederick *lawyer*
wman, John M., Jr. *lawyer*
ols, Howard J.C. *lawyer*
ada, Ronald Shig *lawyer*
Keefe, Francis Ronald *lawyer*
nger, W. James *lawyer*
borne, Frank R. *lawyer, educator, lecturer*
endoff, Stephen Peter *lawyer*
am, John James *lawyer*
s, Zachary T. *lawyer*
obek, Drew Thomas *lawyer*
rlman, Samuel Segel *lawyer, educator*
ry. George Williamson *lawyer*
rzen, Julie Lynn *lawyer*
ino, Thomas Anthony, Jr. *lawyer*
boy, Alvin Michael, Jr. *law librarian, director*
ue, Richard Welch *lawyer*
ock, R. Jeffrey *lawyer*
ka, Andrew Charles *lawyer*
ns, M. Neal *lawyer*
p, Robert Neil *lawyer*
vson, Rachel L. *lawyer*
vson, Robert H., Jr. *lawyer*
ninger, Richard Thomas *lawyer, artist*
pert, Richard Levi *lawyer*
kert, Jeanne Martin M. *lawyer*
erts-Mamone, Lisa A. *lawyer*
enbaum, Jacob I. *retired lawyer*
en, Alan Miles *law educator*
islo, Paul Steve *lawyer*
yer, Raymond Terry *lawyer, consultant, theater producer*
aefer, David Arnold *lawyer*
wieg, Frederic P. *lawyer*
er, Thomas M. *lawyer*
piro, Fred David *lawyer*
eran, Timothy J. *lawyer*
herman, Marvin Allen *lawyer*
ger, Michael Jeffery *law librarian, director*
ith, N. Lindsey *lawyer*
g, Wilton Sherman *lawyer*
omon, Randall Lee *lawyer*
nley, Hugh Monroe, Jr. *lawyer*
nton, R. Thomas *lawyer*
lato, Louis Eugene *lawyer*
vens, Thomas Charles *lawyer*
kes, Louis *lawyer, former congressman*
ne, James Merrill *lawyer*
uch, John L. *lawyer*
efsky, Linda A(nn) *lawyer*
mbu, Victor, Jr. *lawyer*
nan, Richard George *lawyer*
nmers, William Lawrence *lawyer*
rtzbaugh, Marc L. *lawyer*
mmig, Diana Marie *lawyer*
mas, Dynda A. *lawyer*
hey, Brian Frederick *lawyer*
majian, William Martin *lawyer*
Mehren, George M. *lawyer*
deck, John Walter, Jr. *lawyer*
lach, Mark Irwin *lawyer*
son, Richard Thomas *lawyer*
ver, Robin Geoffrey *lawyer, educator*
ler, Jeffry Louis *lawyer*
ite, Gregory A. *prosecutor*
itney, Richard Buckner *lawyer*
ng, Margaret Wai *lawyer*
ng, James Edward *lawyer*
nbie, Allan John *lawyer*
ller, David Louis *lawyer, bank executive*
ck, Gary Alan *lawyer*

eveland Heights
cote, Lee A. *lawyer*

lumbus
er, Alan Scott *lawyer*
lerson, Jon Mac *lawyer, educator*
Aukland, Duncan Dayton *lawyer*
Ayers, James Cordon *lawyer*
Bailey, Daniel Allen *lawyer*
Barnes, Wallace Ray *retired lawyer*
Barnett, Robert B., Jr. *lawyer*
Belton, John Thomas *lawyer*
Bennett, Robert Thomas *lawyer, professional athletics manager*
Berndt, Ellen German *lawyer*
Blackburn, John D. (John David Blackburn) *lawyer, educator*
Booker, James Douglas *retired lawyer, government official*
Bridgman, G(eorge) Ross *lawyer*
Brooks, Richard Dickinson *lawyer*
Brown, Philip Albert *lawyer*
Brubaker, Robert Loring *lawyer*
Buchenroth, Stephen Richard *lawyer*
Carnahan, John Anderson *retired lawyer*
Carpenter, Michael H. *lawyer*
Chappelear, Stephen Eric *lawyer*
Cheap, Richard A. *lawyer, bank executive*
Chester, John Jonas *lawyer, educator*
Crowder, Marjorie Briggs *lawyer*
Cvetanovich, Dan L. *lawyer*
Davis, Julia A. *lawyer, retail executive*
DeRousie, Charles Stuart *lawyer*
Di Lorenzo, John Florio, Jr. *retired lawyer*
Dunlay, Catherine Telles *lawyer*
Fahey, Richard Paul *lawyer*
Fay, Terrence Michael *lawyer*
Ferguson, Gerald Paul *lawyer*
Fisher, Lloyd Edison, Jr. *lawyer*
Fried, Samuel P. *lawyer*
Gall, John Ryan *lawyer*
Geiger, Heather L. *lawyer*
Gibson, Rick J. *lawyer*
Grauer, David W. *lawyer*
Gross, James Howard *lawyer*
Hardymon, David Wayne *lawyer*
Harmon, Phillip Louis *lawyer*
Hatler, Patricia Ruth *lawyer*
Haubiel, Charles W., II, *lawyer*
Hollenbaugh, H(enry) Ritchey *lawyer*
Hutson, Jeffrey Woodward *lawyer*
Jackson, Reginald W. *lawyer*
Johnson, Bruce S. *law librarian, educator*
Johnson, David Lee *lawyer*
Johnson, Mark Alan *lawyer*
Keane, John B. *lawyer, electric power industry executive*
Ketcham, Richard Scott *lawyer*
Kinzer, Allen Shawn *lawyer*
Kirila, Jill S. *lawyer*
Koblentz, Robert Alan *lawyer*
Kuehnle, Kenton Lee *lawyer*
Kurtz, Charles Jewett III *lawyer*
Lancione, Bernard Gabe *lawyer*
Liston, Jefferson Edward *lawyer*
Long, Thomas Leslie *lawyer*
Mann, William Craig *lawyer*
McConnaughey, George Carlton, Jr. *retired lawyer*
McCutchan, Gordon Eugene *retired lawyer, insurance company executive*
McDermott, Kevin R. *lawyer*
McKenna, Alvin James *lawyer*
Miller, Terry Morrow *lawyer*
Minor, Robert Allen *lawyer*
Mirman, Joel Harvey *lawyer*
Moloney, Thomas E. *lawyer*
Moul, William Charles *lawyer*
Nathan, Jerry E. *lawyer*
Nissl, Colleen Kaye *lawyer*
Oman, Richard Heer *retired lawyer*
Petricoff, M. Howard *lawyer, educator*
Phillips, James Edgar *lawyer*
Pigman, Jack Richard *lawyer*
Pressley, Fred G., Jr. *lawyer*
Quigley, John Bernard *law educator*
Radnor, Alan T. *lawyer*
Ramey, Denny L. *bar association executive director*
Ray, Frank Allen *lawyer*
Reasoner, Willis Irl III *lawyer*
Rector, Susan Darnell *lawyer*
Ridgley, Thomas Brennan *lawyer*
Robinson, Barry R. *lawyer*
Robol, Richard Thomas *lawyer*
Rogers, Douglas L. *lawyer*
Rose, Michael Dean *retired lawyer, educator*
Saad, Michael D. *lawyer*
Saxbe, William Bart *lawyer, former United States attorney general*
Schrag, Edward A., Jr. *lawyer*
Shane, Peter Milo *law educator*
Sheward, Richard S. *lawyer*
Shumate, Alex *lawyer*
Sidman, Robert John *lawyer*
Sites, Richard Loren *lawyer, educator*
Sowald, Heather Gay *lawyer*
Stein, Arland Thomas *lawyer*
Stern, Geoffrey *lawyer*
Stinehart, Roger Ray *lawyer*
Sully, Ira Bennett *lawyer*
Swetnam, Daniel Richard *lawyer*
Swift, David A. *lawyer*
Taggart, Thomas Michael *lawyer*
Tait, Robert E. *lawyer*
Tarpy, Thomas Michael *lawyer*
Terakedis, John, Jr. *lawyer*
Thompson, Harold Lee *lawyer*
Todd, William Michael *lawyer*
Tripp, Thomas Neal *lawyer, political scientist*
Turano, David A. *lawyer*
Tyack, Thomas Michael *lawyer*
Vorys, Arthur Isaiah *lawyer*
Walker, Charles Henri *lawyer*
Warner, Charles Collins *lawyer*
Whipps, Edward Franklin *lawyer*
Wightman, Alec *lawyer*
Williams, Douglas Leonard *lawyer*
Winkler, John Frederick *lawyer, educator*
Yeazel, Keith Arthur *lawyer*

Cuyahoga Falls
Jones, John Frank *retired lawyer*

Dayton
Burick, Lawrence T. *lawyer*
Chernesky, Richard John *lawyer*
Conway, Mark Allyn *lawyer*
Farquhar, Robert Nichols *lawyer*
Faruki, Charles Joseph *lawyer*
Hadley, Robert James *lawyer*
Heyman, Ralph Edmond *lawyer*
Jenks, Thomas Edward *lawyer*
Johnson, C. Terry *lawyer*
Krebs, Leo Francis *lawyer*
Lieb, Peter *lawyer*
Lockhart, Gregory Gordon *prosecutor*
Macklin, Crofford Johnson, Jr. *lawyer*
Mues, Robert Leighton *lawyer*
Neltner, Michael Martin *lawyer*
Rion, John Hayes *lawyer*
Saul, Irving Isaac *lawyer*
Taylor, Edward McKinley, Jr. *lawyer*
Vaughn, Noel Wyandt *lawyer*
Watts, Steven Richard *lawyer*

Delaware
Martz, Gary R. *lawyer*

Dublin
Inzetta, Mark Stephen *lawyer*
Maloon, Jerry L. *lawyer, physician*
McCorkle, Leon Marshall, Jr. *lawyer, educator*
Tenuta, Luigia *lawyer*

Eaton
Thomas, James William *lawyer*

Fairlawn
Kitchen, Charles William *lawyer*

Findlay
Kline, James Edward *lawyer*
Kostyo, John Francis *lawyer*

Galena
Greek, Darold I. *lawyer*

Gambier
Leech, Charles Russell, Jr. *lawyer*

Hilliard
Craig, Steve A. *lawyer*
Jungeberg, Thomas Donald *lawyer*

Howard
Lee, William Johnson *lawyer*

Hudson
Withers, Carl Raymond *lawyer*

Independence
Kola, Arthur Anthony *lawyer*

Ironton
Allen, Craig Adams *lawyer, director*

Jackson
Lewis, Richard M. *lawyer*

Kettering
Eubank, David Lynn *lawyer, consultant*

Lakewood
McAndrews, James Patrick *retired lawyer*

Lancaster
Libert, Donald Joseph *lawyer*

Lima
Jacobs, Ann Elizabeth *lawyer*
Robenalt, John Alton *lawyer*

Mansfield
Wolf, Marcus Alan *lawyer*

Marietta
Fields, William Albert *lawyer*

Marysville
Aronowitz, David M. *lawyer, chemicals executive*
Hamilton, Robert Otte *lawyer*

Maumee
Burchinow, Naran U. *lawyer*
Fallat, Dale William *lawyer*
Marsh, Benjamin Franklin *lawyer*
Tuschman, James Marshall *lawyer*
Witherell, Dennis Patrick *lawyer*

Mayfield
Jarrett, Charles Elwood *lawyer, insurance company executive*

Mayfield Heights
Bittenbender, Charles A. *lawyer*

Medina
Tompkins, P. Kelly *lawyer, manufacturing executive*

Miamisburg
Byrd, James Everett *lawyer*

Middletown
Horn, David C. *lawyer*
Rathman, William Ernest *retired lawyer, minister*

Minerva
Martin, Robert Dale *lawyer*

Moreland Hills
Groetzinger, Jon, Jr. *lawyer, pharmaceutical executive, educator*

Mount Vernon
Rose, Kim Matthew *lawyer, educator*

Newark
Hite, David L. *lawyer*
Mantonya, John Butcher *lawyer*
Mencer, Jetta *lawyer*
Meyer, Christopher Richard *lawyer*

North Canton
Dettinger, Warren Walter *lawyer*

Orrville
Harlan, Mary Ann *lawyer*

Painesville
Dean, J. Thomas *lawyer*
Kutz, Alexandra Ellen *prosecutor*

Pepper Pike
Schnell, Carlton Bryce *lawyer*

Perrysburg
Baehren, James W. *lawyer*

Portsmouth
Gerlach, Franklin Theodore *lawyer*

Ravenna
Nolfi, Edward Anthony *lawyer*

Saint Marys
Huber, William Evan *lawyer*
Kemp, Barrett George *lawyer*

Salem
Goll, Geoffrey Steven *lawyer*

Sandusky
Bailey, K. Ronald *lawyer*

Seaman
Young, Vernon Lewis *retired lawyer*

Shaker Heights
Bates, Walter Alan *retired lawyer*

Springfield
Lagos, James Harry *lawyer, small business owner*

Terrace Park
Naylor, Paul Donald *retired lawyer*

Toledo
Anspach, Robert Michael *lawyer*
Bixler, R. Jeffrey *lawyer*
Dalrymple, Thomas Lawrence *retired lawyer*
Gouttiere, John P. *lawyer*
Jackson, Reginald Sherman, Jr. *lawyer, educator*
Krull, Stephen Keith *lawyer*
La Rue, Carl Forman *lawyer*
O'Connell, Maurice Daniel *lawyer*
Pletz, Thomas Gregory *lawyer*
Skiver, Stephen Allen *lawyer, physician*
Spitzer, John Brumback *lawyer*
Strobel, Martin Jack *lawyer, manufacturing and distribution company executive*
Webb, Thomas Irwin, Jr. *lawyer, director*
Wicklund, David Wayne *lawyer*

Troy
Bazler, Frank Ellis *retired lawyer*
Puthoff, Mark Allen *lawyer*

Wadsworth
McIlvaine, James Ross *lawyer*

Warren
Rossi, Anthony Gerald *lawyer*

Westerville
Helvey, Edward Douglas *lawyer*
Young, Sheldon Mike *lawyer, author*

Westlake
Lee, Steven C. *lawyer*
Skulina, Thomas Raymond *lawyer*

Wickliffe
Bauer, Joseph W. *lawyer, chemicals executive*
Crehore, Charles Aaron *lawyer*
Kidder, Fred Dockstater *retired lawyer*

Willoughby
Driggs, Charles Mulford *lawyer*

Wooster
Kennedy, Charles Allen *lawyer*

Worthington
Albert, Robert Hamilton *lawyer*
Brinkman, Dale Thomas *lawyer*
Fisher, Fredrick Lee *lawyer*

Xenia
Chappars, Timothy Stephen *lawyer*

Youngstown
Ausnehmer, John Edward *lawyer*
Briach, George Gary *lawyer, consultant*
Carlin, Clair Myron *lawyer*
Petrony, John Francis *lawyer*
Roth, Daniel Benjamin *lawyer, company executive*

Zanesville
Micheli, Frank James *lawyer*

OKLAHOMA

Alva
Mitchell, Allan Edwin *lawyer*

Bartlesville
Connor, James William *lawyer*
Roff, Alan Lee *retired lawyer, consultant*

Broken Arrow
Jones, Ronald Lee *lawyer, writer*
Stewart, Murray Baker *retired lawyer*

Chandler
Swanson, Robert Lee *lawyer*

Cherokee
Stein, Sam Lee *lawyer*

Claremore
Steidley, Juan Dwayne *lawyer, judge*

Edmond
Angel, Steven Michael *retired lawyer*
Lester, Andrew William *lawyer*
Loving, Susan Brimer *lawyer, former state official*
Wilson, Julia Ann Yother *lawyer*

Enid
Jones, Stephen *lawyer*

Frederick
Evans, Michael D. *lawyer*

Guthrie
Davis, Frank Wayne *lawyer*

Jones
Dean, Bill Verlin, Jr. *lawyer*

Mcalester
Cornish, Richard Pool *lawyer*

Muskogee
Robinson, Adelbert Carl *lawyer, judge*
Sperling, Sheldon J. *prosecutor*
Williams, Betty Outhier *lawyer*

Noble
Winchell, Michael George *lawyer*

Norman
Fairbanks, Robert Alvin *lawyer*
Hastie, John Douglas *lawyer*
Miller, Fred Heins *lawyer, retired law educator*
Talley, Richard Bates *lawyer*

Oklahoma City
Adams, R. Scott *lawyer*
Allen, Robert Dee *lawyer*
Busey, Phil Gordon *lawyer*
Carey, Susan R. *lawyer*
Conger, J. William *lawyer*
Court, Leonard *lawyer, educator*
Cunningham, Stanley Lloyd *lawyer*
Decker, Michael Lynn *lawyer, judge*
Derrick, Gary Wayne *lawyer*
Fenton, Elliott Clayton *lawyer*
Ford, Michael Raye *lawyer*
Gibson, Keith Russell *lawyer, educator*
Gordon, Kevin Dell *lawyer*
Hanna, Terry Ross *lawyer, small business owner*
Homsey, Joseph Richard, Jr. *lawyer*
Hood, Henry J. *lawyer, energy executive*
Isaacs, Garvin Alfred *lawyer*
Johnson, Robert Max *lawyer*
Kenney, John Arthur *lawyer*
Kline, David Adam *lawyer, educator, writer*
Legg, William Jefferson *lawyer*
Lowe, Lyle Justin *lawyer*
MacDougall, Vicki Lawrence *law educator, writer*
Mather, Stephanie June *lawyer*
McCampbell, Robert Garner *lawyer, former prosecutor*
Moler, Edward Harold *retired lawyer*
Necco, Alexander David *lawyer, educator*
Nelon, Robert Dale *lawyer*
Neville, Jack L. (Drew), Jr. *lawyer*
Ogle, James David *lawyer*
Pain, Betsy M. *lawyer*
Paul, William George *lawyer*
Richter, John Charles *prosecutor*
Rockett, D. Joe *lawyer, director*
Ross, William Jarboe *lawyer*
Schwabe, George Blaine III *lawyer*
Smith, (Carl) Michael *lawyer, former federal agency administrator*
Stanley, Brian Jordan *lawyer*
Steinhorn, Irwin Harry *lawyer, educator, corporate financial executive*
Stong, Roger Alan *lawyer*
Stringer, L. E. (Dean) *retired lawyer*
Taylor, Lyndon C. *lawyer, energy executive*
Tompkins, Raymond Edgar *lawyer*
Towery, Curtis Kent *lawyer*
Tuck-Richmond, Doletta Sue *prosecutor*
Walsh, Lawrence Edward *lawyer*
Woods, Harry Arthur, Jr. *lawyer*

Ponca City
Northcutt, Clarence Dewey *lawyer*
Raley, John Wesley, Jr. *lawyer*

Poteau
Sanders, Douglas Warner, Jr. *lawyer, judge*

Pryor
Stinson, Marion Dennis *lawyer, land use planner, judge*

Sayre
Brooks, David Eugene *lawyer*

Seminole
Elsener, G. Dale *lawyer*

Stillwater
Clark, Gary Carl *lawyer*
DeLacerda, Melissa Griner *lawyer*
Fischer, Richard Samuel *lawyer*

Tulsa
Abrahamson, A. Craig *lawyer*
Arrington, John Leslie, Jr. *lawyer*
Barker, John Roy *lawyer, gas industry executive*
Belsky, Martin Henry *law educator, dean*
Bender, James J. *lawyer, oil industry executive*
Biolchini, Robert Fredrick *lawyer*
Bryant, Hubert Hale *lawyer*
Carney, Timothy Alan *lawyer*
Clark, Joseph Francis, Jr. *lawyer*
Cooper, Richard Casey *lawyer*
Eagleton, Edward John *lawyer*
Engel, David Wayne *lawyer, federal official*
Farrell, John L., Jr. *lawyer, consultant, corporate financial executive*
Frey, Martin Alan *lawyer, educator*
Gaberino, John Anthony, Jr. *lawyer*
Gardner, Dale Ray *lawyer*
Givens, Jack Rodman *lawyer*
Hatfield, Jack Kenton *lawyer, accountant*
Haynie, Tony Wayne *lawyer*
Howard, Gene Claude *lawyer, retired state senator*
Huckin, William Price, Jr. *prosecutor*
Huffman, Robert Allen, Jr. *lawyer*
Imel, John Michael *lawyer*
Johnson, Cornelius Raymond *prosecutor*
Kihle, Donald Arthur *lawyer*
Luthey, Graydon Dean, Jr. *lawyer, educator*
Marlar, Donald Floyd *lawyer*
Matthies, Mary Constance T. *lawyer*
Moffett, J. Denny *lawyer*
Murphy, Lawrence R. *lawyer*
O'Meilia, David E. *prosecutor, lawyer*
Plumb, Charles Sumner III *lawyer*
Russell, Irma S. *lawyer, educator*
Slicker, Frederick Kent *lawyer*
Steltzlen, Janelle Hicks *lawyer*
Strecker, David Eugene *lawyer*
Stuart, Harold Cutliff *lawyer, business executive*
Sturdivant, James M. *lawyer*
Tucker, John *lawyer*
Williamson, Walter Bland *lawyer*
Wood, Donald Euriah *retired lawyer*

Vinita
Johnston, Oscar Black III *lawyer*

Weatherford
Beam, Stephen D. *lawyer*

OREGON

Astoria
Haskell, Donald McMillan *lawyer*

Beaverton
Carter, James C. *lawyer, apparel executive*
Stewart, Lindsay D. *lawyer, apparel executive*
Vardavas, Stephanie J. *lawyer*

Brookings
Maxwell, William Stirling *retired lawyer*

Cannon Beach
Hillestad, Charles Andrew *lawyer*

Central Point
Ingraham, Laura *lawyer, political commentator*
Richardson, Dennis Michael *lawyer, educator*

Corvallis
Frohnmayer, John Edward *lawyer, writer*

Dayton
Anderson, Herbert Hatfield *lawyer, farmer*

Eugene
Aldave, Barbara Bader *lawyer, educator*
DuPriest, Douglas Millhollen *lawyer*
Hildreth, Richard G. *lawyer, educator*
Horn, John Harold *lawyer*
Jacobson, Jon L. *law educator*
McCrea, Shaun S. *lawyer*
Scoles, Eugene Francis *lawyer, educator*

Forest Grove
Marvin, Monica Louise Wolf *lawyer*

Jacksonville
O'Connor, Karl William (Goodyear Johnson) *retired lawyer*

Keizer
Stevens, Sharon Cox *lawyer*

La Grande
Joseph, Steven Jay *lawyer*

Lake Oswego
Byczynski, Edward Frank *lawyer, corporate financial executive*
Hill, Gary D. *lawyer*
Kuntz, Joel Dubois *lawyer*
McDonald, Wilson *lawyer*
Rasmussen, Richard Robert *lawyer*

Lincoln City
Arant, Eugene Wesley *lawyer*

Mcminnville
Thompson, Robert Samuel *retired lawyer*

Medford
Carter, William G. *lawyer*
Deatherage, William Vernon *lawyer*
Thierolf, Richard Burton, Jr. *lawyer*

Oregon City
Lounsbury, Steven Richard *lawyer*
Ringle, Philip Hamilton, Jr. *lawyer*

Portland
Abravanel, Allan Ray *lawyer*
Brenneman, Delbert Jay *lawyer*
Cable, John Franklin *lawyer*
Chevis, Cheryl Ann *lawyer*
Cook, Nena *lawyer*
Crowell, John B., Jr. *lawyer, former government official*
Curtis, Michael *lawyer*
Dailey, Dianne K. *lawyer*
Dean, E. Joseph *lawyer*
Dubanevich, Keith Scott *lawyer*
English, Stephen Francis *lawyer*
Epstein, Edward Louis *lawyer*
Ernst, David A. *lawyer*
Feuerstein, Howard M. *lawyer*
Foley, Ridgway Knight, Jr. *lawyer, writer*
Franzke, Richard Albert *lawyer*
Fulsher, Allan Arthur *lawyer*
Glasgow, William Jacob *lawyer, venture capitalist, business executive*
Greene, Herbert Bruce *lawyer, investor, entrepreneur*
Grossmann, Ronald Stanyer *lawyer*
Hanna, Harry Mitchell *lawyer*
Harnden, Edwin A. *lawyer*
Hart, John Edward *lawyer*
Hinkle, Charles Frederick *lawyer, educator*
Hirshon, Robert Edward *lawyer*
Houser, Douglas Guy *lawyer*
Immergut, Karin J. *prosecutor*
Jarvis, Peter R. *lawyer*
Jensen, J. Alan *lawyer*
Johnson, Mark Andrew *lawyer*
Johnston, David Frederick *lawyer*
Jolles, Bernard *lawyer*
Josephson, Richard Carl *lawyer*
Kanter, Stephen *lawyer, educator, dean*
Kennedy, Jack Leland *lawyer*
Kester, Randall Blair *lawyer*
Knoll, James Lewis *lawyer*
Krahmer, Donald Leroy, Jr. *lawyer*
Larpenteur, James Albert, Jr. *retired lawyer*
Livingston, Louis Bayer *lawyer*
Love, William Edward *lawyer*
Maloney, Robert E., Jr. *lawyer*
Menashe, Albert Alan *lawyer*
Meng, Linda *lawyer*
Miller, William Richey, Jr. *lawyer*
Moore, Thomas Scott *lawyer*
Mowe, Gregory Robert *lawyer*
Noonan, William Donald *lawyer, physician*
Nunn, Robert Warne *lawyer*
Paulson, Jane *lawyer*
Purcell, John F. *lawyer*
Richardson, Campbell *retired lawyer*
Richter, Peter Christian *lawyer*
Rosen, Steven O. *lawyer*
Ryan, John Duncan *lawyer*
Savage, John William *lawyer*
Schuster, Philip Frederick, II, *lawyer, writer, educator*
Simpson, Robert Glenn *lawyer*
Sokol, Larry Nides *lawyer, educator*
Stewart, Milton Roy *lawyer*
Stone, Richard James *lawyer*
Strader, Timothy Richards *lawyer*
Sullivan, Edward Joseph *lawyer*
Swenson, Constance Rae *lawyer*
Tucker, Roy W. *lawyer*
Van Valkenburg, Edgar Walter *lawyer*
Waggoner, James Clyde *lawyer*
Westwood, James Nicholson *lawyer*
Whinston, Arthur Lewis *lawyer*
White, Douglas James, Jr. *lawyer*
Williamson, Charles Ready III *lawyer*
Wilson, Owen Meredith, Jr. *lawyer, mediator, arbitrator*
Wood, Marcus Andrew *lawyer*
Yoshida, Stephen P. *lawyer*
Yugler, Richard S. *lawyer*
Zalutsky, Morton Herman *lawyer*

Salem
Abrams, Marc *lawyer, political organization worker*
Breen, Richard F., Jr. *law librarian, educator*
Brown, Eden Rose *lawyer*
Clark, David Scott *law educator, consultant*
Haselton, Rick Thomas *lawyer*
Mannix, Kevin Leese *lawyer, school system administrator*
Nafziger, James Albert Richmond *law educator*
Nicholson, Bradley James *lawyer*
Swaim, Michael E. *lawyer, former mayor*

PENNSYLVANIA

Abington
Bildersee, Robert Alan *lawyer*

Allentown
Brown, Robert Wayne *lawyer*
Brown, W(illiam) Douglas *lawyer*
Grey, Robert J. *lawyer, electric power industry executive*
Holt, Leon Conrad, Jr. *lawyer, chemicals executive*
McGinley, Paul Anthony, Jr. *lawyer*

Allison Park
Ewalt, Henry Ward *lawyer*
Herrington, John David III *retired lawyer, director*
Ries, William Campbell *lawyer*
Rulis, Christopher C. *lawyer*

Ardmore
Heinzen, Bernard George *lawyer*

Bala Cynwyd
Chovanes, Eugene *lawyer*
Garrity, Vincent Francis, Jr. *lawyer*
Kane-Vanni, Patricia Ruth *lawyer, paleontologist, educator*
Mattison, Priscilla Jane *lawyer*
Schwartz, Jeffrey Byron *lawyer*
Weisberg, Richard Charbourn *lawyer*
Wiener, Thomas Eli *lawyer*

Beaver
Petrush, John Joseph *lawyer*

Bensalem
Stern, Colin D. *lawyer, retail executive*

Berwyn
Seidel, Arthur Harris *lawyer*
Watters, Edward McLain III *lawyer*
Wood, Thomas E. *lawyer*

Bethlehem
Rambo, Kelly Clifford *lawyer*
Spry, Donald Francis, II, *lawyer*

Blue Bell
Elliott, John Michael *lawyer*
Potash, Charles *lawyer*
Rounick, Jack A. *lawyer, clothing retail executive*
Siedzikowski, Henry Francis *lawyer*
Sundheim, Nancy Straus *lawyer, computer company executive*
Swansen, Samuel Theodore *lawyer*

Bradford
Hauser, Christopher George *lawyer*

Brookville
Smith, Sharon Louise *lawyer, consultant*

Bryn Mawr
Frick, Benjamin Charles *lawyer*
Narin, Stephen B. *lawyer*

Camp Hill
Kimmel, Mark E. *lawyer*
Mackin, Charles Philip, Jr. *lawyer*
Sari, Robert B. *lawyer, retail executive*

Carlisle
Butler, William Elliott *lawyer, educator*
Turo, Ron *lawyer*

Center Valley
Smillie, Douglas James *lawyer*

Chadds Ford
Cohen, Felix Asher *lawyer*

Chalfont
Hetherington, John Joseph *lawyer*

Chesterbrook
Chou, John G. *lawyer*

Clarks Summit
Beemer, John Barry *lawyer*

Conshohocken
Bramson, Robert Sherman *lawyer*

Cresco
Upright, Kirby Grant *lawyer*

Danville
Gubbiotti, Christine M. *lawyer*

Downingtown
Wusinich, Joseph F. III *lawyer, educator*

Doylestown
Elliott, Richard Howard *lawyer*

Du Bois
Blakley, Benjamin Spencer III *lawyer*

Easton
Brown, Robert Carroll, Jr. *lawyer*
Milgrim, Roger Michael *lawyer*
Noel, Nicholas III *legal company executive, lawyer*

Elkins Park
Myers, Kenneth Raymond *lawyer*

Erie
Tanous, James Joseph *lawyer, insurance company executive*
Van Gorder, Jan Reid *lawyer, insurance comp executive*
Woodard, Jon L. *lawyer*
Zamboldi, Richard Henry *lawyer*

Etters
Steps, Barbara Jill *lawyer*

Exton
Ashton, Mark Randolph *lawyer*

Fayetteville
Molitor, Graham Thomas Tate *lawyer*

Feasterville Trevose
Osterhout, Richard Cadwallader *lawyer*

Frazer
Osborn, John Edward *lawyer, pharmaceutica industry executive, former government offi*

Gibsonia
Benson, Stuart Wells III *lawyer*

Gladwyne
Acton, David *lawyer*
Booth, Harold Waverly *lawyer, finance comp executive*

Glenside
Mermelstein, Jules Joshua *lawyer, educator, commissioner*

Greensburg
Gounley, Dennis Joseph *lawyer*

Grove City
Kochems, Robert Gregory *lawyer*
McBride, Milford Lawrence, Jr. *lawyer*

Harleysville
Browne, Michael Leon *lawyer*
Kauffman, Robert A. *lawyer*

Harrisburg
Adams, Barbara *lawyer*

o, Richard Carmen *lawyer*
ch, David M. *lawyer, former prosecutor*
t, Joel Robin *lawyer*
Andrew Haley *lawyer*
n, James Warren *lawyer, educator*
ey, Brian Patrick *lawyer*
David R. *lawyer*
na, Mark Allan *lawyer*
Joseph Page *lawyer*
Yvette *lawyer, judge*
Robert Edward, Jr. *lawyer*
Michael D. *lawyer*
, David Robert *lawyer*
s, Spero Thomas *lawyer*
on, Sandra L. *lawyer*
r, Leslie Anne *lawyer*
on, J. Michael *lawyer, educator*
non, Anthony *lawyer*
ss, Carleton O. *lawyer*
an, John Cornelius, Jr. *lawyer*
Cile, Philip Taylor III *lawyer, educator*
naw, Allen Charles *lawyer*
James Joseph *lawyer*
on, R. Timothy *lawyer, government ninistrator*
cky, Susan Kline *law librarian*

boro
Robert McClintock *lawyer*
olson, Bruce Allen *lawyer*

erford
ews, Timothy Newlyn *lawyer*
er, Richard Ware *retired lawyer*
r, Jennifer A. *lawyer*
d, James Stanley *retired lawyer*

ertown
Gary Ganesh *lawyer*

leton
nati-Ritz, Genene Marie *lawyer*
avo, Pasco Louis *lawyer*

shey
er, Burton Harold *lawyer*

sham
Franklin Luther, Jr. *lawyer*

tingdon Valley
zanowski, Richard L. *lawyer*

iana
or, John Howard *lawyer*

kintown
s, John Foster III *retired lawyer*
lman, Ralph David *lawyer*
hington, Sandra Boulton *lawyer*

nstown
arick, Jerome John *lawyer*

nett Square
ard, Alfred Fletcher *legal educator*

g Of Prussia
ert, Bruce Rits *lawyer*
neider, Pam Horvitz *lawyer*

gston
er, Martin Jay *lawyer*

e Harmony
nsky, Larry Paul *legal association dministrator*

ncaster
is, Alvin Bower, Jr. *lawyer*
ney, Michael Jay *lawyer*
, Dianne Martha *lawyer*
er, John Frederick, Jr. *lawyer, director*
as, John Nicholas *lawyer*
merman, Donald Patrick *lawyer*

nsdale
anik, Jeffrey Ted *lawyer*

trobe
enfield, David W. *lawyer*

moyne
wart, Richard Williams *lawyer*

wisburg
nsler, John Paul *lawyer*

wistown
in, Allen Joseph *lawyer*

ck Haven
owiss, Alvin L. *lawyer*

alvern
meron, John Clifford *lawyer, health science ssociation administrator*
on, E. A., Jr. *lawyer*
nan, Andrew H. *lawyer*
rshey, Mark A. *lawyer*

c Keesport
cale, Frank Jude *lawyer*

c Murray
custowicz, John Cinq-Mars *lawyer*
erry, John Sebastian *lawyer*

edia
Amico, Andrew J. *lawyer*
rham, James W. *lawyer*
erson, Sterling Jonathan *lawyer*
mlinson, Herbert Weston *lawyer, defender*

endenhall
nert, Norbert Frederick *lawyer, retired hemicals executive*

Monroeville
Cohen, Laura *lawyer*

Mont Alto
Achampong, Francis Kofi *academic administrator*

Moon Township
Alstadt, Lynn Jeffery *lawyer*

Murrysville
Ferri, Karen Lynn *lawyer*

Natrona Heights
Maleski, Cynthia Maria *lawyer*

Nazareth
Stitt, Thomas Paul, Sr. *lawyer*

New Buffalo
Cramer, John McNaight *lawyer*

New Kensington
Wallace, Henry Jared, Jr. *lawyer*

Newtown
Godwin, Robert Anthony *lawyer*

Newtown Square
Kendall, Robert Louis, Jr. *lawyer*

Norristown
Aman, George Matthias III *lawyer*
Britt, Earl Thomas *lawyer*
Gold-Bikin, Lynne Z. *lawyer*
Gregg, John Pennypacker *lawyer*

Philadelphia
Aaron, Kenneth Ellyot *lawyer*
Abramowitz, Robert Leslie *lawyer*
Adamany, David Walter *law and political science educator, former academic administrator*
Albert, Jeffrey B. *lawyer*
Ammon, Gary D. *lawyer*
Anders, Jerrold P. *lawyer*
Angel, Marina *law educator*
Arem, Lawrence Jay *lawyer*
Auten, David Charles *lawyer*
Auten, Donald R. *lawyer*
Bachman, Arthur *lawyer*
Baker, Stephen C. *lawyer*
Barnett, Bonnie Allyn *lawyer*
Barrett, John J(ames), Jr. *lawyer*
Barton, Thomas J. *lawyer*
Beck, Stuart Edwin *lawyer*
Berenato, Mark Anthony *lawyer, insurance company executive*
Berger, Harold *lawyer, electrical engineer*
Berger, Lawrence Douglas *lawyer*
Berger, Lawrence Howard *lawyer*
Berkley, Emily Carolan *lawyer*
Berkman, Richard Lyle *lawyer*
Berlin, Norman B. *lawyer*
Bernabeo, Gregory S. *lawyer*
Bernard, John Marley *lawyer, educator*
Berney, David J. *lawyer*
Bernheim, Daniel S. *lawyer*
Bershad, Jack R. *retired lawyer*
Beyer, Aaron Jay *lawyer*
Black, Allen Decatur *lawyer*
Black, Creed C., Jr. *lawyer*
Blume, Fred *lawyer*
Blumstein, Edward *lawyer*
Bochetto, George Alexander *lawyer*
Boggia, Eugene Stephen *lawyer*
Bogutz, Jerome Edwin *lawyer, educator*
Bonella, Michael J. *lawyer*
Boss, Amelia Helen *lawyer, educator*
Bovaird, Brendan Peter *lawyer*
Brandt, Jennifer Anne *lawyer*
Bressler, Barry E. *lawyer*
Brier, Bonnie Susan *lawyer*
Briscoe, Jack Clayton *lawyer*
Brookman, Marc D. *lawyer*
Brooman, David J. *lawyer*
Brown, Stephen D. *lawyer*
Brown, William Hill III *lawyer*
Browne, Stanhope Stryker *lawyer*
Bryans, Henry S. *lawyer*
Bryce, Teresa Audrey *lawyer*
Buccino, Ernest John, Jr. *lawyer*
Buchholz, Carl M. *lawyer*
Budin, Beverly R. *lawyer*
Burbank, Stephen Bradner *law educator*
Burdumy, Stephen T. *lawyer*
Byler, Anthony J. *lawyer*
Calvert, Jay H., Jr. *lawyer*
Cannon, John III *lawyer, insurance company executive*
Carroll, Mark Thomas *lawyer*
Casper, Charles B. *lawyer*
Chanin, Bernard *lawyer*
Cherken, Harry Sarkis, Jr. *lawyer*
Chimples, George *lawyer*
Chopko, Mark E. *lawyer*
Christenbury, T. Daniel *lawyer*
Clark, Peter S., II *lawyer*
Clark, William H., Jr. *lawyer*
Clauss, Peter Otto *lawyer*
Clothier, Robert Clarkson *lawyer*
Coleman, Robert J. *lawyer*
Colli, Bart Joseph *lawyer*
Collings, Robert L. *lawyer*
Comisky, Hope A. *lawyer*
Congdon, Charles B. *lawyer*
Cooney, J(ohn) Gordon, Jr. *lawyer*
Cooper, Frank G. *lawyer*
Cox, Roger Frazier *lawyer*
Coyne, Charles Cole *lawyer*
Cozen, Stephen Allen *lawyer*
Cramer, Harold *lawyer*
Crawford, James Douglas *lawyer*
Cross, Milton H. *lawyer*
Dabrowski, Doris Jane *lawyer*
Damsgaard, Kell Marsh *lawyer*
D'Angelo, Christopher Scott *lawyer*
Davis, Alan Jay *lawyer*
DeBunda, Salvatore Michael *lawyer*
Delacato, Carl Henry *lawyer*
Del Raso, Joseph Vincent *lawyer*
Devlin, John Gerard *lawyer, writer*
Diamantis, Jennifer *lawyer*
Diaz, Nelson A. *lawyer*
Diaz, Romulo L., Jr. *lawyer*
Dichter, Mark S. *lawyer*
Donohue, James J. *lawyer*
Donohue, John Patrick *lawyer*
Dorfman, John Charles *lawyer*
Dougherty, Brian James *lawyer*
Drake, William Frank, Jr. *lawyer*
Dubin, Leonard *lawyer*
Duffy, Seamus C. *lawyer*
Durant, Marc *lawyer*
Dworetzky, Joseph Anthony *lawyer, city manager*
Epstein, Alan Bruce *lawyer*
Esser, Carl Eric *lawyer*
Ewald, William Bragg III *law educator, philosopher*
Fader, Henry Conrad *lawyer*
Fala, Herman Camillo *lawyer*
Feirson, Steven B. *lawyer*
Feldman, Eric Adam *law educator, academic administrator*
Fickler, Arlene *lawyer*
Fiebach, H. Robert *lawyer*
Fineman, S. David *lawyer*
Finkelstein, Joseph Simon *lawyer*
Fisher, Lane J. *lawyer*
Flanagan, Joseph Patrick, Jr. *retired lawyer*
Floyd, Michael O'S. *lawyer*
Foley, Regina M. *lawyer*
Fox, Richard L. *lawyer*
Frank, Barry H. *lawyer*
Frank, George Andrew *lawyer*
Gallagher, William T. *lawyer, manufacturing executive*
Garcia, Rudolph *lawyer*
Genkin, Barry Howard *lawyer*
George, Paul M. *law librarian, director*
Gerhart, Frederick John *lawyer*
Gershenson, Alan C. *lawyer*
Gilberg, Kenneth Roy *lawyer*
Girard-diCarlo, David Franklin *lawyer*
Goldberg, Joseph *lawyer*
Goldberg, Marvin Allen *lawyer, consultant*
Goldberg, Richard Robert *lawyer*
Goldman, Gary Craig *lawyer*
Goldman, Jerry S. *lawyer*
Goldstein, William Marks *lawyer*
Goodman, Stephen Murry *lawyer*
Gorberg, David J. *lawyer*
Gough, John Francis *lawyer*
Grant, M. Duncan *lawyer*
Grove, David Lavan *lawyer*
Hagan, Mary Ann *lawyer*
Haimm, Neil Keith *lawyer*
Haines, Clifford E. *lawyer*
Haley, Vincent Peter *retired lawyer*
Hamilton, Stephen David Derwent *lawyer*
Hangley, William Thomas *lawyer*
Harkins, John Graham, Jr. *lawyer*
Harris, Judith E. *lawyer*
Harvey, Gregory Merrill *lawyer*
Hickok, D. Alicia *lawyer*
Hickok, Robert L. *lawyer*
Hoelscher, Robert James *lawyer*
Hoffman, Alan Jay *lawyer*
Howard, David Miles *lawyer*
Hunter, James Austen, Jr. *lawyer*
Ivey, Stephen David *lawyer*
James, Jennifer DuFault *lawyer*
Jones, Robert Jeffries *lawyer*
Jordan, Michael B. *lawyer*
Kahn, James Robert *lawyer*
Kaier, Edward John *lawyer*
Kassner, Andrew Charles *lawyer*
Keene, John Clark *lawyer, educator*
Kenty, David Earl *lawyer*
Kessler, Alan Craig *lawyer*
Kiniry, William F., Jr. *lawyer*
Klasko, Herbert Ronald *lawyer, educator, writer*
Klein, Howard Bruce *lawyer, educator*
Kline, Thomas Richard *lawyer*
Klugheit, Mark A. *lawyer*
Knoll, Michael Steven *law educator*
Koc, Lorraine K. *lawyer*
Kopp, Charles Gilbert *lawyer*
Kormes, John Winston *lawyer*
Kraeutler, Eric *lawyer*
Kreimer, Seth F. *lawyer, educator*
Kunz, Michael E. *court administrator*
Kupperman, Louis Brandeis *lawyer*
Laguzzi, Carina *lawyer*
Lasher, Lori L. *lawyer*
Lavorgna, Gregory Joseph *lawyer*
Ledwith, John Francis *lawyer*
Leech, Noyes Elwood *lawyer, educator*
Lefton, Ira S. *lawyer*
Lehr, Michael L. *lawyer*
Leonard, Thomas *lawyer*
Levering, Kathryn H. *lawyer*
Levin, Murray Simon *lawyer*
Lewis, John Hardy, Jr. *lawyer*
Libonati, Michael Ernest *law educator, writer*
Lichtenstein, Robert Jay *lawyer*
Liebenberg, Roberta D. *lawyer*
Lipman, Frederick D. *lawyer, educator, writer*
Lombard, John James, Jr. *lawyer, writer*
Lonergan, Robert A. *lawyer, chemicals executive*
Lord, Geoffrey Craig (G. Craig Lord) *lawyer*
Love, William Allan *lawyer, educator*
Loveless, George Group *retired lawyer*
Luongo, Stephen Earle *lawyer*
MacGregor, David Bruce *lawyer*
Madva, Stephen Alan *lawyer*
Magargee, W(illiam) Scott III *lawyer*
Magaziner, Fred Thomas *lawyer*
Makadon, Arthur *lawyer*
Malloy, Michael P. *lawyer*
Mann, Theodore R. *lawyer*
Mannino, Edward Francis *lawyer, educator*
Mathes, Stephen Jon *lawyer*
Mattoon, Peter Mills *lawyer*
McClure, Matthew N. *lawyer*
McConnel, W. Bruce *lawyer*
McGarrigle, Thomas J. *lawyer*
McGurk, Eugene David, Jr. *lawyer*
McHugh, James Joseph *lawyer*
McKeever, John Eugene *lawyer*
McKenzie, James W., Jr. *lawyer*
McLaughlin, Slade Hayes *lawyer*
McMenamin, Richard F. *lawyer*
McQuiston, Robert Earl *lawyer*
Meehan, Patrick Leo *prosecutor*
Meigs, John Forsyth *lawyer*
Melinson, Gregg R. *lawyer*
Michel, H. John, Jr. *lawyer*
Milbourne, Walter Robertson *lawyer*
Miller, Henry Franklin *lawyer*
Milone, Francis Michael *lawyer*
Mirabello, Francis Joseph *lawyer*
Molitor, Steven John *lawyer*
Moss, Arthur Henshey *lawyer*
Newman, Sandra Schultz *lawyer, former state supreme court justice*
O'Connor, Joseph A., Jr. *lawyer*
Ominsky, Harris *lawyer*
O'Reilly, Timothy Patrick *lawyer*
Pagliaro, James Domenic *lawyer*
Panitch, Ronald Louis *lawyer*
Pappert, Jerry (Gerald J. Pappert) *lawyer, former state attorney general*
Parry, William DeWitt *lawyer*
Petren, Carol Ann *lawyer, insurance company executive*
Pokotilow, Manny David *lawyer, educator*
Pollack, Michael *lawyer*
Pollack, Michael Bruce *lawyer*
Price, Robert Stanley *lawyer*
Promislo, Daniel *lawyer, small business owner*
Putnam, Alfred W., Jr. *lawyer*
Rabinowitz, Mark I. *lawyer*
Rachofsky, David J. *lawyer*
Rackow, Julian Paul *lawyer*
Rainone, Michael Carmine *lawyer*
Ramsey, Natalie D. *lawyer*
Reed, Michael Haywood *lawyer*
Reich, Abraham Charles *lawyer*
Reiss, John Barlow *lawyer*
Reiter, Joseph Henry *lawyer, retired judge*
Reitz, Curtis Randall *lawyer, educator*
Resnick, Stephanie *lawyer*
Rhoads, Nancy Glenn *lawyer*
Rhodes, Alice Graham *lawyer, not-for-profit community development consultant*
Roberts, Carl Geoffrey *lawyer*
Rock, Edward Baron *law educator*
Romano, Carmen J. *lawyer*
Roscher, David K. *lawyer*
Rosenberg, Howell K. *lawyer*
Rosenbloom, Morey Stephen *lawyer*
Ross, Daniel R. *lawyer*
Ross, Murray Louis *lawyer*
Saint-Antoine, Paul Hewitt *lawyer*
Saltz, Jeffrey S. *lawyer*
Samuel, Ralph David *lawyer*
Satinsky, Barnett *lawyer*
Schachtman, Nathan A. *lawyer*
Scher, Howard Dennis *lawyer*
Schneider, Carl William *lawyer*
Schneider, Deena Jo *lawyer*
Schneider, Richard Graham *lawyer*
Schoff, Dennis L. *lawyer*
Schorling, William Harrison *lawyer*
Segal, Robert Martin *lawyer*
Shay, Kathleen M. *lawyer*
Sheils, Denis Francis *lawyer*
Shestack, Jerome Joseph *lawyer*
Shiekman, Laurence Zeid *lawyer*
Shropshire, Kenneth L. *law educator*
Siegel, Bernard L. *lawyer*
Sigmond, Richard Brian *lawyer*
Silverman, David A. *lawyer, finance company executive*
Smith, John Francis III *lawyer*
Solano, Carl Anthony *lawyer*
Sonnenfeld, Marc Jay *lawyer*
Spaeth, Edmund Benjamin, Jr. *retired lawyer, retired law educator, former judge*
Spector, Martin Wolf *lawyer*
Spolan, Harmon Samuel *lawyer*
Sprague, Richard A. *lawyer*
Sproul, Gayle Chatilo *lawyer*
Steinberg, Robert Philip *lawyer*
Stern, Eric L. *lawyer*
Stern, Joan Naomi *lawyer*
Strasbaugh, Wayne Ralph *lawyer*
Strazzella, James Anthony *lawyer, educator*
Strickler, Matthew M. *lawyer*
Stuart, Glen R(aymond) *lawyer*
Stuntebeck, Clinton A. *lawyer*
Summers, Clyde Wilson *law educator*
Suplee, Dennis Raymond *lawyer*
Swain, Clifford H. *lawyer*
Sweet, James M. *lawyer*
Taney, Francis Xavier, Jr. *lawyer*
Temin, Michael Lehman *lawyer*
Thomas, Glen R. *lawyer*
Tiger, Ira Paul *retired lawyer*
Tractenberg, Craig R. *lawyer*
Vaira, Peter Francis *lawyer*
Virelli, Louis James, Jr. *lawyer*
Vogel, Warren *lawyer*
Wachter, Michael L. *law and finance educator*
Wajert, Sean Peter *lawyer*
Webb, William Yerick *lawyer*
Weil, Jeffrey George *lawyer*
Weisberg, Morris L. *retired lawyer*
Wellington, Ralph Glenn *lawyer*
Whinston, Stephen Alan *lawyer*
Whiteside, William Anthony, Jr. *retired lawyer*
Wiener, Ronald Martin *lawyer*
Wild, Richard P. *lawyer*
Wittels, Barnaby Caesar *lawyer, writer*
Wolf, Bruce *lawyer*
Wolff, Deborah H(orowitz) *lawyer*
Wood, Roger F. *lawyer*
Wright, Minturn Tatum III *retired lawyer*
Yaruss, Howard Seth *lawyer*

Zuckerman, Brian David *lawyer*

Pittsburgh
Abbott, Kevin Charles *lawyer*
Acheson, Amy J. *lawyer*
Aderson, Sanford M. *lawyer*
Allen, Rachel Lorey *lawyer*
Aronson, Mark Berne *retired lawyer, advocate*
Artz, John Curtis *lawyer*
Baldauf, Kent Edward *lawyer*
Basinski, Anthony Joseph *lawyer*
Beck, Paul A. *lawyer*
Bellisario, Domenic *lawyer*
Bissoon, Cathy *lawyer*
Bleier, Michael E. *lawyer, director*
Blenko, Walter John, Jr. *lawyer*
Blum, Eva Tansky *lawyer*
Bobby, Theodore N. *lawyer, food products executive*
Bochicchio, Vito Salvatore *lawyer*
Booker, Daniel I. *lawyer*
Boswell, William Paret *lawyer*
Breault, Theodore E(dward) *lawyer*
Brendel, John S. *lawyer*
Brown, David Ronald *lawyer*
Brown, James Benton *lawyer, department chairman*
Brownlee, David A. *lawyer*
Buchanan, Mary Beth *prosecutor*
Burkoff, John Michael *law educator*
Cahouet, Ann P. *lawyer*
Cameron, Douglas E. *lawyer*
Candris, Laura A. *lawyer*
Cheever, George Martin *lawyer*
Cindrich, Robert James *lawyer, retired federal judge*
Colen, Frederick Haas *lawyer*
Coney, Aims C., Jr. *lawyer, labor-management negotiator*
Connors, Eugene Kenneth *lawyer, educator*
Cooper, Thomas Louis *lawyer*
Corcoran, John Paul *lawyer, educator*
Cowan, Barton Zalman *lawyer*
Damico, David A. *lawyer*
Daniel, Robert Michael *lawyer*
Davis, Lewis U., Jr. *lawyer*
DeNinno, David L. *lawyer*
Denys, Sylvia *lawyer, researcher*
Doty, Robert Walter *lawyer*
Dugan, John F. *lawyer*
Ehrenwerth, David Harry *lawyer*
Ellsworth, Laura E. *lawyer*
Evans, Bruce Dwight *lawyer*
Fawcett, David B. III *lawyer*
Finegold, Alan H. *lawyer*
Flechtner, Harry Marshal *law educator*
Flinn, Michael James *lawyer*
Frank, Ronald William *lawyer*
Frolik, Lawrence Anton *lawyer, educator, consultant*
Garraux, James D. *lawyer, metal products executive*
Geeseman, Robert George *lawyer*
Goldberg, Mark Joel *lawyer*
Grupp, Edward A. *arbitrator, prosecutor*
Guadagnino, Frank T. *lawyer*
Hackett, Mary J. *lawyer*
Halpern, Richard I. *lawyer*
Hartman, Ronald G. *lawyer*
Harty, James Quinn *lawyer*
Hellman, Arthur David *law educator, consultant*
Helmrich, Joel Marc *lawyer*
Hershey, Dale *lawyer, educator*
Hershey, Nathan *lawyer, educator*
Hill, John Howard *retired lawyer*
Hitt, Leo N. *lawyer, educator*
Hull, John Daniel, IV, *lawyer, writer*
Hurnyak, Christina Kaiser *lawyer*
Johnson, Robert Alan *lawyer*
Jones, Craig Ward *retired lawyer*
Jones, James M. *lawyer*
Jordan, Gregory B. *lawyer*
Kalis, Peter John *lawyer*
Kenrick, Charles William *lawyer*
Ketter, David Lee *lawyer*
King, Robert Alan *lawyer*
Klett, Edwin L. *lawyer*
Knox, Charles Graham *lawyer*
Krasik, Carl *lawyer, bank executive*
Krebs, Robert Alan *lawyer*
Leech, Frederick C. *lawyer*
Leibowitz, Marvin *lawyer*
Letwin, Jeffrey William *lawyer*
Litman, Roslyn Margolis *lawyer*
Lovett, Robert G. *lawyer*
Mahone, Glenn R. *lawyer*
McCartney, Robert Charles *retired lawyer*
McDevitt, Jerry S. *lawyer*
McGough, Walter Thomas, Jr. *lawyer*
McLaughlin, John Sherman *lawyer*
Meisel, Alan *law educator*
Messner, Robert Thomas *lawyer, bank executive*
Meyers, Jerry Ivan *lawyer*
Murdoch, David Armor *lawyer*
Murdoch, Robert Whitten *lawyer*
Murrin, Regis Doubet *retired lawyer*
Mutterperl, William Charles *lawyer, corporate financial executive*
Naugle, Louis A. *lawyer*
Newlin, William Rankin *lawyer*
Nogay, Arlie R. *lawyer*
Norris, James Harold *lawyer*
Ober, Russell John, Jr. *lawyer*
O'Connor, Edward Gearing *lawyer*
Olson, Stephen M(ichael) *lawyer*
Orsatti, Ernest Benjamin *lawyer*
Perry, Jon Robert *lawyer*
Phillips, Larry Edward *lawyer*
Picadio, Anthony Peter *lawyer*
Plowman, Jack Wesley *lawyer*
Pohl, Paul Michael *lawyer*
Post, Peter David *lawyer*
Powderly, William H. III *lawyer*
Pudlin, Helen Pomerantz *lawyer*
Pusateri, David P. *lawyer*
Rago, John Thomas *law educator*
Randolph, Robert DeWitt *lawyer*
Raynovich, George, Jr. *retired lawyer*
Reed, W. Franklin *lawyer*
Restivo, James John, Jr. *lawyer*
Richey, P. Jerome *lawyer, energy executive*
Ritchey, Patrick William *lawyer*
Rosen, Richard David *lawyer*
Rosenberger, Bryan David *lawyer*
Russell, Richard A. *lawyer*
Scheinholtz, Leonard Louis *lawyer*
Schwab, Arthur James *lawyer*
Schwendeman, Paul William *lawyer*
Shuman, Joseph Duff *lawyer*
Silverman, Arnold Barry *lawyer*
Simon, Jacob Matthew *lawyer*
Singer, Paul Meyer *lawyer*
Smorey-Giger, Marcy *lawyer*
Sokulski, Gary A. *lawyer*
Stepanian, Steven Arvid, II, *lawyer, financial consultant*
Strader, James David *lawyer*
Stroyd, Arthur Heister, Jr. *lawyer*
Sweeney, Clayton Anthony *lawyer, business executive*
Symons, Edward Leonard, Jr. *lawyer, educator, investment advisor*
Tarasi, Louis Michael, Jr. *lawyer*
Thompson, Thomas Martin *lawyer*
Thurman, Andrew Edward *lawyer*
Turner, Harry Woodruff *lawyer*
Ubinger, John Walter, Jr. *lawyer*
Ummer, James Walter *lawyer*
Unkovic, John Clark *lawyer*
Van Kirk, Thomas L. *lawyer*
Vater, Charles J. *lawyer*
Veeder, Peter Greig *lawyer*
Vogrin, Joseph Edward III *lawyer*
von Waldow, Arnd N. *lawyer*
Walton, Jon David *lawyer*
Warman, Guy Lee *lawyer*
Wessels, Daniel L. *lawyer*
Whitehead, Paul *lawyer, labor union administrator*
Wilkinson, James Allan *lawyer, healthcare executive*
Wycoff, William Mortimer *lawyer*
Yang, Wesley *lawyer*
Yorsz, Stanley *lawyer*
Zanic, Michael G. *lawyer*

Plymouth
Musto, Joseph John *lawyer*

Plymouth Meeting
McCausland, Margaret A. *lawyer, educator*

Pottsville
Tamulonis, Frank Louis, Jr. *lawyer*

Presto
Pfaff, Robert James *retired lawyer*

Radnor
Bertolino, Dean A. *lawyer*
Simon, David Frederick *lawyer*

Reading
Brightbill, David John *lawyer, former state legislator*
Duff, Michael A. *lawyer, transportation executive*
Linton, Jack Arthur *lawyer*

Scranton
Burke, Henry Patrick *lawyer*
Haggerty, James Joseph *lawyer*
Howley, James McAndrew *lawyer*
Marino, Thomas A. *prosecutor, lawyer*

Solebury
Cross, Robert William *lawyer, venture capitalist*
Valentine, H. Jeffrey *legal association executive*

Spring House
Rosoff, William A. *lawyer*

Springfield
Maclay, Donald Merle *retired lawyer*

Sunbury
Saylor, Charles Horace *lawyer, judge*

Swarthmore
Elman, Gerry Jay *lawyer*

Uniontown
Coldren, Ira Burdette, Jr. *lawyer*

Valley Forge
Barton, R. Gregory *lawyer, investment company executive*
Knauss, Robert H. *lawyer*
Mesher, John R. *lawyer*
Sprague, William Douglas *lawyer*
Stam, Heidi *lawyer*

Verona
Demmler, John Henry *retired lawyer*

Villanova
Bersoff, Donald Neil *lawyer, psychologist, educator*
Maule, James Edward *law educator*
Murphy, John Francis *law educator, consultant*
Zearfoss, Herbert Keyser *retired lawyer*

Warminster
Hostovich, John Larry *lawyer*

Warren
Ristau, Mark Moody *lawyer, consultant*

Warrington
Sigety, Elizabeth Donnem *lawyer*
Vosik, Wayne Gilbert *lawyer*

Washington
Lerner, William C. *lawyer*
Richman, Stephen I. *lawyer*

Washington Crossing
Kozlowski, Thomas Joseph, Jr. *lawyer, wealth management executive*

Wayne
Binder, David Franklin *lawyer, writer*
Freyer, Charles C. *lawyer*
Guerette, Susan M. *lawyer*
Patterson, Scott David *lawyer*
Silbey, Victoria E. *lawyer*
Wilson, Bruce Brighton *lawyer, retired transportation executive*

West Chester
Archbold, William Cornell, Jr. *lawyer*
Babcock, Charles Witten, Jr. *lawyer*
Donatoni, Robert J. *lawyer*
Ewing, Joseph Neff, Jr. *retired lawyer*
Lamb, William H. *lawyer, former state supreme court justice*
Teti, Louis Nicholas *lawyer*

West Conshohocken
Odell, Herbert *lawyer*
Sager, Margaret E.W. *lawyer*
Teillon, Louis Pierre, Jr. *lawyer*

Wilkes Barre
O'Donnell, Catherine Rose *lawyer*
Roth, Eugene *lawyer*
Ufberg, Murray *lawyer*

Williamsport
Carlucci, William Philip *lawyer*
Knecht, William L. *lawyer*

Wormleysburg
Cherewka, Michael *lawyer*

York
Addison, Brian Michael *lawyer*
Buzzendore, Robert L. *lawyer*
Davis, Jane G. *lawyer*
Hoffmeyer, William Frederick *lawyer, educator*

Youngstown
Love, George H., Jr. *lawyer*

RHODE ISLAND

Barrington
Soutter, Thomas Douglas *retired lawyer*

Bristol
Bogus, Carl Thomas *law educator*

Cranston
Alston, Jametta O. *lawyer*

East Greenwich
Dence, Edward William, Jr. *retired lawyer, bank executive*

Jamestown
Parks, A. Lauriston *lawyer*

Johnston
Pomeroy, John J. *lawyer, insurance company executive*

Little Compton
Caron, Wilfred Rene *retired lawyer*

Newport
McConnell, David Kelso *lawyer*

North Kingstown
Knowles, Charles Timothy *lawyer, state legislator, military officer, educator*

Pawtucket
Kranseler, Lawrence Michael *lawyer*
Nagler, Barry *lawyer*

Portsmouth
Levie, Howard S(idney) *lawyer, educator*

Providence
Berkelhammer, Robert Bruce *lawyer*
Bulman, John *lawyer*
Carlotti, Stephen Jon *lawyer*
Chlebus, Andrew J. *lawyer*
Conley, Patrick T. *lawyer, writer, historian, educator, real estate developer*
Corrente, Robert Clark *prosecutor*
Curran, Joseph Patrick *lawyer*
Donnelly, Kevin William *lawyer*
Farrell, Margaret Dawson *lawyer*
Ferruolo, Stephen Carl *lawyer, historian*
Fogarty, Edward Michael *lawyer*
Gamboli, Michael A. *lawyer*
Gasbarro, Pasco, Jr. *lawyer*
Johnson, Vahe Duncan *lawyer*
Jones, Lauren Evans *lawyer*
Kean, John Vaughan *retired lawyer*
Kraemer, Michael Frederick *lawyer*
Licht, Richard A. *lawyer*
Lipsey, Howard Irwin *lawyer, educator*
Lynch, William Joseph *lawyer*
Marcello, Matthew T. III *lawyer*
Marshall, Jason P. *lawyer*
McAndrew, Thomas Joseph *lawyer*
McCann, Gail Elizabeth *lawyer*
McElroy, Michael Robert *lawyer*
McIntyre, Jerry L. *lawyer*
Medeiros, Matthew Francis *lawyer*
O'Donnell, Terrence *lawyer, multi-industry company executive*
Paster, Benjamin G. *lawyer*
Reilly, Charles James *lawyer, educator, accountant*
Roney, John M. *lawyer*
Salter, Lester Herbert *lawyer*
Salvadore, Guido Richard *lawyer*
Sherman, Deming Eliot *lawyer*
Weinstein, Philip Merrill *lawyer*

Rockville
Walker, Howard Ernest *lawyer*

Scituate
Gorham, Bradford *lawyer*

Warwick
Reilly, John B. *lawyer*
St. Pierre, Michael A. *lawyer*

Westerly
Walsh, Robert Anthony *lawyer*

Woonsocket
Lankowsky, Zenon P. *lawyer, retail executive*
Roszkowski, Joseph John *lawyer*
Spalding, William R. *lawyer, pharmaceutical executive*

SOUTH CAROLINA

Aiken
Pearce, Richard Lee *lawyer*
Rudnick, Irene Krugman *lawyer, educator, former state legislator*

Beaufort
Harvey, William Brantley, Jr. *lawyer, retired lieutenant governor*

Charleston
Bell, James L. *lawyer*
Branham, C. Michael *lawyer*
Cox, Walter Thompson III *lawyer, federal jud educator*
Dominick, Paul Allen *lawyer*
Farr, Charles Sims *lawyer*
Fenno, Edward Thorndike *lawyer*
Freer, Robert Elliott, Jr. *lawyer*
Grant, J. Kirkland *lawyer, educator*
Kahn, Ellis Irvin *lawyer*
Long, Angus Quentin *lawyer, art association administrator*
McCullough, Ralph Clayton, II, *law educator*
Patrick, Charles William, Jr. *lawyer*
Robinson, Neil Cibley, Jr. *lawyer*
Spitz, Hugo Max *retired lawyer*
Waring, Bradish J. *lawyer*

Clemson
Cox, Headley Morris, Jr. *lawyer, educator*

Columbia
Anderson, Charles Hill *lawyer*
Babcock, Keith Moss *lawyer*
Bernstein, Barry Joel *lawyer*
Blanton, Hoover Clarence *lawyer*
Carpenter, Charles Elford, Jr. *lawyer*
Day, Richard Earl *lawyer, educator*
Ellis, F. Earl, Jr. *lawyer*
Finkel, Gerald Michael *lawyer*
Gasser, Jonathan S. *prosecutor*
Gibbes, William Holman *lawyer*
Gray, Elizabeth Van Doren *lawyer*
Handel, Richard Craig *lawyer*
Harvey, Jonathan Matthew *lawyer*
Johnson, Lawrence Wilbur, Jr. *lawyer*
Lambert, Lanneau William, Jr. *lawyer*
Land, John Calhoun III *lawyer, state legislato*
Lloyd, Reginald Ivan *prosecutor, former judg*
Matthews, Steve Allen *lawyer*
McLeod, Walton James *lawyer, state legislato*
Mood, Francis P., Jr. *lawyer, utilities executiv*
Nexsen, Julian Jacobs *lawyer*
Roberts, Pamela J. *lawyer*
Sowell, Thornwell F. (Biff) *lawyer*
Tate, Harold Simmons, Jr. *lawyer*

Conway
Martin, Gregory Keith *lawyer, mayor*
Suggs, Michael Edward *lawyer*

Greenville
Christina, Thomas Michael *lawyer*
Edwards, Harry LaFoy *lawyer*
Estridge, Larry D. *lawyer*
Ferguson, Donald Littlefield *retired lawyer*
Holleman, Frank Sharp III *lawyer*
Horton, James Wright *retired lawyer*
Hutson, Melvin Robert *lawyer*
Lindsay, Ronald Thomas *lawyer, paper comp executive*
Massey, Raymond David *lawyer*
Mauldin, John Inglis *public defender*
Oxner, George Dewey, Jr. *lawyer*
Phillips, Joseph Brantley, Jr. *lawyer*
Riley, Richard Wilson *lawyer, former secreta of education*
Smoak, Lewis Tyson *lawyer*
Talley, Michael Frank *lawyer*
Todd, John Dickerson, Jr. *retired lawyer*
Walters, Johnnie McKeiver *lawyer*
White, Daniel Bowman *lawyer*
Wyche, Cyril Thomas *lawyer*
Wyche, Madison Baker III *lawyer*

Greenwood
Nexsen, Julian Jacobs, Jr. *lawyer*

Hilton Head Island
Becker, Karl Martin *retired lawyer*
Esposito, John Vincent *lawyer*
Hagoort, Thomas Henry *retired lawyer*

Johns Island
Carter, Mary Andrews *paralegal*

Lexington
Lide, Vinton DeVane *lawyer*

Mount Pleasant
Glenn, Edward Vernon Ferrell *lawyer, consul*

e Beach
um, M. Gregory *lawyer*

erry
ge, William Franklin, Jr. *lawyer*

Charleston
rd, Willie Bruce *lawyer, advocate*
a, Lawrence Alexander *lawyer*
, Jarrel L. *lawyer*

Myrtle Beach
s, Albert Eugene *lawyer*

geburg
ell, Charles Brison, Jr. *lawyer*

Hill
, James Carlisle III *lawyer, educator*

anburg
, Terry T. *lawyer*

nerville
Benjamin Harrison, Jr. *solicitor*

erboro
George Wallis *lawyer*

TH DAKOTA

deen
ds, Carlyle Edward *lawyer*

on
, Frank Leroy *lawyer, former governor*

ich
Vaughn Peter *lawyer*

er
er, John Herman *lawyer*

e
s, David Alan *lawyer*
on, Julie Marie *lawyer, lobbyist, judge*
Robert C., Jr. *lawyer*
s, Darla Pollman *lawyer*
pson, Charles Murray *lawyer*

d City
Thomas Harold *lawyer*
er, J. Crisman *lawyer*
, Linda Lea Margaret *lawyer*

x Falls
ey, Martin J. (Marty Jackley) *prosecutor*
on, Richard Arlo *lawyer*
o, Thomas Joseph *lawyer*
hall, Mark F. *lawyer*
en, Michelle G. *prosecutor*
s, Richard L. *lawyer*
, Thomas John *lawyer*

NESSEE

ntville
s, H. Greeley, Jr. *prosecutor*

twood
Creary, James Franklin *lawyer, mediator*
ne, John Calhoun *retired lawyer*
rt, Rachel A. *lawyer*
e, Kim *lawyer*

ttanooga
er, Thomas Maxfield *lawyer*
pbell, Paul III *lawyer*
er, Gary Allan *lawyer*
, Charles L. *lawyer, insurance company ecutive*
e, Hugh Jacob, Jr. *lawyer*
ps, John Bomar *lawyer*
mers, Gerald Howard (Jerry) *lawyer*
, Patricia Best *lawyer*

rksville
ers, David Douglas *lawyer*

lierville
ngfield, James Francis *retired lawyer, banker*

ington
lon, J. Houston *lawyer, political ganization worker*

ssville
low, James Allen *lawyer*

rsburg
ler, James Sampson III *lawyer, judge*

nklin
en, William Warren *lawyer*

rmantown
dell, Phillip Dean *lawyer*

odlettsville
gan, Susan S. *lawyer*

ndersonville
Caleb, Joe Wallace *lawyer*

rmitage
kett, Gerald Arthur *lawyer, musician*

kson
lis, Edwin E., Jr. *lawyer*

nson City
s, James Haws III *lawyer*

Jonesborough
Jenkins, Ronald Wayne *lawyer, mediator, engineer*

Kingsport
Lee, Theresa K. *lawyer, chemicals executive*

Knoxville
Bell, James A.H. *lawyer*
Coleman, Shannon DeShae *lawyer, educator*
Cremins, William Carroll *lawyer*
Dedrick, James R. *prosecutor*
Dillard, W. Thomas *lawyer*
Galligan, Thomas C., Jr. *law educator*
Gentry, Mack A. *lawyer*
Giordano, Lawrence Francis *lawyer*
Holt, Dawn Lizabeth *paralegal*
Howard, Lewis Spilman *lawyer*
Lloyd, Francis Leon, Jr. *lawyer*
McCall, Jack Humphreys, Jr. *lawyer*
Oberman, Steven *lawyer*
Reynolds, Glenn Harlan *law educator, blogger*
Ritchie, Albert *lawyer*
Roach, Jon Gilbert *lawyer*
Routh, John William *lawyer*
Swanson, Charles Walter *lawyer*
Wheeler, John Watson *lawyer*
White, Edward Gibson, II, *lawyer*
Worthington, Robert Fletcher, Jr. *lawyer*

Lebanon
Shoaf, Forrest *lawyer*

Lenoir City
Sproul, Harvey Leonard *lawyer*

Mc Ewen
Williams, John Lee *lawyer*

Memphis
Allen, Newton Perkins *lawyer*
Bobango, John Allen *lawyer*
Broadhurst, Jerome Anthony *lawyer*
Buckner, Thomas Randolph *lawyer*
Carr, Oscar Clark III *lawyer*
Clippard, Richard F. *prosecutor*
Cook, August Joseph *lawyer, accountant*
deWitt, Charles Benjamin III *lawyer, educator*
Doggrell, Henry Patton *lawyer*
Goldsmith, Harry Louis *lawyer*
Haltom, William H. *lawyer*
Harvey, Albert C. *lawyer*
Heiter, Matthew Stephen *lawyer*
Jackson, Thomas Francis III *lawyer*
Johnson, Harry A. III *lawyer, finance company executive*
Kustoff, David F. *prosecutor*
Ledbetter, Paul Mark *lawyer, writer*
Manire, James McDonnell *lawyer*
Masterson, Kenneth Rhodes *lawyer*
McDaniel, A. Stephen *lawyer*
McLean, Robert Alexander *lawyer*
Morgan, Colby Shannon, Jr. *lawyer*
Noel, Randall Deane *lawyer*
Norris, Charles Head *lawyer, manufacturing executive*
Patton, Charles Henry *lawyer, educator*
Pope, Thaddeus Mason *law educator*
Raines, Jim Neal *lawyer*
Rice, George Lawrence, III, (Larry) *lawyer*
Russell, James Franklin *lawyer*
Rutledge, Roger Keith *lawyer*
Scroggs, Larry Kenneth *lawyer, state legislator*
Smith, Maura Abeln *lawyer, paper company executive*
Steinhauer, Gillian *lawyer*
Tate, Stonewall Shepherd *lawyer*
Terry, Joseph Ray, Jr. *retired lawyer*
Trammell, Bradley Ellis *lawyer*
White, Nicholas L. *law educator*
Willet, John *lawyer*
Winchester, Richard Lee, Jr. *lawyer*

Nashville
Barfield, Henry Lee, II, *lawyer*
Barnett, Bruce Edwin *lawyer*
Barrett, George Edward *lawyer*
Bass, James Orin, Sr. *lawyer*
Belton, Robert *law educator*
Blackstock, James Fielding *lawyer*
Blumstein, James Franklin *lawyer, educator, consultant*
Bostick, Charles Dent *retired lawyer*
Bramlett, Paul Kent *lawyer*
Cantrell, Luther E., Jr. *lawyer*
Carr, Davis Haden *lawyer*
Cerjan, Martin *law librarian, educator, dean*
Cobb, Stephen A. *lawyer*
Cohen, William Mark *lawyer*
Conner, Lewis Homer, Jr. *lawyer*
Cooney, Charles Hayes *lawyer*
Covington, Robert Newman *law educator*
Cowart, Richard G. *lawyer*
Dennen, Keith Cameron *lawyer*
Fuchs, Mark *lawyer*
Gannon, John Sexton *lawyer, management consultant, arbitrator, mediator*
Gillmor, John Edward *lawyer*
Goodman, Joe M. *lawyer*
Griffith, James Leigh *lawyer*
Grimes, R. Dale *lawyer*
Habermann, Ted Richard *lawyer*
Hart, Richard Banner *lawyer*
Jakes, William Bryan III *lawyer*
King, David A. *lawyer*
Kohan, Betsy Burns *lawyer*
Ledyard, Robins Heard *lawyer*
Lodge, J. Richard *lawyer*
Lyon, Philip Kirkland *lawyer*
Martin, Henry Alan *public defender*
May, Joseph Leserman (Jack May) *retired lawyer*
Mayden, Barbara Mendel *lawyer*
McDonald, Michael Eugene *lawyer, educator, clergyman*
Quinlan, J(oseph) Michael *lawyer*
Ramsaur, Allan Fields *legal association administrator, lobbyist*
Schreiber, Kurt Gilbert *lawyer*
Sims, Wilson *lawyer*
Soltman, Ronald P. *lawyer*
Summers, Paul G. *lawyer, former state attorney general*
Thomas, Randall Stuart *lawyer, educator*
Thomas, Robert Paige *lawyer*
Torrey, Claudia Olivia *lawyer*
Tuke, Robert Dudley *lawyer, educator*
Viscusi, W(illiam) Gregory Kip *law and economics educator*
Waterman, Robert A. *lawyer*
Winstead, George Alvis *law librarian, director*
Yuspeh, Alan Ralph *lawyer, health company executive*

Newport
Bell, John Alton *lawyer, judge*
Myers, John William *lawyer*

Pigeon Forge
Catron, Stephen Barnard *lawyer, real estate developer, director*

Powell
Hyman, Roger David *lawyer*

Sevierville
Waters, John B. *lawyer*

Soddy Daisy
Leitner, Paul Revere *lawyer*

Springfield
Wilks, Larry Dean *lawyer*

Trenton
Smith, Jeffrey A. *lawyer*

Waverly
Peeler, William James *lawyer*

TEXAS

Abilene
Boone, Billy Warren *lawyer, retired judge*
Robinson, Vianei Lopez *lawyer*
Sartain, James Edward *lawyer*
Suttle, Stephen Hungate *lawyer*
Trimble, Celia Denise *lawyer*

Addison
Beck, Charles Wesley, II, *lawyer*
Epstein, Brooke C. *lawyer*
Mackie, Landon Keller *lawyer*
McKinney, Melissa A. *lawyer*
Wolf, Brandon B. *lawyer*
Zientz, Michael Wayne *lawyer*

Amarillo
Burnette, Susan Lynn *lawyer*
Madden, Wales Hendrix, Jr. *lawyer*

Arlington
Goodman, Toby Ray *lawyer*
Jensen, John Robert *lawyer*
Malorzo, Thomas Vincent *lawyer*
Pierson, Grey *lawyer*
Rosenberry, William Kenneth *lawyer, educator*
Weekley, Frederick Clay, Jr. *lawyer*

Austin
Anderson, David Arnold *law educator*
Baker, Mark Bruce *lawyer, educator*
Blunck, Tedde *lawyer, engineer, engineering company executive*
Bobbitt, Philip Chase *law educator, writer*
Bode, Joyce Scruggs *lawyer*
Botsford, David L. *lawyer*
Brown, Frank Beverly, IV, *lawyer*
Buell, Samuel W. *law educator, lawyer*
Burgess, Kevin L. *lawyer*
Byars, Samuel D. *lawyer*
Cantú, Norma V. *law educator, former federal official*
Carson, Loftus C., II, *law educator*
Clark, Pat English *lawyer*
Cole, Scott L. *lawyer*
Cook, J(ohn) Rowland *lawyer*
Cook, Michael L. *lawyer*
Cruz, Ted *lawyer*
Cunningham, Judy Marie *lawyer*
Davis, Creswell Dean *lawyer, consultant*
Davis, Morris *lawyer*
Davis, Robert Larry *lawyer*
Demond, Walter Eugene *lawyer*
Dickie, Martha S. *lawyer*
Dyer, Cromwell Adair, Jr. *lawyer, legal association administrator*
Ewell, Gary L. *lawyer*
Feazell, Vic *lawyer*
Fernandes, Edward F. *lawyer*
Forbath, William E. *law educator*
Gallerano, Andrew John *lawyer*
Gangstad, John Erik *lawyer*
Gary, James M. *lawyer*
Gehm, Amy K. *lawyer*
Giblin, Pamela M. *lawyer*
Golemon, Ronald Kinnan *lawyer*
Goode, Steven *law educator*
Graglia, Lino Anthony *lawyer, educator*
Graham, Seldon Bain, Jr. *lawyer, engineer*
Greig, Brian Strother *lawyer*
Harrison, Richard Wayne *lawyer*
Helman, Stephen Jody *lawyer*
Henderson, George Ervin *lawyer*
Hernandez, Mack Ray *lawyer*
Hopkins, Bill Everitt *lawyer*
Ikard, Frank Neville, Jr. *lawyer*
Janes, Brandon Chaison *lawyer*
Jansen, Donald Orville *lawyer*
Jentz, Gaylord Adair *law educator*
Keys, Jerry Malcom *lawyer, educator*
Killough, David E. *lawyer*
Kirk, Terrence *lawyer*
Knepp, Christopher A. *lawyer*
Lochridge, Lloyd Pampell, Jr. *lawyer*
Lochridge, Patton G. *lawyer*
Lorenz, Ted R. *lawyer*
Marshall, Richard Paul, Jr. *lawyer*
McCullough, Frank Witcher III *lawyer*
McKetta, John J. III *lawyer*
Mersky, Roy Martin *legal association administrator, educator*
Morton, R. Steven *lawyer*
Moss, Bill Ralph *lawyer*
Moss, Logan Vansen *lawyer*
Mullenix, Linda Susan *law educator*
Osborne, Duncan Elliott *lawyer*
Otto, Byron Leonard *retired lawyer, state agency administrator*
Parrish, William M. *lawyer*
Pena, Richard *lawyer*
Phillips, Thomas Royal *lawyer, former state supreme court chief justice*
Pirkey, Louis Thomas *lawyer*
Roan, Forrest Calvin, Jr. *lawyer*
Robertson, Damon D. *lawyer*
Sampson, John J. *law educator*
Schulze, Eric William *lawyer*
Schuring, Elizabeth *lawyer*
Schuurman, Willem Gerhard *lawyer*
Schwartz, Aaron Robert *lawyer, former state legislator*
Shapiro, David L. *lawyer*
Stephen, John Erle *lawyer, consultant*
Strauser, Robert Wayne *lawyer*
Sturley, Michael F. *law educator*
Stutts, William Floyd, Jr. *lawyer, educator*
Sutton, John F., Jr. *lawyer, educator, dean*
Temple, Larry Eugene *lawyer*
Torres, Gerald *law educator*
Torres, John D. *lawyer*
Tottenham, Terry Oliver *lawyer*
Townsend, Justin C. *lawyer*
Volk, William R. *lawyer*
Watkins, Joe Bill *lawyer*
Weddington, Sarah Ragle *lawyer, educator*
Weinberg, Louise *law educator, writer*
Weintraub, Russell Jay *lawyer, educator*
Wentworth, Earl Jeffrey *lawyer, realtor, state legislator*
West, Royce *lawyer, state legislator*
Westbrook, Jay Lawrence *law educator*
Winters, Sam *lawyer*
Wohlers, Teresa Dahmus *lawyer*
Wood, Donald F. *lawyer*

Beaumont
Black, Robert Allen *lawyer*
Dowell, James Dale *lawyer*
Dryden, Woodson E. *lawyer*
Scofield, Louis M., Jr. *lawyer*

Bellaire
Jacobus, Charles Joseph *lawyer, title company executive, writer*
Soffar, William Douglas *lawyer*

Boerne
Vaughan, Edward Gibson *lawyer*

Borger
Edmonds, Thomas Leon *lawyer, management consultant*

Brenham
Moorman, Richard Hal, IV, *lawyer*

Brownsville
Fleming, Tommy Wayne *lawyer*
Ray, Mary Louise Ryan *lawyer*
Rodriguez, Eduardo Roberto *lawyer*
Weisfeld, Sheldon *lawyer*

Brownwood
Bell, William Woodward *lawyer*

Bryan
Miller, Thomas Eugene *lawyer, writer*

Bullard
Mote, Clyde A *lawyer*

Carrollton
Riggs, Arthur Jordy *retired lawyer*

Cleburne
MacLean, John Ronald *lawyer*

Cleveland
Campbell, Selaura Joy *lawyer*

College Station
Godfrey, Cullen Michael *lawyer, academic administrator*

Colleyville
Whittenberg, Ira Orville *lawyer*

Conroe
Bowersox, Thomas H. *lawyer*
Fleming, Michael Paul *lawyer*

Corpus Christi
Branscomb, Harvie, Jr. *lawyer*
Coover, Ann E. *lawyer*
Fancher, Rick *lawyer*
Klein, Melvyn Norman *lawyer, investment executive*
Miller, Carroll Gerard, Jr., (Gerry Miller) *lawyer*
Potter, Allan L. *lawyer*
Stukenberg, Michael Wesley *lawyer*

Corsicana
McSpadden, Jody Sodd *lawyer*

Daingerfield
Bruster, Anthony K. *lawyer*
Smith, D. Neil *lawyer*

Dallas
Acker, Rodney *lawyer*
Ackerman, Deborah *lawyer*
Adams, Richard Lloyd *lawyer*
Anderson, Barbara McComas *lawyer*
Anderson, E. Karl *lawyer*
Anglin, Michael Williams *lawyer*
Ashby, Danny S. *lawyer*
Askew, Kim Juanita *lawyer*
Babcock, Charles Lynde, IV, *lawyer*
Baggett, Steven Ray *lawyer*
Baggett, W. Mike *lawyer*
Bangs, Nelson A. (Tony Bangs) *lawyer*
Barbour, David A. *lawyer*
Baron, Frederick M. *lawyer*
Becker, Jeffrey M. *lawyer*
Benkowitz, Kevan I. *lawyer*
Bergner, John F. *lawyer*
Beuttenmuller, Rudolf William *lawyer*
Bickel, John W., II, *lawyer*
Biermacher, Kenneth Wayne *lawyer*
Birkeland, Bryan Collier *lawyer*
Bliss, Robert Harms *lawyer*
Blount, Charles William III *lawyer*
Boone, Michael Mauldin *lawyer*
Brainin, Stacy L. *lawyer*
Bramblett, George, Jr. *lawyer*
Brin, Royal Henry, Jr. *lawyer*
Bristol, Murray L. *lawyer*
Bromberg, Alan Robert *lawyer, educator*
Bromberg, John E. *lawyer*
Brooker, Chip *lawyer*
Brooks, Ben A. *lawyer*
Budner, Craig W. *lawyer*
Bumpas, Stuart Maryman *lawyer*
Burke, Carla Michelle *lawyer*
Burke, William Temple, Jr. *lawyer*
Burns, Sandra *lawyer, educator*
Cain, David H. *lawyer, former state legislator*
Caldwell, Bradley W. *lawyer*
Campbell, David *lawyer, utilities executive*
Canada, W. Ralph, Jr. *lawyer*
Cantrill, Thomas H. *lawyer*
Casada, Hilaree A. *lawyer*
Case, Thomas Louis *lawyer*
Clancy, Denyse Finn *lawyer*
Clark, Robert Murel, Jr. *lawyer*
Clements, Jerry K. *lawyer*
Cloutman, Edward Bradbury III *lawyer*
Coggins, Paul Edward, Jr. *lawyer*
Cohen, Harlan P. *lawyer*
Coleman, Robert Winston *lawyer*
Collins, Bruce W. *lawyer*
Colson, Randall Elwin *lawyer*
Conner, Terry W. *lawyer*
Copley, Edward Alvin *lawyer*
Cowan, Barry W. *lawyer*
Cowart, T(homas) David *lawyer*
Cowles, Jim E. *lawyer*
Crain, Russell Jon *lawyer*
Creel, Luther Edward III *lawyer*
Crichton, Thomas, IV, *lawyer*
Crotty, Robert Bell *retired lawyer*
Crowley, James Worthington *retired lawyer, investor, financial consultant*
Daly, Gail M. *law librarian, educator, dean*
Davis, Clarice McDonald *lawyer*
Davis, Joe A. *lawyer*
Davis, Robert Edwin *lawyer*
Dawson, William B. *lawyer*
Deckelman, William L., Jr. *lawyer*
Demarest, Sylvia M. *lawyer*
Doke, Marshall J., Jr. *lawyer*
Dorrill, Jeff W. *lawyer*
Drapkin, Dennis B. *lawyer*
Duddlesten, Kevin M. *lawyer*
Dutton, Diana Cheryl *lawyer*
Dyess, Bobby Dale *lawyer*
Eaton, Michael William *lawyer, educator*
Eichman, John C. *lawyer*
Ellis, Alfred Wright (Al Ellis) *lawyer*
Emery, Herschell Gene *lawyer*
Esserman, Sander L. *lawyer*
Estep, Robert Lloyd *lawyer*
Evans, Roger *lawyer*
Everbach, Otto George *lawyer*
Falk, Robert Hardy *lawyer*
Fankhauser, Mark A. *lawyer*
Fanning, Barry Hedges *lawyer*
Farquhar, Robert Michael *lawyer*
Feld, Alan David *lawyer*
Fenner, Suzan Ellen *lawyer*
Figari, Ernest Emil, Jr. *lawyer, educator*
Fijolek, Richard M. *lawyer*
Fillmore, Robert M. *lawyer*
Fishman, Edward Marc *lawyer*
Flanagan, Christie Stephen *lawyer*
Flegle, Jim L. *lawyer*
Flood, Joan Moore *paralegal*
Forshey, Michael S. *lawyer*
Fortado, Michael George *lawyer*
Fox, Stephen E. *lawyer*
Franze, Laura Marie *lawyer*
Frazier, Charles T., Jr. *lawyer*
Freling, Richard Alan *lawyer*
French, Joseph Jordan, Jr. *lawyer*
Freytag, Sharon Nelson *lawyer*
Frieling, Scott R. *lawyer*
Frisbie, Curtis Lynn, Jr. *lawyer*
Fuller, Kenneth D. *lawyer*
Fuller, Kevin Rice *lawyer*
Galvin, Charles O'Neill *retired law educator*
Gardner, Stephen Henry *lawyer*
Garner, Bryan Andrew *law educator, consultant, writer*
Garner, Daniel C. *lawyer*
Gerberding Cowart, Greta Elaine *lawyer*
Gilchrist, Henry *lawyer*
Girards, James Edward *lawyer*
Glancy, Walter John *lawyer*
Glendenning, Don Mark *lawyer*
Godwin, Donald Everett *lawyer*
Goodstein, Barnett Maurice *lawyer*
Goolsby, Bryan L. *lawyer*
Goolsby, Michelle P. *lawyer, food products executive*
Gores, Christopher Merrel *lawyer*
Goyne, Roderick A. *lawyer*
Greef, Charles E. (Stormy Greef) *lawyer*
Gregory, Louis P. *lawyer, gas industry executive*
Hale, Earl F., Jr. *lawyer*
Hammond, Herbert J. *lawyer, arbitrator, mediator*
Hartnett, Will Ford *lawyer*
Hartt, Grover III *lawyer*
Helfand, Marcy Caren *lawyer*
Henkel, Kathryn Gundy *lawyer*
Hennessy, Daniel Kraft *lawyer*
Henry, Vic Houston *lawyer*
Hensley, Noel M. B. *lawyer*
Hesse, Gregory Getty *lawyer*
Hicks, Marion Lawrence, Jr., (Larry Hicks) *lawyer*
Hinshaw, Chester John *lawyer*
Hirschman, Karen L. *lawyer*
Holmes, James Hill III *lawyer*
Hopkins, Michael B. *lawyer*
Hubach, Joseph F. *lawyer, electronics executive*
Huffman, Gregory Scott Combest *lawyer*
Hughes, Vester Thomas, Jr. *lawyer*
Humble, Monty Garfield *lawyer*
Hurwitz, Ann *lawyer*
Huston, Angela C. *lawyer*
Hutchison, Ray Ray (E. Ray) *lawyer*
Irwin, Ivan, Jr. *lawyer*
Jayson, Melinda Gayle *lawyer*
Jillson, Andrew E. *lawyer*
Johnson, James Joseph Scofield *lawyer, educator, writer, judge*
Johnston, Stephen C. *lawyer*
Jolas, Paul M. *lawyer, diversified financial services company executive*
Jones, James Alton *lawyer*
Jones, Lindy Don *lawyer*
Jordan, Charles C. *lawyer*
Jordan, William Davis *lawyer*
Jung, Peter Michael *lawyer*
Keithley, Bradford Gene *lawyer*
Kennedy, Marc J. *lawyer*
Kent, David Charles *lawyer*
King, Raymund Camilo *lawyer, physician*
Kinnebrew, Jackson Metcalfe *lawyer*
Kinzie, Jack L. *lawyer*
Kitner, David N. *lawyer*
Kneese, Kyle Calvin *lawyer*
Kneipper, Richard Keith *lawyer*
Knott, Jennifer W. *lawyer*
Kobdish, George Charles *lawyer*
Kober, John A. *lawyer*
Koning, Paul Matthew *lawyer*
Kryder, George M. III *lawyer*
Kuhn, Willis Evan, II, *lawyer, mediator*
Lacy, John Ford *retired lawyer*
Ladik, Steven M. *lawyer*
Lan, Donald Paul, Jr. *lawyer*
Leatherbury, Thomas Shawn *lawyer*
LeBlanc, Jennifer Dawn *lawyer*
Lee, Carl B. *lawyer*
Lee, George Terry, Jr. *lawyer*
Lesmes, Stephanie Brooks *lawyer*
Levin, Hervey Phillip *lawyer*
Levy, I. Richard *lawyer*
Lindley, Hamilton P. *lawyer*
Littlejohn, James R. *lawyer*
Long, Sarah Holley *lawyer*
Lowe, John Stanley *law educator*
Lowery, David J. *lawyer*
Makel, Larry A. *lawyer*
Malouf, Stephen Ferris *lawyer*
Mankoff, Ronald Morton *retired lawyer*
Manteuffel, Robert Lee *lawyer*
Mareiniss, Darren Peter *lawyer, physician*
Maris, Stephen S. *lawyer, educator*
Martin, Boe Willis *lawyer*
Mason, Thomas P. *lawyer*
Massman, Richard Allan *lawyer*
Mayo, Thomas William *law educator*
McAleenan, Donald F. *lawyer, construction executive*
McAtee, David Ray *lawyer*
McCombs, David Louis *lawyer*
McCormack, William Arthur *lawyer*
McCurley, Carl Michael *lawyer*
McCurley, Mary Johanna *lawyer*
McDonald, Michael Scott *lawyer*
McDowell, John Henry, Jr. *lawyer*
Mc Elhaney, John Hess *lawyer*
McGowan, Patrick Francis *lawyer*
McKnight, Joseph Webb *lawyer, educator, historian*
McKool, Mike, Jr. *lawyer*
McNamara, Lawrence John *lawyer*
McNamara, Martin Burr *lawyer, former gas industry executive*
McNeil, Barry *lawyer*
McWilliams, Mike C. *lawyer*
Melançon, Renée M. *lawyer*
Melsheimer, Thomas M. *lawyer*
Mendez, Michelle Annette *lawyer*
Micciche, Daniel John *lawyer*
Miers, Harriet Ellan *lawyer, former federal official*
Mighell, Kenneth John *lawyer*
Miller, Charles P. *lawyer*
Miller, Norman Richard *lawyer*
Miller, R. Terry *lawyer*
Mills, Jerry Woodrow *lawyer*
Mitchell, Patrick E. *lawyer*
Montgomery, Matthew L. *lawyer*
Montgomery, Will S. *lawyer*
Moore, Cheryl (Milkes) Jerome *lawyer*
Moore, Edward Warren *lawyer*
Mow, Robert Henry, Jr. *lawyer*
Mueller, Mark Christopher *lawyer*
Murphy, Kathryn J. *lawyer*
Musselman, P. Weston *lawyer*
Nassar, Susan D. *lawyer*
Nelson, Elaine Edwards *lawyer*
Nichols, Henry Louis *lawyer*
Nolan, John Michael *lawyer*
Orwig, Matthew Dane *lawyer, former prosecutor*
Panatier, Christopher J. *lawyer*
Payne, Brett H. *lawyer*
Pennington, Karen Harder *lawyer*
Perkins, Thomas P., Jr. *lawyer*
Peterson, Edward Adrian *lawyer*
Pew, John Glenn, Jr. *lawyer*
Phelan, Robin Eric *lawyer*
Pingree, Bruce Douglas *lawyer*
Pleasant, James Scott *lawyer*
Poole, David P. *lawyer, utilities executive*
Porter, J. Reid *lawyer*
Portman, Glenn Arthur *lawyer*
Powers, Timothy Eugene *lawyer*
Prather, Robert Charles, Sr. *lawyer*
Price, John Aley *lawyer*
Pruessner, David Morgan *lawyer*
Purnell, Maurice Eugene, Jr. *lawyer*
Raggio, Thomas Louis *lawyer*
Redman, Gary Lon, II, *lawyer*
Reid, Rust Endicott *lawyer*
Ribman, James W. *lawyer*
Rice, John S. *lawyer*
Riddle, Michael Lee *lawyer*
Ringle, Brett Adelbert *lawyer, oil and gas industry executive*
Roberts, Harry Morris, Jr. *lawyer*
Robison, Brian E. *lawyer*
Rodgers, John Hunter *lawyer*
Roper, Richard B. III *prosecutor*
Ryan, Dennis Neil *lawyer*
Samuel, Greg R. *lawyer*
Schaeffler, Georg *lawyer, manufacturing executive*
Schreiber, Howard E. *lawyer*
Schreiber, Sally Ann *lawyer*
Schwartz, Charles Morris *lawyer*
Scott, John Roland *business law educator*
Self, Scott W. *lawyer*
Selinger, Jerry Robin *lawyer*
Shank, Mark A. *lawyer*
Sharry, Janice Vyn *lawyer*
Shaw, Curtis S. *lawyer, chemicals executive*
Shepherd, Jon Glen *lawyer*
Simmons, Terry L. *lawyer*
Sims, William D., Jr. *lawyer*
Sinak, David Louis *lawyer*
Sloman, Marvin Sherk *lawyer*
Stalcup, Joe Alan *retired lawyer, dean*
Steinberg, Lawrence Edward *lawyer*
Stewart, Daniel Clark *lawyer*
Stewart, Kenneth L. *lawyer*
Stinnett, Mark Allan *lawyer*
Stockard, James Alfred *lawyer*
Storey, Charles Porter *lawyer*
Strock, William C. *lawyer*
Szuwalski, Andre Michael *lawyer*
Tapscott, William Ken, Jr. *lawyer*
Templin, Donald C. *lawyer*
Thomson, Basil Henry, Jr. *lawyer*
Thomson, Roger F. *lawyer*
Tompkins, Alan W. *lawyer*
True, Roy Joe *lawyer*
Tubb, James Clarence *lawyer*
Turley, Linda *lawyer*
Udashen, Robert Nathan *lawyer*
Urbanowicz, E(ugene) Peter, (Jr.) *lawyer*
Vanden Eykel, Ike *lawyer*
Veach, Robert Raymond, Jr. *lawyer*
Vetter, James George, Jr. *lawyer*
Villareal, Patricia J. *lawyer*
Villarreal, Christie M. *lawyer*
Voyles, Robb Lawrence *lawyer*
Walkowiak, Vincent Steven *lawyer*
Wallace, Anderson, Jr. *lawyer, educator*
Walsh, David M., IV, *lawyer*
Warman, Lynnette R. *lawyer*
Watkins, Craig *prosecutor*
Watler, Paul C. *lawyer*
Welch, Gerald Thomas *lawyer, electrical engineer*
Werbner, Mark S. *lawyer*
Westfall, Constance Courtney *lawyer*
Whitaker, Elizabeth D. *lawyer*
White, James Richard *lawyer*
Wiegand, Robert C. *lawyer*
Will, Clark Bradford *lawyer*
Willingham, Clark Suttles *lawyer*
Wilson, Claude Raymond, Jr. *lawyer*
Wilson, Jonathan C. *lawyer*
Wilson, Robert E. *lawyer*
Wilson, Taylor *lawyer*
Witte, Robert Jay *lawyer*
Wolin, Robert Everett *lawyer*
Woram, Brian J. *lawyer, construction executive*
Wortley, Michael D. *lawyer*
Wright, Alan *lawyer*
Wu, Kathleen J. *lawyer*
Yaeger, Evelyn Ann *lawyer*
Yang, Emeline *lawyer*
Young, Barney Thornton *lawyer*
Young, William D. *lawyer*
Zahn, Donald Jack *lawyer*

Decatur
Boyd, Derrick S. *lawyer*

Denton
Gabriel, Eberhard John *lawyer, bank executive*
Lawhon, John III *lawyer, retired county official*

Dickinson
Neves, Kerry Lane *lawyer*

Dripping Springs
Baker, III, Rex Gavin *lawyer, educator*

Edinburg
Carrera, Victor Manuel *lawyer*

El Paso
Barfield, Lowry *lawyer*
Cox, Sanford Curtis, Jr. *lawyer*
Cross, Clinton Ferguson *lawyer*
Feuille, Richard Harlan *lawyer, director*
Gibson, Sidney Kay *retired lawyer*
Marshall, Richard Treeger *lawyer*
Morton, Fred J. *lawyer*
Smith, Tad Randolph *lawyer*
Yetter, Richard *lawyer*

Eldorado
Kosub, James Albert *lawyer*

Ennis
Swanson, Wallace Martin *lawyer*

Euless
Paran, Mark Lloyd *retired lawyer*

Farmers Branch
Blachly, Jack Lee *lawyer*

Flower Mound
Hunt, David Ford *lawyer*

Fort Worth
Berenson, William Keith *lawyer*
Brown, C. Harold *lawyer*
Brown, Richard Lee *lawyer*
Chalk, John Allen, Sr. *lawyer*
Crumley, John Walter *lawyer*
Dean, Beale *lawyer*
Elkins-Elliott, Kay *law educator*
Elliott, Frank Wallace *lawyer, educator*
Friedman, Walker C. *lawyer*
Goldberg, David *lawyer, retail executive*
Hall, Randy Jarvis *lawyer*
Harbour, Ted Ira *lawyer, construction executi*
Harcrow, Edward Earl *lawyer*
Hart, John Clifton *lawyer*
Hoferer, Paul R. *lawyer, rail transportation executive*
Ingram, Denny Ouzts, Jr. *lawyer, educator*
Keith, Courtney S. *lawyer*
Kelly, Dee J. *lawyer*
Kelly, Raymond Boone III *lawyer*
Larimore, Tom L. *lawyer*
Mack, Theodore *lawyer*
McConnell, Michael Arthur *lawyer*
McDonald, Frank G. *lawyer, energy executive*
Miller, Kleber C. *lawyer*
Minton, Jerry Davis *lawyer, consultant, retire banker*
Munn, Cecil Edwin *lawyer*
Quinn, Francis Xavier *arbitrator, mediator, writer, law educator*
Searcy, Marshall Mayes, Jr. *lawyer*
Shade, Joseph *law educator*
Shannon, Joe, Jr. *lawyer*
Sharpe, James Shelby *lawyer*
Shupe, Dwight A. (Ike) *lawyer*
Streck, Frederick Louis III *lawyer*
Tillman, Massie Monroe *mediator, arbitrator, gallery owner, retired judge*
Wallace, R. H., Jr. *lawyer*
Wallach, David Michael *lawyer*
Watson, Robert Francis *lawyer*
West, Robert Grady *lawyer*

Friendswood
Youngdahl, Jay Thomas *lawyer*

Galveston
Caldwell, Garnett Ernest *lawyer*
O'Toole, Austin Martin *lawyer, mediator*
Salch, Steven Charles *lawyer, mediator, arbitrator*
Vie, George William III *lawyer*

Garland
Irby, Holt *lawyer*

Georgetown
Bryce, William Delf *lawyer*
Olson, Dean A. *lawyer*

Graham
Richie, Boyd Lynn *lawyer*

Grapevine
Franks, Jon Michael *lawyer, mediator*

Harlingen
Pope, William L. *lawyer, judge*

Heath
Kolodey, Fred James *lawyer*

Henderson
Adkison, Ron *lawyer*

Highland Village
Lawrence, William Clarence *lawyer, mediato*

Houston
Addison, Linda Leuchter *lawyer, writer, commentator, columnist*
Adrogué, Sofia *lawyer*
Aguirre, Sarah K. *lawyer*
Allen, Frank Clinton, Jr. *lawyer, chemical engineer*
Allender, John Roland *lawyer*
Amann, Leslie Kiefer *lawyer, educator*
Amdur, Arthur R. *lawyer*
Anani, Tarig *lawyer*
Anderson, Doris Ehlinger *lawyer*
Anderson, Eric Severin *lawyer*
Arnot, William G. III *lawyer*
Asmus, David F. *lawyer*
Asselin, Heather E. *lawyer*
Atlas, Scott J. *lawyer*
Ayers, Howard T. *lawyer*
Bachmann, Richard H. *lawyer, energy execut*
Backus, Marcia Ellen *lawyer*
Baker, C. Mark *lawyer*
Baker, James Addison, III, (Jim Baker) *lawye former secretary of state*
Baker, Robert W. *lawyer*
Ballanfant, Richard Burton *lawyer*
Bankhead, Sherry L. *lawyer*
Barbour, Larry Gregory *lawyer*
Bargfrede, James Allen *lawyer*
Barnett, Edward William *lawyer*
Barton, Sarah Muriel *lawyer*
Bech, Douglas York *retired lawyer, resort executive*
Bechtol, J. Currie *lawyer, oil industry executi*

, Martin Douglas *lawyer*
i, Lawrence Lee *lawyer*
Amie G. *lawyer*
David Howard *lawyer*
Evelyn Hudson *lawyer*
, Bruce R. *lawyer*
shear, A. T., Jr. *lawyer*
, John Lloyd *lawyer*
ett, J. Kevin *lawyer*
vare, Margaret A. *lawyer*
, Maria Wyckoff *lawyer*
, Richard Roland *lawyer*
es, David Manning *lawyer*
on, Gay Creswell, Jr. *retired lawyer*
ky, Donald W. *lawyer*
on, John Soles *lawyer, investor*
ngham, Edwin John III *lawyer*
ey, Vincent H. *lawyer*
, Voris Reagan *mediator, arbitrator, retired*
vyer
Brent Lawrence *lawyer, judge*
rt, David Lee *lawyer*
an, Darryl Michael *lawyer*
, David Alan *lawyer*
n, Joseph Randolph *lawyer*
William John *lawyer*
niss, John Trigg *lawyer*
, Michael Douglas *lawyer*
vell, Richard H. *lawyer*
ur, Matthew W. *lawyer*
in, Dana A. *lawyer*
Edward A. *lawyer*
r, John Francis, II, *lawyer*
r, John Loyd *lawyer*
ez, Rueben Charles *lawyer*
ell, William Howard *lawyer*
dler, Richard E., Jr. *lawyer*
man, Cynthia B. *lawyer*
ez, J. Anthony *lawyer*
vens, Joseph D. *lawyer*
e, Douglas E. *lawyer*
e, Robert Logan *lawyer*
, Lawrence Hubert *lawyer*
ran, Fielding B. III *lawyer*
lan, Kelly Jack *lawyer*
ert, Kevin LeRoy *lawyer*
man, Gregory S. *lawyer*
, Randolph C. *lawyer*
ngs, Chris D. *lawyer*
on, Michael William *lawyer*
en, Heather Marie *lawyer*
elison, Albert Otto, Jr., (Bert Cornelison)
vyer
James Talley *lawyer*
, Alan Rau, Jr. *lawyer, oil industry*
ecutive
on, Gregory Paul *lawyer*
ningham, Tom Alan *lawyer*
eris, Thad Thano *lawyer*
rche, Douglas D. *lawyer*
Jonathan S. *lawyer*
eurin, George Michael, Jr., (Mike DeGeurin)
vyer
eurin, Mike *lawyer*
uerin, Dick *lawyer*
Valle, Teresa Jones *lawyer*
ent, James Alderson, Jr. *lawyer*
in, Francis James *lawyer*
, Joseph Carl *lawyer*
ard, Michael E. *lawyer*
ard, Stephen C. *lawyer*
, Jeff C. *lawyer*
nelly, Rosemarie *lawyer*
glas, James Matthew *law educator, dean*
glass, John Jay *lawyer, educator*
nheller, Anthony D. (Andy) *lawyer*
lop, Fred Hurston *lawyer*
es, Osborne Jefferson III *lawyer*
hardt, William Rudolf III *lawyer*
nd, Gary Wayne *lawyer*
errand, Kenneth G. *lawyer, educator*
nyer, Michael Martin *lawyer*
ank, J. Thomas *lawyer*
nthold, Frances Tarlton *lawyer*
er, Wendy Mineau *lawyer*
sworth, T. Brooke *lawyer*
h, Michael Paul *lawyer*
ung, Richard Denis *lawyer*
l, Thomas W., Jr. *lawyer*
l III, Don D. *lawyer*
er, Charles Crawford *lawyer, educator*
enweider, Donn Charles *lawyer*
non, Stewart Walter *lawyer*
vin, Kerry A. *lawyer, chemicals executive*
es, Stephen Frye *lawyer, oil industry*
ecutive
achis, George Matthew *lawyer*
son, Rex Hilton *lawyer*
oert, Keith Thomas *lawyer, consultant*
dman, Nathan Carliner *lawyer, educator*
aynor, Francis James *lawyer*
ade, Coralyn *lawyer*
edman, Barry Michael *lawyer*
ce, James Martin, Jr. *lawyer*
ving, Richard John *law educator*
y, Robert F., Jr. *lawyer*
enberg, Angela Barmby *lawyer*
essberg, Marc Elias *lawyer*
est, Floyd Emory, Jr. *lawyer*
nter, Joseph Clifford III *lawyer*
l, Charles Washington *lawyer*
nel, Douglas E. *lawyer*
per, A(lfred) J(ohn), II, *lawyer*
rington, Bruce Michael *lawyer, investor*
ris, Warren Wayne *lawyer*
rtrick, Janice Kay *lawyer*
vin, David Tarleton *lawyer*
wes, Clay Erik *lawyer*
ynes, Richard (Racehorse Haynes) *lawyer*
eg, Peggy A. *lawyer, former gas industry*
xecutive
nrich, Randall Wayne *lawyer*
witt, Lester L. *lawyer*
gins, Ryan K. *lawyer*
ton, Paula Weems *lawyer*
vinka, Paul Thomas *lawyer*
g, Matthew *lawyer*

Hollingsworth, Derek S. *lawyer*
Hollingsworth, Lara Hudgins *lawyer*
Holloway, Gordon Arthur *lawyer*
Hollyfield, John Scoggins *lawyer*
Holstead, John Burnham *retired lawyer*
Horrigan, Joseph Stewart *lawyer*
Horton, Donald J. *lawyer*
Hoyt, Mont Powell *lawyer*
Hudson, Franklin *lawyer, real estate developer*
Hudspeth, Chalmers Mac *lawyer, educator*
Hull, Robert Joe *lawyer*
Hunsaker, Barry, Jr. *lawyer*
Hurley, R. Bruce *lawyer*
Irvin, Michael P. *lawyer*
Ivey, Jack Todd *lawyer*
Jacobs, Tonya A. *lawyer*
Jamail, Joseph Dahr, Jr. *lawyer*
Jeske, Charles Matthew *lawyer*
Jewell, Robert V. *lawyer*
Jines, Michael L. *lawyer, energy executive*
Johnson, Arnold J. *lawyer, energy executive*
Joiner, Jamie A. *lawyer*
Jones, Frank Griffith *lawyer*
Jordan, Charles Milton *lawyer*
Jordan, W. Carl *lawyer*
Kaplan, Lee Landa *lawyer*
Kay, Joel Phillip *lawyer*
Kelly, Hugh Rice *lawyer, retired energy executive*
Kelly, T. Mark *lawyer*
Kelly, William Franklin, Jr. *lawyer*
Kennedy, John Edward *lawyer*
Ketchand, Robert Lee *lawyer*
Kline, Allen Haber, Jr. *lawyer*
Koenig, Rodney Curtis *lawyer, rancher*
Kratochvil, L(ouis) Glen *lawyer*
Krebs, Arno William, Jr. *lawyer*
Krieger, Paul Edward *lawyer*
Kristiansen, Eric W. *lawyer*
Kruse, Layne E. *lawyer*
Lacy, Terri *lawyer*
LaFuze, William L. *lawyer*
Lake, Kathleen Cooper *lawyer*
Lannie, Paul Anthony *lawyer, energy executive*
Larkin, Lee Roy *retired lawyer*
Lassetter, Scott D. *lawyer*
Lemmer, William C. *lawyer*
Lewis, Chip *lawyer*
Lewis, Kevin Paul *lawyer*
Liberato, Lynne *lawyer*
Listengart, Joseph *lawyer, energy executive*
Locke, Gene L. *lawyer*
Looser, William Gregory *lawyer*
Lopez, David Tiburcio *lawyer, arbitrator, mediator, educator*
Lott, Marley *lawyer*
Love, Scott Anthony *lawyer*
Lowenberg, Michael J. *lawyer*
Lynch, John F. *lawyer*
Mallett, Edward A. *lawyer*
Marlow, Orval Lee, II, *lawyer*
Marston, Edgar Jean III *lawyer*
Martin, J. Clark *lawyer*
Martin, Jay Griffith *lawyer*
Martin, Paul Edward *lawyer*
Mason, Dwayne L. *lawyer*
Massad, Stephen Albert *lawyer*
Mathers, Paula Janecek *lawyer*
Mattox, Sharon M. *lawyer*
McCarter, Louis Eugene *lawyer*
McClure, Daniel M. *lawyer*
McClure, Jeffrey B. *lawyer*
McCreary, Frank E. III *lawyer*
McDaniel, Jarrel Dave *lawyer*
McFall, Donald Beury *lawyer*
McFarland, Marcie Allred *lawyer*
McLeod, Chanse L. *lawyer*
McQuarrie, Claude Monroe III *lawyer*
Melton, Stephen Reid *lawyer*
Miller, Barry Rixmann *lawyer*
Miller, Gary C. *lawyer*
Minor, Sterling Arthur *lawyer*
Moehlman, Michael Scott *lawyer*
Mohan, Sameer Vijay *lawyer*
Moncure, John Lewis *lawyer*
Moore, Tim *lawyer*
Morgan, Richard Greer *lawyer*
Moroney, Linda L.S. (Muffie) *lawyer, educator*
Moya, Olga Lydia *law educator*
Murphy, Ewell Edward, Jr. *lawyer*
Nacol, Mae *lawyer*
Nathan, Arthur M. *lawyer*
Nations, Howard Lynn *lawyer*
Nelson, Joelle Grace Kenney *lawyer*
Neslage, John E. *lawyer*
Nickens, Jacks Clarence *lawyer*
Niebruegge, Michael E. *lawyer*
Nolen, Roy Lemuel *retired lawyer*
Nugent, Paul C. *lawyer*
Oldham, Darius Dudley *lawyer*
O'Quinn, John M. *lawyer*
Ostendorf, Lance Stephen *lawyer, financial consultant, educator*
Osterberg, Edward Charles, Jr. *lawyer*
Owens, Betty Ruth *lawyer*
Pannill, William Presley *lawyer*
Pate, Stephen Patrick *lawyer*
Pearson, Michael P. *lawyer*
Pector, Michelle D. *lawyer*
Perich, Thomas J. *lawyer*
Peterson, Terry Norris *lawyer*
Pierce, Frank Powell *lawyer, judge*
Pierce, Jesse R. *lawyer*
Pilibosian, Michele Mason *lawyer*
Pitts, Gary Benjamin *lawyer*
Plaeger, Frederick Joseph, II, *lawyer*
Port, P. Allan *lawyer*
Porter, Thomas William III *lawyer*
Pravel, Bernarr Roe *lawyer*
Pugh, William Whitmell Hill III *lawyer*
Raley, John Wesley III *lawyer*
Ramsey, Michael W. *lawyer*
Rapp, Robert David *lawyer*
Ray, Hugh Massey, Jr. *lawyer*
Ray, Hugh Massey III *lawyer*
Reasoner, Barrett Hodges *lawyer*
Reasoner, Harry Max *lawyer*

Rettig, Dwight W. *lawyer*
Rider, Roger Alan *lawyer*
Roach, Robert Michael, Jr., (Randy) *lawyer*
Robin, Alan Jay *lawyer*
Rommel, A. Ross, Jr. *lawyer*
Rosenthal, Gary L. *lawyer*
Rowland, Robert Alexander III *lawyer*
Rozzell, Scott Ellis *lawyer, energy executive*
Runnels, David G. *lawyer*
Rustay, Jennifer Beth *lawyer*
Ryan, Jason Michael *lawyer*
Ryan, Stephen M. *lawyer*
Ryan, Thomas William *lawyer*
Ryan, Vince *lawyer*
Sales, James Bohus *lawyer*
Sarne, Andrew J. *lawyer*
Saunders, Charles Albert *lawyer*
Schaffer, Randy *lawyer*
Schaffer, Stuart F. *lawyer*
Schechter, Arthur Louis *lawyer*
Schick, Robert Michael *lawyer*
Schwartz, Charles Walter *lawyer*
Schwartzel, Charles Boone *lawyer*
Schwind, William F., Jr. *lawyer, oil industry executive*
Seale, Robert Arthur *lawyer*
Secrest, George McCall, Jr., (Mac Secrest) *lawyer*
Segal, Steven E. *retired lawyer*
Shaddock, Carroll Sidney *lawyer*
Shannon, Margaret Barrett *lawyer*
Sheinfeld, Myron M. *lawyer, educator*
Shely, John B. *lawyer*
Sheppard, Ben H., Jr. *lawyer*
Shouse, August Edward *lawyer*
Shu, Glen *lawyer*
Siegler, Kelly R. *lawyer*
Silva, Eugene Joseph *lawyer*
Simmons, Stephen Judson *lawyer*
Sing, William Bender *lawyer*
Smith, Alison Leigh *lawyer*
Smith, E. Ashley *lawyer, insurance company executive*
Smith, Martha Lee *lawyer*
Smith, Walter John *lawyer*
Smith, William Ashley *lawyer, investment banker, energy executive*
Sonfield, Robert Leon, Jr. *lawyer*
Sorrels, Randall Owen *lawyer*
Spalding, Andrew Freeman *lawyer*
Stradley, William Jackson *lawyer*
Streng, William Paul *lawyer, educator*
Stryker, Steven Charles *lawyer*
Sullivan, Charles, Jr. *retired lawyer*
Sullivan, John F. III *lawyer*
Susman, Stephen Daily *lawyer*
Sutton, Neal S. *lawyer*
Swan, Michael K. *lawyer*
Swanson, Roy Joel *lawyer*
Swift, Robert J. *lawyer*
Sydow, Michael David *lawyer*
Szalkowski, Charles C. *lawyer*
Taheri, Marshall M. *lawyer, educator*
Tartt, Blake *lawyer*
Thomas, Byron Andrew *lawyer*
Thompson, Sandra Guerra *lawyer, educator*
Totten, Patricia A. *lawyer*
Touchy, Deborah K.P. *lawyer, accountant*
Townsend, Roger Dale *lawyer*
Tripp, Karen Bryant *lawyer*
Ulmer, Gregory C. *lawyer*
Van Fleet, George Allan *lawyer*
Van Kerrebrook, Mary Alice *lawyer*
Varner, David Eugene *lawyer*
Vassar, Claudia Sue Gee *lawyer*
Vaughan, Jack M. *lawyer*
Vogel, Jennifer L. *lawyer, air transportation executive*
Wagner, Leslie *lawyer*
Wall, Kenneth E., Jr. *lawyer*
Walters, Richard B. *lawyer*
Walton, Dan Gibson *lawyer*
Watson, John Allen *lawyer*
Webb, Jack M. *lawyer*
Weber, Fredric Alan *lawyer*
Weiner, Sanford Alan *lawyer*
Welsh, H. Ronald *lawyer*
Westby, Timothy Scott *lawyer, researcher*
Wheelan, R(ichelieu) E(dward) *lawyer*
Whilden, Robert Harral, Jr. *lawyer*
Whiting, Hugh Richard *lawyer*
Williams, Lowell Craig *lawyer, employee relations executive*
Williams, O'Banion III *lawyer*
Williamson, Peter David *lawyer*
Wittenbraker, Rick L. *lawyer, waste management executive*
Wood, Michael W *lawyer*
Woods, Ronald G. *lawyer, former prosecutor*
Worthington, William Albert III *lawyer*
Wray, Thomas Jefferson *lawyer*
Wynne, John Carlton *lawyer*
Wyrsch, Martha B. *lawyer, energy executive*
Yeates, Marie R. *lawyer*
Yetter, R. Paul *lawyer*
Yokubaitis, Roger T. *lawyer*
Young, Wayne C. *lawyer*
Zager, Stevgn Mark *lawyer*
Zeigler, Ann dePender *lawyer*

Humble
Pickle, George Edward *lawyer*

Hunt
Gambrell, James Bruton III *lawyer, educator*

Huntsville
Vaughn, Michael S. *law educator*

Irving
Beach, Charles Addison *lawyer*
Beasley, Mark V. *lawyer*
Berg, Mark S. *lawyer, oil industry executive*
Lang, Laura Smith *lawyer*
LaSala, Stephen R. *lawyer, oil industry executive*
Mc Cray, Ronald David *lawyer, health products executive*

Molay, Hilary S. *lawyer*
Shuff, Ronald F. *lawyer*
Sudbury, David Marshall *lawyer*
Wenetschlaeger, Patty Strader *lawyer*
Zisman, Barry Stuart *retired lawyer*

Katy
Vickery, Edward Downtain *lawyer*

Kilgore
Rorschach, Richard Gordon *lawyer*

La Marque
Disher, David Alan *lawyer, consultant*

League City
Dupuy, Christopher Michael *lawyer*

Lewisville
Hirschhorn, Robert B. *lawyer*

Llano
Wallis, Olney Gray *lawyer*

Longview
Harrison, Guy Newell *lawyer*
Welge, Jack Herman, Jr. *lawyer*

Lubbock
Beyer, Gerry Wayne *lawyer, educator*
Morton, Harvey Leon *lawyer*
Moseley, Patricia Ann *lawyer*
Phelan, Marilyn Elizabeth *law educator*
Purdom, Thomas James *lawyer*

Magnolia
Bradie, Peter Richard *lawyer, engineer*

Mc Kinney
Albano, Christine Grace *lawyer*
Dowdy, William Clarence, Jr. *retired lawyer*
Roessler, P. Dee *lawyer, educator, mediator, former judge*

Mcallen
Connors, Joseph Aloysius III *lawyer*

Midland
Abney, William K. *lawyer*
Estes, Andrew Harper *lawyer*
MacDonald, Leland Lloyd *lawyer*
Meyers, Alan Hoge *lawyer*
Rowe, Mary R. *lawyer*
Truitt, Robert Ralph, Jr. *lawyer*

Missouri City
Hodges, Jot Holiver, Jr. *retired lawyer, corporate financial executive*

Nacogdoches
Bias, Dana G. *lawyer*

New Braunfels
Benfield, Marion Wilson, Jr. *law educator*

North Richland Hills
Reed, Glenn W. *lawyer*

Odessa
Hendrick, Benard Calvin, VII, *lawyer*

Odonnell
Saleh, John *lawyer*

Plano
Altabef, Peter Anthony *lawyer*
Bober, Joanne L. *lawyer, retail executive*
Bonet, Frank Joseph *retired lawyer*
Gordon, Storrow Moss *lawyer, information technology executive*
Hurley, Rebecca *lawyer*
Korst, Christopher A. *lawyer, rental company executive*
Mondul, Donald David *patent lawyer*
Robertson, Richard L. *lawyer*
Shapiro, Todd D. *lawyer*

Pottsboro
Thomas, Ann Van Wynen *retired law educator*

Richardson
Austin, Ann Sheree *lawyer*
Conkel, Robert Dale *lawyer, consultant*
Martin, Richard Kelley *lawyer*
Olson, Dennis Oliver *lawyer*
Sowers, Wesley Hoyt *lawyer, management consultant*
Stoll, William Frederick, Jr. *lawyer*

Rockport
Porter, Charles Raleigh, Jr. *retired lawyer*

Rockwall
White, Todd William *lawyer, educator*

Round Rock
Tu, Lawrence P. *lawyer, computer company executive*

San Antonio
Armstrong, William Tucker III *lawyer*
Aycock, James J. *lawyer*
Barton, James Cary *lawyer*
Behrens, Kay S. *lawyer*
Bennett, Steven Alan *lawyer, insurance company executive*
Bettac, Robert Edward *lawyer*
Bowers, Kim *lawyer, energy executive*
Bramble, Ronald Lee *lawyer, consultant*
Branton, James LaVoy *lawyer*
Castleberry, James Newton, Jr. *retired law educator, dean*
Chasnoff, Barry A. *lawyer*
Cicconi, James William *lawyer, telecommunications industry executive*
Collins, Kevin Lloyd *lawyer*
Frigerio, Charles Straith *lawyer*

Golden, Stephen L. *lawyer*
Goldstein, Gerald H. *lawyer*
Guenther, Jack Egon *lawyer*
Hardy, Harvey Louchard *retired lawyer*
Henry, Peter York *lawyer, mediator*
Javore, Gary William *lawyer*
Labenz-Hough, Marlene *mediator*
Levin, Andrew W. *lawyer, communications executive*
Lutter, Charles William, Jr. *lawyer*
Maloney, Marynell *lawyer*
Moynihan, John Bignell *retired lawyer*
Parrish, Charles S. *lawyer, oil industry executive*
Patrick, Dane Herman *lawyer*
Perry, Robert Michael *lawyer, consultant, rancher*
Pfeiffer, Philip John *lawyer*
Pipkin, Marvin Grady *lawyer*
Pitluk, Ellen Eidelbach *lawyer, mediator*
Putman, (James) Michael *lawyer*
Reams, Bernard Dinsmore, Jr. *law educator*
Ruttenberg, Frank Z. *lawyer*
Sakai, Peter A. *lawyer*
Schlueter, David Arnold *law educator*
Schmutz, John Francis *lawyer*
Spears, Sally *lawyer*
Steen, John Thomas, Jr. *lawyer*
Sutton, Johnny Keane *prosecutor, lawyer*
Wallis, Ben Alton, Jr. *lawyer*
Watts, Mikal C. *lawyer*
Wells, Tullos *lawyer*
Welmaker, Forrest Nolan *lawyer*
Wheatley, Seagal V. *lawyer, legal association administrator*
Yates, Norris William, Jr. *lawyer*

Southlake
Schwarte, David A. *lawyer, travel company executive*

Spring
Farley, Andrew Newell *lawyer, consultant*

Sugar Land
Greer, Raymond White *lawyer*
Hitchcock, Bion Earl *lawyer*

Temple
Pickle, Jerry Richard *lawyer*

Texarkana
Peck, Leonard Warren, Jr. *lawyer*

The Woodlands
Benedetto, Anthony R. *religious mediator*
Bohannon, Paul M. *lawyer*
Hagerman, John David *lawyer, investment advisor*
Kalish, Bob *lawyer*
Reeves, Robert K. *lawyer, oil industry executive*
Ripley, Charlene A. *lawyer*
Stahl, Craig L. *lawyer*

Trinidad
Conant, Allah B., Jr. *lawyer*

Tyler
Alworth, Charles Wesley *lawyer, engineer*
Dacus, Deron R. *lawyer*
Ellis, Donald Lee *lawyer*
Hadden, Arthur Roby *lawyer, retired judge*
Hester, Sean W. *lawyer*
Patterson, Donald Ross *lawyer, educator*
Thames, E. Glenn, Jr. *lawyer*

Victoria
McKay, Robert Connally *lawyer*

Waco
Mc Swain, Angus Stewart, Jr. *retired law educator*
Morrison, Michael Dean *lawyer, law educator*
Page, Jack Randall *lawyer*
Quarles, Brandon *law librarian*
Smith, Cullen *lawyer*

Weatherford
King, Douglas Michael *lawyer, accountant*

Wichita Falls
Altman, William Kean *lawyer*

Wimberley
Brinsmade, Lyon Louis *retired lawyer*

Yoakum
Williams, Walter Waylon *lawyer, agricultural products supplier*

UTAH

Bountiful
Callister, Louis Henry, Jr. *lawyer*

Cedar City
Slack, Jeffery E *lawyer*

Logan
Daines, N. George *lawyer*
West, Stephen Allan *lawyer*

Manti
Petersen, Benton Lauritz *paralegal*

Murray
Twitchell, E(rvin) Eugene *retired lawyer*

North Salt Lake
Malan, Chris J. *lawyer*

Ogden
Mecham, Glenn Jefferson *lawyer, mayor*
Sullivan, Kevin Patrick *lawyer*

Orem
Schofield, Anthony Wayne *lawyer*

Park City
Armstrong, Roger L. *lawyer*
Chin, Augustus G. *lawyer*

Provo
Ashworth, Brent Ferrin *lawyer*
Hansen, H. Reese *law educator, former dean*
Hill, Richard Lee *lawyer*
Staheli, Kory D. *law librarian*
Thomas, David Albert *law educator, director*

Saint George
Gallian, Russell Joseph *lawyer*
Terry, Gary A. *lawyer, director, former trade association executive*

Salt Lake City
Adams, Joseph Keith *lawyer*
Anderson, Robert Monte *lawyer*
Baldwin, John *legal association administrator, lawyer*
Barusch, Lawrence Roos *lawyer*
Baucom, Sidney George *lawyer*
Bendinger, Gary Frederick *lawyer*
Berman, Daniel Lewis *lawyer*
Bird, David R. *lawyer*
Blackburn, Michael Dale *lawyer, educator*
Christensen, Patricia Anne Watkins *lawyer*
Christensen, Ray Richards *lawyer*
Colessides, Nick John *lawyer*
Conard, Jane Reister *lawyer*
Cornaby, Kay Sterling *lawyer, retired state senator*
Curtis, D. Jay *lawyer*
Dewsnup, Ralph L. *lawyer*
Firmage, Edwin Brown *lawyer, educator*
Greenwood, David A. *lawyer*
Holtkamp, James Arnold *lawyer, educator*
Jensen, Dallin W. *lawyer*
Jepperson, Thomas C. *lawyer*
Kirkham, John Spencer *lawyer, director*
Laursen, Thomas E. *lawyer*
Manning, Brent V. *lawyer*
Matsumori, Douglas *lawyer*
Moore, James R. *lawyer*
Nydegger, Rick D. *lawyer*
Ockey, Ronald J. *lawyer*
Prince, William B. *lawyer*
Rasmussen, Thomas Val, Jr. *lawyer, small business owner*
Reeder, F. Robert *lawyer*
Scruggs, Samuel D. *lawyer, chemicals executive*
Smith, Janet Hugie *lawyer*
Sorenson, Stephen Jay *lawyer*
Swinton, Jeffrey Cheever *lawyer*
Thompson, Neil Daniel *retired lawyer*
Threedy, Debora Lynn *law educator*
Tolman, Brett L. *prosecutor*
Tomsic, Peggy A. *lawyer*
Wickman, Lance B. *lawyer*
Wikstrom, Francis M. *lawyer*
Zimmerman, Michael David *lawyer*

South Jordan
Larson, Bryan Alan *lawyer*

St George
Snow, Vanburen Lowry *lawyer*

Vernal
Judd, Dennis L. *lawyer*

VERMONT

Barre
Koch, Thomas Frederick *lawyer*

Brattleboro
Reid, David G. *lawyer*

Burlington
Anderson, Jon Timothy *lawyer*
Anderson, Thomas D. *prosecutor*
Davis, Christopher Lee *lawyer*
Dinse, John Merrell *lawyer*
Hoar, Samuel Neil, Jr. *lawyer*
Kirby, David V. *prosecutor*
Rendall, Donald James, Jr. *lawyer*
Shattuck, Gary G. *lawyer*

Concord
Norsworthy, Elizabeth Krassovsky *lawyer*

Essex Junction
Sweetser, Susan W. *lawyer, advocate, retired state legislator*

Hyde Park
Sanford, Dianne H. *lawyer*

Middlebury
Robbins, Stephen J. M. *lawyer*

Montpelier
Diamond, M. Jerome *lawyer, retired state attorney general*
Guild, Alden *retired lawyer*
Putter, David Seth *lawyer*
Valerio, Matthew F. *lawyer*

Morrisville
Simonds, Marshall *retired lawyer*

Newport
Pepyne, Edward Walter *lawyer, psychologist, educator*

Rutland
Chapman, Silas Stacy III *lawyer*
Crowley, Arthur Edward, Jr. *lawyer*
Faignant, John Paul *lawyer, educator*

Saint Johnsbury
Gallagher, James C. *lawyer*
Marshall, John Henry *lawyer*

Shelburne
Canfield, Andrew Trotter *lawyer, writer*

South Royalton
Dycus, Stephen *law educator*
Goodenough, Oliver Ramsdell *lawyer, educator*
Wroth, L(awrence) Kinvin *law educator*

Stowe
Siegel, David Burton *lawyer*
Whiteman, Joseph David *retired lawyer, manufacturing company executive*

Warren
Raphael, Albert Ash, Jr. *retired lawyer*

White River Junction
Kainen, Michael Roland *lawyer, state representative*

Woodstock
Zonay, Thomas A. *lawyer*

VIRGINIA

Abingdon
Moore, Suzan E. *lawyer*
Shortridge, Judy Beth *lawyer*

Alexandria
Apperson, Bernard James *lawyer*
Blue, Catherine Anne *lawyer*
Burch, John Thomas, Jr. *lawyer*
Carter, Richard Dennis *lawyer, educator*
Cottrell, James Ray *lawyer*
Dennison, Donald Lee *lawyer*
Drennan, Joseph Peter *lawyer*
Esslinger, John Thomas *lawyer*
Flater, Morris Eugene *lawyer*
Georges, Peter John *lawyer*
Ginsburg, Charles David *lawyer*
Goldfarb, Ronald Lawrence *lawyer, writer, literary agent*
Greigg, Ronald Edwin *lawyer*
Hirschkop, Philip Jay *lawyer, educator*
Hobson, James Richmond *lawyer*
Huckabee, Harlow Maxwell *lawyer, writer*
Hudgins, David Drake *lawyer*
Kelly, Nancy Frieda Wolicki *lawyer*
Kopp, Eugene Paul *lawyer*
Kotlarchuk, Ihor O.E. *lawyer*
Maloof, Farahe Paul *lawyer*
McDowell, Charles Eager *lawyer, retired military officer*
Montague, Robert Latane III *lawyer*
Mossinghoff, Gerald Joseph *lawyer, educator*
O'Hara, John Patrick *lawyer, consultant*
Paturis, E(mmanuel) Michael *lawyer*
Pyle, Howard *lawyer, consultant*
Rosenberg, Chuck (Charles P.) *prosecutor*
Spencer, George Henry *lawyer*
Stevens, Ron A. *lawyer, advocate, surveyor*
Straub, Peter Thornton *lawyer*
Sturtevant, Brereton *retired lawyer, federal official*
Swift, Stephen Christopher *lawyer*
Von Drehle, Ramon Arnold *lawyer*
Walkup, Charlotte Lloyd *lawyer*
Whitaker, Mary Fernan *lawyer*
Williams, John Edward *lawyer*
Winzer, P.J. *lawyer*

Annandale
Jollie, Susan Barbara *lawyer*

Arlington
Anthony, Robert Armstrong *lawyer, educator*
Brenner, Edgar H. *legal association administrator*
Burgess, David *lawyer*
Cohen, Sheldon Irwin *lawyer*
Crouch, Richard Edelin *lawyer*
Doyle, Gerard Francis *lawyer*
Flinn, Charles Gallagher *lawyer, priest*
Gainer, Ronald Lee *lawyer*
Green, Richard Alan *retired lawyer*
Hansen, Kenneth D. *lawyer, ophthalmologist*
Johnson, Charles Owen *retired lawyer*
Keene, Deborah M. *law librarian*
Kelly, John James *lawyer*
Korman, James William *lawyer*
Kosarin, Jonathan Henry *lawyer, consultant*
Lauderdale, Katherine Sue *lawyer*
Leslie, Gregg P. *lawyer*
Lohr, Michael F. *lawyer*
Malone, William Grady *retired lawyer*
Martin, Harry C. *lawyer*
McDermott, Francis Owen *retired lawyer*
Meisel, Michael J. *lawyer*
Mellor, Chip (William H. Mellor) *lawyer*
Nagin, Lawrence M. *lawyer*
O'Sullivan, Lynda Troutman *lawyer*
Parker, Jeffrey Scott *law educator*
Pelton, Erik Michael *lawyer*
Robb, Chuck (Charles Spittal) *law educator, former senator*
Rotunda, Ronald Daniel *law educator, consultant*
Rousselot, Peter Frese *lawyer, consultant*
Rudolph, Lawrence *lawyer*
Schmidt, Paul Wickham *lawyer*
Sloan, Clifford M. *lawyer, publishing executive*
Walker, Woodrow Wilson *retired lawyer, real estate investor, farmer*
Wilderotter, James Arthur *lawyer*
Witort, Janet Lee *lawyer*

Ashburn
Gold, George Myron *lawyer, editor, writer, consultant*

Blacksburg
Jensen, Walter Edward *retired lawyer, educator*

Burke
Bishop, Alfred Chilton, Jr. *lawyer*
Hipfel, Steven J. *lawyer*

Centreville
Etters, Ronald Milton *retired lawyer, former government official*
Fells, Robert Marshall *lawyer*
Kendall, William Melvin *lawyer*

Chantilly
Becker, James Richard *lawyer*
Costello, Daniel Brian *lawyer, consultant*
DeLeon, Charles *lawyer*

Charlottesville
Abraham, Kenneth Samuel *law educator*
Andrews, Minerva Wilson *retired lawyer*
Bonnie, Richard Jeffrey *lawyer, educator, consultant*
Chandler, Lawrence Bradford, Jr. *lawyer*
Dooley, Michael P. *law educator*
Dotson, Donald L. *lawyer*
Fitchett, Taylor *law librarian*
Fox, Charles Dunsmore, IV, *lawyer*
Goetz, Charles John *law and economics educator*
Harrison, John Collier *law educator*
Henderson, Stanley Dale *lawyer, educator, arbitrator*
Hochberg, Bayard Zabdial *retired lawyer*
Hodous, Robert Power *lawyer*
Howard, Arthur Ellsworth Dick *law educator*
Kennedy, Cornelius Bryant *retired lawyer*
Kensington, Andrew Justus *litigation speciali*
Kitch, Edmund Wells *law educator*
Kudravetz, David Waller *lawyer*
Landess, Fred Stone *retired lawyer*
Lane, Mark *lawyer, educator, writer*
Martin, David Alan *law educator*
Meador, Daniel John *law educator*
Menefee, Samuel Pyeatt *lawyer, academic*
Middleditch, Leigh Benjamin, Jr. *lawyer, educator*
Monahan, John T. *law educator, psychologist*
Moore, John Norton *lawyer, educator, diplom*
Nelson, Caleb Edward *law educator*
O'Brien, David Michael *law educator*
O'Connell, Jeffrey *law educator*
Riley, Margaret Foster (Mimi) *law educator*
Robinson, Mildred Wigfall *law educator*
Setear, John K. *law educator*
Slaughter, Edward Ratliff, Jr. *lawyer*
Stroud, Robert Edward *lawyer*
Turner, Robert Foster *law educator, writer*
Wadlington, Walter James *law educator*
Wenger, Larry Bruce *law librarian, educator*
White, George Edward *lawyer, educator*
Whitehead, John Wayne *lawyer, educator, wri*

Chesapeake
Gorry, James A. III *lawyer*

Chester
Connelly, Colin Charles *lawyer*
Gray, Charles Robert *lawyer*

Culpeper
Dulaney, Richard Alvin *lawyer*

Daleville
Butler, Manley Caldwell *retired lawyer*

Danville
Abreu, Luis Alberto *lawyer*
Regan, Michael Patrick *lawyer*
Talbott, Frank III *lawyer*

Fairfax
Anderson, David Lawrence *lawyer*
Arnold, William McCauley *lawyer*
Arntson, Peter Andrew *lawyer*
Baird, Charles Bruce *lawyer, consultant*
Bobzien, David P. *lawyer*
Codding, Frederick Hayden *lawyer*
Dowlut, Robert *lawyer*
Downey, Richard Lawrence *lawyer*
Fagan, John Ernest *lawyer*
Folk, Thomas Robert *lawyer*
Hopson, Everett George *retired lawyer*
Keith, John A(ugustine) C(hilton) *lawyer*
Mackall, Henry Clinton *lawyer*
McGavin, John David *lawyer*
Rieger, Michael Ira *lawyer*
Rust, John Howson, Jr. *lawyer, state legislato*
Sanderson, Douglas Jay *lawyer*
Simpson, Carter B. *lawyer*
Susko, Carol Lynne *lawyer, accountant, educ*

Fairfax Station
Carver, George Allen, Jr. *retired lawyer*

Falls Church
Boehm, Kenneth *legal association administra*
Brady, Rupert Joseph *retired lawyer*
Burroughs, Benton, Jr. *lawyer*
Christman, Bruce Lee *lawyer*
Dewey-Balzhiser, Anne Elizabeth Marie *lawy*
Diamond, Robert Michael *lawyer*
Flaherty, Peter *legal association administrato*
Golden, Wilson *lawyer*
Hardin, Mark A. *legal association administra*
Honigberg, Carol Crossman *lawyer*
Luchini, Joseph S. *lawyer*
Meserve, Richard Andrew *lawyer, administra*
Middleton, J. Howard, Jr. *lawyer*
Perkins, Jack Edwin *lawyer*
Pischke, Vail W. *lawyer, judge*
Savner, David A. *lawyer*
Thomas, William Griffith *lawyer*
Van Cleve, Ruth Gill *retired lawyer*
Ward, Joe Henry, Jr. *retired lawyer*
Waxman, Bruce I. *lawyer*
Wood, John Martin *lawyer*

Fort Belvoir
Harms, John Kevin *lawyer*
Kiechel, Walter, Jr. *lawyer*

Franklin
Watkins, Thomas Linnane *lawyer*

ericksburg
sley, Robert Thaine *lawyer*
n, Herman Harrison, Jr. *lawyer*

Royal
gni, Vincent Francis *lawyer*

Allen
Terrence Raymond *lawyer*
artog, Grace Robinson *lawyer*
Jay J(oseph) *lawyer*
r, Mollie Little *lawyer*

cester
C. Flippo *lawyer*

t Falls
Ronald Andrew *lawyer, former dean*
ell, Roy Shaw *lawyer*
h, George Arthur *lawyer*
n, Charles George *lawyer*
Byrne, Olivia *lawyer*

dy
othlin, Michael Gordon *lawyer*
Clinton Wesley *lawyer*

pton
, Stephen Mark *lawyer*

isonburg
ger, M(elvin) Bruce *lawyer*

s
n, Richard Frederick *lawyer, hotel*
cutive
os, Elizabeth Jason *lawyer, state agency*
ninistrator

market
, Jacob *lawyer*

hsville
erns, Charles Joseph *lawyer*

don
omon, Paul David *lawyer, management*
sultant

n, Donald Thomas *lawyer*
x, Harvey John *lawyer*

wick
ins, Edward J. *retired lawyer*

burg
n, Barbara Purse *lawyer*
ner, Gordon Peter *lawyer*

ngton
s, Frederic Lee *law educator*
t, Sarah Kirsten *law librarian, educator,*
ector

ust Grove
sman, Lawrence Darrow *lawyer, director*

ton
omarco, Dan Ralph *lawyer, consultant*

ettsville
ery, John Philip *lawyer*

chburg
l, James Joseph *lawyer*
y, Joseph Francis, Jr. *lawyer, retired air*
nsportation executive
ert, G(ayla) Beth *retired lawyer*

akin Sabot
t, Craig Bartley *lawyer*

rion
son, Douglas Blaikie *lawyer*

rtinsville
, Douglas Kyle *retired lawyer*
Oeveren, Edward Lanier *lawyer, biologist,*
ysician

Lean
ander, Fred Calvin, Jr. *lawyer*
ler, Thomas L. *lawyer*
utt, Ronald David *lawyer*
r, Keith Leon *lawyer*
rom, Robert Everett *lawyer, finance*
mpany executive
ly, Phillip Donley *lawyer*
vn, Margaret Ann *lawyer*
vn, Thomas Cartmel, Jr. *lawyer*
es, William Joseph *lawyer*
ley, Thomas J. *lawyer*
rch, Randolph Warner, Jr. *lawyer*
ingbould, John *lawyer*
ovan, David P. *lawyer*
all, Richard Osgood *lawyer*
eran, John G., Jr. *lawyer, diversified*
ancial services company executive
scher, Walter Hersch *lawyer*
ter, Jonathan M. *lawyer*
mon, James Alan *lawyer*
gosian, C. Christopher *lawyer*
sman, M. Melissa *lawyer*
s, Lawrence J. *lawyer*
nam, Thomas, Jr. *lawyer*
ge, J. Curtis *lawyer*
s, Adam R. *lawyer*
an, Richard T., Jr. *lawyer*
ersoll, William Boley *lawyer, real estate*
eveloper
son, William Paul, Jr. *lawyer*
bel, John Albert *lawyer, retired government*
gency administrator
hler, Robert H. *lawyer*
dracki, Edward John *lawyer*
ourd, Nancy Susan Oliver *lawyer, writer*

Lewis, James (Jim) M. *lawyer*
Main, David C. *lawyer*
Meltzer, Steven Lee *lawyer*
Miller, David L. *lawyer*
Miller, Donald Eugene *lawyer*
Molineaux, Charles Borromeo *lawyer, arbitrator, columnist, poet*
Morris, James Malachy *lawyer*
Murphy, Thomas Patrick *lawyer*
Olson, William Jeffrey *lawyer*
Porter, Philip Drew *lawyer*
Price, Ilene Rosenberg *lawyer*
Rath, Manik K. *lawyer*
Reiff, Laura Foote *lawyer*
Sack, James M. *lawyer*
Shapiro, Nelson Hirsh *lawyer*
Sirilla, George M. *lawyer*
Stump, John Sutton *retired lawyer*
Tansill, Frederick Joseph *lawyer*
Townsend, Christopher Gordon *lawyer*
Van Lare, Wendell John *lawyer, director*
Wilchins, Howard Martin *lawyer*
Wimmer, Kurt A. *lawyer*
Woolsey, R(obert) James *lawyer, former CIA director*
Zirkle, Warren E. *lawyer*

Middleburg
Beddall, Thomas Henry *lawyer*
Boardman, Harold Frederick, Jr. *lawyer, retired corporate financial executive*

Midlothian
Hall, Franklin Perkins *lawyer, bank executive, state official*
Nuckols, Otis Wills *lawyer, educator*

Newport News
Kamp, Arthur Joseph, Jr. *lawyer*
Saunders, Bryan Leslie *lawyer*
Segall, James Arnold *lawyer*

Norfolk
Albert, Alan Dale *lawyer*
Baird, Edward Rouzie, Jr. *retired lawyer*
Bishop, Bruce Taylor *lawyer*
Corcoran, Andrew Patrick, Jr. *lawyer*
Cranford, Page Deronde *lawyer*
Crenshaw, Francis Nelson *retired lawyer*
Davis, Terry Hunter, Jr. *lawyer*
Dimino, Joseph C. *lawyer*
Drescher, John Webb *lawyer*
Grierson, Kevin William *lawyer*
Hixon, James A. *lawyer, rail transportation executive*
Holloway, John Early *lawyer*
James, Gus John, II, *lawyer*
Martin, Howard W., Jr. *lawyer*
Padgett, John David *lawyer*
Parker, Richard Wilson *lawyer, retired rail transportation executive*
Pearson, John Yeardley, Jr. *lawyer*
Poston, Anita Owings *lawyer*
Rephan, Jack *lawyer*
Russell, C. Edward, Jr. *lawyer*
Ryan, John Morgan *lawyer*
Shannon, John Sanford *lawyer, retired rail transportation executive*
Stillman, Gregory N. *lawyer*
Teal, Gilbert Earle, II, *lawyer, coast guard officer*
Van Buren, William Ralph III *lawyer*
Ware, Guilford Dudley *lawyer*
Weinberg, Jerrold Gladstone *lawyer*

Norton
Jessee, Roy Mark *lawyer*

Oakton
Duesenberg, Robert H. *retired lawyer*
Randolph, Christopher Craven *lawyer*

Petersburg
Baskervill, Charles Thornton *lawyer*
Burns, Cassandra Stroud *prosecutor*
Everitt, Alice Lubin *labor arbitrator*
Spero, Morton Bertram *retired lawyer*

Portsmouth
Moody, Willard James, Sr. *lawyer*

Prince George
Brown, Del M. Mauhrine *lawyer, educator*

Pulaski
McCarthy, Thomas James, Jr. *lawyer*

Purcellville
Sweeny, Peter Michael *lawyer*

Radford
Davis, Richard Waters *lawyer*
Turk, James Clinton, Jr. *lawyer*

Reston
Anderson, Charles Anthony *lawyer*
Bredehoft, Elaine Charlson *lawyer*
Burgujian, Richard V. *lawyer*
Foley, Christopher P. *lawyer*
Fowler, David Lucas *corporate lawyer*
Frankel, Kenneth M. *lawyer*
Hill, David Warren *lawyer*
Kirsch, Mark A. *lawyer*
Lavet, Robert *lawyer*
Lipsey, Charles E. *lawyer*
Lowell, Bret *lawyer*
McBride, Andrew Gerald *prosecutor*
McJunkin, John G. *lawyer*
Myerson, Jay Barry *lawyer*
Plave, Lee Jonathan *lawyer*
Rau, Lee Arthur *lawyer*
Scharff, Joseph Laurent *lawyer*
Tifford, John Mark *lawyer*
Westermeier, John Thomas, Jr. *lawyer, educator*

Richmond
Allen, Jeffrey Rodgers *lawyer*
Bagley, Philip Joseph III *lawyer*
Bagley, Terrence M. *lawyer*
Bates, John Wythe III *lawyer*
Beales, Randolph A. *lawyer, former state attorney general*
Belcher, Dennis Irl *lawyer*
Betts, James Edward *lawyer*
Bing, Richard McPhail *lawyer*
Booker, Lewis Thomas *lawyer*
Brasfield, Evans Booker *lawyer*
Brissette, Martha Blevins *lawyer*
Broadbent, Peter Edwin, Jr. *lawyer*
Brockenbrough, Henry Watkins *lawyer*
Bryson, William Hamilton *law educator*
Buckley, Kevin Joseph *lawyer*
Buford, Robert Pegram *lawyer*
Burke, John K(irkland), Jr. *lawyer*
Burrus, Robert Lewis, Jr. *lawyer*
Carrell, Daniel Allan *lawyer*
Catlett, Richard H., Jr. *retired lawyer*
Cogbill, John Valentine III *lawyer*
Cutchins, Clifford Armstrong, IV, *lawyer*
Denny, Collins III *lawyer*
Derry, William R., Jr. *lawyer*
Dostart, Thomas J. *lawyer*
Dray, Mark Stanley *lawyer*
Edmonds, Thomas Andrew *legal association administrator*
Ellis, Andrew Jackson, Jr. *lawyer*
Fauls, Thomas E. (Ted Fauls) *lawyer*
Flippen, Edward L. *lawyer*
Freeman, George Clemon, Jr. *lawyer*
Gary, Richard David *lawyer*
Gluck, Michelle H. *lawyer*
Goodpasture, Philip Henry *lawyer*
Goolsby, Allen Cunningham III *lawyer*
Gould, Karen A. *lawyer*
Grey, Robert J., Jr. *lawyer*
Hackney, Virginia Howitz *lawyer*
Hall, Stephen Charles *lawyer*
Heaton, Stuart Alan *lawyer*
Hedgebeth, Reginald D. *lawyer, retail executive*
Hettrick, George Harrison *lawyer*
Irwin, Donald Paulding *lawyer*
Johnston, Francis Claiborne, Jr. *lawyer*
Kearfott, Joseph Conrad *lawyer*
Kilgore, Jerry Walter *lawyer, former state attorney general*
King, William H., Jr. *lawyer*
Kissam, Luther C., IV, *lawyer, chemicals executive*
Konvicka, Jason Wade *lawyer*
Landin, David Craig *lawyer*
Ledbetter, David Oscar *lawyer*
Lutz, Jacob A., III, (Jake Lutz) *lawyer*
Marshall, Gary S. *lawyer*
Mathews, Roderick Bell *lawyer*
McClard, Jack Edward *lawyer*
McElligott, James Patrick, Jr. *lawyer*
McFarlane, Walter Alexander *lawyer, educator*
Meath, James V. *lawyer*
Miller, Stephen Wiley *lawyer*
Mims, William Cleveland *lawyer*
Minardi, Richard A. (Rick), Jr. *lawyer*
Moore, T. Justin III *lawyer*
Moore, Thurston Roach *lawyer*
Morris, James Watson III *lawyer*
Pagan, John Ruston *law educator*
Pearsall, John Wesley *lawyer*
Pinckney, Charles Cotesworth *lawyer*
Pollard, Overton Price *retired lawyer*
Pope, Robert Dean *lawyer*
Powell, Lewis Franklin III *lawyer*
Pulley, (J.) Waverly. (III) *lawyer*
Rainey, Gordon Fryer, Jr. *lawyer*
Redmond, David Dudley *lawyer*
Rhoads, Mark B. *lawyer*
Richardson, David L. *lawyer*
Rigsby, Linda Flory *lawyer, director*
Rinaca, James M. *lawyer*
Robertson, Gregory B. *lawyer*
Roday, Leon E. *lawyer, finance company executive*
Rohman, Thomas P. *lawyer*
Rolfe, Robert Martin *lawyer*
Rowe, William L. S. *lawyer*
Rucker, Douglas Pendleton, Jr. *lawyer*
Ryland, Walter H. *lawyer*
Schwarzschild, Jane L. *lawyer*
Sharer, John Daniel *lawyer*
Shiembob, Mark S. *lawyer*
Slater, Thomas Glascock, Jr. *lawyer*
Slaughter, Alexander Hoke *lawyer*
Smith, R. Gordon *lawyer*
Spahn, Gary Joseph *lawyer*
Starke, Harold Eugene, Jr. *lawyer*
Starr, Edward H., Jr. *lawyer*
Stone, Jacquelyn Elois *lawyer*
Strickland, William Jesse *lawyer*
Stutts, James F. *lawyer, energy executive*
Thomas, John Charles *lawyer*
Thompson, Paul Michael *lawyer*
Thro, William Eugene *lawyer*
Traficanti, Joseph J. *lawyer*
Troy, Anthony Francis *lawyer*
Vaughan, C. Porter III *lawyer*
Waddell, William Robert *lawyer*
Walsh, James Hamilton *lawyer*
Walsh, William Arthur, Jr. *lawyer*
Warthen, Harry Justice III *lawyer*
Watts, Stephen Hurt, II, *lawyer*
Wellford, Hill B., Jr. *lawyer*
Whittemore, Anne Marie *lawyer*
Wigner, Preston Douglas *lawyer*
Williams, Amy McDaniel *lawyer*
Witt, Walter Francis, Jr. *lawyer*
Wright, Wiley Reed, Jr. *lawyer, retired judge, mediator*

Roanoke
Anderson, Phillip Verne *lawyer*
Barnhill, David Stan *lawyer*
Bates, Harold Martin *lawyer*
Brownlee, John L. *prosecutor*
Densmore, Douglas Warren *lawyer*
Fishwick, John Palmer *retired lawyer, railroad executive*
Glenn, Robert Eastwood *lawyer*
Lemon, William Jacob *lawyer*
Margolin, Eric Mitchell *lawyer*
Marshall, Heman Alexander III *lawyer*
McGarry, Richard Lawrence *lawyer*
Mundy, Gardner Marshall *lawyer*
Pace, G. Michael, Jr. *lawyer*
Steele, (Margaret) Anita Martin *law librarian, law educator*
Thomson, Paul Rice, Jr. *lawyer*
Woodrum, Clifton A. III *lawyer, retired state legislator*

Salem
Griffith, H(oward) Morgan *lawyer*

South Riding
Murray, Michael Patrick *lawyer*

Spotsylvania
Manthei, Richard Dale *retired lawyer, health products executive*

Springfield
Englert, Roy Theodore *lawyer*

Sterling
Clegg, Roger Burton *lawyer*

Suffolk
Diehl, Richard Paul *lawyer*

Vienna
Cochran, Deborah Donick *lawyer*
Dolan, William D. III *lawyer*
Gary, Stuart Hunter *lawyer*
Mackesey, Daniel R. *lawyer*
Maguire, Margaret Louise *lawyer*
Maiwurm, James John *lawyer*
Peters, Geoffrey Wright *lawyer, fundraising executive*
Schwartz, Philip *lawyer*
Stearns, Frank Warren *lawyer*
Titus, Bruce Earl *lawyer*
Vaughan, Patrick J. *lawyer*
Walsh, William L., Jr. *lawyer*
Whitaker, Thomas Patrick *lawyer*
Yurow, Michael Jay *lawyer*

Virginia Beach
Baldwin, Stanley Forrest *lawyer, insurance company executive*
Barney, Michael E. *lawyer*
Buzard, David Andrew *lawyer*
Christiansen, Margaret Louise *law librarian, lawyer*
Hajek, Francis Paul *lawyer*
Harrell, Charles Lydon, Jr. *retired lawyer*
Jones, Robert Griffith *law educator, mayor*
Pickett, Owen Bradford *lawyer, former congressman*
Sekulow, Jay Alan *lawyer*
Spitzli, Donald Hawkes, Jr. *lawyer*
Swope, Richard McAllister *retired lawyer*

Ware Neck
McVey, Henry Hanna III *retired lawyer*

Warrenton
Howard, Blair Duncan *lawyer*

Williamsburg
Church, Dale Walker *lawyer*
Clark, Morton Hutchinson *lawyer*
Graham, David Browning *lawyer*
Heller, James Stephen *law librarian, educator*
Marcus, Paul *law educator*
Margolin, Robert Jeremy *lawyer*
Merritt, James Edward *lawyer*

Wise
Rogers, Leonard David *lawyer*

Woodbridge
Halagao, Avelino Garabiles *lawyer*
Roberts, Charles Bren *lawyer*
Sandler, Betty Moore *lawyer*

Woodstock
Walton, Morgan Lauck III *lawyer*

WASHINGTON

Anacortes
Cavanaugh, Michael Everett *lawyer, arbitrator, mediator*
Glein, Richard Jeriel, Sr. *lawyer*

Bellevue
Anderson, David Coryell *lawyer, automotive executive*
Hannah, Lawrence Burlison *lawyer*
Kari, Donald G. *lawyer*
Landau, Felix *lawyer*
Morie, G. Glen *lawyer, manufacturing executive*
Schroder, Sigrid Caroline *lawyer, consultant*
Sebris, Robert, Jr. *lawyer*
Sweeney, David Brian *lawyer*

Bellingham
Adelstein, Steven Paul *lawyer*
Anderson, David Bowen *lawyer*
Packer, Mark Barry *lawyer, financial consultant, foundation official*
Raas, Daniel Alan *lawyer*

Bothell
Gustafson, Alice Fairleigh *lawyer*

Bremerton
Cunningham, Gary Allen *lawyer*

Centralia
Buzzard, Steven Ray *lawyer*

East Wenatchee
Hanna, Harold B. *retired lawyer*

Eastsound
Hoagland, Karl King, Jr. *lawyer*
Murray, Michael Kent *lawyer*

Everett
Mestel, Mark David *lawyer*
Ostergaard, Joni Hammersla *lawyer*

Federal Way
McDade, Sandy D. *lawyer, paper company executive*
Nance, John Joseph *lawyer, writer, air traffic controller, announcer, consultant*

Gig Harbor
Thompson, Ronald Edward *lawyer*

Hoquiam
Kessler, Keith Leon *lawyer*

Issaquah
Benoliel, Joel *lawyer*
Oles, Stuart Gregory *lawyer*

Kennewick
Hames, William Lester *lawyer*

Keyport
Treacy, Gerald Bernard, Jr. *lawyer*

La Push
Krueger, Katherine Kamp *lawyer*

Mercer Island
Anderson, Peter MacArthur *retired lawyer*
Medved, Robert Allen *lawyer*

Newcastle
Erxleben, William Charles *lawyer, data processing executive*

Olympia
Isaki, Lucy Power Slyngstad *lawyer*
Miller, Allen Terry, Jr. *lawyer*
Roe, Charles Barnett *lawyer*
Walker, Francis Joseph *lawyer*

Port Angeles
Gay, Carl Lloyd *lawyer*
Taylor, S. Brooke *lawyer*

Pullman
Savage, David William *lawyer*

Redmond
Burt, Thomas William *lawyer*

Renton
Barber, Mark Edward *lawyer*

Seattle
Alkire, John D. *lawyer, arbitrator, mediator*
Alsdorf, Robert Hermann *lawyer*
Alvord, Chase *lawyer*
Andrews, J. David *lawyer*
Aspaas, Jennifer *lawyer*
Bagshaw, Bradley Holmes *lawyer*
Baruffi, Kumi Yamamoto *lawyer*
Batalov, Leo *lawyer*
Benedict, Tim *lawyer*
Berman, Steve William *lawyer, author*
Birk, Ian *lawyer*
Birmingham, Richard Joseph *lawyer*
Blair, M. Wayne *lawyer*
Blom, Daniel Charles *lawyer, investor, retired insurance company executive*
Blumenfeld, Charles Raban *lawyer*
Boeder, Thomas L. *lawyer*
Boggs, Paula Elaine *lawyer, food service executive*
Bridge, Jonathan Joseph *lawyer, retail executive*
Bridgman, Geoff *lawyer*
Bringman, Joseph Edward *lawyer*
Brown, Michael Jay *lawyer*
Burke, William Thomas *lawyer, educator*
Carpenter, Stephen Hayes, Jr. *lawyer*
Carr, Thomas A. *lawyer*
Chapman, Fay L. *lawyer, bank executive*
Char, Patricia Helen *lawyer*
Chicoine, Nicole *lawyer*
Chong, Arthur *lawyer*
Claflin, Arthur Cary *lawyer*
Clausen, Mark A. *lawyer*
Corning, Nicholas F. *lawyer*
Crego, Mary *lawyer*
Cross, Bruce Michael *lawyer*
Cullen, Jack Joseph *lawyer*
Cunningham, Janis Ann *lawyer*
Davis, John MacDougall *lawyer*
Davis, Susan Rae *lawyer*
DeVore, Paul Cameron *lawyer*
Dial, Ellen Conedera *lawyer*
Diamond, Josef *lawyer*
Dillow, John David *lawyer*
Dong, Nelson G. *lawyer*
Dotten, Michael Chester *lawyer*
Dunbar, Jeffrey *lawyer*
Farr, Ross *lawyer*
Favard, Kristi *lawyer*
Ferencz, Garrett R. *lawyer*
Fischer, Thomas Covell *law educator, consultant, writer*
Fisher, Jeffrey L. *lawyer*
Gaffney, Joseph M. *lawyer*
Gerrard, Keith *lawyer*
Giles, Robert Edward, Jr. *lawyer*
Gittinger, D. Wayne *lawyer*
Glover, Karen Elaine *lawyer*
Gores, Thomas C. *lawyer*
Gorton, Slade (Thomas Slade Gorton III) *lawyer, former senator*
Gottlieb, Daniel Seth *lawyer*
Grace, Ryan Thomas *lawyer*
Gradel, James D. *lawyer*
Graham, Stephen Michael *lawyer*
Gray, Marvin Lee, Jr. *lawyer*
Green, William L. *lawyer*
Gustafson, Seth *lawyer*
Haman, Raymond William *retired lawyer*
Hansen, Wayne W. *lawyer*
Hazelton, Penny Ann *law librarian, educator*
Hermsen, James R. *lawyer*
Hill, G. Richard *lawyer*
Hilpert, Edward Theodore, Jr. *retired lawyer*
Hineline, Curt Roy *lawyer*
Holburn, Andrea *lawyer*
Hollinrake, John D., Jr. *lawyer*
Holtan, Ramer B., Jr. *lawyer*
Howshar, Erin *lawyer*
Huston, John Charles *law educator*
Hutcheson, Mark Andrew *lawyer*
Israel, Allen D. *lawyer*
Jackson, Dylan E. *lawyer*
Jaffe, Robert Stanley *lawyer*
Jensen, Jessica *lawyer*
Johnson, Bruce Edward Humble *lawyer*
Jones, Randal R. *lawyer*
Judson, C(harles) James (Jim Judson) *lawyer*
Kane, Alan Henry *lawyer*
Kaplan, Robert David *lawyer*
Keegan, John E. *lawyer*
King, Jeffrey J. *lawyer*
Klein, Otto George III *lawyer*
Knight, W. H., Jr., (Joe Knight) *law educator, former dean*
Koehler, Reginald Stafford III *lawyer*
Koh, Steve Y. *lawyer*
Kraft, James Allen *lawyer*
Kuhrau, Edward W. *lawyer*
Kusunose, Taro *lawyer*
Landefeld, Stewart M. *lawyer*
Leitzell, Terry Lee *lawyer*
Lemly, Thomas Adger *lawyer*
Lisbakken, James Robert *lawyer*
Locke, Gary F. *lawyer, former governor*
Loftus, Thomas Daniel *lawyer*
Loveless, Keith *lawyer, air transportation executive*
Malone, Thomas William *lawyer*
Manning, J. Richard *lawyer*
Marchese, Lisa Marie *lawyer, educator*
Marshall, Toby *lawyer*
McCann, Richard Eugene *lawyer*
McCune, Philip Spear *lawyer*
McKay, John *former prosecutor, lawyer, law educator*
McKay, Michael Dennis *lawyer*
Miles, Anthony R. *lawyer*
Mines, Michael *retired lawyer*
Moore, Cori *lawyer*
Mussehl, Robert Clarence *lawyer*
Nelson, Christina Gerrish *lawyer*
Netterfield, Kyle *lawyer*
Neu, David C. *lawyer*
Neukom, William H. *lawyer*
Niemi, Janice *retired lawyer, state legislator, judge*
Nunn, Todd L. *lawyer*
O'Brien, Kristiana *lawyer*
Oehler, Richard William *lawyer*
Olsen, Harold Fremont *lawyer*
Orth, Andrea *lawyer*
Paget, Joel Hathaway *lawyer*
Palmer, Douglas S., Jr. *lawyer*
Parks, Patricia Jean *lawyer*
Parris, Mark S. *lawyer, professional athletes consultant*
Paul, Thomas Frank *lawyer*
Pedersen, Jamie D. *lawyer*
Peterson, Jan Eric *lawyer*
Petrie, Gregory Steven *lawyer*
Platt, Thomas E. *lawyer*
Prentke, Richard Ottesen *lawyer*
Price, John R. *lawyer, educator*
Pritchard, Llewelyn George *lawyer*
Redman, Eric *lawyer*
Reynvaan, Michael Thomas *lawyer*
Rieke, Paul Victor *lawyer*
Riley, Jessica *lawyer*
Ritter, Daniel Benjamin *lawyer*
Robinson, Jeffery P. *lawyer*
Rondeau, George Charles, Jr. *lawyer*
Rosen, Jon Howard *lawyer*
Rosenthal, Gabriel *lawyer*
Rummage, Stephen Michael *lawyer*
Samiljan, Katriana *lawyer*
Schneider, Harry H., Jr. *lawyer*
Schultheis, Patrick Joseph *lawyer*
Schwab, Evan Lynn *lawyer*
Schwartz, Irwin H. *lawyer*
Scott, Brian David *lawyer*
Scott, Rachel E. *lawyer*
Smith, Scott A. *lawyer*
Soltys, John Joseph *lawyer*
Spitzer, Hugh D. *lawyer*
Squires, William Randolph III *lawyer*
Starr, Isidore *law educator*
Steichen, Randall R. *lawyer*
Stoebuck, William Brees *law educator*
Stokke, Diane Rees *lawyer*
Stross, Cynthia *lawyer*
Takenaka, Toshiko *lawyer, educator*
Terwilliger, Molly *lawyer*
Tessier, Dennis Medward *paralegal, writer*
Tousley, Russell Frederick *lawyer*
Treiger, Irwin Louis *lawyer*
Tune, James Fulcher *lawyer*
Wagoner, David Everett *lawyer, arbitrator*
Walter, Michael Charles *lawyer*
Ward, Ronald R. *lawyer*
Wayne, Robert Jonathan *lawyer, educator*
Wechsler, Mary Heyrman *lawyer*
Williams, J. Vernon *retired lawyer*
Williams, Nancy *lawyer*
Williams, Rebecca Lynn *lawyer, nurse*
Williams-Derry, Amy *lawyer*
Wilson, L. Michelle (Michelle Wilson) *lawyer, information technology executive*
Wilson, Richard Randolph *lawyer*
Zapolsky, David A. *lawyer*

Snohomish
Ellis, Stephen Charles *lawyer*

Spokane
Barnes, Ned Maclin *lawyer*
Clarke, Judy *lawyer*
Connolly, Kenneth Thomas *lawyer*
Eymann, Richard Charles *lawyer*
Harbaugh, Daniel Paul *lawyer*
Koegen, Roy Jerome *lawyer*
Kovacevich, Robert Eugene *lawyer*
McDevitt, James A. *prosecutor, lawyer*
Pontarolo, Michael Joseph *lawyer*
Sayre, Richard Layton *lawyer*
Weatherhead, Leslie R. *lawyer*

Tacoma
Carlisle, Dale L. *lawyer*
George, Nicholas *lawyer, entrepreneur*
Gordon, Joseph Harold *lawyer*
Holt, William E. *lawyer, department chairman*
Homan, Jean P. *lawyer*
Hostnik, Charles R. *lawyer*
Krueger, James A. *lawyer*
Mungia, Salvador Alejo *lawyer*
Waldo, James Chandler *lawyer*
Wesch, Angelia DeAn *lawyer*

Tukwila
Fitzpatrick, Thomas Mark *lawyer*

Tumwater
Edmondson, Frank Kelley, Jr. *lawyer, legal administrator*

Vancouver
Dodds, Michael Bruce *lawyer*

Walla Walla
Hayner, Herman Henry *lawyer*

Wenatchee
Bastian, Stanley A. *lawyer*

Yakima
Larson, Paul Martin *lawyer*
Wright, J(ames) Lawrence *lawyer*

WEST VIRGINIA

Beckley
Rhoades, Marye Frances *paralegal*

Berkeley Springs
Yoho, Billy Lee *lawyer*

Bluefield
Kantor, Isaac Norris *lawyer*

Charleston
Betts, Rebecca A. *lawyer*
Brown, James Knight *lawyer*
Cline, Michael Robert *lawyer*
Combs, Philip Judson *lawyer*
Dissen, James Hardiman *lawyer*
Love, Charles Marion III *lawyer*
Miller, Charles T. *prosecutor*
Neely, Richard *lawyer*
Robinson, E. Glenn *lawyer*
Rowe, Larry Linwell *lawyer, former state senator*
Teare, John Richard, Jr. *lawyer*
Victorson, Michael Bruce *lawyer*
Zak, Robert Joseph *lawyer*

Clarksburg
West, James C., Jr. *lawyer*

Fairmont
Aloi, Michael John *lawyer*

Fairview
Bunner, William Keck *lawyer*

Gassaway
Jones, Jeniver James *lawyer*

Hurricane
Hill, David Lawrence *lawyer*

Lewisburg
Ford, Richard Edmond *lawyer*

Martinsburg
Hill, Philip Bonner *lawyer*
Rice, Lacy I., Jr. *lawyer*

Morgantown
Fisher, John Welton, II, *lawyer, educator, academic administrator*
Fusco, Andrew G. *lawyer*
Hardesty, David Carter, Jr. *law educator, former academic administrator*
Morris, William Otis, Jr. *lawyer, educator*
Ringer, Darrell Wayne (Dan) *lawyer*
Scudiere, Debra Hodges *lawyer*

Oak Hill
Hamilton, Pat R. *retired lawyer, state representative*

Romney
Saville, Royce Blair *lawyer*

Weirton
Fahey, William Thomas, II, *lawyer*

Wellsburg
Viderman, Linda Jean *legal assistant, corporate financial executive*

Wheeling
Hill, Barry Morton *lawyer*
Potter, Sharon Lynn *prosecutor*

WISCONSIN

Black River Falls
Lister, Thomas Edward *lawyer*

Brookfield
Sprague, Charles W. *lawyer, finance company executive*
Winsten, Saul Nathan *lawyer*

Deerfield
Pappas, David Christopher *lawyer*

Delafield
Hausman, C. Michael *lawyer*

Eau Claire
Sands, Dawn M. *lawyer*

Elkhorn
Eberhardt, Daniel Hugo *lawyer*
Sostarich, Mark Edward *lawyer*
Sweet, Lowell Elwin *lawyer, writer*

Germantown
Ehlinger, Ralph Jerome *lawyer*

Grafton
Maynard, John Ralph *lawyer*

Green Bay
Burnett, Ralph George *lawyer*
Nixon, Timothy Francis *lawyer*
Vandenberg, Thomas E. *lawyer, transportatio services executive*
Vandenhouten, Peter G. *lawyer*

Greendale
Vinent-Cantoral, Aida R. *mediator*

Hales Corners
Case, Karen Ann *lawyer*

Janesville
Steil, George Kenneth, Sr. *lawyer*

Kenosha
Higgins, John Patrick *lawyer, mediator, lobby educator*
Marrinan, Susan Faye *lawyer*
Michaelis, Karen Lauree *law educator*

La Crosse
Klos, Jerome John *lawyer, director*
Sleik, Thomas Scott *lawyer*

Lake Geneva
Braden, Berwyn Bartow *lawyer*

Lancaster
Halferty, James Burkhardt *lawyer*

Madison
Anderson, Michael Steven *lawyer*
Bablitch, William A. *lawyer, retired state supreme court justice*
Barkan, Steven M. *law librarian, educator*
Barnhill, Charles Joseph, Jr. *lawyer*
Barnick, Helen *retired judicial clerk*
Basting, Thomas J., Sr. *lawyer*
Behnke, Michelle A. *lawyer*
Bochert, Linda H. *lawyer*
Boucher, Joseph W(illiam) *lawyer, educator, accountant, writer*
Boykoff, Thomas M. *retired lawyer*
Bremer, Howard Walter *lawyer, consultant*
Bugge, Lawrence John *lawyer, educator*
Carnell, Kent I. *lawyer*
Chandler, Richard Gates *lawyer*
Charo, Robin Alta *law educator*
Curtis, Charles G., Jr. *lawyer*
Eldridge, James Francis *lawyer, insurance company executive*
Field, Henry Augustus, Jr. *lawyer*
Hanson, David James *lawyer*
Heymann, S. Richard *lawyer*
Hildebrand, Daniel Walter *lawyer*
Howell, Roberta F. *lawyer*
Langer, Richard J. *lawyer*
Levine, Steven Alan *lawyer*
Linstroth, Tod Brian *lawyer*
MacDougall, Priscilla Ruth *lawyer*
McCallum, Laurie Riach *state government lawyer*
Melli, Marygold Shire *law educator*
Mowris, Gerald William *lawyer*
Peterson, Erik Charles *prosecutor*
Peterson, H. Dale *lawyer*
Pitzner, Richard William *lawyer*
Prange, Roy Leonard, Jr. *lawyer*
Ragatz, Thomas George *lawyer*
Rankin, Gene Raymond *lawyer*
Ranney, Joseph Austin *lawyer*
Rogers, Joel Edward *law, sociology and poli science educator*
Scheller, John C. J. *lawyer*
Schmid, John Henry, Jr. *lawyer*
Schott, Donald Karl *lawyer*
Skilton, John Singleton *lawyer*
Spencer, Christopher S. *lawyer, insurance company executive*
Steingass, Susan R. *lawyer*
Swan, Barbara J. *lawyer, utilities executive*
Temkin, Harvey L. *lawyer*
Vaughan, Michael Richard *lawyer*
Walsh, David Graves *lawyer*
White, William Fredrick *lawyer*

Manitowoc
Jones, Maurice D. *lawyer*
Muchin, Arden Archie *lawyer, director*

Menomonee Falls
Schepp, Richard D. *lawyer, retail executive*

Menomonie
Steans, Phillip Michael *lawyer*

ıon
zky, Joseph George *law educator*
, James Joseph *lawyer, consultant*
ughnessy, James Patrick *lawyer, consultant*
ıan, Stephen Erik *retired lawyer, consultant*
:, George Kenneth, Jr. *lawyer*

lleton
ın, Ronald Charles *lawyer, accountant*

aukee
am, William John, Jr. *lawyer*
son, William H. *lawyer*
r, Wayne E., Jr. *lawyer*
, Thomas Anthony *lawyer*
ıan, Patricia Kling *lawyer*
en, John Thomas *lawyer*
n, Robert J. *lawyer, insurance company*
cutive
ff, Marshall Richard *lawyer*
Michael Melvin *lawyer, writer*
, Joel Wilson *lawyer, retired diplomat*
pic, Steven M. *prosecutor, lawyer*
Peter Charles *lawyer*
Ralf Reinhard *lawyer*
n, Michael Anthony *lawyer, writer*
h, Joseph C. *lawyer*
er, John M. *lawyer*
:, Peter Wayne *lawyer, insurance company*
cutive
n, John Arthur *lawyer, business executive*
on, David Joseph *lawyer*
, John Alexander *lawyer*
er, Richard Henry *lawyer*
tiansen, Keith Allan *lawyer*
, James Richard *lawyer*
olly, Gerald Edward *lawyer*
r, Richard W. *lawyer*
, Frank J(erome) *lawyer*
els, John W., Jr. *lawyer*
ısopoulos, George Allan *lawyer*
hue, John Edward *lawyer*
Dwight Holmes III *lawyer*
uel, John F. *lawyer*
son, Randall J. *lawyer*
heim, Richard Steven *lawyer*
r, Alexander Paul *lawyer*
en, Kurt Herman *lawyer*
schi, Timothy Clark *lawyer*
ert, Robert Howard *lawyer*
man, James Dennis *lawyer*
es, Irving David *lawyer*
nis, John William *lawyer*
ıgher, Richard Sidney *lawyer*
e, Henry Jerome *lawyer*
fuss, C. Frederick, II, *lawyer*
ignani, Joseph Adolph *lawyer*
e, Janine Patricia *law educator*
rdi, James Domenic *lawyer, educator*
lkind, Conrad George *lawyer*
in, D. Michael *lawyer*
erman, F. William *lawyer*
ısh, Robert Lee *lawyer*
eck, William H. *lawyer*
ington, John Timothy *retired lawyer*
, David John *lawyer*
h, Michael Ward *lawyer*
man, Nathaniel A. *lawyer*
:, Harry George *lawyer*
g, Allan Earl *lawyer*
son, Tamara Nicole *lawyer*
an, Stanley S. *lawyer*
Lawrence John *lawyer*
, David Barry *lawyer*
nedy, John Patrick *lawyer, corporate*
ancial executive
her, John Joseph *law educator*
gel, Jerome Howard *lawyer*
eger, Raymond Robert *lawyer*
ale, Bernard Stephen *lawyer*
z, Harvey A. *lawyer*
nner, Beth *lawyer*
udde, Roy Christian *lawyer*
, Jeffrey H. *lawyer*
gley, Grant F. *municipal lawyer*
ne, Herbert *lawyer*
t, William Harold, Jr. *lawyer*
, Alan M. *lawyer*
ne, Gail Ann *lawyer*
ders, Wayne Richard *lawyer*
ch, Michael *lawyer, staffing company*
xecutive
rquis, William Oscar *lawyer*
sterson, Joseph D. *lawyer, partner*
Gaffey, Jere D. *retired lawyer*
Ginnity, Maureen Annell *lawyer*
Keown, James T. *lawyer*
Sweeney, Maurice J. (Marc McSweeney)
wyer
ldman, Robert Edward *lawyer*
lin, Robert Arthur *lawyer*
ten, Matthew John *law educator, lawyer*
lcahy, Robert William *lawyer*
ırma, Jerome D. *lawyer, manufacturing*
xecutive
on, John Marshall *lawyer*
Meara, Stephen Charles *lawyer*
kerman, Bruce Martin *lawyer*
llips, Thomas John *lawyer*
dyck, Bruce Eben *lawyer, corporate financial*
xecutive
ter, Richard H. *lawyer*
ın, Patrick Michael *lawyer*
filippo, Jon *lawyer, court clerk*
telle, James Lewis *prosecutor*
nur, Robert Arnold *lawyer, educator*
ott, Sarah E. *lawyer*
wartz, Carl R. *lawyer*
ivner, Thomas William *lawyer*
nett, Nancy J. *lawyer*
piro, Robyn Sue *lawyer, educator*
iner, Thomas L., Jr. *lawyer*
vik, Donald Harlan *lawyer*
rm, William Charles *lawyer*
ridge, Stephen Zehring *lawyer, writer*
schan, Frank Robert *lawyer*
ly, Catherine T. *lawyer*

Tyson, Joseph B., Jr. *lawyer*
Van Vugt, Eric J. *lawyer*
Wiley, Edwin Packard *retired lawyer*
Will, Trevor Jonathan *lawyer*
Williams, Allen W., Jr. *lawyer*
Williams, Clay Rule *lawyer*
Wynn, Stanford Alan *lawyer*

Monroe
Kittelsen, Rodney Olin *lawyer*

Oak Creek
Giblin, Louis *lawyer*

Oshkosh
Blankfield, Bryan J. *lawyer, automotive executive, accountant*
Curtis, George Warren *lawyer*
Kelly, John Martin *lawyer*
Wilde, William Richard *lawyer*

Pepin
Seymour, Mary Frances *lawyer*

Pewaukee
Ward, James A. *lawyer*

Racine
Coates, Glenn Richard *lawyer*
Du Rocher, James Howard *lawyer*
Gasiorkiewicz, Eugene Anthony *lawyer*
Hecker, David *lawyer*
Rudebusch, Alice Ann *lawyer*

Rhinelander
Saari, John William, Jr. *lawyer*

Ripon
Prissel, Barbara Ann *paralegal, law educator*

Stevens Point
O'Reilly, William M. *lawyer, insurance company executive*

Sturtevant
Brandes, JoAnne *lawyer*

Sun Prairie
Eustice, Francis Joseph *lawyer*

Union Grove
Stern, Walter Wolf III *lawyer*

Waukesha
Arenz, Dale Wesley *lawyer, law educator*
Cauley, James Robert *lawyer*
McCoy, John V. *lawyer*

Wausau
Drengler, William Allan John *lawyer*
Etten, Stewart Louis *lawyer*
Grischke, Alan Edward *lawyer*
Orr, San Watterson, Jr. *lawyer*

Wauwatosa
Alexander, Robert Gardner *lawyer*
Heath, Robert F. *lawyer*
Savage, Thomas Ryan *lawyer*

WYOMING

Buffalo
Kirven, Timothy J. *lawyer*

Casper
Combs, W(illiam) Henry III *lawyer*
Durham, Harry Blaine III *lawyer*
Lowe, Robert Stanley *lawyer*
Sullivan, Michael John *lawyer, former ambassador*

Cheyenne
Burke, E. James *lawyer, state supreme court justice*
Carlson, Kathleen Bussart *law librarian*
Freudenthal, Steven Franklin *lawyer, political organization worker*
Palma, Jack D. *lawyer*
Sansonetti, Thomas L. *lawyer, former federal agency administrator*
Speight, John Blain *lawyer*
White, Daniel Eugene *lawyer*
Wolfe, Lawrence J. *lawyer*

Gillette
Bailey, Daniel B. *lawyer, entrepreneur*
Lubnau, Thomas Edwin, II, *lawyer*

Jackson
Reiniger, Douglas Haigh *lawyer*
Schuster, Robert Parks *lawyer*
Shockey, Gary Lee *lawyer*
Spence, Gerry (Gerald Leonard Spence) *lawyer, writer*

Laramie
Kinney, Lisa Frances *lawyer*
Lauer, Warren A. *lawyer*
Smith, Thomas Shore *retired lawyer*

Riverton
Girard, NettaBell *lawyer*

Sheridan
Cannon, Kim Decker *lawyer*

Wheatland
Hunkins, Raymond Breedlove *lawyer, rancher*

TERRITORIES OF THE UNITED STATES

GUAM

Tamuning
Aguigui, Ignacio Cruz *lawyer*

NORTHERN MARIANA ISLANDS

Saipan
Rapadas, Leonardo M. *prosecutor, lawyer*

PUERTO RICO

Guaynabo
Lasa-Ferrer, Armando *lawyer*

Old San Juan
Weinstein-Bacal, Stuart Allen *lawyer, educator*

San Juan
Corrada del Rio, Baltasar *lawyer, retired former state supreme court justice*
Gil, Guillermo *prosecutor*
Hoglund, Heath *lawyer*
Negron-Garcia, Antonio S. *law educator, former territory supreme court justice*
Pierluisi, Pedro R. *lawyer*
Rodriguez-Diaz, Juan E. *lawyer*
Rodriguez-Velez, Rosa Emilia *prosecutor*
Santos de Alvarez, Brunilda *lawyer*
Wexler, David B. *law educator*

VIRGIN ISLANDS

Charlotte Amalie
Feuerzeig, Henry Louis *lawyer*

Christiansted
Bland, James Theodore, Jr. *lawyer*
Hewlett, Joycelyn Janice *lawyer*
McIntosh, Maxwell David *lawyer*

St Thomas
Caffee, Lorren Dale *lawyer*
Carty, Amos W. *lawyer*
Jenkins, Anthony Jerome *prosecutor*

MILITARY ADDRESSES OF THE UNITED STATES

PACIFIC

APO
Gordon, Carey Nathaniel *lawyer, federal agency administrator*

CANADA

ALBERTA

Calgary
Lougheed, Peter *lawyer, former Canadian premier*
McEwen, Alexander Campbell *legal association administrator, consultant, cadastral studies educator, former Canadian government official, land use planner*
Robottom, David T. *lawyer, energy executive*

BRITISH COLUMBIA

Burnaby
Switlo, Janice Georgina Alice E. *barrister, solicitor, mediator, consultant*
Wainwright, David Stanley *patent agent*

Sooke
Howard, John Lindsay *lawyer*

Vancouver
McEachern, Allan *lawyer*
Penikett, Tony *mediator, negotiator, writer*
Peterson, Leslie Raymond *barrister*

MANITOBA

Winnipeg
Anderson, David Trevor *law educator*
Edwards, Clifford Henry Coad *law educator*
Schnoor, Jeffrey Arnold *lawyer*

NEW BRUNSWICK

Rothesay
Fairweather, Robert Gordon Lee *retired lawyer*

NOVA SCOTIA

Halifax
Dexter, Robert Paul *lawyer*

ONTARIO

Markham
Gulden, Simon *lawyer, management consultant, consultant*

Ottawa
d'Aquino, Thomas *lawyer, educator, entrepreneur*
Pal, Prabir Kumar (Sunny Pal) *lawyer*
Tassé, Roger *lawyer, former Canadian government official*

Toronto
Arthurs, Harry William *lawyer, educator, academic administrator*
Chester, Robert Simon George *lawyer*
Dubin, Charles Leonard *lawyer*
Farquharson, Gordon MacKay *lawyer, director*
Kaufman, Donna Soble *lawyer, director*
Peterson, David Robert *lawyer, former Canadian government official*
Regan, Francis Vincent *lawyer*

West Toronto
Iacobucci, Frank *lawyer, judge, former academic administrator*

QUEBEC

Ile Perrot
Lalonde, Marc *lawyer, former Canadian government official*

Montreal
Popovici, Adrian *law educator*
Pound, Richard William Duncan *lawyer, accountant*
Robb, James Alexander *lawyer*

Quebec City
Dinan, Robert Michael *lawyer*
LeMay, Jacques *lawyer*
Morin, Louis *lawyer*
Prothro, Jerry Robert *lawyer*
Verge, Pierre *legal educator*

Sainte-Foy
Normand, Robert *retired lawyer*

Westmount
Fortier, L. Yves *barrister*

SASKATCHEWAN

Regina
MacKay, Harold Hugh *lawyer*

Saskatoon
Ish, Daniel Russell *law educator, academic administrator*

Montreal
Johnston, Donald James *lawyer, educator*

Toronto
Stanley, Deirdre *lawyer*

MEXICO

Mexico City
Carreto-Chavez, Gerardo *lawyer*

ARGENTINA

Buenos Aires
Walker, Ignacio Jose *lawyer*

AUSTRALIA

Melbourne
Browne, Jeffrey Francis *lawyer*

THE BAHAMAS

Nassau
Beck, Jan Scott *lawyer*

BANGLADESH

Kushtia
Latifur Rahaman, Rasul Boaksh *legal association administrator*

BELGIUM

Brussels
Barnum, John Wallace *lawyer*

BERMUDA

Hamilton
McCormick, Hugh Thomas *lawyer*

Pembroke
Spector, Phillip Louis *lawyer*

CHINA

Beijing
Christianson, Jon L. *lawyer*

Hong Kong
Halperin, David Richard *lawyer*
Nelson, Steven Craig *lawyer*

Shanghai
Lin, Maria C.H. *lawyer*

DENMARK

Copenhagen
Elmer, Michael Bendik *legal administrator*

ENGLAND

Beverley
Edles, Gary Joel *lawyer, educator*

London
Batla, Raymond John, Jr. *lawyer*
Fabricant, Arthur E. *lawyer, corporate financial executive*
Glazer, Barry David *lawyer*
Gottesman, A(rthur) Edward *lawyer*
Hudson, Manley O., Jr. *lawyer*
Lynch, John Edward, Jr. *lawyer*
Montgomery, John Warwick (Baron of Kiltartan and Lord of Morris, Comte de St. Germain de Montgommery) *law educator, theologian*
Phocas, George J. *lawyer*
Plapinger, William A. *lawyer*
Quillen, Cecil Dyer III *lawyer*
Stevens, Robert Bocking *lawyer*
Stojkovic, Dusan *lawyer*
Thomas, Allen Lloyd *lawyer, private investor*
Zonana, Victor *lawyer, educator*

Oxford
Raz, Joseph *philosophy and law educator*

Wiltshire
Sherwin, James Terry *lawyer*
Aufhauser, David D. *lawyer, former federal agency administrator*

FINLAND

Helsinki
Juhani, Erma *lawyer, former stock exchange executive*

FRANCE

Antony
Dahling, Gerald Vernon *lawyer, director*

Paris
Baum, Axel Helmuth *lawyer*
Kammerer, Kelly Christian *lawyer*
Rawlings, Boynton Mott *lawyer*
Reynolds, Stephen Robert *lawyer*
Salans, Carl Fredric *lawyer*

GERMANY

Berlin
Simon, Hans-Joerg Walter *lawyer*

Frankfurt
Simitis, Spiros *legal educator*

GUATEMALA

Guatemala City
Mayora-Alvarado, Eduardo Rene *lawyer, educator*

INDONESIA

Jakarta
Hsi, Edward Yang *lawyer, venture capitalist, industrialist*

ISRAEL

Be'er Sheva
Frenkel, David Arie *law professor*

Ramat-Gan
Aron, Roberto *lawyer, writer, educator*

Tel Aviv
Gross, Joseph H. *lawyer, educator*
Rosenne, Meir *lawyer, federal agency administrator*

ITALY

Rieti
Truini Palomba, Maria Giuseppina *supreme court lawyer, judge*

Rome
McGurn, William Barrett III *lawyer*

JAPAN

Tokyo
Farrar, Stanley F. *lawyer*
Shirai, Shun *law educator, lawyer*

NETHERLANDS

The Hague
Boed, Roman A. *legal administrator*

NORWAY

Oslo
Fitzpatrick, Whitfield Westfeldt *lawyer*

REPUBLIC OF KOREA

Seoul
O'Brien, Timothy James *lawyer*

RUSSIA

Moscow
Tillett, Samuel Raymond *lawyer*

SCOTLAND

Edinburgh
Macneil, Ian Roderick *lawyer, educator*

SIERRA LEONE

Freetown
Rapp, Stephen John *international prosecutor*

SPAIN

Madrid
Herrero Rodriguez de Miñon, Miguel *lawyer, legislator, consultant*

SWITZERLAND

Chateau d'Oex
Berman, Joshua Mordecai *lawyer, manufacturing executive*

Zurich
Hammesfahr, Robert Winter *lawyer*

TAIWAN

Tainan
Chen, Chun-Jen *lawyer, educator*

THAILAND

Phuket
Pianko, Theodore A. *lawyer*

VIETNAM

Ho Chi Minh City
Israel, Barry John *lawyer*

ADDRESS UNPUBLISHED

Abbott, Charles Favour *lawyer*
Abbott, Lawrence E. *lawyer*
Abraham, Alfred Jude *lawyer*
Adams, Arlin Marvin *lawyer, retired judge, arbitrator, mediator*
Adams, Daniel Fenton *law educator*
Adams, Thomas Lawrence *lawyer*
Adams, Thomas Lynch, Jr. *lawyer*
Aikman, Albert Edward *lawyer*
Akindemowo, Olujoke Eniola *law educator, researcher*
Alberger, William Relph *lawyer, former legislative staff, government official*
Albin, Barry G. *lawyer, rabbi*
Aldous, Charla G. *lawyer*
Alemu, Fitsum Achameyeleh *lawyer, researcher*
Alexander, George Jonathon *lawyer, educator, dean*
Alexander, Richard Elmont *lawyer*
Alfred, Stephen Jay *retired lawyer*
Allday, Martin Lewis, Jr. *retired lawyer*
Allen, Toni K. *lawyer*
Allen, William Hayes *lawyer, educator*
Alpern, Andrew *lawyer, architect, historian*
Alters, Jeremy W. *lawyer*
Altman, Louis *lawyer, author, educator*
Altman, Robert Alan *lawyer*
Altsuler, Kent *lawyer*
Amabile, John Louis *lawyer*
Amar, Akhil Reed *law educator*
Ames, Marc L. *retired lawyer*
Anderson, James Francis *lawyer*
Anderson, Jon Eric *lawyer*
Andrews, David Ralph *lawyer*
Ansley, Shepard Bryan *lawyer*
Arbaugh, Jon Halbert *legal assistant*
Areen, Judith Carol *law educator*
Ariyoshi, George Ryoichi *lawyer, business consultant, former governor*
ArmeN, Margaret Meis *lawyer*
Arnold, Alanna S. Welling *lawyer*
Arnold, Charlotte S. *criminal justice agency executive, activist*
Arnold, Jerome Gilbert *lawyer*
Arrowood, Catharine Biggs *lawyer*
Arthur (II), Hugh Thomas *lawyer*
Asai-Sato, Carol Yuki *retired lawyer*
Ashcroft, John David *law educator, former United States attorney general*
Ashe, Bernard Flemming *arbitrator, lawyer, educator*
Ashton, Harris John *lawyer*
Atchison, Rodney Raymond *retired lawyer, arbitrator*
Atkins, William Paul *lawyer*
Auerbach, Ernest Sigmund *lawyer, insurance company executive, writer*
Aune, Debra Bjurquist *lawyer*
Babbin, Jed Lloyd *lawyer, former deputy undersecretary of defense*
Bagley, William Thompson *lawyer*
Bain, William Donald, Jr. *lawyer, chemicals executive*
Baker, Donald *lawyer, director*
Baker, William Thompson, Jr. *lawyer*
Bakken, Gordon Morris *law educator*
Bakkensen, John Reser *lawyer*
Ball, James Herington *retired lawyer*
Bamberger, Phylis Skloot *lawyer, educator, retired judge*
Bandy, Jack D. *lawyer*
Barash, Anthony Harlan *lawyer*
Barger Johnson, Jennifer *law educator, judge*
Barker, Bruce Crichlow *barrister, solicitor*
Barnes, Joy Chappell *lawyer*
Barnhardt, Zeb Elonzo, Jr. *lawyer, mediator, arbitrator*
Barr, Charles F. *lawyer, insurance company executive*
Bartz, David John *lawyer*
Baruch, Hurd *retired lawyer*
Baskins, Ann O'Neil *lawyer, former computer company executive*
Bateman, David Alfred *lawyer*
Battocchi, Ronald Silvio *lawyer*
Baughman, R(obert) Patrick *lawyer*
Baum, Stanley David *lawyer*
Bauman, Frederick Carl *lawyer*
Baumgarten, Jon A. *lawyer*
Bayko, Emil Thomas *lawyer*
Bean, Bruce Winfield *lawyer*
Beck, William Harold, Jr. *lawyer*
Beldock, Myron *lawyer*
Bell, Albert Jerome *lawyer*
Bell, Haney Hardy III *lawyer*
Bell, John William *lawyer*
Belleville, Philip Frederick *lawyer*
Belnick, Mark Alan *lawyer*
Benfield, Ann Kolb *retired lawyer*
Bennett, Bryce Hugh, Jr. *lawyer*
Bennett, Richard Edward *lawyer*
Bergan, Edmund Paul, Jr. *lawyer*
Bergan, William Luke *lawyer*
Berger, Robert Bertram *lawyer*
Berger, Sanford Jason *retired lawyer, securities dealer, real estate broker*
Berger, Steven R. *retired lawyer, state official*
Bergstein, Daniel Gerard *lawyer*
Beringer, William Ernst *mediator, arbitrator, lawyer, retired manufacturing executive*
Berkley, Peter Lee *lawyer*
Berman, Richard Bruce *lawyer*
Berman, Tony *lawyer*
Bernard, Michael Mark *lawyer, city planning consultant*
Bernstein, Merton Clay *law educator, arbitrator*
Berrey, Robert Forrest *lawyer*
Bertram, Manya M. *retired lawyer*
Besing, Ray Gilbert *lawyer, educator*
Best, Laurence Edward *lawyer*
Beukema, John Frederick *lawyer*
Bevelhymer, Darlene Pearl *lawyer, retired secondary school educator*
Bewley, Peter David *lawyer*
Beyer, Marcus Paul *lawyer*
Bidwell, James Truman, Jr. *lawyer*
Bierig, Jack R. *lawyer, educator*
Bigelow, Robert P. *lawyer, arbitrator, mediator, journalist*
Birnbaum, Robby H. *lawyer*
Birne, Kenneth Andrew *lawyer*
Blachman, Michael Joel *lawyer*
Black, William Rea *lawyer*
Blackford, Robert Newton *lawyer, director*
Blake, Elizabeth K. *lawyer*
Blakely, William D. *lawyer*
Blakey, G(eorge) Robert *law educator*
Blatt, Gregory R. *lawyer*
Bleicher, Samuel Abram *law educator, consultant*
Blevins, James Ray *lawyer, insurance company claims executive*
Blevins, Jeffrey Alexander *lawyer*
Blixt, Charles A. *lawyer*
Bloch, Stuart Marshall *lawyer, banker*
Bloomer, Harold Franklin, Jr. *retired lawyer*
Blow, George *lawyer*
Boal, Ellis *lawyer*
Bobrow, Susan Lukin *retired lawyer*
Bodwell, Lori *lawyer*
Bogden, Daniel G. *former prosecutor*
Bokat, Stephen Arthur *lawyer, former business association executive*
Boldt, Kimberly L. *lawyer*
Bondi, Harry Gene *lawyer*
Boner, Eleanor Katz *lawyer*
Bonesio, Woodrow Michael *lawyer*
Booher, Alice Ann *lawyer*
Borenstein, Mark A. *lawyer*
Bork, Robert Heron *law educator, retired federal judge*
Borkowski, John Joseph *lawyer*
Borowitz, Albert Ira *lawyer, writer*
Bosl, Phillip L. *retired lawyer*
Bouvier, Marshall Andre *lawyer*
Bowden, William P., Jr. *lawyer, finance company executive*
Bower, Jean Ramsay *lawyer, writer*
Bowers, Christi C. *mediator, lawyer, writer, poet*
Bowman, Patricia Lynn *lawyer*
Boyd, Joseph Arthur, Jr. *lawyer*
Boyd, William Sprott *lawyer*
Bradley, Amelia Jane *lawyer*
Brady, Edmund Matthew, Jr. *lawyer*
Brady, Edward Thomas, Jr. *lawyer, writer*
Brady, Terrence Joseph *mediator, arbitrator, retired judge*
Brafford, William Charles *lawyer*
Bragg, Michael Ellis *lawyer, insurance comp executive*
Branagan, James Joseph *lawyer*
Branstetter, Cecil Dewey, Sr. *lawyer*
Brantz, George Murray *retired lawyer*
Braun, Jerome Irwin *lawyer*
Brawner, Gerald Andre *paralegal*
Bredehoft, John Michael *lawyer*
Breece, Robert William, Jr. *lawyer*
Brehl, James William *lawyer*
Brennan, James Joseph *lawyer, bank executive*
Brewer, Roy Edward *lawyer*
Brigham, Henry Day, Jr. *retired lawyer*
Brister, Bill H. *lawyer, former bankruptcy jud*
Brodhead, David Crawmer *lawyer*
Brooke, Edward William III *lawyer, retired senator*
Brooks, Patrick William *lawyer, researcher*
Broughton, Phillip Charles *lawyer, director*
Brown, B. Andrew *lawyer*
Brown, Charles Dodgson *lawyer*
Brown, Herbert Russell *lawyer, writer*
Brown, J. E. (Buster Brown) *lawyer, consultar*
Brown, John Robert *lawyer, priest*
Brown, Peter Megargee *lawyer, educator, writ*
Brown, Raymond M. *lawyer, television personality*
Brown, Robert Baldwin III *lawyer*
Brown Spitzmueller, Janiece Marie *lawyer*
Bruess, Charles Edward *lawyer*
Bryson, Nancy Southard *lawyer, former federa agency administrator*
Buchanan, William H., Jr. *retired lawyer, ventu capitalist*
Buchbinder, Darrell Bruce *lawyer*
Buckley, Frederick Jean *lawyer*
Buckley, Kristy Loraine *lawyer, accountant*
Buda, Thaddeus J., Jr. *retired lawyer*
Burack, Michael Leonard *lawyer*
Burgess, Hayden Fern (Poka Laenui) *lawyer*
Burk, Robert S. *lawyer*
Burke, Linda Beerbower *lawyer, mining executive, metal products executive*
Burkey, Lee Melville *lawyer*
Burnstein, Daniel *lawyer*
Burris, Kelly L. *lawyer*
Burris, Steven Michael *lawyer*
Burt, Richard *lawyer*
Burton, Richard Jay *lawyer*
Butler, William Joseph *lawyer, educator*
Buttrey, Donald Wayne *lawyer*
Cacciatore, Ronald Keith *lawyer*
Cades, Stewart Russell *lawyer, communicatior executive*
Calhoun-Senghor, Keith *lawyer*
Calise, William Joseph, Jr. *lawyer*
Cambrice, Robert Louis *lawyer*
Cameron, Jeffrey M. *lawyer*
Camilleri, Michael *lawyer, educator*
Campbell, Frederick Hollister *retired lawyer, historian, retired military officer*
Campbell, George Emerson *lawyer*
Campion, Thomas Francis *lawyer*
Campos-Orrego, Nora Patricia *lawyer, consult*
Caraway, Stephanie Schankerman *prosecutor*
Carey, Jana Howard *lawyer*
Carmack, Mildred Jean *retired lawyer*
Carpenter, Susan Karen *defender*
Carroll, Joseph J(ohn) *lawyer*
Carson, Christopher Leonard *retired lawyer*
Carter, Jeanne Wilmot *lawyer, publishing executive*
Casella, Peter F(iore) *patent and licensing executive*
Casillas, Mark *lawyer*
Casselman, William E., II, *lawyer*
Cassidy, John Harold *lawyer*
Castel, Jean Gabriel *lawyer, educator, international arbitrator*
Castro, Raul Hector *lawyer, retired governor, ambassador*
Cavallini, Donna Francesca *law librarian*
Cazalas, Mary Rebecca Williams *lawyer, nurs*
Cermak, Josef Rudolf Cenek *lawyer, director*
Chaifetz, David Harvey *lawyer*
Chamberlin, Michael Meade *lawyer*
Chance, Steven Kent *lawyer*
Chandra, Subodh *lawyer*
Chapple, Thomas Leslie *lawyer*
Charles, Robert Bruce *lawyer, former federal agency administrator*
Charlton, Paul K. *former prosecutor, lawyer*
Chave, Carol *arbitrator, retired lawyer*
Cheatham, Robert William *retired lawyer*
Cheek, Michael Carroll *lawyer*
Chen, Del-Min Amy *lawyer*
Cherovsky, Erwin Louis *lawyer, writer*
Chiara, Margaret Mary *former prosecutor, lawyer*
China, Daniel William *lawyer*
Chisholm, Tommy *lawyer, utilities executive*
Chopin, Christopher Allen *lawyer*
Christensen, Karen Kay *lawyer*
Christopher, William Garth *lawyer*
Citron, Beatrice Sally *law librarian, educator*
Citron, Diane *lawyer*
Clancy, Patrick L. *lawyer*
Clark, Beverly Ann *retired lawyer*
Clark, Celia Rue *lawyer*
Clark, Donald Otis *lawyer*
Clark, Karen Heath *lawyer*
Clark, Ramsey (William Ramsey Clark) *lawy former United States attorney general*
Closen, Michael Lee *retired law educator*
Clubb, Bruce Edwin *retired lawyer*
Cobb, Miles Alan *retired lawyer*
Coccia, Michel Andre *retired lawyer*
Cohen, Christopher B. *lawyer*
Cohen, Joel J. *lawyer, investment banker*
Cohen, Nelson Craig *lawyer*
Coleman, James Edwin, Jr. *lawyer*

Jordan, Jerry Dale *lawyer, gas industry executive*
Jordan, Katherine D. (Kate Jordan) *lawyer*
Joyce, Joseph James *lawyer, food products executive*
Kahn, Laurence Michael *lawyer, management consultant*
Kantor, Mark Alan *lawyer, arbitrator*
Kantrowitz, Susan Lee *lawyer*
Kaplan, Barry Martin *lawyer*
Kaplan, Helene Lois *lawyer*
Kapner, Lewis *lawyer*
Kapnick, Richard Bradshaw *lawyer*
Karon, Sheldon *lawyer*
Kaster, Laura A. *lawyer*
Katz, Lawrence Sheldon *lawyer*
Katz, Sanford Noah *lawyer, educator*
Kauffman, David Lin *lawyer*
Kaufman, James Jay *lawyer*
Kaye, Stuart Martin *lawyer*
Kearney, Douglas Charles *lawyer, journalist*
Keatinge, Robert Reed *lawyer*
Keaty, Robert Burke *lawyer, business consultant*
Keeling, J(ohn) Michael *lawyer, trade association executive*
Keith, William Douglas *lawyer*
Kelley, James Francis *lawyer*
Kelly, Timothy William *lawyer*
Kempf, Donald G., Jr. *retired lawyer*
Kennedy, Harold Edward *lawyer*
Kennedy, Thomas J. *lawyer*
Kenrich, John Lewis *retired lawyer*
Kent, Matthew *law clerk*
Kerner, Michael Philip *lawyer*
Kestenbaum, Harold L. *lawyer*
Kienitz, LaDonna Trapp *lawyer, librarian, municipal official*
Kilbourn, William Douglas, Jr. *law educator*
Killeen, Michael John *lawyer*
Kim, Michael S. *lawyer*
Kimball, Richard Arthur, Jr. *retired lawyer*
King, David Roy *lawyer*
King, Jack A. *lawyer*
King, Michael Howard *lawyer*
King, Rebecca J. *lawyer, consultant*
King, Robert Lucien *retired lawyer*
Kirchman, Eric Hans *lawyer*
Kirk, John Robert, Jr. *retired lawyer, consultant*
Kirschner, William Steven *lawyer*
Kittrell, Pamela R. *lawyer*
Kitzmiller, Howard Lawrence *retired lawyer*
Klafter, Cary Ira *lawyer*
Klamon, Lawrence Paine *lawyer*
Klaus, Charles *retired lawyer*
Klayman, Larry Elliott *lawyer, legal association administrator*
Klein, Eugene *lawyer*
Klein, Linda Ann *lawyer*
Klein, Paul E. *lawyer*
Klott, David Lee *lawyer*
Knecht, James Herbert *retired lawyer*
Knight, Gary *lawyer, writer, educator*
Koch, Kathleen Day *lawyer*
Kohlstedt, James August *lawyer*
Kojima, Takeshi *law educator, arbitrator, writer, dean*
Kolbert, Kathryn *lawyer, educator*
Kolodny, Stephen Arthur *lawyer*
Kope, Shane Brien *lawyer*
Korn, Michael Jeffrey *lawyer*
Korn, Peter A. *arbitrator, mediator, educator*
Kotcher, Shirley J.W. *lawyer*
Kraft, Henry Robert *lawyer*
Kramer, Paul R. *lawyer*
Kranzow, Ronald Roy *lawyer*
Kratt, Peter George *lawyer*
Kreizinger, Loreen I. *lawyer*
Krivoshia, Eli, Jr. *lawyer*
Krohnke, Duane W. *retired lawyer*
Kubo, Edward Hachiro, Jr. *prosecutor*
Kumble, Steven Jay *lawyer*
Kusma, Kyllikki *retired lawyer*
Lacer, Alfred Antonio *lawyer, educator*
Lackland, John *lawyer, nurseryman*
Laliberte, Brian J. *prosecutor*
Lamborn, LeRoy Leslie *law educator*
Lamel, Linda Helen *lawyer, arbitrator, professional society and retired insurance company executive, college president*
Lanahan, Daniel Joseph *lawyer*
Landry, Paul Leonard *lawyer*
Landy, Lisa Anne *lawyer*
Langenkamp, R. Dobie *lawyer, educator*
Lanier, W. Mark *lawyer*
Lannon, Paul G. *lawyer*
LaRobardier, Genevieve Krause *lawyer*
Lasky, David *lawyer*
Lathrope, Daniel John *law educator*
Latta, Thomas Albert *lawyer*
Laudone, Anita Helene *lawyer*
Lawless, Thomas William *lawyer*
Lawrence, Glenn Robert *arbitrator, mediator, lawyer*
Lea, Lorenzo Bates *lawyer*
Leachman, Russell DeWitt *lawyer*
Leary, Thomas Barrett *lawyer, former federal agency administrator*
LeBlanc, Jonathan M. *lawyer*
Lederer, Peter David *lawyer*
Lee, Marilyn Modarelli *lawyer, retired law library director*
Lefkowitz, Alan Zoel *retired lawyer*
Lempert, Richard Owen *lawyer, educator*
Lentz, Mary A. *lawyer, educator*
Levin, A. Leo *law educator, retired government official*
Levin, William Edward *lawyer*
Levine, Alan *lawyer*
Levinson, Peter Joseph *retired lawyer*
Levy, David *retired lawyer, insurance company executive, consultant*
Lewis, David L. *lawyer*
Libassi, Frank Peter *lawyer*
Lichtenbaum, Peter *lawyer, former federal agency administrator*
Lichtenstein, Natalie G. *lawyer*
Licke, Wallace John *lawyer*
Lidsky, Ella *retired law librarian*
Liebeler, Susan Wittenberg *lawyer*
Lightstone, Ronald *lawyer*
Ligon, Duke R. *lawyer*
Liguori, Robert *lawyer, insurance company executive*
Lilienstern, O. Clayton *lawyer, educator*
Lilly, Thomas Gerald *retired lawyer*
Linde, Maxine Helen *lawyer, corporate financial executive, investor*
Lineen, Edward M. *lawyer, information technology executive*
Linett, David *retired lawyer*
Link, George Hamilton *retired lawyer*
Lippes, Richard James *lawyer*
Lipsky, Burton G. *lawyer*
Lipsman, Richard Marc *lawyer, educator*
Lipton, Robert Steven *lawyer*
Litman, Harry Peter *lawyer, educator*
Lloyd, David Livingstone, Jr. *lawyer*
Locke, William Henry *lawyer*
Logan, James Kenneth *lawyer, retired judge*
Lombard, Richard Spencer *lawyer*
Long, Charles Thomas *lawyer, history professor*
Long, Clarence Dickinson III *lawyer*
Long, James Jay *lawyer*
Longobardo, Guy Alfred *lawyer, department chairman*
Loren, Norman James *lawyer*
Lorne, Simon Michael *lawyer*
Loscalzo, Anthony Joseph *lawyer*
Lotter, Charles Robert *retired lawyer*
Love, Michael Joseph *lawyer*
Lovell, Carl Erwin, Jr. *lawyer*
Lubick, Donald Cyril *lawyer*
Lundgren, Gail M. *lawyer*
Lupin, Louis Martin *lawyer*
Lurie, Alvin David *lawyer*
Lynch, Robert Berger *retired lawyer, judge*
Lynch, Thomas Wimp *lawyer*
Lyon, Bruce Arnold *lawyer, educator*
Mabey, Ralph R. *lawyer*
MacCarthy, John L. *lawyer*
MacDonald, Donald Paul *lawyer*
Macdonald, Lenna Ruth *lawyer, business advisor*
MacKinnon, John Alexander *lawyer*
MacKinnon, Kevin Scott *lawyer*
Magurno, Richard Peter *lawyer*
Mahoney, George LeFevre *lawyer*
Mahoney, George R., Jr. *lawyer*
Malatesta, Mary Anne *lawyer*
Malkin, Michael M. *lawyer*
Malloy, John Richard *lawyer, chemicals executive*
Manne, Henry Girard *lawyer, consultant, economist, educator, retired dean*
Manos, Christopher Lawrence *lawyer, mediator*
Maready, William Frank *lawyer*
Margolis, Daniel Herbert *lawyer*
Marinis, Thomas Paul, Jr. *lawyer*
Marker, Marc Linthacum *lawyer, investor, entrepreneur*
Marsh, Jack, Jr., (John Otho Marsh) *lawyer, former federal agency administrator, congressman*
Marshall, Dante *lawyer*
Marshall, Kathryn Sue *lawyer*
Marshall, Marilyn Josephine *retired lawyer*
Martin, Alice Howze *prosecutor*
Martin, James William *lawyer*
Martin, John William, Jr. *retired lawyer, automotive executive*
Martin, William Edwin *lawyer*
Martineau, Robert John *retired law educator*
Martin Patterson, Connie Ruth *retired lawyer*
Mastandrea, Linda Lee *lawyer*
Mathewson, George Atterbury *retired lawyer*
Mathis, John Prentiss *lawyer*
Matthews, Paul Aaron *lawyer*
Mattson, Stephen Joseph *retired lawyer*
May, Christopher N. *retired law educator*
May, Henry Stratford, Jr. *lawyer*
Mayer, James Joseph *retired corporate lawyer*
McAmis, Edwin Earl *lawyer*
McAvoy, John Joseph *lawyer*
McCabe, Thomas Edward *lawyer, financial software executive*
McCarey, Wilma Ruth *retired lawyer*
McCarthy, J. Thomas *lawyer, educator*
McCarthy, Vincent Paul *lawyer*
Mc Clendon, William Hutchinson III *retired lawyer*
McCobb, John Bradford, Jr. *lawyer*
McConnell, Edward Bosworth *legal association administrator, lawyer*
McConnell, John William, Jr. *lawyer*
McCormack, Douglas P. *lawyer*
Mc Cormack, Francis Xavier *lawyer, former oil company executive*
McCormick, David Arthur *lawyer*
McCormick, Homer L., Jr. *lawyer*
McCoy, John Joseph *lawyer*
McCue, Howard McDowell III *lawyer, educator*
McCurley, Robert Lee, Jr. *lawyer, educator*
McDermott, Kathleen E. *lawyer*
McDonald, Bradley G. *lawyer*
McDonnell, Joseph B. *lawyer*
McGoldrick, John Lewis *lawyer*
McGrath, J. Paul *lawyer*
McIntosh, Terrie Tuckett *lawyer*
McKay, John Douglas *lawyer*
McKean, Robert Jackson, Jr. *retired lawyer*
McKeown, William P. *retired lawyer*
McKinstry, Ronald E. *retired lawyer*
McLaughlin, Joseph *lawyer*
McLendon, Susan Michelle *lawyer*
McMahon, James E. *lawyer, former prosecutor*
McManus, Richard Philip *lawyer, agricultural products executive*
McMillan, Robert Ralph *lawyer*
Mc Quade, Lawrence Carroll *lawyer, investment company executive*
Mead, Matthew Hansen *former prosecutor*
Mehltretter, Kathleen M. *former prosecutor*
Meli, Salvatore Andrew *lawyer*
Meltzer, Jay H. *lawyer, consultant*
Mentz, Lawrence *lawyer*
Mercer, Edwin Wayne *lawyer*
Merrill, Abel Jay *retired lawyer*
Merring, Robert Alan *lawyer, arbitrator, mediator*
Merritt, Bruce Gordon *lawyer*
Merritt, Nancy-Jo *lawyer*
Messier, Pierre *lawyer, manufacturing executive*
Metcalfe, Robert Davis III *lawyer*
Metzger, Jeffrey Paul *lawyer*
Meyer, Max Earl *lawyer*
Meyerson, Ivan D. *lawyer, former corporate financial executive*
Michael, Mark Dixwell *lawyer*
Middleton, James Boland *retired lawyer*
Miles, Donald F. *lawyer*
Miller, Gay Davis *lawyer*
Miller, Kerry Lee *lawyer*
Miller, Lisa Ann *lawyer*
Miller, R. Charles *lawyer*
Miller, Richard Steven *lawyer*
Miller, Robert Joseph *lawyer, former governor*
Miller, Thormund Aubrey *lawyer*
Miller, Warren Lloyd *lawyer*
Millimet, Erwin *lawyer*
Milner, Irvin Myron *retired lawyer*
Minahan, Daniel Francis *lawyer, retired manufacturing executive*
Mingle, James John *lawyer*
Mintz, M. J. *lawyer*
Miquelon, Miriam F. *former prosecutor, lawyer*
Mirabile, Thomas Keith *lawyer*
Missan, Richard Sherman *lawyer, educator*
Mitchell, Carol Ann *lawyer*
Mitchell, David Benjamin *lawyer, arbitrator, mediator*
Mitchell, William Graham Champion *lawyer, corporate officer*
Molinaro, Thomas J. *lawyer*
Monaco, Daniel Joseph *lawyer*
Mooney, Thomas Robert *lawyer*
Moore, Betty Jo *legal assistant*
Moore, Mike (Michael C.) *lawyer, former state attorney general*
Morgan, Timi Sue *lawyer*
Morof, Jeffrey W. *lawyer*
Morris, Roy Leslie *lawyer, electrical engineer, venture capitalist*
Morris, Thomas Bateman, Jr. *lawyer*
Morrison, Donald William *lawyer*
Morse, Robert Harry *lawyer*
Mossawir, Harve H., Jr. *retired lawyer*
Moya, Patrick Robert *lawyer*
Moyer, Craig Alan *lawyer*
Mudd, John O. *lawyer*
Mugridge, David Raymond *lawyer, educator, writer*
Muller, Peter *lawyer, film company and retail executive*
Muller, Scott William *lawyer*
Munsell, Elsie Louise *retired lawyer*
Murchison, David Claudius *lawyer*
Murphy, Daniel Ignatius *lawyer*
Murphy, Kathleen M. *lawyer*
Murphy, Sandra Robison *lawyer*
Murray, William Michael *lawyer*
Musick, Robert Lawrence, Jr. *lawyer*
Myers, Jesse Jerome *lawyer*
Nanda, Ved Prakash *law educator, director, academic administrator*
Naples, Caesar Joseph *lawyer, educator*
Nash, Melvin Samuel *lawyer*
Natcher, Stephen Darlington *retired lawyer, electronics executive*
Nelson, Allyson Lyn *lawyer*
Nelson, Carl Roger *retired lawyer*
Nelson, Roy Hugh, Jr. *mediator, arbitrator, lawyer*
Nesbitt, Charles Rudolph *lawyer, energy executive, consultant*
Neuhaus, Joseph Emanuel *lawyer*
Newman, Carol L. *lawyer*
Newman, Joan Meskiel *lawyer*
Newton, Francis Chandler, Jr. *lawyer*
Nifong, Michael Byron *former prosecutor*
Nikas, Richard John *lawyer*
Nix, Edmund Alfred *lawyer*
Noddings, Sarah Ellen *lawyer*
Nolen, William Giles *lawyer, accountant*
Norton, Gale Ann *lawyer, former secretary of the interior*
Nys, John Nikki *lawyer*
Oakes, Dennis *lawyer, insurance company executive*
Ober, Richard Francis, Jr. *lawyer, director, banker*
O'Brien, J. Willard *lawyer, educator*
O'Brien, William Jerome, II, *lawyer*
O'Connell, Philip Raymond *retired lawyer, paper company executive*
O'Connor, Edward Vincent, Jr. *lawyer*
O'Donnell, John Michael *lawyer*
Oettinger, Julian Alan *lawyer, pharmaceutical executive*
Ogg, Wilson Reid *lawyer, retired judge, poet, curator, publishing executive*
O'Keefe, Edward Franklin *lawyer*
Olmstead, Clarence Walter, Jr. *lawyer*
Olson, Robert Wyrick *lawyer*
O'Meara, John Francis *lawyer*
Onyido, John Chike *lawyer*
Orden, Stewart L. *lawyer*
Orlebeke, William Ronald *retired lawyer, writer*
O'Rourke, C. Larry *lawyer*
O'Shea, Patrick Joseph *lawyer, electrical engineer*
Oshima, Michael W. *lawyer*
O'Sullivan, Judith Roberta *lawyer, writer, artist*
Otis, Lee (Sarah) Liberman *lawyer, educator*
Packard, Stephen Michael *legal association administrator, lawyer*
Page, Rodney Fred *lawyer*
Painter, Richard William *lawyer, educator*
Painton, Russell Elliott *retired lawyer, mechanical engineer*
Pallot, Joseph Wedeles *lawyer*
Parks, Jane deLoach *retired law librarian, legal assistant*
Parode, Ann *lawyer*
Parr, Royse Milton *retired lawyer, writer*
Parrette, Leslie Jackson *lawyer*
Partridge, Bruce James *lawyer, educator, writer*
Pascale, Daniel Richard *lawyer*
Pasco, Hansell Merrill *retired lawyer*
Patrick, Victor Phillip *lawyer, construction executive*
Patton, James Richard, Jr. *lawyer*
Paul, Eve W. *retired lawyer*
Paul, Richard Wright *lawyer*
Pavarini, Peter Alfred *lawyer*
Payne, Leland Howard *lawyer*
Pear, Charles E., Jr. *lawyer*
Peck, Douglas Edward *lawyer*
Peck, Mira P. *lawyer*
Pereyra-Suarez, Charles Albert *lawyer*
Perez, Paul Ignatius *prosecutor, lawyer*
Perkiel, Mitchel H. *lawyer*
Perrin, Michael Warren *lawyer*
Pesch, Ellen P. *lawyer*
Peshkin, Samuel David *retired lawyer*
Peterson, Bruce D. *lawyer, energy executive*
Peterson, Howard Cooper *lawyer, accountant*
Petrillo, Leonard Philip *lawyer, retired investment company executive*
Pettiette, Alison Yvonne *lawyer*
Pfaffenroth, Peter Albert *lawyer*
Phair, Joseph Baschon *lawyer*
Phillips, Dorothy K. *lawyer*
Phillips, James Harold *retired lawyer*
Phillips, Leo Harold, Jr. *lawyer*
Phillips, Robert James, Jr. *lawyer, corporate financial executive*
Pieper, Darold D. *lawyer*
Piga, Stephen Mulry *retired lawyer*
Pinchak, Ann Simcha *lawyer*
Piper, George Chilton *lawyer*
Pitcher, Griffith Fontaine *lawyer*
Pittman, Lisa *lawyer*
Pollard, Dennis Bernard *lawyer, educator*
Pollard, Henry *arbitrator, mediator*
Polon, Ira H. *lawyer*
Polsby, Allen Isaac *retired lawyer*
Pomeroy, Gregg Joseph *lawyer*
Poppe, Laurie Catherine *matrimonial lawyer, social worker, real estate executive*
Poppler, Doris Swords *lawyer*
Porter, J. Ridgely III *lawyer*
Porter, Michael Pell *lawyer*
Portnoy, Sara S. *lawyer*
Posner, Sylvie Pérez *lawyer*
Potter, Tanya Jean *lawyer*
Pound, Frank R., Jr. *lawyer*
Powell, Kathleen Lynch *lawyer, real estate executive*
Powers, Elizabeth Whitmel *lawyer*
Prather, William C. III *lawyer, writer*
Pratt, Robert Windsor *lawyer*
Prem, F. Herbert, Jr. *retired lawyer*
Press, Anthony L. *lawyer*
Prewoznik, Jerome Frank *retired lawyer*
Price, Alfred Lee *lawyer, mining executive*
Prince, Andrew Steven *lawyer, retired government agency administrator*
Purtle, John Ingram *lawyer, former state supr court justice*
Pustilnik, David Daniel *lawyer*
Pytell, Robert Henry *retired lawyer, former ju*
Quarles, James Linwood III *lawyer*
Quay, Thomas Emery *lawyer*
Quillen, Cecil Dyer, Jr. *lawyer, consultant*
Radford, R. S. *lawyer, law educator*
Ragone, Tara Adams *lawyer*
Rainville, Christina *lawyer*
Rappaport, James Wyant *lawyer, real estate developer*
Rash, David C. *lawyer*
Ratner, Michael D. *lawyer*
Rawls, Frank Macklin *lawyer*
Raymond, David Walker *lawyer*
Rea, Anne E. *lawyer*
Reath, George, Jr. *lawyer, mediator, arbitrato*
Reddy, Shyam K. *lawyer*
Redman, Clarence Owen *lawyer*
Reed, Austin F. *lawyer*
Reeder, James Arthur *lawyer*
Reeder, Robert Harry *retired lawyer*
Regenstreif, Herbert *lawyer*
Reich, Laurence *lawyer*
Reiche, Frank Perley *lawyer, former federal commissioner*
Reichs, Kerry E. *lawyer*
Reinhart, Richard Paul *lawyer*
Reiss, Jerome *retired lawyer*
Reiter, Glenn Mitchell *lawyer*
Reveal, Ernest Ira III *retired lawyer*
Rew, Lawrence Boyd *lawyer*
Reynolds, William Bradford *lawyer*
Rhyne, Sidney White *retired lawyer*
Rich, Michael Joseph *lawyer*
Richardson, Arthur Wilhelm *lawyer*
Richardson, John Carroll *lawyer, financial consultant*
Richardson, Margaret Milner *retired lawyer*
Richey, Mary Ellen *lawyer*
Rick, Roseleen P. *lawyer*
Ricks, Joycia Camilla *retired lawyer*
Ring, Renee Etheline *lawyer*
Rissman, Burton Richard *lawyer*
Rivera, Oscar R. *lawyer, educator*
Rivlin, Rachel *lawyer*
Rizowy, Carlos Guillermo *lawyer, educator, political analyst*
Robbins, Norman Nelson *lawyer*
Roberts, William H. *lawyer*
Robinson, Davis Rowland *lawyer, internation arbitrator*
Rochlin, Paul R. *lawyer*
Rodenburg, Clifton Glenn *lawyer*
Roditti, Esther C(laire) *lawyer, writer*
Rodnunsky, Sidney *lawyer, educator*
Rodriguez, Carlos A. *lawyer*
Rodriguez, Carlos Augusto *lawyer*
Rodriguez, Vivian N. *lawyer, accountant*
Roe, Mark J. *law educator*
Rohrbach, Heidi A. *lawyer*
Romanow, Josh *lawyer*

omer, Denise Patrice *lawyer*
ose, Elihu Isaac *lawyer*
osenhouse, Howard *retired lawyer*
osenkranz, E. Joshua *lawyer*
osenn, Harold *lawyer*
osha, Uzi *lawyer*
osky, Burton Seymour *lawyer*
osner, Seth *lawyer, educator*
oss, Harold Anthony *lawyer*
oss, Michael Aaron *lawyer*
oster, Michael *lawyer*
oth, Michael *lawyer*
othman, Howard Joel *lawyer*
owe, Audrey *paralegal*
ubenfeld, Stanley Irwin *lawyer, director, mediator, arbitrator*
ıbenstein, Allen Ira *lawyer*
ıbin, Richard Allan *lawyer*
ıbin, Zick *lawyer, writer, psychology professor*
uddy, Kathy Aakre *paralegal*
ıdolph, Wallace Morton *law educator*
ıffner, Charles Louis *lawyer*
ıhm, Thomas Francis *retired lawyer*
ıbatino, Thomas Joseph, Jr. *lawyer, pharmaceutical executive*
ıck, Sylvan Hanan *lawyer*
ıcripanti, Peter John *lawyer*
Clair, Donald David *lawyer*
Claire, Frank Arthur *lawyer*
literman, Richard Arlen *lawyer*
lvan, Sherwood Allen *lawyer*
lzman, Stanley P. *lawyer*
muels, Janet Lee *lawyer*
ndman, Dan D. *lawyer*
nford, Irene W. *lawyer*
ntman, Leon Duane *lawyer, former federal government executive*
pp, John Raymond *lawyer*
rno, Maria Erlinda *lawyer, chemist*
ttler, Bruce Weimer *lawyer*
unders, Lonna Jeanne *lawyer, newscaster*
unders, Terry Rose *lawyer*
vitt, Susan Schenkel *lawyer, mediator*
x, Joseph Lawrence *lawyer, educator*
acchetti, David J. *lawyer*
haefer, William Goerman *lawyer*
harf, Michael Paul *law educator*
heffler, Stuart Jay *lawyer*
heyer, Daniel *lawyer*
hild, Raymond Douglas *lawyer*
hlozman, Bradley J. *former prosecutor*
hlueter, Linda Lee *law educator*
hmidt, Karl A. *lawyer*
hmidt, Kathleen Marie *lawyer*
hmitz, Joseph Edward *lawyer, former federal agency administrator*
hmoll, Harry F., Jr. *lawyer, educator*
hmults, Edward Charles *lawyer*
hneider, Carl Edward *law educator*
hneidler, Jon Gordon *lawyer*
hor, Suzi *lawyer, psychologist*
hrag, Philip Gordon *law educator*
hram, Ronald Byard *lawyer*
hreiber, Paul Solomon *lawyer*
huchard, Robert L. *lawyer*
hulman, Alan *lawyer*
hultz, Dennis Bernard *lawyer*
hwab, Eileen Caulfield *lawyer, educator*
hwabe, John Bennett, II, *lawyer*
hwartz, Leonard Jay *retired lawyer*
hwerdtner, Frederick Howard *lawyer, retired police commander, real estate broker*
ott, Michael Dennis *lawyer*
udlo, Walter Joseph *lawyer*
abolt, Robert D. *lawyer*
ars, Mary Helen *lawyer*
gal, Phyllis Nichamoff *mediator*
gel, Karen Lynn Joseph *lawyer, tax specialist*
idel, Selvyn *lawyer, educator*
dman, Ellen Shapiro *lawyer, government official*
ymour, Barbara Laverne *lawyer*
kas, Stephen James *lawyer, educator*
affer, Richard James *lawyer, retired manufacturing executive*
affert, Kurt *retired lawyer, chemical engineer*
ambaugh, Stephen Ward *lawyer*
apiro, Edwin Stanley *lawyer, judge*
apiro, Sander Wolf *retired lawyer*
arbaugh, Thomas J. *lawyer*
arkey, Robert Emmett *lawyer*
attuck, Cathie Ann *lawyer, former government official*
aw, Elizabeth Orr *retired lawyer*
aw, L. Edward, Jr. *lawyer*
aw, Nina L. *lawyer*
eeder, Robert Elwood *lawyer*
eils, Paul T. *lawyer*
eldon, Terry Edwin *lawyer, investment advisor*
epard, Michael J. *prosecutor*
ere, Dennis *lawyer, writer, retired publishing executive*
eriff, Seymour *retired lawyer*
erling, Fred W. *lawyer*
ampock, Kathy Elizabeth *lawyer, writer*
adley, Bryan Douglas *lawyer*
ıler, Caroletta Alexis *criminal justice educator*
ıman, Samuel Irving *lawyer, educator*
es, Jack Davis, Jr. *lawyer*
gel, Sarah Ann *lawyer*
kman, Thomas Clement *lawyer*
ner, Deanne Clemence *lawyer*
mon, Joyce Marilyn *lawyer, writer*
ety, Charles Edward *lawyer, financial planner*
erberg, Mark Victor *lawyer, educator*
estri, Gina *lawyer*
non, Robert G. *lawyer*
ıs, John R. *lawyer*
or, Howard Earl, Jr. *lawyer*
, Wang-Ngai *solicitor*
gen, Patricia Sue *lawyer*
lnik, Barnet David *retired lawyer*
vitt, David Walton *retired lawyer*
er, Herbert Jacquemin, Jr. *lawyer*
naker, Norman Dale *lawyer*
ver, William Lewis *lawyer*

Smith, Carole Dianne *retired lawyer, editor, writer, product developer*
Smith, Deirdre O'Meara *lawyer*
Smith, George Patrick, II, *lawyer, educator*
Smith, Jack David *lawyer*
Smith, James A. *lawyer*
Smith, Jules Louis *lawyer*
Smith, Julious Perry, Jr. *lawyer*
Smith, Morton Alan *retired lawyer*
Smith, Robert Michael *lawyer, mediator, arbitrator, writer*
Smith, William Charles *retired lawyer*
Smith, Yolanda Ippolito *law educator, researcher, writer*
Smouse, H(ervey) Russell *lawyer*
Sneeringer, Stephen Geddes *lawyer*
Snow, Tower Charles, Jr. *lawyer*
Snyder, Jean Maclean *lawyer*
Soble, Mark Richard *lawyer*
Sokol, Jan D. *lawyer*
Solkoff, Jerome Ira *lawyer, educator*
Solls, Mark A. *lawyer*
Sorensen, Murray Jim *lawyer*
Sowande, Beverly Folasade *lawyer, educator*
Spander, Deborah L. *lawyer*
Sparks, John Edward *lawyer*
Sparks, Robert Ronold, Jr. *lawyer*
Speaker, Susan Jane *lawyer*
Speers, Roland Root, II, *lawyer*
Spicer, S(amuel) Gary *lawyer, writer, educator*
Spiegel, Jayson Leslie *lawyer, educator, professional society administrator*
Spitzberg, Irving Joseph, Jr. *lawyer*
Springer, Jeffrey Alan *lawyer*
Springer, Paul David *lawyer, film company executive*
Sprung, Arnold *lawyer*
Spurgeon, Edward Dutcher *lawyer, educator, foundation administrator*
Stark, Robert J. *lawyer*
Stead, Edward Benjamin *lawyer*
Stedman, Richard Ralph *retired lawyer*
Stephens, Shand Scott *lawyer*
Stephens, Theodore Reed *lawyer*
Steptoe, Mary Lou *lawyer*
Stern, Joseph A. *lawyer*
Sterrett, Samuel Black *lawyer, former judge*
Stewart, Charles Leslie *lawyer*
Stiefel, Linda Shields *lawyer*
Stiller, Shale David *lawyer, educator*
Stillman, Elinor Hadley *retired lawyer*
Stoiber, Carlton Ray *nuclear law consultant, freelance/self-employed cartoonist*
Stoller, John R. *lawyer*
Stone, Andrew Grover *lawyer*
Stone, Donald Raymond *lawyer*
Stone, Edward Herman *lawyer*
Strantz, Nancy Jean *law educator, consultant*
Stratton, Walter Love *lawyer*
Streb, Paul Gerard *arbitrator*
Street, Erica Catherine *lawyer*
Strick, Gerald Jay *lawyer*
Strutin, Kennard Regan *lawyer, educator, librarian*
Surles, Richard Hurlbut, Jr. *retired law librarian*
Susman, Morton Lee *lawyer*
Sussman, Howard Sivin *lawyer*
Sutter, Laurence Brener *lawyer*
Swacker, Frank Warren *lawyer*
Swanson, Victoria Clare Heldman *lawyer*
Sweeney, Deidre Ann *lawyer*
Taft, Sheldon Ashley *retired lawyer*
Taliaferro, Philip III *lawyer*
Tallman, Ann Marie *lawyer*
Tamen, Harriet *lawyer*
Tanaka, J(eannie) E. *lawyer*
Tancs, Linda Ann *lawyer*
Tanenbaum, Jay Harvey *lawyer*
Tanner, W(alter) Rhett *lawyer*
Taub, Eli Irwin *arbitrator, mediator, lawyer, judicial hearing officer*
Taub, Stephen Richard *lawyer*
Tavrow, Richard Lawrence *lawyer*
Taylor, Job III *lawyer*
Termini, Roseann Bridget *law educator*
Terp, Thomas Thomsen *lawyer*
Terrell, G. Irvin *lawyer*
Thiele, Howard Nellis, Jr. *lawyer*
Thoman, Henry Nixon *lawyer*
Thomas, David Lindsey *lawyer, former state senator*
Thomas, Franklin Augustine *lawyer, consultant*
Thomas, Melissa Ann *lawyer*
Thomas, Patricia Anne *retired law librarian*
Thompson, Holley Marker *lawyer, consultant, marketing professional*
Thompson, James Alexander, Jr. *lawyer*
Thompson, Philip C. *lawyer, investment advisor, educator*
Thorne, William Albert *retired lawyer*
Thumma, Samuel Anderson *lawyer*
Thurmond, J. Strom, Jr. *lawyer, former prosecutor*
Tingle, James O'Malley *retired lawyer*
Tinkelman, Joan *lawyer*
Titus, Christina Maria *lawyer*
Toedt, D(ell) C(harles) III *lawyer*
Tolins, Roger Alan *lawyer*
Tolman, Philip D. *lawyer, corporate financial executive*
Tondel, Lawrence Chapman *lawyer*
Toomey, Richard Andrew, Jr. *lawyer*
Torgerson, Larry Keith *lawyer*
Torre, Gary Jerome *retired lawyer*
Tract, Marc Mitchell *lawyer*
Traeger, Charles Henry III *lawyer*
Treacy, Vincent Edward *lawyer*
Trimble, Phillip Richard *law educator*
Trimble, Sandra Ellingson *lawyer*
Trimble, William Cattell, Jr. *retired lawyer*
Trost, Glenn W. *lawyer*
Trott, Thomas G. *lawyer*
Trotta, Frank P., Jr. *lawyer*
Tucker, Laurey Dan *lawyer*
Tucker, Watson Billopp *lawyer*
Turnage, Fred Douglas *retired lawyer*
Turner, George Mason *lawyer*

Turpening, Patricia Eileen Keller *retired law librarian*
Twardy, Stanley Albert, Jr. *lawyer*
Tyler, Peggy Lynne Bailey *retired lawyer*
Tyndall, Jay Mark *lawyer*
Ulrich, Werner
Underwood, Mark Forest *lawyer*
Uttal, Susan *legal administrator*
Vacco, Dennis C. *lawyer, former state attorney general*
Vachss, Andrew Henry *lawyer, writer, juvenile justice and child abuse consultant*
Vance, Vanessa L. *lawyer*
Van Gorder, John Frederic *lawyer*
Van Vleet, William Benjamin *lawyer, retired insurance company executive*
Venters, Harley Eugene *lawyer*
Vila, Adis Maria *lawyer, business government executive*
Villavaso, Stephen Donald *lawyer, urban planner*
Vinar, Benjamin *lawyer*
von Sauers, Joseph F. *lawyer*
Vosk, Ted W. *lawyer*
Wagner, Arthur Ward, Jr. *lawyer*
Walker, Craig Michael *lawyer*
Walker, Linda Lee *lawyer*
Walker, Mark A. *lawyer*
Walker, Richard Henry *lawyer*
Wallack, Rina Evelyn *lawyer*
Wallison, Frieda K. *lawyer*
Walmer, Edwin Fitch *retired lawyer*
Walpole, Jim (James R.) *lawyer*
Wanger, Eugene Gilkison *retired lawyer*
Warner, Karl K. *former prosecutor*
Warnock, William Reid *lawyer*
Weaver, Delbert Allen *retired lawyer*
Weber, Susan A. *lawyer*
Webster, Robert Kenly *lawyer*
Weil, Peter Henry *lawyer*
Weinman, Glenn Alan *lawyer*
Weinstein, Arthur Gary *lawyer*
Weir, Sir William H. *lawyer, judge, educator*
Weisberg, David Charles *lawyer*
Weisman, Paul Howard *lawyer*
Weiss, Kenneth Andrew *lawyer, educator*
Weldon, Jeffrey Alan *lawyer*
Welnak, Llowell A. *retired lawyer*
Welsh, John Beresford, Jr. *retired lawyer*
Weltchek, Robert Jay *lawyer*
Werthan, Jeffrey Michael *lawyer*
Wessel, Peter *lawyer*
Wessling, Robert Bruce *retired lawyer*
Westfall, David *lawyer, educator*
Weston, Michael C. *retired lawyer*
Wetherill, Eikins *lawyer, investment company executive*
Wheeler, R(ichard) Kenneth *lawyer, educator*
Wheeler, Stephen Frederick *legal administrator*
Whelan, Stephen Thomas, Jr. *lawyer*
White, Jill Carolyn *lawyer*
White, John Joseph III *lawyer*
White, Kendred Alan *lawyer*
White, William Nelson *lawyer*
Whitmore, Bruce G. *lawyer*
Wiehl, Lis W. *legal analyst, educator*
Wiggins, Charles Henry, Jr. *lawyer*
Wilburn, Mary Nelson *lawyer, writer, poet, translator*
Wilcox, Mark Dean *lawyer*
Wildhack, William August, Jr. *lawyer*
Wileman, George Robert *retired lawyer*
Wiley, Richard Arthur *lawyer*
Willard, Richard Kennon *lawyer, former pharmaceutical company executive*
Williams, Paul Robert *lawyer, foreign policy analyst*
Williams, Stephen Edward *retired lawyer*
Willner, Kenneth M. *lawyer*
Wilner, Thomas Bernard *lawyer*
Wilson, John Pasley *retired law educator*
Wilson, Karen Wilkerson *paralegal*
Wilson, Rhys Thaddeus *lawyer*
Wilson, Virgil James III *lawyer, judge*
Winslow, John Franklin *lawyer*
Wittig, Raymond Shaffer *lawyer, intellectual property technology manager*
Wolf, Alan Steven *lawyer*
Wolfson, Michael George *retired lawyer*
Wong, Stova *law firm executive*
Wong-Diaz, Francisco Raimundo *lawyer, educator*
Wood, Robert Charles *lawyer, real estate developer*
Woodard, Joseph Lamar *law librarian, emeritus professor*
Wooldridge, William Charles *lawyer*
Worenklein, Jacob Joshua *lawyer*
Worrell, Stewart Phillip *lawyer, diversified financial services company executive*
Worthington, Daniel Glen *lawyer, educator*
Wray, Wilson E., Jr. *lawyer*
Wright, James Ralph *retired lawyer*
Wright, Robert Payton *lawyer*
Wriston, Kathryn Dineen *corporate director, consultant*
Wruble, Bernhardt Karp *lawyer*
Wunsch Cox, Kathryn Sutherland *retired lawyer*
Wyatt, Robert Lee, IV, *lawyer*
Wyatt, Thomas Csaba *lawyer*
Wyker, Kenneth E. *lawyer*
Yarbrough, Matthew E. *lawyer*
Yeager, Dennis Randall *lawyer*
York, David P. *former prosecutor*
Young, John Hardin *lawyer*
Young, Marlene Annette *lawyer*
Young, Robert Bond *lawyer*
Young, Sherilyn Burnett *lawyer*
Young, Thomas Lee *lawyer*
Yung, Patsy P. *lawyer*
Zarro, Janice Anne *lawyer*
Zeller, Michael Eugene *lawyer*
Zerger, Kirsten Louise *mediator, lawyer*
Ziegler, John Augustus, Jr. *lawyer*
Ziegler, William Alexander *lawyer*
Zimmer, Markus Bernhard *legal association administrator*
Zimmerman, Jean *lawyer*

Zischke, Michael Herman *lawyer*
Zoeller, Donald J. *lawyer*
Zohn, Martin Steven *lawyer*

MEDICINE *See* HEALTHCARE: MEDICINE

MILITARY

UNITED STATES

ALABAMA

Auburn
Tolbert, Clinton Jame *army officer, machinist*

Elberta
Wilkinson, Edward Anderson, Jr. *retired military officer, manufacturing executive*

Enterprise
Parker, Ellis D. *retired military officer*

Gulf Shores
Virden, Frank Stanley *retired military officer*

Huntsville
Burrows, Shania Kay *civilian military employee*
Williamson, Donald Ray *retired career Army officer*

Madison
Parlier, Greg H. *military officer, analyst, engineer, researcher*

Montgomery
Turley, Susan Lynn Welker *military officer*
Uzzell-Baggett, Karon Lynette *career officer*

ARIZONA

Tucson
Cook, Paul Christopher *intelligence officer*
Thurman, Robert Kenneth *retired military officer*
Wickham, John Adams, Jr. *retired army officer*

Yuma
Hudson, John Irvin *retired career officer*

ARKANSAS

Mountain Home
Baker, Robert Leon *military officer*

CALIFORNIA

Arroyo Grande
Oseguera, Palma Marie *retired career officer*

Carlsbad
Kauderer, Bernard Marvin *retired naval officer, consultant*
Smarsh, James David *retired military officer*

Chula Vista
Briggs, Franklin Henry *retired military officer*
Worthington, George Rhodes *retired naval officer*

Coronado
Butcher, Bobby Gene *retired military officer*

El Segundo
Hamel, Michael A. *career officer*

Escondido
Briggs, Edward Samuel *naval officer*

Folsom
Jefferds, William John *military officer*

Healdsburg
Eade, George James *retired military officer, researcher*

La Jolla
Counts, Stanley Thomas *retired military officer, retired electronics executive*

Long Beach
Higginson, John *retired career officer*

Monrovia
Fannin, Daniel Paul Clark *information systems executive*

Monterey
Brook, Douglas Alan *former civilian military employee*
Hoivik, Thomas Harry *military educator, international consultant*
Matthews, David Fort *career officer*
Oliver, Daniel T. *military education administrator, career officer, retired*
Schrady, David Alan *civilian military employee, educator*

Oxnard
Kirschbaum, Alan Ira *air force officer, systems integration specialist*

San Diego
Barr, Edward Sheldon *military officer, writer*

Covey, Dana Curtis *military officer, orthopaedic surgeon*
Darmstandler, Harry Max *retired military officer*
Fernandez, Alfredo Tumbaga, Jr. *military officer*
Koenig, Harold Martin *former United States Navy surgeon general*
Wing, Thomas M. *military officer, systems engineer*

San Marcos
Jones, William Henry *retired military officer*

Santa Barbara
Conley, Philip James, Jr. *retired air force officer*

Santa Maria
Roadarmel, Stanley Bruce *civilian military employee*

Santa Rosa
Andriano-Moore, Richard Count *retired military officer, secondary school educator, elementary school educator*

Seaside
Gales, Samuel Joel *retired civilian military employee, counselor*

Studio City
Williscroft, Robert G. *retired military officer, writer*

Windsor
Sparks, Bennett Sher *military officer*

COLORADO

Colorado Springs
Bowen, Clotilde Marion Dent *retired military officer, psychiatrist*
Renuart, Victor Eugene, Jr., (Gene Renuart) *career military officer*
Skora, Wayne Philip *retired air force officer*
Willis, Frank Edward *retired air force officer*

Denver
Charlip, Ralph Blair *military officer, health facility administrator*

Dillon
Dugan, Michael Joseph *former career officer, health agency executive*

Durango
Fogleman, Ronald Robert *retired air force officer, consultant*

Monument
Breckner, William John, Jr. *retired military officer*
Rokke, Ervin Jerome *military officer, academic administrator*

U S A F Academy
Merchant, P. Glenn, Jr. *military officer, physician*
Westermann, Edward Burton *military officer, analyst, educator*

CONNECTICUT

Groton
Stoddard, Patrick Clare *retired military systems consultant, computer engineer*

Middletown
Fusco, George Matthew *retired military officer, engineer*

New London
Bald, Ronald James *military officer*
Van Sice, James *career military officer, academic administrator*

Niantic
Hunt, Francis Howard *retired navy laboratory official*

Waterford
Hinkle, Muriel Ruth Nelson *naval warfare analysis company executive*

Wilton
Burki, Arde A. *retired military officer*

DISTRICT OF COLUMBIA

Bolling Afb
Dendinger, William J. *career officer, chaplain*

Washington
Allen, Thad William *career military officer*
Anderson, William Carl *civilian military employee, lawyer*
Antony, Paul T. *military officer, physician executive*
Aviles, Dionel Michael *civilian military employee, former federal agency administrator*
Barno, David W. *retired military officer*
Black, Scott C. *career military officer, lawyer*
Bolton, Claude M., Jr. *civilian military employee, retired military officer*
Bowman, Frank Lee (Skip Bowman) *retired military officer*
Bradley, John A. *career military officer*
Buckenmaier, Chester III *military officer, anesthesiologist*
Cartwright, James E. *career military officer*
Casey, George William, Jr. *career military officer*
Chiarelli, Peter W. *career military officer*
Cofer, Jonathan H. *career officer*
Conway, James Terry *career military officer*
Cothron, Tony L. *career military officer*
Crawford, Hunt Dorn, Jr. *retired military officer, educator, diplomat*
Crea, Vivien S. *career military officer*
Cross, Terry M. *career military officer*
Crowe, William James, Jr. *former Chairman of the Joint Chiefs of Staff, international consultant*
Davis, Morris D. *military officer, lawyer*
DuBois, Raymond Francis, Jr. *civilian military employee, former marketing professional*
Dyke, Charles William *retired army officer*
Eastin, Keith E. *civilian military employee, lawyer*
Etter, Delores M. *civilian military employee*
Ford, Nelson M. *civilian military employee*
Fraser, William M. III *career military officer*
Gavrilis, James *military officer*
Geren, Pete (Preston M. Geren III) *civilian military employee, former congressman*
Gibson, Emmitt E. *career officer*
Harvey, John Collins, Jr. *military officer*
Helmly, James R. *career military officer*
Hemingway, Thomas L. *career military officer, lawyer*
Houck, James W. *career military officer, lawyer*
Huston, John Wilson *military officer, historian*
James, Ronald J. *civilian military employee, lawyer*
Kern, Paul John *retired military officer*
King, James C. *retired military officer*
Lakner, George Stephen *military officer*
Leaf, Howard Westley *retired military officer*
Lichte, Arthur J. *career military officer*
MacDonald, Bruce E. *military officer, lawyer*
Mateczun, John Matthew *career military officer*
McGrath, Kevin Michael *military analyst, civilian military employee, researcher*
McNabb, Duncan J. *career military officer*
Moseley, T. Michael (Teed Michael Moseley) *military officer*
Mullen, Michael G. *career military officer*
Navas, William Antonio, Jr. *civilian military employee and retired officer*
Odom, William Eldridge *retired military officer*
O'Reilly, Kenneth William *retired military officer*
Pace, Peter *Chairman of the Joint Chiefs of Staff*
Paige, Kathleen K. *naval officer*
Payton, Sue C. *civilian military employee*
Penn, Buddie J. (B.J. Penn) *civilian military employee*
Ralston, Joseph W. *retired military officer*
Retz, William Andrew *naval consultant, retired naval officer*
Robison, Victor James, Jr. *retired military officer*
Sams, Ronald F. *career military officer*
Schmitt, John K. *army officer*
Schoomaker, Eric B. *career military officer*
Schwartz, Norton A. *career military officer*
Sega, Ronald Michael *civilian military employee, former dean*
Sharp, Walter L. (Gary Sharp) *career military officer*
Sinn, Jerry L. *army officer*
Tabb, Vandoster Langford, Sr. *retired military officer*
Van Antwerp, Robert L., Jr. *career military officer*
Walsh, Patrick M. *career military officer*
Wholley, Michael Christopher *retired military officer, lawyer*
Wilson, Frances C. *career military officer*
Winter, Donald C. *civilian military employee, former science administrator*
Woodley, John Paul, Jr. *civilian military employee, lawyer*
Wright, Daniel V. *career military officer, judge*
Wynne, Michael Walter *civilian military employee*
Zarychta, William Alex *medical officer, physician assistant*
Zinni, Anthony Charles *retired military officer*

FLORIDA

Altoona
Westbrook, Clinton Howard *retired military petty officer, retired protective services official*

Bradenton
Wilburn, Donald Lee *military officer, retail executive*

Celebration
Whelden, Craig B. *retired army officer*

Cocoa Beach
Adkisson, Hubert Keith *military officer*

Eglin Afb
Vail, Thomas Leighton *military officer*

Haines City
Clement, Robert William *retired air force officer*

Indian Harbor Beach
Scanlon, Charles Francis *retired military officer, writer, publisher*

Jacksonville
Delaney, Kevin Francis *retired military officer, consultant*
Folk, David Wilbur *occupational health and safety administrator*

Lake Forest
Ross, Jimmy Douglas *retired military officer*

Longwood
Smyth, Joseph Patrick *retired military officer, physician*

Melbourne
Laposata, Joseph Samuel *army officer*
Simokaitis, Frank Joseph *military officer, lawyer*

Miami
Stavridis, Jim (James George Stavridis) *career military officer*

Miami Gardens
Vangates, Dess *retired military officer*

Naples
Delano, Victor *retired naval officer*
Slaff, Allan Paul *military officer, academic administrator, educator, entrepreneur*

New Port Richey
Miller, Harvey William *retired military officer*

Orlando
Bigum, Randall K. *retired military officer*

Palm Bay
Sheets, Fredrick Sidney *retired military officer, auditor*

Palm Beach Gardens
Giordano, Andrew Anthony *retired naval officer*

Pensacola
Robinson, Harold Gilbert *retired military officer, civilian military employee*

Sarasota
Cooper, William Ewing, Jr. *retired army officer*
Gauch, Eugene William, Jr. *retired air force officer*
Heiser, Rolland Valentine *former army officer, foundation administrator*

Stuart
Slaihem, Ameer Abdullah *career officer*

Tampa
Collins, Jessica Ann *military officer*
Dempsey, Martin E. *career military officer*
Fallon, William Joseph *career military officer*
Haggis, Arthur George, Jr. *retired military officer, educator, publisher*
Matheny, Charles Woodburn, Jr. *former army officer, civil engineer, city official*
Odierno, Raymond T. *career military officer*
Olson, Eric Thor *career military officer*
Petraeus, David Howell *career military officer*

West Palm Beach
Thomashow, Steven Roy *military officer, intelligence officer*

GEORGIA

Alpharetta
DiBattiste, Carol A. *military officer*

Atlanta
Donald, James Edward *retired career officer, government agency executive*
McGuinn, Michael Edward III *retired army officer*
Swift, Charles D. *career military officer, lawyer, educator*

Columbus
Tipton, James D. *retired military officer, education educator*

Douglas
McCrea, Derek Duane *military officer, artist*

Forest Park
Honoré, Russel L. *career military officer*

Fort Benning
Gittins, Timothy *military officer*
Kotwal, Russ Steven *military officer, physician*

Fort Mcpherson
Stultz, Jack C. *career military officer*

Fort Stewart
Stone, Joshua James *military officer*

Jonesboro
Galvin, John Rogers *retired army officer, law educator*

Rome
Sender, James LeRoy *retired military officer, retired federal agency administrator*

Warner Robins
Nugteren, Cornelius *air force officer*

Woodbine
Konetzni, Albert H., Jr. *career officer*

HAWAII

Camp H M Smith
Keating, Timothy J. *career military officer*

Hickam Afb
Paddock, Lori Ann *military officer*

Honolulu
Hays, Ronald Jackson *career officer*
Wellein, Marsha Diane Akau *military educator, director*

Kaneohe
Strang, Nathan Thomas *military officer*

M C B H Kaneohe Bay
Liu, Derek C. *military officer*

Pearl Harbor
Willard, Robert F. *career military officer*

IDAHO

Boise
Clemins, Archie Ray *career officer*

ILLINOIS

Batavia
Brown, Gerald Curtis *retired military officer, engineering executive*

Champaign
Greene, James K. *military officer, educator*

Mattoon
Phipps, John Randolph *retired army officer*

O Fallon
Voellger, Gary A. *business consulting executiv retired air force officer*

Rockford
Borling, John Lorin *military officer*

INDIANA

Madison
Jones, Richard Sheffield *veterans service office*

KANSAS

Fort Leavenworth
Anderson, David Allen *military officer, educat*
Cupp, Orville Shawn *military officer*
O'Neill, Mark E. *military officer*

Manhattan
Myers, Richard Bowman *former joint chiefs o staff chairman, educator*

KENTUCKY

Fort Campbell
Clark, Cecil Lee *military officer*
Griffin, Johnny Lee *military officer*

Ft Campbell
Gutheinz, Michael John *military officer, lawye*

Richmond
Burch, John Russell *retired military officer*

LOUISIANA

Fort Polk
Rolin, Daniel Wayne, Jr. *military officer*

MAINE

Stockton Springs
Snyder, Arnold Lee, Jr. *retired military officer, research director*

MARYLAND

Aberdeen Proving Ground
Halstead, Rebecca S. *career military officer*

Annapolis
Grooms, Bruce Estes *career military officer*
Trost, Carlisle Albert Herman *retired naval officer*

Arnold
Williams, James Arthur *retired military office information technology executive*

Baltimore
Weyandt, Daniel Scott *retired naval officer, engineer, physicist*

Bethesda
Daniel, Charles Dwelle, Jr. *retired military officer*
Kem, Richard Samuel *retired army officer*
Less, Anthony Albert *retired naval officer*
Peck, Edward Lionel *retired foreign service officer, corporate executive*
Schmidt, Raymond Paul *military officer, historian, government agency administrato*

Burtonsville
Hudson, McKinley *retired military officer, re zoological park administrator*

Chevy Chase
Pirie, Robert Burns, Jr. *defense analyst*

Frederick
Albright, Joseph William *civilian military employee*

Lonaconing
Puddy, William (Bill) Curtiss *retired military officer, not-for-profit developer*

Silver Spring
Brog, David *former air force officer, consulta*

Solomons
Dorsey, James Francis, Jr. *naval officer*

Timonium
Sagerholm, James Alvin *retired naval officer*

SACHUSETTS

ngton
Joseph Wendell *retired naval officer*

bridge
n, Jennifer Toby *military officer*

ns
Michael J. *military officer*

com Afb
, David Taylor *civilian military employee*
n, Charles L., II, *military officer*

k
, George David *retired military officer, for-profit executive*

h Oxford
, Roger Francis Xavier *retired military er*

rville
arztraubber, Sayre Archie *former naval er, maritime consultant*

ngfield
Billy Maxwell *retired military officer*

HIGAN

ings
nie, V. Harry *retired military medical vice officer, science educator, ironmentalist*

NESOTA

a
, Bertram George *retired military officer, urities dealer*

nouth
ey, Robert D. *retired army officer*

SISSIPPI

Christian
rdell, James Elton *retired naval officer*

SOURI

Leonard Wood
, Constant Peter *retired military officer, itary analyst, consultant*

erson City
y, David Allen *military officer*

lar Bluff
g, William Webb *military officer, aire rfare specialist, poet*

t Louis
ey, Tracy Elmer, Jr. *army officer, surgeon, alth facility administrator*

NTANA

nilton
ey, Jack Carson *retired military officer*

W HAMPSHIRE

toocook
, Wayne Edward *retired military officer*

W JERSEY

t Dix
ns, Keith Robert *military officer*

t Monmouth
h, John Kenneth *civilian military employee*

sey City
ins, John W., Jr. *retired military officer, chnologist, educator*

nceton
h, Howard K., Jr. *military officer, university dministrator*

W MEXICO

uquerque
rnoy, John Charles, Sr. *retired civilian ilitary employee, officer*
midt, Charles Otto *military officer, engineer*

s Cruces
ur, Paul Keith *retired military officer*

nta Fe
, Randall Dean *military analyst, retired ilitary officer*
ner, Gordon, Jr. *retired military officer*

s
kers, Robert Edwin *retired military officer, istorian, writer*

NEW YORK

Fayetteville
Meigs, Montgomery Cunningham, Jr. *retired military officer, educator*

Fort Drum
Youngs, Michael Theron, Jr. *non-commissioned officer*

Hamburg
Markulis, Henryk John *career military officer*

Malone
Stone, Todd M. *military officer*

Marcellus
Taylor, Robert Wilson *military officer, publishing executive*

Rome
Ferens, Daniel Vincent *retired civilian military employee*

West Point
Boettner, Daisie Dawson *military officer, mechanical engineering educator*

NORTH CAROLINA

Camp Lejeune
Chadwick, Christopher Michael *military officer*

Fort Bragg
Anderson, Curtis Thorwald, II, *military officer*
Fishback, Ian *military officer*

Pinehurst
Carroll, Kent Jean *retired naval officer*

Spring Hope
Hildreth, James Robert *retired air force officer*

Taylorsville
Lewczyk, David C. *military officer*

OHIO

Brookpark
Heil, Michael Lloyd *military officer, academic administrator*

Cincinnati
Randolph, Leonard McElroy, Jr. *career officer*
Smittle, Nelson Dean *military analyst, artist*

Dayton
Jackson, Jason M. *military officer, educator*

Wright Patterson Afb
Cranston, Stewart E. *career officer*
Ray, James Lee *military officer*

OKLAHOMA

Edmond
Hopwood, Howard Hoppy Perry *military officer*

Oklahoma City
Reimer, Dennis J. *retired career military officer*

Tinker AFB
Foote, Wayne C. *military officer*
Goodman, Ernest Monroe *military officer*
Heinz, Jeremy David *military officer*

OREGON

Lake Oswego
McPeak, Merrill Anthony *retired military officer, investor, company director*

PENNSYLVANIA

Annville
Kiehl, Kraig Robert *military officer, law educator*

Bensalem
Long, Robert C. *retired military officer, management consultant*

Carlisle
Huntoon, Maj. Gen. David H., Jr. *military officer*

Clarks Green
Kubic, Charles Richard *civil engineer*

Corry
Chaffee, Philip *retired military officer, retired small business owner*

Evans City
Pagonis, William Gus *retired army general*

Gettysburg
Coughenour, Kavin Luther *career officer, military historian*

Glenshaw
Wilkes, John Michael *military officer, auditor*

Harrisburg
Renner, William Scott *retired military officer*

King Of Prussia
Gallis, John Nicholas *retired military officer, executive leadership training consultant*

Lock Haven
Jamieson, Cynthia Kay *military specialist*

Mechanicsburg
Derr, William James *retired non-commissioned officer*
Sutherly, Curtis Kent *civilian military employee, journalist, writer*

Pittsburgh
Stein, Adam Matthew *military officer*

Rutledge
Senior, Robert Thomas *retired military officer*

RHODE ISLAND

Newport
Carpenter, Stanley Dean MacDonald *military officer, educator*

Portsmouth
Bergstrom, Albion Andrew *retired military officer, educator*

SOUTH CAROLINA

Aiken
Chelberg, Robert Douglas *military officer*

Bluffton
Brown, Dallas Coverdale, Jr. *retired military officer, historian, educator*
Pendley, William Tyler *military officer, educator*

Charleston
Grinalds, John Southy *military officer, retired academic administrator*
Watts, Claudius Elmer III *retired military officer*

Clemson
Clausen, Hugh Joseph *retired army officer*

Columbia
Ellison, Henry Phillips *military officer*
Shuler, Ellie Givan, Jr. *retired military officer, museum administrator*

Hilton Head Island
Brown, Arthur Edmon, Jr. *retired army officer*

Irmo
Parks, Garry Lee *military officer*

Laurens
Gordon, Bobby G. *civilian military employee*

New Zion
Gibbons, Robert Butler, Jr. *retired military officer*

Newberry
Lander, James Albert *retired military officer, controller*

Sumter
Olsen, Thomas Richard, Sr. *air force officer*

Union
Whitener, William Jackson *retired military officer, retired dean*

Wedgefield
McLaurin, Hugh McFaddin III *military officer, museum program director*

York
Blackwell, Paul Eugene, Sr. *military officer*

TEXAS

Alice
Tetlie, Harold *soldier, priest*

Austin
Vande Hey, James Michael *retired air force officer*

Belton
Shoemaker, Robert Morin *retired military officer, commissioner*

College Station
Schunicht, Shannon Anthony *retired military officer, political scientist*

Fort Hood
Metz, Thomas Frederic *career military officer*
Sorenson, Kenneth Raymond *military officer, chaplain*

Fort Sam Houston
Fallert, David Orval *military officer, military analyst*
Goetschius, James Brian *military officer, urban planner*

Fort Worth
Nicholas, Nicholas Constantine *retired military officer*

Houston
Heuser, Mark Charles *military officer, educator*

Lubbock
Huffman, Walter B. *retired army officer, dean, law educator*

Mission
Eyre, Pamela Catherine *retired career officer*

Portland
Soliz, Eusebio *military officer*

Randolph Afb
Ellis, Edward R. *career officer*
Looney, William R. III *career military officer*

Sachse
Eichelberger, Charles Bell *retired career officer*

San Antonio
Kline, John William *retired military officer, management consultant*
Koziol, John Craig (Craig Koziol) *career military officer*
Myers, Paul Walter *military officer, researcher, retired neurosurgeon*
Sculley, Patrick David *retired army officer, director*
Zieres, Carol Lynne *military officer*

Sheppard Afb
Cook, Sharla J. *career officer*

The Woodlands
Jones, Lincoln III *military officer*

Waxahachie
Kiser, Colin Lee *military officer, government contractor*

Wichita Falls
Hamlin, Don Auer *retired military officer, financial health care executive*

UTAH

Dugway
Davis, Vernon Thomas *military officer, researcher*

Hill AFB
Bergren, Scott C. *career officer*
Lohman, Arthur Grover *civilian military employee*

Provo
Baum, Kerry Robert *retired military officer, director*

VIRGINIA

Alexandria
Adams, Ranald Trevor, Jr. *retired air force officer*
Blair, Dennis Cutler *career officer*
Bowman, Richard Carl *defense consultant, retired air force officer*
Brown, Frederic Joseph *military officer*
Burke, Kelly Howard *retired military officer, entrepreneur, philanthropist*
Dunn, Bernard Daniel *former naval officer, consultant*
Edmonds, Albert J. *career officer*
Fedorochko, William, Jr. *retired military officer, military analyst*
Gurke, Sharon McCue *career officer*
Hansen, Jacob Bernard *military officer*
Kroesen, Frederick James *retired army officer, consultant*
Smith, Jeffrey Greenwood *retired military officer*
Wolfe, Thad Allison *air force officer*

Annandale
Tencer, John G. *military officer*

Arlington
Blum, Steven (H. Steven Blum) *career military officer*
DeFilippi, George *retired air force officer*
Dodgen, Larry J. *career military officer*
Graves, Ernest, Jr. *retired army officer, consultant, engineer*
Hokborg, Sven-Olof *military officer*
McCaffrey, Barry Richard *retired military officer*
McKinley, Craig R. *career military officer*
Miller, Kenneth Gregory *retired air force officer*
Nash, Anthony J. *military analyst*
Price, Joseph Maurice *retired military officer*
Putnam, George W., Jr. *retired army officer*
Rogers, Alan Victor *former career officer*
Schultz, Roger C. *career military officer*
Singstock, David John *military officer*
Vaughn, Clyde A. *career military officer*

Dulles
Glacel, Robert Allan *retired military career officer*

Dumfries
Avrit, Richard Calvin *defense consultant, career officer*

Fairfax
Rosenkranz, Robert Bernard *military officer*

Falls Church
Gray, D'Wayne *retired marine corps officer*
Rostker, Bernard *civilian military employee*
Shipko, Janet M. *program director*

Fort Belvoir
Anderson, Frank J., Jr. *retired career officer*
Crenshaw, Horace, Jr. *military officer*

Great Falls
Cowhill, William Joseph *retired naval officer, consultant*

Gum Spring
Dilworth, Robert Lexow *career military officer, educator*

Hampton
Abner, Harold Loyd *military officer, consultant*

Haymarket
Seely, James Michael *retired military officer, defense consultant, small business owner*

Langley Afb
Blalock, Thomas Sullivan, Jr. *military officer*
Corley, John D. W. *career military officer*

Leesburg
Brown, James Robert *retired air force officer*

Lexington
Taylor, Wesley Bayard, Jr. *retired army officer*

Lynchburg
Snead, George Murrell, Jr. *military officer, research scientist, consultant*

Mc Lean
Felman, Marc David *air force officer*
Layman, Lawrence *naval officer*
Yarborough, William Glenn, Jr. *military officer, forester, international business executive*

Merrifield
Earner, William Anthony, Jr. *naval officer*

Millboro
Minetree, James Lawrence III *retired military officer, educator*

Norfolk
Adams, Kevin MacGregor *military officer, educator*
Kern, David Jeffery *military officer*
Quinlan, Kenneth J., Jr. *military officer*
Reason, J. Paul *naval officer*
Roughead, Gary *career military officer*
Smith, Lance L. *career military officer*
Train, Harry Depue, II, *retired naval officer*

Oakton
Frost, S. David *retired naval officer*

Occoquan
Vercauteren, Richard Frank *career officer*

Potomac Falls
Trainor, Bernard Edmund *retired military officer*

Prospect
Picotte, Leonard Francis *naval officer*

Purcellville
Davenport, Aaron Christopher *military officer*

Quantico
Dotto, Peter Attilius *retired marine corps officer, defense consultant*

Radford
Radford, James H. *retired military officer, political science professor*

Reston
Miller, John Edward *military officer, educational association administrator, information technology executive*
Naylon, Michael Edward *retired army officer*

Round Hill
Tice, Raphael Dean *military officer*

Springfield
Ginn, Richard Van Ness *retired military officer, healthcare executive*
Hart, Herbert Michael *military officer*

Suffolk
Baker, Timothy Louis *retired naval officer*

Vienna
Chandler, Hubert Thomas *former army officer*
Jenkins, Robert Gordon *retired military officer, federal official*
Webb, William Loyd, Jr. *retired military officer*

Virginia Beach
Apperson, Jack Alfonso *retired army officer, management executive*
Stansberry, James Wesley *air force officer*

Waynesboro
Alexander, William Woodward, Jr. *military officer*

Woodbridge
Hollingsworth, Bobby G. *career officer*
Messerschmidt, William Harclerode *retired non-commissioned officer, musician*

Woodstock
Sharp, Wayne David *retired military officer*

WASHINGTON

Anacortes
Higgins, Robert (Walter) *career officer, physician*

Lynnwood
Jenes, Theodore George, Jr. *retired military officer*

Spokane
Main, Jack *military officer*

Tacoma
Baxter, Sheila R. *career military officer*

WEST VIRGINIA

Kearneysville
Williams, Solomon Joseph III *military officer*

Mullens
McGhee, William Cleveland *retired military officer, retired transportation engineer*

MILITARY ADDRESSES OF THE UNITED STATES

EUROPE

APO
Lietzau, William Kendall *career officer, lawyer*
Mason, Kevin George *military analyst and officer*
Prendergast, Kenneth Lee Michael, Jr. *career officer*
Yates, Mary Carlin *civilian military employee, former ambassador*

CANADA

ONTARIO

Ottawa
de Chastelain, A(lfred) John G(ardyne) D(rummond) *Canadian army officer, diplomat*
Tellier, Henri *retired Canadian military officer*

Ontario
MacKenzie, Lewis Wharton *military officer*

BELGIUM

Brussels
Baptiste, Thomas L. *career military officer*
Craddock, Bantz John (John Craddock) *career military officer*

GERMANY

APO
Schall, David Gordon *military officer, surgeon*

Damstadt
McNeill, Dan K. *career military officer*

Stuttgart
Ward, William E. (Kip Ward) *career military officer*

SERBIA

Belgrade
Anderson, Joshua Douglas *military officer*

ADDRESS UNPUBLISHED

Abizaid, John Philip *retired military officer*
Aldridge, Donald O'Neal *military officer*
Anderson, Edgar Ratcliffe, Jr. *career officer, physician, health facility administrator*
Astriab, Steven Michael *military officer*
Astroth, Michael Patrick *military officer*
Austin, Robert Clarke *naval officer*
Barber, James Alden *navy officer, educator*
Barbisch, Donna F. *retired military officer*
Bartrem, Duane Harvey *retired military officer, residential designer, consultant*
Blakely, Jesse Alan *military officer*
Block, Emil Nathaniel, Jr. *retired air force officer*
Bowen, James Thomas *career officer*
Braswell, Daniel Edwin *military officer*
Brownlee, Les (Romie Leslie Brownlee) *former civilian military employee*
Buker, Robert Hutchinson, Sr. *army officer, thoracic surgeon*
Carlson, Burford Arlen *retired military officer, pilot*
Carstens, David Henry *military officer*
Cooning, Craig R. *career officer*
Cooper, Charles Donald *military association executive, editor, retired military officer*
Cougill, Roscoe McDaniel *retired military officer*
Darby, Joseph M. *reservist*
Darden, Derrick Carolyle *civilian military employee, educator*
Davis, Charles Memath, Sr. *non-commissioned officer*
Davis, Harley Cleo *retired military officer*
Demson, Philip Henry *military officer*
Dozier, James Lee *former army officer*
Dubik, James M. *career military officer*
Elam, Fred Eldon *retired military officer*
Elgart, Edward Guerry *civilian military employee*
Engel, Richard L. *career officer*
Fargo, Thomas Boulton *retired career military officer*
Fitz-Enz, David G. *retired military officer, television producer*
Floyd, Otis Henry *retired military officer, adult education educator*
Foote, Evelyn Patricia *retired military officer*
Franks, Tommy Ray *retired military officer*
Friskey, Edwin Robert, Jr. *former military specialist*
Gardner, Emerson N., Jr. *military officer*
Garner, Jay Montgomery *retired military officer*
Gerras, Stephen Joseph *military officer, psychologist*
Greco, Richard, Jr. *former civilian military employee*
Griffin, Robert H. *career military officer*
Guilmartin, Eugenia Katherine *military officer*
Gundelfinger, Benjamin Fremont *military officer*
Gutheinz, James O'Leary *military officer, law clerk*
Guthrie, Wallace Nessler, Jr. *naval officer*
Haddock, Raymond Earl *retired career officer*
Harper, Henry H. *retired military officer*
Harrell, John Michael *military officer*
Harvey, Francis J. *former civilian military employee*
Hauck, Frederick Hamilton *retired military officer, retired astronaut, aerospace executive*
Heckman, Gary Walter *military career officer*
Heddings, Raymond Eugene *military officer*
Herlik, Ed *military officer, pilot, small business owner, entrepreneur*
Herriford, Robert Levi, Sr. *retired military officer*
Hodges, Adele E. *career military officer*
Hoffman, Jonathan Frederick *military officer*
Hoover, John Elwood *former military officer, consultant, writer, educator*
Hull, Clifford, Sr. *military officer*
Irby, Eldon Elmore *military officer, banker*
Johnson, Hansford Tillman *former civilian military employee*
Johnson, Joyce *retired military officer*
Johnson, Silas R., Jr. *retired military officer*
Jones, David Charles *retired air force officer, former chairman Joint Chiefs of Staff*
Jumper, John Phillip *retired military officer*
Juskowiak, Terry Eugene *career military officer, computer company executive*
Keene-Burgess, Ruth Frances *military official*
Kellum, Donald Arthur *military officer*
Kelly, Paul Vincent *retired military officer, former federal agency administrator*
Kerwin, Walter Thomas, Jr. *career officer, consultant*
Kiley, Kevin Christopher *retired military officer*
Kutyna, Donald Joseph *air force officer*
LaPorte, Leon Joseph *retired military officer*
Lebras, Paul J. *retired career military officer*
Ledoux, John Lance *military officer*
Leidy, Charlotte *military officer*
Lennox, William James, Jr. *retired military officer*
Limpus, Charles Everett III *non-commissioned officer*
Lindquist, Michael Adrian *career military officer*
Long, Peter Avard Chipman *retired military officer*
Lynch, Jessica *military officer*
Lyons, John W(inship) *retired civilian military employee, chemist, consultant*
Mann, Eric Louis *retired military officer, mathematics professor, researcher*
Marlow, Edward A. *former army officer*
Mc Fadden, George Linus *retired army officer*
McLean, Craig Elliott *retired non-commissioned officer*
Metzger, James W. *career military officer*
Miyagawa, George Robert *retired military officer*
Moloff, Alan Lawrence *retired military officer, physician*
Moore, William Leroy, Jr. *career officer, internist*
Morgan, Thomas Rowland *retired marine corps officer*
Moulitsas Zúniga, Markos *former military officer, blog writer*
Mullen, William Joseph III *military analyst, retired army career officer*
Nabors, Robert L. *military officer*
Netto, Amba Cecile *military officer*
North, Gary L. *career military officer*
Nussbaum, Michael W. *military officer, paramedic*
Nyland, William Lewis *retired military officer*
O'Berry, Carl Gerald *former military officer, electrical engineer*
Palmer, Dave Richard *retired military officer, academic administrator*
Paquin, Gerald Chester *retired military officer, retired registrar*
Parent, Rodolphe Jean *retired Canadian air force officer, pilot*
Price, Joseph Sterling *retired air force officer*
Price, Robert Ira *coast guard officer*
Radzik, Albin F. *federal analyst, military consultant*
Rees, Raymond F. *military officer*
Reinike, Irma *retired civilian military employee, writer, artist, poet, lyricist*
Rigdon, David Tedrick *military officer, geneticist, director*
Riley, James Clifford *military career officer*
Robinson, David Brooks *retired naval officer*
Roche, James Gerard *former civilian military employee*
Rogers, Bernard William *military officer*
Roudebush, James Gordon *career military officer*
Rubenstein, David Aaron *military officer, healthcare administrator*
Ryther, Stephen Glenn *military officer, protective services official*
Sanderson, James Richard *retired naval officer, financial consultant*
San Diego, Armando G. *retired military officer, pathologist, consultant*
Sandkuhler, Kevin M. *military officer*
Scholes, Edison Earl *military officer*
Schoomaker, Peter Jan *retired military officer*
Shalikashvili, John Malchase *former Chairman of the Joint Chiefs of Staff*
Shaw, John Frederick *retired naval officer*
Sheikh, Aatif Manzoor *military officer, pharmacist*
Shelly, Nicholas J. *military officer, international relations scholar*
Shelton, Hugh (Henry Hugh Shelton) *former Chairman of the Joint Chiefs of Staff*
Shinseki, Eric Ken *retired military officer*
Shoemaker, Elizabeth Ellen *retired military officer*
Simmons, Timothy F. *military officer*
Smith, Zannie O. *retired career officer*
Snider, Scott William *civilian military employee*
Springer, Robert Dale *retired air force officer, consultant, lecturer*
Swalm, Thomas Sterling *retired military officer, aviations systems consultant*
Tarantino, David A., Jr. *military officer, emergency physician*
Teets, Peter B. *former civilian military employee*
Truckenbrodt, Yolanda Bernabe *retired air for[ce] officer, consultant*
Van Goor, Anthony Jay *retired military officer, medical executive*
Vessey, John William, Jr. *military officer*
Vincent, Hal Wellman *retired military officer, investor*
Vines, John R. *career military officer*
von Kaenel, Howard J. *army officer*
Webster, William G., Jr. *career military officer*
Weida, Johnny A. *career military officer*
Weyman, Steven Aloysius *retired military offi[cer]*
Wheeler, Albin Gray *retired military officer, retail executive, educator*
Whippo, Scott Dean *consultant*
Wroth, James Melvin *retired military officer*
Yoon, E. Yul *retired career officer*
Zais, Mitchell M. *career military officer*
Zuick, Ernest Ronald, Jr. *career officer, advertising executive*

REAL ESTATE

UNITED STATES

ALABAMA

Birmingham
Coleman, Stephen Beasley, Jr. *real estate bro[ker], writer*
Copeland, Hunter Armstrong *retired real esta[te] company executive*

Montgomery
Cassels, Martha Beasley *realtor, investor*

Tuscaloosa
McFarland, James William *real estate compa[ny] executive, consultant*
McFarland, James William, Jr. *real estate manager*

ALASKA

Girdwood
Trautner, John James *real estate executive*

ARIZONA

Phoenix
Clements, John Robert *real estate company executive*
De Michele, O. Mark *real estate company executive*
Hanneman, LeRoy C., Jr. *real estate executiv[e]*
Lewis, Orme, Jr. *real estate company executi[ve], land use adviser*
Sertich, Kelli Ann *land use planner*

Prescott
Masotti, Louis Henry *real estate educator, consultant*

Scottsdale
Dorrance, Bennett *real estate company execu[tive]*
McCollum, Alvin August *consultant, real est[ate] company executive, real estate developer*

Sedona
Copeland, Suzanne Johnson *real estate comp[any] executive*

Tempe
Jungbluth, Kirk E. *real estate appraiser*
Kim, Joochul *urban planner, educator*

Tucson
Longan, George Baker III *real estate compa[ny] executive*
Tang, Esther Don *real estate developer, consultant, social worker*

West Sedona
Lane, Margaret Anna Smith *property manag[er], real estate developer*

ARKANSAS

Hot Springs National Park
Haupt, Robert J. *hotel and real estate develo[per]*

Rogers
Cooper, John Alfred, Jr. *community developm[ent] company executive*

CALIFORNIA

Apple Valley
Yule, Caroll Jane *real estate broker*

Aptos
Nicholson, Joseph Bruce *real estate develope[r]*

Bakersfield
Chidgey, Guy Clement *marketing executive*

Beverly Hills
Bergman, Nancy Palm *real estate investment company executive*
Glazer, Guilford *real estate developer*
Tamkin, Curtis Sloane *real estate developme[nt] company executive*
Victor, Robert Eugene *real estate company executive, lawyer*

twood
s, Lucia Berta *land developer*

ino
rthy, Brian Nelson *real estate developer*

sbad
oto, Allen M. *real estate company*
cutive

Of Industry
, Edward P., Jr. *real estate developer,*
fessional sports team executive

a Mesa
n, Stanley *commercial real estate developer*

ntain Valley
, Marie Edmonds *real estate agent,*
perty manager

no
ne, Larry M. *real estate broker*

nite Bay
ner, Dorla Dean Eaton (Dorla Dean Eaton)
l estate broker

ne
nley, James Andrew *real estate executive*
ian, Steve *real estate company executive*
, Geoffrey Lawrence *real estate developer*
ell, Kerry Dean *real estate consultant,*
ucator, director, finance educator
sor, Adrian Sharon *real estate broker,*
erature and language professor

Jolla
ony, Harry Antoniades *retired city planner,*
chitect, educator
, L(ewis) Michael *real estate company*
cer

una Beach
uer, Joe Franklin *real estate company*
cer

una Niguel
, James Orison *real estate executive*

g Beach
es, Grace Lucille *real estate educator*

Angeles
man, John C. III *real estate company*
ecutive
iel, Stuart A. *real estate professor, director*
Kenneth Jeffrey *real estate company*
ecutive
k, Michael Stephen *real estate company*
ecutive
on, James Augustus, II, *real estate company*
ecutive, architect
ze, Jeffrey Alan *real estate executive*
ebelen, Pierre *resort planner and developer,*
nsultant
er, Joel *real estate company executive*
ing, Donald T. *real estate mogul,*
ofessional sports team owner
te, Brett *real estate company executive*

ada City
pin-Fleitas, Susan Gail *environmental health*
ecialist, forester

wport Beach
, Donald L. *real estate company executive*
cett, John Scott *real estate developer*
ney, William John, Jr. *real estate developer*
in, Stan *real estate company executive*
aicoff, Igor *real estate company executive*
ner, Jana L. *real estate company executive*

kland
aggio, Debbi *realtor*
ck, Peter H. *conservationist*

tario
itti, James P. *real estate executive*

m Springs
ey, Nancy *real estate broker*

o Alto
n, Robert Nicholas, II, *real estate developer*
ntyre, Robert Wheeler *retired conservation*
rganization executive
ore, Cassandra Chrones *real estate broker*
ng, Y(ing) Wood *real estate investment*
ompany executive, real estate development
ompany executive, venture capital investment
ompany executive

sadena
wley, John Crane *real estate developer*

tterson
ler, David Patrick *real estate broker*

way
t, George Wayne *real estate appraiser*

ncho Mirage
kseth, Timothy *real estate developer*

ncho Santa Fe
ffenbach, Otto Weaver III *real estate*
ompany executive
Driscoll, Margaret Millar (Peggy O'Driscoll)
eal estate broker

dondo Beach
ernethy, Robert John *real estate developer*

ss
holson, William Joseph *energy and*
nvironmental consultant

San Bernardino
Willis, Harold Wendt, Sr. *real estate developer*

San Diego
Oldham, Maxine Jernigan *real estate broker*

San Francisco
Bracken, Thomas Robert James *real estate investment executive*
Freund, Fredric S. *real estate broker and manager*
Shorenstein, Walter Herbert *commercial real estate development company executive*

San Jose
Rothblatt, Donald Noah *urban and regional planner, educator*

San Marcos
Wingert, Hannelore Christiane *realtor, chemicals executive*

San Rafael
Roulac, Stephen E. *real estate consultant*

Santa Barbara
Gunner, Michael Richard *real estate manager, hotel executive*
Perloff, Jean Marcosson *property manager, retired lawyer*

Santa Clara
Berg, Carl E. *real estate developer*

Santa Cruz
Dilbeck, Charles Stevens, Jr. *real estate company executive*
Hersley, Dennis Charles *environmentalist, software systems consultant*

Santa Monica
Wachs, Martin *urban planning educator, author, consultant*

Stockton
Michailoff, Ian Robert *real estate broker, land use planner*

Thousand Oaks
Wolff, Stuart *online real estate executive*

Twain Harte
Kinsinger, Robert Earl *property company executive, educational consultant*

Vista
Cavanaugh, Kenneth Clinton *retired real estate consultant*

Walnut Creek
Ostrander, Willis Frederick *retired real estate appraiser*

Westlake Village
Dalton, Allan D. *real estate company executive*
Yassky, Alan *real estate company executive*

COLORADO

Boulder
Stepanek, Joseph Edward *real estate developer, consultant*

Colorado Springs
Christensen, C. Lewis *real estate developer*

Denver
Considine, Terry *real estate company executive*
Crawford, Joe Jay *real estate company executive*
Kelly, Margaret M. *real estate company executive*
Mandarich, David D. *real estate corporation executive*

Fort Collins
Jensen, Margaret *real estate broker*

Gunnison
Lavigne, Peter Marshall *conservationist, lawyer, educator*

Louisville
Schonbrun, Michael K. *senior housing developer and operator*

Loveland
Harrison, Craig Donald *water rights broker, real estate and land use planner*

Monument
Boggs, Steven Eugene *real estate broker, lawyer*

Parker
McCauley, John Michael *real estate appraiser, consultant*

Vail
Kelton, Arthur Marvin, Jr. *real estate developer*

Woody Creek
Jenkins, Robert Berryman *real estate developer*

CONNECTICUT

Bethel
Kurfehs, Harold Charles *real estate executive*

Danbury
Anderson, Alan Reinold *real estate company and computer security firm executive, consultant*

Greenwich
Urstadt, Charles J. *real estate company officer*

New Haven
Alexander, Bruce Donald *real estate executive, educator*
Harrison, Henry Starin *real estate appraiser, educator, entrepreneur*

North Haven
Westerfield, Carolyn Elizabeth Hess *urban planner*

Norwalk
Soper, Jeannine *real estate agent*

Redding
Addison, Jason Lawrence *multifamily community development executive*

Stamford
Koproski, Alexander Robert *real estate company executive*

Westport
Griggs, Nina M. *retired realtor*

DELAWARE

Dover
Taylor, Suzonne Berry Stewart *real estate broker*

Rehoboth Beach
Little, R. Donald *real estate entrepreneur*

DISTRICT OF COLUMBIA

Washington
Blackwelder, Brent Francis *environmentalist*
Brooks, Jane K. *real estate agent, educator*
Green, Richard K. *real estate company executive*
Hawkins, Philip Linton *real estate executive*
Janes, William Sargent *real estate company executive*
John, Frank Herbert, Jr. *real estate appraiser, investor, marketing executive*
Jones, Susan Dorfman *real estate broker, writer*
Martinez Myers, Frances *real estate company executive*
O'Brien, Greg *real estate company executive*
Siegel, Ned Lawrence *real estate developer*
Stone, Roger David *environmentalist*
Train, Russell Errol *environmentalist*
Wheeler, Douglas Paul *conservationist, state agency administrator, lawyer*
Wilder, James Edward *resident manager*

FLORIDA

Belle Glade
Roberts, Thomas Andrew, II, *development executive*

Boca Raton
Langfield, Raymond Lee *real estate developer*
Wilson, James Laurence *real estate development executive, financial services consultant, educator*

Bonita Springs
Starkey, Jerry L. *real estate developer*

Cedar Key
Starnes, Earl Maxwell *retired urban and regional planner, architect, educator*

Coral Gables
Balzebre, Anthony Francis, Sr. *real estate developer, investor*
Milton, Jose *real estate development company executive*

Fort Lauderdale
Markos, Chris *retired real estate company executive*
Parrish, Lori Nance *property appraiser*
Weiss, David I. *real estate company executive, lawyer, writer*

Gainesville
York, Vermelle Cardwell *retired real estate broker and developer*

Hutchinson Island
Welch, Martha Lynn *environmentalist, educator*

Jacksonville
Aleschus, Justine Lawrence *retired real estate broker*
Bodkin, Ruby Pate *retired real estate broker, educator*
Clarkson, Charles Andrew *real estate investment executive*
Lovett, Radford Dow *marine terminal real estate and investment company executive*

Key West
Taylor, Victoria *real estate rehabilitator, sculptor*

Lake Suzy
Ogan, Russell Griffith *real estate broker*

Lake Worth
Sheehy, Betty Jo *real estate company executive, investment advisor*

Longwood
Gasperoni, Emil, Sr. *realtor, real estate developer*

Lutz
Corbitt, Doris Orene *retired real estate agent, dietician*

Maitland
Vallee, Judith Delaney *environmentalist, writer, not-for-profit fundraiser*

Melbourne
Ward, William Francis, Jr. *real estate investment broker*

Miami
Codina, Armando M. *real estate developer*
Nestor Castellano, Brenda Diana *real estate company executive*
Perez, Jorge M. *real estate developer*
Raffel, Leroy B. *real estate developer*
Salvaneschi, Luigi *real estate developer, management consultant, educator*
West, Macdonald *real estate executive*

Naples
Dorio, Martin Matthew, Jr. *real estate company executive, investor*
Dykstra, David Allen *real estate broker*
Keller, Theodore G., Jr. *investment property owner and manager*
Llewellyn, Leonard Frank *real estate broker, investment company executive*
Stastny, John Anton *real estate executive*

Niceville
Rasmussen, Robert Dee *retired real estate appraiser*

Ocala
Booth, Jane Schuele *real estate company officer, real estate broker*

Ocean Ridge
Mueller, Gerard *realtor, investor, former Internet executive*

Orlando
Gidel, Robert Hugh *real estate investor*

Palm Beach
Bagby, Martha L. Green *real estate holding company executive, writer, publishing executive*
Coudert, Dale Hokin *real estate executive, marketing consultant*
Dillard, Rodney Jefferson *real estate executive*
Klotsche, Charles Martin *real estate company executive, photographer, writer, financial columnist*

Palm Beach Gardens
VanButsel, Michael R. *real estate broker, construction executive*

Palm Coast
Barnes, Judith Ann *real estate company executive*

Saint Petersburg
Hurley, John Kenneth *real estate company and merchant banking executive*
Kanstoroom, David Arnold *real estate developer, entrepreneur*

Saint Petersburg Beach
Hurley, Frank Thomas, Jr. *realtor*

Sebring
Sherrick, Daniel Noah *real estate broker*

Sunrise
Maken, Sonny *real estate company executive, real estate developer*

Tallahassee
Lisenby, Dorrece Edenfield *realtor*

Tampa
Krone, Norman Bernard *real estate developer, lawyer*
Purcell, Henry III *real estate developer*
Schild, Nancy Lois *realtor, music educator*
Stair, Wilson Alfred, Jr. *urban designer, landscape architect*

Titusville
Morton, Craig Richard *real estate investor*

Vero Beach
Freeman, Donald Wilford *real estate developer, horse breeder*

West Palm Beach
Kramer, Eleanor *retired real estate broker, tax specialist, financial consultant*

GEORGIA

Alpharetta
Walker, Thomas H. *real estate developer*
Weitz, John Jerome, Jr. *city planner*

Athens
Melton, Wayne Charles *real estate executive*

Atlanta
Bell, Thomas Devereaux, Jr. *real estate company executive*
Comstock, Robert Donald, Jr. *real estate executive*
Ossewaarde, Anne Winkler *real estate company executive*
Simpson, Allan Boyd *real estate company executive*
Terwilliger, J. Ronald *real estate company executive*
Wieland, John *real estate executive*

Clarkston
Charania, Barkat *real estate consultant*

Folkston
Crumbley, Esther Helen Kendrick *retired real estate agent, retired secondary school educator, councilman*

Forsyth
Coleman, Steven Andrew *surveyor*

Marietta
Carnes, James Donald *real estate manager*

Newnan
Barron, Thomas Willis *real estate broker*

Peachtree City
Clark, James Kermit, Jr. *real estate executive*

Toccoa
Maypole, John Floyd *real estate company executive*

HAWAII

Honolulu
Albano, Andres, Jr. *real estate developer, real estate broker*

Kailua
Wong, Wallace *real estate investor*

IDAHO

Donnelly
Ferensowicz, Michael Jay *real estate company executive*

Eagle
Ricks, Thomas Aaron *real estate developer*

Idaho Falls
Thorsen, Nancy Dain *real estate broker*

ILLINOIS

Aurora
Stephens, Steve Arnold *real estate broker*

Champaign
Guttenberg, Albert Ziskind *planning educator*

Chicago
Berger, Miles Lee *land economist*
Bluhm, Neil Gary *real estate company executive*
Bucksbaum, John *real estate company executive*
Bucksbaum, Matthew *real estate investment trust company executive*
Bynoe, Peter Charles Bernard *real estate developer, lawyer*
Callahan, Timothy T. *real estate company executive*
Campbell, Gavin Elliott *real estate investor and developer*
Daley, Vincent Raymond, Jr. *real estate company executive, consultant*
Daly, Patrick F. *real estate executive, architect*
Darchun, Lino Auksutis *real estate professional*
DeWoskin, Margaret Fogarty *real estate company executive*
Durburg, Jack E. *real estate company executive*
Dyer, Colin *real estate services executive*
Eubanks-Pope, Sharon G. *real estate company executive, entrepreneur*
Ezgur, Michael H. *real estate company executive*
Field, Karen Ann (Karen Ann Schaffner) *real estate broker*
Galowich, Ronald Howard *real estate company executive, venture capitalist, pilot*
Geleerd, James D. (Jake Geleerd) *property manager*
Geoga, Douglas Gerard *real estate developer, lawyer*
Grubbe, Frederick H. *real estate appraisal executive*
Jarrett, Valerie Bowman *real estate company executive, former stock exchange executive*
Kahnweiler, David R. *real estate company executive*
Kincaid, Richard D. *real estate company executive*
Klebba, Raymond Allen *property manager*
Kojaian, C. Michael *real estate company executive*
Martin, Lauralee *real estate company executive*
Matanky, James E. *real estate developer*
Michaels, Robert A. *real estate development company executive*
Neithercut, David J. *real estate company officer*
O'Connor, Pamela Johnson *relocation company executive*
Pappas, Philip James *real estate company executive*
Pehlke, Richard W. *real estate company executive*
Primo, Quintin E. III *real estate company executive*
Riggs, Kenneth P., Jr. *real estate company executive*
Roberts, Peter C. *real estate company executive*
Rose, Mark E. *real estate company executive*
Watts, Michael H. *real estate company executive*
Winslow, Robert A. *real estate company executive*
Wirtz, William Wadsworth *real estate company executive, professional sports team executive*
Zell, Samuel *real estate company executive*

Dekalb
Richoz, Joan Kathryn *real estate agent, retired school nurse*

East Saint Louis
Thomas, Mary Lee *property manager*

Highland Park
Stein, Paula Jean Anne Barton *hotel real estate company executive, real estate broker*

Lake Zurich
Schultz, Carl Herbert *real estate developer*

Northbrook
Levy, Arnold S(tuart) *real estate company executive*
Metz, Adam S. *real estate company executive*
Perelman, Jeffrey E. *real estate company executive*

INDIANA

Elkhart
Vite, Frank Anthony *realtor*

Fort Wayne
Glick, Anna Margaret *real estate broker, consultant*

Indianapolis
Kohart, Mary Beth *real estate company executive*
Mullen, Thomas Edgar *real estate consultant*
Simon, David *real estate company officer*
Simon, Herbert *real estate developer, professional sports team owner*
Simon, Melvin *real estate developer, professional sports team owner*
Sokolov, Richard Saul *real estate company executive*

Jeffersonville
Reisert, Charles Edward, Jr. *realtor, real estate developer*

Newburgh
Tierney, Gordon Paul *real estate broker, genealogist*

IOWA

Cedar Rapids
Baermann, Donna Lee Roth *real estate property executive, retired insurance analyst*

KANSAS

Leawood
Joslin, Janine Elizabeth *preservationist, consultant*

Olathe
Harmon, Roger E. *environmentalist*

KENTUCKY

Lexington
Gable, Robert Elledy *real estate investment company executive*

Louisville
Cafaro, Debra A. *real estate company executive*
Glogower, Michael Howard *real estate company executive, consultant*

Winchester
Cantrell, Georgia Ann *realtor*

LOUISIANA

Covington
Gilman-Anderson, Susan Ellen *real estate company executive, consultant*
Maurin, James E. *real estate executive*

Leesville
Thompson, Darlene Bennett *realtor, musician*

New Orleans
Jones, Glenn Earle *property management executive*

Shreveport
Russell, Robert L. *real estate appraiser*

MAINE

Bangor
Foster, Walter Herbert, Jr. *real estate company executive*

Gardiner
Gosline, Norman Abbot *real estate appraiser, consultant*

MARYLAND

Baltimore
Caplan, Sharon M. *real estate company executive*
D'Alfonzo, Samuel Donald *real estate company executive*
DeVito, Mathias Joseph *retired real estate company executive*
Dewar, Donald John III *property manager*
Gabriel, Donald Albert *real estate company executive*
Millspaugh, Martin Laurence *real estate developer, consultant*

Berlin
Passwater, Barbara Gayhart *real estate broker*

Bethesda
Clark, A. James *real estate company executive*

Chevy Chase
Noonan, Patrick Francis *conservation executive*

Columbia
Deering, Anthony Wayne Marion *real estate developer*
McCuan, William Patrick *real estate company executive*
McGregor, Douglas A. *real estate company executive*

Frederick
Whelihan, Alan Stuart *real estate developer, automotive executive*

North Bethesda
Lerner, Theodore *real estate company executive*

Potomac
Dickerman, Serafina Poerio *real estate broker, consultant*
Eaves, Maria Perry *realtor*

Salisbury
Nutter, David George *city planner*

Silver Spring
McCray, Lora *real estate developer*

Westminster
Erb, Betty Jane *retired real estate agent*

MASSACHUSETTS

Amherst
Bentley, Richard Norcross *regional planner, writer, educator*
Larson, Joseph Stanley *environmentalist, educator*

Boston
Beal, Robert Lawrence *real estate executive*
Holland, James R. *real estate company officer*
Linde, Edward H. *real estate manager*
Lovejoy, George Montgomery, Jr. *real estate company executive*
Lundgren, Richard John *real estate executive, city planner, preservationist*
Radloff, Robert Albert *real estate company executive*
Wigglesworth, Margaret *real estate company executive*

Cambridge
Ross, Matthew Alan *real estate company executive*
Susskind, Lawrence Elliott *urban planner, educator, mediator*
Wood, Richard Robinson *real estate company executive*

Chestnut Hill
Moses, Judy *real estate company executive*

Fairhaven
Hotchkiss, Henry Washington *real estate broker, financial consultant*

Gloucester
Sallah, Majeed (Jim Sallah) *retired real estate developer*

Natick
Strauss, Harlee Sue *environmentalist, consultant*

Newton
Karp, Stephen R. *real estate developer*
Nahigian, Robert John *real estate company executive, consultant*

Shrewsbury
Falter, Robert Gary *real estate broker, educator*
Mastroianni, Anthony Robert *real estate company officer*

Waltham
Nelson, Arthur Hunt *real estate company executive*

Wellesley
Fineberg, Gerald *real estate company executive*

Winchester
Blackham, Ann Rosemary *realtor*

MICHIGAN

Ann Arbor
Clark, Thomas B., Sr. *real estate broker*
Surovell, Edward David *real estate company executive*

Bingham Farms
Robinson, Steve *real estate company executive*
Silverman, Gilbert B. *retired real estate developer, art collector*

Bloomfield Hills
Taubman, Robert S. *real estate developer*

Detroit
Grabowski, Jon *real estate company executive*

East Lansing
Anderton, James Franklin, IV, *real estate company executive*

Flat Rock
Cerasuolo, Jennifer Lyn *preservationist*

Grand Rapids
Vredevoogd Combs, Pat *real estate company executive*

Grosse Ile
Smith, Veronica Latta *real estate company offic*

Grosse Pointe Shores
LaHood, Mary Anne *real estate investor*

Haslett
Hotaling, Robert Bachman *urban planner, educator*

Ithaca
Price, Gregory *environmentalist*

Niles
Tenney, Jane Morris *real estate developer*

Northville
Green, Jody *real estate company executive, rea estate broker*

Royal Oak
Atchison, Steven *real estate company executiv*

Saginaw
Cline, Thomas William *real estate leasing company executive, management consultant*

White Lake
Clyburn, Luther Linn *real estate broker, appraiser*

MINNESOTA

Duluth
Bowman, Roger Manwaring *real estate compa officer*

Minneapolis
Boelter, Philip Floyd *real estate company offic construction executive*
Kreiser, Frank David *real estate executive*
Peltier, Ronald James *real estate corporation officer*

North Oaks
McDonald, Malcolm Willis *retired real estate company executive*

MISSISSIPPI

Vicksburg
Nichols, William Owen *conservationist*

MISSOURI

Ash Grove
Johnson, Iver Christian *retired real estate appraiser*

Chesterfield
Morley, Harry Thomas, Jr. *real estate executiv*

Earth City
Kroenke, E. Stanley *real estate developer, professional sports team owner*

Gray Summit
Desloge, Christopher Davis, Sr. *real estate company, merchant banking and consulting executive*

Holden
Martin, Laurabelle *property manager*

Ironton
Sebastian, Phylis Sue (Ingram) *real estate broker, antiques, appraiser*

Kansas City
Leone, Lawrence Joseph *real estate broker*
Shutz, Byron Christopher *real estate company officer*

Lake Saint Louis
Lang, Danny Robert *planning consultant*
Royal, William Henry *retired real estate developer, architect*

Saint Joseph
Rachow, Sharon Dianne *realtor*

Saint Louis
Drey, Leo *environmentalist*
Meissner, Edwin Benjamin, Jr. *retired real es broker*
Sutter, Jane Elizabeth *conservationist, science educator*

Springfield
Aull, Elizabeth Berryman *real estate development executive*
Carlson, Thomas Joseph *real estate developer lawyer*

MONTANA

Three Forks
Woodriff, Lee *company executive*

NEBRASKA

Lincoln
Tadesse, Tsegaye *climatologist, researcher*
Tavlin, Michael John *real estate company an manufacturing executive*

NEVADA

Las Vegas
Barbagallo, Al T. *real estate company execut*

), Martha L. *real estate broker and esman*
ı, Michael Dean *real estate developer, mer technology entrepreneur*
Theodore Bo *real estate developer*
ran, Christopher David *real estate broker, l estate attorney*

/ HAMPSHIRE

smouth
ngham, Valerie S. *historic preservationist, earcher*

/ JERSEY

ntic Highlands
ey, Joseph. B. *property management ecutive, educator*

e May Point
dler, Marguerite Nella *real estate company ecutive*

rry Hill
etta, Norman George *real estate executive*

nford
, William L. *real estate investment mpany executive*

lewood Cliffs
s, Roberta Paula *real estate finance ecutive*

nington
sky, Douglas George *land use planner*
non, Renay *real estate broker*

vorth
n, Brian J. *real estate company officer*

nasquan
s, Elizabeth Harding *real estate agent, tired elementary school educator*

tune
gomery, John Harold *environmentalist*

vark
ngelo-Bryan, Jeremy Paul *urban planner, ansportation executive*

sippany
Anthony E. *real estate company executive*
, Thomas R. *real estate company executive*
rman, Henry Richard *real estate company ecutive*
h, Richard A. *real estate company executive*

l Bank
nanian, Ara K. *real estate developer*
nanian, Kevork S. *real estate developer*

er Montclair
ı, Dilip K. *retired urban planner*

W MEXICO

uquerque
s, Betty Bourbonia *real estate company ecutive*
l, Jack Leland *real estate company executive*

Cruces
ley, Steven Dwayne *title company executive*

ra
ks, Eugene Ralph *real estate developer, ancher, forester, retired military officer, vestor*

W YORK

oria
fman, George S. *real estate company xecutive*

arcliff Manor
cher, Carolyn *real estate company executive*

onx
ter, Majora J. *urban planner*

ooklyn
nartin, MaryAnne *real estate company xecutive*
iith, Aaron David *real estate broker, onsultant*
ski, Sara *real estate developer*

naan
knap, Michael H. P. *real estate developer*

uglaston
bi, Kenneth Emilio *environmental specialist, esearcher*
ine, Jeffrey E. *real estate developer*

ndee
ler, Ronald K. *real estate broker, educator*

na
th, Sandra Lee *real estate company owner*

nsford
mond, George Marc *city planner, educator*

rrison
one, Michael Jonathan *real estate consultant, awyer, art consultant*

Larchmont
Levi, James Harry *real estate executive, investment banker*

Liverpool
De Long, Jacob Edward *real estate broker*

Melville
Campofranco, Salvatore *real estate company executive*

Mount Vernon
Rossini, Joseph *contracting and development corporate executive*

New York
Barlow, Matthew *real estate company executive*
Beinecke, Frances G. *environmentalist*
Burden, Amanda M. *urban planner*
Close, Michael John *property manager, lawyer*
Colacino, Michael *real estate company executive*
Consolo, Faith Hope *real estate company executive*
Corcoran, Barbara *real estate company executive*
Deutsch, Eric J. *real estate developer, urban planner*
Esposito, Louis *real estate developer*
Farley, Katherine G. *real estate company executive*
Fisher, Arnold L. *real estate company executive*
Fisher, Kenneth *real estate company executive*
Fisher, Steven *real estate company executive*
Fisher, Winston Crawford *real estate company executive*
Garfield, Leslie Jerome *real estate executive*
Glazier, Penny Port *property and event manager*
Gochberg, Thomas *real estate investor, investment banker*
Goldenberg, Charles Lawrence *real estate company executive*
Gordon, Mark J. *real estate company executive*
Gosin, Barry M. *real estate company executive*
Grau, Marcy Beinish *real estate broker, former investment banker*
Gray, Jonathan David *real estate company executive*
Green, Stephen L. *real estate developer*
Gural, Jeffrey R. *real estate company executive*
Hackett, Kevin R. *real estate company executive, lawyer*
Hemmerdinger, H. Dale *real estate executive*
Herman, Dorothy *real estate broker*
Hernstadt, Judith Filenbaum *city planner, real estate and broadcast executive*
Kalikow, Peter Stephen *real estate developer, former transportation and publishing executive*
Kercheval, Michael P. *real estate company executive*
Kogod, Robert P. *philanthropist, former real estate company executive*
Kuhn, James D. *real estate company executive*
Lachman, Marguerite Leanne *real estate investment advisor*
Lenz, Dolly (Idaliz Dolly Lenz) *real estate broker*
Levine, Judy Kendall *real estate broker, interior designer, writer*
Liebman, Pamela *real estate company executive*
Litwin, Leonard *real estate company executive*
Maitland, Wendy *real estate company executive, psychotherapist*
Marshall, Alton Garwood *real estate agent, consultant*
Mathias, Andrew *real estate company executive*
Milstein, Paul *real estate developer*
Mosler, Bruce E. *real estate company executive*
Nichols, Edie Diane *real estate broker*
Pearl, Mary Corliss *wildlife conservationist*
Petz, Edwin V. *real estate company executive, lawyer*
Quinlan, Robert Conrad *real estate developer*
Rampe, Kevin M. *real estate developer*
Resnick, Scott N. *real estate company executive*
Rose, Daniel *real estate company executive, consultant*
Rose, Elihu *real estate executive*
Ross, Stephen M. *real estate company executive*
Roth, Steven *real estate company executive*
Ruben, Lawrence *real estate developer and company executive, lawyer*
Schlang, David *retired real estate company executive, lawyer*
Scott, Stanley DeForest *real estate company executive*
Shvo, Michael *real estate broker*
Siderow, Neil *real estate company executive*
Sigety, Cornelius Edward *real estate developer, director*
Silverstein, Larry A. *real estate developer*
Speyer, Jerry I. *real estate company executive*
Stacom, Tara Irene *real estate company executive*
Steir, Michael S. *real estate company executive*
Stern, Leonard Norman *real estate developer, former pet supply manufacturing company executive*
Tighe, Mary Ann *real estate company executive*
Tishman, John L. *realty and construction company executive*
Weiss, Donald S. *real estate developer*
Yunis, Amira *real estate company officer*

Rochester
Pettinella, Edward *real estate company executive*

Rye
Feinberg, Norman Maurice *real estate company executive*

Southampton
Thomas, Violeta de los Angeles *real estate broker*

Stony Brook
Koppelman, Lee Edward *regional planner, educator*

NORTH CAROLINA

Ararat
Marsh, Joseph Virgil *real estate broker, retired investment advisor*

Boone
Conrad, David Paul *business broker, real estate developer, retired food service executive*

Chapel Hill
Weiss, Shirley F. *retired urban and regional planner, economist, educator*

Durham
Chapman, Robert Lee III *real estate developer*

Raleigh
Willer, Edward Herman *real estate broker*

Statesville
Redman, William Walter, Jr. *retired realtor*

OHIO

Chagrin Falls
Stec, John Zygmunt *retired real estate company officer*

Cincinnati
Randman, Barry I. *real estate developer*
Ten Eyck, Dorothea Fariss *real estate agent*

Cleveland
Jacobs, Richard E. *real estate company executive, sports team owner*
McGinty, Alan J. *real estate company executive*
Swetland, David Wightman *real estate company executive, investment company executive*

Columbus
Coopersmith, Jeffrey Alan *real estate developer*
Pizzuti, Ronald A. *real estate developer*
Pyatt, Leo Anthony *retired real estate broker*
Rouda, Harley, Jr. *real estate company executive*
Schuler, Robert Leo *appraiser, consultant*

Dayton
Wertz, Kenneth Dean *real estate company officer*

Edon
Wilson, Wayne Maurice *real estate broker, auctioneer*

Pepper Pike
Cohen, Judith R. *realtor*

Salem
Barcey, Harold Edward Dean (Hal) *real estate consultant*

Shaker Heights
Solganik, Marvin *real estate executive*

Shelby
Phelan, Martha Armstrong *retired realtor*

Wilmington
Evans, Elizabeth Ann West *retired real estate agent*

Youngstown
Camacci, Michael A. *real estate broker and developer, consultant*
DeBartolo, Edward John, Jr. *real estate developer, former professional football team owner*

OKLAHOMA

Oklahoma City
Binning, Gene Barton *real estate company executive*
Bradford, Dennis Doyle *real estate broker and developer*

Tulsa
Ball, Rex Martin *urban planner, architect*

OREGON

Gladstone
Beals, Herbert Kyle *urban planner, historian, consultant*

Portland
Packard, Robert Goodale III *urban planner*

Springfield
Davis, George Donald *executive land use policy consultant*

PENNSYLVANIA

Allentown
Saab, Deanne Keltum *real estate broker, appraiser*

Bryn Mawr
Pew, Robert Anderson *retired real estate and equipment leasing corporation officer*

Conshohocken
Glazer, William H. *real estate developer*

Erie
Gottschalk, Frank Klaus *real estate company executive*

Harrisburg
Fenstermacher, Joyce Doris *real estate agent, real estate appraiser*

Horsham
Barzilay, Zvi *real estate developer*
Toll, Bruce Elliot *real estate developer*

Langhorne
DiPasquale, John *real estate developer*

Philadelphia
Barnett, Jonathan *urban planner, educator, architect*
Lakhmna, Gagan(deep) *real estate company executive, entrepreneur*
Mellman, Leonard *real estate developer, consultant*
Peck, Robert McCracken *naturalist, historian, writer*
Soens, Peter C. *real estate company executive*

Saint Davids
Bertsch, Frederick Charles III *appraiser, finance company executive*

Wayne
Kolar, Erik E. *real estate company executive*

York
Rebert, Jephrey Lee *urban planner, musician*

RHODE ISLAND

Foster
Sawyer, Mildred Clementina *retired real estate agent*

Warwick
Losek, Darren Thomas *property manager, sales manager*

SOUTH CAROLINA

Aiken
Hallman, Cecilia Ann *real estate consultant*

Columbia
Calk, Stephen Hamilton *environmentalist*
Limehouse, Harry Bancroft, Jr. *real estate developer, transportation consultant*

Greenville
Crawford, William David *real estate broker, consultant*

Hilton Head Island
Gruchacz, Robert S. *real estate company officer*

Saint Helena Island
Yates-Williams, Linda Snow *real estate broker*

Spartanburg
Belenchia, Elizabeth C. *international corporate realtor*

SOUTH DAKOTA

Rapid City
Hamilton, Douglas Warren *real estate executive*

TENNESSEE

Eads
Bogan, John C. *real estate appraiser*

Hendersonville
Spain, Mary Ann *realtor, educator, historian, writer*

Knoxville
Beeler, Sandra Gillespie *realtor*

Loudon
Hicks, Betty Harris *real estate broker, company executive*

Memphis
Crye, Harold *real estate company executive*
Edwards, Martin *real estate company executive*

Nashville
Beck, Robert Beryl *real estate executive*

TEXAS

Addison
Kimbler, Larry Bernard *real estate executive, accountant*
Staubach, Roger Thomas *real estate executive, former professional football player*

Argyle
Stallings, Frank, Jr. *realtor, director*

Austin
Anderson, Mo *real estate company executive*
Nasta, Deep *real estate agent and broker*

Boerne
Daugherty, Linda Hagaman *real estate company executive*

College Station
Jackson, Thomas O. *real estate appraiser, urban planner*

Dallas
Cherry, William Speakman *real estate consultant*
Cook, Virginia *real estate company executive*
Doran, Mark Richard *real estate financial executive*
Marlow, Patricia Bair Bond *realtor*

Solender, Robert Lawrence *retired real estate company executive, retired publishing executive*

Galveston

McLeod, E. Douglas *real estate developer, lawyer*
Shelton, Kenneth R., Jr. *real estate company executive, artist*

Garland

McGrath, James Thomas *real estate investment company executive*

Gonzales

Mosher, Kenneth Vester, II, *property tax appraiser*

Hillsboro

McClendon, Fred Vernon *real estate professional, equity and realty appraiser, financial consultant*

Houston

Barrere, Jamie Newton *real estate company executive*
Blackburn, Sadie Gwin Allen *conservation executive*
Duncan, Robert D. *real estate company executive*
Goldsmith, Billy Joe *real estate broker, rancher*
Hale, C. Robert, III, (Bob) *real estate company executive*
Heard, Larry *real estate company executive*
Johnson, Craig M. *real estate company executive*
Kollaer, Jim C. *real estate executive, architect*
Kurrass, Lisa *real estate company executive*
Morris, Malcolm Stewart *title company executive, lawyer*
Waltrip, Robert L. *environmentalist, funeral company executive*

Irving

Lambert-Saul, Beth *real estate company executive*

Katy

Sadowski, Chester Philip, Jr. *real estate executive*

Lindale

Beckerley, Robert M. *realtor, consultant*

Plano

Hilton, Steven J. *real estate executive*
Landon, John R. *real estate developer*
Perot, Ross (H. Ross Perot, Henry Ross Perot) *real estate company, investment company, data processing executive*
Perot, Ross, Jr., (Henry Ross Perot Jr.) *real estate developer, professional sports team executive*

Port Aransas

Turner, Elizabeth Adams Noble (Betty Turner) *real estate company executive, writer*

Richardson

Lee, Jimmy Che-Yung *urban planner*

San Antonio

Condos, Barbara Seale *real estate broker, developer, investor*
Williamson, Fletcher Phillips *real estate broker*

Waco

Rusling, Barbara N(eubert) *real estate broker*

UTAH

Midvale

Teerlink, J. Leland (Joseph Leland Teerlink) *real estate developer*

VIRGINIA

Appomattox

Beatson, LeGrande Guerry *environmental health specialist*

Arlington

Watkins, Birge Swift *real estate investment executive*

Chesapeake

Owens, Susan Elizabeth *realtor*

Fairfax

Foster, (Paul) Wesley, Jr. *real estate broker*

Falls Church

Cazan, Sylvia Marie Buday (Mrs. Matthew John Cazan) *retired real estate company executive*

Haymarket

Crafton-Masterson, Adrienne *real estate company executive*

Mc Lean

Frazier, Walter Ronald *real estate investment company executive*
McLean, Robert III *real estate company executive*
Nobil, James Howard, Jr. *real estate investor, developer, broker, consultant*
Talbot, Martha Hayne *conservationist, biologist*

Newport News

Goldberg, Stanley Irwin *real estate company executive*

Richmond

Chandler, Theodore Lindy, Jr. *title insurance company executive, lawyer*
Foster, Charles H. *title insurance company executive*
Tuck, Grayson Edwin *real estate agent, gas industry executive*

Roanoke

Edwards, Lacy Lee, Jr. *real estate agent*

WASHINGTON

Bellevue

Scott, J. Lennox *real estate company executive*

Bellingham

Bourm, Roger Michael *real estate broker, investor, property manager*

Edmonds

Bell, Nancy Lee Hoyt *real estate investor, middle school educator, volunteer*

Federal Way

Fulton, Daniel S. *corporate real estate executive*

Seattle

Dillard, Marilyn Dianne *property manager*
Kirk, Judd *real estate development executive*
Sasaki, Tsutomu (Tom Sasaki) *real estate company executive, trade association administrator, consultant*
True, William L. (Bill True) *retired real estate company executive*

Sequim

Jackson, Patrick Joseph *real estate company officer*

Spokane

Covey, Michael J. *forest products and real estate executive*

WISCONSIN

Beaver Dam

Butterbrodt, John Ervin *real estate company officer*
Manthe, Cora De Munck *real estate company executive*

Belgium

Sullivan, Patricia W. (Terry Sullivan) *real estate trainer*

Lake Mills

Lazaris, Pamela Adriane *community planning and development consultant*

Madison

Ring, Gerald J. *real estate developer, insurance company executive*

Wauwatosa

Franke, Brent Douglas *real estate/insurance executive*

WYOMING

Casper

Elliott, Marian Kay *real estate manager*

CANADA

NOVA SCOTIA

Stellarton

Sobey, Donald Creighton Rae *real estate developer*

ONTARIO

Etobicoke

McIntyre, John George Wallace *real estate developer, management consultant*

Toronto

Carrothers, Gerald Arthur Patrick *environmental and city planning educator*
Dimma, William Andrew *real estate executive*
Eagles, Stuart Ernest *real estate company officer*
Tanenbaum, Joey *real estate developer*

ENGLAND

London

Hall, Sir Peter Geoffrey *urban and regional planning educator*

HONG KONG

Hong Kong

Lee, Shau Kee *real estate developer*

KENYA

Nairobi

Maathai, Wangari *environmentalist, consultant*

MONACO

Monte Carlo

Lovett, Laurence Dow *retired real estate and steamship executive*

SPAIN

Adeje

Grindley, Bruce Alan *real estate agency executive*

Valencia

Bañuelos, Enrique *real estate company executive*

ADDRESS UNPUBLISHED

Anderson, Paulette Elizabeth *real estate developer, entrepreneur, retired elementary school educator*
Argyros, George L. *real estate company executive, former ambassador*
Aulbach, George Louis *retired real estate company executive*
Austin, Grant William *real estate appraiser*
Banks, Robert Kaley *real estate and food products executive, lawyer*
Barney, Austin Dunham, II, *real estate developer*
Bartlett, Arthur Eugene *real estate company executive*
Beal, Merrill David *conservationist, museum director*
Bergau, Frank Conrad *real estate, commercial and investment properties executive*
Berliner, Ruth Shirley *real estate company executive*
Bernhardt, Arthur Dieter *urban planner, consultant*
Blackburn, Larry H. *builder*
Brooks, Michael Paul *retired urban planning educator*
Chase, J. Vincent *property manager*
Chesler, Doris Adelle *real estate broker*
Clark, Philip Hart *retired urban and regional planner*
Compton, William Thomas *real estate investor*
Corey, Kenneth Edward *urban planning and geography educator, researcher*
Corkran, Virginia B. *retired real estate agent*
Cox, Linda Smoak *real estate broker*
Cross, Robert Louis *retired realtor, landscape architect, land use planner, writer, real estate appraiser*
Cunningham, Jessie Jerome *real estate investor, import/export company executive, entrepreneur, small business owner*
Davis, John Warren *real estate broker, consultant*
Davis, Mary Byrd *conservationist, researcher*
DeBock, Ronald Gene *real estate company executive*
DeYoung, Marilyn Brant-Chandler *retired urban planner, farmer*
Di Cecco, James *real estate company executive*
Dwyer, William H. *real estate company executive*
Dysart, Benjamin Clay III *conservationist, consultant, engineer*
Ellett, Alan Sidney *real estate developer*
English, Bruce Vaughan *environmentalist, consultant*
Estrin, Richard William *real estate and business broker, retired editor*
Fischer, Michael Ludwig *environmental executive*
Fischer, Zoe Ann *real estate, property and marketing company executive*
Friedman, Howard W. *retired real estate company executive*
Friedman, Jared *realtor*
Furlotti, Alexander Amato *real estate company executive, investment company executive*
Galvis, Camilo Andres *real estate company executive, researcher*
Gasper, Ruth Eileen *real estate executive*
Ghebrhiwet, Freweiny Wendy *real estate broker, consultant*
Gilbert, Frederick E. *development planner, Africanist, consultant*
Glindeman, Henry Peter, Jr. *real estate developer*
Goddess, Lynn Barbara *real estate investor*
Godwin, Ralph Lee, Jr. *real estate executive*
Goldspiel, Arnold Nelson *real estate executive*
Gutstein, Carol Feinhandler *realtor*
Hakala, Karen Louise *retired real estate specialist*
Hatkoff, Craig Mitchell *real estate executive, educator*
Hedreen, Richard C *real estate developer*
Hedrich, Cleda Pollard *real estate broker, writer*
Hefeman, Mark *real estate broker*
Hietala, Valerie Grace *realtor, environmentalist, educator*
Holleb, Doris B. *urban planner, economist*
Horton, Finis Gene *real estate manager*
Howell, William Page *real estate company executive*
Hoyt, Erich *conservationist, writer, researcher*
Ingberman, Sima Blumenfeld *real estate company officer*
Jacobs, Christopher L. *real estate developer, former state official*
Jennison, Brian (Lester) *environmental specialist*
Johnson, Kay Durbahn *real estate manager, consultant*
Kaplan, Barbara Jane *retired city planner*
Karakey, Sherry JoAnne *real estate company executive, interior designer*
Krasnow, Kenneth *real estate company executive*
Kremer, Honor Frances (Noreen Kremer) *real estate broker, small business owner*
Lamy, M. Rebecca (Mary Rebecca Lamy) *consultant, land developer, government official*
Larson, Robert Craig *real estate company officer*
Lax, Philip *land developer, space planner*
Ledford, Janet Marie Smalley *real estate appraiser, consultant*
Lehman, Joan Alice *real estate company executive*
Louargand, Marc Andrew *real estate executive, financial consultant*
MacWilliams, Michael L., Jr. *environmentalist, educator*
Maguire, Robert Francis III *real estate investo*
Maloney, James Henry *community developmen executive, former congressman*
Mann, Clarence Charles *retired realtor*
Mayo, Henry P. *surveyor*
Mayro, Karl R. *realtor*
McGarvie-Munn, Iain Lachlan *real estate agen curator, writer*
McNeil, Edward Warren *real estate company executive*
Mercurio, Renard Michael *real estate company executive*
Messenkopf, Eugene John *real estate develope hotel executive*
Meyer, Daniel Kramer *real estate executive*
Michael, George T. *real estate manager, developer*
Mohamed, Joseph, Sr. *real estate broker, developer, farmer*
Moser, Jeffery Richard *real estate manager*
Page, Patricia (Patty) Newton *real estate broke real estate company executive*
Palow, James Alexander *real estate company executive*
Payne, Daniel Harold (Harold Payne) *real esta developer, small business owner*
Pence, Jean Virginia (Jean Pence) *retired real estate broker*
Phillips, William *real estate company executiv*
Potter, J. Stewart *property manager*
Raven, Patricia Elaine (Penny Raven) *real esta broker, developer, columnist*
Regal, Randall Nathaniel *policy analyst*
Reschke, Michael W. *real estate company offic*
Roberts, Katrina M. *real estate agent*
Sazant, Neil S. *real estate investor and developer*
Schell, Melvin Frank, Jr. *real estate agent*
Smith, Robert J., Jr. *real estate executive*
Stevens, Thomas M. *real estate company executive*
Taubman, A. Alfred *real estate developer*
Thacker, Thomas James *surveyor*
Toshach, Clarice Oversby *real estate develope retired computer company executive*
Trump, Donald John *real estate developer*
van der Harst, John Jay *environmentalist*
Vaughn, Mo (Maurice Samuel Vaughn) *real estate company executive, retired profession baseball player*
Vella, Ruth Ann *real estate executive*
Walker, Margaret Smith *real estate company executive*
Walker, Michael Charles, Sr. *retired services executive*
Whaley, Ross Samuel *environmentalist, educa*
Williams, Phyllis Cutforth *retired realtor*
Woods, Sandra Kay *real estate executive*
Young, James E. *real estate company executiv consultant, engineer*

RELIGION

UNITED STATES

ALABAMA

Andalusia

Patterson, Edwin *minister*

Bessemer

Collins, Patricia Ann *pastor, pastoral counsel*

Birmingham

Hull, William Edward *theology studies educa*

Greensboro

Massey, James Earl *retired clergyman, retired educator*

Hayden

King, Vickie Ruth *minister*

Mobile

Lipscomb, Oscar Hugh *archbishop*

ALASKA

Anchorage

Schwietz, Roger L. *archbishop*

ARIZONA

Duncan

Ouzts, Eugene Thomas *minister, secondary education educator*

Flagstaff

Lapsley, James Norvell, Jr. *minister, educator*

Green Valley

Pike, George Harold, Jr. *religious organizatio administrator, clergyman*

Hereford

Seeland, Arthur David *bishop*

Higley

Chris, Haidet Todd *minister, event producer*

Phoenix

Kuzma, George Martin *retired bishop*
Schenkel, Barbara Ann *minister, nurse, socia worker*

Scottsdale

Coutts, Lawrence Robert *publisher*

City
ilton, Ronald Ray *minister*
lall, Claire *retired religious organization dministrator*

npe
rson, Charles LeRoy *religious studies ucator*

son
s, Rendell Ashton *retired minister, social orker*
am, Charles Owen *priest, educator*

KANSAS

adelphia
berton, Barbara Butler *religious studies ucator*

way
er, Jean Riise *religious organization ministrator*

Dorado
Vernon Roy *minister*

le Rock
pelle, Richard Allen, Sr. *bishop*

rion
es, Michael Randolph *evangelist*

LIFORNIA

adena
ans, Jean Stone *bishop, religious ganization administrator*

ersfield
er, Jo Frances *religious organization ministrator, writer*

lwin Park
ill, James Lawrence *minister*

keley
er, Michael *rabbi*
h, Claude (Raymond) *theology studies ucator*

dbury
bell, Robert Charles *minister, theology dies educator*

bank
er, Richard James *minister*

narillo
r, Theodore *religious organization ministrator, writer, communications ecutive*
rson, Stuart W. *religious raido broadcaster*

tro Valley
son, Glenn Leslie *minister*

remont
eman, Clark Arthur *philosophy and igious studies educator*
ers, James Alvin *retired minister, retired igious studies educator*

ona
l, Brenda Jean *pastor, evangelist*

onado
ya, Deborah Luethje *minister*

a Mesa
nd, Anne (Elizabeth Anne Ortlund) *writer, sician*
ams, William Corey *theology educator, nsultant*

Monte
ng, Tzu-Yang *minister*

ino
weis, Harold Maurice *rabbi*

ndido
y, Verna May *minister, writer*

ntain Valley
ein, Stephen Jan *rabbi*

mont
n, Duane Keith *minister, counselor*

no
g, Tousu Saydangnmvang *minister, theology dies educator*

erton
sque, Paul Joseph *religious studies educator*

den Grove
ler, Robert Harold *minister, writer*

py Camp
, Barbara Ann *publisher*

ywood
ster, Peggy Lindner (Pravrajika hmaprana) *sister, nun*

Jolla
man, David Noel *religious studies educator*
ly, Lawrence Heber *writer*

na Woods
tley, Melvin Ernest, Jr. *retired bishop*

Lakewood
Carr, Firpo Wycoff *bible scholar, educator, writer*

Loma Linda
Sorajjakool, Siroj *religious studies educator, psychology professor*

Long Beach
Prince Crystal, Christina *minister, media specialist*

Los Altos
Marder, Janet *rabbi*

Los Angeles
Berg, Yehuda *rabbi, author, television personality*
Boyd, Malcolm *minister, writer*
Breuer, Stephen Ernest *religious organization administrator, consultant*
Dorff, Elliot *rabbi*
Freehling, Allen Isaac *rabbi*
Hier, Marvin *rabbi*
Levy, Naomi *rabbi*
Mahony, Roger Michael *archbishop*
Miscavige, David *head of religious order*
Ogilvie, Lloyd John *clergyman*
Phillips, Keith Wendall *minister*
Williams, Ronald Dean *minister, religious organization administrator*
Wolpe, David *rabbi*

Malibu
Tyler, Ronald Lee *religious studies educator*

Midway City
Allen, Frances Michael *publisher*

Oakland
Jakubowsky, Frank Raymond *religious writer*

Orange
Brown, Tod David *bishop*
Mc Farland, Norman Francis *bishop*

Palm Desert
Ponder, Catherine *clergywoman*
Stenhouse, Everett Ray *clergy administrator*

Palm Springs
Jones, Milton Wakefield *publisher*

Palo Alto
Forbes, Alfred Dean *religious studies researcher*

Pasadena
Bradley, James Edwin *religious studies educator*
Shuster, Marguerite *minister, educator*
Winter, Ralph D. *Christian world missionary, professor*

Portola Valley
Garsh, Thomas Burton *publisher*

Redlands
Huntley, William Barney *religious studies professor*

Reedley
Dick, Henry Henry *minister*

Sacramento
Cole, Glen David *minister*
Quinn, Francis A. *bishop*

San Bernardino
Del Riego, Rutilio J. *bishop*

San Diego
Brom, Robert H. *bishop*
Hunt, Barnabas John *priest, religious organization administrator*
Lechner, Roger A. *priest*
Mathes, James R. *bishop*

San Francisco
Kelly, James Anthony *priest*
Kushner, Lawrence *rabbi*

San Jose
Beizer, Lance Kurt *priest, lawyer*

San Juan Capistrano
Warren, Rick Duane *minister, writer*

San Leandro
Sawyer, Malcolm James, Jr. *religious studies educator*

Santee
Morris, Henry Madison III *minister, writer, speech professional, consultant*

Sonora
Chandler, Edwin Russell *clergyman, writer*

Stockton
Null, Paul Bryan *minister*

Studio City
Meenan, Alan John *clergyman, theology studies educator*

Thousand Oaks
Hudson, Barbara *writer, actor*

Upland
Jordan, Charles Wesley *retired bishop*

Vallejo
McGowan, Thomas Randolph *retired religious organization administrator*

Valley Village
Finley, Mordecai *rabbi*

Visalia
Levine, Suzin Nancy Leah *religious organization administrator*

COLORADO

Aurora
Nichols, Clyde Richard *minister, consumer products company executive*
Stifel, Frederick Benton *minister, biochemist, nutritionist*

Colorado Springs
Loux, Gordon Dale *philanthropic consultant*

Denver
Chaput, Charles J. *archbishop*
Morgan, David Forbes *minister*
Popham, David Kentner *minister*
Sheeran, Michael John Leo *priest, academic administrator*
Sinoff, Harry *religious studies educator, director*
Wilke, LeRoy *retired church administrator*

Dillon
Follett, Robert John Richard *publisher*

Fort Collins
Chorpenning, H. R. III *minister*
Rolston, Holmes III *theology studies educator, philosopher*

Greeley
van Gorp, Gary Wayne *minister*

Wheat Ridge
Wilcox, Mary Marks *retired Christian education consultant, educator*

CONNECTICUT

Bloomfield
Cronin, Daniel Anthony *emeritus archbishop*

Bridgeport
Lori, William E. *bishop*

Colchester
Nikirk, Susan Silva (Susan Silva) *minister, writer, dancer, consultant*

East Hartford
Jackson, Joseph Essard *religious organization administrator*

Greenwich
Johnson, Herbert Michael *publisher*
Moore, John Plunkett Dennis *publisher*

Hamden
Forman, Charles William *religious studies educator*
Malherbe, Abraham Johannes *retired religious studies educator, writer*
Weinstein, Stanley *Buddhist studies educator*

Hartford
Macaluso, Christie A. *bishop*
Mansell, Henry J. *archbishop*
Markham, Ian Stephen *theology studies educator, dean*
Mattson, Ingrid *theology studies educator, religious organization administrator*
Silk, Mark Reuel *religious studies educator, writer*
Winter, Miriam Therese (Gloria Frances Winter) *nun, religious studies educator*

Lyme
Bessie, Simon Michael *publisher*

Manchester
Scholsky, Martin Joseph *retired priest*

New London
Clarke, Florence Dorothy *minister, educator*

Norwich
Cote, Michael Richard *bishop*
Hart, Daniel Anthony *bishop*

Redding
Begell, William *publisher*

Southport
Twiname, John Dean *minister, human services administrator*

Stamford
Morse, Jonathan Kent *religious organization administrator*

Storrs Mansfield
Baldwin, Carlita Rose *minister*

Torrington
Drobena, Thomas John *minister, educator*

Wilton
Davis, Joel *publisher*

Woodstock Valley
Allaby, Stanley Reynolds *clergyman*

DELAWARE

Middletown
Cataldi-May, Lauren Michelle *head of religious order, music director*

Wilmington
Linderman, Jeanne Herron *priest*
Nichols, George Leon, Jr. *minister*

Saltarelli, Michael A. *priest*

DISTRICT OF COLUMBIA

Washington
Ahmed, Akbar S. *religious studies educator*
Allen, William Jere *minister*
Anderson, Vinton Randolph *bishop*
Baxter, Nathan Dwight *dean*
Burke, John *priest*
Combs, Roberta *religious organization administrator*
Di Lella, Alexander Anthony *biblical studies educator*
Dunn, James Milton *retired religious organization administrator*
Dunton, James Raynor *publisher*
Dyson, Michael Eric *religious studies educator, writer*
Fitzmyer, Joseph Augustine *theology studies educator, priest*
Godsey, John Drew *retired minister, theology educator emeritus*
Harvey, Jane Hull *church administrator*
Jones, Coletta L. *senior pastor*
Leckey, Dolores R. *religious organization administrator, writer*
Lustig, M. Bruce *rabbi*
Marrett, Michael McFarlene *chaplain*
McCrabb, Donald Raymond *pastoral field educator*
Moshier, David Irwin *church administrator*
Outlaw, Wanda Cecelia *priest*
Ross, Robinette Davis *publisher*
Wallis, Jim *religious speaker, activist, writer*
Weigel, George Shillow, Jr. *theologian*
Zikmund, Barbara Brown *minister, religious organization administrator, educator*

FLORIDA

Bartow
Meuser, Fredrick William *retired church administrator, historian*

Boca Raton
Agler, Richard Dean *rabbi*
Laine, Iris Ruth *minister, advertising executive, public relations executive*

Boynton Beach
Meridy, Howard William *rabbi, anesthesiologist*

Bradenton
McRae, Leslie *minister*

Coral Gables
Fitzgerald, John Thomas, Jr. *religious studies educator*

Crawfordville
Brumby, James Remley, III, (Knox Brumby) *retired priest*

Fort Lauderdale
Gray, Phillip Lee *religious studies educator, pastor*
McCormick, Queen Esther Williams *clergyman*

Fort Walton Beach
Williams, Bethtina Qubré *minister*

Jacksonville
Holliday, Patricia Ruth McKenzie *evangelist*
Mueller, Cherone *religious organization administrator, writer, minister*
Taylor, Robert M. *minister*

Leesburg
Genzen, Gary Carl *minister*

Longwood
Hunter, Joel Carl *clergyman, educator*

Miami Shores
Favalora, John Clement *archbishop*

Milton
Collins, Joda Lee *minister*

Naples
Weiss, Daniel Edwin *minister, educator*

New Port Richey
O'Farrell, Mark Theodore *religious organization administrator*

Ocala
Massa, Conrad Harry *retired religious studies educator*

Orlando
Forbes, Daniel Merrill *minister*
Wenski, Thomas Gerard *bishop*

Palm Bay
Elliott, Scott *minister, retired lawyer*

Palmetto Bay
Weeks, Marta Joan *retired priest*

Pensacola
Blankenship, Lawrence L. *retired minister*
Mountcastle, William Wallace, Jr. *retired philosophy and religion educator*
Ricard, John H. *bishop, educator*

Plantation
Harris, Eleanor Lynne K. *theology studies educator*

Saint Augustine
Couture, Sister Diane Rhea *sister, artist, educator*

McCarty, Doran Chester *religious organization administrator*

Saint Petersburg
Lemoi, Brian André *religious organization administrator, religious studies educator, writer*
Petty, M. S. Marty *publisher*

Sarasota
Clough, William Robert *minister, educator*
Hilt, Thomas Harry *minister*
Jones, Tracey Kirk, Jr. *retired minister, educator*
Kerr, Donald Craig *retired minister*
McFarlin, Diane Hooten *publisher*

Venice
Nevins, John J. *bishop*

Vero Beach
Beran, Denis Carl *publisher*

West Palm Beach
Giuffrida, Tom A. *publisher*
Nolan, Richard Thomas *clergyman, educator*
Westman, Steven Ronald *rabbi*

Winter Garden
Reeher, James Irwin *minister*
Stoddart, Mervin *religious studies educator, pastor*

Winter Haven
Boully, LaJuan Bonnie *minister, religious studies educator*

GEORGIA

Americus
Reckford, Jonathan Thomas More *nonprofit organization administrator*

Atlanta
Brelsford, Theodore William, Jr. *theology studies educator*
Bryant, Gregory Alexander *bishop*
Gregory, Wilton D. *archbishop*
Keiller, James Bruce *clergyman, dean*
Patton, Laurie Louise *religious studies educator, writer*
Waters, John W. *minister, educator*

Augusta
Davis, Minnie P. *minister*
MacLeod, James L. *minister, finance company executive, art gallery owner*

Crawford
Spears, Louise Elizabeth *minister, secondary school educator*

Decatur
Clarke, Erskine *religious history professor, writer*

Flintstone
Ragon, Robert Ronald *clergyman*

Hamilton
McEachern, Beverley C. *priest*

Lawrenceville
Brannon, Ronald Roy *retired minister*
Gericke, Paul William *minister, educator*

Macon
Franklin, Roosevelt *minister*
Good, Estelle M. *minister*

Mc Rae
Allen, Annette *minister*

Metter
Guido, Michael Anthony *evangelist*

Norcross
Granger, Philip Richard *minister*

Perry
Jackson, Rutha Mae *pastor, military reserve officer, secondary school educator*

Savannah
Boland, John Kevin *bishop*

Tifton
Roberts, Curtis Creed *minister, writer*

Vidalia
Fountain, Edwin Byrd *minister, librarian, poet*

Woodstock
Collins, David Browning *religious institution administrator*

HAWAII

Honolulu
Merrifield, Donald Paul *ministries coordinator*
Silva, Clarence *bishop*

Kahului
Domingo, Cora Maria Corazon Encarnacion *minister*

Kapaa
Veylanswami, Satguru Bodhinatha *head of religious order*

IDAHO

Nampa
Bowers, Curtis Ray, Jr. *chaplain*

Priest River
Booker, Bruce Robert *rabbi*

ILLINOIS

Barrington
Hybels, Bill *Pastor*

Belleville
Braxton, Edward K. *bishop*
Studer, Louis *priest, religious organization administrator*

Bloomington
Skillrud, Harold Clayton *minister, retired bishop*

Chicago
Almen, Lowell Gordon *church official*
Barbour, Claude Marie *minister, educator*
Betz, Hans Dieter *theology studies educator*
Brummel, Mark Joseph *religious organization administrator*
Farrakhan, Louis (Louis Eugene Walcott) *religious organization administrator*
Gadus, Peg *pastoral associate*
George, Francis Eugene Cardinal *cardinal*
Hanson, Mark S. *bishop*
Jegen, Sister Carol Frances *religious studies educator*
Mansueto, Joseph Daniel *publisher*
Marshall, Cody *bishop*
McDonald, Theresa Beatrice Pierce (Mrs. Ollie McDonald) *church official, minister*
Senior, Donald Paul *religious organization administrator*
Shafer, Eric Christopher *minister*
Snyder, Graydon F. *religion educator*
Thurston, Stephen John *pastor*
Tipton, Margaret Ann *religious organization administrator, writer*
Wall, James McKendree *minister, editor*
Yu, Anthony C. *religion and literature educator*

Deerfield
Schnabel, Eckhard Johannes *theologian, educator*

Elgin
Reimer, Judy Mills *pastor, religious executive*

Flossmoor
Cary, William Sterling *retired church executive*

Galva
Swatos, William Henry, Jr. *priest, sociologist*

Joliet
Kaffer, Roger Louis *bishop*

Kenilworth
Bowen, Gilbert Willard *minister*

Lake Forest
Feinberg, Jeffrey Enoch *religious studies educator, writer*

Lincoln
Wilson, Robert Allen *religion educator*

Moline
Johnson, Mary Lou *lay worker, educator*

Naperville
Raccah, Dominique Marcelle *publisher*

Oak Park
Hiestand, Edgar Leroy *minister*

Peoria
Parsons, Donald James *retired bishop*
Saxon, Randall Lee *pastor, author, educator*

River Forest
O'Meara, Thomas Franklin *priest, educator*

Rochester
Mashbern, William Allen *minister, retired religious organization administrator*

Rockford
Aniol, Scott Michael *pastor*
Doran, Thomas George *bishop*
Gregory, Dola Bell *bishop, customer service administrator*
Schlub, Teresa Rae *minister*

Springfield
Beckwith, Peter Hess *bishop*
Bell, John Perry *minister, religious organization administrator*

Villa Park
Pittelko, Roger Dean *clergyman, theology studies educator*

Wauconda
Gotthardt, Mary Jane *retired religious studies educator*

Wheaton
Pappas, Barbara Estelle *biblical studies educator, author*
Schwanda, Tom *religious studies educator*
Warner, William Kent, Jr. *religious organization administrator, consultant*

INDIANA

Anderson
Conrad, Harold August *retired religious pension board executive*
Lambert, Lloyd Laverne *minister*

Burlington
Roussakis, Peter Ellwood *minister, publisher*

Evansville
Hoy, George Philip *clergyman, county official, state legislator*

Fishers
Christenson, Le Roy Howard *missions mobilizer*

Fort Wayne
Mann, David William *minister*

Fortville
Horner, Sylvia Ann *minister, real estate broker*

Indianapolis
Buechlein, Daniel Mark *archbishop*
Crow, Paul Abernathy, Jr. *retired minister*
Dickinson, Richard Donald Nye *clergyman, theology studies educator*
Enright, William Gerald *religious institute administrator*
French, Tarence Wade, Sr. *minister*
Page, Curtis Matthewson *minister*
Polston, Mark Franklin *minister*
Roger, Janice Lowenstein *cantor*
Smith, Donald Archie *religious business executive, consultant*
Towne, Edgar Arthur *theologian, educator*
Watkins, Harold Robert *minister*
Woodring, DeWayne Stanley *religious organization administrator*

Jasper
Brenner, Raymond Anthony *priest*

Lafayette
Minor, Ronald Ray *minister*

Marion
Walker, Corean Jones *evangelist*

Merrillville
Tlapa, Richard Joseph *retired priest*

Munster
Taylor, Gloria A. *minister, educator*

Noblesville
Wilson, Norman Glenn *church administrator, writer*

Notre Dame
Davis, Stacy Nicole *religious studies educator*
Ladewski, Roman Sebastian *priest, educator*
Williams, Oliver Franklin *priest, educator*

Richmond
Angell, Stephen W. *religious studies educator*

Terre Haute
Chambers, Curtis Allen *clergyman, church administrator*

Winona Lake
Davis, John James *religion educator*
Julien, Thomas Theodore *religious denomination administrator*

IOWA

Cedar Falls
Lindberg, Duane R. *bishop, historian*

Decorah
Farwell, Elwin D. *minister, consultant*

Des Moines
Charron, Joseph L. *bishop*

Dubuque
Burkhart, John Ernest *minister, theology studies educator*
Hanus, Jerome George *archbishop*

Fort Madison
Lorimer, Thomas Harold *minister*

Grinnell
Mitchell, Orlan E. *clergyman, academic administrator*

Iowa City
Baumann, Mark *minister, director*
Bozeman, Theodore D. *religion educator*

Ottumwa
Luman, Richard Gordon *retired religious studies educator*

Waterloo
Waters, Ronald W. *theology studies educator, church administrator, pastor*

West Des Moines
Stines, Fred, Jr. *publisher*

KANSAS

Baxter Springs
Whiteley, Henry Howard *religious studies educator, minister*

Clifton
Compton, Doris Martha *lay worker*

Copeland
Birney, Walter Leroy *religious administrator*

Kansas City
Keleher, James P. *bishop*
Naumann, Joseph F. *archbishop*

Manhattan
Gillispie, Harold Leon *minister*

Marysville
Underwood, Earl Frederick, Jr. *clergyman*

Prairie Village
Vogel, Arthur Anton *clergyman*

Shawnee Mission
Mandl, Herbert Jay *rabbi*

Topeka
Goetz, Roger Melvin *minister*

KENTUCKY

Crestwood
Roy, Elmon Harold *minister*

Glasgow
Whittaker, Bill Douglas *minister*

Hopkinsville
Soberal, Isabel M. *minister, music educator, social worker*

Louisville
Boykin, Gladys *retired religious organizatio administrator*
Dale, Judy Ries *religious organization administrator, consultant*
Fenner, Chris *pastor*
Kelly, Thomas Cajetan *archbishop*
Rainer, Thomas Spratling *pastor*
Zimmerman, Gideon K. *retired minister*

Owensboro
Matally, M. Garswa *minister*
McRaith, John Jeremiah *bishop*

Paducah
Fejes, Robert R. *minister*

Paris
Steffer, Robert Wesley *clergyman*

Richmond
Ballard, Michael Ray (Mickey Ballard) *min music educator*
Wright, John Daniel *minister*

Stanford
Baughman, James Carson *minister, sports o*

Vanceburg
Aker, Duncan Danforth, Jr. *minister, educat*

Wilmore
Kinlaw, Dennis Franklin *clergyman, religiou organization administrator*

LOUISIANA

Alexandria
Gootee, Christy Beck *minister, educator*

Baton Rouge
Koehler, Robert Brien *priest*
Phillabaum, Leslie Ervin *publisher*
Witcher, Robert Campbell, Sr. *bishop*

Crowley
Foreman, Alfred G. *theologian, philosopher*

Denham Springs
Anderson, Alexis *minister*

Donaldsonville
Watson, Stanley Ellis *clergyman, small busi owner*

Gilbert
Bell, Wallace Edward *minister, insurance a*

New Orleans
Carter, James Clarence *pastor, educator*
Hughes, Alfred Clifton *archbishop*
Schulte, Francis B. *retired archbishop*

Ponchatoula
Warden, Waldia Ann *retreat center adminis director*

Shreveport
Webb, Donald Arthur *minister*

Springhill
Morgan, Larry Ronald *minister*

Tioga
Brandow, Stephen Jon *priest*

MAINE

Augusta
Clark, Beth *retired minister*

Brunswick
Visser, Richard Edgar *minister*

Portland
Ives, Samuel Clifton *minister*

South Bristol
Lasher, Esther Lu *minister*

MARYLAND

Baltimore
Byron, William James *minister, retired aca administrator, finance educator*

ıerman Gregory *pastor*
George Paul *minister*
Edwin Frederick *archbishop*
, Carrie *pastor*
, Sally Shoemaker *lay associate*
n, Jill *religious organization*
istrator
d, Marshall Hayward *bishop*

ville
ohn Charles *clergyman, retired theology*
s educator

bia
enjamin George *theologian, educator*
, Charles Kevin *priest, educator*

City
hton, Kenneth John *former publisher*

rsburg
thur Raymond, Jr. *retired minister*
Hoover (Lynn Hoover Rupert) *minister,*

ville
r, Kevin Thomas *religious organization*
istrator
Donald William *archbishop*

ille
rd, Ronald Dawson *minister, educator*

Glen Charles *minister*

el
, Christopher W. *priest*

ellville
r, Lauren Edgar *minister*

ille
z, Sidney Howard *rabbi*

n, Joel Arthur *author, organizational*
ral change facilitator

Spring
Bert Beverly *clergyman*
Reginald *minister*
, Tod Arthur *publisher*
ein, David Nathan *rabbi, lawyer, educator*

ACHUSETTS

rst
David Wood *minister, educator*

rn
der, Robert Stephen *minister*

Harold Russell *retired bishop*

n
Barbara Clementine *bishop*
Gayle Elizabeth *bishop*
ohn William *theology and ecology*
ator
J. Bryan *priest, educator, social services*
inistrator
, Diane Cooksey *religious organization*
inistrator, minister
, Herbert Warren, Jr. *religion and history*
cator, author

ton
ley, Sean Patrick Cardinal *Archbishop of*
on, cardinal

bridge
, Charles Gilchrist *theology studies*
cator, pastor
za, Francis P. *religion educator*
, Peter John *clergyman, educator*
n, William Albert *religious studies and*
ory educator
nan, Gordon Dester *theology studies*
cator
ssler Fiorenza, Elisabeth *theology studies*
cator

tnut Hill
eta, Roberto Segundo *theology studies*
cator
ck, Raymond Glen *priest, educator*
nes, William Charles *priest, academic*
inistrator

aica Plain
-Hammond, Gloria E. *pastor, pediatrician,*
nan rights advocate

rence
er, Peter David *bishop, religious*
anization administrator

blehead
ren, Michele Carol *spiritual director, writer,*
senter, personal coach, retired special
ucation educator

ford
k, Ann Clarisse *minister, counselor*

huen
aughton, William John *retired bishop*

ck
ner, Harold Samuel *rabbi*

th Andover
, Rebecca Sachs *religious studies educator*

Northampton
Derr, Thomas Sieger *religion educator*
Donfried, Karl Paul *theologian, clergyman*

Norton
Worthley, Harold Field *retired minister, educator*

Shelburne Falls
Evelyn, Phyllis *minister*

Squantum
Robertson, Michael Swing *minister*

Vineyard Haven
Kimball, Julie Ellis *small press publisher, humorist, writer*

West Newton
Spitzer, Toba *rabbi*

Weston
Barry, William Anthony *priest, writer*

Westwood
Bier, Louis Henry Gustav *minister*

Williamstown
Eusden, John Dykstra *theology studies educator, minister*

Worcester
Parsons, Edwin Spencer *clergyman, educator*
Reilly, Daniel Patrick *retired bishop*

MICHIGAN

Ann Arbor
Gomez, Luis Oscar *Asian and religious studies educator, clinical psychology educator*
Lightfoot, Albert J. *clergyman*

Bloomfield Hills
Mc Gehee, H. Coleman, Jr., (Harry Coleman McGhhe) *retired bishop*
Syme, Daniel Bailey *rabbi, institution executive*

Dearborn Heights
Ghrist, Catherine Ann *religious organization administrator*

Detroit
Maida, Adam Joseph Cardinal *cardinal*
Vigneron, Allen Henry *theology studies educator, rector, auxiliary bishop*

Farmington
Penberthy, Stanley Josiah, Jr. *publisher*

Farmington Hills
Plaut, Jonathan Victor *rabbi*

Gaylord
Cooney, Patrick Ronald *bishop*

Grand Rapids
Beals, Paul Archer *religious studies educator*
Beeke, Joel Robert *minister, educator, writer*
DeVries, Robert K. *retired publisher, consultant*

Holland
Cook, James Ivan *clergyman, educator*
Van Voorst, Robert E. *theology educator, minister*

Jackson
Popp, Nathaniel *archbishop*

Kalamazoo
Badra, Robert George *theology studies and humanities educator*

Livonia
Gepford, William George *minister*
Haggard, Joan Claire *church musician, piano instructor, accompanist, adjudicator*

Saginaw
Carlson, Robert James *bishop*

Southfield
Willingham, Edward Bacon, Jr. *ecumenical minister, administrator*

Spring Arbor
Bates, Gerald Earl *retired bishop*

Three Rivers
Mundy, B. Jo Ann *minister*

Ypsilanti
Stuppard-Byars, Doris J. *minister*

MINNESOTA

Austin
Alcorn, Wallace Arthur *minister, writer*

Crookston
Balke, Victor H. *bishop*

Edina
Brown, Laurence David *retired bishop*
Worthing, Carol Marie *retired minister*

Excelsior
Fenske, Jerald Allan *minister*

Grand Rapids
Merrill, Arthur Lewis *retired theologian*

Inver Grove Heights
Koenig, Robert August *minister, educator*

Mankato
Orvick, George Myron *religious organization administrator, minister*
Purscell, Keith William *minister*

Minneapolis
Chemberlin, Peg *minister, religious organization administrator*
Hamel, William John *church administrator, minister*
McLaren, Brian *pastor, christian activist*
Miller, William Alvin *clergyman, author, lecturer*

Northfield
Swanson, Stephen Olney *minister, retired English educator*

Rochester
Rinden, David Lee *clergyman*

Rosemount
Aadland, Thomas Vernon *minister*

Roseville
McMillan, Mary Bigelow *retired minister, volunteer*

Saint Paul
Flynn, Harry Joseph *archbishop*
Hopper, David Henry *theologian, educator*

Saint Peter
Jodock, Darrell Harland *minister, educator*

Woodbury
Woodruff, Ellen Louise *chaplain*

MISSISSIPPI

Aberdeen
Forbes, George Neal *minister*

Cleveland
Breland, James Andrew *minister*

Ellisville
McNair, Emma Louise *minister*

Indianola
Matthews, David *clergyman*

Jackson
Carden, Alan L. *hospital chaplain*
Gordon, Granville Hollis *church official*

Mound Bayou
Kamphefner, Pius *minister*

Yazoo City
Woodliff, George Franklin III *priest*

MISSOURI

Ballwin
Ackerson, Charles Stanley *minister, educator, social worker*

Bridgeton
Asma, Lawrence Francis *priest*
Hylla, Linda Kay *sister, social worker*

Excelsior Springs
Mitchell, Earl Wesley *clergyman*

Fayette
Keeling, Joe Keith *religious studies educator, retired dean*

Fenton
Meyer, Joyce *television minister, author*

Florissant
Stormer, John Anthony *retired minister, writer, publisher*

Foristell
Fry, Lowell Lawrence, Jr. *minister*

Independence
Tyree, Alan Dean *clergyman*

Kansas City
Cunningham, Paul George *minister*
Diehl, James Harvey *church administrator*
Finn, Robert W. *bishop*
Petosa, Jason Joseph *publisher*

Lees Summit
Lord, Heaven *consciousness studies educator, minister, translator*

Poplar Bluff
Black, Ronnie Delane *religious organization administrator, mayor*
Carr, Charles Louis *retired religious organization administrator*

Saint Louis
Baumer, Martha Ann *minister*
Brighton, Louis Andrew *religious studies educator*
Burke, Raymond Leo *archbishop*
Kennelly, Sister Karen Margaret *church administrator, nun, retired academic administrator*
Mahsman, David Lawrence *writer, church administrator*
Merrell, James Lee *writer, minister*
O'Donnell, Edward Joseph *bishop, retired editor*
Wiley, Gregory Robert *publisher*
Wilkins, Addi L. *retired lay worker*

Springfield
Given, Mark *religious studies educator*

Trask, Thomas Edward *religious organization administrator*

Wentzville
Park, Young H. *dean*

MONTANA

Billings
Barnea, Uri N. *rabbi, conductor, musician*

Helena
Jones, Charles Irving *bishop*

Kalispell
Vickers, Lee Louise *minister*

NEBRASKA

Blair
Hutton, Delvin Dwayne *retired theology studies educator, minister*

Lincoln
Bruskewitz, Fabian W. *bishop*
Wiersbe, Warren Wendell *clergyman, writer, lecturer*

Omaha
Curtiss, Elden Francis *archbishop*

Papillion
Zuerlein, Damian Joseph *priest*

NEVADA

Las Vegas
Bishop, Leo Kenneth *clergyman, educator*
Dill, Ellen Renée *minister, educator, writer*
Freeman-Clark, J. P. Ladyhawk *vicar, underwater exploration, security and transportation executive, model*
Luckett, Byron Edward, Jr. *chaplain, retired military officer*

Reno
Chrystal, William George *retired minister*
Savoy, Douglas Eugene *bishop, writer, religious studies educator*
Walrath, Harry Rienzi *retired minister*

NEW HAMPSHIRE

Center Sandwich
Booty, John Everitt *retired theology studies educator*

Concord
Robinson, V. Gene (The Right Reverend V. Gene Robinson) *bishop*

Loudon
Moore, Beatrice *religious organization administrator*

West Chesterfield
Garinger, Louis Daniel *retired religion educator*

NEW JERSEY

Atlantic City
Maddox, Odinga Lawrence, II, *head of religious order*

Bloomfield
Glasser, Lynn Schreiber *publisher*

Camden
Galante, Joseph A. *bishop*

Edison
Roskoski, John *religious studies educator, coach*

Englewood
Boteach, Shmuley *rabbi, television personality, author*

Freehold
Jawidzik, Edward Mark *priest*

Hackensack
Burt, Gwynne Elayne *minister, theology studies educator*

Jersey City
Katz, Colleen *publisher*

Lakewood
Levovitz, Pesach Zechariah *rabbi*

Mahwah
Padovano, Anthony Thomas *theologian, literature educator*

Marlton
Clemens, David Allen *minister*

Metuchen
Demkovitz, Russell Bernard *deacon, ceremetary director*

Moorestown
Clark, Maryliz M. *retired minister*

Morris Plains
Spong, John Shelby *retired bishop, writer, columnist*

Morristown
Hastings, Mary Jane *minister*

New Brunswick
Bowden, Henry Warner *religion educator*

Newark
Darmento, Ralph Joseph *religious organization administrator, educator, school system administrator*
Howard, M(oses) William, Jr. *minister*
Hummel, Donald Keith *priest*
Myers, John Joseph *archbishop*

Pomona
Constantelos, Demetrios John *priest, educator*

Princeton
Armstrong, Richard Stoll *minister, educator, poet*
Belshaw, George Phelps Mellick *bishop*
Dougherty, Peter Joseph *publisher*
Miller, Patrick Dwight, Jr. *religious studies educator, minister*
West, Charles Converse *retired theologian*

Ridgewood
Kiernan, Richard Francis *publisher*

Rutherford
Gerety, Peter Leo *archbishop*

Teaneck
Holmes, Miriam H. *publisher*
Meno, John Peter *chorepiscopus*

Tinton Falls
Priesand, Sally J. *rabbi*

Toms River
Donaldson, Marcia Jean *lay worker*

Trenton
Old, Hughes Oliphant *theologian, minister*

Union
Marjanczyk, Joseph Anicetus *priest*

Watchung
Miller, John Ronald *minister*

West Milford
Stelpstra, William John *minister*

West Paterson
Pataki, Andrew *bishop*

West Windsor
Yoseloff, Thomas *publisher*

Woodbury
Doughty, A. Glenn *minister*

NEW MEXICO

Albuquerque
Sheehan, Michael Jarboe *archbishop*

Moriarty
Moonwalker, Tu *minister, counselor, artist*

Portales
Overton, Edwin Dean *retired campus minister, educator*

NEW YORK

Adams Center
Hood, Thomas Gregory *minister*

Albany
Bowen, Mary Lu *ecumencial administrator*
Hubbard, Howard James *bishop*
Kruegler, Catherine A. *sister, parochial school educator*

Albion
Allamon, Karen Henn *minister*

Angola
Green, Gerard Leo *priest, educator*

Baldwin Place
Kurian, George Thomas *publisher*

Brainard
Isaksen, Robert L. *retired bishop*

Bronx
Dulles, Avery *cardinal, theologian*
Grassano, Thomas David *minister*
Hennessy, Thomas Christopher *priest, educator, retired dean*
Hunt, George William *priest, magazine editor*
Parker, Everett Carlton *clergyman*
Weiss, Avi *rabbi*

Brooklyn
Al-Hafeez, Humza *minister, editor*
DiMarzio, Nicholas Anthony *bishop*
Jones, Rudolph *minister*
Krinsky, Yehuda *rabbi*
Teitelbaum, Zalman *rabbi*

Buffalo
Kmiec, Edward Urban *bishop*
McKenzie, Denise *religious organization administrator, academic administrator*

Cambridge
Kriss, Gary W(ayne) *priest*

Centerport
McQueeney, Henry Martin, Sr. *publisher*
Stevens, Martin Brian *publisher*

Coxsackie
Moyna, John Lawrence *priest*

Douglaston
Valero, René Arnold *clergyman*

Elmhurst
Brown, Ronald Joseph *religious studies educator*
Cush, John Patrick *priest, theology studies educator*

Glen Head
Huber, Don Lawrence *publisher*

Hempstead
Zagano, Phyllis *religious studies educator*

Kingston
Tsirpanlis, Constantine N. *theology, philosophy, classics and history educator*

Lakemont
Brothers, Fletcher Arnold *minister, religious organization founder, director*

Larchmont
Rainier, Robert Paul *publisher, consultant*

Mechanicville
Rhodes, Alan Charles *minister*

Melville
Gellman, Marc *rabbi*

Mexico
Halse, Frank Adams, Jr. *retired minister*

Millerton
Welsh, Donald Emory *publisher*

New York
Anderson, Fred Richard *minister, writer*
Ashley, Willard Walden C., Sr. *minister*
Balter, Bernice *religious organization administrator*
Buchwald, Ephraim *rabbi*
Church, Frank Forrester *minister, writer*
Conlon, Peggy Eileen *publisher*
Cowan, Rachel *rabbi*
Demetrios, (Demetrios Trakatellis) *archbishop*
Doherty, Thomas *publisher*
Driver, Tom Faw *theologian, writer, advocate*
Fargis, Paul McKenna *publisher, publishing executive, consultant, book developer*
Forbes, Christopher (Kip Forbes) *publisher*
Friedman, J. Roger *publisher*
Giniger, Kenneth Seeman *publisher*
Ginsberg, Hersh Meier *rabbi, religious organization administrator*
Hirsch, Roseann Conte *publisher*
Hirschfield, Bradley *rabbi*
Hudson, Christopher John *publisher*
Kern, William Bliem, Jr. *minister*
Kleinbaum, Sharon *rabbi*
Matalon, J. Rolando *rabbi*
Molho, Emanuel *publisher*
Neuhaus, Richard John *priest, research institute president*
Ochs, Carol Rebecca *theologian, writer, theology studies educator, philosopher*
O'Keefe, Vincent Thomas *clergyman, educational association administrator*
Olitzky, Kerry Marc *rabbi*
Paley, Michael A. *rabbi*
Powers, Edward Alton *minister, educator*
Reidy, Carolyn Kroll *publisher*
Romanos, John, Jr., (Jack Romanos) *publisher*
Roskam, Catherine S. *bishop*
Ross, Norman Alan *publisher*
Roth, Sol *rabbi*
Rubinstein, Peter J. *rabbi*
Rusch, William Graham *religious organization administrator*
Schneier, Marc *rabbi*
Schori, Katharine Jefferts *bishop*
Schorsch, Ismar *theology studies educator, rabbi*
Simpson, Mary Michael *priest, psychotherapist*
Stolper, Pinchas Aryeh *religious organization executive, rabbi*
Straub, Gregory S. *priest*
Talley, Truman Macdonald *publisher, editor*
Tannenbaum, Bernice Salpeter *national religious organization executive*
Thurman, Robert A.F. *theology studies educator, philosopher*
Tucker, Alan David *publisher*
Whiteman, Douglas E. *publisher*
Wiener, Marvin S. *rabbi, editor, executive*
Yoffie, Erich H. *religious organization administrator*
Yu, Andrew *minister*
Zapata, Angel *pastor*
Zeldin, Richard Packer *publisher*

Newport
Wilson, Eldon Ray *minister*

Niskayuna
Nichols, Albert Myron *retired minister*

North Tonawanda
Majeroni, Ronald L. *pastoral counselor, consultant*

Nyack
Mann, Kenneth Walker *retired minister, psychologist*

Poughkeepsie
Glasse, John Howell *retired philosophy and theology educator*
Harmelink, Herman III *minister, writer, religious studies educator*

Red Hook
Pastrana, Ronald Ray *theology studies educator, science educator, department chairman, psychotherapist, retired school system administrator*

Rochester
Clark, Matthew Harvey *bishop*
Gripe, Alan Gordon *minister*
Middleton, J. Richard *religious studies educator*
Tobin, Barbara Kay *minister*
Webster, Gordon Visscher, Jr. *minister*

Rye
Kaufman, Shirona *cantor, educator*

Saint James
Batule, Robert John *priest, writer*

Scarsdale
Johnson, William Alexander *clergyman, philosophy and theology educator*

Staten Island
Pasciuto, Joseph Doria *priest*

Syosset
Theodosius, *retired leader of the Orthodox Church in America*

Syracuse
Costello, Thomas Joseph *retired bishop*
Emery, Robert Allan *minister*
Jerge, Marie Charlotte *minister*
Moynihan, James M. *bishop*

Troy
Phelan, Thomas *clergyman, academic administrator, educator*

Uniondale
Stewart, Cynthia Willis *minister*

Unionville
Kemnitz, Thomas Milton *publisher*

Verbank
Berry, Maryann Paradiso *minister*

Williamsville
Jones, Robert Alfred *retired clergyman*

Wolcott
Searle, Robert Ferguson *minister*

Yonkers
Gunner, Murray *retired religious organization administrator*

Youngstown
Lamb, Charles F. *retired minister, educator*

NORTH CAROLINA

Brevard
Flory, Margaret Martha *retired religious organization administrator*

Cary
Slaattè, Howard Alexander *minister, philosophy educator*
Taylor, David Wyatt Aiken *retired clergyman*
Vandergriff, Kenneth Lynn *religious studies educator*

Chapel Hill
Chang, Kuk Won *theology educator, researcher, pastor*

Charlotte
Brown, Harold Ogden Joseph *religious studies educator*
Freeman, Sidney Lee *minister*
Graham, Billy (William Franklin Graham) *evangelist*
Graham, Franklin (William Franklin Graham III) *evangelist, missionary*
Grigg, Eddie Garman *minister, educator*
McKay-Wilkinson, Julie Ann *minister, marriage and family therapist*
Oliver, John William Posegate *minister*
Walker, Jewett Lynius *clergyman, church official*

Dunn
Wilson, Douglas Leonard *minister, educator*

Durham
Dorn, Louis Otto *retired minister*
Kort, Wesley Albert *religious studies educator, writer*
Meyers, Eric Mark *religion educator*
Smith, Harmon Lee, Jr. *clergyman, theology studies educator*
Steinmetz, David Curtis *religious studies educator*

Fayetteville
Batts, Dorothy Marie *clergywoman, educator, writer*
Bunting, John Charles *pastoral associate, youth minister*
Soderberg, Herman Albert *minister, educator*

Greenville
Jackson, Bobby Rand *minister*

Hendersonville
Trexler, Edgar Ray *minister, editor*

Lake Junaluska
Tullis, Edward Lewis *retired bishop*

Lexington
Cuthrell, Carl Edward *retired clergyman, lawyer, educator*

Lumberton
Johnson, Judy Van *minister, educator*
Tolar, Anne Melton *minister, music educator*

Monroe
Kyle, John Emery *retired religious organizat administrator*

Pfafftown
Wood, Stephen Wray *minister, educator, legislator, singer, songwriter*

Pilot Mountain
Slomanski-Ward, Patricia Ann *minister*

Smithfield
McClain, Gregory David *chaplain*

Snow Hill
Stevens, JoAnn A. *textile, political leader, author, minister*

Taylorsville
Ross, David Edmond *church official*

Waynesville
Hale, Joe (Joseph Rice) *church organization executive*
Stokes, Mack Boyd (Marion Boyd Stokes) *bishop*

Weaverville
Edwards, Otis Carl, Jr. *theology studies educ*

Wilmington
Conser, Walter Hurley, Jr. *religion and philosophy educator*

Winston Salem
Capps, Richard Henry *retired minister*
Harrelson, Walter Joseph *minister, educator*
Hunt, Ellen *minister, evangelist*
Jenkins, Barbara Alexander *pastor, overseer*
Ludolf, Marilyn Marie Keaton *lay worker*
Rights, Graham Henry *retired minister*
Spach, Jule Christian *church executive*
Winn, Albert Curry *clergyman*

NORTH DAKOTA

Fargo
Foss, Richard John *bishop*

Minot
Eadens, Ethan Ennis *minister, writer*

OHIO

Akron
Malone, Alicia Jane *minister, theologian*

Ashland
Watson, JoAnn Ford *theology studies educat*

Bowling Green
Versteeg, Robert John *minister, actor, writer*

Canton
Mann, John Martin *minister*

Chesterland
Ruble, Bernard Roy *minister, educator, huma resources specialist, labor relations consu*

Cincinnati
Anderson, Joan Balyeat *theology studies educator, minister*
Duffy, Virginia *minister*
Harrington, Jeremy Thomas *priest, publishin executive*
Heiliger, Robert Lee *minister*
Hoffman, Lawrence A. *rabbi*
Pilarczyk, Daniel Edward *archbishop*
Sallquist, Gary Ardin *minister, non-profit executive*
Zola, Gary Phillip *rabbi, historian*

Circleville
Smith, James Leslie *minister, educator, coun*

Cleveland
Buhrow, William Carl *religious organization administrator*
Pilla, Anthony Michael *bishop*
Sherry, Paul Henry *minister, religious organization administrator*
Wedge, Eric *archbishop*

Columbus
Darling, George Curtis *minister, administrat*

Euclid
Obloy, Leonard Gerard *priest*

Findlay
Fry, Charles George *theologian, educator*

Holland
Matthews, Christian William, Jr. *minister*

Ironton
Cremeans, James L. *minister*

London
Hughes, Clyde Matthew *religious denomina executive*

Marblehead
Lis, David Joseph *priest*

Millersburg
Trubee, R. Eldon *minister, writer*

Norwalk
Brewer, Clair Herbert, Jr. *retired minister*

Sebring
Doty, James Edward *minister, psychologist*

nville
Michael *priest, academic administrator*
Gilbert Ignatius *clergyman*

ity
, James Robert *retired minister*

own
Dorothy Daniel *minister*

on
n, Donna J. *minister*

ville
Arthur LeRoy *clergyman, educator*

ffe
Anthony Edward *bishop*

stown
Catherine Mary *clergywoman*

HOMA

sville
Billy Don *bishop, religious organization nistrator*

ny
, James Daniel *bishop*

oma City
Eusebius Joseph *archbishop*
rd, James Leroy *minister, retired theology es educator*
on, Carol McDonald *priest, educator, rian*
, Major Lewis *pastor, religious nization administrator*
Betty Ann *theology studies educator*
White-Grigsby, Queen Deloris *minister, ultant*

nee
, James Clinton *minister, consultant*

, Duane R. *religious studies educator*
Villiam Jackson *retired bishop*
alk, Sister Mary Therese *nun, hospital nistrator*
, La Donna Carol *clergywoman*
s, (Granville) Oral *clergyman*
Frances Tompson *retired publisher*
ay, Ronald Joseph *minister, religious es educator*

n
, Jo Anne *priest*

GON

nd
ter-Shalomi, Zalman *rabbi*

allis
s, John Davison *minister*

ne
no, Margaret A. *chaplain, recreational apist, educational consultant, volunteer*
rs, Jack Thomas *religious studies educator*

and
hamp, E(dward) William *priest, lawyer, ersity administrator, management educator*

er
ff, Ruben Menno *theology studies cator, minister*

onville
ock, Karl Frederick *writer, retired demic administrator*

NSYLVANIA

n
nson, Margery Elsie *missionary, clinical chologist*

town
n, Edward Peter *bishop*

ona
ny, Bertha M. *minister*

lehem
n, Lloyd Howard *minister, religious studies ucator*

r
ell, William Harvey *clergyman*

lford
J. Arthur *minister*

p Hill
ston, Thomas McElree, Jr. *retired church ninistrator*

mbersburg
, Paul Lorenzo *clergy member*

rton
, John Louis (Ivan Minea) *religious studies ucator, archivist*

ton
ot, Mary Lee *minister*

egeville
, Geneva Mae *pastor*

Cranberry Township
Tiller, Olive Marie *retired church worker*

Dover
Hover, Carl Arthur *retired minister*

Drexel Hill
Thompson, William David *minister, educator*

Dunmore
Timlin, James Clifford *bishop*

Elizabethtown
Brown, Dale Weaver *clergyman, theology studies educator*

Erie
Trautman, Donald W. *bishop*

Farrell
Patton-Newell, Janet Lavelle *minister*

Fayetteville
Daywalt, Lee Eric *minister, museum administrator*

Haverford
Kee, Howard Clark *religion educator*

Jenkintown
Black, Thomas Donald *retired religious organization administrator*

Johnstown
Miloro, Protopresbyter Frank *religious organization administrator, theology studies educator*
Smisko, Nicholas Richard *bishop, educator*

Lafayette Hill
Miller, Nancy Lois *senior pastor*

Lancaster
Glick, Garland Wayne *retired theological seminary president*

Lewisburg
Jump, Chester Jackson, Jr. *clergyman, church official*

Malvern
Brighton, Ruth Louise *lay worker, educator*

Marysville
Trigilio, John Patricio *pastor*

New Stanton
Black, Cora Jean *evangelist, wedding consultant*

Philadelphia
Bartlett, Allen Lyman, Jr. *retired bishop*
Burch, Francis Floyd *clergyman*
Carven, John Winslow *priest*
Cortès, Luis *religious organization administrator*
Krych, Margaret A. *religious organization administrator, educator*
Maginnis, Robert P. *bishop*
Marple, Dorothy Jane *retired church executive*
Rigali, Justin Francis Cardinal *archbishop*
Shaw, William J. *religious organization administrator*
Sulyk, Stephen *retired archbishop*
Waskow, Arthur Ocean *theologian, educator*

Pittsburgh
Brauner, Ronald Allan *theology studies educator*
Helminiak, Daniel Albert *theologian, counselor*
Koedel, Robert Craig *minister, historian, educator*
Mason-Hipkins, Patricia *minister*
Miller, William Charles *theological educator, minister*
Schaub, Marilyn McNamara *theology studies educator*
Zeolla, Kim Anne *minister*

Quarryville
Harris, Robert Laird *minister, theology educator emeritus*

Saint Peters
Detterline, Milton E., Jr. *minister*

Sayre
Bentley, Dianne H. Glover *minister, consultant*

Scranton
De Celles, Charles Edouard *theologian, educator*

South Canaan
Herman, *archbishop, head of Orthodox Church in America*

Sunbury
Ely, Donald J(ean) *retired clergyman, secondary school educator*

Swarthmore
Field, Dorothy Maslin *minister*
Frost, Jerry William *religious studies educator, history professor, retired library director, researcher*

Wayne
Rabii, Patricia Berg *retired church administrator*

Waynesboro
Coles, Robert Nelson, Sr. *religious organization administrator*

Wernersville
Koenig, Robert Emil *clergyman*

Wilkes Barre
O'Hara, Thomas J. *priest, academic administrator, educator*

Willow Street
Yrigoyen, Charles, Jr. *retired church denomination executive*

Wyncote
Ehrenkrantz, Dan *rabbi*

Wynnewood
Sider, Ronald J. *theology educator, author*

RHODE ISLAND

East Providence
Spina, Douglas John *priest, educator*

Lincoln
Barlow, August Ralph, Jr. *minister*

Middletown
Demy, Timothy James *military chaplain*

Providence
Frerichs, Ernest Sunley *religious studies educator*
Tobin, Thomas J. *bishop*
Wolf, Geralyn *bishop*

SOUTH CAROLINA

Anderson
Williford, Velma Jean *minister*

Charleston
Salmon, Edward Lloyd, Jr. *bishop*

Columbia
Adams, John Hurst *bishop*

Darlington
Gough, Herbert Frederick, Jr. *minister*

Easley
Sustar, T. David *religious organization administrator*

Florence
Baroody, Albert Joseph, Jr. *pastoral counselor*

Irmo
Branham, Mack Carison, Jr. *retired religious organization administrator, minister*

Spartanburg
Bullard, John Moore *religious studies educator, church musician*

Sumter
McFadden, Lee Vernon *religious organization administrator*

Taylors
Smith, Morton Howison *religious organization administrator, educator*

White Rock
Aull, James Stroud *retired bishop*

SOUTH DAKOTA

Rapid City
Cleveland, Herbert Bruce *minister, consultant*

TENNESSEE

Antioch
Worthington, Melvin Leroy *minister, writer*

Bristol
Hill, Kenneth Clyde *clergyman*

Chattanooga
Milton, Michael Anthony *minister, writer*

Cleveland
Hughes, Ray Harrison *minister, religious organization administrator*
Taylor, William Al *church administrator*

Cordova
Floyd, John David *theology studies educator, minister*

La Follette
Eads, Ora Wilbert *clergyman, church administrator*

Loudon
Hallstrand, Sarah Laymon *denomination executive*
Jones, Robert Gean *religion educator*

Madison
Collins, Joyce A.P. *minister, librarian, educator, realtor*

Memphis
Steib, James Terry *bishop*
Todd, Virgil Holcomb *clergyman, theology studies educator*
Vaughn, Cary Edward *minister, director*
Walker, Randolph Meade *minister*

Murfreesboro
Locke, Gregory Duane *evangelist*

Nashville
Archibald, Chestina Mitchell *minister*
Bigham, Wanda Durrett *religious organization administrator*
Chapman, Morris Hines *denominational executive*
Forlines, Franklin Leroy *minister, educator*
Land, Richard Dale *minister, religious organization administrator*
Page, Frank S. *head of religious order*
TeSelle, Eugene Arthur, Jr. *religion educator*

Sewanee
Parsley, Henry Nutt, Jr. *bishop, academic administrator*

TEXAS

Abilene
Betts, Joe Delton *retired religious studies educator*
Perry, Troy D. *minister, religious organization administrator*

Arlington
Lingerfelt, B. Eugene, Jr. *minister*

Austin
Hitchcock, Joanna *publisher*
Wahlberg, Philip Lawrence *former bishop*

Brownsville
Pena, Raymundo Joseph *bishop*

Dallas
Blue, John Ronald (J. Ronald Blue) *evangelical mission executive*
Carnes, Joseph Sydney *clergyman*
Curran, Charles Edward *theology studies educator, priest*
Daves, Don Michael *minister*
Grahmann, Charles V. *bishop*
Jakes, T(homas) D(exter) *bishop*
Lockridge, Deborah Ann *minister, educator, small business owner*
Pauley, Shirley Stewart *religious organization executive*
Pinson, William Meredith, Jr. *pastor, writer, administrator*
Valentine, Foy Dan *clergyman*
Wiles, Charles Preston *minister*

Duncanville
Lang, James Devore, Jr. *ministry executive*

El Campo
Fisher, Robert Bruce *priest*

Flower Mound
Lowe, J. Allen *minister*

Fort Worth
Gilbert, James Cayce *minister*
Lawson, Carole Jean *religious educator, author, poet*
Rogers, Charles Ray *minister, religious organization administrator*

Happy
Bloodworth, Rick Keith *minister*

Houston
Cooper, Valerie Gail *minister*
DiNardo, Daniel N. *archbishop*
Fiorenza, Joseph A. *retired archbishop*
Foger, Frances Murchison *minister*
Joyce, James Daniel *clergyman*
Karff, Samuel Egal *rabbi*
Montgomery, Cleothus *minister*
Nielsen, Niels Christian, Jr. *retired religious studies educator*
Osteen, Joel *minister*

Jacksonville
Blaylock, James Carl *clergyman, librarian*

Lubbock
Blevins, Stanley Nance *minister, educator*

Richardson
Williams, James Francis, Jr. *religious organization administrator*

San Antonio
Evans, Betty Vaughn *minister*
Gomez, José H. *archbishop*
Mc Allister, Gerald Nicholas *retired bishop, minister*

Schulenburg
Clark, I. E. *publisher*

Spring
Howard, Richard Carl *minister*
Hunt, T(homas) W(ebb) *retired religion educator*
Rex, Lonnie Royce *religious organization administrator*

The Woodlands
Machle, Edward Johnstone *religious studies educator, philosopher*

Victoria
Fellhauer, David E. *bishop*

Waco
Stratton, Margaret Anne *minister*
Talbert, Charles Harold *theologian, educator*

UTAH

Ogden
Harrington, Mary Evelina Paulson (Polly) *writer, educator*

Salt Lake City
Eyring, Henry Bennion *bishop*
Hinckley, Gordon B. *religious organization administrator*
Holland, Jeffrey R. *religious organization administrator*

Monson, Thomas Spencer *religious organization administrator, retired publishing executive*
Niederauer, George H. *bishop*
Smith, Eldred Gee *church leader*

VERMONT

Burlington
Angell, Kenneth Anthony *bishop*
Warneck, Robert Townsend *religious studies educator*

Colchester
Blacketor, Paul Garber *minister*

Middlebury
Ferm, Robert Livingston *religion educator*

Northfield
Wick, William Shinn *clergyman, chaplain, pastor*

Pawlet
Buechner, Carl Frederick *minister, author*

Quechee
Wood, R. Stewart, Jr. *retired bishop*

Wolcott
Fisher, Neal Floyd *religious organization administrator*

VIRGINIA

Alexandria
Devantier, Paul W. *religious organization administrator, broadcast executive*
Sapp, Eric *religious organization executive*
Snyder, Larry *priest, social services administrator*
Vanderslice, Mara *religious organization executive*

Arlington
Coe, Doug *religious organization administrator*
Earl, Sister Patricia Helene *religious studies educator, director*

Blacksburg
Grover, Norman LaMotte *theologian, philosopher*

Charlottesville
Finley, Robert Van Eaton *minister*
Scott, Nathan Alexander, Jr. *minister, educator, critic*

Falls Church
Benton, Nicholas Frederick *publisher*

Front Royal
Andes, Larry Dale *minister*

Glen Allen
Anderson, James Frederick *clergyman*

Gordonsville
Wells, Mary Elizabeth Thompson *deacon, chaplain, spiritual director, iconographer*

Great Falls
Drummond, Alexander R. *priest*

King George
Agnew, Christopher Mack *minister, historian*

Lansdowne
Colson, Charles Wendell *lay minister, writer*

Lexington
Beckley, Harlan R. *religious studies educator*

Lynchburg
LaHaye, Timothy F. *pastor, writer*

Lyndhurst
Dieter, Melvin Easterday *retired minister, educator*

Mechanicsville
Gerrish, Brian Albert *theologian, educator, retired minister*

Mineral
Speer, Jack Atkeson *publisher*

Radford
McNeil, Ramsey English *religious studies educator*

Richmond
DiLorenzo, Francis X. *bishop*
Lee, Peter James *bishop*
Leggett, Gloria Jean *minister*
Slemp, Dennett Clinton *priest, counselor*

Roanoke
Crumley, James Robert, Jr. *retired bishop*
Schumm, Darla Yzonne *religious studies educator*

Springfield
Kalkwarf, Leonard V. *minister*

Sterling
Piper, Thomas Samuel *minister, consultant*

Vienna
Burr, Ronald Edwin *publisher*

Virginia Beach
Christy, Larry Todd *publisher*
Fletcher, Margaret Ann *religious studies educator*
Williams, J.(John) Rodman *theologian, educator, clergyman*

Williamsburg
Holmes, David Lynn *religion educator*

Winchester
Behr, Ken *religious organization administrator*
Nelson, Paul D. *retired religious organization administrator*

Yorktown
Wood, James Edward, Jr. *religion educator, author*

WASHINGTON

Bellevue
Berkley, James Donald *clergyman*

Des Moines
Tuell, Jack Marvin *retired bishop*

Longview
Walston, Rick Lyle *clergyman, seminary executive, educator*

Marysville
Kell, Lyle Nicholas *retired minister, retired real estate broker*

Prosser
Cooper, Lynn Dale *retired minister, retired navy chaplain*

Seattle
Brunett, Alexander J. *archbishop*
Burrows, Elizabeth MacDonald *religious organization executive, educator*
Fluke, Lyla Schram (Mrs. John M. (Lyla) Fluke Sr.) *publisher*
Robb, John Wesley *religion educator*

Spokane
Edwards, James Robert *minister, educator*
Lee, Richard Francis James *evangelical clergyman, media consultant, lawyer*
Polley, Harvey Lee *retired missionary, math and science educator*

Sunnyside
Capener, Regner Alvin *minister, electronics engineer, writer*

Tacoma
Wiegman, Eugene William *minister, academic administrator*

Tukwila
Robinson, Howard Arthur, Jr. *minister*

University Place
Seiber, Richard Allan *retired minister*

Vancouver
Crews, William Odell, Jr. *religious organization administrator*

Walla Walla
Krebs, Keith Ervin *minister*

Yakima
Scott, David Irvin *minister*

WEST VIRGINIA

Beckley
Rehbein, Edward Andrew *minister, geologist, consultant*

Charleston
Prichard, John David *minister*
Scott, Olof Henderson, Jr. *priest*

Clarksburg
Payne, Johnny F. *minister*

Hurricane
Hage, Lillian C. *religious organization administrator, director, dean*

Kingwood
Campbell, Casey Joseph *chaplain*

Pennsboro
Poling, Kermit William *minister*

Wheeling
de Paulo, Craig J. N. *priest, philosopher, educator*
Thurston, Bonnie Bowman *religious studies educator, minister, poet*

WISCONSIN

Bloomer
Prenzlow, Elmer John-Charles, Jr. *minister*

Boscobel
Young, Gary William *minister, educator, retired military officer*

Cottage Grove
Baird, Robert Dahlen *retired theology studies educator*

Green Bay
Geisendorfer, James Vernon *religious writer, researcher*
Harris, John T., IV, *religious organization administrator*

Iola
Mishler, Clifford Leslie *publisher*

Madison
Fitchen, Allen Nelson *publisher*
Fox, Michael Vass *theology studies educator*
Little, George Daniel *clergyman*

Merrill
Goessl, Celine *head of religious order*

Milwaukee
Dolan, Timothy Michael *archbishop*
Weakland, Rembert G. *retired archbishop*

Oshkosh
Barwig, Regis Norbert James *priest*

Racine
Bean, S. Craig *minister, consultant*

Rice Lake
Mueller, Philip Kearns *retired minister*

Sturgeon Bay
Van Duyse, Francis Donald (Fritz Van) *publisher*

Wauwatosa
Stubbe, Ray William *minister, writer*

TERRITORIES OF THE UNITED STATES

AMERICAN SAMOA

Pago Pago
Weitzel, John Quinn *bishop*

FEDERATED STATES OF MICRONESIA

Chuuk
Samo, Amando *bishop*

PUERTO RICO

Barceloneta
Rosado, Jose Elias *religious organization administrator, priest*

San Juan
Aponte Martinez, Luis Cardinal *retired archbishop*
González Nieves, Roberto Octavio *archbishop*

CANADA

BRITISH COLUMBIA

Victoria
Hollis, Reginald *archbishop*

NEWFOUNDLAND AND LABRADOR

Corner Brook
Payne, Sidney Stewart *retired archbishop*

ONTARIO

Brampton
Bastian, Donald Noel *retired bishop*

Cambridge
MacBain, William Halley *minister, theology studies educator, academic administrator*

Kitchener
Winger, Roger Elson *retired church administrator*

Ottawa
Macklem, Michael Kirkpatrick *publisher*
Ryan, William Francis *priest*

Paris
Hooper, Wayne Nelson *retired clergy member*

Sault Sainte Marie
Ferris, Ronald Curry *bishop*

Thorold
O'Mara, John Aloysius *retired bishop*

Toronto
Finlay, Terence Edward *retired archbishop*
Hutchison, Andrew Sandford *archbishop*
Novak, David *theology studies educator, rabbi*

Waterloo
Van Seters, John *retired biblical literature educator*

Willowdale
Irwin, John Wesley *publisher*

Windsor
La Rocque, Eugene Philippe *retired bishop*

QUEBEC

Beauharnois
Lebel, Robert *retired bishop*

Jonquière
Couture, Jean Guy *bishop*

Montreal
Turcotte, Jean-Claude Cardinal *archbishop*

Quebec City
Stavert, Alexander Bruce *archbishop*

Rimouski
Blanchet, Bertrand *archbishop*

Westmount
Coolidge, Robert Tytus *deacon, historian, educator*

North Hatley
Salt, Alfred Lewis *priest*

Vancouver
Packer, James Innell *priest, professor of theo*

MEXICO

Aguascalientes
Godinez Flores, Ramon *bishop*

THE BAHAMAS

Nassau
Harrison, Johnnie Sheppard *religious organization administrator*

ITALY

Rome
Benedict XVI, His Holiness Pope (Joseph A Ratzinger) *Pope of Roman Catholic Churc Bishop of Rome*
Kolvenbach, Peter Hans *priest, head of relig order*
Levada, William Joseph Cardinal *archbishop emeritus, cardinal*

Vatican City
Foley, John Patrick *archbishop*
Stafford, J. Francis Cardinal *Cardinal*
Stafford, James Francis *cardinal*
Szoka, Edmund Casimir Cardinal *archbishop*

JAPAN

Mie
Kitashirakawa, Michihisa *head of religious o*

SOUTH AFRICA

Cape Town
Tutu, Desmond Mpilo *retired archbishop*

ADDRESS UNPUBLISHED

Adams, Sharon Butler *minister, philosopher, researcher*
Allison, Andrew Marvin *church administrato*
Alvis, Joel Lawrence, Jr. *minister*
Ambrozic, Aloysius Cardinal (His Eminence Aloysius Cardinal Ambrozic) *archbishop emeritus*
Anderson, Hugh George *bishop*
Anderson, John Firth *retired religious organization administrator, retired librari*
Anderson, Maurice Elton *minister*
Anjulis, Stanley Joseph *retired church administrator*
Armstrong, (Arthur) James *minister, educato consultant, writer*
Arnesen, Norman Howard *pastor, educator*
Aronson, Jason *publisher*
Banks, Deirdre Margaret *retired church organization administrator*
Barner, Mark E. *minister, consultant*
Baumhart, Raymond Charles *religious organization administrator*
Bayne, David Cowan *priest, educator, lawye*
Beldon, Sanford T. *publisher*
Benbow, Joel Joshua *minister*
Bender, Ross Thomas *minister*
Berman, Saul J. *rabbi*
Bernstein, Edward Charles *rabbi*
Be Vier, William A. *retired religious studies educator*
Bickford, Margaret Wyatt *minister*
Black, Hillel Moses *publisher*
Bodey, Richard Allen *minister, educator*
Bosco, Anthony Gerard *bishop*
Bothwell, John Charles *retired archbishop*
Brenneis, Anne Schaack *religious studies educator*
Britt, Joseph John *religious studies educator*
Broadwater, James E. *publisher*
Brokke, Catherine Juliet *retired mission executive*
Brooks, Babert Vincent *publisher*
Bunkowske, Eugene Walter *religious studies educator*
Capon, Edwin Gould *retired religious organization administrator, minister*
Carlson, Natalie Traylor *publisher*
Cash, Mary Frances *minister, retired civilian military employee*
Castle, Howard Blaine *retired religious organization administrator*
Cates, Dennis Lynn *minister*
Christopher, Sharon A. Brown *bishop*
Clement, John Edward Strausz *retired minis retired religious organization administrato*
Cobb, John Boswell, Jr. *clergyman, educato*
Conn, Sallee J. *minister, educator*

k, Eddie Walton *army chaplain, military fficer*
e, Jeannette Naylor *minister*
bett, Gordon Leroy *minister*
otree, Davida Foy *minister*
ord, Janet Irene *Spiritualist medium, editation consultant*
idson, Diane (Marie Davidson) *publisher*
ko, Thomas Earl *retired minister, religious rganization administrator*
kstader, Deborah Ruth *minister*
oghue, John Francis *archbishop*
ovan, Dennis Dale *priest*
glass, Jane Dempsey *retired theology ducator*
n, Edward Michael Cardinal *archbishop, ardinal*
lish-Anderson, San Dei *minister*
, Eldon Jay *religion educator*
ng, Elisabeth Anne Rooney *priest*
ng, James E. *priest*
o, Evelyn M. *publisher, writer, agent, editor*
egan, Sara Anne (Sara F. Lycett) *publisher*
Gerald, Kyriaki Antonia *theologian, sychologist*
, Carolyn Marie *minister*
t, Larry Claxton, Jr. *publisher*
, Robert Bradley *minister*
kson-Kendrick, Sarah Jane *publisher*
ier, Eloise M. *minister*
nd, William Benedict *bishop*
Hedy *Member of Parliament*
, Edith Kay *retired minister, sychotherapist, social worker*
ignani, Michael Caesar *clergyman, retired athematics professor*
stner, Jonathan Neil *religious studies ducator*
ore, Marshall *bishop*
ny, Jacob Aaron *religious organization dministrator, researcher*
dy, Sandra C. *minister, counselor*
la, Milton *retired publisher*
nt, Leonard Tydings *clergyman*
enberg, Irving *rabbi*
fin, James Anthony *bishop*
wold, Frank Tracy III *retired bishop*
er, Geoffrey John *rabbi*
elstein, Robert Philip *publisher*
, Richard Clyde, Jr. *retired religious ducational administrator*
bidge, Douglas Walter *archbishop*
ilton, David Eugene *minister, educator*
er, Marsha Wilson *religious organization dministrator*
is, Nicholas George *publisher*
is, Rogers Sanders *bishop*
ono, Ignatius Wibisono *writer*
kes, Mary Newgeon *retired minister, ducator*
kins, Harold Stanley *pastor, school director, lice chaplain*
andez, Ramon Robert *retired minister, hool librarian*
e, Reginald Henry *retired bishop*
, Carl Wayne *retired theologian*
ut, Robert Kilborne *clergyman, writer*
strand, Donald Maynard *bishop*
s, William David *retired bishop*
ey, Francis T. *retired archbishop*
n, Roderick Eugene *minister, writer*
acho, David Asonye *campus chaplain*
ch, Joseph Leopold *bishop*
Aura Lee *minister, educator*
ll, Charles Michael *bishop*
son, Gordon Gilbert *theology studies ducator, minister*
son, Jennie *chaplain, social worker, poet*
s, William Augustus, Jr. *retired bishop*
er, William Henry Cardinal *retired cardinal*
ey, Edward Allen *publisher*
er, Helen Mary *minister*
cht, David Freemont *pastor*
se, Edward Charles *priest, educator*
era, Daniel William *retired bishop*
, Irwin James *religious education educator*
aster, Rogers *retired minister*
les, George Miller *biblical studies educator*
lon, John William *retired minister, social orker, educator*
n, Daniel *rabbi*
erdiere, Claudette Marie *nun, head of ligious order*
vsky, Lorna Deane *minister*
y, Herbert Theodore *publisher*
t, Arthur Heath *bishop*
, Dallas *minister*
, Brenda *publisher*
muller, Martin Nicholas *retired bishop*
ey, William Randall *minister*
now, Milo Alvin *clergyman, former church ficial*
kehoelter, Gottlieb Werner (Lee etkehoelter) *retired bishop, clergyman*
, JoyBeth *minister*
nbeel, Edward Elmer *publisher*
in, Benjamin W. *religious studies scholar, litical science scholar*
key, Jeffrey Allen *priest*
rill, Joe Richard, Jr. *religious organization ministrator, minister*
, Paul *publisher, retired management ucator*
y, Martin Emil *theology studies educator*
arrick, Theodore Cardinal *archbishop eritus*
lellan, Larry Allen *minister, educator*
inley, Ellen Bacon *priest*
aster, Belle Miller *religious organization ministrator*
uilkin, John Robertson *theology studies ucator, writer, academic administrator*
wain, Larry Lee *religious studies educator*
r, George Karl III *minister, lawyer*
zek, Dale J. *bishop*
in, Billy Alfred *clergyman*

Messer, Donald Edward *theology educator, administrator*
Metzger, Paul Louis *theologian, director*
Milligan, Sister Mary *theology studies educator, consultant*
Mischke, Carl Herbert *retired religious association executive*
Morris, Mary Elizabeth *pastor*
Muckerman, Norman James *priest, writer*
Muhammad, Claudette Marie *religious organization administrator*
Mulvee, Robert Edward *bishop*
Navasky, Victor Saul *publisher*
Nelson, Reginald (Bob) Wenon, Jr. *minister*
Norgren, William Andrew *retired religious denomination administrator*
Nottingham, William Jesse *retired religious organization administrator, retired minister*
Nunes, Winifred O. *minister, educator*
Nunn, Charles Burgess *retired religious organization administrator*
Oden, William Bryant *bishop, educator*
Oh, Mark Edward *minister*
O'Hare, Joseph Aloysius *priest, editor-in-chief, former academic administrator*
Ortiz, Angel Vicente *church administrator*
Osborne, James Alfred *religious organization administrator*
Osvath, Ludovic Lajos *minister*
Owen-Towle, Carolyn Sheets *clergywoman*
Pagels, Elaine Hiesey *theology studies educator, writer*
Palms, Roger Curtis *writer, educator, minister*
Parker, Robert Chauncey Humphrey *clergyman, publishing executive*
Peck, Paul Lachlan *minister*
Perko, Francis Michael *church administrator, researcher*
Plant, Jackson Vaughn *minister*
Plomp, Teunis (Tony Plomp) *minister*
Post, Avery Denison *retired church official*
Post, Stephen Garrard *theologian, philosopher, educator*
Pressman, Jacob *retired rabbi*
Preus, David Walter *bishop, minister*
Pullen, Bruce Reed *retired pastor*
Ramey, Eudora Malois *minister*
Reynolds, Lewis Dayton *pastor*
Rhodes, Melvin Frank *minister, writer*
Richards, Herbert East *retired minister, commentator*
Righter, Walter Cameron *retired bishop*
Robertson, LaVerne *minister*
Rosser, Essie *minister, counselor, marketing professional*
Scharlemann, Robert Paul *theology studies educator, minister*
Schefter, Ed Queen *minister*
Schroeder, W(illiam) Widick *retired religion educator*
Schuelke, John Paul *religious organization administrator*
Schultz, Clarence John *minister*
Seale, James Millard *retired religious organization administrator, minister*
Shaheen, Shaheen Azeez *minister, textiles executive*
Sharpton, Alfred Charles, Jr. *minister, political activist*
Short, Ray Everett *minister, sociologist, educator, writer*
Shotwell, Malcolm Green *minister*
Sloyan, Gerard Stephen *theology studies educator, priest*
Smith, D(aisy) Mullett *publisher*
Solano, Julio Rafael *priest, educator*
Stackhouse, Max Lynn *religious studies educator*
Staggers, Mary E. *minister*
Taylor, June Ruth *retired minister*
Telushkin, Joseph *rabbi*
Thompson, Richard Lloyd *retired pastor*
Trost, Frederick Richard *retired pastor*
Truehill, Marshall, Jr. *minister*
Unsworth, Richard Preston *minister, educator, director*
Vasko, Peter Theodore Frederick *priest*
Vlazny, John George *archbishop*
Walker, George W. *bishop*
Wantland, William Charles *retired bishop, lawyer*
Weber, Gloria Richie *retired minister, retired state legislator*
Webster, John Crosby Brown *minister, educator*
Weihmuller, Patricia Ann *minister, artist, retired executive secretary*
Weinkauf, Mary Louise Stanley *retired clergywoman, educator*
Welch, Richard L. *priest, lawyer*
Westerhoff, John Henry III *priest, theologian, educator*
Wilkin, Richard Edwin *clergyman, religious organization administrator*
Williams, Ervin Eugene *religious organization administrator*
Wills, Charles Francis *retired religious organization administrator*
Wilson, Lois M. *minister*
Wilson, Warren Samuel *clergyman*
Winslow, David Allen *chaplain, retired military officer*
Wisehart, Mary Ruth *retired religious organization administrator*
Wood, Cheryl Raley *minister, musician*
Woods, J. P. *religious organization administrator*
Wooten, Cecil Aaron *retired religious organization administrator*

Ziegler, Gwendolyn Woods *minister, consultant*

SCIENCE: LIFE SCIENCE

UNITED STATES

ALABAMA

Anniston
Howell, Laura Clark *biologist, educator, small business owner*

Auburn
Ball, Donald Maury *agronomist, consultant*
Klesius, Phillip Harry *microbiologist, researcher*
Kouzmitcheva, Galina A. *molecular biologist, researcher*
Tian, Hanqin *ecologist, educator*

Birmingham
Finley, Sara Crews *medical geneticist, educator*
Janjua, Naveed Zafar *research scientist*
Korf, Bruce Richard *clinical geneticist, neurologist*
Marchase, Richard Banfield *cell biologist, educator, research administrator*
Sabbaj, Steffanie *research scientist*
Schafer, James Arthur *physiologist*

Homewood
Nance, Marione E. *biology educator*

Huntsville
Bearden, Thomas Eugene *research scientist*
Gillani, Noor Velshi *atmospheric scientist, researcher, educator*
Richardson-Weninegar, Loretta Lynne *biologist, educator*
Schwinghamer, Mary Denise *veterinarian*
Wu, Shi Tsan *science research administrator, educator*

Mobile
French, Elizabeth Irene *biology professor, musician*
Taylor, Aubrey Elmo *physiologist, educator*

Montgomery
Sass, Neil Leslie *toxicologist*

Tuscaloosa
Darden, William Howard, Jr. *biology professor*
Lopez-Bautista, Juan Manuel *biology professor, research scientist*

Tuskegee Institute
Datiri, Benjamin Chumang *soil and environmental scientist*

ALASKA

Anchorage
Nielsen, Jennifer Lee *molecular ecologist, researcher*
Parker, Walter Bruce *arctic research specialist, consultant*

Fairbanks
Chapin, F. Stuart III *ecologist*
Kessel, Brina *ornithologist, educator, researcher*
Margraf, Francis Joseph, Jr. *marine biologist, educator*

Juneau
Shepard, Beatrice L. *retired microbiologist, historian*
Siddeek, M. S.M. *marine biologist, educator*

ARIZONA

Flagstaff
Cortner, Hanna Joan *retired political scientist, researcher*
Hammond, Howard David *retired botanist, editor*
Price, Peter Wilfrid *ecology educator, researcher*

Maricopa
Kimball, Bruce Arnold *soil scientist*

Mesa
Schvaneveldt, Roger Wayne *science educator, consultant*

Payson
Stephenson, Larry Kirk *geography educator, financial planner*

Scottsdale
Northey, William Thomas *microbiologist, educator*

Sun City
Joyce, Jeffrey *research scientist, consultant*

Tempe
Adrian, Ronald John *science educator*
Curtiss, Roy III *life sciences professor*
Hölldobler, Berthold Karl *zoologist*
Jacobs, Mark *biology professor, dean*
Page, Robert Eugene, Jr. *biology professor*
Poste, George Henry *biology professor, former pharmaceutical company executive*
Uttal, William R(eichenstein) *psychology and engineering educator, research scientist*

Tucson
Bernstein, Carol *molecular biologist*
Brusca, Richard Charles *biologist, researcher, educator, science administrator*
Enquist, Brian Joseph *ecologist, educator*
Erickson, Robert Porter *genetics researcher, educator, clinician*
Frank, Michael J. *neuroscientist, educator*
Fritts, Harold Clark *botanist, educator*
Gerba, Charles Peter *microbiologist, educator*
Haynes, Caleb Vance, Jr. *geology and archaeology educator*
Hildebrand, John G(rant) *neuroscientist, educator*
Hubbard, William Bogel *planetary sciences educator*
Hughes, Malcolm Kenneth *dendrochronologist, educator, administrator*
Hull, Herbert Mitchell *botanist, researcher*
Jeter, Wayburn Stewart *retired microbiologist, educator*
Johnson, Paula D. *veterinarian*
Macys, Sonja *science association director*
Moran, Nancy A. *ecologist, educator*
Snyder, Richard Gerald *research scientist, administrator, educator, consultant*
Titley, Spencer Rowe *geology educator*
Zegura, Stephen Luke *biologist, anthropologist, educator*
Zhang, Donna D. *toxicologist, educator*
Zou, Changping *research scientist, educator*

Wikieup
Brattstrom, Bayard Holmes *biology professor*

ARKANSAS

Cherokee Village
Hollingsworth, John Alexander *retired science and mathematics educator, writer*

Fayetteville
Bell, Debbie McCulley *science educator*
Brown, Avert Hayden *animal scientist, educator*
Brown, Connell Jean *retired animal science educator*
Morris, Justin Roy *food scientist, consultant*
Musacchia, X(avier) J(oseph) *physiology and biophysics educator*
Musick, Gerald Joe *retired entomology educator*

Jefferson
Schwetz, Bernard Anthony *toxicologist*

Little Rock
Casciano, Daniel Anthony *biologist, educator*
Gealt, Michael A. *environmental microbiologist, educator*
Hinson, Jack Allsbrook *research toxicologist, educator*
Wight, Patricia Anne *neuroscience educator*
Young, Hays Wilson Jorden *research scientist*

Pocahontas
Moss, Linda Elaine *science educator*

State University
Hannigan, Robyn E. *science educator, researcher*

Walnut Ridge
Wheeless, Charlotte Ann *science educator*

Ward
Rudy, Janet Faye Walker *science educator*

CALIFORNIA

Alameda
Earle, Sylvia Alice *research biologist, oceanographer*
Willson, Clyde D. *biologist, educator*

Albany
Meidav, Joshua Sinclair Ethan *ecologist, researcher*
Schwimmer, Sigmund *food enzymologist*

Atherton
Coleman, Robert Griffin *geology educator*

Berkeley
Baldwin, Bruce Gregg *botany educator, researcher*
Barrett, Reginald Haughton *wildlife management educator*
Botchan, Michael R. *molecular biologist, biochemist*
Brenner, Sydney *molecular biologist, researcher*
Casida, John Edward *toxicology and entomology professor*
Chapela, Ignacio H. *biologist, researcher*
Chen, Lu *neurobiologist, biology professor*
Cline, Thomas Warren *geneticist, educator*
Cooper, William Secord *information science educator*
Diamond, Marian Cleeves *neuroscientist, educator*
Fleiszig, Suzanne Mariane Janete *optometry educator*
Hobbs, Christopher Rollin *botanist, writer*
King, Nicole *molecular biologist, educator*
Levine, Mark David *science administrator, director*
Lidicker, William Zander, Jr. *zoologist, educator*
Lipps, Jere Henry *biology and geology professor*
Manga, Michael *earth science educator, geophysicist*
Marletta, Michael A. *biochemistry educator, researcher*
Myrick, Alissa B. *parasitologist, science educator*
Oster, George F. *molecular biologist, environmental scientist*

Patek, Sheila N. *biologist, educator*
Power, Mary Eleanor *biology professor*
Purcell, Alexander Holmes *entomologist, educator*
Quail, Peter Hugh *biologist, educator*
Saraph, Prasad Vaman *research scientist, industrial engineer*
Schekman, Randy W. *molecular biology administrator, biochemist*
Scott, Eugenie Carol *science foundation director, anthropologist*
Seil, Fredrick John *retired neuroscientist*
Sobel, Noam *science educator*
Teeguarden, Dennis Earl *forest economist, educator*
Thorner, Jeremy W. *biology professor*
Wake, Marvalee Hendricks *biology professor*
White, Timothy Douglas *biology professor, educator*

Beverly Hills
Smith, Marilyn Noeltner *retired science educator*

Bodega Bay
Clegg, James Standish *physiologist, biochemist, educator*

Chico
Kistner, David Harold *biology professor*

Claremont
Phillips, M. Ian *physiologist, educator*

Costa Mesa
Allen, Merrill James *marine biologist*
Elliott, Kelli Jeanette *biology professor*
Lattanzio, Stephen Paul *astronomy educator*

Davis
Ardans, Alexander Andrew *veterinarian, educator, lab administrator*
Ball, Barry Allen *veterinarian, researcher*
Barbour, Michael G(eorge) *botanist, educator, ecologist, consultant*
Baskin, Ronald Joseph *biophysicist educator, dean*
Colvin, Harry Walter, Jr. *physiology educator*
Day, Howard Wilman *geology educator*
Enders, Allen Coffin *anatomy educator*
Epstein, Emanuel *plant physiologist*
Greenwood, M. R. C. *biologist, nutrition educator, former academic administrator*
Hess, Charles Edward *environmental horticulture educator*
Holyoak, Marcel *ecologist, educator*
Jones, Edward George *neuroscientist, educator*
Kowalczykowski, Stephen Charles *microbiologist, cellular and molecular biologist, educator*
Langley, Charles Hunt *geneticist, educator*
Meyer, Margaret Eleanor *retired microbiologist*
Moyle, Peter Briggs *marine biologist, educator*
Mukherjee, Amiya K. *metallurgy and materials science educator*
Murphy, Terence Martin *biology professor*
Prokosch, Mark David *research scientist*
Qualset, Calvin O. *agronomist, educator*
Rappaport, Lawrence *plant physiology and horticulture educator*
Rost, Thomas Lowell *retired botany educator*
Roth, John Roger *geneticist, biology educator*
Schoener, Thomas William *zoology educator, researcher*
Sillman, Arnold Joel *physiologist, educator*
Sun, Qiang *botanist*
Turcotte, Donald Lawson *geophysical sciences educator*
Van Alfen, Neal K. *plant pathologist*
Watt, Kenneth Edmund Ferguson *zoology educator*
Yilma, Tilahun Daniel *virologist, veterinarian, educator, researcher*

Del Mar
Farquhar, Marilyn Gist *cell biologist, pathologist, educator*

Duarte
Smith, Steven Sidney *molecular biologist*

Emeryville
Houghton, Michael *geneticist*
White, Raymond Leslie *geneticist*

Encinitas
Hale, David Fredrick *biotechnology executive*

Escondido
Sloan, Anne Elizabeth *food scientist, writer*

Fairfield
Gelpke, Peter Hall *science educator*

Fresno
Burnett, Lynn Barkley *health science educator*
McConnell, Charles Prescott *retired science educator*
Waters, Rosemary R. *biology professor*

Fullerton
Woyski, Margaret Skillman *retired geology educator*

Goleta
Gilbert, Richard Keith *biology professor, researcher*

Healdsburg
Vedros, Neylan Anthony *microbiologist, educator*

Hollywood
Brooks, Lila *animal rights activist, retired hotel executive*

Hopland
Jones, Milton Bennion *retired agronomist*

Huntington Park
Gaines-Page, Rena L. *science educator*

Indio
Olson, Phillip David LeRoy *agriculturist, chemist*

Irvine
Ayala, Francisco José *geneticist, educator*
Catrakis, Haris John *science educator*
Clegg, Michael Tran *genetics educator, researcher*
Demetrescu, Mihai Constantin *research scientist, educator, computer company executive*
Gardiner, David M. *biologist, educator*
James, Anthony Amadé *molecular biologist, educator*
Lenhoff, Howard Maer *biological sciences educator, academic administrator*
Riley, Sally Jean *science educator*
Stanbridge, Eric John *biology professor*
Thigpen, Stephen P. *horticulture products company executive*
Weller, Stephen G. *botanist, educator*

Kensington
Stent, Gunther Siegmund *molecular biologist, educator*

La Jolla
Brooks, Charles Lee III *computational biophysicist, educator*
Chrispeels, Maarten Jan *biology professor*
Elman, Jeffrey Locke *cognitive sciences educator*
Evans, Ronald M. *microbiologist, educator*
Gilbert, James Freeman *geophysics educator*
Guillemin, Roger C.L. *physiologist*
Haxo, Francis Theodore *marine biologist*
Helinski, Donald Raymond *biologist, educator*
Hemingway, George Thomson *marine biologist, educator, priest*
Hunter, Tony (Anthony Rex) *molecular biologist, educator*
Ideker, Trey *computational and molecular biologist*
Kooyman, Gerald Lee *physiologist, researcher*
Lewin, Ralph Arnold *biologist*
Liu, Shumo *molecular biologist*
Macagno, Eduardo R. *biology professor, dean*
Rahman, Yueh-Erh *biologist*
Richman, Douglas Daniel *medical virologist, educator, internist*
Schroeder, Julian Ivan *biology professor*
Sherman, Irwin William *biological sciences educator, academic administrator*
Thomas, Charles Allen, Jr. *molecular biologist, educator*
Vucinic, Dejan *neuroscientist*
Wahl, Geoffrey Myles *biology professor*
West, John Burnard *physiologist, educator*
Wilkie, Donald Walter *retired biologist, aquarium administrator*

La Verne
Izaguirre, George *microbiologist*

Livermore
Anastasio, Michael R. *science foundation director*

Loma Linda
Longo, Lawrence Daniel *physiologist, obstetrician, gynecologist, educator*
Schwab, Ernest Roe III *physiology educator, researcher, academic administrator*
Taylor, Barry Llewellyn *microbiologist, educator*

Long Beach
Mills, Don Harper *pathology and psychiatry educator, lawyer*
Schubel, Jerry Robert *marine scientist educator, dean*

Los Alamitos
Aberman, Harold Mark *veterinarian*

Los Alamos
Daly, John T *research scientist*

Los Altos
King, Chi-Yu *research scientist*

Los Angeles
Agnew, John A. *science educator*
Baker, Robert Frank *molecular biologist, educator*
Banerjee, Utpal *biology professor, research scientist*
Boles, Richard Gregory *clinical geneticist, researcher*
Bottjer, David John *earth science and biology educator*
Butcher, Larry L. *neuroscientist, educator*
Connor-Dominguez, Billie Marie *science information professional*
Craft, Cheryl Mae *neurobiologist, anatomist, researcher*
Daly, Heather Eileen *toxicologist*
De Robertis, Edward M. F. *research scientist, educator*
Diamond, Jared Mason *biologist, writer*
Finegold, Sydney Martin *microbiology educator*
Fischer, Alfred George *geology educator*
Gasson, Judith C. *research scientist*
Gilman, John Joseph *research scientist*
Goldberg, Robert B. *molecular biologist, educator*
Gordon, Malcolm Stephen *biology professor*
Greenberger, Martin *biotechnologist, information scientist, educator*
Grinnell, Alan Dale *neuroscientist, educator*
Guo, Wei *research scientist*
Lee, John Joon *research scientist, minister*
Ljubimov, Alexander V. *molecular biologist, cell biologist, researcher*
Lunt, Owen Raynal *biologist, educator*
Malloy, Courtney L. *research scientist, educator*
Melnick, Michael *geneticist, educator*
Merwine, David Karl *neurophysiologist, educator*
Mohr, John Luther *biologist, environmental consultant*
Orme, Antony Ronald *geography educator*
Plath, Kathrin *biology professor, biomedical researcher*
Rosenfeld, John Lang *geology educator*
Sachs, George *biology professor, physician*
Schopf, James William *paleobiologist, researcher, educator*
Simmons, Donna Marie *neuroscientist, histotechnologist, neuroendocrine anatomist, researcher*
Sonnenschein, Ralph Robert *physiologist*
Szego, Clara Marian *cell biologist, educator*
Taylor, Charles Ellett *biologist, educator*
Thompson, Paul Matthew *neuroscientist*
Villablanca, Jaime Rolando *neuroscientist, medical educator*
Wagar, Elizabeth Ann *microbiologist, director*
Wright, Ernest Marshall *physiologist, consultant*
Xue, Yongkang *science educator*

Malibu
Hunt, Valerie Virginia *electrophysiologist, educator*

Martinez
Thomas, Walter Dill, Jr. *retired forest pathologist, consultant*

Menifee
Aguilar, Shelley Kezer *biology professor, research scientist*

Menlo Park
Lipman, Peter W. *research scientist*

Modesto
Moe, Andrew Irving *veterinarian*

Moffett Field
Friedmann, E(merich) Imre *biologist, educator*
Harper, Lynn D. *biologist*
Kittel, Peter *research scientist*
Lissauer, Jack Jonathan *astronomy educator*

Monrovia
Kimnach, Myron William *botanist, horticulturist*

Monterey
Boger, Dan Calvin *science professor, consultant*
Packard, Julie *aquarium administrator*

Moss Landing
Robison, Bruce H. *marine biologist*

Mountain View
Cabrol, Nathalie Agnes *research scientist*
Schickli, Jeanne Hlavka *virologist, researcher*

Norco
Morrison, James V. *biology professor*

Northridge
Karels, Tim J. *ecology professor*

Oakland
Ames, Bruce Nathan *biochemisty and molecular biology professor, department chairman*
Krauss, Ronald Maxwell *research scientist, endocrinologist, educator*
Masover, Gerald Kenneth *microbiologist*

Orange
Curt, Alan Sandman *neuroscientist, educator*

Palm Desert
Sausman, Karen *zoological park administrator*

Palm Springs
Petermann, Hans Jürgen *research scientist*

Palo Alto
Anderson, Charles Arthur *retired science administrator*
Ernst, Wallace Gary *geology educator, dean*
Johnson, Noble Marshall *research scientist*
Sanders, William John *research scientist*
Tsien, Richard Winyu *biology professor*

Pasadena
Andersen, Richard Alan *physiologist*
Anderson, David J. *biology professor*
Davidson, Eric Harris *molecular and developmental biologist, educator*
Goldreich, Peter Martin *astrophysics and planetary physics educator*
Helou, George *science administrator, educator*
Huang, Alice Shih-hou *biologist, educator, virologist*
Koch, Christof *biologist, educator*
Konishi, Masakazu *neuroscientist, educator*
Lester, Henry Allen *biology professor*
Meyerowitz, Elliot Martin *biologist, educator*
Revel, Jean-Paul *biology professor*
Scott, David Clinton *research scientist*
Steidel, Charles C. *astronomy educator*
Tirrell, David A. *research scientist, educator*
Varshavsky, Alexander Jacob *molecular biologist*
Wang, Jia *research scientist*
Wasserburg, Gerald Joseph *geology and geophysics educator*
Zewail, Ahmed Hassan *chemistry and physics educator, consultant, editor*

Pebble Beach
Neville, Roy Gerald *research scientist, chemical executive, consultant*

Penn Valley
Whitsel, Richard Harry *retired biologist, entomologist*

Pomona
Wagner, Edward John *physiologist, educator*

Porterville
Syrdahl, Rickelle Lyn *biology professor*

Quincy
Hall, Anthony Elmitt *agriculturist, physiolog*

Richmond
Janda, John Michael *microbiologist*

Ridgecrest
Sellers, Claudia Lee *biology professor*

Riverside
Bartnicki-Garcia, Salomon *microbiologist, educator*
Green, Harry Western, II, *geology and geophysics educator*
Hyman, Bradley Clark *biology professor, geneticist*
McHughen, Alan *geneticist, educator*
Millar, Jocelyn G. *entomologist, educator*
Page, Albert Lee *soil science educator, researcher*
Van Gundy, Seymour Dean *plant pathologist, educator*

Roseville
Riepenhoff-Talty, Marie *retired virologist*

Sacramento
Dong, Michael Hon *toxicologist*
Forsyth, Nicole Young *animal scientist*
Rosenberg, Dan Yale *retired plant pathologis*

San Bernardino
Mian, Lal Shah *entomologist, educator*

San Carlos
Wolff, Ronald Keith *toxicologist, researcher*

San Diego
Bartus, Raymond Thomas *neuroscientist, wr pharmaceutical executive*
Bernstein, Sanford Irwin *biology professor*
Crutchfield, Susan Ramsey *neurophysiologis*
Dulbecco, Renato *biologist, educator*
Ecker, Joseph R. *plant molecular and cellula biologist*
Eckhart, Walter *molecular biologist, educato*
Gage, Fred H. *neuroscientist, educator*
Getis, Arthur *geography educator*
Hayes, Claude Quinten Christopher *research scientist, inventor*
Meirowitz, Randy Emil *research scientist, consultant*
Myers, Douglas George *zoological society administrator*
Panetta, Joseph Daniel *biotechnologist, direc*
Rasochova, Lada *research scientist*
Sejnowski, Terrence Joseph *science educator*
Squire, Larry Ryan *neuroscientist, psycholog educator*
Taylor, Marcus Keene *physiologist, research*
Tozer, William Evans *entomologist, educator*
Vause, Edwin Hamilton *research foundation administrator*
Yie, Junming *research scientist*

San Francisco
Alberts, Bruce Michael *cell biologist, former foundation administrator*
Alvarez-Buylla, Arturo *neurobiologist, researcher*
Baxter-Lowe, Lee Ann *science educator*
Clements, John Allen *physiologist*
Ganong, William F(rancis) *physiologist, edu*
Heyneman, Donald *parasitology and tropica medicine educator*
Jan, Lily Yeh *physiology, biochemist*
Kerlikowske, Karla *research scientist*
La Farge, Timothy *retired plant geneticist*
Likova Mineva, Lora T. *research scientist*
Márquez-Magaña, Leticia Maria *biology professor*
McCormick, Frank *research scientist*
Pera, Renee Reijo *biology professor*
Saul-Gershenz, Leslie *entomologist, consulta ecologist, director*
Tlsty, Thea Dorothy *research scientist, educ*
Tricaro, Robert Collet *biologist, educator, ec poet*
Vidwans, Smruti Jayant *microbiologist*
Weiner, Michael W. *neuroscientist, research educator*
Wilkinson, Jeffery Alan *animal scientist*
Wolff, Sheldon *radiobiology educator*
Wyse, Roger Earl *physiologist, department chairman*
Yamamoto, Keith Robert *molecular biologis educator*

San Jacinto
Stange, Sharon (Sherri) *science educator*

San Jose
Zippin, David Benjamin *ecologist, consultar*

San Juan Capistrano
White, Beverly Jane *cytogeneticist*

San Marcos
Fabry, Victoria Joan *biology professor*
Sheath, Robert Gordon *botanist, educator*

San Marino
Benzer, Seymour *neuroscience educator*

Santa Barbara
Badash, Lawrence *science history educator*
Christman, Arthur Castner, Jr. *science advis consultant*
Crowell, John C(hambers) *geology educator, researcher*
Dunne, Thomas *geology educator*

ter, Karl David *retired research scientist*
rdoch, William Wilson *ecologist, educator*
neider, Edward Lee *botanist, researcher*
ker, Shirley Lois Cotter *botanist, educator*

nta Cruz
s, Harland Warren *astronomy educator, optical design consultant*
ssler, David H. *molecular biologist, educator*
key, Harry Douglas *information and omputer science educator*
genheim, Jean Harmon *biologist, educator*
Thorne *geosciences educator*
iams, Terrie M. *biology professor*

nta Monica
dman, Charles A. *science administrator*
eson, Melvin Erwin *management sciences ompany executive, educator*

ntee
ly, Ben(son B.) *orchid nursery executive*

uth San Francisco
dman, Corey Scott *neuroscientist, otechnologist, educator*
wli, Leslie Albert *research scientist, ducator*
Ann L. *biotechnology company executive*
eller, Richard H. *physiologist, science ducator*

nford
n, Ann Margaret *microbiology and nmunology educator, researcher*
lor, Denis Aristide *neuroscientist, educator*
dford, Roger David *science educator*
gs, Winslow Russell *plant biologist, ucator*
wn, Patrick O. *molecular biologist, educator*
pbell, Allan McCulloch *bacteriology ducator*
alli-Sforza, Luigi Luca *geneticist, educator*
en, Stanley Norman *geneticist, educator*
, Linda Katherine *veterinary pathologist, ucator*
y, Gretchen Cara *ecologist, environmental rvices administrator*
y, William J. *computer science educator*
s, Mark M. *microbiologist, educator*
s, Ronald Wayne *genetics researcher, ochemistry educator*
seroth, Karl A. *neuroscientist, educator*
o, Rodolfo *biologist, educator, researcher*
ch, Paul Ralph *biology professor*
ow, Stanley *microbiologist, educator*
cke, Uta *geneticist, educator*
awalt, Philip Courtland *biology professor, searcher*
Connell, Susan K. *neuroscientist*
ley, William C. *neuroscientist*
ney, Harold Alfred *plant ecologist*
ghgarden, Joan E. *biology professor*
piro, Lucy *molecular biology educator*
z, Carla J. *biology professor, researcher*
oter, Eric Manvers *retired neurobiology ofessor, consultant*
erville, Christopher Roland *botanist, ucator*
dich, James A. *biology professor*
ens, Timothy P. *biology professor, geneticist*
rock, Peter Andrew *space science and trophysics educator*
iot, Julie *microbiologist, medical educator*
dell, Brian A. *neuroscientist, educator*
fsky, Charles *retired biology professor*

kton
, Shirley Griffin *science educator, armacist*
ness, Rhonda Ann *retired microbiologist*

set Beach
ham, Thomas Grenville *retired icrobiologist*

Sea Ranch
lick, Leonard *cell biologist, gerontologist, microbiologist, educator, riter*

nga
, Edward Florin *veterinarian*

nut Creek
org, David Michael *evolutionary biologist*

t Hollywood
, Joyce K. *veterinarian*

tminster
yen, Khue Vu *molecular biologist, searcher*

odland
res, Richard Felt *research scientist*

odland Hills
Stuart Ira *physiologist*

LORADO

ada
ers, Christopher Sheridan *science educator, eb site designer*

ora
ey, J. Gordon *food scientist*
din, James Frank *biology professor, searcher*
hlag, Nancy Hansen *environmental and ture resources educator*

lder
strong, David Michael *biology professor*
dy, Radford, Jr. *science administrator*
Clifford, Steven Francis *science administrator, director*
Dubin, Mark William *neuroscientist, educator, academic administrator*
Floyd, Ted *ornithologist, writer*
Guild, Nancy Ann *biology professor*
Knoelker, Michael T.F. *science observatory director*
Meier, Beverly Joyce Loeffler *science educator, educational consultant*
Meier, Mark Frederick *research scientist, educator, artist, small business owner*
Mitchell, Joan LaVerne *research scientist*
Roble, Raymond Gerald *science administrator*
Serafin, Robert Joseph *science center administrator, electrical engineer*
Snow, Theodore Peck *astrophysics educator*
Southwick, Charles Henry *zoologist, educator*
Staehelin, Lucas Andrew *cell biology professor*
Tans, Pieter P. *research scientist*
Tolbert, Margaret A. *geochemistry educator*
Wood, William Barry III *biologist, educator*

Brush
Gabriel, Donald Eugene *science educator*

Carbondale
Cowgill, Ursula Moser *biologist, educator, environmental consultant*

Colorado Springs
Bybee, Rodger Wayne *science administrator*
Driscoll, Lori *neuroscientist, educator*
West, R. Leland *veterinarian*

Denver
Ehret, Josephine Mary *microbiologist, researcher*
Freiheit, Clayton Fredric *zoo director*
McDermott, Sandra *national park administrator*
Taylor, Robert A. *veterinarian*

Fort Collins
Black, William Cormack, IV, *insect geneticist, statistician*
Egger, Erick *veterinarian*
Follett, Ronald Francis *soil scientist*
Johnson, Robert Britten *geology educator*
Keim, Wayne Franklin *retired agronomist, geneticist*
Lumb, William Valjean *veterinarian*
Mortvedt, John Jacob *soil scientist, researcher*
Peng, Junhua *molecular biologist, botanist*
Peterson, Gary Andrew *agronomics researcher*
Seidel, George Elias, Jr. *zoology educator*
Seward, Nathan William *biologist, researcher*

Glenwood Springs
Kelley, Robert Daryl *retired biology professor, mathematics professor*

Golden
Bettinghaus, Erwin Paul *research scientist*
Kazmerski, Lawrence Lee *scientist, research facility executive*
Weimer, Robert Jay *geology educator, energy consultant, civic leader*

Littleton
Vail, Charles Daniel *veterinarian, consultant*

Longmont
Dierks, Richard Ernest *veterinarian, academic administrator*

Northglenn
Hemlock, Roberta Leigh *veterinary technician*

U S A F Academy
Veverka, Donald Victor *science educator*

Westminster
Reynolds-Sakowski, Dana Renee *science educator*

CONNECTICUT

Farmington
Bronner, Felix *physiologist, biophysicist, educator, painter*
Rothfield, Lawrence I. *microbiology educator*

Hamden
Adair, Eleanor Reed *environmental biologist*
Smith, David Martyn *retired forestry educator*

Madison
Kilbourne, Edwin Dennis *virologist, educator*
Stevenson, Robert Edwin *microbiologist, consultant*

Meriden
Lee, Henry C. *forensic scientist*

Mystic
Ballard, Robert Duane *marine geologist*

New Haven
Altman, Sidney *biology professor*
Anderson, John Fredric *science administrator, entomologist, researcher*
Aronson, Peter Samuel *physiologist, researcher*
Behar, Kevin L. *neuroscientist*
Berke, Brett Alan *neuroscientist, research scientist*
Briggs, Derek Ernest Gilmor *science educator*
Brown, Thomas Huntington *neuroscientist*
De Camilli, Pietro V. *cell biologist*
Donoghue, Michael John *biologist, educator*
DuBois, Arthur Brooks *physiologist, educator*
Galston, Arthur William *biology professor*
Kim, Tae Hoon *biology professor*
Mineur, Yann Sébastien *neuroscientist*
Novick, Peter J. *cell biologist, educator*
Pollard, Thomas Dean *cell biologist, educator*
Redmond, Donald Eugene, Jr. *neuroscientist, educator*
Shepherd, Gordon Murray *neuroscientist, educator*
Summers, William Cofield *science educator*
Waggoner, Paul Edward *agricultural scientist*

Newtown
Babbitt, Martha E. *science educator*

North Haven
Glaser, Gilbert Herbert *retired neuroscientist, educator*

Old Greenwich
DeOrchis, Frankie Juanita *forester, writer*

Old Saybrook
Smith, David Clark *research scientist*

Storrs Mansfield
Devereux, Owen Francis *retired metallurgy educator*
Holsinger, Kent Eugene *biology professor, educator*
Laufer, Hans *developmental biologist, educator*
Marcus, Philip Irving *virology educator, researcher*
Rasmussen, Theodore Peter *biology professor*

Wallingford
Dionne, Karen Marie *veterinary technician, educator*
Hartz, Richard Allen *research scientist*

DELAWARE

Greenville
Schroeder, Herman Elbert *scientific consultant*

Millsboro
Bethke, Frederick Randall *microbiologist, researcher*

Newark
Campbell, Linzy Leon *molecular biology researcher, educator*
DeLorme, Michael *toxicologist, researcher*
Sparks, Donald Lewis *soil chemistry educator*

Wilmington
Darko, Denis F. *research scientist, educator, physician*
Hartzell, Charles R. *science foundation director, cell biologist, biochemist*
Sippel-Wetmore, Frances Marie *microbiologist, retired business owner*
Waritz, Richard Stefan *toxicologist, researcher*

DISTRICT OF COLUMBIA

Washington
Affronti, Lewis Francis, Sr. *microbiologist, educator*
Allan, Ronald Gage *academic research coordinator*
Ampy, Franklin Roosevelt *zoologist, educator*
Anand, Rajen S. *physiologist, educator*
Andrews, Peter Michael *biology professor*
Apple, Martin Allen *science executive and educator*
Banks, Richard Charles *ornithologist*
Beehler, Bruce McPherson *research zoologist, ornithologist, conservationist*
Berg, Patricia Elene *molecular biologist*
Carhart, Homer Walter *retired research scientist*
Case, Larry D. *agricultural education specialist*
Challinor, David *retired biologist*
Chamot, Dennis *science policy executive*
Coleman, Bernell *physiologist, educator*
Corell, Robert Walden *science administrator, educator*
Davis, Donald Ray *entomologist*
Davis, Randy Lee *soil scientist*
Elias, Thomas Sam *botanist, author*
Falk, Diane M. *research information specialist, librarian, writer, editor, director*
Feulner, Edwin J., Jr. *research foundation executive*
Harding, Fann *retired science administrator*
Hazen, Robert Miller *research scientist, writer*
Henkin, Robert Irwin *neuroscientist, internist, nuclear medicine physician, medical products executive*
Hope, William Duane *retired zoologist, curator*
Hotez, Peter Jay *research scientist, educator*
Jackson, Margaret Elizabeth *science educator*
Leshner, Alan Irvin *science administrator*
Li, Li *research scientist*
Lovejoy, Thomas Eugene *tropical and conservation biologist, association executive*
McClung, Gwendolyn *soil microbiologist*
Meyers, Wayne Marvin *microbiologist, physician*
Mitchell, Ross Edward *research scientist, educator*
Moore, Donald Emerson III *zoological park administrator, curator, wildlife biologist*
Morse, Larry Eugene *botanist, conservationist*
Nabholz, Joseph Vincent *biologist, ecologist*
Neureiter, Norman P. *science association director*
Nicolson, Dan Henry *retired plant taxonomist*
Nightingale, Elena Ottolenghi *pediatric geneticist, academic administrator, educator*
Pilcher, Carl B. *astrobiologist*
Pyke, Thomas Nicholas, Jr. *science administrator*
Reischauer, Robert D. *research organization executive*
Ridenour, Amy Moritz *research center administrator*
Schimel, David S. *ecologist, science administrator*
Siegel, Frederic Richard *geology educator*
Stern, (Sol) Alan *science administrator, astrophysicist, researcher*
Tidball, M. Elizabeth Peters *physiologist, educator*
Tingus, Steven James *physiologist, researcher*
Torrey, Barbara Boyle *research council administrator*
Ucko, David Alan *science foundation official*
Wasshausen, Dieter Carl *botanist*
West, Robert MacLellan *science educator, consultant*

FLORIDA

Belle Glade
Liang, Lee Z. *biology professor*

Boca Raton
Furman, Mark Evan *neuroscientist*
Lee, Xiaoyang *scientist*
Samuels, William Mason *physiology association executive*

Bradenton
Diana, John Nicholas *physiologist*

Coral Gables
Kohen, Elli *science educator*
Lucà-Moretti, Maurizio *research scientist, nutritionist*

Deland
Benet, Helen Curry *retired toxicologist, artist*

Delray Beach
Chavin, Walter *biological sciences educator, researcher*

Fort Myers
Beever, James William III *biologist*

Fort Pierce
Calvert, David Victor *soil science educator*
Rice, Mary Esther *biologist*
Widder, Edith Anne *biologist*

Gainesville
Arbogast, Richard Terrence *entomologist, researcher*
Besch, Emerson Louis *physiologist, educator, retired dean*
Borkhataria, Rena Rebecca *ecologist, researcher*
Burridge, Michael John *veterinarian, educator, research director*
Cantliffe, Daniel James *horticulture educator*
Dilcher, David Leonard *paleobotany educator, researcher*
Drury, Kenneth Clayton *biologist*
Dunford, James Christopher *entomologist, educator*
Green, Eleanor Myers *veterinarian, educator*
Gridley, Kelly Elizabeth *biotechnologist, researcher*
Grobman, Arnold Brams *retired biology educator, academic administrator*
Gutekunst, Richard Ralph *retired microbiology professor*
Himes, James Albert *retired veterinary medicine educator*
Hoy, Marjorie Ann *entomology educator*
Jones, Richard Lamar *entomology educator*
Mead, Frank Waldreth *taxonomic entomologist*
Nguyen, Ru *entomologist*
Nicoletti, Paul Lee *retired veterinarian, educator*
Oppenheimer, David Gray *botanist, educator*
Price, Donald Dennis *neuroscientist, psychologist*
Purcifull, Dan Elwood *retired plant virologist, retired educator*
Quesenberry, Kenneth Hays *agronomy educator*
Raghavan, Sivakumar *food scientist*
Schmidt-Nielsen, Bodil Mimi (Mrs. Roger G. Chagnon) *retired physiologist, educator*
Skoblar, Barry *neuroscientist*
Soltis, Pamela S. *botanist, educator*
Teixeira, Arthur Alves *food engineer, educator, consultant*
Vierck, Charles John, Jr. *retired neuroscience educator*
Yamamoto, Janet Kazuko *science educator*
Yu, Simon Shyi-Jian *entomologist, educator*

Gulf Breeze
Menzer, Robert Everett *retired toxicologist, educator*

Homestead
Roberts, Larry Spurgeon *biological science educator, zoologist*

Jupiter
Moore, Jon Alistair *biology professor, researcher*
Weissmann, Charles *molecular biologist, educator*

Lake Alfred
Kender, Walter John *horticulturist, educator*

Lakeland
Chapman, Angela Marie *science educator*
Pospichal, Marcie W. *neuroscientist, psychologist, educator*

Melbourne
Storrs, Eleanor Emerett *science administrator, consultant*

Miami
Buchwald, Peter Sandor *science association director*
Gilbert, John Ray *geneticist, researcher*
Goodwin, Kelly Dee *microbiologist, researcher*
Mathee, Kalai *research scientist, educator*
Muench, Karl Hugo *clinical geneticist*
Rodriguez, Irmina Bestard *science educator*

Miami Gardens
Bell, Taunjah Patrease *research scientist*

New Port Richey
Adams, Jean Marie *biology professor*
Day, Peter Rodney *geneticist, educator*

Orlando
Baker, Peter Mitchell *science association director, laser scientist*
Kincaid, John Peter *science educator*
Klemenz, Christine F. *science educator, researcher*
Knowles, Patricia Marie *science educator*

Palm Beach Gardens
Mills, Christopher James *neurophysiologist, electroneurodiagnostic technologist*

Palm Harbor
Calhoun, John Vincent *research scientist*

Panama City
Cortes, Enric *marine biologist*

Port Saint Lucie
Austin, Philip *research scientist*

Punta Gorda
O'Neal, Lyman Henry *biology educator*

Ruskin
Briscoe, Anne M. *retired science educator*

Saint Petersburg
Byrd, Isaac Burlin *retired biologist*
D'Elia, Christopher Francis *marine biologist, educator, academic administrator*
Miller, G(erson) H(arry) *science administrator, mathematician, computer scientist, chemist*
Mueller, O. Thomas *molecular geneticist, pediatrics educator*

Sanford
Dettman, Mary *biology professor*

Sarasota
Clark, Eugenie *zoologist, educator*
Hueter, Robert Edward *marine biologist, researcher*
Mahadevan, Kumar *marine life administrator, researcher*

Spring Hill
Rothenberg, Linda Ann *science educator*

Stuart
Robinson, Michael Hill *retired zoological park director, biologist*

Tallahassee
Anderson, Theresa Ann *science educator*
Khalil, Mohammed K. *research scientist, medical educator*

West Palm Beach
Chimney, Michael John *aquatic biologist/limnologist, consultant*

Winter Haven
Grierson, William *retired agriculturist*

GEORGIA

Adairsville
Dobson, Suzanne *science educator*

Athens
Baile, Clifton A. *biologist, researcher*
Bennetzen, Jeffrey L. *molecular biologist*
Leebens-Mack, James H. *biologist*
Rashleigh, Brenda *ecologist*
Tyler, David Earl *retired veterinary medical educator*
Wessler, Susan R. *biologist, educator*

Atlanta
Circeo, Louis Joseph, Jr. *research scientist, civil engineer*
Compans, Richard W. *microbiology educator*
Cox, Nancy Jane *microbiologist*
de Waal, Frans B.M. *biologist, psychology professor*
Fowler, Bruce Andrew *toxicologist, researcher, public health service official*
Glass, Roger I. *virologist*
Jeffery, Geoffrey Marron *medical parasitologist*
Ly, Hinh *science educator*
Lynn, David G. *biology and chemistry professor*
MacLeish, Peter R. *neuroscientist*
Spitznagel, John Keith *retired microbiologist, immunologist, physician*
Wang, Yuhang *science educator*
Warren, Stephen Theodore *human geneticist, educator*
Yates, Jerome William *scientific administrator, researcher*

Augusta
Baker, Carleton Harold *physiology educator*
Inscho, Edward William *physiology educator*
Kutlar, Ferdane *genetics educator, researcher*

Decatur
Cavallaro, Joseph John *retired microbiologist*

Duluth
Cunningham, Richard Anthony *science administrator*
Johnston, William David *biotechnologist, director*

Gainesville
Lowrey, Alex Andre *biology professor*

Griffin
Doyle, Michael Patrick *microbiologist, educator, director*

Kennesaw
McCoy, R. Wesley *biology educator*

Lithonia
Baxter, Gene Francis *chemical researcher, consultant*

Newnan
Culbreth, Lucretia Joy *science educator*
Krach, Dale James *science educator, athletic trainer*

Norcross
Wagner, Robert Earl *retired agronomist*

Suwanee
Decker, Michael John *neuroscientist*

Woodstock
Barthlow, Michelle Jones *science educator*

HAWAII

Honolulu
Abbott, Isabella Aiona *retired biology educator*
Berg, John Townsend *physiologist, researcher*
Brill, Richard C. *physical science educator*
Fok, Agnes Kwan *retired cell biologist, educator*
Gubler, Duane J. *virologist, educator, researcher*
Hue, Nguyen Van *soil scientist, chemist, educator*
Kamemoto, Fred Isamu *retired zoologist*
Mandel, Morton *molecular biologist*
Owen, Cathy Hesse *science administrator*
Sagawa, Yoneo *horticulturist, educator*

Kailua
Shank, Charles Vernon *science administrator, educator, physicist*

Ocean View
Baglow, David Richard *marine facility administrator*

Waikoloa
Morris, Victor Franklin, Jr. *retired meteorology educator*

IDAHO

Boise
Burton, Timothy Alan *biologist*

Kimberly
Strausbaugh, Carl Alan *plant pathologist*

Moscow
Guy, Stephen Otto *agronomist, educator*
Roberts, Lorin Watson *botanist, educator*
Vaughan, Karen Lynn *soil scientist*

Pocatello
Vailas, Arthur C. *biomechanics educator*

Post Falls
Brede, Andrew Douglas *science administrator, botanist*

ILLINOIS

Argonne
Schriesheim, Alan *science administrator*

Aurora
Elgar, Sharon Kay *science educator*
Lloyd, Johnny Keith *biology professor*

Berwyn
Parker, Alan John *veterinary neurologist, educator, researcher*

Brookfield
Rabb, George Bernard *zoologist, conservationist*
Rudnick, Jamie *geneticist, research scientist*

Carbondale
Burr, Brooks Milo *zoology educator*
LeFebvre, Eugene Allen *zoology educator, ecologist*

Carterville
Krapf, Keith Alan *science educator*

Champaign
Batzli, George Oliver *ecology educator*
Dmitriev, Dmitry A. *entomologist, researcher*
Levin, Geoffrey Arthur *botanist*
Ridlen, Samuel Franklin *agriculture educator*

Chicago
Brown, Joel S. *evolutionary ecologist, educator*
Chakrabarty, Ananda Mohan *microbiologist*
Coyne, Jerry Allen *ecologist, educator*
Crane, Sir Peter Robert *botanist, geologist, paleontologist, educator*
Davidson, Richard Laurence *geneticist, educator*
Desjardins, Claude *physiologist, dean*
Dwivedi, Yogesh *science educator*
Ernest, J. Terry *ocular physiologist, educator*
Frederick, John Eugene *science educator*
Fukui, Yoshio *biology professor*
Goodman, Steven Michael *conservation biologist*
Greenberg, Bernard *retired entomologist*
Howe, Henry Franklin *ecology educator*
Khodarev, Nikolai Nikolaevich *biologist, researcher*
Lerman, Zafra Margolin *science educator, public policy professor*
Mateles, Richard Isaac *biotechnologist*
Mugnaini, Enrico *neuroscience educator*
Niyogi-Salhi, Ruma *science educator*
Olopade, Olufunmilayo Falusi (Funmi Olopade) *geneticist, educator, oncologist, hematologist*

Park, Thomas Joseph *biology researcher, educator*
Pendleton, Elisha Donshell *molecular biologist, researcher*
Pinna, Graziano *biologist, researcher*
Preuss, Daphne *geneticist, biology professor*
Pritchard, Jonathan K. *geneticist, educator*
Provus, Barbara Lee *retired executive search consultant*
Roizman, Bernard *virologist, educator*
Sivananthan, Sivalingam *science educator*
Solaro, Ross John *physiologist, biophysicist*
Yamada, Tohru *biologist, educator, researcher, director*

Coal City
DiGiusto, Elaine Bessie *science educator*

Dekalb
Lotshaw, David Paul *physiologist, educator*

Downers Grove
Brekke, Stewart Ernest *retired chemistry and physics educator*

Edwardsville
Brugam, Richard Blair *biology educator*

Evanston
Dallos, Peter John *neurobiologist, educator*
Enroth-Cugell, Christina Alma Elisabeth *neurophysiologist, educator*
Lamb, Robert Andrew *molecular biologist, virologist, educator*
Novales, Ronald Richards *zoologist, educator*
Weertman, Johannes *materials science educator*
Widom, Jonathan *biology professor*
Wu, Tai Te *biological sciences and engineering educator*

Glen Ellyn
Anderson, Barbara Jean *biology professor*
Poromanska, Margarita Kirilova *science educator, environmental scientist*

Glenview
Kinigakis, Panagiotis *research scientist, engineer, inventor, writer*

Granite City
Cowan, Robert Randall *science educator*

Great Lakes
Bienek, Diane Rose *research scientist*

Lebanon
Jewett, Thomas O. *science educator, writer*

Lisle
Smith, Jared Russell William *research executive, research scientist, consultant, poet*
Ware, George Henry *botanist*

Maywood
Schultz, Richard Michael *biochemistry educator, researcher*

Monmouth
Godde, James Scott *molecular biologist*

Normal
Brown, Lauren Evans *zoologist, researcher, educator*
Stevenson, Cheryl D. *science educator, researcher*

Northbrook
King, Robert Charles *biologist, educator*

Plainfield
Matlock, B. Jane *science educator*

Princeton
Webber, Adam Brooks *science educator*

Robinson
Mallard, Carrie Charlene *science educator*

Rock Island
Anderson, Richard Charles *geology educator*

Round Lake
Bui, Mai Ha *molecular biologist, researcher*

Savoy
Sinclair, James Burton *retired plant pathology educator, consultant*

Skokie
Hong, In Chul *research scientist*

Springfield
Masternak, Michal Mateusz *biotechnologist, educator, molecular biologist, researcher*
Munyer, Edward Arnold *zoologist*

Sugar Grove
DeLay, Larry Gene *science educator, photographer*

Urbana
Berenbaum, May Roberta *entomology educator*
Bernard, Richard Lawson *retired geneticist, educator*
Buetow, Dennis Edward *physiologist, educator*
Chow, Poo *forester*
Crang, Richard Francis Earl *botanist, writer, research scientist*
Crofts, Antony Richard *biochemistry and biophysics educator*
Ehrlich, Gert *science educator, researcher*
Ezeji, Thaddeus Chukwuemeka *microbiologist, educator*
Frazzetta, Thomas Henry *evolutionary biologist, educator*
Greenough, William Tallant *psychobiologist, educator*

Heichel, Gary Harold *agronomist, educator*
Holt, Donald A. *agronomist, consultant, researcher, retired academic administrator*
Kuhlenschmidt, Mark Stuart *microbiologist, researcher*
Larkin, Denis M. *geneticist, researcher*
Meyer, Richard Charles *microbiologist, educ*
Nanney, David Ledbetter *geneticist, educator*
Ra, Hyungshim Yoo *biologist, researcher*
Ridgway, Marcella Davies *veterinarian*
Robinson, Gene Ezia *biologist, educator*
Seigler, David Stanley *botanist, educator, chemist*
Splittstoesser, Walter Emil *botanist, educator*
Tischkau, Shelley Ann *physiologist, educator*
Whitt, Gregory Sidney *evolution educator*
Williams, Martha Ethelyn *information scienc educator*

Vandalia
Jett, Charlene M. *biologist, researcher*

Westchester
Webb, Emily *retired plant morphologist*

Woodstock
Dorn, Diane M. *science educator*

INDIANA

Bloomington
Clevenger, Sarah *botanist, consultant*
Estelle, Mark *biology professor*
Nolan, Val, Jr. *retired biologist, lawyer*
Rieseberg, Loren *botanist, educator*
Ruesink, Albert William *biologist, plant scie educator*
Skosnik, Patrick David *neuroscientist, resear*
Weinberg, Eugene David *microbiologist, educator*

Evansville
Culver, Gregory K. *science educator*

Gary
Schoon, Kenneth James *science educator, wr*

Indianapolis
Babsky, Andriy M. *biologist, researcher*
Banya, Santonino Ku'Caya *science educator*
Burr, David Bentley *anatomy educator*
Ochs, Sidney *neurophysiology researcher, educator*
Rhoades, Rodney Allen *physiologist, educat*
Thomas, Jerry Arthur *soil scientist*

Jasper
Eck, Kenneth James *agronomist*

Kokomo
Roales, Robert R. *natural science educator*

Lafayette
Conley, Shawn *agriculturist*
Nicholson, Ralph Lester *botanist, educator*

Madison
Grahn, Ann Wagoner *retired science administrator*

Muncie
Hendrix, Jon Richard *biology professor*
Henzlik, Raymond Eugene *zoophysiologist, educator*
Mertens, Thomas Robert *biology professor*
Wise, Charles Davidson *science educator*

Notre Dame
Burns, Peter C. *science and engineering educator*
Jensen, Richard Jorg *biologist, educator*
Kulpa, Charles F. *microbiologist, educator*
Pollard, Morris *microbiologist, educator*
Shrader-Frechette, Kristin *science educator*

Pittsboro
Swango, Colleen Jill *science educator*

Valparaiso
Schlender, William Elmer *management scier educator*

West Lafayette
Amstutz, Harold Emerson *veterinarian, edu*
Cuendet, Muriel *research scientist*
Edwards, Charles Richard *entomology and p management educator*
Fouad, Mohamed Raouf *science educator*
Hunt, Michael O'Leary *wood science and engineering educator*
Johannsen, Chris Jakob *agronomist, educato administrator*
Le Master, Dennis Clyde *retired forester, economist, educator*
Nelson, Philip Edwin *food scientist, educato*
Ohm, Herbert Willis *agronomy educator, agriculturist*
Sherman, Louis Allen *biology professor, department chairman*

IOWA

Ames
Anderson, Lloyd Lee *physiologist, educator*
Beran, George Wesley *veterinary microbiol educator*
Blaser, Brock Cameron *agronomist*
Clark, Lynn G. *botanist, educator*
Greve, John Henry *veterinary parasitologist, educator*
Hallauer, Arnel Roy *geneticist*
Hatfield, Jerry Lee *plant physiologist, agricultural meteorologist*
Johnson, Lawrence Alan *cereal technologist, educator, administrator*

ong-Jae *research scientist*
agada, Surya K. *science educator*
ng, William Lloyd *retired veterinarian, gist*
James Walter *entomologist*
Kenneth James *agronomist, educator*
ld, Gary P. *plant pathologist, educator*
, Phillip Aaron *retired veterinarian*
nig, Tanja *veterinary pathologist*
ichard Francis *veterinarian, educator, microbiologist*
Vaughn Allen *retired veterinary logy educator*
son, Louis Milton *agronomy educator, rcher*
Gregory L. *plant pathologist, educator*
n, Richard Lewis *zoology educator*

ville
Mark Aaron *biotechnologist, research tist*

Moines
ll, Stuart *medical entomologist, consulting ician*

dge
ng, Paul R. *sports science educator*

ell
Waldo Sylvester *biologist, educator, emic administrator*

City
a, Michael Allen *microbiologist, educator*
ell, Kevin Peter *physiology and hysics educator*
berger Gilmore, Julie Mae *research ntist*
, David Thomas *microbiology educator*
r, William John, Jr. *microbiologist, ator, public health service officer*
, Russell Forest *research scientist*
Richard Glen *zoology educator*
Ramon (Khe-Siong Lim) *neuroscience cator, researcher*
n, Linda Ellen *biologist, educator*
s, Robert F. *cell biologist*
Jeffrey E. *physiology educator*
Barbara *zoologist, educator*
er, Charles C(ooper) *physiologist, hysicist, educator*

hontas
Sue Kay *science educator*

Des Moines
, Matthew Stephen *retired botanist*

SAS

oria
erg, Marshall David *biology professor*

, Patrick Ivan *physiological ecologist*

as City
In-Young *science educator*

rence
o, Ernest Edward *retired geology and ineering educator*
age, Kenneth Barclay *retired biology fessor*
, George William *retired entomology cator*
er, Christopher Hardin *botany educator*
ton, Richard Fourness *biologist, educator*
wardt, Robert William *mycologist*
ener, Charles Duncan *entomologist, earcher, educator*
kel, Delbert Merrill *microbiologist, logist, educator*

xa
ngs, Gregory Owen *science educator, nsultant*

hattan
m, Khurshida *zoologist, researcher*
riraju, Subramanyam Venkata *entomologist, nsultant*
son, Howard Hugh *veterinarian, physiology ucator*
man, Donald Wayne *research ecologist*
am, M. B. *plant physiologist, educator*
David Andrew *food scientist, educator*
r, Gerry Lynn *agronomist, educator*
enson, Jeffrey Smith *physiologist, educator*

sho Falls
r, Robert Smith *biology and zoology ucator, researcher*

the
lwin, Becky K. *educational technology source educator*

rland Park
z, Kenneth Lee *cardiovascular physiologist, search consultant, writer*

sons
as, Lyle Wayne *agricultural research dministrator, educator*

hita
ks, Melinda Adair *science educator*
, Chan Hyung *cell biologist, physician*

NTUCKY

athiana
lurski, Bruce Lord *retired ecologist, vironmental scientist*

Frankfort
Frye, Wilbur Wayne *retired soil science educator, researcher, administrator*
Gomelsky, Boris *geneticist, educator*
Huebner, Ruth A. *science educator, researcher*

Lexington
Huffman, Gerald P. *science administrator, educator*
Humphries, Asa Alan, Jr. *biologist, educator, dean*
Kasperbauer, Michael John *plant physiology educator, researcher*
Mitchell, George Ernest, Jr. *zoology educator*
Rahman, Shafiqur *neuropharmacologist, scientist, educator*
Robinson, Thomas Christopher *health science educator*
Straus, Robert *behavioral sciences educator*
Timoney, Peter Joseph *veterinarian, educator, virologist, consultant*

Louisville
Foster, William R. *zoological park administrator*
Wiseman, Dennis R. *science educator*

Owensboro
Caplan, Geralyn Marie *biology professor*

Richmond
Branson, Branley Allan *biology professor*

LOUISIANA

Baton Rouge
Besch, Everett Dickman *veterinarian, dean emeritus, educator*
Burns, Paul Yoder *forester, educator*
Hackney, Marcella Wichser *biology professor*
Hansel, William *biology professor*
Head, Jonathan Frederick *cell biologist*
Lopez, Mandi J. *veterinarian, scientist*
Superneau, Duane William *geneticist, physician*
Tipton, Kenneth Warren *retired agricultural administrator, researcher*
Vidal, Martin Andreas *veterinarian*
Wong, Wai Hing *marine biologist, researcher*

Chauvin
Sammarco, Paul William *ecologist, researcher*

Cut Off
Mestayer, Mary Frances *science educator*

Jackson
Kondrup, John Thomas *retired research scientist*

Lafayette
Carolina, Monteiro *ecologist*

New Orleans
Beard, Elizabeth Letitia *physiologist, educator*
Blackwell, James E. *retired science educator*
Ivens, Mary Sue *microbiologist, medical mycologist*
Mitchell, Kenneth David *physiologist, educator*

Shreveport
Hall, Amy Matthews *science educator*

MAINE

Bar Harbor
Leiter, Edward Henry *cell biologist, researcher*

Farmington
Mathews, Linnea Koons *science educator, librarian*

Friendship
Cowan, Diane *research scientist, educator*

Kittery Point
Green, Edward Crocker *research scientist*

Mount Desert
Crawford, Richard Bradway *biologist, biochemist, educator*

Old Town
Ritz, George F. *forester, consultant*

Orono
Causey, Robert Crawford *veterinarian, researcher*

Sangerville
Harris, Norman Edwin *food scientist, consultant*

Walpole
Dorgan, Kelly M. *marine biologist*

MARYLAND

Aberdeen Proving Ground
Kuperman, Roman Gregory *toxicologist, ecologist*
Stuebing, Edward Willis *research scientist*

Baltimore
Allen, Ronald John *astrophysics educator, researcher*
Baskakov, Ilia V. *biotechnologist, researcher*
Brady, Joseph Vincent *behavioral biologist, educator*
Broda-Hydorn, Susan *entomologist*
Brown, Donald David *biology professor*
Colwell, Rita Rossi *microbiologist, former federal agency administrator, medical educator*
Craig, Nancy L. *molecular biologist, educator, geneticist*
Davis, Guy Donald *research scientist*
Dawson, Valina L. *science educator*
Dickfeld, Timm-Michael *electrophysiologist, cardiologist, educator*
Dorsey, Susan G. *neuroscientist, educator*
Gall, Joseph Grafton *biologist, researcher, educator*
Gallo, Robert Charles *research scientist*
Goldberg, Alan Marvin *toxicologist, educator*
Greider, Carol Widney *molecular biologist*
Hansen, Barbara Caleen *physiologist, science educator*
Huganir, Richard Lewis *neuroscientist, educator, researcher*
Littlefield, John Walley *geneticist, cell biologist, pediatrician*
Massof, Robert William *neuroscientist, educator*
McKusick, Victor Almon *geneticist, educator, physician*
Mendell, Joshua T. *molecular biologist, geneticist, educator*
Merchenthaler, Istvan Jozsef *neuroscientist, morphologist*
Mountcastle, Vernon Benjamin *retired neuroscientist*
Nonogaki, Hirofumi *research scientist*
Radhakrishnan, Malathi *biologist, educator*
Rasgon, Jason Laurence *entomologist, microbiologist, educator*
Redfield, Robert R. *virologist, medical educator*
Sack, George Henry, Jr. *molecular geneticist*
Savonenko, Alena *neuroscientist, educator*
Sidransky, David *molecular biologist*
Singh, Om V. *biotechnologist, researcher*
Stewart, Doris Mae *biology professor*
Trpis, Milan *vector biologist, educator*
Trujillo, J. Roberto *virologist*
Wolman, M. Gordon *geography educator*

Beltsville
Bae, Hanhong *molecular biologist, researcher*
Davis, Robert Edward *plant pathologist*
Nemes, Attila *soil scientist, researcher*
Palm, Mary Egdahl *mycologist*
Schneider, Edwin Kahn *research scientist*
Shukla, Jagadish *science educator*

Bethesda
Ahn, Sohyun *neuroscientist, researcher*
Basavappa, Ravi *biophysical science educator*
Bennink, Jack Richard *microbiologist, researcher*
Brady, Roscoe Owen *neurogeneticist, educator*
Bunger, Rolf *physiology educator*
Burns, Drusilla Lorene *microbiologist*
Di Paolo, Joseph Amedeo *geneticist*
Ehrenfeld, Ellie (Elvera Ehrenfeld) *biologist, researcher*
Frank, Martin *physiologist, educator, medical association administrator*
Greenberg, Judith Horovitz *geneticist*
Grisham, Joe Wheeler *cell biologist, educator*
Lorber, Mortimer *retired physiology educator*
Mock, Beverly A. *geneticist, researcher*
Monjan, Andrew Arthur *neuroscientist*
Moss, Bernard *virologist, researcher*
Nussbaum, Robert L. *senior genetics investigator*
Petralia, Ronald Sebastian *entomologist, neurobiologist*
Purcell, Robert Harry *virologist, researcher*
Salmoiraghi, Gian Carlo *physiologist, educator*
Schlom, Jeffrey Bert *research scientist*
Sokoloff, Louis *retired physiologist, neuroscientist*
Webster, Henry de Forest *neuroscientist*
Wolpert-DeFilippes, Mary K. *science administrator*
Woodall, Jerry M. *research scientist, educator*
Yamada, Kenneth Manao *cell biologist*

Chevy Chase
Choppin, Purnell Whittington *science administrator*
Kandel, Eric Richard *neuroscience educator*

College Park
Diener, Theodor Otto *plant pathologist, researcher*
Dylla, H. Frederick *science administrator, physicist*
Fanning, Delvin Seymour *soil science educator*
Izaurralde, Roberto César *science educator, researcher*
Jeffery, William Richard *developmental biology educator, researcher*
Miller, Raymond Jarvis *agronomy educator*
O'Connor, John Dennis *biology professor*
White, Marilyn Domas *information science educator*

Columbia
Nie, Guojun *research scientist*

Frederick
Hughes, Stephen H. *virologist, researcher*
Iverson, Warren Philip *retired microbiologist, research scientist, consultant*
Knisely, Ralph Franklin *retired microbiologist*
Reynolds, Craig W. *research scientist*

Gaithersburg
Aiuto, Russell *science education consultant*
Byers, Christopher Gordon *veterinarian*
Glass, Lawrence *research scientist*
Jiang, Zhi-Gang *neuroscientist*

Garrett Park
Baldwin, Calvin Benham, Jr. *retired science administrator*

Germantown
Byrd, Wyatt *microbiologist, researcher*
Iqbal, Zafar *neuroscientist, biochemist, educator*
Norcross, Marvin Augustus *veterinarian, researcher, retired federal official*
Ritter, Nadine M. *research scientist*

Greenbelt
Comiso, Josefino Cacas *research scientist*

Jefferson
Beall, James Robert *toxicologist, consultant*

Laurel
Harbottle, Heather C. *microbiologist, researcher*
Hoffman, David John *physiologist, ecotoxicologist*
Rorie, Conrad Jonathan *research scientist, retired military officer*

North East
Zatalava, Christine Michelle *science educator*

Oakland
Harman, Yolanda Michelle *science educator*

Olney
Baker, Carl Gwin *retired science administrator, educator*

Princess Anne
Chigbu, Paulinus *fisheries biologist, educator, research scientist*
Johnson, Andrea *biologist, researcher*

Rockville
Baughman, Robert William *neuroscientist, director*
Carlton, Jane M.R. *geneticist*
Chen, Genshe *research scientist*
Gluckstein, Fritz Paul *veterinarian, biomedical information specialist*
Kim, Bong-Jo *molecular biologist, researcher*
Mummaneni, Padmaja *research scientist, educator*
Rosen, Saul Woolf *research scientist, health facility administrator*
Ryan, Kevin William *virologist, clinical research administrator*
Tandon, Narendra Nath *research scientist, director*
Taubenberger, Jeffery Karl *pathologist, molecular biologist*
Um, Ki Sung *research scientist*
Umbreit, Wayne William *bacteriologist, educator*
Venter, J. Craig (John Craig Venter, Craig Venter) *science foundation director, geneticist*

Salisbury
Moultrie, Fred *geneticist, researcher*

Silver Spring
Brandt, Carl David *research virologist*
Brush, Julianna R. *marine biologist*
Corwin, Jeff *biologist, anthropologist, television host*
Guzman, Martha Patricia *science educator*
Kant, Gloria Jean *retired neuroscientist*

Stevensville
Lain, David Cornelius *health scientist, researcher*

Towson
Shah, Shirish Kalyanbhai *computer science, chemistry and environmental science educator*

Wye Mills
Farley, Gregory Scott *biology professor*

MASSACHUSETTS

Amherst
Levin, Robert Eugene *food scientist, educator*
Margulis, Lynn (Lynn Alexander) *evolutionist, educator*

Belmont
Benes, Francine M. *neuroscientist, psychiatrist*

Boston
Altshuler, David Matthew *geneticist, endocrinologist*
Bawa, Kamaljit Singh *biologist, educator*
Broitman, Selwyn Arthur *microbiologist, educator, assistant dean*
Chen, Ching-chih *information science educator, consultant*
Church, George McDonald *geneticist, educator, researcher*
Demidov, Vadim V. *biotechnologist, writer*
DePinho, Ronald *research scientist*
El-Baz, Farouk *science administrator, educator*
Essex, Myron Elmer *microbiology and virology educator*
Fein, Rashi *health sciences educator*
Foote, Warren Edgar *neuroscientist, psychologist, educator*
Gimbrone, Michael Anthony, Jr. *research scientist, pathologist, educator*
Haseltine, William Alan *virology educator, former biopharmaceutical company executive*
Hochedlinger, Konrad *biology professor, biomedical researcher*
Hubel, David Hunter *physiologist, science educator*
Kahn, C. Ronald *research laboratory administrator*
Levy, Stuart B. *molecular biologist, educator, science administrator, researcher*
Liu, Ta-Chiang *research scientist, physician, consultant*
Milunsky, Aubrey *geneticist, pediatrician, educator*
Miron, Alexander *research scientist*
Myers, Richard Hepworth *medical geneticist, educator*
Rapoport, Tom Abraham *cell biology professor*
Ren, Jian-Guo *cell biologist, researcher*
Schwartz, Eric Lee *neuroscientist, educator*
Seidman, Jonathan G. *geneticist, educator*
Sidman, Richard Leon *neuroscientist, educator*
Strahler, Alan H. *geography educator, researcher, writer*
Szostak, Jack William *molecular biologist, educator*

Tabin, Clifford S. *geneticist, educator*
Talarek, Nicolas *geneticist, researcher*
Tosteson, Daniel Charles *physiologist, medical school dean emeritus*
Tullis, Gregory Earl *research scientist*
Walz, Thomas *biology professor*

Boylston
Schofield, Edmund Acton, Jr. *botanist, academic administrator, conservationist, writer*

Burlington
Thayer, Stacy E. *research scientist*

Cambridge
Alcock, Charles Roger *science educator*
Baker, Tania Ann *biology professor, researcher*
Bartel, David *biology professor, researcher*
Bear, Mark Firman *neuroscientist, educator*
Berg, Howard C. *biology professor*
Bizzi, Emilio *neurophysiologist, educator*
Collier, Earl Miller, Jr. *biotechnology company executive*
Dalgarno, Alexander *astronomy educator*
Dowling, John Elliott *biology professor*
Dulac, Catherine *biology professor, researcher*
Eggan, Kevin C. *molecular and cellular biology professor, researcher*
Erikson, Raymond Leo *biology professor*
Fink, Yoel *science educator, researcher*
Fox, James Gahan *veterinarian, educator, researcher*
Fox, Maurice Sanford *retired molecular biologist, educator*
Gilbert, Walter *molecular biologist, educator*
Girguis, Peter Riad *microbiologist, entrepreneur, educator*
Goldberg, Ray Allan *agriculturist, educator*
Grindlay, Jonathan Ellis *astrophysics educator*
Grove, Timothy Lynn *geology educator*
Hastings, John Woodland *biologist, educator*
Hewitt, Jacqueline N. *astronomy educator*
Hopkins, Nancy Haven Doe *biology professor*
Horvitz, Howard Robert *biology professor, researcher*
Hubbard, Ruth *retired biology professor*
Hynes, Richard Olding *biology researcher, educator*
Jaenisch, Rudolf *biologist, educator*
Knoll, Andrew Herbert *biology professor*
Lander, Eric Steven *geneticist, molecular biologist, mathematician*
Langmuir, Charles Herbert *geology educator*
Lauder, George V. *marine biologist*
Levi, Herbert Walter *biologist, educator*
Lindquist, Susan Lee *biology and microbiology professor*
Losick, Richard M. *biology professor*
Marcus, Richard Sargon *research scientist*
Melton, Douglas A. *molecular and cell biology educator*
Murray, Andrew W. *biology professor, researcher*
Narayan, Ramesh *astronomy educator*
Orr-Weaver, Terry L. *cell biologist, educator*
Page, David C. *biologist, educator*
Pardue, Mary-Lou *biology professor*
Petersen, Ulrich *geology educator*
Pierce, Naomi Ellen *biology professor, researcher*
Prinn, Ronald G. *atmospheric science educator*
Sanes, Joshua Richard *neurobiologist, researcher, educator*
Sharp, Phillip Allen *biologist, educator*
Sheng, Morgan Hwa-Tze *neuroscientist, educator*
Sinha, Pawan *research scientist, educator, entrepreneur*
Swager, Timothy Manning *chemistry educator*
Tannenbaum, Steven Robert *toxicologist, chemist*
Tonegawa, Susumu *biology professor*
Walker, Graham Charles *biology professor*
Wheeler, Robert Treide *microbiologist, researcher*
Widnall, Sheila Evans *aeronautical educator, former secretary of air force, university official*
Wilson, Edward Osborne *biologist, educator, writer*
Wurtman, Richard Jay *neuroscientist, educator*
Yannas, Ioannis Vassilios *polymer science educator*
Young, Rick (Richard Allen) *molecular biologist, educator*

Charlestown
Bhide, Pradeep G. *neuroscientist, researcher*
Kovacs, Dora Marta *neuroscientist, researcher, educator*
Moskowitz, Michael Arthur *neuroscientist*
Pittet, Mikael J. *research scientist, director*
Tanzi, Rudolph Emile *neuroscientist, researcher, educator*

Danvers
Butz, Stefan Peter *science association director*

Easthampton
Prattis, Susan Marie *veterinarian, educator*

Falmouth
Milkman, Roger Dawson *genetics educator, molecular biologist, researcher*
Saunders, John Warren, Jr. *biology professor, consultant*

Ipswich
Roberts, Richard John *molecular biologist, consultant, scientific officer*

Lexington
Bazzaz, Fakhri A. *plant biology educator, administrator*
Drouilhet, Paul Raymond, Jr. *retired science administrator, electrical engineer*
Fillios, Louis Charles *retired science educator*
Gibbs, Martin *biologist, educator*

Lincoln
Payne, Roger Searle *zoologist, researcher, science administrator, conservationist*

Lowell
Lustick, David Scott *science educator, mathematics professor*

Medford
Catley, Andrew Paul *veterinarian, researcher*

Natick
Blaha, Michael Douglas *research biologist*

North Grafton
Costa, Lais Rosa Rodrigues *veterinarian, educator, medical researcher*
Schwartz, Anthony *veterinary surgeon, educator*

Northampton
Palser, Barbara F. *retired botanist*

Peabody
Bierman, George William *retired food scientist*

Plymouth
Goldman, Ralph Frederick *research physiologist, educator*

Roxbury
Peters, Alan *anatomy educator*

South Hadley
Burbine, Thomas Hewey *science educator, researcher*
Townsend, Jane Kaltenbach *biologist, educator*

Stoughton
Pitkin, Mark *research scientist*

Waltham
Galinat, Walton Clarence *research scientist*
Hall, Jeffrey Connor *biology educator, behavioral genetics researcher*
Marder, Eve Esther *neuroscientist, educator*
Miller, Christopher *science educator*
Novick, David Kandel *science educator, department chairman*

Watertown
Emerson, Charles P. *research scientist*

Wellesley
Gerety, Robert John *microbiologist, researcher, pediatrician, pharmaceutical executive*
Young, Delano Victor *cell biologist, pharmaceutical scientist, biochemist, educator*

Westborough
Nichols, Guy Warren *retired institute and utilities executive*

Woods Hole
Felzer, Benjamin Seth *ecologist, researcher*
Luyten, James Reindert *research institute director, oceanographer*
Melillo, Jerry M. *ecologist*
Sogin, Mitchell L. *biologist, educator*
Verslycke, Tim *research scientist*
Woodwell, George Masters *ecologist, conservationist*

Worcester
Bagshaw, Joseph Charles *molecular biologist, educator*
Fitzgerald, Katherine *molecular biologist, educator*
Kennedy, Linda Mann *neuroscience educator, researcher*
Venugopal, Thayanithy *biologist, geneticist, researcher*

MICHIGAN

Ann Arbor
Akil, Huda *neuroscientist, educator, researcher*
Atreya, Sushil Kumar *planetary-space science educator, astrophysicist*
Clark, Noreen Morrison *behavioral science educator, researcher*
Clewell, Don B. *microbial geneticist, educator*
Cochran, Kenneth William *toxicologist*
Dawson, William Ryan *zoology educator*
Drach, John Charles *research scientist, educator*
Easter, Stephen Sherman, Jr. *biology professor*
Farrand, William Richard *retired geology educator*
Ginsburg, David *genetics educator, researcher*
Grossman, Esta S. *biology professor*
Hawkins, Joseph Elmer, Jr. *physiologist, educator*
Kaufman, Peter Bishop *biological sciences educator*
Kostyo, Jack Lawrence *physiology educator*
Kothary, Piyush C. *research scientist*
Moore, Thomas Edwin *biologist, educator, museum director*
Neidhardt, Frederick Carl *microbiologist, educator*
Petty, Elizabeth Marie *geneticist*
Sloat, Barbara Furin *cell biologist, educator*
Vandermeer, John H. *ecologist, educator*
Vanderploeg, Henry A. *ecologist, researcher*
Williams, John Andrew *physiology researcher, educator*
Zhang, Youxue *geology educator*

Detroit
Beierwaltes, William Howard *physiologist, educator*
DeRoo, Sally Ann *biology, geology and environmental science educator*
Groves, Odessa Marie *science educator*
Guo, Zhongwu *science educator*
Kaltenbach, James Albert *neurobiologist, educator*
Lerner, Stephen Alexander *microbiologist, physician, educator*
Phillis, John Whitfield *physiologist, educator*
Selyuzhenkov, Ilya *research scientist*
States, J. Christopher *molecular biology educator, researcher*
Wolf, Barry *geneticist, pediatric educator*

East Lansing
Aggarwal, Vaneet *research scientist*
Bromley, Stephen C. *zoology educator*
Bukovac, Martin John *horticulturist, educator*
Cross, Aureal Theophilus *geology and botany educator*
Dennis, Frank George, Jr. *retired horticulture educator*
Fraker, Pamela J. *science educator*
Hackel, Emanuel *science educator*
Lenski, Richard Eimer *evolutionary biologist, educator*
McMeekin, Dorothy *botanist, plant pathologist, educator*
Petrides, George Athan *ecologist, educator*
Root-Bernstein, Robert Scott *biologist, educator*
Sisk, Cheryl *neuroscientist, educator*
Sparks, Harvey Vise, Jr. *physiologist*
Tiedje, James Michael *microbiologist, educator, ecologist*

Edwardsburg
Floyd, Alton David *cell biologist, consultant*

Flint
Wigston, David Lawrence *biologist, dean*

Grand Rapids
Carlotti, Ronald John *food scientist*
Petkus, Alan Francis *microbiologist*

Hickory Corners
Lauff, George Howard *biologist*

Hillsdale
Miller, Robert Raymond, Jr. *biology professor*

Jackson
Graham, Donald James *food technologist, hygienic design consultant*

Kalamazoo
Jayasingh, Preetha *food scientist*
Kujawski, Daniel *science educator*
Marshall, Vincent de Paul *industrial microbiologist, researcher*

Lansing
Nsofor, Leslie Monagolum *food scientist, researcher*

Marquette
Brege, Dorance Charles *biologist*

Midland
Bus, James Stanley *toxicologist*
Davidson, John Hunter *agriculturist*

Millersburg
Bergstedt, Roger Allen *biologist, researcher*

Petoskey
Nicholson, William Noel *clinical neuropsychologist*

Rochester Hills
Unakar, Nalin Jayantilal *biological sciences educator*

Saline
Cruden, Robert William *botany educator*

University Center
Pelzer, Charles Francis *human molecular geneticist, biologist, educator, research scientist*

West Bloomfield
Barr, Martin *science educator, academic administrator*

Wilson
Harris, Mary Lynn *science educator, consultant*

MINNESOTA

Duluth
Johnson, Arthur Gilbert *microbiology educator*

Mapleton
John, Hugo Herman *natural resources educator*

Minneapolis
Adams, John Stephen *geography educator*
Banerjee, Subir Kumar *science educator*
Danielson, James Walter *retired research microbiologist*
Dworkin, Martin *microbiologist, educator*
Georgopoulos, Apostolos P. *neuroscientist, neurologist, educator*
Gorham, Eville *retired ecologist*
Haase, Ashley Thomson *microbiology professor, researcher*
Hensley, Mary Lynne Floyd *academic medical center administrator*
Johnson, Kenneth Harvey *veterinary pathologist*
Moore, Randall Charles *biology professor*
O'Connor, Michael B. *biology professor, researcher*
Porter, Philip Wayland *geography educator*
Sinha, Akhouri A. *cell and development biologist, researcher*
Warman, Eduardo Norberto *research scientist*
Watson, Dennis Wallace *microbiologist, educator*

Morris
Ordway, Ellen *biologist, educator, entomologist, researcher*

Rochester
Maher, L. James III *molecular biologist*
Ordog, Tamas *research scientist, educator*
Van Dyke, Daniel L. *geneticist*

Roseville
Marten, Gordon Cornelius *agronomist, educat federal agency administrator*

Saint Joseph
Kirick, Daniel John *agronomist*

Saint Louis Park
Frestedt, Joy Louise *research scientist, scienc administrator*

Saint Paul
Barnwell, Franklin Hershel *zoology educator*
Busch, Robert Henry *geneticist, researcher*
Cheng, H. H. *soil scientist, agronomic and environmental science educator emeritus*
Davis, Margaret Bryan *paleoecology research educator*
Diesch, Stanley La Verne *veterinarian, educa*
Ek, Alan Ryan *forester, educator*
Hornbach, Daniel J. *biologist, educator*
Kommedahl, Thor *plant pathology educator*
Labuza, Theodore Peter *food science educato*
Leonard, Kurt John *retired plant pathologist, director*
McKinnell, Robert Gilmore *retired zoologist, biology professor, geneticist*
Phillips, Ronald Lewis *plant geneticist, educc*
Roy, Robert Russell *toxicologist*
Sadowsky, Michael J. *microbiologist, educatc*
Speedie, Marilyn Kay *microbiologist, educatc dean*

MISSISSIPPI

Fulton
Mastin, Lynn P. *biology professor*

Jackson
Lewis, Robert Edwin, Jr. *pathology and immunology educator, researcher*
McGuire, Sarah Lea *biology professor*

Mississippi State
Reddy, Kambham Raja *botanist, educator*
Sabanadzovic, Sead *virologist, educator*

Oxford
Keiser, Edmund Davis, Jr. *biologist, educator*
Rego, Cesar *science educator, researcher*

Saucier
Finley, Emma Rosemary *science educator*

Stoneville
Morales-Ramos, Juan Alfredo *entomologist, researcher*
Ranney, Carleton David *retired plant patholo*

University
Duke, Stephen Oscar *physiologist, research scientist, educator*

MISSOURI

Chesterfield
Williams, Luther Steward *research scientist*

Columbia
Blevins, Dale Glenn *agronomy educator*
Brown, Olen Ray *microbiologist, biomedical researcher, educator*
Finkelstein, Richard Alan *retired microbiolog educator, consultant*
Men, Hongsheng *biologist, researcher*
Mitchell, Roger Lowry *retired agronomy educator*
Morehouse, Lawrence Glen *veterinarian, educator, academic administrator*
Mustapha, Azlin *food scientist, educator*
Poehlmann, Carl John *agricultural researche*
Puttler, Benjamin *entomologist*
Roberts, R. Michael *animal scientist, biocher educator*
Van Sambeek, Jerome William *plant physiologist, educator*
Yanders, Armon Frederick *biological science educator, science administrator*

Eureka
Lindsey, Susan Lyndaker *zoologist*

Independence
Burke, Kim Donald *science educator*

Kansas City
Coveney, Raymond Martin, Jr. *geology educ*
Krumlauf, Robert Eugene *neuroscientist, educator*
Lednicky, John A. *virologist, microbiologist*
Neaves, William Barlow *cell biologist, educc*
Spigarelli, James L. *science administrator*

Saint Louis
Ackers, Gary Keith *biophysical chemistry educator, researcher*
Allen, Garland Edward *biologist, professor, writer*
Connor-Ward, Dannette Vaudrilyn *research biologist*
Elgin, Sarah Carlisle Roberts *biology profess researcher*
Engsberg, Jack Robert *science educator, researcher*
Fraley, Robert T. *biotechnologist*
Geslani, Gemma P. *science educator, health researcher*
Green, Maurice *molecular biologist, educato virologist*

ler, James Gegan *research scientist*
nica-Worms, Helen M. *cell biologist, educator*
aal, Barbara Anna *evolutionary biologist, educator*
lkina, Tatyana *botanist, researcher*
npleton, Alan Robert *biology professor*
olsey, Thomas Allen *neuroscientist, biologist*

ringfield
drick, LaRita Denise *science educator*

la Ridge
kowski, Leonard Francis, Jr. *microbiologist*

st Plains
coxson, Roy Dell *plant pathologist, esearcher, educator*

)NTANA

zeman
gan, Peter John Patrick *biologist, researcher*
en, Duncan Theunissen *ecologist educator*
eden, Norman Frank *geneticist, educator*

lena
nson, John Philip *geneticist, researcher*

ssoula
wer, Carol A. *biology professor*

BRASKA

coln
oways, Hugh Howard *systematic biologist, educator*
way, Donald Grant *retired agronomist, educator*
fmann, Richard John *biology professor, dean*
n, Josef *physiology professor*
ssengale, Martin Andrew *agronomist, educator, university president*
ldard, Robert H. *geography educator*
or, Stephen Lloyd *toxicologist, educator, ood scientist*
aver, Anne Marie *plant pathology educator*

aha
eer, Henry Sarkis *physiology educator*
mons, Lee Guyton, Jr. *zoological park irector*

illion
ling, James Anthony *biology professor, chnologist*

VADA

rump
ns, Charles Wayne, II, *biologist, researcher*

no
ord, Gerald Frederic *retired science educator*
ray, Alison Elizabeth *microbiologist, lucator, researcher*

W HAMPSHIRE

rham
ole, Thomas Gordon *microbiology professor, esearcher, department chairman*

nover
ros, Victor R. *geneticist, educator*
zaniga, Michael S. *neuroscientist, ychologist*
ert, John Jouett *aquatic ecologist, educator*
gford, George Malcolm *cell biology educator*
d, Lee Rybeck *biology educator*

anon
ck, Allan Ulf *physiologist, educator*

bornton
nt, Elizabeth Abbott *retired biology rofessor*

W JERSEY

king Ridge
enberger, John Richard *science dministrator*

'ton
Edward Tintai *toxicologist, pharmacologist*

nford
sen, Warren Donald *microbiologist, nsultant*

t Brunswick
browski, Anne Wesseling *retired icrobiologist*

hland Park
erwerker, Elie *biologist, educator*

hlands
y, Norbert Phillip *marine sciences educator*

boken
l, Robert Berger *science administrator*

patcong
n, Robert *retired neuroscientist, consultant*

sey City
tis, Lev Matusovich *test and reliability ientist*

Singer, Howard Jack *biology professor, researcher*
Twersky, Laura Harriet *biologist, educator*

Lawrenceville
Karp, Jonathan D. *biology professor*

Madison
Demain, Arnold Lester *microbiologist, educator*

Marlton
Sidelsky, Patricia Loney *science educator*

Montclair
Chinard, Francis Pierre *physiologist, consultant physician, educator*
Du, Chunguang Charles *biologist, educator*

Mountain Lakes
Wallace, MaryJean Elizabeth *science educator*

New Brunswick
Bennett, Joan Wennstrom *biology educator*
Ehrenfeld, David William *biology professor, writer*
Funk, Cyril Reed, Jr. *agronomist, educator*
Lachance, Paul Albert *food science educator, clergyman*
Maramorosch, Karl *virologist, educator*
Saracevic, Tefko *information science educator*
Smouse, Peter E. *ecologist, educator*
Tedrow, John Charles Fremont *soils educator*
Trivers, Robert L. *bioscience and anthropology educator, evolutionary biologist, sociobiologist*

Newark
Ledeen, Robert Wagner *neuroscientist, educator*
Parveen, Nikhat *microbiologist, educator*
Vatner, Stephen F. *physiologist, researcher, research scientist*
Weis, Judith Shulman *biology professor*
Zaborszky, Laszlo *neuroscientist*

Old Tappan
Lovitch, Joan *science educator, coach*

Piscataway
Arnold, Edward (Eddy Arnold) *research scientist, educator*
Breslauer, Kenneth J. *science educator, researcher*
Denhardt, David Tilton *molecular and cell biology educator*
Dooner, Hugo K. *plant pathologist, educator*
Ebright, Richard High *molecular biologist*
Essien, Francine B. *biologist, educator*
Ferstandig Arnold, Gail *research scientist, educator*
Tischfield, Jay Arnold *genetics educator*
Wang, Tsuey Tang *science educator, venture capitalist*
White, Eileen *science educator, researcher*

Plainfield
Frost, David *retired biology professor, medical editor, consultant*

Port Norris
Canzonier, Walter Jude *shellfish aquaculturist*

Princeton
Altmann, Stuart Allen *biologist, educator*
Ballou, Janice Donelon *research director*
Bassler, Bonnie L. *molecular biologist*
Drakeman, Lisa N. *biotechnologist*
Enquist, Lynn William *molecular biologist*
Gould, Elizabeth *neuroscientist, educator*
Gould, James L. *biology professor*
Grant, Barbara Rosemary *science educator, researcher*
Grant, Peter Raymond *biologist, researcher, educator*
Grigger, Jane Elizabeth *earth science educator, photographer*
Mahmoud, Adel A. *physician, molecular biologist, educator*
Pacala, Stephen W. *ecology educator*
Riehl, Christina Pauline *ecologist*
Schupbach, Trudi M. (Gertrud Schupbach) *biologist, researcher*
Shenk, Thomas Eugene *molecular biology educator, academic administrator*
Silhavy, Thomas Joseph *molecular biology educator*
Wieschaus, Eric F. *molecular biologist, educator*
Witkin, Evelyn Maisel *retired geneticist*

Red Bank
Fred, Rogers Murray III *veterinary oncologist*

River Vale
Verebey, Karl Geza *toxicologist, pharmacologist, educator*

Shrewsbury
Westerman, Liane Marie *research scientist executive*

Somerset
Tsou, Yu-Min *science administrator, chemistry researcher*

Somerville
Hulse, Robert Douglas *biotechnologist*

Stanton
Kille, John William, Jr. *toxicology and biomedical product consultant*

Summit
Barer, Sol Joseph *biotechnology company executive*

Teaneck
Haas, Gerhard Julius *microbiologist, educator*

Tinton Falls
Hoelzler, Michael Gebhard *veterinarian, surgeon*

Union
Chrusciel, Susan Marie *research scientist, molecular biologist*

Wallington
Safira, Barabara *science educator*

Wayne
Patnaik, Pradeep Kumar *science educator*

West Orange
Hwang, Karen *research scientist*

NEW MEXICO

Albuquerque
Bachand, George D. *research scientist*
Brown, James Hemphill *biology professor*
Hager, Gordon Douglas *scientist, engineering educator*
Henderson, Rogene Faulkner *toxicologist, researcher*
Hersee, Stephen Derek *science educator*
Hsi, David Ching Heng *plant pathologist, geneticist, educator*
Mauderly, Joe Lloyd *pulmonary toxicologist*
Polley, Richard Donald *microbiologist, chemist*
Woodward, Joan B. *science association director*

Hondo
Pawley, Ray L. *retired zoological park administrator, curator*

Las Cruces
Tonn, Robert James *retired entomologist*

Los Alamos
Sanbonmatsu, Kevin Y. *molecular biologist, researcher*

Santa Fe
Davis, Tom *biology professor*
Harding, Marie *ecological executive, artist*
Smith, Philip Meek *science administrator, consultant*

NEW YORK

Albany
Flint, Robert Wallace *neuroscientist, educator*
Frank, Joachim *structural biologist, educator, biophysicist*
Mannella, Carmen A. *research scientist*
Schneider, Allan Stanford *biophysics, neuroscience and pharmacology educator, biomedical research scientist*
Shutman, Michael *biologist*

Alexandria Bay
Fisher, Lester Emil *retired zoo administrator*

Annandale On Hudson
Keesing, Felicia *biology professor*

Binghamton
Klir, George Jiri *systems science educator*
Naslund, Howard Richard *geological science educator*

Bronx
Bennett, Michael Vander Laan *neuroscience educator*
Goodrich, James Tait *neuroscientist, neurosurgeon*
Karesh, William B. *science administrator, director, veterinarian*
Long, Gregory R. *botanic garden administrator*
Mukherjee, Asit Baran *geneticist, educator*
Sanderson, Steven E. *science administrator*
Schaller, George Beals *zoologist*
Waelsch, Salome Gluecksohn *geneticist, educator*

Brooklyn
Altura, Bella T. *physiologist, educator*
Altura, Burton Myron *physiologist, educator*
Kramer, Allan Franklin, II, *researcher, botanical garden official*
Lipson, Steven Mark *virologist, microbiologist, environmental scientist, educator*
Medbury, Scot Daniel *botanical garden executive*
Roker, Christopher A. *microbiologist, photographer*
Schiffman, Gerald *microbiologist, educator*

Buffalo
Beutner, Ernst Herman *microbiology educator*
Demant, Peter *geneticist, researcher*
Duax, William Leo *biologist, researcher*
Ghadersohi, Ali *veterinarian, researcher*
Ignatowski, Tracey A. *research scientist, educator*
Ma, Yingyu *research scientist*
Zawicki, Joseph Leo *science educator*

Burnt Hills
DeVries, Robert Charles *research scientist*

Cobleskill
Ingels, Jack Edward *horticulture educator*

Cold Spring Harbor
Hannon, Gregory J. *biology professor, researcher*
Stillman, Bruce *molecular biologist*
Watson, James Dewey *molecular biologist, educator*

Cooperstown
Butts, William Lester *entomologist, researcher*
Harman, Willard Nelson *malacologist, educator*

Cortlandt Manor
Traille, Joy Myra *microbiologist, eldercare service provider*

Floral Park
Isenberg, Henry David *microbiology educator*

Flushing
Commoner, Barry *biologist, educator*

Fredonia
Benton, Allen Haydon *biology professor*

Garden City
Podwall, Kathryn Stanley *biology professor*
Prabhakar, Kumkum *biology professor*

Geneva
Siebert, Karl Joseph *food science educator, consultant*

Great Neck
Gabriel, Mordecai Lionel *biologist, educator*
Puttlitz, Donald Herbert *microbiologist*

Hamilton
Frey, Frank Michael *biology professor*

Homer
Gustafson, John Alfred *biology professor*

Hudson
Geistfeld, James Gordon *veterinarian*

Ithaca
Alexander, Martin *microbiologist, educator*
Cahoon, Richard Stuart *biotechnologist, educator*
Crepet, William Louis *botanist, educator*
Danforth, Bryan Nicholas *entomologist, educator*
Davies, Peter John *plant physiology educator, researcher*
Eisner, Thomas *biologist, educator*
Emlen, Stephen Thompson *zoology educator*
Emr, Scott David *molecular biologist, director*
Fick, Gary Warren *agronomist, educator*
Fitzpatrick, John Weaver *ornithologist, researcher*
Greene, Harry W. *biology professor*
Hairston, Nelson George, Jr. *ecologist, educator*
Henry, Susan Armstrong *biology professor, dean*
Hoy, Ronald Raymond *neurobiology educator*
Jagendorf, André Tridon *physiologist*
Kennedy, Wilbert Keith, Sr. *agronomy educator, retired university official*
Kingsbury, John Merriam *botanist, educator*
Korf, Richard Paul *mycology educator*
Lengemann, Frederick William *retired physiology educator*
Mai, William Frederick *plant nematologist, educator*
Maldonado-Mendoza, Ignacio Eduardo *molecular biologist, researcher*
Mortlock, Robert Paul *microbiologist, educator*
Novak, Joseph Donald *science educator*
Poppensiek, George Charles *retired veterinary scientist, retired educator*
Provine, William B. *biology professor*
Regenstein, Joe M. *food scientist, educator*
Schlafer, Donald Hughes *veterinary pathologist*
Viands, Donald Rex *plant breeder, educator*
Walcott, Charles *neurobiology and behavior educator*
Wasserman, Robert Harold *biology professor*
Welch, Ross Maynard *plant physiologist, educator*
Wootton, John Francis *physiology educator*

Millbrook
Likens, Gene Elden *biology and ecology educator*

Mount Kisco
Laster, Richard *biotechnologist, consultant*

Mount Vernon
Young, Paula Eva *animal shelter director*

Neponsit
Nicastri, Ann Gilbert *science educator*

New Rochelle
Winstead, Melody *science educator*

New York
Abbott, Geoffrey Winston *physiologist, researcher*
Allis, David C. *biologist, educator*
Ausubel, Jesse Huntley *environmental researcher*
Berlin, Heather Ayn *neuroscientist, philosopher, educator*
Bhattacharya, Satyajit *research scientist*
Blobel, Günter *cell biologist, educator*
Bock, Walter Joseph *zoology educator*
Botkin, Daniel Benjamin *biologist, environmental scientist, writer*
Branski, Ryan Comfort *research scientist*
Calame, Kathryn Lee *microbiologist, educator*
Chaganti, Raju S. *geneticist, educator, researcher*
Chalfie, Martin *biology professor*
Chan, Siu-Wai *materials science educator*
Chappell, Richard Lee *biology educator, neuroscientist*
Chen, Xi *research scientist*
Cohen, David Harris *neuroscientist, educator, academic administrator*
Cohen, Joel Ephraim *biologist, educator, demographer*
Covey, Lirio S. *research scientist*
Dales, Samuel *microbiologist, virologist, educator*
Darnell, James Edwin, Jr. *molecular biologist, educator*
Davis, Jessica G. *geneticist*
de Lange, Titia *research scientist, educator*
Delmer, Deborah P. *science educator*
Desnick, Robert John *human geneticist*
Dobrof, Rose Wiesman *gerontology educator*

Eckhardt, Laurel Ann *biologist, researcher, educator*
Einbond, Linda Saxe *biologist, researcher*
Feldman, Samuel Mitchell *neuroscientist, educator*
Fuchs, Elaine V. *molecular biologist, educator*
Giancotti, Filippo Giusto *molecular biologist, educator*
Godson, Godfrey Nigel *molecular geneticist, educator*
Goff, Stephen Payne *molecular biologist, educator*
Greengard, Paul *neuroscientist, educator*
Hirschhorn, Rochelle *genetics educator*
Joyner, Alexandra Leigh *cell biologist*
Keeney, Scott Neal *molecular biologist*
Kelley, Darcy B. *biology professor*
Kelly, Thomas Jesse, Jr. *molecular biologist*
Kilpatrick, Auston Marm (A. Marm Kilpatrick) *research scientist*
Korsten, Susan Snyder *science educator*
Lederberg, Joshua *geneticist, educator*
LeDoux, Joseph E. *neuroscientist, educator*
Lehmann, Ruth *geneticist, educator*
Liao, Martha *geneticist*
Littman, Dan R. *microbiologist*
Llinás, Rodolfo Riascos *neuroscientist, researcher*
Maack, Thomas *physiology professor*
Maas, Werner Karl *microbiology educator*
MacKinnon, Roderick *neuroscientist, educator*
Manley, James L. *molecular biologist, educator*
Marks, Andrew Robert *molecular biologist*
McEwen, Bruce Sherman *neuroscientist, educator*
Mombaerts, Peter *biology professor*
Morrison, John Henry *neuroscientist, educator, lab administrator*
Morse, Stephen Scott *virologist, epidemiologist, immunologist, educator*
O'Donnell, Michael E. *microbiologist, educator*
Pikitch, Ellen Karen *science educator*
Pollack, Robert Elliot *biologist, educator, writer*
Prives, Carol *biologist, educator*
Ptashne, Mark Steven *molecular biology professor*
Quimby, Fred William *pathology educator, veterinarian*
Ravetch, Jeffrey Victor *molecular biologist, immunologist, educator*
Revenkova, Ekaterina *biologist, researcher*
Rice, Charles M. *virologist, educator*
Rothman, James Edward *cell biologist, educator*
Rozen, Jerome George, Jr. *entomologist, curator, researcher*
Segal, Sheldon Jerome *biologist, educator, foundation administrator*
Shelanski, Michael L. *cell biologist, educator*
Silverstein, Samuel Charles *cellular biology and physiology professor, researcher*
Simon, Eric Jacob *neuroscientist, educator*
Stotzky, Guenther *microbiologist, educator*
Tierno, Philip Mario, Jr. *microbiologist, educator, researcher*
Wiesel, Torsten Nils *neurobiologist, educator*
Willner, Judith P. *clinical geneticist, pediatrician, educator*
Windhager, Erich Ernst *physiologist, educator*
Young, Michael Warren *geneticist, educator*
Yuferov, Vadim *research scientist*

Old Westbury
Casares, Federico M. *science educator*

Orangeburg
Yaragudri, Vinod K. *neuroscientist, researcher*

Orchard Park
Urbanski, Jane F. *retired microbiologist*

Owego
Kemp, Eugene Thomas *retired veterinarian*

Palisades
Purdy, G. Michael *observatory director*

Peru
Dawson, James Clifford *environmental science educator, geologist*

Pittsford
Coleman, Paul David *neurobiology educator, researcher*

Port Washington
Kwak, Seung-Keon *research scientist*

Purchase
Ehrman, Lee *geneticist, educator*

Rochester
Alder, Donna Bordelon *biologist, educator*
Clarkson, Thomas William *toxicologist, educator*
Doty, Robert William *neuroscientist, physiologist, educator*
Frisina, Robert Dana *neuroscientist, educator*
Huxlin, Krystel Raluka *neuroscientist, educator*
Rodgers, Suzanne Hooker *physiologist, consultant*
Schanfield, Moses Samuel *geneticist, educator*
Walton, Joseph Paul *neuroscientist, audiologist*

Rome
Simonin, Howard A. *biologist*

Roslyn
Shubin, Joanna *science educator*

Rye
Sales, Mitzi S. *science educator*

Saint Albans
Norfleet, Leontine Sandra *retired biologist*

Schenectady
Fleischer, Robert Louis *geology professor*
Stevens, Roy W. *microbiologist, researcher, photographer*

Staten Island
Chohan, Muhammad Omar *neuroscientist, neurologist*

Stony Brook
Futuyma, Douglas Joel *ecology educator*
Lennarz, William Joseph *research biologist, educator*
Rohlf, F. James *biologist, educator*
Sreebny, Leo M. *oral biology and pathology professor*

Syracuse
Horton, Jason A. *biologist*
Meinig, Donald William *geography educator*
Verrillo, Ronald Thomas *neuroscience educator, researcher*

Troy
Berg, Daniel *science and technology educator*
Ehrlich, Henry Lutz *biology professor*
Watson, E Bruce *science educator*
Zurbenko, Igor Georg *science educator*

Upton
Chaudhari, Praveen *science administrator, materials physicist*
Sutherland, Betsy Middleton *biologist*

Victor
Morris, G. Michael *science educator*

White Plains
Smith, Gerard Peter *neuroscientist*

Yaphank
Narain, Ralph B. *biologist*

Yorktown Heights
d'Heurle, François Max *research scientist, engineering educator*
Wynne, James J. *research scientist*

NORTH CAROLINA

Asheboro
Jones, David M. *zoological park administrator*

Boone
Martin, Vicki Joan *biology professor*

Buies Creek
Hammond, Mark L. *biology professor, academic administrator*

Cary
Timothy, David Harry *retired biology professor*

Chapel Hill
Dangl, Jeffery L. *biology professor*
Farber, Rosann Alexander *geneticist, educator*
Lundblad, Roger Lauren *biotechnology consultant*
Magnuson, Terry R. *geneticist, educator*
Mueller, Nancy Schneider *retired biology professor*
Salmon, Edward Dickinson *cell biologist, educator*
Smithies, Oliver *geneticist, educator*
Stumpf, Walter Erich *cell biology and pharmacology professor, researcher*

Durham
Blum, Jacob Joseph *physiologist, educator*
Gillham, Nicholas Wright *geneticist, educator*
Hogan, Brigid L.M. *molecular biologist*
Jarvis, Erich David *neurobiologist, educator*
Keene, Jack Donald *molecular genetics and microbiology educator*
Malling, Heinrich Valdemar *retired geneticist*
Moehring, Amanda J. *geneticist*
Mushak, Paul *toxicologist, consultant*
Pearsall, Samuel Haff III *ecologist, geographer, foundation administrator*
Pimm, Stuart L. *ecology educator*
Rouse, Doris Jane *physiologist, research scientist*

Elizabeth City
Storie, Eric Duane *science administrator*

Greensboro
Noble, Ralph C. *animal scientist, department chairman*

Greenville
Meggs, William Joel *toxicologist, allergist, emergency physician, educator*
Wiley, John Edwin *cytogeneticist*

Hendersonville
Brittain, James Edward *science and technology educator, researcher*

Morrisville
Bolognesi, Dani Paul *virologist, educator*
Melby, Thomas Edwin *clinical virologist, medical writer*

Raleigh
Aronson, Arthur Lawrence *retired veterinarian, toxicologist, educator, pharmacologist*
Brown, Robert Dale *wildlife science educator, dean*
Burkholder, Joann M. *botany educator*
Cook, Maurice Gayle *soil science educator, consultant*
Cooper, Arthur Wells *retired ecologist, educator*
Davey, Charles Bingham *soil scientist, educator*
Dunphy, Edward James *science educator, crop extension specialist*
Edens, Frank Wesley *physiologist*
Goodman, Major Merlin *botanical sciences educator*
Hardin, James W. *botanist, educator, herbarium curator*
Havlin, John Leroy *soil scientist, educator*
Hodgson, Ernest *toxicologist, educator*
Moreland, Donald Edwin *physiologist*
Sanders, Douglas Charles *horticulturist, researcher, educator*
Stuber, Charles William *retired genetics educator, researcher, director*

Research Triangle Park
Bond, Enriqueta Carter *science administrator*
Haynes, Victoria F. *science administrator*
Mumford, Stephen Douglas *research scientist*
Zeng, Ming *molecular biologist, researcher*

Sanford
Decker, Roger Walter *biologist, researcher*

Wilmington
Fuller, Melvin Stuart *botany educator*
Kelley, Patricia Hagelin *geology educator*
Mintzes, Joel J. *biology professor, researcher*

Winston Salem
Laxminarayana, Dama *geneticist, researcher, educator*
Pollock, Jeffrey *neuroscientist, radiologist*

NORTH DAKOTA

Bisbee
Keller, Michelle R. *science educator*

Bismarck
Niksic, Gwen M. *biology professor*

Fargo
Schmidt, Claude Henri *retired science administrator*

Grand Forks
Carlson, Edward C. *anatomy educator, cell biologist, department chairman*
Seelan, Santhosh Kumar *science educator*

OHIO

Archbold
Henry, Dinah D. *science educator*

Bowling Green
Clark, Eloise Elizabeth *biologist, educator*
Nagi, Lillian S. *biology professor*

Cincinnati
McDaniels, Audrey Evelyn *microbiologist*
Meller, Jaroslaw *biotechnologist, information scientist, educator*
Nebert, Daniel Walter *molecular geneticist, research administrator*
Saal, Howard Max *clinical geneticist, pediatrician, educator*
Schaefer, Frank William III *microbiologist, researcher*
Silberstein, Edward Bernard *nuclear medicine educator, oncologist, researcher*
Souter, Philip Frank *research scientist*
Tan, Ming *research scientist*
Tsuneoka, Yutaka *molecular geneticist*
Ure, Colin *research scientist*

Cleveland
Blackwell, John *science educator*
Dell'Osso, Louis Frank *neuroscience educator*
Lando, Jerome Burton *macromolecular science educator*
Smith, Mark Anthony *neuroscientist, educator*
Taylor, Steve Henry *zoologist*

Columbus
Blanco, Humberto *soil scientist, researcher*
Cheesman, Kerry Lee *biology educator, researcher*
Corbato, Charles Edward *geology educator, academic administrator*
Denlinger, David Landis *insect biology educator*
Faure, Gunter *geology educator*
Floyd, Gary Leon *plant cell biologist*
Foland, Kenneth A. *geological sciences educator*
Foster, Woodbridge A. *medical entomologist, educator*
Fry, Donald Lewis *physiologist, educator*
Glaser, Ronald *microbiologist, educator*
Henkin, Tina M. *science educator, researcher*
Kapral, Frank Albert *microbiologist and immunology educator*
Lee, Kichoon *animal scientist, educator*
Newsom, Gerald Higley *astronomy educator*
Peterle, Tony John *zoologist, educator*
Roth, Robert Earl *ecologist, educator*
Sostaric, Joe Zeljko *research scientist*
Tadesse, Mesfin *botanist, consultant, biology professor, researcher*
Triplehorn, Charles A. *entomologist, educator*
Westman, Judith Ann *clinical geneticist, dean*
Wood, Jackie Dale *physiologist, educator, researcher*
Zartman, David Lester *retired zoology educator, researcher*

Dayton
Gomez-Cambronero, Julian *cell biologist, biochemist, educator*
Gregor, Clunie Bryan *geology educator*

Delaware
Bahrick, Harry Phillip *science educator, researcher*

Elyria
Foote, Nathan Maxted *retired physical science educator*

Hamilton
Munson, Richard Howard *horticulturist*

Highland Hills
Kharina, Nina Yurievna *science educator*

Oberlin
Benzing, David Hill *biologist, educator*
Luck, Dennis Noel *retired biologist, educator, researcher*

Oxford
Eshbaugh, W(illiam) Hardy *botanist, educato*

Powell
Hanna, Jack Bushnell *zoo director*

Springfield
Ryu, Kyoo-Hai Lee *physiologist*

Stow
Rao, Balakrishna *plant pathologist, mycologi botanist*

Toledo
Chakraborty, Joana *physiologist, educator, science administrator*
Chen, Jiquan *ecologist, educator*
Cosentino, Mary Jane *retired science educato*

Wooster
Hoy, Casey William *ecologist, educator*

Wyoming
Cooley, William Edward *research scientist, consultant*

Yellow Springs
Webb, Paul *physiologist, educator, researcher consultant*

Youngstown
Amin, Isam Eldin *science educator, researche*

OKLAHOMA

Ada
Biles, Charles Lee *plant pathologist, physiologist, educator*

Ardmore
Dixon, Richard Arthur *botanist, educator, researcher*

Durant
Rice, Stanley Arthur *biology professor*

Norman
Bluestein, Howard Bruce *meteorology educa*
Hutchison, Victor Hobbs *biologist, educator*
Kessler, Edwin *meteorology educator, consul*
Vaughn, Caryn Carpenter *zoologist, educator*
Zhang, Liang *research scientist*
Zrnic, Dusan S. *research scientist, educator*

Ochelata
Hitzman, Donald Oliver *microbiologist*

Oklahoma City
Branch, John Curtis *biology professor, lawye*
Dubowski, Kurt Max *toxicologist, educator, consultant*
Gunter, James T. *research scientist*
Xu, Jiaqiong *research scientist, statistician*

Park Hill
Yeager, Debra Lyn *science educator*

Pawhuska
Strahm, Samuel Edward *retired veterinarian*

Ponca City
Wann, Laymond Doyle *retired petroleum research scientist*

Sand Springs
Quinn, Art Jay *retired veterinarian, educator*

Stillwater
French, Donald P. *zoologist, educator*
Grischkowsky, Daniel Richard *research scie educator*
Royer, Tom A. *entomologist, educator*

Tonkawa
Ackerson, Rex David *science educator, muse director*

Tulsa
Norvell, John Edmondson III *retired neuroscientist, educator*

Weatherford
Boggs, Lisa Lynn *biology professor*

OREGON

Ashland
Christianson, Roger Gordon *biology professo department chairman*

Beaverton
Wall, Brian Raymond *forest economist, busi consultant, researcher*

Clackamas
Kostow, Kathryn E. *conservation biologist*

Corvallis
Benoit Bird, Kelly J. *science educator*
Chambers, Kenton Lee *botany educator*
Cho, Jang-Cheon *microbiologist, researcher*
Chung, Woon-Gye *toxicologist, researcher*
Frakes, Rodney Vance *plant geneticist, educ*

)er, Joyce E. *plant pathologist, educator*
rita, Richard Yukio *microbiology and ceanography educator*
ry, David Anthony *ecologist*
nar, George Orlo, Jr. *entomologist, science ducator*
stwood, Melvin Neil *horticulturist, omologist*

gene
tthews, Brian W. *molecular biology educator*

rence
rble, Duane Francis *geography educator, esearcher*

nmouth
nderson, Jessica *science educator*

ndleton
pper, Elizabeth Lee *retired physiologist*
chado, Stephen *science educator*

rtland
ners, Wolfhard *physiology and biophysics ducator*
kowiec, Agnieszka Zofia *science educator, esearcher*
ly, Sherry L. *astrobiologist, educator*
enstein, William David *forester, consultant*
lil, Mohammad Aslam Khan *environmental cience educator, engineering educator, hysics professor*
chida, Curtis A. *research molecular eurobiologist, educator*

lem
kson, Ray Charles *retired wildlife biologist*

ent
cMillen, Richard Edward *biological sciences ducator, researcher*

lsonville
don, John Charles *forestry educator*

NNSYLVANIA

oona
ney, Brian B. *environmental eomorphologist, aerial mapping consultant*

nville
noek, Susan Elizabeth *botany educator*

dmore
ers, Willys Kent *geneticist*

la Cynwyd
liss, John Ozro *zoology educator*

hlehem
ama, Kenneth Philip *science educator, cademic administrator*

n Mawr
vford, Maria Luisa Buse *geology educator*

ffalo Mills
pstadt, William Homer *retired botanist, lucator, lay worker*

ylestown
nler, John Milton (Yochanan Menashsheh en Shaul) *science educator, artist*

ton
algo, Ismael J. *pharmaceutical scientist*

ttysburg
drix, Sherman Samuel *biology professor, searcher*

ove City
nner, Frederic James *biology professor, cologist, consultant*

rrisburg
irez, Eneida Sarahi *biology professor*

verford
erardino, Marie Antoinette *developmental ologist, educator*

rshey
ar, Akif *research scientist, biomedical ngineer, educator*
on, Ian Stuart *neuroscience and anatomy lucator, researcher, inventor*

robe
des, Michael E. *biologist, educator*

k Haven
Dongdong *nanoscience educator, physics rofessor*

dia
beck, John Raymond *physiology educator*

fflinville
er, Phillip Andrew *retired biological and llied health sciences educator*

rberth
anson, Neal *virologist, epidemiologist, lucator*

uea
lt, Carol Hargis *microbiologist, researcher*

ladelphia
er, Martin William *neuropharmacologist*
strong, Clay *physiology educator*
ster, Ralph Lawrence *biologist, educator*
van, Vikram H. *zoological park administrator*
Eisenstein, Toby K. *microbiology professor*
Fisher, Aron Baer *physiology educator*
Furth, John Jacob *molecular biologist, educator, pathologist*
Hammond, Benjamin Franklin *microbiologist, educator*
Heber-Katz, Ellen *research scientist, educator*
Hua, Xianxin *cell and cancer biology educator*
Jayadevappa, Ravishankar *science educator*
Kaestner, Klaus H. *genetics educator*
Kaji, Akira *microbiology scientist, educator*
Koprowski, Hilary *microbiologist, educator*
Lambertsen, Christian James *environmental physiologist, physician, educator*
Morrissette, Jennifer J. D. *geneticist*
Okere, Chuma Onyeaghala *neuroscientist*
Patrick, Ruth (Mrs. Ruth Hodge Van Dusen) *botany educator, curator*
Pepe, Frank A. *cell and developmental biology educator*
Pyeritz, Reed Edwin *geneticist, educator, medical researcher*
Rubin, Benjamin Arnold *microbiologist, immunologist, medical educator, researcher*
Scandura, Joseph Michael *neuroscientist, application developer*
Schneider, Adele Sandra *clinical geneticist*
Skalka, Anna Marie *molecular biologist*
Spielman, Richard Saul *genetics educator*
Taniguchi, Tadatsugu *biology professor, researcher*
Testa, Joseph R. *geneticist*
Wang, Jiongjiong *neuroscientist, educator*
White, Howard D. *information science educator*
Wysocki, Charles Joseph *neuroscientist*

Phoenixville
Hanlon, Barbara Jean *family and consumer sciences educator*

Pittsburgh
Amara, Susan *neuroscientist*
Berry, Guy Curtis *polymer science educator, researcher*
Bicchieri, Cristina *science educator*
Cassidy, William Arthur *geology and planetary science educator*
Druzdzel, Marek Jozef *information systems educator, researcher*
Ehrlich, Garth David *molecular biologist*
Feingold, David Sidney *microbiology and biochemistry educator, researcher*
Gollin, Susanne Merle *cell biologist, researcher*
Hall-Stoodley, Luanne *science educator, researcher*
Harrold, Ronald Thomas *research scientist*
Hatfull, Graham F. *microbiologist, educator*
Hollis, Ralph L. *science educator*
Jones, Elizabeth Winifred *biology professor*
Kiger, Robert William *botanist, science historian, educator, researcher*
LaJohn, Lawrence Anthony *research scientist*
Lazo, John Stephen *science educator, director*
Marazita, Mary Louise *genetics researcher*
Moore, Robert Yates *neuroscience educator*
Mutale, Christian Thales *research scientist*
Partanen, Carl Richard *biology professor*
Reddy, Raj *science educator, academic administrator*
Saaty, Thomas Lorie *science educator*
Schatten, Gerald Phillip *stem cell biologist, reproductive biologist, educator*
Seol, Dai-Wu *geneticist, educator*
Willke, Theodore Lawrence *research facility director*
Zeevi, Adriana *microbiologist, immunologist*

Richboro
Dott, John R. *marine life administrator*

State College
Madjid, A. Hamid *retired science educator*

Swarthmore
Gilbert, Scott Frederick *biologist, educator, author*

Swiftwater
Nalli, Sandro *research scientist, consultant*
Shirazi, Arash *research scientist*

Union City
Thomas, Paul Milton *retired science educator*

University Park
Barnes, Hubert Lloyd *geochemistry educator*
Brenchley, Jean Elnora *microbiologist, researcher, science administrator*
Buskirk, Elsworth Robert *physiologist, educator*
Coleman, Michael Murray *polymer science educator*
Cosgrove, Daniel Joseph *biology educator*
Fedoroff, Nina Vsevolod *research scientist, consultant, educator*
Grenfell, Bryan Thomas *biology professor*
Hedges, Stephen Blair *biology professor, researcher*
Roy, Della Martin *materials science educator, researcher*

Valley Forge
Erb, Robert Allan *physical scientist*

Wayne
Krutsick, Robert Stanley *retired science administrator*
Thelen, Edmund *research executive*

Wilkes Barre
Hayes, Wilbur Frank *retired biology professor*

Williamsport
Buckman, Debra Ann *science educator*

Wyndmoor
Strobaugh, Terence Philip, Jr. *molecular biologist, microbiologist*

RHODE ISLAND

Kingston
Hufnagel, Linda Ann *biology professor, researcher*
Markin, Karen Mary *research scientist, journalist*

Narragansett
Goos, Roger Delmon *retired mycologist*

Newport
Chace, Jameson Fales *ecologist, educator*
Koch, Robert Michael *research scientist, consultant, educator*

Providence
Block, Bartley Cavanough *biologist, educator*
Donoghue, John Phillip *neuroscience educator, neurotechnology company executive*
Dowben, Robert Morris *physiologist, researcher*
Forsyth, Donald William *geophysics educator*
Wood, Craig Breckinridge *paleobiologist, natural sciences educator*

SOUTH CAROLINA

Aiken
Bertsch, Paul M. *ecologist, director*

Charleston
Ogretmen, Besim *science educator, molecular biologist, researcher*
Polson, Shawn William *microbiologist, molecular biologist*
Yu, Shan Ping *neuroscientist, educator*

Columbia
Aelion, C. Marjorie *science educator*
Helmuth, Brian *marine biologist, educator*
Koley, Goutam *science educator*
Smith, Theresa Joanne *research scientist, educator*
Watabe, Norimitsu *marine biologist, educator*
Wideman, Ida Devlin *science educator*

Florence
Reay-Jones, Francis Peter Fortnum *entomologist, researcher*
West, Jesse Michael *pediatric neuropsychologist*

Greenville
Cureton, Claudette Hazel Chapman *retired biology professor*
Kupferer, James Leo, Jr. *biotechnologist*

Hilton Head Island
Adams, William Hensley *ecologist, educator*
Lefer, Allan Mark *physiologist*

Mc Cormick
Soni, Jayshri *science educator, director*

Pawleys Island
Kay, Thomas Oliver *agricultural consultant*

Pickens
Lofink, Glenda Jean *science educator*

Prosperity
Long, William McMurray *physiology educator*

Simpsonville
Pratt, Harry Davis *retired entomologist*

Spartanburg
Leonard, Walter Raymond *retired biology professor*

SOUTH DAKOTA

Brookings
Hardwidge, Philip Ross *microbiologist, educator*
Jenks, Jonathan Alden *biologist, educator*
Moldenhauer, William Calvin *soil scientist*

Sioux Falls
Narendranath, Neelakantam V. *microbiologist, researcher*

TENNESSEE

Cookeville
Airhart, Douglas L. *horticulturist, educator*

Fayetteville
Wolfhard, Hans Georg *retired research scientist*

Franklin
Thornsberry, Clyde *microbiologist*

Huntingdon
King, Tracy Lynn *science educator*

Kingsport
Ogbonnaya, Chuks Alfred *entomologist, agronomist, environmentalist*

Knoxville
Chen, James Pai-fun *biology professor, researcher*
Mazur, Peter *physiologist, cryobiologist*
Simberloff, Daniel *biologist, educator*
Wawrzyniak, Cynthia *biology professor*

Loudon
Stafford, William Franklin *veterinarian, educator*

Memphis
Freeman, Bob A. *retired microbiology educator, retired dean*
Howe, Martha Morgan *microbiologist, educator*
Pruitt, Rosalyn Jolena *science educator*
Schoech, Stephan James *biology professor*
Webster, Robert G. *virologist, educator*

Millington
Jones, Lawrence Andrew *research scientist, retired military officer*

Nashville
Catania, Kenneth C. *neuroscientist, educator*
Fanning, Ellen *biology professor, research scientist*
Ike, Justus *biology professor*
Orgebin-Crist, Marie-Claire *retired biology professor, department chairman*
Phillips, John A(tlas) III *geneticist, educator*

Sewanee
Yeatman, Harry Clay *biologist, educator*

TEXAS

Arlington
Smith, Charles Isaac *geology educator*

Austin
Biesele, John Julius *biologist, educator*
Brown, Samuel Paul *biologist*
Chae, Seung-Hyun *research scientist*
Drummond Borg, Lesley Margaret *geneticist*
Fryxell, Greta Albrecht *marine botany educator, oceanographer*
Grant, Verne Edwin *biology professor*
Holz, Robert Kenneth *retired geography educator*
Hubbs, Clark *zoologist, researcher*
Jacobson, Antone Gardner *retired zoology educator*
Liu, Hung-wen (Ben) *science educator, researcher*
Patterson, Donald Eugene *research scientist*
Ramirez Garza, Elizabeth Ann *biology professor, researcher*
Simpson, Beryl Brintnall *botany educator*
Sutton, Harry Eldon *geneticist, educator*

Beaumont
Tarpley, Lee *botanist, educator*

Bogata
Marris, Roy O. *agriculturist, consultant*

Brooks City-Base
Miller, Carolyn Lyons *microbiologist, military officer*

Brownsville
Emilio, Garrido Sanabria Rafael *science educator, researcher*

Bryan
Julson, Amanda Palmer *science educator*
Milford, Murray Hudson *retired soil science educator*
Soonthornpoct, Punnee *biology professor*

Bushland
Payne, William Albert, Jr. *agronomist, educator*

Cedar Park
Albin, Leslie Owens *biology professor*

College Station
Armstrong, Robert Beall *physiologist, educator*
Beaver, Bonnie Veryle *veterinarian, educator*
Borlaug, Norman Ernest *agricultural scientist*
Lancaster, Sarah *research scientist*
McCrady, James David *veterinarian, educator*
Neill, William Harold, Jr. *science educator, researcher*
Swaggerty, Christina L. *microbiologist, researcher*
Tai-Seale, Ming *science educator, consultant*

Corpus Christi
Merritt, Paul *neuroscientist, educator*

Corsicana
Carroll, Ray Dean, Sr. *retired veterinarian*

Dallas
Brown, Michael Stuart *geneticist, educator, science administrator*
Charboneau-McInnis, Janine Joyce *veterinary animal behaviorist*
Goldstein, Joseph Leonard *molecular biologist, educator*
McKnight, Steven Lanier *molecular biologist*
Parada, Luis Fernando *science educator*
Reinert, James A. *entomology educator*
Russell, David W. *molecular geneticist*
Sudhof, Thomas Christian *molecular genetics educator*
Vitetta, Ellen S. *microbiologist, immunologist, educator*
Yanagisawa, Masashi *geneticist, educator, researcher*

Diboll
Fisher, Richard Forrest *research scientist, editor-in-chief*

El Paso
Gill, Thomas Edward *science educator*
Salas, Guillermo *biologist, educator, medical technician*

Fort Worth
Kelly, Janet *science educator*
Lowseth, Lisa Anne *veterinarian*

Galveston
Esenaliev, Rinat Orozbekovich *science educator, lab administrator*
Frederickson, Christopher John *neuroscientist*
Ismail, Nahed *microbiologist, immunologist*
Kanuth, Michelle Susan *science educator*

Leary, James Francis *biomedical research scientist, educator*
Makino, Shinji *virologist, educator*
Markides, Kyriakos Socrates *gerontology educator*
Murphy, Frederick Augustus *virologist, researcher*
Thompson, Edward Ivins Bradbridge *biological chemistry and genetics educator, endocrinologist*
Willis, William Darrell, Jr. *neuroscientist, educator*
Zimmerman, Roger Joseph *fishery biologist*

Georgetown
Deviney, Marvin Lee, Jr. *science administrator, director*
Netsiri, Chaiyapoj *research scientist*

Harlingen
Maupin, Alan Rodger *science educator*

Houston
Butel, Janet Susan *virologist, department chairman, research scientist*
De Bremaecker, Jean-Claude *geophysics educator*
Diamond, Pamela M. *science educator*
Dronamraju, Krishna Rao *geneticist*
Estes, Mary K. *virologist, researcher*
Hossain, Anwar *molecular biologist, educator*
Jurtshuk, Peter, Jr. *microbiologist, educator*
Koul, Dimpy *biology professor, cell biologist, researcher*
Lee, Soo-Kyung *molecular biologist, educator*
Levy, Eugene Howard *planetary sciences and astrophysics educator, researcher*
Mao, Li *molecular biologist, educator*
Massoud, Yehia *science educator*
Mendelson, Robert Allen *polymer scientist, rheologist*
Nelson, David Loren *geneticist, educator*
Oh, Junghwan *biomedical scientist, researcher*
Shetty, Gunapala *biologist, researcher, educator*
Steele, James Harlan *retired veterinarian*
Weinstock, George Matthew *biology educator, researcher*

Kingwood
van Beem, Janny *geneticist, researcher*

Lewisville
Whitney, Sharry Jan *science educator*

Lubbock
Hentges, David John *microbiology educator*
Jackson, Raymond Carl *cytogeneticist*
Skoog, Gerald Duane *science educator*
Wendt, Charles William *soil scientist, educator*

Pearland
Shurtleff, Malcolm C. *plant pathologist, consultant*
Würsig, Bernd Gerhard *marine biology educator*

Plano
MacAlpine, Michelle Lewis *neuroscientist*

Port Aransas
Schake, Lowell Martin *zoology educator, writer*

Prairie View
Cuero, Raul G. *microbiologist, researcher, educator*

Richardson
Atzori, Marco *neuroscientist, educator*
Gray, Donald Melvin *molecular and cell biology educator*
McMechan, George *science educator*
Monti, Paolo *research scientist*

Rockport
Berkebile, Charles Alan *geology educator, hydrogeology researcher*

Round Rock
Schneider, Dennis Ray *microbiology professor, research and development company executive*

San Antonio
Blystone, Robert Vernon *cell biologist, educator*
Burch, James Leo *science research institute executive*
Gracy, Robert *science educator*
Irving, George Washington III *veterinarian, researcher, small business executive*
Mamtani, Manju Rameshlal *geneticist, researcher*
McComas, David John *science administrator, space physicist*
McIntosh, Dennis Keith *veterinarian, consultant*
Perry, George *neuroscientist, educator*
Wahl, Rosemarie *biologist, educator*
Wang, Yufeng *science educator*

Smithville
Scofield, Virginia Lee *research scientist*

Uvalde
Ramsey, Frank Allen *veterinarian, retired army officer*

Vernon
Malinowski, Dariusz Piotr *horticulturist, educator*

Warda
Kunze, George William *retired soil scientist*

UTAH

Brookside
McMahon, James Patrick *ecologist, consultant*

Cedar City
Mayron, Lewis Walter *clinical ecology consultant*

Centerville
Schwartz, Heidi K. *science educator*

Logan
Aust, Steven Douglas *biochemistry, biotechnology and toxicology educator*
McNeal, Lyle Glen *science educator, rancher, consultant*
Rasmussen, Harry Paul *horticulture and landscape educator*

Providence
Vest, Hyrum Grant, Jr. *retired horticultural sciences educator*

Provo
Blake, George Rowland *soil scientist, educator, environmental scientist, researcher*
Bywater, Duncan *biologist, educator*
Crookston, R. Kent *agronomy educator*
Hastriter, Michael Wayne *medical entomologist*
McArthur, Eldon Durant *geneticist, researcher*

Salt Lake City
Bossard, Robert Lee *biologist, educator*
Coley, Phyllis Dewing *biology professor*
Newmark, William D. *conservation biologist*
Olivera, Baldomero M. *biology professor*
Salisbury, Frank Boyer *botanist, educator, writer*

VERMONT

Brattleboro
Ames, Adelbert III *neuroscientist, educator*

Burlington
Heinrich, Bernd *biologist, educator*
Keeton, William Scott *ecologist, educator*

Charlotte
Hamilton, Lawrence Stanley *environmental consultant*
Melby, Edward Carlos, Jr. *veterinarian*

Greensboro
Hill, Lewis Reuben *horticulturist, nursery owner, writer*

Hinesburg
Fay, Glenn Mills, Jr. *science educator*

Morrisville
Lechevalier, Hubert Arthur *microbiology educator*
Lechevalier, Mary Pfeil *retired microbiologist, educator*

VIRGINIA

Alexandria
Borum, Olin Henry *retired research scientist*
Vosbeck, Elizabeth Just *retired geneticist*
Woolley, Mary Elizabeth *science administrator, advocate*

Amissville
Hunter, Beverly Claire *research scientist, educator*

Arlington
Cehelsky, Marta *scientific organization executive*
Chamot, Joshua Andrew *science administrator*
Crosby, Michael P. *science administrator*
Fuchs, Roland John *geography educator, academic administrator*
Glaser, Gerard R. *science administrator*
Harris, William James, Jr. *retired science administrator*
Held, Joe Roger *retired veterinarian*
Markessini, Joan *research scientist, psychologist*
Olsen, Kathie Lynn *science foundation director*
O'Neill, Brian *science administrator*
Ordway, Frederick Ira III *science educator, consultant, researcher, writer*
Sterner, Robert Warner *ecologist, science administrator*

Ashburn
Bawa, Raj *biotechnology educator, nanotechnologist*
Riddiford, Lynn Moorhead *biologist, educator*

Blacksburg
Burkhart, Harold Eugene *forester, educator*
Cowles, Joe Richard *biology professor*
Kelly, James Michael *plant and soil scientist*
Lamb, Ashley Brooks *entomologist*
Sukkariyah, Beshr *soil scientist*

Charlottesville
Chevalier, Roger Alan *astronomy educator, consultant*
Garrett, Reginald Hooker *biology professor, researcher*
Hoffman, Paul Stokes *microbiologist, researcher*
Hornberger, George Milton *environmental science educator*
Menaker, Michael *biology professor*
Molhoek, Kerrington Ramsey *research scientist*
Skrutskie, Michael F. *science educator*
Tuttle, Jeremy Ballou *neuroscientist*

Dublin
Linzey, Juanita Bird *biology professor*

Fairfax
Sun, Donglian *meteorologist*

Falls Church
Hart, C(harles) W(illard), Jr. *zoologist, curator*

Fort Lee
Chumley, Perry Ray *veterinarian, military officer*

Fredericksburg
McGhee, Jay D. *ecologist, educator*

Galax
Dunson, William Albert *biology professor, ecological consultant*

Gloucester Point
Bush, Elizabeth Olney *marine lab technician*

Hampton
Divers, Kevin Samuel *aerospace physiologist*

Haymarket
Katz, Alan Charles *toxicologist*

Keswick
IRafajko, Robert Richard *science administrator*

Lansdowne
Miller, Dorothy Anne Smith *retired cytogenetics educator*

Lexington
Kricorian, Mary Jo Geyer *biology instructor, environmental scientist, consultant*
Spencer, Edgar Winston *geology educator*

Lorton
Ricci, Lisa A. *geneticist, researcher*

Manassas
Isbister, Jenefir Diane Wilkinson *microbiologist, researcher, educator, consultant*
Jong, Shung-Chang *mycologist*

Mc Lean
DeGiovanni-Donnelly, Rosalie Frances *biologist, educator*
Krugman, Stanley Liebert *science administrator, geneticist*
Talbot, Lee Merriam *ecologist, educator, director*

Norfolk
Haoudi, Abdelali *science educator*
Heck, Henry D'Arcy *retired toxicologist, consultant*
Oelberg, David George *neonatologist educator, researcher*

Painter
Lubs, Herbert Augustus *retired genetics educator, administrator*

Reston
Grey, Jerry *science educator*
Shank, Fred Ross *food scientist*

Richmond
Boadle-Biber, Margaret Clare *physiologist, educator*

Triangle
Thomas, Lindsey Kay, Jr. *research ecology biologist, educator, consultant*

Vienna
Liu, Cejun *science educator, researcher, program analyst*

Williamsburg
Griffith, Melvin Eugene *entomologist, public health service officer*
Guastaferro, Angelo *space science administrator, consultant*

Wytheville
Linzey, Donald Wayne *biologist, educator, researcher*

WASHINGTON

Bellevue
Thompson, Winston Mark Obed *entomologist, consultant, writer*
Whatmore, George Bernard *research scientist, writer, internist*

Bellingham
Ross, June Rosa Pitt *biologist, educator*

Longview
Foster, Virginia *retired botany educator*

Lopez Island
Brownstein, Barbara Lavin *geneticist, educator, director*

Olympia
Nadkarni, Nalini Moreshwar *biology professor, researcher*

Prosser
Proebsting, Edward Louis, Jr. *retired horticulturist*

Pullman
Berge, Anna Catharina Björnsdotter *veterinarian, epidemiologist*
Hosick, Howard Lawrence *cell biology professor, academic administrator*
Ibekwe, Abasiofiok Mark *soil scientist, educator*
Thomashow, Linda Suzanne *microbiologist*

Richland
Chou, Charissa J. *staff scientist*

Seattle
Aprikyan, Andranik Andrew Goorgen *molecular biologist, biomedical researcher*
Bassingthwaighte, James Bucklin *physiologist, educator, medical researcher*
Beyers, William Bjorn *geography educator*
Boersma, P. Dee *conservation biologist, educ*
Charlson, Robert Jay *atmospheric sciences educator*
Creager, Joe Scott *geology and oceanography educator*
Daniel, Thomas L. *zoology educator*
Fidel, Raya *information science educator*
Franklin, Jerry Forest *forest ecologist, educat*
Gao, Dayong *science educator*
Greenberg, E. Peter *microbiologist*
Hartwell, Leland Harrison (lee hartwell) *geneticist, educator*
Hellström, Karl Erik *science educator, researcher*
Hendrickson, Anita Elizabeth *biology profess*
Henikoff, Steven *research scientist, educator*
Hille, Bertil *physiology educator*
Hood, Leroy Edward *molecular biologist, educator*
Huey, Raymond B. *zoologist, educator*
Kareiva, Peter Michael *zoology educator, research ecologist*
Kenny, George Edward *pathobiology educato*
King, Ivan Robert *astronomy educator*
King, Mary-Claire *geneticist, educator*
Kirby, Ronald Eugene *fish and wildlife resea administrator*
Kirschner, Marc Alan *neuroscientist*
Kruckeberg, Arthur Rice *botanist, educator*
Kuhl, Patricia K. *science educator*
Lein, Ed *research scientist*
Ning, Xue-Han (Hsueh-Han Ning) *physiologi researcher*
Olstad, Roger Gale *science educator*
Schiffrin, Milton Julius *physiologist*
Senczuk, Anna Maria *cell biologist, research*
Smith, Orville Auverne *physiology educator*
Stifelman, Marc Lee *toxicologist, risk management consultant*
Teemer, Carey *physiologist, medical research*
Ulrich, Cornelia (Neli) *research scientist*
Woods, James Sterrett *toxicologist*

Vancouver
Cushwa, William *biology professor*

Veradale
Keating, Eugene Kneeland *animal scientist, educator*

Washougal
Guillory, Richard John *retired science educa*

Wenatchee
Elfving, Don C. *horticulturist, educator*
Schrader, Lawrence Edwin *plant physiologist educator*

WEST VIRGINIA

Bruceton Mills
Butcher, Fred R. *biochemistry professor, academic administrator*

Kearneysville
Biggs, Alan Richard *plant pathologist, educa*

Morgantown
Cochrane, Robert Lowe *biologist*
Gladfelter, Wilbert Eugene *physiology educa*
Nath, Joginder *genetics and biology educator researcher*
Talukder, Jamil *physiologist, researcher*
Wenger, Sharon Louise *cytogeneticist, researcher, educator*

South Charleston
Bhasin, Madan Mohan *research scientist*

WISCONSIN

Appleton
Maravolo, Nicholas C. *biology professor*

Ashland
Beever, Erik Alan *ecologist, biologist*

Brookfield
Nielsen, Leon *animal scientist*

Clintonville
Primmer, Lillian Juanda *science educator*

Cottage Grove
Lund, Daryl Bert *retired food science educat*

Madison
Amasino, Richard M. *plant physiologist*
Beyer-Mears, Annette *physiologist*
Brock, Thomas Dale *retired microbiology professor*
Carroll, Sean B. *geneticist, biologist, educat researcher, writer*
Cassinelli, Joseph Patrick *astronomy educato*
Dierauf, Leslie Ann *wildlife veterinarian, conservation biologist, consultant*
Easterday, Bernard Carlyle *veterinary medici educator*
Evert, Ray Franklin *botany educator*
Ganetzky, Barry S. *geneticist, science educa*
Goodrich, James A. *veterinarian, researcher*
Greaser, Marion Lewis *science educator*
Handelsman, Jo *plant pathologist, educator*
Hopen, Herbert John *horticulture educator*
Iltis, Hugh Hellmut *botanist, educator, environmental advocate*
Jeanne, Robert Lawrence *entomologist, educ*
Kaesberg, Paul Joseph *virology researcher*
Kawaoka, Yoshihiro *virologist, educator*
Kemnitz, Joseph William *physiologist, researcher*
Marrett, Cora B. *science educator*
Miller, Paul Dean *breeding consultant, geneticist, educator*
Newcomb, Eldon Henry *retired botany educ*

Milton Orville *science educator*
Fabien Andre *research scientist*
rt, Roland Rudyard *retired virologist, ator*
y, Thomas David *botanist, educator*
, Millard *geneticist, educator*
on, James Alexander *molecular biologist, ator*
Monica Goigel *ecologist*
-Hyuk *geneticist, educator*

sha
ng, K. Dubear *biology professor, archer*

monee Falls
Norine Madelyn Quinlan *clinical ratory scientist*

aukee
y, Allen Wilson, Jr. *physiologist*
i, Louis Anthony *science educator, writer*
ne, John P. *anesthesiology and physiology ator*

oygan
Ronald Francis *geography educator*

rior
s, Robert Bradford *natural resources arch scientist*

OMING

son
Paul Alan *ethnobotanist, educator*

mie
, Randolph Vance *molecular biologist, archer*
ovic, Margareta *science educator*

and
nan, Carl *veterinarian, retired demiologist*

RITORIES OF THE UNITED STATES

RTO RICO

adilla
z-Jiménez, Carlos *science educator, robiologist, geneticist*

aguez
rly, Paul Reed *plant pathologist*

Juan
e Samalot, Myrelis *neuroscientist, chologist, consultant*
o, Ana M. *parasitology and immunology cator, researcher*

CANADA

BERTA

ary
, Geoffrey Melvill *physiology research cator*
er, Roger Geoffrey *geology educator, nsultant*

monton
h, Denis Ian *geophysics educator*
ci, Chuji *plant pathologist, educator*
k, Charles Richard *geology educator*

TISH COLUMBIA

ney
low, Margaret Elizabeth Barr (M.E. Barr) *ired botany educator*
rick, William Bryce *biologist, consultant, itor, writer*
n, Cedric Robert *retired science ministrator, oceanographer*

couver
aldson, Edward Mossop *research scientist, arine biologist, consultant*
s, David Robert *retired zoology educator*
sey, Casimir Charles *zoologist, educator*
Lean, Donald Millis *microbiologist, ucator, pathologist, pediatrician*
Neill, John Hugh *pharmaceutical sciences ucator*
man, Murray Arthur *aquarium administrator*
ips, Anthony George *neurobiology searcher*
ips, John Edward *zoologist, educator*
nie, Paul Steven *research scientist, surgeon*
v, Michael *biologist, educator*
lair, Alastair James *geology educator*
ington, William George *entomologist, ologist, educator*

toria
in, David Howard *biologist, educator, cademic administrator*
ary, Urs *neuroscientist, educator*

ANITOBA

nnipeg
aud, Trivedi Vidhya Nandan *anatomy ducator, researcher, consultant*

NEW BRUNSWICK

Fredericton
Saunders, Gary William *biology educator, phycology researcher*

NEWFOUNDLAND AND LABRADOR

Saint John's
Rochester, Michael Grant *geophysics educator*

NOVA SCOTIA

Dartmouth
Mann, Kenneth Henry *marine ecologist*

Halifax
Hall, Brian Keith *biology professor, writer*

ONTARIO

Downsview
Forer, Arthur H. *biology professor, researcher, editor*

Guelph
Beveridge, Terrance James *microbiology professor, researcher*
Bewley, John Derek *botany researcher, educator*
Kasha, Kenneth John *agriculturist, educator*

Hamilton
Blajchman, Morris Aaron *science educator, physician*

Kingston
Leggett, William C. *biology professor, academic administrator*
Wyatt, Gerard Robert *biology professor, researcher*

London
Kang, Chil-Yong *virologist, immunology educator*
Lala, Peeyush Kanti *research scientist, educator*

North York
Davey, Kenneth George *biologist, educator, academic administrator*
Regan, David *neuroscientist*

Ottawa
Baum, Bernard Rene *research scientist*
Carty, Arthur John *science policy advisor, research administrator*
Hughes, Stanley John *retired mycologist*
Perry, Malcolm Blythe *biologist, researcher*
Storey, Kenneth Bruce *biology professor*
Veizer, Ján *geology educator*
Whitehead, J. Rennie *science administrator, consultant*

Peterborough
Hutchinson, Thomas Cuthbert *ecology and environmental educator*

Scarborough
White, Calvin John *zoo executive, zoological association executive, financial manager*

Stittsville
MacLeod, Robert Angus *microbiology educator, researcher*

Toronto
Chandra, Ranjit Kumar *research scientist, educator, physician*
Cook, Stephen Arthur *mathematics and computer science educator*
Dunlop, David John *geophysics educator, researcher*
Liversage, Richard Albert *cell biologist, educator*
MacLennan, David Herman *research scientist, educator*
Masui, Yoshio *zoology educator*
Pawson, Anthony J. *molecular biologist*
Poulsen, Jens Kristian *ultrasonics researcher*
Tobe, Stephen Solomon *zoology educator*

Waterloo
Warner, Barry Gregory *ecologist, educator*

QUEBEC

Laval
Bourget, Edwin Robert *marine ecologist, educator*
Talbot, Pierre Joseph *microbiologist, researcher*

Montreal
Aguayo, Alberto Juan *neuroscientist*
Carroll, Robert Lynn *biology professor, paleontologist, curator, museum director*
Chang, Thomas Ming Swi *research scientist, biotechnologist, educator*
Jolicoeur, Paul *molecular biologist*
Milic-Emili, Joseph *physiologist, educator*
Mysak, Lawrence Alexander *oceanographer, climatologist and mathematics educator*

Pointe-Claire
Lapointe, Lucie *research institute executive*

Quebec City
Potvin, Pierre *physiologist, educator*

Saint Jean Sur Richelieu
Trudel, Marc J. *botanist, educator*

SASKATCHEWAN

Saskatoon
Babiuk, Lorne Alan *virologist, immunologist, researcher*
Huang, Pan Ming *soil science educator*

Sainte Anne de Bellevue
Grant, William Frederick *geneticist, educator*

MEXICO

Cuernavaca
Palacios, Rafael *geneticist*

AUSTRALIA

Woollahra
Hall, Peter Francis *retired physiologist*

BELGIUM

Antwerp
Snyders, Dirk Johan *electrophysiologist and biophysicist educator*

CHINA

Beijing
Yuan, Longping *agronomist*

Wuhan
Cao, Hanqiang *science educator, researcher*

Xi'an
Zhao, Wenming *retired biochemistry and molecular biology educator*

COSTA RICA

San José
Leon Azofeifa, Pedro *molecular biologist*

CZECH REPUBLIC

Prague
Sebek, Michael *research scientist, entrepreneur, educator*

DENMARK

Copenhagen
Jacobsen, Stine *veterinarian, educator*

ECUADOR

Quito
Del Pino, Eugenia M. *biology professor*

EGYPT

Kafr el Sheikh
Saad, Fawzy Ali *molecular geneticist*

ENGLAND

Cambridge
Gurdon, John Bertrand *cell biologist*
Huxley, Sir Andrew (Fielding) *physiologist, educator*
Klug, Aaron *molecular biologist*
Ramakrishnan, Venkatraman (Venki Ramakrishnan) *scientist*
Rees, Martin John *astronomy educator*
Walker, John Ernest *molecular biologist, researcher*

Coventry
Feelisch, Martin *research scientist, consultant*

Kent Cranbrook
Hattersley-Smith, Geoffrey Francis *retired government research scientist*

Leeds
Phillips, Oliver *tropical forest ecologist, researcher*

Leicester
Jeffreys, Sir Alec John *geneticist, educator*

London
Morris, Desmond (John) (Desmond John Morris) *zoologist, writer, artist*

Norwich
Baulcombe, David C. *virologist*

Oxford
Dawkins, Richard (Clinton Richard Dawkins) *ethologist, evolutionary biologist, educator, writer*
Harvey, Paul H. *evolutionary biologist, researcher*
Krebs, John Richard *zoologist, science administrator*

Stoke-on-Trent
Kim, Do Kyung *science educator*

FINLAND

Espoo
Hari, Riitta Kyllikki *neuroscientist*

FRANCE

Compiegne
Dubuisson, Bernard Louis *science educator, administrator*

Gif-sur-Yvette
Duplessy, Jean Claude *research scientist*

Noisy-le-Grand
Le Quéré, Jean François Marie *scientific instrumentation researcher*

Paris
Jacob, François *biologist, educator*
Kourilsky, François Michel *research scientist*
Raharinaivo, André Léon *research scientist, educator*

Saint Etienne
Vergnaud, Jean-Maurice *science educator, researcher*

Vandoeuvre-les-Nancy
Blazy, Pierre François *science educator*

GERMANY

Bad Nauheim
Engel, Felix Benedikt Salomon *cell biologist, researcher*

Leipzig
Pääbo, Svante *molecular biologist, biochemist*

Stuttgart
von Klitzing, Klaus *research facility administrator, physicist*

GHANA

Accra
Jones, Monty P. *science administrator*

INDIA

Bangalore
Gadagkar, Raghavendra *ecologist, educator, entomologist*
Siddiqi, Obaid *retired geneticist*

Chandigarh
Pattipati, Sreenivasulu Naidu *science educator*

Lucknow
Mohan, Dinesh *research scientist*

ISRAEL

Kiryat Shmone
Gophen, Moshe *research scientist*

Rehovot
Sachs, Leo *geneticist, educator*

ITALY

Naples
Tarro, Giulio *virologist*

Pisa
Labardi, Massimiliano *research scientist*

Rome
Levi-Montalcini, Rita *neurobiologist, researcher*

JAPAN

Chiba
Arai, Toshihiko *retired microbiology and immunology educator*
Hattori, Naozo *science educator*

Sapporo
Asari, Eikichi *information sciences educator, researcher*

Tokyo
Ishii, Akira *parasitologist, allergist, malariologist*
Toyoshima, Chikashi *structural biologist, educator*

NEW ZEALAND

Palmerston North
Krone, Cheryl A. *research scientist, consultant*

NORWAY

Kjeller
Maeland, Arnulf Julius *research scientist*

POLAND

Warsaw
Koscielak, Jerzy *research scientist*

REPUBLIC OF KOREA

Seoul
Choi, Won Il *entomologist, researcher*
Chun, Jang Ho *science educator, researcher*
Kim, Yong-Hak *microbiologist*

ROMANIA

Bucharest
Badic, Mihai *research scientist*

SOUTH AFRICA

Thohoyandou
Samie, Amidou *microbiologist, educator, molecular biologist*

SWITZERLAND

Basel
Arber, Werner *microbiologist*
Gehring, Walter Jakob *biology professor, geneticist*

Gland
Leape, James P. *science foundation director*

Zurich
Wüthrich, Kurt *molecular biologist, biophysicist, educator*

TAIWAN

Kaohsiung Hsien
Lin, Yusen Eason *microbiologist, educator*

ADDRESS UNPUBLISHED

Abdullaev, Yalchin *neuroscientist, educator*
Able, Kenneth Paul *biology professor*
Acker, Robert Flint *retired microbiologist*
Addo, Charles Kwame *science educator*
Ahearne, John Francis *science foundation director, researcher*
Ahrens, Franklin Alfred *veterinary pharmacology educator*
Aldridge, Christopher D. *biotechnology executive, consultant*
Alexander, Jeremiah Roy *molecular biologist, researcher*
Alfano, Robert R. *science and engineering educator*
Al-Hajj, Muhammad *biologist*
Andrews, Richard Vincent *physiologist, educator*
Arking, Robert *geneticist, gerontologist, educator*
Arnott, Howard Joseph *biology professor, dean*
Asirvatham, Angela Lily *science educator*
Atkin, J. Myron *science educator*
Aubrey, Douglas P. *ecologist, researcher*
Awomoyi, Agnes Abiola *microbiologist, researcher*
Backus, Elaine Athene *entomologist, educator*
Bandyopadhyay, Ram Shyamal *molecular biologist, researcher*
Baranyi, Lajos *research scientist*
Barefoot, Aldos Cortez, Jr. *retired forester, educator*
Barham, Warren Sandusky *horticulturist*
Barlow, John Sutton *neuroscientist, lexicographer*
Barnard, Donald Roy *medical and veterinary entomologist*
Barnes, Robert F *agronomist*
Barnes-Kempton, Isabel Janet *retired microbiologist, dean*
Barnhart, Charles Elmer *zoology educator*
Beachy, Philip Arden *molecular biology educator*
Beggs, William H. *microbiologist, researcher*
Belfer, Inna *research scientist, medical educator*
Bentley, Charles Raymond *geophysics educator*
Berra, P. Bruce *computer science educator*
Beswick, Ellen J. *research scientist*
Bick, Katherine Livingstone *neuroscientist, educator, researcher*
Bidwell, Roger Grafton Shelford *biologist, educator*
Bilbo, Thomas Earl *biology professor*
Blum, Samuel *retired research scientist*
Bolie, Victor Wayne *molecular biologist, researcher*
Bonner, John Tyler *biology professor*
Borisy, Gary G. *molecular biology professor*
Bose, Santanu *virologist, educator*
Bottone, Edward Joseph *microbiologist, educator*
Bower, James Mason *neuroscientist, educator, science administrator*
Boyle, Tatiana Gennadievna *research scientist*
Braker, William Paul *retired aquarium executive, ichthyologist*
Bremner, John McColl *agronomy and biochemistry educator*
Brown, Harley Procter, Jr. *zoology educator, entomologist, researcher*
Browne, Frederick Douglas *physiologist, educator*
Bryan, Billie Marie (Mrs. James A. Mackey) *retired biologist*
Buia, Calin Ioan *neuroscientist*
Bullard, Ervin Trowbridge *horticulturist*
Burkes, Lionel Seaton *science educator, writer, researcher*
Burton, Lawrence DeVere *agriculturist, educator*
Busse, Paul Lawrence *science educator*
Byun, Youngjoo *research scientist*
Caldwell, Elwood Fleming *food scientist, educator*
Cannizzaro, Linda Ann *geneticist, researcher*
Carter, Kenneth Charles *geneticist*
Carter, Tonya M. *science educator*
Cellarius, Richard Andrew *biology professor*
Cezar, Gabriela *research scientist, entrepreneur*
Chacko, George Kuttickal *management science educator, consultant*
Chang, Susan Marina *neuroscientist*
Cheng, Yue *molecular geneticist, pathologist*
Chitnis, Ashay *research scientist*
Chun, Asaph Y. *research scientist*
Clayton, David A(lvin) *biology professor*
Cleary, Meagan Bayless *ecologist, educator, researcher*
Cohen, Stanley *retired biochemistry educator*
Coleman, Douglas *research scientist, educator*
Conover, Lloyd Hillyard *retired research scientist*
Conway, William Gaylord *zoologist, zoo director, conservationist*
Coughlin, Shaun R. *research scientist*
Cravats, Monroe *science educator*
Creech, John Lewis *botanist, consultant*
D'Alesandro, Philip Anthony *parasitologist, immunologist, retired medical educator*
Dame, Richard Franklin *marine biology educator*
Danehy, Robert Joseph *aquatic biologist*
Darsie, Richard Floyd, Jr. *medical entomologist*
Daves, Glenn Doyle, Jr. *science educator, chemist, researcher*
Davis, Gordon Richard Fuerst *retired biologist, translator*
Deckard, Steve Wayne *science educator, academic administrator*
Decker, Walter Johns *toxicologist*
De Fabo, Edward Charles *photobiologist, research scientist, educator, photoimmunologist*
Despommier, Dickson Donald *microbiology educator, parasitologist*
Dey, Moul *molecular biologist, researcher*
Dickie, Renee *physiologist, researcher*
Doman, Elvira *retired science administrator*
Donahue, J. Kevin *electrophysiologist, researcher*
Doucet, Jennifer *research scientist*
Dragoi, George *research scientist*
Dugan, Patrick Raymond *microbiologist, educator, dean*
Edgar, Robert S. *biology professor*
Edwards, Charles *neuroscientist, educator*
Ellner, Paul Daniel *retired microbiologist*
Eno, Amos Stewart *natural resource foundation administrator*
Erickson, Edward Leonard *biotechnologist, consultant*
Erwin, Donald Carroll *plant pathology educator*
Fa'Bos, Julius Gyuda *retired horticulturist, educator*
Farkas, Daniel Frederick *food science and technology educator*
Feir, Dorothy Jean *entomologist, educator, physiologist*
Fisher, Dale Dunbar *animal scientist, dairy nutritionist*
Fiszer-Szafarz, Berta (Berta Safars) *research scientist*
Flemming, David Paul *biologist*
Fletcher, Ronald Darling *microbiologist educator*
Fotopoulos, Sophia Stathopoulos *medical research scientist, administrator*
Fournier, R. E. Keith *biologist*
Fox, Michael Wilson *veterinarian, animal scientist*
Foy, Charles Daley *retired soil scientist*
Frank, Linda Maria *science educator*
Fuller, Cynthia L. *biologist, researcher*
Gabor-Hotchkiss, Magda *research scientist, librarian*
Gage, Patrick (Leonard Patrick Gage) *biotechnology & pharmaceutical industry consultant*
Gay, William Ingalls *veterinarian, retired health science association administrator*
Gerritsen, Mary Ellen *vascular and cell biologist*
Gift, James Joseph *aquatic toxicologist*
Gilbert, Charles D. *neurobiologist*
Gillett, James Warren *retired ecotoxicology educator*
Giocomo, Lisa *research scientist*
Glysch, Randall Lee *research scientist*
Goldstein, Michael I. *ecologist*
Goldstein, Walter Elliott *biotechnology executive*
Goodall, Jane *zoologist*
Gorham, Robin Wilson *biology professor*
Gowans, Sir James Learmonth *science administrator, immunologist*
Griffin, Leann Creasy *science educator*
Grunder, Hermann A. *science administrator, director, research scientist*
Gruneich, Jeffrey Alan *biotechnologist, director*
Guo, Mingruo *food scientist, educator*
Haber, Ann *biology professor, physiologist*
Habermann, Helen Margaret *botanist, educator*
Hale, Wesley Raymond *research associate, chemical engineer, polymer scientist*
Hamil, Burnette Wolf *science educator*
Hand, Peter James *neurobiologist, educator*
Harlin, Marilyn Miler *marine botany educator, researcher, consultant*
Hauptmann, Randal Mark *biotechnologist*
Hayakawa, Kan-Ichi *retired food scientist*
Heinicke, Ralph Martin *science administrator, consultant*
Helgeson, John Paul *plant pathology and botany educator*
Hemmingsen, Barbara Bruff *retired microbiologist*
Herzog, Jennifer A. *biology professor*
Heyer, Stephanie *science educator*
Hickey, Robert Joseph *research scientist, educator*
Hildebrand, Verna Lee *human ecology educator*
Hill, David Lawrence *research corporation executive*
Hilliard, Sam Bowers *geography educator*
Hillis, William Daniel *biology professor*
Hoffman, Jill M. *neuroscientist, researcher*
Holland, Branti Latessa *science educator*
Hong, Baoming *research scientist, engineer*
Honour, Lynda Charmaine *research scientist, psychotherapist, educator*
Hoskins, Alexander L. (Pete) *retired zoological park administrator*
Houseknecht, Karen L. *research scientist, educator*
Howard-Peebles, Patricia N. *clinical cytogeneticist*
Hoye, Robert Earl *systems science educator*
Hudak, Andrew Thomas *ecologist, forester, researcher*
Huie, Carol P. *information science educator*
Hunt, Carlton Cuyler, Jr. *physiologist, educator*
Huntress, Wesley Theodore, Jr. *research scientist*
Jacobs, Michael Roy *microbiologist, researcher*
Jefferson, Monica Louise *neuroscientist, psychologist*
Jeyaretnam, Benjamin S. *science administrator*
Jo, Mi-Yeoung *neuropsychologist*
Jones, Marvin Lamar *histologist*
Jung, Sangwook *neurobiologist*
Kageyama, Mariko *collections manager*
Kamrin, Michael Arnold *toxicology educator*
Kang, Hyun Wook *research scientist*
Karnauskas, Kristopher Benson *research scientist*
Karp, Gerald Charles *biologist, educator, writer*
Karr, James Richard *ecologist, educator, research director*
Kaye, Edward Michael *biotechnologist, physician, neurogeneticist*
Kelder, Dorothy Mae *science educator*
Kelly, Raymond Crain *toxicologist*
Kennedy, Charles *retired neuroscientist, retired medical educator*
Kim, Charles Wesley *microbiology educator*
Kim, Won Gyu *research scientist*
Kimbrell, Deborah Ann *geneticist, educator*
King, David Alan *ecologist*
King, Megan Christine *cell biologist*
Kirsteuer, Ernst Karl Eberhart *biologist, curator*
Klausner, Richard Daniel *cell biologist, researcher*
Koenig, Maureen Catherine *science educator*
Kolb, James A. *science foundation director, writer*
Kollar, Edward James *retired biology educator*
Krylov, Dmitri *biologist*
Kulnane, Laura Shapiro *geneticist*
Kumako, Kuami Mawunyo *agricultural scientist*
Kung, Patrick Chung-Shu *biotechnologist*
Kushlan, James Anthony *science administrator, educator, conservationist, writer*
Kyesmu, Pius Michael *biology professor, researcher*
LaCrue, Alexis Nichole *parasitologist*
Lafever, Howard Nelson *botanist, educator, geneticist*
Lagna, Giorgio *molecular biologist, researcher*
Langer, Glenn Arthur *cellular physiologist, educator*
Lapiz-Bluhm, Maria Danet Sanchez *neuroscientist, medical/surgical nurse*
Layne, James Nathaniel *retired vertebrate biologist*
Leath, Kenneth Thomas *plant pathologist, educator, agriculturist, consultant*
Leeds, Jennifer Alyson *bacteriologist, researcher*
Lewis, Brian Kreglow *retired physiologist, computer scientist*
Li, Xiang-Yang *science educator*
Lippincott, James Andrew *retired biochemistry and biological sciences educator*
Lotsch, Alexander *scientist*
Low, Morton David *retired neuroscientist, healthcare educator*
Lustyk, Mary Kathleen *neuroscientist, educator*
Lynch, Harry James *retired biologist*
Lynch, John Thomas *retired science administrator, physicist*
Maley, Abigail Joy *zoologist, researcher*
Mark, Hon Fong Louie *cytogeneticist*
Maroni, Donna Farolino *biologist, researcher*
Marshall, Edith *veterinarian*
Martin, Joseph Vinson *neuroscientist, educator*
Martin, Marcia D. *science educator*
Martino, Joseph Paul *research scientist, researcher*
Mathis, Stephanie Charlotte *veterinarian*
Matlock, John Hudson *science administrator, materials engineer*
Mattox, Johnny Lynn *biologist, educator*
Maunder, Addison Bruce *agronomic research company executive*
McCann, Peter Paul *biology researcher, educator*
McClellan, Roger Orville *toxicologist*
McDowell, Elizabeth Mary *retired pathology educator*
McGraw, Donald Jesse *biologist, science historian, writer*
McPherson, Elizabeth Wright *clinical geneticist*
McPherson, John Edwin, Jr. *zoologist, educator, entomologist, researcher*
McShefferty, John *retired research scientist, personal care industry executive, consultant*
McSwain, Byrdie Engle *laboratory scientist, immunohematologist*
Meerow, Alan William *geneticist, horticulturist, botanist*
Menn, Julius Joel *retired research scientist, consultant*
Miekka, Jeanette Ann *retired science educator*
Miftahof, Roustem Narimanovich *science educator, researcher*
Miller, Louis Howard *biologist, researcher*
Miller, Patrick William *research scientist, educator*
Mitchell, John Daniel *taxonomist, ecologist*
Mitchell, John Laurin Amos *biological science educator*
Moon, Il-Ju *marine biologist, educator*
Moore, Thomas Andrew *biotechnology executi*
Moore, Tirin *neuroscientist, educator*
Morden, Robert Dean *biology professor*
Morgan, Bethanye Branch *biology professor*
Moritz, Chad Henry *research scientist*
Moroz, Pavel Emanuel *retired research scienti*
Mosallaei, Hossein *science educator*
Moskovitz, Jackob *biology professor*
Moss, Thomas Henry *science foundation director, physicist*
Mudavanhu, Blessing *research scientist*
Murarka, Shyam Prasad *science and engineer. educator, administrator*
Nakazato, Takuya *ecological geneticist*
Nanda, Navreet K. *research scientist*
Nanos, George Peter, Jr. *science administrator military officer, physicist*
Napoli, Joseph Stephen *horticulturist, conduc*
Nikaido, Hiroshi *microbiologist*
Norman, Thena Monts Durham *microbiologist researcher, health facility administrator*
Nyberg, Stanley Eric *research scientist*
Olshan, Judd David *ecologist*
Onufriev, Alexey *science educator*
Ostlind, Dan A. *retired parasitologist*
Paganelli, Charles Victor *physiologist, educat*
Palade, George Emil *research scientist, educa*
Pan, Ya-Hui Laurie *toxicologist, director*
Paranjpe, Pankaj Vinaykumar *research scienti*
Pearl, Sharrona Hyla *science educator*
Peeples, Mary Anne Baumann *science educat*
Penwell, Rebecca Ann *science educator*
Persad, Anand Bhopraj *entomologist*
Peterson, David Maurice *retired physiologist*
Petkovic, Lucia M. *research scientist*
Pettit, Ghery DeWitt *retired veterinary medic educator*
Pickett, Cecil Bruce *cell biologist*
Pinaud, Raphael *research scientist*
Plotkin, Stanley Alan *virologist*
Purves, William Kirkwood *biologist, educator*
Rabó, Jule Anthony *research scientist, consul*
Radhakrishnan, Ravi *science educator*
Ramirez, Ronaldo Victor *science educator*
Rastogi, Shipra *cell biologist*
Redmon, Larry Allen *agronomist, educator*
Reinardy, Scott Robert *science educator*
Riccio, Angela *science educator*
Richardson, Paul Joseph *food scientist, researcher*
Rodecker, Stephen Bailey *science specialist, secondary school educator*
Roeller, Herbert Alfred *biology professor*
Rogers, Jack David *plant pathologist, educat*
Rogers, Ruth Frances *retired microbiologist*
Romano, Gaetano *research scientist, educator*
Romo, Randulfo *physiologist, educator*
Rose, Michael Robertson *evolutionary biolog educator, consultant*
Russell, James Benjamin *microbiologist, educator, research scientist*
Russell, Liane Brauch *retired geneticist*
Saalfeld, Fred Erich *science educator, researc*
Sabatini, David Domingo *cell biologist, biochemist*
Salkind, Michael Jay *science administrator, metallurgical engineer*
Sanger, Frederick *retired molecular biologist*
Sathaye, Jayant *research scientist*
Sattler, Rolf *retired plant morphologist, educ*
Schaechter, Moselio *microbiology educator*
Schnepf, Harry Ernest *microbiologist, consul*
Schultz, Stanley George *physiologist, educat dean*
Scott, T. Gordon *chemistry and math educat writer*
Setser, Carole Sue *food scientist, educator*
Shahied, Ishak I. *science educator*
Shankar, Maya *research scientist*
Shastry, Suresh *research scientist*
Shaw, Helen Lester Anderson *nutrition educ researcher, retired dean*
Sheehan, D'eane *biology professor*
Shi, Stone D.H. *research scientist*
Shiue, Chyng-Yann *research director, educat*
Simon, Melvin I. *molecular biologist, educat*
Simpson, Frederick James *retired science administrator*
Simpson, Michael Marcial *science specialist, consultant*
Simson, Jo Anne *retired anatomy and cell biology educator*
Sjostrand, Fritiof Stig *biologist, educator*
Slayman, Carolyn Walch *geneticist, educator*
Smith, Catherine Marie *science educator*
Smith, Hamilton Othanel *molecular biologist educator*
Snow, Joel Alan *research director*
Sojka, Gary Allan *biologist, educator, acader administrator*
Sokal, Robert Reuven *biology professor, wri*
Sonntag, Bernard H. *agronomist, researcher, public information officer*
Sperelakis, Nicholas, Sr. *retired physiology a biophysics educator, researcher*
Spiegel, Melvin *retired biology professor*
Sponsler, George Curtis III *science administrator, lawyer*
Štambuk, Nikola *research scientist*
Stark, Nellie May *forester, ecologist, educat*
Steiner, Heinz *science professor, researcher*
Stickle, David Walter *microbiologist*
Stickney, Robert Roy *fisheries educator*
Sullivan, Nicholas G. *science educator*
Sussman, Andrew Louis *research scientist*

tton, Lee *biology professor*
dros, Fawzi M. *educator*
lmage, David Wilson *retired microbiologist, educator, dean*
ndler, Bernard *cell biology educator*
avarthy, Aparna *biologist, researcher*
ylor, Roy Lewis *botanist, educator*
omas, Adrian Wesley *research scientist, director, retired science educator*
omas, Teresa Ann *retired microbiologist, educator*
ompson, Herbert Alden *microbiologist, public health scientist*
omson, Keith Stewart *biologist, author*
dhunter, John Anthony *toxicologist, consultant*
osakal, Erdem *science educator*
emere-Pinaud, Liisa Anne *neuroscientist, educator*
rner, James Benjamin *science educator*
ler, Linda Jean *emergency manager, retired state legislator*
lman, Edwin Fisher *biotechnologist, consultant*
ger, Paul Walter *retired soil scientist*
in, Esther Martinez *science educator*
squez, Jo Anne *retired science educator*
vala, Domenic Anthony *medical research scientist, educator, retired military officer*
nikos, Joan *science organization director*
la-Komaroff, Lydia *molecular biologist, educator, academic administrator*
cent, James Louis *biotechnology company executive*
hniac, Ethan Tecumseh *astronomy educator*
ss, Regis Dale *agronomist, educator*
llace, Douglas C. *geneticist, educator*
n, Julia Chang *retired science educator*
rd, Thomas *research scientist*
instein, Michael P. *marine scientist, administrator*
nstein, Milton Charles *decision scientist, educator*
ller, Milton Webster *wetland ecologist, educator*
n, Yunfei *research scientist*
lcox, Hugh Edward *plant physiologist*
lliams, George Christopher *biologist, ecology and evolution educator*
mut, Ian *biologist*
son, Kenneth Geddes *physics research administrator*
te, Owen Neil *microbiologist, molecular biologist, educator*
odward, James Franklin *science educator*
tt, John Arthur *retired arboretum and botanical garden executive, horticulture educator*
ight, Kristopher *biology professor*
ight, Theodore Robert Fairbank *biologist, educator*
Jonathan T. H. *science educator*
Cecilia Q. *research scientist*
ng, Liufeng *research scientist*
rick, Randy Kregg *science educator*
ler, Kristine E. *molecular biologist, educator*
ng, Judith Anne *animal conservationist*
is, Jorge Jose *anatomy, pathology, and microbiology educator*
aya, Ian A. *biologist, consultant*
o, Xueheng *research scientist*
anov, Boris *research scientist*
, Yong *research scientist*
er, Charles S. *neuroscientist, biology professor*
slocki, Jozef John *neuroscience educator, researcher*

IENCE: MATHEMATICS AND OMPUTER SCIENCE *See also* FORMATION TECHNOLOGY

UNITED STATES

ABAMA

alla
els, Anna Wayne Brothers *retired mathematician, educator*

burn
il, Narendra Kumar *mathematics professor*

mingham
oles, William Dewey, Jr. *mathematics professor*
eeler, Ruric E. *mathematics professor*
gham, Mark Anthony *computer scientist*
odbury, Max Atkin *mathematics professor*

rence
nson, Johnny Ray *retired mathematics professor*

ntsville
s, George Wilson, II, *computer scientist, consultant*
tt, Alice Fay *mathematician, engineer*
ut, Steven Eric *systems analyst, application developer*

ntgomery
cek, John James *mathematics professor*
, Sunil R. *computer scientist, educator*
, Ki Hang *mathematician*

IZONA

ntain Hills
el, Robert Allan *statistician*

Phoenix
Doto, Irene Louise *statistician*

Prescott
Semon, Warren Lloyd *information scientist, educator*

Scottsdale
Drake, Albert Estern *retired statistics educator, farming administrator*

Sierra Vista
Sizemore, Nicky Lee *computer scientist*
Smith, Barbara Jane *computer scientist, educator*

Tempe
Kambhampati, Subbarao *computer scientist, educator*
Smith, Harvey Alvin *mathematics professor, consultant*
Yau, Stephen Sik-sang *computer and information scientist, educator*

Tucson
Moon, Bongki *computer scientist, educator*
Willoughby, Stephen Schuyler *mathematics professor*

Yuma
Hodson, Roy Goode, Jr. *retired logistician*

ARKANSAS

Arkadelphia
Nelson, Leon *retired data processing professional*

Batesville
Carius, Robert Wilhelm *mathematics professor, retired military officer*

Conway
Duan, Qiang *computer scientist, educator*

Fayetteville
Venkatesh, Viswanath *information systems professional, educator, consultant*

Fort Smith
Warner, Carol M. *mathematics professor*

Little Rock
Chiang, Chia-Chu *computer scientist, educator*

Russellville
Barker, Stephanie Anne *middle school mathematics educator*

CALIFORNIA

Bakersfield
Fiedler, Joseph Robert *mathematician, educator*

Berkeley
Agogino, Alice Merner *computer scientist, mechanical engineer, educator*
Arveson, William Barnes *mathematics professor*
Bergman, George Mark *mathematician, educator*
Berlekamp, Elwyn Ralph *mathematics professor*
Bickel, Peter John *statistician, educator*
Brewer, Eric A. *computer science educator*
Chorin, Alexandre Joel *mathematician, educator*
Christ, F. Michael *mathematics professor*
Colella, Philip *mathematician*
Culler, David Ethan *computer science educator*
Dunlop, Neil *computer scientist, department chairman*
Eisenbud, David *mathematics professor*
Gluss, Brian *mathematician, statistician, engineer, systems expert*
Goldberg, Evgueni *computer scientist*
Goldberg, Kenneth Yigael *computer engineering educator, artist*
Graham, Susan Lois *computer scientist, consultant*
Jones, Vaughan Frederick Randal *mathematician, educator*
Osserman, Robert *mathematician, educator, writer*
Patterson, David Andrew *computer scientist, educator, consultant*
Schoenfeld, Alan Henry *mathematics education professor, researcher*
Simon, Horst D. *computer scientist*
Slaman, Theodore A. *mathematics professor*
Smith, Alan Jay *computer science educator, consultant*
Veklerov, Eugene *mathematician, computer scientist*
Voiculescu, Dan Virgil *mathematics professor*
Vojta, Paul Alan *mathematics professor*
Wagner, David *computer scientist, educator*
Wolf, Joseph Albert *mathematician, educator*
Yu, Bin *statistician, educator*
Zelmanowitz, Julius Martin *mathematics professor, academic administrator*

Brea
Painchaud, Phillip Andre *metrologist*

Carlsbad
Halberg, Charles John August, Jr. *mathematics professor*

Castroville
Guglielmo, Eugene Joseph *computer scientist*

Claremont
Coleman, Courtney Stafford *mathematician, educator*
Henriksen, Melvin *mathematician, educator*
Myhre, Janet *mathematician, educator*
Pippenger, Nicholas John *mathematician, researcher, computer scientist, educator*

Davis
Fannjiang, Albert *mathematician, educator*
Tracy, Craig Arnold *mathematics educator*

Elk Grove
McDavid, Douglas Warren *executive research consultant*

Fairfield
Spake, Reuben Michael *mathematics professor, researcher*

Gilroy
McCarty, Robert Clarke *mathematician*

Glendale
Kay, Alan C. *computer scientist, nonprofit organization executive*

Granada Hills
Shoemaker, Harold Lloyd *information scientist*

Hayward
Duncan, Doris Gottschalk *information systems educator*
Sabharwal, Ranjit Singh *mathematician*

Huntington Beach
McKay, David E. *mathematics professor*
Sward, Andrea Jeanne *information and computer scientist, musician*

Irvine
Barsamian, Harut *computer scientist, consultant*
Finkelstein, Mark *mathematician, educator*
Hoffman, Donald David *cognitive and computer science educator*
Jitomirskaya, Svetlana *mathematics professor*
Li, Peter Wai-Kwong *mathematics professor*
Saari, Donald Gene *mathematician, department chairman, economist*
Wan, Frederic Yui-Ming *mathematician, educator*
Yazdi, Ahmad *computer scientist, researcher*

La Jolla
Adams, Marc Anthony *medical statistician, researcher*
Halkin, Hubert *mathematics professor, researcher*
Kehler, Andrew S. *computer scientist, educator*
Linshaw, Andrew Ross *mathematician*
Martin, James John, Jr. *systems analyst, retired research and development company executive*
Rajasekar, Arcot *computer scientist*
Stark, Harold Mead *mathematics educator*
Terras, Audrey Anne *mathematics professor*
Tsybakov, Boris Solomon *information theory and communication networks researcher, educator*
Wallach, Nolan R. *mathematician, consultant*
Wulbert, Daniel Eliot *mathematician, educator*

Long Beach
Moon, Hojin *mathematical statistician, educator*

Los Angeles
Adleman, Leonard M. *computer scientist, educator*
Bekey, George Albert *computer scientist, educator*
Carleson, Lennart A.E. (Lennart Axel Edvard Carleson) *mathematics professor*
Chen, Tony F. *mathematics professor, dean*
Cong, Jason Jingsheng *computer scientist, educator, consultant, researcher*
Dabrowska, Dorota Maria *statistician, educator*
Delaney, Matthew Sylvester *mathematics professor, academic administrator*
Golomb, Solomon Wolf *mathematician, electrical engineer, director, educator*
Gordon, Basil *retired mathematics professor*
Holt, James Franklin *retired numerical analyst, scientific programmer analyst*
Osher, Stanley Joel *mathematician, researcher*
Pearl, Judea *computer scientist, educator*
Port, Sidney Charles *mathematician, educator*
Reinman, Glenn D. *computer scientist, educator*
Roberts, Paul Harry *mathematics professor*
Tao, Terence Chi-Shen *mathematics professor*
Waterman, Michael Spencer *mathematics and biology professor*

Marina Del Rey
Neuman, Clifford *computer scientist, educator*
Swartout, William R. *mathematician, educator, director*

Menlo Park
Bourne, Charles Percy *information scientist, educator*
Neumann, Peter Gabriel *computer scientist*
Sutherland, Ivan E. *computer scientist*

Monterey
Denning, Peter James *computer scientist, engineer*
Neta, Beny *mathematics educator, researcher*

Moss Landing
Lange, Lester Henry *mathematics professor*

Mountain View
Garg, Ashutosh *computer scientist, researcher*

Newport Beach
Wozniak, Steve (Stephen Gary Wozniak) *computer scientist, philanthropist*

Orange
Smith, John LeRoy *mathematician, educator*

Palo Alto
Jacobson, Van *computer scientist, researcher*
Ranganathan, Parthasarathy *computer scientist*

Pasadena
Candes, Emmanuel Jean *mathematics professor*
Holzmann, Gerard Johan *computer science researcher*
Hou, Thomas Yizhao *mathematician*
Keller, Herbert Bishop *mathematics professor*
Knowles, James Kenyon *applied mathematician, educator*

Pearblossom
Goldman, Gary Steven *computer scientist, consultant*

Pomona
Agvanian, Youri *mathematician, educator, physicist*

Portola Valley
Kuo, Franklin F. *computer scientist, electrical engineer*

Rancho Cordova
Mesa, Reinaldo Humberto *information scientist, educator*

Rancho Santa Margarita
Berta, Melissa Rose *mathematics professor*

Redwood City
Mockapetris, Paul V. *computer scientist, information technology executive*

Redwood Valley
Speed, Cynthia Agnes *retired mathematics professor*

Riverside
Ratliff, Louis Jackson, Jr. *mathematics professor*
Shapiro, Victor Lenard *mathematics professor*

Roseville
Reichmann, Péter Iván *mathematics professor*

Sacramento
Crawford, Robert Lawrence *mathematics professor*
Orey, Daniel Clark *mathematics professor*

San Diego
Burgin, George Hans *computer scientist, educator*
Hales, Alfred Washington *mathematics professor, consultant*
Kuniyuki, Ken Toshio *mathematics professor*
Van Tassel, Lowell Thomas *mathematics professor*

San Francisco
Bell, C. Gordon *computer architect and engineer, entrepreneur, researcher*
Goldberg, Adele J. *computer scientist*
Kao, John Sterling *mathematician, educator*
Low, Arnold Kinman *systems executive*

San Jose
Newell, Martin Edward *computer scientist*
Selinger, Patricia Griffiths *computer science professional*
Togasaki, Shinobu *computer scientist*
Zhang, Xinwen *computer scientist, researcher*

San Marino
Lashley, Virginia Stephenson Hughes *retired computer science educator*

Santa Ana
Re Velle, Jack B(oyer) *statistician, consultant*

Santa Barbara
Johnsen, Eugene Carlyle *mathematician, educator*
Minc, Henryk *mathematics professor*
Simons, Stephen *mathematics professor, researcher*

Santa Clara
Kirk, David B. *computer scientist*
Smith, Stephen Allen *mathematician, educator*

Santa Cruz
Stormes, John Max *systems analyst*
Widom, Harold *mathematician, educator*

Santa Monica
Griffith, Arnold Koons *computer consultant*
Sun, Li *statistician*

Stanford
Cottle, Richard Warren *retired operations research educator*
Efron, Bradley *statistician, educator*
Eliashberg, Yakov *mathematician, educator*
Hanrahan, Patrick M. *computer scientist*
Karlin, Samuel *mathematics professor, researcher*
Keller, Joseph Bishop *mathematician, educator*
Knuth, Donald Ervin *computer sciences educator*
Koller, Daphne *computer scientist*
Lai, Tze Leung *mathematician, educator*
Lambers, James Vincent *mathematician, researcher, petroleum engineer*
McCarthy, John *computer scientist, educator*
Penn, Lee *information scientist, consultant, journalist*
Rubin, Karl Cooper *mathematics educator*
Schoen, Richard Melvin *mathematics professor, researcher*
Thrun, Sebastian Burkhard *computer science educator, researcher*
Ullman, Jeffrey David *computer scientist, educator*
Whittemore, Alice *biostatistician*
Widom, Jennifer *computer science and electrical engineering educator*

Sunnyvale
Bowman, Eugene William *retired mathematics professor*

Thousand Oaks
El Fattah, Yousri M. *computer scientist*
Sladek, Lyle Virgil *mathematician, educator*

Torrance
Kerstiens, Gene J. *mathemagenician, consultant*

Westlake Village
Munson, John Backus *computer scientist, retired data processing executive*

Yucaipa
Crise, Robert D., Jr. *mathematics professor*

COLORADO

Boulder
Beylkin, Gregory *mathematician*
Clark, Gary M. *statistician*
Ellis, Homer Godsey *mathematics professor, physicist, researcher*
Glover, Fred William *information scientist, director, educator*
Mycielski, Jan *retired mathematics professor*

Colorado Springs
Fagin, Barry Steven *computer science educator, writer*
Simmons, George Finlay *retired mathematics professor*
Son, Seung Hwan *mathematician, researcher*

Denver
Cherowitzo, William Edward *mathematics professor*
Kuppireddi, Sireesh *computer scientist*
Payne, Stanley E. *mathematics professor*

Fort Collins
Mielke, Paul William, Jr. *statistician, consultant*

Greeley
Miller, Nathaniel Gregory *mathematics professor*

Longmont
Wohler, Wayne L. *information scientist*

Silverthorne
Riley, Mary Jane *computer scientist*

CONNECTICUT

Ansonia
Kerpa, Gary J. *computer science consultant*

Cheshire
Tufte, Edward Rolf *statistician, educator*

Fairfield
Eigel, Edwin George, Jr. *mathematics professor, retired university president*

Groton
Swindell, Archie Calhoun, Jr. *statistician, consultant*

Middletown
Linton, Fred Ernest Julius *mathematics professor, publishing executive*

New Britain
McGowan, Jeffrey *mathematician, educator*
O'Connell, Brian Michael *computer scientist, educator*

New Haven
Coifman, Ronald R. *mathematician, educator*
Feigenbaum, Joan *computer scientist, mathematician*
Fischer, Michael John *computer science educator*
Howe, Roger Evans *mathematician, educator*
Kaplan, Edward H. *operations research specialist*
Margulis, Gregory A. *mathematics and science professor, researcher*
Massey, William S. *mathematician, educator*
Mostow, George Daniel *mathematics professor*
Silberschatz, Abraham (Avi Silberschatz) *computer scientist, educator, researcher*
Zuckerman, Gregg J. *mathematics professor*

Old Lyme
Comfort, William Wistar *mathematics professor*

Ridgefield
Burridge, Robert *former mathematics educator, scientific advisor*

Stamford
Frank, Laura Jean *computer scientist*

Storrs Mansfield
Rajasekaran, Sanguthevar *computer science educator*

West Hartford
Gerjuoy, Herbert George *information scientist, educator, psychologist, consultant, poet*

West Haven
Kyriakides, Tassos Constantino *biostatistician*

Wilton
Brown, James Thompson, Jr. *operations research specialist, information scientist*

DELAWARE

Felton
Vansant, Franklin Steven *mathematician, educator*

Newark
Colton, David Lem *mathematician, educator*
Luke, David Russell *mathematician, educator*

DISTRICT OF COLUMBIA

Washington
Feil, Michael Bruce *statistician*
Freeman, Peter A. *dean*
Frieder, Gideon *computer scientist, educator*
Gray, Mary Wheat *statistician, lawyer*
Hedges, Harry George *retired computer scientist*
Kahlow, Barbara Fenvessy *statistician*
Kotz, Samuel *statistician, educator, translator, editor*
Lutterodt, Clement H. *mathematician, educator*
Perry, Steven Wayne *statistician*
Raphael, Louise Arakelian *mathematician, educator*
Redd, Kenneth Eric *statistician, researcher*
Ryan, David Alan *systems analyst*
Saworotnow, Parfeny Pavlovich *mathematician, educator*
Shaw, William Frederick *statistician*

FLORIDA

Boynton Beach
Warga, Jack *mathematician, educator*
Waterman, Daniel *mathematician, educator*

Clewiston
Griffith, Lonzo, Jr. *technology specialist, educator, farmer*

Coral Gables
Shyu, Mei-Ling *information scientist, educator*

Daytona Beach
Seenith, Sivasundaram *mathematician, educator*

Delray Beach
Hegstrom, William Jean *retired mathematics professor*

Dunedin
Klingbiel, Paul Herman *retired information scientist*

Fort Lauderdale
Albatineh, Ahmed Najeeb *statistician, researcher*
Littman, Marlyn Kemper *information scientist, educator*
Sun, Junping *computer science professor*

Gainesville
Agresti, Alan *statistics educator*
Dinculeanu, Nicolae *mathematician, educator*
Vaidyanathan, Balachandran *operations research specialist, industrial engineer*
Weinrich, Brian Erwin *mathematician, computer scientist*

Key West
Kalb, Chester H. *mathematics professor*

Melbourne
Lakshmikantham, Vangipuram *mathematics professor*

Miami
Clarke, Peter John *computer scientist, educator, educational consultant*
Dimitriou, Dolores Ennis *computer consultant*
España, Lourdes Maria *mathematics professor*
Navlakha, Jainendra *computer scientist, educator, dean*

Milton
McKinney, George Harris, Jr. *training systems analyst*

Orlando
Deo, Narsingh *computer scientist, educator*
Marinescu, Dan Cristian *computer sciences educator, consultant*
Nashed, M. Zuhair *mathematics professor, editor*
Varvak, Mark *mathematician, researcher*
Walker, Roger Craig *mathematics professor*

Palm Harbor
Williams, Thomas Arthur *biomedical computing consultant, psychiatrist*

Patrick Afb
Kohn, Paul Franklin *mathematician*

Pensacola
Ford, Kenneth M. *computer scientist, educator*

Riviera Beach
Berliner, Hans Jack *retired computer scientist*

Saint Augustine
Jurgens, Julie Graham *mathematics professor*

Saint Petersburg
White, June Miller *mathematics professor, educational consultant*

Sarasota
Jacobson, Melvin Joseph *mathematician, educator*

Tallahassee
Gilmer, Robert *mathematics professor*
Kercheval, Alec Norton *mathematician*
Navon, Ionel Michael *mathematics professor*
Nichols, Eugene Douglas *mathematics professor*

Tampa
El-Hadidy, Bahaa *information scientist, educator, consultant*
Murphy, Robin Roberson *computer scientist, robotics engineer*

GEORGIA

Atlanta
Ames, William Francis *mathematician, educator*
Bleicher, Michael Nathaniel *mathematics professor*
Goodman, Seymour Evan *computer science and international studies educator, researcher, consultant*
Huo, Xiaoming *mathematician, educator*
King, K(imberly) N(elson) *computer science educator*
Lim, Sung Kyu *computer scientist, educator*
Oliker, Vladimir *mathematician, educator*
Pan, Yi *computer science educator*
Pu, Calton *computer scientist*
Thompson, Shirley Williams *mathematics professor*
Tighiouart, Mourad *statistician, researcher*
Wilding, Diane *computer scientist, consultant*
Wu, De Ting *mathematics professor, researcher, writer*
Zadeh, Javad Hamadani *mathematics professor*

Jonesboro
Harris, Queen Wiggs *mathematician, educator*

Lovejoy
Onukwuli, Francis Osita *computer scientist, secondary school educator, mathematician*

Statesboro
Kersey, Scott N. *mathematician, educator*

HAWAII

Honolulu
Chyba, Monique *mathematics professor*
Hac, Anna Barbara *computer scientist, educator*
Swanson, Richard William *retired statistician*

Paia
Loomis, James Cook *mathematician, cyberneticist, writer, educator, navigator*

IDAHO

Boise
Chenoweth, Tim *information scientist, educator*

Moscow
Bobisud, Larry Eugene *mathematics professor*
Goetschel, Roy Hartzell, Jr. *mathematician, researcher*

ILLINOIS

Argonne
Lindert, Eric Alton *operations research specialist, small business owner*

Bartlett
Plaskacz, Edward John *computer scientist, engineer, mathematics professor*

Carbondale
Asoh, Derek Ajesam *information scientist, educator*
Headrick, Todd Christopher *mathematical statistician, educator*
Neuman, Edward George *mathematician, educator*

Champaign
Turquette, Atwell Rufus *logician*

Charleston
McBride, Jonica Helene *mathematics professor*

Chicago
Ash, J. Marshall *mathematician, educator*
Bona, Jerry Lloyd *mathematician, educator*
Dardai, Shahid Moinuddin *computer science educator*
Erber, Thomas *mathematics and physics professor*
Foster, Ian Tremere *computer scientist*
Hanson, Floyd Bliss *mathematician*
Hwang, Yujong *information scientist, educator*
Kirkpatrick, Anne Saunders *systems analyst*
Lawler, Gregory Francis *mathematics professor*
Ong, Michael King *mathematician, educator, bank executive*
Smale, Stephen *mathematics professor*
Stigler, Stephen Mack *statistician, educator*
Tangora, Martin Charles *mathematician, educator*
Tartakoff, David Stephen *mathematics professor, researcher*
Thisted, Ronald Aaron *statistician, educator, consultant*
Usiskin, Zalman Philip *mathematics educator*
Wirszup, Izaak *mathematician, educator*

Deerfield
Bialek, Paul Richard *mathematics professor*

Elmhurst
MacInnes, Sally Ackerman *computer education educator*

Evanston
Davis, Stephen Howard *applied mathematics professor*
Devinatz, Allen *retired mathematician, educat*
Ionescu Tulcea, Cassius *research mathematici educator*
Jerome, Joseph Walter *mathematics professor*
Manin, Yuri Ivanovich *mathematician*
Matkowsky, Bernard Judah *mathematician, educator*
Olmstead, William Edward *mathematics professor*
Tanner, Martin Abba *statistician, educator*
Zelinsky, Daniel *mathematics professor*

Glen Ellyn
Cook, Joann Catherine *computer professor*
Nunamaker, Susan Sun *mathematics professor*
Rothmaler, Peter Antell *mathematician, educa*

La Grange Park
Butler, Margaret Kampschaefer *retired compu scientist*

Lemont
Anitescu, Mihai *computer scientist, mathematician*

Lisle
Townsley, Lisa Gail *mathematics professor*

Palatine
Bokhari, Naila Qureshi *mathematician, educational consultant*

Sugar Grove
Del Medico, Amy *mathematics professor*

University Park
Hakala, Reino William *mathematician, educa*

Urbana
Burkholder, Donald Lyman *mathematician, educator*
Carroll, Robert Wayne *mathematics professor*
Henson, C. Ward *mathematician, educator*
Liebman, Judith Rae Stenzel *retired operatio research specialist*
Tondeur, Philippe Maurice *mathematician, educator*

Westchester
Pavelka, Elaine Blanche *mathematics profess*

INDIANA

Bloomington
Buente, Wayne Gerald *information scientist, researcher*
Prosser, Franklin Pierce *computer scientist*
Purdom, Paul Walton, Jr. *computer scientist*
Puri, Madan Lal *mathematics professor*
Smith, David Hunt *systems analyst, educator*
Solomon, Bruce Michael *mathematician, educator*
Temam, Roger M. *mathematician, educator*

Evansville
Kimberling, Clark Hershall *mathematics professor, small business owner*

Fort Wayne
Beineke, Lowell Wayne *mathematics profess*
Stoll, Wilhelm *mathematics professor*

Greencastle
Anderson, John Robert *retired mathematics professor*

Indianapolis
Cliff, Johnnie Marie *mathematics and chemis professor*
Cowen, Carl C. *mathematics professor*
Cravens, Gary Dean *information scientist, physician*
Reid, William Hill *mathematics professor*
Taylor, Nolan J. *information systems educato*
Yovits, Marshall Clinton *information scientis educator, dean*

Kokomo
Ramos, Jamie *information scientist*

Muncie
Ali, Mir Masoom *retired statistician, educato*
Shobe, Franklin Dale *mathematician, educato*

Notre Dame
Kogge, Peter Michael *computer scientist, educator*
Sommese, Andrew John *mathematics profess*

Terre Haute
Bagert, Donald Joseph *computer scientist, educator*

Valparaiso
Mundt, Marvin Glen *retired mathematics professor*

West Lafayette
Abhyankar, Shreeram Shankar *mathematics professor*
Danielli-Garofalo, Donatella *mathematics professor*
Dasgupta, Anirban *statistician, researcher*
Wood, Terry Lee *mathematics educator*
Yu, Jiu-Kang *mathematics professor*

Westville
Serwatka, Judy Ann *computer and informati systems educator*

IOWA

Ames
Dahiya, Rajbir Singh *mathematics professor, researcher*

vid, Herbert Aron *retired statistician, educator*
ler, Wayne Arthur *statistics educator*
llis, Jerry Weldon *computer systems educator, writer*

dar Falls
ack, Joel K. *mathematics professor, academic administrator*

dar Rapids
adur, Birendra *displays research specialist*

rinnell
elberg, Arnold Melvin *mathematics professor, researcher*

wa City
ffitt, James Drake *statistician, educator*
gg, Robert Vincent, Jr. *mathematical statistician, educator*
gensen, Palle E.T. *mathematician, educator*
bertson, Timothy Joel *statistician, educator*

ANSAS

wrence
nmelberg, Charles John III *mathematics professor, researcher*
ner, David Evan *mathematician*
ik-Duncan, Bozenna Janina *mathematics professor, researcher*
benz, James Philip Guenther *computer network scientist*

erland Park
penter, Nancy E. *mathematics professor*

tsburg
ris, James Dean *computer scientist, educator*

awnee Mission
a, Jairus Dale, Jr. *statistician*

NTUCKY

nthiana
ence, Joyce Fritz *mathematics professor*

zard
y, Cynthia Strong *mathematics professor*
wart, Sharon Rose *mathematics professor*

xington
rnigo, Richard John, Jr. *statistician, educator*
stert, Paul Stallings *retired mathematician*

uisville
raoui, Olfa *computer scientist, educator, ectrical engineer*

UISIANA

ton Rouge
ey, James Grieve *mathematics professor*
rtararo, Philip, Jr. *mathematics professor*

y Prong
ain, Paul King *systems analyst*

ayette
, Judith Sharp *mathematics professor, onsultant*
ro, Michael Wayne *information scientist, ducator*

v Orleans
g, DaGang *mathematician, educator*

ston
hran, James J. *mathematics professor, searcher*
, Sumeet *computer scientist, educator*

INE

ermo
erson, Alfred Oliver *mathematician, onsultant*

RYLAND

amstown
all, Charles Stanley *computer scientist, ducator*

napolis
vford, Carol Gloria *mathematician, educator*

ton
h, Kent Ashton *information scientist, nsultant*

timore
am, Hossein *operations research analyst*
dman, John Michael *mathematician, ducator*
udhary, Mohammad Ashraf *biostatistician, searcher*
udhury, Dipa *mathematician, educator*
an, Donald *mathematics professor*
e, Doris Keefe *retired computer science ducator*
nberg, Edwin Harold *systems analyst*
n, Aviel David *computer science educator, riter*
man, Bernard *mathematician, educator*
man, John Charles *mathematician, educator*

hesda
hman, Jack *statistical consultant*
y, Carolyn Bittner *information scientist*

Weiss, George Herbert *mathematician, consultant*
Zheng, Gang *mathematician, statistician, researcher*

Bowie
Buell, Duncan Alan *computer scientist*

College Park
Adams, Jeffrey *mathematics professor*
Antman, Stuart Sheldon *mathematician, educator*
Johnson, Raymond Lewis *mathematician*
Lucas, Henry Cameron, Jr. *information scientist, educator, writer*
Minker, Jack *computer scientist, educator*
Stewart, Gilbert Wright *computer science educator*

Columbia
Gregorie, Corazon Arzalem *operations research specialist*
Tietz, Dietmar Juergen *website engineer, scientist*
Zeng, Dongsong *computer scientist*

Edgewater
Cotter, George R. *retired information scientist*

Fort George G Meade
Schmitt, Robert Lee *computer scientist*

Frederick
McDowell, Eugene Charles *systems analyst, bioethicist*

Gaithersburg
Carasso, Alfred Sam *mathematician*
Rosenblatt, Joan Raup *mathematical statistician*

Hunt Valley
Igusa, Jun-Ichi *mathematician, educator*

Hyattsville
Gonzalez, Joe Fred, Jr. *mathematical statistician, educator*

Kensington
Chiazze, Leonard, Jr. *biostatistician, epidemiologist, educator*

Laurel
Kroshl, William Mark *operations research specialist*
Teeters, Joseph Lee *mathematician, consultant*

Madison
Hoffman, Kenneth Myron *mathematician, educator*

Mount Airy
Spohn, William Gideon, Jr. *mathematician, retired musician*

Potomac
Crowson, Henry Lawrence *mathematician, educator*
Medin, Julia Adele *mathematics professor, researcher*
Navarro, Joseph Anthony *retired statistician, consultant*

Rockville
Levin, Alexander B. *mathematics professor*
Massie, Tammy Jeanne Parliment *statistician*
Nelson, Kevin *statistician*

Silver Spring
Ciment, Melvyn *mathematician*
Sammet, Jean E. *computer scientist*
Sirken, Monroe Gilbert *statistician*
Weiss, Leonard *mathematician, consultant*

Simpsonville
Bluher, Gregory *computer scientist, mathematician*

Towson
Coughlin, James Patrick *mathematician, educator*
Feng, Jinjuan *information scientist, educator*

MASSACHUSETTS

Acton
Smith, Raoul Normand *computer science educator*

Amherst
Cox, David Archibald *mathematics professor*

Belmont
Magidson, Jay *statistician*
Reynolds, William Francis *mathematics professor*

Beverly
Grace, Kathleen M *computer scientist, educator, web site designer*

Boston
Clinger, William Douglas *computer scientist, educator*
D'Agostino, Ralph Benedict *mathematician, statistician, educator, consultant*
Devaney, Robert L. *mathematician, educator*
Falb, Peter Lawrence *mathematician, educator, investment company executive*
Gilmore, Maurice Eugene *mathematics professor*
Hu, Chengcheng *biostatistician, medical researcher*
Hua, Nian Grace *mathematician, researcher*
Noel, Alfred *mathematics professor*
Schoenfeld, David Alan *statistician, educator*
Shtern, Victor *computer scientist, educator*
Weyman, Jerzy Maria *mathematics professor*
Yoshida, Hiroyuki *mathematician, computer scientist, educator, medical science educator*

Cambridge
Adelson, Edward H. *vision science educator*
Bartee, Thomas Creson *computer scientist, educator*
Bertsimas, Dimitris J. *mathematician, researcher, educator*
Blanchet, Jose H. *statistics educator, researcher*
Ciubotaru, Dan *mathematics professor*
Demaine, Erik D. *computer scientist, educator*
Dennis, Jack Bonnell *computer scientist, educator*
Dudley, Richard Mansfield *mathematician, educator*
Goldwasser, Shafrira *computer scientist*
Greenspan, Harvey Philip *applied mathematician, educator*
Gross, Benedict H. *mathematician*
Grosz, Barbara Jean *computer science educator*
Helgason, Sigurdur *mathematician, educator*
Jaffe, Arthur Michael *mathematician, physicist, educator*
Jo, Sungho *computer scientist, researcher*
Kac, Victor G. *mathematician, educator*
Lauga, Eric *physical mathematician, educator*
Leighton, Frank T. *mathematics professor*
Light, Richard Jay *statistician, educator*
Lynch, Nancy Ann *computer scientist, educator*
Mazur, Barry Charles *mathematician, educator*
McMullen, Curtis T. *mathematics professor*
Meinert, Edward *computer scientist, management consultant*
Micali, Silvio *information scientist, educator*
Moses, Joel *computer scientist, educator*
Mrowka, Tomasz *mathematics professor*
Oettinger, Anthony Gervin *mathematician, educator*
Rabin, Michael Oser *computer scientist, educator*
Roberts, Nancy *computer scientist, educator*
Rubin, Donald Bruce *statistician, educator, research and development company executive*
Singer, Isadore Manuel *mathematician, educator*
Stanley, Richard P. *mathematics professor*
Strang, Gilbert *mathematics professor*
Strang, William Gilbert *mathematician, educator*
Stroock, Daniel Wyler *mathematician, educator*
Szolovits, Peter *computer scientist*
Taylor, Richard *mathematics professor*
Toomre, Alar *applied mathematician, theoretical astronomer*
Valiant, Leslie Gabriel *computer scientist, educator*
Vogan, David A., Jr. *mathematics professor*
Welsch, Roy Elmer *statistician, educator*
Wirasinha, Hemamali Anushka *computer scientist, researcher*
Wren, Christopher R. *computer scientist, researcher*
Yau, Shing-Tung *mathematics professor*

Hanscom Afb
Carney, David John *computer scientist, music theorist*

Lexington
Schafer, Alice Turner *retired mathematics professor*

Lincoln
LeGates, John Crews Boulton *information scientist*

Millbury
Yonda, Alfred William *mathematician*

Newton Center
Williamson, Susan *retired mathematician, educator*

North Andover
Kurzweil, Raymond C. *computer scientist, entrepreneur*

Northampton
Robinson, John Alan *information scientist, educator*

Springfield
Murphy, Eileen Bridget *retired mathematics and computer science professor*

Waltham
Brown, Edgar Henry, Jr. *mathematician, educator*
Lian, Bong H. *mathematics professor, department chairman*
Simeonov, Simeon *computer scientist*

Westborough
Schrager, Mindy Rae *operations research specialist*

Westfield
Buckmore, Alvah Clarence, Jr. *computer scientist, ballistician*

Westport Point
Fanning, William Henry, Jr. *computer specialist*

Williamstown
Hill, Victor Ernst, IV, *retired mathematics professor, musician*
Morgan, Frank *mathematics professor*

Worcester
Malone, Joseph James *mathematics professor, researcher*
Varpahovsky, Andrey *computer scientist, educator*
Woolhouse, Maureen Ann *mathematics professor*

MICHIGAN

Adrian
Lamprecht, Elizabeth Ann *mathematics professor*

Ann Arbor
Anupindi, Ravi *operations research specialist, educator*
Bass, Hyman *mathematician, educator*
Beutler, Frederick Joseph *information scientist*
Conway, Lynn *computer scientist, electrical engineer, educator*
Griess, Robert L., Jr. *mathematics professor*
Hill, Bruce Marvin *statistician, educator*
Lazarsfeld, Robert Kendall *mathematician, educator*
Smith, Karen E. *mathematician, educator*
Stembridge, John Reese *mathematics professor*

Bloomfield Hills
Greenwood, Frank *information scientist, educator*

Dearborn
Brown, James Ward *mathematician, educator, author*

Detroit
Dwyer, John M. *mathematician, statistician, computer scientist*
Schreiber, Bertram Manuel *mathematics professor*
Shi, Weisong *computer scientist, educator*

East Lansing
Stapleton, James Hall *retired statistician, educator*

Farmington
Ginsberg, Myron *computer scientist*

Grand Rapids
Becker, Robert Joseph *database consultant, application developer, educator, computer science specialist*

Kalamazoo
Paul, Annegret *mathematics professor*

Manistique
Jeffcott, Janet Bruhn *statistician, consultant*

Novi
Chow, Chi-Ming *retired mathematics professor*

Plymouth
Lou, Zheng (David) *technical specialist*

Southfield
Miller, Nancy Ellen *computer scientist, consultant*

Ypsilanti
Farah, Badie Naiem *computer information systems educator, consultant*

MINNESOTA

Duluth
Gallian, Joseph Anthony *mathematics professor*

Golden Valley
Savitt, Steven Lee *computer scientist*

Minneapolis
Arnold, Douglas Norman *mathematician*
Bingham, Christopher *statistics educator*
Brasket, Curt Justin *systems analyst*
Lipovetsky, Stan(islav) *statistician, mathematician*
Markus, Lawrence *retired mathematics professor*
Petzold, Linda Ruth *computer scientist, educator, researcher*
Santosa, Fadil *mathematics professor*
Serrin, James Burton *mathematics professor*

Moorhead
Heuer, Gerald Arthur *mathematician, educator*

Northfield
Appleyard, David Frank *retired mathematics professor*
Schuster, Seymour *mathematician, educator*
Steen, Lynn Arthur *mathematician, educator*

Saint Paul
Shvartsman, Mikhail Meyer *mathematics professor*

Shakopee
Eliason, Arlene F. *mathematician, educator*

MISSISSIPPI

Mississippi State
Knudson, Kevin Patrick *mathematics professor*

Starkville
Oppenheimer, Bonnie Lou *mathematics professor*

MISSOURI

Bolivar
Harris, Beverly Howard *retired mathematics professor, genealogist*

Canton
Cochell, Gary G. *mathematician, educator*

Columbia
Beem, John Kelly *retired mathematician, educator*
Flournoy, Nancy *statistician, educator*
Li, Y. Charles *mathematician, educator*
Shang, Yi *computer scientist, educator*
Srinivasan, Hema *mathematics professor, researcher*

Hillsboro
Stinson, Stanley Thomas *project manager*

Joplin
Hand, Linda Marie *mathematics professor*

Kansas City
Delaware, Richard Raymond *mathematician, educator*

Reeds Spring
Woods, Dale *retired mathematics professor*

Rolla
Grimm, Louis John *mathematician, educator*
Ingram, William Thomas III *mathematics professor*
Zobrist, George Winston *computer scientist, educator*

Saint Louis
Baernstein, Albert, II, *mathematician, educator*
Boothby, William Munger *retired mathematics professor*
Corich, Evelyn Frances *mathematics professor*
Epner, Steven Arthur *computer consultant*
Mitrophanov, Alexander Yuryevich *mathematician, researcher*
Turner, Jonathan Shields *computer science educator, researcher*
Wilson, Edward Nathan *mathematician, educator*

Union
Boehmer, Ann *mathematics professor*

Warrensburg
Yousef, Mahmoud *mathematics professor, computer scientist, educator*

Winona
Marshall, Lucille Ruth *retired mathematics professor*

MONTANA

Billings
Fried, Michael D. *mathematician, educator*

Missoula
Tonev, Thomas (Toma) V. *mathematics professor*

NEBRASKA

Lincoln
McCutcheon, Allan Lee *statistics educator*

NEVADA

Ely
Daniels, Frank Emmett *mathematician, educator*

Las Vegas
Marcella, Joseph *information scientist*
Snyder, John Henry *computer science educator, consultant*

Reno
Kleinfeld, Erwin *mathematician, educator*
Zaliapin, Ilya *statistician*

Yerington
Price, Thomas Munro *computer consultant*

NEW HAMPSHIRE

Hanover
Kurtz, Thomas Eugene *retired mathematics professor*
Lamperti, John Williams *mathematician, educator*
McIlroy, M. Douglas *computer scientist, educator*
Rockmore, Daniel Nahum *mathematician*

Keene
Pelletier, John B., Jr. *mathematics professor, consultant*

Manchester
Ingraham, Alec *mathematics professor*

Plymouth
Vinogradova, Natalya *mathematician, educator*

NEW JERSEY

Cherry Hill
Levin, Joshua Zev *computer scientist, consultant, transportation engineer*

Cranford
Petryshyn, Wolodymyr V. *retired mathematician*

Cresskill
Jurasek, John Paul *mathematics professor, counselor*

Englewood
Minkoff, John *mathematician, educator*

Highlands
Dann, Emily *mathematics educator*

Hightstown
Hunter, John Stuart *statistician, consultant*

Hoboken
Malek, Manu *information scientist, educator*
Zabarankin, Michael *operations research specialist, educator*

Lakewood
Houle, Joseph E. *mathematics professor*

Matawan
Mayo, Douglas Blake *computer scientist, application developer*
Rivera-Dominguez, Alberto *mathematician, educator, mechanical engineer*

Montclair
Jones, Michael A. *mathematics professor*

Neshanic Station
Muckenhoupt, Benjamin *retired mathematics professor*

New Brunswick
Kahn, Jeffry *mathematics professor*
Kulikowski, Casimir Alexander *computer scientist, engineer, educator*
Scanlon, Jane Cronin *mathematics professor*

Newark
Miura, Robert Mitsuru *mathematician, researcher, educator*
Verkhovsky, Boris *computer scientist, educator*

Ocean City
Culbertson, Jane Young *statistician*

Piscataway
Iwaniec, Henryk *mathematics professor*
Li, Yanyan *mathematician, educator*
Wu, Jian *operations research specialist*
Zhen, Li *systems analyst, researcher*

Princeton
Aizenman, Michael *mathematics and physics professor, researcher*
Bhargava, Manjul *mathematics professor, researcher*
Bombieri, Enrico *mathematician, educator*
Chang, Sun-Yung Alice *mathematics professor*
Deligne, Pierre René *mathematician*
Fefferman, Charles Louis *mathematics professor*
Felton, Edward William *computer scientist, educator*
Gunning, Robert Clifford *mathematician, educator*
Haberman, Shelby Joel *statistician, educator*
Katz, Nicholas M. *mathematician*
Klainerman, Sergiu *mathematics professor*
Kobayashi, Hisashi *computer scientist, dean*
Kollár, János *mathematics professor*
Langlands, Robert Phelan *mathematician, educator*
Lee, Ruby Bei-Loh *multimedia and computer systems architect*
Levin, Simon Asher *mathematician, ecologist, educator*
MacPherson, Robert Duncan *mathematician, educator*
Mirzakhani, Maryam *mathematician*
Nash, John Forbes, Jr. *mathematician, researcher*
Okounkov, Andrei *mathematics professor*
Roetteler, Martin Henri *computer scientist, researcher*
Sarnek, Peter Clive *mathematics professor*
Sinai, Yakov G. *theoretical mathematician, educator*
Singer, Burton Herbert *statistics educator*
Stein, Elias M. *mathematician, educator*
Tarjan, Robert Endre *computer scientist, educator*
Vapnik, Vladimir N. *mathematician, researcher, educator*
Voevodsky, Vladimir *mathematician*
Wiles, Andrew J. *mathematician, educator*

Rivervale
Posamentier, Alfred Steven *mathematics professor, dean*

Teaneck
Chen, Zong *computer scientist, educator*
Zwass, Vladimir *computer science and information systems educator*

Trenton
Deltuvia, John Joseph, Jr. *systems analyst*

Willingboro
Ingerman, Peter Zilahy *systems analyst, consultant*

Yardville
Zweig, Steven Frederick *statistician*

NEW MEXICO

Albuquerque
Bell, Stoughton *computer scientist, mathematician, educator*
Iman, Ronald L. *statistician, consultant*

Las Cruces
Muller, David Eugene *retired mathematics professor, computer scientist, educator*
Salamanca-Riba, Susana Alicia *mathematics professor*

Las Vegas
Mendez, Celestino Galo *mathematics professor, dean*

Los Alamos
Kang, Qinjun *mathematician*
Lipnikov, Konstantin *mathematician*

Santa Fe
Kellner, Richard George *mathematician, computer scientist*

Socorro
Wang, Bixiang *mathematician*

NEW YORK

Albany
Rosenkrantz, Daniel J. *computer science educator*

Alfred
Smith, Mark Arthur *information scientist, educator*

Bayside
Chugh, Om Parkash *mathematics professor, researcher, forensics specialist*

Binghamton
Arcones, Miguel A. *mathematics professor*
Hilton, Peter John *mathematician, educator*

Bronx
Koranyi, Adam *mathematics professor*
Prabhu, Vrunda P. *mathematics professor*
Rose, Israel Harold *mathematics professor*
Seltzer, William *statistician, social science administrator*

Brooklyn
Pennisten, John William *computer scientist, actuary, linguist*
Sakhnovich, Lev Aronovich *mathematics educator, researcher*
Weill, Georges Gustave *mathematics professor*

Buffalo
Coburn, Lewis Alan *mathematics professor*
Hauptman, Herbert Aaron *mathematician, educator, researcher*
Seitz, Mary Lee *mathematics professor*
Shapiro, Stuart Charles *computer scientist, educator*
Vishwanath, Arun *information scientist, educator*
Wiesenberg, Russel John *statistician*
Zhong, Sheng *computer scientist*

Clinton
Redfield, Robert Horace *mathematician, educator*

Endicott
Schreiber, Robert Walter *computer scientist*

Farmingdale
Winn, John Arthur, Jr. *mathematics educator*

Flushing
Brody, Roberta *information science educator*
Mendelson, Elliott *mathematician, educator*

Great Neck
Seckler, Bernard David *retired mathematics professor, translator*

Hamilton
Tucker, Thomas William *mathematics professor*

Hawthorne
Mihaila, George Andrei *computer scientist, researcher*
Ward, Christopher *computer scientist, researcher*

Ithaca
Barbasch, Dan Mihai *mathematics professor*
Billera, Louis J(oseph) *mathematics professor*
Bramble, James Henry *mathematician, educator*
Durrett, Richard T. *mathematics professor*
Earle, Clifford John, Jr. *mathematician*
Gross, Leonard *mathematics professor*
Hartmanis, Juris *computer scientist, educator*
Hopcroft, John Edward *computer scientist, educator*
James, Doug L. *computer scientist, educator*
Kassabov, Martin *mathematics professor*
Kleinberg, Jon M. *computer scientist, educator*
Nerode, Anil *mathematician, educator*
Pantano, Alessandra *mathematics professor*
Shore, Richard Arnold *mathematics professor*
Strogatz, Steven H. *mathematics professor*
Tardos, Eva *computer scientist, educator*
Trotter, Leslie Earl *operations research specialist, educator*
Urazghildiiev, Ildar R. *mathematician*

Jackson Heights
Sohmer, Bernard *mathematics professor, administrator*

Kenmore
Kenny, John Edward *computer analyst*

New York
Aschoff, Lawrence Michael (Mick Aschoff) *computer information scientist*
Barquero, Pedro B. *mathematician, researcher*
Bellovin, Steven M. *computer science educator*
Berger, Marsha J. *computer scientist, educator*
Chichilnisky, Graciela *mathematician, economist, educator, writer*
Christ, Lily Esther Shih *mathematics professor*
Chudnovsky, Maria *mathematician, educator*
Derman, Cyrus *mathematical statistician*
Edwards, Harold Mortimer *mathematics professor*
Finch, Lawrence Nelson, II, *computer scientist, consultant*
Frankel, Martin Richard *statistician, educator, consultant*
Garabedian, Paul Roesel *mathematics professor*
Greegard, Leslie F. *mathematics professor*
Greengard, Leslie F. *mathematician, educator*
Gross, Jonathan Light *computer scientist, mathematician, educator*
Gyles, Robert *mathematics professor*
Kurnow, Ernest *statistician, educator*
Lax, Peter David *mathematician, educator*
Liu, Lewis-Guodo *information scientist, educator*
McKean, Henry P. *mathematics institute administrator*
Morawetz, Cathleen Synge *mathematician*
Moyne, John Abel *computer scientist, linguist, educator*
Newman, Charles Michael *mathematician, physicist, educator*
Nirenberg, Louis *mathematician, educator*
Paik, Myunghee Cho *statistician, educator*
Pnueli, Amir *computer science educator*
Schulhoff, Karen L. *information specialist*
Schulzrinne, Henning G. *computer science educator*
Sellers, Peter Hoadley *mathematician, educatc*
Sloujitel, Jacob Ben *mathematics professor, researcher*
Sullivan, Dennis P. *mathematics professor*
Taylor, Jean Ellen *mathematics professor, researcher*
Traub, J. F. (Joseph Frederick Traub) *compute scientist, educator*
Varadhan, Srinivasa S.R. *mathematics educatc*
Weitzner, Harold *mathematics professor*
Welder, Rachael Mae *mathematician, educato*
Wright, Margaret Hagen *computer scientist, administrator*

Ozone Park
Joanidhi, Zhani *mathematician, educator*

Pittsford
Hollingsworth, Jack Waring *mathematics professor*

Rhinebeck
Scherr, Allan Lee *computer scientist, software executive*

Schaghticoke
O'Connor, Abigail Elizabeth *mathematician, educator, science educator*

Selden
Cook, Lisa Marie *mathematics professor, mathematics learning center coordinator*

Stony Brook
Anderson, Michael Thomas *mathematics professor, researcher, director*
Ebin, David Gregory *mathematician, researcl educator*
Glimm, James Gilbert *mathematician, educat*
Laspina, Peter Joseph *computer resource educator*
Lawson, H(erbert) Blaine, Jr. *mathematician, educator*
Milnor, John Willard *mathematician*
Tucker, Alan Curtiss *mathematics professor*

Syracuse
Crowston, Kevin Ghen *information scientist, educator*
Graver, Jack Edward *mathematics professor*
Malhotra, Yogesh *information scientist, consultant, information technology executi computer engineer*
Pardee, Otway O'Meara *computer scientist, educator*

Tarrytown
Maun, Mary Ellen *computer consultant*

Troy
Acar, Evrim *computer scientist*
Drew, Donald Allen *mathematical sciences educator*
Magdon-Ismail, Malik *computer science professor*
Szymanski, Boleslaw Karol *computer scienti educator, entrepreneur*

West Hempstead
Guggenheimer, Heinrich Walter *mathematicia educator*

Westbury
Sandler, Gerald Howard *computer scientist, information technology executive, educator*

Williamsville
Berner, Robert Frank *managerial statistics educator, administrator*

Yorktown Heights
Hoffman, Alan Jerome *mathematician, educa*
Iyengar, Arun K. *computer scientist*
Lei, Hui *computer scientist*
Winograd, Shmuel *mathematician*

NORTH CAROLINA

Black Mountain
Dalton, Robert Edgar *retired mathematician, computer scientist*

Cape Carteret
Mullikin, Thomas Wilson *mathematics profe*

Cary
Connally, Mark *statistician, psychometrician*

Chapel Hill
Brooks, Frederick Phillips, Jr. *computer scie educator*
Taylor, Michael E. *mathematics professor*

Charlotte
Dienes, Timothy Paul *mathematician, educat*
Wright, Wayne Kenneth *federal agency statistician*
Xu, Mingxin *mathematics professor*

Cullowhee
Willis, Ralph Houston *mathematics professo*

Davidson
Klein, Benjamin Garrett *mathematics profes consultant*

am
, Robert Leamon *mathematics educator*
runner, Herbert *computer scientist, ator, mathematician*
np, Anne Sidlo *statistician, researcher*

teville
, Dothang *information scientist, educator*

isboro
el, William Frederick *information scientist*
Jie *computer science educator*

aville
Soumaya Makdissi *mathematics professor*

rson
n, Arthur Benjamin *mathematics essor, tree farmer*

gh
Wushow *retired computer scientist*
vu, Ethelbert Nwakuche *mathematics essor*
n, John Robert *information scientist*
am, Donald Eric *bioinformatics analyst*

y Mount
n, Thomas M. *mathematics professor, artment chairman*

ington
n, Russell Leland *mathematics, physics essor*

ton Salem
r, John Wesley *retired mathematics and nputer science educator, consultant*

TH DAKOTA

ville
pion, Kathleen Ann *mathematics professor*

O

lzhiev, Khristo Nonev *mathematician, cator, researcher*

ns
Hajrudin *mathematician, educator*
Shih-Liang *mathematics professor*

a
, Richard Allen *mathematics professor, nputer science educator*

innati
ley, Roger *mathematics professor*
Thomas Michael *mathematician, educator, cational association administrator*

eland
cione, Ross Joseph *mathematician, educator*
, Robert Arthur *mathematician, educator*
enzain, Antonio *statistician, consultant*
nan, William *mathematician, educator*
, Richard G. *mathematician, consultant*
k, Stanislaw Jerzy *mathematics professor*
zynski, Wojbor Andrzej *mathematician, ucator*

umbus
drasekaran, Balakrishnan *computer entist, educator*
ing, Thomas Allan *mathematics professor*
man, Avner *mathematician, educator*
er, Mervin Edgar *computer scientist, nsultant, statistician, educator*
Fei-Ran *mathematician, educator*
, Deliang *computer scientist, educator*
en, Stuart Harvey *information scientist, ucator, dean*

ton
ida, Atif *mathematics professor*
Vickie Sue *mathematics professor*

aware
er, Harvey Louis *computer scientist, nsultant, engineering educator*

mont
t, Judith Ann *mathematics professor*

nbier
ener, Judy Ann *mathematics professor, searcher*

ve City
ethu, Susan Wanja *computer specialist, atabase manager*

nt
sal, Arvind Kumar *computer scientist, ucator*
a, Richard Steven *retired mathematics ofessor*

tland
ch, Richard B. *mathematics professor*

nsfield
gory, Thomas Bradford *mathematics ofessor*

wark
rock (Wrentmore), Anita Kay *management d program analyst*

rth Royalton
, Henryk *mathematician, educator*

Salem
Ronshausen, Nina Lorraine *retired mathematics professor, genealogist*

Warren
Dinh, Hai Quang *mathematics professor, researcher*
He, Min *mathematics professor*

Westerville
Brombacher, Bruce E. *mathematics educator*

Wilberforce
Hargraves, William Frederick, II, *mathematics and computer science professor*

Wooster
Geiser, Robert Neil *computer scientist*
Hales, Raleigh Stanton, Jr. *retired mathematics professor, academic administrator*

OKLAHOMA

Edmond
Loman, Mary LaVerne *retired mathematics professor*

Midwest City
Harrell, Beverly Ellen *mathematics professor*

Norman
Apanasov, Boris N. *mathematics professor, researcher*
Trytten, Deborah Anne *computer scientist, educator*

Oklahoma City
Feng, Chengde *mathematician, educator*

Stillwater
Anderson, Cokie Gaston *computer educator, humanities educator*
Binegar, Birne *mathematics professor*
Jaco, William H. *mathematics professor, researcher*
Sarangan, Venkatesh *computer scientist, educator*

Tulsa
O'Sullivan, Cindy Marie *mathematics professor*

OREGON

Albany
Yu, Kitson Szewai *computer science educator*

Corvallis
Parks, Harold Raymond *mathematician, educator*

Hillsboro
Ferguson, James Clarke *mathematician, algorithmist*
Pixley, Carl Preston *mathematician*

Portland
Ahuja, Jagdish Chand *mathematics professor*
Colwell, Robert L. *computer architect, consultant*
Jiang, Bin *mathematician, educator*

Tualatin
Brown, Robert Wallace *mathematics professor, educator*

PENNSYLVANIA

Aston
DiMarco, David *mathematician, educator*

Beaver
High, Keith B. *information scientist*

Bethlehem
Caskie, Grace I. L. *statistics professor*
Ghosh, Bhaskar Kumar *statistics educator, researcher*
King, Jane Connell *mathematics professor*
Schattschneider, Doris Jean *retired mathematics professor*
Styer, Jane M. *computer scientist, consultant*

Blue Bell
Halas, Cynthia Ann *business information specialist*

Bryn Mawr
Ackoff, Russell Lincoln *social systems designer, educator*

Easton
Traldi, Lorenzo *mathematician, educator*

Harrisburg
Pearson, Ronald K. *mathematical data analyst*

Kutztown
Vasko, Francis Joseph *mathematics professor*

Malvern
Liang, Jianming *computer scientist, researcher*

Mansfield
Haner, Matthew S. *mathematics professor, statistician*

Norristown
Brown, Patrick Alan *systems analyst*

Philadelphia
Badler, Norman Ira *computer and information science educator*
Banerji, Ranan Bihari *mathematics professor*
Blaze, Matthew *computer science educator, researcher*
de Cani, John Stapley *retired statistician, educator*
Harbater, David *mathematician*
Iglewicz, Boris *statistician, educator*
Kadison, Richard Vincent *mathematician, educator*
Knopp, Marvin Isadore *mathematics professor*
Mehta, Jatinder S. *mathematics professor*
Mode, Charles J. *mathematician, educator*
Paulos, John Allen *mathematics educator, writer*
Porter, Gerald Joseph *retired mathematician, educator*

Pittsburgh
Balas, Egon *mathematician, educator*
Blum, Lenore *mathematician, computer scientist, educator*
Blum, Manuel *computer science educator*
Buchanan, Bruce G. *computer scientist, educator*
Caginalp, Gunduz *mathematician, educator, researcher*
Carbo, Toni (Toni Carbo Bearman) *information scientist, educator*
Carley, Kathleen M. *computer scientist, educator*
Clarke, Edmund M. *computer scientist, educator*
Cox, Richard James *information science educator*
Fienberg, Stephen Elliott *statistician*
Gurtin, Morton Edward *mathematics professor*
Mason, Matthew Thomas *robotics researcher*
Mazzaferro, Kathryn E. *statistician, researcher*
Phelps, Daniel Christopher *information scientist, researcher*
Valdés-Pérez, Raul E. *computer scientist, researcher*
von Ahn, Luis *computer science educator, computer scientist*

Reading
Rochowicz, John Anthony, Jr. *mathematician, mathematics educator, physics educator*

Schnecksville
Labbiento, Julianne Marie *mathematics professor*
Malozzi, Jason Anthony *mathematics professor*
Schillow, Ned William *mathematics professor*

State College
Boone, Tracy Marie *mathematics professor*
Katok, Anatole *mathematics professor*
Xu, Jinchao *mathematics professor*

Swarthmore
Kelemen, Charles F. *computer science educator*

Tioga
Sullins, Ken *mathematics, science and computer science educator*

Tobyhanna
Lapidus, Arnold *mathematician, educator*

University Park
Andrews, George Eyre *mathematics professor*
Azmy, Yousry Youssef *computational scientist*
Barlow, Jesse Louis *computer scientist, educator*

Villanova
Beck, Robert Edward *computer scientist, educator*
Norton, Douglas Evatt *mathematician, educator*
Sahmoudi, Mohamed *computer scientist*

Wallingford
Morrison, Donald Franklin *statistician, educator*

Wayne
Rush, James Edward *retired information scientist*

Williamsport
Vonada, Nicholas Andrew *information technology educator*

RHODE ISLAND

Providence
Dafermos, Constantine Michael *applied mathematics professor*
Ewing, John Harwood *mathematics professor, department chairman, professional society administrator*
Fleming, Wendell Helms *mathematician, educator*
Freiberger, Walter Frederick *mathematics professor*
Gottlieb, David *mathematics professor*
Kushner, Harold Joseph *mathematics professor*
Mumford, David Bryant *mathematics professor*
Schwartz, Richard Evan *mathematician, educator*
Shu, Chi-Wang *mathematics professor, researcher*
Silverman, Joseph Hillel *mathematics professor*
Upfal, Eliezer (Eli Upfal) *computer scientist, educator*

SOUTH CAROLINA

Aiken
Fadimba, Koffi Baana *mathematics professor*
Li, Rao *mathematician, computer scientist*

Bluffton
Powell, Robert Ellis *mathematics professor, dean*

Charleston
Hoel, David Gerhard *statistician, science educator*
Rollins, John Maxwell *mathematics professor, disc jockey*

Gaffney
Wilde, Edwin Frederick *retired mathematics professor*

Greenwood
Marino, Louis J(ohn) *mathematics educator*

Orangeburg
Bozinovski, Stevo *computer science educator, researcher*

Pendleton
Marshall, Gerald Lee *mathematician, educator*

Spartanburg
Hilton, Theodore Craig *computer scientist, Internet company executive*

SOUTH DAKOTA

Vermillion
Maney, Jack Logan *mathematician, educator*

TENNESSEE

Brownsville
Kalin, Robert *retired mathematics professor*

Chattanooga
Shannon, Jerry Wayne *mathematician, educator*

Germantown
Frantzikinakis, Nikos *mathematics professor*

Jackson
Britt, Timothy *mathematics professor*

Knoxville
Abidi, Besma Roui *information scientist, educator*
Pjesivac-Grbovic, Jelena *computer scientist, researcher*
Wang, Peiling *information scientist, educator*

Memphis
Johnson, Joseph Erle *mathematician*

Murfreesboro
Jih, Wen-Jang *information scientist, educator*

Nashville
Dupont, William Dudley *biostatistician, educator*
McKenzie, Ralph Nelson *mathematician, educator*
Saff, Edward Barry *mathematics professor, dean*
Williams, Marsha Rhea *computer scientist, educator, researcher, consultant*

Oak Ridge
Raridon, Richard Jay *retired computer scientist*

TEXAS

Alpine
Morgan, Raymond Victor, Jr. *mathematics professor*

Arlington
Moore, Marion E. *retired mathematics professor*

Austin
Babuska, Ivo Milan *mathematics professor*
Beckner, William *mathematician*
Caffarelli, Luis Angel *mathematician, educator*
Clark, Charles T(aliferro) *retired statistician*
Doyle, Marcus H. *computer technology educator*
Farkas, Gavril *mathematics professor*
Gillman, Leonard *mathematician, educator*
Moore, J. Strother *computer scientist, educator*
Novak, Gordon S., Jr. *computer scientist, educator*
Starbird, Michael *mathematics professor*
Tate, John Torrence *mathematics professor, researcher*
Uhlenbeck, Karen Keskulla *mathematician, educator*
Xin, Jack *mathematician, educator*

Beaumont
Kemble, Joe David *mathematics professor*

Bedford
Dawes, Robert Leo *mathematician, consultant*

Brownsville
Yi, Taeil *mathematician, educator*

College Station
Hammond, Tracy Anne *computer scientist, educator*
Stroustrup, Bjarne *computer science and engineering professor*
Zheng, Qi *statistician, biomathematician*

Colleyville
Hennessey, Audrey Kathleen *computer researcher, educator*

Denton
Thompson, Frances McBroom *mathematics professor, writer*

El Paso
Foged, Leslie Owen *mathematician, educator*
Quevedo, Hector Adolf *operations research specialist, environmental scientist*

Fort Sam Houston
Wojcik, Barbara Elzbieta *statistician, researcher*

Fort Worth
Doran, Robert Stuart *mathematician, educator*
Sullenberger, Ara Broocks *mathematics professor*
Weaber, Terry Lee *information scientist*

Hewitt
Walbesser, Henry Herman *computer science educator*

Houston
Gardner, Everette Shaw, Jr. *information sciences educator, consultant, author*
Glowinski, Roland *mathematics professor*
Golubitsky, Martin Aaron *mathematician, educator*
Hempel, John P. *mathematics professor*
Hodgess, Erin Marie *statistics educator*
Kakadiaris, Ioannis *computer science educator*
Kavraki, Lydia *computer scientist, educator*
Miller, Charles Rickie *systems analyst, engineering executive*
Scott, David Warren *statistics educator*
Swartz, Michael D. *statistical geneticist*
Tapia, Richard Alfred *mathematics professor*
Tong, Louis Lik-Fu *information scientist*
Veech, William Austin *mathematics professor*
Wang, Chao-Cheng *mathematician, engineer*
Ward, Robin A. *mathematics professor*
Wright, Clark Phillips *computer systems specialist*

Irving
Cherri, Mona Y. *computer scientist, educator, computer scientist, consultant*
Conger, Sue Ann *computer information systems educator*

Laredo
Wu, Fuming *computer science educator*

Lewisville
Ferguson, R. Neil *computer scientist, consultant*

Lubbock
Wilhelm, Jennifer Anne *mathematics and science professor*

Lufkin
Haas, Sally Marie *mathematician, educator*

Mcallen
von Kuster, Lee Norman *retired mathematics professor*

Prairie View
Hritonenko, Natali *mathematics professor, researcher*

Richardson
Dian, Jianwei *mathematician*
Easttom, Chuck *computer scientist, educator*
Overall, Theresa Lynne *computer professor*
Wiorkowski, John James *mathematics professor*

Round Rock
Khalid, Humayun *computer scientist, consultant*

San Antonio
Estep, Myrna Lynne *systems analyst, philosophy educator*
Redfield, Carol Ann Luckhardt *computer scientist, educator*

Sugar Land
Theys, Philippe Paul *data quality professional*

Temple
Bumpus, Floyd David, Jr. *microcomputer analyst*

Texarkana
Mojiri, Ahmad *mathematics professor*

Texas City
Robertson, Paul Francis *mathematician, educator*

Tyler
Bailey, Nan Hutchins *mathematician, educator*

Valley Mills
Odell, Patrick Lowry *retired mathematics professor*

Waco
Rolf, Howard Leroy *mathematician, educator*
Sheng, Qin *mathematics professor*

UTAH

Orem
Moore, Hal G. *mathematician, educator*

Park City
Vance, Dianne Sanchez *mathematician, educator*

Salt Lake City
Livne, Oren Eliezer *mathematician, educator*
Trapa, Peter Engel *mathematics professor*

VERMONT

Burlington
Bongard, Josh Clifford *computer scientist, educator*

North Bennington
Adler, Irving *mathematician*

Norwich
Snapper, Ernst *mathematics professor*

VIRGINIA

Alexandria
Chen, Fen *mathematician, educator, researcher*
Dowling, Dean Edward *information scientist, educator*
Nutile, David Albert *retired information security and systems consultant*

Arlington
Tichenor, Charles Beckham III *operations research analyst*

Blacksburg
Arnold, Jesse Charles *retired statistician*
Good, Irving John *statistician, educator, philosopher*
Hovakimyan, Naira *mathematician, educator*
Posey, Eldon Eugene *mathematician, educator*
Varadarajan, Srinidhi *computer scientist*

Charlottesville
Horgan, Cornelius Oliver *applied mathematics and mechanics professor, engineering educator*
Parshall, Karen Virginia Hunger *mathematician*
Thomas, Lawrence Eldon *mathematics professor*

Chesapeake
Locke, L. Muriel *mathematician, educator*

Clifton
Hoffman, Karla Leigh *mathematician, educator*

Emory
Jones, Jerry Lee *computer educator*

Fairfax
Lillard, Mark Hill III *engineering consultant, retired military officer*
Mulvaney, Mary Frederica *systems analyst*

Falls Church
Hibbs, Ernest G. *computer scientist, engineering executive*

Fort Belvoir
Thompson, Carlynn Jean *information scientist*

Fredericksburg
Hajek, Otomar *mathematician, educator*
McWilliams, Dallas *technical educator*
Mellinger, Keith E. *mathematician, educator*

Hampton
Nazaryan, Hovakim *mathematician, researcher, atmospheric scientist*
Verma, Arun K. *mathematician, educator*

Herndon
Draper, William David *systems engineer*
Hollis, Katherine Mary *information scientist, consultant*

Lexington
Tierney, Michael John *mathematics professor*

Manassas
Bruno, Irene Evelyn *mathematician, educator*

Mc Lean
Ellison, Earl Otto *computer scientist*

Newport News
Summerville, Richard M. *mathematician, academic administrator*

Norfolk
Earl, Archie William, Sr. *mathematician, educator*

Petersburg
Gosciewski, Robert Louis *logistician*
Lakew, Dejenie Alemayehu *mathematician*

Richmond
Bukszár, József *mathematics professor*
Charlesworth, Arthur Thomas *mathematics professor*
Malone, Nicholas Sherlon *systems analyst, consultant*

Roanoke
Wallace, Linda Kay *mathematics professor*

Sterling
Martin, Roger John *computer scientist*

Sweet Briar
Wassell, Stephen Robert *mathematics professor, researcher*

Vienna
Gardenier, John Stark *statistician, philosopher, researcher, writer*
Gardenier, Turkan Kumbaraci *statistician, researcher*

Virginia Beach
Robbins, Reginald L. *mathematician, educator*

Williamsburg
Rodman, Leiba *mathematician*

WASHINGTON

Bellevue
King, Elizabeth Maureen *business systems executive*

Eastsound
de Boor, Carl-Wilhelm R. *mathematician*

Federal Way
Cunningham, John Randolph *project manager*

Kenmore
Sobolewski, John Stephen *computer scientist, director, consultant*

Kennewick
Cochran, James Alan *mathematics professor, department chairman, dean*

Orcas
Greever, John *retired mathematics professor*

Pullman
Kallaher, Michael Joseph *mathematics professor*

Redmond
Allard, J. *computer scientist*
Freedman, Michael Hartley *mathematician, educator*
Lomet, David Bruce *computer scientist*
Oliver, Nuria Maria *computer science researcher*
Smith, Burton Jordan *computer designer*

Richland
Petrini, Fabrizio *computer scientist, researcher*

Seattle
Breslow, Norman Edward *biostatistics educator, researcher*
Criminale, William Oliver, Jr. *applied mathematics professor*
Dang, Chinh *information scientist*
Doran, Charles Francis, Jr. *mathematician, mathematics professor*
Gillispie, Steven Brian *systems analyst, researcher*
Hawrylycz, Michael *information scientist*
Kalet, Ira Joseph *medical computer scientist*
Klee, Victor La Rue *mathematician, educator*
Lee, John Marshall *mathematics professor*
Marshall, Donald E. *mathematics professor*
Mason, Robert McSpadden *information scientist, educator, dean*
Michael, Ernest Arthur *mathematics professor*
Segal, Jack *mathematics professor*

Tacoma
Quinn, Jennifer J. *mathematics professor*
Stuart, Jeffrey L. *mathematics professor, consultant*

Yakima
Jongeward, George Ronald *retired systems analyst*

WEST VIRGINIA

Huntington
Aluthge, Ariyadasa *mathematics professor, researcher*

WISCONSIN

Green Bay
Conley, William Cleland *statistician, educator*

Madison
Askey, Richard Allen *mathematician, educator*
Beck, Anatole *mathematician, educator*
DeWitt, David J. *computer scientist*
Draper, Norman Richard *statistician, educator*
Hibbard, William Louis *computer scientist*
Johnson, Millard Wallace, Jr. *mathematics and engineering professor*
Malkus, David Starr *mathematician*
Mau, Bob *statistician*
Ney, Peter Ernest *mathematician, educator*
Robinson, Stephen Michael *mathematician, educator*

Pleasant Prairie
Biland, Alan Thomas *computer integrated manufacturing executive*

Stevens Point
Barjis, Joseph *computer scientist, educator*

Watertown
Malmanger, Curtis A. *mathematician, educator*

Whitewater
Baica, Malvina Florica *mathematician, educator, researcher*
Nam, Ki-Bong *mathematics professor*

WYOMING

Casper
Wildman, Peter Roberts *mathematics professor*

TERRITORIES OF THE UNITED STATES

PUERTO RICO

Mayaguez
Collins, Dennis Glenn *mathematics professor*

San Juan
Marcano, Mariano *mathematics professor*

MILITARY ADDRESSES OF THE UNITED STATES

EUROPE

APO
Simpson, Sandra Kay *operations research specialist*

CANADA

BRITISH COLUMBIA

Burnaby
Brinkman, Fiona Susan *bioinformaticist, educator, molecular biologist*

Vancouver
Clark, Colin Whitcomb *mathematics profes*
Feldman, Joel Shalom *mathematician*
Granirer, Edmond Ernest *mathematician, educator*
Sion, Maurice *mathematics professor*

Victoria
Manning, Eric *computer scientist, educator, dean, researcher*
Meadow, Charles *information scientist, wri*

NEW BRUNSWICK

Saint Andrews
Anderson, John Murray *operations researcl specialist, consultant, retired academic administrator*

NOVA SCOTIA

Halifax
Fillmore, Peter Arthur *mathematician, educ*

ONTARIO

London
Bauer, Michael Anthony *computer scientist, educator*
Borwein, David *mathematics professor*

Ottawa
Csörgö, Miklós *mathematics and statistics educator*
Dlab, Vlastimil *mathematics professor, researcher*
Fellegi, Ivan Peter *statistician*
Krechetnikov, Rouslan *mathematician, educ*

Toronto
Friedlander, John Benjamin *mathematician, educator*
Gotlieb, Calvin Carl *computer scientist, edu*
Rooney, Paul George *mathematics professor*

Waterloo
Aczél, János Dezsö *mathematician*
Gladwell, Graham Maurice Leslie *mathematician, civil engineering educator*
Paldus, Josef *mathematics professor*
Sprott, David Arthur *statistician, educator, psychologist, educator*

QUEBEC

Montreal
Moser, William Oscar Jules *mathematics professor*
Romanov, Volodymyr Alexeevich *computer science educator, researcher*
Suen, Ching Yee *computer scientist, educato researcher*

SASKATCHEWAN

Regina
Symes, Lawrence Richard *computer science educator, university dean*

Saskatoon
Sowa, Artur *mathematician, researcher*

Ontario
Babulak, Eduard *computer scientist, educato researcher, consultant*

AUSTRIA

Wien
Reichl, Peter *computer scientist, researcher*

BRAZIL

Rio de Janeiro
de Araújo, Aloisio Pessoa *mathematics profe*

BULGARIA

Blagoevgrad
Stefanov, Stefan Minev *mathematics professo researcher*

Sofia
Lazarov, Raicho Dimitrov *mathematician, educator*

CHINA

Beijing
Cheng, Josephine *computer scientist, educato*
Hsieh, Din-Yu *applied mathematics professor*

Shanghai
Lu, Bao-Liang *computer scientist, educator*

CZECH REPUBLIC

no
apka, Jindřich Ludvík *mathematician, physicist, educator, researcher*

ENGLAND

icester
rijan, Ram *technology transfer researcher*

ndon
lenbe, Sami Erol *computer scientist, engineering educator*
lston, Anthony *computer scientist, mathematician, educator*

FRANCE

ris
re, Jean-Pierre *mathematician, scholar*
echiming, Roger Yue Yuen Shing *mathematics professor*

lbonne
ker, Ulrich *computer scientist, researcher*

GERMANY

rlin
hmann, Frank *mathematician*

aunschweig
thelm, Kai *mathematician, researcher*
eberg, Dieter Wolfgang Michael *mathematician*

emen
ls, Raymond O'Neil, Jr. *mathematics professor, researcher*

INDIA

w Delhi
ota, Vijay *mathematics professor*

ISRAEL

usalem
shovski, Ehud *mathematics professor*

mat Aviv
nstein, Joseph *mathematician, researcher, educator*

hovot
mir, Adi *computer scientist*

ITALY

rin
, Michele *mathematics professor*
si, Guido A(ntonio) *mathematics professor, researcher*

JAPAN

u
ada, Kazuyuki *mathematician, educator*

nma
naka, Heisuke *mathematics professor, academic administrator*

raki
be, Tohsuke *mathematics professor, researcher*

sugai
ake, Yasuji *computer science educator*

kyo
Hajime *retired information scientist, educator*
, Shuichi *information scientist, educator*
, Takeo T. *computer scientist, educator*

PORTUGAL

bon
npos, Luís Manuel Braga da Costa *mathematics, physics, acoustics and aeronautics educator*

REPUBLIC OF KOREA

ejeon
, Myung-Ki *computer scientist, researcher*

ul
m, Jong-Hae *mathematician, educator*
Myoungho *computer scientist, educator*
ng, Byeongchan *mathematics professor*

RUSSIA

scow
ikov, Sergei Petrovitch *mathematician*

Romanovski, Mikhail Rem *mathematician*

SCOTLAND

Edinburgh
Atiyah, Sir Michael Francis *mathematician*

SWEDEN

Västerås
Xiong, Ning *computer scientist*

ADDRESS UNPUBLISHED

Adaikkalavan, Raman *computer scientist, educator*
Albrecht, Rebekah S. *mathematician, educator*
Allen, Frances Elizabeth *computer scientist*
Andrews, Byllie D'Amato *retired mathematics professor*
Arciniega, Armando *mathematics professor*
Arden, Bruce Wesley *retired computer scientist, retired engineering educator*
Armstrong, Sonya M. *mathematics professor, researcher*
Ayedun, Kehinde Peter *information systems executive*
Bacon, Leslie Edward *operations analysis manager*
Bailar, Barbara Ann *retired statistician*
Barrett, Lida Kittrell *mathematics professor*
Bender, Virginia Best *computer scientist, educator*
Bentley, Donald Lyon *mathematics professor, minister*
Bhadra, Jayanta *computer scientist, electrical engineer*
Blair, David Clark *information scientist, educator*
Bloch, Anthony Michael *mathematician, educator*
Boardman, Elizabeth Drake *computer security professional*
Bollapragada, Ramesh *information scientist, educator*
Browder, Felix Earl *mathematician, educator*
Bullough, John Donovan *information scientist, educator*
Cable, Charles Allen *mathematician*
Camara, Vincent Antonin Reginald *statistician, educator, researcher*
Cameron, Kirk MacGregor Drummond *statistician*
Caroleo, Linn E. *mathematician, writer*
Carroll, John Millar *computer science and psychology educator*
Cecil, David Rolf *mathematician, educator*
Chang, Samuel Henry *computer scientist, educator*
Chati, Mandar Kalidas *operations research specialist*
Cheeger, Jeff *mathematics educator*
Chen, Shuang *computer science professional*
Choi, Youngok *information science educator*
Chow, Timothy Yi-Chung *mathematician, systems engineer*
Christin, Nicolas *computer scientist, researcher*
Cohen, Michael Paul *statistician*
Commander, Clayton W. *computer scientist*
Comstock, Dale Robert *mathematics professor*
Conn, Richard Lee *computer scientist, educator*
Cooper, Brett D. *mathematician, educator*
Corbett, Lenora Meade *mathematician, community college educator*
Corona, Joseph Anthony *operations research analyst, mathematician, educator*
Cowles, Roger E. *computer consultant*
Daily, Deirdre Lynn *systems analyst*
de Champeaux de Laboulaye, Dennis *computer scientist*
Deng, Li *computer scientist, researcher, electrical engineer*
Deutsch, Alin Bernard *computer scientist, educator*
Dittenhafer, Daniel Webster, II, *computer scientist*
Dixon, Albert Truman *mathematician, educator*
Easton, Roger L. *former operations research specialist, consultant*
Edmunds, Darryl B. *mathematics professor*
Efird, Jimmy Thomas *statistician*
Elble, Joseph M. *computer scientist, researcher*
Elliott, David LeRoy *mathematics and engineering educator*
Exner, Frank Kepler *information scientist, indexer*
Fields-Harris, Deborah Carol *mathematician, educator*
Fossum, Robert Merle *mathematician, educator*
Frankston, Robert M. *computer software executive, developer*
Fulton, William *mathematics professor*
Gehring, Frederick William *mathematician, educator*
Gerson, Donald Jerome *computer scientist, consultant, photographer, small business owner*
Gessaman, Margaret Palmer *mathematician, educator, retired dean*
Gieszl, Louis Roger *mathematician*
Gifford, Marjorie Fitting *mathematician, educator, consultant*
Gletherow, Jamie *computer scientist*
Goldberg, Samuel *retired mathematician, foundation administrator*
Goldstein, Jerome Arthur *mathematics professor*
Gray, James N. *computer scientist*
Greever, Margaret Quarles *retired mathematics educator*
Griffiths, Phillip A. *mathematician, retired academic administrator*
Grothendieck, Alexandre *retired mathematician*
Guild, Jeffrey K. *mathematics professor*
Guinn, Theodore *retired mathematics professor, research scientist*
Gulick, Sidney (Denny) L. III *mathematics professor, writer*
Halberstam, Heini *mathematics professor*
Halitsky, Steve *data analyst, statistician, researcher*
Hamel, Louis Reginald *retired systems analyst*
Hamlen, Kevin William *computer scientist, educator*
Hardie, Michael Howard *mathematician, educator*
Harnedy, Joan Catherine Holland *retired systems analyst*
Hayes, David Ryan *mathematics professor*
Hegamin-Younger, Cecilia *statistician, consultant, educator*
Holford, Theodore Richard *biostatistician, educator*
Holland, Michael James *computer services administrator*
Hollis, Deborah D. *systems analyst, application developer*
Hoppensteadt, Frank Charles *mathematician, educator, dean*
House, Stephen Eugene *information systems consultant*
Hu, Hongde *mathematics professor*
Irick, Michael L. *systems analyst, educator*
Ivie, Evan Leon *computer science educator*
Jackson, Deborah Cheryl *mathematician*
Jacobson, Norman Maron *computer science educator*
Jenkins, Jeffery A. *mathematics professor*
Johnstone, Iain Murray *statistician, educator, consultant*
Jones, Anita Katherine *computer scientist, educator*
Joshi, Madhukar *statistician, consultant*
Kadota, Takashi Theodore *mathematician, electrical engineer*
Karnaugh, Maurice *computer scientist, educator*
Kazanci, Deniz *mathematician*
Kettimuthu, Rajkumar *computer scientist*
Khasawneh, Shadi Turki *computer scientist*
King, Amy Cathryne Patterson *retired mathematics educator, researcher*
Kirshbaum, Jon Alan *systems analyst, consultant, retired systems administrator*
Ko, Kyungduk *statistician, educator*
Konate, Dialla *mathematician, educator*
Krantz, Steven George *mathematics professor, writer*
Kushner, Todd Roger *computer scientist, application developer*
Kvitko, Arkady *mathematician, researcher*
Lampson, Butler Wright *computer scientist*
Lang, Michael *mathematics professor*
Lange, Frederick Edward, Jr. *computer information systems architect*
Leppard, Stephanie Jean *systems analyst, artist*
Lerner, Vladimir Semion *computer scientist, educator*
Levy, Stephen H. *computer scientist, educator*
Lewis, Suford *computer scientist, consultant*
Li, Lide *mathematician, econometrician, consultant*
Litwinowicz, Anthony *information scientist, researcher*
Longstreet, John Charles *retired computer scientist*
Lotspiech, Jeffrey *computer scientist, consultant*
Lynch, Robert Emmett *mathematics professor*
Mandelbrot, Benoit B. *mathematician, research scientist, educator*
March, Michael F. *propulsion systems analyst, consultant*
Masuda, Michele Michi *statistician*
McAuley, Van Alfon *aerospace mathematician*
McCrary, Jonathan Mark *mathematician, educator*
Megiddo, Nimrod *mathematician, computer scientist*
Merritt, Susan Mary *computer science educator, dean*
Mikhelson, Sergei *mathematician, educator*
Mills, Kevin Lee *computer scientist, researcher*
Morris, Daniel S. *computer scientist, researcher*
Nation, David Arthur *retired computer scientist, sculptor*
Neuberger, John William *mathematics professor*
Nguyen, Dong *computer scientist, researcher, software engineer, educator*
Nicoara, Andreea Carina *mathematics professor*
Noh, Jun-yong *computer scientist, researcher*
Norton, Peter K. *retired computer utilities programmer, writer*
Oprea, Dragos *mathematician, educator*
Orr, Richard Clayton *mathematician, retired securities trader*
Orszag, Steven Alan *applied mathematician, educator*
O'Toole, William Edward III *retired computer science and mathematics professor*
Park, Naeun *statistician*
Pasnicu, Cornel *mathematician, educator*
Pepper, Maury *computer consultant*
Peters, Christopher Allen *systems analyst, consultant*
Pittman, Jonathan *computer scientist*
Pollock, Karen Anne *computer analyst*
Ponnapalli, Ramachandra Murty *retired statistician, researcher*
Pruitt Lemley, Cynthia Kaye *computer educator*
Rahal, Imad *computer science educator*
Read, Tony John *information scientist, consultant*
Reece, Julia Ruth *systems analyst, entrepreneur*
Reed, Dale F. *computer scientist, educator*
Reed, David Patrick *information scientist*
Reichenbach, Linda Louise *mathematician, language educator*
Richgels, Glen William *mathematics professor*
Riffenburgh, Robert Harry *biostatistician, researcher*
Roberts, Rodney R. *systems analyst, educator*
Robinson, Molly Jahnige *statistician, educator*
Roitman, Judith *mathematician, educator*
Ronan, Mark A. *mathematician, writer*
Rosen, Judah Ben *computer scientist*
Sahai, Akhil *computer scientist, researcher*
Salahuddin, Parveen *information scientist, researcher*
Scheetz, Bernadette Estelle *elementary mathematics educator*
Schneider, Edgar Rolf Gottfried *retired mathematician, application developer, writer*
Schupp, Russ *computer professor, web site designer*
Sellmann, Meinolf *computer science educator*
Sheppard, John Wilbur *computer research scientist*
Sherman, Jimmie Lee *mathematician, educator*
Shier, Gloria Bulan *mathematics professor*
Shutt, Elsie G. *systems analyst, application developer, consultant*
Sinha, Rakesh Kumar *computer scientist, researcher*
Skiena, Steven Sol *computer scientist, educator*
Sloane, Neil James Alexander *mathematician, researcher*
Souganidis, Panagiotis Emmanuel *mathematician, educator*
Sow, Daby *computer scientist, researcher*
Spinrad, Robert Joseph *computer scientist*
Stager, John C. *information scientist, educator*
Stark, Robert Martin *mathematician, civil engineer, educator*
Štěpánek, Petr *computer science educator*
Suppes, Patrick *statistician, philosopher, psychologist, educator*
Teleman, Silviu *mathematician, educator*
Terzic, Petar *mathematician, educator*
Tobiassen, Barbara Sue *systems analyst, consultant, volunteer*
Tsodikov, Alexander David *biostatistician, educator*
Tymoczko, Julianna Sophia *mathematics professor*
Tyrl, Paul *mathematics professor, researcher*
Urbanski, Joseph V. *mathematics educator*
Vuckovic, Vladeta D *retired mathematics professor*
Wang, Yu-Ping *computer science educator, engineering educator*
Warner, William Hamer *mathematician*
Watkins, Ann Esther *mathematics professor*
Weeks, Jeffrey R. *mathematician, researcher, educator*
Welna, Cecilia *retired mathematics professor, dean*
Wilder, Ksenia A. *systems analyst*
Williams, Ronald Oscar *mathematician*
Wimpffen, Otto Rudolph *mathematics professor*
Winder, Robert Owen *mathematician, computer engineer, geophysicist*
Worthington, Tracy *retired operations research specialist*
Wright, Will *computer game designer*
Yackel, James William *mathematician, academic administrator*
Yeadon, Tammy Pamela *information specialist*
Young, Barry Harrison *retired mathematician, mechanical engineer*
Yuksel, Murat *computer scientist, educator*
Zeilberger, Doron *mathematics professor, researcher*
Zhang, Guili *statistician, educator*
Zierler, Neal *retired mathematician*
Zyroff, Ellen Slotoroff *information scientist, classicist, educator*

SCIENCE: PHYSICAL SCIENCE

UNITED STATES

ALABAMA

Auburn
Neely, William Charles *chemistry professor, consultant, research scientist*

Birmingham
Miyagawa, Ichiro *physicist*
Noah, James William *biochemist, researcher*
Robinson, Edward Lee *retired physics professor, consultant*
Vila-Carriles, Wanda Helena *research scientist*
Vyazovkin, Sergey *chemistry professor*

Huntsville
Allan, Barry David *research chemist, government official*
Brandon, Walter Wiley, Jr. *retired physicist, retired aerospace engineer*
Burko, Lior M. *physicist, educator*
Costes, Nicholas Constantine *aerospace scientist, educator, retired government agency administrator*
Hoover, Richard Brice *astrobiologist*
Jaenisch, Holger Marcel *physicist*
Norman, Ralph Louis *retired physicist, consultant*
Parnell, Thomas Alfred *physicist*
Smith, Robert Earl *space scientist*
Stuhlinger, Ernst *physicist*
Su, Ching-Hua *materials scientist*
Vaughan, William Walton *atmospheric scientist*
Wright, John Collins *retired chemistry professor*

Tuscaloosa
Dixon, David Adams *chemistry professor, researcher*
LaMoreaux, Philip Elmer *geologist, hydrologist, consultant*
Mancini, Ernest Anthony *geologist, educator, researcher*

Periaswamy, Padmini *materials scientist, researcher*
Vincent, John Bertram *chemist, educator*

Tuskegee
Powell, Nichole Larai *chemistry professor, researcher*
Rangari, Vijaya Kumar *chemistry professor, researcher*

ALASKA

Anchorage
Brigham, Lawson Walter *oceanographer, researcher*

Fairbanks
Cahill, Catherine Frances *environmental scientist, educator*
Duffy, Lawrence Kevin *biochemist, educator*
Fathauer, Theodore Frederick *meteorologist*
Kramm, Gerhard *meteorologist, researcher*
Lingle, Craig Stanley *glaciologist, educator*
Roederer, Juan Gualterio *retired physics professor*
Romanovsky, Vladimir Evgeni *physics professor*

Saint Paul Island
Lestenkof, Aquilina Debbie *environmental advocate*

Thorne Bay
Sylvia, Dennis Ashton *geologist*

ARIZONA

Amado
Criswell, Stephen *astronomer*

Chandler
Meieran, Eugene Stuart *materials scientist*

Flagstaff
Herkenhoff, Kenneth Edward *geologist, researcher*
Millis, Robert Lowell *astronomer, science observatory director*
Shoemaker, Carolyn Spellman *planetary astronomer*

Green Valley
Ramette, Richard Wales *chemistry professor*

Litchfield Park
McKeighen, Ronald Eugene *physicist*

Oro Valley
Swalin, Richard Arthur *scientist, company executive*

Phoenix
Bolin, Vladimir Dustin *chemist*
Everett, Paul Marvin *physicist*

Rio Rico
Lowell, J(ames) David *geological consultant, cattle rancher*

Scottsdale
Kinsinger, Jack Burl *chemist, educator*

Sierra Vista
Ponder, Herman *geologist*

Tempe
Bauer, Ernst Georg *physicist, researcher*
Goronkin, Herbert *physicist*
Juvet, Richard Spalding, Jr. *chemistry professor*
McKelvy, Michael John *chemist, research scientist*
Moore, Carleton Bryant *geochemistry educator*
Patel, Vimla L. *research scientist*
Pettit, George Robert *chemist, educator, cancer researcher*
Smith, David John *physicist, researcher*
Theodore, David *research scientist*

Tucson
Angel, James Roger Prior *astronomer*
Barrett, Bruce Richard *physics professor*
Bloembergen, Nicolaas *physicist, researcher*
Crawford, David L. *astronomer*
Davis, Stanley Nelson *hydrologist, educator*
De Young, David Spencer *astrophysicist, educator*
Dunn, Floyd *biophysics and biomedical engineering professor*
Falco, Charles Maurice *physicist, researcher*
Fan, Xiaohui *astrophysicist, educator*
Girardeau, Marvin Denham *physics professor*
Green, Richard Frederick *astronomer*
Gruhl, James *energy scientist, artist*
Gutsche, Carl David *chemistry professor*
Hall, Henry Kingston, Jr. *chemistry professor*
Hays, James Fred *geologist, educator*
Hill, Henry Allen *physicist, researcher*
Hunten, Donald Mount *planetary scientist, educator*
Jannuzi, Buell T. *astronomer*
Jefferies, John Trevor *astrophysicist, director*
Karkoschka, Erich *planetary science researcher, writer*
Kennicutt, Robert Charles, Jr. *astronomer*
Kessler, John Otto *physicist, researcher*
Lamb, Willis Eugene, Jr. *physicist, researcher*
Lunine, Jonathan Irving *astronomer, educator*
Macleod, Hugh Angus McIntosh *optical science educator, physicist, consultant*
Marcialis, Robert Louis *planetary astronomer*
McNulty, Terence Patrick *metallurgist, consultant*
Mould, Jeremy Richard *astronomer*
Neugebauer, Marcia *physicist, researcher*
Neuman, Shlomo P. *hydrologist, educator*
Powers, Linda Sue *biophysicist, educator, biomedical engineer*
Prewitt, Charles Thompson *geochemist*
Rieke, Marcia J. *astronomer, educator*
Roemer, Elizabeth *retired astronomer, educator*
Sprague, Ann Louise *aerospace scientist*
Strittmatter, Peter Albert *astronomer, educator*
Tifft, William Grant *retired physics professor, scientist*
Tollin, Gordon *retired chemistry professor*
Wolff, Sidney Carne *astronomer, science administrator*

ARKANSAS

Batesville
Meinzer, Beverly Anne *chemist, educator*

Bella Vista
Johnson, A(lyn) William *chemistry professor, writer, researcher, consultant*

Fayetteville
King, Jerry Wayne *chemist, researcher, engineer*
Steele, Kenneth Franklin, Jr. *hydrologist*
Wilkins, Charles L. *chemist, educator*

Little Rock
Braithwaite, Wilfred John *physics professor*
Darsey, Jerome Anthony (Jerry Darsey) *chemistry professor, consultant*

Pine Bluff
Walker, Richard Brian *chemistry professor*

CALIFORNIA

Agoura Hills
Currie, Malcolm Roderick *aerospace and automotive executive, research scientist*

Alhambra
Huang, Jia-Sheng Jack *optics scientist, researcher*
Im, Jaemo *research scientist*

Altadena
Mkryan, Sonya *geophysicist, educator, research scientist*

Atascadero
Ogier, Walter Thomas *retired physics educator*

Atherton
Fried, John H. *chemist*
Gill, Stephen Paschall *retired physicist, mathematician*

Auburn
Ferber, Robert Rudolf *retired physics researcher, educator, science administrator*
Hess, Patrick Henry *chemist, researcher*

Bayside
Cocks, George Gosson *retired chemical microscopy professor*

Berkeley
Alivisatos, Armand Paul *chemist, educator*
Attwood, David Thomas *physicist, researcher*
Banfield, Jillian *mineralogist, geomicrobiologist, educator*
Bartlett, Neil *chemist, emeritus educator*
Basri, Gibor *astronomy educator, academic administrator*
Bergman, Robert George *chemist, educator*
Bertozzi, Carolyn R. *chemistry professor*
Bousso, Raphael *physicist, educator*
Bragg, Robert Henry *physicist, researcher*
Bustamante, Carlos J. *biophysicist, educator*
Calendar, Richard Lane *biochemistry educator*
Cerny, Joseph III *chemistry professor, retired dean, director*
Chamberlin, Michael John *retired biochemistry professor*
Chew, Geoffrey Foucar *physicist*
Chu, Steven *physics professor, director*
Clarke, John *physics professor*
Coats, Robert Noyce *hydrologist*
Cuffey, Kurt M. *geophysicist, geochemist, educator*
Delory, Gregory Townsend *aerospace scientist, consultant*
Diamond, Richard Martin *nuclear chemist*
Filippenko, Alexei Vladimir *astrophysicist, educator*
Fleming, Graham Richard *chemistry educator*
Fowler, Thomas Kenneth *physicist*
Fréchet, Jean *chemistry professor*
Freedman, Stuart Jay *nuclear science educator*
Gaillard, Mary Katharine *physicist, educator*
Glaser, Donald Arthur *physicist*
Goldhaber, Gerson *astrophysicist, researcher*
Hahn, Erwin Louis *physicist, researcher*
Haller, Eugene Ernest *materials scientist, educator*
Halpern, Martin Brent *physics professor*
Hearst, John Eugene *retired chemistry professor, consultant, researcher*
Hoffman, Darleane Christian *chemistry professor*
Jackson, J(ohn) David *physicist, researcher*
Jeanloz, Raymond *geophysics educator*
Keasling, Jay D. *chemistry professor, research scientist*
Kerth, Leroy T. *physics professor*
Kirz, Janos *physicist*
Klinman, Judith Pollock *biochemist, educator*
Kurtzman, Ralph Harold, Jr. *biochemist, researcher, consultant*
Langridge, Robert *biophysicist, educator, computational biologist*
Leemans, Wim Pieter *physicist*
Lester, William Alexander, Jr. *chemist, educator*
Lin, Robert Peichung *physicist, educator, researcher*
Linn, Stuart Michael *biochemist, educator*
Ma, Chung-Pei Michelle *astronomer, educator*
Mandelstam, Stanley *physicist*
Marcy, Geoffrey W. *astronomer, physicist, educator*
Markowitz, Samuel Solomon *chemistry professor*
McKee, Christopher Fulton *physicist, astronomer, educator*
Miller, William Hughes *theoretical chemist, educator*
Morris, John William, Jr. *metallurgy educator*
Pavlath, Attila Endre *chemist, researcher*
Perlmutter, Saul *astrophysicist, educator*
Perry, Dale Lynn *chemist*
Pines, Alexander *chemistry educator, researcher, consultant*
Price, Paul Buford *physicist, researcher*
Quinn, Nigel William Trevelyan *research scientist*
Rasmussen, John Oscar *nuclear research scientist*
Raymond, Kenneth Norman *chemistry professor, researcher*
Ritchie, Robert Oliver *materials science educator, department chairman*
Romanowicz, Barbara *geology and geophysics professor*
Roy, Prabir Kumar *physicist*
Sessler, Andrew Marienhoff *physicist*
Shugart, Howard Alan *physicist, researcher*
Smoot, George Fitzgerald III *astrophysicist*
Somorjai, Gabor Arpad *chemist, educator*
Steiner, Herbert Max *physics professor*
Strauss, Herbert Leopold *chemistry professor*
Streitwieser, Andrew, Jr. *retired chemistry professor*
Thompson, Anthony Wayne *metallurgist, educator, consultant*
Townes, Charles Hard *physics professor*
Valentine, James William *paleontologist, educator, writer*
Vega, Reinaldo *research scientist*
Yang, Peidong *material science researcher*

Boron
Fisher, Richard Paul *chemist*

Brea
Xiu, Faxian *research scientist*

California City
Paiva, Clifford Anthony *physicist, consultant*

Camarillo
Gigas, Gunter George *retired physicist, physician*

Canyon Lake
Schilling, Frederick Augustus, Jr. *geologist, consultant*

Carlsbad
Smith, Warren James *optical scientist, consultant, lecturer, author*
Workman, Jerome James, Jr. *chemist*

Chico
Mejia, Barbara Oviedo *retired chemistry professor*

Claremont
Detwiler, Daniel Paul *retired physics professor*
Hansch, Corwin Herman *chemistry professor*
Helliwell, Thomas McCaffree *physicist, researcher*

Concord
Seshadri, Srivatsan *optics scientist*

Corona Del Mar
Britten, Roy John *biophysicist*

Crescent City
Carter, Neville Louis *geophysicist, educator*

Cypress
Cully, Joseph Andrew *hazard substance scientist*

Davis
Burri, Betty Jane *research chemist*
Cahill, Thomas Andrew *physicist, researcher*
Conn, Eric Edward *plant biochemist*
Doi, Roy Hiroshi *biochemist, educator*
Fuhs, G. Wolfgang (Georg Wolfgang Fuhs) *environmental research manager*
Jungerman, John Albert *physics professor*
Liu, Kai *physics professor*
Shackelford, James Floyd *materials science educator, researcher*
Troy, Frederic Arthur, II, *medical biochemistry professor*

El Cerrito
Koths, Kirston Edward *biochemist*

El Dorado Hills
Bartlett, Robert Watkins *metallurgist, educator, consultant*

El Granada
Heere, Karen R. *astrophysicist*

Emeryville
Gombocz, Erich Alfred *biochemist*
Masri, Merle Sid *biochemist, consultant*

Escondido
Tomomatsu, Hideo *chemist*

Foster City
Hotz, Henry Palmer *retired physicist*
Zaidi, Iqbal Mehdi *biochemist, research scientist*

Fountain Valley
Davis, Jeremy Matthew *chemist*

Fremont
Yaoi, Takuro *biochemist*

Fresno
Kauffman, George Bernard *chemistry professo*
Rubingh, Jonathan Patrick *environmental heal specialist*

Fullerton
Shapiro, Mark Howard *physicist, educator, de*

Gardena
Martin, Melissa Carol *radiological physicist*

Glen Ellen
Berkland, James Omer *geologist*

Glendale
Kazarian, Poghos F. *physicist, researcher, educator*

Hemet
Berger, Lev Isaac *physicist, researcher*

Irvine
Bander, Myron *physics professor, dean*
Benford, Gregory Albert *physicist, writer*
Clark, Bruce Robert *geologist, consultant*
Dzyaloshinskii, Igor Ekhielievich *physicist*
Finlayson-Pitts, Barbara Jean *chemistry profes*
Ge, Nien-Hui *chemist, educator*
Manasson, Vladimir Alexandrovich *physicist*
Maradudin, Alexei A. *physics professor*
McLaughlin, Calvin Sturgis *biochemistry professor*
Micic, Miodrag *chemist, researcher*
Nowick, Arthur Stanley *metallurgy and materials science educator*
Phalen, Robert Franklynn *environmental scier*
Randerson, James T. *geophysicist, educator*
Ritz, Thorsten *biophysics professor*
Rose, Irwin A. (Ernie Rose) *biochemist, educator*
Rowland, Frank Sherwood *chemistry professo*
Rynn, Nathan *physics professor, consultant*
Shadpour, Hamed *research assistant*
Shea, Kenneth J. *chemistry professor*
Starostina, Natasha *research scientist*
Wallis, Richard Fisher *physicist, researcher*
White, Stephen Halley *biophysicist, educator*

Kensington
Appelman, Evan Hugh *retired chemist*
Connick, Robert Elwell *retired chemistry professor*

La Canada Flintridge
Baines, Kevin Hays *astronomer, planetary scientist*

La Jolla
Andre, Michael Paul *physicist, educator*
Arnold, James Richard *chemist, educator*
Asmus, John Fredrich *physicist*
Backus, George Edward *theoretical geophysi*
Baran, Phil S. *chemistry professor*
Berger, Wolfgang H. *oceanographer, educato geologist*
Boger, Dale L. *chemistry professor*
Branscomb, Lewis McAdory *physicist, researcher*
Burbidge, E. Margaret *astronomer, educator*
Burbidge, Geoffrey *astrophysicist, educator*
Continetti, Robert E. *chemistry professor*
Cox, Charles Shipley *oceanography research educator*
Davis, Brian Keith *biophysicist, researcher*
Dixon, Jack Edward *biological chemistry professor, consultant*
Driscoll, Charles Frederick *physicist, educato*
Edelman, Gerald Maurice *biochemist, neuroscientist, educator*
Feher, George *biophysicist, educator*
Haymet, Anthony Douglas-John *research scientist, chemistry educator*
Heeb, Mary Jo *biochemist, researcher*
Hendrickson, David Norman *chemistry profe*
Hermann, Thomas C. *chemistry professor*
Itano, Harvey Akio *biochemistry educator*
Kadonaga, James Takuro *biochemist*
Kearns, David Richard *chemistry professor*
Kelly, Jeffrey W. *chemist, educator*
Kennel, Charles Frederick *atmospheric physi professor, academic administrator, governr official*
Khan, Imran *research scientist, educator*
Kitada, Shinichi *biochemist*
Kolodner, Richard David *biochemist, educato director*
Kuperman, William A. *oceanographer, educa*
Lal, Devendra *nuclear geophysics educator*
Lauer, James Lothar *physicist, researcher*
Low, Philip Steven *research scientist, entrepreneur*
Lydon, Nicholas B. (Nick Lydon) *biochemist pharmaceutical executive, researcher*
Ma, Wenxue *medical scientist*
Maple, M. Brian *physics professor*
Marti, Kurt *chemistry professor*
McCammon, James Andrew *chemistry profes*
Molina, Mario Jose *physical chemist, educat*
Nicolaou, K. C. *chemistry professor*
Onuchic, José Nelson *biophysics educator, electrical engineer*
Patton, Stuart *biochemist, educator*
Ride, Sally Kristen *physics professor, researc scientist, retired astronaut*
Rotenberg, Manuel *physics professor*
Schimmel, Paul Reinhard *biochemist, biophysicist, educator*
Sham, Lu Jeu *physics professor, physicist*
Sharpless, K. Barry *chemist, educator*
Shor, George G., Jr. *geophysicist, oceanogra administrator, engineer*
Shuler, Kurt Egon *chemist, educator*
Siegel, Jay Steven *chemistry educator*
Somerville, Richard Chapin James *atmosphe scientist, educator*
Taur, Yuan *physicist, researcher*
Tsien, Roger Yonchien *chemist, cell biologis*

iji, Frederick Ichiro *biochemist, molecular biologist*
n Lint, Victor Anton Jacobus *physicist*
ing, Lei *biochemist*
itson, Kenneth Marshall *physics professor*
olynes, Peter Guy *chemistry researcher, educator*
nmermann, Joerg *biophysicist*

guna Hills
ssiter, Bryant William *chemistry consultant*

vermore
der, Berni Julian *physicist, researcher*
ok, Robert Crossland *chemist, researcher*
wgill, Donald Franklin *physicist*
oper, Edwin Bickford *physicist*
lder, Ray Edward *physicist, consultant*
kwood, Robert Keith *applied physicist*
th, Cecil Eldon, Jr. *retired physicist*
ckolls, John Hopkins *physicist, researcher*
dousky, Harry Brian *physicist*
k, Seymour *nuclear scientist*
ter, Benjamin David *atmospheric scientist*
otts, Wayne J. *nuclear scientist, federal agency administrator*
ller, Eberhard Adolf *physicist, researcher*
ter, Curtis Bruce *physicist, science administrator*
ber, Stephen Vance *physics researcher*
son, James Ricker *physicist, consultant*

ma Linda
tery, Charles Wilbur *biochemistry educator*

ng Beach
er, Roger Duane *chemistry professor, consultant*
Chi Yu *retired physicist, educator*
Gaughey, Charles Gilbert *retired biochemist*

s Altos
knoi, Andrew *astronomer, educator*

s Angeles
derson, W. French (William French Anderson) *biochemist, physician, educator*
son, Sidney William *chemistry researcher*
umik, Mani Lal *physicist*
ver, Paul D. *biochemist, educator*
oi, Myong Yong *chemist, researcher*
, Chi-Cheng *research scientist*
rke, Steven Gerard *chemistry professor*
eman, Paul Jerome, Jr. *physicist, researcher*
nwall, John Michael *physics professor, consultant*
oniti, Ferdinand Vincent *physics and astronomy professor*
vs, David Alan *chemistry professor*
n, Bruce Sidney *materials scientist, educator*
co, Armand John *biochemist*
as, Perry Spiros *physicist*
errez, Carlos G. *chemistry professor*
warth, Robert Willis *physicist, researcher*
k, Kendall Newcomb *chemistry professor*
oby, Neil Herman, Jr. *astronautical scientist, engineer, consultant*
lan, Isaac Raymond *chemistry professor*
sner, Michael Ernest *materials science educator, researcher*
elson, Margaret Galland *physicist*
a, Rokutaro (Rocky Koga) *physicist*
pp, Edwin Charles *astronomer*
ine, Raphael David *chemistry professor*
Yong-Gang Frank *research scientist, educator*
er, Michael Randall *biochemist, educator*
ns, James Richard *research scientist*
ki, Kazumi *physicist, researcher*
kland, Francis Swaby, Jr. *biochemist, educator*
lin, J. David *meteorologist, educator*
feld, Elizabeth Fondal *biochemist, educator*
ni, Marcel Ephraim *biochemistry educator*
n, George Andrew *chemist, educator*
son, Donald Robert *chemistry professor*
g, Weimin *biochemist, molecular biologist*
s, Howard *chemistry professor*
erts, Sidney *biological chemist*
tt, Robert Lane *chemist, educator*
oiro, Jerald Steven *chemist, bank executive*
th, Emil L. *biochemist, educator*
ton, Robert James, Jr. *geologist, educator*
ostin, Aleksandr B. *nuclear scientist, researcher*
wagen, Robert Harwood *biochemistry professor*
ddart, J(ames) Fraser *chemistry professor*
me, Richard Mansergh *physicist*
ible, Stanley Wayne *hydrologist*
, Jennie Ching-I *research scientist, educator*
le, John Emilio *geologist*
ker, Raymond John *physicist*
tten, Charles Alexander, Jr. *physics professor*
ry, David Beryle *physicist, researcher*
odruff, Fay *paleoceanographer, geological researcher*
ght, Edward Leonard *astronomy educator*
g, Henry S. (Hong Yang) *metallurgist, materials engineer*

libu
David Shiao-Kung *research scientist, consultant*
oer, David M. *scientist, educator, writer, inventor, consultant*

rina
ne, William Whitney *astronomer*

kinleyville
nman, Roscoe Edward *physicist, educator*

nlo Park
n, Matthew Arnold *physicist*
stein, Lawrence R. *inorganic chemist, pharmaceutical chemist*

Brodsky, Stanley Jerome *physics educator, consultant*
Bukry, John David *geologist*
Bynum, Gretchen Luepke *geologist*
Crosley, David Risdon *chemical physicist*
Dorfan, Jonathan Mannie *physicist, researcher*
Drell, Persis Sydney *physicist*
Drell, Sidney David *physicist, arms control and national security specialist*
Jaros, John A. *physics professor*
Kuwabara, James Shigeru *research hydrologist*
Mill, Theodore *chemist, researcher*
Penzias, Arno Allan *astrophysicist, information scientist, researcher*
Richter, Burton *physicist, educator*
Ruspini, Enrique Hector *research scientist*
Taylor, Richard Edward *physicist, researcher*

Mission Viejo
Glasky, Alvin Jerald *retired medical research scientist*

Modesto
Morrison, Robert Lee *physical scientist*

Moffett Field
Berenji, Hamid Reza *research scientist, educator*
Chen, Bin *materials scientist*
Glass, Brian Jay *aerospace scientist*
Makeev, Maxim A. *physicist*
Mattioda, Andrew Lige *chemist, researcher, space scientist*

Montecito
Wheelon, Albert Dewell *physicist*

Monterey
Yao, Lihua *research scientist, statistician*

Moss Landing
Brewer, Peter George *ocean geochemist*
Clague, David A. *geologist*
McNutt, Marcia Kemper *geophysicist*

Mountain View
Hoffman, Donald Clinton *physicist, researcher*
Showalter, Mark Robert *astronomer*
Summers, David Patrick *chemist, astrobiologist*

Murrieta
Lake, Bruce Meno *physicist*

Napa
Shin, Ernest Eun-Ho *physicist, educator, researcher*

Newbury Park
Fisk, Charles John *meteorologist, researcher, consultant*

Newport Beach
Kolyer, John McNaughton *materials scientist, retired chemist*

North Hollywood
Thomson, John Ansel Armstrong *biochemist*

Northridge
Smathers, James Burton *medical physicist, educator*

Oakland
Brust, David *physicist*
Carwell, Hattie Virginia *health physicist*
Linford, Rulon Kesler *physicist, electrical engineer*

Oceanside
Miyagawa, Hiroaki *materials scientist, researcher*

Orangevale
Gibson, Gordon Ronald *chemist*

Palo Alto
Andersen, Torben Brender *optical researcher, astronomer, software engineer*
Flory, Curt Alan *research physicist*
Herring, (William) Conyers *retired physicist, educator*
Huberman, Bernardo A. *physicist*
Martin, Robert Bruce *chemistry professor*
Perl, Martin Lewis *physicist, educator, chemical engineer*
Saxena, Arjun Nath *physicist*
Skoog, Douglas Arvid *retired chemistry educator, writer*
Title, Alan M. *astrophysicist*
Varney, Robert Nathan *retired physicist, researcher*

Palos Verdes Estates
Paulikas, George Algis *retired physicist*

Pasadena
Albee, Arden Leroy *geologist, educator*
Allen, Clarence Roderic *geologist, educator*
Anderson, Don Lynn *geophysicist*
Asimow, Paul D. *geophysicist, educator*
Barish, Barry C. *physics professor, researcher*
Barnes, Charles Andrew *physicist, researcher*
Beauchamp, Jesse Lee (Jack Beauchamp) *chemistry professor*
Beer, Reinhard *atmospheric scientist*
Boehm, Felix Hans *physicist, researcher*
Brown, Michael E. *astronomer, astronomy educator*
Byun, Sung Hun *research scientist*
Chahine, Moustafa Toufic *atmospheric scientist*
Chan, Sunney Ignatius *retired chemistry educator*
Cutri, Roc Michael *research scientist*
Dervan, Peter Brendan *chemistry professor*
Dressler, Alan Michael *astronomer*
Duxbury, Thomas Carl *planetary scientist*
Eisenstein, James P. *physicist, educator*
Frautschi, Steven Clark *physicist, researcher*

Freedman, Wendy Laurel *astronomer, educator, director*
Fu, Lee-Lueng *oceanographer*
Golombek, Matthew Philip *research scientist, planetary geologist*
Goodstein, David Louis *physics professor*
Gray, Harry Barkus *chemistry professor*
Grotzinger, John Peter *paleontologist, educator*
Grubbs, Robert Howard *chemistry professor*
Gurnis, Michael Christopher *geological sciences educator*
Heath, James R. *chemistry educator*
Heindl, Clifford Joseph *physicist, researcher*
Helmberger, Donald Vincent *geophysical educator, researcher*
Hitlin, David George *physicist, researcher*
Johnson, William Lewis *materials scientist, educator*
Jun, Insoo *nuclear scientist, researcher*
Kamionkowski, Marc Paul *astrophysicist, educator*
Kanamori, Hiroo *geophysicist, professor emeritus*
Kavanagh, Ralph William *physics professor*
Lange, Andrew E. *astrophysicist*
Lopes, Rosaly Mutel Crocce *astronomer, planetary geologist*
Marcus, Rudolph Arthur *chemist, educator*
Mayo, Stephen L. *biochemist*
McGill, Thomas Conley *physics educator*
Mc Koy, Basil Vincent Charles *theoretical chemist, educator*
Oemler, Augustus, Jr. *astronomer, educator*
O'Linger, JoAnn C. *astronomer*
Politzer, Hugh David *physicist, educator*
Preskill, John Phillip *physics professor*
Roberts, John D. *chemist, educator*
Sandage, Allan Rex *astronomer*
Sargent, Anneila Isabel *astrophysicist*
Sargent, Wallace Leslie William *astronomer, educator*
Schwarz, John Henry *theoretical physicist, educator*
Sekanina, Zdenek *astronomer*
Spilker, Linda Joyce *aerospace scientist*
Stevenson, David John *planetary scientist, educator*
Stone, Edward C. *physicist, researcher*
Thorne, Kip Stephen *physicist, researcher*
Tombrello, Thomas Anthony, Jr. *physics professor*
Vogt, Rochus Eugen *physicist, researcher*
Wilcox, Jaroslava Zitkova *physicist*
Wise, Mark B. *physics professor*
Yeomans, Donald Keith *astronomer*

Pleasanton
Stallings, Charles Henry *retired physicist*

Pomona
Bidlack, Wayne Ross *nutritional biochemist, toxicologist, food scientist*

Rancho Palos Verdes
Silver, Arnold Herbert *retired physicist*

Rancho Santa Fe
Creutz, Edward Chester *physicist, museum director*

Redlands
Clopine, Gordon Alan *consulting geologist, educator*

Redondo Beach
Foster, John Stuart, Jr. *physicist, former defense industry executive*
Mulvey, Gerald John *meteorologist*

Ridgecrest
Bennett, Harold Earl *physicist, optics researcher*
Bennett, Jean Louise McPherson *physicist, research scientist*
St-Amand, Pierre *geophysicist*

Riverside
Rabenstein, Dallas Leroy *chemistry professor*

Rolling Hills Estates
Diaz-Zubieta, Agustin *nuclear physicist, engineering executive*

Sacramento
Purdy, James Aaron *medical physics professor*
Rosenfeld, Arthur H. *physics professor, researcher*

San Carlos
Rathmann, George Blatz *genetic engineering company executive*

San Clemente
Wolfram, Thomas *physicist, educator*

San Diego
Cantor, Charles Robert *biochemistry professor*
Isaac, Charles Edward *environmental scientist, director*
L'Annunziata, Michael Frank *chemist, nuclear scientist, consultant*
Lao, Lang Li *nuclear scientist, physicist*
Pincus, Howard J. *geologist, engineer, educator*
Shneour, Elie Alexis *biophysicist, researcher, historian*
Timoshchuk, Victor Arkadyevich *research scientist*
Verma, Inder M. *biochemist*

San Francisco
Agard, David A. *biochemistry and biophysics educator*
Batterman, Boris William *physicist, educator, academic administrator*
Burlingame, Alma Lyman *chemist, educator*
Cluff, Lloyd Sterling *earthquake geologist*
Cohen, Fred Ehrenkranz *biophysics professor*
DeRisi, Joseph L. *biochemist, educator*

Dill, Kenneth Austin *pharmaceutical chemistry educator*
Fury, Michael Andrew *materials scientist, research and development company executive*
Grodsky, Gerold Morton *biochemistry professor*
Hale, Victoria G. *chemist, pharmaceutical executive*
Hanahan, Douglas *biochemist, educator*
James, Thomas Larry *chemistry professor*
Johnson, Alexander D. *biochemist, molecular biologist, educator*
Julius, David *biochemist*
Marshall, Grayson William, Jr. *materials scientist, biomedical engineer, health sciences educator, dentist*
Nguyen, Ann Cac Khue *pharmaceutical and medicinal chemist*
Sali, Andrej *chemistry professor*
Walter, Peter *biochemist*

San Jose
Craford, M. George *physicist, research administrator*
Madra, Satbir Singh *materials researcher, mechanical engineer*
Parkin, Stuart Stephen Papworth *materials scientist*
Winters, Harold Franklin *physicist*

San Luis Obispo
Grismore, Roger *physics professor, researcher*
Hafemeister, David Walter *physicist*

San Rafael
Pomerantz, Martin Arthur *astronomer, educator, physicist*

Santa Barbara
Ahlers, Guenter *physicist, researcher*
Awschalom, David Daniel *physics professor*
Bazan, Guillermo C. *chemistry and materials professor*
Bowers, Michael Thomas *chemistry professor*
Bruice, Thomas C. *chemist, educator*
Caldwell, David Orville *physics professor*
Evans, Anthony Glyn *materials scientist, educator*
Ford, Peter C. *chemistry professor*
Giddings, Steven B. *physics professor*
Gossard, Arthur Charles *physicist, researcher*
Gross, David Jonathan *physicist*
Heeger, Alan Jay *physicist, educator*
Hubbard, Arthur Thornton *chemist, educator*
Kennedy, John Harvey *chemistry professor*
Kohn, Walter *physicist, retired educator*
Luyendyk, Bruce Peter *geophysicist, educator, academic administrator*
Macdonald, Ken Craig *geophysicist*
Peale, Stanton Jerrold *physics educator*
Pilgeram, Laurence Oscar *biochemist*
Polchinski, Joseph G. *physicist, science educator*
White, Robert Stephen *retired physics professor*
Witherell, Michael S. *physicist, educator*
Young, Michael Kent *physics professor*

Santa Clara
Dafforn, Geoffrey Alan *biochemist*
Dai, Guang-ming George *optics scientist*
Lee, Chan-Yun *physicist, process engineer, educator*
Somani, Seema *optics scientist*

Santa Cruz
Bian, Zhixi *research scientist*
Brown, George Stephen *physics professor*
Bunnett, Joseph Frederick *chemist, educator*
Faber, Sandra Moore *astronomer, educator*
Flatté, Stanley Martin *physicist, researcher*
Griggs, Gary Bruce *oceanographer, geologist, educator, director*
Hill, Terrell Leslie *chemist, researcher, biophysicist*
Kraft, Robert Paul *astronomer, educator*
Margon, Bruce Henry *astrophysicist, educator*
Sands, Matthew Linzee *physicist, researcher*
Wipke, W. Todd *chemistry professor*
Woosley, Stanford Earl *astrophysicist*

Santa Monica
Intriligator, Devrie Shapiro *physicist*

Santa Rosa
Banks, Peter Morgan *physics professor*
Kim, Seung-bum (Sab) *research scientist*

Sherman Oaks
Caren, Robert Poston *aerospace scientist*

Solana Beach
Agnew, Harold Melvin *physicist*

Stanford
Archer, Cristina Lozej *meteorologist*
Baldwin, Robert Lesh *biochemist, educator*
Berg, Paul *biochemist, educator*
Bienenstock, Arthur Irwin *physicist, educator, federal official*
Block, Steven Michael *biophysicist, educator*
Brauman, John I. *chemist, educator*
Brunger, Axel Thomas *biophysicist, researcher, educator*
Bube, Richard Howard *retired materials scientist, educator*
Collman, James Paddock *chemistry professor*
Fayer, Michael David *chemist, educator*
Fetter, Alexander Lees *theoretical physicist, educator*
Harbaugh, John Warvelle *geologist, educator*
Harbury, Pehr A.B. *biochemist, educator*
Harrison, Walter Ashley *physicist, researcher*
Kennedy, Donald *environmental scientist, educator, editor*
Keren, Kinneret *biophysicist*
Kool, Eric T. *chemist, educator*
Kornberg, Arthur *biochemist, educator*
Kornberg, Roger David *biochemist, structural biologist*

Kovach, Robert Louis *geophysics educator*
Lehman, I(srael) Robert *biochemist, educator*
Little, William Arthur *physicist, researcher*
Matson, Pamela Anne *environmental scientist, science educator*
Moerner, William Esco *physical chemist, educator*
Moskalenko, Igor Vladimirovich *physicist, astrophysicist*
Mueller, Holger *physicist*
Osheroff, Douglas Dean *physics professor, researcher*
Quake, Stephen R. *physics professor, researcher*
Rai, Varun *physical chemist*
Ross, John *physical chemist, educator*
Segall, Paul *geologist, educator*
Shenker, Stephen *physics professor*
Solomon, Edward Ira *chemistry professor, researcher*
Stryer, Lubert *biochemist, educator*
Susskind, Leonard *physicist, educator*
Thompson, George Albert *geophysicist, educator*
Trost, Barry Martin *chemist, educator*
Wagoner, Robert Vernon *astrophysicist, educator*
Walt, Martin *physicist, educator*
Wender, Paul Anthony *chemistry professor*
Wojcicki, Stanley George *physicist, researcher*
Zare, Richard Neil *chemistry professor*

Stockton
Samoshin, Vyacheslav Vladimirovich *chemistry professor, science educator, researcher*
Whiteker, Roy Archie *retired chemistry professor*

Sunnyvale
Chang, William Zhi-Ming *research scientist*
Gozani, Tsahi *nuclear physicist*
Uchibori, Chihiro J. *materials scientist, researcher*

Thousand Oaks
Baek, Kwang-Hyun *research scientist*
Bobzin, Steve *chemist, researcher*
Pipes, Gary Dale *biochemist*
Remmele, Richard L., Jr. *research scientist, director*
Zhang, Zhongqi *chemist*

Torrance
Bhargave, Ashish A. *research scientist*
Ibe, Basil Obijiaku *biochemist, educator*
Kim, Keehoon *cybernetic scientist*
Rogers, Howard H. *retired chemist*

Valencia
Levy, Ezra Cesar *aerospace scientist, real estate agent*

Walnut Creek
Wu, Tse Cheng *chemist, researcher*

Westminster
Zeng, Eddy Yongping *chemist*

Woodland Hills
Sharma, Brahama D. *chemistry professor*

COLORADO

Arvada
Mullineaux, Donal Ray *geologist*

Aurora
Grace, William Pershing *petroleum geologist, real estate developer*

Boulder
Bhat, Rajiv *physicist, researcher*
Canup, Robin M. *astrophysicist, science administrator*
Caruthers, Marvin Harry *biochemistry educator*
Chappell, Charles Franklin *meteorologist, consultant*
Clark, Noel A. *physics professor*
Cornell, Eric Allin *physics professor*
DePuy, Charles Herbert *chemist, educator*
Dryer, Murray *physicist, educator*
Dudhia, Jimy *atmospheric scientist*
Faller, James Elliot *physicist, researcher*
Fleming, Rex James *meteorologist*
Garstang, Roy Henry *astrophysicist, educator*
Gosling, John Thomas *space plasma physicist, researcher*
Hall, John Lewis *physicist, researcher*
Hermann, Allen Max *physics professor*
Hill, Mary C. *hydrologist*
Hogg, David Clarence *physicist*
Horikis, Theodoros *research scientist*
Jin, Deborah *physicist, educator*
Joselyn, Jo Ann *space scientist*
Kapteyn, Henry Cornelius *physics professor, engineering educator*
Kellogg, William Welch *meteorologist, researcher*
Killeen, Timothy Laurence *aerospace scientist, science administrator*
King, Edward Louis *retired chemistry professor*
LeMone, Margaret Anne *atmospheric scientist*
Linsky, Jeffrey Lawrence *astrophysicist*
Low, Boon Chye *physicist*
Mahlman, Jerry David *retired meteorologist*
Malde, Harold Edwin *retired federal government geologist*
Nam, Sae Woo *physicist*
Oh, Seongshik *physicist, researcher*
Ostrovsky, Lev Aronovich *physicist, oceanographer, educator*
Pankove, Jacques Isaac *retired physicist, researcher*
Phelps, Arthur Van Rensselaer *physicist, consultant*
Randa, James Paul *physicist, electrical engineer*
Ravishankara, Akkihebal R. *chemist*
Roellig, Leonard Oscar *physics professor*
Smythe, William Rodman *physicist, researcher*
Tatarskii, Valerian Il'Ich *physics researcher*
Templeton, Alexis S. *biogeochemist, educator*
Tolbert, Bert Mills *biochemist, educator*
Trenberth, Kevin Edward *atmospheric scientist*
Tuck, Adrian Francis *meteorologist, physical chemist*
Washington, Warren Morton *meteorologist*
Wieman, Carl E. *physics professor*
Ye, Jun *physicist, researcher*

Brighton
Rinkenberger, Richard Krug *physical scientist, geologist, consultant*

Colorado Springs
Corry, Charles Elmo *geophysicist, not-for-profit developer*
Venugopal, Veerakumar *materials scientist, physicist, researcher*

Denver
Babayev, Djangir Ali Ikram *physicist, researcher*
Bufe, Charles Glenn *geophysicist, researcher*
Cobban, William Aubrey *paleontologist*
Eaton, Gareth Richard *chemistry professor, dean*
Fails, Thomas Glenn *geologist*
Grinspoon, David H. *astrobiologist, writer, museum administrator*
Johnson, Walter Earl *geophysicist*
Landon, Susan Melinda *petroleum geologist*
Morrison, Kendra Ann *environmental scientist*
Neumann, Herschel *retired physics professor*
Ormes, Jonathan Fairfield *astrophysicist, researcher, educator*
Smith, Dwight Morrell *chemistry professor, academic administrator*
Weihaupt, John George *geophysics educator, academic administrator*

Durango
Cristol, Stanley Jerome *retired chemistry professor*

Evergreen
Haun, John Daniel *petroleum geologist, educator*
Heyl, Allen Van, Jr. *geologist*

Fort Collins
Bamburg, James Robert *biochemistry professor*
Fixman, Marshall *chemist, educator*
Meyers, Albert Irving *chemistry professor*
Schumm, Stanley Alfred *geologist, educator*
She, Chiao-Yao *physics professor, researcher*
Thompson, David W.J. *atmospheric scientist, educator*
Zupanski, Dusanka *research scientist*

Golden
DeSanto, John A. *physicist, educator, mathematics professor*
Hamilton, Warren Bell *geologist, geophysicist, educator, researcher*
Krauss, George *metallurgist*
Metzger, Wyatt K. *physicist*
Mocker, Hans Walter *physicist*
Taylor, Philip Craig *physics professor*
Trefny, John Ulric *retired college president*

Greeley
Szczyrba, Igor Nicholas *mathematical physicist, consultant*

Highlands Ranch
Brierley, James Alan *biohydrometallurgy consultant*
Krinsky, Fredda S. *clinical chemist, consultant*

Lakewood
Hansen, Richard Olaf *geophysicist, educator, director*
Quinn, John Michael *physicist, geophysicist*

Littleton
Paull, Richard Allen *geologist, educator*

Livermore
Tkachev, Sergey Nikolayevich *geophysicist*

Lone Tree
Spisak, John Francis *corporation executive*

Louisville
Brault, James William *physicist*

Ridgway
Lathrop, Kaye Don *nuclear scientist, educator*

Windsor
Mayer, Victor James *geologist, educator*

CONNECTICUT

Farmington
Goodson, Richard Carle, Jr. *chemist*
Osborn, Mary Jane Merten *biochemist, educator*
Spencer, Richard Paul *biochemist, physician, educator*

Greenwich
Davenport, Lee Losee *physicist*

Groton
Wager, Carrie Brockway *chemist, researcher*

Ledyard
Chiang, Albert Chinfa *polymer chemist*
Harwood, Harold James, Jr. *biochemist*

Manchester
Galasso, Francis Salvatore *materials scientist*

Middletown
Ettre, Leslie Stephen *chemist*
Starr, Francis *physics professor*

New Haven
Adair, Robert Kemp *physicist, educator*
Baltay, Charles *physicist, educator*
Berson, Jerome Abraham *chemistry professor*
Brudvig, Gary W. *chemistry professor*
Casten, Richard Francis *physicist, educator*
Chupka, William Andrew *chemical physicist, educator*
Curran, Lisa M. *environmental scientist, educator*
DeMille, David P. *physics professor*
Engelman, Donald Max *molecular biophysics and biochemistry educator*
Garen, Alan *biophysicist, educator*
Girvin, Steven Mark *physicist, researcher*
Jaisi, Deb P. *geologist, researcher*
Jorgensen, William L. *chemistry educator*
Korchagin, Vladimir *astrophysicist*
Korenaga, Jun *geophysicist, educator*
Marchesi, Vincent Thomas *biochemist, educator*
Parker, Peter D.M. *physicist, educator, researcher*
Ramirez, Ainissa *materials scientist*
Reed, Mark Arthur *research scientist, educator*
Sandweiss, Jack *physicist, researcher*
Saunders, Martin *chemistry educator, researcher*
Shulman, Robert Gerson *biophysics professor*
Tully, John Charles *research chemical physicist*
Wolf, Werner Paul *physicist, researcher*
Zelitch, Israel *retired scientist*
Zeller, Michael Edward *physicist, researcher*

New Milford
Fabricand, Burton Paul *physicist, researcher*

North Haven
Herzenberg, Arvid *physicist, researcher*

Pawcatuck
Gnanaraj, Joseph Sathiya *scientist*

Ridgefield
Grinberg, Nelu *chemist*

Rocky Hill
Chu, Hsien-Kun *chemist, researcher*

Stamford
Chang, Ted T. *chemist*
Colthup, Norman Bertram *retired spectroscopist*

Storrs Mansfield
Bartram, Ralph Herbert *physicist*
Klemens, Paul Gustav *physicist, researcher*
Marcus, Harris Leon *materials science educator*
Reifsnider, Kenneth Leonard *metallurgist, educator*
Smirnova, Alevtina Leonidovia *physical chemistry educator, researcher*
Stwalley, William Calvin *physics and chemistry professor*

Trumbull
Ouyang, Hao *research scientist*

Waterford
Johnson, Gary William *environmental scientist, consultant*

West Hartford
Gould, Laurence Ira *physicist*

West Haven
Onton, Ann Louise Reuther *chemist*

Willington
Zhang, Heng *research scientist, educator*

Woodbury
Skinner, Brian John *geologist, educator*

DELAWARE

Greenville
Rocek, Jan *retired chemist*

Middletown
Hall, Peter Michael *physics professor, electronics engineer*

Newark
Burmeister, John Luther *chemistry professor, consultant*
Murray, Richard Bennett *retired physics professor*
Rayle, Heather Lynnette *chemist*

Wilmington
Esrey, Elizabeth Gove Goodier *chemist, biologist*
Jaycox, Gary Delmar *research scientist*
Kissa, Erik *retired chemist, consultant*
Kwolek, Stephanie Louise *chemist, researcher*
Marcali, Jean Gregory *retired chemist*
Mukherjee, Partha S. *research scientist*
Parshall, George William *chemist, researcher*

DISTRICT OF COLUMBIA

Washington
Alexander, Joseph Kunkle, Jr. *physicist*
Baldwin, Sheryl Denise *chemist, editor, writer*
Berendzen, Richard *astronomer, educator, author*
Bierly, Eugene Wendell *meteorologist, science foundation director*
Boss, Alan Paul *astrophysicist*
Ciesla, Fred John *astrophysicist, meteoriticist, researcher*
Davidson, Eugene Abraham *biochemist, educator, academic administrator*
Dutro, John Thomas, Jr. *geologist, paleontologist*
El Khadem, Hassan Saad *chemistry professor, researcher*
Esfandiary, Mary S. *physical scientist, operations consultant*
Girard, James Emery *chemistry professor*
Goff, James Franklin *physicist, consultant*
Goldstein, Allan Leonard *biochemist, educator*
Hallgren, Richard Edwin *meteorologist*
Hemley, Russell J. *geophysicist*
Hertz, Paul Louis *astrophysicist*
Hirji, Rafik F. *water resources expert*
Jacobs, David Ernest *environmental health scientist*
Karle, Isabella L. *chemist*
Karle, Jerome *physicist, researcher*
Knopman, Debra Sara *environmental scientist, director, hydrologist, policy analyst*
Komarov, Andrei M. *biophysicist, educator, research scientist*
Ledley, Robert Steven *biophysicist*
Lehman, Donald Richard *physicist, educator, academic administrator*
Lehmberg, Robert Henry *retired research physicist*
Ligler, Frances Smith *biochemist*
Lozansky, Edward Dmitry *physicist, consultar writer*
Mao, Ho-kwang (Dave Mao) *geophysicist, educator*
Maran, Stephen Paul *astronomer*
Meijer, Paul Herman Ernst *physicist, educator*
Montgomery, John A. *physicist*
Mysen, Bjorn Olav *scientist*
Oran, Elaine Surick *physicist*
Pojeta, John, Jr. *geologist, researcher*
Press, Frank *geophysicist*
Rosenberg, Jerome David *physicist*
Ross, Malcolm *minerals consultant*
Sayre, Edward Vale *chemist*
Shamim, Mah Talat *chemist*
Shapero, Donald Campbell *physicist, governr official*
Sheppard, Scott S. *astronomer*
Shuler, James Mannie *health physicist*
Silver, Paul G. *geophysicist*
Singer, Maxine Frank *retired biochemist, scie association director*
Solomon, Sean Carl *geophysicist, lab administrator*
Stanley, Jean-Daniel *geological oceanographe*
Uberall, Herbert Michael Stefan *physicist, researcher*
White, John Arnold *physics professor, researc scientist*
White, Robert Mayer *meteorologist*
Yochelson, Ellis L(eon) *paleontologist*
Youtcheff, John Sheldon *physicist*
Zacharias, Norbert *astronomer*

FLORIDA

Alachua
Schneider, Richard T(heodore) *optics scientis researcher, engineer*

Boca Raton
Louda, J. William *chemist, biochemist, educa*
Weissbach, Herbert *biochemist, researcher*

Bonita Springs
Brown, Theodore Lawrence *chemistry profes*

Boynton Beach
Shang, Charles Yulin *medical physicist*

Bradenton
Brunk, William Edward *astronomer*

Brooksville
Flannery, Michael Sidney *environmental scie*
McBride, Tamera Shawn Dew *geologist*

Clearwater
Platau, Gerard Oscar *chemist, consultant*

Cocoa Beach
Antolik, Michael *geophysicist*

Coral Gables
Einspruch, Norman Gerald *physicist, enginee educator*
Glaser, Luis *biochemistry educator*
Hirschberg, Joseph Gustav *physicist, educato*
Leblanc, Roger Maurice *chemistry professor*
Van Vliet, Carolyn Marina *physicist, research*

Dade City
Burdick, Glenn Arthur *physicist, engineering educator*

Dania Beach
Spieler, Richard Earl *oceanographer, educato*

Daytona Beach
David, Valentina S. *physics professor*

Delray Beach
Simon, Albert *retired physicist, engineer, educator*
Zarwyn, Berthold *physicist, consultant*

Fort Lauderdale
Itkin, Ivan *nuclear scientist, mathematician*

Fort Myers
Curtin, David Yarrow *chemist, educator*
Horecker, Bernard Leonard *retired biochemis professor*
Missimer, Thomas Michael *geologist*

Gainesville
Cousins, Robert John *nutritional biochemist, educator*
Green, Alex Edward Samuel *physicist, mechanical engineering educator*
Hanrahan, Robert Joseph *chemist, educator*
Jacobs, Alan Martin *physicist, researcher*
Katritzky, Alan Roy *chemistry professor*
Kumar, Pradeep *physics professor, researche*
Micha, David Allan *chemistry and physics professor*
Mosier, Arvin Ray *chemist, researcher*

ils Yngve *chemistry and physics ator*
Gregory S. *biochemist*
, John Edward, Jr. *retired environmental tist, consultant*

lez
e, Le Moyne Wilfred *chemist, researcher*

onville
Donald A. *aerospace scientist, ultant*
n, Frederick Cooper *retired biochemist*

r
n, Jerry Irving *biophysicist, theoretical icist, medical researcher*

Vest
ell, Herbert Eugene *retired physicist*

Worth
ch, Howard L. *biochemist*

and
in, Richard Francis *retired industrial ist, researcher*

na
Moses Earl *biochemist, educator*

a
ni, Kavita-Vibha Arun *chemist*

boat Key
on, Harvey James *physics professor*

red William *retired research chemist*

ourne
, Gordon Leigh *chemist, educator*
John H. III *chemical oceanographer, ator*
an, Floyd Landis *chemist*

i
JiuHua *physicist, geophysicist, educator, rials scientist*
n, Mark Anthony *physicist*
Rana Arnold *chemical and physical nographer*
Jose A. *physicist, writer*
, Xiao-Lan *chemist*
rman, Stephen Parker *geologist, educator, er*
eld, (Britt) Max *meteorologist*
s, Christopher Northrup Kennard *physical nographer, educator*
ez, Danmary *research scientist*

es
r, Alfred *retired mathematical physicist, cator, educational film producer*

ndo
iou, Costas John *physicist, educator, archer*
baugh, David Edward *physicist*
an, Elena S. *physicist, physics educator*
, Richard Lawrence *physicist, researcher*
llyn, Ralph Alvin *physics professor*

ond Beach
r, Julian Norman *biochemist, educator*

Beach Gardens
, George *retired chemist*

etto Bay
shima, Tadayoshi *retired biochemist, earcher*

ciana
ams, Donald John *physicist, researcher*

a Gorda
an, Robert Louis *metallurgy consultant*

sota
e, Richard Harry *oceanographer*

ahassee
pin, Gregory Robert *chemistry professor*
r, James Brian *meteorologist, educator*
er, Penny Jane *biochemist, educator*
son, Thomas Alexander *retired eteorologist*
don, Roy Clifford *physicist*
hall, Alan George *chemistry and chemistry educator*
on, Donald *physics professor*
effer, John Robert *physics professor, science ministrator*

pa
son, Anthony O'Leary (Andy Johnson) *eteorologist, consultant*

ice
nann, Edward George *pharmaceutical emist, pharmacologist*

t Palm Beach
Binhe *environmental scientist*
en, John Clifton III *environmental scientist, rector*

ter Park
sey, Erich Carl *chemistry professor*

ORGIA

haretta
ges, Alan Lynn *physicist, researcher, plication developer, computer scientist*

Athens
Black, Clanton Candler, Jr. *biochemistry professor, researcher*
Chu, Chung Kwang *medicinal chemistry professor*
Darvill, Alan G. *biochemist, botanist, educator*
Johnson, Michael Kenneth *chemistry professor*
Law, John Harold *biochemistry educator*
Schaefer, Henry Frederick III *chemistry professor*
Schleyer, Paul von Ragué *chemistry educator*
Yang, Charles Qi-Xiang *chemistry educator, researcher, consultant*

Atlanta
Allison, Stuart Anthony *chemistry professor, researcher*
Ashby, Eugene Christopher *chemistry professor*
Cramer, Howard Ross *geologist, environmental consultant*
Declercq, Nico Felicien *research scientist*
de Heer, Walter A. *physics professor*
Dickinson, Robert Earl *atmospheric scientist, educator, retired science administrator*
Finkelstein, David Ritz *physicist, educator, consultant*
Fox, Ronald Forrest *physicist, educator*
Gonzalez, Ruben Rene *biochemist, researcher, educator*
Howard, Ralph O'Sullivan, Jr. *geologist, researcher*
Kahn, Bernd *radiochemist, educator*
Krishnamurthy, Ramesh Saligrama *environmental scientist, researcher*
Kuklenyik, Zsuzsanna *chemist, researcher*
Lin, Ming-Chang *physical chemistry professor, researcher*
Lynch-Stieglitz, Jean *geophysicist, educator*
McAlister, Harold Alister *astronomer*
Perera, Unil A.G. *physics educator, researcher*
Polk, Malcolm *chemistry professor*
Snyder, Robert Lyman *materials scientist, educator*
Sophianopoulos, Judy Ann *environmental scientist*
Strekowski, Lucjan *chemistry professor*
Wiesenfeld, Kurt Arn *physicist, researcher*
Wong, Ching-Ping *chemist, materials engineer*

Austell
Cohn, Charles Erwin *retired physicist*

Brunswick
Mihal, Sandra Powell *research scientist*

Kennesaw
Kidonakis, Nikolaos *physicist*

Marietta
Berryhill, Henry Lee, Jr. *retired geologist*

Peachtree City
Roobol, Norman Richard *chemistry professor, consultant*

Savannah
Sanders, James Grady *biogeochemist*
Walter, Paul Hermann Lawrence *chemistry professor*
Windom, Herbert Lynn *oceanographer, environmental scientist*

Stone Mountain
Reichert, Leo Edmund, Jr. *biochemist, department chairman, endocrinologist*

HAWAII

Hawaii National Park
Swanson, Donald Alan *geologist*

Hilo
Binder, Philippe-Michel *physicist, educator*

Honolulu
Hawke, Bernard Ray *planetary scientist, researcher*
Hey, Richard Noble *marine geophysicist*
Ihrig, Judson La Moure *chemist*
Jewitt, David *astronomer*
Karl, David Michael *oceanographer, educator*
Keil, Klaus *geology educator, consultant*
Khan, Mohammad Asad *geophysics educator, retired minister, former senator of Pakistan*
Kong, Laura S. L. *geophysicist*
Kudritzki, Rolf-Peter *astronomer, educator*
Lebedev, Konstantin Vladimirovich *oceanographer, researcher*
Mader, Charles Lavern *chemist*
McMurtry, Gary Michael *geochemist, educator*
Pakvasa, Sandip *physicist*
Raleigh, Cecil Baring *geophysicist*
Seff, Karl *zeolite chemist, chemistry educator*
Tiwari, Atul *chemist, researcher*

Kihei
Borchers, Robert Reece *physicist, science administrator*

IDAHO

Emmett
Bennett, Gary Lee *physicist, consultant*

Idaho Falls
Abbott, Michael Lehman *environmental scientist*
Jue, Jan-Fong *materials scientist*
Paviet-Hartmann, Patricia *chemist, researcher*

Moscow
Griffiths, Peter Roughley *chemistry professor, consultant*
Miller, Maynard Malcolm *geologist, educator, science administrator, former state legislator*
Renfrew, Malcolm MacKenzie *chemist, educator*
Shreeve, Jean'ne Marie *chemist, educator*

Pocatello
Bennett, Byron Lee *chemistry professor, researcher*

ILLINOIS

Abbott Park
Jeng, Tzyy-Wen *biochemist, researcher*
Krueger, Allan C. *chemist*

Argonne
Abrikosov, Alexei Alexeyevich *physicist*
Bader, Samuel David *physicist*
Buth, Christian *physicist, researcher*
Derrick, Malcolm *physicist*
Kolesnikov, Alexander Ivanovich *physicist*
Lawson, Robert Davis *theoretical nuclear physicist*
Peshkin, Murray *physicist*
Shpyrko, Oleg G. *physicist*
Steindler, Martin Joseph *chemist*
Sumant, Anirudha *materials scientist, researcher*

Arlington Heights
Rivkin, William B. *physicist*
Smith, Norman Obed *retired physical chemist, educator*

Batavia
Bardeen, William Allan *research physicist*
Jonckheere, Alan Mathew *physicist*
Oddone, Piermaria Jorge *physicist*
Raja, Rajendran *physicist*
Rakhno, Igor *physicist*

Bolingbrook
Sabau, Carmen Sybile *retired chemist*

Carbondale
Oyana, Tonny J. *geoscientist, educator*

Champaign
Balbach, Harold Edward *environmental scientist*
Buschbach, Thomas Charles *geologist, consultant*
Cartwright, Keros *hydrogeologist, researcher*
Gross, David Lee *geologist*
Krug, Edward Charles *environmental scientist*
Rebeiz, Constantin Anis *plant biochemist, educator, lab administrator, foundation administrator*
Wolfram, Stephen *physicist, computer company executive*

Chicago
Chin, Cheng *physicist, educator*
Cronin, James Watson *physicist, researcher*
Eastman, Dean Eric *physicist, researcher*
Farman, Gerrie P. *research scientist*
Freed, Karl Frederick *chemistry professor*
Giger, Maryellen Lissak *medical physicist, educator*
Gomer, Robert *chemistry professor*
Greaves, William Webster *chemist*
Halpern, Jack *chemist, educator*
Harvey, Allison Charmaine *chemist*
Harvey, Ronald Gilbert *research chemist*
Hast, Malcolm Howard *biomedical scientist, educator*
Herzenberg, Caroline Stuart Littlejohn *physicist*
Hildebrand, Roger Henry *astrophysicist, physicist*
Iqbal, Zafar Mohd *biochemist, molecular biologist, pharmacologist, cancer researcher, toxicologist, consultant*
Kadanoff, Leo Philip *physicist, educator*
Kouvel, James Spyros *physicist, educator*
Krawetz, Arthur Altshuler *chemist, science administrator*
Lee, Bao-Shiang Bob *biochemist, researcher*
Lehman, Dennis Dale *chemistry professor, department chairman*
Levy, Donald Harris *chemistry professor*
Liao, Shutsung *biochemist, molecular oncologist*
Makinen, Marvin William *biophysicist, educator*
Nambu, Yoichiro *physics professor*
Newcomb, Martin Eugene, Jr. *chemistry professor*
Oehme, Reinhard *physicist, researcher*
Olsen, Edward John *geologist, educator, curator*
Palmer, Patrick Edward *radio astronomer, educator*
Pilcher, James Eric *physicist*
Reiffel, Leonard *physicist, consultant*
Richter, Frank M. *geophysicist, educator*
Rosner, Jonathan Lincoln *physicist, researcher*
Rosner, Robert *astrophysicist, educator*
Steiner, Donald Frederick *biochemist, physician, educator*
Stroscio, Michael Anthony *physicist, researcher*
Truran, James Wellington, Jr. *astrophysicist, educator*
Turner, Michael Stanley *astrophysics professor, researcher*
Winstein, Bruce Darrell *physics professor*
Yamamoto, Hisashi *chemistry professor*

Dekalb
Dyshkant, Alexander Sergeevich *physicist, researcher*
Kimball, Clyde William *physicist, researcher*

Des Plaines
Pestova, Ekaterina *scientist*

Downers Grove
Green, David William *chemist, educator*
Hubbard, Lincoln Beals *medical physicist, consultant*

Elk Grove Village
Jan, Chwu-Ching Hwang *environmental chemistry consultant*

Evanston
Allred, Albert Louis *chemistry professor*
Brown, Laurie Mark *physicist, researcher*
Cao, Hui *physics and astronomy professor*
Chang, R. P. H. *materials science educator*
Godwin, Hilary A. *chemistry professor, research scientist*
Hoffman, Brian M. *chemistry professor*
Ibers, James Arthur *chemist, educator*
Jennings, Hamlin Manson *materials scientist, educator*
Lambert, Joseph Buckley *chemistry professor*
Margoliash, Emanuel *biochemist, educator*
Marks, Tobin Jay *chemistry educator*
Moore, C. Bradley *chemistry professor*
Oakes, Robert James *physics and astronomy professor*
Sachtler, Wolfgang Max Hugo *chemistry professor*
Schatz, George C. *chemist, educator*
Seidman, David N(athaniel) *materials scientist, engineer, educator*
Silverman, Richard Bruce *chemist, educator, biochemist*
Ulmer, Melville Paul *physics and astronomy educator*
Van Duyne, Richard Palmer *analytical chemistry educator, chemical physics educator*
Wessels, Bruce W. *materials scientist, educator, department chairman*

Galesburg
Schwartzman, Peter David *environmental scientist, educator*

Glen Ellyn
Mooring, F. Paul *physics editor*

Glenview
Rorig, Kurt Joachim *chemist, science association director, educator*

Hinsdale
Kaminsky, Manfred Stephan *physicist*

Homewood
Parker, Eugene Newman *retired physicist, retired educator*

Lake Forest
Weston, Arthur Walter *chemist, consultant, retired chemicals executive*

Lemont
Williams, Jack Marvin *research chemist*

Libertyville
Grote, Jonathan *chemist, researcher*

Lombard
McCoy, Jeanie Shearer *analytical chemist, consultant*

Maywood
Bermes, Edward William, Jr. *biochemist, educator*

Naperville
Arzoumanidis, Gregory G. *chemist*
Sellers, Gregory Jude *physicist*
Sherren, Anne Terry *chemistry professor*

North Chicago
Hutchinson, Douglas K. *chemist*
Loga, Sanda *physicist, researcher*

Northfield
Shabica, Charles Wright *geologist, earth science educator*

Peoria
Chamberlain, Joseph Miles *retired astronomer, educator*
Nielsen, Harald Christian *retired chemist, researcher*

Springfield
Evans, William Kendall *nuclear scientist*

Urbana
Beak, Peter Andrew *chemistry professor*
Ceperley, David Matthew *physics professor*
Granato, Andrew Vincent *physics professor, researcher*
Greene, Joseph E. *material science researcher*
Greene, Laura Helen *physicist*
Gruebele, Martin *chemistry and biophysicist professor*
Iben, Icko, Jr. *astrophysicist, educator*
Jonas, Jiri *chemist, educator*
Kelleher, Neil L. *chemist, educator*
Kieffer, Susan Werner *geologist, educator, media consultant*
Klein, Miles Vincent *physics professor*
Leggett, Anthony James *physics professor, researcher*
Lu, Yi *chemistry professor*
Martinez, Todd J. *chemistry professor*
McFarquhar, Greg M. *meteorologist, educator*
Rowland, Theodore Justin *physicist, researcher*
Schweizer, Kenneth Steven *physics professor*
Snyder, Lewis Emil *astrophysicist, educator*
Song, Xiaodong *geophysicist, seismologist*
Suslick, Kenneth Sanders *chemistry professor*
Switzer, Robert Lee *biochemistry professor*
Watson, William Douglas *astrophysicist*
Woese, Carl R. *biophysicist, microbiology educator*
Xu, Dong *biophysicist, researcher*
Zimmerman, Steven Charles *chemistry professor*

Wadsworth
Ahmad, Moghisuddin *chemist, researcher*

Woodridge
Shen, Sin-Yan *physicist, acoustical engineer, musicologist*

INDIANA

Bloomington
Basu, Abhijit *geologist, educator*
Cameron, John M. *nuclear scientist, educator, administator*
Easton, Susan Dawn *biochemist, educator*
Edmondson, Frank Kelley *retired astronomer*
Hanson, Gail G. *physicist, researcher*
Hattin, Donald Edward *geologist, educator*
Hites, Ronald Atlee *chemist, educator*
Huffman, John Curtis *chemist*
Kauffman, Erle Galen *geologist, paleontologist*
Letsinger, Robert Lewis *chemistry professor*
Macfarlane, Malcolm Harris *physicist, educator*
Peters, Dennis Gail *chemist*
Pollock, Robert Elwood *nuclear scientist*
Poplawski, Nikodem J. *physicist, researcher*
Rocha, Luis M. *physics professor, director*
Smith, Ronald Thomas *environmental scientist*

Brownsburg
Conway, Dwight Colbur *retired chemistry professor*

Chesterton
Crewe, Albert Victor *physicist, researcher, artist*

Elkhart
Free, Helen Murray *chemist, consultant*

Gary
Kilibarda, Zoran *geologist, educator*

Indianapolis
Bein, Frederick L. *geography educator*
Farag, Sherif Shafik *physician scientist, educator*
Fife, Wilmer Krafft *retired chemistry professor*
Kleinhans, Frederick William *biophysicist, educator*
Lau, Pauline Young *chemist*
Li, Shuyu *research scientist*
Mirsky, Arthur *retired geologist, educator*
Olson, Byron Louis *biochemist, educator*
Wong, David T. *biochemist, researcher*

Lafayette
Gartenhaus, Solomon *physicist, educator*
Loeffler, Frank Joseph *physicist, educator*
Porile, Norbert Thomas *chemistry professor*

Madison
Tatera, James Frank *chemist*

Muncie
Call, David Andrew *meteorologist, educator*
Harris, Joseph McAllister *retired chemist*

Notre Dame
Garg, Umesh *physicist, researcher*
Huber, Paul William *biochemistry professor, researcher*
Maurice, Patricia Ann *geochemist, educator*
Meisel, Dan *chemist*
Trozzolo, Anthony Marion *chemistry professor*

Terre Haute
Guthrie, Frank Albert *chemistry professor*
Inlow, Jennifer Kay *chemistry professor, researcher*

Valparaiso
Cook, Addison Gilbert *chemistry professor*

West Lafayette
Abu-Omar, Mahdi M. *chemistry professor*
Adelman, Steven Allen *chemist, educator*
Arabi, Mazdak *hydrologist, researcher*
Barnes, Virgil Everett, II, *physics professor*
Chang, Ching-jer *medicinal chemistry educator*
Cooks, R(obert) Graham *chemist, educator*
Diamond, Sidney *chemist, educator*
Fanwick, Phillip Edward *crystallographer*
Judd, William Robert *engineering geologist, educator*
Lipschutz, Michael Elazar *chemistry professor, consultant, researcher*
McMillin, David Robert *chemistry professor*
Morrison, Harry *chemistry professor*
Negishi, Ei-ichi *chemistry professor*
Overhauser, Albert Warner *physicist*
Rossmann, Michael George *biochemist, educator*
Sanders, David Avram *biochemist, researcher*
Zwier, Timothy S. *chemistry professor*

IOWA

Ames
Angelici, Robert J. *chemistry educator*
Armstrong, Daniel Wayne *chemist, educator*
Barnes, Richard George *physicist, researcher*
Barton, Thomas Jackson J. *chemistry professor, researcher*
Bytautas, Laimutis *chemist, educator*
Clem, John Richard *physicist, educator*
Fritz, James Sherwood *chemist, educator*
Gschneidner, Karl Albert, Jr. *metallurgist, educator, editor, consultant*
Hong, Mei *chemistry professor*
Horowitz, Jack *biochemistry educator*
Jacobson, Robert Andrew *chemistry professor*
Jenks, Cynthia J. *research scientist*
Lo, Chester C.H. *research scientist*
Robyt, John F. *chemistry professor*
Ruedenberg, Klaus *theoretical chemist, educator*
Schlagel, Deborah "Devo" Lynn *chemist, materials scientist*
Smith, John Francis *materials science educator*
Tabatabai, M. Ali *chemist, biochemist*
Yeung, Edward Szeshing *chemist*

Cedar Falls
Koob, Robert Duane *chemistry professor, academic administrator*

Des Moines
Bartschat, Klaus Richard Wilhelm *physics professor*

Grinnell
Swartz, James Edward *chemistry professor, educator, dean*

Iowa City
Baker, Richard Graves *geologist, palynologist, educator*
Bhattacharya, Debashish *environmental scientist, educator*
Burton, Donald Joseph *chemistry professor*
Conway, Thomas William *biochemist, educator*
Donelson, John Everett *biochemistry professor, molecular biologist*
Gurnett, Donald Alfred *physics professor*
MacGillivray, Leonard R. *chemistry professor*
Montgomery, Rex *biochemist, educator*
Prisinzano, Thomas Edward *chemistry professor, researcher*
Titze, Ingo Roland *physics professor*

Le Mars
Rebstock, Theodore Lynn *chemist, educator, retired research scientist*

Panora
Hartman, James Austin *retired geologist*

West Des Moines
Lynch, David William *physicist, retired educator*

KANSAS

Greeley
Fisher, William Ralph *retired geologist*

Kansas City
Drake, Kenneth David *geologist*

Lawrence
Alterman, Michail A. *biochemist, researcher*
Ammar, Raymond George *physicist, researcher*
Dreschhoff, Gisela Auguste Marie *physicist, researcher*
Enos, Paul *geologist, educator*
Gerhard, Lee Clarence *geologist, educator*
Kaesler, Roger L. *paleontologist, educator*
Landgrebe, John Allan *chemistry professor*
Merriam, Daniel F(rancis) *geologist*
Mitscher, Lester Allen *chemist, educator*
Schowen, Richard Lyle *retired scientist*
Stella, Valentino John *chemistry professor*

Manhattan
Klabunde, Kenneth J. *chemistry professor, researcher*
Le, Anh-Thu *physicist, researcher*
Liu, Kelly H. *geophysicist, educator*

Overland Park
Ostby, Frederick Paul, Jr. *meteorologist, retired government official, science administrator*

KENTUCKY

Bowling Green
Slocum, Donald Warren *chemist, researcher*

Frankfort
Zourarakis, Demetrio Periferachis *natural resource scientist*

Georgetown
Wiseman, Frank L., Jr. *chemistry professor*

Lexington
Brock, Carolyn Pratt *chemist, educator*
Ehmann, William Donald *chemistry professor*
Ettensohn, Frank Robert *geologist, educator*
Hamilton-Kemp, Thomas Rogers *organic chemist, educator*
Hojahmat, Marhaba *research scientist*
Kern, Bernard Donald *retired physicist*

Louisville
Belanger, William Joseph *chemist, consultant*
Johnson, Alan Arthur *physicist, educator, consultant*
Yazdanpanah, Mehdi Mohammad *research scientist*

Sturgis
Thornsberry, Willis Lee, Jr. *chemist*

LOUISIANA

Baton Rouge
Mc Glynn, Sean Patrick *physical chemist, educator*
O'Connell, Robert Francis *physics professor*
Robinson, James William *chemistry professor*
Traynham, James Gibson *chemist, educator*
Warner, Isiah Manuel *chemistry professor*
Xu, Feng *research scientist, educator*
Young, David P. *physics professor*
Zhou, Liming *environmental scientist*

Covington
Vercellotti, John Raymond *chemist, researcher*

Hammond
Voegel, Phillip Donovan *chemistry professor*

Lafayette
Harrison, Frank W., Jr. *geologist*
Rout, Bibhudutta *research scientist*

New Orleans
Perdew, John Paul *physics professor*
Prockop, Darwin Johnson *biochemist, medical educator*
Rosensteel, George Thomas *physics professor, nuclear physicist*
Tipler, Frank Jennings III *physicist*

Pearl River
Cantrell, Joseph Sires *chemistry professor*

Pineville
Nanna, Michael Edward *chemist, researcher*

MAINE

Freeport
Panish, Morton B. *retired physical chemist*

Gorham
Sanford, Robert Melvin *environmental scientist, educator*

Kittery
McNally, James Henry *physicist, defense consultant*

Orono
He, Zhongqi *chemist, researcher*
Townsend, David W. *oceanographer, educator*

Peaks Island
Bohan, Thomas Lynch *physicist, lawyer*

Saco
Ames, Ted *environmental scientist*

MARYLAND

Aberdeen Proving Ground
Carrieri, Arthur Helmut *physicist, researcher*
Mackay, Raymond Arthur *chemist*
Steger, Ralph James *chemist*

Adelphi
Agwu, Idika Ume *chemist, educator, reading specialist*
Brandt, Howard Edward *physicist*
Gaunaurd, Guillermo C. *physicist, researcher, engineer*

Annapolis
Bontoyan, Warren Roberts *chemist, lab administrator*
Clotworthy, John Harris *oceanographic consultant*
Hammer, Jacob Myer *physicist, consultant*
Wolf, Alfred A. *physicist, educator*

Baltimore
Beer, Michael *biophysicist, educator, environmentalist*
Deutsch, Robert William *physicist*
Devreotes, Peter Nicholas *biochemistry educator*
Dicello, John Francis, Jr. *physicist, researcher*
Eichhorn, Gunther Louis *chemist, researcher*
Fulton, Thomas *theoretical physicist, educator*
Giacconi, Riccardo *astrophysicist, educator*
Green, Robert Edward, Jr. *physicist, researcher*
Haig, Frank Rawle *physics professor, priest*
Hauser, Michael George *astrophysicist*
Helm, Donald Cairney *geologist, engineer, educator*
Jahren, (A.) Hope *geochemist, educator*
Jones, Hendree Evelyn *research scientist, psychologist*
Judd, Brian Raymond *physicist*
Kaplan, Alexander Efimovich *physics educator, engineering educator*
Krolik, Julian Henry *astrophysicist, educator*
Lee, Yung-Keun *physicist, researcher*
Marsh, Bruce David *geologist, educator*
Mixson, Archibald James *research scientist, internist, endocrinologist*
Moos, H. Warren *physicist, educator, astronomer, director*
Norman, Colin Arthur *astrophysics educator*
Olson, Peter L. *geophysicist, educator*
Posner, Gary Herbert *chemist, educator*
Riess, Adam Guy *astronomer, educator*
Roseman, Saul *biochemist, educator*
Shamoo, Adil Elias *biochemist, educator*
Silverstone, Harris J. *chemistry professor*
Sinha, Neeti *biophysicist, researcher*
Steiner, Robert Frank *biochemist*
Townsend, Craig Arthur *chemistry educator*
Ts'o, Paul On-Pong *biophysical chemist, educator*
Weaver, Kenneth Newcomer *geologist, state agency administrator*

Beltsville
Johnson, Phyllis Elaine *chemist, researcher, federal official*

Berlin
Brodsky, Allen *retired biophysicist*
Passwater, Richard Albert *biochemist, author*

Bethesda
Becker, Edwin Demuth *chemist, director*
Berger, Robert Lewis *retired biophysicist*
Fales, Henry Marshall III *chemist*
Huebner, John Stephen *geologist*
Jacobson, Kenneth Alan *chemist, researcher*
Jamieson, Graham A. *biochemist, researcher, retired organization official*
Kalish, Heather Rachel *chemist, researcher*
Korn, Edward David *biochemist*
Murayama, Makio *biochemist*
Rice, Jerry Mercer *biochemist, consultant, pathologist*
Stadtman, Earl Reece *biochemist, researcher*
Trus, Benes Louis *structural chemist*
Vaughan, Martha *biochemist, educator*
Wickner, Sue Hengren *biochemist*
Wiese, Wolfgang Lothar *physicist, researcher*
Witkop, Bernhard *chemist*
Zoon, Kathryn Christine *biochemist*
Zwanzig, Robert Walter *chemist, physical science educator*

Cabin John
Shropshire, Walter, Jr. *biophysicist, pastor*
Townsend, John William, Jr. *physicist, ret federal agency administrator*

Chevy Chase
Kurochkina, Natalya Alexandrovna *biophy*
Mielke, James Edward *geochemist*
Sinclair, Rolf Malcolm *retired physicist*

College Park
Coffey, Timothy *physicist*
DeFries, Ruth S. *earth system scientist, researcher*
DeSilva, Alan W. *physics professor, resear*
Dragt, Alexander James *physicist, educato*
Dusold, Laurence Richard *chemist, compu specialist*
Farquhar, James *geochemist, researcher*
Fenselau, Catherine Clarke *chemistry prof*
Fisher, Michael Ellis *physicist, educator, c*
Gates, Sylvester James, Jr. *physics profess researcher*
Greenberg, Oscar Wallace *physicist, resear*
Griem, Hans Rudolf *physicist, researcher*
Helz, George Rudolph *chemistry professor*
Korhonen, Fawna J. *geologist, researcher*
Kundu, Mukul Ranjan *physics and astrono professor*
Lubkin, Gloria Becker *physicist*
Misner, Charles William *physics professor*
Nusinovich, Gregory Semeon *physicist, researcher*
Rabin, Herbert *physicist, educator, dean*
Redish, Edward Frederick *physicist, resear*
Rosenberg, Norman Jack *agricultural meteorologist, educator*
Shen, Qing *urban planning educator, resea associate dean*
Silverman, Joseph *chemistry professor*
Walters, William Ben *chemistry professor*
Williams, Ellen D. *physics professor*
Yoo, Jin-Hyeong *research scientist*
Zen, E-an *research geologist, educator*
Zhang, Da-lin D. *meteorologist, educator*

Columbia
Fisher, Dale John *retired chemist, medical investigator*
Khare, Mohan *chemist, researcher*
Terry, Robert Eli *physicist, aerospace scien educator*

Dayton
Fischell, Robert Ellentuch *physicist*

Derwood
Mylonakis, Stamatios Gregory *research sci lawyer*
Stadtman, Thressa Campbell *biochemist*

Edgewater
McCamy, Calvin Samuel *retired optics scie*

Elkton
Xu, Ping *chemist*

Frederick
Carlson, David Emil *physicist, researcher*
Garver, Robert Vernon *retired research phy*
Henderson, Madeline Mary (Berry) *chemist, researcher, consultant*
Lucas, Joe N. *biophysicist, researcher*

Gaithersburg
Boettinger, William J. *metallurgist*
Burnett, John Huszagh *physicist*
Caplin, Jerrold Leon *health physicist*
Caswell, Randall Smith *physicist*
Celotta, Robert James *physicist*
Clark, Charles Winthrop *physicist*
DeRose, Paul Christian *chemist, researcher*
Harman, George Gibson *physicist, consultar*
Jacox, Marilyn Esther *chemist*
Jahanmir, Said *materials scientist, mechanic engineer*
Lynn, Jeffrey Whidden *research physicist, educator*
Phillips, William Daniel *physicist*
Pierce, Daniel Thornton *physicist*
Reader, Joseph *physicist*
Sengers, Johanna M. H. Levelt *physicist*
Tarrio, Charles *physicist*
Tirumala, Vijaya Raghavan *materials scienti*
Weber, Alfons *physicist*
Werner, Samuel Alfred *physicist, educator*

Germantown
Patrinos, Aristides *environmental scientist, federal agency administrator*

Greenbelt
Acuña, Mario H. *astrophysicist*
Danchi, William C. *astrophysicist*
DelloRusso, Neil *astrochemist*
Gehrels, Neil (Cornelius A. Gehrels) *astrophysicist*
Kniffen, Donald Avery *astrophysicist, educat researcher*
Kuchner, Marc Jason *astrophysicist*
Mather, John Cromwell *astrophysicist*
Mumma, Michael Jon *research scientist*
Parkinson, Claire L. *climatologist*
Simpson, Joanne Malkus *meteorologist*
Wollack, Edward J. *astrophysicist*
Wood, H(oward) John III *astrophysicist, astronomer*

Lanham
Degnan, John James III *physicist*
Gavin, James Raphael III *biochemist*

l
Steven Michael *atmospheric scientist, archer*
, Harold Irving, Jr. *research scientist, ultant*
is, Stamatios Mike *physicist, researcher, ator, engineering executive, consultant*
nthony Tat Yin *physicist*
, Richard Hornsby *physicist*
t, Ralph Leroy, Jr. *astrophysicist*

icum Heights
David Eric *physicist, defense analyst, ist, retired military officer*

gomery Village
er, Lawrence Maurice *physical chemist, ultant*
, Peter *retired metallurgist, manufacturing utive*
on, Henry Ward *meteorologist*

Market
, Russell Dawson *physicist, consultant*

Bethesda
r, Stanley Evan *clinical chemist*

ton
rald, Edwin Roger *physicist, researcher*

nac
, Goetz Kuno Heinrich *physicist, essional society administrator*
ze Cheng *aerodynamicist, researcher*

ville
George Stanley *biochemist, physiologist, archer*

erstown
nbaum, Harvey *defense technology sultant*

ville
nan, John Donald *retired nuclear scientist*
Bruce Alan *physicist*
nkun *research scientist*
r, Jerome *materials science educator, sultant*
Potarazu Krishna *environmental consultant*
lone, William Robert *biochemist, educator, medical researcher*
dler, Albert Isadore *physicist, researcher*
ro, Maurice Mandel *nuclear astrophysicist*
Kaizhi *research scientist*
nmeyer, William Anton *retired physicist*

rna Park
ar, James Daniel, II, *physicist, engineer*

r Spring
man, Lucien Morton *retired physicist*
li, Steven J. *chemist*
h, Charles David *physicist*
on, Ralph P. *physicist*
n, Michiko Jeannette *oceanographer, teorologist, educational association ninistrator*
nore, Frank Clifford, Jr. *retired geologist*

land
lain, Edward Fifer, Jr. *retired physicist*

oma Park
li, Alexander John *retired chemist*

ple Hills
ss, Simon Wolf *chemist, materials scientist*

SSACHUSETTS

on
by, Joseph Francis *chemist*

wam
or, Simon William *chemistry professor*

herst
er, Ronald Dean *chemist, educator*
Richard David *chemist, educator*
stein, Joseph Irwin *materials scientist, ucator*
ock, Robert Bruce *physics professor*
Knight, William John *chemist, educator*
in, William Jesse *physics professor*
rson, Gerald Alvin *physics professor*
n, Monroe Stephen Zane *physicist*

lover
gi, Yasuhisa *chemist*

urndale
ow, Saul *radiological physicist, consultant*

ford
ghn, Thomas Joseph *earth science educator, lministrator*

mont
ser, George *biochemist, educator*
n, Richard Harold *physicist, educator*
meyer, John Leopold *chemistry professor*

erly
er, Graeme George *physicist, journalist*

ston
ssimova, Svetlana Vladimirovna *physicist, searcher*
elme, Jean-Pierre Louis Marie *chemist*
cher, Kenneth *astrophysicist, educator*
npbell, David Kelly *theoretical physicist, ngineering educator*
krabarti, Supriya *space astrophysicist*
Cohen, Robert Sonné *physicist, philosopher, educator*
Cohen, Saul G. *chemist, educator*
Edmonds, Dean Stockett, Jr. *physicist, educator, director*
Flomenbom, Ophir *biophysicist, researcher*
Golan, David Eric *biophysicist, pharmacologist, hematologist, medical educator*
Grice, Noreen Alisa-May *astronomer, educator*
Guertin, Robert Powell *physics professor, dean*
Harrison, Stephen Coplan *biochemist, educator*
Kornberg, Sir Hans Leo *biochemist, educator*
Malenka, Bertram Julian *physicist, researcher*
Papisov, Mikhail I. *chemist*
Pardee, Arthur Beck *biochemist, educator*
Shabestari, Khosrow Toutounchi (T. Shabestari) *research scientist*
Small, Donald MacFarland *biophysics professor, gastroenterologist, department chairman, researcher*
Stachel, John Jay *physicist, researcher*
Stanley, Harry Eugene *physicist, researcher*
Stollar, Bernard David *biochemist, educator*
Strominger, Jack Leonard *biochemist*
Trackman, Philip Charles *biochemist, researcher*
Valverde, Paloma *biochemist, educator*
Vodo, Plarenta *physicist, researcher*
von Stackelberg, Katherine Ellen *environmental scientist, consultant*
Yaroslavsky, Anna *biophysicist, educator*
Zhukovsky, Mikhail Andreyevich *biophysicist*

Bourne
Fantozzi, Peggy Ryone *geologist, environmental planner*

Brookfield
Anderson, Theodore Robert *physicist, small business owner*

Brookline
Nash, Leonard Kollender *retired chemistry professor*

Burlington
Maiti, Amitesh *physicist*

Cambridge
Alberty, Robert Arnold *chemistry professor*
Anderson, James Gilbert *chemistry professor*
Arkani-Hamed, Nima *physicist, educator*
Barger, James Edwin *physicist*
Bawendi, Moungi G. *chemist, educator*
Binzel, Richard P. *astrophysicist, educator*
Bloxham, Jeremy *geophysicist, educator*
Bradt, Hale Van Dorn *physicist, x-ray astronomer, educator*
Brecher, Aviva *physicist, researcher*
Burke, Bernard Flood *physicist, researcher*
Canizares, Claude Roger *astrophysicist, educator*
Ceyer, Sylvia T. *chemistry professor*
Chisholm, Sallie Watson *biological oceanography educator, researcher*
Cohn, Daniel Ross *physicist*
Corey, Elias James *chemistry professor*
Cummins, Christopher C. *chemistry professor*
Deutch, John Mark *chemistry professor, former CIA director*
Doty, Paul Mead *biochemist, educator, arms control specialist*
Dresselhaus, Mildred Spiewak *physics and engineering professor*
Eagar, Thomas Waddy *metallurgist, educator*
Ehntholt, Daniel James *chemist*
Emanuel, Kerry Andrew *meteorologist, oceanographer, educator*
Essigmann, John M. *chemistry professor*
Evans, David Albert *chemistry professor*
Feld, Michael Stephen *physics professor*
Feldman, Gary Jay *physicist, researcher*
Ferrari, Raffaele *oceanographer, educator*
Field, Robert Warren *chemistry professor*
French, Anthony Philip *physicist, educator*
Frey, Frederick August *geochemist, researcher, educator*
Friedman, Jerome Isaac *physics professor, researcher*
Fu, Gregory Chung-Wei *chemistry educator*
Gabrielse, Gerald *physics professor*
Garland, Carl Wesley *chemist, educator*
Gebbie, Geoffrey *research scientist, oceanographer*
Geller, Margaret Joan *astrophysicist, educator*
Gingerich, Owen Jay *astronomer, educator*
Glauber, Roy Jay *physics professor*
Goldstone, Jeffrey *physicist, educator*
Greene, Frederick Davis, II, *chemistry professor*
Halperin, Bertrand Israel *physics professor*
Heller, Eric Johnson *physicist, educator, digital abstract artist*
Hernquist, Lars Eric *astronomer, educator*
Herschbach, Dudley Robert *chemistry professor*
Hoffman, Paul Felix *geologist, educator*
Holdren, John Paul *physicist, educator, writer*
Holton, Gerald *physicist, educator, science historian*
Huchra, John Peter *astronomer, educator*
Huth, John E. *physicist, educator*
Jackiw, Roman *physicist, researcher*
Jacobsen, Eric N. *chemistry professor*
Joss, Paul Christopher *astrophysicist, atmospheric physicist, educator*
Kalb, Johannes Andreas *research scientist*
Kamentsky, Louis Aaron *biophysicist*
Kerman, Arthur Kent *physicist, researcher*
Ketterle, Wolfgang *physics professor*
Khorana, Har Gobind *chemist, educator*
Klemperer, Willian *chemistry professor*
Kleppner, Daniel *physicist, researcher*
Knowles, Jeremy Randall *chemist, educator, dean*
Krebs, Hermano Igo *research scientist*
Lee, Patrick A. *physics educator*
Lieber, Charles *chemistry professor, researcher, materials scientist*
Lin, Kai *research scientist*
Lindzen, Richard Siegmund *meteorologist, educator*
Lipscomb, William Nunn, Jr. *retired chemistry professor*
Liu, David Ruchien *biochemist, educator*
Liu, Xiong *atmospheric physicist*
Livingston, James Duane *physicist, researcher*
Lloyd, Seth *physicist*
Loeb, Abraham (Avi Loeb) *astrophysics educator, researcher*
Lomon, Earle Leonard *physicist, educator, consultant*
Long, Alan K. *research administrator*
Marsden, Brian Geoffrey *astronomer*
Martin, Paul Cecil *physicist, researcher*
Meng, Sheng *physicist, researcher*
Meselson, Matthew Stanley *biochemist, educator*
Milner, Richard Gerard *physicist*
Moniz, Ernest Jeffrey *physics professor*
Moran, James Michael, Jr. *astronomer, educator*
Nayeri, Ali *physicist, educator*
Negele, John William *physics professor, consultant*
O'Connell, Richard John *geophysicist, educator*
Oppenheim, Irwin *chemical physicist, educator*
Paul, William *physicist, researcher*
Pettengill, Gordon H(emenway) *physicist, researcher*
Poggio, Tomaso Armando *physicist, educator, computer scientist, researcher*
Pritchard, David Edward *physics professor*
Ramsey, Norman F. *physicist, researcher*
Randall, Lisa *physics professor*
Redwine, Robert Page *physicist, researcher*
Rubin, Lawrence Gilbert *physicist, science administrator*
Sadoway, Donald Robert *materials science educator*
Schrag, Daniel P. *geochemist, educator*
Schrock, Richard Royce *chemistry professor*
Seager, Sara *astronomer, educator*
Seyferth, Dietmar *chemist, educator*
Shapiro, Irwin Ira *physicist, researcher*
Silbey, Robert James *chemistry professor, researcher, consultant*
Soljacic, Marin *physicist, educator*
Soon, Willie Wei-Hock *environmental scientist*
Spaepen, Frans August *physicist, educator*
Steinfeld, Jeffrey Irwin *chemistry professor, educator, writer*
Strandberg, Malcom Woodrow Pershing *physicist*
Tananbaum, Harvey D. *astrophysicist*
Thaddeus, Patrick *physicist, researcher*
Tinkham, Michael *physicist, researcher*
Troccoli, Mariano *astrophysicist, researcher*
Vessot, Robert Frederick Charles *physicist, researcher*
Waugh, John Stewart *chemist, educator*
Weinberg, Robert Allan *biochemist, educator*
Wen, Xiao-Gang *physics professor*
Whitesides, George McClelland *chemistry professor*
Wilczek, Frank Anthony *physics professor*
Wood, John Armstead *planetary scientist, geological sciences educator, artist*
Wu, Tai Tsun *physicist, researcher*
Xie, Xiaoliang Sunney *chemist, educator*
Yi, Wei *physicist*
Zaldarriaga, Matias *cosmologist, physics professor*
Zhuang, Xiaowei *biophysicist, educator*
Zuber, Maria T. *geophysicist, educator*

Chestnut Hill
Kelley, Shana O. *biochemist*

Chilmark
Lazarus, David *physicist, researcher*

Concord
Horwitz, Paul *physicist*
Plummer, William Torsch *optical physicist*

Cotuit
Miller, Robert Charles *retired physicist*

East Longmeadow
Skutnik, Bolesh J. *optics scientist, lay worker, lawyer*

East Orleans
Romey, William Dowden *geologist, educator*

Falmouth
Adelman, William J., Jr. *biophysicist*
Goody, Richard Mead *geophysicist*

Hanscom Afb
Altshuler, Edward Elihu *physicist, researcher*
Mailloux, Robert Joseph *physicist*

Haverhill
DeSchuytner, Edward Alphonse *biochemist, educator*

Ipswich
Herrmann, Robert Lawrence *biochemist, educator*

Leominster
Kerns, Christian Randolph *chemist*

Lexington
Blackwell, William J. *geophysicist*
Dionne, Gerald Francis *research physicist, educator, consultant*
Huang, Robin K. *research scientist*
Silverman, Sam Mendel *physicist, lawyer*

Lowell
Kannenberg, Lloyd Chambers *physicist, researcher*
Pullen, David John *physicist, researcher*

Medford
Cavallaro, Mary Caroline *retired physics professor*
Kumar, Krishna *chemistry professor*
Schneps, Jack *physics professor, department chairman*

Needham
Holt, Stephen S. *astrophysicist*

Newburyport
Robinson, Enders Anthony *geophysicist, educator, writer*

Newton
Dunlap, William Crawford *physicist*
Jeanloz, Roger William *biochemist, educator*
Klyosov, Anatole Alex *biochemist, researcher*
Lichtin, Norman Nahum *chemistry professor*

North Andover
Swallow, Kathleen Clinedinst *chemistry professor*

North Dartmouth
Hsu, Jong-Ping *physicist, educator*
Sauro, Joseph Pio *physics professor*

Peabody
Dobbs, John McGregor *physicist, mechanical engineer*

Roxbury
Simons, Elizabeth R(eiman) *biochemist, educator*

Shrewsbury
Nixon, Eugene Ray *chemist, educator*

South Dartmouth
Mellberg, Leonard Evert *physicist*

South Hadley
Ewing Browne, Sheila *chemistry professor, physical organic chemist*
Williamson, Kenneth Lee *chemistry professor*

Wakefield
Trogolo, Jeffrey A. *research scientist*

Waltham
Abbott, Laurence Frederick *physics educator*
Epstein, Irving Robert *chemistry professor*
Foxman, Bruce Mayer *chemist, educator*
Snider, Barry B. *organic chemist*

Wayland
Brynjolfsson, Ari *nuclear physicist*
Clark, Melville, Jr. *physicist, consultant, electrical engineer*
Wolff, Peter Adalbert *retired physics professor, researcher*

Wellesley
Charpie, Robert Alan *physicist, researcher*
Kato, Walter Yoneo *physicist*
Snitzer, Elias *physicist*

Westford
Paine, Robert J. *environmental scientist, consultant*

Weston
Lin, Alice Lee Lan *physicist, researcher, educator*

Williamstown
Crampton, Stuart Jessup Bigelow *physicist, researcher*
Markgraf, J(ohn) Hodge *chemist, educator*
Park, David Allen *physicist, researcher*
Pasachoff, Jay Myron *astronomer, educator*
Wobus, Reinhard Arthur *geologist, educator*
Wootters, William K. *physics professor*

Wilmington
Lee, Joohan *materials scientist*

Winchester
Milburn, Richard Henry *physics professor*
Winston, Arthur William *physicist*

Woods Hole
Behn, Mark Dietrich *marine geophysicist, educator*
Berggren, William Alfred *geologist, research micropaleontologist, educator*
Burger, Max Marcel *biochemist*
Cohen, Seymour Stanley *biochemist, educator*
Gagosian, Robert B. *chemist, educator*
Hart, Stanley Robert *geochemist, educator*
Ledwell, James R. *oceanographer*
Steele, John Hyslop *marine scientist, oceanographic institute administrator*
Uchupi, Elazar *geologist, researcher*

Worcester
Nelson, Donald Frederick *retired physics educator, researcher*

MICHIGAN

Ann Arbor
Agranoff, Bernard William *biochemist, educator*
Akerlof, Carl William *physics professor*
Ashe, Arthur James III *chemistry professor*
Bartell, Lawrence Sims *chemist, educator*
Blinder, Seymour Michael *chemistry and physics professor, researcher*
Chupp, Timothy Edward *physicist, educator, academic administrator*
Clarke, Roy *physicist, researcher*
Dekker, Eugene Earl *biochemistry educator*
Filisko, Frank Edward *physicist, researcher*
Garneau-Tsodikova, Sylvie *chemistry professor*
Griffin, Henry Claude *retired chemistry professor*
Haddock, Fred(erick) T(heodore), Jr. *retired astronomer*
Hagel, William Carl *metallurgical consultant*
Jones, Lawrence William *retired physicist*

Kesler, Stephen Edward *geology educator*
Krimm, Samuel *physicist, researcher*
Krisch, Alan David *physics professor*
Lin, Hai *physicist*
Merlin, Roberto Daniel *physicist, educator*
Meyers, Philip Alan *geochemistry educator, researcher*
Morris, Michael David *chemistry professor*
Neal, Homer Alfred *physics professor, researcher, academic administrator*
Nordman, Christer Eric *chemistry professor*
Nriagu, Jerome Okon *environmental geochemist*
Oh, So-Ryeok *research scientist*
Pappas, Janice Louise *paleontologist, researcher*
Parkinson, William Charles *physics professor, researcher*
Robertson, Richard Earl *physical chemist, educator*
Roe, Byron Paul *physics professor*
Saltiel, Alan Robert *biochemist*
Sanford, Melanie S. *chemist, educator*
Van der Voo, Rob *geophysicist*
Veltman, Martinus J.G. *retired physics educator*

Belleville
Wilson, David James *chemistry researcher, educator*

Birmingham
Smith, George Wolfram *physicist, researcher*

Chassell
Spain, James Dorris, Jr. *biochemist, educator*

Chelsea
Weinreich, Gabriel *physicist, minister, educator*

Detroit
Bowen, David R. *science and technology educator, consultant*
Drescher, Dennis George *biochemist, researcher*
Frade, Peter Daniel *chemist, educator, administrator*
Gupta, Suraj Narayan *physicist, researcher*
Stewart, Melbourne George, Jr. *physicist, researcher*

East Lansing
Abolins, Maris Arvids *physicist, educator*
Austin, Sam M. *physicist, educator*
Blosser, Henry Gabriel *physicist*
Boehlert, Carl Joseph *materials scientist, educator*
Brown, Boyd Alex *physicist, researcher*
Case, Eldon Darrel *materials science educator*
D'Itri, Frank Michael *environmental research chemist*
Dye, James Louis *retired chemistry professor*
Gelbke, Claus-Konrad *nuclear physics educator*
Harrison, James Francis *chemistry professor, researcher*
Harrison, Michael Jay *physicist, researcher*
Kaplan, Thomas Abraham *physicist, educator*
Kirkpatrick, R(obert) James *geologist, educator*
Preiss, Jack *biochemistry professor*

Farmington Hills
Chapman, Gilbert Bryant *physicist*
Theodore, Ares Nicholas *chemist, researcher*

Grand Rapids
Greenfield, John Charles *biochemist, professional society administrator*
Menninga, Clarence *retired geologist*

Grosse Pointe Park
Orton, Colin George *medical physicist*

Highland
Brown, Ray Kent *biochemist, physician, educator*

Ironwood
Rondeau, Clement Robert *petroleum geologist*

Kentwood
Yovich, Daniel John *chemist, educator*

Leland
Small, Hamish *chemist*

Midland
Chao, Marshall *chemist*
Crummett, Warren Berlin *analytical chemistry consultant*
Dorman, Linneaus Cuthbert *retired chemist*
Nowak, Robert Michael *chemist*

Mount Pleasant
Dietrich, Richard Vincent *geologist, educator*
Mohanty, Dillip K. *chemistry professor, researcher*
Peyrefitte, Ashton George, Jr. *meteorologist, educator*

Negaunee
Hultquist, Thomas Robert *meteorologist*

Okemos
Burnett, Jean B. *biochemist, educator*

Saint Clair Shores
Ugorowski, Philip Brien *nuclear scientist, researcher*

Three Rivers
Boyer, Nicodemus Elijah *chemist, consultant*

Troy
Fritzsche, Hellmut *physics professor*

University Center
Clarey, Timothy Lee *geologist, educator*

Warren
Herbst, Jan Francis *physicist, researcher*

West Bloomfield
Harwood, Julius J. *metallurgist, educator*

Ypsilanti
Barnes, James Milton *retired physics and astronomy professor*
Kolopajlo, Lawrence Hugh *chemistry professor*

MINNESOTA

Bloomington
Bekrenev, Anatoliy *physicist*

Duluth
Minor, Elizabeth Colquitt *chemistry professor*

Mahtomedi
Holmén, Reynold Algott Emanuel *chemist*

Minneapolis
Ackerman, Eugene *biophysics professor*
Carr, Peter William *chemistry professor*
Goldman, Allen Marshall *physics professor*
Halley, James Woods *physics professor*
Kim, Seong Chan *environmental scientist, researcher*
Kohlstedt, David Lee *geophysicist, educator*
Kuhi, Leonard Vello *astronomer, academic administrator*
Lee, Jong Y. *medical scientist, educator*
Marshak, Marvin Lloyd *physicist, researcher*
Muthyala, Ramaiah *chemistry professor, researcher*
Portoghese, Philip Salvatore *medicinal chemist, educator*
Truhlar, Donald Gene *chemist, educator*
Wright, Herbert E(dgar), Jr. *geologist*

Moorhead
Strong, Judith Ann *chemist, educator*

Northfield
Cederberg, James *retired physics professor*

Oakdale
Tran, Nang Tri *research scientist, electrical engineer*

Rochester
Greenleaf, James Fowler *biophysics educator*
Kao, Pai Chih *clinical chemist*
Pang, Yuan-Ping *synthetic and computational chemist*

Saint Paul
Kaliyan, Nalladurai *research scientist*
Newmark, Richard Alan *chemist*
Ouderkirk, Andrew J. *corporate scientist*
Perry, James Alfred *environmental scientist, consultant, science educator, academic administrator*
Prager, Stephen *chemistry professor*
Rubens, Sidney Michel *physicist, consultant*
Van Pilsum, John Franklin *biochemist, educator*
Weisberg, David Steven *environmental scientist*

MISSISSIPPI

Bay Saint Louis
Hurlburt, Harley Ernest *ocean modeling and prediction scientist*

Hattiesburg
Miao, Wujian *chemistry professor*

Ocean Springs
Biber, Patrick D. *oceanographer*

Stennis Space Center
Chin-Bing, Stanley Arthur *physicist, educator*

University
Breazeale, Mack Alfred *research scientist, educator*

Vicksburg
North, Ryan Elliot *geophysicist, researcher*

MISSOURI

Chesterfield
Fujiwara, Hideji *chemist, researcher*

Columbia
Bauman, John E., Jr. *chemistry professor*
Decker, Wayne Leroy *meteorologist, educator*
Gehrke, Charles William *biochemistry professor*
Hawthorne, Marion Frederick *chemistry professor*
Hossain, Maruf *research scientist*
Mashhoon, Bahram *physicist, researcher*
Randall, Douglas D. *biochemist, educator*
Randall, Linda Lea *biochemist, educator*
Weisman, Gary Andrew *biochemist*

Creve Coeur
Bockserman, Robert Julian *chemist*

Ferguson
Chubb, Charles Ray *physicist, researcher*

Independence
Lemon, Leslie Roy *radar meteorologist*

Kansas City
Cheng, Kuang Lu *chemist, educator*
Dias, Jerry Ray *chemistry professor, researcher*
Johnson, Linda Diane *environmental health specialist, biologist*
Kilway, Kathleen Victoria *chemist, educator, researcher*
Parizek, Eldon Joseph *geologist, educator, dean*
Rost, William Joseph *chemist*
Wilkinson, Ralph Russell *retired biochemistry educator, toxicologist*

Kirksville
Festa, Roger Reginald *chemist, educator*

Lees Summit
Hubbard, Harold Mead *energy and environmental systems consultant, retired research executive*

Rolla
Adawi, Ibrahim Hasan *physics professor*
Alexander, Ralph William, Jr. *physics professor*

Saint Louis
Agarwal, Ramesh Kumar *aeronautical scientist, researcher, educator*
Beltcheva (Belcheva), Mariana *research scientist, educator*
Bender, Carl Martin *physics professor, consultant*
Burgess, James Harland *physics professor, researcher*
Cao, Nannan *research scientist*
Clark, John Walter *physics professor*
Colletti, Ronald F. *chemist, researcher*
Concibido, Vergel C. *research and development company scientist, plant geneticist, writer, inventor*
Cowsik, Ramanath *physics professor*
Evans, R. Gregory *bioterrorism researcher, educator*
Fitzpatrick, Susan *biochemist, neurologist, foundation administrator*
Frieden, Carl *biochemist, educator*
Friedlander, Michael Wulf *physicist, researcher*
Gibbons, Patrick Chandler *physicist, researcher*
Gokel, George William *organic chemist, educator*
Gross, Michael Lawrence *chemistry professor*
Hakkinen, Raimo Jaakko *aerospace scientist*
Handel, Peter H. *physics professor*
Israel, Martin Henry *astrophysicist, educator, academic administrator*
Macias, Edward S. *chemistry professor, dean, academic administrator*
Murray, Robert Wallace *chemistry professor*
Norberg, Richard Edwin *physicist, researcher*
Sarder, Pinaki *research scientist*
Sly, William S. *biochemist, educator*
Tibi, Rigobert *seismologist, researcher*
Wallace, Kirk D. *research scientist*
Will, Clifford Martin *physicist, researcher, educator*
Zinner, Ernst K. *physics educator, earth and planetary science educator, researcher*

Springfield
Criswell, Charles Harrison (Harry) *analytical chemist, environmental and forensic consultant, executive*
Thompson, Clifton C. *retired chemistry professor, academic administrator*

Willow Springs
Jordan, Gilbert Fred *geophysicist, physicist*

MONTANA

Billings
Paul, Bessie Margrette *retired weather forecaster*

Bozeman
Grieco, Paul Anthony *chemistry professor*
Han, Jiaping *research scientist*
Horner, John Robert *paleontologist, researcher, curator*
Jacobsen, Jeffrey Scott *environmental scientist*

Butte
Weight, Willis D. *geologist, writer, engineering educator, consultant*

Columbia Falls
Spade-Shenker, George Lawrence (George Shenker) *research scientist*

Dayton
von Volborth, Alex (Alexis) *geochemist, geological engineering educator*

Great Falls
Knudson, Ruthann *environmental consultant, anthropologist, archaeologist*

Missoula
Jakobson, Mark John *retired physics professor*

Monarch
Baker, David Warren *earth scientist*

Twin Bridges
Ruppel, Edward Thompson *geologist*

NEBRASKA

Lincoln
Eckhardt, Craig Jon *chemistry professor*
Jones, Lee Bennett *chemistry professor, academic administrator*
Sellmyer, David Julian *physicist, researcher*
Starace, Anthony Francis *theoretical atomic physicist*
Yoder, Bruce Alan *chemist*

Omaha
Bergt, Gregory Paul *chemist, consultant*
Zepf, Thomas Herman *retired physics professor*

NEVADA

Carson City
Crawford, John Edward *retired geologist, consultant*

Henderson
Anspaugh, Lynn Richard *research biophy*
Holloway, Robert Wester *radiochemist*
Meinel, Aden Baker *optics scientist*
Trivelpiece, Alvin William *physicist, educ consultant*

Las Vegas
Broca, Laurent Antoine *aerospace scienti*
Hua, Fred Huizhong *materials scientist*
Sadineni, Suresh Babu *research scientist*

Reno
Heyvaert, Alan *environmental scientist, e*
Mitchell, David Lancaster *research educa*
Price, Jonathan G. *geologist*
Sladek, Ronald John *physics professor*
Taranik, James Vladimir *geologist, educa*

Sparks
Bonham, Harold Florian *research geologi consultant*

NEW HAMPSHIRE

Durham
Irish, James David *oceanographer, educat*

Glen
Zager, Ronald *chemist, consultant*

Grantham
Grimley, Robert Thomas *chemistry profes*

Hanover
Bel Bruno, Joseph James *chemistry profes*
Curphey, Thomas John *chemist, researche*
Doyle, William Thomas *physicist, retired educator*
Fesen, Robert A. *astronomer, educator*
Kantrowitz, Arthur *physicist, researcher, educator*
Montgomery, David Campbell *retired phys professor*
Wegner, Gary Alan *astronomer*

Jaffrey
Walling, Cheves Thomson *chemistry profe*

Litchfield
Miller, Dawn Marie *retired meteorologist*

Manchester
Durham, Ian Thomas *physicist, educator*

Meredith
Hatch, Frederick Tasker *research scientist*

Nashua
Hahto, Sami K. *physicist*

Salem
Simmons, Marvin Gene *retired geophysics educator*

NEW JERSEY

Annandale
Wu, Margaret *research scientist*

Basking Ridge
Morgan, Samuel P(ope) *physicist, applied mathematician*

Berkeley Heights
Geusic, Joseph Edward *physicist*
Mac Rae, Alfred Urquhart *physicist, electri engineer*

Bogota
Condon, Francis Edward *retired chemistry professor*

Bridgewater
Albrethsen, Adrian Edysel *metallurgist, consultant*

East Brunswick
McDowell, Wilbur Benedict *retired chemist consultant*

East Windsor
Shoemaker, Frank Crawford *retired physicis*

Ewing
Brown, Richard Alexander *chemist*

Highland Park
Brudner, Harvey Jerome *physicist*

Hoboken
Moon, Deok Hyun *research scientist, educa*
Schmidt, George *physicist, educator*

Iselin
Ilinich, Oleg *chemist, researcher*
Liu, Xinsheng *chemist*

Jackson
Arminas, Scott Arnold *chemist, poet, writer*

Jersey City
Koster, Emlyn Howard *geologist, educator*

Kenilworth
Korfmacher, Walter Averill *chemist, research*

Lakewood
Karol, Frederick John *retired industrial chen*

Lawrenceville
Brill, Michael Henry *physicist, editor*

nia
z, Anthony David *physicist*

plewood
son, Dewey, Jr. *retired biochemist*
rek, Alfred Frank *retired chemist, ıvironmental engineer*

ddletown
dgren, Carl William, Jr. *physicist*

rris Plains
ellos, Chris Spiridon *chemist*

untainside
, Susan F. *medicinal chemist*

tune
iar, Adam Martin *chemist, educator*

v Brunswick
enson, Mark Daniel *geologist, educator*
zeo, Anthony R. *chemist*
ley, Ramesh Chandra *chemist, chemicals ecutive*
ock, Alan *meteorology professor*
ıss, Ulrich Paul *chemist, educator*

v Providence
ndross, Edwin Arthur *chemist, consultant*
and, Eugene *chemist*
o, Deborah Lee *materials scientist, searcher*
her, Richart Elliott *physicist, researcher*

vark
ryan, Rubik *chemistry professor, researcher*
zerotti, Louis John *physicist*

ley
Chao-Min *biochemist, biotechnologist, searcher*

wick
elt, John Henry *chemist*

ataway
en, Morrel Herman *physicist, biologist, lucator*
hausser, Charles Michael *physicist, searcher*
James Daniel, Jr. *chemist, educator, ventor, consultant*
, Bernard Henry *materials scientist, nsultant*
h, Paul Larry *physicist, educator, former iversity official*
witz, Joel Louis *mathematical physicist, lucator*
enfeld, Peter *physics professor*
Paul James *environmental health scientist*
owitz, Paul *biochemist, researcher, educator*
bins, Allen Bishop *physics professor*
nlenko, Alexander *research scientist, lucator*
lerbilt, David *physics professor*
witz, Harold *biochemist, nutritionist*
mermann, Frank Martin *physicist, educator, search scientist*

nona
on, Yitzhak Yaakov *physicist, educator*

mpton Plains
mel, Hermann Karl *retired physicist, lab lministrator*

nceton
r, Stephen Louis *physicist*
erson, Philip W. *physicist*
kman, William Frank *physicist, research and velopment company executive*
n, Kirk, Jr. *meteorologist, oceanographer, searcher*
er, Emily Ann *physical chemist, researcher, ucator*
, Robert J. *chemistry professor*
kin, Paul M. *physicist*
, Thomas *mathematical physicist, searcher, educator*
stman, Edward Arthur *physicist*
Jagabandhu *chemist, researcher*
dson, Ronald Crosby *physicist, researcher*
n, Keith W. *meteorologist*
ne, Bruce Thomas *astrophysicist, educator*
n, Freeman John *retired physics professor*
, Nathaniel Joseph *physicist*
, Val Logsdon *physics professor*
ey, Klaus Georg *chemist, pharmaceutical nsultant*
er, Alexander G. *research scientist*
er, Stephen Trent *meteorologist*
dmaine, Joseph Anthony *physicist*
ston, Robert J. *research scientist*
nam, Larry Richard *physicist*
es, John Taylor III *chemist, educator*
ane, F(rederick) Duncan M(ichael) *physics ucator*
ns, Edward Beynon *research astronomer*
mann, Walter Joseph *chemistry professor*
, Elliott Hershel *physicist, mathematician, ucator*
, Frank Wesley, Jr. *chemist*
Millan, David W.C. *chemistry professor*
lacena, Juan Martin *physicist, researcher*
abe, Syukuro *meteorologist*
lure, Donald Stuart *physical chemist, ucator*
gan, William Jason *geophysics educator*
t, Guust *geophysicist*
Nai-Phuan *physicist, educator*
ott, Tullis *microgeologist, geology professor*
enheimer, Michael *physicist*
ker, Jeremiah Paul *astrophysicist, educator*
, Lyman Alexander, Jr. *physicist*
akov, Alexander M. *physics professor*
Ramaprasad, Kackadasam Raghavachar *physical chemist*
Royce, Barrie Saunders Hart *physicist, researcher*
Rutherford, Paul Harding *physicist*
Seiberg, Nathan *physics professor*
Sigman, Daniel M. *geochemist, educator*
Smith, Arthur John Stewart *physicist, researcher*
Spergel, David Nathaniel *astrophysicist, educator*
Sterzer, Fred *research physicist*
Suckewer, Szymon *physics professor*
Taylor, Edward Curtis *chemistry professor*
Taylor, Joseph Hooton, Jr. *radio astronomer, physicist*
Torquato, Salvatore *materials scientist, chemistry professor*
Tremaine, Scott Duncan *astrophysicist*
Van Houten, Franklyn Bosworth *geologist, educator*
Wheeler, John Archibald *physicist, educator*
Wightman, Arthur Strong *physicist, researcher*
Witten, Edward *mathematical physicist*

Rahway
Garcia, Maria Luisa *biochemist, researcher*
Kaczorowski, Gregory John *biochemist, researcher, science administrator*

Raritan
Yong, Guo *chemist, educator*

Secaucus
Puente, Audrey *meteorologist*

Skillman
Diaz, Teresita Perez *chemist*

South Orange
Sahiner, Mehmet Alper *physics professor, researcher*

Stirling
Walsh, Peter Joseph *physics professor*

Summit
Phillips, James Charles *physicist, researcher*

Trenton
Baron, Lisa Ann *environmental scientist*

Union
Zois, Constantine Nicholas Athanasios *meteorologist, educator*

Upper Montclair
Ophori, Duke Urhobo *environmental scientist, educator, research scientist, consultant*

NEW MEXICO

Albuquerque
Emin, David *physicist*
Enke, Christie George *chemistry professor, consultant*
Gander, John Edward *biochemistry educator*
Grady, Dennis Edward *physicist, researcher*
Leeper, Ramon Joe *physicist*
Loftfield, Robert Berner *biochemistry professor*
Paine, Robert Treat *chemistry educator*
Ruiz, Carlos Leon *nuclear scientist, physicist*
Van Devender, J. Pace *research scientist, science administrator*

Las Cruces
Rayson, Gary Donn *chemistry educator*
Richardson, Albert Edward *chemistry professor, researcher*
Sohn, Hansuk *research scientist, educator*

Los Alamos
Atcher, Robert Whitehill *chemist, educator*
Becker, Stephen A. *physicist*
Bergen, Benjamin Karl *research scientist*
Blagoev, Krastan Blagoev *physicist, biophysicist*
Brown, Lowell Severt *physicist, researcher*
Burakovsky, Leonid *physicist, researcher*
Copenhaver, Carl *physicist*
Engelhardt, Albert George *physicist*
Flippo, Kirk *research scientist*
Gibson, Benjamin Franklin *physicist*
Grilly, Edward Rogers *physicist*
Harlow, Francis Harvey *physicist, anthropologist, research scientist, artist*
Huynh, My Hang Vo *chemist, researcher*
Judd, O'Dean P. *physicist*
Keepin, George Robert, Jr. *physicist*
Korber, Bette Tina Marie *chemist*
Kubas, Gregory Joseph *research chemist*
Mead, William Charles *physicist*
Michaudon, André Francisque *physicist*
Mihalas, Dimitri Manuel *astrophysicist, educator*
Nix, James Rayford *nuclear physicist, consultant*
Pack, Russell T. *theoretical chemist*
Picraux, Samuel Thomas *physicist, researcher*
Press, William Henry *physicist, computer scientist*
Rosen, Louis *physicist*
Schwarz, Ricardo B. *research scientist*
Selden, Robert Wentworth *physicist, consultant*
Sharp, David Howland *physicist*
Sickafus, Kurt Edward *materials scientist, researcher*
Smith, James Lawrence *research physicist*
Swadener, John Gregory *research scientist*
Swift, Gregory *physicist*
Terrell, (Nelson) James *physicist*
Thompson, Joe D. *physicist*
Vitev, Ivan Mateev *physicist, researcher*
Wang, Yuejian *research scientist*
Weronski, Pawel *physicist, researcher*

Los Lunas
Seiler, Fritz Arnold *physicist*

Mayhill
Pastor, Stephen Daniel *chemistry professor, researcher, consultant*

Placitas
Long, Timothy Scott *chemist, consultant*

Rio Rancho
Nellessen, James Edward *environmental scientist, consultant*

Santa Fe
Cheetham, Alan Herbert *paleontologist*
Cowan, George Arthur *chemist, bank executive, director*
Fisher, Robert Alan *laser physicist*
Gell-Mann, Murray *theoretical physicist, educator*
Giovanielli, Damon Vincent *physicist, consultant*
Hammer, Charles F. *retired chemistry professor*
Kronberg, Philipp Paul *physicist, educator*
Lee, David Mallin *physicist*
Leibowitz, Jack Richard *physicist, educator*
Lynn, John Eric *nuclear physicist, researcher, consultant*
West, Geoffrey B. *theoretical physicist, physics professor*
White, David Hywel *physics professor, researcher*

Silver City
Buhner, Stephen Harrod *research scientist*
Cunningham, John Edward *retired geologist, educator*

Socorro
Schery, Stephen Dale *physicist*

Sunspot
Keil, Stephen Lesley *astrophysicist*

NEW YORK

Albany
Corelli, John Charles *physicist, researcher*
Frisch, Harry Lloyd *chemist, educator*
Kholodenko, Yuri V. *scientist, educator*
Kim, Jai Soo *retired physicist*
Mekonnen, Ademe *meteorologist*
Schalk, Gerwin *research scientist, software engineer*

Alfred
Pye, Lenwood David *materials science educator, researcher, consultant*

Alfred Station
Condrate, Robert Adam, Sr. *spectroscopy educator*

Amherst
Ismail, Abu Zafar Mohamed *physics professor, researcher*

Amityville
Citrano-Cummiskey, Debra Moira *chemist, network technician*

Ballston Spa
Westbrook, Jack Hall *metallurgist, consultant*

Big Flats
Keck, Donald Bruce *physicist*

Binghamton
Coates, Donald Robert *geologist, educator*
Dimitrov, Nikolay *chemistry professor*
Jones, Wayne Elfed, Jr. *chemist, researcher*
Whittingham, M(ichael) Stanley *chemist*

Briarcliff Manor
Bhargava, Rameshwar Nath *physicist*

Bronx
Engelke, Charles Edward *physics professor*
Hartil, Kirsten *research scientist*
Menthena, Anuradha *research scientist*
Schramm, Vern L. *biochemist, educator*
Yalow, Rosalyn Sussman *biophysicist*

Brookhaven
Kouts, Herbert John Cecil *retired physicist*

Brooklyn
Charton, Marvin *chemist, educator*
Franco, Victor *theoretical physics educator*
Gross, Richard A. *chemist, educator*
Mook, Sarah *retired chemist*
Shcherbakova, Estella *chemist, mathematician, educator*
Shedrinsky, Alexander Mikhail *chemistry professor, conservator, consultant*
Tamir, Theodor *electrophysics researcher, educator*
Wolf, Edward Lincoln *physicist, educator*

Buffalo
Amborski, Leonard Edward *retired chemist*
Baier, Robert Edward *chemist, educator*
Churchill, Melvyn Rowen *chemistry professor*
Jain, Piyare Lal *physics professor*
Patel, Mulchand Shambhubhai *biochemist, researcher*
Reitan, Paul Hartman *retired geologist, educator*
Treanor, Charles Edward *physicist, researcher*

Canandaigua
Lowther, Frank Eugene *research physicist*

Centereach
Alabi, Kehinde *research scientist, mechanical engineer*

Chappaqua
O'Neill, Robert Charles *inventor, consultant*

Clarence
Takeuchi, Esther Sans *chemist*

Clinton
Ring, James Walter *physics professor*

Delmar
Matuszek, John Michael, Jr. *environmental scientist, educator, consultant*

East Hampton
Garrett, Charles Geoffrey Blythe *physicist, consultant*

East Syracuse
Williamson, Carolyn *research scientist*

Elmhurst
Lin, Dahang *medical physicist*

Farmingdale
Nolan, Peter John *physics professor*

Flushing
Goldman, Norman Lewis *chemistry professor*
Hu, Huping *biophysicist, lawyer*
Mirkin, Michael V. *chemistry professor*

Freeport
Pullman, Maynard Edward *biochemist*

Geneva
Roelofs, Wendell Lee *biochemistry professor, consultant*

Hannacroix
Schwebler, Stephen *retired chemist*

Hawthorne
Batstone, Joanna Louise *physicist*

Hempstead
Garuthara, Rohana K. *physics professor*

Ithaca
Ashcroft, Neil William *physics professor, researcher*
Bassett, William Akers *retired geologist, educator*
Bauman, Dale Elton *nutritional biochemistry professor*
Berkelman, Karl *retired physics professor*
Burns, Joseph Arthur *planetary science educator*
Craighead, Harold Gene *physicist, educator*
Csaki, Csaba *physicist*
Fitchen, Douglas Beach *physicist, researcher*
Freed, Jack Herschel *chemist, educator*
Ganem, Bruce *chemistry educator*
Ginsparg, Paul *physicist*
Goldsmith, Paul Felix *astronomy and physics professor*
Hess, George Paul *biochemist, educator*
Hoffmann, Roald *chemist, educator*
Holcomb, Donald Frank *physicist, academic administrator*
Kinoshita, Toichiro *physicist*
Lee, David Morris *physics professor*
Lumley, John Leask *physicist, researcher*
McLafferty, Fred Warren *chemist, educator*
McMurry, John Edward *chemistry professor*
Oliver, Jack Ertle *geophysicist, educator*
Pohl, Robert Otto *physics professor*
Richardson, Robert Coleman *physics professor, researcher*
Salpeter, Edwin Ernest *physical sciences educator*
Scheraga, Harold Abraham *retired physical chemistry professor*
Squyres, Steven Weldon *astronomy educator, planetary geology researcher*
Thomas, Jacob Earl *retired physicist*
Widom, Benjamin *chemistry professor*
Xu, Chris *physicist, educator*

Jamaica
Carter, Timothy Howard *biochemist, educator*
Greenberg, Jacob *biochemist, educator, consultant*

Latham
Stallman, Donald Lee *environmental executive*

Lewiston
Dexter, Theodore Henry *chemist*

Manhasset
Dabideen, Darrin *research scientist*

Manlius
Martonosi, Anthony Nicholas *retired biochemistry professor*
O'Reilly, Mary *environmental scientist, educator*

Melville
Damadian, Raymond Vahan *biophysicist*

New Paltz
Lavallee, David Kenneth *chemistry professor, academic administrator*

New Rochelle
Margolin, Harold *metallurgical educator*

New York
Allison, Michael David *space scientist, educator*
Bederson, Benjamin *physicist, researcher*
Berne, Bruce J. *chemistry professor*
Beshers, Daniel Newson *retired materials scientist*
Birman, Joseph Leon *physics professor*
Bornmann, William Gerard *organic chemist*
Borowitz, Sidney *retired physics professor*
Breslow, Esther May Greenberg *biochemistry professor, researcher*
Breslow, Ronald Charles *chemist, educator*
Briley-Saebo, Karen Catherin *physics professor*
Brus, Louis Eugene *physical chemist*

Campbell, George, Jr. *physicist, university administrator*
Cheh, Huk Yuk *electrochemist*
Chou, Ting-Chao *inventor, educator*
Cohen, Ezechiel Godert David *physicist, researcher*
Cross, George Alan Martin *biochemistry professor, researcher*
Cummins, Herman Zachary *physicist*
Danishefsky, Samuel J. *chemistry professor*
Erickson, Mitchell Drake *chemist, environmental scientist*
Erlanger, Bernard Ferdinand *biochemist, educator*
Fathallah, Hassana *research scientist*
Fraenkel, George Kessler *chemistry professor*
Fusaro, Peter C. *environmental scientist, consultant*
Goulianos, Konstantin *physicist, educator*
Gutzwiller, Martin Charles *theoretical physicist, research scientist*
Haiman, Zoltan *astronomer, educator*
Haines, Thomas Henry *biochemist, educator, researcher*
Hansen, James E. *physicist, meteorologist, federal agency administrator*
Hendrickson, Wayne A(rthur) *biochemist, educator*
Hoffert, Martin Irving *aerospace scientist, educator*
Hoffman, Linda M. *chemist, educator*
Honig, Barry Hirsh *biophysicist, educator*
Kaku, Michio *theoretical nuclear physicist, educator*
Khuri, Nicola Najib *physicist, researcher*
King, Edward Joseph *clinical chemist, laboratory administrator*
Krasna, Alvin Isaac *biochemist, educator*
Kuo, John Tsungfen *geophysicist, educator, researcher*
Lee, Tsung-Dao *physicist, researcher*
Levin, Janna J. *physicist, educator*
Libchaber, Albert Joseph *physics professor*
Lubell, Michael Stephen *physicist, educator*
Mac Low, Mordecai-Mark *astrophysicist*
Marshall, Thomas Carlisle *retired applied physics professor*
McDermott, Ann Elizabeth *chemistry professor*
Middleton, David *physicist, educator*
Moy, Richard L. *research scientist*
Muriel, Amador Cruz *physicist*
Nickoloff, Edward Lee *radiology physicist*
Norell, Mark Allen *paleontologist, curator*
Nye, Bill S. *research scientist, engineer, comedian, writer, inventor*
Oreskes, Irwin *biochemistry educator*
Percus, Jerome Kenneth *physicist, researcher*
Pinczuk, Aron *physicist*
Pope, Martin *chemist, educator*
Roeder, Robert Gayle *biochemist, molecular biologist, educator*
St. Germain, Jean Mary *medical physicist*
Sarachik, Myriam Paula Morgenstein *physics professor, condensed matter physicist*
Sidran, Miriam *retired physicist*
Stork, Gilbert *chemistry professor*
Störmer, Horst Ludwig *physicist*
Stroke, Hinko Henry *physicist, researcher*
Tu, Jiufeng J. *physics professor*
Turro, Nicholas John *chemistry professor*
Tyson, Neil DeGrasse *astrophysicist, museum director*
Upmacis, Rita Karina *chemist*
Werthamer, Nathan Richard *physicist*

Niagara Falls
Bharadwaj, Prem Datta *physics professor*
Knowles, Richard Norris *chemist*

Niskayuna
Edelheit, Lewis S. *research physicist*
Kambour, Roger Peabody *retired polymer physical chemist, researcher*
Varanasi, Kripa Kiran *research scientist*

Oneonta
Hickey, Francis Roger *physicist, researcher*
Horner, Carl Matthew *chemistry professor*

Orangeburg
Hawkins, Pamela Leigh Huffman *biochemist*
Lajtha, Abel *biochemist*

Palisades
Broecker, Wallace S. *geophysicist, educator*
Burckle, Lloyd Henry *geologist, researcher*
Chiu, Tzu-Chien *geologist, researcher*
Kellogg, Herbert Humphrey *metallurgist, educator*
Kent, Dennis V. *earth scientist, educator*
Previdi, Michael *meteorologist, research scientist*
Richards, Paul Granston *seismologist, geophysics educator*
van Geen, Alexander *geochemist, researcher*

Patchogue
Marr, Robert Bruce *physicist, researcher*

Pearl River
Barringer, William Charles *retired chemist*
Lokhnauth, John *chemist, researcher*

Pittsford
Goldstein, David Arthur *biophysicist, educator*

Plainview
Rich, Charles Anthony *hydrogeologist, consultant*

Pleasantville
Shiri-Garakani, Mohsen *physicist, educator*

Potsdam
Fendler, Janos Hugo *chemistry professor*
Islam, Muhammad Azadul *physicist, educator, researcher*
Matijevic, Egon *chemistry professor*
Naik, Sajo P. *physicist, researcher*

Poughkeepsie
Lang, William Warner *physicist*

Rensselaer
Willis, John Patrick *chemist*

Ridge
Adams, Peter David *physicist, writer, editor*
Blume, Martin *physicist*

Rochester
Bigelow, Nicholas Pierre *physicist, researcher*
Blackman, Eric Glen *physics and astronomy professor*
Blanton, Thomas N. *chemist, researcher*
Boeckman, Robert Kenneth, Jr. *chemistry professor, organic chemistry researcher*
Buff, Frank Paul *chemist, educator*
Cain, Burton Edward *retired chemistry professor*
Conwell, Esther Marly *physicist, researcher*
Eisenberg, Richard S. *chemistry professor*
Ferbel, Thomas *physicist, educator*
Houde-Walter, Susan *optics scientist, educator*
Kampmeier, Jack August Carlos *chemist, educator*
Kende, Andrew Steven *chemist, educator*
Knauer, James Philip *physicist*
Knox, Robert Seiple *physicist, researcher*
Kwok, Wingchi Edmund *physicist*
Li, James Chen Min *materials science educator*
Luckey, George William *chemist, researcher*
Makous, Walter Leon *visual scientist, educator*
Melissinos, Adrian Constantin *physicist, researcher*
Meyerhofer, David D. *physicist, educator*
Moore, Duncan Thomas *optics scientist, educator*
Santhanam, Kalathur S. V. *chemist, researcher*
Saunders, William Hundley, Jr. *retired chemist, educator*
Sharma, Gaurav *imaging scientist, electrical engineer*
Sherman, Fred *biochemist, educator*
Szalapski, Robert Francis *theoretical physicist*
Thorndike, Edward Harmon *physicist*
Yip, Kwok Leung *physicist, researcher*

Rockville Centre
Castleman, Louis Samuel *retired metallurgist, educator*

Rouses Point
Weierstall, Richard Paul *retired pharmaceutical chemist*

Scarsdale
Porosoff, Harold *chemist, science administrator, research and development company executive*

Schenectady
Finks, Robert Melvin *paleontologist, educator*
Frost, Robert Edwin *chemistry professor*
Katz, Samuel *retired geophysics educator*
Philip, A. G. Davis *astronomer, educator, editor*

Sherburne
Dodd, Jack Gordon, Jr. *physicist, researcher*

South Setauket
Friedlander, Gerhart *nuclear chemist*

Staten Island
Yang, Song-Yu *medical biochemist*

Stony Brook
Alexander, John Macmillan, Jr. *chemistry professor*
Bonner, Francis Truesdale *chemist, educator, dean*
Brown, Gerald Edward *physicist, researcher*
Geller, Marvin Alan *meteorology educator, researcher*
Ojima, Iwao *chemistry professor*
Swanson, Robert Lawrence *oceanographer, academic program administrator*

Syracuse
Allis, Damian Gregory *chemist, technologist, consultant*
Baldwin, John Edwin *chemistry professor*
Honig, Arnold *physics professor, researcher*
Prucha, John James *geologist, educator*
Schiff, Eric Allan *physics professor*
Smith, Kenneth Judson, Jr. *chemistry professor*
Tolkacheva, Elena *physicist, researcher*
Vook, Richard Werner *retired physics professor*
Winter, William Thomas *chemistry educator*

Troy
Ci, Lijie *materials scientist*
Ferris, James Peter *chemist, educator*
Friedman, Gerald Manfred *geologist, educator*
Giaever, Ivar *physicist*
Levinger, Joseph Solomon *physicist, researcher*
Linhardt, Robert John *chemistry professor*
Medicus, Heinrich Adolf *physicist, researcher*
Persans, Peter David *physics educator, researcher*
Potts, Kevin T. *retired chemistry professor*
Sperber, Daniel *physicist*

Upton
Baltz, Anthony John *physicist*
Bari, Robert Allan *physicist*
Bond, Peter Danford *physicist*
Fowler, Joanna S. *chemist*
Goldhaber, Maurice *physicist, researcher*
Harbottle, Garman *chemist*
Hendrie, Joseph Mallam *physicist, nuclear engineer*
Lindenbaum, S(eymour) J(oseph) *physicist*
Lowenstein, Derek Irving *physicist*
Meinhold, Charles Boyd *health physicist*
Rau, Ralph Ronald *retired physicist*
Samios, Nicholas Peter *physicist*
Setlow, Jane Kellock *biophysicist*
Setlow, Richard Burton *biophysicist, researcher*
Tannenbaum, Michael J(ay) *physicist*
Wei, Xiangdong *physicist, researcher*

Wappingers Falls
Maissel, Leon Israel *physicist, engineer*

Wellsville
Van Tyne, Arthur Morris *geologist*

White Plains
Flanigen, Edith Marie *materials scientist, consultant*
Wittcoff, Harold Aaron *chemist*

Yorktown Heights
Avouris, Phaedon *chemical physicist*
Keyes, Robert W. *physicist, researcher*
Lang, Norton David *physicist*
Lanzerotti, Mary Yvonne *physicist, researcher*
Ning, Tak Hung *physicist, microelectronic technologist*
Tersoff, Jerry David *physicist*

NORTH CAROLINA

Asheville
Haggard, William Henry *meteorologist*
Meyerson, Seymour *retired chemist*

Beaufort
Bonaventura, Celia Jean *biochemist, researcher*

Brevard
Foster, Edward John *engineer physicist*

Cary
Kung, Pang-Jen *materials scientist, electrical engineer*

Chapel Hill
Brookhart, Maurice S. *chemist*
Bursey, Maurice M. *retired chemistry professor*
Davis, Morris Schuyler *astronomer*
Desimone, Joseph M. *chemist, educator*
Eliel, Ernest Ludwig *chemist, educator*
Forman, Donald T. *biochemist, educator*
Frampton, Paul Howard *physics researcher, educator*
Jorgenson, James Wallace *chromatographer, educator*
Klein, Martin Jesse *physicist, science historian, educator*
Lee, Kuo-Hsiung *medicinal chemistry professor*
Ligett, Waldo Buford *chemist*
Macdonald, James Ross *physicist, researcher*
Mersini - Houghton, Laura *physicist, educator*
Merzbacher, Eugen *retired physics professor*
Mitchell, Earl Nelson *physicist, researcher*
Parr, Robert Ghormley *chemistry professor*
Ramsey, John Michael *chemistry professor, researcher*
Rezk, Naser Labeeb *biochemist, researcher*
Sancar, Aziz *research biochemist*
Tsui, Frank *physicist, educator, researcher*

Charlotte
Krueger, Joanna Katherine *chemistry professor, researcher*
Rodite, Robert R.R. *research scientist, finance and computer consultant, educator*

Durham
Fridovich, Irwin *biochemistry professor*
Hammes, Gordon G. *chemistry professor*
Han, Moo-Young *physicist, educator*
Jaszczak, Ronald Jack *physicist, researcher, consultant*
Joklik, Wolfgang Karl *biochemist, virologist, educator*
Meyer, Horst *physics professor*
Mikhailov, Stepan Fedorovich *physicist, researcher*
Modrich, Paul L. *biochemistry professor*
Pearsall, George Wilbur *materials scientist, mechanical engineer, consultant, educator*
Pirrung, Michael Craig *chemistry professor, consultant*
Quin, Louis DuBose *chemist, educator*
Quinn, Jarus William *physicist, former association executive*
Raetz, Christian R. H. *biochemistry professor*
Tselev, Alexander *physicist, researcher*

Greensboro
Clark, Clifton Bob *physicist*

Greenville
Stanfield, Charles Freeman *chemist*

Hayesville
Galloway, David Craig *chemist*

Hendersonville
Saby, John Sanford *physicist, consultant*

Horse Shoe
Roskoski, Robert, Jr. *biochemist, educator, author*

Pinehurst
Huizenga, John Robert *nuclear chemist, educator*
Swanson, Richard Everett *physics professor, dean*

Raleigh
Aspnes, David Erik *physicist, researcher*
Bernholc, Jerzy *physicist, educator*
Gillette, Dale Alan *retired research scientist*
Gould, Christopher Robert *physics professor*
Michielsen, Stephen *chemistry professor*
Mitchell, Gary Earl *physicist, researcher*
Osteryoung, Janet Gretchen *chemistry professor*
Paesler, Michael *physics professor, departme chairman*
Reynolds, C. Lewis, Jr. *materials scientist, educator*
Sudhakar, Nori *materials scientist, researche*
Sun, Ying-Hsuan *research scientist*
Swaisgood, Harold Everett *biochemist, educ*
Whitten, Jerry Lynn *chemistry professor*

Research Triangle Park
Fisher, Robert Perry *environmental scientist, researcher*
Hornberger, Keith Robert *chemist*
Reynolds, Peter James *physicist*
Selkirk, James Kirkwood *biochemist, resear*
Wani, Mansukhlal Chhaganlal *chemist*

Southern Pines
Cooper, Kevin R. *materials scientist*

Wilmington
Pickett, Alicia Euliss *environmental scientist*

Winston Salem
Kerr, William C. *physics professor*
Mokrasch, Lewis Carl *neurochemist, educat*
Rodgman, Alan *chemist, consultant*
Zhang, Lei *physics professor*

NORTH DAKOTA

Fargo
Nasrullah, Mohammed Jaleel *research scien*
Tallman, Dennis Earl *chemistry professor, research scientist*
Wagner, Alexander Johannes *physicist, educ*

Grand Forks
Hoffmann, Mark R. *physical chemist, educa*

OHIO

Ada
Stockert, Amy L. *chemistry professor*

Akron
Gent, Alan Neville *physicist, researcher*
Kennedy, Joseph Paul *chemist, researcher*
Lim, Edward Chol *chemistry professor, researcher*
Ramsey, Sally Judith Weine *chemist, resear and development company executive*

Athens
Nance, Richard Damian *geologist, consultan*

Aurora
Su, Sunyu *physicist*

Beachwood
Krieger, Irvin Mitchell *retired chemistry professor*

Bratenahl
Dunn, Horton, Jr. *organic chemist*

Centerburg
Reynolds, Don William *geologist*

Cincinnati
Briskin, Madeleine *oceanographer, paleontologist*
Francis, Marion David *consulting chemist*
Goodman, Bernard *physics professor*
Iroh, Jude Onwuegbu *chemistry professor*
Jensen, Elwood Vernon *biochemist*
Meal, Larie *chemistry professor, researcher, consultant*
Relyea, Carl Miller *retired hydrologist*
Sullivan, James F. *physicist, researcher*
Witten, Louis *physics professor*

Cleveland
Bidelman, William Pendry *astronomer, educ*
Brazdil, James Frank *chemist, researcher*
Carey, Paul Richard *biophysicist*
Chamis, Christos Constantinos *aerospace scientist, educator*
Chvetsov, Alexei V. *medical physicist, educ*
Colussi, Valdir Carlos *physicist*
Goldstein, Marvin Emanuel *aerospace scier*
Klopman, Gilles *chemistry professor*
Koenig, Jack L. *chemist, educator*
Kowalski, Kenneth Lawrence *physicist, researcher*
Krauss, Lawrence Maxwell *physicist, astron educator, researcher, author*
Lowe, Mark J. *physicist*
Mawardi, Osman Kamel *retired plasma phy*
Meador, Michael Anthony *chemist, research*
Rogers, Charles Edwin *physical chemistry a polymer science professor*
Schuele, Donald Edward *retired physics professor, dean*
Terburg, Bart Paul *physicist, industrial engi*
Wang, Run *research scientist*
Zhang, Nengli *research scientist*

Columbus
Adelson, Edward *physicist, educator, musici*
Behrman, Edward Joseph *biochemistry educ*
Chisholm, Malcolm Harold *chemistry profes*
Cornwell, David George *biochemist, educat*
Daehn, Glenn Steven *materials scientist*
Elliot, David Hawksley *geologist, educator*
Epstein, Arthur Joseph *physics and chemistr educator*
Herbst, Eric *physicist, astronomer, chemist*
Heremans, Joseph Pierre *physicist*
Ling, Ta-Yung *physicist*
Madia, William Juul *chemist*
Miller, Terry Alan *chemistry professor*
Min, David Byong *chemist, educator, resear scientist*
Reibel, Kurt *physicist, researcher*

'e, George Roland, Jr. *materials scientist, eering executive, educator*
Sheldon G. *chemist, educator*
y, Albert Herman *medicinal chemist*
son, Lonnie G. *glaciologist, educator*
ham, Murugesan *research scientist*
Johan Kishen *environmental scientist, 'er, educator*
, John Warren *physics professor*
s, James Case *metallurgist*
ci, Andrew Adalbert *chemist, educator*

y
dward David *chemist, researcher, ultant, inventor*

n
, Rubin *retired chemistry professor*
Shan *materials scientist*
, Philip Edward *physicist, research ıger*
John Austin *physicist*

n
englong *biophysicist, educator*
nxian *chemist, researcher*

ke
ek, Wojciech Lukasz *materials scientist, ırcher*

d
', Michael Brendan *chemist*

orn
Vijay Kumar *retired chemistry professor*

and Hills
'aite, Ormond Dennis *chemistry professor*

nan, Jenny L. *environmental scientist, cator*
Peter Steffen *geologist, educator*

ring
oseph William *materials scientist*

field
ı, David Mark *biochemist, educator*

etta
Albert William *retired chemistry 'essor, academic administrator, research ntist*
n, Robert Ervin *chemist, consultant*

dlefield
en, Karen A. *chemist*

ietown
e, Susan Sonchik *analytical chemist, cator*

nt Vernon
', Joyce Catherine *chemistry professor, earch scientist*

h Canton
, Andrew E. *chemistry professor, earcher*

walk
ann, Richard P(aul) *pharmaceutical ıpany chemist, chemicals executive*

rlin
n, Terry Scott *retired chemist, educator*

ord
on, Gilbert *chemist, educator*
lin, Philip Alan *retired physics professor*

stown
g, John Young Ling *biochemistry professor, earcher*

do
ll, Bruce Alan *chemistry professor*
z, Forrest H. *physicist, educator*

er Arlington
, Ferenc Matyas *chemist*

ton Hills
tt, Stanley B. *chemist, researcher*

kliffe
se, Marjorie N. *biochemist*

ght Patterson Afb
a, Siva S. *research scientist*
elius, Nils Conard *physicist*
cadden, Alan *physicist*

ow Springs
ane, Robert Bruce *biophysical chemist*

LAHOMA

a
ord, Donald Gene *chemistry professor*
g, Mingyu *hydrologist, environmental ientist*

a
lha da Conceicao, Jose Joao *chemistry ofessor, researcher*

tlesville
an, John Paul *chemistry researcher, onsultant*

t Towson
, Thomas Harrison *plant chemist*

Muskogee
Woods, Stuart Henry *environmental scientist, educator*

Norman
Beasley, William H. *meteorology professor*
Cowan, John James *physicist, astronomer, educator*
Droegemeier, Kelvin K. *meteorologist, educator*
Dryhurst, Glenn *retired chemistry professor*
Gourley, Jonathan Joseph *hydrologist*
Pigott, John Dowling *geologist, geophysicist, geochemist, educator, consultant*

Oklahoma City
Alaupovic, Petar *biochemist, educator*
Butnev, Viktor Yurievich *research scientist*
Matsumoto, Hiroyuki *biochemistry professor, researcher*

Skiatook
Harwell, Kenneth E. *chemist, researcher, consultant*

Stillwater
Hubbard, Todd Philip *aerospace scientist*

Tulsa
Blais, Roger Nathaniel *physics professor, academic administrator*
Busch, Daniel Adolph *geologist, educator*
Kozhevnikov, Vladimir F. *physicist, researcher, educator*

OREGON

Ashland
Abrahams, Sidney Cyril *physicist, crystallographer*
Grover, James Robb *chemist, editor*

Corvallis
Dalrymple, Gary Brent *research geologist*
Drake, Charles Whitney *physicist*
Holman, Robert Alan *oceanography educator*
Lee, Yun-Shik *physics professor*
Lubchenco, Jane *environmental scientist, marine ecologist, science association director*
Mathews, Christopher King *biochemist, educator*
Tyavnagimatt, Shanthakumar R. *research scientist, pharmacist*
Van Holde, Kensal Edward *biochemistry educator*
Yeats, Robert Sheppard *geologist, educator*

Eugene
Crasemann, Bernd *physicist, researcher*
Csonka, Paul L. *theoretical physicist, educator*
Deshpande, Nilendra Ganesh *physics professor*
Donnelly, Russell James *physicist, educator*
Griffith, Osbie Hayes *retired chemistry professor*
Maurer, Robert Distler *retired industrial physicist*
Mazo, Robert Marc *retired chemistry professor*
Retallack, Gregory John *geologist, educator*
Richmond, Geraldine Lee *chemist, educator*
von Hippel, Peter Hans *chemistry professor, researcher*
Youngquist, Walter Lewellyn *geologist, consultant*

Kimberly
Fremd, Theodore J. *paleontologist, regional science advisor*

Monmouth
White, Donald Harvey *retired physics professor*

Newport
Peterson, William T. *oceanographer*

Portland
Abel, William Edward *applied physicist, consultant*
Claycomb, Cecil Keith *biochemist, educator*
Cohen, Norm *chemist*
Pearson, David Petri *chemist*
Ruzicka, Alexander Marion *geologist, educator*
Weeks, Wilford Frank *retired geophysics educator, glaciologist*

Salem
Gillette, P. Roger *physicist, systems engineer*

PENNSYLVANIA

Allentown
Orphanides, Gus George *licensing executive*

Berwyn
Devlin, Thomas McKeown *biochemist, educator*

Bethlehem
Heindel, Ned Duane *chemistry professor*
Herman, Richard Gerald *research chemist, consultant, educator*
Koel, Bruce Edward *chemist, educator, researcher*
Lyman, Charles Edson *materials scientist, educator*
Smyth, Donald Morgan *chemistry professor, researcher*

Carlisle
Laws, Kenneth L. *physics professor*
Long, Howard Charles *retired physics professor*

Chadds Ford
Strawhecker, Kenneth Edward *research scientist*

Danville
Chan, Yiumo *biochemist*

Easton
Bose, Ajay Kumar *retired chemistry professor*

Edinboro
Mahmood, Akhtar Hasan *physicist, educator, researcher*

Feasterville Trevose
Dickstein, Jack *chemist*

Harrisburg
Stanley, Edward Alexander *geologist, paleontologist, researcher, retired director, forensic specialist*

Haverford
Gollub, Jerry Paul *physics professor*

Huntingdon Valley
Godfrey, John Carl *medicinal chemist*
Leibholz, Stephen Wolfgang *physicist, information technology executive, entrepreneur*

Indiana
Bencloski, Joseph W. *geography educator*
Kenning, Gregory George *physicist, educator*

Kennett Square
Wilson, Armin *retired chemist*

Lincoln University
Venerable, Grant Delbert, II, *chemist, educator, systems scientist*
Williams, Willie, Jr. *physicist, researcher*

Mc Murray
Mortimer, James Winslow *chemist*

Media
Voltz, Sterling Ernest *physical chemist, researcher*

Mount Joy
Lodde, Gordon Maynard *health physics consultant*

New Holland
Papadakis, Emmanuel Philippos *physicist, consultant*

New Kensington
Ray, Siba Prasad *materials scientist, ceramics scientist*

Orefield
Armor, John N. *chemical company scientist, consultant, research manager*

Philadelphia
Ajzenberg-Selove, Fay *physicist, researcher*
Blumberg, Baruch Samuel *research scientist, educator*
Bortnick, Newman Mayer *research chemist*
Burstein, Elias *physicist, researcher*
Childress, Scott Julius *medicinal chemist*
Cohn, Mildred *retired biochemist, educator*
Dalton, David Robert *chemistry professor*
Dutton, P(eter) Leslie *biochemist, educator*
Englander, Sol Walter *biochemistry and biophysics educator, medical educator*
Fitts, Donald Dennis *chemist, educator*
Frankel, Sherman *physicist, educator*
Glusker, Jenny Pickworth *chemist*
Gogotsi, Yury *materials scientist, educator*
Hameka, Hendrik Frederik *chemistry professor*
Harris, A. Brooks *physicist, researcher*
Hirschmann, Ralph Franz *chemist*
Hochstrasser, Robin M. *chemist, educator*
Hossain, Murshed *physicist, researcher*
Kim, Bum-Jin *research scientist*
Klein, Michael Lawrence *research chemist, educator*
Larson, Donald Clayton *physics professor, consultant*
Lubensky, Tom Carl *physics professor*
Noordergraaf, Abraham *biophysics educator*
Shen, Benjamin Shih-Ping *physicist, educator*
Smith, Amos Brittain III *chemist, educator*
Vitek, Vaclav *materials scientist*
Wales, Walter D. *physicist, researcher*
Wickstrom, Eric *biophysical chemist, educator*
Winkler, Jeffrey D. *chemist*
Yang, Shu *materials scientist*

Pittsburgh
Anderson, Scott Richard *geologist, consultant*
Asher, Sanford Abraham *chemist, educator*
Biondi, Manfred Anthony *physicist*
Bothner-By, Aksel Arnold *chemist*
Carr, Walter James, Jr. *research physicist, consultant*
Choyke, Wolfgang Justus *physicist*
Cohen, Bernard Leonard *physicist, researcher*
Coltman, John Wesley *physicist*
Emmerich, Werner Sigmund *physicist, educator*
Feller, Robert Livingston *chemist, art conservation scientist*
Gerjuoy, Edward *physicist*
Janis, Allen Ira *retired physicist, educator*
Jin, Tao *research scientist*
Kim, Yongbok *physicist*
Laughlin, David Eugene *materials scientist, educator, metallurgist, consultant*
Maher, James Vincent, Jr. *physics professor, academic administrator*
Massalski, Thaddeus Bronislaw *materials scientist, educator*
Matyjaszewski, Krzysztof *chemist, educator*
Morningstar, Colin Jon *physicist, researcher*
Münck, Eckard *chemistry professor*
Nagle, John Frederick *physicist*
Plazek, Donald John *materials scientist, educator*
Rebei, Adnan *physicist, researcher*
Resnick, Robert *physicist, researcher*
Rosenberg, Jerome Laib *chemist, educator*

Sekerka, Robert Floyd *physics and mathematics professor*
Snoke, David Wayne *physicist, researcher*
Star, Alexander *chemist, educator*
Vo, Evanly *organic chemist*
White, Robert Marshall *retired physicist, educator, government official, consultant*
Young, Hugh David *physics professor, writer*

Pottstown
Hergert, Herbert Lawrence *retired consultant*

South Park
Lotze, Barbara *retired physicist*

State College
Garrett, Steven Lurie *physicist*

Swarthmore
Bilaniuk, Oleksa Myron *physicist, researcher*
Pasternack, Robert Francis *chemistry professor*

University Park
Allcock, Harry R. *chemistry professor*
Badding, John Victor *chemistry professor*
Blackadar, Alfred Kimball *meteorologist, educator*
Cahir, John Joseph *meteorologist, educator, educational administrator*
Castleman, Albert Welford, Jr. *physical chemist, educator*
Chan, Moses Hung Wai *physicist, researcher*
Dutton, John Altnow *meteorologist, educator*
Garrison, Barbara Jane *chemistry professor*
Hammes-Schiffer, Sharon *chemist, educator*
Hosler, Charles Luther, Jr. *meteorologist, educator*
Howell, Benjamin Franklin, Jr. *geophysicist, educator*
Jackman, Lloyd Miles *chemistry professor*
Mahan, Gerald Dennis *physicist, researcher*
Mann, Michael E. *physicist, educator, climatologist*
Sen, Ayusman *chemistry professor*
Varghese, Oomman Kulathinthekkethil *materials scientist, researcher*
Weiss, Paul Storch *chemistry educator*
White, William Blaine *geochemist, researcher*
Winograd, Nicholas *chemist*

Villanova
Edwards, John Ralph *retired chemist, educator*
Papaefthymiou, Georgia C. *physicist, educator*
Phares, Alain Joseph *physicist, researcher*

Wallingford
Severdia, Anthony George *chemistry researcher*

Wayne
Kyung, Yun Seung *biochemist, researcher*

Waynesburg
Maguire, Mildred May *retired chemistry professor*

Wexford
Bossart, Paul Nathaniel, Jr. *geologist, geophysicist, consultant*

Wyndmoor
Pfeffer, Philip Elliot *biophysicist*

Wynnewood
Rosen, Gerald Harris *physicist, consultant, educator*

RHODE ISLAND

East Greenwich
Carlson, Shawn Eric *physicist, educator*

Kingston
Fastovsky, David E. *geoscientist, educator*
Reshetnyak, Yana K. *physics professor*

Narragansett
Nixon, Scott West *oceanography science educator*
Pilson, Michael Edward Quinton *oceanography educator*
Rossby, Hans Thomas *oceanographer, educator*

Providence
Avery, Donald Hills *metallurgist, educator*
Briant, Clyde Leonard *metallurgist, educator*
Carpenter, Gene Blakely *crystallography and chemistry educator*
Cooper, Leon N *physicist, researcher*
Dahlberg, Albert Edward *biochemistry professor*
Elbaum, Charles *physicist, educator, researcher*
Estrup, Peder Jan *physics and chemistry professor*
Gerritsen, Hendrik Jurjen *physics professor, researcher*
Head, James William III *geological sciences educator*
Kosterlitz, J. Michael *physics professor*
Lanou, Robert Eugene, Jr. *physicist, researcher*
Levin, Frank S. *physicist, educator*
Stratt, Richard Mark *chemistry researcher, educator*
Valles, James M., Jr. *physics professor*

Wakefield
Moore, George Emerson, Jr. *geologist, educator*

SOUTH CAROLINA

Aiken
Dewberry, Raymond Allen *research scientist, combat engineer*
Dickson, Paul Wesley, Jr. *physicist*

Bluffton
Croft, George T. *physicist*

Charleston
Fragile, Patrick Christopher *physics professor, astrophysicist, researcher*

Clemson
DesMarteau, Darryl Dwayne *chemistry professor*
Lewis, Barbara Sue *chemist*

Columbia
Edge, Ronald Dovaston *physics professor*
Gandy, James Thomas *meteorologist, entrepreneur*
Paleologos, Evangelos *hydrologist, educator*
Samuel, May Linda *environmental scientist*
Shafer, John Milton *hydrologist, consultant, data processing executive*

Florence
Havens, Timothy John *physicist*

Greenville
Belanger, Laura Hewlette *environmental scientist, consultant*
Pepper, Latongia Kenyetta *physicist, curator*

Johns Island
Norton, Norman James *retired exploration geologist, educator*

Mount Pleasant
Thordarson, William *retired hydrogeologist*

Rock Hill
Maheswaranathan, Ponn *physicist, educator*

SOUTH DAKOTA

Brookings
Cervantes Laurean, Daniel *biochemist*
Perumal, Omathanu Pillai *research scientist, medical researcher, educator*

Freeman
Ries, Edward Richard *petroleum geologist, consultant*

Rapid City
Smith, Paul Letton, Jr. *geophysicist*

Sioux Falls
Gerdes, Anthony Martin *research scientist, health science association administrator*
Giri, Chandra Prasad *research scientist*
Viste, Arlen Ellard *chemistry professor*

Spearfish
Erickson, Richard Ames *physicist, emeritus educator*

TENNESSEE

Brentwood
Chappell, Charles Richard *space scientist*
Heiser, Arnold Melvin *astronomer*

Knoxville
Gentry, Robert Vance *physicist, researcher, writer*
Hatcher, Robert Dean, Jr. *geologist, educator*
Nukala, Sirisha Saripalli *research scientist, educator*
Plummer, E. Ward *physics professor*
Qiu, Wulin *chemist, materials scientist, materials engineer*
Renshaw, Amanda Frances *retired physicist, nuclear engineer*
Schweitzer, George Keene *chemistry professor*
Wunderlich, Bernhard *retired physical chemistry professor*
Zhong, Qixin *physical chemist, chemistry professor*

Maryville
Weeks, Robert Andrew *materials science researcher, educator*

Memphis
Crane, Laura Jane *retired chemist*
Desiderio, Dominic Morse, Jr. *chemistry and neurochemistry professor*
Fain, John Nicholas *biochemistry educator*
Franceschetti, Donald Ralph *physicist, educator*

Murfreesboro
Weller, Martha Riherd *physics and astronomy professor, consultant*

Nashville
Chytil, Frank *biochemist*
Feldman, Leonard Cecil *physicist*
Fort, Tomlinson *chemist, chemical engineering educator*
Hamilton, Joseph Hants, Jr. *physicist, researcher*
Hercules, David Michael *chemistry professor, consultant*
Hwang, Jae-Kwang *physicist, researcher*
Inagami, Tadashi *biochemistry professor*
Lukehart, Charles Martin *chemistry professor*
Silberman, Enrique *physicist, director*
Surowiec, Andrew Julius *biophysicist, researcher*
Zavalin, Andrey I. *optics scientist, educator*

Oak Ridge
Bhuiyan, Shafiqur Rahman *materials scientist*
Boatner, Lynn Allen *research physicist*
Borie, Bernard Simon, Jr. *retired physicist, educator*
Carlsmith, Roger Snedden *chemistry and energy conservation researcher*
Han, Qingyou *research scientist, metallurgist*
Harvey, John Arthur *nuclear physicist*
Hu, Zhiyu *research scientist, educator*
Katoh, Yutai *materials scientist*
Krause, Manfred Otto *physicist*
Kronenberg, Andreas *nuclear chemist, radiochemist, nuclear technology consultant*
Larson, Bennett Charles *solid state physicist, researcher*
Liu, C(hain)-T(suan) *materials scientist, researcher*
Maienschein, Fred *retired physicist*
Melnichenko, Yuri B. *physicist*
Nephew, Edmund A. *physicist, retired mayor*
Painter, Gayle Stanford *research physicist, consultant*
Plasil, Franz *physicist*
Schwenterly, Stanley William *physicist, researcher*
Wadsworth, Jeffrey *metallurgist, educator*

Signal Mountain
Howe, Lyman Harold III *chemist, researcher*

TEXAS

Allen
Martin, Patrick Michael *physicist, director*

Amarillo
McGrath, Daniel Andrew *hydrologist*

Arlington
Dasgupta, Purnendu Kumar *chemist, educator, department chairman*
Dollar, David *chemistry professor*
Huang, Junmin *chemist, researcher*
Ray, Asok Kumar *physicist, researcher*
Shanmugam, Ganapathy *geologist, researcher*
Willoughby, Sarah-Margaret C. *retired chemist, educator, chemical engineer, consultant*

Austin
Barbara, Paul Frank *chemistry professor*
Bash, Frank Ness *astronomer, educator*
Bengtson, Roger Dean *physicist, department chairman*
Boggs, James Ernest *chemistry professor*
DeWitt-Morette, Cécile *physicist*
Duncombe, Raynor Lockwood *astronomer*
Erskine, James Lorenzo *physics professor*
Fisher, William Lawrence *geologist, educator, dean*
Folk, Robert Louis *geologist, educator*
Fonken, Gerhard Joseph *retired chemistry professor, academic administrator*
Gangopadhyay, Abhijit *geophysicist*
Gavenda, J(ohn) David *physicist*
Gentle, Kenneth William *physicist*
Griffy, Thomas Alan *physics professor*
Groat, Charles George *geologist, former federal agency administrator*
Hackert, Marvin LeRoy *chemistry professor, biophysical researcher*
Kalmykov, Serguei *physicist*
Krische, Michael J. *chemistry professor*
Lambert, David L. *astronomer, educator*
Lambowitz, Alan Marc *biochemistry educator*
Laubach, Stephen Ernest *research scientist*
Mark, Hans Michael *physicist, former federal agency administrator*
Martin, Stephen F. *chemist, educator, researcher*
McBride, Earle F. *geologist, educator*
Mooney, John Bradford, Jr. *oceanographer, engineer, consultant*
Phillips, Joseph Daniel *geophysicist, oceanographer*
Rossky, Peter Jacob *chemistry professor, chemical engineer, researcher*
Schwitters, Roy Frederick *physicist, researcher*
Sessler, Jonathan Lawrence *chemistry professor*
Stewart, Kent Kallam *analytical biochemistry educator*
Swinney, Harry Leonard *physics professor*
Trafton, Laurence Munro *astronomer, researcher*
Wheeler, John Craig *astrophysicist, writer*
Wilson, Clark R. *geophysicist, educator*
Zeng, Hongliu Henry *geophysicist, geologist*

Beaumont
Bahrim, Cristian *physicist, educator, researcher*

Bryan
McIntyre, John Armin *physics professor*

Calvert
Alemán, Marthanne Payne *environmental scientist, consultant*

College Station
Arnowitt, Richard Lewis *retired physics professor*
Basu, Shabari *research scientist*
Dessler, Alexander Jack *astrophysicist, educator*
Duce, Robert Arthur *atmospheric chemist, oceanographer, educator*
Eaton, Gordon Pryor *geologist, consultant*
Goodman, David Wayne *research chemist, educator*
Hardy, John Christopher *physicist, researcher, educator*
Laane, Jaan *chemistry professor*
McIntyre, Peter Mastin *physicist, researcher*
Nachman, Ronald James *chemist, researcher*
O'Connor, Rod *chemist, consultant, inventor*
Prescott, John Mack *biochemist, retired university administrator*
Sun, Yuefeng *research scientist, educator*
Wild, James Robert *biochemistry and genetics professor*
Xie, Rui-Hua *physicist, researcher*

Dallas
Baxter, Richard Henry Geoffrey *research scientist*
Brooks, James Elwood *geologist, educator*
Deisenhofer, Johann *biochemistry professor, researcher*
Gibbs, James Alanson *geologist*
Marshall, John Harris, Jr. *geologist, oil industry executive*
Ray, Bradley Stephen *petroleum geologist*
Thompson, Keith F. MacKechnie *geochemist, consultant*

Denton
Kim, Hansoo *materials scientist, researcher*
Krokhin, Arkadii *physics professor*

El Paso
Peralta-Videa, Jose R. *environmental scientist, researcher*

Fort Worth
Caldwell, Billy Ray *geologist*
Quarles, Carroll Adair, Jr. *physicist, researcher*
Reinecke, Manfred G. *chemistry professor*
Wampler, Wesley Allen *chemist*
Wicker, Dorothy Baldwin *physicist*

Freeport
Stevens, James C. *chemist*

Galveston
Balaban, Alexandru T. *chemistry professor, researcher*
Estes, Ernest L. *geologist, educator*
Gorenstein, David G. *chemistry and biochemistry professor*

Houston
Abbey, George W. S. *space center executive*
Anderson, Richard Carl *geophysical exploration company executive*
Baker, Stephen Denio *physics professor*
Bakulin, Andrey *geophysicist*
Bally, Albert W. *retired geologist, geology educator*
Bogard, Donald Dale *planetary geochemist*
Bonner, Billy Edward *physics professor*
Brotzen, Franz Richard *materials scientist, educator*
Burke, Kevin Charles Antony *geologist*
Caldwell, Tracy Ellen *surface chemist, researcher*
Chu, Paul Ching-Wu *physicist, director, academic administrator, educator*
Chu, Wei-Kan *physicist, researcher*
Colvin, Vicki Leigh *chemistry professor, educator*
Corley, Larry Steven *chemist*
Curl, Robert Floyd, Jr. *chemistry professor*
Efendi, Riad *biochemist*
Fanchi, John Richard *physicist, educator, consultant*
Forney, Jan Lynette *geophysicist*
Gibson, Everett Kay, Jr. *aerospace scientist, geochemist*
Goloby, George William, Jr. *environmental scientist, editor, ornithologist*
Hoffman, Ronald Bruce *biophysicist, consultant, life scientist*
Hulet, Randall Gardner *physics professor*
Hussain, Moinuddin Syed *geologist, engineer, consultant*
Karner, Stephen Leslie *geophysicist*
Katz, Barry Jay *geologist, researcher*
Kevan, Larry *chemistry professor*
Kinsey, James Lloyd *chemist, educator*
Kit, Saul *retired biochemist, educator*
Kochi, Jay Kazuo *chemist, educator*
Kouri, Donald Jack *chemist, educator*
Lane, Neal Francis *physics professor, retired federal agency administrator*
Lewandowski, Jerome L. *physicist*
Liang, Edison Parktak *astrophysicist, plasma physicist, educator, researcher*
Lucid, Shannon W. *biochemist, astronaut*
Mackwell, Stephen Joseph *geophysicist, educator*
Martinez, David Roger *chemist, researcher*
Meng, Ru-Ling *research scientist*
Reiff, Patricia Hofer *space physicist, educator*
Reso, Anthony *geologist, educator, earth resources economist*
Scuseria, Gustavo Enrique *theoretical chemist*
Spudich, John Lee *biochemist, molecular biologist, chemistry professor*
Talwani, Manik *geophysicist, educator*
Tour, James M. *chemistry educator, researcher*
Weinstein, Roy *physics professor*
Wilson, Thomas Leon *physicist, researcher*
Zhou, Min *geophysicist*

Irving
Eaker, Charles William *chemistry professor*

Kaufman
Hausler, Rudolf Heinrich *research chemist*

Kerrville
Shaw, Alan Bosworth *geologist, retired paleontologist*

Lewisville
Nickon, Alex *chemist, educator*

Lubbock
Adamcik, Joe Alfred *retired chemistry professor, lawyer*

Mc Kinney
Frank, Steven Neil *chemist*

Midland
Berner, Leo De Witte, Jr. *retired oceanographer*

Murphy
Rathmell, Robert D. *physicist*

Nacogdoches
Bowen, Donald Edgar *physics professor, former academic administrator*

Plano
Vempati, Rajan K. *research scientist, educator*

Prairie View
Ciftja, Orion *physicist, researcher*

Richardson
Ishak-Boushaki, Mustapha *research scientist, physicist*
Rutford, Robert Hoxie *geologist, educator*
Salamon, Myron Ben *physicist, educator, dea*

San Antonio
Budalur, Thyagarajan Subbanarayan *chemist, professor*
Cragnolino, Gustavo Adolfo *research scienti*
Datta, Rupali *geochemist, educator*
Goldstein, Jerry *physicist, educator*
Gruber, John Balsbaugh *physics professor*
Lyle, Robert Edward *chemist*
Synek, Miroslav *physicist, chemist, world aff consultant*
Taylor, Ishmael Jay *environmental scientist*
Urbach, Adam Robert *chemistry professor*

Southlake
Herrmann, Debra McGuire *chemist, educator*

Stephenville
Little, Bertis Britt *medical research scientist, obstetrician educator, university administr*

Sugar Land
Downs, Hartley H. III *chemist*
Goodwin, Anthony Robert Holmes *chemist, editor*
Huston, Daniel Cliff *geophysicist*

Temple
Asea, Alexzander *research scientist*

Texas City
Fuchs, Owen George *chemist*

Uvalde
Graham, Robert Albert *physicist, researcher, curator*

Van Alstyne
Hornbeck, Larry J. *physicist, researcher*

Waco
Pedrotti, Leno Stephano *physics professor*

UTAH

Brigham City
Hepworth, John Leonard *chemist, researcher*

Draper
Wright, Stuart I. *materials scientist, material engineer*

Dugway
Phan, Richard Man *chemist*

Holladay
O'Halloran, Thomas Alphonsus, Jr. *retired physicist, retired researcher*

Logan
Schunk, Robert Walter *space physics researc administrator*
Zhu, Lie *physics professor*

Provo
Cheney, Brigham Vernon *physical chemist, consultant*
Deng, Shenglou *chemistry professor*
Henderson, Douglas James *physicist, chemis educator, researcher*
Jones, Steven Earl *physics educator, researc*

Salt Lake City
Bass, Brenda L. *biochemist, educator*
Blair, David F. *biochemist, educator*
Bromley, Benjamin C *physics professor*
Dick, Bertram Gale, Jr. *physics professor*
Foltz, Rodger Lowell *chemistry professor*
Gathogo, Patrick Nduru *geologist, researche*
Gortatowski, Melvin Jerome *retired chemist*
Kim, Sung Wan *chemistry professor*
Louie, Janis *chemistry professor*
Mattis, Daniel Charles *physicist, researcher*
Miller, Jan Dean *metallurgy educator*
Miller, Joel Steven *inorganic and organic materials chemist, educator*
Olson, Ferron Allred *metallurgist, educator*
Poulter, Charles Dale *chemist, educator, consultant*
Salomonson, Vincent Victor *meteorologist, educator*
Stang, Peter John *organic chemist*
Straight, Richard Coleman *photobiologist, natural philosopher*
Velick, Sidney Frederick *research biochemis educator*
Zipser, Edward J. *meteorologist, educator*

VERMONT

Arlington
Pond, Thomas Alexander *physics professor, academic administrator*

Burlington
Nyborg, Wesley Lemars *physics professor*

Guildhall
Resden, Ronald Everett *medical devices pro development engineer*

Lyndonville
Atkins, Nolan Thomas *meteorologist, educa*

Middlebury
Winkler, Paul Frank, Jr. *astrophysicist, educ*

elburne
nite, William North *retired chemistry professor*

etford
agland, Mahlon *biochemist, educator*

RGINIA

exandria
mbardt, John Nicholas *research scientist*
rter, William Harold, Sr. *physicist, researcher, electrical engineer*
nberg, Anthony *physicist*
llet, Arne Woolsey *research scientist*
tsch, William Anthony, Jr. *astronomer*
hlberg, Ira *physicist, mathematician*
ahy, Pat (P. Patrick Leahy) *geologist, former federal official*
nick, Robert Louis *chemist, toxicologist*
asterson, Kleber Sanlin, Jr. *physicist*
uir, Warren Roger *chemist, educator*
mney, Carl F. *seismologist*
ier, Pedro N. *physicist, contractor*
almin, Priestley *retired geologist*

nandale
tuszko, Anthony Joseph *research chemist, administrator, educator*
ab, Harry Frederick, Jr. *retired physicist*

lington
geleisen, Jacob *chemist, educator*
ubb, Talbot Albert *physicist, consultant*
, Karl Albert *physicist, government official*
rgely, Tomas Esteban *astronomer*
tthews, Allan Freeman *geologist*
itcomb, James Hall *geophysicist, foundation administrator*

hburn
nnett, Lawrence Herman *physicist*
bin, Gerald Mayer *biochemistry researcher, educator*

acksburg
yan, Levon V. *physicist, electronics engineer, materials scientist*
utartas, Minodaugas (Mino) Fernand *physical chemist*
Wolf, David Alter *physicist, educator*
aybeal, Jack Daniel *chemist, educator*
, Luke Wei *physicist, researcher*
mittmann, Beate *physics professor*

rke
n, Weixing *meteorologist*

arlottesville
drews, William Lester Self *chemistry educator*
omfield, Louis Aub *physicist, researcher*
ter, William Walton *physicist, researcher*
ser, Cassandra Lynne *chemist, educator*
drick, Laurence William *astronomer, educator*
skin, Felicia *biochemist, educator*
od, Richard Standish *geologist*
mes, Russell Newell *inorganic chemist, educator*
cht, Sidney Michael *chemistry professor*
nt, Donald Frederick *chemistry professor*
Kwok-Yung *astronomer, educator, researcher, administrator*
cDonald, Timothy Lee *chemistry professor*
rshall, James Arthur *chemistry professor*
azin, Craig Leigh *astronomer*
delmann, Paul Kenneth *astronomer, educator*
adberg, Richard Jay *chemistry professor*
aden Bout, Paul Adrian *astronomer, physicist, educator*
ber, Hans Jürgen *physics professor*
es, John Thomas, Jr. *chemistry professor, research scientist*

ase City
nipe, Christopher Howard *environmental health specialist*

esterfield
ng, Kenneth Wayne *environmental health specialist*

hlgren
ssler, Barry Lee *physicist, systems analyst*

irfax
ronov, Yakir *physicist, researcher*
ssam, Abul *chemistry professor*
Jang Wan *research scientist, educator*
rowitz, Harold Joseph *biophysicist, educator*
zer, Victor *physicist, researcher*
ger, Edward Herman *retired chemist*

lls Church
kara, Joseph Augustine *chemist, educator*

mpden Sydney
terfield, William Wendell *chemist, educator*

mpton
zaryan, Vahagn *physics researcher, consultant*
ngumthara, Kunhikrishnan *meteorologist*
pathi, Ram Kishore *physicist, researcher*
lsh, Brian M. *physicist*
nakov, Vesselin Ivanov *aerospace scientist, researcher*

rrisonburg
ker, George Harold III *physicist, educator*

rtfield
nson, Carl Randolph *chemist, educator*

athsville
nkel, Raymond Norman *aerospace scientist, consultant, retired military officer*

Lynchburg
McClenon, John Raymond *retired chemistry professor*
Morgan, Evan *retired chemist*

Mc Lean
Theon, John Speridon *meteorologist, researcher*

Newport News
Cardman, Lawrence Santo *physics professor, researcher*

Norfolk
Noginov, Mikhail A. *physicist, researcher, educator*

Petersburg
Stronach, Carey Elliott *physicist, researcher*

Radford
Zweifel, Paul Frederick *retired physics professor*

Reston
Choudhary, Abdur Rahim *physics professor*
Dickman, Robert S. *aerospace institute administrator, retired military officer*
Hirsch, Robert Maurice *hydrologist*
Kramish, Arnold *physicist, historian, writer*
Naeser, Nancy Dearien *geologist, researcher*
Sato, Motoaki *geologist, researcher*

Richmond
Fenn, John Bennett *chemist, educator*
Reshchikov, Michael A. *physics professor, researcher*
Yeudall, William Andrew *biochemist, molecular oncologist*

Roanoke
Al-Zubaidi, Amer Aziz *physicist, researcher*

Springfield
Benson, William Edward (Barnes) *geologist*
Campbell, Francis James *retired chemist*

Vienna
Bhide, Manohar Gopal *nuclear scientist, educator*
Wiesnet, Donald Richard *retired hydrologist*

Virginia Beach
Hamilton, George Henry, Jr. *geologist, consultant*

Washington
Potts, Richard Bruce *paleoanthropologist*

Williamsburg
Starnes, William Herbert, Jr. *chemist, educator*

Winchester
Ludwig, George Harry *retired physicist, electrical engineer*

WASHINGTON

Bellingham
Brakke, Myron Kendall *retired research chemist, educator*
Cox, David Jackson *biochemistry professor*
Nelson, George Driver *astronomer, educator, former astronaut*

Camano Island
O'Connor, Thomas Edward *petroleum geologist, management consultant*

Ellensburg
Rosell, Sharon Lynn *physics and chemistry professor*

Everett
Brown, Frederick Calvin *retired physics professor*

Freeland
Calio, Anthony John *research scientist, operations specialist*

Friday Harbor
Agosta, William Carleton *chemist, educator*

Lynnwood
Olsen, Kenneth Harold *geophysicist, astrophysicist, historian*

Manchester
Fearon, Lee Charles *chemist*

Olympia
Bloomquist, Rodney Gordon *geologist*

Pullman
Banas, Emil Mike *physicist, researcher*
Hinman, George Wheeler *physics professor*
Ryan, Clarence Augustine, Jr. *biochemistry professor*

Redmond
Meshii, Masahiro *materials science educator*

Richland
Bevelacqua, Joseph John *physicist, researcher*
Elderkin, Charles Edwin *retired meteorologist*
Garrett, Bruce C. *materials scientist, researcher*
Harvey, Scott Douglas *chemist, researcher*
Kathren, Ronald Laurence *health physicist*
Kim, Jin Yong *research scientist*
Moore, Emmett Burris, Jr. *physical chemist, educator*
Onishi, Yasuo *environmental researcher*
Peters, Leonard K. *environmental scientist*
Shin, Yongsoon *research scientist*

Seattle
Andersen, Niels Hjorth *chemistry professor, biophysicist, consultant, researcher*
Atwater, Brian F. *geologist, educator*
Baker, David *biochemist*
Baum, William Alvin *astronomer, educator*
Bernard, Eddie Nolan *oceanographer*
Bichsel, Hans *physicist, consultant, researcher*
Bodansky, David *physicist, researcher*
Brown, Robert Alan *geophysicist, educator*
Brownlee, Donald Eugene, II, *astronomer, educator*
Cahn, John Werner *metallurgist, educator*
Campbell, Charles Taylor *chemistry educator*
Christian, Gary D. *chemistry professor*
Davidson, Ernest Roy *chemist, educator*
Davies, Katherine Stefanie *environmental scientist, educator*
Dehmelt, Hans Georg *physicist, educator*
Deming, Jody Wheeler *oceanography educator*
El-Moslimany, Ann Paxton *paleoecologist, educator, writer*
Engel, Thomas Walter *chemistry professor*
Evans, Bernard William *geologist, educator*
Fischer, Edmond Henri *biochemistry educator*
Fischer, Fred Walter *physicist, engineer, educator*
Halver, John Emil *nutritional biochemist*
Heath, George Ross *oceanographer*
Henley, Ernest Mark *physics professor, retired dean*
Krebs, Edwin Gerhard *biochemistry educator*
Kwiram, Alvin L. *retired chemistry professor, academic administrator*
Lubatti, Henry Joseph *physicist, researcher*
Olmstead, Marjorie Ann *physics professor*
Porter, Stephen Cummings *geologist, educator*
Rabinovitch, Benton Seymour *chemist, educator emeritus*
Reinhardt, William Parker *chemical physicist, educator*
Stern, Edward Abraham *physics professor*
Strunz, Kai *research scientist, educator*
Thouless, David James *retired physicist, educator*
Wilets, Lawrence *physicist, educator*
Wurster, Charles Frederick *environmental scientist, educator*

Silverdale
Walske, M(ax) Carl, Jr. *physicist*

Spokane
Crosby, Glenn Arthur *chemistry professor*

Tukwila
Weidner, Mark *environment research executive*

Walla Walla
Wade, Leroy Grover, Jr. *chemistry educator*

WEST VIRGINIA

Fairmont
Swiger, Elizabeth Davis *chemist, educator*

Morgantown
Han, Runlin *biochemist, researcher*
Seehra, Mohindar Singh *physics professor, researcher*

Parkersburg
Sperati, Carleton Angelo *retired chemist*

Wheeling
Duffy, Norman Vincent *chemistry professor*

WISCONSIN

Eau Claire
King, Frederick W. *chemistry professor, researcher*

Kenosha
Kolb, Vera M. *chemist, educator*

Lake Geneva
Dobray, Alan Michael *theoretical physicist, research scientist*

Madison
Adler, Julius *biochemist, educator, biologist*
Anderson, Louis Wilmer, Jr. *physicist, researcher*
Barger, Amy J. *astronomer, educator*
Barger, Vernon Duane *physicist, educator*
Blackwell, Helen E. *chemistry professor*
Botez, Dan *physicist*
Bruch, Ludwig W. *physicist, researcher*
Burris, Robert Harza *biochemist, educator*
Callen, James Donald *plasma physicist, nuclear engineer*
Cao, Guoping *research scientist*
Christensen, Nikolas Ivan *geophysicist, educator*
Churchwell, Edward Bruce *astronomer, educator*
Clay, Clarence Samuel *acoustical oceanographer*
Cleland, W(illiam) Wallace *biochemistry educator*
Coppersmith, Susan Nan *physicist*
Crim, Forrest Fleming, Jr. *chemist, educator*
Curtiss, Charles Francis *retired chemist, educator*
Dahl, Lawrence Frederick *chemistry professor*
DeWerd, Larry Albert *medical physicist, educator*
Dott, Robert Henry, Jr. *geologist, educator*
Evan, Amato Tomas *climate scientist*
Evenson, Merle Armin *chemist, educator*
Farrar, Thomas C. *chemist, educator*
Frey, Perry A. *biochemistry educator*
Gellman, Samuel Helmer *chemist, educator*
Golovkin, Igor *physicist*
Greenler, Robert George *physics professor, researcher*
Griffin, Martin P.A. *research scientist*
Himpsel, Franz Josef *physicist, researcher*
Hokin, Lowell Edward *biochemist, educator*

Jiang, Eric Y *research scientist, marketing executive*
Khazins, David Mikhailovich *research scientist*
Kiessling, Laura Lee *chemist, researcher*
Kutzbach, John E. *climate scientist*
Lagally, Max Gunter *physics professor*
Lardy, Henry A(rnold) *biochemistry professor*
Lawler, James Edward *physics professor*
Li, Kai *chemist, research scientist*
Lin, Chun Chia *research physicist, educator*
Maher, Louis James, Jr. *geologist, educator*
Morton, Stephen Dana *chemist, consultant*
Mukerjee, Pasupati *chemistry professor*
Pondrom, Lee Girard *physicist, researcher*
Pray, Lloyd Charles *geologist, educator*
Record, M. Thomas, Jr. *biochemist, educator*
Reynolds, Ronald J. *astronomer, educator*
Rich, Daniel Hulbert *retired chemistry professor*
Sazhin, Sergey Victorovich *electrochemist, researcher*
Scherer, Victor Richard *physicist, computer scientist, consultant, musician*
Skinner, James Lauriston *chemist, educator*
Vaughan, Worth Edward *retired chemistry professor*
Yu, Hyuk *chemist, educator*
Zimmerman, Howard Elliot *chemist, educator*

Middleton
Crawford, Mark E. *chemist*

Milwaukee
Bader, Alfred Robert *chemist*
Burch, Thaddeus Joseph, Jr. *physics professor, priest*
Buss, Daniel Frank *environmental scientist*
Griffith, Owen Wendell *biochemistry professor*
Haworth, Daniel Thomas *chemistry professor*
Karkheck, John Peter *physics professor, researcher*
Warejcka, Debra J. *research scientist*

Stevens Point
Droske, John P. *chemistry professor*

Washington Island
Raup, David Malcolm *paleontology educator*

Whitefish Bay
Hendee, William Richard *medical physics educator, academic administrator, radiologist*

Whitewater
Kumpaty, Hephzibah J. *chemistry professor*

Williams Bay
Hobbs, Lewis Mankin *astronomer*

WYOMING

Casper
Ptasynski, Harry *geologist, oil industry executive*
Wold, John Schiller *geologist, former congressman*

Kelly
Knowles, William Standish *retired chemist*

Laramie
Meyer, Edmond Gerald *energy scientist, retired chemistry professor, academic administrator, entrepreneur*
Roark, Terry Paul *astronomer, educator*

TERRITORIES OF THE UNITED STATES

PUERTO RICO

Arecibo
Kerr, Robert B. *astronomer, atmospheric scientist*

San Juan
Bacelo, Daniel Enrique *chemist, educator*

Vega Alta
Matos, Cruz Alfonso *environmental consultant*

CANADA

ALBERTA

Calgary
Campbell, Finley Alexander *geologist, consultant*

Edmonton
Harris, Walter Edgar *chemistry professor*
Kay, Cyril Max *biochemist, educator*
Rutter, Nathaniel Westlund *geologist, educator*

BRITISH COLUMBIA

Delta
Russell, Richard Doncaster *geophysics educator, academic administrator*

Lions Bay
Bartholomew, Gilbert Alfred *retired physicist*

Sidney
van den Bergh, Sidney *astronomer*

Vancouver
Affleck, Ian Keith *physics educator*
Hardy, Walter Newbold *physics professor, researcher*

Vogt, Erich Wolfgang *physicist, academic administrator*

Victoria
Batten, Alan Henry *astronomer*
Best, Melvyn Edward *geophysicist*
Garrett, Christopher J.R. *oceanographer*
Hutchings, John Barrie *astronomer, researcher*
Israel, Werner *physicist, educator*
Leffek, Kenneth Thomas *retired chemist, educator*
Morton, Donald Charles *astronomer*
Wiles, David McKeen *chemist*

West Vancouver
Wynne-Edwards, Hugh Robert *geologist, educator, entrepreneur*

MANITOBA

Winnipeg
Jamieson, James Chilles *biochemist, educator*
Schaefer, Theodore Peter *retired chemistry professor*
Smith, Ian Cormack Palmer *biophysicist*

NEWFOUNDLAND AND LABRADOR

Saint John's
Gibbons, Rex Vincent *geologist*

NOVA SCOTIA

Halifax
Dahn, Jeff Raymond *physics professor*
Hiltz, Arnold Aubrey *retired chemist*
Matta, Chérif Farid *chemistry professor*

Tatamagouche
Roach, Margot Ruth *retired biophysicist, educator*

ONTARIO

Deep River
Davies, John Arthur *retired physics professor, engineering educator, research scientist*
Milton, John Charles Douglas *nuclear physicist, researcher*

Guelph
Dickinson, William Trevor *hydrologist, educator*

Hamilton
Datars, William Ross *physicist, researcher*
Gillespie, Ronald James *chemistry professor, researcher, writer*
Jonasson, Ralph George *chemist, researcher*
Spenser, Ian Daniel *chemistry professor*

Kingston
Ewan, George Thomson *physicist, researcher*
Stewart, Alec Thompson *physicist, educator*
Szarek, Walter Anthony *chemist, educator*

London
Bancroft, George Michael *chemical physicist, educator*
Dreimanis, Aleksis *emeritus geology educator*
Fyfe, William Sefton *geochemist, educator*
Stewart, Harold Brown *biochemist*

Manotick
Hobson, George Donald *retired geophysicist*

North York
Nicholls, Ralph William *physicist, researcher*

Ottawa
Alper, Howard *chemistry professor*
Halliday, Ian *astronomer*
Harington, Charles Richard *vertebrate paleontologist*
Holmes, John Leonard *retired chemistry professor*
Ingold, Keith Usherwood *chemist, educator*
Kates, Morris *biochemist, educator*
Ramsay, Donald Allan *physical chemist*
St-Onge, Denis Alderic *geologist, research scientist, educator*

Owen Sound
Morley, Lawrence Whitaker *geophysicist, consultant*

Toronto
Bohme, Diethard Kurt *chemistry professor*
Brook, Adrian Gibbs *chemistry professor*
Goring, David Arthur Ingham *chemist, educator*
Hofmann, Theo *biochemist, educator*
Kresge, Alexander Jerry *chemistry professor*
Litherland, Albert Edward *physics professor*
Polanyi, John Charles *chemist, educator*
Pritchard, Huw Owen *chemist, educator*
Shepherd, Gordon Greeley *space physics educator, researcher*
Stoicheff, Boris Peter *physicist, researcher*
Sues, Hans-Dieter *paleontologist, zoologist, educator*
Thein, Hla-Hla *research scientist*

Waterloo
Morgan, Alan Vivian *geologist, educator*
Smolin, Lee *physicist, researcher, writer*

Willowdale
Goldberg, David Meyer *retired biochemist*

Windsor
Thibert, Roger Joseph *clinical chemist, educator*

QUEBEC

Kirkland
Baroudy, Bahige Mourad *biochemist, researcher*

Montreal
Barrette, Jean *physicist, researcher*
Das Gupta, Subal *physics professor, researcher*
Eisenberg, Adi *chemist*
Johnstone, Rose Mamelak *biochemistry educator*
Leroy, Claude *physics professor, researcher*
Perlin, Arthur Saul *chemistry professor*
Podgorsak, Ervin B. *medical physicist, educator, administrator*
Solomon, Samuel *biochemistry educator, administrator*
Sourkes, Theodore Lionel *biochemistry professor*
Taras, Paul *physicist, researcher*
Vinet, Luc *physicist, educator*
Whitehead, Michael Anthony *chemistry professor*

Pointe-Claire
Bachynski, Morrel Paul *physicist*

Sherbrooke
Tremblay, André-Marie *physicist*

SASKATCHEWAN

Saskatoon
Kerrich, Robert *geologist, educator*

Sherbrooke
Deslongchamps, Pierre *chemistry professor*

Toronto
Armstrong, Robin Louis *physics professor, physicist*

MEXICO

Saltillo
Anderson, Brooks Doran, II, *geologist, consultant*

AUSTRALIA

Canberra
Taylor, Stuart Ross *geochemist, writer*

Sydney
Hora, Heinrich *physicist*

BELGIUM

Brussels
de Duve, Christian René *chemist, educator*

Liège
Mosora-Stan, Florentina Ioana *physics professor*

BRAZIL

Rio de Janeiro
Davidovich, Luiz *physics professor*

Sorocaba
Martins, Nelson *physics professor*

CHINA

Beijing
Duan, Zhenhao *geochemist, educator, editor*
Yang, Chen Ning Franklin *physicist, educator*
Zhou, Bang Rong *physicist, researcher*

CZECH REPUBLIC

Prague
Čejka, Jiří *retired chemist, researcher*
Kotrla, Miroslav *physicist*

DENMARK

Copenhagen
Mottelson, Ben Roy *physicist*
Pethick, Christopher John *physicist*

ENGLAND

Cambridge
Buckingham, Amyand David *chemistry professor*
Edwards, Sir Samuel Frederick *physicist, researcher*
Hawking, Stephen William *astrophysicist, mathematician, educator*
Lawson, Peter Roderick *physicist, researcher*

Falmer
Cornforth, Sir John Warcup *chemist*

Leeds
Slechta, Jiri *theoretical physicist*

Liverpool
Osetsky, Yuri Nicolai *physicist, researcher*

London
Scott, Raymond Peter William *chemistry professor, writer*
Stelle, Kellogg Sheffield *physicist*

North Yorks
Swan, Robert *explorer, adventurer, foundation administrator*

Oxford
Bell Burnell, S. Jocelyn (Susan Jocelyn Bell) *astrophysicist, physics professor*

Reading
Spencer, David Anthony *geologist, researcher, educator*

FRANCE

Besancon
Boillat, Guy Maurice Georges *mathematical physicist*

Chatenay-Malabry
Evesque, Pierre Henri *physics researcher*

Creteil
Renoux, André *physicist, researcher*

Le Vesinet
Hillion, Pierre Théodore Marie *mathematical physicist*

Orleans
Price, David Cecil Long *physicist, researcher*

Orsay
Friedel, Jacques *retired physics professor*

Paris
Constantin, Emilia *physicist, researcher*
Lehn, Jean-Marie Pierre *chemistry professor*
Tapponnier, Paul *physics professor*

Villefranche-sur-Mer
Legendre, Louis *oceanographer, educator, research scientist*

GERMANY

Augsburg
Kunes, Jan *physicist*

Berlin
Eichler, Hans Joachim *physics professor*
Mantsch, Henry Horst *chemistry professor*

Frankfurt
Greiner, Walter Albin Erhard *physicist*
Michel, Hartmut *biochemist*

Garching
Cesarsky, Catherine *astrophysicist*

Göttingen
Toennies, Jan Peter *research chemical physicist*

Hannover
Allen, Bruce *physicist*

Korschenbroich
Engau, Alexander *research scientist*

Munich
Huber, Robert *biochemist, educator*

Paderborn
Thim, Frank *physicist, astronomer*

Stutensee
Barbian, Otto Alfred *physicist*

Stuttgart
Cardona, Manuel *physics professor*

GREECE

Athens
Miliotis, Demitrios *physics professor*

Piraeus
Papachristou, Costas John *physicist, researcher*

HUNGARY

Budapest
Rakos, Balázs *physicist, researcher*
Szigeti, János *physicist*

Debrecen
Csikai, Gyula *physicist, researcher*

INDIA

Delhi
Mitra, Asoke Nath *retired physicist, educator*

Hyderabad
Shanmugasundaram, Anantharaman *geologist, consultant*

Kanpur
Joglekar, Satish Dinkar *physicist, educator*

IRELAND

Dublin
Coey, John Michael David *physicist, educator*

ISRAEL

Be'er Sheva
Carmeli, Moshe *theoretical physicist*

Netanya
Tsitverblit, Naftali Anatol *physicist, fluid mechanics engineer, researcher*

Ra'anana
Hayon, Elie M. *chemist, educator*

Tel Aviv
Jortner, Joshua *physical chemist, educator*

ITALY

Como
Casati, Giulio *theoretical physics professor*

Rome
Maraviglia, Bruno *physicist, researcher*

JAPAN

Gyoda
Shibasaki, Yoshio *chemistry professor, researc*

Okayama
Ubuka, Toshihiko *biochemist, educator, academic administrator*

Osaka
Ikeda, Kazuyosi *physicist, poet*

Tokyo
Esaki, Leo (Esaki Leona) *physicist, foundatio executive, university president*
Iida, Shuichi *physicist, educator*
Koshiba, Masatoshi *physicist, educator*
Mukaiyama, Teruaki *chemist, educator*
Sakurada, Yutaka *retired chemist*
Suzuki, Akira *physics professor*

Utsunomiya
Yorikawa, Hiroharu *physicist, researcher*
Taketomi, Susamu *physicist, researcher*

MALAYSIA

Petaling Jaya
Wong, Kuok-Shoong Daniel *research scientis*

MOLDOVA

Kishinev
Pyshkin, Sergei L. *physics professor, research*

NETHERLANDS

Utrecht
't Hooft, Gerardus (Gerard 't Hooft) *physicis researcher*

NORWAY

Lilleström
Gjessing, Dag Trygveson *physicist*

Oslo
Birketvedt, Grethe Støa *medical scientist, wri musician*
Gjønnes, Jon Kjell *physics professor*

PANAMA

Balboa
Piperno, Dolores *research scientist*

POLAND

Bydgoszcz
Czajkowski, Gerard Zygfryd *physicist, researcher*

REPUBLIC OF KOREA

Daejeon
Ryu, Ho Jin *materials researcher*

Gyeongsan
Shamsuzzoha, M. D. *research scientist, chem engineer*

Seoul
Ju, Se-Jong *research scientist*
Kim, Chul Sung *physicist, educator*
Oh, Sangyoon *research scientist*

Suwon
Chang, Seunghyuk *physicist, electrical engin*

Taegu
Seok, Jaewook *materials scientist, polymer scientist*

ROMANIA

rest
Nicolae Victor *physicist, researcher*

RUSSIA

Valerey Grigorijevich *physicist,*
rcher

yev, Renat Muzipovich *physicist,*
ator

w
ky, Vladimir Borisovich *physics*
ssor, department chairman
, Vladimir *physicist, researcher*

, Alexander Mikhailovich *physicist,*
ator

SINGAPORE

pore
hn Hon Shing *electronics scientist*

SWEDEN

org
on, Robert Charles Wilhelm *physicist,*
archer

ro
en, Jan R. G. *physicist*

skär
Bert Richard Johannes *atmospheric*
icist, meteorologist, researcher

SWITZERLAND

va
k, Georges *physicist, nuclear scientist*
, Vladimir Dmitrievich *physicist,*
sultant, physics professor
erger, Jack *physicist, researcher*

lon-les-Bains
Peter William *physicist*

h
Richard Robert *chemist, educator*
nmoser, Albert *chemist*

TAIWAN

ei
uan Tseh *chemistry professor*
law-Kuen *physicist*

WALES

liff
David Collingwood *physicist, materials*
nce educator

ADDRESS UNPUBLISHED

nilli, Chowdary B. *research scientist*
ndratos, Spiro Dionisios *chemistry*
fessor, dean
, Edward Lewis *biophysicist, educator*
r, Ralph Asher *physicist, educator*
, Donald Paul *retired air research director*
r, Michael *biophysics professor*
er-Johnson, Betsy *physicist, engineer,*
ired automotive executive
lla, Daniel *biochemist, researcher*
, David *meteorologist, research scientist*
, Charlie A. *physics researcher, inventor*
us, Keriann M. *chemistry scholar, Latin*
erican studies scholar
r, D. James *oceanographer, administrator,*
ence and management consultant
chandran, Priya *environmental scientist*
win, George Curriden *physicist, researcher*
rjee, Gaurab *research scientist*
achyn, Michael R. *chemist*
John Baldwin *chemist, research scientist*
att, Ronald Lee *research biochemist,*
nsultant
ford, Lynn Foster *physicist, engineer*
anager
rseh, Amani Musa *chemist, researcher*
r, Henry Hermann *chemistry and science*
ucator
r, James Monie *aerospace scientist*
hetti, Frederick Daniel, Jr. *physicist,*
searcher
with, Steven Van Walter *astronomy*
ucator
ij, Orest *physicist, investment banker*
endt, John Charles *geophysicist, researcher,*
riter
ens, James William *physicist, administrator,*
thor
ni, Francesco *chemist*
amin, Arlin James *physicist*
nett, Charles Leonard *astrophysicist,*
ducator
nett, William Ralph, Jr. *physicist, researcher*

Benson, Allen B. *chemist, educator, consultant*
Benway, Heather *oceanographer, researcher*
Berlin, Kenneth Darrell *chemistry professor, consultant, researcher*
Bersin, Richard Lewis *physicist*
Biederman, Edwin Williams, Jr. *retired geologist*
Bikales, Norbert M. *chemist, science administrator*
Blackwell, F. Oris *environmental scientist, educator*
Bodanszky, Miklos *chemist, educator*
Bohm, Henry Victor *physicist*
Boschmann, Erwin *chemistry professor*
Bostrom, Carl Otto *physicist, research facility administrator*
Boyer, Herbert Wayne *retired biochemist, biotechnology company executive*
Bradbeer, Clive *biochemistry educator*
Bretthauer, Erich Walter *chemist, educator*
Brickner, Steven J. *chemist*
Brodsky, Marc Herbert *physicist, research and publishing executive*
Browne, John Charles *physicist, researcher, lab administrator*
Bucknum, Michael John *chemist, crystallographer, educator*
Bucksbaum, Philip Howard *physicist*
Bulkley, Gregory Bartlett *fisheries biologist, retired research scientist, academic surgeon, educator, cattle rancher*
Bunyan, Ellen Lackey Spotz *retired chemist*
Butler, James Newton *retired chemist, educator*
Butler, Orton Carmichael *retired climatologist, educator*
Cai, Ming Zhi *chemist, researcher, film producer*
Calvert, Jack George *atmospheric chemist, educator*
Campbell, Mary Stinecipher *retired chemist*
Capasso, Federico *physicist*
Carballo, Juan-Antonio *research scientist*
Casella, Russell Carl *physicist*
Cassel, Robert Uriah *chemist*
Cathou, Renata Egone *chemist, consultant*
Chadsey, Harold A. *astronomer, physicist*
Chandiwal, Amito *research scientist*
Chang, Clarence Dayton *retired chemist*
Chappelle, Emmett W. *physical scientist*
Chiu, Bella Chao *astrophysicist, writer*
Choi, Stephen Sukjun *physicist*
Christoffersen, Ralph Earl *chemist, researcher, director*
Church, Eugene Lent *physicist, consultant*
Clayton, Robert Norman *chemist, educator*
Colbern, Steven Garrett *chemist, researcher*
Colton, John P. *nuclear scientist, engineering executive*
Compton, W. Dale *physicist, researcher, engineer*
Conrath, Barney Jay *astrophysicist*
Cooper, Austin Morris *chemist, consultant, chemical engineer, researcher*
Cotruvo, Joseph Alfred *water, environmental and public health consultant*
Cox, Robert Hames *chemist, consultant*
Crabtree, Robert Howard *chemistry professor, consultant*
Cramer, James Dale *physicist, scientific company executive*
Cuatrecasas, Pedro Martin *research biochemist, pharmaceutical executive*
Daniels, James Maurice *retired physicist*
Daniels, William Burton *retired physicist, educator*
Dash, Sanford Mark *aerospace scientist*
Davids, Robert Norman *retired petroleum exploration geologist*
Day, Richard Allen *retired chemistry professor*
de Planque, E. Gail *physicist*
Deryuga, Vyacheslav O. *nuclear physicist*
Detert, Miriam Anne *chemical analyst*
Dickens, Justin Kirk *nuclear physicist*
Dixon, Gordon Henry *biochemist, educator*
Dodin, Ilya *research scientist*
Dolan, Louise Ann *physicist*
Donaldson, Eva G. *chemist, writer*
Dow, Garnett McCormick *geologist, consultant*
Drahos, Sandra P. *retired chemist*
Dunn, Arnold Samuel *biochemistry educator*
Eberly, Joseph Henry *physics professor, consultant, quantum optics scientist*
Eck, Robert Edwin *retired physicist*
Edwards, Helen Thom *physicist*
Eerkens, Jeff W. *nuclear scientist, educator, laser engineer*
Eguchi, Miharu *chemist, researcher*
Ehrenfeld, John Roos *environmental policy educator*
Eickhorst, Kristin Michele *research scientist*
Einhorn, Martin B. *physicist, educator*
Ensminger, Luther Glenn *retired chemist*
Erdmann, Joachim Christian *retired physicist*
Esquivel, Agerico Liwag *retired research physicist*
Evans, Allan Joseph *research scientist, educator*
Evans, Dennis Hyde *chemist, educator*
Ewen, H. I. *physicist*
Fabiano, Nicola *physicist, researcher*
Farmer, Crofton Bernard *atmospheric physicist*
Fey, Willard *global environmental researcher, educator*
Finlayson, John Sylvester *retired biochemist*
Flinn, Paul Anthony *materials scientist*
Fogleman, Guy Carroll *physicist, mathematician, educator*
Fons, Eric Wallace *physics professor*
Ford, Kenneth William *physicist*
Forsyth, Richard J. *chemist*
Fortner, Rosanne White *environmental scientist, educator*
Fowler, Alan Bicksler *retired physicist*
Fradkin, David Milton *physicist, researcher*
Franz, John E. *bio-organic chemist, researcher*
Franz, Judy R. *physics professor*
French, Julia McAllister (Judy) *environmental consultant*
Friedlander, Charles Douglas (Chuck Friedlander) *aerospace scientist, consultant*

Fukuda, Atsuo *physicist, materials science researcher, educator*
Gabel, Connie *chemist, educator*
Gaffin, David Morris *meteorologist, researcher*
Galloway, Eilene Marie *space and astronautics consultant*
Gandhi, Shaan-Chirag C. *biochemistry and chemistry scholar*
Gangopadhyay, Arup *research scientist*
Gardner, Wilford Robert *physicist, researcher*
Garmany, Catharine Doremus *astronomer*
Garrison, Robert Frederick *astronomer, educator*
Garwin, Richard Lawrence *physicist*
Gelboin, Harry Victor *biochemistry educator, researcher*
Glashow, Sheldon Lee *physicist, researcher*
Glenister, Brian Frederick *geologist, educator*
Gluckstern, Robert Leonard *physics professor*
Golden, David Edward *physicist*
Goldstein, Irving Solomon *chemistry professor, consultant*
Goncharov, Viktor *biochemist, researcher*
Gonzalez, Gabriela Ines *physics professor*
Goodman, Charles David *physicist, researcher*
Goodman, Frederick Denis *retired environmental scientist*
Gorbaty, Martin Leo *chemist, researcher*
Gordon, William Edwin *physicist, educator, electrical engineer, academic administrator*
Gorski, Waldemar *chemist, educator*
Govindjee, *biophysics, biochemistry, and biology professor*
Grady, Lee Timothy *pharmaceutical chemist*
Grandy, Walter Thomas, Jr. *physicist, researcher*
Greenslade, Thomas Boardman, Jr. *physics educator*
Grimes, James Gordon *geologist*
Groh, Sebastien Stephane *materials scientist, researcher*
Gunter, William Dayle, Jr. *physicist, consultant*
Gurvich, Victor Alexander *physicist, engineer*
Haisch, Bernard Michael *astronomer, researcher*
Halada, Richard Stephen *physics educator*
Halasyamani, P. Shiv *inorganic chemist, researcher*
Halpern, Alvin Michael *retired physicist, educator, consultant*
Handschumacher, Robert Edmund *biochemistry professor*
Hanks, Alan R. *retired chemistry professor*
Hanson, Harold Palmer *physicist, editor, academic administrator, government official*
Hardy, Ralph W. F. *biochemist*
Harris, Cyril Manton *physicist, acoustical engineer, engineering and architecture educator*
Harwit, Martin Otto *astrophysicist, writer, educator, museum director*
Hasanyan, Davresh *research scientist, educator*
Haslett, Jared Wooddell *physicist, educator*
Hassan, Sayed Mohammed *chemist*
Heeschen, David Sutphin *astronomer, educator*
Heller, Adam *chemist, researcher*
Hermann, Robert Bell *physical chemist, consultant*
Herzfeld, Charles Maria *physicist, educator*
Hijazi, Yazan S. *research scientist, educator*
Ho, Chih-Ming *physicist, researcher*
Hoeg, Donald Francis *chemist, consultant, research and development company executive*
Hoenig, Steven Lawrence *chemist*
Holmes, Richard Brooks *mathematical physicist*
Holt, William Henry *retired physicist, researcher*
Horton, Robert Carlton *geologist*
Howard, Robert Franklin *observatory administrator, astronomer*
Howell, Everette Irl *physicist, researcher*
Hoyt, Roger Franklin *physicist, consultant*
Hu, Esther Ming *astronomer, educator*
Hubbard, Gregory Scott *physicist*
Hulet, Ervin Kenneth *retired nuclear chemist*
Hulse, Russell Alan *physicist*
Hunsucker, Robert Dudley *physicist, electrical engineer, educator, researcher*
Hunter, James Edward *chemist, consultant*
Huo, Jinshan *materials scientist*
Hwang, Cordelia Jong *retired chemist*
Ignatiev, Alex *physics researcher*
Inlow, Rush Osborne *chemist*
Ishii, Yoshinori *environmental science educator, science writer*
Isley, Sara *chemist, educator*
Ivey, Elizabeth Spencer *retired physicist, educator*
Jackson, Edwin Atlee *retired physicist, educator*
Jackson, Kenneth Arthur *physicist, researcher*
Jan, Yuh Nung *biochemistry and physiology educator*
Jennings, Bojan Hamlin *chemist, former educator*
Jin, Helena *research scientist*
John, Sarah *physicist*
Johnson, Arthur William, Jr. *retired research scientist*
Johnson, Francis Severin *physicist*
Jones, Thornton Keith *chemist, researcher*
Jordan, Kenneth D. *chemistry professor*
Jordan, Robert Reed *retired geologist, educator*
Jordan, Thomas Fredrick *physics professor*
Kamanu, Uchemadu Chee *chemist*
Kapany, Narinder Singh *physicist*
Karplus, Paul Andrew *biochemistry educator*
Kasprzak, Lucian Alexander *physicist, researcher, materials scientist*
Kastner, Marc Aaron *physics professor*
Kawamura, Kenji *aerospace scientist*
Kedes, Laurence Herbert *biochemistry professor, physician, researcher*
Keffer, Charles Joseph *retired physics professor, academic administrator*
Kenney, Melissa A. *environmental scientist, educator*
Keyworth, George Albert *physicist, consulting company executive*
Kirakosyan, Arman *physicist, researcher*
Kistiakowsky, Vera *physical researcher, educator*
Klanderman, Bruce Holmes *retired chemist*

Klein-Seetharaman, Judith *biochemist*
Klema, Ernest Donald *nuclear physicist, educator*
Korn, Jessica Susan *research scientist, educator, program manager*
Kraichnan, Robert Harry *physicist, consultant*
Krakower, Terri Jan *biochemist, researcher*
Kraus, Naomi *retired biochemist*
Krause, Sonja *chemistry professor*
Kravitz, Rubin *chemist*
Krawetz, Stephen Andrew *molecular medicine and genetics scientist, educator*
Kresa, Kent *retired aerospace executive*
Kribel, Robert Edward *consultant, retired physicist, academic administrator*
Kristiansen, Kai de Lange *physicist*
Kroto, Harold Walter *chemistry researcher, educator*
Krueger, Arlin James *physicist*
Kuhlmann-Wilsdorf, Doris *materials scientist, inventor, retired educator*
Kuritsyn, Alexey *physicist, researcher*
Kustin, Kenneth *chemist*
Lagow, Richard James *chemistry professor*
Laporte, Leo Frederic *geologist, educator, paleontologist*
LeBlond, Paul Henri *oceanographer, educator*
Lederman, Leon Max *physicist, researcher*
Lee, Hwan-Soo *materials scientist, researcher*
Lee, Katie N. *biochemistry and chemistry scholar*
Lemieux, Jacob E. *biochemist*
Lemke, James Underwood *physicist*
Leupold, Herbert August *physicist*
Levenson, Marc David *optics and lasers specialist, editor*
Li, Ming *oceanographer*
Limburg-Santistevan, Ellen H. *retired geologist, artist*
Lin, Ray-Qing *physicist, researcher*
Lin, Ronghui *chemist, researcher*
Liu, Yong Cheng *chemist, educator*
Lloyd, Ray Dix *retired health physicist*
Loesch, Arthur Z. *environmental scientist, educator*
Los, Marinus *retired agrochemical researcher*
Louie, Steven Gwon Sheng *physics professor, researcher*
Lovinger, Andrew Joseph *polymer scientist*
Lovins, Amory Bloch *physicist, energy consultant*
Lu, Erdong *research scientist*
Lucas, William Ray *aerospace scientist, consultant*
Lukacs, Michael Edward *electro-optics researcher*
Luke, Karen *chemist, researcher*
Ma, Vu *chemist*
MacCracken, Michael Calvin *atmospheric scientist*
MacQueen, Robert Moffat *solar physicist*
Maddin, Robert *metallurgist, educator*
Makrogiannis, Sokratis *physicist, researcher*
Maling, George Croswell, Jr. *physicist*
Malins, Donald Clive *biochemist, researcher*
Mangasarian, Olvi Leon *research scientist, educator*
Manninen, Peter R. *chemist*
Mantione, Kirk John *research scientist, consultant*
Mantz, Arlan W. *physics professor*
Marcuse, Dietrich *retired physicist*
Marinetti, Guido V. *biochemistry professor*
Mashnik, Stepan G. *physicist*
Mataré, Herbert F. *physicist, consultant*
McCormick, Donald Bruce *retired biochemist, educator*
McKay, Kenneth Gardiner *retired physicist, electronics company executive*
McTague, John Paul *materials scientist, educator, chemist, researcher*
Mehta, Mausmi *oceanographer*
Meinwald, Jerrold *retired chemistry professor*
Melvin, Peter Joseph *astrophysicist, educator*
Mendelson, Sol *physical science educator, consultant*
Meng, Yu-Ju Gloria *research scientist*
Mertz, Aaron F. *physicist*
Metz, Werner Adam *physicist*
Michaud, Georges Joseph *physics professor*
Miller, Phillip Edward *environmental scientist*
Mills, Douglas L. *physics professor*
Mislow, Kurt Martin *chemist, educator*
Mollenauer, Linn Frederick *retired physicist, writer*
Monroe, Frederick Fales *geologist, oceanographer*
Morse, Joseph Grant *chemistry educator*
Moulton, Grace Charbonnet *retired physicist*
Mullis, Kary Banks *biochemist*
Myles, LaToya *research scientist*
Nacht, Sergio *biochemist*
Nagel, Sidney Robert *physics professor*
Nemec, Josef *retired organic chemist, researcher*
Ness, Norman Frederick *retired astrophysicist, educator, administrator*
Nestell, Galina Petrovna *paleontologist, researcher*
Nevill, William Albert *chemistry professor*
Newkirk, John Burt *retired metallurgical research administrator*
Nirenberg, Marshall Warren *biochemist*
Nobles, Laurence Hewit *retired geology educator*
O'Callaghan, Mark Charles *physicist*
Oesterlin, Lovye Gwendolyn *retired chemist, educator, retired educational consultant*
Ogliaruso, Michael Anthony *retired chemist, educator, actor*
Oka, Takeshi *physicist, physical chemist, astronomer, educator*
Onah, Ejembi John *chemist, researcher*
Oort, Abraham Hans *meteorologist, researcher, educator*
Orttung, William Herbert *chemistry professor*
Paik, Ji Hye *research scientist*
Palii, Sergiu Petru *chemist, researcher*

Pan, Deming *chemistry professor*
Pascu, Dan *astronomer*
Patchett, Arthur Allan *medicinal chemist, pharmaceutical executive*
Patterson, Edward Palmer *retired physicist*
Paul, Bipul C. *research scientist*
Paul, Debajyoti *geologist, educator*
Peiris, Suhithi Mahesica *chemist, researcher*
Peleg, Avner *physicist, mathematician*
Petersen, Arne Joaquin *chemist, consultant*
Pettit, Erin *glaciologist*
Phelps, Michael Edward *biophysics professor*
Philander, Samuel George Harker *oceanographer*
Phillips, Julia Mae *physicist*
Pierce, Stephen D. *oceanographer, researcher*
Pirkle, Earl Charnell *retired geologist*
Plummer, Leonard Niel *geochemist*
Pollack, Gerald Leslie *physicist, researcher, educator*
Portis, Alan Mark *physicist, researcher*
Pound, Robert Vivian *physics professor*
Pradzynski, Andrzej Henryk *chemist*
Price, Clifford Warren *retired metallurgist, researcher*
Pristoop, Simon Morris *retired physicist, systems engineer, consultant*
Proctor, Richard James *geologist, consultant*
Proenza, Bill (Xavier William Proenza) *meteorologist, former federal agency administrator*
Profeta, Salvatore, Jr. *chemist, educator*
Pursey, Derek Lindsay *retired physics professor*
Pytlewski, Laura Jean *chemistry professor*
Pytlinski, Jerzy Teodor *physicist, educator, research scientist*
Pytte, Agnar *physicist, retired academic administrator*
Qi, Zhigang *materials scientist, chemist*
Quinn, Helen Rhoda Arnold *physicist*
Qutub, Musa Yacub *hydrogeologist, educator, consultant*
Radmilovic, Velimir *materials scientist, researcher*
Ragent, Boris *physicist*
Read, Virginia Hall *retired biochemistry professor*
Redding, Rogers Walker *physics professor, academic administrator*
Reichmanis, Elsa *chemist*
Reynik, Robert John *materials scientist, consultant, science educator*
Rhyne, James Jennings *condensed matter physicist*
Rice, Kenner Cralle *medicinal chemist*
Rice, Stuart Alan *chemist, educator*
Richards, Austin Ames *physicist, artist*
Richardson, Charles Clifton *biochemist, educator*
Riley, Monica *microbiologist, educator*
Rinebold, Alice June *environmental scientist*
Roberts, Thomas George *retired physicist*
Robertson, John Archibald Law *nuclear scientist*
Robertson, Robert Graham Hamish *physicist*
Roden, Michael Frank *geochemist, educator, director*
Rodgers, Robert Aubrey *physicist*
Rodin, Eugene *aerospace scientist, researcher, engineering educator*
Rohr, Davis Charles *aerospace consultant, retired military officer*
Rokhvarger, Anatoly Efim *materials science and ceramic technology scientist*
Roman, Nancy Grace *astronomer, consultant*
Romanowski, Thomas Andrew *physicist, educator*
Rose, Marian Henrietta *physics researcher*
Rosenkilde, Carl Edward *retired physicist*
Rosenstein, Robert Alan *scientific consultant*
Rosenthal, Joel *chemist, researcher*
Rouxel, Olivier *geochemist, research scientist*
Rubin, Vera Cooper *astronomer, researcher*
Rybczyk, Joseph Anthony *physicist, researcher, writer, inventor*
Sabb, Annmarie Louise *retired chemist*
Sablik, Martin John *research physicist*
Sahrakorpi, Seppo *physicist, researcher*
Salamone, Joseph Charles *polymer chemistry professor*
Sapiano, Mathew Raymond Paul *meteorologist*
Sarkar, Malancha *research scientist, educator*
Sarma, Pallav *research scientist*
Satinover, Jeffrey B. *physicist, psychiatrist, writer*
Sawicki, Mikolaj Ziemislaw *physicist*
Sayre, David *physicist*
Schellman, John A. *chemistry professor*
Schepartz, Alanna *biochemist, educator*
Schneider, Carl Stanley *retired physics professor, researcher*
Schneider, William George *chemist, research consultant*
Schock, Robert Norman *geophysicist*
Schonhorn, Harold *chemist, researcher*
Schutz, Donald Frank *geochemist, environmental corporate executive*
Schwartz, Lyle Howard *materials scientist, science administrator*
Schwartz, Shirley E. *retired chemist, researcher*
Scully, Marlan Orvil *physics professor*
Sengupta, Abhijit *molecular and optical physicist*
Sha, William T. *nuclear scientist, consultant*
Shackelford, Scott Addison *retired chemist, researcher*
Shamatava, Irma *physicist, researcher*
Shapiro, Zalman Mordecai *chemist, consultant*
Shaw, Melvin Phillip *physicist, engineering educator, psychologist*
Sheinin, Rose *biochemist, educator*
Shirley, David Arthur *chemistry professor, science administrator*
Shochet, Melvyn Jay *physicist*
Siavosh-Haghighi, Ali *physical chemist, researcher*
Siganga, Walter *physics professor*
Sikorski, James Alan *research chemist*
Simpson, Robert Homer *meteorologist, consultant*
Sinha, Sunil Kumar *physicist*
Sitnyakovsky, Roman Emmanuil *scientist, writer, inventor, translator*
Slaugh, Lynn H. *retired chemist*
Sloop, Joseph C. *chemistry professor*
Smith, Charles Haddon *geologist, consultant, retired federal agency administrator*
Smith, Christopher T. *environmental health officer*
Smith, H. Morgan *environmental scientist, educator*
Sobolev, Alexandre Andreevich *physicist*
Solomon, Susan *chemist, scientist*
Solon, Leonard R(aymond) *retired physicist, educator, consultant*
Souler, Benjamin Kerwi *retired research chemist, pharmacist, consultant*
Spejewski, Eugene Henry *physicist, consultant*
Squibb, Samuel Dexter *chemistry professor*
Srinivasan, Rangaswamy *chemical physicist*
Stampke, Stuart Reh *physicist, researcher*
Stanley, Steven Mitchell *paleontologist, educator*
Steinhoff, Raymond O(akley) *consulting geologist*
Steitz, Joan Argetsinger *biochemistry professor*
Stern, Robin Lauri *medical physicist*
Stetson, Robert Francis *retired metallurgist*
Stevenson, Paul Michael *physics professor, researcher*
Stever, Horton Guyford *aerospace scientist, educator, aerospace engineer, consultant*
Stief, Louis John *chemist*
Stockbauer, Roger Lewis *retired physicist, researcher*
Straus, Leon Stephan *physicist*
Stringer, John *retired materials scientist*
Stroud, Robert Michael *biophysicist, educator, biotechnologist*
Strouth, Baron Howard Steven *geologist, mining engineer*
Stubbs, Gerald *biochemist, educator*
Subramanian, Tirunelveli Satyanandam *physicist*
Sullivan, Kathryn D. *geologist, former astronaut, former science association executive*
Sullivan, Neil Samuel *physicist, researcher, educator, former dean*
Sunderman, Duane Neuman *chemist, research and development company executive*
Sutin, Norman *retired chemist, researcher*
Suttie, John Weston *biochemist*
Suzuki, Nobutaka *chemistry professor*
Symchowicz, Samson *retired biochemist*
Tabazadeh, Azadeh *environmental scientist, researcher*
Tam, Sunny Wing Yee *physicist*
Tang, Ching Wan *research scientist*
Tangherlini, Frank Robert *physics educator*
Tao, Jing *environmental scientist*
Tao, Mariano *biochemistry educator*
Tauc, Jan *retired physics professor*
Taylor, Kathleen (Christine Taylor) *physical chemist, researcher*
Tevault, David Earl *chemist, researcher*
Texter, John *physical chemist consultant*
Thiara, Parvinder Singh *chemistry scholar*
Thiemens, Mark H. *chemistry professor*
Thomas, John Howard *astrophysicist, mechanical engineer, educator*
Thornton, Rita Louise *environmental scientist, lawyer*
Ting, Samuel Chao Chung *physicist, researcher*
Tolstoy, Maya *marine seismologist*
Tonyushkin, Alexey Alexeyevich *physicist, researcher*
Tripathy, Sucheta *research scientist*
Trocki, Linda Katherine *geoscientist, economist, systems engineer*
Tsigelny, Igor *research scientist*
Tuchman, Avraham (Avi) *physicist, researcher*
Tuul, Johannes *physics professor, researcher*
Uchrin, Christopher George *environmental engineer and scientist*
Ufimtsev, Pyotr Yakovlevich *physicist, electrical engineer, educator*
Upgren, Arthur Reinhold, Jr. *astronomer, educator, writer*
Van Horn, Hugh M. *physicist, astronomer, educator*
Vanier, Jacques *physicist*
Velasquez-Garcia, Luis Fernando *research scientist, consultant*
Velisavljevic, Nenad *physicist*
Veronis, George *geophysics educator*
Vook, Frederick Ludwig *physicist, consultant*
Vugmeister, Boris *physicist, writer*
Wall, Frederick Theodore *retired chemistry professor*
Wallace, Jane House *retired geologist*
Walters, Robert Ancil *physicist, mathematician*
Walther, Adriaan *retired physics professor*
Wang, Jian *materials scientist, researcher*
Wang, Yinmin *materials scientist, educator*
Watkins, George Daniels *physics professor*
Webster, Harold Frank *physicist*
Webster, Owen Wright *chemist*
Weinberg, Steven *physics professor*
Weinreb, Michael Philip *physicist*
Weisburger, Elizabeth Kreiser *retired chemist*
Weiss, Rainer *physics educator*
Weisz, Paul B(urg) *physicist, researcher, chemical engineer*
Wellner, Marcel Nahum *research scientist, educator*
Wells, John Calhoun *retired physics professor*
Westerhout, Gart *retired astronomer*
Wheeler, John Oliver *retired geologist*
Whelan, Colm T. *physicist, researcher*
Wickman, Leslie *research scientist, science administrator*
Wilson, Peggy Mayfield *retired chemist*
Wilson, Robert Woodrow *radio astronomer*
Wolff, Manfred Ernst *chemist, pharmaceutical executive*
Wong, Ah-San *planetary scientist, musician, writer*
Wong, Yanyi Liu *physicist, researcher*
Woodruff, Truman O(wen) *physicist, emeritus educator*
Workman, John Mitchell *chemist*
Wu, Yider *research scientist*
Wyrtki, Klaus *oceanography educator*
Xiang, Hui *biochemist, researcher*
Xue, Yibin *metallurgist, educator*
Yamaguchi, Kenneth Steven *chemistry professor*
Yates, David John C. *chemist, researcher*
Yau, Siu-Tung *physics professor*
Yeliseev, Alexei Arkadievich *biochemist, researcher*
Ying, Jinfa *chemist*
Yoon, Jeong Whan *research scientist, educator*
York, James Wesley, Jr. *theoretical physicist, educator*
Young, David Michael *biochemist, molecular biologist, internist, educator*
Yu, Robert Kuan-jen *biochemistry professor*
Zakim, David *biochemist*
Zaleski, Jan Franciszek *biochemist*
Zhang, Yanwen *physicist*
Zheng, Lingyi Albert *materials scientist, materials engineer, researcher*
Zhou, Dazhuang *aerospace scientist, researcher*
Zhou, Shao Man *chemist, researcher*
Zou, Dekun *research scientist*
Zucker, Alexander *physicist, researcher*

SOCIAL SCIENCE

UNITED STATES

ALABAMA

Arab
Black, Daniel Hugh *retired social studies educator*

Auburn
Clark, Janet Eileen *retired political science professor*
Seroka, James Henry *social studies educator, academic administrator*

Birmingham
Bradley, Laurence Alan *psychologist*
Cockerham, William Carl *sociologist, educator*
Freeman, Arthur Merrimon III *psychology professor, dean*
Nunn, Grady Harrison *retired political science professor*
Taub, Edward *psychology researcher*

Dothan
Wright, Burton *sociologist*

Fairhope
Gwin, John Michael *retired economics professor, management consultant*

Florence
Hansen, Vagn Keith *political science educator, college administrator*

Hartselle
Slate, Joe Hutson *psychologist, educator*

Jacksonville
Chargois, Deborah Majeau *psychology professor, researcher*
Dunaway, Carolyn Bennett *retired sociology professor*

Midfield
Daniels-Rogers, LaTausha *social sciences educator, entrepreneur*

Mobile
Suess, James Francis *retired clinical psychologist*

Montgomery
Wendzel, Robert Leroy *political science professor*

Pell City
Passey, George Edward *psychologist, educator*

Troy
Manners, Pamela Ann *psychology professor*
Rinehart, James Forrest *political science professor, department chairman*

Tuscaloosa
Baklanoff, Eric Nicholas *economist, educator*
Cramer, Dale Lewis *retired economics professor*
Fish, Mary Martha *economics professor*

Tuskegee
Clark, Shawn L. *psychologist, educator*

ALASKA

Anchorage
Lindeman, Janet Claire *psychologist, educator*
Obermeyer, Theresa Nangle *sociology educator*

Fairbanks
Irish, Joel David *anthropologist*
Shier, Juliet Marie *social studies educator*

Juneau
Wessen, Douglas John *psychologist*

ARIZONA

Chandler
Newman, Phyllis *retired counselor, therapist, hypnotist*

Flagstaff
McDonald, Craydon Dean *psychologist*
Pavlik, William Bruce *psychologist, educa*

Fountain Hills
Jan, George Pokung *political science profe*

Gilbert
Metcalf, Virgil Alonzo *economics professo*

Green Valley
Foley, Teresa A. *psychologist*

Mesa
Gordon, Marvin F. *retired social sciences educator*

Oro Valley
Haller, Archibald Orben *sociologist, educa*

Phoenix
Doss, Sylvia M. *psychologist, educator*
Huelster, Jeffery James *social studies educ*
Masters, Jonathan Edward *clinical psychol*
Newman, Donald Lynn *psychologist, cons*
Roberts, Christopher Wayne *psychologist, educational consultant*
Welker, Kristina Diane *psychologist*
Wolf, Irna Lynn *psychologist*

Scottsdale
Baker, Edward Martin *engineering and industrial psychologist*

Tempe
Gordon, Leonard *retired social sciences ed*
Hechter, Michael Norman *sociologist*
Johanson, Donald Carl *physical anthropolo*
Myint, Soe Win *geographer, educator*
Prescott, Edward C. *economist, educator*
Rowley, Beverley Davies *sociologist*
Sackton, Frank Joseph *public affairs educa*
Simon, Sheldon Weiss *political science pro*
Smith, V. Kerry *economics professor*
Weigend, Guido Gustav *geographer, educa*

Tucson
Axinn, George Harold *rural sociology educ*
Block, Michael Kent *economics and law professor, former government official*
Breiger, Ronald Louis *social sciences educ*
Christie, Nancy Gail *psychology professor, department chairman*
Clarke, James Weston *political science prof writer*
Coan, Richard Welton *psychologist, educato*
Larwood, Laurie *psychologist*
Reitan, Ralph Meldahl *clinical neuropsychologist, former educator*
Schwebel, Milton *psychologist, educator*
Serido, Joyce *psychologist, researcher*
Smith, David Wayne *psychologist, educator*
Soren, David *archaeologist, educator, writer filmmaker*
Thompson, Raymond Harris *retired anthropologist, educator*
Underwood, Jane Hainline Hammons *anthropologist, educator*

Yuma
McCarthy, Sherri Nevada *psychologist, educ educational consultant*
Norton, Dunbar Sutton *economic developer*

ARKANSAS

Fayetteville
Costrell, Robert Michael *economist*

Huntsville
Roach, Lonnie Calvin *social studies educato*

Little Rock
Coleman, Marshia Adams *social sciences educator*
Hagen, Jody Lynn *neuropsychologist, educat*
Kaza, Greg John *economist, educator*
Ledbetter, Calvin Reville, Jr., (Cal Ledbetter *political science professor, legislator*

Pine Bluff
Engle, Carole Ruth *aquaculture economics professor*

CALIFORNIA

Alameda
Troll, Lillian Ellman *psychologist, educator*

Anaheim
Gobar, Alfred Julian *retired economic consu educator, investor*

Arcata
Emenhiser, JeDon Allen *political science professor, dean*

Azusa
Miyake, Stephanie Ann *psychology professor director, marriage and family therapist*

Bakersfield
Osterkamp, Dalene May *psychology educato artist*

Banning
Gladden, Garnett Lee *psychologist, educator*

Benicia
Nelson, Elmer Kingsholm, Jr., (Kim Nelson) *political scientist, educator, writer, mediat consultant*

rkeley
garwal, Vinod K. *political science professor*
erlof, George Arthur *economics professor*
adeff, David Albert *economics professor*
erbach, Alan Jeffrey *economist, educator*
mrind, Diana *research psychologist*
lah, Robert Neelly *sociologist, educator*
ndes, Stanley Howard *anthropology educator, writer*
it, Earl Frank *economist, educator*
lier, David *political science professor*
k, Richard Allen *political scientist, consultant, writer, volunteer*
ter, Troy *sociology educator*
lman, Lauren B. *sociologist, law educator*
ansson, Nils Hemming *economist, educator*
ce, Rosemary Alexandria *anthropology educator, department chairman*
abel, Jerome Bernard *sociologist, educator*
ler, Theodore Edwin *retired economics professor*
, Ronald Demos *demographer, economist, educator*
che, John Marion *economist, educator*
slach, Christina *psychology professor*
Fadden, Daniel Little *economist, educator*
r, William Ker, Jr. *political science professor*
ler, Laura *anthropologist, educator*
gaard, Richard Bruce *economist, educator, consultant*
et, Carole Anne *psychologist*
ston, Paul Michael *anthropologist, writer*
gley, John Michael *economist, educator*
sser, Gordon C(lyde) *agricultural and resource economics educator*
ch, Michael *economics professor*
ch, Robert Bernard *political economics educator, former secretary of labor*
ner, David *economics professor*
enzweig, Mark Richard *psychologist, neuroscientist, educator*
tchmer, Suzanne Andersen *economics professor*
lensky, Eugene *economics professor*
oway, Frank Jones *social sciences educator, historian*
on, Laura D'Andrea *economics professor, former dean, federal official*
an, Hal Ronald *economics professor*
r, Margaret *sociologist, political science professor*
ensky, Harold L. *political science professor, sociologist, researcher*
iamson, Oliver Eaton *economics and law professor*
finger, Raymond Edwin *retired political science professor*

Pine
naud-Roepke, Suzanne *psychologist*

nita
ne, Debbe *psychologist, journalist, editor, consultant*
avento, Gary D. *psychologist*

rlingame
wantes, Robert Sidney *international relations executive*

rlsbad
s, Jay Courtney *anthropology educator, art dealer*

rmichael
muth, William Frederick *economics professor*

rpinteria
nidhauser, John Richard *retired political science professor*

rson
ner, Beverly Blazey *psychologist, educator*

stro Valley
ns, Robert William *psychologist, theologian*

ico
Nall, Scott Grant *sociologist, educator, academic administrator*
th, Valene Lucy *anthropologist, educator*

ino Hills
er, Teresa Marie *psychologist, forensic specialist*

remont
endam, Carol Helen *psychologist*
cherding, Thomas Earl *economist*
dekin, Richard Charles Keighley *economics professor*
szentmihalyi, Mihaly *psychology professor*
pern, Diane F. *psychology educator, professional association executive*
ang, Wei-Chin *psychology professor*
a, Harry Victor *political philosophy educator emeritus*
swell, Marcia Lee *psychologist, educator*
ens, James Dean *economics professor*
nan-Blumen, Jean *public policy and organizational behavior educator*
, Cornelis Albertus *economist, finance educator, risk analyst*
sum, Ralph Arthur *political science professor*
al, Daniel Alan *anthropologist, educator*

mpton
w, Sharon Lee *sociologist*
Knight, Carl Phillip *psychologist*

ncord
nbull, Thomas Leigh *social studies educator, secondary school educator*

lver City
tzman, Irving Myron *psychology professor*

Davis
Bower, John Richard Fenn *archaeologist, educator*
Bryant, Brenda K. *psychologist, educator*
Cohen, Lawrence Edward *sociologist, educator, criminologist*
Groth, Alexander Jacob *political science professor*
Knittel, Christopher Roland *economics professor, consultant*
Mason, William A(lvin) *psychologist, educator, researcher*
McHenry, Henry Malcolm *anthropologist, educator*
Musolf, Lloyd Daryl *political science professor, educational association administrator*
Owings, Donald Henry *psychologist, educator*
Simonton, Dean Keith *psychology professor*
Smith, Michael Peter *social sciences educator, researcher*
Spindler, George Dearborn *anthropologist, educator, writer*
Sumner, Daniel Alan *economist, educator*
Wegge, Leon Louis François *retired economics educator*

Del Mar
Quinn, Katherine Sarah *psychologist*

El Segundo
Harwick, Wayne Thomas *economist*

Encinitas
Lougeay, Denruth Colleen *clinical psychologist, educator*

Escondido
Damsbo, Ann Marie *psychologist*

Eureka
Bowker, Lee Harrington *sociologist, educator, writer*

Fairfax
Kadoyama, Margaret *museum educator, management consultant*

Fresno
Dackawich, S. John *sociology educator, academic administrator*
Joseph, James William *political scientist, consultant, educator*
O'Connor, Kevin John *psychologist, educator*

Fullerton
Kaisch, Kenneth Burton *psychologist, priest*
Zettel, Laura A. *psychology professor, researcher*

Granada Hills
Aller, Wayne Kendall *psychologist, educator, computer company executive, property manager*

Granite Bay
Hartmann, Frederick Howard *retired political science professor*

Gridley
Stiles, Owen Rodger *social studies educator*

Guerneville
Mannino, J. Davis *psychologist, educator, author*

Hayward
Reevy-Manning, Gretchen Maria *psychologist, educator*
Staudohar, Paul David *economics professor, labor arbitrator*

Hermosa Beach
Wickwire, Patricia Joanne Nellor *psychologist, educator*

Highland
Miller, R. Warburton *psychologist, farmer*

Hollister
Schallhorn, Charles Dean *social sciences educator, labor union administrator*

Hollywood
Fisher, Joel Marshall *political scientist, educator, wine consultant*

Huntington Beach
Martin, Wilfred Wesley Finny *psychologist, property owner and manager*

Idyllwild
Jones, William Lee, Jr. *psychologist, educator*

Irvine
Aigner, Dennis John *economics professor, consultant*
Burton, Michael Ladd *anthropology educator*
Danziger, James Norris *political science professor*
Feldman, Martha Sue *political scientist, educator*
Gallardo, Miguel E. *psychologist*
Hinderaker, Ivan *retired political science professor*
Huff, C(larence) Ronald *sociologist, criminologist, educator*
Lave, Charles Arthur *economics professor*
Luce, R. Duncan (Robert Duncan Luce) *psychology professor*
Margolis, Julius *economics professor*
Schonfeld, William Rost *political science professor*
Smoot, Skipi Lundquist *psychologist*
Sperling, George *psychologist, educator*
White, Douglas Richie *anthropology educator*

La Jolla
Bellugi, Ursula *neuropsychologist, educator*
Cain, William Stanley *experimental psychologist, educator, researcher*

Coburn, Marjorie Foster *psychologist, educator*
Farson, Richard Evans *psychologist*
Fowler, Raymond Dalton *psychologist, educator*
Granger, Clive William John (Sir Clive Granger) *retired economist*
Harris, Philip Robert *management and space psychologist*
Jacobson, Gary Charles *political science professor*
Machina, Mark Joseph *economist*
Mandler, George *psychologist, educator*
Mandler, Jean Matter *psychologist, educator*
Poole, Keith T. *political science professor*
Rauch, James E. *economics professor*
Schneider, Benjamin *psychology professor, consultant*
Scull, Andrew T. *sociologist, educator*
Starr, Ross Marc *economist, educator*

Laguna Beach
Bent, Alan Edward *political science professor*

Lancaster
Holley, Susan L. *psychologist*

Long Beach
Baber, Walter Franklin *political science professor*
Fiebert, Martin Stephen *psychology professor*

Los Alamitos
Kirkpatrick, James Joseph *psychologist*

Los Angeles
Aberbach, Joel David *political science professor, writer*
Allen, Walter Recharde *sociology educator*
Allen, William Richard *retired economist*
Álvarez, Rodolfo *sociology educator, consultant*
Anawalt, Patricia Rieff *anthropologist, researcher*
Aoki, Masanao *economics professor*
Bennett, Charles Franklin, Jr. *biogeographer, educator*
Champagne, Duane Willard *sociology educator*
Clark, Burton Robert *sociologist, educator*
Darby, Michael Rucker *economist, educator*
Dekmejian, Richard Hrair *political science professor*
Dr. Phil, (Phillip Calvin McGraw) *psychologist, television personality*
Eisenstein, Edward Milton *psychologist, physiologist, radiologist, educator*
Ellickson, Bryan Carl *economics professor*
Emigh, Rebecca Jean *social sciences educator*
Fanselow, Michael Scott *psychology professor*
Forness, Steven Robert *educational psychologist*
Goldberg, Herb *psychologist, educator*
Harberger, Arnold Carl *economist, educator*
Hirabayashi, Lane Ryo *political science professor*
Intriligator, Michael David *economist, educator*
Kaplan, Robert Malcolm *health researcher, educator*
Klein, Benjamin *economics professor, consultant*
La Force, James Clayburn, Jr. *economist, educator*
Levine, Robert Arthur *economist, educator, policy writer*
Malamuth, Neil Moshe *psychology and communication educator*
Montoya, Velma *economist, consultant*
Morgner, Aurelius *economist, educator*
Nelson, Howard Joseph *geographer, educator*
Nilles, John Mathias (Jack Nilles) *futurist*
Nuechterlein, Keith H. *psychology professor*
O'Neil, Harold Francis *psychologist, educator*
Papadopoulos, John K. *archaeology educator*
Raven, Bertram H(erbert) *psychology professor*
Sears, David O'Keefe *psychology professor*
Shearer, Derek Nocross *political science professor, diplomat, academic administrator*
Shneidman, Edwin S. *psychologist, thanatologist*
Sklar, Richard Lawrence *political science professor*
Stanish, Charles *anthropologist, educator*
Steh, Bill Drago *neuropsychologist*
Strack, Stephen Naylor *psychologist*
Taylor, Shelley E. *psychology researcher, educator*
Telles, Cynthia Ann *psychologist*
Thompson, Earl Albert *economics professor*
Thompson, Richard Frederick *psychologist, neuroscientist, educator*
Totten, George Oakley III *political science professor*
Turner, Ralph Herbert *sociologist, educator*
Watson, Sharon Gitin *psychologist*
Wittrock, Merlin Carl *educational psychologist*
Wong, James Bok *economist, chemical engineer, technologist, consultant*
Wood, Nancy Elizabeth *psychologist, educator*
Zame, William R. *economist, mathematician, educator*
Zeitlin, Maurice *sociology educator*

Los Gatos
Ohanjanian, Ruzanna *clinical psychologist*

Madera
Glynn, James A. *sociology educator, writer*

Menlo Park
Vane, Sylvia Brakke *anthropologist, writer*

Mill Valley
Harner, Michael James *anthropologist, educator*

Millbrae
Thomlinson, Ralph *demographer, educator*

Moffett Field
Cohen, Malcolm Martin *psychologist, researcher*

Newport Beach
Whittemore, Paul Baxter *psychologist*

North Hollywood
Totton, Carl Allen, II, *psychologist*

Northridge
Mitchell, Rie Rogers *psychologist, counselor, educator*

Novato
Criswell, Eleanor Camp *psychologist*

Oakland
De Vos, George Alphonse *psychologist, anthropologist*
Neeley, Beverly Evon *sociologist, consultant*
Preston, Elizabeth A. *psychologist*
Theroux, David Jon *economist, educator, research and development company executive*

Oceanside
Hertweck, E. Romayne *psychology professor*

Orange
Stevens, Cherita Wyman *social sciences educator, writer*

Oroville
Barnes, William Wayne *geographer, writer*

Pacific Palisades
Griver, Jeanette A. *psychologist, consultant*
Hoffenberg, Marvin *retired political science professor*
Katz, George Gershon *psychologist, lawyer*
Longaker, Richard Pancoast *retired political science professor, academic administrator*

Palm Desert
Bantz, Jody Lenore *psychologist*

Palo Alto
Beutler, Larry Edward *psychologist, educator*
Card, Stuart Kent *psychologist, researcher*
Flanagan, Robert Joseph *economics professor*
Moos, Rudolf H. *psychologist, researcher*
Scitovsky, Anne Aickelin *economist, researcher*
Sherlock, Phyllis Krafft *psychologist*

Palos Verdes Estates
DiPaul, Christopher *psychologist*

Pasadena
Dimitrius, Jo-Ellan *trial consultant*
Goldschmidt, Walter Rochs *anthropologist*
Ledyard, John Odell *economics professor, consultant*
McAfee, R. Preston *economics professor*
Munger, Edwin Stanton *political geography educator*
Palfrey, Thomas Rossman *economics professor, political science professor*
Plott, Charles Raymond *economics educator*
Scudder, Thayer *anthropologist, educator*
Valone, Keith Emerson *psychologist, psychoanalyst*

Portola Valley
March, James Gardner *social sciences educator*
Ward, Robert Edward *retired political science professor, academic administrator*

Rancho Cucamonga
Shields, Andrea Lyn *psychologist, coach, educator*

Rancho Santa Margarita
Lawson, Thomas Cheney *fraud examiner*

Redondo Beach
McWilliams, Margaret Ann *home economist, educator, writer*

Riverside
Calfee, Robert Chilton *psychologist, educator*
Carpenter, Mark Warren *social sciences educator*
Griffin, Keith Broadwell *retired economics professor*
Mancilla, Faustina Ramirez *retired psychologist*
Petrinovich, Lewis Franklin *psychologist, educator*
Rosenthal, Robert *psychology professor*
Turk, Austin Theodore *social studies educator*

Rocklin
Wiens, Beverly Jo *psychology professor*

Rohnert Park
Byrne, Noel Thomas *sociologist, educator*
Steiner, John Michael *sociologist, educator*

Sacramento
Behrman, Bruce Ward *social sciences educator*
Bruce, Thomas Edward *thanatologist, psychology professor*
Covin, David L. *retired political science professor*
Majesty, Melvin Sidney *psychologist, consultant*
Newland, Chester Albert *public administration educator*
Post, August Alan *retired economist, artist*
Sherwood, Robert Petersen *retired social sciences educator*

San Carlos
Hoffman, Paul Jerome *psychologist, statistician*

San Diego
Bosco, Fernando Javier *geographer, educator*
Callahan, LeeAnn Lucille *psychologist*
Edwards, Darrel *psychologist, researcher*
Hoston, Germaine Annette *political science professor*
Klicperova-Baker, Martina *psychologist, researcher*
Lane, Sylvia *economist, educator*
Lewis, Shirley Jeane *retired psychologist*
Meskell, Kristin Marie *psychologist*
Scott, Richard Malachi *psychologist*

Shedroff, Sharon D. *psychologist, researcher, anthropologist, consultant*
Sheldon-Morris, Tiffini Anne *clinical psychologist, consultative examiner*
Stoessinger, John George *political science professor*
Weeks, John Robert *geographer, social studies educator*

San Fernando
Shannon, George Raymond *gerontologist, educator*

San Francisco
Chase, Alexandra Nin *psychologist, writer*
Cirese, Robert Charles *economist, real estate consultant*
de Vries, Brian *gerontologist, researcher*
Estes, Carroll Lynn *sociologist, educator*
Folkman, Susan *research psychologist*
Fox, Patrick John *sociology educator*
Gamson, Joshua Paul *sociology educator, writer*
Hudson, Darril *political scientist, educator*
Jamison, Dean Tecumseh *economist*
Krippner, Stanley Curtis *psychologist*
Marston, Michael *economist, consultant*
Ratum, Cecilia Bangloy *retired psychologist*
Rice, Dorothy Pechman *medical economist*
Rubin, Seth Isaiah *psychologist*
Satre, Derek Davies *psychologist, researcher*
Sedway, Lynn Massel *real estate economist*
Soh, Chunghee Sarah *anthropology educator*
Sueyoshi, Amy Haruko *social sciences educator*

San Jose
Cedolini, Anthony John *psychologist*
McDowell, Jennifer *sociologist, composer, playwright*
Shao, Otis Hung-I *retired political science professor*
Voth, Alden H. *political science professor*

San Luis Obispo
Fisher, Eric O'Neill *economist*

San Marino
Martin, Olivia Jean *social studies educator*
Medici, Rochelle *psychologist, brain researcher*

San Rafael
Tosti, Donald Thomas *psychologist, consultant*

San Ramon
Kalicki, Jan H. *economist, political scientist, energy executive*

Santa Ana
Klassen, Margreta *clinical psychologist, educator*

Santa Barbara
Aswani, Shankar (Shankar Aswani-Canela) *anthropologist, educator*
Comanor, William S. *economist, educator*
Davidson, Roger H(arry) *political science professor*
Erasmus, Charles John *anthropologist, educator*
Goodchild, Michael Frank *geographer, educator*
Jochim, Michael Allan *archaeologist*
Kendler, Howard H(arvard) *psychologist, educator*
Mack, Judith Cole Schrim *retired political scientist*
Mayer, Richard Edwin *psychology professor*
Sherman, Alan Robert *retired psychologist, educator*
Weidemann, Celia Jean *social sciences educator, management consultant, financial consultant*

Santa Clara
Bell, Genevieve *anthropologist*
Field, Alexander James *economics professor, dean*
Foldvary, Fred Emanuel *economist, educator*
Gilbert, Lucia Albino *psychology professor*
Urdan, Timothy Cameron *psychology professor, consultant*

Santa Clarita
Walker, Robert F. *social studies educator*

Santa Cruz
Chemers, Martin M. *psychologist, educator*
Cheung, Yin-Wong *economics professor*
Langhout, Regina D. *psychology professor*
Machotka, Pavel *psychology and art educator*
Pettigrew, Thomas Fraser *social psychologist, educator*
Pratkanis, Anthony Richard *social psychologist, educator*
Resneck-Sannes, Helen *psychologist*
Roby, Pamela Ann *sociologist, educator*
Smith, M(ahlon) Brewster *retired psychologist, educator*

Santa Monica
Ellickson, Phyllis Lynn *political scientist*
Friedman, Monroe *psychologist, educator, consultant, editor, writer*
Gray, Laura B. *psychology professor, counselor*
Kurtzman, Joel Allan *economist*
Moskos, Charles C. *social studies educator*
Reville, Robert T. *economist*
Smith, James Patrick *economist*
Stiehm, Judith Hicks *political scientist*
Wolf, Charles, Jr. *economist, educator*

Santa Rosa
Jandrey, Becky Lee *psychologist*

Seaside
Mendoza, Ruben G. *anthropologist, educator, archaeologist*

Somerset
Carr, Les *psychologist, educator*

Sonora
Clarke, Paula Katherine *anthropologist, researcher, social studies educator*

Stanford
Arrow, Kenneth Joseph *economist, educator*
Bandura, Albert *psychologist, educator*
Bobo, Lawrence D. *sociologist*
Bower, Gordon Howard *psychologist, educator*
Brody, Richard Alan *political science educator, researcher*
Bulow, Jeremy Israel *economist*
Bunzel, John Harvey *political science professor*
Cook, Karen S. *sociologist, professor*
Damon, William Van Buren *developmental psychologist, educator, writer*
David, Paul Allan *economist, economic historian*
Diamond, Larry *political scientist*
Enthoven, Alain Charles *economist, educator*
Fetterman, David Mark *anthropologist, educator*
Fuchs, Victor Robert *economist, educator*
Gage, Nathaniel Lees *retired psychologist, educator*
Hall, Robert Ernest *economics professor*
Hansen, Peter Reinhard *economics professor*
Hickman, Bert George, Jr. *economist, educator*
Hoxby, Caroline Minter *economics professor*
Huntington, Hillard Griswold *economist*
Inkeles, Alex *sociology educator*
Krumboltz, John Dwight *psychologist, educator*
Kurz, Mordecai *economics professor*
Laitin, David Dennis *political science professor*
Lepper, Mark Roger *psychologist, educator*
Lewis, John Wilson *political science professor*
Maccoby, Eleanor Emmons *psychology professor*
Martin, Joanne *social sciences educator*
McClelland, James Lloyd *psychologist, educator, cognitive neuroscientist*
Mc Lure, Charles E., Jr. *economist, consultant*
Milgrom, Paul Robert *economics educator*
Moore, Thomas Gale *economist, educator*
Noll, Roger Gordon *economist, educator*
Oyer, Paul *economist*
Pearson, Scott Roberts *retired economics professor*
Ricardo-Campbell, Rita *economist, educator*
Roberts, Donald John *economics, business professor, consultant*
Scott, W(illiam) Richard *sociology educator*
Shultz, George Pratt *economics professor, former secretary of state*
Sowell, Thomas *economist, syndicated columnist*
Steele, Claude Mason *psychology professor*
Van Horne, James Carter *economist, educator*
Zimbardo, Philip George *psychologist, educator, writer*
Zitzewitz, Eric *economics professor*

Stockton
McCarty, Lois Leone *retired sociologist*
Roll, Renée F. *retired psychologist, publishing executive*

Trabuco Canyon
Addy, Jo Alison Phears *economist*

Turlock
Ahlem, Lloyd Harold *psychologist*

Union City
Feinberg, Richard Alan *psychologist*

Ventura
Bradley, Jerry Alan *psychologist, consultant*
Naurath, David Allison *engineering psychologist, researcher*

Westlake Village
Lereah, David Alan *economist*

Whittier
Johnson, Julia Marty *psychologist, educator*
McKenna, Jeanette Ann *archaeologist*

COLORADO

Arvada
Yamamoto, Kaoru *retired psychology professor*

Aspen
Manosevitz, Martin *psychologist*
Newman, Ruth Gallert *psychologist*

Aurora
Doze, Maureen Adele (Maureen Adele Mee) *social studies educator*
Olson, Allison W. *social studies educator*

Boulder
Beer, Francis Anthony *political science professor emeritus*
Bourne, Lyle Eugene, Jr. *psychology professor*
Churchill, Ward L. *social sciences educator, advocate*
Cordell, Linda S. *anthropologist, educator, museum director*
Greenberg, Edward Seymour *political science professor*
Jessor, Richard *psychologist, educator, director*
Kintsch, Walter *retired psychology professor*
Menken, Jane Ava *demographer, educator*
Pierce, Christopher A. *neuropsychologist, consultant*
Schneider, Vivian I. *psychologist, researcher*
Walker, Deward Edgar, Jr. *anthropologist, educator*

Castle Rock
Hendrick, Hal Wilmans *human factors educator*

Centennial
Milliken, John Gordon *research economist*

Colorado Springs
Brooks, Glenn Ellis *political science professor, educational association administrator*
Dobson, James Clayton *psychologist, author*
Farrer, Claire Anne Rafferty *anthropologist, educator*
Kane, Robyn A. *economist*
Vandeputte, Dixie Dianne *psychologist, educator*

Denver
Adelman, Jonathan Reuben *political science professor*
Axelrod, Evan M. *psychologist, educator*
Curl, Layton Seth *psychologist, consultant, educator*
Hughes, Brad, Jr. *economist*
Nelson, Sarah Milledge *archaeology educator*
Snyder, Charles Royce *sociologist, educator*
Zimet, Carl Norman *psychologist, educator*

Dolores
Kreyche, Gerald Francis *retired philosophy educator*

Durango
Zeller, Christopher Lee *preservation archaeologist*

Fort Collins
Ahmann, John Stanley *retired psychologist*
Bennett, Thomas LeRoy, Jr. *clinical neuropsychology educator*
Morgan, George Arthur *psychologist*
Sedei Rodden, Pamela Jean *psychologist, director*
Suinn, Richard Michael *psychologist*

Fountain
Hazlett, David Lawrence *social studies educator*

Golden
Petrick, Alfred, Jr. *economist, educator*

Greeley
Hawthorne, Barbara L. *anthropologist, educator*

Highlands Ranch
Sapienza, David Victor *social studies educator*

Lakewood
Kulkarni, Kishore Ganesh *economics professor, consultant*
Winters, Richard Allen *mineral economist*

Longmont
Watkins, John Goodrich *psychologist, educator*

Nederland
Sutton, Philip D. (Philip Dietrich Sutton) *psychologist, educator*

Pine
Jones, David Milton *economist, educator*

CONNECTICUT

Bridgeport
Maloney, Maureen Murphy *social sciences educator*

Chester
Hilsman, Roger *political scientist, educator*

Cromwell
Günther-Stirn, Dagmar Dorothea *retired social sciences educator*

Danbury
Tolor, Alexander *psychologist, educator*

Fairfield
Kleine, Herman *economist*
Morehouse, Sarah McCally *retired political science professor*

Greenwich
Fleming, Martin *economist, strategist*
Grossman, Sanford Jay *former economics professor, financial consultant*

Guilford
Chatt-Ellis, Allen Barrett *psychologist, neuroscientist*
Shelton, Darlene *psychologist, consultant*

Hamden
Dahl, Robert Alan *political science professor*

Hartford
Curran, Ward Schenk *economist, educator*
Giannaros, Demetrios Spiros *economist, educator, state representative*
Gunderson, Gerald Axel *economics professor*

Higganum
de Brigard, Emilie *anthropologist, consultant*

Lebanon
Brodie, Kevin Stuart *social studies educator*

Meriden
Losada-Zarate, Gloria *psychologist*

Middlebury
Phillips, Walter Mills III *psychologist, educator*

Middletown
Bonin, John Paul *economics professor*
Lovell, Michael C. *retired economics professor*
Miller, Richard Alan *retired economist, educator*
Scheibe, Karl Edward *psychology professor*
Wasch, William Karl *gerontologist, consultant*

Milford
Boyer, Carolyn Merwin *school psychologist*
Krall, Vita *psychologist*
Schwartz, Richard Edward Derecktor *retired sociologist, educator*

Naugatuck
Suscovich, David J. *neuropsychologist, marri and family therapist*

New Haven
Andrews, Donald Wilfrid Kao *economics professor*
Bell, Wendell *sociologist, educator, futurist*
Blatt, Sidney Jules *psychology professor, psychoanalyst, investigator*
Bracken, Paul *political science professor*
Brownell, Kelly David *psychologist, educato*
Chevalier, Judith A. *economics professor, fina professor*
Coe, Michael Douglas *retired anthropologist*
Conklin, Harold Colyer *anthropologist, educ*
Crakes, Gary Michael *economics professor*
Ember, Carol R. *anthropology educator, writ*
Ember, Melvin Lawrence *anthropologist, educator*
Erikson, Kai *sociologist, educator*
Errington, James Joseph *anthropology educat*
Evenson, Robert Eugene *economist, educator*
Green, Donald Philip *political scientist, educ*
Heninger, George Robert *psychology professo researcher*
Marks, Lawrence Edward *psychologist, educ*
Marmor, Theodore Richard *political science professor, writer*
Mayhew, David Raymond *political science professor*
McGuire, William James *psychologist, educa*
Mostaghimi, Mehdi *economist, educator*
Phillips, Peter Charles Bonest *economist, educator, researcher*
Pospisil, Leopold Jaroslav *anthropologist, la educator*
Ranis, Gustav *economist, educator*
Roemer, John E. *economics educator*
Rosenbluth, Frances McCall *political scienti educator*
Russett, Bruce Martin *political science profe*
Schowalter, John Erwin *child and adolescent psychiatry educator*
Schultz, T. Paul *economics professor*
Shiller, Robert James *economist, educator*
Shubik, Martin *economics professor*
Skowronek, Stephen Lee *political scientist, educator*
Stevens, Joseph Charles *psychology professo*
Wagner, Allan Ray *psychology professor*
Wynn, Karen *psychologist, educator, researc*
Zigler, Edward Frank *psychologist, educator*

New London
Fainstein, Norman *sociology professor, forme academic administrator*

Norwalk
Brown, William Terrel *psychology professor, educational consultant*
Rosado, Rodolfo Jose *psychologist, educator*

Old Lyme
Johnson, James Myron *psychologist, educato*

Plainville
Perkins-Banas, Melissa Veronica *neuropsychologist*

Ridgefield
Dussan V., Elizabeth B. *scientific adviser*

Sharon
Mesniaeff, Gregory *economist, securities ana*

Southbury
Atwood, Edward Charles *economist, educato*

Stamford
Robins, Robert Sidwar *political science professor, department chairman*
Teeters, Nancy Hays *economist, director*

Storrs Mansfield
Katz, Leonard *psychology professor, researc*
McNeal, Ralph B. *social studies educator*

Stratford
LaDonna, Frank *psychologist*

Voluntown
Thevenet, Patricia Confrey *social studies educator*

Wallingford
Cline, John Carroll *psychologist*

West Hartford
Gitterman, Alex *social work educator*

West Haven
Sacco, Kari Lynn *psychologist*

Westport
Manley, John Frederick *political scientist, educator*

Willimantic
Escoto, Carlos Aurelio *psychology professor, researcher*

DELAWARE

Greenville
Reeder, Charles Benton *retired economic consultant*

Newark
Bilinsky, Yaroslav *political scientist*
Butkiewicz, James Leon *economics professo researcher, consultant*
DiRenzo, Gordon James *sociologist, psychologist, educator*
Smith, Carrie Veronica *psychology professor*

ilmington
netta, Ann H. *psychologist, neuropsychologist*
eavel, Thomas Charles, Jr. *psychologist, educator*

STRICT OF COLUMBIA

ashington
ron, Henry Jacob J. *economics professor*
gel-Urdinola, Diego Fernando *economist*
end, Anthony Clark *social studies educator, academic administrator*
faw, Abay *economist, consultant, research scientist*
und, Anders *economist*
er, Michael Alan *political scientist, educator*
rtlett, Bruce Reeves *economist, columnist*
cker, Mary Louise *political scientist*
rgmann, Barbara Rose *economics professor*
sen, Stanley Martin *economist*
ggs, Jeffrey Robert *political scientist*
amson, Leon *social scientist, educator*
mmer, Andrew Felton *economist, consultant*
ooks, Renana Esther *clinical psychologist, business and political consultant, researcher*
own-Hruska, Sharon *economist, former commissioner*
ezinski, Zbigniew *political science professor, former national security advisor*
lard-Bates, Patricia Carol *psychologist, neuropsychologist*
k, Martha Gertrude *political psychologist*
rtless, Gary Thomas *economist, consultant*
der, Kent Eyring *political science professor, federal agency administrator*
rpenter, Ted Galen *political scientist*
vanagh, John Henry *political economist*
ne, Eric H. *archaeologist, anthropologist, classicist, educator*
ne, William Richard *economist, educator*
ig, John Tucker *economist, consultant*
cker, William Henry *ethnologist, researcher*
nziger, Raphael *political scientist, researcher*
v, Lincoln Hubert *demographer, educator*
kens, William Theodore *economic researcher*
son, Wilton Sterling *anthropologist, foundation administrator*
an, Charles Francis *political scientist, consultant*
wns, Anthony *economist, real estate consultant*
ls, George Curtis *economic consultant*
glish, Richard Allyn *sociologist, educator*
stein, Gerald Lewis *technology and security policy analyst*
hler, William Baldwin *biogerontologist, educator*
ioni, Amitai *sociologist, educator*
bach, Murray *demographer, educator*
dman, Robert Sidney *political science professor*
chtgott-Roth, Harold Wilkes *economist, consultant*
ston, William Arthur *political scientist, educator*
ingham, Robert Fenton *economist, consultant*
dscheider, Frances K. *sociologist, educator*
mlich, Edward Martin *public policy educator, former federal official*
pin, Jacqueline G. *economist*
en, Jeffrey Allan *economist*
perin, Morton H. *political scientist*
perin, Samuel *education and training policy analyst*
ms, Robert Brake *economist*
ss, Stephen *political scientist, writer*
sman, Sally T. *sociologist*
lnut, William Herbert III *political scientist*
dson, Michael Craig *political science professor*
fbauer, Gary Clyde *economist, lawyer, educator*
ghes, Kent Higgon *economist*
obson, Allen Howard *economist*
non, Charles *social sciences educator, dean*
persen, Frederick Zarr *economist*
es, Lauren Patricia *psychologist, not-for-profit developer*
ner, Christopher Clayton *international relations educator*
rns, Mary Hoyt *psychologist*
mp, Geoffrey Thomas Howard *political scientist, consultant*
ndrick, John Whitefield *economist, educator, consultant*
chhar, Kalpana *economist*
vis, Marie-Josee Drouin *economist*
eger, Anne *economist*
lfeld, Ruth Marilyn *anthropologist, educator*
n, Charlotte Virginia *economist*
dy, Nicholas Richard *economist, educator*
Grande, William Mark *political science professor, writer*
ber, Robert James *political science professor*
n, Andrew Bennet *economist*
chester, Paul Brunson *economist*
n, Thomas Edward *political scientist*
rcuss, Rosemary Daly *economist*
rtin, Linda Gaye *demographer, economist*
rtinez, Herminia S. *economist, banker*
shagbeh, Wassel Khalaf *economist*
ggers, Betty Jane *anthropologist, researcher*
llor, John Williams *economist, consultant*
lar, James Robert *economist, educator, university official*
ler, James Clifford III *economist*
ler, Margery *psychologist, educator, speech pathology/audiology services professional, mental health services professional*
stral, Jacques *economist*
ssa, Michael L. *economist, educator*
gorski, Zygmunt *political scientist, writer*
sh, John Davidson, Jr. *economist*
sen, Hart Michael *sociologist, educator*
kanen, William Arthur, Jr. *economist, think-tank executive*
Norquist, Grover Glenn *economist*
O'Connor, Karen *political science professor, researcher, writer*
Orszag, Jonathan Marc *economist, consultant*
Orszag, Peter Richard *economist*
Ortner, Donald J. *biological anthropologist, educator*
Osicka, Teresa D. *health economist, consultant*
Parsons, Donald Oscar *economics professor*
Pasurka, Carl A., Jr. *economist*
Perry, George Lewis *research economist, consultant*
Phillips, Karen Borlaug *economist, rail transportation executive*
Pickenpaugh, Thomas Edward *archaeologist, anthropologist*
Popkin, Joel *economist, consultant*
Prestowitz, Clyde Vincent, Jr. *economist, researcher*
Radner, Roy *economist, educator, researcher*
Randall, Robert L(ee) *ecological economist*
Reich, Bernard *political science professor*
Relyea, Harold Clarence *political scientist, writer*
Reynolds, Robert Joel *economist, consultant*
Richardson, Paul Joseph *economist*
Rivlin, Alice Mitchell *economics professor, former federal official*
Roberts, Markley *economist, educator*
Rosenau, James Nathan *political scientist, educator, writer*
Rosenberg, Joel Barry *economist*
Rupp, Kalman *economist*
Russell, Richard Leavitt *political science professor*
Ryn, Claes Gösta *political science professor*
Sawhill, Isabel Van Devanter *economist*
Scheffman, David Theodore *economist, management educator, consultant*
Schley, Wayne Arthur *political scientist, consultant*
Schneider, Mark *political science professor*
Schorr, Lisbeth Bamberger *sociologist, researcher*
Scott, Charneta Claudetta *psychologist, educator*
Scrivner, Ellen M. *psychologist*
Seifert, Jeffrey W. *political scientist, researcher*
Shambaugh, David Leigh *political scientist, educator, writer*
Snyder, Jed C. *foreign affairs specialist*
Solomon, Elinor Harris *economics professor*
Steinberg, David Isaac *social sciences educator, consultant*
Stelzer, Irwin Mark *economist*
Stent, Angela E. *political scientist, educator, director*
Stephenson, Sherry Madeline *trade economist*
Struelens, Michel Maurice Joseph Georges *political science professor, consultant*
Subbarao, Kalanidhi *economist*
Subiaul, Francys *anthropologist, psychologist, educator*
Teegarden, Lisa A. *psychologist, military officer*
Tenet, George John *diplomacy professor, former CIA director*
Tharp, Roland George *psychology professor*
Trachtenberg, Stephen Joel *political science professor, former academic administrator*
Tsui, Lisa *social scientist, researcher*
Tucker, Jonathan Brin *political scientist*
Turner, John Andrew *economist*
Vigfusson, Robert John *economist*
Weicher, John Charles *economist, research director*
Weinhold, Linda Lillian *psychologist, researcher*
Weintraub, Sidney *economist, educator*
Wilensky, Gail Roggin *economist, researcher*
Willner, Ann Ruth *political scientist, educator*
Willner, Dorothy *anthropologist, educator*
Wongswan, Jon *economist*
Zhang, Zhiwei *research scientist*

FLORIDA

Boca Raton
Joskow, Jules *economic research company executive*
Shalom, Galit *psychologist*

Bradenton
Castro, Valentino *psychologist, counseling administrator*

Cape Coral
Shuman, Carolyn Rae (Thorburn) *psychologist, columnist, writer, nurse*

Clearwater
Peterson, James Robert *engineering psychologist*

Coral Gables
Frohock, Fred Manuel *political science professor*
Humphries, Joan Ropes *psychologist, educator*
Nijman, Jan *geographer, educator*

Deerfield Beach
Panitz, Daniel R. *psychologist, consultant*

Deland
Bailey, T. Wayne *political science professor*

Delray Beach
Dye, Thomas Roy *political science professor*
Levinson, Harry *psychologist, educator*
Make, Isabel Rose *multicultural studies educator, adult education educator, small business owner*

Dunnellon
Dixon, W(illiam) Robert *retired psychologist*

Estero
Routh, Donald K(ent) *psychologist, educator*

Fort Lauderdale
Gagnon Blodgett, Michelle Dawn *psychologist*
McCluskey, Neil Gerard *gerontologist, educator, literary agent*

Fort Myers
Sprinkel, Beryl Wayne *economist, consultant*

Gainesville
Brown, William Samuel, Jr. *communication sciences and disorders educator*
Dewsbury, Donald Allen *psychologist*
Grove, David D. *anthropology professor*
Harrison, Faye Venetia *anthropologist, educator, writer*
Milanich, Jerald Thomas *archaeologist, writer, curator*
Moore, John Hartwell *anthropology educator, consultant*
Opdyke, Neil Donald *geology educator*
Peck, Merton Joseph *economist, educator*
Teitelbaum, Philip *psychologist*
Terza, Joseph Vincent *economics professor*
von Mering, Otto Oswald *anthropology educator*
Wass, Hannelore Lina *educational psychology educator*

Hobe Sound
Snook, Stover Hoffman *social sciences educator, researcher*

Homestead
Armenteros, Eduardo Carlos *psychologist, educator*

Jacksonville
Godfrey, John Munro *economic consultant*
Scott, Kamela Koon *psychologist, educator*

Lakeland
Schultz, David Franklin *psychologist*

Land O Lakes
Wilkinson, Denise V. *psychologist*

Lutz
Ellis, Leslie Elaine *psychotherapist*

Maitland
Von Hilsheimer, George Edwin III *neuropsychologist*

Miami
Arango, Penelope Corey *psychologist, consultant*
Bowden, Helen Frances *psychologist*
Bravo, Irene Maria *psychologist, educator*
Kanet, Roger Edward *political science professor*
Kent, Amy Elizabeth *criminologist*
Rosenbaum, Allan *public administration educator, academic administrator, international governance advisor*
Russell, Elbert Winslow *neuropsychologist*

Miami Beach
Freshwater, Shawna Marie *neuropsychologist, clinical psychologist, cognitive neuroscientist*
Kalsner-Silver, Lydia *psychologist*
Palamara, Sherry A. *psychologist*

Naples
Riggs, Fletcher Eugene *economist, consultant*

Ocala
Mishkin, Michael Lawrence *psychologist, educator*

Orlando
Ashe, Diane Davis *psychology professor, sport psychology consultant*

Panama City
Roberts, Paul Craig III *economics professor, writer, columnist*

Pensacola
Arnold, Barry Raynor *philosophy educator, medical ethicist*
Killian, Lewis Martin *sociology educator*

Plantation
Costa, Paul Joseph *psychologist*

Pompano Beach
Roen, Sheldon R. *psychologist, publishing executive*

Ponte Vedra Beach
Wu, Hsiu Kwang *economist, educator*

Port Charlotte
Von Holden, Martin Harvey *psychologist*

Port Saint Lucie
Augelli, John Pat *geographer, educator, writer, consultant, rancher*

Saint Augustine
Henderson, Hazel *economist, writer*

Saint Petersburg
Felice, William F. *political science professor*
Rosenblum, Zina Michelle Zarin *psychology professor, marketing professional, researcher*

Sanibel
Crown, David Allan *criminologist, educator*

Sarasota
Gordon, Sanford Daniel *economics professor*
Masters, John Christopher *psychologist, educator*
Watson, Joyce Morrissa *forensic and clinical psychologist*

South Miami
Villacian, Vanessa Luisa *psychologist*

Sparr
Tovi, Murray *futurist, research scientist*

Stuart
Grieve, William Roy *psychologist, educator, educational administrator, researcher*

Sun City Center
Petersen, Carolyn Ashcraft *retired psychologist*

Tallahassee
Calhoun, Joseph Patrick *economics professor, researcher*
Guy, Mary Ellen Johnston *political science professor*
Holcombe, Randall Gregory *economics professor*
Laird, William Everette, Jr. *economics professor*
Nam, Charles Benjamin *demographer, sociologist, educator, writer*
Thompson, Gregory Lee *social sciences educator*

Tampa
Berne, Patricia Higgins *psychologist, writer, educator*
Coleman, Rodney Albert *political scientist, consultant*
Forsythe, Robert Elliott *economics professor*
Gironda, Ronald James *psychologist*
Kimmel, Ellen Bishop *psychologist, educator*
MacManus, Susan Ann *political science professor, researcher*
Piper, John Richard *political science professor*
Spielberger, Charles Donald *psychologist, educator*
Weiner, Irving Bernard *psychologist*
Wolfson, Jay *public health and medical educator, researcher, consultant, lawyer*

Tequesta
Swets, John Arthur *psychologist, researcher*

Venice
Delaney, Robert Finley *retired columnist, political sociologist, lecturer*
Gooding, Charles Thomas *psychologist, educator, retired academic administrator*

West Palm Beach
Gold, Bela *economist, educator*

Weston
Alexander, Cynthia Louise *psychologist, educator*
Kortlander, Susan Elizabeth *psychologist*

GEORGIA

Athens
Allsbrook, Ogden Olmstead, Jr. *retired economics professor*
Bertsch, Gary Kenneth *political science professor*
Bullock, Charles Spencer III *political science educator, author, consultant*
Clute, Robert Eugene *political science professor*
Dunn, Delmer Delano *political science professor*
Fincher, Cameron Lane *psychology professor*
Garbin, Albeno Patrick *sociology educator*
Nichols, William Curtis *psychologist, educator, marriage and family therapist, consultant*
Pollack, Robert Harvey *psychology professor*

Atlanta
Bahl, Roy Winford *economist, educator, consultant*
Chiang, Tze I. *economist, researcher, consultant*
Garland, LaRetta Matthews *psychologist, nursing educator*
Gay, Robert Derril *behavioral health consultant*
Harvey, Adia M. *sociology professor*
Kelley, Linda Elaine Spadafora *school psychologist, educator*
Kennedy, Robert *political science professor*
Knapp, Charles Boynton *economist, former university president, educator*
Liu, Zheng *economist, educator*
Luger, Richard *economics professor*
Mialon, Hugo *economics professor*
Muth, Richard Ferris *economics professor*
Nemeroff, Charles Barnet *neurobiology and psychiatry educator*
Shrestha, Ram K. *economist, researcher*
Snarey, John Robert *psychologist, educator*
Speckhart, Dawn Seidner *bone marrow transplant/leukemia psychologist*
Thursby, Jerry Gilbert *economics professor, consultant, department chairman*

Augusta
Davis, Catherine Lucy *psychologist, diabetes researcher*

Bainbridge
Dixon, Lugenia *psychology educator*

Blairsville
Jones, Mary Emma B. *psychologist*

Carrollton
Hunter, Thomas Rogers *political science professor*
Pope, W. Alan *psychology professor, psychotherapist*

Columbus
McFarland, Samuel P., Jr. *psychologist*

Dahlonega
Newman, Thomas Daniel *archaeologist, school system administrator, minister*

Douglas
Vickers, Dana Tate *school psychologist, researcher*

East Point
Johnson, Hardwick Smith, Jr. *school psychologist*

Evans
Zachert, Virginia *retired psychologist*

Fort Stewart
McCarthy, Dorothy A. (Landers) *educator*
Thompson, Frankie Mazie *school psychologist*

Gainesville
Frank, Mary Lou Bryant *psychologist, educator*

Lilburn
Neumann, Thomas William *archaeologist*

Macon
Lewis, Sandra Combs *research psychologist, writer*

Marietta
Dudley, Gary Edward *psychologist*
Fuller, Frank Robert *political scientist, director*
Howard, Bruce Allen *social studies educator*
Huddleston, Connie Marie *archaeologist, consultant*

Norcross
Conway, Hobart McKinley, Jr. *futurist*

Oxford
Cody, William Bermond *political science professor*

Rome
Johnson, Alberta Clark *psychology professor*

Roswell
Klein, John Jacob *retired economist*

Saint Simons Island
Walker, Charls Edward *economist, consultant*

Savannah
Cebula, Richard John *economist, educator*
Martin, Grace Burkett *psychologist*
Mukhtar, Mohamed Haji *social sciences educator*
Rozantine, Gayle Stubbs *psychologist*

Statesboro
Diamanduros, Terry Davis *psychology professor, director*
Henry, Nicholas Llewellyn *public administration educator*
Lloyd, Margaret Ann *psychologist, educator*
Nettles, Saundra R. Murray *psychologist, writer, educator*

Stone Mountain
Farngalo, Rosemarie Merritt *school psychologist*
Torbush, Deborah Nickels *psychologist*

Suwanee
Cox, Albert Harrington, Jr. *retired economist*

Young Harris
March, Boyd Lee *political science professor, researcher*

HAWAII

Hickam Afb
Tallman, Sean Dale *anthropologist*

Holualoa
Scarr, Sandra Wood *retired psychology educator, researcher*

Honolulu
Ahrari, Ehsan M. *political science professor, dean*
Bitterman, Morton Edward *psychologist, educator*
Cho, Lee-Jay *social scientist, demographer*
Finucane, Melissa Lucille *psychologist, researcher*
Fullmer, Daniel Warren *former psychologist, educator*
Ishikawa-Fullmer, Janet Satomi *psychologist, educator*
Kaholokula, Joseph Keaweaimoku *psychologist, researcher*
Laney, Leroy Olan *economist, banker, educator*
Nordyke, Eleanor Cole *demographer, researcher, public health nurse*
O'Brien, Kendra Allen *psychologist, researcher*
Paige, Glenn Durland *political scientist, educator*
Pedersen, Paul Bodholdt *psychologist, educator*
Pinckney, Neal T. *psychologist, retired educator*
Riggs, Fred Warren *retired political science professor*
Staats, Arthur W. *psychology professor*
Streltzer, Jon *psychiatry professor*
Suh, Dae-Sook *political science professor*
Tarui, Nori *economics professor*

Kailua
Stamper, Ewa Szumotalska *psychologist*
Tavares, Samantha *psychologist, educator*

Kamuela
Richards, Phyllis Anderson *psychologist*

Kapaa
Klontz, Bradley T. *psychologist, consultant*

IDAHO

Boise
Overgaard, Willard Michele *retired political scientist*
Pfouts, Ralph William *economist, consultant*
Slaughter, Richard Arthur *political scientist, economist, educator*

Caldwell
Angresano, James *economics professor*

Pocatello
Piland, Neill Finnes *health services economist, researcher, educator*

Sandpoint
Glock, Charles Young *sociologist, writer*
Staff, Jack Robert *economist, author, monk*

Sun Valley
Stewart, John Todd *economist, consultant*

Twin Falls
Wright, Frances Jane *educational psychologist*

ILLINOIS

Arlington Heights
Ammar, Alia N. *neuropsychologist, educator*
Griffin, Jean Latz *political strategist, writer, publisher*
Tongue, William Walter *economics and business consultant, educator*

Aurora
Mitchinson, Milliam J. *social studies educator*

Barrington
Chung, Joseph Sang-hoon *economics professor*
Kunkel, Nancy Angela *psychologist*
Wood, Andrée Robitaille *archaeologist, researcher*

Bellwood
Nader, Nadine Ann *social studies educator*

Belvidere
Mc Nelly, Frederick Wright, Jr. *psychologist*

Carbondale
Benford, Robert Dee *social studies educator, editor*

Champaign
Arnould, Richard Julius *economist, educator, consultant, dean*
Baillargeon, Renee *psychology professor*
Brustein, William Irving *sociology educator*
Cho, In-Koo *economist, educator*
Davis, James Henry *retired psychology educator*
Eriksen, Charles Walter *psychologist, educator*
Roese, Neal J. *psychology professor, consultant*
Triandis, Harry Charalambos *psychologist, educator*

Chicago
Apollo, Brian *psychologist, poet*
Bajich, Milena Tatic *psychologist*
Baum, Bernard Helmut *sociologist, educator*
Becker, Gary Stanley *economist, educator*
Beilock, Sian Leah *psychology professor, psychologist*
Ben-Yoseph, Miriam *social sciences educator*
Bidwell, Charles Edward *sociologist, educator*
Brookens, Carl *psychologist*
Bryant, Fred Boyd *psychology professor*
Coase, Ronald Harry *economist, educator*
Cohler, Bertram Joseph *psychologist, educator*
Cox, Charles C. *economist*
Cropsey, Joseph *retired political science professor*
Dawdy, Shannon Lee *archaeologist, historical anthropologist*
Dawson, Michael C. *political science professor*
Elshtain, Jean Bethke *social sciences educator*
Epstein, Lee Joan *political science and law professor*
Fernandez, James *anthropology educator*
Fogel, Robert William *economist, educator, historian*
Freeman, Leslie Gordon *anthropologist, educator*
Freeman, Susan Tax *anthropologist, educator, culinary historian*
Gal, Susan *anthropologist, educator*
Gannon, Sister Ann Ida *retired philosophy educator*
Giblin, Nan J. *psychologist, educator*
Gibson, McGuire *archaeologist, educator*
Gould, John Philip *economist, educator*
Graber, Doris Appel *political scientist, writer, editor*
Harrow, Martin *psychologist, educator*
Hastie, Reid *psychology professor*
Heckman, James Joseph *economist, educator*
Heinemann, Allen W. *rehabilitation psychologist*
Hollis-Sawyer, Lisa Ann *psychologist, gerontologist, researcher*
Hoogenboom, Carol Annette *clinical neuropsychologist*
Huttenlocher, Janellen *psychology educator, psychologist*
Kaplan, Morton A. *political science professor*
Langman, Lauren *sociology educator*
Larson, Allan Louis *political scientist, educator, lay worker*
Laumann, Edward Otto *sociology educator*
Levitt, Steven D. *economics professor*
Liu, Ben-chieh *economist*
Lowe, Sandra Elveta *psychologist*
Lucas, Robert Emerson, Jr. *economist, educator*
Majer, John M. *psychologist, educator*
McCloskey, Michael *social sciences, psychology, and sociology educator*
McNeill, G. David *psychologist, educator*
Mikesell, Marvin Wray *geography educator*
Morewitz, Stephen John *behavioral scientist, consultant, sociologist, educator*
Murphy, Kevin M. *economics professor*
Myerson, Roger Bruce *economist, educator*
Nicholas, Ralph Wallace W. *anthropologist, educator*
Peltzman, Sam *economics professor*
Rosen, George *economist, educator*
Sanders, Jacquelyn Seevak *psychologist, educator*
Segerstrale, Ullica Christina *social sciences educator, researcher*
Simons, Helen *school psychologist, psychotherapist, educator*
Simpson, Dick Weldon *political science educator*
Smagner, John Patrick *applied behavior analyst, educator*
Smith, Raymond Thomas *anthropology educator*
Smith, Stan Vladimir *economist, finance company executive*
Staller, John Edward *archaeologist, anthropologist, educator*
Taub, Richard Paul *social sciences educator*
Townsend, Robert Morris *economics professor, researcher*
Upshaw, Harry Stephan *psychologist, educator*
Walberg, Herbert John *psychologist, educator, consultant*
Zagar, Robert John *psychologist, researcher*
Zellner, Arnold *economics, econometrics and statistics professor*
Zoloth, Laurie Susan *bioethicist*
Zonis, Marvin *political scientist, educator*

Chillicothe
Tallon, Edward Joseph *social studies educator*

Dekalb
Shernoff, David Jordan *psychology professor*
Slotsve, George Aaron *economist, educator, consultant*

Downers Grove
Feeney, Don Joseph, Jr. *psychologist*

Edwardsville
Browne, Dallas *anthropologist, educator*
DeGarmo, Denise Kay *political scientist, educator*

Evanston
Braeutigam, Ronald Ray *economics professor, educational association administrator*
Gordon, Robert James *economics professor*
Hurter, Arthur Patrick *economist, educator*
Irons, William George *anthropology educator*
Kalai, Ehud *economist, researcher, educator*
Medin, Douglas *psychology professor*
Mills, Edwin Smith *economics professor*
Mineka, Susan *psychology professor*
Oh, John Kie-Chiang *political science professor, academic administrator*
Olszewski, Wojciech *economist, mathematician*
Reiter, Stanley *economist, educator*
Richeson, Jennifer Anne *psychology professor, researcher*
Satterthwaite, Mark A. *economics professor*
Siniscalchi, Marciano *economist*
Weisbrod, Burton Allen *economist, educator*

Glen Ellyn
Emano, Dennis Jose Marmol *psychology professor*
Frateschi, Lawrence Jan *economist, statistician, educator*

Glenview
Farber, Isadore E. *psychologist, educator*
Geller, William Alan *criminologist, consultant, protective services official*

Hinsdale
Dederick, Robert Gogan *economist*

Huntley
Saporta, Jack *psychologist, educator*

Jacksonville
Hardin, Susan Jean *social studies educator, department chairman*

Joliet
Holmgren, Myron Roger *social sciences educator*

Lake Forest
Sadri, Ahmad *sociologist, educator*

Libertyville
Mahoney, Kathleen Marie *social studies educator*

Lincolnwood
Earnest, Craig Hopkins *psychologist, consultant*

Lindenhurst
Eron, Madeline Marcus *psychologist*

Lovington
Duncan, Linda B. *social sciences educator*

Macomb
Ellickson, Jean *anthropology educator*
Merrett, Christopher Douglas *geographer, educator*
Walzer, Norman Charles *retired economics professor*

Maryville
Stark, Patricia Ann *psychologist*

Moline
Penn, J. B. *economist, former federal agency administrator*

Naperville
Cowlishaw, Mary Lou *government educator*
McCallum, Gerald Christopher *clinical psychologist*

Normal
Alferink, Larry Allen *psychology professor*
Brehm, Joan M. *social sciences educator*

Northbrook
Di Spigno, Guy Joseph *industrial psychologis international management consultant*

Orland Park
Antia, Kersey H. *industrial and clinical psychologist, consultant*

Palos Heights
Hassert, Derrick Lawrence *psychology profes*

River Grove
Stein, Thomas Henry *social sciences educator*

Rockford
Clodius, Robert LeRoy *retired economist*
Mottram, Lisa Marie *pediatric psychologist*

Springfield
Phillips, John Robert *political scientist, educa*
Wehrle, Leroy Snyder *economist, educator*

Tinley Park
Freitag, Carol Wilma *political scientist*

Urbana
Althaus, Scott L. *political science professor*
Baer, Werner *economist, educator*
Carmen, Ira Harris *political scientist, educato*
Gabriel, Michael *psychology professor*
Giles, Eugene *anthropology educator*
Gove, Samuel Kimball *retired political scienc professor*
Leuthold, Raymond Martin *agricultural economics professor*
Lüschen, Günther Rudolf Friedo *social scienc educator*
Nettl, Bruno *anthropologist, musicologist, educator*
Resek, Robert William *economist*
Schmidt, Stephen Christopher *agricultural economist, educator*
Thompson, Robert Lee *agricultural economis educator*
Warren, Pamela A. *psychologist*
Wirt, Frederick Marshall *retired political scientist, educator*
Yu, George Tzuchiao *political science profes*

Western Springs
Zamora, Marjorie Dixon *retired political scie professor*

Wheaton
Benson, Bruce Ellis *philosophy educator*
Riley, Betty Anne *psychologist, educator*

Wilmette
Schloss, Nathan *retired economist*
Walker, Ronald Edward *psychologist, educat*

Winnetka
Krueger, Deborah A. Blake *school psycholog consultant*

INDIANA

Bloomington
Becker, William Edward *economist, consulta*
Brehm, Sharon Stephens *psychology professo former academic administrator*
Conrad, Geoffrey Wentworth *archaeologist, educator*
Estes, William Kaye *psychologist, educator*
Guth, Sherman Leon (S. Lee) *psychologist, educator*
Morrison, Clarence Clapp *retired economics professor*
O'Meara, Patrick O. *political science profess*
Ostrom, Elinor *political science professor, researcher*
Ostrom, Vincent A(lfred) *political science professor*
Patrick, John Joseph *social sciences educator*
Peebles, Christopher Spalding *anthropologist, educator, dean, academic administrator*
Reingold, David Ami *sociologist, educator*
Reinisch, June Machover *psychologist, educa researcher*
Rugman, Alan Michael *international busines educator*
Smith, Linda B. *psychology professor*
Thorelli, Sarah V. *economist, researcher*

Carmel
Rychlak, Joseph Frank *psychologist, educator*

Columbus
Williams, Robert Joseph *behavioral health services executive, psychologist*

Granger
Craypo, Charles *labor economics professor*

Greenwood
Hagedorn, Alan Patrick *social studies educat*
Waldkoetter, Raymond Oliver *psychologist, consultant*

Hammond
Fisher, Jeffrey L. *psychologist*

Indianapolis
Cardwell, Sue Webb *psychology professor*
Divita, James J. *retired social studies educat writer, researcher*
Gregg, Stephen Thompson *political scientist, consultant*
Horwitz, Javan Lee *neuropsychologist*
Kessler, Marcia Lynn *school psychologist*
McDonald, Brenna Cathleen *psychologist*
Swindle, Ralph Wilson, Jr. *research psycholo*

Kokomo
Wysong, Earl Edward *sociologist, educator*

afayette
ardin, Lowell Stewart *retired economics professor*
hönemann, Peter Hans *psychologist, educator*
hweickert, Richard Justus *psychologist, educator*

adison
otts, Edward Earl *psychologist, researcher*

arion
eenbergh, Timothy Allen *psychology professor*

uncie
ogg, Richard Allan *sociologist, educator*
neng, Chu Yuan *economics professor*
vartz, B. K., Jr., (Benjamin Kinsell Swartz Jr.) *archaeologist, educator*

otre Dame
nold, Peri Ethan *political scientist*
artell, Ernest *economist, educator, priest*
espres, Leo Arthur *sociologist, anthropologist, educator, academic administrator*
oulet, Denis André *development ethicist*
allinan, Maureen Theresa *sociologist, educator*
rowski, Philip Edward *economics professor*
lenzuela, Julio Samuel *sociologist, educator*
eigert, Andrew Joseph *sociology educator*
elch, Michael R. *sociologist, educator*
ckert, Catherine Heldt *political science educator, writer, editor*

uth Bend
rrington, Michael Davis *criminal justice and security consultant*
owty, Alan Kent *political scientist, educator*

rre Haute
igh, Janis *clinician*

est Lafayette
cirelli, Victor George *psychologist*
nnor, John Murray *economics professor*
rris, Paul Leonard *agricultural economist*
uen, Gerald Elmer *psychologist, educator*
llich, George J. *psychology professor*
rwich, George *economist, educator*
rrucci, Robert *sociologist, educator*
eckel, Paul Veitch *agricultural economics educator, researcher*
u, Raghavendra *economist, educator*
vensen, Clifford Henrik, Jr. *psychologist, educator*
ner, Wallace Edward *agricultural economics educator*
eidenaar, Dennis Jay *retired economics professor*
einstein, Michael Alan *political science professor*

OWA

mes
x, Karl August *retired economist, educator, eco-behavioral scientist*
rl, Neil Eugene *economist, educator, lawyer, writer*

ive
ller, Kenneth Edward *sociologist, educator*

es Moines
morest, Allan Frederick *retired psychologist*
irmbach, Herman Charles *economics professor*

ubuque
gensen, Gerald Thomas *psychologist, educator, lawyer*

wa City
brecht, William Price *economist, educator, government official*
ff, Kevin *neuropsychologist, psychiatry professor*
thke, Gary C. *economics professor, former dean*
ller, John Williams *economics professor*
weke, John Frederick *economics professor*
n, Chong Lim *political science professor*
e, Inah *psychology professor*
ewenberg, Gerhard *political science professor*
than, Peter E. *psychologist, educator*
bert, Calvin D. *economist, educator*
nstad, Anne Helene *psychologist, researcher*
asserman, Edward Arnold *psychology professor*

skaloosa
derson, Roxanna Marion *psychology professor*

est Des Moines
kari, Rosenna *educational psychology professor, consultant*

ANSAS

rn
ssel-Stuke, Donna Jane *psychologist, educator*

nporia
tlett, Robert Bishop *economics professor*

ansas City
nick, Elizabeth C. *psychologist*

ansing
hn, Theresa J. *social studies educator*

awrence
rnett, William Arnold *economics professor*
nga, Otilia M. *psychologist, researcher*

Heller, Francis Howard *retired law and political science educator*
Stull, Donald David *anthropologist, educator*

Manhattan
Babcock, Michael Ward *economics professor*
Barkley, Andrew Paul *economics professor*
Li, Dong *economics professor*
Murray, John Patrick *psychologist, educator, researcher*
Prins, Harald Edward Lambert *anthropologist, educator*
Thomas, Lloyd Brewster *economics professor*
Wesch, Michael *anthropology educator, cultural anthropologist, media ecologist*

North Newton
Eitzen, David Stanley *sociologist, educator*

Saint John
Robinson, Alexander Jacob *retired psychologist*

Shawnee
Poplau, Ronald W. *social studies educator*

Topeka
Spohn, Herbert Emil *psychologist*

Wichita
Moore, Leon, Jr. *social studies educator*

KENTUCKY

Bowling Green
Cangemi, Joseph Peter *psychologist, consultant, educator*

Corbin
Doby, John Thomas *social psychologist*

Frankfort
Rainey, Jo Anne *psychologist, educator*

Georgetown
Bates, Clyde Thomas *retired economics professor*
Lookadoo, Regan *psychology professor*

Highland Heights
Donnelly, Sharlotte K. B. Neely *anthropology educator, writer*

Independence
Hopgood, James F. *anthropologist, educator*

Lexington
Gallagher, Eugene Bennett *sociologist, medical educator*
Hochstrasser, Donald Lee *cultural anthropologist, community health and public administrator*
Miller, Thomas William *psychologist*
Oser, Carrie B. *sociologist, educator*
Reed, Michael Robert *agricultural economist*
Stempel, John Dallas *international studies educator*
Wildasin, David E(arl) *economics professor*
Worell, Judith P. *psychologist, educator*

Louisville
Blandford, Jim, Jr. *social studies educator*
Hua, Shiping *political science professor*
Nahata, Babu L. *economics professor, researcher*
Portes, Pedro René *psychology professor, department chairman*
Stanton, M(orris) Duncan *psychologist, researcher, dean*
Tanguay, Peter Eugene *child and adolescent psychiatry educator*
Tasman, Allan *psychiatry educator*

Morehead
Miller, Green Russell *economist, educator*

Paintsville
Hovee, Mark John *psychologist*

Versailles
Stober, William John, II, *economics professor*

Villa Hills
Giesbrecht, Martin Gerhard *retired economics professor, musician*

LOUISIANA

Alexandria
Thevenot, Maude Travis *retired home economist*

Baton Rouge
Cramer, Gail Latimer *economist*
Guedry, Leo J. *agricultural economics educator*
Sandoz, George Ellis, Jr. *political science educator*

Bossier City
Paris, Norma Jean *psychologist, educator*

Denham Springs
Grimmer, Cindy C. *social studies educator*

Harahan
O'Neal, Edgar Carl *psychology professor*

Metairie
Falco, Maria Josephine *political scientist*
Wood, Jonathan Stuart *economist, educator*

New Orleans
Andrews, E. Wyllys *archaeologist, educator*
Balée, William L. *anthropology educator*
Boudreaux, Kenneth Justin *economist, educator*
Kelly, Eamon Michael *economic development professor, retired university president*

Langston, Thomas Samuel *political science professor*
Moely, Barbara E. *psychologist, educator*
Olson, Richard David *psychology professor*
Thompson, Martyn Philip *political and literary studies educator, translator*
Ukpolo, Victor *economics educator*

Pineville
Thrasher, Fay C. *clinical psychologist*

Ruston
Sale, Tom S. III *financial economist*

Shreveport
Staats, Thomas Elwyn *neuropsychologist*

MAINE

Augusta
Bourque, Bruce Joseph *archaeologist, educator*
Nickerson, John Mitchell *political science professor*

Bath
Galleher, Gay *psychologist*

Brunswick
Fuchs, Alfred Herman *psychologist, educator*

Falmouth
Pierce, Philip Sargent *clinical psychologist*

Little Deer Isle
Mills, David Harlow *psychologist, professional society administrator*

Orono
Cohn, Steven Frederick *sociology educator, consultant*
Goldstone, Sanford *psychologist, educator*

Surry
Pickett, Betty Horenstein *psychologist*

Waterville
Gemery, Henry Albert *economics professor*
Gilkes, Cheryl Louise Townsend *sociologist, educator, minister*
Yeterian, Edward Harry *psychologist, educator, administrator*

MARYLAND

Annapolis
Connolly, Janet Elizabeth *retired sociologist, retired criminal justice educator*

Baltimore
Anderson, Gerard Fenton *economist, academic administrator*
Batten, Sonja Victoria *psychologist, educator*
Bright, Margaret *sociologist*
Catania, A(nthony) Charles *psychologist, educator*
Cooper, Joseph *political scientist, educator*
Dickey, George Edward *economist, educator, lobbyist, federal official*
Franklin, Paula Anne *artist, writer, psychologist*
Green, Bert Franklin, Jr. *retired psychology professor*
Howard, J. Woodford, Jr. *retired political science professor*
Karni, Edi *economics professor*
Kirkhart, Matthew Wayde *psychology professor*
Maccini, Louis John *economist, educator*
Melick, Clifford Francis *sociologist, researcher*
Passley, Josef Antonio *psychologist, educator, writer*
Salamon, Lester Milton *political science professor*
Schwartz, Glenn Martin *archaeologist, educator*
Sorkin, Alan Lowell *economist, educator*
Yantis, Steven George *psychology educator*

Bethesda
Banik, Sambhu Nath *psychologist*
Barton, Jean Marie *psychologist, educator*
Becker, Bruce Clare *clinical psychologist, neuropsychologist, administrator*
de Vries, Margaret Garritsen *economist*
Duncan, Constance Catharine *psychologist, educator, researcher*
Lystad, Mary Hanemann (Mrs. Robert Lystad) *sociologist, writer*
Mishkin, Mortimer *neuropsychologist*
Musil, Robert Kirkland *global environmental politics professor*
Raullerson, Calvin Henry *retired political scientist, consultant*
Solomon, Robert *economist*
Taylor, William Jesse, Jr. *international security studies educator, research institute senior advisor*

Bowie
Bushnell, David Sherman *social psychologist, consultant*
Kardiasmenos, Katrina Suzanne *psychology professor*
Yager, Joseph Arthur, Jr. *economist, consultant*

Chester
Dalrymple, Ronald Gerald *psychologist*

Chestertown
Wendel, Richard Frederick *economist, educator, consultant*

Chevy Chase
Alexander, Arthur Jacob *economist*
Hickman, R(obert) Harrison *political pollster, strategist*
Krupnick, Janice Lee *psychologist, psychotherapist, educator*

Norwood, Bernard *economist*
Norwood, Janet Lippe *economist*
Opper, Barbara Negri *financial economist*

College Park
Destler, I. M(ac) *political scientist, foreign policy writer*
Epstein, Norman B. *psychologist, marriage and family therapist, educator*
Gaylin, Ned L. *psychologist, educator*
Hall, William Sterling *psychology educator*
Hill, Clara Edith *psychologist, educator*
Just, Richard Eugene *economist, consultant, agriculturist, educator*
Lent, Robert William *psychologist*
Nerlove, Marc Leon *economics professor*
Olson, Charles Eric *economist*
Pease, John Alan *sociology educator*
Presser, Harriet Betty *social studies educator*
Presser, Stanley *social sciences educator, researcher*
Quester, George Herman *political science professor*
Schelling, Thomas Crombie *economist*
Sigall, Harold Fred *psychology professor*
Sorenson, Georgia Lynn Jones *political science professor*

Cumberland
Heckert, Paul Charles *sociologist, educator*

Ellicott City
Webster, Sharon B. *economist*

Hampstead
Dotterweich, Patrick Timothy *social studies educator*

Kensington
Oweiss, Ibrahim Mohamed *economist, educator*

Lanham
McClain, George Nelson *economist, lawyer*

Laurel
McConnaughey, James Walter *economist*

Lexington Park
Donely, George Anthony Thomas III *retired economist*

Lutherville
Smith, Michelle Sun *psychologist*

Lutherville Timonium
Muuss, Rolf Eduard *retired psychologist, author*

Mitchellville
Blasier, Cole *political scientist*
Gordon, Lincoln *political economist*

Perry Point
Jones, Scott Nelson *psychologist*

Potomac
Druckman, Daniel *social sciences educator, consultant, researcher*
Reichley, A. James *political scientist*
Rotberg, Iris Comens *social scientist*
Vadus, Gloria A. *scientific document examiner*
Wonnacott, Paul *retired economics professor*

Princess Anne
Brockett, Ramona *criminologist, educator*

Rockville
Banthin, Jessica S. *economist, researcher*
Niewiaroski, Trudi Osmers (Gertrude Niewiaroski) *social studies educator*

Salisbury
Chambers, Dustin Lee *economics professor*

Shady Side
Devine, Donald J. *political science professor, consultant*

Silver Spring
Alexander, Herbert E. *political scientist*
Bate, Marilyn Anne *psychologist*
Hsueh, Chun-tu *political scientist, educator, foundation administrator, historian*
Mohr, Christina *retired economist*
Moon, Marilyn Lee *economist*
Oswald, Rudolph A. *economist*
Rayburn, Carole Ann (Mary Aida) *psychologist, researcher, writer, consultant*
Striner, Herbert Edward *economics professor*

Temple Hills
Smith, Irving *gerontologist*

Towson
Nelson, H. Wayne *gerontologist, advocate*
Zweback, Stanley *psychologist, educator*

Westminster
Madsen, Stephanie D. *psychology professor*
Saxton, Celeste Dawn *social studies educator, consultant*

MASSACHUSETTS

Acton
Evans, Robert, Jr. *economics professor*

Agawam
Sylvester, John Andrew *social studies educator*

Amherst
Averill, James Reed *psychology professor*
Berger, Seymour Maurice *social psychologist*
Daehler, Marvin William *psychology professor*
Klare, Michael Thomas *social sciences educator, director*

Sarat, Austin D. *jurisprudence and political science educator*
Strickland, Bonnie Ruth *psychologist, educator*
Taubman, William Chase *political science professor, writer*
Tropp, Linda R. *psychology professor*
Woodbury, Richard Benjamin *anthropologist, educator*

Babson Park
Genovese, Francis Charles (Frank) *economist, educator, editor-in-chief, writer*

Belmont
Levendusky, Philip George *psychologist, academic administrator, educator*
Raiffa, Howard *economics educator*

Boston
Allinson, Deborah Louise *economist*
Appley, Mortimer Herbert *psychologist, retired academic administrator*
Canning, David *economist*
Dentler, Robert Arnold *sociologist, educator*
Farmer, Paul Edward *medical anthropologist*
Gamst, Frederick Charles *social anthropologist*
Gleason, Jean Berko *psychology professor*
Grossman, Frances Kaplan *psychologist*
Hammond, Norman David Curle *archaeology educator, researcher*
Herzlinger, Regina *economist, educator, writer*
Horrigan, Brian Richard *economist*
Lawrence, Paul Roger *retired psychology professor*
Lundgren, Lena Margareta *social sciences educator, researcher*
Manning, Peter Kirby *criminal justice educator*
Markham, Jesse William *economist, educator*
Mayers, David *political science professor, department chairman, history professor*
Merton, Robert C. *economist, educator*
Newhouse, Joseph Paul *economist, educator*
O'Hern, Jane Susan *psychologist, educator*
Palmer, David Scott *political scientist, educator*
Plotkin, Irving H. (Irving Herman Plotkin) *economist, consultant*
Ra'anan, Uri (Heinz Felix Frischwasser) *international politics educator*
Salinger, Michael Alvin *economist, educator*
Yeager, Peter Cleary *sociologist, educator*

Bridgewater
Kostka, Robert Raymond *social studies educator, department chairman*

Brookline
Buchin, Jacqueline Chase *psychologist*
Cromwell, Adelaide M. *sociology educator*

Cambridge
Acemoglu, Daron (K. Daron Acemoglu) *economics professor*
Alesina, Alberto *economist, educator*
Allison, Graham Tillett, Jr. *political science professor, former federal agency administrator*
Alt, James Edward *political science professor*
Anderson, William Henry *psychobiology educator*
Angrist, Joshua D. *economics educator*
Ansolabehere, Stephen Daniel *political science professor*
Athey, Susan Carleton *economics professor*
Bailyn, Lotte *psychologist, educator*
Bator, Francis Michel *economist, educator*
Berndt, Ernst Rudolf *economist, educator*
Bishop, Robert Lyle *retired economist, educator*
Blackmer, Donald Laurence Morton *political scientist*
Borjas, George J(esus) *economics professor*
Bunn, Matthew G. *political scientist, writer*
Calabrese, Joseph D. *psychologist, educator*
Cestnick, Laurie L. *neuropsychologist, educator, scientist*
Chandra, Satish *psychologist*
Cooper, Richard Newell *economist, educator*
Dominguez, Jorge Ignacio *political scientist, educator*
Eckaus, Richard Samuel *economist, educator*
Ellison, Peter Thorpe *anthropology professor*
Feldstein, Martin Stuart *economist, educator*
Forbes, Kristin J. *economics professor, former federal official*
Friedman, Benjamin Morton *economics professor*
Frisch, Rose Epstein *population sciences researcher*
Gardner, Howard Earl *psychologist, educator, writer*
Gilbert, Daniel *psychology professor*
Glaeser, Edward Ludwig *research economist, educator*
Goldin, Claudia Dale *economics professor*
Greenstone, Michael *economics professor, researcher*
Gruber, Jonathan H. *economist*
Hart, Oliver D'Arcy *economics professor*
Hauser, Marc D. *psychology professor, educator*
Hausmann, Ricardo *economics professor, director*
Hill, Kenneth *demographer, educator*
Hoffmann, Inge Schneier *psychologist, educator*
Holmstrom, Bengt R. *economics professor*
Huntington, Samuel Phillips *political science educator*
Jacoby, Henry Donnan *economist, educator*
Jencks, Christopher Sandys *sociologist, educator*
Jorgenson, Dale Weldeau *economist, educator*
Joskow, Paul Lewis *economist, educator*
Juma, Calestous *international development educator*
Kagan, Jerome *psychologist, educator*
Kaysen, Carl *economics professor*
Keniston, Kenneth *psychologist, educator*
Kennedy, Stephen Dandridge *economist, researcher*
Keyfitz, Nathan *sociologist, educator, demographer*
Kleinman, Arthur Michael *medical anthropology and psychiatry educator*
Kremer, Michael *economist, educator*
Lamberg-Karlovsky, Clifford Charles *anthropologist, archaeologist*
Langer, Ellen Jane *psychologist, educator, writer, artist*
Lieberson, Stanley *sociologist, educator*
Maher, Brendan Arnold *retired psychology educator, editor*
Mankiw, (Nicholas) Gregory *economics professor, former federal official*
Mansbridge, Jane Jebb *political scientist, educator*
McNally, Richard James *clinical psychologist, educator*
Meyer, John Robert *economist, educator*
Mitten, David Gordon *classical archaeologist*
Moore, Sally Falk *anthropology educator*
Newey, Whitney K. *economist, educator*
Newman, J. Bonnie *political science professor, former federal official*
Nye, Joseph Samuel, Jr. *political science professor, former dean*
Parlee, Mary Brown *psychology educator*
Perkins, Dwight Heald *economics professor*
Pilbeam, David Roger *paleoanthropology educator*
Pinker, Steven A. *psychologist, educator*
Poterba, James Michael *economist, educator*
Power, Samantha J. *public policy educator, writer*
Pye, Lucian Wilmot *political science professor*
Rightmire, George Philip *anthropology educator*
Rodrik, Dani *economics and international affairs educator*
Rogoff, Kenneth Saul *economics professor*
Rosenblum, Nancy Lipton *political science professor*
Rosovsky, Henry *economist, educator*
Sampson, Robert J. *sociologist, educator*
Samuelson, Paul Anthony *economist, educator*
Sapolsky, Harvey Morton *political scientist, educator*
Scherer, Frederic Michael *economics professor*
Sen, Amartya Kumar *economist, educator*
Shaheen, Jeanne *political scientist, former governor*
Sidanius, James H. *psychology professor*
Siegel, Abraham J. *economics professor, academic administrator*
Skocpol, Theda Ruth *sociology and political science educator, former dean*
Skolnikoff, Eugene B. *political science professor*
Snyder, James M., Jr. *political science professor, economics professor*
Solow, Robert Merton *economist, educator*
Spelke, Elizabeth Shilin *psychology professor*
Stock, James H. *economics professor*
Thompson, Dennis Frank *political science professor, consultant*
Verba, Sidney *political science professor, retired library director*
Vogel, Ezra F. *sociology educator*
Waters, Mary Catherine *sociology educator*
Willie, Charles Vert *social sciences educator*
Wilson, William Julius *sociology educator*
Yip, Winnie *health economics educator*
Zeckhauser, Richard Jay *economist, educator*
Zeidenstein, George *population educator*
Zinberg, Dorothy Shore *sociologist, educator*

Charlestown
Buckner, Randy L. *psychology professor, neuroscientist*

Dartmouth
Sweeney, Shawna Elizabeth *political science professor, researcher*

Dorchester
Medeiros, Jennifer Lynn *school psychologist, consultant*

Fitchburg
Wellman, Robert Jonathan *psychologist, educator*

Framingham
Coiner, Maryrose C. *psychologist*

Gloucester
McCarl, Henry Newton *economist, geologist, consultant, venture capitalist*

Hopkinton
Newbrander, William Carl *health economist, management consultant*

Ipswich
Jennings, Frederic Beach, Jr. *economist, saltwater flyfishing guide*

Lexington
Balu, Sanjeev *pharacoeconomist*
Horowitz, Morris A. *retired economics professor*
Jordan, Judith Victoria *clinical psychologist, educator*
Levine, Janice R. *clinical psychologist*
Nichols, Albert L. *economic consultant*
Papanek, Gustav Fritz *economist, educator*

Marblehead
Speller, Kerstin G. Rinta *psychologist*

Mashpee
Tarlin, Sara-Fay *school psychologist, consultant*

Medford
Ambady, Nalini *social psychologist, educator, researcher*
Conklin, John Evan *sociology educator*
DeBold, Joseph Francis *psychologist, educator*
Elkind, David *psychology professor*
Miczek, Klaus Alexander *psychology professor*

Melrose
Henken, Bernard Samuel *clinical psychologist, speech pathologist*

Natick
Sedo, Manuel Arturo *psychologist, researcher*

Needham
Boulding, Elise Marie *sociologist, educator*

Newton
Burlage, Dorothy Dawson *clinical psychologist*
Holbik, Karel *economics professor*
White, Burton Leonard *retired educational psychologist, writer, consultant*

Newton Center
Adams, F. Gerard *economist, educator*

North Dartmouth
Barrow, Clyde Wayne *social sciences educator*

Northampton
Rose, Peter Isaac *sociologist, writer, editor*

Orleans
Rappaport, Margaret Mary Williams Ewing *psychologist, physician, writer, pilot, consultant*

Rockport
Harries, James Theodore *psychologist*

Salem
Goss, Laurence Edward, Jr. *geographer, educator*
Higgins, Gina O'Connell *psychologist, writer*

Somerville
Brams, Marvin Robert *economist, mental health counselor, interfaith minister, educator*

Springfield
Harnois, Veronica *psychologist, educator*

Sudbury
Diette, Kelly A. *psychologist*

Waban
Hewlett-Kierstead, Nancy Carrick *psychologist, educator*

Waltham
Altman, Stuart Harold *economist, educator*
Erbil, Can *economist, educator*
McCulloch, Rachel *economist, educator*
Quinn, Michael *economics professor*
Saxe, Leonard *social psychologist, educator*
Sekuler, Robert William *psychologist, educator*
Shepard, Donald Sloane *public policy research educator*

Wellesley
Giddon, Donald B(ernard) *psychologist, educator*
Morant, Ricardo Bernardino *psychology professor*
Sangree, Walter Hinchman *social anthropologist, educator*
Stettner, Edward A. *political science professor*

Westborough
Antalek, Eileen Elizabeth *educational psychologist, consultant*
Staffier, Pamela Moorman *psychologist*

Westfield
Zayac, Linda Mary *sociologist, educator*

Weston
Kraft, Gerald *economist*

Whitinsville
Plaud, Joseph Julian *psychology educator*

Williamstown
Bolton, Roger Edwin *economist, educator*
Cramer, Phebe *psychologist*
Fuller, Renee Nuni *psychologist, educational publisher*
Kassin, Saul *psychology professor*
Sheahan, John Bernard *economist, educator*

Worcester
Dolgon, Corey *sociology educator, political activist*
Mathisen, Howard *psychologist, educator, minister*
Ott, Attiat Farag *economist, educator*

MICHIGAN

Adrian
Weathers, Milledge Wright *retired economics professor*

Ann Arbor
Arlinghaus, Sandra Judith Lach *mathematical geographer, educator*
Behling, Charles Frederick *psychologist, educator*
Bishop, Elizabeth Shreve *psychologist*
Bornstein, Morris *economist, educator*
Brinkman, Michael *neuropsychologist, researcher*
Brown, Donald Robert *psychology professor*
Cain, Albert Clifford *psychologist, educator*
Cohen, Malcolm Stuart *economist*
Converse, Philip Ernest *retired social sciences educator*
Dominguez, Kathryn Mary *economist, educator*
Ellsworth, Phoebe Clemencia *psychology professor*
Frey, William H. *demographer, educator*
Haefner, Don Paul *retired psychology educator*
Hagen, John William *psychology professor*
House, James Stephen *social psychologist, educator*
Irvine, Judith Temkin *anthropologist, educator*
Jackson, James Sidney *psychologist, educator*
Johnston, Lloyd Douglas *social sciences educator*
Kelly, Raymond Case *anthropology educator*
Kim, E. Han *financial economist, educator*
Kingdon, John Wells *political science professo*
Lupia, Arthur W. *political science educator*
Manis, Melvin *psychologist, educator*
Markovits, Andrei Steven *political science professor*
Mitchell, Edward John *economist, retired educator*
Paige, Jeffery Mayland *sociologist, educator*
Parsons, Jeffrey Robinson *anthropologist, educator*
Pedley, John Griffiths *archaeologist, educator*
St. John, Edward P. *social sciences educator*
Schwarz, Norbert *psychology professor*
Shapiro, Matthew David *economist, educator*
Stafford, Frank P. *economist, educator*
Stafford, Frank Peter, Jr. *economics professor, consultant*
Waltz, Susan *political scientist, educator*
Warren, Jane Carol *psychologist*
Whitman, Marina von Neumann *economist, educator*
Williams, David R. *sociologist, educator, senio research scientist*
Williams, Melvin Donald *anthropologist, educator*
Woronoff, Israel *former psychology educator*
Zucker, Robert A(lpert) *psychologist*

Auburn Hills
Etefia, Florence Victoria *retired school psychologist*

Berrien Springs
Hamel, Lorie Ann *psychologist*

Birmingham
Auld, Frank *psychologist, educator*

Detroit
Alexander, Sheldon *psychology educator*
Braid, Ralph M. *economics professor*
Fleming, George Robert *psychologist*
Goodman, Allen Charles *economist, educator*
Jendrzejewski, Roxanne Marie *social studies educator, language educator*
MacDonald, Douglas Andrew *psychologist, educator*
Martin, John E *psychologist, educator*
McArthur, Steven Francis *psychologist, educa*
McCrae, Jocelyn Diane *psychologist*
Pietrofesa, John Joseph *psychologist, educator*

East Lansing
Abeles, Norman *psychologist, educator*
Abramson, Paul Robert *political scientist, educator*
Baillie, Richard Thomas *economist, educator*
Ballbach, Philip Thornton *political consultant, investor*
Crewe, Nancy Moe *retired psychologist*
Gass, Gertrude Zemon *psychologist, researche*
Haider, Steven John *economics professor*
Iglesias, Emma Maria *economics professor*
Koo, Anthony Ying Chang *economist, educat*
Kreinin, Mordecha Eliahu *economics professo*
Manderscheid, Lester Vincent *agricultural economics educator*
Menchik, Paul Leonard *economist, educator*
Press, Charles *retired political science profess*
Winder, Clarence Leland *psychologist, educat*

Farmington Hills
Robinson, Amorie Alexia *psychologist, educa*

Flushing
Lopez Negrete, Kariann May *psychologist*

Grand Rapids
MacDonald, David Richard *industrial psychologist*
Shoemaker, Allen Leslie *psychology professor, consultant*
Tiemstra, John Peter *economics professor*

Holland
Claar, Victor *economist, educator*
Holmes, Jack Edward *political science profess*

Mackinaw City
Evans, Lynn Louise Morand *archaeologist*

Mount Pleasant
Beehr, Terry A. *psychology professor*
Oh-Lee, Justin DoHoon *psychology professor*
Stancato, Franklin Anthony *psychology profes*

Muskegon
Akker, Arlene F. *social sciences educator*
Crummett, Allan Warren *psychologist*

Northport
Thomas, Philip Stanley *economist, educator*

Okemos
Solo, Robert Alexander *economist, educator*

Portage
Cowart, James D. *psychologist*

Rochester
Clark, Jon Brian *psychologist*
Cordes, Mary Kenrick *psychologist, retired*

Saugatuck
Genetski, Robert James *economist*

Sault Sainte Marie
Johnson, Gary Robert *political scientist*

Southfield
Gregory, Karl Dwight *economics professor, consultant*
Hotelling, Harold *economics professor, lawyer*

neose, Kadakampallil George
ologist
Karen Colby (Karen Lynn Colby)
ologist, lawyer

rse City
erger, Betty Lou *psychologist, educator*

rsity Center
an Gordon *sociologist, educator*

Bloomfield
Thomas George *economist*

nti
ein, Jay A. *social sciences educator,*
rcher

NESOTA

ston
h, Alvin Lynard *psychology professor,*
ultant

h
Haim *social sciences educator*
George Robert (Rip Rapp) *geology and*
eology educator

k, Sheridan Mellon *psychologist, director*
man, Irving I. *psychologist, educator*
-Smith, Lilli Ann *biofeedback specialist,*
cator, administrator

t Lake
Cathy Lee *psychologist*

d Marais
, Robert Wilber *political science educator*

e Grove
Deniz S. *psychologist, educator*

eapolis
oft, Ann E. *polar explorer*
eid, Ellen S. *psychology professor, writer,*
archer
ard, Thomas Joseph, Jr. *psychology*
fessor, researcher
, Robert John *social sciences educator,*
sultant
Matthew Kevin *psychology professor*
ian, John Somerset *retired economist,*
cator
hl, Brian Edward *psychologist*
son, W(alter) Bruce *business and*
nomics educator, entrepreneur
dorn, Hildi *psychologist, researcher*
n, Jo-Ida Charlotte *psychology professor,*
earcher
Robert Theodore *political science*
fessor, educator, dean
icz, Leonid *economist, educator*
on, David Wolcott *psychologist, educator*
, David Harmon *sociology educator*
e, Robert Thomas *economist, educator*
, Stephen Richmond, Jr. *economist,*
cator
m, Don *political science professor*
nier, J. Bruce *psychology professor*
Ira Leonard *retired sociology educator,*
ter
iner, John Christian *economics consultant,*
tware publisher
ly, William Phillips *political scientist,*
cator
an, John L. *political science professor*
gen, Auke *retired psychology professor*
, David Allen *sociology educator*
berg, Richard Alan *psychologist, educator*
dyke, James Edward *psychology professor*

rhead
itt, Harding Coolidge *political scientist,*
cator
or, John Felix *retired economics professor*

thfield
, William Hartley *political science*
ofessor

hester
i, Peter J. *psychology professor, researcher*

nt Paul
way, Deborah *psychologist, educator*
n, Robert Lester *sociology educator*
ip, Paul Frederick *financial economist,*
ucator
mann, Jack Eugene *psychologist, educator*
n, Vernon Wesley *agricultural economist,*
ucator

nt Peter
Rostie, Clair Neil *economics professor*

st Saint Paul
ntingale, Edmund Joseph *clinical*
sychologist, educator, consultant

nona
n, Joy Alice *goldsmith, psychology*
rofessor, artist, educator

ung America
cke, Robert Kenneth *social studies educator,*
epartment chairman

SSISSIPPI

nton
son, Martha Gillon *social studies educator,*
onsultant

Hattiesburg
Davis, Charles Raymond *political scientist, educator*

Jackson
Suess, James Francis *retired psychiatry educator*

Morton
Cox, Marlina R. *social studies educator*

Starkville
Westerhold, Ruth Elizabeth *psychologist, educator*

University
Bartee, RoSusan D. *educational leadership educator*
Shughart, William Franklin, II, *economics professor, consultant*

MISSOURI

Advance
Lanpher, Ben Evert *psychologist, researcher*

Bolivar
Brown, Autry *psychology professor, clergyman*

Columbia
Bank, Barbara J. *sociology educator*
Biddle, Bruce Jesse *social psychologist, educator*
Kausler, Donald Harvey *retired psychology professor*
LoPiccolo, Joseph *psychologist, educator, author*
Rowlett, Ralph Morgan *archaeologist, educator*

Edwards
Findley, Kathryn E.C. *psychologist*

Hillsboro
Hollander, Lisa Elizabeth Elena *geographer, educator, history professor*

Jefferson City
Brooks, Sean Christopher *criminologist*

Kansas City
Nagle, Jean Susan Karabacz *retired sociologist, psychologist*
Roosa, Jan Bertorotta *psychologist, writer*

Maryville
Edwards, Carla E. *psychology professor*

Saint Joseph
Boor, Myron Vernon *psychologist, educator*

Saint Louis
Beck, Lois Grant *anthropologist, educator, author*
Browman, David L(udvig) *archaeologist*
Greenbaum, Stuart I. *economist, educator*
Kling, Merle *retired political scientist, retired university official*
Leguey-Feilleux, Jean-Robert *political scientist, educator*
Lenzen, Dana Diane *social studies educator*
Leven, Charles Louis *economics professor*
Le Vine, Victor Theodore *retired political science professor*
Miller, Gary J. *political economist*
North, Douglass Cecil *economist, educator*
O'Connell, Daniel Craig *retired psychologist, educator*
Olney, John William *psychiatry professor*
Ozawa, Martha Naoko *social work educator*
Salisbury, Robert Holt *political science professor*
Shine, Katina Lynniece Wilbon *neuropsychologist, consultant*
Storandt, Martha *psychologist*
Telowitz, Marilyn Marie *English and social studies educator*
Trinkaus, Erik *paleoanthropologist, educator*
Virgo, John Michael *economist, researcher, educator*
Weidenbaum, Murray Lew *economist, educator*
Williams, Mary Alice Baldwin *retired home economist, volunteer*
Witherspoon, William *investment economist*

Springfield
Branstetter, Ann Dyche *psychology professor*
Buttacy, Anthony *social studies educator*
Gill, Angela Sue *clinical psychologist*
Johnson, Eugene Lee *political scientist, history professor*

MONTANA

Billings
DeRosier, Linda Scott *psychologist, educator*

Bozeman
Duffié, Mary Katharine *anthropologist, educator*
Gray, Philip Howard *former psychologist, writer, educator*

Miles City
Gerber, Robin *history and social sciences educator*

Missoula
Lopach, James Joseph *political science professor*
Wollersheim, Janet Puccinelli *psychology professor*

NEBRASKA

Alliance
Haefele, Edwin Theodore *political theorist, consultant*

Bellevue
Evans, Cleveland Kent *psychology professor*

Lincoln
Auld, James S. *educational psychologist*
Deegan, Mary Jo *sociologist*
MacPhee, Craig Robert *economist, educator*

Omaha
Boamah-Wiafe, Daniel *geographer, researcher*
Louisa, Angelo Joseph *social studies educator, researcher*
Maydwell, Robert Mason, Jr. *social sciences educator*
Wilson, Daniel Richard *anthropologist, physician*
Wunsch, James Stevenson *political science professor*

Scottsbluff
Wylie, Guy Stephen *psychologist, educator*

NEVADA

Ely
Alderman, Minnis Amelia *psychologist, educator, small business owner*

Gardnerville
Griffiths, Barbara Lorraine *psychologist, writer, marriage and family therapist*

Incline Village
Jones, Robert Alonzo *economist*

Las Vegas
Cole, Ann Harriet *psychologist, consultant*
Goodall, Leonard Edwin *public administration educator*
Weeks, Gerald *psychologist, educator*

Reno
Chapman, Samuel Greeley *political science professor, criminologist*
Crowley, Joseph Neil *political science professor, former academic administrator*
Cummings, Nicholas Andrew *psychologist*
Hayes, Steven Charles *psychologist, educator*
Kemmelmeier, Markus *sociologist, psychologist, educator*
Leland, Joy Hanson *retired anthropologist, researcher*
Weinberg, Leonard Burton *political scientist*

Yerington
Price, Judith Holm *educational psychologist*

Zephyr Cove
Hudzinski, Leonard Gerard *social sciences educator, researcher*

NEW HAMPSHIRE

Durham
Palmer, Stuart Hunter *sociology educator*
Romoser, George Kenneth *political and social science educator*

Exeter
Schubart, Caren Nelson *psychologist*

Hanover
Bower, Richard Stuart *retired economist*
Demko, George Joseph *geographer*
Fischel, William Alan *economics professor*
Kleck, Robert Eldon *psychology professor*
Lyons, Gene Martin *political scientist, educator*
Masters, Roger Davis *political scientist, educator, toxicologist*
Riggs, Lorrin Andrews *psychologist, educator*
Rutter, Jeremy Bentham *archaeologist, educator*
Slaughter, Matthew J. *economics professor, former federal official*
Starzinger, Vincent Evans *political scientist, educator*

Henniker
Braiterman, Thea Gilda *economics professor, state legislator*

Keene
Baldwin, Peter Arthur *psychologist, educator, author, minister*
Hackett, John Thomas *retired economist and financial executive*

Lebanon
Emery, Virginia Olga Beattie *psychologist, researcher*
Rosenberg, Stanley David *psychologist, educator*

Manchester
Carrier, Celine A. *psychologist*

Plaistow
Libby-Barth, Jennifer *social studies educator*

Portsmouth
Wener, Brian D. *psychologist*

NEW JERSEY

Branchville
MacMurren, Harold Henry, Jr. *psychologist, lawyer*

Burlington
Haws, Elizabeth Anne *psychologist, director*

Camden
Worrall, John Dennis *economics professor, consultant, writer*
Yamada, Tetsuji *health economist, educator*

Chatham
Brodkin, Adele Ruth Meyer *psychologist*

Cranbury
Hawver, Dennis A. *psychologist, consultant*

East Brunswick
Johnson, Edward Elemuel *psychologist, educator*

East Orange
Wolff, Derish Michael *economist*

Edison
Giacino, Joseph T. *psychologist, educator*

Englewood
Kim, Dongsoo *clinical neuropsychologist, researcher*

Englewood Cliffs
Farrell, Patricia Ann *psychologist, educator, writer*

Glassboro
Mukhoti, Bela Banerjee *economics professor*

Hasbrouck Heights
Perham, Roy Gates III *industrial psychologist*

Jackson
Leveson, Irving Frederick *economist*

Jersey City
Ohiwerei, Godwin Oiseozoje *sociologist, educator*
Urso, Ida *psychologist*

Lawrenceville
Evans, Frederick John *psychologist*
Stein, Sandra Lou *educational psychology professor*

Little Ferry
Briggs, Alice *clinical child psychologist*

Livingston
Friedman, Merton Hirsch *retired psychologist, educator*

Lyndhurst
Bunda, Stephen Myron *political advisor, counselor, lawyer, classical philosopher*

Madison
Jennings, George Harold *psychology professor*
Kaboub, Fadhel *economics professor, consultant*

Mahwah
Harth, Marshall Stephen *psychology professor, psychotherapist*

Moorestown
Burnham, Lem *psychologist, think-tank executive*

Morristown
Boodey, Cecil Webster, Jr. *retired political science professor*
Deming, Frederick Wilson *retired economist, banker*

Mount Laurel
Giampetro, Kathleen A. *school psychologist*

Mountain Lakes
Loomis, Rebecca C. *psychologist*

New Brunswick
Alexander, Robert Jackson *economist, educator*
Clauss-Ehlers, Caroline S. *psychologist, educator, journalist*
Elias, Maurice Jesse *psychology educator*
Glasser, Paul Harold *sociologist, educator, social worker, university administrator*
Glickman, Norman Jay *economist, urban policy analyst*
Leventhal, Howard *health psychology educator, researcher*
Mechanic, David *social sciences educator*
Reock, Ernest C., Jr. *retired social studies educator, director*
Rockoff, Hugh Touff *economist, educator*
Rosenberg, Seymour *psychologist, educator*
Russell, Louise Bennett *economist, educator*
Tiger, Lionel *social scientist, anthropology consultant*
Toby, Jackson *sociologist, educator*

Newark
Adler, Freda Schaffer (Mrs. G. O. W. Mueller) *criminologist, educator*
Carroll, John Douglas *mathematical and statistical psychologist, educator*
Collins, Jason L. *psychologist*
Ferguson, Yale Hicks *political scientist, educator*
Hiltz, Starr Roxanne *sociologist, educator, writer, consultant, computer scientist*
Holzer, Marc *public administrator educator*
Kennedy, Leslie W. *criminal justice educator, former dean*
Pagán, Gilberto, Jr. *psychologist*
Patrick, Robert Herbert, Jr. *economist, educator*

North Brunswick
Burge, Micah Benjamin *school psychologist*

Paramus
Hochberg, Lois J. *school psychologist*
Lieberman, Charles *economist*

Piscataway
Gelman, Rochel *psychology professor*
Goss, Mary E. Weber *sociology educator*
Peterson, Donald Robert *psychologist, educator, academic administrator*
Riss, Richard Michael *research economist, church history educator*
Zerubavel, Eviatar *sociologist, educator*

Princeton
Basáñez, Miguel Ebergenyi *political scientist, educator*
Benabou, Roland Jean-Marc *economist, educator*
Blackman, Sue Anne Batey *economics research specialist*
Blinder, Alan Stuart *economist, educator*
Bogan, Elizabeth Chapin *economist, educator*
Christian, Carole Ann *psychologist, academic administrator*
Coffey, Joseph Irving *political scientist, educator*
Cook, Michael Allan *social sciences educator*
Cooper, Joel *psychologist, educator*
Friedberg, Aaron Louis *political science professor*
Girgus, Joan Stern *psychologist, educator, director*
Gordenker, Leon *political science professor*
Gross, Charles Gordon *psychology professor*
Hoebel, Bartley Gore *psychologist, educator*
Johnson-Laird, Philip Nicholas *psychologist*
Kahneman, Daniel *psychology professor*
Kateb, George Anthony *political science professor*
Keller, Suzanne *sociologist, psychotherapist*
Kenen, Peter Bain *economist, educator*
Keohane, Robert Owen *political scientist, educator*
Krueger, Alan B. *economics professor*
Krugman, Paul Robin *economics professor*
Lazarus, Arnold Allan *psychologist, educator*
Lewis, Bernard *retired social studies educator*
Lewis, John Prior *economist, educator*
Malkiel, Burton Gordon *economist, educator*
Maskin, Eric Stark *economics professor*
Miller, George Armitage *psychologist, educator*
Parry, Scott Brink *psychologist*
Quandt, Richard Emeric *economics professor*
Reinhardt, Uwe Ernst *economist, educator*
Rosen, Harvey Sheldon *economics professor, former federal official*
Rozman, Gilbert Friedell *sociologist, educator*
Shapiro, Harold Tafler *economics professor, former academic administrator*
Shear, Theodore Leslie, Jr. *archaeologist, educator*
Spence, Donald Pond *psychologist, psychoanalyst*
Starr, Paul Elliot *sociologist, educator, editor, writer*
Trussell, James *economist, educator, dean*
Von Hippel, Frank Niels *public and international affairs educator*
Walzer, Michael *retired political science professor*
Western, Bruce *sociologist, educator*
Westoff, Charles Francis *demographer, educator*
Willig, Robert Daniel *economics professor*
Willingham, Warren Willcox *psychologist*
Woolfolk, Robert Lee *psychologist, educator*
Zelizer, Viviana *sociologist, educator*

Randolph
Goldman, Phyllis E. *psychology educator*

Red Bank
McWhinney, Madeline H. (Mrs. John Denny Dale) *economist, director*

Ridgewood
Le May, Moira Kathleen *retired psychology educator*

Saddle River
Lasser, Gail Maria *psychologist, educator*

Scotch Plains
Hallard, Wayne Bruce *retired economist*

Somerset
Lichtig, Leo Kenneth *health economist*

Springfield
O'Desky, Ilyse Hope *psychologist, educator*
Shilling, A. Gary *economist, consultant*

Summit
Lovett, Juanita Pelletier *clinical psychologist*

Teaneck
Brudner, Helen Gross *social sciences educator*
Cassimatis, Peter John *economics professor*

Tenafly
Blank, Marion Sue *psychologist, educator*

Titusville
Pandina, Gahan J. *psychologist, researcher*

Trenton
Biskin, Bruce Howard *psychometrician*
Lattanzi, Gregory Denis *archaeologist*

Union
Kim, Youn-Suk Ernest *economist, educator*
Norward, Josephine Norma *social work educator, consultant*

Westfield
Simon, Martin Stanley *economist, consultant*

Westwood
Fabrikant, Craig Steven *psychologist*

NEW MEXICO

Albuquerque
Byers, Steven N. *anthropologist, educator, computer professional*
Calkins, Ralph Nelson *retired economics professor*
Condie, Carol Joy *anthropologist, science administrator*
Harris, Fred R. *political scientist, educator, retired senator*
Jung, Rex Eugene *psychologist, researcher*
May, Philip Alan *sociologist, educator*
McCrady, Barbara Sachs *psychologist, educator*
Schwerin, Karl Henry *anthropology educator, researcher*
Tryon, Patti Ann *school psychologist*

Corrales
Adams, James Frederick *psychologist, academic administrator, educator*

El Prado
Young, Jon Nathan *archaeologist*

Las Cruces
Roscoe, Stanley Nelson *psychologist, aeronautical engineer*

Las Vegas
Riley, Carroll Lavern *anthropology educator*

Los Alamos
Masse, William Bruce *archaeologist*

Santa Fe
Anderson, Darrell Edward *psychologist, educator*
Williams, Stephen *anthropologist, educator*

Silver City
Lopez, Linda Carol *social sciences educator*

NEW YORK

Albany
Capaldi, Elizabeth Ann Deutsch *psychological sciences professor*
Ericson, David Frank *political scientist, educator*
Greenberg, Martin Alan *criminologist, educator*
Langer, Judith Ann *psychologist*
Ley, Ronald *psychologist, educator*
Nathan, Richard P(erle) *political science professor*
Polimeni, John Matthew *economics professor*
Thompson, Frank Joseph *political science professor*
Zimmerman, Joseph Francis *political scientist, educator*

Amherst
Bradford, Michelle M. *social studies educator*

Annandale On Hudson
Papadimitriou, Dimitri Basil *economist, educator, academic administrator*

Auburn
Dello Stritto, Ellen M. *retired social studies educator*
Pelkey, Lawrence Michael *school psychologist*

Averill Park
Haines, Walter Wells *retired economics professor*

Bayside
Ohrenstein, Roman Abraham *economist, educator, rabbi*

Binghamton
Isaacson, Robert Lee *neurobehavioral scientist, educator*
James, Gary Douglas *biological anthropologist, educator, researcher*
Levis, Donald James *psychologist, educator*
Mazrui, Ali Al'Amin *political science professor, researcher*

Brentwood
Liebert, Lynn Langenbach *psychologist, educator*

Bronx
Durglishvili, Nana Z. *psychologist, language educator*
Macklin, Ruth *bioethics educator*
Muller, Katherine Lynn *clinical psychologist*
Rego, Simon Alexander *psychologist*

Brooklyn
Nye, William Roger *psychologist*
O'Doherty, Susan Ann *psychologist, writer*

Buffalo
Frone, Michael R. *psychologist, researcher*
Gort, Michael *economics professor*
Lamb, Charles Moody *political scientist, educator*
Levy, Kenneth Jay *psychology professor, academic administrator*
McCormack, Patricia Lynn *retired psychologist*

Canton
Auster, Nancy Eileen Ross *economics professor*

Chappaqua
Schwarz, Wolfgang *psychologist*

Clinton
Paris, David C. *political science professor*

Conesus
Dadrian, Vahakn Norair *retired sociology educator*

Cornwall On Hudson
Pendley, Stephen *social studies educator, department chairman*

Cortlandt Manor
Lupiani, Jennifer Lynne *school psychologist*

Dobbs Ferry
Kraetzer, Mary C. *sociologist, educator, consultant*

East Meadow
Albert, Gerald *clinical psychologist*
Jeziorski, Michael A. *social studies educator*

Farmingdale
Goodstone, Michael S. *psychology professor, consultant*

Flushing
Beveridge, Andrew Alan *sociologist, educator, consultant*
Pellitteri, John Steven *psychologist, psychotherapist, educator*
Smith, Charles William *social sciences educator*

Freeport
Ferentino, Sheila Connolly *psychologist, consultant*

Fresh Meadows
Male, Ayn Rochelle *psychologist, researcher*

Garden City
Walsh Mitchell, Diana *school psychologist, consultant*

Garrison
Murray, Thomas Henry *bioethics educator, writer*

Geneseo
Olczak, Paul Vincent *psychologist, educator*

Great Neck
Christie, George Nicholas *economist, consultant*
Minkoff, Jack *retired economics professor*

Greenport
Watts, Harold Wesley *economist, educator*

Greenvale
Araoz, Daniel Leon *psychologist, educator*
Kusukawa, Akira *demographer, educator*

Groveland
Battersby, Harold Ronald *retired anthropologist, archaeologist, linguist*

Hamilton
Ammerman, Albert Jay *archaeologist, humanities educator*

Hempstead
Bose, Meena *political science professor*
Shafritz, Keith Michael *psychology professor*
Wattel, Harold Louis *economics professor*

Ithaca
Ascher, Robert *anthropologist, archaeologist, film producer, educator*
Beneria, Lourdes *economist, educator*
Chapman, Lewis Duane *economist*
Darlington, Richard Benjamin *retired psychologist, educator, researcher*
Easley, David *economics professor*
Ehrenberg, Ronald Gordon *economist, educator*
Fireside, Harvey Francis *political scientist, educator*
Jarrow, Robert Alan *economist, educator*
Just, David Ryan *economist*
Kahn, Alfred Edward *economist, educator, government official*
Kennedy, Kenneth Adrian Raine *biological and forensic anthropologist*
Lowi, Theodore Jay *political science professor*
Lyons, Thomas Patrick *economics professor*
Majumdar, Mukul Kumar *economist, educator*
Mueller, Betty Jeanne *social work educator*
Pelto, Gretel H. *nutritional anthropologist, educator*
Pinstrup-Andersen, Per *economist, educator*
Rader, Nancy Louise de Villiers *psychology professor, consultant*
Smidt, Seymour *economics professor*
Smith, Robert John *anthropology educator*
Thorbecke, Erik *economics professor*
Tomek, William Goodrich *agricultural economist*
Vanek, Jaroslav *economist, educator*
Waldman, Michael *economist, educator*

Jamaica
Chirico, Donna M. *psychologist, educator, researcher*
Lees, Francis *economics professor*

Katonah
Wenglowski, Gary Martin *economist*

Lancaster
Schulenberg, Gary Michael *social studies educator*

Larchmont
Siegel, Nathaniel Harold *sociology educator*

Lindenhurst
Kaufman, Susan Shiffman *psychologist*

Manhasset
Savage, Clare Leavy *school psychologist*

Melville
Grayson, Gerald Herbert *economist, educator, arbitrator, writer*

Mexico
Sade, Donald Stone *anthropology educator*

Middletown
Joerger, Jay Herman *psychologist, entrepreneur*

Millbrook
Flexner, Kurt Fisher *economist, educator*

Mount Vernon
Carty, Mary Ellen *psychologist*

Nesconset
Burns-Riviello, Michaela Aileen *social studies educator*

New Paltz
Schnell, George Adam *geographer, educator, demographer*

New Rochelle
Berlage, Gai Ingham *sociologist, researcher*
Rutstein, Eleanor H. *psychologist*

New York
Anderson, Lisa *political science professor, researcher, former dean*
Andreassi, John Lawrence *psychologist, educ*
Bardach, Joan Lucile *clinical psychologist*
Barron, Susan *clinical psychologist*
Beck, Nathaniel L. *political science professor*
Betts, Richard Kevin *political science profess*
Blechner, Mark Jacob *psychologist, educator*
Bond, Alma Halbert *psychoanalyst, author*
Bowers, Patricia Eleanor Fritz *economist*
Braham, Randolph Lewis *political science professor*
Brams, Steven John *political science profess*
Browne, Joy *psychologist, radio personality*
Brusca, Robert Andrew *economist*
Buck, Louise Zierdt *psychologist*
Caraley, Demetrios James *political science professor, writer, editor*
Carr, Arthur Charles *psychologist, educator*
Chelstrom, Marilyn Ann *political science educator, consultant*
Clamar, Aphrodite J. *psychologist*
Cohen, Mitchell S. *political science professor*
Cohen, Stephen Frand *political scientist, writ historian, educator, commentator*
Comitas, Lambros *anthropologist, educator*
Czárán, Lóránt *geographer, consultant*
Dalton, Dennis Gilmore *political science professor*
DeGregorio, Carlo *social studies educator*
deMause, Lloyd *psychologist*
Demeny, Paul George *demographer, research*
Denmark, Florence Harriet Levin *psychology professor*
Dudley, William C. *economist*
Duke, Anthony Drexel *retired sociologist, educator, philanthropist*
Edwards, Franklin Richard *economist, educa consultant*
Elinson, Jack *social sciences educator*
Epstein, Cynthia Fuchs *sociology educator, writer*
Erikson, Robert S. *political science professor*
Feldman, Ronald Arthur *sociologist, educator social worker*
Fischer, Herbert Steven *social studies educat*
Fishman, Steven T. *psychologist*
Fosler, Gail D. *economist*
Fox, Richard Gabriel *anthropologist, educato*
Franklin, Julian Harold *political science professor*
Galanter, Eugene *psychologist, educator*
Gans, Herbert J. *sociologist, educator*
Garzarelli, Elaine Marie *economist*
Gilligan, Carol *psychologist, writer*
Glass, David Carter *psychologist, educator*
Glickman, Michael Richard *social studies educator*
Goldman, George David *psychologist*
Gorenstein, Ethan Ezra *psychologist, educato*
Griffin, Anne *political scientist, educator*
Grody, Deborah *psychologist, director*
Grossman, Michael *economics professor*
Habachy, Suzan Salwa Saba *economist, not-for-profit developer*
Halper, Thomas *political science professor*
Harbeson, John Willis *political science profe*
Heeger, David J. *psychology professor*
Heilbrun, James *economist, educator*
Heyde, Martha Bennett *psychologist*
Holloway, Ralph Leslie *anthropology educat*
Hormats, Robert David *economist, investmen banker*
Hoxter, Curtis Joseph *international economic advisor, public relations executive, communications executive*
Jacoby, Jacob *consumer psychology educator*
Jasso, Guillermina *sociologist, educator*
Jervis, Robert *political science professor*
Kandel, Denise Bystryn *sociologist*
Kaplan, Lawrence Jay *retired economist, educator*
Kaplow, Julie B. *psychologist, educator*
Kavesh, Robert A. *economist, educator*
Kazemi, Farhad *political scientist, educator*
Krauss, Herbert Harris *psychologist*
Kurzweil, Edith *social sciences educator, edi*
Lazarcik, Gregor *economist, educator, financ research company executive*
Leahey, Miles Cary *economist*
Leahy, Robert Louis *psychologist*
Legvold, Robert *political science professor*
Lehman, Edward William *social studies educator, researcher*
Levin, Henry Mordechai *economist, educator*
Lew, Jacob *public administration educator*
Liff, Zanvel A. *psychologist*
Lipsey, Robert Edward *economist, educator*
Lothian, James Robert *economist, educator*
MacLeod, William Bentley *economics, law professor*
Maldonado-Bear, Rita Marinita *economist, educator*
Marable, Manning *social science educator, writer*
Marks, Lillian Shapiro *retired secretarial stu educator, writer, editor*
Marshall, Simone Verniere *psychologist, psychoanalyst*
Mc Cullough, J. Lee *industrial psychologist*
Meyer-Bahlburg, Heino F.L. *psychology professor*
Midlarsky, Elizabeth Ruth *psychologist, educator, researcher*
Miller, Ruby Sills *retired gerontologist*
Mischel, Walter *psychology professor*
Mroz, John Edwin *political scientist*
Muller, Charlotte Feldman *economist, educat*

ıdell, Robert Alexander *economist, educator*
ɔhy, Austin de la Salle *economist, educator, ınker*
ıan, Andrew James *political science educator*
zer, Dick *economics professor*
npo, Jose Antonio *economist, educator, rmer international organization official, rmer Colombian government official*
eill, June Ellenoff *economist*
, Cynthia *sociology educator, consultant*
ck, Hugh Talbot *economist, educator*
., Fred Neil *economist, educator*
y, Shelley *psychologist*
ell, Caroline Hodges *sociologist, educator, ıthor, researcher, consultant*
hesky, Rosalind Pollack *social and political ientist, educator*
ps, Edmund Strother *economics professor*
n, Frances Fox *political scientist, educator*
ɔck, Jefrey Ian *pollster, political consultant*
ıiades, Harry John *political science ofessor*
Gordon Bruce *economist*
Sethuramiah Lakshminarayana *mographer, United Nations official*
nond, Elsa M. *anthropologist*
man, Sophia *psychologist*
Eric *psychologist*
n, Benjamin *political science professor*
ɔck, Stefan Hyman *retired economics ofessor*
ıldo, Renato Ignacio, Jr. *cultural thropology educator*
nthal, Howard Lewis *political science ofessor*
man, Barbara Katz *sociology educator*
ɔini, Nouriel *economics professor*
s, Jeffrey David *economist, educator*
s, Harry *psychologist, health administrator, searcher*
y, Sandra V. *psychologist*
lon, Rosemary *economist*
sa, Joseph Vincent *sociologist, educator, an*
esinger, Stephen Cannon *foreign policy nsultant*
eier, Edward Vincent *political science ofessor*
tter, Andrew Roye *economics professor, nsultant*
vab, George David *social sciences educator, iter*
vartz, Anna Jacobson *economist*
don, Eleanor Harriet Bernert *sociologist, iter*
r, Morris *economist, educator*
n, Jacqueline Albert *political scientist, iter*
l, George LeRoy *geographer, educator*
ki, R. Stefan *anthropologist, educator*
cer, Charles S. *anthropologist*
tz, Joseph Eugene *economics professor, rmer federal official*
ez-Orozco, Carola Elisabeth *psychology ofessor*
ci, Patrick Joseph *clinical psychologist*
, Richard Eugene *economics professor*
ner, Margot Sallop *psychologist, rontologist, psychoanalyst*
r, Lance Jerome *economics professor*
er, Lynn Marsha *gerontologist, educator*
s, Lillian Dick *psychologist, health facility ministrator*
, Ashok *financial economist*
, Estelle B. *psychologist, psychoanalyst*
, Duncan J. *social sciences educator*
berg-Samuels, Janet S. *psychologist*
s, Samuel Abraham *psychologist, ychoanalyst*
e, Lawrence J. *economics professor*
nson, Louise Cherry *psychology professor, an*
, Edward Nathan *economist, educator*
stowski, Stephen Louis *psychologist, ucator*

gara University
rg, Timothy Michael *psychologist, educator, searcher*

ayuna
nt, Theodore Paul, Jr. *political science ofessor*

Westbury
i, Tunch *economics professor*

onta
otra, Ashok Kumar *philosophy educator*
Saal, Walter *psychology professor*

ego
ieri, Lewis Joshua *psychologist, consultant*

ter Bay
ón, Ana *school psychologist*

sford
ner, Robert Julius *political science professor*

sant Valley
hall, Natalie Junemann *economics professor*

Chester
-Dynega, Marlene *psychologist*

ghkeepsie
on, M(aurice) Glen *political science ofessor*
s, Peter A. *psychology professor*

chase
on, Esther Mary *anthropologist, educator*
Edward W. *economics professor*

Park
an, Rachel Beth *psychologist*

Rochester
Aslin, Richard N. *psychology professor, researcher*
Bluhm, William Theodore *political scientist, educator*
Deci, Edward Lewis *psychologist, educator*
Fenno, Richard Francis, Jr. *political scientist, educator*
Hopkins, Thomas Duvall *economics professor*
Johnston, Frank C. *psychologist*
Laties, Victor Gregory *psychologist, educator*
Levy, Harold David *psycholinguist*
Long, John Broaddus, Jr. *economist, educator*
Mapstone, Mark *neuropsychologist, educator*
Mc Kenzie, Lionel Wilfred *economist, educator*
Newport, Elissa L. *psychology professor*
Niemi, Richard Gene *political science educator*
Phelps, Charles Elliott *economics professor, director*
Primo, David Martin *political science professor*
Regenstreif, S(amuel) Peter *political scientist, educator*
Vernarelli, Michael Joseph *economics professor, consultant, academic administrator*
Wagner, Aureen Pinto *psychologist, educator*
Zax, Melvin *psychologist, educator*

Rockville Centre
Lewittes, Don Jordan *psychologist*

Rye Brook
Aquino, Joseph Mario *clinical psychologist*

Saratoga Springs
Miller, Anita Diane *psychologist*

Scarsdale
Cohen, Irwin *economist*

Schenectady
Board, Joseph Breckinridge, Jr. *political scientist, educator*
Huszar, Andrew Louis *school psychologist*

Smithtown
Fritzhand, Irvin Dick *psychologist*

Somers
Trzasko, Joseph Anthony *psychologist, educator*

Staten Island
Caudle, Fairfid Monsalvatge *psychology professor*
Franzone, Eric Scott *psychologist*
Lewis, Carla Susan *psychology educator*
Piegari, James A. *psychologist*
Stolz, Theodora *psychologist*

Stony Brook
Benitez-Silva, Hugo A. *economics professor*
Carr, Edward Gary *psychology professor*
Leakey, Richard Erskine *paleoanthropologist, museum director*
Squires, Nancy *psychology professor*
Stolzberg, Mark Elliott *psychologist*
Stone, Elizabeth Cecilia *anthropology educator*
Tanur, Judith Mark *sociologist, educator*

Syracuse
Birkhead, Guthrie Sweeney, Jr. *political scientist, dean*
Braungart, Richard Gottfried *political scientist, educator*
Han, Jongwoo *political science professor*
Kriesberg, Louis *sociologist, educator*
Monmonier, Mark *geographer, writer*
Smith, Corinne Roth *psychologist*

Tarrytown
Weiner, Max *psychology professor*

Tonawanda
Brunger, Eric Geoffrey *social studies educator, coach*

Troy
Brazil, Harold Edmund *political science professor*

Valhalla
Urban, Diane *psychologist, educator*

West Islip
Theiss, Cynthia C. *home economist, educator*

West Point
Keith, Bruce Edward *sociologist*

Woodbury
Agresti, Miriam Monell *psychologist*

Woodstock
Lieberman, Josefa Nina *retired psychologist, writer*

Yonkers
Lupiani, Donald Anthony *psychologist*

NORTH CAROLINA

Asheville
Dickens, Charles Henderson *retired social sciences educator*
Smith, James Finley *economist, educator*

Biltmore Forest
Sgro, Joseph Anthony *retired psychologist, educator*

Boone
Jones, Dan Lewis *psychologist*

Carrboro
Barbarin, Oscar Anthony *psychologist*

Cashiers
O'Connell, Edward James, Jr. *psychologist, educator, systems administrator, consultant*

Chapel Hill
Baroff, George Stanley *psychologist, educator*
Brown, Frank *social sciences educator*
Campbell, Frances Alexander *psychologist*
Fieleke, Norman Siegfried *economist, educator*
Girdler, Susan Scott *psychologist, educator, researcher*
Gray, Virginia Hickman *political science professor*
Hartlyn, Jonathan *political scientist, educator*
Jones, Lyle Vincent *psychologist, educator*
Latané, Bibb *social psychologist*
Lowman, Robert Paul *psychology professor, academic administrator*
Norton, Edward C. *economist, educator*
Prange, Arthur Jergen, Jr. *psychology and psychiatry professor, neuroscientist*
Rindfuss, Ronald Richard *social studies educator*
Schoultz, Lars *political scientist, educator*
Stenberg, Carl W. III *public administration educator, dean*
Steponaitis, Vincas Petras *archaeologist, anthropologist, educator*
Treml, Vladimir Guy *economist, educator*
Wasik, Barbara Hanna *psychologist, educator*
Wilson, Glenn *economist, educator*
Wright, Deil Spencer *political science professor*

Charlotte
Edmondson, Ruby Johnson *psychologist*
Goolkasian, Paula A. *psychologist, educator*
Kidda, Michael Lamont, Jr. *psychologist, educator*
Neel, Richard Eugene *economist, educator*
Pyle, Gerald Fredric *geographer, educator*
Vazquez Rivera, Ornela Amliv *psychologist*
Webster, Murray Alexander, Jr. *sociologist, educator*

Davidson
Palmer, Edward L. *psychologist, educator, writer*
Ross, Clark Grant *economics professor*

Durham
Aldrich, John Herbert *political science professor*
Blackburn, John Oliver *economist, consultant*
Breland-Noble, Alfiee Matiese *psychologist, researcher*
Conklin, George Henry *sociologist, educator*
Cook, Philip Jackson *economist, educator*
Elliot, Jeffrey M. *political science professor, department chairman*
Guseh, James Sawalla *public administration educator*
Holsti, Ole Rudolf *political scientist, educator*
Kelley, Allen Charles *economist, educator*
Land, Kenneth Carl *sociologist, educator, demographer*
Lockhead, Gregory Roger *retired psychology professor*
McClain, Paula Denice *political scientist, educator*
Simons, Elwyn LaVerne *physical anthropologist, primatologist, paleontologist, educator*
Staddon, John Eric Rayner *psychology professor, neurobiology professor, zoology professor*
Story, Tyler James *psychologist, educator*
Surwit, Richard Samuel *psychology professor*
Talley, Joseph Eugene *psychologist*

Elon
Arcaro, Thomas E. *sociologist, educator*

Greensboro
Chandler, Austin Grace *psychologist*
Goldman, Bert Arthur *psychologist, educator*
Helms-VanStone, Mary Wallace *anthropology educator*
Shelton, David Howard *economics professor*

Greenville
Aziz, Shahnaz *psychology professor*

High Point
Corey, James William *political scientist, educator*

Hillsborough
Goodwin, Craufurd David *economics professor*
Piper, Don Courtney *political scientist, educator*

Jacksonville
Guyer, Charles Grayson, II, *psychologist*

Morganton
Carpenter III, Harry Everett *social sciences educator, history professor*

Pittsboro
Richardson, Richard Judson *retired political science professor*

Raleigh
Allen, Steven Glen *economics and business professor*
Fantz, Janet Nelsen *school psychologist*
Imade, Lucky Osagie *political scientist, educator*
Newman, Slater Edmund *psychologist, educator*
Stroup, Richard Lyndell *economist, educator, writer*

Saluda
Cutright, Phillips *sociologist, educator*

Wilmington
Hines, Elizabeth *geographer, educator*
Snowden, Lynne *sociologist, educator*

Winston Salem
Heckelman, Jac C. *economics professor*

NORTH DAKOTA

Fargo
Hektner, Joel Martin *psychology professor*
Riley, Thomas Joseph *anthropologist, academic administrator*

Grand Forks
Bradley, April Rain *psychology professor*
Russell, Sue Ann *clinical psychologist*

OHIO

Ada
Durkin, Keith Francis *sociologist, researcher*

Akron
Garbrandt, Gail Elaine *political science professor, consultant*
Yardeni, Edward *economist, investment advisor*

Ashland
Ford, Lucille Garber *economist, educator*

Ashtabula
Carrell, Janeen Brown *retired psychologist*

Athens
McNamara, John Regis *psychology educator*
Stump, Earl Spencer *psychologist*
Vedder, Richard Kent *economics professor*

Bath
Coyne, Thomas Joseph *economics and finance professor*

Bowling Green
Berger, Bonnie G. *sport psychologist, educator*
Goza, Franklin William *sociology educator*
Guion, Robert Morgan *psychologist, educator*
Hakel, Milton Daniel, Jr. *psychologist, educator, writer, consultant*
Krane, Vikki *psychology educator*
McCaghy, Charles Henry *retired social sciences educator*

Cambridge
Reisner, Andrew Douglas *psychologist*

Cardington
Linscott, Ross Edward *school psychologist*

Cedarville
Firmin, Michael Wayne *psychology professor*

Cincinnati
Ashley, Lynn *social sciences educator, consultant*
Bieliauskas, Vytautas Joseph *psychologist, educator*
Bishop, George Franklin *political scientist, educator*
Bluestein, Venus Weller *retired psychologist, educator*
Laffitte, Larry James *industrial organizational psychologist, consultant*
Medina, Krista Lisdahl *neuropsychologist, educator*
Tsibulsky, Vladimir Lvovich *psychologist, researcher*

Cleveland
Beall, Cynthia *anthropologist, educator*
Binstock, Robert Henry *public policy educator, writer*
Carlsson, Bo Axel Vilhelm *economics professor*
Carrol, Edward Nicholas *psychologist*
Deal, William Thomas *retired school psychologist*
Detterman, Douglas Kenward *psychologist, researcher*
Hokenstad, Merl Clifford, Jr. *social work educator*
Kolb, David Allen *psychologist, educator*
Lewine, Mark Saul *anthropology professor*
Mayland, Kenneth Theodore *economist*
McHale, Vincent Edward *political science professor*
Myers, Eddie Earl *psychologist*
Sibley, Willis Elbridge *anthropology educator, consultant*

Columbus
Alger, Chadwick Fairfax *political scientist, educator*
Bagnoli, Dannelle M. *school psychologist*
Baird, Leonard Lynn *social scientist, educator, researcher, editor*
Everhart, Velma Vizedom *retired home economics educator, retired real estate agent*
Gilliom, Morris Eugene *social studies and global educator*
Howard, Marilyn Kaye *political science professor*
Johnson, Martha (Marty) Junk (Marty Johnson) *psychology professor*
Johnson, Neal Frederick *psychologist, educator*
Kessel, John Howard *political scientist, educator*
Kiecolt-Glaser, Janice Kay *psychologist*
Larsen, Clark Spencer *anthropology educator*
Millett, Stephen Malcolm *futurist, consultant, historian*
Mirzaie, Ida A. *economics professor*
Mueller, John Ernest *political science professor, dance critic*
Naylor, James Charles *psychologist, educator*
Peterson, Ruth D. *sociologist*
Sporleder, Thomas Lynn *economist, researcher*
Tybout, Richard Alton *economics professor*
Wasserman, Karen Boling *clinical psychologist, nursing consultant*
Weisberg, Herbert Frank *political science professor*

Cuyahoga Falls
Roth, Gregory Edward *social studies educator*

Findlay
Peters, Milton Eugene *retired educational psychologist*

Kent
Feinberg, Richard *anthropologist, educator*
Lovejoy, Claude Owen *anthropologist, educator*
Williams, Donald R. *social sciences educator*
Williams, Harold Roger *economist, educator*

Louisville
Faigley, Joseph Raymond *social studies educator*

Minerva
Grunder, Stuart Edwin *social studies educator*

Moreland Hills
Tolchinsky, Paul Dean *organization design psychologist*

Newark
Federspiel, Howard M. *political science professor*

Oberlin
Taylor, Richard Wirth *retired political science professor*

Oxford
Bergen, Doris *psychologist, educator*
Dawisha, Adeed *political science professor*
Gupta, Barnali *economics professor*
Miller, Norman Calvin *economist*
Rejai, Mostafa *political science professor*

Pataskala
Ripley, Randall Butler *political scientist, educator*

Ripley
Curtis, Russell Glenn *social studies educator*

Shadyside
Weeks, Nancy Kay *psychologist, educator*

Shaker Heights
Ludwig, L(owell) Mark *social studies educator*

Springfield
Seifert, Shelley Elizabeth *psychologist*

Strongsville
Blumer, Frederick Elwin *retired philosophy educator*

Sugar Grove
Dombrowski, Karen S. *social studies and education educator*

Tiffin
Gridley, Mark Charles *psychologist*

Toledo
Funk, Jeanne B. *psychology professor*
Heintz, Carolinea Cabaniss *retired home economist, educator*

University Heights
Eslinger, Kenneth Nelson *social sciences educator*

West Chester
Macks, Ryan Jeffrey *psychologist*

Youngstown
Binning, William Charles *political science professor*

OKLAHOMA

Bartlesville
Jackson, Brian Kelly *economics professor*

Calera
Parker, Marilla J. *school psychologist*

Claremore
Woller, Kevin Marc Peter *psychology professor, researcher*

Norman
Affleck, Marilyn *retired sociology educator*
Henderson, George *educational sociologist, educator*

Oklahoma City
Adams, Russell Lee *neuropsychologist*
Craig, George Dennis *economics professor, consultant*
Morgan, Catherine Marie *psychologist, writer*
Poole, Richard William *economist*
Schroeder, David J. Dean *psychologist*

Stillwater
Chung, Chanjin *economics professor, researcher*
Darcy, Robert Emmett *political science and statistics professor*
Dunlap, Riley Eugene *sociologist*
Finchum, George Allen, II, *geography educator*

Woodward
Fisher, Deena Kaye *social studies education administrator*

OREGON

Ashland
Bornet, Vaughn Davis *social sciences educator, historian, researcher*

Aurora
Meulemans, William Charles *political science professor*

Corvallis
Castle, Emery Neal *economist, educator*
Gillis, John Simon *retired psychologist, educator*
Ray, Edward John *economics professor, academic administrator*

Dallas
Nathan, Gerald Dale *retired psychologist, researcher, writer*

Eugene
Bichsel, Ruth J. *psychologist, educator*
Freyd, Jennifer Joy *psychology professor*
Hunt, Elizabeth Hope *psychologist*
Khang, Chulsoon *economics professor*
Littman, Richard Anton *psychologist, educator*
Neville, Helen J. *psychology professor, neuroscientist*
White, Patricia Marie *psychology professor, researcher*

Forest Grove
Gibby-Smith, Barbara *psychologist, nurse*

La Grande
Thompson, Jo(an) *anthropologist*

Newberg
Adams, Wayne Verdun *pediatric psychologist, educator*
Warford, Patricia *psychologist*

Portland
Anastasiou, Harry *international peace and conflict studies professor*
Harter, Lafayette George, Jr. *retired economics professor*
Kristof, Ladis Kris Donabed *political scientist, writer*
Matarazzo, Joseph Dominic *psychologist, educator*
Matarazzo, Ruth Gadbois *retired psychology professor*
Wiens, Arthur Nicholai *psychology professor*

Salem
Warnath, Maxine Ammer *psychologist, arbitrator*

PENNSYLVANIA

Allentown
Graham, Kenneth Robert *psychologist, educator*

Annville
Lou, Manza *psychology professor*

Bethlehem
Aronson, Jay Richard *economics professor, researcher, academic administrator*
Scheirer, William Kenneth *economist, consultant*
Schwartz, Eli *retired economics professor, writer*
Smolansky, Bettie Moretz *sociology educator*
Wetcher-Hendricks, Debra Elizabeth *social sciences educator*

Bloomsburg
Leitzel, Jeffrey Dale *psychology professor*

Bryn Mawr
Anderson, Eric Edward *psychologist, consultant, healthcare educator*
Newhall, Jane Ward *psychologist*
Porter, Judith Deborah Revitch *sociologist*

Carlisle
Jones, Oliver Hastings *consulting economist*

Coopersburg
Bednar, Charles Sokol *political science professor*

Coplay
Briggs, Chad Michael *political science professor*

Coraopolis
Beaver, William R. *sociology professor*

Coudersport
Kysor, Daniel Francis *psychologist*

Downingtown
Sweeney, Sarina Marie *psychologist, consultant*

Doylestown
Bowers, Nell S. *psychologist*
Ginsberg, Barry Gavrille *psychologist, marriage and family therapist*

Du Bois
Forthun, Larry F. *social sciences educator, consultant*

Easton
Kincaid, John *political science professor, editor*

Erie
Ayrault, Evelyn West *psychologist, writer*
Bennett, Charles Andrew *economics professor, department chairman*
Orton, Geraldine Leitl *psychologist, mental health therapist, educator, author*

Exton
Roth, William McKinley *psychologist*

Fairless Hills
Rosella, John Daniel *clinical psychologist, educator*

Friendsville
Babb, Harold *psychologist, educator*

Glenside
Jones, Elaine F. *psychologist, educator*

Greensburg
Ramm, Douglas Robert *psychologist*

Haverford
Northrup, Herbert Roof *economist*

Indiana
Black, Lynanne *psychologist, educator*
Ciano-Federoff, Lynda *psychologist, educator*
Mc Cauley, R. Paul *criminologist, educator*
Reynolds, Virginia Edith *sociologist, anthropologist, educator, artist*

Kelton
Gulick, Walter Lawrence *psychologist, educator, retired academic administrator*

Kennett Square
Smith, Virginia Eleanore *psychologist, educator*

Kutztown
Gupta, Venu Gopal *psychology professor*

Lancaster
Pavlatos, Arthur L. *retired social studies educator*

Lewisburg
Candland, Douglas Keith *psychology professor*
Dively, Justin Matthew *psychologist*
Hauck, William Edward *retired education educator*
Kinnaman, Thomas Christopher *economics professor, researcher*

Lincoln University
Nwachuku, Levi Akalazu *social sciences and behavioral studies educator*

Mc Veytown
Crosby, Edward George *psychologist*

Meadville
Adams, Earl William, Jr. *retired economics professor*

Minersville
Eisenhuth, Edward George *social studies educator*

Nazareth
Bast, Kimberly Ann *social studies educator*

New Alexandria
Sehring, Hope Hutchison *library science educator*

North Huntingdon
Huszar, Carl George *social studies educator*

Orefield
Langman, Peter Fabbri *psychologist, poet, playwright*

Perkasie
Dillingham, Lee *social studies educator*

Philadelphia
Behrman, Jere Richard *economics professor*
Chrysikou, Evangelia G. *psychology professor*
Clark, John J. *economist, finance educator*
Coché, Judith *psychologist, educator*
Cruess, Dean *psychologist, educator*
Cunningham, Jacqueline Lemmé *psychologist, educator, researcher*
Danien, Elin C. *archaeologist, researcher*
Davey, Adam *gerontologist, researcher*
Diebold, Francis X. *economist, educator*
Eiberson, Jeffrey Lawrence *psychologist, consultant*
Erdmann, James Bernard *educational psychologist*
Evan, William Martin *sociologist, educator*
Fox, Renée Claire *sociology educator*
Frankel, Francine Ruth *political science professor*
Gershenfeld, Matti Kibrick *psychologist*
Goodenough, Ward Hunt *anthropologist, educator*
Guillen, Mauro Federico *sociology and management educator*
Harvey, John Adriance *psychologist, educator, pharmacologist, researcher*
Henisz, Witold Jerzy *social sciences educator*
Klausner, Samuel Zundel *sociologist, educator*
Klein, Lawrence Robert *economist, educator*
Madden, Janice Fanning *economics professor*
Meredith, Lisa Ann Marie *social studies educator, consultant*
Newcombe, Nora *psychology professor*
Orne, Emily Carota *psychologist, researcher*
Perlman, Barry Steven *sociologist, educator*
Postlewaite, Andrew William *economics professor, department chairman*
Rescorla, Robert Arthur *psychology professor*
Rima, Ingrid Hahne *economics professor*
Rutkowski, Duane Joseph *social studies educator*
Sabloff, Jeremy Arac *archaeologist*
Seligman, Martin E.P. *psychologist, educator*
Sharer, Robert James *archaeologist*
Sherman, Lawrence William *criminologist*
Shure, Myrna Beth *psychologist, educator*
Smith, Rogers Mood *political scientist, educator*
Summers, Robert *economics professor*
Wallace, Anthony Francis Clarke *anthropologist, educator*
Zubernis, Lynn Smith *psychologist, counselor*
Zuckerman, Marvin *retired psychologist*

Pittsburgh
Barry, Herbert III *psychologist, educator*
Blumstein, Alfred *urban and public affairs educator*
Cagney, William Robert *psychologist*
Cohen, Sheldon *psychologist, psychology professor*
Curry, Nancy Ellen *psychologist, psychoanalyst, educator*
Dawes, Robyn Mason *psychology professor*
Drennan, Robert D. *archeology educator, researcher*
Eaton, Joseph W. *sociology educator*
Fararo, Thomas John *sociologist, educator*
Fischhoff, Baruch *psychologist, educator*
Holzner, Burkart *retired sociologist, educato*
Klatzky, Roberta Lou *psychologist, educator*
Kydland, Finn E. *economics professor*
Lave, Judith Rice *economics professor*
McCallum, Bennett Tarlton *economist, educ*
Meltzer, Allan H. *economist, educator*
Ogul, Morris Samuel *political science profe consultant*
Perel, James Maurice *pharmacology and psychiatry educator, researcher*
Perloff, Robert *psychologist, educator*
Quinn, Clark Nives *psychologist, consultant*
Schorr-Ribera, Hilda Keren *psychologist*
Strauss, Robert Philip *economics professor*
Sussna, Edward *economist, educator*

Radnor
Rosnow, Ralph Leon *psychologist, educator*
Sicoli, Mary Louise Corbin *psychologist, educator*

Royersford
Krell-Morris, Cheri Lee *psychologist*

Rydal
Heebner, Albert Gilbert *retired economist, educator, bank executive*

Scranton
Parente, William Joseph *political science professor*
Yamanouchi, Midori *social sciences educato*

Shippensburg
France, Olin Kenneth, Jr. *psychologist*

State College
Isenberg, Ann Marie *psychologist*
Klein, Philip Alexander *economist*
Schaie, K(laus) Warner *human development psychology educator*

Swarthmore
Keith, Jennie *anthropology educator, acade administrator, writer*
Marecek, Jeanne *psychologist, educator*
O'Connell, Virginia Adams *sociologist*

University Park
De Jong, Gordon Frederick *demography professor, director*
Ford, Donald Herbert *psychologist, educato*
Humphrey, Craig Reed *social studies educa*
Ray, William Jackson *psychologist*
Roy, Rustum *citizen scientist*

Villanova
Johannes, John Roland *political science professor, dean*
Langran, Robert Williams *political scientist, educator*

Wayne
Stayton, William Ralph *psychologist, educa*

West Chester
Shaffer, Leigh S. *psychology professor*
Zlotowski, Martin *psychologist*

Wyncote
Koppel, Ross *sociology professor, researche*

Wynnewood
Wadden, Thomas Anthony *psychologist, educator*

RHODE ISLAND

Kingston
Alexander, Lewis McElwain *retired geogra educator*
Newman, Barbara Miller *psychologist, educ*
Turnbaugh, William Arthur *archaeologist, educator*

Newport
Brown, David William *economist, educator, consultant*

Pawtucket
Palav, Anjali *neuropsychologist*

Providence
Anderson, James Alfred *cognitive science professor*
Borts, George Herbert *economist, educator*
Chafee, Lincoln Davenport *political science professor, former senator*
Feldman, Allan Maurice *economist*
Goldstein, Sidney *sociologist, educator, demographer*
Heath, Dwight Braley *anthropologist, educ*
Hopmann, Philip Terrence *political science educator*
Houston, Stephen D. *anthropologist, educa*
Marsh, Robert Mortimer *sociologist, educa*
Miller, Linda B. *political scientist*
Paolino, Ronald Mario *clinical psychologis consultant, psychopharmacologist, pharn*
Putterman, Louis G. *economics professor*
Rizzo, Christie J. *psychologist*
Ryder, Harl Edgar *economist, educator*
Shapiro, Ronald Gary *psychologist*
Siqueland, Einar *psychologist, educator*
Stultz, Newell Maynard *retired political sc professor*
Wetle, Terrie Fox *gerontologist, educator, d*

Smithfield
Joseph, Antoine L. *sociologist, educator*

Martin, Janet May *psychologist,*
or

I CAROLINA

lle
A(ngele) Raymond *psychologist*

ston
, Daniel Oliver *retired psychologist*
onald J(ohn) *child psychiatry educator*
, Kenneth Joseph *psychologist*
Kathryn Moye *retired psychologist*

n
Gary Bentley *psychologist, educator*
Paul W. *economics professor*

bia
tty *political scientist, educator*
Charles William, Jr. *political science*
sor
lly Frazier *economics professor*
Jonathan M *archaeologist, researcher*
andra Jean *retired economics and*
ss professor
Robert William *econometrician*
Donald Ashmore *clinical research*
ologist
Ronald Parker *economics professor*

Island
, John David *political science educator*

ville
n, Wallace Dabney *retired economics*
sor, dean
e, Martha Randolph *psychologist,*
ltant

, Thomas Allen *psychologist*

n
, Darrell P. *social studies educator*

Pleasant
ichard A. *economist*

Hill
, Ameda Avrill *social sciences educator*

nburg
el, John Arne *political science professor*

boro
, Roberto *biopsychologist*

H DAKOTA

een
Mark Stephen *clinical psychologist*

ings
Howard Alden *retired economics*
ssor

n
on, Robert Ronald *psychologist,*
ultant

x
o, Larry Kay *psychologist*

Falls
Thomas Charles *psychologist*

llion
Alan Leland *retired political scientist,*
ator

ESSEE

r
Candyace *psychologist*

anooga
Alan A. *economics professor*
, Richard Lee *political science professor*

antown
schmidt, Thomas Orlando *economist,*
ultant

on
Sean *political science professor*

ville
William Marvin III *anthropology educator*
d, Charles Leslie *sociologist, educator*
Diana Koffman *sociologist, educator*
, Isa Maria *political scientist, educator,*
er, writer
ns, Otis Hammond, Jr. *political science*
essor, law educator

phis
Allen Overton, Jr. *psychologist, educator*
n, Jeffrey Scott *psychology professor*
n, Johnny *research psychologist,*
ultant

reesboro
t, Kevin D. *social studies educator,*
archer
Christopher Carnahan *economist*

ville
cao, Erlete Malveira *psychologist,*
cator
Margaret Mendenhall *economist,*
sultant, law educator
Randolph *psychology professor*

Buckles, Stephen Gary *economist, educator*
Cornfield, Daniel Benjamin *sociology educator*
Dillehay, Tom D. *anthropologist, educator*
Fulmer, Douglas Alan *political scientist,*
consultant, journalist
Guinsburg, Philip Fried *alcohol and substance*
abuse counselor
Hargrove, Erwin Charles, Jr. *political science*
professor
Havens, Murray Clark *political scientist,*
educator
Hinshaw, Carroll Elton *economics professor*
Lane, Cornell D. *psychology professor, director*
Lazar, Irving *psychologist*
McCarty, Richard Charles *psychology professor,*
dean
Morton-Young, Tommie *psychology professor,*
writer
Ridley, Carolyn Fludd *retired social studies*
educator
Schoggen, Phil H(oward) *psychologist, educator*
Westfield, Fred Meinhard *economics professor*

Oak Ridge
Colston, Freddie Charles *political science*
professor

TEXAS

Arlington
Brainerd, Charles J(on) *psychologist,*
mathematics professor
Buckner, Joyce *psychologist, educator*
Cole, Richard Louis *political scientist, educator*
Ramsey, Charles Eugene *sociologist, educator*

Austin
Blodgett, Warren Terrell *public affairs educator*
Bost, Jane Morgan *psychologist*
Buchanan, Bruce, II, *political science professor*
Burnham, Walter Dean *political science*
professor
Cooper, William Wager *economics, accounting*
and finance professor, dean
Dumas, Sara Lee *psychologist*
Dusansky, Richard *economist, educator*
Firey, Walter Irving, Jr. *retired sociologist*
Glade, William Patton, Jr. *economics professor*
Hamermesh, Daniel Selim *economics professor*
Hardin, Dale Wayne *political science professor*
Hester, Thomas Roy *anthropologist, educator*
Holtzman, Wayne Harold *psychologist, educator*
Kendrick, David Andrew *economist, educator*
Loehlin, John Clinton *psychologist, educator*
Lowry, Alaire Howard *psychologist*
Magee, Stephen Pat *economics professor, finance*
professor
McFadden, Dennis *psychologist, educator*
Reid, Jackson Brock *psychologist, educator*
Roach, James Robert *retired political science*
professor
Rostow, Elspeth Davies *political science*
professor
Schmitt, Karl Michael *retired political scientist*
Serafine, Mary Louise *psychologist, educator,*
lawyer
Walter, Virginia Lee *psychologist, educator*
Williams, Anna Lassiter *psychologist, researcher*
Williams, Roberton Capell III *economics*
professor

Bellaire
Mayo, Clyde Calvin *psychologist, educator*

Belton
Erlund, Cecilia Wharton *psychology professor,*
small business owner

Brooks City-Base
Villarreal, Roberto Escamilla *retired political*
science researcher, educator, administrator

Brownsville
Soldan, Angelika *political science educator,*
philosopher

Canyon
Hueston, Harry Raymond, II, *criminal justice*
educator, researcher
Thoman, Roy Edward *political scientist,*
educator

Carrollton
Wilson, Kristen Ellen *psychologist*

College Station
Arnold, J(ames) Barto III *marine archaeologist*
Bass, George Fletcher *retired archaeology*
educator
Edwards, George Charles III *political science*
professor, writer
Furubotn, Eirik Grundtvig *economics professor*
Greenhut, Melvin Leonard *economist, educator*
MacOpiyo, Laban Adero *geographer, researcher,*
ecologist
Meier, Kenneth John *political scientist*
Moroney, John Rodgers *economist, educator*
Ory, Marcia Gail *social science researcher*
Phillips, Charles David *gerontologist, researcher,*
medical educator
Van Riper, Paul Pritchard *political science*
professor

Corpus Christi
Cutlip, Randall Brower *retired psychologist,*
university president emeritus

Dallas
Betts, Dianne Connally *economist, educator*
Castillo, Christine Lynn *pediatric*
neuropsychologist
Cochran, Mona Sheinfeld *retired economics*
professor
Free Hosford, Mary Moore *biological and*
medical anthropologist

Freidel, David Alan *archaeologist,*
educator
Kemper, Robert Van *anthropologist, educator,*
minister
Oualline, Viola Jackson *psychologist, consultant*

Dayton
Davis, Kelli Ansley *social studies educator*

Denton
Alexander, Jim R. *social sciences educator*
Belfiglio, Valentine John *political science*
professor
Nievar, M. Angela *social sciences professor*
Ver Duin, D'Arlene K. *sociologist, researcher*
Yang, Philip Q. *sociologist*

Edinburg
Benham, Grant *psychologist, researcher*
Mollick, Andre Varella *economics professor,*
researcher

El Paso
Penley, Julie Anne *psychologist, educator*

Fort Worth
Colaluca, Beth *pediatric neurpsychologist*
Dees, Sandra Kay Martin *psychologist, research*
scientist
Jackson, Donald Wilson *political science*
professor, lawyer
Mullendore, Walter Edward *retired economist*
Simpson, Dennis Dwayne *psychologist, educator*

Fredericksburg
Vinson, David Berwick *neuropsychologist*

Georgetown
Lopreato, Joseph *evolutionary sociologist, writer*
Purdy, Jesse E. *psychology professor*

Glen Rose
Lane, Willa Joan Manes *retired psychologist*

Harlingen
Lytle, Michael Allen *forensic criminologist,*
consultant

Houston
Ayadi, Mary Olufemi *health economist, educator*
Black, Donna Lord *psychologist*
Brito, Dagobert Llanos *economics professor*
Bryant, John Bradbury *economics professor,*
consultant
Carman, Carol A. *psychologist, educator*
Condit, Linda Faulkner *retired economist*
Cuthbertson, Gilbert Morris *political science*
professor
Davidson, Chandler *sociologist, educator*
Demouy, Alyson M. *social studies educator*
Evans, Karen Ann *social studies educator*
Florian-Lacy, Dorothy *psychologist, educator*
Foster, Dale Warren *political scientist, educator,*
real estate agent, accountant, management
consultant
Francis, James Stephen, Jr. *psychology professor,*
psychologist
Grossett, Deborah Lou *psychologist, consultant*
Gutheinz, Joseph Richard, Jr. *criminal justice*
educator, consultant, lawyer
Haensly, Patricia Anastacia *psychology professor*
Jenkins, Sheila Alnita *psychologist*
Justice, (David) Blair *psychology educator,*
writer
Lee, Donghyung *psychologist*
Lehrer, Kenneth Eugene *economic consulting*
company executive
Martin, William C. *social studies educator,*
writer
Miller, Janel Howell *psychologist*
Paul, Gordon Lee *behavioral scientist,*
psychologist
von der Mehden, Fred R. *political science*
professor
Wong-Liang, Eirene Ming *psychologist*
Yatsenko, Yuri Petrovich *economics professor,*
mathematician

Hurst
Mabry, Philip T. *political scientist, consultant*

Laredo
Riggs, William W. *social sciences educator*

Longview
Mann, True Sandlin *psychologist, consultant*

Mcallen
Rebuelta, Avelino Luis *public administration*
educator

Mesquite
Byrd, Kathryn Susan *psychologist, educator*

Midland
Sherpa, Fran Magruder *geography educator*

New Braunfels
Wilson, James Lee *retired geology educator,*
consultant

Olney
Timmons, Gordon David *economics professor,*
farmer

Plano
Glenn, Marshall Andrew *psychologist*
O'Loughlin-Brooks, Jennifer L. *psychology*
professor
Worsfold, Victor Leonard *retired social sciences*
educator

Post
Earl, Lewis Harold *economist, consultant, lawyer*

Prairie View
Prestage, Jewel Limar *political science professor*

Richardson
Andrews, Melinda Wilson *human development*
researcher
Berry, Brian Joe Lobley *geographer, educator,*
urban planner, political economist
Griffith, Daniel Alva *geography educator*
Hicks, Donald Albert *economics professor*
Sandler, Todd Michael *economist, political*
scientist, educator

San Antonio
Anderson, Anita L. *psychology professor*
Austin, Lola Houston *psychologist*
Bellows, Thomas John *political scientist,*
educator
Breit, William *economist, educator, writer*
Fonseca, Joseph Mojica, Jr. *political science*
professor
Furino, Antonio *economist, educator*
Ribble, Ronald George *psychologist, educator,*
writer, behavioral consultant
Spiro, Herbert John *political scientist,*
ambassador

San Marcos
Huber, John D. *psychologist, consultant*

Stafford
Krenek, Mary Louise *political scientist,*
researcher

Sugar Land
Harribance, Sean Lalsingh *parapsychologist*

Victoria
Harrington, Rick *psychology professor*

Waco
Grinols, Earl Leroy III *economist, educator*

UTAH

Boulder
Gove, Walter R. *sociology educator*

Bountiful
Mangum, Garth Leroy *retired economist*

Ogden
Amsel, Eric David *psychology professor*

Provo
Brown, Ralph Browning *sociologist, educator*
Creer, Thomas Laselle *psychologist, educator,*
writer
Gantt, Edwin ElRay *psychology professor*
Hopkins, Ramona O. *psychologist, neuroscientist*
Pedersen, Darhl Max *psychology professor*
Porter, Blaine Robert Milton *sociology professor,*
psychology professor
Sawyer, Melvin Wayne *psychologist*
Seipel, Michael *social sciences educator*

Salt Lake City
Benjamin, Lorna Smith *psychologist*
Bilginsoy, Cihan *economics professor*
Kumpfer, Karol Linda *research psychologist*
Livne, Nava Levia *psychologist, researcher*
O'Connell, James F. *anthropologist, educator*

Sandy
Smith, Willard Grant *psychologist*

Washington
De Vany, Arthur Stacy *economics professor*

VERMONT

Brandon
Farnsworth, Frank Albert *retired economics*
professor

Burlington
Cutler, Stephen Joel *sociologist, educator*
Lawson, Robert Bernard *psychology professor*
Sampson, Samuel Franklin *sociology educator*

Castleton
Roper, Scott Christopher *geographer, researcher*

Charlotte
Naylor, Thomas Herbert *economist, educator,*
consultant

Greensboro
Gilpin, Robert George, Jr. *political science*
professor

Middlebury
Colander, David Charles *economist, educator*
Lamberti, Marjorie *retired social studies*
educator

Montgomery Center
Oktavec, Eileen M. *anthropologist, artist*

Newbury
Doig, Jameson Wallace *political science*
professor

Norwich
Foster, Michael Kirk *anthropologist, linguist*

Wallingford
Gutmann, David Leo *psychology professor*

VIRGINIA

Alexandria
Bezold, Clement *futurist*
Carville, James, Jr., (Chester James Carville)
political scientist, consultant
Corrothers, Helen Gladys *criminal justice official*

Johnson, Edgar McCarthy *psychologist*
Krueger, Gerald Peter *psychologist*
Lindsey, Sara Ann *sociologist, educator*
Matalin, Mary *political consultant*
McConville, Judy Allen *social studies educator*
Revere, Virginia Lehr *psychologist*
Roof, Michael Kitching *demographer, researcher*

Annandale
Bragg, Cheryl Fuller *psychologist*
Carvalho, Julie Ann *psychologist*

Arlington
Boorstein, Laurence *economist, educator*
Buckley, Francis H. *economist, lawyer, educator*
Chipman, Susan Elizabeth *psychologist, researcher*
Clump, Michael Aden *psychologist, educator*
Davis, Lynn Etheridge *political scientist, educator*
Gunn, Joseph Ridgeway III *consulting economist*
Lilenfeld, Lisa Rachelle *psychology professor, psychologist*
Siddayao, Corazón Morales *economist, educator, consultant*
Sundquist, James Lloyd *retired political scientist*
Tolchin, Susan Jane *political science professor, writer*
Vitz, Paul Clayton *psychologist, educator*
von Furstenberg, George Michael *economics professor, researcher*

Blacksburg
Bryant, Clifton Dow *sociologist, educator*
Jannuzi, F. Tomasson *economics professor*

Bluemont
Kobetz, Richard William *criminologist, consultant*

Charlottesville
Abraham, Henry Julian *retired political science professor*
Cornell, Dewey Gene *psychologist*
Elzinga, Kenneth Gerald *economics professor*
Handler, Jerome Sidney *anthropology educator*
Hanft, Ruth S. Samuels *economist, consultant*
Henry, Laurin Luther *public affairs educator*
Hymes, Dell Hathaway *anthropologist, educator*
Keen, Rachel *psychology professor*
Moreno, Jonathan *bioethicist*
Pate, Robert Hewitt, Jr. *counselor educator*
Plog, Stephen E. *anthropologist, educator*
Quandt, William Bauer *political scientist*
Reppucci, Nicholas Dickon *psychologist, educator*
Rhoads, Steven Eric *political science professor*
Sabato, Larry Joseph *political science professor, director*
Sykes, Gresham M'Cready *sociologist, educator, artist*
Wagner, Roy *anthropology educator, researcher*
Whitaker, John King *retired economics professor*
Zelikow, Philip David *public policy educator, former federal official*

Chesapeake
Sari, Dana *psychologist*

Danville
Lea, Robert Lee III *social sciences educator*

Eastville
Williams, Ida Jones *consumer and home economics educator, writer*

Fairfax
Barth, Michael Carl *economist*
Bennett, James Thomas *economics professor*
Buchanan, James McGill *economist, educator*
Cowen, Tyler *economics professor*
Dennis, Rutledge M. *sociologist, educator*
Kash, Don Eldon *political science professor*
Pfiffner, James Price *political science professor*
Pruitt, Dean Garner *psychologist, educator*
Smith, Vernon Lomax *economist, researcher*
Steele, Howard Loucks *economic development consultant, author*
Travis, Toni-Michelle C. *political scientist, educator*
Wagner, Richard E. *economist, educator*

Falls Church
Calkins, Susannah Eby *retired economist*
Clizbe, John Anthony *psychologist, social services administrator*
Fink, Charles Augustin *behavioral systems scientist*
Green, James Wyche *sociologist, anthropologist, consultant, psychotherapist*
Hammerman, Herbert *retired economist*
Roussel, Lee Dennison *economist*
Weiss, Armand Berl *economist, association management executive*

Farmville
Dorrill, William Franklin *political scientist, educator*

Fort Belvoir
O'Kane, Barbara Lynn *research psychologist*

Fort Lee
Leppo, Lisa Marie *forensic anthropologist*

Fredericksburg
Rampersad, Peggy A. Snellings *sociologist, consultant*
Sisk, Fred Dean *retired cartographer*

Glen Allen
Harter, John J. *economic analyst*

Hampton
Holmes, Leonard George *psychologist*
Johnson, Leona Melissa *psychology professor, researcher*

Harrisonburg
Grayson, Joann Hess *psychology professor*

Jamestown
Kelso, William M. *archaeologist*

Jeffersonton
Armor, David J. *sociologist*

Lexington
Elmes, David Gordon *psychologist, educator*
Jarrard, Leonard Everett *psychologist, educator*
Phillips, Charles Franklin, Jr. *retired economist*
Winfrey, John Crawford *economist, educator*

Lynchburg
Duff, Ernest Arthur *political scientist, educator*

Mc Lean
Auerbach, Anita L. *clinical psychologist*
Johnson, Omotunde Evan George *economist*
Nothaft, Frank Emile *economist*
Schneider, Peter Raymond *political scientist*
Zakheim, Dov Solomon *economist, former federal agency administrator*

Mechanicsville
Wells, Mary Julia *psychologist*

Midlothian
Stringham, Luther Winters *retired economist, retired health facility administrator*

Newington
Robertson, Jean Elizabeth *sociology educator*

Newport News
McDougall, Heather Renee *political science professor*

Norfolk
Gómez, Edwin *social sciences educator*
Neumann, Serina Ann Louise *psychologist, researcher*

Portsmouth
Ojeda, Ana Maria *therapist, clinical caseworker*

Purcellville
Grow, Robert Theodore *economist, trade association executive*

Radford
Boyd, Donna Catherine *physical anthropologist, educator*

Reston
Payne, Roger Lee *geographer*

Richmond
Feinstein, Brett *political scientist, consultant*
Geary, David Patrick *criminal justice educator, consultant, writer*
Hall, James Curtis *business professor*
McCall, Shedrick Dwight *psychologist*
Palen, J(oseph) John *social sciences educator*

Springfield
Chatelier, Paul Richard *aviation psychologist*
de Haan, Henry John *research psychologist*

Sterling
Blum, John Curtis *agricultural economist*
Cleveland, Harlan *political scientist, public affairs executive*

Sweet Briar
Miller, Reuben George *retired economics professor*
Shea, Brent Mack *social sciences educator*

Warrenton
Malmgren, Harald Bernard *economist*
Pribram, Karl Harry *neuroscience and psychology educator, brain researcher*

Williamsburg
Kerns, Virginia B. *anthropologist, writer*
Krakauer, Sarah Yael *psychologist*
Lange, Carl James *retired psychology professor*
Smith, Roger Winston *retired political theory educator*

Woodford
Orrock, Robert Dickson *agricultural educator, state legislator*

WASHINGTON

Bellingham
Burdge, Rabel James *sociology educator*

Camano Island
de Vries, Rimmer *economist*

Colville
Culton, Sarah Alexander *psychologist, educator*
Forman, Robert Edgar *retired sociology professor*

Ellensburg
Miller, Maxine Lynch *retired home economist, retired interior designer, educator*

Friday Harbor
MacGinitie, Walter Harold *psychologist, educator*

Granite Falls
Hamilton, Pamela Jane *psychologist, special education educator*

Hansville
Blalock, Ann Bonar *evaluation researcher*

Issaquah
Drazdoff, Nola Gay *psychologist*

La Conner
Garcia, John *psychologist, educator*
Knopf, Kenyon Alfred *economist, educator*

Olympia
Jun, Heesoon *psychology professor*

Pullman
Arthur, Linda Louise *sociologist, educator*
Jussaume, Raymond Adelard *political science professor*
Kohler, Timothy A. *social sciences educator*
McSweeney, Frances Kaye *psychology professor*
Rawlins, V. Lane *economics professor, retired academic administrator*
Warner, Dennis Allan *psychology professor*

Richland
Roop, Joseph McLeod *economist*

Seattle
Borgatta, Edgar F. *sociologist, educator*
Brammer, Lawrence Martin *psychologist, educator*
Fiedler, Fred Edward *retired organizational psychology educator, consultant*
Greenwald, Anthony Galt *psychology educator*
Gross, Edward *retired sociologist*
Hirschman, Charles, Jr. *sociologist, educator*
Olson, David John *political science professor*
Patrick, Donald Lee *sociologist, educator*
Plotnick, Robert David *economic consultant, educator*
Reskin, Barbara F. *sociologist*
Rosenblum, Jeffrey Ira *consulting economist*
Sarason, Irwin G. *psychology professor*
Schwartz, Pepper Judith *sociologist, educator*
Turnovsky, Stephen John *economics professor*
Tuthill, Oliver W., Jr. *psychologist, consultant, independent film producer, director*
van den Berghe, Pierre Louis *sociologist*
Whittaker, James Kevin *retired social sciences educator*

Spokane
Houseman, Gerald L. *political science professor, writer*
May, Richard B. *psychology professor*

Tacoma
Stewart, Susan Marie *psychologist, educator*

University Place
Bourgaize, Robert G. *economist*

Vancouver
Archer, Stephen Hunt *economist, educator*

WEST VIRGINIA

Charleston
DiPino, Raymond Kim *psychologist*

Fairmont
Fulda, Michael *political scientist, educator, space policy researcher*

Morgantown
Bell, Lewis Clay *economics professor, government administrator*
Hayes, Angela Mariw *psychologist*
Kim, Hong Nack *political science professor*
Rieder, Keith Lee *psychologist*
Waller, Stacey *psychologist*
Witt, Tom *economics researcher, educator*

Parkersburg
Branch, Michael Lee *social studies educator, consultant*
McClung, Mary Denise *psychology professor*
McClung, Phil Oran *psychology professor*

WISCONSIN

Beloit
Davis, Harry Rex *political science professor*

Brookfield
Carter, Charlene Ann *psychologist*
Zander, Gaillienne Glashow *psychologist*

Cascade
Baumann, Carol Edler *retired political scientist*

Eau Claire
Dick, Raymond Dale *psychologist, educator*

Fitchburg
Bhargava, Ashok *retired economics professor*

Glendale
Brosio, Richard Anthony *social studies educator*

Green Bay
Alesch, Daniel James *social sciences educator, researcher*

Kenosha
Cyr, Arthur I. *political science and economics professor*

Lancaster
Croft, Candace Ann *psychology professor, academic administrator, small business owner*

Madison
Andreano, Ralph Louis *economist, educator*
Bennett, Kenneth Alan *retired biological anthropologist*
Brock, William Allen III *economist, educator*
Chapman, Loren J. *psychology professor*

Culbertson, Frances Mitchell *psycholog professor*
Davidson, Richard J. *psychology and ps professor, researcher*
Goldberger, Arthur Stanley *economics p*
Graf, Truman Frederick *agricultural ec educator*
Greenfield, Norman Samuel *psychologis educator*
Hansen, W. Lee *economics professor*
Mueller, Willard Fritz *economics profes*
Nichols, Donald Arthur *economist, educ*
Rice, Joy Katharine *psychologist, educa educator*
Sack, Robert David *geography professo*
Shafer, Byron Edwin *American governm educator*
Strier, Karen Barbara *anthropologist, ed*
Thomas, J. Mark *sociologist, educator,*
Viscovich, Nancy Anne *psychologist*
Wilson, Franklin D. *sociology educator*
Wolfe, Barbara L. *economics professor, researcher*
Young, Merwin Crawford *political scien professor*

Middleton
Dorner, Peter Paul *retired economist, ed*

Milwaukee
Baez, JoAnne Marie *school psychologist*
Ksobiech, Kate *sociologist, educator*
Paulson, Belden Henry *political scientist educator*
Quereshi, Mohammed Younus *retired ps professor*
Sinclair, Stephen Lawrence Rabehl *psyc educator*

Oconomowoc
Sieckert, Kristine Ellen *school psycholog consultant*

Oshkosh
Gruberg, Martin *political science profess*

River Falls
LeCapitaine, John Edward *counseling psychology educator, researcher, write*

Stevens Point
Cwiertniak, Robert L. *psychologist, educ consultant*

Superior
Carroll, David William *psychology profe*
Taylor, Winnifred Jane *psychologist*

Waukesha
Franze, Robert Dennis *social studies edu*
Graham, George Andrew, Jr. *psychologis consultant*

Whitefish Bay
Hawkins, Brett William *retired political s professor*

WYOMING

Cheyenne
Newman, Steven David *psychologist, con*

Fairview
Luginbuehl, Marsha Lee *psychologist*

Laramie
Allen, John Logan *geographer, departme chairman*
Chai, Winberg *political science professor, foundation administrator*
Crocker, Thomas Dunstan *economics prof*
Gill, George Wilhelm *retired anthropolog*
Shaffer, Sherrill Lynn *economist*

Wilson
Breitenbach, Mary Louise McGraw *psych chemical dependency counselor*

TERRITORIES OF THE UN STATES

GUAM

Mangilao
Dames, Vivian Loyola *social sciences edu*

PUERTO RICO

Guaynabo
Guisasola Gamez, Elina *psychologist*

Mayaguez
Aguero, Joseph Edward *psychologist, edu*

San Juan
Folch-Serrano, Karen D. *psychologist, con*

CANADA

ALBERTA

Calgary
Stebbins, Robert Alan *sociology educator*

Edmonton
Freeman, Milton Malcolm Roland *anthrop educator*

wn, Lauriston Livingston, Jr. *consulting ychologist*

it Albert
hawa, Bikkar Singh *retired psychologist, ired educator*

ITISH COLUMBIA

naby
tingham, Paul Jeffrey *criminologist, ucator*
ra, Doreen *psychology professor, researcher*

couver
der, Max Sigmund *psychology and ysiology professor, researcher*
er, George Arthur *political science professor*
i, Kalevi Jacque *political scientist, partment chairman*
elman, Jonathan Rhys *economics professor, blic policy researcher*
nce, Jean A. *political scientist, educator*
hak, Maureen Patricia *anthropology and ciology educator, academic administrator*
etz, Peter Newman *economist, researcher, licy analysis educator*
n, Inger Anna *retired psychologist*
rer, Ronald Alexander *economics professor*
feld, Peter *psychologist, educator*
Richard Chisholm *psychology professor, searcher*
er, Michael Angus *economist, director*

oria
, Timothy Milton *political science professor*

t Vancouver
s, Parzival *economist, researcher*

V BRUNSWICK

dericton
on, Gary Michael *gerontologist, educator*

/A SCOTIA

ster Basin
Johnston, Elizabeth *economist, consultant*

fax
sen, Finn *political science professor*
, Denis Winfield *political science professor, partment chairman*

TARIO

milton
ge, Peter James *economist, educator*
, Ellen Bouchard *psychology professor, rontologist*

gston
ki, Stephan Felix *economics professor*
Kinnon, James Gordon *economist, educator*
el, John *political scientist*

don
nport, Paul *economics professor*
er, David Ernest William *economics fessor*
acott, Ronald Johnston *retired economics fessor*

gara-on-the-Lake
, Robert Edward *economist, educator*

th York
, Howard *psychology professor*

wa
ks, David Barry *resource economist*

nto
on, Wendy Kathleen *economics professor*
son, Kingsley George *retired psychologist*
son, Albert Kirk *social studies educator*
ner, Gerald Karl *economics professor*
onald, Hugh Ian *economics professor, blic policy professor, academic ministrator*
o, John Henry Alexander *economics fessor, writer*
Robert Cranford *political scientist, cator*
Jeffrey Raymond *retired economist, public vant, trade unionist*

erloo
ng, Harold Joseph *sociology educator*

BEC

treal
er, Michael *political science professor*
-Smith, Fumiko *anthropologist, educator*
orinis, Kenneth N. *economist*
ack, Ronald *psychology professor*
, Baldev Raj *political science professor*
andeau, Andre Gabriel *criminologist, cator*
T. V. *social sciences educator*
auld, Andre *economist, educator*
rt, Jane *psychology professor*
, Denis *criminologist, educator*
ncourt, Jean-Guy *sociology educator, earcher*
r, Harold Myron *political science professor*

Outremont
Dufour, Jean-Marie *economist, statistician, educator*

Quebec City
Belanger, Gerard *economics professor*

Sainte-Foy
Tremblay, Marc Adélard *anthropologist, educator*

Toronto
Katchanovski, Ivan G. *political scientist, researcher*

MEXICO

Guadalajara
Durand, Jorge *anthropologist*

ARGENTINA

Buenos Aires
Lopez-Murphy, Ricardo Hipolito *economist*

AUSTRALIA

Armadale
Neil, Sandra Eilleen Silverberg *psychologist*

Hackett
Leigh, Andrew Keith *economist, researcher*

DENMARK

Copenhagen
Kurrild-Klitgaard, Peter *political science professor*
Olgaard, Anders *economics professor*

EGYPT

Cairo
Hawass, Zahi *archaeologist, educator, writer*
Lesch, Ann Mosely *political scientist, educator*

ENGLAND

Cambridge
Mirrlees, Sir James Alexander *economics professor*
Renfrew, Andrew Colin (Lord Renfrew of Kaimsthorn) *archaeologist, educator, director*
Richard, Alison Fettes *anthropology educator, academic administrator*

London
Dahrendorf, Lord Ralf Gustav *sociologist, educator*
Junz, Helen B. *economist*
Kuper, Adam Jonathan *anthropologist, educator*
Portes, Richard David *economics professor*

Reading
Dunning, John Harry *economics educator*

ESTONIA

Tallinn
Köörna, Arno *economist, educator*

FRANCE

Paris
Cherkaoui, Mohamed *sociologist*
de Menil, Georges *economist, educator*
Fitoussi, Jean-Paul Samuel *economics professor*

GERMANY

APO
Adams, Julian Timothy *psychologist*

Rostock
Vaupel, James W. *demographer*

GREECE

Athens
Kalamotousakis, George John *economist, merchant banker, educator*

HONG KONG
Roach, Stephen S. *economist*

INDIA

Baner Pune
Ohri, Sangeeta Jean Mary *social studies educator*

Jaipur
Gupta, V. P. *economist, academic administrator*

INDONESIA

Jakarta
Tilaar, Henry A.R. *social sciences educator*

ISRAEL

Arad
Hollander, Samuel *economist, educator*

ITALY

Pisa
Settis, Salvatore *archaeologist, art historian*

Rome
Gros-Pietro, Gian Maria *economics professor*
Scognamiglio Pasini, Carlo *economics and finance professor, senator*
Westley, John Richard *economist*

JAPAN

Kobe
Inoue, Shun *sociologist*
Shrestha, Manoj Lal *economics professor, policy studies researcher*

Mie
Isshiki, Masayuki *sociologist, educator, dean*

Nagoya
Kajitani, Motohisa *sociology educator*

Tokyo
Fukushima, Kiyohiko *economist*
Gyohten, Toyoo *economist*
Hirayama, Eiji *psychologist, educator*
Maki, Atsushi *economics professor*
Nishiyama, Chiaki *economist, educator*

Tsukuba
Hanaki, Nobuyuki *economics professor*

NETHERLANDS

Utrecht
Tielman, Rob A.P. *social sciences educator*

NORWAY

Oslo
Karlsen, Paul Johan *psychologist, researcher, writer*

PHILIPPINES

Cebu City
Bate, Brian R. *retired psychologist*

REPUBLIC OF KOREA

Suwon
Lee, Tong Hun *economics professor*

RUSSIA

Moscow
Grigoriev, Sergei Aleksandrovich *political scientist, researcher*
Saltykov, Boris Georgievich *economist, politician*

SCOTLAND

Aberdeenshire
Talbot, Nyna Lucille *psychologist, writer*

SPAIN

Madrid
Pérez-Díaz, Víctor Miguel *sociology educator*

SRI LANKA

Colombo
Spain, James William *political scientist, writer*

TAIWAN

Pingtung
Fan, Tai-Sheng Allen *social scientist in computer education and computing, educator*

ADDRESS UNPUBLISHED

Adams, Robert McCormick *anthropologist, educator*
Ahmed, Syed Z. *anthropologist*
Aisen, Ari *economist, researcher*
Alberti-Chappell, Roxana Dearing *psychologist*
Alexander, Ascencion (Cency) H. *school psychologist, educator*
Aliber, Robert Z. *economist, educator*
Allen, Bruce Templeton *retired economics professor*
Allen, Jane Folger *psychologist*
Allen, Pamela Smith *retired psychologist, writer*
Allen, William Sheridan *retired social sciences educator*
Allender, Julie Ann *psychologist*
Alpher, Victor Seth *clinical psychologist, consultant*
Altman, Irwin *psychologist, educator*
Alvarez-Corona, Marti *school psychologist, educator*
Amling, Frederick *economist, educator, investment advisor*
Amoroso, Richard Louis *psychologist, educator*
Anderson, Bernard E. *economist*
Anderson, James George *sociologist, educator, communications educator*
Anthony-Perez, Bobbie Cotton Murphy *retired psychology professor*
Aponte, Frances *psychologist, educator*
Aschheim, Joseph *retired economist, educator*
Aumann, Robert John *economics professor*
Austin, Philip Edward *economics professor, former academic administrator*
Avant, Gayle *political scientist, educator*
Aviles, Alice Alers *psychologist*
Axilrod, Stephen Harvey *global economic consultant, economist*
Ayad, Joseph Magdy *retired psychologist*
Baba, Marietta Lynn *anthropologist, academic administrator*
Bacon, Phillip *geographer, author, consultant*
Baez-Feliciano, Doris V. *demographer, educator*
Baker, Marjane L. *social studies educator*
Baker, Paul Thornell *anthropology educator*
Balstad, Roberta *social scientist*
Barker, Richard Alexander *organizational psychologist*
Barnes, Samuel Henry *political science professor*
Bashi, Vilna Francine *sociology professor*
Bateson, Mary Catherine *retired anthropology educator, writer, lecturer*
Becerra Ibanez Pelliza, Julio C. *psychologist, consultant*
Beckett, Faye Trumbo *school psychologist*
Bergeson-Dana, Tonya *psychologist, researcher*
Bergsten, C. Fred *economist*
Bernsen, Harold John *political scientist, educator, retired military officer*
Bethea, Elizabeth *social sciences educator, psychologist, minister*
Blank, Rebecca Margaret *economist*
Bloomfield, Lincoln Palmer *political scientist*
Bluth, B. J. (Elizabeth Jean Catherine Bluth) *sociologist, aerospace technologist*
Boff, Kenneth Richard *engineering research psychologist*
Bonnell, Victoria Eileen *sociologist, educator*
Bourguignon, Erika Eichhorn *anthropologist, educator*
Bradburn, Norman M. *behavioral science educator*
Bredfeldt, John Creighton *economics educator, writer, retired military officer*
Bricker, Harvey Miller *retired anthropology educator*
Bricker, Victoria Reifler *anthropologist, educator*
Briggs, Philip James *political science professor, writer*
Brixiova, Zuzana *economist*
Brooks, Lynda Barbara *psychologist*
Brown, Amira Khalila *neuropsychologist, researcher*
Brown, Candia Post *psychologist*
Buchin, Jean *psychologist, educator*
Bullard, Judith Eve *psychologist, systems engineer*
Burns, Joseph M. *economist*
Burns, Marcelline *retired psychologist, researcher*
Butki, Brian David *psychologist, educator*
Butler, J(ohn) S(cott) *economist, educator*
Cacioppo, John Terrance *psychologist, educator, researcher*
Canes-Wrone, Brandice *political scientist, educator*
Canterbury-Counts, W. Douglas *psychologist*
Canu, William Henry *psychology professor*
Caplow, Theodore *sociologist*
Carfora, John Michael *economics professor, academic administrator*
Carides, George Warren *health economic statistics director*
Carliner, Geoffrey Owen *economist, director*
Carlsen, Mary Baird *clinical psychologist*
Carlson, Janet Frances *psychologist, educator*
Carson, Andrew Doyle *applied psychologist*
Carson, James Wood *psychologist*
Carton, Lonnie Caming *educational psychologist*
Case, Elizabeth Joy *psychology and educational assessment director*
Cavin, Susan Elizabeth *sociologist, writer*
Chang, Won *economist*
Chao, Ruth *psychologist, researcher*
Chatterjee, Anindya *economist, researcher*
Chatterton, Raymond Edward *economics educator*
Chowitz Placzek, Gail Louise *school psychologist*
Christian, James Wayne *economist*
Clark, Caleb Morgan *political scientist, educator*
Clark, William Arthur V. *geographer*
Cochran, John P. *economics professor*
Cohen, Philip N. *sociologist, educator*
Collier, William Gayle *psychology professor, researcher*
Collins, Harker *retired economist, manufacturing and publishing executive*
Cotten, Annie Laura *psychologist, educator*
County, Janis Emerson *school counselor*
Cox, Gary Walter *political science professor*
Culcasi, Karen *geographer, researcher*
Cullari, Salvatore Santino *clinical psychologist, educator, writer*

Daniel, Coldwell III *economist, educator, entrepreneur*
Danielsen, Albert Leroy *economics professor, energy and utilities consultant*
Da Pena, Eileen *psychologist*
David, Martin Heidenhain *economics professor*
Davidson, John Kenneth, Sr. *sociologist, educator, researcher, writer, consultant*
Davis, James Allan *gerontologist, educator*
Dean, Edwin Robinson *economist, educator, consultant*
DeAngelo, LeAnna Marie *research health psychologist, writer*
Dejud, Carlos *psychologist*
Denevan, William Maxfield *geographer, historical ecologist, educator*
DeVaris, Jeannette Mary *psychologist*
Dierickx, Constance Ricker *psychologist, management consultant*
DiPrima, Richard Joseph *neuropsychologist*
Dixit, Avinash Kamalakar *economics professor*
Dobriansky, Lev Eugene *economics professor, diplomat*
Dole, Arthur Alexander *former psychology professor, department chairman*
Dooley, Brendan David *criminologist, researcher*
Dore, Patricia Ann *psychologist*
Dowd, Morgan Daniel *retired political science professor, dean*
Dowling, Edward Thomas *economics professor*
Downen, Robert Lynn *international affairs analyst and political consultant, editor, writer*
Drummond, Dorothy Weitz *geography education consultant, educator, author*
Duckworth, Angela Lee *psychology professor*
Durell, Viviane G. *psychologist, small business owner*
Dwyer, Gerald Paul, Jr. *economist, bank executive*
Dykas, Matthew J. *psychologist*
Earle, Timothy Keese *anthropology educator*
Eberhart, Steven Wesley *psychologist*
Eischen, Donald F. *psychologist, educator, writer*
Eley, Lynn W. *political science professor, retired mayor*
Ellickson, Donald Lien *retired economist, county official*
Engel, Bernard Theodore *psychologist, educator*
Eriksson, Steven *social studies educator*
Eron, Leonard David *retired psychology professor*
Eskew, Henry Lawrence, Jr. *economist, consultant*
Farmer, Christopher J. *political scientist, writer*
Feller, Avi *political science scholar*
Fels, Rendigs *economist, educator*
Finnberg, Elaine Agnes *psychologist, editor*
Fisher, Seymour *psychologist, educator*
Fishman, Joshua Aaron *sociolinguist, educator*
Fontes, Patricia J. *psychologist*
Franklin, Margery Bodansky *psychology professor, researcher*
French, Laurence Armand *social sciences educator*
Friedman, James Winstein *economist, educator*
Frost, Ellen Louise *political economist*
Fu, Yan Cindy *psychologist*
Funseth, Robert Lloyd Eric Martin *international consultant, retired diplomat*
Futrell, Steven *psychologist*
Gaber, Robert *psychologist*
Gallucci-Breithaupt, Adrianne *psychologist, social worker*
Garruto, Ralph Michael *biomedical anthropologist, biologist, educator*
Geake, Raymond Robert *psychologist*
Genis, Sean A. *philosophy, politics and economics scholar*
Ginsburg, Norton Sydney *retired geographer*
Glendening, Terry Sky *psychologist*
Glenn, Norval Dwight *sociologist, educator*
Godinez, Joshua Ray *social sciences educator*
Goldston, Stephen Eugene *community psychologist, educator, consultant*
Goleman, Daniel Jay *psychologist, journalist*
Golub, Sharon Bramson *retired psychologist, educator*
Granott, Nira *psychologist, researcher*
Grant, Carmen Hill *psychologist, psychotherapist*
Greeley, Andrew Moran *sociologist, writer*
Greenberg, Ira Arthur *psychologist*
Greenwood, Janet Kae Daly *psychologist, academic administrator, marketing professional*
Griffith, Monica *psychologist*
Groenheim, Henri Arnold *psychologist, consultant*
Gubser, Peter Anton *political scientist, writer, educator*
Haber, Pierre-Claude *psychologist*
Haber, Ralph Norman *psychology consultant, researcher, educator*
Hahn, Frank Horace *economics professor*
Haines, Richard Foster *retired psychologist*
Haining, Jeane *psychologist*
Hall, Jay *social psychologist*
Hall, John Fry *retired psychologist*
Halmrast, Lynn James *psychologist*
Hammond, Paul Young *political science professor*
Hampton, Lori Beth *psychologist*
Hanushek, Eric Alan *economics professor*
Hardy, Richard Allen, Jr. *psychologist, educator*
Haring-Smith, Whitney *political science scholar*
Harshbarger, Richard B. *retired economics professor*
Hart, Karen E. *psychologist, consultant*
Hartstein, Harold Herman *psychology educator, consultant*
Hartzell, Irene Janofsky *retired psychologist*
Hauner, David *economist*
Hawes, Bess Lomax *retired folklorist*
Haywood, H(erbert) Carl(ton) *psychologist, educator*
Hefferan, Colien Joan *economist*
Helfgott, Roy B. *economist, educator*
Herod, Charles Carteret *Afro-American studies educator*
Hidden-Dodson, Nancy *retired psychologist, consultant, educator*
Hires, William Leland *psychologist, consultant*
Hitz, Frederick Porter *public and international affairs educator*
Hjort, Howard Warren *economist, consultant*
Holmes, Paul Luther *political scientist, educational consultant*
Holmstrom, Lynda Lytle *sociologist, educator*
Holzer, Harry Joseph *economist, educator*
Hope, Kathy Mitchell *social studies educator*
Hopkins, Brenda Luvenia *social sciences educator, minister*
Horn, Wade Frederick *psychologist, former federal agency administrator*
Horner, Althea Jane *psychologist*
Houk, Eric *economics professor*
Howrey, Eugene Philip *retired economics and statistics professor*
Hughes, Ann Hightower *retired economist, trade association administrator*
Hughes, Deanna Elma *psychologist*
Jain, Rachna D. *psychologist, consultant, small business owner*
James, Estelle *economist, educator*
Jefferson, Daisy M. *social studies educator*
Jett, Stephen Clinton *geography and textiles educator, researcher*
Johnson, Albert Wesley *retired political science professor, public official*
Johnson, Benjamin F., VI, *economist, consultant*
Johnson, J(anet) Susan *psychologist*
Johnson, Kimberly Cassandra *psychologist*
Jones, Cleopatra Celeste *retired gerontologist, sociologist, educator*
Jones, Sarah B. *psychologist*
Jordan, Robert Smith *political science professor, civilian military employee*
Juviler, Peter Henry *political scientist, educator*
Kahana, Eva Frost *sociology educator*
Kaliski, Mary *psychologist*
Kane, Michael Barry *social science research executive*
Karayan, Ani A. *psychologist, consultant*
Karim, Muhammad Bazlul *political scientist, educator*
Karson, Samuel *psychologist, educator*
Kaslow, Florence Whiteman *psychologist, educator, family business consultant*
Kauffold, Ruth Elizabeth *psychologist*
Kayser, Brian D. *retired psychologist, writer*
Kellner, Irwin L. *economist*
Kelly, Kathleen Dennis *international government affairs consultant*
Kendrick, Budd Leroy *psychologist*
Kenny, Robert Wade *social sciences and humanities educator, writer*
Kenyon, Daphne Anne *economist*
Keohane, Nannerl Overholser *political scientist, academic administrator*
Kessler, Gale Suzanne *psychologist, educator*
Khavari, Khalil Akhtar *psychology professor*
Kiesler, Charles Adolphus *psychologist, academic administrator*
King, Rosalyn Mercita *social sciences educator, researcher, psychologist*
Klob, Hans Rudolph *economist, consultant*
Kocel, Katherine Merle *psychology professor, researcher*
Konecni, Vladimir J. J. Ch. S. (Graf Konecni) *psychologist, educator, writer*
Kopko, Kimberly Ann *psychologist, researcher*
Kosslyn, Stephen M. *psychologist, educator*
Kostere, Kim Martin *psychologist, consultant*
Kuroda, Yasumasa *political science professor, researcher*
Kvint, Vladimir Lev *economist, mining engineer, finance educator*
Laffer, Arthur Betz *economist*
LaGanke, Allyson Ann *psychologist*
Lancaster, Kirsten Kezar *psychologist*
Landon, William J. *retired intelligence officer*
Lanoue, David J. *political science professor, department chairman*
Lasky, Richard Donald *psychoanalyst, educator*
La Spata, Michelle Gayle *school psychologist*
Laughlin, Louis Gene *economic analyst, consultant*
Lazar, Zoe L. *psychologist*
LeBlanc, Hugh Linus *political science professor, consultant*
Ledbetter, Jennifer Lynn *anthropologist, educator*
Lee, Mordecai *political scientist, educator*
Lee, Tabia (T. Lee) *social studies educator*
Leijonhufvud, Axel Stig Bengt *economics professor*
Leonard, Hasse A. *psychologist, educator*
LeValley, Amber Noel *school psychologist*
Levermore, Monique A. *psychologist, educator*
Levi, Danilo *sociologist, educator, director*
Lewis, Charles Leonard *psychologist*
Lichtblau, John H. *retired economist*
Linde, Armando Steven *economist*
Lindsey, Lawrence Benjamin *economist*
Lipsey, Richard George *economist, educator*
Lipsitt, Lewis Paeff *psychology professor*
Lipson, Abigail *psychologist*
Litrownik, Alan Jay *psychologist, educator*
Locke, Edwin Allen III *retired psychologist, educator*
Loftus, Elizabeth F. *psychology professor*
Long, Ralph Stewart *clinical psychologist*
Lovick, Norma McGinnis *social studies educator*
Lowe, Patricia A. *psychologist, educator*
Ludden, John Franklin *retired economist*
Lundstedt, Sven Bertil *behavioral and social scientist, educator*
Luskin, Frederic Michael *psychologist, educator*
MacHovec, Frank J. *psychologist*
MacLennan, Beryce Winifred *psychologist*
Maehr, Martin Louis *psychology professor*
Magana, Melanie G *psychologist, consultant*
Manfredi, Zachary-John A. *political scientist*
Marcus, Edward *economist, educator*
Marini, Frank Nicholas *political science and public administration educator*
Markovich, Patricia H. *economist*
Matema, Zsun-nee Kimball (Annette K. Miller) *social sciences educator*
Matheny, Adam Pence, Jr. *child psychologist, educator, consultant, researcher*
Maudlin, Robert V. *economics and government affairs consultant*
Maxwell, Sara Elizabeth (Sally) *psychologist, educator, speech pathology/audiology services professional, recording industry executive, director*
Mc Clellan, Catharine *anthropologist, educator*
McDonald, Natasha L. *school psychologist, educator*
McEvoy, Michael Joseph *economist*
McEvoy, Pamela T. *clinical psychologist*
McGough, Duane Theodore *economist, consultant, retired federal official*
McGowan, Bruce Edward *social studies educator, secondary school educator*
McGuire, Amy Catherine *school psychologist*
Mellins, Claude Ann *psychologist*
Mendis, Patrick *diplomat, writer, educator*
Migue, Jean Luc *economics professor*
Miksis, Christina Barbara *psychologist*
Miller, Charles Allen *politics educator*
Mitchell, Steve Harold *psychologist*
Miyata, Sachiko *social scientist, researcher*
Molina, Kevin *social studies educator*
Moore, Stanley Wayne *retired political science professor*
Morse, Gayle Skawennio *psychologist, consultant*
Mospaw, Kathan J. *retired social studies educator*
Muhn, Judy Ann *psychologist, genealogist, trainer*
Murphy, Evelyn Frances *economist*
Mutalipassi, Louis Richard *psychologist, educator*
Myren, Richard Albert *criminologist, consultant*
Nadolski, Dora J. *social sciences educator, researcher*
Nearine, Robert James *educational psychologist*
Newborn, Jud *anthropologist, writer, curator, educator, historian*
Newman, Philip Robert *psychologist*
Nielsen, Morten Ørregaard *economics professor*
Noll, Richard Dean, Jr. *psychologist, educator, historian*
Norman, Donald Arthur *psychologist, educator*
Obara, Ichiro *economics professor*
O'Brien, John Wilfrid *economist, educator, retired university president*
Osowiec, Darlene Ann *clinical psychologist, educator, consultant*
Otis, Jack *social work educator*
Ouyang, Norma M. *psychologist*
Pace, Charles Robert *psychologist, educator*
Palisi, Anthony Thomas *psychologist, educator*
Paredes, James Anthony *anthropologist, educator*
Parish, Thomas Scanlan *psychology professor*
Parker, Melissa Epley *psychologist*
Patino-Brandfon, Sylvia *retired psychologist*
Patterson, Jim *economist, writer*
Patterson, Samuel C. *retired political science professor*
Pearson, Richard Joseph *archaeologist, educator*
Pedersen, Knud George *retired economics professor, academic administrator*
Pepper, Joline Romano *psychologist, educator*
Pepper, Pamela Poe *psychologist*
Peretti, Peter Oral *psychology professor, researcher*
Person, Tammy *psychologist*
Pezeshk, Violet *psychologist, educator*
Pilisuk, Marc *psychology educator*
Pollack, Gerald Alexander *economist, educator, federal agency administrator*
Poser, Ernest George *psychologist, educator*
Power, Mary Susan *political scientist, educator*
Premack, David *psychologist*
Prewitt, Kenneth *political science professor, foundation administrator*
Rabinowitz, Yaron Gil *psychologist, military officer*
Ramsay, J. Russell *psychologist*
Randall, Richard Rainier *geographer*
Randazzo, Marisa R. *psychologist*
Reed, Adam Victor *psychologist, engineer, information scientist*
Reed, Diane Marie *retired psychologist*
Reese, Hayne Waring *psychologist, educator*
Reinleitner, Katherine Mindlin *psychologist, foundation administrator*
Renfro, Charles Gilliland *economist*
Renfro, William Leonard *futurist, lawyer, inventor, entrepreneur*
Repnikova, Maria *international migration scholar*
Reynolds, Clark Winton *economist, educator*
Richard, Robert Carter *retired psychologist*
Richmond, Anthony Henry *sociologist, emeritus educator*
Rickel, Annette Urso *psychology and psychiatry researcher, educator*
Rips, Lance Jeffrey *psychology professor*
Risley, Todd Robert *psychologist, educator*
Robinson, James Arthur *political scientist*
Robinson, Marguerite Stern *anthropologist, educator, consultant*
Robinson, William I. *sociologist*
Rogers, Sally J. *psychologist, educator*
Romanucci-Ross, Lola *anthropologist, educator*
Rosellon, Juan *economist, researcher*
Rowen, Henry Stanislaus *retired economist, former federal agency administrator*
Rudolph, James Robert *psychologist*
Russell, Michael K. *psychology professor, consultant*
Salant, Nira L. *geographer, educator*
Salins, Peter D. *political science professor, academic administrator*
Sanders, Linda E. *psychologist, educator*
Sargent, Thomas Andrew *retired political sc professor*
Schein, Virginia Ellen *psychologist*
Scheinman, Nancy Jane *psychologist*
Schexnider, Virginia Reeves *school psycholo*
Schmandt-Besserat, Denise *archaeologist, educator*
Schneider, Kirk J. *psychologist, writer*
Schull, Natasha Dow *anthropologist, educat*
Schwab, John H. *psychologist*
Sebastian, Peter *political scientist, consultan retired diplomat*
Selders, Jean E. *retired psychology professo*
Serling, Joel Martin *educational psychologis*
Shakow, Alexander *economist, government official*
Shapiro, Leo J. *social researcher*
Sharma, Martha Bridges *geography educato*
Sharpe, William Forsyth *economics professo*
Shaw, Richard Thomas *humanitarian, retire federal agent, retired military officer*
Shen, Yu-Chu *economics professor*
Shepp, Bryan Eugene *psychologist, educato*
Sherry, George Leon *political science profes*
Shipley, Andrew G. *psychology scholar*
Shrum, Robert Matthew *political strategist, educator, journalist*
Sielicki-Korczak, Boris Zdzislaw *political educator, investigative consultant*
Simon, Norma Plavnick *psychologist*
Sims, Kent Otway *economist*
Sinai, Allen Leo *economist, educator*
Sisk, Jane Elizabeth *economist, educator*
Sisley, Emily Lucretia *psychologist, writer*
Skinner, Jonathan Snowden *economics educ*
Sledjeski, Eve Mary *psychologist, researche*
Smelser, Neil Joseph *sociologist*
Smith, Brad M. *political science scholar*
Smith, David Horton *retired social sciences educator*
Smith, Vme Edom (Verna Mae) *social scier educator, freelance photographer, freelan writer*
Smitherman, Todd A. *psychologist, researcl*
Snyder, Marvin *neuropsychologist*
Soileau, Monica Marie *economist*
Soller, Elaine Rita *psychologist, artist*
Sosnick, Stephen Howard *economics profes*
Spangler, Edra Mildred *psychologist*
Splane, Richard Beverley *social work educ*
Spraggins, Johnnie David *sociology and cu studies educator*
Sprinthall, Norman Arthur *psychology educ*
Stengrim, Laura Ann *political scientist, researcher*
Stephenson, Edward *psychology professor*
Stokey, Nancy L. *economist, educator*
Strain, Edward Richard *psychologist*
Strauss, Judy Perkins *psychologist, educato*
Striker, Cecil Leopold *archaeologist, educa*
Studness, Charles Michael *economist*
Stufano, Thomas Joseph *criminologist, auth inventor*
Stumpf, Heinrich Josef *psychometrician, research consultant*
Styer, Denise Marie *psychologist*
Sullivan, Jeremy R. *psychologist, educator*
Sunley, Emil McKee *economist, consultant*
Sussman, Janet I. *social sciences educator*
Swanstrom, Thomas Evan *economist*
Swartz, Jon David *psychologist, educator*
Swint, Kerwin *political science professor*
Szeliga, Victoria I. *retired social studies educator*
Tarr, David Gerald *economist*
Tavares, Samia Costa *economics professor*
Taylor, Charles Henry *psychoanalyst, educa*
Taylor, John Brian *economist, educator, for federal agency administrator*
Taylor, Ronald Lewis *sociology educator*
Teasdale, Brent *sociologist, educator*
Terracciano, Antonio *psychologist, research*
Textor, Robert Bayard *cultural anthropolog educator, writer, consultant*
Thiessen, Delbert Duane *psychologist*
Thomas, Janet Y. *political science professo researcher*
Thompson, Alan Eric *economics professor*
Timmermann, Allan Gilling *management a economics professor*
Tishman, Lynn P. *psychologist, psychoanal*
Titus, Jeffrey Byron *pediatric neuropsychol*
Tonello-Stuart, Enrica Maria *political scien economist*
Tsou, Ming-Hsiang *geographer, educator*
Tubutis, Todd J. *anthropologist*
Turner, Weld W(inston) *industrial psycholo*
Tyler, John Duke *psychologist, educator*
Uchiyama, Craig Lyons *neuropsychologist*
Van Dyk, Frederick Theodore *political scie writer*
Vaux, Henry James, Jr. *economics professo*
Vawter, Marquis Philip *psychologist, resear*
Vayalakkara, Jyothi *neuropsychologist, dire educator*
Vicino, Thomas Joseph *political science professor*
Vojnovic, Igor Zoran *geographer, urban pl educator*
Volcker, Paul A(dolph) *economist, former Chairman of the Board of Governors of Federal Reserve System*
Vost, Kevin Gerard *psychologist*
Walker, Clarence Eugene *psychology profes*
Walton, Andre Pierre *psychologist, consulta*
Wang, Elise *political science scholar*
Watson, Patty Jo *anthropology educator*
Watters, Ann Oliva *psychologist, educator*
Waud, Roger Neil *economist, educator*
Webel, Charles Peter *human science and psychology educator*
Weil, Rolf Alfred *economist, retired univer president*
Weiner, Ferne *psychologist*
Wellisz, Stanislaw *economics professor*
Werner-Jacobsen, Emmy Elisabeth *developmental psychologist*

erfield, Holt Bradford *retired political ientist*
ehead, Tanya Dianne Grubbs *psychologist, lucator, researcher*
inson, Doris *medical sociology educator*
on, Scott Thomas *psychologist, researcher*
Wolfe, Gregory Baker *international relations educator*
Wonders, William Clare *geography educator*
Wrong, Dennis Hume *retired sociologist, educator*
York, Joan Elizabeth Smith *psychologist*
Yost, William Albert *psychology professor*
Zaffino, Michael J. *social studies educator*
Zgaljardic, Dennis Joseph *clinical neuropsychologist*
Zimet, Lloyd *sport psychologist, health educator, program planner and administrator*
Zimmern-Reed, Annette Wacks *psychologist*
Zuckerman, Harriet *sociologist, educator*
Zuiches, James Joseph *sociologist, educator*